Who's Who in the World®

Who's Who in the World®

2001

MARQUIS
Who'sWho
21st Since 1899
Century
Editions
The Chronicle of Human Achievement

18th Edition

MARQUIS
Who'sWho® 121 Chanlon Road
New Providence, NJ 07974 U.S.A.
www.marquiswhoswho.com

Who's Who in the World®

Marquis Who's Who®

Managing Director   Thomas M. Bachmann   **Editorial Director**   Fred Marks

Senior Managing Research Editor   Lisa Weissbard   **Managing Editor**   Eileen McGuinness

Editorial

Senior Editor	Cheryl Rodriguez
Associate Editor	Francine Richardson
Assistant Editors	Alison McGowan
	Deanna Richmond
	Josh Samber
	Lorena Soriano

Editorial Services

Manager	Debra Krom
Creative Project Manager	Michael Noerr
Assistant Creative Project Manager	William R. Miller
Production Supervisor	Jeanne Danzig

Editorial Support

Manager	Debby Nowicki
Coordinator	Mary San Giovanni
Production Assistant	Sola Osofisan

Mail Processing

Supervisor	Kara A. Seitz
Staff	Betty Gray
	Jill S. Terbell

Database Operations

Director, Production & Training	Mark Van Orman
Managing Editor	Matthew O'Connell
Senior Production Editor	Brittany Hartman

Research

Senior Research Editor	Susan Eggleton
Associate Research Editors	Oscar Maldonado
	Stephen J. Sherman
Assistant Research Editor	Lonzy Westbrook

Editorial Systems

Project Manager	Helene Davis
Programmers/Analysts	Sofia P. Pikulin
	Tom Haggerty

Published by Marquis Who's Who, a member of the Lexis-Nexis Group.

President and Chief Executive Officer   Andrew W. Meyer

Vice President and Publisher   Randy H. Mysel

Vice President, Database Production   Dean Hollister

Chief Information Officer   John Roney

Vice President of Information Technology   Gary Aiello

Marquis Who's Who
121 Chanlon Road
New Providence, New Jersey 07974
1-908-464-6800
www.marquiswhoswho.com

WHO'S WHO IN THE WORLD is a registered trademark of Reed Publishing (Nederland) B.V., used under license.
Library of Congress Catalog Card Number 79-139215
International Standard Book Number   0-8379-1125-7 (Classic Edition)
International Standard Book Number   0-8379-1126-5 (Deluxe Edition)
International Standard Serial Number   0083-9825

Table of Contents

Preface

The eighteenth edition of *Who's Who in the World* contains biographical information on important individuals from 215 nations and territories and virtually every professional field. As technology advances, and as governments, cultures, and economies become more interrelated and interdependent, the need for reference material on significant international figures likewise increases. With sketches profiling over 60,000 globally noteworthy persons, *Who's Who in the World* facilitates the work of researchers, historians, students, and other interested readers.

The book encompasses a broad range of professional endeavors. Most prominent are heads of state and others holding influential governmental positions. Sketches of national leaders were repeatedly revised until the book went to press in order to provide the most up-to-date information. Included are sketches of religious leaders of denominations from across the world. Coverage of business professionals includes all industries. Careful research has ensured inclusion of prominent scholars, scientists, and educators. Physicians and healthcare professionals, media representatives, artists, philanthropists, and athletes who are recognized around the world have their life's achievements chronicled in thorough biographical detail.

Selection of a name for inclusion in *Who's Who in the World* is based on reference value. Some individuals become eligible for listing because of position, while others have distinguished themselves through notable achievements in their fields. Many of the Biographees qualify by virtue of both position and professional excellence.

In the editorial evaluation that resulted in the ultimate selection of names for this directory, it was a person's achievements that determined eligibility. An individual's desire to be listed was not sufficient reason for inclusion. Similarly, wealth and social position were not criteria; only occupational stature or achievement influenced selection.

Most of the Biographees listed have furnished their own data, thus ensuring a high degree of accuracy. As in previous editions, Biographees were provided with prepublication proofs to ensure the sketches were correct. In some cases where individuals of great reference interest failed to supply information, Marquis staff members profiled these persons through careful, independent research. Sketches compiled in this manner are denoted by an asterisk.

In an effort to make this reference volume as useful as possible, Marquis editors and researchers have attempted to standardize the English spellings and alphabetization of names originating in non-Roman alphabets. This process is described under *Alphabetical Practices* on page xv.

Also included in the eighteenth edition of *Who's Who in the World* is a Professional Index. With the index, each Biographee is listed alphabetically by occupation. This reference tool makes it easier than ever for interested readers to find Biographees in any given profession.

Marquis Who's Who editors and researchers have exercised diligent care in the preparation of each biographical sketch. Despite all precautions, however, errors occasionally occur. Users of this directory are invited to notify the publisher of such errors so that corrections can be made in a subsequent edition.

With the eighteenth edition of *Who's Who in the World*, Marquis Who's Who continues the tradition of excellence established in 1899 with the publication of the first edition of *Who's Who in America*. The essence of that tradition is the continuing effort to produce reference works that are responsive to the needs of their users. The biographies found in *Who's Who in America*, *Who's Who in the World* and 18 other Marquis titles can also be accessed in *The Complete Marquis Who's Who on CD-ROM*.

Standards of Admission

The foremost consideration in selecting Biographees for *Who's Who in the World* is the extent of an individual's reference interest. Such reference interest is judged on either of two factors: (1) the position of responsibility held, or (2) the level of achievement attained by the individual.

Admissions based on the factor of position include:

Heads of state and other key government officials

High-ranking military officers

Principal officers of selected international business organizations and corporations

Heads of major universities and colleges

Selected members of national academies of science and of the humanities

Heads of international and national health organizations

Directors of major national cultural, educational, and scientific organizations, such as museums, opera companies, libraries, and research institutes

Chief ecclesiastics of the principal religious denominations

Editors and program directors from international media agencies

United Nations officials

Principal officers of selected international financial institutions, central banks, and stock exchanges

Recipients of major international awards, such as the Nobel Prizes and Cannes International Film Festival Awards

Admission for individual achievement is based on qualitative criteria. To be selected, a person must have attained conspicuous achievement.

Key to Information

[1] **CARLSSON, MATS,** [2] banker; [3] b. Uppsala, Sweden, Aug. 22, 1939; [4] s. Lars Odvar and Ingrid (Lindblad) C.; [5] m. Sigrid Søderstrom, Oct. 10, 1966; [6] children: Eric, Gunnar. [7] Grad. Umeå U., 1959. [8] Chartered Accountant. [9] Supervising acct. Svenskabanken, Stockholm, 1962-75, asst. v.p., 1975-78, v.p. 1978-85, pres., CEO, 1985-90, chmn. bd., 1991—, chmn. exec. com., 1993—; [10] dir. Staatsbank, Zürich, Switzerland, Bekaert-Belgium, Brussels, Barrère et Cie., Paris; adj. prof. Stockholms Universitet, 1980-85.[11] Author: Studies in World Monetary Balance, 1982, Common Market Strategies for the Nineties, 1988. [12] Mem. Riksdag, 1977-85; mem. Mayor's Com. Environ. Control, Stockholm, 1987—, chmn., 1990-95; bd. dirs. Stockholm Trade Fair. [13] Served with Swedish Army, 1959-62. [14] Civic Svc. award City of Stockholm, 1997. [15] Mem. Swedish Bankers Assn., City Club, Rotary (Stockholm). [16] Christian Democrat. [17] Lutheran. [18] Home: Strandvægen 85, 115 27 Stockholm, Sweden [19] Office: Svenskabanken, Blasieholmstorg 15, 103 228 Stockholm, Sweden

KEY

[1]   Name
[2]   Occupation
[3]   Vital statistics
[4]   Parents
[5]   Marriage
[6]   Children
[7]   Education
[8]   Professional certifications
[9]   Career
[10]   Career-related
[11]   Writings and creative works
[12]   Civic and political activities
[13]   Military service
[14]   Awards and fellowships
[15]   Professional and association memberships, clubs and lodges
[16]   Political affiliation
[17]   Religion
[18]   Home address
[19]   Office address

Table of Abbreviations

The following abbreviations and symbols are frequently used in this book.

*An asterisk following a sketch indicates that it was researched by the Marquis Who's Who editorial staff and has not been verified by the Biographee.

A Associate (used with academic degrees only)

AA, A.A. Associate in Arts, Associate of Arts

AAAL American Academy of Arts and Letters

AAAS American Association for the Advancement of Science

AACD American Association for Counseling and Development

AACN American Association of Critical Care Nurses

AAHA American Academy of Health Administrators

AAHP American Association of Hospital Planners

AAHPERD American Alliance for Health, Physical Education, Recreation, and Dance

AAS Associate of Applied Science

AASL American Association of School Librarians

AASPA American Association of School Personnel Administrators

AAU Amateur Athletic Union

AAUP American Association of University Professors

AAUW American Association of University Women

AB, A.B. Arts, Bachelor of

AB Alberta

ABA American Bar Association

ABC American Broadcasting Company

AC Air Corps

acad. academy, academic

acct. accountant

acctg. accounting

ACDA Arms Control and Disarmament Agency

ACHA American College of Hospital Administrators

ACLS Advanced Cardiac Life Support

ACLU American Civil Liberties Union

ACOG American College of Ob-Gyn

ACP American College of Physicians

ACS American College of Surgeons

ADA American Dental Association

a.d.c. aide-de-camp

adj. adjunct, adjutant

adj. gen. adjutant general

adm. admiral

adminstr. administrator

adminstrn. administration

adminstrv. administrative

ADN Associate's Degree in Nursing

ADP Automatic Data Processing

adv. advocate, advisory

advt. advertising

AE, A.E. Agricultural Engineer

A.E. and P. Ambassador Extraordinary and Plenipotentiary

AEC Atomic Energy Commission

aero. aeronautical, aeronautic

aerodyn. aerodynamic

AFB Air Force Base

AFL-CIO American Federation of Labor and Congress of Industrial Organizations

AFTRA American Federation of TV and Radio Artists

AFSCME American Federation of State, County and Municipal Employees

agr. agriculture

agrl. agricultural

agt. agent

AGVA American Guild of Variety Artists

agy. agency

A&I Agricultural and Industrial

AIA American Institute of Architects

AIAA American Institute of Aeronautics and Astronautics

AIChE American Institute of Chemical Engineers

AICPA American Institute of Certified Public Accountants

AID Agency for International Development

AIDS Acquired Immune Deficiency Syndrome

AIEE American Institute of Electrical Engineers

AIM American Institute of Management

AIME American Institute of Mining, Metallurgy, and Petroleum Engineers

AK Alaska

AL Alabama

ALA American Library Association

Ala. Alabama

alt. alternate

Alta. Alberta

A&M Agricultural and Mechanical

AM, A.M. Arts, Master of

Am. American, America

AMA American Medical Association

amb. ambassador

A.M.E. African Methodist Episcopal

Amtrak National Railroad Passenger Corporation

AMVETS American Veterans of World War II, Korea, Vietnam

ANA American Nurses Association

anat. anatomical

ANCC American Nurses Credentialing Center

ann. annual

ANTA American National Theatre and Academy

anthrop. anthropological

AP Associated Press

APA American Psychological Association

APGA American Personnel Guidance Association

APHA American Public Health Association

APO Army Post Office

apptd. appointed

Apr. April

apt. apartment

AR Arkansas

ARC American Red Cross

arch. architect

archeol. archeological

archtl. architectural

Ariz. Arizona

Ark. Arkansas

ArtsD, ArtsD. Arts, Doctor of

arty. artillery

AS American Samoa

AS Associate in Science

ASCAP American Society of Composers, Authors and Publishers

ASCD Association for Supervision and Curriculum Development

ASCE American Society of Civil Engineers

ASHRAE American Society of Heating, Refrigeration, and Air Conditioning Engineers

ASME American Society of Mechanical Engineers

ASNSA American Society for Nursing Service Administrators

ASPA American Society for Public Administration

ASPCA American Society for the Prevention of Cruelty to Animals

assn. association

assoc. associate

asst. assistant

ASTD American Society for Training and Development

ASTM American Society for Testing and Materials

astron. astronomical

astrophys. astrophysical

ATLA Association of Trial Lawyers of America

ATSC Air Technical Service Command

AT&T American Telephone & Telegraph Company

atty. attorney

Aug. August

AUS Army of the United States

aux. auxiliary

Ave. Avenue

AVMA American Veterinary Medical Association

AZ Arizona

AWHONN Association of Women's Health Obstetric and Neonatal Nurses

B. Bachelor

b. born

BA, B.A. Bachelor of Arts

BAgr, B.Agr. Bachelor of Agriculture

Balt. Baltimore

Bapt. Baptist

BArch, B.Arch. Bachelor of Architecture

BAS, B.A.S. Bachelor of Agricultural Science

BBA, B.B.A. Bachelor of Business Administration

BBB Better Business Bureau

BBC British Broadcasting Corporation

BC, B.C. British Columbia
BCE, B.C.E. Bachelor of Civil Engineering
BChir, B.Chir. Bachelor of Surgery
BCL, B.C.L. Bachelor of Civil Law
BCLS Basic Cardiac Life Support
BCS, B.C.S. Bachelor of Commercial Science
BD, B.D. Bachelor of Divinity
bd. board
BE, B.E. Bachelor of Education
BEE, B.E.E. Bachelor of Electrical
   Engineering
BFA, B.F.A. Bachelor of Fine Arts
bibl. biblical
bibliog. bibliographical
biog. biographical
biol. biological
BJ, B.J. Bachelor of Journalism
Bklyn. Brooklyn
BL, B.L. Bachelor of Letters
bldg. building
BLS, B.L.S. Bachelor of Library Science
BLS Basic Life Support
Blvd. Boulevard
BMI Broadcast Music, Inc.
BMW Bavarian Motor Works (Bayerische
   Motoren Werke)
bn. battalion
B.&O.R.R. Baltimore & Ohio Railroad
bot. botanical
BPE, B.P.E. Bachelor of Physical Education
BPhil, B.Phil. Bachelor of Philosophy
br. branch
BRE, B.R.E. Bachelor of Religious
   Education
brig. gen. brigadier general
Brit. British, Brittanica
Bros. Brothers
BS, B.S. Bachelor of Science
BSA, B.S.A. Bachelor of Agricultural Science
BSBA Bachelor of Science in Business
   Administration
BSChemE Bachelor of Science in Chemical
   Engineering
BSD, B.S.D. Bachelor of Didactic Science
BSEE Bachelor of Science in Electrical
   Engineering
BSN Bachelor of Science in Nursing
BST, B.S.T. Bachelor of Sacred Theology
BTh, B.Th. Bachelor of Theology
bull. bulletin
bur. bureau
bus. business
B.W.I. British West Indies

CA California
CAA Civil Aeronautics Administration
CAB Civil Aeronautics Board
CAD-CAM Computer Aided Design–
   Computer Aided Model
Calif. California
C.Am. Central America
Can. Canada, Canadian
CAP Civil Air Patrol
capt. captain
cardiol. cardiological
cardiovasc. cardiovascular
CARE Cooperative American Relief
   Everywhere
Cath. Catholic
cav. cavalry
CBC Canadian Broadcasting Company
CBI China, Burma, India Theatre of
   Operations
CBS Columbia Broadcasting Company
C.C. Community College
CCC Commodity Credit Corporation
CCNY City College of New York

CCRN Critical Care Registered Nurse
CCU Cardiac Care Unit
CD Civil Defense
CE, C.E. Corps of Engineers, Civil Engineer
CEN Certified Emergency Nurse
CENTO Central Treaty Organization
CEO chief executive officer
CERN European Organization of Nuclear
   Research
cert. certificate, certification, certified
CETA Comprehensive Employment Training
   Act
CFA Chartered Financial Analyst
CFL Canadian Football League
CFO chief financial officer
CFP Certified Financial Planner
ch. church
ChD, Ch.D. Doctor of Chemistry
chem. chemical
ChemE, Chem.E. Chemical Engineer
ChFC Chartered Financial Consultant
Chgo. Chicago
chirurg. chirurgical
chmn. chairman
chpt. chapter
CIA Central Intelligence Agency
Cin. Cincinnati
cir. circle, circuit
CLE Continuing Legal Education
Cleve. Cleveland
climatol. climatological
clin. clinical
clk. clerk
C.L.U. Chartered Life Underwriter
CM, C.M. Master in Surgery
CM Northern Mariana Islands
CMA Certified Medical Assistant
cmty. community
CNA Certified Nurse's Aide
CNOR Certified Nurse (Operating Room)
C.&N.W.Ry. Chicago & North Western
   Railway
CO Colorado
Co. Company
COF Catholic Order of Foresters
C. of C. Chamber of Commerce
col. colonel
coll. college
Colo. Colorado
com. committee
comd. commanded
comdg. commanding
comdr. commander
comdt. commandant
comm. communications
commd. commissioned
comml. commercial
commn. commission
commr. commissioner
compt. comptroller
condr. conductor
Conf. Conference
Congl. Congregational, Congressional
Conglist. Congregationalist
Conn. Connecticut
cons. consultant, consulting
consol. consolidated
constl. constitutional
constn. constitution
constrn. construction
contbd. contributed
contbg. contributing
contbn. contribution
contbr. contributor
contr. controller
Conv. Convention
COO chief operating officer

coop. cooperative
coord. coordinator
CORDS Civil Operations and Revolutionary
   Development Support
CORE Congress of Racial Equality
corp. corporation, corporate
corr. correspondent, corresponding,
   correspondence
C.&O.Ry. Chesapeake & Ohio Railway
coun. council
CPA Certified Public Accountant
CPCU Chartered Property and Casualty
   Underwriter
CPH, C.P.H. Certificate of Public Health
cpl. corporal
CPR Cardio-Pulmonary Resuscitation
C.P.Ry. Canadian Pacific Railway
CRT Cathode Ray Terminal
C.S. Christian Science
CSB, C.S.B. Bachelor of Christian Science
C.S.C. Civil Service Commission
CT Connecticut
ct. court
ctr. center
ctrl. central
CWS Chemical Warfare Service
C.Z. Canal Zone

D. Doctor
d. daughter
DAgr, D.Agr. Doctor of Agriculture
DAR Daughters of the American Revolution
dau. daughter
DAV Disabled American Veterans
DC, D.C. District of Columbia
DCL, D.C.L. Doctor of Civil Law
DCS, D.C.S. Doctor of Commercial Science
DD, D.D. Doctor of Divinity
DDS, D.D.S. Doctor of Dental Surgery
DE Delaware
Dec. December
dec. deceased
def. defense
Del. Delaware
del. delegate, delegation
Dem. Democrat, Democratic
DEng, D.Eng. Doctor of Engineering
denom. denomination, denominational
dep. deputy
dept. department
dermatol. dermatological
desc. descendant
devel. development, developmental
DFA, D.F.A. Doctor of Fine Arts
D.F.C. Distinguished Flying Cross
DHL, D.H.L. Doctor of Hebrew Literature
dir. director
dist. district
distbg. distributing
distbn. distribution
distbr. distributor
disting. distinguished
div. division, divinity, divorce
divsn. division
DLitt, D.Litt. Doctor of Literature
DMD, D.M.D. Doctor of Dental Medicine
DMS, D.M.S. Doctor of Medical Science
DO, D.O. Doctor of Osteopathy
docs. documents
DON Director of Nursing
DPH, D.P.H. Diploma in Public Health
DPhil, D.Phil. Doctor of Philosophy
D.R. Daughters of the Revolution
Dr. Drive, Doctor
DRE, D.R.E. Doctor of Religious Education
DrPH, Dr.P.H. Doctor of Public Health,
   Doctor of Public Hygiene
D.S.C. Distinguished Service Cross

DSc, D.Sc. Doctor of Science
DSChemE Doctor of Science in Chemical Engineering
D.S.M. Distinguished Service Medal
DST, D.S.T. Doctor of Sacred Theology
DTM, D.T.M. Doctor of Tropical Medicine
DVM, D.V.M. Doctor of Veterinary Medicine
DVS, D.V.S. Doctor of Veterinary Surgery

E, E. East
ea. eastern
E. and P. Extraordinary and Plenipotentiary
Eccles. Ecclesiastical
ecol. ecological
econ. economic
ECOSOC Economic and Social Council (of the UN)
ED, E.D. Doctor of Engineering
ed. educated
EdB, Ed.B. Bachelor of Education
EdD, Ed.D. Doctor of Education
edit. edition
editl. editorial
EdM, Ed.M. Master of Education
edn. education
ednl. educational
EDP Electronic Data Processing
EdS, Ed.S. Specialist in Education
EE, E.E. Electrical Engineer
E.E. and M.P. Envoy Extraordinary and Minister Plenipotentiary
EEC European Economic Community
EEG Electroencephalogram
EEO Equal Employment Opportunity
EEOC Equal Employment Opportunity Commission
E.Ger. German Democratic Republic
EKG Electrocardiogram
elec. electrical
electrochem. electrochemical
electrophys. electrophysical
elem. elementary
EM, E.M. Engineer of Mines
EMT Emergency Medical Technician
ency. encyclopedia
Eng. England
engr. engineer
engring. engineering
entomol. entomological
environ. environmental
EPA Environmental Protection Agency
epidemiol. epidemiological
Episc. Episcopalian
ERA Equal Rights Amendment
ERDA Energy Research and Development Administration
ESEA Elementary and Secondary Education Act
ESL English as Second Language
ESPN Entertainment and Sports Programming Network
ESSA Environmental Science Services Administration
ethnol. ethnological
ETO European Theatre of Operations
Evang. Evangelical
exam. examination, examining
Exch. Exchange
exec. executive
exhbn. exhibition
expdn. expedition
expn. exposition
expt. experiment
exptl. experimental
Expy. Expressway
Ext. Extension

F.A. Field Artillery
FAA Federal Aviation Administration
FAO Food and Agriculture Organization (of the UN)
FBA Federal Bar Association
FBI Federal Bureau of Investigation
FCA Farm Credit Administration
FCC Federal Communications Commission
FCDA Federal Civil Defense Administration
FDA Food and Drug Administration
FDIA Federal Deposit Insurance Administration
FDIC Federal Deposit Insurance Corporation
FE, F.E. Forest Engineer
FEA Federal Energy Administration
Feb. February
fed. federal
fedn. federation
FERC Federal Energy Regulatory Commission
fgn. foreign
FHA Federal Housing Administration
fin. financial, finance
FL Florida
Fl. Floor
Fla. Florida
FMC Federal Maritime Commission
FNP Family Nurse Practitioner
FOA Foreign Operations Administration
found. foundation
FPC Federal Power Commission
FPO Fleet Post Office
frat. fraternity
FRS Federal Reserve System
FSA Federal Security Agency
Ft. Fort
FTC Federal Trade Commission
Fwy. Freeway

G-1 (or other number) Division of General Staff
GA, Ga. Georgia
GAO General Accounting Office
gastroent. gastroenterological
GATE Gifted and Talented Educators
GATT General Agreement on Tariffs and Trade
GE General Electric Company
gen. general
geneal. genealogical
geod. geodetic
geog. geographic, geographical
geol. geological
geophys. geophysical
geriat. geriatrics
gerontol. gerontological
G.H.Q. General Headquarters
GM General Motors Corporation
GMAC General Motors Acceptance Corporation
G.N.Ry. Great Northern Railway
gov. governor
govt. government
govtl. governmental
GPO Government Printing Office
grad. graduate, graduated
GSA General Services Administration
Gt. Great
GTE General Telephone and ElectricCompany
GU Guam
gynecol. gynecological

HBO Home Box Office
hdqs. headquarters

HEW Department of Health, Education and Welfare
HHD, H.H.D. Doctor of Humanities
HHFA Housing and Home Finance Agency
HHS Department of Health and Human Services
HI Hawaii
hist. historical, historic
HM, H.M. Master of Humanities
HMO Health Maintenance Organization
homeo. homeopathic
hon. honorary, honorable
Ho. of Dels. House of Delegates
Ho. of Reps. House of Representatives
hort. horticultural
hosp. hospital
H.S. High School
HUD Department of Housing and Urban Development
Hwy. Highway
hydrog. hydrographic

IA Iowa
IAEA International Atomic Energy Agency
IATSE International Alliance of Theatrical and Stage Employees and Moving Picture Operators of the United States and Canada
IBM International Business Machines Corporation
IBRD International Bank for Reconstruction and Development
ICA International Cooperation Administration
ICC Interstate Commerce Commission
ICCE International Council for Computers in Education
ICU Intensive Care Unit
ID Idaho
IEEE Institute of Electrical and Electronics Engineers
IFC International Finance Corporation
IGY International Geophysical Year
IL Illinois
Ill. Illinois
illus. illustrated
ILO International Labor Organization
IMF International Monetary Fund
IN Indiana
Inc. Incorporated
Ind. Indiana
ind. independent
Indpls. Indianapolis
indsl. industrial
inf. infantry
info. information
ins. insurance
insp. inspector
insp. gen. inspector general
inst. institute
instl. institutional
instn. institution
instr. instructor
instrn. instruction
instrnl. instructional
internat. international
intro. introduction
IRE Institute of Radio Engineers
IRS Internal Revenue Service
ITT International Telephone & Telegraph Corporation

JAG Judge Advocate General
JAGC Judge Advocate General Corps
Jan. January
Jaycees Junior Chamber of Commerce
JB, J.B. Jurum Baccalaureus

JCB, J.C.B. Juris Canoni Baccalaureus
JCD, J.C.D. Juris Canonici Doctor, Juris
    Civilis Doctor
JCL, J.C.L. Juris Canonici Licentiatus
JD, J.D. Juris Doctor
jg. junior grade
jour. journal
jr. junior
JSD, J.S.D. Juris Scientiae Doctor
JUD, J.U.D. Juris Utriusque Doctor
jud. judicial

Kans. Kansas
K.C. Knights of Columbus
K.P. Knights of Pythias
KS Kansas
K.T. Knight Templar
KY, Ky. Kentucky

LA, La. Louisiana
L.A. Los Angeles
lab. laboratory
L.Am. Latin America
lang. language
laryngol. laryngological
LB Labrador
LDS Latter Day Saints
LDS Church Church of Jesus Christ of Latter
    Day Saints
lectr. lecturer
legis. legislation, legislative
LHD, L.H.D. Doctor of Humane Letters
L.I. Long Island
libr. librarian, library
lic. licensed, license
L.I.R.R. Long Island Railroad
lit. literature
litig. litigation
LittB, Litt.B. Bachelor of Letters
LittD, Litt.D. Doctor of Letters
LLB, LL.B. Bachelor of Laws
LLD, L.L.D. Doctor of Laws
LLM, L.L.M. Master of Laws
Ln. Lane
L.&N.R.R. Louisville & Nashville Railroad
LPGA Ladies Professional Golf Association
LPN Licensed Practical Nurse
LS, L.S. Library Science (in degree)
lt. lieutenant
Ltd. Limited
Luth. Lutheran
LWV League of Women Voters

M. Master
m. married
MA, M.A. Master of Arts
MA Massachusetts
MADD Mothers Against Drunk Driving
mag. magazine
MAgr, M.Agr. Master of Agriculture
maj. major
Man. Manitoba
Mar. March
MArch, M.Arch. Master in Architecture
Mass. Massachusetts
math. mathematics, mathematical
MATS Military Air Transport Service
MB, M.B. Bachelor of Medicine
MB Manitoba
MBA, M.B.A. Master of Business
    Administration
MBS Mutual Broadcasting System
M.C. Medical Corps
MCE, M.C.E. Master of Civil Engineering
mcht. merchant
mcpl. municipal
MCS, M.C.S. Master of Commercial Science

xii

MD, M.D. Doctor of Medicine
MD, Md. Maryland
MDiv Master of Divinity
MDip, M.Dip. Master in Diplomacy
mdse. merchandise
MDV, M.D.V. Doctor of Veterinary
    Medicine
ME, M.E. Mechanical Engineer
ME Maine
M.E.Ch. Methodist Episcopal Church
mech. mechanical
MEd., M.Ed. Master of Education
med. medical
MEE, M.E.E. Master of Electrical
    Engineering
mem. member
meml. memorial
merc. mercantile
met. metropolitan
metall. metallurgical
MetE, Met.E. Metallurgical Engineer
meteorol. meteorological
Meth. Methodist
Mex. Mexico
MF, M.F. Master of Forestry
MFA, M.F.A. Master of Fine Arts
mfg. manufacturing
mfr. manufacturer
mgmt. management
mgr. manager
MHA, M.H.A. Master of Hospital
    Administration
M.I. Military Intelligence
MI Michigan
Mich. Michigan
micros. microscopic, microscopical
mid. middle
mil. military
Milw. Milwaukee
Min. Minister
mineral. mineralogical
Minn. Minnesota
MIS Management Information Systems
Miss. Mississippi
MIT Massachusetts Institute of Technology
mktg. marketing
ML, M.L. Master of Laws
MLA Modern Language Association
M.L.D. Magister Legnum Diplomatic
MLitt, M.Litt. Master of Literature, Master
    of Letters
MLS, M.L.S. Master of Library Science
MME, M.M.E. Master of Mechanical
    Engineering
MN Minnesota
mng. managing
MO, Mo. Missouri
moblzn. mobilization
Mont. Montana
MP Northern Mariana Islands
M.P. Member of Parliament
MPA Master of Public Administration
MPE, M.P.E. Master of Physical Education
MPH, M.P.H. Master of Public Health
MPhil, M.Phil. Master of Philosophy
MPL, M.P.L. Master of Patent Law
Mpls. Minneapolis
MRE, M.R.E. Master of Religious Education
MRI Magnetic Resonance Imaging
MS, M.S. Master of Science
MS, Ms. Mississippi
MSc, M.Sc. Master of Science
MSChemE Master of Science in Chemical
    Engineering
MSEE Master of Science in Electrical
    Engineering

MSF, M.S.F. Master of Science of Forestry
MSN Master of Science in Nursing
MST, M.S.T. Master of Sacred Theology
MSW, M.S.W. Master of Social Work
MT Montana
Mt. Mount
MTO Mediterranean Theatre of Operation
MTV Music Television
mus. museum, musical
MusB, Mus.B. Bachelor of Music
MusD, Mus.D. Doctor of Music
MusM, Mus.M. Master of Music
mut. mutual
MVP Most Valuable Player
mycol. mycological

N. North
NAACOG Nurses Association of the
    American College of Obstetricians and
    Gynecologists
NAACP National Association for the
    Advancement of Colored People
NACA National Advisory Committee for
    Aeronautics
NACDL National Association of Criminal
    Defense Lawyers
NACU National Association of Colleges and
    Universities
NAD National Academy of Design
NAE National Academy of Engineering,
    National Association of Educators
NAESP National Association of Elementary
    School Principals
NAFE National Association of Female
    Executives
N.Am. North America
NAM National Association of Manufacturers
NAMH National Association for Mental
    Health
NAPA National Association of Performing
    Artists
NARAS National Academy of Recording
    Arts and Sciences
NAREB National Association of Real Estate
    Boards
NARS National Archives and Record Service
NAS National Academy of Sciences
NASA National Aeronautics and Space
    Administration
NASP National Association of School
    Psychologists
NASW National Association of Social
    Workers
nat. national
NATAS National Academy of Television
    Arts and Sciences
NATO North Atlantic Treaty Organization
NATOUSA North African Theatre of
    Operations, United States Army
nav. navigation
NB, N.B. New Brunswick
NBA National Basketball Association
NBC National Broadcasting Company
NC, N.C. North Carolina
NCAA National College Athletic Association
NCCJ National Conference of Christians and
    Jews
ND, N.D. North Dakota
NDEA National Defense Education Act
NE Nebraska
NE, N.E. Northeast
NEA National Education Association
Nebr. Nebraska
NEH National Endowment for Humanities
neurol. neurological
Nev. Nevada
NF Newfoundland

NFL National Football League
Nfld. Newfoundland
NG National Guard
NH, N.H. New Hampshire
NHL National Hockey League
NIH National Institutes of Health
NIMH National Institute of Mental Health
NJ, N.J. New Jersey
NLRB National Labor Relations Board
NM New Mexico
N.Mex. New Mexico
No. Northern
NOAA National Oceanographic and
    Atmospheric Administration
NORAD North America Air Defense
Nov. November
NOW National Organization for Women
N.P.Ry. Northern Pacific Railway
nr. near
NRA National Rifle Association
NRC National Research Council
NS, N.S. Nova Scotia
NSC National Security Council
NSF National Science Foundation
NSTA National Science Teachers Association
NSW New South Wales
N.T. New Testament
NT Northwest Territories
nuc. nuclear
numis. numismatic
NV Nevada
NW, N.W. Northwest
N.W.T. Northwest Territories
NY, N.Y. New York
N.Y.C. New York City
NYU New York University
N.Z. New Zealand

OAS Organization of American States
ob-gyn obstetrics-gynecology
obs. observatory
obstet. obstetrical
occupl. occupational
oceanog. oceanographic
Oct. October
OD, O.D. Doctor of Optometry
OECD Organization for Economic
    Cooperation and Development
OEEC Organization of European Economic
    Cooperation
OEO Office of Economic Opportunity
ofcl. official
OH Ohio
OK Oklahoma
Okla. Oklahoma
ON Ontario
Ont. Ontario
oper. operating
ophthal. ophthalmological
ops. operations
OR Oregon
orch. orchestra
Oreg. Oregon
orgn. organization
orgnl. organizational
ornithol. ornithological
orthop. orthopedic
OSHA Occupational Safety and Health
    Administration
OSRD Office of Scientific Research and
    Development
OSS Office of Strategic Services
osteo. osteopathic
otol. otological
otolaryn. otolaryngological

PA, Pa. Pennsylvania

P.A. Professional Association
paleontol. paleontological
path. pathological
PBS Public Broadcasting System
P.C. Professional Corporation
PE Prince Edward Island
pediat. pediatrics
P.E.I. Prince Edward Island
PEN Poets, Playwrights, Editors, Essayists
    and Novelists (international association)
penol. penological
P.E.O. women's organization (full name not
    disclosed)
pers. personnel
pfc. private first class
PGA Professional Golfers' Association of
    America
PHA Public Housing Administration
pharm. pharmaceutical
PharmD, Pharm.D. Doctor of Pharmacy
PharmM, Pharm.M. Master of Pharmacy
PhB, Ph.B. Bachelor of Philosophy
PhD, Ph.D. Doctor of Philosophy
PhDChemE Doctor of Science in Chemical
    Engineering
PhM, Ph.M. Master of Philosophy
Phila. Philadelphia
philharm. philharmonic
philol. philological
philos. philosophical
photog. photographic
phys. physical
physiol. physiological
Pitts. Pittsburgh
Pk. Park
Pky. Parkway
Pl. Place
P.&L.E.R.R. Pittsburgh & Lake Erie
    Railroad
Plz. Plaza
PNP Pediatric Nurse Practitioner
P.O. Post Office
PO Box Post Office Box
polit. political
poly. polytechnic, polytechnical
PQ Province of Quebec
PR, P.R. Puerto Rico
prep. preparatory
pres. president
Presbyn. Presbyterian
presdl. presidential
prin. principal
procs. proceedings
prod. produced (play production)
prodn. production
prodr. producer
prof. professor
profl. professional
prog. progressive
propr. proprietor
pros. atty. prosecuting attorney
pro tem. pro tempore
PSRO Professional Services Review
    Organization
psychiat. psychiatric
psychol. psychological
PTA Parent-Teachers Association
ptnr. partner
PTO Pacific Theatre of Operations, Parent
    Teacher Organization
pub. publisher, publishing, published
pub. public
publ. publication
pvt. private

quar. quarterly
qm. quartermaster

Q.M.C. Quartermaster Corps
Que. Quebec

radiol. radiological
RAF Royal Air Force
RCA Radio Corporation of America
RCAF Royal Canadian Air Force
RD Rural Delivery
Rd. Road
R&D Research & Development
REA Rural Electrification Administration
rec. recording
ref. reformed
regt. regiment
regtl. regimental
rehab. rehabilitation
rels. relations
Rep. Republican
rep. representative
Res. Reserve
ret. retired
Rev. Reverend
rev. review, revised
RFC Reconstruction Finance Corporation
RFD Rural Free Delivery
rhinol. rhinological
RI, R.I. Rhode Island
RISD Rhode Island School of Design
Rlwy. Railway
Rm. Room
RN, R.N. Registered Nurse
roentgenol. roentgenological
ROTC Reserve Officers Training Corps
RR Rural Route
R.R. Railroad
rsch. research
rschr. researcher
Rt. Route

S. South
s. son
SAC Strategic Air Command
SAG Screen Actors Guild
SALT Strategic Arms Limitation Talks
S.Am. South America
san. sanitary
SAR Sons of the American Revolution
Sask. Saskatchewan
savs. savings
SB, S.B. Bachelor of Science
SBA Small Business Administration
SC, S.C. South Carolina
SCAP Supreme Command Allies Pacific
ScB, Sc.B. Bachelor of Science
SCD, S.C.D. Doctor of Commercial Science
ScD, Sc.D. Doctor of Science
sch. school
sci. science, scientific
SCLC Southern Christian Leadership
Conference
SCV Sons of Confederate Veterans
SD, S.D. South Dakota
SE, S.E. Southeast
SEATO Southeast Asia Treaty Organization
SEC Securities and Exchange Commission
sec. secretary
sect. section
seismol. seismological
sem. seminary
Sept. September
s.g. senior grade
sgt. sergeant
SHAEF Supreme Headquarters Allied
    Expeditionary Forces
SHAPE Supreme Headquarters Allied
    Powers in Europe
S.I. Staten Island

S.J. Society of Jesus (Jesuit)
SJD Scientiae Juridicae Doctor
SK Saskatchewan
SM, S.M. Master of Science
SNP Society of Nursing Professionals
So. Southern
soc. society
sociol. sociological
S.P.Co. Southern Pacific Company
spkr. speaker
spl. special
splty. specialty
Sq. Square
S.R. Sons of the Revolution
sr. senior
SS Steamship
SSS Selective Service System
St. Saint, Street
sta. station
stats. statistics
statis. statistical
STB, S.T.B. Bachelor of Sacred Theology
stblzn. stabilization
STD, S.T.D. Doctor of Sacred Theology
std. standard
Ste. Suite
subs. subsidiary
SUNY State University of New York
supr. supervisor
supt. superintendent
surg. surgical
svc. service
SW, S.W. Southwest
sys. system

TAPPI Technical Association of the Pulp and
　　Paper Industry
tb. tuberculosis
tchg. teaching
tchr. teacher
tech. technical, technology
technol. technological
tel. telephone
Tel. & Tel. Telephone & Telegraph
telecom. telecommunications
temp. temporary
Tenn. Tennessee
Ter. Territory
Ter. Terrace
TESOL Teachers of English to Speakers of
　　Other Languages
Tex. Texas
ThD, Th.D. Doctor of Theology
theol. theological

ThM, Th.M. Master of Theology
TN Tennessee
tng. training
topog. topographical
trans. transaction, transferred
transl. translation, translated
transp. transportation
treas. treasurer
TT Trust Territory
TV television
TVA Tennessee Valley Authority
TWA Trans World Airlines
twp. township
TX Texas
typog. typographical

U. University
UAW United Auto Workers
UCLA University of California at Los
　　Angeles
UDC United Daughters of the Confederacy
U.K. United Kingdom
UN United Nations
UNESCO United Nations Educational,
　　Scientific and Cultural Organization
UNICEF United Nations International
　　Children's Emergency Fund
univ. university
UNRRA United Nations Relief and
　　Rehabilitation Administration
UPI United Press International
U.P.R.R. United Pacific Railroad
urol. urological
U.S. United States
U.S.A. United States of America
USAAF United States Army Air Force
USAF United States Air Force
USAFR United States Air Force Reserve
USAR United States Army Reserve
USCG United States Coast Guard
USCGR United States Coast Guard Reserve
USES United States Employment Service
USIA United States Information Agency
USMC United States Marine Corps
USMCR United States Marine Corps Reserve
USN United States Navy
USNG United States National Guard
USNR United States Naval Reserve
USO United Service Organizations
USPHS United States Public Health Service
USS United States Ship
USSR Union of the Soviet Socialist Repub-
　　lics
USTA United States Tennis Association

USV United States Volunteers
UT Utah

VA Veterans Administration
VA, Va. Virginia
vet. veteran, veterinary
VFW Veterans of Foreign Wars
VI, V.I. Virgin Islands
vice pres. vice president
vis. visiting
VISTA Volunteers in Service to America
VITA Volunteers in Technical Assistance
vocat. vocational
vol. volunteer, volume
v.p. vice president
vs. versus
VT, Vt. Vermont

W, W. West
WA Washington (state)
WAC Women's Army Corps
Wash. Washington (state)
WATS Wide Area Telecommunications
　　Service
WAVES Women's Reserve, US Naval
　　Reserve
WCTU Women's Christian Temperance
　　Union
we. western
W. Ger. Germany, Federal Republic of
WHO World Health Organization
WI Wisconsin
W.I. West Indies
Wis. Wisconsin
WSB Wage Stabilization Board
WV West Virginia
W.Va. West Virginia
WWI World War I
WWII World War II
WY Wyoming
Wyo. Wyoming

YK Yukon Territory
YMCA Young Men's Christian Association
YMHA Young Men's Hebrew Association
YM & YWHA Young Men's and Young
　　Women's Hebrew Association
yr. year
YT, Y.T. Yukon Territory
YWCA Young Women's Christian
　　Association

zool. zoological

Alphabetical Practices

Names are arranged alphabetically according to the surnames, and under identical surnames according to the first given name. If both surname and first given name are identical, names are arranged alphabetically according to the second given name.

Surnames beginning with De, Des, Du, however capitalized or spaced, are recorded with the prefix preceding the surname and arranged alphabetically under the letter D.

Surnames beginning with Mac and Mc are arranged alphabetically under M.

Surnames beginning with Saint or St. appear after names that begin Sains, and are arranged according to the second part of the name, e.g. St. Clair before Saint Dennis.

Surnames beginning with Van, Von, or von are arranged alphabetically under the letter V.

Compound surnames are arranged according to the first member of the compound.

Many hyphenated Arabic names begin Al-, El-, or al-. These names are alphabetized according to each Biographee's designation of last name. Thus Al-Bahar, Neta may be listed either under Al- or under Bahar, depending on the preference of the listee.

Also, Arabic names have a variety of possible spellings when transposed to English. Spelling of these names is always based on the practice of the Biographee. Some Biographees use a Western form of word order, while others prefer the Arabic word sequence.

Similarly, Asian names may have no comma between family and given names, but some Biographees have chosen to add the comma. In each case, punctuation follows the preference of the Biographee.

Parentheses used in connection with a name indicate which part of the full name is usually deleted in common usage. Hence Chambers, E(lizabeth) Anne indicates that the usual form of the given name is E. Anne. In such a case, the parentheses are ignored in alphabetizing and the name would be arranged as Chambers, Elizabeth Anne. However, if the name is recorded Chambers, (Elizabeth) Anne, signifying that the entire name Elizabeth is not commonly used, the alphabetizing would be arranged as though the name were Chambers, Anne. If an entire middle or last name is enclosed in parentheses, that portion of the name is used in the alphabetical arrangement. Hence Chambers, Elizabeth (Anne) would be arranged as Chambers, Elizabeth Anne.

Where more than one spelling, word order, or name of an individual is frequently encountered, the sketch has been entered under the form preferred by the Biographee, with cross-references under alternate forms.

Who'sWho in the World®
Biographies

AABAD, A. M. M., multi-media consultant; b. Calcutta, India. BSc with honors, Calcutta U., 1945. Advisor on developing countries ITU Unesco, 1980; dir. Tech. Ctr. Asia Pacific Broadcasting Union(ABU), 1981-90; cons. Dhaka, Bangladesh, 1990—. editor: Technical Development of Broadcasting in Asia-Pacific, 1964-84. Comdr. (L) BNVR, Bangladesh, retired. Mem. Inst. Elec. Electronics Engrs. London (group), mem. RTS (Royal Television Soc.). Home: PO Box G-3373, Dhaka 1000, Bangladesh

AADAHL, JORG, business executive; b. Trondheim, Norway, June 16, 1937; came to U.S., 1966; s. Ottar P. and Gurli (Lockra) A.; MS in Mech. Engring., Tech. U. Norway, 1961; MBA, U. San Francisco, 1973; m. Inger R. Holst, July 13, 1973; children: Erik, Nina. Rsch. fellow Tech. U. Norway, Trondheim, 1961-62; mgr. arc welding devel. NAG, Oslo, 1964-66; mfg. engr. Varian Assocs., Palo Alto, Calif., 1966-67; sr. tech. writer Lynch Comm. Sys., 1967-69; indsl. engr., project mgr., 1969-74, bus. mgr. United Airlines, San Francisco, 1974-75, sr. systems analyst, 1976-81; strategic planning specialist Magnex Corp., San Jose, 1981-82; cons. in mgmt., 1982-84; founder, pres. Safeware, Inc., San Mateo, Calif., 1984—; founder, prin. CampuSafe Sys., 1996—; dir. Safeware Sys. Ltd., U.K., 1990—. Developer Safechem Hazardous Chem. Mgmt. Sys. Recipient Cert. of Honor, San Francisco Bd. Suprs., 1973. Mem. Leif Erikson League (pres. 1973), Norwegian Soc. Profl. Engrs. Club: Young Scandinavians (v.p. 1971), Environment and Safety Data Exch. (founding mem., dir.). Author: Strength Analysis, Welded Structures, 1967; contbr. articles in various fields to profl. jours.; editor Nordic Highlights, 1972. Office: Safeware Inc PO Box 6745 2575 Flores St San Mateo CA 94403-2366

AADNESEN, CHRISTOPHER, railroad company executive, consultant; b. Salt Lake City, Nov. 2, 1948; s. Grant C. and Helen Jane (Ray) A.; m. Helen Elizabeth Twelves, Aug. 14, 1973 (div. 1988); children: Aric Paul, Brian James, Nicholas Twelves; m. Betty Jean DeLeon, Aug. 19, 1988; children: Brooke Bingham, Brad Bingham. BA in English, U. Utah, 1971, MBA, 1973; PMD, Harvard U., 1990. Gen. mgr. and founder Thaddeus Duncan Co., Salt Lake City, 1968-72; divsn. supt. Western Pacific R.R., Sacramento, 1978-82; gen. supt. of transp. Mo. Pacific R.R., Spring, Tex., 1983-84; asst. gen. mgr. So. Region Union Pacific R.R., Spring, Tex., 1984-88; gen. dir. pers. svcs. Union Pacific R.R., Omaha, 1988-89, asst. v.p. ops. adminstrn., 1989-90, asst. v.p. employee devel. and involvement, 1990-91, sr. asst. v.p. field ops., 1992-93, sr. asst. v.p. transp., 1993-95, pres. capitol city group, pres. capitol city mgmt. assocs., 1996—; chief oper. officer Transp. Ferroviara Mexicana, S.A. de C.V., 1996-99, exec. v.p., 1999—; exec. v.p., COO Tex. Mexican Ry. Co., 1999—; chmn. Port Terminal R.R. Assn., 2000—; bd. dirs. Brownsville and Matamoros Bridge Co., Brownsville, Tex., 1992-95. Campaign mgr. County Commr., Quincy, Calif., 1978. With USN, 1967-69. Mem. Am. Assn. R.R. Supts., Field Club of Omaha, Happy Hollow Country Club, Berry Creek Country Club, Greater Austin C. of C., Round Rock C. of C., Georgetown C. of C., Beta Theta Pi. Republican. Episcopalian. Avocations: guitar, piano, golf, fishing, bowling. Home: 30205 Oak Tree Dr Georgetown TX 78628-1143 Office: The Capitol City Group 3007 Dawn Dr Ste 104 Georgetown TX 78628-2864 also: TFM SA de CV, Av Manuel C Barragan, 4850 Norte Col Hidalgo, Monterrey Mexico

AAKJER, THOMAS, electrical engineer; b. Grindsted, Jylland, Denmark, May 21, 1969. MSEE, Tech. U. Denmark, 1992, PhD, 1995. Rschr. Denmark Tech. U., Lyngby, Denmark, 1992-95; rsch. and devel. Digital Switching Corp. Comm. A/S, Denmark, 1995-98, Nat. Semiconductor, Germany, 1998-2000, Dialog Semiconductor, Germany, 2000—. Contbr. articles to profl. jours. Office: Dialog Semiconductor, Industriestrasse 1, D-82110 Germering Germany

AAKVAAG, TORVILD, petroleum company executive; b. Baerum, Norway, Jan. 18, 1927; s. Torvild and Dagny (Rivertz) A.; m. Dagen Dahl, 1952; m. Ruth Kleppe, 1990. Attache Norwegian Ministry Fgn. Affairs, 1951-56; joined legal dept. Norsk Hydro, 1956, head legal dept., 1967-70, gen. mgr. Petroleum Div., 1970-75, exec. v.p., 1975-77, dep. pres., 1977-84, pres., 1984-92, chmn. bd., 1992—. Office: Norsk Hydro A/S, Bygdoy Alle 2, N-0240 Oslo 2, Norway*

AALBAEK-NIELSEN, BENT, publishing executive; b. Ollerup, Denmark, Mar. 27, 1934; s. Rask and Vilna (Aalbaek) Nielsen; m. Bodil Vejby, June 4, 1958; children: Lars, Nanna. Cert., State Tng. Coll., Jelling, Denmark, 1955. Tchr. Secondary Sch., Oure, Denmark, 1955-83; mgr. Aerospace Publs., Gudme, Denmark, 1983—. Editor: Propel, 1970—; author, editor (aerospace yearbook) Luft- og Rumfartsårbogen, 1982—. Capt. Royal Danish Air Force Home Guard, 1978-90. Dubbed Knight of Dannebrog The Queen of Denmark, 1985; recipient Order of Merit The Danish Home Guard, 1987. Mem. Danish Air Force Assn. (hon.). Home and Office: Danish Aerospace Publs, Kastanievj 4, DK-5884 Gudme Denmark

AALL, CHRISTIAN BERGENGREN, software company executive; b. St. Louis, Dec. 7, 1955; s. Christian Hiorth Aall and Ruth (Bergengren) Perkins; m. Esther Drugowitsch, Aug. 5, 1983; children: Christian Daniel, Nathalie Caroline. MME, Swiss Fed. Inst. Tech., Zürich, Switzerland, 1980; MBA, Internat. Mgmt. Devel. Inst., Lausanne, Switzerland, 1987. Project mgr. Cementos Apasco S.A., Apasco, Mex., 1981-82; cons. Holderbank (Switzerland) Mgmt. & Cons. Ltd., 1982-86; mgr. systems and strategic planning GM Europe Parts and Accessories, Zürich, 1988-91; comptr. GM Europe Parts & Accessories, Ruesselsheim, Germany, 1991-92; comptr. sales Adam Opel AG, Ruesselsheim, Germany, 1992-95; mng. dir. Opel Master Lease GmbH, Ruesselsheim, Germany, 1996-98; pres. Daidalos Cons., Wellesley, Mass., 1998—; dir. internat. ops. Daidalos Unternehmensberatung GmbH, Wolfratshausen, Germany, 1998—. Bd. trustees Frankfurt Internat. Sch., 1995-97, chmn. bldgs. and grounds com., treas., chmn. fin. com. 1997-98; treas. IMD Alumni Deutschland e.V., 1995-99. Office: Daidalos Cons PO Box 81058 Wellesley MA 02481-0001

AANDERAA, STÅL OLAV, retired mathematics educator; b. Beitstad, Trondelag, Norway, Feb. 1, 1931; s. Johannes and Margrete (Refsdal) A.; m. Kari Lien, Dec. 28, 1960; children: Gjøa Krintine, Olav Stål, Anne Kari, Birgit, Sigurd Johan. MS, U. Oslo, 1959; PhD, Harvard U., 1967. Tchg. asst. U. Oslo, 1959-68, univ. lectr. math., 1966-78, prof., 1978-96; ret., 1999; rsch. asst. Harvard U., Cambridge, Mass., 1963-66; guest investigator Rockefeller U., N.Y.C., 1970; prof., rsch. fellow Norges Forskningsråd, Oslo, 1996-99; guest sppkr. Nordic Math. Congress, 1984, Math. Scis. Rsch. Inst., Berkeley, Calif., 1989. Contbr. articles to sci. jours., including Bull. Am. Math. Soc., Jour. Assn. Computer Machinery, Trans. Am. Math. Soc., Jour. Symbolic Logic, Arch. Math. Logik, chpts. to books. Rsch. fellow IBM Thomas J. Watson Rsch. Ctr., Yorktown Heights, N.Y., 1972-73. Home: Sørbråtveien 27, N-0891 Oslo Norway Office: U Oslo Dept Math, PO Box 1053, Blindern, N-0316 Oslo Norway

AANENSON, ERIC EVAN, food products executive; b. Mpls., Feb. 2, 1944; S. Vernon Oliver and Margaret (Holk) A.; m. Marjorie Alice Carter, June 24, 1963 (div. 1974); children: Chad Eric, Marc Quentin; m. Donna Faye Pulliam, Feb. 13, 1981. B in Physics, U. Minn., 1967; MBA, U. Santa Clara, 1970. Exptl. engr. Lockheed Missile and Space Co., Sunnyvale, Calif., 1967-69; sr. ops. analyst Liquid Air, Inc., San Francisco, Calif., 1970-74; v.p. Old Dutch Foods, Inc., St. Paul, Winnipeg (Can.), 19745; dir. Enterprise Investments, St. Paul, 19865; cons. Warrior Distbg. (Zubaz), St.Paul, 19885. Named All Am. in trapshooting Sports Afield mag., 1961. Mem. Potato Chip Snack Food Assn. (chmn. tech. com. 1978-80), Can. Potato Chip Snack Food Assn. (pres. 1977-79, 81), Touchdown Club U. Minn. (dir.), Ferrari Club Am. Republican. Avocations: tennis, classical piano, photography. Office: Old Dutch Foods 2375 Terminal Rd Saint Paul MN 55113-2577

AARESTAD, JAMES HARRISON, retired educational administrator, army officer; b. Mpls., Dec. 3, 1924; s. Selmer Emil and Myrthel Perline (Olson) A.; m. Mary-Jo Finn, Oct. 20, 1951; 1 child, Elizabeth Boe. BA, U. Minn., 1949; MA, Georgetown U., 1959; postgrad., Commd. and Gen. Staff Coll., Ft. Leavenworth, Kans., 1960-61, Nat. War Coll., Washington, 1970-71. Commd. 2d lt. U.S. Army, 1949, advanced through grades to col., 1970; comdr. 2d Squadron, 11th Cav., U.S. Army, Vietnam, 1969; dir. strategy and policy War Plans Div., Washington, 1970; chief staff Hdqrs. 1st Armored Div., Fed. Republic Germany, 1971-72; comdr. 2d Brigade, 3d Armored Div., Fed. Republic Germany, 1972-74; dir. nat. security seminar Army War Coll., Carlisle Barracks, Pa., 1974-76; ret., 1976; dep. dir. indsl. devel. N.C. Dept. Commerce, Raleigh, 1976-79; sec., bus. mgr. Dover (Pa.) Area Sch. Dist., 1979-92; ret., 1992; sr. strategy cons. Ketron Corp., Malvern, Pa., 1980—. Bd. dirs., vice chmn. York County Econ. Devel. Corp., 1980-84, chmn. bd., 1986-88, treas., 1988-96, dir. emeritus, 1997—; chmn. mgmt. com. CYPER Ctr., York, 1990-97; bd. dirs., mem. exec. com. Better York, 1989-97; charter mem. Mil. Heritage Found., 1999; bd. dirs. Susquehanna Conf.; vet. WWII, Korea, Vietnam wars. Decorated Silver Star, Legion of Merit with 3 oak leaf clusters, DFC, Bronze Star, Air medal with 9 oak leaf clusters, Presdl. Unit Citation; recipient cert. of appreciation Gov. State of N.C., 1976, 79, resolution of appreciation York County Indsl. Devel. Corp., 1988. Mem. Nat. Assn. Sch. Bus. Ofcls. (registered sch. bus. adminstr.), Pa. Assn. Sch. Bus. Ofcls. (regional pres. 1982-83, citation 1986), Ends of Earth Club (N.Y.C.), Cavalry and Guards Club (London), Army-Navy Country Club (Arlington, Va.), Officers of the First Divsn. 11th Cavalry Vets. of Vietnam and Cambodia, U.S. Cavalry Assn., Rotary, Sigma Alpha Epsilon. Republican. Episcopalian. Avocations: golf, gardening, military history, travel. Home: 1200 Stratford Dr Carlisle PA 17013-3543 Office: York County Econ Devel Corp 160 Roosevelt Ave Ste 300 York PA 17404-3333

AARI, JAMILUDDIN, writer; b. Delhi, India, Jan. 1, 1926; came to Pakistan, Aug. 1947.; s. Amiruddin and Jamira (Begum) A.; m. Tayyaba Bano, Jan. 19, 1920; children: Huhaira, Zulqarnain, Jamir, Nasuruddui, Rabia, Manad Jewf. BA, Dehli U., 1944; LLB, Karachi U., 1976. Inspector internal revenue Govt. Pakistan, 1952-66; sec. Nat. Press Trust of Pakistan, 1964-66; head corp. planning divsn. Nat. Bank Pakistan, 1967-88; senator Pakistan Senate, 1997—. Author: (book) Destination Beyond Destination. Recipient Hilal-E-Imtiaz in Literature, Govt. of Pakistan, 1998. Avocation: reading, writing. Home: Fl 14 Bloch, 602 A Bon Vista Apts, 75600 Karachi Pakistan Office: Senate of Pakistan, Parliament House, Islamgliau Pakistan

AARINOLA, PETER KOFOWOROLA, chemical engineer, researcher; b. Ilora, Oyo, Nigeria, Jan. 4, 1963; s. Iyanda Olawale and Wuraola Aduni (Adeniran) A.; m. Inna Yurievna Balakireva, Sept. 20, 1994; 1 child, Jesse Olufemi. MSc, grad. cert. tchg. Russian, Mendeleev Inst. Chem. Tech., Moscow, 1990, PhD, diploma of rschr., 1995. Cert. profl. engr.; cert. adult edn. tchr. Engring. trainee AZLK (Moskvich) Autoconstrn. Co., Moscow, 1989; chem. engr. Nigerian Nat. Petroleum Corp., Lagos, Nigeria, 1990-91; jr. rsch. fellow Mendeleev U., Moscow, 1991-95; prin. rschr., project mgr. MP ECOMED Engring. Ltd., Moscow, 1996—; lab. asst. Mendeleev Inst., Moscow, 1987-90; tech. sales mgr. SKIF Internat. Ltd., Moscow, 1992-93; cons., rsch. engr. TEP-MHTI Ltd., Moscow, 1992-96; tech. cons. Aquastel Advanced Tech. Unit Ltd., Edinburgh, Scotland, 1997—. Transl.: Electroplating & Surface Treatment; patentee in field. V.p. Nigerian Students' Union, Moscow, 1988-89; students' leader Fgn. Students' Union, Mendeleev U., Moscow, 1987; presiding officer Fed. Elec. Commn., Nigeria, 1983; pres. Royal Amb., Nigeria, 1978, 81. Undergrad. scholar Nigerian Fed. Govt., 1983-90, grad. scholar, 1991-95; postdoctoral fellow Mendeleev U. Chem. Tech., 1997. Avocations: outdoor sports, traveling, environmental protection, music, community development services. E-mail: kofo.aarinola@excite.com. Home: Block 1 Apt 36, Dokukina St House 9, 129226 Moscow I-226, Russia Office: MP ECOMED Engring Ltd, Selscokhoziastvennaya 12-3, 129226 Moscow Russia

AARKROG, ASKER, radioecologist, researcher; b. Aarhus, Denmark, Jan. 5, 1932; s. Asker Jens Peder and Ketty (Vinderslev) A.; m. Tove Bryrup, Aug. 9, 1957; children: Vibe, Peter Asker. MSc, Denmarks Tech. Univ., 1955; DSc, Univ. Copenhagen, 1981. Scientist Risoe Nat. Lab., Roskilde, Denmark, 1957-61; deputy head of dept. Riso Nat. Lab., Roskilde, Denmark, 1961-93, head of program, 1961-99; ret. Contbr. articles to profl. jours. With Royal Danish Air Force, 1956-57. Recipient N.V. Timofeev-Ressovsky medal Russian Acad. Medical Sci., 1996. Mem. Internat. Union of Radioecologist (pres. 1986-90), Nordic Soc. Radiation Protection (pres. 1996-99). Avocations: ornithology, modern art. Home: Mosehojvej 10A, DK 2920 Charlottenlund Denmark Office: Riso Nat Lab, NUK 114 PO Box 49, DK 4000 Roskilde Denmark

AARON, BENJAMIN, law educator, arbitrator; b. Chgo., Sept. 2, 1915; s. Henry Jacob and Rose (Weinstein) A.; m. Eleanor Opsahl, May 24, 1941; children: Judith, Louise. A.B., U. Mich., 1937; LL.B., Harvard U., 1940; postgrad., U. Chgo., 1940-41. With Nat. War Labor Bd., 1942-45; mem. labor adv. com. to Supreme Comdr. Allied Powers, Tokyo, 1946; research assoc. Inst. Indsl. Relations; lectr. labor law, dept. econs. UCLA, 1946-51, assoc. dir., 1957-60, dir., 1960-75, prof. law, 1960-86, prof. emeritus, 1986—; faculty mem. Salzburg (Austria) Seminar in Am. Studies, 1958, 67; arbitrator labor-mgmt. disputes, 1946—; pub. mem. WSB, Washington, 1951-52; mem. Statutory Arbitration Bd. in R.R. Dispute, 1963-64; chmn. Calif. Farm Labor Panel, 1965-66; mem. Nat. Commn. on Tech., Automation and Economic Progress, 1965-66; pub. mem. Adv. Council on Employee Welfare and Pension Benefit Plans, 1966-68; vis. prof. Harvard U., 1972, U. Mich., 1979; mem. pub. rev. bd. U.A.W., 1975—; mem. arbitration services adv. com. Fed. Mediation and Conciliation Service, 1974-82; mem. ILO Com. of Experts on Application of Convs. and Recommendations, 1986-94; charter emeritus fellow Coll. of Labor and Employment Lawyers, 1996—. Author: Legal Status of Employee Benefit Rights Under Private Pension Plans, 1961; Editor: The Employment Relation and The Law, 1957, Labor Courts and Grievance Settlement in Western Europe, 1970, Comparative Labor Law jour, 1979-85; co-editor: Industrial Conflict: A Comparative Legal Survey, 1972; Public-Sector Bargaining, 1979; editorial bd., Internat. Labor Law Reps., 1974—. Fellow Center for Advanced Study in Behavioral Sciences, 1966-67; vis. fellow Clare Hall, Cambridge (Eng.) U., 1973, Australian Nat. U.; named First Southwestern Legal Found. Research Fellows' Disting. Scholar in Residence, 1971; first Howard W. Wissner Meml. Lectr. Tulane U., 1971; Phi Beta Kappa vis. scholar, 1978-79. Mem. ABA (sec. sect. labor rels. law 1975-76), AAUP, Internat. Soc. Labor Law and Social Security (chmn. U.S. nat. com., internat. exec. com. 1967-83, v.p. N.Am. region 1982-85, pres. 1985-88, hon. pres. 1988—), Nat. Acad. Arbitrators (pres. 1962, bd. govs.), Indsl. Rels. Rsch. Assn. (exec. bd. 1965-68, pres. 1972, mem. CCH labor law reports panel of experts 1987-92), Am. Arbitration Assn. (mem. adv. coun. L.A. 1975-76, Disting. Svc. award 1981). Home: 316 18th St Santa Monica CA 90402-2406 Office: UCLA 405 Hilgard Ave Los Angeles CA 90095-9000

AARON, FRANCISC DIONISIE, physicist; b. Cluj-Napoca, Romania, May 10, 1953; s. Francisc and Ana (Mucea) A.; m. Simona Maria Gaicu, Aug. 29, 1981; children: Andrei, Mihai. BSc, U. Bucharest, 1975, MSc, 1977, PhD, 1992. Physicist Inst. Physics & Radiation Devices, Bucharest, Romania, 1978-82; from asst. prof. to assoc. prof. U. Bucharest, 1982—. Mem. Optical Soc. Am., N.Y. Acad. Sci., Jockey Club. Roman Catholic. Avocations: history, tourism, yoga.

AARON, JEAN-JACQUES, chemist, educator; b. Fontainebleau, France, Oct. 25, 1939; s. Michel and Marie (Deloustal) A.; m. Paulette Chabriere, Dec. 7, 1961; children: Hélène, Emmanuel. Licence es Sciences, Faculty Sci., Paris, 1961; Doctorate, Faculty Scis., Paris, 1965, Doctorat d'Etat, 1968. Asst., then asst. prof. Faculty Sci., Paris, 1962-70; postdoctoral fellow U. Fla., Gainesville, 1971-72; sci. attaché French Gen. Consulate, Houston, 1972-75; prof. U. Dakar, Senegal, 1976-85; prof. chemistry U. Paris 7 and Marne la Vallée, 1985—. Contbr. chpts. to books, articles to sci. jours. Grantee NATO, Brussels, 1971, 87-93. Mem. Am. Chem. Soc., French Soc. Chemistry, European Photochemistry Assn. Achievements include patent on protection of metals against corrosion, development of new analytical methods for determination of traces of pollutants and drugs; new technique for monitoring electropolymerization on solid surfaces. Home: 44 Elysée 2, 78170 La Celle St Cloud France Office: Itodys Univ Paris 7, 1 Rue Guy de la Brosse, 75005 Paris France

AARONS, STEPHEN D., lawyer; b. St. Louis, Nov. 23, 1954; s. Donale E. and Teddye W. Costello; m. Doris A. Valdez, Apr. 12, 1993; 1 child, Ian. BA, George Washington U., 1976; MA, Oxford (Eng.) U., 1984; JD, St. Louis U., 1979. Bar: N.Mex., U.S. Supreme Ct. VISTA lawyer Mont. Legal Svcs., Gt. Falls, 1979-80; judge advocate U.S. Army Intelligence Command, Augsburg, Germany, 1980-83; chief capital trial def. counsel N.Mex. Pub. Defender Dept., Santa Fe, 1984-89; assoc. Jones, Snead, Wertheim, Santa Fe, 1989-92; mng. atty. Aarons Law Firm, PC, Santa Fe, 1992—; mem. faculty Nat. Inst. Trial Advocacy. Nat. pres. Coll. Dems. of Am., Washington, 1975-77. Lt. col. USAR, 1980—. Office: Aarons Law Firm PC 300 Catron St Santa Fe NM 87501-1807

AARONS-HOLDER, CHARMAINE MICHELE, lawyer; b. Kingston, Jamaica, Jan. 24, 1959; came to U.S., 1982; d. Alan and Berly-Mae Aarons; m. Lisle Anthony Holder, 1982. LLB honors, U. W.I., Barbados, 1980; Cert. Legal Edn., Norman Manley Law Sch., Kingston, 1982; JD cum laude, U. Houston, 1987. Bar: Barbados 1982, Tex. 1987, U.S. Dist. Ct. (so. dist.) Tex. 1988, U.S. Ct. Appeals (5th cir.) 1996. Participating assoc. Fulbright & Jaworski, Houston, 1987-94; atty. Wickliff & Hall, Houston, 1994-99; sr. atty. Equiva Svcs., LLC, Houston, 1999—. Co-editor, co-author: The Texas Environmental Law Handbook, 1989, 2nd edit., 1990, 3rd edit., 1993. Mem. ABA, Tex. Bar Assn., Houston Bar Assn. (chair campaign for homeless com. 1996-97), Houston Young Lawyers Assn. (chair hunger relief com. 1994-95), Order of Coif, Order of Barons. Democrat. Avocations: swimming, sailing. Office: Equiva Svcs LLC 910 Louisiana St Houston TX 77002-4916

AARONSON, DAVID ERNEST, law educator, lawyer; b. Washington, Sept. 19, 1940; s. Edward Allan and May (Rosett) A.; m. Laura Dine, 1991; stepchildren: Dara Prushansky, Jared Prushansky. B.A. in Econs, George Washington U., 1961, M.A., 1964, Ph.D., 1970; LL.B., Harvard U., 1964; LL.M. (E. Barrett Prettyman fellow), Georgetown U., 1965. Bar: D.C. bar 1965, Md. bar 1975, U.S. Supreme Ct. bar 1969. Research asst. Office of Commr., Bur. Labor Stats., U.S. Dept. Labor, Washington, 1961; staff atty. legal intern program Georgetown Grad. Law Center, Washington, 1964-65; research assoc. patent research project dept. econs. George Washington U., Washington, 1966; assoc. firm Aaronson and Aaronson, Washington, 1965-67; ptnr. Aaronson and Aaronson, 1967-70; prof., B.J. Tennery Scholar Am. U. Law Sch., Washington, 1970—; prof. Sch. Justice, Coll. Public and Internat. Affairs, 1981-92; dep. dir. Law and Policy Inst., Jerusalem, Israel, summer, 1978; interim dir. clin. programs Md. Criminal Justice Clinic, 1971-73, founder prosecutor criminal litigation clinic, 1972, co-dir. trial practice litigation program, 1982—; vis. prof. Law Sch. of Hebrew U., Jerusalem, summer, 1978; trustee Montgomery-Prince George's Continuing Legal Edn. Inst., 1983—. Author: Maryland Criminal Jury Instructions and Commentary, 1975, (with N.N. Kittrie and D. Saari) Alternatives to Conventional Criminal Adjudication: Guidebook for Planners and Practitioners, 1977, (with B. Hoff, P. Jaszi, N.N. Kittrie and D. Saari) The New Justice: Alternatives to Conventional Criminal Adjudication, 1977, (with C.T. Dienes and M.C. Musheno) Decriminalization of Public Drunkenness: Tracing the Implementation of a Public Policy, 1981, Public Policy and Police Discretion: Processes of Decriminalization, 1984, (with R. Simon) The Insanity Defense: A Critical Assessment of Law and Policy in the Post-Hinckley Era, 1988, Maryland Criminal Jury Instructions and Commentary, 2d rev. edit., 1988; contbr. articles to legal and public policy jours. Mem. council Friendship Heights Village Council, 1979. Recipient Outstanding Community Service award, 1980; Outstanding Tchr. award Am. U. Law Sch., 1978, 81, Scholar/Tchr. of the Year award Am. U., 1989; Pauline Ruyle Moore scholar in Pub. Law, 1983. Mem. ABA (mem. criminal justice sect. rules of cr. prof. and evid. com. 1991—), D.C. Bar Assn. (chmn. criminal code rev. com. 1971-73), Md. State Bar Assn. (criminal law sect. coun. 1984—, chairperson 1989-90, Robert C. Heeney award 1999), Assn. Am. Law Schs. (elected to sect. coun., criminal justice sect. 1999—), Montgomery County (Md.) Bar Assn., Soc. for Reform of Criminal Law, Am. Law Inst., Phi Beta Kappa. E-mail: daarons@wcl.american.edu. Office: Am U Law Sch 4801 Massachusetts Ave NW Washington DC 20016-8196

AAS, I. H. MONRAD, researcher; b. Steinkjer, Norway, Oct. 21, 1948. DDS, U. Oslo, 1973, Lic. Odontology, 1979, D in Odontology, 1983. Rschr. U. Oslo, 1976-84, Norwegian Inst. Hosp. Rsch., Trondheim, Norway, 1985-1990, Nordic Sch. Pub. Health, Göteborg, Sweden, 1990-95, The Work Rsch. Inst., Oslo, 1995—. Contbr. articles on health svcs. rsch. to profl. jours. Lt. Norwegian Air Force, 1974-75. Mem. Norwegian Ch. Avocations: jogging, music, theatre. Office: The Work Rsch Inst, Box 8171 Dep, 0034 Oslo Norway

AASERUD, FINN, science historian; b. Fredrikstad, Norway, May 18, 1948; arrived in Denmark, 1989; s. Olaf Andreas Olsen and Ingrid Aaserud; m. Gro Synnoeve Naes, June 10, 1986; children: Andreas, Karen. Cand. Real, U. Oslo, 1976; PhD, Johns Hopkins U., 1984. Assoc. historian Am. Inst. of Physics, N.Y.C., 1985-89; dir. Niels Bohr Archive, Copenhagen, 1989—; cons. Smithsonian Instn., Washington, 1987-88, Am. Inst. Physics,

N.Y.C., 1989—. Author: Redirecting Science, 1990. Rsch. grantee NSF, 1986, 88, Sloan Found., 1986, MacArthur Found., 1988, Am. Coun. of Learned Socs., 1993; By-fellow Churchill Coll., 1996. Mem. Soc. for Social Studies of Sci., Brit. Soc. for History of Sci., History of Sci. Soc., Danish Nat. Com. on History and Philosophy of Sci. (chmn. archives 1990—), European Phys. Soc. (history of physics group). Avocations: music, reading, spending time with family. Office: Niels Bohr Archive, Blegdamsvej 17, DK-2100 Copenhagen Denmark

AASURI, MURALI KRISHNAMACHARY, ophthalmologist; b. Hyderabad, India, Apr. 3, 1965; s. Srinivasa Rangachary and Sulochana Aasuri; m. Agatha Chary, Apr. 17, 1997. B Medicine, B Surgery, Osmania Med. Coll., Hyderabad, 1988; MD in Ophthalmology, All India Inst. Med. Scis., New Delhi, 1992. Diplomate Nat. Bd. Ophthalmology. Sr. resident R.P. Ctr. All India Inst. Med. Scis., New Delhi, 1992-93; fellow L.V. Prasad Eye Inst., Hyderabad, 1994, rsch. ophthalmologist, 1995, faculty mem., 1996—; in charge of Indian contact lens edn. program L.V. Prasad Eye Inst., Hyderabad, 1996-99, in charge of phacoemulsification tng., 1998-99. Author: (book chpt.) Current Opinion in Ophthalmology, 1999; contbr. articles to sci. jours. Eye surgeon Sri Geeta Bhavan Trust, Haryana, 1990, Rotary Club, Uttar Pradesh, 1991. Recipient Best Paper award Asia Pacific Soc. Refractive Surgery, 1998; fellow Internat. Assn. for Contact Lens Educators; travel grantee for Young Investigator's award Bausch & Lomb, 1999. Mem. Internat. Contact Lens Soc. of Ophthalmologists (mem. bylaws com. 1999). Avocations: cricket, carroms, movies, music. Fax: 91-40-3548271. E-mail: mkchary@yahoo.com. Home: 214-B Block, Paragon Venkatadri Apts, Hyderabad 500 027, India Office: L V Prasad Eye Inst, L V Prasad Marg Banjara Hls, Hyderabad 500 034, India

AAVIKSAAR, AAVO, research institute administrator, researcher; b. Türi, Järva, Estonia, Sept. 20, 1941; s. Arthur and Juuli (Lutsius) A.; m. Elme Roomeldi, Dec. 22, 1967; children: Iiris, Tõnis. MA cum laude, Tartu (Estonia) U., 1965, PhD in Chemistry, 1969; DSc in Chemistry, Inst. Chem. Physics, Moscow, 1985. Cert. in chemistry. Rsch. scientist Tartu U., 1965-73; head of biochemistry dept. Inst. Cybernetics, Tallinn, Estonia, 1973-80; head of lab. of bioorganic chemistry Inst. Chem. Physics and Biophysics, Tallinn, Estonia, 1980-91; dir. Inst. Exptl. Biology, Harku at Tallinn, 1991—; tech. cons. Biokungla Ltd., Tallinn, 1990—; sci. coun. Inst. Chemistry, Tallinn, 1991-98. Inventor in field; contbr. articles to profl. jours. Mem. coun. Union Estonian Scientists, Tallinn, 1992—. Mem. Estonian Biochem. Soc. (pres. 1989—), Estonian Chem. Soc. (mem. coun. 1996—). Avocation: medicinal plants. Home: Raja Str 7A-29, 12616 Tallinn Estonia Office: Inst Exptl Biology, Instituudi Tee 11, 76902 Tallinn Estonia

AAVIKSOO, JAAK, former minister of education of Estonia; b. Tartu, Jan. 11, 1954; married; 3 children. Grad., Tartu State U., 1976; PhD in Physics, Estonian Acad. Scis., 1981. Jr., sr., leading rsch. assoc. Inst. Physics, Estonian Acad. Scis., 1976-81; vis. rschr. Novosibirsk Thermophysics Inst., 1981-86; guest prof. Paris U., 1991-93; rsch. prof. Osaka (Japan) U., 1993; prof. optics, spectroscopy U. Tartu, Estonia, 1992-95, 97—; former min. edn. Govt. Estonia. A.V. Humboldt Rsch. fellow, 1987-88. Office: U Tartu, 18 Ulikooli St, Tartu EE 2400, Estonia

ABADIE, JEAN M., mathematician, educator, researcher; b. Mirande, Gers, France, Oct. 19, 1919; s. Maurice C. and Persephone (Theophanides) A.; m. Julia Lalayannis, Aug. 24, 1961; 1 child, Alexandre J. Baccalaureat, Lycee Henry IV, Paris, 1942; Licence, U. Lyon, France, 1947, D.E.A., 1948; Agregation (Math.), U. Paris, 1950. Statistician, Water and Forestry Research Ctr., Nancy, France, 1950-55; head math. group Electricité de France, Paris, 1955-63, sci. adviser, 1963-79; prof. Statis. Inst., U. Paris, 1959-69, prof. U. Paris VI, 1979—, research dir. U. Paris-Dauphine, 1969—; vis. prof. Case Western Res. U., U. Calif.-Berkeley, Stanford U., U. Chgo. Essec, French rep. to spl. com. on systems sci. NATO, Brussels, 1978-83. Editor: Nonlinear Programming, 1967; Integer and Nonlinear Programming, 1970; editor-in-chief RAIRO-Ops. Research Jour., 1970—; assoc. editor various jours.; contbr. articles to sci. jours. and internat. meetings. Inventor GRG Method of Optimization. Decorated Chevalier Ordre des Palmes Académiques. Mem. Math. Programming Soc. (chmn. 1980-83), Inst. Mgmt. Sci. (mem. council 1968-70, 80-82), Internat. Statis. Inst., Societe Mathematique de France, Am. Math. Soc., PEN Club. Home: 29 Blvd Edgar Quinet, 75014 Paris France Office: U Pierre et Marie Curie Paris VI, Dept Computer Sci 4 Place Jussieu, 75005 Paris France

ABÁDI-NAGY, ZOLTÁN, English language educator; b. Abádszalók, Hungary, Nov. 16, 1940; s. Zoltán Nagy and Irén Polyák; m. Katalin Katona, Dec. 12, 1964 (div. 1998); 1 child, Katalin. Degree in English, Kossuth U., Debrecen, Hungary, 1965, Dr.univ., 1970; PhD, Hungarian Acad., Budapest, 1979, DSc, 1993. Cert. English tchr. Instr., mentor Kossuth U., Debrecen, 1965-71, from asst. prof. to assoc. prof., 1971-93, prof., 1993—; Fulbright prof. U. Minn., Mpls., U. Okla., Norman, U. Calif., Irvine, 1987-90; disting. vis. lectr. Tex. Christian U., Ft. Worth, 1998-2000; pres. Kossuth U., Debrecen, 1993-95, dean humanities and social sci., 1992-93, head Inst. of English Am. Studies, 1991-92, chair N.Am. dept., 1991-92, chair English dept., 1990-91; chair Hungarian Fulbright Commn., 1998. Author: (books) Swift, a szatirikus és a tervező, 1973, Válság és komikum: a hatvanas évek amerikai regénye, 1982, Az amerikai minimalista próza, 1994, Mai amerikai regénykalauz, 1995, Világregény-Regényvilág: Amerikai Íróinterjúk, 1997; editor: Hungarian Jour. of English and Am. Studies; mem. editl. bd. Filológiai Közlöny, Modern Nyelvoktatas. Mem. bd. trustees Széchenyi Profs. Fellowship, 1996-98, Ministry of Edn., Budapest, Soros Found. Com. for Higher Edn., Budapest, 1997-98. Recipient Albert Szent-Györgyi prize Ministry of Edn., 1997, Decoration for Excellence, 1985; exch. scholar Brit. Coun., U. Leeds, Eng., 1967-68; ACLS fellow Duke U., 1972-73. Fellow Royal Hist. Soc. (hon.); mem. Hungarian Soc. for Study of English (pres. 1995-99), Hungarian Assn. for Am. Studies (co-pres.), Hungarian Acad. (co-pres. com. for modern philology 1997-99, com. for lit. 1999—). Avocations: music, photography. E-mail: abnagyzo@tigris.klte.hu. Office: Inst English & Am Studies, U Debrecen, 4010 Debrecen Hungary

ABADIR, KARIM MAHER, econometrics and statistics educator; b. Cairo, Jan. 6, 1964; s. Maher and Shahira (Naguib-Mahfouz) A. BA in Econs., Am. U. Cairo, 1985, MA in Econs., 1990; PhD in Econs., Oxford (Eng.) U., 1992. Lectr. econs. Lincoln Coll., Oxford U., 1988-92; rsch. fellow in econs. Am. U. Cairo, 1992-93; sr. lectr. stats. Exeter U., 1993-94, reader econometrics, 1994-96; prof. econometrics and stats., head stats. group U. York, Eng., 1996—; external assessor for recruitments and promotions; econometrics external examiner; external examiner Inst. Math. Stats., Copenhagen, London Sch. Econs., U. Oxford, U. Warwick; dir. Nacita Corp., Forex Corp.; condr. confs. and seminars, 1993—; referee proposals stats. and probability sect., econs. sect., NSF, Econ. and Social Rsch. Coun., Cambridge U. Press, Springer-Verlag, Oxford Univ. Press; organizer, co-founder Econometric Theory Seminars, Exeter, 1994-96; joint organizer Rsch. Workshops, Exeter, 1994-96, Bristol-Exeter Seminars, 1995-96; program com. Econometric Soc. European Meeting, 1995-96; founder Stats. Seminars, York, 1996; dir., co-founder BA, BSc in Econs. and Math., Econs., Econometrics & Fin., MSc in Econometrics and Econs., York. Assoc. editor Rev. Econ. Studies, 1994—, Econometric Theory; joint editor U. Exeter Discussion Papers in Econs., 1994-96; referee Econometric Revs., Econometric Theory, Econometrica, Econ. Jour., Annals of Statistics, Annals of the Inst. Statis. Math., Internat. Econ. Rev., Jour. Applied Econometrics, Jour. Applied Stats., Jour. Bus. and Econ. Stats., IEEE Transactions, Jour. Cultural Econs. Jour. Econometrics, Jour. Royal Statis. Soc. B., Jour. Time Series Analysis, Oxford Bull. Econs. and Stats., Oxford Econ. Papers, Bull. Econ. Rsch., Econometrics Jour., Jour. Econ. Dynamics and Control, Jour. Statis. Computation and Simulation, Rev. Econ. Studies; contbr. articles to profl. jours. V.p. Student Union, 1982-84. Recipient Econometric Theory Multa Scripsit award; Econ. and Social Rsch. Coun. grantee. Mem. Royal Econ. Soc. (founding editor Econometrics Jour.), Econometric Soc., Inst. Math. Stats., Profl. Assn. Diving Instrs. Avocation: diving. Office: U York, U York Dept Math and Econs, Heslington, York Y010 5DD, England

ABADJIEV, VALENTIN IVANOV, engineering educator, researcher; b. Rasgrad, Bulgaria, Sept. 8, 1946; s. Ivan Nikolov and Ludmila Hristova (Triphonova) A.; m. Evdokia Stoyanova, Oct. 10, 1972; 1 child, Emilia. MSME, Tech. U., Rousse, Bulgaria, 1970; PhD in Applied Mechanics, Bulgarian Acad. Scis., Sofia, 1985. Registered mech. engr. Rsch. fellow Inst. Motors and Cars, Sofia, 1972-83; asst. prof. Inst. Mechanics Bulgarian Acad. Scis., Sofia, 1983-88, assoc. prof. Inst. Mechanics, 1988—; bd. dirs. Edn./Sci. Co., Sofia, 1997—. Author: (book) contbr. Freight Containers—Design, Manufacture and Repair, 1978; contbr. numerous articles to sci. publs.; patentee in field. Mem. Regional Mcpl. Coun., Sofia, 1995-99. Recipient nat. medal for inventions State Com. Sci., 1987, 3d Competitive Session Sci. award Ministry of Edn. and Sci., 1997, also numerous rsch. grants. Mem. Nat. Tech. Com. of Standardization (chmn. 1993-98), Bulgarian Acad. Scis. (mem. sci. coun. Inst. Mechanics 1993—, mem. tech. coun. Inst. Mechanics 1989—), High Testimonial Com. (mem. spl. sci. coun. 1998—). Democrat. Avocations: farming, design of farming mechanisms. Office: Inst Mechanics Bulg Acad Sc, Acad G Bonchev Str Bl 4, 1113 Sofia Bulgaria

ABAGNALE, FRANK WILLIAM, JR., document security company executive; b. Apr. 27, 1948; s. Frank William and Paulette Noel (Anton) A.; m. Kelly Anne Welbes, Nov. 6, 1976; children: Scott, Chris, Sean. Cert. spkg. profl. Pres., CEO Abagnale & Assocs., Washington, 1976—, document verification mgr., 1997—; pub. spkr. Author: Catch Me If You Can, 1980; author, pub.: Abagnale Advisor Newsletter, 2000. Republican. Roman Catholic. Home: PO Box 701290 Tulsa OK 74170-1290

ABAH, OGA STEVE, theater educator, researcher; b. Onyuwei, Nigeria, July 15, 1953; s. Abah and Ogba (Ewache) Emaikwu; m. Alache Ametu Ekesi, Apr. 19, 1980. BA with honors, Ahmadu Bello U., Zaria, Nigeria, 1978, MA, 1982; PhD, U. Leeds, U.K., 1987. Grad. asst. Ahmadu Bello U., Zaria, 1979-82, sr. lectr., 1990-93, assoc. prof., 1993—; head drama Ahmadu Bello U., 1988-94, head dept., 1994-96. Author: Performing Life: Case Studies in the Practice of Theatre for Development, 1997; editor: Debates in the Practice of Theatre, 1999; editor Na We jour., 1991. Pres. Nigerian Popular Theatre Alliance, Zaria, 1989—; chairperson Nigerian Participatory Action Rsch. Network, Ibadan, 1994-96; programme coord. Second Chance Orgn. Nigeria, Zaria, 1996—. Fellow Chgo. Humanities Inst.; mem. Nigerian Popular Theatre Alliance (pres. 1989—), African Assn. Theatre for Devel. Avocations: jogging, badminton, saxophone. Office: Ahmadu Bello Univ, PO Box 542 Dept English, Samaru Zaria Nigeria

ABAK, ALI TOYGAR, engineering researcher; b. Istanbul, Turkey, Aug. 15, 1973; s. Feti and Necla A. BS in Electronics and Comm. Engr., Istanbul Tech. U., 1995; MS Elec. and Electronics, Bogazici U., Istanbul, 1998. Researcher TUBITAK (Scientific and Tech. Rsch. Coun. Turkey), Marmara, Kocaeli, 1996—. Contbr. articles to profl. jours. Mem. IEEE (student mem. Computer Soc., Signal Procesing Soc.), SPIE. Avocations: aikido, ta'i chi, Latin dances. Office: TUBITAK-Marmara Rsch Ctr, PK 21 Gebze, Kocaeli 41470, Turkey

ABAKANOWICZ, MAGDALENA, artist, sculptor; b. Falenty nr. Warsaw, Poland, June 20, 1930; d. Konstanty and Helena (Domaszowska) A.; m. Jan Kosmowski, Sept. 22, 1956. Grad., Warsaw Acad. Fine Arts, 1954; Dr. (hon.), Royal Coll. Art, London, 1974, R.I. Sch. Design, 1992, Acad. of Fine Arts, Lódz, Poland, 1998, Pratt Inst., N.Y.C., 2000. Prof. Acad. Fine Art, Poznan, Poland, 1965, 1979. Works include monumental space forms of woven fibres, cycles of figurative sculptures of burlap, wood, metals, stone and clay drawings, paintings; exhibited in one-woman shows at Kunsthaus Zurich, 1968, Nationalmuseum Stockholm, 1970, Pasadena (Calif.) Art Mus., 1971, Dusseldorf Kunsthalle, 1972, Whitechapel Art Gallery, London, 1975, Nat. Gallery of Victoria, Melbourne, 1976, Muzeum Sztuki, Lodz, Poland, 1978, Musee d'art Modern de la Ville de Paris, 1982; Mus. of Contemporary Art, Chgo., 1982, Musee d'Art Contemporain, Montreal, 1983, Portland Art Mus. (Oreg.), 1984, Dallas Mus. Fine Arts, 1984, Xavier Fourcade Gallery, N.Y.C., 1985, Turske & Turske Gallery, Zürich, Mücsarnok Palace, Budapest, 1988, Städel Kunstinstitut, Frankfurt, 1989, Marlborough Gallery, N.Y.C., 1989, Sezon Mus., Tokyo, 1991, Mus. Modern Art, Shiga, 1991, Art Tower, Mito, 1991, Hiroshima Art Mus., 1991, Walker Art Ctr., Mpls., 1992, Inst. Contemporary Art P.S. 1 Mus., N.Y., 1993, BWH Kraków, 1993, Hiroshima City Mus. Contemporary Art, 1993, Kordegarda, Warsaw, 1994, Muzeum Sztuki Łódź, 1994, Marlborough Gallery, Madrid, 1994, Fundacio Mira a Mallorca, 1994, Ctr. Polish Sculpture, Oronsko, 1995, Yorkshire Sculpture Park, 1995, Manchester City Art Galleries, 1995, Ujazdowski Castle, Warsaw, 1995, Galerie Marwan Hoss, Paris, 1996, Charlottenborg Exhbn. Hall, Copenhagen, 1996, Oriel Mostyn, Wales, 1996, Doris Freedman Plaza, N.Y., Marlborough Gallery, N.Y., 1997, Galerie Marvan Moss, Paris, 1997, Gallery Starmach, Krakow, 1998, Met. Mus. Art, N.Y., 1999, Jardins du Palais Royal, Paris, 1999; exhibited in group shows Internat. Biennale de Tapisserie, Lausanne, 1962-79, Internat. Biennale of Art, Sao Paulo, 1965, 79, Venice Biennale, 1968, 80, ROSC, Dublin, 1980, Nat. Gallery, Berlin, 1983, ARS '83, Helsinki, 1983, Mus. Moderner Kunst Vienne, 1984, Nürnberg Triennale of Drawing, 1985, Sydney Biennale of Art, 1986, Olympic Pk., Seoul, 1988, Mus. Modern Art, N.Y.C., 1987, County Mus., 1987, Hirshorn Mus., Washington, 1988, Museu Nacional de Belas Artes, Rio de Janeiro, 1992, Fuji San Kei Biennial, Japan, 1993, Europa-Europa, Bonn, Germany, 1994, Muzeum Narodove, Warsaw, 1994, Centro Galego De Arte Contemporanea Santiago De Compostela, 1994, Royal Festival Hall, London, 1995, Mus. Ludwig, Cologne, 1995, Les Champs Elysees, Paris, 1996; A Century of Sculpture, The Nasher's Collection, Guggenheim Mus., New York, 1997, opening exhibition Guggenheim Mus., Bilbao, 1997-98, Sculpture Park, Cologne, 1997, Musee D'Art Moderne De La Ville de Paris, 1997, Arco Madrid, 1998, Nat. Gallery Jeu de Paume, Paris, 2000; represented in collections Muzeum Sztuki Lodz, Mus. Modern Art, N.Y.C., Mus. Modern Art, Kyoto, Japan, Stedelijk Mus., Amsterdam, Australian Nat. Collection, Canberra, Centre Georges Pompidou, Paris, Mus. Contemporary Art, Chgo., Nat. Mus., Stockholm, Met. Mus., N.Y.C., L.A. County Mus., Israel Mus., Jerusalem, Mus. Moderner Kunst, Vienna, Spazzi d'Arte, Italy, Va. Mus. Fine Art, Richmond, W. Lehmbruck Mus., Duisburg, Storm King Art Ctr., N.Y., Mus. Ludwig, Köln, Germany, Hess Collection, Napa, Calif., Nasher Collection, Tex., Mus. Nacional Centro fe Arte Reina Sofia, Madrid, Musee D'Art Moderne De La Ville De Paris, Paris, Nelson-Atkins Mus. Art, Mo., Nat. Gallery Art, Washington, others. Mem. Presdl. Coun. for Culture, 1992—. Decorated officier de l'Ordre des Arts et Lettres (France), 1999, Comdr. Cross with Star, Order of Polonia Restituta, 1998; recipient prize 1st class Min. of Culture, Poland, 1965, Gold medal VIII Biennale of Art, Sao Paulo, 1965, Polish State prize Stiftung F.V.S. Hamburg, Vienna, 1979, Alfred Jurzykowski prize, 1982, award for distinction in sculpture, N.Y., 1993, Leonardo da Vinci World award of Arts, 1997, Cavaliere Nell Ordine Al Merito Della Republic Italiana, 2000, Orden Pour le Merite fur Wissenschaften und Kunste Berlin, 2000. Mem. Am. Acad. Arts and Letters (hon.), Polish Assn. Authors. Address: Bzowa 1, 02-708 Warsaw Poland

ABAKUMOV, GEORGY ALEKSANDROVICH, physicist, researcher; b. Shatsk, Russia, Nov. 9, 1933; s. Aleksandr Sergeevich and Aleksandra Aleksandrovna (Sinitsina) A.; m. Zinaida Nikolaevna 'Ievleva, Jan. 5, 1957; 1 child, Evguenia Georgievna Matveeva. MSc in Physics, Moscow State U., 1959, PhD in Physics and Math., 1971, DSc in Physics and Math., 1992. Engr. Radio-Electronics Rsch. Inst., Moscow, 1959-62; jr. scientist L. Ya. Karpov Phys. Chemistry Rsch. Inst., Moscow, 1965-75, sr. scientist, 1975-90, lead scientist, 1990—, mem. sci. coun. for PhD and DSc degree recommendation, 1994—; cons. rschr. Moscow State U., 1968—. Contbr. articles to sci. and profl. jours.; patentee in field of laser technology. Grantee Internat. Sci. Found., 1993, Russian Fundamental Rsch. Found., 1993-95, 96-98. Mem. Mendeleev Russian Chem. Soc., Moscow House of Scientists (book sect. 1979-91). Russian Orthodox. Avocations: books in Russian and foreign langs. E-mail: perov@cc.nifhi.ac.ru. Home: Ul Akad Volgina 13-94, 117485 Moscow Russia Office: Karpov Phys Chem Rsch Inst, Vorontsovo Pole 10, 103064 Moscow Russia

ABAN, JEFFREY DERICK CHRISTOPHER, executive; b. Bridgetown, Barbados, Jan. 11, 1954; s. Gouldan and Sylvia (Lewis) A.; m. Apr. 16, 1989 (div. 1997); 1 child; m. Enid Bissoon. Dir., shareholder Ideal Traders Ltd., St. George, Grenada, 1970-80; with Nat. Importers Ltd., St. George, Grenada, 1980—; dir. A & A Trading Co. St. Pauls, St. Georges, Grenada; mng. dir. Nat. Importers Ltd., St. George's, Grenada, 1980—. Avocations: wrestling, reading. Office: Nat Importers ltd, PO Box 153 Richmond & Hill, Saint Georges Grenada

ABANTE, BIENVENIDO MIRANDO, JR., missionary, pastor; b. Manila, July 15, 1951; s. Bienvenido Oliver Sr. and Priscilla (Mirando) A.; m. Marie Paz Toledo, June 14, 1977; children: Priscilla Marie, Rita Antonia, Benny Fog III. BS, Far Eastern U., Manila, 1971; grad. in Theology, Bapt. Bible Coll., Makati, The Philippines, 1973; BS in Theology, Citadel Bapt. Coll., 1985; M in Govt. Mgmt., Pamantasan Ng Lungsod, Manila, 1996; M in Theology (hon.), Citadel Bapt. Coll., 1985; D of Theology (hon.), Indpls. Bapt. Coll., 1987. Collector E.S. Baltao & Co., Manila, 1969-70; office auditor E.S. Balboo & Co., Manila, 1970-77; youth leader Bapt. Youth Impact, Manila, 1970-75; pastor, missionary Met. Bible Bapt. Ch., Manila, 1975—; pres. Met. Lighthouse Theol. Sch. and Inst., Quezon City, The Philippines, 1985—; adminstr. Met. Internat. Christian Acad., Manila, 1985—; city councilor City of Manila, 1992-95; commr. Presdl. Commn. for Urban Poor, Manila, 1996-98; spl. asst. to nat. chmn. Nat. Union of Christian Dems., Philippines, 2000—; founder/pres. Bible Believers League for Morality and Democracy, Manila, 1986—, Christian Profls. Evangelism Fellowship, Manila, 1980—; founder, CEO Bapt. Internat. Lighthouse Relief and Rescue Mission, Inc., Manila, 1991—. City councilor manila City Coun., 1992-95; founder/pres. Movement Against Jueteng, Jai-Alai & Lotto, Manila, 1992—. Recipient Keeper of the Faith award Bapt. Bible Fellowship of The Philippines, 1993, Tower of Excellence award Manila TV and Radio, 1994, Outstanding Councilor Manila, Manila Hall Press Club, 1994. Avocations: chess, reading and writing, singing and choir directing, basketball, swimming. Office: Met Bible Bapt Ch, 2330 Revellin St Sta Ana, Manila 1009, The Philippines

ABASAEED, AHMED ELHAG, science educator; b. Gabait, Sudan, June 28, 1954; arrived in Saudi Arabia, 1989; s. Abasaeed Elhag Elfaki and Fatima Ibrahim Elkhawad; m. Naima Mohamed Khier, May 30, 1981; children: Abasaeed, Iman, Inas, Ahad. BS with honors, U. Khartoum, Sudan, 1978; MS, U. Fla., 1982; PhD, Auburn U., 1987. From rsch. asst. to sr. rsch. asst. Energy Rsch. Inst., Khartoum, 1978-83, from rschr. to sr. rschr., 1983-90, assoc. rsch. prof., 1990-94; from asst. prof. to assoc. prof. King Saud U., Riyadh, Saudi Arabia, 1990-99, prof., 1999—; project leader Nat. Energy Adminstrn., Khartoum, 1987-89; cons. Almajd Factory, Riyadh, 1999. Contbr. numerous rsch. papers to profl. jours. Avocations: football, movies, sightseeing, walking. Fax: 966-1-470-1338. E-mail: abasaeed@ksu.edu.sa. Office: King Saud U, PO Box 800 Chem Eng Dept, Riyadh 11421, Saudi Arabia

ABAYA, EFREN FLORES, engineering educator, telecommunication consultant; b. Manila, Philippines, Oct. 29, 1955; s. Bonifacio Acosta and Virginia (Flores) A.; m. Jane Gerardo, Jan. 11, 1997. BS in Elec. Engring. summa cum laude, U. Philippines, 1977; MS in Engring., U. Tex., 1980, PhD in Elec. Engring., 1982. Registered engr., Philippines. Prof. elec. engring. U. Philippines, Quezon City, 1977—, chmn. dept. elec. engring., 1986-89; cons. Computer Info. Sys., Metro Manila, 1983-97; comms. officer Comprehensive Nuclear Test Ban Treaty Orgn., 1998—; exch. scientist Tokyo Inst. Tech., 1984, 95. Editor-in-chief The Elec. Engr. Mag., Philippines, 1984, 92-94; contbr. chpt. to book, articles to profl. jours. Trustee Philippine Sci. H.S. Found., 1988, 97; chmn. scholarship com. NEC Found., Inc., Philippines, 1987-97; mem. continuing profl. edn. coun. Profl. Regulations Commn., 1995-97; chmn. tech. com. on elec. engring. Commn. on Higher Edn., Philippines, 1996-97. Named Outstanding Young Scientist, Nat. Acad. Sci. and Tech. Philippines, 1989; UNDP-UNESCO fellow, 1979-82. Mem. IEEE (chmn. Philippine sect. 1994-95, Inst. Integrated Elec. Engrs. Philippines (sr. mem.; v.p. 1988-90), Philippine Nat. Sci. Soc. (info. tech. sect.). Roman Catholic. Avocation: reading. Home: Loessweg 4/26/16, 1220 Vienna Austria Office: Comprehensive Nuclear Test Ban Treaty Orgn, Vienna International Centre, Vienna 1220, Austria

ABAZA, MOHAMED HILMY, physician, consultant, researcher; b. Desouk, K. Sheikh, Egypt, Dec. 11, 1933; s. Hafez Ismail and Salma Mohamed (Gharini) A.; m. Nagwa Hassan Negm, Aug. 11, 1968 (dec. Aug. 1983); children: Amr, Ghada, Tarek; m. Sanaa Anwar Sorour, June 28, 1988; 1 child, Mohammed. MB ChB, U. Alexandria, 1959, diploma in tropical medicine, 1961, diploma in medicine, 1962, MD, 1967. House officer Alexandria U. Hosps., 1959-60, resident, 1960-62; clin. demonstrator faculty of medicine Alexandria U., 1962-67, lectr. faculty of medicine, 1967-72, asst. prof., 1972-77, prof., 1977—; head dept. tropical medicine, Faculty of Medicine, Alexandria U., 1980-94; head Diabetes Ctr., Tripoli, Libya, 1973-75; cons. internal medicine Tripoli Ctrl. Hosp., Libya, 1973; vis. prof. Strathclayde U., Glasco, U.K., 1989-90. Author: Common Endemic Diseases, 1980, Immunology of Schistosomiasis, 1998, Handbuch der Inneren Erkrankungen Band 5, 1983, (with others) Hepatology, 1996. Recipient Medal Gen. Syndicate, 1993, U. Alexandria, 1992, Pan Arab Congress of Hepatology. Fellow Royal Soc. of Tropical Medicine; mem. Egyptian Soc. of Hepatology (pres.), Egyptian Soc. of Hepatology and Infectious Diseases (v.p.), Egyptian Soc. of Hepatology, Rotary Club, Soc. of the Disabled (v.p.), Sporting Club. Avocations: reading, squash, football, swimming. Home: 600 Horeya St Zizinia, Alexandria Egypt Office: 5 Abdel Hamid Badawi St, Ramleh Station, Alexandria Egypt

ABAZA, MOHAMED MAHER, Egyptian government official; b. Sharkia, Egypt, Mar. 12, 1930; married; two children. BSc in Elec. Power Engring., Cairo U., 1951. Engr. dept. hydro-electric power Ministry of Pub. Works, 1951-61, sr. engr. Office of Elec. Projects, 1961-64; mgr. dept. elec. network studies Egyptian Gen. Electricity Authority, 1964-66, dir. gen. dept. elec. network projects, 1968-72; dir. gen. dept. elec. network projects Ministry of Electricity, 1966-68; inspector gen. Rural Electrification Authority, 1972-73; mng. dir. studies and projects Egyptian Gen. Electricity Authority, 1973-74; first under-sec. of state Ministry of Electricity and Energy, 1975-80; Min. Electricity and Energy, 1980-99; chmn. Mid. East Oil Tankage & Pipelines Co., Midor Electricity Co.; vice-chmn. Mid. East Oil Refinery Co., East Mediterranean Gas Co., 1999—; bd. dirs. Faculty of Engring., Cairo U., Investment Authority. Mem. Egyptian Soc. Elec. Engrs. Office: MIDOR/MIDTAP, 22 El Badia St, Heliopolis Cairo, Egypt

ABBADO, CLAUDIO, conductor; b. Milan, Italy, June 26, 1933. Hon. degree, Aberdeen, 1986, Ferrara, 1990, Cambridge, 1994. Music dir. Teatro alle Scala Milano, 1968-86, London Symphony Orch., 1979-88, Vienna (Austria) State Opera, 1986-91; generalmusikdirektor City of Vienna, 1987—; artistic dir., prin. condr. Berlin Philharm. Orch., 1989—; founder European Commn. Youth Orch., 1978; founder, artistic dir. Gustav Mahler Jugend Orch., 1988, WIEN MODERN Festival Contemporary Art, 1988, Encounters in Berlin Chamber Music Festival, 1992, Competitions of the Salzburg Easter Festival, 1994; artistic advisor Chamber Orch. of Europe; artistic dir. Easter Festival Salzburg, 1994. Recipient Mozart medal Mozart Gemeinde, Vienna, 1973, Golden Nicolai medal Vienna Philharm. Orch., 1980, Std. Opera award Covent Garden, London, 1989, Gold medal Internat. Mahler Soc., 1985, internat. prizes for recs.; decorated with Gran Croce of the Italian Rep., 1984, French Legion D'Honneur, 1988, Bundesverdienstkreuz, Germany, 1992, Ehrenring der Stadt Wien, 1994, Goldenes Ehrenzeichen Österreich. Office: Berliner Philharm Orch, Matthaikirchstrasse 1, D-10785 Berlin Germany also: care Columbia Artists Man Inc 165 W 57th St New York NY 10019-2201*

ABBAS, ADEL MOHAMMED ALI, microbiology consultant; b. Cairo, Egypt, Nov. 11, 1931; s. Mohammed Ali and Sania Mohammed (El-Bakley) A.; m. Patricia Ann Logan, May 5m 1965; children: Hany, Ehab, Colin Stuart, Martin Patrick. MBCHB, Ain Shams Med. Sch., 1955; MPH, High Inst. Pub. Health, 1961; PhD, Med. Sch., 1965. Lectr. High Inst. Pub. Health, Alexandria, Egypt, 1961-68; sr. registrar Pub. Health Lab. Svcs., Middlesborough, Eng., 1971-72; asst. prof. TATA Faculty Medicine, Egypt, 1968-76; sr. registrar St. Mary's Hosp. London U., 1974-75; microbiologist, cons. Gen. Hosp., Rotherham, Eng., 1975-96; hon. clin. lectr. Sheffield (England) U., 1975-96; clin. dir. lab. medicine Rotherham Gen. Hosp., 1996—, mem. hosp. mgmt., chmn. ethics com., chmn. COSHH and control of infection coms. Author: Principals of Medical Microbiology, 1970, His Throne was on Water, 1996; contbr. articles to profl. jours. Bd. govs. Sheffield U. Recipient Distinction award Pres. Nasar, Egypt, 1961, Distinction & Meritorious award British Govt. Fellow Pathology Soc. Gt. Britain & Ireland, Assn. CLin. Pathologists; mem. British Med. Assn. (chmn.), Assn. Domestic Mgrs. (nat. pres.),. Office: Rotherham Dist Gen Hosp, Moorgate Rd, Rotherham S60 2UD, England

ABBAS, ALI EL-SAYED, oil company executive, researcher; b. Cairo, Heliopolis, Egypt, Sept. 9, 1968; s. El-Sayed Saleh and Raifa Ali (Salama) A. Gen. cert. edn., U. London, 1985; BSc, Ain Shams U., Cairo, 1990; MSc, Stanford Univ., 1998, postgrad., 1998—. Tchg. asst. U. Hamburg, 1990-91; lectr. Ain Shams U., Cairo, 1991-92; operating engr. Schlumberger, Muscat, Oman, 1993-94; rschr., tng. instr. Schlumberger, Dubai, United Arab Emirates, 1994-95; ops. mgr. Schlumberger, Sinai, Egypt, 1995—; cons. Egyptian Army, Cairo, 1991. Author: Electromagnetic Propagation Tools, 1993, Optical Fluid Analysis, 1995 (award 1995). Head students union English Sch., Cairo, 1985. Recipient Ideal Lectr. award Ain Shams U., 1990. Mem. IEEE, Soc. Petroleum Engrs., Stanford Alumni Assn. Avocations: writing poetry, web navigating and publishing, reading. Home: PO Box 15025 Stanford CA 94309-5025 Office: Schlumberger Ltd, 7 A Cornich El Nile Dallah, 11728 Cairo Egypt

ABBAS, HUSAIN, civil engineering educator, consultant, researcher; b. Amroha, India, Sept. 12, 1960; s. Mazahir Husain and Aquela Khatoon Abbas; m. Neelam Naqvi, Oct. 23, 1991 (div. 1999); 1 child, Abid. BS in Civil Engring., Z.H. Coll. Engring. and Tech., Aligarh, India, 1982, MS in Bldg. Engring., 1984; PhD in Structures, U. Roorkee, India, 1993. Lectr. civil engring. Aligarh Muslim U., 1984-93, reader civil engring., 1993-2000, prof. civil engring., 2000—; asst. dir. Ctrl. Water Commn., New Delhi, 1987; expert Mahab Ghodss Consulting Engrs., Tehran, 1995-98. Contbr. articles to profl. jours.; inventor in field. Mem. Amnesty Internat., India, 1995—. Recipient Khosla Rsch. prize, 1996, Khosla award, 1998. Mem. Instn. Engrs. India, Indian Soc. Earthquake Tech., Indian Soc. Wind Engring. Avocations: developing softwares, table tennis, travelling, badminton. Home: 4/1175-F Sir Syed Nagar, Aligarh UP 202002, India Office: Aligarh Muslim Univ, Dept Civil Engring, Aligarh UP 202002, India

ABBAS, KHALED ABDELAZIM, engineering educator, researcher, consultant; b. Moscow, May 13, 1963; s. Abdelazim Abbas Sayed and Somaia Mohamed Moussa Afifi; m. Nadia Mohamed Al-Hussieny Abou Farha, July 19, 1997; 1 child, Reem. Gen. cert. edn., British Coun.-U. London, Cairo, 1979; BSCE, Ain Shams U., Cairo, 1984; postgrad., U. Newcastle-upon-Tyne, Eng., 1987, PhD in Transport Engring. and Ops., 1991. Asst. prof. Nat. Inst. of Transport-Ministry of Transport, Cairo, 1991-97, assoc. prof., 1997—; asst. prof. Egyptian Mil. Coll., Cairo, 1993-94; assoc. prof. Egyptian Traffic Police, Cairo, 1999-2000; cons. UN Econ. Commn. Africa, Addis Ababa, 1994; sr. transport/traffic planner, economist Dar Al-Handasah Cons., 1994-99; transport/traffic expert Tech. Cons. Bur., Cairo, 1998-99, Egyptian Traffic Police, Cairo, 1996-99, Nat. Inst. Transport, Cairo, 1997-99, Transport Rsch Ctr.- Ain Shams U., 1999—. Contbr. articles to profl. jours. including Transp. Rsch., Jour. Transp. Engring., Transp. Revs., others, also papers to confs. Capt. jr. football teams, 1975-81. Recipient Best Group Presentation award Harvard Inst. Internat. Devel., 1996; Fulbright scholar U. Tex., Austin, 1995; Overseas Devel. Adminstrn. fellow Newcastle-upon-Tyne, U.K. Mem. Egyptian Expert Sys. Interest Group, Arab Assn. for Roads, Arab Sci. Assn. Transport, Egyptian Syndicate of Engrs., Instn. Hwys. and Transp. U.K., Chartered Inst. Transport U.K., Orgn. Tchrs. Transport Studies U.K., Sys. Dynamics Soc. U.S., Inst. Transp. Engrs. USA, Fulbright Commn. (com. mem.), Internat. Symposium Automotive Tech. and Automation (com. mem.), Egyptian Hwy Code (com. mem.), Union Soc. U. Newcastle-upon-Tyne (hon. life mem.). Avocations: volleyball, tennis, table-tennis, swimming. Office: Nat Inst Transport Nasr Rd, Nasr City Box 34 Abbassia, Cairo Egypt

ABBASI, GHALEB YOUSEF, engineering educator; b. Arbid, Jordan, Feb. 25, 1958; s. Yousef Suliman and Nawal Saleem Abbasi; m. Rihab Salman; children: Fares, Amira, Nawal, Yousef. BSCE, Cairo U., 1980; MEA, George Washington U., 1984, DSc, 1988. Asst. project engr. Alia Housing Project, Amman, Jordan, 1980-81; project engr. Mitsubishi Corp., Amman, 1981-82; head tech. dept. Cities and Villages Devel. Bank, Amman, 1982-83; instr. George Washington U., Washington, 1986-87, vis. rsch. scholar, 1992; asst. prof. engring. U. Jordan, Amman, 1988—; cons. Internat. Ctr. for Sys. and Mgmt. Sci., Amman, 1989—, Outreach Cons. Project, Amman, 1994—; lectr., trainer Team-Engring. Mgmt. Cons., Amman, 1993—. Author: Basics of Integrated Project Management, 1995, also textbook in field, 1996. Avocations: swimming, walking, squash. Home: PO Box 850797, Amman 11185, Jordan Office: U Jordan, Faculty Engring and Tech, Amman Jordan

ABBE, ELFRIEDE MARTHA, sculptor, graphic artist; b. Washington; d. Cleveland Jr. and Frieda (Dauer) A. Student, Art Inst. Chgo., 1937; B.F.A., Cornell U., 1940; postgrad., Syracuse U., 1947. Author and illustrator: books including The Plants of Virgil's Georgics, 1965; One-woman exhbns. include Carnegie-Mellon U., 1962, 69, Cornell U., 1963, Trinity Coll., Hartford, 1964, Arts Club of Washington, 1972, Cornell Club of N.Y., 1977, Copley Soc. Boston, 1978, Woods-Gerry Gallery, R.I. Sch. Design, 1983; represented in permanent collections Met. Mus. Art., Watson Library, Boston Mus. Fine Arts, Cin. Art Mus., Dumbarton Oaks, Washington, Houghton Library, Harvard U., Hunt Library, Carnegie-Mellon U., N.Y. Pub. Library, Rosenwald Collection Nat. Gallery, Kew Gardens Library, Royal Bot. Garden, Edinburgh, Nat. Library, Canberra, Australia; sculpture placed in Mann Library, Kroch Library and Morrison Hall, Cornell U., McGill U., N.Y. Bot. Gardens, Hunt Library, Pitts., Pres.'s Office, Keene (N.H.) State Coll., Herzog August Bibliothek, Wolfenbüttel, Fed. Republic Germany (bronze bust of founder). Recipient Gold medals Pen and Brush, N.Y.C., 1964, Margaret Sussman Meml. award 1987, Gold medals Nat. Arts Club, 1970, Gold medals Acad. Artists Assn., Springfield, Mass., 1976, Founders' Prize Pen and Brush, 1977; Bd. Dirs. award Salmagundi Club N.Y., 1978; Elliot Liskin award, 1979, Catherine Lorillard Wolfe Club award, 1993. Fellow Nat. Sculpture Soc. (Barrett-Colea prize 1984); mem. Nat. Soc. Mural Painters, Phi Kappa Phi.

ABBEY, KAREN DIANE, clothing company executive; b. Falmouth, Mass., Nov. 23, 1965; d. Chetwynd Arnold and Joyce Cecelia (Wordell) A. BS in Computer Math., Keene (N.H.) State Coll., 1987; MBA, Plymouth (N.H.) State Coll., 1994. Applications programmer MARKEM Corp., Keene, N.H., 1987-88; programmer Brookstone, Peterborough, N.H., 1989-90; sr. programmer analyst Holstein Assn. USA, Brattleboro, Vt., 1990-95; project mgr. L.L. Bean Inc., Freeport, Maine, 1995—; Registered Maine guide. Mem. fin. com. Cheshire Housing Trust, Keene, 1991-93; mem. steering com. New Eng. Christian Singles, Lexington, Mass., 1995-99; treas. Maine St. Bapt. Ch., 1998—. Mem. Appalachian Trail Club (membership com. 1997—). Evangelical Christian. Avocations: bible study, sea kayaking, biking, hiking. Home: 77 Hildreth Rd Harpswell ME 04079-2828 Office: LL Bean Inc Taylor Bldg Freeport ME 04033-0001

ABBOTT, BEVERLY STUBBLEFIELD, artist; b. Greensboro, N.C., Dec. 12, 1940; d. Robert L. and Helen W. Stubblefield; m. Ira H.A. Abbott, May 7, 1960; children: Ira Robert, Leslie Ann. Represented by Gallery Jamel, Waldorf, Md., Blue Skies Gallery, Hampton, Va., Gray Wolf Gallery, Woodbridge, Va., Rappahannock Hang-Ups, Kilmarnock, Va., Seaside Art Gallery, Nags Head, N.C. Exhibited in group shows at Leigh Yawkey Woodson Art Mus., 1996, 97, Seaside Art Gallery Internat. Art Show, 1996, 97, 98, 99, Village Gallery Internat. Show, 1997, 98, 99, 2000, Germantown Gallery, 1999, Fla. Wildlife Art Expo, 1999, 2000. Mem. Hampton Arts League (Merit award 1997), Atlantic Wildfowl Heritage Mus. (Appreciation award 1990), James River Camera Club (pres. 1994), Langley Kennel Club (life, show chmn. 1977, 84). Avocations: traveling, photography. Home: 13 Delta Cir Newport News VA 23601-3117

ABBOTT, CHARLES FAVOUR, lawyer; b. Sedro-Wolley, Wash., Oct. 12, 1937; s. Charles Favour and Violette Doris Abbott; m. Oranee Harward, Sept. 19, 1958; children: Patricia, Stephen, Nelson, Cynthia, Lisa, Alyson. BA in Econs., U. Wash., 1959, JD, 1962. BAr: Calif. 1962, Utah 1981. Law clk. Judge M. Oliver Koelsch, U.S. Ct. Appeals (9th cir.), San Francisco, 1963; assoc. Jones, Hatfield & Abbott, Escondido, Calif., 1964; pvt. practice Escondido, 1964-77, Provo, Utah, 1983-93; of counsel Mueller & Abbott, Escondido, 1997—; ptnr. Abbott, Thorn & Hill, Provo, 1981-83, Abbott & Abbott, Provo, 1993—. Author: How to Do Your Own Legal Work, 1976, 2d edit., 1981, How to Win in Small Claims Court, 1981, How to Be Free of Debt in 24 Hours, 1981, How to Hire the Best Lawyer at the Lowest Fee, 1981, The Lawyer's Inside Method of Making Money, 1979, The Millionaire Mindset, 1987, How to Make Big Money in the Next 30 Days, 1989, Business Legal Manual and Forms, 1990, How to Make Millions in Marketing, 1990, Telemarketing Training Course, 1990, How to Form A Corporation in Any State, 1990, The Complete Asset Protection Plan, 1990, Personal Injury and the Law, 1997, Fen-Phen Fallout--The Medical and Legal Crisis, 1998; mem. editl. bd. Wash. Law Rev. and State Bar Assn. Jour., 1961-62; bd. editors Phen-fen Litigation Strategist, 1998—; contbr. articles to profl. jours. Mem. ATLA, Utah Bar Assn., Calif. Bar Assn., U.S. Supreme Ct. Bar Assn. Home: 2830 N Marrcrest Circle Provo UT 84058 Office: Abbott & Abbott 3651 N 100 E Ste 300 Provo UT 84604-4521

ABBOTT, JOHN RODGER, electrical engineer; b. L.A., Aug. 2, 1933; s. Carl Raymond and Helen Catherine (Roche) A.; m. Theresa Andrea McQuaide, Apr. 20, 1968. BS with honors, UCLA, 1955; MSEE, U. So. Calif., 1957. Registered profl. engr. Calif.; cert. tchr. Calif. Advanced study engr. Lockheed Missile Systems, L.A., 1955-56; B-58 aircraft doppler radar systems engr. Hughes Aircraft Co., L.A., 1956-59; devel. engr. F-104 aircraft air data computer Garrett Airesearch Co., L.A., 1959-63, instr. in-plant tng. program, 1962-63; asst. project engr. Litton Industries, L.A., 1963; space power systems engr. pioneer 6 TRW Systems, L.A., 1963-65; engr. specialist L.A. Dept. Water and Power, 1965-92, Abtronix, 1992—; frequency coordination chmn. Region X, Utilities Telecommunications Coun., 1977-79, sec.-treas. Utilities Telecommunication Coun., 1979-80; instr. amateur radio course L.A. City Schs., Birmingham High Sch., Van Nuys, Calif., 1965-66, Los Feliz Elem. Sch., Hollywood, Calif., 1990—. Author, pub.: Ride The Airwaves with Alfa & Zulu and DIT & DAH Card and Dice Games; contbr. articles to profl. jours. Mem. IEEE, Am. Radio Relay League (Pub. Svc. award 1971), Tau Beta Pi. Office: Abtronix PO Box 220066 Santa Clarita CA 91322-0066

ABBOTT, PAMELA ANN, sociology educator, academic administrator; b. London, June 27, 1947; d. William Henry and Ida May (Goodman) A.; children: Alasdair, Francesca, Nicole. BSc in Sociology, U. London, 1970; MSc in Sociology, Birkbeck Coll., London, 1975, PhD in Sociology, 1982. Postgrad. cert. in edn. Lectr. U. Brighton, Eng., 1984-85, U. Plymouth, Eng., 1985-92; prof. sociology U. Derby, Eng., 1992-95; dir. social scis. U. Teesside, Middlesbrough, Eng., 1995-2000; vice chancellor Glasgow Caledonian U., 2000—; chair Quality Assurance Agy. for Higher Edn., Sociology Bench Making Group,1 999—; mem. Higher Edn. Funding Coun. Rsch. Assessment Exercise Sociology Panel, 1999—. Author: Research Methods for Nurses and Caring Professions, 1998, An Introduction to Sociology: Feminist Perspectives, 1996, Social Policy for Nurses, 1996, The Family and the New Right, 1992, Women and Social Class, 1987. Fellow Royal Soc. Arts; mem. Brit. Sociol. Assn. (exec. com. 1997—, hon. gen. sec. 1998—). Office: Glasgow Caledonian Univ, Glasgow G4 0BA, Scotland

ABBOTT, RICK JOSEPH, broadcast executive; b. Anaheim, Calif., Oct. 26, 1962; s. Leonard Delman and Maria Carmen A.; m. Angela Renee Abbott, Nov. 15, 1997; children: Grace Elizabeth, Lauren Melissa. BA in Journalism, U. Minn., 1988. Player Milw. Brewers Baseball Club, Milw., 1983-85; prodr. ABC Sports, N.Y.C., 1987-92; prodn. mgr. ValueVison, Eden Prarie, Minn., 1992-95; dir. on-air programming U.S. Satellite Broadcasting, St. Paul, 1995-99; v.p. programming Hubbard Media Group, St. Paul, 1999-2000; sr. v.p. Movie Watch Network, St. Paul, 2000—. Author: Bottom of the Ninth, 1999. Recipient Emmy award NATAS, 1991, Golden Eagle award CINE, 1997, Golden Statue award PROMAX, 1998, 7 Telly awards for promotion, 1996-98. Mem. Assn. Ball Players of Am. Avocations: outdoor activities, reading, sports. E-mail: rabbott@hbi.com. Office: Hubbard Media Group 3415 University Ave W Saint Paul MN 55114-1019

ABBOTT, STEPHEN JOHN, secondary education educator; b. Southsea, Eng., Oct. 10, 1957. BSc, U. Birmingham, Eng., 1980; MSc, Open U., Eng., 1990. Tchr. math. Alexandra H.S., Tipton, Eng., 1981-84; lectr. math. and stats. Stockport (Eng.) Coll. Further and Higher Edn., 1984-90; head math. faculty Farlingaye H.S., Woodbridge, Eng., 1990-96; dep. head tchr. Claydon H.S., Ipswich, Eng., 1997—. Mem. Math. Assn. (editor Math Gazette 1994—, pres. 2000—). Mem. Labour Party. Office: Claydon HS, Church Lane, Claydon Ipswich IP6 0EG, England

ABBOTT, WILLIAM SAUNDERS, lawyer; b. Medford, Mass., June 2, 1938; s. Charles Theodoric and Evelyn (Saunders) A.; m. Susan Shaw, June 24, 1961; children: Cathryn, Stephen, David. AB, Harvard U., 1960, LLB, 1966. Bar: Mass. 1967, U.S. Dist. Ct. Mass., U.S. Ct. Appeals (D.C. cir.). White House fellow, 1966-67; regional coord., U.S. Agrl. Programs, Asia, USDA, 1967-68; gen. counsel Cabot, Cabot & Forbes Co., Boston, 1968-77; prin. Simonds, Winslow, Willis & Abbott, Boston, 1977—; bd. dirs. Bay Tower Restaurant, Arlington Bd. Selectmen, 1970-73; pres. Plymouth County Wildlands Trust, 1984-90, 96-97; pres. Nat. Found. to Improve TV, 1970—. Mem. Harvard Law Rev. Lt. USN, 1963-66. Mem. Mass. Bar Assn., Boston Bar Assn., Phi Beta Kappa. E-mail: wabbott1@aol.com. Home: 33 Herring Way Plymouth MA 02360-3225 Office: Simonds Winslow Willis & Abbott 50 Congress St Ste 925 Boston MA 02109-4075

ABBOTT, WILLIAM THOMAS, claim specialist; b. Guthrie, Okla., Jan. 6, 1938; s. Benjamin Franklin and Eva Mae (Lattin) A.; m. Jerri Evelyn Stacy, Apr. 20, 1974. BS, Cen. State U., Okla., 1960; Casualty Claim Law Assoc., Am. Edn1. Inst., 1975. Cert. Fraud Examiner, Assn. Cert. Fraud Examiners, 1996. Claim adjuster Crawford and Co., Lubbock, Tex., 1964-67, Tulsa, 1967-70; sr. claim specialist State Farm Ins. Co., Tulsa, 1970—; bd. dirs. Okla. Arson Adv. Coun., chmn., 1996—. Mem. Young Reps., 1967, Tulsa Met. Ministries, 1971-75, Tulsa Mental Health Hotline, 1971-73, Okla. Hist. Soc. With USMC, 1960-64. Mem. Am. Legion, Internat. Assn. Arson Investigators (bd. dirs. Okla. chpt. 1985-93, pres. 1991), Assn. Cert. Fraud Examiners (Tulsa chpt.), Tulsa Claims Assn. (pres. 1981, Claimsman of Yr. 1979), pres. Mt Carmel Cemetery Assn., Noble Co., Okla., Internat. Assn. Spl. Investigation Units (bd. dirs. Okla. chpt. 1998—), Profls. Against Confidence Crime (assoc.), Investigative Reporters and Editors (assoc.), Santa Fe Trail Assn., Blue Goose, Fire Marshal Assn. Okla. (assoc.), League Am. Bicyclists (life), Adventure Cyclists, Tulsa Bicycle Club, Nat. Off-Road Bicycle Assn., Adventure Club N.Am. Republican. Methodist. Avocations: bicycling, state and regional history, writing. Office: State Farm Ins Co 12222 State Farm Blvd Tulsa OK 74146-5402

ABBOUD, EMAD BISHARA, ophthalmologist, vitreoretinal specialist; b. Cairo, May 1, 1957; s. Bashara Assad Abboud and Renee Antoun Haggar; m. Odile Simone Bastide, May 17, 1985; children: Alexandre, Marion, Eric. CES in Opthalmology, Pierre et Marie Curie U., Paris, 1986. Diplomate Am. Bd. Ophthalmology. Resident in ophthalmology U. Chgo., 1986-89; fellow in vitreoretinal diseases Wills Eye Hosp., Thomas Jefferson U., Phila., 1989-91; cons. vitreoretinal surgeon King Khaled Eye Specialist Hosp., Riyadh, Saudi Arabia, 1992-95, chief vitreoretinal divsn., 1992-95, assoc. med. dir., 1999—. Fellow Am. Acad. Ophthalmology; mem. French Soc. Ophthalmology, PanArab Coun. Ophthalmology. Avocations: swimming, bowling, reading. Fax: 966-1-4821234x3456. E-mail: emabboud@shabakah.net.sa. Office: King Khaled Eye Spec Hosp, PO Box 7191, 11462 Riyadh Saudi Arabia

ABBRUZZESE, PIETRO ANGELO, cardiac surgeon; b. Taranto, Italy, June 27, 1950; s. Cosimo and Anna (De Pace) A.; m. Alessandra Napoleone, Aug. 8, 1987; children: Carlo, Benedetta, Cosimo. MD, Pisa (Italy) U., 1976, specialist in gen. surgery, 1981; specialist in cardiac surgery, Torino (Italy) U., 1984; specialist in vascular surgery, Cagliari (Italy) U., 1989. Asst. in cardiac surgery Ospedale S. Carlo, Potenza, Italy, 1977-78; fellow in cardiothoracic surgery Oreg. Health Scis. U., Portland, 1979, resident in cardiothoracic surgery, 1980-82; asst. in cardiac surgery Ospedali Riuniti, Bergamo, Italy, 1982-86; asst. in cardiac surgery Ospedale Maggiore, Novara, Italy, 1986-87; assoc. in cardiac surgery Ospedale Brotzu, Cagliari, 1987-92, assoc. and acting chief, 1992-95; chief cardiac surgery Ospedale Infantile Regina Margherita, Torino, 1996—, chief dept. cardiology and cardiac surgery, 1998—. Author: (books) Operative Surgery, Cardiac Surgery, 1986, Trattato Delle Malattie Cardiovascolari, 1987; contbr. numerous articles to med. jours. Named Famous Citymen, City of Taranto. Fellow European Bd. Thoracic and Cardiovasc. Surgeons; mem. Soc. Thoracic Surgeons. Avocations: tennis, traveling. Office: Ospedale Infantile Regina M, Piazza Polonia 94, 10126 Torino Italy

ABDALLAH, MAYSSA AMIN, engineering educator; b. Alexandria, Egypt, June 7, 1960; d. Amin Hassan Abdallah and Nabiha Mohammed Hanafy. BSc, Alexandria U., 1983, MSc, 1987, PhD, 1993. Instr. Faculty Engring., Alexandria, 1983-87, lectr., 1988-93, asst. prof., 1993—; postdoctoral fellow U. Miami, Fla., 1998. Mem. Engrs. Syndicate. Avocation: music. Home: 405 A Tarik El-Horia St, Moustafa Kamel, Alexandria Egypt Office: Fac Engring Dept Engring, Alexandria Univ, 21544 Alexandria Egypt

ABD-EL-BARR, MOSTAFA IBRAHIM, computer science educator, computer engineering educator, researcher, educator; b. Cairo, Mar. 29, 1950; s. Ibramin Abd-El-Barr; m. Ebtesam Abd-El-Basset, Aug. 19, 1975; children: Muhammad, Abd-El Rahman, Ibrahim. BSc, Cairo U., 1973, MSc, 1979; PhD, U. Toronto, Ont., Can., 1986. Registered profl. engr., Can. Rsch. engr. Atomic Energy Computer Ctr., Cairo, 1974-77; tchg. asst. King Saud U., Riyadh, Saudi Arabia, 1977-82; asst. prof. U. Sask., Saskatoon, Can., 1986-88, assoc. prof., 1988-93, prof., 1993-96, adj. prof., 1996—; prof. computer engring. King Fahd U. Petroleum and Minerals, Dhahran, Saudi Arabia, 1996—, cons. Rsch. Inst., 1998-99; mem. Adv. Com. on Establishment Pvt. U. in Riyadh, 1998-99; internal auditor Quality Mgmt. Sys., 1998. Contbr. about 100 articles to profl. jours. and symposium procs. Mem. Interfaith Com., Saskatoon, 1989-92; pres. Islamic Assn. Sask., Saskatoon, 1990-93. Open fellow U. Toronto, 1982-85; strategic grantee Can. Microelectronic Corp., Saskatoon, 1991. Mem. IEEE (cert., sr.), Assn. for Computing Machinery (sr.), Profl. Engrs. Can. With Egyptian Army, 1973-76. Avocations: travel, soccer, reading, fishing. Fax: (965) 532-9417. E-mail: mostafa@ccse.kfupm.edu.sa. Home and Office: King Fahd U Petroleum-Mins, Dept Comp Engring POB 1579, Dhahran 31261, Saudi Arabia

ABDEL-FATTAH, KAMAL IBRAHIM, physiologist, researcher; b. Monofeya, Egypt, Feb. 17, 1953; s. Ibrahim Abdel-Fattah El-Sayed and Saadia Omer Abdel-Rahman; m. Hekmat Mohammed Abou-Safy. BSc, Ain Shams U., Cairo, 1975, MSc, 1985; PhD, Acad. Agr., Cracow, Poland, 1991. Asst. rschr. Acad. Scis., Cairo, 1976-77; asst. rschr. Nat. Ctr. for Radiation Rsch. and Tech., Cairo, 1977-91, rschr., 1991—; head Animal Physiology Lab., Radiation Biology Dept. Nat. Ctr. for Radiation Rsch. and Tech. Mem. AAAS, Sic. Professions Syndicate, N.Y. Acad. Scis. Achievements include research on metabolic effect of reverse triiodothyronine in chickens, physiological role of some chemical and biochemical radioprotectors. Office: Nat Ctr Radiation Rsch Tech, PO Box 29, Nasser City Cairo Egypt

ABDEL-FATTAH, MOATAZ MOHAMMED, medical statistician, educator; b. Damietta, Egypt, Nov. 21, 1960; s. Mohammed Abdel-Halim Abdel-Fattah and Soad El-Sayed El-Emam; m. Azza Moktar Kasem, Oct. 10, 1991; children: Ahmed, Hadeer, Kareem. MB, BChir, Faculty Medicine, Alexandria, Egypt, 1984; MPH, High Inst. Pub. Health, Alexandria, Egypt, 1993, PhD in Pub. Health, 1997. Ho. officer U. Hosp., Alexandria, 1985-86; physician Ministry Health, Alexandria, 1986-87, Mil. Hosp., Cairo, 1987-89; demonstrator med. stats. Med. Rsch. Inst., Alexandria, 1989-92, asst. lectr. med. stats., 1992-97, lectr., 1997—; vis. scientist Mario Negbri Sud, Chieti, Italy, 1993-96. Contbr. articles to profl. jours. Mem. Alexandria Cancer Registry, Arabic Assn. for Cancer Registration and Control. Office: Med Rsch Inst, 165 Al-Horria Ave, Alexandria Egypt

ABDELGADER, HAKIM SALEM, engineering researcher; b. Tarhuna, Libya, Apr. 20, 1964; s. Salem Abdelgader and Eisha Elfarjani; children: Fathma, Aiya, Salem. BSc, Al-Fath U., Tripoli, Libya, 1988; MSc, Tech. U. Gdansk, Poland, 1990, PhD, 1996. Sec. fgn. econ. affairs Liaison Ctr. for Fgn. Grads. of Polish Univs., Lodz, Poland, 1994-96; rschr. Gdansk (Poland) Tech. U., 1996—. Author: Cement and Concrete Research, 1999; contbr. articles to profl. jours. Mem. Am. Concrete Inst. Avocations: sports, history. E-mail: hakimsa@poczta.onte.pl. Home: Ul Wojska Polskiego 52/5, 80-268 Gdansk Poland Office: Tech U Gdansk, Ul Narutowicza 11/12, 20-952 Gdansk Poland also: PO Box 377, Tripoli Libya

ABDEL HADI, AHMED, veterinarian; b. Bara, Sudan, Jan. 1, 1957; s. Ahmed Abdel Hadi Farah and Khiwaidim Abdel Quaom Fadl Alla; m. Samira Elhag Mohamed, Aug. 8, 1985; 6 children. BVS, Khartoum (Sudan) U., 1982, PhD in Vet. Sci., 1987. Vet. officer Ministry of Animal Resources, Khartoum, 1982-83; tchg. asst. Khartoum U., 1983-87; lectr. Juba (Sudan) U., 1987-90; analytical chemist Vet. Dept., United Arab Emirates, 1990-94; camel racing expert, chemist Camel Racing Lab., Abu Dhabi, United Arab Emirates, 1994—; cons. Agrl. Material Co., Alain, 1993—, Camel Racing Assn., 1994—. Contbr. articles to profl. jours. Mem. Orgn. Offl. Racing Chemists, Intenrat. Orgn. Forensic Toxicologists, Suda Pharm. Soc., Sudanese Environ. Conservation Assn., Khordofan Sons Assn., Traditional Reviving Soc., Sudan Vet. Assn. Avocations: football, camel racing, horse racing, traditional nomad life in the desert. Office: Camel Racing Forensic Lab, PO Box 253, Abu Dhabi United Arab Emirates

ABDEL-HALIM, IBRAHIM ABDEL-MONEIM, electrical engineering educator; b. Cairo, Dec. 3, 1946; s. Abdel-Moneim Abdel-Halim Imam and Anisa Abdel-Halim El-Attar; m. Ragaa Abdel-Kader, Dec. 13, 1947. BSEE, Ain-Shams U., Cairo, 1968; MSEE, Cairo U., 1973; PhD in Elec. Engring., Loughborough (Eng.) U. Tech., 1978. Tchg. asst. Helwan U., Cairo, 1969-73, lectr., 1973-74; lectr. Benha br. Zagazig U., Cairo, 1973-78, asst. prof., 1978-81, assoc. prof., 1981-85, prof., 1985—, head elec. engring. dept., 1981-83, 91-95, 2000—, cons. faculty engring., 1993—; chmn. elec. machines stds. com. Ministry of Industry, Cairo, 1990—. Contbr. articles to profl. jours. Recipient State Prize in Engring. Acad. Sci. Rsch. and Tech., 1992, medal of excellence 1st class Pres. of Egypt, 1995. Fellow Inst. Elec. Engrs. London; mem. Syndicate Engrs. Egypt. Avocations: jogging, gymnastics, classical music. Office: Zagazig U Faculty Engring, 108 Shoubra St, Cairo Egypt

ABDEL-LATIF, ATA ABDEL-HAFEZ, biochemistry and molecular biology educator; b. Ramallah, Palestine, Jan. 22, 1933; came to U.S., 1951, naturalized, 1963; m. Iris K. Graham, Sept. 10, 1957; children: Rhonda, David, Joseph, Rhadi. BS in Biology and Chemistry, DePaul U., Chgo., 1955, MS in Chemistry, 1958; PhD in Biochemistry, Mt. Sinai Med. Rsch. Found., Ill. Inst. Tech., 1963; postgrad. in Neurochemistry, U.Ill. Coll. Medicine, 1963-65. Rsch. assoc. dept. psychiatry U. Ill., 1963-67; med. rsch. scientist V, Dept. Mental Health State of Ill., 1963-67; assoc. prof. biochemistry and molecular biology Med. Coll. Ga., Augusta, 1967-74, prof., 1974-87, Regents' prof., 1987—; vis. prof. U. Nottingham, 1975-76; rschr., spkr. in field. Contbr. articles to profl. publs. NIH fellow, 1959-63; NIH grantee, 1965—; recipient Award for Outstanding Contbn. to Vision Rsch. Alcon Rsch. Inst., 1990, Merit award NIH, 1989. Mem. Am. Soc. Biol. Chemists, Am. Physiol. Soc., Am. Soc. Pharmacology and Exptl. Therapeutics, Am. Soc. Neurochemistry, Soc. Exptl. Biology and Medicine, Internat. Soc. for Eye Rsch., AAAS, Assn. Rsch. in Vision and Opthalmology. Office: Med Coll Ga Dept Biochemistry And Augusta GA 30912

ABDEL-MEGIED, MOHAMED, mathematician, educator; b. Assiut, Egypt, June 28, 1941; m. Anissa Ahmed Hussein, July 30, 1978; 1 child, Ahmed. BSc, Assiut (Egypt) U., 1962, MSc, 1967; PhD, Humboldt U., Berlin, 1972. Rsch. asst. dept. theoretical physics Atomic Energy Establishment, Cairo, Egypt, 1962; rsch. asst. dept. math. Assiut U., 1963-68, lectr. dept. math., 1972-75; grad. asst. dept. math. Humboldt U., Berlin, 1968-72; asst. prof. dept. math. U. Riyad, Saudi Arabia, 1975-78, assoc. prof., 1978-81; prof. Minia U., El-Minia, Egypt, 1981—, vice dean faculty of sci., 1982-85, head math. dept., 1982-95; vis. prof. Inst. Math. & Informatics, Max-Planck Inst. Physics and Astrophysics, Munich, Germany, 1981-82, Kassel (Germany) U., 1986, U. Aberdeen, Scotland, 1986, 87, U. Newcastle upon Tyne, England, 1987, U. of United Arab Emirates, 1991-92, Greifswald U., 1998, Albert Einstein Inst. Potsdam, Berlin, 1998; cons. Ministry of Edn., Egypt, 1988-94; lectr. in field. Contbr. articles to profl. jours.; editl. bd. El-Minia Sci. Bulletin. Mem. Internat. Soc. Gen. Relativity, Am. Math. Soc., London Math. Soc., Egyptian Math. Soc.. Moslem. Home: 5 Al-Horia St, 61111 El Minia Egypt Office: Minia Univ Faculty of Sci, Math Dept, 61111 El Minia Egypt

ABDEL-MOGIB, MAMDOUH, science educator; b. Nawasa El Bahr, Dakahlia, Egypt, Apr. 24, 1959; p. Mohamed Ibrahim Abdel-Mogib and Fatma Ahmed Aboul Amayem; m. Hanaa Mohamed Ragheb, July 30, 1987; children: Mohamed, Basmah, Ramy. BSc in Chemistry, Mansoura (Egypt)

U., 1981, MSc in Organic Chemistry, 1986, PhD in Chemistry of Natural Products, 1990; PhD in Chemistry of Natural Products, Tech. U., Berlin, 1990. Demonstrator Faculty Sci., Mansoura U., 1983-86, asst. lectr., 1986-88, lectr., 1990-94; asst. prof. Faculty Sci., King Abdulaziz U., Jeddah, Saudi Arabia, 1994-96; assoc. prof. Faculty Sci., King Abdulaziz U., Jeddah, 1996—; co-investigator rsch. project King Abdulaziz U., Jeddah, 1998-99, prin. investigator in rsch. project, 1999—. Author: Natural Products Chemistry, 1988. Soldier Egyptian Army, 1981-83. Mem. Chemists League, Saudi Chem. Soc. Avocations: walking, running, drawing. E-mail: mamdouh m@hotmail.com. Fax: 00966 2 6952292. Office: King Abdulaziz U, Abdullah Alsulaiman St, Jeddah 21413, Saudi Arabia

ABDEL-RAHMAN, ABDEL A., pharmacology educator; b. Alexandria, Egypt, Oct. 16, 1947; s. Ahmed and Fatma Abdel-R.; m. Shadia Abdel-Rahman, Jan. 1, 1976; children: Rania, Rehab, Ahmed, Heba. BS, Alexandria U., 1970, MS, 1973; PhD, Leeds U., Eng., 1979. Instr. dept. pharmacology Alexandria U., 1970-74, asst. prof., 1979-82, 84-85; instr. dept. pharmacology Leeds U., 1974-79; vis. scientist East Carolina U., Greenville, N.C., 1982-84; asst. prof. dept. pharmacology East Carolina U., Greenville, 1985-89, assoc. prof., 1989-94, prof., 1994—; East Carolina U. Sch. of Med. del. Pharmacopeial Conv., 1991—. Mem. Am. Soc. Pharmacol. Exptl. Therapeutics, Am. Heart Assn. (rsch. rev. subcom. 1989-91, rsch. rev. com. 1992—), Am. Soc. Hypertension, Am. Physiol. Soc., Soc. Neurosci., Am. Autonomic Soc. Avocations: soccer, table tennis, basketball. Office: East Carolina U Sch Med Dept Pharmacology Greenville NC 27858

ABDEL-RAHMAN, SUSAN M., pharmacy and medicine educator; b. Cortland, N.Y., Sept. 9, 1971; d. Mohamed Abdel-Rahman and Janine Edgar. BS in Pharmacy, Rutgers U., 1994, PharmD, 1995. Rsch. asst. BASF-AgChem, Durham, N.C., 1990-92; rsch. assoc. Duke U., Durham, 1992; postdoctoral fellow Ohio State U., Columbus, 1995-97; asst. prof. pharmacy U. Mo. Sch. Pharmacy, Kansas City, 1997—; adj. asst. prof. pediat. U. Mo. Sch. Medicine, Kansas City, 1998—. Contbr. several chpts. to books and more than 30 articles to profl. jours. Mem. planning com. Habitat for Humanity, N.J., 1988-90. Edward J. Bloustein Disting. scholar, 1989-93, Anthony J. Derosa Meml. scholar, 1994-95, Seymour A. Lubman Meml. scholar, 1994-95, Rutgers U. Alumni Assn. scholar, 1993-94, Medco scholar, 1993-94. Mem. Am. Coll. Clin. Pharmacy, Am. Assn. Colls. Pharmacy, Am. Soc. for Clin. Pharmacology and Therapeutics, Lambda Kappa Sigma (profl. chair 1991-92, pres. 1992-93), Rho Chi (pres. 1993-94), Golden Key. E-mail: srahman@cmb.edu.

ABDELRAHMAN, TALAAT AHMAD MOHAMMAD, financial executive; b. Kafr Saqr, Sharkia, Egypt, Sept. 13, 1940; came to U.S., 1970; s. Ahmad Mohammad and Zeen Elmahdi (Hassan) A.; m. Soher T. Ali (Dec. Feb. 1979); children: Manar, Neven, Nancy, Amon; m. Ekram T. Kandil (div. May 1994); m. Moushira El Shafei, Jan. 1996. BS in Mgmt., Cairo U., 1965, BA in Law, 1969, PhD in Fin., 1987; MBA in Acctg., NYU, 1974. Fin. analyst Nat. Bank Egypt, Cairo, 1965-70; Euro-dollar specialist Bankers Trust Co., N.Y.C., 1970-74; sr. cost acct. Phelps Dodge Cable & Wire, Yonkers, N.Y., 1974-75; fin. cons. East Orange, N.J., 1975-76; asst. treas. ITT Fed. Electric, Paramus, N.J., 1976-82; fin. mgr. ITT Fed. Electric, Jed, Saudi Arabia, 1982-86; corp. fin. mgr. ITT Fed. Electric, Paramus, 1987-91; gen. dir., chmn. Franconia Pediat. & Family Med. Ctrs., Alexandria, Va., 1997—; bd. dirs. ITT Howard/Egypt, Cairo, Talkan USA, Inc., Morganville, N.J.; owner 7-Eleven Franchise, Wood Ridge, N.J., 1991-96, Hackensack, N.J., 1992-96, Family Food Store Inc., T/A Broadway Stop & Shop, Fair Lawn, N.J., 1993-95. Contbr. articles to profl. jours. Pres. Bergen County Islamic Ctr., 1995-96. Avocations: windsurfing, swimming. Home: 13468 Bregman Rd Silver Spring MD 20904-1240 Office: Franconia Pediat & Family Med Ctr 6078 Franconia Rd Ste B Alexandria VA 22310-1719

ABD ELRAZAK, MOHAMED ALY, rheumatologist; b. Cairo, Egypt, May 27, 1945; s. Aly Abd Elrazak and Atyat Farrag; m. Nehad Shalaby, Sept. 26, 1971; children: Shahirs, Shareef, Deena. Diplomate Am. Bd. Internal Medicine, Am. Bd. Rheumatology. Fellow Cleve. Clinic, 1980-82; head rheumatology/immunology hosps., Saudi Arabia, 1983-98; internist, rheumatologist Aramco, Saudi Arabia, 1998—. Fellow Am. Coll. Physicians, Am. Coll. Rheumatology. Home: Box 5790 Udhiliyah, 31311 c/o Aramco Saudi Arabia

ABD EL-SALAM, MOHAMED EL-HUSSEINY, engineering executive; b. Sirs El-Layn, Egypt, Apr. 25, 1930; s. Abdel-Salam Mohamed El-Teeh and Fatma Ossman Ismael; m. Leila Mohamed El-Naggar, Jan 1, 1958; children: Mahmoud, Ossama, Omar. BSCE, Cairo U., 1952; diploma, Inst. Mil. Engring., Kent, Eng., 1955; MSCE, Cairo U., 1961. Cert. civil engr. With Corps of Egyptian Mil. Engrs., 1952-78, dep. dir., 1979-80, dir., 1981; chief of staff Mil. Engring. Orgn., Cairo, 1981-82; chmn. Nile Co. for Rd. Constrn., Egypt, Nat. Authority for Tunnels, Cairo, 1983-98; tech. advisor Egyptian Minister of Transport, 1998-2000; chmn. Bur. Egyptien de Conseils Techniques (BECT), Nasr City, Cairo, Egypt, 2000—; bd. dirs. Gen. Assembly Rds. and Bridges, Cairo, Gen. Assemblies of Constrn. Cos., Transp. Planning Authority of Egypt. Author books on mil. bridges; contbr. articles to profl. jours. Cert. in civil engring. Decorated grade chevalier, grade officier Legion of Honor, French Govt.; recipient Drawl badge, 1955, Independence badge, 1956, Victory badge, 1956, 10th Revolution Anniversary, Tng. 1st class badge, 1971, Duty badge 1st class, 1972, Republic badge, 1974, others. Fellow Nasser Mil. Acad.; mem. Egyptian Tunnelling Soc. (chmn. 1992—), Internat. Tunnelling Assn. (bd. dirs. 1990-97). Avocations: sports, music, reading, writing articles and books. Home: Heliopolis, 17 Sabry Abo-Alam, 11341 Cairo Egypt Office: BECT/Youssef Abbas St, El Mohandseen El Arkareyeen, Bldg 1 Nasr City, Cairo Egypt

ABDELSAMAD, MOUSTAFA HASSAN, dean; b. Mar. 12, 1941. B in Commerce with honors, Cairo U., 1961; MBA, George Washington U., 1965, DBA, 1970. Assoc. dean Va. Commonwealth U., Richmond, Va., 1977-88; dean, finance prof. U. Mass., N. Dartmouth, Mass., 1988-91; prof. fin. Tex. A&M U., Corpus Christi, Tex., 1991—, dean Coll. Bus., 1991—; cons. in field. Editor-in-chief SAM Advanced Mgmt. jour., 1985—. Mem. Fin. Mgmt. Assoc., Soc. Advancement Mgmt. (mgmt. excellence award, 1991, 1998, pres. excellence award, 1996, Phil Carroll Advancement Mgmt. finance award, 1989, internat. pres. 1983-86, 96—), Tex. Coun. Coll. Bus. Edn., So. Bus. Adminstrn. Assoc. Office: Dean Coll Business Tex A&M U Corpus Christi Corpus Christi TX 78412

ABDELSAYED, WAFEEK HAKIM, accounting educator; b. Fayoum, Egypt, Aug. 16, 1958; came to U.S., 1970; s. Fr. Gabriel H. and Tahani (Mikhael) A. BBA, Hofstra U., 1979; MBA, Adelphi U., 1983, MS, 1984; PhD, U. Conn., 1996. CPA Fla., N.Y.; cert. fraud examiner Assn. of Cert Fraud Examiners; cert. fin. mgr. Staff acct. KPMG Peat Marwick, L.I., N.Y., 1981-82, Deloitte & Touche, L.I., 1983-84; prof. acctg. dept. So. Conn. State U., New Haven, 1984—. Contbr. rsch. papers to profl. publs. (Competitive Paper award 1991, Becker's Outstanding Rsch. award 1991). Mem. bd. deacons Virgin Mary Coptic Orthodox Ch. Recipient scholarship N.Y. State Soc. CPAs, 1983. Mem. AICPA, N.E. Bus. and Econs. Assn. (bd. dirs.), Am. Acctg. Assn., Inst. Mgmt. Accts. (cert. mgmt. acct., cert. fin. mgmt.), Inst. Internal Auditors (cert. internal auditor), Cert. Govt. Financial Mgr., Assn. of Govt. Accts, Conn. Soc. CPAs, Beta Gamma Sigma, Beta Alpha Psi. Egyptian/Christian Orthodox. Avocations: coin and stamp collecting, photography. Home: PO Box 170 North Haven CT 06473-0170 Office: So Conn State U Sch Bus 501 Crescent St New Haven CT 06515-1330

ABDEL WAHAB, SAMIHA MOHAMED, chemistry educator, researcher; b. Cairo, Feb. 14, 1921; d. Mohamed Abdel Wahab Mahgoub; m. Abdel Fattah Ali Ismail, Sept. 10, 1942; children: Mohamed, Nabila. BSc 1st class with distinction, Foad 1st U., Cairo, 1941, BSc in Spl. Chemistry, 1941; PhD in Organic Chemistry. Demonstrator Cairo U., 1941-44; asst. lectr. Faculty of Sci., Alexandria, Egypt, 1945-53, lectr., 1954-56; lectr. Univ. Coll., Cairo, 1957-62, asst. prof., 1963-69, head chemistry dept., 1972-77, dean, 1977-81, prof. organic chemistry, 1982—; prof. organic chemistry Ain-Shams U., Cairo, 1969—; established chemistry dept., prof. organic chemistry Kuwait U., 1966-72, head chemistry dept., 1966-72. Contbr. numerous articles to profl. jours. Mem. Univs. Grads. Orgn., Gezira Sport Club, Shooting Club. Avocations: reading, classical music, gardening, walking. Home: Faculty of Girls for Art, 16 Yemen St, Mohandessin Cairo Egypt Office: Ain-Shams U, Khalifa El-Mamoon, Cairo Egypt

ABD EL-WAHED, MOSHIRA MOHAMED, physician, researcher; b. El-Mahala El-Kobra, Kharbia, Egypt, Jan. 7, 1964; s. Mohamed Abd El-Wahed Abou El-Magd and Afaf Mohamed Othman; m. Abdou Saad El-Tabl, Aug. 6, 1992; children: Mohamed Abdou Saad El-Tabl and Amer Abdou Saad El-Tabl. BS, Faculty of Medicine, Menoufiya, Egypt, 1987, MS in Pathology, 1992; PhD in Pathology, Faculty of Medicine and, Menoufiya and Tex., 1997; Cert., M.D. Anderson Cancer Ctr., 1995. Demonstrator pathology dept. Faculty of Medicine Menoufiya (Egypt) U., 1989-92, asst. lectr. pathology dept. Faculty of Medicine, 1992-94, 1995-97, lectr. pathology dept. Faculty of Medicine, 1997—, cons. pathology dept. Faculty of Medicine, 1998—; observer M.D. Anderson Cancer Ctr., Houston, 1994-95. Mem. El-Watany Party, 1996—. Mem. Club Egyptian Pathologists. Avocations: researching, reading, swimming, drawing. Home: Gamal Abd El-Naser St, Dr El-Seedy Bldg No 5, Shebin El-Kom Menoufiya, Egypt Office: Fac Medicine Pathology Dept, Menoufiya U Shebin El-Kom, Shebin El-Kom Menofiya, Egypt

ABDI, HERVÉ, psychology educator; b. Belfort, France. M Psychology, U. Franche Comté, France, 1975; M in Neurobiology, U. Strasbourg, France, 1976; M in Economy, U. Clermond Ferrand, France, 1977; PhD in Math. Psychology, U. Aix en Provence, France, 1980. Asst. prof. U. Franche Comté, 1979-83; assoc. prof. U. Bourgogne, 1983-87, prof., 1988-98; prof. U. Tex., Dallas, 1990—; vis. prof. cognitive sci. Brown U., Providence, 1987-88. Author: Experimental Data Analysis, 1987, Neural Networks, 1996; editor: Neural Networks, 1994, Computational Methods, 1996, Neural Networks for Face Processing, 1997, Neural Networks, 1999. Scientist French Navy, 1979-80. Fulbright scholar. E-mail: herve@utdallas.edu. Office: U Tex Dallas Program in Cognition MS GR 41 Richardson TX 75083-0688

ABDIN, MARIA, research service executive, publisher; b. Washington. AA, Pima C.C., Tucson, 1982; student, U. Ariz., U. Wash. Owner Prensa Samizdat Rsch. Svc./Pubs., various locations, 1974—; Native Am. sacred clown. Contbr. articles to profl. jours. Bd. sec., outreach, Com. de Vecinos Internat.; creator ednl. and social svcs. program Peoples Involvement Corp. Office: Prensa Samizdat Rsch Svc PO Box 21521 Seattle WA 98111-3521

ABDO, SAAD, orthopedic surgeon, researcher; b. Kfifan, Lebanon, Dec. 11, 1952; arrived in France, 1972; B in Math., Lebanon, 1972; medicine faculty, Montpellier, France, 1982, Rouen, France, 1984, Marseille, France, 1981. Nat. Medicine Order cert. diploma in surgery; corporeal damage expert. Gen. surgeon asst. U. Rouen, 1983-84; gen. and orthop. surgeon Ctr. Hosp. de Fecamp, France, 1984-88, Ctr. Hosp. de Bernay, France, 1988-90, Clinique St. Dominique, Brioude, France, 1991-92; gen. and orthop. hosp. surgeon Ctr. Hosp. de la Ferte Bernard, France, 1992-95, Ctr. Hosp. Ambert, France, 1995-2000. Home: 5 allée des lilas, 63600 Ambert France Office: Ctr Hosp, Svc de chirugie, 63600 Ambert France

ABD-RABOU, SHAABAN MAHMOUD, entomologist, researcher; b. Cairo, Feb. 23, 1959; s. Mahmoud Abd-Rabou and Fawsiya Tolba Kalaf; m. Aza Mohammad Arafa, May 27, 1993; children: Mahmoud, Yasmin, Basant, Amr. BS, Ain Shams U., Cairo, 1982; MS, Ain Shams U., 1990, PhD, 1994. Splst. in agr. Cairo, 1983-87; asst. rsch., leader whiteflies unit Plant Protection Rsch. Inst. Dokki, Cairo, 1987-90, asst. researcher, prin. investigator, 1990-94, researcher, 1994-99, cons., 1998-99, sr. researcher, 1999—. Contbr. articles to profl. jour.; inventor. Grantee Common Fund Commodities, 1998, 99, Israel, 1999. Office: Plant Protection Rsch Inst, 7 Nadi El-Seid, Giza Egypt

ABDUL, MANNAN, airline executive; b. Comilla, Bangladesh, Mar. 13, 1951; s. Haji M. Worish Mollah and Mollah Jabeda Khatoon; m. Nazma Begum, Mar. 13, 1977; children: Fathama Nahid, Arshal Arafat, Ahanab Arafat. Diploma in engring., Comilla Poly. Inst., Bangladesh, 1969; diploma in naval arch., MDTC, Narayanganj, Bangladesh, 1972; degree in naval arch., AOTS, Tokyo, 1974; quality control, Assn. Tech. Scholarship, Tokyo, 1982. Asst., foreman instr. BUET, Dhaka, 1972-79; cons. Asian Devel. Bank, Manila, 1979-82; mng. dir. Mollah Group of Industries, Dhaka, 1983-95, Bismillah Airlines Ltd., Dhaka, 1995—; chmn. bishmillah-Ogden Aviation Svcs. Co. Ltd., Dhaka, 1997—; cons. ADB, Karachi, Dhaka, 1980-95, World Bank, 1977-85, IMO, 1979-89. Author: Rule of Ships Bangladesh, 1979, Navigation of Waterways, 1983; editor: Marine Bulatin, 1979-85. Fellow Internat. Digonatic Engring., Brit. Mgmt. Inst.; mem. Assn. Tech. Scholarship. Office: Bismillah Airlines Ltd, 94 DIT Rd Mailbag, Dhaka 1217, Bangladesh

ABDULAGATOV, ILMUTDIN MAGOMEDOVICH, thermophysics researcher; b. Makhachkala, Russia, Nov. 30, 1953; s. Mogamed Baitullaevich Abdulagatov and Edei Abdurazakova; m. Gulinaz Murtuzalievna Zairbekova, Sept. 7, 1974; children: Aziz Ilmutdinovich, Alisa Ilmutdinovna. MS, Dagestan (Russia) State U., 1976; PhD, Moscow Power Inst., 1992. Rschr. Inst. Physics Dagestan Sci. Ctr., Russian Acad. Scis., 1976-80, head thermophysics divsn., 1986—; guest rschr. NIST, Boulder, Colo., 1998—; prin. investigator NATO/Russian Sci. Found., 1993-96, 96—; reviewer internat. and nat. sci. jours.; mem. working group on thermophys. properties of fluids and fluid mixtures in the vicinity of critical points Russian Acad. Sci., 1986—. Author monographs in field. Capt. arty. Soviet armed forces, 1971-76. Recipient Dagestan State Prize in field of sci. and tech., 1991, Hon. award for outstanding achievements in sci. rsch. and thermophysics Dept. Energy Russian Acad. Scis., 1994-98. Mem. Internat. Assn. Properties of Water and Stream. Fax: (303) 497 5224. E-mail: mangur@datacom.ru. Home: Yaragskogo 75A/93, 367030 Makhachkala Dagestan Russia Office: Inst Geothermal Problems, Shamilya 39A, 367030 Makhachkala Dagestan Russia

ABDULAI, YESUFU SEYYID MOMOH, international agency executive; b. June 19, 1940; s. Momoh and Haijia Fatimah A.; m. Zene Makonnen, 1982; 4 children. Degree, Mount Allison U., McGill U. Tech. asst. to exec. dir. African Group I, World Bank Group, Washington, 1971-73, advisor to exec. dir., 1973-78, alternate exec. dir., 1978-80, exec. dir., 1980-82, vice chair audit com., exec. bd., 1980-82; chair sec. African exec. dirs. World Bank Group and IMF, 1975-77; mgn. dir., CEO Fed. Mortgage Bank of Nigeria, 1982-83; dir. gen., CEO OPEC Fund for Internat. Devel., 1983—. Avocations: sports, reading, photography, music. Office: OPEC Fund Internat Devel, Parking 8 PO Box 995, A-1011 Vienna Austria*

ABDULATIPOV, RAMAZAN, Russian government official; b. 1946. Dep. prime min. Ethnic Policy; min. Ministry of Nationalities Affairs, Moscow, from 1998, now acting min. without portfolio. Address: Krasnopresnenska Nab 2, 103274 Moscow Russia Office: Ministry Nationalities, ul Ivana Babushkina 16, Moscow 117292, Russia*

ABDUL GHANI, ABDUS SALAM, electric company engineer; b. Lahore, Pakistan, May 1, 1943; s. Mohammad Din and Hajrah Abdul Ghani; m. Shagufta Latif, Apr. 30, 1972; children: Ahsan Hammad, Aminah Nusheen, Aysha Sabeen. BS in Engring., U. Engring. and Tech., Lahore, 1967. Shift engr. Hydel Power Plant, Wapda, Pakistan, 1967, Power Control, Wapda, Pakistan, 1968-73; sr. shift engr. Thermal Power Plant, Wapda, Pakistan, 1973-75; asst. dir. Power Control, Wapda, Pakistan, 1975-79; shift engr. LDC Sceco, Jeddah, Saudi Arabia, 1979-97; chief engr. ops. Sceco, Jeddah, Saudi Arabia, 1997—. Mem. IEEE. Home: 4-M Model Town (Ext), Lahore Pakistan Office: PO Box 20443, Jeddah 21455, Saudi Arabia

ABDUL HAMID, JAMAL HAMDI, diagnostic industry sales executive; b. Aldelnjat, Behara, Egypt, June 14, 1967; s. Hamdi Abdlhamid Alkarsh; m. Mona Hamdi Riyad, July 14, 1999. BSc in Biochemistry and Chemistry, Ein Shams U., Cairo, 1989. Med. rep. Randox Lab. Ltd., Cairo, 1990-93, United Diagnostics Industries, Riyadh, Saudi Arabia, 1993-96; products specialist United Diagnostics Industries, Dammam, Saudi Arabia, 1996-99, sales exec., 1999—. Contbr. articles to newspapers. Capt. Egyptian armed forces, 1990-91. Mem. Clin. Lab. Internat. Internat. Lab., Lab. Medica. Avocations: football, tennis, swimming. Office: United Diagnostics Industry, Area 71 PO Box 7011, Dammam 31462, Saudi Arabia

ABDUL-HAMID, TALAAT ASAAD, marketing and advertising educator, consultant; b. Mansoura, Egypt, Nov. 13, 1944; s. Asaad Abdul-Hamid Albanna and Dawlat Deyarby; m. Salwa Selim Salem, Dec. 27, 1972; children: Amr, Yousra. BBA, Cairo U., 1965, MBA, 1975; PHD, Mansoura (Egypt) U., 1977. Banker Nat. Bank Egypt, Cairo, 1965-75; lectr., assoc. prof. Mansoura U., 1975-82, assoc. prof., 1987-91, prof. mktg., 1994—; mktg. cons. Riyadh C. of C., 1991-94; mktg. tng. cons., 1977—; head Arab Bur. for Creativity and Devel., Giza, 1993—. Author: Effective Marketing, 1986, 10th edit., 2000; Effective Sales Manager, 1997, 4th edit., 2000 (Ahram Book of Yr. award 1998), Effective Selling Techniques, 1990, 6th edit., 2000, (books and software) Effective Marketing Plan, 2000; dep. chief editor Al Mal Waltegarah mag., 1977—; mng. editor Mktg. and Advt. mag., 1997—. Mgr. tng. ctr. Mansoura, 1987-92. Recipient Book of Yr. award Ahram Instn., 1998. Mem. Am. Mgmt. Assn., Am. Mktg. Assn., Egyptian Mgmt. Assn. (bd. dirs. 1980-96), Intenrat. Advt. Assn., Egyptian Advt. Assn. (dir. tng. activities 1998—). Avocations: computers, sports, reading, scientific writing. E-mail: tasaad@menanet.net. Home: 169 Ahram St, 12111 Giza Egypt Office: Mansoura U, Faculty Commerce, Mansoura Egypt

ABDULLA, WALIED YOUSIF, anesthesiologist; b. Basrah, Iraq, July 1, 1945; arrived in Germany, 1963; s. Yousif and Kanda (Khalil) A.; m. Regina Eckhardt, Dec. 12, 1979; children: Susanne, Sina. MD, U. Mainz, 1973, ScD, 1979. Assoc. prof. U. Mainz, 1979-82, U. Tex. Southwestern Med. Sch., Dallas, 1982-83; prof., chmn. dept. anesthesiology U. Basrah, 1984-91; prof. dept. anesthesiology U. Heidelberg, 1991-92; prof., chmn. dept. anesthesiology Intensive Care Bernburg, Germany, 1992—; exec. dir. Rescue Svcs., Gulf War, Basrah, 1985-91, chief of staff 1992—; v.p. bd. mgmt. German Red Cross, Bernburg, 1993—. Author: ABC of Burns, 1977, Blood Transfusion and Blood Coagulation, 1982, Principles of Resuscitation and Intensive Care, 1989, Ministry of Higher Educational and Scientific Research, Interdisciplinary Intensive Care, 1999. Mem. German Red Cross, 1993—. Mem. Am. Soc. of Anesthesiologists, German Soc. of Anesthesiology and Intensive Care, Iraqi Med. Soc. Avocations: recreational activities, reading. Office: Klinikum Bernburg, Kustrenaer Strasse 98, 06406 Bernburg Germany

ABDULLAEV, YALCHIN G., neuroscientist, educator; b. Baku, Azerbaijan, Aug. 19, 1960; s. Gulhuseyn Huseynoglu Abdullaev and Almas Abdullaev; m. Naida Velieva, Nov. 24, 1987; 1 child, Mikail. MS, Azerbaijan State U., Baku, 1982; PhD, Inst. Exptl. Medicine, St. Petersburg, Russia, 1987; MD, St. Petersburg Med. Acad., 1994. Rsch. asst. Inst. Physiology, Azerbaijan Acad. Scis., Baku, Azerbaijan, 1982-84; grad. stud. Inst. Exptl. Med., St. Petersburg, 1984-87, jr. rsch. scientist, 1987-89; sr. rsch. scientist Inst. Exptl. Medicine, St. Petersburg, 1989-90, Brain Ctr., St. Petersburg, 1990-94; asst. prof. U. Oreg., Eugene, 1994-96; asst. prof. dept. psychiatry U. Louisville, 1996—; mem. grad. faculty U. Louisville, 1997—; rsch. dir. Cognitive Neurosci. Lab., 1996—. Mem. editl. bd. Internat. Jour. Psychophysiology, 1992-96; contbr. articles to profl. jours. Mem., Amer. Psych. Soc., Soc. for Neuroscience, Internatl. Org. for Human Brain Mapping. E-mail: yalchin@louisville.edu. Office: U Louisville Dept Psychiatry 500 S Preston St Louisville KY 40202-1702

ABDULLAH, ABDULLAH AHMAD, mathematics educator; b. Makkah, Saudi Arabia, May 15, 1959; s. Ahmad Abdullah Mohammad and Mariam Kasem Abdu; m. Latifa Isaaq Khayyat, Setp. 1, 1984; children: Esam, Ammar, Abdularahman, Ahad, Moaaz. BS, Umm Al-Qura U., Makkah, Saudi Arabia, 1981; MS, Glasgow U., 1987, PhD, 1990. Programmar Computer Ctr. Umm Al-Qura Univ., Makkah, 1981-83, tchg. asst. math. dept., 1983-90, asst. prof., 1990-96, assoc. prof., 1996—; head of info. dept. Hajj Rsch. Ctr., Makkah, 1993-96; vice-dean of adminstrn. and registration, Umm Al-Qura U., 1996—. Office: Umm Al-Qura Univ/Fac Appl S, PO Box 3711, Makkah Saudi Arabia

ABDULLAH, JAFRI MALIN, neurosurgeon, educator, researcher; b. Kuantan, Pahang, Malaysia, Dec. 5, 1962; s. Abdullah Samsudin and Norleni (Mohamed Salleh) A.; m. Siti Fatimah Abdul Rahman, Dec. 5, 1987; children: Amirul Jafni Malin, Mohammmed Amir Hariz, Siti Amirah Hana, Mohammad Adam Hafiz, Siti Sara Aishah. MD, U. Sains Malaysia, Penang, 1986; diplomate in neurosurgery, U. Ghent, Belgium, 1994, PhD in Biomed. Scis. magna cum laude, 1995. House officer Hosp. U. Sci. Malaysia, Kubang Kerian, 1986-87, med. officer, 1988-89; resident in neurosurg. U. Ghent, 1989-94, fellow in neurosurgery and neurophysiology, 1994-95; fellow in functional neurosurgery Inst. Karolinska, Stockholm, 1994-95; instr., examiner Cardiopulmonary Resuscitation Group, Kubang, Kelantan, 1987-89; cons. Malaysia Nat. Tissue Bank, Kubang, Kelantan, 1996-98. Contbg. author: Minimal Invasive Neurosurgery, 1994; contbr. articles to profl. jours. including Acta Neurochirurgica and Acta Neurologica Scandanivica. Pres. Malaysian Soc. Ghent, 1990-91, U. Sci. Malaysia, Med. Doctors Alumni Soc., 1986—. Mem. Am. Assn. Neurol. Surgeons, Congress Neurol. Surgeons, Acad. Medicine Malaysia, Belgium Neurosurg. Soc., Internat. Soc. for Pediat. Neurosurgery. Islam. Avocations: collecting antique furnishings, stamps, and old pictures of towns, tennis, international camping. Office: Univ Science Malaysia, Jalan Sultanah Zainab II, Kelantan Kubang Kerian 16150, Malaysia

ABDUL-RAHIM, SHAREEF, professional basketball player; b. Dec. 11, 1976. Forward, guard Vancouver Grizzlies. Named to NBA All-Rookie First Team, 1996-97, Third Team All-Am., AP. Avocations: pool, collecting basketball jerseys, movies. Office: Vancouver Grizzlies, 800 Griffiths Way, Vancouver, BC Canada V6B 6G1

ABDUL RAHMAN, AFAF SHABAN, microbiology educator; b. Cairo, Nov. 13, 1951; d. Shaban Abdul Rahman Ahmed and Fawzia Ahmed (Salama); m. Mansour Mohammed Abdul Ghani, Feb. 16, 1978; children: Abdul Hady, Khlood, Abdul Rahman, Hoor, Niera. MB, BCh, Ain Shams U., Cairo, 1976; MS, Ain Shams U., 1981, PhD, 1988; MS in Ob-Gyn., Azhar U., Cairo, 1988. Demonstrator microbiology Ain Shams U., 1978-82, asst. lectr. microbiology, 1982-88, lectr. microbiology, mycology, 1988-93, asst. prof., 1993—; cons. Mobarak Hosp., Ryiadh, Saudi Arabia, 1988-92, Ganzory Hosp., Cairo, 1995—; rschr. molecular biology U. Mich., Ann Arbor, 1997. Contbr. articles to profl. jours. Recipient award for diagnosis of viruses NAMURO, Cairo, 1984, award for diagnostic methods in immunology NAMURO, 1984, award for diagnostic methods of mycotoxins, Nat. Rsch. Ctr., 1995. Mem. Egyptian Soc. Med. Microbiology, Nasr City Club, Ahly Club. Avocations: draw sewing, poetry, reading, writing poetry, handmade sewing. Home: Dr Mohamed Ahmed Kamal 12, from Abass Elakad St, Nasr City Cairo, Egypt Office: Faculty of Medicine Abbassia, Ain Shams U, Cairo Egypt

ABDULRAZZAQ, YOUSEF MOHAMED, pediatrics educator; b. Dubai, United Arab Emirates, Mar. 29, 1952; s. Mohamed Abdulrazzaq Bastaki and Khadija Mohamed Kazem; m. Suad Ahmed Mohamed-Haji Ahmed, Dec. 3, 1980; children: Abdulla, Jinan, Faisal, Fahad. MD, Shiraz (Iran) U., 1979; PhD, U. London, 1985, DPP, 1996. Resident paediatrician Ministry of Health, Dubai, 1979-80; teaching asst. United Arab Emirates U., Al Ain, 1980-85, asst. prof., 1985—, assoc. prof., 1997—; rsch. fellow St. George's Hosp., London, 1981-85, hon. sr. house officer, 1981-82, hon. registrar, 1982-85; cons. paediatrician Tawan Hosp. & Al Ain Hosp., 1985—. Author and editor: Diabetes Mellitus and Its Complications, 1993, Morphometry: Applications to Medical Sciences, 1997, Clinical Genetics, 1996, Human Heredity, 1996, Pediatric Neurology, 1997, Teratology, 1997; (jour.) Physiol., 1983, Early Human Devel., 1988, Med. Tchr., 1991, 93, Allergy, 1994, Jour. Asthma, 1994, 95, others; editor Emirates Med. Jour. Mem. AAAS, British Med. Assn., European Assn. Sci. Editors, Emirates Med. Assn. (pres. Paediatrics divsn. 1990-92), Coun. Sci. Editors, Royal Coll. Pediatrics and Child Health. Avocations: reading, lawn tennis, table tennis, soccer. Home: PO Box 24, Dubai United Arab Emirates Office: United Arab Emirates U, PO Box 17666, Al-Ain United Arab Emirates

ABDULSALAM, RUKAIYAH HILL, writer; b. Sacramento, Jan. 16, 1959; arrived in Saudi Arabia, 1992; d. Calvin Heywood Hill and Jane Marie Maciel; m. Mohammad Ismail Abdulsalam, July 12, 1991; children: Ismail, Sarah. Student, Morehead State U., 1989-90; cert. interior design/decoration, Florence Tech. Inst. Office mgr. Chapple & Assocs., 1982-85; freelance crafts/interior decorator Tempe, Ariz., 1989-90; mem. ins. underwriting support staff Scottsdale (Ariz.) Ins., 1990-92; editor, freelance writer Jeddah,

Saudi Arabia, 1992-99; editor Abul-Qasim Pub. Ho., Jeddah, 1998. Author: Women's Ideal Liberation, 1998. Mem. Morehead Coalition Homeless, 1989-90; vol. visitor Morehead Treatment Ctr., Ky., 1990. Mem. Univ. Women's Writers Club. Muslim. Avocations: watercolor, travel, aerobics, reading. Home and Office: PO Box 1627, Jeddah 21441, Saudi Arabia

ABDULSAMAD, ESAM OMAR, paleontologist, researcher; b. Benghazi, Libya, Jan. 16, 1961; s. Omar R. and Aminah (Mangush) A.; m. Hend Hamid Yosef Abdulsamad, Feb. 2, 1993; 1 child, Aminah. BS, Garyonis U., Benghazi, Libya, 1986; MS, Southampton (U.K.) U., 1991; PhD, Bologna (Italy) U., 1999. Tchr. Benghazi (Libya) Sch., 1986-89; rsch. assoc., asst. lectr. Garyounis U., Benghazi, Libya, 1992-94; staff mem. earth sci. dept. Garyonis U., Benghazi, Libya, 1994—. Avocations: history, sports, photography, fossil collecting. E-mail: abdul@geomin.unibo.it. Office: U Garyounis Earth Sci Dept, PO Box 9480, 40126 Benghazi Libya

ABE, HIROKI, marine biochemistry educator; b. Tokamachi, Niigata, Japan, May 3, 1944; s. Teiji and Kumiko (Samata) A.; m. Shizuko Akashima, June 29, 1969; children: Yuya, Haruka. BA, U. Tokyo, 1969, MA, 1971, PhD, 1974. Lectr. Kyoritsu Women's U., Tokyo, 1974-78, assoc. prof., 1979-91, prof., 1992-97; prof. U. Tokyo, 1997—; vis. prof. B.C. U., Vancouver, 1983-84. Author: (book) Fish Science, 1994, Food Chemistry of Fishes, 1987; contbr. chpt. to book and numerous articles to profl. jours. Recipient Award for Sci. Progress, Japanese Fisheries Soc., 1996. Mem. AAAS, N.Y. Acad. Sci. Office: U Tokyo Agrl Life Sci, Bunkyo-ku, Tokyo 1138657, Japan

ABE, HIROYUKI, mechanical engineering educator; b. Tokyo, Oct. 9, 1936; s. Yoshio and Mine A.; m. Hiroko Imai, May 15, 1966; children: Yoshikatsu, Motoyuki. B Engring., Tohoku U., Sendai, Japan, 1959, D Engring., 1967. Lectr. Faculty of Engring. Tohoku U., Sendai, 1967-68, assoc. prof., 1968-77, prof., 1977—, senator, 1989-91, dean Faculty of Engring., 1993—, pres.; vis. researcher Northwestern U., Evanston, Ill., 1975-76; dir. internat. house, Tohoku U., 1991-93. Contbr. articles to profl. jours.; patentee in field. Mem. Japan Soc. Mech. Engrs. (medals 1975, 85, 92), ASME, other socs. Home: Taihakuku, 1-5-6 Yagiyamaminami, Sendai Japan Office: Office Pres Tohoku Univ, 2-1-1 Katahira, Aoba Sendai 980-8577, Japan*

ABE, HITOSHI, political science educator; b. Ohta, Tokyo, Japan, June 28, 1933; s. Seiji and Yano Abe; m. Nobuko Hayashi, 1957 (div. 1976); children: Itaru, Yukari; m. Kyo Nakata, Feb. 28, 1977. BA, U. Tokyo, 1957, MA, 1959, PhD, 1963. Assoc. prof. Seikei U., Tokyo, 1966-70, prof., 1970-77; prof. U. Tsukuba, Ibaraki, 1977-85, U. of the Air, Chiba, 1985—. Author: The American Presidency, 1972, Logic of Democracy, 1973, Contemporary American Politics, 1986, Contemporary Politics and Political Science, 1989, Contemporary Political Theories, 1991, Introduction to Political Science, 1996. Fellow Am. Coun. Learned Socs., 1966-68; Fulbright scholar, 1988-89. Mem. Japanese Assn. for Am. Studies (pres. 1996-98), Japanese Polit. Sci. Assn. (dir. 1980-89), Japanese Soc. for Pub. Adminstrn. Avocations: watching a Bunraku puppet show, reading a mystery novel. Home: 5-241-2 Shinmatsudo, Matsudo Chiba 270-0034, Japan Office: U of the Air, 11 2-Chome Wakaba, Mihama Chiba Chiba 261-8586, Japan

ABE, JIN, admissions administrator; b. Yokohama, Japan, Jan. 18, 1964; s. Masayuki and Kazuko Abe; m. Mami Takata, Sept. 11, 1993; 1 child, Jun. Degree in journalism, U. Minn., 1988; postgrad. in counseling in higher edn., Western Mich. U., 1996-99. Mktg. specialist IBM, Osaka, Japan, 1989-96; overseas ednl. advisor Studylink U.S.A., Osaka, 1996; grad. asst. Western Mich. U., Kalamazoo, 1996-98, admissions program specialist, 1998—, instr., 1997. Grantee Assn. Coll. and Univ. Housing Officers, 1997, Assn. Internat. Educators, 1998. Mem. NAFSA-Assn. Internat. Educators (region V MicroSig liaison 1999—), Am. Coll. Pers. Assn. (bd. dirs. 1997—, rsch. grantee 1997). Avocations: paragliding, investing, football, web publishing. Fax: (616) 387-5899. E-mail: jin.abe@wmich.edu. Office: Western Mich U A 411 Ellsworth Hall Kalamazoo MI 49008

ABE, KANJI, statistics educator; b. Changchen, China, Feb. 18, 1939; s. Masao and Harumi Abe; m. Abe Fukuda, Jan. 10, 1969; 3 children: Tomoyuki Fukuda, Yayoi Abe, Chiharu Abe. B., Tokyo U., 1963, M., 1965, D., 1968. Rsch. assoc. Tokyo Inst. Tech., 1970-72; assoc. prof. Kyushu U., Fukuoka, Japan, 1972-77; asst. prof. Tokyo U., 1977-87, prof. stats., computer programing, energy resources, 1987-99; prof. computer simulation Teikyo Heihei U., 1999—. Author: Engineering Mathematics, 1976, Excise in Fluid Dynamics, 1982, Differential Equation, 1991, Dynamics, 1990. Home: Matsuba chou 6-37-4, Kashiwa shi 277, Japan

ABE, KENJI, pathologist, researcher; b. Yamagata, Japan, Oct. 11, 1953; s. Zen-ichi and Yaeko A.; m. Satoko Makino, Mar. 20, 1984; 2 children. DVM, Nippon Vet. and Animal Sci. U., Tokyo, 1972; PhD Sch. Medicine, Nihon U., Tokyo, 1985. Rsch. fellow dept. pathology U. Tokyo, 1976-80; asst. prof. Nihon U., 1977-82; sr. rschr. Nat. Inst. Infectious Diseases (formerly Nat. Inst. Health), Tokyo, 1982—; vis. scientist Lab. Virology, Lindsley F. Kimball Rsch. Inst., N.Y.C., 1990-92. Rsch. prize Japanese Assn. Study of Liver, 1988, Viral Hepatitis Rsch. Found. Japan, 1989, Uehara Meml. Found. Japan, 1990. Fax: 030-3-5285-1189. E-mail: kenjiabe@nih.go.jp. Office: NIID Dept Pathology, Toyama 1-23-1, Tokyo Shinjuku-ku 162-8640, Japan

ABE, MASAYUKI, engineering executive; b. Inawashiro, Fukushima, Japan, Jan. 7, 1941; s. Kihachiro and Miyuki Abe; m. Kasumi Nakamura, May 22, 1973; children: Mika, Mari, Yuki. B in Engring., Osaka (Japan) U., 1967, M in Engring., 1969, PhD, 1973. Group leader Fujitsu Labs. Ltd., Atsugi, Japan, 1973-80; sect. mgr. Fujitsu Labs. Ltd., Atsugi, 1981-85, mgr., 1986-93, gen. mgr., 1994-97; vice dir. Kansai Rsch. Inst. (KRI), Kyoto, Japan, 1998—. Author: GaAs VLSI Technology for High-Speed Computers, 1985, Ultrahigh-Speed HEMT LSI Circuits, 1989, HEMT Devices, 1993; guest editor IEEE Transactions on Electron Devices, 1986. Recipient internat. prize Salone dell'Informatica della Telematica della Orgn. Aziendale, Italy, 1987, Disting. Contributed Paper award Laser Soc. of Japan, 1980. Fellow IEEE, Japan Soc. Applied Physics (bd. dirs. 1994—), Inst. Electronics, Info. and Comm. Engrs. of Japan. Avocations: fishing, playing with Irish setter. Home: 3-10-6 Shibusawa, Hatano 259-1322, Japan Office: Kansai Rsch Inst Kyoto Rsch Park, 17 Chudoji-Minami Shimogyo, Kyoto 600-8813, Japan

ABE, SHUZO, marketing educator; b. Nagao-cho, Japan, Nov. 23, 1944; s. Akira and Chiyoko (Dokan) A.; m. Emiko Tada, Jan. 28, 1973; 1 child, Hiroshi. BCommerce, Meiji U., Tokyo, 1967; MCommerce, Hitotsubash U., Tokyo, 1969, postgrad., 1969-72; postgrad., UCLA, 1981-82. Rsch. asst. Hitotsubashi U., 1972-74; lectr. Nihon U., Tokyo, 1974-77, assoc. prof., 1977-79; assoc. prof. Yokohama (Japan) Nat. U., 1979-87, prof., 1987—; adv. Assn. Consumer Rsch., U.S., 1994-96. Co-author: Global Perspective in Cross-Cultural and Cross-National Consumer Research, 1996; mem. editl. bd. Asian Jour. Mktg., Psychology and Mktg.; contbr. articles to profl. publs. Chmn. Large Retail Stores Coun., Kanagawa, Japan, 1997—. Mem. Japan Assn. Consumer Studies (pres. 1995), Japan Inst. Mktg. Sci. (bd. dirs. 1987—), Japan Soc. Mktg. and Distbn. (pres. 2000—). Buddhist. Avocation: gardening. Office: Yokohama Nat U, 79-4 Tokiwa-dai, Hodogaya Yokohama Kanagawa, Japan

ABE, YUMIKO, obstetrician-gynecologist, educator; b. Yokohama, Japan, Apr. 12, 1956; s. Yoshio and Tatsu Abe. MD, Gunma U. Sch. Medicine, Maebashi, Japan, 1982, PhD, 1990. Med. res. Tokyo Fuchyu Hosp., 1982-83; internal medicine res. Tokyo Women's Hosp., 1983-85; clin. fellow in ob-gyn. Gunma U. Sch. Medicine, 1985-86; assoc. physician Haramachi Red Cross Hosp., Japan, 1990; postdoctoral rsch. fellow, dept. biochemistry Tex. U. Southwestern Med. Ctr., Dallas, 1990-93; adj. ast. prof. ob-gyn. Gunma U. Sch. Medicine, 1994-97, asst. prof. ob-gyn., 1997—. Home: Tonya 2-14-8, Imperial Hts A106, Maebashi 371-0855, Japan Office: Gunma U Sch Medicine, 3-31-22 Showa, Maebashi 371-8511, Tokyo

ABEBA, KADIDJA, court of appeals president. Pres. Ct. of Appeal of Djibouti. Office: Court of Appeal, PO Box 12, Djibouti Djibouti*

ABECASSIS, FERNANDO MARIA DE GAMBOA, engineering executive, educator; b. Venice, Italy, Apr. 1, 1939; s. Alberto Abecassis and Ana Maria Da Costa De Sousa De Macedo De Gamboa Bandeira de Melo; m. Marie Isabelle D'Orey Marchand, Apr. 10, 1965. MA, Lisbon U., Portugal, 1963; diploma in econs., Oxford U., 1971, DPhil, 1974. Profl. civil engr., economist. Exec. dir., CEO Sofamar, Lisbon, 1974-77; engr. Hidrotecnica Portuguesa, Lisbon, 1977-84, exec. dir., 1989-95; exec. dir. EPAL, Emp Aguas de Lisboa, Lisbon, 1984-86; dir. Luso Am. Found., Lisbon, 1986-93; exec. v.p., CEO W.S. Atkins, Lisbon, 1995-2000; prof. U. Lusofona, Lisbon, 1986-2000; asst. prof. U. Nova, Lisbon, 1983-93. Author: Os Desaparecidos, 1989, Project Analyses, 1983, 88, 92, 2000, Agua: O Desafio Vital, 1998. Lt. Army Corp of Engrs., 1962-66, Mozambique. Mem. Ordem des Engrs., Grenio Lit. (dir.), Circulo Eca De Queiroz. Roman Catholic. Avocations: yachting, fencing. Home: Costa Do Castelo 2 2d, 1100 Lisbon Portugal Office: WS Atkins Portugal, R Soeiro P Gomes n 7, 1600 Lisbon Portugal

ABEDI, MEHRDAD, electrical engineering educator; b. Tehran, Iran, Oct. 10, 1948; s. Rahim and Etrah (Ghoreshi) A.; m. Parivash Refahi, June 21, 1979; children: Raha, Nahal. BS, Tehran U., 1970; MS, London U., 1974; PhD, NewCastle U., U.K., 1977. Cert. elecitrical engr. Engr. G.E.C. Co., Stafford, England, 1977-78; asst. prof. Amirkabir U., Tehran, Iran, 1978-88; assoc. prof. Amirkabir U., Tehran, 1988-93, prof., 1993—; chief cons., Ministry of Energy, Tehran, 1980—. Co-editor: (jour.) Amirkabir Jour. Science and Technology. 2nd Lt., Army, 1970-72. Islam. Avocation: swimming. Phone: 0098-21-2564882. Home: Yakhcahal St, Hedayat Ave St No 5, 19497 Tehran Iran Office: Amirkabir U Elec Engring, Hafez Ave, Tehran Iran

ABEDIN, SULTANAL, research phytotaxonomist; b. Ghaziabad, India, Apr. 29, 1937; arrived in Pakistan, 1964; s. Zainal and Muqaddas (Khatoon) A.; m. Tasawwur Khattoon, Feb. 21, 1970; children: Massood Al-Abedin, Mansoor Al-Abedin, Shamaila Abedin. BSc, Muslim U., Aligarh, India, 1958, MSc, 1964; MSc, Karachi (Pakistan) U., 1967, PhD, 1976; DSc, Alternative Medicine Inst., Colombo, Sri Lanka, 1997. Lectr. Karachi U., 1964-68, 76-79, rschr., 1968-76, asst. prof. botany, 1979-81; asst. prof. botany King Saud U., Riyadh, Saudi Arabia, 1981-89, rschr., 1989—; chmn. dept. pharmacognosy, U. Karachi, 1979-81; warden Quaid-i-Azam Hostel, U. Karachi, 1976-80. Author: Know the Plants Around You, 1968; contbr. articles to profl. jours.; patentee in field of new species, subspecies, varieties and new ranks of various taxa. Pres. Aligarh Muslim U. Student Union, 1957-58. Fellow Linnaeus Soc., Royal Soc. Health (London), Pakistan Acad. Pharm. Scis.; mem. Pakistan Pharmacol. Soc. Avocations: travel, bridge, reading, TV. Home: A-459/1 Gulshane Iqbal, Karachi 75300, Pakistan Office: U Karachi, Dept of Botany, Karachi 75270, Pakistan

ABEKAWA, SUMIO, bank executive; b. Tokyo, 1947. Degree, Tokyo U. Dir. Daiwa Bank Ltd., 1968-71, head office bus. dept. to gen. mgr., 1968-69, gen. affairs dept. to gen. mgr., 1969-71, gen. planning divsn. to sr. dep., 1970-71, mng. dir., 1971-75, sr. mgn. dir., 1975-77, dep. pres., 1977-84, pres., 1984-91, chair, 1991-97; bd. dirs., advisor Daiwa Banl Ltd., Osaka. mem., Rohm Music Foundation, Japan. Office: Daiwa Bank Ltd, 2-2-1 Bingo-machi, Chuo-ku Osaka 541, Japan*

ABEL, EDWARD WILLIAM, chemist and educator; b. Kenfig Hill, Glam, Wales, Dec. 3, 1931; s. Sydney John and Donna Maria (Grabham) A.; m. Margaret Rosina Edwards, Aug. 6, 1960; children: Christopher, Julia. BSc, U. Wales, Cardiff, 1952; PhD, No. Poly., London, 1957; DSc, U. London, 1967. Rsch. assoc. Imperial Coll., London, 1957-59; lectr./reader Bristol (U.K.) U., 1959-72; prof. inorganic chemistry Exeter (U.K.) U., 1972-95, dep. vice-chancellor, 1991-94; Chmn. phys. scis. com. Univ. Grants Com., 1986-89, Coun. for Nat. Acad. Awards, 1987-91. Editor: Comprehensive Organometallic Chemistry, 9 vols., 1984, Supplement COMCII, 14 Vols., 1995, Specialist Periodical Reports—Organometallic Chemistry, Vols. 1-25, 1970-96; contbr. articles to profl. jours. Chair UGC Phys. Scis. Com., 1986-89, CNAA Phys. Scis. Com., 1987-91. Decorated comdr. Brit. Empire. Fellow Royal Soc. Chemistry (Main Group Chemistry award 1976, Tilden medal 1981, pres. Dalton divsn. 1987-89, chair sci. affairs bd. 1990-95, pres. 1996-98). Ch. of Eng. Avocation: gardening. Office: U Exeter, Dept Chemistry, Exeter EX4 4QD, England

ABEL, ELIE, reporter, broadcaster, educator; b. Montreal, Que., Can., Oct. 17, 1920; s. Jacob and Rose (Savetsky) A.; children: Mark, Suzanne; m. Charlotte Page Abel, July 2, 1995. B.A., McGill U., 1941, LL.D., 1971; M.S. in Journalism, Columbia U., 1942; LL.D., U. Western Ont., 1976. Reporter Windsor (Ont.) Star, 1941; asst. city editor Montreal Gazette, 1945-46; fgn. corr. N.Am. Newspaper Alliance, Berlin, 1946-47; UN corr. Overseas News Agy., 1947-49; nat., fgn. corr. N.Y. Times, 1949-59; Washington bur. chief Detroit News, 1959-61; with NBC, 1961-69, chief London bur., 1965-67; diplomatic corr. NBC News, Washington, 1967-69; Godfrey Lowell Cabot prof., also dean Grad. Sch. Journalism, Columbia U., N.Y.C., 1969-79; Harry and Norman Chandler prof. Stanford U., 1979-91; Bd. govs. Am. Stock Exchange, 1974-78. Author: The Missile Crisis, 1966, (with Marvin Kalb) Roots of Involvement, The U.S. in Asia 1784-1971, 1971, (with Averell Harriman) Special Envoy to Churchill and Stalin, 1941-46, 1975, Leaking: Who Does It? Who Benefits? At What Cost?, 1987, The Shattered Bloc: Behind the Upheaval in Eastern Europe, 1990; editor: What's News: The Media in American Society, 1981. Recipient George Foster Peabody award for outstanding radio news, 1968; Overseas Press Club award for best interpretation of fgn. news, 1969. Mem. Coun. Fgn. Rels., Cosmos Club (Washington).

ABEL, MICHAEL L., marketing executive; b. New London, Wis., Jan. 15, 1952; s. William A. and Delores R. (Shuey) A.; m. Monica L. Miller, Dec. 18, 1971; children: Richard M., David M. AAS, Joliet (Ill.) Jr. Coll., 1975; BA in Bus. Adminstrn., Lewis U., 1977, MBA, 1979. Lab. technician No. Petrochem. Co., Morris, Ill., 1975-76, tech. specialist, 1976-80; nat. account rep. No. Petrochem. Co., Des Plaines, Ill., 1980-82; product mgr. Enron Chem. Co., Omaha, 1982-85, mktg. mgr., 1985-87; sr. account exec. Quantum Chem. Co., Rancho Mirage, Calif., 1987-89; sr. v.p. N.Am. ops. Intac Automotive Products, Inc., Lemont, Ill., 1989—; pres., chief exec. officer Desert Leisure Devel. Corp., Palm Springs, 1991—, bd. dirs.; bd. dirs. Palm Cts. Assn., Rancho Mirage, 1988-97, The Kids Business, Inc., Rancho Mirage, 1996—. Patentee in chem. engring. field. Pres. Palm Ct. Owners Assn., Rancho Mirage, 1988-97; mem. Rep. Presdl. Task Force, 1990—. Mem. ASTM, Soc. Automotive Engrs., Nat. Assn. Corrosion Engrs. (sec. 1981-82), Internat. Platform Assn. Republican. Lutheran. Home: 36845 Palm Ct Rancho Mirage CA 92270-2206

ABEL, WOLFGANG OTHENIO, botany educator; b. Berlin, Apr. 4, 1932; s. Wolfgang Lothar and Juliane (Versluys) A.; m. Gisela Franziska Frischeisen, Aug. 19, 1958; children: Brigitte, Norbert, Gernot. PhD, U. Vienna, Austria, 1956. Asst. U. Cologne, Germany, 1956-59, Max-Planck-Inst., Heidelberg, Germany, 1959-71; prof. U. Heidelberg, 1971-75, U. Hamburg, 1975—; dean faculty biology U. Heidelberg, 1972-74; mng. dir. Inst. Gen. Botany, U. Hamburg, 1977-81, 91-96. Roman Catholic. Home: Pichlgut Au 36, A-5311 Loibichl Austria Office: Univ Hamburg Inst Botany, Ohnhorststr 18, D-22609 Hamburg Germany

ABELL, RICHARD BENDER (RICHARD LON WELCH), lawyer, federal judicial official; b. Phila., Dec. 2, 1943; s. Lon Edward Welch, Jr. and Charlotte Amelia (Bender) A., stepfather Ernest George Abell; m. Lucia del Carmen Lombana-Cadavid, Dec. 2, 1968; chldren David, Christian, Rachel. BA in Internat. Affairs, George Washington U., 1966, JD, 1974. Bar: Pa. 1974. Vol. Peace Corps, Colombia, 1967-69; assoc. Reilly & Fogwell, West Chester, Pa., 1974-80; asst. dist. atty. Chester County, Pa., 1974-79; staff mem. U.S. Senator Richard Schweiker, Washington, 1979-80; dir. Office of Program Devel. Peace Corp., Washington, 1981-83; dep. asst. atty. gen. U.S. Dept. Justice, Washington, 1983-86, asst. atty. gen., 1986-90; special master U.S. Ct. Fed. Claims, 1991—; mem. adj. faculty Del. Law Sch., Wilmington, 1975-77, West Chester State U., 1976; bd. dirs. Fed. Prison Industries, Inc., 1985-91; chmn. Nat. Crime Prevention Coalition, 1986-90; mem. adv. bd. Nat. Inst. Corrections, 1986-90; co-chmn. adv. com. Nat. Ctr. for State and Local Law Enforcement Tng., 1987-90; vice chmn. rsch. and devel. rev. bd. Dept. Justice, 1987-89; mem. nat. drug policy bd. Enforcement Coordinating Group and Coordinating Group for Drug Abuse Prevention and Health, The White House, Washington, 1988-89. Author: Peter Smith of Westmoreland County, Va. (Died 1741) and Some Descendents, 1996, Sojourns of a Patriot: Field and Prison Papers of An Unreconstructed Confederate, 1998. Chmn. Young Rep. Nat. Fedn., Washington, 1979-81; mem. exec. com. Rep. Nat. Com., 1979-81; mem. fed. coordinating coun. on Juvenile Justice and Delinquency Prevention, 1986-90; mem. Pres.'s Task Force on Adoption, 1987-88; mem. Pres.'s Commn. on Agrl. Workers, 1988-93. With U.S. Army, 1969-71. Decorated Purple Heart, Army Commendation medal for heroism, Air medal; recipient Jefferson Davis Hist. gold medal, 2000. Episcopalian. Home: 8209 Chancery Ct Alexandria VA 22308-1514

ABELLAN, JOSÉ LUIS, humanities educator; b. Madrid, May 19, 1933; s. José M. Abellan and Angela M. Gonzalez. M, U. Complutense, Madrid, 1960; PhD, U. Complutense, 1961. Prof. U. P.R., 1961-63, U. Belfast, Ireland, 1963-65, U. Madrid, 1966—; corr. N.Am. Acad. Spanish Lang., 1993—; rep. of Spain to exec. bd. UNESCO, 1983-85. Author: (7 vols.) History of Spanish Thought, 1979-82, Nat. Essay prize, 1981, Erasmism in Spain, 1976, Theldea of America, 1972; editor: (5 vols.) Spanish Exile of 1939, 1976-78. Grantee Juan March Found., 1976. Fellow Soc. Spanish and Spanish-Am. Studies Nebr. U. Avocations: walking, photography. Home: Gravina 7, 28004 Madrid Spain Office: Facultad de Filosofia, Univ Complutense, 28040 Madrid Spain

ABELS, HERBERT, mathematics educator; b. Aachen, Germany, May 4, 1941. Dr. rer. nat., U. Würzburg, Fed. Republic Germany, 1965, habilitation, 1971. Asst. U. Bochum, Fed. Republic Germany, 1965-71; rsch. fellow U. Calif., Berkeley, 1966-67; prof. U. Bielefeld, Fed. Republic Germany, 1972—; vis. prof. Cornell U., 1987-88. Author: Finite Presentability of S-arithmetic Groups, Compact Presentability of Solvable Groups, 1987. Office: U Bielefeld Postfach 100131, U Bielefeld Postfach 100131, Fakultät Mathematik, D-33501 Bielefeld Germany

ABELSHAUSER, WERNER LUDWIG, educator; b. Wiesloch, Baden, Germany, Nov. 24, 1944; s. Franz Josef and Gertrud (Mangold) A.; m. Petra-Monika Jander, Jan. 11, 1974; 1 child, Hans. Diploma Volkswirt, U. Mannheim, 1970; PhD, U. Bochum, 1973, D Phil habil., 1980. Prof. U. Bochum, 1983-88, U. Bielefeld, Germany, 1991—; dean faculty, 1994-96; bd. dirs. Inst. for European Labor Movement Studies, 1985-88; prof. EUI-Florence, Florence, Italy, 1989-91. Author: Wirtschaftsgeschichte der BRD, 1983, der Ruhrkohlenbergbau seit 1945, 1984, die Weimarer Republik als Wohlfahrtsstaat, 1987, Revolution in Rheinland und Westfalen, 1988, Wirtschaft und Rüstung in den 1950er Jahren. 1997; co-editor: Geschichte und Gesellschaft, 1992—. Fellow St.Antony's Coll., Oxford, European U. Inst., Florence, U. Mo. at St. Louis, U. N.S.W., Sydney. E-mail: werner.abelshanser@geschichte.uni-bielefeld.de. Office: U Bielefeld, Postfach 100131, D-33501 Bielefeld 1 Germany

ABENG, TANRI, diversified industry executive; b. Selayar, Celebes, Indonesia, Mar. 7, 1942; s. Palehe and Kinriati A.; m. Farida Nasution, Oct. 13, 1968; children: Emil, Edwin. BBA, U. Hasanuddin, Indonesia, 1965; MBA, SUNY, Buffalo, 1968. Office mgr., chief acct. PT Union Carbide Indonesia, Jakarta, 1969-71, sec., treas., 1971-76; mktg. ops. mgr. Union Carbide Singapore Pte. Ltd., 1976-79; pres., CEO PT Multi Bintang Indonesia, Jakarta, 1980—; min. of state for reform of state enterprises Indonesia; supr. PT Lucent Techs., Jakarta; bd. dirs. PT Perusahaan Limun Indonesia Jakarta, 1981—, Malayan Breweries Ltd., Singapore, 1982—; commr. PT Food Specialities Indonesia, 1985—. Mem. Indonesian Mgmt. Assn. (pres. 1983—), Bina Antar Budaya (vice chmn. 1985—), Indonesian Inst. Mgmt. Devel. (mem. adv. bd.), Asia Soc. (mem. internat. coun. 1984—), Indonesian C. of C. (chmn. environ. dept. 1985—), Indonesian Lawn Tennis Assn. (chmn. 1986—). Avocation: tennis. Office: GKBI Tower, Semanggi, Central Jakarta Indonesia*

ÅBERG, TORKEL HAMPUS JOHAN, cardio-thoracic surgeon; b. Mexico City, Mar. 31, 1939; arrived in Sweden, 1945; s. Karin S.G. Huldt Åberg; m. Gun Wallin. MB, Karolinska Inst., Stockholm, 1959, lic. medicine, 1965, MD, 1974; specialty degree in thoracic surgery, U. Uppsala, Sweden, 1975. Cons. dept. thoracic surgery Upsala Akademiska sjukhus, 1988-92; head dept. thoracic and cardiovascular surgery Umeå (Sweden) Univ. Hosp., 1988, 95—, Univ. Hosp., Lund, Sweden, 1994; dir. heart ctr. Umeå (Sweden) Univ. Hosp., 1997. Author: Lower Costs, Better Health Care, 1992; contbr. over 200 articles to profl. jours. Cons. Swedish Bd. Health and Welfare, 1983-94, mem. adv. bd. for cardiac and cardiovascular diseases. Served with Swedish mil. Mem. Am. Assn. Thoracic Surgery, Soc. Thoracic Surgeons, Soc. Cardiothoracic Surgeons of Gt. Britain and Ireland (hon.), European Assn. Cardio-Thoracic Surgery (sec. gen. 1992—, sec. CTSNet, bd. dirs. 1999—). Office: Heart Ctr, Univ Hosp, S-90185 Umeå Sweden

ABERNETHY, ROBERT JOHN, real estate developer; b. Indpls., Feb. 28, 1940; s. George Lawrence and Helen Sarah (McLandress) A. BA, Johns Hopkins U., 1962; MBA, Harvard U., 1968; cert. in real estate fin. and constrn., UCLA, 1974. Asst. to chief scientist Phoenix missile program Hughes Aircraft Co., L.A., 1968-69, asst. program mgr. Iroquois night fighter and night tracker program, 1969-71, asst. to contr. space and comm. group, 1971-72, contr. tech. divsn., 1972-74; pres. Am. Std. Devel. Co., L.A., 1974—, Transit Cmty. Devel. Corp., 1997—; bd. dirs., chmn. audit com. Pub. Storage, Inc., Glendale, Calif., Marathon Nat. Bank, L.A., Tech Net, L.A. Bancorp, Met. Water Dist., So. Calif., Met. Transp. Authority, L.A. County; pres. Self Svc. Storage Assn., San Francisco, 1978-83. Asst. to dep. campaign mgr. Humphrey for Pres., Washington, 1968; commr. L.A. Planning Commn., 1984-88, L.A. Telecom. Commn., 1992-93, Calif. Transp. Commn., 1999—, Calif. State Bd. Edn., 2000—; vice chmn. L.A. Econ. Devel. Coun., 1988-93; chmn. Ctr. for Study Dem. Inst., Santa Barbara, Calif., 1986—; bd. dirs. Met. Transp. Authority Los Angeles County, South Bay Civic Light Opera, World Children's Transplant Fund, French Found. for Alzheimers Rsch., Pacific Coun. on Internat. Policy; adv. bd. mem. Peabody Conservatory, 1992—, Ctr. Talented Youth, 1992—, Nitse Sch. Advanced Internat. Studies, 1993—, Harvard Ptnrs., 1996—, Inst. Acad. Achievement of Youth, 1999—; bd. vis. Davidson Coll.; bd. dirs. L.A. Theatre Ctr., 1986-92, YMCA; trustee Johns Hopkins U., 1991—; mem. Coun. on Fgn. Rels., L.A. Com. on Fgn. Rels. Lt. USNR, 1962-66. Mem. So. Calif. Planning Congress (bd. dirs.), Parker Found. (bd. dirs.), California Club, St. Francis Yacht Club, Jonathan Club, Calif. Yacht Club, Alpha Lambda. Address: 5221 W 102nd St Los Angeles CA 90045-6001

ABETZ, ERIC, senator; b. Stuttgart, Germany, Jan. 25, 1958; arrived in Australia, 1961; s. Walter and Irmgard (Seitz) A.; m. Michelle Ann Oates, Oct. 5, 1991; children: Laura, John, Jeremy. BA, U. Tasmania, Australia, 1979, LLB, 1981. Ptnr. Abetz, Curtis & Docking, Australia, 1987-94; liberal senator for Tasmania Govt. of Australia, Hobart, 1994—; barrister, solicitor Supreme Ct. of Tasmania, 1983—, High Ct. of Australia, 1986—; commr. Supreme Ct. of Tasmania, 1987-94; legal cons. Abetz & Co. in conjunction with Shields Heritage, Australia, 1994—. State pres. Tasmanian divsn. Liberal Party of Australia, 1990-94; fed. pres. Australian Liberal Student's Fedn., 1980-81. Mem. Rotary Internat. Mem. Reformed Ch. Avocations: gardening, bush walking. Office: Govt of Australia, GPO Box 1675, Hobart TAS 7001, Australia

ABHARY, KAZEM, mechanical and manufacturing engineering educator, researcher, consultant; b. Tehran, Iran, Apr. 22, 1947; s. Fazlollah and Shamsi (Soleimani-Moghaddam) A.; m. Tahereh Ziaian, June 11, 1976; children: Sabahat, Sotoodeh. BS in Mech. Engring., Tehran U., 1969, MS in Mech. Engring., 1970; MS in Mech. Engring., U. Manchester Inst. Sci. and Tech., Eng., 1973, PhD in Mech. Engring., 1975. Mech. engr. Steel Mill of Iran, Tehran, Esfahan, 1970-72; asst. prof. Tehran U., 1975-85, assoc. prof., 1985-87; sr. lectr. U. Tech., Lae, Papua New Guinea, 1987-88; sr. lectr. U. South Australia, 1988-98, assoc. prof., 1999—; vis. prof. Machine Tool Mfg. Co., Tabriz, Iran, 1980-81, U. NSW, Sydney, Australia, 1986-87, Tehran U., 1990-91; mem. coun. chancellorship Tehran U., 1979-80; mem. supreme coun. Dept. Edn., Iran, 1980-82; mem. directing bd. Iranian Aviation Industry, Tehran, 1981-82; bachelor course coord. U. South Australia, Sch. Mfg. and Mech. Engring., 1992-94, masters course coord., 2000—, head sch., 1998; consulting engr. numerous industries, Iran and Australia, 1975—; spkr. SBS radio, Australia, 1993—; mem. organising com./adv. bd. numerous internat. engring. confs. Author: Vector Mechanics, Dynamics, 1971, Applied Mathematics, 1971, Vocabulary of Mechanical Engineering, English-Persian, Persian-English, 1997; translator: Some Applications of Mechanics in Mathematics, 1982; editor-in-chief Mech. Engring. Publs., Iran Univ.

Press, 1984-86; assoc. editor: Engineering Design and Automation; contbr. numerous articles to engring. jours.; inventor rotary press for mfg. small insulators. Mem. coun. South Australian Secondary Sch. Langs., Adelaide, Australia, 1992—; mem. adv. com. Sr. Secondary Assessment Bd. South Australia, Adelaide, 1992—; dep. mem. Multicultural Edn. Coordinating Com., South Australia, 1994-99, mem. multicultural edn. com., 2000—; mem. Stds.-Australia/Std.-New Zealand Mech. Engring. Com., 1994—. Recipient scholarship Tehran U., 1972-75. Mem. ASME, Internat. Inst. Acoustics and Vibration, Australasian Assn. for Engring. Edn., Am. Soc. for Engring. Edn. Avocations: poetry, classical music, sports, philosophy of science, yoga. Office: U South Australia, Dept Adv Mfg and Mech Engring, The Levels Campus Mawson Lakes SA 5095, Australia

ABHYANKAR, KRISHNA DAMODAR, retired astronomy educator; b. Indore, India, June 21, 1928; s. Damodar Keshav and Sarajabai Abhyankar; m. Shalaja Krishna Kelkar Leela, May 5, 1960. BS, Agra U., India, 1949, MS in Physics, 1951; PhD in Astronomy, U. Calif., Berkeley, 1959. Lectr. in physics Holkar Coll., Indore, India, 1951-52; sr. rsch. fellow Kodaikanal Obs., India, 1952-54; Lick obs. fellow U. Calif., Berkeley, 1955-58; jr. rsch. astronomer U. Calif., 1958-59; prof. astronomy Osmania U., Hyderabad, India, 1960-88; emeritus prof. U. G.C., New Delhi, 1989-91; postdoctoral fellow David Dunlap Obs., Toronto, 1963-64; postdoctoral resident rsch. assoc. Jet Propulsion Lab., Pasadena, Calif., 1967-70; head astronomy dept., dir. Nizamiah & Japal Rangapur Obs. Osmania U., 1961-63, 73-81, 86-88. Author: Astrophysics: Stars and Galaxies, 1992, Astrophysics of the Solar System, 1999, (collection of Marathi poems) Belaché Paan, 1999; editor: Bull. Astron. Soc. India, 1992-94. Pres. Vivekananda Negar Welfare Assn., Hyderabad, 1984-90. Fellow Royal Astron. Soc., Indian Nat. Sci. Acad., Indian Acad. Sci., Nat. Acad. Sci.; mem. Astron. Soc. India (pres. 1980-82), Astron. Soc. Pacific, Internat. Astron. Union. Avocations: bridge, popular lectures, radio talks, poetry. Home: 5 76 Vivekananda Habshiguda St 8/26, Hyderabad 500007, India

ABID, ALI, artist, caricaturist; b. Tunis, Tunisia, 1938; married; 9 children. Caricaturist several Tunisian newspapers, Dialogue Mag. Exhibited in group shows in Tunis, 1972, Cite Internationale des Arts, Paris, 1974, Internat. Salon Humour, Bordighera, Italy, Internat. Salon Caricature, Montreal, Can. Recipient 1st prize La Marsa Commune, Salon Caricature Arabe, 1981, Prize Arab Union of Journalists, 1993. Mem. Nat. Union Plastic and Graphic Arts. Avocation: graphic arts. Home: 27 Rue de la Menthe, Cité Ezzouhour, Tunis Tunisia

ABID, RUHUL, geneticist, researcher; b. Dhaka, Bangladesh, May 27, 1961; s. Abdul Ghafoor and Razia Begum; m. Tahamma Abid, May 19, 1985; children: Faisal, Tanaz. MD, Dhaka U., 1986; PhD in Genetics, Nagoya U., 1997. Resident Dhaka Med. Hosp., 1986-87; med. officer Duncan Hosp., Dhaka, 1988-91; group med. officer Cmty. Hosp., Dhaka, 1991-92; rsch. assoc. Nagoya (Japan) U., 1993-94; postdoctoral rschr. La. State U., Shreveport, La., 1997-99; genetic rschr. Harvard U., Boston, 1999—; advisor PhD com., Nagoya U., 1997-98. Contbr. articles to sci. and profl. jours. Sci. fellow, Japanese Govt., 1993-97. Mem. AAAS, Am. Assn. Cancer Rsch., Molecular Biolog. Assn. Avocations: tennis, travel, music, history. Home: 19 Maple St Belmont MA 02478-1935 Office: Harvard U E/RW 663 330 Brookline Ave Boston MA 02215-5400

ABIDI, SYED KAZIM HUSAIN, management executive; b. Lucknow, India, May 31, 1939; s. S.B.H. and S.B. Abidi; m. Tatheer Abidi, Aug. 15, 1968; children: Ghizal, Farhal. BA in Econs., Karachi (Pakistan) U., 1959, MA in Econs., 1961. Vice prin. Model High Sch., Karachi, 1959-61; lectr. econs. and stats. Nat. Coll., U. Karachi, 1961-62; math. tchr. Wimbledon High Sch., London, 1962-68; supr. stats. and o.r. techniques Chiswick Poly., London, 1968-74; dir. rsch., consultancy and tng. West London Inst. Higher Edn., 1978-83; sr. assoc. cons. Royal Inst. Pub. Adminstrn., London, 1983-85; prin. cons. Mgmt. Consultants Internat., London, 1983-85; chief exec. Mgmt. Advisors London, 1986—; vis. lectr. Bedford Coll., U. London, Royal Inst. Pub. Adminstrn.; cons. London boroughs of Camden, Ealing, Greater London Coun., Croydon, Hammersmith, Houslow, Westminster and Royal Borough of Kensington, Chelsea, Uniliver, Glaxo, Beecham, Westminster Bank; overseas cons., Indonesia, Pakistan, Egypt, Malaysia. Author: Mathematical Analysis for Management Decisions, 1986, Mathematics of Work Management, 1988, Statistics as an Aid to Management, 1990; contbr. articles to profl. jours. Fellow Royal Statis. Soc., Am. Biograph. Rsch. Inst., Am. Biograph. Inst. (lifetime dep. gov.); mem. Inst. Stats., Brit. Inst. Mgmt. Avocations: football, cricket, tennis. Office: Willow House, 47 West St, Surrey Sutton SM1 1SJ, England

ABIKO, YOSHIMITSU, dental studies educator; b. Taipei, Taiwan, Nov. 26, 1947; parents Gyokusan and Shima Abiko; m. Noriko Abiko Endo, Mar. 20, 1975; children: Rieka, Yurika. DDS, PhD, Nihon U., Surugadai, Tokyo, 1977. Cert. dentist, Tokyo. From instr. to asst. prof. to assoc. prof. Nihon U., Matsudo, Chiba, 1971-92; prof. Nihon U., Matsudo, 1992—; vis. asst. prof. Ala. U., 1978-80; advisor Japanese Assn. Dental Rsch., Osaka, 1998—; dir. Japanese Oral Biology Assn., Tokyo, 1997—. Named Hakuyuukai Outstanding Rschr., Tokyo, 1986. Mem. Internat. Assn. Dental Rsch., Am. Biol. Chemistry and Molecular Biology Assn. Avocations: music, tennis, traveling. Fax: 81-47-360-9329. E-mail: yabiko@mascat.nihon-u.ac.jp. Home: 3-401 Shinmatsudo, Matsudo Chiba 270-0034, Japan Office: Nihon U, 2-870-1 Sakaecho-nishi, Matsudo Chiba 271-8587, Japan

ABI-SAD, SERGIO CALDAS MERCADOR, diplomat; b. San Fidelis, Rio de Janeiro, Brazil, Mar. 2, 1942; s. José Mercador Abi-Sad and Ana Caldas Mercador. LLD, U. Brazil, 1966; postgrad., Diplomatic Sch. Brazil, 1964-66, Inst. for Univ. Studies, Geneva, 1983. Lic. lawyer; cert. diplomat. 3rd sec. Ministry for Foreign Affairs, 1966-69, 2nd sec., 1969-76, 1st sec., 1976-84, counselor, 1989—, head western European divsn., 1993-95; alternate mem. Brazilian delegation Internat. Atomic Energy Agy., Vienna, Austria, 1996-97; assignments abroad Ministry Fgn. Affairs include Genoa, Italy, 1969-71, Kabidjan, Ivory Coast, 1971-74, Sofia, Bulgaria, 1974-75, Ottawa, Can., 1977-81, Bern, Switzerland, 1981-87, Ankara, Turkey, 1989-91, Peking China, 1991-93, Vienna, Austria, 1996—; tchr. diplomatic sch. Brasiun, 1975-76, 94-95; lectr. Air Force Sch., Rio de Janeiro, Brazil, War Sch., Rio de Janeiro, 1994; Brazilian rep. Orgn. for Complete Nuclear Test-Ban, 1996-98, UN Commn. for Outer Space, 1996-98; mem. Latin Am. and Caribbean Group IAEA, 1996-98, del. Nuclear Supplies Group, 1996-98; v.p. diplomatic conf. on nuclear liability, Vienna, 1997. Author: The Power of the Dragon, 1996, The Wall and the Myth, 1996; The Rebel Angels and the Celestial Peace, 1997. Brazilian del. to Germany, Eng., Portugal, European Union, 1993-95. Named comdr. Nat. Orders of Germany, Italy, Portugal and Côte D'Ivoire; recipient medal Brazilian Navy, Brasilia, 1988. Avocations: jogging, swimming, collecting stamp and rare books. Home: Shin QL 15 Cons 8 Casa 2, Lago Norte Brazil Office: Brazilian Embassy, Itainen Puistotie 4-B-1, 00140 Helsinki Suomi, Finland

ABITBOL, WILLIAM, foreign diplomat; b. Paris, Sept. 6, 1949. Mem. European Parliament, 1999—, vice chmn. com. on econ. and monetary affairs, substitute com. on constnl. affairs; mem. Union for Europe of the Nations Group; mem. delegation for relations with Switzerland, Iceland and Norway. Office: Rassemblement pour la Franc, 159 rue Charles de Gaulle, F-92200 Neuilly France*

ABIVARDI, CYRUS, scientist, researcher, educator; b. Shiraz, Fars, Iran, Dec. 22, 1940; arrived in Switzerland, 1981; s. Gholam-Reza and Khomar (Gorguin-Pour) A.; m. Homa Jahanshahi, Sept. 14, 1966; children: Haleh, Golnar, Aslan. Degree agricultural engring., Shiraz (Iran) U., 1963; PhD, U. Calif., Davis, 1968. Instr. Shiraz U., 1963-65, asst. prof., 1968-71, assoc. prof., 1972-79, prof., 1980; scientific cooperator ETH, Zurich, Switzerland, 1983-84, scientific collaborator, 1986-91, sr. scientist, 1992—; scientific cooperator Sandoz, Witterswil, Switzerland, 1984-85; prof. agrobiology Ciba-Geigy, Basel, Switzerland, 1985-86; rsch. cons. Dept. Environtl. Protection, Tehran, Iran, 1973-74; vis. prof. Colo. State U., Ft. Collins, 1976-77; assoc. dean Coll. Agrl. Shiraz U., 1978-79; dir. agrl. rsch. ctr. Coll. of Agrl., 1978-79, chair dept. plant protection, 1979-81. Assoc. editor: Iranian Jour. of Agrl. Rsch., 1971-76, Nematologia Mediterranea, Bari, Italy, 1971-76; author: An Introduction to Iranian Entomology 2 volumes, 2000; Founder: The first rose garden of Iran (Eram Garden, Shiraz, Iran); contbr. articles to profl. publs. Scholarship Ministry of Sci., 1965-68. Mem. Entomol. Soc. of Am., Swiss Entomol. Soc., Assn. of Applied Biologists. Avocations: music, reading, writing, ping-pong. Office: Swiss Fed Inst Tech, Zurhichberg Str #38, Ch-8044 Zurich Switzerland

ABIYEV, SAFAR, government official; b. Baku, Azerbaijan, 1950; married; 2 children. Grad., Baku All-Mil. Officers' Sch., 1971. Min. of def. Govt. Azerbaijan, Baku, 1992—. Office: Ministry of Defense, Azizbeyou prospekri 3, Baku 370073, Azerbaijan*

ABKEN, HINRICH JOHANN, biochemist, immunologist, researcher; b. Esens-Ostfriesland, Germany, Apr. 23, 1958; m. Juliane Fluck. MD, U. Essen, Germany, 1985. Postdoctoral in cancer rsch. U. Essen, 1983-88; group leader in cancer rsch. U. Bonn, Germany, 1988-93; prof. cancer genetics and cell biology U. Cologne, Germany, 1993—; co-founder AbGen GmbH. Patentee in field of tumor markers and growth control; contbr. articles to profl. jours. Office: Medizinische Klinik, Tumor Gen/Lfl E4 Uni-Klinik, Cologne D-50924, Germany

ABLE-THOMAS, URIEL LYTTON, engineering executive; b. Banjul, The Gambia, Sept. 25, 1957; s. Samuel Charles and Kezia Susannah Able-Thomas; m. Jean Able-Thomas, June 8, 1991. BSc with honors, Bolton (Eng.) Inst. Higher Edn, 1983; MSc, U. Wales, Cardiff, 1987; PhD, U. Northumbria, Newcastle Upon Tyne, Eng., 1994. Hydrometrist Water Resources Dept., Banjul, 1978-80; electronic cadet Civil Aviation Dept., Yundum, The Gambia, 1980-83; electronics engr. Civil Aviation Dept., Yundum, 1983-90, sr. electronics engr., 1990-91, engring. dir., 1994—; rsch. engr. Northumbri U., Newcastle Upon Tyne, 1991-94; sr. staff counselor The Salvation Army, Ashford, Conn., 1982; rsch. engr. Inst. Ctr. for Theoretical Physics, Trieste, Italy, 1993; cons. Gambia Renewable Energy Ctr., Kanifing, 1994—; engring. adviser Internat. Civil Aviation Orgn., Dakar, Senegal, 1995. Contbr. articles to profl. jours. Recipient Reliability prize Govs. Gambia H.S., Banjul, 1976, Lawn Tennis prize The Gambia Tennis Assn., Banjul, 1990, Table-Tennis prize Organizing Com. Gambia Civil Aviation Authority, Yundum, 1995. Mem. Instn. Elec. Engrs. (corp. mem.), World Renewable Energy Congress (internat. steering com.), Engring. Coun. (chartered engr.). Anglo-Catholic. Avocations: sports, farming, traveling. Office: Gambia Civil Aviation Auth, PO Box 285, Banjul The Gambia

ABLIN, RICHARD JOEL, immunologist, educator; b. Chgo., May 15, 1940; s. Robert Benjamin and Minnie Edith (Gordon) A.; m. Linda Lee Lutwack; 1 son, Michael David. AB, Lake Forest Coll., 1962; PhD in Microbiology, SUNY, Buffalo, 1967. Diplomate Am. Bd. Clin. Immunology and Allergy; cert. specialist in pub. health and med. lab. microbiology Nat. Registry Microbiologists of Am. Acad. Microbiology. Grad. asst. dept. biology SUNY-Buffalo, 1963-65, research asst., summer 1963, research fellow, 1965-66; USPHS postdoctoral fellow dept. microbiology Sch. Medicine, lectr., lab instr., 1966-68; instr., research asst. Rosary Hill Coll., 1965-66; research cons. program med. edn. AID, Paraguay, 1968; dir. div. immunology Millard Fillmore Hosp. Rsch. Inst., Buffalo, 1968-70; head sect. immunology, renal unit Meml. Hosp. of Springfield, 1970-73; dir. sect. immunobiology div. urology dept. surgery Cook County Hosp. and Hektoen Inst. for Med. Research, Chgo., 1973-75, sr. sci. officer div. immunology, 1976-83; sr. mem. sci. staff, clin. immunologist Cook County Hosp., 1973-75; asst. prof. medicine So. Ill. U., 1971-73; assoc. prof. microbiology Univ. Health Sci. (Chgo. Med. Sch.), 1973-74; research assoc. prof. urology, dir. immunology unit dept. urology SUNY, Stony Brook, 1983-89; pres., dir. Robert Benjamin Ablin Found. for Cancer Rsch., Evergreen Park, Ill., 1979—; dir. sci. investigation Innapharma, Inc., Suffern, N.Y., 1991—; mem. Univ. Senate, 1986-89, 89-92, Univ. Governing Coms., 1984-92; acad. del. United Univ. Professions, 1986-88, 88-90; organizer, presenter, instr., participant numerous nat. and internat. profl. meetings, symposia, seminars. Editor: Allergologia et Immunopathologia, 1980-84; contbg. editor: Current Perspectives in Allergology and Immunopathology, 1974-84; assoc. editor Jour. Investigational Allergology and Clin. Immunology (formerly Allergologia et Immunopathologia), 1985-95, Seminars in Immunopathology and Oncology, Ill. Med. Jour., 1975-88; adv. editor: Jour. Cancer, 1976—; assoc. editor: Low Temperature Medicine, 1975—; mem. internat. editl. staff: Medikon, 1974—; mem. editl. bd. Advances in Therapy, 1999—, Am. Jour. Reproductive Immunology and Microbiology, 1980-91, Annals Clin. and Lab. Sci., 2000—, Bratislava Med. Jour., 1999—, Current Oncology, 1998—, Immunology and Allergy Practice, 1979-95, Cellular and Molecular Biology, 1985-87, Early Pregnancy: Biology and Medicine, 1995—, Prostate Jour., 1999—, Procs. Soc. Exptl. Biology and Medicine, 2000—; mem. sci. bd. Chemistry Today, 1991-97, TumorDiagnostik and Therapie, 1980-98; mem. editl. acad. Internat. Jour. of Oncology, 1996—; mem. editl. adv. bd. Med. Sci. Rsch., 1984—; contbr. numerous articles to profl. jours. and texts. Chief Sangamo Nation Y-Indian Guides, Springfield, 1972-73; mgr. Skokie Indians' Boys' Baseball, Ill., 1973-74, 77, 80, 81, bd. dirs., 1979-83, exec. v.p., 1981-82; mgr. Little League Three Villages, Setauket, N.Y., 1986; cubmaster N.W. Suburban coun. Boy Scouts Am., 1974-78, asst. scoutmaster, 1975-77; mem. exploring divsn. Suffolk County coun. Boy Scouts Am., 1985-88; pres., dir. Spirit of Chgo. Hockey Club Found., Evergreen Park, Ill., 1982—. Recipient Nat. Pres. Leader's Dist. Boy Scouts Am., 1975; named Cubmaster of Yr. Boy Scouts Am., 1977. Fellow Am. Coll. Allergy and Immunology, Am. Coll. Cryosurgery (v.p. 1977-79, parliamentarian 1977-79, adv. bd. 1977-78, 80-81, 84-99), Indian Cryogenics Coun. (hon.), Assn. Clin. Scientists; mem. AAAS, Am. Assn. Cancer Rsch., Am. Assn. Immunologists, Am. Soc. Microbiology, Assn. Med. Lab. Immunologists, Brit. Assn. Surg. Oncology, Buffalo Collegium Immunology, Ernest Witebsky Ctr. for Immunology, Internat. Soc. Andrology, Internat. Soc. Chronobiology, Internat. Soc. Cryosurgery (pres. 1977-80, hon. life pres.), Internat. Soc. Immunology Reprodn., Japan Soc. Low Temperature Medicine, N.Y. Acad. Scis., Soc. Leukocyte Biology, Soc. Cryobiology, Soc. Protozoologists, Soc. Study Reprodn., Soc. Exptl. Biology and Medicine, Transplantation Soc., Cryoimmunotherapeutic Study Group (chmn.), Sigma Xi, Phi Beta Kappa (Theta of Ill. at Lake Forest Coll.). Achievements include identification of prostate specific antigen (PSA), used as tumor marker (diagnosis) in prostate cancer, and of human thymic specific antigen providing means for differentiation of thymic lymphocytes from other lymphoid cells and the development of antithymocyte globulin (selectively immunosuppressive for thymocytes) used in renal allograft (transplant) recipients; and development of concept of cryoimmunotherapy for treatment of cancer. Office: Innapharma Inc Suffern NY 10901

ABOAGYE, SAMPSON YAW, medical educator; b. Akim Tumfa, Ghana, Aug. 20, 1945; s. Foster Kwabena Anane and Grace Pankyee; m. Elizabeth Appiah, June 21, 997; children: Jnr, Stephanie. Gen. cert. edn., Aristotle U., Thessaloniki, Greece, 1968; MD, Athens (Greece) U., 1982. Med. clk. internal medicine U. Turku (Finland) Med. Sch., 1977; houseman pediat., gen. surgery and internal medicine 37 Mil. Hosp., Accra, Ghana, 1983-85; med. officer 37 Mil. Hosp., Accra, 1985-86; resident Chest Clinic Sismanogleio Gen. Hosp., Athens, 1986-90; sr. med. officer pulmonology and tuberculosis Korle-Bu Tchg. Hosp., Accra, 1990—, acting head dept. Chest Clinic, 1996—; chest physician specialist head chest dept. Korle-Bu Tchg. Hosp., 1999; facilitator Nat. Tuberculosis Control Program, Ghana Internat. Asthma Coun., Internat. Union Against Tuberculosis and Lund Diseases; Ghana Med. Assn. rep. Greater Accra Prisons Com.; lectr. in field. Contbr. articles to profl. jours. Founder Kindness Club Ghana, 1966-68; med. adviser Environ. Restoration Orgn., Accra, 1996, Okwawuman Congress, Accra, 1997. Ghana Govt. scholar, Salonica, Greece, 1974-82, Athens U., Greece, 1986-90. Mem. Hellenic Thoracic Soc., Nat. Tuberculosis Programme Ghana. Avocations: traveling, table tennis, current affairs, nature. Home: PO Box 3989, Accra Ghana Office: K Bu Tchg Hosp Chest Dept, PO Box 77, Accra Ghana

ABOALSAMH, DUAÁ ABDULRAHMAN, endodontist, researcher; b. Cairo, Nov. 3, 1964; d. Abdulrahman Abdulzaher Aboalsamh and Amina Mohamed Abdulghani. BS/DDS, King Saud U., Riyadh, Saudi Arabia, 1989, MS in Dental Sci. with honors, 1995, cert. in endodontics, 1995. Gen. dentist Security Forces Hosp., Riyadh, 1988-89, Hada (Saudi Arabia) Mil. Hosp., 1989-94; specialist endodontist Riyadh Mil. Hosp., 1994—; lectr. King Saud U., 1991-95. Mem. ADA, Saudi Dental Soc. Avocations: painting, swimming, writing. Home: PO Box 829, 11421 Riyadh Saudi Arabia Office: Riyadh Military Hospital, Solimania, Riyadh Saudi Arabia

ABOLO, EMMANUEL MOORE, economist; b. Sapele, Nigeria, Dec. 25, 1961; s. David Umukata and Edje Maryn (Eyefia) A.; m. Endurance Inikori Akponeware, Oct. 19, 1996; children: Terrence, Onome, Neville, Hurwiz. BSc, U. Lagos, Nigeria, 1984, MSc, 1986, PhD, 1994. Cert. economist. Fin. exec. Credit Alliance Fin. Svcs. Ltd., Lagos, 1987-88; asst. fellow Nat. Ctr. for Econ. Mgmt. and Adminstrn., Ibadan, Nigeria, 1988-89; mgr. Jet Fin. and Cons. Ltd., Lagos, 1989; head corp. fin. New Horizons Fin., Lagos, 1989-90; head spl. projects FP Comm. Ltd., Lagos, 1990-91; sr. cons. Coopers & Lybrand, Lagos, 1991-95; head corp. planning and implementations monitoring First Bank of Nigeria, Lagos, 1995—; bd. dirs. Terrence Moore & Assocs., Lagos Ctr. for Rsch. in Bus. and Govt. Policy, Lagos Datanomics Info. Investments Ltd., Lagos; assoc. lectr. dept. econs. U. Lagos, 1996-99; fellow Inst. Credit Adminstrn., 1997, Inst. Ind. Membership Mgmt. Nigeria, 1997, Inst. Ind. Mktg. Mgrs. Nigeria, 1999; assoc. Cert. Inst. Mktg. Nigeria, 1999; mem. bd. acad. advisers Grad. Sch. Credit Adminstrn., Lagos, 1998—. Author: Economics for SSS/Students, 1994; contbg. editor Air Commerce Nigeria, Quarterly Mgmt. and Bus. Jour., 1997—; mem. editl. bd. Nigeria Environment Forum; contbr. articles to profl. jours. Mem. Nat. Youth Svc. Corps, Porthacourt, 1985; asst. sec. Nigeria Econs. Students Assn., Lagos, 1982. Recipient Nat. Merit award Fed. Govt. of Nigeria, 1982. Mem. Inst. of Chartered Accts. of Nigeria, Chartered Inst. Bankers of Nigeria, Nigeria Inst. Mgmt. (assoc.), Nigerian Econ. Soc. Avocations: football, table tennis, athletics, lawn tennis, reading. Home: PO Box 3113, Shomolu Lagos Nigeria Office: First Bank of Nigeria Plc, 35 Marina 11th Fl, Lagos Nigeria

ABONYI, GEORGE, international development consultant; b. Miskolc, Hungary, Apr. 8, 1948; arrived in Can., 1959; s. Andor and Irene (Grosz) A.; m. Thora Kristin Broughton, Apr. 9, 1983; children: David B., Benjamin A. BA with honors in Econs., U. Toronto, Ont., Can., 1971; MA in Econs., York U., Toronto, 1972; PhD, UCLA, 1978. Prof. strategic mgmt. faculty adminstrn. U. Ottawa, Ont., 1977-91; sr. advisor Nat. Econs. and Social Devel. Bd., Office Prime Min., Bangkok, 1983-86, 88-92, 96-99; sr. advisor Asia Pacific region Can. Internat. Devel. Agy., Singapore, 1992-94; sr. advisor, mem. core coord. group, econ. coop. program Greater Mekong Region (GMS) Asian Devel. Bank, 1994—, sr. advisor strategy & policy dept., 1999-2000; team leader Strategy for Silk Rd. Area Devel. Program UN Devel. Program, 1997-98; vis. prof. Grad. Sch. Mgmt., UCLA, 1980-81; sr. rsch. fellow, vis. prof. Ctr. Applied Studies in Devel., U. South Pacific, Suva, Fiji, 1982; sr. vis. fellow Masters in Publ Policy Programme, Nat. U. Singaport, 1994-98; assoc. sr. fellow Inst. Southeast Asia Studies, Singapore, 1996—; exec. dir. Asia Strategy Forum; cons., team leader, project dir. various projects including Asian Devel. Bank, UN, Royal Thai Govt., Govt. Can., Govt. Spain, Govt. Ghana. Contbr. articles to profl. jours., chpts. to books. Named Comdr. of Most Exalted Order of White Elephant, His Royal Majesty King Bhumipol Adulyadej of Thailand, Bangkok, 1992; recipient Can. Coun. doctoral fellowship, 1973-77. Avocations: judo, swimming, Tai Kwon Do.

ABORESHAID, SALEH, director, engineering educator; b. Jeddah, Saudi Arabia, Aug. 1, 1966; child of Abdulrahman and Zainab Ahmad Al-Ruba; m. Munerah Al-Bdaiwi, Jan. 1, 1991; children: Zainab, Abdulrahman. BSEE, King Saud U., Riyadh, Saudi Arabia, 1990; MSEE, U. Saskatchewan, Saskatoon, Can., 1993, PhD in Elec. Engring., 1997. Asst. lectr. Riyadh Coll. Tech., 1990-91, lectr., 1993-94, asst. prof., head dept. elec. engring., 1997-98, dep. dean student affairs, 1998-99, prof.; tchg. asst. U. Saskatchewan, Saskatoon, 1991-93, 94-97; dir. gen. curricula Gen. Orgn. Tech. Edn. and Vocat. Tng., Riyadh, 1999—; dir. Student Activity Ctr. Riyadh Coll. Tech., 1997—. Contbr. articles to profl. jours. Scholar Saudi Govt., 1991, 94, U. Saskatchewan, 1993; Pres. grantee U. Saskatchewan, 1996. Mem. IEEE. Muslim. Fax: 966-1-456-1197. Office: Riyadh Coll Tech, PO Box 22870, Riyadh 11416, Saudi Arabia

ABOU-ALLAM, RAGAA MAHMOUD, psychologist, educator; b. Fowa, Egypt, Jan. 28, 1927; s. Abdel-Fattah and Mariam Abdou (Barakat) Abou-A.; m. Nawal Mohamed Hagras, Sept. 15, 1966; children: Nassma, Sherouk. BA, Cairo U., 1950; MA, Columbia U., 1962; PhD, NYU, 1965. Cons. Min. Edn., Kuwait, 1967-74; from assoc. prof. to prof., chmn. dept. Kuwait U., 1974-96; prof. emeritus Cairo U., 1996—; chmn. Exec. Office for Gifted, Kuwait, 1986-93; bd. trustees Gifted Project, Kuwait, 1986-93; spl. edn. cons., Kuwait, 1993-96. Author: Measurement and Evaluation of Academic Achievement, 1987, Introduction to Educational Research, 1989, Methods of Research in Psychology and Education, 1998, 2nd edit., 1999; contbr. articles to profl. publs. Mem. Nat. Assn. Gifted Children. Avocation: music. Home: 2 Rd 259, New Maadi Cairo 11435, Egypt Office: Cairo U, Inst Ednl Rsch, Giza Cairo Egypt

ABOULAFIA, ELIE D., vascular surgeon; b. Jerusalem, June 16, 1928; s. David and Mathilda (Yeshaya) A.; m. Miriam Bernstein, May 19, 1953 (dec. June 1960); children: Diane Dalya, David Michael, Albert Jonathan; m. Eileen Helman, May 2, 1965. BSc in Medicine, U. Geneva, 1949, MD, 1953; MSc in Surgery, Tufts U., 1960. Diplomate Am. Bd. Surgery with subspecialty in gen. vascular surgery. Intern Michael Reese Hosp., Chgo., 1953-54; resident in surgery NYU-Bellevue Med. Ctr., N.Y.C., 1954-56; surg. rsch. fellow Tufts-New Eng. Med. Ctr., Boston, 1958-59, chief surg. resident, 1959-61; dir. surg. rsch. Sinai Hosp., Detroit, 1961-63; head sect. vascular surgery Betsford Gen. Hosp., Farmington Hills, Mich., 1963-95; dir. surg. edn. Highland Park (Mich.) Gen. Hosp., Detroit, 1969-73; dir. vascular med. svcs. DMC/Sinai-Grace Hosp., Detroit, 1995—; clin. prof. surgery Mich. State U., East Lansing, 1977—; clin. prof. medicine Wayne State U., Detroit, 1998—. Mem. editl. bd. Internat. Jour. Surgery, 1972-95, Internat. Jour. Angiology, 1992—; contbr. articles to profl. jours. Bd. trustees Jewish Mus. of Greece, Athens, 1991—; bd. trustees Friends of Israel Def. Forces, N.Y.C., 1997—. Lt. comdr. USN-R, 1956-58. Fellow Internat. Coll. Surgeons (pres. 1991, emeritus fellow 1995, Disting. Svc. award 1992), Soc. Clin. Vascular Surgery, Midwest Vascular Surg. Soc., Mich. VascularSurg. Soc.; mem. U.S./Internat. Coll. Surgeons (pres. 1991), Internat. Coll. Angiology (vice chair sci. coun. 1994—), Mich. State Med. Soc. (Spl. Recognition Leadership award 1991), Southeastern Mich. Surg. Soc. (pres. 1984-85), Maimonides Med. Soc. (pres. 1966-68), Sigma Xi. Home: 27501 W 14 Mile Rd Farmingtn Hls MI 48334-1812 Office: Detroit Med Ctr/Sinai Grace Hosp 6071 W Outer Dr Detroit MI 48235-2624

ABOUL-ATA, ABOUL-ATA EL-NADY, phytovirologist, educator, researcher; b. El-Saadieen, Sharkia, Egypt, Mar. 22, 1948; s. El-Nady Aboul-Ata El-Saied and Sekina Mohammed El-Gaar; m. Ferial Abdel-Moniem El Azrak, Sept. 2, 1978; children: Islam Aboul-Ata El-Nady, Ramy Aboul-Ata El-Nady. BS in Agr., Ain Shams U., Cairo, 1971; MS, Cairo U., 1978, PhD in Plant Virus-Vector Relationship, 1983. Rsch. asst. plant virus sect. Plant Pathology Inst., Cairo, 1973-78, rsch. assoc. Agrl. Rsch. Ctr., 1978-83, researcher Agrl. Rsch. Ctr., 1983-89, sr. researcher Agrl. Rsch. Ctr., 1989-94, 1989-94, chief rsch. Agrl. Rsch. Ctr., 1994—; prin. investigator cereal viruses activity Aphid/Virus Network Nile Valley and Red Sea Rsch. Project, 1993—; mem. team Virus-Free Stone Fruits, Egypt and France, 1994-98, Cereal Viruses Epidemiology Cairo U.-ARC, 1986-88; vis. prof. U. Ky. Nat. Agrl. Rsch. Project, 1993, Cornell U., Ithaca, 1996, Ohio Agrl. R&D Ctr., Ohio, Wooster, 1986. Contbr. articles to profl. jours. Mem. Am. Phytopathology Soc., N.Y. Acad. Scis. Avocations: painting and drawing, writing, history-religion relation. Fax: 202-5728099. Home: 30 D Pass 11 El-Karama St, Alf Maskan PO Box 11321, Cairo Egypt Office: Plant Path Rsch Inst ARC, PO Box 11777, Giza Egypt

ABOUL GHEIT, AHMED AL, Egyptian diplomat. Rep. to UN for Egypt N.Y.C. Office: Permanent Mission of Egypt to UN 304 E 44th St New York NY 10017-4402*

ABOUL GHEIT, AHMED KADRY, chemist, educator; b. Tanta, Gharbeia, Egypt, Jan. 1, 1936; s. Mohamed Aboul Gheit and Doreiya Hassan Khadr; m. Sohair Mohamed Abdel Hamid, May 18, 1966; children: Amr, Noha. BS, Cairo U., 1958, PhD, 1969; MS, Ain Shams U., 1964. Chemist Wadi El Natrun (Egypt) Projects, 1959-60; asst. rschr., rschr. Nat. Rsch. Ctr., Cairo, 1960-74; assoc. prof. Egyptian Petroleum Rsch. Inst., Cairo, 1974-79, prof., 1979—; rschr. Inst. Francais du Petrole, Rueil Malmaison, 1971-72; assoc. prof. Coll. Engring. Baghdad (Iraq) U., 1975-79; prof. Applied Sci. and Engring. Umm Al Qura U., Makkah, Saudi Arabia, 1983-90; part-time instr. Coll. Petroleum & Minerals Engring., Suez Canal U., Faculty

of Sci., Ain Shams U., Cairo. Author: Properties of Petroleum and Natural Gas, 1982, Petrochemicals-Science and Technology, 1990; contbr. numerous articles to profl. jours. Mem. Sci. Professions Syndicate, Am. Chem. Soc., Egyptian Chem. Soc., European Assn. Solids (elected). Avocations: boxing, rowing, swimming, painting. Home: 7th Region Nasr City, 63 Moh Farid Abo Hadid St, Cairo Egypt Office: Egyptian Petrol Rsch Inst, Ahmed El Zomor St Nasr City, Cairo 11787, Egypt

ABOUZAYD, SHAFIQ BAHJAT, educational foundation executive; b. Mlikh, Jezzine, Lebanon, May 12, 1954; arrived in the United Kingdom, 1982; s. Bahjat and Emilie Abouzayd. Lebanese Baccalaureat, Coll. des Apotres, Jounieh, Lebanon, 1974; MA, Fribourg (Switzerland) U., 1981, ThD, 1987; PhD, Oxford U., 1994, MA, 1998. Ordained priest The Maronite Church, 1987. Chmn. ARAM Soc. for Syro-Mesopotamian Studies, Oxford, Eng., 1987—; founder ARAM Soc. Oxford U., 1986, Harvard U., Cambridge, Mass., 1991, Am. U. Beirut, Lebanon, 1993; mem. faculty oriental studies U. Oxford, 1998. Author: Ihidayutha, 1993; editor The Nabataeans, 1990, The Syriac-Arabic Cultural Interchange during the Abbasid Era, 1991, The Decapolis, 1992, Syriac Studies, 1993, The Arab-Byzantine-Syriac Cultural Interchange during the Umayyad Era, 1994, Palmyra, 1995, Trade Routes in the Near East, 1996, The Mamluks in Bilad Al-Sham, 1997, Cultural Interchange in the Arabian Peninsula, 1997, The Early Ottoman Period in Bilad Al-Sham, 1998, Antioch and Edessa, 1999, The Mandaeans, 2000. Avocations: classical music, natural medicine, vegetarian. Office: The Oriental Inst Oxford U, Pusey Ln, Oxford OX1 2LE, England

ABRAHAM, ARTHUR, history educator; b. Daru, Sierra Leone, July 12, 1945; m. Fatu Veronica Sesay, Jul. 10, 1976; children: Bao, Abdul Hassan, Nadiya. BA (hons.), Durham Univ., 1967; MA, Univ. Sierra Leone, 1971; PhD, Birmingham Univ., U.K., 1974; DSocSc, World Univ. RoundTable, 1986. Lectr, sr. lectr., prof., dean Univ. Sierra Leone, Freetown, 1973-97; assoc. prof. Cuttington Univ. Coll., Liberia, 1978-80; mins. of state Gov. of Sierra Leone, 1992-93; prof. Va. State Univ., Petersburg, Va., 1999—; vis. prof. L.I. Univ., N.Y., 1997-99; exec. chmn. Abco Limited, Seirra Leone, 1986-92; bd. dirs. Nat. Ins. Co., 1990-94, Nat. Agricultural Coordinating Coun., 1992-96. Author: Topics in Sierra Leone History, 1976, Mende Government and Politics, 1978, Development Problems in Sierra Leone, 1994; co-author: The Sierra Leone Army, 1986. Dir. SOS Children's Village, Lumley, Sierra Leone, 1982-88, Daru Rural Bank, Sierra Leone, 1988-97; chmn. Daru Rural Water Supply Project, 1990-95; pres. Kortright Lawn Tennis Club, 1987-96; justice of the peace State of Sierra Leone, 1992. Mem. African Studies Assn., The Historical Soc., African Assn. of Political Sci., Historical Soc. of Sierra Leone (editor, 1976-86, exec. mem.). Avocations: lawn tennis, cycling, gardening. E-mail: aabraham@vsu.edu. Office: Va State Univ Petersburg VA 23806

ABRAHAM, F(AHRID) MURRAY, actor, educator; b. Pitts., Oct. 24, 1939; s. Fahrid and Josephine Abraham; m. Kate Hannan, 1962; two children. Student, U. Tex., El Paso, 1959-61. Actor Broadway, Off-Broadway, children's theater, musicals, film, TV; prof. Bklyn. Coll., 1985—; dir. No Smoking Please, N.Y.C., Time & Space Ltd. Theatre, N.Y.C. Profl. stage debut in The Wonderful Ice Cream Suit, Coronet Theatre, L.A., 1965; Broadway debut in The Man in the Glass Booth, Royale Theatre, 1968; appeared in numerous Broadway plays including 6 Rms RivVu, 1972-73, Bad Habits, 1974, The Ritz, 1976, Teibele and Her Demon, 1979; other stage appearances include Landscape of the Body, 1977, The Master and Margarita, 1978, The Golem, 1984, King Lear, 1981, Frankie and Johnny in the Claire de Lune, 1987, A Month in the Country, 1995; films include: They Might Be Giants, 1971, Serpico, 1974, The Sunshine Boys, 1975, All the President's Men, 1976, The Ritz, 1976, The Big Fix, 1979, Scarface, 1983, Amadeus, 1984 (Academy award best actor 1984, Golden Globe award best actor 1984), The Name of the Rose, 1986, Russicum, 1989, An Innocent Man, 1989, Bonfire of the Vanities, 1990, Cadence, 1991, Mobsters, 1991, National Lampoon's Loaded Weapon I, 1993, By the Sword, 1993, Last Action Hero, 1993, Surviving The Game, 1994, The Case, 1994, Nostradamus, 1994, Jamila, 1994, Fresh, 1994, Mighty Aphrodite, 1995, Dillinger and Capone, 1995, Baby Face Nelson, 1995, Looking for Richard, 1996, Children of the Revolution, 1996, Mimic, 1997, Eruption, 1997, Laurel and Hardy: For Love or Mummy, 1998, Star Trex IX, 1998, Falcone, 1999, Esther, 1999, Muppets From Space, 1999, Finding Forrester, 2000; narrator Herman Melville, Damned in Paradise, PBS, 1985; appeared in PBS Masterpiece Theatre prodn.: Silas Marner, 1987, Noah's Ark, 1999, Star Trek: Insurrection, 1998; TV mini-series Larry McMurtry's Dead Man's Walk, 1996; TV spl. Einstein Revealed (voice), 1996, TV movie Sex and the Married Woman, 1978, Color of Justice, 1997, Noah's Ark, 1999, Esther, 1999; TV series Love of Life. Recipient Obie award for Uncle Vanya 1984; Los Angeles Film Critics award, 1985. Mem. Actors Equity, AFTRA, Screen Actors Guild.

ABRAHAM, GEORGI KOODATHUMMURIYIL, physician, medical educator; b. Vennikulam, Kerala, India, Oct. 27, 1950; s. Eapen and Mariamma (Varkey) A.; m. Rene George, May 29, 1979. MBBS, T.D. Med. Coll., Alleppey, India, 1975; MD, Kasturba Med. Sch., Mangalore, India, 1979. House surgeon T.D. Med. Coll. Hosp., Alleppey, India, 1974-75; sr. house surgeon C.M.C. Hosp., Vellore, India, 1975-76; resident Govt. Wenlock Hosp, Mangalore, India, 1976-79; rsch. fellow C.M.C. Hosp., Vellore, India, 1979-80; house surgeon, registrar NHS Hosps., U.K., 1980-84; sr. registrar Nubarakal Mubayak-al Kabeer Hosp., Kuwait, 1984-86; sr. clin. fellow Toronto (Ont., Can.) Western Hosp., 1986-89; cons. Alhada Armed Forces Hosp, Taif, Saudi Arabia, 1989-90, Tamil Nad Hosp., Chennai, India, 1990-96; prof. medicine Sri Ramachandra Med. Coll. & Rsch. Inst., Chennai, 1996—. Editor Indian Jour. Operitoneal Dialysis, 1997; mem. editl. bd. Peritoneal Dialysis Internat., Advances in Renal Replacement Therapy. Founder, trustee Tanker, Chennai, 1993—. Fellow Royal Coll. Physicians London, Royal Coll. Physicians and Surgeons Glasgow; mem. Peritoneal Dialysis Soc. of India (pres. 1997-99). Orthodox Christian. Home: 9/2 15th Ave, Harrington Rd, Chennai India Office: Ramachandra Med Coll, Porur, Chennai 600116, India

ABRAHAM, HENRY JULIAN, political science educator; b. Offenbach am Main, Germany, Aug. 25, 1921; s. Fredrick and Louise (Kullmann) A.; m. Mildred Kosches, Apr. 13, 1954; children: Philip F., Peter D. AB summa cum laude, Kenyon Coll., 1948, LHD (hon.), 1972; MA, Columbia U., 1949; PhD, U. Pa., 1952; LLD (hon.), U. Hartford, 1982, Knox Coll., 1982; LittD (hon.), St. Joseph's U., 1987; LLD (hon.), Old Dominion U., 1996. Mem. faculty U. Pa., 1949-72, prof. polit. sci., 1962-72; Doherty prof. govt. and fgn. affairs U. Va., 1971-78, James Hart prof., 1978-97, James Hart prof. emeritus, 1997—; vis. prof. Swarthmore Coll., CCNY, Colo. U., Columbia U., U. Richmond Law Sch., U. Copenhagen, U. Stockholm, Aarhus U., Lund U., U. Göteborg, U. Oslo, U. Helsinki, U. Uppsala, U. Amsterdam, U. London; cons. in field, 1956; Fulbright prof., Denmark, 1959-60. Author: Compulsory Voting, 1955, Government as Entrepreneur, 1956, Courts and Judges, 1959, Elements of Democratic Government, 1964, Essentials of National Government, 1971, Justices & Presidents, 1992, American Democracy, 1990, Justices, Presidents and Senators, 1999, The Judiciary, 1997, The Judicial Process, 1998, Freedom and the Court, 1998. Mem. com. on nondiscrimintion Phila. Bd. Edn., 1962; mem. vis. com. on govt. Lehigh U., 1967-71; trustee fedn. Jewish Agys. Greater Phila., 1970-72, Kenyon Coll., 1987-93; mem. Va. Commn. on Bicentennial of Constn. of U.S., 1985-92, Va. Coun. on Human Rights, 1999—. Recipient award excellence undergrad. teaching U. Pa., 1959, 67, Kite and Key Teaching award, 1967, award excellence undergrad. teaching U. Va., 1978, Thomas Jefferson award U. Va., 1983, U. Va. Alumni Teaching award, 1986, Disting. Svc. award Va. Social Sci. Assn., 1982, Disting. Prof. award U. Va. Alumni Assn., 1986, First Lifetime Achievement award, org. sec. on law & courts, Am. polit., sci. Assn., 1993, others; NEH, 1975, 76, 78, 80, 81, NSF fellow, 1965, fellow Am. Philos. Soc., 1961-67, 79, Rockefeller Found. fellow, 1978, Earhart fellow, 1984, Bradley Found., 1989-97. Mem. Fellows in Am. Studies (pres. 1966), Am. Polit. Sci. Assn. (v.p. 1980-82), Raven Soc., Am. Soc. for Legal History, So. Polit. Sci. Ass. (rec. sec. 1980-81), Soc. of Fellows, Met. Opera Guild, Nat. Trust, Golden Key, Greencroft Club (v.p. 1985-87, Charlottesville, Va.), Z Club (U. Va.), Imp Club (U. Va.), Yale Club (N.Y.C.), Phi Beta Kappa (vis. scholar 1970-71), Pi Sigma Alpha, Pi Gamma Mu, Omicron Delta Kappa. Fax: 804-924-3359. Home: 906 Fendall Ter Charlottesville VA 22903-1617 Office: Univ Va 232 Cabell Hall Charlottesville VA 22903

ABRAHAM, JACOB, delivery service executive; b. Ayroor, Kerala, India, Jan. 22, 1968; s. Oonukalil Chacko and Annamma Chacko Abraham; m. Elizabeth Thachirathu Sally, July 5, 1993; children: Abel, Robin. BA, U. Bombay, 1989; diploma in air cargo, Internat. Air Transport Assn., Geneva, 1991, diploma in air cargo rating, 1992. Airport ops. staff Blue Dart Express, Bombay, 1986-88, sr. courier, 1988-92, sales exec., 1992-93, sr. sales exec., 1993; mktg. officer Al Mousim Air Cargo, Riyadh, Saudi Arabia, 1993-94; tng. specialist FedEx, Riyadh, 1994-96, nat. ops. mgr., 1996—. Mem. Toastmaster Internat. (gulf champion pub. speaking 1998). Avocations: reading, writing, public speaking. Fax: 00-066-1-419-2375. Home and Office: SMSA/FedEx, PO Box 63529, Riyadh 11526, Saudi Arabia

ABRAHAM, JOSEPH, management consultant, educator; b. Kfar-Saba, Israel, May 6, 1950. BA, Tel Aviv U., 1975; MA, Fresno State U., 1977; DSc, Technion, 1993. Owner mobile home factory Israel, 1978-85, pvt. practice mgmt. cons., 1985—; lectr. Technion, Haifa, Israel, 1990—. Author book on creative tchg.; contbr. articles to profl. publs. Capt. Israeli Def. Forces, 1971. Avocation: international travel. Home: 109/1 Morad-Hagai, 20100 Carmiel Israel Office: 6 Simtat-Haktima St, Pardes-Hanna 37000, Israel

ABRAHAM, TONSON, chemist, researcher; b. Bombay, Dec. 21, 1948; came to U.S., 1970; s. Thykadavil Jorge and Annie (Joseph) A.; m. Iona Marianne Joseph, June 17, 1978; children: Akash, Kavi. B in Tech., Indian Inst. Tech., Kanpur, India, 1970; PhD in Organic Chemistry, Cath. U. Am., 1976. Fellow NRC, Washington, 1976-78; postdoctoral fellow No. Ill. U., DeKalb, 1978-79; vis. asst. prof. Ill. State U., Normal, 1979-80; polymer scientist Wright-Patterson Air Force Base, Fairborn, Ohio, 1980-86; sr. scientist Owens-Corning Fiberglas, Granville, Ohio, 1986; R & D assoc. B.F. Goodrich Co., Brecksville, Ohio, 1987-94; polymer chemist Argonne (Ill.) Nat. Lab., 1994-96; sr. rsch. specialist Advanced Elastomer Sys., Akron, Ohio, 1996—. Contbr. articles to profl. jours. Mem. Am. Chem. Soc. Roman Catholic. Achievements include patents in synthetic polymer and organic chemistry; research in the synthesis and applications of thermoplastic elastomers, biodegradable polymers, water swellable and water soluble polymers, synthesis of high temperature, oil resistent elastomers, fluoroelastomers, hydrogenation of polymers, homogeneous hydrogenation catalysts, thermosetting resin precursors for aerospace composites and in the chemistry of indoles. Home: 16936 Deer Path Dr Strongsville OH 44136-6260 Office: Advanced Elastomer Sys 388 S Main St Ste 600 Akron OH 44311-1065

ABRAHAM-FROIS, GILBERT, educator; b. Bayonne, France, Oct. 11, 1934; m. Michele De Coccola, May 25, 1962; children: Marianne, Nicolas. DS, Paris, 1960. Asst. U. Paris, 1962-63; charge de cours U. Caen, France, 1963-64; prof. U. Rabat, Casablanca, Morocco, 1965-68, U. Poitiers, France, 1968-69, U. Paris X, Nanterre, 1969—. Author: Dynamique Economique, 1995, Prices, Profits and Accumulation Rhythms, 1997; editor: Non Linear Analysis and Endogenous Cycles, 1998. Sgt. French Mil., 1959-62. Mem. Assn. Sci. & Econs. France (v.p. 1997-99, pres. 1999-2000), N.Y. Acad. Scis. Office: U Paris X, 200 Ave Republique, 92001 Nanterre Cedex France

ABRAHAMSEN, PÅL, psychiatrist, consultant; b. Oslo, Norway, Oct. 30, 1943; s. Odd H. and Jenny B. (Ruud) A.; (div. 1990); children: Øystein, Geir, Bjarne, Line. MD, U. Bergen, Norway, 1968, degree in sociology, 1969. Resident, rsch. fellow U. Bergen, 1969-70, 1971-72, 1973-76; advanced resident Beth Israel Hosp., Boston, 1972-73; med. officer Gaustad Hosp., Ullevål Hosp., Oslo, 1976-83; med. supt. Oslo Hosp., 1983-90; med. cons. Ostensjo Family Guidance Clin., Oslo, 1990—; pvt. practice Oslo, 1990—; med. supt. DPS, Hadeland, Gran, Norway, 1997—; intern Hosp. & Dist., 1969-70; assoc. prof. U. Oslo Inst. Behavioral Scis. in Medicine, 1976-80; police psychiatrist, Oslo, 1979-93; forensic psychiatrist, cons., 1979—. Author: People in Dispair, 1982, others; contbr. articles to profl. pubs. Capt. Norwegian Army, 1974-75. Fellow Harvard U., 1972-73; Fulbright grantee Fulbright Assn. Norway, 1972. Mem. Norwegian Med. Assn., Norwegian Psychiatric Assn., Norwegian Assn. Family Therapy (gen. sec. 1983—, editor Metaforum), Norwegian Assn. Non-fiction Authors. Home and Office: Seilduksinst AS, Markveien 23, N-0554 Oslo Norway

ABRAHÃO-NETO, JOSÉ, enzymology educator; b. Jacareí, Brazil, July 11, 1953; s. Antonio josé and Francisca Ferreira Abrahão. M in Fermentation Tech., U. São Paulo, 1986, PhD in Biochemistry, 1991. Cert. in pharm. biochemistry. Analyst Boehringer Ingelheim, Itapecerica, Da Serra, Brazil, 1979-80, supr., 1980; pedagogical asst. FCF/U. São Paulo, 1981-86, asst. to prof., 1986-91; rep. dept. in graduation commn. U. São Paulo, 1998, PhD rep. of counseling dept., 1993-2000; cons. São Paulo Pharm. Session of Sci., 1996. Contbr. sci. articles and papers to profl. jours. Vol. Found. FEBEm, São Paulo, 1983-85. Rsch. grantee Found. Help to Rsch. Sao Paulo's State and Nat. Coun. Sci. and Technol. Devel., 1991, 92, 94, 95, 97, 98, 99, 2000. Mem. Brazilian Soc. Biochemistry and Molecular Biology, Brazilian Soc. Microbiology, São Paulo Pharmacy and Chemistry Soc. Worker's Party. Avocations: reading, carpentry, electronics. Home: PCA Miguel Ortega 180 161, 06754160 Taboão da Serra Brazil Office: U São Paulo, Av Prof Lineu Prestes 580, 05508900 São Paulo Brazil

ABRAHM, JANET LEE, hematologist, oncologist, educator; b. San Francisco, Mar. 14, 1949; d. Paul Milton and Helen Lesser Abrahm; m. David Rytman Slavitt, Apr. 16, 1978. Student, U. Calif., Berkeley, 1969; BA, U. Calif., San Francisco, 1970, MD, 1973. Diplomate Am. Bd. Internal Medicine, Hematology & Oncology. Intern and resident medicine Mass. Gen. Hosp., Boston, 1973-75, hematology fellow, 1975-76; chief resident medicine Moffitt Hosp. U. Calif., San Francisco, 1976-77; hematology/oncology fellow Hosp. U. Pa., Phila., 1977-80; postdoctoral fellow medicine U. Pa., Phila., 1977-78, postdoctoral trainee medicine, 1977-80, asst. prof. medicine, 1980-86; asst. prof. medicine Hosp. U. Pa. and VA Med. Ctr., Phila., 1986-89, assoc. prof. medicine, 1989—; attending physician Hosp. U. Pa., Phila., 1980-93, 98—; staff physician Phila. VA Med. Ctr., 1982—, dir. Hematology/Oncology Clinic, 1983-94, chief hematology and oncology sect., 1984-94, med. oncologist Hospice Consultation Team, 1993-97, chief med. svc., 1994-97, faculty scholar Project Death in Am., 1997—; med. dir. Wissahickon Hospice UPHS, 1998—; prin. investigator Palliative Care Fellowship Grant, 1996-2001; mem. concensus panel on End-of-Life Care, ACP, 1997—; chmn. adv. com. Cancer Care VA Dist. 4, 1987-90; sec. subspecialty bd. hematology Am. Bd. Internal Medicine, 1987-92, sec. SEP subcom. hematology, 1993-95; vis. asst. prof. medicine Med. Coll. Pa., 1988-97; adj. asst. prof. clin. pharmacy Phila. Coll. Pharmacy and Sci., 1988—; mem. tech. adv. group Cancer Care Region 1, 1990-95; med. oncology cons. cancer pain consultation panel Ctr. for Continuing Edn. U. Pa. Sch. Nursing, 1990—; mem. quality of life and cancer edn. com. Pa. Cancer Adv. Bd., 1994-97; mem. human resources coun. of VHA VISN, 1996-97, councillor Region 1, AVOCOM, 1996-97; invited lectr. Mt. Zion Med. Ctr., U. Calif., San Francisco, 1992, 95, Women in Medicine, Phila., 1993, 98, Med. Coll. Pa., Phila., 1993-96, Mercy Cath. Med. Ctr., 1995, Mt. Sinai Med. Ctr., Miami, 1995, U. Chgo. Med. Sch., 1995, Northwestern U. Sch. Medicine, Chgo., 1995, U. Calif., San Diego, 1995, Stanford U., 1995, Tulane U. Sch. Medicine, 1996, Lehigh Valley Hosp., 1997, U. Okla. Med. Sch., 1997, Bethlehem, Pa., 1998, Coatesville, Pa., 1998, Columbia U. Coll. Physicians Surgeons, 1998, Am. Acad. Hospice and Palliative Medicine, 1999, 2000, ACP, 2000, others. Author: Clinical Care of the Terminal Patient, 1982, Yearbook of Medicine, 1984, Yearbook of Cancer, 1984, Pain Management in Hematology: Basic Principles and Practice, 1990, 94, 99, Internal Medicine for Dentistry, 2d edit., 1990, Pain Management in Kelley W. Textbook of Internal Medicine, 1996, 2000, Anemia, Pain Management in Geriatric Secrets, 1996, 2000, A Physician's Guide to Pain and Symptom Management in Cancer Patients, 2000; contbr. (booklets) Caring for the Terminally Ill Patient at Home - A Guide for Family Caregivers, 1986, Caring for the Cancer Patient at Home - A Guide for Patients and Families, 1986; reviewer JAMA, Cancer, Archives Internal Medicine, Annals Internal Medicine, Jour. Cancer Edn., Resident and Staff Physician, Palliative Medicine; contbr. numerous articles to profl. jours. Mem. edn. com. Greater Phila. Pain Soc., 1993. Recipient Manual award Merck, 1973; Fife Medicine scholar, 1973. Fellow ACP (lectr. Pa. chpt. 1994, consensus panelist on end-of-life care 1997—, invited lectr. ann. meeting 1999); mem. Am. Soc. Hematology, Am. Fedn. Clin. Rsch., Am. Soc. Clin. Hypnosis, Am. Soc. Clin. Oncology, Am. Assn. Cancer Edn. (program com. 1993), Am. Pain Soc., Am. Assn. Hospice and Palliative Medicine (invited lectr. 1999), Phi Beta Kappa, Alpha Omega Alpha. Home: 523 S 41st St Philadelphia PA 19104-4501 Office: Hosp of U Pa 514 Maloney Bldg 3400 Spruce St Philadelphia PA 19104-4206

ABRAM, JOSEPH, architect, painter; b. Cairo, Apr. 21, 1951; s. David and Renée (Azgour) A.; m. Marie-Claude Atlan, 1971 (div. 1980); children: Abram Hélène, Abram Florence; m. Jeanine Ferber-Gennari, 1981; stepchildren: Caroline Gennari, Alexandre Gennari. Architect, Sch. Archtecture, Nancy, 1975; DEA, History Art, 1991. Prof. Sch. of Architecture, Nancy, 1975—, Sch. of Art, Metz, France, 1981-95, Inst. of Architecture, Geneva, 1995—; rschr. History Lab. Contemporary Architecture, Nancy, 1985—; lectr. in univs., sch. of arts and architecture, France, Eng., Germany, U.S., Spain, Italy, Finland, Czech Republic, Greece, Belgium, Portugal, Turkey, Switzerland; cons. in field; curator archtl. exhbns. at Inst. French Inst. Architecture, Paris, 1985, Mus. Architecture, Basel, 1989, others. Author: Perret et l'Ecole du Classicisme Structurel, 1985, Political Will and the Cultural Identity Crisis in Late Twentieth Century French Architecture, 1998, L'architecture Moderne en France: 1940-1966, 1999; (with others) Oscar Nitzchké, 1985, Diener and Diener: From City to Detail, 1992, The Filter of Reason: Work of Paul Nelson, 1990, Albert Flocon: du Bauhaus à la perspective curviligne, 1992, Devanthéry and Lamunière, 1996, others; architect scenograhies for exbhns. Cité des Scis. de la Villette, Inst. Français d'Architecture, 1986; designer cast-iron furniture; paintings and sculptures exhibited Found. Septentrion, Marq-en-Baroeul, France, Grande Halle de la Villette, 1988, Musée des Arts Décoratifs, Paris, 1988, also in Strasbourg, Paris, Geneva; curator exhbns. Cooper Union Sch., N.Y.C., 1985, Columbia U., N.Y.C., 1989, Centre G. Pompidou, Paris, 1991; mem. editl. bd. Faces, Geneva, 1996—; contbr. articles to profl. jours. Home: 59 Rue De La Mutualité, 54600 Villers les Nancy France Office: Ecole D Architecure Nancy, 2 Rue Bastien LePage, 54001 Nancy France

ABRAM, ZOLTAN SAMOIL, medicine educator; b. Seini, Maramures, Romania, Dec. 9, 1963; s. Samoil Abram and Lydia (Idem) Sarkozi; m. Noemi Bako, Apr. 1, 1989; children: Peter, Endre, Noemi. Degree in Medicine, U. Medicine and Pharmacy, Targu Mures, Romania, 1989; degree in Journalism, Balint Gyorgy Journalist Sch., Budapest, Hungary, 1991. Physician City Hosp., Targu Mures, 1990-91; asst. lectr. U. Medicine and Pharmacy, 1991-96, lectr., 1996—. Author: Hungarians Around the World, 1995, The Muddy Nyarad, 1996, In Memorial of Communitas, 1996, Environmental Protection, 1997, Szentegyhaza, 1998, Dietetics, 1999, Lifestyle-Health, 2000; contbr. articles to profl. jours. and newspapers. Bd. dirs. Hungarian Youth Assn., 1990-92; co-pres. Hungarian Folk H.S. Soc., 1992—; co-pres. Rhododendron Ecol. Assn., 1993—. Recipient Pro Hygiene award Fodor József Nat. Inst., 1999. Mem. Romanian Hygiene and Pub. Health Soc. (sec. 1992—), Transilvanian Med. Soc. (sec. 1992—), N.Y. Acad. Scis., Preventio Health Promotion Assn. (pres. 1998). Mem. UDMR. Avocations: photography, civic activities, cultural management, literature. Home: Borsos Tamás 25, 4300 Targu Mures Romania Office: U Medicine and Pharmacy, Gh Marinescu 38, 4300 Targu Mures Romania

ABRAMCZUK, TOMASZ, computer image processing specialist; b. Warsaw, Poland, Aug. 4, 1954; arrived in Sweden, 1972; s. Kazimierz and Krystyna (Bozek) A.; m. Barbara Dunia, May 12, 1984; 1 child, Monika. MSc, Royal Inst. Tech., Stockholm, 1979; lic. in technology, Royal Inst. Tech., 1989. Rsch. engr. Royal Inst. Tech., Stockholm, 1982-83; researcher Royal Inst. Tech., 1983-85, sr. researcher, 1985-87; chief exec. of R & D Sydat Automation, AB, Stockholm, 1988—; also bd. dirs. Sydat Automation, AB; chief exec. officer Poltra AB, Stockholm, 1991—, also bd. dirs.; cons. in field. Author: Image Processing, 1984; contbr. articles to profl. pubs. Mem. IEEE, Swedish Elec. Engring. Orgn., Internat. Assn. Polish Experts and Cons. (co-founder 1991, bd. dirs. 1991—), N.Y. Acad. Scis., Royal Inst. Tech. Radio Club. Avocations: sailing, motor sports. Office: SYDAT Automation AB, Gökottestigen 17, 163 47 Spånga Sweden

ABRAMENKO, VALENTINA IZOSIMOVNA, astronomer, educator; b. Arkhangelsk, Russia, Sept. 21, 1950; arrived in Ukraine, 1973.; d. Izosim Pavlovich and Klaudia Moisseevna (Nekrasova) V.; m. Vladimir Alexandrovich Abramenko, Apr. 27, 1973; children: Tanja, Konstantin. Bachelors, Leningrad (USSR) U., 1973; PhD, Ioffe Inst., Leningrad, 1990. Rschr. Crimean Astrophysics Obs., Nauchny, Ukraine, 1975—; lectr. Crimean Astrophysics Obs., Nauchny, 1982—. Contbr. over 40 articles to profl. jours. Dep., City Assembly, Bakhchisarai, Crimea, 1989-95. Grantee Internat. Astron. Union, 1992, European Phys. Soc., 1993, European Union, 1996. Avocations: traveling, clothes designing. Home: Bl 14 Apt 7, 334413 Nauchny Crimea, Ukraine Office: Crimean Astrophys Obs, 98409 Nauchny Crimea, Ukraine

ABRAMO, MIGUEL ANGEL, lawyer; b. Monterrey, Nuevo Leon, Mex., Dec. 13, 1966; s. Gerardo Torres A. and Maria de Guadalupe Gonzalez Martinez; m. Sonia Angelica Perez, Apr. 3, 1992; children: Miguel Angel, Marcelo, Ana Paula. Lic. en Derecho y Ciencias Juridicas, U. Automoma Nuevo Leon, Monterrey, Mex., 1990; LLM, U. Ill., 1993. Assoc. Notary Pub. #64, Monterrey, Nuevo Leon, Mex., 1985-87; assoc. Santos Elizondo Garcia, S.C., Monterrey, Nuevo Leon, Mex., 1987-93, jr. ptnr., 1993-99, ptnr., 1999—. Mem. ANADE, Mex.-Tex. Bar Assn., 1995. Avocations: playing soccer, horseback riding, reading, walking. Office: Santos Elizondo Garcia SC, Ave Lazaro Cardenas 2400 Losoles, San Pedro Gza Gcia Monterrey 66250 NL, Mexico

ABRAMOV, YORAM, obstetrician, gynecologist, researcher; b. Jerusalem, Dec. 25, 1964; s. Abraham and Ayala (Wertheimer) A.; m. Anat Freidkin, Feb. 23, 1995; children: Yftah, Na'ama. MD, Hebrew U., Jerusalem, 1993. Phys. dept. ob-gyn. Hadassah Med. Ctr., Jerusalem, 1993—. Contbr. articles to med. jours., including Fertility and Sterility, Human Reprodn., Am. Jour. Obstetrics and Gynecology. Capt. Israel Def. Force, 1983-86. Avocations: jogging, swimming. E-mail: abramo@md2.huji.ac.il. Office: Hadassah Med Ctr, Dept Ob-Gyn, 91120 Jerusalem Israel

ABRAMOVA, LUDMILA ARKADIEVNA, chemist, researcher; b. Moscow, Russia, Jan. 15, 1941; d. Arkadii Mikhailovich and Alexandra Mikhailovna (Zaznobina) A.; m. Sixto Octavio Murguia, Oct. 15, 1966 (dec. 1978); 1 child, Maxim. Diploma in chemistry, Moscow State U., 1963; PhD, Zelinskii Inst. Organic Chem., Moscow, 1978. Prof., educator Friendship U., Moscow, 1963-67; chem. rschr. Zelinskii Inst. Organic Chemistry Russian Acad. Scis., Moscow, 1967-98, sr. rsch. scientist Zelinskii Inst. Organic Chemistry, 1999—. Contbr. articles to profl. jours. including Jour. Catalysis, Jour. Phys. Chem. Solids, Mendeleev Comms., among others. Grantee Internat. Sci. Found., 1993, 94, Russian Found. for Basic Rsch., 1995, 1999, Internat. Sci. and Tech. Ctr., 1996. Home: AP 27, 22-1 Tarusskaia St, 117588 Moscow Russia Office: ND Zelinskii Inst Org Chem, Leninsky Prospect 47, 117913 Moscow Russia

ABRAMOVIĆ, BILJANA FRANJA, chemistry educator; b. Novi Sad, Vojvodina, Yugoslavia, Dec. 15, 1952; d. Franja Budimir and Zorka Spasoje (Poček) Jeftović; m. Borislav Krsto Abramović, Aug. 14, 1976; 1 child, Gordana. BSc in Chemistry, U. Novi Sad, 1975, MSc in Chemistry, 1979, PhD in Chemistry, 1983. Jr. asst., then sr. asst. Inst. Chemistry U. Novi Sad, 1976-84, asst. prof., 1984-90, assoc. prof., 1990-95, prof., 1995—. Author: Selected Topics of Microanalysis, 1989, Practical Exercises in Microanalysis, 1995, Microanalysis, 2000; assoc. editor chem. series Rev. of Rsch.; contbr. more than 60 articles to sci. and profl. jours. Mem. Serbian Chem. Soc. Home: Vojvodina, Fruškogorska 30, 21000 Novi Sad Yugoslavia Office: U Novi Sad Faculty Sci, Trg Dositeja Obradovica 3, 21000 Novi Sad Vojvodina, Yugoslavia

ABRAMOVICH, FELIX, statistics researcher; b. Moscow, June 28, 1964; arrived in Israel, 1987; s. Pavel Abramovich and Marta Balashinsky. MSc in Applied Math., Moscow Oil and Gas Inst., 1986; PhD in Stats., Tel Aviv U., 1993. Instr. Tel Aviv U., 1988-94; rsch. assoc. in math. Bristol U., Eng., 1994-95; lectr. Tel Aviv U., 1995-99, sr. lectr., 1999—. Contbr. articles to profl. jours. Cpl. Israeli Def. Forces, 1992-93. Mem. Am. Statis. Assn., Inst. Math. Stats., Royal Statis. Soc. Avocations: music, sports. Office: Tel Aviv U, Dept Stats, 69978 Tel Aviv Israel

ABRAMOVITCH, RUDOLPH ABRAHAM, chemistry educator; b. Alexandria, Egypt, July 19, 1930; came to U.S., 1977; s. Lazare W. and Elise

Abramovitch; m. Liliane E. Abramovitch, July 1952 (div. 1976); children: Daniel Y., Michael Alan (dec.); m. Dorota A. Abramovitch, Feb. 4, 1977; children: Paula, Anna. BSc in Chemistry with honors, U. Alexandria, 1950; BSc, U. London, 1950, DSc (hon.), 1964; PhD, King's Coll., London, 1953. Sr. tchr. sci. and math. Menasce H.S., Alexandria, 1946-48, prin., 1948-51; rsch. chemist Weizman Inst., Rehovot, Israel, 1955; Imperial Chem. Industries rsch. fellow King's Coll., 1956-57; prof. chemistry U. Sask., Saskatoon, 1957-67, U. Ala., Tuscaloosa, 1967-77; head dept. chemistry and geology Clemson (S.C.) U., 1977-81, prof., 1981—. Editor: (book series) Pyridine and Its Derivative, 1974-76, Reactive Intermediates, Vols. 1-3, 1981-84; contbr. numerous articles to sci. jours. V.p. Temple Emmanuel, Tuscaloosa, 1976. Fulbright Found. scholar, France, 1983. Fellow Chem. Inst. Can. (chmn. organic divsn. 1966-67); mem. Am. Chem. Soc., B'nai B'rith (pres. Moses Temerson lodge 1975), Sigma Xi. Avocations: reading, music, tennis, fishing. E-mail: raa@clemson.edu. Office: Clemson Univ Dept Chemistry Clemson SC 29634-0001

ABRAMOVITZ, ANITA ZELTNER BROOKS (MRS. MAX ABRAMOVITZ), writer; b. Long Island, N.Y., Jan. 7, 1914; d. Charles Frederick and Amelia (Koch) Zeltner; m. Thomas Vail Brooks, Sept. 25, 1937 (div. July 1957); children: Antoinette Brooks-Floyd, Cora Vail Brooks, Henry Stanford Brooks II; m. Max Abramovitz, Feb. 29, 1964. Grad., Sarah Lawrence Coll., 1932, BA, 1962. Editl. asst. The New Yorker mag., N.Y.C., 1943-46; editor alumni mag. Sarah Lawrence Coll., 1947-48, asst. to prof. history, 1958-60, asst. in writing to lectr. courses, 1960-62, tchr. remedial reading, 1950; asst. to dir. Sarah Lawrence Paris Summer Sch., 1963. Author series Picture Aids to World Geography, Picture Book of Fisheries, 1961, Picture Book of Tea and Coffee, 1962, Picture Book of Grains, 1963, Picture Book of Salt, 1964, Picture Book of Oil, 1965, Picture Book of Timber, 1966, A Small Bird Sang, 1967, Winifred, 1970, Picture Book of Metals, 1972, People and Spaces: A View of History Through Architecture, 1979; contbr. stories to children's books. Democratic Party Insp. 18th Dist. Hastings-on-Hudson, N.Y., 1958-61; founding mem. Village League, 1950. Home: 176 Honey Hollow Rd Pound Ridge NY 10576-1105

ABRAMOVITZ, MAX, architect; b. Chgo., May 23, 1908; s. Benjamin and Sophia (Maimon) A.; m. Anne Marie Causey, Sept. 4, 1937 (div.); children: Michael John, Katherine Paul; m. Anita Zeltner Brooks, Feb. 29, 1964. BS, U. Ill., 1929; MS, Columbia U., 1931; postgrad., Ecole des Beaux Arts, 1932-34; DFA (hon.), U. Pitts., 1961, U. Ill., 1970. Ptnr. firm Harrison & Abramovitz, Architects, 1945-76, Abramovitz-Harris-Kingsland, Architects, N.Y.C., 1976-85, 85—; asso. prof. Yale U. Sch. Fine Arts, 1939-42; dep. dir. UN Hdqrs. Planning Office, 1947-52; Cons. Brandeis U., U. Pitts. Prin. works include U.S. Steel Bldg, Pitts., Nationwide Ins, Columbus, Ohio, Assembly Hall and Krannert Center Performing Arts, U. Ill.-Urbana; chapels Brandeis U; major campus devel. La Banque Rothschild, Paris, France, Groupe des Assurances Nationales, LaDefense, France, Jewish Chapel, U.S. Mil. Acad., West Point, N.Y., Rockeller U. Rsch. Lab., N.Y.C.;. Served with C.E. AUS, 1942-45; col. 1950-52; spl. asst. to asst. sec. air force Mar. 1952-July 1952. Recipient Legion of Merit; fellow Brandeis U., 1963; Achievement award U. Ill. Alumni Assn., 1963. Fellow AIA; mem. Am. Soc. C.E., Regional Plan Assn. (chmn. bd. 1966-68), Archtl. League N.Y. Club: Century Assn. (N.Y.C.). Home: 176 Honey Hollow Rd Pound Ridge NY 10576-1105

ABRAMOVSKY, ABRAHAM, law educator, lawyer; b. Jerusalem, Aug. 12, 1946; came to U.S., 1956; s. Abba and Ahuva (Kruglikov) A.; m. Deborah Lee Wright, Sept. 21, 1970; children: Aviva, Abba, Ari, Dov. BA, Queens Coll., 1967; JD cum laude, SUNY, Buffalo, 1970; LLM, Columbia U., 1971, JSD, 1976. Bar: N.Y. 1971, U.S. Dist. Ct. (so. and ea. dists.) N.Y. 1982, U.S. Supreme Ct. 1982. Pvt. practice N.Y.C., 1971-72, 73-75; asst. prof. Coll. of Law U. Toledo, 1975-77; assoc. prof. Sch. Law Pace U., White Plains, N.Y., 1977-79; prof. Sch. Law Fordham U., N.Y.C., 1979—, dir. Internat. Criminal Law Ctr., 1990—. Editor: Federal Criminal Law and the Corporate Counsel, 1979; columnist N.Y. Law Jour., N.Y.C., 1982—; guest host Cable TV, N.Y.C.; interviewee CBS Nightwatch, ABC News, Daily News, Newsday, L.A. Time, N.Y. Times, San Francisco Chronicle; contbr. articles to profl. jours. Fordham U. grantee, 1987; vis. fellow U. Warwick Sch. of Law, Coventry, Eng., 1976; Charles Evans Hughes fellow Columbia U., 1972-73. Mem. ABA (vice chair internat. criminal law com.), Anti-Defamation League (bd. dirs. L.I. chpt.). Jewish. Office: Fordham U Sch Law 140 W 62nd St New York NY 10023-7407

ABRAMOWICZ, ADAM ZBIGNIEW, electrical engineering educator, researcher; b. Michałowo, Poland, Dec. 6, 1958; s. Eugeniusz and Bronisława (Gryko) A. MSEE, Warsaw (Poland) U. Tech., 1982, PhD in Electronics, 1993. Devel. engr. Fit-Messtechnik GmbH, Bad Salzdetfurth, Germany, 1996-97; rsch. asst. Warsaw U. Tech., 1983-86, asst. prof. elec. engring., 1986-96, 97—; cons. ATV, Lodz, Poland, 1994-95. Co-author: (in Polish) Dielectric Resonators and Their Applications, 1990; contbr. articles to sci. jours., including IEEE Trans. on MTT, Bull. Polish Acad. Sci.; co-patentee for method of measuring microwave ferrite parameters. Sgt.-cadet Polish Army, 1982-83. Recipient award Polish Min. Nat. Edn., 1991, 95; postdoctoral fellow Japan Soc. for Promotion Sci., 1996. Mem. IEEE (sr. mem., chpt. sec.-treas. 1996—), Internat. Union Radio Scientists (nat. com., Young Scientist award 1993). Roman Catholic. Avocations: soccer, tennis, reading. Home: Mikołajczyka 12/102, 03-894 Warsaw Poland Office: Warsaw U Tech, Nowowiejska 15/19, 00-665 Warsaw Poland

ABRAMOWITZ, ISRAEL, vascular surgeon, educator, consultant; b. Johannesburg, South Africa; m. Julia Aires; children: Roslyn, Linda, Mark. MB, BCh, Witwatersrand U., Johannesburg, 1951. Intern Johannesburg Hosp., 1952-54, resident, 1956-61; lectr. depts. anatomy and surgery Witwatersrand U., 1954—; pvt. practice, Johannesburg, South Africa, 1964—; cons. Mines Benefit Hosp., Johannesburg, 1982-90. Contbg. author: Surgical Anatomy, 12th edit., 1986; contbr. numerous articles to med. and sci. jours. Past pres. and chmn. South African Jewish Bd. Deps. Fellow ACS, Coll Medicine South Africa, Royal Coll. Surgeons (Edinburgh); mem. B'nai B'rith (pres. South Africa).

ABRAMS, FAITH (FAITH WHITE), sculptor; b. N.Y.C., Apr. 7, 1950; d. Edward and Faith-Hope (Green) Kahn. BA summa cum laude, L.I. U., 1971; studied woodcarving, with Nathaniel Burwash, Cambridge, Mass., 1976, with Joseph Wheelwright, Boston, 1977-94. Freelance sculptor Boston, 1971—, N.Y.C., 1995—; adminstrv. asst. to dean of students Grahm Jr. Coll., Boston, 1972-74; exec. sec. to New Eng. regional mgr. Bur. of Nat. Affairs, Inc., Boston, 1974-77; asst. to dir. New Eng. Aquarium, Boston, 1977-80, dir. pers., 1980-82; guest juror for travel grant Boston Visual Artists Union, 1994; show mgr. Sculpture and Large Works, The Copley Soc. of Boston, 1992; instr. woodcarving The Eliot Sch., Jamaica Plain, Mass., 1992-94; tchg. artist Very Spl. Arts program Mus. of Sci., Boston, 1992, 93; project coord. First Night, Boston, 1986, 87, 88; judge Sr. Panel Carving competition Belmont (Mass.) Hill Sch., 1985; docent Hands-On Sculpture show New Eng. Sculptors Assn. at Mus. of Sci., Boston, 1984. One-woman show at Mills Gallery, Boston, 1987; two-person invitational show at The Copley Soc. of Boston, 1994; other exhbns. include Boston Ctr. for Arts, 1984, 85, Boston Visual Artists Union Gallery, 1985, Concord Art Assn., 1985, Cambridge Art Assn., 1986, The Copley Soc. of Boston, 1984, 85, 88, 89, 91, 92, 93, 94, 95, 96, 98, 99, 2000 (including holiday invitationals for award winners 1988, 91, 92), Fed. Res. Bank of Boston Gallery, 1989, with Copley Masters, 1994, Howard Yezerski Gallery, 1989, 90, 91, 92, 93, 94, 95, 96, 97, 98, 99, Libr. Ctr., Newport, Mass., 1990, Landau Gallery, Belmont Hill Sch., 1991, Attleboro (Mass.) Mus., 1992, Gallery NAGA, Boston, 1992, others; represented in permanent collection Sherrill House, Boston. Liaison between mission com. Trinity Ch., Boston and vol. program Sherrill House Nursing Home, 1987-94. Mem. The Copley Soc. of Boston (Copley Master 1992), New Eng. Sculptors Assn. (bd. dirs., mem.-at-large 1985-86, 88-89). Episcopalian. Avocation: fitness training.

ABRAMSON, EDWARD ALLAN, American literature educator; b. N.Y.C., Jan. 14, 1944; arrived in Eng., 1969; s. Arthur Aaron and Emily (Markowitz) A.; m. Avril Nicola Brown, Dec. 17, 1974; children: Elise, David, Dorian. BA, CUNY, 1965; MA, U. Iowa, 1966; PhD, U. Manchester, Eng., 1977. Instr. English East Carolina U., Greenville, N.C., 1966-69; from asst. lectr. to lectr. U. Hull, Eng., 1971-92, sr. lectr. Am. studies, 1993—, head dept. Am. studies, 1994-97; vis. prof. English Coll. William and Mary, Williamsburg, Va., 1986-87; sr. tutor for humanities and European langs. and cultures U. Hull, Eng., 1991-94. Author: Chaim Potok, 1986, Bernard Malamud Revisited, 1993, The Immigrant Experience in American Literature, 1982 (pamphlet). Mem. Brit. Assn. for Am. Studies, Assn. Univ. Tchrs. Avocations: sailing, swimming, hiking, cycling. Office: U Hull, Dept Am Studies, Hull HU6 7RX, England

ABRAMSON, ELAINE SANDRA, graphic designer, crafts artist; b. Cleve., Aug. 27, 1942; d. Norman Morris and Ruth Lea (Glassman) Splaver; m. Martin Stanley Abramson, May 27, 1977; children: Deborah Sue, Mitchell Lee. Hebrew tchr. cert., Hyam Greenberg Inst., Jerusalem, 1961; BS in Edn., Kent State U., 1964; fine and decorative arts appraising cert, Cleve. Inst. Art, 1965, NYU, 1990. Illustrator Ednl. Rsch. Coun., Cleve., 1964-65; tchr. art Cleve. Bd. Edn., 1965-67; owner A & A (formerly Create-A-Craft), Ft. Worth, 1967—; author, spkr. affects of copyright law and politics on the artist, 1991—; apptd. dir. Animagic Internat. Animation Studio Sch., Vancouver, Can., 1997-99; founding artist, publicity designer Sassy Cat, Chagrin Falls, Ohio, 1967-71; adviser Women's Am. ORT Collection, Houston, 1983-84; designer Golden Gourmet dolls Hobby Industries Am., Dallas, 1981-85; intern, columnist Appraisers Assn. Am., 1990; cons. appraising and decorative arts for copyright law. Author: (syndicated column) Appraisals by Abramson, (cartoons) Rojo the Red Lobster, Cow-town, Alley Gator, Rock-a-Pearl Band, Santa Cow, Sports Cows, Political Cows, Star Staples, Collegiate Crunchies, Culinary Court, Gallant Gators, Library Loonies, Granny Greatness, Billy Joe Cow, Cindy Sue Cow, Cow Chip Crew, Papa Bull, Hillary and Harvey Horse, The Golden Gourmets; editor, art dir. Art Forum, 1991—; creator, lic., author: Those Characters from Cowtown (citation Tex. Ho. of Reps. 1987, Tex. Senate Proclamation, 3 Mayor of Ft. Worth Proclamations including 1st Woman State Artist of Tex. 1993, numerous letters to stimulate Tex. tourism, used in Richards for Gov. campaign 1990, used in State Artist Competition); creator (characters) RomantiCat appearing on Pixelon Network, 2000; one-woman shows include Kent State U., 1963-64, Ctrl. Nat. Bank Cleve., 1961-66, Md. Pub. TV Arts Exhibits, 1972-77, Tex. State Artist Competition; group shows of illustration, soft crafts, toys, enamelling including Cleve. Mus. Art, 1964, Cleve. Inst. Art, 1964-71, Towson Courthouse, Md., 1972-77; designer, inventor, creator craft kits, toys games, 1967—. Advisor Jr. Achievement, Ft. Worth. Scholar Practicing Law Inst., 1992; named Tex. Woemn Hall of Fame in Art, 1989-91, Guinness Book of Records, 1991, Internat. Woman of the Yr. in Art, 1993, 96, State Artist Tex., 1993-94. Mem. Am. Crafts Coun., Am. Mus. Natural History, Nat. Enamelists Guild, Nat. Geographic Soc., Nat. Assn. Self-Employed, Soc. Craft Designers (in Dallas Showcase of Designers 1985), Md. Art League (bd. dirs., workshop chmn.), Nat. Assn. TV Prodrs. and Execs., Graphic Artists Guild (bd. dirs. 1991-94, founder Tex.-at-large chpt. 1991, first chpt. dir., sr. adv.), Cartoonists Guild, Orgn. for Internat. Historic Preservation, Composers, Authors and Artists in Am., Tex. Accts., Lawyers for Arts, Graphic Artists Guild (founder Tex. chpt. 1991), Authors and Artists of Am., Nat. League Advt. Agys., Am. Film Inst., Nat. Writers Club, Nat. Mus. Women in Arts, Tex. Accts. and Lawyers for the Arts (cons. for lawyers on copyrights and appraising fine and decorative arts 1991—), Bus. Profl. Women's Found., Delegation for Friendship among Women Writer's Workshop, Dallas Soc. Illustrators, Soc. Children's Book Writers and Illustrators, Nat. League of Am. Pen Women (pres. 1996, 2000—, art judge Nat. Book Prodn. Buyer's Guide art and photo contest, founding editor, art dir. newsletter 1996), Advt. Club. Ft. Worth, Am. Advt. Fedn., Zonta. Jewish. Avocations: sewing, painting, reading, travel. Office: A & A PO Box 941293 Plano TX 75094-1293

ABRAMSON, RACHEL, psychologist; b. Melbourne, Australia, May 15, 1959; d. Abraham Samuel and Esther (Friedman) Welber; m. Michael John Abramson, Nov. 23, 1986; children: Phillip Justin, Simon Joseph. BA, Chisholm Inst. Tech., Australia, 1985, grad. diploma in applied psychology, 1987; diploma in solution oriented hypnosis, Ctr. of Effective Therapy, Australia, 1994, diploma in solution oriented counseling, 1996; M of Applied Psychology Occupl., Monash U., 1998. Registered psychologist. Profl. officer pediatrics dept. Univ. Newcastle, Australia, 1987-88; tutor dept statistics Univ. Melbourne, 1989; session tutor dept. hospitality & tourism mgmt. V.U.T., Australia, 1990-93; session lectr. dept. psychology & intellectual disability R.M.I.T., Australia, 1995; prin. psychologist Rachel Abramson & Assocs., Australia, 1993—. Contbr. numerous articles to profl. jours.; produced Person and Profl. Development Program News, Careers Quarterly and Head Quarters. With Army Res., 1990-92. Mem. Australian Psychological Soc.(Coll. Orgn. Psychologists editor 1994-95, divsn. indp. practicing psychologists profl. devel. officer 1994-97, mem. com. 1998—), Australian Assn. Career Counsellors (nat. membership officer 1997-99), Australian Inst. Mgmt. Avocations: sewing, gardening, cycling, computers, breadmaking. Office: Rachel Abramson & Assocs, PO Box 300, Caulfield South 3162, Australia

ABRANCHES, JOSÉ MENDES, pharmaceutical marketing executive; b. Coimbra, Portugal, July 13, 1955; s. António César and Elsa Cavaleiro (Mendes) A. BBA, U. Coimbra, 1981. Sales coord. ACCS Abbott Lab., Lisbon, Portugal, 1993-96; product mgr. Abbott Labs., Lisbon, Portugal, 1996—; ptnr. Topbizz, Ltd., Coimbra, 1984-95; fin. adviser Argent Internat., Cascais, Portugal, 1982-83; gen. mgr. Top Bizz Ltd, 1984-94; cons. Assn. Comml. and Indsl. of Coimbra, 1992-96; CECOA, Lisbon, Portugal, 1992-96, Instituto de Força de Vendas, Lisbon, Portugal, 1995. Author: The Quality in the Sales Network, 1992; contbr. articles to profl. publs. Mem. Cruz Vermelha Portuguesa, Lisbon, 1990, Amnesty Internat., Lisbon, 1990, Portuguese New Philharm. Orch. Recipient prize of honor Bissaya Barretto Found., Coimbra, 1989, Best Presentation prize of honor Iberian Quality Congress, Madrid, 1992, Bronze medal Univ. World Judo Championship, 1980. Mem. Assn. Nat. Jovens Empresarios (bd. dirs. 1993), Am. Mgmt. Assn., Portuguese Assn. Mgmt., Portuguese Assn. Quality (bd. dirs. 1993), XVIIIth Century Portuguese Soc., Club of Clubs., Exec. Club Internat. Avocations: golf, judo, photography, bridge, reading. Office: Abbott Labs, PO Box 7520, 2720 Alfragide Portugal

ABRAO, MARISIA, psychologist, educator; b. Cumari, Goias, Brazil, Jan. 3, 1943; d. Abdala and Rita Goncaloes A.; m. Elias Helou, May 31, 1961 (dec. June, 1987); children: Sami, Eduardo. Diploma, Cath. U. Goias, Brazil, 1978; Masters, Cath. U. Sao Paulo, Brazil, 1996, State U. Campinas, Brazil, 1998. Tchr. Cath. U. of Goias, Goiania, Brazil, 1979—; clinic supr. Cath. U. of Goias, Goiania, 1979—; psychoanalyst pvt. clinic, Goiania, 1979—. Mem. Internat. Psychoanalytical Assoc. Avocation: gardening. Home: Rua 82 #279/ap201, 7408310 Goiania Brazil Office: Rua 10 # 250 Room 7 S Oeste, 74120020 Goias Brazil

ABRASHEV, MIROSLAV VERGILOV, physicist, educator; b. Tutrakan, Ruse, Bulgaria, May 2, 1963; s. Vergiliy Nikolov and Maria Trifonova (Iovkova) A.; m. Antonia Petkova Petkova, Dec. 15, 1999; children: Maria, Nikolai, Yasen. MSc, Sofia (Bulgaria) U., 1988, PhD, 1993. Physicist Sofia U., 1988-93, asst. prof. physics, 1994—. Contbr. articles to Phys. Rev. Alesander von Humboldt Found. rsch. fellow, Bonn, Germany, 1996; Bulgarian Nat. Sci. Fund grantee, 1996. Orthodox Christian. Avocations: bridge, backgammon, hiking, synthesizers. Office: Sofia Univ, Faculty Physics, BG-1126 Sofia Bulgaria

ABREU, GREGORIO BENITO, pharmaceutical executive; b. Manila, Philippines, May 9, 1928; s. Jose C. and Andrea J. (Mariano) A.; m. Cornelia Morelos, July 7, 1951; children: Gregorio, Antonio, Enrique, Cristina. BS in Chemistry cum laude, U. Philippines, Diliman, Quezon City, 1950; Grad. studies, Harvard U., Cambridge, 1951. Exec. Shell Co. Philippines, Manila, 1951-53; prod. mgr. E.R. Squibb and Sons, Makati, Philippines, 1953-61; pres. Mabuhay Feeds Inc., Quezon City, Phillippines, 1961—, Inphilco Inc., Quezon City, 1963—. Mem. Philippine Assn. Feed Millers Inc., Philippine Vet. Drug Assn., Philippine Assn. Animal Health Industry (bd. dirs.). Roman Catholic. Clubs: Baguio Country (Baguio City, Philippines), Valle Verde Country (Pasig, Metro Manila), Canlubang Country (Canlubang, Philippines). Avocation: traveling.

ABRIE, PIETER LUCAS, engineering company executive, software developer, educator; b. Brakpan, South Africa, May 4, 1953; s. Johannes Jacobus and Mona (van der Westhuizen) A.; m. Hilda Grundlingh, July 5, 1980; children: Albert, Dewald, Willem. B in Elec. Engring., Pretoria (South Africa) U., 1976, B in Engring. with honors, 1981, M in Engring., 1983, D in Engring., 1986. Engr.-in-tng. UKOR, Pretoria, 1976-77; lectr. U. Pretoria, 1977-87, assoc. prof. engring., 1988-89; mgr. Ampsa CC, Pretoria, 1989-96; mng. dir. Ampsa (Pty.) Ltd., Somerset West, South Africa, 1996—; extraordinary prof. engring. U. Pretoria, 1996—. Author: The Design of Impedance-Matching Networks for Radio-Frequency and Microwave Amplifiers, 1985, Design of RF and Microwave Amplifiers and Oscillators, 1999; author Multimatch Impedance-Matching, Amplifier and Oscillator Synthesis software, 1985—, Q-Match Lumped-Element Impedance-Matching Software, 2000; contbr. articles to profl. jours. Mem. IEEE Microwave Theory and Techniques. Home: 6 Francolin St, 7130 Somerset West South Africa Office: Ampsa (Pty) Ltd, 76 Andries Pretorius St, 7130 Somerset West South Africa

ABRIKOSOV, ALEKSEI ALEKSEYEVICH, physicist; b. Moscow, June 25, 1928; s. Aleksey Ivanovich and Fanny Davidovna (Vulf) A.; m. Svetlana Yuriyevna Bun-kova, 1977; 3 children. Degree, Moscow U., 1948; DS in Physics and Math., Inst. Phys. Problems, Moscow, 1955; DS (hon.), Lausanne U., 1975. Postgrad. rsch. assoc., sr. scientist Inst. Phys. Problems USSR Acad. Scis., Moscow, 1948-65, head dept. L.D. Landau Inst. Theoretical Physics, 1965-88; dir. Inst. High Pressure Physics, Moscow, 1988-91; disting. sci. Argonne Nat. Lab., Ill., 1991—; asst. prof., prof. Moscow U., 1951-68; prof. Gorky U., 1971-72; prof. Moscow Phys. Engring. Inst., 1974-75; head chair Theoretical physics Moscow Inst. Steel and Alloys, 1976-92. Author: Quantum Field Theory Methods in Statistical Physics, 1962, Introduction to the Theory of Normal Metals, 1972, Fundamentals of the Theory of Metals, 1987; contbr. articles to profl. jours. Recipient Lenin prize, 1966, Fritz London aweard, 1972, Landau prize Acad. Sci. USSR, 1982, State prize USSR, 1989, Internat. John Bardeen award, 1991. Fellow Am. Physics Soc.; mem. NAS Am. Acad. Arts and Scis. (fgn. hon. mem.), Russian Acad. Scis. Office: Argonne Nat Lab 9700 Cass Ave Argonne IL 60439-4803

ABRIL, VICTORIA, actress. Stage appearances include Obras de Mihura, 1977, Viernes día de libertad, 1977, Nuit d'Ivresse, Paris, 1986; TV appearances; films include Obsesión, 1975, Robian and Marian, 1976, Robin Hood, 1976, Caperucita Roja, 1975, Cambio de sexo, 1975, La bien plantada, 1976, Doña Perfecta, 1976, Esposa y Amante, 1977, La muchacha de las bragas de oro, 1979, Asesinato en el Comité Central, 1981, La Guerrillera, 1981, La Colmena, 1982, La batalla del porro, 1982, Le Bastard, 1982, La Lune dans le Caniveau, 1982, Sem Sombra de pecado, 1981, J'ai Epousé un ombre, 1982, Rio Abajo, 1982, Bajo el signo de Piscis, 1983, Le Voyage, 1983, Las bicicletas son para el verano, 1983, L'Addition, 1983, 84, Rouge George, 1983, La noche más hermosa, 1984, Padre Nuestro, 1984, After Dark, 1984, La hora bruja, 1985, Tiempo de Silencio, 1985, Max mon Amour, 1985, Vado e torno, 1985, El Lute, 1987, El placer de matar, 1987, Barrios altos, 1987, El juego más divertido, 1987, Ada dans la jungle, 1988, Baton Rouge, 1988, Sandino, 1989, Atame, 1989, A solas contigo, 1990, Amantes, 1990, Tie Me Up! Tie Me Down, 1991, High Heels, 1992, Kika, 1993, Gazon Maudit, 1996, La Femme du Cosmonaute, 1997, Entre las piernas, 1999, Mon père, ma mère, mes frères et mes soeurs, 1999, 101 Reykajavik, 2000. Office: care JFPM, 11 rue de Chanez, 75781 Paris Cedex 16, France*

ABRUKOV, VICTOR SERGEYEVICH, physicist, educator; b. Kazan, Tatar, ASSR, Jan. 11, 1952; s. Sergey Andreyevich and Lidiya (Arsentjevna) A.; m. Galina Vasiljevna, July 12, 1975; children: Anna, Sergey. Degree in physics, Leningrad (Russia) State U., 1974, Chuvash State U., Cheboksary, Russia, 1974; Candidate in Physics and Math., Acad. Scis. Soviet Union, Moscow, 1985; D in Physics and Math., Russian Acad. Scis., Moscow, 1995. Assoc. prof. All-Soviet Union Poly. Inst. (now Moscow State Open U.), 1986-94, prof., 1994-96, head Cheboksary Study Ctr., 1986-96; rschr. subfaculty of physics of heat Chuvash State U., 1974-76, sr. rschr., 1976-86, prof., chairperson physics of heat, 1996—; vice chmn. combustion diagnostics commn. Sci. Coun. for Combustion, Russian Acad. Scis., 1990—; chief rschr. problem-oriented sci. rsch. lab. of physics of non-stationary combustion Chuvash State U., 1995—, vice dir., mem. sci. coun. Natural Scis. Inst., mem. sci. coun. physics of engring. faculty, 1997—; chmn. expert advice of Chuvash State U., 1998—. Author: Interferometric Techniques in Combustion, Gas Dynamic and Heat Transfer Research, 1997; co-author: Optical Holography and Its Application, 1985; reviewer Jour. Physics Combustion and Explosive, 1999; contbr. articles to profl. publs. Russian Found. Basic Rsch. grantee, Moscow, 1993-95, 98-99, George Soros Internat. Sci. Found. travel grantee, N.Y., 1993, Volga Region grantee, Moscow-Cheboksary, 1999-00. Mem. Internat. Combustion Inst. (Russian sect.). Avocations: football, chess, playing cards, travel. E-mail: victor@chuvsu.ru. Office: Chuvash State Univ, Moskovsky Prosp 15, 428015 Cheboksary Chuvash, Russia

ABSALOM, DOUGLAS JOHN, linguistics educator; b. Taree, NSW, Australia, Aug. 1, 1945; s. John Cedric and Betsy Jean (Shepherd) A.; m. Christine Marilyn Wamsley, Aug. 17, 1968 (div. 1985); children: Sharon Elizabeth, Michael Douglas; m. Lynne Maree Wilson, Oct. 3, 1987; children: David Scott, Lauren Ashleigh. BA with honors, U. Newcastle, Australia, 1966, diploma in edn., 1967, MA, 1969, PhD, 1976, B in Edn. Studies, 1979; MLitt, U. New England, Australia, 1988. Secondary education educator Dept. Sch. Edn., NSW, Australia, 1971-72; lectr. Mitchell Coll. of Adv. Edn., Bathurst, NSW, Australia, 1972-76; lectr., prin. lectr. Newcastle Coll. Adv. Edn., 1976-89; prin. lectr. to assoc. prof. edn. U. Newcastle, 1989—; Found dir. Elicos Ctr., U. Newcastle, 1988-93; mem. Higher Sch. Edn. Syllabus Com., Dept. Sch. Edn., NSW, 1978-90; comm. cons. Nat. Safety Coun., NSW, 1983-90; found. tchr. Aboriginal Edn. Ctr., U. Newcastle, 1982-86, lectr. and presented papers at acad. conf. in Sweden, Holland, Eng. U.S.A, Korea, China, Bangkok, Finland, and Hong Kong. Joint editor Australian Jour. Linguistics, 1997—; co-editor AALIT Jour., 1996-97; contbr. articles to profl. jours. Bd. dirs., Hunter Valley Theatre Co., Newcastle, 1979-95; pres. Hunter br. English Tchrs. Assn., 1985-86. Mem. Australian Linguistic Soc. (treas. 1977—), Applied Linguistics Assn. Australia (found. mem., exec. liaison officer 1976—), Australian Coll. Edn., Newcastle Rugby Club (life). Office: U Newcastle, Faculty of Edn, Newcastle NSW 2308, Australia

ABSAR, NURUL, biochemistry educator; b. Feni, Bangladesh, Jan. 2, 1951; s. Nabalak Mea and Hosneara Begum; m. Tahmina Akhter; children: Rafi Bin, Rubaiya Absar. BS, Dhaka U., Bangladesh, 1971, MS, 1972; M in Agr., Kyushu U., Japan, 1982, D in Agr., 1985. Lectr. U. Rajshahi, Bangladesh, 1976-79, asst. prof., 1980-85, assoc. prof., 1986-91, prof., 1992—. Contbr. articles to profl. jours. Provost Madar Baksh Hall, Rajshahi, 1992-95. Recipient Monbusho scholarship, Japanese Govt., 1980-86, Cida-Nserc fellowship Can. Govt., 1990-91. Mem. Bangladesh Med. Rsch., Bangladesh Biochem. Soc. Avocation: tennis. Office: Dept Biochemistry, Univ Rajshahi, 6205 Rajshahi Bangladesh

ABSHAGEN, ULRICH WOLFGANG PETER, consultant, phamacology educator; b. Würzburg, Bavaria, Germany, July 18, 1943; s. Wolfgang and Irmgard (Tratt) A.; m. Ursula Marie Proestler, Oct. 19, 1967; children: Christian Constantin, Constanze Catherina. MD, U. Wüzburg, 1968, PhD, 1970; Habilitation, Free U. Berlin, 1974. Cert. German Bd. Pharmacology, German Bd. Internal Medicine. Sci. asst. in clin. pharmacology Free U. Berlin, 1970-73, sci. asst. dept. internal medicine, 1973-77; head dept. clin. pharmacology Boehringer Mannheim (Germany) GmbH, 1977-82, dir. divsn. product devel., 1982-85, mem. bd. mgmt., 1985-92; pres. Therapeutics Corange Ltd. Hamilton, Bermuda, 1987-93; mng. dir. Abshagen Cons. GmbH, Mannheim, 1995—; prof. clin. pharmacology U. Heidelberg, Germany, 1981—; chmn. bd. Boehringer Mannheim Pharm. Corp., Rockville, Md., 1986-93; mem. exec. com. Corange Ltd., London, 1992-93; organizer IV World Conf. Clin. Pharmacology and Therapeutics, Mannheim-Heidelberg, 1989. Editor, author: Handbook of Experimental Pharmacology, Vol. 76, Clinical Pharmacology of Antianginal Drugs, 1985; mem. editl. bd. Clin. Pharmacology, 13 vols.; contbr. over 200 articles to sci. jours. Chmn. bd. dirs. Paul Martini Found., 1987-92. Mem. German Soc. Pharmacology and Toxicology (chmn. sect. clin. pharmacology 1982-88, mem. mng. bd. 1992-95), German Pharm. Soc. (Fritz Külz award 1971), also numerous other nat. and internat. sci. socs. Roman Catholic. Avocations: skiing, diving, reading. Home: Burgunderweg 8, D-69469 Weinheim Germany Office: Abshagen Cons GmbH, Neustadter Strasse 41, D-68309 Mannheim Germany

ABSMEIER, ALBERT FRANZ, publisher; b. Safferstetten, Bavaria, Germany, Nov. 10, 1958; s. Albert and Gisela (Fett) A.; m. Brigitte Susanne Elizabeth Braun, May 26, 1983; children: Evelyn, Isabelle. Dipl. Ing. in Physics, Fachhochschule Munich. Editor Markt & Technik, Munich, Germany, 1983-84, sr. editor, 1984-86, editor in chief, 1986-94; pub. Magnamedia, Munich, 1995—. Avocations: golf, fitness, skiing. Office: IT Mgmt, Arnibastr 2 Str 2, 85635 Hoehenkirchen Germany

ABT, CLARK C., social scientist, executive, engineer, publisher, educator; b. Cologne, Germany, Aug. 31, 1929; came to U.S., 1937, naturalized, 1945; m. Wendy Peter, Nov. 3, 1971; children: Thomas, Emily. BS, MIT, 1951, PhD, 1965; MA, Johns Hopkins U., 1952. Instr. Johns Hopkins U., Balt., 1951-52; mgr. advanced systems dept. Raytheon Co., Bedford, Mass., 1957-64; pres., treas. Abt Assocs., Inc., Cambridge, Mass., 1965-86, chmn., 1986—; pres., publisher Abt Books Inc., Cambridge, 1987-94; prof., dir. Ctr. for Study of Small States Boston U., 1991-93, rsch. prof. internat. rels., 1991-94, dir. Def. Tech. Conversions Ctr., 1993-96; vis. lectr. Harvard U., 1968-69; vis. prof. SUNY, Binghamton, 1975-76; adj. prof. mgmt. U. Mass., 1991-93; dir. Russian Am. Boston Workshop on Def. Tech. Conversion, 1992, dir. Moscow Workshop, 1993; faculty dir. Moscow Entrepreneurial Workshop, 1993, 95; assoc. Ctr. for Sci. and Internat. Affairs Harvard U., 1991—. Author: Serious Games, 1970, The Evaluation of Social Programs, 1977, The Social Audit for Management, 1977, Applied Research for Social Policy: The U.S. and the Federal Republic of Germany Compared, 1978, Costs and Benefits of Applied Social Research, 1979, A Strategy for Terminating a Nuclear War, 1985, AIDS and the Courts, 1990, Drugs and Crime CD-ROM Library, 1990, International Drug Library CD-ROM, 1990, National Portrait Gallery Permanent Collection of Notable Americans on CD-ROM, 1990, The Future of Energy, 1999, Solar-Powered Econmomic Growth, 1999, others. Served with USAF, 1952-57. Recipient grand prize Thoreau award for landscape architecture, 1975. Clubs: Cosmos, MIT of Boston. Home: 19 Follen St Cambridge MA 02138-3502 also: Abt Assocs Inc 55 Wheeler St Cambridge MA 02138-1192

ABU-AKEL, FAHED LABEEB, religious organization executive; b. Kuffer-Yessif, Palestine, Apr. 13, 1944; s. Labee Elias Abu-Akel and Adlah Heriez Shehadeh; m. Mary Shibly Zumot, Aug. 30, 1980. BA, Southeastern Coll., 1970; MDiv, Columbia Theological Seminary, 1973; D in Ministry, McCormick Theological Seminary, 1983. Youth minister First Presbyn. Ch., Atlanta, 1975-77; founder, exec. dir. Atlanta Ministry with Internat. Students Inc., Atlanta, 1978—; Mem. mission staff First Presbyn. Ch., Atlanta, 1990—. Recipient Arab Am. Cmty. award Atlanta, 1984, Leadership award Jewish and Christian Interfaith, Atlanta, 1997, Peacemaker award Greater Atlanta Presbytory, Atlanta, 1998. Mem. Nat. Assn. for Internat. Educators (Ga. chpt., Region VII chpt.), Northside Kiwanis Club (pres. 1996-97, chmn. internat. understanding 1998-00, outstanding leadership award 1998). Avocations: travel, reading, walking, speaking. E-mail: fabu-akel@firstpresatl.org. Fax: 404-228-7760. Office: AMIS Inc 1328 Peachtree St NE Atlanta GA 30309-3209

ABU-ARAB, MAHMOUD, psychologist; b. Majd El-Korum, Acre, Israel, Sept. 3, 1953; arrived in Australia, 1988; parents Mohammad and Zena (Askari) Abu-Arab; m. Zlatica Minichova, Mar. 21, 1981 (div. Apr. 1993); children: Maria, Silvia; m. Mariola Zuk, Jan. 27, 1999; 1 child, Adam. MA, Comenius U., Bratislava, Slovakia, 1981, PhD, 1985. Psychologist Bratislava City Coun., 1982-83, Psychiat. Hosp., Pezenok, Slovakia, 1984; lectr. Ibrahimieh Coll., Jerusalem, 1985-88; dir. Palestinian Counseling Ctr., Jerusalem, 1986-88; rsch. officer Arab Studies Soc., Jerusalem, 1987-88; counsellor Granville Tafe Coll., Sydney, NSW, Australia, 1988—; head dept. psychology Al-Amal Hosp., Jeddah, Saudi Arabia, 1993-94; pvt. practice, 1994—; spkr., presenter in field. Author standardization Psychol. Screening Inventory on Slovak Population, 1984, Psychol. Test on Palestinian Population, 1988; contbr. articles to profl. jours. Justice of the peace Min. for Justice, NSW, 1992; rep. Palestinian Charity Instns. Week of Peace Conf., Tokyo, 1987, Drug Abuse Prevention Conf., 1988. Mem. Australian Psychol. Soc., NSW Counsellors Assn., Nat. Acupuncture Detoxification Assn., Coll. Independently Practising Psychologists, Coll. Counselling Psychologists, Australian Assn. for Applied Psychophysiology and Biofeedback, Coll. Health Psychology, Australian Pain Soc. Avocations: bushwalking, snow skiing, travel, reading. Home: PO Box 391, Granville Sydney NSW 2142, Australia Office: Granville Coll of Tafe, 136 William St, Granville Sydney NSW 2142, Australia

ABU-ARAFEH, ISHAQ AHMAD, pediatric neurology consultant, educator, researcher, lecturer; b. Jerusalem, Feb. 8, 1955; arrived in Eng., 1983; s. Ahmad and Hikmat Abu-Arafeh; m. Ghada Abu-Omar, Sept. 15, 1983; children: Ahmad, Hashem. MB, BChir, U. Jordan, Amman, 1980; MD, U. Aberdeen, Scotland, 1996. Intern Makassed Hosp., Jerusalem, 1980-81; med. officer Caritas Baby Hosp., Bethlehem, 1981-83; sr. house officer/fellow Leeds (Eng.) Gen. Infirmary, 1983-84; sr. house officer U. Hosp. of Wales, Cardiff, 1985-86, Jessop Hosp., Sheffield, Eng., 1986-87; registrar Royal Aberdeen Children's Hosp., 1987-91; rsch. fellow U. Aberdeen, 1991-93, lectr., 1993-95; cons. pediatrician Stirling (Scotland) Royal Infirmary, 1995—. Contbr. articles to profl. jours. and books. Med. advisor Cyclical Vomiting Syndrome Assn., Eng., 1995—; pres. Palestinian Soc., Scotland, 1996—. Fellow Royal Coll. Pediat. and Child Health; mem. Royal Coll. Physicians (Ireland), Scottish Pediat. Neurology Group (sec. 1996—). Avocations: soccer, current affairs. Office: Stirling Royal Infirmary, Livilands, Stirling FK8 2AU, Scotland

ABU-ARAFEH, WAEL MAHMUD, physician, consultant in urology; b. Jerusalem, Israel, Aug. 9, 1958; s. Mahmud Izhag and Siret (Abed) Abu-A.; m. Abeer Daoud Asmar, July 15, 1988; children: Samah, Gassan, Muhamad. MD, Med. Sch., Bucharest, Romania, 1984. Resident in gen. surgery Caplan Hosp., Rehovot, Israel, 1988-90; resident in urology Shaare Zedek Hosp., Rehovot, Israel, 1990-93, cons. in urology, 1993—; urology adviser Auguste-Victoria, Jerusalem, 1997-99; lectr. Faculty of Medicine, Jerusalem, 1999—. Mem. Am. Urol. Assn., European Assn. Urology, Intenrat. Assn. Urology, N.Y. Acad. Scis. Avocations: poetry, sports (tennis, gymnastics).

ABUBAKAR, ABBULSALAMI AMINU, pharmacist; b. Jos, Plateau, Nigeria, June 2, 1956; s. Abdussalam and Nafisatu Abubakar; m. Karimatu Aminu, Aug. 27, 1982; children: Abdussalam Jr., Nafisatu Jr., Hauwa'u, Abu Ubaidah. BSc in Pharmacy, Ahmadu Bello U., 1979; MSc in Pharmacology, Ahmandu Bello U., 1965; PhD in Exptl. Pathology, St. Andrews (Scotland) U., 1990. Intern pharmacist Hosps. Mgmt. Bd., Bauchi, Nigeria, 1979-80; sr. pharmacist Health Mgmt. Bd., Bauchi, 1982-83, prin. pharmacist, 1985-86, dep. chief pharmacist, 1990-91, chief pharmacist, 1991-92, dir. pharm. svcs., 1993—; head of state Fed Rep of Nigeria. Contbr. articles to profl. jours. Mem. Overseas Soc. St. Andrew U. Avocations: reading, table tennis, travelling, listening to music. Office: Hosps Mgmt Bd, GRA Rd PO Box 1127, Bauchi Nigeria*

ABUBAKR, SAID MOHAMMED, chemical engineering educator; b. Irbid, Jordan, Sept. 23, 1948; came to U.S., 1977; s. Abdellatif and Khaireh (Hrais) A.; m. Doha M. Serieh, Jan. 24, 1984; children: Haniene, Tamer, Maher, Majdy. BS in Petroleum Engring., Moscow Inst. Petrochems., 1974; MSChemE, Mich. State U., 1981, PhD in Chem. Engring., 1982. Prodn. engr. Jordan Petroleum Refinery, Zarga, 1974-77; instr. Mich. State U., East Lansing, 1977-82; asst. prof. Yarmouk U., Irbid, 1982-84; asst. prof. U. Wis., Stevens Point, 1984-87, from assoc. prof. to prof., 1987-93; project leader USDA Forest Products Lab., Madison, Wis., 1993—; mem. adv. bd. U. Wis.-Stevens Point Gesell Inst., 1988-93, U. Wis.-Stevens Point, 1993—. Editor: Anthology of Paper Recycling, 1996; contbr. more than 100 sci. papers to profl. publs., author/co-author four books. Recipient Tchg. Excellence award U. Wis., 1987, Sec.'s Honor award USDA, 1995-97, Tech. Transfer award Forest Svc. Chief, 1997. Fellow TAPPI (mem. divsn. coun. forestry bd. 1997—, vice chair fiber recycling 1997—); mem. AIChE. Achievements include research in area of paper recycling and removal of contaminants from recycled paper using enzymatic deinking, fiber loading and fractionation; inventions in field. Office: USDA Forest Products Lab One Gifford Pinchot Dr Madison WI 53705

ABU DAIA, JEHAD MOHAMAD, pediatric surgeon; b. Gaza, Palestine, Mar. 28, 1956; s. Mohamad and Zinab Ahmed Abu Daia; m. Sama Jamil Ashour, Apr. 27, 1984; children: Mohamad, Majed, Waleed, Jamil. B Medicine and Surgery, Alexandria (Egypt) U., 1981. Med. officer King Fahid Specialist Hosp., Al Qassim, Saudi Arabia, 1983-89, resident in surgery, 1989-91, sr. registrar, pediat. surgeon, 1992-95, cons. pediat. surgeon, 1995-96; pediat. surgeon King Faisal Specialist Hosp. and Rsch. Ctr., Riyadh, Saudi Arabia, 1996-98, pediat. urologist, 1998—; dir. primary health care Tirak, Burgdah, Qassim, 1983-89; med. edn. and rsch. coord. King Fahd Specialist Hosp., 1992-95. Contbr. articles to profl. jours. Fellow Royal Coll. Surgeons Edinburgh, Internat. Coll. Surgeons; mem. Arab Assn. Pediat. Surgeons, Asian Assn. Pediat. Surgeons. Avocations: swimming, running. Address: King Faisal Spec Hosp, MBC 83 PO Box 3354, Riyadh 11211, Kingdom of Saudi Arabia

ABUDO, JOSE IBRAIMO, government official. Min. justice Govt. of Mozambique, Maputo, 1994—. Office: Min of Justice, Avenida Julius Nyerere 33, Maputo Mozambique*

ABUDULMAJID, IMAN See **IMAN**

ABU ESLEIH, MAHMOUD MOHAMMAD, internist; b. Zaita, Palestine, Mar. 9, 1958; s. Mohammad Ahmad and Safieh Okasheh (No'man) Abu E.; m. Basema Ahmad Al-Sayyed, Dec. 27, 1984; children: Ayah, Bará, Obadah, Walá, Bayan, Hadeel. MD, Faculty Medicine, Iasi, Romania, 1983; specialist internal medicine, Al-Makassed Hosp., Jerusalem, 1995; diploma in epidemiology, U. Oslo, 1997. Lic. to practice medicine, Jordan; diplomate Jordan Bd. Internal Medicine; Ednl. Commn. for Fgn. Med. Grads. cert. Gen. practitioner Health Dept., Nablus, Palestine, 1985-86; resident Ittihad Hosp., Nablus, 1986-87; gen. practitioner Shifa Clinic, Qalqilia, Palestine, 1987-88; med. resident Makassed Hosp., Jerusalem, 1989-93; internist Al Ahli Hosp., Hebron, Palestine, 1993-94, Tulkarm (Palestine) Hosp., 1995-98, Al Razi Hosp., Jenin, Palestine, 1998—; dir. sci. com. Alahli Hosp., Hebron, 1993-94. Mem. Jordan Med. Assn., Assn. Internists, N.Y. Acad. Sci. Home: Tulkarm-Atil, West Bank Israel Office: Al Razi Hosp, PO Box 1000, Jenin West Bank Israel

ABU-HAIMID, ABDULRAHMAN IBRAHIM, civilian military deputy; b. Riyadh, Saudi Arabia, Apr. 17, 1947; s. Ibrahim Mohamad Abu-Haimid; 6 children. BA in Acctg., Bus. Adminstrn., King Saud U., Saudi Arabia, 1971; MA in Acctg., Bus. Adminstrn., Ea. N.Mex. U., 1974. Deputy head gen. comml. registration Ministry Comml. and Industry, Riyadh, 1963-66; dir. gen. training affairs Inst. Pub. Adminstrn., Riyadh, 1966-78; asst. dep. for tech. affairs Nat. Guard, Riyadh, 1978-80, dep. for tech. affairs, 1980-93, dep., 1994—; mem. Supreme com. of Nat. Guard Modernization Program; bd. dirs. Al Jazeerah Newspaper for Printing and Publishing. Mem. supervising com. Nat. Guard Mag., 1980—; contbr. articles to profl. jours. Mem. King Abdul Aziz Libr., Riyadh; bd. dirs. King Abdul Aziz Al Saud Found. for Islamic and Human Sci. Studies, Casablanca, Morocco, Prince Salman Soc. Ctr. Recipient Medal of Merit-2nd grade HM the Custodian of Two Holy Mosques, 1984. Mem. Am. Accts. Assn., Inst. Pub. Adminstrn. Mag. Editors, Saudi Accts. Assn., Saudi Accts. Soc., Am. Acctg. Soc. Home: PO Box 5794, Riyadh 11432, Saudi Arabia

ABUL-AZM, AHMED GAMAL, marine engineer; b. Ismailia, Egypt, Feb. 14, 1959; s. Gamal Mahmoud and Hamida Sedky (Said) A.; m. Iman Roushdy Abdelsalam, Aug. 14, 1983; children: Omar, Amina, Mariam. BS, Cairo U., 1980, MS, 1983; PhD, U. Houston, 1988. Teaching asst. Cairo U., 1980-83; rsch. asst. U. Houston, 1983-88; rsch. engr. Single Buoy Moorings, Inc., Monaco, Monte Carlo, 1989-90; asst. prof. Cairo U., 1990-95, assoc. prof., 1995-98; head environ. mgmt. sector Egytian Environ. Affairs Agy., 1998—; vis. asst. prof. U. Houston, 1988-89; dir. Engring. Co. Marine Affairs, Cairo, 1990—; cons. in field. Contbr. papers to profl. jours. Mem. ASCE. Avocations: reading, rowing, squash. Office: E C M A, PO Box 148, Cairo 11431, Egypt

ABUL-HAJ, ELIZABETH, art and antique appraiser; b. Erie, Pa., Jan. 15, 1924; d. George Elias and Sarah (Muffett) Abood; m. Suleiman K. Abul-Haj, Feb. 11, 1948; children: Charles, Alan, Cary. Student, John Huntington Polytech., Cleve., 1942-45, Cleve. Art Sch., 1945-46, San Francisco Art Inst., 1946-48. Office supr. pub. works dept. Naval Supply Ctr., Oakland, Calif., 1951-52; tech., sec. Bur. of Mines/U. Calif., Berkeley, 1952-53; med. office supr. Cancer Divsn. U. Calif., San Francisco, 1953; office mgr. Henry and Charles Mock, M.D., Chgo., 1955-56; v.p., sec. Path. Svc. Med. Group, Ventura, Calif., 1971-83; v.p. Clin. Path. Svc. Group, Ventura, Calif., 1971-83; owner, appraiser Appraising, Elizabeth Abul-Haj, Ventura, Calif., 1968—. Author: Charles Andre Boulle for ASA, 1970s. Bd. dirs. Am. Cancer Soc., Ventura, 1967-72; bd. dirs., sec. Forum of Arts, Ventura, 1968-70, YWCA, Ventura; bd. dirs., pres. Vis. Nurses Assn., 1970-83, Ventura Med. Soc. Aux., 1978-80; pres., mem. Ventura Med. Soc., 1979-80; mem. Assistance League, Ventura Heart Assn., Children's Home Soc. Recipient Disting. Svc. award Am. Cancer Soc., Ventura. Mem. Am. Soc. Appraisers (bd. dirs. 1971-89, pres. 1971-89, sr. mem. Ventura Santa Barbara br.), World's Affair Coun., Channel Island Club. Republican. Avocations: collecting antiques, books, reading, swimming, tennis. Home: 105 Encinal Way Ventura CA 93001-3317

ABUL-HAJ, SULEIMAN KAHIL, pathologist; b. Palestine, Apr. 20, 1925; came to U.S., 1946, naturalized, 1955; s. Sheik Khalil and S. Buteina (Oda) Abul-H.; m. Elizabeth Abood, Feb. 11, 1948; children: Charles, Alan, Cary. BS, U. Calif., Berkeley, 1949; M.S., U. Calif., San Francisco, 1951, MD, 1955. Intern Cook County Hosp., Chgo., 1955-56; resident U. Calif. Hosp., San Francisco, 1949, Brooke Gen Hosp., 1957-59; chief clin. and anatomic pathology Walter Reed Army Hosp., Washington, 1959-62; assoc. prof. U. So. Calif. Sch. Medicine, L.A., 1963-69; sr. surg. pathologist Los Angeles County Gen. Hosp., 1963; dir. dept. pathology Cmty. Meml. Hosp., Ventura, Calif., 1964-80, Gen. Hosp. Ventura County, 1966-74; dir. Pathology Svc. Med. Group, 1970—; cons. Calif. Tumor Tissue Registry, 1962-96, Camarillo State Hosp., 1964-70, Tripler Gen. Hosp., Hawaii, 1963-67, Armed Forces Inst. Pathology, 1960-69. Contbr. articles to profl. jours. Bd. dirs. Tri-Counties Blood Bank, Am. Cancer Soc. Maj., M.C., U.S. Army, 1956-62. Recipient Calif. Honor Soc. award, 1949, Borden award, 1955, Achievement cert. Surgeon Gen. Army, 1962. Fellow Coll. Am. Pathologist; mem. Internat. Coll. Srgeons, World Affairs Coun. Achievements include research in cardiovascular disease, endocrine, renal, skin diseases, also cancer. Home and Office: 105 Encinal Way Ventura CA 93001-3317

ABULHASAN, MOHAMMAD ABDULLA, ambassador; b. Kuwait, Jan. 12, 1943; m. Sabeeha Haji, Jan. 21, 1969; children: Mohammed, Maysoun, Amani, Arwa, Miriam. BA, U. Cairo, 1965. Joined Kuwaiti Ministry Fgn. Affairs, 1965; mem. mission to UN, GEneva, 1968-73; 1st sec. Embassy, Tehran, Iran, 1973-75; Kuwaiti amb. to People's Republic of China, 1975-78, Hungary and East Germany, to Yugoslavia, 1978-81, Cuba, Argentina and Mex., 1981—; A.E. and P. to UN, 1981—, non-resident amb. to the Bahamas, 1999—, v.p. 55th session gen. assembly, 2000—; chmn. social, humanitarian and cultural com. Gen. Assembly, 1988, v.p. 44th session, 1989; pres. Pledging Conf. Devel. Activities, 1988, High Level Com. on Rev. TCDC, 1989. Decorated Order of Flag (Yugoslavia). Office: UN Permanent Mission of Kuwait 321 E 44th St New York NY 10017-4401

ABULKAIROVA, EVGENIA DZHUMADILOVNA, library director; b. Pavlodar, Kazakhstan, May 15, 1940; d. Abulkairov Dzhumadilda and Nurzhigitova Kulbaram. Degree in libr. sci., Kazakh State Woman's Pedag., Almaty. Bibliographer Kazakh Poly. Inst., Almaty, 1966, head info. dept., 1968, asst. dir., 1973-90; dir. Al-Farabi Kazakh Nat. State U. Libr., Almaty, 1990—. Author: The Scientific Library, 1934-94, 1994; editor: A Guidebook Library of Polytechnical Institute, A Bibliographical Index of Scientific Research Works. Recipient medal Vet. of Labour. Mem. Interdepartmental Counsel of Rep. of Libr. Affairs, Counsel Dirs. Inst. Libr. (chmn.). Islam. Avocations: reading, sewing, knitting. Home: Al-Farabi Kazakh St U Ctrl Libr, Micro-raion Koktem 1-16-38, 480100 Almaty 480070, Kazakhstan Office: Al-Farabi Kazakh Nat U, Sovetskaya Ul 28, 480100 Almaty Kazakhstan also: Almaty City Adminstrn Bldg, 71 Al-Farabi St, 480078 Kazsu Kazakhstan*

ABU-MANSOUR, MAHASEN HASAN, linguistics educator; b. Makkah, Saudi Arabia, Jan. 3, 1953; d. Hasan Muhammad and Khadija Hamed (Abu-Shok Harasani) Abu-M. BA, King Abdulaziz U., Makkah, Saudi Arabia, 1975, diploma in curriculum, 1977; MA, U. Fla., 1982, PhD, 1987. Asst. lectr. Umm Alqura U., Makkah, Saudi Arabia, 1975-87; asst. prof. Umm Alqura U., Makkah, 1988-95, head of English dept., 1988-93, assoc. prof., 1996—, dean of admissions and registrations (women's campus), 1995-99; vis. scholar U. Mass., Amherst, 1993-94, 2000—. Contbr. articles to profl. jours. First Pl H.S. Grad. award Govt. Saudi Arabia, 1971; Scholarship to U.S., Govt. Saudi Arabia, 1979-87. Mem. Arabic Linguistic Soc., Linguistic Soc. Am., Linguistic Assn. Can. and U.S. Muslim. Avocations: travel, reading. Home: PO Box 1222, Makkah Saudi Arabia

ABU-MOUSTAFA, ADEL H., medical educator, dean; b. Cairo, Egypt, Nov. 18, 1939; came to U.S., 1962; s. Abdulhamid and Zanab (Ayad) Abu-moustafa; m. Magda Ismail Kabbany, Oct. 10, 1962; children: Heidi, Sally, Sherief. BSc, Cairo U., 1960; MA, Harvard U., 1964; PhD, Boston U., 1969. Instr. Boston Coll., Chestnut Hill, Mass., 1964-67; from asst. prof. to assoc. prof. Salem (Mass.) State Coll., 1967-70, prof., 19770-72, dean undergrad studies, 1972-74, acting acad. dean, 1974-76, dean acad. svcs., 1976-79, exec. v.p., 1979-83; adminstrv. counselor King Faisal U., Saudi Arabia, 1983-86; dir. svcs. to higher edn. Acad. for Ednl. Devel., Washington, 1983-87; dir. assoc. dean internat. health affairs Tufts U. Sch. Medicine, Boston, 1987-97, dean internat. health affairs, 1983-87; team leader consortium of U.S. Univs. and U.S. Dept. Treasury, U.S. Saudi Commn. on Econ. Cooperation to assist King Faisal U., Saudi Arabia, 1983-87. Contbr. articles to profl. jours. Mem. exec. com. Fletcher Sch. Law and Diplomacy, 1987—. Mem. Arab Am. Physicians. Muslim. Avocation: politics. Office: Tufts U Sch Medicine 136 Harrison Ave Boston MA 02111-1817

ABU-MUSA, ANTOINE ALBERT, physician; b. Broumana, Lebanon, Mar. 10, 1959; s. Albert Abdallah and Nazle Habib (Karam) Abu-M.; m. Huda Bassil, Nov. 12, 1997; 1 child, Ghadi. BS, Am. U. Beirut (Lebanon), 1980, MD, 1984; PhD, Shimane (Japan) Med. U., 1993. Med. Diplomate; DPhil. Rsch. fellow Shimane (Japan) Med. U., 1987-89, dr. course fellow, 1989-93; asst. prof. Am. U. Beirut, 1993-99, assoc. prof., 1999—. Contbr. numerous articles to profl. jours. Mem. Nat. Heritage Found. Recipient Organon Middle East Fertility Rsch. award Middle East Fertility Soc., 1994. Mem. Am. Soc. Reproductive Medicine, European Soc. Human Reproduction and Embryology, Lebanese Fertility Soc. (co-founder), Hosp. Assn. for Pediat. Interest (co-founder). Avocations: photography, nature appreciation, classical music, archeology. Home: Gladys Karam Bldg Main St, Broumana Lebanon Office: Am U Beirut Ob-Gyn, 113-6044-6A, Beirut Lebanon

ABU NIMAH, HASAN, former ambassador; b. Battir, Jerusalem, Jordan, Sept. 11, 1935; s. Abdul Rahim and Fatima Othman (Oweinah) Abu N.; m. Samira, Dec. 25, 1965; children: Ruba, Maye, Ali. Student, Al-Ummah Coll., Bethelehem, 1952-55; BA in History, Am. U., Beirut, Lebanon, 1959. Polit. commentator Amman (Jordan) Broadcasting Svc., 1963-65; 3rd sec. Jordanian Embassy in Kuwait, 1965-67; 2nd sec. Jordanian Embassy in Baghdad, Iraq, 1967-70; 1st sec. Jordanian Embassy in Washington, 1970-72; with Fgn. Ministry, Amman, 1972-73; counsellor Jordanian Embassy, London, 1973-77; amb. Jordanian Embassy, Belgium and Netherlands, 1978-90; permanent rep. of Jordan EEC, European Parliament, Coun. Europe, 1978-90; amb. Jordanian Embassy, Luxembourg, 1990; amb., permanent rep. of Italy, Portugal, San Marino FAO, Internat. Fund for Agrl. Devel., World Food Program, Rome, from 1990; permanent rep. of Jordan to the UN N.Y.C., 1995-99; Jordanian non-resident amb. to Panama, 1996, to Cuba, 1997—; lectr., edn. instr. UN Relief and Works Agy., UNESCO Tchr. Tng. Ctr., Ramallah, 1959-63; mem. UN Gen. Assembly Session, 1977; dean Arab Diplomatic Corps Belgium and Luxembourg, 1987-90. Recipient medal Pope Paul VI, 1964, Order al-kawkab Jordan, 1966, Order Independence Jordan, Grade I, 1988, Grand Cross Crown Belgium, 1989, Order of Grand Cross of Merit, Italy, 1995. Mem. Euro-Arab Club (pres. 1987-90). Muslim. Office: Permanent Mission Hashemite Kingdom of Jordan to UN 866 U N Plz Rm 550-552 New York NY 10017-1822*

ABUSHABAN, LULU M.T., pediatric cardiologist; b. Kuwait, Kuwait, Feb. 1, 1958; d. Mohammed Taher Abushaban and Rawda Ahmed Lababidi; m. Nabil Nassar Alayyoubi, Dec. 16, 1981; children: Saad, Firas, Yasmin, Farah. B Medicine B Surgery third rank, Baghdad (Iraq) Med. Sch., 1981; DCH, Nat. U., Ireland, 1988. Asst., registrar Ministry of Health, Kuwait, 1981-84, sr. registrar in pediats., 1984-89; sr. registrar, fellow Children's Hosp./U. Dublin, Ireland, 1989-93; cons. pediat. cardiologist Chest Hosp., Kuwait, 1993-97; asst. prof. pediat. cardiology Kuwait U., 1997—; lectr. Children's Hosp., Dublin, 1990-92; cons. pediat. cardiac cases Chest Hosp., 1993—; rschr. in field. Contbr. articles to profl. jours. Fellow Royal Coll. Physicians Ireland; m. Royal Coll. Physicians London, Kuwait Heart Found., Kuwait Med. Assn. Avocations: swimming, world travel, reading. Fax: 965-5338940. Office: Kuwait U Faculty Medicine, PO Box 24924, Kuwait 13110, Kuwait

ABU SHADY, MOHAMMAD RAMADAN, microbiology educator, consultant, researcher; b. Tanta, Gharbia, Egypt, Jan. 1, 1943; s. Ramadan Ibrahim and Shafia Mohammed (El-Essawy) Abu S.; m. Nadia Mohammed El-Beih, Jan. 10, 1970; children: Manal, Hala, Nancy, Shrief. BSc, Ain Shams U., 1966, MSc in Microbiology, 1969, PhD in Microbiology, 1972. Demonstrator Ain Shams U., Cairo, 1966-69, asst. lectr., 1969-72, lectr., 1972-78, assoc. prof., 1978-84, prof. microbiology, 1984—, vice dean, 1993-96, head microbiology dept., 1996—; cons. Inst. of Chest and Allergy, 1984—. Mem. El-Shams Club. Avocations: photography, trips. Home: 142 El-Merghani St, Cairo Heliopolis Egypt Office: Ains Shams U, Fac of Sci, Cairo Abbasia Egypt

ABU-ZIDAN, FIKRI MAHMOUD, surgeon; b. Derna, Libya, May 19, 1957; arrived in New Zealand, 1995; s. Mahmoud Abdallah and Faheema Mousa (Salman) A.; m. Iman Ahmad Raad, Mar. 27, 1989; children: Mohammad, Yousef, Omar. MD, Aleppo (Syria) U., 1981; FRCS, Glasgow, Scotland, 1987; PhD, Linköping (Sweden) U., 1995; diploma in applied stats., Massey (New Zealand) U., 1999. Intern Allepo U. Hosp., 1980-81; anatomy demonstrator Faculty of Medicine, Kuwait, 1981-83; surgeon Univ. Hosp., Kuwait, 1983-93; residency in surgery Mubarak Alkabeer Teaching Hosp., Kuwait, 1985-90; rsch. fellow Linköping U., 1993-95; sr. rsch. fellow in surg. sci. Auckland (N.Z.) U. Hosp., 1996—; reviewer European Jour. Surgery. Contbr. numerous articles and abstracts to profl. jours. Lions Rsch. Found. grantee, 1994, Auckland Med. Rsch. Found. grantee, 1998. Fellow Royal Coll. Physicians and Surgeons U.K. Avocations: football, learning languages, swimming, reading. Office: Auckland Hospital Univ, Park Rd Bag 92024 dept Surg, Auckland New Zealand

ABYAD, ABDULRAZAK M.B., geriatrician; b. Tripoli, Lebanon, Apr. 7, 1959; s. Bachir Toufik and Nazak H. (Alaaf) A. BSc in Biology with Distinction, Am. U. of Beirut, Lebanon, 1982, MD, 1986, MPH, 1988. Intern and resident in family medicine Am. Univ. of Beirut, Lebanon, 1986-90; fellowship program in faculty devel. U. Ariz., Tucson, 1991-92, fellowship in geriatric, 1991-93; instr. Dept. Family Medicine Am. Univ. of Beirut, 1990-91; asst. clin. lectr. Ariz. Ctr. on Aging U. Ariz. Health Scis. Ctr., Tucson, 1991-92, 92-93; asst. prof. Am. Univ. of Beirut, 1993-96; dir. Abyad Med. Ctr., 1997; coord. Ain & Zein Comprehensive Geriatric Program Ain & Zein Hosp., Chouf, Lebanon, 1995; peer reviewer of manuscripts for various groups; book reviewer The Jour. of the Am. Bd. of Family Practice; cons. in Health Edn. Rsch. Unit in Dept. Pub. Health, Am. Univ. of Beirut, 1990-91, Univs. of Eng. Consortium for Internat. Activities, 1994; internat. and scholarly presentations in the field. Author: (computer chpts. and software) The 5-Minute Clinical Consult, Cellulitis, Part I and II, 1995-2000, Superficial Thrombophlebitis, 1995-2000, (monographs) Motivating People to take appropriate Family Planning Measures, Strategies for Family Health Program: Care of the Elderly, Strategies for Family Health Program: Primary health care psychiatry in Lebanon; mem. editorial bd. Mature Medicine CANADA, 1998—; contbr. over 40 articles to profl. jours. Fellow Am. Soc. Geriatrics; founding mem. Lebanese Assn. Epidemiology, SALMAR (v.p.), Lebanese Geriatric Soc. (v.p.); mem. World Homecare Hospice Orgn., Lebanese Order of Physicians, Am. Soc Gerontology, Am. Soc. Tchrs. Family Medicine, Am. Acad. Family Physicians, Lebanon Family Planning Assn., Internat. Soc. Gen. Practice, Internat. Physicians for Prevention of War, Soc. Pub. Health (U.K.), World Med. Assn., N.Am. Primary Care Rsch. Group, Lebanese

Family Medicine Assn., Intenrat. Gerontology Soc. Avocations: tennis, swimming, stamp collection, travel. Office: Abyad Med Ctr, PO Box 618 Azmi St ABDO Ctr, Tripoli Lebanon

ACAMPORA, RALPH JOSEPH, brokerage firm executive; b. N.Y.C., Oct. 2, 1941; s. Ralph J. and Teresa (Fusco) A. BA, St. Joseph's Sem., Yonkers, N.Y., Iona Coll. With Harris, Upham & Co. (merged with Smith Barney), N.Y.C., 1969-80; sr. v.p., tech. analyst Kidder Peabody & Co., N.Y.C., 1980-90; sr. v.p., tech. analyst Prudential Securities, N.Y.C., 1990—, mng. dir. tech. rsch.; tchr. N.Y. Inst. Fin., 1970—; panelist on TV show Wall St. Week with Louis Rukeyser. Author: The Fourth Mega Market, 2000. Mem. Market Technicians Assn. (chartered, founder 1970s, pres. 1979-80, founder assn. libr. 1975, hon. award 1987), Internat. Fedn. Technician Analysts (founder, former and first chmn. 1986-92), N.Y. Soc. Security Analysts (bd. dirs.). Republican. Roman Catholic. Avocation: study of World War II. Home: 350 Albany St Ph 1 New York NY 10280-1415 Office: Prudential Securities 1 New York Plz New York NY 10004-1901

ACCARDI, LUIGI, mathematics educator; b. Naples, Italy, Aug. 13, 1947; s. Vittorio and Ida (De Filippis) A.; m. Daniela Dohrn, Mar. 30, 1972; 1 child, Alessio. Laurea, U. Naples, 1970; Kandidat Nauk, U. Moscow, 1974. Rschr. Consiglio Nazionale Delle Richerche, Naples, 1971-79; prof. U. Rome, 1980—. Office: U Rome Torvergata Facolta di Economia, Centro V Volterra Via di Torvergata, 00133 Rome Italy

ACCARDO, SALVATORE, violinist; b. Turin, Italy, Sept. 26, 1941; s. Vincenzo and Ines Nea Accardo; m. Resy Corsi, 1973. Student, Conserv S. Pietro a Majella, Naples, Accademia Musicale Chigiana, Siena. 1st profl. recital, 1954; repertoire includes concertos by Bartók, Beethoven, Berg, Sibelius, Stravinsky, Tchaikovsky; performed with Amsterdam Concertgebouw, Berlin Philharm., Boston Symphony, Chgo. Symphony, others; appeared as soloist/dir. English, Scottish and Netherlands Chamber Orchs.; artistic dir. Naples Festival; recs. include Paganini Concertos and Caprices, concerts by Beethoven and Brahms, concertos by Mendelssohn, Sibelius and Tchaikovsky, others. Recipient 1st prize Geneva Competitionat age 15, 1st prize Paganini Competition at age 17, Caecillia prize, Brusssels, Italian Critics' prize for rec. of Six Paganini Concertos, Diapuson d'Or for rec. of Sibelius Concerto. Avocations: electronics, sports, cooking. Office: care Van Walsum Mgmt, 4 Addison Bridge Plz, London W14 8XP, England*

ACCONCI, VITO (HANNIBAL), conceptual artist; b. Bronx, N.Y., Jan. 24, 1940; s. Amilcare Privato and Catherine (Colombo) A. A.B., Holy Cross Coll., Worcester, Mass., 1962; M.F.A., U. Iowa, 1964. Mem. faculty Sch. Visual Arts, N.Y.C., 1968-71, 77, N.S. Coll. Art and Design, Halifax, 1971-72, 78, Calif. Inst. Art and Design, Valencia, 1976. Author: Pulse: From my Mother, Multiplicata, 1972, Ten-Point Plan for Video, Video Art, 1976, Think/Leap/Rethink/Fall, 1977; contbr. to Conceptual Art, 1972; featured in issue of Avalanche mag., 1972; one-person shows include John Gibson Gallery, N.Y.C., 1971, Sonnabend Gallery, N.Y.C., 1972, 73, 75, 76, 77, Galeria Schema, Florence, Italy, 1973, Galeria A. Castelli, Milan, Italy, 1974, Modern Art Agency, Naples, Italy, 1977, Wright State U., Dayton, Ohio, 1976, Centre d'Art Contemporain, Geneva, Mus. Contemporary Art, Chgo., 1980, U. Mass., 1982, Gallery Nature Morte, N.Y.C., 1984, La Jolla Mus. Contemporary Art, 1987, Mus. Modern Art, N.Y.C., 1988, Barbara Gladstone Gallery, 1991, Centre d'Art Contemporain, Grenoble, 1991, Museo Luigi Pecci, Prto, 1992, Mus. für Angewandte Kunst, Vienna, 1993, Mus. d'Art Modern, Saint-Etienne, France, 1994; group shows include Documenta V, Kassel, Germany, 1972, Contemporanea, Rome, 1973, Mus. Modern Art, N.Y.C., 1976, Venice Biennale, 1976, 78, 80, Whitney Biennial, N.Y.C., 1977, Documenta VI, Kassel, 1977, 82, Inst. Contemporary Art, U. Pa., 1980, 83, Whitney Mus. Am. Art, N.Y.C., 1981, Kunsthaus, Zurich, Switzerland, 1981, Padighione d'Arte Contemporaine, Milan, Italy, 1981, Mus. Contemporary Art, Chgo., 1981, Weatherspoon Gallery, U. N.C.-Greensboro, 1981, Hirschhorn Mus., N.Y.C., 1981, High Mus. Art, Atlanta, 1982, Centre d'Art Contemporaine, Geneva, 1982, Stedlijk Mus., Amsterdam, 1982, Mus. d'Art Contemporaine, Toronto, Ont., Can., 1982, Parc Lulain, Geneva, 1985, World Fin. Ctr., N.Y.C., 1988, Whitney Biennial, 1991, Zoetemeer, The Netherlands, 1992, Mus. Modern Art, San Francisco, 1993, Royal Coll. Art, London, 1994; pub. commns. Coca-Cola, Atlanta, 1987, St. Aubin Pk., Detroit, 1990, Embarcadero Promenade, San Francisco, 1991, Chgo. Dock & Canal, 1992, Arvada Art Ctr., 1992, N.Y. City Sch. System, 1993, Queens Coll., N.Y., 1993, storefront for Art & Arch, N.Y., 1993. Grantee N.Y. State Council, 1976, Nat. Endowment Arts, 1976. Home: 39 Pearl St Brooklyn NY 11201-1132 Office: Barbara Gladstone Gallery 515 W 24th St New York NY 10011-1104*

ACEBES, ANGEL, federal official. Min. of pub. adminstrn., 1999-2000; min. of justice Spain, 2000—. Office: Ministry of Justice, San Bernardo 62, 28071 Madrid Spain*

ACERA, MANUEL MARTIN-MERINO, physics educator; b. Salamanca, Spain, July 28, 1972; s. Gonzalo Martin Merino and Carolina (Santos) A. Degree in physics, U. Salamanca, 1996. Tchr. Sch. Computer Sci. Pontifical U. Salamanca, 1996—. Author: Tutorial for Middle Education, 1997; contbr. articles to profl. jours. Recipient Leonardo award European Union, 1996. Mem. IEEE. E-mail: manuel@upsa.es. Office: Pontifical U Salamanca, Compania 3, Salamanca Spain

ACERET, PRIMITIVO SAGUIBO, nematologist, researcher; b. Bacarra, Ilocos N., The Philippines, Apr. 16, 1952; arrived in Australia, 1989; s. Ciriaco and Regina (Saguibo) A.; m. Teresita Beleta Llaguno, Apr. 20, 1979; children: Jennifer Regina Maureen, James Robert, Jacqueline Rose. BS, Far Eastern U., Manila; MS, U. The Philippines, Los Baños, 1989; PhD, Ctrl. Queensland U., Rockhampton, Australia, 1998. Cert. civil svc. career profl.; cert. fishery biologist. From instr. to rsch. assoc. U. The Philippines, 1973-82, econ. rschr., 1982-89, univ. rschr., 1989-91; interpreter Migrant Resource Ctr., Dept. Social Svcs., Townsville, Australia, 1991-92; rsch. assoc. James Cook U., Townsville, 1990-92; nematologist Ctr. Tropical Agr., Queensland Dept. Primary Industries, Mareeba, Australia, 1997—, animal ethics coord., 1999—; cons. Plant Pathology Diagnostic Ctr., Mareeba, 1997—; mem. learning group com. Animal and Plant Health Svc. North Region, Mareeba, 1999—. Author: (handbook) Root Knot Nematodes of Mareeba-Dimbulah Tobacco Farms, 1999. Mem. Barron River Catchment Mgmt. Assn., Mareeba, 1999—; Mareeba Multicultural Soc., 1997—, U. The Philippines Los Baños Supervisors Assn., 1984-89; exec. sec., newsletter editor Filipino-Australian Assn. North Queensland, Townsville, 1991-93. Staff devel. program scholar U. The Philippines, 1986-89, postgrad. scholar Ctrl. Queensland U., 1994-96; plantability farms and gardens rsch. grantee Ctrl. Queensland U., 1994-96. Mem. Am. Microscopical Soc., Australian Plant Pathology Soc., Internat. Assn. Meiobenthologists, Australasian Assn. Hematologists. Roman Catholic. Avocations: tennis, table tennis, bowling, music. Home: 19 Peters St, Mareeba QLD 4880, Australia Office: Qnsld Dept Primary Industry, 28 Peters St, Mareeba QLD 4880, Australia

ACERET, TERESITA LLAGUNO, science educator, researcher; b. Quezon City, The Philippines, Feb. 3, 1956; arrived in Australia, 1989; d. Sixto Malacad and Maura (Beleta) Llaguno; m. Primitivo Saguibo Aceret, Apr. 20, 1979; children: Jennifer Regina, Maureen, James Robert, Jacqueline Rose. BS in Zoology, U. Philippines, Quezon City, 1976; MS in Zoology, U. Philippines Los Baños, 1987; MS in Chemistry, James Cook U. North Queensland, Australia, 1991, PhD, 1995. Cert. civil svc. careerist The Philippines, pub. svc. careerist Australia. Rsch. asst. U. Philippines, Quezon City, 1976-77; instr. U. Philippines Los Baños, 1978-89, asst. prof., 1990—; rsch. officer James Cook U. North Queensland, Townsville, Australia, 1990-93; rsch. officer Ctrl. Queensland U., Rockhampton, Australia, 1994-96, math., scis. tutor ATAS, DEET, 1997-99; lectr. U. Papua, New Guinea, 1999—; sci. media resource person Quezon City, The Philippines, 1986-89. Author articles for Sci. Club Mag.; contbr. articles to profl. jours. Sec. Filipino Australian Assn. No. Queensland, Townsville, Australia, 1990-91; cathechist Rockonia Parish, Rockhampton, Australia, 1994-97, Mareeba Parish, Australia, 1998—; pres. Mareeba Multicultural Soc., 1998—. Rsch. fellow Ctrl. Queensland U., Rockhampton, Australia, 1996-97; scholar U. Philippines Los Baños, 1982-87, IDP Australia, 1989-94. Mem. Australian Marine Scientists Assn., Haribon (Philippine Wildlife Soc.), N.Y. Acad. Scis., Mareeba Multicultural Soc. Roman Catholic. Avocations: reading, movies, aromatherapy, gardening. E-mail: acerett@fastinternet.net.au.

ACERO, JULIO J., surgeon, educator; b. Madrid, Sept. 6, 1957; s. Julio Acero and Angeles Beatriz Sanz; m. Maria Angeles Jimenez, July 2, 1983; children: Belen, Julio. MD, Autonoma U., Madrid, 1980, PhD, 1992; D in Dental Surgery, Complutense U., Madrid, 1982. Rsch. fellow FISS, Madrid, 1981-82; med. resident Ramon y Cajal Hosp., Madrid, 1982-85, staff specialist, 1985; sr. staff specialist Gregorio Maranon Hosp., Madrid, 1985—; assoc. prof. Complutense U., Madrid, 1994—; guest prof. European U., Madrid, 1999. Co-author: Tratado de Odontologia, 1998, Oncologia Medica, 1999; contbr. articles to profl. jours. Recipient Health fellowship Coun. Europe, 1992, Sci. Coop. fellowship Reg. Govt. Madrid, 1995. Fellow European Bd. Oro-Maxillofacial Surgery; mem. Spanish Assn. Oro-Maxillofacial Surgeons (sec. gen. 1991-95, elect pres. 1999—), Spanish Assn. Head Neck Surgery (mem. coun.), European Assn. Craniomaxillofacial Surgery, Internat. Assn. oral and Maxillofacial Surgery, German Assn. Maxillofacial Surgery (extraordinary mem.). Avocations: classical music, books, tennis. Office: Inst Cirugia Maxillofacial, C Velazquez 27 20, 28001 Madrid Spain Address: C Velazquez 27, 2 IZQ, 28001 Madrid Spain

ACEVEDO, GUILLERMO, pathologist, educator; b. Bogota, Colombia, Oct. 1, 1938; came to U.S., 1964; s. Guillermo Sr. and Teresa (De Francisco) A.; m. Consuelo Sanz, Dec. 12, 1964; children: Guillermo, Mauricio, Juan Camilo. MD, Univ. Javeriana, Bogota, Colombia, 1964. Cert. anatomical pathology and clin. pathology Am. Bd. Pathology. Intern St. Joseph's Hosp., Providence, 1966; resident The Hosp. of St. Raphael, New Haven, Conn., 1967-68; fellow clin. pathology MD Anderson Hosp., Houston, 1971-72; staff pathologist Meth. Hosp., Dallas, 1973-75; asst. prof. Univ. Janveriana, Bogota, Colombia, 1975-77; chair labs. Clinica Barraquer, Bogota, Colombia, 1977—; full prof. Escuela Supr. Oftalmologia, Bogota, Colombia, 1977—. Maj. U.S. Army Med. Corps., 1969-70. Fellow Coll. Am. Pathologists; mem. Sociedad Colombiana Patologia, Sociedad Americana Oftalmologia. Roman Catholic. Avocations: music, golf. Office: Clinica Barraquer, Apt Aereo 90404, Bogota Colombia

ACEVEDO, ROBERTO, chemistry educator, researcher; b. Santiago, Chile, Nov. 30, 1950; s. Germán Acevedo and Rosa Ester Llanos; m. Lucia Cecilia Moya; children: Roberto Jr., Ruby Cecilia, Sissi Brigitte, Alfredo William, Colin David. MSc, U. Chile, Santiago, 1974; PhD, U. London, 1981. Asst. prof. chemistry U. Chile, 1974-81, assoc. prof., 1981-91, prof., 1991—, chmn. dept. basic chemistry, faculty phys. and math. scis., 1982-87; hon. rsch. fellow U. London, 1984, 85, 90, 91; vis. scholar U. Va., Charlottesville, 1982, 91, rsch. fellow, 1993; vis. prof. City U., Hong Kong, China, 1996, Inst. for Low Structure Rsch., Wroclaw, Poland, 2000, Inst. Physics, Nicholas Copernicus U., Torun, Poland, 2000; part-time prof. Diego Portales; rschr. in field. Author: Atoms and Molecules, 1996, Introductory Elements in Atomic and Molecular Spectroscopy. Applications to Systems of Spectroscopic Interest, 2000; mem. editl. bd. Asian Jour. Spectroscopy, 1997—; editor Ciencia Abierta; co-editor Ciencia al dia Internacional; contbr. articles to profl. jours. Fellow Brit. Coun., 1978-81. Mem. AAAS, N.Y. Acad. Scis. Avocations: reading, writing, music. Home: Casa 2950, Froilán Roa 5833, Macul Santiago Chile Office: Fac Ciencias Fisicas Math, U Chile, Santiago Chile

ACEVES-PASTRANA, PATRICIA, chemistry educator, researcher, editor; b. Mexico City, Mex., Apr. 9, 1948; d. Modesto and Alicia (Pastrana) Aceves-Barrera; m. Isaac Schifter, Nov. 30, 1970 (div. 1991); children: Liliana, Daniel. B in Chemistry cumma cum laude, UNAM, Mexico City, 1969, M in History, 1988, postgrad., 1999—; PhD, U. Claude Bernard, Lyon, France, 1975; D (hon.), U. Complutense Madrid. Asst. lab. prof. U. Nat. Autónoma Mex., Mexico City, 1971-73, assoc. prof., 1976-77, lectr. prof., 1989—, sr. prof., 1991—, pres., 1998—; assoc. prof. U. Autónoma Met., Xochimilco, 1979-90; sci. referee Nat. Coun. Sci. and Tech., Mexico City, 1992—; gen. coord. Internat. Network History Chem. and Biol. Scis., Mexico City, 1992—; mem. internat. sci. com. Revue Scis. et Techniques en Perspective, Nantes, France, 1995—. Author: Chemistry, Botany, and Pharmacy in the New Spain, 1993 (Beecham V Centenario prize 1991); co-author: (with others) Lavoisier in European Context: Negotiating a New Language for Chemistry, 1995; editor, contbr.: Study History Chemistry and Biology Sciences, 5 vosl., 1994-99; editor Stud. Hist. Chem. & Biol. Scis., 1994—; contbr. articles to profl. jours. Fellow Brit. Soc. for History Sci., N.Y. Acad. Scis., Club de la Chimie; mem. Nat. Sys. Rsch., Nat. Acad. Scis. Avocations: dance, music, decoration, collecting Mexican crafts. Home: Privada de San Francisco 46, casa 41, Col. Pueblo Nuevo, 10500 Mexico City Mexico Office: UAM, Calzada del Hueso 1100, 04960 Col Villa Quietud Mexico

ACHALU, ONUEGBU EMMANUEL, university administrator, health educator; b. Aguluzigbo, Nigeria, Dec. 20, 1945; s. Peter Nwankwo and Alice Chiagowuo (Nsorah) A.; m. Dorathy Ifeyinwa Adigwe, July 29, 1979; children: Chisom, Tosi, Chinwe, Nkechi, Chika. BSc, Dana Coll., 1976; MSc, So. Ill. U., 1979, PhD, 1982. Head dept. health edn. U. Cross River State, Uyo, 1986-91; head dept. health edn. U. Uyo, 1991-95, dir. Inst. of Edn., 1996—. Author: Drug Abuse Resource Handbook: A Guide to Drug Literature in Nigeria, 1950-91, 1992, Bibliography of Drug Related Reports in Some Nigerian Newspapers, 1974-91, 1992, (with others) Introduction to Special Education in Nigheria, 1988, Sports Development in Nigerian Universities, 1990, Sociology of Education: A Book of Readings, 1992, Special Education: An Introduction, 1992, In the Microbial World, 1994, others; editl. bd. Sch. Health Edn. Jour., Jour. of Health Edn., Health and Movement Edn. Jour., Akamkpa Jour. of Sci. and Math. Edn.; contbr. articles to profl. jours. Trustee Uyo Club, 1985—; patron Aguluzigbo Devel. Union, 1984—, Man O'War Cadet Club, Uyo; chmn. PTA Christ the King Internat. Sch., Uyo, 1986-98. Recipient Knight of St. Christopher Anglican Diocese of Uyo. Mem. Nat. Assn. of Phys. and Health Edn., Sch. Health Assn. of Nigeria, Nat. Assn. of Health Edn. Tchrs. Avocations: lawn tennis, listening to good music, travelling. Home: PO Box 1786, Uyo Nigeria Office: Dept Health Edn U Uyo, PMB 1017, Uyo Nigeria

ACHAM, KARL, sociology educator; b. Leoben, Austria, Nov. 15, 1939; s. Karl and Hildegard (Pichler) A.; m. Britta Sophie Valentin, June 19, 1965; children: Andreas Leonhard, Stephan Raimund, Gilbert Alexander. PhD, U. Graz, 1964. Asst. prof. U. Graz, Austria, 1964-71, assoc. prof., 1971-74; prof. U. Berne, Austria, 1974, U. Graz, Austria, 1974—; vis. prof. U. Hamburg, 1973, 74, U. Waterloo, Ont., 1987, 91, U. Wuhan, 1991, São Paulo, 1992, Tsinghua U., Beijing, 1997; rsch. fellow Japan Soc. for the Promotion of Sci., Japan, 1995; vis. fellow Inst. for Human Scis., Vienna, 1995. Author: Reason and Commitment, 1972, Analytical Philosophy of History, 1974, Philosophy of the Social Sciences, 1983, The Demand of Reason and the Pressure of Expectations, 1989, History and Social Theory, 1995; editor: Methodological Problems of Social Sciences, 1978, Societal Processes, 1983, History of Human Sciences in Austria, Vols. 1-3, 1999-2000; co-editor: Part and Whole, 1991, Gaines and Losses of Scientific Discovery, 1998. Recipient Koerner prize, 1972, Innitzer prize, 1972, 98, Styrian Rsch. prize, 1996, Austrian hon. award Scis. and Arts. Mem. Austrian Acad. of Scis., others. Home: Am Rehgrund 20, A-8043 Graz Austria Office: U Graz Dept Sociology, Universitaetsstrasse 15, A-8010 Graz Austria

ACHARD, PIERRE, international finance administrator; b. Paris, Dec. 27, 1934; s. Paul and Hilda (Janssens) A. Diploma, Inst. of Polit. Studies, Paris, 1957; degree in law and econ., Paris U., 1957; degree, Nat. Sch. of Adminstrn., Paris, 1965. Econ. and Fin. Ministry Govt. of France, Paris, 1965-69; Chargé de mission for European Affairs SGCI, 1969-72, sec. gen. adjunct for European Affairs, 1972-75; adviser, then head adviser Minister for Coop. and to Minister for Fgn. trade, 1976-78; spl. advisor to Prime Minister R. Barre and Sec. Gen. for European Affairs, 1979-82; Minister for Fin. Affairs French Embassy, Rome, 1983-92; Minister for Fin. Affairs for Germany and No. Europe French Embassy, Bonn, Germany, 1992-99; insp. gen. of fin. French Embassy, Bonn; prof. Inst. d'Etudes Politiques de Paris, 1980—; bd. dirs. Credit Lyonnais, 1994-99, Conseil Gen. of Banque de France, 1993. Officer Naval Res., 1961-62. Mem. Automobile Club of France, Le Siècle, Maxims Bus. Club. Avocations: music, mountain climbing, skiing. Home: 23 rue de Tournon, 75006 Paris France Office: Ministry Econ and Fin, 139 rue de Bercy, 75012 Paris France

ACHARYA, SHABD SWAROOP, economist; b. Raipur, Rajasthan, India, May 9, 1939; s. Ram Chandra Acharya and Koyal Devi Trivedi A.; m. Chandra Sharma, June 21, 1958; children: Rajesh, Sheel. BS in Agr., U. Rajasthan, Udaipur, India, 1959; MS in Agr., Punjab Agrl. U., Lundhiana, India, 1966; PhD, Indian Agrl. Rsch. Inst., New Delhi, 1973. Agrl. ext. officer Govt. of Rajasthan, 1959-66; project dir. Govt. of Rajasthan, Jaipur, 1979-80; asst. prof. Rajasthan Agrl. U., Udaipur, 1966-71; assoc. prof. Rajasthan Agrl. U., Jobner, 1971-79; prof. Rajasthan Agrl. U., Udaipur, 1980-91; mem. Commn. for Agrl. Costs and Prices, New Delhi, 1991-92, chmn., 1992-96; dir. Inst. of Devel. Studies, Jaipur, 1996—; head dept. Rajasthan Agrl. U., Udaipur, 1973-91, dir. planning, 1989-91; chmn. Agr. HAQ Cons., Jaipur, 1989-91; mem./sec. zonal planning team, planning commn., New Delhi, 1988-90; mem. task force planning commn., 1996. Author: Green Revolution, 1982, Agricultural Marketing in India, 1987, 89, 92, 94, 98, Agricultural Production, Marketing and Price Policy in India, 1988, Applied Econometrics for Agricultural Economists, 1988, Marketing of Milk and Milk Products in India, 1992, Agricultural Prices - Analysis and Policy, 1994. Pres. Alumni Assn., Jobner, 1974-75, Udaipur, 1981-82; hon. sec. Consumers Coop. Store, Jobner, 1976, Vikas Samiti, Udaipur, 1983-85. Recipient honours Punjab Agrl. U., 1967, gold medals Indian Agrl. Rsch. inst., 1973. Fellow Indian Coun. Agrl. Rsch.; mem. Indian Soc. Agrl. Economics (life, v.p. 1987-88, pres. 1996), Indian Soc. Agrl. Mktg. (life, pres. 1994, chief editor 1988—), Internat. Assn. Agrl. Economists, Agrl. Econs. Rsch. Assn. of India (life). Avocations: writing, reading, gardening, TV. Office: Inst Devel Studies 8-B, Jhalana Instnl Area, 302004 Jaipur/Rajasthan India

ACHARYA, VIDYA NARAYAN, medical educator, consultant nephrologist; b. Chickballapur, Karnataka, India, Jan. 8, 1938; d. Narayan Gopal and Jaya Narayan A. Intersci. student, Elphinston Coll., Bombay, 1955; MB, BS, Seth G.S. Med. Coll., Bombay, 1961, MD, 1964. Fellow Acad. Med. Scis., Delhi, India, 1980; Fellow Indian Coll. Physicians, Pune, 1989. Tutor in medicine K.E.M. Hosp., Seth G.S. Med. Coll., Bombay, 1964-67, asst. prof. medicine, 1967-71, prof. medicine, head divsn. nephrology, 1971-78, prof. medicine, head dept. medicine, 1978-86, prof. medicine, head dept. nephrology, 1986-96; prof., dir. postgrad studies nephrology Muljibhai Patel Nephro-Urol. Hosp., Nadiad, India, 1996—. Sectional editor: (textbook) API Texbook of Medicine, 1992, 1994; assoc. editor: (monogram) Essentials of Nephrology and Urology, 1994. Nominated Best Citizen of India, 1998, Woman Yr., 2000; fellow Nat. Acad. Med. Scis., 1980. Fellow Am. Biog. Inst.; mem. N.Y. Acad. Scis., Indian Soc. Nephrology (pres. 1973-75), Nat. Coun. Hypertension (pres. 1985-86), Indian Soc. Organ Transplantation (pres. 1991-93, Lifetime Achievement award 1996), Nat. Kidney Found. (chmn. 1996—), Consumer Guidance Soc. India, Asian Pacific Soc. Nephrology. Avocations: photography, Indian classical music. Office: Bombay Inst Prev Kidn Dis, Gita-B Pandita Ramabai Rd, Gamdevi Bombay 400 007, India

ACHATZ, HANS, computer science researcher; b. Zuckenried, Bavaria, Fed. Republic Germany, July 13, 1964; s. Johann and Maria (Fleischmann) A.; m. Petra Niederau, Mar. 10, 1990. MS, U. Passau, Bavaria, 1989, DrRerNat, 1995. Rsch. asst. U. Passau, 1989—. Avocations: skiing, golf, tennis. Office: U Passau, Innstr 29, D-94032 Passau Germany

ACHEAMPONG, ROBERT KWABENA, investment consultant; b. Nyakrom, Ghana, Sept. 17, 1962; came to U.S., 1982; s. Yeboa and Hanna (Hayford) A.; m. Dina Cardoso, May 27, 1989; children: Bobby Simao, Celicia Hanna. BSBA, Berea (Ky.) Coll., 1985; MBA, U. Dayton, 1992; postgrad., Case Western Res. U., Cleve., 1995-96. CPA, Ohio. Mgr. trainee Kobacker Cos., Columbus, Ohio, 1985-87; fin. advisor/account rep. Horace Mann Cos., Columbus, 1988-93; agy. mgr./exclusive agt. Allstate Ins. Cos., Columbus, 1992-93; bus. opportunity cons. AT&T Corp., Cleve., 1994-96; mng. cons. Monymax Cons. Group, Cleve., 1995—; adj. faculty Bryant & Stratton Coll., Cleve., 1997—; prin. Acheampong & Assocs., CPAs, Cleve., 1996—. Bus. advisor Minority Owned Bus., Cleve., 1994—; cons. advisor Watoes Outreach Program, Canton, Ohio, 1994—. Recipient Nkrumah Parker Leadership award Berea Coll., 1985. Mem. AICPAs, Ohio Soc. CPAs, N.E. Ohio Soc. CPAs (minority devel. com. 1996—). Avocations: reading, travel. Office: Moneymax Consulting Group PO Box 43011 Highland Hgts OH 44143-0011

ACHEBE, CHINUA, writer, humanities educator; b. Ogidi, Nigeria, Nov. 16, 1930; s. Isaiah Okafo and Janet N. (Iloegbunam) A.; m. Christie Chinwe Okoli, Sept. 10, 1961; children: Chinelo, Ikechukwu, Chidi, Nwando. Student, Univ. Coll., Ibadan, Nigeria, 1948-52; BA, U. London, 1953; DUniv, Stirling U., U.K., 1975, Open U., U.K., 1989; DLitt (hon.), Dartmouth Coll., 1972, U. Southampton, Eng., 1975, U. Ife, Nigeria, 1978, U. Nigeria, Nsukka, 1981, U. Kent, Canterbury, Eng., 1982, Mt. Allison U., Sackville, Can., 1984, U. Guelph, Canada, 1984, Franklin Pierce Coll., 1985, Ibadan (Nigeria) U., 1989, Skidmore Coll., 1991, CCNY, 1992, Fitchburg State Coll., 1994; DLitt, Harvard U., 1996, BinghamtonU., 1996, Bates Coll., 1996, Syracuse U., 1997, Brown U., 1998, Ohio Wesleyan U., 1999, Trinity Coll., 1999; LLD (hon.), U. Prince Edward Isl., Canada, 1976, Georgetown U., 1990, Port Harcourt (Nigeria) U., 1991; LHD (hon.), U. Mass., 1977, Westfield Coll., 1989, New Sch. for Social Rsch., 1991, Hobart and William Smith Coll., 1991, Marymount Manhattan Coll., 1991, Colgate U., 1993, Brown U., 1998. Prodr., contbr., dir. Nigerian Broadcasting Co., Lagos, 1954-66; sr. rsch. fellow in African studies U. Nigeria, 1967-72, prof. dept. English, 1976-81, emeritus prof., 1985—; vis. prof. English U. Mass., Amherst, 1972-75, U. Conn, Storrs, 1975-76, Afro-Am. studies U. Mass., Amherst, 1987-88; pro-chancellor Anambra State U. Tech., Enugu, Nigeria, 1986-88; Regent's lectr. UCLA, 1984; dir. Heinemann Ednl. Books (Nigeria) Ltd.; vis. fellow and Ashby lectr. Clare Hall, Cambridge (Eng.) U., 1993. Author: (novels) Things Fall Apart, 1958, No Longer at Ease, 1960, Arrow of God, 1964, A Man of the People, 1966, Anthills of the Savannah, 1988; (poetry) Christmas in Biafra, 1975; (short stories) Girls at War, 1972; (essays) Morning Yet on Creation Day, 1975; (children's stories) The Flute, 1978, The Drum, 1978, The Trouble with Nigeria, 1983, Hopes and Impediments-Selected Essays, 1965-87, 1988; (essay and poems) Another Africa, 1998; (non-fiction) Home and Exile, 2000. Mem. coun. Lagos (Nigeria) U., 1966; mem. East Ctrl. State Libr. Bd., 1971-72, Anambra State Arts Coun., 1977-79; Goodwill amb. UN Population Fund, 1998—. Recipient Lit. award New Statesman, 1965, Commonwealth Poetry prize, 1973, Nat. Creativity award Nigeria, 1999, St. Louis Literary award 1999; Rockefeller fellow, 1960-61; UNESCO fellow, 1963. Fellow MLA (hon.), Royal Soc. Lit. (London), Nigerian Acad. Letters; mem. Am. Acad. Arts and Letters (hon.), Nonino Risit D'Aur, Royal African Soc. (hon. v.p. London, 1998). Office: Bard Coll Dept Lang and Lit Annandale On Hudson NY 12504

ACHGILL, RALPH KENNETH, retired research scientist; b. Indpls., June 17, 1938; s. Kenneth and Lois Ann (Philips) A.; m. Virginia Ann Swisher, July 21, 1956 (dec. Nov. 1992); children: Kenneth Edward, Douglas Alan, Kerry Wayne, Bridget Marie; m. Diane K. McCauley, Dec. 26, 1993. Student, Purdue U., 1956-60. Rsch. scientist Eli Lilly & Co., Indpls., 1956-93, internat. tech. coord., 1974-93; ret., 1993. Patentee in field. Mem. Masons (past master), Optimist Club (charter pres.). Republican. Avocation: philatelic dealer and auctioneer. Home: PO Box 6508 Lafayette IN 47903-6508

ACHI, PETER BENSON UCHECHUKWU, mechanical engineer; b. Urualla, Nigeria, Oct. 18, 1950; s. Benjamin and Celina (Agbasi) A. BS, U. Nigeria, 1975; MSc, U. Aston, 1978, PhD, 1981. Asst. lectr. U. Aston, England, 1979-81; lectr. U. Nigeria, Nsukka, 1981; sr. lectr. Asutech, Nigeria, 1981-83; from sr. lectr. to prof. Fed. U. Technology, Owerri, Nigeria, 1983-92, head dept. mech. engring., 1992-96; coord. Student Indsl. Work Experience Scheme, 1984; chmn. Academic Staff Union, 1981-83, 90-93; mem. Univ. Governing Coun., 1993-96; dir. Univ. Computer Ctr., 2000. Home: Block 3 Futo Estate Works Layout, Owerri Imo, Nigeria Office: Fed U Technology, DMB 1526, Owerri Imo, Nigeria

ACHILLES, RICARDO ALFREDO, power system consultant, researcher, educator; b. San Juan, Argentina, Oct. 22, 1945; s. Konrad Martin and Gisela (Holtz) A.; m. Susana Maria Villafañe, July 30, 1971; children: Alfredo Sebastian, Tamara Aime. EM technician, Nat. U. Tucuman, Argentina, 1964; BSEE, Nat. U. Cuyo, San Juan, 1971; MSc in Hydroelec. Engring., U. Buenos Aires, 1972. Tchr. asst. in elec. engring. Nat. U. Cuyo, Comahue, San Juan, Neuquen, Argentina, 1968-79; sr. engr. power equipment div. Hidronor S.A., Neuquen, 1972-80; sr. engr. power sys. studies,

mem. ops. and mgmt. staff Hidronor S.A., Cipolletti, Argentina, 1980-93; power sys. cons., Neuquen, 1993—; lectr. in electromagnetics, electric machinery and control systems at U. Tecnológica Confluencia, Neuquen, 1995—. Contbr. articles to profl. jours. With Argentina Army, 1966-67. Mem. Power Engrng. Soc. of IEEE (sr., working group on torsional issues), N.Y. Acad. Scis. Methodist. Avocations: tennis, listening to music, reading fiction. Office: Belgrano 147 Ste 5A, Q8300HVC Neuquen Argentina

ACHIMASTOS, ARISTARQUOS IOANNIS, hemobiologist; b. Lefcas, Greece, Nov. 10, 1932; s. Spyridon and Lamprini (Themeli) A.; m. Eleni Andreadou, June 1, 1958; children: Spyridoy, Nicolas. Diploma in mil. medicine, U. Salonica, Thessaloniki, Greece, 1956; MD, U. Athens, Greece, 1962; diploma in hematology, U. Paris, 1964. Commd. 2d lt. Greek Army, 1956, maj. gen. Health Svc., 1956-85; dir. blood bank and hematology lab. Army Med. Rsch. Ctr., Athens, 1964-67, 68-70; dir. lab. hematology Mil. Hosp., Athens, 1971-74; dir. ctrl. labs. NIMTS Vets. Hosp., Athens, 1975-79, 83-85; dir. gen. Army Med. Rsch. Ctr., Athens, 1982-83; dir. hematology lab. Hygeia Hosp., Athens, 1984-98; ret. Health Svc. Greek Army, 1985; dir. gen. Ctrl. Labs. Hygeia Hosp. Athens, 1998—; asst. prof. Sch. Medicine U. Athens, 1976; Greek nat. del. Euromed, 1976-84; comdr. Army Tng. Ctr. Health Svcs., Greek Army, Arta, 1981-82; educator U. Ioannina, 1979-82. Contbr. articles to profl. jours. including Nature and Hellenic Army Forces Med. Rev., among others. Fellow French Govt., 1962-64, Can. Govt., 1970-71; decorated Golden Cross (2), Mil. Merit medal, Brigadier of Bn. of Honor. Mem. N.Y. Acad. Scis. Avocations: music, gardening. Fax: (01) 6845089. Home: Dem Soutsou 39, 11521 Athens Greece

ACHIME, NWABUEZE HYACINTH, health economics educator; b. Enugu, Nigeria, Apr. 20, 1954; s. Chief Eze Nwano and Ekenma Nwauduchukwu A.; m. Christy Ebea, Feb. 28, 1987; children: Emeka Nwabueze Jnr., Ugonna, Amaka, Nnamdi, Afamefuna. BS in Econs., U. Sci. and Arts, Okla., 1978; MA in Econs., U. Tex., 1980, MS in Polit. Econ., 1982; PhD, U. Benin, Nigeria, 1993. Mgr. Sears & Roebuck, Dallas, 1978-80; dir. A&P Transnat. Col., Dallas, 1980-82; asst. dir. Inst. Substance Abuse, Benin City, Nigeria, 1983—; coord. Postgrad. Prog. uniben, Benin City, Nigeria, 1985—; sr. lect. U. Benin, Benin City, Nigeria, 1991—; cons. UNICEF Cuso, Fed. Ministry of Health, Nigeria, 1989—; chmn. Presdl. Task Force, Nigeria, 1992-93; chmn. Evaluation Team, Nigeria, 1991-93; senator U. Benin, 1992—; cons. in field.. Contbg. or co-author several books, including: Imminization through Community Education and Mobilization, 1989, Rotational Presidentialism, 1987, Rotational Presidentialism and Two Political Parties for Nigeria, Business Ownership under SAP, 1987, Investment Policy Analysis and the Nigerian Economic System: Investment and Government, 1996, Investment Policy Analysis and The Nigerian Economic System, 1996, others; contbr. articles to profl. jours. Pres. Nigerian Students Union, Okla., 1976-78, Bapt. Students Union, Okla., 1976-78; pres. Nigeria Am. Trained Grad., 1983-93. Mem. Nigerian Econ. Soc. (life, nat. publicity sec. 1988-92), Nigerian Polit. Sci. Assn, others. Anglican. Avocations: table tennis, long tennis, soccer, reading, literature. Home: U Benin, Inst Pub Adminstrn Ext Svcs, Benin City PMB 1154, Nigeria

ACHIN, MILOS KOSTA, historian, writer; b. Knjazevac, Yugoslavia, Feb. 28, 1915; came to U.S., 1950; s. Kosta Sava and Vuka (Vujic) A.; divorced; children: Vuka, Kosta. Student, Mil. Acad., Belgrade, 1934, Air Force Sch., Pancevo, 1938. Capt., editor Yugoslav Guerrila, Free Mountains, 1941-44; dir. UN IRO Ctr., Trieste, Gorica, 1948-50; writer Free Serbian Press, 1950—. Author: Srbija Gori, 1960, Prolog Buducnosti, 1963, Branioci Kosova, 1973, Kosovski Kristali, 1976, Povratak Suncu, 1982, Koreni & Iskorenjeni, 1982, Vremeplov, 1984, Od Kosmaja do Kosmosa, 1989, 95, 100 Strele do Stratospere, 1994, General Mihailovic and Ravna Gora, 19 Vols., 1996, Tales of Socialist Yugoslavia, Yugoslavia in Our Time, 1991, Yugoslavia Dismembered, 1992, Draža Mihailović: A Biography, 3 Vols., 1997, numerous other books, essays, short stories and articles. Capt. Royal Yugoslav Air Force, 1938-41. Rankovich Charitable and Ednl. Fund grantee, 1988, 89. Mem. Soc. Serbian Writers and Artists Abroad, N.Am. Soc. Serbian Studies. Home and Office: 6221 Walhonding Rd Bethesda MD 20816-2138

ACHIS, CHRISTOS GEORGE, insurance company executive; b. Piraeus, Greece, Dec. 5, 1910; s. George C. and Helen A. (Francou) A.; m. Maro T. Polymeropoulou, Dec. 29, 1946; children: George, Theodore. Law degree, Athens U., 1935; degree advanced dr. econ. studies, Paris U., 1939; dr. degree, Athens High Sch. Econs. Sr. ofcl. Ministry Mercantile Marine, 1930-54; chief exec. ins. cos., 1955-68, undersec. state fin., 1969-71; gov. Nat. Bank Greece, 1971-74; chmn. Horizon Ins. Co. S.A., Athens, 1974—. Served to comdr. Greek Navy, WWII. Decorated grand officer Order of PHolenix, comdr. Order George I; grand officer Order Nat. Merit (France). Fellow Internat. Bankers Assn.; mem. Internat. Maritime Law Assn., Athens Rotary, Hellenic Yachting Club. Home: 8 Nymfon St, 26 V Amalias Ave, 105-57 Athens Greece Office: 26A Amalias Ave, 1055-57 Athens Greece

ACHKAR, MARIA, language professional, educator; b. Minas, Camaguey, Cuba, July 14, 1926; came to U.S. 1960, naturalized 1971; d. Ased Amin and Hanne (Seade) Achkar. BA, Instituto Camaguey, Cuba, 1947; postgrad., U. Havana, Cuba, 1952-55; PhD, U. Havana, 1958. Cert. Spanish translator. Pvt. Spanish lang. tutor, 1980; instr. Spanish lang. Youngstown (Ohio) State U., 1979-87, instr. dept. human ecology, 1987—; author, compiler, developer numerous course materials, Youngstown State U., 1984—, co-advisor Spanish club, 1979-80; cons. Youngstown Bilingual Rsch. Project, 1987-88; bd. dirs. Choffin Career Ctr. Dept. Cosmetology Youngstown City Schs., 1992-98; participant UN Assn. Leadership Conf., State Dept., Washington, 1981; presenter Ann. Conf. on Teaching of Fgn. Langs. and Lits., Youngstown State U., 1980, others. Editor, Spanish cons.: The Spanish Holiday Workbook, 1982, The Easy Foreign Language Holiday Activity Workbook, grades 4-7, 1995; translator The Client's Rights, Ohio Dept. Mental Health, 1984. Bd. dirs. UN Assn., 1980-83, 90—, Junta de Communicacion Hispana, 1980-81, Ea. Mental Health, 1993, Pillars of Stambaugh (exec. mem.), 1993; mem. Citizens League, 1990; study/analysis condr. in civic edn. City Index, 1990—; trustee YWCA, Youngstown, 1987—, mem. fin. devel., pub. rels. and battered person's shelter coms., co-chair 10th ann. celebration women's artist com., 1991; mem. steering com. N.E. Ohio Internat., 1994, citizen adv. bd. Woodside Receiving Hosp., Youngstown, 1984—, pres. 1995-96. Mem. Am. Assn. Tchrs. Spanish & Portuguese, Fedn. Cuban Educators in U.S., Ohio Modern Lang. Tchrs. Assn., Ohio Assn. Bilingual & Multicultural Edn., Sigma Delta Pi. Home: 2821 Belmar Dr Apt 1 Youngstown OH 44505-2149 Office: Achkar Jewelers Mfrs Inc 7313 South Ave Youngstown OH 44512-5718

ACHKASOVA, VALENTYNA NYKYFORIVNA, curator; b. Uman, Ukraine, Jan. 12, 1928; d. Nykyfor Georgiyovych and Liudmyla Yevgrafivna (Stebliak) A.; m. Vitaly Ivanovych Yushko, Aug. 12, 1966. Diploma in arch., Inst. of Civil Engring., Kiev, Ukraine, 1951. Arch. Teploelektroproekt, Kiev, 1952-57, sr. engr., 1957-61, head of designing team, 1961, dep. arch.-in-chief, 1961-65, arch.-in-chief, 1965-67; dir., chief curator Nat. Sofiysky Hist. & Archtl. Mus., Kiev, 1967-2000; pres. The St. Sophia Philanthropic Found., 2000—; sci. sec. Adv. Bd. Reconstrn. Important Monuments History and Culture to Pres. Ukraine, 1996—; cons., mem. acad. coun. Com. Preservation and Restoration of Archtl. Monuments of Kiev, 1990—. Contbr. articles to profl. jours. Chmn. Inspection com. Ukrainian Soc. Preservation of Hist. and Cultural Monuments, 1970—. Recipient Hon. Worker in Field of Culture The Supreme Rada of Ukraine, 1987, Order of Princess Olga Presdl. award, 1998. Mem. Internat. Coun. Monuments & Sites. Orthodox. Avocations: travelling, photography, poetry, music.

ACHMADI, UMAR-FAHMI, public health physician, educator; b. Cilacap, Indonesia, Oct. 5, 1948; s. Ahmad and Sartini (Sudjari) A.; m. Endang-Pamularsih Soedarman, Nov. 21, 1977; children: Febiani, Samatha. MD, U. Indonesia, Jakarta, 1973; MPH, U. Philippines, Manila, 1976; Phd, Griffith U., Brisbane, Australia, 1985. Tchg. staff U. Indonesia, Jakarta, 1975—, prof., 1991—, chmn. dept., 1991-96, chmn. Inst. for Health, 1993-98; dir. gen. Ministry of Health, Jakarta, 1997—; mem. adv. com. WHO-Kobe (Japan) Ctr., 1997—; mem. sci. working group WHO-Regional, S.E. Asia, 1998. Author, editor: Occupational Health for Informal Sector, 1990; contbr. articles to profl. jours. Recipient award for Twenty Yrs. Svc., Govt. of Indonesia, 1995. Mem. Indonesian Med. Assn. for Occupational Health (pres. 1992-95, 95-98), Indonesian Assn. for Pub. Health (v.p. 1990-94), Indonesian Assn. for Environ. Health (dir. expert com. 1996—), Japan Soc. for Air Pollution. Islamic. Avocations: natural recreation, reading. Home: Jl Damai 54, Jatiwaringin 04-9, 17411 Jakarta Indonesia Office: Ministry of Health, Jl Percetakan Negara 29, 10560 Jakarta Indonesia

ACHRAFI, HADI, cardiologist, consultant; b. Nichaboore, Iran, May 24, 1941; s. Massih and Hachmat (Arbabe) A.; m. Michele LeRwyet, Nov. 28, 1978; children: Farchad, Soraya. MD, U. Paris, 1973, diploma cardiology, diplome nat. med. aero. and spatiale. Intern, then resident dept. cardiology Ctrl. Gen. Hosp., Troyes, France, 1969-72; assoc. prof. Nat. U. Teheran, Iran, 1978-80; cardiac ressucitation cardiologist Nat. U. Teheran, Paris, 1981; pvt. practice Chartres, France, 1982—. Contbr. articles to profl. jours. including Lancet, Internat. Jour. Cardiology, Actualité Medicale Belge, Cardiologie Jour., Stimulation Cardiac Cath. Lab. Digest, Province Med., Info. Cardiologie, Actualite Med. Internat., Cardiologie Pratique, Hypdertension Cardinal, others. Recipient Physician's award Mass. Postgrad. Med. Inst., 1988. Mem. AAAS (invited), Am. Heart Assn. (sci. coun.), French Soc. Cardiology, European Soc. Cardiology, Assn. Echocardiographiie, French Coll. Cardiac Stimulation, N.Y. Acad. Scis., Filiale Echocardiographie. Fax: 0237214462. Office: Residence Topaze, 8 Rue GD Faubourg, 28000 Chartres France

ACHTZIGER, NORBERT RAINER, physics educator, researcher; b. Selb, Bavaria, Germany, May 27, 1962; s. Gerhard and Helga (Benker) A.; m. Claudia Ingrid Hartl, Apr. 20, 1991; children: Florian, Katrin. Physics diploma, U. Erlangen, Germany, 1988, PhD, 1991; habilitation, U. Jena, 1998. Rsch. scientist U. Erlangen, 1991-94; instr. physics, rschr. U. Jena, Germany, 1995-2000; rschr. physics and high frequency electronics Fraunhofer Inst. IIS, Erlangen, Germany, 2000—; spokesman collaboration at CERN, Geneva, 1992-96. Contbr. and referee articles to profl. jours. including Phys. Rev. B., Applied Physics Letters, Phys. Rev. Letters, also chpt. to book. Recipient Young Scientist award European Materials Rsch. Soc., 1991. Mem. German Phys. Soc. Avocations: bicycle trips, mountaineering, skiing. Office: Fraunhofer IIS, Am Weichselgarten 3, D-91058 Erlangen Germany

ACIERNO, LOUIS JOSEPH, medical educator, researcher; b. N.Y.C., June 30, 1920; s. Michelangelo and Anna (Brienza) A.; m. Dorothy Theresa Monahan, June 6, 1948; children: M. Barry, Denise. BS, Manhattan Coll., 1941; MD, Georgetown U., 1944, Bologna (Italy) U., 1974. Diplomate Am. Bd. Internal Medicine. Intern Kings County Hosp., Bklyn., 1944-45, resident, 1945-46, 48-50; NIH post-doctoral rsch. fellow in cardiology SUNY-Downstate, 1950-51; prof. cardiopulmonary scis. U. Ctrl. Fla., 1979—. Author: Cardiac Rehabilitation and Prevention, 1984, The Human Machine: How It Breaks Down, History of Cardiology, 1994, Digest of Chest Diseases, 1997, Elements of Cardiac Pharmacology, 1998. Capt. U.S. Army, 1946-48. Fellow ACP, Am. Coll. Cardiology (Gifted Tchr. of Yr. award 1997). Republican. Roman Catholic. Avocations: reading, writing. Home: 245 Salvador Sq Winter Park FL 32789-5618 Office: University of Central Florida Orlando FL 32816

AÇIMUZ, METIN OSMAN, naval officer; b. Çorum, Turkey, Mar. 26, 1944; s. Zeki Açimuz and Nigar (Çetintas) Turan; m. Aynur Sezener, Dec. 27, 1975; 1 child, Bige. Grad., Naval Acad., 1965, postgrad., 1965-67; grad., Turkish Naval War Coll., 1977, Armed Forces Staff Coll., 1984. Commd. ens. Turkish Navy, 1965, advanced through grades to rear adm., 1995, comms. officer, gunnery officer; comms. officer Destroyer TCG Adatepe, navigations and ops. officer Destroyer Tinaztepe, 2d comdr. officer Destroyer TGC M.F. Çakmak, comdr. Destroyer TCG Piyalepasa, 1985-86, comdr. amphibious divsn., 1991-92; chief of staff Turkish Navy; naval attache Turkish Navy, Algeria, 1986-89; naval base comdr. Turkish Navy, Iskenderun, 1995-97; Istanbul strait comdr. Turkish Navy, 1999—.

ACKER, ANDREW FRENCH, III, mathematics educator, researcher; b. New London, Conn., May 9, 1943; s. Andrew French Jr. and Miriam Luce (Woodhull) A.; children: Denise, Marcella, Joseph, Laurel; m. Melissa Ann Stanton, Aug. 10, 1991; children: Michael, Christian. BS, Union Coll., Schenectady, 1965; PhD, Boston U., 1972; Prof Dr, Karlsruhe U., Germany, 1982. Lectr. Boston U., 1969-72; asst. prof. La. State U., New Orleans, 1972-73; asst. U. Karlsruhe, 1973-83; assoc. prof. math. Iowa State U., Ames, 1983-87; assoc. prof. math. Wichita (Kans.) State U., 1987-91, prof., 1991—; guest rschr. U. Heidelberg, Germany, summer 1987. Contbr. articles to math. jours. Mem. Am. Math. Soc., Sigma Xi, Pi Mu Epsilon. Achievements include contributions to the analytical treatment of free boundary problems in elliptic partial differential equations, especially flow-surface and flow-interface problems in fluid dynamics, with emphasis on the existence, uniqueness, convexity and geometry of solutions; development of operator methods for successive approximation of free boundaries. Home: 1213 Farmstead St Wichita KS 67208-2628 Office: Wichita State U Dept Math Wichita KS 67260-0001

ACKERET, CHRISTOPH MARTIN, real estate company executive, urban development consultant; b. Zurich, Switzerland, Feb. 18, 1945; s. Robert Friedrich and Cornelia Louise (Spaltenstein) A.; m. Katrin Baumgartner, Sept. 11, 1976; children: Markus, Adrian. Diploma in Architecture, Swiss Fed. Inst. Tech., Zurich, 1970; MBA, Internat. Inst. Mgmt. Devel., Lausanne, Switzerland, 1975. Registered engr. Asst. arch. Stücheli Archs., Zurich, 1970-74; bldg. site mgr. Nordfinanz-Bank, Zurich, 1971-74; mgmt. asst. Spaltenstein Group, Zurich, 1976-80; pres. Spaltenstein Immobilien Ag, Zurich, 1981-98; chmn., CEO, co-owner real estate companies, 1998—; bd. dirs. Spaltenstein Immobilien Ag, Zurich; chmn. World Trade Ctr. Zurich Ltd., 1992—, Lerch Immobilien Ag, Winterthur, Switzerland, 1995—, Colliers CSLAG, 1998—; chmn. Casatip Holding AG, 1999—. Project mgr. Stadelhofer Passage Zurich, 1977-84 (Outstanding Bldg. 1985); project chmn. Galleria Opfikon-Zurich, 1982-93. Mem. Bldg. Permission Bd., Zollikon, Switzerland, 1990—. Mem. Swiss Soc. Engrs. and Archs. (cert.), European Engrng. Soc. for Urban Devel. (chmn. 1988—), Internat. Inst. Mgmt. Devel., Alumni Assn., Internat. Family Bus. Network (chmn. Swiss German chpt. 1997—). Avocations: traveling, jogging, cross country skiing, history, arts. E-mail: christoph.ackeret@colliers.ch. Home: Alfred Ulrich Strasse 6, CH-8702 Zollikon Zurich, Switzerland Office: Siewerdtstrasse 8, CH-8050 Zurich Switzerland

ACKERLY, THOMAS VINCENT, investment advisor, financial advisor; b. Jersey City, Oct. 4, 1947; s. Vincent Raymond Ackerly and Irene Teresa McCabe; m. Frances Sue Passero, Sept. 22, 1973; children: Karen, Lisa, Tracey. Grad. H.S., Jersey City. Pres. GS Fin. Svcs., Inc., N.Y.C., 1984-97; sr. advisor UN Devel. Programme, N.Y.C., 1997-99; pres. Opportunity Mgmt., Inc., N.Y.C., 1997—. Sgt. U.S. Army, 1966-68. Named one of Fifty Top Wall St. Irish Ams., Irish Am. Mag., N.Y.C., 1998. Mem. Acad. Polit. Sci., N.Y. Stock Exch. Luncheon Club, N.Y. Friars Club. E-mail: tvagstv@aol.com. Fax: 212-635-4177. Office: Opportunity Mgmt Inc PH #3 45 Wall St Ph 3 New York NY 10005-1961

ACKERMAN, BRIAN MICHAEL, marine engineer, consultant; b. Bklyn., Dec. 19, 1968; s. Stephen David and Shirley Ester (Kress) A. BS in Marine Engring., U.S. Mcht. Marine Acad., 1990; MSME, U. New Haven, 1996. Marine engr. USN, 1990—, chief engr., 1995—; tech. cons., lectr., adj. prof. U.S. Mcht. Marine Acad., Kings Point, N.Y., 1995—. Mem. Soc. Naval Architects and Marine Engrs. (life), F&AM Huguenot Lodge 381. Avocations: sailing, rowing. Office: Am Maritime Officers 2 W Dixie Hwy Dania FL 33004-4312

ACKERMAN, BRUCE ARNOLD, law educator, lawyer; b. N.Y.C., Aug. 19, 1943; s. Nathan and Jean (Rosenberg) A.; m. Susan Gould Rose, May 29, 1967; children: Sybil Rose, John Mill. BA summa cum laude, Harvard U., 1964; LLB with honors, Yale U., 1967. Bar: Pa. 1970. Law clk. U.S. Ct. Appeals (2d cir.), New York, 1967-68; law clk. to assoc. justice John M. Harlan U.S. Supreme Ct., Washington, 1968-69; prof. law and public policy analysis U. Pa., Phila., 1969-74; prof. law Yale U., New Haven, 1974-82, Sterling prof. law and polit. sci., 1987—; Beekman prof. law and philosophy Columbia U., N.Y.C., 1982-87. Author: Private Property and the Constitution, 1977, Social Justice in the Liberal State, 1980 (Gavel award ABA), (with Hassler) Clean Coal/Dirty Air, 1981, Reconstructing American Law, 1984, We the People: Foundations, 1991, The Future of Liberal Revolution, 1992, (with Golove) Is NAFTA Constitutional?, 1995, We the People: Transformations, 1998, (with others) The Uncertain Search for Environmental Quality, 1974 (Henderson prize Harvard Law Sch.). Guggenheim fellow, 1985. Fellow Am. Acad. Arts and Scis.; mem. Am. Law Inst. Office: Yale U Law Sch PO Box 208215 New Haven CT 06520-8215

ACKERMAN, F. DUANE, telecommunication industry executive; b. 1942; m. Kappy Ackerman; 4 children. BS, Rollins Coll., MS; MS, MIT. With Bell South Corp., Orlando, Fla., 1964-91, vice-chmn., group pres., 1991-95, vice-chmn., COO, 1995-97, pres., CEO, 1997-98; chmn., CEO Bell South Corp., Atlanta, 1998—; bd. dirs. Am. Heritage Life Ins. Corp., Am. Bus. Products. Bd. dirs. Ctrl. Atlanta Progress, The Commerce Club; trustee Rollins Coll. Mem. Atlanta C. of C. Office: BellSouth Corp 1155 Peachtree St NE Atlanta GA 30309-3610

ACKERMAN, ROBERT LLOYD, chemical engineer, environmental tree farmer; b. Greensburg, Pa., Sept. 3, 1925; s. Lloyd William and Anne Stella (Saul) A.; m. Margaret Dorothy Ansty, May 30, 1959; children: Julia Anne Ackerman Glenister, Janet Deborah Ackerman Fuhrmeister, Robert Peter. BSChE, U. Pitts., 1947. Tech. supr. Pittsburgh Plate Glass Co., Creighton, Pa., 1948-52; chem. engr. Koppers Co., Inc., Pitts., 1952-57; sr. chem. engr. Arabian Am. Oil Co., N.Y.C., also Saudi Arabia, 1957-75; sr. commg. engr. 8 oil desalting plants Oil Svc. Co. of Iran, Ahwas, Iran, 1975-77; sr. design-commg. engr. Balikpapan oil refinery, Murchison and Beryl B Northsea oil/gas producing platforms, also Ok Tedi gold/copper refinery, Bechtel Internat., Inc., London, Indonesia, Papua New Guinea, 1978-84; tree farmer New Alexandria, Pa., 1984—. Author: A Short History of Andrico, A Coal Patch. Patentee mfg. device used in glass industry; inventor of a graphical method used as a basis to plan and control daily operating parameters for an oil refinery-marine shipping complex. V.p. Westmoreland Woodlands Improvement Assn., Greensburg, Pa., 1990—; assoc. dir. Westmoreland Conservation Dist., Greensburg, 1993—; treas. Penn West conf. United Ch. of Christ, Greensburg, 1994-2000. Recipient Maurice K. Goddard State award Pa. Assn. Conservation Dists., 1993, Outstanding Conservation Svc. award Westmoreland Conservation Dist., 1999. Mem. Sigma Tau. Mem. United Ch. of Christ. Avocations: reading, hunting, hiking, genealogy. Home: PO Box 339 New Alexandria PA 15670-0339

ACKERMAN, ROY ALAN, research and development executive; b. Bklyn., Sept. 9, 1951; s. Jack A. and Estelle (Kuchlik) A.; m. Janet Sharon Ostrow, July 4, 1974 (div. 1984); children: Shanna Avrah, Shira Batya; m. Kathleen T. Smith, 1989; 1 child, Daniel Jacob. BSChemE, Poly. Inst. of N.Y., 1972; MSChemE, MIT, 1974; PhD, U. Va./U. B.H., 1986. Chem. engr. Tri-Flo Rsch. Labs., Bellmore, N.Y., 1972-74; sr. project engr. Thetford Corp., Ann Arbor, Mich., 1975; dir. R & D Applied Sci. Through Rsch. and Engring. (now ASTRE), Ann Arbor, 1976-77, ASTRE Cons. Corp., Charlottesville, Va., 1978-81; tech. dir. ASTRE Corp. Group, Charlottesville, 1981-89, Alexandria, Va., 1989—; bd. dirs. Indsl. Microgenics Ltd., Charlottesville, Automated Bus. Conss.; chmn. Bicarbolyte Corp., Alexandria, Va. Author: Water Reuse and Recycle, 1981; patentee in field. Lay leader Congregation Beth Israel, Charlottesville, 1979-89. Scholar Samuel Ruben Found., 1968-72. Fellow Am. Inst. Chemists; mem. Water Pollution Control Fedn., Am. Assn. Rsch. Cos., Sigma Xi, Tau Beta Pi. Avocations: reading, swimming, tennis, politics, dancing. Office: ASTRE PO Box 25766 Alexandria VA 22313-5766

ACKERMANN, JUERGEN ERNST, research institute administrator, researcher; b. Bochum, Germany, Oct. 5, 1936; s. Ernst Rudolf and Ilse (Gittermann) A.; m. Christa Witz, Nov. 6, 1961; children: Lutz, Karin, Beate, Birgit. Dipl.-Ing., Tech. U., Darmstadt, Fed. Republic Germany, 1961, Dr.-Ing., 1967; MS, U. Calif., Berkeley, 1964; Dr.-Ing.habil., Tech. U., Munich, Fed. Republic Germany, 1974. Asst. Deutsches Zentrum fuer Luft und Raumfahrt, Oberpfaffenhofen, Fed. Republic Germany, 1962-69, head of control systems group, 1969-71, dir., Inst. Robotics and Mechatronics, 1971—; vis. prof. U. Ill., Urbana, 1978-79, U. Calif., Irvine, 1989-90; coun. mem. Internat. Fedn. Automatic Control, 1990-96; senate mem. DLR, 1990-98; chief reviewer Deutsche Forschungsgemeinschaft, 1988-95; adj. prof. Tech. U. Munich. Author: Sampled Data Control, 1972, 3d rev. edit., 1988 (VDE award 1973), transl. Polish, Eng. and Chinese, 1976, 85, 91; editor: Uncertainty and Control, 1985, Robust Control, 1993; contbr. numerous articles to profl. jours. Recipient Johann Maria Boykow award, 1970; Otto Lilienthal fellow, 1989; recipient Nathaniel Nichols medal IFAC, 1996. Fellow IEEE (chmn. CSS Tech. Award com. 1990-91, assoc. editor-at-large Trans-Automatic Control, 1990-94, bd. govs. 1992-95, Hendrik Bode prize 1996), European Community Control Assn. (founding mem.), VDI./VDE Ges. Mess. und Automatisierungs-technik, Verein Deutscher Studenten. Home: Madeleine Ruoff Str 14C, 82211 Herrsching Germany Office: DLR-OP-RM, 82230 Wessling Germany

ACKERMANN, LOTHAR AUGUST, radiologist; b. Würzburg, Bavaria, Germany, Dec. 22, 1923; s. Ludwig Adam and Karoline Maria (Mainberger) A.; m. Renate Ulrich, May 12, 1967; children: Gerd-Armin, Karen. MD, U. Würzburg, 1951; cert. radiologist, Düsseldorf, Germany, 1957. German cert. radiologist. Intern U. Würzburg, 1951-55; head physician St. John's Hosp., Duisburg, 1955-57; rsch. radiologist Adox-Fotowerke, Frankfurt, Germany, 1957-63; staff radiologist Du Pont de Nemours, Frankfurt, 1963-89; pvt. rschr. Königstein, Germany, 1989—. Author: The Personal File of W.C. Röntgen, 1959, Encyclopedia of Medical Radiology, 1968, Summa Radiologica, 1972, Planning of X-Ray Departments, 1975; inventor in field. Auditor German X-Ray Mus., Lennep, Germany, 1964-85; active Help for Children, Duisburg, 1980—. Pvt. 1st class Med. Corps German Air Force, 1942-46. Mem. German X-Ray Soc. Avocations: medical-social projects for self-help of indigenous people in Guatemala and Chile. Home: Friedrich-Bender-Str 12, D-61462 Königstein Ts Hesse, Germany

ACKERS, GARY KEITH, biophysical chemistry educator, researcher; b. Dodge City, Kans., Oct. 25, 1939; s. Leo Finley and Mabel Ida (Hostetler) A.; children: Lisa, Sandra, Keith. BS in Chemistry and Math., Harding Coll., Searcy, Ark., 1961; PhD in Physiol. Chemistry, Johns Hopkins U., 1964. Instr. physiol. chemistry Johns Hopkins U. Sch. Medicine, Balt., 1965-66, prof. biology and biophysics, 1977-89, dir. Inst. Biophys. Rsch., 1987-89; asst. prof. biochemistry U. Va. Sch. Medicine, Charlottesville, 1966-67, assoc. prof., 1967-72, prof. biochemistry and biophysics, 1972-77; prof. biochemistry and molecular biophysics Washington U., St. Louis, 1989—, head dept. biochemistry and molecular biophysics, 1989-96; instr. physiology Marine Biol. Labs., Woods Hole, Mass., 1974-76; chmn. Gordon Conf. on Proteins, 1985; disting. lectr. Red Cell Club, 1997—. Mem. editorial bd. Analytical Biochemistry, 1970-79, Biophys. Chemistry, 1973-78, Proteins, Structures, Functional Genetics, 1991—; contbr. over 150 articles to sci. jours. Guggenheim fellow, 1972-73; recipient NIH Merit award, 1987. Fellow Biophys. Soc. (coun. 1972-74, 80-83, pres. 1984-85, Cole rsch. award 1994); mem. Am. Chem. Soc. (program chair biol. chem. divsn. 1994), Am. Soc. Biochem. Molecular Biology. Office: Washington U Med Sch Dept Biochem and Molecular Biophysics 660 S Euclid Ave Saint Louis MO 63110-1010

ACKERSON, CHARLES STANLEY, minister, social worker; b. St. Louis, June 19, 1935; s. Charles Albert and Glenda Mae (Brown) A.; m. Carol Jean Stehlick, Aug. 18, 1957; children: Debra Lynn, Charles Mark, Heather Sue. AB, William Jewell Coll., 1957; MDiv, Colgate Rochester Div. Sch., 1961. Ordained to ministry Am. Bapt. Ch., 1961; lic. clin. social worker. Pastor Glens Falls (N.Y.) Friends Meeting, 1961-65; assoc. pastor Delmar Bapt. Ch., St. Louis, 1965-68; resource dir. Block Partnership, St. Louis, 1968-71; group home supr. St. Louis Juvenile Ct., 1973-74; program dir. Youth Opportunities Unltd., casework supr. St. Louis County Juvenile Ct., 1974-83; youth svcs. specialist St. Louis County Dept. Human Svcs., 1985-94; assoc. dir. Gen. Protestant Children's Home, 1994-99; residential dir. Mo. Bapt. Children's Home, 1999—; instr. adminstrn. of justice and human svcs. Mo. Bapt. Coll., St. Louis, 1980—; asst. pastor St. Jordan's and St. John's United Chs. of Christ, 1976—; exhibit coord. Dog Mus., 1989-91; cons. Am. Youth Found., 1990—; mem. ordination coun. area V, Great Rivers region Am. Bapt. Chs. U.S.A., 1982-84; chmn. youth focus group Interfaith Partnership Met. St. Louis, 1985-88; chmn. St. Louis Area Youth Svcs. Network, 1987-89. Chmn. group home com. Mo. Coun. on Criminal Justice, 1973-75; chmn. cts. and instns. subcom. Juvenile Delinquency Task Force for Gov. Mo. Action Plan for Pub. Safety, 1976. Mem. Nat. Coun. Juvenile and Family Ct. Judges, Mo. Juvenile Justice Assn. (v.p., chmn. tng.

com.), Am. Correctional Assn., Nat. Audubon Soc., Smithsonian Instn. Assn., Cairn Terrier Club Am., Three Rivers Kennel Club of Mo. (past pres.), mo. Conservation Fedn., Lambda Chi Alpha. Democrat. Baptist. E-mail: cackersn@swbell.net. Home: 1221 Havenhurst Rd Ballwin MO 63011-4402

ACKLEY, ROBERT O., lawyer; b. Chgo., July 24, 1952; s. William O. and Jeannette E. (Mitchell) A.; m. Patricia Ann Cerney, May 24, 1980; children: Matthew, Allison, Elizabeth, Anne, Kathryn, Kimberly. BA, No. Ill. U., 1974; MA., No. Mich. U., 1977; JD, John Marshall Law Sch., Chgo., 1988. Bar: Ill. 1988, U.S. Dist. Ct. (no. dist.) Ill. 1988. Adminstrv. intern, asst. to city mgr. City of Marquette, Mich., 1976-77; adminstrv. asst. to town mgr. Town of Glastonbury, Conn., 1978; supr. Continental Bank, Chgo., 1979; chief methods analyst dept. fin. City of Chgo., 1980-81, chief supr. ops. dept. revenue, 1981-84; pres. Ackley & Assocs., Chgo., 1984-88; law clk., adminstrv. asst. to chief justice Thomas J. Moran Supreme Ct. of Ill., Lake Forest, 1988-90; atty. Cassiday, Schade & Gloor, Chgo., 1990-91; pvt. practice Chgo., 1991—; bd. dirs. Ill. Pro Bono Ctr.; adj. prof. Roosevelt U., Chgo., 1989-90; mem. panel arbitrators Cir. Ct. of 19th Jud. Cir., 1991-97, Cir. Ct. Cook County, 1993-97; detention screening atty. pretrial svcs. Cir. Ct. of Cook County, 1991—; drugs panel atty. Office of State Appellate Defender, 1992—. Bd. dirs. Bryn Mawr-Broadway Ridge Mchts. Assn., Chgo., 1984-87; panel mem. Capital Resource Ctr., 1991, Community Econ. Devel. Law Project. Fellow Ill. Bar Found.; mem. ABA, Nat. Assn. Counsel Children, Ill. Bar Assn., Chgo. Bar Assn., Lake County Bar Assn., Ill. Appellate Lawyers Assn., Acad. Polit. Sci. (life). Home: 606 Buckingham Pl Libertyville IL 60048-3326 Office: 500 N Lake St Ste 109 Mundelein IL 60060-1860

ACKROYD, NORMAN, art educator; b. Leeds, U.K., Mar. 26, 1938; s. Albert Ackroyd and Clara Briggs; m. Sylvia Buckland, 1963 (div. 1975); two children; m. Penelope Hughes Stanton; two children. Degree, Ctrl. Sch. Art and Design. Tutor in etching Ctrl. Sch. Art and Design, 1965—; adj. prof. U. Ind., 1970. Exhbns. include Mickelson Gallery, Wash., 1973, 77, 79, 82, 84, 88, Anderson Oday Gallery, London, 1979, 88, Dolan Maxwell Gallery, Phila., 1981, 83, 85, 87, 89;. Avocations: British history, archaeology, cricket. Office: care Royal Acad Arts, Piccadilly London W1J OBD, England*

ACKROYD, PETER, writer; b. London, Oct. 5, 1949. Grad. with honors, Clare Coll., Cambridge, Eng., 1971. Literary editor The Spectator mag., London, 1973-77, mng. editor, 1977-81; free-lance writer London, 1981—; chief book reviewer The Times, London, 1986—. Author: (poetry) London Lickpenny, 1973, Country Life, 1978, The Diversions of Purley, 1987; (literary criticism) Notes for a New Culture, 1976; (sociological study) Dressing Up, 1979, Exra Pound and His World, 1980, The Great Fire of London, 1982, The Last Testament of Oscar Wilde, 1983, T.S. Eliot, 1984, Hawksmoor, 1985, Chatterton, 1987, First Light, 1989, Dickens, 1990, English Music, 1992, The House of Doctor Dee, 1993, Dan Leno and the Limhouse Golem, 1994, Blake, 1995, Milton in America, 1996, The Life of Thomas More, 1998, The Plato Papers, 1999, The Biography, 2000. Mellow fellow Yale U., 1971-73; recipient Somerset Maugham prize, 1984, Whitbread prize for best biography, 1984-85, Guardian Fiction award, 1985, Whitbread prize for best novel, 1986. Fellow Royal Soc. Lit. Office: care Anthony Sheil, 43 Doughty St, London WC1N 2LF, England

ACOSTA, ANTONIO MONREAL, composer; b. Murcia, Spain, July 16, 1975; s. Antonio Monreal and Enriqueta Acosta. Student, Murcia Conservatory. Composer: Pane Lucrando. Home: c/ Princesa no8-2 dcha, 30 002 Murcia Spain

ACOSTA, MARIO, pharmaceutical educator, consultant, researcher; b. Mexico City, Mex., Apr. 16, 1963; Mario Acosta and Isabel Mejia; m. Mirian Coterillo, Nov. 7, 1986; children: Myriam, Giovanna, Mario. MD with honors, Univ. Mex., 1985, M in Neuro Sci., 1989; PhD in Pharm. Sci. with honors, Cambridge U., U.K., 1995. Gen. dir. med. svcs. U. Mex., 1988-90, sr. prof. med. maj., 1990-97, clin. rschr., 1991-93; clin. rschr. Adenbrook Hosp. U. Cambridge, 1993-95; chmn. clin. rsch. Boehringer Mannheim Inst., Mex., 1991-93; founder, pres. Pharm. Sci. Coll., Mex., 1996—. Contbr. articles to profl. jours. Recipient Youth award, Mex., 1984. Mem. AAAS, Internat. Pharmacology Soc., Internat. Assn. Study Pain, N.Y. Acad. Scis. Avocations: piano, ballroom dancing. Home: Urdaneta No 56, Navegantes Cd Mexico 53120, Mexico Office: Blvd San Mateo No 22, Naucalpan 53140, Mexico

ACOSTA, MARTHA M., physical therapist, educator; b. Lafayette, La., Sept. 19, 1950; children: Jesse Curtis, Marie Camille. B in Pre-Medicine, U. Southwestern La., 1972; B in Phys. Therapy, U. Tex. Med. Br., 1973; M in Healthcare Adminstrn., Southwest Tex. State U., 1994. Lic. phys. therapist Tex. Staff phys. therapist Charity Hosp., New Orleans, 1974-75, Travis State Sch., Austin, Tex., 1975-77; dir. phys. therapy San Marcos (Tex.) Treatment Ctr., The Ranch Treatment Ctr., Austin, 1977-91, Ctrl. Tex. Med. Ctr., San Marcos, 1991-92, Rio Vista Rehab. Hosp., El Paso, Tex., 1992-94; asst. prof. U. Tex., El Paso, 1994—; adv. bd. mem. El Paso C.C., 1992-98; mem. Kellogg faculty Inst. Border Cmty. Partnerships, El Paso, 1994—. Contbr. book revs. in field. Sec. Southwest Tex. State Alumni Assn., West Tex. chpt., 1994-96; mem. WestPoint Parents' Club, El Paso, 1997—, Raza Faculty, El Paso, 1999—; liaison U. Tex. Med. Br. Alumni Assn., El Paso, 2000—. Mem. Am. Phys. Therapy Assn. (edn., neurology and geriatric sects., treas. Greater El Paso dist. 1993-95, del. 2000—, bd. cert. clin. specialist 1997). Avocations: exercise, gardening, hiking, dancing. E-mail: maracost@utep.edu. Home: 604 Dorsey Dr El Paso TX 79912-7064 Office: U Tex 1101 N Campbell St El Paso TX 79902-4238

ACTON, EDWARD DAVID JOSEPH, historian, educator; b. Harare, Zimbabwe, Feb. 4, 1949; s. John and Daphne (Strutt) A.; m. Stella Conroy, Apr. 8, 1972; children: Helen Marie, Natalie Elizabeth. BA in History with honors, U. York, Eng., 1971; PhD in History, U. Cambridge, Eng., 1975. Grad. trainee Bank of Eng., 1975-76; lectr. U. Liverpool, Eng., 1976-86, sr. lectr., 1986-88; sr. lectr. U. Manchester, 1988-91; prof. U. E. Anglia, 1991—. Author: Alexander Herzen, 1979, Russia: The Present and the Past, 1986, Tsarist and Soviet Legacy, 1995, Prethinking the Human Revolution, 1990; contbr. articles to profl. jours. Research grantee Brit. Acad., 1983, 86, 95, Brit. Council, 1983, Leverhulme Trust, 1987. Fellow Royal Hist. Soc.; mem. Hist. Assn. (pres. Liverpool and dist. br. 1984-87). Roman Catholic. Avocations: bridge, tennis, racing. Home: 24 Moss Lane, 365 Unthank Rd, Norwich Norfolk NR4 7PG, England Office: U Manchester Dept History, U East Anglia, Norwich Norfolk NR4 7TJ, England

ACZÉL, JÁNOS DEZSÖ, mathematics educator; b. Budapest, Hungary, Dec. 26, 1924; s. Dezsö and Irén (Adler) A.; m. Susan Kende, Dec. 14, 1946; children: Catherine, Julie. MA, U. Budapest, 1947, PhD, 1947; DSc, Hungarian Acad. Sci., 1957; Dr. honoris causa, U. Karlsruhe, 1990, U. Graz, 1995, Silesian U. Katowice, 1996, U. Miskolc, 1999. Faculty U. Szeged, Hungary, 1948-50; prof. math. Tech. U., Miskolc, 1950-52, Kossuth U., Debrecen, Hungary, 1952-65, U. Waterloo, Ont., Can., 1965-93; disting. prof. U. Waterloo, 1969-93, disting. prof. emeritus, 1993—; vis. prof. U. Fla., Gainesville, 1963-64, 81, Stanford U., 1964, U. Koln, Germany, 1965, U. Giessen, 1966, 70, Ruhr U., 1968, Fla. Atlantic U., 1968, U. Pavia, 1968, 69, Ist. Naz. Alta Matematica, Rome, 1971, Monash U., Clayton, Victoria, Australia, 1972, Ahmadu Bello U., Zaria, Nigeria, 1975-76, Calif. Inst. Tech., 1978, Karl-Franzens U., Graz, Austria, 1979, 86, 91, 93, 99, Okayama U. (Japan), 1984, U. Milan, 1985, 91, U. Hamburg, 1985, U. Politécnica Catalunya, Barcelona, 1986, 92, U. Berne, Switzerland, 1986, U. Karlsruhe, Germany, 1992, 98, U. Calif., Irvine, 1994, 96—; cons. Naval Ocean Systems Ctr., San Diego, 1979-81; chmn. Internat. Symposium Functional Equations, 1962-96, hon. chmn., 1997—;. Author: (with S. Golab) Funktionalgleichungen der Theorie der geometrischen Objekte, 1960, Vorlesungen über Funktionalgleichungen und ihre Anwendungen, 1961, Ein Blick auf Funktionalgleichungen und ihre Anwendungen, 1962, Lectures on Functional Equations and Their Applications, 1966, On Applications and Theory of Functional Equations, 1969, (with Z. Daróczy) On Measures of Information and Their Characterizations, 1975, A Short Course on Functional Equations Based Upon Recent Applications to Social and Behavioral Sciences, 1987, (with J. Dhombres) Functional Equations in Several Variables with Applications to Mathematics, Information Theory and to the Natural and Social Sciences, 1989; editor: Functional Equations: History, Applications and Theory, 1984, Aggregating Clones, Colors, Equations, Iterates, Numbers and Tiles, 1995; editor jours. Rendiconti di Matematica e delle sue Applicazioni, Inequalities and their Applications, Mathematica Japonica, Results of Mathematics, Mathware and Soft Computing; hon. editor-in-chief Aequationes Mathematicae; editor: Theory and Decision Library, Series B; also numerous articles. Recipient M. Beke award J. Bolyai Math. Soc., 1961, Hungarian Acad. Scis. award, 1962, Cajal medal Spanish Nat. Council Sci. Research, 1988. Fellow Royal Soc. Can., Hungarian Acad. Scis. (fgn.); mem. Can. Math. Soc., Am. Math. Soc., N.Y. Acad. Scis., Austrian Math. Soc. Achievements include initiation of modern theory of functional equations; gave gen. theorems and applications to geometry, algebra, analysis, econs., mathematical psychology, utility, decision, probability, and info. theory; theories of mean values, measurement, and webs. E-mail: jdaczel@math.uwaterloo.ca. Home: 97 McCarron Cres, Waterloo, ON Canada N2L 5M9 Office: U Waterloo, Pure Math Dept, Waterloo, ON Canada N2L 3G1

ADACHI, NOBUHIRO, educator; b. Kyoto, Japan, Feb. 8, 1944; s. Tsutomu and Takeko (Hyo) A.; m. Megumi Fujimoto; children: Shiori, Tomoki. BA, Kansai U., Osaka, Japan, 1968; MA, U. Hawaii, 1973, U. Hawaii, 1978; PhD, Kansai Gaidai U., 1995. Passenger svc. officer Cathay Pacific Airways, Osaka, Japan, 1967-69; assoc. prof. Kansai Jr. Coll. Fgn. Studies, Osaka, Japan, 1979-89; exch. prof. Gustavus Adolphus Coll., St. Peter, 1985-88; prof. Kansai Gaidai U., Osaka, 1989—; vis. scholar U. Hawaii, Honolulu, 1993-94; dean acad. affairs Kansai Gaidai U., 1995-99. Author: Linguistic Americanizatin of Japanese-Americans, 1996; co-author: A Handbook for Teaching English at Japanese Colleges and Universities, 1993, Wars and Japanese Immigrants, 1997. Spark Matsunaga grantee, Honolulu, 1994, The Young-Tae Kim grantee, Honolulu, 1997. Mem. Assn. Asian-Am. Studies, Ctr. Asia-Pacific Exch. Avocations: travel, bicycling, treking, reading, jazz. Office: Kansai Gaidai U, 16-1 Kitakatahoko-cho, Osaka 573-1001, Japan

ADACHI, SHINYA, surgeon, educator; b. Oita, Japan, June 5, 1957; s. Tsugiya and Umeno (Goto) A.; m. Nahomi Toshimitsu, May 1, 1982; children: Kana, Kyosuke. MD, U. Tsukuba, 1982, D in Med. Sci., 1990. Resident Tsukuba U. Hosp., 1982-88; chief surgeon Kinu Med. Assn. Hosp., Mitsukaido, Japan, 1988-94; asst. prof. U. Tsukuba, 1994—. Contbr. articles to profl. jours. Mem. Internat. Gastric Cancer Assn., Internat. Gastro-Surg. Club, Japanese Gastric Cancer Assn. (coun.). Avocations: golf, baseball, gardening. Office: Inst Clin Med U Tsukuba, 1-1-1 Tennodai, Tsukuba 305-8575, Japan

ADACHI, YUKIHIKO, medical educator; b. Nagaokakyo, Kyoto, Japan, Sept. 22, 1943; s. Masao and Yoshiko Adachi; m. Miwa Ozaki, Mar. 14, 1971; children: Emi, Yuri. MD, Kyoto U., 1968, PhD, 1976. Asst. prof. Kinki U. Sch. Medicine, Osakasayama, Osaka, Japan, 1975-91, assoc. prof., 1991-97; direct prof. Mie U. Sch. Medicine, Tsu, Mie, Japan, 1997—. Contbr. med. rsch. articles to profl. jours. Recipient Mitsukoshi award for Young Med. Researchers, Mitsukoshi Enterprise for Social Welfare, 1974. Mem. Internat. Soc. Clin. Enzymology, Am. Assn. Study of Liver Diseases, European Assn. Study of the Liver, Japan Soc. Clin. Biochemistry and Metabolism (councilor 1992—), Japan Soc. Hepatology (councilor 1990—, guidance physician 1989—), Japan Soc. Gastroenterology (councilor 1986—, guidance physician 1988—, award of encouragement 1988), Japanese Soc. Internal Medicine (guidance physician 1988—, councilor 1998—), Internat. Assn. Study of the Liver. Buddhist. Fax: 81-59-231-5223. Home: 604-282 Kan-nonji-cho, Tsu 514-0062, Japan Office: Mie U Sch Med , 3d Dept, Int Med, 2-174 Edobashi, Tsu 514-8507, Japan

ADALBERT, PER, artist; b. Stockholm, Dec. 4, 1953; m. Diana M.C.U. Bjorkman, Sept. 6, 1980; children: Greta, Per Jr., Malcolm, Sten. hon. sec. Artist Union, Kro, Sweden, 1994-96; chmn. Montparnasse, Inc., Sweden, 1994—. Exhbns. include Liljevalchs, Stockholm, 1983, Krasnapolsky, Copenhagen, 1986, Art/London, 1989, Great White Eagle, Antwerp, 1989, Pierre Cardin, Paris, 1990, Millesgarden, Stockholm, 1991, Art Revolution, Tokyo, 1996, Volvo Showroom, Stockholm, 1997, Galerie Jansen o Kooy, Amsterdam, 1997; artist: (book) Black Period of Adalbert, 1988 (Goldbook of Paris 1988, Jacques Chirac.), Projection Metaphysique, 1990, Cosmos and Chaos, 1991, The Management Orchestra, 1994,, Art Revolution, 1996, Je suis ici, 1998; represented in collections Prinz von undzu Liechtenstein, Gianni Versace, Absolut Vodka, Prestige Mourlot, Museu Comarcal Barcelona, Rausing Collection, London. Home: Rosenhird, 640 60 Akers Styckebruk Sweden

ADAM, ANDRÉ, ambassador; b. Brussels, Sept. 10, 1936; married; four children. Diploma Pub. Adminstrn., U. Brussels, 1958, degree polit. sci., 1958. Jr. trainee Bank Lambert, Brussels, 1960; rsch. asst. dept. applied econs. U. Brussels, 1961-64; various diplomatic posts Belgian Embassy, Havana, Paris, Kinhasha, London, 1964-79; chef de cabinet of Minister Henri Simonet Minister of Fg. Affairs, 1979-80, head Energy Divsn., 1980-82; consul gen. L.A., 1982-86; amb. Algiers, 1986-90, Kinshasa, 1990-91; dir. gen. for polit. affairs Ministry of Fgn. Affairs, 1991-94; amb. to U.S. Belgian Embassy, Washington, 1994-98; rep. to the UN N.Y.C., 1998—; chmn. European Polit. Com., 1993; Olympic attache for Belgium during 1984 Olympic Games in L.A.; chmn. non-profit orgn. in Calif. for Belgian Olympic team in U.S. Grand Officer in Order of the Crown, Belgium, Order of the Falcon, Iceland, Commdr. in the Order of Merit, Poland, Order of Leopold, Belgium. Mem. Internat. Inst. for Strategic Studies. Avocations: tennis, swimming, horseback riding; fluent in several langs., including French, Dutch, English, German and Spanish. Office: Belgian Mission to the UN 823 United Nations Plz 345 East 46th St 4th Fl New York NY 10017

ADAM, CHRISTOPHER, retired pharmaceuticals executive; b. Warsaw, Sept. 7, 1940; s. Ignacy Adamczewski and Maria Sophia (Wroblewska) Moss; m. Georgina Caroline Potter, Dec. 16, 1967; children: Alexander, Olivier, Benjamin. BSc in Biochemistry, U. London, 1965; sr. exec. program, Stanford U., 1983. Market rsch. exec. Fisons Ltd., Felixstone, 1965-67; personal asst. to CEO Fisons Ltd., London, 1967-68; sales and mktg. exec. Fisons Pharm., London, 1968-70; comml. dir. SOV-Fisons, Lyon, France, 1970-71; mng. dir. Lab. Fisons SA, Paris, 1971-83; chmn., CEO Lab. Glaxo SA, Paris, 1983-90; dir. internat. mktg. Glaxo Group, London, 1990-92, dir. comml. strategy, 1992-95; regional dir. Japan Glaxo Wellcome PLC, 1995—; ret., 2000. Decorated Chevalier Légion d'Honneur (France). Mem. Stanford U. Alumni Assn. Avocations: golf, bridge, chess.

ADAM, CHRISTOPHER MICHAEL, economics educator; b. Suva, Fiji, Aug. 31, 1951; s. Roy Sivyer and Shirley Ruth (Cole) A.; m. Wendy Moorhead, July 9, 1977; children: Jennifer Katherine, Murray James. B. in Econs. with honors, U. Western Australia, 1974; MA, Harvard U., 1976, PhD, 1977. Lectr. U. NSW, Sydney, 1977-81, sr. lectr., 1981-88; assoc. prof., assoc. dean Bond U., Gold Coast, Australia, 1989-92; prof. U. Sydney, 1992—. Contbr. articles to profl. jours. Mem. Econometric Soc. (life), Am. Econ. Assn., Asia-Pacific Fin. Assn., Acad. Internat. Bus., Harvard Club of Australia. Avocations: history, tennis. Home: 10 Paul St, Bondi Junction NSW 2022, Australia Office: U NSW, Australian Grad Sch Mgmt, New South Wales 2052, Australia

ÁDÁM, ÉVA, microbiologist, educator; b. Ujpest, Hungary, Sept. 20, 1946; d. János and Gizella (Meinx) Á. Pharmacist, Semmelweis U., Budapest, 1973, PharmD, 1975, PhD, 1981, Acad. DMS, 1992. Lic. pharmacist. Mem. Inst. Microbiology, Semmelweis U., 1973, dep. dean, 1993-99; assoc. prof. Inst. Med. Microbiology, Budapest, 1985-92; prof. Inst. Microbiology, Budapest, 1992—. Contbr. articles to sci. publs. Mem. Hungarian Soc. Microbiology (bd. dirs.). Avocation: virology. Home: Madzsar J u 25, H-1039 Budapest Hungary Office: Inst Microbiology, Nagyvárad tér 4, H-1089 Budapest Hungary

ADAM, GEORGE, physician; b. Lodz, Poland, Jan. 9, 1946; came to U.S., 1948; arrived in Eng., 1974; s. James and Lucille A.; m. Susan Frances Elizabeth Trevett, Jan. 29, 1972; children: Alexandra, Ross. AB, NYU, 1967; MD, George Washington U., 1971. Diplomate Nat. Bd. Med. Examiners, Am. Bd. Internal Medicine. Med. intern USPHS Hosp., S.I., 1971-72, med. resident, 1972-74; surg. intern Farnborough Hosp., Kent, Eng., 1975; trainee family practice Forest Hill Rd. Group Practice, London, 1975-76, primary care physician, 1976—; clin. asst. chest disease Queen Mary's Hosp., Sidcup, Kent, Eng., 1981-93; clin. asst. cardiology Guy's and St. Thomas' Hosps., London, 1993—. Advising editor Cardiology in Practice, 1982-83. Lt. comdr. USPHS, 1971-74. Mem. ACP. Avocations: art history, ice skating. Fax: 020 82990200. Email: gadam007@aol.com. Office: Forest Hill Rd Group Pract, 1 Forest Hill Rd, London SE22 0SQ, England

ADAM, GUNTER ERNST KURT, chemist; b. Muhlhausen, Thuringia, Germany, Dec. 8, 1932; s. Kurt and Eva (Beck) A.; m. Marga Erna Alma Kellner, Apr. 19, 1958; children: Christiane Riedel, Ernest Adam. Diploma, Friedrich-Schiller U., Jena, Germany, 1959, PhD, 1962; Habilitation, Martin-Luther U., Halle, Germany, 1967; Prof., Acad. Scis., Berlin, 1979. Rsch. scientist Acad. Agr., Mühlhausen, Germany, 1959-61, Inst. Cultivated Plants, Gatersleben, Germany, 1961-69; head of lab. Inst. Plant Biochemistry, Halle, 1969-77, head rsch. dept., 1977-98; lectr. Martin Luther U., Halle, 1977-89, prof. 1994-98; dir. Inst. Plant Biochemistry, Halle, 1990-98; guest prof. U. Baghdad, Kuwait, Milan, Hanoi, Reims, Tokyo, N.Y. and Peking. Co-editor: Brassinosteroids-Chemistry Biochemistry Application, 1991; contbr. articles to profl. jours. Recipient Leipniz medal Acad. Scis., 1975. Mem. Gesellschaft Deutscher Chemiker (Friedrich Wöhler prize 1968), DECHEMA (bd. com./Frankfurt), Gesellschaft Deutscher Naturforscher, Phytochemical Soc. Europe, Gesellschaft fur Arzneipflanzenforschung. Lutheran. Office: Inst Plant Biochemistry, Weinberg 3 PO Box 110432, D-06018 Halle Germany

ADAMANTOPOULOS, KONSTANTINOS, lawyer, consultant; b. Sparta, Greece, Oct. 31, 1959; s. Adamantios and Maria (Masgana) A.; m. Aspa Savvidou; 2 children. Law degree, U. Athens, Greece, 1982; European law degree, U. Saarland, Saarbruecken, Germany, 1983, LLD, 1987. Bar: Athens, 1984. Asst. lawyer Law Office of Takis Zachopoulos, Athens, 1982-84; pvt. practice Athens, 1984-87; asst. legal svc. European Econ. Community, Luxembourg, 1987-88; assoc. Stanbrook and Hooper, Brussels, 1988-90, ptnr., 1991-93; ptnr. Dagtoglou, Mavros-Adamantopoulos, Athens, 1991-93, Hammond Suddards, Brussels, 1993—. Author: Subventionsrecht-Gatt, 1988, EEC Anti-Dumping Law, 1990, The Anatomy of the World Trade Organisation, 1997; contbr. articles to profl. jours. Mem. Rotaract, Athens, 1978-85; pres. local adminstrn. Greek New Democrat Party, Saarbruecken, 1984-88; rep. Greek industry fedn. Union Indsl. and Employers Confedns. Europe. Mem. Air Transport Law Assn., European Trade Law Assn., Hellenic Fedn. European Law, Greek-German Lawyers Assn., Belgian-Hellenic C. of C. (v.p.), European Aviation Club. Greek Orthodox. Avocations: jogging, skiing, wind surfing, cinema, music. Office: Hammond Suddards, Ave Louise 250 bte 65, B-1040 Brussels Belgium

ADAMANY, DAVID WALTER, law and political science educator; b. Janesville, Wis., Sept. 23, 1936; s. Walter Joseph and Dora Marie (Mutter) A. AB, Harvard U., 1958, JD, 1961; MS, U. Wis., 1963, PhD in Polit. Sci., 1967; LLD (hon.), Adrian Coll., 1984; AAS (hon.), Schoolcraft Coll., 1986; D. Engrng. (hon.), Mich. Tech. U., 1987; D in Pub. Svc. (hon.), Ea. Mich. U., 1997. Bar: Wis. 1961. Spl. asst. to atty. gen. State of Wis., Madison, 1961-63, exec. pardon counsel, 1963; commr. Wis. Public Service Commn., 1963-65; instr. polit. sci. Wis. State U., Whitewater, 1965-67; asst. prof., then assoc. prof. Wesleyan U., Middletown, Conn., 1967-72; dean coll. Wesleyan U., 1969-71; assoc. prof., then prof. polit. sci. U. Wis., Madison, 1972-77; v.p. acad. affairs, prof. Calif. State U., Long Beach, 1977-80, U. Md., College Park, 1980-82; disting. prof. law and polit. sci. Wayne State U., Detroit, 1982-2000, pres., 1982-97, pres. emeritus, 1997; CEO Detroit Pub. Schs., 1999-2000; pres. Temple U., Phila., 2000—; chmn. Wis. Coun. Criminal Justice, 1973-75, Wis. Elections Bd., 1976-77; sec. Wis. Dept. Revenue, 1973-75; advisor to Gov. Patrick J. Lucey, State of Wis., 1972; bd. dirs. Caraco Pharm. Ltd., Thyssen Inc. Author: Financing Politics, 1969, Campaign Finance in America, 1972; co-author Borzoi Reader in American Politics, 1972, American Government: Democracy and Liberty in Balance, 1975, Political Money, 1975; editorial bd.: Social Sci. Quarterly, 1973—, State and Local Govt. Rev., 1974-80; contbr. articles to profl. jours. Mem. exec. com. Detroit Med. Ctr., 1982-97; chmn. Mich. Bicentennial of U.S. Constrn. Commn., 1986-88; bd. dirs. Detroit Inst. Arts Founders Soc., 1983-92, Detroit Symphony Orch., 1983-89, Detroit Econ. Growth Corp., 1984-92, Karmanos Cancer Inst., 1982-97, New Detroit, 1982-95, Blue Cross Blue Shield Found. Mich., 1995-2000, Gilmour Fund, 1996—, HOPE Fund of Cmty. Found. of S.E. Mich., 1995-2000; mem. Wis. Gov.'s Commn. on Campaign Fin. Reform, 1996-97; mem. Mich. Civil Svc. Commn., 1996-99. Mem. ACLU, ABA (commn. on coll. and univ. legal studies 1992-95), Wis. Bar Assn., Am. Polit. Sci. Assn., Pres.'s Coun. State Univs. (chmn. 1986-88), Can.-U.S. Fulbright Commn. (bd. dirs. 1993-97), Nat. Adv. Com. on Institutional Quality and Integrity (U.S. dept. edn.). Democrat. Office: Temple U Law Sch Philadelphia PA 19122

ADAMATZKY, ANDREW, researcher, consultant; b. St. Petersburg, Russia, Oct. 10, 1965; s. Igor and Ludmila (Zhuiko) A.; m. Svetlana Kalinina, May 31, 1992; children: Kristian, Sebastian. MSc in Biology, Physiology, & Biophysics, St. Petersburg U., 1987, MSc in Maths., 1990; DSc in Physics and Maths., Inst. Program Sys., Pereslavl-Zallesky, Russia, 1996. Jr. rsch. fellow St. Petersburg U., 1987-90, rsch. fellow, 1990-93, sr. rsch. fellow, 1994-97; sr. rsch. fellow U. of the West of England, Bristol, 1997—; chief lab. Galafox Rsch. Corp., St. Petersburg, 1989-92; cons. Def. Industry, Russia, 1991-93, Adia-m Pub. Co., St. Petersburg, 1992—, Nanotechnology Devel. Corp., Tex., 1997—, NanoComputer Dream Team, 2000—. Author: Identification of Cellular Automata, 1994; contbr. articles to profl. jours.; mem. editl. bd. Internat. Jour. Multiple-Valued Logic and Kybernetes, 1997—. Recipient gold medal Exhibition of Industry and Sci., Moscow, 1979; grantee Soros Found., 1996, USAF, 1996, Santa Fe Inst., 1996. Fellow Inst. Nanotechnology; mem. European Assn. for Theoretical Computer Sci. Office: U of the West of England, Frenchay Campus, BS16 1QY Bristol England

ADAMATZKY, IGOR ALEKSEEVICH, publishing company; b. Leningrad, Russia, Jan. 27, 1937; s. Alexei Osipovich and Maria Ivanovna Gul A.; m. Ludmila Stefanovna Lisenko, Oct. 17, 1964 (div. 1984); 1 child, Andrew; m. Nadezhda Eduardovna Varnina, May 7, 1999. Diploma, Leningrad State U., 1968. Rschr. All-Russian Soc. of Knowledge, 1968-71; tchr. in Russian lang., 1971-91; pres. of pub. ctr. ADIA-M, 1991—; chief editor Dean Pub. Co., 1995—. Author: (novels) including Begstvo po Krugu, 1961, Natyurmort z Zhenschionoi, 1971, Byl vecher, budet utro 1971, Posleslovie, 1972, Ekivoka, 1987, others.

ADAMCZAK, EUGENIUSZ, publisher; b. Leszno, Poland, Aug. 30, 1935; s. Wladyslaw and Helena (Tomaszewska) A.; m. Teresa Jedrasiak, Nov. 18, 1958 (div. Oct. 1965); m. Krystyna Marte, Dec. 22, 1966 (div. June 1972); children: Arkadiusz, Joanna; m. Miroslawa Reichel, Feb. 8, 1981; children: Magdalena, Barbara. M Natural Sci., U. Wroclaw, Poland, 1958. Dir. Ossolineum, Wroclaw, 1969-92; dir. br. office Romer Polish Cartographical Pub. House, Wroclaw, 1992—; editor yearbook Ossolineum, Wroclaw, 1976, mem. sci. council of library, 1984-92; chmn. Panorama Raclawicka council, Wroclaw, 1986-90; mem. philol. commn. Polish Acad. Sci., Wroclaw, 1986-90; mem. sci. council Inst. Lit. Research, Warsaw, Poland, 1987-89. Head editor ann. Wroclaw calendar, 1971-76; mem. staff Ze Skarbca Kultury, 1977-90. Mem. head council Polish Students Assn., Warsaw, 1959-64, pres. local council Wroclaw, 1961-63; mem. hdqrs. Univ. Sports Assn. Poland, Warsaw, 1960-62. Decorated knight of Polonia Restituta Order, 1977, commandery of Polonia Restituta Order, 1985; recipient Golden Cross of Merit People's State Council, 1970, award Minister of Culture and Art, 1972, medal Com. Nat. Edn./Minister of Edn., 1980, Golden Medal of Merit, 1987. Mem. Polish Pubs. Assn. (officer 1976—, v.p. 1979-80). Avocations: tennis, basketball, collecting medals and books. Home: Agrestowa 41, 53-006 Wrocław Poland Office: Romer Polish Cartographical Pub House, Sw Jadwigi 12, 50-266 Wrocław Poland

ADAMEC, PŘEMYSL, Russian linguistics educator; b. Bohutice, Znojmo, Czech Republic, Aug. 15, 1930; s. Jaromír and Helena (Vališová) A.; m. Pavla Berglová, May 27, 1937; children: Filip, Vít. Master, Masaryk U. Brno, Czech Republic, 1953; PhD, Charles U., Prague, Czech Republic, 1960, DSc, 1988. Asst. Inst. Russian Lang. and Lit., Prague, 1953-63; docent Charles U., 1964-88, prof., 1989-95; prof. emeritus, 1995—; assoc. prof. UCLA, 1968-69; vis. prof. Goethe U., Frankfurt, Germany, 1991-92. Author: Porjadok slov v sovremennom russkom jazyke, 1966, Očerk funkcionalno-transformacionnogo sintaksisa, 1973, 2d vol., 1975, Obrazovanie

predloženij iz propozicij, 1978. Mem. Linguistic Soc. Czech Republic (v.p.), Circle linguistique de Prague, Czech Assn. Russicists. Home: Manesova 8, CZ-12000 Praha Czech Republic

ADAMENKO, VICTOR GREGORY, biophysics researcher and educator; b. Krasnodar, Russia, June 10, 1936; arrived in Greece, 1988; s. Gregory Emilian and Nadejda Vladimir (Belikevitch) A.; m. Alla Michael Vinogradova, Oct. 15, 1960 (div.); 1 child, Tatiana; m. Eda Vittoria Marangoni, July 25, 1987, separated 1991. Diploma in electronic engring., Radio-Engring. Inst., Taganrog, U.S.S.R., 1962; PhD in Physics, Byelorussian Acad. Scis., Minsk, 1975. Sr. engr. Sci. Rsch. Inst. Ministry of Electronic Industry, Moscow, 1962-70, sr. rsch. assoc. Sci. Rsch. Inst. automated systems, 1972-74; sr. rsch. assoc. Inst. Neurophysiology Acad. Med. Sci. USSR, Moscow, 1974-78; sr. rsch. assoc. ORION, Moscow, 1981-84; prof. U. Crete, Rethimno, Greece, 1988-92; sci. rsch. assoc. in biophysics U. Athens, Greece, 1994—. Author: Introduction to Psychobiophysics; mem. editorial adv. bd. Internat. Jour. Paraphysics, 1971; mem. editorial bd. Internat. Jour. Psychoenergetic Systems, 1977; contbr. numerous articles to profl. jours. Member Better World Soc., Washington, 1990. Mem. AAAS, Moscow Soc. Explorers of Nature, Found. Rsch. on the Nature of Man, Parapsychol. Assn. (assoc.), Planetary Soc., Cooperazione Sanitaria Complementare Interuropea, Internat. Soc. Study of Subtle Energies and Energy Medcine, Soc. for Psychical Rsch., London, N.Y. Acad. Scis. Home: 27 Archelaoy Str, 27 Archelaoy Str Pagrati, 116 35 Athens II635, Greece Office: U Athens Dept Biology, Panepistimiopolis, Kouponia, 15701 Athens Greece

ADAMIA, SHOTA, geologist, researcher; b. Tbilisi, Georgia, Jan. 25, 1929; s. Alexander and Nadejda (Natsvlishvili) A.; m. Cecilia Kishmareishvili, Dec. 29, 1950; children: Revaz, Marina. Grad., Tbilisi (Georgia) State U., 1953, postgrad., 1953-55, candidate geol. sci., 1958, D in Geol. Sci., 1969. Rsch. worker Geol. Inst. Acad. Sci. Georgia, Tbilisi, 1955-71, head of dept., 1971-76, dep. dir., 1976-88, dir., 1988-95; min. of environ. protection Govt. of Georgia, Tbilisi, 1992-95; cons. dept. geology Tbilisi State U., 1985—, prof. faculty of geology, 1991-93. Author: Prejurassic Formations of the Caucasus, 1968; contbr. articles to profl. jours. Active Citizen's Union, Georgia, 1994. Grantee G. Soros Internat. Sci. Found., 1993, rsch. grantee, 1994; recipient Djanelidze prize laureate Acad. Sci. Georgia, 1986, Signe of Honor award USSR Govt., 1988. Mem. Geol. Soc. Georgia (pres. 1991-95). Avocations: sports, classical music. Home: 28 Griboedov, 380008 Tbilisi Georgia Office: Geol Inst Acad Sci Georgia, M Aleksidzc 1/9 Geof, 380093 Tbilisi Georgia

ADAMIETZ, IRENAEUS A., physician, researcher; b. Murcki, Katowice, Poland, Mar. 17, 1955; arrived in Germany, 1981; s. Arnold J. and Ursula M. (Pytel) A.; m. Elisabeth J. Kwiecien, Dec. 18, 1980; children: Raphael, Katharina. Physician, Med. Acad., Warsaw, Poland, 1979, Reg. Physician, 1981; Specialist in Radiology, Med. Sch., Hannover, Germany, 1989, Specialist in Radiotherapy, 1989. Asst. physician dept. diagnostic radiology Regional Hosp., Wetzlar, Germany, 1981-84, asst. physician dept. radiooncology, 1984-86; sr. staff, lectr. dept. radiotherapy and spl. oncology Med. Sch., Hannover, Germany, 1986-91; vice chmn., assoc. prof. in radiation oncology Johann Wolfgang Goethe U., Frankfurt/Main, Germany, 1991-97; dir., chmn. Clinic Radiotherapy and Radio-Oncology Ruhr-U. Buchum, 1998—; med. dir. Marienhospital U., Bochum, 2000—; vis. prof. dept. radiation oncology and nuclear medicine Hahnemann U., Phila., 1994. Author some 250 sci. presentations and some 220 sci. publs. in radiation oncology. Mem. German Soc. Radiation Oncology (chmn. working party on palliative radiotherapy 1996—, chmn. working party of radiation treatment technicians 2000—), German Cancer Soc. (treas., sec. working party on supportive treatment in oncology), Multinat. Assn. of Supportive Care in Cancer, others. Roman Catholic. Avocations: crafts, sports (tennis, diving, sailing, skiing), gardening, painting. Office: U Clinic Radiotherapy & Radio Oncology, Hoelkeskampring 40, D-44625 Herne Germany

ADAMKIN, DAVID HOWARD, pediatric medicine educator; b. N.Y.C., Apr. 4, 1948; s. Joseph and Julie (Termin) A.; m. Carol Ann Seyfferth, Aug. 18, 1979; children: Stephanie Merete, Michelle Rachel, Matthew David. BS in cum laude, Ohio State U., 1970; MD, Upstate Med. Coll., 1974. Diplomate Am. Bd. Pediatrics; diplomate Sub-Bd. Neonatal-Perinatal Medicine, Am. Bd. Pediatrics. Pediatric resident Upstate Med. Ctr., Syracuse, N.Y., 1974-76; neonatalology fellow U. Louisville (Ky.) Sch. Med., 1976-78, asst. prof. pediatrics, asst. prof. obstetrics, 1978-85, assoc. prof. pediatrics, assoc. prof. obstetrics, 1985—, prof. pediatrics, 1992—; vis. prof. U. Ill., Chgo., 1984, Ind. U., Riley-Children's Hosp. and the Ind. Perinatal Assn., Indpls., 1985, La. State U., Baton Rouge, 1987; mem. adv. com. Gov.'s Conf. on Infant Mortality, Frankfort, Ky., 1989; dir. Divsn. Neonatal Medicine, U. Louisville, 1994—; dir. nurseries Kosair Children's Hosp., Louisville, Women's Pavilion, The Norton Hosp., Louisville, 1994—; staff mem. U. Louisville (Ky.) Hosp.; various coms. and adv. positions Kosair Children's Hosp., 1980—; presenter in field. Contbr. chpts. to books and textbooks and articles to profl. jours.; manuscript reviewer Jour. of Perin, Ped Rsch., Jour. of Am. Coll. of Nutrition; med. reviewer AMA. Active March of Dimes State Coun., Mid-Am. Region for Maternal and Child Health, 1989—, rev. panel for Phys. and Devel. Environ. of High Risk Inf.; bd. dirs. Ronald McDonald House, 1996. Grantee Abbott Labs., 1978-83, 85, 87, 91, WHAS-TV Crusade for Children, 1979, 82, 87, 88, 90, 92-98, Travenol Labs., 1981, Mead Johnson, 1982, 91, 92, 93, Ross Labs., 1984, 85, 87, 90, 96, 98, Nat. Eye Inst. NIH, 1989, Alliant Cmty. Trust, 1990, 93, Wyeth-Ayerst, 1995, 96. Fellow Am. Coll. Nutrition; mem. Am. Pediatric Soc., Am. Acad. Pediatrics, Subsection Neonatal/Perinatal Medicine-Am. Acad. Pediatrics, Am. Soc. for Parenteral and Enteral Nutrition (Pediatric planninc com. 1989), Nat. Perinatal Assn. (coun. 1989-91), So. Soc. for Pediatric Rsch. (instn. rep. 1982—), Ky. Perinatal Assn. (organizer 1988, first pres. 1988-91, Disting. Leadership award 1991, Outstanding Leadership and Founder award 1993), Ky. Sect. Acad. Pediatrics, Ky. Med. Assn., Jefferson County Med. Soc. Jewish. Avocations: jogging, basketball, sports events, volleyball, cooking. Home: 9109 Brookwood Path Louisville KY 40241-2417 Office: 571 S Floyd St Ste 300 Louisville KY 40202-3829

ADAMKUS, VALDAS V., president; b. Kaunas, Lithuania, Nov. 3, 1926; m. Alma Adamus. Student, U. Munich; degree in constrn. engring., U. Ill., 1960; D (hon)., Vilnius U., 1989. Dep. regional dir. Ohio Basin region Fed. Water Pollution Co EPA, Cin., 1970-71; dep. regional adminstr. region V EPA, Chgo., 1971-81, regional adminstr., 1981-97; pres. Govt. Lithuania, 1997—. Founder Lituanica, 1951; chair bd. dirs. Santara Ctr. Lithuanian Students in U.S.,1957-58; vice-chmn. Santara-Sviesa Fedn., 1958-65, chmn., 1967; bd. dirs. Lithuanian Cmty. in Am., 1961-64, vice chmn. ctrl. bd., mem., chmn. Am. Lithuanian Coun.; chmn. organizing com. World Lithuanian Games, 1983; founder Internat. Tech. Assistance Program for Baltic States, 1990; mem. Lithuanian Environ. Coun.; founder Lithuanian environ. award, 1990; active polit. campaigns, Lithuania, 1993, 96; commr. Ohio River Sanitary Commn.; head U.S. del., chief U.S. negotiator Gt. Lakes Water Quality Agreement, Internat. Joint Commn. on Gt. Lakes; U.S. del. 1st environ. agreement between U.S. and USSR, 1972; lectr. EPA, USSR, 1974, U. Vilnius, U. Kaunas; advisor WHO, Poland, 1977. Recipient Godl medal EPA. Office: Office of Pres, S Daukanto Square 3, 2001 Vilnius Lithuania*

ADAMO, MARIO ANTONIO, beverage company executive, pharmacist; b. Innisfail, Queensland, Australia, Sept. 25, 1961; s. Dionigi and Guiseppina (Vaccaneo) A.; m. Julie Anne Watt. B in Pharmacy, U. Queensland, Brisbane, Australia, 1981; B in Bus., U. So. Queensland, Toowoomba, Australia, 1991; MBA, U. Melbourne, 1993; grad. diploma applied fin./investment, Securities Inst. Australia, Melbourne, 1998. Registered practising pharmacist. Pharmacist Payless Chemists, Cairns, Australia, 1982-90; rsch. assoc. Pacific Dunlop, Melbourne, 1992-93; mgr. fin. and adminstrn. Carlton & United Breweries, Brisbane, Australia, 1994-95; mgr. prodn. purchasing and fin. support Carlton & United Breweries, Melbourne, 1996-97, mgr. prodn. strategic devels., 1997-98, bus. devel. mgr. bioresources, 1998—. Pres. Woree Squash Club, Cairns, 1984-87. Melbourne Bus. Sch. Found. scholar, 1991-93; Pharmacy Rsch. grantee Australian Coll. Pharmacy Practice, U. Sydney, 1991-93. Fellow Australian Inst. Pharmacy Mgmt. (assoc.); mem. Australian Inst. Mgmt., Pharmacy Soc. Australia. Avocations: squash, cycling, waterskiing, musician, golf. Home: PO Box 3010, Port Melbourne VIC 3207, Australia Office: Carlton & United Breweries, 77 Southbank Blvd, Melbourne VIC 3005, Australia

ADAMOV, MOISEY NAUMOVITCH, physicist, chemist, consultant; b. Leningrad, USSR, Apr. 18, 1920; s. Naum Moiseyevitch and Sarra Mironovna (Davidova) A.; m. Olga Pavlovna Bordodimova, June 9, 1957 (div. March, 1996); 1 child, Svetlana Adamova-Sussman. MD, U. Leningrad (USSR), 1948, Cert. Sr. Sci. Researcher, 1961, PhD in Physics and Maths., 1971. cons. Sci. Rsch. Inst., St. Petersburg, 1990—. Leading scientific researcher U. St. Petersburg (Russia), 1961—. Contbr. articles to profl. jours. Decorated Commemorative Medal 250 Ann. St. Petersburg, 1953, 275th Ann. St. Petersburg, 1999. Avocations: music, computer, theatre, collecting literary and musical works. Home: 47 Galernaya St App No 16, 190000 Saint Petersburg Russia Office: Rsch Inst Physics at Univ, 1 Ulianovskaya St, 198904 Saint Petersburg Russia

ADAMOV, YEVGENIY OLEGOVICH, Russian government official; b. Moscow, Apr. 28, 1939. Grad., Moscow Aviation Inst., 1962; DS, 1984. Nuclear scientist; dir. Power Techs. Rsch. Inst., 1998; min. Atomic Energy, 1998—. Mem. Russian Acad. Engring. Scis. Office: Ministry Atomic Energy, ul Bolshyaya Oroynka 2426, 101000 Moscow Russia*

ADAMOVICH, LUDWIG, judge. Pres. Constl. Ct. Austria. Office: Verfassungsgerichtshof, Judenplatz 11, Vienna Austria

ADAMOWICZ, MIECZYSLAW, agricultural economist, consultant; b. Zarzecze, Zamosc, Poland, Apr. 20, 1939; s. Feliks and Marianna (Artymiak) A.; m. Wieslawa Anna Stefaniuk, June 3, 1967; children: Tomasz, Jacek. Technician, Tech. Agrl. Sch., Zamosc, 1957; MSc, Warsaw Agrl. U., 1962, PhD, 1969, Dr.Habil., 1975. Inspector Ministry of Fgn. Trade, Warsaw, 1962-65; rschr./educator faculty agrl. econs. Warsaw Agrl. U., 1965—, dep. dean, 1978-81, dean, 1981-87, prof. dept. world agr., 1988-91, head dept. agrarian policy and mktg., 1992—, head high sch. agrl. mktg. coop., 1992—, head grad. studies mgmt. and mktg. in agrl. bus., 1995—, mem. senate, 1993—; rschr. Inst. Agrl. and Rural Devel., Polish Acad. Scis., 1988-92, dep. chmn. agrl. econs. com., 1993-95; supplementary work High Commerce Sch., Kielce, 1998—; mem. adv. bd. Agrl. Mkt. Agy., Warsaw, 1996—; mem. social coun. for regional policy of econ. com. Coun. Ministers, Poland, 1995—, mem. rural devel. expert group, 1999—; cons. agrl. policy programs various polit. bodies and agrl. orgns. Author: Foreign Trade and Agriculture, 1988, Agriculture in the Process of Integration of Poland with the European Union, 1996; contbr. articles to profl. jours.; editor, co-author books. Chmn. Apt. Constrn. Coop., Warsaw, 1978-90. Decorated Gold Cross of Merit, The State Coun., Poland, 1979, Cavalier Cross of Renaissance Order of Poland, 1986; recipient Medal of Nat. Edn., Minister of Nat. Edn., 1996, Gold medals Warsaw Agrl. U., 1989, Gödöllö U., Hungary, 1989. Mem. European Assn. Agrl. Economists, Internat. Assn. Agrl. Economists, Polish Econ. Soc., Assn. Agr. and Agribus. Economists, Soc. Internat. Devel., N.Y. Acad. Scis., U.S. Nat. Assn. of Colls. and Tchrs. in Agrl. Roman Catholic. Avocation: gardening. Home: Nowoursynowska 135H, 02-797 Warsaw Poland Office: Warsaw Agricultural Univ, Nowoursynowska 166, 02-787 Warsaw Poland

ADAMS, A. JOHN BERTRAND, public affairs consultant; b. Liverpool, Eng., Nov. 22, 1931; came to U.S., 1962, naturalized, 1971; s. Wilfrid and Francine Sophia (Bertrand) A.; m. Vibeke Dinsen, June 3, 1963 (div. 1975); m. Judith Ann Duff, Oct. 15, 1978; 1 dau., Caroline Louise. Corr. London Daily Telegraph, 1952-56; editor, bur. chief, asst. dir. news Radio Free Europe, Bonn and Munich, W.Ger., 1956-62; Africa corr. ABC News, 1963; writer, exec. CBS News, N.Y.C., 1964-70; assoc. dir. advt. and pub. rels. Investment Co. Inst., 1971-72; dir. pub. affairs U.S. Price Commn., Washington, 1972-73; pres. John Adams Assocs., Inc., Washington, 1973—; founding chmn. The WORLDCOM Group, N.Y.C., London, Tokyo, 1987; bd. dirs. King Comm. Group, Washington. Author: (with J.M. Burke) Civil Rights: A Current Guide to the People, Organizations and Events, 1970; editor: Energy Policy: Industry Perspectives, 1975. Bd. dirs. Psychiat. Inst. Found., Washington, 1974-79, Nat. Coun. Fireworks Safety, 1986-96, Radio Free Europe Radio Liberty Fund, 1987—, Am. Com. for Aid to Poland, 1989-97, Am. Friends of Queen Mary Coll., U. London, 1990—, Friends of Benjamin Franklin House, London, 1990—; exec. dir. Eviron. Industry Coun., 1975-80; mem adv. bd. Gallaudet Coll. for Deaf, Washington, 1977-79. Lt. King's Shropshire Light Inf., Brit. Army, 1951-52, Korea. Recipient Knight's Cross, Order of Merit, Govt. of Poland, 1998, Disting. Svc. award U.S. Price Commn., 1973. Mem. Pub. Rels. Soc. Am. (Silver Anvil award 1978, 84, Hall of Fame, 1999), Nat. Press Club, Fed. City Club (Washington), Severn River Yacht Club (Annapolis, Md.). Home: 12204 Meadow Creek Ct Potomac MD 20854-1408 Office: John Adams Assocs 655 National Press Building Washington DC 20045-1601

ADAMS, ALFRED BERNARD, JR., environmental engineer; b. Asbury Park, N.J., Oct. 15, 1920; s. Alfred Bishop and Julia Ruth (Wiseman) A.; m. Claudia Neff, Dec. 28, 1942; children: Alfred B. III, Tamara Adams Harris, Carla Adams York. BSChemE, Ga. Inst. Technol., 1943; postgrad., Wayne State U., 1946-48, U. Ala., Birmingham, 1986-88, Jefferson State C.C., 1989-95. Registered profl. engr., Ala., Mich., Fla., Ga., N.C.; Diplomate in Am. Acad. Environ. Engrs. Project engr. Pennwalt, Wyandotte, Mich., 1946-50; sales mgr., design engr. Goslin-Birmingham Div., Birmingham, Ala., 1950-61; field engr. & Sales Elmco Corp., Birmingham, Ala., 1961-62; prin. engr. Morton-Thiokol Corp., Brunswick, Ga., 1962-64; tech. mgr. Rust Internat., Birmingham, 1964-86; pres., owner Adams Cons. & Engring. Svcs., Birmingham, 1986—; cons. Goslin divsn. Therma Black Clawson Pkg., 1989-98; cons. in field. Contbr. tech. papers to profl. publs. Pres. Woodhaven Lakes Property Owners Assn., Pinson, Ala., 1980-82, Lake Park Neighborhood Assn., 1996-98; mem. Pub. Health Com., Birmingham, 1975-78. 2d lt. U.S. Army Chem. Corps, 1943-53. Mem. Air & Waste Mgmt. Assn., Tech. Assn. Pulp & Paper Industries. Presbyterian. Avocations: travel, photography, golf. Fax number: (205) 870-3685. Home and Office: Adams Cons & Engring Svcs 400 University Park Dr Apt G17 Birmingham AL 35209-6787

ADAMS, BARBARA, English language educator, poet, writer; b. N.Y.C., Mar. 23, 1932; d. David S. Block and Helen (Taxter) Block Tyler; m. Elwood Adams, June 6, 1952; (dec. 1993); children: Steven, Amy, Anne, Samuel. BS, SUNY, New Paltz, 1962, MA, 1970; PhD, NYU, 1981. Prof. English Pace U., N.Y.C., 1984—, dir. bus. comm., 1984—; poet in residence Cape Cod Writers' Conf., 1988. Author: Double Solitaire, 1982, The Enemy Self: The Poetry & Criticism of Laura Riding, 1990, Hapax Legomena, 1990, Negative Capability, 1999 (1st Prize for Fiction); contbr. poems, stories, articles to various mags. and jours. Recipient 1st prize for poetry NYU and Acad. Am. Poets, 1975, 1st prize for fiction Negative Capability contest, 1999; Penfield fellow NYU, 1977. Mem. PEN, Poetry Soc. Am., Poets and Writers. Home: 59 Coach Ln Newburgh NY 12550-3818 Office: Pace U Pace Plz New York NY 10038

ADAMS, BERNARD STANLEY, Hungarian-English literary translator; b. Wordsley, Stafford, Eng., Jan. 2, 1937; s. William Stanley and Florence Adelaide A.; m. Patricia Jones, Oct. 28, 1966. BA, Pembroke Coll., Cambridge, 1961, MA, 1964. Tchr. King Edward Sch., Aston, Birmingham, Eng., 1963-64; fellow in Turkish Sch. of Oriental and African Studies, London, 1964-67; housemaster Highgate Sch., London, 1967-91; Hungarian-English literary translator Brecon, 1991—. Transl.: Relations (Zs. Móricz), 1997, The Princess That Saw Everything, 1998, Letters from Turkey (K. Mikes), 2000, Memoirs of D.S. Likhachev, 2000, The Hungarian Hussar (J. Zachar), 2000, The Dogs of Hungary (T. Buzády), 2000. Mem. Inst. of Linguists, Royal Airforce Club. Avocations: music, literature. Home: 42 Orchard St, Brecon/Powys LD3 8AL, United Kingdom

ADAMS, CHARLES FRANCIS, advertising and real estate executive; b. Detroit, Sept. 26, 1927; s. James R. and Bertha C. (DeChant) A.; m. Helen R. Harrell, Nov. 12, 1949; children: Charles Francis, Amy Ann, James Randolph, Patricia Duncan. BA, U. Mich., 1948; postgrad., U. Calif., Berkeley, 1949. With D'Arcy-MacManus & Masius, Inc., 1947-80, exec. v.p., dir., 1970-76, pres., chief operating officer, 1976-80; pres. Adams Enterprises, 1971—; exec. v.p., dir. Washington Office, Am. Assn. Advt. Agys., 1980-84; chmn., chief exec. officer Wajim Corp., Detroit; past mem. steering com. Nat. Advt. Rev. Bd.; mem. mktg. com. U.S. Info. Agy.; pres. Internat. Visitors Ctr. of the Bay Area, 1988-89. Author: Common Sense in Advertising, 1965, Heroes of the Golden Gate, 1987, California of the Year 2000, 1992, The Magnificent Rogues, 1999. Past chmn. exec. com. Oakland U. Mem. Am. Assn. Advt. Agys. (dir., mem. govt. relations com.), Advt. Fedn. Am. (past dir.), Nat. Outdoor Advt. Bur. (past chmn.), Theta Chi, Alpha Delta Sigma (hon.). Republican. Roman Catholic. Clubs: Bloomfield Hills Country; Carmel Valley Ranch (Calif.); Nat. Golf Links Am. (Southampton, L.I.); Olympic, The Family (San Francisco). Home: 2240 Hyde St # 5 San Francisco CA 94109-1509 Office: 10 W Long Lake Rd Bloomfield Hills MI 48304-2707

ADAMS, CHARLES PAUL, communications engineer; b. Kansas City, Mo., June 20, 1955; s. Henry Robert and Corlyn Leola (Holbrook) A.; m. Lanita Jill Christy, July 14, 1979 (div. 1998); children: Allison Denise, Robert Benjamin. BA, Southwestern Okla. State U., 1978. Cert. quality auditor, Am. Soc. Quality Control. Analytical chemist Mosites Rubber Co., Ft. Worth, 1978-79, Alcon Labs., Inc., Ft. Worth, 1979-82; analytical rsch. chemist Johnson and Johnson Med., Inc., Arlington, Tex., 1982-84; lead avionics quality engr. Northup-Grumman, Inc., Dallas, 1985-91; lead quality engr. EG&G Inc. (Super Conducting Super Collider Lab.), Waxahachie, Tex., 1991-95; sr. radio frequency design engr. Nokia Networks, Inc., Irving, Tex., 1995—; v.p. Adams Mgmt. Svcs., Inc., Ft. Worth, 1980-85; radio frequency cons. Midcom, Inc., Irving, 1982—; spl. cons. NFL, N.Y.C., 1996, Dallas Cowboys Football Club for Wireless Sys., 1998. Pub. Tex. 220, 1981-83; contbr. articles to profl. jours. Tech. advisor Tarrant County Radio Amateur Civil Emergency Svc., Ft. Worth, 1978—; mem. event mgmt. team, comm. team leader Ft. Worth Main St. Arts Festival, Ft. Worth Parade of Lights, Ft. Worth Fourth of July, 1991—. Recipient Pub. Svc. award Ft. Worth Fire Dept., 1980, 82, 84, 87, 88, 89, 90, 91; cert. commendation Ft. Worth-Tarrant County Office Civil Def., 1992, 93, 98, 99. Mem. Tex. VHF-FM Soc., Inc. (life mem., frequency coord. 1982-92, pres. 1984-85, v.p. 1985-86), Radio Club Am., Phi Mu Alpha. Republican. Achievements include pending patents in the telecommunications and cellular areas. Home: 4613 Collinwood Ave Fort Worth TX 76107-4160 Office: Nokia Networks Inc 6000 Connection Dr Irving TX 75039-2600

ADAMS, CHRISTOPHER BERTLIN, neurosurgeon; b. Birkenhead, Lancashire, England, Apr. 7, 1939; s. Geoffrey Turner and Dora Eileen (Bertlin) A.; m. Sarah Isobel Holland, Jan. 12, 1957; children: Nicholas, Justin, Sam, Poppy, Henry, Belinda, George, Alex, Tom, Arabella, Matthew. Student, Cambridge (Eng.) U., 1957-61, Guys Hosp., London, 1961-66. Resident Nat. Hosp., Queens Square, London, 1967, Dept. of Neurosurgery, Oxford, Eng., 1968; sr. resident neurosurgical dept. Guys-Maudsuey Hosp., London, 1969-71; cons. neurosurgeon Radcliffe Infirmary, Oxford, 1972—. Found. scholar Pembroke Coll., Cambridge, 1957. Fellow Royal Coll. Surgeons, Green Coll. Oxford (emeritus); corr. mem. Am. Assn. Neurol. Surgeons, Soc. British Neurosurgeons. Avocations: swimming, travel, children. Home: 29 Charlbury Rd, Oxford OX2 GUU, England Office: Felstead House, 23 Banbury Rd, Oxford OX2 6NX, England

ADAMS, CORLYN HOLBROOK, nursing facility administrator; b. Beloit, Kans., Sept. 28, 1926; d. Charles Benjamin and Hazel Marian (Brokaw) Holbrook; m. Henry Robert Adams, Oct. 28, 1961; 1 child, Charles Paul. Grad., U. Kans., 1948. Lic. nursing facility adminstr. Clk. bd. edn. Beloit (Kans.) City Schs., 1945-48; adminstr. Stanford Conv. Ctrs., Fort Worth, 1973-79; adminstr., owner Four Nursing Homes, Fort Worth, 1979-84. Author, editor: The Jose Family, 1994; contbr. Pioneer Women of Faith and Fortitude, Vol. IV, 1986, Women of Faith and Fortitude, 1998. Mem. Order of Ea. Star, DAR, Nat. Soc. New England Women (sec. 1975), Nat. Hugenot Soc., Gen. Soc. Mayflower Descendents, Daus. of Utah Pioneers. Republican. Avocations: geneaology, music-playing piano.

ADAMS, DEAN (LEWIS ADAMS), theater director; b. Seattle, July 22, 1957; s. Brockman and Mary Elizabeth (Scott) A.; m. Kristin Cook Gilbert, June 20, 1981. BA in Drama and English, Tufts U., 1980; MA in TV-Film, U. Md., 1986. Stage prodn. mgr. Shakespeare and Co., Washington, 1975-79; asst. stage mgr. Arena Stage, Washington, 1976; tech. dir. St. Albans Sch., Washington, 1980-82; dir. theater Loomis Chaffee Sch., Windsor, Conn., 1982-88, Westminster Sch., Simsbury, Conn., 1989-99; artistic dir. Centennial Theater Festival, 1999—; freelance theater dir.; artistic dir. Centennial Theater Festival, Simsbury, 1989—. Dir. (U.K. tour) Dining Room, 1985; dir., producer (1st Chinese tour of Am. mus.) Once Upon a Mattress, 1987. Bd. dirs. Farmington Valley Music Found. Grantee Ford Found., 1984; scholar Tufts U., 1978-80. Mem. Internat. Brotherhood Magicians, Soc. Am. Magicians, Soc. of Stage Dirs. and Choreographers, New Eng. Presenters, Assn. of Performing Arts Presenters. Democrat. Episcopalian. Home and Office: 3211 Horseshoe Trl Tallahassee FL 32312-5064 Office: Westminster Sch 995 Hopmeadow St Simsbury CT 06070-1880

ADAMS, DEBORAH ROWLAND, lawyer; b. Princeton, N.J., July 28, 1952; d. Bernard S. and Natalie S. Adams; m. Charles L. Campbell, June 16, 1990. BA, Colo. Coll., Colorado Springs, 1974; JD, U. Colo., 1978. Bar: Ind. 1978, Colo. 1978, U.S. Dist. Ct. Colo. 1978. Atty. Legal Svcs. Orgn. Ind., Indpls., 1978-79, Pikes Peak Legal Svcs., Colorado Springs, 1979-80, Pub. Defender's Office, Colorado Springs, 1980-81; assoc. Ranson, Thomas, Cook and Livingston, Colorado Springs, 1982-84, Ranson, Thomas, Adams, Petinga and Yukawa, Colorado Springs, 1984; pvt. practice Colorado Springs, 1985—; mem. state Jud. Nominating Commn. for 4th Jud. Dist., 1994-99; Colo. State Grievance Com., 1997-98, atty. regulation com., 1999. Bd. dirs. Domestic Violence Prevention Ctr., 1980-86, pres., 1982-84; bd. dirs. Pikes Peak Legal Svcs., 1983-88, pres., 1986-87, pro bono advocacy sch. faculty, 1990-92; co-chairperson Colo. Springs Devel. Com., Colo. Women's Found., 1987, mem. grant selection com., 1988, 90; bd. dirs. Vis. Nurses Assn., 1989-91, Colo. Coll. Bus. and Cmty. Alliance Bd., 1999—, Citizens Project Bd., 1999—; bd. dirs. CASA, 1999—, Chins Up, 1991-97, pres., 1997-98; co-chairperson El Paso County sect. COLTAF Fundraising Com. for benefit of Colo. Legal Aid Found., 1991-99, chairperson, 1994-95; mem. state bd. dirs. Legal Aid Found., 1994-2000, v.p., 1997-99. Recipient Pro Bono award Pikes Peak Legal Svcs., 1988; named Atty of Yr. El Paso County Legal Secs. Assn., 1990; selected to attend First Colo. Springs Leadership Class, Colorado Springs Leadership Inst., 1997. Mem. Colo. Bar Assn. (family law sect. 1991-99, conciliation panel subcom. of profls. com. 1992, bd. govs. 1994-97, exec. com. 1995-97, nominating com. 1996), Colo. Bar Found., Colo. Women's Bar Assn., El Paso County Bar Assn. (pres.-elect 1994-95, pres. 1995-96, Trial Advocacy Sch. faculty 1990, 94, Moot Ct. judge 1992, 95, fee arbitration dispute com. 19905), Women Lawyer's Assn. Fourth Jud. Dist.(chairperson jud. nominating com. 1991-93, Portia award 1992), Zonta Club Colorado Springs (pres. 1989-90, co-chairperson dist. 12 regional conf. 1991-92, Zontian of Yr. 1990-91). Democrat. Avocations: reading, skiing, tennis, running, mountain biking. Office: 2 N Cascade Ave Ste 1010 Colorado Springs CO 80903-1629

ADAMS, DEE BRIANE, hydrologist, civil engineer; b. Provo, Utah, Feb. 6, 1942; s. Dee B. and Helen Beth (Henrichsen) A.; m. Julie Dian Herbert, June 15, 1962; children: Andrew Briane, Sarah, Aaron Thomas. Student, Snow Coll., Ephraim, Utah, 1960-61; BS cum laude, U. Utah, 1971; MS, MIT, 1974. Engr. technician Thiokol Chem. Corp., Brigham City, Utah, 1962-64; hydrologic technician water resources divsn. U.S. Geol. Survey, Salt Lake City, 1964-71, civil engr., 1971-73; hydrologist U.S. Geol. Survey, Denver, 1974-77; sr. hydrologist U.S. Geol. Survey, Grand Junction, Colo., 1977-82; chief hydrologic studies U.S. Geol. Survey, Tampa, Fla., 1982-87; dist. chief for Ala. U.S. Geol. Survey, Tuscaloosa, 1987-90; for S.E. region U.S. Geol. Survey, Atlanta, 1990—; also nat. tech. cons. U.S. Geol. Survey; com. mem. Water, Energy and Biogeochemical Budgets Global Change Rsch. program. Contbr. tech. reports and articles to profl. jours. Leader Boy Scouts Am., Colo., Fla., Ala., Ga., 19775; bd. dirs. Colo. Fed. Credit Union, Grand Junction, 1981-82, Panorama Improvement Dist., Grand Junction, 1981-82; tech. com. mem. Ala. Gov.'s Water Resources Study Commn., 1989-91; mem. So. Appalachian Man and Biosphere Coop., 1997; bd. Dirs., 1993—, chmn., 1993-96, exec. com., 1991—; gen. chmn. Applications and Mgmt. of Geog. Info. Sys. in Hydrology and Water Resources Internat. Symposium, Mobile, Ala., 1993; mem. Ga. Gov.'s RiverCare 2000 Com., 1996—; fed. co-chair water resources sector U.S. Nat. Assessment: The Potential Consequences of Climate Variability and Change, 1997—. With U.S. Army, 1966-68. U.S. Geol. Survey fellow, 1973-74; recipient Hammer award Vice-Pres. Gore, 1997. Fellow Am. Water Resources Assn. (coms. 19875, organizer, pres. Ala. sect. 1988-89, chmn. promotion com., bd. dirs. 1994-97); mem. ASCE (com. model water code 1991-96), ASTM (vice chmn., mem. com. D18.01.08 on global change 1991-95), Am. Geophys. Union, Am. Inst.

Hydrology (registered profl., pres. Fla. sect. 1986-87, conf. orgn. com. 1986), Tau Beta Pi, Chi Epsilon. Mem. LDS Ch. Avocations: outdoor sports, car building, woodworking. Home: 2272 Westridge Dr Snellville GA 30078-3169 Office: Office Regional Hydrologist Spalding Woods Ofc Pk # 160 3850 Holcomb Bridge Rd Norcross GA 30092-5223

ADAMS, DOUGLAS NOEL, writer; b. Cambridge, England, Mar. 11, 1952; s. Christopher Douglas and Janet (Donovan) A.; m. Jane Belson, 1991; 1 child, Polly Jane Rocket. BA and MA in English Lit., Cambridge (Eng.) U., 1974. Author: The Hitchhiker's Guide to the Galaxy, 1979 (Best books for Young adults list ALA 1980), The Restaurant at the End of the Universe, 1980, Life, The Universe and Everything, 1982, So Long, And Thanks for All the Fish, 1984, The Original Hitchhiker's Radio Scripts, 1985, Dirk Gently's Holistic Detective Agency, 1987, The Long Dark Tea Time of the Soul, 1988, More Than Complete Hitchhiker's Guide, 1990, (with Mark Carwardine) Last Chance to See..., 1990, Mostly Harmless, 1992, The Illustrated Hitchhiker's Guide to the Galaxy, 1994; (with John Lloyd) The Meaning of Liff, 1983, The Deeper Meaning of Liff, 1993; (with others) Not 1982: Not the Nine O'Clock News Rip Off Annual, 1981; editor (with Peter Fincham) The Utterly Utterly Merry Comic Relief Christmas Book, 1986; freelance comedy scriptwriter for BBC Radio; script editor TV series Doctor Who, 1978-80; creator, author: (CD Rom) Starship Titanic, 1998; creator n2g2.com, 1999. Office: c/o h2g2 Ltd, 11 Maiden Ln, London WC2E 7NA, England

ADAMS, FREDDY, university rector; b. Lede, Belgium, July 10, 1938; s. Achiel and Johanna (Muland) A.; m. Denise Van Den Bergh; children: Anne, Michele. Licentiate, State U. Ghent, Belgium, 1960, Doctorate, 1963. Research assoc. NFWO, Brussels, 1960-65; teaching asst. Free U. Ghent, 1965-72; prof. U. Antwerp, 1972—, rector, 1983-95; chmn. Flemish Interuniv. Council, Brussels, 1985-87; bd. dirs. Nat. Fund of Sci. Research, Brussels, 1983—. Author: Applied Gamma Ray Spectroscopy, 1971; contbr. numerous articles to profl. jours. Home: Rijvissche Park 17, B-9052 Ghent Belgium Office: U of Antwerp, B-2610 Antwerp Belgium

ADAMS, GEORGE BELL, lawyer; b. N.Y.C., Sept. 16, 1930; s. George Bell and Mary Josephine (Smith) A.; m. Lucy Elizabeth Ahearn, Sept. 10, 1952; children—Lucy S., Marea F., George B. Jr., Alison E. BA, Yale U., 1952; LLB cum laude, Harvard U., 1957. Bar: N.Y. 1957, U.S. Dist. Ct. (so. and ea. dists.) N.Y. 1965, U.S. Ct. Appeals (2d cir.) 1973. Assoc. Debevoise, Plimpton, Lyons & Gates, N.Y.C., 1957-65; ptnr. Debevoise & Plimpton, N.Y.C., 1966-97, chmn. corp. dept., 1988-93; mng. ptnr. Debevoise & Plimpton, London, 1993-96; of counsel Debevoise & Plimpton, N.Y.C., 1998—; pres. Greater N.Y. Fund, N.Y.C., 1981-84, also bd. dirs. Trustee Sarah Lawrence Coll., Bronxville, N.Y., 1977—, chmn. bd. trustees, 1987-91, vice chmn., chmn. exec. com., 1981-87; bd. dirs. United Way of N.Y.C., 1982-95; dir. Lawyers Alliance for World Security, 1989-98, mem. adv. bd., 1999—; fellow Pierpont Morgan Libr., N.Y.C., 1977—, coun. of fellows, 1983-87; mem. Yale U. Coun., 1983-90, chmn. Yale alumni publs., 1979-83; trustee Am. Trust for the Brit. Libr., 1998—; bd. dirs. New Amsterdam Singers, 1997—. 1st lt. U.S. Army, 1952-54. Fellow Davenport Coll., Yale U., 1983-90. Fellow Am. Bar Found.; mem. ABA, Assn. of Bar of City of N.Y., Internat. Bar Assn., Am. Arbitration Assn. (mem. panel arbitrators), Pilgrim Soc., Am. Assn. Internat. Com. on Jurists (dir. 1996—), Law Soc. (Eng. affiliate mem.), Cosmos Club, Racquet & Tennis Club. Office: Debevoise & Plimpton 875 3rd Ave Fl 25 New York NY 10022-6225

ADAMS, GREGORY JAMES, insurance company executive; b. Pitts., May 14, 1955; s. James Edward and Dolores (Cook) A.; m. Rosemary Stopper, May 28, 1977; children: Giselle, Brooke, Gregory II. BS, BA, Geneva Coll., 1977; student, Coll. Fin. Planning, 1993. CFP. Acct. exec. Roger Bouchard Ins., Clearwater, Fla., 1978-79; ins. agt., pres. Adams & Assocs. Ins. Inc., Palm Harbor, Fla., 1979-89; office mgr. James Adams Agy., Monroeville, Pa., 1989-91; ins. agt. State Farm, Pitts., 1991-96; pres. Greg Adams Ins. Agy., Monroeville, Pa., 1996—. Pres. Heather Highlands Civic Assn.; bd. dirs. Youth for Christ, v.p., 1988-89. Mem. Alle-Kiski Profl. Bus. Assn. (bd. mem.), Internat. Assn. Fin. Planning, Lions (past pres. 1985), Rotary. Avocations: golf, bowling, racquetball, fishing.

ADAMS, JAY WILLETTE, chemist, consultant; b. Portland, Maine, Apr. 1, 1953; adopted parent Katherine Margaret Adams. BGS, Suffolk U., 1987. Chemist Burgess Fobes Paint Co., Portland, 1972-77; lab. mgr. Dampney Co., Inc., Everett, Mass., 1978-87; tech. svc. mgr. Tego Chemie Svc. U.S.A., Hopewell, Va., 1987-93; mgr. country devel. Tego Hdqtrs., Essen, Germany, 1993—. Contbr. articles to Paint & Coatings Industry mag., Jour. Coatins Tech., Am. Paint and Coatins Jour. Mem. ASTM, Fedn. Socs. for Coatings Tech., Nat. Assn. Corrosion, Steel Structures Painting Coun. Episcopalian. Achievements include development of Thurmalox 250, numerous coatings for product finishing, corrosion-resistant and military applications. E-mail: Jay.Adams@Tego.de. Office: Goldschmidt Tego Chem Svc, Gerlingstrasse 64, Essen D-45139, Germany

ADAMS, JIMMY WAYNE, osteopath; b. Rockymount, Va., July 21, 1953; s. Mose Chitwood and Nellie June (Hall) A.; m. Mary Virginia Hunter, May 19, 1996. BA in Psychology, Roanoke Coll., Salem, Va., 1982; DO, Kirksville Coll. Osteo. Med., 1991. Diplomate Am. Bd. Osteo. Med. Examiners, Am. Acad. Pain Mgmt. Family med. intern Doctors Hosp., Columbus, Ohio, 1991-92, resident in diagnostic radiology and nuclear medicine, 1992-94; resident in phys. medicine and rehab. Med. Coll. Va., Richmond, 1994-96, attending physician episodic care unit, emergency dept., 1994-95; med. dir. Commonwealth Diagnostics and Rehab., Richmond, 1995-98; attending physician in pain mgmt. Albemarle Pain Ctr., 1996-2000; attending physician Family Practice Specialists Richmond, 1997—, Huntingting Spine Rehab. and Pain Mgmt. Ctr., Huntingtion, 2000—; mental helth therapist Roanoke Valley Psychiat. Ctr., Salem, 1982-85; clin. instr. Ohio U. Coll. Osteo. Medicine, Columbus, 1993-94. Squadron comdr. North Ctrl. Mo. Composite Squadron, CAP USAF Aux., Kirksville, Mo., 1988-90. Mem. AMA, Am. Osteo. Assn., Christian Med. and Dental Soc., Am. Osteo. Acad. Sports Medicine, Am. Acad. Phys. Medicine and Rehab., Va. Osteo. Med. Assn., Am. Acad. Pain Mgmt., Am. Pain Soc., Albemarle County Med. Soc., Am. Coll. Osteo. Family Practitioners, Med. Soc. Va., Soc. Pain Practice Mgmt., Psy Chi, Pi Gamma Mu, Iota Tau Sigma. Roman Catholic. Avocations: flying, running, hiking, canoeing, photographer. Home and Office: 1 Sheppe Dr Barboursville WV 25504-2249

ADAMS, JO-ANN MARIE, lawyer; b. L.A., May 27, 1949; d. Joseph John and Georgia S. (Wein) A. AA, Pasadena C.C., 1968; BA, Pomona Coll., 1970; MA, Calif. State U., L.A., 1971; MBA, Pacific Luth. U., 1983; JD, Santa Clara U., 1996. cert. in telecom. and info. resource mgmt. Secondary tchr. South Pasadena (Calif.) Unified Schs., 1970-71; appraiser Riverside County (Calif.) Assessor's Office, 1972-74; systems and procedures analyst Riverside County Data Processing Dept., 1974-76, supr. systems analyst, 1976-79; systems analyst computer Boeing Computer Svcs. Co., Seattle, 1979-81; sr. systems analyst Thurston County Ctrl. Svcs., Olympia, Wash., 1981-83, data processing systems mgr., 1983-84; data processing systems engr. IBM Corp., 1984-87; realtor assoc. Dower Realty, 1987-92; corp. sales rep. UniGlobe Met. Travel, 1988-89; project mr. Servco Pacific, 1989-90, Scott Software Systems, 1990-91; systems analust Dept. Atty. Gen., 1991-93; pvt. practice, 1986—; cons. in field, 1993—; law clerk HiTech Law, 1995-96, Law Offices Thomas R. Hogan, 1995; instr. Riverside City Coll., 1977-79; vis. lectr. Santa Clara U., 1997-2000. Chair legis. task force Riverside/San Bernardino chpt. NOW, 1975-76, chpt. co-chair, 1978; mem. ethics com. Calif. NOW, Inc., 1978; alt. del. Calif. Dem. Caucus, 1978. Mem. ABA, SCCBA (mem. rainbow com. 1994—, chair 1998, minority access com. 1999—, nominating com. 2000), NAFE, Pomona Coll. Alumni Assn., Santa Clara U. Alumni Assn. Home: 1200 Ranchero Way Apt 80 San Jose CA 95117-3155 Office: 19925 Stevens Creek Blvd Cupertino CA 95014-2305

ADAMS, JOSEPH BRIAN, operations research engineer, mathematics educator; b. Lancaster, Pa., Apr. 23, 1961; s. Laurence John and Ann (Onufrak) A. BS in Nuclear Engring., Pa. State U., 1983, M in Engring. Sci., 1987; M of Mech. Engring., U. Del., 1993, PhD in Ops. Rsch., 1997. Registered profl. engr., Pa. Radiol. engr. Phila. Electric Co., 1983-88; instr. math. U. Del., Newark, 1988-91; pres. J.B. Adams & Assocs., Lancaster, Pa., 1993—; adj. asst. prof. math. scis. Lebanon Valley Coll., Annville, Pa., 1997-00; lectr. math. and engring. Widener U., Chester, Pa., 1987-91; adj. prof. math., stats. and engring. Pa. State U., 1992—; lectr. in ops. rsch. U. Del., 1996; pres. J.B. Adams & Assocs., 1993—; adj. asst. prof. math. Franklin & Marshall Coll., Lancaster, Pa., 2000—. Mem. AAUP, NSPE, Math. Assn. Am., Informs, Aircraft Owners and Pilots Assn. Roman Catholic. Home and Office: 23 Ramsgate Ln Lancaster PA 17603-5975

ADAMS, KIM HASTINGS, artist, sculptor; b. Edmonton, Alta., Can., Dec. 17, 1951; s. Alvin Clarence and Harriet Maud Adams; m. Barbara Fischer, June 5, 1983. Student, U. Victoria, 1979. Works exhibited in solo and group shows in major galleries and mus. in Can., U.S. and Europe including 19th Sao Paulo Internat. Biennial, 1987, Can. Biennial Contemporary Art, Nat. Gallery Can., 1989, Skulptur Projekte 97, Münster, Germany, In Site, San Diego, 1997; represented in pvt. and pub. collections. Office: c/o Wynick-Tuck Gallery, 80 Spadina Ave, Toronto, ON Canada M5V 2J4

ADAMS, LILIANA OSSES, music performer, harpist; b. Poznan, Poland, May 16, 1939; came to U.S., 1978, naturalized, 1990; d. Sylwester and Helena (Koswenda) O.; m. Edmund Pietryk, Sept. 4, 1965 (div. Aug. 1970); m. Bruce Meredith Adams, Feb. 3, 1978. MA, Music Acad. Poznan, Poland, 1971. Prin. harpist Philharm. Orch. of Szczecin, Poland, 1964-72, Imperial Opera and Ballet Orch., Tehran, Iran, 1972-78; pvt. music tchr. Riyadh, Saudi Arabia, 1979-81; soloist Austrian Radio, 1981-86; solo harpist, pvt. tchr. harp and piano Antioch, Calif., 1986—; music cons. Schs. and Librs., Calif., 1991—. Contbr. articles to profl. jours. Mem. Am. Fedn. of Musicians, Am. Harp Soc., Music Tchrs. Assn. Calif., Internat. Soc. of Harpers, U.K. Harp Assn., Internat. Harp Ctr. (Switzerland). Fax: 925-778-0174. E-mail: harpliliana@home.com. Home: PO Box 233 Antioch CA 94509-0023

ADAMS, MAERITA ELAINE OWEN, early childhood educator; b. Asheville, N.C., Aug. 11, 1946; d. Troy Everette and Ethel Melinda (Rhodes) Owen; m. Charles Ronald Adams, Mar. 4, 1967; 1 child, Charles Ronald II. Diploma T-4 Early Childhood Edn., Valdosta State Coll., 1968, Diploma T-5 Early Childhood Edn., 1976, T-6 Specialist in Early Childhood Edn., 1980. Cert. mid. sch. tchr. Tchr. Lowndes County Sch. System, 1969-71, S.E. Elem. Sch., 1971-73, South St. Kindergarten, 1973-78, W.G. Nunn Elem., Valdosta, Ga., 1978-93, J.L. Newbern Mid. Sch., 1993-00; ret., 2000; edn. fair chmn. W.G. Nunn Elem., 1989-91. Poll worker Charles Hatcher Campaign, Valdosta, 1988. Mem. Ga. Assn. Educators, NEA, Valdosta Assn. Educators (legis. chmn. 1989-91), Internat. Reading Assn., Phi Delta Kappa (historian 1989-91). Republican. Baptist. Avocations: reading, stitchery, travel, plants. Office: JL Newbern Mid Sch 2015 E Park Ave Valdosta GA 31602-4418

ADAMS, MARTIN DAVID, robotics research scientist, educator; b. Swindon, Wiltshire, Eng., Dec. 10, 1966; arrived in Switzerland, 1992; s. Norman and Marlene (Kallenbach) A. BA in Engring. Sci., U. Oxford, 1988, PhD of Engring. Sci., 1992. Rsch. scientist Alcan R&D Labs., Banbury, U.K., 1986-87; rsch. assoc., lectr. ETH Zurich, Switzerland, 1992-96; rsch. scientist ESEC, Cham, Switzerland, 1996—; asst. prof. NTU, Singapore, 2000—; prof. Neu Tech. Buchs, Switzerland, 1994-95; tutor U. Oxford, U.K., 1988-92; guest prof. ocean engring. Fla. Atlantic U. Author: Sensor Design, Modelling and Data Processing for Autonomous Navigation, 1999; inventor in field; contbr. articles to profl. jours. Grantee SERC, 1988, Sasakawa Found., 1991, Fellowship Engring., 1989-90. Mem. IEEE (reviewer jour.), Profl. Assn. Diving Instrs. Conservative. Baptist. Avocations: scuba diving, underwater photography, skiing, cycling, travel. Home: Neuhofstrasse 30, CH-8708 Maennedorf Switzerland Office: Nanyang Technol U, Sch Elec & Electronic Engrn, Singapore Singapore

ADAMS, MICHAEL FRED, university president, political communications specialist; b. Montgomery, Ala., Mar. 25, 1948; s. Hubert W. and Jean (Taylor) A.; m. Mary Lynn Ethridge, June 7, 1969; children: David Winston, Stephen Taylor. BA, Lipscomb U., 1970; MA, Ohio State U., 1971, PhD, 1973. Asst. prof. Ohio State U., 1973-74; chief of staff for Sen. Howard Baker, Washington, 1975-79; advisor to gov. State of Tenn., Nashville, 1981-82; v.p. Pepperdine U., Malibu, Calif., 1982-88; pres. Centre Coll. Ky., Danville, 1988-97, U. Ga., Athens, 1997—; chmn. Nat. Assn. Ind. Colls. and Univs., 1995-96; bd. dirs. Ky. Ctr. Pub. Issues, Assoc. Colls. of South; mem. coun. for advancement and support of edn. NCAA Pres. Commn., 1992-94; chmn. Commn. on Colls. of So. Assn. Colls. and Schs.; vice chmn. task force that founded Coun. for Higher Edn. Accreditation; bd. dirs. Am. Coun. on Edn. Author: Rhetorical Strategies of Howard Baker, 1973; contbr. articles to various publs. Pres. Circle K Internat., Chgo., 1970; nominee for U.S. Congress, Nashville, 1980; mem. site host com. 1984 Olympiad, L.A.; elder Christian Ch. Recipient Bronze Quill award Internat. Assn. Bus. Communicators, 1986, Excellence award Nat. Sch. Pub. Relations Soc., 1985; Ohio State U. grad. fellow, 1970-73. Mem. Young Pres. Orgn., Speech Comm. Assn., Ctr. for Study of Presidency, Univ. Club (N.Y.C.). Republican. Avocations: golf, reading, travel. Office: U Ga Lustrat House Athens GA 30602

ADAMS, MICHAEL JOHN, air force non-commissioned officer; b. Buffalo, May 20, 1958; s. Raymond Francis and Ruth Margaret A.; m. Heidi Luise Gehling, June 5, 1998. AS in Bus. Adminstrn., Onondaga C.C., Syracuse, N.Y., 1980; AS in Comm. Ops. Tech., Community Coll. of the Air Force, 1983. Enlisted USAF, 1981, advanced through grades to tech. sgt., 1996; operator giant talk radio ops. 2006th Communications Group, SAC, Incirlik Air Base, Turkey, 1982-83; frequency mgr. combat crew communications 2019th Communications Squadron, Griffiss AFB, N.Y., 1983-85; frequency mgr. info. network USAF in Europe, Comiso Air Sta., Sicily, Italy, 1985-86; supr. mil. affiliate radio system 2045th Communications Group, Andrews AFB, Md., 1986-87, supr. ops. satellite communications, 1987-89; unit tng. mgr. 2045th Communications Group, 1989-91; sr. operator Global Command and Control Sta., 1956th Communications Group, Yokota Air Base, Japan, 1991-93; mgr. unit tng. 374th Comm. Squadron (PACAF), Yokota AFB, Japan, 1993-95; unit tng. mgr. 374th Maintenance Squadron, Yokota AFB, Japan, 1995-96; noncommd. officer-in-charge tng. systems mgmt., distance lng., civilian pers. tng. 3d Comm. Squadron, Elmendorf AFB, Alaska, 1996-99, interactive video teletng. coord., 1998-99; chief tng. systems mgmt. and Air Force testing proctor 31st Spl. Ops. Squadron,, OSAN AB, Korea, 1999—. Vol. local food bank. Mem. VFW, Am. Soc. Tng. and Devel., U.S. Distance Learning Assn., Air Force Sgts. Assn., Assn. for Quality and Participation, Internat. Pers. Mgmt. Assn., Am. Legion. Republican. Lutheran. Avocations: computers, fishing, hunting.

ADAMS, MICHAEL KEITH, military officer; b. Trappe, Md., Aug. 7, 1948; s. Maurice Tarbutton and Erva Harrison Adams; m. Rebecca J. BA, Salisbury State U., 1975; MS, U. Md., 1982. Registered environ. profl. Nat. Registry of Environ. Profls. Environ. project mgr. Md. Environ. Svc., Annapolis, 1983-84; environ. engr. David Taylor R&D, Annapolis, 1984-90; commd. 2d lt. U.S. Army, 1970, advanced through grades to col., 1997; environ. officer Office Chief Army Res., Washington, 1990-95; environ. divsn. chief U.S. Army Res. Command, Atlanta, 1995-97; dep. asst. commandant U.S. Army Engr. Ctr., Ft. Leonard Wood, Mo., 1997-99; asst. chief of staff Maneuver Support Ctr.-AR, Ft. Leonard Wood, 1999—; adj. faculty mem. Park Coll., Ft. Leonard Wood, 1998. Mem. Am. Def. Preparedness Assn., Army Engr. Assn. (named to Hall of Fame 1998), Beta Beta Beta. Achievements include patent for low flow fluid separator. Avocations: hiking, camping, water skiing, skeet shooting. Home: PO Box 747 Fort Leonard Wood MO 65473-0747

ADAMS, NORMAN, artist, educator; b. London, Feb. 9, 1927; s. Albert Henry Adams and Winifred Elizabeth Rose; m. Anna Teresa Butt, 1947; two children. Student, Royal Coll. Art, London, 1948-51. Tchr. St. Albans, Maidstone, Hammersmith Art Schs., 1952-61; head painting Manchester Coll. Art and Design, England, 1962-71; prof. fine art U. Newcastle Upon Tyne, 1981-86; keeper of arts Royal Acad. Arts, London, 1986-95, prof. painting, 1986-99, prof. emeritus, 1999—. Public collections include Tate Gallery, London, Scottish Nat. Gallery Modern Art, Edinburgh, Ulster Mus., Belfast, Ireland, Nat. Gallery New Zealand, Wellington, St. Mary's Roman Cath. Ch., Manchester, 1995; illustrator: (written by Glyn Hughes) Alibis and Convictions (Glyn Hughes), 1978, A Decade of Painting, 1971-81, 1981, (written by A. Adams) Angels of Soho, 1988, Island Chapters, 1991, Life on Limestone, 1994. Avocations: art, music, literature. Home: Butts Horton-in-Ribblesdale, Settle N, Yorkshire BD24 0HD, England Office: 6 Gainsborough Rd, Chiswick W4 INJ, England

ADAMS, PETER GORDON, solicitor; b. Twickenham, England, Dec. 11, 1946; s. George and Marjorie (Gordon) A.; m. Alice Elizabeth Cromie, June 2, 1979; children: Charles, Henry. Student, Wellington Coll. Articled clk. Warmingtons & Hasties, England, 1965-70; asst. silicitor Gregory Rowcliffe & Co., England, 1971-72; legal adviser Cleveland Petroleum Co., England, 1972-75; asst. gen. counsel Esso Petroleum Co., England, 1975-91; head legal svcs. AGAS Ltd., England, 1991-2000; head law and regulation Total Fina Elf Gas & Power U.K. Ltd., 2000—. Mem. Law Soc. Home: 5 Osten News, London SW7 4HW, England Office: 33 Cavendish Square, London England

ADAMS, PETER WILLIAM, diabetologist, endocrinologist, physician; b. London, Sept. 22, 1937; s. Walter and Tatiana (Makarova) A.; divorced; children: Elena, Anna, Paul; married; children: Nicholas, Marianna. MB BChir, U. Cambridge, Eng., 1961, MA, 1962. House surgeon dept. thoracic surgery London Hosp., 1961-62, house physician pediatrics, 1962; house physician gen. medicine Bedford (Eng.) Gen. Hosp., 1962-63; house surgeon ob-gyn. Cuckfield (Sussex, Eng.) Hosp., 1963, sr. house officer gen. medicine, 1963-64; resident med. officer pediatrics Royal Alexandra Hosp. for Sick Children, Brighton, Sussex, 1964-66; registrar gen. medicine Prospect Park Hosp., Reading, Berks, Eng., 1966-69; lectr. metabolic unit St. Mary's Hosp., London, 1969-79; cons. physician Ashford (Middlesex, Eng.) Hosp., 1979—; pvt. practice London, 1979—; clin. dir. dept. medicine Ashford (Middlesex, Eng.) Hosp., 1992—. Contbr. rsch. articles to med. jours. Fellow Royal Coll. Physicians; mem. Royal Coll. Obstretricians (diploma), Royal Coll. Surgeons (diploma child health), Royal Soc. Medicine, Brit. Med. Assn. (powar 1986—), Internat. Diabetic Fedn., Brit. Diabetic Assn. (mem. sci. sect.). Russian Orthodox. Avocations: water sports, traveling, painting, gardening, steam engines. Home: 25 Castelnau, London SW13 9RP, England Office: Pvt Cons Rms, 44 Wimpole St, London WIM 7DG, England

ADAMS, RICHARD GEORGE, writer; b. Newbury, Berkshire, Eng., May 9, 1920; s. Evelyn George Beadon and Lilian Rosa (Button); m. Elizabeth Acland, Sept. 26, 1949; children: Juliet Vera Lucy, Rosamond Beatrice Elizabeth. M.A., Oxford U., 1948. With Brit. Home Higher Civil Svc. Ministry Housing and Local Govt., 1948-74; asst. sec. Dept. Environ., 1968-74; writer-in-residence U. Fla., 1975, Hollins Coll., 1976. Author: Watership Down, 1972 (Guardian award Children's Lit. 1972, Carnegie Medal 1972), Shardik, 1974, (with Max Hooper) Nature Through the Seasons, 1975, The Tyger Voyage, 1976, The Adventures and Brave Deeds of the Ship's Cat on the Spanish Main: Together with the Most Lamentable Losse of the Alcestis and Triumphant Firing of the Port of Chagres, 1977, The Plague Dogs, 1977, (with Max Hooper) Nature Day and Night, 1978, Introduction to Faithful Ruslan, 1979, The Unbroken Web: Stories and Fables, 1980, Voyage Through the Antarctic, 1982, The Girl in a Swing, 1980, Maia, 1985, The Bureaucats, 1985, A Nature Diary, 1985, The Legend of Te Tuna, 1986, Traveller, 1988, The Day Gone By, 1990, Tales from Watership Down, 1996, The Outlandish Knight, 2000; editor, contbr. Occasional Poets, 1986. Served with Brit. Army, 1940-46. Fellow Royal Soc. Lit., Royal Soc. Arts; mem. Royal Soc. for Prevention of Cruelty to Animals (former pres.). Mem. Ch. of Eng. Home: 26 Church St, Whitchurch Hampshire, England

ADAMS, ROBERT DAVID, mechanical engineering educator, consultant; b. Stoke-on-Trent, U.K., Apr. 13, 1940; s. William Peter and Marion Adams; m. Susan Waite, Sept. 26, 1963; children: Rosemary Frances, Jocelyn William. BS in Engring., London U., 1962; PhD, St. John's Coll., Cambridge, Eng., 1967; DSc in Engring., London U., 1986. Rsch. fellow Inst. Sound and Vibration Rsch. Southampton U., U.K., 1966-67; lectr. U. Bristol, U.K., 1967-73, reader, 1973-86, prof., 1986—, head dept. mech. engring., 1994-98, dean grad. studies, 1998—; Franqui professorship Vrieje U., Brussels, 1991. Author: Structural Adhesive Joints in Engineering, 1984, 2d edit., 1986; co-author: Structural Adhesive Joints in Engineering, 1997; editor-in-chief Internat. Jour. Adhesion and Adhesives; 12 patents in field; contbr. over 250 articles to confs. and profl. jours. Mem. Rotary Club Clifton (Bristol, pres. 1999-2000). Avocations: wine, gardening, travel. Office: Univ Bristol, Dept Mech Engring, Bristol BS8 1TR, United Kingdom

ADAMS, ROBERT EDWARD, journalist; b. Geneseo, Ill., Apr. 27, 1941; s. Horace Mann and Florence (Beidelman) A. BS, U. Ill., 1963. Reporter Champaign-Urbana Courier, 1962-64; reporter, city staff St. Louis Post-Dispatch, 1966-72, Washington corr., 1972-93, asst. Washington bur. chief, 1981-83, Washington bur. chief, 1983-93; Washington commentator Sta. KMOX, St. Louis, 1984—; founding mem. St. Louis Journalism Rev., 1970. Recipient reporting award Nat. Civil Service League, 1975, polit. reporting award Lincoln U., Jefferson City, Mo., 1984, Raymond Clapper Meml. award for Washington Corr., 1987, citation for excellence Overseas Press Club, for series on Soviet Union, 1988; co-recipient Fgn. Corr. award Overseas Press Club Am., 1984, Nat. Headliner award, 1986. Mem. Nat. Press Club, Internat. Platform Assn., Com. to Protect Journalists, Washington Ind. Writers, The Gridiron Club, Sigma Delta Chi (Outstanding Young Reporter award St. Louis chpt. 1969). Roman Catholic. Home: 2500 Wisconsin Ave NW Washington DC 20007-4504 Office: 529 14th St NW Washington DC 20045-1000

ADAMS, ROBERT MCCORMICK, anthropologist, educator; b. Chgo., July 23, 1926; s. Robert McCormick and Janet (Lawrence) A.; m. Ruth Salzman Skinner, July 24, 1953; 1 dau., Megan. PhB, U. Chgo., 1947, MA, 1952, PhD, 1956; DSc (hon.), U. Pitts., 1985, Dartmouth Coll., 1989; LHD (hon.), Hunter Coll., CUNY, 1986, Coll. William and Mary, 1989, Brandeis U., 1992; LD (hon.), Harvard U., 1992. Archaeol. field tng. in Jarmo, Iraq, 1950-51, Yucatan, Mex., 1953; field studies history irrigation and urban settlement Iraq, Saudi Arabia and Iran, 1956-77; reconnaissance and excavation ancient Mayan settlement patterns Chiapas, Mex., 1958-61; mem. faculty dept. anthropology Oriental Inst. U. Chgo., 1955-84, assoc. prof. Oriental Inst., 1961-62, prof., 1962-84, dir. Oriental Inst., 1962-68, 81-83, dean div. social scis., 1970-74, 79-80, provost, 1982-84; sec. Smithsonian Instn., Washington, 1984-94; Homewood prof. dept. anthropology and near ea. studies Johns Hopkins U., 1984-94; adj. prof. U. Calif., San Diego, 1993—; fellow Inst. for Advanced Study, Berlin, 1995-96; resident dir. Baghdad Sch., Am. Schs. Oriental Rsch., 1968-69; chmn. assembly behavioral and social scis. NRC, 1972-76, chmn. commn. on behavioral and social scis. and edn., 1987-93. Author: Land Behind Baghdad, 1965, The Evolution of Urban Society, 1966, (with H.J. Nissen) The Uruk Countryside, 1972, Heartland of Cities, 1981, Paths of Fire: An Anthropologist's Inquiry into Western Technology, 1996; editor: (with C. H. Kraeling) City Invincible: A Symposium on Urbanization and Cultural Development in the Ancient Near East, 1960, (with C.S. Schelling) Corners of a Foreign Field, 1979, (with N.J. Smelser and D.J. Treiman) Behavioral and Social Science Research: A National Resource, 1982. Trustee Nat. Opinion Ctr., 1970-94, Nat. Humanities Ctr., 1976-83, Russell Sage Found., 1978-91, Santa Fe Inst., 1984—, Am. U. Beirut, 1989-94, Morehouse Coll, 1989-94, German Am. Acad. Coun., 1993-99. Recipient medal UCLA, 1989, Great Cross of Vasco Núñe de Balboa, Panama, 1993. Fellow AAAS, Am. Anthrop. Assn., Am. Acad. Arts and Scis., Mid. East Studies Assn., Iraqi Acad. (assoc.); mem. NAS, Soc. Am. Archaeology (Disting. Svc. award 1996), German Archaeol. Inst., Am. Philos. Soc., Coun. Fgn. Rels., Sigma Xi.

ADAMS, RONALD G., middle school educator; b. Boston, July 7, 1948; s. Russell Lawrence and Alice Gertrude (LeCorn) A.; m. Patricia Marie Sullivan, Mar. 15, 1950; children: Ronald Patrick, Michael Joseph, Kevin Russell. BS, U. Mass., 1975; MEd, Cambridge Coll., 1992. Cert. tchr. English, reading, adult basic edn., Mass. Tchr. English Quincy (Mass.) Pub. Sch., 1975-81, tchr. grade 7, 1983—; tchr. grade 7/8 Lincoln (Mass.) Pub. Schs., 1981-83; mem. adv. bd. Mass. Carnegie Coun.: Turning Points, Dept. Edn., Mass., 1991-93; founding mem. Internat. Space Educators Coun., Huntsville, Ala., 1992-93. Prodr. TV documentary Quincy Shipbuilding, 1989 (award Dept. Edn. 1990); co-author: (booklet) Not Me, I Can Handle It, 1985 (Gov.'s award 1986); cons. TV series A Century of Women, TBS, 1994 (A&E Cable award 1992). Founder Winnie the Welder Day, City of Quincy, 1991-93; coach Houghs Neck Women's Softball League, Quincy, 1980-85; vol. Cub Scouts, Weymouth, Mass., 1989-93; mem. edn. steering com. Amnesty Internat., Somerville, Mass., 1989-93; mem. adv. bd. U.S. Naval Shipbldg. Mus., Quincy, 1992-93. Recipient Nat. Edni. award Cable in

Classroom, 1992, George Washington medal Freedoms Found., 1992, Young Prodr.'s award Continental Cablevision, 1992, A World of Difference Tchr. award Anti-Defamation League, 1994, Giraffe award, Reebok Internat. Youth-in-Action Human Rights award, 1995, Minn. Advocates for Human Rights award, 1997, Domestic Partnership award US AID, 1998, Anti-defamation League's Global Activism award 1998, 99, Darryl Williams Human Rights Leadership award Northeastern U., 1999, Bearer of Light award Union of Am. Hebrew Congregations, 1999, Global Edn. award The Peace Corps, 2000; named Tchr. of Yr., Mass. Dept. Edn., 1992, Nat. Consumers League Trumpeter award, 1998, Citizen of the Yr. 2000, Quincy Sun Newspaper. Fellow Mass. Acad. Tchrs. (history coord. 1992-93), Boston Writing Project; mem. NEA (Human and Civil Rights award 2000Applegate/Dorros Peace and Global Edn. award 2000), Nat. State Tchrs. of Yr., Nat. Coun. Social Studies, Nat. Coun. Tchrs. English, Mass. Tchrs. Assn. (Human Rights award 1991), Quincy Edn. Assn. (exec. bd. 1980-81). Avocation: N.Y. Giants football. Home: 8 Coolidge Ave Weymouth MA 02188-3605 Office: Broad Meadows Middle Sch 50 Calvin Rd Quincy MA 02169-2516

ADAMS, THOMAS TILLEY, lawyer; b. Orchard Park, N.Y., Oct. 9, 1929; s. Floyd Tilley and Clara Elizabeth (Potter) A.; m. Virginia Rives Smith, Sept. 1, 1956; children: Julia, Janet, Claire, Douglas. BA, U. Buffalo, 1951; JD, Cornell U., 1957. Bar: N.Y. 1957, U.S. Ct. Appeals (2d cir.) 1962, U.S. Supreme Ct. 1962, Conn. 1964. Tchr. Lake Shore Cen. Sch., Angola, N.Y., 1953-54; assoc. Davies, Hardy & Schenck, N.Y.C., 1957-63; prin. Gregory & Adams P.C., Wilton, Conn. and N.Y.C., 1963—; lectr. Cornell U. Law Sch., Ithaca, N.Y., 1962-65, emeritus mem. adv. coun., 1990—; adj. assoc. prof. law Fordham U., N.Y.C., 1973-76; adviser Dana Fund Internat. and Comparative Legal Studies, Toledo, 1976-91; assoc. bd. dirs. Union Trust Co., Stamford, Conn., 1982-94; mem. adv. bd. Norwalk Savs. Soc., 1993-97. Town counsel Town of Wilton, 1966-71; pres. Five Town Found., Norwalk, Conn., 1983-85, trustee, 1989-91; chmn. bldg. com. Wilton High Sch., 1966; bd. dirs. Woodcock Nature Ctr., Wilton-Ridgefield, Conn., 1997-99, trustee Wilton Library Assn., Inc., 2000—, Norwalk Hosp., 1974. Recipient Silver Beaver award Boy Scouts Am., 1980, Disting. Alumnus award Cornell Law Sch., 1990. Mem. ABA, Am. Judicature Soc. (dir. 1991-92), Norwalk/Wilton Bar Assn. (pres. 1990), Stamford/Norwalk Regional Bar Assn. (bd. dirs. 1991-93), Conn. Bar Assn. (ethics com. 1970-75, 92-93, mem. coun. bar pres.'s 1988-90), N.Y. Bar Assn., Silver Spring Country Club (gov. 1998—), Cornell Club (N.Y.), Phi Delta Phi. Episcopalian. Fax: 203-834-1628. Home: 55 Deer Run Rd Wilton CT 06897-1204 also: Rogers Rock Clb Ticonderoga NY 12883 Office: Gregory & Adams PC 190 Old Ridgefield Rd Wilton CT 06897-4023

ADAMS, TRACEY LINDEN, artist, educator; b. L.A., Nov. 2, 1954; d. Edwin Robert and Berna Berry Linden; m. John Stockton Adams, June 25, 1983. BA, Mt. St. Mary's Coll., 1978; MusM, New Eng. Conservatory, Boston, 1980. One-woman shows include U. Calif., Santa Cruz, 1995, Monterey (Calif.) Peninsula Coll., 1996, Winfield Gallery, Carmel, Calif., 1998, Andrea Schwartz Gallery, San Francisco, 1999, Kathryn Markel Fine Arts, N.Y.C., 2000; exhibited in group shows Winfield Gallery, Carmel, 1994, 95, 96, 97, 98, 99, Monterey Peninsula Coll., 1993, 94, Pacific Grove (Calif.) Art Ctr., 1994, Marjorie Evans Gallery, Carmel, 1994, Carl Cherry Center for Arts, Carmel, 1995, 98, Valdosta (Ga.) U., 1995, Miriam Perlman Gallery, Chgo., 1995, Brand Art Gallery, Glendale, Calif., 1995, Andrea Schwartz Gallery, San Francisco, 1995, Monterey Mus. Art, 1995, 96, 97, 98, 99, Calif. State U., Chico, 1995, Cabrillo Coll., Aptos, Calif., 1996, Pope Gallery, Santa Cruz, Calif., 1996, The Print Ctr., Phila., 1996, L.A. County Mus. Rental and Sales Gallery, 1996, Olga Dollar Gallery, San Francisco, 1996, 97, Nancy Solomon Gallery, Atlanta, 1996, Artspace II, Birmingham, Mich., 1997, Mt. St. Mary's Coll., 1998, Solomon Projects, Atlanta, 1998, 99, Finer Things Gallery, Nashville, 1999, Locus Gallery, St. Louis, 1999, 2000, Kathryn Markel Fine Arts, N.Y.C., 1999, 2000, Hunter Mus. Am. Art, Chatanooga, 2000; represented in permanent collections Adobe Systems, AFL-CIO Housing Investment Trust, Alza Pharms., BEA Systems, Beverly Hills Pub. Libr., Broadvision, Canon Systems Globalization, Canon, Inc., Caribe Hilton, The Chubb Group, Clarify, Inc., Fidelity Investments, Ford Motor Co., Four Seasons Hotel, Fujitsu, Galaxi, GE Corp., Hambrecht and Quist, Hilton Hotel, Kaiser-Permanente Hosp., Macy's, Manatt, Monterey Mus. Art, Phelps and Phillips, Marcus and Millichap, Marriott Associa, Marshall Fields, MGM Grand Hotel and others. Mem. L.A. Printmaking Soc. Avocations: tennis, gardening. E-mail: adams@montereybay.com. Home: PO Box 223093 Carmel CA 93922-3093

ADAMS, TUCKER HART, economic research company executive; b. Prescott, Ark., Jan. 11, 1938; d. Hugh Ross and Mildred (Dunn) Hart; m. Daniel Williams Adams, Sept. 6, 1957; children: Virginia Schoenthaler, Carolyn, Catherine Adams-Gravley, Anne Green. BA in Math., Wellesley Coll., 1959; MA in Econs., U. Colo., 1977, PhD in Econs., 1979. V.p., chief economist United Banks of Colo., Denver, 1978-88; pres., chief exec. officer The Adams Group, Inc., Colorado Springs, Colo., 1988—; pres. Am. Russian Collaborative Enterprises, LLC, 1994—; bd. dirs. Mortgage Analysis Corp., Mont. Power Co., Ag Am., Tax Free Fund Colo., Rocky Mountain Equity Fund. Bd. dirs. Colo. Health Facilities Authority, Denver, Denver Found., U. Colo. Found., Boulder. Pendleton scholar Wellesley Coll., 1955; grad. fellowship U. Colo., 1977. Mem. Colo. Womens Forum (pres. 1988), Internat. Womens Forum. Republican. Presbyterian. Avocations: adventure travel, gardening, needlework, grandchildren. Office: The Adams Group Inc 4822 Alteza Dr Ste 300 Colorado Springs CO 80917-4002

ADAMS, WARREN LYNN, publisher, business consultant; b. Clarksville, Ark., Jan. 11, 1955; s. Warren Earnest Adams and Doris Anita (Reed) Crandall; m. Pamela Jo Sullivan, Sept. 9, 1978 (div. 1995); children: Lindsay Nichelle, London Reed; m. Brenda Kay Pettigrew, Feb. 3, 1996; children: Kristin Lea Haney, Phillip Kollin Haney, Kasey Kay Haney. BA, U. Ctrl. Okla., 1978, BS, 1994; MBA, Oklahoma City U., 1996. Dir. pub. rels. Oklahoma City Zoo, 1979-80; dir. sports info. Oklahoma City U., 1980-82; chief operating officer Fite-Davis & Assocs., Oklahoma City, 1982-84; pres., CEO Lynn Adams & Assocs., Oklahoma City, 1984-88; pub. rels. technician Runkle-Moroch Advertising, Oklahoma City, 1988-89; chief operating officer Jim Fite Mktg. and Mgmt. Resources, Edmond, Okla., 1989-92; administrator Okla. Ctr. for Alcohol and Drug-Related Studies, Oklahoma City, 1992—; publ. cons. 1st Bapt. Ch., Oklahoma City, 1984-95; bus. cons. Adams Assocs., Ninnekah, Okla., 1995—; pub., bus. mgr. Real Estate Exec. Mag., Chickasha, Okla., 1996-99, Builder/Architect Mag., Chickasha, 1996-99. Contbr. articles to profl. jours. Master mason Ancient, Free & Accepted Masons, Oklahoma City, 1981—; 32 Mason Okla. Scottish Rite, Guthrie, 1982—; recreation coord. First Baptist Ch., 1984-95; sec., bd. deacons 1988-90. Named Gov.'s Non-Profit Corp. of Yr., Okla. Fedn. of Parents for Drug-Free Youth, Oklahoma City, 1994. Mem. Outstanding Young Men of Am. (named Outstanding Young Men of Am. 1987, 88, 89, 92; mem. nat. nom. com.), U. Okla. Health Scis. Ctr. (OUHSC) Staff Senate. Democrat. Mem. Christian. Ch. (Disciples of Christ). Avocations: antiques, science fiction, travel, lighthouses, covered bridges. Home: RR 2 Box 6 Ninnekah OK 73067-9504 Office: Okla Ctr for Alcohol & Drug-Related Studies 800 NE 15th St Ste 410 Oklahoma City OK 73104-4602

ADAMSKI, PETER J., automotive executive. BA, Rutgers U., 1976; MBA, Rutgers U., Newark, 1977. CPA. Auditor Arthur Andersen, Newark, 1977-79; divsn. controller Johnson & Johnson, New Brunswick, N.J., 1979-95; dir. corp. bus. devel. Baush & Lomb, Rochester, N.Y., 1995-98; v.p. fin., CFO Hahn Automotive, Rochester, 1998—. Mem. AICPA, Inst. Mgmt. Accts., N.J. Soc. CPAs (trustee 1991-92). Office: Hahn Automotive Warehouse Inc 415 W Main St Rochester NY 14608-1944

ADAMSON, JOYCE ROBERTS, physician; b. Bklyn., Jan. 14, 1945; d. Robert B. and Muriel (Aust) R.; m. David R. Adamson, June 5, 1966; children: Glenn Douglas, Peter Scott. BA, Brandeis U., 1965; MD, Boston U., 1969. Diplomate Am. Bd. Internal Medicine. Pvt. practice, 1978—; chair dept. medicine Winchester (Mass.) Hosp., 1992-98; mem. profl. adv. com. Middlesex East VNA. Mem. Bd. Health, Stoneham, Mass., 1975-78. Democrat. Mem. Unitarian-Universalist Ch. Office: 61 Main St Stoneham MA 02180-3364

ADAMSON, MICHAEL ROBERT, business consultant; b. Kenosha, Wis., Sept. 20, 1962; s. James Cantwell and Rita Marie Adamson; m. Carol Janice Adamson, June 6, 1992; children: Rachel Lynn, Samuel James. BBA, U. Wis., Milw., 1984; MBA, Ariz. State U., 1986; MA, U. Calif., Santa Barbara, 1996, PhD, 2000. Sr. Andersen Cons., Phoenix, 1986-89; sr. assoc. Coopers & Lybrand, San Francisco, 1989-90; bus. application cons. Synon, Inc., Larkspur, Calif., 1990-94; ind. cons., 1994—. Author govt. publs.; contbr. article to profl. jours. Humane studies fellow Inst. for Humane Studies, 1998-99, Econ. History Rsch. fellow All-U. Calif. Econ. History Group, 1998, grad. fellow U. Calif., Santa Barbara, 1999. Mem. Hist. Assn., Soc. for Historians of Am. Fgn. Rels., Am. Hist. Assn. Libertarian. Avocations: soccer and golf, running, reading, mountain biking, travel. E-mail: caroladamson@compuserv.com.

ADAMU, YUSUF MUHAMMAD, geography educator, writer; b. Katsina, Nigeria, Mar. 9, 1968; s. Muhammad Nata'ala Adamu and Gambo Sambo Muhammad; m. Amina Isma'il Yusuf, Nov 11, 1991; children: Khadijah, Muhammad, Abdurrashid. BSc in Geography, Usmanu Danfodio U., Sokoto, Nigeria, 1990; MSc in Geography, U. Ibadan, Nigeria, 1994; PhD in Geography, Bayero U., Kano, Nigeria, 2001. Cert. med. geographer. Asst. lectr. geography Bayero U., 1995-97, lectr., 1997—, admissions officer dept. geography, 1998—; assoc. cons. Inter-Tropical Cons., Kano, Nigeria, 1998—; survey coord. Ctr. for Gender Studies, Ife, Nigeria, 1996-97; chmn. Kano Resource Ctr., 1999—; hon. vis. fellow Ctr. for African and Asian Studies, U. Sussex. Author: Idan So Cuta Ne, 1989, Dukan Ruwa, 1990 (Kaduna Arts Coun. award 1990), Butterfly and Other Poems, 1995; co-editor: Study on Inequality in Nigeria, 2000. Chmn. Ilmi Trust Fund, Kano, 1997—. Hon. vis. rsch. fellow U. Sussex, Eng., 1998. Mem. Nigerian Geog. Assn., Assn. Nigerian Authors, Social Sci. Acad. Nigeria. Islam. Avocation: photography. Office: Dept Geography PMB 3011, Bayero U, Kano Kano, Nigeria

ADAN, ANA, psychophysiology educator; b. Barcelona, Spain, Dec. 14, 1962; d. Juan Antonio Adan and Magdalena Puig; m. Albert Lluch, Sept. 10, 1983; 1 child, Albert. Grad. in Edn., Specialty Scis., U. Barcelona, Spain, 1983; Grad. in Psychology, U. Barcelona, 1988, PhD in Psychology, 1994; Grad. Catalan Lang., U. Autonoma of Barcelona, 1984. Grad. fellow Spanish Ministry of Sci. and Edn., 1989-92. Author: (books) Els Fossils A L'escola, 1986, Seguridad y Tolerancia En El Uso de Aines en Reumatologia, 1996, Resultados del Estudio de Farmaco/vigilancia de Citalopram en el tratamiento de Espisodios Depresivos, 1998, Resultados del estudio de farmaco/vigilancia de Mirtazapina en el tramamiento de episodios depresivos, 1999, others; contbg. author 10 books in field; contbr. numerous articles to profl. jours. and publs. Recipient 1st award of 7th competition on reports about psychology divulgation, Psychology Coll. of Catalonia, Barcelona, 1996, 2d award Psychology Coll. Catalonia, 1999. Mem. Internat. Soc. for Chronobiology, Spanish Soc. for Psychophysiology, Colegio Oficial de Psicologos. Avocations: psychobiology, chronobiology, addictive behavior. Fax: 34 93 402 15 84. E-mail: aadan@psi.ub.es. Home: Marques de Sentmenat 70 5-2, 08029 Barcelona Spain Office: Dep Psiquiatria/U Barcelona, Passeig Vall D'Hebron 171, 08035 Barcelona Spain

ADANIYA, KEVIN SEISHO, lawyer; b. San Francisco, Sept. 24, 1968; s. Roy Seijin and Lavern Gay Adaniya. BA in Polit. Sci., U. Calif., Santa Barbara, 1990; JD, U. of the Pacific, Sacramento, 1995. Bar: Hawaii 1996, U.S. Dist. Ct. Hawaii 1997. Law clk. State of Hawaii, Hilo, 1995-96; sole practitioner Honolulu, 1996—; mem. faculty Inst. for Paralegal Edn., 1999; facilitator, recorder Ohana Conferencing, 1999—. Co-author: Paralegals in Family Law Practice, 1999. Vol., Kids First Program, Honolulu, 1998—, Vol. guardian Ad Litem Program, Honolulu, 1998—; atty. mem. AmeriCorps/Students and Advs. for Victims of Domestic Violence, 1996-97, 98-99. Recipient cert. of spl. commendation Vol. Legal Svcs. Hawaii, 1997, Outstanding Local V.P. award U.S. Jr. C. of C., 1998. Mem. ABA, ATLA, Hawaii State Bar Assn. (dir. young lawyers divsn. 1999, 2000), Hawaii Bus. Jaycees (v.p. 1997—, Edward R. Nakano Meml. award 1998, Daniel K. Inouye award 1999). Office: 33 S King St Ste 140 Honolulu HI 96813-4319

ADANYINA, JOHN ELVIS, journalist; b. Chiana, Ghana, Nov. 27, 1952; s. Kutira and Kasinga (Ayi) A.; m. Fella Patricia Azumah, Apr. 12, 1981; children: Nancy, Ernest, Aaron, Kenneth. Diploma in journalism, Ghana Inst. of Journalism, 1973; diploma in news agy. journalism, Indian Inst. Mass Comm., New Delhi, 1995. Cert. in radio and TV prodn., BBC London, population and comm. mgmt., Ghana Inst. Mgmt. Pub. Admin., 1984. Reporter Info. Svcs. Dept., 1973-75, sr. pubs. asst., 1976-78, asst. info. officer, 1978-80, info. officer, 1980-84, sr. info. officer, 1984-90, pub. rels. officer, 1990—, prin. info. officer, 1992-98, asst. dir., 1998—; Reporter BBC Network Africa Programme, 1975-81. Asst. editor (newspaper) Labaare, 1975. Apptd. regional info. officer Upper East Region, Ghana, 1994—; mem. nat. planning com. Nat. Festival of Arts and Culture, 1998; mem. Regional Ministerial Adv. Bd.; mem. bd. govs. Chiana Sr. Secondary Sch., 1996—; mem. Regional Disaster Mgmt. Com.; mem. Regional Tourism Devel. Planning Com.; mem. Population Adv. Com.; exec. mem. Chiana Youth Aassn.; mem. Friends of India Soc., 1995. Mem. Ghana Journalists Assn. (asst. regional sec., reg. chmn., 1996), Navrongo Devel. Club (orgn. sec. 1991, sec. 1994). Avocations: reading, travel, table tennis, debating, meeting people. Office: Info Svcs Dept, PO Box 49, G1000 Bolgatanga Ghana

ADASKIN, GORDON, artist, educator; b. Toronto, Ont., Can., June 7, 1931; s. Harry Adaskin; children: Jon, Susan. Apprentice of Frank Lloyd Wright, 1951; grad., Vancouver (Can.) Sch. Art, 1952, Prov. Normal Sch. Vancouver, 1955. Docent, asst. curator Vancouver Art Gallery, 1955-56; art tchr., counselor Vancouver Sch. Sys., 1956-62; instr. drawing, painting, anatomy and art history Alta. (Can.) Coll. Art, Calgary, 1963-66; asst. prof. environ. studies U. Man., Can., 1966; prof. U. Man., 1971, chair basic design, 1975; instr. drawings Banff Sch. Fine Art, 76; painting instr. Banff Sch. Fine Arts, summers 1964, 65, 70, instr. drawing, summers, 1975, 76; lectr. basic design Banff Ctr. Theatre Crafts, 1972-77, edn. program cons. to theatre divsn., 1977; instr. in design U. Alta., summers 1963, 66; guest lectr. U. B.C., 1973. One-man shows include London House, 1953, Maison Canadienne, Paris, 1954, Tempus Gallery, Vancouver, 1963, Banff Sch. Fine Arts, 1964, 65, Applied Arts Ctr. Gallery, 1965, Little Gallery, 1966, U. Man., 1967, 69, 80, Griffiths Gallery, Vancouver, 1967, 68, 69, Studio Gallery West, Vancouver, 1973, Pvt. Studio Shows, Vancouver, 1973, Banff, 1975, Winnipeg, 1976, Peter Whyte Gallery Banff, 1976, Bau-Xi Gallery, Vancouver, 1981, Melnychenko Gallery, Winnipeg, 1981; exhibited in numerous group shows; represented in pub. and pvt. collections. Home: 844 Oceanmount Blvd, Gibons, BC Canada V0N 1VB

ADCOCK, MURIEL W., special education educator; b. Chgo.. BA, U. Calif. Sonoma State, Rohnert Park, 1979. Cert. spl. edn. tchr., Calif., Montessori spl. edn. tchr. Tchr. The Concordia Sch., Concord, Calif., 1980-85; tchr., cons. Tenderloin Community Children's Ctr., San Francisco, 1985-86; adminstr. Assn. Montessori Internat.-USA, San Francisco, 1988, tchr., advisor, 1989—; course asst. Montessori Spl. Edn. Inst., San Francisco, 1985-87, tchr. spl. edn., 1990, tchr. cons., 1991—, rschr. 1992—. Contbr. articles to profl. jour. Sec. Internat. Forum World Affairs Coun., San Francisco, 1990-95, program chair, 1993-95. Mem. ASCD, Nat. Assn. Edn. Young Children, Am. Orthopsychiat. Assn., Internat. Soc. Sys. Scientists, Assn. Montessori Internat., N.Am. Montessori Tchrs. Assn., Assn. Childhood Edn. Internat., Smithsonian Assocs., N.Y. Acad. Scis., Internat. Sys. Inst., Menninger Found., Club of Budapest (pres. 2000—). Avocations: general evolutionary systems theory, sustainable development, educational systems design, ethical leadership.

ADDAI, FREDERICK KWAKU, anatomy educator, research scientist; b. Buoyem, Ghana, May 28, 1958; s. Anthony Arden and Comfort Yaa (Pokuaa) A.; m. Cecilia Akosua Ataa, May 8, 1987; children: Caroline Serwaa-Adusei, Mark, Abena Addai-Pokuaa. BSc with honors, U. Ghana, 1982; PhD, U. Leicester, Eng., 1987. Teaching asst. U. Ghana, Legon, 1982-83; sr. rsch. asst. U. Ghana Med. Sch., Korle-Bu, 1983-84, lectr., 1987-94, sr. lectr., 1994—; cons. mortician U. Ghana Med. Sch., 1988—; lectr. Sch. Med. Scis., Kumasi, Ghana, 1988-91; item-resource person West African Exams. Coun., Accra, Ghana, 1989—; postgrad. tutor U. Ghana Med. Sch., 1988—; vis. prof. Tulane U. Med. Ctr., 1997-98. Contbr. articles to profl. jours. Brit. Coun. scholar, 1984-87; Wellcome Trust fellow, 1991; Wellcome Trust Travel grant, 1993, Brit. Coun. grant, 1993. Mem. AAAS, N.Y. Acad. Scis., Ghana Sci. Assn. (sec. 1990-91), Anat. Soc. West Africa, Internat. Soc. Poets, Nat. Geographic Soc. Avocations: reading, gardening, film, singing, cycling. Home: Korle-Bu, # 5 Staff Rd Box KB 305, Korle-Bu, Accra Ghana Office: U Ghana Med Sch, U Ghana Med Sch Dept Anatom, Box 4236, Accra Ghana

ADDINGTON, DAVID JOHN, legal administrator, arbitrator; b. London, July 11, 1947; s. Walter Robert and Evelyn Franklin A.; m. Moira Louise Meiklejohn, May 20, 1972 (div. June 29, 1988); children: Juliet Louise, Holly Somers Lindsay; m. Mary Ann Mitchelson, Apr. 29, 1989; children: Robert Iain, Emily Margaret Mary. Student, Hampstead Sch., London, 1959-63, Poly. Ctrl. London, 1963-64. Mng. clk. Field Fisher Waterhouse, London, 1963-71; litigation mgr. D. Miles Griffiths Piercy & Co., London, 1971-73, Rubinstein Callingham, London, 1973-75, S. Rutter & Co., London, 1975-77, Appleby Spurling & Kempe, Bermuda, 1977-94, Mello, Jones & Martin, Bermuda, 1994—; mem. law reform com. Bermuda Supreme Ct. rules, 1989—; mem. com. Bermuda Mediation and Arbitration Ctr., 1994—. Contbr. articles to profl. jours. Master Lodge Civil and Mil., Bermuda, 1995—; sec. Anglican Ch. Synod, Bermuda, 1996; diocesan reader, 1995, ordinand, 1998; vice chmn. Bermuda Sailors Home Inc., 1998—. Fellow Inst. Legal Execs. (chmn. Bermuda branch 1982—), Chartered Inst. Arbitrators; mem. Inst. Mgmt., Mariners Club, Bermuda Zone Internat. Assn. Lions Club (chmn. 1992-93). Anglican. Avocations: sailing, music, literature. Home: Ken-Ogle 11, Wreck Rd, Somerset Bridge SB01, Bermuda Office: Mello Jones & Martin, Reid House 31 Church St, Hamilton HM12, Bermuda

ADDISON, JASON LAWRENCE, retirement community development executive; b. Westmount, Que., Can., Aug. 10, 1967; came to U.S., 1995; s. Victor Robert Addison and Erla Marie Daly; m. Diane St. Laurent, July 20, 1991 (div. 1995); m. Marie-Pascale Louise Addison, Nov. 6, 1997; children: Mathieu, Olivia. Civil Engring. Technologist, Dawson Coll., Montreal, Can., 1992; B in Commerce, McGill U., Montreal, Can., 1994; MSc in Real Estate Devel., MIT, 1996. Real estate sales rep. Century 21, Hamilton, Ont., Can., 1986-88, Re/Max, Hamilton, 1988-90; land surveyor Daniel Lacroix, Montreal, 1991-94; land planning coord. Intrawest Corp., Mt. Tremblant, Que., Can., 1994-95; sr. assoc. Ocwen Fin. Corp., West Palm Beach, Fla., 1996-97; project devel. mgr. Life Care Svcs. LLC, Des Moines, 1997—. Mem. Urban Land Inst. Avocations: scuba, alpine skiing, viticulture. Home: 3634 NW 75th Pl Ankeny IA 50021-9128

ADDO, NELSON OTU, sociology and demography researcher; b. Adukrom, Ghaha, Nov. 4, 1933; d. Gottfried Charles Nyako Otu and Mary Anyankwabea (Ayisi) Otu; married; 5 children. BS in Sociology, U. Ghana, Legon, 1962; MS, London Sch. Econs., 1964, PhD, 1969. Agrl. officer Ghana Ministry Agr., 1952-59; mem. faculty U. Ghana, 1965—, assoc. prof. sociology, 1975-82, prof., 1982—, also dir. population dynamics program; rsch. cons. Ghana Manpower Bd., Ministry Econ. Planning; vis. scholar U. N.C. Population Centre, 1976; Commonwealth vis. prof., Smuts vis. fellow Cambridge U., also vis. fellow Clare Hall, 1977-78; cons. to UNESCO; ILO expert regional advisor on population and employment policy and research for English-speaking Africa, 1983-95; pvt. cons. in the field of population policy and devel., 1996—. Author papers in field, editor jours. and books. Trustee, chmn. research com. Ghana Rural Reconstrn. Movement; 1st sec. Planned Parenthood Assn. Ghana; past mem. Ghana Eastern Regional Planning Com.; chmn. ISSER Endowment Trust, U. Ghana, 1998—. Fellow Population Council, 1962-65, 68-69. Mem. Internat. Union Sci. Study Population, Population Assn. Africa (mem. council, sec. planning com.), Assn. African Statisticians, Ghana Sociol. Assn. (hon. sec. 1972-77). Presbyterian. Office: care Internat Labor Office Africa, PO Box 2788, Addis Ababa Ethiopia

ADDY, MARIAN EWURAMA, biochemist; b. Nkawkaw, Ghana, Feb. 7, 1942; d. Samuel Joseph and Angelina (Kwofie) Cole; m. Ebenezer Charles Addy, Mar. 21, 1970; children: Nah Lamiley, Lamiorkor Esi. BSc, U. Ghana, 1966; MSc, Pa. State U., 1968, PhD, 1971. Assoc. prof. Howard U., Washington, 1972-76; lectr. U. Ghana, Legon, 1976-82, sr. lectr., 1982-92, assoc. prof. biochemistry, 1992-97, head of biochemistry dept., 1993-98, full prof., 1997—; cons. UNDP, Accra, Ghana, 1994; head chem. pathology unit NMIMR, Legon, 1983-85. Contbr. articles to profl. jours. Univ. rep. UNESCO Nat. Commn., 1992-96; mem. Third World Orgn. for Women in Sci., Trieste, Italy. Fulbright African Sr. Rsch. scholarship CIES, 1990; internat. seminar fellowship SAREC and UNESCO, 1985-86; Named Africa Am. Inst. Disting. Alumna for Excellence, 1998, Winner of UNESCO Kalinga prize, 1999, Winner of Nat. Millennium Excellence award for Ednl. Devel., 1999. Mem. Ghana Biochem. Soc. (pres. 1993-95), Women in Sci. and Tech. (pres. 1989—). Anglican. Avocations: tennis, designing clothes. Home: 31 Legon Hill, Legon Ghana Office: Univ Ghana, Dept Biochemistry, PO Box 54, Legon Ghana

ADDY, TRALANCE OBUAMA, healthcare company executive; b. Kumasi, Ghana; s. Matthew Biala Addy and Docea Larteley Baddoo; m. Jo Alison Addy, May 26, 1979; children: Nii Mantse, Miishe, Dwetri, Naakei. BA in Chemistry, BSME, Swarthmore Coll., 1969; MSME, U. Mass., 1974, PhD, 1974. Sr. rsch. project engr. Scott Paper Co., Phila., 1973-76, rsch. scientist, 1976-79, program mgr., 1979-80; dir. applied rsch. Surgikos Inc., subs. Johnson & Johnson, Arlington, Tex., 1980-85, dir. tech. and venture devel., 1985-88; v.p. rsch., gen. mgr. Advanced Sterilization Products divsn. Johnson & Johnson Med., Arlington, 1988-90; v.p., gen. mgr. Advanced Sterilization Products divsn. Johnson & Johnson Med., Irvine, Calif., 1990-95, divsn. pres., 1995-98; internat. v.p. Johnson & Johnson, New Brunswick, N.J., 1998—; mem. exec. com. Adaptive Bus. Leaders, Irvine, 1997—. Contbr. articles to sci. and profl. jours. Bd. dirs. Sickle Cell Disease Assn. Am., 1997—, Orange County United Way, 1998—; tchr., vol. Upward Bound Program, Swarthmore Coll., U. Mass., 1966-73. Fellow Am. Inst. Med. Biol. Engring.; mem. ASME, AAAS, Sigma Xi. Avocations: tennis, running, anthropology. Office: Johnson & Johnson Tech Ventures 33 Technology Dr Irvine CA 92618-2346

ADE, WOLFGANG ROLAND, physician, medical advisor; b. Stuttgart, Germany, Jan. 15, 1947; arrived in Japan, 1981; s. Roland Gotthilf and Gretl (Niebling) A.; m. Shizuko Okawa, Nov. 22, 1981; 1 child, Eruna. Degree in applied managerial econs., Fachschule Betriebswirtschaft, Stuttgart, 1974; MD, Ruprecht Karl U., Heidelberg, Germany, 1982. Med. diplomate, Germany. Computer programmer Brauerei Rob. Leicht AG, Stuttgart, 1966-72; rsch. fellow Tokyo Women's Med. Coll., 1982-87, lectr. 1st dept. surgery, 1987-89; med. advisor Nippon Roussel/Roussel Morishita/Hoechst Marion Roussel, Tokyo, 1983—; mem. adj. staff, rsch. and sci. officer Juro Wada Commemorative Heart and Lung Inst., Tokyo, 1987—; trustee Japan chpt. Pan-Pacific Surg. Assn., Tokyo, 1991—. Contbr. articles to profl. jours.; editor Jour. Cardiovascular Surgery, Torino, Italy, 1994—; mem. editl. bd. Cardiovascular Engring., Lengerich, Germany, 1996—. Served with German Air Force, 1967. Fellow World Soc. Cardio-Thoracic Surgeons (sec. gen., sec. steering com., trustee Japan chpt. 1991—); mem. Japanese Assn. Thoracic Surgery, World Artificial Organ, Immunology and Transplantation Soc. (sec. 1993—). Mem. New Apostolic Ch. Avocation: poetry. E-mail: whlij@attglobal.net. Office: Juro Wada Commemorative Heart & Lung Inst, IPO Box 5048, Tokyo 100-3191, Japan

ADEBAYO, STEPHEN OLUYEMI, engineering educator; b. Ire-Ekiti, Ekiti, Nigeria, Oct. 9, 1956; s. Elijah and Mary Ariyeke (Falowo) A.; m. Cecilia Olajumoke Olusuyi, Feb. 27, 1961; children: Caleb, Cornelius, Victor, Mary. Higher nat. diploma, Fed. Poly., Ado-Ekiti, Nigeria, 1982; postgrad. diploma, Anambra State U. Tech., Enugu, Nigeria, 1990; postgrad., Fed. U. Tech., Akure, Nigeria, 1999. Cert. engring. and engring. geology, State of Nigeria. Jr. tutor Ayede Grammar Sch., Ayede-Ekiti, Nigeria, 1975-77; paymaster Ministry Lands and Housing, Akure, 1978; road maintenance officer Ministry of Works, Azare, Nigeria, 1982-83; sr. tutor Ayedun Comp. H.S., Akure, 1983-84; lectr. Fed. Poly., Ado-Ekiti, 1984—, coord., 1998—; cons. Maurice Project Ltd., Lagos, Nigeria, 1980, 81; chmn. bldg. com. GFMI, Ado-Ekiti, 1987—. Author of poems. Ordained elder Gospel Faith Mission Internat., Ibadan, Nigeria, 1987. Mem. Internat. Assn. Engring. Geology, Nigerian Soc. Engrs., Nigerian Assn. Engring. Geology. Pentecostal. Avocations: writing poems, table tennis, farming, fine art work, reading. Home: Ang High Sch Rd, Ado-Ekiti Ekiti, Nigeria Office: Civil Engring Dept, The Fed Poly, Ado-Ekiti Ekiti, Nigeria

ADEBAYO, YINKA ROTIMI, environmental scientist, diplomat; b. Owu, Kwara, Nigeria, Jan. 17, 1959; s. Alabi Moses and Ajoke Deborah Adeoye; m. Adebisi Oluwafeyisayo Adebayo Ariyo, Sept. 27, 1988; children: Eniafe, Tiwatope, Bankole. BS, U. Ibadan (Nigeria), 1980, MS, 1982, PhD, 1985. Asst. lectr. Ogun State U., Ago-Iwoye, Nigeria, 1983-85; lectr. U. Ilorin, Nigeria, 1985-88; sr. lectr. Kenyatta U., Nairobi, Kenya, 1988-90; environ. program officer UN, Nairobi, 1990—; cons. environ. program UN, Nairobi, 1989-90. Fellow Royal Meteorol. Soc. (Eng.). Office: UN Environ Programme, Limuru Rd, Nairobi Kenya

ADEBIMPE, VICTOR ROTIMI, psychiatrist; b. Iji, Kwara, Nigeria, Nov. 6, 1945; came to U.S., 1972; s. Solomon Olawepo and Bolaji Adebimpe; m. Folasade Oluremi Ogunlana, Apr. 29, 1972; children: Oluseyi, Babatunde, Olajumoke. BS, U. Ibadan, Nigeria, 1968; MD, U. Ibadan, 1971. Intern Bapt. Hosp., Ogbomosho, Nigeria, 1971-72; resident Mo. Inst. Psychiatry, St. Louis, 1972-75; attending psychiatrist U. Pitts., 1975-79; med. dir. No. Commn. Mental Health Ctr., Pitts., 1979-82; sr. lectr. U. Ilorin, Ilorin, Nigeria, 1982-84; dir. psychiatry St. Johns Health & Hosp. Ctr., Pitts., 1984-90; med. dir. Charles R. Drew Community Mental Health Ctr., Phila., 1987-92; dir. adult psychiatry Mercy Psychiat. Inst., Pitts., 1990-95, pres. med. staff, 1992-95; adj. asst. prof. psycniatry Allegheny U. Health Scis., 1996; attending psychiatrist Mercy Providence Hosp., Pitts., 1996. Contbr. articles to profl. jours. Med. dir. Luth. Youth & Family Svcs., Zelienople, Pa., 1996. Mem. AAAS, Am. Psychiat. Assn., Nat. Med. Assn. Baptist. Office: Allies Behavioral Ctr 275 Gateway Twrs Pittsburgh PA 15222-1616

ADEDEJI, ADEBAYO, economist, former government official; b. Ijebu-Ode, Ogun, Nigeria, Dec. 21; came to Ethiopia, 1975; s. L.S. and Adeola Adedeji; m. Aderinola Ogun, Aug. 11, 1957; children: Adedoyin, Funso, Adekunle, Adeleke, Adeniyi, Adeola, Adefunke, Adeyinka, Adepoju, Adedipe, Adeoye. Diploma in Local Govt. Adminstrn., Univ. Coll., U. Ibadan, 1953-54; B.Sc. in Econs., Leicester U. Coll., 1958; M.P.A., Harvard U., 1961; Ph.D. in Econs., U. London, 1967; Litt.D. (hon.), Ahmadu Bello U., 1976; LL.D. (hon.), U. Dallhousie, 1984, U. Zambia, 1984, U. Calabar, 1987; DSc (hon.), Obafemi Awolowo U., 1989. Sr. asst. sec. for revenue Nigerian Civil Service, 1958-63; dep. dir. Inst. Adminstrn. U. Ife, 1963-67, dir. Inst. Adminstrn., prof. pub. adminstrn., 1967-75; fed. commr. Ministry for Econ. Devel. in Reconstrn. Nigeria, 1971-75; under-sec.-gen., exec. sec. UN Econ. Commn. for Africa, Addis Ababa, Ethiopia, 1975-91; dir. African Ctr. for Devel. and Strategic Studies; mem. Ad Hoc Com. of Experts of Fins. of UN and its Specialized Agys., 1965; mem. Expert Com. on Restructuring Econ. and Social Sectors of UN System, 1975; chmn. senate UN Inst. for Namibia, 1975-90; trustee dept. econs. Boston U., 1978—; chmn. Western Nigerian Govt. Broadcasting Corp., 1966-67; mem. Nigerian Nat. Manpower Bd., 1968-71; chmn. Directorate of Nat. Youth Service Corps of Nigeria, 1973-75; founder and exec. dir. African Ctr. for Devel. and Strategic Studies, 1991—; mem. U.N. panel of high level experts on the restructuring of the U.N., chmn. devel. program, 1994. Author books, the most recent being: Africa, The Third World and the Search for a New Economic Order, 1976; Africa: The Crisis of Development and the Challenge of a New Economic Order, 1977; The Political Class, the Higher Civil Service and the Challenge of Nation Building, 1981; The Deepening International Economic Crisis and its Implications for Africa, 1982; editor: Indigenization of African Economies, 1981; Economic Crisis in Africa: African Perspectives on Development Problems and Potentials, 1985, Towards The Dawn of the Third Millenium and the Beginning of the 21st Century, 1986, Towards a Dynamic African Economy, 1989, Preparing Africa for the Twenty-First Century: Agenda for the 1990's, 1991, Africa Within the World: Beyond Disposession and Dependence, 1993, South Africa and Africa: Within or Apart?, 1996. Decorated grand officer Order of Mono (Togo); comdr. Order of Merit of Islamic Republic Mauritania; grand comdr. Order of Disting. Service First Class (Zambia); Grand Comdr. Order of the Lion (Senegal), 1987; recipient Gold Mercury Internat. award, 1982. Fellow Nigerian Inst. Mgmt. (dir. 1968-75), Nigerian Econ. Soc. (pres. 1971-72), African Assn. for Pub. Adminstrn. and Mgmt. (v.p. 1971-74, pres. 1975-85); mem. African Acad. Sci. Home: Asiwaju Ct GRA Erunwon Rd PO Box 203, Ijebu Ode Nigeria Office: African Ctr Devel Strategic Studies, PO Box 203, Ijebu Ode Nigeria*

ADEGBITE, SAMUEL IGBAYILOLA, banker; b. Ibadan, Nigeria, Jan. 3, 1940; s. Joel and Alice Sijuwola (Adapele) A.; m. Comfort Monilola Olawoyin, Mar. 3, 1963; children: Adeyinka, Adewale, Adegoke, Ademola, Adeyemi. LLB with honors, U. London, 1969. Clk. First Bank Plc, Nigeria, 1961-63; bank officer Nat. Bank Ltd., Nigeria, 1971, bank mgr., 1972-74; dept. head Nat. Mcht. Bank, Nigeria, 1980-81; exec. dir. WEMA Bank Plc, Nigeria, 1981-83, dep. mng. dir., 1983, mng. dir., CEO, 1983-98; exec. vice chmn. NBM Bank Ltd., 1999—; chmn. investigating panel and br. devel. divsn., CIBN, Nigeria, chmn. and pres. of coun. Author: Path to Greater Heights-Facts Behind WEMA Bank's Turnaround Years, 1982-92, Current Developments in Nigerian Commercial Law-Essays in Honour of Chief S.I. Adegbite. Fellow Chartered Inst. Bankers, Chartered Inst. Secs. and Adminstrs., Nigerian Inst. Mgmt.; mem. Oluyole Club, Met. Club. Avocations: lawn tennis, swimming, jogging, golfing, reading. Home: 15 Adekunle Fajuyi Str, Lagos Nigeria Office: NBM Bank Ltd, 77 Awolowo Rd PO Box 52463, Ikoyi Lagos Nigeria

ADEGBOLA, RICHARD ADEBAYO, microbiologist, researcher; b. Ibadan, Oyo State, Nigeria, Dec. 3, 1951; s. Amusa Olasupo and Adebisi (Adejinmi) A.; m. Modupe Olubisi Falade, May 29, 1976; children: Temitope, Adekunbi, Oluranti, Anuoluwapo. MSc, U. Dundee, Scotland, 1981, PhD, 1983. Med. technologist Lagos U. Tchg. Hosp, Lagos, Nigeria, 1976-79; microbiologist Lagos U. Tchg. Hosp, Lagos, 1983-84; sr. lectr., head unit Lagos State U., 1985-90; unit bacteriologist, head sect. microbiology Med. Rsch. Coun. Labs. Fajara, Banjul, The Gambia, 1990—; mem. governing bd. Lagos State U., 1988-90; mem. sci. coord. com. Med. Rsch. Coun. Labs., Banjul, 1990—, chmn. safety com., 1992—, mem. local mentoring com., 1993-96, mem. hib vaccination focal mentoring com. Author, editor: Questions and Model Answers in Medical Bacteriology, 1990; contbr. articles to profl. jours. Mem. Nat. Drug Formulary Com. and Nat. Task Force for Epidemic Preparedness, Ministry of Health The Gambia, Banjul, 1996. Recipient Overseas Rsch. Students awards Com. Vice-Chancellors and Prinx. of Brit. Univs., U.K., Dundee, 1981-83; Nigerian Govt. Postgrad. scholar Oyo State Govt., 1979-83. Fellow Royal Coll. Pathologists U.K., Inst. Biomed. Scis., Tropical Medicine Hygiene U.K.; mem. N.Y. Acad. Sci. Roman Catholic. Avocations: lawn tennis, table tennis, reading. Office: MRC labs, Fajara Atlantic Rd, Banjul The Gambia

ADEGBUYI, OLATUNDE, geologist, geochemist, educator; b. Ijebu-Igbo, Nigeria, Dec. 2, 1954; s. Solomon Mofolorunso and Racheal Asabi (Suleiman) A.; m. Omowumi Olayide Oriola, Jan. 16, 1992; children: Oluwatosin Emmanuel, Oluwatobi Rebecca, Oluwadamilola Samuel, Oluwafunmito Esther. BSc with honors, U. Ibadan, Nigeria, 1978, MSc in Mineral Exploration, 1981; diploma in geothermal energy tech., U. Auckland, New Zealand, 1989. Sr. geologist Nat. Steel Raw Materials Agy., Kaduna, Nigeria, 1979-85; lectr. II Ogun State U., Ago-Iwoye, Nigeria, 1985-91; lectr. II/I Ondo State U., Ado-Ekiti, Nigeria, 1991—; assoc. lectr. Fed. U. Tech., Akure, Nigeria, 1990-91, 98-99. Co-author: Ancient Banded Iron Formations, 1990, Advances in Geology and Geophysics Research in Africa, 1998. Mem. Nigeria Mining and Geosci. Soc., Assn. Geoscientists for Internat. Devel., Internat. Assn. Geochemistry and Cosmochemistry. Avocations: reading, praying. Home: Oke-Sopin, Mosalasi Jimo St, 21 Ijebu-Igbo Nigeria Office: Ondo State Univ, PMB 01 Geology Dept, Akungba-Akoko Nigeria

ADEKSON, MARY OLUFUNMILAYO, therapist, counselor educator; b. Ogbomoso, Nigeria; came to U.S., 1988; d. Gabriel and Deborah Williams; children: Adedayo, Babatunde. BA in English and Am. Lit., Brandeis U., 1975; MEd in Guidance and Counseling, Obafemi Awolowo U., Ile-Ife, Nigeria, 1987; PhD, Ohio U., 1997. English tchr. Ctrl. Sch. Bd., Ibadan, Nigeria, 1968-88; acting prin. Abe Tech. Coll., Ibadan, 1978; coord. guidance svcs. Min. Edn., Ile-Ife, 1984-88; part-time lectr. Obafemi Awolowo U., Ile-Ife, 1986-88; vice prin. Olubuse Meml. H.S., Ile-Ife, 1987-88; grad. asst. Ohio U., Athens, 1988-91; vol. contract worker, trainer Careline, Tri-County Mental Health Ctr., Athens, 1988-92; vol. My Sister's Place, Athens, 1989, Good Works Athens, 1989, Montgomery County Hotline, 1994; contract worker Tri County Activity Ctr., Athens, 1989-92, therapist II Woodland Ctr., Gallipolis, Ohio, 1991-92; part-time lectr. U. Md., 1993, coord. tutorial svcs.; dir. Christian Book Ctr., Ile-Ife; vol., part-time counselor DWI program Prince George's County Health Dept., Hyattsville, Md.; counselor Potomac Healthcare Found. Mountain Manor Treatment Program; adj. prof. Bowie (Md.) State U. Counseling Program, 1997-98; asst. prof. St. Bonaventure U., 1998—; faculty adviser Chi Sigma Iota, Phi Rho chpt. Vol. Montgomery County Police Dept.; mem. Alcohol and Other Drug Abuse Adv. Coun., Montgomery County, Md.; mem. adv. com. Germantown (Md.) Libr.; mem. Gaithersburg (Md.) City Adv. Com.; chmn. bd. dirs. Faith Enterprises; dir. Faith Consultancy Group. Recipient Gold medal West African Athletic Assn., 1965; Internat. Peace scholar P.E.O., 1990-91, Wien Internat. scholar Brandeis U., 1973-75. Mem. ACA, Am. Mental Health Counselors Assn. Network on Children and Teens (membership chair 1991-92, chair 1993-98), Am. Assn. Counseling and Devel. (award for internat. grad. students 1990), Counseling Assn. Nigeria (planning com. 1986), Am. Rehab. Counselors Assn., Am. Mental Health Counseling Assn., Assn. Multicultural Counseling and Devel., Oyo State Nigeria Assn. Guidance Counselors (chmn. Oranmiyan local govt. area 1986-88), Chi Sigma Iota (program coord. Ohio U. chpt. 1990, faculty advisor Phi Rho chpt.). Avocations: meeting people from around the world, jogging, walking, playing tennis, reading.

ADELT, BRUNO, automotive company executive. CFO Volkswagen AG, Wolfsburg, Germany, now mem. mgmt. bd., dir. controlling and auditing. Office: Brieffach 1848-2, Wolfsburg 38436, Germany*

ADELT, DIETER, physician, spine surgeon; b. Castrop-Rauxel, Germany, Mar. 3, 1950; s. Fred Hans and Maria Theresia (Ohlberger) A.; m. Petra Koester, May 8, 1982; children: Julia Catharina, Alina Christine. Staatsexamen medizine, Tech. U. Aachen, 1978. Resident Tech. U., Aachen, Germany, 1978-84, cons., 1984-90; cons. U. Hosp., Essen, Germany, 1990-94; head dept. of neurosurgery Ostsee Klinik, Damp, Germany, 1995—. Author: Advances in Neurosurgery, 1986; contbr. articles to profl. jours. Mem. Deutsche Gesellschaft Neurochirurgie. Avocations: wine collecting, cooking. Office: Dept Neurosurgery, Ostseeklinik, D-24349 Damp Germany

ADEMOROTI, CHRISTOPHER M. ADEREMI, chemistry educator; b. Ilesa, Osun, Nigeria, Dec. 25, 1938; s. Samuel Kayode Adedokun and Felicia Omileye (Odubade) A.; m. Beatrice Boladale Ajenifuja, Dec. 24, 1967; children: Adekemi, Adebusola, Olufemi, Adeola, Adejumoke. BSc in Chemistry with honors, U. London, 1973, PhD in Chemistry, 1979. From chem. analyst to rsch. officer II Nat. Cereals Rsch. Inst., Ibadan, Nigeria, 1970-74; sci. officer I Min. Works, Housing and Enviroment, Ibadan, 1974-77, sr. sci. officer, 1977-79, prin. sci. officer, 1979-80, asst. chief sci. officer, 1981-83; sr. lectr. U. Benin, Benin City, 1983-89, prof., 1989—; cons. WHO/UN Devel. Program, Ibadan, 1974-75, Ford Found./Nigerian Environment Study Team, Benin, 1984-85, 94-96, Shell Petroleum Devel. Co., Nigeria, 1985—, UNESCO, 1988-90; pub. analyst, cons. Fed. Republic Nigeria, 1982—. Author: Chemical Thermodynamics, 1995, Environmental Chemistry and Toxicology, 1996, Standard Methods for Water and Effluents Analysis, 1996; contbr. articles to profl. jours. Mem. Internat. Assn. on Water Quality, Inst. Chartered Chemists Nigeria (chmn. Benin chpt. 1988-89), Chem. Soc. Nigeria (chmn. Benin chpt. 1988-89), Chartered Inst. Chemistry. Methodist Church Nigeria. Achievements include invention of fluidized bed techniques for water and wastewater treatment under aerobic conditions. Avocations: lawn tennis, swimming, gardening, photography, itenerant evangelism. Home: KPU 2 Ademoroti St, Oke-Opo GRA, Ilesa Osun, Nigeria Office: U Benin Chemistry Dept, PMB 1154, Benin City Edo, Nigeria

ADENE, DANIEL FOLUSO, veterinary poultry specialist, educator; b. Owo, Ondo, Nigeria, June 21, 1944; s. John Monday and Dorcas Funke (Oladele) A.; m. Esther Abiodun Adesida, Oct. 30, 1973 (div. Oct. 1986); children: Sola, Ayo, Adewslu; m. Oluyomi Taiwo Olayanju, Aug. 5, 1989; children: Tolu, Debo, Simi. DVM, U. Ibadan, Nigeria, 1970, PhD, 1980; M in Vet. Sci., U. Liverpool, Eng., 1974. Vet. officer Ministry Agr., Ibadan, 1970-72; lectr. II U. Ibadan, 1972-76, lectr. I, 1976-78, sr. lectr., 1978-82, assoc. prof., 1982-86, prof., 1986—; senate mem. U. Ibadan, 1982—; founder, agr. dir. Vet. Tchg. Hosp., Ibadan, 1982-84; resource person, advisor Am. Soybean Assn., U.S. Feed Grains, Lagos, Nigeria, 1982-85; chief cons. V.T.H., Ibadan, 1986—. Contbr. articles to profl. jours. Patron Students Farm Found., Unibadan, 1990-98, grand patron, 1998—. Commonwealth Acad. fellow ACU, U.K., 1982, Fulbright Sr. Rsch. fellow CIES, 1985-86; CSIRO Travel grantee, Australian, 1995-96, Nat. Agr. Rsch./World Bank Rsch. grantee, Nigeria, 1996-98. Fellow Coll. Vet. Surgeons Nigeria, Nigerian Vet. Med. Assn.; mem. World Vet. Poultry Assn., World's Poultry Sci., N.Y. Acad. Scis. Anglican. Avocation: lawn tennis. Home: University Campus, 13 Amina Way, Ibadan Oyo, Nigeria Office: Dept Vet Medicine, Univ Ibadan, Ibadan Oyo, Nigeria

ADENEY, HOWARD MARTIN, public relations executive; b. Jerusalem, Palestine, Sept. 7, 1942; s. Arthur Webster and Edith Marjorie (Blagden) A.; m. Ann Valerie Corcoran, Dec. 18, 1971; children: Samuel John Stanton Moore, William Edward, Thomas Henry. BA, Queens Coll., Cambridge, Eng., 1965. Reporter Guardian Newspapers, Manchester and London, 1965-72; labour corres. Guardian Newspapers, London, 1972-77; feature writer Colombo Plan, 1968-69; indsl. corres. Sun. Telegraph, London, 1977-78; labour corres. BBC-TV, London, 1978-82, indsl. editor, 1982-89; group pub. rels. mgr. ICI, London, 1989—, v.p. pub. affairs, 1997-2000; prin. Martin Adeney Assn., London, 2000—. Author: (with John Lloyd) The Miner's Strike: Loss Without Limit, 1986; The Motormakers, 1988, Nuffield: A Biography, 1993.

ADENIRAN, ADESHOLA, plastic and reconstructive surgeon, consultant; b. Lagos, Nigeria, June 11, 1958; s. Adejumobi Emmanuel and Aduke Stella (Adebowale) A.; m. Adedayo Otunla, Mar. 1, 1986; children: Adedapo, Adefolaranmi. MBBS, U. Lagos, 1981. House officer State Specialist Hosp., Ibadan, Nigeria, 1981-82, med. officer, 1983-84; med. officer Nat. Youth Svc. Corps, Lagos, Nigeria, 1982-83; jr. and sr. resident Univ. Coll. Hosp., Ibadan, 1985-90; trainee NHS Hosps., Bristol and Salisbury, Eng., 1990-96; plastic and reconstructive surgeon St. Georges Tchg. Hosp., London, 1996-97. Contbr. articles to Jour. Hand Surgery, Jour. Bone and Joint Surgery, Burns, others. Fellow Internat. Coll. Surgeons, West Africa Coll. Surgeons, Royal Coll. Surgeons Glasgow; mem. N.Y. Acad. Sci., Internat. Soc. for Burn Injuries. Avocations: music and arts, football, athletics. Home and Office: 56 Brook Rd, Newbury Park, Ilford IG2 7EY, England

ADEOLA, ANTHONY OLUKEMI, management educator, researcher, management consultant; b. Ilupeju-Ekiti, Nigeria, Sept. 29, 1949; arrived in Lesotho, 1996; s. Johnson Olaiya and Comfort Omoleye (Ibimiluyi) A.; m. Lucy Adefunke Afuye, Dec. 8, 1978; children: Ademola, Adeniyi, Adebola, Oluwabukola. BSc, U. Ife, Ile-Ife, Nigeria, 1977; MA, U. Ife, 1983, PhD, 1986. Head of sci. Modakeke (Nigeria) H.S., 1980-83; vice-prin. St. David's Grammar Sch., Ile-Ife, 1983-87; lectr. U. Ibadan, Nigeria, 1987-96, U. Botswana, Gaborone, 1993-95; sr. lectr. Nat. U. Lesotho, 1996—; part-time lectr. U. Ife, 1986-87; dir. Roadside Mechanic Project, Ibadan, 1991-92; dep. dean Fac. Edn., 1999—. Author: Organisation and Administration of Adult Education, 1991, Management Techniques in Adult Education, 1997. Adminstr. Internat. Found. for Edn. and Self-Help, Ibadan, 1989-93. Mem. Internat. Coun. for Univ. Adult Edn., Nat. Assn. Ednl. Adminstrn. and Planning, Lesotho Ednl. Rsch. Assn. Avocations: soccer, athletics, gardening, reading, table tennis. Home: H16 Isiwo St, Ilupeju-Ekiti Nigeria Office: Nat U Lesotho Dept Edl Funds, PO Roma 180, Lesotho Lesotho

ADEPOJU, ADERANTI, demographer, educator; b. Oyan, Osun, Nigeria, July 17, 1945; s. Afolabi Joseph and Oladunni Ester Adepoju; m. Adunola Adeyemi, Nov. 25, 1972; children: Abiola, Adegboyega, Aboyepe, Adegoke. BSc, U. Ife, Nigeria, 1969; MSc, London Sch. Econs., 1970, PhD, 1973. Reg. advisor ILO, Addis Ababa, Ethiopia, 1977-78; prof., head dept. Univ. Ife, Ile-Ife, Nigeria, 1980-84; UN prof. Univ. Swaziland, Kwaluseni, 1985-86; prof., dean Univ. Lagos, Nigeria, 1984-88; tng. coord. UN Population Fund, Dakar, Senegal, 1988-98; mem. panel on population of sub-Saharan Africa, com. on population Nat. Acad. Scis. Author, editor: The Impact of Structural Adjustment, 1993; contbr. articles to profl. jours. Mem. Union for African Population Studies (pres. 1991-95), Internat. Sociol. Assn., Population Assn. Nigeria, World Social Prospects Assn., Nigeria Econ. Soc., Internat. Assn. Survey Statisticians, Internat. Union for Sci. Study of Population, NAS (population com.). Avocations: squash, jogging. Office: HRDC 16a Dany Estate, Makoko Rd, Yorba Lagos, Nigeria

ADEROBA, ADEYEMI ADEGBEMISIPO, mechanical engineer educator, industrial engineer; b. Ondo, Ondo, Nigeria, Mar. 5, 1949; s. Samuel Adeyoriju and Comfort Omonubi (Obayangbon) A.; m. Agnes Ibukun Akinnola, Nov. 30, 1974; children: Tayo, Niyi, Fadeke, Gbenga. B in Tech. with honours, Loughborough (Eng.) U., 1973; MS, U. Ill., 1975, PhD, 1977. Chartered engr., Gt. Britain; Coren registered engr., Nigeria. Grad. rsch. and tchg. asst. U. Ill., Urbana, 1973-75, rschr. dept. mech. and indsl. engring., 1975-77; lectr., sr. lectr. U. Benin, Benin City, Nigeria, 1977-82, coord. indsl. tng., 1978-82; prodn. mgr. Nigeria Machine Tools, Oshogbo, 1982-84; chmn., mng. dir. Besade (Nigeria) Ltd., Ondo, 1984-86; assoc. prof. mech. engring. Fed. U. Tech., Akure, Nigeria, 1986—, head dept., 1992-95, prof. dept. mech. engring., 1997—; external examiner U. Benin, 1986-91, U. Ibadan, Nigeria, 1995=96; Commonwealth expert, London, 1993; chmn. Ondo State Bd. for Tech. Edn., Akure, 1997-99. Author: Basic Machining Techniques, Vols. I-III, 1991-93, Engineering Project Management, 1995; editor-in-chief Nigerian Jour. of Engring. Mgmt., 2000—; contbr. articles to profl. jours., including Jour. Info. Decision Techs. Scholar Shell-B.P., Lagos, Nigeria, 1969-73; fellow Assn. Commonwealth Univs., London, 1995-96. Mem. Nigerian Soc. Engrs. (tech. sec. 1979-81), Ondo Divsnl. C. of C., Mines and Agr. (treas. 1984-86), Ondo United Friends Club (treas. 1990-95). Anglican. Avocations: chess, table tennis. Home: 26 Olajide St, PO Box 603, Ondo Ondo, Nigeria Office: Fed U Tech, Dept Mech and Prodn Engring, Akure Nigeria

ADESINA, ADESOJI ADEDIRAN, engineering educator; b. Ijebu-Ode, Ogun, Nigeria, Apr. 2, 1959; arrived in Australia, 1991; s. Adolphus Adediran and Bernice Adetoun (Oyelaja) A.; m. Bolajoko Titilola Oni, Nov. 12, 1988; children: Fopefoluwa, Fiyinfoluwa, Folafoluwa. BSc with honors, U. Lagos, Nigeria, 1980; MASc, U. Waterloo, Can., 1984, PhD, 1986; grad. cert. higher edn., U. NSW, Australia, 1992. Cert. profl. engr.; chartered chemist. Well-site petroleum engr. Shell, Pt. Harcourt, Nigeria, 1980-81; asst. lectr. U. Pt. Harcourt, 1981-86, lectr., 1986-89; vis. fellow U. Waterloo, Can., 1989-90; from lectr. to sr. lectr. U. NSW, 1991-99, assoc. prof., 1999—. Contbr. articles and papers to profl. jours. and confs. Doctoral scholar Can. Commonwealth Coun., 1984. Mem. Royal Australian Chem. Inst., Inst. Engrs. Australia. Office: U NSW, Sch Chem Eng & Ind Chem, 2052 Sydney NSW, Australia

ADETIBA, MAYEN MODUPEOLA, civil engineer, consultant; b. Ilorin, Kwara, Nigeria, Apr. 17, 1951; d. Okon Nyakpa and Bassey Okon (Akaba) Eshiett; m. Bamidele Aderemi Adetiba, Nov. 19, 1979; children: Adekemi, Bamidele Jr., Aderemi Jr. BS in Engring., Columbia U., 1975; MCE, Cornell U., 1976. Pupil engr. Struct-Engring., Lagos, Nigeria, 1976-77; engr. Nigerconsults, Lagos, 1977-78, DHV (Dutch Consulting Engrs.), Lagos, 1978-80; assoc. ptnr. O. Ogunshola & Partners, Lagos, 1980-82; prin. ptnr. Derkem Assocs., Lagos, 1983—; chmn., mng. dir. Mayad Ltd., Lagos, 1986—; bd. mem. Bata Shoe Co. Nigeria Ltd., Unex Securities. Recipient Presidl. Merit award Nigerian Soc. of Engrs. Fellow Nigerian Soc. Engrs.(vice chmn. nat. publicity), Nigerian Inst. Mgmt., Assn. of Profl. Women Engrs. of Nigeria (bd. dirs.); mem. ASCE, Assn. Consulting Engrs., Coun. of Registered Engrs. of Nigeria, Zonta Internat. Club Lagos II (v.p.), Ibeno Women Forum (pres.). Avocations: travelling, music, reading news, sports. Office: Delkem Assocs, PO Box 5067, Marina Lagos Nigeria

ADETILOYE, PHILIP OMONIYI, agronomist; b. Ise-Ekiti, Nigeria, Oct. 18, 1952; s. Gabriel Adetiloye Akingbade and Veronica Aarinola Adelabu-George A.; m. Catherine Monisola Ogundipe; children: Seun, Taiwo and Kehinde, Tope and Tomi. BS in Plant Soil Sci., U. Nigeria, 1976, PhD in Crop Sci., 1980. Lectr. O.A. Univ., Ile-Ife, Nigeria, 1981-89; sr. lectr., dept. head Univ. Agr., Abeokuta, Nigeria, 1990—; vis. scientist IITA, Ibadan, Nigeria, 1988-89, USDA, Md., 1992-93; dir. Future World Ctr. Project. Author: Humankind, Religion, Science and the Future, 1996, Geometic Art for Creative Thinking, 1996; contbr. articles to profl. jours. Scholar Govt. Nigeria, 1972; rsch. fellow Ford Found., 1977-80, IITA; grantee Fed. Ministry, 1984, 96. Mem. Soc. Sci. Exploration, Nigerian Agrl. Soc. Roman Catholic. Avocations: writing, reading, modeling 3-D regular spaces. E-mail: poadeti@unaab.ng.edu.

ADEY, CHRISTOPHER, conductor; b. London, Feb. 19, 1943; m. Catherine Cave, 1965 (div. 1985); 1 child. Ed., Royal Acad. Music, London. Violinist with Hallé Orch., 1963-65, London Philharm. Orch., 1967-71; assoc. condr. BBC Scottish Symphony Orch., 1973-76, Ulster Orch., 1981-83; condr., prof. Royal Coll. Music, 1979-83, dir. orchestral studies, jr. dept., 1973-80; freelance condr., appearing as guest condr. with maj. orchs. U.K., U.S., Can., Europe, Mid. East; condr., The National Youth Orchestra of Wales. Author: Orchestral Performance: A Guide for Conductors and Players, 1998. Recipient Czechoslovakian Commemorative medal, 1986. *

ADÊYOKUNNU, ADETUNJI ADEMUYIWA, pediatrician, consultant; b. Ilesha, Oyo, Nigeria, May 26, 1938; s. Omolade and Marian Wende (Adefemike) A.; m. Tomilayo Olufolake Falohun (div. May, 1978); children: Abayomi (dec.), Jokotade; m. Adefunke Julianah Adesokan; Oct. 17, 1979; children: Aderemi, Aderinola, Adeboye. MBBS, Univ. Coll., London, 1965; DCH, U. Glasgow, 1969; MRCP, Royal Coll. Physicians, 1972. Resident in tng. Univ. Coll., Ibadan, Nigeria, 1965-68; commonwealth registrar Royal Sick Child Hosp., Glasgow, Scotland, 1969-72; sr. registrar, lectr. U. Ibadan, Nigeria, 1973-76, from sr. lectr. to prof., 1976-86; sr. rsch. fellow U. London, Eng., 1976-77; prof., sr. staff physician Nat. Guard Hosp., Riyadh, Saudi Arabia, 1986-96; chief dept. pediatrics Al Fanateer Hosp. Jubail, Industrial City, Saudi Arabia, 1997—; prof. and head of pediatrics U. Ibadan, Nigeria, 1983-86; vice chmn. med. adv. com., dir. clin. svcs. and tng. Univ. Coll. Hosp., Ibadan, Nigeria, 1984-86; program dir. pediatrics King Fahad Nat. Guard Hosp., Riyadh, Saudi Arabia, 1989—, prof. pediatrics, dep. chmn., head divsn. pediatrics, 1993-96. Contbr. articles to profl. jours., chpt. to Concise Textbook on Principles and Practice of Community Health in Africa, 1985. Nat. treas. Pediatric Assn. of Nigeria, Lagos, 1973-76; regional sec., nat. treas. Sickle Cell Club of Nigeria, Kaduna, 1979-83; dep. chmn. Comty. Chest, Oyo State Br., Nigeria, 1978-81; v.p. Genetic Soc. Nigeria, Lagos, 1977-80; justice of the peace, State Govt. Oyo, Nigeria, 1983. Capt. Marine Commando Unit, Nigerian Army, 1968. Recipient Commonwealth Scholarship, Brit. Govt., Eng., 1968, Heinz Fellowship award Brit. Pediatric Assn., London, 1977. Fellow Royal Coll. Physicians Glasgow, Royal Coll. of Physicians London; mem. AAAS, Brit. Med. Assn., N.Y. Acad. Sci. Anglican. Avocations: tennis, hunting, music. Office: Al Fanateer Hosp, PO Box 11720, Jubail Industrial City 31961, Saudi Arabia

ADHAM, SAMER, environmental engineer; b. Riyadh, Saudi Arabia, Nov. 21, 1965; s. Said Fawzi and Shuhra Faiz Adham. BSCE, King Fahd U. Petrol. & Min., Dhahran, Saudi Arabia, 1987, MS in Environ. Engring., 1989; PhD in Environ. Engring., U. Ill., 1993. Prin. engr. applied rsch. dept. Montgomery Watson, Pasadena, Calif., 1993—; guest spkr. UCLA, 1994, U. So. Calif., 1994, U. Ill., Urbana-Champaign, 1995; presenter. Contbr. articles to profl. jours. Mem. ASCE, Am. Water Works Assn. (mem. rsch. com., reviewer Jour. Am. Water Works Assn.), Water Environment Fedn., Internat. Desalting Assn., Arab Scientists & Technologists Abroad. Office: Montgomery Watson 250 N Madison Ave Pasadena CA 91101

ADHAMI, EFTIM JOSIF, anesthesiologist; b. Tirana, Albania, Sept. 3, 1966; s. Josif Eftim and Albertina Jorgji (Papailia) A.; m. Phoebe Anastasios Manuben, June 8, 1997. MD, Tirana Med. Sch., 1989, U. Athens, Greece, 1991. Gen. practice rschr. Spitalior 5, Tirana, 1989-90; gen. dr. Levkos Stauros, Athens, 1991-92; anesthesiologist Tzanio Hosp., Pireus, Greece, 1992-97; rschr. cardiac arrhythmias U. Memphis, 1997-98, tchr., 12000—. Author: Albanian Grammar, 1995; contbr. articles to med. jours. With Albanian Army, 1989. Mem. Albanian Med. Assn., Greek Med. Assn. Mem. Church of Christ. Avocations: soccer, Ping-Pong, swimming, chess, volleyball. Home: 1277 Wedgewood St Memphis TN 38111-8160

ADHIKARI, DILIP KUMAR, scientist; b. Calcutta, Apr. 4, 1952; s. Manmatha Kumar and Santimaye A.; m. Ketaki Mukherjee, May 9, 1979; children: Hema, Kunal. BS in Chemistry with honors, Calcutta U., 1972; BTechin Food Tech. & Biochem. Engring., Jadavpur U., 1978; MTech, IIT

Delhi, 1981; PhD in Chem. Engring., MS U. of Baroda, India, 1993; Postdoctoral fellow, U. Wis.; Cert., Inst. Biochem. Tech./USDA, Madison, Wis. Chemist Hindusthan Breakfast Foods Corp., Delhi, 1981-82; scientist Indian Inst. Petroleum, Dehradun, India, 1982—; project leader petroleum Biotech., India, 1992-99; exec. com. mem. IIChE, Calcutta, 1993-96; vis. faculty Jiwaji U., Gwalior, India. Inventor in field. Spiritual discourse Ramkrishna Mission, Dehradun, 1999. Mem. IIChE (life), ISAS (life), Tribology Soc. India. Avocations: classical music, sports, sci. edn. for rural people. E-mail:dilipadhikara@hotmail.com. Office: Indian Inst Petroleum, PO IIP, 248005 Dehrandun India

ADHIKARI, GOVIND RAJ, scientist, researcher; b. Dang, Nepal, Jan. 22, 1951; s. Ram Mani and Sumitra Devi Adhikari; m. Indira Dhital. ISc, Trichandra Coll., Nepal, 1971; MSc in Mining, People's Fellowship U., Moscow, 1979; PhD in Civil Engring., Mangalore (India) U., 1997. Mining engr. Dept. Mines and Geology, Kathmandu, Nepal, 1979-84; rsch. assoc. CMRS, Dhanbad, India, 1984-85, scientist, 1986-90; scientist 3 Nat. Inst. Rock Mechs., Kolar Gold Fields, India, 1990-95, scientist 4, 1995—; cons. in field. Mem. adv. bd. Internat. Jour. Rock Blasting and Fragmentation; contbr. articles to profl. jours. Mem. ISRM, ISEE, ISRM&TT, MEAI. Office: Nat Inst Rock Mechs, Champion Reef Post, Kolar Gold Fields India

ADHIKARI, RAJU, molecular scientist; b. Dang, Rapti Zone, Nepal, Feb. 24, 1958; arrived in Australia, 1995; s. Jagannath and Tara Adhikari; m. Susan Pokhrel, Nov. 24, 1988; 1 child, Sambridhi. BSc, U. Garwhal, India, 1977, MSc, 1980; PhD, U. Delhi, India, 1986. Sr. rsch. scientist Univ. Grants Commn., Delhi, 1985-86; in-charge Ctrl. Rsch. Lab. Royal Nepal Acad. Sci. and Tech., Kathmandu, Nepal, 1986-90; postdoctoral fellow Commonwealth Sci. and Indsl. Orgn. Molecular Sci., Victoria, Australia, 1992-93; rsch. scientist Commonwealth Sci. and Indsl. Rsch. Orgn. Molecular Sci., Victoria, 1995-98, sr. rsch. scientist, 1999—; vis. fellow Deutscher Akademischer Austauschdienst, Stuttgart, Germany, 1993; in-charge Natural Products Project, Royal Nepal Acad. Sci. and Tech., Kathmandu, 1988-91, project chief TWAS Grant, 1990-91, UNESCO Grant, 1989-91; chief bioorganic divsn. Nepal Chem. Soc., Kathmandu, 1989-90. Inventor, patentee in field. Pres. Nepali Assn. Victoria, 1997—; sec. Internat. Symposium Natural Products Chemistry, Kathmandu, 1990; v.p. Nepal Chem. Soc., 1991-92. Recipient Sitaram Agrawal Chemistry award Nepal Chem. Soc., 1990, Gold medal His Majesty's Govt. Nepal, 1988. Mem. Nepal Chem. Soc., Royal Australian Chem. Inst., Australian Biomaterial Soc., AAAS. Avocations: reading, bushwalking, sports, social activities, driving. Fax: 61-3-95458050. E-mail: R.Adhikari@molsci.csiro.au. Home: 9 Basil Crescent, Wheelers Hill VIC 3150, Australia Office: CSIRO Molecular Sci, Bayview Ave Bag 10, Clayton S Victoria, Australia

ADIE, WILLIAM ANDREW CHARLES (IAN ADIE), management consultant; b. London, Feb. 21, 1926; s. William John and Lorraine Charlotte Patullo (Bonar) A.; m. Francoise Galy, Sept. 7, 1965; children: Antony William, Alistair John, Chantal Mireille, Annabelle. BA with honors in Literae Humaniores, Oxford U., 1951, MA, 1953. Postgrad. sr. scholar St. Antony's Coll., Oxford, 1954-59; 2d sec. Fgn. Svc., U.K., 1956-59; rsch. to sr. rsch. fellow Oxford U., 1960-71; sr. rsch. fellow internat. rels. Australian Nat. U., 1971-75; sr. pvt. sec. to Minister for Spl. Trade Representations/Govt. Australia, 1978-80; mem. dir. staff Australian Mgmt. Coll., 1981-91; cons. Australian Exec. Svc. Overseas Program, 1993—; rsch. fellow Faculty of Arts, Deakin U.; assoc. Asia Inst.; assoc. dept. bus. and econs. Monash U., Melbourne; vis. prof. and fellow, Inst. Internat. Studies, U. S.C. and U. NSW, 1976-77; adv. bd. New Lugano Rev., Asia Quar., others; adviser to media: London Observer, Telegraph, and others, 1965-70; cons. in field. Editor: The Practising Manager; mem. various editorial bds. jours. in field, including Internat. Jour. of Commerce and Mgmt./USA; contbr. articles to profl. jours., monographs, also chpts. to books. Served U.K. and Indian Armies Intelligence Corps, 1944-48. Mem. Gray's Inn (life/London), Internat. Assn. Schs. and Inst. Adminstrn./Brussels, Australian Inst. Internat. Affairs, Australia-New Zealand Acad. of Mgmt., Assn. Devel. Rsch. and Tng. Insts. of Asia and Pacific/Kuala Lumpur, Contemporary European Studies Assn. of Australia, Australian-Asian Assn., Policy Studies Orgn., Asian Studies Assn. Australia, Inc. Australian Coun. for Europe (founding mem.), Oxford Soc., Travellers Club (London), others. Avocations: collecting early printed books in Latin and Greek, Chinese calligraphy. Home: 76 Canadian Bay Rd, Mount Eliza VIC 3930, Australia also: 12 Impasse des Pecheurs, La Menouniere Saint Pierre d'Oleron 17310, France

ADIKANE, HARSHVARDHAN VISHVANATH, research biochemist; b. Banosa, India, Oct. 28, 1958; s. Vishvanath Asaram and Jijabai Vishvanath (Gondane) A.; m. Vijaya Yeshwantrao Narnawre, May 23, 1986; children: Neha, Vihang. BSc, Marathwada U., Aurangabad, India, 1978, MSc, 1980, PhD, 1986. Biochemist Delhi (India) Adminstrn., 1985-88; asst. dir. Ctrl. Labour Inst., Ministry Labor, Bombay, 1988-89; scientist Nat. Chem. Lab., Pune, India, 1989—. Contbr. articles to scientific jours., inventor in field. Avocation: writing poetry. Office: Nat Chemical Lab, Chem Engring Divsn Pashan Rd, Pune 411 008, India

ADINNA, EMMANUEL NNANYELU, geography educator, consultant; b. Umumba Ndiagu, Enugu, Nigeria, Dec. 31, 1942; s. Adinna Ozoajulu and Amudu Ozochicke; m. Mary Obioma Onwuzu, Oct. 25, 1975; children: Eunice, Pamela, Judith, Juliet, Ifeoma, Nonye. BS in Geography, U. Nigeria, Nsukka, 1972, MS in Indsl. Location, 1984; PGDipEd, Ahmadu Bello U., Zaria, Nigeria, 1979; PhD in Environ. Resources Mgmt., U. Jos (Nigeria), 1992. Tchr. Primary Sch. Mgmt. Bd., Enugu, Nigeria, 1962-66; head dept. social scis. Mt. St. Michael's Secondary Sch., Aliade, Benuu, Nigeria, 1972-76; head dept. social scis., geography tchr. Sch. Basic Studies, Makurdi, Nigeria, 1977-81; sr. lectr. geography, head geography dept. Coll. Edn., Eha-Amufu, Nigeria, 1981-92; reader in geography Coll. Edn., Eha-Amufu, 1991-92; sr. lectr. Enugu State U. Sci. and Tech., 1992—, head dept. geography, 1996—; prin. cons., dir. ADEMBO Consult, Nigeria, 1996-98. Author, co-editor: Environment and Social Harmony, 1994, Ecology, Environment and Politics, 1996; editor-in-chief: Enugu State U. Tech. Jour. of Environ. Mgmt., 1997; contbr. articles to profl. jours. Pres. Gen. Umumba Ndiagu (Nigeria) Town Union, 1998—; chmn. abuses com. Presdl. Com. on Tertiary Sch. Indiscipline Coll. Edn., Eha-Amufu, Nigeria, 1986-92; mem. Ezeagu Leaders of Thought Ezeagu local govt., 1986-98; mem. Emene (Nigeria) Vanguard for provision of social infrastructure in Emene suburban area, 1998. Mem. Nigerian Geograph. Asssn. (mem. coun. 1995-98). Roman Catholic. Avocations: photography, excursions, drawing. Home: PO Box 2298, Enugu Nigeria Office: Enugu State U Sci & Tech, Dept Geography & Meteorology, PMB01660 Enugu Nigeria

ADJANI, ISABELLE, actress; b. June 27, 1955; 1 son, Barnabe. Films include: Faustine ou le bel été, 1972, la Gifle, 1974, l'Histoire d'Adèle H., 1975 (best actress N.Y. Critics 1976), le Locataire, 1976, Barocco, 1977, Violette et François, 1977, Driver, 1977, Nosferatu, 1978, les Soeurs Bronté, 1978, Possession, 1980 (best actress Cannes 1981), Clara et les chics types, 1980, Quartet, 1981 (best actress Cannes 1982), l'Année prochaine si tout va bien, 1981, Antonieta, 1982, l'Eté meurtrier, 1983 (best actress César 1984), Mortelle randonné, 1983, Subway, 1985, Ishtar, 1987, Camille Claudel, 1988 (best actress César 1989), Queen Margot, 1994; theater: la Maison de Bernarda, 1970, 74, l'Avare, 1972-73, l'Ecole des femmes, 1973, Port-Royal, 1973, Ondine, 1974; TV: le Petit bougnat, 1969, le Secret des flamands, 1972, l'Ecole des femmes, 1973, Top à Sacha Distel, 1974. Address: care Irene Murroni, 33 rue Marbeuf, 75008 Paris France

ADKINS, FREDRICK EARL, III, financial consultant, educator; b. Florence, Ala., Oct. 12, 1952; s. Frederick Earl and E. Virginia (Beavers) A.; m. Maureen Blackburn, Aug. 10, 1974; children: Sarah C., Laura E. BS in Mgmt., Harding Coll., 1975; MBA, U. Miss., 1976; cert. in Fin. Planning, Coll. for Fin. Planning, Denver, 1986. CLU, ChFC, CFP; admitted to Registry of Fin. Planning Practitioners, 1987. Mgmt. trainee Met. Life, Little Rock, 1976-79; tng. supr. Conn. Mutual Life Ins., Little Rock, 1979-82, gen. agt., 1982-84; pres. Ark. Fin. Group, Inc., Little Rock, 1984—; adjunct prof. fin. U. Ark., Little Rock, 1990—. Co-author: Guide to Investment Advisory Services, 1997. Pres. Little Rock Founders Lions Club, 1986-87, Ctrl. Ark. Life Underwriters, 1984-85; bd. dirs. Ark. Eye Bank and Lab., Inc., Little Rock, 1986-95, pres., 1989-90, Jones Eye Inst., U. Ark. Med. Scis. Campus, 1993—; Whitbeck Beyer chair Ins. and Fin. Svcs. Adv. Bd., 1994—. Melvin Jones fellow, 1996; named One of Am.'s Top 250 Fin. Advisors Worth mag., 1997, One of the 120 Best Fin. Advisors for Doctors, Med. Econs. Mag., 1998. Mem. Am. Soc. CLU and ChFC (pres. Ark. chpt. 1989-90), Internat. Assn. Fin. Planning (pres. Ark. chpt. 1991-92), Beta Gamma Sigma, Omicron Delta Epsilon. Mem. Ch. of Christ. Avocations: tennis, computers. Home: 364 Valley Club Cir Little Rock AR 72212-2916 Office: Ark Fin Group Inc 225 E Markham St Ste 375 Little Rock AR 72201-1632

ADKINS, GREGORY D., higher education administrator; b. Charleston, W.Va., May 20, 1941; s. Wondel Lafayette and Corda Christenia (Carnes) A.; m. Dolores June Lowe, Sept. 9, 1961; children: Christenia Lea, Angela Dawn. BS, U. Charleston, 1962; MEd, Fla. Atlantic U., 1966; M.C.S., U. Miss., 1968, EdD, 1970. Assoc. prof. edn. Palm Beach Atlantic Coll., West Palm Beach, Fla., 1972-74, chair dept. edn., 1972-73, chair div. profl. studies, dir. tchr. edn., 1973-74; assoc. dean career edn. W.Va. No. Community Coll., Wheeling, 1974-75, dean acad. affairs, 1975-79; coordinator instrn. and planning Colo. State Bd. C.C.s. and Occupational Edn., Denver, 1979-81; pres. So. W.Va. Community Coll., Logan, 1981-88, Bluefield (W.Va.) State Coll., 1988-93, Franklin County Schs., Frankfort, Ky., 1993-94, Jefferson Coll., Hillsboro, Mo., 1994—; vice chmn. adv. coun. of pres. W.Va. Bd. Regents, 1986-87; chair legis. affairs com., 1986-87; bd. dirs. Missourians for Higher Edn., Mo. Coordinating Bd. for Higher Edn. Com. on Transfer and Articulation, 1997—, Jefferson Coll. Found. Inc. Mem. Gov.'s Labor/Mgmt. Coun., Charleston, 1986-93, W.Va. Enterprise Zone Authority, Charleston, 1987-93, Mercer County Econ. Devel. Authority, 1989-93; bd. dirs. Bluefield Regional Med. Ctr., 1988-89, W.Va. Joint Commn. for Vocat. and Occupational Edn., 1989-93, Missourians for Higher Edn., 1996—; mem. coms. on transfer and articulation Mo. Coordinating Bd. for Higher Edn., 1996—. Recipient Alumnus of Yr. award U. Charleston, 1984, award VFW, Chapmanville, 1987; NSF grad. fellow 1967-68, Richard Weaver fellow Intercollegiate Studies Inst., 1969-70. Mem. W.Va. Assn. Coll. and Univ. Pres. (pres. 1984-85), W.Va. C.C. Assn. (pres. 1985-86), Mo. C.C. Assn. (bd. dirs. 1995-97, adv. coun. of pres. 1994—), North Ctrl. Assn. (cons., evaluator 1984—, commr.-at-large 1984-90), Kiwanis, Rotary Internat., Chi Beta Phi (pres.). Mem. Ch. of Christ. Avocations: outdoor sports, gardening. Office: Jefferson Coll 1000 Viking Dr Hillsboro MO 63050-2440

ADKINS, LESLEY, archaeologist, author; b. East Sussex, Eng., Apr. 6, 1955; m. Roy Adkins, Aug. 12, 1978. BA with honors in Archaeology and Ancient History, Latin, U. Bristol, Eng., 1976; M in Philosophy, U. Surrey, Guildford, Eng., 1982. Archaeol. asst. Milton Keynes (Eng.) Devel. Corp., 1976; field officer Surrey Archaeol. Soc., London, 1977-83; sr. archaeologist Mus. of London, 1983-87; archaeol. cons. Somerset, Eng., 1987—; extra-mural lectr. U. London, 1982-83, U. Bristol, 1988-90; adult edn. lectr. London Borough of Croydon, 1983-84. Author: A Thesaurus of British Archaeology, 1982, Under the Sludge, Beddington Roman Villa, 1986, Archaeological Illustration, 1989, An Introduction to Archaeology, 1989, Talking Archaeology, 1990, Abandoned Places, 1990, Introduction to the Romans, 1991, A Field Guide to Somerset Archaeology, 1992, Handbook to Life in Ancient Rome, 1994, Dictionary of Roman Religion, 1996, Handbook to Life in Ancient Greece, 1997, The Keys of Egypt, 2000. Fellow Soc. Antiquaries; mem. Soc. Authors, Inst. Field Archaeologists, Soc. for Promotion of Roman Studies. Avocations: archaeology, gardening. Home and Office: Ten Acre Wood, Whitestone Devon EX4 2HW, England

ADKINS, THOMAS SAMUEL, library director; b. Portsmouth, Ohio, Oct. 24, 1965; s. Millard Elwood and Ruth Caroline (Shultz) A. BS, Ohio U., 1988; MLS, Kent (Ohio) State U., 1993. Tchr. Cmty. Action Agy., Portsmouth, Ohio, 1988, Scioto County Schs., Portsmouth, 1988-89; ext. svcs. coord. Portsmouth Pub. Libr., 1989-95; dir. G.A. Wilson Pub. Libr., Waverly, Ohio, 1996—; chairperson Libr. Adv. Coun., Wellston, Ohio, 1997. Author: Lucasville Cemeteries, 1988; editor: A Backward Glance, vol. 1, 1987, vol. 2, 1990. Mem. Cmty. Svcs. Coun., Waverly, Ohio, 1996—; treas. Lucasville (Ohio) Hist. Soc., 1986—; mem. Valley Alumni Scholarship Com., Lucasville, 1990—; govt. rels. com. OLC, 1998—; participant Libr. Leadership Inst., Snowbird, Utah, 1999. Recipient Diana Vescelius Meml. award, 1998. Mem. ALA (Emerging Leaders 2000), Ohio Libr. Coun., Rotary Club Pike County, Pike County C. of C. (bd. dirs.). A. Avocations: book collecting, local history, movies, travel.

ADKINS, WILLIAM LLOYD, state official; b. Emporia, Kans., May 19, 1959; s. James Lloyd and Elaine (Staples) A.; m. Sheri Jo Brown, May 19, 1984; children: Brian Patrick, Erica Michelle. BA in Psychology, Washburn U., Topeka, Kans., 1981; MA in Adminstrn. of Justice, Wichita State U., 1996. Toll collector Kans. Turnpike Authority, Topeka, 1976-79; biofeedback technician VA, Topeka, 1979-81; career counselor U. Kans., Lawrence, 1981; resdl. coord. Dodge City (Kans.) Mental Health, 1982-83; vault adminstr. Kans. Lottery, Topeka, 1987-88; corrections officer Kans. Dept. Corrections, Lansing, 1988-91; corrections specialist I Kans. Dept. Corrections, El Dorado, 1991, corrections counselor II, 1991—. Contbr. articles to profl. jours. Crisis counselor Headquarters, Inc., Lawrence, 1981-83; cadet advisor Towanda Law Enforcement, 1993-99; jail steering com. Butler County, El Dorado, 1995-96; mem. Butler County Sheriff Res., 1999—; CPR and first aid instr. ARC. With U.S. Army, 1983-87. Mem. VFW, Hostage Negotiators of Am., Kans. Correctional Assn. (facility rep. 1991—), Correctional Peace Officers Found., Kans. Peace Officers Assn., Am. Correctional Assn. (pub. screening com. 1991—), Charles F. Menninger Soc. Avocation: walking dog. Office: El Dorado Correctional Facility PO Box 311 El Dorado KS 67042-0311

ADKISON, LINDA RUSSELL, geneticist, consultant; b. Columbia, S.C., Apr. 28, 1951; d. George Palmer Russell, Jr. and Annie Frances (Ingram) White; m. Daniel Lee Adkison, Jan. 28, 1978; children: Emily Kathleen, Seth Adams Russell. BS, Ga. So. U., 1973, MS, 1977; PhD, Tex. A&M U., 1986. Lab. tech. VA Hosp., Gainesville, 1973-75, Shands Teaching Hosp., Gainesville, Fla., 1973-75; grad. teaching asst. Ga. So. U., Statesboro, 1975-77; rsch. assoc. U. South Ala. Med. Sch., Mobile, 1978-80; instr. St. Mary's Dominican Coll., New Orleans, 1980-81; grad. rsch. asst. Tulane Med. Sch., New Orleans, 1980-82, Tex. A&M U., College Station, 1982-86; postdoctoral fellow Jackson Lab., Bar Harbor, Maine, 1986-89; asst. prof. genetics Mercer U. Sch. Medicine, Macon, Ga., 1989-94, assoc. prof. genetics, 1994-99, prof. genetics, 1999—, assoc. prof. ob-gyn., 1995-99, asst. prof. ob-gyn., 1991-95, prof. ob-gyn., 1999—. Vol. Girl Scouts Mid. Ga., Macon, 1990—, Abnaki Girl Scout Coun., Bar Harbor, 1986-89, Ctrl. Ga. Boy Scouts, Macon, 1993—. Exec. Leadership in Acad. Medicine for Women fellow, Phila., 1999-2000. Mem. AAAS, Am. Coll. Med. Genetics, Am. Soc. Human Genetics, Grad. Women in Sci., Internat. Mammalian Genome Soc., S.E. Regional Genetics Group, Genetics Soc. Ga. (bd. dirs. 1990-97, sec. 1997—), Ga. Acad. Sci., Sigma Xi. Achievements include research in gene mapping mutational analyses, Chromosome 2 physical mapping, X-inactivation. Avocations: running, gardening, softball. Home: 1699 Wesleyan Bowman Rd Macon GA 31210-1037 Office: Mercer Univ Sch Medicine 1550 College St Macon GA 31207-1500

ADLBAUER, KARL, zoologist; b. Graz, Styria, Austria, Aug. 21, 1949; s. Fritz and Josefa (Steiner) A.; m. Edeltraud Ambros, Sept. 19, 1992; 1 child, Wolfgang. PhD, U. Graz, Austria, 1986. Joiner Joinery, Graz, Austria, 1963-70; worker Synthetic Material Factory, Graz, 1970-73; tech. asst. Commonwealth Inst. Biol. Control, Delemont, Switzerland, 1974-75, Inst. Nature Protection, Graz, 1976-80; asst. Government Austria, Graz, 1986-87; zoologist Mus., Graz, 1987—, dept. head, 1990—. Editor Zoolog. Jour., 1990—, Faunistical Periodical, 1990—; contbr. numerous articles on entomol. subjects to profl. jours. Mem. Austrian Entomol. Soc., Naturwissenschaftlicher Verein für Steiermark (Graz), Wiener Koleopterologen-Verein. Roman Catholic. Avocations: entomology, travel. Home: Kasernstrasse 84, A-8041 Graz Styria, Austria Office: Landesmuseum Joanneum, Raubergasse 10, A 8010 Graz Styria, Austria

ADLEMO, ANDERS, science educator; b. Malmö, Sweden, Aug. 11, 1957; s. Eric Vilhelm Andersson and Inger Birgitta (Svensson) A.; m. Rina Maria Navarro Viadana, June 25, 1983; children: Tania Citlali, Vanessa Xanat, Melissa Istacu. MSc, Lund Inst. Tech., Sweden, 1981; PhD, Chalmers U. Tech., Göteborg, Sweden, 1993. Engr. ABB, Västerås, Sweden, 1981-83, Ericsson Telecom, Stockholm, 1984-87; with Ericsson Hewlett-Packard Telecom, Mölndal, Sweden, 1993-96; assoc. prof. Chalmers U. Tech., 1996—. Co-author: Modern Manufacturing: Information Control and Technology, 1994, Balanced Automation Systems, 1995, Balanced Automation Systems II, 1996. Pvt. Swedish Army, 1976-77. Saab scholar Saab Scania, 1990, NUTEK, 1993, Volvo, 1996. Conservative. Roman Catholic. Home: Slätskäddegatan 2A, SE42658 Frölunda Sweden Office: Chalmers U Tech Dept EE, Hörselgången 4, PO Box 8873, SE40272 Lindholmen Göteborg, Sweden

ADLER, ADRIENNE EDNA-LOIS, art dealer, gallery owner, publisher; b. Stillwater, Okla., Mar. 9, 1947; d. Wayne L. Brake and Lois K. (Fisk) Kyle; m. Gary G. Wilcox, Aug. 4, 1964 (div. 1974); children: Troy V., Trisha J.; m. Frederick Peter Adler, Oct. 11, 1991. Butler County Jr. Coll., Richland Coll. From asst. to pres. H.J. Gruy & Assocs., Dallas, 1972-75; from asst. to v.p. econs. dept. DeGolyer and MacNaughton, Dallas, 1975-80; sales mgr. Telecom. Specialists, Inc., Dallas, 1980-85; dir. various art galleries in Calif., Wash., Colo., Tex. & Hawaii, 1985-90; owner Genestar Internat., Santa Barbara, Calif., 1990-95, Galerie Adrienne & Adrienne Editions, San Francisco, La Jolla,, San Diego, 1995—. Chmn. tri-counties adv. bd. Jefferson Ctr. Character Edn., Santa Barbara 1993-95; v.p., pres. women's bd. Santa Barbara Mus. Art, 1995; v.p., chmn. of ball Symphony League, Santa Barbara, 1994-95; advocate, mem. Calif. Assn. Mentally Ill, 1993—. Mem. NAFE, The Commonwealth Club Calif., San Francisco Mus. Art, World Affairs Coun. No. Calif., San Diego Mus. Art, Contemporary Art Mus. San Diego. Avocations: walking, reading, theatre, symphony, opera.

ADLER, CHARLES SPENCER, psychiatrist; b. N.Y.C., Nov. 27, 1941; s. Benjamin H. and Anne (Greenfield) A.; m. Sheila Noel Morrissey, Oct. 8, 1966 (dec.); m. Peggy Dolan Bean, Feb. 23, 1991. BA, Cornell U., 1962; MD, Duke U., 1966. Diplomate Nat. Bd. Med. Examiners, Am. Bd. Psychiatry and Neurology. Intern Tucson Hosps. Med. Edn. Program, 1966-67; psychiat. resident U. Colo. Med. Sch., Denver, 1967-70; pvt. practice medicine specializing in psychiatry and psychosomatic medicine Denver, 1970—; chief divsn. psychiatry Rose Med. Ctr, 1982-87; co-founder Applied Biofeedback Inst., Denver, 1972-75; prof. pro tempore Cleve. Clinic, 1977; asst. clin. prof. psychiatry U. Colo. Med. Ctr., 1986—, chief psychiatry and psychophysiology Colo. Neurology and Headache Ctr., 1988-95; med. dir. Colo. Ctr. for Biobehavioral Health, Boulder, 1994—; bd. dirs. Acad. Cert. Neurotherapists. Author: (with Gene Stanford and Sheila M. Adler) We Are But a Moment's Sunlight, 1976, (with Sheila M. Adler and Russell Packard) Psychiatric Aspects of Headache, 1987; contbr. (with S. Adler) sect. biofeedback med. and health ann. Ency. Britannica, 1986; chpts. to books, articles to profl. jours.; mem. editorial bd. Cephalalgia: an Internat. Jour. of Headache, Headache Quar. Emeritus mem. Citizen's Adv Bd. Duke U. Ctr. Aging and Human Devel. Recipient Award of Recognition, Nat. Migraine Found., 1981; N.Y. State regents scholar, 1958-62. Fellow Am. Psychiat. Assn.; mem. AAAS (rep. of AAPB to med. sect. com.), Am. Assn. Study Headache, Internat. Headache Soc. (chmn. subcom. on classifying psychiat. headaches), Am. Acad. Psychoanalysis (sci. assoc.), Colo. Psychiat. Soc., Biofeedback Soc. Colo. (pres. 1977-78), Assn. for Applied Psychophysiology and Biofeedback (rep. to AAAS, chmn. ethics com. 1983-87, bd. dirs. 1990-93, Sheila M. Adler cert. honor 1988). Jewish. Office: 955 Eudora St Apt 1605 Denver CO 80220-4341

ADLER, EDWARD I., media and entertainment company executive; b. N.Y.C., Jan. 12, 1954; s. Walter S. and Justine (Rosenberg) P.; m. Shari Goldman; children: Alexander Justin, Jillian Haly. BA, Vassar Coll., 1976; MA in Journalism, NYU, 1979. Reporter Time Mag. subs. Time Inc, N.Y.C., 1976-79; sports programming exec. Home Box Office Inc. subs. Time Inc., N.Y.C., 1979-81; news editor TV-Cable Week Mag. subs. Time Inc., N.Y.C., 1981-83; sr. assoc. corp. pub. affairs Time Inc., N.Y.C., 1983-88; mgr. media rels. corp. communications Time Warner Inc., N.Y.C., 1989-93, dir. media rels. corp. comm., 1993-97, v.p. corp. comm., 1997-2000, sr. v.p. corp. comm., 2000—; bd. dirs. N.Y. Cares. Democrat. Office: Time Warner Inc 75 Rockefeller Plz New York NY 10019-6990

ADLER, ERWIN ELLERY, lawyer; b. Flint, Mich., July 22, 1941; s. Ben and Helen M. (Schwartz) A.; m. Stephanie Ruskin, June 8, 1967; children: Lauren, Michael, Jonathan. B.A., U. Mich., 1963, LL.M., 1967; J.D., Harvard U., 1966. Bar: Mich. 1966, Calif. 1967. Assoc. Pillsbury, Madison & Sutro, San Francisco, 1967-73; assoc. Lawler, Felix & Hall, L.A., 1973-76, ptnr., 1977-80; ptnr. Rogers & Wells, L.A., 1981-83, Richards, Watson & Gershon, L.A., 1983—. Bd. dirs. Hollywood Civic Opera Assn., 1975-76, Children's Scholarships Inc., 1979-80. Mem. ABA (vice chmn. appellate advocacy com. 1982-87), Calif. Bar Assn., Phi Beta Kappa, Phi Kappa Phi. Jewish. Office: Richards Watson & Gershon 333 S Hope St Bldg 38 Los Angeles CA 90071-1406

ADLER, IRVING, mathematician; b. N.Y.C., Apr. 27, 1913; s. Marcus and Celia (Kress) A.; m. Ruth Relis, June 2, 1935 (dec. 1968); children: Stephen L., Peggy A.; m. Joyce Lifshutz, Sept. 16, 1968 (dec. 1999). BS, CCNY, 1931; MA, Columbia U., 1938, PhD, 1961; DSc (hon.), St. Michael's Coll., 1990. Tchr. pub. high schs., N.Y.C., 1932-46; chmn. dept. math. Textile High Sch., N.Y.C., 1946-52; instr. math. Columbia U., N.Y.C., 1957-60, Bennington Coll., North Bennington, Vt., 1961, So. Vt. Coll., Bennington, 1983; researcher in math. biology North Bennington, 1972—; lectr. in field. Author 49 books; co-author 34 books; contbr. numerous articles to profl. jours.; contbg. editor Sci. and Society, 1981—; mem. editl. bd. Sci. and Nature, 1978-89. Recipient awards for outstanding sci. books for children Children's Book Coun. and Nat. Sci. Tchrs. Assn., 1972, 75, 80, 90, Townsend Harris medal for outstanding achievement CCNY Alumni Assn., 1993. Fellow AAAS, Vt. Acad. Arts and Sci.; mem. Am. Math. Soc., Math. Assn. Am., Nat. Council Tchrs. Math., Soc. for Indsl. and Applied Math., Authors League, Townsend Harris Hall of Fame, 1996, Phi Beta Kappa, Sigma Xi. Democrat. Jewish. Avocations: vegetable gardening. Home: 297 Cold Spring Rd North Bennington VT 05257-9748

ADLER, JACQUES, history educator; b. Paris, Nov. 28, 1927; s. Szymon Jacob Adlersztejn and Mindla Fajgenbaum; m. Ruth Kurop, Nov. 3, 1949; children: Paul, Louise. BA in History, Tel Aviv U.; PhD in History, U. Melbourne, Australia, 1982. Assoc. fellow U. Melbourne, 1982-98, sr. fellow, 1999—. Author: Face à la Persecution, 1984, The Jews of Paris and the Final Solution, 1987; contbr. entries to the Holocaust Encyclopedia, 1990. Sgt. French inf., 1944-45. Jewish. Home: PL 2-3/431 St Kilda Rd, Melbourne Victoria 3004, Australia Office: U Melbourne, Grattan St, Carlton Victoria 3052, Australia crw

ADLER, MORTIMER JEROME, philosopher, author; b. N.Y.C., Dec. 28, 1902; s. Ignatz and Clarissa (Manheim) A.; m. Caroline Sage Pring, 1963. Ph.D., Columbia U., 1928; B.A., Columbia Coll., 1983. Instr. Columbia U., 1923-30; asst. dir. People's Inst., N.Y.C., 1927-29; assoc. prof. philosophy of law U. Chgo., 1930-42, prof., 1942-52; dir. Inst. for Philos. Research, 1952-95; pres. San Francisco Prodns., Inc., 1954-94; chmn. bd. editors Ency. Brit., 1974-95; chmn. emeritus, 1995—; hon. chair, co-founder Ctr. for the Study of Great Ideas, 1990—; vis. lectr. St. John's Coll., Md., 1937—, visitor emeritus, 1985—; university prof. U. N.C., Chapel Hill, 1988-91; hon. trustee The Aspen Inst., 1973—. Author: Dialectic, 1927, (with Jerome Michael) Crime, Law and Social Science, 1933, (with Maude Phelps Hutchins) Diagrammatics, 1932, Art and Prudence, 1937, What Man Has Made of Man, 1938, 94, How To Read a Book, 1940 (with Charles Van Doren), rev. edit., 1972, Problems for Thomists, The Problems of Species, 1940, A Dialectic of Morals, 1941, How to Think About War and Peace, 1944, 95, (with Louis Kelso) The Capitalist Manifesto, 1958, 75, The New Capitalists, 1961, 75, (with Milton Mayer) The Revolution in Education, 1958, The Idea of Freedom, Vol. I, 1958, Vol. II, 1961, Great Ideas from the Great Books, 1961, The Conditions of Philosophy, 1965, The Difference of Man and the Difference It Makes, 1967, 1993, The Time of Our Lives, 1970, 95, The Common Sense of Politics, 1971, 95, (with William Gorman) The American Testament, 1975, Some Questions About Language, 1976, 1991, Philosopher at Large, 1977, 1992, Reforming Education, 1977, Aristotle for Everybody, 1978, 1991, How To Think About God, 1980, 91, Six Great Ideas, 1981, The Angels and Us, 1982, The Paideia Proposal, 1982, Paideia Problems and Possibilities, 1983, How to Speak/How to Listen, 1983, 1985, The Paideia Program, 1984, A Vision of the Future, 1984, Ten Philosophical Mistakes, 1985, 87, A Guidebook to Learning, 1986, We Hold These Truths, 1987, Reforming Education: The Opening of the American Mind, 1989, Intellect: Mind Over Matter, 1990, 93, Truth in Religion, 1990, Haves

Without Have-Nots, 1991, Desires Right and Wrong, 1991, A Second Look in the Rearview Mirror, 1992, 94, The Great Ideas: A Lexicon of Western Thought, 1992, The Four Dimensions of Philosophy, 1993, Art, the Arts, and the Great Ideas, 1994, 95, Adler's Philosophical Dictionary, 1995; editor: (with Charles Van Doren) Great Treasury of Western Thought, 1977; assoc. editor: Great Books of the Western World, 1945-52, editor in chief 2d edit., 1990, Syntopicon, 1952, 90; gen. editor: The Idea of Happiness, The Idea of Justice, The Idea of Love, The Idea of Progress, 1967; editor in chief: The Annals of America, 21 vols., through 1986, How to Think About the Great Ideas, 2000. Mem. Am. Catholic philos. assn., Am. Maritain Assn, Internat. Listening Assn. Home: 555 Laurel Ave Apt 510 San Mateo CA 94401-4153 Office: Ctr for Study of Great Ideas 845 N Michigan Ave Ste 950W Chicago IL 60611-2221

ADLER, NORMAN T., dean, psychologist, educator; b. Chgo., June 7, 1941; s. Arthur and Mary (Tenner) A.; m. Sheila Stein; children: Shira, Tanya, Ari, Kiva, Tahg. BA, Harvard U., 1962; MA in Endocronology, U. Calif., 1967. Rsch. prof. dept. elec. engring., 1985-93; prof. psychology in psychiatry sch. medicine U. Pa., 1988-93, assoc. dean coll. Sch. Arts and Scis., 1989-93; vice provost rsch. Northeastern U., 1993-95; prof. psychology Yeshiva U., N.Y.C., 1995—, dean, 1995—. Mem. Am. Assn. (organizer roundtable liberal), Grad. Group Anatomy, Grad. Group Neurosci., Exec. Com. Inst. Address: Northern Univ 407 Huntington Ave Apt 27 Boston MA 02115-5406

ADLER, PIERRE MICHEL, researcher, scientist, consultant; b. Roanne, Loire, France, July 8, 1948; s. Henry and Blanche (Gatti) A.; m. Michèle Geneviève Vignes, Dec. 3, 1974; children: Laurent, Danièle. Engr., Ecole Centrale de Paris, 1970; DSc in Physics, U. Paris VI, 1975; Doctorate (hon.), Acad. Gubkine, Moscow, 1997. Attaché de rsch. Nat. Ctr. Sci. Rsch., 1971-80, chargé de rsch., 1981-85, dir. rsch., 1985—; vis. prof. U. Rochester, 1980-81. Author: Porous Media: Geometry and Transport, 1992, Fractures and Fracture Networks, 1999; editor: Multiphase Flow in Porous Media, 1995; prin. editor Jour. PhysicoChem. Hydrodynamics, 1988-90; assoc. editor Applied Mechanics Reviews, 1999; mem. editl. bd. Transport in Porous Media; contbr. articles to profl. jours. Head Laboratoire de Phénomènes de Transport dans les Mélanges, CNRS, Poitiers, 1992-94; cons. Compagnie Générale des Eaurx, Air Liquide, Saft, Gaz de France, Inst. Français du Pétrole, Millipores. Office: IPGP, 4 Place Jussieu, 75252 Paris France

ADLER, POSY (ROSLYN), artist, educator; b. Chgo., Feb. 6, 1916; d. Leon and Julia (Sonnenschein) Woolf; m. Leon Adler, Nov. 1, 1937 (dec.); children: Larry, Janet. BE, Nat. Coll. Edn., Evanston, Ill., 1975; MFA in Sculpture, Goddard Coll., Plainfield, Vt., 1975; studied with Roger Armstrong, Eliot O'Hara, Barbara Neijna, Robert Stoetzer. Art tchr. Miami (Fla.)-Dade Coll., Miami, Fla., 1964-84; sculpture tchr. Saddleback Coll., Mission Viejo, Calif., 1984—; art tchr. Newport Harbor Mus., Irvine Fine Arts Ctr., Met. Art Ctr., Dade County C.C., New Sch. Fine Arts. Exhibited sculpture and watercolors in shows at Art Angles, Calif., Artist's Unlimited, Fla., Bacardi Art Gallery, Fla., Blunt Gallery, Ctr. for the Arts, Boca Raton, Fla., Design Ctr. South, Calif., Grove House Gallery, Fla., Jockey Club Art Gallery, Fla., U. Fla. Lowe Art Gallery, Fla., Met. Art Ctr., Fla., Mus. Science, Miami, Neiman Marcus Art Gallery, Rauchbach Galleries, Tolley Gallery, Turnberry Gallery; commissions include: Sherman Gardens, Calif., Sports Clinic, Laguna Hills, Calif., Temple Or Olom, Miami. Ind. state v.p. Mental Health Soc., Frankfort, 1954-55, bd. dirs., Miami, Fla., 1957-62; hospice vol., Laguna Hills, Calif., 1990-99; vol. Adult Day Care Ctr., Laguna Hills, 1999. Mem. Am. Crafts Coun., Costa Mesa Art League, Ceramic League Miami, Creative Arts Guild, Dana Point Coastal Arts Coun., Florida Craftsman, Laguna Arts Assn., Miami Cultural Arts Alliance, Nat. League Am. Penwomen, Nat. Mus. Women in the Arts, Niguel Art Assn., Sculptors of Fla., Women's Caucus for Art. Democrat. Jewish. Avocations: travel, sculpting, painting, craft work.

ADLER, RAPHAEL, educator emeritus, speech pathologist; b. N.Y.C., Feb. 21, 1922; s. Marcus and Celia (Kress) A.; m. Minna Adler, Sept. 23, 1948; children: Ava Dee, Roxanne, Margo Celeste. BA, Wayne State U., 1953, M in Edn., 1962; PhD, Walden U., 1981. Cert. tchr. secondary schs., Mich.; cert. speech pathologist Am. Speech and Hearing Assn. Tchr. dept. English/ speech Berkley (Mich.) Sch. Dist., 1954-68; prof. Oakland C.C., Union Lake, Mich., 1968-92; prof. emeritus Oakland C.C., Union Lake, 1992—; dir. speech and hearing St. Joseph Mercy Hosp., Pontiac, Mich.,1965-84; owner, dir., pres. Speech Pathology Svcs., Southfield, Mich., 1972-86; cons. hosps., nursing homes, VNA, S. Oakland County Health Dept.; bd. dirs. Motion Picture Inst. Mich. Com. mem. Am. Heart Assn. of Mich.; chmn., bd. trustees State of Mich . Stroke Com. Recipient many speaking citations and awards, 1953-62, Toastmasters Internat. 1971, Mrs. Horace Elgin Dodge award Am. Heart Assn. Mich., 1989, 92, 95. Avocations: reading, dancing, gardening, volunteering, writing. Office: Oakland Cmty Coll 7350 Cooley Lake Rd Waterford MI 48327-3864

ADLER, SARA, arbitrator, mediator; b. Chgo., Jan. 26, 1942; d. Matthew Michael and Mildred Paula (Eckhaus) Lewison; m. James N. Adler, Aug. 19, 1967; children: Michael, Philip, Matthew. AB, U. Chgo., 1961; JD, UCLA, 1969. Bar: Calif. Cons. Inst. Criminal Justice Adminstrn. U. Calif., Davis, 1969-71; assoc. Law Office of Sara Radin, L.A., 1971-72; assoc. dir. Paralegal Tng. Inst. U. So. Calif., L.A., 1972-74; assoc. Wyman, Bautzer, et al, L.A., 1974-78; arbitrator, mediator Dispute Resolution Svcs., L.A., 1978—; pres. Resolution Resources. Fellow Coll. Labor and Employment Lawyers; mem. ABA (neutral co-chair ADR in Labor/employment Law 1995-98, neutral mem. coun. Labor & Employment Law sect., coun. 2000—), Am. Arbitration Assn. (bd. dirs., exec. com., mem. labor mgmt. law task force, employment ADR steering com.), Nat. Acad. Arbitrators (regional chair 1994-96, bd. govs. 2000—), Indsl. Rels. Rsch. Assn. (pres. so. Calif. 1991-92), L.A. County Bar Assn. (chmn. labor and employment sect. 1997-98). Avocations: travel, theater, bridge. Office: Dispute Resolution Svcs 1034 Selby Ave Los Angeles CA 90024-3106

ADLER, SAUL, lawyer; b. N.Y.C., May 30, 1944; s. Tov and Elena Adler; m. Penny Slepkow. LLB, NYU, 1967. Bar: N.Y. 1967, R.I., 1969. Mng. ptnr. law practice Cranston, R.I., 1969—. Office: PO Box 8998 Cranston RI 02920-0988

ADLER, YEHUDA, cardiologist; b. Tel-Aviv, Israel, Nov. 21, 1962; s. Shmuel and Rachel (Levcovich) A.; m. Shuly, May 27, 1993; children: Shir, Roy. MD, B in Med. Sci., Hadassah Ein-Kerem, Jerusalem, 1990; Internal Medicine, Tel-Hashomer Hosp., Israel, 1994; Cardiology, Beilinson Campus, Israel, 1999; Sr. in Cardiology, Rehab. Cardiology Ctr., Tel Hashomer, Israel; lectr. degree in cardiology, Tel-Aviv U. Intern Tel-Hashomer Hosp., sr. cardiology, 1999—; tutor MD students thesis. Contbr. articles to profl. jours. Mem. bd., exec. com., chmn. internat. and pub. rels. com., med. com. Magen David, Israel. Lt. Israel Def. Force Med. Corps. Office: Corning Rehab Ctr, Chaim Sheba Med Ctr, Tel Hashomer 52621, Israel

ADLERCREUTZ, KARIN ELSA INGA, legal educator; b. Lund, Sweden, Sept. 26, 1931; d. Elmo Gottfrid and Karin Svenborg (Larsson) Lindholm; m. Axel Hugo Gustaf Adlercreutz; children: Patrick, Catharina, Mariana. ML, Lund U., Sweden, 1954. Dist. ct. clerk Malmö, Sweden, 1954-56; lectr. pvt. law Lund U., 1965-75, asst. prof., 1975-99; dir. of studies Lund U., 1976-82; vice dean of law faculty, 1983-92; bd. mem., 1986-92; warden of one of the students union, 1979—. Author: Evaluation Report to the Board of Universities on Legal Studies in Sweden, 1982. Mem. of local bldg. com. Lund, 1982-88, mem. bd. of chief Guardians, Lund, 1988-91; chmn. election com. Swedish Assn. Univ. Tchrs., 1982-99. Avocations: literature, walking. Home: Olshögsvägen 10, Lund 224 60 Sweden Office: Lund U Faculty of Law, Lilla Grabrödersgatan 4, Box 207 Lund 22100, Sweden

ADLER-KARLSSON, GUNNAR, philosopher, social scientist; b. Karlshamn, Sweden, Mar. 6, 1933; arrived in Italy, 1968; s. Herbert and Elsa (Andersson) A.; m. Marianne Ehrnford, Dec. 27, 1960. Student, Harvard U., 1960-61, U. Calif., Berkeley, 1961-62; D of Law, Stockholm U., 1962, PhD in Econs., 1968. Prof. Roskilde U. Ctr., Denmark, 1974-88; exec. dir. Capri Inst. for Internat. Social Philosophy, Italy, 1979—. Author books in field; contbr. articles to profl. jours. E-mail: adler.karlsson@capri.it. Home: Via Donna Olimpia 20, I-00152 Rome Italy Office: Inst Internat Social Philosophy, CP 79, I-80071 Anacapri Italy also: Norrtullsgatan 55, S-11345 Stockholm Sweden

ADLERSHTEYN, LEON, naval architect, engineer, educator, researcher; b. St. Petersburg, Russia, Oct. 28, 1925; s. Tsalim and Judith (Shusterovich) A.; m. Irina Bereznaya, Feb. 24, 1962. MS in Shipbuilding, Shipbuilding Inst., St. Petersburg, 1951; DSc in Engring., Ctr. Rsch. Inst. Shipbuilding Tech., St. Petersburg, 1970. Foreman, dep. chief of the hull shop Baltic Shipyard, St. Petersburg, 1951-63; chief technologist Ctrl. Rsch. Inst. for Shipbuilding Tech., St. Petersburg, 1963-65, leader of the team, 1965-74, chief rschr., 1993-94; head of the dept. Acad. of Shipbuilding, St. Petersburg, 1974-88, prof., 1988-94; ret., 1994; chmn. state examination commn. State Marine Tech. U., St. Petersburg, 1989-94; coun. mem. Acad. of Shipbuilding, St. Petersburg, 1974-94, Ctrl. Rsch. Inst. for Shipbuilding Tech., St. Petersburg, 1963-94. Co-author, author 11 books on shipbuilding technology; contbr. over 140 articles to profl. jours. Chmn. coun. sect. Union of Scientists and Engrs., St. Petersburg, 1992-94, mem. bd., 1990-94. Pvt. Russian Army, 1943-45, WWII veteran. Decorated 12 mil. medals Pres. of USSR Supreme Soviet and Pres. of Russian Fedn., 1945-99, 3 mil. awards Am. Legion and Am. Assn. of Invalids and Vets. of WWII, 1995-2000; recipient Order of the Patriotric War 1st Class Pres. USSR Supreme Soviet, 1985, Medals Russian Nat. Indsl. Exhbn., 1955-93. Fellow Inst. of Marine Engrs. (U.K.); mem. Soc. of Naval Architects and Marine Engrs., Union of Scientists and Engrs., Russian Soc. of Shipbuilders (various prizes 1955-93), Am. Assn. Invalids and Vets. of WWII from the former USSR. Achievements include 9 Russian patents on shipbuilding technology; creation and leadership in development of the theory of accuracy in ship hull manufacturing; designed and developed mechanized means for ship manufacturing. Home: 72 Montgomery St Apt 1510 Jersey City NJ 07302-3827

ADLI, HABIB EL, administrator; b. Mar. 1, 1938; married. Grad., Police Acad., 1961. 1st asst. Ministry Interior, Cairo, 1993-97, min., 1997—. Office: Ministry Interior, Sharia Sheikh Rihan, Bab al-Louk Cairo, Egypt*

ADOLPHS, HANS-DIETER, urology educator; b. Raeren, Eupen, Germany, Aug. 7, 1942; s. Bernhard and Helene (Huppertz) A.; m. Heidel Pfennings, May 18, 1977; children: Julia,Claudia, Stephan. MD, U. Duesseldorf, 1968. Intern Univ. Hosps., Duesseldorf, Fed. Republic Germany, 1968-70, East Orange, N.J., 1968-70; asst. in internal medicine, surgery, immunology and urology Univ. Hosp., Aachen, Fed. Republic Germany, 1970-76; asst., then asst. prof. dept. urology U. Bonn (Fed. Republic Germany), 1976-83, assoc. prof., 1983—; chief dept. urology St. Ansgar Hosp., Hoexter, Fed. Republic Germany, 1983—. Contbr. over 100 articles on basic sci., exptl. immunology and urology to med. jours. Ministry Rsch. and Tech. grantee, 1979, 8l. Mem. German Cancer Assn., Assn. Immunology, German Assn. Urology, European Assn. Urology, Am. Urol. Assn., German TNM Com., Lions. Avocations: tennis, skiing, music, sailing. Office: St Ansgar Hosp, Brenkhaeuser Strasse 71, D-37671 Hoexter Germany

ADOOR, GOPALAKRISHNAN, filmmaker; b. Adoor, Kerala, July 3, 1941; s. Madhavan Unnithan and Gouri Kunjamma; m. R. Sunanda, 1972; 1 child. Mem. Working Group on Nat. Film Policy, 1979-80; dir. Nat. Film Devel. Corp., 1980-83; mem. faculties of fine arts U. Kerala, Calicut and Mahatma Gandhi Univs., 1985-89; chair film and TV Inst. of India, 1987-89, 93-98; chair 7th Internat. Children's Film Festival of India, 1991; adv. com. Nat. Film Archive of India, 1988-90; mem. Jury Internat. Film Festival of India, 1983, Venice Internat. Film Festival, 1988, Bombay Internat. Festival, 1990. Film maker: Swayamvaram, 1972, Kodiyettam, 1977, Elippathayam, 1981 (British Film Inst. award), Mukhamukham, 1984 (Internat. Film Critics prize), Anantaram, 1987 (Fipresci prize), Mathilukal, 1989 (Fipresci prize), Vidheyan, 1993 (Fipresci prize), Kathapurushan, 1995 (Fipresci prize), more than 24 short and documentary films; plays include Vaiki vanna velicham, 1961, Ninte rajyam varunnu, 1963, (collection of essays) The World of Cinema, 1983. Recipient numerous internat. film awards. Office: Darsanam Trivandrum, Kerala 695 017, India

ADREES, MUHAMMAD, chemical industry executive; b. Faisalabad, Punjab, Pakistan, Mar. 15, 1958; s. Haji Bashir Ahmed and Naziran Begum; m. Rukhsana Adrees, Dec. 10, 1982; 1 child, Haseeb Ahmed. Grad., Punjab U., Lahore; diploma in higher bus. mgmt., London Poly., 1982; postgrad., PIM Lahore, 1986, 88, 97, LUMS Lahore, 1990-, 92. Dir. export Sitara Textile Industries, Faisalabad, 1982-83; chief exec. Sitara Chem. Industries, Faisalabad, 1983—; bd. dirs. Sitara Energy Ltd., Sitara Textile Industries, Sitara Spinning Mills Ltd., Yasir Spinning Mills. Contbr. articles, revs. to profl. publs. Mng. trustee Aziz Fatimah Trust Hosp., Faisalabad, 1981, Aziz Fatimah Girls H.S., Faisalabad; trustee Ghafoor Bashir Children's Hosp., Faisalabad. Recipient European Quality award, 1993, Top 25 Cos. award Karachi Stock Exch., 1996. Mem. Assn. Industrialists of Shahkot (vice chmn.), Inst. Engrs. Pakistan, Pakistan Chem. Engrs., Caustic Soda Mfg. Assn. (chmn.), Faisalabad Lions Club (regional chmn. 1993-94, spl. assoc. to dist. gov. 1994-95, vice dist. gov. 1995-96, dist. gov. 1996-97, Best Dist. Gov. of Yr. 1996-97), Chenab Club (hon. sec.). Avocation: badminton. Home: Sitara House 139-C, Peoples Colony, Faisalabad Punjab, Pakistan Office: Sitara Chem Industries Ltd, PO Box 442, Faisalabad Punjab, Pakistan

ADRIAENS, PATRICK ANDRÉ, periodontist, consultant, educator; b. Oostende, Belgium, July 23, 1953; s. André and Yvonne (Vandewalle) A.; m. Anne Pannier, Apr. 23, 1977; children: Laurence, Barnabé, Charline. B in medical scis., U. Ghent, Ghent, Belgium, 1974; Lic. Dental Scis., U. Ghent, Belgium, 1976, D in Dentistry, 1982, PhD in Dentistry, 1988. Specialist in periodontology. Asst. prof. U. Ghent, 1977-90; vis. scientist U. Bergen, Bergen, Norway, 1983, U. Aarhus, Aarhus, Denmark, 1983, U. Erfurt, Erfurt, Germany, 1983; asst. prof. U. Mich., 1984-85; lectr. in oral microbiology U. Ghent, 1988-90; chmn., dept. head of periodontology Head & Neck Cen., Brussels, Belgium, 1988-95; prof., chmn. dept periodontology U. Brussels, 1990—; vice dean edn. U. Brussels, 1991—; cons. Ministry of Health, Brussels, 1991—; dir. Internat. Ctr. for Periodontology and Oral Implants, 1995—. Author 10 books, 60 scientific papers in field; co-editor profl. jours. Recipient Dr. Priem prize Dr. Priem Found., 1982, 88, Pfizer award Royal Belgian Acad. Medicine, 1984-85, Fogarty fellowship N.I.H., Bethesda, 1984-85, Internat. Rsch. fellow public health, N.I.H., 1986. Fellow Internat. Coll. Dentists, Delta Sigma Delta; mem. Internat. Assn. Dental Rsch., European Orgn. Caries Rsch., Belgian Soc. Electron Microscopy, Belgian Soc. Cellular Biology, Belgian Soc. Periodontology (pres. 1991-96, Fluocaril prize 1984-85), Tothfriendlypres. 1992—), Belgian Rsch. Group for Oral Biology (pres. 1994—). Avocations: modern art, skiing, tennis, music. Home: Cafmeyerstraat 16, B-1970 Wezembeek-Oppem Belgium Office: ICPOI, 47 Rue de la Vanne, B-1000 Brussels Belgium

ADRIAN, FRANCES See POLLAND, MADELEINE A(NGELA CAHILL)

ADRIAN, JIM, retired mechanical engineer; m. Cecilia Adrian; 3 children. BSME, 1974. Mech. and nuclear engr. Puget Sound Naval Shipyard, 1974-97; ret., 1997; adv. com. U. Wash., Tacoma, 1996—; bd. dirs. Salvation Army. Charter, founding mem. Puget Rental Owners Assn., past pres., past bd. dirs.; coun. mem. City of Bremerton, Wash., 1983-85, internal audit com.; bd. dirs. Kitsap Cmty. Action, 1983-84, YMCA, 1991; com. mem. Bremerton Sch. Dist. Initiative, 1986—; active PTA, Bremerton Solid Waste Adv. Com., 1990-92, Kitsap County Fire Safety Adv. Com., 1998—; v.p., sec. Bremerton Mainstreet Bd., 1987-89; co-chmn. Com. to Protect City Parks, Bremerton, 1989; adv. com. U.S. Senator Slade Gortons Kitsap County, 1998—. Mem. Puget Sound Naval Bases Assn. (bd. dirs., 1st v.p., past sec.). E-mail: cnjadrian@sinclair.net.

ADRIAN, MANUELLA, research scientist, administrator. BA, McGill U., Montreal, Can., 1968; MS in Hygiene, U. Pitts., 1973. Cons. Orgn. Controle Endemies en Afrique Ctrl., Ctrl. African Republic, Chad and Cameroon, 1973; prof. Coll. Algonquin, Ottawa, Ont., 1973-74; policy analyst Ministry State Sci. and Tech., Ottawa, 1974-75; rsch. economist, sociologist Dept. Health and Welfare Can., Ottawa, 1975-78; sr. scientist, head statistical rsch. program Addiction Rsch. Found., Toronto, 1978-96; sr. rsch. scientist, dir. health behavior rsch., dir. rsch. Kans. Health Inst., Topeka, 1996-98; with dept. health svcs. rsch. U. Kans., Overland Park, 1998—; cons. WHO, Geneva, 1982-95, Pan Am. Health Orgn., 1988; adj. rsch. prof. dept. preventive medicine U. Kans., Wichita, 1996-98, lectr. dept. anthropology U. Kans., Lawrence, 1996—. Author, editor: (textbook) Canadian Women's Use of Tobacco, Alcohol and Other Drugs, 1996; guest editor: Jour. Substance Use and Misuse, spl. issue, 1996, 2000; contbr. articles to profl. jours., Can. World Almanac, Ency. of Alcoholism, State of Health Atlas.; mem. editl. bd. Toxicomanies, 1980—, Jour. Substance Use and Misuse, 2000—. Com. mem. United Way, Toronto. Grantee Nat. Health and Rsch. Devel. Program, Can. Mem. Am. Pub. Heatlh Assn. (rev. Alcohol, Tobacco and Other Drugs 1991-99). Office: 300 Bayview Dr Apt 1507 Miami FL 33160-4746

ADRIANOPOLI, BARBARA CATHERINE, librarian; b. Fort Dodge, Iowa, Jan. 27, 1943; d. Daniel Joseph and Mary Dolores (Coleman) Hogan; m. Carl David Adrianopoli, June 28, 1968; children: Carlin, Laurie. BS, Mundeline Coll., 1966; MLS, Rosary Coll., 1975; student, Ozark Rsch. Inst., 1999-2000. Cert. in Pranic Healing and Dowsing Ozark Rsch. Inst. Tchr. Father Bertrand H.S., Memphis, 1966-68; caseworker Dept. Pub. Aid, Chgo., 1968; tchr. North Chgo. Jr. H.S., 1968-70, Austin Mioddle Sch., Chgo., 1970-73; libr. Barrington (Ill.) Pub. Libr., 1976-79, Schaumburg Twp. (Ill.) Dist. Libr., 1979—; mem. diversity com. N. Suburban/Suburban Libr. Sys., Wheeling, Ill., 1995—. Columnist local newspaper, 1995—; contbr. articles to profl. jours. Mem. com. Schaumburg Twp. Disabled, 1981—; historian Village of Hoffman Estates, 1986-99; adv. com. Hoffman Estates Sister Cities, 1988-96; advisor Boy Scout Am. handicapped badge, Schaumburg Twp., 1981—; mem. adv. bd. Cmty. Nutrition Network, 1994—; organizer, mem. Northwest Corridor-St. Patrick's Day Parade com., 1986—; bd. dirs. Children's Mus. and Imaginasium, 1990-93; trainer A World of Difference Anti-Defamation League, 1994; spkr. on libr. outreach svcs., 1995—; me. Com. For Choices For Success-Seminars For Young Women, 1996—. Grantee Sears Cmty. Project for Literacy, Choices for the 21st Century, 1998; recipient Hoffman Estates Citizen of Yr. award VFW, 1995, Libr. Advocate award North Suburban Libr. Sys., 1998. Mem. ALA, Ill. Libr. Assn.úú. Democrat. Roman Catholic. Home: 1105 Kingsdale Rd Schaumburg IL 60194-2378 Office: Schaumburg Twp Pub Libr 130 S Rosedale Rd Schaumburg IL 60193

ADRIANSEN, INGE O., museum curator, historian; b. Skanderborg, Jutland, Denmark, July 27, 1944; d. Børge Mathias and Karen Kristine (Rasmussen) O.; m. Svend Ravn Adriansen (dec. June 26, 1969); children: Hanne Kirstine, Gunnar Christian. Teacher, Denmark Teachers' Sch., 1969; PhD, U. Copenhagen, 1988. Asst. Mus. in Sønderburg Castle, Denmark, 1969-85, curator, 1985—; external examiner U. Copenhagen, 1989-94; chair Johanne Hansen's Legacy; cons. to Dansk Kvindebiografisk Leksion. Author (books) Faedrelandet, Folkeminderne og Modersmaalet, 1990, Ivan from Odessa, 1991, Deutsch Oder Dänisch Bilder Zum Nationalen Selbstverständnis aus dem Jahre 1920, 1992, De forenede Teglvarker i Egernsund, 1894-1994, Sønderjysk Kogebog, 1996, Krig og Kaerlighed i 1864, 1998; contbr. over 100 articles to profl. jours. Recipient from Col. Parkov's Endowment, 1991, Kulturpris (Mark of Honour) County of Slesvig Aabenraa, 1992, Literary mark of honor, Sønderjysk Sprogforening, Aabenraa, 1993, H.V. Clausens legat til danskhedens Fremme, 1999. Mem. Historisk Samfund for Sønderjylland (com. mem.), Skandinavisk Museumsforbund (com. mem.), Danmarks Folkeminder (com. mem.). E-mail: adriansen@adr.dk. Home: Kyshøj 24, DK 6470 Sydals Denmark Office: Museet paa Sønderborg, Slot, DK 6400 Sønderborg Denmark

ADROUNIE, V. HARRY, public health administrator, scientist, educator, environmentalist; b. Battle Creek, Mich., Apr. 29, 1915; s. Haroutune Asadour and Dorthy (Kalaidjian) A.; m. Emalea Riley, June, 1943 (div. Jan. 1980); children: Harry Michael, Vee Patrick; m. Agnes M. Slone, June 26, 1981. BS, St. Ambrose U., 1940, BA, 1959; MS in Environ. Health, Western States U. Profl. Studies, 1984, PhD in Environ. Health, 1984, PhD in Pub. Health, 1984. Diplomate Am. Bd. Indsl. Hygiene, Am. Acad. Sanitarians; registered sanitarian, Calif., Mich., Pa. Enlisted U.S. Army, 1941, commd. 2nd. lt., 1943; advanced through grades to lt. col. USAF, ret., 1968; founder, tech. dir. ARA Environ. Svcs., 1968; dir. environ. health div. Chester County (Pa.) Health Dept., 1971-75, Berrien County (Mich.) Health Dept., 1975-78; prof. environ. health Sch. Pub. Health U. Hawaii, Manoa, 1978-80; dean, prof. Sch. Pub. Health, Western States U. Profl. Studies, Mo., 1980-83; ret., 1983; vis. prof. environ. and pub. health Am. U., Armenia, 1995; USAF rep. U.S. Interdepartmental Com. on Nutrition for Nat. Def., 1959-61; cons. Health Mobilization Program USPHS Surgeon Gen., 1957-61; mem. USAF Surgeon Gen.'s med. goodwill tour all S.Am. countries, 1960; chmn., vis. assoc. prof. dept. environ. health, faculty med. scis. Am. U. Beirut, 1963-66, chmn. dept. environ. health, 1964-66; charter mem. RSH-UN Welfare Relief Agy. Pub. Health Examining Bd. for Mid. East, 1963-66, UNWRA cons., 1964-66; founder, coord. 1st and 2d Environ. Health Symposium of Mid. East, 1965-66; mem. Mich. Hazardous Waste Policy Com., 1990-91, Mich. Mustfa Fin. Policy Bd., 1994—; adj. instr., mem. adv. com. environ. health Ferris State Coll., Big Rapids, Mich., 1974-75, 77-78. Contbr. numerous articles to profl. jours.; author many manuals and tng. booklets for USAF and several books. Chmn. Barry County Solid Waste Planning and Oversight com., 1981—; mem. Barry County Family Independence Agy., 1996—, vice chmn., 1998—; vice chmn. Hastings City Planning Commn., 1984—; mem., co-founder sci. adv. and policy bd. Mich. Ground Water Survey, Inc., 1983-90, chmn., 1988-91; chmn. adv. coun. South Ctrl. Mich. Commn. on Aging, 1981-91; charter mem. UL Underwriters adv. coun. environ. and pub. health, 1996—; appointed mem. Vision 2020 Com., St. Ambrose U., 2000—; past adult leader Boy Scouts Am. Decorated Legion of Merit, USAF; named Alumnus of Yr., Hastings H.S., 1961; recipient Walter S. Mangold award Nat. Environ. Health Assn., 1963, spl. recognition Mich. Environ. Health Assn., 1980, Concerned Citizen award World Safety Orgn., 1992, Safety Person of World Safety Orgn., 1992, Safety Person of Yr. award World Safety Orgn., 1991, State of Mich. White Pine award, 1998. Mem. VFW (life), APHA (emeritus v.p., emeritus conf. 1993, pres.-elect 1994-95, pres. 1995-97, immediate past pres. 1997-99), Mich. Assn. Local Environ. Health Adminstrs. (pres., founder 1976), Nat. Environ. Health Assn. (life, pres. 1961-62), Assn. Mil. Surgeons U.S. (life), Internat. Pub. Health Soc. (charter-emeritus), Global Health Assn., NRA (life, cert. rifle marksmanship instr.), World Safety Orgn. (bd. dirs. 1986-95, cert. bd. 1987—, editl. bd. 1988—), Mich. Environ. Health Assn. (pres. 1991-92), Air Force Assn., Am. Legion (comdr. post 45 1989-90), Indonesian Environ. Health Assn. (co-founder 1979), Lions, Elks (Tyre, Lebanon chpt., life), Moose, Kiwanis (Hasings, Mich. chpt. pres. 1985-86). Home: 1905 N Broadway Hastings MI 49058-1086

ADU-GYAMFI, JOSEPH JACKSON, agricultural research scientist, plant physiologist; b. Kumasi, Ashanti, Ghana, May 15, 1959; s. Benedict Adu-Gyamfi and Helina Aseiduaa; m. Comfort Achiaa; 1 child, Ursula. BSc in Agr., U. Ghana, Accra, 1982; MSc, Hiroshima U., Japan, 1988, PhD, 1991. Asst. rschr. Soil Rsch. Inst., Kumasi, Ghana, 1982-84, scientist, 1991-96; project mgr. Regional Devel. Corp., Kumasi, 1984-85; scientist Internat. Crops Resch. Inst. Semi-Arid Tropics, Hyderabad, India, 1994-97, prin. scientist, team leader, 1997—, cons., 1994. Office: Int Crops Rsch Inst, Semi Arid Tropics, Patancheru AP 502 324, India

ADUM, DAVORIN MATE, geometry researcher, artist, engineer; b. Sibenik, Dalmatia, Croatia, Jan. 18, 1929; arrived in Denmark, 1965; s. Mate Ante and Olga Edmund (Tiller) A.; m. Mira Georg Hauer, Sept. 28, 1958; children: Danica, Mate, Milena. Degree in Philosophy and Langs., U. Belgrade, former Yugoslavia, 1957; cert. in photogrametry, U. Milan, 1957; student, 1975. With Inst. Photogrametry, former Yugoslavia, 1949-65, UN Tech. Assistance Bur. Author: Deciphering the Circle, 1996; designer sciatica protecting super trousers, Super Healthy Featherbed, 1996; exhbns. include Foto Gallery, Croatia, 1989, Social-Pedagogisk Seminarium, 1992, Det Nordjyske landsbibliotek medborgerhuset udstillingslokale, 1993, Thorshavn, Faroe Islands, 1994, Shambala Gallery, Copenhagen, 1996, Medborgerhuset, Copenhagen, 1996, Aalborg (Denmark) Hallen, 1996. Assoc. Danish Red Cross, 1994; cultural mediator Danish Refugee Coun., Aalborg, 1996. Achievements include discovery of intrinsic trigonometry of spiral galaxy; video film made on manuscript The Circle and Beyond (in English). Avocations: astronomy, science fiction translations. Office: Box 1541, 9100 Ålborg Denmark

ADURODIJA, OJO FREDERICK, physicist, educator, researcher; b. Ugboshi-Afe, Akoko-Edo, Nigeria, May 23, 1962; s. Bariki George and Folayemi Ojuolape (Gbadamashi) A. BSc in Physics, Edo State U.,

Ekpoma, Nigeria, 1987; PhD in Physics, U. Northumbria, Newcastle upon Tyne, Eng., 1994. Tchr. Nat. Youth Svc. Corps, Otun-Ekiti, Nigeria, 1987-88; grad. asst. Edo State U., 1988-95, lectr. physics dept., 1995—, chmn. staff welfare physics dept., 1995; postgrad. rsch. asst. U. Northumbria, 1990-95; vis. rschr., cons. Korea Inst. Energy Rsch., Taejon, 1996-98. Contbr. numerous articles to profl. jours. Postgrad. fellow Brit. Overseas Devel. Assn., 1990, New Energy and Indsl. Devel. Orgn. rsch. fellow Hyogo Prefectural Inst. Indsl. Rsch., Kobe, Japan, 1998—. Mem. Inst. Physics (London) (chartered). Achievements include solar cell materials and devices, electronic materials, application of lasers in material processing. Avocations: sports, music, photography, traveling, Christian activities.

ADVANI, LAL K., government executive, former journalist, social worker; b. Karachi, Pakistan, Nov. 8, 1927; s. Kishinchand and Gyani Advani; m. Kamala Jagtiani, 1965; 2 children. Ed., Nat. Coll., Hyderabad, Sind., Govt. Law Coll., Bombay. With Rashtriya Swayam Sevak Sangh social work orgn., New Delhi, 1942, sec. Karachi br., 1947; with Bharatiya Jana Sangh, New Delhi, 1951; party worker Rajasthan, 1951-58; sec. Delhi (India) State Jana Sangh, 1958-63, v.p., 1965-67, mem. cen. exec. com., 1966; organizer joint edit. of Bharatiya Jana Sangh paper New Delhi, 1960-67; interim mem. Met. Coun., New Delhi, 1966; leader Jana Sangh Group, New Delhi, 1966; chmn. Met. Coun., 1967; mem. Rajya Sabha, New Delhi, 1970—; head Jana Sangh parliamentary group, New Delhi, 1970; pres. Bharatiya Jana Sangh (incorporated in Janata), New Delhi, 1973-77; prisoner, 1975-77; gen. sec. Janata party, New Delhi, 1977; min. info. and broadcasting New Delhi, 1977-79; gen. sec. Bharatiya Janata party, New Delhi, 1980-86, pres., 1986—; now min. fgn. affairs Govt. of India, New Delhi. Author: A Prisoner's Scrap-Book, the People Betrayed. Avocations: theatre, cinema, books. Office: Ministry Fgn Affairs, N Block 1 Rm 26, New Delhi 110 001, India also: C-1/6, Pandara Park, New Delhi India*

AEBERHARD, JOHN P., public relations consultant; b. London, Mar. 6, 1937; s. Armin and Winifred Florence (Ryland) A.; m. Penelope Jane Rankin, Sept. 5, 1964; children: Matthew John, Daniel Edwin, Peter Joseph. MA with honors, Oxford U., 1961. Press officer Michelin Tire Co. Ltd., London, 1962-66, English Elec. Computers Ltd., London, 1966-68; corp. press officer Internat. Computers Ltd., London, 1968-69; cons. Carl Byoir & Assocs., Inc., London, 1969-75; dir. pub. rels. Honeywell Info. Systems, Inc./Honeywell Ltd., Bracknell, Brentford, Eng., 1975-78; dir. pub. rels. and advt. Honeywell Info. Systems, Inc., Waltham, Mass., 1978-80; chmn. A Plus Group Ltd., London, 1981-96; trustee/dir. AbilityNet Ltd. Contbr. articles to profl. jours. Mem. Brit. Computer Soc. Disability Group (bd. dirs.). Avocations: travel, walking, history, architecture. Home: Millstones Egypt Ln, Millstones Egypt Ln, Farnham Common Bucks SL2 3LF, England

AEBERHARDT, ANDRE AUGUSTE, physician radiobiologist; b. Saint-Imier, Berne, Switzerland, Feb. 18, 1916; s. Auguste Ernest and Clara Cécile (Grimm) A.; m. Esther Lydie Feugnet, Apr. 26, 1943; children: Marianne, Catherine, Jean-Paul. MD, Faculté de Médecine, Lyon, France, 1943; PhD, Faculté des Scis. Sorbonne, Paris, 1961; Docteur ès lettres Histoire, Faculté des Lettres, Tours, France, 1983; Maître Recherches Svc., Santé de Armées. Médecin-lt. Service de Santé des Armées, 1942—; médecin général, 1969-76; chef du lab. de radiopathologie Commissariat Energie Atomique, Paris, 1962-68; dir. Service Mixte de Contrôle Biologique, 1964-71; dir. Centre de recherches du Service de Santé des Armées, Paris, 1971-76, retired, 1976; expert med. N.B.C., NATO, 1964—; expert N, Finabel, 1966-76. Contbr. articles to Internat. Jour. Radiation Biology, Health Physics and other profl. jours. Légion d'Honneur, Officier, Ordre du Mérite National, Commandeur, Croix de guerre 1940-45. Mem. N.Y. Acad. Scis., Soc. Nat. des Antiquaires de France (mem. corr. 1985—). Home: 112 Bd Béranger, 37000 Tours France

AEBISCHER, NICHOLAS JOHN, biometrician, researcher; b. Vevey, Switzerland, Mar. 9, 1957; s. René Olivier and Jennifer (Broadbent) A.; m. Helen Clare Cradock, Apr. 16, 1994; children: Sebastian, Zoë. Lic. in math. sci., U. Lausanne, Switzerland, 1980; PhD, U. Durham, Eng., 1985. Rsch. asst. U. Durham, 1984-85, sr. rsch. asst., 1985-87; biometrician Game Conservancy Trust, Fordingbridge, Eng., 1987-90; head biometrics Game Conservancy Trust, 1990-98, dir. biometrics, 1998-99, dep. dir. of rsch., 2000—. Mem. editl. panel Ibis, Eng., 1996—, Game & Wildlife, France, 1993—; contbr. numerous articles to profl. jours. Mem. Brit. Trust Ornithology, Brit. Ornithologists Union (coun. 1996-00), Internat. Biometric Soc., Internat. Union Conservation of Nature (conservation specialist groups), Brit. Ecol. Soc. Avocations: bird watching, classical music, badminton. Office: The Game Conservancy Trust, Fordingbridge SP6 1EF, England

AEHLERT, BARBARA JUNE, health services executive; b. San Antonio, June 17, 1956; d. Bobby Ray and Ronella Su (Light) Mahoney; m. Dean A. Aehlert, Sept. 6, 1980; children: Andrea, Sherri. AA in Nursing, Glendale (Ariz.) C.C., 1976; BS in Profl. Arts, St. Joseph's Coll., Windham, Maine, 1997. Cert. ACLS instr., affiliate faculty, BLS instr., Basic Trauma Life Support instr., emergency med. tng./paramedic instr., ATLS course coord. Gen. mgr. Hosp. Ambulance Svc., Phoenix, 1982-83; critical care nurse Samaritan Health Svcs., Phoenix, 1978-80, coord. patient transp., 1980-82, mgr. clin. programs, 1983-92; dir. emergency med. svcs. edn. EMS Edn. and Rsch., 1992-97; pres. S.W. EMS Edn. Inc., Glendale, Ariz., 1997—. Author: ACLS Quick Review Study Guide, 1994, ACLS Quick Review Slide Set, 1994, ACLS Quick Review Study Cards, 1994, PALS Study Guide, 1994, ECGs Made Easy, 1995, ECGs Made Easy Lesson Plans, 1996, Mosby's Computerized Paramedic Test Generator, 1996, Aehlert's EMT Basic Study Guide, 1997. Republican.

AERTS, DIEDERIK EMIEL, physics educator, science center administrator; b. Heist-Op-Den.Berg, Flanders, Belgium, Apr. 17, 1953; s. Karel Jozef A. and Juliette Emilia Claes; m. Natalia Argüelles Caranza, Aug. 5, 1995; 1 child, Johannes. Candidate Math. Physics, Free U. Brussels, 1973, Grad. Theoret. Physics, 1975, Doctorate, 1981. Researcher Belgium Fund Scientist Rsch. HFWD, Brussels, 1976-81, rsch. assoc., 1981-85, sr. rsch. assoc., 1985—, dir. Ctr. Leo Apostel, 1995—; head rsch. group Fund Free U. Brussels, 1996—; organizer internat. conf. Einstein Meets Magritte, Belgium, 1995. Author: De Muze Van Het Leven, 1993; co-author: World Views, 1994, Perspectives of the World, 1995; editor-in-chief: Foundations of Science Kluwer International, 1998—. Mem. Internat. Quantum Structure Orgn. (sec. 1996—). Office: Free U Brussels CLEA Fund, Pleinlaan 2, 1050 Brussels Belgium

AERTS, LUC M.T.K., barrister; b. Brecht, Antwerp, Belgium, June 6, 1959; s. Robrecht and Maria (Van Dongen) A.; m. Claudine Keleman, Mar. 3, 1984; children: Koenraad, Goedele. B of Common Law, Cath. U. of Louvain, Belgium, 1981, Licentiate of Laws, 1982; M of Laws, U. London, 1983. Asst. prof. internat. law Cath. U. Louvain, 1983-85; barrister Antwerp, 1983—. Home and Office: Vaartstraat 81, 2960 Brecht Antwerp, Belgium

AESCHLIMANN, EDSEL ANDRÉS, telecommunications company executive; b. Córdoba, Argentina, Nov. 15, 1965; s. Edsel Delfor Aeschlimann and Stella Maris Nardelli; m. María Sabina Uribarren; children: Sabina María, Virginia. Diploma in electronic engring., Nat. U. Córdoba, 1991. Designer, mfr. electronic equipment Villa Carlos Paz, Argentina, 1983-94; spl. projects engr. Antena Comm. Villa Carlos Paz, Córdoba, 1991-94; prof. Nat. U. Córdoba, 1992-97; sr. engr. Co. Telfonos Interior, 1994-97; mgr. radio frequency planning Nextel Argentina, Buenos Aires, 1997—. Mem. IEEE, Consortium Prof. Telecom., Electronic and Computer Engrs., Soc. Cable Telecom. Engrs. Roman Catholic. Avocations: wind surfing, swimming, cross country running. Office: Nextel Argentina, Palestina 977, 1182 Buenos Aires Argentina

AEUGLE, THOMAS, semiconductor development researcher; b. Heidenheim, Germany, July 15, 1960; s. Rudolf and Brigitte (Faigle) A.; m. Petra Fuerst, Mar. 1993. Physics diploma, U. Ulm, 1986, PhD, 1991. Semiconductor rschr. U. Ulm, 1987-91; quality ins. Siemens-Nixdorf, Augsburg, Germany, 1991-93; Silicon process tech. Siemens, Munich, 1993—; project mgr. Siemens, Munich, 1995—, mobile phones mgr., 1999—. Contbr. articles to profl. jours.; patentee in field. Mem. IEEE. Avocations: music, sports, long distance travel. Home: Albert Schweitzer Str 38, 81735 Munich Germany Office: Siemens at men, Grillpatzerstr 12a, 81675 Munich Germany

AFANASEV, IGOR BORISOVITCH, chemist; b. Moscow, May 25, 1935; m. Vera Mamaeva; 1 child, Ilya. Engr.-technologist, Chem.-Technol. Inst., Moscow, 1958; PhD in Chemistry, Inst. Element Organic Chem., Moscow, 1963; D of Chem. Sci., Inst. Chem. Physics, Moscow, 1972; prof. chem. kinetics, Moscow, 1980. Rschr. Inst. Nitrogen Industry, Moscow, 1958-64, sr. rschr., 1964-66, head of lab., 1966—. Author: (books) Superoxide Ion: Chemistry and Biological Implications, Vol. I, 1989, Vol. II, 1991, Lipoic Acid in Health and Disease, 1997, Antioxidants in Disease: Mechanisms and Therapy, 1997. Mem. Soc. for Free Radical Rsch. (chmn. nat. com.). Avocation: reading. E-mail: iafan aha.ru. Home: Efremova Str 12/70, Moscow 119048, Russia Office: Vitamin Rsch Inst, Nauchny pr 14A GSP-7, Moscow 117820, Russia

AFANAS'EV, VALERY VASILIJEVITCH, physicist; b. Nizhneudinsk, Siberia, Russia, Mar. 31, 1960; s. Vasili Fedorovitch and Ninel Petrovna (Fadeeva) Afanas'ev; m. Olga Borisovna Grishina-Berdnikova, Sept. 2, 1993; children: Andrei, Daniil. MSc, U. Leningrad, 1982, PhD, 1985. Rsch. assoc. U. Leningrad, Russia, 1985-92; rsch. fellow Tech. U. Delft, The Netherlands, 1992-94, U. Erlangen, Germany, 1994-95; sr. rsch. fellow U. Leuven, Belgium, 1995—; cons. Simon-Freeman Assocs., Inc., Landover, Md., 1994, Indsl. Microelectronic Ctr., Kista, Sweden, 1996. Fellow A. von Humboldt Found., 1994. Office: Cath U Leuven Semicondr Lab, Celestijnenlaan 200 D, B-3001 Leuven Belgium

AFANASIEV, ANDREI NIKOLAEVICH, executive economist, designer; b. Klin, Moscow Reg, Nov. 23, 1950; s. Nikolai Aleksandrovich and Lidia Feliksovna (Lampe) A.; m.Tatiana Bentsionovna Nevedomskaia, Mar. 26, 1976; children: Egor, Timofei. Engr., Moscow Power Inst., 1975; economist, Bus. Sch. VNIKI, Moscow, 1991. Engr. Electro-Mech. factory, Solnechnogorsk, Russia, 1975-84; master Angstrem Factory, Zelenograd, Russia, 1984-86; exec. Gosstandart, Klin, Russia, 1986-90, Termopribor factory, Klin, 1990—. Home: 47 Gagarina St Apt 24, 141600 Klin Russia Office: Termopribor Joint Stock Co, 44 Volokoiamskoe shosse, 141600 Klin Russia

AFANASYEV, BORIS NIKOLAEVICH, chemist, researcher; b. Leningrad, USSR, Sept. 9, 1937; s. Nikolay Aleksandrovich Afanesyev and Ekaterina Alekseevna Vasilyeva; m. Galina Adnreevna Shasholina, Oct. 12, 1965; 1 child, Lyudmila; m. Yulia Petrovna Akulova, May 4, 1996. Degree, Karlov U., Prague, Czechoslovakia, 1961; PhD, Tech. Inst., Leningrad, 1965, DSc, 1977. Cert. chemist. Asst. lectr. Tech. Inst., Leningrad, 1961-68, assoc. prof., 1968-79, prof., 1979—; cons. Poly. Inst., Havana, Cuba, 1981-82, Kabul, Afghanistan, 1986; Soros prof. Internat. Soros Sci. Edn. Program, N.Y., 1999. Avocation: travel. Home: Dimitrov st. 4-I-293, 192239 Saint Petersburg Russia Office: Tech Inst, Moskovskii pr., 26, 198013 Saint Petersburg Russia

AFIFI, ASHRAF MOHAMED EL-SADEK, neonatologist, pediatrician; b. Egypt, Aug. 22, 1954; s. Mohamed El-Sadek Afifi. B Medicine B Surgery, Cairo U., 1977, M Pediats., 1981, PhD in Pediats., 1986. Intern Cairo U. Hosp., 1978-79; pediat. resident Cairo U. Children's Hosp., 1979-82, asst. pediat. lectr., 1983-85; neonatology fellow Children's Hosp. Med. Ctr./George Washington U., Washington, 1985-87; pediat. resident fellow U. Md. Hosp., Balt., 1987-89; attending in neonatology Washington Hosp. Ctr., 1989-90; neonatology attending, pediat. instr. Johns Hopkins Bay View Med. Ctr., Balt., 1990-92; cons. neonatology attdneing Saudi Aramco/Dhahran (Saudi Arabia) Health Ctr., 1992—. Contbr. articles to profl. publs. Rsch. grantee Children's Hosp. Med. Ctr., 1985-87. Fellow Am. Acad. Pediats., Am. Bd. Neonatal-Perintal Medicine, Egyptian Neonatology Assn. (hon.); mem. AMA. Avocations: walking, jogging, computers, gardening. Fax: 9663-877-3792. E-mail: afifiam@aramco.com.sa. Office: Saudi Aramco Med Svcs Orgn, Saudi Aramco Box 11985, Dhahran 31311, Saudi Arabia

AF KLINTEBERG, BRITT G. E., psychology educator; b. Falun, Sweden, May 19, 1942; d. Gösta and Gerd (Ytterberg) Werner; m. Sten Ludvig Humble; children: Pontus, Paula, Christa. BA in Edn., French and Econs., Stockholm U., 1979, PhD in Psychology, 1988. Tchr. phys. edn. Stockholm Schs., 1964-79; investigator Conscientious Objectors Bd., Stockholm, 1978-80; rsch. asst. Karolinska Inst., Stockholm, 1982; rsch. asst. Stockholm U., 1983-84, lectr., rschr., 1988-91, assoc. prof. dept. psychology, 1992-98, prof., 1998—; dep. rep., dept. of psychology, Stockholm U., 1993—, dep. head divsn. biol. psychology, 1994—; mem. initiative com. Med. Rsch. Coun., Stockholm, 1997—; organizer, sec. Divsn. Biol. Psychology and Neuropsychology, 1989-91. Contbr. articles to profl. jours., chpts. to books. Rsch. fellow European Sci. Found., 1990. Mem. N.Y. Acad. Scis., Internat. Soc. for Study of Individual Differences, Internat. Soc. for Study of Personality Disorders, Swedish Alcohol Rsch. Fund (bd. dirs.). Avocations: music, art, reading. Office: Stockholm U Dept Psychology, Frescati Hagvag 14, S-106-91 Stockholm Sweden

AFONIN, EDUARD ANDRIYOVYCH, librarian, sociologist; b. Kungur, Molotovska, Russia, Nov. 29, 1948; m. Oksana Tymofiivna Afonina; m. Laryssa Yuriivna Osypenko, Mar. 14, 1975; children: Kostiantyn, Serhiy, Kateryna. Tchr. in physics, State Pedagogic Inst., Taganrog, Russia, 1970; lawyer, High Sch. Com. State Security, Minsk, USSR, 1973; expert in patents and lics., Inst. Intell. Property Protec., Kyiv, Ukraine, 1993; DSc in Sociology, State U., Kharkiv, Ukraine, 1996. Cert. sociologist. Sec. City Com. of Union of Youth of Ukraine, Chervonograd, USSR, 1971-72; co-worker Com. of State Security, Minsk-Lviv-Kyiv-Moscow, 1972-91; acad. sec. Nat. Acad. Sci. of Ukraine, Kyiv, 1991-94; asst. to spkr. of parliament Verkhovna Rada, Kyiv, 1994-96, head of info. and libr. dept., 1996—; expert State Program of Govt., Kyiv, 1992-95; expert, mem. supervision bd. Nat. Soros Found., Kyiv, 1993-98. Author: (monograph) Ukrainian Army Raise Up: Social and Psychological Problems, 1994; co-author: (handbooks) Social and Psychological Study, Prognostication and Correction of Behavior of Serviceman's Contract, 1994, The Actual Issues of Legislative Activity, 1998, Parliament of Ukraine: Elections '98, 1998, Ukraine and the World: Problems and International Cooperation and Collective Security, 1999, President of Ukraine: Reference Index (1991-1999), 2000, Politics and Politicians fo Ukraine in the Mirror of Periodics, Vols. 1 and 2, 2000, Social Development A.D., 2000. Pres. Ukrainian Social Innovations Soc., 1995. Soldier Soviet Army, 1970-71. Named. Hon. Citizen, Lincoln, Nebr., 1995. Mem. Nat. Libr. Assn. Ukraine, Sociologist's Assn. Ukraine. Orthodox. Avocations: dancing, swimming, traveling. Fax: 380 44 226 2145. E-mail: afonin@rada.gov.ua. Home: Apt 23 Bl 4 Chekistiv Ln, Kyiv 01024, Ukraine Office: Verkhovna Rada of Ukraine, 5 Hrushevskoho Str, Kyiv 01008, Ukraine

AFRIDI, MUHAMMAD ALI, oncologist, consultant; b. Peshawar, Pakistan, Aug. 14, 1947; s. Muhammad Hanif and Safia (Begum) A.; m. Riffat Sultana Nawaz, Sept. 22, 1977; children: Amina, Waffiyah, Sameera, Hajirah. MBBS, Khyber Med. Coll., Peshawar, Pakistan, 1969. Diplomate Am. Bd. Radiology. Demonstrator pharmacology dept. Khyber Med. Coll., Peshawar, 1969-71; intern Ellis Hosp., Schenectady, N.Y., 1972-73; resident in radiation oncology Roswell Park Meml. Cancer Ctr., Buffalo, 1973-76; fellow in radiation oncology Hosp. U. Pa., Phila., 1976-77; cons. radiation oncologist, asst. prof. U. Pitts., 1977-82; cons. radiation oncologist Vassar Bros. Hosp., Poughkeepsie, N.Y., 1982-92; cons. radiation oncologist, head dept. radiation oncology Shifa Internat. Hosp., Islamabad, Pakistan, 1993—; also bd. dirs., 1997—; mem. edn. coun. Shifa Coll. Medicine, Islamabad, 1998—. Contbr. articles to profl. jours. Vis. scholar Nuffield Found., 1968. Mem. Am. Coll. Radiology, Am. Soc. Therapeutic Radiology and Oncology, Pakistan Med. Assn. (Rawalpindi). Avocations: reading, watching sports, sightseeing. Home: House # 22 St # 28 F-10/1, Islamabad Pakistan Office: Shifa Internat Hosp, Sector H-8/4, Islamabad Pakistan

AFSHAR, AMIR ASLAN, former Iranian government official; b. Tehran, Iran; s. Amir Massoud and Amir Banou A.; m. Camilla Saed, Feb. 19, 1950; children: Fatima, Mohammad. D Polit. Sci., U. Vienna, 1943; HHD, U. Utah, 1971. Joined Iranian Fgn. Svc., 1948; service in Netherlands, civil aide to Shah, 1957-79, dep. of Parliament, 1956-60, amb. to Austria; chmn. bd. govs. Internat. Atomic Energy Agy., Vienna, 1967-69; amb. to U.S., 1969-73, amb. to Mexico, 1970-73, amb. to Fed. Republic Germany, 1973-77, grand master of ceremonies of The Shah, 1977-79; del. UN gen assemblies, 1957, 58, 60, dep. gov. Am. Biograph. Inst., 1985—; head delegation of Iran to INTERSAT, Rd and Trafic, Unido and 15 other internat. confs. Author: (in German) The Possibilities of the Development and Expansion of the Iranian Economy; (in Farsi) The Fall of the Third Reich, Iran's Participation in International Organizations, God Created the World, The Dutch Built Holland; (in English) Report on America; German Law and Constitution of the Third Reich; also studies in German on German law. Decorated order Homayoun 1st and 2d class, Order Taj 3d, 4th and 5th class, medal of Farhang 2d class, Medal of Pas 1st class, Commemorative medal, Coronation medal, 2500 Ann. Founding Persian Empire medal, Fifty Years Pahlavi Dynasty medal; also 20 fgn. 1st class decorations; Eisenhower exch. fellow, U.S., 1955-56. Home: 38 Promenade des Anglais, F-0600 Nice France

AFSHAR, FARHAD, neurosurgeon; b. Dec. 1941; s. Aziz Afshar Yazdi and Btoul Ameli; m. Lucille Anne Afshar, Aug. 23, 1968 (div. 1983); children: Iain, Daniel, Brett, Nina. BSc with honors, Lord Wandsworth Coll., Hants; MB BS with honors, London Hosp. Medicine Coll.; MD, U. London. Fellow Royal Coll. Surgeons, England; fellow in neurosurgery Ohio State U., 1975-76; cons. neurosurgeon, sr. lectr. neurosurgery London Hosp., 1975-85; sr. registrar in neurosurgery London and St. Bartholomew's Hosp., 1977; cons. neurosurgeon St. Bartholomew's Hosp., 1985—; sr. cons. neurosurgeon Royal London Hosp.; examiner in surgery U. London. Author: Stereotaxic Atlas of Human Brain Stem and Cerebellar Nuclei, 1978; contbr. numerous chpts. to books, articles to med. jours. Fellow Royal Soc. Medicine, Royal Coll. Surgeons (licentiate); mem. Soc. Brit. Neurosurgeons, Congress Am. Neurosurgeons, Euro and World Stereotaxic Surgeons, World Pituitary Surgeons. Avocations: photography, natural history, walking. Fax: 0207-935-7245. E-mail: fary afshar@fsmail.net. Office: St Bartholomew's Hosp, Dept Neurosurgery, London E1 1BB, England also: Royal London Hos, Whitechapel, London E1 1BB, England

AFTERMAN, ALLAN B., accountant, educator, researcher, consultant; b. Chgo., Jan. 25, 1944; s. Joseph and Ruth Gertrude (Jacobson) A.; m. Joan Elaine Hoffman, Apr. 30, 1974; children: Debra, Lori, Julie, Robin. BBA, Roosevelt U., 1964; PhD, U. Birmingham, Eng., 1989. CPA, Calif. Asst. dir. securities exchange com. practices Alexander Grant & Co., Chgo., 1967-70; nat. staff mgr. Touche Ross & Co., Chgo., 1970-73; nat. tech. dir. Practice Devel. Inst., Chgo., 1977-82; acctg. prof. U. Ill., Chgo., 1983-88, dir. exec. edn.; mem. faculty grad. sch. bus. U. Chgo., 1992-99; cons. to govts. Author: Accounting and Auditing Disclosure Manual, 1982, Compilation and Review, 1983, Accounting and Auditing Update, 1984, SEC Accounting and Reporting Update, 1985, GAAP Practice Manual, 1985 (best loosleaf bus. reference award profl. and scholastic divsn. Assn. Am. Pubs. 1985), Accounting and Tax Highlights, 1986, Handbook of SEC Accounting and Disclosure, 1987, Credit Analyst's Report, 1988, Financial Reporting and Disclosure Manual in the United Kingdom, 1989, Public Accounting Practice Manual, 1990, Governmental Accounting & Auditing Disclosure Manual, 1991, Nonprofit Accounting and Auditing Disclosure Manual, 1992, Auditing Standards and Practices in Poland, 1993, SEC Regulation of Public Companies, 1994, International Financial Accounting, Reporting & Analysis, 1994, U.S. Securities Regulation of Foreign Issuers, 1995, Charities Accounting and Auditing Disclosure Manual in the United Kingdom, 1996, Nonprofit GAAP Practice Manual, 1998, Audit Committee Governance Report, 2000. Mem. AICPA, Am. Acctg. Assn., Practicing Law Inst., N.Y. Soc. CPAs. Jewish. Home: 3900 Mission Hills Rd Apt 302 Northbrook IL 60062-5721 Office: 3330 Dundee Rd Ste N6 Northbrook IL 60062-2329

AF TROLLE, MARIKA ELISABETH, artist; b. Österåker, Sweden, Jan. 13, 1952; d. Georg Herman and Ingrid Maria (Gullberg) af T.; m. Ulf af Trolle, Nov. 2, 1977; 1 child, Kristina Marika. Degree, Österalm U., 1970. Artist Sweden, France, 1970-85; musical art video films Sweden France, Ireland, Japan, 1985—; electronic painting and installations Sweden, France, Finland, 1985—. Author and editor of catalogues. Creator, chmn., Assn. for Protection of Children Against Violence in TV, 1993—; hon. citizen The Coun. of Tholonet, Le Tholonet France, 1988. Avocations: physics, information technology, eastern philosophy, religion. Home: Campagne Ripert, 13100 Le Tholonet France

AFWERKI, ISAIAS, president of Eritrea; b. Asmara, Feb. 2, 1946; married; 2 children. Student, U. Addis Ababa, 1965-66. Combattant Eritrean Liberation Front, 1966-70, dep. divsn. commdr., 1967-70; founding mem. Eritrean People's Liberation Front, 1970, dep. sec. gen., 1977-87, sec. gen., 1987-91; sec. gen. Provisional Govt. Eritrea, Asmara, 1991-93, pres., 1993—; chmn. Nat. Assembly, People's Front for Democracy and Justice. Office: Office of Pres, PO Box 257, Asmara Eritrea*

AFXENTIOU, AFXENTIS COSTA, bank executive; b. Larnaca, Cyprus, Dec. 11, 1932; s. Costas and Terpsichore (Panayi) A.; m. Stella Vanezis, 1957 (dec. 1974); 2 children: Maria, Costas; m. Egli Markides, 1981. Student, Athens (Greece) Sch. Econs. and Bus Sci.; MA in Econ., U. Ga. With Hellenic Mining Group, Nicosia, Cyprus, 1955-62; econ. officer to dir.-gen. Ministry of Fin., Nicosia, Cyprus, 1962-79, minister of fin., 1979-82; gov. Ctrl. Bank of Cyprus, Nicosia, 1982—; gov. for Cyprus IMF, 1982—. Mem. Cyprus Econ. Soc. Avocations: reading, walking, swimming. Office: Ctrl Bank Cyprus, POB 5529 80 Kennedy Ave, 1395 Nicosia Cyprus

AFZAL, MOHAMMAD, physician, consultant; b. Jalundhar, Punjab, India, Dec. 28, 1945; arrived in Saudi Arabia, 1984; s. Shah Mohammad and Sardar (Bibi) A.; m. Shazia Nasir, Oct. 19, 1984; children: Mohammad Ahmad, Abdullah, Amnah. Degree in pre-med. studies, Govt. Coll., Jhang, Pakistan, 1964; MB BS, Nishter Med. Sch., Multan, Pakistan, 1969. Diplomate Am. Bd. Pathology. House officer in medicine and surgery Nishter Hosp., Multan, 1970-71; physiology instr. Nishter Med. Sch., Multan, 1971-72; intern Doctors Hosp., Washington, 1972-73, resident in surgery, 1973-74; resident in pathology VA Hosp. and NYU, N.Y.C., 1974-78; assoc. pathologist Clin. Pathology Lab., Des Moines, 1978-80, St. Joseph Hosp., Port Charles, Fla., 1980-84; head histopathology dept. Ctrl. Lab., Riyadh, Saudi Arabia, 1984-99; cons. pathologist Advanced Lab., Riyadh, Saudi Arabia, 1999. Contbr. more than 30 articles to profl. jours. Fellow Coll. Am. Pathologists, Am. Assn. Clin. Pathologists. Avocations: reading, indoor games. Home: PO Box 60179, Riyadh 11545, Saudi Arabia Office: Advanced Lab, PO Box 92267, Riyadh 11653, Saudi Arabia

AFZALNIA, MOHAMMAD REZA, psychologist; b. Tehran, Iran, Jan. 23, 1950; arrived in England, 1988; s. H. Aziz and Nezam-Abadi; m. Parvin Firouzi, May 18, 1954; children: Arash, Shadi, Shirin. BA, Shiraz Univ., Iran, 1973; BA in Lit., Shiraz Univ., 1978; MA in Comparative Lit., Tehran Univ., Iran, 1980; EdS, Ind. Univ., 1980; MA in Psychology, Keele Univ., Eng., 1992. Radio producer Nat. RTV, Iran, 1976-78, researcher, cons., documentary film producer, 1981-83; lectr. Sch. of TV & Cinema, Iran, 1983-86, sr. lectr., dept. head, 1986-88; researcher Keele U., England, 1988-92, U. East London, 1994-95, U. Manchester Met., Eng., 1995—; lectr. Tehran U., Tabatabaii U. Tchrs. Coll., North Midland Coll., Newcastle Coll., Ahwaz Univ., Nat. Univ., Tehran U. Sch. Cinema, Tchrs. Coll., Iran. Editor Jong-e-Dast, 1969-73; acitivist Islamic Leftwing, Shiraz, 1969-70; contbr. articles to profl. jours. With Iranian Mil., 1973-75. Mem. British Psychol. Soc. Avocations: reading, writing, computers, music, photography. Home: 16 Thistleberry Ave, Newcastle ST5 2LT, England Office: U Manchester Met, Dept Psychology, Manchester M13 OJA, England

AFZELIUS, BJÖRN ARVID, cell biology educator; b. Stockholm, Sweden, June 30, 1925; s. Nils Arvid and Margarethe (Thirring) A.; m. Ulla Elisabeth Fogelberg, May 24, 1957; children: Görel T.E., Boel A.M. PhD, Stockholm U., Sweden, 1957; MD (hon.), Karolinska Inst., Stockholm, 1981; PhD (hon.), U. Siena, Italy, 1986. Rsch. fellow Johns Hopkins U., Balt., 1957-58; lectr. Stockholm U., 1958-68, prof., 1968—. Author: Anatomy of the Cell, 1966, AB Maunsbach and BA Afzelius: Biomedical Electron Microscopy, 1999. Avocations: reading, writing. Home: Docentbacken 15, S-10405 Stockholm Sweden

AGA, NAOZER JAMSHED, financial executive; b. Mumbai, Oct. 22, 1941; s. Jamshed Burjor and Shirin Jamshed (Cooper) A.; m. Sheila Naozer Chawla, Dec. 4, 1966; children: Armand, Ayesha. BSc with honors, St. Xavier's Coll., Mumbai, 1962. Mgmt. trainee Voltas Ltd., Mumbai, 1962-64, mktg. asst., 1964-69, All India product mgr., 1969-72; chmn., bd. dirs.

Armayesh Group of Cos., Mumbai, 1972—; bd. dirs. Mohan Three Wheelers, Mumbai, 1997—; joint promoter, founder, mng. dir. Rodal Circaprint Electronics Ltd., Mumbai, 1985-89. Mem., hon. sec. Indian Liberal Group, Mumbai, 1984—. Recipient Winner's Cup, Loltegaon Motor Sports Club, 1963. Mem. All India Mgmt. Assn. (life), Inst. Dirs. (London), Willingdon Wports Club, Royal Western India Turf Club, Lions Club Internat. (life, Outstanding Chmn., social svc. membership devel., others), Grand Lodge India (Ritual Working Competition trophy regional Grand Lodge Western India 1973). Zoroastrian. Avocations: motor sports, reading. Fax: 91-22 3634352. Office: Armayesh Group Cos, Sir P Mehta Rd, Mumbai 400 001, India

AGA, RENÉ L., retired petrochemical company executive; b. St. Agatha Berchem, Brabant, Belgium, Mar. 26, 1935; arrived in Spain, 1971, naturalized, 1975; s. Petrus and Gabriella (Van Zeebroeck) A.; m. Azucena Aguirre; children: Daniel, Eva, Magdalena, Susana. Lic. in Chemistry, U. Louvain, Belgium, 1957, DSc in Chemistry, 1959. Project leader rsch. lab. Petrofina, Brussels, 1961-71; mgr. tech. svcs. dept. Petronor, Bilboa, Spain, 1972-94; mgr. conceptual and basing engring. dept. REPSOL, Bilboa, 1994-2000; ret.; mem. coun. Basque Total Quality Found., Bilbao, 1992-95; corr. for Spain, Applied Catalysis, Netherlands, 1980s; ind. cons. petroleum refining and petrochem. industry; mem. panel experts European Refining Tech. Conf., 1999. Contbr. articles to profl. jours.; patentee process for purification of light petroleum distillates. Mem. Chemici Lovanienses, Cath. Corp. of Ex-Students, Real Club Jolaseta. Roman Catholic. Avocations: tennis, walking, travel, swimming, video camera.

AGAG LONGO, ALEJANDRO, member European parliament; b. Madrid, Sept. 18, 1970. Mem. European Parliament, Bruxelles, 1999—; mem. Group of the European People's Party (Christian Democrats) and European Democrats, com. on econ. and monetary affairs, com. on budget, delegation to the EU-Bulgaria Joint Parliamentary, vice-chmn. Mem. People's Party. Office: 67 rue Arlon, B-1040 Bruxelles Belgium*

AGAJANIAN, GILDA, pianist; b. Apr. 3; d. Oganes and Azatuhi (Tosunian) A. BA, U. So. Calif., 1973, Grad. Study, 1974-76; Diploma, Am. Coll. of Musicians, Austin, Tex., 1981, Artist Diploma, 1984. Russian educator Calif., 1976-81; music educator Gilda Agajanian Piano Studio, La Habra Heights, Calif., 1987—; profl. classical pianist Calif., 1985—; entrepreneur, ptnr. Aggie's Restaurants, Calif., 1981-89. Mem. Westshore Musicians Club (pres. 1992-95), Music Tchrs. Nat. Assn., Calif. Assn. of Profl. Music Tchrs. (chmn. recitals 1992—), Dominant Club (sec. 1994-96), nat. Guild of Piano Tchrs., AAUW, Woman's Club of Hollywood. Avocations: Slavic langs. and lits., exotic birds, dogs, cats, horticulture. Office: Gilda Agajanian Piano Studio 2039 N Cypress St La Habra Hgts CA 90631-8243

AGAM, YAACOV, artist; b. May 11, 1928. Ed., Bezalel Acad. Arts and Design, Jerusalem, 1945-49; pvt. study, Zurich, 1949-51; PhD (hon.), U. Tel Aviv, 1975. guest lectr. advanced exploration visual comm. Carpenter Ctr. Visual Arts Harvard U., 1968. One-man shows include Paris, 1953, 56, 58, Belgium, 1958, Israel, 1958, Switzerland, 1959, 62, London, 1959, N.Y.C., 1966, 71, 80, Tokyo, Osaka, Kawasaki, 1989, Tampa Mus. Fine Arts, 1995, Philharmonic Ctr. Arts, Naples, Fla., 1996, Museo Nacional de Bellas Artes, Buenos Aires, 1996, Fundacion Arte y Tecnologia, Madrid, 1997-98; numerous group exhbns., 1954—; exptl. films, 1956-58; retrospective exhbn. Musée National d'Art Modern, Paris, Städtrische Kunsthale, Düsseldorf, Fed. Republic Germany, Stedelijk Mus., Amsterdam, Tel Aviv Mus., 1972-73; represented in permanent collections including Mus. of Modern Art, N.Y.C., Hirshhorn Mus., Washington, Pompidou Ctr., Paris, Tel Aviv Mus., Israel Mus.; most recent works include Forum Leverkusen, 1970, monumental sculpture Lincoln Ctr., N.Y.C., 1971, sculpture Pres. Residence, Israel, 1972, Salon Pompidou Elysée Palace, Paris, 1972, Plaza with Fountain, La Défense, Paris, 1975, Villa Regina, sculpture Chgo., 1983, mural Port Authority Bus Terminal, N.Y.C., 1984, Miami (painting of entire apt. bldg.), Homage to Mondrian, L.A., 1984, Dan Hotel, Tel Aviv, 1985, monumental Firewater fountain, Dizengof Sq., Tel Aviv, 1986, sculpture Kennedy Airport, N.Y.C., 1986, Grand Prix Artec, 1989, cruise ship M.S. Fantasy, 1990, 2 computer art murals cruise ship Maasdam, 1994; retrospective exhbn. Guggenheim Mus., N.Y.C., 1980; author 36 visual edn. manuals. Decorated chevalier Ordre des Arts et des Lettres, 1974, comdt. Ordre des Arts et Lettres, 1985; recipient prize for artistic rsch. Saô Paulo Bienale, 1963, Palette d'Or, Internat. Festival of Cagnes-sur-Mer, 1971, medal Council of Europe, 1977, Grand Pris of the 1st Artech, Nagoya, 1989, Amos Comenius medal of UNESCO, 1996. Office: Artful Enterprises 658 Front St #7277 Lahaina HI 96761 also: 26 rue Boulard, 75014 Paris France*

AGAMA, GODFRIED KPORTUFE, banker; b. Asidovui-Agava, Tongu Dist., Volta, Ghana, Apr. 28, 1936; m. Comfort Henrietta Agama; 4 children. Student, McGill U. and Toronto U., Montreal; PhD, McGill U. Rsch. asst. bus. fin. divsn. Dominion Bur. of Statistics, 1964-65; rsch. fellow Econ. Devel. Inst., Nigeria U., Enugu, 1965-66; lectr. dept. econs. Econ. Devel. Inst., Nigeria U., 1966-71; mem. of parliament, mem. coun. of state South Tongu, Ghana, 1969-72, 79-81; chmn. external debt com. Ministry Fin. and Econ. Planning, 1972-75; mem. Nat. Econ. Planning Coun., 1974-78, Nat. Econ. Adv. Com., 1978-79, Nat. Devel. Commn., 1980-81; chief rsch. officer Cocoa Mktg. Bd., 1972, dep. exec chmn., 1972-73, 1st dep. chief exec., 1973; chmn. fin. com. Internat. Cocoa Orgn., 1974-75; chmn. bd. dirs. Bank of Ghana, 1986-88, gov., 1988—; mem. electoral commn., Ghana, 1966-68, govt. econs. com., 1967, nat. adv. com., 1967-68, Constituent Assn., 1968-69, assoc. bd. Econ. Bull. of Ghana, 1968; rep. gen. coun. Commonwealth Parliament Assn., 1969-70; mem. State Enterprises Commn., 1976-78, chmn., 1978-79; chmn. exch. and clearing com. West Africa Clearing House. Author: Structural Changes in the Economy of Ghana, 1966, The Growth of Money and Debt in Ghana, 1968, Prospects for Cocoa, 1968, Population and Manpower Development in Ghana, 1969, Taxation for African Development, 1971, The International Cocoa Agreement, 1973, A New Direction in Economic Policy for Ghana, 1985; mem. editorial bd. Legon Observer, 1967-69. Office: Bank of Ghana, PO Box 2674, Accra Ghana*

AGAR, ROBERT ALEXANDER, geologist, consultant; b. Cleethorpes, Eng., Nov. 25, 1951; arrived in Australia, 1987; s. Maurice Norman and Jean (Clark) A.; m. Elizabeth Hilda Noblet, July 26, 1975; children: Graham, Alexandra, Stephen. BSc with distinction, U. Liverpool, Eng., 1973, BSc with honors in geology, 1974, PhD in Geology, 1978. Rsch. asst. Brit.-Peruvian Tech. Assistance Program, Peru, 1974-78; exploration geologist Minex, Lusaka, Zambia, 1978-79; geologist Geol. Survey, Lusaka, 1979-81; prin. geologist D.G.M.R., Jedda, Saudi Arabia, 1981-86; cons. geologist Greenwich Resources, Egypt, 1986-87; exploration mgr. Carrboyd Minerals Ltd., Perth, Australia, 1987-90; gen. mgr. Geoscan Pty. Ltd., Perth, 1990-94; mng. dir. Australian Geol. and Remote Sensing Svcs., Perth, 1994—, Bayley Resources N.L., Perth, 1997—; dir. Amigo Pty. Ltd., Perth, 1998—. Fellow Australasian Inst. Mining and Metallurgy, Geol. Soc. London (chartered geologist); mem. Instn. Mining and Metallurgy (London)(treas. Western Australia br.), Australian Inst. Geoscientists, Australian Inst. Co. Dirs. (grad.), Kalamunda Cricket Club (jr. cricket coord.). Roman Catholic. Avocations: cricket, natural history, scuba, photography, music.

AGARWAL, ASHUTOSH, chemist, researcher; b. Allahabad, India, July 19, 1958; s. Rameshwar Dayal and Ramsumarni (Agarwal) A.; m. Neerja Bansal, Dec. 24, 1982; children: Anindita, Vinyak. BS, Ewing Christian Coll., Allahabad, 1975; MS with honors, U. Allahabad, 1977, PhD, 1980; Assoc. (hon.), Instn. of Chemists, Calcutta, 1981. Rsch. asst. trainee Shriram Inst. for Indsl. Rsch., Delhi, India, 1980-81; R&D chemist Atul Products Ltd., Valsad, India, 1981-85; R&D mgr. and works mgr. (tech.) Chemiequip Ltd., Thane, India, 1985-91; R&D mgr. Magatul Industries Ltd., Vapi, India, 1991-95; dep. gen. mgr. (organic chem. bus.) Ballarpur Industries, Karwar, India, 1995-98; gen. mgr. (R&D) VAM Organic Chems. Ltd., Gajraula, India, 1998—; lectr. M.L.N.R. Engring. Coll., Allahabad, 1977-78. Mem. Am. Chem. Soc., Rotary. Avocations: reading, table tennis, badminton, music, touring. Office: VAM Organic Chems Ltd, Bhartiagram, 244 223 Gajraula India

AGARWAL, G., engineering educator, consultant; b. Ajmer, Rajasthan, India, Sept. 5, 1952; s. B.R. and Gyanwati (Gyanwati) A.; m. Rajni Goyal, Mar. 5, 1979; children: Gunjan, Robin. BE with honors, B.I.T.S., Pilani, India, 1973; MSc in Engring., Kurukshetra U., India, 1977; PGDBM, Bhartiya Vidya Bhawan, Jaipur, India, 1984; PhD, Indian Inst. Tech., Bombay, 1993. Chartered engr., India. Asst. indsl. engr. M/S Cimmco Ltd., Bharatpur, India, 1974-75; tchg. asst. R.E.C., Kurukshetra, 1977-78; lectr. in mech. engring. U. Jodhpur, India, 1979; reader in mech. engring. Engring. Coll., Kota, India, 1984-96; lectr. in mech. engring. M.R. Engring. Coll., Jaipur, 1979-84, prof. mech. engring., 1996—. Fellow Instn. of Engrs. India (life), ISTE (life). Avocations: reading, watching television, cricket, swimming, photography. Home: B-6 MREC Campus, Jaipur 302017, India Office: Malaviya Regl Engring Coll, 302017 Jaipur Rajasthan, India

AGARWAL, GHANSHYAM DAS, association executive; b. Kanpur, U.P., India, Aug. 17, 1956; s. Udai Kishan and Munni Devi (Poddar) A.; m. Neeta Agarwal, Nov. 28, 1981; children: Arpit, Ankit. B Comm., Kanpur (India) U., Kanpur, 1976, M Comm., 1980. Chartered acct., India. Accounts officer M.K. Industries, Kanpur, 1980-85, M.P. Udyog Ltd., Kanpur, 1985-87; tax mgr. Kailash Motors, Kanpur, 1987—; pres. Rainbow Internat., Kanpur, 1978—. Editor Rainbow Bull., 1983 (Soc. award 1983). Mem. World Peace Rally, Rainbow Internat., Kanpur, 1987, Peace on Wheel, Kanpur to Kathmandu, 1987, signature campaign, Washington, 1988, world books and photo exhbn., Kanpur, 1988. Recipient merit scholarships U.P. Bd., Allahabad, 1972, 74, nat. scholarship Kanpur U., 1976. Mem. IPJET, Internat. Bus. Travelers Club, Japan Assn. Travel Agts. Mem. Bhartiya Janta party. Mem. Rashtriya Swayam Sewak Sangh. Avocations: music, singing, painting, reading, writing. E-mail: gdrainbow@yahoo.com. Office: Rainbow Internat, Post Box 43, Kanpur 208001, India

AGARWAL, RAM KUMAR, chemistry educator, researcher; b. Meerut, India, Apr. 5, 1949; s. Madhu Sudan and Urmila Agarwal; m. Pushpa Agarwal, Feb. 18, 1972; children: Jain Payal, Himanshu. BSc, Meerut U., 1967, MSc, 1969, PhD, 1980, DSc, 2000; postgrad., Charles U., Prague, Czechoslovakia, 1981. Lectr. Meerut Coll., 1969-70; lectr. Lajpat Rai Coll., Sahibabad, India, 1970-83, reader, 1983—; vis. fellow Indian Nat. Sci. Acad., 1992-93. Editor-in-chief Asian Jour. Chemistry, 1989—. Post-warden CD of India, Sahibabad, 1986—. Univ. Grants Commn. New Delhi nat. assoc., 1982-84. Fellow Indian Chem. Soc. (life), Instn. of Chemists (life); mem. Indian Coun. Chemists (zonal sec. 1996—), Indian Thermal Analysis Soc., Indian Assn. Nuclear Chemists and Allied Scientists, Lions Club Internat. (joint sec. 1995-96, sec. 1996-97, v.p. 1997-2000, pres. 2000—). Home: Sector 3, 11/100 Rajendra Nagar, 201005 Sahibabad Ghaziabad, India Office: Lajpat Rai Coll, 201005 Sahibabad India

AGARWAL, SHIV KUMAR, chemist, researcher; b. Lucknow, India, July 15, 1952; s. Raghunath Prasad and Kishan Devi Agarwal; m. Vinod Kumari Agarwal, Dec. 10, 1974; children: Neelima, Kailash. BSc, Lucknow U., 1971, MSc, 1974, PhD, 1981. Scientist Ctrl. Drug Rsch. Inst., Lucknow, 1981-88, sr. scientist, 1988-93, asst. dir., 1993-95; head basic rsch. Wockhardt Rsch. Ctr., Aurangabad, India, 1995—; vis. fellow Queen's U., Belfast, No. Ireland, 1989-90, postdoctoral fellow, 1983-85; NIH vis. fellow NIADDK, Bethesda, Md., 1985-86. Recipient Wockhardt Significant Performance award, 1997-98. Mem. Indian Chem. Soc. (v.p. Lucknow chpt. 1993-95, sec. 1991-93, joint sec. 1988-91), Indian Pharm. Assn., Am. Chem. Soc. Avocations: reading, photography, tourism, playing cards, movies. Office: Wockhardt Rsch Ctr, D-4 MIDC Area Chikalthana, Aurangabad 431210, India

AGARWAL, SURAJ PRAKASH, pharmacy educator; b. Bareilly, Uttar Prad, India, Apr. 28, 1940; s. Oudh Behari Lal and Sukh Devi Shinghal; m. Uma Agarwal, July 10, 1967; children: Rohinee, Sharad, Anita. BPharm, U. Rajasthan, Pilani, India, 1960; MPharm, Benaras Hindu U., Varanasi, India, 1962; MS, U. Ill., 1965, PhD, 1969. Registered pharmacist, Delhi. Lectr. Ahmadu Bello U., Zaria, Nigeria, 1970-72; sr. lectr. U. Nigeria, Nsukka, 1972-76, reader, 1976-86, prof., 1986-87; reader Jamia Hamdard U., New Delhi, 1988—; head dept. pharmaceutics, Nsukka, 1984-86, dept. pharm. technology, 1986-87, dept. pharmaceutics Jamia Hamdard U., New Delhi, 1989-92. Author: Pharmaceutical Jurisprudence, 1997, Pharmaceutics, 1997, Physical Pharmacy, 2000; contbr. articles to profl. jours. Pres. Resident Welfare Assn., Saket, New Delhi, 1997; mem. exec. coun. Jamia Hamdard U., 1994-96. Travel awardee Dept. of Sci. and Tech., India, 1990; fellow Brit. Coun., Manchester, U.K., 1979. Mem. Indian Pharm. Assn. (exec. councillor 1996—). Hindu. Home: J-194 Saket, 110017 New Delhi India Office: Jamia Hamdard Univ, Hamdardnagar, 110062 New Delhi India

AGARWALA, BASANT KUMAR, science educator; b. Calcutta, India, Jan. 1, 1954; s. Trilok Chand and Ram Piyari Agarwala; m. Pushpa Agarwal, July 1, 1979; children: Vandana, Sarad, Rajat. BSc with honors, U. Calcutta, 1972, MSc, 1974, PhD, 1980. Sr. rsch. fellow U. Calcutta, 1976-78, rsch. assoc., 1978-81; lectr. U. Calcutta, Agartala, India, 1981-86; sr. lectr. Tripura U., Agartala, 1986-94, reader, 1994-99, prof., 1999—; prin. investigator ICAR, Agartala, 1983-86, DST, Agartala, 1986-89, CSIR, Agartala, 1990-94, CSIR/DST/ICAR, Agartala, 1994-98; vis. scientist INSA Royal Soc., 1997-98; invited fellow Japan Soc. for Promotion of Sci., 2000-01. Co-author: (book) Fauna of India: Aphididae: VI Vol., 1996; inventor in field. Commonwealth rsch. fellow Commonwealth Scholarship Commn., 1989-90. Fellow Philol. Soc.; mem. Entomology Assn. (life), Aphidological Soc. (exec. mem.). Avocations: popular writings, debates, science fiction. Office: Tripura U, PO Agartala Coll, 799004 Agartala Tripura, India

AGARWALA, SANJAY, orthopaedic surgeon; b. Varanasi, India, Oct. 18, 1954; s. Rajendra Prasad Gayaprasad and Prabha Rajendra A.; m. Nisheeta Kantilal Sanjay Parekh, May 10, 1979; children: Anisha, Arjun. MBBS, G.S. Med. Coll., Mumbia, India, 1978; D of Orthopaedics, Coll. Physicians & Surgeons, Bombay, India, 1981; MS in Orthopaedics, U. Bombay, 1982; MCh in Orthopaedics, U. Liverpool, England, 1985. Cert. orthopaedic and trauma surgeon. Jr. resident, med. officer King Edward Meml. Hosp., Mumbai, India, 1978-79, resident, med. officer, 1979-80, registrar in orthopaedics and traumatology, 1980-82; profl. fellow, registrar The Robert Jones and Agnes Hunt Orthopaedics Hosp., U.K., 1982-83; hand fellow, registrar Derbyshire Royal Infirmary Assoc. Hosps., U.K., 1983; Stanley Johnson Microsurg. Fellowship/Orthopaedic Registrar Northwick Park Hosp./Clin. Rsch. Ctr., U.K., 1984; assoc. fellow Liverpool U., U.K., 1985; acting sr. registrar orthopaedics and traumatology Hartshill Orthopaedic Hosp., U.K., 1986; cons. orthopaedic and trauma surgeon P.D. Hinduja Nat. Hosp., Mumbai, 1986-92, head orthopaedics and traumatology, 1992, chief surgery, 1998—. Contbr. articles to profl. jours. Grad. fellow Rotary Found., Evanston, Ill., 1982, Stanley Johnson Microsurg. fellow Northwick Park Hosp., England, 1984; recipient Norman Roberts prize U. Liverpool, 1985, others. Mem. Indian Assn. Laser Surgery & Medicine, Indian Rheumatology Assn., Indian Orthopaedic Assn. Home: Agarwal House, 61-D Rd Churchgate, Mumbai 400 020, India Office: PD Hinduja Nat Hosp, Veer Savarkar Marg, 400 016 Mumbai Bombay 400 016, India

AGARWALLA, ARVIND, computer company executive; b. Calcutta, India, Aug. 26, 1961; s. Chandrakumar and Sushiladevi (Kajaria) A.; m. Vandana Toshniwal, Mar. 11, 1986; children: Vaidehi, Vidisha. B in Comm., U. Calcutta, 1983. CEO Vedika Software PVT LTD, Calcutta, 1987—; dir. Fact Sys. Malaysia SDN BHD, Kuala Lumpur, 1993—; CEO Fact Software Internat. PTE LTD, Singapore, 1993—, AllIndia.com. Ltd., Calcutta, 1996—, Vedika Internat. PVT LTD, Calcutta, 1996—. Mem. Asia Pacific Internet Assn. (adv. group 1997—). Avocations: reading, photography, driving, surfing the internet. Home and Office: Internat Plaza, 10 Anson Rd # 38-01, Singapore 079903, Singapore

AGARWALLA, VIPIN, pediatrician; b. Dhanbad, Bihar, India, May 12, 1960; s. Bishwanath and Savitri Devi Agarwalla; m. Usha Sharraf, Dec. 5, 1987; children: Anant, Anjali. MB BChir, Rajendra Med. Coll., Ranchi, Bihar, 1986; MD in Pediats., Patna (Bihar) Med. Coll., 1991. Resident in pediats. and neonatology Shotley Bridge Gen. Hosp., Newcastle-Upon-Tyne, Eng., 1993-94, Birmingham Children's Hosp., Manchester, Eng., 1994-95, Kingston Hosp., Kinston-Upon-Thames, Eng., 1995-96; staff grade in pediats. and neonatology Newcross Hosp., Wolverhampton, Eng., 1995-97; resident in pediats. and neonatology Wythenshawe Hosp., Manchester, 1997-98; resident in neonatology St. Mary's Hosp., Manchester, 1998-99; resident in pediat. endocrinology Royal Manchester Childrens Hosp. Birmingham Childrens Hosp., Manchester, 1999; resident in pediats. Brookdale U. Hosp. and Med. Ctr., Bklyn., 1999—. Contbr. articles to profl. jours. Univ. scholar Ranchi U., 1981. Fellow AMA (resident), Am. Acad. Pediats. (resident); mem. Royal Coll. Physicians (London), Royal Coll. Pediats. and Child Health, Indian Acad. Pediats. (life). Avocations: child health, self-improvement, philosophy, yoga. E-mail: vipusa2000@aol.com. Office: Brookdale U Hosp Med Ctr Dept Pediats One Brookdale Plz Brooklyn NY 11212

AGASSI, ANDRE KIRK, professional tennis player; b. Las Vegas, Nev., Apr. 29, 1970; s. Mike and Elizabeth Agassi; m. Brooke Shields, April 19, 1997 (div. 1999). Mem. U.S. Davis Cup team, 1988—. Owner found. for children. Winner tournaments including Itaparica, 1987, Memphis, 1988, Charleston, 1988, Forest Hills, 1988, Stuttgart, 1988, Stratton Mountain, 1988, Livingston, 1988, Orlando, 1989, San Francisco, 1990, Key Biscayne, 1990, Washington, 1990, ATP Tour World Championship-Frankfurt, 1990, Orlando, 1991, Washington, 1991; Wimbledon champion, 1992, U.S. Open champion, 1994, Australian Open champion, 1995; gold medal U.S. Olympics, 1996; winner French Open/Grand Slam, 1999, U.S. Open, 1999, Australian Open, 2000. Address: International Mgmt Group 1 Erieview Plz Ste 1300 Cleveland OH 44114-1715*

AGATHOCLEOUS, NICOS, permanent delegate. Perm. rep. of Cyprus to UN N.Y.C., 1995-97; permanent del. of Cyprus European Union, Brussels, 1997—; ambassador to Belgium and Luxembourg, 1999—. Office: Square Ambiorix 2, 1000 Brussels Belgium*

A. GAZEE, MOHD. YUSOFF, oil company executive; b. Gemas, Malaysia, July 16, 1949; s. Abd Gazee and Sarah Hussain; m. Suhainy A. Manan, Nov., 1974; children: Emma Suzainy, Ezlin, Emilia, Ezreena. Student, Sekolah Menengah Tuanku Abtul, Rahman, Gemas, N.S., 1961-67; BSc in Mech. Engring., Sekolah Menengah Tuanku Abdul Rahman, 1967. Steelmaker Malayawata Perai, 1968-75; mech. technician Esso Refinery, Port Dickson, 1975-82; rotating specialist integrated machinery inspection Petronas Refinery; with Petronas Penapisan (T) Sdn. Bhd., Terengganu, Malaysia. King scout Boy Scout Assn., Malaysia. Fellow Instn. Diagnostic Engrs. (U.K.); mem. Am. Soc. Mech. Engring., Am. Welding Soc. Avocations: music, art, computers. Home: 18 Jalan 59 Rantau Petronas, Kerteh Terengganu 24300, Malaysia Office: Petronas Penapisan (T) Sdn, Kerteh, Terengganu 24300, Malaysia

AGAZZI, EVANDRO, journalist, educator; b. Bergame, Italy, Oct. 23, 1934; s. Aldo and Emma (Carminati) A.; m. Lucia Castelli, Sept. 26, 1967; children: Isolda, Siviero, Aldo, Arianna; m. Lourdes Velazquez, July 20, 1998. MA, Cath. U., Milan, 1957; libera docenza in philosophy of sci., 1963, libera docenza in math. logic, 1966; hon. doctorate, U. Cordoba, Argentina, 1991, U. Santiago del Estero, Argentina, 1997, U. Ricardo Palma, Lima, Peru, 2000. Author over 24 books, 1961-95. mem. Italian Philos. Soc. (pres. 1978-80), Internat. Acad. Philos. Sci. (pres. 1978—), Internat. Fedn. Philos. Soc. (pres. 1988-93), Internat. Inst. Philos. (pres. 1993-96), Rotary (recipient Morelli-prize 1962, Prince of Liechtenstein prize 1993). Avocations: playing piano, traveling, skiing. Office: U Genoa Dept Philos, Via Balbi 4 116124, Genoa Italy

AGBANDJE-MCKENNA, MAVIS, research scientist; b. Orogun, Nigeria, Apr. 11, 1963; d. Samuel Agbandje and Rachel Ebu Ogwa; m. Robert McKenna, Nov. 5, 1988; children: Sean Thomas, Nicole Mary. BSc (hons.), Univ. Hertfordshire, Hatfield, Eng., 1985; PhD, Univ. London, 1989. Postdoc. rsch. asst. Purdue Univ., West Lafayette, Ind., 1989-92; rsch. asst. Purdue Univ., 1992-93, asst. rsch. scientist, 1993-95; rsch. fellow Univ. Warwick, Coventry, Eng., 1995-97, sr. rsch. fellow, 1998-99; asst. prof. Univ. Fla., Gainesville, 1999—; cons. Purdue Univ., 1996. Recipient grants. Mem. British Crystallographic Assn. Avocations: reading, travel, physical fitness. Fax number: 352 392 3422. E-mail: mckenna@ufl.edu. Office: Univ Fla Dept biochemistry & mol biology Gainesville FL 32610-0245

AGBENIN, JOHN, soil scientist, educator; b. Ubiaja, Edo State, Nigeria, Apr. 3, 1959; s. Asika and Angelina (Ezehi) A.; m. Nnennaya Ogechi Udemba, July 16, 1994. BS with honors, Ahmadu Bello U., Zaria, Nigeria, 1984, MS, 1988; PhD, U. Saskatchewan (Can.), 1993. Asst. lectr. Ahmadu Bello U., 1987-90, lectr. II, 1990-93, lectr. I, 1993-96, sr. lectr., 1996-97; collaborating scientist Internat. Inst. Tropical Agr., Ibadan, Nigeria, 1996-97; rsch. scientist Alexander Von Humboldt, Giessen, Germany, 1996—; vis. soil scientist, Inst. Agronomy, Campinas Sao Paolo, Brazil, 1997-98; rsch. scientist Justus Liebig U., Giessen, Germany, 1998-2000. Contbr. articles to profl. jours. Assoc. fellow Third World Acad., 1997, rsch. fellow Alexander Von Humboldt, 1998. Mem. Soil Sc. Am., Am. Soc. Agronomy, African Soil Soc. Avocations: lawn tennis, reading, classical novels, gardening. Home: Area E ABU Staff Qtrs, PMB 1044, Zaria Kaduna, Nigeria Office: Ahmadu Bello U Fac Agr, Dept Soil Sci PMB 1044, Zaria Kaduna, Nigeria

AGBENORKU, PIUS THOMAS, plastic surgeon, educator, consultant; b. Lakpo-Dabala, Ghana, Feb. 25, 1956; s. Nanenu Awuku and Akua (Treba) A.; m. Margaret Yawo Adzokpa-Mensah, July 30, 1983; children: Elikplimi, Manolo, Mayvor. MD, Lvov (Ukraine) Med. Inst., 1985; PhD, Wroclaw (Poland) Med. Acad., 1992. Diplomate in plastic and reconstructive surgery. Med./surg. house officer Korle-Bu Tchg. Hosp., Accra, Ghana, 1985-86, med. officer, 1986-89; resident in gen. surgery State Ry. Hosp., Wroclaw, 1989-90, resident in plastic and reconstructive surgery, 1990-93; lectr. and cons. plastic surgeon UST Sch. Med. Scis./Komfo Anokye Tchg. Hosp., Kumasi, Ghana, 1993—; part-time med. practitioner Cathedral Clinic, Accra, 1987-88; vol. med. practitioner Akplale (Ghana) Clinic, 1988-89; vis. trainee in plastic surgery St. Markus Krankenhaus, Frankfurt, Germany, 1991; vis. trainee in burn surgery Unfal Klinik, Duisburg, Germany,1991; vis. cons. in plastic surgery St. Martin's Hosp., Agroyesum, Ghana, 1994—, E.P. Ch. of Chana Hosp., Krapa-Ejisu, Ghana, 1995—. Contbr. articles to profl. jours. Pres. Nat. Union Ghanaian Students, Lvov, 1983-85; mem. missionary com. Accra Chapel Trust, Korle-Gu, Accra, 1985-89; founder, patron Christian Students Assn. Internat., Wroclaw, 1989-93; co-founder, med. dir. E.P. Ch. of Ghana Hosp, 1995—. Recipient 1st prize Dist. Sci. Fair, Ghana Nat. Assn. Sci. Tchrs., 1977, 1st prize Regional Sci. Fair, 1977, 2d prize Lvov State Med. Inst., 1983, 1st prize Lvov State Med. Inst., 1983. Fellow Internat. Coll. Surgeons, West African Assn. Plastic Surgeons (exec. mem. 1995—), Ghana Surg. Rsch. Soc.; mem. Ghana Med. Assn., Internat. Christian Med. and Dental Assn., Christian Med. Fellowship of U.K. Mem. Evang. Presbyterian Ch. of Ghana. Avocations: football, volleyball, lawn tennis. Home: 6A Allotei Konuah Est, Beposo Rd UST Campus, Kumasi Ghana Office: UST Sch Med Scis, Komfo Anokye Tchg Hosp, Kumasi Ghana

AGBETOYE, LEO AYODEJI, agricultural engineer, educator; b. Igogo, Ekiti, Nigeria, Apr. 11, 1965; s. Michael Ajigbotoge and Veronica Obebe (Esan) A.; m. Mercy Olufunmilayo Orisasona, Oct. 11, 1993; children: Seun, Toyin. B in Tech., Fed. U. Tech., Akure, Nigeria, 1987, M in Engring., 1992; PhD, Cranfiel U., Silsoe, U.K., 1996. Cert. agrl. engring. Agrl. engr. Sarda, Gusau, Nigeria, 1987-88; tutor United Secondary Sch., Usiekiti, Nigeria, 1989; examiner West Africa Exam Coun., Lagos, Nigeria, 1989-91; grad. asst. Fed. U. Tech., Akure, 1989-92, asst. lectr., 1992-97, lectr. I, 1997-2000, sr. lectr., 2000—; co-designer fruit processing machines F.U.T.A., Akure, 1998—, designer cocoyam harvester, 1998-99. Contbr. articles to profl. jours. Pres. Afonbierin Movt., Igogo, 1984-88; patron Igogo Students Union Ado, Nigeria, 1989—. Scholar IITA, Ibadan, 1985, Postgrad. scholar Fed. Govt. Nigeria, Abuja, 1990-91, ACU scholar Commonwealth Commn., U.K., 1991-94. Mem. IAgE (U.K.), Nigerian Soc. Agrl. Engrs. Roman Catholic. Avocations: football, singing, swimming, reading, watching movies. Home: Isaba St K63, Igogo Ekiti Moba Lga, Nigeria Office: Fed U Tech Dept Agrl Engr, PMB 704, Akure Ondo, Nigeria

AGBETUYI, SEGUN, banker; b. Iddo, Osi, Nigeria, June 30, 1953; s. Agboola and Eunice Agbetuyi; m. Titlayo Agbetuyi; 2 children. Student, Ekiti Parapo Coll., Iddo-Ekiti, Ahmadu Bello U., Zaria; profl. and mgmt. tng., Manchester (Eng.) Bus. Sch., Harvard U. Bus. Sch., Lagos Bus. Sch. Banking trainee Arab Bank (now Nigeria-Arab Bank), Bank of Am. (now Savannah Bank); credit and mktg. mgr., then area credit mgr. for no. region IBWA (currently Afribank), Lagos; pioneer exec. Nigerian-Am. Merchant Bank, 1980; various positions to v.p. Bank of Boston, various locations, 1984-86; country risk mgr., gen. mgr. credit and bus. strategy Nigerian-Am.

Merchant Bank, Lagos, 1987-89, dep. mng. dir., 1989-93; mng. dir., CEO Owena Bank (Nigeria) Plc, 1993—; asst. lectr. dept. acctg. Ahmadu Bello U.; mem. governing coun. Fin. Instns. Tng. Ctr., 1990-92. Patron Banking Students Assn. of Ahmadu Bello U., Ondo State Students Assn. of Lagos State U.; grand patron Econs. Students Assn. of U. Ilorin; hon. auditor St. Andrew's Anglican Ch., Usi-Ekiti. Fellow Chartered Inst. Bankers in London and Nigeria, Inst. Mgmt. Specialists Eng.; mem. London Inst. Bankers (assoc.), Inst. Dirs. Eng., Inst. Dirs. Nigeria, Am. Mgmt. Assn., Rotary Club Victoria Island East (past pres 1989-90, Paul Harris fellow). Avocations: golf, classical and church music, minimalism, human nature, evangelism. Office: Owena Bank (Nigeria) Plc, PMB 80134 Victoria Island, Lagos Nigeria

AGBONOGA, JOHN EDELEFO, urban and regional planning educator, researcher; b. Iyamoh-Uzairue, Nigeria, June 20, 1960; s. Arone Obo and Florence Ogie (Salomo) A.; m. Bridget Emoshioke Oshiomogho, Mar. 5, 1985; 5 children. BS in Geography, U. Benin, Nigeria, 1984, MS in Urban and Regional Planning, 1990, PhD in Geography, 1993. Registered town planner, Nigerian Inst. Town Planners. Tchr. Iyamoh-Uzairue (Nigeria) H.S., 1980-84; dept. head Idanre (Nigeria) H.S., 1984-91; lectr. Kaduna (Nigeria) Poly. U., 1991-94, sr. lectr., 1994—; dir. Agbons Assocs., Kaduna, 1990—; prin. ptnr., CEO Balasama Urban Planners, Kaduna, 1994—; dir. Fevic Nigerian Internat. Ltd., Benin, 1990—. Contbr. chpt. to book, articles to profl. jours. Sec. dist., youth wing Nat. Party, Estako, Nigeria, 1982; exec. dist.-wing Social Democratic Party, Kaduna, 1991. Recipient Contbn. to Devel. award Etsako Cmty., Edo, Nigeria, 1993, Excellence award Uzairue Social Club, Edo, 1994, award for Meritorious Svcs. Edo State Govt., 1995. Fellow Otu Movement (chmn.); mem. Nigerian Geographical Assn., Environ. Behavior Soc. Nigeria (sec. 1993-95, merit award 1996), Rotary Club. Christian. Avocations: reading, travel, football, basketball, charity work. Home: No 10 Gadani St Narayi, Kaduna Nigeria Office: Kaduna Poly Dept Urban Plan, Coll Environ St PMB 2026, Kaduna Nigeria

AGBORUCHE, WILLIAM, accountant, educator, philosopher, biologist; b. Oviri-Okpe, Bendel, Nigeria, Apr. 27, 1954; came to U.S., 1975; s. Jacob and Alice Agboruche; m. Jacqueline D. Martin, Aug. 5, 1986 (div.). BS in Acctg., Eastern Mich. U., 1980; MEd, Wayne State U., 1982, postgrad., 1985—; MS in Acctg., Walsh Coll., 1985. CPA, Mich. Audit mgr. Wilkerson & Co. CPA's, Detroit, 1984-86; internal auditor Electronic Data Sys. Corp., Southfield, Mich., 1986—; pres. Gen. Assets Corp., Oak Park, Mich., 1990; tng. cons. Human Energy Am., Grosse Pointe, Mich., 1984—; pres. William Agboruche & Co., CPAs, 1988—; pres., bd. dirs. Am. Techs. Inst., Detroit, 1989. Mem. AICPA, Mich. Assn. CPAs, Nat. Assn. Accts. (mem. coun.), Assn. Govt. Accts. (assoc.), Assn. MBA Execs., Rosicrucian Order, Phi Theta Kappa. Avocations: tennis, poetry, writing and reading philosophy. Office: William Agboruche & Co CPAs PO Box 47603 Oak Park MI 48237-5303

AGELIDIS, VASSILIOS GEORGIOS, electrical engineer; b. Serres, Greece, Oct. 17, 1965; arrived in Australia, 1993; s. Georgios Vassilios and Chrisi Christos (Siopi) A. B in Engring., Democritus U., 1988; M in Applied Sci., Concordia U., 1991; PhD in Engring., Curtin U., 1997. Rsch. and teaching assoc. Concordia U., Montreal, 1989-93; assoc. lectr. Curtin U., Perth, Australia, 1993-94, lectr., 1995-98; sr. lectr. Curtin U., Perth, 1999-00, CERPD Univ. Glasgow, 2000—; dep. dir. CRESTA, Perth, 1996-97; tech. dir. Australis Promotions and Techs., Perth, 1995-97; dir. Unitronics Pty Ltd., Perth, 1996-97. Contbr. articles to profl. jours. Mem. Inst. Engrs. Australia, IEEE, Inst. Engrs. Greece (Excellence award 1988). Greek Orthodox. Avocations: bicycling, swimming, body building, tennis, golf. Office: U Glasgow Ctr Econ Renew Pw, 72 Oakfield Ave, Glasgow G12 8LT, Scotland

AGEMA, RICK RIENTS, transport logistics company executive; b. Den Helder, The Netherlands, Apr. 2, 1939; s. Pieter Sjoerd Agema and Nelly Willy Alida (Van de Wetering) De Rooy; m. José Marie Schyvens, 1966; children: Erik Pieter Johannes, Dagmar Natasha Maria, Marit Kerstin. Grad. H.S., Rotterdam, The Netherlands. Trainee various orgns. in transp. field, 1961-65; mgr. ops. L. Th. De Bruyn, Rotterdam, Frankfurt/Main, 1966-69; gen. mgr. Goedkoop & De Geus, Rotterdam, 1970-75; gen. mng. dir. Van Amerongen, Barneveld, The Netherlands, 1976-84; mng. dir. Müller Thomsen Stevedoring, Rotterdam and Antwerp, The Netherlands and Belgium, 1984-90; gen. mng. dir. Internat. Distbn. Sys. B.V., Woerden, The Netherlands, 1990-98; cons. mgr. rsch. transport logistics; mem., bd. mem., chmn. Transfrigo Route NOB Wegtransport, Nesotra, Intertsjech, Trailstar, 1976-84; sec. I.D.S. Holding, Woerden, 1992-98; bd. mem. Dutch Internat. Distbn. Coun., The Hague, The Netherlands, 1958-60. 1st lt. Dutch Infantry, 1958-60. Mem. Dutch Ctr. of Dirs., Marine Club Rotterdam. Roman Catholic. Avocations: sailing, gardening, reading. Fax: (31) 180-669138. E-mail: contrra@capitolonline.nl.

AGEYEV, VALENTIN VASILIEVITCH, psychology educator; b. Murmansk, Russia, Apr. 1, 1947; s. Vasilii Konstantinovitch and Anfisa Sergeevna (Sannikova) Ageev; m. Anna Petrovna Slabodzinskaya, June 8, 1987 (div. Mar. 14, 1992); m. Ekaterina Leonidovna Koturga, Mar. 17, 1992; 1 child, Koturga Leonid. Grad. in Phys. Engring., Moscow Engring. and Phys. Inst., 1973; D of Psychology, Acad. Pedagogical Scis., Moscow, 1987. Sr. rsch. worker Inst. Gen. and Pedagogical Psychology, Acad. Pedagogical Scis., 1981-86; dep. head sci. Inst. Tchrs. Tng., Voronezh, Russia, 1988-89; head Rsch. Ctr., Alma-Ata, Russia, 1989-91; head sci. Pvt. Exptl. Ednl. Instn., Volgodonsk, Russia, 1992-95; head rsch. dept. IInst. Tng. Ofcls., Govt. Republic of Kazakhstan, Almaty, Russia, 1996; dep. dean sci. dept. philosophy and politics Nat. U. Kazakhstan, 1997—; sr. tchr./lectr. psychology Moscow Regional Pedagogical Inst., Moscow, 1984-87; vice prof. dept. psychology Kazalkh Pedagogical Inst., Alma-Ata, , 1989-91; head rsch. lab. Inst. Pedagogical Scis., Alma-Ata, 1990-92; expert Soros-Kazakhstan Found., Aimaty, 1996-97. Author: Psychology of Creation, 1994; contbr. articles to profl. jours.; patentee in field. Recipient diploma Min. of Edn. of Kazakhstan, 1991, grant Soros-Kazakhstan Found., 1996, 99. Mem. (internat. affiliate) APA, CPA. Avocations: reading (detective stories, Russian classics), TV (Am. western films). Home: 124-24 Furmanov St Almaty, 480091 Kazakhstan Russia

AGGARWAL, AMRIT LAL, engineer executive; b. Punjab, India, Sept. 3, 1937; s. Tara Chand and Kaushalya (Devi) A.; m. Parul Aggarwal; 1 child. Diploma in Civil Engring., Punjab Govt. Sch. of Engring., Nilokheri, India, 1958; degree in civil engring., Instn. of Engrs., India, 1963. Overseer Pub. Works Dept., Punjab, 1958-60; jr. engr. Mcpl. Corp. of Delhi, Delhi, 1961-69, asst. engr., 1969-78, exec. engr., 1978-87, supr. engr., 1987-95, chief engr., 1995; arbitrator Panel of Indian Coun. of Arbitration, Delhi. Contbr. articles to profl. jours. Recipient IRC medal Min. of Shipping Surface & Transport Govt. of India, 1975, ASIAD award Govt. of India, 1982. Fellow ASCE, Instn. of Engrs., Instn. of Civil Engrs., Instn. of Values, Indian Coun. Arbitration; mem. Indian Roads Congress, Internat. Assn. Bridge and Structural Engrs. Home: Block No C4A Flat No 1A, Janak Puri, New Delhi 110058, India

AGGARWAL, MADAN MOHAN, physics educator, researcher; b. Hoshiarpur, Punjab, India, Aug. 23, 1950; s. Krishan Das and Saroj Rani A.; m. Asha Rani, Jan. 1, 1964; children: Madhusudan, Pooja. BSc, Panjab U., Chandigarh, India, 1972, MSc, 1973, PhD, 1980. Rsch. fellow Panjab U., Chandigarh, India, 1974-78, rsch. assoc., 1978-80; rsch. assoc. SUNY-Buffalo, 1980-85; pool officer C.S.I.R. Panjab U., Chandigarh, 1985-88; lectr. Panjab U., Chandigarh, 1988-94, reader, 1994—; Co-authored numerous papers for profl. jours. Mem. Indian Physics Assn., Indian Assn. Physics Tchrs. Avocations: table tennis, playing cards. Office: Physics Dept, Panjab U Sector 14, Chandigarh 160014, India

AGGARWAL, NAND LAL, computer sciences educator; b. Amritsar, Panjab, India, Apr. 10, 1936; arrived in France, 1962; s.Rakharam and Shamdevi Aggarwal. BA, Panjab U., India, 1955, MA, 1958; PhD, Pierre & Marie Curie U., Paris, 1965; DSc, U. de Franche-Comte, Besançon, France, 1974. Collaborator technique U. de Franche-Comte, Besançon, France, 1965-67, lectr., 1967-70, asst. prof., 1970-92, prof., 1992—. Contbr. articles to profl. jours. Mem. Internat. Fuzzy Sys. Assn., French Assn. for Artificial Intelligence. Avocations: tennis, cheiromancy. Office: Nand Lal Aggarwal Sci Econ, Ave de l'Observatoire, 25030 Besançon Cedex, France

AGGARWAL, NARINDER KUMAR, physician, educator; b. Dhariwal, Punjab, India, Dec. 19, 1957; s. Yash Paul and Sudarshan Kumari A.; m. Sneh Garg, Nov. 18, 1986; children: Saurabh, Ashish. M.B.B.S., U. Coll. Med. Scis., New Delhi, India, 1979; MD, U. Coll. Med. Scis., Delhi, India, 1987. Registered med. dr. Med. Coun. India. Demonstrator U. Coll. Med. Scis., New Delhi, 1982-88, lectr., 1988-89, sr. lectr., 1989-92; reader U. Coll. Med. Scis., Delhi, 1992—, G.T.B. Hosp., Delhi, 1992—; lectr. Indian Med. Assn., New Delhi. Contbr. articles to profl. jours., chpt. to book. Mem. Indian Acad. Forensic Medicine (life), Delhi Psychiatric Soc. (life). Hindu. Avocations: cricket, stamp collecting, reading. Home: WZ 283/15 Vishnu Garden, ext 1, New Delhi 110018, India Office: U Coll Med Scis Dept Foren, Dilshad Garden, Delhi 110095, India

AGGARWAL, NEAL, medical information scientist; b. Nairobi, Kenya, Dec. 26, 1960; s. Baldev and Trina Philomena (Raymond) A.; m. Ami Patel, June 22, 1983; children: Acacia, Gaia. M.B.Ch.B., U. Nairobi, 1985. Physician Intel Electronics Ltd., Nairobi, 1987-95; CEO, chief web developer Cybercoll Ltd., Nairobi, 1995—; CEO, CIO, chief systems analyst Sofscript Kenya Ltd., Nairobi, 1998—; sr. lectr. Intel Computers Data Processing, Nairobi, 1990-95; sr. technician Intel Electronics, Nairobi, 1989-95. Author: A Microelectronics Workbook, 1992, C/C Programming Workbooks, vols. 1-4, 1995; author CD-ROM: Cybercoll Distance Learning Course, 1998; author software: Codeblue - SQL Based Medical System, 1999. Vice chmn. Nyari residents Welfare Soc., Nairobi, 1997, 98, 99, environmental officer, 1997-99; com. mem. Pegasus Flyers Ltd., Nairobi, 1992-98. Fellow Inst. for the Mgmt. of Info.; mem. IEEE, Brit. Computer Soc., Assn. for Computing Machinery, MCSE, MCDBA. Avocations: tennis, weight training, rally driving, flying. Home and Office: #15 Nyari Estate, Nairobi Kenya

AGGARWAL, RAJESH KUMAR, ophthalmic surgeon, consultant; b. Aurusha, Tanzania, Sept. 18, 1959; came to U.S., 1967; s. Krishan Dev and Vimla Vati Aggarwal; m. Alison Sarah Wall; children: Jessica, Nina, Jay. MB, U. Southampton, Eng., 1983. Sr. house officer in gen. medicine Southampton Hosp., 1985-87; sr. house officer in ophthalmology Addenbrookes Hosp., Cambridge, Eng., 1987-89; from registrar to sr. registrar in ophthalmology Birmingham (Eng.) and Midland Eye Hosp., 1989-94; anterior segment fellow Flinders Med. Ctr., Adelaide, Australia, 1994-95; anterior segment and cataract fellow Moorfields Eye Hosp., London, 1995-96; cons. ophthalmologist Southend (Eng.) NHS Trust Hosp., 1996—. Contbr. articles to profl. jours. Fellow Royal Coll. Surgeons, Royal Coll. Ophthalmologists; mem. Royal Coll. Physicians, Midlands Ophthal. Soc., Am. Acad. Ophthal., European Cataract and Refractive Surgery Assn. Home: 47 Burlescoombe Rd, Southend-on-Sea SS1 3QE, England Office: Southend NHS Trust Hosp, Prittlewell Chase, Southend-on-Sea Essex, England

AGGARWAL, SATISH KUMAR, electrical engineer, government official; b. New Delhi, Nov. 2, 1938; came to U.S., 1967; s. Damodar Das and Balwanti (Devi) A.; m. Renu Aggarwal, June 13, 1969; children: Angela, Monica, Neil. BSc, Delhi (India) U., 1957, BE in EE, 1961; MSEE, N.J. Inst. Tech., 1969; MBA, NYU, 1970; postgrad., Columbia U., 1968-69, George Washington U., 1971, U. Md., 1972. Registered profl. engr., N.Y., Md., Ga. Project engr. Siemens, Bombay, India, 1961-63; exec. engr. GE, Bombay, 1964-67; project engr. Consol. Edison, N.Y.C., 1967-70; engr. supr. Bechtel Power Corp., Gaithersburg, Md., 1970-76; chief. elec. engring. U.S. Army Corps Engrs.-Facilities Engring. Support Agy., Ft. Belvoir, Va., 1977-81; sr. program mgr. U.S. NRC, Washington, 1981—; vis. prof. USDA, Washington, 1979-80; chmn. Internat. Nuclear Power Plant Aging Workshop, 1982, Symposium, 1988, Conf., 1992. Author nuclear power plant regulations and regulatory guides; contbr. articles to profl. jours. Recipient Presdl. commendation for outstanding contbns. to nuclear power plant aging, 1988, Spl. Achievement award for Tech. Leadership, U.S. Dept. Def., 1980, Md. Gov. commendation for tech. leadership in power engring. 1999, Presdl. Commendation for Profl. Achievements, 2000. Fellow Instn. Elec. Engrs. (India, Eng.); mem. IEEE (sr., bd. dirs. Washington sect. 1982-84, mem. nuclear power engring. com. 1988—, mem. standards bd. 1991—, vice chmn. Washington sect. 1997-98, chmn. 1998-99, vice chair nat. capital area coun. 2000—, Standards Medallion 1998, 3d Millennium medal 2000), Inustry Application Soc. of IEEE (chpt. chmn. 1980-82), Nuclear Plasma Soc. of IEEE (chpt. chmn. 1982-83), Indo-Am. Cultural Soc. (pres. 1989). Democrat. Hindu. Home: 11101 Smoky Quartz Ln Potomac MD 20854-1214 Office: NRC Washington DC 20555-0001

AGGARWAL, SUDESH KUMAR, mechanical engineer, educator; b. Jalandhar, Punjab, India, Aug. 1, 1942; s. Ram Parkash and Janak Dulari (Gupta) A.; m. Shashi Bala Gupta, Mar. 1, 1970; children: Sonu, Ankur. BSMechE, Panjab U., Chandigarh, India, 1964; ME in Machine Design, U. Roorkee, India, 1967, PhD, 1980. Sr. fellow U. Roorkee, 1964-67, lectr., 1967-69; assoc. prof. mech. engring. Punjab Engring. Coll., Chandigarh, 1969-82, prof. mech. engring., 1982—, head dept. mech. engring., 1987—; dir. tech. edn. U.T., Chandigarh, 1998—; cons. Bur. Indian Standards, New Delhi, 1982—, Chandigarh Transport, 1989—, Chandigarh Med. Coll., 1995—; mem. editl. adv. bd. Jour. of Comm. and Instrumentation, 1995—. Contbr. articles to profl. jours. Writer The Tribune, Chandigarh, 1992—, Indian Express, Chandigarh, 1993—. Fellow Inst. Engrs. India. Avocations: writing, social service, listening to music. Home: House No 1619 Sector 35B, Chandigarh 160022, India Office: Dept Mech Engring, Punjab Engring Coll, Chandigarh 160012, India

AGGELIS, GEORGE, agricultural educator; b. Livanates, Fthiotida, Greece, July 24, 1959; s. Dimitrios and Ioanna (Kougiatsou) A.; m. Theodora Mazioti, Mar. 13, 1983; children: Dimitra, Lyda. BS in Agr., U. Athens, Greece, 1982; MSc, U. Sci., Tech., Lang., Montpellier, France, 1986; PhD tres honorable, U. Sci., Tech., Lang., 1989. Profl. cert. in oenology, agrl. scis. Vis. prof. Harokopion U., Athens, Greece, 1989-93; rschr. Argl.U., Athens, 1989-93, lectr., 1993-97; asst. prof. Agrl. U., Athens, 1997—; cons. Logonmotiv S.A., Paris, 1989-93, Damia, S.A., Athens, 1992-96, Athina, S.A., Athens, 1994-95; mem. senate Agrl. U. Athens, 1993-97. Contbr. more than 45 papers, articles, rsch. to profl. jours. Mem. Assn. FrancoHellenique Sci. Technique, Greek Biotech. Soc., Greek Food Sci. Tech. Soc. Avocations: music, tennis, chess. Home: Agias Marinas 5, 141-21 Athens Heraklion Attikis, Greece Office: Agrl U Athens, Iera Odos 75, 118-55 Athens Greece

AGGERBECK, LAWRENCE PAUL, medical researcher, research scientist, educator; b. Chgo., Aug. 26, 1945; arrived in France, 1989; s. Lawrence John and Ruth Anne (Filline) A.; m. Martine Suzanne Yates, May 14, 1977; children: Valerie Ruth, Christopher Lawrence, Jonathan Francis. BA in Chemistry, St. Olaf Coll., 1967; MD, U. Chgo., 1974, PhD in Biochemistry, 1974. Diplomate Nat. Bd. Med. Examiners. Resident in medicine Evanston (Ill.) Hosp., 1977-78; chargé de recherche Centre Nat. de la Recherche Scientifique, Gif-Sur-Yvette, 1980-90, dir. rsch., 1990—; pres. com. on hygiene and security Centre de Genetique Moleculaire, 1994—, dep. dir., 2000—; mem. editl. com. Sci. Chimique et Scis. de la Vie Centre Nat. de la Recherche Scientifique, Gif-Sur-Yvette, 1991—; sci. dir. DNA Microarray Facility, Gif/Orsay, 1999—; vis. assoc. rsch. biochemist U. Calif., San Francisco, 1986-88; guest scientist Lawrence Livermore Lab., U. Calif., Berkeley, 1987; vis. scientist Gladstone Found. Lab. for Cardiovasc. Rsch., U. Calif., San Francisco, 1985-88; mem. sci. coun. Group d'Etudes et de Recherche Sur Les Lipides, Soc. Francaise de Biochemie et Biologie Moleculaire, Paris, 1989—; sci. adv. bd. Lab. de Enzymologie, CNRS, Gif-Sur-Yvette, 1990-94. Contbr. articles to profl. jours. including Sci., Nature, Jour. of Molecular Biology, Jour. Biol. Chemistry, Gene, Jour. Clin. Investigation, Jour. Lipid Rsch., among others. Mem. Sch. Bd., Athis-Mon, 1989; mem. ch. coun. Evang. Luth. Ch., Massy-Palaiseau, 1994—. Recipient Hon. Student award Am. Oil Chemists Soc., Mex., 1974; recipient numerous grants. Fellow Coun. on Atherosclerosis, Am. Heart Assn.; mem. Am. Chem. Soc., Soc. Francaise de Biochimie et Biologie Moleculaire, Soc. Francaise de Biophysique, Soc. Francaise de Biologie Cellulaire, Comité Français de Coordination des Recherches sur L'Atherosclerose et le Cholestérol, Blue Key Nat. Honor Fraternity, Sigma Pi Sigma, Phi Beta Kappa. Lutheran. Avocations: reading, gardening, computer science. Home: 4 Impasse des Trois Ormes, 91200 Athis-Mons France Office: Cen de Genetique Mol/Cen Nat de la Recherche Scien, Avenue de la Terrasse, 91198 Gif-Sur-Yvette France

AGHASSI, WILLIAM J., mechanical engineer, consultant; b. N.Y.C., July 3, 1948; s. Norman H. and Violette (Solomon) A.; m. Marion Weston, June 17, 1979; children: Rachel, Eli. BSME, Polytech. U. Bklyn., 1969; MS in Environ. Engring., N.J. Inst. Tech., 1975. Registered profl. engr., N.Y.; cert. asbestos investigator, N.Y.C. Engr. Combustion Engring., Windsor, Conn., 1969-71, City of N.Y., 1971-74, Leeds and Northrup Co., N.Y.C., 1974-82; prin. W.J. Aghassi Cons. Engrs., N.Y.C., 1982—; developer engring. curricula for h.s. Recipient Environ. Quality award EPA, 1998. Mem. ASME, ASHRAE, Am. Water Works Assn. Avocations: hiking, biking, outdoor activities. Home: 180 Cabrini Blvd New York NY 10033-1138

AGHDASI, FARZIN, science educator; b. Kashmar, Khorasan, Iran, Oct. 17, 1954; arrived in South Africa, 1995; s. Djahangeer and Eshraghieh (Muhajerin) A.; m. Fariba Farzaneh, Jan. 2, 1982; children: Bayan, Carmel. BSc in Engring. with honors, U. London, 1977; MBA, U. Portland, 1979; PhD, U. B.C., Vancouver, Can., 1994. Chartered profl. engr. Design engr. Tektronix Inc., Beaverton, Oreg., 1976-78; lectr. U. Zimbabwe, Harare, 1979-88; rsch. fellow B.C. Cancer Rsch. Ctr., Vancouver, 1989-92; product devel. mgr. Xillix Techs. Corp., Vancouver, 1992-95; sr. lectr. U. Witwatersrand, Johannesburg, South Africa, 1995—; cons. Eskom Nat. Utility, Johannesburg, 1998-00, Securicor Inc., Johannesburg, 1998—; dir. Relief Svcs., Luanda, Angola, 1985-89. Author: (books) State of the Art in Digital Mammographic Image Analysis, 1994, Biomedical Image Processing, 1993; contbr. articles to profl. jours. and conf. procs. Mem. aux. bd. Bahá'i Faith, Zimbabwe, 1980-89; sec. Spiritual Assembly of Bahá'is of Greater Vancouver, 1990-95. Commonwealth scholar Can. Govt., Vancouver, 1990-94; grad. fellow U. B.C., 1990-94. Mem. IEEE, Inst. Elec. Engrs. U.K. (corp. mem.), South African Inst. Elec. Engring. (sr. mem.). Bahá'i. Avocations: reading, movies. Home: PO Box 30169, Kyalami 1684 South Africa Office: U Witwatersrand, 1 Jan Smuts Ave, 2050 Johannesburg South Africa

AGHION, PHILIPPE MARIO, economist; b. Paris, Aug. 17, 1956; s. Raymond and Gabriella Aghion; m. Beatriz Armendariz, July 4, 1986; children: Mikhaela, Eduardo. PhD in Econs., Harvard U., 1987. Asst. prof. MIT, Cambridge, Mass., 1987-89; rschr. Ctr. Nat. Recherche Scientifique, Paris, 1989-91; prof. econs. Harvard U. at Univ. Coll. London, 2000—. Mem. editorial bd. Rev. Econ. Studies, 1990—, Econometrica, 1993. Official fellow Nuffield Coll., Oxford, 1992. Fellow Econometric Soc. E-mail: p.aghion@ucl.ac.uk. Office: Univ Coll London Dept Econs, Gower St, London WC2A 16B, England also: Harvard U Dept Econs Cambridge MA 02138

AGIER, JEAN M., civil law consulting company executive; b. Poitiers, Vienne, France, Dec. 8, 1929; s. Ernest R. and Radegonde E. (Chauveau) A.; m. Monique H. Gagneraud, June 15, 1964; children: Christine, Robert and Francis (twins). Lic. in law, U. Paris, 1953. Notaire Agier, Paris, 1963-87; chmn., CEO Mannkraft Corp., Newark, 1987-93; mgr. Fagimo, Paris, 1994—, Agier Conseils, civil law cons., Paris, 1998—. Lt. French Air Force, 1954-57. Mem. Internat. Acad. Estate and Trust Law, Automobile Club France. Avocations: golf, skiing. Home: 5 Rue de L'Alboni, 75016 Paris France Office: Agier Conseils, 88 Ave de Villiers, 75017 Paris France

AGIOBENEBO, TAMUNOPRIYE JONES, economics educator, researcher, consultant; b. Bakana, Rivers State, Nigeria, Feb. 28, 1953; s. Sam Jones and Lilian March (Agiobenebo) Jones-Agiobenebo; m. Ada Omoni Braide, Sept. 2, 1960; children: Tamuno-Tonye Emilia, Ibiba, Queen Beneboba, Odumye, Opubo. BS in Econs., Ahmadu Bello U., Zaria, Nigeria, 1976; MA in Econs., U. Pitts., 1981, PhD in Econs., 1986. Asst. lectr. U. Sci. and Tech., Pt. Harcourt, 1977-80; lectr. II U. Pt Harcourt, 1982-86, lectr. I, 1986-89, sr. lectr., acting head of econs., 1989-91, sr. lectr., dir., 1991-95, sr. lectr. econs., 1989—; cons., sec. relocation com. NNPC, Finima, Nigeria, 1988-89; external examiner UME, Lagos, Nigeria, 1992-96; mem. Rivers State Tech. Com. on Environ. Guide Lines and Stds., 1999-2000, chmn. socioeconomics subcom., chmn. rev. com., 2000. Author: Microeconomics: Theory and Applications, 1996, Public Sector Economics, 1998, Introductory Mathematical Methods, vol. 1, 1998, vol. 2, 1999, Inductory Microeconomics: Theory and Applications, 2d edit., 1999, Public Sector Economics, vol. 1, 2d edit., 2000; editor-in-chief Jour. Bus. and Econ. Rsch.; editor African Jour. Theoretical and Applied Econs. chmn. caretaker com. SDP, Degema, 1992-93; mem. gov. coun. Nigerian Econ. Soc., 1994—; adviser PHCIMA, Pt. Harcourt, 1992-93; dir. gen. The Cir., Bakana, 1995—. Univ. scholar Fed. Govt. Nigeria, 1973, postgrad. scholar Rivers State Govt., 1978, Postgrad. scholar U. Sci. and Tech., Port Harcourt; tchg. fellow U. Pitts., 1979, 84. Mem. NES (life, coun. mem. 1994-96), ISAN (life, sec. 1992—), Am. Econ. Assn. Eckankar. Avocations: athletics, long and high jumping, table and lawn tennis, badminton. Home: 334 Uniport Post Office, Port Harcourt Rivers State, Nigeria Office: U Pt Harcourt, Dept Econs, PMB 5323 Port Harcourt Rivers State, Nigeria

AGLI, STEPHEN MICHAEL, English language educator, literature educator; b. Yonkers, N.Y., Feb. 11, 1942; s. Michael Joseph and Pauline Joanna (Perrone) A. AB summa cum laude, Fordham Coll., 1965; AM, Harvard U., 1968, EdM, 1972; postgrad., CUNY, 1995—. Cert. secondary sch. English tchr., N.Y. Resident tutor Quincy House, Harvard Coll., Cambridge, Mass., 1968-73; instr. humanities Berklee Coll. Music, Boston, 1971-73; mem. curriculum devel. com., teaching fellow in expository writing Harvard U., Cambridge, 1973-77, tutor in expository writing Bur. of Study Counsel, 1977-81; tchr., chmn. English dept. Jewish H.S. South Fla., North Miami Beach, 1982-83, St. Sergius H.S., N.Y.C., 1983-84; tchr. secondary sch. English Columbia Grammar and Prep. Sch., N.Y.C., 1984-85; coll. counselor, ednl. adminstr. St. Sergius Acad., 1994-95; bd. Freshman advisers Harvard Coll., 1970-77; counselor, ednl. cons., Cambridge, Mass., N.Y.C., 1977-82; ednl. rsch. and cons., N.Y.C., 1985—; adj. instr. English N.J. Inst. Tech., Newark, 1987-88, CUNY, 1992—; conf. session chmn. Soc. for Textual Scholarship, 1993; presenter rsch. papers Rockhurst Coll., Kansas City, Mo., 1989, St. Louis U., Gerard Manley Hopkins Centennial Celebration, 1989, Malone Soc. Centennial Conf., Stratford-upon-Avon, Eng., 1990; spkr. St. Sergius H.S. commencement, 1992-93; lectr. Gerard Manley Hopkins lecture series, various locations, U.S., 1999—. Alumni rep. Harvard U., 1982-90. Recipient Woodrow Wilson fellowship Woodrow Wilson Found. to Harvard U., 1965-66, CUNY travel and rsch. awards to confs. and librs. in U.S. and Europe, 1988-90, 95; fellow NDEA Dept. Celtic Langs. and Lit., Harvard U., 1967-70, CUNY, 1986-90, N.E. MLA, London and Oxford, 1990. Mem. MLA, N.E. MLA, Celtic Studies Assn. N. Am. (speaker annual meeting 1989), Phi Beta Kappa. Home: 65 Central Park Ave Apt 1M Yonkers NY 10705-4707

AGLIETTA, MASSIMO, medical educator; b. Biella, Italy, Dec. 30, 1951; s. Attilio Aglietta and Iride Baietto; m. Franca Fagioli, 1993; children: Anna, Vittoria. MD, Turin (Italy) Med. Sch., 1976, specialist in internal medicine, 1981; specialist in oncology, Parma (Italy) Med. Sch., 1986. Rsch. fellow Radiobiol. Inst., Rijswijk, The Netherlands, 1976-78, Favretto Found., Turin, 1978-80; from asst. prof. to assoc. prof. U. Turin Med. Sch., 1980-90, prof., 1990-96; head dept. hematology oncology Mauriziano Inst. Cancer Rsch. & Treatment U. Turin Med. Sch., 1996—. Author: Myeloproliferative Diseases, 1987; contbr. over 180 articles to profl. jours. Recipient Banno prize, 1989. Mem. Italian Soc. Cancer (v.p. 1994—), Italian Soc. Ematologia Sp. (v.p. 1991-94), Internat. Soc. Hematology, Internat. Soc. Exptl. Hematology. Avocations: tennis, skiing, swimming. Home: Silvio Pellico 31, 10125 Turin Italy Office: IRCC, Strada Provinciale 142, 10060 Candiolo (TO), Italy

AGNAMEY, PATRICE, parasitologist, researcher; b. Cove, Zou, Benin, Mar. 16, 1951; s. Jules and Jeanne (Ayinadou) A. BS, U. Bordeaux (France), 1980, Lecturship, 1981, DSc, 1985. Chemist. In charge of rsch. IMPM, Yaounde, Cameroon, 1986-91; 2nd asst. Ctr. Hospitalier Universitaire, Rouen, France, 1992—; tchr. U. Rouen, 1993-95. Home: 5 Rue du Clos Thirel, 76000 Rouen France Office: Hopital Charles Nicolle, 1 rue Germont, 76031 Rouen France

AGNELLI, GIOVANNI, industrial executive; b. Turin, Italy, Mar. 12, 1921; s. Edoardo and Princess Virginia Bourbon del Monte Agnelli; m. Princess Marella Caracciolo di Castagneto; children: Edoardo, Margherita. LLD, U. Torino, 1943. With Fiat Co., 1943—, vice chmn. bd., 1943-66, mng. dir., 1963-66, chmn., 1966-96, hon. chmn., 1996—; chmn. IFI Istituto Finanziario Industriale, Exor Group S.A.; chmn. Giovanni Agnelli Found; bd. dirs.

Eurafrance; internat. adv. coun. Chase Manhattan Corp. Mem. adv. bd. Bilderberg Meetings; hon. co-chmn. Coun. for the U.S. & Italy; assoc. mem. Moral and Polit. Scis. Acad. of Inst. de France; life mem. Italian Senate; chmn. Editrice La Stampa Spa. With Italian Army, 1940-45. Decorated Cross Mil. Valour, grand cross Royal Order of the No. Star; comdr. Legion of Honor (France). Mem. Italian Stock Cos. Assn. (dir.), Turin Indsl. Assn. (dir.), Confedn. Italian Industry (mem. exec. bd.), Assn. Monetary Union Europe (hon. v.p.). Office: Fiat Spa, Via Nizza 250, 10126 Turin Italy

AGNELLI, UMBERTO, industrialist; b. Lausanne, Switzerland, Nov. 1, 1934; s. Edoardo and Virginia Bourbon del Monte Agnelli; m. Allegra Caracciolo, 1974; three children. Law degree U. Coord. Fiat Internat., Turin, Italy, 1968-70; mng. dir. Fiat SpA, 1970-76, vice chmn, 1976-79, vice chmn., mng. dir., 1979-80, vice chmn. 1980—; vice chmn. Fiat Auto SpA, 1979-80, chmn., 1980-90; vice chmn, mng. dir. Istituto Finanziario Industriale; chmn. IFIL, Carfin; vice chmn., bd. dirs. Giovanni Agnelli Found.; bd. dirs. Danone. Vice-chmn. Internat. Coun. for New Initiatives in East-West Coop.; co-chmn. Italy Japan Bus. Group; chmn. Internat. Vienna Coun.; mem. adv. com. Allianz Versicherungs AG; mem. European adv. com. N.Y. Stock Exchange; mem. Italian Group of Trilateral Commn. Senator of the Italian Republic, 1976-79. Decorated chevalier Legion of Honor, grand officer Order of Merit (Italian Republic). Office: IFI SpA, Corso Matteotti 26, 10121 Turin Italy*

AGNEW, CHRISTOPHER MACK, minister, historian; b. Santa Barbara, Calif., Aug. 7, 1944; s. Jack and Agnes Emma (Mack) A.; m. Suzanne Marie Souder, June 1, 1974 (div.); m. Elizabeth Lewis Lyddane, Apr. 25, 1998. AB, Bucknell U., Lewisburg, Pa., 1967; MA, U. Del., Newark, 1975, PhD, 1980; STM, Gen. Theol. Sem., N.Y.C., 1991. Ordained to ministry Episcopal Ch. as deacon, 1991, as priest, 1992. Reference libr. Dover (Del.) Pub. Libr., 1969-72; tchg. asst. dept. history U. Del., Newark, 1972-76; manuscript libr. Hist. Soc. Del., 1979-81; asst. prof. history and Can. studies SUNY, Plattsburgh, 1981-84; registrar Diocese of Del., Wilmington, 1985-89; deacon St. Thomas' Ch., Newark, 1991-92; assoc. ecumenical officer Episcopal Ch., N.Y.C., 1989-94; priest assoc. All Angels Ch., N.Y.C., 1992-95; interim rector All Hallows, Wyncote, Pa., 1995, St. Michael's, Litchfield, Conn., 1995-97, Ch. of the Ascension, Norfolk, Va., 1997, St. Peter's in Great Valley, Paoli, Pa., 1997-99; priest in charge St. Paul's, Owens, Va., 2000—; mem. staff Anglican-Roman Cath. Consultation, Standing Commn. Ecumenical Rels., 1989-94, Episcopal Russian Orthodox Joint Coord. Com., 1990-94; mem. Faith and Order Commn., 1991-95; mem. NCC Christian-Muslim Rels. Commn., 1989-91, NCC Christian-Jewish Rels. Commn., 1989—, chmn. 1991—; mem. Parliament of the Worlds Religions, 1993, NCC Interfaith Working Group, 1990-95, Interfaith Rels. Commn., 1996—, Planning Com., Nat. Workshop on Christian Unity, 1990-94. Editor: The Ecumenical Bull., 1989-94, Anglican Statements on the Church: Selected Documentary Sources for a Study of Anglican Ecclesiology, 1994; author: God With Us, 1986; contbr. articles to profl. jours. Mem. Nat. Episc. Historians Assn. (mem. exec. bd. 1995-99), Hist. Soc. Episc. Ch., Order Crown Charlemagne U.S. (asst. chaplain 1997—), Orgn. Am. Historians, Am. Hist. Assn., N.Am. Acad. Ecumenists, Can. Hist. Assn., Assn. Can. Studies in U.S., Mil. Order of Loyal Legion of U.S. (chaplain-in-chief 1995—), Mil. Order of Stars and Bars, Soc. Colonial Wars, N.Am. Guild of Change Ringers. Home: 12433 Richards Ride King George VA 22485-5435 Office: 5486 Saint Paul's Rd King George VA 22485

AGNEW, JANET BURNETT, secondary education educator; b. Spartanburg, S.C., Aug. 29, 1936; d. James and Ruby Evelyne (Burnett) A.; 1 child, James Gilmour. BA, U. N.C., Greensboro, 1958; MA in Teaching, Converse Coll., Spartanburg, S.C., 1966; postgrad., Clemson (S.C.) U., 1970-72, U. S.C., Columbia, 1990—. Cert. tchr., prin., math. supr. Tchr. gen. math. and algebra Greensboro Schs.-Aycock, 1958-60; tchr. coll. prep. math. Air Force Dependent H.S., Stevenville, Nfld., Can., 1960-61; tchr. gen. math. and algebra Roebuck H.S. Spartanburg Schs. #6, 1962; tchr. gen. phys. sci. Campobello Sch. Spartanburg Schs., 1962-63, tchr. math. and algebra, 1965-68, substitute tchr., 1975-76; tchr. gen. math. and algebra Pacolet & Broome H.S., 1976-98; corp. sec. Delagrave Co., Spartanburg, 1963-75; instr. math. Spartanburg Meth. Coll., 1968-75; ret., 1998; cons., 1998—. Contbr. articles to profl. jours. Pres. Gen. Fedn. Women's Clubs-S.C., Columbia, 1978-80, chmn. trustees, 1985-87, 88-91, 91-97, 1999-2000, chmn. scholarship com., 1991-93, 95-97, 97-03, sec.-treas. so. region, 1990-92, v.p., 1992-94, pres. 1994-96, sec., 2000—. Recipient Svc. award Spartanburg March of Dimes, 1967, 68. Mem. NEA-R (life), Nat. Coun. Tchrs. Math., S.C. Edn. Assn.-R (life, del. assembly 1987-98, Rep. dist. dir. # 3 1999-01, chmn. by-laws and policies com.), S.C. Tchrs. Math. (life), Spartanburg County Assn. Educators (dist. dir. 1988-91, v.p, pres. elect 1991-92, pres. 1992-93, rep. to del. assembly and NEA assembly,), Spartanburg Country Club Woman's Golf Assn., Spartanburg Coun. Federated Woman's Clubs (pres. 1989-92, 2000—), Jubilee Club (pres. 1996-2000), Piedmont Jr. Woman's Clubs (pres. 1974, 76, Clubwoman of Yr. 1974, 75, 76), Delta Kappa Gamma (Sigma Theta Alpha chpt. v.p. 2000—). Democrat. Presbyterian. Avocations: crafts, travel. Home: 140 Burnett Dr Spartanburg SC 29302-3402

AGNEW, JOHN BROUGHTON, chemical engineering educator, consultant; b. Sydney, Australia, Oct. 27, 1933; s. James Broughton and Ada Winifred (Burgess) A.; m. Elizabeth Mary Hitt, Aug. 15, 1959; children: James Broughton, Michael John, Robert Edward. B of Engring., U. Sydney, Australia, 1955; PhD, Monash U., Australia, 1967. Chartered engr., U.K.; registered profl. engr., Australia. Chem. engr. Brit. Petroleum Ltd., 1955-61; lectr. in chem. engr. U. Melbourne, Australia, 1961-64; sr. lectr. chem. engring. Monash U., 1964-70, assoc. prof. chem. engring., 1971-83; prof., head chem. engring. U. Adelaide, Australia, 1983-94, dean engring., 1988-90, 95-98, head divsn. engring. and math. scis., 1996-98; emeritus prof. U. Adelaide, 1999—; vis. fellow U. Cambridge, Eng., 1967-68; vis. prof. U. Conn., 1986-87, U. Wyo., 1999. Contbr. over 115 articles to profl. jours. Commr. Environ. Resources and Devel. Ct., South Australia, 1995—; exec. officer Australian Coun. Engring. Deans, 1999—. Fellow Instn. Chem. Engrs. (Award of Excellence 1991), Australian Acad. Tech. Scis. and Engring., Instn. Engrs. Australia (hon., chmn. Coll. Chem. Engrs. 1988-89, chmn. South Australia divsn. 1992, John A. Brodie medal 1982, Chemeca medal 1997), Royal Australian Chem. Inst., Australian Inst. Energy. Avocations: reading, gym, music, travel. Home: 12 Fowlers Rd, Glen Osmond 5064, Australia Office: U Adelaide, Dept Chem Engring, Adelaide 5005, Australia

AGNEW, KENNETH MALCOLM, design educator; b. London, June 7, 1933; s. Lionel Patrick and Alice (Mann) A.; m. Jean Helen Miller, Dec. 10, 1970; 1 child, Giles Edmund. Cert. in Architecture, U. Coll., London, 1959; Des RCA, Royal Coll. of Art, London, 1961, M Des RCA with Distinction, 1969. Fellow Chartered Soc. Designers. Consular clk. Fgn. Office, London, 1950-55; archtl. asst. Riches & Blythin, London, 1955-56; rsch. worker Royal Coll. Art, London, 1961-78; pvt. practice Agnew Assocs., Norfolk, 1978-83; prof. of design U. Ulster, Belfast, 1984-98; cons. Simple Systems, London, 1983-84, Cambridge Comms., 1982-83, Brit. Steel, London, 1974-78. Designer: Kings Fund Hospital Bed, 1966 (Sci. Mus. Collection 1996), Solar Panel and Ground Heat Recovery, 1976; designer/builder: Horizons solar house and swimming pool, 1986. 2nd lt. Royal Artillery, Germany, 1952-54. Recipient Silver Medal for Indsl. Design, RCA, London, 1961, IBM/Aspen fellow, N.Y.C., 1966; Churchill fellow, London, 1970. Fellow Royal Soc. Arts, Chartered Soc. of Designers. Avocations: photography, fgn. travel, chess. Home: Horizons, Church Rd, Wreningham Norfolk NR16 1BA, England

AGNEW, RUDOLPH ION JOSEPH, mining company executive; b. Mar. 12, 1934; s. Rudolph John and Pamela Geraldine (Campbell) A.; m. Whitney Warren, 1980. Ed. pub. schs., Eng. With Consolidated Gold Fields, 1957—; chief exec. officer Amey Roadstone Corp., 1974-78, chmn., 1974-77; group chief exec. Consolidated Gold Fields, London, 1978-89, chmn., 1983-89; chmn. Stena Line, 1990—; non-exec. dir. Gold Mines of Sardinia Ltd., Perth, Australia. Fellow Game Conservancy. Served with His Majesty's 8th Royal Irish Hussars, 1953-57. Avocation: shooting. Office: Gold Mines Sardinia Ltd, 145 Stirling Hwy Ste 3, Nedlands Perth WA 6009, Australia*

AGNEW, THEODORE LEE, JR., historian, educator; b. Ogden, Ill., Dec. 21, 1916; s. Theodore Lee and Agnes (Faris) A.; m. Jeanne Starrett LeCaine, Dec. 25, 1942 (dec.); children: Theodore (dec.), Theodore Lee III, Susan Elizabeth (Mrs. Tom Balestreri), Hugh LeCaine, Peter Wallace, Marion Jeanne. B.A., U. Ill., 1937, M.A., 1938; A.M., Harvard U., 1939; Ph.D., Harvard, 1954. Grad. research asst. U. Ill., 1938; asst prof. history Okla. State U., Stillwater, 1947-54, assoc. prof., 1954-60, prof., 1960-84, prof. emeritus, 1984—; vis. prof. history Emory U., summer 1964, 66-67; adj. prof. Meth. history Phillips Grad. Sem., Tulsa, 1992, 94; mem. World Meth. Coun., 1976-91, 96—, exec. com., 1981-86; del. United Meth. Gen. Conf. and South Ctrl. Judisdictional Conf., 1976, 80, 84, 88, 92, 96, mem. gen. commn. on archives and history, 1972-80, commn. to study ministry, 1972-76, 88-92, commn. on Christian unity and interreligious concerns United Meth. Ch., 1980-88, gen. coun. on ministries, 1984-88; mem. bds. South Ctrl. Jurisdiction and Okla. Ann. Conf., Okla. Conf. of Churches; lay mem. Okla. Ann. Conf., 1971—, mem. joint adminstrv. bd. Meth. Theol. Sch. in Ohio and United Theol. Sem.; lay consultation coun. St. Paul Sch. Theology; bd. dirs. Frances E. Willard Home, Tulsa. Author: The South Central Jurisdiction 1939-1972, 1973,; contbr. articles to profl. jours. and biog. dictionaries. Served from ensign to lt. USNR, 1942-46, comdr. Res. ret. Mem. AAUP (mem. coun. 1960-63), Am. Hist. Assn., Orgn. Am. Historians, So. Hist. Assn., Am. Soc. Ch. History, Am. Studies Assn., Midcontinent Am. Studies Assn. (pres. 1982), Okla. and Ill. Hist. Socs., Phi Beta Kappa, Phi Kappa Phi, Phi Alpha Theta, Alpha Kappa Lambda. Democrat. Home: 1216 N Lincoln St Stillwater OK 74075-2749

AGNIHOTRI, ROHIT, information technology executive, consultant; b. Kanpur, Uttar Pradesh, India, July 26, 1961; s. Ram Sut and Shail Bala (Pandey) A.; m. Priti Misra, Dec. 1, 1991. BE in Electronics & Comm. Engring., U. Roorkee, India, 1982. Exec. H.A.L., Hyderabad, India, 1982; sr. mgr. CMC Ltd., Chandigarh, India, 1982—. Author: Computer-EK-Parichay, 1987 (1st Nat. award 1988); editor: (mag.) Electroniki, 1989; contbr. articles, poetry to mags., newspapers. Exec. Madhya Pradesh Vigyan Sabha, Bhopal, 1985. Mem. IEEE, Computer Soc. India (sr.), Soc. for Electronics and Computer Tech. (v.p. 1985). Home: 3A/36 Azadnagar, Kanpur 200002, India Office: CMC Ltd, SCO 156-158 Sector 17C, Chandigarh 160017, India

AGNOLI, JOHANNES, retired political science educator; b. Valle di Cadore, Veneto, Italy, Feb. 22, 1925; arrived in Germany, 1948; s. Pietro and Margherita (Da Ponte) A.; m. Barbara Gorres, June 14, 1938; children: Babette Magherita, Niccolò Pierin Agnolo. PhD, U. Tübingen, Germany, 1956. Asst. U. Tübingen, Germany, 1957-58, U Cologne, Germany, 1960-62; asst. U. Berlin, 1962-69, asst. prof. polit. sci., 1970-72, prof. in ordinary, 1972-91, prof. in ordinary emeritus, 1991—; tchr. Trade Union Sch., Berlin, 1963-65; co-publisher (polit. revs.) Das Argument, Berlin, 1966-67, Critica del Diritio, Rome, 1974-86. Author: (books) Transformation Der Demokratie, 1967, 90, Überlegungen zum Bürgerlichen Staat, 1975, 95, Subversive Theorie, 1996, Faschismus ohne Revision, 1997, 1968 und die Folgen, 1999, Geschichte und Politik, 2000; (essays) Zur Faschismus Diskussion, 1968, 97, Zur Kritik der Politik, 1989, 90. Mem. SPD Tübingen and Cologne, Germany, 1957-61; co-foundr Republicanischer Club, Berlin, 1967. Avocations: mountaineering, cooking. Home: Via Dei Bevilacqua 133D, 55060 San Quirico Moriano Italy

AGNON, AMOTZ, earth science researcher; b. Haifa, Israel, Feb. 5, 1955; s. Hemdat and Pnina (Sperling) A.; m. Daphna Golan, June 1984; children: Gali, Uri. BS, Hebrew U., Jerusalem, 1980, MS, 1983; PhD, U. Calif., Berkeley, 1988. Asst. Hebrew U., Jerusalem, 1980-83, U. Calif., Berkeley, 1983-88; lectr. Hebrew U., 1990-96, sr. lectr., 1996—; adj. lectr. Hebrew U., 1988-90. Assoc. editor Israel Jour. Earth Sci., 1992—. Mem. Yesh-Gvul (Israeli Res. Soldiers Refusing to Serve in Opressive Activities), 1989—, Am. Friends Yesh Gvul, Berkeley, 1988. With Israeli Defense Forces, 1973-76. Fulbright scholar, 1983-88. Mem. Am. Geophys. Union, Israel Geol. Soc., European Union Geosci. Avocations: listening to jazz music, soccer. Home: 38 Habanai St, 96264 Jerusalem Israel Office: Hebrew U, Inst Earth Scis, 91904 Jerusalem Israel

AGORASTOS, THEODOROS, obstetrics and gynecology educator; b. Drama, Macedonia, Greece, Dec. 31, 1951; s. Agorastos and Paraskevi (Kassimidou) A.; m. Ioanna Ikonomou, July 27, 1977; 1 child, Agorastos. Diploma in medicine, Aristotelian U. Thessaloniki, Greece, 1975; MD U. Aachen, Germany, 1979. Jr. registrar dept. ob-gyn U. Aachen, 1975-81; lectr. Aristotelian U. Thessaloniki, 1982-87, asst. prof., 1987-98, assoc. prof., 1998—. Author, editor: Fetale Epidermis und Vernix c., 1989, Handbook of Cardiotocography, 1991, Carcinogenesis in Female Genital Trct, 1997, 1999, Primary and Secondary Prevention of Gynecologic Cancer, 1999. With Greek Navy, 1981-82. Scholar Aristotelian U. Thessaloniki, 1970-71, German Acad. Exch. Svc., 1984, 86; fellow Alexander von Humboldt Found., Graz, Austria, Aachen, Stockholm, 1989-90; grantee Volkswagen Found., 1991. Mem. European Soc. Human Reprodn. and Embryology, European Assn. Gynecologists and Obstetricians, German Soc. Ob-Gyn, Greek Soc. Ob-Gyn, Greek Soc. Gynecologic Oncology. Avocations: reading, painting, music. Home: 87 Mitropoleos St, 546 22 Thessaloniki Greece Office: Hipprokrateion Hosp, 49 Konstantinoupoleos St, 54642 Thessaloniki Greece

AGOSTINI, MICHAEL DAVID, retired oil company executive engineering educator; b. St. Augustine, Trinidad, Jan. 20, 1939; arrived in Australia, 1972; s. Joseph Emmanuel and Marie Rita (Tardieu) A.; m. April Lynn Cox, Aug. 31, 1963; children: Jennifer, Antoinette, Christopher. BSc, N. C. State U., 1963. Registered profl. engr. Petroleum engr. Woodside Offshore Petroleum, Perth, Australia, 1972-79, chief engr., 1979-85, mgr. offshore ops., 1985-89, gen. mgr., 1994-95; gen. mgr. Woodside Offshore Petroleum, Karratha, Australia, 1991-99; lead strategy analyst Shell Internat., The Hague, Holland, 1989-91; ret., 1999; adj. prof. engring. U. Western Australia. Br. pres. Liberal Party Australia, Perth, 1975-77, divsn. v.p., 1977-87, divsn. pres., state exec., 1987-89. Mem. Inst. Engrs. Australia, Soc. Petroleum Engrs. (divsn. chmn. 1988-89). Roman Catholic. Avocation: golf.

AGOSTINI, NICOLANTONIO, ornithologist; b. Marina di Gioiosa Jonica, Italy, Sept. 15, 1964; s. Michele and Maria Carmela (Michelotti) A. Degree in Natural Sci., U. Parma, Italy, 1987. Intern U. Parma, 1988-89, U. Calabria, Cosenza, Italy, 1990-93, McGill U., Montreal, Can., 1994; profl., 1995—; mem. sci. coordination com. Italian League for the Protection of Birds, 1988-91. Contbr. articles to profl. jours. Promoter of actions against poaching for the protection of birds of prey, Italian League for the Protection of Birds, Straits of Messina, 1985-91. Mem. Italian Soc. Natural Sci., Raptor Rsch. Found. Home: Via Carlo Alberto 4, 89046 Marina di Gioiosa Jonica Italy

AGOSTONI, EMILIO, physiologist; b. Milan, Italy, Mar. 18, 1929; s. Giuseppe Agostoni and Elena Fonio; m. Ada Ferrario; children: Giuseppe, Lucia, Stefano, Marco, Elena. MD, U. Milan, 1953. Hon. rschr. asst. dept. physiology Univ. Coll., London, 1954; asst. Inst. Human Physiology U. Milan, Italy, 1954-66, prof., chmn. Inst. Human Physiology, 1972—; prof., chmn. Inst. Human Physiology U. Ferrara, Italy, 1966-72; councilor Internat. U. Physiol. Scis., 1974-83, chmn. Com. Respiratory Physiology, 1977-83. Mem. editl. bd. Respiration Physiology, 1966-73; contbr. articles to profl. jours., chpts. to books. Fellow NIH, Rochester, N.Y., 1958-59, Buffalo, 1959. Mem. Nat. Acad. Lincei, Italian Physiol. Soc. (chmn. 1973-76). Office: U Milan Dept Physiology, Via Mangiagalli 32, 20133 Milan Italy

AGRANOVSKY, ALEXEY ANATOLIEVICH, virologist, researcher; b. Moscow, June 23, 1953; s. Anatoly Abramovich and Galina Fedorovna (Kamanina)A.; m. Alexandra Pavlovna Gretchina, Sept. 10, 1977; 1 child, Maria. BSc, Moscow State U., 1975, PhD, 1981, DSc, 1994. Rsch. asst. Moscow U., 1975-82, rsch. officer, 1982-84, sr. rsch. officer, 1987-91, head virus molecular biology sector, Dept. Virology, 1993—; sr. rsch. officer Sci. Phytopathol. Lab. of USSR Ministry of Agr., Ambo, Ethiopia, 1984-86; rsch. fellow humboldt Found., Braunschweig, Germany, 1991-93. Contbr. articles to profl. jours. Avocations: playing blues music in band. Office: Belozersky Inst, Physico-chem Biology, 119899 Moscow Russia

AGRAWAL, ANUPAM, research scientist; b. Shikohabad, India, Nov. 5, 1969; s. Hari Om and Prem Kanti Agrawal; m. Vandana Agrawal, Dec. 5, 1992; 1 child, Shivam. BSc in Physics, Chemistry and Math., Allahabad (India) U., 1986, MSc in Computer Sci., 1988; M Tech. in Computer Sci. and Engring., Indian Inst. Tech., Madras, 1995; postgrad., U. Roorkee, India, 1999—. Scientist B DRDO, New Delhi, 1989-91; scientist B DRDO, Dehradun, India, 1991-94, scientist C, 1994-2000; scientist D DRDO, Dehradun, 2000—; mem. dipta project DEAL, Dehradun, 1991-95, mem. sarvadrista project, 1996—. Contbr. articles to profl. jours. Mem. ISTE, IETE, CSI (sr.). Avocations: music, badminton, travel, reading, writing technical articles. Home: 1/5 Married Scientist Hostl, Raipur Rd DEAL Colony, Dehradun India

AGRAWAL, ARUN KUMAR, scientist; b. Moradabad, India, Nov. 15, 1947; s. Brij Kumar and Prabha Kumari Agrawal; m. Madhu Agrawal, Feb. 16, 1975; children: Arty, Mohit. BSc, Agra U., India, 1968, MSc, 1970; PhD, Delhi (India) U., 1983. Cert. in chem. scis. Sr. sci. asst. Nat. Phys. Lab., New Delhi, 1977-81, scientist A, 1981-82, scientist B, 1982-87, scientist C, 1987-92, scientist EI, 1992-97, scientist E II, 1997, head Indian Reference Materials Sect., 1994—. Editor: Jour. Metrology Soc. India, 1997; mem. editl. bd. Acean Chemistry Letters, 1998.; patentee in field. Fellow Instn. Chemists (life), Metrology Soc. India (life), Indian Chem. Soc. (life). Avocation: books. E-mail: aka@csnpl.ren.nic.in. Home: 38 Scientist Apt NPL Colony, 110060 New Delhi India Office: Nat Phys Lab, Dr K S Krishman Rd, 110012 New Delhi India

AGRAWAL, BIJAYA KRISHNA DAS, chemical engineering educator; b. Varanasi, India, May 2, 1935; m. Pushpa Agrawal, Jan. 20, 1964; children: Rajat D., Rajeev. BScChemE, Banaras Hindu U., Varanasi, 1959, PhDChemE, 1973; MSChemE, U. Wis., 1961. Rsch. asst. U. Wis., Madison, 1960-61; tchg. asst. U. Windsor, Ont., Can., 1967-70; lectr. chem. engring. Banaras Hindu U., 1961-73, reader, 1973-79, prof., 1979-97; ret.; head dept. chem. engring. Banaras Hindu U., 1981-83; instr. Tex. Tech U., Lubbock, 1970-71; standing com. Harcort Butler Tech. Inst., Kanpur, India, 1985; judge Khosla award U. Roorkee, India, 1990-95; coord. rsch. project Setting Lab. for Computerized Indsl. and Process Control, Ministry Human Resource and Devel., New Delhi, 1992-94; nat. adv. com. Nat. Symposium on Advances in Chem. Reaction Engring., 1997; mem. expert selection coms. univs. and govt. orgns. Shahjalal U. of Sci. and Tech., Bangladesh; presenter in field; vis. prof. Indian Soc. for Tech. Edn., 1994-95, 99; expert COSIST Chem. Tech. of U.G.C., New Delhi, 1999. Mem. Indian Inst. Chem. Engrs. (life, chmn. congress tech. sessions 1990), Indian Soc. for Tech. Edn. (life), Oil Tech. Assn. India (life), Indian Assn. for Air Pollution Control (life, treas. 1983). Avocations: listening to music, travel, helping others. Home: 5 1/4 Kabir Nagar Durgakund, 221 005 Varanasi Utt Prad, India

AGRAWAL, HARI NARAYAN, finance educator, researcher; b. Tigaria, India, Sept. 27, 1943; s. Mohan Lal and Gandi Devi (Agrawal) A.; m. Vimla Agrawal, June 30, 1963; 4 children. BCom, Rajasthan U., Jaipur, India, 1964, MCom, 1966, Phd, 1977. Lectr. Govt. Colls., Ajmer, India, 1966-81; assoc. prof. Saurashtra U., Rajkot, India, 1981-89, prof., 1989-95, prof., head dept., 1995—; mem. commerce desk panel, Univ. Grants Commn., 1997-2000. Author: A Portrait of Nationalised Banks, 1979; contbr. articles to profl. jours. Govt. of India Nat. scholar, 1964-65; Govt. of Rajasthan Merit scholar, 1961-63. Mem. Indian Commerce Assn. (life; exec. mem. 1981-84, 94-97), Indian Acctg. Assn. (life). Home: 81 Ruda Nagar II, 360005 Rajkot, Gujarat India Office: Saurashtra U, 360005 Rajkot, Gujarat India

AGRAWAL, JAI PRAKASH, chemist, researcher; b. Bisaula, U.P., India, June 16, 1944; s. Bishamber Dayal and Shanti Agrawal; m. Sushma Rastogi, Nov. 30, 1973; 2 children. BSc, Lucknow (India) U., 1965; MSc, Gorakhpur (India) U., 1967, PhD, 1971. Jr. rsch. fellow Gorakhpur U., 1967-71; jr. sci. officer Inspectorate of Gen. Stores, New Delhi, 1971-74; sr. sci. officer grade I, Explosives R&D Lab., Pune, India, 1974-80; asst. dir. scientist D, High Energy Materials Rsch. Lab., Pune, 1980-84, dep. dir. scientist E, 1984-90, joint dir. scientist F, 1990-98, assoc. dir. scientist G, 1998—; advisor Union Pub. Svc. Commn., New Delhi; expert CSIR and DRDO selections; PhD examiner for Indian univs.; lectr. in field; mem. rsch. panel Armament Rsch. Bd., Ministry of Def.; mem. sub-com. on tech. and R&D, Coun. for Devel. of Explosives Industry; chmn. nat. expert com. on armaments, high explosives and pyrotechnics. Author: (monograph) Composite Materials, 1991; contbr. over 125 articles to profl. jours.; mem. editl. bd. Jour. Popular Plastics and Packaging, 1989-91, Indian Jour. Engring. and Material Scis.; referee internat. CSIR jours.; patentee and designee in field. Mem. adminstrv. staff Coll. of India Alumni Assn. (life). Recipient Cash award and commendation, Sci. Advisor, Def. Ministry and Sec., Govt. of India, 1989, Dr. Gorakh Prasad Vigyan prize, 1995, Def. Rsch. & Devel. Orgn. Tech. award, 1996; Marie-Curie rsch. fellow Cambridge U., Indo-French High Level Rsch. fellow. Fellow Royal Soc. of Chemistry (U.K.); mem. Indian Soc. for Composite Materials (joint sec. 1985-93). Avocations: social service, badminton. Home: 6 Priyanka Park Sanewadi, Pune 411007, India Office: High Energy Matl Rsch Lab, Pune 411021, India

AGRAWAL, POONAM, scientist, educator; b. Lucknow, India, Jan. 3, 1958; d. Bishambher Nath and Shanti (Vaish) A. BSc, Udaipur (India) U., 1977; MSc, Pantnagar (India) U., 1980; PhD, Indian Agr. Rsch. Inst., New Delhi, 1985; postgrad., U. Düsseldorf, Germany, 1985-87. Part-time tchg. assoc. Pantnagar U., 1977-78, 79-80; asst. prof. Rajasthan Agr. U., Udaipur, 1983-91; sci. officer U. Düsseldorf, 1987; sr. sci. officer Ministry Sci. and Tech., New Delhi, 1988-89; assoc. prof. C.S. Azad U. Agr. and Tech., India, 1991-95; prof. Pandit Sunderlal Sharma Ctrl. Inst. Vocat. Edn. Nat. Coun. Ednl. Rsch. and Tng., Govt. of India, Bhopal, 1995—; dean H.Sc. Pantnagar India Univ., India, 2000—; Indian Agr. Rsch. Inst. jr. rsch. fellow, 1983-85; German Acad. Exch. Svc. postdoctoral fellow, 1985-87; mem. bd. studies Rajasthan Agr. U., 1989-91; mem. bd. studies Kanpur (India) U., 1995-96, expert mem. R & D com., 1997—; acad. facilitator Nat. Open Sch., Bhopal, 1997; chairperson sci. sessions various nat. and internat. confs. Contbr. articles to sci. jours.; inventor fields of nutrition, agr., diabetes, antioxidants. 1st sec. Overseas Students Coordination, Aachen, Germany, 1986. Recipient award for diabetes rsch. S. Bhagwati Rastogi Trust, Vishakhapatnam, India, 1991. Mem. Nutrition Soc. India (life, cert. of merit 1990, 91), Assn. Food Scientists and Technologists (life), Indian Assn. Ednl. Planning and Adminstrn. (life), Soc. Plant Biochemistry and Biotech. (life), Internat. Coll. Nutrition (life), Lions. Avocations: writing poetry, painting, playing sitar, travel. Office: PSSCIVE, NCERT, 131, Zone II, M P Nagar, Madhya P Bhopal 462011, India

AGRAWAL, RAKESH, industrial researcher; b. Ara, Bihar, India, Nov. 3, 1953; came to U.S., 1975; s. Girdhar Lal and Bimla; m. Manju Agrawal, June 18, 1980; children: Udit, Numit. BTech, Indian Inst. Tech., Kanpur, 1975; MChE, U. Del., 1977; ScD, MIT, 1980. From process engr. to process mgr. Air Products and Chems., Allentown, Pa., 1980-90; sr. engring. assoc. Air Products and Chems., Allentown, 1990-92, prin. engring. assoc., 1992-96, chief engr. process synthesis, 1996—; trustee Cache Corp., Austin, 1997—. Contbr. over 60 articles to profl. jours.; holder over 400 patents in field. Mem. AIChE (mem. chem. engring. tech. coun. 1999—, cons. editor Separations 1999—, Inst. award for Excellence in Indsl. Gases Tech. 1998). Avocations: exercise, photography, reading. E-mail: agrawar@apci.com. Office: Air Products and Chems 7201 Hamilton Blvd Allentown PA 18195-1526

AGRAWAL, SATISH CHANDRA, botany educator; b. Varanasi, India, Oct. 20, 1955; s. Santosh Kumar and Sarda Devi Agrawal; m. Sushma Agrawal, Feb. 12, 1981; children: Niket, Neha. BSc, Banaras Hindu U., Varanasi, 1974, MSc, 1976, PhD, 1980. Postdoctoral fellow Banaras Hindu U., Varanasi, 1980-82; lectr. botany U. Allahabad, India, 1983-88; sr. lectr. botany U. Allahabad, 1988-96, reader botany, 1996—. Author: Limnology, 1999; contbr. chpt. to book. Grantee U. Grants Commn., New Delhi, 1990, 97. Mem. Phycol. Soc. India. Achievements include inventor of folia microbiologica. Avocations: reading subject books, writing manuscripts, field collecting. Office: Dept Botany, Univ Allahabad, Allahabad 211002, India

AGRAWAL, SATYENDRA KUMAR, metallurgical engineering educator; b. Ramnagar, U.P., India, Apr. 28, 1944; s. Shivraj Sharan and Kamla Devi A.; m. Sudha Agrawal, Nov. 25, 1969; children: Angira, Varishu, Avantika. BS, Meerut Coll., India, 1963; B Engring., U. Roorkee, India, 1967; M Engring., U. Baroda, India, 1977. Profl. engr. India. Asst. lectr. L.D. Coll. Engring., Ahmedabad, Gujarat, India, 1967-70; lectr. metall. engring. dept. M.S. U. of Baroda, 1970-79, reader metall. engring., 1979-84, prof. metall. engring., 1984—, head metall. engring., 1997—; cons. Gandhi Tube, Halol, Gujarat, 1991-93, Apar Ltd., Baroda, 1994-97; coord. U. Grants Commn., New Delhi; mem. adv. com. Dept. Rsch. Support, UGC, 1991—; investi-

gator-in-charge Bd. for Rsch. in Nuclear Sci., 1988-93; coord. Instnl. Network Sch. for Devel. of Welding Lar., 1992-94; investigator Grain Refinement of Aluminium Studies, Indian Aluminium, Calcutta, 1980-82, Failures in Thermal Power Plant, 1980-83. Chmn. Inst. of Ind. Foundrymen, Baroda chpt., 1988-90; vice-chmn. Ind. Soc. for Non-Desructive Test, 1986—, The Ind. Inst. of Metals, 1993-99. Fellow Indian Inst. of Welders, Instn. Engrs.; mem. Inst. Indian Foundrymen. Avocations: photography, travel, nature conservation, gardening. Office: Met Engring Dept/Fac Tech, MS Univ Bardoa, Baroda/Gujarat 390001, India

AGRAWAL, YADVENDRA KUMAR, chemistry educator, researcher; b. Mandla, India, Sept. 19, 1943; s. Gopal Prasad and Annapurna Agrawal; m. Sandhya Gupta, July 6, 1976; 1 child. BS, Govt. Sci. Coll., Jabalpur, India, 1964, MSc, 1966; PhD, R.S. U., Raipur, India, 1970; DSc, Awdesh Pratap Singh U., Rewa, India, 1979. Head dept. chemistry Govt. Poly., Ujjain, India, 1971-72; sci. officer Bhabha Atomic Rsch. Ctr., 1972-77; reader Maharaja Sayaji Rao U., Baroda, 1977-80; prof. M.S. U., Baroda, 1980-90, head pharmacy, 1981-90; prof., head Gujarat U., Ahemdabad, 1990—; dir. Stanzan Pharms. India, 1994—. Mem. editl. bd. Indian Drugs, Jour. Pharm. Scis., H.K. Sen Meml. award, 1998; contbr. over 300 articles to profl. jours. Recipient Hariom Ashram award Saurashta U., India, 1993. Fellow Royal Chem. Soc. London; mem. Royal Chem. Soc. (cert.). Home: Gujarat Univ Campus, 9 Prof Qr, Ahmedabad 380009, India Office: Gujarat Univ, Dept Chemistry Sch Scis, Ahmedabad 380009, India

AGRAZ, FRANCISCO JAVIER, SR., lawyer, public affairs representative; b. Laredo, Tex., Aug. 21, 1947; s. Jose Jesus and Irene (Garcia-Gomez) A.; m. Rosalinda Varela, Aug. 23, 1969 (div. Feb. 1980); children: Francisco Javier Jr., Raquel Jeanne; m. Ruth Urquidi, Jan. 1, 1984. BA in Journalism, U. Tex. at El Paso, 1970; JD, U. Houston, 1987. Bar: Tex. 1988, U.S. Dist. Ct. (so. dist.) Tex. 1988. Anchor reporter KENS-TV, San Antonio, 1970; corr. ABC Capital Cities Comms., Chgo., Houston, N.Y., 1970-77; pub. affairs analyst Exxon Corp., Houston and Memphis, 1977-83; assoc. Wood, Burney, Cohn & Bradley, Corpus Christi, Tex., 1987-89, Redford, Wray & Woolsey, P.C., Corpus Christi, 1989-91; pres., atty. at law Francisco J. Agraz P.C., Houston, 1991—; gen. mgr. The MRAM Co., Houston, 1996-98; pub. affairs officer FBI, Houston, 1998—. Bd. govs. United Way of Coastal Bend, Corpus Christi, Tex., 1987-91. Mem. State Bar of Tex. (grievance com., pub. rels. com.). Roman Catholic. Avocations: Spanish translator. E-Mail: agrazfj@worldnet.att.net.

AGREEN, LINDA KERR, secondary education educator; b. Washington, Aug. 29, 1949; d. Elton Clare and Barbara Ann (Wilson) Kerr; m. Russell Warren Agreen, June 26, 1971. BS, U. Md., 1971, MEd, 1974. Cert. secondary math. tchr., Md. Tchr. Marley Jr. H.S., Glen Burnie, Md., 1971-75, DuVal H.S., Seabrook, Md., 1975-76; math. tchr. coord. Eleanor Roosevelt H.S., Greenbelt, Md., 1976-96; coach math. team, Greenbelt, 1975-98; team leader Sch. Based Supervision Team, Greenbelt, 1976-98; mem., chmn. Faculty Adv. Com., Greenbelt, 1976-98; math. tchr. Queen Anne's County H.S., Centreville, Md., 1996-98; math. coord. Kent Island H.S., Stevensville, Md., 1998—, NHS advisor, 1998—. Choir mem. Unitd Bapt. Ch., New Carrollton, Md., 1988-98; choir, Sunday Sch. tchr., supt. Trinity Bapt. Ch., Adelphi, Md., 1966-88. Named Agnes Meyer Outstanding Tchr., Washington Post, 1984, Outstanding Educator, Cornell U., Ithaca, N.Y., 1990; recipient Presidential award NSF, Washington, 1992. Mem. Nat. Coun. Tchrs. Math. (publicity com.), ASCD, Math. Assn. Am., NEA, Md. Coun. Tchrs. Math. (local arrangements chair competitions com. 1989), Md. Assn. Tchr. Educators, Prince George's County Educators Assn., Queen Anne's County Educators Assn. Democrat. Avocations: needlepoint, golf, skiing, reading, music. Office: Kent Island HS 900 Love Point Rd Stevensville MD 21666-2120

AGREITER, ANTON JOSEF, priest; b. Brixen, Bozen, Italy, Mar. 18, 1934; arrived in Falkland Islands, 1986; s. Josef and Maria (Clara) A. D of Canon Law, Gregorian U., Rome, 1964; diploma in liturgy, Inst. for Liturgy, Trier, Germany, 1969. Instr. canon law and liturgy Mill Hill Missionaries, London, 1962-68, Nat. Seminary, Kampala, Uganda, 1969-77; sec. gen. Hdqs. of Mill Hill Missionaries, London, 1977-85; apostolic prefect Roman Cath. Ch. in South Atlantic Ocean, Stanley, Falkland Islands/St. Helena, 1986—, Stanley, Tristan Da Cunha, 1986—; judge Met. Tribunal of Roman Cath. Archdiocese of Westminster, London, 1963-68. Author: Die Anstellung der Kooperatoren im Bistum Brixen, 1963. Avocations: watch repairs, gardening, photography. Home and Office: St Mary's Presbytery, Ross Rd, Stanley Falkland Islands

AGRELLOS, JOSÉ CARLOS, bank executive; b. Beira, Mozambique, Dec. 15, 1943; arrived in Portugal, 1947; s. Manuel Carlos and Maria José (Sousa-Pinto) A.; m. Marjorie Kathleen Durham, Mar. 21, 1968; children: Carlos, Luis, Miguel. Degree in Econs., Oporto U., Portugal, 1967. Trainee Banco Portugues Do Atlantico, Oporto, Portugal, 1972-73, asst. mgr. to dep. mgr., 1973-79; sr. mgr. Banco Portugues De Investimento, Oporto, Portugal, 1981-87, ctrl. gen. mgr., pvt. banking, 1988—, bd. dirs., 1995—; head of the cabinet of the Sec. of State for Planning, 1980. Mem. Douro Soc. Corretora De Valores Mobiliarios Sa (chmn. 1987-97), Oporto Golf Club (chmn. 1995-99), Oporto Cricket Lawn Tennis Club, Lawn and Tennis Club Da Foz, Club Portuense, Royal and Ancient Golf Club St. Andrews. Roman Catholic. Avocations: shooting, golf, tennis, water and alpine skiing.

ÅGREN, GÖRAN INGEMAR, ecologist, researcher, educator; b. Borlänge, Dalarna, Sweden, Feb. 2, 1945; s. Karl Edvard Henrik and Ruth Elin (Wikman) Å.; m. Elisabeth Ann Andréasson, Dec. 14, 1979; children: Åsa, Emma, Sofia. MS, Chalmers U. of Tech., Gothenburg, Sweden, 1969; PhD, Chalmers U. of Tech., Gotheburg, Sweden, 1975. Asst. prof. sys. ecology Swedish U. of Agrl. Scis., Uppsala, 1980-86, prof. sys. ecology, 1986—, head dept. ecology and environ. rsch., 1989-93. Author: (with Ernesto Bosatta) Theoretical Ecosystem Ecology-Understanding Element Cycles, 1996; editor: (with A.I. Breymeyer, D.O. Hall and J.M. Melillo) Global Change-Effects on Coniferous Forests and Grasslands, 1996. Office: Swedish U Agrl Sci, Box 7072 Dept Ecology, SE-75007 Uppsala Sweden

AGRUSS, NEIL STUART, cardiologist; b. Chgo., June 2, 1939; s. Meyer and Frances (Spector) A.; m. Janyce Zucker; children: David, Lauren, Michael, Joshua, Susan, Robyn, Bryan. BS, U. Ill., 1960; MD, 1963. Diplomate Am. Bd. Internal Medicine. Resident in internal medicine, 1964-65, 67-68; fellow in cardiology Cin. Gen. Hosp., 1968-70; dir. coronary care unit, 1971-74, dir. echocardiography lab., 1972-74; dir. cardiac diagnostic labs. Ctr. DuPage Hosp., Winfield, Ill., 1974—; asst. prof. medicine U. Cin., 1970-74, Rush Med. Coll., 1976—; chmn. coronary care com. Heart Assn. DuPage County, 1974-76. Author: co-author publs. in field. Active Congregation Beth Shalom, Naperville, Ill. Capt. M.C. U.S. Army, 1965-67. Fellow ACP, Am. Coll. Cardiology, Am. Coll. Chest Physicians, Coun. Clin. Cardiology, Am. Heart Assn.; mem. AMA, DuPage County Med. Soc., Ill. Med. Soc., Am. Fed. Clin. Rsch., Chgo. Heart Assn. Office: 454 Pennsylvania Ave Glen Ellyn IL 60137-4418

AGUERREVERE-R, GONZALO, electrical engineer, management consultant; b. Caracas, Venezuela, July 16, 1946; s. Santiago Aguerrevere-V and Ana Ruiz de Aguerrevere; m. Morela Arraiz, Dec. 17, 1972; children: Gonzalo Rafael, Juan Andres, Daniel Ignacio. Elec. Engr., U. Ctrl. de Venezuela, Caracas, 1970; Spec. in Color TV, Ministry of Basic Sci., Bonn, Germany, 1971; Radio Comm. T., Ministry of Comm., Caracas, 1973. Prof. U. Simon Bolivar, Caracas, 1974-81; TSD mgr. Summa Corp., Caracas, 1981-83; engring. mgr. Videodacta, Caracas, 1983-88, Siemens, Caracas, 1988-94; owner, v.p. OFAIN, Caracas, 1986—; owner, pres. Equielec. Svcs., Caracas, 1995—; cons. Invedi-USB, Caracas, 1976-81; designer DICA, Caracas, 1979-81; cons. E de C, Caracas, 1994-96; cons., prof. INC, Caracas, 1996; cons. C.A.V.TV, 1997-99, T.S.M. Tallard Tech. Inc., Caracas, 1999—; bd. dirs. Fundei-Metropolitane, Caracas, 1998-99. Pres., Maintenance Com. of Fundei, Caracas, 1992-96, ACINTEL, Caracas, 1995-97. Mem. IEEE (sr.), Colegio de Ingenieros de Venezuela. Roman Catholic. Achievements include patent for diagonal television. Fax: 58-2-2841505. Office: Aguerrevere Ing Con, Apartado 60606, Caracas 1060A, Venezuela

AGUIAR, ADAM MARTIN, chemist, educator; b. Newark, Aug. 11, 1929; s. Joaquim Ramahlo and Emilea Andrada (Nunes) A.; m. Laura E. Brand, Sept. 2, 1980; children: Justine Diane, David Laurence, Adam Albert, Erick Arthur, Aaron Benjamin, Evan Joaquim. BS, Fairleigh Dickinson U., 1955; MA, Columbia U., 1957, PhD, 1960. Chemist Otto B. May, Newark, 1948-55; asst. prof. Fairleigh Dickinson U., Rutherford, N.J., 1959-63; asst. prof. chemistry Tulane U., New Orleans, 1963-65, assoc. prof., 1965-67, prof., 1967-72, head dept. chemistry Newcomb Coll. div., 1970; dean grad. and research programs William Paterson Coll., Wayne, N.J., 1972-73; research prof. Rutgers U., Newark, 1973-75; prof. chemistry Fairleigh Dickinson U., Madison, N.J., 1975-93, chmn. dept. chemistry/geol. scis., 1984-89; pres. Seltox Corp., N.J., 1980—; adj. prof. chemistry Monmouth U., West Long Branch, N.J., 1993—; cons. chem. firms in La. and N.J. Contbr. articles to profl. jours. Union Carbide fellow, 1957; NIH fellow, 1959; recipient other grants. Mem. AAUP, Am. Chem. Soc., AAAS, N.Y. Acad. Sci., Ctr. for Profl. Advancement, Sigma Xi, Phi Lambda Epsilon, Phi Omega Epsilon. Home: 37 Wyncrest Ln Neptune NJ 07753-7421

AGUIAR, ANTONIO JOSÉ DE ARAUJO, veterinary medicine educator; b. Belém, Pará, Brazil, Feb. 3, 1965; s. Hélio de Araujo and Maria Glória (Cunha) A.; m. Flávia de Rezende Eugênio, Sept. 28, 1991; children: Fernando E.A. Bachelors degree, FCAP, Belém, 1985; specialist in vet. anesthesiology, Sao Paulo State U., Botucatu, Brazil, 1989, MSc, 1992, PhD, 1999. Asst. prof. São Paulo State U., Botucatu, Brazil, 1989-93; asst. prof. São Paulo State U., Araçatuba, Brazil, 1993-98, assoc. prof., 1999—. Recipient Fundunesp grant, Newmarket, Eng., 1992, Abbott grant Abbott Inc., Giessen, Germany, 1993; grantee UNESP, Greece, 1997, Ghent, Belgium, 1998, ZENECA, 1997. Mem. AAAS, Assn. Vet. Anaesthetists, Assn. Equine Pracitioners, Nat. Geog. Soc., Soc. Numismática Brasileira, N.Y. Acad. Scis. Avocations: numismatics, philately. Home: Aclimação, Tupinambás 1188, 16020130 Morumbi S Paulo, Brazil Office: DCCRA, Medicine Vet-UNESP, Rua Clovis Pestana, 793, 16050680 Araçatuba S Paulo, Brazil

AGUIAR, CRISTINA M., diplomat, educator; b. Santo Domingo, Dominican Republic, Nov. 25, 1950; came to U.S., 1997; d. Francisco E. Aguiar and Maria Cristina Quezada; divorced; 1 child, Laura Aurelina. PhD in Law, U. Paris, 1996; Dr. Honoris Causa, U. Pro-Accion y Cultura, Santo Domingo, 1998. Atty. Paris Bar, 1979-96; amb. ext. plenipotentiary European Union, Paris and Brussels, 1996-97; amb. permanent rep. for Dominican Republic UN, N.Y.C., 1997—; prof. law Ecole des Hautes Etudes Internat., Paris, 1992-97. Author: (book) Human Rights in Latin America, 1999. V.p. Women's Polit. Com. for Election of LEonel Fernandez, 1996/. Avocations: collecting art books, painting furniture. E-mail: cag7736972@aol.com. Office: Permanent Mission of the Dominican Republic 4th Fl 144 E 44th St Fl 4 New York NY 10017-4008

AGUILAR, GLENN, engineering educator; b. Iloilo, Philippines, Dec. 23, 1963; s. Salvador P. and Ester Doromal A.; m. Riza Ordonio, Dec. 28, 1992; 1 child, Arielle Rae. BS in Fisheries, U. Philippines, Diliman, Quezon City, 1984; MS in Engring., U. Wash., Seattle, 1988; Doctor Engring., U. Tokyo, 1995. Asst. prof. U. Philippines, Visayas, 1989—, asssoc., 1996—; dir. Inst. Marine Fisheries and Oceanology U. Philippines, Ilolo, 1998—. Avocations: scuba diving, soccer, tennis. Home: UPV #27, Miagao 5023, Philippines Office: Inst Marine Fisheries/Ocean, UP in the Visayas, Miagao 5023, Philippines

AGUINALDO, JORGE TANSINGCO, chemical engineer, water treatment consultant; b. Paniqui, Tarlac, The Philippines, Feb. 22, 1952; s. Andres Pagaduan and Lydia Obcena (Tansingco) A.; m. Juliet Sibal, May 10, 1978; children: Janice, Jeremy. BSChemE, Adamson U., Manila, 1973; postgrad., De La Salle U., Manila, 1977-82, Calif. State U., Sacramento, 1990-91. Registered chem. engr., Philippines. Supr. Paniqui (Tarlac) Sugar Corp, 1973-77; product mgr. water treatment and pollution control Alpha Machinery & Engring. Corp., Manila, 1977-83; sr. project engr. Metito Saudi Arabia Ltd., Riyadh, 1983-85, Metito Engring., Ltd., Nicosia, Cyprus, 1985-86; sr. project engr. Metito Arabia Industries Ltd., Riyadh, 1986-89, project mgr., 1989-90; proposals mgr. Am. Engring. Svcs., Inc., Tampa, Fla., 1991—; bd. dirs. Bios Trading & Mgmt. Svcs. Corp., Manila; cons. J.M. Templa & Assocs., Manila, 1980—. Adult leader Boy Scouts Am. Troop 176 Gulfridge Coun., Tampa. Mem. AIChE, Soc. Indsl. Microbiology, Am. Chem. Soc., Instrument Soc. Am. (sr.), Am. Water Works Assn., Soc. Indsl. Microbiology, Water Environ. Fedn., Philippine Inst. Chem. Engrs., Indsl. Computing Soc., Knights of Columbus, Tampa Bay Fossil Club. Roman Catholic. Avocations: paleonthology, photography, computers. Office: 5912 Breckenridge Pky Ste F Tampa FL 33610-4200

AGUIRRE, FRANCISCO, business educator; b. Temple, Tex., Aug. 21, 1943; s. Eugenio and Maria (Quinteros) A.; m. Linda M. Lopez (1969); children: Christina, Francisco Javier. BBA, Tex. A&I U., 1972; MBA, Sul Ross State U., Alpine, Tex., 1974; MA, N.Mex. State U., 1978. Enlisted USAF, 1962, advanced through grades to chief master sgt., 1980; ret., 1992; assoc. prof. bus. N.Mex. State U., Alamogordo, 1992—. Recipient Tchg. Excellence award Mediterranean region Embry-Riddle Aero. U., 1990. Mem. Nat. Bus. Educators Assn., VFW, Hispanic C. of C., Alamogordo C. of C., Air Force Sgts. Assn., Kiwanis (bd. dirs. Alamogordo 1995). Republican. Roman Catholic. Avocations: gardening, travel. Home: 7435 Highway 54 70 Alamogordo NM 88310-9146 Office: NMex State U 2400 Scenic Dr Alamogordo NM 88310-3722

AGUIRRE, MANUEL ANTONIO, mathematical researcher, educator; b. Rosario, Carazo, Nicaragua, Feb. 7, 1948; arrived in Argentina; s. Manuel Aguirre and Ernestina Téllez; m. Laura Alicia Rebora, Feb. 3, 1950; children: Eloy, Emilio. Lic. in edn., UNAN, Managua, Nicaragua, 1974; lic. in math., U. Buenos Aires, 1976, D in Math., 1984. Full prof. UNAN, Managua, 1976-78; assoc. prof. U. Catolica, Argentina, 1979; asst. prof. U. Belgrano, Argentina, 1979; assoc. prof. U. Nat. del Centro, Argentina, 1980-85, full prof., 1985—; prof. U. Centro Am., Nicaragua, 1976-78; dean math dept. Faculty Ex. Sc., Tandil, Argentina, 1983-85, 96—, vice-decano, 1991-96, dir. Rsch. Inst., 1993—. Author: Integral Serie and Fourier Hans Forum, 1980, Logic and Set Theory Applications, 1984. Fellow OEA, U. Buenos Aires, 1974, 76. Mem. AAAS, CIC, Union Mathematics Argentina. Roman Catholic. Achievements include research in functional analysis-distributions thepry. Avocations: traveling, walking, watching baseball games. Home: Tierra del fuego 928, 7000 Tandil Argentina Office: Dept Math Fac Ex Sc, UNCPBA Pinto 399, 7000 Tandil Argentina

AGUIRRE, ROBERTO RAMON IGNACIO, engineering executive; b. Cordoba, Argentina, Oct. 1, 1950; s. Roberto Tito and Ines Maria del Carmen (Soria) A.; m. Magdalena Celina Ruiz Guinazu, Dec. 4, 1981; children: Roberto, Magdalena, Ignacio, Rosario, Agustina. Engr., U. Catolica Argentina, 1974. Design asst. transp. engr. Grimaux Cons. Assn., Buenos Aires, 1970-74; founder, pres. Aguirre Pinasco S.A., Buenos Aires, 1975; founder, CEO Upstream Svcs. S.A., 1988; project developer Norpacifico LNG Project, Argentina, 1989-92. Contbr. articles to profl. jours. Mem. Argentine Engring. Assn., Marayui Country Club, Jockey Club. Roman Catholic. Home: Warnes 315, 1609 San Isidro Buenos Aires Argentina Office: Esmeralda 155 7th Flr, 1035 Buenos Aires Argentina

AGUIRRE-BACA, FRANCISCO, publisher, consultant; b. León, Nicaragua, Jan. 7, 1920; came to U.S., 1947; s. Horacio and Pilar (Baca) Aguirre-Muñoz; m. Gladys Sacasa Aguirre, Dec. 27, 1941; children: Gladys, Francisco Xavier, Mariangeles, Rafael Eugenio, Guiomar, Alejandra. JD, U. Granada, Nicaragua, 1947. Various sr. positions Nicaraguan Armed Forces, 1940-47; rep., coord. numerous L.Am. newspapers and mags. Washington, 1947-53; co-founder, co-pub. Diario Las Americas, Miami, Fla., 1953—; founder Francisco Aguirre & Assocs. Latin Am. Newspapers and mag., Washington, 1960; dir. Pan Am. Divsn. Am. Road Builders Assn., Washington, 1948-53; co-founder, co-pub. Diario Las Americas, Miami, Fla., 1953; founder Francisco Aguirre & Assoc., Washington, 1960; amb. to III Summit Iberoamerican Chiefs of State Del. Dominican Republic, Salvador, Bahia, Brazil, 1993, amb. to IV Summit Iberoamerican Chiefs of State, 1994; amb. to IV Summit Iberoamerican Chiefs of State Del. Republic Panama, Cartajena, Colombia, 1994; amb. to IV Summit Iberoamerican Pres. and Heads of States Nicaraguan Del., Santiago, Chile, 1996; amb. to official visit to His Holiness John Paul II Nicaraguan Del., Vatican City, Italy, 1996; amb. to Summit of the Ams. Nicaraguan Del., Santa Cruz, Bolivia, 1997; amb. to inauguration new Pres. Nicaragua Arnoldo Aleman Lacayo U.S. Del., Managua, Nicaragua, 1997; amb. to official visit to Republic China Nicaraguan Del., Taiwan, 1998; amb. II Summit of the Ams. Nicaraguan Del., Santiago, Chile, 1998; amb. XXVIII Gen. Assembly OAS Nicaraguan Del., Caracas, Venezuela, 1998; internam. cons. Ambassador Extraordinary and Pleinpotenciary of Nicaragua in Spl. Missions. Bd. dirs. Panamerican Divsn., Am. Rd. Builders Assn., 1948. Knight Order of St. Gregory, Sovereign Order of Malta; decorated by govts. of Argentina, Ecuador, Panama, Dominican Republic, Spain, Nicarauga, Republic of China (Taiwan). Mem. Hist. Georgetown Club, City Club, Nat. Press Club, Univ. Club, Congl. C.C. Republican. Roman Catholic. Home: 4951 Rockwood Pkwy NW Washington DC 20016-3247

AGUIRRE-BATTY, MERCEDES, Spanish and English language and literature educator; b. Cd Juarez, Mex., Dec. 20, 1952; came to U.S., 1957.; d. Alejandro M. and Mercedes (Péon) Aguirre; m. Hugh K. Batty, Mar. 17, 1979; 1 child, Henry B. BA, U. Tex., El Paso, 1974, MA, 1977. Cert. online tchr., Calif. Instr. ESL Paso del Norte- Prep Sch., Cd Juarez, 1973-74; tchg. asst. ESL and English U. Tex., El Paso, 1974-77; instr. ESL English Lang. Svcs., Bridgeport, Conn., 1977-80; instr. Spanish and English, coord. modern lang. Sheridan (Wyo.) Coll., 1980—, pres. faculty senate, 1989-90; pres. faculty senate, chair dist. coun. No. Wyo. C.C. Dist., 1995-96; planning com. No. Wyo. C.C. Dist., 1996-97; mem. advanced placement faculty Spanish cons. Coll. Bd. Ednl. Testing Svc., 1996-99; adj. prof. Spanish, U. Autonoma Cd Juarez, 1975; adj. prof. Spanish and English, Sacred Heart U., Fairfield, Conn., 1977-80; spkr. in field. Bd. dirs. Wyo. Coun. for the Humanities, 1988-92; translator county and dist. cts., Sheridan; vol. Wmen's Ctr.; translator Sheridan County Meml. Hosp.; del. Citizen Ambassador Program, People to People-India, 1996. NEH fellow, 1991-92; Wyo. State Dept. Edn. grant, 1991. Mem. MLA (del. assembly 1998—), Wyo. Fgn. Lang. Tchrs. Assn. (pres. 1990-92), Am. Assn. Tchrs. Spanish and Portuguese (founder, 1st pres. Wyo. chpt. 1987-90), TESOL, Sigma Delta Mu (v.p. 1992-99, pres. 2000—), Sigma Delta Pi (pres. 1974-75). Avocations: travel, reading, archeology, languages, geography. Office: Sheridan Coll NWCCD 3059 Coffeen Ave Sheridan WY 82801-9133

AGUNBIADE, SHADRACH OLUDARE, food scientist; b. Omuo, Ekiti, Nigeria, June 5, 1946; s. Emmanuel and Ajayi (Aribisala) A.; m. Christianah Bamidele Osadiya, Apr. 4, 1976; children: Ayoola, Ayodeji, Ayowole, Ayokunle, Ayoyinka. BSc, U. Ife, Nigeria, 1972; PhD, U. Ibadan, Nigeria, 1992; MSc in Food Tech., U. Reading, Eng., 1979. Head dept. sci. Ekiti Tchrs. Coll., Ikere, Nigeria, 1972-74; lectr. The Poly., Ibadan, 1975—; liaison officer The Poly., Ibadan, 1983, head dept. biology, 1995-96, head dept. food sci. & tech., 1998-99. Contbr. articles to profl. jours. Fed. Govt. scholar, Nigeria, 1969-72, 78-79; UNICEF fellow, 1974-75. Mem. UKIFST (award 1979), Nigeria IFST (award 1979), Omuo Tennis Club. Anglican. Avocations: football, badminton, lawn tennis, reading, singing. Home: c/o Emmanuel Anglican Ch, Eduglesbreet PO Box 66, Omuo Nigeria Office: The Poly, PO Box 22, Ibadan Nigeria

AGUNLOYE, EMMANUEL IDOWU, research scientist, chemist, parasitologist; b. Ikare-Akoko, Ondo State, Nigeria, June 21, 1958; s. Olorunmowe Moses and Ibukun Comfort (Olorunda) A.; m. Ebun Olumide Olowofila, Aug. 22, 1992; children: Boluwatife, Oluwatosin, Ayomide. Tchr.'s cert., St. Peter's Coll., Akure, Nigeria, 1976; Associate degree in clin. chem., U. Coll. Hosp., Ibadan, 1982, Fellow in med. and veterinary parasitology, 1992. Head lab. Gamma Labs., Ibadan, 1982, Alafia Hosp. Suleja, Niger, 1982-83, Holy Trinity Hosp., Ikeja, Lagos, Nigeria, 1984-85; head lab. State Health Ctr., State U., Ado-Ekiti, 1984-99, Akungba Akoko, Nigeria, 1999; advisor to state assn. Assn. Med. Lab. Scientist of Nigeria, Ado-Ekiti, 1996—; lab. cons. Trinity Med. Ctr., Ado-Ekiti, 1986—, Alafia Hosp., 1990—; dir. Ebman Enterprises, Ikare-Akoko, 1998; bd. dirs. Adebitola Nigeria Ltd.; creator radio program Consider Your Way, 1999. Author: The Fear of God, 1998; contbr. articles to profl. jours. Bd. dirs. Ile-Abiye Hosp., 1999; field rep. Full Gospel Businessmen Fellowship Internat., Ado-Ekiti, Akoko, Owo, Ifon, Ondo State, Nigeria, 1996; state coord. Intercessors for Nigeria, Ekiti State, Ado-Ekiti, 1997; mem. Chaplain Fountain of Hope Internat., Ado-Ekiti, 1997. Fellow Inst. Med. Lab. Sci. and Tech. Nigeria; mem. N.Y. Acad. Scis. Anglican. Avocations: reading science facts, preaching the gospel of Jesus Christ, praying for the world, conflict resolution, farming. E-mail: agunloye@workmail.com. Home: 41/43 Main Ave, PO Box 1353, Ado-Ekiti Nigeria Office: State U Path Lab Health Ctr, PMB 01, Akungba-Akoko, Ondo State Nigeria

AGUSTONI, GILBERTO CARDINAL, archbishop; b. Schaffhausen, Switzerland, July 26, 1922. Prelate auditor Roman Rota, 1970-86; ordained titular archbishop Caorle, 1987; sec. Congregation for Clergy, 1986-92; proprefect Apostolic Signatura, 1992-94; prefect Supreme Tribunal of the Apostolic Signatura, 1994—; created and proclaimed cardinal, 1994. Address: 00120 Vatican City State Vatican City State*

AGUTTER, JENNY, actress, dancer; b. Taunton, Eng., Dec. 20, 1952; d. Derek Brodie and Catherine (Lynam) Agutter; m. Johan Tham, 1990; 1 child. Ed., Elmhurst Ballet Sch. Actress in TV films, dramas, and series; actress on stage RSC and Nat. Theatre. Appeared in plays including Tempest, Spring Awakening, Hedda Gabler, Betrayal, The Unified Field, Breaking the Code, Love Labours Lost, 1996, Peter Pan in Nat. Theatre, 1998; films include Ballerina, 1964, I Start Counting, The Railway Children, 1969, Walkabout, Logan's Run, 1975, The Eagle Has Landed, Equus (Brit. Acad. award Best Support Actress), Man in the Iron Mask, The Survivor, 1980, An American Werewolf in London, 1981, Secret Places, 1983, Dark Tower, 1987, Child's Play 2, 1991, Freddie as Fro 7, 1993, Blue Juice, 1995, Mothers and Daughters, 1998; appeared on TV in Amy, 1980, The Good Guys, 1991, Heartbeat, 1994, September, 1995, The Buccaneers, 1995, Snow Goose (Emmy award), And The Beat Goes On, 1996, A Respectable Trade, 1997, Bramwell, 1998, The Railway Children, 2000. Avocation: photography. Office: JY Publicity, 54A Ebury St, London SW1W 0LU, England Mailing: Marmon Mgmt, 308 Regent St Langham House, London Weston R5 AL, England*

AHARONI, HERZL, engineering educator, researcher; b. Haifa, Israel, Feb. 20, 1937; s. Bechor and Sara (Chanimov) A.; m. Miriam Rosenberg Aharoni, Aug. 18, 1964; children: Sigalit, Avinoam, Nurit, Alon. BS, Technion IIT, Haifa, Israel, 1964, MS, 1967, diploma in Engring., 1970, DSc, 1972. Asst., instr. Technion ITT, Haifa, Israel, 1965-73; vis. prof. U. Calif., San Diego, 1978-79; rsch. assoc. Jet Propulsion Lab., Pasadena, Calif., 1979-80; rschr. Solar Energy Rsch. Inst., Golden, Colo., 1984-86; vis. prof. dept. elec. engring. U. Pretoria SA, 1993-94; prof. Tohoku U., Sendai, Japan, 1994-96; prof. dept. elec. and computer engring. Ben-Gurion U. Negev, Beer-Sheva, Israel, 1973—; senate mem. Ben-Gurion U., Beer-Sheva, Israel, 1984—. Author (poetry): Poems in the Rain, 1989, Poems from Heaven and Earth, 1993; pantntee: Indirect Bandgap Semiconductor Optoelectronic Device, Multi-Terminal Optoelectronic Device, 1996; contbr. over 120 articles to profl. jours. and confs. Electronics instr. Air Force Tech. Sch., 1958-61, Haifa, Israel. Recipient Applied Electronics prize The Polish Jewish Ex-Servicemen's Assn. London, U.K., 1997-98, Student's Assn. Esteemed Tchr. award 1988-89, School Engring. Best Tchr. award, 1987, 88, Ben-Gurion U., Beer-Sheva, Israel; named Disting. Rsch. Prof. Rand Afrikaans U., Johannesburg, South Africa, 1990-93. Mem. IEEE (sr. mem.), Israel Vacuum Soc., Israel Crystal Growth Soc. Jewish. Avocations: sight-seeing, writing poetry, reading literature and philosophy. Home: 13 Hazait St, Omer 84965, Israel Address: New Industtry Creation, Hitachi Ctr Tohoku Univ, Sendai 980-8579, Japan

AHAVI, ATSU KOKU, physicist, researcher; b. Agou-Nyogbo, Togo, Dec. 11, 1963; s. Komi and Abra (Adah) A.; m. Francoise Abra Savary Ahavi, Apr. 15, 1995; children: Paul, Christelle. BS, U. Benin, Lome, Togo, 1987; PhD, U. Abidjan, Cote, D'Ivoire, 1995. Rschr. Inst. Rsch. sur les Energies Nouvelles, Abidjan, Cote D'Ivoire, 1991-95; math. tchr. Coll. St. Dominique, Guingamp, France, 1996-98; computer scientist Applications des Sys. Info. par Carte Enterprises, Paris, 1999—. Contbr. articles to profl. jours. Mem. N.Y. Acad. Sci. Avocations: music, sports. Home: 12 rue De La Mairie, Pommerit-Le-Vicomte 22200, France

A'HEARN, MICHAEL FRANCIS, astronomer, educator; b. Wilmington, Del., Nov. 17, 1940; m. Maxine Ramold, 1963; children: Brian J., Kevin P., Patrick N. BS, Boston Coll., 1961; PhD, U. Wis., 1966. From asst. prof. to assoc. prof. U. Md., College Park, 1966-72, prof. astronomy, 1982—, acting.

dir. astronomy program, 1985-87, acting chmn. dept. astronomy, 1991-93; adj. astronomer Lowell Obs., 1987—. Fellow AAAS; mem. Am. Astron. Soc. (chmn. planetary sci. divsn. 1993-94), Inst. Navigation, Internat. Astron. Union (v.p. 1990-93, pres. com. 15 1994-97, pres. divsn. III, 1997-2000, Asteroid named in honor). Office: U Md Dept Astronomy College Park MD 20742-0001

AHEDO, ALEJANDRO, electronics executive; b. El Paso, Tex., July 9, 1929; divorced; six children. Grad. high sch., La Mesa, N.M. Owner Alex Electronics, El Paso, 1933—.

AHERN, BERTIE, Prime Minister of Ireland; b. Dublin, Ireland, Sept. 12, 1951; s. Cornelius and Julia Ahern; m. Miriam P. Kelly (separated); 2 children. Ed., Rathmines Coll. Commerce, Dublin, Univ. Coll., Dublin. Acct. Mater Hosp., Dublin; mem. Dail, Dublin, 1977—, City Coun., Dublin, 1979; Lord Mayor Dublin, 1986-87; min. state Dept. Taoiseach and Def., Dublin, 1982; min. labour Dept. Labour, Dublin, 1987-91; min. fin. Dept. Fin., Dublin, 1991, 1993-94; pres. Fianna Fail, 1994—; Prime Minister, Govt. of Ireland, Dublin, 1997—; mem. bd. govs. IMF, World Bank, European Investment Bank, European Bank for Reconstrn. and Devel. Chmn. Orgn. for Econ. Cooperation and Devel. Ministerial, 1994; v.p., treas. Fianna Fail. Decorated Grand Order of Order of Merit with star and sash (Germany). Mem. Fianna Fail. Avocations: sports reading. Home: St Luke's Ave, 161 Lower Drumcondra Rd, Dublin Ireland Office: Office of Prime Minister, Upper Merrion St, Dublin 2, Ireland

AHERN, DERMOT, government minister; b. Drogheda, Ireland, 1955. Student, Marist Coll., U. Coll., Dublin. Elected to Dail, 1987, asst. govt. whip, 1988-91; chief govt. whip, min. Ministry State Dept. Defense, 1991-92; min. Dept. Social, Cmty. & Family Affairs, 1997—. Office: Dept Social Welfare, Aras Mhic Dhiarmada, Dublin Ireland

AHLBECK, KARSTEN MAGNUS, anesthesiologist; b. Borgholm, Sweden, May 16, 1969; s. Jan-Olof Ahlbeck and Uta (Löwe) Förster; m. Christine Margareta Glader, June 25, 1993; 1 child, Tilde Amanda Margareta Ahlbeck Glader. Exam. Med. Sch., Umeå (Sweden) U., 1996. Intern Vasternorrlands Landsting, Omskoldsnik, Sweden, 1996-98; resident in anesthesia and intensive care Norrlands Univ., Umeå, 1998-2000; anesthesiologist Anestesikliniken Karolinska Sjukhuset, Stockholm, 2000—; owner computer bus. Vol. Youth for Understanding, Umeå, 1988-95. Named Hon. Dep., Lubbock (Tex.) Police Dept., 1988. Home: Upplandsgatan 86, 113 44 Stockholm Sweden Office: Anestesikliniken, Karolinska Sjukhuset, 117 76 Stockholm Sweden

AHLBERG, ÅKE KARL MARTIN, orthopedic surgeon, researcher; b. Orkelljunga, Sweden, June 26, 1925; s. Martin and Marta (Nuhma) A.; m. Mona Matson; children: Birgitta, Goran, Michael. MD, U. Lund, Sweden, 1953, PhD in Medicine, 1965, docent in Orthpaedics, 1966. Med. diplomate, specialist in orthopaedics. Asst. prof. Malmo (Sweden) Univ. Hosp., 1967-69, assoc. prof. orthopaedics, 1970-80; prof., chmn. orthopaedics King Faisal U., Dammam, Saudi Arabia, 1980-95; head Swedish Red Cross Amputation Ctr., Algeria, 1966-67; lectr. World Fedn. Haemophelia Work Shops, Teheran U., 1978, Kuwait U., 1985, New Delhi, 1985; co-dir. Internat. Haemophelia Tng. Ctr., Malmo Univ. Hosp., 1972-80. Author: (monograph) Haemophilia in Sweden: incidence, treatment and prophylaxis of arthropathy and musculo-skeletal manifestations in Haemophelia A and B, 1965; author some 100 articles mainly on orthopaedics in haemophilia and on joint replacement. Recipient Prix Internat. de l' Assn. Francaise des Hemophiles, Paris, 1985. Mem. Swedish Orthopaedic Assn., World Fedn. of Haemophilia, Travellers Club Malmo.

AHLBERG, LARS ÅKE, military officer; b. Knäred, Sweden, Oct. 25, 1955; s. Bo Verner and Ruth Maria (Sultan) A. Commdr. Halland Infantry Brigade, Halmstad, Sweden, 1990-96, maj., 1992—, with dep. tng. unit, 1997—, with brigade staff, 1998-2000, mem. AA regiment staff, planning and logistics officer, 2000—. Contbr. articles to profl. jours. Mem. Soc. Nautical Rsch., U.S. Naval Inst., Internat. Naval Rsch. Orgn. Home: Tuskaftgangen 4B, Halland Halmstad S 302 44, Sweden Office: Lv 6, Box 515, Halland Halmstad S 301 80, Sweden

AHLBERG, RICHARD ERIC, physician, researcher; b. Stockholm, Sweden, Feb. 9, 1962; s. Eric and Marianne Inger (Rosenquist) A.; m. Gabrielle Daniela Ottoson, Sept. 9, 1989; children: Alexandra, Eric. MD, Karolinska Inst., Stockholm, 1986, PhD, 1993. Resident Dept. Internal Medicine, Karolinska Hosp., Stockholm, 1991-96; postdoctoral Hospital Necher, Paris, 1993-94; cons. Dept. Hematology Karolinska Hosp. Home: Angsvagen 5, 18274 Stockholm Sweden Office: Dept Hematology, Karolinska Hosp, 17176 Stockholm Sweden.

AHLERT, DIETER, economics educator; b. Stassfurt, Fed. Republic Germany, Feb. 19, 1944; s. Dietrich and Theodora Ahlert; m. Heide Marie Wacker. B. Commerce, U. Cologne, Fed. Republic Germany, 1967; D., Engring. Coll., Aachen, Fed. Republic Germany, 1971, Habilitation, 1974. Prof. in ordinary U. Münster, Fed. Republic Germany, 1975—; mng. dir. Inst. Retail Mgmt., Münster, Germany, Internat. Ctr. for Franchising & Coop., Münster, Germany; dir. Marketing Ctr. Münster, Germany; mng. dir. Textile Rsch. Ctr., Münster, Germany. Author: Industrial Accounting, 5th edit., 1992, Features of Economics, 6th edit., 1991, Contractual Distribution Systems, 1981, Management of Distribution, 3d edit., 1996, Legal Features of Marketing, 1989, 2d edit., 1996, Integrated Merchandising Systems and Retail Controlling, 3d edit., 1998, Information Systems for Retail Management, 1998, Internet & Co., 2000, Process Management in Vertical Marketing, 2000, Brand Management in Retail Business, 2000. Avocations: skiing, riding, tennis, dancing. Home: Siebenstücken 80, 48308 Senden Germany Office: Inst Econs Distbn Retailing, Am Stadtgraben 13-15, 48143 Münster Germany

AHLERT, GUENTER WERNER, biogerontologist, researcher; b. Berlin, Mar. 6, 1933; s. Arthur and Amalie Margarete (Woischnik) A.; m. Ilse Morgner, May 2, 1959; children: Thorsten, Kerstin. MD, Humboldt U, Berlin, 1958. Sci. asst. Pathology Inst., Humboldt U., Berlin, 1959-60, med. asst. Internal Med. Clinic Charité, 1961-66, sr. physician Internal Med. Klinik Charité, 1966-73; med. dir. Eli Lilly Co., Homburg, 1973-81, LVA, Frankfurt, 1982-89; pvt. rschr. in gerontology Oberursel, 1990—; cons. med. dir. Shionogi-Comp., Dusseldorf, Germany and Osaka, Japan, 1982-89. Author: Altern-Ergebnis Oekolog. Anpassung, 1996, (with others) Praktische Geriatrie, 1970, Innere Medizin, 1970; editor Infection, 1975, 78, 79; contbr. more than 50 articles to profl. jours. Avocations: athletics, running, chess. Home and Office: Eschenweg 14, 61440 Oberursel Hessen, Germany

ÅHLSTRÖM, PER G., editor; b. Surahammar, Sweden, May 15, 1946; s. Gunnar E. and Elsa (Jansson Andersson) Å; m. Anna-Greta Sjölander; m. Eva Andersson, Aug. 24, 1968 (div. July 1993); 1 child, Lisa. Student, Chalmers Tech. U., Gothenburg, Sweden, 1967-69; diploma, Gothenburg Sch. Journalism, 1971. Info. officer Vattenfall, Stockholm, 1971-73; journalist Metallarbetaren, Stockholm, 1973-78, editor-in-chief, 1978-82; press sec. to min. energy Ministry of Industry, Stockholm, 1983-84; editor-in-chief Nya Norrland/Dagbladet, Härnösand, Sweden, 1985-99; polit. editor Tidnigen Angermanland, 2000—. Author: Jegna Hander, 1998. Recipient North Sweden Journalism award Norrlandsforbundet, 1990. Mem. Swedish Assn. Newspaper Pubs. (bd. dirs. 1994-99), Press Club Sweden (regional pres. 1992-95). Social Democrat. Avocation: cars.

AHLSTROM, THERESA P., accountant; b. Bklyn., Jan. 15, 1962; d. Peter and Amelia Palamaro; m. Robert J. Ahlstrom Jr., Oct. 5, 1991. BS in Acctg., St. John's U., Jamaica, N.Y., 1983. CPA, N.Y. Ptnr. KPMG LLP, Melville, N.Y., 1982—. Treas. Adults and Children with Learning and Developmental Disabilities, Bethpage, N.Y., 1998—; v.p. Women Econ. Developers of L.I., 1998-2000, treas., 2000—; bd. dirs., chair fin. com. Cath. Charities of Diocese of Rockville Centre, 1996—; bd. dirs. L.I. chpt. Nat. Multiple Sclerosis Soc., 1994—. Named to Acad. of Women Achievers, YWCA, 1998, Top 50 Women, L.I. Bus. News, 2000. Roman Catholic. Office: KPMG LLP 1305 Walt Whitman Rd Melville NY 11747-4300

AHLUWALIA, DALJIT SINGH, mathematics educator; b. Sialkot, India, Sept. 5, 1932; came to U.S., 1962; m. Devinder Kaur; children: Gurpreet, Jasjit, Gurinder, Muninder. MA in Math., Punjab U., India, 1955; MS in Physics, PhD in Applied Math., Ind. U., 1965. From asst. prof. to prof. Courant Inst. NYU, 1968-86; dir. Ctr. Applied Math. and Statistics N.J. Inst. Tech., Newark, 1986—, chairperson math. sic. dept., 1986-89, 96—. Mem. Am. Math. Soc., Soc. Indsl. and Applied Math. (rep. Nat. Congress on Theoretical and Applied Mechanics). Office: NJ Inst Tech Math Scis Dept 323 Martin Luther King Blvd Newark NJ 07102

AHMAD, ABOBAKR SULTAN, information systems specialist; b. Cairo, Egypt, May 21, 1938; s. Sultan and Zakeya (Alshayeb) A. BS, U. Cairo, Egypt, 1961; MS, U. Al-Azhar, Egypt, 1973; PhD, U. Leeds, U.K., 1990. Engr. quality control ElNasr Co., Cairo, 1961-63, sr. engr., 1963-66; dep. mgr. rsch. and devel. ElNasr Co., 1966-69, head final inspection, 1969-71, mgr. quality control, 1971-75; rsch. asst. King Saud U., Riyah, 1975-97, rschr., 1997—; cons. Islamic Devel. Bank, Jrddah, Saudi Arabia, 1998, A.M. Farid & Co., Riyadh, 1999—. Translator: (book) Wireless Personal Communications, 1997; co-author: (book) Dc Conduction and Physicochemical Characteristics of Transformer Oils, 1999; contbr. articles to profl. jours. Recipient Best Paper award, IEE, U.K., 1988. Mem. IEEE (Egpytian com. 1974, sr. mem. 1981—), Egyptian Orgn. Standardization, Applied Physics and Electronic Conf., Acad. Sci. and Tech. (mem. rsch. commn.). Avocations: swimming, tennis, music, history. Office: King Saud U, PO Box 800, Riyadh 11421, Saudi Arabia

AHMAD, ADIL MUSTAFA, architect, educator; b. Umm-Durman, Khartoum, Sudan, May 1, 1946; s. Ibrahim Mustafa A.; m. Muna Khalid Mahgoub, June 1, 1978; children: Umaima, Dina, Mustafa. BSc in Arch., U. Khartoum, 1969; Diploma in Devel. and Tropical Studies, Archtl. Assn./Sch. Arch., London, 1971; PhD, U. London, 1975. Tchg. asst. U. Khartoum, 1969-70, lectr., 1975-81, assoc. prof., 1981-95, prof., 1995—; sr. scholar U. London, 1970-75; prof. Coll. Arch. and Art U. Petra, Amman, 1998-2000, dean Coll. Arch. and Art, 2000—; head dept. architecture, U. Khartoum, 1984-87, dir. and co-founder Sudanese Group for the Assessment of Human Settlements, 1987-89; vis. scholar Aga Khan Program for Islamic Architecture, Harvard U., MIT, 1991; celebrity spkr. Royal Inst. of Brit. Architects, London, 1987; regional coord. Arab African countries for affordable housing working group Shimberg Ctr. Affordable Housing U. Fla., Gainesville, 1996—. Contbr. articles to profl. jours.; mem. adv. bd. Environment & Urbanization Jour., Internat. Inst. for Environ. and Devel., London, 1989—. Mem. N.Y. Acad. Scis., Brit. Soc. Aesthetics, Soc. of Archtl. Historians. Avocations: photography, gardening. Office: Coll of Architecture and Art, U Petra POB 961343, Amman Jordan

AHMAD, IRSHAD, physicist, nuclear chemist; b. Azamgarh, India, Nov. 1, 1939; came to U.S., 1962; s. Aquil and Tahira (Khatoon) A.; m. Fauzia Mazhar, Jan. 23, 1969; children: Fahim, Mateen, Sabina. MS, U. Pacific, 1965; PhD, U. Calif., Berkeley, 1966. Postdoctoral fellow Lawrence Berkeley (Calif.) Lab., 1966; postdoctoral fellow Argonne (Ill.) Nat. Lab., 1966-68, asst. chemist, 1968-71, chemist, 1971-85, physicist, 1985—. Contbr. articles to Phys. Rev. Letters, Revs. Modern Physics, Ann. Rev. of Nuclear Particle Sci. Mem. Am. Phys. Soc., Am. Chem. Soc., Sigma Xi. Office: Argonne Nat Lab D 203 9700 Cass Ave Argonne IL 60439-4803

AHMAD, KHALIL, mathematician, educator; b. Bilgram, UP, India, July 15, 1949; s. Abid and Sakina Ali; m. Safia Sultana, June 11, 1970; 4 children. BS, Kanpur U., 1968, MS, 1970; MPhil, A.M.U. Aligarh, 1976; PhD, Delhi U., 1982. Lectr., reader Jamia Millia Islamia, New Delhi, India, 1975-93; prof. Jamia Millia Islamia, New Delhi, 1994—. Author: Functional Analysis, 1995. Home: 275/10 Zakir Nagar, New Delhi 110 025, India Office: Dept Mathematics, Jamia Millia Islamia, New Delhi 110 025, India

AHMAD, MANJUR SARWAR, mechanical engineer; b. Comilla, Bangladesh, Jan. 1, 1964; s. Shahid Uddin Ahmad and Saleha Akhter; m. Tulin Rahman Talukder, Oct. 19, 1995. BSc in Mech. Engring., BIT, Chittagong, Bangladesh, 1988; postgrad. diploma indsl. mgmt., BMDG, Dhaka, Bangladesh, 1995. Mech. engr. K.N. Cold Storage Ltd., Comilla, 1988-89; asst. mgr. Beximco Pharma, Tongi, Bangladesh, 1989—; mgr. Beximco Infusions Ltd., Tongi, 1989—; quality auditor Beximco Infusions Ltd., Tongi, 1996-97. Mem. ASME, Canadian Soc. Mech. Engrs., Jaycees Internat. Office fax: 880-2-9800711. E-mail: mjr@bpl.net; msahmad@citecho.net. Home: Taj Cottage 32/6/Kha, Dhaka 1217, Bangladesh Office: Beximco Pharma, Tongi Gazipur, Dhaka Bangladesh

AHMAD, M-NOR AZHARI, artist; b. Ipoh, Perak, Malaysia, Oct. 28, 1955; s. Puteh Nor and Isa (Ramlah) A.; m. Rahman Norsita, Oct. 10, 1987. Student, Mara Inst. Tech. Sch. Art, 1973-74. Graphic artist The Lang. and Literary Agy., Kuala Lumpur, Malaysia, 1975-77, The New Straits Times Press, Kuala Lumpur, 1977-87. One-man shows include Park Royal Hotel, Kuala Lumpur, 1996, Space 2324, Kuala Lumpur, 1997, Balai Seni Maybank, Kuala Lumpur, 1997, Regent Hotel, Kuala Lumpur, 1998, The Stonor Ctr., Kuala Lumpur, 1999; exhibited in group shows at Berita Pub., Kuala Lumpur, 1984, Nat. Art Gallery, Kuala Lumpur, 1985, Merlin Hotel, Kuala Lumpur, 1985, APS Gallery, Kuala Lumpur, 1985, 86, 88, Nat. Art Gallery, Kuala Lumpur, 1986, 87, 88, 91, 93, 94, 98, On Tai Gallery, Kuala Lumpur, 1986, Gallery Kia Peng, Kuala Lumpur, 1988, Nat. Gallery, Kuala Lumpur, 1989, Galeriwwan, Kuala Lumpur, 1990, Galeriwan, Kuala Lumpur, 1992, 94, Baze Discotheque, Kuala Lumpur, 1992, Balai Seni Maybank, Kuala Lumpur, 1998, PWTC, Kuala Lumpur, 1998, Langkawi, Kedah, 1999. Recipient Winner logo design competition Malaysian Indsl. Devel. Authority, 1980, Maj. award Berita Pub. Sdn. Bhd., 1984. Islam. Avocations: reading, writing, talking to visitors. Home and Office: 220 Lorong Maarof Bangsar, Kuala Lumpur Malaysia

AHMAD, MOHAMMAD, physicist, researcher; b. Quetta, Bluchistan, Pakistan, Sept. 7, 1964; s. Mohammad Shafi and Amtur Rashid; m. Tahira Ahmad, July 27, 1995; children: Myra Nayab, Mahnur. BSc, Punjab U., Lahore, Pakistan, 1984, MSc, 1988; MPhil, Quaid-i-Azam U., Islamabad, Pakistan, 1990; PhD, Manchester (Eng.) U., 1996. Jr. rsch. asst. Quaid-i-Azam U., 1988-90, sr. rsch. asst., 1990-92; rsch. assoc. in laser photonics Manchester (Eng.) U.; instr. MSc class Taleem-ul-Islam Coll., Rabwam, Pakistan, 1988. Contbr. articles to sci. jours. Recipient talent award Ahmadiyya Cmty., London, 1993; grantee Fauji Found., Rawalpindi, Pakistan, 1986-88. Ahmadi Muslim. Avocations: writing novels, hiking, mountain climbing. Home: 68 Lonsdale Rd, Manchester M19 3FL, England also: 18/10 Dar-Ul-Nasar Gharbi, Rabwah 35460, Pakistan Office: Manchester U Laser Photonic, Physics Dept, Manchester M13 9PL, England

AHMAD, NAZAR OTHMAN, architect, urban planner, consultant; b. Mosul, Iraq, Nov. 12, 1945; s. Othman Ahmad and Saadiya Khayat; m. Shaween Khayat, Feb. 4, 1984; children: Delan, Neeyan. BArch, U. Liverpool, Eng., 1969; MA in Urban and Regional Planning, Nottingham (Eng.) U., 1972. Arch. Liverpool City Housing Dept., 1969-70; lectr. Ctr. Urban and Regional Planning, Baghdad, Iraq, 1972-73, dep. dir., 1973-74; head regional planning sect. Iraqconsult, Baghdad, Iraq, 1974-75; co-founder, sr. ptnr. Planar, Baghdad, Iraq, 1975-87, Abu Dhabi, United Arab Emirates, 1978—; nominator Agha Khan award for architecture, Geneva, Switzerland, 1983—; external lectr. architecture Baghdad U., 1972-74; planning advisor Ministry of Planning, Baghdad, 1974-75; co-dir. Pax Internat., London, 1984-88. Editor, coord. (planning report) Northern Iraq Regional Development Plan, 1975; co-editor (planning report) Upper Euphrates Resettlement Plan, 1979. Mem. Nat. Geog. Soc., Iraqi Engrs. Union, United Arab Emirates Soc. Engrs. Avocations: painting, reading.

AHMAD, SALAHUDDIN, nuclear scientist; b. Sylhet, Bangladesh, Nov. 25, 1954; arrived in Can., 1978; came to U.S., 1990; s. Jalal and Momtaz (Begum) A.; m. Munawar Sultana, June 1, 1978; 1 child, Nahid Rubaba. MSc, Dhaka U., Bangladesh, 1975; PhD, U. Victoria, B.C., Can., 1981. Lectr. Dhaka U., 1978; postdoctoral rsch. assoc. U. Victoria, 1981; rsch. scientist U. Paris South, Orsay, France, 1982-83; profl. rsch. assoc. U. Sask., Saskatoon, Can., 1983-84; rsch. assoc. Triumf Nat. Lab., Vancouver, 1984-86, U. B.C., Vancouver, 1987-89; faculty fellow Rice U., Houston, 1990-96; rsch. assoc. MD Anderson Cancer Ctr., U. Tex., Houston, 1996-98; instr. radiology Baylor Coll. Medicine, Houston, 1999—; physicist VA Med. Ctr., Houston, 1999—. Contbr. more than 120 articles to sci. jours. and conf. procs., including Physics Letters, Phys. Rev., Phys. Rev. Letters. Bangladeshi rep. World Muslim Youth Conf., Abha, Saudi Arabia, 1977; founder, pres. Bangladesh-Can. Cultural Assn., Vancouver, 1988-89, Bangladesh-Am. Lit., Art and Cultural Assn., Houston, 1992-95, 98-99. Raja Kalinarayan scholar U. Dhaka, 1974-75; fellow Can. Commonwealth Fellowship Com., 1978-81. Mem. Am. Assn. Physicist in Medicine (jr.). E-mail: sahmad@bcm.tmc.edu. Office: VA Med Ctr Radiotherapy 190 2002 Holcombe Blvd Houston TX 77030-4211

AHMAD, SHAKIL, education educator, researcher; b. Gorakhpur, India, Dec. 1, 1941; s. Khalil Ahmad and Taiyeba Khatoon; m. Nigar Fatma, May 20, 1973; children: Khalid Shakil, Asma Shakil, Ayesha Shakil. BS, U. Lucknow, India, 1961, MS, 1964; PhD, U. Roorkee, India, 1971. Rsch. fellow Ctrl. Drug Rsch. Inst., Lucknow, India, 1964-67; rsch. scholar U. Roorkee, India, 1967-69; lectr. Jamia Millia Islamia, New Delhi, India, 1969-80, Al-Fateh U., Sebha, Libya, 1980-83; reader Jamia Millia Islamia, New Delhi, India, 1983-98, prof., 1998—. Author: Nutrition, 1982; inventor: Indian Jour. of Chemistry, , 1997, J. Indian Chem. Soc., 1997, Bulletin of Medico-Ethno Botanical Rsch., 1997. Sec. Zakir Bagh Housing Soc., New Delhi, India, 1979. Fellow Indian Chem. Soc. Office: Jamia Millia Islamia Dept Chem, Jamia Nagar, New Delhi 110025, India

AHMAD, SHEIKH RAFI, optics scientist, educator; b. Kishoreganj, Bangladesh, Feb. 4, 1944; arrived in U.K., 1967; s. Khursheid Uddin and Mollika Aktar (Khatoon) A.; m. Estelle Baker; children: Sakhina, Emma, Tariq. BSc with honors, Dhaka U., Bangladesh, 1964, MSc, 1966; PhD, Oxford (Eng.) U., 1972. Sci. officer AEC, Dhaka, 1966-67; rsch. fellow Oxford U., 1967-72; grad. demonstrator Royal Mil. Coll. Sci., U.K., 1972-74; sr. sci. office Royal Mil. Coll. Sci./Cranfield U., Swindon, U.K., 1974-94; head optics and sensors group Cranfield U., Swindon, U.K., 1994-98; head Ctr. for Applied Laser Spectroscopy Cranfield U., Swindon, 1998—; cons. Dhaka U./Birdem, 1983-84. Author: Laser Beam, 1965; contbr. articles to profl. jours. Trustee Thamesdown Islamic Assn., Swindon, 1976—; mem. exec. com. Aliah Madrasha Orphange, Kisoregani, Bangladesh, 1990—; pres. Asian Ctr., Swindon, 1994—. Islamic. Avocations: badminton, swimming, reading. Home: 15 Vicarage Ln Shrivenham, Swindon Wiltshire SN6 8DT, England Office: Cranfield Univ RMCS, Environ and Ordnance Dept, Shrivenham SN6 8LA, Snindon United Kingdom

AHMAD, TOHEED, diplomat, writer; b. Lahore, Punjab, Pakistan, Oct. 15, 1947; s. Mureed Ahmad and Iftikhar Begum; m. Nausheen Ahmad, Dec. 22, 1983; children: Shameel, Mureed. BA, Forman Christian Coll., Lahore, 1967; MA, U. Punjab, 1969. Staff reporter The Pakistan Times Daily, Lahore, 1969-71; 3rd sec. trainee Pakistan Embassy, Paris, 1972-73; 3rd sec. Pakistan Embassy, Tunis, 1973-76; 2nd sec. Pakistan Embassy, Hanoi, 1976-79; sect. officer, dir. Min. Fgn. Affairs, Islamabad, 1979-84; 1st sec. Pakistan Embassy, Damascus, 1984-87; counsellor, min. Pakistan Embassy, Brussels, 1987-91; dir. gen., acting additional sec. Min. Fgn. Affairs, Isbd, 1991-96; high commr. Pakistan Embassy, Singapore, 1997—. Author: Conversation on the Informatics Revolution; translator: What Do Managers Do?. Avocations: translating technology writings into Urdu, reading, information technology, European classical music. Office: High Commn Pakistan, 1 Scotts Rd Shaw Ctr 240204, Singapore 228208, Singapore

AHMAD, YUSUF WAHBI, hotel facility executive; b. Singapore, Mar. 24, 1959; s. Ahmad Lazim and Supiah Tak; m. Maisuriyathi Marzuki, Dec. 22, 1986; 3 children. Asst. maitre 'd Sheraton Hotel, Brunei, 1981-83; mgr. restaurant Emporium Holding, Brunei, 1983-84; mgr. asst. banquet Hyatt Borneo, Brunei, 1985—, mgr. banquet, 1986—, mgr. food & beverage, 1991—. With Singapore Armed Forces, 1977-79. Avocations: badminton, soccer, squash. Home: No 186, Jalan Sungai Hanching Baru, Simpang 528 Bandar Seri Begawan Brunei Office: Hyatt Borneo Mgmt Svcs, Seri Complex Jalan Tutong, 2604 Bandar Seri Begawan Brunei

AHMAD, ZAKI X., materials science and corrosion educator; b. Indore, India, 1943; arrived in Pakistan, 1946; Pakistani citizen.; s. Wali Ahmad and Hafeez-Un Nisa. BS with honors, U. Karachi, Pakistan, 1960; Diploma E, Leeds U., U.K., 1968, PhD, 1971. FIM, FIMF/U.K. Assoc. prof. AMUT, Tehran, 1972-78; group leader GKSS, Tesperhude, Germany, 1978-80; assoc. prof. KFUPM, Dhahran, 1980—; cons. IDO, Tehran, 1975-79; dir. Corrosion Lab, KFUPM, Dhahran. Pres. Internat. Student Orgn., Leeds, 1968-69, Islamic Soc., Leeds, 1968-70. Fellow Inst. Materials, Inst. Metal Finishing; mem. European Fedn. Corrosion. Muslim. Avocation: photography. Home: KFPUM Box # 1748, 31261 Dhahran Saudi Arabia Office: King Fahd U Petroleum/Minrl, Dhahran Saudi Arabia

AHMADI-ABHARI, SEYED-ALI, psychiatrist, educator; b. Tehran, Feb. 4, 1946; s. Seyed Shamseddin Ahmadi-Abhari and Sakineh Ansari; m. Mahnoush Dorrizadeh, Jan. 9, 1975; children: Salomeh, Golnoush, Sina. BS, Tehran U., 1968; MEd, Fla. Agrl. and Mech. U., 1973, 1973; MS in Pub. Health, Tehran U., 1976; MD, Iran U., 1983; specialist degree in psychiatry, Tehran U. Med. Scis., 1986. Educator Fla. A&M U., Tallahassee, 1971-73, Tehran U., 1973-74, Tehran Tchrs. Tng. U., 1975-84; asst. prof. Ahwaz (Iran) U. Med. Sci., 1986-87; asst. prof. Tehran U. Med. Sci., 1987-93, assoc. prof., 1993—; chief adminstr. Roozbeh Hosp., Tehran, 1991-96; head dept. psychiatry, Tehran U. Med. Sic., 1991-96; adminstr. students guidance and counseling ctr., Tehran U., 1990-97, dep. rsch. affairs dept. psychiatry, 1998—; mem. adv. bd. Jansen-CILAG Pharm. Co., Switzerland, 1999; mem. promotion bd. psychiatry, Ministry of Health, Iran, 1998. Contbr. articles to sci. and profl. jours. Lt. Iranian Army, 1968-70. Recipient award Islamic Republic Iran Razi Med. Festival, 1999, Ministry of Health, 2000, Tehran U. Med. Scis., 2000. Mem. N.Y. Acad. Sci. Avocations: computers, music, cinema, theater. Home: Opp Gas Sta Niavaran, #5 Mahtab Alley Jashin St, Tehran 19787, Iran Office: Roozbeh Hosp, Kargar Jonoobi St, Tehran 13185, Iran

AHMED, ABDALLA HASSAN, bank executive. Gov. Bank of Sudan, min. internat. coop. and investment. Office: Bank of Sudan, Gamea Ave PO Box 313, Khartoum Sudan*

AHMED, ABDUL WAHAB EL KHIDIR, food scientist, consultant chemist, quality assura; b. Atbara, Sudan, Apr. 25, 1938; arrived in United Arab Emirates, 1983; BSc in Agr. with honors, U. Khartoum, Sudan, 1966; MSc in Food Sci., U. Reading, Eng., 1971, PhD in Food Sci., 1980. Cert. in analytical quality assurance, food control and food safety. Asst. insp. horticulture Dept. Horticulture, Ministry of Agr., Khartoum, 1966-67; asst. food dehydration specialist Food Rsch. Ctr., Khartoum, 1967-69, head edible oils and fats sect., 1971-77, 80-83, asst. dir., 1975-83, dep. dir., 1981-83; head Ctrl. Food Control and Consultancy Lab. Food Lab., Sharjah Municipality, Sharjah, United Arab Emirates, 1983—; cons. UN-WHO, Amman, Jordan, 1995, Baghdad, Iraq, 1998, Food Safety, North Governorates, Iraq, 1999. Contbr. articles to profl. jours. Fellow Inst. Food Sci. and Tech. (U.K.); mem. AOAC Internat., Leatherhead Food RA. Home: 79 Khalid Ben Mohammed St, Sharjah United Arab Emirates Office: Ctrl food Control/Cons Lab, Box 22 Sultan Ben Saqr El Qasmi St, Sharjah United Arab Emirates

AHMED, AHMED ABDULLA, medical administrator, ophthalmologist; b. Manama, Bahrain, Feb. 19, 1943; s. Abdulla Ahmed Mohamed and Aysha Mohammed Noor; m. Balquees Ahmed Fakhro, Nov. 23, 1972; children: Esmat, Yousif. BSc, Am. U. Beirut, Lebanon, 1966, MD, 1970; MPH, Johns Hopkins U., 1981; postgrad., U. South Fla., 1991. Diplomate Am. Bd. Ophthalmology. Intern Am. U. Med. Ctr., Beirut, 1969-70, resident dept. ophthalmology, 1970-73; clin. fellow in ultrasonography dept. ophthalmology U. Iowa, Iowa City, 1973-74; cons. ophthalmologist Salmaniya Med. Ctr., Bahrain, 1976—, chmn. dept. ophthalmology, 1977-84, dep. chief med. staff, 1978-80, chief med. staff, 1984-89, chmn. dept. ophthalmology, 1993—; assoc. prof. Sch. Medicine and Med. Scis. Arabian Gulf U., Bahrain, 1987—, chmn. human structure divsn., 1989-95; head planning unit Ministry of Health, Manama, Bahrain, 1989-94, asst. undersec. for tng. and planning, 1995—; postgrad. fellow Sch. Hygiene and Pub. Health Johns Hopkins U., Greater Balt. Med. Ctr., 1981; chmn. exam. com. Arab Bd. Ophthalmology, 1994—. Mem. internat. adv. bd. Mid. East Jour. Ophthalmology; mem. editl. bd. Bahrain Med. Bull., 1984-90; contbr. articles to profl. jours. Fellow Am. Acad. Ophthalmology; mem. Proctor Fellowship Assn., Iowa Hosps. Fellowship Assn., Johns Hopkins Fellow Assn., Amiri

Acad. Med. Specialists (sec. 1986-89), Bahrain Med. Soc. (mem. editl. bd. jour. 1992—), Bahrain Sports Assn. (mem. exec. com.), Bahrain Archeol. Soc., Rotary (sr.), Am. U. Beirut Alumni Assn., Alumni Club Bahrain. Avocations: photography. Home: 330 Ave 29, Jurdab 729, Bahrain Office: Min Health, PO Box 12, Manama Bahrain

AHMED, AKHTAR, neurologist, educator; b. Warangal, Deccan Hydrabad, India, Feb. 9, 1935; arrived in Pakistan, 1948; s. Azizuddin and Begum (Lateefunnisa) Muhammad; m. Shamom Fatima, 1958; children: Yasmin, Zarina, Mona, Erum Naz. MD, Dow Med. Coll., Karachi, Pakistan, 1957; degree in Edn., Inst. Neurology, Queen Square, London, 1962. House officer Dow Med. Coll., Karachi, Pakistan, 1957-58; med. resident Cuyahoga County Hosp., Cleve., 1959-60; sr. house officer Dist. Gen. Hosp., Grantham, Eng., 1960-61; res. med. officer Westminster Auxiliary Hosp., Swanley, Kent, 1961-62; rsch. officer in charge Jinnah Postgraduate Med. Ctr., Karachi, 1964-70; from asst. prof. to prof. Dow Med. Coll. and Civil Hosp., Karachi, 1970-79; prof. Dow Med. Coll. & Civil Hosp., Karachi, 1979-97; dean postgrad. clin. studies Ziauddin U. Hosp., North Nazimabad Karachi, 1997-99; cons. Neurologist Specialists' Clinic III-A/16, Nazimabad, Karachi; mem. mng. com. Ida Rieu Poor Welfare Assn., 1994-98; med. dir. Ma Ayesha Meml. Ctr., 1988-95; dean faculty neurology Coll. Physicians and Surgeons, Pakistan, 1994-97. Editor: (jour.) Mental Retardation in Pakistan, and others. Recipient Mistry Golg medal U. Karachi, 1957, W.H.O. fellow in Neurology, 1979. Fellow Royal Soc. Medicine; mem. Am. Acad. Neurology, Assn. British Neurologists, Pakistan Med. Assn. (life), Pakistan Acad. Neurol. Scis. (past pres.). Moslem. Avocation: astronomy. Office: Specialist's Clinic, Nazimabad, Karachi 74600, Pakistan

AHMED, BELAL, agronomist; b. Dhaka, Bangladesh, June 1, 1949; arrived in Jamaica, 1988; s. Hafiz Uddin Ahmed and Rezia Sarker Khatun; m. Sultana Afroz, June 14, 1981. BSc with hons., U. Dhaka, Bangladesh, 1969; MSc, U. Dhaka, 1970; PhD, U. W.I., St. Augustine, Trinidad and Tobago, 1978. Postdoc. fellow U. West Indies, St. Augustine, 1978; forage agronomist Caribbean Agrl. Rsch. and Devel. Inst., St. Augustine, 1978-87, Mona, Jamaica, 1988-89; agronomist Scientific Rsch. Coun., Mona, 1990-91; mgr. Planning Inst. Jamaica, Kingston, 1996-99; freelance cons., 2000—; cons. USAID, St. Lucia, St. Vincent, 1986, Caroni, Trinidad and Tabago, 1988, 89, UN Devel. Program, Dhaka, 1992. Author: Political Economy of Food and Agriculture in the Caribbean, 1996; contbr. articles to profl. jours. Sec. Bengali Popularisation Movement, Dhaka, 1966. Grantee Petro Can., 1977, Internat. Devel. Rsch. Ctr., 1980. Mem. Internat. Soc. Soil Sci., Internat. Assn. Studying Common Property, Agronomy Soc. Am. Avocations: eco-tourism, reading, swimming, hiking. Home and Office: 29 College Common, Mona Kingston, Jamaica

AHMED, FATHELRAHMAN ELAWAD, pediatric educator, consultant; b. Shendi, Nile, Sudan, Jan. 1, 1953; s. Elawad Elawad and Alnakhil Othman Sultan; m. Hanan Abotalib Arif, Nov. 9, 1982; children: Nashwa, Nasreen, Najah, Namariq, Abobakr, Mohmmad, Noran, Nayrah. MB, BS, U. Khartoum, Sudan, 1978. Resident in pediatrics Khartoum Tchg. Hosp., 1979-81, King Faisal U., Khobar, Saudi Arabia, 1981-86; pediatric specialist Air Base Hosp., Dahran, Saudi Arabia, 1986-87, pediatric cons., 1987-89; pediatric cons. Mil. Hosp., Tabuk, Saudi Arabia, 1989-96, pediatric educator, 1996—. Contbr. articles to med. jours., including Pediat., Acta Pediatrica, Annals Saudi Medicine, Practitioner East Mediterranean. Mem. Royal Coll. Physicians (London), N.Y. Acad. Sci., Nat. Geog. Soc. Avocations: football, swimming. Office: Military Hospital, PO Box 100, Tabuk Saudi Arabia

AHMED, GHIASUDDIN, banker; b. Jhenidah, Bangladesh, Oct. 1, 1933; s. Al-haj Jalaluddin Ahmed and Al-haj Zubaida Khatoon; m. Fahima Ghias, July 14, 1967; 1 child, Zuby. BA, Dhaka Coll., Dhaka, Bangladesh, 1953; MA in Econs., U. Dhaka, 1955; LLB, U. Karachi, 1963. Rsch. officer Ministry Labor, Govt. of Pakistan, Karachi, Lahore, 1957-61; asst. sec., gen. mgr., acting mng. dir. Pakistan Indsl. Fin. Corp., Indsl. Devel. Bank Pakistan, Bangladesh Shilpa Bank, Karachi, Dhaka, 1961-85; mng. dir. Bangladesh Shilpa Rin Sangstha, Dhaka, 1985-88, Investment Corp. Bangladesh, Dhaka, 1988-89; dir. Bangladesh Inst. Bank Mgmt., Dhaka, 1989-90; chief BBCI cell Bangladesh Bank, 1992; cons. Nathan Assocs. Inc., 1992-93; adviser Kader Synthetic Fibres Ltd./Dutch Bangla Bank Ltd., 1993-95; cons. Ea. Bank Ltd., World Bank, 1996-97; adminstr. (chief exec.) Al-Arafah Islamic Bank Ltd., 2000—. Mem. Bangladesh Econ. Assn., Dhaka Club. Avocations: reading, gardening, listening to music. Home: House No 95 Rd No 13, Block E Banani, Dhaka 1213, Bangladesh

AHMED, IQBAL, chemist; b. Kulaura, Bangladesh, May 12, 1950; came to U.S., 1982; s. Abdus and Shamsun Nahar (Khanam) Salam; m. Syeda Afsa Khatun, May 27, 1984; children: Samie Ifran, Saadi Imad. BS in Chemistry with honors, U. Chittagong, Bangladesh, 1971; MS in Applied Chemistry, U. Dhaka, Bangladesh, 1973; PhD in Polymer Chemistry, North East London Polytech., 1981. Asst. chemist Natural Gas Fertilizer Factory, Fenchugonj, Bangladesh, 1973-76; sr. rsch. chemist Phillips Petroleum Co., Bartlesville, Okla., 1987-99; sr. rsch. scientist Stockhausen, Inc., Greensboro, N.C., 1999—. Author: (with others) Water Soluble Polymers for Petroleum Recovery, 1988, Polymeric Materials Encyclopedia, 1996, Current Topics in Polymer Science, 1987; contbr. rsch. articles to profl. jours. Grad. student fellow Brit. Coun., London, 1977-81, postdoctoral rsch. fellow U. Lowell, Mass., 1984-87. Mem. Am. Chem. Soc., Royal Soc. Chemistry. Democrat. Islam. Achievements include 43 patents in polymer and catalysis field. Avocations: reading, research, gardening, travel. Home: 3605 Chance Rd Greensboro NC 27410-8449 Office: Stockhausen Inc 2401 Doyle St Greensboro NC 27406-2911

AHMED, JAVED, consumer products company executive; b. Karachi, Pakistan, Feb. 10, 1960; came to U.S., 1986; s. Ziauddin and Haseena Ahmed; m. Talat Naila Hasan, July 11, 1985; children: Sara Unzila, Ayesha Duha. BA magna cum laude, Williams Coll., Williamstown, Mass., 1982; MBA, Stanford U., 1984. Directeur du marche Procter & Gamble AG, Geneva, 1984-86; mgr. Bain & Co., Inc., Boston, 1986-90, Bain & Co., U.K. Ltd., London, 1990-91; sr. mgr. Bain & Co., Inc., Boston, 1991-92; pres. Can. Benckiser Consumer Products Can., Inc., Conn., 1992-95; mng. dir. Benckiser Ltd., Wiltshire, United Kingdom, 1995-99; sr. v.p., regional dir. No. Europe Reckitt Benckiser plc, Wiltshire, Eng., 1999—. Patron Afganistan Refugee Relief Fund, Chgo., 1986-92. Haystack scholar Williams Coll, 1978-81, Harry A. Garfield scholar Williams Coll., 1981-82, Rhodes scholarship finalist, 1982; fellowship grantee Stuart Found., 1982. Mem. Phi Beta Kappa. Mem. Moslem faith. Avocations: reading, long-distance running, travel. Home: 277 Beacon St Boston MA 02116-1271 Office: c/o Benckiser Ltd, Electra House Farnsby St, Swindon Wiltshire SN1 5AH, England

AHMED, KAZI MATIN UDDIN, hydrogeologist; b. Ratanpurvillage, Bangladesh, Sept. 21, 1960; s. Kazi Siraj Uddin and Zobaeda (Khatun) A.; m. Rofiqua Binte Zahed, Nov. 23, 1995' 1 child, Kazi Rafid. BS with honors, Dhaka U., Bangladesh, 1982; MS, Dhaka U., 1985; PhD, U. Coll. London, U.K., 1994. Asst. hydrogeologist Master Plan Orgn., Dhaka, 1985; geologist Bangladesh Atomic Energy Commn., Dhaka, 1985-87; lectr. Dhaka U., 1987-94, asst. prof., 1994-99, assoc. prof., 1999—. Sec. Welfare Assn., Ratanpur, 1980-85, U. Coll. London Bangla Soc., 1993-94; v.p. Bangladesh Students Network, 1992-93. Recipient scholarship, Comilla Found., 1980-84, Dhaka U., 1983-84. Fellow The Geological Soc., Bangladesh Geological Soc. (life), Internat. Assn. Hydrogeologists. Avocations: travel, reading, swimming. Home: House No 18 Rd No 4, Pisciculture Houseing Soc, Mohammadpur 1207, Bangladesh Office: Dept Geology, Curzon Hall Campus Dhaka U, Dhaka 1000, Bangladesh

AHMED, MAINUDDIN, astrophysicist; b. Jalangi, India, Aug. 1, 1943; arrived in Bangladesh, 1965; s. Taibuddin and Thanda (Bibi) Fakir; m. Rokeya Khatun, June 26, 1969; children: Rokonuddin, Murshida, Munira. BS with honors, Krishnath Coll., 1964; MS, Rajshahi U., 1967; PhD, Imperial Coll., 1983. Lectr. Bangladesh Agrl. U., 1968-72, Rajshahi (Bangladesh) U., Bangladesh, 1973-75; asst. prof. Rajshahi (Bangladesh) U., 1975-86, assoc. prof., 1986-92, prof., 1992—, chmn. dept. math., 1994—. Inventor in field. Recipient King Faisal Found. award, Riyadh, Saudi Arabia, 1983. Office: Rajshahi U, Dept Math, Rajshahi 6205, Bangladesh

AHMED, MUBARIK RAJPOOT, secondary education educator; b. Lahore, Pakistan, Nov. 11, 1937; arrived in Norway, 1968; s. Majeed Abdul and Hajrah Begum (Chugtai) Rajpoot; m. Kera Aleksandrova Ahmedova (div. 1973); 1 child, Regina Nargis; m. Astrid Emilie Nordahl (div. 1984); children: Osamah, Hamzah; m. Robina Sonam Latif; children: Khozemah, Sidrah, Zoyah, Hirah. BSc, various schs., Oslo, 1975. Tchr. Urdu AOF Evening Sch., Oslo, 1973-93; bilingual tchr. Skolesjefen Secondary Sch., Oslo, 1973—; freelance journalist, photographer. Author: Urdu Compendium, 1973, Laer Urdu, 1988; editor (weekly Urdu newspaper) Akhbar-E-Pakistan, 1973; broadcasting dir. (radio/TV) Islam Ahmadiyya, 1981, marketing writing proj. for Norwegian Dictionary. Mem. Oslo Journalist Club. Office: Pb 233 Sentrum, N-0103 Oslo Norway

AHMED, PESHIMAM NISAR, Arabic educator; b. Vaniyambadi, Tamil Nadu, India, Dec. 3, 1950; s. Peshimam Muhammad Zubair and Peerji Zakira. m. Khateeb Saliha Begum, Apr. 14, 1974; children: Tanweer Ahmed, Zakira Begum, Muneer Ahmed, Baseer Ahmed, Kausar Ahmed, Munawar Ahmed, Safeer Ahmed, Sabeel Ahmed. BA in Econs., U. Madras, India, 1971, MA in Arabic, 1973, MLitt in Arabic, 1977, PhD in Arabic, 1984. Lectr. in Arabic U. Madras, 1977-85, reader, 1985-91, prof. Arabic, 1991—, chmn. bd. studies in Arabic and Persian, 1993—; chmn. bd. studies in Persian Calicut (India) U., 1999—; chmn. bd. studies in Arabic and Urdu, Bharati Dasan U., India, 1999—; rector Acad. Islamic Scis., Vaniyambadi, 1980—. Author: Studies in Quranic Sciences, 1987, Arab Thought During the 20th Century, 1989, Al Jameel Tamil Arabic Dictionary, 1996, others. Mem. Muslim Ednl. Soc., Anjuman-e-Danish mandan-e-urdu, MEDNET. Avocations: collecting material on space sciences and Islamic studies. Office: U Madras, Dept Arabic Persian & Urdu, Madras Tamil Nadu 600005, India

AHMED, RASHEED, environmental health executive; naturalized Canadian citizen; s. Mas Jeelani and Rahmathunissa A.; m. Fouzia Ahmed; children: Umar, Aminah. BS, Mysore U., India, 1969; M in Edn., Gannon U., 1973; cert. pub. health inspection, Ryerson U., Can., 1978. Environ. health officer City of North York Pub. Health Dept., Toronto, Ont., Can., 1977-86; environ. health supr. Royal Commn. for Jubail (Saudi Arabia) Project, 1987—; lectr. univs. and pub. svc. orgns., Karnataka, India. Recipient citation USMC, 1990. Mem. Am. Acad. Sanitarians (cert. diplomate), Pub. Health Assn. (Can.) (cert. pub. health inspector), Nat. Environ. Health Assn. (cert. sanitarian and environmentalist). Avocations: reading, travel. Office: Health Svcs Dept/Royal Comm, PO Box 10001, Jubail Indsl City 31961, Saudi Arabia

AHMED, SADDIQUE, sales manager; b. Hari Pur, Hazara, Pakistan, July 14, 1963; s. Mohammed and Jamila Sadiq; m. Farzana Noor Ahmed, Jan. 1, 1999; children: Aishaa Sadique, Samir Asad Anees. Degree in bus. mgmt., 1980. Sales mgr. Interlink Express, High Wycombe, 1983-89; mng. dir. Discount Avionics Ltd., Bedford, U.K., 1989-91; sales mgr. Air Transport Avionics Ltd., Slough, U.K., 1991—. Presenter: (radio show) Saaz Aur Awaz. Muslim. Avocations: radio presenter, PA engineer, singing. Home: 70 Dunchurch Dale, Walnut Tree Milton Keynes, Bucks MK7 7BU, England

AHMED, SHAHABUDDIN, president of Bangladesh; b. 1930; s. Talukder Risat A. Bhuiyan; 5 children. BA (hon.) in Econs., Dhaka U., 1951; MA in Internat. Rels., Fazlul Haq Hall, 1952; student, Oxford U. Sub-divisional officer Gopalganj, Natore; additionaldy comnr. Faridpur; additional dist. and session judge Dhaka, Barisal; dist., sessions judge Comilla, Chittagong; registrar of high court East Pakistan, bench of high court; judge of the Appellate Divsn. Supreme Ct. of Bangladesh; chmn. Commn. of Inquiry, 1983, Nat. Pay Commn., 1984; chief justice Bangladesh, 1990-95, pres., 1996—; chmn., Labour Appelate Tribunal, Bangladesh Red Cross Soc., vice pres., League of Red Cross and Red Crescent Soc. (Geneva); acting pres., Bangladesh, 1990-91, pres., 1996—, master, Hon'ble Soc., Gray's Inn, London. •

AHMED, SHAIKH FAIZ UDDIN, civil engineering educator; b. Khulna, Bangladesh, June 1, 1970; p. Shaikh Idel Hossain and Feroza Begam. BSc in Civil Engring., Bangladesh Inst. Tech., Khulna, 1993; M in Engring. Structural, Asian Inst. Tech., Bangkok, 1998; postgrad., Nat. U. Singapore, 1999—; cert. materials engring., Nihon U., Koriyama, Japan, 1999. Design engr. Stapatya Koushal Ltd., Dhaka, Bangladesh, 1993-94; structural design engr. Sthapati Sangsad Ltd., Dhaka, 1994; lectr. civil engring. Khulna U. Contbr. articles to profl. jours. Mem. ASCE (assoc.), Inst. Engrs. Bangladesh. Avocations: football, cricket, music, movies. E-mail: shaikhfa@rocketmail.com and engp9621@nus.edu.sg. Fax: 65 874-2248. Office: Nat Univ Singapore, 10 Kent Ridge Crescent, Singapore 119260, Singapore

AHMED, SHEIKH SARFUDDIN, plant breeder; b. Hitampur, Bangladesh, Feb. 1, 1944; s. Sheikh Mohiuddin and Mossammet Rejia (Khatun) A.; m. Begum Jahanara, Dec. 12, 1970; children: Shahed, Saeed, Sadiq, Ashek. ISc, Daulatpur BL Coll., Khulna, 1958, BS, 1963; MS, Rajshahi Varsity, 1967. Rsch. asst. Pakistan Cen. Jute Com., Rangpur, 1968-71; jr. rsch. officer Bangladesh Jute Rsch. Inst., Tarabo, 1972-75; scientific officer Bangladesh Jute Rsch. Inst., Monirampur, 1976-78; sr. scientific officer Bangladesh Jute Rsch. Inst., Dhaka, 1979-95, principal scientific officer, 1996-98, chief scientific officer, 1999. Contbr. articles to profl. jours. Mem. Bangladesh Plant Breding Soc., Bangladesh Botanical Soc. Avocations: fishing, reading, writing. Home: 643 Shewrapara, Dhaka Bangladesh Office: Bangladesh Just Rsch Inst, Manik Mia Ave, 1207 Dhaka Bangladesh

AHMED, SYED MANZOOR, chemicals company executive; b. Calcutta, India, Mar. 11, 1954; s. Syed Mahmud and Sultana Begum; m. Rezina Manzoor Khandokar, Dec. 8, 1986; 1 child, Refa'at Bin Manzoor. BS in Chemistry with honors, U. Dhaka, Bangladesh, 1977, MS in Applied Chemistry, 1979; MBA, Inst. Bus. Adminstrn. U., Dhaka, 1983. Chemist Fisons, Dhaka, until 1979; chemist Pfizer, Dhaka, 1980, sr. market rsch. officer, 1981-87; dept. mgr. BASF, Dhaka, 1987-93, dir. mktg., 1993-97, gen. mgr., 1997—, also bd. dirs. Team leader Notre Dame Coll., Dhaka, 1972. Recipient 2d prize debate competition Pakistan Cultural Coll., 1968. Avocations: reading, cricket, traveling, listening to music. Office: BASF Chem/Polymers Pakistan, 46-A Block 6 P E C H S, 75400 Karachi Sindh, Pakistan

AHMED, SYED Z., anthropologist; b. Meerut, India, Aug. 19, 1923; s. Syed Riazuddin and Shah Jehan Begum; m. Susan Ahmed, Feb. 20, 1944; 1 child, Suraiya. PhD, Eng. Leader Sahara Recon Expdn., North Africa; prodr. 40 scientific documentary films for TV, Europe; pres., exec. prodr. Xploration Internat.; rschr., traveler numerous expdns. worldwide. Author: Twilight of an Empire in India, Twilight of an Empire in China, Twilight on the Silk Road, Ruwenzori: A Land Journey Through Europe to Central Africa, Twilight on Caucausus, Incredible Journeys Around the World, Tales of Imperial China and Asia, 1997, Travel in Shangri-La, 1998, East of Tien Shan, 1998, An Imperial Affair, 1999, I Was a Geisha, 1999. Islamic.

AHMED, ZAKARIA, microbiologist; b. Dhaka, Bangladesh, Dec. 14, 1970; s. Ibrahim Bhuiyan and Rawshan Ara Begum. BS, Dhaka U., 1991, MS, 1992; postgrad., Ehime U., Matshuyama, Japan. Fellow Min. of Sci. and Tech., Dhaka, 1995; sci. officer Bangladesh Jute rsch. Inst., Dhaka, 1996—; rsch. asst. Kagawa (Japan) U., 1998-99, tchg. asst., 1998-99, 99—; part-time microbiologist Sonear Labs., Dhaka, 1994-95. Contbr. articles to profl. jours. Jr. H.S. scholar Bangladesh Govt., 1983-86, Dhaka U. scholar, 1989-92, Monbusho scholar Japan Govt., 1997—. Mem. Am. Soc. for Microbiology, Soc. for Fermentation and Bioengring., Asiatic Soc. of Bangladesh. Avocations: music, playing football, tourism, friendship. Home: B14 Sci Lab Quarter, Dhaka-1205, Dhaka Bangladesh Office: Bangladesh Jute Rsch Inst, Shere-Bangla Nagar, 1207 Dhaka Bangladesh

AHMET, ZERIN, research scientist; b. Nicosia, Cyprus, Apr. 20, 1951; arrived in Eng., 1961; d. Ahmet Hassan Kaya and Faika (Zihni) Hassan Kaya. Ordinary nat. cert. in biol. scis., Tottenham Tech. Coll., London, 1971; higher nat. cert. in biol. scis., Paddington Tech. Coll., London, 1974; MS in Biomolecular Orgn., U. London, 1988. Trainee technician U. Coll. Hosp., London, 1969-75; technician The London Hosp. (now named Royal London Hosp.), 1977-79, sr. med. lab. scientist, 1979-85; chief med. lab. scientist Chelsea Hosp. for Women/Queen Charlotte's and Chelsea Hosp., London, 1985-90; sr. rsch. sci. Queen Charlotte's and Chelsea Hosp., London, 1991-95, sr. clin. sci. Karim Ctr. Meningitis Rsch., 1995-96; tng./teaching microbiology rsch. supr. The London Hosp., 1979-85, Queen Charlotte's and Chelsea Hosp., London, 1985-95. Contbr. rsch. articles to profl. jours. including Jour. Infection, Lancet Jour. Antimicrobial Chemotherapy, Brit. Jour. Obstetrics and Gyn., Jour. Clin. Med. Microbiology, Jour. Clin. Pathology and Jour. Hosp. Infection, Sexually Transmitted Diseases, (book article) Recent Advances in Chemotherapy, 1985. Chmn. Turkish Women's Philanthropic Assn., London, 1975-77; participant TV debate The Right to Reply; speaker TV show Comment, London Turkish Radio. Conservative. Muslim. Avocations: opera, classical music, embroidery, walking. Office: Queen Charlottes and Chelsea Hosp, Tooting Broadway, London SW17, England

AHN, CHANGHYUN, physicist, researcher; b. Seoul, Korea, Oct. 24, 1960; s. Youngwoong and Youngja (Kim) A.; m. Mikyoung, Aug. 18, 1993; 1 child, Jiyoon. BA, Yonsei U., Seoul, 1986; PhD, SUNY, Stony Brook, 1992. Postdoctoral fellow Joint Inst. for Nuclear Rsch., Dubna, 1993-95, Kyunghee U., Seoul, 1995-97, Seoul Nat. U., Seoul, 1997—; vis. Postech, Pohang, Korea, 1997, Asia Pacific Ctr. for Theoretical Physics, Seoul, 1997. Contbr. articles to profl. jours. including Physics Letters B. With Korean mil., 1981-82. Office: Dept of Physics, Kyungpook Nat U, Taegu 702-701, Korea

AHN, CHUNG-SI, political science educator; b. Sangju-Si, Kyungbukdo, Korea, May 7, 1944; s. Sup-Mo and Ki-Joon (Kim) A.; m. Bong-Sook Sohn, Nov. 20, 1969; children: Jung-Hyun, Jung-Mihn. BA, Seoul Nat. U., 1967, MA, 1971; PhD, U. Hawaii, 1977. Asst. prof. Inst. Fgn. Affairs and Nat. Security, Seoul, 1977-79; prof. Seoul Nat. U., 1979—, dir. Inst. Social Scis., 1994-96, dir. Inst. Korean Polit. Studies, 2000—; vis. prof. Princeton (N.J.) U., 1988-89, Nat. U. Singapore, 1996-97, Inst. S.E. Asian Studies, Singapore, 1996-97. Author: Social Development and Political Violence, 1981; editor: The Local Political System in Asia, 1987, Korean Democracy in Transition: 1987-92, 1993, Koreans and Korean Business Interests in Central Europe and CIS Countries, 1998, Politics and Economy of Regime Transformations: Korea and Central European Countries, 1999; co-author: Political Economy of ASEAN, 1993, Major Theories of Political Economy, 2000. Mem. Korean ASEAN 21st Century Commn., Ministry of Fgn. Affairs, 1996-98, mem. policy adv. com., 1995—, mem. presdl. com. on the 21st Century, 1989-94; mem. policy adv. com. Ministry of Home Affairs, 1995-96. Lt. (j.g.) Korean Navy, 1967-70. Grantee U.S. Inst. Peace, 1996, Asia Fond., 1984, Fulbright-Hays Fond., 1988. Mem. Korean Assn. S.E. Asian Studies (pres. 1995-97), Jacob Internat. Soc. for Collaborative Studies (pres., bd. dirs. 1995-98), Internat. Polit. Sci. Assn., Korean Polit. Sci. Assn., Korean Assn. Internat. Studies. Office: Seoul Nat U, Dept Polit Sci, Seoul Korea

AHN, DUCK KYOON, plastic surgeon, educator; b. Seoul, Korea, Feb. 4, 1956; s. Byung Woo and Hyun Sook (Cho) A.; m. Tammy Kim, Nov. 21, 1986; children: Sook Young, Jong Seok. BA, Han Yang U., Seoul, 1977, MD, 1981, M, 1984, PhD, 1987. Cert. Nat. Bd. Plastic Surgery, Korea. Intern Han Yang U. Hosp., Seoul, 1984-85, resident dept. plastic surgery, 1985-89, assoc. prof., 1995-2000, prof., 2000—; asst. prof. Konkuk U. Hosp., Chung Ju, Korea, 1989-94; rsch. fellow Mass. Gen. Hosp., Boston, 1993-95. Contbr. articles to profl. jours. Lt. Korean Army, 1981-84. Recipient Acad. award Korean Microsurg. Soc., 1996. Mem. Korean Soc. Plastic Surgeons (sec. treasury 1997—), Internat. Confedn. Plastic Surgery, Oriental Soc. Aesthetic Plastic Surgery, Am. Soc. Plastic and Reconstructive Surgeons, Pan-Pacific Assn. Surgeons. Presbyterian. Avocations: golf, tennis, travel, climbing, cooking. Office: Han Ynag U Hosp, Kyomoon-Dong 249-1, 471-020 Kuri Republic of Korea

AHN, DUCKSUN, plastic surgeon; b. Seoul, Korea, Aug. 26, 1953; s. Kiyoung Ahn and Chishik Kim; m. Hyung Im, Nov. 17, 1982; children: Eusang, Eujee. MD, Korea U., Seoul, 1978. Intern Korea U. Hosp., Seoul, 1981-82; residetn in surgery U. Toronto, Ont., Can., 1983-88, clin. fellow, 1988-90; asst. prof. Korea U. Med. Coll., Seoul, 1990-94, assoc. prof., 1994-99, prof., 1999-2000, chmn. dept. med. edn., 1999—; head dept. plastic surgery Korea U. Hosp., 1993-98. Corr. author: Plastic and Reconstructive Surgery, 1999; contbr. articles to profl. jours. Capt. Korean Army, 1978-81. Internat. Med. Edn. fellow, Washington, 1998, fellow Edn. Commn. for Fgn. Med. Grad. Fellow Royal Coll. Surgeons; mem. Am. Soc. Plastic and Reconstructive Surgery. Avocations: hiking, music. Office: Korea U Hosp 126-1, 5KA Anamdong Sungbukku, 136-705 Seoul Korea

AHN, JOONG HO, systems analyst, educator; b. Kimhae, Korea, Jan. 15, 1951; m. Bong Sun Han, Dec. 16, 1978; children: Minna, Sung Hyun. BA, Seoul (Korea) Nat. U., 1975, MPA, 1980; MPhil, NYU, 1985, PhD, 1987. Cert. systems profl. Officer Korea Army Engring. Corps, Korea, 1975-77; asst. prof. Fordham U., N.Y.C., 1986-87; assoc. prof. U. Balt., 1987-88; prof. Coll. of bus. Seoul (Korea) Nat. U., 1989—, assoc. dean Office of Rsch. Affairs, 1994-96; exec. dir. electronic commerce program, adviser to pres. Boram Bank, Seoul, 1992—, Chohung Bank, Seoul, 1993—, Samsung Data Systems Co., Seoul, 1994—. Author: (book) Business Data Processing, 1990, Information Technology & Management, 1993, Business Data Communications, 1994, Internet & Electronic Commerce, 2000, Management & Information Systems, 2000. Dir. Office Environment Betterment Promotion Agy., Seoul, 1993; mem. mgmt. evaluation team for govt. enterprises, Ministry of Fin. and Economy, 1993—. Recipient Rotary Found. scholarship Rotary Internat. Found., 1980. Mem. Assn. for Computing Machinery, Japanese Soc. of OA Studies, Korea Facilities Mgmt. Acad. (pres. 1995—), Korea Soc. Mgmt. Info. Systems (v.p. 1993-95, pres. 1999—), Korea Med. Informatics Soc. (bd. dirs. 1992). Office: Seoul Nat U, Shinrim-Dong San 56-1, Seoul 151-742, Republic of Korea

AHN, JUNG-HO, engineering educator, scientist; b. Daejeon, South Korea, Jan. 31, 1954; s. Young-Whan Ahn and Jeong-Nyong Lee; m. Ok Seon Kim, Sept. 19, 1982. DSc in Naturelles Appliquées, U. Cath. Louvaine, Belgium, 1988, licencie scis. appliquées, 1984; B of Engring., Sungkyunkwan U., Seoul, Korea, 1981. Sr. rschr. Korea Inst. of Machinery and Metals, Changwon, Korea, 1989-95; prof. Andong (Korea) Nat. U., 1995—; vis. scientist Nat. Inst. for Metals, Tsukuba, Japan, 1994. Assoc. editor: Jour. of Metastable and Nanocrystalline Materials, 1999—; contbr. articles to profl. jours. Office: Andong Nat U Materials Engr, Songchun-dong 388, Andong 760-749, South Korea

AHN, KYU-HONG, science educator; b. Seoul, Republic of Korea, July 21, 1952; s. Byung-Chull Ahn and Sook-Hee Hwang; m. Sang-Hee Lee, June 10, 1980; children: Daniel, Edward. BS, Seoul Nat. U., 1976; MS, Cornell U., 1981, PhD, 1983. Rsch. fellow Korea Inst. Sci. & Tech., Seoul, 1983-91, sr. rsch. fellow, 1991-99, dir. gen., 1999—; vis. faculty Asian Inst. Tech., Bangkok, 1987-89, U. Hawaii at Manoa, Honolulu, 1997; adj. prof. Korea U., Seoul, 1990—; cons. CDG, Bangkok, 1987-89, UNDP, Vienna, Austria, 1992-95, CH2M Hill Internat. Co., Seoul, 1993-98, World Bank, Washington, 1994-97. Contbr. articles to profl. jours. V.p. Environ. Sci. and Tech., Seoul, 1994—; mem. Korea Peaceful Reunification, Seoul, 1999. Mem. WEF (sec.-treas. 1985-88), IAWQ, Pax Koreana. Achievements include invention of method for preparing porous membranes. Avocation: golf. Home: 32-603 Han Yang Apt, Apgujung-Dong Kang Nam-Gu, Seoul Republic of Korea Office: Korea Inst Sci & Tech, 39-1 Hawolgok-Dong, Sungbuk-Gu Seoul, Republic of Korea

AHN, SEI-HYUN, breast surgeon, educator, researcher; b. Seoul, Mar. 3, 1957; s. Eung-Gul and Yoon-Jin A.; m. Soon-Won Ahn; children: Yoo-Ri, Yoo-Mi. MD cum laude, Seoul Nat. U., 1981, MS, 1986, PhD, 1992. Intern Seoul Nat. U. Hosp., 1981, resident in surgery, 1982-86; fellow Asan Med. Ctr., Seoul, 1989-90; instr. surgery U. Ulsan, Seoul, 1990-92, asst. prof., 1992-96, assoc. prof., 1996—; vis. scientist M.D. Anderson Cancer Ctr., Houston, 1994-95; breast cancer rschr. Ministry Health and Welfare, Seoul, 1996-98; breast cancer investigator Korean Rsch. Fund, Seoul, 1997. Author: The Breast, 1999. Capt. Ministry Nat. Def., 1986-89. Mem. Korean Breast Cancer Soc., Am. Soc. Clin. Oncology, Am. Soc. Breast Disease. Presbyterian. Office: Asan Med Ctr Dept Surgery, Poongnap-Dong 388-1, Songpa-ku Seoul 138-040, Republic of Korea

AHN, YONG CHAN, radiation oncologist, educator; b. Seoul, Korea, Oct. 6, 1959; s. Chong Nam and Chae Sun Lee; m. Chi Yeun Yoon, June 10,

1983; children: Hyoungchin, Haren. MD, Seoul Nat. U., 1984, M in Med. Sci., 1992. Rotating intern Seoul Nat. U. Hosp., 1984-85, resident in therapeutic radiology, 1989-92; assisting physician Bupyung Ahn's Hosp., Incheon, Korea, 1985-86; rsch. physician Roswell Pk. Cancer Inst., Buffalo, 1992-93; clin. fellow in radiation oncology B.C. Cancer Agy., Vancouver, Can., 1993-94; radiation oncologist Samsung Med. Ctr., Seoul, 1994—; asst. prof. Sungkyunkwan U., Seoul, 1997—; Diplomate Korean Bd. Therapeutic Radiology. Capt. Rep. Korea Army, 1986-89. Mem. Internat. Soc. Sterotactic Radiosurgery, European Soc. Therapeutic Radiology and Oncology, Am. Soc. Therapeutic Radiology and Oncology, Korean Soc. Therapeutic Radiology and Oncology (editor 1995). Avocation: badduk, golf. Fax: 82-2-3410-2619. Office: Samsung Med Ctr, 50 Ilwon-dong, Kangnam-ku, Seoul 135-710, Republic of Korea

AHN, YOUNG-CHEOL, chemical engineer, educator; b. Seoul, Korea, Jan. 17, 1957; s. Byoung-Ok and Byoung-Im (Yoon) A.; m. Sung-Hee Kim, Jan. 15, 1995; children: Kye-Hyoung, Yerin. BSc, Hanyang U., Korea, 1979; MSc, Seoul Nat. U., 1981; PhD in Chem. Engring., SUNY, Buffalo, 1991. Rschr. Hyosung T&C Corp., Korea, 1981-84; tchg. asst. SUNY, Buffalo, 1987-89, rsch. asst., 1989-90; rsch. assoc. Hanwha R&E Ctr., Korea, 1991-94; lectr. chem. engring. Kyungnam U., 1994-96, asst. prof. chem. engring., 1996-2000, assoc. prof. chem. engring., 2000—. Contbr. articles to profl. jours. Korea Min. of Edn. scholar, 1985-87. Mem. AIChemE, Soc. Plastics Engrs., N.Y. Acad. Scis., Korean Inst. Chem. Engrs. Avocations: Korean chess, swimming, hiking, gardening, floriculture. Home: 393-2 Yochang-ri Chindong-myun, Hye-Chang Apt 102-2201 Kyungnam, Masan 631-810, Republic of Korea Office: Kyungnam U, 449 Wolyoung-dong Happo-gu, Masan 631-701, Republic of Korea

AHNERT, FRANK, geomorphologist, educator; b. Wittgensdorf, Germany, Dec. 12, 1927. DPhil, U. Heidelberg, 1953. Postdoctoral rsch. fellow U.S. NRC, 1954-56; from asst. prof. to prof. geography U. Md., 1956-74; prof. phys. geography Geographisches Inst. Tech. U., RWTH, Aachen, Germany, 1974-93, prof. emeritus, 1993—. Author: Einführung in die Geomorphologie, 1996, 2d edit., 1999, Introduction to Geomorphology, 1998; editor: Quantitative Slope Models, 1976, Geomorphological Models—Theoretical and Empirical Aspects, 1987, Landforms and Landform Evolution in West Germany, 1989; mem. editl. bd. Earth Surface Processes and Landforms, 1982-99, Catena, 1972-94, Springer Series in Physical Environment, 1985—, Geomorphology, 1992—; also articles in field. Grantee German and U.S. rsch. founds. Mem. Deutscher Arbeitskreis Geomorphologie, Brit. Geomorphological Rsch. Group. Home: Karl-Christ-Str 15a, 69118 Heidelberg Germany Office: Geog Inst Tech Univ, Templergraben 55, S-52056 Aachen Germany

AHO, YAO MESSAN, bank executive. Dir. Banque Centrale des Etats de l'Afrique de l'Ouest, Lome, Togo. Office: Banque Ctrl Etats l'Afrique, Ave de Sarakaqa, BP 120 Lomé Togo*

AHOKAS, HANNU OLAVI, researcher, educator; b. Ähtäri, Finland, May 13, 1947; s. Aarne Olavi and Hilja (Jääskeläinen) A.; m. Marja Tuulikki Saura, June 7, 1976; children: Lari, Laura. Candidate of Sci., U. Helsinki, Finland, 1973, Candidate of Philosophy, 1974, Licenciate of Philosophy, 1984, PhD, 1984. Tchg. asst. U. Helsinki, 1970—; rsch. asst. Acad. Finland, Helsinki, 1975-81, sr. rschr., 1984-89; advanced rschr. Agr. Rsch. Ctr., Jokioinen, Finland, 1989—; docent plant genetics U. Helsinki, 1984—. Contbr. articles to profl. jours. Office: Agr Rsch Ctr Crops & Soil, Myllytie 10, FIN31600 Jokioinen Finland

AHRENBERG, SVEN-GOSTA THEODOR, retired athletics professional; b. Gothenburg, Sweden, June 12, 1939; s. Theodor Ossian and Birgit Liljan (Israelsson) A.; m. Anna-Greta Nilsson, Nov. 9, 1974; children: Per Gustaf Theodor, Anna Maria Theodora. Grad., Solbacka Boarding Sch., Sweden, 1964. Cert. sportmaster U. Royal Swedish Sportacademy. Capt. Logistics Corps Traffic Br. Res. Swedish Army, 1969—; head sports Trollhattan Sch., Sweden, 1974-2000. Mem. local community coun., Trollhattan, 1981—; mem. local police bd., North Alvsborg County, 1985—. Recipient medals UN Cyprus, 1973, UN/Observe Mid. East, 1980-81, The Swedish Union of Officers in the Res., 1994. Mem. The Black Eagle Soc., Rotary (Paul Harris fellow), Masons, Ordre Souverain et Militaire du Temple de Jerusalem. Mem. Conservative Party. Lutheran. Avocations: orgn., adminstrn., leadership. Home: North Alvsborg County, Torsbogatan 27, S-461 57 Trollhattan Sweden

AHRENDS, GÜNTER, English language educator; b. Wilhelmshaven, Germany, Dec. 27, 1937; s. Erich and Erika (Kr) A.; m. Evelyn Buschmann, Dec. 15, 1965. DPhil, U. Bonn, Germany, 1965, DPhil Habilitation, 1975. Asst. U. Bonn, 1965-75; prof. U. Bochum, Germany, 1975—. Author: Traumwelt und Wirklichkeit im Spätwerk Eugene O'Neills, 1978, Die amerikanische Kurzgeschichte, 1980, 3d rev. edit., 1996; editor: Forum Modernes Theater, 1986—, (book) Konstantin Stanislawski Neue Aspekte und Perspektiven, 1992. Mem. Deutscher Anglistenverband, Deutsche Gesellschaft für Theaterwissenschaft, Deutsche Shakespeare-Gesellschaft. Home: Hahnenfussweg 26, 44797 Bochum Germany Office: Ruhr-Univ Bochum, Universitätsstr 150, 44801 Bochum Germany

AHRENS, WILLIAM HENRY, architect; b. N.Y.C., May 12, 1925; s. John Karl and Sophie (Hashage) A.; m. Joyce Nolan, Mar. 27, 1951. Student, R.I. Sch. Design, 1946; A.B. in Architecture, Princeton U., 1950, M.F.A. in Arch. and Urban Planning, 1953; postgrad., Tehran U., 1960. Chief architect Litchfield, Whiting, Bowne, Iran, 1958-61, Rome, 1961-64; dir. internat. ops. Whiting Assos., Rome, 1964-67; architect William H. Ahrens, AIA, Rome, Italy. Prin. archtl. works include ITT Sheraton Hotels, Tunisia and Iraq, Marriott Hotels, Egypt and Iran, Esso Hotels, Bologna, Italy and Bordeaux, France, Holiday Inn at Salalah Oman, Univ. of Dallas Rome Campus, various projects for NATO, Pontifical N.Am. Coll., Vatican Cuty State. Trustee John Cabot U.; mem. adv. bd. U. Dallas, U. Rome; bd. regents Marymount Internat. Sch., Rome. With USAAF, World War II, PTO. Recipient award AIA, 1953, Pub. Svc. award Tehran Lions Club, 1961, Rector's award Pontifical N.Am. Coll., Rome, 1994. Mem. AIA, Princeton Club (N.Y.C.), John's Island Club, Circolo del Golf Club (Rome), Knight of Malta, Knight of St. Gregory, Met. Club (N.Y.C.). Home: John's Island 371 Silver Moss Dr Vero Beach FL 32963-3430

AHRONOVITCH, YURI, conductor; b. Leningrad, May 13, 1932; Left USSR to settle in Israel, 1972.; s. Michael Ahronovitch and Anna Eskina; m. Tamar Sakson, 1973. Student, Leningrad Conservatorium with Kurt Sanderling and Nathan Rachlin. Conductor, Saratov Philharmonic Orchestra, 1956-57, Yaroslav Symphony Orchestra 1957-64; Chief Conductor Moscow Radio Symphony Orchestra 1964-72; opera debut in Europe, Cologne 1973; debut Royal Opera House Covent Garden (Boris Godunov) 1974' Chief Conductor Gurzenich Orchestra, Cologne 1975-98, Stockholm, Philharmonic Orchestra 1982.

AHTIAINEN, ANTTI ANTERO, sociologist; b. Kotka, Finland, Nov. 29, 1961. B in Social Sci., U. Orebro, Sweden, 1995. Survey mgr. Stat Sweden, Orebro, 1990—. Co-author: Minska Bortfallet, 1997; contbr. articles to profl. jours. Office: Stat Sweden, 701 89 Orebro Sweden Address: Stats Sweden, Survey Unit, 701 89 Orebro Sweden

AH-TYE, KIRK THOMAS, lawyer; b. L.A., Mar. 31, 1951; s. Thomas and Ruth Elizabeth (Liu) Ah-T.; m. Deborah Ann Wells, Jan. 31, 1981; 1 child, Torrey Ann. BA, U. Calif., Santa Barbara, 1973; JD, Boston Coll., 1976. Bar: Calif. 1977, U.S. Dist. Ct. (cen. dist.) Calif. 1978, U.S. Dist. Ct. (ea. dist.) Calif. 1994, U.S. Ct. Appeals (9th cir.) 1978, U.S. Supreme Ct. 1981. Co-exec. dir., mng. atty. Channel Counties Legal Svcs. Assn., Santa Barbara, 1977—; expert witness Assembly Com. on Edn., Calif. Legis., Sacramento; panelist Ctr. for the Study of Dem. Instns., Santa Barbara; panelist, instr. CLE approved classes; past legal cons. Santa Barbara chpt. calif. Assn. Bilingual Educators; inaugural prodr., moderator Santa Barbara Law, Sta. KTMS-AM, 1994—. Editor (bar newsletter) Santa Barbara Lawyer, 1992-93, (monthly legal series) Santa Barbara News-Press; contbr. articles to profl. jours. Trustee Montessori Ctr. Sch., Santa Barbara, 1991-93; bd. dirs., v.p. Santa Barbara Internat. Film Festival, 1991-93; chair adv. bd. Santa Barbara Regional Health Authority, 1985; mem. blue-ribbon com. County Bd. Suprs., Santa Barbara, 1988; chair Santa Barbara County Affirmative Action Commn., 1987-88; mem. grant-making com. Fund for Santa Barbara, 1988-92. Recipient Local Hero award Santa Barbara Ind., 1988. Master Santa Barbara Am. Inns of Ct.; mem. State Bar Calif. (state resolutions com. to state bar conf. of dels. 1994-96, exec. com. to conf. dels. 1997, ann. legal svcs. achievement award for so. Calif. 1997, Achievement award for legal svc. 1997), Santa Barbara County Bar Assn. (jud. svc. award com. 1992, chmn. pro bono com. 1993, bd. dirs., sec., CFO 1992—, pres. 1997-98), Lawyer Referral Svc. Santa Barbara (bd. dirs., pres. 1992). Avocations: sports, film, literature, weights, tennis. Office: Channel Counties Legal Svcs Assn 324 E Carrillo St Ste B Santa Barbara CA 93101-7438

AHUJA, CHANDER SHEKHAR, non-profit association administrator; b. New Delhi, India, May 8, 1956; s. Arjan Lal and Radha Rani A.; m. Indu Chowfin, Nov. 1, 1980 (dec. Apr. 1996); 1 child, Zarul. Profl. Diploma in Visual Comm., Nat. Inst. of Design, 1981. Cons. Org Operation Rsch. Group, Baroda, India, 1980, UNICEF Project Support Comm. Sect., New Delhi, India, 1980-81; chief deisgner UNICEF Transp. and Eq. Section, New Delhi, 1981-82; chief design cons. UNICEF Water Sect., New Delhi, 1981-83; chief designer, chief exec. Soc. Healing Anaemic Disorders and Emotional Support, New Delhi, 1984—, pres., 1996-98; cons. USHA Shriram Group, New Delhi, 1984-86, Electrogard, Ambala, India, 1986-94; designer NDTV Ltd., 1988-2000; works dir. Mayar Printers, New Delhi, 1988-92; graphic examiner Jamia U., New Delhi, 1987-90; hon. lectr. Sch. Planning and Architecture, New Delhi, 1996-98. Chief designer periodicals and posters for UNESCO; designer for All India Inst. Med. Schs. Nat. Med. Jour. Avocations: swimming, driving, photography. Fax: 91 11 5449246. E-mail: shekharshade@hotmail.com. Studio: A-32 Mansarover Gardens, New Delhi 110 015, India Office: SHADE 1st Fl, 3/15 Asaf Ali Rd, New Delhi 110 002, India

AHUJA, HARJIT KAUR, animal scientist; b. Ambala, Haryana, India, Apr. 3, 1955; d. Hara Singh and Wiran Wali (Sawhney) Anand; m. Gursharan Singh Ahuja, Nov.. 22, 1981; 1 child, Amandeep Singh. BSc, Dyal Singh Coll., Karnal, India, 1974; MSc, Nat. Dairy Rsch. Inst., Karnal, India, 1976, PhD, 1982. Scientist S-1 Nat. Dairy Rsch. Inst., Karnal, 1978-84, scientist S-2, 1984-86, sr. scientist in animal nutrition, 1986—; lectr. and presenter in field. Contbr. over 64 articles to profl. jours. CSIR Jr. Rsch. fellow, 1974; World Bank/NARP Project grant, 1995. Mem. Animal Nutrition Assn. (life), Indian Soc. for Nuclear tech. in Agr. and Biology (life), Animal Nutrition Soc. of India (life, mem. editl. bd.). Mem. Sikh Religion. Office: Nat Dairy Rsch Inst, Dairy Cattle Nutrition Div, Karnal 132001, India

AHUJA, VEENA MEHTA, physiology educator; b. Delhi, India, Aug. 26, 1944; d. Karam Chand and Sushila Devi Mehta; m. Harish Kumar Ahuja, Jan. 9, 1982. MB, BS, Maulana Azad Med. Coll., Delhi, 1968, MD in Physiology, 1974. Cert. Edn. Commn. for Fgn. Med. Grads. Resident Lok Nayak Jai Prakash Narain Hosp., Delhi, 1969-70; demonstrator Maulana Azad Med. Coll., Delhi, 1970-75; asst. prof. Maulana Aazd Med. Coll., Delhi, 1985-88; assoc. prof. Maulana Azad Med. Coll., Delhi, 1988-93, prof., 1993—; lectr. U. Coll. of Med. Scis., Delhi, 1975-85; lectr. USM, Penang, Malaysia, 1980-81; mem. expert com. for recruitment of scientists Def. Inst., Delhi, 1992-95; mem. expert com. for recruitment asst. profs. M.P. State Govt. Med. Colls. Contbr. articles to profl. jours. Pres. Ayudham Soc. sr. citizens home, Delhi, 1993-96. Fellow India Assn. Biomed. Scientists (life), Found. Integrated Medicine; mem. India Habitat Ctr. (New Delhi), Indian Med. Assn., Assn. Physiologists and Pharmacologists (life), Soc. Rsch. in Reprodn. and Fertility (life), V.V. Club (New Delhi). Avocations: reading, music, theatre, gardening. Home: Shanti-Niketan, 4th St House 20, New Delhi 110021, India Office: Maulana Azad Med Coll, B S Zafar Marg, New Delhi 110002, India

AHVENAINEN, JORMA JUHANI, history educator; b. Helsinki, Finland, Jan. 12, 1930; s. Aarne Johannes and Martta Irene (Huhtiainen) A.; m. Ritva Sinikka Kemiläinen, July 12, 1958 (dec. 1976); children: Helena, Tuula; m. Marja Selma Kristiina Juti, May 5, 1984. MA, U. Helsinki, 1956, PhD, 1963. Sr. history lectr. Rovaniemi Grammar Sch., 1959-62; history lectr. U. Jyväskylä, 1966-72, assoc. prof. in econ. history, 1972-90, prof. in world history, 1990-97. Author: Dutch Traders in Lapland and Russia, 1967, The History of the Far Eastern Telegraphs, 1981, The History of Sawmills in Finland, 1984, The History of the Caribbean Telegraphs, 1996. Recipient Olaus Magnus award The Oulu Hist. Soc. Mem. Finnish Bus. Archives (chmn. 1980—). Avocations: forestry, riding. Home: Kuurolantie 825, 32800 Kokemäki Finland

AI, HSIAO-BAI (XIAO-BAI AI), theoretical physicist; b. Zhenjiang, Jiangsu, China, Sept. 5, 1943; s. chang-geng and Shu (Lu) Ai; m. Mei-ying Shen, Dec. 14, 1974; 1 child, Mier. BA, Harbin (China) Engring. Coll., 1967; MA, U. Mass., Dartmouth, 1983; PhD, CUNY, 1988. Technician, engr. Chengdu Shuguang Med. Co., Chengdu, 1967-78; assoc. prof. Shanghai Inst. Nuclear Rsch./Chinese Acad. Scis., 1988-98, prof., 1998—. Contbr. articles to profl. jours. Dist. congressman Shanghai Jiading People's Congress, 1990—. Mem. N.Y. Acad. Scis. Avocations: reading, writing, swimming, travel. E-mail: mrsaic@online.sh.cn. Home: 645 Fengshun Rd Apt 74-401, Shanghai 201108, China Office: Shanghai Inst Nuclear Rsch, PO Box 800-204, 201800 Shanghai 201800, China

AIACHE, JEAN MARC, pharmaceutical educator; b. Algiers, Algeria, Sept. 27, 1938; arrived in France, 1962; s. Maurice and Lucie Aiache; m. Simone Sudaka, 1962; 1 child, Martine. M in Pharmacy, U. Algiers, 1961; PhD of Pharm. Tech., U. Clermond-Ferrand, 1968. Intern Hosp., Algiers, Algeria, 1961; asst. prof., prof. Sch. Pharmacy U. Clermont-Ferrand, France, 1962—; biologist Sabourin Hosp., Clermont-Ferrand, 1964—, head biopharmaceutics dept. Sch. Pharmacy U. Clermont-Ferrand, France, 1972—; cons. WHO, European Pharmacopoeia; mem. Commn. of Standardization of Spray Devices, French Pharmacopoeia. Author: Initiation à la Connaissance du Mèdicament, 3d edit., 1999; co-author: (with G. Legrand) Manuel du Prèparateur en Pharmacie, 1992, (with P.P. LeBlanc) Traitè de Biopharmacie, 3rd edit., 1997. Recipient prize French Cosmeceutics Soc., 1969, Silver medals Acad. Medicine for Tuberculosis and Respiratory Diseases and Health Edn., 1974, 76, Pierre Velon prize French Soc. Cosmetology, 1981. Fellow Am. Coll. Clin. Pharmacology; mem. Internat. Pharm. Fedn. (past pres. acad. sect.), Internat. Soc. Aerosols in Medicine (past pres.), Acad. Pharm. Scis., Soc. Therapeutics and Pharmacodynamics, French Soc. Immunology, Am. Pharm. Assn., Am. Assn. Pharm. Scientists, Acad. Pharmacy (corr., Argentina, Chile, Peru). Avocations: tennis, stamp collecting, medals related to history of pharmacy. Office: U Clermont-Ferrand Sch of Pharmacy, 28 Place H Dunant, 63001 Clermont-Ferrand France

AIBA, NOBUYASU, physician; b. Uozu, Toyama, Japan, July 5, 1960; s. Kin-ichi and Kumi (Doi) A.; m. Yoshiko Tanaka, May 23, 1993. MD, Toyama Med. and Pharm. Univ., 1985, PhD, 1989. Resident third dept. of internal medicine Toyama Med. and Pharm. U. Hosp. and Assoc. Hosp., 1989-91, 93; rsch. fellow dept. virology Toyama Med. and Pharm. U., 1991-93, asst. third dept. of internal medicine faculty of medicine, 1995-98; rsch. fellow dept. of medicine St. Mary's Hosp. Med. Sch., London, 1993-95; asst. dir. Seiyu Hosp., Toyama, 1998-2000, dir., 2000—; expert U. of Campinas, Brazil, 1993, 97. Contbr. articles to profl. jours. Fellow Japanese Soc. Internal Medicine; mem. Japan Gastroenterol. Endoscopy Soc., Japanese Soc. Gastroenterology (Award 1990), Japan Soc. Hepatology, Japan Geriatrics Soc. Avocation: reading historical novels. Office: Medical Corp Seiyu Hosp, 103 Kamisenbyo, Toyama 939-8134, Japan

AIBONI, VICTORIA UDOGHOREYON, soil scientist, educator; b. Warri, Fine, Nigeria, July 15, 1945; d. Peter and Meniafor (Awani) Akumagba; m. Sam Amaize Aiboni; children: Gloria, Faith, Sam, Tosan. MSc in Agronomy, Moscow (USSR) Friedship U., 1971; M. in Agrl. Sci., U. Reading, England, 1972; PhD, U. IFE, Ile-Ife, Nigeria, 1985. Clerk, cashier Barclays Bank D.C.O., Warri, Nigeria, 1963-65; clerk Greater London Council, Bromley, Bow, E. London, England, 1965-66; rsch. officer Ministry of Agrl., Benin, Nigeria, 1971-85; lectr. Bendel State Sch. Agr., Asaba, Nigeria, 1972-78, Bendel State U., Ekpoma, Nigeria, 1986-96, U. Agr., Abeoiluta, Nigeria, 1997—; cons. Shell Nigeria Ltd., Warri, Nigeria, 1986-92, EEC, Ekpoma, Nigeria, 1986, 87, 89, Inst. Rsch. Training, Ibadan, Nigeria, 1996-97. Fellow Internat. Tropical Agr., Ibandan, Nigeria, 1971-72, Fed. Govt., Benin, Nigeria, 1971-74, Bendel State Govt., Benin, 1980-85; scholar Fed. Ministry Edn., Lagos, Nigeria, 1966-71. Mem. Soils Sci. Assn., Nigeria Soc. Soils Sci. Roman Catholic. Avocations: reading, gardening, travel. Home: 27A Ivbhare St, Ozalla Owan West Local Area, Ozalla Owen West Nigeria

AICHBHAUMIK, DIBYAJYOTI, metallurgical engineer; b. Netrokona, Bangladesh, Jan. 5, 1944; came to U.S., 1971, naturalized, 1977.; s. Dibyenda and Jyotsna (Goon) A.; m. Nilu Datta, Feb. 4, 1971; 1 child, Niladri. BS, U. Calcutta, India, 1965; MS, Wayne State U., 1972, PhD, 1976. Foundry trainee Howrah Iron and Steel Corp., Calcutta, summers 1963-65; from jr. engr. to project engr. Kuljian Corp., Calcutta, 1965-71; fellow, rsch. asst., mem. faculty Wayne State U., Detroit, 1971-76; rsch. engr. Nat. Steel Corp., Weirton, W.Va., 1976-79, sr. rsch. metallurgist, 1979-80, supr. metall. engring. rsch., 1980-85, mgr. uncoated products/process, 1985-87; chief metall. engr. Weirton Steel Corp., 1987-89, mgr. rsch. and tech., 1989-90, mgr. quality assurance, 1990-92, mgr. metall. engring. and customer assurance, 1992-97, sr. fellow, 1997-98; tech. leader, sr. mgr., v.p. tech. Thomas Steel Strip, Weirton, 1998-99; cons. Debo Aichbhaumiks Assocs., Weirton, 1999—. Contbr. articles to profl. jours. Mem. AAAS, AIME, ASME, Am. Soc. Metals, Metall. Soc., Indian Inst. Metals, Sigma Xi. Hindu. Home and Office: 105 Freedom Ct Coraopolis PA 15108-9020

AIDA, ICHIRO, production and operations management educator; b. Shinjuku-ku, Tokyo, May 2, 1932; s. Haruo and Tome (Kawahara) A.; m. Keiko Suzuki, Apr. 1, 1964; children: Masashi, Miwako, Satoshi. BA, Sch. Commerce, Meiji U., Tokyo, 1955; MA, Meiji U., 1957. From asst. to prof. prodn. and ops. mgmt. Sch. Commerce, Meiji U., 1957—. Mem. Japan Soc. Bus. Adminstrn., Japan Acad. Soc. for Venture and Entrepreneur, Japan Indsl. Mgmt. Assn. Buddhist. Office: Meiji U Sch Commerce, 1 Chome Kanda-Surugadal, Chiyo da-ku Tokyo 101-8301, Japan

AIDLEY, DAVID JOHN, biologist, educator; b. Manchester, U.K., Feb. 5, 1937; m. Jessica Murrell, July 3, 1971; children: Timothy, Richard, Katie, Jack. MA, Cambridge U., 1964, PhD, 1964. Dept. demonstrator, zoology Oxford U., Eng., 1963-67; lectr. biol. scis. U. East Anglia, Norwich, Eng., 1967-79, sr. lectr., 1979-98; sr. fellow U. East Anglia, Norwich, 1998—; vis. prof. Bayero U., Kano, Nigeria, 1981-82. Author: Physiology of Excitable Cells, 1998, Ion Channels, 1996; editor: Animal Migration, 1981. Ch. warden, Ch. of England, Morley St. Botolph, Norfolk, 1990—. Mem. Physiol. Soc., British Ornithologists Union. Avocation: birdwatching. Office: U East Anglia, Sch Biol Scis, NR4 7TJ Norwich England

AIDMAN, EUGENE V., psychologist, educator; b. Saratow, Russia, Feb. 7, 1962; arrived in Australia, 1991; s. Vladimir I. Aidman and Loudmila N. Karmacheva; m. Marina A. Romanovsky, July 19, 1985; 1 child, Anna. PhD, Moscow State U., 1987. Lic. psychologist. Rsch. officer Moscow State U., 1985-87, asst. prof., 1987-91; rsch. assoc. Latrobe U., Australia, 1991-92; lectr. psychology U. Ballarat, Mt. Helen, Victoria, Australia, 1992—; specialist cons. Fiji Nat. Olympic Com., 1995-96. Co-author: (book) Jogging the Brain, 1996, 2d edit., 1997, (software) Self-Appreciation Test, 1999, others; contbr. rsch. articles to profl. jours. Vol. counselor Chernobyl Relief Fund, Victoria, 1994-95. Mem. APA (internat. affiliate), Australian Psychol. Soc. (mem. emerging telecomms. techs. and practice of psychology task force 1997-99), Australian Psychol. Soc. Coll. Sports Psychologists. Avocations: poetry, classical music, athletics. Office: U Ballarat, Gear Ave, 3350 Mount Helen Victoria, Australia

AIGINGER, JOHANNES, physics educator; b. Vienna, Austria, Apr. 12, 1937; s. Josef and Hilda (Hanusch) A.; m. Waltraud Eder, June 7, 1967. Cert. matriculation, Tech. Coll., Vienna, 1956; M. in Engring., Tech. U., Vienna, 1961; Dr. Tech., Tech. U., 1963, Habilitation, 1969. Univ. asst. Tech. U., Vienna, 1961-69; asst. prof. Tech. U., 1970-72, prof., 1973—, dean of studies in tech. physics, 1998-2000; vis. prof. Agrl. U., Vienna, 1971—; cons. Office for Pub. Bldgs., Vienna, 1976-89. Pres. Österreichischer Akademikerbund, Vienna, 1983-88; v.p. Austrian Assn. Radiation Protection, Seibersdorf, Austria, 1974—. Recipient Innitzer award Sci. Bd., Vienna, 1969, Bunsen-Kirchhoff award, 1991. Mem. Austrian Physical Soc. (sci. sec. Internat. Congress on Radiation Protection 1996). Avocations: sci. and soc., polit. impact sci., hist. sites and monuments. Home: Auhofstrasse 77 7 1, A 1130 Vienna Austria Office: Atominstitut, Schuettelstrasse 115, A 1020 Vienna Austria

AIGNER, THOMAS, pathologist; b. Erlangen, Bavaria, Germany, Nov. 24, 1962; s. Alois and Erika (Schubert) A. PhB, Coll. of Philosophy, Munich, 1984; BTh, U. Munich, 1985; MD, U. Erlangen, Germany, 1992, U. Erlangen, 1993. Postdoctoral fellow Max-Planck Soc., Erlangen, 1992-94; asst. in pathology U. Erlangen, 1994—. Contbr. articles to profl. jours. Head Cath. Youth Orgn., Nuernberg, Bavaria, 1980-86. Recipient award European League Against Rheumatism, 1991. Mem. Am. Orthopaedic Soc., Endocrinology Soc., European Soc. of Matrix Biology, Am. Soc. Bone and Mineral Rsch., N.Y. Acad. Scis. Roman Catholic. Avocations: philosophy, theology. Office: Univ Erlangen/Pathology, Krankenhausstr 8-10, Erlangen D-91054, Germany

AIGRAIN, JACQUES A., banker; b. Paris, Aug. 15, 1954; arrived in Eng., 1991; s. Pierre R. and Françine E. (Bogard) A.; m. Nicoletta I. Gentinetta, Apr. 16, 1983; children: Florian, Laurène. BA in Law, Pantheon, Paris, 1975; M of Econs., Dauphine, Paris, 1976; PhD in Econs., Sorbonne, Paris, 1980. Registered SFA. Cons. Orgn. for Economic Cooperation & Development, France, 1979-80; analyst J.P. Morgan, N.Y.C., 1981-82; asst. treas. J.P. Morgan, Paris, 1982-85; v.p. J.P. Morgan, N.Y.C., 1986-91; v.p. J.P. Morgan, London, 1991-93, mng. dir., 1993-96; chmn. J.P. Morgan SA, Paris, 1996-98; worldwide head energy, chem., healthcare J.P. Morgan SA, London, 1998—, co-head worldwide M&A, head healthcare, chem. and energy, 1998—, co-head investment banking, 2000—. Contbr. articles to fin. publs. Lt. French Navy, 1977-78. Avocations: skiing, windsurfing, mountain climbing. Home: 167 E 71st St New York NY 10021-4322 Office: J P Morgan 60 Wall St New York NY 10260-0001

AIHARA, JUN-ICHI, chemistry educator; b. Tokyo, July 2, 1941; s. Tsutomu and Masako (Shinohara) A.; m. Akiko Yoshimura, Apr. 20, 1969; 1 child, Yoichiro. BSc, U. Tokyo, 1965, MSc, 1967, DSc, 1970. Asst. prof. Hokkaido U., Sapporo, Japan, 1970-81; assoc. prof. Shizuoka (Japan) U., 1981-89, prof. chemistry, 1989—; councilor Shizuoka U., 1999—. Contbr. articles to profl. jours. Recipient Sci. prize IBM Japan, Ltd., Tokyo, 1987, Grand prize Shizuoka Asahi TV, 1992. Mem. Am. Chem. Soc., Chem. Soc. Japan. E-mail: scjaiha@ipc.shizuoka.ac.jp. Home: 2-3-3 Kusanagi-Sugimichi, Shimizu, Shizuoka 424-0885, Japan Office: Shizuoka U Dept Chemistry, Faculty of Science, Oya Shizuoka 422-8529, Japan

AIHARA, KEN-ICHI, engineering educator; b. Yokohama, Kanagawa, Japan, July 10, 1945; s. Ken Aihara and Fumiko (Nagase) Terasaka; m. Itsuko Fujimoto, Mar. 22, 1975. BS, Waseda U., Tokyo, 1969, MS, 1971, PhD, 1974. Sr. rsch. engr. NTT, Yokosuka, Japan, 1974-88, sr. mgr., 1991-97; v.p. NTT Am., N.Y.C., 1988-91; prof. Nagoya U. Commerce and Bus. Adminstrn., 1997—; vis. prof. Musashino Art U., Tokyo, 1995-97. Co-author: High Speed Broadband Networking, 1994, ATM Technology, 1995; contbr. articles to profl. publs. Fellow IEEE (regional coord. 1992-95), Assn. Computing Machinery, Asynchronous. Transfer Mode Forum (v.p. 1994-96, Ambassador Excellence award 1996), Inst. Electronic Info. and Comm. Engrs. in Japan, Japan Soc. for Mgmt. Info. (regional rep. 1999—). Avocations: driving, sightseeing, music.

AIKAWA, JERRY KAZUO, physician, educator; b. Stockton, Calif., Aug. 24, 1921; s. Genmatsu and Shizuko (Yamamoto) A.; m. Chitose Aihara, Sept. 20, 1944; 1 son, Ronald K. AB, U. Calif., 1942; MD, Wake Forest Coll., 1945. Intern, asst. resident N.C. Baptist Hosp., 1945-47; NRC fellow in med. scis. U. Calif. Med. Sch., 1947-48; NRC, AEC postdoctoral fellow in med. scis. Bowman Gray Sch. Medicine, 1948-50, instr. internal medicine, 1950-53, asst. prof., 1953; established investigator Am. Heart Assn., 1952-58; exec. officer lab. service Univ. Hosps., 1958-61, dir. lab. services, 1961-83, dir. allied health program, 1969—, assoc. dean allied health program, 1983—, pres. med. bd.; assoc. dean clin. affairs asst. prof. U. Colo. Sch. Medicine, 1953- 60, asso. prof. medicine, 1960-67, prof., 1967—, prof. bi-

ometrics, 1974—, assoc. dean clin. affairs, 1974—; Pres. Med. bd. Univ. Hosps. Fellow ACP, Am. Coll. Nutrition; mem. Western Soc. Clin. Research, So. Soc. Clin. Research, Soc. Exptl. Biology and Medicine, Am. Fedn. Clin. Research, AAAS, Central Soc. Clin. Research, AMA, Assn. Am. Med. Colls., Phi Beta Kappa, Sigma Xi, Alpha Omega Alpha. Home: 3233 Lake Albano Cir San Jose CA 95135-1467 Office: U Colo Sch Medicine 4200 E 9th Ave Denver CO 80220-3706

AIKAWA, NAOKI, surgeon, educator; b. Kanagawa, Japan, Feb. 22, 1944; s. Toshio and Sadako (Kiozumi) A.; m. Taka Ishii; 1 child, Yoshiko. MD summa cum laude, Keio U., Tokyo, 1968; D Med. Scis., Keio U., 1981. Diplomate Japanese Bd. Surgery, Japanese Bd. Emergency and Critical Care Medicine. Rsch. fellow Harvard Med. Sch., Boston, 1973-76; clin. and rsch. fellow Mass. Gen. Hosp., Boston, 1973-76; chief surgeon Saiseikai Kanagawa Hosp., Yokohama, Japan, 1978-80; assoc. prof. Sch. Medicine Keio U., 1988-92, prof., chmn. dept. emergency and critical care medicine, 1992—; dir. emergency and critical care and trauma svcs. Keio U. Hosp., Tokyo, 1992—; post med. advisor U.S. Embassy, Tokyo, 1991—; hon. med. advisor Can. Embassy, Tokyo, 1992—; sr. com. mem. rsch. comm. com. Sci. Coun. Japan, 1999—; chmn. exam com. Nat. Med. Bd. Japan, 1999—; mem. Ctrl. Drug Adminstrn. Com., Japanese Govt., 1992—; hon. prof. 3rd Mil. Med. Coll., Pla, China. Editor-in-chief Keio Jour. Medicine, 1995—, Jour. Japanese Assn. Acute Medicine, 1996—; sr. dep. editor Japanese Jour. Surgery, 1993-95; mem. editl. bd. Burns, 1994—; assoc. editor The Lancet, Japanese edit., 1991-93; mem. editl. com. Stedman's English Japanese Dictionary, 1980, 2d edit., 1985; editl. bd. JAMA Japanese edit. 1999—. Recipient Harvard prize Harvard Club of Japan, 1961, Everet Idris Evans Lectureship award Am. Burn Assn., 1995. Fellow ACS; mem. Japan Shock Soc. (trustee 1986), N.Y. Acad. Scis., Internat. Soc. for Burn Injuries (pres.-elect 1998—), Japanese Soc. for Burn Injuries (pres. 1995-96). Office: Keio U Sch Medicine, 35 Shinanamochi, Shinjuku 160-8582, Japan

AIKEN, JOAN (DELANO), author; b. Rye, Sussex, Eng., Sept. 4, 1924; d. Conrad Potter and Jessie (MacDonald) A.; m. Ronald George Brown, July 7, 1945 (dec. 1955); children: John Sebastian, Elizabeth Delano; m. Julius Goldstein, Sept. 2, 1976. Staff BBC, London, 1942-43; libr. UN Info. Ctr., London, 1943-49; sub-editor, features editor Argosy mag., London, 1955-60; copywriter J. Walter Thompson, London, 1960-61. Author: (juvenile fiction) All You've Ever Wanted and Other Stories, 1953, The Kingdom and The Cave, 1960, Black Hearts in Battersea, 1964, The Whispering Mountain, 1968 (Guardian award, 1969), Night Fall (Mystery Writer's of Am. award, 1972), Winterthing: A Child's Play, 1970, The Cuckoo Tree, 1971, All and More, 1971, A Harp of Fishbones and Other Stories, 1972, The Skin Spinners, 1976, The Spiral Stair, 1979, The Shadow Guests, 1980, Up The Chimney Down, 1985, Give Yourself a Fright, 1989, A Foot in the Grave, 1990, Is, 1992, A Creepy Company, 1993, numerous others; (adult fiction) The Silence of Herondale, 1964, Beware of the Boquet, 1966, The Ribs of Death, 1967, The Embroidered Sunset, 1970, Castle Barebane, 1976, Last Movement, 1977, The Smile of the Stranger, 1978, The Weeping Ash, 1980, Foul Matter, 1983, Mansfield Revisted, 1984, If I Were You, 1987, Blackground, 1989, Jane Fairfax, 1990, The Shoemaker's Boy, 1991, The Midnight Moropus, 1993, Cold Shoulder Road, 1995, A Handful of Gold, 1995, Emma Watson, 1996, The Cockatrice Boys, 1996, The Jewel Seed, 1997, Moon Caie, 1998, The Youngest Miss Ward, 1998, others; (trans.) The Angel Inn, (Contessa de Ségur, 1976), Moon Cake, 1998, The Youngest Miss Ward, 1998, The Way to Write for Children, 1998, Dangerous Games, 1999, Lady Catherine's Necklace, 2000, In Thunder's Pocket, 2000. Address: The Hermitage, East St Petworth, West Sussex GU28 0AB, England

AIKEN, LINDA HARMAN, nurse, sociologist, educator; b. Roanoke, Va., July 29, 1943; d. William Jordan and Betty Philips (Warner) Harman; children: June Elizabeth, Alan James. BSN, U. Fla., 1964, M in Nursing, 1966; PhD in Sociology, U. Tex., 1973. Nurse Med. Ctr. U. Fla., Gainesville, 1964-65, instr. coll. nursing, 1966-67; instr. sch. of nursing U. Mo., Columbia, 1967-70, clin. nurse specialist sch. of nursing, 1967-70; program officer Robert Wood Johnson Found., Princeton, N.J., 1974-76, dir. rsch., 1976-79, asst. v.p., 1979-81, v.p., 1981-87; Claire M. Fagin Leadership prof. nursing, prof. sociology U. Pa., Phila., 1988—, dir. Ctr. for Health Svcs. and Policy Rsch., 1988—; rsch. assoc. population studies ctr. U. Pa.; mem. Sec. Health and Human Svcs. Commn. on Nursing, 1988, Pres. Clinton's Nat. Health Care Reform Task Force, 1993; commr. Physician Payment Rev. Commn. nat. adv. coun. U.S. Agy. for Health Care Policy and Rsch. Author: Health Policy and Nursing Practice, 1981, Nursing in the 1980s, 1982, Applications of Social Science to Clinical Medicine and Health Policy, 1986, Evaluation Studies Rev. Ann., 1985, Charting Nursing's Future, 1991, Hospital Restructuring in North America and Europe, 1997; contbr. articles to profl. jours. Mem. Adv. Council Social Security, 1982-83. Recipient Joint Secretarial commendation U.S. Dept. Health and Human Services and HUD, 1987; NIH Nurse Scientist fellow, 1970-73. Mem. ANA (Jessie M. Scott award 1984), Am. Acad. Arts and Scis., Assn. Health Svcs. Rsch. (Disting. Investigator), Inst. Medicine, Nat. Acad. Scis., Nat. Acad. Social Ins., Am. Acad. Nursing (pres. 1979-80), Am. Sociol. Assn. (chair med. sociology sect. 1983-84), Sociol. Rsch. Assn., Coun. Nurse Rschrs. (Nurse Scientist of Yr. 1991), Sigma Theta Tau, Phi Kappa Phi. Home: 2209 Lombard St Philadelphia PA 19146-1107 Office: U Pa 420 Service Dr Philadelphia PA 19104-4210

AIKING, HARRY, environmental toxicologist; b. Amsterdam, The Netherlands, June 11, 1949; s. Harm and Godeliva Rosalia (Kooiker) A.; m. Marijke Jeanne Brandenburg, Sept. 16, 1977. MSc, U. Amsterdam, 1973, PhD, 1977. Rschr. U. Amsterdam, 1973-77; rsch. assoc. Ind. U., Bloomington, 1978-79; rsch. fellow Netherlands Ctrl. Blood Bank Lab., Amsterdam, 1980; sr. rschr. Vrije U., Amsterdam, 1980—, coord. sector environ. quality, 1993-95, program mgr. environ. resource mgmt., 1996-99; program mgr. Protein Foods, Environment, Tech. and Soc., 1999—; cons. to The Netherlands atty. gen. in cases of soil pollution Vrije U. Inst. for Environ. Studies, Amsterdam, 1987—; participant mission to establish Sino-Dutch environ. collaboration, 1996. Editor: (Dutch) Mosaic of Environmental Problems, 1982, Environmental Health Impact Assessment, 1989; contbr. articles to profl. jours. Mem. Royal Dutch Chem. Soc., Netherlands Soc. of Toxicology (registered toxicologist), Dutch Microbiol. Soc., Dutch Biotechnol. Soc., Dutch Environ. Soc. Avocations: table tennis, computers, war gaming. Office: Vrije Univ Inst Environ Studies, De Boelelaan 1115, 1081 HV Amsterdam The Netherlands

AIKMAN, ALBERT EDWARD, lawyer; b. Norman, Okla., Mar. 11, 1922; s. Albert Edwin and Thelma Annette (Brooke) A.; m. Shirley Barnes, June 24, 1944; children: Anita Gayle, Priscilla June, Rebecca Brooke. B.S., Tex. A&M U., 1947; J.D. cum laude, So. Meth. U., 1948, LL.M., 1954. Bar: Tex. (no. dist.) 1948, U.S. Supreme Ct. 1956, U.S. Ct. Appeals (5th dist.), U.S. Tax Ct. Staff atty. Phillips Petroleum Co., Amarillo, Tex., 1948-49; sole practice, Amarillo, 1949-53; tax counsel Magnolia Petroleum Co. (Mobil) Dallas, 1953-56; ptnr. Locke, Purnell, Boren, Laney & Neely, Dallas, 1956-71; sole practice, Dallas, 1973-81; of counsel Pickens Energy Corp., Dallas, 1981-96; couns. Ptnrs. In Exploration, LLC, Dallas, 1997—. Served with inf. U.S. Army, 1943-45. Mem. ABA, Tex. Bar Assn., Dallas Bar Assn. Methodist. Contbr. articles in field to profl. jours.

AIKMAN, ROBERT EDWIN, oil and gas company executive; b. Oklahoma City, Feb. 7, 1932; s. Claud Edwin and Gladys (Jesse) A.; m. Rachel Elizabeth Stockton, may 18, 1950; children: James Stockton, Meredith Elizabeth, Melinda Elaine, Amy Jean. BBA, U. Okla., 1952. Cert. petroleum landman. Petroleum landman Cities Svc. Oil Co., Jackson, Miss., 1952-56, Amarillo, Tex., 1952-56; v.p. Petroleum Exploration, Inc., Amarillo, 1956-57; pres. Aikman Bros. Corp., Amarillo, 1957-69, Mana Resources, Inc., Calgary, Alberta, Can., 1969-72, Dorcester Exploration, Inc., Dallas, 1972-76, Energy Resources Corp., Amarillo, 1982-95; chmn. OGP Energy Cos., Inc., Dallas, 1997—; chmn., pres. Lazy G Ranch, Amarillo, 1989—; chmn. Provident Comm., Inc., Dallas, Washington, 1995—, Wham Technologies, Inc., Dallas, 1998—. Potter/Randall County Fin. chmn. Republicans for Ford, Amarillo, 1976; mem. Gov.'s Energy Coun., Austin, 1980-82. Mem. Panhandle Petroleum and Royalty Assn., Ind. Petroleum Assn. of Am., Tex. Ind. Producers and Royalty Owners, Panhandle Petroleum Landmans Assn., Am. Assn. Petroleum Landmen, Dallas Petroleum Club, Dallas Country Club, Amarillo Country Club. Republican. Episcopalian. Avocations: hunting, travel. Office: Aikman Cos 2201 Civic Cir Ste 300 Amarillo TX 79109-1841

AI-LIAN, LING, chemistry educator; b. Shanghai, July 23, 1940; s. Ling Jian-ming and Chen Shi-fang; m. Li Ze-ren; children: Gao, Li. Diploma, Hua-dong Chem. Engring. Inst., Shanghai, 1962. Asst. Beijing Polytechnic U., 1962-78, 1978-86, lectr., 1986-94, vice prof., 1994—; prof. Chang-Shu Hoisting Jack Factory, Jiang Su, China, 1980-83; mem. coun. Beijing Membrane Inst., 1991-94, Chinese Inst. of Sea Water Desalination and Water Resue, Chinese Chemistry Inst. Contbr. articles to profl. jours. Recipient Nat. Invertery award People's Rep. of China Sci. and Tech. Com., 1983, Govt. Spl. Alowance, People's Republic of China, 1993, others. Avocations: readings, Beijing opera. Home: Nang guang south rd 1-5-201, 100021 Beijing China Office: Beijing Polytechnic Univ, Ping Le yuan 100, 100022 Beijing China

AILLONI-CHARAS, DAN, marketing executive; b. Ploiesti, Rumania, May 22, 1930; came to U.S., 1950, naturalized, 1960; s. Max and Felicia (Lupescu) Charas; m. Miriam C. Taytelbaum, Oct. 8, 1957; children: Ethan, Benjamin, Orrin, Adam. AB with honors, U. Calif., Berkeley, 1952, MA, 1953; PhD, NYU, 1968. Mem. editl. staff San Francisco Call Bull., 1953-54; exec. sec. TAHAL, 1955-57; project dir. Marplan divsn. Interpub., N.Y.C., 1958-60; supr. advt. studies NBC, N.Y.C., 1960-62; dir. consumer and comm. rsch. Forbes Rsch., Inc., N.Y.C., 1962-63; mgr. market rsch. Chesebrough-Pond's, Inc., N.Y.C., 1963-64, new products mgr., 1964-68, mgr. internat. mktg. services dept., 1968-69; pres. Stratmar Sys., Inc., Port Chester, N.Y., 1969-91, chmn., CEO, 1991—; asst., then prof. mktg. Pace U., 1963-85; mem. adv. bd. Premium Incentive Show, 1986-92, Nat. Premium Incentive Show, 1987-92; lectr. Israel Inst. Tech., 1956-58, dir. extension divsn. no. region, 1956-58. Author: Promotion: A Guide to Effective Promotional Planning, Strategies and Execution, 1984; editor: Mktg. Rev., 1960-63, Proc. 1st Ann. Conf. on Rsch. Design, 1964, New Directions in Research Design, 2d Conf., 1965, Planning, 1968-71; bd. editors Jour. Consumer Mktg., 1982—, Jour. of Brand and Product Mgmt., 1991—, Jour. Svc. Mktg., 1992—; contbr. to Brandweek, Marketime News, Chain Drug Rev., MMR, New Product News. Trustee Inst. Advanced Mktg. Studies, 1965-66, Philharmonic Symphony of Westchester, 1977-80; bd. dirs. Young Men's Bd. Trade, 1960-63, state dir., N.Y. StatJr. C. of C., 1962-63; bd. advisers Ad Expo, 1978; 1st v.p. Student World Affairs Coun. Northern Calif., 1953-54, chmn. Asilomar World Affairs conf., 1954; founder Israel Assn. Grads. Social Scis. & Humanities, 1955; pres. Haifa Jr. C. of C., 1956-57. Coro Found. fellow, 1953; Univ. honors scholar NYU, 1968. Mem. Am. Mktg. Assn. (pres. N.Y. chpt. 1965-66, nat. v.p. 1970-71), Promotion Mktg. Assn. Am. (bd. dirs. 1978-98, chmn. edn. com. 1979-81, 82-91, chmn. premium show com. 1982-91, exec. com. 1986-87, 89-93, 94-95, 96-97, 99-2000, chmn. nat. conf. 1988, 96, v.p. 1989-93, 94-95, chmn. retailers and mfrs. conf. 1992, 93, chmn. in-store mktg. coun. 1993-94), N.Am. Soc. Corp. Planning (bd. dirs. 1970-72), Nat. Assn. Chain Drug Stores (nat. industry adv. bd. 1992—), Am. Friends of the Coll. Mgmt. (chmn. 1999—), Soc. Profl. Journalists, Nat. Arts Club, Can. Club, The Deadline Club, Can. Club, Coro Alumni Assn. (nat. bd. dirs. 1989-95), Sigma Delta Chi, Phi Sigma Alpha. Home: 23 Woodland Dr Rye Brook NY 10573-1723 Office: Stratmar Bldg 109 Willett Ave Port Chester NY 10573-4232

AIM, KAREL VACLAV, chemist; b. Prague, Czech Republic, Oct. 16, 1947; s. Karel Vaclav and Zdenka Anna (Ticha) A.; m. Helena Duronova, July 31, 1971 (div. 1975); 1 child, Martin; m. Jindriska Schmidtova, Oct. 7, 1976; children: Dagmar, Irena. MS in Chemistry, Inst. Chem. Tech., 1971; PhD in Phys. Chemistry, ICPF Czech Acad. Sci., 1977. Asst. rsch. scientist Inst. Chem. Process Fundamentals, Czech Acad. Sci., Prague, 1975-77; rsch. scientist inst. Chem. Process Fundamentals, Czech Acad. Sci., Prague, 1977-91; asst. prof. computer sci. Agrl. U., Prague, 1977-81; sr. rsch. scientist Inst. Chem. Process Fundamentals, Czech Acad. Sci., 1991—; abstractor Chem. Abstracts Svc., Columbus, Ohio, 1972—; elected sci. bd. Inst. Chem. Process Fundamentals, 1990—, deputy head dept. thermodynamics, 1992—, chmn. sci. bd., 1992—; lectr. Inst. Chem. Tech., 1988—; mem. bd. govs. Joint Rsch. Centre of the European Commn., 1999—. Co-author: Vapor-liquid Equilibrium at Normal and Low Pressures, 1982; contbr. articles to profl. jours. Sgt. Czech Mil., 1974-75. Rsch. fellow Tech. U. Denmark, Lyngby, 1981-82, U. Trieste, Italy, 1989. Mem. AiChE, Czech Chem. Soc., Czech Soc. Chem. Engring., Acad. Sci. Czech Republic (elected acad. assembly). Roman Catholic. Avocations: hiking, travel, chess, literature. Home: Stehlikova 476, 165 00 Prague 6 Czech Republic Office: Inst Chem Process Fundament, Rozvojova 135, 165 02 Prague 6 Czech Republic

AIMÉ, JEAN-CLAUDE, United Nations official; b. Haiti, Sept. 10, 1935; s. Christian F. Aimé and Carmen Amelia Gautier; m. Elizabeth B. Bettinson, 1963 (div. 1991); m. Lisa M. Buttenheim, 1992. Student, Harvard Coll., U. of Pa. Asst. sec.-gen., chief of staff Exec. Office of Sec.-Gen., UN, N.Y.C., 1992-97, exec. sec. compensation com., 1997—. Avocations: music, reading, squash, hunting. Office: care United Nations Diplomatic Pouch Rm S-3800E New York NY 10017*

AIN, MICHAEL, lawyer; b. N.Y.C., Feb. 22, 1949; s. Herbert and Victoria Ain; m. Esther Luskin, June 18, 1972; children: Andrew, Stacie. BA, SUNY, Buffalo, 1971; JD (hon.), George Wash., 1975. Bar: U.S. Dist. Ct. Md., Wash. Assoc. Keilp Law Firm, Vienna, Va., 1975-83, Giordano Bus. Villareale & Vaughn, Upper Marlboro, Md., 1983-85; joint practice Jean D O'Malley, Wash., 1985-86; pvt. practice Wash., 1986—; lectr. Paralegal Inst. Phila., 1984, Wash. Bar. Master Am. Inns of Ct.; mem. ATLA. Avocations: reading, history, tennis, baseball.

AINARDI, SYLVIANE H., foreign diplomat; b. Ugines (Savoie), France, Dec. 19, 1947. Mem. European Parliament, 1999—, mem. com. on employment and social affairs, substitue com. on regional policy, transport and tourism; mem. bur. Confederal Group of the European United Left/Nordic Green Left; mem. delegation for relations with South Africa. French Communist Party. Office: 1 allée Marc Saint Saens, BP 1157, F-31036 Toulouse France*

AINDOW, MARK, engineering educator; b. Barrow-in-Furness, Cumbria, Eng., June 23, 1964; s. Joseph Charles and Brenda Ann A.; m. Tai-Tsui Cheng, Mar. 23, 1991; children: Ann, Jay. BEng in Metallurgy and Materials Sci., U. Liverpool (Eng.), 1985, PhD in Materials Sci. and Engring., 1989. Rsch. fellow Case Western Res. U., Cleve., 1989, Ohio State U., Columbus, 1990; lectr. U. Birmingham (Eng.), 1990-96, sr. lectr., 1996-99; assoc. prof. U. Conn., Storrs, 1999—. Office: U Conn Dept Metallurgy & Materials 97 N Eagleville Rd Dept & Storrs Mansfield CT 06269-9011

AINLAY, THOMAS ERNEST, JR., direct marketing professional, writer, publisher; b. Longview, Wash., Oct. 6, 1951; arrived in Japan, 1976; s. Thomas Ernest Sr. and Betty Jean (Herd) A.; m. Shizue Takahashi, Dec. 20, 1978; children: Tessera, Shina. BA, DePauw U., 1973. Cert. neurolinguistic programming practitioner U. Calif., Santa Cruz. Tchr. math. U.S. Peace Corps, Kuantan, Malaysia, 1973-75; journalist Press Internat., Tokyo, 1976-80; copy chief Asia Advt. Agy., Tokyo, 1980-85; gen. mgr. McCann Direct, Tokyo, 1985-95; dir. consumer mktg. Time Inc., North Asia, Tokyo, 1995-98; chmn. Breakthrough Enterprises, Inc., 1998—; pub. Legacy Memoirs, 1998—; pres. AZ Way Books, 2000—; bd. dirs. Japan Telemarketing Assn., Tokyo, 1989-90; founder, coord. Tokyo English Lit. Soc., 1977-86. Author: The Last Book, 1984, The Door, 1982; editor: Printed Matter, 1978. Vice chmn. Dem. Abroad Japan, Tokyo, 1995-97; judge USDMA Echo awards, N.Y.C., 1993-96; treas. Dem. Party Com. Abroad, 1997-99; torchbearer Olympics, Nagano, Japan, 1998. Recipient Signal award-gold, Japan Direct Mail Assn., 1987, silver, 1990, Asian Direct Mktg. award-gold, 1992, bronze, 1993. Mem. Am.-Japan Soc., Japan P.E.N. Club, Internat. Soc. Japanese Philately, World Literary Acad. (fellow), European Direct Mktg. Assn. (bd. dirs.), U.S. Direct Mktg. (adv. coun.), Am. C. of C. (bd. govs.), Nat. Eagle Scout Assn. (life, Eagle award 1966). Avocations: writing, stamp collecting, computers, cooking. Home: 5-2-11 Chuo Nakano-ku, Tokyo 164, Japan

AINSA, FRANCIS SWINBURNE, lawyer; b. El Paso, Tex., Jan. 7, 1915; s. Frank S. and Roselle (McNamee) A.; m. Evelyn Fraser, Jan. 14, 1941; children: Dorothy, Francis Jr., Michael, Mary, Kathleen, Richard, Barbara, Stephen. AB, Georgetown U., 1936; LLB, Harvard U., 1940; postgrad., U.S. Army Sch. Mil. Govt.; postgrad ethnology, archaeology, U. Tex., El Paso. Legal officer sup. hq. AEF Mission to Luxembourg, 1944-45; pvt. practice law, El Paso, Tex., 1947-99; ret., 1999. Bd. chmn. Mary L. Peyton Found., El Paso, 1955-77; mem. zoning bd. of adjustment, El Paso, 1960. Maj. U.S. Army Cavalry, 1942-46 ETO. Decorated Bronze Star, 1946, Croix de Guerre (Luxembourg), 1946; named Officer Order of Couronne de Chene (Luxembourg), Officer Order of Leopold II (Belgium), 1946, Knight of St Gregory, Holy See, 1965, Knight Grand Comdr. Equestrian Order of Holy Sepulchre Jerusalem, 1985. Roman Catholic. Avocations: photography, automotive. Home and Office: 525 Corto Way El Paso TX 79902-3817

AINSCOW, ROBERT MORRISON, former British government official, independent consultant; b. Salford, Eng., June 3, 1936; s. Robert M. and Hilda (Cleminson) A.; m. Faye Bider, 1965; children: Katharine Lara, Matthew Robert. BA in Econs. with honors, Liverpool (U.K.) U., 1957. Econ. statistician Govt. of the Fedn. of Rhodesia and Nyasaland, 1957-61, UN Secretariat, N.Y.C., 1961-65, 66-68, Dept. of Econ. Affairs, London, 1965-66; econ. adviser Ministry of Overseas Devel., London, 1968-70; sr. econ. advisor Overseas Devel. Adminstrn., London, 1971-76, head South Asia dept., 1976-79, under sec. edn. and tech. coop., 1979-80, prin. fin. officer, under sec., 1980-86, dep. permanent sec., 1986-96; chmn. Working Party on Fin. Aspects of Devel. Assistance, OECD/DAC, Paris, 1982-86; mem. World Bank Task Force on Concessional Flows, 1983-85, mem. devel. com. task force on multinat. devel. banks, 1994-96; cons. to UN World Bank OECD, UKDFID, Irish Aid and ODC Washington, 1996—. Trustee Brit. Red Cross, 2000—. Decorated companion Order of the Bath. Avocations: film, theatre, modern novel, travel, walking.

AINSWORTH, JAMES PETER, art historian; b. Lancaster, Eng., May 30, 1932; arrived in Australia, 1967; s. James and Patricia (Cronshaw) A.; m. Doreen Waugh; children: Sarah Louise, Paul James, Mark James. BA, U. London, 1959, MA, 1961; PhD, British Museum, 1995. Chartered dir. Constable Police, Yorkshire, Eng., 1953-62; detective Police, Lancashire, Eng., 1962-66; bodyguard Commonwealth of Australia, 1969-70; consuting dir., 1970; bodyguard British Royal Family, Yorkshire, 1957-60; chmn. Rombolds Holdings Ltd., Australia, 1971-94; lectr. in field. Mem. N.Y. Acad. Sci., Valuers, Assessors, Art Restorers Australia.

AIRAKSINEN, MAUNO MATTI, retired medical educator, researcher; b. Karttula, Finland, May 2, 1930; s. Pekka Juho and Edla (Karttunen) A.; m. Eila Marjatta Neuvonen, June 21, 1958; children: Marja Hartikainen, Pekka, Matti, Paavo, Liisa. B Medicine, U. Helsinki, 1955, MD, 1959, PhD, 1964. Instr., dept. pharmacology U. Helsinki, 1956-63; rsch. fellow Nat. Med. Rsch. Coun., Helsinki, 1962-65; asst. prof., dept. pharmacology U. Helsinki, 1963-68; rsch. specialist Tex. Rsch. Inst. Mental Sci., Houston, 1966-68; assoc. prof. pharmacology & biological stds. of drugs U. Helsinki, 1968-73; prof. pharmacology, head dept. pharmacology and toxicology U. Kuopio, Finland, 1973-94; specialist mem. Nat. Drug Registration Bd., Helsinki, 1968-96 (vice chmn. 1994-96); consulting expert Nat. Agy. of Medicines, Finland and European Agy. for Evaluation of Drugs, London, 1996—; mem., chmn. drug sect.-social med. adv. bd., Social Ins. Instn. Finland, 1971-95; various activities U. Kuopio including mem., chmn. Univ. Coun., dean of med. faculty, vice dean and dean of pharmaceutical faculty, 1979-87. Contbr. articles to profl. jours. Bd. dirs., chmn. 2 yrs. local fund of Finnish Cultural Fund, 1984-90. Recipient Advanced Scientist's award Acad. of Finland, 1977, 80, 81, 87, various rsch. grants from other sources, White Rose of Finland, 1985. Home: Kuvelammentie 24, FIN70800 Kuopio Finland Office: U Kuopio Dept Pharmacology Toxicology, PO Box 1627, FIN70211 Kuopio Finland

AIRLIE, CATHERINE See MACLEOD, JEAN SUTHERLAND

AISTOV, ANDREY VALENTINOVICH, physics and economics educator; b. Gorky, USSR, June 10, 1962; s. Valentin Mikhailovich and Vera Nikolaevna (Kiselyeva) A.; m. Oksana Vladimirovna D'yachenko, May 5, 1984 (div. Oct. 1989); 1 child, Aleksandr; m. Elena Alekseevna Protsak, Mar. 21, 1992; children: Ol'ga, Kseniya. Grad., Gorky (USSR) State U., 1984; Kandidat in Radiophysics, U. Nizhni Novgorod, Russia, 1994. Engr. Gorky State U., 1984-85, lectr., 1985-91; sr. instr. gen. physics U. Nizhni Novgorod, 1994-98; asst. prof. gen. physics, 1998-99; dir. radiophysics postal courses U. Nizhni Novgorod, 1994-96, dir. Radiophysics Sch., 1996-98; asst. prof. econs. U. Higher Sch. Econs., 1998—. Grantee Soros Found., 1993; sci. scholar Govt. of Russia, 1994. Mem. Internat. Union Radio Scientists (corr., award for young scientists 1996). Avocation: playing badminton. Home: Ankudinovskoe sh 26-a KV 53, 603144 Nizhni Novgorod Russia Office: Higher Sch Econs., Subsidiary Bolshaya Pechorskaya St 25, 603600 Nizhni Novgorod Russia

AÏT-ABDELKADER, NADRA FADHILA, biologist, researcher; b. Constantine, Algeria, May 7, 1951; arrived in France, 1988; d. Ammar and Simoucha (Boussouf) A.-A. Grad. Engr., INA, Algiers, Algeria, 1970; DEA, U. Paris, 1978, PhD, 1982; Doctorat d'Université, U. Marseille, France, 1993. Engr. Agrl. Ministry, Constantine, 1974-75; asst. U. Constantine, 1974-78, lectr., 1978-89, dir. Inst. of Nutrition, 1983-89; rschr. CNRS/U. Marseille, 1993—. Home: 19/21 rue Brandis, 13005 Marseille France Office: U Aix Marseille 1 CNRS, 163 ave de Luminy, 13288 Marseille 9, France

AITKEN, RUTH ELAINE WILLSON, educational consultant. BS in Secondary/Vocat. Edn., Indiana U. of Pa.; MS, Pa. State U., postgrad. Cert. ednl. and vocat. instr., Pa. Dir. field placements Pa. State U., University Park, 1972-83, field placements coord., 1972-83; edn./mktg./mgmt. cons. Aitken Assocs., State College, Pa., 1983—; owner, mgr. Carnegie On-Call, State College, 2000—; substitute tchr. bus. edn., computer literacy, English, sci., life arts classes, 1985-94; substitute tchr. dept. continuing edn. Pa. State U., instr. dept. ind. learning, 1985-94. Regional chair Am. Cancer Soc., Arthritis Found.; mem. Centre Region Health Coun.; membership com. Centre County Coun. on Human Svcs. Recipient Nat. Women of Excellence award. Mem. NAFE, Am. Mgmt. Assn., Am. Coun. on Consumer Interests, Nat. Coun. Consumer Involvement, Pa. State Alumni Assn. (univ.-alumni-faculty task force com.), Coll. Human Devel. Alumni Assn. (bd. dirs. nominations com., chair), Individual and Family Studies Undergrad. Student Orgn. (advisor), Bus. and Profl. Women (state and dist. conv. del., newsletter editor, founds. chair), Chamber of Bus. and Industry of Centre County, Toastmasters Internat., Soroptomist Club (youth scholarship com.), Kappa Omicron Nu, Alpha Kappa Delta. Avocations: community leadership and service projects. Office: Aitken Assocs 124 S Patterson St State College PA 16801-3911

AITKIN, DONALD ALEXANDER, university administrator; b. Sydney, Australia, Aug. 4, 1937; s. Alexander George and Edna Irene (Taylor) A.; m. Janice Wood, Dec. 20, 1958 (div.); children: Susan Jill, Lesley Jennifer, Gabrielle Vanessa, Alexander Lewis; m. Susan Tracy Elderton, May 20, 1977 (div. 1991); 1 child, Max David; m. Beverley Ann Berger, Dec. 20, 1991. BA with honors, U. New Eng., Armidale, Australia, 1959, MA, 1961; PhD, Australia Nat. U., Canberra, 1964. Research fellow Australia Nat. U., 1965-68, sr. research fellow, 1968-71; found. prof. politics Macquarie U., Sydney, Australia, 1971-79; prof. pol. sci., head of dept. Research Sch. Soc. Scis. Australia Nat. U., 1980-88; chmn. Australian Research Council, 1988-90; vice chancellor, pres. U. Canberra, 1991—; Mem. Australian Sci. and Technol. Council, Canberra, 1986-92, Nat. Research Fellowship Adv. Com., 1986-88; mem. Australian Research Grants Com., Canberra, 1984-88, chmn. 1986-88. Author: The Colonel, 1969, Stability and Change in Australian Politics, 1977, 2d edit., 1982; co-author Australian Political Institutions, 1980, 6th edit., 2000. Councillor Canberra Bus. Coun., 1992—; chmn. ACT Schs. Legis. Rev., 1998-2000; mem. bd. Australian Higher Edn. Indsl. Assn., 1999—. Fellow Australian Coll. Edn., Acad. Social Scis. in Australia; mem. Australasian Polit. Studies Assn. (life, pres. 1979, treas. 1981-88). Avocations: bushwalking, tennis, music, cooking. Office: U Canberra, ACT 2601, Australia

AITMAN, DAVID CHARLES, solicitor; b. London, Apr. 11, 1956; s. Gabriel and Irene Bertha A.; m. Marianne Lucille Atherton, Mar. 26, 1983; children: Lauren Jane Mary, Marcus Jon, Polly Beatrice. Licentiate, Royal Acad. Music, London, 1977; BA, Sheffield (Eng.) U., 1978; hon. degree, Clifton Coll., Bristol, Eng. Ptnr. Denton Wilde Sapte, London, 1980—; bd. dirs. Bertelsmann U.K., Ltd., London. Co-author: Butterworth's

Encyclopedia of Competition Law, 1990, Bellamy and Child's Common Market Law of Competition; contbr. Practical Intellectual Property Law, 1991, Yearbook of Media Law, 1995-2000. Avocations: music, literature, skiing, windsurfing. Office: Denton Wilde Sapte, 1 Fleet Pl, London EC4M 7WS, England

AIZAWA, SHIRO, English and comparative literature educator; b. Kitakami, Japan, Apr. 24, 1931; s. Takeji and Kimi (Ozawa) A.; m. Etuko Oikawa, Nov. 22, 1957; children: Hujiko, Takeshi. BA, Aoyamagakuin U., Tokyo, 1955, MA in Lit., 1957. Lectr. English and comparative lit. Tokai U., Tokyo, 1963-65, asst. prof., 1966-74, prof., 1975—; standing dir. Mus. Contemporary Japanese Poetry, Kitakami, Japan, 1990—; dir. Modern Japanese Poetry Studies Internat. Network, Tokyo, 1992—. Author: (lit. criticism) Roses and Illusionary Fields, 1974, (cultural criticism) Culture on the Back, 1976, (poetry anthologies in Tohoku dialect) Akuro-oh, 1977, One-eyed Gods, 1990, Songs of the North-Eastern Folk, 1998, (plays) Two Old Men, 1986, Home-Coming, 1992. Recipient Y. Maruyama Modern Poetry prize. Mem. Assn. Modern Japanese Poets. Avocations: camera, sports, listening to folk music. Home: 275-5 Kamituruma, 228 Sagamihara Japan Office: Tokai U, 1117 Kitakaname, 259-12 Tokyo Japan

AIZAWA, YOSHINORI OR HISASHI, retired law educator; b. Matsushima-cho, Miyagi, Japan, June 25, 1915; s. Suekichi and Haruno (Kayaba) A.; m. Yoshiko Masumoto, July 16, 1937; m. Koko Takeuchi, June 21, 1945 (dec. Dec. 1993). LLB, Tokyo (Japan) U., 1941; LLD, Tohoku (Japan) U., 1962. Asst. prof. Fukushima (Japan) Nat. U., 1953-57; asst. prof. Sophia U., Tokyo, 1958-63, prof., 1964-86, prof. emeritus, 1986—, chief postgrad. law sch., 1975-76, dean law dept., 1977-78; guest prof. Cologne (Germany) U., 1964-65; vis. prof. Ateneo de Manila U., 1980, De LaSalle U., 1985-86; lectr. Bonn. U., 1988, Nat. Saitama U., 1988—; mem. The Coun. Religious Corp. of Japanese Govt., 1972-82; mem. rep. conf. Cause of Separation of Religion and Politics, 1984-94. Author: Religion and Politics in the Present State, 1966, A Critical Study of Current Theories on the Japanese, 1976, State and Religious Organizations, 1977, Gypies, An Introduction, 1980, Jurisprudence and Political Science, An Interdisciplinary Study, 1986, Viewpoints of the Japanese People, 1987, Gypsies, Sufferers and Wanderers, 1989, Roma, Viewed in Anthropology, 1996, Experience of a Too Straightforward Man in Wartime, 1998, also 55 treaties, 7 transls., and 6 collaborations. Mem. rescue operation of the atom bomb victims. Sgt. Japanese Infantry, 1942-43. Recipient spl. prize of the jury in reciting contest for Goethe poems, Tokyo, 1987, 3d Order of Merit, 1988. Mem. Peace-loving Christian Soc., Religious Law Rsch. Assn. (bd. dirs. 1980-96). Avocations: reciting poems, hiking. Home: Inogashira 4-26-5, Mitaka Tokyo 181-0001, Japan

AIZENBERG, ALEXANDER, family practice physician; b. Lvov, Ukraine, May 22, 1959; arrived in Israel, 1990; s. Simcha and Svetlana (Shtarcman) A.; m. Natalie Pleshkevich, June 10, 1983; children: Illya, Sharon, Avital. MD, Med. Faculty, Krasnoyarsk, Russia, 1981. Intern, resident High Med. Sch., Krasnoyarsk, 1981-84, rsch. worker, 1985-87; otolaryngologist Univ. Hosp., Krasnoyarsk, 1984-85; otolaryngologist dept. otolaryngology, face and jaw surgery Dept. Neurosurgery, Krasnoyarsk, 1987-90; intern Dept. Family Medicine, Beersheva, Israel, 1992-97; family practitioner, Beersheva, 1997-98; head Primary Care Clinics, Ashqelon, Israel, 1998—; instr., preceptor Ben-Gurion U. of the Negev, Beersheva, 1997—. Author: Laser Techniques and Optoelectronics, 1984; contbr. articles to profl. jours.; inventor in field. Capt. Israeli Def. Force, 1993—. Mem. AAAS, Israeli Family Practitioners Assn., N.Y. Acad. Scis. Avocation: practical shooting. Home and Office: Irus Ha-Negev 115, 84851 Beer Sheva Israel

AIZENBERG, GUSTAVO ELIAS, electronics research specialist; b. Montevideo, Uruguay, July 27, 1959; arrived in Israel, 1986; s. Jacobo and Teresa (Blank) A.; m. Edna Shaked, Feb. 9, 1989; children: Karen, Yair, Shahar. MSc in Telecom., U. Buenos Aires, 1984; MSc in Semiconductors, Ben Gurion U., Beer Sheva, Israel, 1990; PhD in Semiconductors, Rand Afrikaans U., Auckland Park, S. Africa, 1993. Cert. elec. engr.; cert. computer engr. Devel. engr. Entel Telecom, Buenos Aires, 1983-84; electronics engr. SICOM, Buenos Aires, 1984-86; rsch. asst. Ben Gurion U., Beer Sheva, 1986-90; rschr. Rand Afrikaans U., Auckland Park, 1991-93; rsch. officer Scholand Rsch. Ctr. for Nuc. Scis., Johannesburg, 1993; scientist Applied Materials, Rehovot, Israel, 1994-2000; electronics R&D mgr. Applied Materials, Rehovot, 2000—; ad-honorem asst. U. Buenos Aires, 1983-85. Contbr. articles to profl. jours. Recipient Young Scientist award European Materials Rsch. Soc., Strasbourg, France, 1992, Sec. of Comms. award IEEE Argentina, Buenos Aires, 1984. Mem. IEEE (sr.), Israeli Register of Engrs. and Archs., Argentine Ctr. of Engrs. Jewish. Avocations: philately, numismatics, fishing, riding bicycles. Home: 33/1 Meir Herman St, 74014 Ness Ziona Israel

AIZPURU, JUANA DE, art gallery director; b. Valladolid, Spain, Aug. 22, 1933; d. Teodosio Domínguez and Concha Manso; d. Juan Aizpuru, June 19, 1958 (dec. 1997); children: Margarita, Cristina, Concha. Degree in History and Philosophy, Complutense U., Madrid, 1957. Dir. Juana de Aizpuru Gallery, Seville, Spain, 1970—, Madrid, 1983—; founder, dir. Internat. Art Fair ARCO, Madrid, 1980-87. Pres. Soc. for the Prevention of Cruelty to Animals and Plants, Sevilla, 1974-84; subscriber Green Peace, Madrid, 1976. Recipient Fine Arts medal Ministry Culture, Cairo, 1978, Fine Arts Dedalo prize Diario 16, 1980, Fine Arts Gold medal Junta de Andalucía, 1995, Fine Arts Gold medal Spanish Govt., 1998. Mem. Spanish Assn. Contemporary Art Galleries (pres. 1991-99). Office: Juana de Aizpuru Gallery, C/ Barquillo 44 1o, 28004 Madrid Spain

AIZYATULOV, RUSHAN FATICHOVICH, physician, educator; b. Donetsk, Ukraine, USSR, Sept. 14, 1951; s. Fatich Hasenovich and Zyagrya Naginovna (Takhtashova) A.; m. Elmira Maxutovna Mavletdinova, Aug. 4, 1984; children: Rinat, Dinara. Grad., Med. Inst., Donetsk, 1974, MD, 1990. Med. diplomate. Asst. Donetsk Med. Inst., 1978-90; sr. lectr. Donetsk Med. Inst., Ukraine, 1990-92, prof. Author: Syphilis, 1998, Sexual Transmitted Diseases, 1999; contbr. articles to profl. jours. Maj. Soviet Army, 1975-77. Mem. Ukrainian Soc. Dermatologists and Venerologists, Charkov Sci. Rsch. Inst. Dermatology (mem. specialized coun.), N.Y. Acad. Scis. Fax: 8-062-337-76-76. Home: 3/41 Mira Ave, 83050 Donetsk Ukraine Office: Donetsk Med U, 16 Illyacho Ave, 83003 Donetsk Ukraine

AJAI-IKHILE, DADA FREDERICK EHI, advertising and communications company executive; b. Lagos, Nigeria; s. Jonathan Ajai and Ebun Ikeke (Obarein) I.; m. Elsie Iruo-Oghene Okposo, Dec. 19, 1998; 1 child, Olohireme Oghene Fego. BA in Theatre Arts, U. Benin, Benin City, Nigeria, 1987. Advt. exec. Top News Mag., Lagos, 1988-89, Quality Mag., Lagos, 1989-90; sr. media exec. SOLU Ltd., Lagos, 1990-92; group head media Prima Garnet, Lagos, 1992-98; head media, dir. USP Comm. Ltd., Lagos, 1998—. Lead role Eshu and the Vagabond Minstrels, 1986, Merchant of Venus, 1988; dir. Tales By Shakespeare, 1989. Mem. APCON (assoc.), NIMARK, NIPR. Pentecostal. Avocations: broadcasting, counseling, dancing, reading, travel. Home: Ire Akari Estate, 7 Bayo Olumide St, Lagos Nigeria Office: USP Comm Ltd, Ikeja, 73A Opebi Rd Box 15088, Lagos Nigeria

AJAREM, JAMANN SAID, zoologist; b. Maleha, Saudi Arabia, Oct. 25, 1950; s. Dais and Haleema (Al-Khalofa) A. BS, Coll. Sci., Riyadh, Saudi Arabia, 1975; MPhil, Nottingham U., England, 1982; PhD, U. Wales, 1985. Teaching asst. King Saud U., Riyadh, Saudi Arabia, 1975-77, asst. prof., 1985-92, assoc. prof., 1992—. Co-author: Cross-Disciplinary Studies on Aggression, 1986. Postdoctoral fellow British Coun., 1990. Mem. Saudi Birds Banding Com., Internat. Coun. Bird Conservation (Saudi nat. sect. 1991—). Avocations: reading, swimming, travel, football. Office: King Saud U Coll Scis, Dept Zoology PO Box 2455, Riyadh 11451, Saudi Arabia

AJDANLIJSKY, GEORGE KRASTEV, stratigraphy educator; b. Varna, Bulgaria, Dec. 4, 1964; s. Krasto Georgiev and Jordanka Petrova Ajdanlijska. MSc in Geology, U. Mining and Geology, Sofia, Bulgaria, 1989. Rsch. fellow Bulgarian Acad. Sci.-Geol. Inst., Sofia, 1989-90; asst. prof. U. Mining and Geology, Sofia, 1990-93, sr. asst. prof., 1993—; vis. expert internat. geology expedition, Cen.-East Sudan, 1996. Contbr. papers to profl. jours. Recipient Gustavus E. Archie Internat. grant-in-aid, 1997. Mem. Am. Assn. Petroleum Geologists, Soc. Econ. Paleontologists and Mineralogists (Soc. Sedimentary Geology), European Assn. Petroleum Geologists. Avocations: mineralogy-lapidary, jewelry, dogs.

AJELLO, EDITH H., state legislator; b. Apr. 26, 1944; d. Kenneth Aaron and Rozella Christina (Ewoldt) Hanover; children: Linell, Aaron. BA, Bucknell U., 1966. Store mgr. V George Rustigian Rugs, Inc., 1981-93, 94—; interim exec. dir. Providence Schs., 1993; mem. R.I. Ho. of Reps., 1993—; with V. George Rustigian Rugs, 1994—. Democrat. Home and Office: 29 Benefit St Providence RI 02904-2743

AJIT, CHANNAGIRI, computer scientist; b. Bangalore, India, Sept. 15, 1950; m. Sharada Rao, Sept. 19, 1977; children: Tejaswi, Samartha. BSc, U. Mysore, 1969; B in Engring., Indian Inst. Sci., Bangalore, 1972; M in Tech., Indian Inst. Tech., Bombay, 1974. From att. exec. engr. to chief engr. ITI Ltd., Bangalore, 1974-99; addittional dir. Electronics R&D Ctr. of India, Calcutta, 1999—. Mem. Computer Soc. India. Avocations: listening to music, reading the classics. Home: 100 42d Cross Jayanagar, 560082 Bangalore India Office: ITI Ltd, Electronics R&D Ctr India, 000 000 Calcutta 700 091, India

AJIWO, ENOCH OLUFEMI, laboratory technology educator; b. Epinmi, Ondo, Nigeria, Mar. 3, 1946; s. Emmanuel Alabi and Janet Oyinlola (Arewa) A.; m. Stella Olusola Bamimeke, Jan. 7, 1971; children: Ololade Cordelia, Abayomi Osagbelimi, Abolade Osavolomi. Higher diploma, Yaba (Lagos State) Coll. Tech., 1974; specialist diploma, Nigeria Inst. Tech., Ibadan, Oyo State, 1984. Assoc. mem. Nigerian Inst. Sci. Tech., Ibadan, 1975-83, mem., 1984—; chmn. Ilaro br. Nigerian Inst. Sci. Tech., Ogun State, 1986—; mem. exam. bd. Nigerian Inst. Sci. Tech., Ibadan, 1982-86, mem. rsch. and refresher course, 1982-86. Author: Safety in Laboratories and Workshops, 1992, Laboratory Hazards, 1992. Mem. Am. Chem. Soc., N.Y. Acad. Sci. Achievements include beverage development from Blighia Sapida. Home: 25 Old Lagos Rd, Badagry Lagos, Nigeria Office: Fed Polytechnic, Oja Odan Rd, Ilaro Ogun, Nigeria

AJMERA, AROON, financial company executive, management consultant; b. Morvi, Saurashtra, India, Aug. 18, 1938; s. Shantilal and Ramalaxmi (Parekh) A.; m. Sumi Shah, Dec. 3, 1962; children: Radhika Hookway, Sarupa Lane. B.Com., Podar Coll. Commerce/Econs., Bombay, India, 1959; MBA, NYU, 1961. Field rep. The coca-Cola Export Corp., New Delhi, India, 1961-64; owner property bus. Bombay, 1965-67; mng. ptnr. Clean-A-Car Svcs., London, 1968-74; mgmt. cons. Meghraj Group Ltd., London, 1974-98, Meghraj Bank Ltd., London, 1998—; Feng Shui cons. Feng Shui Designs, London, 1998—; Feng shui tchr., London, 1999—. Author: Feng Shui & Your Home, 2000. Mem. Fin. Intermediaries, Mgrs. and Brokers Regulatory Assn., Inst. Pers. Devel., Feng Shui Soc. U.K. (exec. com.). Avocations: interior design, photography, music, reading, art collecting. Office: Feng Shui Designs Sarika, 57 Armitage Rd, London NW11 8QT, England

AJURIA, SERGIO, chemical engineer, researcher; b. Mexico City, Oct. 23, 1936; s. Luis Mario and Isabel (Garza) A.; m. Maria Arcelia Guerra, Aug. 7, 1963; children: Sergio Arturo, Alejandra Arcelia. Grad. in Chem. Engring., Nat. U. Mex., 1962; MS in Chemistry, U. Calif., Berkeley, 1965. Chemist Nat. Commn. Nuclear Energy, Mexico City, 1962-63; rsch. engr. Anaconda Co., Tucson, 1965-72; head dept. extractive metallurgy Nat. Inst. Nuclear Rsch., Mexico City, 1972-81; head nuclear fuel cycle area Nat. Commn. Nuclear Safety and Safeguards, Mexico City, 1981-83; metall. engr. Internat. Atomic Energy Agy., Vienna, Austria, 1983-89; head dept. radioactive waste Nat. Inst. Nuclear Rsch., Mexico City, 1989-94; sci. attaché Permanent Mission of Mex. to Internat. Atomic Energy Agy., 1994-97; dep. dir. for internat. orgns. Secretaría de Energía, Mexico City, 1998—; cons. Uranio Mexicano, Mexico City, 1981-82. Co-author, editor: Manual on Laboratory Testing for Uranium Ore Processing, 1990; co-author, co-editor Analytical Techniques in Uranium Exploration and Ore Processing, 1992; co-author: Uranium Extraction Technology, 1993, 12 other books; contbr. articles to profl. jours. Grantee Consejo Nacional Ciencia Technologia, Mexico City, 1972, 92-93, Internat. AEA, Mexico City, 1977, Vienna, 1982. Fellow Mex. Acad. Engring.; mem. Am. Chem. Soc., Mex. Soc. Radiation Protection. Presbyterian. Avocations: aviation, travel, opera, classical music. Office: Sec Energy Dir Gen Asuntos Internat, Insurgentes Sur 890 12th Fl, 03100 Mexico City Mexico

AK, COSKUN, foreign language educator; b. Erzurum, Turkey, May 22, 1947; s. Hakki and Safiye A.; m. Maide Kunduzcu, Feb. 16, 1974; children: Bugra, Burcin. PhD, Ataturk U., Erzurum, Turkey, 1977; Asst. Prof., Uludag Univ., Balikesir, Turkey, 1989. Tchr. Urfa H.S., Turkey, 1969-72, Karacabey H.S., Bursa, Turkey, 1972-73; asst. to a prof. Ataturk U., Erzurum, 1973-83; staff mem. Uludag U., Balikesir, Turkey, 1983-89, 1990—; dean of faculty, Faculty of Theology, Bursa, 1990-93, vice-dean Uludag U., 1984-87. Author: (books) Muhibbi Divani, 1987, Muhibbi Farsca Divan, 1995, Bagdatli Ruhi, 1989, Nedim, 1989. Avocations: reading, watching movies, theatre, football. Office: Uludag Univ Fen-Edebiyat, Fak Turk Dili Ve Edebiyati, AOS Kampusu/Bursa 16120, Turkey

AKAGBOSU, FIDELIS THOMAS, infertility consultant, gynecologist/obstetrician; b. Benin-City, Nigeria, Apr. 24, 1955. BS with honors, U. Ife, Nigeria, 1976, MB, BChir, 1979; M in Med. Sci., U. Nottingham, U.K., 1994. Diplomate U. Ife. Gen. practice med. officer Eko Hosp., Lagos, Nigeria, 1981-84; resident in ob/gyn. U. Benin Tchg. Hosp., Benin-City, Nigeria, 1984-87, sr. registrar, 1987-89; sr. house officer ob/gyn. Gravesend (U.K.) Hosp., 1989-90; registrar ob/gyn. North Middlesex Hosp., London, 1990-93; rsch. fellow assisted conception unit Fazakerley Hosp., Liverpool, U.K., 1994-95; infertility cons. Bourn (U.K.) Hall Clinic and Ares Serono Internat., 1995—. Co-author: (chpt.) Handbook of Intrauterine Insemination, 1997; contbr. articles to profl. jours. Fellow West African Coll. Surgeons; mem. Royal Coll. Obstetricians and Gynecologists, Faculty Family Planning and Reproductive Health Care, Brit. Med. Assn., Brit. Fertility Soc., European Soc. for Human Reproduction and Embryology, Am. Soc. Reproductive Medicine, European Assn. Gynecologists and Obstetricians, ALPHA-Scientists in Reproductive Medicine. Avocations: travel, photography. Office: Bourn Hall Clinic, High St, CB3 7TR Bourn United Kingdom

AKAHOSHI, KAZUYA, gastroenterologist; b. Kitakyushu, Japan, Aug. 15, 1960; s. Genya and Takako (Totoki) A.; m. Akiko Haraguchi, Nov. 28, 1987; children: Kazuaki, Haruna, Hikaru. MD, Kagoshima U., 1986; PhD, Kyushu U., 1993. From resident to rschr. Kyushu Univ. Hosp., Fukuoka, Japan, 1986-91; physician Nat. Nakatsu Hosp., Japan, 1991-93, Fukuoka Prefectual Kaho Hosp., 1993-94; asst. prof. Kyushu U., 1994-97; head gastroenterology Aso Iizuka Hosp., Japan, 1997—. Fellow Japanese Soc. Gastroenterology, Japan Gastroenterol. Endoscopy Soc. Avocations: climbing, model trains. Fax: 81-948-8747. Office: Aso Iizuka Hosp, 3-83 Yoshio-cho, 820 Iizuka Fukuoka, Japan

AKAIKE, MASAMI, communications technology educator; b. Kamakura, Japan, Oct. 15, 1940; s. Saburo and Suiko Akaike; m. Aya Murata, Nov. 16, 1971; 1 child, Makoto. B of Engring., U. Tokyo, 1964, M of Engring., 1966, D of Engring., 1969, PhD of Engring (hon.). Rsch. engr. Nippon Telegraph and Telephone Co., Tokyo, 1969-72, sr. rsch. engr., 1972-81, sect. head, 1983-89; dept. head ATR Optical and Radio Comms. Rsch. Labs., Kyoto, Japan, 1989-92; prof. Sci. U. of Tokyo, 1992—; vice-chmn. URSI Japanese Commn., Tokyo, 1996—. Author: Introduction to Microwave and Optical Wave Engineering, 1989; contbr. articles to profl. jours. Fellow IEEE MTT Soc. (Tokyo chpt. vice-chmn. 1986-90, chmn. 1993-95, assoc. editor Transactions on IEEE MTT, 1984-91), Inst. Electronics, Info. and Comms. Engrs. (Yonezawa Meml. prize 1972). Avocations: playing tennis, swimming, growing plants. E-mail: akaike@ee.kagu.sut.ac.jp. Home: 1-36-15 Kaminomiya, Tsurumi-ku, Yokohama 230-0075, Japan Office: Sci Univ of Tokyo, 1-3 Kagurazaka Shinjuku-ku, Tokyo 162-8601, Japan

AKAL-STRADER, AYCA, chemistry and biochemistry educator; b. Ankara, Turkey, Feb. 10, 1970; came to U.S., 1994; d. Mehmet Rifat Akal and Latife Hafize Kocoglu; m. Michael Brad Strader, May 16, 1997. BSc in Chemistry, Middle East Tech. U., Ankara, 1993; MSc in Biochemistry, U. Tenn., 1997. Tour guide Dolmabahce Palace, Istanbul, Turkey, 1989; rschr. in product devel. Procter & Gamble, Istanbul, 1993; rsch. asst., grad. rsch. fellow Fulbright/Internat. Inst. Edn., Knoxville, Tenn., 1994-97; tchg. asst. U. Tenn., Knoxville, 1998—. Avocations: classical music, piano, drums, scientific reading. E-mail: ayca akal@hotmail.com and astrader@utk.edu. Fax: 865-974-6306. Home: 521 Balsam Dr Knoxville TN 37918-3004 Office: U Tenn Dept BCMB Walters Life Scis Bldg # E308 Knoxville TN 37996-0001

AKAM, MICHAEL EDWIN, biologist; b. Bromley, Kent, U.K., June 19, 1952; s. William Edwin and Evelyn Warriner (Thorne) A.; m. Margaret Madeleine Bray, Apr. 1979; children: Thomas, Simon. BA, Cambridge U., 1974; PhD, Oxford U., 1978. Coll. lectr. Magdalen Coll., Oxford, 1978; MRC postdoctoral fellow MRC Lab. Molecular Biology, Cambridge, 1978-79; rsch. fellow Kings Coll., Cambridge, 1978-86; Runyan/Winchell cancer fellow dept. biochemistry Stanford (Calif.) U., 1979-81; Med. Rsch. Coun. sr. fellow dept. genetics Cambridge U., 1982-89; Wellcome prin. fellow Wellcome/CRC Inst., Cambridge, 1990-97, rsch. prof. developmental genetics, 1997; prof. zoology, dir. U. Mus. Zoology, Cambridge, 1997—. Mem. editl. bd. Biology, Evolution and Development, others; editor: The Evolution of Developmental Mechanisms, 1994; contbr. articles to profl. jours. Sci. scholar Royal Inst., 1970; scholar Kings Coll., Cambridge, 1971-74. Fellow Royal Entomol. Soc., Linnean Soc., Royal Soc.; mem. Genetical Soc. Gt. Brit., Brit. Soc. Devel. Biology (chmn. 1989-94), European Molecular Biology Orgn. Achievements include analysis of Homeotic genes of Drosophila; development of in situ hybridization techniques. Office: U Mus Zoology, Downing St, Cambridge CB2 3EJ, England

AKANDE, JOHN ADEBAYO, environmental company executive, educator, researcher, consultant; b. Abeokuta, Ogun, Nigeria, Nov. 24, 1953; s. Joseph Oluwole and Felicia Folorunso (Ajibola) A.; m. Folake Yetunde Opo-Osun, Dec. 17, 1983; children: Olaide, Rotimi. BS, U. Ibadan, Nigeria, 1978; MS, SUNY, Syracuse, 1982, PhD, 1988; diploma, Nat. Inst. Rural Devel., India, 1992. Rsch. asst. prof. W.Va. U., Morganton, 1989-90; asst. chief forest officer Forestry Mgmt. and Environ. Coordinating Unit, Ibadan, Nigeria, 1991-93; sr. lectr. U. Agr., Abeokuta, Nigeria, 1994-96; vis. scientist Forestry and Forest Products Rsch. Inst., Tsukuba, Japan, 1996-97; leader environ. study group Ctr. Tech. Policy, Lagos, Nigeria, 1997-98; chmn., CEO Ctr. Resource and Environ. Mgmt., Ibadan, 1998—; mktg. and utilization expert Formecu, Ibadan, 1991-93; cons. Fed. Coll. Edn., Osiele, Abeokuta, Nigeria, 1994, Geomatics Nigeria Ltd., Ibadan, 1995; external examiner PhD thesis def. U. Ibadan, 1995. Contbr. articles to profl. jours. Mem. Operation Feed the Nation team, Abeokuta, 1975-76, Nat. Youth Svc. Corps, Kaduna, Nigeria, 1978-79, Social Dem. Party, Ibadan, 1993; assoc. Coolidge Ctr. Environ. Leadership, Boston, 1987. Recipient grant U.S. Dept. Agr., 1989, 90, Rsch. grant U. Agr., Abeokuta, 1994, fellowship Sci. and Tech. Agy., Japan, 1996. Fellow Kegites Club U. Ibadan; mem. Forestry Assn. Nigeria (editl. bd. Jour. Forestry 1992-95), N.Y. Acad. Scis. Baptist. Avocations: hiking, bicycling, volleyball, landscaping, movies. Home: No 3 Oluga St New Bodija, Ibadan Oyo Nigeria Office: U Ibadan Ctr Resource Envir, PO Box 21715, Ibadan Oyo Nigeria

AKANE, ATSUSHI, medical educator; b. Matsue, Shimane, Japan, Feb. 20, 1960; s. Hiroshi and Kazuko Akane; m. Reiko Ashizawa, Oct. 12, 1991; 1 child, Yuki. MD, Shimane Med. U., Izumo, Japan, 1984, PhD, 1988. Med. diplomate. Instr. dept. legal medicine Shimane Med. U., Izumo, 1988-93; lectr. dept. legal medicine Kansai Med. U., Moriguchi, Osaka, Japan, 1993, prof., 1993—. Fellow The Medico-Legal Soc. Japan; mem. AAAS, N.Y. Acad. Sci., Molecular Biology Soc. Japan, Japan Soc. Human Genetics. Home: Ikeda-Shin-machi 12-1-207, Osaka Neyagawa 572-0038, Japan Office: Kansai Med U Dept Legal Med, Fumizono-cho 10-15, Osaka Moriguchi 570-8506, Japan

AKANJI, OMOLARA OLOLADE, banker, researcher; b. Lagos, Nigeria, Dec. 5, 1948; d. Daniel Adesanya and Betarice (Oyebowale) Banjoko; m. Michael Olusola Akanji, Dec. 14, 1974; children: Oto-Ola, Olusegun, Olufemi. BSc, U. Ibadan, Nigeria, 1973; MSc, U. Reading, Eng., 1977; cert. in computing, U. Canterbury, Eng., 1986; cert. in mgmt., U. Sheffield, Eng., 1993. Dep. dir. Ctrl. Bank of Nigeria, 1978—; rsch. asst. U. Ibadan, 1973-74, U. Reading, 1976. Contbr. articles to profl. jours. including Econ. and Fin. Rev. Mem. exec. com. African Farm Mgmt., Nairobi, 1996. Mem. Internat. Statis. Soc. Roman Catholic. Avocations: reading, writing. Home: Plot 5B LSDPC Estate, Isolo Lagos Nigeria Office: Ctrl Bank of Nigeria, Garki Abuja PMB 0187, Abuja Nigeria

AKASE, MASAKO, humanities educator; b. Tokyo, Nov. 25, 1933; d. Tashiro and Haru (Mori) A. BA, Waseda U., 1957, MA, 1959; diploma of phonetics, Paris U., 1962. Lectr. Momoyama Gakuin U., Osaka, Japan, 1968-70, assoc. prof., 1970-74, prof., 1974—, prof. grad. course, 1993—. Author: Kafu Nagai and French Literature, 1976, Development of Comparative Studies, 1983, Kafu Nagai-Comparative Study, 1986, Comparative Literature Comparative Culture, 1995, Kafu Nagai and French Culture, 1998; author, editor: Kafu Nagai-Bibliographical Study, 1990. Recipient Mozume Sakuin prize, 1990. Mem. Japanese Comparative Lit. Assn. (trustee), France-Japanese Hist. Studies Assn. (trustee), Pen Club, French Lang. and Lit. Assn., Japanese MLA. Avocations: ballroom dance, Latin dance, yoga, kiko. Home: 50-1-307 Kamikatsura, Maedacho Nishikyoku, Kyoto 6158223, Japan Office: Momoyama Gakuin U, 1-1 Manabino Izumishi, Osaka 5941198, Japan

AKASHAH, SAEDELDEEN AHMAD, executive; b. Nablus, Palestine, June 1947; arrived in Kuwait, 1951; s. Ahmad Mohamed and Munefa Hafz (Sharabi) A.; m. Sohal Yousef Al-Fulaij; children: Mey, Omar, Ali, Fatema. BSCE, Fri State U., Angola, 1972; MSCE, Okla. State U., 1978, PhD, 1980. Indsl. planner Min. of Industry, Kuwait, 1972-75; asst. prof. U. Kuwait, 1980-83; dept. mgr. Kuwait Inst. Sci. Rsch., 1983-84, divsn. dir., 1984-88, sr. rsch. scientist, 1988-93; sr. transp. PAAC, Kuwait, 1993-95; sr. engring. cons. Arab Fund, Kuwait, 1995-97; chmn., CEO Kuwait Catalyst Co., 1997—; spkr. & cons. in field. Catalyst in Petroleum Refining, 1990; patentee in field. UN fellow, 1973, 74. Mem. Kuwair Soc. Engring., Kuwait Red Crescent Soc., Oxford Energy Policy Club, Omega Chi Epsilon, Tau Beta Pi, Omicron Delta Kappa, Phi Kappa Psi. Kuwait Democrat. Collation. Moslem. Avocations: reading, writing poetry, tennis, swimming. Office: Kuwait Catalyst Co, PO Box 12305, 71654 Shamieh Kuwait

AKASHI, HIDEAKI, research scientist; b. Shichinohe-Machi, Aomori, Japan, Nov. 20, 1951; s. Hidetoshi and Miyo (Sasaki) A.; m. Masako Ota, Oct. 14, 1982; 2 children. BS, Iwate U., Morioka-Shi, Japan, 1974, MS, 1976. Cert. tchr. From asst. to rschr. Multidisciplinary Rsch. Coun. Japan, Tokyo, 1976-94, exec. dir., 1988—; guest rschr. Met. Areas Rsch. Devel. Assn., Tokyo, 1997—. Author: An Introduction to Interdisciplinary Research, 1997; contbr. articles to profl. jours. Fellow Japanese Assn. Rsch. on Care and Welfare, Japan Info.-Culture Soc. Avocations: horses, fishing. Fax: 81-3-5687-6052. Office: Multidisciplinary Rsch Coun, Iwamoto-Cho 2-14-3 Miki Bld, Tokyo Chiyoda-ku 101-0032, Japan

AKAYEV, ASKAR, Kyrgyz government official; b. Nov. 10, 1944; s. Akai Tokoyev and Aselj Tokoyeva; m. Mairam Akayeva, 1970; children: Bermet, Aydar, Saadat, LLim. Prof. Frunze Politech. Inst., 1972-73, chair, 1976-86; prof. Inst. Precise Mechanics and Optics, 1973-76; head dept. sci. and edn. Kyrgyz Ctrl. Com., 1987-89; pres. Kyrsyzstan Govt. Offices, Frunze, 1990, 91—; lectr. Leningrag Inst., Frunze Polytech. Inst. Recipient Unity Internat. Found. award, 1995; named Hon. Akademician Internat. Engring. Acad, 1996, named Hon. Akademician Internat. Acad. Creation., 1996. Fellow N.Y. Acad. Scis.; mem. Kyrgyzstan Acad. Scis. (v.p. 1987-89, pres. 1989-90), Internat. Acad. Edn. Industry Scis. and Arts (hon.). Office: Office of Pres, Government House, 720003 Bishkek Kyrgyzstan*

AKAZAWA, KOHEI, statistician; b. Morioka, Iwate, Japan, Sept. 17, 1959; s. Shingo and Yoko (Baba) A.; m. Emiko Okubo, Apr. 29, 1987; children: Fumiaki, Sayumi. PhD in Biostats., Kyushu U., Fukuoka, 1993; PhD in Statistics, Kyushu U., 1999. Asst. prof. Kyushu U., 1985-94, assoc. prof., 1994-99; prof. Niigata U., 1999—. Avocations: fishing, badminton. Office: 1-754 Asahimachi-Lori, Niigata 951-8520, Japan

AKBAR, SHER, education educator; b. Zhob, Pakistan, Nov. 12, 1950; s. Said Afzal and Roshan Jan; m. Zahida Akbar, Nov. 25, 1974; children: Rafia, Shazia, Zahid, Jahan Zeb, Khan Zeb, Noor, Saddiq, Farooq. BSc, Govt. Degree Coll., Quetta, Pakistan, 1970; MSc, Govt. Coll., Lahore, Pakistan, 1972; PhD, U. Bradford, Eng., 1980. Sci. tchr. Govt. H.S., Sanjavi, Pakistan, 1973-74; lectr. Govt. Coll., Zhob, Pakistan, 1974-75; from lectr. to assoc. prof. Balochistan U., Quetta, Pakistan, 1975-94, prof., 1994—. Merit scholar Govt. Pakistan, 1968-72. Mem. Chem. Soc. Pakistan (life), N.Y. Acad. Scis. Home: B-11 Balochistan U Colony, Quetta Pakistan Office: Balochistan Univ, Sariab Rd Dept Chemistry, Quetta Pakistan

AKBAR, SYED ALI, chemical engineer; b. Thatta, Sindh, Pakistan, Apr. 17, 1971; s. Syed Ali (Najma) Aichtar. B Chem. Engring., Nedvet, Karachi, Pakistan, 1994. Prodn. engr. Anwar Zaib White Cement Ltd., Kotri, Pakistan, 1994, FFC-Jordan Fertilizer Co., Karachi, 1994-95, Engro Asahi Polymer & Chem. Ltd., Karachi, 1998—. Avocation: installation, commissioning and operation of large chemical plants. Home: E-211 Commercial-I, Gulshan-E-Shamin FB Area 08, Karachi Pakistan

AKBARI, SHAHEEN AHMED, financial executive; b. Patna, Bihar, India, Apr. 11, 1973; arrived in United Arab Emirates, 1980; s. Shakil Ahmed Akbari and Najma Shakil Nikhat; m. Ayesha Shaheen Akbari, Feb. 22, 1998. Intermediate of sci. with honors, Emirates English, Dubai, United Arab Emirates, 1993, BS, 1994. Asst. to gen. mgr. Century Fin. Brokers, Dubai, 1994-95, comml. and trading dealer, 1995-96, forex dealer, 1996-98, sr. supr. ops., 1999—; fin. cons. Century Fin. Brokers, Dubai, 1998-99. Artist: (catalog of paintings and drawings) United Arab Emirates— Past & Present, 1995 (Gold medal 1995); designer (model) Missiles of the Future, 1993-94. Local sports developer, Dubai, 1994; organizer-in-charge DCC Cricket Com., Dubai, 1995. Named Artist of United Arab Emirates '94, Ministry of Edn., 1994, Outstanding Personality of Yr. in Sports and Academics, Dubai Schs. Com., 1994. Mem. Dubai Cricket Assn. (organizer 1994-95). Avocations: drawing, painting, cricket, movies, computer games. Home: Al Mankhool St PO Box 9126, Dubai United Arab Emirates Office: Century Fin Brokers, Mankhool St PO Box 9126, Dubai United Arab Emirates

AKCHURIN, RAUF KHAMZINOVICH, material science and engineering educator; b. Aktubinsk, USSR, Feb. 10, 1945; s. Khamza Khasanovich and Ainulkhaiat Izmailovna A.; m. Svetlana Petrovna Zharova, Oct. 22, 1968. BS, Moscow Inst. Elec. Engring., 1977, PhD, 1993. Engr. State Inst. Nonferros Metals, Ust-Kamenogorsk, Kazakhstan, 1967-69, State Inst. Rare Metals, Moscow, 1969-73; rschr. Moscow Inst. Elec. Engring., 1973-78; rschr. Moscow Inst. Fine Chem. Tech., 1978-96, educator, 1996—, head dept. semiconductor materials tech. Author: (with V.B. Ufimstev) Physicochemical Bases of Liquid Phase Epitaxy, 1983, (with others) Physics and Materials Science of Semiconductors with Deep Levels, 1987; contbr. articles to profl. jours. and reviews. Home: Tcherniakhovskogo 5-1-89, 125319 Moscow Russia Office: Moscow State Acad Fine Chem, Tech Vernadskogo av 86, 117571 Moscow Russia

AKEBONO, TARO (CHAD ROWAN), professional sumo wrestler; b. Oahu, Hawaii, May 8, 1969; s. Jan and Randy Rowan; m. Christine Kalina, Oct., 1998; 1 child. Student, Hawaii Pacific Coll. Sumo wrestler, 1988—, named yokozuna, 1993. Winner 10 Makuuchi Divsn. Championships, 4 awards for outstanding performance, 2 Fighting Spirit prizes. Office: care Japan Sumo Assn, 1-3-28 Yokozuna Sumidaku, Tokyo 130, Japan*

AKEEL, HADI ABU, robotics executive; b. Cairo, Egypt, Apr. 9, 1938; came to U.S., 1961; s. Kobaisi Aly Abu-Akeel and Zeinab Makhlouf; m. Sofia Sarwat; children: Shereef, Nezar. BS in Mech. Engring., Cairo U., 1959; MS in Applied Mechanics, UCLA, 1963; PhD in Mech. Engring., U. Calif., Berkeley, 1966. Cert. mfg. engr. Acting instr. U. Calif., Berkeley, 1963-66; analytical specialist Bendix Corp., South Bend, Ind., 1966-69; assoc. prof. Ain Shams U., Cairo, 1969-74; sr. staff engr. GM Mfg., Warren, Mich., 1974-76; program mgr. GM Corp., Warren, 1976-78; dept. head mfg. staff GM, Warren, 1978-80, chief engr. flexible automation systems, 1980-82; v.p., chief engr. GMFanuc Robotics Corp., Auburn Hills, Mich., 1982-92; sr. v.p. Fanuc U.S.A., 1992-96, also bd. dirs., vice chmn., 1992-98; gen. mgr. Berkeley Lab. Fanuc Am. Corp., Union City, Calif., 1992—; sr. v.p. Fanuc Robotics N.A., Inc., 1996-98; tech. advisor FANUC Ltd., Japan, 1992—; advisor Mgmt. of Tech. Program U. Calif., Berkeley, 1988-92; chmn. bd. dirs. Robotics Internat. of SME, Dearborn, Mich., 1992-93;. Author: Machine Design, 1972; contbr. articles to profl. jours.; holds over 55 U.S. and fgn. patents. Soccer coach Am. Youth Soccer Orgn.; mem. bd. advisors Sch. Engring., U. Mich., Dearborn, 1991—; chmn. bd. visitors Sch. Engring., Oakland U., 1991-92. Recipient Joseph F. Engleberger award Robotic Industries Assn., 1989, Mich. Sci. Trailblazer award State Mich., 1989. Fellow ASME, Soc. Mfg. Engrs. (internat. dir.); mem. IEEE, Nat. Acad. Engring. Republican. Muslim. Avocations: tennis, swimming, camping, travel, machine shop. Office: Fanuc Robotics Corp 3900 W Hamlin Rd Rochester Hls MI 48309-3253

AKEL, OLLIE JAMES, oil company executive; b. Harlan, Ky., Aug. 14, 1933; s. William M. and Jameleh (Raffih) A.; m. Mona, June 11, 1966; children: Omar James, Amanda Dalal, Roanna Lyn. BSME, U. Ky., 1954; M in Aero. Engring., Rensselaer Polytech. Inst., 1955; MS in Mgmt., Mass. Inst. Tech., 1967. Thermodynamic engr. North Am. Aviation, Columbus, Ohio, 1958-59; engr. Middle East Airlines, Beirut, Lebanon, 1959-65, Exxon Corp., N.Y., London, Arabia, 1967-80; pres. Exxon Chem. Mideast and Africa, Brussels, 1981-86, Exxon Chem. Belgium, Brussels, 1986-88; dir. corp. comm. Exxon Chem. Internat., Brussels, 1988-89; pres. Exxon Saudi Arabia, Riyadh, 1989-92; pres. Exxon Mexicana, Mex., 1993-96, ret., 1997; pres. AB Assocs.LLC, 1998—. Author: Driving According to Oliver, 1999, Prisoners of Circumstances, 1999. Dir. United Way, Brussels, 1988-89. 2d lt. U.S. Army, 1956-58. Mem. Am. C.C. Mex. (bd. dirs., pres. 1995), Am. Businessmen's Group of Riyadh (steering com. 1979-81, 90-92), Tau Beta Pi, Pi Tau Sigma. Protestant.

AKELIS, VINCAS, book publisher; b. Marijampole, Lithuania, July 9, 1946; s. Vincas and Marija (Brizgyte) A.; m. Birute Raisyte, June 5, 1965; two children. Grad. in engring., Kaunas Poly. Inst., 1976. Sect. chief Hydrometeorol. Svc., Lithuania, 1963-75, Tng. Enterprises Unification, Lithuania, 1976-86, Info. Inst., Lithuania, 1986-91; dir. Lithuanian Writers Union Publs., 1991—. Mem. Lithuanian Publ. Assn. Office: Lithuanian Writers Union, K Sirvydo 6, 2600 Vilnius Lithuania

AKER, SUSAN K., elementary education educator; b. Bklyn., Aug. 4, 1951; d. Mike and Rose Kriegsman; m. David Aker, Sept. 1, 1974; children: Michael, Jessica. BA, CUNY, 1973, MS, 1975; MS, Long Island U., 1976, Long Island U., 1991, Coll. New Rochelle, 1998. Cert. in early childhood edn., elem. edn., spl. edn., libr. sci., sch. adminstrn. and supervision. Tchr. 4th grade Yeshiva of Crown Heights, Bklyn., 1974-75; tchr. 6th grade Hebrew Acad. of Nassau County, Bethpage, N.Y., 1975-76; libr. Jericho (N.Y.) Jewish Ctr., 1978-81, Half-Hollow Hills Pub. Libr., Dix Hills, N.Y., 1978-81; libr. media specialist Uniondale (N.Y.) Free Sch. Dist., 1989-90, Hempstead (N.Y.) Union Free Sch. Dist., 1990-92; tchr. P.S. 105 N.Y.C. Bd. Edn., Bronx, 1993—; adj. prof. Mercy Coll., Yorktown; internal geography cons. N.Y.C. Bd. Edn., 1996—, staff devel. workshop presenter, 1996—. Contbr. articles to TeacherLink. Grantee United Fedn. Tchrs., 1997, N.Y. Geographic Alliance, 1998, 99. Mem. ASCD, N.Y. Geographic Alliance, N.Y. Reading Assn., Phi Delta Kappa. Home: 23 Southern Rd Hartsdale NY 10530-2128

ÅKERBLOM, MALIN JOHANNA BRÄNDÉN, science administrator; b. Växjö, Sweden, Feb. 4, 1940; d. Bengt Valdemar and Inga Cecilia (Cassel) Å.; m. Lars Yngve Terenius, 1964 (div. 1987); children: Olof Yngve, Bengt Petter; m. Carl-Ivar Brändén, Feb. 15, 1992. BSc, Uppsala (Sweden) U., 1962; PhD, Swedish U. Agrl. Scis., 1990, assoc. prof., 1996. Asst. Plant Protection Inst., Sweden, 1964-68; rsch. asst. Swedish U. of Agrl. Scis., Sweden, 1968-76; head pesticide unit Swedish Lab. Agrl. Chemistry, 1976-93, scientist, 1993-95; head unit environ. organic chemistry, dept. environ. assess. SUAS, 1995-97; dir. internat. program in chem. scis., internat. sci. prog. Uppsala U., 1997—. Author: (book) Environmental Monitoring of Pesticide Residues: Guidelines for the SADC Region, 1995; contbr. chpts. to books, articles to profl. jours. Fellow Internat. Union of Pure and Applied Chemistry.

AKERS, JAMES ERIC, medical practice marketing executive; b. Jonesboro, Ark., Oct. 14, 1945; s. Ward Eldridge and Dorothy Catherine (Erb) A.; 1 child, William Eric; m. Marie Oreigr, Aug. 31, 1991. BA in Social Sci., Vanderbilt U., 1968; MDiv in Strategic Planning, Louisville Presbyn. Theol. Sem, 1971. Gen. mgr. TGI Fridays, Nashville, 1972-73, Annie Tigues Restaurant & Bar, Jacksonville, Fla., 1973-77; sales rep. Northwestern Mut. Life Ins. Co., Jacksonville, 1977-79, Peter Gregg Mercedes-Benz, Jacksonville, 1979-80; dir. life flight Bapt. Med. Ctr., Jacksonville, 1980-83, dir. spl. projects, 1983-84; dir. mktg. Jacksonville Faculty Practice Assn., 1984-88, v.p. planning, devel. and mktg., 1988—; v.p. mktg. Profl. Biling Systems Inc. subs. JFPA, 1986—, Fin.-Med. Mgmt. Svcs., 1989—, Physician Bus. Svcs. Inc., 1990; pres. Healthcare Mktg. Cons., Jacksonville, 1990-2000; dir. of ops. Health Screen Am., 2000. Master of ceremonies Children's Miracle Network Telethon, Jacksonville, 1983, 84, 89, Am. Heart Assn., Jacksonville, 1988-90; chief auctioneer Sta. WJCT-TV, PBS, Jacksonville, 1983-98; campaign mgr. Senator Bill Bankhead, Jacksonville, 1984; pres. bd. dirs. Suicide Prevention Svcs., Jacksonville, 1983-89. Col. U.S. Army, 1966-96. Mem. Med. Group Mgmt. Assn., Acad. Practice Assembly, Am. Soc. Hosp. Based Emergency Air Med. Svcs. (bd. dirs.), Am. Coll. Healthcare Mktg., Alliance for Healthcare Strategy and Mktg., Acad. Health Svcs. Mktg., N.G. Officers Assn., Ye Mystic Revellers (team leader), Rotary (sec. Mandarin, Fla. 1983-84, Paul Harris fellow 1990). Republican. Presbyterian. Avocations: mountain climbing, flying, whitewater rafting. Home: 8629 Royalwood Dr Jacksonville FL 32256-8447 Office: Health Sereen Am 4555 Emerson St Ste 200 Jacksonville FL 32207-4958

AKERS, NICOLAS PAUL, electronics engineer, physicist; b. Norwich, Eng., Feb. 26, 1953; s. Leslie William and Jean Elizabeth (Bavington) A.; m. Janet Elizabeth Kiln, Apr. 10, 1982; children: Eleanor Jane, Clare Rebecca, Jennifer Lucy. BSc with honors, U. Liverpool, 1975; MSc, U. Portsmouth, 1976, PhD, 1981. Chartered physicist. Sr. engr. Marconi Space and Def., Frimley, Eng., 1980-82; rsch. fellow U. Portsmouth, Eng., 1982-84; sr. prin. engr. Plessey Avionics, Havant, Eng., 1984-90; prin. engr. Continental Microwave Tech., Luton, Eng., 1990-95; engr. Nera, Ltd., 1995—. Contbr. articles to profl. jours. Trustee Robert Kiln Charitable Trust, Hertford, Eng., 1989—. Mem. IEEE, Inst. of Physics. Anglican. Avocations: amateur archaeology, watercolor painting, tennis, badminton. Office: Nera Ltd Telecomms, 171 Camford Way Sundon Park, Bedfordshire LU3 3AN, England

AKGUN, KEMAL, computer support professional, consultant; b. Adana, Turkey, Apr. 12, 1960; s. Huseyin and Meryem (Colak) A.; m. Binnaz Gultekin, Dec. 9, 1983 (div. 1992). BS, Bosphorus U., 1983. Bottle design engr. Sisecam, Mersin, Turkey, 1983-85, CAD/CAM engr., 1986-93; control engr. Turkish Army, Erzurum, Turkey, 1985-86; computer support svcs. mgr. Sisecam, Istanbul, Turkey, 1993—. Author: Culture Personal Computer, 1992; editor CAD/CAM Mag., 1990—, Sys. & Automation mag., Computer mag. Mem. Computer Soc., IT Mgrs. Club, Bosphorus Univ. Alumni Assn. Avocations: chess, writing, reading, trekking, photography. Office: Sisecam, Barbaros Bulvari 125, 80706 Istanbul Turkey

AKHATOV, ISKANDER SHAUKAT, physicist, educator; b. Bashkortostan, Russia, Aug. 18, 1956; s. Shaukat Nurligayan Akhatov and Rauza Abdulla Saydasheva; m. Gouzel Ramazan Yanbekova, Aug. 10, 1984; 1 child, Adelya. MS, Lomonosov Moscow U., 1979; PhD, Russian Acad. Scis., Moscow, 1983; DSc, Lavrentyev Inst. Hydrodynamics, Novosibirsk, 1991. Cert. physicist. Asst. prof. Bashkir U., Ufa, Russia, 1983-85, assoc. prof., 1985-89, full prof., head of dept., 1991—; v.p. Ufa br. Russian Acad. Scis., 1993-2000; dir. Inst. Mechanics of Ufa Branch of Russian Acad. Scis., 2000—; mem. sci. com. 3d Internat. Conf. on Multiphase Flow, France, 1998. Contbr. papers to profl. jours. Mem. Acoustical Soc. Am. Office: UFA Br Russian Acad Scis, K Marx Str 6, 450000 Ufa Russia

AKHEDJAKOVA, LIYA MEDJIDOVNA, actress; b. Dniepropetrovsk, USSR, June 9, 1938; d. Medjid Salekhovich and Yulia Aleksandrovna Akhedjakova; m. Vladimir Nikolayevich Persyanov. Student, State Inst. Theatre Art. Actress Moscow Theatre of Young Spectator, 1953-71, Sovremennik Theatre, 1971—. Leading roles in plays of Shakespeare, Tenessee Williams; appeared in films Garage, Office Romance, Blessed Heaven, Twenty Days Without War, Lost Bus. Named People's Artist of Russia; recipient State prize, Nice prize, People's Art of Russia prize. Address: Udaltsova Str 12 Apt 153, 117415 Moscow Russia

AKHIEZER, ALEXANDER NAUMOVICH, research scientist; b. Kiev, Ukraine, Mar. 26, 1928; s. Naum Il'ich and Zoya (Lvovna) A.; m. Irina Vladimirovna Ushakova; 1 child, Tatyana. Radio engr., Moscow Energy Engring. Inst., 1949; cand. sci. in physics and math., Ukrainian Phys. and Tech. Inst, 1954. Rsch. scientist Ukrainian Phys. and Tech. Inst., Kharkov, 1949-53, Kharkov State Inst. Measures and Instruments, 1953-54, Kharkov State Inst. Metrology, 1954-89; leading rsch. scientist State Scientific & Indsl. Assn. Metrology, 1989—. Author: Investigations in Quasioptical Beams, 1969; inventor in field; contbr. articles to profl. jours. Office: State Sci and Indsl Assn, 42 Mironositskaya St, 610022 Kharkov Ukraine

AKHIYEZER, ALEXANDR SAMYILOVICH, philosopher, sociologist, anthropologist; b. Moscow, Sept. 22, 1929; s. Samuil Alexandrovich and Esther Vladimrovna (Shmidt) A.; m. Izolda Julievna Fridman, Sept. 21, 1957 (div. Sept. 1984); children: Helen, Olga; m. Susanna Jakovlevna Matveyeva, May 5, 1990. Higher edn., State Econ. Inst., Moscow, 1953; postgrad., Inst. People's Economy, Moscow, 1955, Inst. Mgmt., Moscow, 1962, Inst. High State Planning Com., Moscow, 1964; PhD, Inst. of People's Economy, Moscow, 1967. Cert. economist, philosopher, culturologist; cert. in math. methods in industry, economy planning. Chmn. planning commn. Exec. Com., Zaoksk, 1953-56; editor Cen. Union of Coops., Moscow, 1956-57; technologist Moscow-Light Engring. Co., 1957-60; head of dept. Inst. Agrl. Constrn., Moscow, 1960-62; main engr., head of group Inst. Urban Constrn., Moscow, 1962-69; main rschr. Inst. Comparative Politology Russian Acad. Scis., Moscow, 1969-91, Inst. Problems of Employment RAN, Moscow, 1991-93; sr. rschr. Inst. Rsch. Econ. Forecasting Russian Acad. Scis., Moscow, 1993—. Author: (books) Scientific and Technological Revolution and Some Problems of Production and Management, 1974, Ecological Problems Discussed by the Congress of People's Deputies of the USSR, 1990, Russia: A Critique of Historical Experience, 1991, 2d edit., 1997-98, Socio-cultural Problems of the Development of Russia, 1992, From the Past to the Future, 1994, Opening of the Closed Society, 1997 (2d prize Inst. Open Soc. 1997), (book chpts.) Change of Labor Content and Social Functions of the Working Class under Capitalism, 1974, Ecological Problems of a Capitalist City, 1985, co-author: (books) Recommendations on the Application of Mathematical Methods and Computers in City Building, 1965, Reforms and Controreforms in Russia, Cycles of Modernization Process in Russia, 1996, (book chpt.) Modernization and Conflict of Values in Russia, 1994, Russian State: Sources, Traditions and Perspectives, 1997, Russian Uniqueness as a Research Problem//Russian Studies in History, Vol. 36, No. 1 & 2, 1997; contbr. articles to profl. jours. Grantee Interdisciplinary Acad. Ctr. for Social Scis.-Intercenter, 1993, 94, Humanitarian Russian Sci. Found., 1994-96, Soros Found., 1994, Open Soc. Inst., 1996, John S. and T. MacArthur Found., others. Mem. Russian Philosophic Soc., Russian Sociologic Soc., Russian Acad. Humanitarian Scis., K. Popper Soc., N.Y. Acad. Scis. Office: Rm 1304 Nakhimowsi pr. 47, 117418 Moscow Russia

AKHMETZIANOV, MARAT KHALIKOVICH, mechanical engineer, educator, research scientist; b. Kazan, Tatarstan, Russia, Oct. 13, 1932; s. Khalik and Gainia (Aukhadeeva) A.;m. Galina Petrovna Naidenova, June 21, 1957; children: Andrew, Roxana. M in Engring. Mechanics, Railway Engring. Inst., Novosibirsk, Russia, 1956, PhD, 1963, DSc, 1970. Mgr. Strength Problems Lab. Railway Engring. Inst., Novosibirsk, 1956-65, assoc. prof., 1965-70, prof., 1970—, head theoretical mechanics dept., 1970-83, head engring. mechanics dept., 1983—, v.p. for rsch., 1974-83, head sci. coun., 1975-94; fellow sci. coun. Inst. Theoretical and Applied Mechanics, Russian Acad. Sci., Siberian divsn., 1978—. Co-author: Photomechanics, 1973, Measurement of Static and Dynamic Parameters of Structures and Materials, 1987; contbr. articles to profl. jours. Recipient Badge of Hon. Supreme Soviet of USSR, 1975, State prize Coun. Mins. USSR, 1980, Hon. Scientist award, 1983. Mem. Russian Transport Acad. (academician 1991—). Avocation: fishing. Office: Siberian U Transport, 191 D Kovalchuk St, 630049 Novosibirsk Russia

AKHTAR, JUNAID, engineering researcher; b. Karachi, Sind, Pakistan, Apr. 30, 1969; s. Muhammad Shamsul Haque and Noor Aysha (Khatoon). BS, NED U, Pakistan, 1992; postgrad., Wayne State U., Detroit, 1996-97. Registered profl. engr., Mich. Asst. mgr. R&D NS Industries, Karachi, Pakistan, 1992-94; design engr. Trans Mobile, Karachi, Pakistan, 1994-96; rsch. engr. Ford Motor Co., Dearborn, Mich., 1997—. 4D. Mem. ASME, Pakistan Engring. Coun. Avocations: tourism, meeting people from different cultures. Address: 9953 Pelham Rd Apt 7 Allen Park MI 48101-1265

AKHTAR, MUHAMMAD, education educator; b. Batala, Punjab, India, Feb. 23, 1933; s. Muhammad Azeem Chaudhry; m. Monika E. Schurmann, Aug. 3, 1963; children: Marcus Imran, Daniel Azeem. MS, Punjab U., Pakistan, 1954; PhD, Imperial Coll., London, 1959; DS (hon.), Karachi U. Rsch. scientist Inst. for Med. and Chemistry, Cambridge, Mass., 1959-63; lectr. and sr. lectr. biochemistry Sch. Biochem. and Physiol. Sci., Southampton, 1963-68, reader in biochemistry, 1968-73, prof. biochemistry, 1973-98, prof. emeritus biochemistry, chmn., 1983-87; chmn. Inst. Biomolecular Sci., Southampton, 1989-90; head dept. biochemistry Southampton U., 1978-93; dir. SERC Molecular Recognition Centre, Southampton, 1990-93. Contbr. articles to profl. jours. Recipient MS Gold Medalist, U. Punjab, Pakistan, 1954, Sitara-I-Imtiaz, Govt. of Pakistan, 1981, Flintoff medal Royal Soc. Chemistry, 1993; TWAS medal lectr., 1996; grantee SERC, MRC, Wellcome. Fellow Royal Soc., Third World Acad. Sci. (founding fellow, treas., mem. coun. 1992-98, v.p. 1998—). Office: Dept Biochemistry, U Southampton Bassett Crescent E, S09 3TU Southampton England

AKHTAR, SHAMIM, obstetrician, gynecologist; b. Hyderabad, Deccan, India; s. Syed Zahid and Wazir (Fatima) Hussain; m. Akhter Ahmed, Nov. 28, 1958; children: Yasmeen, Zarina, Mona, Erum. MBBS, Dow Med. Coll., Karachi, Pakistan, 1957; Diploma in Gynecology and Obstetrics, Trinity Coll., Dublin, Ireland, 1961; Lic. for Midwifery, Rotunda Hosp., Dublin, 1961; Diploma in Ob-Gyn., Royal Coll. Ob-Gyn., London, 1962. House surgeon dept. gen. surgery Civil Hosp. Karachi, 1957-58; intern gen. medicine Evang. Deaconess, Cleve., 1959; resident gen. medicine High View Hosp., Cleve., 1959-60; house officer Banbury (Eng.) Hosp., 1961-62; resident med. officer Lady Dufferin Hosp., Karachi, 1962; cons. obstetrician Mohammadi Hosp., Karachi, 1962-64; med. supt. ob/gyn, originator nurse tng. program Akram Khatoon All Pakistan Women's Assn. Hosp., Karachi, 1964-73; owner, med. dir., dir. ob-gyn well woman & neonatal care svc Specialist's Clinic and Zayem Neurol. Clinic, Karachi, 1973—; cons. in field. Mem. Pakistan Soc. Obstetricians and Gynecologists, Pakistan Med. Assn. (life). Avocation: cooking.

AKHTER, JAVED, virologist; b. Karachi, Sindh, Pakistan, Aug. 25, 1958; s. Mohammed Yamin and Ateqa Begum. Higher nat. diploma, Sheffeild Hallam U., S. Yorks, Eng., 1979; BSc in Biol. Scis., Wolverhampton U., W. Midlands, Eng., 1981; PhD, Leicester (Eng.) U., 1995. Lab. scientist J. H. Heinz Co. Ltd., Uxbridge, Eng., 1982; med. lab. sci. officer Chesterfield (Eng.) and N. Derbyshire Royal Hosp., 1982-85; virologist King Faisal Specialist Hosp. and Rsch. Ctr., Riyadh, Saudi Arabia, 1985—. Reviewer Saudi Med. Jour.; contbr. articles to profl. jours. Fellow Inst. Biomed. Scis.; mem. Am. Soc. Clin. Pathologists (specialist 1999), Toastmasters Internat. Avocations: tennis, squash, chess, hiking. Fax: 9661-442-4331. Office: King Faisal Specialist Hosp & Rsch Ctr Dept Pathology & Lab, Dept Pathology PO Box 3354, Riyadh 11211, Saudi Arabia

AKHTYRTSEV, BORIS PAVLOVICH, soil science educator; b. Repievka Voronezh, Russia, Jan. 1, 1929; s. Pavel Jakovlevich and Anna Andreevna (Butyvskaja) A.; m. Nadezhda Ivanovna Skrinnikova; children: Anatolly Borisovich, Elena Borisovna. MSc, U. Voronezh, Russia, 1952, Candidate Biol. Scis., 1955, DSc in Biology, 1968. Asst. U. Voronezh, 1955-56, lectr., 1957-60, sr. lectr., 1961-70, prof., 1971—, head dept., 1976—; chmn. trade union com. Voronezh U., 1974-84, leader soil sci. expedition, 1976-97. Author: Grey Forest Soils, 1979, Meadow-chernozemic Soils of the Central Regions of Russia, 1981; contbr. articles to profl. jours. Decorated medal for varliant labour Presidium of the USSR Supreme Soviet, 1970; recipient Order Sign of Honour, Presidium of the Supreme Soviet of the USSR, Moscow, 1981, decoration for excellent work achievements Ministry Higher Edn. USSR, 1983; named Honoured Scientist of the Russian Fedn., 1999; grantee Russian Acad. Scis., 1994-96, 97—, Ministry of Gen. Edn. of Russian Fedn., 1994-97, 98—, Internat. Sci. Fund, 1993. Mem. Internat. Soc. Soil Scientists, All-Union Soc. Soil Scientists USSR and Russia, Geographical Soc. USSR and Russia. Avocation: family activities. Home: Teatralnaja 19-48, 394000 Voronezh Russia Office: Voronezh State Univ, Universitetskaja Pl 1, 394693 Voronezh Russia

AKHUTINA, TATIANA VASILYEVNA, neuropsychologist; b. Dzerjinsk, Gorky, Russia, Aug. 15, 1941; d. Vasiliy Ivanovich Ryabov and Elena Nikolayevna Gruzintseva; m. Anatoliy Valerianovich Akhutin, Jan. 15, 1972; 1 child, Fedor. Diploma, Moscow Lenin Pedagog. Inst., 1963, grad. diploma, 1968; PhD, M.V. Lomonsov State U., Moscow, 1970, DSc, 1989. Speech therapist N.N. Burdenko Neurosurgery Inst., 1963-64; jr. rsch. worker Russian Lang. Ctr. Moscow State U., 1966-72, sr. rsch. worker dept. psychology, 1972-92; head of lab. dept. psychology M.V. Lomonsov State U., Moscow, 1992—. Author: Dynamic Aphasia, 1975, Production of Speech: Neurolinguistic Analysis of Syntax, 1989; co-author: The Method of Evaluating Speech in Patients with Aphasia, 1981, School of Attention: The Method of Development and Correction of Attention in Children, 1997. Grantee Soros Found., 1995. Mem. Internat. Assn. for Study of Child Lang. (exec. com.), Soc. of Psychologists of Russia. Avocations: reading, walking. Home: Profsoyuznaya 2/22-33, 117292 Moscow Russia Office: Moscow MV Lomonsov State U, Mokhovaya 8-5, 103009 Moscow Russia

AKI, KEIITI, seismologist, educator; b. Tokyo, Japan, Mar. 3, 1930; came to U.S., 1966, naturalized, 1976; s. Koichi and Humiko (Kojima) A.; children: Shota, Zenta, Kajika, Uka. B.S., U. Tokyo, 1952, Ph.D., 1958; hon. degree in engring., Colo. Sch. Mines, 1991; hon. degree, U. Grenoble, 1993. Research fellow Calif. Inst. Tech., 1958-60, vis. assoc. prof., 1963; instr. Internat. Inst. Seismology and Earthquake Engring., 1961-62; assoc. prof. U. Tokyo, 1964-66; prof. geophysics MIT, Cambridge, 1966-84, R.R. Shrock prof. earth and planetary scis., 1982-84; WAE geophysicist U.S. Geol. Survey, 1967-75; vis. scientist Royal Norwegian Council for Sci. and Indsl. Research, 1974; cons. Sandia Corp., 1976-78; vis. scientist Los Alamos Sci. Labs., U. Calif., 1977, cons., 1977—; W.M. Keck Found. prof. geol. scis. U. So. Calif., 1984—; cons. Del Mar Assos., 1977-78, Nuclear Regulatory Commn., 1978—, UN, 1979, Time-Life, Inc., 1980-81, NSF, 1981-84; sci. dir., chmn. bd. dirs. Southern Calif. Earthquake Ctr., 1991-96; vis. prof. U. Chile, 1970, 72, U. Paris, 1983, U. Kyoto, 1990; vis. scientist Japan Soc. Promotion of Sci., 1978, 90, Nat. Rsch. Ctr. for Disaster Prevention, Japan, 1988; chmn. com. on seismology Nat. Acad. Sci., 1978-79, chmn. panel on seismic hazard analysis, 1984; Disting. vis. prof. U. Alaska, 1981-88; mem. Nat. Council for Earthquake Prediction Evaluation, 1980—, Calif. Council for Earthquake Prediction Evaluation, 1984—; chmn. earthquake subcom. of adv.com. to U.S. Geol. Survey, 1988-89; mem. com. on earthquake engring. NRC, 1988-92. Author: Stochastic Phenomena in Physics, 1956, Quantitative Seismology: Theory and Methods, Vols. I and II, 1980; editor in chief: Pure and Applied Geophysics, 1982-88; mem. editorial com.: Tectonophysics, 1974-84; assoc. editor: Geophys. Research Letters, 1977-82; adv. editor: Jour. Physics of Earth and Planetary Interiors. Mem. earth scis. adv. bd. Stanford U., 1987-90; mem. vis. com. Carnegie Instn. Washington, 1989; mem. Bd. of Earth Scis. and Resources, 1989-91. Fulbright postdoctoral fellow, 1958-60, European Union Geol. Scis. Fgn. Hon. fellow, 1986; recipient Thorarinsson medal Internat. Assn. Volcanology and Chemistry of Earth's Interior, 2000. Fellow Am. Acad. Arts and Scis.; mem. NAS, Am. Geophys. Union (mem. com. fellows 1975-76, pres. seismology sect. 1980), Seismol. Soc. Am. (dir. 1971-74, v.p. 1978, pres. 1979, Soc. Medal 1986, hon. mem. 1988), Seismol. Soc. Japan, Royal Astron. Soc. Home: 19 Bis Rue des Abeilles, 97430 Le Tampon La Reunion, France

AKIBA, RYOJIRO, aerospace institute administrator, engineering educator; b. Musashino, Tokyo, Japan, Sept. 8, 1930; s. Masuji and Toshiko Akiba; m. Masako Sakurai, Apr. 2, 1959; children: Mami, Yoshie, Eri. D. Engring., U. Tokyo, 1959. Assoc. prof. U. Tokyo, 1961-74, prof., 1974-81; prof. Inst. Space and Astronautical Sci. (ISAS), Tokyo, 1981-88; prof. Inst. Space and Astronautical Sci. (ISAS), Sagamihara/Kanagawa, Japan, 1988-91, dir. gen., 1992-96; mem. Space Activities Commn., Chiyodaku, Tokyo, 1997—; prof. Hokkaido Inst. Tech., 1996-98; bd. dirs. Nat. Space Devel. Agy., Minatoku, Tokyo, 1991; cons. Inst. for Unmanned Expt. Free Flyer (USEF), Chiyodaku, Tokyo, 2000—. Contbr. articles to profl. jours. Mem. Internat. Acad. Astronautics, AIAA, Japan Soc. for Space and Astronautical Sci., Japanese Rocket Soc. Achievements include development of space launch vehicles for Japanese scientific satellites. Fax: 81 42253 6008. Home: 3-13-14 Kichijoji-Kitamachi, Musashino 180-0001, Japan Office: Shinko Bldg, 2-12 Kanda-Ogawamachi, Chiyoda-ku Tokyo 101-0052, Japan

AKIHITO, EMPEROR, Emperor of Japan; b. Tokyo, Dec. 23, 1933; s. Emperor Hirohito and Empress Nagako Kuni; m. Michiko Shoda, Apr. 10, 1959; children: Crown Prince Naruhito, Prince Fumihito, Princess Sayako. Ed., pvt. tutors; grad., Gakushuin U., 1956. Invested as Crown Prince of Japan, 1952; succeeded late father Emperor Hirohito, 1989; crowned Emperor of Japan, 1990; hon. pres. Eleventh Pacific Sci. Congress, 1966, Japan World Expn., Osaka, 1970, Internat. Sports Games for the Disabled, 1964, Internat. Skill Contest for Disabled, 1981, Third Asian Games, 1958, U. Tokyo, 1967, Second Internat. Conf. on Inds-Pacific Fish, 1985. Co-author: Fishes of the Japanese Archipelago; contbr. numerous articles to profl. jours. Collar of the Supreme Order of the Chrysanthemum, 1989. Mem. Ichthyological Soc. Japan, Linnean Soc. of London (hon.), Rsch. Assoc. of Australian Mus. (hon.). Avocations: tennis, horseback riding, cello. Office: Imperial Household Agy, 1-1 Chiyoda Chiyoda-ku, Tokyo 100-8111, Japan*

AKIKUSA, NAOYUKI, computer company executive. CEO, Fujitsu Ltd., Tokyo, 1998—. Office: Fujitsu Ltd, 1-6-1 Marunouchi Chiyoda-ku, Tokyo 100-8211, Japan*

AKIMARU, HARUO, university educator; b. Miyazaki Prefecture, Japan, Apr. 17, 1927; s. Jiro and Miki (Mori) A.; m. Nobuko Nagata, May 25, 1955; children: Mariko, Machiko. B Engring., Tohoku (Japan) U., 1950, D Engring., 1962. Head toll switching sys. Nippon Telegraph & Telephone Corp., Tokyo, 1966-68, head switching and signaling, 1968-74, dir. info. and patent, 1974-78; prof. Toyohashi (Japan) U. Tech., 1978-92; prof. Asahi U., Gifu, Japan, 1992—, dean bus. adminstrn., 1994-98; pres. Info. Network Rsch., Tokyo, 1992—. Author: Cross Bar C8 System, 1964, Modern Switching Engineering, 1979, Introcution to Probability Theory, 1983, Teletraffic-Theory and Applications, 1993. Fellow IEEE; mem. Inst. Electronic, Info. and Comm. Engrs., Info. Processing Soc. Avocations: golf, writing, Internet, personal computing, ballroom dancing. Home: Hakusan 16-9, Nishitakashi, Toyohashi 441-8154, Japan Office: Asahi U, Hozumi 1851, Motosugun, Gifu 501-0296, Japan

AKIMASA, SAKANO, computer scientist; b. Kobe, Japan, Aug. 24, 1949; s. Noboru and Kazue (Haneda) S.; m. Harumi Yukawa; 4 children. B of Info. Tech., Osaka U., 1973. With scientific dept. Osaka, 1973-93; gen. mgr. tech. market rsch. dept. Japan Rsch. Inst., Ltd., Osaka, 1993-94, joint gen. mgr. Advanced Info. Tech. Ctr., 1997—, sys. cons., 1985—; sr. rschr. Kansai Inst. Info. Sys., 1996-98. Mem. IEEE, Info. Processing Soc. of Japan (fin. sec. Kansai br. 1997-98, 2000—). Avocations: reading, movies, driving a car, cooking. Home: 2-7-12 Nakayamadai, Takarazuka-city 665-0876, Japan Office: Japan Rsch Inst Ltd, 1-6-3 Shin-machi Nishi-ku, Osaka 550, Japan

AKIMOTO, YOSHIAKI, oral and maxillofacial surgeon; b. Tokyo, Sept. 21, 1952; s. Masanosuke and Taki (Masuko) A.; m. Emi Saito, Mar. 28, 1986; children: Mai, Shou. DSc, Nihon U., Matsudo, Japan, 1977, PhD, 1981. Diplomate dental. Instr. Nihon U., 1981-84, asst. prof., 1984-94, assoc. prof., 1994—. Author: Recent Advances in Chemotherapy, 1985, 91, 93, Clinical Basis for Oral Surgery, 1994. Mem. N.Y. Acad. Scis., Internat. Assn. of Oral and Maxillofacial Surgeons. Avocation: fishing. Office: Nihon U Sch Dentistry Second Dept Oral Surgery, 2-870-1 Sakaecho-Nishi, Matsudo Chiba 271-8587, Japan

AKIMOV, MIKHAIL NIKOLAEVICH, physicist; b. Kilia, Ukraine, May 6, 1957; s. Nikolay Petrovich and Galina Georgievna (Zakharova) A.; m. Tatiana Yurievna Bobyleva Akimova, July 20, 1982; 1 child, Natalia. Student, Leningrad State U., USSR, 1974-80, postgrad., 1980-83, PhD, 1984. Cert. physicist. Rsch. scientist Leningrad (USSR) State U., 1984-87; prof. Leningrad (USSR) Tech. Sch. Physics, 1987-95; deputy chief St. Petersburg (Russia) Tech. Sch. of Fire Investigation, 1995-97; prof. St. Petersburg (Russia) Inst. of Fire Safety, 1997-98, St. Petersburg U. Ministry Internal Affairs Russia, 1998—. Author: Electricity and Magnetism, 1995; contbr. articles to profl. jours. Lt. col. Min. Internal Affairs of Russia, 1987—. Recipient Honorary Emblem, Min. of Internal Affairs of Russia, 1996. Mem. D.I. Mendeleev Chem. Soc. Mem. Russian Orthodox Ch. Avocation: gardening. E-mail: amn@MA4215.spb.edu. Home: Koroleva 24 k 36, 197349 Saint Petersburg Russia

AKINGBADE, ADEBAYO ABEL, agricultural studies educator, nutritionist; b. Ibi, Taraba, Nigeria, Nov. 4, 1963; s. Oladele and Kehinde Abigail A.; m. Oyekemi Abigail Afon, May 21, 1994; 2 children. BAS, OAU Ile-Ife, Nigeria, 1988; MSc, U. Aberdeen, Scotland, 1993; postgrad., UNP, South Africa, 1999—. From grad. asst. to asst. lectr. Lautech., Ogbomosho, Nigeria, 1991-97, lectr. II, 1997—; rschr. in field. Councillorship race ward 10 Nat. Rep. Conv., Ilesa local govt. area, 1990. Recipient Odasss award ODA and U. Aberdeen, 1992-93. Avocations: football, community service. Home: PO Box 1787, Ogbomoso Nigeria Office: Lautech Dept Animal Prodn, PO Box 4000, Ogbomoso Nigeria

AKINLUSI, MOTOLANI AHDIJAT, lawyer; b. Lagos, Nigeria, Apr. 4, 1965; d. Muhammed Adio and Taybat Ayoka Akinlusi. Higher sch. cert., Fed. Sch. Arts and Sci., Lagos, 1985; LLB with honors, U. Lagos, 1989; BL, Nigerian Law Sch., Lagos, 1990. Legal adviser Multibond Ins. Brokers, Lagos, 1993-94; group legal adviser Harrongate Group, Lagos, 1995-97; prin. ptnr. Motolani Akinlusi & Co., Lagos, 1997—; bd. dirs. Plata Estates Ltd., Lagos, Tecsa Travels, Lagos, Harrogate Group, Lagos. Com. mem. Islami Mission Orgn., Lagos, 1999. Named One Star Officer, Islami Mission Orgn., Lagos, 1999. Mem. Internat. Bar Assn., Nigerian Bar Assn. Avocations: traveling, reading, swimming. Home: 27 Irepodvn Ave PO Box 1665, Lagos Nigeria Office: Mutolani Akinlusi & Co, 8-10 Broad St 16th Fl, Lagos Nigeria

AKINRINMADE, JOSEPH FADEYEMI, veterinary surgeon, educator, consultant; b. Odigbo, Ondo, Nigeria, Sept. 30, 1954; s. Emmanuel Bayode and Esther Bolanle (Awoditire) A.; m. Dorcas Olubukola Osundina, Dec. 15, 1984; children: Moradeke, Omolade. DVM, U. Ibadan, Nigeria, 1980; M in Vet. Medicine, U. Ibadan, 1986. Vet. officer Ministry of Agr. and Natural Resources, Ondo, 1981-82; lectr. grade II dep. vet. surgery U. Ibadan, 1982-86, lectr. grade I, cons., 1986-92, sr. lectr., cons., 1992—; coord. Nigerian Inst. Sci. Tech., 1986-91, 95—, Vet. Tchg. Hosp., U. Ibadan, 1999—; subdean Faculty of Vet. Medicine, Nigeria, 1991-94; chmn. Faculty Field Sta., Nigeria, 1996—. Mem. Nigerian Vet. Med. Assn. (chmn. 1996—), N.Y. Acad. Scis. Avocations: tourism, sports, wildlife. Office: Dept Vet Surgery & Reprodn, U Ibadan, Ibadan Nigeria

AKINS, MARTIN T., clergyman; b. Cleburne, Tex.; s. Ferris Franklin and Grace Ramona Akins; m. Deborah Akins, Aug. 20, 1983; children: Danisha, Marleah, Tilatha. AA, Temple Coll., 1982; BA, Howard Payne U., 1984; MDiv, Southwestern Bapt. Theol. Sem., Ft. Worth, 1988, PhD in O.T., 1995. Ordained to ministry Bapt. Ch. Min. youth 1st Bapt. Ch., Bronte, Tex., 1980; pastor Liberty Bapt. Ch., Brady, Tex., 1983-84, Dunn Meml. Ch., McKinney, Tex., 1985-88, 1st Bapt. Ch., Weatherford, Tex., 1988-92; sr. pastor 1st Bapt. Ch., Alvarado, Tex., 1992-94, Snyder, Tex., 1994—. Office: 1st Bapt Ch PO Box 860 1701 27th St Snyder TX 79550-0860

AKINS, VAUGHN EDWARD, retired engineering company executive; b. Gowanda, N.Y., Sept. 28, 1934; s. Elsworth D. and Alice (Carlton) A.; m. Muriel M. Hoglund, May 15, 1960 (dec. 1992); children: Sonja L., Coleen R., Joseph E.; m. Beverly J. Martin, Apr. 5, 1997. Student, U.S. Naval Schs., 1956-57, IBM Engring. Sch., 1961-65. Lab. specialist IBM, Poughkeepsie, N.Y., Boulder, Colo., East Fishkill, N.Y., 1959-65; test mgr. Semi, Phoenix, 1969-74; mgr. computer-aided mfg. and test engring. semicondr. R&D Motorola Corp., Mesa, Ariz., 1974-84; applications mgr. (SIM) Motorola Corp. New Enterprises Group, Mesa, 1984-86; mgr. computer integrated mfg. semicondr. products sector Motorola Corp., Phoenix, 1986-87; with start-up team SEMATECH, Inc., Austin, Tex., 1988-93, dir. internat. standards programs, 1989-93, mgr. incubator programs, 1992; mgr. strategic integration Motorola Ctr. Advanced Computer Products, Austin, 1993-96; ret. Motorola Wireless Sys. Ctr., Austin, 1996-98; cons. strategic mktg., 2000—. Precinct committeeman N.Y. State Conservative Party, 1963; instr. first aid ARC, 1971-78; chair U.S. exec. com. S.E.M.I., Inc., mem. exec. com. internat. standard program. With USNR, 1956-59. Mem. IEEE (sr.), NRA, Mensa, Electrochem. Soc. (cons. to exec. bd., chmn. founding com. Automation in Mfg. chpg., exec. com. electronics divsn. 1985-92). Republican. Fundamentalist. Home: 270 W Oak Loop Cedar Creek TX 78612-3265

AKINTUNDE, IFEDAYO, civil engineer; b. Ondo, Nigeria, Nov. 2, 1933; s. James Rotimi and Felician Adebolajo A.; m. Florence Oluremi Opeke, Apr. 20, 1963; children: Yemisi, Ifeolu, Akinola. Inter BSc, U. Coll., Ibadan, Nigeria, 1956; BSc, Woolwich Poly. U., London, 1959; MSc, U. Birmingham, 1961, U. Newcastle-Upon-Tyne, 1971. Civil engr. Sir Lindsay Parkingson & Co., London, 1959-60; materials engr. Western State Min. Works, Ibadan, 1962-65; from divsnl. engr. to prin. engr. Western State Min. Works, 1965-73; asst. project mgr. World Bank Assisted Road Program, Ibadan, 1973-74; chief engr. L.A.O. Banjoko & Sons Ltd., Ibadan, 1974-76; chief exec. Profen Cons. Inc, Ibadan, 1976—; mem. faculty bd. tech. Obafemi Awolowo U., Nigeria, 1978—; dir. Nigerian Gas Co., Inc., 1988-91, project devels. Projects Devel. Inst., Inst. Nat. Sci. & Engring. Infrastructures, Nigeria, 1987-94; mem. bd. Projects Devel. Agy., 1989-94. Author: Technological Development Through Self-Reliance, 1994. Engr. Ondo Diocese, 1975—. Fellow Br. Instn. Civil Engrs.; mem. ASCE, World Fedn. Engring. Orgn. (v.p. 1991-97, 99, exec. com.), Fedn. African Orgn. Engrs. (exec. com.), Nigerian Soc. Engrs. (pres. 1987-88, merit award 1983). Anglican. Avocations: table tennis, music, traveling, reading, social welfare work. Home: Old Ife Rd 17 S Ade Ojo Estate, Ibadan Oyo, Nigeria Office: Profen Cons, PO Box 6331 Agodi Gate, Ibadan Oyo, Nigeria

AKIO, TERUMASA, company executive; b. Tokyo, Oct. 7, 1942; s. Kiyoshi and Tomiko (Yokoyama) A.; m. Linda I. Corbett (div. 1987); children: Kohei, Machie Irene. BA, Waseda U., Tokyo, 1966. Pres. Minsai Ctr., Tokyo, 1987—, Hokubei, Tokyo, 1987—, Exch.: Japan, Mich., 1987—; v.p. Edn. for Devel. Found., Thailand, 1987—; pres. Darunnee Found., Mich., 1995—, EDF-Laos, 1995—; vice chairperson Janic, Tokyo. Author: Me and Alves, 1985; co-author: Guide for International Exchange, 1996. Avocations: reading, travel. Home: Nerimaku, 18-12 Tatenomachi, 177-0054 Tokyo Japan Office: Minsai Ctr Ikeda Bldg # 702, 1-15 Shin-Ogawamachi, 162-0814 Tokyo Japan

AKIRA, MASANORI, radiologist; b. Higashiosaka, Osaka, Japan, June 22, 1955; s. Ichiro and Sachiko (Ohashi) A. MD, Yamaguchi U., 1982; PhD, Osaka U., 1990. Cert. radiologist, 1994. Resident radiology, med. staff Osaka (Japan) U., 1982-86; med. staff radiology Kinki Chuo Hosp., Sakai, Japan, 1986-92, chief dept. radiology, 1992—; cons. Dept. Labor, Tokyo, 1993-95. Mem. Japanese Soc. Radiology, Japanese Soc. Chest Diseases, Am. Roentgen Ray Soc. Avocation: travel. Home: 39-12 Minamigaoka, Osaka Kawachinagano 586, Japan Office: Nat Kinki Chuo Hosp, 1180 Nagasonecho, Osaka Sakai 591, Japan

AKIRA, TOSHIAKI, scientist; b. Osaka, Japan, Dec. 19, 1955; s. Norimichi and Emiko Ichimichi Akira; m. Yukari Akira Matsubara, Feb. 10, 1985; children: Mayuko, Hideaki. BSc, Kyoto U., 1980, MSc, 1982, PhD, 1989. Asst. rschr. The Green Cross Corp., Osaka, Japan, 1982-89, sr. scientist, 1993-98; prin. scientist Alpha Theraputic Corp., L.A., 1990-91; rsch. scholar UCLA Brain Rsch. Inst. and Dept. Neurology Sch. Medicine, 1991-93; rsch. scientist VA Med Ctr. Epilepsy Rsch., Sepulveda, Calif., 1991-93; sr. scientist, team head, circulatory disorder team, drug discovery rsch. labs. Yoshitomi Pharm. Industries, Ltd., Hirakata, 1998-99, dep. head; sr. prin. rschr., dept. head, inflammation allergy disease, exploratory rsch. II, drug discovery labs., Welfide Corp., Hirakata, 2000—. Recipient Sofamor Danek award Internat. Soc. of Study for the Lumbar Spine, 1998. Avocations: baseball, traveling, music. Fax: 81-72-868-9597. E-mail: tedakira@welfide.co.jp. Office: Drug Discovery Rsch Lab, Welfide Corp 2-25-1 Shodai-Ohtani, Hirakata 573-1153, Japan

AKIWUMI, AKIWUSI ABIOLA, physician, consultant; b. Accra, Ghana, Apr. 6, 1923; s. Augustus Molade Akiwumi and Grace Chochoe Aryee; m. Doreen Catchpole, May 1952 (div. 1965); children: Karen Ayodele Akiwomi-Tanoh, Mark William Babatunde, Hazel Bernice Modukpe Akiwumi-Anderson; m. Joanna Teikvor Caesar, June 30, 1973; children: Gillian Mobayode. MB, ChB, Edinburgh (Scotland) U., 1950; DTM&H, Liverpool (Eng.) U., 1955. House officer Gen. Hosp., Nottingham, 1950-52; med. officer Ministry of Health-Gold Coast, 1953-58; specialist physician, med. supt. Sekondi-Takoradi Hosps., 1958-67; dep. dir. Health Svcs., Ghana, 1967-70; physician in charge Tudu Clinic, Accra, 1970—; registrar Med. and Dental Bd., Ghana, 1967-70; mem. Stds. Bd., Ghana, 1967-70; leader delegation WHO Regional Com. Africa, 1968-69; mem. mgmt. com. pharm. divsn. Ghana Indsl. Holding Corp., 1970-80; mem. Pharmacy Bd., Ghana, 1976-84; insp. gen. Rose Croix Dist., Ghana, 1990—; bd. dirs. Crusader Ins. Co. (Ghana) Ltd.; bd. govs. W. Africa Secondary Sch., 1983-2000. Founder Chapel Hill Prep. Sch., Takoradi, 1960; treas. bd. govs. North Ridge Lyceum, Accra, 1978-88; bd. govs. West Africa Secondary Sch., 1983—. Fellow Royal Coll. Physicians, West African Coll. Physicians, Ghana Med. Assn. (chmn. western divsn. 1959-66, v.p. 1964-65, Silver Jubilee citation 1983); mem. Ghana Soc. Pvt. Med. Practitioners (chmn. pension and group life assurance scheme, Silver Jubilee citation 1993), United Grand Lodge Eng. (dep. dist. grand master Ghana dist. 1988—, dep. grand supt. Grand chpt. 1998-2000), Ghana Club. Methodist. Avocations: reading, music, German Shepherd dogs. Office: Tudu Clinic, PO Box 2052, Accra Ghana

AKIYAMA, FUMINORI, educator; b. Peking, China, Dec. 23, 1940; s. Fumichika and Ayako (Nakagiri) A.; m. Michiko Morishita, Sept. 21, 1969; children: Tomoko, Yoshiko, Hiroshi. B, Tohoku Univ., Sendai, Japan, 1963, M, 1965; D in engr., Osaka Univ., Osaka, Japan, 1968. Rsch. assoc. Tohoku Univ., 1971-85, assoc. prof., 1985—. Author: Polymeric Materials Encyclopedia, 1996. Mem. Chemical Soc. Japan, Soc. Synthetic Organic Chemistry Japan, Soc. Polymer Sci. Japan. Avocations: music composition, bamboo flute playing. Office: Tohoku Univ, Katahira 2-chome, 980 Sendai 980-8577, Japan

AKIYAMA, KAYO, neuroscientist, researcher; b. Sapporo, Hokkaido, Japan, May 11, 1960; d. Kazumasa and Hisako (Shiota). BS, Hokkaido U., 1983; PhD in Health Sci., Kitasato U., Japan, 1991. Rschr. U. Tsukuba, Japan, 1983—, chief officer, 1996—; cons. Nikon Corp., Tokyo, 1984—, Taisho Pharm. Co. Ltd., Tokyo, 1999—, Yamato Sci. Co. Ltd., Tokyo, 2000—. Contbr. articles to profl. jours. Fellow Japanese Pharmacol. Soc., Japanese Soc. Neuropsychopharmacology; mem. AAAS, N.Y. Acad. Scis. Avocations: classical music, cycling, gardening. Office: U Tsukuba Inst Med Sci, 1-1-1 Tennoudai, Tsukuba Ibaraki 305-8575, Japan

AKIYAMA, MASAYUKI, educator; b. Kaminokawa, Tochigi, Japan, Feb. 5, 1930; s. Tokumatsu and Masa A.; m. Sakiko Higashijima, Mar. 10, 1958; children: Risa, Yuka, Mika. BA, Nihon U., 1952; postgrad., U. Oreg., 1964-65; PhD, Nihon U., 1999. Instr. Jr. Coll. Nihon U., 1956-63, instr. Coll. Humanities and Sci., 1963-66, asst. prof., 1966-74, prof. English and comparative lit., 1974-2000, dean acad. affairs Coll. Internat. Rels., 1979-85, vice dean, 1987-90, dean, 1990-91, 94-99, v.p., 1997-98, standing trustee, 1999—; trustee Nihon U., 1990-91, 94—, standing trustee, 2000—; vis. prof. U. Ill., 1975-76. Author: American Way of Life, 1963, Henry James: His World, His Thought, His Art, 1981; East-West editorial bd. Comparative Lit. Studies. 1980—; contbr. articles to profl. jours. Dir. Mishima Assn. Fgn. City Affiliation; trustee Nihon U., 1990-91. Nihon U. grantee, 1980. Mem. Am. Lit. Soc. Japan, English Lit. Soc. Japan, Japanese Comparative Lit. Assn. (rep. dir. 1999—), Am. Comparative Lit. Assn., MLA, Henry James Soc. Home: 1-3-1 Kataseyama, Fujisawa, Kanagawa 251, Japan Office: Nihon U, Kudan-minami 4-chome, Chiyoda-ku Tokyo 102-8275, Japan

AKIYAMA, YOSHIHISA, utility company executive. Vice chmn., dir. Kansai Electric Power Co., Inc., Osaka, Japan, now pres., dir. Office: Kansai Electric Power Co, 3-22 Nakanoshima 3-chome, Kita-ku Osaka 530-8270, Japan also: Kansai Electric Power Co Inc 375 Park Ave Ste 2607 New York NY 10152-2699*

AKKOR, GUNDOGDU, hospital architect, architectural and engineering services executive; b. Ankara, Turkey, Apr. 3, 1936; s. Omer Faruk and Servet A.; m. Inci Ayse Benler, Oct. 11, 1962; children—Gunin, Gun. Architect, Istanbul Tech. U., 1955, Engr. M.S., 1961. Chief hosp. planning group Hacettepe Sci. Center Archtl. Office, Ankara, 1961-70; mgr. building. design group SISAG Co. Ltd., Ankara, 1970-76, also dir.; mgr. archtl. and engring. services group TEKSIS Co. Ltd., Ankara, 1976-81, also dir.; dir. 2 Hacettepe Found. cos. and UCME Archtl. and Engring. Co. Ltd., 1981—; instr. Middle East Tech. U., 1971; cons. to Turkish State Planning Orgn., 1965, 70. Archtl. works include: Gen. Teaching Hosp., Hacettepe U, Ankara, 1963, Children's Hosp., Hacettepe U., 1967, Turkish Gen. Hosp., Nicosia-Cyprus, 1971, Gen. Teaching Hosp., Istanbul U., Edirne, Turkey, 1975, also 10 other teaching hosps. in Turkey, 1975-85. Vice pres. bd. trustees Bilkent Univ. Served to 2d lt. Armoured Divs., Turkish Armed Forces, 1972-74. WHO fellow, 1963. Mem. Union Chamber of Turkish Engrs. and Architects. Home: Bilkent Univ, Housing Blocks 25/1 Bilkent, 06533 Ankara Turkey Office: Bilkent Univ Vice Pres Bd Trustees, PO Box 174 06572 Maltepe, Ankara Turkey

AKKOYUNLU, MUSTAFA, physician, scientist; b. Yozgat, Turkey, Mar. 1, 1960; came to U.S., 1997; s. Sezai and Zeliha Akkoyunlu. MD, Ankara (Turkey) U., 1988; PhD, Lund U., Malmö, Sweden, 1997. Dist. doctor Social Security Dept., Amasra, Turkey, 1988-89; trainee Lund (Sweden) U., 1989-97; postdoctoral fellow Yale U., New Haven, 1997—. Recipient Med. award Swedish Med. Rsch. Coun., 1994; Travel grantee European Soc. Clin. Microbiology and Disease, 1992; James Hudson Brown-Alexander B. Coxe fellow, 1998. Avocations: world politics, basketball, traveling. Home: 13 Linden St New Haven CT 06511-2526 Office: Dept Internal Medicine Sect Rheumatology 333 Cedar St # LCI 604 New Haven CT 06510-3206

AKOMEAH, PAUL OSEI, export company executive, consultant; b. Accra, Ghana, Nov. 1, 1965; s. Osei Kwame Felix and Felicia Afua Akyaa; m. Lucy Agyei Akosua, May 1, 1994; 1 child, George. BA in Sociology, U. Ghana, Accra, 1991. Export officer Gelina Co. Ltd., Accra, 1992-93, export mgr., 1994—. Author: Attitude Towards Family Planning Methods, 1991 (Best Writer award 1991). Family planning advisor Dist. Adminstrn., Juaso, Ashanti, 1991. Recipient certs. Coun. for Family Planning Devel., Accra, 1992, Assn. Plan-Parenthood, Accra, 1992. Mem. Lions' Club (sec. 1993-95, cert. 1994), Pentym Club (patron 1992-95, cert. 1994). National Patrotic Party. Mem. Pentecost Church. Avocations: stamp collecting, football, photography, reading, sports. Home and Office: PO Box 1636, Kaneshie Accra Ghana

AKOPOV, ANDREI, surgeon, researcher; b. Tbilisi, Georgia, USSR, Oct. 7, 1966; s. Leonid and Liana (Stepanian) A.; m. Ioulia Terentieva, Aug. 6, 1988; children: Ann, Marina. Physician, 1 Pavlov Med. U., St. Petersburg, Russia, 1989; thoracic surgeon, State Rsch. Ctr. Pulmonology, St. Petersburg, 1991, pulmonologist, 1997, Candidate of Med. Sci. (hon.), 1993. Cert. thoracic surgeon, pulmonologist. Rsch. worker State Rsch. Ctr. Pulmonology, St. Petersburg, 1991-94, sr. rsch. worker, 1994-99, chief physician, 1999—; thoracic surgeon Pavlov Med. U., St. Petersburg, 1992-96, tchr. surgery, 1994-96; cons. Pub. Health Dept., St. Petersburg, 1993-99. Author: (book) Plasmapheresis and Laser Irradiation in Thoracic Surgery, 1993; patentee in field, contbr. articles to profl. jours. State sci. grantee Acad. Sci. of Russia, 1994-96, tng. grantee European Assn. Cardiothoracic Surgery, 1997, rsch. grantee Pavlov Med. U., 1999. Fellow European Respiratory Soc.; mem. Pirogov's Surgeons Soc. Avocations: mountain skiing, football, classical music, art. Home: 30 Bolshaya Monetnaya 15, 197061 Saint Petersburg Russia Office: State Rsch Pulmonology, 12 Rentgen St, 197089 Saint Petersburg Russia

AKOPYAN, VALENTIN BABKEN, biophysicist, educator; b. Tbilissi, Georgia, USSR, May 17, 1941; s. Babken Tigran and Maria Levon Mnjoyan; m. Alla Stepanyan, June 5, 1970; children: George, Alexander. MS in Physics, Tbilissi State U., 1964; PhD in Biophysics, USSR Inst. Balneology, Moscow, 1970, DSc in Biophysics, 1984. Jr. scientist Physics Inst. Acad. Sci. Georgia, 1965-70; sr. scientist Inst. Balneology and Phys. Therapy, Tbilissi, 1970-72; from scientist to sr. scientist Phys. Chemistry Inst. Acad. Sci., Moscow, 1972-92; head physics and biophysics depts. Moscow Veterinary Acad., 1992—; rsch. prof. Protein Biosynthesis Inst., Moscow, 1988-91, Moscow State U. of Environmental Engrg., 1998—; head Soviet-Bulgarian joint project on ultrasound, 1992-93; vis. prof. Valencinnes U., 1984—; editl. bd. Soviet Med. Ency., 1984. Recipient silver medal Exhbn. Nat. Achievement, Moscow, 1987; holder 19 patents in field. Office: Proteines Biosynthesis Inst, B Kommunisticheskaya 27, 109004 Moscow Russia

AKOR, MATTHIAS EDOKA, economics educator, consultant; b. Ogenago-Imane, Nigeria, May 3, 1956; s. Akor and Elamma (Adehi) Ayegba; m. Felicia Abiba Awulu, Aug. 25, 1982; children: Iye Akor, Nugwa Akor, Nimi Akor, Chide Akor. BS, A.B. U. Zaria, Nigeria, 1978; MA, Ohio U., 1981. Asst. lectr. U. Jos, Nigeria, 1981-83; lectr. II U. Jos, 1983-86, lectr. I, 1986-89, sr. lectr., 1989-92, head dept. econs., 1994—; bd. dirs. Lobi Bank of Nigeria Ltd., Makurdi, 1990-93; mem. U. Jos senate, 1993-95. Author: Government and Business in Nigeria, 1990; editor: Readings in Contemporary Economic Issues, 1995; co-editor: Rural Development in Nigeria, 1996; contbr. articles to profl. jours. Recipient fed. scholarship, 1974-75, Benue State scholarship, 1976-78, Perotti African award Ohio U., 1980-81. Mem. Nigerian Econ. Soc. (sec. gen. Unijos chpt. 1990-95), Nigerian Polit. Sci. Assn., Sociology Assn. Nigeria, Rural Sociology Assn. Nigeria, Nigerian Soc. Internat. Affairs, Social Scis. Rsch. Coun. Nigeria. Roman Catholic. Avocations: reading, discussing, watching football on TV. Office: U Jos, Dept Econs, Jos Nigeria

AKOTOYE, HUGH KOMRA, botany educator, researcher; b. Lolobi Kumasi, Volta, Ghana, Apr. 1, 1948; s. Nyawuame and Matilda Kudzisi (Egbi) A.; m. Margaret Afi Atidamah, Feb. 1, 1975; children: Francis, Kofi, Thomas Kweku. BSc with honors, U. Cape Coast, Ghana, 1974, MSc in Botany, 1977; PhD in Botany, U. Benin, Nigeria, 1988. Tchg. asst. U. Cape Coast, 1974-77; sci. officer Ghana Atomic Energy Commn., Accra, 1977-78; lectr. Coll. Edn., Port Harcourt, Nigeria, 1979-82, U. Benin, 1983-90; sr. lectr. Ondo State U., Ado-Ekiti, 1990-92; sr. lectr. U. Cape Coast, 1992—, curator Mus. and Herbarium, 1992—; curator of herbarium Ondo State U., 1990-92; mem. exch. student program Internat. Assn. for the Exch. of Students for Tech. Experience, 1974. Contbr. more than 35 articles to profl. jours. including Feddes Repertorium, Italian Jour. Botany, Leucaena Rsch. Reports, and Korean Jour. Botany. Recipient scholarship U. Cape Coast, 1975-77. Fellow Ghana Inst. Biologists; mem. Ghana Sci. Assn. Roman Catholic. Avocations: soccer, reading, traveling. Home: 208 UCC Staff Quarters, Cape Coast Ghana Office: U Cape Coast Dept Botany, Univ Post Office, Cape Coast Ghana

AKOVBIAN, VAGAN ARMAISOVICH, physician; b. Tashkent, Uzbekistan, USSR, May 29, 1941; s. Armais Aristagesovich and Vera Aleksandrovna (Muromtzeva) A.; m. Galina Aleksandrovna Polyakova, Oct. 26, 1968; children: Gaspar, Armais. PhD, Tashkent Med. Inst., 1969, Sci. Fellow, 1974; MD, Central Inst., 1988. Faculty mem. Tashkent Med. Inst., Tashkent, U.S.S.R., 1958-64; asst. dept. pathology Tashkent Med. Inst., 1964-71, asst. dept. dermatol., 1971-86; dir. Uzbek Sci. Rsch. Inst., Tashkent, 1986-92; head STD's dept. Ctr. Inst. Skin Venerial Dis., Moscow, 1992-99; dep. dir. Ctr. Inst. Skin Venerial Dis., 1999—. Editor: Atlas of STD's, 1998. Recipient Silver Medal 850 Years of Moscow, Moscow, 1999. Mem. Supreme Council. Avocations: travelling, jazz music. Office: Central Rsch Inst, 3 Korolenko Str, 107076 Moscow Russia

AKPAKA, PATRICK EBERECHI, physician; b. Mbaise, Owerri, Nigeria, Mar. 15, 1960; s. Canice Ihekoronye Akpaka and Appolonia Akuwueze A. MBBS, U. Nigeria, 1990. Med. officer U. Ilorin, Nigeria, 1992-93, Nat. Chest Hosp., Jamaica, 1994—. Regional dir. Children's Evangelism Min., The Caribbean, 1996—, nat. coord., 1994—. Recipient Meritorious award Nat. Youth Svc. Corps. Niger State, 1991. Mem. Med. Assn. Jamaica, Jr. Doctors Assn. Avocations: games, sports, listening to gospel musics, watching moves, traveling. Office: Nat Chest Hosp, 36 1/2 Barbican Rd, Kingston 6, Jamaica

AKPAKPAN, BASSEY AKPAN, accounting educator; b. Ikot Osong, Nigeria, Sept. 27, 1948; s. Akpan Usanga and Adiaha (Ekpo) A.; m. Mfon Bassey Inyang, Dec. 27, 1987; children: Ekemini, Sisong, Menyeneabasi Abasiekeme. BBA, North Tex. State U., 1975; MBA, East Tex. State U., 1977; EdS, East Tenn. State U., 1980, EdD, 1982. Cert. prin., supt., Tenn. Indsl. worker, mem. tng. staff Sherwood, Commerce, Tex., 1976-78; grad. asst. East Tenn. State U., Johnson City, 1979-80, postgrad. fellow, 1980-82; lectr. U. Cross R. State, Uyo, Nigeria, 1984-91, U. Uyo, 1991-97, U. Calabar, Nigeria, 1997—; tchr., rschr., East Tenn. State U., 1980-82, U. Uyo, 1984—. Author: Guideline in Project Writing, 1987, Book of Reading in Education, 1989, Accounting for Beginners, 1999, Books Used in Accounting Work, 1999. Treas. Ch. of Christ, Ikot Ekpene, Nigeria, 1987-91; examiner Joint Admissions and Matriculation, Labos, Nigeria, 1994—; organizaer, sec. Youth Assn., Ikot Osong, Nigeria, 1984—. Recipient plaque Bristol (Tenn.) Sch. Bd., 1981 . Mem. Econ. Assn. Nigeria, Nigerian Econ. Soc., Nat. Acctg. Students Assn. (cert. appreciation 1991-99, cert. merit 1997, patron/advisor), MBA Execs. Avocations: reading, writing, travel, badminton, counselling. Home: No 19 Gibbs St, Uyo Akwa Ibom Nigeria Office: U Uyo Dept Acctg, PMB 1017, Uyo Akwa Ibom Nigeria

AKRAMULLAH, SHAHRIAR MOHAMMAD, engineer; b. Dhaka, Bangladesh, Jan. 1, 1967; s. Mohammad Sultanuddin and Amena (Sultana) A.; m. Ferdousi Rahman, Dec. 22, 1995; 1 child, Abdullah Faiyaz. BSc in Engring., Bangladesh Inst. Tech., Chittagong, 1991; MPhil, Hong Kong U. Sci. and Tech., 1995, PhD, 1999. Lectr. BIT, Chittagong, 1991-93; rsch. asst. Hong Kong U. Sci. and Tech., 1996-99, rsch. assoc., 1999—. Contbr. articles to profl. jours. Commonwealth scholar Hong Kong, 1993-95. Mem. IEEE, Inst. of Engrs. (Bangladesh), Assn. Computing Machinery. Islamic. Home: 43/1 Bishnu Charan Das St, Dhaka Bangladesh 1205 Office: Hong Kong U Sci and Tech, Clear Water Bay Dept EEE, Kowloon Hong Kong China

AKSAKOGLU, GAZANFER HUSEYIN, community medicine educator; b. Ordu, Turkey, Feb. 4, 1950; s. Abdullah Kesfi and Piraye (Acar) A.; m. Iltekin Cagatay, July 19, 1974; children: Zeynep Ceren, Cansu Pelin. BSc, Hacettepe U., Ankara, Turkey, 1970, MD, 1975, specialist in cmty. medicine, 1979. Med. diplomate. Lectr. Liverpool (Eng.) U., 1979-80; specialist Hacettepe U., Ankara, 1980-82; asst. prof. Dokuz Eylul U., Izmir, 1982-84, assoc. prof., 1984-91, prof., 1991—, vice dir. Inst. Postgrad. Health Scis., 1984-89, bd. dirs., 1996-98; med. dir. Narlidere Dist., Ministry of Health, Izmir, 1982-94; cons. UNICEF, Ankara, 1984, WHO, Geneva, 1989; med. dir. Univ. Hosp., 1996-98, head dept. pub. health, 1996—. Author: Principles of Controlling Communicable Diseases, 1983, 2nd edit., 1996; Research Methods and Analytical Techniques in Health, 2000; co-author: Health Centre Administration, 1982, 9th edit., 1997, AIDS Prevention: Guidelines for MCH Workers, 1990; editor (spl. issue) Health Systems, 1994-95. Active Internat. Epidemiol. Assn., London, 1984, Assn. for the Study of Med. Edn., Edinburgh, Scotland, 1988, World Fedn. for Med. Edn., Ottawa, Can., 1988, Nat. Geog. Soc., Washington, 1997. Lt. Turkish Ministry of Def., 1981-82. Mem. Turkish Med. Assn. Avocation: photography. Home: 1747 Sokak 44/4, 35530 Karsiyaka Izmir, Turkey Office: Dokuz Eylul Univ, Sch Medicine, 35340 Inciralti Izmir, Turkey

AKSENENKO, NIKOLAY YEMELYANOVICH, federal official; b. 1949. Dep. min. Ministry of Transp., 1997; min. Ministry of Railways, Moscow, 1997—. Office: Ministry of Railways, ul Novo-Basmannaya 2, Moscow 107174, Russia*

AKTAN, SAMIYE GÜLDEREN, ophthalmologist, consultant; b. Ankara, Turkey, Dec. 12, 1958; d. Mehmet Resat and Emine (Altuniç) A. MD, U. Ankara, 1982. Physician Ministry of Health, Ankara, 1982-84; resident U. Ankara Med. Sch., 1985-91, cons. ophthalmologist, 1991—. Contbr. articles to profl. jours. Mem. Ophthalmology Soc. Ankara (Top Rsch. award 1996). Avocations: piano, sports, travel, reading, art. Home: Bülten sok 50/12, 06700 Ankara Turkey

AKULA, SURYA KUMARI, history educator, department head; b. Vijayawada, Andhra Pradesh, India, Dec. 20, 1942; d. Lokavana Rao and Lakshmi Bhrathamma A. BA, Andhra U., Tenali, India, 1960; MA, Sri Venkateswara U., Tirupathi, Andhra Pradesh, India, 1962, PhD, 1967. Rsch. asst. Sri Venkateswara U., Tirupathi, 1962-67; lectr. J.M.J. Coll. Women, Tenali, 1968-76; prof., head P.G. dept. history St. Mary's Coll., Tuticorin, India, 1976-85; reader Mother Teresa Women's U., Kodaikanal, 1985-86, prof., head, 1986—, registrar-in-charge, 1989, 95-96; registrar-in-charge, 1997-98, controller exams., 1996—; mem. exec. coun. Tamil Nadu History Congr.; v.p. South Indian History Congress; nodal officer Tamil Nadu State Coun. for Higher Edn.; mem. standing com. on Nehruvian studies U. Grants Commn., New Delhi, India; mem. Madurai divsn. Tamil Nadu Archives; mem. various bds. numerous univs. in India; organizer workshops and seminars. Author: History of Japan since 1850, 1979, History of Russia from 1845 to 1964, 1980, History of Kallar Tribe, 1986, Uplift of Women in South India, 1986, (monograph) Women Stone Breakers of Tamil Nadu, 1989, The Temple of Andhradesa, 2nd edit., 1989, Cultural History of South East Asia, 1992, (monograph) Echoes from the Past - Quit India Movement, 1992, Woemn's Studies- An Emerging Academic Discipline, 1993, Quality of Rural Women's Life for Employment Around Kodaikanal, 1996; contbr. numerous articles to profl. jours. Mem. Internat. Colloquium on Peace and Disarmament, 1990. Fellow 8th Ann. Conf. Washington on Connecting Rsch. and Policy: Women's Rights, 1989, 4th Nat. Women's Studies Assn. Conf., 1989, fellow Mt. St. Vincent U., Halifax, N.S., Can., 1989; recipient award Nat. Coun. Rsch. on Women, 1989. Mem. Indian Assn. Women's Studies (life), South Indian History Congress (v.p. 1996—), Tamil Nadu History Coun. (patron, exec. mem.), Rotary, Red Cross Soc. Avocations: tennis, badminton, table-tennis, Carnatic music drama. Home: Babu Rex 4th St, 624 102 Kodaikanal Tamilnadu, India Office: Mother Teresa Women's U, 4th St Anandagiri, 624 102 Kodaikanal Tamilnadu, India

AKULIN, VLADIMIR MIKHAILOVICH, physicist; b. Moscow, July 28, 1953; s. Mikhail S. and Diana K. A.; 1 child, Larissa Simonova. MS, Moscow Inst. Physics and Tech., 1976; PhD, Lebedev Inst., Moscow, 1979; DS, Landau Inst., Moscow, 1989. Jr. rschr. Lebedev Inst., Moscow, 1976-83; sr. rschr. Gen. Physics Inst., Moscow, 1984-89; assoc. prof. Moscow Inst. Physics and Tech., 1984-94; dir. rsch. Lab. Aime Cotton, Orsay, France, 1994-96; prof. U. Marne la Vallee, Noisy le Grand, France, 1996—. Author: (book) Intense Resonant Interactions in Quantum Electronics, 1991; contbr. numerous articles to profl. jours. Recipient Nat. prize in physics, USSR, 1978. Office: Lab Aime Cotton, Bat 505 Campus d'Orsay, Orsay 91405, France

AKURUGODA, SANGADASA, electrical engineer, consultant; b. Matara, Sri Lanka, May 19, 1944; arrived in New Zealand, 1995; s. Liveris and Sisilin (Munasinghe) A.; m. Manel Gaminige, July 8, 1976; 3 children. IESL (Part III), Instn. of Engrs., Sri Lanka, 1974. Chartered engr., U.K. Elec. engr. Ceylon Steel Corp., Sri Lanka, 1974-78; sr. asst. engr. Zambia Consol. Copper Mines Ltd., 1978-84; chief engr., constrn. Lanka Electricity Co. Ltd., Sri Lanka, 1984-93; design and contracts engr. Fiji Electricity Authority, 1993-95; sr. elec. engr. Beca Carter Hollings and Ferner Ltd., New Zealand, 1995-97; design engr. Gooder Constrn. Ltd., New Zealand, 1997-98, Electrix Ltd., New Zealand, 1998-2000; sr. engr. Powercor Ltd., Australia, 2000—. Mem. Instn. Elec. Engrs. (U.K.); fellow Inst. of Engrs. (Sri Lanka), IPENZ (New Zealand). Avocations: gardening, reading. Home: 311 Blackburn Rd, Burwood E, Melbourne Vic 3151, Australia Office: Powercor Australia Ltd, 40 Market St, Melbourne City Victoria, Australia

AKUTSU, HIDEO, biophysical chemist, educator; b. Tokyo, Mar. 21, 1944; s. Yashichi and Hideyo (Mashima) A.; m. Junko Sato, Mar. 26, 1973; children: Shiho, Miho, Chihiro. BS, U. Tokyo, 1967, MS, 1969, DS, 1973. Instr. Osaka (Japan) U., 1972, assoc. prof., 1985-86, vis. assoc. prof., 1987-88; assoc. prof. Yokohama (Japan) Nat. U., 1985, prof., 1991—, chmn. div. material scis. and chem. engring. Grad. Sch., 1994-96; prof. Osaka (Japan) U., 2000—; vis. scientist U. Basel, Switzerland, Japan Soc. for Promotion Sci., 1978, European Molecular Biology Orgn. fellow, 1979-80; vis. prof. U. Ariz., Tucson, 1989. Contbr. articles to profl. jours. Grantee Japan Ministry Edn., Sci. and Culture, 1985-86, 89-94, 97—; rsch. grantee New Energy and Indsl. Tech. Devel. Orgn., Tokyo, 1995-97. Mem. Biophys. Soc. Japan (steering com. 1993-94, 99—), Japanese Biochem. Soc., Chem. Soc. Japan. Achievements include Japanese patent for a lipid membrane structure containing muramyldipeptide; the determination of the polar head group of lipid bilayers by 2H-NMR. Home: 1928-4 Kawashimacho, Asahi-ku Yokohama 241-0011, Japan Office: Osaka U Inst Protein Rsch, 3-2 Yamadaoka, Suita 565-0871, Japan

AKUTSU, YOSHIHIRO, communications educator; b. Utsunomiya, Tochigi, Japan, Apr. 13, 1932; s. Miyoshi and Fumi (Owada) A.; m. Masako Ota, May 3, 1963. BA, Internat. Christian U., Mitaka, Tokyo, 1958, MA in Edn., 1960; PhD in Communication, Mich. State U., 1969. Instr. Internat. Christian U., 1969-71, asst. prof., 1971-74, assoc. prof., 1974-77, prof., 1977—; chmn. divsn. edn. Internat. Christian U., 1980-82, dir. pub. info. office, 1985-87, dean of students, 1988-90, dean Coll. of Liberal Arts, 1991-93. Co-author: Explorations in Mass Communication, 1970, Public Communication, 1975; editor Jour. Communication, 1976. Advisor social edn. Mitaka-City, 1983-91. Mem. Japan Soc. for Study of Audio-Visual Edn. (bd. dirs. 1972-94), Japan Soc. for Study of Radio-TV Edn. (bd. dirs. 1977-94), Japan Soc. Ednl. Sociology (bd. councillors 1987-97), Japan Assn. for Ednl. Media Study (bd. dirs. 1994—), Japan Soc. for Child Study (bd. dirs. 1994—). Avocations: Noh song, Go. Home: 4-12-11 Josuiminami, Kodaira Tokyo 187-0021, Japan Office: Internat Christian U, 3-10-2 Osawa, Mitaka Tokyo 181-8585, Japan

AKWAR, EMMANUEL C., laboratory staff; b. Bamenda, Cameroon, Dec. 25, 1972; came to the U.S., 1994; s. John Ndi Akwar and Mary Idam Agwu. BS in Biology, U. Tex., San Antonio, 1999. Residential asst. CaLab, Inc., San Antonio, 1997—; lab. asst. U. Tex., San Antonio, 1998—; proprietor Corp. Asst. Living, San Antonio, 1999—. MBRS scholar NIH, Md., 2000. Mem. AAAS, U. Tex. San Antonio Sci. Club (adv. com. 1998—). Presbyterian. Avocations: playing soccer, going to movies, volunteer work, traveling, reading. E-mail: eakwar@hotmail.com. Home: 3434 Oakdale St Apt 203 San Antonio TX 78229-2428

AKYARLI, ADNAN OGUZ, civil engineer, educator; b. Adapazari, Sakarya, Turkey, Sept. 4, 1949; s. Hasan and Muyesser (Gulyuva) A.; m. Aytulu Artuc, July 20, 1976; children: Aysegul, Aysin. MSc in Civil Engring., Istanbul Tech. U., 1971; PhD in Coastal Engring., Ege U., Izmir, 1975. Rsch. asst. Ege U., Izmir, 1972-75, asst. prof., 1975-76, 78-80, assoc. prof., 1980-81; rsch. fellow Hydraulic Rsch. Ltd., Wallingford, U.K., 1976-77; assoc. prof. Dokuz Eylul U., Izmir, 1981-87, prof., 1987—, vice dir. Inst. Marine Sci. and Tech., 1982-87, head marine tech. divsn., 1988-98; top mgr. Ozture-Kimtas Group, 1998—; head Dept. Civil Engring., Denizli, 1987-88. Author: GIS in Coastal Zone Management, 1994, Fluid Mechanics, 1999; editor: Marine Disposal Systems, 1995; editor Aegean Culture, 1994-98. Mem. esthetics com. Met. Mcpl., Izmir, 1995—; mem. environ. adv. coun. Chamber of Industry, Izmir, 1994-98; chmn. infrastructure com. CESME, Izmir, 1995—; v.p. Found. Aegean Culture, Izmir, 1994-98. Recipient scholarship Hurriyet Pubs., Inc., 1966-71; grantee Turkish Sci. and Rsch. Coun., 1995-96, Chamber of Industry, 1995. Mem. Internat. Assn. Water Quality (U.K.), Internat. Soc. Polar and Offshore Engring. (U.S.) (charter), Turkish Lime Assn. (v.p., chair tech. com.). Avocations: traveling, reading, fishing, photography. Home: Mithatpasa Cad 628/4, 35260 Izmir Turkey Office: Ozture Holding, Sehit Nevres Bey Bul 3/7, 35210 Izmir Turkey

AKYOL, FADIL HUSNU, radiation oncologist; b. Ankara, Turkey, Mar. 10, 1954; s. Bulent and Perihan (Duzguner) A.; m. Behiye Koldakoc, Mar. 10, 1987; 1 child, Asli. BS in Biology, Hacettepe U., Ankara, 1975, MD, 1977. Cert. in radiation oncology, Turkish Bd. Radiology. Resident gen. surgery Ege U., Izmir, Turkey, 1977-78; resident radiation oncology Hacettepe U., 1978-81; registrar, radiotherapy and oncology Royal Marsden Hosp., London, 1981-82; asst. prof. radiation oncology Hacettepe U., 1986-90, assoc. prof. radiation oncology, 1990-96, prof. radiation oncology, 1996—. Contbr. articles to profl. jours. 1st lt. (med. cons.), Gulhane Mil. Sch. Medicine, 1983-85, Ankara. Mem. European Soc. for Therapeutic Radiology and Oncology, Turkish Assn. Cancer Rsch. and Control, Turkish Soc. Radiation Oncology. Office: Hacettepe U Fac Medicine, Dept Radiation Oncology, 06100 Ankara Turkey

ALA'ALDEEN, DLAWER, microbiologist, educator; b. Koya Arbil, Kurdistan, Iraq, Nov. 28, 1960; arrived in Eng., 1984; parents Abdul'Aziz and Nasreen (Masum) Ala'A; m. Sundis Muaid Abdul-Wahid; children: Kardo, Aryan, Avesta. MB ChB, Sch. Medicine, Baghdad, Iraq, 1983; MSc, Sch. Hygiene Tropical Medicine, London, 1987; D Tropical Medicine and Hygiene, Royal Coll. of Medicine, London, 1987; PhD, Med. Rsch. Coun., London, 1992; postgrad. in Pathology, Royal Coll. Pathologists, London, 1994—; MSc in Clin. Microbiology, London U. Clinician trainee Arbil (Iraq) Hosp., 1983-84, London Hosps., 1985-86; scientist Clin. Rsch. Ctr., Med. Rsch. Coun., London, 1992-94; clin. lectr. Univ. Hosp., Nottingham, Eng., 1994-98, reader, cons. in clin. microbiology, 1998—, head meningococcal rsch. group; mem. PHLS Meningococcus Forum, London, 1996—; module convenor MSc in Molecular Med. Microbiology; chmn. Genetic Manipulation Assessment com. Sch. Clin. Lab. Scis., post-grad student advisory Sch. Clin. Lab. Scis. Author: (book) Death Clouds, 1991; editor: (book) Molecular and Clinical Aspects of Bacterial Vaccine Development, 1995; editor (newsletter) KSMA News Bull., 1989—. Mem. Royal Coll. Pathologists, Kurdish Sci. and Med. Assn. London (founding mem., sec.), Hosp. Infection Soc. (travel fellow 1996), Soc. Gen. Microbiology (mem. clin. microbiology com. 2000—), Pathol. Soc. Great Britain and Ireland (com. mem.), Brit. Soc. Infection, Med. Protection Soc., Assn. Med. Microbiology. Avocations: travel, football, keyboard music. Office: Univ Hosp QMC, Microbiology Divsn, Nottingham NG7 2UH, England

AL-ABED, NAZMIEH SALIM, principal; b. Tarchiha, Palestine, Feb. 9, 1942; arrived in United Arab Emirates, 1975; d. Salim Mahmoud Khorchid and Najieh Mohammad Faisal; m. Ibrahim Abdul-Rahman Al-Abed, Sept. 19, 1965; children: Bassem, Hanan, Samar. BA, Beirut Arab U., Lebanon, 1967. Tchr. Choueifat Sch., Lebanon, 1962-75, Govt. Sch., Abu Dhabi, United Arab Emirates, 1976-79, Choueifat Sch., Abu Dhabi, 1979-82; prin. Al-Worood Sch., Abu Dhabi, 1982—; lectr. in field. Mem. AAAS, TESOL Arabia. Avocations: reading, socializing, embroidery, cooking. Office: Al-Worood Sch, New Airport Rd POB 46673, Abu Dhabi United Arab Emirates

AL-ABED AL-HAQ, FAWWAZ M., English studies educator; b. Qafgafa, Jarash, Jordan, Apr. 1, 1957; s. Mohammed Al-Rashed and Humeideh (Suleiman) Al Abed Al-H.; m. Firyal Abdel-Kareem Abu-Dalbouh; children: Mohammad, Al-Baraa, Abraar, Thanan, Suhaib, Sundus. BA in English Lang. and Lit., U. Jordan, 1978; MEd, Yarmouk U., 1982; MA in Linguistics, U. Wis., 1985, PhD in Linguistics, 1985. Asst. prof. Yarmouk U., Irbid, 1986-95, assoc. prof., 1985-99, acting chmn. English Dept., 1989, acting chmn. Ctr. for Jordanian Studies, 1995, prof., 1999—; lectr., spkr. on problems in tchg. and learning English lang.; TOEFL tchr. various groups; presenter Yamouk U., 1988, 89, Bani Kananah Directorate of Edn., Irbid, 1988, Mafraq Directorate of Edn., 1988, Ibn Khaldun C.C., 1987, Al-Mazar Comprehensive Sch., 1989, Ajlun C.C., 1989, Irbid Secondary Schs. for Girls, 1990, U. Wis., MAdison, 1996, Imam Muhammad Ibn Saud Islamic U. Contbr. articles to profl. jours. including Internat. Jour. Islamic and Arabic Studies, Korean Assn. Islamic Studies, Lang. Scis., Studies and Rsch. in Arabic Lang. and Social Scis. Jour., World Englishes, others; author: Undoing and Redoing Corpus planning, 1997. Recipient scholarship Ministry of Edn., 1979-82; grantee King Hussein Royal Ct., 1982-85, Fulbright, 1996-97, among others. Mem. TESOL, Lang. Planning and Lang. Problems, Internat. Inst. Islamic Thought, Jordanian Translators Assn., Forum Assn. Linguistics. Fax: 00-962-2226302. Office: Yarmouk U, Dept English Lang and Lit, Irbid Jordan

ALABI, BABATUNDE, mechanical engineer, educator; b. Ibadan, Nigeria, Mar. 22, 1950; s. Adegbindin and Ajibike A.; m. Abisoye, Feb. 20, 1982; children: Toluloipe, Omolola, Babajide. BSc, U. Lagos, 1976; MSc, U. London, 1976, PhD, 1979. Registered profl. engr. Mech. engr CFAO Motors, Lagos, 1974-75; sr. lectr. mech. engring. U. Ibadan, Nigeria, 1984-87; fellow U. Southampton, England, 1987-88; head mech. engring. U. Ibadan, 1988-90; fellow automotive engring. ctr. U. Birmingham, England, 1993-94; prof. mech. engring. U. Ibadan, 1994—. Avocations: chess, tennis, table tennis, photography, music. Office: Mech Engring Dept, U Ibadan, Ibadan Nigeria

ALABSI, JALAL M., dermatovenerologist, researcher; b. Ebb, Yemen, Sept. 26, 1969; arrived in Russia, 1984; s. Mohmmed A. Alabsi and Fatima A. Keshafa; m. Tatiana I. Khristoforova. D in Med. Scis., Stavropol State Med. Acad., Russia, 1996, specialization of dermetovenerology, 1998, Masters Degree, 1998, PhD, 1999. Physician Hosp. Elthoura, Ebb, Yemen, 1996; dermetovenerology Stavropol C.H., 1996-98, 1998—, rsch. dermetovenerology, 1997—; rschr. Stavropil State Med. Acad., 1998—. Contbr. articles to profl. jours. Mem. N.Y. Acad. Scis. Avocation: tennis. E-mail: azhon@usa.net. Home: PO Box 1630, Oktyabarsky Revolutsiya 10/12, 350035 Stavropol Russia

AL-ADEL, FIDA FOUAD, physics educator, laser spectroscopy researcher; b. Damascus, June 22, 1947; s. Fouad and Inayat (Dalatieh) Al-A.; m. Latifa T. El-Hamyani, Dec. 18, 1974; children: Mahdi, Farah, Fadwa, Ahmad. PhD, U. Paris VI, 1981. From asst. prof. to prof. physics King Fahd U., Dharan, Saudi Arabia, 1982-95; head laser rsch. King Fahd U., Dhahran, Saudi Arabia, 1985-97, mgr. energy resources divsn., 1995-97. Sr. editor Asian Jour. Spectroscopy; contbr. more than 25 articles to profl. jours. Recipient Chevalier/Ordre Des Palmes Academiques award French Prime Min., 1992, Distinction in Rsch. award Prince Mohammad Bin Fahd, Saudi Arabia, 1995. E-mail: ffadel@kfupm.edu.sa. Home and Office: KFUPM, Box 732, 31261 Dhahran Saudi Arabia

ALAFOUZO, ANTONIA, marketing and business strategy professional; b. Cairo, Egypt, Oct. 13, 1952; came to U.S., 1982; d. Pano Antony and Agni-Maria (Ranos) A.; m. Thomas D'Ambola Jr., May 29, 1988; 1 child, Tatiana Maryana. BSC in Econs., Brunel U., London, 1975; Diploma in Econs. and Politics, Oxford (Eng.) U., 1977, M of Philosophy, PhD, 1980. Staff reporter The Economist, London, 1973-75, contbg. writer, 1975-82; mktg. exec. Rubenstein, Wolfson Co., N.Y.C., 1982-87; founder, pres. Markcom Ltd., N.Y.C., 1987—; contbg. writer Fin. Report, London, 1975-82; cons. writer Fin. Times, London, 1980-82; cons. communications and econs. World Gold Council, N.Y.C., 1982—. Contbr. reports to fin. publs. Mem. Inst. Journalism Internat., Oxford Union Soc. Avocations: travel, languages, tennis, marksmanship, horse riding. Office: Markcom Ltd 270 Lafayette St New York NY 10012-3327

ALAGAPPA, ALEX VAIRAVAN, solicitor; b. Penang, Malaysia, July 19, 1944; arrived in Eng., 1964; s. Sithambaram Vairavan and Pattammal Iyengar; m. Ann Margaret Slade, Aug. 5, 1972; 1 child. LLB, London U., 1970; TEP, London, 1995. Solicitor Supreme Ct. of Eng. and Wales, 1983. Trust adminstrn. Barclays Bank, London, 1966-69; sr. examiner Inland Revenue, London, 1970-80; solicitor Stephensons', Ruislip, 1981-83; ptnr. Edward Mackie, London, 1983-87; sr. ptnr. Alex Alagappa, Ruislip, 1988—; justice of peace, Middlesex, 1975; magistrate, Uxbridge/Brent, Eng., 1975—; chmn. Magistrates Assn., 1989-92, British Legal Assn. London, 1996-99; part-time immigration judge, 1999—. Editor Middlesex Magistrates Newsletter, 1989-92; contbr. articles to profl. jours. Chmn. Liberal Party, Ruislip-Northwood, 1981-83; parliamentary candidate liberal, 1983. Fellow Royal Soc. Arts; mem. Law Soc. Avocations: reading, writing, debating, overseas travel. Home: 1 Park Farm Close, HA5 2QP Pinner England Office: Alex Alagappa & Co, 4 Kingsend, HA4 7DA Ruislip England

ALAGAPPA, MUTHIAH, international politics researcher; b. Apr. 14, 1942. Diploma, U. Lancaster, U.K., 1977, MA, 1978; PhD, Tufts U., 1985. Sr. fellow Inst. Strategic Studies, Kuala Lumpur, Malaysia, 1986-89; vis. sr. fellow East-West Ctr., Honolulu, 1989-90; vis. prof. Columbia U., N.Y.C., 1990-91; sr. fellow East-West Ctr., 1991-98, dir. Ctr. for Politics and Security, 1996-98, dir. studies, 1998—. Author, editor: Political Legitimacy in South East Asia, 1995, Asian Security Practice, 1998; co-editor: UN and Management of International Security, 1999; mem. editl. bd. The Pacific Review, The Australian Jour. Internat. Affairs. Recipient Abe fellowship Ctr. for Global Partnership, 1996-97, grant Smith-Richardson Found., 1998—, grant Ford Found., 1998—, grant US-Japan Found., 1999—. Mem. Internat. Studies Assn., Am. Polit. Sci. Assn., Assn. Asian Studies. Avocations: ALAGAPPM@ewc.hawaii.edu. Office: East West Ctr 1601 E West Rd Honolulu HI 96848-1601

ALAHIOTIS, STAMATIS NIKOS, geneticist, educator; b. Asfendiou, Kos, Greece, May 24, 1944; s. Nikos C. and Sophia S. (Hantzigeorgally) A.; m. Thalia A. Giannakou; children: Sophia, Nikos. BS in Biology, U. Thessaloniki, 1969; PhD in Genetics, U. Patras, 1975. Rsch. assoc. Dartmouth Coll., 1976-77, Brandeis U., 1979; rsch. asst. Patras (Greece) U., 1972-79, lectr. in genetics, 1976-82, asst. prof., 1982-84, assoc. prof., 1984-88, prof., 1988—; chmn. divsn. genetics dept. biology Patras U., 1985-86, chmn., 1989-94, rector, 1994—. organizer Internat. Conf. Biochem. and Devel. Genetics, Kos, Greece, 1983, 5th Internat. Congress on Isozymes, Kos, 1986; author textbooks; contbr. articles to profl. jours. Pres. sci. coun. Nat. Ctr. Marine Rsch., Athens, Greece; mem. Nat. Rsch. Adv. Coun., Athens; former pres. adminstrv. coun. IHTHIKA, Neohori, Greece; pres. local steering com. Inst. Strategic and Devel. Studies, Audreas Papandreou, Athens. Fellow Dartmouth Coll., Brandeis U. Mem. Am. Genetic Assn., Genetics Soc. Am., Soc. for Study of Evolution, Hellenic Soc. Biol. Scis. (organizer 5th ann. conf. 1983, 10th ann. conf. 1988). Avocation: soccer. Home: Navmahias Ellis 37-39, 26441 Patras Greece Office: U Patras, Panepistimioupoli, 26500 Patras Greece

ALAHUHTA, MATTI JUHANI, telecommunications executive; b. Alaharma, Finland, June 22, 1952; married; children: Tiina, Teemu. MSc, Helsinki U. Tech., Espoo, Finland, 1976, DEng, 1990. R&D engr. Nokia Electronics, Helsinki, 1975-79; team mgr. Info. Systems, Nokia Electronics, Helsinki, 1980-82; sales dir. Rank Xerox, Helsinki, 1982-84; sales dir. Transmission Systems, Nokia Telecomms., Espoo, 1984-86, v.p. Dedicated Networks, 1986-90, sr. v.p. Pub. Networks, 1990-92, exec. v.p., 1992, pres., 1993-98; pres. Nokia Mobile Phones, Espoo, 1998—; mem. group exec. bd. Nokia Group, Helsinki, 1993—. Office: Nokia Group, Keilalahdentie 4, FIN02150 Espoo Finland

ALAÏA, AZZEDINE, fashion designer; b. Tunis; arrived in France, 1957;; Ed., Ecole des Beaux Arts, Tunis; student of sculpture, student of dressmaking. With Christian Dior, Paris, Guy Laroche, Paris; founder dressmaking bus. Paris, 1960s; founder atelier in Faubourg St. Germain, 1965-84; opened Azzedine Alaïa boutique, Beverly Hills, Calif., 1983, Marais dist. Paris, 1984. Exhibited in retrospective at Mus. Modern Art, Bordeaux, 1985; definative retrospective Groninger Mus., Groningen, The Netherlands, 1997; work represented in book entitled Alaïa, 1998. Named Designer of Yr., French Ministry of Culture, 1985. Office: 18 rue de la Verrerie, 75004 Paris France*

ALAIN, MARIE-CLAIRE, organist; b. St.-Germain-en-Lye, France, Aug. 10, 1926; d. Albert and Madeleine (Alberty) A.; m. Jacques Gommier, 1950; 2 children. Student, Inst. Notre Dame, St.-Germain-en-Laye, Cons. Nat. Superieur Musique, Paris; DHL (hon.), Colo. State U.; DMus (hon.), So. Meth. U.; postgrad., Boston Conservatory. Organ tchr. Cons. Musique de Paris; lectr. Summer Acad. for Organists, Haarlem, The Netherlands, 1956-72; lectr. at univs. throughout the world; expert on organology Min. Culture. Appeared in numerous concerts; artist over 250 recordings, including complete works of J. Alain, C.P.E. Bach, J.S. Bach, C. Balbastre, G. Böhm, N. Bruhns, D. Buxtehude, L.N. Clérambault, F. Couperin, L.C. Daquin, C. Franck, N. de Grigny, J.A. Guilain, G.F. Handel, J. Haydn, F. Mendelssohn, A. Vivaldi, others. Recipient numerous prizes for recs. and performances, including Buxtenhudepreis, Fed. Republic Germany, Prix

Léonie Sonning, Copenhagen, Prix Franz Liszt, Budapest, Commandeur Légion d'Honneur, Ordre du Mérite, Arts et Lettres. Address: 4 rue Victor Hugo, 78230 Le Pecq France

ALAJBEG, ANDA, chemist, researcher; b. Udovicic-Sinj, Dalmatia, Croatia, July 29, 1944; d. Petar and Ana (Pavic) Omrcen; m. Slobodan Alajbeg, Apr. 10, 1971; children: Ivan, Josip. Chemistry engr., U. Zagreb, Croatia, 1968, MS, 1977, DSc, 1982. Rsch. asst. Industrija narfte-Organska Kemijska Industrija, Zagreb, 1969-73, young rschr., 1973-75; rschr.-specialist INA R&D, Zagreb, 1976-88, mem. R&D mng. bd., 1988-92, coord. rsch. projects, 1992-98, expert in petroleum rsch., 1988—; sci. assoc. U. Zagreb, 1986, sr. sci. assoc., 1992; vis. rschr. Ecole Poly., Pallaiseau, France, 1975, 77, 78, U. Cardiff, Wales, 1981, Chevron, COFRC, COPI, La Habra and San Ramon, Calif., 1989; devel. cons. Herbos, Sisak, Croatia, 1995—; invitee Gordon Rsch. Conf., Holdeners Sch., N.H., 1981-85, N.Y. Acad. Sci., 1996. Co-author: (book) Biological Markers in Sediments and Petroleum, 1992; contbr. articles to profl. jours. Grantee Sci. Exch. Agreement, 1975, 77, 78. Mem. Croatian Geoscientists Assn., Croatian Acad. Sci. and Art (mem., founder geochemistry com. 1992). Avocations: skiing, sailing, native Mediterranean vegetation. Office: INA R&D, Savska C 41/X, 10000 Zagreb Croatia

AL-AJLAN, SALEH BIN ABDULRAHMAN, science educator; b. Bal Jurashi, Saudi Arabia, Nov. 18, 1963; s. Abdul Rahman Garamah Al-Ajlan and Azza Abdullah Al-Ghoneem; m. Aysha Ali Al-Heneedi; 4 children. BS in Engring., King Abdulaziz U., Saudi Arabia, 1986; M of Solar Hydrogen Energy, U. Miami, 1988; MS in Renewable Energy and Environment, Reading (Eng.) U., 1991, PhD in Energy, 1994. Asst. project mgr. HYSOLAR project energy conservation engr. King Abdulaziz City for Sci. and Tech. Energy Rsch. Inst., Riyadh, 1989-90, asst. rsch. prof. energy conservation engring., 1995, acting head energy and bldg. dept. energy conservation engr., 1995, acting head R&D dept. energy rsch. engring., 1995, head solar energy dept. comprising thermal unit and PV unit, 1996; dir. applied rsch. divsn. King Abdulaziz City for Sci. and Tech. Energy Rsch. Inst., Riyadh, Saudi Arabia, 1996-97; prin. investigator solar distillation project King Abdulaziz City for Sci. and Tech. Energy Rsch. Inst., Riyadh, 1997, prin. investigator solar date dryer, 1997, prin. investigator solar flat plate collector, 1997, dir. conventional energy rsch. divsn., 1997—, prin. investigator thermal insulation rsch. project, 1999; lectr., presenter in field. Contbr. articles to profl. jours. Recipient Cash award Saudi Amb. to USA, 1998, First prize Solar Energy Conf., 1998. Mem. ASHRAE, Internat. Fedn. Inventors Assn., World Energy Congress (study group), World Renewable Energy Congress (mem. steering com., nat. com.). Avocation: reading books. E-mail: Salajlan@KACST.edu.sa. Home: KACST Camps, PO Box 6086, Riyadh 11442, Saudi Arabia Office: KACST, Riyadh 11442, Saudi Arabia

AL-ALAWI, SALEH MAHDI, physics educator; b. Bahrain, Dec. 25, 1954; s. Mahdi Kadhim and Haseena (Hashim) A.; m. Maheen Ghuloom Dairi; children: Noor, Mohammed. BSc in Physics, U. Basrah, Iraq, 1979; MSc, U. Strathclyde, Glasgow, Eng., 1981, PhD, 1987. Instr. physics Bahrain U., 1981-83; demonstrator physics U. Strathclyde, Glasgow, 1983-87; asst. prof. Bahrain U., 1987-95, assoc. prof., 1995—; lectr. in physics to secondary schs. in Bahrain. Contbr. numerous articles to profl. jours. Recipient Brit. Ambassador fellowship Brit. Coun., 1991, Bahrain Ctr. for Studies & Rsch., 1991. Mem. Inst. of Physics, Biochemistry Soc., Bahrain Astron. Soc. Avocations: reading, travel. Office: U Bahrain Physics Dept, PO Box 32038, Isa Town Bahrain

AL-ALOUSI, LOUAY MUHIELDDIN, forensic scientist; b. Baghdad, Iraq, July 1, 1952; s. Muhielddin Abdullah and Kamila Ali al-Alousi; m. Sahar Mohammad Zeki Abdurrazzak, June 4, 1984; children: Salam Louay, Ramiya Louay. B Medicine B Surgery, Coll. Medicine, Baghdad, 1976; postgrad., Medico-Legal Inst. Baghdad, 1980; PhD, U. Glasgow, Scotland, 1987. DMJPath, Soc. Apothecaries, 1989. Sr. med. officer Medico-legal Inst. Baghdad, 1978-82; rsch. fellow U. Glasgow, 1982-86; histopatologist Hairmvres, East Kilbride, U.K., 1986-89; sr. lectr., cons. home office pathologist U. London, 1989-94; sr. lectr. forensic medicine, cons. forensic pathologist, 1994—; mem. faculty medicine U. Glasgow, 1995—; forensic rsch. coord. U. London, 1992-94. Contbr. articles to profl. jours.; inventor reference graph ruler for estimating the post-mortem interval. Fellow Royal Coll. Pathologists; mem. AAAS, Am. Coll. Forensic Examiners, N.Y. Acad. Scis., Brit. Acad. Forensic Scis., Am. Acad. Forensic Sci., Assn. Clin. Pathologists, Assn. Police Surgeons. Avocations: medical photography, drawing, reading. E-mail: L.M.al-alousi@formed.gld.ac.uk.

ALALUF, RAFAEL, structural engineer, consulting company executive; b. Izmir, Turkey, May 13, 1966; s. Leon and Matilda (Benyakar) A.; m. Melis Evrenol; one child: Melda Evrenol. BSCE, Bosphorus U., Istanbul, Turkey, 1989; MS in Structural Engring., Stanford U., 1990. Reg. profl. engr., Calif. Tchg. asst. Stanford U., 1989-90; structural engr. H.J. Degenkolb Assocs., San Francisco, 1990-94; tech. mgr. YESA Constn. Co., Istanbul, 1994—; pres. A & E Engrs., Inc., Istanbul, 1998—. Contbr. articles to profl. jours. Mem. ASCE, Earthquake Engring. Rsch. Inst. (profl.), Structural Engrs. Assn. No. Calif., Am. Concrete Inst. E-mail: alaluf@alumni.stanford.org; alaluf@attglobal.net. Home: Matbuat Sokak 31 Esentepe, Istanbul 80300, Turkey Office: A E E Engrs Inc, Hikaye Sokak 28 Esentepe, Istanbul 80300, Turkey

ALAM, BADRUL, accountant; b. Rajshahi, Bangladesh, July 1, 1945; s. Mohammad Abdul and Akhter (Banu) Quddus; m. Shelley Alam, May 11, 1973; children: Munazah, Nabeela. B Commerce, Dhaka (Bangladesh) U., 1964. Chartered acct., Pakistan. Sr. qualified acct. A Qasem & Co., Chartered Accts., Dhaka, 1969-70; sr. dep. dir. State Bank Pakistan, Karachi, 1970-72; sr. dep. chief officer Bangladesh Bank, Dhaka, 1972-77; fin. advisor Ras Lanuf (Libya) Oil & Gas Processing Co. Inc., 1977-86; mem. Nat. Wages & Productivity Commn., Govt. Bangladesh, Dhaka, 1990-91; ptnr. B. Alam & Co. Chartered Accts., Dhaka, 1987—; owner Nagwa Corp., Dhaka, 1988—; cons. Macdonald Mott Internat., 1990; mng. dir. Nabeela Garments Ltd., Dhaka, 1991—; prin. Golden Rays Tutorial, Dkaha, 1999—. Fellow Inst. Chartered Accts. Bangladesh; mem. Bangladesh Taxes Bar Assn. Avocations: postgage stamps, coins, tourism, music, gardening. E-mail: nalam@bangla.net. Home: 17 New Bailey Rd, Dhaka 1217, Bangladesh Office: B Alam & Co Chartered Accts, B Alam & Co Chtd Accts, 78/E Purana Paltan Ln 2d Fl, Dhaka 1000, Bangladesh

ALAM, IMTIAZ, gastroenterologist, hepatologist; b. Patna, India, Jan. 30, 1963; came to U.S., 1989; s. Maswood and Anwer Alam; m. Shanawar A., July 21, 1990; children: Imran, Irfan. BMSc with honors in Pharmacology, Dundee (Scotland) U., 1985, MBChB, 1988. Diplomate Am. Bd. Internal Medicine, Am. Bd. Gastroenterology. Med. intern Ninewells Univ. Hosp., Dundee, 1988-89; surg. intern York (Eng.) Dist. Hosp., 1989; med. res. Lehigh Valley Hosp., Allentown, Pa., 1989-90, Hahnemann U. Hosp., Phila., 1990-92; chief med. res. Lehigh Valley Hosp., 1992-93; gastroenterology and hepatology fellow U. Calif., San Francisco, 1993-96; asst. prof. medicine Tex. A&M Coll. Medicine, VA Med. Ctr., Temple, Tex., 1996-98; med. dir. Austin (Tex.) Diagnostic Clinic, 1998—. Contbr. articles to profl. jours., chpt. to book; oral presenter, poster presenter in field. NIH grantee, 1994-96. Mem. AMA, Am. Gastroenterol. Assn., Am. Assn. Study of Liver Disease. Avocations: sports, music, movies. E-mail: ialam.adclinic.com. Office: Austin Diagnostic Clinic 12221 N Mopac Expwy Austin TX 78758

ALAM, MANSOOR, computer science and engineering educator; b. Ratsar, U.P., India, Mar. 1, 1947; came to U.S., 1989; s. Mohammad Ishaque and Zulekha Khatoon; m. Sajida Mansoor, Mar. 13, 1975; children: Suhail, Nadia, Shadia, Tariq. BSEE, Aligarh Muslim U., India, 1969; MSEE, Indian Inst. Sci., Bangalore, 1971, PhD, 1974. Lectr. dept. elec. engring. Aligarh Muslim U., India, 1974-75; rsch. fellow U. Liverpool, Eng., 1975-76; post doctoral fellow U. Saskatchewan, 1976-77; asst. prof. dept. elec. engring. U. Petroleum and Minerals, Dhahran, Saudi Arabia, 1977-80, assoc. prof., 1980-82; assoc. prof. sch. computer sci. U. Windsor, 1982-85, prof., 1985-91, acting dir. sch. computer sci., 1985-87; prof. computer sci. and engring. dept. U. Toledo, 1991-95, prof., grad. dir. dept. elec. engring. and computer sci., 1995-98, prof., undergrad. dir., 1998—; cons. dept. comms., Ottawa, 1983-85. Contbr. articles to profl. jours. Grantee NSF, Washington U., 1998. Mem. IEEE (sr.). Avocations: reading, comparative religion, philosophy books. E-mail: malam@eecs.utoledo.edu. Office: U Toledo Dept EE and Computer Sci 2801 W Bancroft St Toledo OH 43606-3328

ALAM, MOHAMMAD JAHANGIR, engineering educator; b. Chandanaish, Chittagong, Bangladesh, Nov. 30, 1960; s. Mohammad Monir Ahmed and Rashida Begum; m. Roksana Mannan Lipi, Apr. 11, 1997; 1 child, Sathila. Student, Chittagong Govt. Coll., 1978; BSCE, U. Chittagong, 1984; M in Structural Engring., Anna U., Madras, India, 1991, PhD in Civil Engring., 1994. Cert. civil engr. From lectr. to asst. prof. Bangladesh Inst. Tech., Chittagong, 1984-99, assoc. prof., 1999—; advisor DDC-PCI Airport, Chittagong, 1999—; investigator Instn. Engrs., Chittagong, 1997, Ministry of Edn., Dhaka, 1998; cons. in field. Fellow UNESCO, 1989, Inst. for Internat. Sci. and Tech. Coop., Ministry of Sci., Macedonia, 1999, Netherland fellow Asian Inst. Tech. Mem. ASCE, N.Y. Acad. Scis., Asian Ctr. for Engring. Computations and Software, Indian Soc. Earthquake Tech. Islam. Avocations: engineering articles, news, music, cricket, football. Office: Bangladesh Inst Tech, Civil Engring Dept, 4349 Chittagong Bangladesh

ALAM, QAISER ZOHA, English educator, researcher; b. Patna, Bihar, India, Mar. 16, 1941; s. Syed Manazir and Sultan Ara Alam; m. Naheed Mohsin, June 8, 1969; children: Azfar, Saba. MA in English, Ranchi U., 1963, PhD, 1968. Lectr. in English St. Columba's Coll., Hazaribagh, 1964-65, Birsa Coll., Khunti, 1965-68; lectr. in English Ranchi Coll. of Edn., 1958-76, 78-80, reader in English, 1980-86, Univ. prof. English, 1985-95, prof. postgrad. dept. English, 1995—; head dept. English, dean faculty humanities Ranchi U., 2000—; reader in English Regional Coll. of Edn., NCERT, 1976-78. Author: Issues: Linguistic and Pedagogic, 1983, The Dynamics of Imagery, 1994, English Language Teaching in India, 1995, Language and Literature: Divers Indian Experiences, 1996, Commonwealth Language and Literature, 1997, Sharar-e-Justajoo, 1983; contbr. articles to profl. publs. Mem. Internat. Soc. for Humor Studies, Am. Book Club of India, Linguistic Soc. of India, Indian Assn. for English Studies, English Lang. Tchrs. Assn. of India, Indian Assn. for Commonwealth Lit. and Lang. Studies. Office: Dept English Ranchi U, Ranchi 834002, India

ALAM, S. KAISAR, electrical engineer. B of Tech. with honors, Indian Inst. Tech., Kharagpur, India, 1986; MS, U. Rochester, 1991, PhD, 1996. Lectr. dept. elec. and electronic engring. Bangladesh Inst. Tech., Rajshahi, 1986-89; postdoctoral fellow dept. radiology U. Tex. Med. Sch., Houston, 1995-98; mem. rsch. staff Riverside Rsch. Inst., N.Y.C., 1998—. Contbr. papers to profl. jours. and confs.; reviewer manuscripts for scholarly internat. jours.; patentee in field. Govt. of India scholar Indian Inst. of Tech., 1982-86. Mem. IEEE (sr.), Am. Inst. Ultrasound in Medicine, Acoustical Soc. Am., Sigma Xi (shared 1st prize 1997). Avocations: reading, music, tennis, photography.

ALAM, SULTAN SALAHUDDIN ABDUL AZIZ HISHAMUDDIN, Sultan of Selangor; b. Istana Bandar, Kuala Langat, Malaysia, Mar. 8, 1926; s. Sultan Hisamuddin 'Alam Shah; m. Raja Saidatul Hisham, 1943; 7 children; m. 2d, Tengku Rahimah, 1956; 2 children. Student, Malay Coll., Kuala Langsar, 1936-41, Sch. Oriental and African Studies, U. London, Kuala Langsar, 1947. Pres. Council of Regency, Selangor, 1952; regent, 1960; sultan of Selangor, 1960—; col. Royal Malaysian Air Force, 1966; chancellor U. Agr. Malaysia, 1977; dep. paramount ruler Malaysia, from 1994, now paramount ruler. Office: Jalan Istana, Istana Negara, 50500 Kuala Lumpur Malaysia*

ALAM, SHAHIN, hypertension physician; b. Dhaka, Bangladesh, Nov. 26, 1962; arrived in Australia, 1991; s. Shafiul Alam and Mohsena Begum; m. Sofia Sultana Ali, Jan. 14, 1992. MB BChir, Sir Salimullah Med. Coll., Dhaka, 1986; M in Tropical Health, U. Queensland, Australia, 1995; PhD in Cardiovasc. Medicine, U. Queensland, 1999. Postgrad. tng. in medicine Lewisham Hosp., London, 1988-89; cmty. practitioner People Health Ctr., London, 1988-91; sr. med. officer Internat. Med. Cons., Dhaka, 1991-92; clin. and rsch. fellow John Curtin Sch. Med. Rsch. Woden and Valley Hosp., Australia, 1993-94; clin. fellow Princess Alexandra Hosp., Brisbane, 1995-99; specialist in hypertension U. Hosp. Carl Gustav Carus, Dresden, Germany, 1999—. Contbr. papers to profl. jours. Herdsman postgrad. med. fellow, 1997-99; HECS postgrad. scholar U. Queensland, 1996-99, undergrad. med. scholar Dhaka U., 1980-86. Mem. Bangladesh Assn. of Brisbane Inc. (pres. 1997-99). Muslim. Avocations: gardening, working out, reading. Office: Princess Alexandra Hosp, Woolloongabba Ipswich Rd, 4102 Brisbane Australia

ALAM, SYED MAHBUBUL, finance executive, accountant; b. Chittagong, Bangladesh, Feb. 14, 1956; s. Mohammed Ezharul Haque and Kulsum Begum; m. Lubna Sheikh, Jan. 15, 1988; children: Syeda Maisha Musarrat Mahbub, Syeda Nashita Mahbub. B in Commerce, Govt. Coll. Commerce, Chittagong, Bangladesh, 1975; MBA, U. Dhaka, Bangladesh, 1979. Sr. officer Bangladesh Shilpa Bank, Dhaka, 1980-81; asst. project acct. Fisons (Bangladesh) Ltd., Dhaka, 1981-84, cost acct., 1985-89; mgr. fin. and acctg. Partex Group of Industries, Dhaka, 1989-90, dep. gen. mgr. fin. and acctg., 1991-92; fin. mgr. Beximco Pharms. Ltd., Dhaka, 1992-98, sr. fin. mgr., 1999—. Contbr. articles to profl. jours. Fellow Inst. Cost and Mgmt. Accts. Bangladesh (treas. Dhaka chpt. 1987, vice chmn. 1990), U. Dhaka Inst. Bus. Adminstrn. Alumni Assn. Avocations: reading, travelling, cricket, tennis. Home: Dhanmondi Res Area, Apt B-3 House 57/1 Rd 12/A, Dhaka 1205, Bangladesh Office: Beximco Pharms Ltd, 17 Dhanmondi Rsch Area Rd #2, Dhaka 1205, Bangladesh

ALAM, SYED NURUL, toxicologist; b. Kushtia, Bangladesh, Jan. 1, 1936; came to U.S., 1971; s. Syed Abdul and Nurunnessa Quddus; m. Rashida Alam, Jan. 18, 1959; children: Runa, John, Tony. BSc with honors, Dhaka (Bangladesh) U., 1956, MSc, 1957; PhD, McMaster U., Hamilton, Ont., Can., 1964. Rsch. assoc. U. Iowa, Iowa City, 1971-77; rev. pharmacologist, toxicologist FDA, Rockville, Md., 1977-94, acting supervisory pharmacologist, 1994, expert rev. pharmacologist, 1994-98; assoc. dir. Otsuka Pharms., Inc., Rockville, 1998—; rsch. assoc. U. Goettingen, Germany, 1966-69. Contbr. articles to profl. jours. Commonwealth scholar Can. Govt., 1960-64. Mem. AAAS, Assn. Govt. Toxicologists. Avocations: reading, fishing, singing, photography. E-mail: syedal@mocr.oapi.com. Home: 8817 Bells Mill Rd Potomac MD 20854-4284 Office: Otsuka Pharms Inc 2440 Research Blvd Rockville MD 20850-3238

ALAMEDA, RUSSELL RAYMOND, JR., radiologic technologist; b. San Jose, Calif., Oct. 13, 1945; s. Russell Raymond and Rose Margaret (Manzone) A.; m. Gayle Evileen Allison, Feb. 16, 1969 (div. 1975); children: Lynda Rae, Anthony David. Student, San Jose City Coll., 1963-65. Served with U.S. Navy, 1966-75; x-ray technician VA Hosp., Palo Alto, Calif., 1975-78; office mgr. Orthopedic Surgery, Mountain View, Calif., 1978-99; radiologic technologist Desert Orthopedic Ctr., Rancho Mirage, Calif., 2000—; owner, operator Ren-Tech, San Jose, 1982-87; radiologic technologist San Jose (Calif.) Med. Clinic, 1982-93; part-time fin. analyst Primerica Fin. Svcs., Newark, Calif., 1998—. Mem. DeFrank Community Ctr. Recipient Mallinckrodt Outstanding Achievement award Mallinckrodt Corp., 1971. Mem. DAV (life), ACLU, NOW, Am. Registry of Radiologic Technologists, Lamda Legal Def., Calif. Soc. Radiologic Technologists, Am. Soc. Radiologic Technolgoist. Democrat. Lutheran. Home: 1840 S Caliente Rd Palm Springs CA 92264-9202 Office: Orthopedic Surgery 2500 Hospital Dr Ste 7 Mountain View CA 94040-4115 also: Primerica Fin Svcs 39899 Balentine Dr Ste 175 Newark CA 94560-5357

ALAND, BARBARA EDITH, religious studies educator; b. Hamburg, Germany, Dec. 4, 1937; d. Ludwig and Edith (Repsold) Ehlers; m. Kurt Aland, July 1972 (dec. Apr. 1994). PhD, U. Frankfurt, Germany, 1964; lic., Istituto Biblico Pontifico, Rome, Italy, 1969; DLitt (hon.), Wartburg Coll., Waverly, Iowa, 1988; DD (hon.), Mt. St. Mary's, Emmitsburg, Md., 1989. Prof. U. Muenster, Germany, 1980—, dir. Inst for Neutestamentliche Textforschung, 1983—. Co-editor: Novum Testamentum Graecum, 1997, The Greek New Testament, 4th edit., 1993; editor: Das Neue Testament in Syrischen Uberliefenung, Vol. I, 1991, Vol. 2, 1995. Recipient Paulus-Plakette, City of Muenster, 1998. Mem. Hermann Kunst-Stiftung Förderung der neutestamentlichen Textforschung, Verwaltungsrat of the German Bibl. Soc., Kuratorum Stiftung Bibel und Kultur. Lutheran. Office: Inst Neutestamentliche Text, Georgskommende 7, 48143 Muenster Germany

AL-ANI, MAJEED RASHEED, nutritionist; b. Ana, Anbar, Iraq, May 3, 1941; s. Rasheed Abdullah and Sabria Macky Al-Ani; m. Lamia Abulrazzak Al-Ubaidi, June 19, 1976; 1 child, Dahlia. BSc, U. Baghdad, Iraq, 1963; MSc, Purdue U., 1970, PhD, 1972. Rsch. asst. U. Baghdad, 1963-68, instr., 1972-76, asst. prof., 1978-93, head dept. biochemistry, 1981-85, prof. coll. of medicine, 1993—; rschr. London U./Charing Cross Hosp., 1976-78; prof. nutrition Jordan U. Sci. & Tech., 1999; cons. Nutrition Inst., Baghdad, 1980-81. Author: Diabetes Mellitus, 1994; contbr. 27 papers to profl. jours. Avocation: reading. Office: Jordan U Sci & Tech, PO Box 3030, Irbid 22110, Jordan

ALAPPA, RAMA KRISHNA, food products engineering executive; b. Mysore, India, July 1, 1958; s. Mysore Kapanaiah and Puttaboramma (Mysoreboraiah) A.; m. Savitha Alappa, Aug. 18, 1994; 2 children, Supritha Ramakrishna, Sourabh Ramakrishna. B in Mech. Engring., S.J. Coll. Engring., Mysore, 1990, M in Tech., 1993. Scientist def. food rsch. lab. Def. Rsch. and Devel. Orgn., Mysore, 1984—; thermal processing and packaging foods specialist; mem. faculty food analysis and quality assurance, 1992—; student adv.; co-investigator numerous def. R & D projects. Inventor in field including design of food processor, thermoplastic heat sealing machines; contbr. articles to profl. jours. Mem. ASME, Assn. Food Sci. Tech. India, Inst. Engrs. India (Best Sci. Worker 1988, Best Outstanding Engr. 1990). Avocations: reading, swimming, pen pals, drawing, hiking. Home: # 659 F 90, Basabeswara Main Rd, Kille Mohalla 570 004, India Office: Def Food Rsch Lab, TN Pur Rd, Mysore 570 011, India

AL-AQEEL, AIDA IBRAHIM, pediatrician; b. Burydaha, Qassim, Saudi Arabia, Aug. 25, 1960; d. Ibrahim Mohammed and Nazira Ibrahim Al-Aqeel. BSc in Biochemistry, Kuwait U., 1978, BSc in Med. Scis., 1980, MD, 1983. Resident in pediat. Riyadh (Saudi Arabia) Armed Forces Hosp., 1984-86, registrar in pediat., 1986-88; fellow in inborn errors of metabolism and endocrine sys. King Faisal Specialist Hosp., Riyadh, 1988-90; cons. in pediatric inborn errors genetics & endocrinology Riyadh Armed Forces Hosp., 1991—; postdoctoral fellow in molecular genetics Northwestern U., Chgo., 1995; postdoctoral fellow in clin. biochem. and molecular genetics Yale U., New Haven, 1995-96; mem. ethical rsch. com. Riyadh Armed Forces Hosp., 1996—. Reviewer: Which Test for my Unborn Baby, 1992, Practical Genetic Counseling, 1994; contbr. articles to profl. jours. Fellow Royal Coll. Physicians; mem. Soc. Study of Inborn Errors of Metabolism, Soc. Inherited Metabolic Disorder, Am. Soc. Human Genetics. Office: Armed Forces Hosp W951, King Abdulaziz Rd PO 7879, Riyadh 11159, Saudi Arabia

ALARCON, CONSUELO G., communications advisor, commercial specialist; b. Dolores, Tolima, Colombia, July 20, 1945; s. Ricardo Alarcon and Sixta Elena Guzman. BBA, Univ. de los Andes, Bogota, 1973. Adminstrv. asst. IRS, Bogota, 1972-74; fin. analyst U.S. AID, Bogota, 1975-78; sr. comml. specialist U.S. Dept. Commerce, Bogota, 1979-99. Contbr. articles to profl. jours. Recipient Bronze medal U.s. Dept. Commerce, 1989. Felow Uniandinos Bogota; mem. Global Telecom Women's Network. Mem. Liberal Party. Roman Catholic. Avocations: riding horses, singing. Home: Calle 125 41-26, Bogota Colombia Office: US Dept Commerce, Calle 22D bis 47-51, Bogota Colombia

ALARCON VERA, ANTONIO LUIS, agricultural educator, counselor, researcher; b. Murcia, Spain, June 21, 1969; s. Antonio Alarcon and Carmen Vera; m. Consuelo Egea Nicolas, Feb. 17, 1969. BS in Chemistry, U. Murcia, Spain, 1992; Envrion. Mgmt. Master, Inst. Investigaciones Ecols, Malaga, Spain, 1995; PhD in Chemistry, U. Murcia, 2000. Rschr. U. Murcia, 1992-96; chemist Soivre, Cartagena, Spain, 1993-95, Cice, Murcia, 1995-96; educator Columbares Assn., Murcia, 1996-98; prof. U. Murcia, 1998-99, Polytechnique U. Cartagena, 2000—; tech. dir. Cifacita S.L., 1999—; rschr. projects U. Murcia, 1992-2000; tech. dir. Novedades Agricolas Rev., Mazarron, Spain, 1999—; participant over 20 nat. and internat. rsch. projects; coord. internat. ann. master about plant nutrition, internat. ann. course about tech. transfer in intensive agr. Contbr. articles to profl. jours., over 60 chpts. to books; author, coord. Office: Polytechnique U Cartagena, Paseo Alfonso XIII no 52, 30203 Cartagena/Murcia Spain

AL-ASHTAL, ABDALLA SALEH, ambassador; b. Addis Ababa, Ethiopia, Oct. 5, 1940; children: Lamees, Azal. B.B.A., Am. U. Beirut, 1966; M.A., NYU, 1973. Asst. dir. Yemeni Bank, Sanaa, Yemen Arab Rep., 1967-68; mem. supreme peoples council Hadramout province People's Democratic Republic Yemen, 1967-68, mem. gen. command nat. liberation front, 1968-70, polit. adviser permanent mission to UN, 1970-72, sr. counsellor permanent mission, 1972-73, non-resident ambassador to Mex., 1975-79, Can., 1974—, Brazil, 1984, Argentina, 1988; permanent rep. to UN, 1973—. Office: UN Permanent Mission Republic of Yemen 413 E 51st St New York NY 10022-6403*

AL-ASSAF, IBRAHIM ABDULAZIZ, banker; b. Ayon Al-Jawa, Gassim, Saudi Arabia, Jan. 28, 1949; s. Abdulaziz Abdulla and Hussah (Al-Mante) Al-A.; m. Rogayah Al-Manie, Sept. 8, 1978; children: Abdulaziz, Moneerah, Mai, Faisal. BA in Econs. and Polit. Scis., Riyadh (Saudi Arabia) U., 1971; MA in Econs., U. Denver, 1976; PhD in Econs., Colo. State U., 1982. Teaching asst. King Abdulaziz Mil. Acad., Riyadh, 1971-82; chmn. dept. adminstrv. scis., asst. prof. econs. Saudi Fund for Devel., Riyadh, 1982-86, econ. advisor, 1982-86; alt. exec. dir. IMF, Washington, 1986-89; exec. dir. World Bank Group, Washington, 1989-95; min. fin. and nat. economy Govt. of Saudi Arabia, Riyddh, 1995—; vis. lectr. Staff's Acad., Riyadh, 1982-83; bd. trustees Saudi Islamic Acad., Washington, 1986—. Mem. Arab Internat. Studies Assn. of Washington, Saudi Econ. Assn., Arab Soc. for Econ. Rsch. Avocations: reading, swimming, gardening. Office: Min Fin & Nat Economy, Airport Rd, Riyadh 11177, Saudi Arabia*

ALATHEL, ABDULLAH M., diplomat, commerce and trade consultant; b. Alruss, Saudi Arabia, Dec. 2, 1953; s. Mohammad Nasser Alathel and Monerah Suliman Alassaf; m. Feryal Ali Almojhed, Mar. 19, 1987; children: Shahad, May, Yara. BS, So. Oreg. State U., 1981, MS, 1984. Asst. prof. King Abdulaziz Mil. Acad., Riyadh, Saudi Arabia, 1981-82; office dir. commerce Dep. Min. Commerce, Riyadh, Saudi Arabia, 1985-87; asst. Fgn. Trade Dept., Riyadh, Saudi Arabia, 1987-89; comml. attache Saudi Arabian Embassy, Washington, 1989—; exec. com. U.S.-Saudi Arabia Bus. Coun., Washington, 1998—. Mem. U.S.-Arab C. of C. (exec. com. Washington 1993—). E-mail: aathel@resa.org. Home: 2271 Kings Garden Way Falls Church VA 22043-2558 Office: Royal Embassy Saudi Arabia 601 New Hampshire Ave NW Washington DC 20037-2405

ALATIQI, IMAD MOHAMMAD, chemical engineering educator; b. Kuwait, Kuwait, Jan. 25, 1956; s. Mohammad Abdulazeez and Fatima Abdulqader Alatiqi; m. Iman Abdulah Alateeqi, Oct. 1978; children: Abdulazeez, Mohammad, Huda, Sulaiman, Abdullah, Saleh, Yusef. BSc, Alexandria U., 1978; MSc, Lehigh U., 1982, PhD, 1985. Asst. prof. Kuwait U., 1985-88, dir. rsch. adminstrn., 1991-94, prof., 1997—, dean Coll. Engring. and Petroleum, 1998—; dir. petroleum divsn. KISR, Kuwait, 1988-91; pres. Alatiqi Cons., Kuwait, 1997—; vis. prof. U. Louisville, Ky., 1994-96; mem. Supreme Petroleum Coun., 1990—; cons. Techno-Econ. divsn. Kuwait Inst. for Sci. Rsch., 1986-88; chmn. Planning Com. for Cmty. Colls. Co-author: Research Developments at Kuwait University, 1994. Lt. Kuwaiti Army, 1986-87. Mem. AIChE, Kuwait Engrs. Soc., Market Technicians Assn., Assn. Profl. Genealogists. Moslem. Avocations: swimming, Taekwondo, reading, writing. Office: Alatiqi Cons, PO Box 17, 72861 Faiha Kuwait

AL-ATTAS, SYED MUHAMMAD AL-NAQUIB, philosopher, educator; b. Bogor, Java, Indonesia, Sept. 5, 1931; s. Syed Ali and Sharifah Raguan (Al-Aydrus) Al-A.; m. Latifah (Moira Maureen O'Shay) Oct. 9, 1961; children: Sharifah Faizah, Syed Ali Tawfik, Sharifah Shifa, Syed Haydar. Student, Royal Mil. Acad., Sandhurst, Eng., 1953-55, U. Malaya, 1957-59; MA, McGill U., 1962; PhD, London U., 1965; DLitt (hon.), U. Khartoum. Lectr. then sr. lectr., reader classical Malay Islamic lit. U. Malaya, 1964-69, dean faculty arts, 1969-70; co-founder Nat. U. Malaysia, 1970; prof. Malay lang. and lit., dean faculty arts, founder Inst. Malay Lang., Lit. and Culture/Nat. U. Malaysia, 1970—; state guest scholar Inst. Vostokovedenia, Moscow, 1970; vis. scholar, vis. prof. Temple U., Phila., 1976-77; disting. prof., Tun Abdul Razak chair S.E. Asian studies disting. prof. Islamic studies Ohio U., 1981-82, prof. Islamic Thought and Civilization Internat. Islamic U., Kuala Lumpur, 1987-90, designer, landscaper, interior decorator, founder, dir. In-

ternat. Inst. Islamic Thought & Civilization, 1991, Al-Ghazali chair in Islamic thought, 1993; del. internat. philos. congresses; prin. cons. World of Islam Festival; spkr. Internat. Islamic Conf., London, 1976; UNESCO expert on Islamic history and civilization; lectr. in field. Author: RANGKAIAN Rubaiyat, 1959, Some Aspects of Sufism as Understood and Practiced Among the Malays, 1963, Raniri and the Wujudiyyah of 17th Century Acheh, 1966, The Origin of the Malay Shair, 1968, Preliminary Statement on a General Theory of the Islamization of the Malay-Indonesian Archipelago, 1969, The Mysticism of Hamzah Fansuri, 1970, Concluding Postscript to the Origin of the Malay Shair, 1970, The Correct Date of the Trengganu Inscription, 1971; Islam dalam Sejarah dan Kebudayaan Melayu, 1971, Buku Panduan Jabatan Bahasa dan Kesusasteraan Melayu, 1972, Risalah Untuk Kuam Muslimin, 1973, Comments on the Reexamination of al-Raniri's Hujjatu'l-Siddiq: A Refutation, 1975, Islam: The Concept of Religion and the Foundation of Ethics and Morality, 1976, Islam: Faham Agama dan Asas Akhlak, 1977, Islam and Secularism, 1978, The Concept of Education in Islam, 1980, Islam dan Sekularisme, 1981, Konsep Pendidikan dalam Islam, 1984, Islam, Secularism and the Philosophy of the Future, 1985, A Commentary on the Hujjat-al-Siddiq of Nural-Din al-Raniri, 1986, The Oldest Malay Manuscript: A 16th Century Translation of the Aqaid of al-Nasafi, 1987, Islam and the Philosophy of Science, 1989, The Nature of Man and the Psychology of the Human Soul, 1990, The Intuition of Existence, 1990, On Quiddity and Essence, 1990, The Meaning and Experience of Happiness in Islam, 1993, The Degrees of Existence, 1994, Prolegomena to the Metaphysics of Islam, 1995, others; editor Aims and Objectives of Islamic Education, 1979. Contbr. to Ency. of Islam, also numerous articles to publs.; inventor Arabic calligraphic panel for Tropen Mus., Amsterdam; discovered, established true and correct date of Trengganu inscription. Served with Malay Inf., 1950-56. Can. Council fellow, 1960-62, Commonwealth fellow, 1963; Brit. Coun. and Asia Found. grant, 1963-64, Asia Found. grant, 1971; recipient Iqbal Centenary Commemorative medal Pres. Pakistan, 1979, IRCICA award Pres. Turkey, 2000. Fellow Imperial Iranian Acad. Philosophy; mem. Am. Philos. Assn., Soc. Thomiste Internat., Royal Acad. Jordan. Islam. Home: 11 14-47A Petaling Jaya, Selangor Malaysia Office: Internat Inst Islamic Thought, Civ ISTAC, Kuala Lumpur Malaysia

AL-ATTIYAH, ABDALLAH KHALID, banker. Gov. Ctrl. Bank Qatar. Office: Qatar Central Bank, PO Box 1234, Doha Qatar*

ALATZAS, GEORGE, delivery service company executive; b. Salonika, Greece, Sept. 30, 1940; came to U.S., 1954; s. Gus Alatzas and Georgia Karayanidou; m. Ida Elizabeth Feldman, Sept. 26, 1965; children: Dennis, Ari. AA in Liberal Arts, Middlesex Community Coll., 1979; student, Rutgers U. Dept. mgr. Bamberger's N.J. div. Macy's Dept. Store, Newark, 1959-61, 63-65; buyer Koos Bros., Rahway, N.J., 1965-67; sales rep. Bassett (Va.) Furniture, 1967-69; store mgr. W&J Sloane, Union, N.J., 1969-72, Steinbach & Co., Freehold, N.J., 1972-78; owner, pres. Lawyers & Corp. Messenger Svc., Middlesex, N.J., 1978-84; pres., chief exec. officer Pegasus Delivery Systems, Inc., Somerville, N.J., 1984—; pres. Just In Time Inc. fin. mgmt. and support svcs.; bd. dirs. Alternarives Inc. Instr. swimming Am. Legion Children's Camp, Newburgh, N.Y., 1957-58; instr. marksmanship reservation Boy Scouts Am., Yards Creek, and Blairstown, N.J., 1980-83; pres. Office Condominium Assn. Ctr. at Raritan. With U.S. Army, 1961-63; Command Sgt. Maj. USAR, 1973—. Recipient Somerset County Businessman of Yr. award, 1999; Paul Harris fellow. Mem. Assn. U.S. Army, Nat. Alliance Businessmen, 78th Divsn. NCO Assn., 78th Divsn. Vets. Assn., N.J. Bus. and Industry Coun., Rotary (Somerville chpt. bd. dirs.). Greek Orthodox. Avocations: tennis, golf, walking. Office: Pegasus Delivery Systems Inc 1124 Us Highway 202 Ste B14 Raritan NJ 08869-1475

ALAVALAPATI, JANAKI R.R., forester, educator; b. Agadur, India, June 1, 1953; came to the U.S., 1998; s. Veera Reddy and Balanagamma Alavalapati; m. Renuka D. Mamilla, Dec. 14, 1975; children: Ram K., Rahul. MS, Sri Venkateswara U., Tirupati, India, 1975, U. Alta., Edmonton, Alta., Can., 1990; PhD, U. Alta., Edmonton, Alta., Can., 1995. Resource economist Foothills Model Forest, Edmonton, 1995-98; rsch. assoc., vis. asst. prof. Can. Forest Svc., U. Alta., Edmonton, 1995-98; asst. prof. U. Fla., Gainesville, 1998—. Mem. Soc. Am. Foresters (cert.), Assn. Environ. and Resource Economists, Fla. Forestry Assn., Xi Sigma Pi. Avocations: tennis, hiking, traveling, watching movies. E-mail: janaki@.ufl.edu. Office: Univ Fla PO Box 110410 Gainesville FL 32611-0410

ALAVANOS, ALEXANDROS NICOLAOS, economist, international government official; b. Athens, May 22, 1950; s. Nilolaos Constantinos and Loukia (Tsapalira) A.; m. Ekaterini Charalabaki, July 20, 1977; children: Loukia, Eleftheria. Student Sch. Econs., Athens U. Mem. European Parliament, Brussels, 1981—, alt. mem. fgn. affairs com., 1999—; mem. culture, edn. and audui-visual com. European Parliament, Brussels, 1999—; pres. common del. European Parliament and Bulgarian Parliament, 1997—. Author: Notes on European Left, 1989, Environmental Policy of Etc, 1994, Greeks of Constantinople, 1994. Office: European Parliament, Rue Wiertz 97, 1047 Brussels Belgium

ALAVI, GHASEM, biogeophysicist, researcher; b. Sabzevar, Chorasan, Iran, Sept. 8, 1957; arrived in Sweden, 1983; s. Ali-Mohammad and Esmat Alavi. MS in Engring., Royal Inst. Tech., Stockholm, 1991; Tech. Licentiate in Hydrotechnique, Swedish U. Agrl. Scis., Uppsala, 1995, PhD in Environ. Physics, 1999. Guest rschr. Forest Rsch. Inst., Rotorua, New Zealand, 1996; rschr. Swedish U. of Agrl. Scis., Uppsala, 1997—. Author: Radial Stem Growth and Transpiration of Norway Spruce in Relation to Soil Water Availability, 1995, Climate, Leaf Area, Soil Moisture and Tree Growth in Spruce Stands in Southwest Sweden-Field Experiments and Modelling, 1999. Mem. Dem. Students Orgn., Iran, 1978-86. Mem. Swedish Biogephysicists. Avocations: soccer, reading. Home: Djäknegatan 11-350, S-75423 Uppsala Sweden Office: Swedish U of Agrl Scis, Dept Soil Scis Box 7014, S-75007 Uppsala Sweden

ALAWANA See WALDMAN, ALAN I.

AL-AYOUB, ABDULLAH KHALED, lawyer; b. Kuwait, Kuwait, July 17, 1947; s. Khalid Ayoub Al-Ayoub and Lolua Hasan Al-Manae; m. Nora Abdullah Al-Blayees, 1967; children: Waleed, Osama, Ahmed, Maha, Shamlan, Abdulaziz. LLB, Kuwait U., 1975. Lic. atty. Kuwait. Dist. atty. Kuwait, 1975-78; asst. faculty of law Kuwait U., 1976; assoc. Al-Essa & Abu Zayed, Kuwait, 1977-82; ptnr., founder Al-Ayoub & Ptnrs., Kuwait, 1982—; chmn. Legal Ethics Com., Kuwait, 1984-86; arbitrator GCC Comml. Arbitration Ctr. Editor mag. Lawyer. Bd. dirs. Martyrs Com., Kuwait; mem. Kuwaiti Resistance during Iraqi invasion, 1990-91. Mem. ABA (assoc.), World Jurist Assn., Arab Lawyers Union (bd. dirs.), Kuwait Bar Assn. (pres. 1994), Arab. Assn. for Internat. Arbitration. Avocations: humanitarian service and social welfare, music, reading. Office: Abdullah Kh Al-Ayoub & Asso, Fahed Al-Salem St PO 1714, 13018 Safat Kuwait

AL-AZMEH, AZIZ, history of religion educator; b. Damascus, Syria, July 23, 1947; s. Malak and Salma (Nabulsi) Al-A.; m. Nadia Al-Bagadi; 1 child, Omar. License-ès-lettres, Beirut Arab U., 1971; MA, Eberhard-Karls U., Tübingen, 1973; D. of Philosophy, U. Oxford, 1978. Lectr. U. Kuwait, 1981-83; fellow dept. Arabic and Islamic studies U. Exeter, Eng., 1983-84, Sharjah prof. Islamic studies, 1985-95; Zayed prof. Am. U., Beirut, 2000—; vis. prof. Yale, Columbia, Georgetown; cons. BBC TV, BBC Svc., various univs., project for translation of Arabic lits. UNESCO, ALESCO, UNITAR; bd. dirs. Arts Worldwide, London. Author: Ibn Khaldun in Modern Scholarship, 1981, Ibn Khaldun: An Essay in Reinterpretation, 1982, Historical Writing and Historical Culture (in Arabic), 1983, Arabic Thought and Islamic Societies, 1986, The Politics and History of Heritage (in Arabic), 1987, (in Arabic) Arabs and Barbarians, 1991, (in Arabic) Secularism, 1992, Islams and Modernities, 1993, Muslim Kingship, 1997; gen. editor Arabic and Islamic Studies; mem. editorial bd. Review of Middle East Studies. Chmn. Arab Orgn. for Human Rights, London, 1986. Fellow Inst. Advanced Study, Berlin, 1994-95, 96-98; decorated Order of Merit Svcs. to Arab Culture President of Tunisia, 1993. Office: Am Univ Beirut, Bliss St, Beirut Lebanon

AL-AZZAWI, FAROOK ABDUL LATIF, gynecologist, consultant, educator; b. Baghdad, Iraq, Mar. 21, 1951; s. Abdul Latif Muhiddin and Fatima Mensi Al-Azzawi; m. Saffana Abdul Jabbar Shawket; children: William, Andrew. MB, BChir, Baghdad U., 1974; PhD, U. Strathclyde, Glasgow, U.K., 1988; MA (hon.), U. Cambridge, U.K., 1988. Registrar in ob-gyn. Stobhill Hosp., Glasgow, Scotland, 1982; rsch. fellow, hon. registrar in ob-gyn. Western Infirmary and Stobhill Hosp., Glasgow, 1985; clin. lectr. dept. ob-gyn. Cambridge U., 1985—; hon. sr. registrar East Anglian Regional Health Authority, 1985—; sr. lectr., hon. cons. Ob-gyn. Leicester Royal Infirmary, 1990—. Author: Atlas of Childbirth and Obstetric Technique, 2d edit., 1998. Fellow Royal Coll. Ob-gyn. Avocation: tennis. Office: U Leicester Dept Ob/gyn Royal Infirmary, Clin Scis Bldg, Leicester England

ALBA, RICHARD DENIS, sociologist; b. N.Y.C., Dec. 22, 1942; s. Richard and Mary Theresa (O'Sullivan) A.; m. Gwen Lova Moore, Dec. 31, 1976; children: Michael Moore, Sarah Dina Moore. AB summa cum laude, Columbia U., 1963, PhD, 1974. Asst. prof. sociology CUNY, 1974-77; asst. prof. Cornell U., Ithaca, N.Y., 1977-80; assoc. prof. SUNY, Albany, 1980-85, prof. sociology and pub. affairs and policy, 1985—; dir. Ctr. for Social and Demographic Analysis, Albany, 1981-90. Author: (with others) Right Versus Privilege, 1981; Italian Americans: Into the Twilight of Ethnicity, 1985, Ethnic Identity: The Transformation of White America, 1990; editor: Race and Ethnicity in the U.S.A., 1985. Guggenheim fellow, 2000—; recipient Fulbright awards, 1986-87, 93-94. Mem. Am. Sociol. Assn. (v.p. 2000-01), Ea. Sociol. Soc. (pres. 1997-98), Population Assn. Home: 45 Union Ave Delmar NY 12054-1628 Office: SUNY Sociology Dept 1400 Washington Ave Albany NY 12222-0100

ALBACETE CARREIRA, ALFONSO, artist; b. Málaga, Spain, Mar. 14, 1950; s. Alfonso and Maria Albacete Carreira; m. Luisa Gómez, 1986; 2 children. Studied with Juan Bonafé; studied painting, Valencia, Spain, 1969, Paris. Asst. Juan Bonafé's Studio, 1967-69. One-man shows include Madrid, 1972, Museo de Arte Contemporaneo, Madrid, 1986, Basilea, 1989, Galeria Maeght, Barcelona, 1993, Sala Robauera, 1994, Babel Murcia, 1995, 10 of the Best Jakarta, 1997, Palacio Almudt, 1998, Circulo de Bellas Artes, Madrid, 1999, Espacio c Povreus, 2000; group exhbn. at Ctr. for Contemporary Art, Chgo., 1989, Giuspels Fils Madrid, 1995, Medievogs Castelo Fortomaier, 1995, Fundesco, 1996, ARCO 22nd Biennal Ljubljana, Slovenia, 1997, Spanish Art Fin de Siede Mus., 1999, Würth Alemania, 1999, Labyrint Prage, 1999; represented in numerous pub. and pvt. collections. Avocations: botany, architecture. Address: Blasco de Garay 86 6oA, 28015 Madrid Spain

ALBACH, RICHARD ALLEN, microbiology educator; b. Chgo., Mar. 31, 1930; s. Maurice and Martha (Silverman) A.; m. Janice Elaine Boewe, Jan. 23, 1962; children: Michael, Karren, Kimala, David, Brian, Julie, Barry. BS, U. Ill., 1956, MS, 1958; PhD, Northwestern U., 1963. Asst. prof. U. Health Scis., Chgo. Med. Sch., North Chicago, Ill., 1968-69; assoc. prof. U. Health Scis., Chgo. Med. Sch., North Chicago, 1969-73, prof., 1973—, vice chmn., 1975-82, acting chmn., 1982-83; editl. cons. Yearbook Med. Pubs., Chgo., 1975-81; vis. prof. St. George's U. Sch. Medicine, Grenada, 1992—. Contbr. articles to profl. jours. With U.S. Army, 1953-55. Recipient Trustees Rsch. award Chgo. Med. Sch., 1968, Tchg. Prof. of Yr. award, 1976, 78, 82; fellow Abbott Found., 1961; grantee NIH, 1965-78. Fellow Am. Acad. Microbiology; mem. Am. Soc. Microbiology, Soc. Protozoologists (exec. com. 1984-89, chmn. awards com. 1995—), Am. Soc. Parasitologists, Ill. Soc. Microbiology (membership chmn. 1969-70). Achievements include research in biology of parasitic protozoa. Office: U Health Sci Chgo Med Sch 3333 Green Bay Rd North Chicago IL 60064-3037

AL BAKRI, DHIA, environmental geoscience educator; b. Baghdad, Iraq, Sept. 27, 1949; arrived in Australia, 1992; p. Hamza and Hasiba Al Bakri; m. Taghrid Al-Hussaini, Aug. 13, 1982; children: Sarah, Samar. BSc in Geology, Mosul U., Ninava, Iraq, 1971; MSc in Geomorphology, Sheffield (Eng.) U., 1975, PhD in Sedimentology, 1980. Cert. in geology. Asst. lectr. Mosul U., 1971-73; rsch. assoc. Sheffield U., 1974-80; rsch. scientist Kuwait Inst. for Sci. Rsch., 1980-91; lectr. U. New Eng., Orange, NSW, Australia, 1992-94; sr. lectr. U. Sydney, Orange, 1996—; cons. Regional Orgn. for the Protection of Marine Environment, Arabian Gulf Region, Kuwait, 1982-84, EPA-Kuwait, 1985-90. Contbr. articles to profl. jours. Scholar Mosul U., 1973-75, Ministry of Higher Edn., Iraq, 1976-79. Mem. Geosci. Inst. Australia, Environ. Inst. Australia, Geol. Soc. of Australia. Avocations: reading, walking, swimming. E-mail: albakri@orange.usyd.edu.au. Fax: 61-2-6360 5590. Office: Univ Sydney, Leeds Parade, Orange NSW 2800, Australia

AL-BANAWI, MOHAMMED ISMAIL, industry executive; b. Jeddah, Saudi Arabia, Jan. 12, 1957; s. Ismail Mohammed Al-Banawi and Lutfia Abdul Latif; 5 children. BBA, King Abdulaziz U., Jeddah, 1976. Acct. Banawi Agys., Jeddah, 1976-77, sales rep., 1978-79, adminstrn. mgr., 1980-85, dep. gen. mgr., 1985—. Contbr. articles to profl. publs. Mem. Gulf Mktg. Assn. Avocations: reading, swimming, volleyball. Office: Banawi Agys Shobukshi St, Al-Hamra PO Box 84, 21411 Jeddah Saudi Arabia

ALBANESE, DOMENICO, chemist, researcher; b. Milan, Italy, Oct. 10, 1962; s. Pietro and Livia (Scarpetta) A.; m. Lucia Schweiger, 1999. Degree in indsl. chemistry, U. Degli Studi di Milano, 1988, PhD, 1992, diploma in organic synthesis, 1994. Postdoctoral fellow U. Degli Studi di Milano, 1994—; vis. rschr. Tech. U. Denmark, Lyngby, 1992, Imperial Coll., London, 1997; cons. Exxon Chem. Mediterranea, Milan, 1988-89, Recordati, Milan, 1993, ACS-Dobfar, 1994-2000. Contbr. articles to profl. jours. including Jour. Organic Chemistry, Chem. Comm., Tetrahedron, Tetrahedron Letters, Synthesis, Synlett, Jour. Chem. Soc. Lance cpl. Italian Armed Forces, 1989-90. Grantee U. Degli Studi di Milano, 1992-94, 94-96, Accademia Nazionale Dei Lincei and Royal Soc. Chemistry (London), 1997. Fellow Touring Club Italiano. Mem. Liberal Party. Roman Catholic. Avocations: painting, traveling, rowing, swimming, reading. Home: via Pastorelli 4d, 20143 Milan Italy Office: U Degli Studi di Milano, Via Golgi 19, 20133 Milan Italy

ALBANESE, THOMAS, food industry executive, consultant; b. Passaic, N.J., June 27, 1930; s. Charles and Viola (Gueritey) A.; m. Theresa Mary Perez, Aug. 8, 1953; children: Thomas II, John, Theresa Lynn, Richard Charles, Michael Quintin. Grad. high sch., Garfield, N.J. Pres. Thomas Albanese Inc., Clifton, N.J., 1958-60; founder, pres. Albanese Products Inc., Las Vegas, Nev., 1960—; exec. cons. The Norlen Co., Las Vegas, 1971—; exec. dir. The Las Vegas Chili Co., Las Vegas, 1982—; owner The Chef Tomal Co., Las Vegas, 1995—. Creator Gourmet Chili Meals and Desserts-La Chilafesta, 1982, Mr. B's Hang All Kit, 1971; patentee plumbing sys. Founder Double TT Rancho, dir., 1986—. With USAF, 1951-55. Mem. United Assn. Plumbers and Pipefitters, Plumbers and Pipefitters Local 525. Avocations: designing, inventing. Home and Office: 700 Sunny Pl # 804 Las Vegas NV 89106-3632

ALBANI, ROBERTO, pediatrician, consultant; b. Asmara, Ethiopia, Aug. 21, 1943; s. Ernesto and Assunta (Riccio) A.; m. Maria Nella Mason, Jan. 13, 1968 (div. 1985); children: Odette, Marta. MD, Rome U. "La Sapienza", 1969. Intern in pediatrics Montefiore Hosp., N.Y.C., 1970-71; resident in pediatrics Flower & Fifth Ave. Hosp., N.Y.C., 1971-73; fellow in pediatric gastroenterology Albert Einstein Coll. Medicine, N.Y.C., 1973-76; cons. pediatric gastroenterology Rome Med. Sch., 1976—; sci. advisor SFERA Pub., Milan, 1985—. Author: Understanding Your Child, 1985, Treating Your Child, 1989, Feeding Your Child, 1996, How to Talk to Your Children, 1998; contbr. numerous articles to profl. jours.; author: (video) Parents Today, 1995. Pres. Sch. for Parents, Rome, 1990—. Fellow Am. Acad. Pediatrics (bd. cert.). Office: Via Livenza 6, 00198 Rome Italy

ALBANI, THOMAS J., manufacturing company executive; b. Hartford, Conn., May 3, 1942; s. Charles A. and Marie F. Albani; m. Suzanne Beardsley, Sept. 3, 1966; children: Karin, Steven. B.A., Amherst Coll., 1964; M.B.A., Wharton Sch. U. Pa., 1967. Asst. product mgr. Gen. Mills, Inc., Mpls., 1967-69; dir. mktg. Am. Can Co., Greenwich, Conn., 1969-73; mgmt. cons. McKinsey and Co., Inc., N.Y.C., 1973-78; gen. mgr. Gen. Electric Corp., Bridgeport, Conn., 1978-84; group v.p. Black & Decker, Inc., Bridgeport, 1984; pres. Sunbeam No. Am. Appliance Div. Allegheny Internat., Oak Brook, Ill., 1984-86; pres. appliance bus. Allegheny Internat. Inc., Pitts., 1986, exec. v.p., chief operating officer, 1986-89; prin. New England Cons. Group, Westport, Conn., 1990-91; pres., chief exec. officer Electrolux Corp., Atlanta, 1991-98; bd. dirs. Select Comfort Corp., Mpls., Dyersburg Corp., Charlotte, N.C., Doskocil Mfg. Co., Inc., Dallas, Tex. Mem. Nat. Housewares Mfrs. Assn. (bd. dirs. 1985-90), Assn. Home Appliance Mfrs. (bd. dirs. 1985-87), Chgo. Assn. Commerce and Industry (bd. dirs. 1986).

ALBANIS, TRIADAFYLLOS ATHANASIOS, chemistry educator, researcher; b. Thessaloniki, Greece, Mar. 3, 1956; s. Athanassios and Dimitra (Papazoglou) A.; m. Maria-Eleni Lekka, Dec. 4, 1984; children: Orestis, Dimitra. 1st deg. in Chemistry, Poly. Sch., Thessaloniki, 1979; Diplome, Mediterranean Agr. Inst., Zaragosa, Spain, 1983; PhD in Chemistry, U. Ioannina, 1987. Asst. rschr. Poly. Sch., Thessaloniki, 1980-81; asst. rschr. U. Ioannina, Greece, 1981-86, lectr., 1987-89, asst. prof., 1992-98, assoc. prof., 1998—, chmn. dept. applied agroecology, 1998—. Editor: Modelling in Environment Chemistry, 1991; contbr. articles to profl. jours. Postdoctoral fellow U. Tex., San Antonio, 1989-90. Mem. Greek Chem. Soc., Am. Chem. Soc. (agrochems. divsn.), Internat. Assn. Environ. Analytical Chemistry, Internat. Assn. Water Pollution Rsch. Control. Achievements include development of analytical techniques for pesticide determination in environment; physical and chemical procedures for micropollutants removal from water; pesticide fate and transportation in environment; photolysis and photocatalytical degradation of pesticides in water and soils. Office: U Ioannina, Dept Chemistry, 45110 Ioannina Greece

ALBANO, ANTHONY WILLIAM, retired career officer, secondary school educator; b. Atlanta, Dec. 6, 1953; s. Rocco Louis and Ida Elizabeth (White) A. AA, Manatee Jr. Coll., 1973; BA, U. Fla., 1975; MA, Cen. Mich. U., 1979. Commd. 2d lt. USAF, 1975, advanced through grades to maj., 1979, ret., 1993; tchr. Venice (Fla.) Area Mid. Sch., 1995—. Scoutmaster Boy Scouts Am., Rochester, N.H., 1984-86, Ramstein AB, Germany, 1986-88, asst. dist. commr., Mt. Holly, N.J., 1988-92; vestry mem. St. Albans Episcopal. Congregation, Ramstein AB, 1986-88. Mem. Air Force Assn., Order Daedalians, Mil Order of World Wars, Elks. Republican. Avocations: hiking, skiing, water skiing, camping, boating, travel. Home: 711 Albee Farm Rd N Nokomis FL 34275-2411

ALBANO, PASQUALE CHARLES, management educator, management and organization development consultant; b. Bayonne, N.J., Dec. 3, 1941; s. Armando and Marie (Fasulo) A.; m. Norma Agnes Eichholz, July 16, 1960; children: Donna, Nancy, Susan, Carol. BS in Edn.-Social Sci. cum laude, Monmouth U., 1967; postgrad., Rutgers U., 1969-70; MA in Mgmt. magna cum laude, Pepperdine U., 1976; cert. in orgnl. cons., U.S. Army Tng. Ctr., 1979; EdD in Leadership and Policy summa cum laude, Temple U., 1987. Cert. tchr. social scis., N.J.; orgn. devel. cons. Personnel-employee devel. specialist Hdqs. Army Comm.-Electronics Command, Ft. Monmouth, N.J., 1967-69; chmn. mgmt. devel. dept. army edn. ctr. Hdqs. Army Comm. Command, Ft. Monmouth, N.J., 1969-75, dir. northeastern U.S. regional tng. ctr., 1975-78, orgnl. effectiveness officer R & D ctr., 1978-81, chief orgnl. effectiveness office, 1981-85, chief leadership rsch. office, 1985-87, chief orgnl. conulting office, 1987-94; pvt. practice cons., 1993—; tchr. U.S. Army Pers. Mgmt. Program, Ga., Washington, Pa., N.J., Ala., Ariz., Va., N.Y., Okla., S.C., Panama, 1976-78, Internat. Assn. Quality Circles, Internat. Pers. Mgmt. Assn., Info. Resource Mgmt. Assn., USAR, 1981-91, Am. Mgmt. Assn., 1995—, Ctr. for Bus. and Inds., Monmouth and Ocean Counties, 1995; adj. prof. mgmt. and social psychology small bus. mgmt. Kean Coll., Union, N.J., 1981-96, Brookdale C.C., N.J., 1975-93, Pepperdine U., L.A., 1977-81, Temple U., Phila., 1987-88, grad. sch. bus. Fairleigh Dickinson U., 1990—; adj. prof. tchr. mgmt. and orgnl. psychology in MBA and spl. corp. onsite edn. programs Rutgers U., 1997—; tchr. interpersonal rels. Ocean County Coll., 1971-73; creative thinking Brookdale C.C., 1972-73; mem. small bus. adv. coun., 1996; cons. Mut. UFO Network, 1998. Author: Transactional Analysis on the Job, 1974, Retention of Engineers and Scientists, 1983, Effects of an Experimental Program, 1987, Value-Adding Leadership, 1988; developer mgmt. tng. curriculum for Monmouth and Ocean County Adult Edn. Commn., 1996, also instnl. materials for tng. telephone crisis hotline ctr. workers Contact USA, 1996, ednl. programs for lab. software engrs. and orgnl. surveys of U.S. Army, 1995; merger, mgmt. and original design tng. programs, 1996—; contbr. world wide web articles to numerous publs. Tchr. human rels. ednl. assns. Monmouth and Ocean Counties, 1970-74, Fed. Women's Program, 1980, ESL Cmty. and Family Svcs., Monmouth, 1990-93; pvt. tutor English Citizenship; vol. Habitat for Humanity Internat., 1995-96, Contact USA, 1995-96, Presbyn. Youth Program, 1965; mem. NAACP, 1963-64; mem. Small Bus. Adv. Coun., Ocean County Coll., 1996. With U.S. Army, 1958-60. Recipient Bernard Watson award William Penn Found., 1987, Quality Circle Devel. commendation U.S. Army, 1981, Devel. Sci. Pers. commendation, 1983, Creative Edn. Techniques commendation, 1988, ESL Textbooks commendation U.S. Army Materiel Command, 1992, Mgmt. Devel. Curriculum commendation, 1992, numerous World Wide Net awards for creative writing, 1998. Mem. ASTD, Creative Edn. Found., Internat. Transactional Analysis Assn., Adult Edn. Assn., Nat. Assn. Retired Fed. Employees, Nat. Speleol. Soc., Archaeol. Inst. of Am., Soc. Advancement of Mgmt., Acad. Mgmt., World Future Soc., Assn. of U.S. Army, Internat. Platform Assn. (elected), Jersey Shore Quality Coun., Inst. Noetic Sciences, Acad. of Am. Poets, Planetary Soc. (cons. mutual UFO network 1998), Mensa, Phi Alpha Theta, Phi Delta Kappa. Avocations: investigating mysteries, exploring caves and ancient ruins, digging fossils, inventing, writing poetry. Home and Office: Adaptive Leadership 805 Woodwild Dr Point Pleasant NJ 08742

ALBARN, DAMON, singer, songwriter; b. London, Mar. 23, 1968; s. Keith and Hazel Albarn. Vocalist, keyboard player, songwriter Blur (formerly Seymour), 1989—. Albums include Leisure, 1991, Modern Life is Rubbish, 1993, parklife, 1995, The Great Escape, 1995, Blur, 1997; numerous singles, including Sunday Sunday, 1993, Girls and Boys, 1994, Parklife, 1994, End of a Century, 1994, Country House, 1995, Universal, 1995, Charmless Man, 1995, Beetlebum, 1997, Song 2, 1997, On Your Own, 1997, MOR, 1997, Tender, 1999, Coffee & TV, 1999, No Distance Left To Run, 1999; composer original score (films): Ravenous, 1998, Ordinary Decent Criminal, 1999, 101 Reykjavik, 2000; appeared in film Face, 1997. Recipient Gold and Platinum Discs, U.K. Avocations: football, tae kwon do. Address: CMO Unit 32 Ransomes Dock, 35-5 Parkgate Rd, London SW11 4NP, England

AL-BASHIR, UMAR HASAN AHMAD, Sudanese president; b. 1935. Chmn. Revolutionary Command Council for Nat. Salvation, Khartoum, Sudan, 1989—; head of state, pres., min. of def. Khartoum, Sudan, 1989—, min. culture and info., 1992-93. Office: Office of President, The Palace, Khartoum Sudan*

ALBECK, MICHAEL, chemist, educator; b. Berlin, Oct. 15, 1934; arrived in Israel, 1935; s. Chanoch and Henya (Weiss) A.; m. Shulamith Firanko, Mar. 16, 1955; children: Amnon, Dan, Yael, Ruth. MSc, Hebrew U., Jerusalem, 1959; PhD, Hebrew U., 1962. Prin. investigator Inst. Fiber Forest Products, Jerusalem, 1962-64; head chem. lab. Mekorot Water Co. Israel, Tel Aviv, 1964-65; prof. Bar Ilan U., Ramat Gan, 1965—; dean natural scis. Bar Ilan U., Ramat Gan, Israel, 1967-79, 72-75; rector Bar Ilan U., Ramat Gan, 1982-86, pres., 1986-89. Patentee in field; contbr. over 90 articles to profl. jours. Maj. Israeli Def. Force, 1952-55. Mem. Israel Chem. Soc. (pres. 1978-80). Avocations: painting. Home: 8 Harel, 52223 Ramat Gan Israel Office: Bar Ilan U, Ramat Gan 52100, Israel

ALBEE, EDWARD FRANKLIN, author, playwright; b. Mar. 12, 1928; s. Reed A. and Frances (Cotter) Albee. Student, Trinity Coll., 1946-47. Messenger Western Union, 1955-58; lectr. Brandeis U., Johns Hopkins U., Webster U., others. Plays written include The Zoo Story, 1958, The Death of Bessie Smith, 1959, The Sandbox, 1959, The American Dream, 1960, Who's Afraid of Virginia Woolf?, 1961-62, The Ballad of the Sad Cafe (adaption of Carson McCullers' novella), 1963, Tiny Alice, 1964, Malcolm, 1966, A Delicate Balance, 1966 (Pulitzer Prize for drama 1967), Everything in the Garden, 1968, Box, Quotations from Chairman Mao, 1970, All Over, 1971, Seascape, 1975 (Pulitzer prize for drama 1975), Counting the Ways, 1976, Listening, 1977, The Man Who Had Three Arms, 1983, The Lady from Dubuque, 1978-79; adaptation of Lolita (Nabokov), 1980, Finding the Sun, 1982, Marriage Play, 1986-87, Three Tall Women, 1990-91 (Pulitzer Prize for drama 1994), Fragments, 1993, The Play about the Baby, 1996; dir. plays, including Happy Days, 1993, Alley Theatre, Houston, 1991. pres. Edward F. Albee Found. Recipient gold medal in drama Am. Acad. and Inst. Arts and Letters, 1980; inducted into Theater Hall of Fame, 1985, Nat. Medal of Arts, 1996; Kennedy Ctr. honoree, 1996. Mem. Nat. Inst. Arts and Letters,

Dramatists Guild Coun. Address: 14 Harrison St New York NY 10013-2842

ALBE FESSARD, DENISE GABRIELLE, educator; b. Paris, May 31, 1916; d. Jacques and Marie Louise (Teisseire) Albe; m. Fessard, July 1942; 1 child, Jean. Ingenieur, Ecole de Physique et Chime, Paris, 1937; DSc, U. Paris, 1950. Rsch. fellow CNRS, Paris, 1938—; with Ecole Pratique des Hautes Etudes, Paris, 1950—; prof. neurophysiologie U. Paris, 1957—, hon. prof., 1985—. Named Officer de l'ordre du merite, France, 1979. Mem. Internat. Assn. Pain Rsch. (1st pres. 1974-77). Home and Office: 29 rue des Peupliers, 92100 Boulogne France

ALBEGOVA, IRINA FYODOROVNA, psychologist, educator; b. Yaroslavl, Russia, July 27, 1954; d. Fyodor Lukyanovitch and Lidia Pavlovna (Ovetchkina) Reminnik; m. Georgy Jigitovitch Albegov, May 7, 1948 (div. 1976); 1 child, Fyodor Georgievitch. BS, Yaroslavl (Russia) U., 1976; Candidate of Sci., Moscow State Pedagog. Inst., 1982. Lectr. Yaroslavl State U., 1982-83; sr. lectr. Yaroslavl State U., Yarlslavl, 1983-84, asst. prof., 1984—. Author: The Influence of Changes of Social Structure, 1983; editor: Yaroslavl NGO: Problems of Development, 1998, Social Work: History, Theory, Technology, 1999. Pres. polit. orch. Sotsium, Yaroslavl, 1996—; chmn. coun. Ctr. Support for Yaroslavl Non-govtl. Orgns., Yaroslavl, 1999—. Avocations: travel, nature protection. Home: Apt 133, Mashinostroiteley St 19/14, 150051 Yaroslavl Russia

AL-BELTAGUI, MAMDOUH AHMED, Egyptian government official; b. Cairo, Apr. 21, 1939; married; 1 son. LLB, Cairo U., 1958; PhD in Econs., Sorbonne U., France, 1973, PhD in Polit. Scis., 1975, certs. in Fin. and Polit. Sci., 1970. Asst. prosecutor through counsellor Ct. of Appeals, Cairo, 1958-75; mem. Secretariats Coun. of Radio and TV Union; chmn. Bd. Dirs. of Newspapers; min. plenipotentiary for info. Egyptian Embassy in France, 1975-82; chmn. State Info. Svc., 1982; sec. gen. Nat. Dem. Party, 1992; mem. Shura Coun., 1992; mem. Secretariat Gen. Nat. Dem. Party, 1994—; Min. Tourism Govt. of Egypt, 1993—. Office: 110 al-Kasr al-Eini St, Misr Tourism Tower Abbasia, Cairo Egypt*

ALBER, PHILLIP GEORGE, lawyer; b. Lansing, Mich., Dec. 10, 1948; s. Phillip Karl and Audrey Irene (Putnam) A.; m. Shari Thornton; children: Emily Nicole, Phillip George, Elisabeth Whitney, Christian Thornton. BA magna cum laude, U. Mich., 1971; JD cum laude, Wayne State U., 1974. Bar: Mich. 1975, U.S. Dist. Ct. (ea. dist.) Mich. 1975, U.S. Ct. Appeals (6th cir.) 1978, U.S. Dist. Ct. (we. dist.) Mich. 1982. Assoc. Harvey, Kruse, Westen & Milan, Detroit, 1975-79, ptnr., 1979-85; ptnr. Mager, Mercer and Alber, Detroit, 1985—; lectr. Ill. Inst. Continuing Edn., Chgo., 1980. Mem. ABA (torts ins. practice sect., vice chair fidelity and surety law com.), Detroit Bar Assn. (pub. adv. com. 1979—, cir. ct. com. 1978—), Mich. Bar Assn. (rep. assembly 1970-80), Internat. Assn. Def. Counsel (fidelity and surety com. 1984—), Surety Claims Inst., Nat. Bd. Claim Assn. (pres. 1992-94, program chair 1990—), Assn. Def. Trial Counsel, Detroit Athletic Club, Hundred Club, Goodfellows Old Newsboys Club (Detroit). Republican. Roman Catholic. Home: 655 Rivard Blvd Grosse Pointe MI 48230-1253 Office: Mager Mercer & Alber 755 W Big Beaver Rd Ste 1700 Troy MI 48084-4906

ALBER, RICHARD LAWRENCE, quality assurance professional; b. Troy, N.Y., Aug. 5, 1947; s. Norman Lawrence and Jane Frances (Procak) A.; m. Janet Carol Pakatar, Oct. 28, 1967; children: Michael, David. AS, Hudson Valley C.C., Troy, 1975; grad. mgmt. devel., Rensselaer Polytechnic Inst., 1992. Cert. lead quality auditor. Machinist Watervliet (N.Y.) Arsenal, 1966-72; intern quality assurance specialist Dept. Army, Washington, 1972-75; quality assurance specialist Watervliet Arsenal, 1975-86, supr. quality assurance specialist, 1986—. Mem. Am. Soc. for Quality (cert.), U.S. Water Polo (referee), Mt. Zion Free and Accepted Masons Lodge #311 (master 1992-93). Avocations: swimming, biking, travel, Greek language, computers. Home: 42 Whiteview Rd Wynantskill NY 12198-7832 Office: SIOWV-ODP-M Watervliet Arsenal Watervliet NY 12189

ALBER, SIEGBERT, international justice; b. 1936. Student, U. Tübingen, U. Berlin, U. Paris, U. Hamburg, U. Vienna, U. Turin, Cambridge U. Mem. Bundestag, 1969-80; mem. European Parliament, 1977; mem., chmn. Com. on Legal Affairs and Citizens' Rights, 1993-94; chmn. Del. for Rels. with Baltic States, Subcom. Data Protection & Poisonous or Dangerous Substances; v.p. European Parliament, 1984-92; advocate gen. Ct. of Justice of European Cmtys., 1995—. Office: Ct Justice European Cmtys, Palais de Cour de justice, Kirchberg L-2925, Luxembourg*

ALBERANI, VILMA, library and editorial service director; b. Rome, Oct. 3, 1933. Degree in fgn. lang., U. Rome, 1958. Chief libr. and documentation ctr. physics lab. Istituto Superiore Sanità, Rome, 1958-75, asst. to dir. gen., 1976-81, with libr. editl. sect., 1982-87; dir. editl. svc. Inst. Superiore Sanità, Rome, 1988—, dir. libr., 1996-2000. Author: The Grey Literature, 1992, Italian Official Publications, 1996; co-editor: The Grey Literature 2d National Meeting, 1996; editor Annals of Istituto Superiore di Sanità, 1990—. Mem. Internat. Fedn. Libr. Assn., Italian Libr. Assn. Office: Ist Superiore Sanità, Viale Regina Elena 299, 00161 Rome Italy

ALBERIGO, GIUSEPPE, religious studies educator; b. Varese, Italy, Jan. 21, 1926; s. Giovanni and Eugenia (Banfi) A.; m. Angela Nicora, Jan. 7, 1950; children: Anna, Stefano, Paola. Jurisprudence, Cath. U., Milan, Italy, 1948; Ecumenical Theology, Evang. Faculty of Theology, Munchen, Germany, 1990, Cath. Faculty Theology, Strasbourg, France, 1996, Cath. Faculty, Münster, Germany, 1999. Full prof. U. Modena, Italy, 1951-54; lectr., full prof. U. Florence, Italy, 1954-67; univ. prof. U. Bologna, Italy, 1967—; sec. gen. Istituto Per Le Scienze Religiose, Bologna, 1962—, Found. per le Scienze Religiose "Giovanni XXIII", Bologna, 1990—, Cath. Hist. Rev., Rev. des Scis. Religieuses; assoc. editor Concilium, Nijmegen, Olanda, 1980-95; editor sci. jour. Cristianesimo Nella Storia, Bologna, 1980—. Author: (book) I Vescovi Italiani al Concilio, 1959, Cardinalato e Collegialita', 1969, Chiesa Conciliare, 1981; editor: (book) Conciliorum Oecumenicorum Decreta, 1962, 73, Les Conciles Oecumeniques, 1994, Concilium, 1996; dir. The History of Vatican II, 1959-65, 1995—. Home: Via Mazzini 82, 40138 Bologna Italy Office: Inst Religious Sci, Via San Vitale 114, 40125 Bologna Italy

ALBERS, GERD, city and regional planner; b. Hamburg, Germany, Sept. 20, 1919; s. Ernst and Bertha (Rohr) A.; m. Ingrid Maria Keup, June 11, 1952; 1 child, Martin. MS, Ill. Inst. Tech., 1950; diploma in engring., Tech. Hochschule, Hannover, Germany, 1951; DEng E.H. (hon.), U. Karlsruhe, Germany, 1958; D. in Engring. E.H. (hon.), U. Karlsruhe, Fed. Republic of Germany, 1986. Asst. planner City of Ulm, Germany, 1952-54; head planning dept. City of Trier, Germany, 1954-59; head all tech. svcs. City of Darmstadt, Germany, 1959-62; prof., chair city and regional planning Tech. U. Munich, 1962-88. Author: Was wird aus der Stadt, 1972, Entwicklungslinien, 1975, Stadtplanung 1945-80, 1984, Stadtplanung, 1988, Zur Entwicklung der Stadtplanung in Europa, 1997. Lt. comdr. German Navy, 1937-46. Recipient Fritz Schumacher prize City of Hamburg Senate, 1973, Camillo Sitte prize Vienna Tech. U. Mem. German Acad. City and Regional Planning (pres. 1985-91), Bavarian Acad. Fine Arts (pres. 1974-83), Internat. Soc. City and Regional Planners (pres. 1975-78), Acad. Regional Scic. and Planning, Royal Town Planning Inst. London (hon., corr.). Lutheran.

ALBERT, HIS MAJESTY II, King of the Belgians; b. Brussels, June 6, 1934; s. King Léopold III and Queen Astrid (formerly the Princess of Sweden); m. Donna Paola Ruffo Di Calabria, 1959; children: Prince Philippe, Prince Laurent and Princess Astrid. Pres. Caisse Générale d'Epargne et de Retraite, 1954-92, Belgian Office Fgn. Trade, 1962-93; pres. Belgian Red Cross, 1958-93, formerly Prince de Liège, succeeded to the throne 9 following death of his brother King Baudouin I, Aug. 1993, King of the Belgians, 1993—. Office: H M the King, Royal Palace Rue Brederode 16, B-1000 Brussels Belgium*

ALBERT, HANS, retired philosopher; b. Cologne, Germany, Feb. 8, 1921; s. Viktor and Bertha (Kehrein) A.; m. Margarete v. Pacher-Theinburg, Oct. 27, 1957; children: Max, Kurt, Gert. Dipl Kfm, U. Cologne, 1950, Dr rer pol, 1952, Privat-Dozent, 1957. Asst. U. Cologne, 1952-58, dozent, 1958-63; prof. sociology and philosophy of sci. U. Mannheim (Fed. Republic Germany), 1963-89, prof. emeritus, 1989—. Author: Traktat über kritische Vernunft, 1968, Traktat ü rationale Praxis, 1978, Die Wissenschaft und die Fehlbarkeit der Vernunft, 1982, Kritik der reinen Hermeneutik, 1994, also others. Lt. arty. German Army, 1939-45. Recipient Ernst Hellmut Vits prize, 1976, Arthur Burkhardt prize, 1984. Mem. Am. Econ. Assn., Friedrich List Gesellschaft, Internat. Vereinigung für Rechts-und Sozialphilosophie, Deutsche Gesellschaft für Soziologie, Gesellschaft für Wirtschafts-und Sozialwissenschaften. Home: Freiburgerstrasse 62, 69126 Heidelberg Germany

ALBERT, JAMES SPURLING, curator, zoology educator; b. L.A., Jan. 15, 1964; s. Samuel H. Albert and Anne L. Samuelson; m. Sara Holmberg. BS, U. Calif., Berkeley, 1986; PhD, U. Mich., 1995. Asst. prof. Nippon Med. Sch., Tokyo, 1995-99; curator Fla. Mus. Natural History, Gainesville, 1999—. Contbr. articles to profl. jours. Mem. Am. Soc. Ichthyologists and Herpetologists, Soc. for the Study of Evolution, Soc. Systematic Biology. Office: Fla Mus Natural History Univ Fla Gainesville FL 32611-7800

ALBERT, MANUEL JOHN, microbiologist; b. Kaliyickakuzhi, Tamil Nadu, India, May 28, 1950; arrived in Australia, 1983; s. David and Lysol (Gnanadeepam) Manuel; m. Emely Philip-John, Dec. 17, 1983; children: David John, Davina John, Daniel John. BSc, Madurai U., India, 1970; MSc, Madras U., 1973, PhD, 1979. Rsch. fellow Adelaide (Australia) Children's Hosp., 1984-85, Royal Children's Hosp., Melbourne, Australia, 1985-87, Melbourne U., 1988-89; rsch. microbiologist Alice Springs Hosp., Australia, 1989-99; head dept. lab. rsch., lab. sci. divsn. Internat. Ctr. Diarrhoeal Disease Rsch., Dhaka, Bangladesh, 1994-99; prof. microbiology Kuwait U., 2000—; cons. microbiologist Harvard Inst. Internat. Devel., Boston, 1991, WHO, Geneva, 1993, 95, 96, 97, 98. Contbr. articles to profl. jours., chpts. to books; patentee live oral rotavirus vaccine; discoverer Vibrio Cholerae 0139 Bengal. Mem. Australian Soc. Microbiology. Avocations: tennis, squash, jogging, reading. Office: Kuwait U Dept Microbiology, PO Box 24903, Safat 13110, Kuwait

ALBERT, MICHEL MAURICE LOUIS DELPHIN, bank executive; b. Fontenay-le-Comte, Vendée, France, Feb. 25, 1930; s. Maurice Albert and Marie-Louise Perrotin; m. Claude Balland; children: Jean-Marc, Eric, Pierre-Emmanuel, Christophe. Diplome, Inst. d'etudes politique, Paris; JD, École Nat. d'Adminstrn., 1954. Fin. insp., 1956-59; sec.-gen. Com. Rueff-Armand, 1959; insp. gen. Moroccan Finances, 1960; dep. dir.-gen. Nat. Bank for Econ. Devel. of Rabat, Morocco, 1961-63; dep. dir. Banque Européenne d'Investissement à Brussels, 1963-66, dir., 1966-70; dir. structure and econ. devel. Commn. de la Communauté Économique Européenne à Brussels, 1966-69; v.p. Express-Union, 1969-70; v.p. oversight coun. Groupe Express, 1970-71; fin. insp. first class Unicredit, 1971, dir., 1973-79, dir.-gen.; dir.-gen. Union d'Études et d'Investissements, 1972-75; dep. commr., govt. planning officer, 1976—, commr. gen., 1978-81; pres: Groupe Assurances Générales de France, 1982-94, Centre d'Études Prospectives et d'Informations Internat., 1983-95; elected mem. l'Académie des Scis. Morales et Politiques, 1994. Writings include: Ciel et terre, 1970, Les vaches maigres, 1975, Le pari français, 1982 (Prix Aujourd'hui), Un pari pour l'Europe, 1983, Crise Krach Boom, 1988, Capitalisme contre capitalisme, 1991. Decorated officier Legion of Honor (France), grand officer l'Ordre Nat. du Merite (France), officer Ouissam Alaouite (France), comdr. l'Ordre Saint-Charles, comdr. Merite de la République Fed. d'Allemagne (Germany). Office: Banque de France, 9.11 rue de Valois, 75001 Paris France

ALBERT, SUZANNE DICKSON, artist; b. Cleve., Apr. 24, 1946; d. Alvin Kenneth and Doris Lustig Dickson; m. Philip Charles Albert, Oct. 9, 1999. BS in Math., Ohio U., 1968, MA in German Lit., 1970; MAE in Painting, R.I. Sch. Design, 1978; JD, Roger Williams U., 1999. Tchr. math. Barrington (R.I.) Pub. Schs., 1991-94; paralegal intern R.I. Commn. Human Rights, Providence, 1993-94; corp. paralegal Hasbro, Inc., Pawtucket, R.I., 1994-97; faculty rsch. asst. Roger Williams U. Sch. Law, Bristol, R.I., 1998; law clk. David E. Maglio & Assocs., 1999; rule nine intern juvenile criminal divsn. Atty. Gen. R.I., 1999; law clk. to judge Howard Lipsey Washington County Ct., R.I., 1999; leader profl. workshops in pastel. One person shows include DeBlois Gallery, Newport, R.I., Vet.'s Meml. Auditorium, Providence, Attleboro (Mass.) Mus., Providence Art Club, Wheeler Gallery, Providence, Newport Art Mus.; exhibited in group shows at Hydrangea Gallery, Newport, Greenhut Gallery, Portland, Maine, Deer Isle Art Assn., Deer Island, Maine, Providence Art Club (Grumbacher award), Gallery 401, Providence, Vincent Smith Mus., Springfield, Mass., Pittsfield (Mass.) Cmty. Art Ctr., Ariel Gallery, N.Y.C., Milford (Conn.) Fine Arts Coun., Virginia Lynch Gallery, Tiverton, R.I., William Hart Benton Mus., Storrs, Conn.; represented in permanent collections in Raytheon, Sudbury, Mass., Cambridge (Mass.) Savings Bank, Berkshire Ptnrs., Inc., Boston, Linsco/Pvt. Ledgers, Boston, Brigham and Woman's Hosp., Boston, Testa, Herwitz & Thibeault, Boston, Morrison, MaHoney & Miller, Boston, Kates Properties, Providence, Nabisco Co., Newark, Price Waterhouse, Boston, Fed. Nat. Mortgage Assn., Atlanta, Putnam Investments, Boston, Roger Williams Hosp., Providence, Fidelity Investments, N.Y.C. Recipient Grumbacher award Grumbacher Art Supply, 1988. Mem. R.I. Bar Assn. (student), Providence Art Club, Delta Theta Phi. Avocation: tennis. Home: 9 Wicklow Rd Westerly RI 02891-3645

ALBERTINI, DEMETRIO, professional soccer player; b. Besana, Brianza, Italy, Aug. 23, 1971. Midfielder AC Milan, Italy. Mem. 1994 and 1998 World Cup squads; winner 5 Italian titles and European Cup. Office: Milan Assn Calcio SpA, Via Turati 3, 20121 Milan Italy*

ALBERTS, BRUCE MICHAEL, federal agency administrator, foundation administrator, biochemist; b. Chicago, Ill., Apr. 14, 1938; s. Harry C. and Lillian (Surasky) A.; m. Betty Neary, June 14, 1960; children: Beth L., Jonathan B., Michael B. AB in Biochemical Scis. summa cum laude, Harvard Coll., 1960; PhD in Biophysics, Harvard U., 1965. Postdoctoral fellow NSF Institut de Biologie Moleculaire, Geneva, 1965-66; asst. prof. dept. chemistry Princeton (N.J.) U., 1966-73, assoc. prof. dept. biochemical scis., 1971-73, Damon Pfeiffer prof. life scis., 1973-76; prof., vice chmn. dept. biochemistry and biophysics U. Calif., San Francisco, 1976-81, Am. Cancer Soc. Rsch. prof., 1981-85, prof., chmn., 1985-90, Am. Cancer Soc. Rsch. prof. of biochemistry, 1990-93; pres. NAS, Washington, 1993—; chrm. NRC, Washington, 1993—; trustee Cold Spring Harbor Lab., 1972-75; adv. panel human cell biology NSF, 1974-76; adv. coun. dept. biochemical scis. and molecular biology Princeton U., 1979-85; chmn. vis. com. dept. biochemistry and molecular biology Harvard Coll., 1983-86; com. mapping and sequencing the human genome Nat. Rsch. Coun. Com., 1986-88; bd. sci. couns. divsn. arthritis and metabolic diseases NIH, 1974-78, molecular cytology study sect. 1982-86, chmn. 1984-86; program adv. com. NIH Human Genome Project, 1988-91; sci. adv. bd. Jane Coffin Childs Meml. Fund for Med. Rsch., 1978-85, Markey Found., 1984—, Fred Hutchinson Cancer Rsch. Ctr., Seattle, 1988—; com. mem. corp. vis. dept. biology MIT, 1978—, dept. embryology Carnegie Inst., Washington, 1983—; faculty rsch. lectr. U. Calif., San Francisco, 1985; sci. adv. com. Marine Biological Lab., Woods Hole, Mass., 1988—; bd. dirs. Genentech Rsch. Found., Fed. Am. Socs. for Experimental Biology; adv. bd. Bethesda Rsch. Labs. Life Tech. Inc., Nat. Sci. Resources Ctr., Smithsonian Inst., 1990—; com. mem. adolescence and young adulthood/sci. standards, Nat. Bd. Profl. Teaching Standards, 1991—. Co-author: The Molecular Biology of the Cell, 1989; editor: Mechanistic Studies of DNA Replication and Genetic Recombination, 1980; editorial bd. Jour. Biological Chemistry, 1976-82, Jour. Cell Biology, 1984-87; assoc. editor Annual Reviews Cell Biology, 1984—; essay editor Molecular Biology of th Cell, 1991—; contbr. numerous articles to profl. jours. including Saunders Sci. Publ., Current Sci., Ltd. Fellow NSF, 1960-65; recipient Eli Lilly award in biological chemistry Am. Chemical Soc., 1972, Baxter award for Disting. Rsch. in Biomedical Scis. Assn. Am. Med. Colls., 1992; named Lifetime Rsch. Prof. Am. Cancer Soc., 1980, Outstanding Vol. Coord. Calif. Sch. Vol. Partnership, 1993. Gairdner Foundation InternationalAward, 1995. Fellow AAAS; mem. NAS (commn. life scis. Nat. Rsch. Coun. 1988—, chmn. 1988-93, adv. bd. Nat. Sci. Resources Ctr. 1990—, Nat. Com. Sci. Edn. Standards and Assessment 1992—, com. mem. Nat. Edn. Support System for Tchrs. and Schs. 1992—, U.S. Steel Found. award 1975), Am. Chemical Soc., Am. Soc. for Cell Biology, Am. Soc. for Microbiology, Genetics Soc. Am., Am. Soc. Biochemistry and Molecular Biology (councilor 1984—), Am. Philos. Soc., European Molecular Biology Orgn. (assoc.), Phi Beta Kappa. Office: National Academy of Sciences/NRC Office of the President 2101 Constitution Ave NW Washington DC 20418-0006

ALBERTS, HAROLD, lawyer; b. San Antonio, Apr. 3, 1920; s. Bernard H. and Rose Alberts; m. Rose M. Gaslin, Mar. 25, 1945; children: Linda Rae, Barry Lawrence. LLB, U. Tex., 1942. Bar: Tex. 1943, U.S. Supreme Ct. 1950, U.S. Ct. Mil. Appeals 1959. Tchr. U. Tex., 1942; instr. U. Tex., Austin, 1941-42; legal officer Chase Field, 1944; sole practice Corpus Christi, Tex. Pres. Jewish Welfare Fund, Corpus Christi, 1948; chmn. S.W. Regional Anti-Defamation League, Tex. and Okla., 1970-71, chmn., 1969-72, chmn. Brotherhood Week, 1957; chmn. Nueces County (Tex.) Red Cross, 1959-61; mem. campaign exec. com., chmn. meetings United Cmty. Svcs., 1961; v.p. Little Theatre, Corpus Christi, 1964; chmn. Corpus Christi NCCJ, 1967-69, nat. dir., 1974-76; bd. dirs. Tex. State Assn. Mental Health; pres. Combined Jewish Appeal, Corpus Christi, 1974-76; moderator Friday Morning Group, 1975, 96. Served to lt. (sr. grade) USNR, 1942-46. Mem. ABA, Tex. Bar Assn., Corpus Christi Bar Assn., Kiwanis (pres. 1962), B'nai B'rith (pres. 1955), Masons (32d degree). Home: 5314 Hulen Dr Corpus Christi TX 78413-2247 Office: PO Box 271477 Corpus Christi TX 78427-1477

ALBERTS, LAURENCE, physicist; b. Port Elizabeth, South Africa, Oct. 30, 1923; s. Pieter Jacobus and Susanna (Johanna) van Dalen; married, Dec. 3, 1948; children: Philip, Albert, Johannes, Sonnette. MSc, U. Rhodes (South Africa), 1945; DSc, U. Orange Free State, Bloemfontein, South Africa, 1952, DSc in Physics (hon.), 1985; DSc in Engring. (hon.), U. Natal, Durban, South Africa, 1985; DSc in Physics, Rand Afrikaans U., Johannesburg, South Africa, 1988. Prof. physics U. Orange Free State, Bloemfontein, 1961-67, Rand Afrikaans U., Johannesburg, 1967-71; v.p. South Africa Atomic Energy Commn., Pretoria, 1971-77; pres. South Africa Coun. Mineral Tech., Johannesburg, 1977-84; dir. gen. Dept. Mineral & Energy Affairs, Pretoria, 1984-87; cons. in pvt. practice Menlo Park, South Africa, 1987—; bd. dirs. E.L. Bateman, Boksburg, South Africa, Lanok, Paarl, South Africa. Contbr. articles to profl. jours. Chmn. Rustenberg (South Africa) Ch. Conf.; facilitator South Africa Peace Accord, Johannesburg, 1992. Col. South African Army, 1978-80. Fellow Inst. of British Inst. of Physics, South African Inst. of Mining and Metallurgy, Royal Soc. of South Africa; mem. Sci. Adv. Coun., South Africa Inst. of Physics (hon. life mem.). Mem. Dutch Reformed Ch. Home: Ruimtesig F5, Pretoria South Africa Office: PO Box 35705, Menlo Park 0102, South Africa

ALBERTSEN, KEN, writer, philosopher; b. Copenhagen, 1952. Self-employed web site designer Calif., 1994-98; owner Wonderfull.com, 1995, Adventure 1.com, 1996; spkr. at seminars, Calif., 1995-98. Author: Metaphysical and Paranormal Hocus Pocus, Key to the Airways, Worldwide Diplomatic Contacts, Worldwide English Language Periodicals. Coord., benefactor No. Thailand Girls Football League. Mem. Green party. Buddhist. Avocations: bouldering, rock climbing. Home: Poste Restante, Chiang Rai 57000, Thailand

ALBERTSON, CHRISTIERN GUNNAR (CHRIS ALBERTSON), broadcaster, music critic, writer; b. Reykjavik, Iceland, Oct. 18, 1931; came to U.S., 1957, naturalized, 1963; s. Thordur and Yvonne (Broberg) A.; m. Hanne Elisabeth Christensen, 1954 (div. 1958). Student, Kent Coll., Canterbury, England, 1947-49; grad., Acad. Merc. Art, Copenhagen, 1952. Gen. mgr. Storyville Club, Copenhagen, 1952-54; producer, writer U.S. Armed Forces Radio and TV, Iceland, 1954-57, WCAU Radio, Phila., 1957-58; disc jockey WHAT-RM Radio, Phila., 1958-60; producer Riverside Records, N.Y.C., 1960-62; continuity dir. WNEW Radio, N.Y.C., 1963-64; gen. mgr. WBAI-FM Radio, N.Y.C., 1964-66; dir. BBC programs HArtwest Prodns., N.Y.C., 1966-67; co-producer, host weekly TV series The Jazz Set, PBS Network, 1972-73; pres. Video One, Inc., 1976-79; producer, co-host weekly cable TV weries Doin' It, 1976-77; entertainment editor Beauty Trade Mag., 1978-79; producer Bessie Smith blues series Columbia Records, 1970; U.S. jazz reporter Danish Radio, 1972-75; U.S. music corr. Berlingske Tidende, Copenhagen, 1960-64; talent cons. Dupont Show of Week, 1961. Author: Bessie-The Life of Bessie Smith, 1972, rev. edit., 2000, Empress of the Blues, 1974; contbg. author: Bluesland, 1992, Jazz: A Listener's Companion, 2000; contbg. editor: Oxford Biographical Encyclopedia of Jazz, 1998; writer story and script The Alberta Hunter Story, TV mini-series, 1980, (film) Really The Blues, 1997, (TV documentary) My Castle's Rockin', 1988, The Story of Jazz, 1994; contbg. editor Stereo Review, 1973-99, A Plus Mag., 1983-96, Sound & Vision, 1999-2000; editl. cons. Routes Mag., 1978-80, 91-95; contbr. articles to Down Beat, Saturday Rev., Rolling Stone, N.Y. Times, Jazz Forum, Sound & Image, MacWeek, N.Y. Amsterdam News, Timeline, others; assoc. producer, cons. (film) Bessie, 1974; music cons. (film) Buddy Can You Spare A Dime, 1974. Mem. adv. bd. N.Y. Jazz Mus., 1972-75. Recipient Grand Prix du Disque, Montreux Jazz Festival, 1971, Trendsetter of Yr. award Billboard, 1971, CEBA award for distinction, 1964, Critics Poll Best Liner Notes award Living Blues Mag., 1993. Mem. Nat. Acad. Rec. Arts & Scis. (Grammy award 1971, Trustees award 1971, Grammy nominations 1977, 97). E-mail: fugl@rcn.com. Address: 444 Central Park W New York NY 10025-4378

ALBERTZ, RAINER, religious studies educator; b. Roestfelde, Germany, May 2, 1943; s. Heinrich and Ilse (Schall) A.; m. Helke Hainig, Sept. 5, 1964; 1 child, Anuschka. Protestant Theology, U. Heidelberg, 1969, Doctorate in Protestant Theology, 1972, Habilitation in Old Testament, 1977. Prof. Old Testament and Oriental history of religion U. Heidelberg, 1980-83; prof. bibl. theology U. Siegen, Germany, 1983-95; prof. Old Testament, U. Muenster, Germany, 1995—; spkr. in field. Author: Weltschoepfung und Menschen-schoepfung, 1974, Persoenliche Froemmigkeit und Offizielle Religion, 1978, Der Gott des Daniel, 1988, A History of Israelite Religion in Old Testament Times, 2 vols., 1994, Zorn über der Unrecht, 1996, Religion und Gesellschaft, 1997. Elder Reformist Ch., Hilchenbach, 1988-95. Recipient Publ. award Bibl. Archaeol. Soc., 1995. Mem. Social Dem. Party. Avocation: amateur radio. Home: Am Stenpatt 8, D-48341 Altenberge Germany Office: U Münster Evangelisch-Theologische Fakultaet, Universitaetsstr 13-17, D-48143 Münster Germany

ALBERY, NICHOLAS, social inventor, editor; b. St. Albans, U.K., July 28, 1948; s. Donald and Heather (Boys) A.; m. Josefine Speyer, May 19, 1991; 1 child, Merlyn. BA, N.E.L.P., 1985; diploma, Inst. Psychotherapy and Social Studies, 1986. Dir. Natural Death Ctr., London, 1991—; gen. sec. Coun. for Posterity, 1993—; editor Global Ideas Bank (www.globalideasbank.org), 1994—; dir. ApprenticeMaster Alliance, 1994—, Poetry Challenge, U.K., 1995—; chair Inst. for Social Inventions, London, 1985—. Editor Social Inventions Jour., Poem for the Day; editor: Book of Visions-An Encyclopedia of Social Innovations, 1993, New Natural Death Handbook, 1997, Creative Speculations, 2000, Time Out Book of Country Walks, 1997, 1,001 Health tips, 1999, Social Dreams and Technological Nightmares, 1999, The Book of Inspiration, 2000; editor DoBe participative events website, 2000—. Recipient Award Schumacher Soc., 1994. Avocations: learning a poem for every day of the year, walking with friends. Office: Inst for Social Inventions, 20 Heber Rd, London NW2 6AA, England

ALBERY, TIM, theatre and opera director; b. May 20, 1952. Dir. plays including War Crimes, 1981, Secret Gardens, 1983, Venice Preserv'd, 1983, Hedda Gabler, 1984, The Princes of Cleves, 1985, Mary Stuart, 1988, As You Like It, 1989, Berenice, 1990, Wallenstein, 1993, Macbeth, 1996, Attempts on Her Life, 1997; dir. operas including (for. English Nat. Opera) Billy Budd, 1988, Beatrice and Benedict, 1990, Peter Grimes, 1992, Lohengrin, 1993, From the House of the Dead, 1997, (for Opera North) The Trojans, 1986, Don Giovanni, 1991, Don Carlos, 1992, Kara Kabanova, 1999, (for Welsh Nat. Opera), The Trojans, 1987, (for Scottish Opera) The Midsummer Marriage, 1988, Fidelio, 1994, das Rheingold, 2000, (for Australian Opera) The Marriage of Figaro, 1992, (for Netherlands Opera) Benvenuto Cellini, 1991, La Wally, 1993, (for Royal Opera House), Cherubim, 1994, Nabucco, 1995, (for Met. Opera) Midsummer Night's Dream, 1996, (for Santa Fé Opera) Beatrice and Benedict, 1998, The Merry Widow, 2000, others.

ALBES, JOHANNES, thoracic and cardiovascular surgeon; b. Vechta, Germany, Mar. 21, 1960; s. Maximilian Johannes and Maria (Wergen) A. MD, Hannover (Germany) Med. Sch., 1985. Bd. cert. gen. surgeon, thoracic and cardiovascular surgeon. Intern and resident divsn. thoracic,

cardiovascular surgery Hannover (Germany) Med. Sch, 1987-93; chief resident Hannover (Germany) Med. Sch., 1993-95; staff surgeon U. Tuebingen, Germany, 1995-98; asst. prof. U. Tuebingen, 1998-99, U. Jena, Germany, 1999—. Contbr. articles to profl. jours. Mem. Soc. Thoracic Surgeons, German Soc. Thoracic and Cardiovasc. Surgery, German Transplantation Soc., European Soc. Heart and Lung Transplantation, Internat. Soc. Heart-Lung Transplantation. Avocations: jazz, running, squash. Office: Friedrich-Schiller U, Dept Thoracic Cardiac Vasc Surgery, Jena Germany

ALBINI, ADRIANA, chemist, researcher; b. Venice, Italy, Sept. 2, 1955; d. Umberto and Giovanna (Martini) A.; m. Douglas M. Noonan, May 23, 1987; children: Thomas, Silvia. BA, Liceo Colombo, Genoa, Italy, 1974, PhD in Chemistry, 1979. Postdoctoral fellow Max Planck Inst., Munich, 1980-82; vis. scientist NIH, Bethesda, Md., 1985-88; rsch. asst. Nat. Cancer Inst., Genoa, 1980, rsch. scientist, 1983-85, sr. investigator, 1988-97, sect. chief tumor progression Advanced Biotech. Ctr., 1997—, dir. molecular biology lab., 1999—; advisor Superior Oncology Sch., Genoa, 1996—; over 400 presentations at sci. meetings, 1980—. Author: (novel) A Clone in the Suitcase, 1995 (Premio Gronchi award); mem. editl. bd. Invasion and Metastasis, Forum, Pathology Oncology Rsch., Internat. Jour. Oncology; contbr. over 120 articles to internat. sci. jours.; patentee in field. Mem. Internat. Metastasis Soc. (bd. dirs. 1997—), Italian Soc. Cancerology (bd. dirs. 1997—), Am. Assn. for Cancer Rsch., Am. Soc. Cell Biology, Società Italiana Patologia. Avocations: writing novels, fencing, skiing. E-mail: albini@ermes.cba.unige.it. Home: Salita Provvidenza 14-1B, 16134 Genoa Italy Office: Nat Cancer Inst (1st) CBA, Largo R Benzi 10, 16132 Genoa Italy

ALBINI, UMBERTO, humanities educator; b. Savona, Liguria, Italy, May 3, 1923; s. Giovanni and Bianca Maria (Panconi) A.; m. Giovanna Martini; children: Adriana, Francesca. BA, Liceo Chiabrera, 1941; MA, U. Genova, 1945; PhD, U. Rome, 1955. Tchr. H.S., Savona, Italy, 1945-50; libr. Biblioteca Nazionale Centrale, Florence, Italy, 1950-65; prof. U. Genova, 1966-98; prof. h.c. U. Budapest, 1977; asst. prof. U. Bonn, Germany, 1952-54, U. Florence, 1958-65; dir. Studi Ital. Filologia Classica, Florence, 1983—; pres. Istituto Nazionale Dramma Antico, 1995-98. Author: Nel Nome Di Dioniso, 1991, Atene: L'Udienza e' Aperta, 1994, Riso alla Greca, Aristofane, 1997, Testo e Palcoscenico, 1998, Euroipide o dell'invenzione, 2000. Recipient Golden medal for culture, Budapest, 1978, Golden medal for rsch., Rome, 1996, Ostia Antica prize, 1999; Paul Harris fellow, 1998. Fellow Hungarian Acad. Lit. (hon.).

ALBIZUREZ, FRANCISCO, writer, educator; b. Guatemala City, Dec. 1, 1935; s. Herlindo Albizurez and Catalina Palma; m. Marta Gil, Mar. 4, 1962; children: Monica, Pamela. Lic., San Carlos U., Guatemala, 1961; PhD in Philology, Complutense U., Spain, 1965. Prof., rschr. U. San Carlos, 1962-90; editor Banco de Guatemala, 1989-97. Author: Historia de la literatura Guatemala, 3 vols., 1981-87 (Gold Quetzal award 1981). Fulbright grantee, 1987, 91. Mem. Academia Guatemalteca de la Lengua. Home: 30 Calle 18-72, 01012 Guatemala City Guatemala

ALBIZURI, FRANTZISKO XABIER, computer science educator; b. Donostia, Spain, Jan. 28, 1963; s. Jesus and Josefa (Irigoyen) A. MSc in Physics, Basque Country U., 1987, PhD in Computer Sci., 1995. Assoc. prof. Basque Country U., Spain, 1989—. Contbr. articles to profl. jours. Mem. IEEE Computer Soc. Social Democrat. Avocations: history, philosophy, mountaineering. Office: Informatika Fakultatea, PO Box 649, 20080 Donostia Spain

ALBLAS, BERNARD PIETER, physical chemist, researcher; b. Utrecht, The Netherlands, Dec. 27, 1953; s. P and Ch. E. (Verheul) A. DSc, U. Utrecht, 1978; PhD, State U. Groningen, The Netherlands, 1983. Rschr. State U. Groningen, 1978-83, Tech. U. Twente, The Netherlands, 1983-85, Applied Sci. Rsch. (TNO), Soesterberg, The Netherlands, 1985-90; mgr. Phys. and Chem. Lab., Ctr. Tech. Rsch. and Consulting (COT) bv, Haarlem, The Netherlands, 1990—. Patentee in field. Mem. Dutch Royal Chem. Soc. (KNCV), Dutch Phys. Soc. (NNV), Dutch Orgn. Paint Technicians (sec. 1992), Eurolab. Home: Looiersgracht 103, 1016 WC Amsterdam NHolland, The Netherlands Office: COT bv, PO Box 98, 2050 AB Overveen NHolland, The Netherlands

ALBOROUGH, JEZ, children's book author; b. Kingston-upon-Thames, Surrey, Eng., Nov. 13, 1959; s. John Warmen and Cecily (Gathercole) A.; m. Rikke Buhl, July 18, 1987. Degree in graphic design, Norwich Sch. Art, 1981. Writings include: Bare Bear, 1984, Running Bear, 1985, Willoughby Wallaby, 1986, The Grass in Always Greener, 1987, Esther's Trunk, 1988, Hillary Hic-cup, 1988, The Candle Story, 1988, The Clock Story, 1988, The Umbrella Story, 1988, The Mirror Story, 1988, Cupboard Bear, 1989, Beaky, 1990, Shake Before Opening, 1991, Where's My Teddy?, 1992, Cuddly Dudley, 1993, Clothesline, 1993, Hide and Seek, 1994, It's the Bear, 1994, Can You Peck Like a Hen?, 1996, Can You Jump Like a Kangaroo?, 1996, Watch Out! Big Bro's Coming, 1997, Balloon, 1998, My Friend Bear, 1998, Duck in the Truck, 1999, HUG, 2000; illustrator Can You Hear Me, Granddad?, 1986, The Canterville Ghost, 1987, Martin's Mice, 1988. Office: Walker Books, 87 Vauxhall Walk, London SE11 5HJ, England

ALBRACHT, MANFRED, software developer; b. Bergheim, Germany, Mar. 11, 1963; s. Josef and Gertrud (Arnolds) A. Diploma, Tech. U., Aachen, Germany, 1990. Cert. computer scientist. Gen. mgr. MAITD, Aachen, 1988-92, DTP Software Albracht, Aachen, 1992—. Author: True Type Designer, 1993; author of software. Avocation; hang gliding. Office: DTP Software Albracht, DTP Software Albracht, Am Handwerkerzentrum 7, 52756 Monschan Germany

AL-BRAIKAN, HAZEM KHALID, global fund manager; b. Kuwait, July 16, 1972; s. Khalid AbdulAziz Al-Braikan. BS in Fin. and Banking with distinction, U. Kuwait, 1995. Portfolio mgr. Kuwait Investment Projects Co., 1995—, fund mgr., 1996—; bd. dirs. United Assets Mgmt. Co., Luxembourg, United Fisheries of Kuwait, The Dragon Fund Mgmt. Co., Luxembourg, Al-Razi Investment Co., Kuwait. Author: Kuwait...Where It Stands, 1995. Served with Kuwait mil., 1990-91. Recipient medal of honor Gulf War Coalition Forces, Saudi Arabia, 1991, Kuwait medal of honor, Pres. of Kuwait, 1991. Mem. Kuwait Forex Assn., Internat. Securities Market Assn. Avocations: fishing, swimming.

ALBRECHT, FRANK MATTHIAS, antiquarian bookseller; b. Hamburg, Germany, Sept. 15, 1959; s. Wilhelm and Ruth (Gensch) A. Apprentice Buchhandlung Schaumburg, Stade, Germany, 1981-82; with Auktionshaus Tenner, Heidelberg, Germany, 1983-85; gen. mgr. Verlag and Antiquariat, Schriesheim, Germany, 1985—. Author: (bibliography) Krieg und Frieden, 1988-97. Chmn. Stadtjugendring, Buxtehude, Germany, 1976-77. Mem. PEN, Verband Deutscher Antiquare. Home and Office: Verlag und Antiquariat, Panoramastrasse 4, 69198 Schriesheim Germany

ALBRECHT, GUDRUN, mathematician, researcher, adult educator; b. Munich, Germany, May 17, 1965; d. Rüdiger and Edelgard (Weihmann) A. M in Math., Munich U. Tech., 1990, PhD in Math., 1993, habilitation in math., 1999. Sci. employee Munich U. Tech., 1990-93, asst. prof., 1993-95, 97—, dept. math. women's rep., 1992-94; vis. rsch. fellow U. Kaiserslautern, Germany, 1995-96, Ariz. State U., Tempe, 1996-97. Contbr. articles to profl. jours. including Jour. Geometry. Fellow German Sci. Found., 1995-97. Mem. Soc. Indsl. and Applied Math. Avocation: languages. Office: Munich U Tech, Dept Math, 80290 Munich Germany

ALBRECHT, HEINZ, psychiatrist; b. Molln, Germany, Sept. 29, 1948; arrived in New Zealand, 1981; s. Werner A. and Irmgard Albrecht Schehl; m. Deborah Thomas, Jan. 26, 1986; children: Tessa, Bonnie. MD, U. Gottingen, Germany, 1976. Psychiatrist Auckland Hosp. Bd., New Zealand, 1981-86, Regional Forensic Psychiatry Svcs., Auckland, 1986-98; sr. lectr. U. Auckland Med. Sch., 1989-98, asst. to dir., 1992-97; clin. dir. Acute Care/Crisis Cmty. Team, Gold Coast, Queensland, Australia, 1999—; mem. adv. bd. criminology Bond U., Gold Coast, vis. adj. prof. Ctr. Applied Psychology and Criminology. Asst. co-author: Caught Up with His Past, 1995; contbr. articles to profl. jours. Am Field Svc. Exch. Student scholar, 1969. Fellow Australian and New Zealand Coll. Psychiatrists; mem. Am. Acad. Psychiatry and Law, Am. Acad. Forensic Scis., Australian and New Zealand Soc. Psychology, Psychiatry, Law, Australasian Soc. Emergency Medicine, Am. Acad. Emergency Medicine. Lutheran. Avocations: jogging, jet skiing. E-mail: 17dolphin@one.net.au.

ALBRECHT, JOIE, television and film producer, director, writer; b. Denver; d. Alfred Emil and Virginia Lee Albrecht; m. Scott N. Garen, Sept. 17, 1979 (div. Aug. 1989). Student, U. Colo., 1976-78, U. Calif., Bakersfield, 1979. V.p. Garen/Albrecht Prodns. Inc., Santa Monica, Calif., 1980-88; owner, pres. Albrecht & Assocs., Inc., Topanga, Calif., 1989—; guest lectr. Am. Film Inst., L.A., 1981, Women's Image Network, L.A., 1994; judge Emmy awards, L.A., 1985—; producer, writer, dir. Scandals, pilot for ABC/Stephen J. Cannell Prodns.; producer, dir., writer CBS Comedy Bloopers; author Adam's Guide to Eve. Prodr. (nat. syndication) The Cliffwood Avenue Kids'; prodr., dir. Up Close HBO series; co-creator, developer, prodr.: (TV spl.) Sixty Years of Seduction, cable spl. Carole King: One to One; prodr., writer TV's Bloopers and Practical Jokes--NBC; developer, prodr., writer: (TV spls.) Television's Greatest Commercials; creator, prodr., writer, dir.: Down and Out with Donald Duck, 1987; prodr., writer, co-dir.: Mickey's 60th Birthday, Totally Minnie--Disney/NBC; prodr., writer, dir.: (TV spl.) Comedy Bloopers. Recipient Belding Bowl for outstanding contbn. to advt. Belding Awards, 1984, gold award for Smart Investing, N.Y. Film Festival, 1986, bronze award for outstanding achievement in film and TV music video category Cindy Awards,; talent scholar U. Colo. Mem. AFTRA, ASCAP, SAG, Dirs. Guild Am. (women's com. 1991—), Writers Guild Am., Women in Film, Topanga Assn. for Scenic Cmty., Old Topanga Homeowners Assn. Democrat. Avocations: spiritual pursuits, crafts, travel. Office: PO Box 8626 Calabasas CA 91372-8626

ALBRECHT, RONALD FRANK, anesthesiologist; b. Chgo., Apr. 17, 1937; s. Frank William and Mabel Dorothy (Cassens) A.; children: Ronald Frank II, Mark Burchfield, Meredith Ann. A.B., U. Ill., 1958, B.S., 1959, M.D., 1961. Diplomate Am. Bd. Anesthesiology. Intern U. Cin. Hosp., 1961-62; resident in anesthesiology U. Ill. Hosp., Chgo., 1962-64, attending physician, 1966-73, 89—; clin. assoc. NIH, Bethesda, Md., 1964-66; practice medicine specializing in anesthesiology Chgo., 1966—; asst. prof. anesthesiology U. Ill., Chgo., 1966-70, clin. assoc. prof., 1970-73, prof. anesthesiology, head dept. Coll. Medicine, 1989—; chief dept. anesthesiology U. Ill. Hosp., Chgo., 1989—, pres. med. staff, 1999—; chmn. dept. anesthesiology Michael Reese Med. Ctr., Chgo., 1971—; prof. anesthesiology U. Chgo., 1973-89. Contbr. articles to profl. jours. Served to lt. comdr. USPHS, 1964-66. Fellow Am. Coll. Anesthesiologists; mem. AMA, Internat. Anesthesia Rsch. Soc., Am. Soc. Anesthesiologists, Assn. Anesthesists Gt. Britain and Ireland, Am. Physiol. Soc., Soc. Acad. Anesthesiology Chairs, Assn. Anesthesiology Program Dirs. (pres. 1991-93), Ill. Soc. Anesthesiologists (pres. 1980-81), Ill. State Med. Soc., Chgo. Med. Soc., Chgo. Soc. Anesthesiologists (pres. 1986-90), Assn. Univ. Anesthesiologists. Presbyterian. Home: 1020 Chestnut Ave Wilmette IL 60091-1732 Office: U Ill Chgo Coll Medicine Dept Anesthesiology MC/515 1740 W Taylor St Ste 3200 Chicago IL 60612-7232

ALBRECHT, RONALD LEWIS, financial services executive; b. Derby, Conn., Dec. 30, 1935; s. Lewis Davis and Gladys Imogene (Spear) A.; m. Mikyong Kim, Dec. 28, 1968; children: Rondi Kim, Kathryn Lynn, Karen Ann. BS in Agr., U. Vt., 1957; BBA in Bus. Mgmt., Baylor U., 1966; MA in Bus. Mgmt., Cen. Mich. U., 1975. Commd. 2d lt. USAF, 1957, advanced through grades to lt. col., 1973; comdr. detachment USAF, Sioux City AB, Iowa, 1957-60; air traffic control officer USAF, Cheveston, Eng., 1960-62; dir. air traffic control HQ12 USAF, Waco, Tex., 1962-66; comdr. detachment USAF, Kimpo AB, Korea, 1967-68; comdr. squadron Sewart AFB USAF, Tenn., 1969-70; comdr. squadron Holloman AFB USAF, N.Mex., 1970-73; staff officer, air traffic control HQ air force systems command USAF, Andrews AFB, 1973-75; dep. comdr. group USAF, Pentagon, 1975-77; staff officer electronics HQ joint staff USAF, Yongson, Korea, 1977-79; staff officer air traffic control communications area USAF, Rome, N.Y., 1979-80; retired USAF, 1980; real estate broker Bangor, Maine, 1980—; retirement, investment and fin. planning exec. Bangor (Maine) Savs. Bank, 1981-87; pres. Maine Fin. Mgmt. Svcs.,Inc. and Albrecht Fin. Svcs., Bangor, 1987—; instr. Los Angeles Community Coll., Seoul, Korea, 1977-79, Husson Coll. Bangor, 1981-84. Mem. loaned exec. bd. div. planning com. United Way of Penobscot Valley, Bangor, 1981—, Rep. Party, Bangor, 1981—. Hood Dairy scholar U. Vt., 1955. Mem. Internat. Assn. Fin. Planning (v.p. programs, co-founder 1985, pres. Maine chpt. 1988-89), Inst. Cert. Fin. Planners, Internat. Cert. Fin. Planners (bd. standards and practices), Ret. Officers Assn., Am. Assn. Ret. Persons, Air TrafficControl Assn., Armed Forces Communications Electronics Assn., Kiwanis (2d and 1st v.p. Bangor Club, pres. 1987-88), Masons, Anah Temple, Valley of Tokyo, Orientof Japan and Korea. Avocations: reading, hiking, gardening, travel. Home: 98 Judson Blvd Bangor ME 04401-2542

ALBRECHT, THEO, business executive; b. Mar. 28, 1922; m. Cilli Albrecht; children: Theo, Berthold. Grad., secondary sch. Owner grocery bus. eventually covering, all of Ruhr area, Germany, 1946—; founder, propr., mng. ptnr. Albrecht KG, Herten, Germany, 1961—; opened first Aldi market, Dortmund, Germany, 1962; acquired by Albrecht Group in USA, 1977; mng. ptnr. Aldi GmbH & Co., Mülheim, Germany; co-CEO, Aldi Group, Essen, Germany. Served with German Army, World War II; Am. prisoner of war. Avocations: golf, growing orchids. Office: Aldi Group, Eckenbergstr 16 PB 13 01 10, D-45291 Essen Germany also: Otto-Suhr-Allee 26/28, 10585 Berlin Germany*

ALBRECHT, WALTER, urologist, researcher; b. Vienna, Austria, Feb. 27, 1954; s. JOhann and Hertha (Roetzer) A.; married, May 8, 1982; 1 child, Iris. MD, U. Vienna, Austria, 1982. Attending physician KFJ-Hosp., Vienna, 1982-84; resident in urology Rudolfstiftung, Vienna, 1985-90, attending urologist, 1991-96, chief uro-oncologist, 1992 , vice chmn., 1996—. Contbr. articles to profl. jours. Recipient Michalowski medal U. Cracow, Poland, 1994. Fellow European Bd. Urology; mem. European Orgn. Rsch. and Treatment of Cancer (study coord. prostate cancer com. 1993 , treas. 1993), European Group on Tumor Markers, Austrian Uro-Oncology Group (chmn. 2000), Austrian Soc. Urology (vice sec. 1988-90), Viennese Testis Cancer Group. Roman Catholic. Avocations: music, Austrian history, travel. Office: Juchgasse 25, A-1030 Vienna Austria

ALBRECHT-OLSEN, PETER MIKAEL, orthopedic surgeon; b. Copenhagen, June 18, 1954; s. Eyvin Henning and Else (Albrecht-Beste) Olsen; m. Maha Fuad Aref Sleem, July 4, 1987; children: Nuha Nathalie, Sixten Alexander. MD, U. Copenhagen, Denmark, 1981. Cert. orthopedic surgeon. Chief orthopedic surgeon, head of dept. Hilleroed Hosp., Denmark. Inventor in field; co-inventor meniscus repair device Meniscus Arrow Bionx. Recipient innovation prize European Soc. for Sport Traumatology, Knee Surgery and Arthroscopy, Berlin, 1994. Mem. Danish Orthopedic Soc., Danish Sports Medicine Soc. Avocations: jogging, skiing. E-mail: pealol@Fa.Dk. Home: Slotsvej 69, 2920 Charlottenlund Denmark

ALBRIGHT, JOSEPH WILLIAM, army officer; b. Chillicothe, Ohio, Feb. 3, 1954; s. Herman LeRoy and Catherine Regina (Rieder) A.; m. Deanna Wells, Aug. 13, 1989; children: Andrea Lyn, Jason Michael; stepchildren: Jennifer Charlene, Tammy Darlene. BME, U. Dayton, 1976; grad., U.S. Army War Coll., 2000. Commd. 2nd lt. Ordnance br. U.S. Army, 1976; advanced through grades to col. Ordnance br. U.S. Army, 1999; accountable officer 9th ordnance co. 9th Ordnance Co., Germany, 1977-79, ops. officer, 1979-80; rsch. engr., chief integrated logistic support office large caliber weapon sys. lab., 1980-82; material officer 3rd ordnance bn. 59th ordnance brigade 3d Ordnance Bn., 59th Ordnance Brigade, 1982-85; Dept. of Army coord. for ammunition logistics Dept. of Army, 1985-87; asst. exec. officer to dep. commanding gen. Material Readiness Army Material Commd., 1987-88; commdr. 96th ordnance co. 96th Ordnance Co., 1988-90; inspector gen. Tech. Insp. divsn. Army Material Command Tech. Insp. divsn. Army Materiel Command, 1990-93, chief program mgmt. divsn., 1993-94; comdr. Milan Army Ammunition Plant Milan Army Ammunition Plant, Tenn., 1994-96; dep. support ops. officer 3rd corps support command V U.S. Army Corps, 1996-98; depot maintenance project chief Hdqrs., Dept. of Army, 1998-99, indsl. ops. project chief, office dep. chief staff logistics, 2000—. Decorated Legion of Merit, Meritorious Svc. medal with 5 oak leaf clusters, Army Commendation medal with oak leaf cluster, Army Achievement medal; named Disting. Mil. Grad., 1976, Disting. Grad. Ordnance Officer Advanced Course, 1980. Mem. ASME, Pi Sigma Tau. Home: 219 Diamond Dr Walkersville MD 21793-9145 Office: Dep Chief Staff Logistics Supply & Maintenance Direct 500 Army Pentagon Washington DC 20310-0500

ALBRIGHT, JUDITH ANNE, writer; b. Toldeo, Ohio; d. Matthew M. and Margaret Fern McMahon; m. Bill Eugene Albright, Aug. 15, 1964; children: Mary Sheila, Michael James. Tchr. Peoria, Ill., 1964, Concord Sch. System, Elkhart, Ind., 1965-67, Dows Ln. Sch., Irvington, N.Y., 1967-69, Capistrano Unified Schs., San Juan Capistrany, Calif., 1980-89; owner, dir. Albright Presch., Mission Viejo, Calif., 1984-86; tchr. St. Edwards Sch., Dana Point, Calif., 1986-87; cons., spkr. in field of religion. Author: Our Lady of Medjugorje, 1988, Neustra Senora de Medjugorje, 1988, Mary and the Children of Medjugorje, 1989, Our Lady of Garabandal, 1992. Roman Catholic. Avocations: travel, reading, writing, boating. Home: 201 Internat Dr #313 Cape Canaveral FL 32920

ALBRIGHT, KENDRA SUZANNE, research professional; b. Bloomington, Ind., Apr. 13, 1956; d. Joseph F. and Marcia L. (Geckler) Albright; children: Brynne, Darcy. BS, U. Tenn., 1979, MS in Libr. Sci., 1985, postgrad., 2000—. Bus. info. ctr. mgr. Whittle Communications LTd., Knoxville, 1985-86; cons. pvt. practice Oak Ridge, Tenn., 1986-92, 99—; tech. libr. Oak Ridge Nat. Lab., 1986-92; mgr. Info. Internat. Assocs., Inc., Oak Ridge, 1992-96, 2000. Contbr. articles to profl. jours. Mem. Am. Libr. Assn., Soc. Competitive Intelligence Profls., Am. Soc. for Info Sci. Home and Office: 131 Chestnut Hill Rd Oak Ridge TN 37830-7185

ALBRIGHT, MADELEINE KORBEL, secretary of state; b. Prague, Czechoslovakia, May 15, 1937; d. Josef and Anna (Speeglova) Korbel; m. Joseph Medill Patterson Albright, June 11, 1959 (div. 1983); children: Anne Korbel, Alice Patterson, Katharine Medill. BA with honors in Polit. Sci., Wellesley Coll., 1959; student, John's Hopkins U.; MA, Columbia U., 1968, cert.Russian Inst., 1968, PhD, 1976. Washington coord. Maine for Muskie, 1975-76; chief legis. asst. to U.S. Senator Muskie, 1976-78; mem. staff NSC, 1978-81, White House, 1978-81; sr. fellow in Soviet and Eastern European Affairs Ctr. for Strategic and Internat. Studies, Ctr. for Strategic and Internat. Studies, 1981; fellow Woodrow Wilson Internat. Ctr. for Scholars, Washington, 1981-82; Research prof. internat. affairs, dir. women in fgn. service Sch. Fgn. Service Georgetown U., 1982-93; pres. Ctr. for Nat. Policy, 1985-93; fgn. policy coord. Mondale for Pres. campaign, 1984, to Geraldine A. Ferraro, 1984; vice chmn. Nat. Dem. Inst. for Internat. Affairs, Washington, 1984-93; perm. rep. of the U.S. UN, N.Y.C., 1993-97; Sec. U.S. Dept. of State, 1997—; sr. fgn. policy advisor Dukakis for Pres. Campaign, 1988; mem. Pres.'s Cabinet, NSC. Author: Poland: The Role of the Press in Political Change, 1983; contbr. articles to profl. jours., chpts. to books. Bd. dirs. Beauvoir Sch., Washington, 1968-76, chmn., 1978-83; trustee Black Student Fund, 1969-78, 82-93, Dem. Forum, 1976-78, Williams Coll., 1978-82, Wellesley Coll., 1983-89; mem. exec. com. D.C. Citizens for Better Pub. Edn., 1975-76; bd. dirs. Washington Urban League, 1982-84, Atlantic Coun., 1984-93, Ctr. for Nat. Policy, 1985-93, Chatham House Fedn., 1986-88. Mem. Council Fgn. Relations, Am. Polit. Sci. Assn., Czechoslovak Soc. Arts and Scis. Am., Atlantic Council U.S. (dir.), Am. Assn. for Advancement Slavic Studies. Office: Office of the Secretary of State 2201 C St NW Washington DC 20520-0001

ALBU, ION, anatomist, educator; b. Căstău-Orăstie, Romania, Oct. 4, 1920; s. Dionisie and Valeria (Daniil) A.; m. Sylvia Ghitescu, Nov. 30, 1961; 1 child, Silviu. D of Medicine and Surgery, U. Cluj., Romania, 1945; BA, U. Cluj, Romania, 1949. Probating asst. dept. anatomy sch. medicine U. Medicine, Cluj-Sibiu, 1941-45, asst. prof., 1945-49; lectr. U. Medicine, Timsoara, Romania, 1949-63; reader, prof., head dept. anatomy U. Medicine, Cluj, 1963-65, 65-90, cons. prof. dept. anatomy, 1995—; prof. head dept. anatomy Ecol. U., Bucarest, Romania, 1990-92; advisor in anatomy and histology, 1968—; jr. surgeon ob-gyn. U. Hosp., Timisoara, 1956, sr. surgeon, 1959; prof. anatomy Sch. of the Arts, Cluj, 1946-48; dir., prof. anatomy Postgrad. Med. Coll., Timisoara, 1949-51. Author: Papilian's Textbook of Anatomy, 1974-98; co-author: (with R. Georgia) Surgical Anatomy Textbook, 1994-98, Manual of Practical Anatomy, 1996, 19 manuals of anatomy for med. students, (with others) Human Anatomy Textbook, 1996; contbr. articles to profl. jours.; mem. editl. bd. Acta Anatomica. Rsch. bd. advisors Am. Biog. Inst., 1999. Named Disting. Physician, Ministry of Health, Romania, 1956, Disting. Univ. Prof., Ministry of Edn., Romania, 1984. Mem. Romanian Acad. Med. Scis. (emeritus), Anatomische Gesellschaft, European Teratology Soc., Soc. Morphology (heading com., editl. bd. jour.), Vertebrate Directory. Avocations: history, classical music, travel. Home: Calea Turzii nr 44, 3400 Cluj Romania

ALBUQUERQUE, SUSANA, lawyer; b. Lisbon, Portugal; d. José Ferreira Picado and Maria Ribeiro Albuquerque. LLB, U. Lisbon, 1993; specialization in securities, Clifford Chance, London, 1995. Bar: Portugal, Supreme Ct. Eng. and Wales. Assoc. A.M. Pereira, Leal E Assocs., Lisbon, 1993—. Editor European Lawyers Assn. Newsletter, 1998—. Mem. Law Soc. Eng. and Wales (solicitor), Portuguese Law Soc. (adv.), Portuguese Assn. Fin. Houses (dir. 1997—), European Lawyers Assn. (vice chmn. 1999—). Avocations: sailing, hiking, swimming, painting, dancing. Office: Portuguese Assn Finance, Houses Rua Filipe Folque2-7, 1050 Lisbon Portugal

ALBURY, WILLIAM RANDALL, university administrator, educator; b. Sept. 14, 1944; arrived in Australia, 1973; s. William Arthur Jr. and Marcia Mae (Packard) A.; m. Rebecca Ann McClure, Oct. 30, 1966 (div. 1980); children: Katherine M., Alicia F.; m. Barbara Helen Altorjai, Apr. 30, 1983; 1 child, William M. BA with honors, Johns Hopkins U., 1968, PhD with distinction, 1972. Lectr. history and philosophy of sci. U. NSW, Sydney, Australia, 1973-78, from sr. lectr. to assoc. prof., 1978-86, head Sch. of History and Philosophy of Sci., 1984-88, prof., 1986-98, head Sch. Sci. and Tech. Studies, 1989-91, 94-95, exec. head Kensington Colls., 1989-90, assoc. dean faculty arts and social sci., 1995-98; dean faculty arts U. New Eng., Armidale, NSW, Australia, 1998—; head Philip Baxter Coll., Kensington, 1985-93; vis. prof., rsch. assoc. Johns Hopkins U., Balt., 1981; vis. scholar U. N.C., Chapel Hill, 1992; cons. Edn. Commn. NSW, Sydney, 1984; mem. Australian Govt. Recombinant DNA Monitoring Com., Canberra, 1985-88, Australian Govt. Genetic Manipulation Adv. Com., 1988-92. Author: The Politics of Objectivity, 1983; transl., editor: Condillac's Logic/La Logique, 1980; editor: (jours.) Metasci., 1984-90, Social Studies of Sci., 1985-88, 91-94; contbr. articles to profl. jours. Woodrow Wilson Found. fellow, 1971-72, Macy Found. postdoctoral fellow, 1972-73; Am. Philos. Soc. Penrose Rsch. grantee, 1981. Mem. History of Sci. Soc., Am. Assn. History of Medicine, Australasian Assn. History Philosophy and Social Studies of Sci., Australia Soc. History of Medicine, Soc. Social Studies of Sci. Avocations: hiking, camping, theater, concerts, opera. Office: U New England, Armidale NSW 2351, Australia

ALBUS, MARGOT IRENE, psychiatrist; b. Mindelheim, Germany, Mar. 14, 1951; d. Hans and Maria (Froehlich) A.; 1 child, Mathias. Grad. in Psychology, U. Munich, 1977, grad. in Medicine, 1978, Habilitation in Psychiatry, 1990. Specialist in psychiatry, neurology, psychotherapy. Fellow dept. neurology Max-Planck-Inst. Psychiatry, Munich, 1979-80; fellow Psychiat. Hosp. U. Munich, 1980; fellow State/Mental Hosp., Regensburg, Germany, 1981; fellow Psychiat. Hosp. U. Munich, 1981-83, fellow dept. neurology, 1983-84; vis. scientist NIMH, Bethesda, Md., 1984-85; sr. fellow Psychiat. Hosp. U. Munich, 1986-89; head div. tchg. and rsch. State Mental Hosp. Haar, Germany, 1989—, head acute inpatient hosp., 1989—. Inventor in field. Mem. Arbeitsgemeinschaft fuer Neurologie und Psychiatrie. Roman Catholic. Avocations: skiing, tennis, windsurfing. Office: State Mental Hosp, Vockestr 72, D-85529 Haar Germany

ALCAMO, FRANK PAUL, retired educational administrator; b. South Fork, Pa., May 25, 1920; s. Carmelo and Antonia (Trifiro) A.; m. Josephine Giusto, June 22, 1944; 1 child, Antoinette. Student, Johnstown Coll., 1938-39; BS, Indiana U. Pa., 1942; MEd, Pa. State U., 1954. Tchr. math. and sci. Wilmore (Pa.) H.S., 1942-54, Beaverdale (Pa.)-Wilmore H.S., 1954-56; tchr. math. South Fork-Croyle H.S., 1956-61, Triangle Area H.S., Sidman, Pa., 1961-62; asst. prin. Windber (Pa.) Area H.S., 1962-63, prin., 1963-81; ret., 1981; bd. dirs. Allegheny Ridge Corp. Author: The Windber Story, 1983, The South Fork Story, 1987, The Summerhill Story, 1992. Treas. Windber Summer Playground Assn., 1963; chmn. Windber Police CSC, 1964-81; bd. dirs., pres. Mid-State Automobile Club Johnstown, Pa., 1965—; bd. dirs.

Johnstown-Windber Indsl. Devel. Assn., Cambria County Hist. Soc., 1988-93, Sr. Activities Ctr. Cambria County, Inc., 1994-98; founder, dir. CBW Schs. Fed. Credit Union, 1956—; v.p. Windber Pub. Libr., 1976-81; bd. dirs. Windber Recreation Assn., treas., 1974-80; bd. dirs., v.p. Johnstown Area Heritage Assn., 1985—; instr., site coord. counselor IRS Tax Counseling for Elderly, 1984-96. Lt. (j.g.) USNR, 1944-46. Named to Windber Hall of Fame, 1984. Mem. NEA (life), ARC (historian Keystone chpt.), Pa. Edn. Assn. (local br. com. 1966-70, dept. adminstrn. pres. 1971-75, pres. Windber 1965-66), Somerset County Secondary Prins. Assn. (pres. 1965-66), Nat. Secondary Sch. Prins. Assn., Pa. Secondary Sch. Prins. Assn., Pa. Interscholastic Athletic Assn. (dist. treas. 1970-80), Greater Johnstown Assn. Sch. Retirees (pres. 1983-85, 88-91, 95-96), Sons of Italy, Pa. Assn. Sch. Retirees, Automobile Club So. Pa. (bd. dirs. 1988—), Rotary (dir. Windber 1964-69, pres. 1968-69), Phi Delta Kappa, Sigma Tau Gamma. Democrat. Roman Catholic. Avocations: playing the trombone Swing City Johnstown, model railroading. Home: 603 Harshberger St Johnstown PA 15905-3129

ALCARAZ, JOSE LUIS, engineering educator; b. Hellin, Spain, July 3, 1963; s. Luis and Soledad (Tafalla) A. BA, Maristas La Merced, Murcia, Spain, 1981; grad. in indsl. engring., U. Poly., Valencia, Spain, 1988; D in Indsl. Engring., U. De Navarra, San Sebastian, Spain, 1993. Assoc. prof. U. Poly., 1988-89; asst. prof. U. De Navarra, 1989-93; assoc. prof. U. Del Pais Vasco, Bilbao, Spain, 1993-94, prof. titular interino, 1994-97, prof. titular, 1997—; cons. Asepeyo, Valencia, 1988, Tabacalera, S.A., Valencia, 1988, Tubacex, Llodio, Spain, 1990-93. Author: Theory of Plasticity and Applications, 1994, Elasticity and Strength of Materials, 2nd edit., 1997, Advanced Course on Strength of Materials, 2d edit., 1997; contbr. articles to profl. jours. Recipient Engring. Grad. Outstanding award Fin De Carrera, ETS Indsl. Engrs., Spain, 1989, Rsch. Tng. award Ministry Edn. Y Ciencia, Madrid, 1990-93. Mem. European Mechanics Soc., European Structural Integrity Soc., Spanish Assn. Mech. Engrs. Avocations: running, reading, languages. Office: Escuela De Ingenieros, Alameda Urquijo S/N, 48013 Bilbao Spain

ALCAZAR, JUAN LUIS, physician; b. Malaga, Spain, Sept. 7, 1966; s. Francisco and Ana (Zambrano) A.; m. Ana Jimenez, June 29, 1991; children: Boria, Beatriz, Teresa. MD, Navarre U., Spain, 1990. Attending physician C.U.N., Pamplona, Spain, 1991—. Contbr. articles to profl. jours. Mem. Am. Inst. Ultrasound Medicine, Am. Soc. Reproductive Medicine, Intenat. Soc. Ultrasound Ob-gyn. Home: Benjamin de Tudela 35 1-B, E 31008 Pamplona Spain Office: Clin U Navarra, Avenida PIO XII 36, 31008 Pamplona Spain

AL-CHALABI, MAHBOUB, geophysicist, consultant; b. Baghdad, Iraq, June 6, 1938; arrived in U.K., 1954; s. Mahmoud and Zainab (Al-Hakeem) A.; m. Sumaya Al-Wattari, July 29, 1964; children: Ammar, Zainab, Thawab. BSc with honors, U. Birmingham, Eng., 1959, MSc, 1961; diploma in engring., French Petroleum Inst., Rueil-Malmaison, 1965; PhD, U. Durham, Eng., 1970. Geophysicist Min. of Oil, Baghdad, 1962-64, Iraq Nat. Oil Co., Baghdad, , 1966-67; rsch. geophysicist Brit. Petroleum, Sunbury-on-Thames, England, 1970-73; sr. geophysicist Brit. Petroleum, London, The Hague, Tunis, , 973-83; advisor Petroleos de Venezuela/BP, Caracas, , 1983-89; dir. Petrotech Consultancy, Ascot, , Eng., 1990—; cons. geophysics, lectr. in field. Author: Popular Mural Art in Venezuela, 1987, 2d edit., 1995; assoc. editor Jour. of European Assn. of Geoscientists and Engrs., 1998; contbr. articles to profl. jours.; patentee in field. Gulbenkian Found. fellow, Lisbon, 1967-70; Iraq Petroleum Co. scholar, 1954-59. Fellow Geol. Soc. U.K.; mem. Royal Inst. Internat. Affairs, Inst. of Petroleum U.K., Soc. of Exploration Geophysicists, European Assn. Geoscientists and Engrs. Avocations: travel, photography, art and literature, calendars and methods of time reckoning. Home: 25 Prince Consort Dr, Ascot Berkshire SL5 8AW, England

ALCHORNE, MAURÍCIO DE OLIVEIRA DE AVELAR, physician; b. Sao Paulo, June 22, 1966; s. Mauricio M.A. and Alice O.A. Alchorne; m. Debora Moreira de Alvar, Nov. 20, 1993; children: Isabella, Maurício. MD, HCFMUSP, Sao Paulo, 1989, postgrad., 1994. Emergency rm. supr. Hosp. Vila Maria, Sao Paulo, 1994-95; med. coord. Hosp. Santa Marcelina, Sao Paulo, 1996-98; med. dir. Blue Life HMO, Sao Paulo, 1999—; regulation ofcl. Cassi, Sao Paulo, 1996-98; auditory specialist Generali Seguros, Sao Paulo, 1998-99; lectr. in field. Author curriculum materials in field. Officer Brazilian Army, 1990-91. Mem. Brazilian Coll. Surgeons, Brazilian Soc. Trauma, Brazilian Med. Coun. (cert.), Brazilian Med. Soc. Health Adminstrn.

ALCOCK, ANTONY EVELYN, international relations educator; b. Valletta, Malta, Sept. 12, 1936; s. Gilbert St. Aubyn and Maria Theresa (Berky) A.; m. Mary Catherine Wedgewood, Jan. 4, 1975; children: Alexander, Charlotte, Caroline. BA in History and Politics, McGill U., Montreal, Can., 1961; MA in History, Stanford U., 1962; PhD in Internat. Rels., Geneva Grad. Inst. Internat. Studies, 1970. Translator OECD, Paris, 1963; historian, internat. civil servant ILO, Geneva, 1968-71; internat. civil servant UNITAR, N.Y.C., 1971-72, EEC, Brussels, 1972-74; tchr. U. Ulster, Coleraine, U.K., 1974—; prof. European studies U. Ulster, Coleraine, 1984; cons. bd. dirs. Internat. Inst. for Nationality Rights and Regionalism, Munich, 1978—. Author: History of the South Tyrol Question, 1970, History of the International Labour Organisation, 1971, Südtirol Seit Dem Paket, 1982, Understanding Ulster, 1994, A Short History of Europe, 1998, A History of the Protection of Regional Cultural Minorities in Europe, 2000; editor: The Future of Cultural Minorities, 1979. Coun. mem. Ulster Unionist Party, Belfast, 1988—, chair European com., 1995—, mem. No. Ireland forum, 1996-98, negotiator in all party talks on future of No. Ireland, 1997-98. 2d lt. Brit. Army, 1955-57. Recipient Gold medal for history McGill U., 1961, Woodrow Wilson fellowship W.W. Found., 1961, Calouste Gulbenkian scholarship C.G. Found., Geneva, 1963-68. Mem. Ulster Soc. (pres. 1990—), No. Ireland Bridge Union (rep. No. Ireland at internat. and Irish Inter-provincial level). Mem. Ch. of Eng. Avocations: bridge, chess, gardening, squash rackets. Home: White Lodge 9 Roselick Rd, Portstewart NIreland BT55 7PP, United Kingdom Office: Univ Ulster, Cromore Rd, Coleraine North Ireland BT52 1SA, United Kingdom

ALCOCK, VIVIEN (DOLORES), children's author; b. Worthing, Eng., Sept. 23, 1924; d. John Forster and Molly (Pulman) A.; m. Leon Garfield, Oct. 23, 1947; 1 child, Jane Angela. Student, Ruskin Sch. Drawing and Fine Arts, Oxford, Eng., 1940-42, Camden Arts Ctr. Artist Gestetner Ltd., London, 1947-53, mgr. employment bur., 1953-56; sec. Whittington Hosp., London, 1956-64. Writings include: The Haunting of Cassie Palmer, 1980, The Stonewalkers, 1981, The Sylvia Game (A Novel of the Supernatural), 1982, Travellers by Night, 1983 (Horn Book Honor list 1985, Notable Book of Yr. ALA 1985), Ghostly Companions: A Feast of Chilling Tales, 1984, The Cuckoo Sister, 1985 (Notable Book of Yr. ALA 1986), Wait and See, 1986, The Mysterious Mr. Ross, 1987, The Monster Garden, 1988 (Voice of Youth Advocate Best Sci. Fiction Book 1988, Notable Book of Yr. ALA 1988), The Thing in the Woods, 1989, The Trial of Anna Cotman, 1990, A Kind of Thief, 1991, The Dancing Bush, 1991, Singer to the Sea God, 1992, Othergran, 1993, The Wrecker, 1994, Face at the Window, 1994, The Red-Eared Ghosts, 1996, The Silver Egg, 1997, A Gift on a String, 1998, Ticket to Heaven, 2000. Served as ambulance driver Brit. Army, 1942-46. Mem. Authors Soc. Mem. Ch. of Eng. Avocations: painting, patchwork, reading. Office: John Johnson Ltd Clerkenwell Ho, 45-47 Clerkenwell Green, London EC1R 0HT, England

ALCON, CHARLES ARTHUR, JR., technical company executive; b. Lafayette, Ind., June 20, 1964; s. Charles Arthur and Kathryn Marie Alcon; 1 child, Madelyn. BS, U. Wis., Eau Claire, 1987. Account mgr. Rorke Data, Eden Prairie, Minn., 1987-92; v.p. Microboards Tech., Chanhassen, Minn., 1993—; bd. dirs. Microboards Tech., Chanhassen, DST, N.Y.C., DRT, Phoenix. E-mail: calconjr@microboards.com. Home: 9882 Brighton Ln Eden Prairie MN 55347-3173 Office: Microboards Tech 1721 Lake Dr W Chanhassen MN 55317-8580

ALCORN, DAINE, research biologist, educator; b. Adelaide, Australia, July 3, 1949; d. Henry Arthur and Gwendolyn Ison (Giddings) A.; m. Trevor William Davey, Oct. 8, 1977; 1 child, William Edwin. MSc, U. Melbourne, 1975, PhD, 1978. Rsch. fellow U. Melbourne, Australia, 1979-82, lectr., 1983-87, sr. lectr., 1988-92, assoc. prof., reader, 1992-95, prof., 1995—, dept. head, 1996—. Office: U Melbourne, Dept Anatomy Cell Biology, Parkville 3010, Australia

ALCORN, WALLACE ARTHUR, minister, writer; b. Milw., Aug. 29, 1930; s. William Keith and Dora Mildred (Brazee) A.; m. Ann Margaret Carmichael, June 5, 1958; children: John Mark, Allison Alcorn-Oppedahl, Stephen Paul. Student, Marquette U., 1950; AB, Wheaton Coll., 1952; MDiv, Grand Rapids Bapt. Theol. Sem., 1959; AM, Wheaton Grad. Sch. Theology, 1959; postgrad., Mich. State U., 1959-60, U. Mich., 1960-61; ThM, Princeton Theol. Sem., 1965; PhD, NYU, 1974; cert. in clin. pastoral edn., Fitzsimons Army Med. Ctr., 1975; postgrad., U. Minn., 1980-81. Ordained to ministry Gen. Assn. Regular Bapt. Chs., 1957; cert. advanced mediator Am. Arbitration Assn. Pastor Caddy Vista Bapt. Ch., Caldonia, Wis., 1955-57; tchr. Wyoming (Mich.) Schs., 1958-60; pastor Bloomfield Hills (Mich.) Bapt. Ch., 1960-61; English tchr. Waterford-Kettering H.S., Drayton Plaines, Mich., 1961-62; pastor Community Bapt. Ch. Shark River Hills, Neptune, N.J., 1962-67, 1st Bapt. Ch., Austin, Minn., 1976-83; prof. bible Moody Bible Inst., Chgo., 1967-73; assoc. prof. N.T. N.W. Bapt. Sem., Tacoma, 1974-76; clin. pastoral care specialist Madigan Army Med. Ctr., Tacoma, 1974-76; police chaplain Tacoma, 1974-76, Austin, Minn., 1976—; prin. Wallace Alcorn Assocs., Austin, 1983—; pastoral counselor New Life Family Svcs., Rochester, Minn., 1987-92; radio tchr. Moody Radio Network, 1968-74; radio commentator Sta. KTIS and Northwestern Coll. Network, 1987-98; syndicated newspaper columnist, 1993—; adj. faculty Riverland C.C., 1994—; chmn. Minn. Assn. Regular Bapt. Chs., 1980-83; pres. Faith Acad., Fridley, Minn., 1986; cons. U.S. Dept. Edn., 1953-54, N.J. Dept. Edn., 1964-67. Author: The Bible as Literature, 1965, Elijah, Prophet of God, 1972, The Life of Christ Visualized, 1973, Knowing and Using the Bible, 1975, Momentum, 1986; nat. editor Christian Life, 1956-60, Mil. Life, 1983-86; N.T. editor Living Bible Commentary, 1974-76, The Book We Love, 1994; contbr. Wycliffe Bible Ency., 1974, Tyndale Family Bible Ency., 1976, New Commentary on the Whole Bible, 1990, Stones of Remembrance, 1995; contbr. numerous articles to profl. jours. Mem. citizen's adv. coun. Neptune (N.J.) Bd. Edn., 1965-67; chair Austin Human Rights Commn., 1989-98; mem. profl. adv. coun. Pub. Edn. Religion Studies Ctr., Wright State U., 1972-76; pub. mem. 10th Jud. Dist. Ethics. Com., 1993—; dir. The Good News Hour, Austin, 1976-83, Minn. Human Rights Commn., 1990-98, Coop. Solutions Mediation Ctr., Austin, Minn., 1995-99. With USNR, 1947-52, U.S. Army, 1952-54, USAR, 1954-57, chaplain, col., 1957-90. Recipient Amy Writing award, 1988. Mem. Evang. Theol. Soc., Evang. Press Assn., Nat. Assn. Religious Broadcasters, Soc. of Profl. Journalists, Assn. of Former Intelligence Officers, Mil. Chaplains Assn. (pres. Chgo. chpt. 1970-74), hist. socs. Wis., Ohio, S.C. E-mail: waalcorn@smig.net. Home: 1010 7th Ave NW Austin MN 55912-2153 Office: PO Box 733 Austin MN 55912-0733

ALDA, ALAN, actor, writer, director; b. N.Y.C., Jan. 28, 1936; s. Robert and Joan (Browne) A.; m. Arlene Weiss; children: Eve, Elizabeth, Beatrice. BS, Fordham U., 1956, hon. degree, 1978; hon. degree, Drew U., 1979, Columbia U., 1979, Conn. Coll., 1980, Kenyon Coll., 1982. Ind. actor stage, screen, TV, 1956—; tchr. Compass Sch. Improvisation. Actor: (Broadway plays) including The Apple Tree (nominated Tony award), The Owl and the Pussycat, Purlie Victorious, Fair Game for Lovers, Jakes Women (Tony award nominee), Art, (films) including Gone Are the Days, 1963, The Moonshine War, Paper Lion, 1968, The Extraordinary Seaman, 1968, Jenny, 1970, The Mephisto Waltz, 1971, To Kill a Clown, 1972, California Suite, 1978, Same Time, Next Year, 1978, Crimes and Misdemeanors, 1989 (D.W. Griffith award, N.Y. Film Critics award), Whispers in the Dark, 1992, Manhattan Murder Mystery, 1993, Canadian Bacon, 1995, Flirting With Disaster, 1996, Everyone Says I Love You, 1996, Murder at 1600, 1997, Mad City, 1997, The Object of My Affection, 1998; (TV movies) include The Glass House, 1972, Marlo Thomas and Friends in Free to be...You and Me, 1974, 6 Rms Riv Vu, 1974, Kill Me If You Can, And The Band Played On, 1993 (Emmy nomination, Supporting Actor - Special, 1994), White Mile, 1994; star: (TV series, as Benjamin Franklin "Hawkeye" Pierce) M*A*S*H, 1972-83 (5 Emmy awards, 5 Golden Globe awards, Humanitas award for writing); creator: (TV series) We'll Get By, 1975, The Four Seasons; writer,(narrator) Scientific American Frontiers, 1993—; actor TV series ER; actor: (film) The Seduction of Joe Tynan, 1979; actor, writer, dir.: (films) The Four Seasons, 1981, Sweet Liberty, 1986, A New Life, 1987, Betsy's Wedding, 1990. Presdl. appointee Nat. Commn. for Observance of Internat. Women's Yr., 1976; co-chair Nat. ERA Countdown Campaign, 1982; trustee Mus. of TV and Radio, 1985, Rockefeller Found., 1989. Recipient Theatre World award for Fair Game for Lovers, 7 People's Choice awards; elected to TV Acad. Hall of Fame, 1994. Mem. AFTRA, Dirs. Guild Am. (awards 1977, 82), Writers Guild Am. (award 1977), Screen Actors Guild, Actors Equity Assn.

ALDAG, JORN P., manufacturing executive; b. Kampen, Germany, Feb. 22, 1959. MBA, European Bus. Sch., 1982; postgrad., Harvard U., 1994. Dir. controlling MAN Roland Ah, Offenbach, Germany, 1985-91; bus. dir. Treuhandanstalt, Berlin, 1991-95; CFO MAN GHH AG, Oberhausen, Germany, 1995-97; CFO, pres. EVOTEC Biosystems AG, Hamburg, Germany, 1997—. Office: EVOTEC AG, Schnackenburgallee 114, 22525 Hamburg Germany

ALDAHHAN, ABDULMONEM ABDULLAH, electrical engineer, consultant; b. Qatif, Saudi Arabia, Dec. 27, 1970; s. Abdullah Ahmad and Ma'Soumah Saeed A. BS, King Fahd U. Petroleum/Mins., Dhahran, Saudi Arabia, 1994. Elec. engr. Alkhobar Municipality, Saudi Arabia, 1995—. Mem. IEEE, Math. Assn. Am. Avocations: reading, football, running. Home: PO Box 1328, Qatif 31911, Saudi Arabia Office: Alkhobar Municipality, Alkhobar Saudi Arabia

AL-DAKHIL, BADR YOUSEF, computer programmer; b. Riyadh, Saudi Arabia, Dec. 8, 1961; s. Yousef Ali and Hossa N. (Mutawa) Al-D.; m. Nasseba A. Murjan, Nov. 25, 1985; children: Ala's, Wala, Wa'ad, Hussa. Diploma in Computer Info. Sys., Ctrl. Mo. State U., Warrensburg, 1985; diploma in Exec. Assistance Devel. Prog., Inst. Banking, Riyadh, 1994. Letter of credit rep. Saudi Arabian Monetary Agy., Riyadh, 1980-83, programmer software applications, 1985—, computer user's trainer, 1986-87, software application testing and integration, 1987, exec. asst. computer dept., 1994-95. Avocations: music, travel, making new friends, swimming, cars. E-mail: Badr01@hotmail.com. Home: PO Box 42607, Riyadh 11551, Saudi Arabia Office: PO Box 2992, Riyadh 11169, Saudi Arabia

ALDAKHILALLAH, KHALID ABDULLAH, business and economic educator, researcher; b. Kharj, Saudi Arabia, Jan. 1, 1966; s. Abdullah and Fatemh A.; m. Haya Mohammad Al-Swailem; 1 child, Abdullah. BC, King Saud U., Saudi Arabia, 1988; MBA, Drake U., Des Moines, Iowa, 1991; MS, SUNY Sch. Engring., Buffalo, 1996, PhD, 1997. Teaching asst. King Saud U., Saudi Arabia, 1988, SUNY, Buffalo, 1995-97; chmn. computer sci. King Saud U., Saudi Arabia, 1999—, vice dean Coll. Sci., 1999—, asst. prof., 1997—; dir. Computer Sci. Ctr. King Saud U., Saudi Arabia, 1998-99. Contbr. numerous papers in field. Recipient Robert F. Berner award for Excellence in Statistics, SUNY, 1994; named Dean;s List, King Saud U. Mem. Inst. for Ops. Rsch. and the Mgmt. Scis. (INFORMS), Am. Soc. Quality Control, Inst. Ops. Rsch. and Mgmt. Scis., Prodn. and Ops. Mgmt. Soc., Sigma Iota Epsilon, Beta Gamma Sigma. Avocations: reading, painting. Office phone: 966 380 1586. Home: PO Box 1844, Kharj 11942, Saudi Arabia Office: King Saud U, PO Box 6033, Qassim Saudi Arabia

AL-DAWOOD, KASIM MOHD, medical educator; b. Al-Jubail, Saudi Arabia, Jan. 7, 1961; s. Mohd Saleh Al-Dawood and Fatima Ali Al-Otaish; m. Sita Abdulla Al-Otaish; children: Reem, Fatima, Mohd, Abdul Rahman, Hisham, Fay. MB BChir, King Faisal U., Dammam, Saudi Arabia, 1985. Demonstrator Coll. Medicine and Med. Scis., King Faisal U., Dammam, 1987-91, fellow, 1991, asst. prof., 1991-93, assoc. prof. family and cmty. medicine, 1993—, chmn. dept. family and cmty. medicine, 1994-96; cons. Gen. Orgn. Social Ins., Dammam, 1991—, Islamic Relief Orgn., Dammam, 1991—, World Assembly Moslim Youth, Dammam, 1991—. Editor: Family and Comty. Medicine newsletter, 1991—; reviewer sci. jours. Fellow CMMS-King Faisal U., 1991. Mem. AAAS, Internat. Epidemiol. Assn., Islamic Soc. Statis. Scis. Avocations: soccer, jogging. Home: PO Box 2290, Al-Khobar 31952, Saudi Arabia Office: King Faisal U Coll Med, PO Box 2144, Dammam 31451, Saudi Arabia

ALDAZ, ANTONIO, physical chemistry educator; b. Murcia, Spain, Apr. 25, 1943; s. Enrique and Josefa (Riera) A.; m. Marian Carroll, Apr. 3, 1973. BS, U. Murcia, 1965, PhD, 1968. Lectr. U. Autonoma, Madrid, 1968-72, assoc. prof., 1973-80, prof. electrochemistry, 1980-82; assoc. prof. U. Sevilla, Spain, 1971-73; prof. phys. chemistry U. Alicante, Spain, 1987—. Mem. Internat. Soc. Electrochem., Electrochem. Soc. Office: U Alicante Apdo 99, Dept Phys Chemistry, 03080 Alicante Spain

ALDCROFT, STEWART ROBERT KENNETH, marketing and sales executive; b. Beckenham, England, Sept. 16, 1950; s. Kenneth and Muriel A.; m. Connie Man Yu Fung, Feb. 24, 1996. Regional mgr. Schroder Fin. Mgmt., London, 1976-85; assoc. dir. Schroders Asia Ltd., Hong Kong, 1986-89; exec. dir. HSBC Asset Mgmt., Hong Kong, 1989-94; mktg. and sales dir. Templeton Franklin Investment Svcs., Hong Kong, 1994-99; head bus. devel. and mktg. Standard Chartered Bank, Group Investment Svcs., 1999-2000; mng. dir. Investec Asset Mgmt. Asia Ltd., Hong Kong, 2000—.

ALDÉN, ERIK MAGNUS, physicist, researcher; b. Uppsala, Sweden, July 21, 1966; s. Gunnar Alexander and Lillemor (Söderlund) A.; m. Malin Viktoria Ekman, Mar. 26, 1994; children: Josefin, Ludvig. MSc, Uppsala U., 1990, PhD, 1994. Cons. Cap Gemini, Stockholm, 1994-95, 1996; postdoctoral rschr. Max Planck Inst. Festkörperforschung, Stuttgart, Germany, 1995-96; rschr. Telia AB, Stockholm, Sweden, 1996—. Contbr. rsch. articles to sci. publs. Recipient postdoctoral stipend Swedish Natural Rsch. Coun., Stuttgart, Germany, 1995-96. Avocations: classical music, aviation, sailing. Home: St Göransgatan 102, 11245 Stockholm Sweden Office: Telia Mobile, 131 86 Nacka Strand, Stockholm Sweden

ALDERMAN, CHARLES WAYNE, university dean; b. Mobile, Ala., Oct. 10, 1950; s. Charles B. and E. Mae (Henderson) A.; m. Mary Noel Perritt. BS, Auburn U., 1971, MBA, 1972; D in Bus. Adminstrn., U. Tenn., 1977. CPA, cert. internal auditor. Sr. auditor Ernst & Young, Birmingham, Ala., 1973-75; asst. prof. U. Tex., 1978-79; asst. prof. Auburn (Ala.) U., 1979-82, assoc. prof., 1982-87, Coopers & Lybrand prof., dir. Sch. Accountancy, 1987-89, assoc. dean Coll. Bus., 1990-93, dean bus., south trust endowed prof., 1993—; bd. dirs. Auburn Bank. Co-author: Accounting Information Systems, 1982, 86, 90, Auditing, 1987, 90, 93, 96, 99; contbr. articles to profl. jours. Ernst & Young grantee, 1976-77. Mem. AICPA (bd. examiners 1995-98), Ala. Soc. CPAs, Am. Acctg. Assn., Mortar Board, Omicron Delta Kappa, Phi Gamma Delta (faculty advisor 1982-99). Presbyterian. Office: Auburn U Coll Bus Auburn AL 36849

ALDERMAN, GEOFFREY, academic administrator; b. Hampton Court, England, Feb. 10, 1944; s. Samuel and Lily (Landau) A.; m. Marion Freed, Sept. 9, 1973; children: Naomi, Eliot. BA, U. Oxford, 1965, DPhil, 1969. Rsch. asst. Univ. Coll., London, 1968-69; lectr. Univ. Coll., Swansea, UK, 1969-70; rsch. fellow U. Reading, UK, 1970-72; lectr., reader, prof. Royal Holloway Coll., Egham, UK, 1972-94; head acad. devel. & quality assurance unit Middlesex U., London, 1994—, pro vice chancellor, 1996-99; v.p. internat. programs Touro Coll., N.Y.C., 2000—. Author: The Jewish Community in British Politics, 1983, Modern Britain 1700-1983, 1986, Britain: A One-Party State?, 1989, Modern British Jewry, 1992. Fellow Royal Hist. Soc., Royal Soc. Arts; mem. Inst. Quality Assurance. Jewish. Avocations: reading, music. Office: Touro Coll 50 W 23rd St Fl 17 New York NY 10010-5205

ALDERTON, IAN WILLIAM, mathematics educator; b. Middleburg, Mpumalanga, South Africa, Feb. 21, 1952; s. Robert Frank and Margaret (Fawdry) A.; m. Pierott-Cosimo Ashley Le Roux, Mar. 9, 1996. BSc, U. South Africa, Pretoria, 1978, BSc with honors, 1980, MSc, 1984, PhD, 1986. Lectr. U. South Africa, Pretoria, 1982-87, sr. lectr., 1987-91, assoc. prof. math., 1992-99, prof., 2000—, head dept. math., 1999—. Contbr. articles to profl. jours. Chair U. South Africa Sexual Orientation Forum, Pretoria, 1998—. Recipient Bronze medal South African Assn. Advancement of Sci., 1985. Mem. Am. Math. Soc., South African Math. Soc. (sec. 1993-95), Pi Mu Epsilon. Avocations: piano, gardening. Office: Dept Math, PO Box 392, Unisa 0003, South Africa

AL-DHOBAIB, AHMED MOHAMMAD, academic administrator. Pres. King Saud U., Riyadh, Saudi Arabia. Offife: POB 2454, 11451 Riyadh Saudi Arabia*

ALDISS, BRIAN (WILSON), writer; b. East Dereham, Norfolk, Eng., Aug. 8, 1925; s. Stanley and May (Wilson) A.; children from previous marriage: Clive, Caroline Wendy; m. Margaret Christie Manson, Dec. 11, 1965 (widowed Nov. 1997); children: Timothy Nicholas, Charlotte May. LittD (hon.), U. Reading, Eng., 2000. Lit. editor Oxford Mail, 1957-69; editor sci. fiction novels Penguin Books Ltd., London, 1961-64; art corr. The Guardian, London, 1971-80; judge Booker-McConnell Prize, 1981; v.p. West Buckland Sch., 1997—. Author: (novels) The Brightfount Diaries, 1955, Non-Stop, 1958 (Prix Jules Verne 1977), Starship, 1959, Vanguard from Alpha, 1959, Bow Down to Nul (published in Eng. as The Interpreter, 1961), 1960, The Male Response, 1961, The Primal Urge, 1961, The Long Afternoon of Earth (published in Eng. as Hothouse, 1962), 1962 (Hugo award for best short fiction World Sci. Fiction Conv. 1962), The Dark Light Years, 1964, Greybeard, 1964, Earthworks, 1965, The Saliva Tree, and Other Strange Growths, 1966 (Nebula award for best novella Sci. Fiction Writers Am. 1966), An Age, 1967 (published as Cryptozoic!, 1968), Report on Probability A, 1968, A Brian Aldiss Omnibus, 1969, Barefoot in the Head: A European Fantasia, 1969, The Hand-Reared Boy, 1970, A Soldier Erect, 1971, Brian Aldiss Omnibus 2, 1971, Frankenstein Unbound, 1973, The Eighty-Minute Hour: A Space Opera, 1974, The Malacia Tapestry, 1976, Brothers of the Head, 1977, A Rude Awakening, 1978, Enemies of the System: A Tale of Homo Uniformis, 1978, Life in the West, 1980, Moreau's Other Island, 1980 (published as An Island Called Moreau 1981), Helliconia Spring, 1982 (John W. Campbell Meml. award for best novel 1982, Brit. Sci. Fiction Assn. award for best fiction 1982, Kurd Lasswitz award 1984), Helliconia Summer, 1983, Helliconia Winter, 1985 (BSFA award best novel 1986), The Year Before Yesterday: A Novel in Three Acts, 1987, Ruins, 1987, Forgotten Life, 1988, Cracken at Critical: A Novel in Three Acts, 1989, Dracula Unbound, 1992, Remembrance Day, 1993, Somewhere East of Life, 1994, White Mars Or, The Mind Set Free, 1999; (non-fiction) Cities and Stones: A Traveller's Yugoslavia, 1966, The Shape of Further Things, 1970, Billion Year Spree: The History of Science Fiction, 1973 (BSFA Spl. award 1974, Coneta D'Argento Italy, 1977, Eurocon III award 1976), Science Fiction Art, 1975, This World and Nearer Ones: Essays Exploring the Familiar, 1979, Pile: Petals from St. Klaed's Computer, 1979, The Pale Shadow of Science, 1985, ...And the Lurid Glare of the Comet, 1986, (with David Wingrove) Trillion Year Spree: The History of Science Fiction, 1986, Bury My Heart at W.H. Smith's, 1990 (Hugo award Best Nonfiction 1987, Locus award Best Nonfiction 1987, J. Lloyd Eaton Meml. award Best Critical Work of Yr. 1988), Home Life with Cats, 1992, At the Caligula Hotel, 1995, The Detached Retina, 1995, Songs from the Steppes of Central Asia, 1996, The Twinkling of an Eye, 1998, When the Feast if Finished, 1999, The Squire Quartet, 1999, Art After Apogee, 2000; (story collections) Space, Time and Nathaniel, 1957, The Canopy of Time, 1959, No Time Like Tomorrow, 1959, Galaxies Like Grains of Sand, 1960, The Airs of Earth, 1963, Starswarm, 1964, Best Science Fiction Stories of Brian Aldiss, 1965 (published as Who Can Replace a Man?, 1966), Intangibles Inc., and Other Stories: Five Novellas, 1969, Neanderthal Planet, 1969, The Moment of Eclipse, 1971 (Brit. Sci. Fiction Assn. award 1972), The Book of Brian Aldiss, 1972 (published in Eng. as Comic Inferno, 1973), Last Orders and Other Stories, 1977, New Arrivals, Old Encounters, 1979, Foreign Bodies, 1981, Seasons in Flight, 1984, Best Science Fiction Stories of Brian W. Aldiss, 1988, Science Fiction Blues: The Show that Brian Aldiss Took on the Road, 1988, A Tupolev Too Far, 1993, The Secret of This Book, 1995, Common Clay, 1996; co-editor several anthologies including SF Master series, 1976-79, Best Science Fiction annuals, 1967-75, Decades SF, 1975-77, World Omnibus of Science Fiction, 1986; played roadshow Science Fiction Blues, 1986-95; appeared in own play Kindred Blood, Kensington Gore, Fla. and London, 1992, Poitiers, France, 1999; contbr. numerous stories to periodicals and books. Served Brit. Army, Indian Army, 1943-46. Decorated Burma Star; recipient Observer award for sci. fiction, 1956, Ditmar award for world's best contemporary sci. fiction author, 1970, James Blish award for excellence in sci. fiction criticism, 1977, Internat. Assn. for Fantastic in the Arts Disting. Scholarship award, 1986; named Most Promising New Author of Yr., World

Sci. Fiction Conv., 1958. Fellow Royal Soc. Lit.; mem. Internat. Inst. Study of Time, Internat. Assn. for the Fantastic in Arts, World Sci. Fiction Soc. (pres. 1982-84), Brit. Sci. Fiction Assn. (pres. 1960-64, Britain's Most Popular Sci. Fiction Author Spl. award 1964), Sci. Fiction Writers Am. (Grand Master of Sci. Fiction 2000), Sci. Fiction Rsch. Assn. (Pilgrim award 1978), Soc. Authors (chmn. 1977-78, Arts Coun. Gt. Britain (lit. panelist 1978-80), Cultural Exchs. Com. (chmn.)., Sci. Fiction Theatre of Liverpool (officer mem.), H.G. Wells Soc. (pres. 1994—, Prix Utopia award 1999). Office: Hambelden, 39 St Andrews Rd Old Headington, Oxford OX3 9DL, England

AL-DOBAIAN, SAAD ABDULLAH, library science educator, researcher; b. Rwaidah Al'Ard, Saudi Arabia, July 4, 1943; s. Abdullah Ibrahim Al-Dobaian and Norah Abdullah Al-Rabi'ah; m. Norah Saad Al-Dhwaiyan; children: Abdullah S., Amal S., Haifa S., Sahar S., Samar S., Bader S., Dina S., Khalid S. BA, King Saud U., Riyadh, Saudi Arabia, 1972; MA, U. Denver, 1978; PhD, Loughborough U., Leicestershire, Eng., 1995. Tchr. Ministry Edn., Riyadh, 1963-66; with Ministry Social Affairs, Riyadh, 1966-68, Riyadh Water Supply Dept., 1968-72; tchg. asst. King Saud U., Riyadh, 1972-78, lectr., 1978-85, asst. prof., 1985-91, assoc. prof., 1991—; head dept. libr. sci. Coll. of Arts King Saud U., 1985-87, dean of librs., 1992-97, mem. coun., 1992—; cons. Ministry of Edn., Riyadh, 1997—. Author: Copyright in the Kingdom of Saudi Arabia, Analytical and Comparison Study, 2d edit., 1994, A Brief History of Public Libraries in Saudi Arabia with Directory, 1994, Directory of Public Libraries in the Kingdom of Saudi Arabia, 1994, Studies on the Public Libraries in the Kingdom of Saudi Arabia, 1995; translator: Islamic Books, 1990, Saudi Aramco mobile libr., present and future prospects U. Riyadh, 2000, Coll. Tchrs. Librs in Saudi Arabia, King Fahd natl. libr., Riyadh, 2000. ; contbr. articles to profl. jours. Head 2d Riyadh Internat. Book Fair, King Saud U., 1979, 3d Book Fair, 1980, 4th Book Fair, 1981, chmn. organizing com. 7th Book Fair, 1993. Scholar King Saud U., 1975, 82; grantee Saudi Edn. Mission, 1985. Mem. ALA, Libr. Assn. (Eng.). Avocations: reading, writing, sports, music, travel. Office: King Saud U, PO Box 3744, Riyadh 11481, Saudi Arabia

ALDREES, ABDULMOHSEN MOHAMMED, manufacturing executive; b. Artawiah, Saudi Arabia, June 12, 1945; s. Mohammed Assad Aldrees and Lulwa Suliman Al Aqeel; m. Hessa Abdulaziz Al-Rabiah, July 4, 1980; children: Abdullah, Nawaf, Lulwa, Sarah, Nouf, Mishaal, Meshaael, Reem, Ghadah. BS, U. Fla., 1972; MSc, U. Okla., 1977; postgrad. in bus. adminstrn., Kennedy Western U. Mgr. Aldrees Tools & Equipment, Riyadh, 1977-78; mng. dir. Mohammed Assad Aldrees & Sons Co., Riyadh, 1978—; chmn. Saudi Am. Glass Factory, Riyadh, 1979—; owner Al El Al Internat., Riyadh, 1983—; part-time salesman, Riyadh, 1957-60; part-time sales mgr., Riyadh, 1961-66. Author: Analysis of Forehead Skin Temperature, 1977 (master's thesis). Mem. Saudi Benevolent Assn. for Handicapped Children, Patient's Friends Assn., Riyadh. Mem. Riyadh C. of C. and Industry (bd. dirs.), Islamic C. of C., Nat. U.S.-Arab C. of C., Saudi Econ. Soc., Saudi Natl. Committee for Internat. C. of C., U.S.-Saudi Arabian Bus. Coun., Saudi-Can. Jt. Bus. Coun., Saudi-Japanese Bus. Coun., Saudi Arabian-Chinese Friendship Assn. Office: Mohammed Assad Aldrees & Sons Co, PO Box 609, Riyadh 11421, Saudi Arabia

ALDREN, CHRISTOPHER PHILIP, otolaryngologist, surgeon, consultant; b. Guisborough, Cleveland, Eng., Feb. 27, 1962; s. Aleck Robinson and Jean Dorothy (Brooks) A.; m. Hege Hoffart, July 11, 1987; children: Alexander, Thomas, Benjamin. BA, U. Cambridge, Eng., 1983, MA, 1987; MB, BS, U. London, 1986. Head departmental anatomy demonstrator U. Cambridge, 1987-89; sr. house officer in head and neck surgery The Royal Marsden Hosp., London, 1990-91; registrar in ear, nose and throat surgery Freeman Hosp., Newcastle, Eng., 1991-94; fellow in head and neck surgery Princess Alexandra Hosp., Brisbane, Australia, 1994-95; sr. registrar Freeman Hosp., Newcastle, 1995-97; cons. surgeon Wexham Pk. Hosp., Eng., 1997; cons. The Princess Margaret Hosp., Windsor, Eng., 1997—. Contbr. articles to profl. jours. Traveling fellow Ethicon Found., Eng., 1994, TWJ Found., Eng., 1996. Fellow Royal Coll. Surgeons, Royal Soc. Medicine; mem. Brit. Med. Assn., Brit. Assn. Otolaryngologists/Head and Neck Surgeons, Young Cons. in Otolaryngology, Head and Neck Surgery Great Britain (pres. 1999—). Avocation: violin. Office: The Princess Margaret Hosp, Osborne Rd, Windsor SL4 3SJ, England

ALDRICH, C. ELBERT, real estate broker; b. Rosebud, Tex., Sept. 12, 1923; s. Murdock Collins and Mamie (Mock) A.; m. Dorothy Ann Cox, June 30, 1947; children: Ann Aldrich Dunn, Amy Aldrich Thomas. Student, Temple Jr. Coll., 1946-47. Co-owner M.C. Aldrich & Son, Temple, Tex., 1946-65; pres. Elbert Aldrich Realtor, Inc., Temple, 1965—; bd. dirs. 1st Fed. Savs. & Loan, Temple, Temple Indsl. Found. Served with USN, 1942-46, PTO. Decorated D.F.C.; named Realtor of Yr., Temple Bd. Realtors, 1971, 73, 77, Farm and Land Broker of Yr., Tex. chpt. Farm and Land Inst., 1979. Mem. Realtors Land Inst. (regional v.p. 1977-79, pres. Tex. chpt. 1978), Soc. Indsl. Realtors (pres. South Cen. Tex. chpt. 1989-90), Realtors Nat. Mktg. Inst. (cert.), Tex. Assn. Realtors (bd. dirs. 1965), Nat. Assn. Realtors, Temple C. of C. (v.p. 1973-75), Sons of Republic of Tex. Baptist. Lodges: Rotary, Masons, Shriners, Descendents of San Jacinto. Home: 510 Blackfoot Dr Temple TX 76504-3727 Office: 18 N 3rd St Temple TX 76501-7617

ALDRICH, DAVID LAWRENCE, public relations executive; b. Lakehurst Naval Air Sta., N.J., Feb. 21, 1948; s. Clarence Edward and Sarah Stiles (Andrews) A.; m. Benita Susan Massler, Mar. 17, 1974. BA in Communications, Calif. State U.-Dominguez Hills, 1976. Pub. info. technician City of Carson (Calif.), 1973-77; pub. rels. dir./adminstrv. asst. Calif. Fed. Savs., L.A., 1977-78; v.p., group supr. Hill & Knowlton, L.A., 1978-81; v.p., mgr. Ayer Pub. Rels. western div. N.W. Ayer, L.A., 1981-84; pres. Aldrich and Assocs. Inc., L.A., 1984—; bd. dirs., exec. com. Drum Corps Internat. Bd. dirs. Long Beach (Calif.) Housing Devel. Co.; mayor's task force for strategic planning Long Beach; docent Long Beach Aquarium of the Pacific; bd. govs. Theatre League Alliance of L.A. Home: 25 15th Pl Unit 704 Long Beach CA 90802-6061 Office: Aldrich & Assocs 110 Pine Ave Ste 620 Long Beach CA 90802-4423

ALDRICH, FRANK NATHAN, banker; b. Jackson, Mich., June 8, 1923; s. Frank Nathan and Marion (Butterfield) A.; m. Edna Dora DeJan, Nov. 21, 1956; children: Marion Dolores, Clinton Pershing. Student, U. Md., summer 1943; A.B. in Govt, Dartmouth Coll., 1948; postgrad., Harvard U., summer 1948. Sub-mgr. First Nat. Bank of Boston, Havana, Cuba, 1949-60, Rio de Janeiro, Brazil, 1961-62; sub-mgr. First Nat. Bank of Boston, Sao Paulo, Brazil, 1963-64, mgr., 1965, exec. mgr. Rio de Janeiro, 1966, v.p. Brazilian brs., 1966-69; v.p. overseas ops. First Nat. Bank of Boston, Boston, 1969-70; v.p. Latin Am.-Asia-Africa-Middle East div., Boston, 1970-73; sr. v.p. Latin Am. div., Boston, 1973-88; pres., CEO McLaughlin Bank N.V., Netherland Antilles, 1989-96; CEO Amicorp N.V., Netherlands Antilles, 1996—; dir. Paradigm Fin. Svcs., Netherlands Antilles; prin. Mitan Capital Corp., N.Y.C. Trustee Pan Am. Devel. Found., Washington. With USAAF, 1943-46. Decorated Air medal with 4 oak leaf clusters, D.F.C. U.S.; Medalha Marechal Candido Mariano da Silva Rondon (Brazil); Ordem Nacional do Cruzeiro do Sul (Brazil). Fellow Brit. Interplanetary Soc.; mem. Air Force Assn., Res. Officers Assn., Confederate Air Force, Inst. Navigation, Royal Astron. Soc. Can., Soc. of the Cin., Sphinx Soc., Vets of Battle of the Bulge, Squadron A Assn. of N.Y., Disting. Flying Cross Soc., Harvard Club (Boston), Dartmouth Coll. Club, Yale Club (N.Y.C.), Army and Navy Club (Washington), Wellesley (Mass.), Country Club, Wellesley Coll. Club, Masons, Shriners., Beta Theta Pi. Home: 3 Indian Spring Rd Dover MA 02030-2331

ALDRICH, GEORGE HOOVER, judge, arbitrator; b. St. Louis, Feb. 25, 1932; s. Emmett Porter and Hettie Barbara (Hoover) A.; m. Rosemary Margaret Balmforth Aldrich, June 6, 1959; children: Edward, Stephen, Robert. BA, DePauw U., 1954; LLB, Harvard Law Sch., 1957, LLM, 1958. Bar: Ind., 1958. Atty. Dept. Navy, Washington, 1959-60, Dept. Def., Washington, 1960-63; legal adv. U.S. Delegation to NATO, Paris, 1963-65; asst. legal adv. Dept. State, Washington, 1965-69, deputy legal adv., 1969-77, amb., deputy spl. rep. to pres., 1977-81; judge Iran-U.S. Claims Tribunal, The Hague, The Netherlands, 1981—; U.S. amb. for Laws of War Negotiations, Geneva, Switzerland, 1974-77; mem. UN Internat. Law Commn., Geneva, Switzerland, 1981, Bd. editors Am. Jour. Internat. Law, 1987—; prof. Leiden U., The Netherlands, 1990-97. Author: The Jurisprudence of the Iran-United States Claims Tribunal, 1996; author, negotiator: The Protocols to the 1973 Vietnam Peace Agreement.; contbr. articles to profl. jours. Pres. Exec. com. of Am. Sch. of The hague, 1987-88. Named Disting. Sr. Exec. President Carter, 1980. Mem. Coun. on Fgn. Rels., Am. Soc. Internat. Law, Internat. Inst. Humanitarian Law. Avocations: tennis, sailing. Home: 24389 Oakwood Park Rd Saint Michaels MD 21663-2543 Office: Iran-US Claims Trib, Parkweg 13, 2585 JH The Hague The Netherlands

ALDRICH, JORGEN, editor, writer; b. Vallekilde, Denmark, Apr. 24, 1941; s. Niels Henry and Ingrid (Sorgenfrey) A. JD, Sch. of Journalism, Aarhus, Denmark, 1993; Cert. in Internat. Studies, NYU, 1996. Sub-editor Sjaellands Tidende, Slagelse, Denmark, 1966-68; sub-editor Fyens Stiftstidende, Odense, Denmark, 1968-79, fgn. editor, 1979—. Fellow Winewriters' Assn. (pres. 1984-91). Home: Vesteraagade 5, DK-5672 Broby Denmark Office: Fyens Stiftstidende, Blangstedgaardsvej 2-6, DK-5220 Odense SO, Denmark

ALDRICH, RICHARD EDWARD, education educator; b. London, June 10, 1937; s. George Arthur and Kathleen Emily (Barnes) A.; m. Deirdre Jane Forrest, July 11, 1959 (div. 1980); children: Simon, Stuart, Matthew; m. Jean Averil Aldrich, Sept. 25, 1980. BA, Cambridge (Eng.) U., 1958, MA, 1962; MPhil, U. London, 1970, PhD, 1977. Postgrad. cert. edn., London, 1959. History tchr. Godalming County Sch., Surrey, Eng., 1959-65; lectr., sr. lectr. Southlands Coll., Wimbledon, Eng., 1965-73; lectr., sr. lectr., reader, prof. Inst. Edn. U. London, 1973—; pres. sr. common room U. London, 1988-90, chair acad. bd., 1990-93, chair dept. history, humanities and philosophy, 1991-95; internat. lectr. Author: Sir John Pakington and National Education, 1979; An Introduction to the History of Education, 1982; co-author: (with Patricia Leighton) Education: Time for a New Act?, 1985, (with Peter Gordon) Dictionary of British Educationists, 1989; (with Peter Gordon and Dennis Dean) Education and Policy in England in the Twentieth Century, 1991; editor: History in the National Curriculum, 1991, School and Society in Victorian Britain, 1995; editor: In History and in Education, 1996, Education for the Nation, 1996, (with Peter Gordon) Biographical Dictionary of North American and European Educationists, 1997, The National Curriculum Beyond 2000, 1998, (with David Crook and Davis Watson) Education and Employment: the DFEE and its Place in History, 2000, (with Crook) History of Education for the Twenty-first Century, 2000; mem. editl. bd. Education Today, History of Education, History of Education Review, Historical Studies in Education, Paedagogica Historica, Welsh Jour. Edn., History of Edn. Quar., Am. Ednl. Rsch. Jour.; contbr. over 80 book chpts. and articles to profl. jours. Sec. U.K. History of Edn. Soc., 1981-85, pres., 1988-92; pres. Internat. Standing Conf. for History of Edn., 1994-97; dir. Gen. Tchg. Coun. Co. for Eng. and Wales, 1990-2000. Rsch. grantee Leverhulme Found., 1993-95, Nuffield Found., 1997-99. Fellow Royal Soc. Arts, Royal Hist. Soc. Avocations: soccer, poetry, gardening. Office: Inst Edn, 20 Bedford Way, London WC1H 0AL, England

ALDRICH, ROBERT JOSEPH, economic history educator; b. N.Y.C., July 29, 1954; arrived in Australia, 1981; s. Chester Robert and Frances (Callaway) A. BA, Emory U., 1975; MA, Brandeis U., 1977; PhD, 1980. Instr. Boston Coll., 1979-80; lectr. Harvard U., Cambridge, Mass., 1980, 81; Mellon fellow Washington U., St. Louis, 1980-81; lectr. U. Sydney (Australia), 1981-84, sr. lectr., 1985-88, assoc. prof., 1989—. Author: Economy and Society in Burgundy since 1950, 1984, The French Presence in the South Pacific, 1842-1940, French and the South Pacific Since 1940, 1993, The Seduction of the Mediterranean: Writing, Art and Homosexual Fantasy, 1993, Greater France: A History of French Overseas Expansion, 1996; co-author: An Economic and Social History of Europe, 1890-1939, 1987, An Economic and Social History of Europe from 1939 to the Present, 1987, France's Overseas Frontier: Departements et Territoires d'Outre-Mer, 1992, The Last Colonies, 1998; contbr. articles to profl jours. Office: U Sydney, Dept Econ History, Sydney New South Wales 20006, Australia

ALDRICH, YVETTE M., writer, educator; b. May 23, 1971. BA, Lincoln U. Co-founder, instr. Historiconnections, Inc., Balt., 1997—; tchr. WAWC/TAPP Elem. Sch., Balt., 1997—, Catonsville (Md.) Sr. H.S., 1997—. Author: RED, Ten Little Shorts; contbr. articles to various mags.; reader of poetry in cafes, night clubs, museums, etc. Recipient 2d pl. for poetry Balt. Book Festival, 1998. Mem. Md. Writer's Assn., Journey: African-Am. Outdoor Sports Assn. (hike instr. 1998—).

ALDRIDGE, SANDRA, civic volunteer; b. Iowa, Apr. 22, 1939; d. Maurice D. and Maureen M. (Bennett) Anderson; m. Guy E. Seymour, Jan. 8, 1960 (div. Oct. 1966); m. Victor E. Aldridge, Jr., Nov. 11, 1970 (dec. May 1995); 1 child, Victor E. III. Student, Millikin U., Decatur, Ill., 1957-58. Pres. Crawford Sch. PTA, 1976-78, Terre Haute Lawyers Aux., 1979; pres., dir. Wabash Valley Assn. for Gifted and Talented Children, 1981-83, Vigo County Task Force for Alcohol and Drug Abuse, 1983-84; treas., dir. Union Hosp. Svc. League; bd. dirs. YWCA of Terre Haute, Inc., 1987-89; v.p., fin. chair, mem. exec. coun. Wabash Valley coun. Boy Scouts Am., Inc.; mem. Vigo County Tax Adjustment Bd., 1986-88; mem. Class IX Leadership Terre Haute, 1985; bd. trustees Vigo County Sch. Corp., Terre Haute, 1985-97, v.p., 1992-93, 96; sec. Ernie Pyle Chapter, The Ret. Officers Assn., 1998-2000; active Children's Theatre, United Way of Wabash Valley. Mem. Ind. Assn. Gifted Children, Swope Art Gallery, Vigo County Hist. Soc., Women's Dept. Club, Arts Illiana, Elks Women's Golf League. Democrat. Episcopalian. Home: 2929 Winthrop Rd Terre Haute IN 47802-3443

AL DURI, ZAID, orthopaedic surgeon, researcher; b. Baghdad, Iraq, Jan. 1, 1952; arrived in England, 1977; s. Abdul Aziz and Rajiha Amin. MBChB, Cairo U., 1975; MSc in Orthopaedic, London U., 1990. Surg. trainee Prince of Wales Gen. Hosp., 1978-79; surgeon St. Ann's Gen. Hosp., 1980, Princess Alexandra Hosp., 1982-83, North Middlesex Hosp., Edmonton, 1983; sr. house officer, acting registrar St. Ann's Gen. Hosp., 1982-85, Ealing Hosp., 1986-87; registrar in Orthopaedics The West Middlesex U. Hosp., 1988-90; clin. asst. in Orthopaedics Westminster Hosp., 1991; assoc. specialist in orthopaedic surgery The Wellington Knee Surgery Unit, 1992; Locum Cons. Orthopaedic Surgeon Chase Farm Nat. Health Trust, 1995. Author: (with Aichroth, Dilworth Cannon, Dipak V. Patel) Knee Surgery-Current Practice, 1992; numerous presentations on anterior knee pain syndrome and knee fat pad; contbr. articles to profl. jours. Mem. Brit. Assn. Surgery of the Knee (assoc.), Royal Soc. Medicine, Patella Femoral Study Group. Fax 020 7483 5241. E-mail: kneesurgery@columbiahealthcare.co.uk. Office: Wellington Hosp Knee Surgery Unit, Wellington Pl, London NW8 9LE, England

AL-EDRUS, HABEEB NIZAMUDIN, marketing communications consultant; b. Bangalore, Karnataka, India, Apr. 6, 1969; s. Habib Omer and Quamar Fathima. B of Commerce, St. Joseph's Evening Coll., Bangalore, 1990; postgrad. diploma in mkrg. mgmt., St. Joseph Coll. Bus. Admin., Bangalore, 1993. Project coord. Emgee Assocs., Bangalore, 1991-93; response officer Times of India, Bangalore, 1993-94; sr. media buyer Ogilvy & Mather, Mumbai, 1994-96, media supr. TV, 1996-97, media supr. integrated media buying, 1997-98, assoc. media dir., 1998—; advisor Media India, Mumbai; cons. UTV, Mumbai. Creator: (ad film) Dove, 1995, (media innovations) Pidilite-Sholay, 1996 (Gold Abby award for media innovation of yr. 1997), Kodak Moments, 1998 (Gold Lion award for media innovation 1999). Named Media Profl. of the Future, Assn. Advt. Profls., 1997. Avocations: writing, painting, traveling. Fax: 91 022 4913866. E-mail: habeeb.nizamudin@ogilvy.com. Home: 607-B wing Janakdeep, 7 Bungalows Andheri West, Mumbai 400061, India Office: Ogilvy & Mather Trade Ctr, Senapati Bapat Marg, Mumbai 400013, India

ALEINIKOV, GENNADY, bank executive; b. Minsk, Belarus, Nov. 10, 1947; m. Olga Aleinikova; children: Maxim, Pavel, Alexander. Degree in econ., Belarussian State Inst. Nat. Economy, 1977; degree in internat. econ. rels., Moscow Acad. Fgn. Trade, 1985. Loan officer, dep. mgr., mgr. Minsk dist. brs. USSR State Bank, Minsk, 1977-87, dep. chmn. dist exec. com., 1987-89; vice chmn. bd., CEO dept. econ. USSR Vnesheconombank Belarussian Br., 1989-91; pres., chmn. of bd. Bank Fgn. Econ. Affairs, Rep. of Belarus, 1991-97; chmn. Nat. Bank of Rep. Belarus, 1997-98, Internat. Trade and Investment Bank, Minsk, 1998—. Named Disting. Economist of Rep. of Belarus, 1997. Fax: 375-017-220-17-00. Office: ITI Bank, Sovetskaya Str 12, 220050 Minsk Belarus

ALEISSA, KHALID A., nuclear engineering researcher; b. Taif, Saudi Arabia, 1961; s. Abdulaziz I. and Hussah A. Aleissa; m. Huda N. Alsarkan; children: Nwaf, Ghadah, Joud. BSc in Civil and Environ. Engring., King Saud U., Riyadh, Saudi Arabia, 1983, MSc in Nuclear Engring., 1987; PhD in Nuclear Engring., Oreg. State U., 1997. Sci. rschr. atomic energy rsch. King Abdul Aziz City Sci. Tech. Inst., Riyadh, 1983-88, lab. supr., 1988-93, sect. head, 1997—. Mem. AAPM, RSS, HPS. Avocations: football, biking. Home: PO Box 26298, Riyadh 11486, Saudi Arabia Office: King Abdul Aziz City Sci, Tech Inst, PO Box 6086, Riyadh 11442, Saudi Arabia

ALEIXO DA SILVA, JOSÉ A., forestry educator, researcher; b. Caruaru, Brazil, Oct. 3, 1951; s. Antônio S. da Silva and Ivanise Aleixo; m. Lucia Sousa, Apr. 17, 1976; children: Sahib, Grazielle, Baidhy. Diploma in Agronony Engring., U. Fed. Rural Pernambuco, Brazil, 1975; MS in Forest Mensuration, U. Fed. de Viçosa, Brazil, 1977; PhD in Forest Biometrics, U. Ga., 1986, post-doctorate in Forest Biometrics, 1993; Didactic Merit (hon.), U. Fed. Rural Pernambuco, Brazil, 1990. Aux. prof. U. Fed. Rural de Pernambuco, Recife, 1976-77, asst. prof., 1978-85, adj. prof., 1986—; vis. prof. U. Fed. de Viçosa, 1977, Sch. of Forest Resources, U. Ga., Athens, 1991-93; vice dean agronomy dept. U. Fed. Rural de Pernambuco, 1987-88, dean, 1989-91. Author: Princípios Básicos de Dendrometria, 1979, Estatística Experimental Aplicada à Ciência Florestal, 1982, 2d edit., 1995, Métodos Estatísticos Aplicados à Pesquisa Científica: Uma Abordagem para Profissionais da Pesquisa Agro pecuária, 1999. Mem. Alumni Cpt. U. Ga./Brazil (pres. 1987-99), Conselho Regional de Engenharia e Arquitetura, WWF, Brazilian Soc. for Advancement Sci. (regional sec., rsch. 2A of CNPq). Avocation: soccer. Office: U Fed Rural Pernambuco, Rua D Manoel Medeiros S/N, Dois Irmaos Recife 52171030, Brazil

ALEJANDRO, GIRALDO, physician; b. Feb. 25, 1948. MD, U. Nat. Medicne, Bogota, Colombia, 1973; MPH, Johns Hopkins U., 1988. Dir. Fundacion Gillow, Bogota, 1993; asst. prof. human genetics U. Nat. Bogota, 1997; vice-chmn. Colombian Nat. Inst. Health, Bogota, 1976-93. Contbr. articles to profl. jours. Office: Calle 100 No 11A-12, Bogota Colombia

ALEKHIN, VLADIMIR NICHOLAEVICH, civil and structural engineering executive; b. Yekaterinburg, Sverdlovsk, Russia, Feb. 21, 1953; s. Nicholai Alekseevich and Nina Ivanovna (Chulkova) A.; m. Olga Bruno Martens, July 7, 1978; 1 child, Alekhina Maria Vladimirovna. MSc, Urals State Tech. U., 1975, PhD, 1981. Sr. structural engr. Ctrl. R&D Inst. of Metal Structures, Yekaterinburg, Russia, 1975-78; asst. prof. Urals State Tech. U., Yekaterinburg, 1982-84, assoc. prof., 1984-92, head of dept., 1992—; gen. dir. Techcon Tech., Yekaterinburg, 1991—, JV Duntek, Yekaterinburg, 1997—; dir. Ingras-Pro Ltd., Yekaterinburg, 1996—; dep. dir. AMA Ltd., Yekaterinburg, 1993—. Author: (with others) International Handbook of Earthquake Engineering, 1994; inventor connection of floor system to column; contbr. articles to profl. jours. Sr. lt. Urals Mil. Dist., 1981—. Mem. Ecol. Acad. of Russia (corr.), N.Y. Acad. Scis., Assn. of Civil Engring. Inst. of CIS. Avocations: basketball, English, reading, music, history. Home: 12 Piekhanova St, 620034 Yekaterinburg Russia Office: Urals State Tech U, 19 Mira St, 620002 Yekaterinburg Russia

ALEKNA, VIRGILIJUS, Olympic athlete; b. Terpeikiai, Lithuania, Feb. 13, 1972. Winner Silver Medal World Championships Athens, 1997; winner Gold Medal discus throw Sydney, 2000. First man to throw discus 70 meters in 2000; recorded throw of 70.39 meters, Tartu, Estonia, 2000. Office: Lithuanian Athletic Found, Zemaitis 6, LT-2675 Vilnius Lithuania*

ALEKSANDROV, ALEKSEI ALEKSANDROVICH, engineering educator; s. Aleksandr Timopheevich and Zinaida Konstantinovna (Kozlovskaja) A.; m. Irina Sergeevna Fedoseeva, Dec. 30, 1955 (div. June 1976); 1 child, Marina; m. Asija Yanovna Essalnek, Oct. 15, 1976. Degree in engring., Moscow Power Engring. Inst., 1956, Candidate Tech. Scis., 1962, D in Tech. Scis., 1982. Cert. engr. Rschr. Moscow Power Engring. Inst., 1956-57, asst., 1960-63, lectr., 1963-83, prof., 1983—. Author: (with V.A. Zubarev, V.S. Okhotin) Practicum on Technical Thermodynamics, 1965, 71, 86, (with M.P. Vucalovich, S.L. Rivkin) Tables of Thermophysical Properties of Water and Steam, 1969, (with V.N. Popov) Calculations of Thermophysical Properties of Substances, 1972, (with S.L. Rivkin) Steam Tables, 1975, 78, 84, 88, (with S.L. Rivkin, E.A. Kremenevskaja) Thermodynamics Derivatives for Water and Steam, 1977, 78, (with M.S. Trakhtengerts) Thermophysical Properties of Water at Atmospheric Pressure, 1977, (with S.L. Rivkin) Thermophysical Properties of Water and Steam, 1980, (with B.A. Gzigozieb) Tables of Thermophysical Properties of Water and Steam, 1999. Recipient prize on sci. and tech. USSR Coun. of Mins., 1987, State prize of Russia, Pres. of Russia, 1996. Fellow Internat. Assn. Properties of Water and Steam (hon.); mem. Nat. Com. Properties of Water and Steam (sci. sec. 1964-92, chmn. 1992). Home: Karamzina 9 fl 279, 117463 Moscow Russia Office: Moscow Power Engring Inst, Krasnokazarmennaja 14, 111250 Moscow Russia

ALEKSANDROV, GEORGIJ NIKOLAEVICH, electrical engineering educator, researcher; b. St. Petersburg, Russia, Jan. 7, 1930; s. Nikolaj Vladimirovich and Beatrisa Aleksandrovna (Dikhof) A.; m. Natalia Pavlovna Bashkatova, May 1954 (div.); children: Andrej, Maria, Pavel; m. Galina Nikolaevna Kirpicheva, July 9, 1983. Grad. in Engring., Leningrad (Russia) Poly. Inst., 1953, Candidate of Tech. Sci., 1957; D of Tech. Sci., All Union Electrotech. Inst., Moscow, 1967. Asst. Leningrad Poly. Inst., 1953-57, sci. worker, 1957-62, dozent, 1962-71, prof., 1971—, head dept., 1974—, Prorector in sci., 1977-82; cons. Electrosetisolazia, Moscow, 1995—. Author: Corona Discharge on Transmission Lines, 1964, Electrical Strength of External High Voltage Insulation, 1969, A.C. Electrical Energy Transmission, 1990; author, editor: Designing of Extra-High Voltage Transmission Lines, 1983. Fellow IEEE (sr.); mem. Russian Acad. Sci. Avocations: growing and service of fruit trees, invention. Home: Nekrasova str 31 app 2, 194902 Saint Petersburg Russia Office: St Petersburg State Tech U, Polytechnicheskaja str 29, 195251 Saint Petersburg Russia

ALEKSANDROVSKII, ANATOLII NIKOLAEVICH, physicist, researcher; b. Kharkov, Ukraine, July 26, 1946; s. Nikolai Nikolaevich and Claudia Stepanovna (Tsygankova) A.; m. Nina Grigorievna Scorokhodova, July 23, 1969; children: Oksana, Elena. Physicist, State U. Kharkov, 1972; PhD in Physics and Math., Inst. Low Temp. Phys./Eng., Kharkov, 1980. Jr. rschr. Inst. Low Temperature Physics and Engring., Kharkov, 1972-84, sr. rschr., rsch. group leader, 1984—. Patentee in engring. field; contbr. articles to profl. jours. Mem. Phys. Soc. Home: Apt 2, 27 Str Transformatornaya, 310066 Kharkov Ukraine Office: Inst Low Temp Physics/Eng, 310164 Kharkov Ukraine

ALEKSANDROWICZ, DARIUSZ LEOPOLD, philosopher; b. Wroclaw, Poland, Oct. 30, 1949; s. Zygmunt and Maria Magdalena (Dluzniewska) A.; m. Izabela Kiszczynska, Oct. 13, 1973; children: Paula, Lech, Ewa. MA in German Philology, U. Wroclaw, 1972, MA in Philosophy, 1974, PhD, 1976, D. habil. Philosophy, 1982. Jr. asst. U. Wroclaw, 1972-74, asst. lectr., 1974-76, tutor, 1976-83, assoc. prof. philosophy, 1983-93, chmn., 1977-81; prof. philosophy Europa U., Viadrina Frankfurt, 1993—; mem. senate U. Wroclaw, 1983-84, dean faculty, 1984-87; research fellow Etvös Lorand U., Budapest, Hungary, 1979, U. Mannheim, Fed. Republic Germany, 1982-84, U. Kassel, Fed. Republic Germany, 1988; vis. prof. U. Graz, Austria, 1992; mem. adv. bd. Geschichte und Gegenwart, Graz, Initial, Berlin. Author: (books) Knowlege and Criticism, 1979 (ministry of higher edn. award 1980), Philosophical Foundations in Lukacs Theory of Knowledge, 1983 (Rectors award 1984), Hegel and Aftermath, 1990 (Rectors award 1991), You Shall Know the Truth, 1993; contbr. numerous articles to profl. jours. Mem. Inst. Internat. de Philosophie Politique (Paris, bd. dirs.), Interdisziplinaeres Zentrum fuer Ethik (Frankfurt), Frankfurter Inst. fuer Transformationsstudien. Home: Lessingstr 16, 15230 Frankfurt Germany Office: Europa U Viadrina, PSF 1786, 15207 Frankfurt Germany

ALEKSEEV, BORIS FEDEROVICH, physics educator, researcher; b. City Krasnojarsk, Russia, Jan. 26, 1942; s. Fedor Alekseevich and Ol'ga Stepanovna (Laneva) A.; m. Tatiana Michailovna Gerasimova, June 27, 1967; children: Julia, Ol'ga. BS in Engring., Electrotech. Inst., Leningrad, Russia, 1965, PhD, 1972. Asst. Electrotech. Inst., Leningrad, Russia, 1968-74; assoc. prof. Electrotech. U., 1974—. Co-author, co-editor: (book) Radiospectroscopy of Natural Substances, 1987; co-author: (book) Laboratory Practicum on Physics, 1988; contbr. articles and rev. to profl. jours.

Recipient award St. Petersburg (Russia) Phys. Soc., 1992; grantee: Soros, 1995, 97; named Soros Assoc. Prof., 1995. Mem. N.Y. Acad. Scis., Internat. EPR Soc., Russian Phys. Soc. Office: State Electrotech Univ, Prof Popov Str 5, 197376 Saint Petersburg Russia

ALEKSEEV, IGOR EVGENIEVICH, chemist; b. Leningrad, Soviet Union, Jan. 14, 1960; s. Evgeny Nikolaevich and Tamara Ivanovna (Vladimirova) A.; m. Saida Ruslanovna Tharkahova, Oct., 19, 1985; 1 child, Vikenty. MS in Chemistry, State U., Leningrad, Soviet Union, 1982; PhD, State U., 1990. Engr. Mechanobr Inst., Leningrad, Soviet Union, 1982-84; rschr. State U., Leningrad, 1984-91, St. Peterburg, Russia, 1991-2000; chief dep. radiation safety State Univ., St. Petersburg, Russia, 2000—; dep. dir. Technolab Bus. Ltd., St. Petersburg, 1994—; adv. Central Rsch. Inst. Structural Materials Prometey, St. Petersburg, 1995—. Contbr. articles to profl. jours., patents in field. Mem. Soc. Nuclear Med. Avocations: Russian literature, St. Bernard dogs. Office: St Petersburg St U, 7/9 Universitetskaya Emb, 199034 St Petersburg Russia

ALEMÁN, (JOSE) ARNOLDO, president of Nicaragua; b. Managua, Nicaragua, Jan. 23, 1946; widowed; 4 children. Grad., U. Nat. Autonoma, León, Nicaragua, 1967. Atty. Nicaragua, 1968-79; mayor Managua, 1990; pres. Govt. Nicaragua, 1995—; lectr. Fla. Internat. U., Miami, Tulane U., New Orleans, Ctrl. Am. Inst. Bus. Adminstrn., Managua. Pres. Liberal Constn. Party, 1990-91, 93-96. Recipient Nat. Order of Merit with Grand Cross, Colombian Govt., Isabel la Catolica decoration King of Spain, Grand Order Belgranian Cross, Govt. Argentina, Key to City, Taipei, China; Hon. Citizen New Orleans. Mem. Coffee Growers Assn. Managua (pres. 1983-86), Nat. Farmers Union (pres. 1986-90), Ctrl. Am. Fedn. City Couns. (pres. 1992-93), Mcpl. Fedn. Ctrl. Am. Citie (pres. 1993-95). Office: Office of Pres, Casa de Gobierno Apdo 2398, Managua Nicaragua*

ALEMÁN, MARTHANNE PAYNE, environmental planner, consultant; b. Houston, Dec. 3, 1938; d. Charles Franklin and Evelyn Inez (Dudley) Payne; m. Samuel Garza Alemán, July 5, 1968. BS in Landscape Arch. magna cum laude, Tex. A&M U., 1988; MS in Interdisciplinary Studies, Tex. Tech. U., 1989; PhD in Urban and Regional Sci., Tex. A&M U., 1995. Engring. aide City of Austin, 1966-69, Bryant-Curington Engrs., Austin, 1969-72; entrepreneur Rio Verde Farm, San Benito, Tex., 1972-83; rsch. asst. Tex. Tech. U., Lubbock, 1988-91, Tex. A&M U., College Station, 1993-94; cons. Rio Verde Land & Investment Corp., Calvert, Tex., 1995—; sec./treas., bd. dirs. Tex. Avocado Growers Assn., Weslaco, 1979-83. Author: Soil Salinity in the Texas Lower Rio Grande Valley: Cause for Concern, 1987, Export-Driven Development of Soil and Water Resources: Barrier to Sustainable Development and Inducement to Desertification, 1995. Mem. and active participant Robertson County Hist. Commn., Calvert, 1980-83. Smithsonian Instn. intern, Washington, 1987, Presdl. scholar U.S. Fed. Register, 1993; recipient Nat. Collegiate Archtl. and Design award, U.S. Achievement Acad., Lexington, Ky., 1989. Mem. Am. Planning Assn., Soil and Water Conservation Soc. of Am. (vol. Heart of Tex. chpt., Waco, Tex.). Avocations: breeding, showing, and training collies. Office: Rio Verde Land and Investment Corp 201 Browning Calvert TX 77837

ALEMDAROGLU, KEMAL, university official. Rector Istanbul U. Office: Istanbul Univ, Beyazit, Istanbul Turkey*

ALENCAR, MARCELO SAMPAIO DE, electrical engineering educator; b. Serrita, Pernambuco, Brazil, Oct. 11, 1957; s. José I Sampaio De and Gilvoneide (Sampaio De) A.; m. Silvana Lucia Tavares de Alencar, Dec. 25, 1982; children: Thiago, Raphael, Marcella. B in Engring., UFPE, Recife, Brazil, 1980; MSc, UFPB, Campina Grande, Brazil, 1988; PhD, U. Waterloo, Can., 1993. Profl. elec. engr. Asst. prof. FEJ/UDCSC, Joinville, Brazil, 1982-84; prof. UFPB, Campina Grande, Brazil, 1984—; cons. Fed. Agy. for the Sponsorship of Studies and Projects, Brasilia, Brazil, 1985-87, Embratel, Recife, Brazil, 1989; vice chmn. Dept. Elec. Engring./Fed. U. Paraiba, Campina Grande, 1985-87; chmn. industry univ. com., Campina Grande, 1994—. Author: (book) Digital Telephony, 1998, Principles of Communication, 1999; author Jour. Selected Areas of Communication, 1994. Recipient scholarship Nat. Coun. for Sci. and Tech. Rsch., Recife, 1980, Waterloo, Ont., 1990-93; tchg. assistantship U. Waterloo, 1992. Mem. IEEE (sr.), Soc. Brasileira Telecom., Soc. Brasileira Microondas. Avocations: soccer, tennis, volleyball, basketball, classical music. Home: R Maria de Sousa, Ribeiro 129, CP 547 58100 Campina Grande Brazil Office: U Federal da Paraiba, Av Aprigio Veloso 882, 58100 Campina Grande Brazil

ALENIKOFF, FRANCES, choreographer, performer, writer, dancer, artist; b. N.Y.C., Aug. 20, 1920; d. Clement Jack Lipman and Ruth (Alder) Taylor; m. Martin Freedman, 1936 (div. 1973); children: Francesca Rheannon. BA, Bklyn. Coll., 1940. founding mem. Dance Theatre Workshop, N.Y., 1968—. Soloist and company at colls., univs., theaters, in festivals and community ctrs. in U.S. and abroad, 1959-93; soloist in films including Frekoba, 1969, Alenka, 1968, Episodes On The Edge, 1973, Shaping Things, 1978; soloist at Lincoln Ctr., 1985; choreographer for Zaide, 1956, L'Histoire Du Soldat, 1957, Josephine Baker Show On Broadway, 1964, Joan and the Devil, 1978; performer Dream Play, 1970, Oddfellows Players, 1991-95; participant in various art festival, 1966-86; dir. Eden's Expressway, 1975—; dance critic Dance News, 1970-82; staff writer Craft Horizons Mag., 1971-74; actress in Witness, Blood Summer Rituals, 1994; dancer, choreographer St. Mark's Dancespace, 1996, 98, 2000, Frederick Loewe Theater, 1996, Dance Theatre Workshop, 1996, 97, Soho Arts Festival, 1996, 97, Judson Ch., N.Y.C., 1997, Downtown Arts Festival, 1998, 99, Dixon Place, Merce Cunningham Studio, 2000, Lifetime TV, 2000, Tribeca Performing Arts Ctr., 2000; contbr. articles to profl. jours. Recipient Grant N.Y. State Coun. on the Arts, 1972-80, NEA, 1973-74, N.Y. City Cultural Coun., 1978, Meet the Composer, 1980, N.J. State Coun. on the Arts, 1972, Cine Internat. Golden Eagle award, 1978; named Pick of Yr. for Best in Dance, Village Voice, 1997. Mem. Dancers Over Forty. Home: 537 Broadway New York NY 10012-3930

ALESHIN, ANDREI NIKOLAEVICH, physicist; b. St. Petersburg, Russia, Nov. 16, 1956; s. Nikolai and Ludmila (Smirnova) A.; m. Galina Rotova, Jan. 18, 1986; 1 child, Peter. MS, St. Petersburg Tech. U., 1980; PhD, I.F. Ioffe Phys-Tech. Inst., St. Petersburg, 1989. Jr. physicist State Optical Inst., St. Petersburg, Russia, 1980-83; from jr. physicist to sr. physicist Ioffe Phys-Tech. Inst., 1983—. Mem. Materials Rsch. Soc. Avocations: cycling, skiing, walking. Home: 3 Marinesko str #48, 198096 Saint Petersburg Russia

ALESHIN, VLADIMIR PAVLOVICH, nuclear physicist; b. Donetsk, Ukraine, May 9, 1944; s. Pavel and Zoja (Pishchita) A.; m. Valeria Anatolievna, May 9, 1964; two children. MSc, Dnepropetrovsk State U., 1966; DSc, Joint Inst. Nuclear Rsch., Russia, 1992. Engr. Inst. Physics, Kiev, 1967-92; from engr. to leading scientific rschr. Inst. Nuclear Rsch., Kiev, 1970—. Office: Inst Nuclear Rsch, Prospect Nauki 47, 03680 Kiev Ukraine

ALESI, JEAN, race car driver; b. Avignon, France, June 11, 1964; divorced; children: Charlotte Marcelle, Helena. Race car driver, 1983—. Winner Renault 5 Turbo Cup, 1983, 2-time winner, French Formula 3, 1986, champion, 6-time consecutive winner French Formula 3, 1987, 3-time winner Formula 3000, 1989, 1 win Formula 1, 1989—. Avocations: skiing, golf, tennis. Office: Rte de St Saturnin, 84279 Vedene France

ALESKEROV, MURTUZ NADZHAF OGLU, Azerbaijan government official; b. Gyandzha, Sept. 20, 1928; married; 2 sons, 1 daughter. Grad., Azerbaijan State U. Sr. lectr. Azerbaijan State U., 1954—, head of chair of state law, 1965—, prof., 1969, rector, 1993-96; chmn. Nat. Assembly (Milli Majlis), Baku, Azerbaijan; dep. chair Party Yeni Azerbaijan; mem. Polit. Coun.; elected dep. Milli Majlis, 1995, chair, 1996—. Contbr. about 200 articles to profl. jours.; author several monographies, textbooks on internat. and constl. law. Mem. Int. Juridical Assn. *

ALESSANDRI, FRANCISCA COHN, journalist, educator; b. Santiago, Chile, Jan. 7, 1957; d. Arturo Alessandri and Nancy (Cohn) A.; m. Francisco Bezanilla Vial, Oct. 25, 1980; children: Francisco, Amelia, Jose Domingo, Barbara, Valentina. M in political sci., Chile, 1987. Prof. sch. journalist U. Catolica, Chile, 1979, dir. asst. sch. journalist, 1991—, dir. sch. journalist dept., 1993-97. Author: Arturo Alessandri: El Leon De Tarapaca, 1994. Roman Catholic. Home: Fray Bernardo, 11835 Santiago Chile Office: Univ Catolica, J Guzman, 3300 Santiago Chile

ALESSI, ROBERT JOSEPH, lawyer, pharmacist; b. Rome, N.Y., Aug. 22, 1958; s. William John and Mary Jean A.; m. Ellen Mary Paczkowski, May 21, 1988; children: Laura C., Grace E. BS in Pharmacy, Union U., 1982; JD cum laude, Albany Law Sch., 1985. Bar: N.Y. 1986, U.S. Dist. Ct. (no. dist.) N.Y. 1986, U.S. Dist. Ct. (we. dist.) N.Y. 1986, U.S. Dist. Ct. (ea. dist.) N.Y. 1993, U.S. Dist. Ct. (so. dist.) N.Y. 1993, U.S. Ct. Appeals (2d cir.) 1995, U.S. Supreme Ct. 1996. Assoc. Nixon, Hargrave, Devans & Doyle, Albany, N.Y., 1985-90; assoc. LeBoeuf, Lamb, Greene & MacRae, Albany, 1990-93, ptnr., 1994—, mng. ptnr., 1999—; adj. prof. law Albany Law Sch., 1989-94. Co-author: Year 2000 Deskbook, 1998. Mem. master plan com. Town of Bethlehem, Delmar, N.Y., 1989-89, mem. planning bd. counsel, 1990-94. Mem. N.Y. State Bar Assn., Albany Law Sch. Environ. Alumni Group, Rockefeller Found. (advisor Pocantico roundtable consensus on brownfields). Avocations: tennis, fitness training, reading. Fax: 518-626-9010. E-mail: ralessi@llgm.com. Home: 8 Partridge Rd Delmar NY 12054-3919 Office: LeBoeuf Lamb Greene & MacRae LLP One Commerce Plz Ste 2020 99 Washington Ave Albany NY 12210

ALEX, VOLKER ERNST, physicist, researcher; b. Magdeburg, Germany, July 26, 1939; s. Ernst Otto and Erna (Rödel) A.; m. Bettina Margarete Kriebitzsch, May 26, 1978; 1 child, Jördis Margot. Diploma in physics, U. Halle, Germany, 1964, PhD in Physics, 1970. Cert. radiation protection inspector. Asst. U. Halle, 1968-73; rschr. Acad. Scis., Berlin, 1973-91, Leibniz-Cmty., Berlin, 1992—. Contbr. (book) Dynamical Interference Theory, 1976. Mem. German Phys. Soc., German Soc. Crystallography, German Soc. Crystal Growing and Growth. Achievements include patent Goniometer Head, patent Device for Circle Guide with Small Set Angles, and patent Device for Circle Guide with Moment-of-Rotation Fine Setting. Office: Inst fuer Kristallzuechtung, Max-Born-Strasse 2, D-12489 Berlin Germany

ALEXA, DIMITRIE, electrotechnical engineer, educator; b. Cernauti, Romania, Nov. 5, 1938; s. Ioan and Elisabeta (Stiasny) A.; m. Maria Carciuleanu, July 30, 1966. MSEE, Tech. U. Iasi, Romania, 1960, PhD, 1975. Rschr. Ctr. Physics. Rsch., Iasi, 1960-70; lectr. Tech. Univ., Iasi, 1970-81, prof., 1981, dean faculty electronics and telecomm., 1992—. Author: Inverters and Rectifiers with High Energetical Parameters, 1986, Power Static Converters Applications, 1989, Power Converters with Resonant Circuits, 1998; contbr. articles to profl. jours. Recipient Acad. award Power Electronics, 1991. Mem. IEEE (sr.), N.Y. Acad. Scis. Russian Orthodox. AvocationsL chess, classical music. Home: Bloc H5 Ap 9, Titu Maiorescu St 24A, 6600 Iasi Romania Office: Tech Univ Faculty Electonic and Telecom, Blvd Copou 11, 6600 Iasi Romania

ALEXAKHIN, ROUDOLF MIKHAILOVICH, agricultural executive; b. Korolev, Russia, Dec. 15, 1936; s. Mikhail Timofeevich Alexakhin and Valentina Mikhailovna Alexakhina; m. Tatjana Ivanovna Palievskaya, Dec. 12, 1970. Diploma, Moscow State U., 1959; postgrad., Inst. Forest Sci., Moscow, 1963; DSc, Ministry Mid. Machine Bldg., 1974; diploma in agrl. scis., Russian Acad. Agrl. Scis., 1988, Agrarian Acad. Scis., Ukraine, 1995. Jr. rsch. assoc. Moscow State U., 1959-61, USSR Acad. Sci., 1961-66; sci. sec. Ministry Mid. Machine Bldg., Moscow, 1966-75; dir. Russian Inst. Agrl. Radiol. Agroecolog., Obinsk, Russia, 1975—; mem. ICRP com. 4, 1977-84, 97—, USSR (Russia) Delegation UNSCEAR, 1974-98. Contbr. articles to profl. jours. Recipient USSR Govt. award, 1974, Russian Honoured Scientist, 1997; named to Order Peoples Friendship, 1980. Mem. Russian Sci. Com. Radiolog. Protection (vice-chmn. 1990—), Internat. Union Radioecology. Office: Russian Inst Agrl Radiology Agroecology, Kievskoe str, 249020 Obninsk Kaluga Region, Russia

ALEXAKIS, ALEXANDRE, chemistry educator; b. Alexandria, Egypt, July 22, 1949; s. Constantin and Jeannette (Banoun) A.; m. Lucienne Galinier, July 30, 1971; children: Camille, Marc. Diploma, U. Paris (France), 1969, M in Biochemistry, 1971, PhD, 1975. Rsch. assoc. CNRS, Paris, 1977-85, dir. rsch., 1985-96; prof. chemistry U. Pierre & Marie Curie, Paris, 1996-98, U. Geneva, 1998—. Contbr. over 150 articles to profl. jours. Ministry of Fgn. Affairs grantee, France, 1969-74. Mem. French Chem. Soc. (bd. dirs. organic chemistry divsn.), Swiss Chem. Soc., Am. Chem. Soc., Royal Chem. Soc. Avocations: classical music, fishing, squash. Home: 44 bis av Krieg, 1208 Geneva Switzerland Office: U Geneva Dept Organic Chem, 30 quai Ernest Ansermet, 1211 Geneva Switzerland

ALEXANDER, ANNA MARGARET, artist, educator; b. Greenville, Tex., Jan. 26, 1913; d. Samuel Jefferson and Elizabeth (Smith) Fooshee; m. Joseph C. Jake Alexander, Feb. 12, 1936 (dec. 1988); children: Joanna, Ellen Stein, Mardi. BA, Rice U., 1933. Cert. tchr. Tchr., Klein, Tex., 1933-38; fashion artist, writer, adv. mgr. Smart Shop, Houston, 1938-43; fashion artist, writer Kreeger's, New Orleans, 1943-45, Everitt Buelow Ralph Rupley, 1953-68; art tchr. Spring Branch, Houston, 1968-74; founder Historic Outdoor Art Gallery, New Braunfels, TX. Vol. literacy program, ch., hist. socs., sr. citizen groups, children's mus., food bank; leader, camp counselor Girl Scouts U.S.A., Houston, 1956-60; pres. Girl's Booster Club, Houston, 1966-68; bd. dirs. St. Francis Episc. Day Sch., 1965-70; Sunday sch. tchr. St. Francis Ch., Houston, 1958-62; active PTA. Mem. Advt. Club Houston, Univ. Women Houston, DAR, Colonial Dames New Braunfels, Garden Club, Ret. Tchrs. Assn., C. of C. Vis. Bur. (downtown design rev. commn.), others. Avocations: ecology, church activities, gardening, volunteerism, travel, family activities. Home: 909 Allen Ave New Braunfels TX 78130-4903

ALEXANDER, BARTON, consumer products company manager; b. Toledo, Dec. 8, 1951; s. Barton and Marian (Gordon) A. BA magna cum laude, Harvard U., 1973; MSc, London Sch. Econs., 1975. Exec. dir. Toledo Coalition, 1970; policy analyst U.S. Dept. HEW, 1971-72; spl. asst. Mass. Dept. Mental Health, 1973-74; analyst/sr. policy budget analyst Colo. Gov. Office, 1975-77; acting dir. Adams Co. (Colo.) Dept. Social Svcs., 1978-79, asst. dir., 1977-80, dir. program devel., 1980-83; dep. dir. to acting exec. dir. Colo. Dept. Labor and Employment, 1983-87; dep. dir. Colo. Dept. Local Affairs Govs. Econ. Devel. Offices, 1987-88; exec. dir. Jobs for Colorado's Future, Denver, 1988-89; mgr. alcohol issues Coors Brewing Co., Golden, Colo., 1990-92, group mgr. corp. and alcohol issues, 1993-97, dir. pub. affairs, 1997—; bd. dirs. Bacchus, Internat. Ctr. for Alcohol Policies, Spring Inst. for internat. Understanding; cons. in field. Bd. dirs. Capital Hill Cmty. Svcs. Gates Found. Pub. Leadership fellow, 1986, Rotary Internat. fellow. Mem. London Sch. Econs. Soc. Democrat. Avocations: mountain climbing, skiing, theatre, food, music. Home: 3330 Oak St Wheat Ridge CO 80033-5457

ALEXANDER, BILL, theater director; b. Hunstanton, Eng., Feb. 23, 1948; s. Bill and rosemary Paterson; m. Juliet Harmer, 1978; 2 children. Student, St. Lawrence Coll., Ramsgate U., Steele U. Dir. Bristol Old Vic; with Royal Shakespeare Co., 1977—, assoc. dir., 1984-91, artistic dir., 1991—; artistic dir. Birmingham (Eng.) Repertory Theatre; with Notting ham Playhouse, Royal Court Theatre, Victory Theatre, N.Y. and Shakespeare Theatre, Washington. Prodns. include Tartuffe, Richard III, 1984, Volpone, The Accrington Pals, Clay, Captin Swing, School of Night, A Midsummer Night's Dream (Olivier award for Best Dir. 1986), Othello, The Snowman, Macbeth, Dr. Jekyll and Mr. Hyde, The Alchemist, Awake and Sing, Hamlet, Merchant of Venice, The Tempest, Twelfth Night. Avocation: tennis. Home: Rose Cottage, Tunley Glos GL7 6LP, England Office: Birmingham Repertory, Broad St, Birmingham B1 2EP, England

ALEXANDER, CARL ALBERT, ceramic engineer, educator; b. Chillicothe, Ohio, Nov. 22, 1928; s. Carl B. and Helen E. Alexander; m. Dolores J. Hertenstein, Sept. 4, 1954; children: Carla C., David A. B.S., Ohio U., 1953, M.S., 1956; Ph.D., Ohio State U., 1961. Mem. staff Battelle Columbus Labs., 1956—, research leader, 1974—, mgr. physico-chem. systems, 1976—; mem. faculty Ohio State U., 1963—, prof. ceramic and nuclear engring., 1977—; sr. research leader, chmn. tech. council of Biol. and Chem. Scis. Directorate, 1987—, chief scientist, 1987; prof. materials sci. and engring, 1988—;. Author; patentee in field. Served to lt. (j.g.) USNR, 1951-54. Recipient Merit award NASA, 1971, IR-100 award, 1987, R&D-100 award, 1988; citations Dept. Energy, citations AEC, citations ERDA. Mem. Am. Soc. Mass Spectrometry, Keramos, Sigma Xi. E-mail: alexandc@battelle.org. Home: 4249 Haughn Rd Grove City OH 43123-3216 Office: 505 King Ave Columbus OH 43201-2696

ALEXANDER, CLIFFORD JOSEPH, lawyer; b. New Orleans, Oct. 2, 1943; s. Charles Ernest and Lois Primus (Boley) A.; m. Elizabeth McAnany, June 11, 1966; children: Brian, Heather, Rachel. AB, Rockhurst Coll., 1966; JD, Georgetown U., 1969. Bar: Mass. 1970, D.C. 1977. Mem. staff SEC, Washington, 1967-70; assoc. Gaston Snow & Ely Bartlett, Boston, 1970-75; mem. staff U.S. Senate Banking Com., Washington, 1975-77; mem. Kirkpatrick & Lockhart LLP (formerly Kirkpatrick, Lockhart, Hill, Christopher & Phillips, and predecessor), Washington, 1977—. Co-editor: Money Managers Compliance Manual. Mem. ABA (corp., banking and bus. law sect.), Boston Bar Assn., Fed. Bar Assn. (securities and banking law sects.), D.C. Bar Assn., Mass. Bar Assn., U.S. Supreme Ct. Bar. Home: 8721 Bluedale St Alexandria VA 22308-2307 Office: Kirkpatrick & Lockhart 1800 Massachusetts Ave NW Fl 2 Washington DC 20036-1806

ALEXANDER, DAVID RITCHIE, lawyer; b. Hasting, New Zealand, Sept. 29, 1948; arrived in Australia, 1979; s. Robert Ritchie and Evelyn Constance A.; divorced; children: Ben, Claire. BA, We. State Coll., Gunnison, Colo., 1970; LLB, Auckland (New Zealand) U., 1974. Lawyer Lawson Jones & Fulton, Brisbane, Australia, 1980-81, A. W. Bale & Son, Brisbane, Australia, 1981-82; pvt. practice Brisbane, Australia, 1982-84; solicitor J. Brynes, Brisbane, Australia, 1985-86; sr. ptnr. Blackwell Appleyard, Maroochydore, Australia, 1987-93; pvt. practice D.R. Alexander & Co., Maroscldyove, Australia, 1993—. Contbr. articles to profl. jours. Rev. com. Legal Aid Office, Maroochydore, 1989—. Mem. Law Coun. Australia, Old Queensland Law Soc., Assn. Family Law Mediators. Avocations: tennis, golfing, stamp collecting, gardening. Office: 15/27 Evans St, Maroochy Dove 4558 QLD, Australia

ALEXANDER, ELLIN DRIBBEN, financial marketing company executive; b. Albany, N.Y., July 20, 1955; d. Irving S. and Helen (Meyer) Dribben; m. Richard D. Alexander, May 18, 1984; children: Evan R., Elisabeth D., Hannah Claire. BA, St. Lawrence U., 1977; postgrad., Boston U., 1978—. Asst. dir. devel. Northea. Assn of the Blind, Albany, 1979-80; mktg. rep. Newkirk, Albany, 1980-85, asst. v.p., 1985—, mgr. trust info. and comm. sys., 1990-98, product mgr. will files and direct mail programs, 1998—; bd. dirs. Albany Dist. Postal Customer Coun. Fundraiser Am. Cancer Soc., Albany, 1988-92; bd. dirs. Arbor House, Albany, 1980-88; bd. dirs. ARC N.E. N.Y., 1992-99, chairperson bd. dirs., 1995-97; mem. N.Y. State Svc. Coun., ARC, 1997—; campaign divsn. chmn. United Way of N.E. N.Y., bd. dirs., 1990-95. Mem. N.Y. State Realtors Assn., Albany County Bd. Realtors, Jr. League Albany (bd. dirs. 1980-81, 83, 86, 88, 90-95), Phi Beta Kappa, Omega Delta Kappa. Roman Catholic. Avocations: gardening, theatre, volunteer work, driving. Office: Newkirk 15 Corporate Cir Albany NY 12203-5177

ALEXANDER, ELMORE ROSEBUR, III, business educator, dean; b. Florence, S.C., July 14, 1952; m. Pamela C. Alexander. BA, Wake Forest U., 1974; MA, U. Ga., 1976, PhD, 1978. Prof. mgmt. U. Memphis, 1977-89; prof. Am. U., Washington, 1989-96, chair mgmt. dept., 1989-93, assoc. dean Kogod Coll. Bus. Adminstrn., 1993-96; prof., dir. divsn. bus. mgmt. Johns Hopkins U., Balt., 1996-98; prof., dean Sch. Bus. Adminstrn. Phila. U., 1998—. Contbr. articles to profl. jours. Methodist. Avocations: golf, tennis. Fax: 215-951-2652. Home: 348 Valley Rd Merion Station PA 19066-1520 Office: Phila U School House Ln & Henry Ave Philadelphia PA 19144-5497

ALEXANDER, HAROLD CAMPBELL, insurance consultant; b. Houston, Dec. 11, 1920; s. Henry Campbell and Essie Mae (Gilbert) A.; m. Dorothy Emma Schraub, Aug. 21, 1925; children: Linda Carol, Beverly Lynn Whitworth, Daniel James Alexander, William Campbell. BS, Miss. State U., 1938-42; postgrad., South Tex. Sch. Law, 1954-56, Harvard U., 1943, Navy Fin. and Supply Sch., 1942-43. Asst. div. credit mgr. Continental Emsco Co., Houston, 1953-56; gen. agt. and mgr. United Founders Life Ins. Co., 1956-69; mgr. Holt & Bridges Ins., Houston, 1960-69; owner, pres. Holt & Alexander Ins. Agy., Inc., Houston, 1969-85; ins. cons. Lawrence Ilfrey & Co., Houston, 1985—; adv. bd. dirs. NBC Bank. Pres. Meyerland Cmty. Improvement Assn., 1969. Served as lt. commdr. USN, 1942-46, 1950-52. Mem. Profl. Ins. Agts. Tex. (state bd. dirs. 1973-74), Soc. Cert. Ins. Counselors. Republican. Presbyterian. Club: Pine Forest Country, Club of Houston. Avocation: golf. Home and Office: 8727 Manhattan Dr Houston TX 77096-1318

ALEXANDER, JAMES WESLEY, surgeon, educator; b. El Dorado, Kans., May 23, 1934; s. Rossiter Wells and Merle Lydia Alexander; m. Maureen L. Strohofer; children: Joseph, Judith, Elizabeth, Randolph, John Charles, Lori, Molly. Student, Tex. Technol. Coll., 1951-53; MD, U. Tex., 1957; ScD, U. Cin., 1958-64; postgrad., U. Minn., 1966-67. Diplomate Am. Bd. Surgery, Am. Bd. Thoracic Surgery; lic. physician, Ohio. Intern Cin. Gen. Hosp., 1957-58; resident U. Cin.-Cin. Gen. Hosp., 1958-64; mem. faculty Coll. Medicine, U. Cin., 1962-64, 66—, prof. surgery, 1975—, dir. transplantation div., dept. surgery, 1967-99, dir. surg. immunology lab., 1967—; dir. research Shriners Burns Inst., 1979-90; practice medicine and surgery Cin., 1966—; mem. staff U. Cin. Hosp., Bethesda Hosp., Cin. Children's Hosp., Christ Hosp., Good Samaritan Hosp., Jewish Hosp.; mem. study sect. NIH, 1983-87, 89-93, chmn., 1990-93, ad hoc com., 1990-99. Author: (with R.A. Good) Fundamentals of Clinical Immunology, 1977; mem. editl. bd. Annals of Surgery, 1975—, Jour. Burn Care and Rehab., 1979—, Burns, Including Thermal Injury, 1985-98, Graft, 1998—, Jour. Parenteral and Enteral Nutrition, 1991-99, Nutrition, 1991—, Transplantation Sci., 1991-94, Transplantation, 1994—, Jour. Trauma, 1998—; contbr. more than 650 articles to profl. jours. Served as capt. M.C., U.S. Army, 1964-66. Mem. AAAS, Am. Assn. for Surgery of Trauma, Am. Assn. Immunologists, Am. Burn Assn. (pres. 1984-85), ACS, Am. Soc. Transplant Surgeons (sec. 1985-87, pres. elect 1987-88, pres. 1988-89), Am. Soc. Parenteral and Enteral Nutrition, Am. Surg. Assn., Assn. for Acad. Surgery, Central Surg. Assn., Cin. Acad. Medicine, Cin. Surg. Soc., Halsted Soc., Internat. Soc. Surgery, Colombian Coll. Surgeons (hon.), Peruvian Acad. Surgery (hon.), St. Paul Surg. Soc. (hon.), Ohio Med. Assn., Soc. Univ. Surgeons, Surg. Biology Club, Surg. Infection Soc. (sec. 1981-84, pres.-elect 1985-86, pres. 1986-87), Tranplantation Soc., Shock Soc., Mont Reid Surg. Soc., Alpha Omega Alpha, Alpha Chi, Alpha Epsilon Delta, Phi Eta Sigma. Home: 757 Riverwatch Dr Crescent Springs KY 41017-4480 Office: U Cin Coll Medicine 231 Bethesda Ave Cincinnati OH 45229-2827

ALEXANDER, JANE, federal agency administrator, actress, producer; b. Boston, Oct. 28, 1939; d. Thomas Bartlett and Ruth (Pearson) Quigley; m. Robert Alexander, July 23, 1962 (div. 1969); 1 child, Jason; m. Edwin Sherin, Mar. 29, 1975. Student, Sarah Lawrence Coll., 1957-59, U. Edinburgh, 1959-60; LHD, Wilson Coll., 1984; DFA (hon.), The Julliard Sch., 1994, N.C. Sch. Arts, 1994, N.C. Sch. Arts, 1994, U. Pa., 1995; PhD (hon.), U. Pa., 1995; DFA (hon.), The New Sch. Social Rsch., 1996; PhD (hon.), Duke U., 1996; LHD (hon.), The Coll. of Santa Fe, 1997; PhD, Sarah Lawrence Coll., 1998; DFA (hon.), Smith Coll., 1999, Pa. State U., 2000. Ind. TV, film and theatrical actress, 1962—; chmn. Nat. Endowment for Arts, Washington, 1993-97; guest artist in residence Okla. Arts Inst., 1982, tchr. adult theatre workshop, 1984, 91, tchr. master class, 1990; bd. trustees Wildlife Conservation Soc., 1997—, Am. Bird Conservancy, 1995-98, The MacDowell Colony, 1997—. Author: (with Greta Jacobs) The Bluefish Cookbook, 5 edits., 1979-95, ; translator: (with Sam Engelstad) The Master Builder (Henrik Ibsen), 1978; appeared in prodns.: Charles Playhouse Boston, 1964-65, Arena Stage, Washington, 1965-68, 70—, Am. Shakespeare Festival; plays include Major Barbara, Mourning Becomes Electra, Merry Wives of Windsor, Stratford, Conn., summers 1971-72; Broadway prodns. include The Great White Hope, 1968-69 (Tony award 1969, Drama Desk award, Theatre World award), 6 Rms Riv Vu, 1972-73 (Tony nomination), Find Your Way Home, 1974 (Tony nomination), Hamlet, 1975, The Heiress, 1976, First Monday in October, 1978 (Tony nomination), Goodbye Fidel, 1980, Monday After the Miracle, 1982, Night of the Iguana, 1988, Shadowlands, 1990-91, The Visit, 1992 (Tony nomination), The Sisters Rosensweig, 1993 (Drama Desk award 1992-93, Tony award nomination, Obie award 1993), Honour (Tony nomination), 1998; also appeared in plays The Time of Your Life, Present Laughter, 1975, The Master Builder, 1977, Losing Time,

1980, Antony and Cleopatra, 1981, Hedda Gabler, 1981, Old Times, 1984, Approaching Zanzibar, 1989, Mystery of the Rose Bouquet, 1989, The Cherry Orchard, 2000, An Actress in the Theatre of Politics, 2000; appeared in films The Great White Hope, 1970 (Acad. award nomination), A Gunfight, 1970, The New Centurions, 1972, All the President's Men, 1976 (Acad. award nomination), The Betsy, 1978, Kramer vs. Kramer, 1979 (Acad. award nomination), Brubaker, 1980, Night Crossing, 1981, Testament, 1983 (Acad. award nomination), City Heat, 1984, Sweet Country, 1986, Square Dance, 1987, Glory, 1989, The Cider House Rules, 1999; appeared in TV films Welcome Home Johny Bristol, 1971, Miracle on 34th Street, 1973, Death Be Not Proud, 1974, This Was the West That Was, 1974, Eleanor and Franklin, 1976 (Emmy nomination), Eleanor and Franklin: The White House Years, 1977 (Emmy nomination, TV Critics Circle award), Lovey, 1977, A Question of Love, 1978, Playing for Time, 1980 (Emmy award 1980), Calamity Jane: The Diary of a Frontier Woman, 1981, Dear Liar, 1981, Kennedy's Children, 1981, In the Custody of Strangers, 1982, When She Says No, 1983, Mountainview, 1989, Daughter of the Streets, 1990, A Marriage: Georgia O'Keeffe and Alfred Stieglitz, 1991; appeared in TV spls. A Circle of Children, 1977, Blood and Orchids, 1986, Calamity Jane, 1984 (Emmy nomination), Malice in Wonderland, 1985 (Emmy nomination), In Love and War, 1987, Open Admissions, 1988, A Friendship in Vienna, 1988, Stay the Night, 1992. Recipient Achievement in Dramatic Arts award St. Botolph Club, 1979, Israel Cultural award, 1982, Western Heritage Wrangler award, 1985, Helen Caldicott Leadership award, 1984, Living Legacy award Women's Internat. Ctr., San Diego, 1988, Environ. Leadership award Eco-Expo, 1991, Muse award N.Y. Women in Film, 1993, Torch of Hope award, 1992, Lectureship award NIH, 1994, Houseman award The Acting Co., 1994, medal UCLA, 1994, Outer Critics Circle award Disting. Voice in Theatre, 1994, Helen Hayes award Am. Express Tribute, 1994, Women of Achievement award Anti-Defamation League, 1994, Margo Jones award, 1995, Mass. Soc. award, 1995, N.Am. Mont Blanc de la Culture award, 1995, Common Wealth award, 1995, Creative Coalition: Christopher Reeve award, 1998, Outstanding Leadership for Advancement in Arts, People for Am. Way, 1998, Lifetime Achievement award Americans for Arts and U.S. Conf. Mayors, 1999, Harry S. Truman award for pub. svc., Independence, Md., 1999; named to Theatre Hall of Fame, 1993. Mem. AFTRA, SAG, Actors Equity Assn., Acad. Motion Picture Arts and Scis., Actors Fund, Wildlife Conservation Soc. (bd. trustees 1997—). Office: William Morris Agy c/o Samuel Liff 1325 Avenue of Americas New York NY 10019

ALEXANDER, JEFFREY CHARLES, sociology educator; b. Milw., May 30, 1947; s. Frederick Charles and Esther Leah (Schlossman) A.; children: Aaron, Benjamin. BA, Harvard Coll., 1969; PhD, U. Calif., Berkeley, 1978. Lectr. U. Calif., Berkeley, 1974-76; asst. prof. UCLA, 1976-81, prof., 1981—; chair dept. sociology UCLA, 1989-92, dir. social sci. collegium, 1992-97; prof. U. Bordeaux, France, 1994; vis. prof. Inst. Advanced Studies, Vienna, Austria, 1995. Author: Theoretical Logic in Sociology, vols. I-IV, 1982-83, Twenty Lectures: Sociological Theory Since World War Two, 1987, Action and Its Environments: Towards a New Synthesis, 1988, Structure and Meaning: Relinking Classical Sociology, 1989, Teoria Sociologia E Mutamento Sociales, Un Analisi Multidemensionale della Modernita, 1990, Soziale Differenzierung und Kultureller Wandel Studien zur Neofunktionalistischen Gesellschafstheorie, 1993, Fin-de-Siecle Social Theory: Relativism, Reduction and the Problem of Reason, 1995, Neofunctionalism and After, 1998, (Japanese trans.) Neofunctionalism and Civil Society, 1996, Cultural Trauma, 2000; editor: Neofunctionalism, 1985, Durkheimian Sociology: Cultural Studies, 1988, Real Civil Societies, 1997; co-editor: The Micro-Macro Link, 1987, Differentiation Theory and Social Change: Historical and Comparative Perspectives, 1990, Rethinking Progress: Movements, Forces and Ideas at the End of the Twentieth Century, 1990, Culture and Society: Contemporary Debates, 1990, Diversity and Its Discontents, 1999, The New Social Theory, 2000. Guggenheim fellow, 1979-80; Travel and Study fellow Ford Found., 1980; Princeton Inst. for Advanced Studies fellow, 1985-86; Swedish Colloquium for Advanced Study in the Social Scis., 1992, 96; Ctr. for Advanced Studies in the Behavioral Scis., 1998-99. Mem. Am. Sociol. Assn., Internat. Sociol. Assn. (founder, co-chair rsch. com. sociol. theory 1990-94), Sociol. Rsch. Assn. Democrat. Jewish. Avocations: photography, tennis, skiing. Home: 722 Copeland Ct Apt 4 Santa Monica CA 90405-4445 Office: U Calif Dept Sociology Los Angeles CA 90024

ALEXANDER, JOHN ANDREW, academic administrator; b. Glasgow, Scotland, July 8, 1948; s. Andrew White and Margaret Frame (Park) A. BS, U. Edinburgh, Scotland, 1970. Adminstrv. asst. U. Glasgow, 1976-82, adminstr. Office for Internat. Programmes, 1982-98, asst. dir. student recruitment and admissions svc., 1998—; asst. registrar Strathclyde (Scotland) Regional Coun., 1974-76. Office: U Glasgow, Student Recruitment, Glasgow Scotland

ALEXANDER, JOHN INNIS, anesthesiologist; b. Dublin, Ireland, Mar. 17, 1942; came to Eng., 1946; s. William Bahudur and Winifred Edith (Cottle) A.; m. Hilary Hunter-Smith, Apr. 20, 1967 (div. Jan. 1974); m. Susan Diane Taylor, Apr. 22, 1978; children—Phyllida Jane, Christopher James. M.B., B.S., Univ. Coll. Hosp. Med. Sch., London, 1965. Cons. anesthetist Bristol Health Authority, Eng., 1974—, cons. algologist, 1974—; clin. lectr. U. Bristol, 1976—. Contbr. articles to med. jours. Covenant sec. Parochial Ch. Coun., Frampton Cotterell, Avon, Eng., 1983-97; mem. ct. U. Bristol, 1984-85. Fellow Royal Coll. Anaesthetists; mem. Royal Coll. Surgeons (Eng.), Royal Coll. Physicians London (licentiate), Royal Coll. Obstetricians and Gynecologists (diploma in obstetrics, chmn. local rsch. ethics com. 1993—), Back Pain Assn. (pres. Bristol br. 1985), Assn. Anesthetists, Intractable Pain Soc., Internat. Assn. for Study of Pain (founder mem.), Anesthetic Research Soc. Mem. Ch. of England. Avocation: gardening. Home: 278 Church Rd Frampton Cotterell, So Gloucestershire BS36 2BH, England Office: Bristol Royal Infirmary, Anesthetic Dept, Bristol BS2 8HW, England

ALEXANDER, LESLIE M., ambassador; b. Frankfurt, Germany, Nov. 9, 1948; s. Leslie M. and Ginette Chevalon Alexander; m. Deborah A. McCarthy, 1992; children: Margaret, Natalia. BA, U. Md., 1970; MS, Salve Regina U., 1986; MA, U.S. Naval War Coll., 1991. Officer U.S. Fgn. Svc., 1971—; various assignments in Washington and abroad, 1971—; prin. officer U.S. Consulate Porto, Alegre, Brazil, 1983-85; econ. coun. U.S. Embassy, Rome, 1986-89; dep. dir. Caribbean Affairs, U.S. Dept. State, 1989-91; dep. chief of mission Haiti, 1991-92; U.S. chargé d'affairs, 1992-93, U.S. amb. to Comoros & Mauritius, 1993-96, U.S. amb. to Ecuador, 1996—. Office: US Amb Ecuador US Embassy Quito Ave 12 de Octobre y Avenida Patria APO AA 34039

ALEXANDER, LEWIS MCELWAIN, geographer, educator; b. Summit, N.J., June 15, 1921; s. Harry Louis and Laura (Stryker) A.; m. Jacqueline Peterson, Dec. 30, 1950; children: Louise Anne, Lance Stryker. A.B., Middlebury (Vt.) Coll., 1942; M.A., Clark U., 1948, Ph.D., 1949. Instr. geography Hunter Coll., 1949-50; asst. prof. geography Harpur Coll., State U. N.Y., 1950-57, asso. prof., 1957-60; prof. geography U. R.I., Kingston, 1960-80, 83-91, prof. emeritus, 1991—, chmn. dept., 1960-80; dir. marine affairs program U. R.I., 1968-80, dir. Ctr. for Ocean Mgmt. Studies, 1983-89; cons. State Dept., 1963-80; dir. Office of Geographer, 1980-83; exec. dir. Law of Sea Inst., 1965-73, mem. exec. bd., 1973-82, 85-91; mem. ocean affairs adv. com. Dept. State, 1973-80; dep. dir. Pres.'s Commn. on Marine Sci., Engring. and Resources, 1967-68; cons. Nat. Coun. for Marine Resources and Engring. Devel., 1969-70; mem. adv. com. on law of sea Interagy. Law of Sea Task Force, 1973-80; mem. ocean policy com., ocean affairs bd. NRC, 1973-76; maritime boundary cons. Govt. of Bahrain, 1998—. Author: World Political Patterns, 2d edit, 1963, Offshore Geography of Northwestern Europe, 2d edit, 1966, The Northeastern United States, 2d edit., 1976, Regional Cooperation in Marine Science, 1979, Navigational Restrictions within the New Los Context: Geographical Implications for the United States, 1986; mem. editorial bd. Ocean Devel. and Internat. Law Jour., 1973-99, Ocean Mgmt., 1973-87, Marine Policy, 1976-98; editor: (with J. Charney) International Maritime Boundaries, 3d edit., 1998. Served with USAAF, 1942-46. Recipient Ann. award Sea Grant Assn., 1979, U. R.I. Acad. Achievement award, 1986; Office Naval Rsch. grantee, 1958, 62, 66, 76. Mem. Assn. Am. Geographers (Honors award 1980), Am. Geog. Soc., Am. Soc. Internat. Law, Marine Tech. Soc. Club: Cosmos. Home: 66 Beech Hill Rd Peace Dale RI 02879-2524 Office: U RI Washburn Hall Kingston RI 02881

ALEXANDER, LISA D., nursing administrator; b. Jonesville, La., Dec. 20, 1964; d. J.D. Jr. and Martha Rea (Ainsworth) A.; 1 child, Jessica Lee Boothe. Diploma, La. State U., Alexandria, 1986; BSN, Northwestern Stae U., Natchitoches, La., 1995. RN, La.; cert. BLS instr., ACLS instr.; cert. in home health care ANCC. Staff nurse St. Frances Cabrini Hosp., Alexandria, 1987-89; charge nurse, staff nurse ICU Natchez (Miss.) Cmty. Hosp., 1989-91; staff surg. nurse Natchez Regional Med. Ctr., 1989-91; dir. edn. Natchez Cmty. Hosp., 1991-93, dir. quality mgmt., 1993-95; dir. clin. svcs. Four Rivers Home Care, Inc., Pineville, La., 1995—. Mem. AACCN, Nat. Assn. Healthcare Quality, Am. Heart Assn., Sigma Theta Tau. Baptist. Avocations: travel, horseback riding, basketball, swimming, skiing. Home: HC 86 Box 24A Harrisonburg LA 71340-9707

ALEXANDER, MANFRED, history educator; b. Paderborn, Germany, Oct. 10, 1939; s. Otto and Ilse (Mueckenheim) A.; m. Dorota Zuzanna Skibka, Aug. 4, 1967; children: Vera, Martin. PhD, U. Cologne, 1968. Prof. history U. Cologne, 1983—. Author: German-Czechoslovak Arbitrage Treaty 1925, 1970, Der Petrashevskij-Prozess, 1979; editor: Deutsche Gesandtschafts-berichte aus Prag, 1983, 98. Mem. Collegium Carolinum. Avocations: languages, music. Home: Leipziger Ring 11A, 50374 Erftstadt Germany Office: Univ Cologne, Kringsweg 6, 50 931 Cologne Germany

ALEXANDER, MARJORIE ANNE, artist, hand papermaker, art consultant; b. Chgo., Apr. 16, 1928; d. Alexander and Nancy Rebecca (Cordrey) Roberts; m. Harold Harman Alexander, June 13, 1948; children: Jeffrey C., Cassandra J., Peter B., Timothy C., Patrick J. Student, Wilson Jr. Coll., 1945-47; MFA in Painting, U. Ill., 1968, MA in Art Edn., 1972. cert. tchr. K-12: Ill., Minn. Graphic artist Barry Martin Studio, Rumson, N.J., 1963-65; instr. painting, drawing U. YMCA, Champaign, Ill., 1968-72; teaching asst. U. Ill., Urbana, 1968-72, rsch. assoc., 1972-76; instr. art Champaign High Sch., 1973-75, Urbana High Sch., 1976-80, Concordia Acad., St. Paul, Minn., 1982-84, U. Minn., Mpls., 1984-87; design, housing and apparel artist in residence U. Minn., St. Paul, 1984-88; craft cons. and educator tech. asstance program USAID, OAS, U. Minn., Kingtson, Jamaica, 1986—; design cons. J.A.M. Corp., Mpls., 1988—; tech. cons. OAS, Kingston, 1990-91, Blandin Found. grantee, Minn., 1989—; rsch. and product devel. agrl. unilization rsch. inst., 1992-95; tech. cons. Zabbaleen Paper Project, Assn. for the Protection of the Environment, Cairo, 1993—, St. Lucia Paper project Weyerhauser Found., 1994—, paper project YMCA, Jamaica, W.I., 1997—; co-curator Paper Trivia and Treasure exhibit Goldstein Mus. Design/U. Minn., St. Paul, 2000. Works have appeared in over 34 solo shows, 1960—, over 64 invitational shows nationally and internationally, 1985—; work chosen for inclusion 1996 Internat. Calendar Papierfabak Schfufelen Lenningen, Germany; work chosen for poster paper exhibit Leopold-Hoesch Mus., Doren, Germany, 1999; traveling exhibit, Bavaria, Germany, Geneva; represented in permanent collection Imadate, Fukui, Japan, U. Ill., U. Minn., So. Cross U., NSW, Australia, Montclair (N.J.) Art Mus., Am. U, Cairo, other univs. and colls. and corp. collections; co-author (book): Selected Papers, 1994, Handcrafted paper and Paper Products Made from Indigenous Plant Fibers, 1997; contbr. articles to profl. jours. Vestry mem. St. John's Episcopal Ch., Champaign, 1975-78, St. Matthew's Episcopal Ch., St. Paul, 1989—. Recipient Celebrity award Minn. State Fair, 1984, book First award 1986, Honorable mention 3rd Onn/Off Paper Nat., Wis., 1984; grantee Blandin Found. U. Minn., 1989-90, OAS, 1990-91, Agrl. Utilization Rsch. Inst. grantee, 1992-95, Weyerhauser Found., 1997, Minn. Arts Bd., 1999. Mem. Nat. League Am. Penwomen (Minn. art chair 1990-94, state v.p. 1994-96), Internat. Assn. Hand Papermakers and Paper Artists, Friends of Dard Hunter Paper Mus. (com. chair 1990-95). Episcopalian. Avocations: swimming, cooking, theatre, travel. Home: Graybridge 3251 Fernwood St Arden Hills MN 55112

ALEXANDER, ROBERT JACKSON, economist, educator; b. Canton, Ohio, Nov. 26, 1918; s. Ralph S. and Ruth (Jackson) A.; m. Joan O. Powell, Mar. 26, 1949; children: Anthony, Margaret. B.A., Columbia U., 1940; M.A., Columnbia U., 1941; Ph.D., Columbia U., 1950. Asst. economist Bd. Econ. Warfare, 1942, Office Inter-Am. Affairs, 1945-46; mem. faculty Rutgers U., 1947—, prof. econs., 1961-89, prof. emeritus, 1989—; mem. Pres.-elect Kennedy's Latin Am. Task Force, 1960-61. Author 37 books including Juan Domingo Peron: A History, 1979, Romulo Betancourt and the Transformation of Venezuela, 1982, Bolivia: Past, Present and Future of Its Politics, 1982, Biographical Dictionary of Latin American and Caribbean Politics, 1988, Juscelino Kubitschek and the Development of Brazil, 1991, International Trotskyism 1929-85, 1991, The ABC Presidents, 1992, The Bolivarian Presidents, 1994, The Presidents of Central America, Mexico, Cuba and Hispaniola, 1995, Presidents, Prime Ministers and Governors of the English Speaking West Indies and Puerto Rico, 1997, The Anarchists in the Spanish Civil War, 1999, International Maoism in the Developing World, 1999. Mem. nat. bd. League Indsl. Democracy, 1955—; mem. nat. exec. com. Socialist Party-Social Dem. Fedn., 1957-66; bd. dirs. Rand Sch. Social Sci., 1951-56; mem. exec. com. Open Door Student Exch., 1970-94. Decorated officer Order Condor of the Andes Bolivia. Mem. Am. Econ. Assn., Latin Am. Studies Assn., Mid. Atlantic Coun. Latin Am. Studies (v.p. 1986-87, pres. 1987-88), Coun. Fgn. Rels., Interam. Assn. Democracy and Freedom (chmn. N.Am. com. 1970-87), Phi Gamma Delta. Home: 944 River Rd Piscataway NJ 08854-5504 Office: Rutgers U Dept Econs New Brunswick NJ 08903

ALEXANDER, ROLAND E., musician, educator; b. Cambridge, Mass., Sept. 25, 1935; s. Benjamin and Vera (Sullivan) A.; m. Judith E. Jordan, June 4, 1997; children: Denise Phillips, Taru. MusB, Boston Conservatory Music, 1958. Musical dir. Charlie Persip's Band, N.Y.C., 1959-60; traveling musician Philly Joe Jone's Band, 1961-63, Beaver Harris' Band, 1964-65, Lloyd Price's Band, 1965-66; freelance musician N.Y.C., 1967-74; band dir. New Muse- Children's Mus., Bklyn., 1974-84; music cons. N.Y. Housing Authority, N.Y.C., 1991—; instr. Jazz Mobile, N.Y.C., 1995-96. Musician (John Coltrane record) Trane's Strain, 1957, (film) School Daze, 1986; composer, musician: Pleasure Bent, 1961; Jazz composer NEA, 1973; composer: (opera) Hodges & Company, 1978, Black Cowboys, 1978; (suite) Malcolm X Suite, 1980; (songs) King, 1996, Kojo Time, 1996; interviewee, musician (TV show) Jazz Corner, 1997. Recipient award for composition N.Y. Found. for Arts, 1996. Mem. SoFocus (music cons. 1996—). Avocation: aviation.

ALEXANDER, STEPHEN WINTHROP, sales executive; b. Port Washington, N.Y., Apr. 18, 1941; s. Eben Roy and Mary Louise (Webb) A.; m. Marian Susan Burda, Oct. 27, 1962; children: Stephen, Kevin, Jennifer, Bryan, David, Matthew, Reagan, Christopher. BS in History, St. Louis U., 1962. With advt. sales dept. Time, N.Y.C., 1965-67, 72-76, Cleve., 1967-69, Pitts., 1969-72; Midwest sales mgr. Time, Chgo., 1976-82, 87-89; U.S. sales mgr. Time, N.Y.C., 1982-87; v.p. sales The Sporting News, Chgo., 1990-93; v.p. advt. sales SRDS, Wilmette, Ill., 1993-95; assoc. pub. dir. Modern Maturity and The AARP Bull., 1995-97; pub. Chgo. Home and Garden, 1997—; bd. dirs. Better Bus. Bur., Chgo., 1987-89. Chmn. CCD program St. Mary's Ch., Lake Forest, Ill., 1980-82. Capt. USMC, 1962-65. Mem. Chgo. Advt. Club (bd. dirs. 1986-87). Roman Catholic. Avocations: family activities, golf, swimming. Home: 790 Coventry Dr Lake Forest IL 60045-2765 Office: Chgo Home and Gardens 825 S Waukegan Rd Lake Forest IL 60045-2696

ALEXANDER, VEDHAMONICKOM, chemistry educator, researcher; b. Chathencode, Tamilnadu, India, Oct. 23, 1956; s. Mariaarulappan Vedhamonickom and Ammal Lysammal; m. Margaret Thangaraj, June 7, 1990; children: Criscilla, Carlson. BS, Christian Coll., Martandam, India, 1976; MEd, St. Xavier's Coll., Palayamkottai, India, 1979; MSc, St. Joseph's Coll. Edn., Trichy, India, 1981; PhD, U. Madras, India, 1987. Jr. rsch. fellow U. Madras, 1981-83, sr. rsch. fellow, 1983-84; asst. prof. Am. Coll., Madurai, India, 1985; asst. prof. Loyola Coll., Chennai, 1985-95, prof., 1995—; asst. dir. Loyola Coll. Hostels, Chennai, 1985-87; mem. bd. studies several and examiner univs. and autonomous colls. in India, 1985—; lectr. in field. Contbr. articles to internat. chem. jours.; inventor in field. Recipient Veddanapalli award; rsch. grantee Dept. Sci. and Tech., Govt. of India, 1989, 96, Dept. Atomic Energy, Govt. of India, 1990, 97, Coun. of Sci. and Indsl. Rsch., Govt. of India, 1997, Def. Rsch. and Devel. Orgn., Govt. of India, 1998. Fellow Indian Chem. Soc.; mem. Am. Chem. Soc., Royal Soc. Chemistry. Avocations: reading, writing reviews. Home: Flat 8 Redbrick Leela, 30 Tank Bund Rd Nungabakkam, Chennai 600034, India Office: Loyola Coll, Nungambakkam, 600034 Chennai India

ALEXANDER, WILLIAM M., educator, researcher, writer; b. Hood River, Oreg., Nov. 26, 1925; s. George M. and Lorena M. A.; m. Anna M. Alexander, Sept. 9, 1950; children: William, John, Lorena. BS, Oreg. State U., 1949; MA, Pa. State U., 1953; PhD, U. Oreg., 1962. Prof. food politics Calif. Polytechnic State U., San Luis Obispo, Calif., 1958-88; prin. investigator Food First Inst., Oakland, Calif., 1988-99, Earthwatch Expdn., Cambridge, Mass., 1990-93. E-mail: walexander@calpoly.edu. Home: 637 Bambi Ln Santa Rosa CA 95409-3101

ALEXANDRAKIS, GEORGE, military officer, model; b. Athens, Greece, Aug. 12, 1970; s. Alexander Alexandrakis and Kalliope Tsaggaraki. Degree in comm., Naval Acad., Athens, 1990, degree in biochem. war, 1991; cert. flight deck dir., Helicopter Sch., Athens, 1993; MBA in Law, Brentwick U., 2000. Cadet Naval Acad., Athens, 1989-92; class leader Naval Coll., San Antonio, 1996-97; mgr. comm. Hdqs., Athens, 1997; model, Athens, 1994; boxer Panellinios, Athens, 1987-97; tchr., Athens, 1997. Hellenic Orthodox. Avocations: boxing, fashion shows, trips, reading. Home: Ouranoupoleos 23B, 111-42 Athens Greece

ALEXANDRATOS, SPIRO DIONISIOS, chemistry educator; b. N.Y.C., Dec. 11, 1951; m. Olga Pantos; 1 child, Jonathan. BS, Manhattan Coll., 1973; PhD, U. Calif., Berkeley, 1977. Sr. rsch. chemist Rohm and Haas Co., Phila., 1977-81; from asst. prof. to assoc. prof. U. Tenn., Knoxville, 1981-92, prof. chemistry, 1993-2000, Paul and Wilma Ziegler prof. chemistry, 2000—; collaborating scientist U. Tenn./Oak Ridge Nat. Lab., 1998—. Holder 12 patents in field; mem. editorial adv. bd. Reactive and Functional Polymers, Separation Science and Technology, Solvent Extraction and Ion Exchange. Recipient Hoechst-Celanese Rsch. award, 1993, R & D 100 award R & D Mag., 1994, Tech. Achievement award Lockheed-Martin, 1999. Mem. Am. Chem. Soc. (chmn. divsn. indsl. engring. chemistry 1993-94, chmn. subdivsn. separation sci. 1991-92; assoc. editor Jour. of Indsl. and Engring. Chemistry Rsch.), Gordon Rsch. Conf. Reactive Polymer (chmn. 1995-97), Sigma Xi, Phi Beta Kappa (cert. merit 1993). Home: 2137 Cherokee Blvd Knoxville TN 37919-8342 Office: U Tenn Dept Chemistry Knoxville TN 37996-0001

ALEXANDRE, GÉRARD-EUGENE, orthopedic surgeon; b. Paris, Jan. 13, 1930; s. André-Maurice and Marcelle (Blum) A.; m. Liliane Martha Pierre, June 13, 1956; children: Fabienne-Jacqueline, Dominique Liliane. MD, U. Paris, 1963. Intern Hosp. of Paris, 1961-66, head surg. orthopedic clinic, 1966-69; cons. surgeon Nat. Inst. Disabled Ministry of War Veterans, 1963-74; asst. dept. child surgery St. Vincent-de-Paul Hosp., Paris, 1967; asst. dept. orthopedic surgery Hosp. Cochin, Paris, 1969-82; orthopedic surgeon Clininque de Marly, Marly le Roi, France, 1969-95, dir. massage, physiotherapy and chiropody sch., 1963—; cons. orthopedic surgery Emile Roux Hosp. Eaubonne, 1997—. Contbr. articles to profl. jours. Mem. Conseil Supérieur Professions Paramédicales, Health Ministry, 1973-81, 86-91. Mem. Nat. Orgn. Dirs. Physiotherapy Schs. (sec. gen. 1969-89), French Soc. Surgical Orthopedy, Nat. Coll. Orthopedic Surgeons, French Assn. Artificial Limb Supply, Hand Study Group, West Orthopedic Soc. Lodge: Rotary. Avocations: Skiing, windsurfing. E-mail: alexandregerard.e@wanadoo.fr. Home: 59 Ave de Briens, Villennes Sur Seine 78670, France Office: Institut d'Assas, 56 Rue de l'Eglise, Paris 75015, France

ALEXANDRE DU PORTAL, LUC JEAN, banker; b. Orange, Vaucluse, France, May 12, 1941; s. Jean Ludovic and Antoinette (de Leamont) Alexandre du P.; m. Nadege Forestier, July 7, 1973; children: Cedric, Lydwine. Baccalaureat, Ecole St. Exupery, Melun, France, 1959; MBA, EDCAE, Paris, 1966; postgrad., NYU, N.Y.C., 1967-68. Trainee Union Bank of Switzerland, Geneva, 1966; asst. v.p. Hayden Stone, N.Y.C., 1967-70; investment officer Brown Bros. Harriman, N.Y.C., 1970-73; v.p. Credit Comml. de France, Paris, 1973-80; 1st v.p. Banque Nationale de Paris, 1980-98; ptnr. Eurosearch Group, Paris, 1998—; bd. dirs. Interecu, Luxemborg, 1985. Treas., bd. dirs. Polo de Paris Assn., 1983. Mem. French Fencing Acad. (hon.). Avocations: archaeology, photography, tennis, skiing. Home: 71 Quai Branly, 75007 Paris France Office: Eurosearch Group, 12 Rue de Castiglione, 75001 Paris France

ALEXANDROFF, MIRRON (MIKE ALEXANDROFF), retired college president; b. Chgo., Mar. 3, 1923; s. Norman and Cherrie (Phillips) A.; m. Anna C. Avgerin, Dec. 22, 1947 (dec.); children: Niki Alexandroff Gray, Pam Alexandroff Eidenberg; m. Jane Ann Legnard, Jan. 27, 1962 (dec.); 1 child, Norman. BA, Roosevelt U., 1947; MA, Columbia Coll., Chgo., 1948; D of Humane Letters (hon.), DePaul U., 1992. Pres. Columbia Coll., 1961-92, pres. emeritus, 1992—; chmn. Chgo. Met. Higher Edn. Coun., 1981-90; bd. dirs. Bank Bellwood, Ill. Adv. com. Chgo. Dept. Cultural Affairs, 1985-92; pres. Grant Park Cultural and Ednl. Cmty., 1985-92. Sgt. U.S. Army, 1942-45, PTO. Recipient Sydney R. Yates Advocacy award, 1991, Clarence Darrow award for leading svc. in cause of social justice, 1984, Louis Lerner award Ill. Pub. Action., 1992, Disting. Urban Fellow award Assn. Urban Univs. 1992, Outstanding Contbr. to Latin Am. TV award Mex. Nat. Assn. Broadcasters, 1980. Mem. Am. Assn. Urban Univs. (chmn. 1986-88), Fedn. Ind. Ill. Coll. and Univs. (exec. com. 1978-92). Office: Columbia College 600 S Michigan Ave Fl 5 Chicago IL 60605-1996*

ALEXANDROV, ALEXANDER HARALANOV, forester; b. Stara Zagora, Bulgaria, Sept. 24, 1938; s. Haralan Alexandrov and Tsvetanka Dobreva (Savova) Todorova; m. Bistra Nevenova Tomova, Aug. 14, 1966; children: Haralan, Elena. B in Forestry Engring., Higher Inst. Forestry, Sofia, Bulgaria, 1961, DSc, 1984; PhD, Forest Rsch. Inst., Sofia, Bulgaria, 1967. Head of forest range State Forestry, Tsonevo-Varna, 1961-63; researcher Forest Expt. Sta., Velingrad, 1964-66; researcher Forest Rsch. Inst., Sofia, 1967-75, sr. rschr., 1976-85, rsch. prof., 1986—, dep. dir., 1986-88, dir., 1989, 91-93, head dept. genetics and physiology, prof. phytogeography, 1996—; corr. mem. Bulgarian Acad. Scis., 1995—, prof. ecology, 1999—. Author: Genetics and Breeding, 1990, Forest and Forest Products Country Profile: Bulgaria, UN, 1994, Pinus Peuce, 1998, Corylus colurna L, 1995, Aesculus hippocastanum L, 1996, Noble Hardwoods Genetic Resources in Bulgaria, 1998, Structure and Dynamics of High-Mountain Ecosystems in Rila-Rhodopes Massif, 1999, Genetic Resources of Fagus spp. in Southeastern Europe, 2000; co-author: Formation of Productive Forests, 1982 (Union prize 1983), Coniferous Forests in Bulgaria, 1988; mem. editl. bd. Forest Genetics, Forest Sci. Bulgaria, Jour. Balkan Ecology, Ecoman: Biotechnology & Biotechnology Equipment. Min. of environment Coun. of Mins., Sofia, 1990; dep. chmn. Assn. Bulgarian Ecologists; nat. coord. EUFORGEN, 1998; mem. rsch. bd. advisors ABI-NC-USA, 1997; mem. Civil Soc. Devel. Found. Bulgaria, 1997. Recipient Ministry of Forestry, 1979, Fedn. of Socs. of Scientists and Engrs., 1991. Mem. Internat. Coun. of Internat. Union of Scientists (chmn. forestry sect. 1994—), Forestry Soc. (dep. chmn. 1987-93), Nat. Found. for Rsch., Balkan Ecol. Fedn. (v.p. 1994-96, pres. 1997—), Internat. Eurasian Acad. Scis. (academician 1996—), Nat. Ecol. Club (chmn. 1998—), IPPS. Office: Forest Rsch Inst, 132 Kliment Ohridski Blvd, BG-1756 Sofia Bulgaria

ALEXANDROV, BORIS SERGEEVITCH, physicist, researcher; b. Moscow, Feb. 9, 1941; s. Sergei Andreevitch and Maria Vasiljevna (Azhgibkova) A.; m. Olga Mihailovna Istrashenko, June 30, 1971; children: Sergei, Constantin. Physicist, State U., Leningrad, Russia, 1963, postgrad., 1966; Candidate of Phys.-Math. Sci. (hon.), Moscow U., 1988. Jr. scientist Russian Sci. Ctr. Applied Chemistry, Leningrad, 1966-71, sr. scientist, 1971—. Contbr. papers to profl. jours. Grantee Russian Found. Basic Rsch., Internat. Sci. Tech. Ctr. Avocations: music, gardening. Home: Fl 15 h 46, Bolshaja Pushkarskaja St, 197101 Saint Petersburg Russia Office: Russian Sci Ctr Appld Chem, 14 Dobrolubov Ave, 197 198 Saint Petersburg Russia

ALEXANDROV, ERIC LEONIDOVICH, physicist; b. Krasnoyarsk, Russia, May 22, 1928; s. Leonid Alexandrovich and Elena Fedotovna (Krikina) A.; m. Antonina Constantinovna Ilyina, Feb. 15, 1958; 1 child, Khudoleeva Natalia Ericovna. Physicist, Moscow Chem. and Tech. Inst., 1952, PhD, 1956. Scientist Inst. Applied Geophysics, Moscow, 1956-68; scientist Inst. Exptl. Meteorology Russia, Obninsk, 1968-70, lab. head, 1970—. Author, editor: Man and Stratospheric Ozone, 1979, Atmospheric Ozone and Global Climate Changes, 1982, Earth's Ozone Shield and Its Changes, 1992; contbr. articles to profl. jours. Grantee Russian Found. Basic Rsch., 1994. Home: 34 Lenin Ave Apt 19, 249020 Obninsk Kaluga,

Russia Office: Inst Exptl Meteorology, 82 Lenin Ave, 249020 Obninsk Kaluga, Russia

ALEXANDROV, VICTOR MIKHAILOVICH, science administrator; b. Rostov-on-Don, Russia, Jan. 1, 1936; s. Mikhail Petrovich and Anna Amajakovna (Artsatbanjan) A. Univ. degree, Rostov State U., Russia, 1958, PhD, 1963, DSc, 1972, prof., 1974. Cert. mechanician-rschr. Asst. Rostov State U., 1961-64, dotzent, 1964-72, prof., 1972-78; leading rschr. Inst. of Russian Acad. of Scis., Moscow, 1978-86, head of dept., 1986—; prof. Moscow State U., 1980—. Author: (books) Contact Problems for Bodies with Thin Coatings and Layers, 1983, Problems with Mixed Boundary Conditions in Continuum Mechanics, 1986, Thin Stress Concentrators in Elastic Bodies, 1993, Non-Classical Contact Problems in 3D for Elastic Bodies, 1998. Mem. Russian Acad. Natural Scis. Office: Inst Problems in Mechanics, pr Vernadskogo 101 Bldg 1, 117526 Moscow Russia

ALEXANDROV, YURI ANDREEVICH, physicist; b. Karsun, Russia, May 26, 1929; s. Andrei Ivanovich and Elizaveta Terentievna (Timofeeva) A.; m. Ljudmila Ivanovna Shmakova, July 1950 (div. 1957); 1 child (dec.); m. Svetlana Sergueevna Karjukina, Jan. 27, 1968; 1 child. Engr.-Physicist, Phys. Inst., Moscow, 1952; PhD in Physics and Math., Inst. Physics & Power Engring., Obninsk, Russia, 1959; DSc in Physics and Math., Joint Inst. for Nuclear Rsch., Dubna, Russia, 1987. Scientist dept. physics Inst. Physics & Power Engring., Obninsk, Russia, 1952-59; sr. scientist dept. physics Inst. Physics & Power Engring., Obninsk, 1959-62; sr. scientist Lab. Neutron Physics, Joint Inst. for Nuclear Rsch., Dubna, 1962-65, sector leader, 1965-89; group leader Frank Lab. Neutron Physics, Joint Inst. for Nuclear Rsch., Dubna, 1989—. Author: Fundamental Properties of the Neutron, 1976, 82, 92; co-author: Diffraction Methods in Neutron Physics, 1981; referee Phys. Rev. and Phys. Rev. Letters, 1994—; contbr. more than 100 articles to profl. jours. Decorated medal Valiant Labour during the Gt. Patriotic War 1941-45, medal 50 Years of the Victory in the War 1941-45, medal 850 Years of Moscow, 20th Century award for Achievement. Mme. N.Y. Acad. Scis., Neutron Scattering Soc. Am., Sci. Club Dubna. Orthodox. Home: Saharov Str 21, 141980 Dubna, Moscow Russia Office: Frank Lab Neutron Physics, Joint Inst for Nuclear Rsch, 141980 Dubna, Moscow Russia

ALEXANDROVICH, SEREGIN ARTUR, physicist, researcher; b. Voronezh, Russia, Dec. 27, 1941; s. Alexandr Nikitovich and Praskov'ya Alexeevna (Kruglova) S.; m. Elean Andreevna Khodyakova, Jan. 28, 1967; children: Nadezhda, Lyubov. Grad., U. Vororezh, 1964; Cand. Physics/Math. Scis., U. Moscow, 1970; D of Physics/Math. Scis., JINR, Dubua, Russia, 1990. Sr. lab. asst. Inst. Physics and Power Engring., Obnisk, 1965-69, jr. sci. worker, 1969-73, sr. sci. worker, 1973-93, chief sci. worker, 1993—. Contbr. articles to profl. jours.; patentee in field. Avocations: tennis, tourism. Office: Inst Physics/Power Engring, Bondarenko Sq 1, Obninsk 249020, Russia

ALEXANDRU, HORIA V., physicist, educator, researcher; b. Racari, Dimbovita, Romania, Aug. 22, 1939; s. Vanghele A. and Elena (Balasescu) A.; m. Ioana Maria Marinescu, Mar. 10, 1973; children: Radulescu, Radu, Cristian. Diploma in physics, Bucharest U., 1963, PhD in Physics, 1974. Asst. lectr. Pedagogic Inst., Bucharest, 1963-67; prof.'s asst. Bucharest U., 1967-90, lectr., 1990-91, assoc. prof., 1991-99, prof., 1999—; vis. prof. U. Manchester, Inst. of Sci. and Tech., Eng., 1993, vis. prof., Lawrence Livermore Natl. Lab., Calif., 1998; presenter in field. Author: Materials Science and Technology; editor Jour. Optoelectronics and Advanced Materials, 1999—; contbr. articles to profl. jours. Mem. Assn. of Scientists in Romania, Romanian Phys. Soc., Romanian Materials Sci.-Crystal Growth Soc. (pres., founding mem. 1994—), Internat. Orgn. for Crystal Growth (councillor rep. nat. orgn. 1995—), European Phys. Soc., Nat. Geog. Soc. Avocations: travel, fishing, photography, ancient history. Fax: 401-746-5066. Home: Block Z6 Ap 34, Str Valea Rosie 7, 77478 Bucharest Romania Office: Alexandru PO Box 74-165, 77400 Bucharest Romania

ALEXEENKO, IHOR ROSTISLAVOVICH, publishing executive; b. Donetsk, Ukraine, Sept. 13, 1947; s. Rostislav and Zinaida (Pridannikova) A.; m. Natalia Shelina, Jan. 26, 1974; children: Sviatoslav, Maria, Anastasia. MD, Med. Inst., Kyiv, Ukraine, 1971; PhD in Biology, Inst. Biochemistry, Kyiv, Ukraine, 1977. Lab. asst. inst. biochemistry Nat. Acad. Sci. Ukraine, Kyiv, 1970-75, engr., 1975-77, jr. rschr., 1977-80, scientific sec. dept. biochemistry, physiology, 1980-85, sr. rschr., 1980—, scientific sec. editl. pub. bd., 1985-94; dir. Naukova Dumka Pub., Kyiv, 1994—. Author: Extremal Factors and Bioobjects, 1989, Regulation Mechanisms of Vector Enzymes of Biomembranes, 1990, Biosphere and Civilization, 1992, Surfactants as Instruments of Membranes Study, 1993, The Last Civilization?, 1997. Avocations: reading, sports. Home: 77 apt, 64/56 Geroev Stalingrada St, 04213 Kyiv Ukraine Office: Naukova Dumka Pub, 3 Tereshchenkivska St, 01601 Kyiv 1, Ukraine

ALEXEEV, BORIS VLADIMIROVICH, physicist, educator; b. Orechovo-Zuevo, USSR, May 2, 1938; s. Vladimir Markovich Raymist and Lidia Sergeyevna A.; 1 child, Tatyana Borisovna. Degree in physics, engring., Moscow Inst. Physics Tech., 1961, PhD, 1964; DSc, USSR Acad. Scis., 1973. Sr. rsch. scientist USSR Acad. Sci., Moscow, 1964-73; head physics dept. Moscow Aviation Inst., 1973-83, Moscow Fine Chem. Tech. Inst., 1983—; expert Highest Attestation Commn. USSR, Moscow, 1975-81; mem. com., head Moscow regional com., organizing com. Russian Acad. Scis., Moscow, 1991; vis. prof. U. Provence, Marseille, France, 1992-95, U. Ala., Huntsville, 1995, 97. Author: Boundary Layer with Chemical Reactions, 1967, Mathematical Kinetics of Reacting Gases, 1982, Generalized Boltzmann Physical Kinetics, 1997; co-author: Transport Processes in Reacting Gases and Plasma, 1994. Recipient Meritorious Sci. Technics Worker of Russia award Pres. Russia, 1989, Meritorious Worker of Higher Profl. Edn. of Russia award, 1998. Mem. Internat. Higher Edn. Acad. Scis., Russian Nat. Com. on Theoretical and Applied Mechanics, N.Y. Acad. Scis. Fax: 095 242 11 69. Home: 3d Frunzenskaya H 9 Ap 130, 119270 Moscow Russia Office: Moscow Fine Chem Tech Inst, Prospekt Vernadskogo 86, 117571 Moscow Russia

ALEXEEV, DMITRI KONSTANTINOVICH, pianist; b. Moscow, Aug. 10, 1947; s. Konstantin and Gertrude (Bolotina) A.; m. Tatiana Sarkisova, 1970; 1 child. Studied with Dmitri Bashkirov, Moscow Conservatoire. Pianist performing USSR, U.K., Europe, U.S., touring Australia, Japan, Hong Kong, others; pianist London Philharm. Orch., Berlin Philharm., Berlin Radio Symphony Orchs., Chgo. Symphony Orch., Phila. Orch., London Symphony Orch., St. Petersburg Philharm. Orch., Royal Concertgebouw of Amsterdam, Munich Bavarian Radio Orch., Orchestre de Paris, City of Birmingham Symphony Orch., Royal Philharm. Orch., Israel Philharm.; recordings include concertos by Schumann, Grieg, Rachmaninov, Prokofiev, Shostakovich, Scriabin, Medtner and solo works by Brahms, Rachmaninov, Schumann, Chopin, Liszt; performed at recitals in Munich, Florence, Rome, London, St. Petersburg, and Helsinki among others; worked with conductors such as Ashkenazy, Boulez, Dorati, Giulini, Muti, Rozhdestvensky, Tennstedt, Temirkanov, Tilson Tomas, and Jansons, among others. Recipient top honours Marguerite Long Competition, Paris, 1969, George Enescu Competition, Bucharest, 1970, Tchaikovsky Competition, Moscow, 1974, first prize 5th Leeds Internat. Piano Competition, Eng., 1975, Edison award The Netherlands, 1994. Office: IMG Artists/Lovell House, 616 Chiswick High St, London 5RX UK, England*

ALEXENBERG, MEL, artist, art educator; b. N.Y.C., Feb. 24, 1937; s. Abraham and Jeanne (Kahn) A.; m. Miriam Benjamin, Oct. 25, 1959; children: Iyrit, Ari, Ron, Moshe. BS, Queens Coll., CUNY, 1958; MS, Yeshiva U., 1959; EdD, NYU, 1969. Sci. tchr. N.Y.C. Pub. Schs., Queens, 1959-61; sci. supr. Manhasset (N.Y.) Pub. Schs., 1961-65; asst. prof. Adelphi U., L.I., N.Y., 1965-69; sr. lectr. Tel Aviv U., 1969-73; assoc. prof. Columbia U., N.Y.C., 1973-77; pres. Ramat Hanegev Coll., Yeroham, Israel, 1977-84; assoc. prof. Bar Ilan U., Ramat Gan, Israel, 1978-84; rsch. fellow MIT, Cambridge, Mass., 1984-88; chmn. dept. fine arts Pratt Inst., Bklyn., 1985-90; dean New World Sch. Arts, Miami, Fla., 1990-2000; prof. Coll. of Judea and Samaria, Ariel, Israel, 2000—; chair. com. on design. edn. Israel Ministry Edn., 1983-84. Author: Light and Sight, 1969, A Semiotic Taxonomy of Contemporary Art Forms, 1976, Aesthetic Experience in Creative Process, 1981, Art with Computers: The Human Spirit and the Electronic Revolution, 1988, Miami in Ecological Perspective, 1994, Art Thrones and Legacy Scrolls, 1998; art editor Visual Computer: Internat. Jour. Computer Graphics; works include Lights Orot, 1987-89, Digitized Homage to Rembrandt, 1989-90, Four Corners of Am., 1995-96, Centers: Lebanon (Kansas) and Jerusalem (Israel), 1996, Art Thrones, Intergenerational Pub. Art with Miriam Benjamin, 1997, Legacy Scrolls, 1998, Trees of Good Deeds & Wisdom, Synagogue Designed with Arch. K. Treister, 1999, Danish Lights, Charlottenborg Mus., Copenhagen, 2000, Divine Retribution, Coll. of Santa Fe, N.Mex., 2000; represented in permanent collections Met. Mus. Art, N.Y.C., Mus. Modern Art, N.Y.C., Princeton (N.J.) Art Mus., Del. Art Mus., Wilmington, Phila. Mus. Art, Balt. Mus. Art, Tel Aviv Mus., Victoria and Albert Mus., London, Mus. Moderner Kunst, Vienna, Austria, Museo de Arte Contemporaneo, Caracas, Venezuela, Israel Mus., Jerusalem, Haags Gemeentemuseum, The Netherlands, Malmo (Sweden) Mus., High Mus. Art, Atlanta, Museo Nacional de Artes Plasticas Montevideo, Uruguay. Bd. trustees Torah Sch. for Environ. Studies, Mitzpeh Ramon, Israel. Recipient award for art direction Am. Film Festival, 1964; Founders Day award NYU, 1969; MIT rsch. fellow, 1984-88. Mem. Internat. Soc. Edn. Through Art, Nat. Art Edn. Assn., Israel Soc. Painters and Sculptors. Jewish. Office: Coll of Judea and Samaria, 300 NE 2nd Ave, Ariel 44837, Israel

ALEXIADOU, VEFA, publisher; b. Volos, Greece, Mar. 19, 1933; d. Odysseas and Angeliki (Ioanidis) Boulgaris; m. Constantinos Alexiadis, May 17, 1959; children: Angie, Alexia. Advanced diploma in violin, Nat. Conservatory, Volos, Greece, 1949; BS in Chemistry, Aristotelion U., 1955. Chemist N. Kralis Chem. labs., Thessaloniki, Greece, 1956-69; comml. rep. sci. instruments, free-lance agts. Thessaloniki, 1969-79; pub., author Editions Vefa Alexiadou, Thessaloniki, 1979—; bd. dirs. Alba Editions, Athens, Vefa's House Kitchenware Mail Order Co.; TV chef Antena TV, Athens, 1990—; cons. caterer Elena's Gourmet, Thessaloniki, 1996—; food tester numerous gourmet food festivals, 1990—; author and pub. cookbooks. Recipient Diplome D'Honneur for best merchandising 20 booklet series Livre Gourmand Perigrieux, 1998. Mem. Internat. Assn. Culinary Profls., Greek Pubs. Assn., Internat. Women's Orgn. (pres. welfare com. 1965—), Azchestratos Ctr. for Preservation and Advancement of Traditional Greek Gastronomy. Avocations: cooking, decorating food, travel, meeting people, swimming. Home: 17A Chymaras Str, 146-71 Athens Greece Office: Alexiadou Editions, 4 Leonidou Str, 14452 Athens Greece

ALEXIOU, GEORGE PHILIP, computer engineer, educator, researcher; b. Germa, Kastoria, Greece, Oct. 18, 1953; s. Philippos and Zoe Alexiou; m. Maria Kordaki, July 21, 1983; children: Carolina, Melissa. BSc in Physics, U. Patras, Greece, 1976, PhD in Electronics, 1981. Rschr. U. Patras, 1976-80, adj. scientist, 1983-84, lectr., 1984-87, asst. prof., 1987-94, assoc. prof., 1994—; sr. rschr. C.T.I., Greece, 1985—; rschr. U. Tex., Dallas, 1988, R.T.I., Research Triangle Park, N.C., 1989. Contbr. articles to profl. jours. Nat. Rsch. Found. Greece scholar, 1987-88. Home: 13 Karaiskaki Str, 26500 Rion Achaia, Greece Office: Univ of Patras, Dept Computer Engring, 26500 Patras Achaia, Greece

ALEXIS, MICHEL, artist; b. Paris, July 1, 1950; s. Edmond Barrie and Jeanne Pereira; m. Nathalie Laborde Barrie, July 17, 1993; 1 child, James-Raphael. One-man shows include Double Rocking G Gallery, Calif., 1985, Joslyn ctr. ARts, Calif., 1986, M. Ivey Gallery, Calif., 1987, 88, R. 86, Bachofner Gallery, Calif., 1992, 95, 97, 99, Espace Malraux, Chambery, France, 1993, Dahn Gallery, N.Y.C., 1995, E. Wimmer Gallery, N.Y.C., 1997, U. Denver, 1997; group shows include L.A. County Mus., 1985, Musee Dauphinois, France, 1991, Artist Space, N.Y.C., 1992, Drawing Ctr., N.Y.C., 1993, Bronx Mus. of the Arts, 1993, 1995, Dortmunder Kunstverein Mus., Germany, 1995, Rosenberg & Kaufman Gallery, N.Y.C., 1997, U. R.I., 1999; represented in permanent collections Denver Art Mus., Long Beach Mus., Dortmunder Kunstverein Mus., L.A. County Mus. Recipient Pollock-Krasner Found. award, 1994. Address: 6 Rue Faidherbe, 94160 Saint Mande France

ALEXOPOULOS, ARGYRIOS DIMITRIOS, career officer; b. Athens, Greece, Jan. 23, 1973; s. Dimitrios Argyrios and Christine Aris (Aggelatos) A. Lt. Greek Army, 1996—. Mem. AFCEA, Old Crows, Amauteur. Avocation: amateur radio. Home: HRAS 58, 83100 Vathi Greece Office: Army, 79 NDBEO Malagari, 83100 Samos Greece

ALEXY, PATRIARCH II (ALEXEI MIKHAILOVICH RIDIGUER), patriarch of Moscow and Russia; b. Tallinn, Estonia, Feb. 23, 1929; s. Mikhail Aleksandrovich and Yelena Iosifovna (Pisareva) R. Cand. Theology, Sankt-Petersburg Theol. Acad., 1953, DTh, 1984; DDiv with hons., Theol. Acad. of Reformed, Ch. in Hungary, Debrecen, Jan Komensky Theol. Faculty, Prague, Gen. Seminary of the Episcopal, Ch. in USA, 1991, St. Vladimir's Theol. Seminary, of Orthodox Ch. in Am., N.Y., 1991, St. Tikhon's Theol. Seminary, of the Orthodox Ch. in Am., 1991, Alaska Pacific U., 1993; D of Philology with hons., St. Petersbourg State U., Russia, 1994; DDiv with hons., The Theol. Faculty of the, Serbian Orthodox Ch., Beograd, Serbia, 1994. Ordained priest Russian Orthodox Ch., 1950. Psalm-reader Tallinn, 1946-47; priest Estonia, 1950-61; bishop Tallinn, 1961-64, archbishop, 1964-68, metropolitan, 1968-86; patriarch Moscow and All Russia, 1990—; dean Theophanias-parish, Jõhvi, Estonia, 1950; mem. ctrl. com. World Coun. Chs., 1961-68; vice chmn. dept. external chs. rels. Moscow Patriarchate, 1961-64; chancellor, mem. tchg. com. Moscow Patriarchate, 1964-86; pres., mem. Presidium Conf. of European Chs., Geneva, 1964-92; chmn. Presidium Conf. of European Chs., Geneva, 1987-92; chmn. of ednl. com. Moscow Patriarchate, 1965-86, metropolitan of Leningrad and Novgorod, 1986-90, primate of the Russian Orthodox Ch., 1990; U.S.S.R. People's dep., 1989-91. Contbr. articles to profl. jours. Permanent mem. Holy Synod. Russian Orthodox. Avocation: gathering mushrooms. Office: Moscow Patriarchate Danilov, Monastery 22 Danilovsky val, Moscow 113191, Russia*

ALEYNIKOV, SERGEY MIKHAYLOVICH, geotechnics educator; b. Voronezh, Russia, Jan. 6, 1954; s. Mikhail Arkhipovich Aleynikov and Klara Borisovna Belen'kaya. MSc, Voronezh State U., 1975; PhD, Heat and Mass Transfer Inst., Minsk, Belorussia, 1982. Rsch. assoc. State U., Voronezh, Russia, 1976-78, Luikov Heat and Mass Transfer Inst., Minsk, 1978-81; lectr. Civil Engring. Inst., Voronezh, 1982-92; rsch. assoc. Inst. Physics of the Earth, Moscow, 1992-95; lectr. Acad. Architecture and Constrn., Voronezh, 1995—; vice dean Faculty Civil Engring. and Tech., Civil Engring. Inst., Voronezh, 1984-90. Author: Rheological Constitutive Equations, 1981, Theory of Complex Variable Functions, 1993, Boundary Element Method in Contact Problems for Elastic Spatial-and-nonhomogeneous Bases, 1999; patentee in field. Recipient 1st degree sci. prize Siberian dept. Russian Acad. Scis., 1981; named Soros assoc. prof., Soros Found., 1999. Mem. Internat. Soc. Soil Mechanics and Geotech. Engring. (European regional tech. com.), Internatl. Soc. for Boundary Elements. Home: Plekhanovskaya 1-93, 394018 Voronezh Russia Office: Voronezh State Acad Architechture & Constrn, 20 Letiya Oktaybrya 84, 394006 Voronezh Russia

AL-FALAHI, LAITH ABDULLA, mechanical engineer; b. Baghdad, Iraq, Nov. 3, 1955; s. Abdullah Ali and Thamina (Ali) A. BSc in Mech. Engring. with honors, U. Baghdad, 1977; PhD in Orthop. Mechanics, U. Salford, U.K., 1984. Rsch. assoc. in rheumatology biomed. physics dept. U. Manchester, Eng., 1984-87; adj. prof. dept. biomed. tech. Coll. Applied Med. Scis., King Saud U., Riyadh, Saudi Arabia, 1987—; orthop. and rehab. bioengring. cons., rsch. corrd. rehab. Joint Ctr. for Rsch. in Prosthetics & orthotics, Riyadh, 1987—; v.p. Islamic World Coun. on Disability and Rehab., Riyadh, 1996—, mem. sci. and tech. adv. bd., 1996—; cons. Med. and Rehab. Consultancy House, Riyadh, 1995—; mem. med. and sci. com. Prince Sultan Bin Abdulaziz City for Humanitarian Svcs., 1994-96; mem. sci. com. 1st conf. Saudi Benevolent Assn. for Disabled Chidlren, Riyadh, 1992. Assoc. editor Saudi Jour. Disability and Rehab.; contbr. numerous articles to profl. jours. Mem. Internat. Soc. for Prosthetics and Orthotics Denmark, Soc. for Clin. Densitometry, Rehab. Engring. Sco. N.Am. Avocations: tennis, swimming, bridge. Office: Joint Ctr Rsch in Prosthet, PO Box 27240, Riyadh 11417, Saudi Arabia

ALFARES, HESHAM KAMAL, engineering educator; b. Qatif, Saudi Arabia, Apr. 15, 1960; s. Kamal Muhammad Alfares and Batool Husain Al-Awwami; m. Hannan Hassan Al-Qatari, July 2, 1987; children: Layla, Eman, Husain, Sarah, Muhammad. BS in Elec. and Computer Engring., U. Calif., Santa Barbara, 1982; MS in Indsl. Engring., U. Pitts., 1984; PhD in Indsl. Engring., Ariz. State U., 1991. Indsl. engr. Saudi Aramco, Dhahran, Saudi Arabia, 1983, 84, 95,97, cons., 1999-2000; lectr. King Fahd U. Petroleum and Minerals, Dhahran, 1984-91, asst. prof., 1991-2000, assoc. prof., 2000—; vis. rschr. U. Warwick, Coventry, Eng., summer 1993, U. Nottingham, Eng., summer 1998. Contbr. articles to sci. publs., including IIE Transactions, Computers & Operations Rsch., Computers & Indsl. Engring. Rsch. grantee British Coun., 1993, 98. Mem. Inst. Ops. Rsch. and Mgmt. Scis., Alpha Pi Mu. Avocations: reading, poetry, basketball. Home: PO Box 738, Qatif 31911, Saudi Arabia Office: Sys Engring Dept, King Fahd U Petro Minerals, Dhahran 31261, Saudi Arabia

ALFARO, ANDREV, sculptor; b. Valencia, Spain, Aug. 5, 1929; s. Andrés Alfaro and Teresa Hernández; m. Dorothy Hofmann, 1954; 3 children. Studio artist, 1958—. One-man shows include Sala de la Dirección Gen. de Bellas Artes de Madrid, 1967, Galerie Dreiseitel, Cologne, Germany, 1974, Ministry of Culture, Palacio Velázquez, Parque del Retiro de Madrid, 1979, U. Complutense de Madrid, 1981, Antic Mercat del Born de Barcelona, 1983; other exhbns. include Bienal Venezia, 1966, 76, 95, Paris and Madrid, 1989, Cologne and Frankfort, 1990, retrospective exhbn. Inst. Valenciano de Arte Moderno, 1991, Barcelona, 1993, Madrid, 1994, Cologne, Valencia, 1995, XLVI Biennal of Venezia, 1996, Valencia, Madrid, Barcelona, 1997-98, Roma, Girona, 1999; monumental open-air sculptures in Valencia, Barcelona, Madrid, Nüremberg, Cologne, Frankfurt, Munich, N.Y.; author: El Arte visto por los artistas, 1987, Doce artistas de vanguardia en el Museo del Prado, 1991; contbr. articles to profl. jours. Recipient Gold medal Salón Internat. de Marzo Valencia, 1964, Premio Nat. de Artes Plásticas, 1981, Creu de Sant Jordi, 1982, Premi Alfons Roig, 1991, Premio de Urbanismo, Arquitectura y Obra Pública del Ayto de Madrid, 1991, Premio Tomás Francisco Prieto, 1995, Casa de la Moneda, Madrid. Home: 138R, Urbanizacion Sta Barbara, 46111 Rocafort Valencia, Spain

ALFARO, GUILLERMO HANNE, geology educator, consultant; b. Lebu, Arauco, Chile, June 19, 1942; s. Guillermo Rodriguez Alfaro and Edith Koch Hanne; m. Maritza Frost Hoeneisen; children: Diego Rodrigo, Gonzalo Guillermo, Arturo Alejandro. Degreee geology, U. Chile, Santiago, 1966; PhD, U. Tohoku, Sendai, Japan, 1984. Geologist Minera Tocopilla, Chile, 1967-69, Geol. Survey, Antofagasta, Chile, 1970-72; chief geologist Geol. Survey, Concepcion, Chile, 1972-81; prof. U. Concepcion, 1981—; rschr. U. Heidelberg, Germany, 1984; cons. Carbonifera Catamuton, La Union, Chile, 1986—, Minera La Union, Santiago, 1986-95. Scholarship MMAJ-JICA, 1978, Von Humboldt Found., 1984. Mem. Geol. Soc., Soc. of Econ. Geologists. Avocation: yachting. Home: Nonguen 249, Concepcion Chile Office: U Concepcion, 160-3 Concepcion 3, Chile

ALFARO, MIGUEL E., plastic surgeon, surgery educator; b. San Jose, Costa Rica, Nov. 30, 1942; s. Leonidas and Maria (Davila) A.; m. Sylvia Escalante, Dec. 13, 1967; children: Monica, Andrea, Leonardo, Alberto. MD, U. Costa Rica, 1968. Resident gen. surgery U.S. and Costa Rica, 1974; resident plastic surgery U.S., 1974-76; attending surgeon Social Security Sys.-Hosp. San Juan de Dios, Costa Rica, 1976-84; chief plastic surgery-burn unit Social Security Sys.-Hosp. San Jurnte Dios, Costa Rica, 1984—; prof. surgery U. Costa Rica, 1977—; sponsorship prof. U. Toronto, ON, Canada, 1980, U. Melbourne, 1981; sci. com. Colegio de Médicos, Costa Rica, 1979-83; mem. mal praxis com., Costa Rica, 1993-95; organizer med. meetings, 1979-99. Opera singer Costa Rica Lyric Co.; contbr. articles to profl. jours. Mem. Nat. Bioethical Com., Costa Rica, 1998—, Nat. Rescue of Values Com., Costa Rica, 1998—, Nat. Com. Med. Social Assistance, 1988-92. Mem. Costa Rican Coll. Surgeons, Costa Rica Assn. Plastic Surgery, Costa Rica Assn. Oncology, Costa Rica Assn. Mastology, Iberolatino Am. Soc. Plastic Surgery, Internat. Coll. Surgeons, Internat. Soc. Burn Injuries, Am. Soc. Aestetic Plastics. Liberacion. Roman Catholic. Avocations: singing opera and popular. Home: PO Box 1813-1000, San Jose Costa Rica

ALFASSI, HAVIV, business executive; b. Maknas, Morocco, Aug. 12, 1947; arrived in Australia, 1971; s. Hanania and Sima Alfassi. Student, Bar-Ilan U., 1996-97. Inspector Ministry of Def., Tel-Aviv, 1967-68; clk. Bank Leoni, Tel-Aviv, 1968-70; bus driver NSW Govt., Sydney, 1972-73; bus. exec. Sydney, 1974-94; dir. Sparo Pty. Ltd., Sydney, 1982—; co-dir. Sparo P/L, Sydney, 1982—. With Israeli Def. Force, 1964-66. Mem. Nat. Rds. Motorist Assn., South Sydney J.L. Club, City Tattersaus Club (Sydney). Mem. Liberal Party. Jewish. Avocations: water sports, piloting, travel, skiing, breeding animals. Home and Office: 93 Old South Head Rd, Bondi Junction NSW 2026, Australia

AL FAYED, MOHAMED, entrepreneur; b. Alexandria, Egypt, Jan. 27, 1933; s. Aly Aly Fayed; m. Samira Khashoggi, 1954 (div. 1956); 1 child, Emad (dec.); m. Heini Wathen; 4 children. Founder company Alexandria, 1956; oil trading, constrn., gas and oil concessions businessman Haiti; owner Ritz Hotel, Paris, 1979—, also chmn. bd. dirs.; owner Harrods, Ltd., London, 1994—, also chmn. bd. dirs.; active shipping and constrn. industry; chmn. Fulham Football Club. Decorated Order of Merit (Italy), officer Legion of Honor (France); recipient Le Grande Medaille de la Ville de Paris, 1985, Plaque de Paris, 1989. Office: Harrods Ltd, Brompton Rd, Knightsbridge London SW1X 7XL, England*

ALFEROV, ZHORES I., physicist, researcher; b. Vitebsc, Byelorussia, USSR, Mar. 15, 1930; s. Ivan Karpovich and Anna Vladimirovna (Rosenblum) A.; m. Tamara Georgievna Darscaya, Nov. 11, 1967; 1 child, Ivan Zhoresovich. Degree in Engring., Electrotechnical Inst., Leningrad, USSR, 1952; Degree in Sci. and Tech., Ioffe Physico-Tech. Inst., Leningrad, 1961; DSci in Physics and Math., Iosse Physical Tech. Inst., Lenningrad, 1970. Cert. engr. Jr. scientist Ioffe Physico-Tech. Inst., Lenningrad, 1953-64, sr. scientist, 1964-67, head lab., 1967-87, dir., 1987—; v.p. Acad. Scis. of the USSR, Moscow and Leningrad, 1990-91, Russian Acad. Scis., Moscow and St. Petersburg, 1991—. Author numerous books; contbr. articles to profl. jours.; inventor in field. People dep. of USSR People's Congress of the USSR, 1989-92. Recipient Ballantyne medal Franklin Inst., 1971, Lenin prize Govt. USSR, 1972, Hewlett-Packard Europhysics prize EPS, 1978, State Prize Govt. USSR, 1984, GaAs Symposium award, Interna. GaAs Symposiun, 1987, H. Welker medal, 1987, A.P. Karpinskii prize Shifting FVS, 1989, Nobel Prize, 2000. Mem. Russian Acad. Scis. (full mem., academician), 1979, Life Fellow of the Franklin Inst., 1971, Foreign mem. German Acad. Scis., 1987, Hon. Prof. of the Havana U., Cuba, 1987, Foreign mem. of the Polish Acad. of Sciences, 1988, Foreign Assoc. of the Nat. Acad. Engring., 1990, Foreign Assoc. of the Nat. Acad. Scis., 1990. Office: A F Ioffe Phisico-Tech Inst, Politekhnicheskaya Ul 26, 194021 Saint Petersburg Russia

ALFIERI, SERGIO, surgeon, researcher; b. Rome, Dec. 28, 1966; s. Giuseppe and Helga (Katalinič) A. Degree in medicine, Cath. U., Rome, 1992; diploma in gen. surgery, Gemelli Hosp., Rome, 1997. Resident in surgery Gemelli Hosp., Rome, 1992-97, gen. surgeon, 1997—; asst. dept. digestive surgery Gemelli Hosp. Cath U., Rome, 1998—. Contbr. articles to profl. jours. Mem. World Assn. Hepato-Pancreato-Biliary Surgery, Italian Sailing Fedn. Roman Catholic. Avocations: sailing, skiing. Home: Via Radiotelegrafisti 28, 00143 Rome Italy Office: Cath U Sacred Heart, L Go Agostino Gemelli 8, 00168 Rome Italy

ALFONSECA, MANUEL, computer scientist, educator; b. Madrid, Apr. 24, 1946; s. Manuel and Carmen (Moreno) A.; m. Maria Angel Cubero, Nov. 24, 1971; children: Maria de los Angeles, Enrique. Dr. in Electronics Engring., Poly. U. Madrid, 1971, MS in Computer Sci., 1976. Researcher Ministry of Edn., Madrid, 1970-71; computer scientist U. Computing Ctr., Madrid, 1971-72; asst. prof. Poly. U., Madrid, 1971-86, prof., 1986-93; researcher IBM, Madrid, 1972-86, sr. tech. staff mem., 1986-94; prof. Autonomous U., Madrid, 1993—; sci. collaborator La Vanguardia newspaper, Barcelona, Spain, 1983-97, Santillana Pub., Madrid, 1985-87, Espasa Calpe Pub., Madrid, 1992-96. Author 20 books for children and juveniles, translated into 3 languages, 1986— (Lazarillo award 1988), 8 books on computer sci., 7 books on sci., 1978—, 22 software products, 1979—; contbr. articles to profl. jours. Recipient Nat. Graduation award Spanish Govt., 1970, Cross of Alfonso X El Sabio award Spanish Govt., 1970. Mem. IEEE Computer Soc., N.Y. Acad. Scis., Spanish Assn. Telecommunication, Spanish Assn. Sci. Journalists, Assn. Computer Machinery, British APL

Assn. Roman Catholic. Avocations: piano playing, classical music, writing for children. Home: Belianes 2, 28043 Madrid Spain Office: Univ Autonoma, Dept Ingenieria Informatica Cantoblanco, 28049 Madrid Spain

ALFONSO-FAUS, ANTONIO, engineering educator, researcher; b. Onteniente, Valencia, Spain, Jan. 9, 1939; s. Alfredo and Maria Alfonso-F.; m. Carmen Garcia-Ortubia, Apr. 30, 1964; children: Antonio, Javier, Miguel, Alicia. MSc in Physics, U. Minn., 1967, PhD in Physics, 1968; degree in aero. engring., Esquela Tecnica Superior Ingenieros Aeronautica, Madrid, 1964; PhD in Aero. Engring., Esquela U. De Ingemeria Tecnica Aeronautica, Madrid, 1969. Prin. investigator Instituto Nacional Detecnica Aeroespacial, Madrid, 1968-73; engring. coord. Iberia Airlines, 1973-78, plant engr., 1978-81, devel. engr. chief, 1981-87, total quality dir., 1988-91, devel. dir., 1991-94; engring. educator Universidad Politecnica De Madrid, Madrid, 1974-94; prof. UPM, Madrid, 1995—. Contbr. articles to profl. jours. including Jour. Geophysics Rsch., Plantetary and Space Sci., and Internat. Jour. Theoretical Physics. Fellow European Space Rsch. Orgn., 1964, NASA-European Space Rsch. Orgn., 1965. Avocation: cosmology. Home: Bravo Munillo 23, 28015 Madrid Spain Office: EUIT Aeronautica, Plz Cardonal Cisneros 3, 28040 Madrid Spain

ALFORD, MARGIE SEARCY, lawyer, author; b. Tuscaloosa, Ala., Dec. 20, 1949; d. Joseph Alexander and Margaret Tyler (Zehmer) Searcy; m. Andrew Ray Alford, Sept. 4, 1992. BS, U. Ala., 1967-69, 70-71; student, U. Ams., Mexico City, 1969, Emory U., Atlanta, 1970; JD, U. Ala., 1974. Bar: Ala. 1974; U.S. Dist. Ct. (no. dist.) Ala. 1975. Assoc. univ. counsel U. Ala., Tuscaloosa, 1974-75; pvt. practice Tuscaloosa, 1975-92, Birmingham, Ala., 1992—. Editor-in-chief, prin. author: Matthew Bender's A Guide to Toxic Torts, 4 vols., 1986; contbg. author: Matthew Bender's Drug Product Liability, 4 vols.; contbr. numerous articles to legal jours., freelance writer for numerous publs. Group leader Ea. Area Diabetes Support Group, 1997—; vol. tchr. Ch. Cir., 1996—; mem. Trussville Area C. of C., bd. dirs., 2000—. Named Most Outstanding Young Career Woman in Ala. Ala. Bus. and Profl. Women, 1986. Mem. ATLA (twice nat. chair environ. and toxic tort law sect., twice nat. chair of women trial lawyers caucus), Ala. Media Profls., Women's Bus. Ownership Coun. Democrat. Presbyterian. Avocations: collecting antique furniture and paintings, chow chow dog breeder, gardening, traveling. Fax: (205) 520-5083. E-mail: margialfor@aol.com. Office: PO Box 610781 Birmingham AL 35261-0781

ALFORD, NEILL HERBERT, JR., retired law educator; b. Greenville, S.C., July 13, 1919; s. Neill Herbert and Elizabeth (Robertson) A.; m. Elizabeth Talbot Smith, June 26, 1943; children: Neill Herbert III, Margaret Dudley, Eli Thomas Stackhouse. BA, The Citadel-Mil. Coll. S.C., 1940; LLB, U. Va., 1947; JSD, Yale U., 1966. Bar: Va. 1954. Mem. faculty law U. Va. Law Sch., Charlottesville, 1947-61, 62-90; Doherty Found. prof. U. Va. Law Sch., 1966-74, spl. cons. to pres. univ., legal adviser to rector and bd. dirs., 1972-74; Joseph Henry Lumpkin prof., dean Law Sch. U. Ga., Athens, 1974-76; Percy Brown Jr. prof. law U. Va., 1976-90; state reporter Supreme Ct. Va., 1977-84; counsel Woods, Rogers & Hazelgrove, Charlottesville, 1991-97; prof. chair internat. law Naval War Coll., 1961-62, cons. 1962-68; spl. counsel Va. Code Commn. 1954-57; dir. Va. Bankers Assn. Trust Sch., 1958-61; summer tchr. George Washington U., U. N.C.; chmn. bd. dirs. U. Va. Press, 1970-74, 87-89; prof. law emeritus U. Va., 1990—; Lehmann Disting. vis. prof. law Washington U., St. Louis, 1991; Hofstedler prof. Ohio State U. Law Sch., 1992; prof. Washington and Lee Law Sch., 1992. Author: Cases and Materials on Decedents Estates and Trusts, 8th edit, 1993, Modern Economic Warfare: Law and the Naval Participant, 1967; Contbr. articles to profl. jours. Comdr. civil affairs group U.S. Army Res., 1947-66. Lt. col. inf. AUS, 1941-46, ETO; col. inf. AUS; ret. 1968. Decorated Bronze Star, Combat Inf. badge.; Sterling fellow Yale U., 1950-51, Ford fellow U. Wis., 1958. Fellow Va. Law Found., Am. Bar Found.; mem. ABA, Selden Soc., Am. Soc. Legal History, Am. Judicature Soc., Am. Law Inst., Va. State Bar, Va. Bar Assn., Raven Soc., Colonnade Club, Order of Coif, Phi Alpha Delta, Omicron Delta Kappa. Home: 1868 Field Rd Charlottesville VA 22903-1619

ALFRED, R. See BEATTY, ROBERT ALFRED

ALFSTAD, TORE, telecommunications engineer; b. Oslo, Norway, June 1, 1958; s. Oddvar Marius adn Kari Marie (Ravn) A. Student, Sofienberg Tech. Sch., Oslo, 1978-79, Grimstad Telecomm. Sch., 1988. Cert. telcomm. engr. Svc. technician Storm and Storm A/S, Oslo, 1976-77, Grundig Norway, Oslo, 1979, Noratom Instruments, Drammen, Norway, 1979-80; telecomm. technician Norwegian Telecomm., Oslo, 1980-96; owner Alfatek, Norway, 1996—. Mem. Norwegian Radio Relay League, Planetary Soc. Avocations: computers, ham radio, boating, UFO logy, astronomy. Office: ALFATEK, Storåsveien 5, 1169 Oslo Norway

ALFVEGREN, LARS BERTIL, foreign language educator; b. Visby, Gotland, Sweden, Aug. 10, 1925; s. Bertil Karl and Greta Julia (Högvall) A.; m. Marianne Dorotea Lindeberg, 1951 (dec. 1983). PhD, U. Uppsala, Sweden, 1958. Asst. prof. U. Uppsala, 1959-62; headmaster Coll. Journalism U. Göteborg, Sweden, 1962-90. Author several sci. books in Swedish. Sgt. Swedish Inf., 1944-45. Recipient Nordstjerneorden, 1973. Mem. Royal Bacherlors' Club. Home: Molinsgatan 9, 41133 Göteborg Sweden

AL-GARNI, ABDULLAH MOHAMMED, civil engineering educator, researcher, consultant; b. Al-Obaid, Saudi Arabia, Jan. 1, 1959; s. Mohammed Abdullah and Norah Saeed Al-Garni; m. Sabah Saeed Al-Ghamdi, July 1, 1964; children: Aljowharah, Mohammed, Mohannad, Moayed, Raghad. BSc in Engring., King Saud U., Riyadh, Saudi Arabia, 1984; MSc in Engring., Ohio State U., 1986, MSc in Geodetic Sci. and Surveying, 1991, PhD, 1992. Tchg. asst. King Saud U., 1983-84, asst. prof. civil engring., 1992-96, assoc. prof. civil engring., 1996—; cons. Saudi Ministry Def. and Aviation, Riyadh, 1993-95, King Abdulaziz City Sci. and Tech., Riyadh, 1997—; dir. photogrammetry project Beeah Co., Riyadh, 1996-98; civil engring. rep. Rsch. Ctr. Coll. and Engring., Riyadh, 1996—; GIS dir. Prince Sultan Co., Riyadh, 1994—. Contbr. articles to profl. jours. (Best Rsch. award 1983, Edward Dolezal award 1996, Coun. Arabia Mins. Environment award 1997); mem. editl. bd. Jour. Photogrammetry and Remote Sensing, 1985—. Rsch. grantee Ctr. Coll. & Engring., Saudi Arabia, 1997. Mem. Desert Studies Ctr. Avocations: swimming, football, TV, books. Office: King Saud U Coll Engring, PO Box 800, 11421 Riyadh Saudi Arabia

AL-GARNI, AHMED ZAFER, aerospace engineer, educator; b. Al-Khobar, Saudi Arabia, May 14, 1953; s. Zafer Ali Al-Garni and Sharefa Ahmed Al-Sada; m. Fetha Mana Al-Amri; children: Zafer, Abdallah, Sharefa, Mohamad, Abdalrahman. BS in Aerospace Engring., U. Ariz., 1981, MS in Aerospace Engring., 1983; MS in Aerospace Engring., U. Mich., 1987; PhD in Aerospace Engring., U. Md., 1991. Aerospace engr. Royal Saudi Air Force, Saudi Arabia, 1975-84; lectr. in aerospace engring. King Fahd U. Petroleum and Minerals, Dhahran, Saudi Arabia, 1984-91, asst. prof. aerospace engring., 1991-96, assoc. prof. aerospace engring., 1996—; aeronautic group coord. King Fahd U. Petroleum and Minerals, 1992—, chmn. aerospace engring. program, 1994—, founder, dir. Aerospace Eng. Prog., 1998. Contbr over 40 articles to profl. jours. Mem. (sr.) AIAA. Muslem. Achievements include establishment of aeronautical/aerospace engineering program at King Fahd U. Petroleum and Minerals. Home and Office: King Fahd U Petrol Minerals, Box 842, Dhahran 31261, Saudi Arabia

ALGERS, BO FREDRIK, veterinarian, educator; b. Stockholm, Jan. 5, 1950; s. Börge and Ulla (Ljungberg) A.; m. Anita Frick, 1976 (div. 1988); children: Johanna, Malin; m. Anne Rasmussen, 1990; children: Maria, Jonas. DVM, Royal Vet. Coll., Stockholm, 1974; PhD, Swedish U. Agrl. Sci., Uppsala, 1989. Rsch. asst. Royal Vet. Coll., Skara, Sweden, 1975-76; rsch. mgr. Swedish U. Agrl. Sci., Skara, 1977-94, asst. prof. vet. medicine, 1990-94, prof. vet. medicine, 1994—, head dept. animal hygiene, 1993-96, head dept. animal environ. and health, 1997—. Achievements include research on biological effects of electromagnetic fields on dairy cow fertility, maternal behavior and mother offspring interactions in pigs, environmental effects on health and behavior of laying hens. Recipient Guldtackan award Landbrukarnas Riksforbund, Sweden, 1988. Mem. AAAS, Am. Soc. for Animal Sci., Internat. Soc. for Applied Ethology, Internat. Soc. for Animal Hygiene (mem. coun.), Swedish Animal Welfare Coun. E-mail: bo.algers@hmh.slu.se. Office: Swedish U Agrl Scis, PO Box 234, S-53223 Skara Sweden

ALGHAFERI, MUNEERA YOUNUS, health facility administrator; b. AbuDhabi, United Arab Emirates, Dec. 13, 1971; d. Younus Abdullah AL-ghaferi and Fatima Mohd Alsulaimi. AS, Navarro Coll., 1994; BS in Microbiology, N.C. State U., 1997. Lab. technologist Zayed Mil. Hosp., AbuDhabi, 1997-98, technologist and officer in charge microbiology dept., 1998—; tutor for freshman N.C. State U., Raleigh, 1995-96, genetic lab. asst., 1996, genetic/microbiology rsch. lab. asst., 1997; vol. worker lab. Rex Hosp., Raleigh, 1996-97. Lt. Zayed Mil. Hosp., 1997—. Mem. Am. Soc. Microbiology. Muslim. Avocations: reading, learning new cultures, traveling. E-mail: alghamunizmh@hotmail.com. Office: Zayed Mil Hosp, Box 3744, AbuDhabi United Arab Emirates

AL GHAMDI, ABDUL-LATIF SAEED, business owner; b. Al-Tarafain, Al-Baha, Saudi Arabia, Apr. 19, 1950; s. Saeed Abdullah and Hasana Abdullah Al-Ghamdi; m. Fawziyah Al Quhaiz, 1976; children: Reem, Raied. BSCE, U. Petroleum and Minerals, Dhahran, Saudi Arabia, 1975; postgrad., Georgetown U., 1989. Field engr. Santa Fe Corp., Rastanura, 1972-73; civil engr. Saudi Arabian Oil Co., Dhahran, 1975-78; sr. project engr. Saudi Arabian Oil Co., Abgaiq, Saudi Arabia, 1978-80, Aramco Svcs. Co., Houston, 1980-82; chief surveying svcs. Saudi Aramco, Dhahran, 1983-86; project mgr. Saudi Aramco, Dhahran, Saudi Arabia, 1986-88; sr. project mgr. Saudi Aramco, Ras Tanura, Saudi Arabia, 1988-90; mgr. projects Saudi Aramco, L.A., 1990-92; mgr. oil and gas projects Saudi Aramco, Dhahran, 1992-94; pres., gen. mgr. A.S. Alghamdi Trading Corp., Al Khobar, Saudi Arabia, 1994—. Mem. ASCE, Nat. Geog. Soc. Avocations: general sports, travel, writing science subjects, music. Office: PO Box 3631, 31952 Al Khobar Saudi Arabia

AL-GHUSAIN, IBRAHIM AHMAD NOURI, engineering educator, researcher, consultant; b. Kuwait, Aug. 6, 1964; s. Ahmad Nouri Al-Ghusain and Nazeerah Yousef Alkhateeb; m. Lina Husni Dairanieh, Jan. 1, 1987; children: Faisal, Talah. BS in Civil Engring., Kuwait U., 1986; MS, U. Md., 1989, PhD, 1993. Lab. engr. Kuwait U., 1986-87, instr. in scholarship, 1987-93, asst. prof., 1994—, vice dean for consultation Coll. Engring., 1999—; cons. Ministry Pub. Works, Kuwait, 1994-96, Regional Orgn. Protection of the Marine Environment, Kuwait, 1995-97; cons., shareholder Nat. Environ. Svcs. Co., Kuwait, 1997—; vice dean, Coll. Engring., Kuwait U., 1999—. Contbr. articles to profl. jours. Sgt. Kuwait Armed Forces, 1997-98. Kuwait U. scholar, 1987, 89. em. ASCE, Internat. Assn. Water Quality, Water Environment Fedn. Avocations: motoring, boating, flying, computers. Home: PO Box 38062, 72251 Abdullah Al Salem Kuwait Office: Kuwait U Civil Engring Dept, PO Box 5969, 13060 Safat Kuwait

ALHABIBI, YASSER ALI, mechanical engineer; b. Cairo, Apr. 24, 1955; s. Ali Alsaid and Zeinab Mohamed Alhabibi; m. Nagwa Almasry, Jan. 18, 1987; children: Mohamed, Ahmed. BSME, Ain Shams U., 1974; MSc in CBIS, U. Sunderland, 1998. Vehicles sales rep. Alhamrani United Co., Jeddah, Saudi Arabia, 1981-82, incharge of sec., 1982-85, asst. mgr., 1985-87, 88-92, br. sales coord., 1987-88, plan and inventory control mgr., 1992-99; plan, inventory control mgr. Elmashreq Trading & Industry SAE-Seoudi Group, Dokki, Giza, Egypt, 1999—; cultural lectr. Army, Cairo, 1980-81; sales instr. AUC Co., 1989-91, incharge of Decision Support Sys., ESS, 1993—, GCC 2000 mem., 1993—. Cultural mem. Student Union, 1970; dep. dir. gen. Internat. Biog. Ctr., 1998; mem. Al Shams Social Club, 1987, Al Ahaly Social Club, 1993. Mem. AAAS, IEEE, ASME, Egyptian Syndicate of Engring., Saudi Computer Soc., Brit. Computer Soc., Egyptian Computer Soc., Nat. Geog. Soc., Planetary Soc., N.Y. Acad. Scis. Muslim. Fax: 3365815. E-mail: alhabibi@elmashreq.com. Home: 14 Tripoli St 6th Dist, Nasr City, Cairo Egypt Office: Elmashreq Trading Industry, 131 El Tahrir St, Dokki Egypt

AL-HADI, ABD AL-RAB MANSUR, Yemeni government official; b. Abyan Governorate, al-Ghadir, Yemen, 1944; 5 children. MA, Nasir Acad., Egypt, USSR. Chief of staff Armored Corps War Coll., commdr. ops. sector, dir. supplies and logistics. Adviser V.P., 1990; min. def. Govt. Yemen, 1994, v.p., 1994—. Office: Presdl Coun, Zubairy St, Sana'a Yemen*

AL-HAFEEZ, HUMZA, minister, editor; b. N.Y.C., Feb. 28, 1931; s. Asa Mose and Rose Mae (Danielson) Weir; children: Jacqueline, Yuhanna, Rasul, Bismillah, Habib, Wardi, Larry, Don, Mariama. Student, Food Trades Vocat. Sch., 1947-48. Patrolman N.Y.C. Police Dept., from 1959; chmn. Temple of Islam, Inc.; founder Nat. Soc. Afro-Am. Policemen Inc.; also past pres.; cons. community relations to chief insp. N.Y.C. Police Dept., to; U.S. Dept. Justice; investigator of corruption among N.Y.C. police officers Knapp Commn.; undercover narcotic officer, investigator Manhattan office Dist. Atty.; investigator Office of 1st Dep. Policy Commr.; undercover investigator U.S. Dept. Justice.; insp. N.Y. State Athletic Commn.; Lectr. Princeton U., Mich. State U., N.Y. State U., Pace Coll., Bklyn. Coll., U. Chgo., NYU, Satellite Acad., N.Y.C., Kinlock Mission for Blind, City N.Y. Police Acad., Nassau Community Coll.; others. Appeared on radio and TV.; Editor-in-chief: Your Muhammad Speaks newspaper; author The Slanderer, 1987. Pastoral bd. Interfaith Hosp.; chaplain Frackville (Pa.) Correctional Facility, 1995—. Recipient Father of Yr. award Kinlock Freedom Found. for the Blind, 1973; Community Service award United Council of Chs., 1975; named Person of Yr. Nat. Assn. Black Policemen, 1982. Mem. Internat. Platform Assn. Mem. Nation of Islam; minister Muhammad's Temple of Islam, Bklyn. Home: 361 Clinton Ave Apt 12C Brooklyn NY 11238-1145 Office: 1211 Atlantic Ave Brooklyn NY 11216-2709

ALHAJRI, ABDULLAH DHAFFER, government official; b. Alaflaj, Riyadh, Saudi arabia, July 7, 1945; s. Dhaffer Mohammad and Gozail Hammad (Aldosary) A.; m. F.M. Alhajri, July 17, 1962; children: Sarah, Yacrob. BA, U. Riyadh, 1975; M.Devel. Adminstrn., Western Mich. U., 1986. Asst. mgr. adminstrn. Med. Svcs. Def., Riyadh, 1975-78; tchr. Ministry of Def., Riyadh, 1979-80; mgr. Ministry of Fin., Riyadh, 1981—; ind. investor. Mem. Am. Assn. Individual Investors, Highlander Club. Avocations: sports, travel, reading. Office: PO Box 88566, Riyadh 11672, Saudi Arabia

AL HAMDANI, ABDULKARIM MOHAMED, health facility administrator, physician, internist, consultant, cardiologist; b. Taiz, Yemen; arrived in Saudi Arabia, 1981; s. Mohamed and Takia (Eisa) M.; m. Khadija Abdulla, Mar. 19, 1981 (div. 1997); m. Ghaza Almorisi, July 13, 1995; children: Mohamed, Wisam. Cert. MD, MB, ChB., Jeddah, Saudi Arabia. Chief registar Fing Fahad Hosp., Al Bahaa, KSA, 1989-93; registar King Fahad Hosp., Al Bahaa, KSA, 1989-93, St. George's Hosp., London, 1993; cons. internist, cardiologist Al Thowa Hosp., Sanaa, Yemen, 1993-95, Dr. chief med. and ICU dept., 1994-95; cons. internist, cardiologist United Dr.'s Hosp., Jeddah, KSA, 1995—, head cardiovasc. unit, 1998—, head edn. program, 1999—. Fellow ACA; mem. ACC, ADA, Med. Coun. (Jordanian bd. dirs.). Achievements include doing the 1st permanent pacemaker implantation in Yemen. Avocations: traveling, table-tennis. Office: United Dr's Hosp, Al Corniche, 33692 Jeddah 21458, Saudi Arabia

ALHAMID, ABDULAZIZ A., hydraulics specialist, educator, researcher; b. Thurmada, Saudi Arabia; s. Abdullah I. and Monerah A. (Alyosef) A.; m. Amal S. Alfehaid, Nov. 15, 1988; children: Hadeal, Anfall, Osamah, Ghadear. BS, King Saud U., Riyadh, Saudi Arabia, 1984, MS, 1987; PhD in Civil Engring., U. Birmingham, Eng., 1991. Tchg. asst. King Saud U., 1984-87, lectr., 1987-89, asst. prof. civil engring., 1991-96, assoc. prof., 1996—, chmn. dept. civil engring., 1999—; cons. Arriyadh Devel. Authority, Riyadh, 1994—. Mem. ASCE, Internat. Assn. Hydraulic Rsch. Avocations: reading, swimming, camping. Office: King Saud U Dept Civil Engr, PO Box 800, Riyadh 11421, Saudi Arabia

ALHEGELAN, FAISAL AL-ABDUL-AZIZ, Saudi Arabian government official; b. Jeddah, Saudi Arabia, Oct. 7, 1929; s. Abdul-Aziz Abdul-Rahman Alhegelan and Fatima Abdullah Al-Eissa; m. Nouha Rushdi Tarazi, 1961; children: Khalid, Hisham, Omar. BA in Law, Fouad U., Cairo, 1951. Chief of protocol Saudi Arabian Fgn. Office, Riyadh, 1958-60; polit. advisor to King Sa-ud Govt. of Saudi Arabia, Riyadh, 1960-61; amb. to Spain, Madrid, 1961-68; amb. to Venezuela and Argentina Caracas and Buenos Aires, 1968-75; amb. to Denmark Copenhagen, 1975-76; amb. to Eng. London, 1976-79; amb. to U.S., Washington, 1979-83; min. of state and mem. coun. mins. Govt. of Saudi Arabia, Riyadh, 1984—; min. of health, authorized rep. King Faisal Spec. Hosp. & King Khalid Eye Spec. Hosp., Riyadh, 1984-95; amb. to France Paris, 1996—. Chmn. bd. dirs. Saudi Red Crescent Soc., Riyadh, 1984—, Saudi Anti-Smoking Soc., Riyadh, 1985—; chmn. bd. trustees Saudi Coun. Health Spltys., 1992—. Decorated Order of King Abdulaziz, grand cross Cordon of King Abdul Aziz (Saudi Arabia), Order of Isabela la Catolica (Spain), gran cordon Orden del Libertador (Venezuela), grande ofcl. Orden Riobranco (Brazil), May Grand Decoration (Argentina), hon. knight Order of Brit. Empire. Avocations: bridge, golf. Office: Royal Embassy Saudi Arabia, 5 av Hoche, 75008 Paris France

AL-HEJAILAN, JAMIL IBRAHIM, international organization executive. Sec.-gen. Coop. Coun. Arab States of the Gulf, Riyadh, Saudi Arabia. Office: Coop Coun ASG, PO Box 7153, 11462 Riyadh Saudi Arabia*

AL-HELAL, HUSSEIN SAUD, psychology educator, researcher; b. Naam, Saudi Arabia, Dec. 8, 1962; s. Saud Hussain and Nora Mohammed Al-Helal; m. Lamya Saleh Al-Owain, Mar. 15, 1991; children: Saud, Faisal. BA, King Saud U., Riyadh, 1983; MS, U. Bridgeport, 1988; PhD, U. Warwick, Coventry, Eng., 1996. Grad. asst. King Saud U., Riyadh, 1983-96, asst. prof., 1996—. Grantee King Saud U., 1983, 91. Mem. APA, Saudi Soc. Psychology and Edn., Phi Kappa Phi. Avocations: travel, playing volleyball, reading, watching TV news. Home: PO Box 30433, 11477 Riyadh Saudi Arabia Office: King Saud U, Dept Psychology, 11458 Riyadh Saudi Arabia

AL-HERABI, ZAID M. ABBAD, health facility administrator; b. Onaizah, Al-Quaseem, Saudi Arabia, July 1, 1942; s. Mohammed A. Abbad Al-Herabi and Aisha Nisser Al Jowaed; m. Noorah Mohammed Al-Buthi, Nov. 14, 1964; children: Moneerah, Mohammed, Ameen, Muna. BA in Lit., Riyadh (Saudi Arabia) U., 1970; postgrad. cert. hosp. adminstrn., Ga. State U., 1976; cert. hosp. adminstrn., Shal Hosp., Atlanta, 1976; diploma, King Abdul Aziz U., Jeddah, 1977. Adminstrv. dir. King Abdul Aziz Hosp., Riyadh, 1972-73; hosp. dir. Ministry of Health, Jeddah, 1976-77; adminstr. tchg. hosp. project F. Mikaau, Jeddah, 1977-79; gen. mgr. med. svcs. Saudia, Jeddah, 1979-85, Gen. mgr. health affairs, 1985-91, adv. med. projects, 1991—. Contbr. articles to profl. jours. Fellow Alexander Hamilton Inst. (cert.); mem. Oxford Club (life, chmn.'s cir. 1993—), Saudi Mgmt. Assn., Highlander Club. Avocations: sports, reading, writing, poetry. Home: PO Box 35134, Jeddah 21488, Saudi Arabia

ALHO, OLLI, broadcast executive; b. Sääksmäki, Finland, Feb. 25, 1943; s. Matti Adrian and Elin Alexandra (Koivula) A.; m. Mari Annikki Lautamatti, Dec. 29, 1978. PhD, U. Turku, Finland, 1976. Sr. asst. ethnology U. Jyväskylä, Finland, 1974-76; acting prof. folklore U. Turku, 1976-79; dir. Finnish Film Archive, Helsinki, 1979-89; dir. radio Finnish Broadcasting Co., Helsinki, 1990-94, dir. programming, 1994—; advanced scholar Acad. Finland, 1987-88; adj. prof. comparative religion U. Helsinki, 1978—; adj. prof. cultural anthropology U. Jyväskylä, 1979—. Author: Religion of the Slaves, 1976, Defence of Madness, 1988, Serfs and Masters, 1979, Guardians of the Universe, 1988. Mem. State Rsch. Coun., Helsinki, 1978-82, Ctrl. Commn. of the Acad. Finland, 1980-85, chmn. standing com. for the humanities, 1980-85; chmn. Lahti Internat. Writers Reunion, Finland, 1981-89; chmn. Finnish Nat. Commn. for UNESCO, 1999—. Office: YLE, PO Box 58, 00024 Yleisradio Finland

AL-HOMOUD, MOHAMMAD SAAD, architectural engineer, educator, consultant; b. Abha, Saudi Arabia, Jan. 22, 1964; children: Fatimah, Abdullah, Saad, Ruwaidah. BS with honors Archtl. Engring., King Fahd U. Petrol. and Minerals, Dhahran, Saudi Arabia, 1986; MS in Archtl. Engring., Pa. State U., 1989; PhD, Tex. A&M U., 1994. Asst. prof. archtl. engring. King Fahd U. Petroleum and Minerals, Dhahran, 1994—, coord. profl. devel. short courses, 1995—, asst. prof. archtl. engring., 1994—, coord. profl. devel. short courses, 1995—. Contbr. articles to profl. jours. Ednl. officer Saudi students house TAMU, College Station, Tex., 1991, pres. 1992. Mem. ASHRAE, Assn. Energy Engrs., Internat. Facility Mgmt. Assn., Archtl. Engring. Inst. (founding mem.). Home and Office: KFUPM, PO Box 689, Dhahran 31261, Saudi Arabia

ALHOZAB, ADEL ABDULLA, dean, educator; b. Alhassa, Saudi Arabia, June 6, 1958. BSc, King Faisal U., Alhassa, 1981; MSc, U. Ariz., 1985; PhD, Oreg. State U., 1990. Cert. univ. prof. Asst. prof. King Faisal U., Alhassa, 1990-99, chmn. dept. animal sci., 1995-97, dean libr. affairs, 1997—. Contbr. articles to sci. jours. Mem. Internat. Goat Assn., Soc. for Study of Reproduction. Fax: 009663-5801247. E-mail: ahozab@kfu.edu.sa. Home: PO Box 55016, Alhassa 31982, Saudi Arabia Office: King Faisal U, Dept Animal Sci, Alhassa 31982, Saudi Arabia

AL-HUSSEINI, AMEEN ABDULLAH, automobile trading company executive; b. Sana'a, Yemen, July 28, 1971; s. Abdullah Hamoud and Fatima Mohammed (Raghib) Al-H.; m. Kawkab Ahmed Jubary, Sept. 5, 1996; children: Hasna Ameen, Fayrooz. Student, Sch. Internat. Tng., Brattleboro, Vt., 1990-91, Boston U., 1991, Sanaa Univ., Sana'a, 1993. Acad. dir. Yemen Students Union, Sana'a, 1987; import mgr. A.H.A., Sana'a, 1993-94; asst. gen. mgr. Volkswagen, Sana'a, 1994-97; gen. mgr. Sons Corp., Sana'a, 1997-98; founder Ameen Trade Co., Sana'a, 1995—. Editor, contbr. Yemen Times. Dir. rels. Nat. Com. Yemen, 1994—. Avocations: tennis, writing, watching CNN. Home: University St, Box 14540, San'a Yemen Office: Sons Corp, Zubairy St Box 14540, Sana'a Yemen

ALI, AHMAD MOHAMED, banker; b. Medina Munawarah, Saudi Arabia, 1934; m. Ghada Mahmood Masri; 4 children. BA, Cairo U., 1957; MA, U. Mich., 1962; DPA, SUNY, Albany, 1967. Dir. Sci. and Islamic Inst., Aden, 1958-59; dep. rector King Abdul Aziz U., Jeddah, Saudi Arabia, 1967-72; dep. min. edn. for tech. affairs Govt. of Saudi Arabia, 1972-75; sec. gen. Muslin World League, Makkah al-Mukarramah, 1993-95; pres. Islamic Devel. Bank, Jeddah, 1975-92, 95—, also chmn. bd. dirs.; mem. adminstrv. bd. Saudi Credit Bank. Contbr. articles to profl. jours. Bd. dirs. coun. King AbdulAziz U., King Saud U., Riyadh, Saudi Arabia, Oil and Mineral U., Dhahran, Saudi Arabia, Islamic U., Medina, Saudi Arabia, Imam Mohamed Ben Saud U., Riyadh; mem. advminstrv. bd. Saudi Fund for Devel. Avocations: cycling, walking. Office: Islamic Development Bank, PO Box 5925, Jeddah 21432, Saudi Arabia also: care Muslim World League, PO Box 537-358, Makkah Saudia Arabia*

ALI, AHMED, physicist; b. Saharanpur, India, Apr. 6, 1946; s. Akhtar and Jameela (Saeed) A. MS, Karachi U., 1966; MPhil, Islamabad U., 1968, PhD, 1971. Rsch. fellow Internat. Ctr. for Theoretical Physics, Trieste, Italy, 1972-73; assoc. Stevens Inst. of Tech., Hoboken, N.J., 1973-75; Alexander v. Humboldt fellow U. Hamburg, Germany, 1975-76, rsch. asst., 1976-78; rsch. assoc. CERN, Geneva, 1983-84, 93-94; staff assoc. ICTP, Trieste, 1991-93; staff mem. DESY, Hamburg, Germany, 1978—; dir. Internat. Nathiagali Coll. on Physics and Contemporary Needs, Pakistan, 1995—; mem. internat. adv. com. Particle Data Group Lawrence Berkely Lab., 1995-99; vis. prof. dept. physics UCLA, 1988; prof. Ludwig-Maximillian U., 1989-90, Hamburg U., 2000—. Editor European Physical Jour., 1999—; contbr. articles to profl. jours. Avocations: tennis, cricket. E-mail: ali@theopc4.desy.de. Office: DESY, Notkestrasse 85, D-22603 Hamburg Germany

ALI, DJAMA MOHAMED, bank executive. Gov. Banque Nationale de Djibouti. Office: Banque Nationale de Djibouti, PO Box 2118, Djibouti Djibouti

ALI, EMADADEEN M., engineering educator; b. Riyadh, Saudi Arabia, Nov. 11, 1961; s. Mostafa K. Ali and Naiema M. Sultan; m. Naiema B. Mohammad, Aug. 8, 1987; children: Ahmed, Duha, Shatha, Omar. BSc, King Saud U., Riyadh, 1986; MSc, U. Pitts., 1989; PhD, U. Md., 1996. Cert. in engring. Tchg. asst. King Saud U., Riyadh, 1986-96, asst. prof., 1996-2000, prof., 2000—; cons. Saudi Arabian Co. for Basic Industries, Riyadh, 1997—. Contbr. sci. papers to profl. jours. Scholar King Saud U., 1986; rsch. grantee King Abdul Aziz City for Sci. and Tech., 1998, Saudi Arabian Bask Industries Co., 1998. Avocations: soccer, volleyball, computer programming. Fax: (9661) 467-8770. Office: King Saud U, Chem Eng Dept PO Box 800, Riyadh 11421, Saudi Arabia

ALI, HAIDER, research scientist; b. Chuadanga, Bangladesh, Jan. 3, 1963; s. Buddhu Shaik and Gadari Bibi; m. Lilima Arshad, Mar. 7, 1991; children: ahmed Zubaer, Ihmed Imtiaz. BSc, U. Dhaka, Bangladesh, 1987, MSc, 1989; postgrad., Toyohashi U. Tech., Japan, 1996—. Registered profl. engr. Sci. officer Atomic Energy Commn., Bangladesh, 1990-95; asst. prof. Shahjalal U. Sci. and Tech., Bangladesh, 1995—. Author rsch. papers in field. Rsch. grantee Hori Found., Japan, 1998-99. Mem. Inst. Electronics, Info. and Comm. Engrs. (student mem.), Bangladesh Computer Soc. (assoc.). Avocation: swimming. E-mail: haider@mmip.tutics.tut.ac.up. Home: AK Rd, Chuadanga, Bangladesh 7200, Bangladesh Office: Toyohashi U Tech, Tempaku-cho, Toyohashi 441-8580, Japan

ALI, KHAYYAM, SR., elementary education educator. BA in Econs., CUNY, 1982, MEd, 1993; M Edn. Adminstrn., Coll. New Rochelle, 1999. Tchr. N.Y.C. Bd. Edn., Bronx, 1986-97, Hempstead (N.Y.) Pub. Schs., 1997—; radio talk show guest spkr.; motivational spkr. Editor: Ten Girls on the Write Way to College, Doing the Write Thing; playwright: A Fast Life, Lord Give Me Strength; editor, contbr. to profl. publs.; inventor pneumatically controlled toilet seat and flusher.

ALI, KHWAJA MOHAMMED, aeronautical engineer; b. Lahore, Punjab, Pakistan, June 13, 1948; came to U.S., 1989; s. Khwaja Mohammed and Rashida Savi; m. Yasmin Khan, Aug. 7, 1976; children: Mehvash, Babar. B Aero. Engring., U. Karachi, Pakistan, 1970; MBA in Aviation Mgmt., Dowling Coll. Registered profl. engr., Pakistan. Supr. Pakistan Internat. Airlines, Karachi, 1970-74, aircraft engr., 1974-75, devel. engr., 1975-78; sta. engr. Pakistan Internat. Airlines, Islamabad, Pakistan, 1979-82; programs engr. Pakistan Internat. Airlines, Karachi, 1982-89; maintenance mgr. Pakistan Internat. Airlines, N.Y.C., 1989-93; maintenance engr. Pakistan Internat Airlines, 1993-94; maintenance programs engr. Emirates Airlines, Dubai, 1995-97; prin. engr. maintenance program engring. Boeing, 1997-2000, regional dir. mktg., 2000—; project advisor for engring. univ. students on Hovercraft and Cockpit Armour Protection. Contbr. articles to profl. publs. Bd. dirs. Adventure Found. Pakistan, Karachi, 1986-88; pres. Marine Club, Karachi, 1988-89; leader Indus River Expedition, Pakistan, 1978, Swat White River Expedition, Pakistan, 1981. Fellow Instn. Engrs. (vice chmn. 1984-89); mem. AIAA (sr. mem.), Royal Aero. Soc. (aero. program sec. 1985-89), Delta Mu Delta. Islam. Achievements include design and fabrication of single seater aircraft. Home: 4303 NE 6th Pl Renton WA 98059-4741 Office: The Boeing Co PO Box 3707 MC21-33 Seattle WA 98124

ALI, MAHJABEEN, librarian; b. Karachi, Pakistan, Oct. 30, 1972; d. Umer Draz and Mateena Begum. BA, Govt. Coll. for Women Saudabad, Karachi, 1995; BLS, Karachi U., 1996, MLS, 1997. Libr. SPDC, Karachi, 1997—. Mem. Pakistan Libr. Assn. Home: R-400 Pak Kausar Town Ext, Karachi 75080, Pakistan Office: SPDC, 15 Maqbool Coop Housing Soc, Karachi 775400, Pakistan

ALI, MD MOHSIN, radiation chemist; b. Rajshahi, Bangladesh, Nov. 30, 1956; s. Md Shahabuddin and Mst Fatema Khatun; m. Mst Mahfuza Khatun, May 10, 1988; children: Mushfiq, Shahriyar. HSC, Bhawanigonj Coll., Bangladesh, 1974; BS with hons., Rajshahi U., Bangladesh, 1979; MS, Rajshahi U., 1980; D Sci., Hiroshima U., Japan, 1993. Scientific officer Bangladesh Atomic Energy Commn., 1984-91, sr. scientific officer, 1991—. Recipient fellowship Internat. Atomic Energy Agy., China, 1986, Royal Soc. London, 1996; scholarship Govt. Japan, 1989. Mem. N.Y. Acad. Scis., Radiation Soc. Japan, Bangladesh Atomic Energy Sci. Assn. Avocations: travel. Office: Inst Nuclear Sci & Tech, AERE Savar PO Box 3787, Dhaka Bangladesh

ALI, MOHAMMAD SABER, fertilizer company executive; b. Rajshahi, Bangladesh, Sept. 1, 1944; s. Mohammad Wazed and Sofia Begum A.; m. Meherun Nesa Saber, Nov. 30, 1986; children: Sadia, Monkasir. BSc in Chem. Engring., Bangladesh U. Engring. & Tech., 1968. Mng. dir. Urea Fertilizer Factory, Narsingdi, 1990-93; dir. ops. Karnaphuli Fertilizer Co., Chittagong, 1993—. Avocation: stamp collecting. Home: Islam Bagh, Dinajpur Bangladesh Office: Karnaphuli Fertilizer Co, GPO Box 1010, Chittagong 4000, Bangladesh

ALI, MOHAMMED, chemistry educator; b. Kurikhera, India, July 5, 1947; s. Mohammed Siddique and Hafijan Begum; m. Nooran-nisha Begum, June 10, 1972; children: Shahnaz, Shaheen. BSc with honors, Aligarh (India) Muslim U., 1970, MSc in Chemistry, 1972, MPhil in Chemistry, 1974, PhD, 1976; DSc, Internat. Open U., Sri Lanka, 1997. Rsch. scholar Aligarh Muslim U., 1972-77; lectr. Jamia Millia U., New Delhi, 1977-79; scientists pool Coun. Sci. and Indsl. Rsch., New Delhi, 1979-82; scientist Reg. Rsch. Lab., Jammu Tawi, India, 1982-90; asst. prof. Hamdard U., New Delhi, 1990—. Author: Textbook of Pharmacognosy, 1994, Textbook of Pharmaceutical Organic Chemistry, 1995, Textbook of Pharmaceutical Inorganic Chemistry, 1996, Practical Pharmaceutical Chemistry, 1997, Hospital and Clinical Pharmacy, 1997, Dictionary of Pharmacy, 1998, Vigyanic Jigyasa, 1998, Pharmacy Entrance Guide, 1998, Techniques in Triterpenoid Identification, 1998; co-author: Drug Store and business Management, 1996; editl. sec. Oriental Jour. Chemistry, 1984-90; contbr. some 150 articles to profl. jours.; presenter at confs. Mem. Indian Assn. for Study of Traditional Asian Medicine (exec. com. 1996—), CSIR Scientists Welfare Soc. (exec. com. 1987-89), Saifi Assn. for Higher Edn. and Tng. (pres. 1992—), Indian Pharma. Assn. (life), Indian Chem. Soc., Muslim Assn. for Advancement of Sci. (hon.), Indian Soc. Pharmacognosy (life), Assn. Pharm. Tchrs. of India (life), Indian Sci. Congress. Avocations: plantation, walking, social reform, collecting books. Office: Jamia Hamdard U Pharmacy, Sch PO Hamdard Nagar, New Delhi 110 062, India

ALI, SHOWKAT, economist, educator; b. Kayerpara, Chowgacha, Bangladesh, Aug. 15, 1953; came to the U.S., 1981; s. Ahmed and Hamida Begum Ali; m. Ruhina Tasmin, Aug. 31, 1965; children: Farzana Tasmin, Ibrahim Ahmed Showkat. BA with honors, U. Chittagong, Bangladesh, 1977; diploma, Columbia U., 1981; MA in Econs., CUNY, N.Y.C., 1986; PhD in Econs., Fordham U., 1996; cert. fin. engr., Poly. U. Adj. asst. prof. Fordham U., N.Y.C., 1993—, CUNY, 1994—; cons. economist Voice of Am., Washington, 1998; chmn. Fast Svcs. Internat. Mem. Am. Econ. Assn., Assn. Fin. Engrs., Global Assn. for Risk Analysis Profls., Bangladesh Journalists and Writers Assn. N.Am. (pres.). Avocations: human rights, religious rights, womens rights, immigrant rights. E-mail: showkat3@aol.com. Home: 111 16th St # 1 Brooklyn NY 11215-4710

ALI, SYED ABID, chemist; b. Karachi, Sindh, Pakistan, Aug. 1, 1966; s. Syed Shakir Ali and Zarina Bano. BS, U. Karachi, 1989; MS, Islamabad (Pakistan) U., 1991; PhD, U. Karachi, 1997. Cert. scientist, Pakistan. Sr. rsch. fellow Internat. Ctr. for Chem. Scis. U. Karachi, 1992-97; postdoctoral fellow Physiol. Chem. Inst. U. Tuebingen, Germany, 1997-99; vis. scientist Daresbury Lab., Warrington, Cheshire, Eng., 1997-98. Contbr. sci. articles to profl. jours. Deutscher Akademischer Austauschdienst rsch. scholar, 1996, Coun. for the Ctrl. Lab. of the Rsch. Couns. scholar, 1997. Mem. Internat. Soc. Neurosci., Chem. Soc. Pakistan, Pakistan Soc. Biochemistry and Molecular Biology, Am. Chem. Soc. Muslim. Avocations: music, poetry, soccer, reading books. E-mail: saali66@hotmail.com. Home: R-25 Bl 10A Manin Rashid Rd, Gulshan-e-Iqbal, Karachi Sindh Pakistan Office: U Tuebingen Phys Chem Inst, oppe-Seyller-Str 4, D-72076 Tuebingen Germany

ALI, SYED AHMED, chemical engineer, researcher; b. Hyderabad, India, Aug. 8, 1959; s. Syed Ameer and Zahra Begum (Bahauddin) A.; m. Anjum Waheed, Aug. 9, 1987; children: Amjad, Akram, Zahra, Ajmal. B of Tech., Osmania U., Hyderabad, 1981; MS, King Fahd U. Petroleum and Minerals, Dhahran, Saudi Arabia, 1984; PhD, Hokkaido U., Sapporo, Japan, 1997. Rsch. asst. dept. chem. engring. King Fahd U. Petroleum and Minerals, 1981-84; engr. II Rsch. Inst., King Fahd U. Petroleum and Minerals, 1984-90, engr. I, 1990-96, rsch. engr., 1996—; project mgr. numerous rsch. projects; lectr. in field. Contbr. articles to profl. jours.; patentee in field. Recipient Distinctive Performance award Osmania U., Hyderabad, 1981. Mem. Am. Chem. Soc. (Saudi Arabia chpt.). Avocations: music, table tennis. Home: King Fahd Univ, PO Box 341, Dhahran 31261, Saudi Arabia Office: King Fahd U, Rsch Inst, Dhahran 31261, Saudi Arabia

ALI, SYED SAEED, chemist, researcher; b. Sindh, Pakistan, Sept. 10, 1962; s. Syed Mehfooz Ali and Hafiz Jamal; m. Farida Naz Syed, Oct. 25, 1999. BSc, U. Sindh, Jamshoro, Pakistan, 1982, PhD, 1999; MSc, U. Karachi, Pakistan, 1985. Chemist 7-Up Lab., Kotri, Pakistan, 1986; med. rep. Fisons Pharm. Co., Hyderabad, Pakistan, 1986-90; med. info. officer Merck Pharm. Co., Hyderabad, 1990-91; lectr. in chemistry Edn. Dept. of Govt. of Sindh, 1991—. Contbr. articles to profl. jours. Sec. gen. Muslim Student Orgn., Cookeville, Tenn., 1999, Sindh Lectr. and Prof. Assn., Hyderabad, 1996. Mem. Am. Chem. Soc., Pakistan Chem. Soc. Home: H#2455 A-114, Hirabad, 71000 Sindh Pakistan Office: Govt Coll Hyderbad, Kali Mori, 71000 Hyderabad Pakistan

ALI, HER MAJESTY WIJDAN, Princess of Jordan, art historian; b. Baghdad, Iraq, 1939; d. Sherif Fawaz Muhana and Sherifa Nafaa Jamil; m. His Royal Heir Prince Ali Bin Nayef, 1966; 4 children. BA in History, Beirut U. Coll., 1961; PhD in History of Art, U. London, 1993. 1st woman with Jordanian Fgn. Svc., 1962; 1st woman to represent Jordan UN Gen. Assembly, N.Y.C., 1962; bd. govs. Internat. Ctr. Islamic Studies, London; mem. Arab Thought Forum, Amman; mem. World Affairs Coun., Amman. Exhibited in group shows in London, West Berlin, Washington D.C., Madrid, Karachi, Assilah-Morocco, Tunis, Moscow, Amman; author: Taarif Bil Fan al-Islami, 1988, Contemporary Art from the Islamic World, 1989, The Status of Islamic Art in the Twentieth Century in Muqarnas, vol. 9, 1992, An Overview of Arab Art in Forces of Change: Artists of the Arab World, 1994, Modern Art in Jordan, 1996, Modern Islamic Art: Development and Continuity, 1997, Waht is Islamic Art, 1998, Arab Contribution to Islamic Art, 1999; editor, contbr.: Problems of Art Education in the Islamic World, 1991, The Dictionary of Art, 1996, Development of Islamic Art, 1998, Challenges of Peace Support Into the 21st Century, 1999; editor Jour. Royal Inst. Religious Studies, 1998. Bd. govs. Internat. Child's Coun., 1984-98, Internat. Ctr. Islamic Studies, London, 1984-98; bd. dirs. McMullen Mus., Boston, 1996; v.p. Internat. Coun. Philosophy and Humanistic Studies, 1997; mem. adv. bd. Internat. Congress Asian and N. African Studies, Budapest, 1997. Mem. Royal Soc. Fine Arts. Avocations: horseback riding, swimming, traveling to exotic places. Office: PO Box 2296, Amman Jordan

ALIA, VALERIE, humanities educator, writer; b. N.Y.C., Dec. 20, 1942; d. Julius Abraham and Bertha (Fenyves) Graber; m. Sal P. Restivo, 1967 (div. 1984); children: David Owen Restivo, Daniel Olam Restivo; m. Pete Steffens, 1998. BA, U. Cin., 1965; MA, Mich. State U., 1967; PhD, York U., Toronto, Ont., 1989. Dance critic Boston Herald Traveller, 1971-72; dance and music critic Times Union, Knickerbocker News, Albany, N.Y., 1974-79; reporter, photographer Rutland (Vt.) Herald, 1979-81; instr. U. Toronto, summer 1989; broadcast coord., prof. U. Western Ont., London, 1989-96; Disting. prof. Can. culture Western Wash. U., Bellingham, 1996-98; sr. lectr. journalism, media and cultural studies U. Sunderland, England, 1999—, reader in media ethics and culture, 2000—; assoc. Scott Polar Rsch. Inst. U. Cambridge, 2000—; mem. Ctr. for Rsch. in Media and Cultural Studies, Sunderland, 2000—; cons. faculty of environ. studies York U., 1987-88, Inst. Environ. Rsch., Toronto, Yukon Govt., Whitehorse, 1990-91, Royal Commn. on Electoral Reform and Party Financing, Can., 1990-92, Native Computer Comm. Network; mem. awards panel NSF, Washington, 1997-99; rsch. assoc. Ctr. Can.-Am. Studies, Fairhaven Coll. and Western Wash. U., Bellingham, 1998-99; spkr. Birkbeck Coll., London, 2000. Author: Names, Numbers & Northern People, 1994, Deadlines & Diversity, 1996, Un/covering the North, 1999. spkr., panelist U. Haifa, Israel, 1997; spkr. Investiture of Fed. Judge Susan P. Graber, Portland, Oreg., 1998. Strategic grantee in media ethics Social Scis. and Humanities Rsch. Coun. of Can., 1994-96, Workshop grantee Western Wash. U. Diversity Fund, 1998, Ethics/Values Studies and Arctic Social Sci. Program grantee NSF, 1998-99; grantee in aboriginal media Can. High Commn., 2000—; rsch. fellow Fairhaven Coll., Belllingham, 1998-99. Mem. Can. Fedn. for Humanities Women's Caucus (co-chair 1994-96), The Writers' Union of Can., Native News Network of Can. (founding, bd. dirs. 1990-95, mem. adv. bd.), Arctic Inst. N.Am., Internat. Arctic Social Scis. Assn. (founding), Internat. Coun. Onomastic Scis., Humanities and Social Scis. Fedn. Can. Women's Issues Network. Jewish. Avocations: travel, gardening. E-mail: valerie.alia@sunderland.ac.uk. Office: U Sunderland Sch Arts Design Media, Forster Bldg Chester Rd, Sunderland SR1 3SD, United Kingdom

ALIAS, LUIS JOSE, mathematician, educator, researcher; b. Molina de Segura, Murcia, Spain, Mar. 21, 1967; s. Luis Josafat and Purificacion (Linares) A.; m. Maria Del Carmen Candel, May 21, 1994; children: Carmelila, Esperanza. BSc, U. Murcia, 1990, MSc, 1991, PhD, 1994. Asst. prof. math. U. Murcia, 1993-96, prof. math., 1996—, sec. dept. math., 1998, vice-dean fac. math., 1998—; postdoctoral fellow U. Durham, Eng., 1994-95. Reviewer Math. Revs., U.S., 1996—, Zentralblatt für Math., Germany, 1996—; contbr. articles to profl. jours. Recipient First Nat. award in math. Spanish Ministry Edn. and Sci., 1991, Extraordinary Bachelor award U. Murcia, 1991, Extraordinary Doctorate award, 1995. Mem. London Math. Soc., Real Soc. Math. Española, Am. Math. Soc. Roman Catholic. Avocations: sports, reading, playing with children, walking. Office: U Murcia, Dept Math, 30100 Espinardo Murcia Spain

AL-IBRAHIM, ABDULRAHMAN MOHAMMED, research educator; b. Taif, Saudi Arabia, June 2, 1964; s. Mohammed Abdulrahman and Haya Nasser (Al-Rashid) Al-I.; m. Sara Abdulaziz Al-Rashid; children: Reem, Ruaa, Tariq, Mohammad,. BSc in Mech. Engring., King Abdulaziz U., Jeddah, Saudi Arabia, 1986; MSc in Mech. Engring., U. Wis., 1991, PhD in Mech. Engring., 1997. Project mgr. Energy Rsch. Inst., King Abdulaziz City for Sci. and Tech., Riyadh, Saudi Arabia, 1986-87, asst. rsch. prof., 1997—, asst. dir. info. internat. cooperation dept., 1998—. Contbr. articles to profl. jours. Govs. Energy fellow State of Wis., 1995. Muslim. E-mail: aibrahim@kacst.edu.sa. Office: KACST Prince Abdullah Rd, PO Box 6086, 11442 Riyadh Saudi Arabia

ALICIAS, EDUARDO REZONABLE, JR., education educator, researcher; b. Vigan, Ilocos Sur, The Philippines, Aug. 10, 1945; s. Eduardo Ferido Sr. and Martina Refuerzo (Rezonable) A.; m. Teresita Siazon Raquepo, Dec. 24, 1968; children: Lillian, Irma, Eugene. BS in Edn., Divine Word Coll. Vigan, 1967; MA in Edn., Mariano Marcos State U., Laoag City, The Philippines, 1977; EdD, U. of the Philippines, Quezon City, 1981; diploma of edn., U. London, 1986. Tchr. Divine Word Coll. Vigan, 1968-69; tchr. Immaculate Conception Minor Sem., Vigan, 1969-71, prin., 1971-77; instr. U. No. Philippines, Vigan, 1977-78; instr. U. of the Philippines, Quezon City, 1979-81, asst. prof., 1981-88, assoc. prof., 1988—, Melquiades Castro chair ednl. adminstrn., 1988-89; cons. Bur. of Nonformal Edn., Dept. Edn., Culture & Sports, Metro Manila, 1989-91, Bur. of Secondary Edn., 1992—, Alicias Data Svcs., Quezon City, 1993—; founder, pres. Gasat Devel. Corp., 1999—. Author: Data Organization and Analysis in a Computer Environment, 1995, 97, Classroom Observation and Related Fallacies: Lessons for Educational Administration, 1996, Humor and Madness, 1997; founding editor The Search Jour., 1989. Grantee Brit. Coun., London, 1985-86; Guiness World Records record holder for longest preface relative to total book length. Mem. Soc. Ednl. Adminstrs. and Rschrs. (founder, pres. 1988—), U. of the Philippines Rsch. Orgn. for Better Edn. (founder). Roman Catholic. Avocations: reading, writing, lecturing, farming, computing. Home: UP Campus, AB4-201 Hardin Ng Rosas, Diliman Quezon City The Philippines Office: Coll of Edn, Univ of the Philippines, Diliman Quezon City The Philippines

ALIGIA, ARMANDO ANGEL, physicist, researcher; b. Buenos Aires, Argentina, July 7, 1955; s. Armando Giuseppe and Catalina (Diez) A.; m. Ana Gladis Rojas; children: Marcos, Ruben, Adrian, Javier. Tech. in chem., Otto Krause, Buenos Aires, 1968-73; student, Univ. Buenos Aires, 1974-75; M in physics, Inst. Balseiro, Bariloche, 1979, PhD in physics, 1984. Dir. of theoretical divsn. Centre At, Bariloche, 1994-96; prof. physics Inst. Balseiro, Bariloche, 1989—; staff mem. Centro Atomico Bariloche, Bariloche, 1983—. Contbr. numerous articles to profl. jours. Mem. Movement to Socialism, Bariloche, 1982-90. With Ground Army, 1975-76. Recipient several research grants, 1990—; Alexander Von Humboldt fellowship, 1985-87. Avocations: sports, kayak, jogging, soccer, swimming, bicycle, triatlon. Office: Centro Atomico, 8400 Bariloche Argentina

ALIJAH, FARHANG ALEXANDER, chemistry educator; b. Burnham, Eton, Eng., Oct. 11, 1958; s. Feroze Muzaffar and Christiane (Schubert) A. Diploma in chemistry, U. Bielefeld, Germany, 1984, Dr.Rer.Nat., 1988, Habilitation, 1996. Postdoctoral rsch. fellow U. Strathclyde, Glasgow, Scotland, 1988-90; postdoctoral rsch. fellow U. Bielefeld, 1990-96, pvt. docent, 1996—; vis. prof. U. de Coimbra, Portugal, 1999. Contbr. articles to profl. jours. Avocations: classical music, piano, theater, budo. Home: Schlosshofstr 108, 33615 Bielefeld Germany Office: U Bielefeld Dept Chemistry, Universitaesstr, 33615 Bielefeld Germany

ALIKHANI, HOSSEIN, oil industry executive, researcher, writer; b. Tehran, Iran, Dec. 22, 1944; arrived in Cyprus, 1979; s. Habib and Sonat (Yousefi) A.; m. Jula Farmarzi, Sept. 21, 1971; children: Helia, Borna, Dana. BA in Advanced Lit., Tehran (Iran) U., 1975. Sales mgr. Iran Book Mgr., Tehran, 1973-75; mng. dir. Iran Book Mgr., 1975-79, Polygon Co. Ltd., Tehran, 1980—; dir. Ctr. Bus. Studies, Eng., 1994; pres. Ctr. World Dialogue, Cyprus, 1997. Author: The Claw of the Eagle, 1995. Mem. Am. Soc. Internat. Law, Iran Assn. Energy Econs., Acad. Polit. Sci. Avocations: reading, painting. Home: 14 Queen Olga St, 2001 Nicosia Cyprus Office: Polygon Co Ltd Apt 202, 20 Stassicratous str, 1065 Nicosia Cyprus

ALIKI (ALIKI LIACOURAS BRANDENBERG), author, illustrator children's books; b. Wildwood Crest, N.J., Sept. 3; d. James Peter and Stella (Lagakos) Liacouras; m. Franz Brandenberg, Mar. 15, 1957; children: Jason, Alexa Demetria. Grad., Mus. Coll. Art, 1951. Muralist, commercial artist Phila. and N.Y.C., 1951-56. Author, illustrator Story of William Tell, 1960, My Five Senses, 1962, My Hands, 1962, The Wish Workers, 1962, The Story of Johnny Appleseed (Jr. Lit. Guild, World of Reading Readers' Choice award Silver Burdett & Ginn 1989), George and the Cherry Tree, 1964, The Story of William Penn (Jr. Lit. Guild), A Weed is a Flower: The Life of George Washington Carver, 1965, Keep Your Mouth Closed, Dear (Omar's Book award 1986), Three Gold Pieces: A Greek Folk Tale (Boys' Clubs Am. Jr. Book award 1968), New Year's Day, 1967, (editor) Hush Little Baby: A Folk Lullaby, 1968, My Visit to the Dinosaurs, 1969, The Eggs: A Greek Folk Tale, 1969, Diogenes: The Story of the Greek Philosopher, 1969, Fossils Tell of Long Ago, 1972, June 7, 1972, The Long Lost Coelacanth and Other Living Fossils, 1973, Green Grass and White Milk, 1974, Go Tell Aunt Rhody, 1974, At Mary Bloom's (Am. Inst. Graphic Arts Children's Book Show, Jr. Lit. Guild), 1976, Children's Book Coun. for Children's Book Showcase), Corn Is Maize: The Gift of the Indians (Children's Sci. Book award N.Y. Acad. Scis.), The Many Lives of Benjamin Franklin, 1977, Wild and Woolly Mammoths, 1977, rev. edit., 1995, The Twelve Months, 1978, Mummies Made in Egypt (Silver Slate Pencil award Dutch Children's Book Coun., Garden State (N.J.) Children's Book award), The Two of Them, 1979, Digging Up Dinosaurs, 1981, We Are Best Friends, 1982, Use Your Head, Dear, 1983, A Medieval Feast, 1983, Feelings (Prix du Livre pour Enfants Geneva), Dinosaurs Are Different, 1985, How a Book Is Made, 1986, Jack and Jake, 1986, Overnight at Mary Bloom's, 1987, Dinosaur Bones, 1988, King's Day: Louis XIV of France, 1989, My Feet, 1990, Manners, 1990, Christmas Tree Memories, 1991, I'm Growing, 1992, Milk: From Cow to Carton, 1992, Communication, 1993, My Visit to the Aquarium, 1993, The Gods and Godesses of Olympus, 1994, Tabby, 1995, Best Friends Together Again, 1995, Hello, Good-Bye, 1996, Those Summers, 1996, My Visit to the Zoo, 1997; illustrator: Who Lives Here?, 1961, Cathy Is Company, 1961, Listening Walk, 1961, What's for Lunch, Charley?, 1961, What Can I Buy?, 1962, A Book to Begin On: Alaska, 1962, The Lazy Little Zulu, 1962, This Is the House Where Jack Lives, 1962, The Horse That Liked Sandwiches, 1962, Archmedes and His Wonderful Discoveries, 1962, Computers at Your Service, 1962, New Ways in Math, 1962, Television and How It Works, 1962, Electricity in Your Life, 1963, Mister Moonlight and Omar, 1963, That's Good, That's Bad, 1963, Bees and Beelines, 1964, More New Ways in Math, 1964, Sherlock on the Trail, 1964, Everything Has a Size, 1964, Everything Has a Shape, 1964, One Day It Rained Cats and Dogs, 1965, Five Dolls in a House, 1965, Is It Blue as a Butterfly?, 1965, Mother's Day, 1965, I Want to Read!, 1965, Is That A Happy Hippomatus?, 1966, Everything Has a Shape and Everything Has a Size, 1966, Five Dolls in the Snow, 1967, Five Dolls and the Monkey, 1967, Five Dolls and Their Friends, 1968, Five Dolls and the Duke, 1968, Mrs. Neverbody's Recipes, 1968, At Home: A Visit in Four Languages, 1968, Oh Lord, I Wish I Was a Buzzard, 1968, Birds at Night, 1968, Weighing and Balancing, 1970, On the Other Side of the River, 1972, Ears and Tails and Common Sense: More Stories from the Caribbean, 1974, Averages, 1975, Evolution, 1987, Mommy's Briefcase, 1995; illustrator books by Franz Brandenberg: I Once Knew a Man, 1970, Fresh Cider and Pie, 1973, No School Today!, 1975, A Secret for Grandmother's Birthday, 1975, A Robber! A Robber!, 1976, I Wish I Was Sick, Too!, 1976, What Can You Make of It?, 1977, Nice New Neighbors, 1977, A Picnic, Hurrah!, 1978, Six New Students, 1978, Everyone Ready?, 1979, It's Not My Fault!, 1980, Leo and Emily, 1981, Leo and Emily's Big Idea, 1982, Aunt Nina and Her Nephews and Nieces, 1983, Aunt Nina's Visit, 1984, Leo and Emily and the Dragon, 1984, The Hit of the Party, 1985, Cock-a-Doodle-Doo, 1986, What's Wrong with a Van?, 1987, Aunt Nina, Good Night!, 1989; Marianthe's Story: Painted Words & Spoken Memories, 1998 (Double Book, Jane Addams Peace prize 1999), William Shakespeare and the Globe, 1999 (Boston Globe-Horn Book Honor Book 1999), All By Myself, 2000, One Little Spoonful, 2000. Recipient citation Drexel U. and Free Libr. Phila., 1991, recognition for outstanding contbns. in field lit. Pa. Sch. Libr. Assn., 1991. Avocations: gardening, theater, museums, travelling, reading. Office: Greenwillow Books 1350 Avenue Of The Americas New York NY 10019-4702

ALIMARDONOV, MURODALI, bank executive; b. Hissor Region, Tajikstan, Mar. 20, 1960; m. Alimardovna Zulaiho; children: Abduali, Lutphiddin, Marziya, Zilola, Zaitunat. Grad., Tajik State U., 1983. Economist, credit divsn. Frunze's br. State Bank Duchanbe, Tajikstan, 1983-85; sr. economist, head Credit Divsn. of Hissar Region, Tajikstan, 1985-88; dep. gov. Joint-Stock Comml. Bank Agroprombank, Hissar Region, 1992; gov. Shahrinav's br. Joint-Stock Comml. Bank Agroprombank, Shahrinav Region, 1992; gov. bd. Joint-Stock Comml. Bank Agroprombank Shark, Dushanbe City, 1992-94; chmn. Nat. Bank of Tajikstan, Dushanbe, 1994—. Office: Nat Bank of Tajikistan, ul Rudaki 23/2, Dushanbe 734004, Tajikistan*

ALIMBAROVA, LUDMILA MIKHAYLOVNA, virologist, researcher; b. Moscow, Aug. 13, 1966; d. Mikhail Stepanovich and Anna Alexandrovna (Strukova) A. MD with honors, I.M. Sechenov 1st Med. Inst., Moscow, 1989; PhD in Med. Sci., D.I. Ivanovsky Inst. Virology, Moscow, 1994. Jr. rsch. scientist Inst. Virology Russian Acad. Med. Sci., Moscow, 1989-94, sr. rsch. scientist, 1994—; med. sci. cons. indsl. enterprise, Moscow, 1995—. Contbr. articles to profl. jours. Grantee Russian Acad. Sci., 1997. Mem. Scientific Soc. Virologists (Moscow). Avocation: music. Office: DI Ivanovsky Inst Virology, Gamalei Str, 16, 123098 Moscow Russia

ALIMOV, ALEXANDER, zoologist, researcher, science director; b. Leningrad, Russia, Nov. 9, 1933; s. Fyodor and Vera (Rodziontkovskaya) A.; m. Lora Chigirik, May 17, 1958; 1 child, Igor Alimov. Grad., Leningrad State U., 1960; PhD in Biol. Scis., Zool. Inst. USSR Acad. Scis., Leningrad, 1964. Jr. rschr. Zool. Inst. USSR Acad. Scis., Leningrad, 1965-72, sr. rschr., 1972; dep. dir. Zool. Inst. Russian Acad. Scis., St. Petersburg, 1979-94, dir., 1995—, head lab. exptl. freshwater hydrobiology, 1987—. Author: Functional Ecology of Freshwater Bivalves, 1981, Introduction to Production Hydrobiology, 1989; editor: (book) Biotic Relationships in the Ecosystem of Fish Culture Lakes, 1993, State of Environment of the North-Western and Northern Regions of Russia, 1995. Mem. Russian Acad. Scis., Russian Hydrobiol. Soc. (pres. 1991—), vice-chmn. sci. coun. ecology 1995—). Avocation: oil painting. Fax: 812-328-29-41, 812-114-04-44. E-mail: aaf@zisp.spb.su. Home: Nalichnaya St 40 1 151, 199397 Saint Petersburg Russia Office: Zool Inst Russian Acad Scis, Univ Embankment 1, 199034 Saint Petersburg Russia

ALIMOV, ANDREI, molecular geneticist, researcher; b. Kaunas, Lithuania, Apr. 9, 1963. MSc in Molecular Genetics & Gene Engring, Lomonsov State U., 1987; PhD in Molecular Biology, Engelhardt Inst., Moscow, 1992. Jr. rsch. fellow Inst. Biochemistry, Russia, 1985-87; jr. rsch. fellow Engelhardt Inst. Molecular Biology, 1990-92, rschr., 1992-98; vis. scientist Karolinska Inst., Stockholm, 1995-97, sect. urology, 1998-2000. Contbr. articles to jours. in field. Grantee Russian Acad. Scis., 1994; fellow EMBO, 1994, Karolinska Inst., 1995-96, Wenner-Gren, 1996-97. Mem. AAAS, European Assn. Cancer Rsch., Russian Assn. Tereology.

ALINE, DAVID PAUL, language educator; b. San Jose, Calif., June 21, 1959; s. Peter Glover and Minnie (MacLennan) A.; m. Yoko Yamaki, June 27, 1990. BA in English and History, Portland Stte U., 1984; MA, Columbia U., 1992; EdD, Temple U., 1999. Cert. in tchr. ESL. Instr. Hotel New Otani, Tokyo, 1991-93, Tokai U. Jr. Coll., Tokyo, 1991-99, Meikai U., Urayasu, Japan, 1993-96, Sophia U., Tokyo, 1993—, Tokyo Internat. U., Saitama, Japan, 1995-96, Waseda U., Tokyo, 1995-96, Kanagawa U., Yokohama, 1999—; mem. com. Applied Linguistics Colloquium, Temple U., Tokyo, 1998. Co-author: Psycholinguistics: Language, Mind and World, 2d edit.; contbr. articles to profl. jours. Mem. TESOL, Japan Assn. Lang. Tchrs., Japan Assn. Coll. English Tchrs. E-mail: aline@cc.kanagawa-u.ac.jp. Home: Shioyaki 4-10-3-713, Ichikawa Chiba 272-0114, Japan Office: Kanagawa Univ, 3-27-1 Rokkakubashi, Kanagawa-ku Yokohama Japan

AL-IRYANI, ABD AL-KARIM ALI, Yemeni prime minister; b. Iryan, Yemen, Feb. 20, 1935; s. Qadi Ali al-Iryani; married, Feb. 1969; children: Rasha, Rabab. Student, U. Tex., U. Ga.; Ph.D. in Biochem. Genetics, Yale U. Dir. Wadi Zeid Agrl. Project, 1968-69; head Ctrl. Planning Orgn., 1972-74, 74-77; min. devel. Govt. of Yemen Arab Republic, Sana'a, 1974-77, min. edn., 1976-79, min. agr., 1979-80, prime min., 1980-83, min. fgn. affairs, dep. prime minister, 1984—, dep. prime min. and min. fgn. affairs, now prime min.; pres. Sana's U., 1976-79. Office: Ministry Fgn AffairsOffice Prime Min, St of 26th September, Sana'a Yemen*

AL-ISMAIL, SAAD ABDUL-DAIM, hematologist, consultant; b. Baghdad, Iraq, June 9, 1947; arrived in U.K., 1974; s. Abdul-Daim Abdul-Razzaq and Sabiha Ibrahim (Dawood) Al-I.; m. Fatin Yousif, Jan. 17, 1974; 1 child, Deana. MB, BChir, Coll. Medicine, Baghdad, 1970. Med. diploma Royal Coll. Physicians, U.K. and Ireland. Sr. house physician Baghdad (Iraq) Tchg. Hosp., 1970-72; registrar in gen. medicine Basrah (Iraq) Tchg. Hosp., 1972-75; rsch. registrar haematology U. Hosp. Wales, Cardiff, 1976-77, sr. registrar haematology, 1978-80; lectr. in haematology U. Hosp. Wales/Coll. Medicine, Cardiff, 1980-82, clin. tchr., 1982—; cons. clin. haematologist West Glamorgan Health Authority, Swansea, Wales, 1982—; head haematology West Glamorgan Health Authority, Swansea, 1984—; dir. Haemophilia Ctr., Swansea, 1984—; chmn. West Glamorgan Pathology Com., Swansea, 1987-89. Contbr. articles to profl. jours. Fellow Royal Coll. Physicians London, Royal Coll. Pathologists London (med. diploma); mem. Internat. Soc. Haematology. Office: Swansea NHS Trust, Sketty, Swansea SA2 8QA, Wales

ALIYEV, HEYDAR, Azerbaijani government official; b. Nakhiehevan, Azerbaijan, May 10, 1923; m. Zarifa Aziz gizi Aliyeva (dec. 1985); 2 children: Sevil, Ilham. Diploma, Azerbaidzhan State U., 1957; PhD (hon.), Baku State U., 1994, Hojjat-Tapu U., Ankara, Turkey, 1994. Ofcl. of security forces and mem. Council of Ministers of Nakhichevan Autonomous Republic, 1941-49; leading ofcl. of Ministry of Internal Affairs and Com. of State Security (KGB) of Azerbaidzhan S.S.R.; dep. chmn., 1964-67; chmn. with rank of maj.-gen. 1967-69; cand. mem. Central Com. of Communist Party of Azerbaidzhan (CPA), 1966-69, mem. Cen. Com., 1969—, mem. Bur., 1969—, 1st sec. Central Com., 1969-82; mem. Communist Party of Soviet Union, 1945—, mem. Central Com., 1971-89, cand. mem. Politburo of Central Com. 1976-82, mem., 1982-87; dep. to USSR Supreme Soviet, 1970-74; vice chmn. Soviet of the Union, 1974; 1st dep. chmn. USSR Council of Ministers, 1982-87, chmn. bur. social devel. until 1987; chmn. Supreme Majlis, Nat. Assembly, 1990-93; dep. speaker Supreme Soviet of Azerbaijan, 1990-93; speaker Supreme Soviet, acting pres., 1993; pres. Supreme Soviet, comdr.-in-chief Armed Forces, 1993—; chmn. Supreme Meilis Nakmichevan Autonomous Republic, 1991-93, dep. sprk. Supreme Soviet Azerbaijan, 1991-93, pres. Republic Azerbaijan, 1993—. Recipient Order of Lenin (2), and others. Office: Istiglal kuc 19, Baku 370066, Azerbaijan*

ALIYEV, IRSHAD, government official; b. Gurzalar Village, Azerbaijan, June 30, 1944; married; 3 children. Engr., Agrl. Acad. Azerbaijan, 1970. Mem. CP of Azerbaijan, 1968-91, chmn. refugees com., 1992-94, cons. in presdl. office, 1992; dep. Supreme Soviet of Azerbaijan, 1985-90, 91-95; min. agr. and produce Azerbaijani Republic, 1994—. Office: Ministry of Agr and Produce, Shykhali Gurbanov Kuc 4, Baku 370078, Azerbaijan*

AL JALOUD, ALI ABDULLAH, soil water management specialist; b. Al Gasseem, Saudi Arabia, Mar. 27, 1952; s. Abdullah Ali and Sara Hamad (Al Nagmosh) Al J.; m. Moneerah Ali, Oct. 11, 1955; children: Hisah, Sara, Abdullah, Mishal, Mishary. BS, King Saud U., Riyadh, Saudi Arabia, 1977; MS, Calif. State U., 1983; PhD, Ghent State U., Belgium, 1988. Rsch. asst. Natural Agrl. & Water Rsch. Ctr., Riyadh, Saudi Arabia, 1977-80, rsch. assoc., 1983-85; sect. head Soil and Irrigation Dept., 1988-90; tech. dir. Natural Agrl. Water Rsch. Ctr., 1988-90; asst. prof. King Abdulaziz City Sci. & Tech., Riyadh, Saudi Arabia, 1990-94, asst. dir., 1991-94; dir. Natural Resources & Environ. Rsch. Inst., Riyadh, Saudi Arabia, 1994-96; assoc. prof. King Abdulaziz City Sci. & Tech., 1994—; cons. and rschr. in field. Author: Farming Related Horsescope in Saudi Arabia, 1994; contbr. articles to profl. jours. Mem. Am. Soc. Agronomy, Indian Soil Soc., Saudi Biol. Soc., Soil Sci. Soc. Am., Internat. Soil Sci. Soc., Internat. Assn. Optimization of Plant Nutrition, Soil & Water Conservation, Water Sci. & Tech. Assn. Avocations: reading, travel. Home: PO Box 28322, Riyadh 11437, Saudi Arabia Office: King Abdulaziz City Sci Tech, PO Box 6086, Riyadh 11442, Saudi Arabia

AL JAMMAZ, IBRAHIM JAMMAZ, research scientist; b. Riyadh, Saudi Arabia, Dec. 30, 1964; s. Jammaz Muhammad Al Jammaz and Sarah Ibrahim Al Yahya; m. Huda Faris Al Abdulkarim; children: Faisal, Bandar. BS, King Saud U., 1988; PhD, U. Surrey, 1997. Chartered chemist. Radio chemist II King Faisal Special Hosp., Riyadh, 1987-90, radio chemist I, 1990-92, assoc. scientist, 1997—; course dir. IAEA, Riyadh, 1999; scientist Johns Hopkins Hosp., Balt., 1998. Inventor in field; contbr. articles to profl. jours. Rsch. grantee KACST, Riyadh, 1999-00. Mem. Am. Chem. Soc., Royal Soc. Chemistry. Avocations: camping, travel, soccer. Office: King Faisal Spec Hosp/Rsch, PO Box 3354, Riyadh 11211, Saudi Arabia

AL-JARALLAH, MOHAMMED BIN IBRAHIM, federal official; b. 1944. BSc in Civil Engring., Riyadh (Saudi Arabia) U., 1972; MSc in Civil Engring., Stanford U., 1974; PhD in Civil Engring., Mich. State U., 1978. Tchg. asst. King Saud U., dir. projects, mem. staff; gen. mgr. Saudi Real Estate Fund; min. Ministry of Mcpl. and Rural Affairs, Riyadh, 1995—; bd. dirs. Saudi Devel. Fund; mem. Saudi-British Joint Com. Office: Ministry Mcpl Rural Affairs, Nasseriya St PO Box 955, Riyadh 11136, Saudi Arabia*

AL-JIHANI, ALI BIN TALAL, Saudi Arabian government official; b. 1945. BSc in Bus. Adminstrn., 1970, MSc in Math. Econs., 1973; PhD in Econs., U. Calif., 1977. Lectr., asst. analyst to dir. of budget Bank of Am., Saudi Arabia; lectr. Princeton U.; asst. prof. King Fahd U., 1978, dean dept. indsl. mgmt., 1980; sec. gen. Pub. Corp. Mil. Industries, 1986; econ. rschr. Ministry of Planning; min. Ministry of Posts, Telegraphs and Tel., Riyadh, Saudi Arabia, from 1995; now min. of state Royal Ct., Riyadh. Office: Royal Ct, Riyadh 1112, Saudi Arabia*

AL-JIHIMI, TAHIR, Libyan government official. Sec. economy and trade Govt. of Libya, Tripoli, until 1996; gov. Ctrl. Bank of Libya, Tripoli, 1996—. Office: Ctrl Bank of Libya, POB 1103 Sharia al-Malik Seoud, Tripoli Libya*

AL-JUNAYD, MUHAMMAD AHMAD, Yemeni government official; b. Hodeida, Yemen, 1934; married, Oct. 1965; 1 child. BS in Engring., London U. Dir. tech. sect. Hodeida Pub. Works Office, 1964-65; dep. tech. dir. Yemen Petroleum Co., 1965, also bd. dirs., 1965; under-sec. Ministry Pub. Works, 1967; min. agr. Govt. of Yemen, 1968-71, min. devel., 1971-72, min. treasury and fin., 1973, dep. prime min. for econ. and fin. affairs, 1977, min. electricity, water and sewerage, 1982-84, now min. finance, 1995-96, min. civil svc. & adminstrn. reform, 1996—; gov. Ctrl. Bank Yemen, Sanaa, 1995-96; chmn. agrl. devel. bd., 1968. Office: c/o Ministry Civil Svc/Admin, PO Box 1992, Sana'a Yemen*

AL-KAHTANI, MOHAMMED MOFAREH, geography educator, researcher; b. Mathab, Asir, Saudi Arabia, Feb. 13, 1956; s. Mofareh Shebli Al-Kahtani and Monirah Mohammed Al-Bishri; m. Hadba Mohammed Al-Bishri. BA, King Saud U., Saudi Arabia, 1982; PhD, Southampton U., United Kingdom, 1989. Tchg. asst. King Saud U., Riyadh, Saudi Arabia, 1982-89; asst. prof. King Saud U., Riyadh, 1989-95; assoc. prof. King Saud U., Abha, Saudi Arabia, 1995-99, King Khalid U., Abha, Saudi Arabia, 1999—; dir. rsch. ctr. King Saud U., Abha, 1990-93; chmn. dept. geography King Saud U., Abha, 1993-99. Author: Tourism in Asir Region, 1996; contbr. articles to profl. jours. Scholar King Saud U., 1982, Am. Rsch. Fellow Program, 1994, British Coun., 1996. Mem. Coll. Coun., Abha's Cultural Club. Avocations: swimming, hunting, photography. Office: Coll of Edn Dept of Geography, Coll of A Sand Adm/Geograph, King Khalid U Po Box 1183, Abha Saudi Arabia

ALKALAY-GUT, KAREN HILLARY, lecturer, poet; b. London, Mar. 29, 1945; came to U.S., 1948, arrived in Israel, 1972; d. Louis and Doris (Kaganovich) Rosenstein; m. Nissim Alkalay, July 4, 1967 (div. mar. 1979); children: Orit, Oren; m. Ezra David Gut, July 26, 1980. BA, U. Rochester, N.Y., 1966, MA, 1967, PhD, 1975. Instr. S.U. N.Y. @ Geneseo, N.Y., 1967-70; lectr. Ben Gurion U. Negev, Beer Sheva, Israel, 1972-76, Bar Ilan U., Ramat Gan, Israel, 1976-79, Tel Aviv U., Ramat Aviv, Israel, 1977—; chair Israel Assn. Writers in English, 1980-84, 87—, Israel Am. Studies Assn., 1989-94; bd. PEN Israel, 1996—. Author: Making Love: Poems, 1980, Alone in the Dawn, 1988, Mechitza, 1983, Ignorant Armies, 1994, The Love of Clothes and Nakedness, 1999, In My Skin, 2000. Mem. Fedn. Writers Assn. (governing bd. 1987—vice chair 1997—). Avocations: sculpture, music, poetry. Office: Dept English, Tel Aviv University, Ramat Aviv Israel

AL KHADHRAWI, MOHAMMAD RADHI, chemist, geochemist; b. Qudaih, Qatif, Saudi Arabia, Apr. 12, 1966; s. Radhi Mohammad and Alawia (Hashim) A.; m. Qadriyah Abdullah Alghomgham, Aug. 29, 1993. BS in Indsl. Chemistry, King Fahd U. Petroleum/Mineral, Dhahran, Saudi Arabia, 1991, MS in Chemistry, 1996. Tech. brand mgr. Modern Industries Co./Procter and Gamble, Jeddah, Saudi Arabia, 1991; lab. scientist Saudi Aramco, Dhahran, 1991—. Author: (with others) The Geochemistry of the Jurassic Petroleum System in Eastern Saudi Arabia, Pangea: Global Environments and Resources, 1994; presenter in field. Bd. dirs. Mudhar Charitable Soc. Edn. Program, Qudaih, 1992-93. Mem. Am. Chem. Soc., Am. Assn. Petroleum Geologists (assoc.). Muslim. Avocations: computers, volleyball, photography. E-mail: mrkhadhrawi@visto.com. Home: PO Box 9304, Dhahran 31311, Saudi Arabia Office: Saudi Aramco, Lab R&D Ctr Box 62, Dhahran 31311, Saudi Arabia

ALKHADRA, FOUAD FAWZI, engineering consulting company executive; b. Kuwaiti National, Mar. 6, 1945; s. Fawzi A. and Fawzia A. (Arab) A.; children: Amro, Osama, Fahed. BSc, St. Louis U., 1968; MS, Rutgers U., 1971; PhD, Univ. Econs. & Sci., Berlin, 1989. Planning engr. Kuwait Airways, Kuwait, 1969; inspector Dir. of Civil Aviation, Kuwait, 1969-72; dep. mng. dir. Petrochem. Industries Co. of Kuwait, 1972-86; pres., CEO Nat. Cons. Bur., Kuwait, 1986—; cons. to many internat. trading, mfg. & constrn. cos.; mem. adv. bd. Kuwait Inst. for Sci. Rsch. Petroleum, Kuwait, 1982-86; mem. Kuwait Petroleum Corp. Higher Tender Com., Kuwait, 1983-86, OAPEC 4th Coun. Conf., Kuwait, 1985-86. Contbr. articles to profl. jours. Mem. AICE, ASME, Am. Mgmt. Assn. Muslem. Office: Nat Cons Bur, PO Box 5092, Safat 13051, Kuwait

AL-KHALIFA, ABDALLAH BIN KHALID, Bahraini government official; b. 1922. Head Dept. Municipalities and Agriculture, 1949; pres. Rifa'a Municipality, 1967, Manama Municipality, 1967; mem. State Coun., 1970; min. commerce and agriculture Govt. of Bahrain, 1971-72, acting min. commerce and agriculture, 1975-76, now min. justice and Islamic affairs, min. housing, municipalities and environment. Office: Diplomatic Area POB 450, Manama Bahrain*

AL-KHALIFA, SHEIKH HAMAD BIN ISA, Crown Prince of Bahrain; b. Al Riffa, Bahrain, Jan. 28, 1950; s. Shaikh Isa Bin Salman A.; m. Sheikha Sabeeka bint Ibrahim, 1968; 10 children. Ed., Cambridge U.; student, Mons Officer Cadet Sch., Aldershot, Eng.; grad., U.S. Army Command and Gen. Staff Coll., Ft. Leavenworth, Kans., 1972; M in Mil. Sci., Armed Forces Indsl. Coll., 1972. Formed Bahrain Def. Force, 1968, comdr.-in-chief, head def. dept., 1968—, raised Def. Air Wing, 1978; mem. State Adminstrv. Council, 1970-71; min. of def. Govt. of Bahrain, 1971-88, dep. to Amir, 1974, crown prince, Amir; dep. pres. Family Council Al-Khalifa, 1974—; created Hist. Documents Center, 1976. Founder-mem., pres. Bahrain High Council Youth and Sports, 1975—; initiated Al-Areen Wildlife Parks Rev., 1976; founder Sulman Falcon Centre, 1977, Amiri Stud Bahrain, 1977; founder, pres. Bahrain Equestrian and Horse Racing Assn., 1977—; founder, chmn. Bahrain Ctr. Studies & Rsch., 1981. Decorated 1st class Order Star Joradan, 1967; 1st class Order Al-Rafidain (Iraq), 1968; 1st class Order Nat. Def. Kuwait, 1970; 1st class Order Al-Muhammedi (Morocco), 1970; 1st class Order Al-Nahdha (Jordan), 1972; 1st class Order Qiladat Gumhooreeya (Egypt), 1974; 1st class Order Taj (Iran), 1973; 1st class Order King Abdul-Aziz (Saudi Arabia), 1976; 1st class Order Republic Indonesia, 1977; 1st class Order Republic Mauritania, 1969; 1st class Order El-Fateh Al-Adheem (Libya), 1979; hon. knight comdr. Order St. Michael and St. George (U.K.), 1979; hon. mem. Helicopter Gt. Brit. Avocations: horse riding, golf. Office: The Amiri Ct Rifaa Palace, PO Box 555, Rifaa Bahrain*

AL-KHALIFA, SHEIKH KHALIFA BIN SALMAN, prime minister of Bahrain; b. Bahrain, 1935; married; 3 children. Pres. Edn. Council, 1957-60, head of fin., 1960-66; dir. fin. and pres. Electricity Bd., 1961; pres. Adminstrn. Council, Bahrain, 1966-70, State Council, Bahrain, 1970-73; prime minister of Bahrain, 1973-75, 78—; chmn. Bahrain Monetary Agy. Address: Office of Prime Min, Govt Rd PO Box 1000, Manama Bahrain*

AL-KHALIFA, SHEIKH MUHAMMAD BIN MUBARAK, Bahraini government official; b. 1935; s. Sheikh Mubarak Bin Hamad Al-Khalifa; married; 2 children. Student, Am. U., Beirut, Oxford (Eng.) U.; diploma in modern history and internat. law, U. London. Candidate for bench Bahrain Cts., 1961; dir. info. Govt. of Bahrain, 1962—; head Polit. Bur., 1968—, Dept. Fgn. Affairs, 1969—; apptd. to State Council, 1970; min. of fgn. affairs Govt. of Bahrain, 1971—. Office: Ministry Fgn Affairs, POB 547 Govt House Govt Rd, Manama Bahrain*

AL-KHALIFA, SHEIKH MOHAMED BIN KHALIFA HAMID, Bahrain government official; b. 1937; s. Khalifa Bin Hamed Bin Issa Al-Khalifa; married, 1959; children: Fawaz, Tallal, Lamia, Amani. Grad., Royal Mil. Acad., Sandhurst, Eng. Police insp. Dept. Pub. Security, Bahrain, 1959—, dep. dir. gen., 1970-73; dir. immigration and passports Govt. of Bahrain, 1966—, min. of the interior, 1973—. Office: Ministry of the Interior, PO Box 12, Manama Bahrain*

AL-KHALIQ, MUSTAFA ABD, judge; b. Yemen, 1945. LLB, Baghdad Univ. Sec. of Aden Municipality, prosecutor People's Ct. in the First Governorate; sec. Yemen- USSR Friendship Assn., 1970, min. of justice, waqfs, 1971-73; amb. to USSR, 1973-74; mem. People's Supreme Coun. of Yemen; pres. People's Supreme Ct. Yemen. *

AL-KHARRAT, EDWAR, writer; b. Alexandria, Egypt, Mar. 16, 1926; s. Kolta Faltas Youssef Al-Kharrat; children: Ehab, Ayman. B of Law, U. Alexandria, 1946. Storehouse asst. Royal Navy Victualling Dept., Alexandria, 1944-46; clk. Nat. Bank Egypt, Alexandria, 1946-48, Nat. Ins. Co., Alexandria, 1950-55; dir. tech. affairs Afro Asian People's Solidarity Orgn., Cairo, 1959-67, asst. sec. gen., 1967-83, pres., cons., 1967—. Author: (short stories) High Walls, 1959, Hours of Pride, 1972 (State prize), Suffocations of Love and Mornings, 1983; (novels) Rama and the Dragon, 1979, The Railways' Station, 1985, Saffron Dust, 1986, The Ribs of Desert, 1987, Girls of Alexandria, 1990, Creations of Flying Desires, 1990, Waves of the Nights, 1991, Stones of Bobello, 1992, Penetrations of Love and Perdition, 1993, My Alexandria, 1994, Ripples of Salt Dreams, 1994, Fire of Phantasies, 1995, Soaring Edifices, 1997, The Certitude of Thirst, 1997, Throes of Facts and Folly, 1998, Boulders of Heaven, 2000; (criticism) The New Sensibility, 1994, From Silence to Rebellion, 1994, Transgeneric Writing, 1994, A Hymn to Density, 1995, Assault on the Impossible, 1996, Enticing the Impossible, 1997, Beyond Reality, 1999, Voices of Medernity in Fiction, 1999, Modernist Poetry in Egypt, 2000; (poetry) Interpretations, 1996, Wings of Your Bird Struck Me, 1996, Why? Extracts of a Love Poem, 1996, Tyranny of the Internal, 1996, Cry of the Unicorn, 1998, Seven Clouds, 2000; editor: Anthology of Egyptian Short Stories of the Seventies, 1982; editor Lotus mag.; editorial bd. Gallery 68 mag.; translated many creative works into Arabic. Recipient: Franco-Arab Friendship prize, 1991, Oweiss prize, 1996, Cavifis prize, 1998, State Merit award, 2000. Mem. Afro Asian Writer's Assn. (asst. sec. gen. 1967-72), Egyptian Writers' Union, Egyptian Assn. Men of Letters, Egyptian Story Club, Egyptian PEN. Mem. Orthodox Coptic Ch. Avocation: travel. Home: 45 Ahmed Heshmat St, Cairo Egypt

AL-KHASAWNEH, AWN SHAWKAT, judge; b. Feb. 22, 1950. MA, Cambridge U., LLM. With Jordanian diplomatic svc., 1975; 2nd sec., then 1st sec. Permanent Mission to Jordan to the UN, N.Y., 1976-80; with Ministry of Fgn. Affairs, 1980-85, head leagl dept., 1985-90; legal adviser to Crown Prince El-Hassan bin Talal, amb., 1992, 95, apptd. adviser to king, adviser to state on internat. law; chief Royal Hashemite Ct., 1996-98; judge Intl. Ct. of Justice (the Hague), Netherlands; mem. Arab Internat. Law Commn., 1982-89; mem. subcommn. on prevention of discrimation and protection of minorities Commn. on Human Rights, 1984-93; chmn. commn. IV UNESCO Gen. Conf., 1993; mem. Internat. Law Commn., 1986; mem. Jordanian Royal Commn. on Legis. and Adminstrv. Reform, 1994-96; chmn. Jordanian Nat. Group on the Implementation of Internat. Humanitarian Law, 1988; lectr. in acad. seminars and various univs. Bd. editors Palestine Yearbook of Internat. Law; contbr. articles to profl. publs. Recipient Istiqlal Order, First Class, 1993, Kawkab Order, First Class, 1996, Nahda Order, First Class, 1996, Légion d'Honneur, Grand Officer, 1997. Mem. Internat. Law Assn. Office: Internat Ct of Justice, Peace Palace, 2517 KJ The Hague The Netherlands*

ALKHATEEB, ARWA, business educator; b. Irbid, Jordan, Nov. 17, 1958; came to the U.S., 2000; d. Moh'd and Hiyam (Karmi) A.; m. Harald Georg Singer, Feb. 27, 1992; 1 child, Hani. BA in Mgmt. and Info. Sys., Beirut U., 1984; MBA, Nagoya (Japan) U., 1992; PhD in Med. Info. Sys., Kyoto (Japan) U., 1999. Sys. analyst Royal Sci. Soc., Amman, Jordan, 1979-89; lectr. Hannan U., Osaka, Japan, 1999—; rschr. Kyoto U. Hosp. Grantee Kyoto Perfectural Office/Jordan-Japan Friendship Amb., 1996, ISO Corp. Fund for Top Female Rschrs., Tokyo, 1996, Japanese Ministry Edn., Tokyo, 1998, Suzuken Meml. Funds, Nagoya, 1998. Mem. Internat. Soc. for Telemedicine, Japanese Soc. Med. Informatics, Japanese Office Automation Soc., N.Y. Acad. Sci. Avocations: swimming, tennis, reading, traveling, cooking. E-mail: arwa singer@yahoo.com. Fax: 1-781-278-9668. Home: 64 George St Norwood MA 02062-2302

AL-KHATIB, MAHMOUD ABED, language educator; b. Irbid, Jordan, Feb. 21, 1952; s. Abed Ahmad and Arifeh Mohamad (Abu-Hamad) Al.; m. Ibtisam Mustafa Hamad, Jul. 18, 1980; children: Sami, Rana, Ola, Tariq. BA, Ain Shams U., Cairo, 1978; MA, Durham U., Eng., 1985, PhD, 1988; cert. in teaching, Lancaster U., Eng., 1993. Translator KOCC, Saudi Arabia, 1979-80, Keum Kang Ltd., Riyadh, Saudi Arabia, 1980-84; asst. prof. linguistics and English Univ. Sci. and Tech., Irbid, Jordan, 1990-96, head English lang. unit, 1993-96, assoc. prof. linguistics and English, 1996—, head dept. English for applied studies, 1996-98; dean sci. rsch., acting dean faculty arts and sci. Irbid Nat. U., 1998-99, head dept. English for applied studies, 1999—; cons. Students English Lang. Soc., 1995-97. Co-author: A Course of English for the Students of Science & Technology, 1989-93; contbr. articles to profl. jours. Recipient TCT award The British Coun., 1993. Avocations: playing football, tennis. Home: PO Box 1260, Irbid Jordan Office: Univ Sci & Tech, Dept Eng for Applied Studie, Irbid Jordan

AL-KHAWASHKY, MOHAMMAD ISHAQ AHMAD, health organization representative, consultant; b. Jerusalem, Palestine, Mar. 1, 1931; arrived in Saudi Arabia, 1957; s. Ahmad Yehya and Bahiya Tawfik Tamini Al-H.; m. Soheila Ameen Tamimi; children: Hazem, Mazen, Samer; m. Naela Hussein Murtagi, Oct. 27, 1985; m. Salwa Rizk Ibrahim, June, 1991. MB, Faculty of Medicine, Cairo, 1956; diploma in anesthesiology, Faculty of Medicine, Copehnagen, 1961; diploma in medicine, Faculty of Medicine, Cairo, 1975, D in Anesthesiology, 1977. Resident anesthesiology Ministry of Health, Riyadh, Saudi Arabia, 1958-60, anesthesiologist, 1962-64, chief anesthesiology dept., 1965-74, chief anesthesiology and intensive care depts., 1978-82, spl. advisor, exec. dep. minister, 1982-83; dir. gen. Riyadh Cen. Hosp., 1977-82; mem. Kasr El-Eini faculty medicine, coun. Cairo U., Egypt, 1991-98; bd. mem., cons. Faculty of Allied Helath Scis., Riyadh, 1978-82; cons. road traffic accidents Arab Health Ministers of Gulf, Saudi Arabia, 1978-82; cons. Red Crecent, Riyadh, 1975-82, WHO, Eastern Mediterranean Regional Office, Alexandria, Egypt, regional advisor orgn. health care svcs., 1983-89, WHO rep. in Egypt, 1989-98; spl. advisor to regional dir. WHO/EMIRO, 1999—. Author: Principles of Anaesthesia, 1978; contbr. articles to profl. jours.; author, assoc. aeidor: Saudi Medical Journal, 1980, 81. Recipient Outstanding Achievements in Traffic Medicine award Internat. Assn. Accident and Traffic Medicine, Helsinki, 1992, Egyptian Med. Syndicate Shield, 1996, Cert. of Appreciation and Recognition of Med. and Humanity Svcs., 1996. Mem. Saudi Anaesthetic Assn. (bd. dirs. 1990—), Club of Alexandria, Gezira Sporting Club, Alexandria Sporting Club. Moslem. Avocations: reading, music, tennis, walking. Office: World Health Orgn, PO Box 1517, 21563 Alexandria Egypt

ALKIRE, BETTY JO, artist, commercial real estate broker, marketing consultant; b. Kansas City, Mo., June 20, 1942; d. Robert Emmitt and Gladys Faye (Craigg) Sharp; m. Daniel Wayne Hedrick, Nov. 15, 1958 (div.); children—Diane Laurie, Lisa Kay, Brett, Darin, Julie; m. William Edgar Alkire, Sept. 23, 1975. Tchr. art Independence Adult Edn., Mo., 1967—; portrait artist Silver Dollar City Nat. Crafts Festival, 1971—; owner, operator portrait artist's concession Kansas City Worlds of Fun, 1972-96 ; tchr. pvt. art classes, 1970—; tchr., lectr. mktg. art U. Mo. Extension Program, 1982—; cons. mktg. and life-planning for artists; broker and cons. comml. investment real estate. Contbr. articles in field to various mags. Mem. Bur. of Tourism, Tri-Lakes Bd. of Realtors Edn. com., R.B. Bd. of Planning and Zoning; chmn. R.B. Park and Mus. Bd. Mem. Mo. Arts Council, Table Rock Art Guild, Independent Profl. Artists Assn. (pres. 1980—), Branson Mo. C. of C. (mem. leadership program). Methodist. Clubs: Rockaway Beach Ladies, Rockaway Beach Booster (Mo.). Avocations: local art and history, antiques, real estate. Home: Historic Taneywood Rockaway Beach MO 65740

AL-KODMANI, NASSER, civil engineer; b. Damascus, Syria, Jan. 1, 1961; s. Mohammad Tyseer and Huda (Al-Reefi) A.; m. Rima Haj Ebrahim, Jan. 5, 1989; children: Khaled, Mohammad. BSCE, Damascus U., 1985. Structural engr. Gen. Co. for Engring. and Cons., Damascus, 1986-91; project engr. Arabian Constrn. Co., Abu Dhabi, United Arab Emirates, 1991—. Lt. Syrian Armed Forces, 1986-88. Mem. ASCE, Syrian Engrs. Syndicate, Soc. Engrs. (United Arab Emirates). Mouslem-Sunni. Avocations: swimming, football. Fax: 009712 770513. Office: Arabian Constrn Co, PO Box 2113, Abu Dhabi United Arab Emirates

AL-KOFAHI, MAHMOUD MEJALLI, physicist, educator; b. Barha, Irbid, Jordan, Jan. 19, 1951; s. Mejalli Al-Refai and Khadeeja Mahmoud; m. Khetam Ahmed, July 23, 1976; children: Majd, Osameh, Ahmed, Jafar, Khalid, Mejalli. BS in Physics, Jordan U., 1973, MS in Nuclear Physics, 1977; PhD in Nuclear Physics, Mass. Inst. Tech., 1982. Instr. physics Amman (Jordan) Tchr. Tng. Coll., 1974-77; prof. physics Yarmouk U., Irbid, Jordan, 1982-86, assoc. prof. physics, 1986—; rsch. scientist U. Petroleum & Minerals, Dharhan, Saudi Arabia, 1986-90; dir. dir. sci. & tech. Arab Atomic Energy Agy., Tunis, Tunisia, 1990-95; prof. physics Yarmouk U., Irbid, Jordan, 1995—. Author: Electricity & Magnetism, 1985; editor: Proceedings of 1st Arab Conference on the Peaceful Applications of Atomic Energy, 1993. Mem. Am. Physics Soc., Jordan Physics Soc., Jordan Radio Amateur Club. Muslim. Avocations: computer applications, interfacing, electronics, microprocessor control. Home: PO Box 226, Irbid Jordan Office: Yarmouk U, Dept Physics, 21163 Irbid Jordan

ALKUHAIMI, SIHAM ABDULAZIZ, physicist, educator; b. Beirut, Lebanon; d. Abdulaziz and Hafsa Mahmood A. BS, Girl's Coll. Edn., 1977, MS, 1984, PhD, 1987. From head physics dept. to prof., supr. energy rsch. Girl's Coll. Edn., Riyadh, Saudi Arabia. Mem. AAAS, Saudi Chem. Soc., N.Y. Acad. Scis. Fax: 009661-4020594. Home: PO Box 18003, Riyadh 11415, Saudi Arabia

ALLABY, JOHN MICHAEL, writer; b. Belper, Eng., Sept. 18, 1933; s. Albert Theodore and Jessica May (King) A.; m. Ailsa Marthe McGregor, Jan. 3, 1957; children: Vivien Gail, Robin Graham. Student, Birmingham (Eng.) Sch. Speech Tng. and Dramatic Art, 1954-55. Police cadet Birmingham City Police, 1950-51; freelance actor London, 1955-64; editor The Soil Assn., Haughley, Suffolk, London, 1964-72; mng. editor The Ecologist, Wadebridge, Cornwall, and Haughley Suffolk, 1970-73; freelance writer Wadebridge, Cornwall, 1973-2000, Argyll, Scotland, 2000—. Author: The Eco-Activists, 1971, Who Will Eat?, 1972, Ecology, 1975, Inventing Tomorrow, 1976, World Food Resources, Actual and Potential, 1977, Animals that Hunt, 1979, Wildlife of North America, 1979, Making and Managing a Smallholding, 1979, The Politics of Self-Sufficiency, 1980, A Year in the Life of the Field, 1981, Le Foreste Tropicali, 1981, Animal Artisans, 1982, Dutch edit., 1983, The Changing Uplands, 1983, The Food Chain, 1984, Japanese edit., 1984, Out in the Country: Where You Can Go and What You Can Do, 1985, 2040, 1985, Your Child and the Computer, 1985, The Woodland Trust Book of British Woodlands, 1986, Ecology Facts, 1986, The Ordnance Survey Outdoor Handbook, 1987, A Pony's Tale, 1987, Conservation at Home: A Practical Handbook, 1988, Guide to Gaia, 1989, Living in the Greenhouse, 1990, Into Harmony with the Planet, 1990, The Concise Oxford Dictionary of Zoology, 1991, 2d edit., 1999, Elements-Air, 1992, Elements-Water, 1992, The Concise Oxford Dictionary of Botany, 1992, Dictionary of Plant Sciences, 2d rev. edit., 1999, Elements-Earth, 1993, Elements-Fire, 1993; (with Floyd Allen) Robots Behind the Plow, 1974; (with Marika Hanbury-Tenison, John Seymour and Hugh Sharman) The Survival Handbook, 1975; (with Colin Tudge) Home Farm, 1977; (with Peter Crawford) The Curious Cat, 1982; (with James E. Lovelock) The Great Extinction, 1983, Spanish edit., 1986, The Greening of Mars, 1984, German edit., 1985; (with Jane Burton) Nine Lives, 1985, A Dog's Life, 1986; (with Ailsa Allaby) The Concise Oxford Dictionary of Earth Sciences, 1990, 2d edit., 1999; (with Neil Curtis) Planet Earth: A Visual Factfinder, 1993, How the Weather Works, 1995, Facing the Future, 1995, How it Works: The Environment, 1996; (with Michael Kent) Collins Pocket Reference Biology, 1996, Basic Environmental Science, 1996, 2d edit. 2000, Dangerous Weather: Hurricanes, 1997, Dangerous Weather: Tornadoes, 1997, Dangerous Weather: Blizzards, 1997, Dangerous Weather: Drought, 1997, Dangerous Weather: Floods, 1997, Dangerous Weather: A Chronology of Weather, 1997, Ecosystem: Temperate Forests, 1999, Ecosystem: Deserts, 2000; gen. editor: A Dictionary of the Environment, 1977, Spanish edit., 1984, 4th rev. edit., 1994, The Oxford Dictionary of Natural History, 1986; editor: Thinking Green: An anthology of essential ecological writing, 1989. Pilot RAF, 1952-54. Mem. Soc. for History of Natural History, Planetary Soc., N.Y. Acad. Scis., Assn. Brit. Sci. Writers, Soc. Authors, Inst. Biology (assoc.). Avocations: walking, swimming, reading, movies. Home: Braehead Tighnbruaich, Argyll PA21 2ED, Scotland

ALLAERTS, WILFRIED, biologist, researcher; b. Brussels, June 13, 1958; arrived in The Netherlands, 1990; s. Josephus Ludovicus and Leona (De Hondt) A.; m. Maria Catherina Van Boxel, Oct. 24, 1981 (div. 1994); children: Jan Herman Daan, Dries Jakob Neel; m. Diane Liliane Lemmers, Aug. 10, 1995; children: Daniel, Noah. MSc in Zoology, U. Louvain, Belgium, 1980, PhB, 1987, PhD, 1989. Fellow Inst. for Sci. Rsch. in Industry and Agr., 1980-83; tchr. biology and chemistry Secondary Sch., Brussels, 1983-84; rsch. asst. U. Louvain, Belgium, 1985-90; rschr. U. Leiden, The Netherlands, 1990-91, U. Rotterdam, The Netherlands, 1991-95; rsch. assoc. U. Nijmegen, The Netherlands, 1995-98; sec. Fedn. Med. Sci. Assns. The Netherlands, 1999—; innovation cons. U. Twente, Enschede, The Netherlands, 1999; sec.-treas. Soc. for Study and Protection Mammals, Belgium and The Netherlands, 1984-87. Editor Mediator, 1999—; contbr. articles to profl. jours. Recipient Laureate, Belgian Work Against Cancer, Brussels, 1990, Neuro-Immuno-Endocrinology award Ipsen Found. Paris, 1994. Mem. AAAS, Soc. for Immunology/Endocrinology, Soc. of Neuroendocrinologie Experimentale, Dutch Neurofedn. (sec. 2000—). Avocations: flutist. Office: Erasmus U Rotterdam, Josephine Nefkens Inst PO Box 1738, 3000 DR Rotterdam The Netherlands

ALLAHVERDI, ALI, engineering educator, industrial engineer, researc; b. Gevas, Van, Turkey, May 14, 1965; s. Mehmet and Mahcebin A.; m. Hatice Altin, Aug. 5, 1990; children: Fatima Zehra, Muberra. BS, Istanbul (Turkey) Tech. U., 1986; MS, Rensselaer Polytechnic Inst., Troy, U.S.A., 1990, PhD, 1992. Rsch. asst. Technical U., Istanbul, 1987-88; rsch. asst. Rensselaer Polytechnic Inst., Troy, N.Y., 1989-91, tchg. asst., 1991-92; asst. prof. Marmara U., Istanbul, 1993-95; asst. prof. Kuwait U., 1995-99, assoc. prof., 1999—. Contbr. articles to profl. jours. Recipient Dissertation prize Rensselaer Polytechnic Inst. Troy, N.Y., 1993; Fellow Turkey's Ministry of Edn., 1988-93, Rensselaer Polytechnic Inst., 1989-92. Mem. Inst. Operations Rsch. and MS, Operational Rsch. Soc. (U.K. and Turkey chpts.). Avocations: reading, swimming. Home: Area 3 St 5 Apt 385 1st Fl, Salwa Kuwait Office: Kuwait U Dept Mech Indsl En, PO Box 5969, 13060 Safat Kuwait

ALLAIN, HERVE JEAN, neurologist, pharmacologist, medical educator; b. St. Brieuc, France, Feb. 11, 1950; s. Joseph and Yvonne (Le Mounier) A.; m. Nicole Jeanne Doe de Maindreville, Apr. 23, 1973; children: Pierre-Yves, Bertrand, Solenn, Baptiste. MD, U. Rennes, 1977. Prof. pharmacology U. Rennes (France) Med. Sch., 1982—; head dept. pharmacology Rennes (France) Med. Sch., 1992—; mem. French Medicine Agy., Paris, 1992—, local ethics com., Rennes, 1985—; expert in EMEA, London, 1994—; project leader European Alzheimer Clearing House, 1997. Contbr. articles to profl. jours. Mem. CINP, ECNP, French Assn. Clin. Pharmacologists, French Neurosci. Soc., French Pharm. Soc. Roman Catholic. Avocations: music, windsurfing. Home: 27 bis rue E Rostand, 35700 Rennes France Office: Faculty of Medicine, 2 Ave Pr L Bernard, 35043 Rennes France

ALLAIN, LOUIS, literature educator, scientific advisor; b. Brest, France, June 28, 1933; s. Louis and Louise (Nicolas) A.; m. Annie Luc, May 21, 1964; children: Andree-Lise, Juliette, Laurence, Alexandre. B Degree, Ecole Normale Superieure, Paris, 1958, Agregation, 1957; Doctorate, Sorbonne, Paris, 1979. Sch. tchr. Lycee Lakanal, Paris, 1961; asst. lectr. Sorbonne, 1961-63, sr. lectr., 1963-69; mng. lectr. Univ. Lille, 1969-81, prof., head dept. Slavic langs., 1981-98, prof emeritus, 1998—; contbr. Acad. Sci., Hungary, 1988, Russia, 1988, 90, 94, 96, Israel, 1994, Poland, 1995, 96, 97, 98, Montenegro, 1996, U. Houston, 1989, Cornell U., 1994, Columbia U., 1998, Dostoevsky Symposium, Cerisy-la-Salle, 1983, Ljubljana, 1989, Oslo, 1992, Kartause Gaming, 1995, N.Y. 1998, Gumilev Symposium I & II, Glasgow, 1986, St. Petersburg, 1996, Chekhov Symposium I & II, Badenweiler, 1985, 94, From Dissidence to Democracy, Paris, 1996., Jerusalem in Slavic cultures and religious traditions, 1996, others. Author: Dostoievski et Dieu, 1981, Dostoievski et l'Autre, 1984, Etiudy o russkoi literature, 1989, Dostoevsky i Bog, 1993, F.M. Dostoevsky: Poetika, mirooshchushchenie, bogoiskatel'stvo, 1996, Skvoz' prizmu vekov, 1998, Shtrikhi k portretu F.M. Dostoevskogo, 1998; editor: B. Poplavsky, I&II, 1993, N. Otsup, 1993-95, G. Adamovich, 1993, G. Ivanov, 1993, V. Vishnjak, 1993, V.V. Rozanov, (study), 1993, A. Remizov, 1994, N. Plevitskaya, 1994, N. Fedorova, 1994, V. Gippius, 1994, V. Zen'kovsky, 1994, I. Napelbaum, 1995, M. Voloshin (study), 1996, F. M. Dostoevsky: Poetika, mirooshchushchenie, bogoiskatel'stvo, 1996, Skvoz' Prizmu Vekov, 1998, Shtrikhi k portretu F.M. Dostoevskogo, 1998; co-editor: Jews and Slavs, vol. 2, 1994; contbr. articles to profl. jours. Lt. French Navy, 1958-61, France. Comdr. of Acad. Palms, French Ministry of Edn., 1990, medal City of Lille, 1994, Melanges offerts au Professeur Louis Allain, Lille, 1996. Mem. Alumni Ecole Normale Superieure, Intra-Marine/France, Internat. Dostoevsky Soc., Inst. Slavic Studies, Paris. Avocations: cooking, gardening. Home: Rue Jules Guesde 408, Villeneuve d'Ascq 59650, France Office: Charles de Gaulle Univ, BP 149, Villeneuve d'Ascq Cedex 59653, France

ALLAIN, YVES-MARIE, radiotherapist; b. Carhaix, Finistère, France, Mar. 14, 1927; s. Yves and Perrine (Le Bloas) A.; m. Annie Derché, Dec. 5, 1940; 1 child, Louis. Doctorat, Ecole du Service de Santé et Faculté de Medecine, Lyon, 1953. Asst. Hôpitaux Des Armées, Paris, 1958-63; electroradiologiste Hôpitaux Militaires, Paris; chef de service de radiologie Hôpital Begin, 1963-68; chef de service de radiotherapie Cen. Anticancereux, Rennes, France, 1968-70; chef de service de radiologie Hopital N.D. de Bon Secours, Paris, 1970-72; chef de service de radiotherapie Hopital Des Peupliers, Paris, 1972-75, Cen. Anticancereux, Angers, France, 1976-92; main prof. D.T.S. IMRT, Angers, 1993-2001. Named Chevalier de l'ordre, Nat. Du Mérite, 1967. Roman Catholic. Avocation: golf. Office: 29 Blvd Malesherbes, 75008 Paris France

ALLAIRE, PAUL ARTHUR, office equipment company executive; b. Worcester, Mass., July 21, 1938; s. Arthur E. Allaire and Elodie (LePrade) Murphy; children: Brian, Christiana. BSEE, Worcester Poly. Inst., 60; MSIA, Carnegie-Mellon U., 1966. Fin. analyst Xerox Corp., Rochester, N.Y., 1966-70; dir. fin. analysis Rank Xerox Ltd., London, N.Y., 1970-73; dir. internat. ops. fin. Xerox Corp., Stamford, Conn., 1973-75; chief staff officer Rank Xerox Ltd., London, 1975-79, mng. dir., 1979-83; sr. v.p., chief staff officer Xerox Corp., Stamford, Conn., 1983-86, pres., 1986-90, CEO, 1990-99, chmn. bd., 1991—, also. chmn. exec. com., CEO, bd. dirs., 2000—; bd. dirs. Sara Lee Corp., J.P. Morgan, N.Y. City Ballet, Catalyst, SmithKline Beecham plc, Lucent Techs., The Ford Found., Priceline.com; mem. Coun. on Competitiveness. Trustee Worcester Poly. Inst., Carnegie Mellon U. Mem. Coun. on Fgn. Rels. (bd. dirs.), Nat. Acad. Engring., Tau Beta Pi, Eta Kappa Nu. Democrat. Office: Xerox Corp PO Box 1600 800 Long Ridge Rd Stamford CT 06904

ALLAIS, MAURICE-FELIX, economist; b. Paris, May 31, 1911; s. Maurice and Louise (Caubet) A.; m. Jacqueline Bouteloup, Sept. 6, 1960; 1 child, Christine. Grad. 1st pl., Poly. Sch., Paris, 1933; grad., Nat. Higher Sch. Mines, Paris, 1936; D Eng, Faculty of Scis., Paris, 1949; D honoris causa, U. Groningen, The Netherlands, 1964, U. Mons, Belgium, 1992, Am U., Paris, 1992, U. Lisbonne, Portugal, 1993; diplome d'Honneur Hautes Etudes Commls., U. Paris, Paris, 1993. Engr. Dept. Mines and Quarries, 1937-43; dir. Bur. Documentation and Stats., 1943-48, Econ. and Social Rsch. Group, Paris, 1944-70; prof. econ. analysis Nat. Higher Sch. Mines, Paris, 1944-88; dir. Econ. Analysis Ctr., Paris, 1944—; prof. econ. theory Inst. Stats. U. Paris, 1947-58, dir. Ctr. Clement Juglar for Monetary Analysis, 1970-85; dir. rsch. Nat. Ctr. Sci. Rsch., Paris, 1954-79; prof. Grad. Inst. Internat. Studies, Geneva, 1967-70; disting. vis. scholar Thomas Jefferson, U. Va., Charlottesville, 1958-59; mem. energy commn. Econ. Coun., Paris, 1960-61; chmn. com. of experts for study of options in transport tariff policy EEC, Brussels, 1963-64. Author: A la Recherche d'une Discipline Economique, 1943, 2d edit. Traité d'Economic Pure, 1952, 3d edit., 1994, Abondance ou Misère, 1946, Economie et Intérêt, 1947, 2d edit., 1998, La Gestion des Houillères Nationalisées et la Théorie Economique, 1949, Les Fondements Comptables de la Macroéconomique, 1954, 2d edit., 1992, Fondements d'une Théorie positive des choix comportant un risque, 1955, Notes to French Academy of Sciences on the Anomalies in the Movements of the Paraconic Pendulum, 1957-58, Should the Law of Gravitation Be Reconsidered?, 1959, L'Europe Unie, Route de la Prospérité, 1959 , L'Algérie d'Evian, 1962, 2d edit. 1999, The Role of Capital in Economic Development, 1963, Reformulation de la Théorie Quantitative de la Monnaie, 1965, L'Impôt sur le Capital, 1966, Les Conditions de l'Efficacité dans l'Economie, 1967, Growth Without Inflation, 1968, Growth and Inflation, 1969, La Libéralisation des Relations Economiques Internationales, 1970, 2d edit., 1995, Les Théories de l'Equilibre Economique Général et de l'Efficacité Maximale, 1971, Inégalité et Inégalités, 1971, Inequality and Civilizations, 1973, L'Inflation Française et la Croissance, 1974, Inflation, Income Distribution and Indexation, 1976, L'Impôt sur le Capital et la Réforme Monétaire, 1977, 2d edit., 1988, Expected Utility Hypothesis and the Allais' Paradox, 1979, La Théorie Générale des Surplus, 1980, 2d edit., 1989, Frequency, Probability and Chance, 1982, Foundations of Utility and Risk Theory, 1983, Détermination de l'Utilité Cardinale suivant un modèle intrinsèque invariant, 1984, Credit Mechanism, 1984, The Empirical Approaches of the Hereditary and Relativistic Theory of the Demand for Money, 1986, The Concepts of Surplus and Loss and the Reformulation of the General Theory of Economic Equilibrium and Maximum Efficiency, 1986, The General Theory of Random Choices in Relation to the Invariant Cardinal Utility Function and the Specific Probability Function, 1986, The Equimarginal Principle: Meaning, Limits and Generalization, 1987, Les Conditions Monétaires d'une Economie de Marchés, 1987, My Life Philosophy, 1988, Autoportraits, 1989, Pour l'Indexation, 1990, Pour la Réforme de la Fiscalité, 1990, L'Europe face à son avenir-Que Faire?, 1991, De l'Europe des Douze à la Grande Europe, 1992, Erreurs et Impasses de la Construction Européenne, 1992, Cardinalism, 1994, Combats pour l'Europe 1994, L'anisotropie de l'espace, 1997, la crise mondiale d'aujourithui, 1999, L'umon Europeeune la Fouidobiation et le chóurage, 1999, Globalization, the Destruction of Employment and Growth: The Empirical Evidence, 1999; also sci. papers on risk and utility theory; editorial bd. Polit. Econ. Rev., 1952—. Lt. arty., French Army, 1939-40. Named Laureate French Acad. Scis., 1933, French Acad. Moral and Polit. Scis., 1954, 59, 83, 84; recipient Lanchester prize Johns Hopkins U. and Operational Rsch. Soc. Am., 1958, Great Prize of Atlantic Community, 1959, Galabert prize French Astronautical Soc., 1959, Gravity Rsch. Found. prize, 1959, Grand Prix André Arnoux, 1968, Zerilli Marimo prize, 1984, Gold medal Soc. for Promotion of Nat. Industry, 1971, French Nat. Ctr. for Sci. Rsch., 1978, Prix Spl. Jury Dupuit-de Lesseps, 1987, Nobel prize in econ. scis., 1988, medal U. Paris-X, 1989, Gold medal City of Paris, 1989, Great Gold medal City of Nancy, 1990, Gold medal Etoile Civique, 1990, Amis de François Quesnay, 1994; decorated Officer of Palmes Académiques, 1949, Chevalier Nat. Economy Order, 1962, Comdr. Legion of Honor, 1989, Grand Officier Ordre Nat. du Mérite, 1998. Fellow Ops. Rsch. Soc. Am., Internat. Econometric Soc. (editorial bd. 1959-69), mem. NAS (assoc.), Nat. Acad. Scis., Morales et Politiques, Acad. Nat. dei Lincei (assoc.), Acad. Scis. Russia, French Assn. Econ. Sci. (chmn. 1972), Am. Econ. Assn. (hon.), Internat. Statis. Inst., Statis. Soc., Racing Club Paris. Avocations: history, theoretical and experimental physics. Home: 15 rue Des Gate-Ceps, 92210 Saint Cloud France Office: Econ Analysis Ctr, 60 Blvd Saint Michel, 75272 Paris France*

ALLAKHVERDOV, GRANT RANTOVICH, chemist, researcher; b. Moscow, July 11, 1941; s. Rant A. and Larisa A. (Baltaga) A.; m. Tatjana A. Matkovskaya, May 26, 1972; 1 child, George. Degree in engring., Moscow Inst. Fine Chem. Tech., 1967; DSc, State Inst. Chem. Reagents, Moscow, 1972; prof., Gorky U., 1986. Engr. State Inst. Chem. Reagents and Pure Chem. Substances, Moscow, 1965-72, head of lab., 1972-83, head of dept., 1983—. Contbr. over 100 articles to profl. jours.; inventor in field. Mem. Russian Acad. Engring. Scis., N.Y. Acad. Scis. Home: Sumskoy proezd 4-4-304, Moscow 113208, Russia Office: State Inst Chem Reagents & High Purity Substances, Bogorodsky val 3, Moscow 107076, Russia

ALLAL, ABDELKARIM SAID, radiation oncologist, researcher; b. Tlemcen, Algeria, Nov. 11, 1960; arrived in Switzerland, 1991; s. Boumediene Allal and Zoubeida Haffaf; m. Amina Berrached; children: Sonia, Nihed. MD, Inst. des Scis. Medicales, Oran, Algeria, 1985; degree in radiation oncology, Cath. U. Louvain, Belgium, 1990. Fellow Ctr. George François Leclerc, Dijon, France, 1990-91; chief of clinic Cantonal U. Hosp. of Geneva, Geneva, 1991-92, 93-98; head dept. Hosp. Frantz Fanon, Blida, Algeria, 1992-93; assoc. physician Cantonal U. Hosp. of Geneva, 1998—. Contbr. articles to sci. and profl. jours. Grantee Ministry of Edn., Algeria, 1986, Geneva League Against Cancer, 1997. Mem. Am. Soc. Therapeutic Radiology and Oncology, European Soc. Therapeutic Radiology and Oncology, European Sch. Oncology. Office: Cantonal U Hosp of Geneva, 1227 Geneva Switzerland

ALLAM, SCHAFIK, Egyptology educator; b. Benha, Egypt, Dec. 9, 1928; came to W. Ger., 1954.; BA, Cairo U., 1949, diploma of archaeology, 1952; PhD, U. Göttingen, Fed. Republic Germany, 1960; habilitation, U. Tübingen, Fed. Republic Germany, 1968. Asst. Cairo U., 1953-54; lectr. Göttingen U., 1955-61; asst. U. Tübingen, 1961-69, prof., 1972—; reader Sorbonne/Paris, France, 1970-71. Author: Beiträge zum Hathorkult, 1963, Urkunden zum Rechtsleben im Altägypten, 1973—, Untersuchungen zum Rechtsleben im Altägypten, 1973—. Home: Weissdornweg 14/85, 72076 Tübingen Germany Office: Aegyptologisches Inst, Schloss, D-72070 Tübingen Germany

ALLAMI, SHAMSI, pediatrician, educator; b. Kermanshah, Iran, Jan. 4, 1942; d. Abbas and Iran Allami; m. Arshad Mirza Shahid, May 14, 1988. MD, Mashaad (Iran) U., 1972. Trainer in pediat. Mashaad U., 1968-71, Tehran (Iran) U., 1971-72; pediatrician Iranian Ministry Oil, Tehran, 1972, Social Security Clinic and Pediat. Hosp. No. 4, Tehran, 1971-77; with Iranian Ministry Health Clinic, Tehran, 1977-78, Baharloo Hosp., Tehran, 1978-79; chief of ward Pediat. Akhwaan Hosp., 1985-97; asst. prof. Azaad Med. U., Tehran, 1991-97; cons., chief of ward, Takhti Hosp., Tehran, 1979-85, Tehran Med. U. Akhwaan Hosp., Tehran, 1992-97, Azimabaad Med. Ctr., 1997-98, Zyayaan Hosp., Tehran, 1998—. Contbr. articles to med. jours. Scholar Tehran U. Med. Scis., 1992-98. Mem. Iranian Pediat. Soc. Avocations: historical stamps, travel, studying latest journals. Home: PO Box 14155-5747, Tehran 14, Iran Office: Zyaxaan Hosp, Abuzaar St, Tehran Iran

ALLAN, GEORGE WILLIAM, computer scientist, educator; b. Aberdeen, Scotland, Dec. 30, 1945; s. George and Williamina (McCullouch) A.; m. Sharon Peggy Bramson, Mar. 25, 1967 (div. 1986); children: Andrea, James, Gordon, Cameron, Bradley. BS, U. Reading, Eng., 1967; MA in Edn., U. Portsmouth, Eng., 1997. Commd. sub-lt. Royal Navy, 1974, advanced through grades to lt. comdr., 1978; Univ. lectr. Royal Naval Engring. Coll., Manadon, Eng., 1976-80; dep. tng. mgr. Def. Automatic Data Processing Tng. Ctr., Blandford Forum, Eng., 1980-84; project leader Ministry of Def., London, 1984-86, project mgr., 1986-89; project dir. Ctr. for Weapon Analysis and Trials, Portsmouth, 1989-91; ret. Royal Navy, 1990; sr. lectr. U. Portsmouth, 1991—; dir. Deepwood Co., Fareham, Eng., 1990—; mng. dir. P.M.A., Fareham, 1992—; dep. chair, configuration mgmt. specialist group, 1995-99. Author: A Systems Approach to Project Management; acad. editor Computer Auditors Jour., 1994-99. Lt. comdr. Royal Navy, 1974-90. Mem. IEEE, Brit. Computer Soc. (examiner profl. exams. body, dep. chair C.M.S.G. 1995-99), Inst. Quality Assurance, Mensa. Roman Catholic. Avocations: bridge, golf, choral singing. Office: U Portsmouth, Dept Info Sys, Portsmouth PO1 3AE, England

ALLAN, JOHN STEELE, marketing professional, educator; b. Aberdeen, Scotland, Apr. 3, 1941; s. Andrew Allan and Agnes Whitelaw (Morrison) A.; m. Veronica Edmonds; children: Caroline Rose, Tavia Katriona, Peter, Alexandra, Flora. MA, Cambridge (Eng.) U., 1962. Cert. Inst. Mktg., Inst. Work Study. Prodn. mgr. Beyford Ltd., Manningtree, Eng., 1962-64; buyer Boots Co. PLC, London, 1964-69; sales mgr. Granada Group, London, 1969-71; sr. buyer John Lewis PLC, London, 1971-78, 82-95; mng. dir. Dundale Group, 1978-82. Author: 3 NVY Level 3 Book 1, 1992, Team Management, 1994, Motivating People, 1996, How to Cut Costs in Business, 1997. Methodist. Avocations: trout fishing, gardening, motorbikes. Home: 1 Manor Rd, Herts Tring HP235DA, England

ALLAN, JONATHAN DAVID, autograph dealer, pop culture historian; b. Grasmere, N.H., July 23, 1948; s. David Nisbet and Natalie Mary (Chandler) A.; m. Barbara Lauderbach, 1966 (div.); 1 child, Jonathan David II; m. Nancy Page, 1982. BA magna cum laude, U. N.H., 1972. Registered dealer. Bookseller, book buyer, columnist, book reviewer, freelance writer, 1972-81; co-owner, pres. Elmer's Nostalgia, Inc., Sanford, Maine, 1981—. Author: The Rock Trivia Book, 1976; columnist; mem. adv. bd. Autograph Collector Mag., 1986-92. N.H. chmn. Nat. Com. to Reopen the Rosenberg Case, 1973-77; vol. York County Shelters, Alfred, Maine, 1993—. Served with USNR, 1966-67. Mem. ACLU, NAACP, Ams. United for Separation Ch. and State, Universal Autograph Collectors Club (Outstanding Autograph Dealer award 1998), Am. Polit. Items Collectors, Maine People's Alliance, Planned Parenthood, People for the Am. Way, So. Poverty Law Ctr., Amnesty Internat., McFarlane Clan Soc., Phi Beta Kappa. Mem. Socialist Party U.S.A. Avocations: collecting autographs and historical ephemera, painting, gardening, doing historical research. E-mail: jon@elmers.net. Office: Elmer's Nostalgia Inc 3 Putnam St Sanford ME 04073-2024

ALLAN, LYLE JAMES, political science educator; b. Melbourne, Victoria, Australia, Jan. 12, 1944; s. Olliver and Mavis Allan. BCom, U. Melbourne, 1969, MA, 1981. Coord. flexible lng. Victoria U. Tech., 1975-98; dir. Edn. Credit Union Ltd., Melbourne, 1981-85. Author: Introduction to Australian Government, 1994; contbr. articles to profl. jours., chpts. to books. Pres. Australian Labor Party Disputes Tribunal, Melbourne, 1991-99; treas. Melbourne Unitarian Peace Meml. Ch., 1995-2000. Rsch. scholar, Monash U., 1999—. Mem. Australian Coll. Edn., Australasian Polit. Studies Assn., Lions. Mem. Australian Labor Party. Unitarian. Avocation: reading. Office: Monash U Sch Polit Inquiry, 13 Beavers Rd, Northcote 3070 VIC, Australia

ALLAN, PERCY, consultant; b. London, July 24, 1946; arrived in Australia, 1953; s. Emil Allan and Bodil Bach Hansen. B of Econs., Sydney (Australia) U., 1968, M of Econs., 1971. Sr. econs. officer Bank of New South Wales, Sydney and London, 1971-75; officer in charge indsl. devel. divsn. Dept. Labour and Industry, Port Moresby, New Guinea, 1975-76; asst. chief economist New South Wales Treasury, Sydney, 1976-80; sr. policy advisor to state treas. Sydney, 1981-85; sec. New South Wales Treasury, Sydney, 1985-94; chmn. NSW Treasury Corp., 1985-94; fin. dir. Boral Ltd., Sydney, 1994-96; vis. prof. grad. sch. mgmt. Macquarie U., 1997—; dir. Allen Consulting Group, Sydney, 1997-98; prin. Percy Allan and Assocs. Pty Ltd., Sydney, 1998—; chmn. NSW Premier's Coun. on Cost and Quality of Govt., Sydney, 1999—, Constellation Capital Mgmt. Ltd., Sydney, 1999—. Contbr. articles to profl. jours. Convener The Reform Club, 1994—; trustee Com. Econ. Devel. Australia, 1997—. Decorated Order of Australia. Fellow Australian Inst. Mgmt., Australian Soc. CPAs, Australian Inst. Co. Dirs.; mem. Inst. Pub. Adminstrn. (pres. NSW br. 1993-94), Amnesty Internat. (NSW parliamentary br., treas. 1988-94). Avocations: films, theater, art, economic and current affairs. Home: 10 Saint Marys St, Balmain NSW 2041, Australia

ALLAOUCHICHE, BERNARD, anesthesiologist; b. Marseille, France, Nov. 10, 1960; s. Jean and Daniele (Borra) A.; m. Patricia Adrienne Genis, Aug. 22, 1987; 1 child, Lauriane. MD, U. Claude Bernard, Lyon, France, 1991, M in Biology, 1995. Intern, resident Edouard Herriot Hosp. and Croix-Rousse Hosp., Lyon; fellow Hospices Civils de Lyon, France, 1985-91, 91-95, assoc. prof. medicine, 1996—. Contbr. articles to profl. jours. Recipient Infectious Diseases Investigation award French Soc. Critical Care Medicine, 1993. Mem. Soc. Critical Care Medicine, Soc. Anesthesiology (assoc.). Avocations: music, sport, cinema. Home: Le Village, 38080 Saint Marcel Bel Acc France Office: Pavilion N Hosp L E Herriot, Intensive Care Unit, 69437 Lyon 03, France

ALLARDICE, DAVID JOHN, fuel technologist; b. Melbourne, Victoria, Australia, June 26, 1941; s. Kenneth John and Melva Jean (Brewster) A.; m. Alison Nethercote, Aug. 21, 1965; children: Geoffrey John, Lachlan David. BSc with honors, U. Melbourne, 1962, MSc with honors, 1964, PhD, 1967. Chartered chemist, chartered engr. Rsch. assoc. Pa. State U., State College, 1967-70; rsch. scientist State Electricity Commn. of Victoria, Melbourne, 1970-82; mgr. devel. Victorian Brown Coal Coun., Melbourne, 1982-85; mgr. bus. devel. and rsch. Coal Corp., Victoria, Melbourne, 1985-93; gen. mgr. Coal Corp., Melbourne, Victoria, Australia, 1993-95; mgr. coal tech. HRL Ltd., Mulgrave, Victoria, Australia, 1995-99; mng. dir. Allardice Cons., Vermont, Australia, 1999—; mem. Nat. Energy Coun., Canberra, ACT, 1989-91; dir. Australian Coal Industry Rsch. Labs., Sydney, 1987-91. Recipient Pub. Svc. medal Australian Govt., 1994. Fellow Australian Inst. Energy (pres. 1988-89), Royal Australian Chem. Inst., Inst. Energy. Achievements include research in brown coal science and utilization technology; internationally recognized expert on low rank coal. Office: HRL Ltd Allardice Cons, 10 Arcady Grove, Vermont VIC 3133, Australia

ALLARDT, ERIK ANDERS, academic administrator, educator; b. Helsingfors, Finland, Aug. 9, 1925; s. Arvid and Marita I. (Heikel) A.; m. Sagi E. Nylander; children: Jörg, Monica, Barbro. MA, U. Helsinki, Finland, 1947, PhD, 1952; PhD (hon.), U. Stockholm, 1978, Abo Acad., Finland, 1978, U. Uppsala, Sweden, 1984, U. Bergen, 1996, U. Copenhagen, 2000. Instr. sociology U. Helsinki, 1948-53; rsch. asst. bur. of applied social rsch. Columbia U., 1954; rsch. dir. Helsinki Sch. of Social Scis., 1955-57; prof. U. Helsinki, 1958-70, 80-85; rsch. prof. Acad. of Finland, 1970-80, pres., 1986-91; chancellor Abo Acad. Univ., 1992-94; vis. prof. U. Calif., Berkely, 1962-63, U. Ill., Urbana, 1966-67, U. Wis., Madison, 1970, U. Mannheim, Fed. Republic of Germany, 1985; vis. scholar Wilson Ctr., Washington, 1978-79. Author: Drinking Norms and Drinking Habits, 1957, About Dimensions of Welfare, 1973, Implications of the Ethnic Revival in Industrialized Society, 1979, (with Lysgaard and Sorensen) Sociologin i Sverige, vetenskap, miljo och organisation, 1988, The History of Social Sciences in Finland 1828-1918, 1997; author, editor: (with Y. Littunen) Cleavages, Ideologies and Party Systems, 1964, (with S. Rokkan) Mass Politics, 1970, Acta Sociologica, 1968-71, Scandinavian Polit. Studies, 1975-76, (with M. Alestalo, A. Rychard and W. Wesolowski) The Transformations of Europe, 1994. Chmn. Finnish sect. Amnesty Internat., Finland, 1977-78, Tampere Inst. for Peace and Conflict Research, Finland, 1977-78, Coms. for Devel. of Future Studies, Finland,

1988-89. Mem. The Norwegian Acad. Sci. and Letters (fgn. mem. 1986—), European Sci. Found. (exec. coun. 1987-92, v.p. 1990-92), Academia Europaea (founder mem. 1988—), Finnish Soc. Scis. and Letters (hon. mem. 1988—, chmn. 1985-86), Scandinavia-Japan Sasakawa Fond. (bd. dirs. 1987-96), Royal Swedish Acad. Letters, History and Antiquities (fgn. 1992—), Polish Sociol. Assn. (hon. mem. 1996—). Home: Unionsgatan 45 B 40, FI-00170 Helsinki Finland Office: U Helsinki Comparative Soc, Rsch Group Box 18, FI-00014 Helsinki Finland

ALLARS, PETER DAVID, retired contractor; b. London, Apr. 17, 1930; s. Herbert Charles and Sybil Anness (Whitby) A.; m. Doreen Daphne Hall, June 27, 1953; children: Nicholas, Gregory, Alastair. Diploma, East Ham Tech. Coll., 1952. Surveyor James Longley Crawley, Sussex, Eng., 1952-59; mgr. J. M. Jones, Maidenhead, Eng., 1959-62, McAuley McIlroy, Bangor, 1962-65; mgr. Shepherd Constrn., York, Eng., 1965-81, dir., 1981-88; ret., 1988; Chmn. Shepherd/Haden Joint Venture, Petersborough City Hosp., 1984-88; founder, chmn. Quality Brickwork Award, London, 1985-87. Author: (booklet) Financial Management for Contractors, 1986, (book) The Practice of Site Management, 1992; contbr. various articles to profl. jours. Treas. Conservative Grantham, 1977-80. Mem. Nat. Fedn. Nottingham (pres. 1978-79), Bldg. Trades Employers Assn. Avocations: golf, bridge. Home: Holly House, Mill Ln, Martin LN4 3QZ, England

ALLATT, JAMES PETER, management consultant; b. Halifax, Yorkshire, Eng., Sept. 15, 1934; s. Harry and Winifred (Thacker) A.; m. Patricia Armitage, July 23, 1966; 1 child, Jonathan. BA in Mech. Sci., St. John's Coll., Cambridge, Eng., 1953, MA in Mech. Sci., 1956. Tech. trainee, machine designer S. Hodgson & Co., Ltd., Halifax, 1958-62; mgmt. trainee Crompton Parkinson Ltd., Guiseley, Eng., 1962-66; works mgr. Crompton Parkinson Ltd., Newport, Wales, 1966-68; operating cons. Orr & Boss and Ptnrs., Ltd., London, 1968-73, supervising cons., 1973-76; mng. dir. Crompton Parkinson Vidor, Ltd., Guiseley, 1976-84; CEO CBL Ceramics, Ltd., Milford Haven, Wales, 1985-90; prin. Peter Allat Assocs., Durham, Eng., 1990-94; chmn. no. counties br. Inst. Dirs., Newcastle-upon-Tyne, Eng., 1992-95; bus. counsellor Entrust, Newcastle-upon-Tyne, 1984-85; dir. Orr & Boss and Ptnrs. Pension Fund Trustee Co., Ltd., London, 1974-76. Mem. coun. St. Williams Found., York, 1995—. With Royal Navy, 1957-58. Fellow Inst. Mgmt. Cons. (cert.); mem. Inst. Elec. Engrs. (chartered). E-mail: peter@allatt.com. Home & Office: Hoppy Acres Brancepeth, Durham DH7 8EL, England

ALLAVENA, MARCEL, physical-chemistry researcher; b. Nogent sur Marne, France, Aug. 21, 1930; s. Marcel and Madeleine (Dorangeon) A.; m. Josette Levy, Mar. 23, 1961; children: Stephane, David. Lic. scis., U. Sorbonne, Paris, 1958, doctorat 3 degree cycle, 1960, doctorat scis., 1965. Stagiaire de recherches Centre Nat. de la Recherche Scientifique, Paris, 1959-60, chargé de recherches, 1960-70, dir. recherches, 1970—; com. nat. Centre National de la REcherche Scientifique, 1980-86, chargé de Mission dept. chimie, 1990-93, dir. Lab. of Dynamique des Interactions Moleculaires, 1984—. Contbr. articles to profl. jours. Mem. Societe Française de Chimie. Home: 7 Ter Rue Louis Xavier de Ricard, 94120 Fontenay Sous Bois France Office: Univ P & M Curie Ctr Nat Recherche Scientif, 4 Place Jussieu, 75252 Paris France

ALLAWALA, S.M. IDREES, cosmetics executive; b. Delhi, India, Oct. 22, 1931; arrived in Pakistan, 1947; s. S.M. Ismail and Fatima Bi A.; m. Naseema Begum, 1955; children: Anjum, Mansoor, Imran, Kamran, Naeem. Grad., Cambridge U., Delhi, 1947. Mng. dir. Kohinoor Chem. Co. (Pvt.) Ltd., Karachi, 1960—; bd. dirs. Kohinoor Chem. Co. (Pvt.) Ltd., Kohinoor Container (Pvt.) Ltd., Mercantile Industries (Pvt.) Ltd., Allawala Bros. (Pvt.) Ltd.; mng. dir. Admiral of N.Y., Karachi, 1976—; chief exec., dir. Al-Mansoor Trading Agys. (Pvt.) Ltd., Karachi, 1978—; mng. dir. Internat. Consumer Products (Pvt.) Ltd., Karachi, 1986—; chmn., dir. Idrees Textile Mills Ltd., 1990—; chief exec., dir. Bilal Omair Textile Mills Ltd., 1992—. Mem. Karachi Boat Club, Karachi Golf Club. Home: 289/290 Delhi Mercantile, Housing Soc, Alamgir Rd, Karachi 74800, Pakistan Office: Al-Mansoor Trading Agys Pvt, 5th Fl Tibet Centre, MA Jinnah Rd, Karachi Karachi 74400, Pakistan

ALLDIS, JOHN, musical director; b. London, Aug. 10, 1929; s. William James and Nell (Bennet) A.; m. Ursula Mason, July 23, 1960; children: Dominic, Robert. MA, Cambridge (U.K.) U., 1956. Musical dir. John Alldis Choir, London, 1960-85; prof. Guildhall Sch. of Music, London, 1966-77; founder, condr. London Symphony Chorus, 1966-69; condr. London Philharm. Choir, 1969-82, Danish Radio Choir, 1971-77, Cameran Singers, Israel, 1986-88, Group Vocale de France, Paris, 1978-83, London Philharm. Choir, 1969-82; com. mem. Vaughan Williams Trust, London, 1974—. Decorated Chevalier Arts and Letters (France). Fellow Royal Soc. Arts, Royal Coll. Organists (assoc.), Westminster Choir Coll. (Princeton, N.J.)(hon.). Avocations: swimming, reading. Home and Office: 3 Wool Rd, London SW20 OHN, England

ALLEGRA, LUIGI SALVATORE, medicine educator, researcher; b. Palermo, Italy, Apr. 15, 1938; s. Bartolomeo N. and Elena (Gattuso) A.; m. Layla M. Rigazzi, Jan. 21, 1963; children: Elena Désirée, Daniela. MD, U. Palermo, 1961, PhD, 1966. Tng. in respiratory disease U. Palermo, 1961-64; rsch. asst. U. Montreal, Que., Can., 1963-64; asst. prof. respiratory diseases U. Milan, 1968-73, assoc. prof., 1973-81, prof., 1981—, dean Med. Sch., 1984-90, dir. Inst. Respiratory Diseases, 1988—, dir. Sch. Specialization in Respiratory Diseases, 1992—; sci. dir. Italian Jour. Thoracic Diseases, 1980—. Editor: The Trilogy of Bronchial Mucology, 1988, 89, 90, Methods in Asthmology, 1994 (best Italian sci. book award 1995), Chlamydia Pneumoniae Infection, 1996, Chlamydia Pneumoniae, Heart and Lung, 1998, Asthma and Gastroesophageal Reflux, 1999; patentee device for studying gas exchs. in asthma. Recipient C. Forlanini gold medal Italian Fedn. Against Tb, 1990, Trinacria Scientifica award City of Palermo, 1991. Mem. European Respiratory Soc. (pres. 1984-85), European Soc. Clin. Respiratory Physiology (v.p. 1977-79), Italian Soc. Respiratory Medicine (pres. 1993-96). Avocations: geography, ethnology. Office: U Milan Inst Respir Dis, Via F Sforza 35, 20122 Milan Italy

ALLEGRE, MAURICE, retired public company executive; b. Antibes, France; s. Guy and Renee-Lise (Bermond) A.; m. Catherine Pierre, Feb. 16, 1962; children: Frederic, Mathilde. Student Ecole Polytechnique, Paris, 1951; student, Ecole des Mines, 1954, Ecole du Petrole, 1956; Lic. en Droit, U. Paris, 1956. Oil exploration/prodn. Ministere de l' Industrie, Paris, 1957-62; dir. des mines Organisne Saharien, Alger, Algeria, 1962-64; personal adviser of ministry of fin. Paris, 1965-67; del. informatics French Govt., Paris, 1967-74; dir. gen. French Petroleum Inst., Paris, 1975-81; dir. innovation Ministere de la Recherche, Paris, 1981-84; dir. gen. to pres. BRGM, Paris, 1984-92; pres. Andra, Chatenay-Malabry, France, 1993-98; ret., 1998; cons. in energy and nuclear waste. Decorated chevalier de Legion d'Honneur, officer de L'Ordre du Merite (France). Roman Catholic. Avocations: photography, sailing, hiking, opera.

ALLEGRETTI, EDWARD PHILIP, electrical construction company executive; b. San Jose, Calif., Jan. 31, 1962; s. John Michael and Shirley Bernal Allegretti. BS in Bus. Adminstrn. with distinction, San Jose State U., 1984. Loan and collection mgr. BayTech Fed. Credit Union, Santa Clara, Calif., 1993-95; corp. credit mgr. MCI WorldCom, Hayward, Calif., 1995-98; dir. credit and fin. svcs. The Brix Group, Inc., Campbell, Calif., 1998-2000; dir. credit Rosendin Electric, Inc., 2000—. Chmn. San Jose City Coun. Salary Setting Commn., 1987-88; dir. Burbank Sanitary Dist., Santa Clara County, 1992-93. Mem. Internat. Credit Assn. San Jose (pres. 1999-2000), Founders of Santa Clara County (bd. dirs. 1999-2000), Los Californianos (bd. dirs. 1999), San Jose Country Club. Republican. Home: 10981 Edgemont Dr San Jose CA 95127-1740

ALLEGRI, RICARDO FRANCISCO, physician, researcher, consultant, educator; b. Buenos Aires, Dec. 9, 1958; s. Norberto Carlos and Marta Alica (Valicenti) A.; m. Mirta Lidia Cragnolino, Oct. 26, 1984; children: Agostina, Antonella. Bachelor, San Martin Nat. Sch., Buenos Aires, 1975; grad. in Medicine, U. Buenos Aires, 1981; grad. in Neurology, Ministry of Pub. Health and Environ., Argentina, 1989; MD, U. Buenos Aires, 1993. Fellow dept. neurology Posadas's Nat. Hosp., Buenos Aires, 1983-86, chief fellows dept. neurology, 1986-87; fellow in behavioral neurology dept. neurology U. St. Etienne, France, 1989; head behavioral neurology unit dept. neurology Buenos Aires Brit. Hosp., 1990—; head neurology svc. Zubizarreta Hosp., 1992—; head neuropshychology unit CEMIC Hosp., 1991—; rschr. CONICET, 1996—. Fellow Am. Acad. Neurology (corr.); mem. Internat. Neuropsychol. Soc., Internat. Psychogeriatric Assn., Internat. Neuropsychiatric Assn., Argentinean Neurol. Soc., Argentinean Neuropsychol. Soc., Argentinean Soc. Clin. Rsch., Behavioral Neurology Soc. Roman Catholic. Avocations: sailing, windsurfing. E-mail: allegri@jede.net. Office: CEMIC, Galvan 4102, 1431 Buenos Aires Argentina

ALLEMAND, VALERIE, veterinarian; b. Paris, Nov. 24, 1971; d. Jean-Pierre and Annick (Rablade) A. BS, Ecole Nat. Veterinaire, Toulouse, France, 1996. Veterinarian clinics, France, 1996—. Avocations: fitness, reading books, movies, theater. Home: 78 bd de la Marquette, 31000 Toulouse France

ALLEN, ALGERNON S.B.P., government official; b. Nassau, Bahamas, Apr. 16, 1950; married; 5 children. BA Law, London U. Called to Brit. and Bahamas bar, 1973. Pres. Key Club; mem. for Marathon Ho. of Assembly, Nassau, 1987—, min. youth and culture, 1992-97; min. housing and social devel. Cabinet, Nassau, 1997—. Pres. Young People's Christian Movement. Mem. Free Nat. Movement. Office: Min Housing & Social Devel, PO Box N-3206F, Nassau Bahamas*

ALLEN, ALICE, communications and marketing executive; b. N.Y.C., May 31, 1943; d. C. Edmonds and Helen (McCreery) A.; 1 child, Helen. Student, Conn. Coll., 1961. Pres. Alice Allen, Inc., N.Y.C., 1970-83; sr. v.p. Robert Marston, N.Y.C., 1983-84, Cunningham & Walsh, N.Y.C., 1984-86, Carl Byoir (acquired by Hill & Knowlton), N.Y.C., 1986; sr. v.p., dir. comms. and corp. mktg. Hill & Knowlton, N.Y.C., 1986-88; pres., owner Allen Comms. Group, Inc., N.Y.C., 1988-95, Alice Allen Comms, 1995—. Bd. dirs. Family Dymanics, N.Y.C., 1976-78, Veritas, 1980-85; v.p. Jr. League, N.Y.C., 1975-76; Mem. adv. bd. Enterprise Found., 1992—. Mem. Pub. Rels. Soc. Am., Pub. Publicity Assn. (pres. 1969-71), Women's Media Group, Comm. Network. Office: Alice Allen Comms 320 E 72nd St New York NY 10021-4769

ALLEN, ALPIAN, Saint Vincentian government official; married; 3 children. Cert., Secondary Sch. Mgmt.-Internat. Tng. Inst., Sydney, Australia; diploma in Edn., St. Vincent Tchrs' Coll.; cert. in Edn., U. West Indies. Mem. Parliament, 1989—; parliamentary sec. Ministry Health and Environment Govt. of St. Vincent and the Grenadines, Kingstown, min. health and environment; min. fgn. affairs, tourism and info. Govt. of St.nt Vincent and the Grenadines, Kingstown, from 1994, now min. edn., culture, womens and ecclesiastical affairs. Office: Ministry Education, Govt Bldgs, Kingstown Saint Vincent and the Grenadines*

ALLEN, BARRY JOHN, physicist; b. Melbourne, Australia, June 10, 1940; s. William Parker Allen and Louisa Arendina Boschart; m. Cynthia Diane Pike, Feb. 26, 1969; children: Juliet, Nicole. BS, U. Melbourne, 1961, MS, 1963; PhD, U. Wollongong, 1974; DSc, U. Melbourne, 1981. chmn. Experimental Radiation Oncology info. meetings, 1993—, In Vivo Composition info. meetings, 1994—; rsch. staff Oak Ridge (Tenn.) Nat. Labs., 1969-72. Prin. rsch. scientist Australian Atomic Energy Commn., 1963-86; chief rsch. scientist Nuclear Sci. & Tech. Orgn., 1987-94; prin. hosp. scientist St. George Hosp., Kogarah, Australia, 1994—. Contbr. chpts. to books, over 230 articles to sci. jours. including Stellar Nucleosynthesis, Resonance Neutron Physics, Cancer Therapy, Body Composition. Grantee over 25 rsch. projects, 1985—. Fellow Australian Inst. Physics, Am. Phys. Soc., Australasian Coll. Physicists and Engrs. in Medicine (v.p. 1996, pres. NSW br. 1995-97, pres. coll. 1998-90); mem. Internat. Soc. Neutron Capture Therapy (pres. 1988-90), Clin. Oncology Group Australia (chmn. cancer rsch. group 1996—, melanoma and skin group 1995-96). Avocations: weight training, sailing, travel. Office: St George Cancer Care Ctr, Gray St, Kogarah NSW, Australia

ALLEN, BRIAN PHILIP, physicist; b. Derby, U.K., July 4, 1954; s. Clifford William and Jessie Audrey (Revill) A.; m. Carol Margaret Allen, Aug. 9, 1975; children: Simon Roger, Claire Nicole. BSc with honors, Reading Univ., Eng., 1975, PhD, 1980. Chartered physicist. Elect. devel. engr. GEC Reactor Equipment Ltd., Leicester, Eng., 1975-77; sr. scientist deBeers Ind. Diamond, Johannesburg, South Africa, 1980-83; systems engr. Bae Air Weapons Divsn., Hatfield, Eng., 1983-86; ops. mgr. Centronics Ltd., London, 1986-88; med. imaging mgr. EEV Ltd., Chelmsford, Eng., 1988-99; strategy mgr. Marconi Applied Tech., Chelmsford, 1999—. Mem. Inst. of Physics. Achievements include patent in reducing colour of diamond; creation in the laboratory of the natural diamond impurity structures, digital panoramic dental detection. Home: 30 Church Ln, Toppesfield CO9 4DS, England

ALLEN, CHARLES RICHARD, retired financial executive; b. Cleve., Mar. 10, 1926; s. Charles Ross and Jennie (Harmon) A.; m. Marion Elizabeth Taylor, Aug. 17, 1946; children: Kathleen Allen Templin, Jeanne Allen Duffy, Kenneth. Student, Occidental Coll., 1942-43; BS, UCLA, 1945. Acctg. supr. N.Am. Aviation, Inc., Los Angeles, 1946-55; div. controller TRW, Inc., Los Angeles, 1955-61, dir. fin., 1961-64; asst. controller TRW, Inc., Cleve., 1964-66, controller, 1966-67, v.p., 1967-77, exec. v.p., 1977-86, chief fin. officer, 1967-86; bd. dirs. Titan Corp., San Diego. Trustee Maritime Mus. San Diego; mem. San Diego World Affairs Coun. Served with USNR, 1943-46. Mem. Fin. Execs. Inst., Univ. Club, City Club of San Diego. Home: 1730 Avenida Del Mundo Coronado CA 92118-3021

ALLEN, CLAXTON EDMONDS, III, investment banker; b. N.Y.C., Aug. 27, 1944; s. C. Edmonds and Helen (McCreery) A. BA, Washington and Lee U., 1964, JD, 1967. Bar: N.Y. 1969. Assoc. Simpson Thacher & Bartlett, N.Y.C., 1967-70; assoc. gen. counsel GE Credit Corp., N.Y.C., 1970-71; investment banker Merrill Lynch, Pierce, Fenner & Smith, Inc., N.Y.C., 1971-72; pres. Gloucester Internat. Ltd., N.Y.C., 1972-82, Comanche Exploration Corp., N.Y.C., 1981-86, Compass Internat. Corp., N.Y.C., 1982—, Horizon Coal Corp., Mineral Res. Corp., N.Y.C., 1982-85, Compass Coal Corp., N.Y.C., 1986-91, Overseas & Fgn. Investors, Inc., N.Y.C., 1990—; bd. dirs. Purbrook Ltd., Cranwood Investments Ltd., L&H Internat. Ltd. Mem. Met. Club. Home: 405 E 54th St New York NY 10022-5123 Office: 123 E 54th St 8th Fl New York NY 10022-4506

ALLEN, DAVID, government official; b. York, Maine, May 15, 1942; s. Pliny Arunah and Tillie (MacQuinn) A.; m. JoAnn Moeckly, 1968 (div. 1975); children: Torrie, Heather; m. Robin Lee Perry, Mar. 11, 1983; children: Rebecca, Patrick. BA, Lake Forest Coll., 1965; MA, U. Ariz., 1967, PhD, 1968. Asst. prof. dept. psychology S.D. State U., Brookings, 1968-71; rsch. psychologist CIA, Washington, 1971-78; chief rsch. br. CIA, 1978-85, dep. chief psychol. svcs. divsn., 1985-87; chief rsch. and info. systems divsn. CIA, Washington, 1987-90, trustee investment plan, 1988-92, investigator Office of Insp. Gen., 1990-92, chief info. systems Latin Am. divsn., 1992-95; chief electronic messaging divsn., program dir. Enterprise Messaging Svcs., Office of Comm. CIA, Washington, 1995-97; dir. program devel./mktg. for Ctr. for Sci. and Tech. Mitretek Sys., Inc., 1998—. Contbr. articles to profl. jours. Rsch. fellow USPHS, 1967-68; rsch. grantee NSF, 1970-71; recipient U.S. Govt. Career Intelligence medal, CIA, 1997. Republican. Avocations: choral singing, amateur radio, cosmology, mathematics, high technology. Home: 905 N Emerson St Arlington VA 22205-2562

ALLEN, DAVID ELLISTON, research administrator; b. Southport, Lancashire, Eng., Jan. 17, 1932; s. Gerald Elliston and Alice Joan (Davis) A.; m. Gillian Clare Archibald, May 13, 1972. BA, MA, U. Cambridge, Eng., 1953, PhD, 1988; D of Univ. (hon.), U. Essex, Eng., 1995. Exec. Brit. Market Research Bur. Ltd., London, 1956-57; research mgr. Dorland Advt. Ltd., London, 1957-65; com. sec. Econ. and Social Research Council, London, 1967-86; co-ordinator of history of medicine programme The Wellcome Trust, London, 1987-97. Author: British Tastes, 1968, The Victorian Fern Craze, 1969, The Naturalist in Britain: a Social History, 1976, The Botanists, 1986, Flora of the Isle of Man, 1986. Fellow Linnean Soc. London (H.H. Bloomer medal 1981); mem. Bot. Soc. of Brit. Isles (hon. gen. sec. 1967-69, pres. 1985-87), Soc. for History of Natural History (pres. 1977-80, Founders' medal 1998), Brit. Soc. for History of Sci. (council 1978-81). Avocation: field botany. Home: Lesney Cottage, Middle Rd, Winchester, Hampshire SO22 5EJ, England

ALLEN, DONALD GEORGE, retired diplomat; b. London, June 26, 1930; s. Sidney George and Doris Elsie (Abercrombie) A.; m. Sheila Isobel Bebbington, Mar. 5, 1955; children: Stephen George (dec.), David Martin, Mark Andrew. Cert., Southall Grammar Sch., 1948. With Her Majesty's Diplomatic Svc., London and abroad, 1948-80; dir. investigations Parliamentary Commr.'s Office, London, 1980-82, dep. ombudsman, 1982-90; ret., 1990. Commr. Broadcasting Complaints Commn., London, 1990-97. Named Companion of the Order of St. Michael and St. George, The Queen of England, 1981. Mem. Brit. and Irish Ombudsman Assn., Vets. Squash Club of Gt. Britain (v.p. 1980—), Royal Automobile Club. Mem. Ch. of England. Avocations: squash, golf, tennis. Home: 99 Parkland Grove, Ashford TW15 2JF, England

ALLEN, DONALD VAIL, investment executive, writer, concert pianist; b. South Bend, Ind., Aug. 1, 1928; s. Frank Eugene and Vera Irene (Vail) A.; m. Betty Dunn, Nov. 17, 1956. BA magna cum laude, UCLA, 1972, MA, 1973, D (hon.), 1973. Pres., chmn. bd. dirs. Cambridge Investment Corp.; music editor and critic Times-Herald, Washington; music critic L.A. Times; lectr. George Washington U., Am. U., Washington, Pasadena City Coll. Transl. works of Ezra Pound from Italian into English; author of papers on the musical motifs in the writings of James Joyce; specialist in works of Beethoven, Chopin, Debussy, Liszt, and Scriabin; premiere performances of works of Paul Creston, Norman dello Joio, Ross Lee Finney, appearances in N.Y., L.A., Washington; represented by William Matthews Concert Agy., N.Y.C.; selected by William Steinway and Sascha Greiner of Steinway Piano Co. as an exclusive Steinway concert artist. Pres. Funds for Needy Children, 1974-76. Mem. Ctr. for Study of Presidency, Am. Mgmt. Assn., Internat. Platform Assn., Nat. Assn. Securities Dealers, Am. Guild Organists, Chamber Music Soc., Am. Mus. Natural History. Avocations: languages, music, travel, writing, stock market. Home: 670 W Via Rancho Pkwy Escondido CA 92029-7313

ALLEN, DWAYNE LEROY, information systems specialist; b. Sumter, S.C., Aug. 13, 1961; s. LeRoy and Charity (White) A.; m. Jennifer Marie Jackson, Nov. 28, 1992. BA in Comms., U. Va., 1984; postgrad., Yale U., 1993; MBA, George Washington U., 1996. Mgr. info. systems Roy Rogers divsn. Restaurant Ops. group Marriott Internat., Inc.; dir. corp. systems devel. info. systems and tech. divsn. reengring. Marriott Internat., Inc., Washington, dir. Marriott Yr. 2000 Project; v.p. info. tech. First Union Corp., Charlotte, N.C.; chief tech. advisor Hill Ventures, Detroit; mem. adv. bd. Am. Visions, Washington. Deacon, mem. pastoral search com. Heritage United Ch. of Christ, Reston; mem., cons. Greater Washington Cultural Alliance; vol. mentor Fairfax County Juvenile and Domestic Ct. Sys. Mem. Washington D.C. Electronic Data Interchange Users Group, Alpha Phi Alpha. Avocations: travel, sports, art, theater, basketball, golf. Office: First Union Corp 1 Marriott Dr Washington DC 20058-0001

ALLEN, FERGUS HAMILTON, writer, retired government official; b. London, Sept. 3, 1921; arrived in Ireland, 1922; s. Charles Winckworth and Marjorie Helen (Budge) A.; m. Margaret Joan Gorman, Aug. 1, 1947; children: Mary FitzGerald, Elizabeth Colclough. BA, U. Dublin, Ireland, 1944; M of Engring., Trinity Coll./U., Ireland, 1948; ScD, Trinity U. Dublin, Ireland, 1966. Dir. hydraulics rsch. Dept. Sci. and Indsl. Rsch., Wallingford, Eng., 1958-65; chief sci. officer Cabinet Office, London, 1965-69; first civil svc. commr. Civil Svc. Dept., London, 1974-81; cons. Boyden Internat. Ltd., London, 1982-86. Author: (poetry collections) The Brown Parrots of Providencia, 1993; Who Goes There?, 1996, Mrs. Powers Looks Over the Bay, 1999. State honoree as Companion of Order of the Bath, 1969. Fellow Instn. Civil Engrs. (mem. coun. 1962-71, Telford Gold medal 1958), Royal Soc. Lit., Athenaeum. Home: Dundrum, Wantage Rd Streatley, Reading, Berks RG8 9LB, England

ALLEN, GERALD (GERRY ALLEN), spirits company executive; b. Canton, Ohio, June 26, 1941; s. Tillman and Claudia Elva Allen; m. Donetta Lee Liggens, Sept. 15, 1963; children: Gerald, Terald, Sheryl; m. Patricia Ann Haegele, Apr. 6, 1993. BS, U. Nebr., 1965; MS in Stats., Morgan State U., 1971. Dir. EEO programs Foster Wheeler, Livingston, N.J., 1972-75; dir. human resources Johnson & Johnson, New Brunswick, N.J., 1975-78; dir. labor rels. GM, Detroit, 1978-85; v.p. human resources Gannett, N.Y.C., 1985-93; dir. indsl. rels. Joseph E. Seagram & Sons, N.Y.C., 1993—. Trustee United Food Comml. Workers, Englewood, N.J. Staff sgt. USAF, 1960-62. Home: 300 Taconic Rd Greenwich CT 06831-2847 Office: Joseph E Seagram & Sons 3 Gannett Dr Ste 1 White Plains NY 10604-3409

ALLEN, GERALD CAMPBELL FORREST, management consulting company owner; b. Boston, Jan. 1, 1924; s. Charles Francis and Sarah Ann (Campbell) A.; m. Anne Elisabeth Conrad, May 23, 1944; children: Katherine Sarah Anne, Ethan William John Campbell, Elisabeth Amy Martha Joan. BA, MA, Harvard U., 1945-49; PhD, U. Chgo., 1952. Ency. editor Consol. Book Pub., Chgo., 1952-54; advt. exec. Chgo. Tribune, 1954-59; pres. Gerald Allen Co., Chgo., 1960-66; v.p. Klau-Van Pietersom-Dunlap, Inc., Milw., 1967-71; v.p., dir. Unidex Pub. Co., Inc., Milw., 1971-80; chmn., CEO Allen Mgmt. Group, Inc., Milw., 1980—; pres. Psychologists in Advt., Chgo., 1965; instr. mktg. and bus. adminstrn. U. Wis., 1967-68; v.p., dir. Benchmark Mfg. Co., Inc., Milw.; cons. Kellett Commn. on Higher Edn. Mem. ad hoc Low Income Energy Task Force, State of Wis.; mem. energy crisis planning com. City of Milw. Capt. royal arty. Brit. Army, 1944-45, ETO. Fellow Royal Hort. Soc.; mem. Am. Mktg. Assn., Am. Statis. Assn., AAAS, Am. Econ. Assn., N.Y. Acad. Scis., Harvard Club of Wis., Harvard Club of Chgo., Mensa. Republican. Home: 13 Linden Manor Kewaunee WI 54216-1735 Office: Allen Mgmt Group Inc 1204 Forth St Kewaunee WI 54216-1777

ALLEN, HOWARD NORMAN, cardiologist, educator; b. Chgo., Nov. 19, 1936; s. Herman and Ida Gertrude (Weinstein) A.; children: Michael Daniel, Jeffrey Scott. BS, U. Ill., Chgo., 1958, MD, 1960. Diplomate Am. Bd. Internal Medicine, Am. Bd. Cardiovascular Disease, Nat. Bd. Med. Examiners. Intern Los Angeles County Gen. Hosp., L.A., 1960-61; resident in internal medicine Wadsworth VA Med. Ctr., L.A., 1961, 64-66; fellow in cardiology Cedars-Sinai Med. Ctr., L.A., 1966-67, dir. cardiac care unit Cedars of Lebanon Hosp. div., 1968-74, dir. Pacemaker Evaluation Ctr., 1968-89, dir. Cardiac Noninvasive Lab., 1972-88; Markus Found. fellow in cardiology St. George's Hosp., London, 1967-68; attending physician cardiology svc. Sepulveda (Calif.) VA Med. Ctr., 1972-86; pvt. practice Beverly Hills, Calif., 1988—; asst. prof. medicine UCLA, 1970-76, assoc. prof., 1976-84, adj. prof., 1984-88, clin. prof., 1988—; cons. Sutherland Learning Assocs., Inc., L.A., 1970-75; cardiology cons. Occidental Life Ins. Co., L.A., 1972-86. Contbr. articles to med. jours., chpts. to books. Commr. L.A. County Emergency Med. Svcs., 1989-91. Capt. M.C., U.S. Army, 1962-63, Korea. Fellow NSF, 1958, NIH, 1966-67. Fellow ACP, Am. Coll. Cardiology (Calif. chpt. dist. councilor, 1999—); mem. Am. Heart Assn. (fellow coun. on clin. cardiology, pres. Greater L.A. affiliate 1987-88, bd. dirs. 1979-94, Heart of Gold award 1994), U. Ill. Alumni Assn. (life, Loyalty award 1996), Cedars-Sinai Alumni Assn. (sec., treas. 2000—, exec. bd. 1999—), Big Ten Club So. Calif. (bd. dirs.), Alpha Omega Alpha, Pi Kappa Epsilon. Office: 414 N Camden Dr Ste 1100 Beverly Hills CA 90210-4532

ALLEN, JAMES CHARLTON, career officer; b. Columbus AFB, Miss., Sept. 8, 1965; s. James Robert and Henrietta Helene Allen; m. Laura Ann Keathley, Sept. 3, 1994; children: James (Jay) Robert II, Megan Ann. BS in Aerospace Engring., U. Kans., 1989. Commd. lt. comdr. USN, 1989; student naval flight officer USN, Pensacola, Fla., 1989-91, electronic counter measures officer, 1991-95; student aviator USN, various, 1995-97; pilot USN, NAS Whidbey Island, Wash., 1997—. Lutheran. Avocations: skiing, physical fitness.

ALLEN, JESSE OWEN, III, development manager; b. Albany, Ga., Apr. 7, 1938; s. Jesse Owen Jr. and Erma Hazel (Pearson) A.; children by previous marriage: Charlotte Renee, Garrett Owen, Cheryl Hazel; m. Barbara Joanna Smith Ozment, May 23, 1987; 1 stepchild, Pamela Ozment Cartee. LLB, LaSalle Law Sch., 1967; AS, U. State N.Y., Albany, 1978, BS in History, Lit. and Bus., 1986; MA in Philosophy, Calif. State U., 1987; PhD in Organizational Behavior, The Union Grad. Sch., 1991; postgrad., Oxford U.,

England, 1997. Founder, pres. Specific Action Corp., Greensboro, N.C., 1971—; pres. Inst. for Christian Studies, Inc., Greensboro, N.C., 1987—; bd. dirs. ECA Internat.; pres. Worldwide Travel, Greensboro, N.C., 1994—; lectr., cons. in field internat. Author: (book, manual, course) Weatherization Production Control, 1978, Personal Profile Labs, 1980, Management Power: The Specific Action Way, 1985, Personality Power: The Specific Action Way, 1988, Master of Personal Excellence Program, 1994; contbr. articles to profl. jours., Specific Action Management System, 1996, Specific Action Personality System, 1996, Specific Action Team System, 1997; patentee Allen valve, 1967. Named to Hon. Order of Ky. Cols., Commonwealth of Ky., 1978, Hon. Adm. State of Nebr., 1978. Mem. Am. Soc. Tng. and Devel. (pres. 1976, Best Chpt. award 1976), Nat. Speakers Assn. (cert. speaking profl. 1988), Greensboro City Club, Inst. Mgmt. Cons. (cert. 1989). Republican. Home: 520 Lindley Rd Greensboro NC 27410-4933 Office: Specific Action Corp PO Box 19125 Greensboro NC 27419-9125

ALLEN, JOHN, organic chemist; b. Torquay, Devon, Eng., Apr. 18, 1947; arrived in France, 1976; s. Stanley Allandale and Eileen Estelle (Andrews) A.; m. Patricia Joan Henderson, Oct. 16, 1976; children: Emma Elizabeth, Thomas John, George Michael. BTech., Brunel U., London, 1969; PhD, London U., 1972. Rsch. chemist Union Internat. Rsch.-U.K., St. Albans, 1972-74; team leader Amersham (Eng.) Internat.-U.K., 1974-76; rsch. group leader Synthelabo Rsch., Chilly, Mazarin, France, 1976-98; head dept. Synthelabo Rsch., Chilly, 1998-99; internat. dept. dir. Sanafi-Synthelabo, Chilly-Mazarin, France, 1999—; mem. adv. bd. Jour. of Labelled Compounds and Radiopharms., N.Y., 1987—; sci. chmn., organizer 5th Internat. Symposium of the Synthesis and Applications of Isotopes and Isotopically Labelled Compounds, Strasbourg, France, 1994. Editor: Synthesis and Applications of Isotopes, 1994, Jour. Labelled Compounds and Radiopharmaceuticals, 1998—; contbr. more than 100 articles to profl. jours. Mem. Royal Soc. Chemistry, Am. Chem. Soc., Internat. Isotope Soc. (exec. bd. dirs. 1991-2000, pres. 1992, 97, sec. 1998-2000), Soc. for Drug Rsch., Internat. Soc. for the Study of Xenobiotics. Office: Synthelabo Rsch 1 Ave Pierre Brossolette, 91385 Chilly-Mazarin France

ALLEN, JOHN ANTHONY, marine biologist; b. West Bridgford, U.K., May 27, 1926; s. George Leonard John and Dorothy Mary (Willoughby) A.; m. Marion Ferguson Crow (div. 1983); children: Hamish John, Elspeth Ferguson; m. Margaret Porteous Aitken (Aug. 12, 1983); 1 stepchild, Andrew Murdoch. BS, U. London, 1950, PhD, 1956, DS, 1963. Rschr. Scottish Marine Biol. Assn., 1950-51; asst. lectr. U. Glasgow, 1951-54; sr. lectr., reader U. Newcastle-upon-Tyne, 1954-76; prof. U. London, 1976-91, prof. emeritus, 1991—; dir. U. Marine Biol. Sta., Millport, 1976-91; hon. rsch. fellow U. Marine Biol. Sta., 1991—; John Murray Travel student Royal Soc. London, 1952-54; vis. prof. U. W.I., 1976, U. Wash., 1968, 70-71; guest investigator Woods Hole Oceanographic Instn., 1965—. Contbr. articles to profl. jours. Coun. mem. Natural Environ. Rsch. Coun. U.K., 1977-83, chmn. univ. affairs com. 1978-83; coun. mem. Nature Conservancy Coun. U.K., 1982-90, chmn. scientific adv. com. 1984-90; mem. Brit. Nat. Com. for Oceanic Rsch., 1988-90; mem. life sci. bd. Coun. for Nat. Acad. Awards, U.K., 1981-84. Sgt. Royal Army Med. Corps, 1945-48. Grantee Nat. Environment Rsch. Coun., 1965—. Fellow Royal Soc. Edinburgh, Inst. Biology; mem. Marine Biol. Assn. of the U.K., Scottish Marine Biol. Assn., Malacol. Soc. of London (pres. 1982-84), Challenger Soc. of U.K. Avocations: flower photography, travel, bird watching, gardening. Home: Drialstone, Isle of Cumbrae KA28 OEP, Scotland Office: U Marine Biol Sta/Millport, Isle of Cumbrae KA23 OEG, Scotland

ALLEN, JOHN EDWARD, engineering educator, plasma physicist; b. Devonport, England, Dec. 6, 1928. B Engring., U. Liverpool, Eng., 1949, PhD, 1953, DEng, 1963; MA, Cambridge (Eng.) U., 1964, U. Oxford, Eng., 1965; DSc, U. Oxford, Eng., 1975. Sci. officer, sr. sci. officer Atomic Energy Rsch. Establishment, Harwell, Eng., 1952-58; cons. CNEN Lab. Gas Ion, Italy, 1958-64; prof. U. Rome, 1958-64; asst. dir. rsch. Cambridge U., 1964-65; fellow Univ. Coll. Oxford U., 1965-96, emeritus fellow, 1996, univ. reader engring. sci., 1990-96, prof. engring. sci., 1996, prof. emeritus, 1996. Contbr. articles to sci. jours.; patentee for improved RF plasma reactor. Fellow Inst. Physics, Instn. Elec. Engrs., Am. Phys. Soc.; mem. IEEE Nuclear and Plasma Soc. (affiliate). Office: Oxford U, Engring Sci Dept, Oxford OX1 3PJ, England

ALLEN, JOHN ELLISTON, aeronautical engineer, educator, consultant; b. London, U.K., Feb. 7, 1921; s. Alfred Arthur and Phoebe Maud (Elliston) A.; m. Margaret Isobel Heath, May 26, 1948 (dec. June 1987); children: David John, Peter Trevor. BSc in Engring. with honors, London U., 1941; diploma with honors, Northampton Engring. Coll., Eng., 1941. Sci. officer Royal Aircraft Establishment, Farnborough, U.K., 1941-44, Farnborough, 1950-54; sr. sci. officer Marine Aircraft Expt. Establishment, Felixstone, U.K., 1944-50; head projects, weapons div. AVRO, Woodford, U.K., 1954-63; dep. chief engr. Hawker Siddeley Advanced Projects, Kingston, U.K., 1963-69; chief future project engr. Hawker Siddeley, Kingston-upon-Thames, 1969-83; prof. Cranfield Inst. Tech., Bedfordshire, Eng., 1977—; bd. dirs. Watt Com. on Energy, London, 1977-81; chmn. The Interdisciplinary Com., London, 1981; cons. Raychem. U.K., 1983-87, Rolls Royce, U.K., 1983-86, Lotus, U.K., 1983—, Brit. Aerospace; vis. prof. faculty tech. Kingston U., 1999—. Author: Aerodynamics; Space Age Survey, 1963, rev. edit., 1969, Future of Aeronautics, 1970, Transport Control, 1970, Aerodynamics, Science of Air in Motion, 1982, rev. edit. 1986. Chmn. Arts and Crafts Soc., Westcott Surrey, 1968, Blythburgh Soc., 1992; freeman City of London. Recipient Bronze medal Swedish Soc. Engrs., 1973. Fellow Royal Aero. Soc. (hodgson 1959), Royal Soc. Arts, Royal Geog. Soc., Instn. Mech. Engrs., Offshore Futures Club (pres. 1982-86). Achievements include patents on City Centre Airport, on Relevance Dodecahedron. Home: The Gabriels, Angel Ln, Blythburgh Suffolk 1P19 9LU, England

ALLEN, JOHN POLK, environmental scientist; b. Carnegie, Okla., May 6, 1929; s. Paul Benight and Opal (Wall) A. Student, Northwestern U., Stanford U., Oklahoma U., 1946-49; BS, Colo. Sch. Mines, 1957; MBA, Harvard U., 1962. Supervising metallurgist Allegheny Ludlum Steel, Brackenridge, Pa., 1957-59; crushing, leaching dept. head Union Carbide Nuclear, Uravan, Colo., 1959-60; asst. v.p. Devel. & Resources Corp., N.Y.C., 1961-63; pres. Mountain & Manhattan, N.Y.C., 1963-66; head metallurgist Meadows Gold, Santa Fe, N.Mex., 1966-67; co-founder, dir. Inst. Ecotechnics, London, 1968—; co-founder, chmn. Biospheric Design, Santa Fe, 1978—; exec. chmn. Space Biospheres Ventures, Oracle, Ariz., 1984-94; co-founder, chmn. Planetary Coral Reef Found., Santa Fe, N.Mex., 1991—; chmn. Global Ecotechnics, Santa Fe, N.Mex., 1998—, Off the Road, 2000. Author: The Human Experiment, 1989, Space Biospheres, 1986, Off the Road, 2000; inventor in field. Organizer UPWA-CIO Dist. 10, Chgo., 1950-52; pres. student body Colo. Sch. Mines, 1956-57. Pvt. U.S. Army Engrs., 1952-53. Hon. Citizen City of Ft. Worth, 1989; Baker scholar high distinction Harvard U. Bus. Sch., 1962; Outstanding Senior Colo. Sch. Mines Tau Beta Pi, 1957. Fellow Linnean Soc. London, Royal Geographic Soc.; mem. AAS. Achievements: created 1st closed life sys. with 100% recycle of waste, water and 90% of air per year. Avocations: expeditions to remote areas, theater, cultures, the game of GO. Office: Global Ecotechnics Corp 7 Silver Hills Rd Santa Fe NM 87505-4488

ALLEN, JOHN THOMAS, JR., lawyer; b. St. Petersburg, Fla., Aug. 23, 1935; s. John Thomas and Mary Lita (Shields) A.; m. Joyce Ann Lindsey, June 16, 1958 (div. 1985); children: John Thomas III, Linda Joyce, Catherine Lee (dec.).; m. Janice Dearmin Hudson, Mar. 16, 1987. BSBA with honors, U. Fla., 1958; JD, Stetson U., 1961. Bar: Fla. 1961, U.S. Dist. Ct. (mid. dist.) Fla. 1962, U.S. Ct. Appeals (5th cir.) 1963, U.S. Ct. Appeals (11th cir.) 1983, U.S. Supreme Ct. 1970. Assoc. Mann, Harrison, Mann & Rowe and successor Greene, Mann, Rowe, Davenport & Stanton, St. Petersburg, 1961-67, ptnr., 1967-74; sole practice St. Petersburg, 1974-95; pvt. practice Allen & Maller, P.A., 1996-98, Gulfport, Fla., 1998—; counsel Pinellas County Legis. Del., 1974-75; counsel for Pinellas County as spl. counsel on water matters, 1975-98. Mem. Com of 100, St. Petersburg, 1975-98. Mem. ABA, Fla. Bar Assn., St. Petersburg Bar Assn., St. Petersburg C. of C., Lions, Beta Gamma Sigma. Republican. Methodist.

ALLEN, KEITH WILLIAM, retired chemist, educator; b. Reading, England, Apr. 9, 1926; s. Clifford and Dora (Harding) A.; m. Marguerite Florence Woods, July 16, 1955; children: Paul, Mary, Elizabeth, Anne, Ruth. BSc, U. Reading, 1949; MSc, U. London, 1958; DSc, City Univ. London, 1994. Chartered chemist, physicist. Lectr. City Univ. London, 1949-83, dir. adhesion studies, 1984-92; vis. sr. rsch. fellow Oxford Brookes Univ., England, 1990-98, vis. prof., 1998—. Editor: (book series) Adhesion 1 - Adhesion 15, 1977-91; editl. bd. Jour. Adhesion, Internat. Jour. Adhesion & Adhesives, Materials Sci. and Tech.; contbr. articles to profl. jours. Elder, lay preacher United Reformed Ch. Livery of Worshipful Co. of Horners and Freeman, City of London; recipient meritorious svc. award Plastics and Rubber Inst. London, 1992, Ellinger-Gardonyi medal Oil & Colour Chem. Assn., 1999. Fellow Royal Soc. Chemistry, Inst. Materials (adhesives sect. com. 1971—), Tech. of Surface Coatings; mem. Inst. Physics., Soc. Adhesion & Adhesives (founder). Avocations: walking, reading. Home: Ranworth Tydehams, Newbury RG14 6JT, England

ALLEN, LEON ROBERT, food products executive; b. Apr. 21, 1939; married: three children. BA in English and History, Stanford U., 1961. Mktg., gen. mgr. Procter & Gamble, Venezuela, Mex., U.S.,, Spain and Austria, 1961-79; v.p. Europe, Middle-East, Africa Clorox, 1979-82; v.p. Lat. Am. Del Monte and Canada Dry RJR Nabisco, 1982-86; regional dir. no. Lat. Am. Internat. Nabisco brands, 1986-88, pres., CEO Del Monte Foods Europe, 1988-90; chmn., CEO Del Monte Foods Internat. Ltd., 1990-92; chmn. Devro Internat. plc, 1992-98; chmn., CEO The Tetley Group Ltd., 1995-99; bd. dirs. Abbey Nat. plc; chmn. bd. The Braes Group Ltd. E-mail: leon.allen@bigfoot.com.

ALLEN, LESLIE, physics educator; b. London, Oct. 22, 1935; s. James Herbert and Beatrice May (Blunden) A.; m. Barbara Russell, July 22, 1957 (div. Nov. 1989); children: Michael John, Carol Ann, Jennifer Lesley, David Philip; m. Polly Barnes, Dec. 23, 1991. BSc, U. London, 1957; DIC, diploma Imperial Coll., PhD, 1960; DSc, U. London, 1973; assoc., Royal Coll. Sci., 1957. Chartered physicist. Asst. lectr. Royal Holloway Coll., U. London, 1960-62; lectr. U. Sussex, 1962-69; reader U. Sussex, Brighton, 1969-85; dep. rector Polytechnic East London, London, 1986-91; vis. prof. U. Leiden, The Netherlands, 1991-92; Donders prof. U. Utrecht, The Netherlands, 1994—; hon. prof. U. St. Andrews, 1995-99; hon. rsch. fellow U. Glasgow, 1999—; vis. lectr. U. Ife, Nigeria, 1966; vis. sr. rsch. assoc. U. Rochester, N.Y., 1968-69, 72, 74, 77, 79; vis. prof. Indian Inst. Tech., Delhi, 1975, U. Sussex, 1989-92, 2000—, U. Essex, 1992-98; rsch. fellow Leverhulme Trust, 1992-93, emeritus 1999—; rsch. fellow J.I.L.A. U. Colo., 1995-96; emeritus prof. U. East London, 1992—; physics advisor Assn. Commonwealth Univs. Scholarship Commn., 1987-91; mem. sci. bd., nuclear physics bd. Sci. and Engring. Rsch. Coun., 1989-92; mem. com. for rsch. Coun. Nat. Acad. Awards, 1987-91; treas. Brit. Pugwash Group, London, 1989-93; coord. SERC non-linear optics initiative, 1992-94. Author: Essentials of Lasers, 1969; co-author: Principles of Gas Lasers, 1967, Optical Resonance and Two-Level Atoms, 1975, 87, Concepts of Quantum Optics, 1983; editl. advisor Progress in Optics, 1975-88; contbr. 110 articles to profl. jours. Mem. exec. com. Coun. for Edn. in Commonwealth, 1987-88. Sci. and Engring. Rsch. Coun. rsch. grantee, 1971, 77, 78, 82, 85, 93, 94, 96, 97, Royal Soc. Travel grantee. Fellow Royal Soc. Arts, Inst. Physics; mem. Surrey County Cricket Club, Millwall Football Club. Avocations: theater, art, opera, jazz. Home: Taunton Lodge Wattisfield Rd, Walsham-le-Willows Bury St, Edmunds 1P31 3BD, England

ALLEN, LINDA LEE, administrative assistant; b. Bowden, Ga., Apr. 20, 1940; d. Paul Hughen and Jessie Estelle (Huddleston) Lee; m. James Harrell Mosley, June 8, 1958 (div. Nov. 1968); children: Cynthia L. Mosley-Mizushima, Suzanne R. Mosley Goldston; m. Calvin Theodore Allen, Mar. 1, 1987. Exec. Sec. Cert., Massey Draughons Jr. Coll., Atlanta, 1960. Cert. Profl. Sec. Profl. Secs. Internat. Inst. for Cert. Legal sec. Am. Soc. of Composers, Authors & Pubs., Atlanta, 1964-69, Valley Forge Corp., Atlanta, 1969-74, Met. Life Ins. Co., Atlanta, 1982-84; adminstrv. asst. WANG Labs., Inc., Dayton, Ohio & Montgomery, Ala., 1984-86, Ala. Dept. Indsl. Rels., Montgomery, 1989-92, Ala. Office of Water Resources, Montgomery, 1992—; com. chair Exec. of Yr. in State Govt., Montgomery, 1994-95, 97-98; mem. planning com. Profl. Devel. Conf. for State Secs. and Office Profls., Montgomery, 1995-96, Ann. Seminar for State Secs., Montgomery, 1992-94. Mem. profl. staff recruitment com. Macedonia Bapt. Ch., Union Springs, Ala., 1994-98, mem. ann. 4th of July and homecoming celebration com., 1995, 97, vol. shut-in outreach sr. program, 1996-98. Sec. of Yr. in State Govt., State Capital Chpt., Profl. Secs., Internat., Montgomery, 1995 (chpt. pres. 2000-2001). Mem. Am. Water Resources Assn., Tri-Rivers Waterway Devel. Assn., Ala. Rural Water Assn., Am. Soc. Notaries. Avocations: genealogy, fishing, needlework, reading. Office: Ala Office of Water Resources 401 Adams Ave Ste 434 Montgomery AL 36104-4325

ALLEN, MARYON PITTMAN, former senator, journalist, lecturer, interior and clothing designer; b. Meridian, Miss., Nov. 30, 1925; d. John D. and Tellie (Chism) Pittman; m. Joshua Sanford Mullins, Jr., Oct. 17, 1946 (div. Jan. 1959); children: Joshua Sanford III, John Pittman, Maryon Foster; m. James Browning Allen, Aug. 7, 1964 (dec. June 1978). Student, U. Ala., 1944-47, Internat. Inst. Interior Design, 1970. Office mgr. for Dr. Alston Callahan, Birmingham, Ala., 1959-60; bus. mgr. psychiat. clinic U. Ala. Med. Center, Birmingham, 1960-61; life underwriter Protective Life Ins. Co., Birmingham, 1961-62; women's editor Sun Newspapers, Birmingham, 1962-64; v.p., ptnr. Pittman family cos., J.D. Pittman Partnership Co., J.D. Pittman Tractor Co., Emerald Valley Corp., Mountain Lake Farms, Inc., Birmingham; mem. U.S. Senate (succeeding late husband James B. Allen), 1978; dir. pub. rels. and advt. C.G. Sloan & Co. Auction House, Washington, 1981; feature writer Birmingham News, 1964; writer syndicated column Reflections of a News Hen, Washington, 1969-78; feature writer, columnist Maryon Allen's Washington, Washington Post, 1979-81; columnist McCall's Needlework Mag., 1993—; owner The Maryon Allen Co. Cliff House (Restoration/Design), Birmingham. Contbg. editor So. Accents Mag., 1976-78. Mem. Ladies of U.S. Senate unit ARC, Former Mems. of Congress, Ala. Hist. Commn., Blair House Fine Arts Commn.; charter mem. Birmingham Com. of 100 for Women; trustee Children's Fresh Air Farm; trustee, deacon, elder Ind. Presbyn. Ch., Birmingham; Democratic Presdl. elector, Ala., 1968. Recipient 1st place award for best original column Ala. Press Assn., 1962, 63, also various press state and nat. awards for typography, fashion writing, food pages, also several awards during Senate service; sponsor, U.S. Navy Nuclear submarine, U.S.S. Birmingham, S.S.N. 695, launched Newport News, Va., 1977, commissioned 1978. Mem. Nat. Press Club, 1925 F Street Club, 91st Congress Club, Congl. Club, Birmingham Country Club. Home: Cliff House 3215 Cliff Rd S Birmingham AL 35205-1405

ALLEN, MEREDITH CLAYTON, lawyer; b. Atlanta, Nov. 25, 1971; d. James Norwood and Linda Weeks Clayton; m. Jeffrey Roberts Allen, May 1, 1999. BA in Psychology, Spanish, Austin (Tex.) Coll., 1993; JD, U. Tex., 1998. Bar: Tex., 1998, U.S. Dist. Cts. (no. dist., 1999, ea. dist., 1999, so. dist., 1999) Tex. Assoc. Cowles & Thompson, Dallas, 1998-2000, Hermes Sargent Bates L.L.P., 2000—. Notes editor The Review of Litigation, 1997-98. Mem. State Bar Tex., Dallas Bar Assn., Dallas Assn. Young Lawyers, Tex. Young Lawyers Assn. Methodist. E-mail: meredith.allen@hsblaw.com. Office: Hermes Sargent Bates LLP 1717 Main St Ste 3200 Dallas TX 75201-7347

ALLEN, MERRILL JAMES, marine biologist; b. Brady, Tex., July 16, 1945; s. Clarence Francis and Sara Barbara (Finlay) A. BA, U. Calif., Santa Barbara, 1967; MA, UCLA, 1970; PhD, U. Calif., San Diego, 1982. Cert. jr. coll. tchr., Calif. Asst. environ. specialist So. Calif. Coastal Water Rsch. Project, El Segundo, 1971-77; postdoctoral assoc. Nat. Rsch. Coun., Seattle, 1982-84; oceanographer Nat. Marine Fisheries Svc., Seattle, 1984-86; sr. scientist MBC Applied Environ. Scis., Costa Mesa, Calif., 1986-93; prin. scientist So. Calif. Coastal Water Rsch. Project, Long Beach and Westminster, Calif., 1993—; tech. adv. com. Santa Monica Bay Restoration Project, Monterey Park, Calif., 1989—; steering com. So. Calif. Bight Pilot Project, 1993-98, So. Calif. Bight 1998 Regional Marine Survey, 1998—; affiliate asst. prof. sch. fisheries U. Wash., Seattle, 1985-89; mem. sci. rev. panel for marine ecol. reserves rsch. program Calif. Sea Grant Coll., 1996-97; adj. prof. dept. biology Calif. State U., Long Beach, 1996—. Mem. AAAS, Am. Inst. Fisheries Rsch. Biologists (dir. So. Calif. dist. 1991-93), Am. Fisheries Soc., Am. Soc. Ichthyologists and Herpetologists. Achievements include development of most comprehensive atlas of marine fishes from Bering Sea to Mexico; description of state of contamination of Santa Monica Bay. Office: So Calif Coastal Water Rsch Project 7171 Fenwick Ln Westminster CA 92683-5218

ALLEN, MICHAEL RICHARD, anthropologist, educator, researcher; b. Dublin, Ireland, Nov. 11, 1928; arrived in Australia, 1954; s. William Arthur and Beatrice Adelaide (Pim) A.; m. Shirley Patricia Jessop, Feb. 8, 1964 (div. 1994); children: Kerry Patricia, Catherine Elizabeth, Fiona Beatrice. BA with honors, Trinity Coll., Dublin, 1950; PhD, Australian Nat. U., Canberra, 1964. Tchg. fellow Sydney (Australia) U., 1964-65, from lectr. to prof., 1965-93; overseas fellow Churchill Coll., Cambridge (Eng.) U., 1973-74; vis. prof. U. Calif., San Diego, 1982-83, Maynooth (Ireland) Coll., 1990, James Cook U., Townsville, Australia, 1994-95; vis. fellow Australian Nat. U., Canberra, 1983. Author: Male Cults and Secret Initiations in Melanesia, 1967, The Cult of Kumari: Virgin Worship in Nepal, 1975; editor: Vanuatu: Politics, Economics and Ritual in Island Melanesia, 1981, Women in India and Nepal, 1981, Anthropology of Nepal: Peoples, Problems and Places, 1994, Ritual, Power and Gender: Ethnographic Explorations in Vanuatu, Nepal and Ireland, 2000, (jour.) The Australian Jour. of Anthropology, 1993—. Grantee Australian Rsch. Coun., 1967-74, 88-93, Wenner-Gren Anthrop. Found., 1993. Fellow Australian Acad. Social Scis., Australian Anthrop. Soc., Assn. Social Anthropologists of Commonwealth; mem. Am. Anthrop. Assn. Avocations: cooking, swimming, carpentry. Home: 21 Pashley St, Balmain NSW 2041, Australia Office: U Sydney, Dept Anthropology, Sydney NSW 2006, Australia

ALLEN, MYLES ROBERT, climate researcher; b. Farnham, Surrey, Eng., Aug. 11, 1965; s. Hubert J.B. and Phoebe C.V. (Stoney) A.; m. Irene M.C. Tracey, Sept. 10, 1994; 1 child, Colette Phoebe. BA in Physics and Philosophy, Oxford (Eng.) U., 1987, PhD in Physics, 1993. Tech. mgr. Bellerive Found., Nairobi, Kenya, 1987-89; cons. UN Environ. Program, Nairobi, 1989; NOAA global change fellow MIT, Cambridge, 1994-95; Atlas rsch. fellow Rutherford Appleton Lab., U. Oxford, 1993-94, 96-97, Nat. Environ. Rsch. Coun. advanced rsch. fellow, 1997—; cons. UN Environ. Program World Meteorol. Orgn., Geneva, 1991—. Contbr. articles to sci. jours.; inventor key analysis techniques. Open scholar St. Johns Coll., Oxford, 1984; Global Change fellow Univ. Corp. for Atmospheric Rsch., Boulder, Colo., 1994. Mem. Am. Geophys. Union, European Geophys. Soc. (convenor 1996-97). Anglican. Avocations: bicycling, hiking. Office: Rutherford Appleton Lab, Space Sci and Tech Dept, Chilton OX11 0QX, England also: Oxford U, Dept Physics, Oxford England

ALLEN, NEWTON PERKINS, lawyer; b. Memphis, Jan. 3, 1922; s. James Seddon and Sarah (Perkins) A.; m. Malinda Lobdell Nobles, Oct. 4, 1947 (dec. Nov. 1986); children: John Lobdell, Malinda Allen Lewis, Newton Perkins, Cannon Fairfax; m. Malinda Lobdell Crutchfield, June 23, 1990. AB, Princeton, 1943; JD, U. Va., 1948. Bar: Tenn. 1947, N.C. 1990. Assoc. Armstrong, Allen, Prewitt, Gentry, Johnston & Holmes, Memphis, 1948, ptnr., 1950-95; assoc. Dann & Allen, 1996—. Contbr. articles to profl. jours. Mem. Chickasaw coun. Boy Scouts Am., 1958-60, exec. bd. mem., 1961-69; trustee LeBonheur Children's Hosp., Memphis, 1964-72, vice chmn. bd., 1965; mem. alumni coun. Princeton, 1954-64, 90-93; pres. bd. trustees St. Mary's Episcopal Sch., 1966-67, v.p., 1972-73; chmn. Greater Memphis Coun. on Crime and Delinquency, 1976-80; co-chmn. Memphis conf. Faith at Work, 1975, bd. dirs., 1976-79; bd. dirs. Memphis Orch. Soc., pres., 1979-81. Mem. ABA (editl. bd. sr. lawyers divsn. 1990, publs. com. chair 1993-95, coun. mem. 1994-95, chair travel and leisure com. 1995-96, vice chair 1996-97, chair-elect 1997-98, chair 1998-99), Am. Coll. Trust and Estate Coun., Tenn. Bar Assn., Memphis Bar Assn., Tenn. Def. Lawyers Assn., N.C. Bar Assn., Princeton Alumni Assn. Memphis (pres. 1992), Memphis Lions (pres. 1956). Republican. Office: Dann & Allen 6263 Poplar Ave Ste 1103 Memphis TN 38119-4724

ALLEN, NORMA ANN, librarian; b. Balt., Jan. 22, 1951; d. James Crawley and Thelma Agusta (Keaton) Ghee; children: Lamont Ricardo Ghee, Alissa S. Allen, Avery O. Allen. BA in Adminstrn. Mgmt., Sojourner Douglass Coll., Balt., 1987; MS in Instrnl. Tech., Towson State U., 1999. Instr. data processing PSI Inst., Balt., 1987-88; acquisition technician Social Security Adminstrn., Balt., 1987-89, reference librarian, 1989-91, acquisitions librarian, 1991—; instrnl. developer Computer Asst. Instrn., Towson U., 1995—; freelance floral designer/arranger, freelance instr. basic writing skills and computer literacy. Sec., bd. dirs. New Image Child Care Facility, Balt., 1992; instr. active reading literacy program Enoch Pratt Libr., Balt., 1992; instr. United Missionary Bapt. Conv., 1997. Multicultural scholar Towson U., 1995-96. Mem. ALA, Spl. Libraries Assn. Office: Social Security Adminstrn 6401 Security Blvd Rm 571 Baltimore MD 21235-0001

ALLEN, PAUL G., computer executive, professional sports team owner. Student, Wash. State U. Co-founder Microsoft Corp., Redmond, Wash., 1975, exec. v.p., 1975-83; founder Asymetrix Corp., Bellevue, Wash., 1985—, Starwave Corp., Bellevue; founder, chmn. Intervas Rsch., Palo Alto, Calif.; CEO Vulcan Ventures, Bellevue, 1987—; owner, chmn. Seattle Seahawks; owner, chmn. bd. Portland (Oreg.) Trail Blazers, 1988—; bd. dirs. Egghead Discount Software, Microsoft Corp., Darwin Molecular, Inc.

ALLEN, ROBERT EDWARD, JR., physician assistant; b. Omaha, Mar. 27, 1950; s. Robert Edward and Virginia (Connor) A.; m. Christine Ann Rahm, July 16, 1985; children: Sean Edward, Erin Christine. Student, Brooke Army Hosp., San Antonio, 1968-69, St. Anthony Ctrl. Hosp., Denver, 1984, 86. Cert. Nat. Bd. Orthopaedic Physician Assts.; cert. EMT, vocat. tchr., Colo.; lic. physician asst., Colo.; cert. BLS. Mem., patroller, instr. Nat. Ski Patrol, 1974-90; orthopaedic physician asst., orthopaedic technician Luth. Med. Ctr., Wheatridge, Colo., 1980-85, instr. EMT program, 1983-89; physician asst., mem. staff St. Joseph Hosp., Denver, 1985-87; physician asst. Denver Orthopedic Clinic and Inst. for Limb Preservation, 1987-96, Advanced Orthopedics Assoc., 1996—; part-time EMT, Golden, Colo., 1980-84; lectr. continuing med. edn. Colo. Emergency Med. Svcs. Sys., also nursing staffs; manuscript reviewer William and Wilkins, Balt., 1993—; splty. lectr. oncology Clinicians Rev., Clifton, N.J., 1993—; insvc. lectr. in field. Exec. prodr. instrnl. videos; contbr. articles to profl. publs.; designer saw blade for arthroscopic anterior crucial ligament reconstrn.; co-designer antibiotic bead maker; patent Pin Site Care Kit. Vol. Toys for Tots, Denver, 1992—. With Spl. Forces, U.S. Army, 1968-71, Vietnam. Recipient 2nd place in best case study for alkaptonuria/ochrunosis Advance PA mag., 1997. Fellow Am. Soc. Orthopedic Physician Assts.; mem. Am. Acad. Physician Assts., NRA. Lutheran. Avocations: scuba diving, hunting, fishing, water and snow skiing. Home: 14650 E Floyd Ave Aurora CO 80014-3803 Office: Advanced Orthopedics Assocs 360 S Garfield St Ste 630 Denver CO 80209-3136 also: 4500 E 9th Ave Ste 150S Denver CO 80220-3932

ALLEN, ROBERT EUGENE BARTON, lawyer; b. Bloomington, Ind., Mar. 16, 1940; s. Robert Eugene Barton and Berth R. A.; m. Cecelia Ward Dooley, Sept. 23, 1960 (div. 1971); children: Victoria, Elizabeth, Robert, Charles, Suzanne, William; m. Judith Elaine Hecht, May 27, 1979 (div. 1984); m. Suzanne Nickolson, Nov. 18, 1995. BS, Columbia U., 1962; LLB, Harvard U., 1965. Bar: Ariz. 1965, U.S. Dist. Ct. Ariz. 1965, U.S. Tax Ct., 1965, U.S. Supreme Ct. 1970, U.S. Ct. Customs and Patent Appeals 1971, U.S. Dist. Ct. D.C. 1972, U.S. Ct. Appeals (9th cir.) 1974, U.S. Ct. Appeals (10th, and D.C. cirs.) 1984, U.S. Dist. Ct. N.Mex., U.S. Dist. Ct. (no. dist.) Calif., U.S. Dist. Ct. (no. dist.) Tex. 1991, U.S. Ct. Appeals (fed. cir.) 1992, U.S. Dist. Ct. (ea. dist.) Wis. 1995. Ptnr., dir. Allen & Price, Phoenix; spl. asst. atty. gen. Ariz. Ct. Appeals, 1978, judge pro-tem, 1984, 92, 99; Nat. pres. Young Dems. Clubs Am., 1971-73, mem. exec. com. Dem. Nat. Com., 1972-73, Ariz. Gov.'s Kitchen Cabinet working on a wide range of state projects, bd. dirs. Phoenix Bapt. Hosp., 1981-83, Phoenix and Valley of the Sun Conv. and Visitors Bur., United Cerebral Palsy Ariz., 1984-89, Planned Parenthood of Cen. and No. Ariz., 1984-87, Internat. Coun. Ariz. Heart Inst. Found., 1998—, Cordell Hull Found. for Internat. Edn., 1996—, Ariz. Aviation Futures Task Force, chmn. Ariz. Airport Devel. Criteria Subcom., mem. Apache Junction Airport Rev. Com., Am. rep. exec. bd. Atlantic Alliance of Young Polit. Leaders, 1971-76, 81-85, mem. Am. delegations to Germany, 1971, 72, 76, 79, USSR, 1971, 76, 88, France, 1974, 79, Belgium, 1974, 77, Can., 1974, Eng., 1975, 79, Norway, 1975, Denmark, 1976, Yugoslavia and Hungary, 1985, Am. observer European Parlimentary elections, Eng.,

France, Germany, Belgium, 1979, Moscow Congrssional, Journalist delegation, 1989, NAFTA Trade Conf., Mexico City, 1993, Atlantic Assembly, Copenhagen, 1993, , trustee Environ. Health Found., 1994-97, Friends of Walnut Canyon, 1991-94. Contbr. articles on comml. litigation to profl. jours. Mem. ABA, Ariz. Bar Assn., Maricopa County Bar Assn., N.Mex. State Bar, D.C. Bar Assn., Am. Judicature Soc., Fed. Bar Assn., Am. Arbitration Assn., Phi Beta Kappa, Harvard Club. Democrat. Episcopalian (lay reader). Office: Allen & Price 3131 E Camelback Rd Phoenix AZ 85016-4500

ALLEN, SHEILA HILL, nursing executive, counselor, consultant; b. Imperial, Nebr., Sept. 28, 1935; d. Roger William and Lois Marion (Clayton) Hill; children: Steven Morgan, Lee-Ann Hill, Todd Everett, Andrew James. RN, St. Lukes Sch. Nursing, 1958; BS, U. Denver, 1959. Cert. alcohol drug counselor, calif. Asst. head nurse St. Lukes Hosp., Denver, 1959-62; dir. nursing Ridge Vista Mental Health, San Jose, Calif., 1973-75; dir. nursing svcs. Westwood Mental Health, Fremont, Calif., 1975-89; DON, Chem. Dependency Inst. No. Calif., Campbell, Calif., 1989-90; program dir. O'Connor Hosp. Recovery Ct., San Jose, 1991-94; health facilities evaluator nurse State of Calif. Dept. Health Svcs. Licensing/Certification, 1995—; bd. dirs., sec., Health Acctg. Svcs., Calif., 1984-89; co-founder, partner Health Acctg. Svcs., Fremont, 1984-89; co-owner Westwood Mental Health, 1984-89. Contbr. articles to profl. jours. Mem. Nat. Assn. Alcoholism and Drug Abuse Counselors, Nat. Consortium Chem. Dependency Nurses, San Francisco Acad. Hypnosis, Nat. Coun. Alcoholism and Drug Dependence, Am. Adoption Congress, Search-Finders of No. Calif., Delta Gamma.

ALLÉN, STURE, academic administrator, linguistics educator; b. Göteborg, Sweden, Dec. 31, 1928; s. Bror G. and Hanna (Johanson) A.; m. Solveig Janson, June 5, 1954; children: Karin, Eivor, Ingemar. BA, U. Göteborg, 1954, lic. philosophy, 1961, PhD, 1965; PhD (hon.), Åbo (Finland) U., 1988. Asst. prof. Scandinavian langs. U. Göteborg, 1965-70, prof. computational linguistics, 1979-93, pro-rector, 1980-85, rector, 1986, founder dept. computational linguistics, 1972, founder Swedish Lang. Bank, 1975; assoc. prof. computational linguistics Human Research Council, 1970-72; prof. Human Rsch. Coun., 1972-79; permanent sec. Swedish Acad., Stockholm, 1986-99; bd. dirs. Chalmers U. Tech., Göteborg. Author: Graphemic Analysis 1-2, 1965, (with others) Frequency Dictionary of Present-Day Swedish 1-4, 1970-80, (with others) Swedish Dictionary, 1986, 3d edit., 1999, (with others) Dictionary of the Swedish National Encyclopaedia 1-3, 1995-96; editor: Data Linguistica, 1970—. Bd. dirs. Nobel Found., Stockholm, 1987-99. Served with Swedish Royal Coast Artillery, 1948-49. Recipient Henrik Ahrenberg prize U. Göteborg, 1966, Lang. Cultivation prize, Swedish Acad., 1979, Erik Wellander prize Swedish Lang. Com., 1980, Golden Ladder award Studema, 1987, H.M. King's medal King Charles XVI Gustavus, 1987, Chester Carlson Rsch. prize, 1988, medal of Merit City of Göteborg, 1994; named Knight Comdr Order of White Rose Finland, 1994. Mem. Soc. Linguistica Europeae, Nordic Assn. Linguists, Assn. for Literary and Linguistic Computing (bd. dirs. 1977-89), Swedish Lang. Com. (vice chmn. 1979-99), Royal Soc. Arts and Scis. of Göteborg, Royal Acad. Letters, History and Antiquities, Swedish Acad. (Margit Pahlson linguistic prize 2000), Royal Swedish Acad. Engring. Scis., Academia Europaea, Soc. Swedish Lit. in Finland, Icelandic Soc. Scis., Norwegian Acad. Scis. and Letters. Lutheran. Avocations: music, sports. Office: Swedish Acad, PO Box 2118, S-103 13 Stockholm Sweden

ALLEN, THOMAS WESLEY, medical educator, dean; b. Chgo., Sept. 13, 1938; s. Thomas and Helen Irene (Spitler) A.; m. Annette Faye Power, June 23, 1962 (div. 1988); children: Roderick Nelson, Andrea Jane; m. Keith Mayo Capen, Oct. 16, 1988; 1 stepchild, Hilary Tate. BA, Ottawa (Kans.) U., 1960; DO, Midwestern U., Chgo., 1964; DHL (hon.), U. New Eng., Biddeford, Maine, 1989. Diplomate internal medicine with subspecialty in pulmonary medicine, Am. Osteo. Bd. Internal Medicine. Intern Met. Hosp., Grand Rapids, Mich., 1964-65; resident in internal medicine Hosps. Chgo. Coll. Osteo Medicine, 1965-68; fellow in pulmonary medicine Northwestern U., 1969-70; from asst. to prof. medicine Chgo. Coll. Osteo. Medicine, 1968-87; pvt. practice Chgo., 1970-78; dean and v.p. acad. affairs and prof. medicine Midwestern U. Coll. Osteo. Medicine, Chgo., 1978-87; assoc. dean for acad. and clin. affars, prof. medicine U. Medicine and Dentistry of N.J. Coll. of Osteo. Medicine, 1987-91; provost, dean, prof. medicine Okla. State U. Coll. Osteo. Medicine, Tulsa, 1991-99, v.p. for health affairs, dean, 1999—; mem. Nat. Adv. Coun. on Nat. Health Service Corps, Washington, 1994-97, Nat. Adv. Coun. on Health Professions Edn., Washington, 1986-90. Editor-in-chief Jour. Am. Osteo. Assn., 1987-98. Civic unit chair Tulsa Area United Way, 1995; trustee Village of Western Springs, Ill., 1981-85. Col. USAR, 1988—. Recipient Outstanding Achievement award Chgo. Coll. Osteo. Medicine Alumni Assn., 1993. Fellow Am. Coll. Osteo. Internists, Am. Coll. Chest Physicians; mem. Am. Osteo. Assn., Am. Assn. Colls. Osteo. Medicine, Am. Osteo. Acad. Sports Medicine, Am. Coll. Sports Medicine, Phi Kappa Phi. Episcopalian. Avocations: running, horseback riding. Home: 8911 S Florence Pl Tulsa OK 74137-3333 Office: Okla State Univ College Osteopathic Med 1111 W 17th St Tulsa OK 74107-1800

ALLEN, W. WAYNE, retired oil industry executive; b. 1936. BS, Okla. State U., 1959, MME, 1969. With Phillips Petroleum Co., 1961-84, regional mgr. U.K., 1984-85, gen. mgr. exploration and prodn. western divsn., 1986-89, sr. v.p. exploration and prodn., 1989-91, pres., COO, 1991-94, chmn. bd., CEO, 1994-99; ret., 1999. Capt. U.S. Army, 1959-61. Office: Profl Bldg 117 W 5th St Ste 401 Bartlesville OK 74004-0001*

ALLEN, WILLIAM ANTHONY, banker; b. Croydon, Surrey, Eng., May 13, 1949; s. Derek William and Margaret Winifred (Jones) A.; m. Rosemary Margaret Allen, July 29, 1972; children: Rosalind Jane, Edmund James, Lucy Ruth. BA in Math., Oxford (Eng.) U., 1970; MS in Econs., London Sch. Econs., 1972. Staff mem. econ. intelligence dept. Bank of Eng., 1972-77, staff mem. cashiers dept., 1977-78; staff mem. monetary and econ. dept. Bank Internat. Settlements, Switzerland, 1978-80; asst. adviser econs. div. Bank of Eng., London, 1980-82, mgr. gilt-edged divsn., 1982-86, head money market ops. divsn., 1986-90, head fgn. exch. divsn., 1990-94, dep. dir. monetary analysis, 1994-98, dep. dir. market ops., 1999—; part time adviser Nat. Bank of Poland, 1990—. Avocations: gardening, jazz. Office: Bank of Eng, Threadneedle St, London EC2R8AH, England

ALLEN, WILLIAM DOUGLAS, physicist; b. Mussooree, India, July 27, 1914; s. John Howard and Clara Helen (Padman) A.; m. Gwenduline Genevieve Thomspn, Noc. 15, 1939; children: Catherine Elspeth, Margaret Gillian, David Douglas, James Richard Alexander. BS, Adelaide U., Australia, 1932, BS in Physics, 1935; DPhil in Physics, Oxford U., England, 1940. Sr. officer, sr. officer, sr. sci. officer Min. Aircraft Prodn., Malvern, England, 1939-44; sr. sci. officer Uranium Isotope Suparation Tube Alloys, Berkeley, Calif., 1944-45; rsch. officer Electron Acceleration, Sydney, Australia, 1945-46, prin. sci. officer, 1946-61; sr. prin. sci. officer Electron Acceleration, Harwell, England, 1946-61; dep. chief sci. officer Chilton, 1961-77; prof. dept. elec. engring. Reading, 1976-78, Southampton, 1979-81. Author: Newtron Detection, 1949. Chmn. N. Berks Music Festival, 1960-683. Mem. England Phys. Soc., Probus Club. Avocation: gardening. Home: Quirang, Burcot, Abingdon OX14 3DP, England

ALLEN, WILLIAM JERE, minister; b. Greenville, Miss., Apr. 23, 1934; s. Marion Goodman and Gradie Lee (Yates) A.; m. Lorena Faye Franklin, June 24, 1960; children: Lorena Lynn Brickson, Jennifer Dawn Moradi, William Jere Allen Jr. B of Bldg. Constrn., Auburn U., 1956; BDiv, So. Bapt. Theol. Sem., 1963; DMin, Union Theol. Sem., 1973. Ordained to ministry First Bapt. Ch., 1960. Pastor 45th Street Mission, Ashland, Ky., 1959-60, Rose Hill Bapt. Ch., Ashland, 1960-62, Colonial Ave. Bapt. Ch., Roanoke, Va., 1962-67, Bainbridge St. Bapt. Ch., Richmond, Va., 1967-71, Bainbridge Southampton Bapt. Ch., Richmond, 1972-75; cons., dir. spl. missions dept. Ala. Bapt. State Conv., Montgomery, 1975-79; assoc. then dir. met. mission dept. Home Mission Bd., So. Bapt. Conv., Atlanta, 1979-91; exec. dir., min. D.C. Bapt. Conv., Washington, 1992—; mega focus cities cons. Home Mission Bd., So. Bapt. Conv., Atlanta, 1982—; bd. trustees Bapt. Sr. Adult Ministries, Washington, 1993—. Co-author: Shaping a Future for Church in Changing Community, 1981, Church and Community Diagnostic Workbook, 1986; author: (with others) Shooting the Rapids: Efective Ministry in a Changing World, 1990, Faith and Social Ministry: Ten Christian Perspectives, 1990. Mem. Interfaith Conf., Washington, 1992—, Dem. Nat. Com., 1993—. Capt. USAF, 1956-62. Mem. Assn. of So. Bapt. Exec. Dirs., Regional Exec. Ministries Coun., Am. Bapt. Chs. (gen. exec. coun.), Faith Group Leaders of Washington. Avocations: jogging, reading, family travel, golf. Home: 3041 Chestnut St NW Washington DC 20015-1407 Office: DC Bapt Conv 1628 16th St NW Washington DC 20009-3099

ALLEN, WILLIAM RICHARD, veterinary science educator; b. Auckland, New Zealand, Aug. 29, 1940. Fax: 01638 667207. Office: TBA Equine Fertility Unit, Mertoun Paddocks Wooditton Rd, Newmarket, Suffolk CB8 9BH, England

ALLEN, WOODY (ALLEN STEWART KONIGSBERG), director, actor, writer; b. N.Y.C., Dec. 1, 1935; s. Martin and Nettie (Cherry) Konigsberg; m. Louise Lasser (div.); 1 child (with Mia Farrow), Satchel; adopted children: Moses, Dylan; m. Soon-Yi Previn, 1997. Student, NYU, 1953, CCNY, 1953. Writer TV comedy for Sid Caesar, 1957, Art Carney, 1958-59, Herb Shriner, 1953; appeared in numerous nightclubs, TV shows, from 1961; author screenplay, also appeared in motion picture What's New Pussycat?, 1964-65; screenplay, dir., actor Take the Money and Run, 1969, Bananas, 1971, What's Up Tiger Lily?, 1966, Everything You Always Wanted to Know About Sex But Were Afraid to Ask, 1972, Sleeper, 1973, Love and Death, 1975, The Front, 1976, Manhattan (Brit. Acad. award 1979, N.Y. Film Critics award), Stardust Memories, 1980; writer, dir., prodr., actor films Annie Hall (N.Y. Film Critics Circle award for Best Dir. and Best Screenplay 1977, Acad. awards for best film, best direction, Nat. Soc. Film Critics Screenwriting award), Zelig, 1983, Broadway Danny Rose, 1984, Hannah and Her Sisters, 1986 (Acad. award for best screenplay, D.W. Griffith award for best dir. Nat. Bd. Rev. of Motion Pictures), Oedipus Wrecks, 1989, Mighty Aphrodite, 1995 (Acad. award nominee for best screenplay 1996), Everyone Says I Love You, 1996, Deconstructing Harry, 1997, Count Mercury Goes to the Suburbs, 1997, Celebrity, 1998, Sweet and Lowdown, 1999, Small Town Crooks, 2000; writer, dir., narrator film Radio Days, 1987; screenplay, dir. films Interiors, 1978, Purple Rose of Cairo, 1985, A Midsummer Night's Sex Comedy, 1982, September, 1987, Another Woman, 1988, Crimes and Misdemeanors, 1989, Alice, 1990, Shadows and Fog, 1992, Husbands and Wives, 1992, Manhattan Murder Mystery, 1993, Bullets Over Broadway, 1994, Mighty Aphrodite, 1995; author play: Don't Drink the Water, 1966 (actor, dir. of TV movie, 1994), The Floating Lightbulb, 1981, (one act) Death Defying Acts, 1995; play, screenplay Play It Again, Sam, 1969, film, 1972; actor, film King Lear, 1988, Scenes From a Mall, 1990, Cannes...les 400 coups, 1997, Waiting for Woody, 1998, Impostors, 1998, AFI's 100 Years...100 Movies, 1998, Antz, 1998, Wild Man Blues, 1998, Stuck on You, 1998, Company Man, 1999 Picking Up the Pieces, 1999; author: Getting Even, 1971, Without Feathers, 1975, Side Effects, 1980; guest appearances (TV) Just Shoot Me, The Tonight Show; contbr. numerous pieces to Playboy, New Yorker, other mags. Recipient Sylvania award, 1957; Spl. award Berlin Film Festival, 1975; nominated for Emmy award as TV writer, 1957. Democrat. Office: 48 E 92nd St New York NY 10128-1316

ALLEN-CLAIBORNE, JOYCE G., psychologist; b. Feb. 23; d. Homer W. Jr. and Berneda C. Allen; m. Andrew J. Claiborne, Nov. 20, 1976 (dec.); 1 child, Jomo Abd-Allah Kenyatta Claiborne. BA cum laude, Spelman Coll., 1970; MA, U. Pitts., 1972; PhD, 1975. Lic. clin. psychologist; cert. sch. psychologist. Tchg. fellow U. Pitts., 1972; rsch. assoc., 1975-77; clin. psychologist Hillcrest Children's Ctr., Washington, 1977-78; pvt. practice Washington, 1980-90, Albany, Ga., 1995—; lead psychologist psychol. svcs. Dougherty County Sch. Sys., 1998—; psychologist, Region D, D.C. Pub. Schs., Washington, 1979-90; adj. prof. Union Grad. Sch., Clin., 1980-83; mem. rev. bd. Nat. Register Health Svc. Providers in Psychology, 1987-90; psychologist Dougherty County Sch. Sys., 1990—; instr. dept. psychology, sociology, social work Albany State U., 1995-96. Mem. adv. bd. Albany Group Home, 1998—. Pub. health fellow NIMH, 1972-74. Mem. APA, Assn. Black Psychologists, Spelman Coll. Alumnae Club (pres. Albany chpt. 1996-99), Delta Sigma Theta. Baptist. Home: 601 Freemont St Albany GA 31707-4507 Office: PO Box 1470 Albany GA 31702-1470

ALLENDE, ISABEL ANGELICA, writer; b. Chile, Aug. 2, 1942; d. Tomas and Francisca A.; m. Miguel Frias, 1962 (div. 1987); children: Paula (dec.), Nicolas; m. William Gordon, 1988. LLD, N.Y. State U., 1991, Dominican Coll., 1994; Prof. Lit. honoris causae, U. Chile, 1991; LLD, Bates Coll., 1994; hon. doctorate, Mills Coll., 2000, Lawrence U., 2000. Sec. FAO, Santiago, Chile, 1959-65; journalist Paula mag., Santiago, Chile, 1967-74, Mampato mag., Santiago, Chile, 1969-74; TV interviewer Canal 13/Canal 7, 1970-75; worked on movie newsreels, 1973-75; journalist El Nacional newspapers, Venezuela, 1975-84; adminstr. Colegio Marroco, Caracas, Venezuela, 1979-82; lectr. U.S.A., Europe, and Latin Am., lit. workshops, U.S.A.; speaker, lectr. univs. and colls.; tchr. lit. U. Va., Charlottesville, Montclair (N.J.) Coll., U. Calif., Berkeley. Author: Civilice a su troglodita: los impertinentes de Isabel Allende, 1974, La casa de los espíritus, 1982 (pub. as The House of Spirits, 1985), La gorda de porcelana, 1984, De amor y de sombra, 1984 (pub. as Of Love and Shadows, 1987; L.A. Times Book prize nomination 1987), Eva Luna, 1987, Los cuentos de Eva Luna, 1990 (pub. as The Stories of Eva Luna, 1991), El plan infinito, 1991 (pub. as The Infinite Plan, 1993), Paula, 1995, Afrodita, 1997, Daughter of Fortune, 1999; writer short stories for children and humor books, Chile, 1972-73, theater plays in Chile El Embajador, 1971, La Balada del Medio Pelo, 1973, Los Siete Espejos, 1974; contbr. articles to newspapers and mags. U.S.A., Europe, Latin Am. Recipient Panorama Literario award (Chile), 1983, Grand Prix d'Évasion (France), 1984, Point de Mire (Belgium), 1985, XV Premio Internazionale I Migliori dell'Anno (Italy), 1987, Mulheres best fgn. novel award (Portugal), 1987, Before Columbus Found. award, 1988, Best Novel award (Mexico), 1985, Author of Yr. award (Germany), 1986, Freedom to Write Pen Club award, 1991, XLI Bancarella Lit. award (Italy), 1993, Ind. Fgn. Fiction award (Eng.), 1993, Brandeis U. Major Book Collection award, 1993, Critic's Choice award, 1996, Gabriela Mistral Recognition award (Chile), 1994, Chevalier dans l'Ordre des Arts et des Lettres award (France), 1994, Feminist of Yr. award Feminist Found., 1994, Read About Me Literary award, 1996, Books to Remember award ALA, 1996, Gift of Hope award, 1996, Harold Washington Lit. award, 1996, Malaparte award Amici di Capri, Italy, 1998, Donna Citta Di Roma Lit. award Italy, 1998; named Hon. Citizen of City of Austin, 1995, Mem. Academia de Artes y Ciencias (P.R.), 1995. Office: Carmen Balcells, Diagonal 580, 08021 Barcelona Spain

ALLENDE, JORGE EDUARDO, biochemist, molecular biologist; b. Cartago, Costa Rica, Nov. 11, 1934; s. Octavio Allende and Amparo Rivera; m. Catherine C. Connelly, 1961; 4 children. Student, La. State U., Yale U. Rsch. assoc. Rockefeller U., N.Y.C., 1961-62; asst. prof. biochemistry U. Chile, Santiago, 1963-68, assoc. prof., 1968-71, prof. biochemistry and molecular biology, 1972—, also dir. Inst. Biomed. Scis. dept. medicine; regional coord. L.Am. Network Biol. Scis., 1975—; pres. Pan Am. Assn. Biochem. Socs., 1976; mem. exec. com. Internat. Cell Rsch. Orgn., 1976—, Internat. Union Biochemistry, 1982-91; mem. exec. bd. Internat. Coun. Sci. Unions, 1986-90; fgn. assoc. Inst. Medicine, NAS. Contbr. articles to profl. jours. Fogarty scholar-in-residence NIH. Fellow Third World Acad. Scis.; mem. Chilean Acad. Scis. (pres. 1991—), Chilean Acad. Medicine (hon.). Office: Chilean Acad Scis, Clasificador 1349, Correo Central Santiago Chile*

ALLEN-JONES, CHARLES MARTIN, solicitor; b. Hazel Grove, Eng., Aug. 7, 1939; s. John Ernest and Margaret Ena (Rix) Allen-Jones; m. Caroline Beale, June 25, 1966; children: Christopher, Nicola, Anna. Degree, Clifton Coll. Ptnr. corp. fin. and capital markets Linklaters & Paines, Eng., 1968-76; head Hong Kong office Linklaters & Paines, Hong Kong, 1976-81; head internat. fin. dept. Linklaters & Paines, Eng., 1981-83, head corp. dept., 1985-91, head corp. group, 1991-96; sr. ptnr. Linklaters & Alliance, various locations, 1996—, co-chmn., 1998—. Trustee Br. Mus., 2000—; mem. Barbican Adv. Coun., 1997—. Mem. The Law Soc. (chmn. Far East subcom. 1996-99). Avocations: tennis, gardening, theatre, reading, traveling. Office: Linklaters & Alliance, One Silk St, London EC2Y 8HQ, England

ALLENMARK, STIG GERHARD, chemistry educator, researcher, consultant; b. Stockholm, Feb. 9, 1936; s. Axel Gerhard and Anna Charlotta (Carlsson) A.; m. Anna-Greta Persson, Oct. 1, 1960 (div. Feb., 1980); 1 child, Erik; m. Maria Elisabeth Heikkilä, Dec. 19, 1981; 1 child, Fredrik. BSc, U. Lund, Sweden, 1959, MSc, 1963; PhD, U. Uppsala, 1966. Asst. prof. U. Uppsala, Sweden, 1968-69, 70-76; acting prof. U. Umeå, Sweden, 1969-70; sr. rsch. engr. U. Linköping, Sweden, 1978-82, acting prof., 1982-83; prof. U. Göteborg, Sweden, 1984—. Mem. editl. bd. Chromatographia, Jour. of Chromatography B, Analytical Pharmacology, Chirality, Enantiomer, Molecules; author: Chromatographic Enantioseparation, 1988, rev. edit., 1991; inventor Columns for chiral liquid chromatography, 1983, 92. Mem. Am. Chem. Soc., Swedish Chem. Soc. Avocations: mountain walking, fishing, music, tennis. Home: Östra Björnvägen 4, S-429 30 Kullavik Sweden Office: Univ Göteborg, Dept Organic Chemistry, S-41296 Göteborg Sweden

ALLEN-MEARES, PAULA G., dean, social work educator; b. Buffalo, N.Y., Feb. 29, 1948; d. Joseph N. Allen and Mary T. Hienz; m. Henry O. Meares, June 8, 1974; children: Tracey, Nichole, Shannon. BS, SUNY, Buffalo, 1970; MSW, U. Ill., 1971, PhD, 1975; cert., Harvard U., 1990; mgmt. cert., U. Mich., 1994. Faculty U. Ill., Champaign-Urbana, 1978-93, dir. doctoral program, 1985-89, dean, 1990-93; dean, prof. U. Mich., Ann Arbor, 1993—. Editor-in-chief Jour. Social Work Edn., 1997-2000. Mem. NASW (chair commn. on edn. 1982-88, comm. com. 1990—), Coun. on Social Work Edn. (bd. dirs. 1989-91), Delta Mu, Delta Kappa Gamma. E-mail: pameares@umich.edu. Office: Univ Mich Sch Social Work 1080 S University Ave Ann Arbor MI 48109-1106

ALLEN-MITCHELL, ARLENE, public relations executive; b. Nassau, Bahamas, Mar. 6, 1966; d. George Phillip and Hazel Adelaide Allen; m. Marcus Ralston Mitchell, Jan. 7, 2000. BA, U. West Fla., 1988; MPA, Ga. State U., 1996. Comm. officer Barnett Bank South Fla., Miami, 1988-91; dir. pub. rels. Fla. Meml. Coll., Miami, 1991-94; pres. Write Angles, Snelville, Ga., 1994-98; mktg. adminstr. Tropical Fed. Credit Union, Miami, 1996-97; dir. office pub. rels. City of Hollywood, Fla., 1998—. Mem. exec. com. Leadership Miami, 1990-92. Mem. Internat. Assn. Bus. Communicators (treas. 1997, v.p. programs 1998, pres. Miami chpt. 1998-99). Democrat. Roman Catholic. Avocation: traveling. E-mail: aallen@hollywoodfl.org. Office: City of Hollywood 2600 Hollywood Blvd Ste B Hollywood FL 33020-4800

ALLESCHER, HANS-DIETER, internist, gastroenterologist; b. Cham, Germany, Nov. 11, 1958; s. Erich and Ludmilla (Troppmann) A.; m. Doris Kath; children: Julia, Hannah, Simon. MD, Tech. U. Munich, 1985. Rsch. fellow Tech. U. Munich, 1985-86; postdoctoral fellow McMaster U., Hamilton, Canada, 1986-87; rsch. fellow Tech. U., Munich, 1988-93, sr. cons., 1993-94, assoc. prof., 1994—. Mem. Am. Gastroenterol. Assn., German Gastroenterol. Assn. Office: Tech U Med Dept, Ismaningerstr 22, 81675 Munich Germany

ALLEYNE, MERVYN (C.), linguist; b. Trinidad, June 13, 1933; s. Coleridge F. and Carmen (Lindo) A.; m. Beverley Hall, Dec. 26, 1984; children: Trevor, Malou, Taji, Micha, Malene. BA with honors, U. West Indies, 1957; Doctorat, U. Strasbourg, 1960. Prof. sociolinguistics U. West Indies, Kingston, Jamaica, 1960—; vis. prof. Yale U., SUNY, Buffalo, Ind. U., Bloomington, U. Kans., U. Puerto Rico, U. Amsterdam. Author: Les Noms des vents en Gallo-Roman, 1962, Krio Language Training Manuel, 1965, Comparative Afro-American, 1980, Theoretical Issues in Caribbean Linguistics, 1984, Studies in Saramaccan Language Structure, 1987, The Roots of Jamaican Culture, 1988, Syntaxe Historique Créole, 1995, The Folk Medicine of Jamaica, 1997; contbr. articles to acad. jours. Mem. Comite Internat. d'Etudes Creoles (pres.), Soc. Caribbean Linguistics. Office: Univ of West Indies, Mona Kingston 7, Jamaica*

ALLEZ, ANTOINE EMILE, lawyer; b. Paris, Feb. 29, 1964; s. Marc and Christine (Lemoine) A.; children: Alexandre, Arthur. LLB, U. London, 1988; LLB (French), The Sorbonne, Paris, 1988, DESS Commerce Ext., 1989, DESS Droit Affairs Fiscalite, 1990. Cert. adv., France, Czech Republic. Adv. Clifford Change, Paris, 1990-2000; ptnr. Andersen Legal Office, Paris, 2000—. With French Navy, 1989. Recipient: Prix Cojura, Paris, 1990. Avocations: sailing, diving, horses.

ALLHUSEN, JAMES J., financial servies executive; b. Rockville Centre, N.Y., Dec. 16, 1948; s. John Theodore and Harriet Martha (Morgan) A.; m. Susan Starr, Oct. 1, 1983; children: Robert, Brett, Eric, Jennifer, Lauren. BA, Colgate U., 1971; Cert. in Bank Mktg., Colo. U., 1977; Cert. in Banking, Rutgers U., 1981. Pres. Franklinton Fin. Svcs., Columbus, Ohio, 1980-85; pres. Midwest divsn. Household Bank, Columbus, Ohio, 1985-90; global group exec. Std. Chartered Bank, Hong Kong, Singapore, Dubai, 1990-95; pres., CEO Advanta Nat. Bank, Phila., 1995-98; exec. v.p., group exec. Equifax Inc., Atlanta, 1998-99; COO Internat. Payment Svcs., LLC, Atlanta, 1999—. Dir. Ballet Met., Columbus, 1980-90, Ctr. for Sci. and Industry, Columbus, 1985—, Annenberg Ctr., Phila., 1996-98. E-mail: jallhusen@intlps.com. Office: Internat Payment Svcs LLC 3060 Peachtree Rd NW Ste 750 Atlanta GA 30305-2240

ALLIANCE, DAVID, apparel executive; b. June 1932. LLD (hon.), U. Manchester, 1989; DSc (hon.), Heriot-Watt U., 1991. Companion Inst. Mgmt., Textile Inst. Owner Thomas Hoghton, Oswaldtwistle, 1956, Spirella, 1968, Vantona Ltd. (merged to form Vantona Group), 1975, Carrington Viyella (merged to form Vantona Viyella), 1983, Nottingham Mfg., 1985, Coats Patons (merged to form Coats Viyella), 1986; chmn. Coats Viyella, 1989—, group CEO, 1975-90; chmn. N. Brown Group, 1968—, Tootal Group, 1991—. Named Knight Brit. Empire, 1989, Comdr. Order of Brit. Empire, 1984. Fellow Royal Soc. Arts, U. Manchester Inst. Sci. and Tech. (hon.), Shenkar Coll. Textile Tech. and Fashion (Israel), City and Guilds of London Inst. Office: 53 Dale St, Manchester M60 6ES, England*

ALLIKMETS, KRISTINA, cardiologist, researcher; b. Tallinn, Estonia, Dec. 26, 1965; d. Jüri and Aino (Tamm) Kann; m. Erik Allikmets, Sept. 4, 1987; children: Kaija, Silvia. MD, U. Tartu, Estonia, 1989, PhD, 1997. Asst. U. Tartu Med. Faculty, 1990-94; rsch. asst. U. Tartu, 1989-91, postgrad., 1991-96, resident in cardiology, 1997-2000. Co-author: Arterial Hypertension: Practical Aspects, 1995; contbr. articles to profl. jours. Mem. Estonian Soc. Hypertension (sec. 1995-99), Estonian Soc. Cardiology. Office: U Tartu Dept Cardiology, 18 Ülikooli St, EE 2400 Tartu Estonia

ALLINE, HENRI-MARIE, communications company executive; b. Ermont, France, Sept. 5, 1948; s. Augustin and Arlette (Burtschell) A.; m. Catherine Berranger; children: Mathilde, Jean-Baptiste, Pierre-Etienne. Comml. mgr. Electrolux, France, 1970-73; vocat. tng. mgr. Infotec, France, 1973-75; comm. dir. Hoechst, France, 1975-90, Rhone Poulenc Chimie, Herts, Eng., 1997—. Chmn. La Pierre d'Angle, France, 1990—; CEO Union des Journalistes & Journaux de France. With French mil., 1968-70. Roman Catholic. Avocation: opera. Home: 38-40 Rue du Docteur Roux, 95110 Sannois France

ALLINSON, JOHN, human resources professional; b. Hussein-Dey, Algeria, Apr. 5, 1948; arrived in France, 1962; s. Frank and Gisele Agathe Marie (Baeza) A.; m. Jelena Zovko, Aug. 9, 1969; children: Gordon, Gregory, Jennifer. Diploma, Ecole Superieure de Journalism, Paris, 1971, Hautes Etudes Internat., Paris, 1971; lic. in geography and history, U. Sorbonne, Paris, 1972; diploma, Mgmt. Inst., Lyon, France, 1989. With dept. compensation and benefits TOTAL, Paris, 1968-71; head pers. rsch. group ITT France, Paris, 1971-75; head dept. pers. and adminstrn. ITT Algeria, Algiers, 1975-79; head dept. indsl. rels. ITT France, Paris, 1979-81; dir. human resources FORACO, Aix en Provence, France, 1981-85; human resources dir. ELF Internat. Svcs., Geneva, Switzerland, 1985-2000, mng. dir.; head internationalization and expatriation Total Fina ELF, Paris, 2000—; mng. dir. ELF Internat. Svcs., Annecy, France; v.p. human resources IPMSC Ltd., Guernsey, Channel Islands, 1993-2000; chmn. Eurowage SA, Geneva, 1996-97. Author: Croatia's Independence War, 1996, Croatia's Liberation War, 1997. Mem. European Ctr. for Social Studies, European Coun. on Benefits and Compensation (conf. bd.). Avocations: news, RV building, photography, painting, history. Office: ELF Internat Svcs, PO Box 1476, 1211 Geneva Switzerland

ALLIO, ROBERT PAUL, management consultant; b. Troy, N.Y., Nov. 3, 1956; s. Robert John and Barbara Maria (Littauer) A.; m. Beate Barbara Freter, Nov. 28, 1981 (div. Oct. 31, 1997); children: Christopher, Devon,

Nicole. BA, York U., Toronto, Can., 1979; postgrad., Am. Univ., 1980. Bus. mgr. Planning Rev., Cambridge, Mass., 1981-83; v.p. Robert J. Allio and Assocs., Cambridge, 1982-89; tchg. fellow Harvard U., Cambridge, 1984-88; dir. corp. mktg. Paul C. Rizo & Assocs., Pitts., 1990-92; chief adminstrv. officer Nicholson Constrn. Corp., Atlanta, 1993-96; sr. v.p. Robert J. Allio and Assocs., Santa Fe, N.Mex., 1997-99; dir. Mid. Market Bus. Consulting Price Waterhouse-Coopers, Atlanta, 1999—. Mem. Strategic Leadership Forum, Strategic Planning Soc., Brit. Am. Bus. Group. Avocations: tennis, Tae Kwon Do (instructor). Home: 3562 Piedmont Rd NE Atlanta GA 30305-7000 Office: Price Waterhouse Coopers 400 Northridge Rd Ste 1000 Atlanta GA 30350-3328

ALLISON, BROOKE HASTINGS, artist; b. N.Y.C., Feb. 12, 1940; s. Frederick Gay and Miriam Lorraine (Watkins) Hastings; m. John Borden Allison, Dec. 17, 1966 (dec. 1996); children: Brooke Allison Scannell, Jaime Joy; stepchildren: Jeffrey Clark, Jay Borden, Jerrianne Allison Anderson, Jane Sue. Student, Shimer Coll., 1957-58, Art Inst. Chgo., 1958-60, 81-82, Am. Acad. Art., 1960-61, Lake Forest Coll., 1961. Instr. Dunedin (Fla.) Fine Art Ctr., 1984-2000. Exhibited in groups shows Tampa Mus. Art, 1997, Jacksonville (Fla.) Mus. Art, 1998, works featured in 200 Great Painting Ideas, 1998, Artist Mag., 1998, St. Petersburg Arts Ctr., 1999 (J. Brown Meml. award), Ridge Art 50th Ann. Nat. Competition, 2000 (2d prize, 1st prize graphics), Broome St. Gallery, 1999, 2000; curator Artists of the 3d Age, Octagon Gallery, Clearwater, Fla. Pinellas County Artists Resource grantee, 1999; recipient award Catharine L. Wolfe Exhbn., 1993-94, others. Mem. Pastel Soc. Am. (signature), Pastel Soc. of West Coast, Midwest Pastel Soc., Profl. Assn. Visual Artists (past. pres. 1992-94), Fla. Artist's Group, Catherine Lorillard Wolfe Art Club. Presbyterian. Avocations: reading, service work. Home: 1654 Mckay Ct Dunedin FL 34698-3529

ALLISON, DAVID GEORGE, microbiologist; b. Edinburgh, Scotland, U.K., Oct. 30, 1959; s. William and Margaret (Forrest) A.; m. Angela Bramwell, Sept. 5, 1987; 1 child, Alesha Holly. BSc, U. Edinburgh, 1981, PhD in Microbiology, 1985. Postdoctoral fellow Imperial Chem. Industries Pharms., Macclesfield, England, 1984-87, Aston U., Birmingham, England, 1987-89; lectr. Manchester U., England, 1990; sr. lectr. Manchester U., Eng., 2000—. Grantee Nuffield Found., Manchester, 1991, 92, Royal Soc., Manchester, 1992, Sci. and Engring. Rsch. Coun., Chgo., 1994. Mem. Am. Soc. Microbiology, Soc. for Gen. Microbiology, Soc. for Applied Bacteriology, Biofilm Club. Avocations: hockey, hiking, wine, traveling, gourmet dining. Office: U Manchester Pharmacy Dept, Oxford Rd, Manchester M13 9PL, England

ALLISON, JOHN ROBERT, lawyer; b. San Antonio, Feb. 9, 1945; s. Lyle (stepfather) and Beatrice (Kaliner) Forehand; m. Rebecca M. Picard; 1 child, Katharine. BS, Stanford U., 1966; JD, U. Wash., 1969. Bar: Wash. 1969, D.C. 1973, Minn. 1994, U.S. Supreme Ct. 1973. Assoc. Garvey, Schubert & Barer, Seattle, 1969-73; ptnr., 1973-86; prin. Betts, Patterson & Mines, P.S., 1986-94; sr. counsel Minn. Mining & Mfg. Co., 1994-2000, asst. gen. counsel, 2000—; lectr. bus. law Seattle U., 1970, U. Wash., 1970-73; judge pro tem, King County Superior Ct., 1983-94. Mem. ABA (vice chmn. toxic and hazardous substances and environ. law com. 1986-91, chair elect 1991-92, chair 1992-93), Minn. Bar Assn., Seattle-King County Bar Assn. (chmn. jud. evaln. polling com. 1982-83), Wash. State Bar Assn. (bd. bar examiners 1984-94), D.C. Bar Assn., Nat. Inst. Pollution Liability (co-chmn. 1988), Order of the Coif, Wash. Athletic (Seattle). Office: Minn Mining & Mfg Co 3 M Ctr Saint Paul MN 55144-0001

ALLISON, JONATHAN, retired lawyer; b. Washington, Pa., Apr. 17, 1916; s. Albert Johnson and Etta (Tucker) A. BS, Washington and Jefferson Coll., 1937; JD, U. Pa., 1940; postgrad., Harvard Grad. Bus. Adminstrn., 1940-41. Bar: Pa. 1942. Pvt. practice Washington, 1946-95; ret., 1995. Maj. AUS, 1941-46. Mem. ABA, Pa. Bar Assn., Washington County Bar Assn., Duquesne Club (Pitts.), Southpointe Golf Club, St. Clair Country Club (Upper St. Clair). Republican. Presbyterian. Home: 20 Fairmont Ave Washington PA 15301-3509 Office: 438 Washington Trust Bldg Washington PA 15301

ALLISON, LAIRD BURL, business educator; b. St. Marys, W.Va., Nov. 7, 1917; s. Joseph Alexander and Opal Marie (Robinson) A.; m. Katherine Louise Hunt, Nov. 25, 1943 (div. 1947); 1 child: William Lee; m. Genevieve Nora Elmore, Feb. 1, 1957 (dec. July 1994). BS in Personnel and Indsl. Relations magna cum laude, U. So. Calif., 1956; MBA, UCLA, 1958. Chief petty officer USN, 1936-51, PTO; asst. prof. to prof. mgmt. Calif. State U., L.A., 1956-83; asst. dean Calif. State U. Sch. Bus. and Econs., L.A., 1971-72, assoc. dean, 1973-83, emeritus prof. mgmt., 1983—; vis. asst. prof. mgmt. Calif. State U., Fullerton, 1970. Co-authored the Bachelors degree program in mgmt. sci. at Calif. State U., 1963. Mem. U.S. Naval Inst., Navy League U.S. Ford Found. fellow, 1960. Mem. Acad. Mgmt., Inst. Mgmt. Sci., Western Econs. Assn. Internat., World Future Soc., Am. Acad. Polit. Social Sci., Calif. State U. Assn. Emeriti Profs., Calif. State U. L.A. Emeriti Assn. (program v.p. 1986-87, v.p. adminstrn. 1987-88, pres. 1988-89, exec. com. 1990-91, treas. 1991—), Am. Assn. Individual Investors, Am. Assn. Ret. Persons, Ret. Pub. Employees Assn. Calif. (chpt. sec. 1984-88, v.p. 1989, pres. 1990-92), Am. Legion, Phi Kappa Phi, Beta Gamma Sigma, Alpha Kappa Psi. Avocations: history, travel, photography, hiking. Home: 2176 E Bellbrook St Covina CA 91724-2346 Office: Calif State U Dept Mgmt 5151 State University Dr Los Angeles CA 90032-4226

ALLISON, MARVIN JEROME, pathologist, anthropologist; b. Schenectady, N.Y., Jan. 6, 1921; s. Arthur Jerome and Jessie May A.; m. Esther Allison, Dec. 13, 1955; children: Arthur Felix, Jessie; m. Nancy Eudosia Allison, Dec. 3, 1984; 1 child: Rachel Christine. BA, Coll. William and Mary, 1942; MS, U. Pa., 1947, PhD, 1960. Clin. lab. dir. Md. State Lab., Balt., 1947-48; dir. lab. Firestone Hosp., Harper, Liberia, 1948-50, Talara Hosp., Peru, 1950-55; rsch. assoc. pathology Henry Phipps Inst., Phila., 1960-61; prof. pathology Med. Coll. Va., Richmond, 1961-83; prof. emeritus pathology Med. Coll. Va., 1983—; prof. anthropology U. Tarapaca, Arica, Chile, 1983-88; lab. cons. Vets. Hosp., Richmond, 1965-70; clin. lab. supr. Derby Hosp., Seymour, Conn., 1956-58, St. Vincent de Paul Hosp., Bridgeport, Conn., 1955-56. Contbr. articles to profl. jours.; author numerous book chpts. Fulbright fellow, Peru, 1970, Chile, 81, Am. Thoracic Soc. fellow, U. Pa., 1960-61; named hon. prof. pathology Sch. of Medicine San Luis Gonzaga, Ica, Peru, 1996, Officer Soc. Bernardo O'Higgens, Pres. Pinachel, Chile, 1989. Mem. Internat. Acad. Pathology. Avocations: ancient medieval history, languages, biking, collecting masks and African artifacts. E-mail: mallison@hsc.vcu.edu. Home: 8705 Playground Ct # 1 Richmond VA 23237-2378 Office: Med Coll Va Marshall St Dept Pathology Richmond VA 23298

ALLISON, ROBERT JOSEPH, software engineer; b. Corby, Eng., Dec. 12, 1955; s. Robert Rennie and Elizabeth (Maguire) A. BSc in Applied Physics with honors, Strathclyde U., Glasgow, Scotland, 1977; PhD, U. Kent, Canterbury, Eng., 1984. Chartered software engr., Eng. Software engr. Comart Computers, St. Neots, 1984; leading engr. Brit. Aerospace, Stevenage, 1985; team leader, software quality engr. Thorn EMI Micrologic, Bedford, 1985-88; sys. analyst Yanbu (Saudi Arabia) Petromin Refinery, 1988-90; software cons. Zergo Sys., Basingstoke, Eng., 1991-93; software group leader RMS Comms., Odiham, Eng., 1993-97, sr. sys. developer, 1997-98; software group leader Motorola, Basingstoke, Eng., 1999—. Contbr. articles to profl. jours. including Planetary and Space Sci.; co-inventor mains signalling sys. Mem. Brit. Computer Soc., Assn. for Computing Machinery, IEEE Computer Soc. Avocations: reading, swimming, music appreciation. Office: Motorola CGISS Jays Close, Viables Industrial Estate, Basingstoke Hampshire RG22 4PD, England

ALLISON, ROY ANTHONY, international relations administrator, educator; b. London, July 6, 1957. BA with 1st class honors, U. Exeter, Eng., 1978; DPhil, Oxford (Eng.) U., 1983. Lectr. U. Birmingham, 1987-92; sr. assoc. mem. St. Antony's Coll. U. Oxford, 1991-93; sr. lectr. Russian def. and internat. security policy U. Birmingham, Eng., 1992-99; head Russia and Eurasia program Royal Inst. Internat. Affairs, London, 1993—. Author: (books) Finland's Relations with the Soviet Union, 1944-1984, 1985, The Soviet Union and the Strategy of Non-Alignment in the Third World, 1988, (booklet) Military Forces in the Soviet Successor States, 1993; editor: (books) Superpower Competition and Crisis Prevention in the Third World, 1990, Radical Reform in Soviet Defence Policy, 1992, Challenges for the Former Soviet South, 1996; co-author: (book) Internal Factors in Russian Foreign Policy, 1996; co-editor: (book) Security Dilemmas in Russia and Eurasia, 1998; mem. editl. bd.: Internat. Affairs, 1995—, Cambridge Russian Soviet and Post-Soviet Studies, 1994-2000. Postdoctoral fellow Econ. and Social Rsch. Coun., St. Antony's Coll., Oxford U., 1983-86; grantee for project Soviet Def. and Arms Control Policies, 1985-2000, Ford Found., 1990-93, grantee for project Keeping the Peace in the CIS, 1994-99, Russian-NATO Rels. and Peacekeeping, MacArthur Found., 2000—, Russian and Iron in Ctrl. Asia, Econ. and Social Rsch. Coun., 2000—. Mem. Internat. Inst. for Strategic Studies. Avocations: traveling in Asia, trekking, photography. Office: Royal Inst Internat Affairs, 10 St James's Sq, London SW1Y 4LE, England

ALLISON, STEPHEN GALENDER, broadcast executive; b. Springfield, Mo., Dec. 11, 1952; s. Edgbert Allcorn and Naomi Louise (Chamless) A.; m. Linda Lavelle, June 6, 1974 (div. Dec. 1981); children: Julie Ann, Jennifer Erin; m. Tara Rae Foster, Aug. 20, 1986 (div. Aug. 1994). Cert. radio mktg. cons. Radio Advt. Bur. On-air personality Sta. WSBB, New Smyrna, Fla., 1971-72, Sta. WMFJ-AM-FM, Daytona Beach, Fla., 1972-75, Sta. KADI-FM, St. Louis, 1975-76, Sta. KAUM-FM, Houston, 1976-79, Sta. WKYS-FM, Washington, 1979-81; gen mgr. Sta. KSTM-FM, Phoenix, 1981-85; pres. Allison Broadcasting Co., Inc., Phoenix, 1985—, Allison Broadcast Group, Inc., Dallas, Del Mar, Calif., 1987—; owner Stas. KGRX-FM/ KIKO, Phoenix, 1986-91, Sta. KDGE-FM, Dallas, 1989-94, WLVX-FM, Gainesville, Fla., 1994-95; mgr. talk/bus./ESPN programming ABC Radio Networks, Dallas, 1996-97; dir. Clear Channel Comms., Tampa, 1997-98; nat. dir. mktg. Metro Networks, Phoenix, 1998-99; sr. exec. analyst George S. May Internat. Co., San Jose, Calif., 1999—; mktg. cons. St. Louis Post-Dispatch, 1975-76, Houston Chronicle, 1976-79, Washington Star, 1980-81; advt. cons. Celebrity Theatre, Phoenix, 1985-86; pres. JFM Branson (Mo.) Inc., 1993—; owner Doc Severinsen Theater. Bd. dirs. Desert-Mt. Foothills Assn., Scottsdale, Ariz., 1981-91, 98—, Alwun House Cultural Ctr., Phoenix, 1982—, Film in Ariz., Phoeniz, 1985-93, Ariz. Commn. on the Arts, Phoenix, 1986-89; active Nat. Rep. Congl. Com., 1988-93, No. Tex. Commn. Mem. Nat. Assn. Broadcasters, Ariz. Broadcasters Assn., Tex. Assn. Broadcasters, Phoenix Active 20-30 Club, Internat. Platform Assn., Las Colinas Sports Club, Pointe Royale Country Club, Preston Trails Country Club, The Heritage Club. Avocations: collecting classic cars, traveling, racquetball, golfing, boating. Home: 1747 E Northern Ave Apt 212 Phoenix AZ 85020-3992 Office: Metro Networks 14605 N Airport Dr Ste 330 Scottsdale AZ 85260-2460

ALLMAN, AVIS ASIYE, artist, poet, Turkish and Islamic culture educator, human rights activist; b. Phila., Dec. 27, 1954; d. William Berthold and Margo (Hutz) A. BFA in Painting, Windham Coll., 1975; MBA in Arts, SUNY, Binghamton, 1978; postgrad., Hunter Coll., 1983, NYU, 1987-88, 91-95. Devel. officer The Bklyn. Mus., 1977; program analyst N.Y. State Coun. Arts, N.Y.C., 1977-80, dir. spl. projects, 1980-81; dir. adminstrn. Mus. Broadcasting, N.Y.C., 1981; sr. fin. analyst CBS TV Network, N.Y.C., 1981-82; rsch. cons. Am. Coun. on Arts, N.Y.C., 1983-84; fin. analyst Cmty. Svc. Soc., N.Y.C., 1983-84; pres. Allman Fin. Svcs., Bklyn., 1985—; artist-in-residence (tiles) Canakkale Ceramics, Istanbul, Turkey, 1991-96, (carpets) Net Holding, Izmir, Turkey, 1989, (painter, poet) Zaman Newspaper, Ankara, Turkey, 1997; rsch. assoc. Georgetown U. Muslim-Christian Understanding, 1998-99. One-woman shows include Mus. Turkish/Islamic Arts, Istanbul, 1987, 90, 92, French Cultural Ctr., Izmir, 1992, Women's Libr., Istanbul, 1996, Mus. Calligraphy, Istanbul, 1996; exhibited in group shows at Müsiad/IBF Forum, Istanbul, 1997, Altinpark, Ankara, 1997; represented in permanent collections at Vatican, Mus. Turkish/Islamic Arts, Indpls. Mus. Art; author: Road to Democracy, 1997, Religious Freedom in Turkey, 1999, Turkey Is Crying, 1999, Human Rights, Democracy and Islam in Turkey, 2000. Sr. Rsch. Fulbright scholar U.S. Info. Agy, 1988-89; vis. scholar NYU, 1991-94; recipient Exhbn. grants U.S. Info. Svc., Ankara, 1987, Greek Consulate, Izmir, Turkey, 1992, Kale Group, Istanbul, 1992, 96, Glaxo Wellcome, Istanbul, 1996. Democrat. Muslim. Avocations: dancing, praying to God, Mediterranean Sea, walking. Studio: 202 State Rd West Grove PA 19390-8906 Office: Allman Fin Svcs 20 Henry St Apt 3G Brooklyn NY 11201-1348

ALLMAN, MARGARET ANN LOWRANCE, counselor; b. Carmel, Calif., June 2, 1938; d. Edward Walton and Rhoda Elizabeth (Patton) Lowrance; m. Jackie Howard Hamilton, Dec. 21, 1959 (div. May 1976); children: John Scott, David Lee, Dennis Lynn; m. Jack Fredrick Allman, Dec. 22, 1977; stepchildren: John Frederick, James Paul, Jeffrey Lee. AA, Christian Coll., 1958; BA in Spanish, U. Mo., 1960, MEd, 1971, EdD, 1994. Tchr. Spanish Neosho (Mo.) H.S., 1961-62, asst. prin., 1974-77; florist Wallflower Shop and Greenhouse, Joplin, Mo., 1962-69; dean girls Joplin Sr. H.S., 1967-69; florist, bookkeeper Mueller's Garden Ctr., Columbia, Mo., 1969-71; instr. edn., asst. dean of students Columbia (Mo.) Coll., 1971-74; dir. guidance Am. Cmty. Sch., Buenos Aires, 1978-81; tchr. Spanish, psychology Ava (Mo.) H.S., 1982-84; tchr. Spanish, social studies McDonald County H.S., Anderson, Mo., 1984-88; counselor Mo. So. State Coll., Joplin, 1988—; mem. adv. bd. Adult Basic Edn., Joplin, 1992—; cons. Mo. So. State Coll., 1990—, mem. internat. task force, 1994-96; presenter Ctr. for Applications of Psychol. Type Internat. Conf., 1996. Recipient William D. Phillips Music award 1st Christian Ch., Columbia, 1956; named to Outstanding Young Women of Am., 1972. Mem. Mo. Sch. Counselor Assn., Southwest Mo. Sch. Counselor Assn. (sec. 1994-97, v.p. 1992-94, 99—, mem. governing bd., chmn. publs. and rsch. com. 1997—), Kappa Delta Pi, Phi Theta Kappa, Sigma Phi Gamma, Delta Eta Chi, Phi Sigma Iota (romance lang., pres 1959-60), Sigma Delta Pi. Avocations: music, photographer, sketch artist, needlecrafts, jewelry crafts. Home: 1214 Circle Dr Neosho MO 64850-1301 Office: Mo So State Coll 3950 Newman Rd Joplin MO 64801-1512

ALLMAN, WILLIAM BERTHOLD, musician, engineer, consultant; b. Phila., Feb. 16, 1927; s. Drue Nunez and Blanche (Oppenheimer) A.; m. Margo Hutz, Feb. 19, 1954; children: Avis Louise, David Drue. BSEE, Drexel U., 1949; MBA, U. Pa., 1951. Registered profl. engr., Pa. Contract engr. Atlantic Refining, Phila., 1951-55, E.I. DuPont de Nemours & Co., Inc., Wilmington, Del., 1955-58; constrn. engr. Niagra Falls, N.Y., 1958-59; cons. engr. Wilmington, 1959-82, Allman Assocs., West Grove, Pa., 1982—; owner, mgr. Allman Bldgs., Phila., 1965-87. Contbr. numerous articles on plastic pipe to profl. mags.; drummer, washboard player with Allman, Melton and Co. band; performed with various musicians including Lionel Hampton, Brownie McGhee, Mississippi Fred McDowell, Sonny Terry. Mem. Bi-racial com. City of Newark, Del., 1963-71, chmn. 1965, London Grove Township Mcpl. Authority, Chester County, Pa., 1985-89, chmn. 1986; Dem. committeeman, Del., 1964-71, chmn., 1968; candidate Mayor City of Newark, 1970; adv. coun. Neighborhood Svcs. Ctr., Oxford, Pa., 1989—. With USNR, 1945-46. ETO. Mem. Am. Assn. Individual Investors, Del. Ctr. Contemporary Arts, Del. Art Mus., Phila. Mus. Art, Nature Conservancy. Democrat. Unitarian. Avocations: painting, music, gardening, traveling, reading. Home and Office: 202 State Rd West Grove PA 19390-8906

ALLMAND, LINDA F(AITH), retired library director; b. Port Arthur, Tex., Jan. 31, 1937; d. Clifton James and Jewel Etoile (Smith) A. BA, North Tex. State U., 1960; MA, U. Denver, 1962. Clerical asst. Gates Meml. Libr., 1953-55; libr. asst. Houston Pub. Libr., 1955-58; children's libr. Denver Pub. Libr., 1960-63; children's coord. Anaheim Pub. Libr., Calif., 1963-65; br. mgr. Dallas Pub. Libr, 1965-71, chief br. svcs., 1971-81; dir. Ft. Worth Pub. Libr., 1981-98; instr. North Tex. State U., Denton, 1967—; instr. Dallas County C.C., 1981; bldg. cons. Dallas Pub. Libr., 1974-80, Hurst Pub. Libr., 1977-78, Jacksonville (Tex.) Pub. Libr., 1976-79, Carrollton Pub. Libr., 1979-81, Haltom (Tex.) City Pub. Libr., 1984, Iowa Park (Tex.) Pub. Libr., 1985, S.W. Regional Libr., Ft. Worth, 1987. Author: 1981-2000, Ft. Worth Public Library—Facilities and Long-Range Planning Study, 1982; contbr. chpts. to books, articles to profl. jours. Bd. dirs. City of Dallas Credit Union, 1973-81, Sr. Citizen's Ctrs., Inc., 1982; com. chmn. Goals for Dallas, 1967-69; mem. Forum Ft. Worth, 1983; mem. Edn. Info. Task Force, Downtown Fort Worth, Inc., 1992-93. Pilot Club of Port Arthur scholar, 1954, Libr. Binding Inst. scholar, 1958; recipient Disting. Alumnus award North Tex. State U., 1983, U. North Tex., 1998, Leadership Ft. Worth, 1982-83; named Tarrant County Newsmaker of the Yr., 1984, Outstanding Leader, Ft. Worth Star Telegram, 1989, Outstanding Woman of the Yr., Mayor's Commn. on Status of Women, 1989, North Tex. Pub. Adminstr. of the Yr., 1990. Mem. ALA, AAUP, AAUW (Tarrant County pres.-elect 1998, pres. 1999), Tex. Libr. Assn. (pres. pub. libr. divsn. 1980-81, chmn. planning com. 1982-84, pres.-elect 1985-86, pres. 1986-87, Libr. of Yr. award 1985, North Tex. Pub. Adminstr. of Yr. award 1990), Tarrant Regional Librs. Assn., Am. Mgmt. Assn., Dallas County Librs. Assn. (pres. 1968-69), Downtown Ft. Worth (mem. edn. info. task force 1992-93), Freedom to Read Found., Ft. Worth C. of C. (bd. dirs. 1993-95), Rotary, Sister Cities, Inc., Ft. Worth Pub. Libr. Found. Home: 701 Timberview Ct N Fort Worth TX 76112-1715

ALLMER, STEPHEN DALE, agricultural products executive; b. Greeley, Colo., June 16, 1954; s. Floyd Allmer and Lillian Christine Dye-Allmer; m. Penny Lou Spilman, May 24, 1975; children: Rebecca Sue, Matthew Stephen. AA in Acctg., Northeastern Jr. Coll., Sterling, Colo., 1974. Cert. pastor, Calif. Auditor, jr. acct. Canteen Food & Vending, Denver, 1974; asst. feed prodn. mgr. Farmer's Mktg. Assn., Denver, 1975; project foreman Don Allmer Plumbing, Lancaster, Calif., 1977-79; master plumber Allen Plumbing, Greeley, Colo., 1979-81; project mgr., estimator Robert Dougan Constrn. Co., Denver, 1981-91; prin. Allmer & Co., Fairfield, Calif., 1991-98; CFO, COO, pres. Guided By God, Inc., Vacaville, Calif., 1992-93. Elder, mem. adv. bd. Living Faith Foursquare Ch., Fairfield, 1993—; elder, fin. advisor, pastor Liberty Christian Ctr., Fairfield, 1994-98; youth pastor Liberty Christian Ctr., Fairfield. Avocations: sports, reading, family activities.

ALLMON, CHARLES W., investment advisor; b. East Liverpool, Ohio, Feb. 9, 1921; s. E. Floyd Allmon and Josephine T. Tate; m. Gwen D. Allmon, Apr. 15, 1954; children: Kathy Allmon Goodrich, Jane Allmon Heath. BS, Purdue U., 1941, PhD, 1994. With rsch. dept. United Fruit Co., Honduras, 1941-42; supt. divsn. Firestone Rubber Co., Liberia, 1943-46; freelance photographer, writer various mags., 1947-53; asst. editor illustrations Nat. Geographic Mag., Washington, 1953-69; pres., editor Growth Stock Outlook, Inc., Bethesda, Md., 1965—; speaker in field. Interviewee over 1600 radio and T.V. programs, 1975—. Mem. citizen's com. North Chevy Chase, Md., 1962-65; trustee Alexander Graham Bell Assn. Deaf, Washington, 1972-98. Mem. Explorers Club N.Y., Masons. Presbyterian. Avocations: photography, international travel. Office: Growth Stock Outlook Inc 4405 E West Hwy Bethesda MD 20814-4522

ALLNUTT, F. C. THOMAS, biologist; b. Frederick, Md., June 27, 1954; s. Benoni Dawson and Sarah Thomas Allnutt; m. Virginia Pierce Allnutt, June 26, 1987; children: B. Dawson, Annie Lee, Mary Alice. BS in Biology, Va. Poly. Inst., 1976, MS in Microbiology, 1979; PhD in Biology, U. Pa., 1985. mentor biotech. Bus. and Edn. as Mentors-Howard County, Columbia, 1996—. Postdoctoral assoc. Purdue U., West Lafayette, Ind., 1985-87; postdoctoral assoc. Rutgers U., New Brunswick, N.J., 1987-88, coadjutant, lectr., 1989; microbiology group leader Martek Biosci. Corp., Columbia, Md., 1989-94, sci. mgr., 1994-97, mgr. fluorescent products, 1997-98, dir. fluorescent products, 1998—. Contbr. articles to profl. jours. Grantee NSF, 1996—, NIH, 1992-95. Mem. Am. Soc. Microbiology, Soc. Biomolecular Screening, Soc. Indsl. Microbiology, Am. Assn. Plant Physiology, Sigma Xi. Avocations: gardening, sports, outdoors. E-mail: t allnutt@compuserve.com. Office: Martek Biosci Corp 6480 Dobbin Rd Ste J Columbia MD 21045-4701

ALLONES, PANFILO AMBOY, research company executive, mechanical engineer; b. Alimodian, The Philippines, Sept. 26, 1948; s. Alipio Albila and Pacencia Alomia A.; m. Betty Lozada, Sept. 12, 1976; children: Junette, Lionel, Filbeth, Cheryl. Student, We. Inst. Tech., Iloilo, The Philippines, 1966-71, De La Salle U., Bacolob, The Philippines, 1981-84. From head boiler sect. to supt. planning and mktg. Lopez Sugar Corp., Sagay, The Philippines, 1975-95, head tng. and rsch., 1995—. City councilman, Sagay, 1995-98, mcpl. councilman, 1992-95; dir. Peoples Econ. Coun., Sagay, 1991. Recipient Golden Excellence award United Group Charities and Human Devel. Inc., Quezon City, The Philippines, 1991. Mem. Toastmasters (pres. 1995-96), Rotary (pres. Sagay chpt. 1989-90, Gov's award 1991). Roman Catholic. Avocations: reading, furniture & cabinet making, current events. Home: Sarromar Subdivsn, 6122 Sagay City The Philippines Office: Lopez Sugar Corp, Fabrica 6123, Sagay City The Philippines

ALLPORT, JOHN MARTIN, mechanical engineer; b. Accrington, U.K., Feb. 12, 1963; s. Anthony John and Catherine Mary (Hargreaves) A.; m. Geraldine Frances Corcoran, July 16, 1988. B in Engring., U. Nottingham, Eng., 1985; PhD, U. Bradford, Eng., 1994. Engring. scholar Nat. Coal Bd., Yorkshire, Eng., 1981-86; tech. asst. Newlands Coal Pty, Glenden, Australia, 1985; devel. engr. Thomas Broadbent & Sons Ltd., Huddersfield, Eng., 1986-89; devel. engr. Holset Engring. Co. Ltd., Halifax, Eng., 1989-93, sr. project engr., 1993-94, prin. engr., 1994-98; tech. specialist Simpson Internat. Ltd., Halifax, Eng., 1998—; hon. vis. rsch. fellow U. Bradford, Eng., 1994—. Patentee in field. Troop leader Scout Assn., Elland, Eng., 1987—, dist. exec. mem., 1991—. Indsl. fellowship Royal commn. for the Exhbn. of 1851, 1991-94. Mem. Mensa. Achievements include development of practical C.A.E. techniques for elastomeric materials. Office: Holset Engring Co Ltd, Simpson Internat, 131 Parkinson Ln, Halifax HX13 RD, England

ALLRED, KEITH JOHNS, naval officer; b. El Paso, Tex., Jan. 4, 1955. BA with high honors, Brigham Young U., 1979; student, Univ. Wash., 1982-85; JD, U. Wash., 1985; student, DePaul Univ., Chicago, 1994-95; LLM, DePaul U., 1995. Bar: Wash. 1985, Ct. Mil. Appeals 1987. Gunnery officer, navigator USS Towers (DDG-9), 1979-82; trial lawyer San Diego, 1985-89; attorney Commander Fleet Air, Carribbean, Puerto Rico, 1989-92; staff judge advocate Battle Force Seventh Fleet, Yokosuka, Japan, 1992-94, Carrier Strike Force U.S. Seventh Fleet, Yokosuka, Japan, 1992-94; gen. counsel Naval Med. Ctr., San Diego, 1995-97; exec. officer Naval Legal Svc. Office Southwest, San Diego, 1997-99; cir. mil. judge Western Pacific Jud. Cir., 1999—; instr. Keller Grad. Sch. Mgmt., San Diego, 1997—. Contbr. articles to profl. jours.; asst. case note editor: Jour. Health & Hosp. Law, 1994-95. ensign, US Navy, 1979, lt. (j.g.), 1981, lt., 1984, lt. comdr., 1990, comdr., 1995. Office: Western Pacific Judicial Circuit PSC 473 Box 14 FPO AP 96349

ALLSEBROOK, MARY NESBIT, writer, researcher; b. Hanover, N.H., Aug. 25, 1910; arrived in U.K., 1940; d. Charles Henry and Harriet (Boyd) Hawes; m. John Colin Pole Allsebrook, Feb. 24, 1940; children: Duncan Lloyd, Anne Boyd. BA, Radcliffe Coll., 1933. Statis. rschr. in bituminous coal Nat. Recovery Adminstrn., Washington, 1934-35; rschr. on U.S. trends Internat. Labor Office, Washington, summer 1935; jr. economist, jr. legal asst. Consumer Project, Dept. Labour, Washington, 1935-38; roving corr. Washington Post, Ctrl. Europe, 1939; advisor on food availability in Europe U.S. Embassy, London, 1942-45; writer, spkr., 1967—. Author: Born to Rebel, 1992; editor: Weekley Precis, Am. Outpost, 1940-42, Prototypes of Peacemaking: The First 40 Years of the UN, 1986; contbr. articles to profl. jours. Mem. exec. and polit. coms. United Nations Assn., London, 1970s and 80s; founder, trustee Oxford (Eng.) Project for Peace Studies, 1980-94. Democrat. Quaker. Avocations: Minoan archaeology, furthering awareness of pioneering work of Harriet Boyd Hawes, house design.

ALLSOP, JOHN LESLIE, neurologist, consultant; b. Sydney, NSW, Australia, Apr. 12, 1924; s. Leslie Thomas and Irene Margaret (Nattrass) A.; m. Philippa Gordon Bain, Aug. 30, 1947; children: Richard John Bain Allsop, James Leslie Bain Allsop, Philippa Ann Allsop. MB BS, U. Sydney, 1946, MD (hon.), 1992. Fellow Royal Australasia Coll. Physicians. Resident Royal Prince Alfred Hosp. Camperdown, Sydney, 1946-50; clin. supt. Royal Prince Alfred Hosp. Camperdown, 1950-53, hon. asst. physician, 1953-63, hon. physician, 1963-70, vis. neurologist, 1970-89, cons. neurologist, 1989—; bd. dirs. Royal Prince Alfred Hosp. Camperdown, 1972-85, chmn., 1973-84. Contbr. articles to profl. jours. Decorated Order of Australia; chevalier de l'Ordre Nat. du Merite (France). Mem. Australian Assn. Neurologists, Royal Sydney Golf Club, Australian Club, French Soc. Neurology (fgn. mem.). Anglican. Avocations: woodwork, golf. Home: 703/170 Ocean St, 2027 Edgecliff Australia Office: Royal Prince Hosp Alfred Med Ctr, 100 Carillon Ave, Newtown 2042, Australia

ALLSOP, RICHARD EDWARD, transport educator; b. Derby, Eng., May 2, 1940. MA, Queens' Coll., Cambridge, Eng., 1962; PhD, U. Coll., London, 1970, DSc, 1995. Sci. officer Road Rsch. Lab., Harmondsworth, Eng., 1964-66; rsch. fellow U. Coll., London, 1967-69, lectr. Transport

Studies, 1970-72, prof., 1976—; dir. transport ops. rsch. group U. Newcastle upon Tyne, Eng., 1973-76; vis. scientist Transport & Road Rsch. Lab. Traffic Group, Crowthorne, Eng., 1987-92. Contbr. numerous articles profl. jours.; programmer software for traffic signal calculations;. Convenor Road Environ. Working Party Parliamentary Adv. Coun. Transport Safety, London, 1987-93, dir., 1995—; chmn. rd. infrastructure working party European Transport Safety Coun., 1993—; mem. Road Traffic Law Review, Eng., 1985-88. Fellow Chartered Inst. Transport (coun. mem. 1981-84), Instn. Highways and Transp. (coun. mem. 1987-96), Instn. Civil Engrs., Royal Acad. Engring., Inst. Logistics and Transport. Episcopalian. Office: U Coll London, Gower St, WC1E 6BT London England

ALLSOPP, RONALD JAMES, solicitor; b. Oxford, Eng., May 12, 1947; s. Alfred Thomas and Primrose Ethel (Bollen) A.; m. Greta Jane Vincent, Sept. 3, 1977; children: James, Katherine. LLB, St. Andrews U., Scotland, 1968. Solicitor, 1972. Lectr. The Coll. of Law, Guildford, 1971-73; asst. solicitor Penningtons, London, 1973-74, ptnr., 1974—, head of co. and comml. dept., 1986-92, 97—, chmn. exec. bd., 1992-96, chmn., partnership com., 1996—; lectr. on strategic planning and corp. legal issues to staff and clients. Mem. Law Soc., City of London Solicitors Co., Brit. Assn. for Shooting and Conservation. Conservative. Avocations: shooting, fishing, wine, cooking, family. Office: Penningtons Solicitors, Bucklersbury H 83 Cannon St, London EC4N 8PE, England

ALLUMS, JAMES A., retired cardiovascular surgeon; b. Kountze, Tex., Sept. 28, 1937; m. Elizabeth Dee Walton, June 24, 1961; children: Ann Elizabeth, Sarah Dee, Benjamin Walton. BA, U. Tex., 1959; MD, U. Tex. Med. Br., 1962. Diplomate Am. Bd. Med. Examiners, Am. Bd. Surgery, Gen. Vascular Surgery, Am. Bd. Thoracic Surgery. Rotating intern Phila. Gen. Hosp., 1962-63; resident gen. surgery Med. Br. U. Tex., Galveston, 1963-66, 68-69; ptnr. Thoracic and Cardiovascular Surg. Assocs., Beaumont, Tex., 1971-97; clin. asst. prof. dept. thoracic and cardiovascular surgery U. Tex. Med. Br., Galveston, ret., 1997; active physician St. Elizabeth Hosp., chief of staff 1976-77, 87-88; active Beaumont, Bapt. Hosp. of S.E. Tex., Beaumont, Beaumont Regional Med. Ctr., Beaumont Regional Med. Ctr., Park Place Hosp.; courtesy staff St. Mary Hosp., Port Arthur, Mid Jefferson Hosp., Nederland, Tex.; cons. staff U. Tex. Med. Br. Hosp., Galveston; mem. cardiovascular com. Bapt. Hosp., 1991-93, 1996, physician, nurse ad hoc com., 1992; clin. asst. prof. Dept. of Surgery U. Tex. Med. Br. Hosp., 1993-94; OR com. St. Elizabeth Hosp., Beaumont, 1990-91, 93-94, cardiovascular quality assurance subcom., 1991-92, cardiovascular/coronary care com., 1990-91, 92-93, CCU quality assurance subcom. Contbr. articles to profl. jours. Capt. U.S. Army, 1966-68. Recipient J.C. Crager award Am. Heart Assn., 1992, Mr. East Tex. award Tyler County Dogwood Festival, 1993. Fellow ACS (gov. 1989-94, pres. South Tex. chpt. 1987), Am. Coll. of Angiology, Am. Coll. of Cardiology, Am. Coll. of Chest Physicians, Beaumont Acad. of Medicine; mem. AMA, Assn. of Am. Physicians and Surgeons, Bapt. Hosp. P.H.O., Beaumont Regional P.H.O., Jefferson County Med. Soc., Singleton Surg. Soc., Soc. of Thoracic Surgeons, So. Assn. for Vascular Surgery, So. Med. Assn., So. Thoracic Surg. Assn., St. Elizabeth Hosp. P.H.O., Tex. Med. Assn. (coun. on med. edn. 1985-92), Tex. Surg. Soc., Alumni Assn. of the U. of Tex. Med. Br. (pres. 1984-85)Phi Eta Sigma, Alpha Epsilon Delta.

ALLWOOD, MICHAEL JOHN, retired clinical physiologist; b. Stoke-on-Trent, Eng., July 31, 1925; s. Edgar Henry and Florance (Nicholson) A.; m. Rosemary Marguerite Harrison, July 15, 1950 (dec. 1983); 5 children. MB BS, U. London, 1950, PhD, 1959, MD, 1970. Diplomate Eng. Bd. Med. Examiners. Rschr. Nat. Inst. Med. Rsch., London, 1951-53, Inst. Aviation Medicine, Farnborough, 1963-67; lectr. U. London, 1953-63; cons. Walsgrave Gen. Hosp., Coventry, 1967-90; ret., 1990; hon. lectr. U. Birmingham, 1967-76. Contbr. articles to profl. jours. Served to surg. capt. Eng. Naval Res., 1949-82. Decorated Vol. Res. decoration with clasp. Mem. Interallied Confedn. Med. Res. Officers (U.K. rep. 1974-82, pres. 1980-82, cons. 1984), Midland Naval Officers Assn. (chmn. 1983-89), Res. Forces Assn. (coun. 1977-83), Naval Club. Mem. Ch. of Eng. Home: Ridge Barn, Ufton Fields, Leamington Spa CV33 9PE, England

ALM, JAN EVAN ROBERT, psychologist, researcher; b. Hudiksvall, Sweden, Oct. 25, 1947; s. Emil Per and Elin Gunborg (Carlsson) A.; m. Rüya Ayse Elizabeth Storm, Dec. 19, 1989; children: Christina, Helena. Lic. psychologist. Psychologist Falun Hosp. Psychiat. Clinic, 1972-74; pvt. practice psychology, 1974-81, mgr. family bus., 1982-86; psychologist Swedish Nat. Labour Market Adminstrn., 1986-96; head Swedish Inst. for Psychol. Assessment, Inc., Uppsala U., 1996—; mem. sci. com. 4th World Congress on Dyslexia, Macedonia, Greece, 1997; presenter in field. Mem. editl. bd. U.S. Jour. Rsch. in Schs.; contbr. articles to profl. jours. Mem. Internat. Acad. for Rsch. in Learning Disabilities, European Dyslexia Acad. for Rsch. and Tng. (founder, bd. mem.), Swedish Dyslexia Assn. (bd. mem.). Avocations: golf, history, traveling, Eastern philosophy. E-mail: jan.alm@p-syk.uu.se. Home: Skolgatan 31, 75311 Uppsala Sweden Office: SPU Inc, Vaksalagatan 6, 75320 Uppsala Sweden

ALMADANY, ISMAIL MOHAMED, environmental scientist, educator; b. Bahrain, Bahrain, July 29, 1956; s. Mohamed Ahmed Almadany and Fatima Mohamed Ismail; m. Ahmed Mohamed Fatima, 1985. BSc, U. Tex., Austin, 1979; MSc, U. Manchester Inst. Sci. Tech., Eng., 1982, PhD, 1984. Asst. prof. Bahrain U., 1984-86; asst. prof., dir. student affairs Arabian Gulf U., Bahrain, 1986-89, assoc. prof., dir. student affairs, 1989-94, prof., 1994—; cons. environ. program, devel. program UN, Gulf Orgn. for Indsl. Cons., Arab Bur. Edn. Gulf States; columnist Al Khaleej News, 1990—. Author: Sewage Water, 1989, Towards Environmental Awareness in the Gulf, 1989, domestic Waste Utilization Methods, 1992, Out Environment is in Danger, 1995, Our Resources are Threatened, 1997, Sport and Environment, 1998, Cars: Problem and Solution, 1999, Tubli Bay, 2000; contbr. over 200 articles to profl. jours. Cons. Ministry of Housing Municipality and Environment. Recipient Award for Outstanding Achievement State of Bahrain, 1992, Land Crown Prince award Best Sci. Rsch., 1996, Arab Environ. Patron award, 1997. Mem. Youth and Environment Soc. (chmn. 1990—), Bahrain Nat. Com. for Protection of Wildlife (sec.-gen.). Avocation: Tae Kwon Do. E-mail: bncftpw@batelco.com.bh. Home: 1255 Rd 4618, A'ali 746, Bahrain Office: Arabian Gulf U, Nat Commn Wildlife Protect, Box 28690, Bahrain Bahrain

AL-MADHI, FAHAD TURKI, physician, medical attache; b. Oct. 30, 1940; came to U.S., 1994; s. Turki Al-Madhi and Noriah Mallah; m. Salwa Abdulhameed Al-Khateeb, Aug. 10, 1971; children: Mohannad, Fargad, Forgan, Morooge, Tameem. B Medicine B Surgery, Ain Shams U., Cairo, 1970, diploma in internal medicine, 1973. Head med. dept. Border Guards, Riyadh, Saudi Arabia, 1971-75; gastroenterologist Riyadh Ctrl. Hosp., 1975-80; med. attache Ministry of Health, London, 1980-86; dir. gen. health affairs Riyadh, 1986-88, Makkah, Saudi Arabia, 1988-91; dir. gen. Ctrl. Riyadh Hosp., 1991-93; dir. gen. med. com.. Ministry of Health, Riyadh, 1993-94; med. attache Royal Embassy of Saudi Arabia, Washington, 1994—. Author: Diabetes Metallus, 1986; editor daily mag. Min/Mothakkarat Turki Al-Madhi, 1999; contbr. to weekly mag. Al-Yamamah. Avocations: photography, reading, writing, travel. Home: PO Box 58177 Washington DC 20037-8177 Office: Royal Embassy of Saudi Arabia 601 New Hampshire Ave NW Washington DC 20037-2405

ALMAGOR, YARON, cardiologist; b. Hadera, Israel, July 19, 1953; s. Saul Lither and Ruth (Segal) A.; m. Rivka Zimmerman, Sept. 10, 1974 (div. 1995); m. Marzia Bernati, May 25, 1997; children: Ben, Daniel, Yonatan. MD, U. Milan, 1981. Fellow in cardiology Tel-Aviv, 1982-86; fellow in interventional cardiology, 1986-90; co-dir. Columbus Heart Ctr., Milan, 1990-93; dir. interventional cardiology Jerusalem, 1993—. Office: Shaare Zedek Med Ctr, 12 Hans Beyth PO Box 3235, 91031 Jerusalem Israel

AL-MAHAYNI, MOHAMAD KHALED, Syrian government official, finance educator; b. Damascus, Syria, May 30, 1943; s. Salim Al-Mahayni; m. Falak Sakkal, 1966; children: Suzan, Salim, Rima, Tarek. PhD in Econs., Damascus U., 1991; doctorate in commerce and econs. Fin. dir. various pub. establishments, 1961-76; auditor, 1970—; dir. pub. debt fund dept. Ministry of Fin., Damascus, 1977-79, dir. computerized fin. data processing dept., 1979-80, dir. pub. enterprises affairs, 1981-84, dep. min. fin., 1984-87, min. fin., 1987—; prof. econs. Damascus U., 1992—; mem. Uniform Acctg. Sys., Coun. Mins., Econ. Com., Higher Coun. Planning, Higher Coun. Pub. Constrns., Higher Coun. Tourism; fin. dir. numerous pub. enterprises, Damascus, 1961—; bd. govs. IBRD,1987—, Arab Bank for Econ. Devel. in Africa, 1989—. Author: Methodology of the General State Budget in the Syrian Arab Republic, 1994, Supplementary Policies for Financial Planning, 1995, Government Accounting, 1996, Public Finance and Tax Legislation, 1999; contbr. articles to profl. publs. Mem., specialized Ministerial Comms. and The Cabinet; Permanent Comms. of Uniform Acctg. System, 1987—, Counc. of Minsters; Economic Comm., Higher Counc. Planning, Higher Counc. of Public Constructions, Higher Counc. of Tourism. Avocations: reading, computers. Fax: (963) (11) 2224701. E-mail: mof@net.sy. Office: Ministry of Finance, PO BOX 13136 Jule Jamal St, Damascus Syria

AL-MAHMEED, AHMED SALEH, engineering educator; b. Kuwait City, Kuwait, Oct. 25, 1954; s. Saleh M. Al-Mahmeed and Khadija Saleh Khalaf; m. Buthainah AbdulAziz Al-Hashash, July 1, 1989; children: Mariam, Sara, Esra'a, Fatimah. BS, U. Dayton, 1981, MS in Engring., 1984; PhD in Computer Sci., U. Strathclyde, Glasgow, Scotland, 1994. Cert. in engring. and sci. Elec. engr. Kuwait TV, 1976-79, Civil Aviation, Kuwait, 1979-81; prof. Pub. Authority for Applied Edn. and Tng., Kuwait, 1981—; cons. Regional Consulting Co., Kuwait, 1995-97; adviser Ministry of Edn., Kuwait, 1996-99. Author: (book) Meta-Heuristics: Theory and Applications, 1995; contbr. rsch. articles to projects and profl. publs. Lt. Ground Engring., 1987-88. Scholar Ministry of Higher Edn., 1990. Mem. IEEE, IEEE Computer Soc., Assn. Computing Machinery, Kuwait Soc. Engrs. Avocations: traveling, reading, computers, chess. Fax: 965 551 8097. E-mail: mahmeed@netscape.net. Home: PO Box 15084, Dayiah 35451, Kuwait Office: Pub Authority Appl Edn/Tng, PO Box 36, Sabah Al-Salem 44401, Kuwait

AL-MAHMOUD, SHEIKH ABDULLAH BIN SAID, judge; b. Bani Tamim Province, Saudi Arabia, 1909. Studied Islamic and Arabic studies, Islamic Shari'a. Chief judge Qatar, 1939; now pres. Shari'a Cts. and Islamic Affairs. Contbr. articles to profl. jours. Office: Shari'a Courts & Islamic Affairs, Office of Pres PO Box 232, Doha Qatar*

ALMAHROOS, HUSSAIN MOHAMED HASAN, engineering educator; b. Manama, Bahrain, Jan. 4, 1960; s. Mohamed Hasan Almahroos and Ghalya Mahmood Awad Kazerooni. B Engring. with distinction, Concordia U., Montreal, Quebec, Can., 1983; M Applied Sci., U. Waterloo, Ontario, Can., 1985; postgrad., Pa. State U., 1986-87; PhD, U. Cin., 1992. Rsch. asst. Concordia U., Montreal, 1980-83; rsch. and tchg. asst. U. Waterloo, Ontario, 1984-85, Pa. State U., Univ. Park, 1986-87, U. Cin., 1987-93; tech. dir. M. H. Al-Mahroos, Bahrain, Bahrain, 1993-98; asst. prof. U. Bahrain, 1994-98; dir. indsl. and engring. divsn. M.H. Al-Mahroos, Bahrain, 1998—; area mgr. TECNOMARE, Italy, 2000—; area sales mgr. BROAD, People's Republic of China, 2000—. Sec. and treas. The Aerospace Engring. and Engring. Mechs. Grad. Students Assn., U. Cin., 1990-91. Recipient scholarship Caltex Petroleum Co., USA/Bahrain, 1980-86, grad. scholarship U. Waterloo, Can., 1984-85, Pa State, 1986-87, U. Cin., 1987-92. Mem. AIAA, ASME. Avocations: travel, tennis, horseback riding. Home: PO Box 65, Manama Bahrain

ALMAKKY, GHAZY ABDULWAHED MAKKY, diplomat, geography educator; b. Al Madina Al Mounawara, Saudi Arabia, Mar. 25, 1950; s. Abdulwahed Makky and Fatima Mohammed (Al Hesnawi) A.; m. Wafaa Ismail Daghustani, Aug. 25, 1960; children: Abeer, Hana, Rawa, Mohammed, Anas. BA in Geography, King Saud U., Riyadh, Saudi Arabia, 1972; MA in Urban Geography, Mich. State U., 1976, PhD in Urban Geography, 1981. Trainer King Saud U., 1972-81, asst. prof. geography, 1981-88, assoc. prof., 1978—, prof. geography, 1998—; dir. rels. Saudi Arabian Cultural Mission, U.S.A., 1992-95; cultural attaché Saudi Arabian Cultural Mission, Can., 1995—; rschr. Hajj Rsch. Ctr., Jeddah, Saudi Arabia, 1981-86, cons., 1982; cons. Riyadh Higher Commn. for Devel., 1984-86, Civil Def., Ministry of Interior, Riyadh, 1986; mem. st. naming and ho. numbering com. Riyadh Municipality, 1985—. Author: Mecca: The Pilgrimage City, A Study of Pilgrimage Accommodation, 1978; editor: Education in Saudi Arabia, 2nd edit., 1995; contbr. articles to profl. publs.; pub. maps of City of Riyadh (award Municipality and Emirate of Riyadh). Mem. Assn. Am. Geographers, Assn. Saudi Geographers. Moslem. Avocations: jogging, soccer. Office: Saudi Arabian Cultrl Missn, 99 Bank St Ste 1144, Ottawa, ON Canada K1P 6B9

AL-MAKTUM, SHEIKH HAMDAN BIN RASHID, United Arab Emirian government official; b. 1945; s. Sheikh Rashid al-Maktum. Dep. prime min. Govt. of United Arab Emirates, Abu Dhabi, 1971-73, min. of fin. and industry, 1973—; pres. Dubai Mcpl. Coun., 1973; mem. gov. bd. Rashid Port, Dubal, 1973—; rep. at IMF, OPEC; chmn. United Arab Emirates Currency Bd., Abu Dhabi, 1973-80; gov. Islamic Devel. Bank. Office: Ministry Fin & Industry, PO Box 433, Abu Dhabi United Arab Emirates*

AL-MAKTUM, SHEIKH MAKTUM BIN RASHID, United Arab Emirian government official, ruler of Dubai; b. 1943; s. Sheikh Rashid bin Said al-Maktoum; married, 1971. Dep. ruler Dubai, United Arab Emirates; prime min. Govt. of United Arab Emirates, Abu Dhabi, 1971-79, 1991—, dep. prime min., 1979-90; v.p. Govt. United Arab Emirates; ruler of Dubai, 1990—. Office: Office of Prime Min, PO Box 899, Abu Dhabi United Arab Emirates*

ALMALIK, MANSOUR SALEH, petroleum engineering educator, researcher; b. Al Russ, Saudi Arabia, Dec. 20, 1954; s. Saleh Hamad Almalik and Nora Salem Aljoaib; m. Hessah Mohammed Almalik; children: Shatha, Lama, Saud, Sultan, Nada. BSc, King Saud U., Riyadh, Saudi Arabia, 1978; M in Engring., Tulane U., 1982; PhD, Tex. A&M U., 1988. Asst. prof. engring. King Saud U., 1988—; adviser Ministry of Petroleum, Saudi Arabia, 1990-94. Mem. Soc. Petroleum Engrs. Moslem. Avocations: sports, arts, travel. Home: PO Box 26022, 11486 Riyadh Saudi Arabia Office: King Saud U, PO Box 800, 11421 Riyadh Saudi Arabia

ALMANE, KHALID ABDULATIF, pediatric radiologist, consultant; b. Basrah, Iraq, Sept. 5, 1955; s. Abdulatif Ibrahim and Asma Mohamad (Alesa) A.; m. Nazira Mohamed Alkhuwaiter, July 5, 1984; children: Asma, Asra, Ala, Elaf. MD, U. Basrah, 1978; diploma in Med. Radiology, U. London, 1990, Riyadh U., Saudi Arabia, 1993. Sr. house officer Riyadh Mil. Hosp., 1980-83, 84-89, sr. registrar, 1990-97; sr. house officer Queen Elizabeth Hosp., Adelaide, Australia, 1983-84; registrar U. Wales, Cardif, 1989-90; cons. pediat. radiologist King Fahad Nat. Guard Hosp., Riyadh, 1997—; mem. Saudi Coun., Riyadh, Saudi Arabia, 1999—; examiner Saudi Bd. Exam. Pediat., Riyadh, 1998—; fellow radiology, London, 1993, Riyadh, 1994; fellow pediat. radiology, Riyadh, 1996. peer reviewer Saudi Med. Jour., 1997—; contbr. articles to profl. jours. Recipient letter of appreciation Nat. Guard Health Affairs, 1999. Mem. Soc. Pediat. Radiology, Saudi Radiology Club. Avocations: playing tennis, painting. Office: King Fahad Nat Guard Hosp, PO Box 22490, Riyadh 11426, Saudi Arabia

ALMANSA PASTOR, ANGEL F., chest physician; b. Malaga, Idem, Spain, Sept. 12, 1934; s. Salvador Almansa de Cara and Paula Pastor Roda; m. Isabel Mendez Peña, May 16, 1970; children: Maria Isabel, Angel, Paloma. Student Agustinos Coll., Malaga, 1943-47, Salesianos Coll., 1948-51; U. Grad., F. Medicine, Granada, 1957, Specialist Thoracic Surgeon, 1965, Specialist Pneumologie, 1980, Specialist Cardiologie, 1980. Diplomate Spain Bd. Med. Examiners. Asst. Hosp. Princesa, Madrid, 1958-59, Speziallungenklinik Hemer, Westfalhem, Fed. Republic Germany, 1969-76, U. Chirurg Klinik, Düsseldorf, 1961-65; chief pneumology Hosp. Civil Privincial, Malaga, 1966-75; med. dir. Hosp. Torax, Malaga, 1975—; prof. pneumologie Diputacion Provincial, Malaga, 1966, Valencia, 1965. Patentee blood circulation activator. Contbr. articles to profl. jours. Served with Spain Mil. Service, 1956-57. Pre-Univ. Grad. with honors, U. Granada, 1952; Med. Grad. with honors, F. Medicine, 1957. Fellow Am. Coll. Chest Physicians; mem. Coll. Internat. Angyologiae, Soc. Spain Patology A. Respiratorio, Soc. Spain Cardiologia, Soc. Andaluza Cardiologia, Soc. Spain Geriatria, Assn. Med. Naturistas. Roman Catholic. Club: Mediterraneo. Avocations: tennis; golfing. Office: San Lorenzo 2, Malaga 29001, Spain

AL-MANSOURI, HANAA MOHAMMED, family physician; b. Dahran, Saudi Arabia, Mar. 26, 1960; d. Mohammed Sadaga and Ehsan (Hamouda) A.; m. Anas Zubier Sambas, 1989; children: Rakan, Mohammed, Al-Zubier. MBchB, King Abdul Aziz U., Jeddah, Saudi Arabia, 1987; M, King Abdul Aziz U., Riyadh, 1992; PhD, Rykyu U., Okinawa, Japan, 1997. House officer King Abdulaziz U. Hosp., Jeddah, 1987-88; physician King Khalid Nat. Guard Hosp., Jeddah, 1989-90; resident King Faud U., Riyadh, 1990-92; rschr. Ryukyu U., Okinawa, Japan, 1993-97; asst. cons. Nat. Guard Hosp., Riyadh, 1997—. Author: (book) Forceps Delivery, 1992. Recipient scholarship, Momboshow, Japan, 1995-97. Mem. Family Medicine Club, Saudi Arabia. Avocations: art, crafts, reading. Home: PO Box 53957, Riyadh 11593, Saudi Arabia

ALMA'R, IVAN FERENC, astronomer; b. Budapest, Hungary, Apr. 21, 1932; s. György and Lili (Veszprémi) A.; m. Erzsebet Illés, Aug. 3, 1959; children: Edit, A'kos. PhD, Eötvös U., Budapest, 1959; DSc, Hungarian Acad. Scis., Budapest, 1980. Researcher Konkoly Observatory, Budapest, 1954-72, dep. dir., 1982-92; dir. Satellite Geodetic Observatory, Budapest, 1972-82; pres. Sci. Coun. on Space Rsch., 1997—; v.p. Internat. Astronautical Fedn., 1982-84. Editor-in-chief: Encyclopaedia of Astronautics, 1980; guest editor: Multilingual Space Dictionary, 1995. mem. Internat. Acad. Astronautics, Hungarian Astronautical Soc. (pres. 1972-97, hon. pres. 1997—), N.Y. Acad. Scis. Office: Konkoly Observatory, PO Box 67, H 1525 Budapest Hungary

ALMAZAN, ANSELMO DOLOR, mathematician, consultant; b. Lupao, The Philippines, Nov. 4, 1933; s. Mariano Hidalgo Almazan and Alipia Umipig Dolor; m. Cecilia Peralta Alalan, Jan. 30, 1960 (dec. June 1981); children: Angelo, Anselmo II, Archimedes, Anselmo III. BS in Civil Engring., Nat. U., Manila, 1957; BS in Geodetic Engring., U. The Philippines, Quezon City, 1962, MS in Civil Engring., 1972; MS in Math., Far Ea. U., Manila, 1964; PhD in Math., Centro Escolar U., Manila, 1977. Reg. profl. engring. educator, The Philippines. Pres. St. Louis Coll., Tuguegarao, The Philippines, 1976-80, Almazan Constrn. Engring. Svcs., Quezon City, 1978-88; prof. engring. U. The Philippines, Quezon City, 1986—, chmn. dept. geodetic engring., 1988-92, dir. tng. ctr. applied geodesy photogrammetry, 1989-92; cons. Land Brokerage Devel., Quezon City, 1987—, Trans-Asia Geodetic Civil Engring. Consultancy, Quezon City, 1989—, Cmty. Devel. Land Tech. Matters, Quezon City, 1991-93, U.P. Rsch. Devel. Found., Quezon City, 1992—, Continuing Profl. Edn. Coun., Manila, 1995—; chmn. U.P. Remote Sensing Project, Quezon City, 1990-92. Contbr. articles to Euclidean Geometry, Applied Math., Math. Rsch., Algebraic Rsch. Chmn. Adults and Non-formal Edn., Cagayan, The Philippines, 1982; pres. YMCA, Cagayan, 1992-95. Mem. ASCE, Philippine Inst. Civil Engrs. (life, chmn. civil engring. law com. 1995, pres. chpt. 1994, Merit award, 1995), Soc. Filipino Geodetic Engrs. (pres. 1992—, Merit award), Geodetic Engrs. Philippines (life, Outstanding Geodetic Engr. 1993), Rotary (pres. 1980-81), Masons (worshipful master 1982). Roman Catholic. Home: Tchrs Village West, 24 Mahabagin St, Diliman Quezon City 1101, The Philippines Office: Coll Engring, U The Philippines, Diliman Quezon City 1101, The Philippines

ALMAZAN, MAURICIO A., obstetrician/gynecologist; b. Oaxaca, Mexico, May 28, 1943; s. Angel and Lucila (Diaz) A.; m. Jacqueline Jean, Oct. 20, 1966; children: Mauricio, Alejandro, Eduardo. MD, U. Mex., 1967. Diplomate Am. Bd. Ob-Gyn. Resident in ob-gyn. SUNY Nassau Hosp., Stony Brook, 1969-73; prof., chief endoscopy Mexican Inst., 1974-80; chief rsch. Min. Health/WHO, Mexico, 1981-82; pvt. practice ob-gyn. Mexico City; prof. pharmacology U. Mexico, 1967; med. dir. Assn. Profl. Maternal Health, Mex., 1977-78; internat. advisor George Washington U., 1977; found. Mex. Assn. Endoscopic Surgery, 1991, Gynecol. Endoscopy Assn., 1982. Recipient physician's recognition award AMA, 1972, 77, 80. Fellow Am. Coll. Surgeons, Am. Coll. Obstetricians and Gynecologists; mem. Royal Soc. Medicine London. Roman Catholic. Avocations: swimming, jogging, motorcycling, water skiing, reading. Office: Ob-Gyn Office, 735 Ave Palmas Ste 801, 11000 Mexico City Mexico

ALMEDA, BORIS RAOUL, solar energy executive; b. Gibraltar, Oct. 14, 1936; s. Braulio and Elena Araceli (Cassano) A.; m. Leta Ferguson Nunn, June 5, 1972. Grad., Admiralty Tech. Coll., Gibraltar, 1953. Shipwright Admiralty Dockyard, Gibraltar, 1953-58; fireman Admiralty Fire Service, Gibraltar, 1958-64; guitar soloist various locations, 1964-80; mng. dir. High Chaparral Holdings Ltd., Gibraltar, 1980—; cons. High Chaparral Cons., 1985—, Gib-Office Mgmt., Gibraltar, 1987—; dir. Bodel Ltd., Gibraltar, 1987—, Telesis Ltd., Gibraltar, 1988—; participant inauguration ceremony for world's first solar breeder, Frederick, Md., 1982. Author: Introducing Photovoltaics, 1985. Mem. Gibraltar Red Cross, 1985—, Assn. for the Advancement of Civil Rights, Gibraltar, 1986—. Served with Gibraltar Regiment, 1958-59. Mem. Gibraltar Ornothol. and Natural History Soc., UN Assn. Gibraltar, Gibraltar Heritage Trust, Assn. Energy Engrs. Jewish. Avocations: reading, cats, cosmological research. Home: 8 Morellos Ramp, Gibraltar Gibraltar Office: High Chaparral Holdings Ltd, PO Box 486, Gibraltar Gibraltar

AL-MEGUID, AHMAD ESMAT ABDEL, international organization executive. Sec. gen. League of Arab States, Cairo, Egypt. Office: League Arab States Midan Attahir, Tahrir Sq PO Box 11642, Cairo Egypt*

ALMEIDA, JOSE JORGE ALCAZAR, diplomat; b. Buenos Aires, Argentina, Nov. 29, 1952; s. Jorge de sa and Carmen (Alcazar) A. BSc in Fgn. Svc., Georgetown U., 1974; postgrad., Inst. Brazilian Fgn. Svc., Brasilia, 1979; MA in Internat. Econs. Rels., London Sch. Econs., 1984. Dep. consul gen. Brazilian Embassy, London, 1981-84; dep. head of mission Embassy of Brazil, Abu-Dhabi, United Arab Emirates, 1984-86, Athens, Greece, 1986-90, Beirut, Lebanon, 2000; first sec. Ministry Fgn. Affairs, Brasilia, 1990-95; dep. head of mission Embassy of Brazil, Riyadh, Saudi Arabia, 1993-95, Beirut, 2000—; alt. permanent rep. to UN Brazilian Mission, Vienna, Austria, 1990—, chmn. Group of 1977, China task force, 1998, chmn. Group L.Am. and Caribbean, pensions fund com. UNIDO, 1999, mem. pensions fund com. UNIDO, 1999; commd. counselor Beirut, 2000; presenter in field. Mem. innovative project tng. 150 schs. Ctrl. Am., 1999, Volos, Greece, 1989. Decorated Order of Phoenix, Govt. Greece; Chevalier of Sovereign Order of St. John of Jerusalem Knights of Malta, 2000. Avocations: hiking, reading. Home: Brazilian Embassy, Antonins St 70 PO Box 40242, 1010 Beirut Lebanon

ALMEIDA, OSBORNE FRANCISCO XAVIER, biologist, researcher; b. Nakuru, Kenya, July 28, 1954; s. Brigido Luis Caetano and Olga Maria Angela (Sousa) A.; m. Isabel Forgas y Moya, 1995; 1 child, Leila Olga Miguela Rocio. BS, U. London, 1976; MS, U. Wales, U.K., 1979; PhD, U. Edinburgh, Scotland, 1982; dr. habil., Faculty of Biology, U. Munich, 1995. Rsch. officer Reproductive Biology Unit Med. Rsch. Coun., Edinburgh, 1981-82; vis. scientist Nat. Inst. Child Health & Human Devel., NIH, Bethesda, Md., 1982-84; rsch. scientist Max Planck Inst. Psychiatry, Martinsried, Fed. Republic of Germany, 1984-89; acad. counselor vet. faculty U. Munich, 1987-90; basic science group leader Max Planck Inst. Psychiatry, Munich, 1991—; lectr. Zoology Inst. U. Munich, 1992-96; guest prof. Natural History Mus., Paris, 2000; vis. prof. Inst. Anatomy Med. Faculty U. Porto, Portugal, 1996; cons. Tokyo Metropolitan Inst. Neurosci., 1995; vis. scientist Nat. Mus. Natural History, Paris, 1998. Author, editor: (with T.S. Shippenberg) Neurobiology of Opioids, 1991, (with V.K. Patchev) Steroid Hormone-Dependent Organization of Neuroendocrine Functions, 1999; mem. editl. bd. Assisted Reproductive Tech.-andrology, 1986-91, Life Sci. Advances, 1986-91, Jour. Neuroendocrinology, 1989-97, Neuroendocrinology, 1990-97; contbr. over 90 articles to profl. jours. Fulbright fellow, 1982-84, Fogarty internat. fellow, 1982-84, travel fellow Internat. Soc. for Neuroendocrinology, 1986; rsch. grantee Sir Richard Stapley Trust, 1979, German Rsch. Soc., 1984—, German Academic Exch. Svc., 1986—, European Sci. Found., 1988-90, Max Planck Soc., 1992-94, SmithKline Beecham Stiftung, 1993, Commn. European Cmtys., 1994-96, Ministry for Sci. and Tech. Rsch., 1994-99, European Union, 2000—. Mem. Soc. Endocrinology U.K., Soc. for Study Fertility U.K., German Soc. Pharm. Toxicology, Soc. for Neurosci., German Neurosci. Soc., German Endocrine Soc., German Soc. Neuro-pharmacopsychiatry. Roman Catholic. Avocations: mountain walking, nature, literature. Fax: 49-89-30622-461. Home: Tuerkenstr 61, 80799 Munich Germany Office: Max Planck Inst Psychiatry, Kraepelinstr 2-10, 80804 Munich Germany

ALMEIDA BOSQUE, JUAN, Cuban government official, musical composer; b. Havana, Cuba, Feb. 17, 1927; s. Juan and Rosario (Bosque) Almeida; m. Pubila Garcia, 1960 (div. 1976); children: Juan Juan, Beatriz, Brenda, Belinda; m. Gudelia Beuballet, 1977 (div. 1981); children: Juan Antonio, Berta, Rosario; m. Berta Maria Gonzalez, 1982; children: Diana Teresa, Juan Guillermo. Grad., Escuela Artes y Oficios, Havana, 1949, Higher Acad. Revolutionary Armed Forces, Havana, 1966. Chief mechanized regiment Revolutionary Armed Forces, Havana, 1959, air force chief, 1959, nat. army chief, 1959-61, ctrl. army chief, 1961-63; first dep. min. Ministry of Armed Forces, Havana, 1963-68; polit. bur. rep. Contstrn. Sector, Havana, 1968-70, Ea. Provinces, 1970-76; v.p., comdr. armed forces Coun. of State, Havana, 1976—. Author: Contra El Agua y El Viento, 1985 (Casa de Las Americas award 1985), La Unica Ciudadana, 1985, El General en Jefe Maximo Gomez, 1986, Presidio, 1987, Exilio, 1987, Desembarco, 1988, La Sierra, 1989, Por Las Faldas del Turquino, 1992, Atención! Recuento!, 1992, Algo Nuevo en el Desierto, 1994, La Sierra Maestra y más allá, 1995; author poems; composer over 300 musical works. Polit. bur. Cuban Communist Party, 1965—; dep. Nat. Assembly, 1976—. Decorated Orden de Camilo Cienfuegos, Orden Liberación de Primer Grado, Orden de Maximo Gomez de Primer Grado; recipient Raul Gomez Garcia award, Illiteracy Campaign medal, Anniversary XX and XXX medals Revolutionary Armed Forces, Tercer Frente Oriental medal. Mem. Cuban Assn. Music Writers and Composers, Union Writers and Artists of Cuba. Avocations: sports, volley ball, baseball. Office: Consejo Estado Palacio Revolucion, Office of Pres Council of State, Havana Cuba*

ALMEN, LOWELL GORDON, church official; b. Grafton, N.D., Sept. 25, 1941; s. Paul Orville and Helen Eunice (Johnson) A.; m. Sally Arlyn Clark, Aug. 14, 1965; children: Paul Simon, Cassandra Gabrielle. BA, Concordia Coll., Moorhead, Minn., 1963; MDiv, Luther Theol. Sem., St. Paul, 1967; LittD (hon.), Capital U., 1981; DD (hon.), Carthage Coll., 1989, Concordia Coll., 1994. Ordained to ministry Luth. Ch., 1967. Pastor St. Peter's Luth. Ch., Dresser, Wis., 1967-69; asso. campus pastor, dir. communications Concordia Coll., Moorhead, Minn., 1969-74; mng. editor Luth. Standard ofcl. publ. Am. Luth. Ch., Mpls., 1974-78; editor Luth. Standard, 1979-87; sec., officer Evangelical Luth. Ch. Am., Chgo., 1987—. Author: Old Songs for a New Journey, 1990, One Great Cloud of Witnesses, 1997; author, co-editor: The Many Faces of Pastoral Ministry, 1989; editor: World Religions and Christian Mission, 1967, Our Neighbor's Faith, 1968. Recipient Disting. Alumnus award Concordia Coll., 1982; Bush Found. grantee, 1972. Office: Evang Luth Ch 8765 W Higgins Rd Chicago IL 60631-4101

ALMENDROS MARTIN, GONZALO, soil biochemist, researcher; b. Madrid, Sept. 21, 1955; s. Francisco Almendros and Amparo Martín. BS in Biol. Scis. with hons., U. Complutense, Madrid, 1977, PhD in Biol. Scis., 1980. Postgrad. rschr. Consejo Superior de Investigaciones Científicas, Madrid, 1978-85, rschr., 1985-90, sr. rschr., 1990—; prof. internat. course of soil sci. Mexico U., 1992—; mem. ofcl. commn. for organic fertilizers Ministry of Agr., Spain, 1995—; project leader various nat. and internat. programs, 1983—; rschr. in field. Contbr. over 160 articles to profl. jours. Rsch. fellow Min. Edn. Ciencia, Consejo Superior Investigaciones Científicas, 1978-85. Roman Catholic. Avocations: reading, gardening, computer programming, family, music. E-mail: humus@ccma.csic.es. Home: Joaquín María López 60, E 28015 Madrid Spain Office: Ctr of Environ Scis, Serrano 115 bis, E 28006 Madrid Spain

ALMÉRAS, PHILIPPE CHARLES, writer, educator; b. Paris, Jan. 4, 1930; s. Joseph Alméras and Irène Marie (Alberte) d'Essigny. Baccalaureat, Coll. Stanislas, Paris, 1949; PhD, U. Calif., Santa Barbara, 1969; LittD, U. Paris, 1987. Assoc. editor Réalités, Paris, 1955-61; editor in chief L'Action, Paris, 1961-63; asst. prof. U. Colo., Boulder, 1969-72, assoc. prof., 1972-74; dir. French-Am. Study Ctr., Lisieux, 1974-85, pres., 1985—. Author: Les Catholiques Français, 1963, Les Idées De Céline, 1987, 2d edit., 1992, Celine, 1994, Lettres Des Années Noires, 1995, Un Francais Nommé Petain, 1995, Vichy-Londres-Paris, 1997, Retours sum ie siecle, 1999. With French Mil., 1954-55. Roman Catholic. Avocations: farming. Home & Office: c/o FASC, 12 Blvd Carnot, 14104 Lisieux France

ALMIRALL, PEDRO, psychologist; b. LaHabana, Marianao, Cuba, July 26, 1949; s. Juan and Miedalia (Hernandez) A.; m. Nancy Palenzuela, Apr. 22, 1978; 1 child, Monica. Student, U. LaHavana, 1973; MD, Occupl. Health Inst., 1986. Diplomate Psychology. Head psychologist Occupl. Health Inst., Havana, Cuba, 1977—. Author: Advances in Neurobehavioral Toxicology, 1990, Manual de Neurotoxicologia, 1987; contbr. articles to profl. jours. Mem. Cuban Soc. Psychology (sec. 1974-96). Avocations: playing volleyball, movies, music, visiting museums. Home: 43 19026 e/ 190y194, 11500 La Lisa La Habana Cuba

ALMOAYYED, FAROUK YOUSUF, conglomerate executive; b. Bahrain, May 26, 1944; s. Yousuf Khalil and Aisha (Ahmad) A.; m. Fadia Algosaibi, Dec. 27, 1973; children: Mashael, Mohamed, Hala, Yousuf. BME, Loughborough Engring. Coll., Eng., 1966. Chmn. Y.K. Almoayyed & Sons, Manama, Bahrain, 1966—; mng. dir. Algosaibi Travel Agy., Bahrain, 1973; vice chair Bahrain Hotels Co., 1977; chmn. Ashraf Bros., 1994—; chmn. Almoayyed Internat., Almoayyed Computers, Comnet E.C., Almoayyed Electronics, Almoayyed Trading and Contracting, Almoayyed Comml. Services, Almoayyed Comm., Apple Centre, Bahrain, 1979, Bahrain Duty Free Shop Complex Co., 1990; propr. Arabian Establishment for Tech. Contracting, 1976; dep. chmn. Nat. Bank Bahrain; bd. dirs. Gulf Union Ins. and Reins. Co., B.S.C., Bahrain; chmn. Ibn Khuldoon Nat. Sch., Bahrain, 1979; mem. Bahrain Consultative Coun. Mem. Bahrain Soc. Engrs., Skal Club, Rotary Internat. Moslem. Avocations: tennis, boating, fishing, reading. Office: Y K Almoayyed & Sons BSC, Government Rd PO Box 143, Manama Bahrain

AL-MODHHI, ADEL ZAID, electrical engineer; b. Al-Khobar, Saudi Arabia; s. Zaid Mohammad and Asma (Ali) A.; m. Kholood Hussain; children: Doaa, Hawraa, Mohammed. BS, KFUPM, Dhahran, 1997. Tng. specialist Lucent Tech. Internat., Saudi Arabia, 1997—; comm. specialist Arab Nat. Bank., Riyadh, Saudi Arabia, 1997. Mem. IEEE. Avocations: reading, swimming. Home: PO Box 5782, 31982 Hofof Saudi Arabia Office: Tng & Documentation, PO Box 4945, 11412 Riyadh Saudi Arabia

ALMODÓVAR, PEDRO, filmmaker; b. Calzada de Calatrava, Spain, Sept. 25, 1949. Theater group actor: Los Goliardos; short films include: Salome, 1978-83; films: Pepi, Luci, Bom y otras chicas del monton, 1980, Laberinto de pasiones, 1980, Dark Habits, 1983, What Have I Done to Deserve This?, 1985, Matador, 1986, Law of Desire, 1987, Women on the Verge of a Nervous Breakdown, 1988 (Felix award 1988), Tie Me Up, Tie Me Down, 1990, High Heels, 1991, Kika, 1993, The Flower of My Secret, 1995, Live Flesh, 1997, All About My Mother, 1999 (Best Dir., Cannes Film Festival, 1999, Best Fgn. Lang. Film, Acad. Awards 2000); pub. Fuego en las entrañas, 1982, Patty Diphusa and Other Stories, 1992. Address: El Deseo SA, Ruiz Perello 15, Madrid 28028, Spain*

ALMOG, JOSEPH, forensic scientist; b. Tel Aviv, Israel, Feb. 4, 1944; s. Haim and Guta (Halperin) Appelbaum; m. Elinoar Youngman, Nov. 7, 1950; children: Uri, Oded. BS, The Hebrew U., Jerusalem, 1964, MS, 1968, PhD, 1972; postgrad., Imperial Coll., 1973. Instr. The Hebrew U., Jerusalem, 1968-72; deputy dir. rsch. & devel. divsn. Israel Police, Jerusalem, 1974-82, dir. divsn. identification & forensic sci., brigadier gen., 1984-2000; vis. scientist MIT, Cambridge, Mass., 1973-74; vis. prof. Tel Aviv U., 1993—, The Hebrew U., 1993—. Co-author: (chpt.) Advances in Fingerprint Technology, 1991; contbr. articles to profl. jours. Capt. Israel Defence Forces, 1970. Postdoctoral fellow Imperial Coll., London, 1972-73. Achievements include research in physico-chemical methods for latent fingerprint development, forensic field tests, explosives detection and identification. Office: Israel Police, Sheikh Jarrah, 91906 Jerusalem Israel also: The Hebrew Univ, Casali Inst of Applied Chem, 91904 Jerusalem Israel

AL-MOGBEL, ABDULLAH ABDULRAHMAN, government executive; b. Riyadh, Saudi Arabia, Feb. 13, 1955; s. Abdul Rahman Mohammad and Joharah Abdullah Al-Mogbel; m. Wafa Ibrahim Al Khuzaim. BS in Civil Engring. with honors, King Fahd U. Petroleum & Minerals, Dhahran, 1978. Supervisory engr. Ministry Commn., Riyadh, Saudi Arabia, 1978-81, gen. supr. Riyadh Rd. Projects and Kingdom Expressways, 1981-88, dir. gen. design and studies dept., 1988-91, asst. dep. min. comm. tech. affairs, 1991-97, dep. min. rds., 1997—; nat. coord. UN Devel. Program, Riyadh, 1986—; mem. High Commn. for the Devel. Riyadh City, 1996—; chmn. bd. dirs. Saudi Arabian Pub. Transport Co., 1997—; presenter in field. Contbr. articles to profl. jours. Recipient Letter of Appreciation, Mayor of Riyadh, 1986, Letter of Appreciation, H.R.H. Gov. Riyadh, 1987, Armor of Appreciation, U.S. Dept. Transp., 1990, Cert. Appreciation, Cornell U., 1991, Letter of Appreciation, Fed. Hwy. Adminstrn., U.S. Dept. Transp., 1991, Armor of Appreciation, UN Devel. Program, 1994, Armor of Appreciation, Al Ain Municpality, United Arab Emirates, 1997, Armor of Appreciation, Arab Inst. for City Devel., 1997, Mars 2001 Lander Participation cert. NASA; Eisenhower scholar for sci. and cultural coop., 1984. Fellow Inst. Transp. Engrs.; mem. Internat. Rd. Fedn. (dir., world exec. bd. mem.), Internat. Tunnel Assn., Am. Soc. Intelligent Transport Sys., Transp. Rsch. Bd., Transp. and Rds. Documentation Program Orgn. for Econ. Cooperation and Devel. Avocations: reading, swimming, table tennis. Office: Ministry Comm, Old Airport Rd, Riyadh 11178, Saudi Arabia

ALMOHANDIS, AHMED A., geology educator, consultant; b. Medina, Saudi Arabia, Dec. 21, 1949; s. Abdulkader Mahmoud and Fatima Hamza (Abdulfattah) A.; m. Fayzah Abdulmohsen Mamlook, June 21, 1973; children: Lamis, Hani, Lamya, Sultan. BSc, King Saud U., Riyadh, Saudi Arabia, 1970, MSc, 1972, PhD, 1974; MSc, Manchester (Eng.) U., 1974, PhD in Earth Scis., 1977. Prof. King Saud U., 1992—, vice-dean, 1992-95, chmn. dept. astronomy, 1994-96, chmn. dept. geology, 1990-92, dir. Translation Ctr., 1997—; cons. Ministry of Planning, Riyadh, 1996—. Author: Principles of Geology, 1986; editor: Geologists Working in Saudi Arabia, 1988; translator: Metamorphic Geology, 1998; contbr. some 100 articles to nat. and internat. jours. Fellow Geol. Soc.; mem. Mineral. Soc., Saudi Earth Scis. Soc. (v.p. 1993-96). Avocations: reading, writing, travel, driving. Office: King Saud U Coll Scis, PO Box 2455, Riyadh 11451, Saudi Arabia

AL-MOMANI, FOUAD ABDELAZIZ, microbiologist; b. Ajlun, Jordan, Jan. 1, 1957; s. Abdelaziz Suliman and Faliha Suliman Al-momani; m. Ebtisam Ali Al-Kodah, Dec. 31, 1993; 3 children. BSc in Biology, Jordan U., Amman, 1979; MSc in Biology, Yarmouk U., Irbid, Jordan, 1986; PhD in Biology, U. Punjab, Lahore, Pakistan, 1991. Biology tchr. Min. of Edn., Amman, 1979-87; rsch. asst. Yarmouk U., Irbid, 1984-87; part-time lectr. Jordan U. of Sci. and tech., Irbid, 1991-92, rschr., 1992-93, lectr., 1993-97, asst. prof. microbial biotechnology, 1997—. Home: Main St, 64441232 Ajlun Jordan Office: Jordan U of Sci and Tech, Irbid Amman 22110, Jordan

ALMOND, JEFFREY WILLIAM, microbiologist; b. Thirsk, Yorkshire, U.K., June 28, 1951; s. Stanley Peter and Joyce Mary (Fountain) A.; m. Karen E. Batley, Aug. 8, 1976; children: Max, Gemma, Adam. BSc, Leeds U., 1973; PhD, Cambridge U., 1977. Rsch. scientist Sandoz, Vienna, 1977-79; lectr. U. Leicester, U.K., 1979-85; prof. U. Reading, 1985-99; sr. v.p. R&D Aventis Pasteur, Marcy-L'etoile, France, 1999—; chmn. virology divsn. Internat. Union Microbiol. Socs., 1996-99. Contbr. articles to profl. jours. Mem. Spongiform Encephalopathies Adv. Com. of U.K. Govt., 1996-99. Mem. Soc. Gen. Microbiology (internat. sec. 1996—). Office: Aventis Pasteur, 1541 Ave Marcel Mérieux, 69280 Marcy-L'etoile RG6 6AJ, France

ALMOND, PAUL, film director, producer, screenwriter; b. Montreal, Que., Can., Apr. 26, 1931; s. Eric and Irene Clarice (Gray) A.; m. Joan Elkins, Sept. 11, 1976; 1 son, Matthew James. Student, McGill U., Montreal, 1948-49; B.A., Balliol Coll., Oxford, 1952, M.A., 1954. TV producer-dir. CBC, Toronto, also in Los Angeles, N.Y.C., London, 1954-67; pres. Quest Films, Montreal, 1967—. Writer, producer, dir.: feature films Isabel, 1968 (DGA nomination Best Feature Dir.), Act of the Heart, 1970 (Genie-Best Cand. Dir.), Journey, 1972, Ups & Downs, 1982, The Dance Goes On, 1991; dir. Captive Hearts, 1984; subject of book: (Janet Edsforth) Paul Almond, The Flame Within, 1973; author: La Vengeance des Dieux, 1999. Recipient Spl. diploma of merit Prague for Seven Up, 1963; Genie as Best Can. TV drama dir., 1980. Mem. Dirs. Guild Am., Dirs. Guild Can. (hon. life), Royal Can. Acad. Arts. Anglican. Home: 54 Malibu Colony Malibu CA 90265-4637

ALMOND, RICHARD J., psychiatrist; b. Chgo., Jan. 19, 1938; s. Gabriel Abraham and Dorothea Kaufmann Almond; m. Barbara Rosenthal Almond, Dec. 16, 1962; children: David, Michael, Steven. AB, Harvard Coll., 1959; MD, Yale U., 1963. Bd. cert. Am. Bd. Psychiatry and Neurology. Clin. assoc. NIMH, Bethesda, Md., 1967-69; asst. prof. psychiatry Stanford (Calif.) Med. Sch., 1969-73; pvt. practice Palo Alto, Calif., 1973—; tng. analyst San Francisco Psychiat. Inst., 1999—, trees., 1997-00. Author: (books) The Healing Community, 1974, The Therapeutic Narrative, 1996; contbr. papers to profl. jours. Office: # 339 550 Hamilton Ave Ste 339 Palo Alto CA 94301-2031

ALMORE-RANDLE, ALLIE LOUISE, special education educator; b. Jackson, Miss., Apr. 20; d. Thomas Carl and Theressa Ruth (Garrett) Almore; m. Olton Charles Randle, Sr., Aug. 3, 1974. BA, Tougaloo (Miss.) Coll., 1951; MS in Edn., U. So. Calif., L.A., 1971; EdD, Nova Southeastern U., 1997. Recreation leader Pasadena (Calif.) Dept. Recreation, 1954-56; demonstration tchr. Pasadena Unified Schs., 1956-63; cons. spl. edn. Temple City (Calif.) Sch. Dist., 1967; supr. tchr. edn. U. Calif., Riverside, 1971; tchr. spl. edn. Pasadena Unified Sch. Dist., 1955-70, dept. chair spl. edn. Pasadena H.S., 1972-98, also adminstrv. asst. Pasadena H.S., 1993-98; ind. rep. Am. Comm. Network, Inc., 1997—; supr. Evelyn Frieden Ctr., U. So. Calif., L.A., 1970; mem. Coun. Exceptional Children, 1993—; ednl. cons. Shelby Renee Ednl. Ctr., Gardena, Calif., 2000—. Organizer Northwest Project, Camp Fire Girls, Pasadena, 1963; leader Big Sister Program, YWCA, Pasadena, 1966; organizer, dir. March on The Boys' Club, the Portrait of a Boy, 1966; pub. souvenir jours. Women's Missionary Soc., AME Ch., State of Wash. to Mo.; mem. NAACP, Ch. Women United, Afro-Am. Quilters L.A., established Dr. Allie Louise Almore-Randle Scholarship Award, Pasadena H.S., 1998; co-established Theressa Garrett Almore Music Scholarsip award Jackson State U., Jackson, Miss., 1989. Recipient Cert. of Merit, Pasadena City Coll., 1963, Outstanding Achievement award Nat. Coun. Negro Women, Pasadena, 1965, Earnest Thompson Seton award Campfire Girls, Pasadena, 1968, Spl. Recognition, Outstanding Community Svc. award The Tuesday Morning Club, 1967, Dedicated Svc. award AME Ch., 1983, Educator of Excellence award Rotary Club of Pasadena, 1993, Edn. award Altadena NAACP, 1994; named Tchr. of Yr., Pasadena Masonic Bodies, 1967, Woman of the Yr. for Community Svc. and Edn., Zeta Phi Beta, 1992; grad. fellow U. So. Calif., L.A., 1970, recognition Uniformly Excellent Work and Exceptional Commitment and Dedication to Altadena/Pasadena Communities, Pasadena African Amer. Sch. Administr., 1998, Cert. Achievment in Educational Leadership, First AME Ch., 1998, Fran Cook Salute Great Inspiring Educator Award, United Tchrs. of Pasadena, 1998, Named Outstanding Educator, Nat. Sorority Phi Delta Kappa, 1998. Mem. NAACP (bd. mem., chmn. ch. workers com. 1955-63, Fight for Freedom award West Coast region 1957, NAACP Edn. award Altadena, Calif. chpt. 1994), ASCD, Calif. Tchrs. Assn., Calif. African Am. Genealog. Soc., Nat. Coun. Negro Women, African Pan Am. Doctoral Scholars, L.A. World Affairs Coun., Phi Delta Gamma (hospitality chair 1971—), Phi Delta Kappa, Alpha Kappa Alpha (membership com.), Phi Delta Phi (founder, organizer 1961), Phi Delta Kappa. Democrat. Mem. AME Ch. Avocations: wedding director, photography, gardening, arts and crafts, sewing. Fax: 626-797-5549. E-mail: akainger@acninc.net. Home: 1710 La Cresta Dr Pasadena CA 91103-1261

AL-MOSHAIKAH, MOHAMED SULAIMAN, dean, education educator; b. Buraidaii, Qassim, Saudi Arabia, Aug. 4, 1951; s. Sulaiman Hamoud Al-Moshaikh and Lulwa Abdulaziz Al Amer; m. Hind Fahad Al-Bidah; children: Shahinaz, Nizar, Zyad, Nada. BA, King Saud U., Riyadh, Saudi Arabia, 1974, diploma, 1977; Master of Edn., Ind. U., 1980; PhD in Edn., U. Pitts., 1982. Dep. dean Deanship of Admissions, Qassim, Saudi Arabia, 1983; supr. dept art edn. King Saud U., 1983-86, prof., 1989—, chmn. ednl. tech. dept., 1993-94, head ednl. tech. dept., 1994-97, vice dean Coll. Edn., 1995—; cons. and lectr. in field. Scholar King Saud U., 1977-80, 80-82. Mem. AECT, ETEC, Egyptian Assn. Ednl. Tech., Assn. for Edn. and Psychology Saudi Arabia. Islam. Avocations: drawing, swimming, football. Home: PO Box 85371, Riyadh 11691, Saudi Arabia Office: PO Box 2458, Riyadh 11451, Saudi Arabia

AL-MOUALEM, WALID, diplomat; b. Damascus, Syria, July 17, 1941; m. Sawsan Al-Khayat; 3 children. BA in Econs., Cairo U. Amb. to U.S. Syria, Washington, 1990—. Author: Palestine and Armed Peace, 1970, History of Syria: 1946-58, 1983, Syria: The Road to Freedom, 1916-1946, 1986, Syria in the Days of Al-Zaim: The First Coup; The World and the Middle East in the American Perspective, 1987. Office: Syrian Embassy 2215 Wyoming Ave NW Washington DC 20008-3991*

AL-MOUSAWI, FASISAL RAHDI, Bahraini government official; b. Manama, Bahrain, Apr. 6, 1944; married. MB ChB, U. Cairo, 1966. Cons. orthopedic surgeon Salmaniya Med. Ctr., chmn. dept. surgery; asst. prof. Coll. Medicine and Med. Scis. Arabian Gulf U.; asst. undersec. med. svcs. Ministry of Health Govt. of Bahrain, Salmaniya, min. of health, 1995—. Fellow Royal Coll. Sci. (Ireland and Edinburgh). Office: Ministry of Health, PO Box 12, Manama Bahrain*

ALMSTROM, HARALD NILS HARALDSSON, obstetrician, gynecologist; b. Stockholm, Sweden, May 2, 1950; s. Harald R. and Marianne J.B. (Westermark) A.; m. Ann-Cathrin E. Lindstrand, 1981; children: Charlotte, Robert. MD, Karolinska Inst., 1975, PhD, 1995. Physician dept. ob-gyn. Danderyd Hosp., Stockholm, Sweden, 1975-80; physician dept. surgery Karolinska Hosp., Stockholm, Sweden, 1980-81, physician dept. urology, 1981; cons. dept. ob-gyn. Danderyd Hosp., Stockholm, Sweden, 1982-91; dir. Ultra Gyn. Med. Ctr., Stockholm, Sweden, 1991—; cons. in field; auditor of the Scandinavian Fedn. of Obstet. and Gynecology, 1996—. Rsch. fellow Karolinska Inst., 1990—. Fellow AAAS, Royal Soc. Medicine, Swedish Soc. Medicine (auditor 1998—); mem. Swedish Med. Assn. (sec. 1983-87, vice chmn. 1987-90), Swedish Soc. Ob-gyn. (bd. dirs. 1995—, treas. 1996—), Internat. Soc. Ultrasound Ob-gyn. Avocations: golf, skiing, wine, gardening. Office: Ultra Gyn Med Ctr, Odengatan 69, 11322 Stockholm Sweden

AL-MUBARAK, AHMAD BIN ABDUL AL-AZIZ, judge; b. Saudi Arabia, 1910; s. Abdulaziz al-Mubarak; married; 5 children. Qadi (Islamic law judge) Saudi Arabia, 1950-58; chief qadi, advisor for religious affairs to HH the head of state; chief Sharia judge Union Supreme Ct., Abu Dhabi, United Arab Emirates; mem. Islamic Union, Makkah, Saudi Arabia. Author: (Arabic) Islamic Education, the Mosque: About Islam and Muslims, etc. Avocations: hunting, religious and Islamic affairs, lit., poetry. Office: Union Supreme Ct, PO Box 7, Abu Dhabi United Arab Emirates*

AL-MUBARAK, AHMED I., chemical company executive; b. Jubail, Saudi Arabia, Sept. 13, 1939; s. Ibrahim A. Rahman Al-Mubarak and Sarah M. Al-Otaibi; m. Othman Ahmed Al-Mubarak; children: Yasmin, Ibrahim, Sarah, Nassir, Mansor. BS, Ariz. State U., 1973; AS, Contra Costa Coll., San Pablo, Calif., 1969. Dir. gen. Royal Commn., Jubail Industrial City, 1984-92.

AL-MUHANDIS, BATOOL ALI, nurse educator; b. Manama, Bahrain, May 7, 1953; d. Ali Mohsen and Zahra Ghulam (Bahrain) Al-M.; m. Abdul Hadi Khalil Ebrahim, Oct. 11, 1977; five children. Diploma in Nursing, Bahrain Nursing Sch., 1973; Registered Gen. Nursing Cert., Bd. of Trainees, Dublin, 1977; Adminstrn. and Hosp. Mgmt. Degree, Mgmt. Inst., Dublin, 1977; Diploma in Tchg. and Tng., Coll. of Health Scis., Bahrain, 1982, BSN, 1986; MSN, U.K., 1993. Staff nurse Salmaniya Hosp., Bahrain, 1973-76; nurse instr. Coll. of Health Scis., Bahrain, 1977-79, lectr., 1980-86, sr. lectr. in nursing, 1995-2000, dean, 2000—; head of h.s. nursing program, Coll. of Health Scis., 1982-84, counterpart to the head of nursing, 1986-88, coord. for clin. nursing courses, 1991-95. Contbr. articles to profl. jours. Mem. Nursing Gulf Coop. Coun., 1995—. Recipient Silver medal His Highness The Ameer of Bahrain, 1982, 86, 94. Mem. Bahrain Nursing Soc. (founder, pres. 1996-99), Internat. Coun. Nurses. Home: 3119 Villa No 956, Manama 331, Bahrain

AL-MUKHTAR, AYAD, information technology executive; b. Baghdad, Iraq, Apr. 6, 1956; arrived in Eng., 1974; s. Asad and Firdous (Zaki) Al-M.; m. Elaine Wendy Ford, Jan. 31, 1981 (div. 1994); m. Christine Anne Wain, Feb. 1, 1999; 1 child, Sara Alexandra. BSc in Engring. (1st), Imperial Coll., London, 1979, diploma, 1984, PhD, 1984. Chartered engr. Cons. Logica U.K. Ltd., London, 1984-85; tech. dir. Technocrat Ltd., Maidenhead, 1985-87; pvt. practice cons. London, 1987-89; project mgr. Electronic Data Systems, Telford, 1989-97, Cap Gemini, London, 1997—. U. London scholar, 1979. Mem. IEEE, Brit. Computer Soc., Fedn. European Assn. Nat. Engrs., Assn. Project Mgmt. Avocations: French, German, bridge, pistol shooting. Home: 3 The Sandlings, School Rd, Saltwood Hythe Kent CT21 4PL, England Office: Cap Gemini UK PLC, Cap Gem, Hse, 130 Shaftesbury Ave, London W1V 8HH, England

AL-MUTAIRI, SAJED METEB, occupational health physician; b. Ahmadi, Kuwait, Apr. 11, 1970; s. Meteb Mejed Al-Mutairi and Jamala Mattrood Jahel; m. Manal Ahmed Al-Saleh, July 1, 1992; children: Al-Faisal, Fares, Farah. B in Medcicine and Surgery, Kuwait U., 1996; MSc in Occupl. Health, U. Birmingham, Eng., 1999. Physician Farwaniya Hosp., Kuwait, 1996-97; network mgr. Kuwait Med. Assn., 1997; occupl. health physician Ministry Health, Kuwait, 1997-99. Avocations: digital imaging, computer art, designing, internet webmastering. Home: PO Box 957, 45710 Surra Kuwait Office: Indsl Med Ctr, PO Box 10098, 65451 Shuaiba Kuwait

ALMY, EARLE VAUGHN, JR. (BUDDY ALMY), real estate executive; b. July 29, 1930; s. Earle Vaughn and Minnye Ruth (Rounsaville) A.; m. Gorden Yetive McGowan, July 31, 1964 (div. 1967). BS in Animal Husbandry, Tex. Tech. U., 1952; postgrad., Am. Inst. Banking, 1956-62. Cert. Realtors Inst., 1977, real estate brokerage mgr.; accredited land cons.; cert. real estate appraiser, Texas State Certified General Real Estate Appraiser. Credit analyst First Nat. Bank, Fort Worth, 1956-62; dir. finance and poultry feed sales Burrus Feed Mills, Saginaw, Tex., 1963-69; pres., mgr. Almy and Co., Hurst, Tex., 1970-79, Granbury, Tex., 1979—; v.p., dir. Northeast Tarrant County Bd. of Realtors, Hurst, Tex., 1972-74; pres. Almy and Co. Realtors, Weatherford, Tex., 1973-78; instr. appraisal of farms and ranches Weatherford Coll., 1986-89; state dir. Texas Realtor's Inst., 2000—. Mem. Fort Worth Farm and Ranch Club; usher Acton United Meth. Ch.; pres. Rep. Club Hood County, 1991. With USAF, 1952-56. Sears Roebuck scholar, 1951. Mem. Nat. Assn. Realtors, Tex. Assn. Realtors, Granbury Assn. Realtors, Nat. Realtors Land Inst., Tex. Realtor's Inst. (state dir.), Tex. Realtors Land Inst., Nat. Assn. Real Estate Appraisers (cert. real estate appraiser), Pecan Plantation Country Club. Republican. Avocations: golf, hunting, fishing, boating, swimming. E-mail: almyco@hcnews.com. Home: PO Box 129 Granbury TX 76048-0129

AL-NACHAWATI, HICHAM MUSTAPHA, statistician; b. Damascus, Syria, Aug. 25, 1949; s. Mustapha Mohamad and Atia Mohamad (Al-Hlabi) Al-N.; m. Said Bakri Al-Nahas; children: Abdulrahman, Yaman, Radwan, Samah. BS in Math., U. Damas, Damascus, 1974; PhD, U. Grenoble, 1985. Asst. U. Damascus, Syria, 1975-76, U. Tebessa, Algeria, 1985-89; asst. K.S.U., Riyadh, Saudi Arabia, 1989-97, assoc. prof., 1997—. Contbr. articles to profl. jours. Mem. Saudi Assn. Math. Scis. Home: 1511-335 Webb Dr, Dariya, Mississauga, ON Canada Office: Nat Water Rsch Inst, PO Box 5050 867 Lakeshore, Burlington, Canada L7R 4A6

AL-NAHHAS, ADIL MOOSA, nuclear medicine physician; b. Baghdad, Iraq, Mar. 12, 1951; came to U.K., 1980; s. Moosa Mohammed and Fatima (Mahmood) A.; m. Elham Amin Hilali, Feb. 6, 1976; children: Saif, Ahmed. M.B.Ch.B., Coll. of Medicine, Baghdad, 1974; MSc in Nuclear Medicine with distinction, U. London, 1981. Registrar Hammersmith Hosp., London, 1980-81; head cons. Hosp. Nuclear Medicine, Baghdad, 1981-85; sr. rsch. fellow St. Barts, London, 1985-90; sr. registrar Royal Marsden Hosp., London, 1991-95; cons., head dept. nuclear medicine Derriford Hosp., Plymouth, 1995—; expert Internat. Atomic Energy Agy., Vienna, 1998—. Contbr. articles to profl. jours. Advisor Brit. Thyroid Found., Plymouth, 1996—. Fellow Royal Coll. Physicians Dublin; mem. Brit. Nuclear Medicine Soc., European Assn. Nuclear Medicine, Soc. Nuclear Medicine. Avocations: reading, classical music, computing. Office: Derriford Hosp, Derriford Rd, Plymouth PL6 8DH, England

ALNAHI, HAITHAM GHALIB, electrical engineering educator; b. Basrah, Iraq, June 20, 1956; arrived in England, 1986; s. Ghalib Abdul Moutalib and

Assia Assaf Alnahi; m. Najla'a Salman Loaibi, June 29, 1991; children: Assia, Zahra. BSc, Basra, Iraq, 1978; MSc, York, England, 1988; PhD, London, 1993. Rsch. fellow Basra (Iraq) U., 1979-83, rsch. assoc., 1983-85, lectr., 1985-87; computer cons. Key West Co., England, 1987-88; researcher dept. elec. engring. Brunel U., Uxbridge, England, 1988-93, lectr. dept. elec. engring., 1993—; exec. Genetic Engring. Inst., Oxford (Eng.) U., 1995—; chancellor Oman Embassy, London, 1999; dir. Protein Engring. Ctr., 2000—; cons. Brookstone Ltd., England, 1986-88, Keywest Traveller, England, 1988-96; dir. Oxford Centre Culture and Tech. Author 5 books; contbr. numerous articles to profl. jours. Mem. IEEE, Am. Assn. Artificial Intelligence, N.Y. Acad. Scis. Achievements include invention of the predicting protein multiple structures using information theory to predict protein secondary structure. Avocations: reading historical books, photography, traveling, meeting famous people. Home: 72 Charterhouse Ave, Wembley Middx HRO 3DB, England Office: Brunel Univ, Oman Embassy, 64 Ennismore Gards, London SW7 11VH, England

AL NAHYAN, SHEIKH ZAYED BIN SULTAN, president of United Arab Emirates, ruler of Abu Dhabi; b. Al Ain, Abu Dhabi, United Arab Emirates, 1918; s. Sheikh Sultan bin Zayed Al Nahyan; married; children include Crown Prince Sheikh Khalifa bin Zayed Al Nahyan. Gov. Al Ain Province, 1946-66; ruler of Abu Dhabi, 1966—; pres. Trucial States, 1969-71, United Arab Emirates, 1971—; mem. Arab Gulf Cooperation Coun., 1981—; founder Zayed Rehab. Agrl. Project, 1996, Marriage Fund, 1992, Zayed Herbal Ctr., Sir Bani Yas Island Nature Res., Worldwide Fund for Nature, (Golden Panda award 1997). Decorated knight comdr. Hon. Order of Garter (U.K.). Muslim. Address: Office of the President, Presidential Ct PO Box 280, Abu Dhabi United Arab Emirates*

AL-NAIMI, ALI BIN IBRAHIM, government official; b. 1935. BSc in Geology, LeHigh U., 1962; MSc in Geology, Stanford U., 1963. Supr., prodn. mgr. ARAMCO, Abqaiq, 1963-69, asst. dir., dir. prodn. no. province, 1972-75, v.p. prodn. affairs, 1975, sr. v.p. petroleum affairs, 1978, bd. dirs., 1980, exec. v.p. ops., 1982, pres., 1984, CEO, 1988; min. petroleum and mineral resources Govt. of Saudi Arabia, 1995—. Office: Min Petroleum and Resources, PO Box 757, Airport Rd, Riyadh 11189, Saudi Arabia also: Embassy of Saudi Arabia 601 New Hampshire Ave NW Washington DC 20037-2405*

AL-NAJJAR, MOHAMMED FAROUK IBRAHIM AS'AD, economist; b. Nablus, West Bank, Palestine, Feb. 18, 1944; s. Ibrahim As'ad Al-Najjar and Moyassar Dawood Halaweh. BS in Econs. and Politics, Beirut Arab U., 1975. Tchr. Ministry Edn., Nablus and Amman, Palestine and Jordan, 1966-73; translator, interpretor Royal Saudi Air Force Base, Dhahran, Saudi Arabia, 1973-75; econ. advisor Alzahid Ests/Co's, Dammam, Saudi Arabia, 1976-78; mktg. and transport gen. mgr. Fakeeh Est., Jeddah, Saudi Arabia, 1979-80; econ. analyst Cities and Villages Devel. Bank, Amman, 1980-83; Yehia Ismail sponsor Jeddah, 1983-87; dir. Poliecons Econ. Ctr., Nablus, 1987—; lectr. Unrwa Amman Tng. Ctr., 1985-86, Hittin C.C., Amman, 1986-87; econs. cons., Amman, 1985-87; founder U. Palestine. Author: The Love Is the Life, 1985; contbr. articles to newspapers and mags. Main founder ptnr. Beirut Arab Est., Amman, 1979; mem. control com. Beirut Arab U. Grad. Assn., Amman, 1980-82. Recipient Silver medal Coll. Tchrs., Irbed, Jordan, 1968. Mem. Arab Economists Assn., Beirut Arab U. Grads. Club, Highlanders Club. Mem. Arab Nationalist Movement/Palestine Liberation Orgn. Avocations: sports, music, singing, movies, writing. Home and Office: Al Hijaz St # 8 PO Box 1158, Nablus Palestine

ALNAKHLI ALMUZANI, ABDULKAREEM ALI, auditor; b. Al Med-dina, Saudi Arabia, Jan. 7, 1961; s. Ali Mohammed and Jawza Hamzah (Al Muzaini) A.; m. Qamar Hasan Sharaf, Dec. 12, 1988; children: Fatimatuzahra, Ali, Wala. B of Acctg., King Abdulaziz U., Jeddah, Saudi Arabia, 1984. Telephone asst. Ministry of P.T.T., Jeddah, 1979-84; operation supr. Saudiamerican Bank, Jeddah, 1984; acct. Saudi Arabian Monetary Agy., Riyadh, 1984-88, auditor, 1988-94, sr. internal auditor, 1994—; exchange auditor Ernst Young, Milw., 1989-91; writer Riyadh newspaper, 1995-96; columnist Aljazirah newspaper, 1996-97; contbr. numerous Saudi newspapers. Mem. (past) Am. Inst. Internal Auditors, Saudi Orgn. for CPA's. Muslim. Avocations: writing, reading, swimming, lecturing, traveling. Home: PO Box 15537, Riyadh 11454, Saudi Arabia Office: Sadi Arabian Monetary Agy, PO Box 2992, Riyadh 11169, Saudi Arabia

AL NAMLAH, ABDULAZIZ MOHAMED, construction executive; b. Riyadh, Saudi Arabia, Mar. 6, 1954; s. Mohamed Sulaiman Al Namlah and Fatimah Ali Al Barrak; m. Munirah Abdulaziz Al-Omair, June 30, 1977; children: Mohamed, Al Danah, Nouf, Modhi, Ali. BSc in Civil Engring., U. Denver, 1975, MPA, 1976. Dir. Constrn. & Maintenance Saudi Marine Forces, Dhahran, Saudi Arabia; asst. dir. Gen. Directorate Mil. Works, Riyadh; asst. dir. Engring. & Housing Directorate Riyadh Royal Saudi Air Def. Forces, Riyadh, dir. Saudi Strategic Storage Program, dir. directorate O&M; chmn., CEO Contractors Svcs. Co., Riyadh. Recipient Kuwait Liberation Brevet medal Prince of Kuwait. Home and Office: PO Box 29880, Riyadh 11467, Saudi Arabia

AL-NASSER, IBRAHIM ABDULRAHMAN, biochemist, educator; b. Dawadmi, Saudi Arabia, Sept. 1, 1953; s. Abdulrahman Abdullah Al-Nasser; m. Norah Abdulla Al-Gaith, Jan. 6, 1982; children: Rana, Abdulrahman, Rawan, Majed, Khalid, Rema, Yasser. B in Biochemistry, King Saud U., Riyadh, Saudi Arabia, 1978; M in Biochemistry, U. London, Eng., 1983, PhD, 1987. Demonstrator King Saud U., Riyadh, 1978-79, asst. prof., 1987-95, chmn. biochemistry dept., 1991-92, assoc. prof., 1995-99, prof., 1999—; referee for rsch. proposals King Abdulaziz U., Jeddah, Saudi Arabia, 1993. Author: Biochemistry for Health Control, 1988, Principles of Practical Biochemistry (in Arabic), 1995; contbg. author: Intracellular Calcium Regulation, 1983; contbr. articles to profl. jours. Achievements include founder of Ca2+ activated pore in rat liver inner mitochondrial membranes; research of the occurence of an identical pore in mitochondria from various sources and characterization of several features of this pore activity. Home: PO Box 75250, Riyadh 11578, Saudi Arabia Office: King Saud U Dept Biochem, PO Box 2455, Riyadh 11451, Saudi Arabia

AL-NUAYMI, RASHID BIN ABDALLAH, United Arab Emirian government official. Min. fgn. affairs Govt. of United Arab Emirates, Abu Dhabi, 1992—. Office: Ministry Fgn Affairs, POB 1, Abu Dhabi United Arab Emirates*

AL-NUHAYYAN, HAMDAN BIN ZAYID, United Arab Emirian government official. Min. state for fgn. affairs Govt. of United Arab Emirates, Abu Dhabi. Office: Ministry Fgn Affairs, PO Box 1, Abu Dhabi United Arab Emirates*

ALOFF, MINDY, writer; b. Phila., Dec. 20, 1947; d. Jacob and Selma (Album) A.; m. Martin Steven Cohen, June 16, 1968 (div. June 2000); 1 child, Ariel Nikiya. AB in English, Vassar Coll., 1969; MA in English, SUNY, Buffalo, 1972. Asst. prof. English U. Portland, Oreg., 1973-75; editor Encore Mag. of the Arts, Portland, 1977-80, Vassar Quar., Poughkeepsie, N.Y., 1980-88; free-lance writer Bklyn., 1988—; coord. Portland Poetry Festival, 1974-75. Author: (poems) Night Lights, 1979; author essays and revs. theatrical dancing and lit. for N.Y. Times Weekend, Book Rev. and Arts & Leisure, New Republic mag., Nation mag., Threepenny Rev., Dance mag., New Yorker mag., ann. Ency. Britannica, others. Recipient Whiting Writers award Mrs. Giles Whiting Found., N.Y.C., 1987; Woodrow Wilson Found. fellow, 1969, Woodburn fellow SUNY-Buffalo, 1972, Am. Dance Festival Dance Critics Inst. fellow, New London, Conn., 1977, John Simon Guggenheim Meml. Found. fellow, 1990. Mem. Nat. Book Critics Circle (bd. dirs. 1988-91), Phi Beta Kappa.

ALOIA, PATRICK C., computer company executive; b. Miami, Fla., Feb. 21, 1965; s. Patrick A.; m. Iris R., Feb. 25, 1995; childre: Gregory, Corey, Keil. Grad., Def. Lang. Inst., 1985; AA, U. Alaska, 1997. Programmer, analyst iCat Corp., Seattle, 1996-98; bus. systems mgr. Intel Corp., Seattle, 1998—. Tech. editor Online Auctions at Ebay, 1999, 2d edit., 1999, Create Your First Web Page in a Weekend, 3d edit., 1999, Electrify Your Web Page. Sgt. USAF, 1985-91. Office: Intel Corp 1420 5th Ave Ste 1800 Seattle WA 98101-4088

AL-OMAIR, SALEH, trade association administrator. Chmn. governing bd. OPEC Fund Internat. Devel., Vienna, Austria. Office: OPEC Fund Internat Devel, PO Box 995, A-1011 Vienna Austria*

ALONEFTIS, ANDREAS, venture capitalist, investment executive, former Cypriot government official; b. Nicosia, Cyprus, Aug. 24, 1945. BA, Sch. Accountancy and Bus. Studies, Glasgow, Scotland, 1973; MBA, So. Meth. U., 1978; postgrad., N.Y. Inst. Fin., 1982, Henley Mgmt. Coll., U.K., 1996—. Acct. Cyprus Devel. Bank, Nicosia, 1966-72, chief acct., 1972-76, mgr. fin., 1976-78, sr. mgr. investments, 1978-82; gen. mgr., chief executive officer Cyprus Investment and Securities Corp., Nicosia, 1982-88; minister of def. Republic of Cyprus, 1988-93; chief exec. Am. Life Ins. Co., Nicosia, Cyprus, 1993-95; mng. dir. CypriaLife Ins., Nicosia, Cyprus, 1995-99, group gen. mgr. ins., 1999-2000; mng. dir., CEO Lambousa Venture Capital and Olympos Investments, Nicosia, 2000—; sec. Cyprus Stock Exchange Interim Com., 1980-82. Contbr. articles to profl. jours. and newspapers. 2nd lt. Cyprus N.G., 1964-66. Fulbright Found. grantee, 1977-78; So. Meth. U. fellow, 1977-78. Fellow Assn. Internat. Accts. (mem. coun.). Greek Orthodox. Lodge: Rotary Club, Propeller Club of the U.S. Avocations: music, reading, cinema, jogging. Home: 10 Kastellorizo St, Nicosia 2108, Cyprus Office: Lambousa Venture Capital, PO Box 21744, Nicosia 1589, Cyprus

ALONI, RONI, botany educator; b. Israel, Dec. 2, 1944; s. Mordechai and Chava (vardi) A.; m. Orna Aloni, Aug. 10, 1965; children: Erez, Miri, Daphna. BSc, Hebrew U., 1968, MSc, 1970, PhD, 1974. Instr. Hebrew U., Jerusalem, 1972-73; lectr. Israel Inst. Tech., Haifa, 1973-77; lectr. Tel Aviv (Israel) U., 1976-79, sr. lectr., 1979-85, assoc. prof., 1985-91, prof., 1992—; vis. fellow Princeton (N.J.) U., 1974-76; Bullard rsch. fellow Harvard U., Cambridge, Mass., 1982-83, vis. prof. U. Waterloo, Ontario, Can., 1988-90, adj. prof. U. Waterloo, 1989—. Co-author: (book) Vascular Differentiation and Plant Growth Regulators, 1988; editor (jour.) Trees Structure and Function, 1990—; contbr. articles to profl. jours., chpts. to books; mem. editorial bd. Internat. Jour. of Plant Sci., Physiologia Plantarum, Tree Physiology, Jour. of Plant Rsch. Sgt. Israeli Army, 1962-65. Recipient rsch. fellowship Princeton (N.J.) U., 1974-76, Harvard U., Cambridge, 1982, awards Nat. Scis. and Engring. Rsch. Coun. Can. (Ont.), 1988, 89, 90; Visiting award U.K., 1994; elected world leader Working Party on Formation of Wood, Internat. Union of Forestry Rsch. Orgns. Fellow Internat. Acad. Wood Sci.; mem. Botanical Soc. Israel (pres. 1996-98). Achievements include 5 patents on methods to increase fiber and wood production. Avocations: swimming, painting. Home: 10 Rav Ashi, Tel Aviv 69395, Israel Office: Tel Aviv Univ, Dept Plant Scis, Tel Aviv 69978, Israel

ALONSO, ANTONIO ENRIQUE, lawyer; b. Havana, Cuba, Aug. 31, 1924; came to U.S., 1959; s. Enrique and Inocencia (Avila) A.; m. Daisy Ojeda, July 20, 1949; children: Margarita, Antonio, Enrique, Jorge. JD, U. Habana, Cuba, 1946; PhD, U. Habana, 1952; student, U. Fla., 1974-76. Bar: Fla. 1976. Pub. defendant High Ct. Las Villas, Cuba, 1946-49; atty. Provincial Gov., Cuba, 1950-52; under sec. Treasury, Cuba, 1952-54; mem. House of Reps. Congress of Cuba, 1954-58; prof. U. Jose Marti, 1952-58, Inst. Soc. Action, 1964-65; prof. modern lang. Coll. St. Teresa, 1968; sole practice Miami, 1976—; adj. prof. St. Mary's Coll., Minn., summers, 1968-73. Author: (with others) Violation of Human Rights in Cuba, 1962, History of the Communist Party of Cuba, 1970; weekly columnist on real estate and law Diario Las Ams. newspaper; contbr. articles to profl. jours. Recipient Field Svc. Program award Nat. Assn. Student Affairs, 1973. Mem. AAUP, Am. Assn. Tchrs. Spanish and Portuguese, Fla. Bar Assn. Republican. Roman Catholic. Home: 1900 SW 12th Ave Miami FL 33129-2613 Office: 1699 Coral Way Ste 315 Miami FL 33145-2860

ALONSO, IGNACIO FRANCISCO, manufacturing executive; b. Gijon, Spain, June 19, 1947; s. Joaquin and Olvido (Garcia) A.; m. Margarita Castellet Alonso, July 25, 1980; children: Ignacio, Borja. MS, Tech. Inst. Engring., Bilbao, Spain, 1972; doctoral studies, Gijon, Spain, 1973-74; environ. studies, Inst. Catalan Tech., Barcelona, Spain, 1989. Chartered engr. Tech. dir. Indsl. Alonso S.A., Gijon, Spain, 1972-74; tech. and comml. dir. Ind. Alonso S.A., Gijon, Spain, 1975-76; v.p., 1977-79; gen. mgr. Puerto Rico Casting Steel, San Juan, 1979-81, Talleres Castellet S.A., Barcelona, Spain, 1982-85; mng. dir., 1986—; prof. engring. Tech. Inst. Engring., Gijon, Spain, 1972-76. Contbr. articles to profl. jours. pres. Rotary Club Barcelona-Mediterraneo, Spain, 1997-98; treas. bd. dirs. Serafransa Owners Orgn., Barcelona, 1988—; 2nd lt. Spanish Army, 1973, Gijon. Mem. Coll. Engrs., European Assn. Normalization for Tanks to Transport Dangerous Goods, Real Club De Polo. Avocations: tennis, skiing, reading, music, travel. Office: Talleres Castellet SA, Feixa Llarga 15-17, 08040 Barcelona Spain

ALONSO, MODESTO M., clinical psychologist; b. Buenos Aires, July 21, 1944; s. Modesto and Berta Elena (Araldi) A.; m. Isabel E. Insua, Jan. 27, 1972; 1 child, Veronica. Lic., U. Buenos Aires, 1975; psicoterapeuta, Escuela de Psicoterapia, 1978. Psychotherapist Centro de Psicoterapia, Buenos Aires, 1976—, clin. psychologist, 1976—; clin. psychologist Centro de Psicoterapia, Santa Rosa, La Pampa, 1976—; rschr. Instituto Nacional de Medicina Aeronáutica y Espacial, Buenos Aires, 1994-96; tchr. U. Buenos Aires, 1993—, tchr. aviation psychology, 2000—; tchr., prof. Escuela de Psicoterapia, 1980—; tchr. Asoc de Psiquiatras Argentinos Inst. Postgrad., 1990—; coord. Centro de Psicoterapia, Buenos Aires, 1984-91, Santa Rosa, La Pampa, 1980—; dir. Programa Salud Mental Mirot, Buenos Aires, 1991-98; rsch. dept. Assn. Argentine Psicoterapia, Buenos Aires, 1991—, pres., 2000—; sec. Asociacion Arg de Psicoterapia, Buenos Aires, 1986-98; nat. Rep. Sociedad Interamericana de Psicologia, Buenos Aires, 1992—; cons. in field. Co-author, editor 4 books and numerous papers in field. Mem. APA, World Fedn. for Mental Health, Soc. for Psychotherapy Rsch., N.Y. Acad. of Scis., World Coun. for Psychotherapy, Psychotherapy Assn. Republic of Argentina, Soc. Interamericana de Psicología, Asociación de Psicólogos Buenos Aires, Internat. Fedn. for Psychotherapy, Colegio de Psicólogos de la Pampa, Interam. Soc. Aero. Psychology, Assn. Aviation Psychologists, Assn. Agrengine Psychologists. Avocation: private pilot. Fax: 54 011 4781-8907. E-mail: alonso@ssdnet.com.ar.

ALONSO-AMELOT, MIGUEL ENRIQUE, chemistry educator; b. Caracas, Venezuela, Dec. 30, 1946; s. Ramón and Christiane (Amelot) Alonso; m. María Adela Tarnawiecki, Aug. 13, 1971; 1 child, Gabriel Alejandro. Lic. in Chemistry, U. Central de Venezuela, Caracas, 1968; PhD, Ind. U., 1974. Technician in chemistry IVIC-Sección de Química, Caracas, Venezuela, 1967-68, profl. chemist, 1968-70; assoc. researcher IVIC Centro de Petróleo y Química, Caracas, Venezuela, 1975-86; assoc. prof. U. Los Andes, Mérida, Venezuela, 1986—; vis. scholar Cornell U., Ithaca, N.Y., 1982; vice dean of grad. students IVIC Ctr. of Advanced Studies, Caracas, 1980-82; vis. prof. Ill. State U., Normal, 1993-94; cons. in field. Author: Art of Problem Solving in Org., 1987; contbr. over 65 sci. articles on organic and ecol. chemistry to profl. jours. Recipient Best Chemistry Work award CONICIT, Caracas, 1978, 81, Lorenzo Mendoza Fleury award Polar Found., 1985; grantee CONICIT, 1978-91, Interam. Devel. Bank, 1992-97, 97—. Mem. Internat. Soc. Chem. Ecology, Asociación venezolana para el avance de la Ciencia, Internat. Bracken Group. Avocations: piano, harpsichord, mtn. trailing. E-mail: alonso@ciens.ula.ve.

ALONSO-BETANZOS, AMPARO, computer science educator; b. Vigo, Spain, Oct. 10, 1961; d. Eugenio Eduardo and Carmen (Pura) B.; m. Vicente Moret-Bonillo, July 23, 1988. BSChemE, U. Santiago, Spain, 1984, MSChemE, 1985, PhD in Physics, 1988; Postdoctoral Fellow, Med. Coll. Ga., Augusta, 1990. Predoctoral fellow U. Santiago, Spain, 1985-88, Med. Coll. Ga., Augusta, 1988-90; asst. prof. U. Santiago, 1990; assoc. prof. U. Coruña, 1990—. Contbr. articles to profl. jours. and chpt. to book. Recipient Outstanding Thesis award Faculty of Physics, Santiago, 1988, Award of Merit, Jour. Clin. Engring., 1990. Mem. IEEE, N.Y. Acad. Scis., Assn. Computing Machinery. Roman Catholic. Avocations: phys. tng., music, travel, films. Office: U Coruña, Campus Elviña, 15071 Coruna Spain

ALONSO DE PINA, GLORIA MARIA, marine biologist; b. Pigue, Argentina, July 10, 1950; d. Galo Antonio and Amelia (Gil) A.; m. Victor Alfredo Pina, Jan. 18, 1988. M in Ecology/Systematics of Crustacea, U. Buenos Aires, 1977, DSc, 1984. Rschr. CONICET (Bs.As). Contbr. articles to profl. internat. and sci. jours. Avocations: movies, reading, gardening, travel, biking. Office: Mus Argentino Natural Scis Bernarolino Rivadavia, Av Angel Gallardo 470, 1405 Buenos Aires Argentina

ALONSO-FERNANDEZ, ROBERTO, microbiologist, molecular biologist; b. Madrid, June 24, 1965; s. Angel Alonso and Josefa Fernandez; m. Maryluz Campillo, Sept. 17, 1991. BS, Complutense U., Madrid, 1988, PhD, 1991. Asst. prof. U. Las Palmas, Spain, 1992-94; microbiologist Hosp. Gregorio Haranon, Madrid, 1994—. Mem. ASM. Avocations: horse riding, music, reading. Office: DP Microbio Hosp G Maranon, C/Dr Esquerdo 46, 28028 Madrid Spain

ALONSO-LEJ, FERNANDO, cardiothoracic surgeon; b. Zaragoza, Spain, Jan. 27, 1927; s. Fernando Alonso-lej and Damiana De Las Casas; m. Madeleine Genty, May 20, 1955 (div. 1980); 1 child, Chantal; m. Mercedes Pascual, Oct. 3, 1983; 1 child, Raquel. BS, U. Zaragoza, 1945, MD summa cum laude, 1951. Diplomate Am. Bd. Gern. Surgery, Am. Bd. Thoracic Surger. Intern James Walker Meml. Hosp., Wilmington, N.C., 1952-53; resident in surgery Balt. City Hosp., 1953-56; assoc. resident in surgery Mercy Hosp., Balt., 1956-57, chief resident, 1957-58; asst. resident thoracic surgery U. Md. Hosp., 1958-59, chief resident thoracic surgery, 1959-60; chief cardiothoracic surgery Hosp. Gen. Asturias, Spain, 1964-75, Hosp. Miguel Servet, Zaragoza, 1975-97; chief cardiac surgery Clinica Montpellier, Zaragoza, 1990—. Co-author: Recent Progess in Mitral Valve Disease, 1984; contbr. numerous articles to profl. jours. Mem. Soc. Thoracic Surgeons (founding mem.), Soc. Cardiosurgeons (former pres.), Aragonesa de Cardiologia, Spanish Soc. Cardiovasc. Surgery (former pres.), Spanish Soc. Cardiology. Home: Manuel Lasala 40-4, 50006 Zaragoza Spain

ALÓS-FERRER, CARLOS, economic researcher, educator; b. Moncófar, Spain, Nov. 22, 1970; arrived in Austria, 1998; s. Vicente Alós-Alós and Loreto Ferrer-Presencia; m. Olivia Ortells-Alós, Oct. 28, 1988 (div. 1998); 1 child, Veronica Alós-Ortells. MSc in Math., U. Valencia, Spain, 1992; PhD in Econs., U. Alicante, Spain, 1998. Numerical processes contr. Garcia-Ballester, Burriana, Spain, 1992-93; asst. prof. U. Alicante, 1993-96; rsch. fellow Ministry of Sci., Alicante, 1996-97; asst. prof. U. Vienna, Austria, 1998—. Contbr. articles to books and profl. jours. Recipient Award to Young Economists, Austrian Econ. Assn., 1999, Extraordinary Master award Maths. Faculty, 1992. Mem. Austrian Math. Soc., German Econ. Soc., Econometric Soc. Avocations: science fiction, role-playing games, Japanese manga. Office: U Vienna, Hohenstaufengasse 9, A-1010 Vienna Austria

ALPAN, SADRETTIN H., mining engineer; b. Aksehir, Turkey, June 22, 1924; s. Bahri and Mebrure Alpan; m. Annie Mary Heal, Nov. 5, 1952; 1 child, Kenan. BS with honors, Birmingham (Eng.) U., 1948, PhD, 1951. Assoc. prof. Tech. U., Istanbul, Turkey, 1954; chief engr. Mineral Rsch. and Exploration Inst. Turkey, Ankara, 1951-55, dir. exploration dept., 1955-58, dep. gen. dir., 1958-60, gen. dir., 1960-78; interregional adviser Divsn. Natural Resources and Energy UN, N.Y.C., 1979-91; chmn. bd. trustees Mid. East Tech. U., Ankara, 1960-70; mem. AEC, Turkey, 1960-75; part-time lectr. Istanbul Tech. U., Istanbul U., Ankara U., Trabzon Tech. U., Ege-Izmir U., Haceteppe U., Mid. East Tech. U., 1955-79. Contbr. papers on mining prodn. and mineral resources to publs. Res. officer Turkish Armed Forces, 1951-52. Recipient Victor prize Inst. Mining Engrs., Eng., 1950. Mem. Chamber of Engrs. Ankara-Turkey, Geol. Soc. Ankara-Turkey, Internat. World Mining Congress (organizing com.). Muslim. Office: 8 Kisim B-34 Blok Apt 27 Atakoy, 34750 Istanbul Turkey

ALPAR, JOHN J., ophthalmologist, educator; b. Sopron, Hungary, Dec. 28, 1925; s. Géza and Margit A.; m. Elizabeth Klara Alpar, Aug. 6, 1952; children: Andrea, Andrew, Alan, Anita, David, Elizabeth. Student in metallurgy, Tech. U. Mining, Metallurgy and Forestry, 1944-45; MD, Royal Hungarian Peter Pazmany U. Sch. Med., 1950; MA in English, West Tex. State U., 1969. Diplomate Am. Bd. Ophthalmology. Rotating intern County Hosp. Sopron, Czechoslavakia, 1949-50; resident in internal medicine, ophthalmology, and surgery County Hosp. Sopron; resident in ophthalmology Univ. Eye Clin., Budapest, Hungary, 1950-51, County Hosp. Miskolc, Czechoslavakia, 1952-53; rotating intern Del. Hosp., Wilmington, 1957-58, resident in ophthalmology, 1957-59; pvt. practice ophthalmologist Amarillo, Tex., 1959—; assoc. clin. prof. ophthalmology Tex. Tech U., 1973-83, clin. prof., 1983—; active staff Bapt.-St. Anthony's Health Sys., Amarillo; affil. staff Northwest Tex. Healthcare Sys., Amarillo; cons. staff VAMC, Amarillo. Co-author: (with Paul U. Fechner) Grundlagen and Operationslehre, 1984, Fecnher's Intraocular Lenses, 1986, Intraocular Lenses, 1986, (with Arthur Linksz) Fighting the Third Death, 1986; contbr. over 150 articles to med. jours., including Ophthalmic Surgery, Jour. Ophthalmology, Pakistan Jour. Ophthalmology, others; contbr. chpts. to books. Fellow Am. Acad. Ophthalmology (Honor award 1989), Am. Coll. Surgeons, Barraquer Inst. Barcelona, Internat. Coll. Surgeons; mem. AMA (Physicians Recognition awards 1973—, Am. Soc. Cataract and Refractive Surgery (former mem. sci. adv. bd.), Tex. State Med. Assn., Am. Viennese Med. Assn., Glaucoma Assn. of Pan-Am. Assn. Ophthalmology, Pan.-Am. Assn. Ophthalmology, Internat. Glaucoma Assn., Internat. Corneal Soc., Royal Soc. Health, others. Avocations: reading, music, medival history. E-mail: stlukei@arn.net. Office: 5311 W 9th Ave Amarillo TX 79106-4161

ALPAY, MERAL, library science educator, library director; b. Izmir, Turkey, Oct. 21, 1938; d. Ahmet Kamil and Zeynep (Turut) Senöz; m. Yurdakul Alpay; children: Menekse, Egemen. MA, Istanbul (Turkey) U., 1963, Doctorate, 1968. Cert. German lang. and lit. Assoc. prof. Istanbul U., 1973-81, prof., 1982—, head of chair libr. sci., 1983—, head dept. libr. sci., 1993-98, head Ctrl. Libr., 1994—; head Assn. Turkish Librs., Istanbul Br., 1970-73; visitor Brit. Coun., London, Manchester, Birmingham, 1981—, Assn. Austrian Writers in Vienna, 1982—; head orgn. com. 1st and 2nd Internat. Books Fair for Children, Istanbul; head local com., mem. nat. com. Internat. Fedn. Libr. Assns. Instns. Conf., Istanbul, 1995. Author: Harf Devriminin Kütüphanelerde Yansimasi, 1976, Kinderbucher Aus Der Turkei Ju Joslawien-Griechenland, 1984, Studies on Research in Reading and Libraries, 1991, H.Ü. Kütüphanecilik Bölümü 25 Yila Armagan, 1997; advisor Jour. Kirmizifare, 1999. Mem. Instn. for Ataturks Prins. and History Turkish Revolution (bd. dirs. 1988—), Assn. Writers and Illustrators for Childrens Lit., Sect. Libr. Theory and Rsch. (corr.), Assn. for Ataturk's Ideas (founder 1989—). Social Democrat. Islam. Avocations: visiting art exhibitions, cooking. Office: Istanbul Univ, Merkez Kütüphanesi, 34452 Beyat-Istanbul Turkey

ALPEN, EDWARD LEWIS, biophysicist, educator; b. San Francisco, May 14, 1922; s. Edward Lawrence and Margaret Catherine (Shipley) A.; m. Wynella June Dosh, Jan. 6, 1945; children: Angela Marie, Jeannette Elise. B.S., U. Calif., Berkeley, 1946, Ph.D., 1950. Br. chief, then dir. biol. and med. scis. Naval Radiol. Def. Lab., San Francisco, 1952-68; mgr. environ. and life scis. Battelle Meml. Inst., Richland, Wash., 1968-69, assoc. dir., then dir. Pacific N.W. div., 1969-75; dir. Donner Lab., U. Calif., Berkeley; also assoc. dir. Lawrence Berkeley Lab., 1975-87; prof. biophysics emeritus U. Calif., Berkeley, 1975—; prof. radiology emeritus U. Calif., San Francisco, 1976—; dir. study ctr. U. Calif., London, 1988-90; councillor, dir. Nat. Council Radiol. Protection, 1969-92; exec. v.p., tech. dir. Neutron Tech. Corp., Berkeley, 1990-93; mem. Gov. Wash. Council Econ. Devel., 1973-75; bd. dirs. Wash. Bd. Trade, 1973-76. Author books, papers, abstracts in field. Served to capt. USNR, 1942-46, 50-51. Recipient Navy Sci. medal, 1962, Disting. Service medal Dept. Def., 1963, Sustaining Members medal Assn. Mil. Surgeons, 1971; fellow Guggenheim Found., 1960-61; sr. fellow NSF, 1958-59. Fellow Calif. Acad. Scis.; mem. Bioelectromagnetics Soc. (pres. 1979-80), Radiation Rsch. Soc., Soc. Exptl. Biology and Medicine, Biophys. Soc., Brit. Inst. Radiology, Am. Philatelic Soc., Sigma Xi (nat. lectr. 1994-96). Episcopalian. Home: 1182 Miller Ave Berkeley CA 94708-1755

ALPER, ANNE ELIZABETH, professional association executive; b. Montreal, Que., Can., Nov. 7, 1942; d. John S. and Emma (Flynn) Fairhurst; m. Howard Alper, June 4, 1966; children: Ruth and Lara (twins). BS in Chemistry with honors, Marianopolis Coll., Montreal, 1962; PhD in Organic Chemistry, McGill U., Montreal, 1966. Rsch. assoc. Textile Rsch. Inst., Princeton, N.J., 1968-69; mgr. publs. Chem. Inst. Can., Ottawa, Ont., 1981-86, exec. dir., 1986-98; exec. dir. Can. Rsch. Mgmt. Assn., Ottawa, 1996-98; officer Panel B Info. Techs., Panel G New Directions NSERC; team leader Nat. Sci. Engring. Rsch. Coun., 1998—; bd. dirs. MITE-RN. Office: Nat

Scis Engring Rsch Coun Chem Inst Can, 350 Albert St, Ottawa, ON Canada K1A 1H5*

ALPERIN, GOLDIE GREEN, consulting librarian, lawyer; b. Des Moines, Aug. 16, 1905; d. Morris and Bessie (Miliwer) Green; LL.B., Drake U., 1927; m. Moses Alperin, Dec. 25, 1930 (dec. 1950); children—Herschel Burton, Judith Miriam. Admitted to Iowa bar, 1927, U.S. Supreme Ct. bar, 1959; practice in Des Moines, 1927-30; law librarian Chgo. Bar. Assn., 1951-63; dir. Def. Information Office, Chgo., 1963-65; librarian book selections Northwestern U. Law Sch. Library, 1966-72; ret., 1972. Named one of 20 rep. U.S. women lawyers of various phases practice Women's Adjustment Bd., London, Eng., 1957; One of Outstanding Women of Am. Bicentennial, Austin (Tex.) Bicentennial Com., 1976; cert. religious sch. tchr. Bd. Jewish Edn., Chgo., 1951. Mem. Am. (sec. 1960-65), Chgo. (past exec. bd., editor 1958-59) assns. law libraries, Nat. Assn. Women Lawyers (regional) dir. 1960-64). Jewish religion. Asst. editor Women Lawyers Jour., 1961-67, exec. bd., 1961-67. Home: 3100 N Lake Shore Dr Apt 1512 Chicago IL 60657-4953

ALPERIN, IRWIN EPHRAIM, clothing company executive; b. Scranton, Pa., Apr. 29, 1925; s. Louis I. and Bessie (Wickner) A.; m. Francine Leah Friedman, Dec. 5, 1948; children: Barbara Joy, Jane Leslie. Cert. Mech. Engring., Pa. State U., 1945; BS in Indsl. Engring., Lehigh U., 1947; DHL (hon.), U. Scranton, Pa., 1991. Mgmt. trainee Mayflower Mfg. Co., Scranton, 1947-49, sec., 1952-79, pres., 1980-91; with Triple A Trouser Mfg. Co., Inc., Scranton, 1952, v.p., treas., 1958-79, pres., 1980-91; with Gold Star Mfg. Co., Inc., Scranton, 1956, pres., 1956-91; sec. Astro Warehousing, Inc., Scranton, 1962-91; sec.-treas. Bondeal, Inc., Scranton, 1978-89, pres., 1989—; v.p. RCO, Inc., 1989-91; vice chmn. Montage, Inc., 1979-92; sec. Alperin, Inc., 1982-91, pres., 1991—; sec. All Star Industries, Inc., 1989-92, pres., 1993—; treas. Calvin Clothing Co. Inc., 1996—. Bd. dirs. Econ. Devel. Coun. N.E. Pa., Avoca, 1974-96, v.p., 1978-83; bd. dirs. ARC, Scranton, 1968-88, pres. spl. adv. bd., 1988—; bd. dirs. Jewish Home Ea. Pa., Scranton, 1970—, treas., 1981-97; pres. Elan Gardens, 1995-2000, pres. emeritus, 2000—; bd. dirs. Jewish Cmty. Ctr., Scranton, 1971-86, now life mem.; bd. dirs. Pa. United Way, Harrisburg, 1973-78, Scranton Counseling Ctr., 1975-78, trustee, 1979-95; pres. Planning coun. Social Svcs. Lackawanna County, 1972-74, now life mem.; pres. Jewish Family Svc. of Lackawanna County, 1967-70, now life bd. mem.; v.p. United Way Lackawanna County, 1974-78, exec. com., 1978-86; pres. Alperin Found., Scranton, 1962-93; treas. Scranton-Lackawanna Jewish Fedn., 1973-75, life mem. bd. dirs.; trustee Amos Lodge Found., 1982—, v.p., 1989-91; trustee Found. Jewish Elderly, 1994—, v.p., 1985—; trustee Pocono N.E. Devel., 1983—, sec., 1986-95, pres., 1995-96; pres. Temple Hesed, 1969-71, life mem., bd. dirs., Scranton; mem. Lackawanna County Libr. Bd., 1983-85; treas. Lackawanna Regional Cultural Coun., 1988-91, bd. dirs. 1988-93; bd. dirs. Broadway Theatre League Lackawanna County, 1989-2000, vice chmn., 1994-99; bd. dirs. Masonic Temple Civic Ctr. Found., 1989-93; trustee U. Scranton, 1991-97. With C.E. AUS, 1944-46. Recipient Americanism award, 1982; named Man of Year, Jewish Community Ctr., 1973, Disting. Pennsylvanian, Phila. C. of C., 1982. Mem. Am. Inst. Indsl. Engrs. (sr.), Glen Oak Country Club (Clarks Summit, Pa.), Wave Oak Realty (Clarks Summit) (v.p. 1989-91), Masons, Shriners, Elks, B'nai B'rith (trustee, Man of Yr. 1982). Home: 1010 Victoria Ln Clarks Summit PA 18411-9248

ALPERIN, RICHARD MARTIN, clinical social worker, psychoanalyst; b. Mt. Vernon, N.Y., Oct. 16, 1946; s. Israel and Sara A.; children: Heather Nicole, Alexander Scott. BBA, Western Mich. U., 1968; MSW, Fordham U., 1974; DSW, Columbia U., 1982; postdoctoral diploma in psychotherapy and psychoanalysis, Adelphi U., 1988. Cert. social worker, N.Y.; lic. clin. social worker, N.J.; diplomate Am. Bd. Examiners in Clin. Social Work; cert. group psychotherapist Nat. Registry Cert. Group Psychotherapists. Cons. Mt. Vernon Youth Bd., 1972-76; adj. faculty Marymount Manhattan Coll., N.Y.C., 1974-76; psychotherapist Riverdale Mental Health Clinic, N.Y.C., 1974-77; psychol. counselor, psychotherapist Ctr. Counseling and Psychol. Svcs. Ramapo Coll. of N.J., 1976-81, adj. faculty, 1977-86, moderator evening forums, 1978, 80; counselor, psychotherapist Ctr. Counseling and Psychol. Svcs. SUNY, Purchase, 1981-82, 84-85, acting dir., 1982-84; clin. cons. Westside Ctr. for Family Svcs., N.Y.C., 1985-87; guest lectr. Cabrini Med. Ctr., 1979; pvt. practice psychotherapy and psychoanalysis Riverdale, N.Y., 1977—, Teaneck, N.J., 1980—, N.Y.C., 1984—; guest lectr. grand rounds dept. psychiatry, Brookdale Hosp. Med. Ctr., 1996; field instr. Sch. Social Work-Columbia U., 1983-85; adj. assoc. prof. Sch. Social Svc.-Fordham U., 1985—; adj. asst. prof. Grad. Sch. Social Work-NYU, 1989-91; mem. faculty, dean curriculum Rockland Inst. for Psychoanalysis and Psychotherapy, 1990-95; mem. faculty Advanced Inst. Analytic Psychotherapy, 1992-95, Object Rel. Inst. Psychoanalysis and Psychotherapy, 1992—, Psychoanalytic Psychotherapy Study Ctr., 1994—, N.J. Inst. for Tng. in Psychoanalysis, 1994—. Co-editor: The Impact of Managed Care on the Practice of Psychotherapy: Innovation, Implementation, and Controversy, 1996; contbr. articles to profl. jours.; rsch. on psychotherapy, suicide and provision of preventative svcs. Nat. Jewish Welfare Bd. fellow Fordham U., 1972-74. Trainee NIMH Columbia U., 1978. Mem. NASW, N.Y. State Soc. Clin. Social Work (chair com. on psychoanalysis 1991-96, diplomate 1997), Adelphi Soc. Psychoanalysis and Psychotherapy, Am. Group Psychotherapy Assn., Inc., Ea. Group Psychotherapy Soc., Acad. Cert. Social Workers (cert.), Nat. Fedn. Soc. Clin. Social Work, Nat. Membership Com. Psychoanalysis Clin. Social Work (chair N.Y.-N.J. area 1992-94, treas. 1991-93), Alliance for Universal Access to Psychotherapy (founder, membership chair, mem. steering com. 1994-96), Nat. Study Group on Social Work and Psychoanalysis, N.J. Coalition Mental Health Profls. and Consumers (mem. adv. bd.). Office: 175 Cedar Ln Teaneck NJ 07666-4315

ALPERIN, STANLEY I., publisher, writer, editor, consultant; b. Boston, Jan. 3, 1931; s. Herman and Esther (Gorovitz) A.; m. Sondra Price, Sept. 8, 1957; children: Lisa Alperin Rose, Marlene Alperin Hochman, Hillary Baker. Pub., pres. U.S. Directory Service, Miami, Fla., 1966-91; pres. Unicol, Inc., Miami, 1991—; cons. U.S. Directory Svc., Macmillan Pub., Reed Reference Pub. Author: Careers in the Health Care Field, Careers in Nursing, U.S. Medical Directory, Directory Medical Schools Worldwide, The Hospital Phone Book, The Federal Hospital Phone Book, Insurance Phone Book & Directory, Hospital Telephone Directory, University & College Phonebook, Discover America Directory; editor, researcher numerous medical directories. Home: 8821 SW 103rd St Miami FL 33176-3053 Office: UNICOL Inc PO Box 1690 655 NW 128th St Miami FL 33168-2735

ALPERN, LINDA LEE WEVODAU, health agency administrator; b. Harrisburg, Pa., July 16, 1949; d. William Irvin Wevodau and Maretia Christine (Mills) Staley; m. Neil Stephen Alpern, Apr. 12, 1985; 1 child, Philip Wevodau. BS in Edn., Shippensburg (Pa.) U., 1971. Unit program coord. Pa. Div. Am. Cancer Soc., Harrisburg, 1973-75, unit exec. dir., 1975-76, div. svc. dir., 1976-81; div. med. affairs dir. Pa. Div. Am. Cancer Soc., Hershey, 1981-83; div. crusade dir. Md. Div. Am. Cancer Soc., Balt., 1983-87, div. v.p. for field ops., 1988, div. dep., exec. v.p. ops., 1988-95, divsn. chief oper. officer, 1995-96; sr. v.p. field ops. Mid-Atlantic divsn. Am. Cancer Soc., Balt., 1997—. Bd. dirs., sec. Cmty. Assn.; treas., v.p., pres. PTA; trustee Balt. Hebrew-Congregation Day Sch.; bd. electors Balt. Hebrew Congregation, nominating com. Democrat. Methodist. Avocations: photography, gardening, reading. Home: 4108 Colonial Rd Baltimore MD 21208-6042

ALPEROVICH, MARK, chemist; b. Moscow, Russia, May 25, 1931; arrived in Israel, 1993; s. Abram A. and Berta Kisber; m. Alexandra Burda, Dec. 18, 1955; 1 child, Irena. MS, Inst. Fine Chem., Moscow, 1953; PhD, Rsch. Photo Inst., Moscow, 1960, DS, 1981. Head organic lab. Cincma-Photo Inst., Shostka, Russia, 1953-57, dep. dir. sci., 1957-65; head dept. organic & photochem. Inst. Moscow, 1965-93; dir. comp.studyes Tech. Ctr., Grat, Israel, 1994-96; head chem. dept. C-TRI Ltd., Rehovot, Israel, 1994—. Contbr. articles to profl. jours.; inventor in field. Mem. Am. Chem. Soc. Office: C-TRI D Israel Ltd. 2 Prof Bergman Park Rabin, 76327 Rehovot Israel

ALPERT, JONATHAN EDWARD, psychiatrist, researcher; b. Bklyn.; s. Harold and Alice Lila (Goldman) A.; m. Wendy Lee, Sept. 3, 1989; 1 child, Samuel Jeremy. BA, Yale Coll., 1977; MD, Yale U., 1986; PhD, U. Cambridge, England, 1987. Diplomate Am. Bd. Psychiatry and Neurology. Intern in pediats. Childrens Hosp., Boston, 1986-87, resident in pediats., 1987-89; resident in psychiatry McLean Hosp., Belmont, Mass., 1989-92; assoc. dir. depression clinic and rsch. program Mass. Gen. Hosp., Boston, 1992—; asst. prof. Harvard Med. Sch., Boston, 1997—; med. adv. Jonathan O. Cole Mental Health Consumer Resource Ctr., Belmont, Mass., 1994—; clin. rsch., patient care, tchr. Mass. Gen. Hosp., 1992—. Contbr. articles to profl. jours. Marshall scholar Marshall Commemorative Commn., England, 1980. Mem. APA, Am. Soc. Clin. Psychopharmacology, Mass. Psychiatric Soc. Avocations: piano, reading, travel. E-mail: jalpert@partners.org. Office: Mass Gen Hosp Acc 812 15 Parkman St Boston MA 02114-3117

ALPERT, MARTIN JEFFREY, chiropractic physician; b. N.Y.C., Apr. 22, 1951; s. Sheldon Lee and Beatrice (Ostrager) A.; m. Elyse Shelly Sherman, Dec. 26, 1976, (div.); children: Chad, Mitchell, Eva. BA, Syracuse U., 1972; D Chiropractic, N.Y. Chiropractic Coll., 1976; MS, U. Bridgeport, 1979. Diplomate Am. Bd. Disability Analysts, Am. Acad. Pain Mgmt., Am. Bd. Profl. Disability Cons., Am. Acad. Experts in Traumatic Stress. Pvt. practice, Yonkers, N.Y., 1977-84, Hollywood, Fla., 1985, Coconut Creek, Fla., 1987-92, Miami, Fla., 1992-95, Ft. Lauderdale, Fla., 1985—, Orlando, Fla., 1994—. Lt. col., SC, USAR, 1970-2000. Fellow Am. Back Soc.; mem. Am. Chiropractic Assn., Internat. Chiropractors Assn., Am. Coll. Sports Medicine, Fla. Chiropractic Assn., N.Y. Acad. Scis., Am. Public Health Assn., World Fedn. Chiropractic. Democrat. Avocations: jogging, chess, basketball, piano. Home: 357 Lakeview Dr Weston FL 33326-1342 Office: Third Ave Chiropractic Ctr Inc 300 W Sunrise Blvd Ste 7 Fort Lauderdale FL 33311-6200

ALPERT, PINHAS, atmospheric scientist; b. Jerusalem, Sept. 28, 1949; s. Shimon and Sara (Weber) A.; m. Rachel Safrai, Dec. 21, 1971; eight children. BSc, Hebrew U., 1970, MSc, 1972, PhD, 1980. Forecaster Israeli Def. Forces, 1972-77; postdoctoral fellow Harvard U., Cambridge, Mass., 1980-82; full prof. Tel-Aviv U., 1983—; postdoctoral fellow U. Okla., Norman, 1983; vis. scientist NASA, Greenbelt, Md., 1986-87, sr. assoc., 1995-97, NASA/TOMS sci. team, 1998—; head NASA-Earth Observing System, Data Imfo. Systems Regional Ctr., Israel, 1998—. Mem. Am. Meteorol. Soc., Israel Meteorol. Soc. Jewish. Avocation: Bible study.

ALPERT, WARREN, oil company executive, philanthropist; b. Chelsea, Mass., Dec. 2, 1920; s. Goodman and Tena (Horowitz) A. BS, Boston U., 1942; MBA, Harvard U., 1947; DBA (hon.), Bryant Coll. Mgmt. trainee Standard Oil Co. of Calif., 1947-48; financial specialist The Calif. Oil Co., 1948-52; pres. Warren Petroleum Co., 1952-54; now chmn. bd.; founder, pres., chmn. bd. Warren Equities, Inc., from 1954; chmn. emeritus Ritz Tower Hotel, 1995—; chmn. bd. Kenyon Oil Co., Inc., Mid-Valley Petroleum Corp., Puritan Oil Co., Inc., Drake Petroleum Co., Inc.; mem. of U.S. Com. for UN, 1958; exec. com. Small Bus. Adminstrn., 1958; adminstr. for adminstrn. U.S. AID, 1962; former trustee, mem. exec. com. Boston U.; trustee Emerson Coll.; former v.p. Petroleum Mktg. Edn. Found.; bd. dirs. Assocs. of Harvard Bus. Sch., Mass. Life; mem. com. for resource and devel. Harvard Med. Sch., bd. fellows. Bd. dirs. World Coun. Synagogues; bd. overseers Albert Einstein Med. Sch.; founder Warren Alpert Found.; bd. fellows Harvard Med. Sch.; former trustee Boston U., Emerson Coll. Andrew Wellington Cordier fellow Sch. Internat. Affairs, Columbia U.; Harvard Med. Sch. Rsch. Ctr. Bldg. named in his honor, 1993. Mem. Am. Petroleum Inst. (dir. mktg. divsn.), Harvard Bus. Sch. Club (exec. com., dir., bd. govs., pres. 1960-61), Am. Petroleum Industry 25 Year Club, Young Presidents Orgn. (past dir.), Harvard Club (N.Y.C., mem. house com.), Marco Polo Club, Met. Club, University Club. Office: Warren Equities Inc 375 Park Ave Ste 2502 New York NY 10152-2595

ALPHONES, AROKIASWAMI, electronics and information science educator; b. Coimbatore, Tamil Nadu, India, May 2, 1959; s. Arokiaswami and Lourdumary A.; m. Josephine Mala, Jan. 21, 1988; 1 child, Maria Margret. BSc in Applied Scis., U. Madras, India, 1979; BTech, Anna U., India, 1982; MTech, Indian Inst. Tech., Kharagpur, 1984; PhD, Kyoto (Japan) Inst. Tech., 1992. Rsch. fellow Indian Inst. Tech., Kharagpur, 1984-87, sr. rsch. asst., 1987-88; vis. faculty mem. Anna U., Madras, 1988; asst. prof. Pondicherry (India) Engring. Coll., 1992—; vis. scholar dept. electronics and info. sci. Kyoto (Japan) Inst. Tech., 1996-98; chief investigator project planning and executing; referee papers in field. Named Rsch. fellow Mombosho, Japan, 1988-92; recipient Post Doctoral Fellowship award Japan Soc. for Promotion of Sci., 1996—. Fellow Optical Soc. India; mem. IEEE (sr., aerospace electronic systems, comm. sects. 1996),. Avocations: cricket, music, gardening. Office: Ctr Wireless Comm Nat U Sin, 20 Science Park II, Matsugasaki Singapore 117674, Singapore

ALPINI, DARIO CARLO, otolaryngologist, researcher; b. Milan, July 27, 1958; s. Falstaff Alpini and Ameda Garini; m. Maria Rosella Barone, Sept. 19, 1983; children: Alberto, Alessandro, Benedetta. MD, U. Milan, 1983, specialization in ear-nose-throat, 1986, specialization in audiology, 1989. Cons. Ear, Nose and Throat dept. Hosp. Melegnano, Milan, 1984-85; asst. in Ear, Nose and Throat dept. Hosp. Busto, Arsizio, Italy, 1985-94; head Ear, Nose and Throat-Otoneurology Svc. Sci. Inst. of Santa Maria Nascente, Milan, 1994—; clin. prof. U. Milan, 1997—; head, dept. otolaryngology Hosp. S. Rita, Milan, Italy, 1999—; cons. in multiple sclerosis, Univ. Ctr., Milan, 1987-94, Tribunal, Milan, 1987. Editor: Equilibrum Disorders: Brainstem and Cerebellar Pathologies, 1994, Whiplash Injuries, 1996; author: Rehabilitation of Vertigo and Dizziness, 1998, (handbook) Disturbi Dell'Equilibrio Nellanziano, 1997, Terapia Delle Vertiaini e del Disequicibrio, 2000. Fellow Italian Soc. of Ear, Nose and Throat Physicians; mem. Neuro-otologic Soc., Italian Acad. Neuro-otology (founder). Avocations: reading, sports. Home: Via Tallone 01, 20133 Milan Italy Office: Sci Inst St Maria Nascente, Via Capecelatro 66, 20148 Milan Italy

ALPTEKIN, CEM, linguistics and foreign language educator; b. Istanbul, June 15, 1942; s. Mehmet and Bedia (Canga) A.; m. Margaret Jean Weiler, Jan. 6, 1975. BA, Bogazici U., 1965; MA, So. Ill. U., 1975; MPhil, NYU, 1978, PhD, 1980. Instr. U. Ill., Urbana, 1979-81; coord., lectr. Ohio State U., Columbus, 1981-84; sr. lectr. Eastern Mediterranean U., Cyprus, 1984-86; prof. Bogazici U., Istanbul, 1986—, chair dept. fgn. lang. edn., 1993-96, dean sch. edn., 1993—. Contbr. articles to profl. jours. Rsch. grantee Bogazici U., 1988, 91, travel grantee Oxford U. Press, 1992, The British Coun., 1997. Mem. TESOL Internat., Internat. Assn. Tchrs. English as a Fgn. Lang. Office: Bogazici U Faculty Edn, Bebek, Istanbul 80815, Turkey

AL-QADHAFI, MUAMMAR ABU MINYAR, Libyan government official; b. Sirta, Libya, 1942; s. Mohamed Abdulsalam Abuminiar and Aisha Ben Niran; married, 1970; 4 sons, 2 daus. Student, U. Libya, Benghazi, grad. mil. acad., 1965. Chmn. Revolutionary Command Council, Libya, 1969-77; comdr. in chief Armed Forces, Libya, 1969—; leader of 1969 Revolution Libya, prime minister, 1970-72, minister of def., 1970-72, leader, 1977—; sec. gen. of Gen. Secretariat of Gen. People's Congress, 1977-79; mem. Pres. Council, Fedn. of Arab Reps., 1971—; rank of Maj. Gen., 1976, still keeping title of col. Author: The Green Book (3 vols), Military Strategy and Mobilisation, The Story of the Revolution. Served with Libyan Army, 1965—. Address: Office of Leader, care Sec Gen People's Com, Tripoli Libya*

ALQANNOOR, NASSER MUHAMMAD, linguist, educator; b. Kuwait, Shamiyah, Kuwait, Oct. 15, 1947; s. Muhammad Nasser AlQannoor and Rifa Ghareeb AlRasheedi; m. Sarah Mubarak AlQannoor; children: Amal, Huda, Muhammad, Fatimah, Omar, Aminah, Faysal. BA, Kuwait U., 1974; H.Dip., Moray House Coll., Edinburgh, Scotland, 1976; MA, U. Coll. Dublin, Ireland, 1980; PhD, U. London, 1983. English lang. tchr. Kuwait U., 1974-81, chmn. dept., 1984-86, prof., 1983—; lectr., examiner Ministry of Edn., Kuwait, 1989; cons. Arab Bur. Edn., 1992. Editor curriculum materials: English for Emirates, 1992, Our World Through English, 1992, English for Saudia Arabia, 1992; contbr. articles to profl. jours., a book. Bd. dirs. Kuwait U. Faculty Assn., 1992-94; active human rights group, 1992; mem. Group of 45 Rise for Constitution, Kuwait, 1989-90. Mem. Linguistic Soc. Am., Chronicle of Higher Edn. Avocations: camping, travel. Fax: (965) 4893388. Office: Kuwait U Dept English, PO Box 23558, 13096 Kuwait Kuwait

AL-QASIMI, SHEIKH SULTAN BIN MUHAMMAD (SHEIKH SULTAN BIN MUHAMMAD AL-QASIMI), Emir of Sharjah; b. July 6, 1939; s. Shaikh Mohammed Bin Bin Saqur Al-Qasimi; married; 6 children. BSc in Agr., Cairo U., 1971; PhD in Arabic and Islamic Studies, Exeter U., 1985, LittD, 1993; DSc, U. Agriculture, Faisalabad, Pakistan, 1983; LLD (hon.), Khartoom U., Sudan, 1986; PhD in Polit. Geography, Durham U., 1999. Tchr. Sharjah Tech. Tng. Sch.; min. of edn. Govt. of United Arab Emirates, 1960-63, 71-72; ruler of Sharjah, 1972—; mem. Supreme Ct. of Rulers, 1972—. Hon. fellow Ctr. Middle Eastern and Islamic Studies, 1992, Afro-Asian Studies Inst., Khartoum U., 1977. Mem. Arab Historian's Union, Sharjah Humanitarian Soc. Avocation: reading. Office: Rulers Office, Sharjah United Arab Emirates also: Supreme Coun Rulers, Rulers Palace, Abu Dhabi United Arab Emirates

AL-QATAM, ABDULLA ABDALI, Arabic poetry educator; b. Kuwait, Kuwait, Apr. 12, 1947; s. Abdali Ali and Maryam Hasan (Al-Mu'ayli) Al-Q.; m. Maryam Ahmad Faras; children: Muhammad, Ali, Husain, Isa, Dawud, Lamis. BA, Kuwait U., 1980; MA, UCLA, 1986; PhD, U. Utah, 1992. Tchr. Ministry of Edn., Kuwait, 1969-82; asst. rschr. Kuwait U., 1987, asst. prof. classic Arabic poetry, 1992—. Author: Writing of Arabic Names in Latin, 1995; Editor: Arabic Book ofr High Sch., 1994—; author Lexicons in Kuwait, A Critical Viewpoint, Kuwaiti short stories about Iraqi invasion, Political Poetry of Abdullah al-Faraj, 1998, Love poetry of Muhammad al-Fayiz, 1999. Mem. Middle East Studies Assn., Kuwaiti Writers Assn., Faculty of Univ. Assn. Avocations: walking, jogging. Home: Block 3 4th St No 25, 40003 Mishref Kuwait Office: Kuwait U Dept Arabic, PO Box 23558, 13096 Safat Kuwait

AL-QUBATI, YASIN ABDUL ALEEM, health association administrator; b. Al-Kabeitah, Yemen, Nov. 6, 1949; s. Abdul Aleem Mohammed Al-Qubati and Ulof Murshid Ibraheem; m. Siham Taha Al-Sakaaf (div. July 1990); children: Dalia, Saleh, Lyla; m. Iman Yasin Kaid, Nov. 22, 1990; children: Fatima, Nagib. MB, BChir, Cairo U., 1976, MSc, 1980. Dir. Malaria Control, Taiz, Yemen, 1977-78, Environ. Health & Sanitation, Taiz, 1980-82, Al-Gomhoria Hosp., Taiz, 1983-88, Nat. Leprosy Control Programme, Taiz, 1988-2000; resident dermatologist Kasr Al-Aini Hosp., Cairo, 1979-80; gen. sec. Yemen Leprosy Elimination Soc., Taiz, 1992—; part-time dir. Nat. Leprosy Control Programme, 1983-88; temporary advisor WHO Ind. Nat. Leprosy Elimination Programme Evaluation Govt. India, New Delhi, 1995, IV Mtg. Steering Com. Spl. Action Programme Elimination Leprosy, Geneva, 1996, 98, 99, Informal Consultation Monitoring Drug Supply & MDt Coverage, 1996, coordination mtg. Progress Elimination Leprosy in Region, Damascus, Syria, 1996, Leprosy Elimination Monitoring, Indonesia, 1997, Sub-Regional Workshop Elimination Leprosy Arab Countries of Gulf, Muscat, Oman, 1997, short-term cons. Nat. Leprosy Control Programme, libya, 1997; participant joint ILEP/WHO Workshop, Geneva, 1998. Author: Together for Elimination of Leprosy, 1994; contbr. articles to profl. jours. Head Com. Environ. Health & Sanitation, Taiz, 1992—; bd. dirs. Soc. Water Resources & Devel., Taiz, 1996—; bd. sec. Kat Compating, Taiz, 1998—; mem. Nasirist Polit. Party, Yemen, 1969-78. Recipient Person of Yr. Yemen Times, Sana'a, 1994, award sci. & arts Hayel Saeed Anam Soc., Taiz, 1998. Fellow Royal Soc. Tropical Medicine & Hygiene; mem. Internat. Leprosy Assn., Pan Arab League Dermatologists (bd. dirs. 1998—), Yemen Leprosy Elimination Soc. (gen. sec. 1992—), Yemen Dermatology Andrology Soc., Asian Dermatol. Assn., Internat. Soc. Dermatology (adv. coun. 1997-98), N.Y. Acad. Scis. Fax: 967-4-218113. E-mail: alkobati@yahoo.com. Home: PO Box 6330, Taiz Yemen Office: Nat Leprosy Control, PO Box 55722, Taiz Yemen

AL-RAMADI, BASEL KHALIL, microbiologist, educator; b. Jerusalem, Sept. 3, 1959; came to U.S., 1995; s. Khalil Yousef Al-Ramadi and Zakia Qassim Mo-Touk; m. Maria-Jesus Fernandez-Cabezudo; 1 child, Khalil B. Ramadi. BSc, Edinburgh (Scotland) U., 1984; PhD, Temple U., 1990. Postdoctoral assoc. Yale U., New Haven, 1990-93, assoc. rsch. scientist, 1993-97; assoc. prof. United Arab Emirates U., Al Ain, 1997—. Contbr. articles to profl. jours. Recipient Swebilius Cancer Rsch. award Yale Comprehensive Cancer Ctr., New Haven, 1994, Pilot Rsch. award Nat. Multiple Sclerosis Soc., 1996, Terry Fox Cancer Fund rsch. award, 1999. Mem. Am. Assn. Immunologists, Am. Soc. Microbiology. Avocations: international travel, reading, racketball, swimming. Office: Dept Med Microbiol PO 17666, United Arab Emirates U, Al-Ain United Arab Emirates

AL-RAMAHI, WADEE, engineering executive; b. Makkah, Saudi Arabia, Nov. 29, 1970; s. Hamzah H. and Rawdah Al-Ramahi; m. Lewa M. Al-Ramahi, Aug. 25, 1993; 1 child, Hamzah. BSc in Indsl. Engring., U. Jordan, Amman, 1988. Cert. engr. Indsl. engr. Y.M.W.A., Amman, 1993-95; bus. devel. mgr. O & K Group, Amman, 1995—; cons. Badiah Engring. Co., Amman. Mem. Inst. Indsl. Engrs., Jodanian Engring. Assn. Avocations: fishing, reading. Fax: 962-6-5412348. Home: Dabooq, PO Box 142070, Amman 11844, Jordan Office: O & K Group, Um Al-Semaq, Amman 11821, Jordan

AL-RASHEED, MUHAMMAD BIN AHMAD, federal official; b. 1944. BA in Arabic, Al-Imam Muhammad bin Saud Islamic U., 1964; MSc in Personnel Mgmt., U. Ind., 1969; PhD in Higher Edn. Mgmt., U. Okla., 1972. Tchg. asst. King Saud U., 1964-65, asst. prof., 1972-79, assoc. prof., 1979-89, assoc. dean faculty edn., 1976-79, dean, 1979-88; founder Gulf U., Bahrain, Saudi Arabia, 1979-88; min. Ministry of Edn., Riyadh, Saudi Arabia, 1995—. Office: Min Edn, PO Box 3734 Airport Rd, Riyadh 11148, Saudi Arabia*

AL-RASHEED, TURKI FAISAL, agricultural products company executive; b. Riyadh, Saudi Arabia, Aug. 5, 1954; s. Faisal and Munira Ghazi (Al Shammari) Rasheed; m. Mashael Muteb Rasheed, Dec. 29, 1979; children: Faisal, Haya, Abdullah, Meshal. B of Agrl. Engring., U. Ariz., 1978. Pres. TFIC, Riyadh, Saudi Arabia, 1980—; chmn., pres. Golden Grass Inc., Riyadh, Saudi Arabia, 1984—; deputy chmn. Horizon Travel, Riyadh, Saudi Arabia, 1990-91; pres. Al-Mahara, Riyadh, Saudi Arabia, 1990—, Hail (Saudi Arabia) Pesticide Co., 1993—, Saudi Fruit Co., Hail, 1993—; bd. dirs. NADEC, Riyadh; mem. agrl. com. Riyadh C. of C., 1990-93. Mem. Assn. Agrl. Engring. Avocations: reading, walking, travel, swimming, basketball. E-mail: tfrasheed@goldengrass.com.sa. Home and Office: Golden Grass Inc, PO Box 25306, Riyadh 11466, Saudi Arabia

AL-RASHEID, KHALED ABDULLAH, zoology educator; b. Jeddah, Saudi Arabia, Apr. 9, 1966; s. Abdullah Sulaiman Al-Rasheid and Wedad Mohammed Ali; m. Danyah Alroy, Oct. 1990; children: Gasim, Isra, Sameera, Wedad. BSc, King Saud U., Riyadh, Saudi Arabia, 1987; PhD, Southampton (U.K.) U., 1992. Tchg. asst. King Saud U., Riyadh, 1987-88, asst. prof., 1992-98, assoc. prof., 1998—; DAAD vis. prof. Bonn (Germany) U., 1996, Tubingen (Germany) U., 1999; vis. prof. Salzburg U., 1998. Author: Practical Zoology, 1996; contbr. articles to profl. jours. Mem. Soc. Protozoologists, Est. Coast Sci. Assn., Saudi Biol. Soc. Avocations: computing, swimming, drawing. E-mail: krasheid@ksu.edu.sa. Fax: 4678514. Office: King Saud U Coll Sci, PO Box 2455, Riyadh 11451, Saudi Arabia

AL-RIFAI, KHAWLA MUSTUFA, biologist, microbiologist; b. Kuwait, Aug. 13, 1963; d. Mustufa Muhmoud Al-Rifai and Faiza Ahmed Qunibi; m. Ali Ibraham Al-Omari, July 30, 1990; children: Farah, Ghassan, Ragad, Duha. BSc in Natural Sci. and Biol. Analysis, Jordan U., Amman, 1986. Environ. technologist Royal Scientific Soc., Amman, 1986-89; food microbiologist Jordanian Ministry Health, Amman, 1989-92, water microbiologist, 1992-94, environ. microbiologist, 1994-96, clin. analyst, 1996-98, head water microbiology lab., 1998—. Mem. N.Y. Acad. Sci., Jordan Soc. Biol. Sci. Avocations: painting, reading, writing. Home: Jabal Al-Hussein, PO Box 212113, PO Box 212113, Amman Jordan Office: Amman Health Directorate, Tabal Alhussein, Amman Jordan

ALRUBAIE, TALAL HAMDI, psychiatrist, psychotherapist, consultant. MBChB, Bagdhad U., Iraq, 1976; MD, Vienna U., Austria, 1986; diploma in human sexuality, London U., 1994, MSc in Human Sexuality, 1997. Specialist in psychiatry Min. Health, Vienna, 1988, Brit. GMC Specialist Register, 1997. Psychiatrist Univ. Hosp., Vienna, 1982-90, Royal Coll. Psychiatrists, London, 1990-92; psychotherapist London, 1993—; asst. prof. U. Vienna, Austria, 2000—; asst. prof. U. Vienna; rsch. coord. European Jour. Psychotherapy, Counseling and Health. Editl. bd. European Jour. Clin. Hypnosis, 1994, Changes: An Internat. Jour. of Psychology and Psychotherapy,. Austrian Acad. Sci. grantee, London, 1990. Fellow Royal

Soc. medicine; Mem. U.K. Coun. Psychotherapy (rsch. com.), Ctrl. Register Advanced Hypnotherapists, Austrian Acad. Sci., Assn. Iraqi Acads. (exec. com.). Home and Office: Schlossgasse 14/12, 1050 Vienna Austria

ALS, CLAUDINE, physician, clinician, researcher; b. Luxembourg, Luxembourg, Apr. 27, 1959; arrived in Belgium, 1979, Switzerland, 1991.; d. Georges and Françoise (Dupont) A. MD, Free U. Brussels, 1985, Specialist Nuclear Medicine, 1990, PhD, 1996. Resident Free U. Brussels, 1990-91; resident Inselspital U. Berne, Switzerland, 1991-95, clin. rschr., 1995—. Contbr. articles to profl. jours. Recipient Jubilee awrd Swiss Soc. Med. Radiology, 1995. Mem. European Assn. Nuclear Medicine, Belgian Assn. Nuclear Medicine (Van Vaerenbergh-De Visscher prize 1991), Swiss Assn. Nuclear Medicine, German Assn. Nuclear Medicine, French Assn. Nuclear Medicine, European Thyroid Assn. Avocation: amateur theatre. Office: Inselspital, Inselspital U Berne, 3010 Berne Switzerland Office: Clinique STE Therese, L-2763 Luxembourg

AL-SABAH, SHEIKH JABIR AL-AHMAD AL-JABIR, Emir of Kuwait; b. Kuwait City, Kuwait, June 29, 1926; s. His Highness Sheikh Ahmad Al-Jabir Al-Sabah; married. Student, Al-Mubarikiyyah Sch. Gov. of Ahmadi and oil areas Kuwait, 1949-59; pres. Dept. Fin. and Economy, Kuwait, 1959; minister of fin., industry and commerce Govt. of Kuwait, 1963, 65, prime minister, 1965-67; crown prince Kuwait, 1966-77; amir of Kuwait, 1978—; chmn. Supreme Def. Council, Kuwait, Supreme Petroleum Coun.; chmn. 5th session Orgn. of Islamic Conf., 1989—. Chmn. bd. dirs. Kuwait Fund for Arab Econ. Devel., Kuwait Found. for Sci. Advancement; chmn. Supreme Com. for Master Plan and Maj. Projects, Kuwait. Home: Sief Palace, Amiry Diwan Kuwait Office: care Press Attache Embassy State Kuwait 2940 Tilden St NW Washington DC 20008-1149*

AL-SABAH, MOHAMMED SABAH AL-SALIM, ambassador; b. Oct. 10, 1955; m. Shaikha Feryal D. Al-Sabah; 4 children. BA in Econs., Claremont McKenna Coll.; MA, PhD in Econs., Harvard U. Former prof. econs. Kuwait Univ.; chymn. Kuwait's Econ. Com. Higher Planning Coun., 1987—; vice chmn. Kuwait Trading, Contracting and Investment Co., 1988—; mem. higher consultative ocun. Kuwaiti Govt. in Exile, 1990-91; amb. to U.S. Kuwaiti Govt., 1993—. Founding mem. Kuwaiti-Am. Found. Office: Embassy of State of Kuwait 2940 Tilden St NW Washington DC 20008-1193

AL-SABAH, SHEIKH SAAD AL-ABDALLAH AL-SALIM, Crown Prince of Kuwait, prime minister of Kuwait; b. 1929; married. Pvt. edn., Kuwait. With police dept. Kuwait, 1945-53; trained at Met. Police Coll. Hendon, U.K., 1953-54; dep. head Kuwait Met. Police, 1954-59; dep. pres. Police and Public Security Dept., 1959-61; min. of interior, 1961-77, min. of def., 1965-77; head Ministerial Com. on Labor Problems, 1975-78; Crown Prince, 1978—, prime min. of Kuwait, 1978—. Address: Office of HH The Crown Prince, POB 4 Safat, Kuwait 13001, Kuwait also: Amiri Diwan, PO Box 799, Safat Kuwait 13008*

AL-SABAH, SHEIKH SALEM ABDUL AL-AZIZ AL-SAUD, banker; b. Kuwait, Nov. 1, 1951. BA in Econs., Am. U., Beirut, Lebanon, 1977. Econ. analyst studies sect. fgn. ops. dept. Cen. Bank Kuwait, 1977-78, head studies sect. fgn. ops. dept., 1978-80, head investment and studies sects., dep. mgr. fgn. ops. dept., 1980-84, head inspection sec., dep. mgr. banking supervision dept., 1984, mgr. banking supervision dept., 1984-85, exec. dir. banking supervision and monetary policy, 1985-86, dep. gov., 1986, gov., chmn. bd., 1986—; chmn. bd. dirs. Inst. Banking Studies, 1986—; bd. dirs. KUwait Investment Authority; mem. Supreme Planning Bd., 1987—. Office: Ctrl Bank Kuwait, PO Box 526, Abdullah al-Salem St, 13006 Safat Kuwait Kuwait*

AL-SABAH, SHAIKH SAUD NASSER, federal agency administrator, gas, oil industry executive; b. Kuwait, Oct. 3, 1944; married; 5 children. Barrister at Law, Gary's Inn, London, 1968. Lawyer legal dept. Ministry Fgn. Affairs Govt. Kuwait, Safat, 1969-75; ambassador to Sweden, Denmark, Norway Govt. of Kuwait, Safat, 1975-80, ambassador to UK, 1980-81, ambassador to U.S.A., Can., Venezuela, 1981-92, minister of info., 1992-98, min. oil, 1998—; chmn. bd. dirs. Kuwait Petroleum Corp. Office: Ministry of Oil, PO Box 5077, Safat 13051, Kuwait

AL-SAID, ANWAR GHALIB, educational administrator, education educator; b. Amman, Jordan, Apr. 6, 1954; s. Ghalib Abdul-Sami and Raesa Abdul-Moutee (Al-Khateeb) Al-Said; m. Dawlat abdel-Rahman Saleh, Dec. 24, 1989; children: Ghalib, Firas. BA, U. Jordan, Amman, 1977; MA, Calif. State U., Pomona, 1979; EdM, Columbia U., 1985, EdD, 1987. Diploma in edn., tchg. cert. Traffic officer Royal Airlines, Amman, 1977-78; elem. tchr. Glendora Sch. Dist., 1979-80; ednl. cons. Saudi Ednl. Mission, Houston, 1982-83, L.A., 1980-82; prof. edn. U. Jordan, Amman, 1988—, asst. dean, 1995-98, assoc. prof. edn.; occasional contract rschr. UNESCO regional office, Jordan, Ministry Edn., Jordan; occasional contract cons. pvt. schs., Jordan; mem. univ. coun. U. Jordan, 1995-96; asst. dir. UN U./Internat. Leadership Acad., 1998-2000. Translator into Arabic lang.: Analytical Tools for Sector Work in Education, by Alan Mingat and Jee-Peng Tan, 1996, Economics of Education, by Geraint Johnes, 2000; contbr. articles to profl. jours. Mem. adv. com. Ctr. Phonetics Rsch., Jordan, 1996; mem. Local Charity Orgn., Amman, 1990. Guest prof. grantee DAAD, Germany, 1994, doctoral study grantee King Faisal Found., Saudi Arabia, 1984, undergrad. univ. grantee Govt. Jordan, 1973. Mem. Comparative and Internat. Edn. Soc., Internat. Coun. Edn. for Tchg., Am. Univs. Alumnus Assn. Avocations: volunteer and charity works, travel, nature adventures, tennis. Home: PO Box 13338, Amman 11942, Jordan

AL-SALAMI, ALAWI SALIH, banker. Min. fin. Yemen Arab Republic, Sana'a, 1989-94, 97—; gov. Ctrl. Bank of Yemen, Sana'a, 1994-97. Office: Min of Fin, Ring Rd POB 190, Sanaa Yemen*

AL-SALEH, DAWOOD MUSAAD, Kuwaiti government official; b. Kuwait, Nov. 27, 1926; s. Musaad Al-Saleh and Shaikha Yousif Al-Easa; m. Nasima Sultan Al-Easa, Nov. 20, 1933; children: Zaher, Ziad, Zahra, Mohammad. Student, Manchester, Eng., 1952; PhD in Bus. Adminstrn., Kennedy Western U., Idaho, 1992. Chmn. dir. MS&S Contracting, Kuwait, 1968-75; chmn. MS&S Investment, Kuwait, 1975-84; chmn., mayor Kuwait Municipality, 1984-86; chmn. Coun. Governorate, Hawalli, 1988-990; gov. State of Kuwait, Hawalli, 1991-94, 95-99, 2000—; v.p., founder Constrn. Mat. Ind, Oman, 1980-87, Union Bank, Oman, 1980-86; dir. Gulf Bank, Kuwait, 1970-84, exec. dir., 1982-84; founder, part-owner Al Watan Newspaper, 1974. Author: Administration in Kuwait, 1955; translator (Al Gore) The Best Kept Sectrets in Government, 1997; contbr. papers to profl. publs. Head Kuwait Peace Del., 1990. Mem. Kuwait Grad. Club (sec. 1958), Gazal Club, The Oxford Club. Avocations: traveling, walking, reading. Office: PO Box 28483, 13145 Safat 13145, Kuwait

AL-SALIH, ALI SALIH ABDALLAH, Bahrain minister of commerce; b. Dec. 28, 1942; married; 3 children. B Com., Ain Shams U., Cairo, 1966. Min. commerce Govt. of Bahrain, 1995—; chmn. Bahrain Stock Exch., Bahrain Promotion and Mktg. Bd., Bahrain Internat. Exhbn. Ctr. Bd., Stds. and Metrology Com. Trustee Bahrain Ctr. Studies and Rsch. Office: Ministry of Commerce, PO Box 5479 Diplomatic Area, Manama Bahrain*

AL-SALIH, MOHAMMED MALDI, minister of trade; b. Rawah, al Anbar, Iraq, 1947. Grad., Baghdad U. Sch. of Edn., 1968; MA in Econs., Manchester U., Eng., 1976, PhD in Regional Planning, 1978. Tchr. Iraq Schs., 1968-73; officer ministry of planning Govt. of Iraq, Baghdad, 1978-80, chief regional planning sect. ministry of planning, 1980; gen. dir. Republican Pres. Economic Office, Baghdad, 1981-83; chief econ. sect. Presdl. cabinet Govt. of Iraq, Baghdad, 1983; dep. chief Presdl. cabinet for econs., agrl., fin., indsl. offices Govt. of Iraq, Baghdad, 1985-87; minister of trade Govt. of Iraq, Baghdad, 1987—. Office: Ministry of Trade, Reinsurance Co Bldg, Jamhuriyah St, Khullani Sq, Baghdad Iraq*

AL-SALLOUM, NASER BIN MOHAMMAD, federal official; b. 1938. BSc in Civil Engring., Cairo U., 1964; MSc in Civil Engring., U. Ariz., 1968, PhD in Civil Engring., 1973. Engr. Ministry of Comm., Riyadh, Saudi Arabia, 1964; dir. rsch. dept., asst. dir. gen. tech. dept. Ministry of Comm., Riyadh, dir. gen. projects dept., 1973, asst. dep. min. tech. affairs, 1974, dep. min., 1976, min., 1995—. Office: Ministry Comm Transp, Airport Rd, Riyadh 11178, Saudi Arabia

AL-SALMAN, MUSSAAD MOHAMMED SALEH, medical educator, surgeon; b. Oniza, Saudi Arabia, Jan. 11, 1959; s. Mohammed Saleh and Rokia (Humidan) Al-S.; m. Fatima Abdullah Al-Agla, Sept. 23, 1985; children: Yara, Madouie, Shadin, Fahad. MB BS, KSU Sch. of Medicine, 1981. Demonstrator King Saud U., Saudi Arabia, 1982-84, chief resident, 1988—, asst. prof., 1992-96, assoc. prof., 1996-2000; vascular fellow U. B.C., 1989-91; prof. King Saud U., 2000—; cons. KFNGH, Riyadh, 1993-95, Al Habib Med. Ctr., Riyadh, 1995—, King Saud U., 1993—. Contbr. articles to profl. jours. Fellow Royal Coll. of Can., Am. Coll. of Angiology, Internat. Coll. of Surgeons; mem. Internat. Soc. of Cardio Vascular Surgery (S.A. agt.). Avocations: walking, swimming. Home: PO Box 59199, Riyadh 11525, Saudi Arabia Office: King Khalid U Hosp, PO Box 7805, Riyadh 11472, Saudi Arabia

AL-SAMAWI, AHMED ABDULRAHMAN, government official; b. Otomah, Dhamar, Yemen, June 12, 1946; s. Abduirahman Ali and Asma Mohammed Al-Samawi; m. Amal Mohammed Al-Zabadi, Aug. 23, 1973; children: Najla, Hoda, Mohammed, Mona, Faris. Hons. degree in Econs., Alex U., Egypt, 1968; postgrad. diploma, U. Kuwait, 1970, U. Manchester, Eng., 1976. Asst. gen. dir. Ministry of Economy, Sanaa, Yemen, 1968-70, dir. gen., 1970-72; chmn. Ctrl. Budget Bur., Sanaa, 1972-75; dep. fin. min. Sanaa, 1975-78, min. fin., 1978-80; dir. Prime Min. Office, Sanaa, 1980-83; exec. dir. Arab Monetary Fund, Abu Dhabi, United Arab Emirates, 1983-85; chmn. Yemen Bank, Sanaa, 1985-91; adviser Presidency, Sanaa, 1991-97; gov. Ctrl. Bank of Yemen, 1997—. Author: Foreign Aid for Economic and Social Development in Yemen, 1970, Journey to Al-Anualus (Spain), 1980, Journey to Istanbul (Turkey), 1988, Journey to Bali (Indonesia), 1989. Mem. Supreme Election Com., Yemen, 1992-93; mem. People's Gen. Congress, Yemen, 1982—; bd. dirs. UBAF, Paris, 1985-91; gov. Arab Monetary Fund, Abu Dhabi, United Arab Emirates, 1974-80. Avocation: chess. Office: Ctrl Bank of Yemen, PO Box 59, Sana'a Yemen

ALSANIE, SALEH IBRAHIM, psychology educator; b. Buraidah, Qassim, Saudi Arabia, Jan. 11, 1959; s. Ibrahim Abdullatif Alsanie and Latifah Sulaiman Alnasir; m. Shikha Ibrahim Alsaif; children: Faisal Saleh, Ahmad Saleh, Atheer Saleh. BA, King Saud U., Riyadh, 1982; MA, Ind. U., 1985; PhD, Imam U., Riyadh, 1989, Cert., 1994, 96; Cert., Saudi Psychol./Ednl. Assn., Riyadh, 1994. Elem. tchr. Ministry of Edn., Riyadh, 1977-79; prin. Nat. Guard Dept. Edn., Riyadh, 1979-82; asst. instr. King Saud U., Riyadh, 1982-85; lectr. Imam U., Riyadh, 1985-89, asst. prof., 1990-94, assoc. prof., 1994—; vice dean Deanry of Acad. Counseling, Riyadh, 1994-96; cons. Badr Pvt. Schs., Riyadh, 1991-94. Author: Religiousity as a Therapy for Crime, 1993, Studies on Islamization of Psychology, 1995, Religiousity and Psychological Health, 2000; author rsch. papers in field. Mem. Am. Psychol. Assn., World Fedn. for Mental Health, Saudi Psychol. and Ednl. Assn. (exec. com. 1992-94, sec. exec. com. 1998—). Avocations: swimming, reading, social activities. Home: PO Box 86161, 11622 Riyadh Saudi Arabia Office: Immam U Coll Social Scis, Psychology Dept, Riyadh Saudi Arabia

AL-SAQAT, TARIK MOHAMMAD ARABI, infectious diseases physician; b. Makkah, Saudi Arabia, Jan. 20, 1961; s. Mohammad Arabi Al-Saqat and Aydah Mohammad Abdulzaher; m. Amal Salah Abduljabbar; children: Reem, Mohammad, Maram, Husam. B Medicine B Surgery, King Saud U., Rihadh, Saudi Arabia, 1983; MS, Liverpool Sch. Tropical Med., U.K., 1988. Diplomate Arab Bd. Internal Medicine. Physician King Khalid U. Hosp., Riyadh, 1982-84; physician Security Forces Hosp. Program, Riyadh, 1984—, chmn. mil. med. com., 1995-99, dir. edn. and tng. affairs, 1999—, vice chmn. infection control com. Recipient Prince Naif award for med. security Ministry of Interior, Saudi Arabia, 1992. Mem. Am. Soc. Tropical Medicine and Hygiene, Infectious Disease Soc. Am., Am. Microbiology Soc. Avocations: table tennis, snooker. Home: Po Box 26372, Riyadh 11481, Saudi Arabia Office: Security Forces Hosp Prog, Sitteen St PO Box 3643, Riyadh 11481, Saudi Arabia

AL-SAUD, PRINCE ABDALLAH BIN ABD AL-AZIZ, Saudi Arabian government official; b. Riyadh, 1924; s. King Abdul-Aziz ibn Saud. Dep. min. defense Govt. of Saudi Arabia, Riyadh, 1962-63, second dep. prime min., 1975, dep. prime min., 1982—; comdr. Nat. Guard, Riyadh, Saudi Arabia, 1963—, head, 1982—; mem. Saudi dels. to Arab and Islamic Summit Confs., state visits and UN Gen. Assembly sessions; chmn. Supreme Com. for Adminstrv. Reform; v.p. Supreme Council Higher Edn. Office: Dep Prime Min, Royal Court, Riyadh Saudi Arabia*

ALSAUD, ALWALEED BIN TALAL BIN ABDULAZIZ, investment company executive; married; 2 children. Grad., Menlo Coll.; postgrad., Syracuse U. Avocations: exercise, reading. Office: Kingdom Holding Co, PO Box 2, Riyadh 11321, Saudi Arabia

AL-SAUD, FAHD BIN ABD AL-AZIZ, King of Saudi Arabia; b. Riyadh, 1923; s. King Abdul Aziz ibn Saud. Min. edn., 1953, min. interior, 1962-75, 2d dep. prime min., 1967-75, 1st dep. prime min., 1975-82, prime min., 1982—, crown prince, 1975, king of Saudi Arabia, 1982—, assumed title Custodian of the Two Holy Mosques, 1986. Office: Royal Court, Riyadh 11111, Saudi Arabia*

AL-SAUD, PRINCE NAYIF BIN ABDUL-AZIZ AL BIN ABDULRAHMAN, Saudi Arabian minister of interior; b. Taif, Saudi Arabia, 1934; s. King Abdul-Aziz; married; 10 children. Pvt. studies in religious sci.; hon. doctorate politics, China; hon. doctorate in law, South Korea. Former dep. Riyadh, Saudi Arabia; Amir Riyadh, 1954—; vice min. interior Saudia Arabia, from 1974, min. state internal affairs, from 1975, min. interior, 1975—; hon. chmn. Coun. Arab Mins. Interior; chmn. bd. Arab Ctr. Security Studies and Tng., Manpower Coun., High Commn. Info., High Commn. Civil Def.; pres. High Commn. Civil Def.; Hajj High Commn.; v.p. Nat. Commn. Wildlife Conservation and Devel.; mem. High Coun. Youth Welfare. Recipient King Abdulaziz sash, Blessed Clouds sash, Legion of Honor, France, Planet medal, Jordan, Great Reliever medal, Venezuela, Pub. Safety medal, South Korea, Lebanese Cedar medal. Office: Ministry of Interior, PO Box 2933 Airport Rd, 11134 Riyadh Saudi Arabia*

AL-SAUD, PRINCE SAUD AL-FAYSAL BIN ABD AL-AZIZ, Saudi Arabian government official; b. Riyadh, Saudi Arabia, 1941; s. King Faisal. BA in Econs., Princeton U. Former dep. min. petroleum and mineral resources Govt. of Saudi Arabia, 1971-74, min. state for fgn. affairs, 1975, min. fgn. affairs, 1975—; leader Saudi del. to UN Gen. Assembly, 1976; spl. envoy diplomatic efforts to resolve Algerian-Moroccan conflict over Western Sahara, and civil war in Lebanon; mem. Saudi del. to Arab restricted summit, Riyadh, 1976, also to Summit Conf., Arab League, 1976. Founding mem. King Faisal's Internat. Charity Soc. Avocation: reading. Office: Min Fgn Affairs PO Box 495, Nasseriya St, Riyadh 11124, Saudi Arabia*

AL SAUD, PRINCE SULTAN IBN ABDULAZIZ, Saudi Arabian government official; b. Riyadh, Saudi Arabia, 1928; s. King Abdulaziz. Student, Royal Ct. Gov. City of Riyadh, Saudi Arabia; min. agr. Govt. of Saudi Arabia, 1953, min. transp., min. def. and aviation, insp. gen., 1963, second dep. prime min., min. def. and civil aviation, insp. gen., 1982—; mem. Saudi del. to Arab and Islamic Summit Confs., state visits and UN Gen. Assembly; chmn. of supreme Com. for Adminstrv. Reform; v.p. Supreme Coun. of Edn. Policy. Decorated Orders of Merit. Office: Ministry Def and Aviation, PO Box 26731 Airport Rd, Riyadh 11165, Saudi Arabia*

AL-SAWAHRI, KHALIL HUSSEIN, writer, publishing executive; b. Jerusalem, 1940; s. Hussein Sawahri; married; 5 children. BA in Philosophy and Sociology, Damascus U., 1965. Gen. mgr. Dar al-Karmel Pub. and Distributing. Author numerous books, including 5 short story books. Recipient Palestinian Short Story award, Irani Short Story award, Jordan, Short Story award Arab Ednl., Cultural and Sci. Orgn., 1977. Mem. Jordanian Writers Soc. (chmn. 1984-85), Palestinian Writers Union (sec. gen. 1969-70). Office: Dar al-Karmel Pub/Distrib, PO Box 17067, Amman Jordan

AL-SAWWAF, MONQIDH MOHAMMED, surgeon; b. Baghdad, Iraq, 1950; s. Mohammed Mahmmod and Noria (Najmaldeen) Al-S. Student, Pahlavi U. Coll. of Medicine, Shiraz, Iran, 1967-70, MD, 1976. Diplomate Am. Bd. Surgery, Am. Bd. Surg. Critical Care. Resident Harlem Hosp., N.Y.C., 1976-81, fellow, 1981-83, asst. attending physician, 1983-86, assoc. attending physician, 1986-88, attending physician, 1988—, co-chief surgey ICU, 1987-89, chief surgey ICU, 1989—; instr. surgery Columbia U., N.Y.C., 1983—, asst. clin. prof., 1989—; researcher in clin. critical care Harlem Hosp., N.Y.C., Columbia U., N.Y.C., 1983—; lectr. in critical care. Contbr. articles to profl. jours. V.p. United Drs. Assn., 1990—. Mem. Am. Soc. Gastrointestinal Endoscopy, Internat. Coll. Surgeons, Soc. Critical Care Medicine. Office: Harlem Hosp Dept Surgery 506 Lenox Ave Dept Surgery New York NY 10037-1889

AL-SAYYARI, HAMAD SAUD, Saudi Arabian government official; b. Dhurma, Saudi Arabia. MA in Econs., U. Md., U.S., 1971. Sec. gen. Pub. Investment Fund, Riyadh, Saudi Arabia, 1973-74; dir. gen. Saudi Indsl. Devel. Fund, Riyadh, 1977-79; vice gov. Saudi Arabian Monetary Agy., Riyadh, 1980-83, gov., 1983—; bd. dirs. Pub. Investment Fund, Pension Fund, Petramin, Riyadh. Office: Saudi Arabian Monetary Agy, PO Box 2992, Mather St, Riyadh 11169, Saudi Arabia*

AL-SHAALI, MOHAMMAD BIN HUSSEIN, diplomat; b. Ajman, 1950; married; 4 children. B.Commerce, Adminstrn. and Economy, Beirut U., Lebanon, 1974. With Dept. Polit. Affairs Diplomatic and Consular Svc., Abu Dhabi, UAE, 1974-77; chargé d'affaires Vienna, 1977-78, Tunis, 1978; former acting dir. Dept. Polit. Affairs; former chief Arab and Gulf Affairs Divsn.; former acting dir. Dept. Adminstrn. and Fin.; dir. Arab world dept. Ministry of Fgn. Affairs, Abu Dhabi, 1982-85; permanent rep. UN, 1985-92, pres. Security Coun., 1986; del. spl. sessions Gen. Assembly UN, N.Y.C., 1978, 80, 82; dep. chair delegation UN, 1984, head delegation Gulf Cooperation Coun.; now United Arab Emirates amb. to U.S. Washington; ret., 1999—. Office: Embassy of United Arab Emirates 1255 22d St NW Ste 7000 Washington DC 20037-1217

AL-SHABANAH, OTHMAN ABDULLAH, pharmacologist, educator; b. Al-Majma, Saudi Arabia, July 10, 1952; s. Abdullah and Minerah (Twejeria) A.-S. BS in Pharmacy, King Saud U., 1976; MS, U. Pacific, 1981, PhD, 1988. Asst. prof. King Saud U., Saudi Arabia, 1989-93, assoc. prof., 1993-98, chmn. dept. pharmacology, 1998—, prof., 1999—; mem. drug registration adv. com. Ministry of Health, Saudi Arabia, 1991-96. Grantee Rsch. Ctr. Coll. Pharmacy King Saud U., 1993; recipient J. William Fulbright award, 1996. Mem. Am. Soc. Pharmacology and Exptl. Therapeutics, Am. Assn. Pharm. Scientists, Am. Pharm. Assn., Am. Assn. Coll. Pharmacy, Saudi Pharm. Soc. (bd. dirs. 1992—, chmn. scientific rsch. and continuing edn. com. 1992—). Home: PO Box 50721, Riyadh 11533, Saudi Arabia

AL-SHAIKH, ABDALLAH MUHAMMAD IBRAHIM AL, Saudi Arabian government official; b. 1949. BA, Shari'ah Coll., Imam Mohammed bin Saud U., Saudi Arabia, 1975; MA, Al-Azhar U., Cairo, 1980; PhD, Imam Mohammed bin Saud U., 1987. Tchg. asst. Imam Mohammed bin Saud U., Saudi Arabia, 1975, asst. prof., 1988; min. of justice Govt. of Saudi Arabia, Riyadh, 1992—. Office: Ministry of Justice, University Street Main Ministry, Riyadh 11137, Saudi Arabia*

AL-SHARA, FAROUK, Syrian government official; b. Daraa, Syria, Jan. 17, 1938; s. Hussein and Farha (Hariri) Al-Shara; m. Amal Marouf, Sept. 29, 1964; children: Mudar, Nuwaar. B.A. in English Lit., Damascus U., 1963; student internat. law, U. London, 1971-72. Regional mgr. Syria Air, London, 1968-72; comml. dir. Syria Air, Damascus, 1972-76; Syrian ambassador to Italy Rome, 1976-80; min. of state for fgn. affairs Govt. of Syria, Damascus, 1980-84, fgn. min., 1984—. Mem. cen. com. Baath Arab Socialist Com., Damascus, 1985. Avocations: reading, art, literature, chess. Office: Ministry Fgn Affairs, Shora Ave, Damascus Syria*

ALSHARIF, ADNAN A., geologist; b. Gaza, Saudi Arabia, Oct. 27, 1949; s. Abdulraouf Y. and Kawther Y. (Alami) A.; m. Diala S. Shawwa, Aug. 21, 1980; children: Raouf, Dana, Rami. BS, Am. Univ. of Beirut, 1973, MS, 1975. Adminstr. Exploration, Dhahrand, Saudi Arabia, 1986-89, chief hydrologist, 1989-97, chief geologist, 1997—. Mem. Nat. Groundwater Assn., Nat. Geographic Soc., Soc. Petroleum Engring. E-mail: sharifaa@aramco.com.sa. Office: Saudi Aramco, Box 842, Dhahran 31311, Saudi Arabia

AL SHAYE, MOHAMED A., engineering executive; b. Al Zulfi, Saudi Arabia, June 21, 1944; s. Ali S. Alshaye and Muhrah A. Yahya; m. Muneerah A. Al Duhaim; children: Muhra, Nora, Asma, Abeer, Ali, Abdul Rahman, Abdullah. BSCE, BA in Math., St. Martin's Coll., Olympia, Wash., 1971. Personnel officer Royal Saudi COE, Khamis Mushayt, Saudi Arabia, 1971-73; constrn. supr. U.S. Army COE, Livorno, Italy, 1973-74; liaison officer Mil. Works, Jeddah, Saudi Arabia, 1974-75; chief project mmgt. Mil. Works, Riyadh, Saudi Arabia, 1975-84; dir. ops. and maintenance, maj.-gen. King AbdulAziz Mil. City, Tabuk, Saudi Arabia, 1984-97; maj. gen. Corps of Engrs. Hdqs., 1997—. Reception The Perfection medal His Royal Highness The Min. of Def. and Aviation, Tabuk, 1996. Achievements include the creation of a manmade lake for treated sewage water, introducing sea life as a recreational site. Avocations: reading, travel, sports. Address: PO Box 9006, Riyadh Saudi Arabia Office: Dir Operation & Maintenance, Cmdr Royal Saudi Corps Engr, King AbdulAziz Mil City, Tabuk Saudi Arabia

AL-SHAZLY, KAMAL (MOHAMMED) EL-, Egyptian government official; b. Monoufia, Egypt, Feb. 16, 1934; married; 4 children. BA in Law, Cairo U., 1957. Mem. NAt. Assembly al-Bagour, 1969, 71, People's Assembly, 1979; organizing sec. gen. NDP, 1981; min. Ministry State People's Assembly and Shura Coun. Affairs, 1993—. Office: Office of Prime Min, Sharia Magles al-Sha'ab, Cairo Egypt*

ALSHEHABI, ALI SALEH, contractor; b. Bahrain, Bahrain, Nov. 27, 1948; s. Saleh Ali and Takeyyah A. Shaheed Alshehabi; m. Badreyya Abdulla Abdul Latif, 1963; children: Amal, Hussain, Fatheyya, Jaffar. BSc, Somerset (Eng.) U., 1982, DSc, 1984. Cert. in engring. and mgmt. Supr. Oil Co., Bahrain, 1967-71; lectr. Tech. Inst., Bahrain, 1971-75; mng. dir. Contn. Co., Bahrain, 1975-92, Sayhat, Saudi Arabia, 1992—. Fellow Inst. D, IMgt., IIM, IEM, AMA; mem. IRTE, IMI, ASE, BASE. Avocation: reading. Office: Moa'azir Cont Est, PO Box 846, 31972 Sayhat Saudi Arabia

AL-SHEHRY, GARAMAH-YAHYA, surgeon, consultant, health facility administrator; b. Taif, Makka, Saudi Arabia, July 1, 1960; s. Yahya Gharamah and Fatma Ali Al-shehry; m. Hend Yahya Al-shehry, June 1, 1989; children: Motasem, Asem, Mohammad, Mariam, Tomader. Degree, King Abdelaziz U., Jeddah, Saudi Arabia, 1986; degree in surgery, 1996. Specialist RMC, Riyadh, Saudi Arabia, 1992-93; cons., chief or surgery Bisha (Saudi Ababia) Hosp., 1993-96, med. dir., 1996-97, med. asst. to gen. supr., 1996-97; med. dir. Assir Ctrl. Hosp., Abha, Saudi Arabia, 1999—; cons. Assir Ctrl. Hosp., 1997-99; assoc. lectr. King Khalid U., Abha, 1995—; rep. nat. program for cancer registry, external examiner Med. Abha Coll., 1998—. Contbr. articles to profl. jours. Dep. commdr. Nat. Guard, 1996. Mem. Assir Jour. Club (chief 1997—). Avocations: poetry, tourism, sports, reading. E-mail: fouadkarami@hotmail.com.

ALSHUAIB, WALEED BAKER, neurobiology educator, researcher; b. Kuwait, Jan. 1, 1958; s. Baker Yaqoob and Meriam (Mohamed) A.; m. Jessica Amal Maksaereekul, Jan. 28, 1981; children: Yousif, Eesa. BS in Biomedical Engring., U. So. Calif., 1981, MS in Edn. Adminstrn., 1982, MS in Biomedical Engring., 1985, PhD in Neurobiology, 1990. Biomedical engr. Ministry Pub. Health, Kuwait, 1982-83; rsch. assoc. U. So. Calif., L.A., 1985-90, postdoctoral, 1991-92; prof. Kuwait U., Safat, 1992—; cons. Mubarak Hosp., Kuwait, 1992—; dir. Kuwait Animal Resources Ctr., 1999—. Contbr. articles to profl. jours. Rsch. grantee Kuwait U., 1996, 99. Mem. Soc. Neuroscience, Internat. Brain Rsch. Orgn. Muslim. Avocations: swimming, golf, soccer, camping, fishing. Home: PO Box 65032, 25551 Rumathia Kuwait Office: Kuwait U., Dept Physiology, PO Box 24923, 13110 Safat Kuwait

AL-SHU'ALA, ABDUL NABI ABDULLA, Bahraini government official; b. Manama, Bahrain, May 15, 1948; married; 3 children. BA in Politics and Pub. Adminstrn. Businessman, 1974—; mem. Shura (consultative) Coun., mem. exec. com. State of Bahrain; min. labor and social affairs Govt. of Bahrain, Isatown, 1995—. Mem. Bahrain C. of C. and Industry (mem. bd. 1982-85). Office: Ministry Labor & Social, POB 32333, Isa Town Bahrain*

ALSIP, CHERYL ANN, owner, manager business services company; b. Jersey City, Aug. 1, 1957; d. Clarence and Louise Rose (Grier) L.; m. Manuel Edward Alsip, May 23, 1992 (dec. Oct., 1992); 1 child, Jeremy Tyler. Student, Bergen C.C., Paramus, N.J., 1979-82, Broward C.C., Coconut Creek, Fla., 1983-84; AS in Electronic Engring., NEC-Bauder, Ft. Lauderdale, Fla., 1988; AS in Acctg., Internat. Corr. Sch., Scranton, Pa., 1997. Various clerical positions N.Y.C. and N.J., 1979-81; pers. mgr. Universal Merchandising, Inc., Clifton, N.J., 1981-82; store mgr. Travelers Transp. Inc. doing business as The Gift Shop, Deerfield Beach, Fla., 1983; gen. mgr. Travelers Transp. Inc. doing business as Budget Rent-A-Car, Pompano Beach, Fla., 1982-84; various office and technical positions Fla., 1985-91; ind. contractor Mary Kay, Pompano Beach, Fla., 1991-92; customer svc. rep. Taleigh, Inc., Boca Raton, Fla., 1992; tech. writer, technician various Fla. Cos., 1992-93; owner, operator CALA Distinctive Enterprises, Salcha, Alaska, 1992-99; prin. Bus. Svcs., Alaska, 1999-2000. Commr. Boy Scouts of Am., 1992—; mem. Comty. Emergency Response Team, Pompano Beach, Fla., 1997-98—; vol. Aux. Police Dept., Pompano Beach, 1997-98; mem. CAP, 1996— With U.S. Army, 1975-78. Mem. Internat. Soc. Cert. Electronic Technicians, Navy League of the U.S. Republican. Roman Catholic. Avocations: camping, handcrafts, reading. Home and Office: PO Box 140097 Salcha AK 99714-0097

AL-SMADI, SAMI AHMAD, marketing professional, educator; b. Amman, Jordan, Jan. 2, 1959; s. Ahmad Mohammad and Ameneh Mohammad Al-Smadi; m. Asma Khalaf, 1986; children: Baker, Ahmad, Moath, Roqia. BA, Yarmouk U., 1985; MBA, Strathclyde U., 1988; PhD, Heriot-Watt U., 1992. Tchg. asst. Yarmouk U., Jordan, 1985-87, asst. prof., 1992—; rschr., cons., trainer, 1992—. Squash referee. Mem. Squash Fedn. Avocation: squash. Home and Office: Mktg Dept, Yarmouk Univ, Irbid Jordan

AL-SOHAIBANI, MOHAMMED OMAR, pathology educator; b. Al-Kharj, Riyadh, Saudi Arabia, Sept. 9, 1949; s. Omar Mohammad Al-Sohaibani; m. Munira Nassar Al-Sohaibani; children: Omar, Zakaria, Maaz, Assem, Rayed, Aisha, Noora, Nassar, Abdullah. MB BChir, U. Riyadh, 1976. Diplomate Am. Bd. Pathology. Intern Riyadh, 1976-77; fellow dept. pathology Ottawa (Can.) U., 1979-80; resident in pathology McGill U., 1980-84; chmn. pathology dept. King Khalid U. Hosp., Riyadh, 1993—; head histopathology King Khalid U. Hosp. and KAUH, Riyadh, 1993—; bd. dirs. Coll. Medicine, dir. postgrad. studies pathology KSU, Riyadh, 1993—, dir. univ. med. labs., acad. supr. Coll. Medicine, 1995—; cons. pathologist King Khalid U. Hosp., Riyadh, 1991—; part-time cons. histopathologist KFNGH, Riyadh, 1993-95, Alhammadi Hosp., Riyadh, 1995—; cons. histopathologist KFUH, Alkhobar, Saudi Arabia, 1984-91. Contbr. articles to profl. jours. Fellow Royal Coll. Pathologists. Office: King Khalid U Hosp, Dept Pathology PO Box 2925, 11461 Riyadh Saudi Arabia

ALSOP, MAUREEN AURORA SEAN, psychologist; b. Pontiac, Mich., Oct. 12, 1969; arrived in Australia, 1996; d. Robert Eugene and Barbara Ann (Boyle) Mehoke; m. Steven Thomas Alsop, Oct. 31, 1996. BA in Psychology and English, Mich. State U., 1991; MS, Radford U., 1993, Ednl. Splst., 1994; postgrad., James Cook U., Townsville, Australia, 1998—. Resident asst. Mich. State U., E. Lansing, 1990-91; counselor Radford (Va.) U., 1991-93; sch. psychologist N.C. Pub. Schs., Charlotte, 1993-96; mgr., psychologist Supported Options in Lifestyle Acces Svc., Townsville, Queensland, 1996-97; cmty. liaison officer, coord. mental health program No. Queensland Rural Divsn. Gen. Practice, Townsville, 1997-99; rsch. fellow Australian Inst. Suicide Rsch. and Prevention Griffith U., Brisbane, Queensland, 1999—. Contbr. article to profl. jour. Mem. Australian Psychol. Soc., Nat. Assn. Sch. Psychology, Am. Assn. Sociology. Avocations: painting, writing, hiking, poetry, swimming. Home: 1/19 Alexandra St, Townsville QLD, Australia 4810

ALSTON, PHILIP, international law educator; b. Melbourne, Australia, Jan. 23, 1950; s. Robert Bruce and Sheila Gertrude (MacKenzie) A.; m. Helen Brien, May 6, 1978; children: Sylvie Leila, Theresa Helen. LLB with honors, U. Melbourne, 1972, B in Comm., 1976, LLM, 1976; JSD, U. Calif., Berkely, 1980. Prin., pvt. sec. Min. for Capital Terr., Australia, 1974-75; legal officer UN, Geneva, 1978-84; assoc. prof. Fletcher Sch. of Law and Diplomacy, Boston, 1984-89; lectr. Harvard Law Sch., Boston, 1984-89; prof. Australian Nat. U., Canberra, Australia, 1989-95; prof. internat. law, head law dept. European U. Inst., Florence, 1996—; vis. prof. Harvard Law Sch., Boston, 1993, U. Mich. Law Sch., Ann Arbor, 1993; vis. prof. global law program NYU, 1998—; dep. dean A.N.U. Law Sch., 1994-95; human rights commr. Australian Capital Terr., 1992-94; cons. Min. for Fgn. Affairs, Canberra, 1994-95. Editor: The United Nations and Human Rights, 1992, 2d edit., 2000, The Best Interests of the Child, 1994, Towards an Australian Bill of Rights, 1994, Promoting Human Rights Through Bills of Rights, 1999, International Human Rights in Context, 1996, 2d edit., 2000, The EU and Human Rights, 1999; editor-in-chief European Jour. Internat. Law, 1996—. Chairperson com. on econ. and social rights UN, Geneva, 1991-98. Office: European Univ Inst, CP No 2330, 50100 Florence Italy

ALSTON, RICHARD, administrator; b. Perth, Australia, Dec. 19, 1941; married; 2 children. B of Laws, U. Melbourne, Australia, 1964, BA, 1968; M of Law, Monash U., Australia, 1983, MBA, 1989. Apptd. Australian Senate, 1986; shadow min. Dept. Comm., Australia, 1989-90, 93-96, Dept. Social Security, Child Care & Retirement Invomes, Australia, 1990-92, Dept. Superannuation & Child Care, Australia, 1992-93; deputy leader of Govt. Australian Senate, 1997—; min. Dept. Comm., 1997—. Office: Dept Comm, Parliament House Ste MF 70, Canberra ACT 2600, Australia*

ALSTRØM, PREBEN, physicist, researcher; b. Frederiksberg, Denmark, Jan. 17, 1957; s. Tage Alex and Anna Louise (Pedersen) A.; m. Marianne Ingeborg Skov, July 4, 1987; children: Jette, Lena. PhD, U. Copenhagen, 1986. Nordita fellow Copenhagen, 1985-87; rsch. assoc. Boston U., 1987-89; rsch. asst. prof. U. Copenhagen, 1989-92, rsch. assoc. prof., 1992-98; dir. CORE A/S, Copenhagen, 1999—; adj. prof., U. Copenhagen, 1999—; rsch. cons. Cobrain, Copenhagen, 1995—. Adv. editor Physica A, 1995—; contbr. more than 80 articles to profl. jours.; inventor/patentee adaptive performance networks. Fulbright fellow, 1987-89, Carlsberg fellow, 1987-89. Office: Niels Bohr Inst, Blegdamsvej 17, DK-2100 Copenhagen Denmark

AL-SUDAIRY, ZIAD A., government official, lawyer; m. Monera K., 1974; children: Tariq, Jawaher, Sara, Abdulrahman, Khalid. BA with hon. and distinction, U. Az.; JD, U. Va., 1980. Legal adv. Ministry of Interior, Saudi Arabia, 1981-83; ptnr. Al-Sudaiary & Fahad Law Office, Riyadh, 1983-88; mem. cons. assembly Meglis Shoura Coun., 1993—; ptnr./pres. Badrahn Enterprises, Riyadh; chmn. United Gulf Group Co., Ltd.; bd. dirs. Al-Rajhi Banking & Investment Corp. Bd. dirs. Sultan Bin Abdulaziz Charity Found.; mgn. dir. Abdulrahman Alsudairy Found. Office: Badrahn Enterprises, PO Box 10071, Riyadh 11433, Saudia Arabia

AL-SULTAN, FAWZI HAMAD, United Nations official; b. Kuwait, 1944; married; 3 children. BA, Am. U. of Beirut, Lebanon, 1966; MA, Yale U., 1970. With Kuwait Fund for Arab Econ. Devel., 1966-77; mng. dir. Bank of Kuwait and Mid. East, 1971-81; chmn. Interant. Fin. Advisors KSC, Safat, Kuwait, 1981-84; exec. dir. World Bank, Washington, 1984-93; pres., chmn. exec. bd. Internat. Fund for Agrl. Devel., Rome, 1993—; bd. dirs. United Bank of Kuwait and Ifabanque S.A., Paris. Mem. Kuwait Economists Soc. Office: Internat Fund Agrl Devel, Via del Serafico 107, 00142 Rome Italy

ALSUP, KAREN, nurse; d. Lee B. Barnes and Mary Ann Gose; m. Harry Alsup, Dec. 17, 1993. BSN, U. Tenn., 1993. RN. Crit. care staff nurse Meth. Med. Ctr., Oak Ridge, Tenn., 1993-99; acute care unit shift mgr. Meth. Med. Ctr., Oak Ridge, 1999—. Mem. Humane Soc. of U.S., Roane County Humane Soc. Recipient Organic Chemistry Achievement award Roane State C.C., 1998. Mem. AACCN, Am. Chem. Soc., Sigma Theta Tau, Phi Kappa Phi. Avocations: gardening, skydiving, reading, tennis. Office: Meth Med Ctr Turnpike Oak Ridge TN

AL-SUWAIDI, JAMAL SANAD, political scientist; b. Dubai, United Arab Emirates, July 30, 1959; s. Ali Sanad and Fatima (Muhammad) A.-S. BS in Polit. Sci., Kuwait U., 1981; MA, U. Wis., 1985, PhD, 1990. Assoc. prof. dept. polit. sci. United Arab Emirates U., Al Ain, 1990—, head adminstrv., fin. and econ. rsch. and consultation dept., 1991, dep. dean grad. studies faculty, 1992; advisor to chief of staff Armed Forces, Abu Dhabi, 1993—, secondment to the armed forces, 1994—; dir., founder Emirates Ctr. for Strategic Studies and Rsch., Abu Dhabi, 1994—; cons. Fed. Nat. Coun., Abu Dhabi, 1991, Ministry of Edn., Abu Dhabi, 1992, Ministry of Fgn. Affairs, Abu Dhabi, 1992. Editor: ECSSR Emirates Occasional Papers, ECSSR Strategic Studies, ECSSR International Studies; contbg. author: Democracy, War and Peace in the Middle East, 1995; editor: The Yemeni War of 1994: Causes and Consequences, 1995, Iran and the Gulf: A Search for Stability, 1996; contbr. articles to profl. jours. Mem. Midwest Polit. Sci. Assn., Am. Polit. Sci. Assn., Middle East Studies Assn. N.Am. Home and Office: PO Box 4567, Abu Dhabi United Arab Emirates

AL-SUWAYDI, SULTAN BIN NASIR, banker. Gov. Ctrl. Bank United Arab Emirates. Office: Ctrl Bank United Arab Emirates, PO Box 854, Abu Dhabi United Arab Emirates*

ALT, ECKHARD U., physician, educator; b. Pforzheim, Fed. Republic Germany, Nov. 9, 1949; s. Theodor and Lore A.; m. Uta Alt; children: Christopher, Fabian, Valerie, Sarah. MD, U. Heidelberg, 1974. Rsch. fellow Tech. U., Munich, 1973-75, cardiologist, 1976—, assoc. prof. internal medicine, 1976-92, prof., 1992—. Author 4 books; contbr. more than 300 articles to profl. jours.; patentee in field of electrophysiology and interventional cardiology. Recipient Rsch. award European Soc. Cardiothoracic Surgery, 1986; named Best Exptl. Rschr. in Interventional Cardiology Erasmus U. Rotterdam, 1997. Mem. German Working Group on Cardiac Pacing (chmn.), European Soc. Cardiology (bd. dirs.), Internat. Soc. Cardiac Pacing and Electrophysiology (pres.). Office: Tech U Munich, Med Clinic, 81675 Munich Germany

ALT, HELMUT GUIDO, chemistry educator, researcher; b. Schwansdorf, Germany, Dec. 3, 1944; s. Gustav Wilhelm and Waltraut Stefanie (Hampel) A.; m. Susan Heidi Kovacs, May 29, 1975; children: Andreas, Matthias, Elisabeth, Helene. D Natural Scis., Tech. U. Munich, 1973; D Rer. Nat. Habil., U. Bayreuth, 1980. Postdoctoral fellow U. Mass., Amherst, 1973-74; sci. asst. Tech. U. Munich, 1975-78; sci. asst. U. Bayreuth, Germany, 1978-87, prof. chemistry, 1987—. Contbr. numerous articles to sci. and profl. jours.; patentee in field. Mem. Gesellschaft Deutscher Chemiker. Roman Catholic. Avocations: skiing, travelling, collecting stamps. Home: Wacholderweg 27, D-95445 Bayreuth Germany Office: Univ Bayreuth, Universitatsstrasse 30, D-95440 Bayreuth Germany

ALT, KARIN, philology educator; b. Dresden, Germany, May 7, 1928; d. Hermann and Leonie (Kyber) A. Degree in Edn., U. Tubingen; Dr Phil, Frankfurt U., 1953; Dr Phil Habil, Berlin Free U., 1970. Mitarbeiter Thesaurus Linguae Latinae, Munich, Germany, 1956-58; lectr. Free U., Berlin, 1958-70, prof., 1971—. Editor: Euripides, Helena, 1964; author: Philosophie Gegen Gnosis, 1990; Weltflucht und Weltbejahung, 1993. Lutheran. Home: Thielallee 18, D-14195 Berlin Germany

ALTADILL-FELIP, DAVID, geophysicist, researcher; b. Tortosa, Spain, Sept. 23, 1966; s. Jose Altadill-Espuny and Maria Cinta Felip-Bertomeu; m. Catalina Cordero Gonzalez, July 22, 1995; 1 child, Carla Altadill Cordero. B in Physics, U. Barcelona, Spain, 1991; D in Physics, U. Ramon Llull, Spain, 1997. Cert. geophysicist. Prof. secondary sch. Dept. Edn. of Generalitat of Catalonia, Tortosa-Tarragona, Spain, 1990-91; award holder Geophys. Inst. Bulgarian Acad. Scis., Sofia, 1992-93, 93-94; colaborator Observatori de l'Ebre, Roquetes, Spain, 1994-97; award holder France Telecom/CNET, Lannion, France, 1996; prof. Observatori de l'Ebre, Roquetes, Spain, 1997—, head ionospheric dept., 1999—; rsch. commn. U. Ramon Llull, 1998—; org. com. nat. congress History of Sci. and Tech. Observatori de l'Ebre, 1998. Mem. adv. bd. Bulgarian Geophys. Jour., 2000—; contbr. articles to profl. jours. Recipient 191.4 Bulgaria, 1992-93, 192.1 Bulgaria, 1993-94, Foreing Min., Sofia, Bulgaria, 1996 BEAI200002 Commn. for Univs. and Rsch. of Catalonia, Lannion, France, 1996. Mem. Com. on Space Rsch. (assoc.). Avocations: farmer, stockbreeder. E-mail: ebre.daltadill@readysoft.es. Fax: 34977504660. Office: Observatori de l'Ebre, Horta Alta No 38, E-43520 Roquetes Spain

ALTAISKY, MIKHAIL VICTOROVICH, nuclear scientist, physicist; b. Sebastopol, Ukraine, USSR, July 26, 1964; s. Victor Ivanovich and Elena Alexeevna (Zabusik) A.; m. Lioubov Ivanovna Ermakova, June 17, 1988; 1 child, Ekaterina. MSc, Kharkov (Ukraine) U., 1987; PhD, Joint Inst. Nuclear Rsch., Dubna, Russia, 1992. Lic. physicist. Engr. Space Rsch. Inst., Moscow, 1987-89, jr. scientist, 1989-91, scientist, 1991—; sr. scientist Joint Inst. Nuclear Rsch., Dubna, 1993—; vis. prof. Birla Sci. Ctr., Hyderabad, India, 1995—. Contbr. articles to profl. jours. ISF grantee, Soros, 1993. Avocations: yoga, Hindu culture. Office: Joint Inst Nuclear Rsch, 141980 Dubna Russia

AL-TAMEEMI, AMER THEYAB, manufacturing executive; b. Kuwait, Kuwait, Sept. 3, 1944; s. Theyab Bader Al-Tameemi and Hussah Mohammed Yousef; m. Mai Abdul Malek Al-Nouri, June 14, 1970; children: Hend, Hadeel, Mohammed, Theyab, Hussah. BS in Econs., Clarkson U., 1968; diploma in stats., U.S. Census Bur., Washington, 1973. Contr. Ctrl. Stats. Office, Kuwait, 1968-75; dep. gen. mgr. Kuwait Real Estate Investments, 1975-82; sr. v.p. for direct investment Kuwait Fgn. Trd. Cont. & Invs., 1982-88; asst. gen. mgr. for rsch. and mktg. Kuwait Invst. Projects, 1988-96, advisor top mgmt., 1996-97; chmn., mng. dir. United Industries Co., 1997—. Contbr. articles to newspapers. Decorated knight Moroccan Govt., 1982. Mem. Kuwait Econ. Soc. (chmn. 1993—), Kuwait Cinema Club (chmn. 1992-99).

ALTAN, M(USTAFA) CENGIZ, mechanical engineering educator; b. Ankara, Turkey, Dec. 26, 1963; s. A. Rifki and Nursel Altan; m. Betul S. Marmara, July 4, 1992. BSME, Mid. East Tech. U., Ankara, 1985; PhD in Mech. Engring., U. Del., 1989. Tchg. asst. U. Del., Newark, 1985-86, rsch. asst., 1986-89; asst. prof. mech. engring. U. Okla., Norman, 1989-95, assoc. prof., 1995—. Editor: (conf. procs.) Developments in Non-Newtonian Fluid Mechanics, 1993, Intelligent Manufacturing and Material Processing, 1995; contbr. articles to profl. jours. Recipient rsch. initiation award Soc. Mfg. Engrs., 1990, Regents' award for superior tchg. U. Okla., 1998; rsch. grantee Okla. Ctr. for Advancement Sci. and Tech., 1991, NASA, 1996, Seagate Techs., 1996, Hawthorne York Internat., 1999. Mem. ASME (assoc., chmn. materials processing com. materials div. 1994-97), Soc. R heology, Internat. Polymer Processing Soc., Am. Soc. Engring. Edn., Am. Phys. Soc., Am. Soc. for Composites, Pi Tau Sigma (hon., Most Outstanding Prof. award for U. Okla. 1997). Achievements include patents on computer-controlled curing of composite materials. Office: U Okla Sch Aero-Mech Eng 865 Asp Ave Rm 212 Norman OK 73019-1029

ALTARELLI, GUIDO, theoretical physicist; b. Rome, July 12, 1941; s. Angelo and Carmelita (Lavaggi) A.; m. Rita Di Paolo, Sept. 19, 1966 (div. 1988); children: Claudia, Fabrizio; m. Monica Pepe, Oct. 29, 1988; children: Giulia, Marco. D Physics, U. Rome, 1963, postgrad., 1965. Prof. U. Florence, Italy, 1965-68; rsch. asst. NYU, 1968-69, Rockefeller U., 1969-70; prof. incaricato, asst. ordinario U. Rome, 1970-80, prof. ordinario, 1980—; mem. staff theory divsn. CERN, Geneva, 1987—. Co-editor: Collider Physics, 1987; author: The Development of Perturbative QCD, 1994; contbr. over 220 articles to profl. jours. and books. Office: CERN Theory Divsn, 1211 Geneva 23, Switzerland

AL-TAYIR, AHMAD BIN HUMAYD, United Arab Emirian government official; b. United Arab Emirates, 1950; s. Hamid a.; married. BA in Econs., Cairo U. Dir. econ. dept. Ministry Fin. and Industry, 1973-74, dir. gen., 1974-78, asst. under sec., 1978-86; min. state Ministry Fin. and Industry, Abu Dhabi, United Arab Emirates, 1986—; min. comm.; vice chmn. Arab Investment and Fgn. Trade Bank; bd. dirs. Amman Ins. Co.; alt. gov. Internat. Monetary Fund and World Bank, Islamic Devel. Bank, United Arab Emirates; chmn. Emirates Indsl. Bank, Comml. Bank of Dubai Ltd. Avocations: football, literature, science, economics. Office: Min Comm, PO Box 900, Abu Dhabi United Arab Emirates*

ALTENBERGER, ANDRZEJ RYSZARD, physical chemist; b. Warsaw, Poland, Sept. 19, 1942; came to U.S., 1980; s. Gustav Stanislav and Maria (Myszkorowski) A.; m. Alicja Sitek, Sept. 30, 1972. MSc in Nuclear Chemistry, U. Warsaw, 1966; PhD in Phys. Chemistry, Polish Acad. of Scis., 1972. Rsch. assoc. U. Warsaw, 1966-68; rsch. assoc. Inst. of Phys. Chemistry, Polish Acad. of Scis., Warsaw, 1968-72, rsch. group leader, sr. scientist, 1973-80; rsch. assoc. chemistry dept. MIT, Cambridge, 1972-73; vis. scientist, lectr. SUNY, Stony Brook, 1980-82; vis. asst. prof. chem. engring. and material sci. U. Minn., Mpls., 1982—. Contbr. articles to profl. jours. Mem. Am. Chem. Soc. Roman Catholic. Avocations: judo, karate, tennis. Home: 2311 Territorial Rd Saint Paul MN 55114-1613 Office: U Minn Dept Chem Engring Minneapolis MN 55455

ALTENBURGER, OTTO ANDREAS, accountant, educator; b. Vienna, Austria, Oct. 29, 1951; s. Otto Leopold and Gertraud Eva M. (Hofer) A.; m. Veronika Maria Weber, June 26, 1981; children: Angelika Johanna, Dorothea Christine, Eleonore Judith, Konstanze Maria, Agathe Gabriele. MBA, Vienna U. Econs. and Bus. Adminstrn., 1975, Dr. rer. soc. econs. (ring of honor), 1979; postgrad., Miami U., Oxford, Ohio, 1976; habilitation, Vienna U. Econs. Bus. Adminstr, 1990. CPA, Austria. Research and teaching asst. Vienna U. Econs. and Bus. Adminstrn., 1974-79, 81-88; auditor Alpen-Treuhand Co., Vienna, 1979-81; mng. clk. Alpenlaendische Treuhand Co., KPMG Austria, Vienna, 1989-90; prof. U. Gegensburg, Germany, 1991—; lectr. Vienna Bd. Trade, 1975-78, Vienna U. Econs. and Bus. Adminstrn., 1975-92, Austrian Chamber Accts., 1976—, U. St. Gallen for Bus. Adminstrn., Econs., Law and Social Scis., Switzerland, 1982—, U. Linz, Austria, 1989; external examiner U. Limerick, Ireland, 1999—. Author: Elements of a Theory of Production of Services, 1980 (Cardinal Innitzer Encouragement award 1981), Commentary on the Austrian Financial Reporting Act, 1993, Financial Accounting and Uncertainty, 1995; editor: Achievements in Accounting, 1999, 2d edit., 2000; contbr. articles to jours. and books. Served to 1st lt. Austrian armed forces. Recipient W. Wilfling Rsch. Encouragement award, 1990. Mem. Austrian Soc. Ins. Sci., German Assn. Ins. Sci., Assn. Univ. Tchrs. Bus. Adminstrn. Roman Catholic. Avocations: music, theater, gymnastics. Home: Desingweg 8, D-93049 Regensburg Germany Office: Alpenlaer lische Treuhand Co, U Regensburg, D-93040 Regensburg Germany

ALTENHOFEN, KATRINA BETH, emergency medical services coordinator; b. Belleville, Ill., Sept. 16, 1961; d. Charles William and Carolyn Sue Rentfro Und; m. Michael Roger Altenhofer, Sept. 24, 1983; children: Dustin Michael, Shamus Cody, Benjamin Joseph. MPH in Adminstrn., LaSalle U., Mandeville, La., 1999. Cert. emergency med. tech., deputy county coord. Workshop dir. Washington County Devel. Ctr., Washington, Iowa, 1983-85; teaching assoc. St. James Elem. Sch., Washington, Iowa, 1985-87; adminstrv. asst. Southeast Iowa Emergency Med. Svcs., Washington, Iowa, 1993—; adjunct faculty Southeastern C.C., Burlington, Iowa, 1989—; edn. dir. Washington County Emergency Med. Avcs. Assn., Washington, Iowa, 1990—; state coord. Iowa Dept. Pub. Health, Iowa, 1995—. Author: I Am The Child You Saved, 1998, Vilunteer Recruitment and Retention, 1997. Recipient Iowa Spirit of Jr. Miss, 1980, Emergency Med. Svcs. for Children award maternal Child Health Bur., 1996—; named Dean list honor student Kirkwood C.C., LaSalle U., 1991-99. Mem. Iowa Lyne Disease Assn., West Chester 1st Responder, St. James Ch., Iowa Emergency Med. Svcs. Assn., Washington County Emergency Med. Svcs. Assn., Critical Illness and Trauma Found. E-mail: kaltenho@health.state.ia.us. Office: IDPH Bur of EMS PO Box 24 Washington IA 52353-0024

ALTENMULLER, ECKART OTTMAR, music physiologist; b. Rottweil, Germany, Dec. 19, 1955; s. Theodor and Margarete (Timm) A.; m. Barbel Winker, May 4, 1987; children: Heinrich, Konrad, Charlotte. MD, U. Freiburg, 1983; MA in Performing Arts, Musikhochschule, 1985. Rsch. asst. U. Freiburg (Germany), 1983-85; rschr., intern U. Tubingen (Germany), 1985-92, asst. prof., 1992-94; dir., prof. U. Hannover (Germany), 1994—; dir. Inst. Music Physiology, Hannover, 1994. Editor: Event Related Potential, 1996; contbr. articles to profl. jours. Mem. AAAS, European Brain and Behavior Soc., Deutsche Gesellschaft Musik Med. Musikphysiology, European Soc. Cognition Music. Avocations: piano, reading, bicycling. Home: Rosengasse 9, 31303 Burgdorf Germany Office: Hannover Acad Music/Drama, Plathnerstr 35, 30175 Hannover Germany

ALTÉUS, ÅKE, foundation administrator. Dep. exec. dir. The Nobel Found., Stockholm. Office: The Nobel Found, Sturegatan 14 Box 5232, SE-10245 Stockholm Sweden*

ALTFEST, LEWIS JAY, financial and investment advisor; b. N.Y.C., Oct. 14, 1940; s. Sam and Ruth (Zwang) A.; m. Karen Caplan, Dec. 25, 1966; children: Ellen Wendy, Andrew Gamer. BBA with honors, CCNY, 1962; MBA, NYU, 1970; PhD, CUNY, 1978. CPA, N.Y.; chartered fin. analyst; cert. fin. planner, personal fin. specialist. Sr. investment analyst Wertheim and Co., N.Y.C., 1969-75, Lehman Bros., N.Y.C., 1975-76; dir. research, gen. ptnr. Lord Abbett and Co., N.Y.C., 1976-82; pres. L.J. Altfest and Co., Inc., N.Y.C., 1982—; assoc. prof. fin. Pace U. Grad. Sch. Bus., N.Y.C., 1984—; dir. fin. planning and investments program New Sch. for Social Rsch., N.Y.C., 1988—; arbitrator Nat. Assn. Securities Dealers, Am. Arbitration Assn., 1985-88; bd. dirs. Consumer Fin. Edn. Found., 1994-95. Author: (with others) Introduction to Business, 1978, Capital Budgeting Handbook, 1986; author: Lew Altfest Answers Almost All Your Questions About Money, 1992, revised edit., 1994; contbr. articles to profl. jours. Pres. 240 E. 79th Coop. Bd., N.Y.C., 1983-86; bd. dirs. Consumer Fin. Edn. Found., 1993-97. With U.S. Army, 1962-63. Named one of best fin. planners in U.S. Money Mag., 1987, one of best fin. advisors Worth Mag., 1996, 97, 98, one of best advisers for physicians, Med. Econs., 1998; recipient Disting. Alumni award Ph.D. Alumni Assn. CUNY, 1992. Mem. Nat. Assn. Personal Fin. Advisors (bd. dirs. 1985-89, Outstanding Leadership award 1989), AICPA, Internat. Assn. for Fin. Planning (bd. dirs. N.Y. chpt. 1987-93), Inst. Chartered Fin. Analysts, Am. Fin. Assn., Fin. Analysts Fedn., Fin. Mgmt. Assn., N.Y. Soc. Security Analysts, Registry Fin. Planning Practitioners, CCNY Bus. Alumni Assn. (bd. dirs. 1983-87), Acad. of Fin. Svcs. Office: L J Altfest & Co Inc 116 John St Rm 1120 New York NY 10038-3305

AL-THANI, SHEIKH ABDALLAH BIN KHALIFA, prime minister of Qatar. Min. of interior Doha, Qatar, 1989, acting min. of fin. and petroleum; prime minister Qatar, Doha, 1996—. Office: Office of Prime Minister, PO Box 923, Doha Qatar*

AL-THANI, AHMAD BIN SAYF, Qatari government official; b. Qatar, 1946; s. Saif al-Thani; married. Diploma in Pub. Adminstrn., London, 1971. Qatar amb. to Ct. of St. James London, 1971-77; min. of justice, past min. of state for fgn. affairs Govt. of Qatar, Doha, until 1995, min. of state, 1995—. *

AL-THANI, HAMAD BIN JASIM BIN JABIR, Qatari government official; b. Doha, 1959. Former min. agr. and mcpl. affairs Govt. of Qatar, Doha, former acting min. electricity and water, now min. fgn. affairs. Office: Min Foreign Affairs, PO Box 250, Doha Qatar*

AL-THANI, SHAIKH HAMAD BIN KHALIFA, Qatari government official; b. Doha, Qatar, 1952; s. Shaikh Khalifa Bin Hamad al-Thani; married; 3 children. Grad., Royal Mil. Coll., Sandhurst, U.K., 1971. Major, comdr. Moving Detachment I Qatar Armed Forces, 1971-72; major-gen., comdr.-in-chief Qatar Armed Forces, Doha, 1972—; heir apparent, 1977-95; min. def. Govt. of Qatar, Doha, 1977—, comdr.-in-chief, 1977—, prime min., 1995-96, amir, 1995—. Chmn. Higher Coun. Planning, 1989; founder Qatar Found. Edn., Sci, and Cmty. Devel. Decorated Knight Grand Cross of Order St. Michael and St. George U.K., 1979; named to Order Francisco de Miranda Venezuela, 1977, Grand Officer de la Legion d' Honneur France, 1980, Grand-Croix de la Legion D'Honneur France, 1998, Ordre Nat. du Lion Senegal, 1998, Des Grosskreuzes Germany, 1999, Ordinul Nat. Steaua

Romaniei Romania, 1999, Cavaliere di Gran Croce Italy, 2000; recipient Medal of Oman, 1975, The Nile Sash Egypt, 1976, King Abdul-Aziz medal Saudi Arabia, 1976, Diagam Tanda Kehormation Indonesia, 1977, Al-Muhammadi medal Morocco, 1981, Sash of Merit Lebanon, 1986, Al-Hussain Bin Ali Necklace Jordan, 1995, Medal of Merit Sultanate of Oman, 1995, Medal of 7th Nov. Republic of Tunis, 1997, Nishan-i-Pakistan, 1999, Nat. CEDAR medal of order of greatest sash Lebanon, 2000. Mem. Higher Coun. for Youth Welfare (chmn. 1979-91), Internat. Mil. Sporting Assn. (founder). Office: Office of the Amir, PO Box 923, Doha Qatar

AL-THANI, MUHAMMAD BIN KHALIFA, Qatari government official; b. Doha, 1965. BS, George Washington U., D.C., 1987. Sec. of state, Ministry Finance and Petroleum Govt. of Qatar, Doha, 1989-92, undersec., Ministry Finance, 1992, min. finance, econ. and trade, 1992-98, dep. prime minister, 1998—. Office: Ministry of Finance Economy and Trade, Office Prime Min PO Box 923, Doha Qatar*

ALTHAUS, ALFREDO ALBERTO, lawyer; b. Rosario, Santa Fe, Argentina, Nov. 8, 1938; s. Arnoldo Guillermo Nicolás and Elisa Catalina (Juchli) A.; m. Susana Altschuler, Mar. 16, 1989. LLB, U. Nat. Litoral, Santa Fe, 1960, JD, 1972. Legal adviser Caja de Créditos Rosario, Argentina, 1964-79, Banco Udecoop C.L., Rosario, 1979-86, Instituto Movilizador de Fondos Cooperativos C.L., Rosario, 1968—; prof. Law Sch. U. Nat. Rosario, 1984—, Law Sch. U. Nat. Litoral, Santa Fe, 1987-99; sr. ptnr. Estudio Schujman & Althaus, Rosario, 1961—; bd. dirs. Law Sch. Rosario Nat. U., 1986-92; bd. dirs. Rosario Nat. U., 1994-98, acad. jury, 1994—; pres. Coop. Law Inst. Colegio de Abogados Rosario, 1981-84, 95-99. Author: Treatise on Cooperative Law, 1974, 2nd edit., 1977; contbr. articles to profl. jours. Recipient Bonow Internat. Coop. Alliance, London, 1982. Mem. Internat. Assn. Coop. Law (pres. Argentine br. 1990—), Argentine Assn. Comparative Law (mem. bd. Rosario br. 1975—), Inter-Am. Bar Assn. Office: Estudio Juridico Schujman & Althaus, Av Corrientes 763 P3 Of 308, 2000 Rosario Santa Fe, Argentina

ALTHAUS, DAVID STEVEN, chemical research company executive, controller; b. Massilon, Ohio, Dec. 25, 1945; s. James Horace and Mary Jane (Horan) A.; m. Joan Elizabeth Wrenn, Aug. 4, 1973; children: D. Steven Jr., Matthew, Beth Anne; foster children: James, Elise. BA, Miami U., Oxford, Ohio, 1967; cert., Def. Lang. Inst., Monterey, Calif., 1969; MBA, Miami U., Oxford, Ohio, 1976. CPA, N.C., Ohio. Internal auditor Harris Corp., Cleve., 1976-77; sr. staff acct. Harris Corp., Rochester, N.Y., 1977-78; acctg. supr. Imperial Group Ltd., Wilson, N.C., 1978-80; dir. planning Am. Mortgage Ins. Cos., Raleigh, N.C., 1980-83; asst. v.p., budget mgr. Gen. Electric Mortgage Ins. Cos., Raleigh, 1983-84; contr., asst. treas. Chem. Industry Inst. Toxicology, Research Triangle Park, N.C., 1984—, mgr. human resources, 1984-90, asst. sec., 1989—. Cubmaster Boy Scouts Am., 1986-90, asst. scoutmaster, 1990-95. Capt. USMC, 1968-74, Vietnam. Decorated Cross of Galantry, Rep. of Vietnam, Da Nang, 1970. Mem. AICPA, Inst. Mgmt. Accts., Am. Compensation Assn., Contr.'s Coun., Soc. for Human Resources Mgmt. Baptist. Office: Chem Industry Inst Toxicology PO Box 12137 Durham NC 27709-2137

ALTHEIDE, PHYLLIS SAGE, computer scientist, software engineer; b. St. Louis, Apr. 13, 1963; d. Paul D. and Alvera Sage; m. Richard W. Altheide, Aug. 1984 (div. June 1999); children: Martha Elizabeth, Paul William. BS in Computer Sci., U. Mo., Rolla, 1985, MS in Computer Sci., 1992. GS-12 computer scientist U.S. Geol. Survey, Rolla, 1988-95, GS-13 computer scientist, 1996-98, GS-13 supervisory computer specialist software engring sect., 1998-2000, sci. mgr. geographic and cartographic rsch. and applications, 2000—; lead developer Spatial Data Transfer Standard Task Force, Rolla, 1990-95; presenter workshops Australia, 1995, New Zealand, 1995, Malaysia, 1997; technical expert ISO working group on geospatial stds., 1998—. Author: (with others) GIS Data Conversion: Strategies, Techniques, Management, 1998. Recipient Superior Svc. Honor award Dept. of Interior, 1997. Mem. IEEE Computer Soc. Lutheran. Avocations: photography, travel, walking.

ALTIER, WILLIAM JOHN, management consultant; b. Drexel Hill, Pa., July 22, 1935; s. William John and Gertrude (Soule) A.; m. Mileen Rishel Bower, June 21, 1958; children: William Clark, Dwight Douglas. BA, Lafayette Coll., 1958; MBA, Pa. State U., 1962. Assoc. Kepner-Tregoe Inc., Princeton, N.J., 1964-68, Applied Synergetics Ctr., Waltham, Mass., 1968-69; dir. mktg. Comstock & Wescott Inc., Cambridge, Mass., 1969-70; gen. mgr. divsn. Princeton Rsch. Press, 1970-75, sr. assoc., 1975-76; pres. Princeton Assocs. Inc., Buckingham, Pa., 1976—; grad. asst. Dale Carnegie Courses; lectr. Assn. for Media-Based Continuing Edn. for Engrs.; guest lectr. Grad. Sch. Mgmt., New Sch. for Social Rsch., Wharton Sch., U. Pa., Pa. State U.; bd. dirs., vice chmn. Inst. Mgmt. Cons., also exec. editor IMC Newsletter. Author: The Thinking Manager's Toolbox, 1999; editor, pub. The PA Perspective; abstractor Jour. Product Innovation Mgmt.; mem . editl. rev. bd. Jour. Managerial Issues; contbg. author: Management Consulting, 3d edit., 1996, The Art of M&A Integration: A Guide to Merging Resources, Processes, and Responsibilities, 1997; contbr. articles to profl. jours.; patentee in field. Co-chmn. indls. divns. United Cmty. Fund, Carlisle, Pa., 1963; elder Doylestown Presbyn. Ch.; exec. v.p. Bucks County br. ARC, also mem. planning com. Southeastern Pa. chpt.; vol. worker civic orgns. Fellow Inst. Mgmt. Cons. (cert.); mem. Acad. Mgmt., Am. Chem. Soc., Am. Vacuum Soc., Armed Forces Comm. and Electronics Assn., Am. Mgmt. Assn., Product Devel. and Mgmt. Assn. (v.p.), Nat. Spkrs. Assn., Liberty Bell Spkrs. Assn., Indsl. Mgmt. Club, Inst. Mgmt. Cons. (participative process cons. spl. interest group), Am. Arbitration Assn. (panel arbitrators), U. So. Calif. Ctr. for Futures Rsch., Assn. Mng. Cons. (trustee, editor newslette UPDATE II), Union League Phila., Mensa, Ctrl. Bucks C. of C., Tech. Coun. Greater Phila., Pa. Innovation Network, World Affairs Coun. Phila., Am. Creativity Assn., Exch. Club (bd. control 1960-64), Doylestown Toastmasters (v.p.), Nat. Spkrs. Assn., Liberty Bell Spkrs. Assn., 1000 Club, Kappa Sigma Alumni Corp. (chpt. pres.). Office: PO Box 820 Buckingham PA 18912-0820

ALTIN, SEDAT, medical educator, medical administrator; b. Gan, Turkey, Apr. 4, 1965; s. Kenan and Zeynet (Kaya) A.; m. Sükran Batur, July 29, 1989; children: Hamdi, Kerem. Student, Med. Faculty Cerrahpasa, Istanbul, Turkey, 1981-87. Cert. assoc. prof. in pulmonary diseases and tuberculosis. Asst. dr. Yedikule Pulmonary Diseases State Hosp., Istanbul, 1987-91, chief asst. dr., 1991-96, assoc. prof. dr., asst. dir. of hosp., 1996—, clinic dir., 1999—. Avocation: playing electrical organ. Office: Yedikule Pul Dis State Hosp, Belgratkapi Yolu # 11, 34760 Istanbul Turkey

ALTMAN, IRWIN, psychology educator. BA, NYU, 1951; MA, U. Md., 1954, PhD, 1957. Asst. prof. psychology Am. U., Washington, 1957-58, sr. rsch. scientist, assoc. prof., 1960-62, adj. prof., 1962-69; rsch. scientist in human scis. Arlington, Va., 1958-60; rsch. psychologist Naval Med. Rsch. Inst., Bethesda, Md., 1962-69; adj. prof. U. Md., 1968-69; prof. U. Utah, Salt Lake City, 1969-79, chmn. dept. psychology, 1969-76, dean Coll. Social and Behavioral Sci., 1979-83, v.p. for acad. affairs, 1983-87, disting. prof., 1987—. Author: (with J.E. McGrath) Small Groups, 1966, (with D.A. Taylor) Social Penetration, 1973, Environment and Social Behavior, 1975; (with M. Chemers) Culture and Environment, 1980; (with J. Wohlwill) Human Behavior and Environment: Vol. I, 1976, Vol. II, 1977, Vol. III, 1978, Vol. IV, 1980, Vol. V, 1981, Vol. VI, 1983, Vol. VII, 1984, (with C. Werner) Vol. VIII, 1985, (with A. Wandersman) Vol. IX, 1987, (with E. Zube) Vol. X, 1989, (with K. Christensen) Vol. XI, 1990, (with S. Low) Vol. XII, 1992, (with A. Churchman) Women and the Environment, Vol. XIII, 1994; (with D. Stokols) Handbook of Environmental Psychology, Vols I and II, 1987; (with J. Ginat) Polygamous Families in Contemporary Society, 1996; mem. editl. bds.: Small Groups, 1970-79, Man-Environment Systems, 1969-73, Jour. Applied Social Psychology, 1973-85, Sociometry, 1973-76, Environment and Behavior, 1975, Jour. Personality and Social Psychology, 1974-83, Contemporary Psychology, 1975-86, Environ. Psychology and Nonverbal Behavior, Psychology, 1976-90, Am. Jour. Cmty. Psychology, 1978-81, Population and Environment, 1979, Jour. Environ. Psychology, 1982, Computers and Human Behavior, 1985, Internat. Jour. Applied Social Psychology, 1984, Communication Monographs, 1992-95; assoc. editor Am. Jour. Cmty. Psychology, 1988-92; co-editor Jour. Environ. Psychology, 1990-98; contbr. articles to profl. jours. 1st lt. Adj. Gen. Corps, AUS, 1954-56. Mem. APA (pres. divsn. population and environment), AAAS, Soc. Exptl. Social Psychology, Soc. Psychol. Study of Social Issues, Soc. Personality and Social Psychology (pres.), Environ. Design Rsch. Assn., Am. Psychol. Soc.

ALTMAN, JACOB ABRAM, physiologist, educator; b. Kishniev, Moldova, Russia, July 15, 1930; s. Abram Jacob and Haya Idel (Berman) A.; m. Elena Alexander Radionova, Mar. 8, 1990; 1 child, Alla. MD, Med. Inst. Vladicavcas, 1954; PhD, Pavlov Inst. Physiology, St. Petersburg, 1962, DSc, 1970. Physician Hosp. Kostroma, USSR, 1954-57; sci. worker Pavlov Inst. Physiology, St. Petersburg, 1960-72, head lab. of hearing physiology, 1972—; prof. physiology U. St. Petersburg, 1996—. Author: Localization of Sound, 1972, English edit., 1977, Neurophysiological Mechanisms of Sound Source Localization, 1975, Localization of Moving Sound Sources, 1983; co-author: (with S.F. Vaitulevich) Human Auditory Evoked Potentials and Sound Source Localization, 1993. Named Emeritus Sci. Worker of Russia, Pres. of Russia, 1995. Mem. Internat. Brain Rsch. Orgn., Russian Acad. Scis. (corr., IM Sechenov Gold medal 1994), Russian Physiol. Soc. Home: Shepetovskaya St 3 Apt 2, 195027 St Petersburg Russia Office: IP Pavlov Inst Physiology, nab Makarova 6, 199034 St Petersburg Russia

ALTMAN, ROBERT B., film director, writer, producer; b. Kansas City, Mo., Feb. 20, 1925; m. Kathryn Altman; children: Robert, Matthew; children by previous marriage: Michael, Stephen, Christine. Student, U. Mo., 3 years. Owner Sandcastle 5 Prodns. Writer, prodr., dir.: (TV) Kraft Theatre; writer, prodr., dir.: (TV pilot) The Long Hot Summer; co-prodr.: (film) The James Dean Story, 1957; dir.: (films) The Delinquents, 1957, Countdown, 1968, That Cold Day in the Park, 1969, M*A*S*H, 1970 (Grand Prix award Cannes Film Festival 1970, Best Film, Nat. Soc. Film Critics 1970), Popeye, 1980, Come Back to the 5 & Dime, Jimmy Dean, Jimmy Dean, 1982, Streamers, 1983, Beyond Therapy, 1987, The Gingerbread Man, 1997, (TV series) Gun, 1997; producer: The Late Show, 1977, Welcome to L.A., 1977, Rich Kids, 1979, Remember My Name, 1979, Mrs. Parker and the Vicious Circle, 1994; prodr. and dir.: A Wedding, 1978, Quintet, 1979, A Perfect Couple, 1979, Secret Honor, 1985, The Player, 1992 (Best Dir. citation Cannes Film Festival, 1992), After Glow, 1997; prodr., dir., screenwriter: Three Women, 1977, Health, 1979; dir., screenwriter: Brewster McCloud, 1970, McCabe and Mrs. Miller, 1971, Images, 1972, The Long Goodbye, 1973, Thieves Like Us, 1974, California Split, 1974, Buffalo Bill and the Indians, 1976, Fool for Love, 1985, Short Cuts, 1993 (Best Dir. Acad. award nominee 1993), Ready to Wear (Prêt-à-Porter), 1994, Kansas City, 1996, Cookie's Fortune, 1999; dir. for stage: (Broadway) Come Back to the 5 & Dime, Jimmy Dean, Jimmy Dean, 1982, (Lyric Opera of Chgo.) McTeague, 1993; prodr., dir.: (TV) The Laundromat, 1984, The Dumb Waiter, 1987, The Room, 1987, Caine Mutiny Court Martial, 1987, Tanner '88, 1988; dir. film Vincent and Theo, 1990; prodr., dir. Nashville, 1976; actor: (TV movie) Frank Capra's American Dream, 1997. Served with AUS, 1943-47. Mem. Dirs. Guild Am. Office: Sandcastle 5 Prodns 502 Park Ave Ste 15G New York NY 10022-1108 also: ICM 8942 Wilshire Blvd Beverly Hills CA 90211-1934

ALTMAN, SIDNEY, biology educator; b. Montreal, Que., Can., May 7, 1939. BS, MIT, 1960; PhD in Biophys., U. Colo., 1967; DSc (hon.), McGill U., Montreal, 1991, York U., U. Colo., U. Montreal, U. B.C. Teaching asst. Columbia U., 1960-62; Damon Runyon Meml. Fund cancer rsch. fellow in molecular biology Harvard U., 1967-69; Anna Fuller Fund fellow, then Med. Rsch. Coun. fellow Med. Rsch. Coun. Lab. Molecular Biology, 1969-71; from asst. to assoc. prof. Yale U., New Haven, 1971-80, prof. biology, 1980—, Sterling prof. biology, 1990—, prof. chemistry, 1994—, chmn. dept., 1983-85; dean Yale Coll., 1985-90; tutor Radcliffe Coll., 1968-69; researcher effects of acridines on T4 DNA replication, mutants, precursors of tRNA processing by catalytic RNA and ribonuclease function. Author: Transfer RNA, 1978. Recipient Nobel Prize in Chemistry, 1989. Fellow AAAS; mem. Am. Soc. Biol. Chemists, Genetics Soc. Am., Nat. Acad. Scis., Am. Philos. Soc. (Rosenstiel award 1989). Office: Yale U Kline Biology Tower PO Box 208103 New Haven CT 06520-8103

ALTMANN, KONRAD, software development company executive, consultant; b. Munich, Germany, Jan. 24, 1941; s. Herbert and Berta (Gaub) A.; m. Erika Pfeifer, Nov. 2, 1979; 1 child, Georg. Diplom in Physics, Ludwig-Maximilian U., Munich, 1972, Dr, 1975. Diplomate in physics. Rsch. engr. Messerschmitt-Bölkow-Blohm AG, Munich, 1977-91; optics cons. German Aerospace, Munich, 1991-92; computational physics cons. Daimler-Benz AG, Munich, 1992-93; pres. Micro Systems Design Dr. Altmann GmbH, Munich, 1993—. Contbr. articles to profl. jours.; patentee laser amplification system. Recipient Comml. Tech. Achievement award Laser Focus World, 2000; Bavarian Rsch. Found. grantee, 1998. Mem. Optical Soc. Am. Avocations: music (piano), metal sculpturing. Office: Micro Sys Design Dr Altmann, Brunhildenstrasse 9, D-80639 Munich Germany

ALTMANN, OLIVIER, advertising agency executive; b. Lyon, France, May 6, 1964; s. Paul and Anne (Kleinberg) A.; m. Helene Gresset, Sept. 9, 1995; children: Leonard, Joseph and Samuel (twins). BS, Ecole Alsacienne, Paris, 1982; Veterinarian, Coll. Sainte Barbe, 1983; diploma in Comm., Inst. Univ. Tech., Paris, 1986. Copywriter FCB, Paris, 1987, 89-92, Australie, Paris, 1988, BDDP, Paris, 1992-98; creative dir. BDDP and FILS, Paris, 1998—. Recipient Bronze Lion, Cannes Internat. Advt. Festival, 1990, 95, Gold Lion, 1996. Avocations: diving, skiing. Office: BDDP and FILS, 5 bis rue Mahias BP 210, 92108 Boulogne Billancourt France

ALTON, ERIC WALTER FREDERICK WOLFGANG, respiratory medicine academic; b. London, Mar. 6, 1957; s. Ernest Eric and Eva Irene Antonio (Dörner) A.; m. Karen Pamela Turner, Sept. 23, 1989; children: Rebecca Amy, William Eric. BA with honors, Cambridge (Eng.) U., 1978, MA, 1998; MB BS, London U., 1981, MD, 1990. Sr. house officer Hammersmith/Whittington/Royal Brompton Hosps., London, 1982-85; registrar Whittington Hosp., London, 1985-86, Royal Brompton Hosp., London, 1986-90; lectr. Nat. Heart & Lung Inst., London, 1990-94; sr. lectr./hon. cons. physician Nat. Heart & Lung Inst./Royal Brompton Hosp., 1994—, prof. respiratory medicine and gene therapy, 1999—. Contbr. articles to profl. jours. Titular scholar Jesus Coll., Cambridge, 1978; recipient Geoffrey Holt award Brit. Med. Assn., 1987; Med. Rsch. Coun. Tng. fellow, 1988, HC Roscoe fellow Brit. Med. Assn., 1991, Intermediate fellow Brit. Heart Found., 1991, Sr. Clin. fellow Wellcome Trust, 1994. Fellow Royal Soc. Medicine; mem. Royal Coll. Physicians, Brit. Thoracic Soc., Am. Thoracic Soc., European Thoracic Soc. Avocations: bridge, music, philately. Office: Nat Heart & Lung Inst, Manresa Rd, London SW3 6LR, England

AL TRAIF, IBRAHIM HAMAD, physician, consultant; b. Oneizah, Saudi Arabia, Dec. 19, 1960; s. Hamad Abdullah and Hessah Sulaiman (Al Keid) A.; m. Mona Mohammed Al Khenaini; children: Soundos, Mohammed, Sara, Manaf. MBBS, King Faisal U., Saidi Arabia, 1985; MRCP, London, 1989, FRCP, 1999. Fellow in medicine. Intern Armed Forces Hosp., Riyadh, Saudi Arabia, 1985-86; resident Nat. Guard Hosp., Riyadh, Saudi Arabia, 1986-89, specialist, 1989-90; fellow U. Alberta, Edmonton, Can., 1990-92, U. Toronto, Can., 1992-93; cons. King Fahad Nat. Guard Hosp., Riyadh, Saudi Arabia, 1993—; dir. Endoscopy unit, 1995-97, co-dir. liver transplantation, 1993-94, King Fahad Nat. Guard Hosp., Riyadh, Saudi Arabia. Author: Liver Disease and Transplantation, 1999; contbr. over 50 abstracts and 32 scientific articles to profl. jours. Recipient Teaching award U. Toronto, 1993. Fellow Royal Coll. Physician; mem. Am Assn. Liver Disease, Saudi Gastroenterology Assn. Avocations: travel, music, writing, poetry. Home phone: 966 1 237 0754. Home: PO Box 59908, Riyadh 11535, Saudi Arabia Office: King Fahad Nat Guard Hosp, PO Box 22490, Riyadh 11426, Saudi Arabia

ALTSHULER, NINA SEMENOVNA, physics educator, researcher; b. Kazan, Russia, Apr. 25, 1947; d. Semen Alexandrovich Altshuler and Evgenia Pavlovna Kharitonova; m. Alexander Leonidovich Larionov, June 19, 1971; 1 child, Igor. PhD, Kazan U., 1974. Rsch. asst. prof. U. Kazan, 1973-75, asst. prof., 1975-81, assoc. prof., 1981—; dir. student physics competition physics faculty U. Kazan, 1984-97. Contbr. articles to profl. jours. Grantee Russian Fund Basic Rsch., 2000. Avocations: reading, travelling, theaters. Home: St Butlerov 45 ap 9, 420012 Kazan Russia Office: Kazan VI Lenin State U, St Kremlevskay 18, 420008 Kazan Russia

ALTUKHOV, PAVEL DMITRIEVICH, physicist; b. Khabarovsk, Russia, May 20, 1946; s. Dmitrii Nikolaevich Altukhov and Zoya Alekseevna Koshkina; m. Evgeniya Mikhailovna Ushakova, Oct. 28, 1981 (div. 1986); 1 child, Nikolai Pavlovich. PhD, Ioffe Inst., Leningrad, Soviet Union, 1979; DSc, Ioffe Inst., 1988. Engr. Ioffe Inst., Leningrad, Soviet Union, 1973-76; from jr. rschr. to lead rschr. Ioffe Inst., 1976—. Contbr. articles to profl. jours. Recipient State prize of the Soviet Union, 1988. Avocations: bicycling, gardening, music, skiing, fishing. Office: AF Ioffe Inst, Politekhnicheskaya St 26, 194021 St Peterburg Russia

ALTUKHOV, YURI PETROVICH, geneticist; b. Elan'-Koleno, USSR, Oct. 11, 1936; s. Pyotr Kornilovich and Alexandra Mikhailovna (Andreeva) A.; m. Rimma Gerasimovna Domrina, June 19, 1958 (div. Jan. 1966); 1 child, Mikhael; m. Elena Pavlovna Volkova, Nov. 2, 1966; 1 child, Dmitry. MSc, Fisheries Inst., Moscow, 1959; PhD, Moscow State U., 1964; DSc, Russian Acad. Scis., Moscow, 1972. Jr. rschr. Karadag Biol. Sta., Krimea, Ukraine, USSR, 1959-62; sr. rschr. Moscow State U., 1964-67; head lab. Marine Biology Inst. Russian Acad. Sci., Vladivostok, 1967-72, head lab. Gen. Genetics Inst., 1972—; prof. Gen. Genetics Inst. Russian Acad. Sci., 1976—, dir. Gen. Genetics Inst., 1992—; Soros prof. Open Soc. Inst., N.Y., 1994—; mem. adv. bd. jour. Selection, Evolution, Paris, 1993-97, Sarsia, Bergen, 1997—. Author: Population Genetics of Fish, 1974 (diploma 1978), Genetics Processes in Populations, 1983, Population Genetics: Diversity and Stability, 1990, Population Genetics of Salmonid Fishes, 1997; inventor method of artificial propogation of local animal populations (Gold medal 1973); dep. editor-in-chief Russian Jour. Genetics, 1993—; editor-in-chief jour. Advances in Modern biology, 1995—, Forest Genetics, 1995—. Recipient State Sci. & Tech. prize, 1996; grantee Russian Found. Basic Rsch., 1993-2000, Internat. Sci. Found., 1994-95, Open Soc. Inst., Internat. Soros Sci. Edn. Program, 1994-97; named hon. prof. Moscow State U., 1999. Mem. Internat. Acad. Sci., Sci. Coun. for Genetics and Selection, Marine Biology Inst.-Russian Acad. Sci. (hon.), Vavilov Soc. for Genetics and Breeding (v.p. 1994—), Russian Acad. Scis. (academician 1997). Avocations: music, literature, philosophy, history. Home: 43-2-415 Profsoyznaya St, 117420 Moscow Russia Office: Vavilov Inst Gen Genetics, 3 Gubkin St, 117809 Moscow Russia

AL-TURAIKI, MOHAMMED HOMOD, biomedical technologist; b. Zulfi, Saudi Arabia, Feb. 23, 1955; s. Homod Soliman and Miznah Abdulaziz (Al-Misnid) Al-T.; m. Norah Saud Al-Misnid, Ratibé Hassan Saleh; children: Isra, Eman, Najla, Ahmed, Danyah, Homod, Abdulaziz, Misnah, Merna. BSc, U. Lancaster, 1980; PhD, U. Salford, 1984. Diplomate Am. Bd. Profl. Disability Consultants. Rsch. asst. prof. King Abdulaziz City for Sci. and Tech., Riyadh, Saudi Arabia, 1984-86; asst. prof. orthopedic bioengring. and rehab. Coll. Applied Med. Scis., King Saud U., Riyadh, 1986-90, assoc. prof., chmn. biomed. tech. dept., 1990-97, full prof., 1996—; vis. prof. Northwestern U. Med. Sch., Chgo., 1989; prin. investigator, dir. gen. Joint Ctr. for Rsch. in Prosthetics & Orthotics and Rehab. Programs, Riyadh, 1987—; pres. med. and rehab. cons. house Riyadh, 1995—; prin. investigator, dir.-gen. Nat. Rsch. Project on Disability and Rehab. and Cmty. Based Rehab.; advisor, team leader Prince Sultan Bin Abdulaziz City for Humanitarian Svcs., 1994; cons. Prince Mohammed Bin Fahd Ctr. for Rehab. Tech.; cons. in field. Author, editor over 23 textbooks and references including: The Human Knee: Functional Anatomy, Biomechanics and Instabilities and Assessment Techniques, 1986, The Knee Book, 1988, Manual of Prosthetics and Orthotics, 1988, Handling the Handicapped, 1988, Pre-Prosthetic Care for Above-Knee Amputees, 1990, Pre-Prosthetic Care for Below-Knee Amputees, 1990, Orthotics and Prosthetics Digest, 1990, The Rights of the Disabled, 1991, Disabled Village Children, 1994, Critical Stages in the Development of Systems and Strategies of Disability and Rehabilitation in Saudi Arabia, 1997; editor-in-chief Saudi Jour. Disability and Rehab., The Disability and Rehabilitation Periodical, Disability World, The Scientist; author, contbr. more than 70 articles to profl. jours.; patentee of 2 inventions in field. Mem. bd. trustees Am. Lebanese Ill. Univ.; pres. Islamic World's Coun. of Disability and Rehabilitation USA; dep. v.p. Rehab. Internat. for Arab Region. Recipient Best Paper Gold medal award Ann. Conf. Indian Assn. Phys. Medicine and Rehab., 1996, Leadership award Temple U. Sch. Podiatric Medicine, 1998. Mem. AAAS, Internat. Soc. Prosthetics and Orthotics, Biol. Engring. Soc., Br. Orthopaedic Rsch. Soc., Instn. Mech. Engrs. Address: PO Box 65, Al-Zulfi 11932, Saudi Arabia Office: Joint Ctr Rsch Prosthetics, PO Box 27240, Riyadh 11417, Saudi Arabia

AL-TURKI, ABDUL AZIZ ABDALLAH, oil industry association executive; b. Jeddah, Saudi Arabia, Aug. 12, 1936; s. Abdalla al-T.; married; 2 children. BBA, Cairo U., 1964. With ARAMCO, Saudi Arabia, 1954-66, bd. dirs., 1980-89; dir. Office of the Min. of Petroleum and Mineral Resources, Saudi Arabia, 1966-68, dep. min., 1975-90; dir. gen. affairs Directorate of Mineral Resources, Saudi Arabia, 1968-70; asst. sec. gen. Orgn. Arab Petroleum Exporting Countries, 1970-75, sec. gen., 1990—; bd. dirs. Petromin, 1975-89; sec. gen. Supreme Adv. Coun. Petroleum and Mineral Affairs, Saudi Arabia, 1975-90; gov. OPEC, Saudi Arabia, 1975-90; bd. dirs. Arabian Oil Co. Ltd., 1980-89; chmn. bd. dirs. Arab Maritime Petroleum Transport Co., Kuwait, 1981-87; chmn. Petromin-Mobil Yanbu Refinery Co. Ltd., 1982-89; bd. dirs. Saudi Ports Authority, 1987-89. Avocations: tennis, swimming. E-mail: oapec@qualitynet.net. Office: Orgn of Arab Petroleum, PO Box 20501, Safat 13066, Kuwait

AL-TURKI, ABDULRAZAQ ALI, marketing professional; b. Al-Khobar, Saudi Arabia, Apr. 8, 1961; s. Ali Abdulrehman Al-T. and Noora Ahmed Al-Hawas; m. Khadeeja Saeed Al-Helali. BS in Internat. Studies/Sociology, U. Oreg., 1986; MS in Spl. Edn., Am. U., 1988, MA in Internat. Affairs, 1992. Human resources devel. mgr. A.A.Alturki Corp., Dammam, Saudi Arabia, 1988-90; chmn. info. com., dir. pub. rels. Ea. Province Rehab. Soc. for Disabled Persons, Dammam, 1992-98; dir. mktg. Namma Cargo Svcs. Co. Ltd., Al-Khobar, Saudi Arabia, 1992—; polit. analyst Saudi Arabian Embassy, Washington, 1992-98. Author: Saudi Arabian-Japan Relationship, Closing the Gap Between Rich and Poor Nations, Indonesia: Politics, Economy and Culture, Die But with Dignity, Capital Punishment in Islamic Religion, Woman's Rights in Islam, Meeting Saudi Arabian Manpower Needs, Expatriate Education and Training, The Art of Marketing, The Reasons of Failure of the Companies, The Strategic Marketing, others. Coord. Internat. Health Day, Enivrontl. Day, Internat. Deaf Day; active Internat. White Cane Day, Internat. Handicapped Week, Kingdom's Nat. Day; mem. exec. bd. Saudi Charitable Soc. Edn. and Rehab. of Down Syndrome, Omni Conf., London, First Internat. Conf. for Arabic-African Non-Govtl. Orgns., Libya. Mem. Saudi Arabian Spl. Edn. Bd., Handicapped Sports Club in Al-Hassa, Safe Environment, Inst. Sales and Mktg. Mgmt. (London), Arabian World of Handicapped (exec.), Arab Regional Conf. of Rehab. Internat. Avocations: organizing public meetings, world politics. Address: Namma Cargo Services Co Ltd, PO Box 31678, Al-Khobar 31952, Saudi Arabia

ALTWEGG, PETER, mechanical engineer; b. Zürich, Switzerland, May 26, 1954; m. Marie L. Altwegg; children: Jan Pascal, Pamela Aida Maria. Diploma in Mechanics, Fed. Inst. Tech., Zürich, Switzerland, 1980. Comissioning engr. Sulzer, Zürich, Switzerland, 1980-83; tchr. DEH, Lausanne, Switzerland, 1983-85; sales project mgr. BBC, Baden, Switzerland, 1985-90; project mgr. Tuma Turbomach, Mezzovico, Switzerland, 1990-91; devel. mgr., 1991-92, tech. dir., 1992—. Office: Tuma Turbomach SA, via Cantonale, CH-6805 Mezzovico Switzerland

ALTY, JAMES LENTON, computer science educator; b. Haslingden, Lancs., Eng., Aug. 21, 1939; s. William Graham and Annie (Beharrel) A.; m. Mary Eleanor Roberts, Jan. 16, 1965; children: Gareth Thomas, Carys Ann, Sian Cathryn, Graham James. BSc with 1st class honors, U. Liverpool, 1961, PhD in Nuclear Physics, 1966. Rsch. fellow U. Liverpool, 1963-65, 66-68; systems engr. IBM (UK) Ltd., 1968-71, sales exec., 1971-72; dir. Computer Lab., U. Liverpool, 1972-82; prof. computer sci. U. Strathclyde, Glasgow, 1982-90; exec. dir. Turing Inst., Glasgow, 1984-90; prof. computer sci. Loughborough (England) U., 1990—, head dept., 1991-96, 98—; bd. dirs. Turine Inst., Glasgow, 1984-92; mem. computer bd. for univs., 1975-81. Author 6 books on computing; composer musical compositions; contbr. over 80 articles to profl. jours. Esprit (CEC) grantee, 1984-89, 89-93, 93-95, 94-99, Engring. and Phys. Sci. Rsch. Coun. grantee, 1994-97, 2000—. Fellow Brit. Computer Soc., Inst. Elec. Engrs. Avocations: skiing, musical composition. Home: 168 Station Rd, Cropston LE7 7HF, England Office: Loughborough U, Dept Computer Sci, Loughborough LE11 3TU, England

ALUSIK, STEFAN, physician, rheumatologist; b. Úbrež, Michalovce, Czechoslovakia, Oct. 23, 1947; s. Štefan Alušik and Mária (Halamková) Alušiková; m. Marie Dubnová, Feb. 24, 1973; children: Andrea, Tomáš. MD, U. P.J. Safarik, Košice, Czechoslovakia, 1971; PhD, U. Palacky, Olomouc, Czechoslovakia, 1983, asst. prof., 1994. Resident physician Dist. Hosp., Zlín, Czechoslovakia, 1971-75, Faculty Hosp., Olomouc, Czechoslovakia, 1975-85; head physician Inst. Rheumatology, Prague, Czechoslovakia, 1985-92, Hosp. Ma Micnkach Prague, 1992-98; assoc. prof. Inst. Postgrad. Medicine, Prague, 1998—. With Army of Czechoslovakia, 1972-73. Home: Malešická 26, 108 00 Prague Czech Republic Office: Faculty Thomayer Hosp, Vídeňská 800, 148 00 Prague Czech Republic

ALVÁN, GUNNAR, medical products executive, researcher; b. Stockholm, Feb. 25, 1945; s. Martin and Kerstin (Skårman) A.; m. Katarina Györffy, May 22, 1971; children: Mattias, Maria. MB, Karolinska Inst., Stockholm, 1966, LM, 1971, MD, PhD, 1977. Diplomate Karolinska Inst. Rsch. asst. Karolinska Inst., 1973-77, assoc. prof., 1977, prof. clin. pharmacology, 1997—; assoc. head physician Huddinge U. Hosp., Stockholm, 1978-91, dir. dept., 1991-96, head physician, 1996-99; dir. gen. Swedish Med. Products. Agy., Uppsala, 1999—; mem. Swedish Adverse Drug Reaction Com., Uppsala, 1981-85; project vice chmn. European Cooperation in Field of Sci. and Tech. Rsch. Project B1 Commn. European Cmtys., Brussels, 1986-98; dep. dir. WHO Collaborating Ctr., Stockholm, 1994-99. Editor: European Consensus Conf. on Pharmagogenetics, 1990, Clin. Pharmacokinetics, 1986—, Brit. Jour. Clin. Pharmacology, 1988-94, 97—, European Jour. Clin. Pharmacology, 1997—, Thèrapie, 1990—; contbr. over 250 articles to sci. and med. jours. Recipient Paul Martini prize Paul Martini Stiftung, Germany, 1990, award for rsch. in cystic fibrosis Glaxo, Sweden, 1993. Mem. Swedish Soc. Med. Scis., Swedish Assn. for Clin. Pharmacology (chmn. 1978-84), Brit. Pharmacological Soc. Avocation: music. Home: Högúddsvägen 31, S-181 62 Lidingö Sweden Office: Läkemedelsverket, Box 26, S-751 03 Uppsala Sweden

ALVARADO, CAROL, legislative executive; b. Houston, Oct. 26, 1967; d. Frank Sr. and Ida Alvarado;. BA, U. Houston, 1992. Project coord. S.W. Voter Registration Edn. Project, Houston, 1998; clerk Harris County Constables, Houston, 1989-92; legis. asst. U.S. Ho. of Reps, Washington, 1993-94; exec. dir. Magnolia Comml. Revitalization Project, 1994-97; coord. Mayor-Elect Brown's Trans. Team City of Houston. Mem. steering com. Al Gore Presdl. Campaign, Houston; mem.-at-large Dem. Nat. Com. Washington, 1998—; mem. exec. com. Texas Dem. Party, 1998—; mentor Latinas on the Rise, 1998—; mem. adv. bd. Hispanic Women in Leadership, 1999—; bd. dirs. Planned Parenthood Action Fund, Houston, 1997—, Habitat for Humanity, Houston, 1998—. Recipient Humanitarian award Harris County Dem. Party, 1997, Adv. Yr. award Houston Hispanic C. of C. Mem. Am. Leadership Forum (Class XVIII). Roman Catholic. Home: 9213 E Avenue L Houston TX 77012-2727 Office: City Hall Mayor's Office 901 Bagby St Fl 3D Houston TX 77002-2526

ALVARADO, JUAN DE DIOS, food engineering educator, researcher; b. Quito, Pichincha, Ecuador, Sept. 4, 1946; s. Lola Alvarado A.; m. Gladys Cecilia Navas Miño, Apr. 7, 1972; children: Sylvia Cristina, Paul Santiago. coord. Area foods CONACYT-BID, Quito, Ecuador, 1993-94, Nat. RIPFADI, Ecuador, 1992-97. Author: (book) Principles of Engineering Applied to Foods, 1996; mem. editl. bd.: Latin Am. Applied Rsch., 1988, 1997, Latin. Am. Archives of Nutrition, 1990. Pres. Nat. Coll. Food Engring., Ecuador, 1986-89. Named Joaquin Lalama Mcplty. Ambato, Ecuador, 1995, Pedro V. Maldonado Mcplty., Quito, 1997. Mem. Ecuadorian Acad. Scis., Latin Am. Soc. Heat and Mass Transfer (sec. 1985-91). Avocations: lecturing, mountaineering, basketball. Office: U Ténica de Ambato, Cuidadela Ingahurco Fcial, 18010334 Ambato Tgurahua, Ecuador

ALVAREZ, A(LFRED), writer; b. London, Aug. 5, 1929; s. Bertie and Katie (Levy) A.; m. Ursula Graham Barr, 1956 (div. 1961); 1 child, Adam Richard; m. Audrey Anne Adams, 1966; children: Luke Lyon, Kate. BA, Oxford (Eng.) U., 1952, MA, 1956; DLitt (hon.), U. East London, 1998. Sr. rsch. scholar Corpus Christi Coll. Oxford U., 1952-55, tutor English, 1954-55; Procter vis. fellow Princeton (N.J.) U., 1953-54, Gauss seminarian, vis. lectr., 1957-58; vis. fellow Rockefeller Found., N.Y.C., 1955-56, 58; poetry editor, critic Observer, London, 1956-66; D.H. Lawrence fellow U. N.Mex., 1958; drama critic New Statesman, 1958-60; vis. prof. Brandeis U., Waltham, Mass., 1960-61, SUNY, Buffalo, 1966. Author: Stewards of Excellence, 1958 (pub. in Eng. as The Shaping Spirit 1958), The End of It, 1958, The School of Donne, 1961, Under Pressure: The Writer in Society, Eastern Europe and the U.S.A., 1965, Lost, 1968, Twelve Poems, 1968, Beyond All This Fiddle: Essays, 1955-1967, 1968, 69, Apparition, 1971, The Savage God: A Study of Suicide, 1971, 72, Samuel Beckett, 1973 (pub. in Eng. as Beckett 1973), Hers, 1974, Autumn to Autumn and Selected Poems, 1953-1976, 1978, Hunt, 1978, Life After Marriage: Love in an Age of Divorce, 1982 (pub. in Eng. as Life after Marriage: Scenes from Divorce 1982), The Biggest Game in Town, 1983, Offshore: A North Sea Journey, 1986, Rain Forest, 1988, Feeding the Rat: Profile of a Climber, 1989, Day of Atonement, 1991, Night: Night Life, Night Language, Sleep and Dreams, 1995, Where Did It All Go Right?, 1999, 2000; (screenplay) The Anarchist, 1969; author: (with others) The Penguin Book of Contemporary Verse, 1918-1960, 1962, Penguin Modern Poets 18, 1970; editor, author introduction The New Poetry, 1962, Faber Book of Modern European Poetry, 1992; adv. editor Penguin Modern European Poets series, 1966-78; contbr. to numerous Am. and Brit. periodicals. Recipient Vachel Lindsay prize for poetry, 1961. Mem. Climbers' Club, Alpine Club, Beefsteak Club. Avocations: poker, classical music. Office: Gillon Aitken Assocs, 29 Fernshaw Rd, London SW10 0TG, England

ALVAREZ, BLANCA MAGRASSI, educational director, psychotherapist; b. Tampico, Mex., Nov. 29, 1923; d. Camilo and Magdalena (Scagno) M.; m. Luis Hector Alvarez; children: Luis Jorge, Blanca Estela. BA, Incarnate Word Coll., San Antonio, 1944; MA, N.Mex. State U., Las Cruces, 1967; PhD, Union Grad. Sch., Cin., 1977. Sch. psychologist Inst. Femenino, Chihuahua, Mex., 1967-72; pvt. practice Chihuahua, Mex., 1967—; founder, dir. Inst. Psychology Studies, Chih, Mex., 1968-86; coord. Bilingual and Multiculture Divsn. Southwest Ednl. Lab., Austin, Tex., 1977; personal devel. dir. Women D.I.F. Mcpl., Chih, Mex., 1984-86; founder, dir. Instrn. Program, Chih, Mex., 1979-86, Edn. Cultural Arts, Chih, Mex., 1992—; lectr. Social Work Sch., Chihuahua, Mex., 1967-71; sch. guidance Colegio Montessori, Chihuahua, Mex., 1968-70; founder Difusion Educativa y Cultural, Chihuahua, Mex., 1985, Escuela Miguel Ahumada, Chihuahua, Mex., 1981. Mem., 1956, mem. nat. coun., 1967—, candidate for mayor, 1968, candidate for senator, 1994, Partido Accion Nacional, Chihuahua, Mex. Named Disting. Contbn. Consejo Nacional de Ensenanza e Investigacion Psicologica, Mex., 1982, Inst. Superior de Ciencia y Tech. de La Laguna, Torreon, Coahuila, 1982, Woman of Yr., Profl. Womens Assn., Chihuahua, Mex., 1996. Mem. APA, Psychol. Mex. Assn., Internat. Sch. Psychology Assn. Avocations: travel, reading. Home: Dakota Del Norte 3213, 31250 Chihuahua Mexico Office: Educacion Cultura Artes, 1 de Mayo 1609D, 31020 Chihuahua Mexico

ALVAREZ, RAFAEL GONZALEZ, anesthesiologist; b. Durango, Mex., Feb. 26, 1936; s. Rafael Gamiz Alvarez and Guadalupe Gonzalez; m. Maria Luisa Ancira, Jan. 17, 1963; children: Maria Luisa, Maria Elena, Maria Alejandra, Rafael, Octavio, Maria Guadalupe. MD, Nat. Autotoma U. Mex., Mexico City, 1962. Diplomate Am. Bd. Anesthesiology. Intern Robert B. Green Meml. Hosp., San Antonio, 1963, resident in anesthesia, 1964-67; mem. staff ABC Hosp., Mexico City, 1967—; assoc. prof. Nat. Inst. Cardiology, Mexico City, 1967-68, cons., 1968-69. Contbr. articles to med. jours., including Ibero Am. Jour. Surgery, Anesthesia in Mex. Mem. Am. Coll. Anesthesiology, Anesthesia Assn. ABC Hosp. (pres. 1996-98). Roman Catholic. Avocations: swimming, fitness, movies, music. E-mail: alex@infoabc.com. Home: Amargura 105 Casa 20, Jardines de la Herradura, 52785 Huixquilucan Mexico Office: ABC Hosp, Sur 136 No 116 Las Americas, 01120 Mexico City Mexico

ALVAREZ, ROBERTO, agronomy educator, researcher; b. Buenos Aires, June 13, 1957; s. Enrique and Nelida (Braeckman) A. Bachelor degree, Reconquista, Buenos Aires, 1975. Cert. agronomy engr. Asst. faculty agronomy U. Buenos Aires, 1981-88, asst. prof. faculty agronomy, 1988-90, prof., 1990—. Editor-in-chief Ciencia del Suelo jour., 1993-98; mem. sci. com. Argentine Jour. Microbiology; contbr. articles to profl. jours. Mem. Internat. Soc. Soil Sci., Am. Soc. Agronomy, Argentine Soc. Soil Scis. (sec. 1996-97), Argentine Soc. Microbiol. Home: Capdevila 3050, 1431 Buenos Aires Argentina Office: Univ Buenos Aires Faculty Agronomy, Av San Martin 4453, 1417 Buenos Aires Argentina

ALVAREZ, THOMAS, producer, performing company executive, consultant; b. Ft. Wayne, Ind., Jan. 1, 1948; s. Raul and Felicitas (Vargas) A. Student, Purdue U., 1965-69. Producer, dir. McGraw-Hill Broadcasting Co. Inc./WRTV-TV, Indpls., 1973-88; pres. The Alvarez Group Inc., Indpls., 1988-98; mng. dir. Edyvean Repertory Theatre, 1998-99; pres. Alvarez Resource Group, Indpls., 1999—; freelance journalist Indpls. Star, Indpls. Monthly, Nuvo, Arts Inc., Ind. Bus. Mag., Indpls. New Times; arts reporter Across Ind., WFYI-TV, 1991-93, mem. adv. coun.; mem. cmty. adv. coun. Sta. WRTV, 1993-96, Sta. WFYI-FM, 1991-93; adj. faculty dept. journalism Ind. U., Indps., 1995-97. Prodr., dir. (documentaries) A Portrait of La Gente, 1975, Dave Baker: A Medley, 1976, Concord Today, 1977, Nine Leaves on a Sprig: The Story of Madame C.J. Walker, 1977, Domestic Violence, 1977, 500 Miles: Yesterday and Today, 1979, Tuckaway, 1982, Under the Influence, 1983, Rag to Bop: A Memoir of Indianapolis Jazz, 1984, A Woman's Story, 1985, Indiana State Museum: Living the Legend, 1986, Indiana Repertory Theatre: The First Fifteen Years, 1986, Solid Gold Years, 1987; prod. James Dean & Me: Nineteenth Star, 1995 (Telly award 1997, Emmy award 1997), The Rythm Makers: A Chronicle of Indiana Jazz, 1996. Bd. dirs. Phoenix Theatre, Indpls., 1982-85, First Step Inc.,1 988-90, Ind. Film Soc., 1988-90, ARC, 1989, United Way Cen. Ind., Greater Indpls. Coun. on Alcoholism, 1993; founder, chair Festival of New Can. Cinema, 1988, 89; mem. Ind. Cares, Inc., 1991-93; active Indpls. Men's Chorus; bd. dirs. Damien Ctr., 1996-98; mem. adv. com. Arts. Coun. Indpls., 1996. Recipient Casper award Community Svcs. Coun. Indpls., 1974, CEBA award of merit Advt. and Comm. to Black Communities Inc., 1981, Nat. Coun. on Family Rels. award, 1984, Arti award, 1991, Minority Bus. and Profl. Achievers award 1999; fellow media arts, Ind. Arts Commn. Avocations: travel, cinema, running, gardening, photography. Home and Office: 316 N East St Indianapolis IN 46202-3611

ALVAREZ-CASCOS FERNANDEZ, FRANCISCO, Spanish government official; b. Madrid, Oct. 1, 1947. City councilman City of Gijón/Asturias, 1979, City of Gijón, 1983; popular group spokesman, mem. principality of Asturias autonomous parliament, 1979, 83; AP senator Spanish Parliament for Asturias, 1982, CP mem., 1986; sec.-gen. Popular Group, 1986, PP mem., 1989—, spokesman com. on interior, 1989—; rep. Parliamentary Assembly of Coun. of Europe, 1990—, mem. com. on polit. affairs, 1990—; also sec.-gen. PP, v.p., min. of presidency; now min. devel. Govt. of Spain, Madrid. Author: Testimonio de una crisis, 1982, Discursos politicos, 1984, Los parlamentarios asturianos en el reinado de Fernando VII, 1985, Rasgos y riesgos del desencanto astur, 1987, Europa asignatura pendiente, 1989. Office: Prime Min's Chancellery, Complejo de la Moncba Edif INIA, 28071 Madrid Spain*

ALVAREZ-ESTRADA, RAMON FERNANDEZ, physicist, physics educator; b. Gijon, Asturias, Spain, June 9, 1943; s. Ramon Fernandez and Isabel Alvarez-E.; children: Gabriel, Rebeca. PhD in Phys. Scis., U. Complutense, Madrid, 1968; PhD, U. Faculty Scis. d'Orsay, Paris, 1971. Rschr. theoretical physics Junta de Energia Nuclear, Madrid, 1965-69, 71-75; assoc. prof. U. Autonoma, Madrid, 1971-73; assoc. prof. U. Complutense, Madrid, 1975-82, prof. theoretical physics, 1982—; vis. postdoctoral fellow U. Faculty Scis. d'Orsay, Paris, 1969-70, European Ctr. for Nuclear Rsch., Geneva, 1970-71; leader rsch. group theoretical physics U. Complutense, 1987—, head dept. theoretical physics I, 1996-97. Co-author: Models of Hadron Structure Based on Quantum Chromodynamics, 1986, Particulas Elementales, 1988, Fisica Cuantica, 2 vols., 1991, 100 Problemas de Fisica Cuantica, 1996; contbr. articles to sci. jours. Sr. Fulbright fellow at Lawrence Berkeley Lab., Berkeley, Calif., 1985-86. Achievements include research on macromolecular theory. Office: U Complutense Faculty Scis, Dept Theoretical Physics I, 28040 Madrid Spain

ALVAREZ GARDEAZABAL, GUSTAVO, writer; b. Tuluá, Valle, Colombia, Oct. 31, 1945. Letras, U. del Valle, Cali, Colombia, 1970. Author: La Tara Del Papa, 1971, Condores NoEntierran Todos Los Dias, 1972, Dabeiba, 1972, La Boba Y El Buda, 1973, El Bazar De Los Idiotas, 1974, El Titiritero, 1977, Cuentos Del Parque Boyaca, 1979, Los Mios, 1981, Pepe Botellas, 1985, El Divino, 1986, El Ultimo Gamonal, 1987, Los sordos ya no hablan, 1991, Las cicatrices de don Antonio, 1997, Perorata, 1997, Prisionero de la Esperanza, 2000. Alderman, Mcpl. Council of Cali, 1978-82, Tuluá, 1984-86; dep. State Duma, Cali, 1982-84; maj. Tuluá, 1988-94; gov. Dept. of Valle del Cauca, 1998—. Guggenheim fellow, 1984-85. Mem. Am. Orchid Soc. Avocations: orchids, dogs, geese. Home: Aptdo 400, Tulua Colombia

ALVAREZ-VAZQUEZ, LINO JOSE, mathematician, educator; b. Vigo, Spain, May 7, 1964; s. Jose Alvarez and Ana Vazquez; m. Aurea Maria Martinez-Varela, Apr. 8, 1990; children: Lino Jose, Aurea. Degree in math., U. Santiago, Spain, 1987, PhD, 1991. Assoc. prof. U. Santiago, 1989-93; prof. math. U. Vigo, Spain, 1993—. Contbr. articles to profl. jours. Avocations: music, oil painting, reading. Office: U Vigo, ETSI Comm, 36200 Vigo Spain

ALVEAR VALENZUELA, MARIA SOLEDAD, Chilean government official; b. Sept. 17, 1950. Asst. U. Chile, 1970-73, prof. law, 1973-75, lawyer, 1994; lawyer Financial Cooperative Inst., 1975-76; cons., legal advs. FAO, 1987, 89-90; prof. civil law U. Andres Bello, 1990, chmn. dept. civil law, 1990; dir. preparatory com. Nat. Svc. for Women, 1990, min. dir., 1992—; mem. govt. Pres. Patricio Aylwin; min. justice Govt. of Chile, Santiago, from 1994, now min. fgn. rels.; mem. Inter-American Com. of Women, OAS, 1990-93; adv. Solidarity and Social Investment Found., 1991—; dir. Nat. Com. for Family, 1992; coordinator Nat. Com. of Intrafamily Violence, 1992-93; mem. Interministerial Com. of Devel., 1992-93. Office: Ex Edificio del Congreso, Morande 441, Santiago Chile*

ALVES, DIÓGENES SALAS, engineering researcher, engineer; b. São Paulo, May 17, 1957; s. Joaquim and Maura Alves; m. Ana Lucia Vivero, Mar. 26, 1983; children: Anna, Sofia. Doctorate, U. Paris VI, 1983; Dr. in Engring., U. São Paulo, 1989. Systems analyst Itautec, Brazil, 1984-87; rschr. Nat. Inst. Space Rsch., Brazil, 1987—; vis. prof. U. N.H., 1993-94. Author: (with others) Climate Change, 1994, 1995, Changes in Land Use and Land Cover, 1994; contbr. articles to profl. jours. Office: INPE, Av Astronautas 1758, 12227010 Sao Jose dos Campos Brazil

ALVES, FERNANDO JORGE LINO, engineering educator, researcher; b. Porto, Portugal, Oct. 10, 1961; s. Albino Fernando Ascensao and Maria Prazeres (Lino) Alves; m. Maria Ines Carvalho, Sept. 29, 1990; children: Ana Francisca, Sara. Lic., Faculdade de Engenharia, Porto, 1985, M, 1991; PhD, Lehigh U., 1997. Rsch. asst. Faculdade de Engenharia, Porto, 1985-91, asst. prof., 1997—; tech. mgr. INEGI, Porto, 1997—; vice coord. INEGI-CETECOFF, Porto, 1997—; mem. pedagogic commn. FEUP/DEMEGI, Porto, 1998—. Contbr. articles to profl. jours. 2nd lt. Portuguese Army, 1986-87. Mem. Am. Ceramic Soc. (2nd place ceramographic competition 1994), Am. Soc. Metals, Soc. Mfg. Engring. Avocations: coin collector, badminton player, gardening. Home: Largo da Igreja 70, 4445-460 Ermesinde Portugal Office: Faculdade de Engenharia, Rua dos Bragas, 4099 Porto Portugal

ALVES, HARLEY, military officer; b. Belo Horizonte, Brazil, Mar. 11, 1959; s. Raimundo Gregorio and Helena Gertrudes Alves; m. Eliane Moreno Guimaraes, Jan. 31, 1960; children: Natascha Guimaraes Alves, Amanda Helena Guimaraes. Maj. Brazilian Army, 1977—. Roman Catholic. Home: Pca Gen Tiburcig 83, Apt 1002, 2223900 Rio de Janeiro Brazil Office: ECEME, Pca Gen Tiburcio 125, 22010020 Rio de Janeiro Brazil

ALVES, JOAQUIM PAREDES, hotel executive; b. Mealhada, Aveiro, Portugal, Dec. 9, 1922; s. Adelino Rodrigues Paredes and Madalena Rosário Alves; m. Gilda Nunes de Abreu, Nov. 19, 1947; children: Luis Miguel, Joana, João. Diploma, Cornell U., 1962, Inst. Estudios Turisticos, Madrid, 1963. Chief acct. Hotel Avenida, Coimbra, Portugal, 1939-46; gen. mgr Palacio Hotel & Casino, Espinho, Portugal, 1946-50, Hotel Astória, Monfortinho, Portugal, 1950-55, Hotel Embaixador, Lisbon, Portugal, 1955-57; mgr., owner Hotel Eduardo VII, Lisbon, 1957—, Curitiba, Brazil, 1975—; mgr., owner Hotel Continental, Luanda, Angola, 1958—, Hotel turismo, Abrantes, Portugal, 1981—; pres. Best Western Hotels, Portugal, 1986—, Fed. Fortuguesa Skäl Clubs, 1970-72; v.p. Skäl Club Lisbon, 1966-70; pres. Confrerie Gastronomique "Chaine des Rotisseurs" Portugal. Author: Modern Systems of Accounts for Hotels, 1969; editor: Who's Who in Tourism and Hotels in Portugal, 1984; contbr. articles to profl. jours. V.p. Assn. Intercontinental Estudos Turisticos Culturais, Lisbon, 1977-80. Recipient Merit Order of Tourism award Portuguese Govt., 1982. Mem. Portuguese Hotels Dirs. Assn., Internat. Hotels Assn., Portuguese Hotels Assn., Portuguese Travel Agts. Assn., Portuguese Golf Fedn. (treas. 1982-86), Am. Soc. Travel Agts.,. Roman Catholic. Clubs: Golf (Estoril and Cascais, Portugal), Grémio Literário (Lisbon). Avocation: golf. Home: Rua D Afonso Henriques 1590, 2765 Estoril Portugal Office: Eduardo VII Hotels, Eduardo VII Hotels, 5 Ave Fontes P de Melo, 1069-114 Lisbon Portugal

ALVES, JÜRGEN, biochemist, educator; b. Osnabrück, Germany, July 3, 1955; s. Günther and Ella (Schulze) A. BS, U. Hannover, Germany, 1981, D Natural Sci., 1984; Habilitation, Medizinische Hochschule, Hannover, 1990. Cert. biochemist. Postdoctoral fellow Medizinische Hochschule Hannover, 1984-90, assoc. prof., 1990-95, asst. prof. biochemistry, 1995—, temporary head dept., 1996—. Office: Medizinische Hochschule, Hannover Zentrum Biochemie, D-30623 Hannover Germany

ALVES PEREIRA, JOSE DE ALMEIDA, lawyer; b. Agueda, Aveiro, Portugal, Feb. 25, 1945; s. Jose Alves P. and Maria Jose (Almeida) Oliveira; m. Maria Joao Amaral, Aug. 20, 1970; children: Joao Pedro, Monica Maria. Licentiate in Law, Classic U., Lisbon, Portugal, 1968. Lawyer, dep. pub. prosecutor Portuguese State, Mozambique, 1968-70; assoc., jr. ptnr. Gonçalves Pereira, Lisbon, Portugal, 1970-81; sr. ptnr. Jose Alves Pereira e Associados, Lisbon, 1981-99, Barrocas & Alves Pereira, Lisbon, 2000—; dir., ptnr. various cos. Contbr. articles to profl. jours. Mem. ABA, IBA, Portuguese Bar Assn. (v.p.), Mozambique Bar Assn. Avocations: sailing, tennis. Office: Barrocas & Alves Pereira, Amoreiras Torre 2 16 Andar, 1070-274 Lisbon Portugal

ALVINE, ROBERT, industrialist, entrepreneur, international business leader; b. Newark, Aug. 25, 1938; s. James C. and Marie Alvine; m. Diane C. Marzulli, May 6, 1961 (div. 1995); children: Robert James, Laurie Anne. BS, Rutgers U., 1960; postgrad., Syracuse U., 1968-69; grad. PMD, Harvard Bus. Sch., 1972; DHL (hon.), U. New Haven, 2000. With Celanese Corp., 1960-77; bus. mgr. nylon products Celanese Plastics Co., Newark, 1967-69, bus. mgr. polyolefin products, 1969-72; dir. mktg. and ops. Celanese Piping Systems and Fabricated Products Co., Hilliard, Ohio, 1972-75; v.p., gen. mgr. comml. Celanese Polymer Spltys. Co., Louisville, 1975-77, Uniroyal Inc., 1977-87; v.p., dir. strategy planning and bus. devel. Uniroyal-Chem., Naugatuck, Conn., 1977; v.p. corp. planning and devel. Uniroyal Inc., Middlebury, Conn., 1978; v.p., gen. mgr. Uniroyal Tire Co., 1979-80; pres. Uniroyal Merchandising Co., 1979-84; pres., CEO, Uniroyal Devel. Co., 1980-82; CEO, COO, group v.p. Uniroyal Engineered Products & Svcs., Worldwide, 1982-87; pres. Uniroyal Plastics Co., Uniroyal Footware Columbia, Uniroyal Power Transmission Co., Uniroyal Indsl. Products Cos., 1982-87; also corp. sr. v.p., corp. worldwide officer responsible for mergers and acquisitions and corp. strategic planning Uniroyal, Inc., 1979-87, and sr. corp. officer and major prin. and team leader in mgmt. leverage buy-out of Uniroyal, Inc., 1985; founder, chmn., CEO I-Ten Mgmt. Corp., Woodbridge, Conn., 1987—; founder, chmn., CEO, I-Ten Capital Corp., Woodbridge, 1987, Aim Capital Group, Woodbridge, 1987—; chmn., CEO, prin. shareholder Charter Power Sys. (now C&D Techs. Inc.), Blue Bell, Pa., 1988-94; entrepreneur, prin. Charterhouse Group Internat., Inc., N.Y.C., 1988-95; vice chmn., CEO, major shareholder AP Parts Mfg. Co., Toledo, 1989-93; prin., dir. Internat. Automobile Products Holdings Corp., N.Y.C., 1993-95; prin. Uniroyal Holdings, Waterbury, Conn., 1985—; trustee Uniroyal Liquidating Trust; bd. dirs. E.D.O. Corp., N.Y.; chmn. compensation com., strategic com., exec. com., chair spl. com. bd. Jackson Labs., Bar Harbor, Maine, mem. capital campaign, rsch. resources and philantropy coms., 1998, mem. bd. Tax Rsch. Sys.; mem. adv. bd. Polaris Fund, N.Y.C., 1996-99; mem. bd. govs. U. New Haven, 1998, mem. chair audit com., chmn. exec. com., chmn. commn. on future of U. New Haven, chmn. bd. trustees, 2000—, chmn. bd. govs. and chmn. exec. com., 2000—; chmn. Henry Lee Inst. Forensic Scis., 1998; sr. oper. ptnr., mem. investment com. Desai Capital Mgmt. Pvt. Equity Investors Fund, 2000—. Mem. Rep. Presdl. Task Force, Pres.'s Roundtable, Citizens AgainstGovt. Waste, Presdl. Legion of Merit; bd. dirs., trustee Nat. Theater of the Deaf, Chester, Conn., 1994—, chmn. bd. dirs., 1995—, Wildlife Conservation Soc., N.Y., trustee, Long Wharf Theatre, New Haven, mem. exec. fin. com., chmn. bus. devel. com., strategy com., trustee; mem. adv. bd. Arts Scis. Coun., Rutgers U., N.J.; mem. Navy War Coll. Found.; mem. sch. bus. adv. bd. U. New Haven. With U.S. Army, 1962-68. Recipient numerous citations and recognitions including Disting. Bus. Achievement and Svcs. to the Nations award, Presdl. Legion Merit, Honor grad. Southeastern Signal Sch., 1962, Proclamation for Supreme Achievement Within the Internat. Cmty.; named Ky. Col., Gov. Ky., 1976. Mem. Nat. Assn. Corp. Dirs., Pres.'s Assn., Nat. Adv. Coun., Assn. Governing Bds. of Univs. and Colls., Am. Inst. Mgmt., Internat. Bus. Coun., World Affairs Coun.-Conn., Nat. Planning Inst., Nat. Assn. Corp. Growth, Rubber Mfrs. Assn., Battery Coun. Internat., Newcomen Soc. Am. (Conn. com.), Soc. Plastics Industry (sr., past dir.), Soc. Plastics Engrs. (past dir.), Mfg. Chemists Assn., Societe de Chemie Industriale, Nat. Paint and Coatings Assn., Coun. of Ams., Nat. Maritime Hist. Soc., Nat. Trust for Hist. Preservation, New Haven Colony Hist. Soc., Columbus House, Rutgers Alumni Assn., Harvard Bus. Sch. Alumni Assn., Harvard Bus. Sch. Club Greater N.Y. (honor roll mem.), So. Conn., Ellis Island Found. (charter), U.S. Navy Meml. Found., WWII Meml. Found. (charter), Oaklane Country Club, Renaissance Club, Am. Legion, Commanders Club, Chi Phi. Mem. Ch. of Christ. E-mail: ialv@aol.com. Fax: 203-389-5153. Home: 55 N Racebrook Rd Woodbridge CT 06525-1407

ALVIS, JOEL LAWRENCE, JR., minister; b. Memphis, Nov. 12, 1955; s. Joel Lawrence Sr. and Martha Jean (Lowe) A.; m. Vicki Lynn Welch, Aug. 12, 1978; children: Joel Lawrence III, Mark Thomas. BA, Samford U., 1977; MA, U. Miss., 1980; PhD, Auburn U., 1985; MDiv, Louisville Presbyn. Theol. Sem, 1989. Ordained to ministry Presbyn. Ch. (U.S.A.), 1989. Local ch. history and records adminstr. Presbyn. Hist. Found., Montreat, N.C., 1982-86; rsch. assoc. Louisville Presbyn. Sem., 1986-89; pastor St. Pauls (N.C.) Presbyn. Ch., 1989-97; assoc. pastor St. Luke's Presbyn. Ch., Dunwoody, Ga., 1998—; mem. com. on ministry Coastal Carolina Presbytery, 1990-93, moderator of Presbytery, 1997. Author: (with others) Diversity of Discipleship, 1991, Religion and Race: Southern Presbyterians, 1946-1983, 1994. Mem. Com. on Disabled, St. Pauls, 1991, John Walker Meml. Fund, St. Pauls, 1990; treas. Robeson County Ch. and Cmty. Ctr., 1992-95. Recipient Nelson R. Burr prize Hist. Soc. of Episcopal Ch., 1981, Book award N.C. Presbyn. Hist. Soc., 1995; Univ. fellow U. Miss., 1977-78, Anderson fellow Louisville Presbyn. Theol. Sem., 1991. Office: St Lukes Presbyn Ch 1978 Mount Vernon Rd Atlanta GA 30338-4617

ALWASIAK, JANUSZ FRANCISZEK, pathologist; b. Pabianice, Lodz, Poland, Dec. 3, 1932; s. Michal and Janina (Kolodziejczyk) A.; m. Barbara Maria Pacha, Oct. 19, 1957; children: Elzbieta, Hanna, Joanna, Rafal. D. Med. Acad., Lodz, 1957, Med. Acad., Lodz, 1969. Asst. Dept. Pathological Anatomy Med. Ac., Lodz, 1964-75, Sci. Rsch. Ctr.-Med. Acad., Lodz, 1976-78; asst. prof. Dept. Oncology Med. Acad., Lodz, 1978-90; head Dept. Oncological Pathology, Med. Ac., Lodz, 1996-98; ret., 1999; mem. Com. Neurooncology Polish Acad. Sci., Warsaw, 1984—. Mem. Internat. Soc. Neuropathology, European Acad. Pathology. Avocations: recreational activities, gardening, skiing. Home: 173 Moniuszki Street, 95-200 Pabianice Poland Office: Dept Oncological Pathology, 4 Paderewski Street, 93-509 Lodz Poland

ALWORTH, CHARLES WESLEY, lawyer, engineer; b. Buenos Aires, Aug. 23, 1943; s. Cecil Dwight and Kathleen Mary (Whitaker) A.; m. Sally Ann Wells, Dec. 21, 1967 (div. Nov. 1981); m. Madeline E. Wilson, Feb. 14, 1983; children: Cecil Dwight II, Barbara Diane. BSEE, U. Okla., 1965, M in Elec. Engring., 1967, PhD, 1969; JD, U. Tulsa, 1992. Bar: U.S. Patent

Bar Office 1989, Tex. 1993, U.S. Dist. Ct. (ea. dist.) Tex. 1993; registered profl. engr., La., Okla., Tex. Tchg. asst. elec. engring. U. Okla., Norman, 1965, grad. asst. elec. engring., 1965-67, spl. instr. elec. engring., 1967-68; asst. prof. elec. engring. Tex. A&M U., College Station, Tex., 1968-74; chief, prin. cons. Conoco, Inc., Ponca City, Okla., 1974-90; rsch. assoc. profl. engr. U. Tulsa, Okla., 1990—; chief engr. Alworth Cons., Tyler, Tex., 1990—; of counsel Sefrna & Assocs., Tyler, 1993-95; prin. Charles W. Alworth Engr. & Atty. at Law; assoc. prof. and head elec. engring. U. Tex., Tyler, 1997-98. Patentee in field; contbr. articles to profl. jours. Mem. Phi Delta Phi, Tau Beta Pi, Eta Kappa Nu, Sigma Xi. Episcopalian. Avocations: aviation, woodworking, gardening. Home: 502 Cumberland Rd Tyler TX 75703-9324

ALY, OMAR FERNANDES, thermal power plant engineer; b. Sao Paulo, Brazil, Aug. 12, 1955; s. Omar and Dulce (Fernandes) A. Degree in Mech. Engring., Politécnica Da USP, Sao Paulo, Brazil, 1977; postgrad., Energy and Nuclear Rsch. Inst., 1999—. Mech. engr. Eletropaulo de Sao Paulo, Sao Paulo, Brazil, 1978—; maint. specialist Electropaulo, Sao Paulo. Brazil, 1986-99; collaborator ISTLI, Tech. U. Vienna. Author: (film) Brasil O Novo Mundo De Albert Eckhout, 1995, Tema E Variacao Primeira, 1992. Avocations: poetry, photography, movie critics, bibliophily, literature, music, arts. E-mail: ofaly@uol.com.br.

AL-YAWER, RIYADH JALAL, lawyer; b. Erbil, Iraq, Sept. 25, 1940; arrived in the U.K., 1984; s. Jalal Daoud and Najia Hussein Awni (Al'Mumaiez) Al-Y.; m. Sana Muhammad Al'Dabbagh, Jan. 11, 1980; children: Farah, Hussein. BA, Baghdad (Iraq) U., 1962, MA, 1973. Solicitor Al-Yawer & Ptnrs., Baghdad, Iraq, 1962-63; mgr. in charge of studies Iraq Reinsurance Co., Baghdad, 1963; diplomat Iraqi Ministry for Fgn. Affairs, Baghdad, 1964-70; consul gen. Iraqi Embassy, London, 1966-67; mgr. legal studies and rsch. dept. Ministry of Planning, Baghdad, 1970-73; chmn., pres. Middle East Transport and Trade Co., W.L.L., Baghdad, 1973-80. Author: Fundamental Change in International Treaties, 1973. V.p. Iraqi Free Coun., London, 1991; founding mem. Iraqi Nat. Congress, Vienna, Austria, 1992; mem. exec. coun. Iraqi Nat. Congress, Salahuddin, Iraq, 1993; elected to presdl. coun. Iraqi Nat. Congress, 1999. Muslim. Avocations: reading, photography, boating, sports. Home: 2 Greenoak Way, Wimbledon London SW19 5EN, England

ALYOSHIN, ALEXANDER M., science organization executive; b. Donetsk, Ukraine, Sept. 29, 1955; s. Michael T. and Klaudia M. Alyoshin; m. Laura A. Panchenko, May 13, 1978; children: Alex, Serge. Master's degree, Air Force Acad., Kiev, Ukraine, 1977, PhD, 1990; academician, Ukrainian Internat. Acad. Original Ideas, Kiev, 1992. Cert. in electromech. engring. Regiment chief engr. Ukrainian Air Force, 1977-84; docent Air Force Acad., Kiev, 1984-98; v.p. Adron, Kiev, 1998—; cons. Arsenal, Kiev, 1998—. Mem. Ukrainian Internat. Acad. Original Ideas (advisor 1992—, sec. 1999—). Avocations: electronics, skydiving. Fax: (38044) 246 1522. E-mail: sturenko@adron.kiev.ua. Home: Ivana Pulyuya 5a 34, Kiev 03048, Ukraine Office: Adron Co, Laboratorny per 1 off 180, Kiev 252133, Ukraine

ALYOSHIN, NICHOLAS EUGENE, biologist, researcher; b. Krasnodar, USSR, Sept. 23, 1954; s. Eugene Paul and Tamara Alexander (Sedletskaya) A.; m. Nina Vladimir Scherbakova, Feb. 11, 1983; children: Vladimir, Nike. MS, Kuban U., Krasnodar, USSR, 1977; PhD in Biology, Usbek Acad. Sci., Tashkent, USSR, 1980; PhD in Agr., Moscow U., 1982; DSc in Econ. and Social Scis. (hon.), U. Ferrara (Italy), 1995; DSc in Agr., Russia Attestation Com., Moscow, 1996. Prof. inplant breeding, 1996; cert. Russia Pres. Acad. State Svc., 1995. Asst. prof. Kuban Agrl. Inst., Krasnodar, USSR, 1977-81, 81-84; dep. dir. All-Russia Rice Rsch. Inst., Krasnodar, 1984-91, exec. dir., 1991-99; dir. gen. Krasnodar Agrl. Biotechnol. Ctr., 1991—; dir. Advanced Learning Biotech. Inst., Krasnodar, USSR, 1991—. Author: Rice, 1993, 2d edit., 1997, Biology Against Obscurantism, 1996, Land of Adygs, 1996, God-chosen Royal Priesthood, 1999; inventor rice varieties (Medal USSR Exhibn.). Endorser Nuclear Age Peace Found., Calif., 1989; pres. Scientists for Responsibility, Scientists for Democracy, Krasnodar, USSSR, 1983. Recipient Medal Chinese Assn. Advanced Sci., 1989, Meml. Medal Internat. Rice Rsch. Inst., 1991, Gold Medal Russia Ministry of Edn., 1972. Fellow Russia Acad. Aquaculture Scis.; mem. Russia Acad. Technol. Sci. (corr.), Internat. Network Genetic Evoln. of Rice (mem., founder steering com. 1995—), State Assn. Rice (exec. dir. gen. 1991-99), Ind. Trade-Union Rice Growers (pres. 1996). Avocation: writing sonnets. Home: Dlinnaya W 108 f W1, 350000 Krasnodar Russia

ALYSSANDRAKIS, KONSTANTINOS, member European Parliament; b. Athens, Greece, Aug. 27, 1948. Mem. European Parliament, Brussels; mem. com. on indsutry, external trade, rsch. and energy, com. on culture, youth, edn. the mdeia and sport, vice chmn. substitute del. to European Union-Cyprus Joint Parliamentary Com. Mem. Confed. Group of European United Left/Nordic Green Left. Mem. Communist Party Greece. Office: KKE, Leof Irakliou 145, GR-14231 North Ionia Greece*

AL-ZADJALI, HAMOOD SANGOUR, banker; b. Muscat, Oman, Aug. 15, 1947; s. Sangour Hashim and Mafoodha Faqir Al-Zadjali; m. Fatma Taj Mohd Saleh Al-Raisi, Jan. 1, 1973; children: Kamil, Mutassim, Mohamed, Mayasa, Zayana, Shaima, Khulood. BS, Boston U., 1981. Mgr. British Bank of the Middle East, Muscat, Oman, 1969-75; mgr. Ctrl. Bank of Oman, Muscat, Oman, 1975-78, sr. v.p., 1978-85; gen. mgr. Oman Housing Bank, Muscat, Oman, 1985-90; dep. exec. pres. Ctrl. Bank of Oman, Muscat, Oman, 1990-91, exec. pres., 1991—. Office: Ctrl Bank of Oman, PO Box 1161, Ruwi Muscat 112, Oman

AL-ZANATI, MUHAMMAD, Libyan government official. Sec.-gen. Gen. People's Congress, Tripoli, Libya. *

ALZAYED, NASER S., academic administrator, educator; b. Al Qasr, Qasim, Saudi Arabia, Aug. 20, 1960; p. Saleh A. and Nora M. Al Rayes; m. Badriah Al Reshoodi, July 21, 1984; children: Saleh, Omar, Anas, Rand, Rasha, Abdulaziz. BS, King Saud U., Riyadh, Saudi Arabia, 1984; MS, Ohio U., 1988; PhD, U. Kans., 1994. Adminstr. King Saud U., Riyadh, 1984-94, asst. prof., 1995—. Author: Internet Using Email, 1998. Islam. Avocations: computers, internet programing, reading. E-mail: nalzayed@ksu.edu.sa. Fax: 966-1-467-3656. Office: King Saud Univ, PO Box 2455, Riyadh 11451, Saudi Arabia

ALZEBDEH, KHALID IBRAHIM, structural engineer, consultant; b. Kafr-Sur, Tulkarm, Jordan, July 3, 1964; came to U.S., 1990; s. Ibrahim Abdul-Rahim Alzebdeh and Wasilah Ibrahim Saadeh; m. Suha Samir Abu-Tayeh, Dec. 29, 1992; 1 child, Osama Khalid. BSCE, Yarmouk U., Irbid, Jordan, 1986; MSCE, Jordan U. Sci. and Tech., Irbid, 1990; PhD in Engring. Mechanics, Mich. State U., 1994. Rsch. assoc. Mich. State U., East Lansing, 1994-97; stress analyst locomotive divsn. GM, Chgo., 1997-98; structural engr. Ergotron, Inc., St. Paul, 1998—; rsch. cons. Inst. Paper Sci. and Tech., Atlanta, 1997—. Contbr. articles to sci. jours., including Jour. Applied Mechanics, others; inventor in field. Thoman fellow Mich. State U., 1993, postdoctoral fellow Ga. Inst. Tech., Atlanta, 1997; Jordan Govt. scholar Yarmouk U., 1982. Mem. ASME. Avocations: sports, camping. E-mail: kalzebdeh@yahoo.com. Office: Ergotron Inc 1181 Trapp Rd Saint Paul MN 55121-1266

AMADASUN, PATRICK I., financial consultant, author; b. July 21, 1955. BSc in Biology and Medicine, U. Ibadan, Nigeria, 1977; MBA in Fin. and Acctg., Atlanta U., 1981; PhD in Fin., Kennedy Western U., Boise, Idaho, 1992. Exec. chmn. 1st Continental Ins. Co., Lagos, Nigeria, 1992-99; chmn. Internat. Grains, Lagos, 1995-99; fin. cons., Stone Mountain, Ga., 1999—. Author: 20 Ways You Could Become A Millionaire, 1997, Evolution: The Theory of Absolutism, 1998. Office: 406 W Country Dr Duluth GA 30097-5907

AMADIO-BACKOWSKI, THERESE MARIE, small business owner; b. Cleve., May 10, 1949; d. Henry Joseph and Therese Eleanor (Nicoll) Backowski; m. Alex Villena (div. 1974); m. Blase S. Amadio (div. 1986); children: Elizabeth Angelique, Charles Aaron, Angelo Benjamin, Margaret Eleanor, Jessica MariRose. Diploma, Erasmus Hall. Lic. vet. technician Ohio State Vet. Bd. Vet. technician Animal Med. Clinic, Dublin, Ohio, 1974-78; acct. Credit Bur. Svcs., Mansfield, Ohio, 1980-82; pres. Park Ave. Pets Inc., Mansfield, 1982—; grooming judge Groom Expo West, Burbank, Calif., 1992; tchr. dog obedience Madison H.S. Adult Edn., Mansfield, 1984-94; animal trainer for film Shawshank Redemption, Castle Rock Pictures, 1994; freelance writer; spkr. in field. Editor: Off Lead Magazine. Mem. bd. advisors Madison Adult Edn. Divorced Homemakers to Work Program, 1985-91, Richland County 4-H, Mansfield, 1991-97; mem. block grant com. HUD, Mansfield, 1982-85, chmn., 1984-85; pres. Poplar St. Neighborhood Assn., Mansfield; leader Heritage Trail coun. Girl Scouts U.S., Mansfield, 1981-85. Named Employer of Yr. Mansfield City Schs., 1987-88. Mem. NAFE, Nat. Dog Groomers Assn., Richland County Kennel Club. Republican. Roman Catholic. Avocations: horseback riding, fishing, reading, swimming. Home: 142 Poplar St PO Box 5289 Mansfield OH 44901-5289 Office: Park Ave Pets Inc 166 Park Ave W Mansfield OH 44902-1637

AMADO, HONEY KESSLER, lawyer; b. Bklyn., July 20, 1949; d. Bernard and Mildred Kessler; m. Ralph Albert Amado, Oct. 24, 1976; children: Jessica Reina, Micah Solomon, Gabrielle Beth. BA in Polit. Sci., Calif. State Coll., Long Beach, 1971; JD, Western State U., Fullerton, Calif., 1976. Bar: Calif. 1977, U.S. Dist. Ct. (ctrl. dist.) Calif. 1981, U.S. Ct. Appeals (9th cir.) 1981, U.S. Supreme Ct. 1994. Assoc. Law Offices of Jack M. Lasky, Beverly Hills, Calif., 1977-78; pvt. practice Beverly Hills, Calif., 1978—; lectr. in field. Contbr. articles to profl. jours.; mem. editl. bd. L.A. Lawyer mag., 1996—, articles coord., 1999-2000, chair, 2000—. Mem. Com. Concerned Lawyers for Soviet Jewry, 1979-90; nat. v.p. Jewish Nat. Fund, 1995-97; bd. dirs. Jewish Nat. Fund L.A., 1990—; sec. L.A. region, bd. dirs. , 1991-94, Am. Jewish Congress, Jewish Feminist Ctr., 1992-99, co-chair steering com., 1994-96; mem. Commn. on Soviet Jewry of Jewish Fedn. Coun. Greater L.A., 1977-83, chmn., 1979-81, commn. on edn., 1982-83, cmty. rels. com., 1979-83. Mem. Calif. Women Lawyers (bd. govs. 1988-90, 1st v.p. 1989-90, jud. evaluations co-chair 1988-90), San Fernando Valley Bar Assn. (family law mediators and arbitrators planel 1983-94, judge pro-tem panel 1987-94), Beverly Hills Bar Assn. (family law mediators panel 1985-94), L.A. County Bar Assn. (family law sect., appellate cts. com. 1987—, chmn. subcom. to examine reorgn. Calif. Supreme Ct. 1990-94, judge pro tem panel 1985-95, appellate jud. evaluations com. 1989—, editl. bd. L.A. Lawyer mag. 1996—, articles coord. 1999—, dist. 2 settlement program 1996—), Calif. State Bar, Calif. Ct. Appeal. Democrat. Jewish. Office: 261 S Wetherly Dr Beverly Hills CA 90211-2515

AMAGASA, MASAHARU, neurosurgeon; b. Kiryu, Japan, Feb. 6, 1959; s. Itsue Amagasa; m. Sumiko Moriya; children: Hiroshi, Jin. MD, Tohoku U., Sendai, Japan, 1982, PhD, 1990. Med. staff Yamagata City Hosp., Japan, 1991—. Mem. Soc. Neurosci., Japan Neurosurgery Soc., Japan Soc. Brain Tumor Pathology. Avocation: personal computer. Home: 1-4-25 Nishida, Yamagata 990-0831, Japan Office: Yamagata City Hosp, 1-3-26 Nanokamachi, Yamagata 990-0831, Japan

AMAKO, KAZUNOBU, bacteriologist, medical educator; b. Fukuoka, Japan, Sept. 10, 1933; s. Tamikazu and Sakiko (Maeda) A.; m. Kuni Aso, Oct. 10, 1960; children: Tomoko, Yutaka, Minoru. MD, Kyshu U., Fukuoka, 1959, PhD, 1964. Rsch. assoc. Kyushu U., 1964-73, asst. prof. bacteriology, 1973; prof. bacteriology Fukuoka U., 1973-82; prof. bacteriology Kyushu U., 1983-97, ret., 1997, prof. emeritus, 1997—; chmn. cholera panel U.S.-Japan Med. Cooperative Program, 1993-95; mng. dir. Fukuoka Women's Jr. Coll., 1997-99; pres. 69th Nat. Meeting Japan Bacteriologist, 1996, 2nd Japan-Korea 2d Internat. Symposium of Microbiology, 1994. Editor: (jours.) Microbiology Immunology, Jour. Electron Microscopy, (textbook) Toda's New Bacteriology, 1997. Mem. Japanese Soc. Electron Microscopy (bd. mem. 1985-86, Seto award 1977), Japanese Soc. Bacteriology (bd. mem. 1988-93, pres. 1996, Asakawa award 1994). E-mail: amako@mxw.mesh.ne.jp.

AMAL, ICHLASUL, academic administrator. Rector U. Gehjah Mada, Vogyakarta, Indonesia. Office: Gadjah Mada U, Burksumur, Vogyakarta 55281, Indonesia*

AMALSAD, MEHER DADABHOY, writer, speaker, seminar leader; b. Karachi, Pakistan, Sept. 12, 1958; s. Dadabhoy and Nancy A.; m. Katayoon Amalsad; 1 child, Anahita Meher. BS in Engring., Nadirshaw Edulgee Dinshaw Engring. Univ., Karachi, Pakistan, 1982; MS in Engring., Northrop Univ., 1987. Program mgr. Hughes Aircraft Co., Rancho Santa, Calif., 1988-95; dist. mgr. ICM, Garden Grove, Calif., 1995-97; pres., CEO Starmasters, Garden Grove, Calif., 1997—; mem. acad. svcs. com. The Pegasus Sch., Huntington Beach, Calif., 1991-98. Author: Gifts That Lift, Shift and Uplift, 1996, Bread for the Head, 1997, In Search of Your Quest, How to Be Your Best, 1995, Love Grows and Shows Only When it Flows, 1995; co-author: (with Shahriar Shahriari) SOUL (Success Out-of Understanding Love), 1998, Bread for the Parents' Head, 1997; inventor. Chairperson First World Zoroastrian Youth Congress, 1993, First North Am. Zoroastrian Youth Congress, 1987, Helping Hands Com. of Fedn. of Zoroastrian Assns. N.Am., 1987-93; pres. Hughes Toastmasters, 1995. Mem. Profl. Speakers Network, Relationship Building Network (sponsor), Leads Club. Avocations: music, writing, dancing, speaking, inventing, creative cooking. Home: 15842 Villanova Cir Westminster CA 92683-7616

AMANAR, SIMONA, olympic athlete; b. Constanta, Romania, Oct. 7, 1979; d. Vasila and Sofika A. Mem. gymnastics team Romania; winner gold World Championship, 1995, 97, winner team gold, 1999, winner silver in vault and floor exercise, 1999; winner gold in vault Olympics, Atlanta, 1996, co-winner bronze in all-around, 1996, winner silver in floor exercise, 1996; winner gold individual all-around Olympics, Sydney, Australia, 2000, winner team all-around, 2000. Office: Romanian Gymnastics Ctr Romanian Studies, Ofcl Postal I Casuta Postala 108, 6600 Iasi Romania*

AMAND, JEAN-CLAUDE HENRI, chemist; b. Chimay, Hainaut, Belgium, Sept. 11, 1950; s. Henri Gaston and Madeleine Ghislaine (Cantinaux) A.; m. Nadine Andree Tambour, Apr. 28, 1973; children: Christophe, Nathalie. Grad. Chemist, I.P.E.T.S.E., Leuze, Belgium, 1970; Engring. in Chemistry, U. Nancy, France, 1982. Chemist diplomate. Chemist Sucreries de Donstiennes, Belgium, 1970-71, C.C.B., Gaurain, Belgium, 1973, Technicon Chems., Tournai, Belgium, 1973-74; prodn. supr. Idem, Belgium, 1974-75, prodn. mgr. asst., 1975-76, prodn. mgr., 1976-92; prodn. mgr. Bayer Diagnostics Mfg., Idem, Belgium, 1992-95; chemist, safety officer level 2 UCL, Louvain-la-Neuve, Belgium, 1997-99; safety officer level 1 faculty medicine U. Cath. de Louvain, Bruxelles, Belgium, 2000—. Author: Safety Synergy to a Zero Injury Target, 1994, (with A. Regibeau) Mixed Waste: Practical Experience with Belgian Regulation, 1998, Machinery Conformity Upgrade in Compliance with Belgian Regulation, 1999. Pres. Essor Luna Marquain, 1980—. With Med. Unit, 1972-73, Germany. Home: 30 Rue Rene Delrue, 7522 Blandain Belgium

AMANN, GABRIELE M., psychologist; b. Salzburg, Austria, July 8, 1960; d. Anton and Hildegard A. PhD, U. Salzburg, Austria, 1984; PD, U. Dortmund, Germany. Asst. U. Salzburg, 1984-99, prof., 1999—; psychotherapist Salzburg, 1988. Editor: Zeitschrift "Verhaltenstherapie & Verhaltensmedizin", Germany; editor: Sexual Abuse: A Survey of Research, Consulting and Therapy, 1997, Health Promotion: A Multidimensional Field, 1998. Mem. adv. bd. of youth welfare, regional govt., 1999—. Recipient Erwin Schroedinger award Fund of Sci. Rsch., Austria, 1986. Mem. Arbeitsgemeinschaft Verhaltensmodification, Deutsche Gesellschaft Psychologie. E-mail: gabriele.amann@sbg.ac.at. Office: Univ Salzburg/Inst Psych, Hellbrunnerstr 34, Salzburg 5020, Austria

AMANN, LESLIE KIEFER, lawyer, educator; b. Pensacola, Fla., Dec. 21, 1955; d. Robert C. and Marilyn Joan (Franklin) K.; m. Colin B. Amann, Apr. 12, 1985; children: Augustus Kiefer, Nicholas Jacob. BMEd, S.W. Tex. State U., 1976; JD, U. Houston, 1987. Bar: Tex. 1987, U.S. Dist. Ct. (so. dist.) Tex. 1988, U.S. Ct. Appeals (5th cir.), 1991, U.S. Dist. Ct. (no. dist.) Tex. 1992. Legis. aide to Lindon Williams Tex. State Senate, Austin, 1977-81; tchr. The Lincoln Sch., Guadalajara, Mex., 1979-82; legal asst. Koons Rasor Fuller & McCurley, Dallas, 1983-84; clk., assoc., participating assoc. Reynolds, Allen, Cook, Reynolds & Cunningham, Houston, 1984-93; shareholder Cunningham & Amann, Houston, 1993-94; asst. gen. counsel Charter Bank, Houston, 1995-96; fiduciary counsel Bank of America, Houston, 1996—; adj. faculty Law Sch., U. Houston, 1988—; mem. faculty Tex. Bankers Assn. Trust Sch., 1998, 99, 2000. Contbr. articles to profl. jours. Mem. adv. bd. Probate and Trust Law Inst., South Tex. Coll. Law, Houston, 1998, 99, 2000; vol. Annunciation Orthodox Sch., Houston, 1996; vol. Greater Houston Partnership Texas Scholars, 2000. Recipient Adj. Faculty award Univ. Houston Law Sch., 1999. Fellow Tex. Bar Found.; mem. Houston Bar Assn. (vol. lawyers in pub. schs. 1998), Tex. State Bar., Women Attys. in Tax and Probate. Republican. Methodist. Avocations: writing, reading, book collecting. Office: Bank of America PO Box 2518 700 Louisiana 6th Fl Houston TX 77252-2518

AMANO, MASAHARU, science educator; b. Hoten, Manchuria, Nov. 23, 1935; s. Shoichi and Ise (Mushiake) A.; m. Harue Matsumoto, Dec. 7, 1965; 1 child, Reiko. BS, Tokyo U. Edn., 1958, MS, 1960, PhD, 1965. Cert. H.S. tchr., Japan. Asst. Tokyo U. Edn., 1964-66; rschr. Nat. Inst. Ednl. Rsch., Tokyo, 1966-86, dir. rsch. dept., 1985-86; prof. U. Tsukuba, Japan, 1985-99, prof. emeritus, 1999—; prof. U. Seitoku, Japan, 1999—; rsch. fellow Textbook Rsch. Ctr., Tokyo, 1986—. Author: Education in Germany Today, 1978, What Education in West Germany Tells Us, 1981, Internationalization of Education in Japan and Germany, 1993, Intercultural Education in Germany, 1997. Recipient Continuous Svc. award Nat. Inst. Ednl. Rsch., 1984, U. Tsukuba, 1994. Mem. Ctrl. Rsch. Inst. Edn. (trustee 1989-98), Japan Soc. for Study of Edn. (trustee 1989—, chief sec. 1998—), Japan Comparative Edn. Soc. (trustee 1981—, chmn. 1997-99), Japanese Soc. for Philosophy of Edn. (trustee 1989—), Intercultural Edn. Soc. Japan (trustee 1991—), Japan Assn. Internat. Edn. (trustee 1995—). Buddhist. Avocations: reading, travel, tennis. Home: 1-36-17 Sakuradai, Nerima-ku Tokyo-to 176-0002, Japan Office: U Seitoku, 550 Iwase Matsudo-shi, Chiba-ken 271-8555, Japan

AMANZE, CHINENYE DOM, business educator, procurement consultant; b. Mbaise, Imo State, Nigeria, Dec. 22, 1954; s. Michael Odichukwu and Regina (Iroagalachi) A.; m. Kenny Adeshola; children: Nwadima, Obinna. BSc, Unilag, Lagos, Nigeria, 1985; MBA, A.A.U., 1990. Cert. in procurement mgmt. Purchasing mgr. IBRU, Nigeria, 1982-84; materials dir. Drek Ltd., Lagos, 1985-90; sr. lectr. Kano (Nigeria) State Poly. Sch. Mgmt. Studies, 1990—; CEO, Aman Assocs., Kano, 1995—; procurement cons. KNSG, Kano, 1991-93; cons. internat. multi-group, Nigeria, 1993—. Author: Advancing a New Procurement Initiative, 1991, Use of Mathematics in Inventory Control, 1993. Cmty. leader MFU, Imo, Nigeria. Mem. CIPS (sec. local br. 1992—), NIGP. Jehovah's Witness. Avocations: horticulture, cycling, classical music. Home: PO Box 12340, Kano Nigeria Office: Kano State Poly Sch Mgmt St, PMB 3404, Kano Nigeria

AMARAL, HELENA GALVÃO (LENAGAL, artist; b. San Miguel, Azores, Portugal, June 7, 1957; d. Manuel Vitorino Amaral and Olga Bettencourt Galvão; m. João Lourenco Victória, Feb. 17, 1997. Student, Portuguese Engravers Coop., Lisbon, 1987, Nat. Soc. Fine Arts, Lisbon, 1991, Art and Visual Comm. Ctr., Lisbon, 1992. Works exhibited in group shows at Gallery Pop Cave, Barcelos, Portugal, 1995, U. Mass.-Portuguese Am. Women's Assn., Dartmouth, 1997, Gallery One Capital Hill, Providence, R.I., 1998, Centro Cultural E. Bettencourt Governo Regional, Funchal, Portugal, 1999, U. S.C. Spartanburg Performing Arts Ctr. Gallery, 1999. Donator AMI Internat. Med. Assn., Lisbon, 1997, Portuguese-Am. Scholarship Found., Inc., R.I. and Mass., 1998, 99, Alzheimer Portuguese Assn., Lisbon, 1999. Recipient Silver medal Acad. European Desarts, Paris, 1996, citation The R.I. Ho. of Reps., Providence, 1998, diploma of excellence Art Addition Internat. Gallery, Stockholm, 1998. Avocations: music, dance, yoga, jogging, reading. Home and Office: R João de Deus 4-1 esq, 2735-285 Cacém Portugal

AMARAVADI, VEDADRI NARASIMHAM, physicist; b. Balemarru, India, June 24, 1935; s. Peravadhani and Saradamba Amaravadi. BSc, Andhra U., 1954, MSc, 1957; AINP, Indian Inst. Technology, Madras, 1960; PhD, Indian Inst. Technology, 1970. From lectr. to prof. physics Indian Inst. Technology, 1964-95; spkr., rschr. in field. Contbr. over 75 articles to profl. jours. Achievements include research in dielectrics, dielectric ultrasonics, theoretical and solid state physics. Home: 6 III St I Main Rd III Colo, Narayanapuram Pallikkaranai, Madras 601302, India

AMARCHAND, DEEPCHAND, commerce educator; b. Ajmer, Rajasthan, India, Nov. 18, 1941; s. Jain Deepchand and Kanwar Patang; m. Bai Vasantha, Feb. 17, 1964; three children. M in Commerce, U. Calcutta, India, 1962; LLB, U. Calcutta, 1964; MLitt, Annamalai U., India, 1965; PhD, Annamalai U., 1973. Lectr. Annamalai U., 1968-76; reader U. Madras, India, 1976-82; prof. U. Madras, 1982—, registrar, 1996-98. Author: Promotion and Control of Private Industry in India, 1976, Government and Business, 1994; editor Bus. Spectrum, 1989-93. Mem. All India Commerce Assn. (life). Jain. Avocations: conducting training course in quality of life, ethics. Home: 0-1 Lotus Colony First St, Nandanam Chennai Tamilnadu 600 035, India Office: Dept Commerce, Univ Madras, Chepauk Chennai 600 005, India

AMATI, PIETRO, computer and video engineer; b. Rome, Feb. 7, 1954; s. Pasquale and Rita (Alibrandi) A.; m. Marisa Papaluca, June 25, 1986; children: Federica, Alessandro. Degree in Engring., U. Rome, 1982. Cert. engr. Svc. mgr. Ampex, Rome, 1979-89; broadcast sales JVC, Rome, 1989-90; sales mgr. BTS, Rome, 1990-91; gen. mgr., owner Advanced Video Tech., Rome, 1991—, London, 1995—. Office: AVT Advanced Video Tech, Via Mosca 77, 00142 Rome Italy

AMAT LE COZ, JACQUELINE, Latin educator; b. Brest, France, Jan. 27, 1934. DSc (hon.), U. Paris, 1980. Prof. Lycée, St. Quentin, France, 1959-61, Lycié, Nantes, France, 1961-63; asst. U. Rennes, France, 1963-65, matire asst., 1965-72; maitre de conf. U. Brest, France, 1972-80, prof. Latin, 1980—; dir. rsch. Sur l'Antiquite Tardive. Author: Dreams and Visions in Late Antiquity, 1985, Dreams and Visions, 1996; editor: Califanius Siculus, 1991, Panio Peyetual and Felicitatio, 1993, Consdatio ad Leviem, Elgiae um Maecenatem, Bucolics of Euseldein, 1991. Roman Catholic. Avocation: sports. Home: 26 rue de Denver, 29200 Brest France Office: Faculte Lettres V Segalen, rue Duquesne, 29200 Brest France

AMATO, GUILIANO, Italian prime minister; b. Turin, Italy, May 13, 1938; married; 2 children. LLB, U. Pisa, Italy, 1960; M in Comparative Constitutional Law, Columbia U., 1963. Asst. prof. Italian and comparative constitutional law U. Rome, 1964-69; head legis. office Ministry Budget and Econ. Programming, Rome, 1967-68, 73-74; prof. constl. law U. Perugia, Italy, 1970-74; prof. law U. Florence, Italy, 1974-75; prof. U. Rome, 1975—; M.P. Rome, 1983—; under sec. state to pres. Coun. Mins., Rome, 1983-87, v.p., 1987-88; min. treasury Rome, 1987-88, 89-92; prime min., pres. Coun. Mins., Rome, 1992-93; min. treasury and budget Rome, from 1999; now prime minister Govt. of Italy, Rome; chmn. Commn. for Reorgn. of Presidency of Coun. Mins., 1979, Commn. for Reform of Pub. Industry, 1980; nat. dep. sec. Italian Socialist Party, 1988-92. Office: Palazzo Chigi, Piazza Colonna 370, 00100 Rome Italy*

AMATO, MARISA CAMPOS MORAES, cardiologist; b. São Paulo, Brazil, Sept. 8, 1953; d. Irany Novah and Fulvia Odylea Campos Neto Moraes; m. Salvador Jose De Toledo Arruda Amato, Apr. 7, 1978; children: Alexandre, Marcelo, Fernando. MD, Santo Amaro U., São Paulo, 1977; M of Medicine, São Paulo U., 1984, MD, 1991, private docent, 1999. Cert. med. dr. São Paulo. Asst. dr. Heart Inst. São Paulo U. Med. Sch., 1980-91; dir. cardiology divsn. Jaragua Hosp., São Paulo, 1980—; owner Vascular Cardio Ctr., São Paulo, 1993—; supr. cardiologists AMESP, São Paulo, 1980—; coord. MD residency cardiology and internal medicine Jaragua Hosp., São Paulo, 1991—; supr. health dept. Ibero-Am. U., São Paulo, 1996—; rsch. asst. Heart Inst., São Paulo U. Med. Sch., 1985-91. Author: (books) Diagnosis by Dynamic Imaging, 1996, Change of Life-Style, 1997; co-author: (book) Cardiologic Valve Disease, 1998; co-editor, author: (book) Health Problems in Brazil, 1995; co-editor: (mag.) Inst. for Devel. of Health Scis. and Med. Acads. of São Paulo, 1995—; editl. cons.: (mag.) Carisma, 1980-97, Brit. Med. Jour., 1997—. Recipient Best Study of Yr. in Cardiac Surgery award FUNCOR-BIOLAB, XLII Congress of Brazilian Cardiol. Soc., 1991, Best Book of Yr. in Nature and Med. Scis. Jabuti award; rsch. grantee Alexander Von Humboldt Found., 1992-93. Mem. Med. Acads. Soc. São Paulo (adj. sec., gen. sec. 1991-92, 93-94, 95-96, 97-98), Brazilian Med. Soc., Cardiol. Soc. São Paulo, Club of Humboldt Grant Receivers of Brazil (counselor, gen. sec. 1987-89, 95—). Fax: 55-11-50510233. E-mail: checkup@originet.com.br. Office: Vascular Cardio Ctr, Avenida Juriti 144, São Paulo 04520000, Brazil

AMAWATTANA, EMAVARDHANA TIPAWADEE, psychology educator; b. Nontaburi, Thailand, May 20, 1946; d. Samuth Emavardhana and Nualsri (Panichkul) Amawattana. BA with honors in Psychology, Thammasat U., Bangkok, 1970; M Psychology, Flinders U., Adelaide, South Australia, 1974; PhD, U Mo., 1985. Cert. counseling psychology, clin. psychology. Lectr. Thammasat U., Bangkok, 1970-76, asst. prof., 1976-83, assoc. prof. psychology, 1983—; cons. Internat. Labour Orgn., Bangkok, 1986-96; guest spkr. Univs., Bangkok; trainer pharm. cos., Bangkok, 1992-96; trainer, cons. pub. health, Payao, Loburi, Thailand, 1992—. Author, translator: How to Bring Up Your Parents, 1976 (award 1980, Thai translation version). Recipient scholarship Am. Field Svc., Sebastopol, Calif., 1964, award Nat. Coun. Social Welfare of Thailand, 1980; scholar Ctr. AIDS Prevention Studies, U. Calif., San Francisco, 1991. Mem. APA, Internat. Coun. Psychologists. Avocation: gardening. Office: Thammasat U Dept Psychology, Faculty Liberal Arts, Bangkok 10200, Thailand

AMBACH, GORDON MAC KAY, educational association executive; b. Providence, Nov. 10, 1934; s. Russell W. and Ethel (Repass) A.; m. Lucy DeWitt Emory, Mar. 9, 1963; children: Kenneth Emory, Alison Repass, Douglas Mac Kay. BA, Yale U., 1956; MA, Harvard U. Grad. Sch. Edn., 1957, cert. advanced study, 1966. Tchr. social studies 7th and 8th grades East Williston Sch. Dist., L.I., N.Y., 1958-61; asst. program planning officer U.S. Office Edn., Washington, 1961-62, asst. legis. specialist, 1962-63, exec. sec. Higher Edn. Facilities Act Task Force, 1963-64; adminstrv. asst. to mem. Boston Sch. Com., 1964-65; staff seminar mgr., mem. staff Harvard U. Grad. Sch. Edn., Cambridge, Mass., 1966-67; spl. asst. to commr. for long range planning N.Y. State Edn. Dept., Albany, 1967-69, asst. commr. for long range planning, 1969-70, exec. dep. commr., 1970-77; commr. edn. and pres. U. State N.Y., Albany, 1977-87; exec. dir. Coun. Chief State Sch. Officers, Washington, 1987—; del., chmn. resolutions com. The White House Conf. on Librs. and Info. Scis., 1991; mem. Nat. Coun. on Edn. Standards and Testing; chmn. nat. adv. panel Ctr. Student Testing, Evaluation and Standards, Rsch. Ctr. on Learning Techs.; mem. adv. com. Getty Edn. Inst. for Arts; mem. Nat. Bd. Internat. Comparative Studies in Edn., U.S. rep. to Internat. Assn. for Evaluation of Edn. Achievement, mem. standing com. With USAR, 1957-63. Mem. Acad. Polit. Scis., Am. Assn. Sch. Adminstrs., PEW Forum on Edn. Reform, Phi Delta Kappa. Office: Coun Chief State Sch Officers One Massachusetts Ave NW Ste 700 Washington DC 20001

AMBACHE, NACHMAN, medical researcher; b. Ismailia, Egypt, July 8, 1917; came to Eng., 1929; s. Simha and Lea (Steinberg) A.; m. Stella Cornes, Sept. 14, 1942; children—Jonathan (dec.), Jeremy, Diana. B.A. in Natural Scis., Trinity Coll., Cambridge, Eng., 1939. Lectr. pathology Guy's Hosp., London, 1943-47; lectr. physiology Univ. Coll., London, 1947-48; Med. Research Council staff Inst. Ophthalmology, London, 1948-59; external staff, dir. Med. Research Council, Royal Coll. Surgeons, London, 1959-82. Contbr. chpts to books, articles to profl. jours.; editor Jour. Physiology, 1959-66, Brit. Jour. Pharmacology, 1967-71. Recipient Sr. scholarship Trinity Coll., 1938. Fellow Royal Soc. Medicine; mem. Physiol. Soc., Brit. Pharm. Soc. Avocations: chamber music; violin restorations.

AMBARISHA, BABU MULLANGI, scientist; b. Kalakada, India, July 1, 1956; s. Seshaiah Mullangi and Mullangi (Subbarathnamma) Seshaiah; m. Ambarish Sreelatha, Mar. 29, 1978; children: Shilpa Ambarish, Vinesh Ambarish. B of Tech., S.V.U. Engring. Coll., Tirupati, India, 1978; M of Tech., J.N.T. U., Kakinada, India, 1980. Lectr. K.O.R.E. Coll., Cuddapah, India, 1980; scientist "C" Indian Space Rsch Orgn., Sriharikota, India, 1980-85; scientist "D" Indian Space Rsch Orgn., Bangalore, India, 1985-90, scientist "E", 1990-97, scientist "F", 1997—. Avocations: reading, sports, TV, swimming. Home: 46 3d Main Manjunatha Nagar, 2d Phase Bangalore 560 010, India

AMBARTSOUMIAN, EUGENIA NICKOLAEVNA, physicist, researcher; b. Tambov, Russia, Oct. 23, 1940; d. Nickolai Petrovitch and Zinaida Georgievna (Baraboshkina) Galkin; m. Rafael Victorovitch Ambartsoumian, Oct. 16, 1962; children: Shagane, Andrey. Diploma in physicist experimentator, Moscow State U., 1958-64; postgrad., USSR Acad. Scis., 1972-76, PhD Inst. High Temps., 1981. Engr. spl. constructor Tech. Bur., Moscow, 1964-66; jr. sci. rschr. High Temperature Inst. Russian Acad. Scis., Moscow, 1966-78; sr. rschr. scientist Inst. for Problems in Mechanics, Moscow, 1978—; head of sci. rsch. group Inst. for Problems in Mechanics, Moscow, 1981—. Inventor in field; contbr. over 60 articles to profl. jours. Grantee Found. Fundamental Investigations of Russia, 1995-99. Mem. Soc. Znanie, Mendeleev Sci. Soc., N.Y. Acad. Scis. Avocations: tennis, skiing, working in garden, theater, conservatory. Home: Academic Vargi str 24-52, 117133 Moscow Russia Office: Inst for Problems in Mechanics, Vernadskogo prospect 101, 117526 Moscow Russia

AMBER, DOUGLAS GEORGE, lawyer; b. East Chicago, Ind., Apr. 15, 1956; s. George and Margaret (Watson) A. BA in Polit. Sci., Ind. U., 1978; JD, U. Miami, 1985. Bar: Fla. 1985, US. Ct. Claims 1986, U.S. Ct. Internat. Trade 1986, U.S. Tax Ct. 1986, U.S. Ct. Appeals (11th cir.) 1986, U.S. Dist. Ct. (mid. and so. dists.) Fla. 1987, U.S. Ct. Mil. Appeals 1987, U.S. Ct. Appeals (fed. cir.) 1987, Ind. 1988, U.S. Dist. Ct. (no. and so. dists.) Ind. 1988, U.S. Ct. Appeals (7th cir.) 1989, U.S. Supreme Ct. 1989. Dep. prosecutor 31st Jud. Cir. Ind., Crown Point, 1988-93; pvt. practice Munster, 1993—; adj. prof. polit. sci. Purdue U., 1997—. Mem. exec. bd. dirs. Calumet coun. Boy Scouts Am., 1994-96. Mem. ABA, Acad. Legal Studies in Bus., Nat. Dist. Attys. Assn., South Lake County Bar Assn., Ind. State Bar Assn., Lake County Bar Assn. (bd. dirs. 1990-96), Ind. Trial Lawyers Assn., Audio Engring. Soc., Soc. Audio Cons. (cert. video and audio cons.), Mensa, Delta Theta Phi. Avocations: bicycling, weight training. E-mail: amber@axp.calumet.purdue.edu. Office: Amber Golding & Hofstetter 9250 Columbia Ave Ste E-2 Munster IN 46321-3530

AMBER, LAURIE KAUFMAN, lawyer; b. N.Y.C., Apr. 15, 1954; d. Martin and Barbara (Schiffman) Kaufman; m. Henry Michael Amber, June 18, 1977; children: Ian, Kyle. BS, Cornell U., 1974, MBA, 1975; JD, U. Miami, 1978. Bar: Fla. 1978, U.S. Dist. Ct. (so. dist.) Fla. 1978, U.S. Tax Ct. 1978, U.S. Ct. Appeals (5th cir.) 1979, U.S. Ct. Customs and Patent Appeals 1979, U.S. Customs Ct. 1979, U.S. Ct. Appeals (11th cir.) 1981, U.S. Ct. Internat. Trade 1981, U.S. Supreme Ct. 1982, U.S. Claims Ct. 1985; cert. circuit mediator Supreme Ct. Fla.; cert. family mediator Supreme Ct. Fla. Staff mgr. Proctor & Gamble Mfg. Co., Staten Island, N.Y., 1975; adj. asst. prof. Nova U., Fort Lauderdale, Fla., 1976-77; atty., labor arbitrator Amber & Amber, P.A., South Miami, Fla., 1978—; arbitrator nat. labor panel Am. Arbitration Assn., Miami, 1982—, Grievance Arbitration Panel of Fla. PERC, Tallahassee, 1979—; hearing examiner pers. appeals County of Dade, Miami, 1985-91, 2000—; dir. Kids That Care Pediat. Cancer Fund, 1996—. Pres. Office Village Condominium Assn., South Miami, 1994, Children's Cancer Fund, 1996-2000; bd. dirs. Jackson Meml. Found., 1996-2000, Kids That Care Pediatric and Cancer Fund, 2000—. Named Woman of Yr. ABWA, 1983. Mem. ABA, Zonta (bd. dirs. Coral Gables, Fla. club 1988). Office: Amber & Amber PA 7731 SW 62nd Ave Ste 202 Miami FL 33143-4908

AMBERS, HENRY JOHN, writer; b. June 24, 1916; s. Stanley Ambers and Maria Balsikiewicz. Student, U. Mo., 1943-44; BA, U. Calif., Berkeley, 1949. Enlisted U.S. Army; clk.-typist U.S. 9th Army Hdqs.; food ops. chief U.S. Mil. Govt., Berlin. Author: The Dirigible and the Future, 1970, rev. edit., 1981, The Waltzer, 1970, The Unfinished Building, 1974. Home and Office: 405 E 63d St New York NY 10021

AMBIRAJAN, SRINIVASA, economics educator; b. Jan. 10, 1936; s. Srinivasa Iyengar and Padmasani Ambirajan; m. Prabha Dorasamy; children: Amrit, Neela. BA with honors, Andhra U., Waltair, Andhra Pradesh, India, 1955, MA with honors, 1957, PhD, 1960; PhD, Manchester (Eng.) U., 1964. Lectr. U. Queensland, Brisbane, Australia, 1964-66; sr. lectr. U. NSW, Sydney, Australia, 1966-74, assoc. prof., 1974-81; prof. Indian Inst. Tech., Madras, 1981-96; hon. prof. Madras Sch. Econs. Author: Taxation of Corporate Income in India, 1964, Classical Political Economy and British Policy, 1978, Political Economy and Monetary Management: India 1766-1914, 1984, Good People Bad Times: Views from Periphery, 1998. Hallsworth fellow U. Manchester, 1961-64, Simon sr. fellow, 1980. Mem. Am. Econ. Assn., History of Econs. Soc. Hindu. Home: Sydney House 277-B TTK Salai, Madras Tamilnadu India 600018 Office: Madras Sch Econs, Gandhi Mandapam Rd, Madras 600025, India

AMBLER, ZDENĚK, neurologist, educator; b. Pilsen, Czechoslovakia, Dec. 2, 1940; s. Josef and Vlasta (Hodková) A.; m. Věra Novotná, Nov. 23, 1974; children: Tomás, Martina. MD, Charles U., Prague, 1963, PhD, 1980; DSc, Palacky U., Olomouc, Czech Republic, 1988. Diplomate Bd. Electromyography, Bd. Neurology. Physician Mil. Hosp., Pilsen, Czechoslovakia, 1963-71; asst. prof. Sch. Medicine, Charles U., Pilsen, 1971-84, assoc. prof., 1984-90, prof., chmn. dept. neurology, 1990—; vis. fellow Uppsala (Sweden) U., 1984; vis. prof. U. London, U. Nijmegen, The Netherlands, U. Edinburgh, Scotland, Oxford (Eng.) U., Duke U., Harvard U., 1991-95; rschr. on neuromuscular disorders, cerebrovascular disorders; nat. coord. Internat. Stroke Trial, 1991-96. Mem. editl. bd. Ces Slov Neurol Neurochir jour.; author: Ces a Slov Neruol. Neurochir, Electroenceph Clin. Neurophysiol; contbr. articles to profl. jours. Mem. Czech Soc. Neurology (mem. com. 1990—, chmn. sec. for neuromuscular disorders), Czech Soc. for Clin. Neurophysiology (mem. com. 1990—), European Fedn. Neurol. Socs. (mem. task force for continuous med. edn.), World Fedn. Neurology (nat. rep. 1996—), N.Y. Acad. Scis. Avocations: skiing, travel, arts, music. Office: Univ Hosp Dept Neurology, alej Svobody 80, 304 60 Pilsen Czech Republic

AMBROS, PETER FRIEDRICH, geneticist; b. Vienna, June 21, 1953; s. Franz and Inge Ambros; m. Inge M. Schratter, June 11, 1988; children: Raphael, Magdalena. Degree in philosophy, U. Vienna, 1984. Asst. dept. cytogenetics Inst. Botany, Vienna, 1976-80; postdoctoral rschr. human genetics unit MRC, Edinburgh, Great Britain, 1984-85; scientist dept. molecular biology Austrian Acad. Sci., Salzburg, 1985-86; co-dir., scientist Children's Cancer Rsch. Inst., Vienna, 1988—. With Austrian Mil., 1975. Home: Carl Reichertgasse 26, A-1170 Vienna Austria Office: Childrens Cancer Rsch Inst, Kinderspitalgasse 6, A-1090 Vienna Austria

AMBROS, ROBERT ANDREW, pathologist, educator; b. Passaic, N.J., May 21, 1959; s. Henry and Adele (Ruta) A.; m. Maryla Warszawa, Aug. 22, 1981; children: Robert, Janek, Julia. MD, Copernicus Acad. Medicine, 1982. Resident in surgery Morristown (N.J.) Meml. Hosp., 1983-85; resident in pathology N.J. Med. Sch., Newark, 1985-89; fellow in gynecologic pathology Johns Hopkins Hosp., Balt., 1989-91; asst. prof. pathology Albany (N.Y.) Med. Coll., 1991-96, asst. prof. ob-gyn., 1993-96, assoc. prof. pathology, ob-gyn., 1996—; cons. in gynecologic pathology Albany Med. Coll., 1991—. Contbr. articles to profl. jours.; editor: Internat. Jour. Gynecol. Pathology, 1994—. Clin. oncology fellow Am. Cancer Soc., 1990; recipient Basic Oncology Rsch. award Am. Cancer Soc., 1988. Fellow Coll. Am. Pathologists; mem. AAAS, Internat. Soc. Gynecol. Pathologists, Internat. Acad. Pathology, N.Y. Acad. Scis., Johns Hopkins Med. and Surg. Assn. Achievements include research in the surgical and molecular pathology of gynecologic malignancies. Office: Albany Med Coll Dept Pathology 43 New Scotland Ave Albany NY 12208-3412

AMBROSE, DUNSTON PHILOMAN, entomology educator, researcher; b. Melamanakudy, India, Feb. 23, 1955; s. Philoman and Nambikkai Mary (Philoman) A.; m. Annie Dunston, May 6, 1981; children: Sarah Aveline, Kiruba Angeline. BSc, Scott Christian Coll., Nagercoil, India, 1974; MSc, Am. Coll., Madurai, India, 1976; PhD, U. Madras, Coimbatore, India, 1980; DSc, Madurai Kamaraj U., India, 1999. Field biologist BNHS, Point Calimere, India, 1980-81; asst. prof. zoology St. Joseph's Coll., Trichy, India, 1981-82; lectr. zoology St. Xavier's Coll., Palayankottai, Tamil Nadu, India, 1982—; dir. entomology rsch. unit St. Xavier's Coll, 1982—. Author: (monograph) Assassin Bugs, 1999; editor: Biological and Cultural Control of Insect Pests, 1996; contbr. numerous articles to sci. publs. Recipient Spkr. award XIX Internat. Congress Entomology, Beijing, 1992, Career award Univ. Grants Commn., India, 1993, St. Xaveriah Rsch. award, 1997, 98, 99, 200. Mem. Heteropterist Assn. (U.S.), Biocontrol Advancement. Mem. Assembly of God Ch. Avocations: evangelism, philately, gardening. Home: Jesus Abides, 644 B 15th Cross St, Tirunelveli Thiyagarajanagar India 627 011 Office: St Xavier's Coll, Entomology Rsch Unit, Taml Ndu Palayamkottai 627 002, India

AMBROSE, THOMAS ALBERT, II, orthopaedic surgeon; b. Las Vegas, Nev., Apr. 2, 1957; s. Thomas Anthony and Ida Ambrose; m. DeniseLynn Trimmer, Sept. 18, 1993; 1 child, Hunter Blair. BA, UCLA, 1979; MD, Ohio State U., 1983. Diplomate Nat. Bd. Med. Examiners, Am. Bd. Orthopaedic Surgery. House staff Riverside Meth. Hosp., Columbus, Ohio, 1983-88, Ohio State U. Hosp., Columbus, 1983-88, Columbus Children's Hosp., 1986-88; fellow The Children's Hosp., Denver, 1988-89; assoc. prof. Ind. U. Sch. Medicine, Indpls., 1989—; fellow AO/ASIF, Hannover, Germany, Basel, Switzerland, 1989. Fellow ACS, Am. Acad. Orthopaedic Surgeons; mem. AMA, Orthopaedic Trauma Assn., Mid Am. Orthopaedic Assn., Ind. Orthopaedic Soc. Avocations: golf, big game and waterfowl hunting, scuba diving, sailing. Office: Associated Orthopaedic Surgeons 541 Clinical Dr Ste 600 Indianapolis IN 46202-5233

AMBROSI, GERHARD MICHAEL, economics educator; b. Berlin, Mar. 27, 1943; s. Gerhard Michael and Maria-Elisabeth (Koch) A.; m. Marlene Beuttenmueller, Dec. 11, 1987; 1 child, Christine. Diploma in econs., Free U., Berlin, 1968, PhD in Econs., 1979. Rschr., organizing asst. Cambridge U., England, 1969-70; asst. to commissary A. Spinelli European Cmty., Belgium, 1970-71; rschr. U. Constance, Germany, 1971-72; lectr. Wagner Coll. Study Program, Bregenz, Austria, 1972-76; rschr., assoc. prof. Free U., Berlin, 1976-92; prof. European econ. policy Trier U., Germany, 1992—; organizing asst. 2d World Congress, Econometric Soc., Cambridge, 1970; v.p. Study Reform for Econs., Baden-Wuerttemberg, Germany, 1972; vis. prof. Fudan U., Shanghai, 1996; head dept. econs. U. Trier, 1995-97; hon. prof. U. Transilvania, Brasov, Romania. Author: Payments Union and Transformation, 1993; contbr. articles to profl. jours. Acad. dir. European Documentation Ctr., U. Trier, 1996—. Mem. European Cmty. Studies Assn., Verein Socialpolitik, Deutscher Hochschulverband, European Soc. History Econ. Thought. Avocations: history, violin. Office: Trier U FB IV VWL, D-54286 Trier Germany

AMBROSIADIS, IOANNIS, veterinarian, food scientist, educator; b. Thessaloniki, Greece, Sept. 13, 1952; s. Aristidis and Eleni (Vavoura) A.; m. Zoumboulio Petkoglou; children: Aristidis, Evdoxia. DMV, U. Thessaloniki, 1976; postgrad., Fed. Meat Rsch. Inst., Kulmbach, Germany, 1977-79; PhD, Free U. Berlin, 1981. Scientific contbr. Fed. Inst. Meat Tech., Kulmbach, 1981-83; prodn. supr. Kreser Meat Industry, Serres, Greece, 1986-89; food control lab. staff Agr. Ministry, Rhodes, Greece, 1986; lectr. vet. medicine U. Aristotle, Thessaloniki, 1989-94, asst. prof. vet. medicine, 1994—; scientific cons. Confedn. Agr., Germany, 1978-83, Kreser Co., 1989-93. Author: Meat Technology, 1999; contbr. articles to internat. profl. jours. and mags. With Greek Mil., 1983-85, Thessaloniki. Mem. Greek Food Tech. Soc., Greek Vet. Soc., Greek Hygienists Soc. Home: Ellis 6, GR-57019 Peraia Greece Office: Aristotle U Fac Vet Med, Univ Campus, GR-54006 Thessaloniki Greece

AMBROSO, GUIDO CLAUDIO, United Nations official; b. Milan, Oct. 20, 1961; s. Alessandro and Liana (Ruberl) A.; m. Nayma Moussa Ahmed, Feb. 13, 1994; children: Emanuele Eli, Micol Sagal. BA in Anthropology/Geography with honors, U. London, 1983, PhD in Geography, 1987. Tutor U. Coll. London, 1986; protection officer UN High Commn. for Refugees, Kampala, Uganda, 1988-90; field officer UN High Commn. for Refugees, Sanandaj, Iran, 1991; protection officer UN High Commn. for Refugees, Djibouti, 1992, Jijiga, Ethiopia, 1993-95; field officer UN High Commn. for Refugees, Azerbaijan, 1995-97; field/repatriation officer UN High Commn. for Refugees, Hargeisa, Somalia, 1997—; European affairs officer Brussels, 1999. Author chpt. to book and articles to profl. jours. Recipient Radcliffe-Brown award Royal Anthrop. Soc. London, 1987. Avocations: studying history of Horn of Africa, listening to Latin jazz and Bossa Nova. Office: UNHCR Pouch Hargeisa (Somalia), PO Box 2500, CH-1211 Geneva 2, Switzerland

AMBROZAITIS, ARVYDAS, medical educator, researcher; b. Vilnius, Lithuania, May 16, 1948; s. Kazys and Birute (Kucinskaite) A.; m. Jurate Visockaite Ambrozaitiene, June 28, 1975; children: Milda, Birute. MD, U. Vilnius Med. Faculty, Lithuania, 1972; PhD, Inst. Virology Med. Acad., Moscow, 1981; Habil. Dr., U. Vilnius, Lithuania, 1995. Assoc. investigator U. Vilnius, Lithuania, 1972-75; asst. prof., 1975-90, assoc. prof., 1990-98, prof. medicine, 1998—; chmn. Dept. Infectious Diseases U. Vilnius, Lithuania, 1990—. Mem. Vilnius-Madison Sister Cities, Inc., 1995—. Fulbright scholar U. Wis., 1997; recipient Outstanding Contbns. in Rsch. award Vilnius Med. Soc., Lithuania, 1992, 96. Mem. Lithuanian Soc. For Infectious Diseases (chmn.), European Assn. for Study of Liver, Internat. Soc. Infectious Diseases, European AIDS Clin. Soc. Avocations: languages, travel, tennis. E-mail: arvydas.ambrozhitis@elnet.lt. Office: U Vilnius Dept Infect Diseases, Birutes 1, LT-2004 Vilnius Lithuania

AMBROZIC, ALOYSIUS CARDINAL (HIS EMINENCE ALOYSIUS CARDINAL AMBROZIO), cardinal archbishop; b. Gabrje, Slovenia, Jan. 27, 1930; s. Aloysius and Helen (Pecar) A. Student, St. Augustine Sem., 1955; S.T.L., U. San Tommaso, Rome, 1958, Sacrae Scripturae Licentiatus, Biblicum, Rome, 1960; Th.D., U. Wurzburg, 1970. Ordained priest Roman Cath. Ch., 1955. Ordained aux. bishop of Roman Cath. Ch., Toronto, 1976; appointed coadjutor archbishop of Toronto, 1986, archbishop of Toronto, 1990—, created cardinal, 1998; parish work Port Colborne, Ont., Can., 1955-56; faculty St. Augustines Sem., Scarborough, Ont., Can., 1956-76, dean studies, 1971-76; prof. N.T. exegesis Toronto Sch. Theology, 1970-76; apptd. to Pontifical Coun. for Pastoral Care of Migrants and Itinerant People, 1990, Vatican Congregation for Clergy, 1991, Pontifical Coun. for Culture, 1993, Vatican Congregation for Divine Worship and Discipline of Sacraments, 1999, Congregation for Oriental Chs., 1999; rep. Synod on the Formation of Priests, Rome, 1990, Synod on Religious Life, Rome, 1994. Author: The Hidden Kingdom: A Redaction-Critical Study of the References to the Kingdom of God in Mark's Gospel, 1972, Remarks on the Canadian Catechism, 1974; former columnist Cath. Register.

AMBRUS, JULIAN L., physician, medical educator; b. Budapest, Hungary, Nov. 29, 1924; came to U.S., 1949, naturalized, 1955; s. Alexander and Elizabeth Ambrus; m. Clara M. Bayer, Feb. 18, 1945; children: Madeline (Mrs. David Lillie), Peter, Julian, Linda (Mrs. Edward Broenniman), Steven, Katherine (Mrs. Thomas Cheney), Charles. Student, U. Budapest, 1942-47; MD., U. Zurich, 1949; postgrad., Sorbonne, 1949-50; PhD in Med. Sci, Jefferson Med. Coll., 1954; ScD (hon.), Niagara U., 1984. Diplomate: Am. Bd. Clin. Chemistry, Am. Acad. Pain Mgmt. Research asst., instr. histology and med. biology U. Budapest, 1943-45, demonstrator pharmacology, 1946-47; asst. pharmacology U. Zurich, 1947-49; asst. dept. therapeutic chemistry, virology and tropical medicine Inst. Pasteur, Paris, 1949; asst. prof., asso. prof., prof. Phila. Coll. Pharmacology and Sci., 1950-55; prin. cancer research scientist Roswell Park Meml. Cancer Inst. and Hosp., 1955-65; asst. to the dir. Roswell Park Meml. Inst. and Hosp., 1961-65; dir. Springville Labs., 1965-75, dir. cancer research, head dept. pathophysiology, 1975-89, mem. dept. medicine, 1989-92; asst. prof. pharmacology U. Buffalo Med. Sch., 1955-61, asso. prof. pharmacology, 1961-65, prof., 1965-72; chmn. Roswell Park div. exec. com. Grad. Sch., 1955-65; assoc. in internal medicine SUNY, Buffalo, 1961-64, asst. prof. internal medicine, 1964-66, prof. biochem. pharmacology, 1964-80, assoc. prof. internal medicine, 1966-71, prof., 1971—; prof., chmn. dept. exptl. pathology Grad. Sch., 1972-92; prof. emeritus, 1992—; attending physician Roswell Park Meml. Cancer Hosp., 1955-92, prof. emeritus Roswell Park Cancer Inst., 1992—; attending physician Buffalo Gen. Hosp., Erie County Med. Ctr., Children's Hosp. Buffalo, 1983—; cons. Millard Fillmore Hosp., Sisters of Charity Hosp., Buffalo, 1983—; dir. Instnl. Cancer Tng. Program, USPHS, 1956-65; mem. com. Thrombolytic agts. USPHS-NIH, 1960-66; cons. adv. com. on thrombosis AMA Coun. Drugs; Blood Coagulation Components, Protein Found., Cambridge, Mass.; Bur. Drugs FDA, WHO, Geneva; commr. Lake Erie chpt. U.S. Pony Clubs, mem. intercollegiate polo com. Editor-in-chief: Revs. of Hematology Jour. Medicine; contbr. articles to profl. jours. Trustee Calasanctius Prep. Sch. for Acad. Gifted, 1964-92. Decorated Order of Alexander the Great (France), knight comdr. Equestrian Order Holy Sepulcher of Jerusalem; recipient first prize med. student paper Hungarian Med. Sch., 1947, 1st prize surgery U. Budapest, 1947, Nelson lectureship and medal U. Calif. Davis, 1972, George F. Koepf award in biomed. rsch. Hauptman-Woodward Med. Rsch. Inst., 1997, Heart and Hand award EUA, 1997, Louis A. and Ruth Siegel award SUNY Buffalo Sch. Medicine, 1997; named Disting. Alumnus Thomas Jefferson U., 1990. Fellow ACP, AAAS, Am. Coll. Nuclear Physicians, Am. Coll. Angiology, Royal Soc. Medicine, Am. Coll. Pharmacology and Chemotherapy, Coun. on Clin. Cardiology, Am. Heart Assn., Internat. Coll. Angiology, Am. Geriat. Soc., N.Y. Acad. Sci., Internat. Soc. Hematology; mem. NAS (fgn. mem. Hungary), Am. Soc. Hematology, Am. Soc. Pathologists, Am. Soc. Nuclear Medicine, Am. Soc. Pharmacology and Exptl. Therapeutics, Am. Soc. Physiology, Am. Assn. Cancer Rsch., Am. Soc. Clin. Oncology, Fedn. Clin. Rsch., Soc. Exptl. Biology and Medicine, Assn. Am. Med. Colls., Cath. Physicians Guild (pres. 1985-86, 93-96), Sigma Xi, Rho Chi, Physiol. Soc. Phila., Radiation Rsch. Soc., Buffalo Zool. Soc. (chmn. Sci. Com. 1965-66), Buffalo Acad. Medicine (pres. 1976-77). Home: 143 Windsor Ave Buffalo NY 14209-1020 also: West Hill Farm Emmerling Rd Boston NY 14025 Office: Buffalo Gen Hosp Kaleida Health Sys SUNY/B 100 High St Buffalo NY 14203-1154

AMBUJAM, N.K., agricultural engineering educator; b. Chennai, Tamil Nadu, India, Mar. 8, 1962; s. N. Kanniperumal and V.S. Vimala; m. M. Madhusoothanna, May 27, 19184; children: Manu Vaasanthi, Vimala Madhangi. B Engring., Tamil Nadu Agrl. U., Coimbatore, India, 1984; PhD, Anna U., Chennai, 1993. Asst. engr. Dept. Agrl. Engring., Chennai, 1984-85; lectr. Anna U., 1990-94, sr. lectr., 1994—; cons. W.R.O., Chennai, 1999—, Sipcot, Chennai, 1998. Tchg. rsch. fellow C.W.R., 1986, sr. rsch. fellow CSIR, 1989, travel fellow Swedish Inst., 1992. Mem. Inst. Engrs. (assoc.), Indian Water Resources Soc. Hindu. E-mail: nkamguj@annauniv.edu. Home: No 3 Temple Ave, Sri Nagar Colony, Saidapet Channai 600 015, India Office: Anna U, Ctr Water Resources, Chennai Tamil Nadu 600 025, India

AMDUR, ARTHUR R., lawyer; b. Houston, Jan. 19, 1946; s. Paul S. and Florence Amdur; m. Dora B.; children—Josh, Jonny, Shira. B.A., 1967; J.D., 1970; LL.M., 1974. Bar: Tex. 1970, D.C. 1974; cert. immigration law Tex. Bd. Legal Specialization, 1988 . pvt. practice, Houston and Washington, 1970-76; asst. U.S. atty, Houston, 1976-82; pvt. practice, Houston, 1982—, lectr. on immigration law ; adj. prof. law South Tex. Coll. Law, Houston. Bd. dirs. YMCA Internat. Refugee Ctr., 1985—; spl. asst. to gen. counsel Republican Nat. Com., Washington, 1974. Named Adj. Law Prof. of Yr., South Tex. Coll. Law, 1983. Mem. Fed. Bar Assn. (pres. 1981), Tex. State Bar Assn., Am. Immigration Lawyers Assn., Immigration Law Examiner, State Bar Tex. (bd. legal specialization 1997—). Jewish. Club: Georgetown U. Alumni (pres. 1984) (Houston). Office: Amdur Law Office 6161 Savoy Dr Ste 450 Houston TX 77036-3379

AMEDURI, BRUNO MICHEL, materials researcher; b. Marseille, France, Aug. 20, 1961; s. Louis Virgilio and Raymonde Therese (Moureau) A.; m. Catherine Marie-Pierre Destampes, Aug. 7, 1993; children: Damien, Julien. Diploma in chem. engring., Ecole Nat. Superieure Chimie, Montpellier, France, 1984; MSc, U. Laval, Que., Can., 1986; PhD, U. Montpellier, 1988. Rschr. IBM, San Jose, Calif., 1986, Ecole Nat. Superieure Chemistry, Montpellier, 1986—; dir. rsch. CNRS; rschr. U. Prague, Czech Republic, 1992; referee Jour. Fluorine Chemistry, Macromolecular Chem. Physics, Polymer Internat., Chem. Materials. Treas. Montpellier Tandem Club Handisport, 1995—. Mem. French Polymer Soc., French Chem. Soc., Am. Chem. Soc. Roman Catholic. Achievements include research in synthesis of fluorinated monomers, telomers, polymers and elastomers. Avocations: tandem biking with the blind, hiking, swimming, skiing. Home: 28 rue Treille Muscate, 34090 Montpellier France Office: Ecole Nat Superieure Chimie, 8 rue Ecole Normale, 34296 Montpellier Cedex 5, France

AMEEN, FAWZI ABDULLA, physician; b. Muhurraq, Bahrain, Mar. 30, 1955; s. Abdulla Ameen Mohamed and Mariam (Hamed) Al Mahmeed; m. Ashjan Ahmed Almahmeed, July 4, 1985. MB, Cairo U., Cairo, 1977; family practice cert., Am. U., Beruit, 1982; Diploma in Tropical Medicine and Hygiene, Liverpool U., Eng., 1983; MPH, Johns Hopkins U., Balt., 1987; PhD, Leeds U., 1998. Resident in family medicine Salmaniya Med. Ctr., Bahrain, 1979-81, sr. resident, 1981-83; physician in charge Sh. Sulman Health Ctr., Bahrain, 1984; dep. chief of staff for family and community health Primary Health Care, Bahrain, 1985—; asst. prof. faculty medicine Arabian Gulf U., 1990—. Contbr. articles to profl. jours. Chmn. 1st aid

com. Bahrain Red Cross Soc., 1980—, undersec. assistance for internal affairs, 1981—. Mem. Bahrain Med. Soc. (research prize 1983), Royal Coll. Gen. Practitioners, Royal Soc. Tropical Medicine, Am. Pub. Health Assn. Club: Muhurraq Sports. Office: Ministry of Health, Ministry of Health, PO Box 22118, Manama State of Bahrain

AMELAR, RICHARD DANIEL, urologist, andrologist; b. N.Y.C., July 9, 1927. BA, NYU, 1946, MD, 1950. Resident urology NYU Med. Ctr.; pvt. practice urology N.Y.C.; mem. faculty NYU, prof. clin. urology, 1977—; dir. Male Infertility Clinic, Bellevue Hosp., 1970. Cons. editor Urology; assoc. editor Internat. Jour. Fertility; editl. bds. Fertility and Sterility, Jour. Andrology Internat. Jour. Nephrology, Urology, Andrology. Grantee Irene Heinz Give and John La Porte Given Found. and N.Y. Found., 1970; ecipient Disting. Andrologist award Am. Soc. Andrology, 1999. Mem. Am. Soc. Andrology, Soc. Sci. Study Sex (pres. 1970-71), Soc. Reproductive Surgeons, Soc. for Study of Male Reprodn., Am. Urol. Assn. Home: 526 Bull Mill Rd Chester NY 10918-4706

AMER, MOHAMED AMIN, dermatologist, educator; b. Cairo, Egypt, Dec. 27, 1941; s. Mohamed Amin and Bossina Ali (Marei) A.; m. Susan Abdulhamid Ibrahim; children: Amin, Susan. MB BCh, Ain Shains, Cairo, 1964; diploma in venereology and dermatology, Ain Shains, 1969, diploma in medicine, 1972, MD in Dermatology and Venereology, 1974. Dermatologist Ministry of Health, Kuwait, 1966-74; lectr. dermatology and venereology Zagazig (Egypt) U., 1975-79, asst. prof., 1979-83, chmn. dept., 1983-93, v.p., 1995—, dermatology cons., 1975—; pres. The African Assn. for Dermatology, 1997; vis. prof. Thomas Jefferson U., Phila., 1988, Tulane U., New Orleans. Author: Global Dermatology, 1994, Pediatric Dermatology, 1989, (with others) Management of Dermatologic Patient, 1986; editor-in-chief African Jour. Dermatology, 1988-95. Mem. com. health Dem. Nat. Party, Egypt, 1979—; mem. Supreme Coun. Dermatologic Edn., Cairo, 1995—; chmn. Com. of Professorial Selection, Cairo, 1995-98; cons. Supreme Coun. of Youth and Sports, Egypt, 1993—. Recipient Nat. award for Med. Rsch., Ministry of Rsch., 1983, 1991. Mem. Am. Acad. Dermatology, Internat. Soc. Pediat. Dermatology, Zamalek Sporting Club (bd. dirs. 1988-96). Mem. Nat. Dem. Party. Moslem. Avocations: sports, tennis, football, arts, music. Home: 9 Gabalaya St, 11211 Cairo Egypt Office: 86 Ahmed El Zyat St, Cairo Dokki Egypt

AMERASINGHE, TERENCE PERCIVAL, English educator; b. Hakmana, Sri Lanka, Apr. 27, 1917; s. Bernard Perera and Elaine Lillith (Poulier) A.; m. Seelawatie Bird Borella Arachige, Apr. 2, 1950 (dec. May 1993); children: Chitra, Tilak. BA in History with honors, U. London, 1939, MA in History, 1954; D in Edn., Hamilton State U., 1956; JD, 1990; JD honoris causa, John Dewey U., 1994. Bar: Sri Lanka 1954. Prin. Nat. Inst. Higher Studies, Colombo, Sri Lanka, 1941-54; pres. World Constitution and Parliament Assn., Colombo, 1960—, co-pres., 1970—; pres. Universal Love and Brotherhood Assn., Colombo, 1979—, English Speaking Union Sri Lanka, Colombo, 1981—; bd. dirs. English Lang. Sch., Colombo, Grad. Sch. World Studies, Lakewood, Colo.; advisor English studies Dushanbe, Tajikistan, World Federalist Movement Asian Ctr., Osaka, Japan, 1990—. Editor Ceylon Jour. Adult Edn., 1941-45, 44, Colombo City News, 1944-48, Aizen World, 1982 (honours 1982). Gen. sec. Ceylon Literacy Campaign, Mahara, Kadawata, Sri Lanka, 1950; pres. Soc. for the Protection of the Rights of the Child, Colombo, 1981, Miyake Home for Orphan Childre, Colombo. Recipient Artists Embassy medal, San Francisco, 1994; Smith-Mundt Fulbright scholar U.S. Govt., Washington, 1954; fellow Carleton Coll. Pub. Adminstrn., Can., 1956. Fellow Asian Artists and Spkrs. Bur. (chmn. 1959-80); mem. Royal Orchid. Mem. World Federation of Religions. Avocations: English poetry, Asian history, cricket, human rights, music. Home: Mahara Walauwa Mahara, Kadawata Sri Lanka Office: English Speaking Union, 234 Galle Rd, Colombo 3, Sri Lanka

AMES, JAMES BENJAMIN, biochemistry educator, researcher; b. Flint, Mich., July 10, 1963; s. James Frederick and Diane Ames. BS, U. Mich., Flint, 1986; PhD, U. Calif., Berkeley, 1992. Postdoctoral rschr. Stanford (Calif.) U., 1993-97; asst. prof. U. Md., Rockville, 1998—. Office: Ctr Advanced Rsch 9600 Gudelsky Dr Rockville MD 20850-3479

AMES, JOHN LEWIS, lawyer; b. Norfolk, Va., July 15, 1912; s. Harry Lee and Catherine I. (Betty) A.; m. Margaret Kilbon, Apr. 8, 1939 (dec. Sept. 1996); children: Margaret Lee, John Lewis. AB, Randolph-Macon Coll., 1933; JD, U. Richmond, 1937; postgrad., NYU, 1939-40. Bar: Va. 1936, N.Y. 1940. Mem. tax div. Home Life Ins. Co., N.Y.C., 1937-38; trial atty. Tanner, Sillocks & Friend, N.Y.C., 1938-41; house counsel Ruthrauff & Ryan, Inc., N.Y.C., 1941-42, house counsel and asst. to pres., 1945-48, sec., counsel, 1948-50, v.p., sec., 1950-55, v.p., sec., treas., 1955-57, also dir.; v.p., sec. Erwin, Wassey, Ruthrauff & Ryan, Inc., 1957-59; asst. dir. bus. affairs CBS TV Network, Inc., N.Y.C., 1959-62; v.p., sec., treas. Kudner Agy., Inc., 1962-65, also dir.; sr. v.p. adminstrn. and fin. West, Weir & Bartel, Inc., N.Y.C., 1966, exec. v.p., dir., until 1968; v.p., sec. Lennen & Newell, Inc., 1968-73; v.p. bus. and legal affairs Dancer-Fitzgerald-Sample, Inc., 1973-83, legal cons. Saatchi & Saatchi DFS Inc., 1983-96; dir. Carroll Products, Inc.; spl. agt. FBI, Washington and N.Y.C., 1942-45; spl. dep. atty. gen. N.Y. State, 1946-48; mem. Nassau County N.Y. Crime Commn., 1973-83. Trustee, Randolph-Macon Coll., 1955-85, trustee emeritus, 1985—. Mem. Massapequa Bd. Edn., 1952-79, pres., 1957-78; past pres. Nassau-Suffolk Sch. Bds. Assn. Past chmn. trustees Am. Assn. Advt. Agencies Group Ins; trustee, pres. men's club, chmn. adminstrv. bd. White Stone United Methodist Ch. Mem. N.Y. County Lawyers Assn., Am. Arbitration Assn. (mem. nat. panel), Soc. Former Spl. Agts. FBI (past nat. sec.), Alumni Soc. Randolph-Macon Coll. (past pres.), Lancaster County Crime Solvers, Inc. (pres. 1991-94), Indian Creek Yacht and Country Club, Windmill Point Yacht Club, Phi Kappa Sigma, Omicron Delta Kappa, Tau Kappa Alpha. Methodist. Home: PO Box 727 White Stone VA 22578-0727 Office: 375 Hudson St New York NY 10014-3658

AMES, SANDRA PATIENCE, sales executive; b. Quincy, Calif., May 23, 1947; d. Bruce Ray Richards and Margaret Elizabeth (Steiner) Richards Johnson; m. Martin P.M. Bettenhausen, Dec. 10, 1965 (div. 1972); m. Thomas William Ames, Nov. 28, 1975. Student, Yuba City Jr. Coll., 1965-66. Sales corr. Nat. Can Corp. (now Am. Nat. Can Co.), Seattle, 1974-76, Lehigh Valley, Pa., 1976-79; nat. acct. sales corr. Nat. Can Corp. (now Am. Nat. Can Co.), Chgo., 1979-81, dist. sales office mgr., 1981-82; sales analyst I Nat. Can Corp. (now Am. Nat. Can Co.), Oakbrook, Ill., 1982-84; regional sales office mgr. Nat. Can Corp. (now Am. Nat. Can Co.), Oakbrook, 1984-86, mgr. regional sales office, 1987-89, mgr. ctrl. sales adminstrn., 1989-93, inside sales assoc., 1993-95; inside sales assoc. Silgan Containers, Rosemont, Ill., 1995-98, office adminstr., 1998—. Mem. NAFE. Office: Silgan Containers Mfg Corp 9700 W Higgins Rd Ste 820 Rosemont IL 60018-4736

AMES, SUSAN, astrophysicist; b. Biloxi, Miss., Aug. 18, 1945; d. Irving M. and Ann (Fisher) A. BA, Bryn Mawr Coll., 1967; MA, U. Calif., Berkeley, 1969, PhD, 1972. Rsch. asst. Radioastronomy Div. Observatory of Paris, Meudon, France, 1967; rsch. asst. Radioastronomy Lab. U. Calif., Berkeley, 1967-69; rsch. asst. Nat. Radioastronomy Observatory, Charlottesville, Va., 1969; staff mem. Inst. for Advanced Study, Princeton, N.J., 1972-74, Los Alamos (N.Mex.) Scientific Lab., 1974-77; scientific assoc. Max-Planck Inst. for Nuclear Physics, Heidelberg, Fed. Republic Germany, 1977-81; vis. researcher Radioastronomy Inst., U. Bonn, Fed. Republic Germany, 1982—. Fellow Royal Astron. Soc.; mem. Am. Astron. Soc., German Astron. Soc. Office: Radioastronomy Inst, Auf Dem Hugel 71, 53121 Bonn Germany

AMET, SIR ARNOLD K., judge. Chief justice Supreme Ct. Papua New Guinea, Boroko. Office: Supreme Ct, POB 7018, Boroko NCD Papua New Guinea*

AMETANI, AKIHIRO, engineering educator; b. Nagasaki, Japan, Feb. 14, 1944; s. Kaoru and Shinobu (Itoh) A.; m. Rimiko Matsumoto, Apr. 3, 1982; children: Mariko, Asumi. BSc, Doshisha U., Kyoto, Japan, 1966, MSc, 1968; PhD, Manchester (Eng.) U., 1973. Royal Chartered engr., U.K. Asst. Univ. Manchester Inst. of Sci. and Technology, Manchester, 1971-74; asst. Doshisha U., Kyoto, 1968-71, lectr., 1974-76, assoc. prof., 1976-85, prof., 1985—; cons. Bonneville Power Adminstrn., Portland, Oreg., 1976-81; prof. Cath. U. Leuven, Belgium, 1988; dir. Sci. and Engring., Inst. Doshisha U., Kyoto, 1996-97, dean Libr. and Computer/Info. Ctr., 1998—. Author: Electrical Energy System Engineering, 1988, Electrical Engineering Handbook, 1988, Electrical Circuit Theory, 1989, Distributed-Parameter Circuit Theory, 1990. Mem. Kyoto Industries and Info. Ctr., 1992. Recipient prize to new devel. New Tech. Devel. Fund, Tokyo, 1984, Paper prize Inst. Electrical Engrs., Tokyo, 1976, Inst. Illuminating Engrs., Tokyo, 1996. Fellow IEEE, Inst. Elec. Engrs. (U.K.); mem. IEE Japan. Budhism. Avocations: composing poems, hiking, fishing. Home: 349-4 Aoji-cho Kusatsu-shi, Shiga 525, Japan Office: Doshisha Univ, Kyo-Tanabe, Kyoto 610-0321, Japan

AMEXO, KWAKU, internist; b. Accra, Ghana, Nov. 6, 1957; came to U.S., 1992; MD, Vinnitsa Med. Inst., 1987. Diplomate Am. Bd. Internal Medicine. Intern Brookdale Med. Ctr., Bklyn., 1992-93; resident Presbyn. Med. Ctr., Phila., 1993-95, asst. clin. instr., 1993-95; fellow Temple U. Hosp., Phila., 1995-96, clin. instr., 1995-96; pvt. practice Phila., 1997—; with Pa. Hosp., Phila., Mercy Hosp. of Phila. Mem. ACP, AMA. Office: 930 Washington Ave Philadelphia PA 19147-3840

AMIARD, JEAN-CLAUDE ARSENE, ecotoxicologist, researcher; b. Paris, Apr. 27, 1947; s. Arsene Gustave and Gilberte Desiree (Trimoreau) A.; m. Claude Louise Triquet, Feb. 9, 1973. Spl. doctorate, U. Paris, 1972, PhD, 1978; habilitation rsch., U. Nantes, 1987. Chef de svc. CNRS U. Nantes, 1989; dir. rsch., 1988, head of rsch., 1987, 1979; ingenieur CEA, 1973; v.p. Soc. Toxicology, Nantes, France, 1988—; mem. nat. com. Rsch. Sci., Paris, 1980-83; cir. coun. Station Biology Rsch., 1980-83. Author: La radioecologie des Milieux Aquatiques, 1980, Le Littoral ses contraintes et ses conflits, 1992, Les Biomarqueurs, 1997, Utilisation dos biomarqueurs, 1998. Capt. Marines, 1972-73, France. Mem. Union Oceanography of France (pres.), Found. Med. Rsch., Inst. of Substances and Organisms, Acad. Environment. Office: CNRS ISOmer Nantes Svc Eco, 2 R Houssinieère, BP 92208 44322 Nantes Cedex 3, France

AMICHETTI, DENNIS JOSEPH, advertising executive; b. Phila., Apr. 24, 1946; s. Frank and Margret H. (Ziegler) A.; m. Elizabeth Keefe, June 27, 1970; children: Christine, Karen. BS, Drexel U., 1969, MBA, 1973. Mfg. engr. Gen. Electric Co., Phila., 1969-70; mgr. mktg. devel. ESB, Inc., Phila., 1970-74; asst. v.p., dir. mktg. Phila. Sav. Fund Soc., 1974-78; v.p. SE Nat. Bank, Malvern, Pa., 1978-79; sr. v.p. Mel Richman Inc., Bala Cynwyd, Pa., 1979-83; v.p. Beneficial Corp., Wilmington, Del., 1983-86; pres. Amichetti Lewis & Assocs., Exton and Wayne, Pa., 1987—. Planning commn. East Goshen Twp., Pa., 1977-83. Recipient Gold Effie award for fin. advt. Mem. Am. Mktg. Assn., Acad. for Health Services Mktg., Direct Mktg. Assn., Beta Gamma Sigma. Republican. Roman Catholic. Avocations: music, theater, golf. Home: 814 Wetherill Ln Wayne PA 19087-2072 Office: Amichetti Lewis & Assocs Inc 300 N Pottstown Pike Ste 120 Exton PA 19341-2235

AMICK, JAMES H., JR., financial consultant; b. Charleston, S.C., June 22, 1961; s. James Henry and Lillie (Thomason) A.; m. Mary Kathryn A., Apr. 14, 1984; children: Mary Robbins, Jamie Lynn. BA in English Lit., Wofford Coll., 1983. Acct. exec. Harris 3M Corp., Columbia, S.C., 1987-89; nat. sales dir. Richtex Corp., Columbia, S.C., 1989-91, regional mgr., 1991-93; asst. v.p. Merrill Lynch, Charleston, S.C., 1993—. Bd. dirs. Trident United Way, Charleston, Edn. Found., Charleston, Charleston Metro C. of C.; chmn. profl. adv. com. Trident United Way, 1998—; chmn. Workplace Inst. for Educators, Charleston, 1996—. 1st Lt. U.S. Army, 1984-87. Mem. Rotary Club St. Andrews (bd. dirs., club svc. dir. 1997-99, cmty. svc. dir. 1996-97), Charleston Met. C. of C. (bd. dirs. 1995-97, v.p. edn., leadership chmn. 1996-97). Republican. United Methodist. Avocations: adult soccer league, adult basketball league. E-mail: amick1@home.com. Home: 10 Brigadoon Pl Charleston SC 29414-7342 Office: Merrill Lynch 17 Lockwood Dr Ste 200 Charleston SC 29401-1194

AMIDA, BARON OF See BERGHOLM, ERNST TAUNO HERMAN

AMIEL, ANTOINE, executive; b. Paris, Mar. 11, 1969; s. Claude and Janet (Hendricks) A.; m. Stephanie Domont, Apr. 8, 1995; 1 child, Samuel. BA in Economy, Sorbonne, Paris, 1992; M of Corp. Fin., Dauphine, Paris, 1993. Deputy treas. Essilor Internat., Paris, 1993; market analysis Essilor of Am., Tampa, Fla., 1994-95; fin. controller Essilor Far East, Hong Kong, 1995-97; v.p., CFO Essilor Nidek, Tokyo, 1998—; CFO Nikon Essilor Group, 2000—; dir. Paris Lunnettes Corp., Tokyo, 1998—, Essilor Japan, Tokyo, 1998—, Varilux Japan, Tokyo, 1998—, Aichi Nikon KK, Nasu Nikon KK. Avocations: violin, sailing, car racing. Home: 1-1-22 Minamu Azabu, Tokyo 106 0047, Japan Office: Essilor Nidek, 2-1-10 Dabashi, Tokyo 102, Japan

AMIEL, MICHEL JEAN, radiologist, educator; b. Setif, Algerie, France; s. Felix and Adrienne (Pomes) A.; m. Arlette Jourdan, Feb. 1958; children: Pierre-Michel, Fabienne. MD, Faculty of Medicine, Alger, 1960. Resident Hosp. of Lyon, France, 1963-66, asst., 1966-69; prof. agrige U. Lyon, 1970-79, prof. and chmn. dept. radiology, 1975—; dir. rsch. unit CNRS 5515, Lyon, 1984-98, mem. sci. com., Paris, 1992—; mem. adv. bd. Biomed. 2, Brussles, 1993—. Author: Heart and Great Vessels - Radiology, 1979, Selective Bronchography, 1979, Coronary Artery Diseases, 1986; editor: Contrast Media in Radiology, 1989. Adminstr. Hosp. Civil de Lyon, 1989-90. Ltd. French Army, 1960-62. Decorated Chevalier, Palmes academiques, France, 1986. Mem. French Univ. Profs. of Radiology (pres. coun. 1984-88), French Soc. Radiology (pres. 1996-99), European Soc. Cardiovascular Radiology (bd. dirs. 1986-96), European Congress Radiology. Office: Hospital Cardiology Radiology Svc, 59 Bd Pinel, 69395 Lyon France

AMIGO, LOURDES, food scientist; b. Valladolid, Spain, Aug. 24, 1958; d. Felix and Ma Concepción (Garrido) A.; m. Santiago Biec, July 25, 1987; children: Teresa, Santiago, Carlos. Degree in Biology, U. Complutense, Madrid, 1985; PhD in Chemistry, Autonoma, Madrid, 1989. Predoctoral fellow Spanish Coun. Sci. Rschrs., Madrid, 1985-89, postdoctoral fellow, 1991-92, jr. rschr., 1993—; doctoral fellow Spanish Govt., Madrid, 1989-90. Contbr. articles to profl. jours. Mem. Internat. Dairy Fedn. (standing com. on farm mgmt. and phyisicochemical methods of analysis). Home: Pedro Rico 31 2o I, 28029 Madrid Spain Office: Inst Fermentawciones Indsl, Juan de la Cierva 3, 28006 Madrid Spain

AMIN, ABU TAHER MOHAMMED NURUL, economics educator, researcher; b. Barjalia, Bangladesh, Feb. 1, 1948; s. Abul Hashem Sikdar and Rahima Khatoon; m. Mirza Rehena, Feb. 28, 1979; children: Sara Nuzhat, Seema Nusrat. BA with honors, U. Dhaka, Bangladesh, 1969, MA, 1970; MA, U. Man., Winnipeg, Can., 1976, PhD, 1982. Lectr. Jahangirnagar U., Dhaka, 1973-75; from asst. to assoc. prof. Jahangirnagar U., 1982-86; tchg. asst. U. Man., 1975-78; asst. prof. Asian Inst. Tech., Bangkok, 1987-88; assoc. prof. Asian Inst. Tech., 1988-98, prof., 1998—; chmn. divsn. human settlements devel. Asian Inst. Tech., 1991-93, coord. urban environ. mgmt. program, 1996-99; provost Mir Mosharref Hossain Hall, Jahangirnagar U., 1985-86; cons. Internat. Labour Orgn.- Asian Regional Team for Emloyment Program, Bangkok, 1990-91, team leader, Jakarta, Indonesia, 1989-93. Contbr. chpts. to books and articles to profl. jours. Gen. sec. Jahangirnagar U. Tchrs. Assn., 1985; pres. East Pakistan Student Union Jinnah Hall Br., Dhaka, 1969. Recipient IDRC award, 1978; Sr. fellow UN Ctr. for Regional Devel., Nagoya, Japan, 1994, fellow Brit. Coun., Dhaka, 1986. Mem. Bangladesh Econ. Assn. (life, gen. sec. 1986). Moslem. Avocations: reading newspapers, periodicals and journals, swimming, walking. Home: Faculty House # 17 AIT Campus, Km 42 Paholyothin Hwy, Klong Luang Pathumthani Thailand 12120 Office: Asian Inst Tech, GPO Box 4, Bangkok Thailand

AMIN, ANEEM, marketing research official; b. Rawalpindi, Punjab, Pakistan, Jan. 29, 1971; s. Ullah and Bilquis Nagi Amin. B Com, Hailey Coll., Lahore, Pakistan, 1993; MBA, NCBA&E, Lahore, 1997. Asst. adminstrv. mgr. Ijaz Enterprises, Lahore, 1992-93; asst. mkgt. and customer svc. mgr. Fortress Products Inc., Lahore, 1993-98; mktg. rsch. officer Total Lubricants, Lahore, 1999—. Avocations: net surfing, business books, collecting currency and perfume. Home: 64 Eden Ave-Defence Rd, Lahore Punjab, Pakistan Office: Total Atlas Lubricants, 1 McLeod Rd, 54000 Lahore Punjab, Pakistan

AMIN, MASSOUD, executive, systems science and mathematics educator; b. Tabriz, Iran, July 4, 1961; came to U.S., 1978; s. Mohammad Shafi and Nahid (Loghman-Adham) A.; m. Elizabeth Ambrose, May 28, 1994. BSEE, U. Mass., 1982, MS in Elec. and Computer Engring., 1985; MSc, Washington U., 1986, DSc, 1990. Rsch. assoc. elec. and computer engring. U. Mass., Amherst, 1982-84, tchg. assoc. elec. and computer engring. dept. math, 1983-85; lectr., rsch. assoc. systems sci. and math. Washington U., St. Louis, 1987-92, sr. fellow Ctr. for Optimization and Semantic Control, 1990-94, asst. prof. systems sci. and math., 1992-97, assoc. prof., 1997-98, assoc. dir. Ctr. for Optimization and Semantic Control, 1994-98; mgr. math., info. sci. Electric Power Rsch. Inst., Palo Alto, Calif., 1998—; co-chair conf. Internat. Fedn. Operational Rsch. Soc., St. Louis, 1995; advisor grad. theses and sr. projects Washington U., 1990-98; referee, reviewer jours. in field. Guest editor Math. and Computer Modelling, 1995, 98, Internat. Transactions in Operational Rsch., 1998, IEEE Control Sys. Mag., 2000; editl. bd. of four acad. jours.; contbr. numerous articles to profl. jours. Vol. Orgn. for Aged in St. Louis, 1988-91; vol. instr. Washington U. Kenpo Club, 1992-96. Mem. AIAA (Young Profl. award 1990), IEEE (liaison to neural network coun., assoc. editor Control Systems mag. 1998, Best Session Paper Presentation awards Am. Control Conf. 1997), Inst. Ops. Rsch. & Mgmt. Scis., Soc. Indsl. and Applied Math., N.Y. Acad. Scis., AAAS, Sigma Xi, Eta Kappa Nu, Tau Beta Pi (chief advisor Mo. Gamma chpt. 1994-98). Achievements include work as principal investigator or co-principal investigator on several collaborations with industry and government, original contributions to research and design of decision-aiding system for advanced tactical aircraft as well as cross-disciplinary contributions in intelligent control and optimization, research on development and application of the Semantic Control Paradigm; successful creation and launch of a 28-Univ. complex interactive networks research intiative. Avocations: books, travel, athletics, Kenpo karate. E-mail: mamin@epri.com. Office: EPRI 3412 Hillview Ave Palo Alto CA 94304-1395

AMIN, MOHAMMAD NURUL, political science educator; b. Madaripur, Bangladesh, Apr. 3, 1954; s. MD. Rabiullah and Ogifa (Khatun) Bepari. BA in Polit. Sci. with honors, Dacca U., Bangladesh, 1975, MA in Polit. Sci., 1976, MPhi. in Polit. Sci., 1980. Lectr. Dacca U., Bangladesh, 1980-84, asst. prof., 1984-87, assoc. prof. polit. sci., 1987—. Contbr. articles to profl. jours. Mem. Bangladesh Polit. Sci. Assn., Asiatic Soc. Bangladesh. Avocation: fishing. Office: Dacca U Dept Polit Sci, Dacca Bangladesh

AMIN, MOHAMMAD RUHUL, engineering educator, researcher; b. Dhaka, Bangladesh, Apr. 10, 1954; came to U.S., 1981; s. Abdus Salam and Mahmuda Begum; m. Shadmani Malik, July 30, 1984; children: Ruhani, Raima. BS in Mech. Engring., Bangladesh U., Dhaka, 1977; MS, U. Tenn., Chattanooga, 1983; PhD, U. Tenn., Knoxville, 1989. Registered profl. engr., Mont. Adj. asst. prof. Mont. State U., Bozeman, 1989-91, asst. prof., 1991-97, assoc. prof., 1997è. Contbr. articles to profl. jours. Mem. ASME (faculty advisor 1990—), Sigma Xi. Avocations: fishing, running. Office: Mont State U 220 Roberts Hl Bozeman MT 59717-0001

AMIN, MOHAMMED NURUL, chemist, researcher; b. Mohanpur, Bangladesh, Dec. 21, 1942; s. Fazlul Karim Mian and Arafatun Nessa Karim; m. Hosne Ara Begum, July 19, 1970; children: Engineer Saiful Amin, Sarah Thasin Noor, Farah Nowreen Noor. BSc in Chemistry with honors, Dhaka U., Bangladesh, 1963, MSc in Chemistry, 1964, PhD in Chemistry, 1986. From scientific officer chief scientific officer Bangladesh Jute Rsch. Inst., Dhaka, 1966-99, chief scientific officer, 1999—; nat. project leader Internat. Jute Orgn., Dhaka, 1992-96; founder Samaj-O-Sanskriti Sangha, Mohanpur, 1961; prin. investigator Bangladesh Agrl. Rsch. Coun., 1999—. Mem. editl. bd. Bangladesh Jour. of Jute & Fibre Rsch., 1997—; contbr. articles to profl. jours.; patentee in field; convenor Sonali Ansh Pub., 1987, Abstracts of Tech. Reports on Rsch. Project (1979-88), 1991. UNIDO fellow StrathClyde Univ., Glasgow, Scotland, 1980-81, Ida World Bank fellow Jute Technological Rsch. Labs., Calcutta, India, 1988. Mem. Bangladesh Jute Rsch. Scientist Assn. (pres. 1987), Bangladesh Chem. Soc. (exec. mem. 1980-81), Bangladesh Assn. Scientists and Scientific Profession. Avocations: reading scientific journals, religious books. E-mail: amin@bdcom.com. Office: Bangladesh Jute Rsch Inst, Manik Miah Ave, Dhaka 1207, Bangladesh

AMIN, MUHAMMAD NURUL, botanist, educator; b. Dhamoirhat, Bangladesh, May 1, 1953; s. Mohammed Daimuddin Mondol and Akimun Nessa; m. Suhely Yeasmin, Nov. 25, 1979; children: Somala, Ishtiaq Mahmood. BSc with honors, Rajshahi (Bangladesh) U., 1975, MSc, 1976; PhD, Banaras (India) Hindu U., 1988; internat. diploma, Royal Botanic Gardens, Kew, U.K., 1999. Rsch. fellow Rajshahi U., 1979-81, lectr., 1981-84, asst. prof., 1984-89, assoc. prof., 1989-94, prof. botany, 1994—; vis. biotech. fellow Agrl. U. Malaysia, 1992-93; students' hall provost Rajshahi U., 1995-98; project dir. Ministry Sci. and Tech., 1999-2000. Contbr. articles to profl. jours. Indian Govt. Doctoral scholar, 1984; UNESCO biotech. fellow, France, 1992; Rsch. grant Bangladesh Agrl. Rsch. Coun., 1992, Ministry Sci. and Tech., 1999, Bangladesh Rural Advancement Com., 1998-2000. Mem. Bangladesh Bot. Soc. (life), Bangladesh Assn. Plant Tissue Culture (life), Bangladesh Hort. Soc., Bangladesh Assn. Advancement of Sci., N.Y. Acad. Sci. Islam. Avocations: ancient history, table tennis, computer paint and design, TV. Office: Dept Botany, U Rajshahi, Rajshahi 6205, Bangladesh

AMIN, PRAFULL BHOGILAL, pathologist, consultant; b. Ahmedabad, Gujrat, India, Oct. 12, 1939; s. Bhogilal Manilal and Kamla (Bhogilal) A.; m. Neelam Kapoor, July 20, 1970; children: Sonal, Noopur. MBBS, G.S. Med. Coll., Bombay, 1961, MD in Pathology and Bacteriology, 1966. Diplomate in pathology, India. Lectr. pathology Seth G.S. Med. Coll., Bombay, 1963-66, asst. prof. pathology, 1966; dep. chief pathologist Bombay Hosp., 1967-68, 71-78; asst. resident pathology Sinai Hosp., Balt., 1968-70; fellow cytopathology Johns Hopkins Hosp., Balt., 1970-71; cons. pathologist Dr. Amin's Pathology Lab., Bombay, 1979—, dir., 1982-99. Author: SMA-12 (Diagnostic Interpretation), 1974, Pacer-26 (Diagnostic Interpretation), 1983. Life patron Inst. Shri Krishna Consciousness, Bombay, 1997. Fellow Am. Soc. Clin. Pathologists; mem. Indo-Am. Soc., Bharatiya Vidya Bhavan, Am. Soc. Cytopathology, Am. Soc. Clin. Chemistry. Avocations: Indian music, computer software science, reading. Office: 901-902 Tulsiani Chambers, 212 Nariman Point, Bombay 400 021, India

AMIN, SHAHID, civil engineer; b. Lahore, Pakistan, Apr. 14, 1945; s. Mohnammad and Munawar (Sultana) A.; m. Shahida Amin; children: Imran Shahid, Uszma Shahid. BSCE, Kingston Polytech., London, 1971; degree (hon.), MICE, London, 1975, MBIM, London, 1985. Tech. asst. London Transport, 1971-72; design Engr. Costain (E.J. Cook), London, 1972-73; project engr. Costain, London, 1973-75; chief engr. Minstry of Pub. Works, Jeddah, Saudi Arabia, 1976-84; tech. dir. Kara Constrn., Jeddah, Saudi Arabia, 1984—. Pres. Jeddah Cricket League, 1977—. Mem. Inst. Mgmt. London, Inst. Civil Engrs., Coun. Engring. Insts. Avocations: cricket, photography. Home: 14 Granard Avenue, London SW15 6HJ, England Office: Kara Constrn, PO Box 7038, Jeddah 21462, Saudi Arabia

AMINI, FARSHAD, engineering educator, consultant; b. Tehran, Iran, Feb. 5, 1959; came to U.S., 1977; s. Mohammadreza Amini and Baghi Nikzad; m. Azarm Sadeghpour-Koleveri, Mar. 8, 1992. BS, U. Kans., 1981, MS, 1982; PhD, U. Md., 1986. Cert. profl. engr. Project engr. Driggs Corp., Capital Heights, Md., 1983-85; sr. geotechnical engr. Soil Cons., Inc., Chantilly, Va., 1986-89; prof. U. D.C., 1989—; geotechnical cons. Soil Cons., Inc., Manassas, Va., 1989—. Author: Neural Networks, 1997; contbr. articles to profl. jours. Mem. ASCE (mem. editl. bd. Jour. Getechnical Engring. 1990—). Avocations: reading, jogging. Office: U DC MB4202 Dept Civil Engring Washington DC 20008

AMINU, BELLO, management company executive, consultant; b. Yola, Adamawa, Nigeria, Aug. 8, 1964; s. Aminu Modibbo and Aisha Dikko Aminu; m. Bilkisu Bello Idrisu, Oct. 17, 1992; children: Rahima, Aisha, Khadija. BSc in Architecture, Ahmadu Bello U., Zaria, Kaduna-Nigeria, 1987, MSc in Architecture, 1989. Registered arch., Nigeria. Arch. Arch-Design Assocs., Calabar, Nigeria, 1989-90, Afri-Projects Consortium, Yola, Adamawa, Nigeria, 1990-91; projects mgr. Afri-Projects Consortium, Yola, Nigeria, 1991-92; mgr. dir. Aminu & Assocs., Yola, 1992-94; cons. Afri-Projects Consortium, Abuja, Nigeria, 1994-99; mng. dir. Mega Projects Internat. Ltd., Abuja, 1999—; bd. dirs. CyberNet Nigeria Ltd., Abuja.

Contbr. articles to profl. publs. Mem. Nigerian Red Cross Soc., Yola, 1973. Fellow Inst. Constrn. Industry Arbitrators Nigeria; mem. Nigerian Inst. Mgmt., Internat. Facility Mgmt. Assn. Nigeria. Islam. Avocations: long distance hiking, travel, photography, adventure. Fax: 234-5237197. E-mail: cpc@hyperia.com. Home: Block 4, Sirasso Crecent, Off Kigoma St, Wuse Zone 7, Abuja FCT, Nigeria Office: Mega Projects Internat Ltd, 1 Sirasso Cres, Off Kigoma, Abuja FCT, Nigeria

AMIR, HASSAN, surgeon; b. Zanzibar, Tanzania, Sept. 14, 1950; p. Amirali Alli and Fatemah Amirali (Jessa) Alli; m. Waheeda Mohamed Husien Kermali, Jan. 21, 1982; children: Taha, Mohamed. MB BS, U. Kashmir, India, 1976; M of Surgery, Muslim U., Aligarh, India, 1980. Intern Med. Coll. Hosp., Aligarh, 1976-77, resident in surgery, 1977-80; cons. surgeon Dubai Med. Ctr., Red Crescent Soc. I.R. Iran, 1981-88; lectr., cons. surgeon Muhimbili U. Coll. Health Scis., Dar-Es-Salaam, Tanzania, 1988-92; sr. lectr., cons. surgeon Muhimbili U. Coll. Health Scis., Dar-Es-Salaam, 1992-97, assoc. prof. surgery, 1997—; chairperson rsch. dept. surgery Muhimbili U. Coll. Health Scis., Dar Es Salaam, 1997—. Vice chmn. sci. adv. bd. Austral-Asian Jour. Cancer; contbr. articles to profl. jours. Grantee Internat. Union Against Cancer, Geneva, 1991. Fellow Assn. Surgeon of East Africa, Tanzania Surg. Assn.; mem. Med. Assn. Tanzania, Assn. Internat. Union Against Cancer Fellows (life). Achievements include research in cancer in African population; breast cancer in African population; Karposi's sarcoma in African population; HIV-asociated cancers. Fax: 255 (51) 152137. Home: 73 Elvira Crescent, London, ON Canada N6E 2N1

AMIR, JONATHAN, agriculture educator; b. Wien, Austria, Mar. 7, 1915; arrived in Israel, 1935; s. Hermann and Hansi (Nebenzahl) Reiss; m. Amir Sarah David, May 1949; children: Amram, Hanoch, Avinoam (dec.). Student, Tech. U. Haifa, Israel. Farmer, tchr. agr. h.s., ret. With Israel def. Force. The Socialist Party. Avocation: studying history. Home: Kibutz Sha'ar Ha'amakin, Sha'ar Ha'amaqim 30-097, Israel

AMIR, RABAH, economist, educator; b. Algiers, Algeria, Feb. 4, 1957; came to U.S., 1976;. BS, U. Ill., 1980, PhD, 1985. Rsch. fellow Yale U., New Haven, Conn., 1985; asst. prof. SUNY Stony Brook, 1986-90; vis. scholar Cath. U., Louvain, Belgium, 1990-91, 94, U. Dortmund, Germany, 1991-93, U. Ariz., Tucson, 1993-94; sr. fellow WZB, Berlin, 1995-97; prof. dept. econs. Odense U., Denmark, 1997—. Contbr. articles to profl. jours. Mem. Am. Econ. Assn., European Assn. Rsch. Indsl. Econs., Royal Econ. Soc. Office: Odense U Dept Econs, 5230 Odense Denmark

AMIROU, MUSTAPHA, physician; b. Draa-Ben-Khedda, Kabylie, Algeria, Feb. 19, 1963; s. Said Amirou and Ouardia Saidj; m. Corinne Thomasset, May 1, 1965; children: Emilie Lylia, Noemie Assireme. MD, Grenoble, France; Specialization in Nephrology, Lyon, France, Pediatrics in France; Specialization in Nephrology; Artificial Nutritionist, Paris. Medical diplomat. Intern CHU, Grenoble, 1990-93; asst. Hosp., Gap, France, 1993-98, Montluson, France, 1998-99. Contbr. articles to profl. jours. Mem. Rural and Uremique Assn., 1999. Mem. Am. Soc. Nephrology (assoc.), European Renal Assn., French Soc. Nephrology. Avocations: tennis, golf. Office: Hosp de Montluson, BP 1148 Montluson 03113 France

AMIS, MARTIN LOUIS, author; b. Oxford, Aug. 25, 1949; s. Kingsley and Hilary (Bardwell) A.; m. Antonia Phillips, 1984 (div. 1996); 3 children. BA in English with honors, Oxford U., 1971. Editorial asst. Times Literary Supplement, London, 1972-75; asst. literary editor New Statesman, London, 1975-79; spl. writer The Observer, 1980—. Actor: (film) A High Wind in Jamaica, 1965; author: The Rachel Papers, 1973 (Somerset Maugham award 1974), Dead Babies, 1975 (pub. as Dark Secrets, 1977), Success, 1978, Other People, 1981, Invasion of the Space Invaders, 1982, Money: A Suicide Note, 1984, The Moronic Inferno and Other Visits to America, 1986, Einstein's Monsters, 1987, London Fields, 1989, Time's Arrow, 1991, Visiting Mrs. Nabokov and Other Excursions, 1994, The Information, 1995; co-author: (with others) My Oxford, 1977; screenwriter: Saturn 3, 1980. Address: The Wylie Agy, 36 Parkside 52 Knightsbridge, London SW1X 7JP, England

AMJAD, IMRAN MCSOOD, insurance executive; b. Demerara, Guyana, South America, Mar. 13, 1957; s. Mohamed Hassan and Bibi (Hassan-Shakoor) A.; m. Farina Ayesha Khan, Aug. 26, 1979; children: Reza, Tariq. Tchr. Ministry of Edn., Georgetown, Guyana, 1974-75; asst. mgr. GTM Group of Cos., Georgetown, Guyana, 1975-82; gen.mgr. NAGICO Ins., St. Maarten, Netherlands Antilles, 1982—, dir., shareholder, 1990—; bd. dirs. Antilles Banking Corp., Paradise Car Rental, St. Martin, French West Indies, 1986—. Mem. Chartered Ins. Inst. (chartered, assoc., corres. 1981—), St. Maarten Ins. Assn. (founder, edn. chmn.), St. Maarten Cricket Assn. (founder, v.p. 1986-97, pres. 1997—). Moslem. Office: NAGICO Ins, CA Cannegieter St, Philipsburg Netherlands Antilles

AMLER, BARBARA, physician; b. Hilden, Germany, Oct. 14, 1961; d. Heinrich-Otto and Ursula (Ohrenschall) Weiss; m. Marc Georg-Richard Amler, Feb. 16, 1989; children: Ann-Sophie, Nicholaus- Ferdinand. Exam. of histology, chemistry, zoology, Riju U., Gent, 1981-83; student, U. Madison, 1985; staats examen, U. Heidelberg, 1991. Intern and resident in internal medicine Solingen, Germany, 1993-94; jr. house officer ATOS Klinik, Germany, 1991; exec. mgr., chairholder MID-Verlags GmbH, 1994-96, Weiss-Amler Hausverwaltung GmbH, 1992-96, MIV-Verlag, 1996—. Contbr. articles to newspapers. Mem. Lions (founder, pres. 97-98), Steuben-Schurz, N.Y. Acad. Sci., Soc. for Right and Politics in Health Soc., Deutsch-Chinesche Gesellschaft, Chinese-German Med. Soc. of Medicine. Avocations: music, literature, philosophy. Home: Goetheallee 4, 01309 Dresden Germany Office: Goethealle 4, MIV Verlages GmbH, 01309 Dresden Germany

AMMANN, JEAN-CHRISTOPHE, art director; b. Berlin, Jan. 14, 1939. PhD, U. Fribourg, Switzerland, 1966. Asst. Kunsthalle Bern, Switzerland, 1967-68; dir. Kunstmuseum, Lucerne, Switzerland, 1968-77, Kunsthalle, Basle, Switzerland, 1978-88; dir. Mus. für Moderne Kunst, Frankfurt, Germany, 1989—, prof., 1998—; commr. German Pavillion of Biennial of Venice, Italy, 1995; lectr. U. Frankfurt/M. and Giessen, 1992—. Author: Rèmy Zaugg—Discussion with Jean-Christophe Ammann, 1994, (with Harald Szeemann) Von Hodler zur Antiform, 1968, Louis Moilliet: Das Gesamtwerk, 1972, Bewegung im Kopf. Vom Umgang mit der Kunst, 1993, Kulturfinanzierung, 1995, Annäherung. Über die Notwendigkeit von Kunst, 1996, Remy Zaugg-Conversation with Jean Christophe Ammann, French edit., 1990, German edit., 1994, Das Glück Zu Sehen, 1998; co-organizer of documenta 5, Kassel, 1972. Office: Museum für Moderne Kunst, Domstrasse 10, 60311 Frankfurt Germany

AMMANN, LILLIAN ANN NICHOLSON, writer, small business owner; b. Pearsall, Tex., June 20, 1946; d. Harvey Franklin and Annie Laura (Matthews) Nicholson; m. Jack Jordan Ammann Jr., May 31, 1967; 1 child, William erik. BA magna cum laude, Southwestern U., 1968. Mgr. inventory Kelley AFB, San Antonio, 1967-70; employment counselor Tex. Employment Commn., San Antonio, 1970-75; owner, operator Lillie's Lovely Little Gardens, San Antonio, 1975-77; owner, operator Lillie's Interior Landscapes, San Antonio, 1980-82, pres., 1983-96; sec. Jack Ammann Inc., 1983-87; pres. Lillie's & Sherry's Plants & Pottery, San Antonio, 1977-80; ind. bus. owner, diamond dir. Rexall Showcase Internat., 1996—. Author: Lillie's Lovely Little Gardening Book, 1976, Look Beyond Tomorrow: The Carola Spencer Story, 1998, Stroke of Luck, 1999; editor: A Bouquet of Recipes from the Diocese of the Southwest, Anglican Church in America, 1998. Vol. All Saints Anglican Ch., Caring Connections San Antonio. Mem. Women in Bus. (past pres.), Alamo City Rep. Women's Club, World Romance Wr iters, Electronically Published Internet Connection Digital Women (Alamo chpt.). Fax: 210-344-1958. E-mail: lillie@ammann.com. Home and Office: 603 Mauze Dr San Antonio TX 78216-3711

AMMAR, MAGDA, librarian; b. Ismailia, Egypt, Mar. 25, 1951; d. Ammar Ahmed and Hanim Aly Osman; m. Mamdeuh Mostafa Sultan, July 18, 1977; children: Mostafa, Aly, Omar. Lic., Cairo U., 1973. Human resources profl. Arab Contractors Co., Egypt, 1973-74, exec. sec., 1974-75, clk. main libr., 1975-78, asst. libr., 1979-85, libr. main libr., 1986-90, chief libr., 1991—. Mem. Egyptian Assn. for Info. and Libr. Sci., Arab Fedn. for Libr. and Info., Spl. Librs. Assn. Avocations: reading, painting, music, meditation. Office: Arab Contractors Main Libr, 120 Mohi Eldin Abu Elezz St, Box 177 Dokki Egypt

AMMATURO, VINCENZO, physician; b. Naples, Campania, Italy, June 18, 1937; s. Diego Leonida Ammaturo and Maria Nappi; m. Anna Maria Guardascione, Dec. 21, 1966; children: Maria, Daniela, Bianca. MD, Naples U., Italy, 1962. Vol. asst. U. Naples, 1962-64, permanent asst., 1964-71, lectr. clin. microscopy, 1971-81, assoc. prof. pathophyology, 1981-98, assoc. prof. hematology, 1998—. Editor/author: Le Cellule del Sangue, 1982, Citochimica Ematologica, 1991; author: Teeniche Ematologiche, 1985, Medicina Transfusuale, 1992. Mem. Italian Soc. Internal Medicine, Italian Soc. Hematology, Lions. Roman Catholic. Avocations: tennis, soccer. Office: 2th Univ, Largo Madonna Delle Graziel, 80138 Naples Italy

AMMERMAN, GALE RICHARD, organization executive, retired educator; b. Sullivan, Ind., Mar. 6, 1923; s. Lyman Sylvanious and Iva Mae Amerman; m. Jane Loretta Burke, Sept. 26, 1943; children: Kathleen, John, Joseph, Mark, Christopher. BS, Purdue U., 1950, MS, 1953, PhD, 1957. Asst. prof. Purdue U., Lafayette, Ind., 1958-60; dir. food rsch. Liby McNeill & Libby, Chgo., Ind., 1960-67; prof. food sci. Miss. State U., Starkville, 1967-85, dept. head, 1985-88, prof. emeritus, 1990—, mem. grad. coun., 1984-85; pres. Aliceville C. of C., 1997—. Author: Careers in Food Technology, 1975, Home Canning, 1978; contbg. author: Channel Catfish Culture, 1985; contbr. over 125 articles on food sci. to profl. jours. 1st lt. USAAF, 1941-45, ETO. Decorated Dutch Orange Lanyard (The Netherlands). Fellow Inst. Food Technologists (chmn. Chgo. sect. 1964-65, pres. Magnolia sect. 1987-88, Calvert Willey award 1988); mem. Coun. for Agr. Sci. and Tech. (pres. 1985-86, bd. dirs. 1977-87), Phi Kappa Phi, Phi Tau Sigma (pres. 1984-85). Democrat. Roman Catholic. Achievements include patent for fish skinning process. Avocations: hunting, fishing, writing. E-mail: ammerman@pickens.net. Home: 210 Quail Trail Aliceville AL 35442 Office: Aliceville C of C 416 Broad St NE Aliceville AL 35442-2142

AMMERMANN, DIETER F., zoologist; b. Hannover, Germany, Mar. 30, 1937; s. August and Hildegard (Holtz) A.; m. Elisabeth M. Elfers; children: Kathrin, Heidi, Heiko, Inyo, Volker. PhD, U. Tuebingen, 1965, Habilitation, 1971. Head dept. cell biology U. Tuebingen, 1972—, prof., 1973—. Home: Lindenstr 17, D-72119 Ammerbuch Germany Office: Univ of Tuebingen, A D Morgenstelle 28, 72076 Tuebingen Germany

AMMON, HERMANN PHILIPP THEODOR, pharmacologist, educator; b. Nuremberg, Bavaria, Germany, Jan. 24, 1933; s. Theodor and Käthe (Schatz) A.; m. Helga Ursula Grummt, Aug. 3, 1963; children: Susanne, Christiane. MD, U. Erlangen-Nuremberg, Fed. Republic of Germany, 1963, privat dozent, 1968. Rsch. fellow U. Erlangen-Nuremberg, Fed. Republic of Germany, 1965-70; asst. prof. Dept. Pharmacology, U. Erlangen, Nuremberg, Fed. Republic of Germany, 1971-74; instr. medicine Harvard Med. Sch., U. Harvard, Cambridge, Mass., 1970-71; assoc. prof. pharmacology Inst. Pharm. Scis., U. Tuebingen, Fed. Republic Germany, 1974-76; prof. U. Tübingen, Fed. Republic Germany, 1976—; dir. Inst. Pharm. Scis., U. Tuebingen, 1986-89, 95-98. Author, editor: (handbook) Arzneimittelneben und Wechselwirkungen, 1981, 86, 91; editor, co-editor over 15 sci. jours. and books; contbr. 180 articles to profl. jours. Com. mem. Bundesgesundheitsamt, Berlin, 1978; bd. reviewers Deutsche Forschungsgemeinschaft, Bonn, Bad Godesbuerg, Fed. Republic of Germany, 1988. Recipient Gold Medal Chamber of Pharmacists Baden-Wurttemberg, 1992, Verdienstorden der Bundesrepublik Deutschland am Band, 1999, Lesmuller-Medal, Arbeitsgemeinschaft Deutscher Apothekerverbande, 2000. Mem. German Soc. for Exptl. and Clin. Pharmacology, Toxicology, German Diabetes Assn. (bd. dirs. 1989, pres. 1994-95), German Pharm. Soc. (bd. dirs. 1986, pres. 1996-99), Am. Diabetes Assn., Endocrine Soc. (U.S.), European Soc. for Study Diabetes, Lions (pres. Tuebingen 1983-84, gov. dist. IIISM 1992-93). Achievements include research in biochemistry of insulin secretion, antidiabetic drugs, pharmacology of medicinal plants, boswellic acids (from francincense) with anti-inflamatory and antitumor activity. E-mail: sekretariat.ammon@uni-tuebingen.de. Home: Im Kleeacker 30, D-72072 Tübingen Germany

AMOAH, JAMES KWAME, artist, educator; b. Agona, Ghana, July 3, 1943; s. Kwame Amoah and Yaa Dufie; m. Mary Bissue, Febr. 10, 1972; children: Sarah, Akua Pokua, James Jr., Gerhard. Diplom, Gesamthochschule, Kassel, Germany, 1993; BA in Art, UST, Kumasi, Ghana, 1996. Asst. rsch. fellow Coll. Art., UST, Kumasi, 1966-69, lectr., 1971-82, sr. lectr., 1982—. Mem. Ghana Assn. Visual Arts, Gideons Internat. Avocation: fish farming. Home: 11 Bruboro Rd, Kumasi Ghana Office: Coll Art-UST, PO Box 50, Kumasi Ghana

AMOAKO, KINGSLEY Y., international organization administrator. Exec. sec. Econ. Commn. Africa, Addis Ababa, Ethiopia. Office: Africa Hall, PO Box 3005, Addis Ababa Ethiopia*

AMOAKO-NUAMA, CHRISTINE, Ghana government official; b. Bekwai, Ashanti, Ghana, Feb. 3, 1944; 4 children. Student, U. Sci. and Tech., Kumasi, Ghana, 1965; BSc in Zoology and Botany, U. Ghana, 1966, MS in Mycology, 1969; PhD in Plant Pathology and Microbiology, U. Western Ont., London, Can., 1974. Tchr. biology Opoku Ware Secondary Sch., Kumasi, Ghana, 1966-67; grad. tchg. asst. U. Ghana and U. Western Ont., 1968-74; fellow, instr. U. Western Ont., 1974-76; lectr. U. Ghana, Legon, 1976-84, mem. acad. bd., faculty sci. bd., agrl. rsch. stas. br., 1978-83; assoc. prof. U. Liberia, 1984-90; sr. programs officer EPA, Accra, Ghana, 1990-93, dep. dir.; min. of state responsible for environ. Govt. of Ghana, Accra, 1993-94, min. of state of environ., sci. and tech., 1994-97, min. for edn., 1997-98, min. for lands and forestry, 1998—; mem. Ghana Export Promotion Coun., 1992-94; mem. acad. planning com. U. Liberia Sci. Coll., 1984-90. V.p. Green Forum for Devel: Environ. Journalists and Communicators, Ghana; trustee Iwokrama Internat. Ctr. for Rain Forest Conservation and Devel. of Commonwealth, Guyana, Ctr. for Internat. Forestry Rsch.; joint patron Ghana Girl Guides Assn. Mem. Legon Soc. Nat. Affairs (editl. bd., observer 1978-82), Ghana Inst. Biology, Ghana Sci. Assn., Ghana Biodiversity Assn., Ghana Assn. Cons., Internat. Assn. Tropical Forsters, Fedn. African Women Educationalists, Women in Sci. and Tech. Mem. Nat. Dem. Congress. Office: Ministry Lands & Forestry, PO Box M 212, Accra Ghana

AMODIO, PIERLUIGI, mathematician, researcher; b. Bari, Italy, Apr. 8, 1965; s. Michele and Evelina (Cimadomo) A.; m. Luisa Belsito, July 22, 1992; 1 child, Francesco. Degree in computer sci., U. Bari, 1988. Rschr. U. Bari, 1990-98, assoc. prof., 1998—. Author: (with D. Trigiante) Elementi di Calcolo Numerico, 1993; contbr. over 30 articles to profl. publs. Consiglio Nazionale Delle Ricerche scholar, 1988-90. Mem. Soc. Indsl. and Applied Math. Roman Catholic. Avocations: collector, sports. Home: Piazza Mercantile 10, 70122 Bari Italy Office: U Bari Dept Math, Via Orabona 4, 70125 Bari Italy

AMOLOCHITIS, GEORGE, sales executive; b. Athens, Greece, Feb. 6, 1951; s. Emmanuel and Dimitra (Paraskevopoulou) A.; m. Marguerite Gabrielian, Sept. 27, 1979; children: Emmanouil, Natalia. M of Chemistry, U. Athens, 1981, M of Computer Sci., 1984. Tech. chemist BASF A.G., Ludwigshafen, 1978; wine chemist Schaan Vinimex, 1981-84; product specialist Bacacos S.A., Athens, 1984-88; sales support exec. Hewlett-Packard S.A., Athens, 1988-89; registration mgr. Middle East and Africa regional offices Novo-Nordisk A.S., Athens, 1989—. Mem. Assn. Greek Chemists, Greek Stats. Inst., Hellenic Assn. Ops. Research. Avocation: foreign languages. Office: Novo-Nordisk A/S Athens Tower, Athinas Ave Status Ctr, GR 11671 Athens Vouliagmeni Greece

AMON PARISI, CRISTINA HORTENSIA, mechanical engineering educator, researcher; m. Carmelo Parisi, Dec. 6, 1980; children: Andreina, Gabriel. Degree in mech. engring. summa cum laude, U. Simon Bolivar, Caracas, Venezuela, 1981; MS, MIT, 1985, PhD, 1988. Instr., researcher U. Simon Bolivar, Caracas, 1981-83; asst. prof. Carnegie-Mellon U., Pitts., 1988-93, assoc. prof., 1993-97, prof., 1997—, dir. Inst. Complex Engineered Sys., 1999—. Assoc. editor: IEEE CPMT, Heat Mass Transfer; contbr. articles to profl. jours. Recipient Rsch. Initiation award NSF, 1989, G.T. Ladd award CIT, 1991, Ednl. award Ladd, 1998. Fellow AIAA (assoc.), ASME (Pitts. Engr. of Yr. 1999, Gustus L. Larson Meml. award 2000); mem. IEEE (sr.), Soc. Automotive Engring. (R. Teetor Ednl. award 1994), Sci. Rsch. Soc., Am. Soc. Engring. Edn. (North Ctrl. Sect. Outstanding Tchr. award 1995, Best Campus Rep. award 1996, George Westinghouse award 1997, Teare award 1998), Soc. Women Engrs. (Distig. Educator award 1999), Soc. Hispanic Profl. Engrs., Sigma Xi. Office: Carnegie Mellon U Dept Mech Engring Pittsburgh PA 15213

AMOR, JAMES MICHAEL, dentist, actor; b. Bklyn., Apr. 10, 1959; s. James and Louisa (Piñeiro) A.; m. Patricia Elvira Mancuso, Sept. 25, 1988; children: William Anthony, James Patrick. BS in Biology, Fairleigh Dickinson U., 1980, DMD, 1984. Lic. dentist, N.Y., N.J., Pa. Staff dentist Internat. Longshoremen's Assn. - N.Y. Shipping Authority, Hoboken, N.J., 1985-87, AFL-CIO Teamsters Union Local Dental Facility, Elmsford, N.Y., 1989-90; clin. assoc. Office of Thomas Doran, DDS, Huntington, N.Y., 1985-90; ptnr. Wolfe-Amor Dental Svcs., New Holland, Pa., 1990-95; owner New Design Dental Assocs., New Holland, 1995—; assoc. prof. Sch. Dentistry Fairleigh Dickinson U., Hackensack, N.J., 1985-89; dental cons. Ephrata (Pa.) Manor Nursing Home - U.C.C. Homes, 1992-95, Zerbe Sisters Nursing Home, Narvon, Pa., 1990-95, Luther Acres Nursing Home-Luth. Homes, Lititz, Pa., 1991-95. Mem. cast in Nutcracker, Fulton Opera House, Lancaster, Pa., 1997, 98, 00, Pa. Renaissance Faire, 1998, 99, 2000. Mem. ADA, Lancaster County Dental Soc. (mem. comprehensive cmty. care com. 1992-95), Acad. Gen. Dentistry, Hispanic Dental Assn., Kiwanis (pres. New Holland club 1999), Psi Omega. Roman Catholic. Avocations: classic cars, heraldry, Arthurian legend, photography, computers. Home: PO Box 6 New Holland PA 17557-0006 Office: New Design Dental Assocs 121 E Main St New Holland PA 17557-1227

AMOR, SIMEON, JR., photographer; b. Lahaina, Hawaii, Apr. 24, 1924; s. Simeon and Victoria Amor. Grad. high sch., Hilo, Hawaii. Post commdr. Engrs. Post #22, Am. Legion, Honolulu, 1952-53; approp. acct. Hawaii Air Nat. Guard, Honolulu, 1953-64; prodn. control supr. Svc. Bur. Corp., Honolulu, 1964-73; prodn. control computer ops. Bank of Hawaii, Honolulu, 1973-86; owner, propreitor Image Engring., Honolulu, 1986—; historian VFW Dept. Hawaii, Honolulu, 1987-90, 96-97, First Filipino Infantry Regiment Hawaii Connection; treas. DAV Dept. Hawaii, Honolulu. Tech. advisor: (film documentary) Untold Triumph, Saga of the American Filipino Soldier. Cpl. U.S. Infantry, 1943-46, master sgt. USNG, 1952-64. Recipient Disting. Svc. award Nat. Disabled Am. Vet., 1992-94, Oahu chpt. Disabled Am. Vet., 1992-94. Mem. Am. Photographer's Internat., VFW. Home: 1634 Kino St Honolulu HI 96819-2651

AMORIM, CELSO LUIZ NUNES, government official. Student, Rio-Branco Inst., Diplomatic Acad. Vienna, London Sch. Econs. Amb. UN, Geneva, 1991-93; min. Ministry Fgn. Affairs, Brasilia, Brazil, 1993-94; permanent rep. Brazil UN, N.Y.C., 1995-99, Geneva, 1999—; spl. asst. to Ministry Sci. & Tech.; asst. prof. dept. polit. sci. and internat. rels. U. Brasilia, permanent mem. dept. internat. affairs Inst. Advanced Studies. Contbr. articles to profl. jours. Ofice: Permanent Mission Brazil/UN, 1218 Grand Sacconex, Geneva Switzerland

AMORY, CHRISTINE MARIE EUGENIE, physicist, researcher; b. Boulogne, France, Oct. 10, 1949; d. Rigobert and Marie Therese Simone (Cagnioncle) A.; divorced. M in Physics, U. Paris VI, 1972, PhD in Geophysics, 1974; degree in mgmt., U. Paris I, 1979; D degree, U. Paris VI, 1983. Tchr. Edn. Nationale, Paris, 1971-76; engr. Centre A l'Energie Atomique, Bruyères le Chatel, 1976-78; rschr. Centre Nat. de la Recherche Scientifique, Paris, 1978—; mem. numerous worldwide sci. projects. Contbr. articles to profl. jours. including Geophysic Periodic, Magnetism, and Meteorology. Mem. Confédération Française dÉmocratique des Travailleurs, Paris, 1971-96; vice-chairwoman Assn. Cultuelle du Temple Pyramide, 1992-95, Cité Sainte de Mandarom Shambhasalem, La Baume, Castellane, France; chairwoman Assn. Vajra Triomphant, 1995—. Mem. Assn. Vajra Triomphant (chairwoman 1995), Comité Nat. Francais de Geophysique et Geodésie, 1984—, Comité Nat. Francais de Recherches Antartiques, N.Y. Acad. Scis. Avocations: music, riding, swimming. Office: CETP, 4 Ave de Neptune, 94107 Saint-Maur-des-Fosses France

AMOS, BETTY GILES, restaurant company executive, accountant; b. Lebanon, Mo., July 18, 1941; d. Clarence Edgar and Clara Mae (Gann) Giles; m. E.L. Amos, Sept. 18, 1959 (div. Oct. 1965); 1 child, Jeffrey Lee; m. Thomas R. Righetti, Jan. 2, 1983. BBA magna cum laude, U. Miami, Coral Gables, Fla., 1973, MBA, 1976; D of Bus. Adminstrn. honoris causa, Johnson & Wales U., 1990. CPA, Fla. Sec. City of Lebanon, 1959-63; dept. head Empire Gas Co., Lebanon, 1963-68; fin. analyst asst. Biscayne Assocs., Ltd., Miami, Fla., 1968-73; investment mgr. Universal Restaurants Inc., Miami, 1973-77; pvt. practice accountant, investment mgr. Miami, 1977-83; pres. The Abkey Cos., Miami, 1983—; founder, Mega Bank, Miami, 1983-94; adv. com. Fuddruckers, Inc., Boston, 1986—. Trustee Miami Project, 1986-89, United Fund of Dade County, 1992—; pres. Humane Soc. Greater Miami, 1994-2000, bd. dirs., 1993-2000; mem. pres. coun. U. Miami, 1994—, mem. founder's soc., 1994—, bd. trustees, 1997—; mem. presdl. search com. U. Miami, 2000—. Recipient Philip J. Romano Founders award, 1988. Mem. AICPA, Fla. Inst. CPAs, Am. Women's Soc. CPAs, Coconut Grove C. of C. (trustee 1988—), Nat. Assn. Women Bus. Owners (Outstanding Woman Bus. award 1993), U. Miami Alumni Assn. (nat. pres. 1999—), Iron Arrow. Republican. Roman Catholic. Avocations: snow skiing, water skiing, scuba diving, tennis, windsurfing. Home: 13724 SW 92nd Ct Miami FL 33176-6858 Office: The Abkey Cos 3444 48 Main Hwy 3d Floor PO Box 330927 Miami FL 33233-0927

AMOS, FRANCIS JOHN CLARKE, academic administrator; b. London, Sept. 10, 1924; s. Frank and Alice Mary (Clarke) A.; m. Geraldine Mercy Sutton; children: Zephyr Lucie, Gideon John. Diploma in architecture, London Poly., 1951; diploma in town planning, Sch. Planning, London, 1952; BSc, London Sch. Econs., 1955. Architect Harlow New Town Devel. Corp., Essex, Eng., 1951; urban planner London County Council, 1952-53; regional planning officer Ministry Housing and Local Govt., London, 1957-59, 61-62; gen. tech. adviser Govt. Ethiopia, 1959-61; city planning officer Liverpool City Council, Merseyside, 1962-73; chief. exec. Birmingham City Council, West Midlands, 1973-77; sr. fellow U. Birmingham, West Midlands, 1977—; cons. various internat. banks and govts., 1977—; commr. London and Metropolitan Govt. Staff Commn., 1983-86; asst. commr. Local Govt. Boundary Commn., 1987-93. Mem. Exec. Com. Action Resource Ctr., 1976-86, Nuffield Inquiry into Town and Country Planning, 1984-87; trustee Community Projects Found., 1978-89; adviser Dept. Internat. Devel., 1991—. Served to capt. Indian Army, 1942-47. Named Comdr. British Empire, Her Majesty the Queen. Mem. Royal Inst. British Architects, Royal Town Planning Inst. (pres. 1971-72, hon. sec. 1979-90), Royal Soc. Arts. Home and Office: 20 Westfield Rd, Edgbaston, Birmingham B15 3QG, England Office: U Birmingham Sch Pub Policy, Gefford Warminster Coach House Aston, Willshire BA12 ONX, England

AMOUR, SALMIN, Tanzanian government official. Pres. of Zanzibar Govt. of Tanzania, Zanzibar, chmn. revolutionary coun. Office: Pres of Zanzibar, PO Box 776, Zanzibar Tanzania*

AMPEL, ROMAN, astronomer, researcher, educator; b. Wojnica, Wolyn, Poland, Aug. 6, 1929; s. Leon and Marta (Majstruk) A.; m. Teresa Dominiak, May 7, 1954; children: Miroslawa, Leszek. MS, N. Copernicus U., Torun, Poland, 1955, DSc, 1958. Postdoctoral fellow Stockholm Observatory, 1959-60; prodean Pedagogical U., Rzeszow, 1966-72, 92-99, dean, 1974-75, 81-91, prorector, 1975-78. Editor Scis. Papers of Rzeszow Sci. Soc., 1968-78, Physics Papers of Pedagogical U., 1970-78. Pres. 500th Anniversary of N. Copernicus Birthday, Rzeszow, 1968-73, 200th Anniversary of Polish Edn. Com., Rzeszow, 1972-74. Decorated Cross of Merit Polonia Restituta Ilocation; recipient medal N. Copernicus 500th Birthday, 1973, 200th Anniversary of Polish Edn. Com., 1973. Mem. Rzeszow Sci. Soc. (pres. sci. dept. 1966-92), European Phys. Soc., Polish Astron. Soc., Polish Phys Soc. Avocation: apiculture. Home: Jalowego 28a/7, 35010 Rzeszów Poland Office: Pedagogical U, Rejtana 16a, 35310 Rzeszów Poland

AMPHOUX, CHRISTIAN-BERNARD, research philologist, educator; b. Vannes, France, July 17, 1943; s. André Pierre and Simone Marguerite France (Lerch) A.; m. Luce Jeanneret, Dec. 23, 1967; children: Pauline, Laure, Hèloise, Amielle. Lic. de lettre, U. Paul Valéry, Montpellier, France,

1964, agrégation de grammaire, 1967; D 3d cycle, U. Sorbonne, Paris, 1981. Prof. de lettre Lycée de l'Arc, Dole, France, 1967-69, Lycée Stanlislas, Wissembourg, France, 1969-70, Gymnase J. Sturm, Strasbourg, France, 1970-74; rsch. asst. Nat. Ctr. Sci. Rsch. (CNRS), Dijon, France, 1974-79; dir. rsch. Nat. Ctr. Sci. Rsch. (CNRS), Paris, 1981-89, Montpellier, 1990-93, Aix-Marseille, France, 1994—; course dir. Inst. Cath., Lyon, France, 1982—, Inst. Protestant, Montpellier, 1975—. Author: La Parole qui devint Évangile, 1993, Év. Matthieu, Codex de Bèze, 1996; co-author: Initiation à la Critique Textuelle du Nouveau Testament, 1986, English edit., 1991; co-author, co-editor: Codex Bezae (Lunel colloquium), 1996, Lecture Liturgique des Ép. Catholiques, 1996, Premières Traditions de la Bible, 1996, Evangile de Maic, recherches su les versions du text, 1999. Co-organizer Acad. of Langs., Saintes, France, 1986-99, Lille, France, 2000—, Colloque Codex Bezae, Lunel, France, 1994, intervenant daus la série télévisée Corpus Christi diffusée, 1997, 98, concernant l'histoire de Jésus. Home: 5 rue Subleyras, F-34000 Montpellier France Office: Ctr Paul-Albert Février Espace Jean-Duplacy, 30 rue des Caladons, F-34400 Lunel France

AMR, SHERIF MAMDOUH, orthopedist; b. Alexandria, Egypt, Mar. 31, 1961; s. Mamdouh Abdel-Hafez and Faiza (Abdel-Razek) A. MB BCh, Cairo U., 1985, MSc, 1989, MD, 1996, postdoctoral, 1996—. Bd. Orthopedics and Traumatology. Intern Sch. Medicine Cairo U., Cairo, 1986-87, resident dept. orthopedics Sch. Medicine, 1987-90, asst. lectr. dept. orthopedics Sch. Medicine, 1990-96, lectr. Sch. Medicine, 1996—; vis. resident dept. of plastic surgery MHH, Hannover, Germany, 1992-94; guest rschr. dept. biomechanics Tech. U. Hamburg, 1997; founder, rschr. Lab. of Orthopaedic Biomechanics, Dept. Orthopedics Cairo U. Contbr. articles to profl. jours. Fellow Soc. of Exptl. Surgery; mem. Egyptian Med. Syndicate, German Acad. Exchange Svc. Muslim. Avocations: biking, cooking, swimming, history, foreign languages. Home: 63 King Abdel Aziz El-Soud, Str Manial PO Box 11451, Cairo Egypt

AMSCHLER, DENISE H., health science educator; b. Alton, Ill., Aug. 1, 1950; d. Victor V. and Delphine L. Amschler; m. Neal E. Lambert, Apr. 27, 1985. BS, So. Ill. U., 1972, MS, 1973, PhD, 1975. Adj. asst. prof. Southern Ill. U., Carbondale, 1975-76; asst. prof. Ball State U., Muncie, Ind., 1976-83, assoc. prof., 1984-93, full prof., 1994—. Contbr. articles to profl. jours. Fellow Am. Sch. Health Assn.; mem. APHA, Jacobs Inst. for Womens Health, Eta Sigma Gamma (life, editor-in-chief The Health Educator jour. 1977-92, Disting. Svc. award 1985, Warren E. Schaller Presdl. citation 1993). E-mail: damschler@gwbsu.edu. Office: Dept Physiology/Health Sci Ball State U Muncie IN 47306-0001

AMSEL, BRAM JULES, cardiologist; b. Amsterdam, Netherlands, Mar. 3, 1949; s. Naftali Hersch and Ruth Henriette (Simons) A.; 1 child, Alon. SB in Applied Math. cum laude, Brown U., 1971; MD, U. Amsterdam, 1977, cert. in cardiology, 1983. Cardiologist-in-charge dept. cardiac surgery Univ. Hosp., Antwerp, Belgium, 1984—; lectr. U. Antwerp, Belgium, 1994—. With med. corps Army of Netherlands, 1977-78. Office: U Hosp of Antwerp, Wilrijkstraat 10, Edegem B-2650, Belgium

AMTMANN, HANS HENRY, aeronautical engineer, naval architect; b. Sande, Prussia, Germany, Oct. 15, 1906; came to U.S., 1946; s. August Johann and Charlotte Mathilde (Bode) A.; m. Margret Suberg; children: Jürgen, Dieter, Gunter, Sylvia. BS, State Tech. Sch., Hamburg, Germany, 1928. Lic. naval arch. Design engr. Junkers Aircraft Co., Dessau, Germany, 1928-33; pre-design engr. Ernst Heinkel Aircraft Co., Warnemünde, Germany, 1933-34; chief pre-design Blohm & Voss Aircraft Divsn., Hamburg, 1934-45; with Project Paperclip, Wright Field, Ohio, 1946-51; design specialist Convair, San Diego, 1951-61; staff engr. Gen. Atomic, La Jolla, Calif., 1961-71, cons. engr., 1971-81; cons. engr. Inesco, La Jolla, 1981-83, Sparta Inc., Del Mar, Calif., 1984-86; pvt. cons., Del Mar, 1988; ret., 1988. Author: The Vanishing Paperclips, 1988; contbr. articles on aircraft to profl. jours. Elder Village Ch., Rancho Santa Fe, Calif., 1952-55. Decorated War Merit Cross (Germany). Fellow Inst. Aerospace Sci. (assoc.). Republican. Presbyterian. Achievements include inventions in aircraft and nuclear reactors. Avocations: art, painting, violin, stamp collecting, writing. Home: PO Box 714 Rancho Santa Fe CA 92067-0714

AMUSATEGUI DE LA CIERVA, JOSÉ MARIA, bank executive; b. San Roque, Cadr, Spain, Mar. 12, 1932; m. Amalia de Leon, Apr. 29, 1988 (div.). Student, Colegio Huerfarnos de la Armada, Cadiz; LLB, U Ctrl. Madrid, 1954. State lawyer Fin. Ministry, Gerona, Spain, 1959-70; dep. chmn. Inst. Nacional Industria, Madrid, 1970, Prodinsa, Madrid, 1974, Inst. Nacional Hidrocarburos, Madrid, 1981-85; chmn. Campsa, Madrid, 1982-85; exec. dep. chmn. Banco Hispano Americano, Madrid, 1985, mng. dir., 1985-88, chmn., CEO, 1990; chmn. Banco Ctrl. Hispano, Madrid, 1992-99; joint chmn. BanCo Santander Ctrl. Hispano, 1999—. Recipient Spain's Grand Cross of Civil Merit, 1971. Avocations: motorcycling, astronomy, botany. Fax: 34 91 7 25 74 75. Office: Banco Ctrl Hispano Plz Canadejas 1, Alcalá 49, 28014 Madrid Spain

AMYES, EDWIN WESTBY, neurosurgeon; b. Edinburgh, Scotland, Nov. 2, 1920; came to U.S., 1921; s. Herbert Westby and Ruth Frieda Amyes; children: Nina, Christopher. BS, Pacific Union Coll., 1941; MD, Loma Linda U., 1944. Diplomate Am. Bd. of Neurosurgery. Intern White Meml. Hosp., Loma Linda, 1943, resident in psychiatry and neurology, 1944; staff physician St. Francis Hosp., Lynwood, Calif., 1946-48; pvt. gen. practice Huntington Park, Calif., 1946-48; resident, sr. resident in neurology U. So. Calif.-Loma Linda U., 1948-50; resident in neurosurgery L.A. County Hosp./White Meml. Hosp., 1950-53; with Rancho Los Amigos, 1955-65, organizer, designer neurosci. svcs., chief of neurosurgery, chief of staff; neurosurgeon Loma Linda U./White Meml. Hosp., St. Francis Hosp., Lynwood; staff neurosurgeon Hoag Meml. Hosp. Presbyn., Newport Beach, Calif., 1972—; asst. prof. neurol. surgery Loma Linda U., L.A.; chief of neurosurgery Loma Linda U. at L.A. County Hosp., 1953-56; assoc. clin. prof. neurol. surgery U. Calif./Irvine Med. Ctr., 1972—; cons. in neurosurgery; pres., CEO Bioelectronics, Inc., Lynwood. Contbr. articles to profl. jours. 1st lt. U.S. Army, 1944-46. Mem. Coun. of State Neurol. Socs. (founder, 1st chmn. 1975-80), Am. Assn. Neurol. Surgeons. Fax: (949) 642-6326. Home: 3640 5th Ave Corona Del Mar CA 92625-2537 Office: 320 Superior Ave Ste 310 Newport Beach CA 92663-2742

AMZAR, DINU, mathematician, writer; b. Berlin, Mar. 11, 1943; s. Dumitru Christian and Maria (Bernea) A.; m. Moiken Friederike Bossung, Dec. 28, 1982; 1 child, Cornelius. BS, U. Mainz, 1967, diploma in math., 1972. Scientist Fed. Office of Statistics, Govt. of Germany, Wiesbaden, 1973-83. Author: Sehübungen an Rebengerippen, 1975, Gebiete den Grillen zu schweigen, 1979, Langholzabfuhren, 1990, In Sätzen, in Ketten, 1999. Home and Office: Lenaustrasse 2, 72488 Sigmaringen Germany

AN, HAEJUNG, food technology educator; b. Seoul, Republic of Korea, May 13, 1958; came to U.S., 1981; d. Sung-Ho Ahn and Seung-Ah Park; m. Thomas A. Seymour, June 18, 1986; 1 child, Jillian A. BS, Seoul Nat. U., 1981; MS, La. State U., 1984; PhD, U. Fla., 1989. Postdoctoral U. Fla., Gainesville, 1989-90; asst. prof. Oreg. State U., Astoria, 1991-97, assoc. prof., 1997-2000; assoc. prof. Auburn (Ala.) U., 2000—. Contbr. articles to profl. jours. Grantee Oreg. State U., 1991-93, Sea, 1993-97, 99-2000, USDA, 1993—. Mem. Am. Inst. Fishery Rsch. Biologists, Inst. Food Technologists, Am. Chem. Soc. Home: 325 N Cedarbrook Dr Auburn AL 36830-2651 Office: Auburn U Dept Nutrition and Food Scis Spidle Hall 328 Auburn AL 36849

AN, JUNLING, environmentalist; b. Haiyuan County, China, Mar. 15, 1967; s. Yaode and Yulian (Zhang) A.; m. Lijuan chen, Aug. 4, 1995; 1 child, Miaorui. BS, Nanjing Inst. Meteorology, 1989; MS, Lanzhou Inst. Plateau, Atmospheric Physics/Chinese Acad. Scis., Lanzhou, 1992; PhD, Chinese Acad. Scis., Beijing, 1996. Diploma in Envrion. Scis. and Atmospheric Physics. Scientist Inst. Atmospheric Physics/Chinese Acad. Scis., Beijing, 1995-98, State Key Lab. Atmospheric Bounday Layer/Chinese Acad. Scis., 1998—; advisor Beijing Mcpl. Environ. Protection Bur., Beijing, 1998-99; cons. World Bank, Beijing Mcpl. Environ. Protection Bur., Beijing, 1999—. Contbr. articles to profl. jours. (3rd award for Natural Scis. Chine Acad. of Scis. 1994). Recipient awards Nanjing Inst. Meteorology, 1987, 88. Mem. Bejing Mcpl. Environ. Protection Bur. Avocations: music, basketball, badminton. E-mail: anjil@mailcity.com. Office: State Key Lab Phys/Chem, Chinese Acad Scis, Qijiahuozi/Beijing 100029, China

AN, YUEHUI HUEY, orthopaedic surgeon, educator; b. Shenyang, China, Oct. 23, 1960; came to the U.S., 1991; s. Rongkai An and Yanyun Wang; m. Tianhua Ge, Jan. 20, 1986 (div. Aug. 1988). MB, Harbin (China) Med. U., 1983; M in Medicine, Beijing Inst. Orthopaedics, 1986. Orthop. resident Beijing Ji Shui Tan Hosp., 1984-88, chief resident, 1988-90; hand fellow Sydney (Australia) Hosp., 1990-91; post-doctoral fellow orthop. Med. U. S.C., Charleston, 1991-93, asst. prof. orthop., 1993-98, assoc. prof. orthop., dir. orthop. rsch. lab., 1998—; adj. asst. prof. bioengring. Clemson (S.C.) U., 1996—; cons. Cardiovasc. Tissue Techs., Charleston, 1997—, Organ Recovery Systems, Charleston, S.C., Cambridge Sci., Inc., Boston, 1997—. Editor: Animal Models in Orthopaedic Research, 1999, Mech. Testing of Bone and the Bone-Implant Interface, 2000, Handbook of Bacterial Adhesion—Principles, Methods and Applications, 2000; contbr. articles to Jour. Bone Joint Surgery, Clin. Orthop., Jour. Orthopaedic Rsch., Jour. Biomed. Material Rsch., Jour. Material Sci., Biomaterials, others. Chmn. Ji Shui Tan Hosp., Bicycle Sports Assn., Beijing, 1990-91. Mem. Am. Soc. Biomechanics, Soc. for Biomaterials, Soc. Tissue Engring., Orthopaedic Rsch. Soc. Achievements include international patent for thermally reversible gelling cell culture media; U.S. patent for adjustable ligament anchor; 6 patent disclosures. Avocations: long distance bicycling, fishing, hunting, traveling. E-mail: any@musc.edu. Home: Apt 1103 2284 Ashley River Rd Charleston SC 29414-4746 Office: Med Univ SC Orthopaedic Surgery QC 302B 51 Albert B Sabin St Charleston SC 29403-5816

ANAGLI, JOHN YAO, biomedical research scientist, consultant; b. Denu, Volta, Ghana, Nov. 4, 1956; came to the U.S., 1996; s. Joseph Kwaku and Edith Adzo (Sallah) A.; m. Carine Josee Cambier, Oct. 9, 1984; children: Victor, Bryan, Tracy. MSc in Chem. Scis., Cath. U. Louvain, Louvain-La-Neuve, Belgium, 1986; postgrad., Free U. Brussels, 1987; PhD in Biochemistry, U. Basel, Switzerland, 1991. Rsch. asst. Ciba Geigy/Friedrich Miescher Inst., Basel, 1987-88; rsch. asst. Friedrich Miescher Inst., Basel, 1988-91, rsch. assoc., 1991-92; asst. prof. Swiss Fed. Inst. Tech., Zürich, 1992-96; sr. staff investigator Henry Ford Health Sys., Detroit, 1996—; v.p. Molecular Solutions Internat., Royal Oak, Mich., 1998—. Sec. The Ghana Union Switzerland, Zürich, 1994-96. Recipient Rsch. award Parke-Davis Pharm., Ann Arbor, Mich., 1997, rsch. grant-in-aid Am. Heart Assn., Lathrup Village, Mich., 1998; Josephine Ford Cancer Ctr. rsch. grantee, Detroit, 1998. Mem. Am. Soc. for Biochemistry and Molecular Biology, Am. Peptide Soc. Achievements include inventor of a method for treating tissue damaged from Ischemia; research on the effects of specific cysteine protease inhibitors on experimental cerebral ischemia; invented a method to reduce infarct volume in an animal model of middle cerebral artery occlusion. Avocations: traveling, jazz music, soccer, table tennis. Office: Henry Ford Health Sys Ste 5D One Ford Pl Detroit MI 48202

ANAGNOSTAKIS, EMMANUEL ALEXANDER, physicist, educator; b. Athens, Greece, Feb. 3, 1961; s. Alexander Emmanuel and Ioanna Panagiotis (Makellarakis) A.; m. Despina Symeon, Nov. 4, 1995; 1 child, Ioanna Emmanuel. BSc in Physics, U. Athens, 1982, MSc in Electronics, 1984, PhD in Optoelectronic Semicondr. Devices, 1990. Rschr. Hellenic Air Force Rsch. and Tech. Ctr., Glyfada, Greece, 1989-91; vis. prof. Hellenic Air Force Acad., Dekelia, Greece, 1987-98; prof. Hellenic Army Acad., Vari, Greece, 1992—, coord. physics lab., 1992—; coord. Hellenic Centre for Study of Optoelectronics, Athens, 1996—. Referee jour. Inst. of Physics, 1998—, internat. rsch. jour. Thin Solid Films, 1998—. Fellow Hellenic Phys. Soc. (sci. affairs officer 1997—); mem. European Phys. Soc., Optical Soc. Am. (rsch. monograph reviewer 1999—), Electrochem. Soc. Greek Orthodox. Avocations: swimming, ancient Greek studies, poetry composition. E-Mail: emmanagn@otenet.gr. Office: Hellenic Army Acad, 72 Cyprus St, Athens GR112 57, Greece

ANAGNOSTAKIS, YANNIS EMMANUEL, pharmacist; b. Heraklion, Crete, Greece, May 19, 1966; s. Emmanuel Ioannis and Irene Emmanuel (Vidaki) A.; m. Christina Ioannis Dervou, Jan. 18, 1997. D of Pharmacy, U. Thessaloniki, 1988; PhD, U. Crete, 1992. Lectr. U. Crete, Heraklion, 1989-94; pres. Materia Analytica, Heraklion, 1994-95, Opus-Materia Ltd., Athens, Greece, 1996—; R&D dir. A. Dervos-G. Dimitrakopoulos SA, Athens, 1996—; gen. dir. G. Dimitrakopoulos & Co. OE, Athens, 1996—; pres. Genoma Ltd., Athens, 1996—. Contbr. articles to profl. jours. Mem. New Dem. Party, 1990—. Pharmacist Health Divsn. Greece, 1994. Mem. Panhellenic Pharmicist Union, Greek Soc. Neurosci. Avocations: playing Cretan mandoline, singing Cretan traditional, sailing, cultivating vineyards and olive trees. Home: 33 Paleologou Str, 17564 P Faliron Athens, Greece Office: Opus Materia Ltd, 33 Paleology Str, 17564 P Faliron Athens, Greece

ANAGNOSTOPOULOS, JOHN PANAGIOTOU, electrical engineer, researcher; b. Athens, Attika, Greece, May 15, 1951; s. Panagiotis I. and Catherine T. (Perivolaraki) A. BS in Engring. Sci., CUNY, 1975; MS in Elec. Engring., Poly. U. N.Y., N.Y.C., 1977. Cert. profl. engr. Rsch. engr. Fellows Corp., Springfield, Vt., 1977-79; cons. Athens, 1979-87; project engr. KEETHA Rsch. Ctr., Thrakomacedones, Athens, 1987-92; spl. scientist KETES Rsch. Ctr., Thrakomacedones, 1992—; TV mfg. svc. and fin. support Telefex Corp., Athens, 1981-86. Fellow Tech., Epimeleterion, Elados. Avocations: electronics projects, tennis, ping pong, swimming, learning foreign languages. E-mail: a@tee.gr. Home: 13 Anaxagora Str, 17778 Athens Greece

ANAGNOSTOU, EMMANOUIL NIKOLAOS, civil and environmental engineering educator; b. Athens, Greece, Feb. 27, 1968; came to U.S., 1992; s. Nikolaos Emmanouil Aganostou and Ekaterini Koraki; m. Svetlana Kalnova, July 9, 1998. Diploma, Nat. Tech. U., Athens, 1990; MS, U. Iowa, 1994, PhD, 1997. Registered profl. engr., Tech. Chamber of Greece. Rsch. asst. Nat. Tech. U., Athens, 1990-92; grad. rsch. asst. Iowa Inst. Hydraulic Rsch., Iowa City, 1992-97; vis. scientist NASA, Greenbelt, Md., 1997-98; asst. prof. U. Conn., Storrs, 1999—; sci. team mem. NASA, 1998—; tech. advisor Nat. Obs., Athens, 1999—. Recipient Marie Curie award European Union Environ. and Climate Program, 1998. Mem. ASCE, Am. Geophys. Union, Am. Meteorol. Soc., Greek Soc. Civil Engrs. Avocations: skiing, basketball, watersports. E-mail: manos@engr.uccon.edu. Office: U Conn 261 Glenbrook Rd Unit U-37 Storrs Mansfield CT 06269-2037

ANAGNOU, NICHOLAS P., molecular biologist, hematologist; b. Dire-Dawa, Ethiopia, Nov. 15, 1947; s. Panayotis and Angela (Karlovasitou) A. MD, U. Athens, 1972, PhD, 1977. Intern Samos Gen. Hosp., Greece, 1973-74; resident U. Hosp., U. Athens, 1974-77; fellow in hematology U. Athens Hosp., 1977-79; postdoctoral fellow NIH, Bethesda, Md., 1980-83; rsch. assoc. NIH, 1983-86; asst. prof. medicine U. Wash., Seattle, 1986-88; assoc. prof. molecular biology, chief Lab. Molecular Biology U. Crete, 1989-98, chmn. dept. basic scis., 1990-91, 93-95, prof. molecular biology, 1993-99; prof. molecular biology U. Athens Sch. Medicine, 1999—; mem. Com. Gene Therapy, Nat. Adv. Coun. on Rsch.; nat. expert adv. com. Biomed Program, European Union, 1992-98. Mem. editl. bd. Hemoglobin, Haema, Hellenic Jour. Human Genetics; contbr. articles to profl. jours. Fogarty Internat. Ctr. fellow, 1980-83; Found. State Scholarship of Greece rsch. fellow, 1973-75, others. Mem. Am. Soc. Clin. Investigation, Am. Fedn. Clin. Research, AAAS, Am. Soc. Cell Biology, Am. Soc. Hematology, Internat. Soc. Exptl. Hematology, Am. Soc. Human Genetics, Am. Soc. Gene Therapy, Human Genome Orgn., European Soc. Gene Therapy, Rotaract Club. Office: U Crete, Inst Molecular Biol and Biotech, Crete Greece 711 10

ANAH, CHRISTIAN ONYEKPANDU, cardiologist, consultant, educator; b. Ihiagwa-Owerri, Imo, Nigeria, July 24, 1936; s. John and Lucy (Anokam) A.; m. Abigail Onyegecha Ubah, July 20, 1963; children: Chukwuma, Chiaka, Ogechi, Kechinyere. MB, BS, U. London, 1961. Intern Gen. Hosp, Lagos, Nigeria, 1962; registrar in cardiology Univ. Coll. Hosp., Ibadan, Nigeria, 1963-64; U.K. commonwealth fellow Assn. Commonwealth Univs., London, 1965-67; registrar Bernhard Baron Meml. Rsch. Labs. Queen Charlotte's Maternity Hosp., London, 1968; registrar, then sr. registrar United Oxford (Eng.) Hosps./Churchill Hosp., 1969-72; from lectr. to prof. medicine, cons. physician U. Benin Hosp., Benin City, Nigeria, 1973-84; prof., cons. physician U. Port Harcourt (Nigeria) and Hosp., 1985—; past head dept. medicine U. Benin; past head dept. medicine U. Port Harcourt, provost Coll. Health Scis., 1986-92; mem. governing bd. Univ. Hosp. Benin, 1977, Univ. Hosp. Port Harcourt, 1986-92. Contbr. articles to sci. jours. Fellow Royal Coll. Physicians (London), Internat. Coll. Angiology (N.Y.). Home: Umuokwo, Ihiagwa, Owerri Imo, Nigeria Office: U Port Harcourt Coll Health, PMB 1 Choba, Dept Medicine, Port Harcourt Rivers, Nigeria

ANAM, EDET MATTHEW, chemistry educator, researcher; b. Calabar, Nigeria, July 21, 1946; s. Akabom Matthew and Iquo Matthew (Anamiakan) A.; m. Rosemary Edet Eyo, Apr. 21, 1986; children: Ene Edet, Ikpeme Edet, Akabom Edet. BSc, U. Calabar, 1981, MSc, 1984, PhD in Organic Chemistry, 1991. Tchg. asst. The Poly., Calabar, 1974-77; asst. lectr. U. Calabar, 1984-86, lectr., 1987-92, sr. lectr., 1993-95, reader, 1996—; coord. consultancy U. Calabar, 1993-95. Contbr. articles to Planta Medica, Phytochemistry, Indian Jour. Chemistry, others. Mem. Civil Svc. Commn., Calabar, 1989-91. Mem. Inst. Med. Lab. Technologists (assoc.), Sci. Assn. Nigeria, Chem. Soc. Nigeria, Polyphenol Soc. Christian. Avocations: singing, table tennis, lawn tennis, boxing, fishing. Office: U Calabar Dept Chemistry, PMB 1115, Calabar Nigeria

ANAND, ADARSCH SEIN, judge; b. Jan. 11, 1936. BsC, GGM Sci. Coll., Jammu, India; LLB, Lucknow (India) U.; PhD, Univ. Coll., London. Enrolled adv. Bar Coun., from 1964; practice crimina., consl., election law Punjab and Haryana High Ct., Chandigar, India; additional judge Jammu and Kashmir High Ct., 1975-76, permanent judge, 1976-85, chief justice, 1985-89; judge Madras High Ct., 1989-91; judge Supreme Ct. India, New Delhi, 1991—, now chief justice. Office: Supreme Ct, Tilak Marg, New Delhi 110 011, India*

ANAND, ARUN VEER, airport executive; b. Karachi, India, Sept. 19, 1942; s. Ganga Ram and Shakuntla (Sethi) A.; m. Neelam Bhayana, Oct. 14, 1970; children: Rimi, Anubhav. BSc, Christ Church Coll., Kanpore, India, 1961, MSc, 1963; cert. air traffic controller, sr. exec., Henley Staff Coll. U.K. Dep. airport dir. Internat. Airport Authority India, Delhi, 1978-82; airport dir. Internat. Airport Authority India, Calcutta, 1982-85; chief ops. Internat. Airport Authority India, Delhi, 1985-86, airport dir., 1986; airport dir. Internat. Airport Authority India, Bombay, 1986-90; exec. dir. Airport Authority India, New Delhi, 1990—; airport ops. mgmt. expert Internat. Civil Aviation Orgn., Entebbe, Uganda, 1991-92, 94, chmn. FAL divsn., Montreal, Can., 1995. Fellow Aero. Soc. India (life); mem. Auto. Assn. India (life), Airports Coun. Internat. (Asian rep. for world environ. com. 1992—), Loss and Prevention Assn. India (life). Avocations: badminton, table tennis, reading, vocal music, socializing. Office: Airports Authority India, Gurgaon Rd, New Delhi 110037, India

ANAND, PAWAN KUMAR, bank officer; b. Jabalpur, India, Nov. 16, 1964; s. Amar Nath and Ved Kumari (Kohli) A.; m. Asha Sethi, Mar. 6, 1980; 2 children. BAS, P.A.U., Ludhiana, India, 1974; MAgr, P.A.U., 1980. Bank officer Syndicate Bank, Meerut, U.P., India. Avocation: singing. Home: D-115 Shastri Nagar, 250004 Meerut India Office: Syndicate Bank, H-0 Manipal, 250004 Meerut India

ANAND, RAJESH KUMAR, animal scientist, researcher; b. Mussoorie, Dehradoon, India, Oct. 15, 1952; s. Suraj Parkash and Kailash Rani (Sabharwal) A.; m. Minoo Suri, Feb. 24, 1979; 1 child, Akshay. BSc in Zoology with honors, Panjab U., Chandigarh, India, 1973, MSc in Zoology with honors, 1975, PhD in Zoology, 1979. Postdoctoral fellow zoology dept. Panjab U., Chandigarh, 1979-80, rsch. assoc. zoology dept., 1980-82; staff scientist II Nat. Inst. Immunology, New Delhi, 1982-85, staff scientist III, 1985-90, sr. staff scientist IV, 1990-95, sr. staff scientist V, 1995—; cons. Span Diagnostics, Surat, India, 1990-92, Pharmax, New Delhi, 1992-94, Ranbaxy Rsch. Labs., New Delhi, 1994-96, Inst. Microbial Tech., Chandigarh, 1998—; rsch. assoc. Indian Coun. Med. Rsch., New Delhi, 1980-82. Patentee in field. Recipient jr. rsch. fellowship Coun. Sci. and Indsl. Rsch., New Delhi, 1975-77, sr. rsch. fellowship, 1977-79. Mem. Internat. Soc. Immunology and Reproduction, Indian Immunology Soc. (life, treas. 1997-99), Lab. Animal Sci. Assn. India (life). Avocations: music, reading, movies, animals, travel. Office: Nat Inst Immunology, Aruna Asaf Ali Rd, New Delhi 110067, India

ANANDAN, SAMIREDDY PALLE, animal scientist; b. Chittoor, India, Jan. 25, 1966; p. Janakiraman and Tulasi Samireddy Palle; m. Rani Uma, Feb. 7, 1997. B of Vet. Sci., Andhra Pradesh Agrl. U., Hyderabad, 1988, M of Vet. Sci., 1991; PhD, Indian Vet. Rsch. Inst., India, 1994. Asst. exec. Nat. Dairy Devel. Bd., India, 1990-91; scientist Nat. Inst. Animal Nutrition & Pysiology, Karnataka, India, 1995—. Contbr. articles to profl. jours. Mem. Animal Nutrition Soc., Animal Nutrition Assn., Veterinary Coun. India. Avocations: gardening, reading. Home: H No 19 Maruthi Nagar, 560 068 Bangalore India Office: Nat Inst Animal Nutr & Phys, Adugodi, 560 030 Karnataka India

ANAPLIOTIS, SPYROS JOHN, physician, consultant; b. Xanthy, Thrace, Greece, May 5, 1945; s. John and Kyriaki (Kazan) A.; m. Sofia Aspasia Ethnopoulou, Mar. 8, 1973; children: Domenika, Zina. Diploma in medicine, Med. Sch., Thessaloniki, Greece, 1971, diploma ob-gyn., 1978. Sr. house officer Hammersmith Hosp., Birmingham, Eng., 1974-76; sr. house officer Hammersmith Hosp., London, 1977-78, registrar, 1978; registrar West Middlessex Hosp., London, 1979-80; specialist U. Thessaloniki, 1980-84; cons. UN/Ministry of Health, Greece, 1984-87, In Vitro Fertilization and Infertility Ctr., Blue Cross, Thessaloniki, 1987—; trainer of trainers UNFPA/Ministry of Health, Athens, 1985. Author: Training of Doctors in Family Planning, 1984; contbr. articles to profl. publs. Mil. doctor Greek Army, 1971-73. Scholarship UN, 1984, WHO, 1984. Mem. ESHRE (life), British Med. Assn. Avocations: sculpture, photography. Office: Dr SI Anapliotis, 99 Metropoleos St, 546 22 Thessaloniki Greece

ANASTASESCU, MICHAEL, administrator; b. Constanta, Romania, July 31, 1953; arrived in Belgium, 1990; s. George and Ioana A.; m. Beatrice Porta; 1 child, Alexandra. MD, Sch. Medicine, Bucharest, 1979. Gen. physician Dept. Hosp., Constanta, Romania, 1979-82, Topalu, Romania, 1982-83; orthopaedic splty/ Mcpl. Hosp., Bucharest, 1983-86; orthopaedic surgeon Dept. Hosp., Constanta, 1986-90; tech. mgr. Bone & Tissue Bank, Brussels, 1991—; presenter in field. Avocations: wind surfing, skiing, music. Home: Rue E Claus 15 b1, 1050 Brussels Belgium

ANASTASSIADES, EFTHYVOULOS GEORGE, nephrologist; b. Nicosia, Cyprus, May 22, 1952; s. George and Valentina (Paraskevaides) A.; m. Jacqueline Darling, Oct. 1, 1992. BSc with honors in Physiology, U. Manchester, Eng., 1972, MB, ChB with honors, 1975, DM, 1988. Accreditated in internal medicine and nephrology Gen. Med. Coun. Registrar in medicine Royal Hallamshire Hosp., Sheffield, Eng., 1979-80, Hammersmith Hosp., London, 1980-82; lectr. medicine Charing Cross Hosp. Med. Sch., London, 1982-86; sr. registrar Manchester Royal Infirmary, 1986-90; cons. nephrologist King's Coll. Hosp., London, 1991-93, Larnaka (Cyprus) Gen. Hosp., 1994—; hon. cons. nephrologist King's Coll. Hosp., London, 1993—. Contbr. articles to profl. jours. Fellow Royal Coll. Physicians (London). Fax: 357-4-663959. E-mail: anastass@spidernet.com.cy. Office: Larnaka Gen Hosp, Larnaca Cyprus

ANASTASSIADIS, KYRIAKOS, civil engineering educator; b. Lipohor, Edessa, Greece, Jan. 1940; s. Konstantinos and Parthenopi (Anthopoulou) A.; m. Efthymia Taxiarhopoulou, Aug. 16, 1970; children: Parthenopi, Konstantina, Konstantinos-Vassilios. Degree civil engring., Aristotle U., Thessaloniki, Greece, 1964, PhD, 1971; postgrad., Centre de Hautes Etudes Constn, Paris, 1973-74. Asst. to reinforced concrete sect. Aristotle U., 1969-71, lectr., 1972-76, sr. lectr., 1977-81, asst. prof., 1982-83, assoc. prof., 1983-86, prof., 1987—; com. pres. Ministry of Environ. Phys. Planning and Pub. Works, Athens, 1994-98; bd. dirs. Ogrn. of Aseismic Planning and Protection, Athens, 1993-98; com. pres. Ministry of Transport, Athens, 1998-99; v.p. Inst. of Tech. Seishology of Aseismic Structures, Thessaloniki, 1993-99. Author: Dynamics of Structures, vol. 1, 1983, Aseismic Structures, vols. 1-2, 1989; contbr. articles to profl. jours. 2d lt. Corps of Engrs., 1965-67. Mem. Tech. Chamber of Greece, Assn. of Civil Engrs. of Greece, Assn. Francaise de Genie Parasismique. Avocations: cinema, theatre, reading, writing, walking. Home: 124 Konstantinou Karamanli, 54248 Thessaloniki Greece Office: Aristotle U of Thessaloniki, Dept Civil Engring, 54006 Thessaloniki Greece

ANATI, EMMANUEL, archaeologist, educator; b. Florence, Italy, May 14, 1930; s. Ugo and Elsa (Castelnuovo) A.; m. Ariela Fradkin, 1962; children: Daniel, Miriam. BA in Hist. Geography, Hebrew U., Jerusalem, 1953, MA in Archaeology, 1955; AM in Anthropology and Social Rels., Harvard U., 1959; D.Lettres, Sorbonne, 1960. Archaeologist Israeli Dept. Antiquities, 1950-55; rsch. fellow Ctr. Nat. Rsch. Sci., Paris, 1955-58, Hebrew U., 1961-66; sr. lectr. Tel Aviv U., 1964-68; prof. prehistory Tel Aviv U., Israel, 1968-72; founder, exec. dir. Centro Camuno di Studi Preistorici, Capo di Ponte, Italy, 1964—; prof. palaeo-ethnology U. Lecce, 1980-99; mem. permanent coun. Union Internat. des Scis. Prehistoriques, 1972-78; gen. sec. Internat. Symposia Prehist. and Tribal Art, 1987—; founder, 1st chmn. exec. bd., pres. internat. com. on rock art Internat. Coun. Monuments and Sites, 1980-90; pres. Institut des Arts Prehistoriques et Ethnographiques, Paris, 1992—; leader numerous archaeol. expdns.; gen. sec. nat. and internat. symposia; cons. in field. Author: La Grande Roche de Naquane, 1959, La Civilisation du Val Camonica, Paris, 1960, Camonica Valley, 1961, Palestine Before the Hebrews, 1963, Naquane: Decouverte d'un Pays et d'une Civilisation, 1966, Arte Prehistorica in Valtellina, 1967, Origini della Civilta Camuna, 1968, Arte Rupestre nelle regioni Occidentali della Penisola Iberica, 1968, Rock Art in Central Arabia (4 vols.), 1972-75, Le Statue stele dell'Italia Settentrionale, 1972, Hazorea I, 1973, Evolution and Style in Camunian Rock art, 1976, Methods of Recording and Analysing Rock Engravings, 1977, L'art rupestre du Negev et du Sinai, 1979, Le Statue Stele delle Lunigiana, 1981, I Camuni alle Radici della Civilta Europea, 1982, Gli Elementi Fondamentali della Cultura, 1983, Har Karkom, Montagna sacra nel deserto dell'Esodo, 1984, La Prehistoire des Alpes, 1986, The Mountain of God, 1988, Origini dell'arte e della concettualita, 1988, Les Origines de l'Art, 1989, 10,000 Anni di storia in Valcamonica, 1990, Felsbilder Wiege der Kunst und des Geistes, 1991, Le Radici della Cultura, 1992, Har Karkom In the Ligh of New Discoveries, 1993, World Rock Art: The Primordial Language, 1993, Valcamonica Rock Art: A New History for Europe, 1994, La Religione delle Origini, 1995, Les Racines de la Culture, 1995, Brescia Preistorica, 1995, Il Museo Immaginario della Preistoria: L'arte Rupestre nel Mondo, 1995, I segni della storia, 1997, Esodo tra mito e storia, 1997, L'art rupestre dans le monde L'imaginaire de la prehistoire, 1997, Höhlenmalerei, 1997, La religion des origines, 1999, Har Karkom, Vent Anni Di Richerce Archeologie, 1999, Les Mystères du mont Sinai, 2000, over 70 volumes and numerous monographs. Decorated Cavaliere al Merito della Repubblica (Italy); recipient Kennedy gold medal, 1970; named hon. citizen of Capo di Ponte, 1967; Fulbright fellow, 1958-59. Mem. Explorers Club, Rotary. Fax: 0039 0364 42572. E-mail: ccspreist@globalnet.it. Address: Centro Camuno di Studi, Preistorici, Capo di Ponte, 25044 Valcamonica Italy

ANBAR, MICHAEL, biophysics educator; b. Danzig, June 29, 1927; came to U.S., 1967, naturalized, 1973; s. Joshua and Chava A.; m. Ada Komet, Aug. 11, 1953; children: Ran D., Ariel D. MSc, Hebrew U., Jerusalem, 1950, PhD, 1953. Instr. chemistry U. Chgo., 1953-55; sr. scientist Weizmann Inst. Sci., 1955-67; prof. Frienberg Grad. Sch., Rehovoth, Israel, 1960-67; sr. rsch. assoc. NASA Ames Rsch. Ctr., 1967-68; dir. phys. sci. SRI Internat., Menlo Park, Calif., 1968-72; dir. mass spectrometry research ctr. SRI Internat., 1972-77; prof. biophysical sci., chmn. dept. Sch. Medicine, SUNY, Buffalo, 1977-90, Faculty prof., dir. Interdeptl. Clin. Biophysics Group, 1990—, exec. dir. Health Instrument and Device Inst., 1983-85; assoc. dean applied research Sch. Medicine, SUNY, 1983-85; v.p. R & D AMARA Inc, Amherst, N.Y., 1992—; rsch. prof. surgery Sch. Medicine, SUNY, 1998—. Author: The Hydrated Electron, 1970, The Machine of the Bedside: Strategies for Using Technology in Parient Care, 1984, Clinical Biophysics, 1985, Computers in Medicine, 1986, Quantitative Dynamic Telethermometry in Medical Diagnosis and Management, 1994; editor-in-chief: Thermology, 1993; contbr. articles to profl. jours. With Israeli Air Force, 1947-49. Grantee in field. Mem. IEEE, AAAS, IEEE Computer Soc., IEEE Engring. in Biology and Medicine Soc., Assn. Am. Med. Colls., Am. Inst. Physics, Am. Chem. Soc., Am. Inst. Ultrasound in Medicine, Am. Assn. Clin. Chemistry, Am. Assn. Dental Rsch., Am. Assn. Mass Spectrometry, Am. Acad. Thermology, Am. Assn. Med. Systems Informatics, N.Y. Acad. Scis., Internat. Assn. Dental Rsch., Radiation Rsch. Soc., Internat. Med. Informatics Assn., Isternat. Soc. Optical Engring. Office: SUNY 118 Cary Hall Buffalo NY 14214-3023

ANBE, YOSHIHARU, control system executive; b. Hita City, Japan, Feb. 15, 1939; s. Nobuhei and Hatsue (Chihara) A.; m. Atsuko Fukuo, May 5, 1966; children: Yukiko, Tetsuro. BA, Osaka (Japan) U., 1962, MA, 1964, PhD, 1981. From rschr. to sr. fellow Toshiba Corp., Tokyo, 1964-95, chief fellow, 1995—. Co-author: Power Electronics and Control System, 1991, Theory and Application of Control System, 1992. Avocations: fishing, golf, tennis. Home: 1-859-5 Ogawa Cho, 187 Kodaira Japan Office: Toshiba Corp, 1 Toshiba Cho, 183-8511 Fuchu Japan

ANBUMOZHI, VENKATACHALAM, environmental science educator, researcher; b. Samudram, Tamilnadu, India, July 30, 1967; s. Venkatachalam J. and Padmajothi A.; m. Anbumozhi Gomathi, June 29, 1997; children: Anbumozhi Adhityan. BE, Tamilnadu Agrl. U., Coimbatore, India, 1989; MEng, Asian Inst. Tech., Bangkok, 1991; PhD, U. Tokyo, 1995. Rschr. Tamilnadu Agrl. U., Coimbatore, 1989-90, Asian Inst. Tech., Bangkok, 1990-92; mgr. Pacific Cons. Internat., Tokyo, 1995-99; prof. U. Tokyo, 1999—; dep. dir. Pacific Cons., Tokyo, 1998-99. Editor: Paddy Fields in the World, 1995; inventor in field; contbr. articles to profl. jours. Recipient Sci. Encouragement award Japanese Soc. for Promotion of Sci., Tokyo, 1995; scholar Norwegian Govt., 1989; named Best Asian Student in Agrl. Engring. Asian Inst. Tech., 1991. Fellow. Am. Soc. Agrl. Engrs.; mem. Japanese Soc. Irrigation and Drainage Engrs., Asian Assn. for Agrl. Engrs. (life), Internat. Red Cross Soc. (Tokyo), Asia Frendship Soc. (Tokyo, sec. gen. 1995-98). Avocations: cricket, book reading, sports, human watching. Office: U Tokyo Grad Sch Frontier S, 7-3-1-Hongo Bunkyo-Ku, Tokyo 206 0002, Japan

ANCHA, SRINIVASAN, agronomist, crop scientist, consultant; b. Guntur, India, June 19, 1962; s. Raghavaiah and Anasuya (Kalluri) A.; m. Uma Devi Kanagala, Feb. 23, 1989; 1 child, Phanindraja. BSc in Agr., Andhra Pradesh Agrl. U., 1981; MSc in Agronomy, Indian Agrl. Rsch. Inst., 1984; PhD, U. Cambridge, 1988. Postdoctoral rsch. fellow Internat. Crops Rsch. Inst. for Semi-Arid Tropics, Patancheru, India, 1989-92; sci. and tech. agy. fellow Hokkaido Nat. Agrl. Exptl. Sta., Sapporo, Japan, 1992-93; vis. scientist Japan Internat. Rsch. Ctr. for Agrl. Scis., Ishigaki, 1993-95; sr. researcher Regional Sci. Inst., Sapporo, 1995—; cons. Godrej Soaps Ltd., Bombay, 1991, Gromore Fertilizers Ltd., Hyderabad, India, 1990-91; mem. Devel.Edn. Exch. Svc. of the Food and Agrl. Orgn. of the UN, 1992—. Contbr. articles to profl. jours.; reviewer articles and books; editor conf. procs. Active Vols. in Tech. Assistance, Arlington, Va., 1992—, Nat. Social Svc., Bapatla, India, 1977-81. Recipient Gold medal Indian Agrl. Rsch. Inst., New Delhi, 1984, Fgn. and Commonwealth Office award Brit. Coun., London, 1984, Eisaku Sato Meml. Found. prize, 1998. Fellow Cambridge Commonwealth Soc.; mem. Soil Sci. Soc. Am., Am. Soc. Agronomy and Crop Sci. Soc. Am., Global Grain Legume Drought Rsch. Network, Precision Farming Consortium. Avocations: gardening, community service, think tank activities. Home: Apt #1-50-506 Hiragishi 4jo, 18 chome Toyohira-ku, 062-0934 Sapporo Japan Office: Regional Sci Inst, 4-13 Kita 24 Nishi 2 Kitaku, 001-0024 Sapporo Japan

ANCHETA, F. E. CALDITO, fragrance company manager; b. Pozzorubio, The Philippines, May 30, 1953; parents Teofilo Rilloraza and Felicidad Caldito Ancheta. BS in Food Tech., U. of The Philippines, Quezon City, 1975. R&D project leader CFC-Universal Robina Corp., Pasig, The Philippines, 1976-78; rsch. asst. Griffith Labs., Makati, The Philippines, 1978-79; tech. asst. Wise & Co. Inc., Pasig, 1979-80, sales rep., 1980-83, mktg. asst., 1983-85; mktg. asst. Bush Boake Allen Phils Inc., Pasig, 1985-88, sales devel. mgr., 1988-94, bus. unit mgr., 1994-98, gen. mgr., 1998—.

ANCHEV, PANKO KIRILOV, literary critic, publisher, journalist; b. Varna, Bulgaria, Mar. 25, 1946; s. Kiril Ivanov and Todorka Panajotova (Dimitrova) A.; m. Donka Koleva Hristova, June 1, 1975; children: Kalin, Vesselin. MA, U. Veliko Tarnovo, Bulgaria, 1971. Editor Radio Varna, 1972-73; editor G. Bakalov Pub., Varna, 1973-76, editor-in-chief, 1976-86, chief, 1986-90; chief Andina Pub., Varna, 1990—, Bulgarian TV, Varna, 1996—. Author: Authors and Words, 1982, The Man in Words, 1986, The Conscience of Words, 1989; editl. bd. Literaly newspaper, 1988-89, Contemporary mag., 1988-90, Scope mag., 1988-90. Cpl. Mil. Sch. Bulgaria, 1965-67. Mem. Bulgarian Writers Union, Bulgarian Journalists Union. Bulgarian Socialist Party. Orthodox christian. Avocation: chess. Home: Str Vladislav bl 24 flat 2, 9009 Varna Bulgaria Office: Andina Pub House, 10 Tsar Simeon 1 St, 9000 Varna Bulgaria

ANCHEYTA-JUÁREZ, JORGE, petroleum engineer, educator; b. Ciudad Hidalgo, Chiapas, Mex., Aug. 4, 1965; s. Antonio Ancheyta-Aguilar and Gumercinda Juárez-Gálvez; m. Norma Cristina Segovia-Gamboa, Oct. 12, 1989; children: Jorge A. Ancheyta-Segovia, Jorge L. Ancheyta Segovia. Diploma, Esiquie-Ipn, Mex., 1989, MSc, 1993; MBA, Esia-Ipn, Mex., 1997; PhD, UAM, Mex., 1998. Project leader Mexican Petroleum Inst., 1989—; lectr. Nat. Poly. Inst., Mex., 1992—; vis. dr. LGPC-CPE, Lyon, France, 1999-00. Author: Kinetics for Homogeneous Systems, 1999. Mem. Am. Chem. Soc. Roman Catholic. Achievements include patents for HDT Process for Middle Distillates, HDT Process for Vacuum Gas Oils, HDT Process for Heavy Crude Oils. Avocation: swimming. Home: Lataounga 809-4, 07300 Mexico City Mexico Office: Inst Mexicano Petróleo Col San Bartolo Atepehuacan, Eji Central Lázaro Cárdenas 152, Mexico City 07730, Mexico

ANCIAUX, BERT, lawyer; b. Merksem, Belgium, Sept. 11, 1959; s. Vic Anciaux and Lies Decoster; m. Damienne Tant, Apr. 6, 1991; children: Lien, Stijn, Britt. LLB, Vrije Univ., Brussels, 1984. Pvt. practice Brussels, 1984—; Flemish minister Culture, Youth, Brussels Affairs and Devel. Corp., Brussels, 1999—. Author: De Vergeten Vernieuwing, 1992, Kinderen Van De Hoop, 1997, Alles in beweging, 1999. City councillor, Brussels, 1987-95, alderman, 1992-95; provincial councillor, Brabant, Belgium, 1991-92; pres. Volksunie, 1992-98, VU & ID, 1998-99; Senator, Belgium, 1995-99. Home: Korte Groenweg 127, 1120 Neder over Heembeek Belgium Office: Flemish Min Culture Youth, Martelaarsplein 7, 1000 Brussels Belgium

ANDACHT, HERMAN WILLIAM, retired educator and counselor; b. Milw., July 28, 1920; s. Edna (Sell) A.; m. Dorothy Mae DeLang, Sept. 10, 1941; children: Diana Sue, Cindi D. BS, Carroll Coll., 1948; MEd, Marquette U., 1957, postgrad., 1966-72. High sch. tchr. Menomonee Falls (Wis.) Pub. Schs., 1948-51; supervising prin. Glenbeulah (Wis.) Pub. Sch., 1952-53; elem. sch. prin. Dousman (Wis.) Pub. Schs., 1955-56; asst. prof. Milw. Sch. Engring., 1956-72; guidance counselor Sheboygan (Wis.) Pub. Schs., 1966-82; retired, 1982; owner, operator Drive Inn Restaurants, Pewaukee, Wis., 1948-71; pvt. practice clin. testing, Wis., 1958-81. Chmn. Pewaukee Civil Svc. Commn, 1969-81; chmn. Planning Commn., Town of Delafield, Wis., 1985-87. With US Marine Corps, 1941-45, PTO, Iwo Jima. Decorated Purple Heart. Mem. DAV (life), VFW (life), Am. Def. Preparedness Assn. (life), Shriners. Republican. Methodist. Avocations: real estate management, hunting, fishing, reading, stocks. Home: W298N 2777 Shady Ln Pewaukee WI 53072-4208 also: W298n2777 Shady Ln Pewaukee WI 53072-4208

ANDELMAN, FANI, neuropsychologist, speech therapist; b. Tartu, USSR, Nov. 21, 1951; arrived in Israel, 1973; d. Shmuel and Mira (Zigelbaum) Spungin; m. David Andelman, July, 1978; children: Guy, Michal. BA, Tel Aviv U., 1977, MA, 1979; MA, Boston U., 1984; PhD, CUNY, 1990. Cert. rehab. psychology. Intern in psychology Lewinstein Rehab. Hosp., 1989-91; psychologist Tel Aviv Ednl. Svc., 1991-94; neuropsychologist Tel Aviv Med. Ctr., 1996—. Mem. APA (fgn. affiliate), Internat. Neuropsychological Soc., Israeli Psychol. Soc. Office: Sourasky Med Ctr, 6 Weizmann St, 64239 Tel Aviv Israel

ANDENYANG, IKUN HABU, education educator; b. Kwesati, Lissam, Nigeria, Apr. 14, 1958; p. Agbu and Wadaki A. BSc in Chemistry with honors, AB U., Zaria, Nigeria, 1981, MSc in Analytical Chemistry, 1986, postgrad., 1999—. Lectr. NYSC, Igueben, Nigeria, 1981-82; master II, dept. head Tech. Coll., Yola, Nigeria, 1982; asst. lectr. Coll. Prelim Studies, Yola, Nigeria, 1982; grad. asst. Fed. U. Tech., Yola, Nigeria, 1983-84, from lectr. II to lectr. I, 1987—; from asst. lectr. to lectr. II Modibbo Adama Coll./U. Maiduguri, Yola, Nigeria, 1984-87; vis. acad. rschr. dept. pure and applied chemistry U. Strathclyde, Glasgow, Scotland, 1996-97; presenter, cons. in field. Contbr. articles to profl. jours. Gongola State scholar, 1978-81, Gongola State Govt. scholar, 1978-81, Nigerian Fed. Govt. scholar, 1984-86; Study fellow Fed. U. Tech., 1994-95. Mem. Chem. Soc. Nigeria, Nigeria Soc. Chem. Engrs., Linguistic Assn. Nigeria, Sci. Tchrs. Assn. Nigeria, Curriculum Orgn. Nigeria. Mem. Reformed Ch. of Christ. Avocations: gardening, reading, writing. Home: Bisaula Rd, Lissam Nigeria Office: Fed Univ Adamawa State, PO Box 2076 Dept Tech, Yola Nigeria

ANDERBERG, ROY ANTHONY, journalist; b. Camden, N.J., Mar. 30, 1921; s. Arthur R. and Mary V. (McHugh) A.; m. Louise M. Brooks, Feb. 5, 1953; children: Roy, Mary. AA, Diablo Valley Coll., 1975. Enlisted USN, 1942, commd. officer, 1960, ret., 1970; waterfront columnist Pacific Daily News, Agana, Guam, 1966-67; pub. rels. officer Naval Forces, Mariana Islands, 1967; travel editor Contra Costa (Calif.) Times, 1968-69; entertainment and restaurant editor Concord (Calif.) Transcript, 1971-75; entertainment editor Contra Costa Advertiser, 1975-76; dining editor Rossmoor News, Walnut Creek, Calif., 1977-78; free-lance non-fiction journalist, 1976—. Recipient Best Feature Story award Guam Press Assoc., 1966. Mem. VFW, DAV, U.S. Power Squadron, Ret. Officers Assn., Am. Legion, U.S. Submarine Vets. WWII (state comdr., regional dir., nat. 2d v.p.), Naval Submarine League (XO), Martinez Yacht Club (charter), Rossmoor Yacht Club (commodore 1995), Toastmasters. Democrat. Home: 1840 Tice Creek Dr Apt 2228 Walnut Creek CA 94595-2460

ANDERER, FRIEDRICH ALFRED, biochemist, researcher; b. Ravensburg, Baden-Wuerttenberg, Germany, June 4, 1926; s. Rainhard Alfred and Katharina Augusta (Prinz) A.; m. Johanna Tatjinka Aust, Mar. 16, 1956; children: Fred Boris, Tatjana Isabell. Diploma in organic chemistry, U. Tuebingen, Fed. Republic Germany, 1953; doctorate, U. Tuebingen, 1956. Sci. asst. Max-Planck Inst. for Virusforschung, Tuebingen, 1957-67, head dept., 1969-72; sci. mem. Max-Planck Assn., Munich, 1967—; dir. Friedrich-Miescher lab. Max-Planck Assn., Tuebingen, 1972—; prof. biochemistry U. Tuebingen, 1972—. Contbr. articles to profl. jours.; patentee in field. Corr. mem. European Acad. Arts, Scis. and Humanities, Paris, 1989—. Recipient Fritz Merck prize Merck Found., 1967, Felix Haffner prize Thomae Co. Found., 1969, E.K. Frey prize Bayer Found., 1973. Mem. European Peptide Soc., Assn. for Biologische Chemie, Assn. for Immunologie, Assn. Deutscher Naturforscher and Aertze, Deutsche Krebs Assn., Am. Assn. for Cancer Rsch. (corr. mem.), N.Y. Acad. Scis. Avocation: painting. Office: Max Planck Assn, 37 39 Spemannstrasse, D-72076 Tübingen Wuerttenberg, Germany

ANDERLIND, MARTIN LARS, internet consultancy executive, communications; b. Washington, Nov. 8, 1968; s. Lars Einar and Lisa Margareta (Svensson) A.; m. Charlotta Emy Sofia Strömberg, June 27, 1998. MScBA, Uppsala (Sweden) U., 1994. Dir. lang. camps and Discover Am. tours EF Edn., Cambridge, Mass., 1994-95; co-founder, bd. mem. Netsolutions, Sweden, 1995-99; v.p. market comm. FRAMFAB, Sweden, 1999—. Active Mil. Police, 1988-89, Sweden. Avocations: architecture, skiing, golfing, sailing. Home: Dragarstigen 8B, SE-13336 Saltsjöbaden Sweden Office: FRAMFAB, Kungsgatan 27 Box 5494, 11484 Stockholm Sweden

ANDERS, BRENDA MICHELLE, communications professional; b. Washington, July 9, 1971; d. Stephen R. and Mary (Phillips) A. BA, Smith Coll., 1993. Mem. advance staff Clinton/Gore '92, Little Rock, 1992; confidential asst. Sec. U.S. Dept. Edn., Washington, 1993-94; dir. scheduling and advance Alan Wheat for U.S. Senate, Kansas City, Mo., 1994; splty. press coord. The White House, Washington, 1995-96; press sec. to Tipper Gore Clinton/Gore '96, Washington, 1996; radio and spl. projects coord. The White House, Washington, dir. TV prodn., 1998—; dir. pub. affairs Lifetime TV, N.Y.C., 2000—. Democrat.

ANDERS, NISSLING, fisheries biologist; b. Stockholm, Sweden, May 28, 1957; s. Sven-Eje and Birgit (Axelsson) N. BS, Uppsala U., 1983; PhD, Stockholm U., 1995. Cons. K-Konsut, Stockholm, 1987-88; rsch. asst. Stockholm U., 1989-94; rschr. Fishery Bd. Sweden, Lysekil, 1995-98, Gotland Univ. Coll., Visby, 1999—. Home: Karlbergsvagen 68, S-11335 Stockholm Sweden

ANDERS, NORBERT, ophthalmologist, researcher, educator; b. Weidenberg, Bavaria, Germany, Apr. 6, 1960; s. Erwin and Gertrud (Sinner) A.; m. Christina-Patricia Stolze, Sept. 11, 1992; children: Sophie-Isabelle, Leandra-Laetitia. MD, Friedrich-Alexander U., Erlangen, Germany, 1985, D, 1986. Asst. dr. Klinikum Rudolf Virchow, Berlin, 1987-91; asst. med. dir. Virchow Klinikum, Berlin, 1991-96, asst. prof., 1996-99; prof. Virchow Klinikum, 2000—; cons. Virchow Klinikum, Berlin, 1991—, charité, Berlin, 1996—. Co-author: Auge und Orbita, 1995; contbr. articles to profl. jours. Served with German mil., 1985-87. Mem. Am. Soc. Cataract & Refractive Surgery, Assn. Rsch. in Vision & Ophthalmology, German Ophthalmology Soc. Home: Argentinische Allee 1, D-14163 Berlin Germany Office: Charite Campus Virchow-Ulin, Augustenburger Platz 1, D-13353 Berlin Germany

ANDERSEN, BODIL NYBOE, bank executive; b. Copenhagen, Oct. 9, 1940; d. Poul Nyboe and Ditte (Raben) A.; m. Henning Holten; divorced; children: Kasper Holten, Johan Holten. MSc in Econs., U. Copenhagen, 1966. Asst. prin. Min. for Econ. Affairs, Copenhagen, 1966-68; assoc. prof. U. Copenhagen, 1968-80; mng. dir. Andelsbanken, Copenhagen, 1981-90; group mng. dir. Unibank and Unidanmark, Copenhagen, 1990; mem. bd. govs. Danmarks Nationalbank, Copenhagen, 1990—, chmn. bd. govs., 1995—; mem. bd. govs. The Denmark-Am. Found., 1993—, Velux Fonden of 1981, 1994—; chmn. bd. of Govs., 1995—, gov. for Denmark to the Internat. Monetary Fund, 1995—, Coun. of European Monetary Inst., 1995-98; chmn. Danmarks Nationalbanks Anniversary Found. of 1968, 1995—, The Danish Fgn. Policy Soc., 1995—; gen. coun. mem. European Sys. of Cen. Banks, 1998—. Office: Danmarks Nationalbank, Havnegade 5, DK-1093 Copenhagen Denmark

ANDERSEN, FRANK ANGELIUS, principal dancer, ballet company artistic director; b. Copenhagen, Apr. 15, 1953; s. Carl Angelius and Sonja (Jensen) A.; m. Eva Kloborg, May 14, 1983; 1 child, Sebastian. Grad. ballet course (high sch. level), The Royal Danish Ballet Sch., Copenhagen, 1960-71. Dancer The Royal Danish Ballet, 1971-77, prin. dancer, 1977—, dir., 1985-94; artistic dir. Royal Swedish Ballet, 1995—. Co-producer: Bournonville ballet A Folk Tale, Napoli. Named Knight of Dannebrog, 1984; recipient King Olav order, 1991. Home: Gammel Vartovvej 10, DK-2900 Hellerup Denmark Office: Royal Swedish Ballet, Royal Theatre PO Box 16094, S 10322 Stockholm Sweden

ANDERSEN, HUGO, executive; b. Dec. 31, 1946. Grad. polit. scis., U. Copenhagen, 1975. Head dept. Fallesbanken, Denmark, 1975-78; head investment dept., deputy gen. mgr. Topsikring, Denmark, 1978-83; exec. v.p. Provinsbanken, Copenhagen, 1984-86, Den Danske Bank, Copenhagen, 1987-89; group mng. dir. Nykredit, Copenhagen, 1990-97; pres., CEO Tryg-Baltica, Ballerup, Denmark, 1997—. Office: Tryg-Baltica, Klausdalsbrovej 601, DK-2750 Ballerup Denmark

ANDERSEN, IB, sociologist, researcher, educator, consultant; b. Silkeborg, Jutland, Denmark, Sept. 1, 1943; s. Joergen and Karen Marie (Steffensen Hansen) A.; m. Greta Lilian Nilsson, Feb. 27, 1966; children: Louise Boel, Rasmus Rune. M in Sociology, U. Copenhagen, 1972. Rsch. fellow Denmarks Tech. U., Lyngby/Copenhagen, 1970-72; rsch. fellow Copenhagen Bus. Sch., 1972-78, assoc. prof., 1972-87, 88-94, head dept. orgn. and indsl. sociology, 1981-83, dir., 1994—; chief cons. Danish Inst. Orgnl. Studies, 1987-88, chmn., 1988—; cons. WHO, Geneva, 1989. Co-author: The Course of Life of Drug Addicts, 1984, The Art of Doing Field Studies, 1995, The Incarnate Reality--A Social Science Methodology, 1997; co-author, editor: The Methodology of Organizational and Sociological Investigation, 1990. Avocations: history, gastronomy, tennis, yachting. Home: Tøxensvej 30, 4600 Køge Denmark Office: Copenhagen Bus Sch, Grundtvigsvej 37, 1864 Frederiksberg Denmark

ANDERSEN, JENS RIKARDT, gastroenterologist; b. Copenhagen, Feb. 8, 1947; s. Arnold Rikardt and Rita (Christiansen) A.; m. Birgitte Weile, May 26, 1981; children: Christian, Julie. MD, U. Copenhagen, 1974, Specialist Gastroenterology, 1984, Specialist Internal Medicine, 1987. Intern Bispebjerg Hosp., Copenhagen, 1977-78, registrar in medicine, 1979; registrar in gastroenterology Univ. Hosp., Hvidovre, Denmark, 1980-81, sr. registrar in gastroenterology, 1982-85; sr. registrar in medicine Saint Elisabeth Hosp., Copenhagen, 1986-87; sr. registrar in gastroenterology County Hosp., Gentofte, Denmark, 1988-91, cons. in gastroenterology, 1992; chief gastroenterology Ctrl. Hosp., Nykøbing Falster, Denmark, 1993—, chief internal medicine, 1996—; coun. mem. Alcohol Rsch. Ctr., Copenhagen, 1987—, chmn. 1996—; lectr. in medicine U. Copenhagen, 1981-94; organizer numerous postgrad. courses, several internat. congresses on biol. alcohol rsch.; chmn. postgrad. edn. Stomstroma County, 1993-99, chmn. edn. TQA-advisors, 1999—; inspector internal medicine Danish Nat. Health Authorities, 1997—. Contbr. many articles and papers to internat. sci. jours. Mem. exec. com. Social-Liberal Party, Denmark, 1990—, chmn. party orgn. Copenhagen County, 1990-95, mem. leading polit. com., 1994—; mem. parliament com. Alcohol Politics, Denmark, 1994—; mem., bd. dirs. Gentofte Mcpl. Soc. for Social Housing, 1993—, chmn., 1996—; mem. Coun. Copenhagen Gen. Coop. Housing Soc., 1997—. Lt. Air Force, 1976-77, Denmark. Mem. Nordic Soc. for Biol. Alcohol Rsch. (coun. mem. 1991—). Social-Liberal. E-mail: jra@post3.tele.dk and jra@chf.stam.dk. Home: Fragariavej 13, DK-2900 Hellerup Denmark Office: Central Hosp, Dept Gastroenterology, 4800 Nykøbing Falster Denmark

ANDERSEN, JENS ULRIK, physics educator; b. Tørring, Jylland, Denmark, Sept. 2, 1941; s. Svend Aage and Helga (Nielsen) A.; children: Marie-Louise, Svend Bjarke, Anne Sophie. Magister, U. Aarhus, Denmark, 1965. Guest scientist, then mem. tech. staff Bell Labs., Murray Hill, N.J., 1967-69; asst. prof. physics U. Aarhus, 1966-67, assoc. prof., 1969-77, prof., 1977—; dir. Aarhus Ctr. for Atomic Physics, 1994—; vice chmn. Com. for Evaluation of Danish Physics, 1990-91. Chmn. bd. dirs. Danish Space Rsch. Inst., 1995—. Carlsberg fellow Cavendish Lab., Churchill Coll., Cambridge, Eng., 1985. Mem. Royal Danish Acad. Scis. and Letters, Danish Rsch. Coun. for Natural Scis. (chmn. 1991-93, chmn. coun. of chairmen for Danish Rsch. Couns. 1992-93). Fax: 45 8612 0740. E-mail: jua@ifa.au.dk. Home: Hamphøjvej 15, 8270 Højbjerg Denmark Office: Aarhus Ctr Atomic Physics, Inst Physics and Astronomy, 8000C Århus Denmark

ANDERSEN, K(ENT) TUCKER, investment executive; b. Manchester, Conn., June 5, 1942; s. Alfred Hans and Dorothy Emily (Ray) A.; m. Karen Ann Kirchofer, Oct. 11, 1963; children: Heather Michele, Kristen Eileen. Student, Phillips Exeter Acad., N.H., 1957-59; BA, Wesleyan U., 1963. Chartered fin. analyst. Actuarial student Travelers Ins. Co., Hartford, Conn., 1963-66; security analyst Smith Barney & Co., N.Y.C., 1968-69; ptnr. Rudman Assocs., N.Y.C., 1969-72; ptnr. Cumberland Assocs. LLC, N.Y.C., 1972—, mng. ptnr., 1982-96, chief investment strategist, 1997—. Bd. dirs. Cato Inst., Washington, 1987—, exec. com., 1992—; trustee YWCA of Montclair, North Essex, N.J., 1980—, 1st United Meth. Ch., Montclair, 1976-94, Martin Luther King Scholarship Fund Montclair, 1989-94, Phillips Exeter Acad., 1989—, chmn. investment com., 1992—, bd. v.p. and chmn. exec. com., 1993—, admissions rep. N.J. area, 1983-93; exec. com. GOPAC, 1993—, bd. dirs., 1995—. With USPHS, 1966-68. Recipient Disting. Alumnus award Wesleyan U., 1988. Mem. Soc. Actuaries, N.Y. Soc. Security Analysts, Inst. Chartered Fin. Analysts, Polit. Club for Growth (mem. exec. com. 1984-94), Kappa Nu Kappa (pres. 1963). Republican. Avocation: N.Y.C. marathons. Office: Cumberland Assocs 38th Fl 1114 Avenue Of The Americas New York NY 10036-7703

ANDERSEN, KIM VALDEMAR LEANDER, information science educator; b. Aalborg, Denmark, June 29, 1966; s. Hardy V. and Ruth A. MA, Copenhagen U., 1988, PhD, 1994. Asst. prof. Aalberg U., Denmark, 1994-97; assoc. prof. Copenhagen Bus. Sch., Denmark, 1997—; vis. rschr. U. Calif., Irvine, 1991-93, Tokyo U., 1996-97; cons. Danish Labor Market Agy., 1994—, EU, 1992. Editor: (books) EDI in the Public Sector, 1997, Economic Modeling in the Public Sector, 1995. Postdoctoral fellow Japan Soc. for Promotion of Sci., Japan, 1996-97; grantee Danish Rsch. Coun., Denmark, 1994-97, Danish Rsch. Acad., Denmark, 1991-93. Mem. Danish Fedn. of Economists and Lawyers, Internat. Assn. Info. Systems Profs. Avocations: tennis, computers, reading, hiking, biking. E-mail: andersen@cbs.dk. Office: Copenhagen Bus Sch, Howitzvej 60, DK-2000 Frederiksberg Denmark

ANDERSEN, MOGENS, painter, author; b. Copenhagen, Aug. 8, 1916; s. Einar F. T. and Erna Ingeborg (Andersen) A.; m. Inger Therkildsen, Nov. 28, 1947; children: Christian, Benedicte. Student, P. Rostrup Boyesen, Copenhagen. Tchr. art Copenhagen, 1952-59; mem. art faculty Academie de la Grande Chaumiere, Paris, 1963, Royal Acad. Fine Arts, Copenhagen, 1970-72; pres. Danish State Art Found., Copenhagen, 1977-80. Author: Moderne Fransk Kunst, 1948, Omkring Kilderne, 1967, Nødigt, Men Dog Gerne, 1976, Ungdoms Rejsen, 1979, Huset, 1986, Punktum, Punktum, Komma, Streg, 1994; paintings in European Mus. Mem. Coun. Danish Radio and TV, 1968-74. Decorated knight Legion d'honneur, officier Art et Lettres (France); knight of Dannebrog (Denmark); recipient Eckersberg medal Royal Acad. Fire Arts, 1949, Thorvalden medal, 1984.

ANDERSEN, PAUL KENT, linguist, educator; b. Omaha, Nebr., Aug. 10, 1948; s. Milton Huxley and Vera Faye (Krick) A.; m. Gun Lisbet Gustafson, July 31, 1981. BS, U. Colo., 1972; PhD, U. Freiburg, Federal Rep. Germany, 1970; Habilitation, U. Bielefeld, Federal Rep. Germany, 1988. Asst. prof. dept. linguistics U. Bielefeld, 1980-88; prof., 1988—; lectr. U. Munster, Fed. Republic Germany, 1981-86, numerous other univs. throughout the world. Author: Word Order Typology and Comparative Consturctions, 1982, Minor Rock Editcts of Ashoka, critical edit., 1987, contextual criticism, 1988, Studien zur Anwendung funktionaler Theorien auf die Syntax älderer Sprachen des indischen Kulturbereiches, 1987; contbr. articles to profl. jours. Mem. Am. Oriental Soc., Linguistic Soc. Am. Office: Fakultat der Univ, D 4800 Bielefeld Germany

ANDERSEN, TORBEN BRENDER, optical researcher, astronomer, software engineer; b. Naestved, Denmark, May 17, 1954; came to U.S., 1983; U.S. citizen, 1994; s. Bjarne and Anna Margrethe (Brender) A.; children: Iris, Erik. PhD, Copenhagen U., Denmark, 1979. Rsch. fellow Copenhagen U., 1980-82, sr. rsch. fellow, 1982-85; optical cons. Nordic Optical Telescope Assn., Roskilde, Denmark, 1985; optical systems analyst Telos Corp., Santa Clara, Calif., 1985-88; rsch. scientist Lockheed Martin Missiles and Space, Palo Alto, Calif., 1988-93, staff scientist, 1993-95, sr. staff scientist, 1995-96; staff software engr. Lockheed Martin Missiles and Space, 1996—; vis. scholar Optical Scis. Ctr., U. Ariz., Tucson, 1983-85. Editor: Astronomical Papers Dedicated to Bengt Strömgren, 1978; contbr. articles to Jour. Quantitative Spectroscopy Radiation Transfer, Applied Optics, Astronomische Nachrichten. Mem. Optical Soc. Am., Internat. Astron. Union, Soc. Photo-Optical Instrumentation Engrs. Achievements include development of method for computing optical aberration coefficients to arbitrarily high orders; discovery of set of differential equations for the Voigt function; contributing to optical design software. Office: Lockheed Martin Advanced Tech Ctr O/L9-23 3251 Hanover St # B201 Palo Alto CA 94304-1121

ANDERSON, ALBERT SYDNEY, III, lawyer; b. Atlanta, July 7, 1940; s. Albert S. Jr. and Constance S. (Spalding) A.; children: Judith, William. BA in Math., Emory U., 1962; MS in Physics, Stanford (Calif.) U., 1964, PhD in Physics, 1968, JD, 1977. Bar: Ga. 1978, U.S. Patent and Trademark Office 1980, U.S. Supreme Ct. 1981. Assoc. Stokes & Shapiro, Atlanta, 1978-81, Kutak, Rock & Huie, Atlanta, 1981-84; ptnr. Jones & Askew, Atlanta, 1984-96; pvt. practice Norcross, Ga., 1996—; asst. atty. gen. State of Ga., Atlanta, 1984-88. Elder Trinity Presbyn. Ch., Atlanta, 1978-81; chmn. bd. trustees Trinity Sch., Atlanta, 1971-74. Mem. Am. Phys. Soc. Avocations: golf, hiking, music. Office: Patent Law Offices 35 Technology Pkwy S Ste 170 Norcross GA 30092-2928

ANDERSON, ALLAN CURTIS, pharmaceuticals researcher; b. Miles City, Mont., Mar. 6, 1955; m. Natalie R. Cramer, Jan. 15, 1976; children: Brandie N., Jessica L. AA in Med. Sci., Miles C.C., Miles City, 1989; BS in Pharmacy, U. Mont., 1992; PharmD, SUNY, Buffalo, 1994. Photo lithography engr. Intel, Aloha, Oreg., 1978-80; engr. Crowley Maritime, Seattle, 1981-86; rsch. assoc. U. Mont., Missoula, 1989-92; forensic toxicology technician Mont. Dept. Justice, Missoula, 1991-92; clin. rschr. Clin. Phamacokinetics Lab., Buffalo, 1992-94; program dir. gastrointestinal rsch. Clin. Phamacokinetics Lab., 1995-99; pharmacist Good Samaritan Pharmacy, New Brighton, Minn., 1994-95; postdoctoral fellow U. Minn., Mpls., 1995; dir. R & D Dynamic Concepts, Tonawanda, N.Y., 1995-99; dir. clin. rsch. Gastrotarget Corp., Tonawanda, 1995-99; dir. pharmacy core rsch. lab. Tex. Tech. U. Health Sci. Ctr. Sch. Pharmacy, Amarillo, 1998—, asst. prof. critical care and infectious disease, 1998—, vice-chair dept. pharmacy practice, 2000—. Contbr. articles to profl. jours. Recipient Rsch. award Upjohn Pharmacy, 1991. Mem. Am. Coll. Clin. Pharmacy, Am. Soc. Health Sys. Pharmacists, Biomed. Engring. Soc., Am. Coll. Clin. Pharmacy, Am. Soc. Health System Pharmacists, Kappa Psi, Sigma Xi. Achievements include patents for novel medical devices and agriculture, devel. of comml. applications of mil. tech., devel. of mfg. sys. for Intel Corp. Office: Tex Tech Univ Health Sci Ctr Sch Pharmacy 1300 Coulter Dr Rm 206 Amarillo TX 79106-1712

ANDERSON, ALLAN R., psychotherapist, educator; b. Melbourne, Fla., Mar. 4, 1944; s. Donald Piper and Martha Anderson; m. Sandra L. Anderson, June 9, 1984. BA, Morningside Coll., 1972; MS, Okla. State U., 1992, PhD, 1999. Lic. profl. counselor, Okla. Dir. drug/alcohol unit Meadowlake Hosp., Enid, Okla., 1986-89; therapist, dir. Crossroads Halfway Ho., Enid, 1989-93; asst. dir. Youth and Family Svcs., Enid, 1993-96; prof. No. Okla. Coll., Enid, 1996—; therapist Anderson Counseling Assocs., Enid, 1999—; pres. Enid faculty No. Okla. Coll., 1999—; legis. liaison Youth Coordinating Coun., Enid, 1994—. With U.S. Army, 1967-69, ETO. Mem. Assn. Cmty. Colls. (sec. 1998—), Phi Kappa Phi. Avocation: fishing. E-mail: al4moc@hotmail.com. Office: No Okla Coll 100 S University Ave Enid OK 73701-6439

ANDERSON, ARTHUR J., clinical psychologist, researcher; b. Buffalo, N.Y., Mar. 29, 1956; s. John M. and Elizabeth K. (Callahan) A. BS in Social and Orgnl. Behavior, U. Md., 1981, BA in Psychology, 1982; MA in Behavioral Psychology, George Washington U., 1984; MA in Psychology, New Sch. for Social Rsch., N.Y.C., 1993; PhD in Clin. Psychology, Saybrook Inst. and Rsch. Ctr., San Francisco, 1998. Dir. clin. program devel. and homeless svcs. Bellevue Hosp. Ctr., N.Y.C., 1986-94; sr. cons. psychologist U.S. State Dept., The Honduras, 1994-97; pub. health analyst U.S. Dept. HHS, Washington, 1997-98; dual diagnosis coord. C&I Brithish Nat. Health Svc., London, 1998—. Contbr. articles to profl. jours. Mem. APA, British Psychol. Soc., World Assn. for Psycho-social Rehab.

ANDERSON, BARRY, chemist; b. London, Mar. 2, 1947; s. William George Stephen and Olive Emily (Norris) A.; m. Pauline Anne Holt, Apr. 5, 1969; children Mark Robert, Nicola Claire. BSc in Chemisty with Honors, Hull U., Nottingham, Eng., 1974. Svc. officer U.K. Chem. Info. Svc. Nottingham U., 1974-76, mktg. officer U.K. Chem. Info. Svc., 1976-79; sales sect. head Royal Soc. Chemistry, Cambridge, England, 1979-84; sales & promo. mgr. Royal Soc. Chemistry, 1984-98; sales, 1999—. Organizer Boy Scout activities, Bingham, Eng., 1982. Avocations: gardening, fishing, chess, reading, painting. Office: Royal Soc Chemistry, Milton Road, Cambridge England

ANDERSON, BRUCE JAMES, electrical engineer, consultant; b. Springfield, Mass., Oct. 16, 1962; s. Bruce James and Frances (Cirillo) A.; m. Susan Patricia Bauer, Apr. 28, 1990. BSEE, Western New Eng. Coll., 1984. Sr. engr. Lockheed, Plainfield, N.J., 1984-90; mng. dir. digital TV and entertainment Sarnoff Corp., Princeton, N.J., 1990—. Patentee in field. Mem. IEEE, Assn. of Computng Machines. Achievements include co-design of Grand Alliance High Definition TV Sys. Office: Sarnoff Corp 201 Washington Rd Princeton NJ 08540-6449

ANDERSON, BRUCE MORGAN, computer scientist; b. Battle Creek, Mich., Oct. 8, 1941; s. James Albert and Beverly Jane (Morgan) A.; m. Jeannie Marie Hignight, May 24, 1975; children: Ronald, Michael, Valerie, John, Carolyn. BEE, Northwestern U., 1964; MEE, Purdue U., 1966; PhD in Elec. Engring., Northwestern U., 1973. Rsch. engr. Zenith Radio Corp., Chgo., 1965-66; assoc. engr. Ill. Inst. Tech. Rsch. Inst., Chgo., 1966-68; sr. electronics engr. Rockwell Internat., Downers Grove, Ill., 1973-75; computer scientist Argonne (Ill.) Nat. Lab., 1975-77; mem. group tech. staff Tex. Instruments, Dallas, 1977-88; sr. scientist BBN Systems and Techs., Cambridge, Mass., 1988-90; systems engr. Lockheed Martin, Denver, 1990-94; sr. scientist CTA Inc., Englewood, Colo., Colo., 1994-97; sr. program mgr. SAIC, Englewood, 1997-98; sr. tech. mgr. TRW, Denver, 1998—; lectr. computer sci. U. Tex.-Arlington and Dallas; adj. prof. computer sci. N. Tex. State U.; vis. indsl. prof. So. Meth. U.; computer systems cons. Info. Internat., Culver City, Calif., HCM Graphic Systems, Gt. Neck, N.Y.; computer cons. depts. geography, transp., econs., sociology and computer sci. Northwestern U., also instr. computer sci.; expert witness for firm Burleson, Pate and Gibson. Contbr. articles to tech. jours. NASA fellow Northwestern U., 1973. Mem. IEEE Computer Soc. (chmn. Dallas 1984-85), Am. Assn. Artificial Intelligence, Assn. Computing Machinery (publs. chmn. 1986 fall joint computer conf. IEEE and Assn. Computing Machinery), Toastmasters Internat., Sigma Xi, Eta Kappa Nu, Theta Delta Chi. Home: 3473 E Euclid Ave Littleton CO 80121-3663 Office: 1999 Broadway Denver CO 80202-3025

ANDERSON, BRUCE RAY, school superintendent; b. Morris, Ill., Aug. 18, 1937; s. Millard Orvin and Rachel Karina (Tweet) A.; m. Carol Ann Davis, Dec. 22, 1959; children: Gregory Bruce, Julie Lynn, Matthew Owen, Rachel Alicia. BA, Wheaton Coll., 1959; MEd, U. Ill., 1962, EdD, 1967. Cert. social sci. tchr., prin., supt., Ill., Minn.; cert. prin., supt., Tex. Tchr. Elgin (Ill.) Pub. Schs., 1959-61; from tchr. to adminstrv. asst. Champaign (Ill.) Pub. Schs., 1961-68; from asst. supt. to supt. schs. Richfield (Minn.) Pub. Schs., 1968-79; supt. schs. Coll. Sta. (Tex.) Ind. Schs., 1979-82, West St. Paul (Minn.) Ind. Sch. Dist. 197, 1982-92, Moorhead (Minn.) Ind. Sch. Dist. 152, 1992-2000; cons. Search Inst., Mpls., 1982—; rsch. project on ednl. change, Instituto Americano, Cochabamba, Bolivia, 1966; trainer, Peer Counseling, Mpls., 1986—. Contbr. articles to profl. jours. Ruling elder, Hope Presbyn. Ch., Richfield, 1990—; bd. dirs. YMCA, 1992-2000, Healthy Cmty. Initiative, 1993-2000. Fellow Bush Found., St. Paul, 1984. Mem. Am. Assn. Sch. Adminstrs., Tex. Assn. Sch. Adminstrs., Minn. Assn. Sch. Adminstrs., Suburban Sch. Supts., Kiwanis (pres. West St. Paul 1990-91), Rotary Internat. Presbyterian. Avocations: tennis, racquetball, Spanish, Russian, international affairs. Home: 7052 Oak Grove Blvd Richfield MN 55423-3039

ANDERSON, CAMPBELL MCCHEYNE, business executive; b. Sydney, Australia, Sept. 17, 1941; s. Allen Taylor Anderson and Ethel Catherine Rundle; m. Sandra Maclean Harper, 1965; 3 children. B in Econ., U. Sydney, 1964. Audit clk. Priestley and Morris, 1958-59; with Boral Ltd., 1962-69; from gen. mgr. to mng. dir. Reef Oil Ltd. and Basin Oil Ltd., 1969-72; with Burmah Oil Australia Ltd., 1972-73, N.Y.C., 1973-74; from divsn. dir. to CFO Burmah Oil Trading Ltd., Eng., 1974-75; dir. Burmah Oil Co. Ltd., 1975-76, exec. dir., 1976-82; mng. dir. Burmah Oil PLC, 1982-85; mng. dir. Renison Goldfields Consolidated Ltd., 1985, mng. dir., CEO, 1986-93; dir. Consolidated Gold Fields PLC, 1985-89; chmn. Ampolex Ltd., 1991-96; mng. dir. North Ltd., 1993-98; chair Energy Resources Australia Ltd., 1993—; pres. Bus. Coun. Australia. Mem. Australian Soc. Accts. (assoc.). Avocations: golf, shooting, horse racing, swimming. Office: 193 Domain Rd, South Yarra VIC 3041, Australia Office: Bus Coun Australia, GPO Box 1472 N, Melbourne VIC 3000, Australia*

ANDERSON, CARL DENNIS, lawyer; b. Mt. Vernon, N.Y., July 4, 1942; s. Carl and Ellen Anderson; m. Karen A. Anderson, Aug. 21, 1965; children: Christopher P., Michael L., Kate K. BA, JD, U. Conn., 1967. Bar: Conn. 1967. Atty. Brown, Jacobson, Jewett & Laudone, P.C., Norwich, Conn., 1967-88; pres. Carl D. Anderson & Assocs., Norwich, 1988-92, Anderson, Laffey, Eckert & Ferdon, P.C., Norwich, 1992-94, Anderson & Ferdon, P.C., Norwich, 1994—; corporator Jewett City Savs. Bank, 1970—; consul Finland, State of Conn., 1977—; trial referee, fact finder State of Conn. Jud. Sys., 1996—. Chmn. Dem. Town Com., Voluntown, Conn., 1972—; sec. Voluntown Planning and Zoning Commn.; legal counsel indian trails coun. Boy Scouts Am., 1972-97. Mem. ATLA, ABA, Am. Quarter Horse Assn., Conn. Trial Lawyers Assn. (mem. bd. govs. 1968—), Conn. Bar Assn., Conn. Quarter Horse Assn., New London County Bar Assn., Snake Meadow Club, Tamarack Lodge, Inc. (pres.). Avocations: quarter horse breeder and exhibitor, gardening, fly fishing. Home: 880 Pendleton Hill Rd Voluntown CT 06384-2202 Office: Anderson and Ferdon PC 101 Water St Norwich CT 06360-5730

ANDERSON, CHARLES HILL, lawyer; b. Chattanooga, June 16, 1930; s. Ray N. and Lois M. (Entrekin) A.; div.; children: Eric S., Alicia L., Burton H.; m. Shirley Roach, May 17, 1996. JD, U. Tenn., 1953. Bar: Tenn. 1953, U.S. Dist. Ct. Tenn. 1953, U.S. Ct. Appeals (6th cir.) 1956, U.S. Supreme Ct. 1956, U.S. Ct. Mil. 1964. Pvt. practice Chattanooga, 1953-59; assoc. gen. counsel Life & Casualty Ins. Co. Tenn., Nashville, 1960-69; dist. atty. U.S. Dept. Justice, Nashville, 1969-77; pvt. practice Nashville, 1977-79, 87—; asst. adj. gen. State of Tenn., Nashville, 1979-87. Mem. U.S. Atty. Gen. Adv. Com., Washington, 1973-77; del. Tenn. Constl. Conv., Nashville, 1965-66; dir. Nashville Pub. TV Coun., 1994-99; chmn. Met. Bd. of Equalization, 1998—. Brig. gen. USAR, ret., 1987. Mem. ABA, Tenn. Bar Assn., Nashville Bar Assn., Fed. Bar Assn. (pres. Nashville chpt. 1972), Am. Arbitration Assn. (arbitrator), Assn. Life Ins. Counsel (mediator, approved Tenn. Supreme Ct., U.S. Dist. Ct.), Cumberland Club (pres. 1981-82), The Federalist Soc. Presbyterian. Home: 221 Diane Dr Madison TN 37115-2565 Office: BNA Corp Ctr Bldg 200 404 Bna Dr Ste 304 Nashville TN 37217-2582

ANDERSON, CLAIRE W., computer gifted and talented educator; b. Albuquerque, May 22, 1930; d. Wentworth Henry and Clara Lea (Magruder) Corley; m. William James Young (div.); children: Gayle L. Mirkin, D. Young, Sherry B. Butler; m. Wallace L. Anderson. Student in Engring., U. Miss., 1946; BA, Rice U., 1951, postgrad., 1993; MEd, U. Houston, 1962, postgrad., 1963; postgrad., Carnegie Mellon U., Tex. A&M, 1992. Cert. elem. and secondary tchr., early childhood, exceptional children tchr., Tex. Tchr. Golfcrest Elem. Shc., Houston, 1959-60, Montrose, Poe Elem. Sch., Houston, 1960-62, St. Mark's Private Sch., Houston, 1962-63; substitute teaching Spring Branch Ind. Sch. Dist., Houston, 1965-68; tchr. Meml. Hall, Houston, 1968-73; instr. English, math. Internat. Hispanic U., Houston, 1971-74; tchr. Dogan Elem. Sch., Houston, 1971-74, Lanier Mid. Sch., Houston, 1974-79, High Sch. Health Profl., Houston, 1979-90, Clifton Mid. Sch., Houston, 1990-91, Jesse H. Jones Sr. High Sch., Houston, 1992—; adj. tutoring David Livingston and Assoc., Houston, 1960-65; instr. Internat. Hispanic U., Houston, 1971-74, Houston C.C., 1984—, Internat. Edn. Comm. Ctr., High Point, N.C., 1990, Houston C.C. Sys., 1991; invited judge Kiev, Ukraine Math. and Sci. Competitions, 1989; facilitator Tex. Coun. of Women Sch. Execs. Summer Conf., 1994—; active The Rice/HISD Sch. Writing Project; acad. sponsor secondary edn. svc. and sci. clubs. Pres. bd. dirs. Women for Justice, 1990-94; active Houston Photography Ctr., Mus. Fine Arts, Houston Health Objectives 2000, Children's Mus.; coord. study and enrichment tutoring program, 1994. Recipient Tex. award for Excellence in Tchg. and Outstanding Svc. to the Cmty., 1994; scholar Precalculus Design Team, Dow Jones scholar Pa. State, Advance Placement scholar Tex. A&M, Woodrow Wilson; grantee NSF, Impact II. Mem. IEEE, Nat. Coun. Tchrs. Math., Nat. Coun. Tchrs. English, Am. Acoustic Soc., Assn. Calculating Machinery, Assn. for Early Childhood Edn. (internat. chairperson), Tex. Assn. Edn. Tech., Tex. Computers Educators Assn., N.Y. Acad. Sci., Internat. Coun. Computers in Edn., Phi Delta Kappa. Office: 7414 Saint Lo Rd Houston TX 77033-2732

ANDERSON, CLARENCE AXEL FREDERICK, retired mechanical engineer; b. Muskegon, Mich., Dec. 14, 1909; s. Axel Robert and Anna Victoria (Wikman) A.; m. Frances K. Swem, Apr. 9, 1934; children: Robert Curtis, Clarelyn Christine Anderson Schmelling, Stanley Herbert. Student, Muskegon Jr. Coll., 1929, Internat. Corr. Schs., 1934. With Shaw-Walker Co., Muskegon, Mich., 1928-78, mech. engr., 1940-65, project engr., 1965-70; chief engr. Shaw-Walker Co., Muskegon, 1970-78, ret., 1978. Mem. Forest Park Covenant Ch., 1953—, Christian edn. bd. Forest Park Covenant Ch., 1959-61, 67-73, usher, 1953-86, trustee, 1985, 86, chmn. bd. trustees 1986; co-chmn. Jackson Hill Oldtimers Reunion, 1982, 83, 85. Mem. NRA, AARP, Holland (Mich.) Beagle Club (life, pres. 1966-96). Home: 5757 Sternberg Rd Fruitport MI 49415-9740

ANDERSON, DALE, philanthropist; b. N.Y.C., Jan. 13, 1943; d. Bernard I. and Esther Leviton; m. Douglas C. Anderson, May 5, 1977; children: Michael Feld, Barrie Birge, Melisa Mykytiuk; m. Douglas C. Anderson, May 5, 1977. Grad., New Lincoln H.S., N.Y.C., 1961. Trustee Creative Glass Ctr. Am., Millville, N.J., 1990-96, Art Alliance for Contemporary Glass, 1991—, Pilchuck Glass Sch., Seattle, 1991—; mem. adv. bd. Internat. Glass Mus., Tacoma, Wash., 1996—; mem. arts com. Norton Mus. Art, W. Palm Beach, Fla., 1995-97; mem. founder's cir. Minot Mus. Craft and Design, Charlotte, N.C., 1998—; chair collector's cir. Am. Crafts Mus., N.Y.C., 1990-98; mem. adv. coun. Westum Mus. Art, Racine, Wis., 1995—; dir. coll. program Mayor's Vol. Action Ctr., N.Y.C., 1974-77. Recipient Mayor's award N.Y.C., 1977, Svc. to Field Contemporary Glass award Urbanglass, 1996. Avocation: collecting art. Home: 100 Worth Ave Palm Beach FL 33480-6710

ANDERSON, DALE A., electric power industry executive; b. Hettinger, N.D., Jan. 5, 1950; s. Kenneth E. and Norma Anderson; m. Kathie s. Anderson, Oct. 7, 1972; children: Shane, Amber. Student, Ea. Mont., 1976-78; cert. power plant technician, MCC, Miles City, Mont., 1982. Optician Benson Optical, Billings, Mont., 1972-78; power plant operator Mont. Power Co., Colstrip, Mont., 1979-86, insdl. instr., 1986-94, dir. safety & tng., 1995, steam electric sta. ops. & maintenance supr., 1995—. Editor: CPD Safety Manual, 1991. With U.S. Army, 1969-72, Vietnam. Mem. VFW (sr. vice comdr. 1990—). Home: 645 Starlight Dr Billings MT 59101-6835 Office: PO Box 38 Colstrip MT 59323-0038

ANDERSON, DANA CUNNINGHAM, director, teacher, artist; b. Schenectady, N.Y., Aug. 17, 1951; d. Harold Gene Anderson and Jo Lee Wilsher; m. William Emmett Barton, Sept. 4, 1971 (div. Jul. 1979). BA in French/Comparative Lit., U. Sci. & Art Okla. (formerly Okla. Coll. Liberal Arts), 1972; MS in Counseling, East Tex. State U., 1983; Certificate in Marriage and Family Therapy, Southwest Family Inst., 1985. Certified Marriage and Family Therapist. Editor-in-chief Windsor Comms., Inc./Impressions Magazine, Dallas, 1977-78; editor Barton & Burns, Inc., Dallas, 1979-81; freelance editor Spring Publications (under James Hillman, PhD), Dallas, 1979-81; marriage and family therapist pvt. prac., Dallas, 1983-92; founder/dir. The Inner Door Personal Growth Ctr, Cannon Beach, Oreg., 1993-95, The Inner Door Personal Growth Ctr., Gearhart, 1995—; instr. Clatsop Cmty. Coll., Astoria, Oreg., 1994-99; designer/artist ArtLight Media, Gearhart, Oreg., 1998—; dir. Tools for Conscious Living, Gearhart, 1998—; cons. Living Enrichment Ctr./The Living Enrichment Circles Program, Wilsonville, Oreg., 1998-99. artist Polaroid slide transfer artist's print, 1994, In the Silence,1987, The Safety of Arms, 1986; editor/designer webpage for calendar and card design ArtLight Media.com, 2000, quotation calendar, 1995-2000; contbr. article to profl. jour. Cmty.-at-large rep., screening com. Clatsop Cmty. Coll., 1998, 97; co-founder The Spiritual Network, Dallas, 1990—; co-founder Dallas Adult Children of Alcoholics, 1984; sponsor Aquarius Club Alateen Group, Dallas, 1983-85. Mem. Am. Assn. Marriage and Family Therapy, Oreg. Assn. Marriage and Family Therapy, Inst. Noetic Scis., Assn. Holotropic Breathwork Internat. E-mail: danderso@teleport.com. Office: ArtLight Media Co PO Box 2485 Gearhart OR 97138-2485

ANDERSON, DANITA RUTH, minister; b. Chgo., Nov. 5, 1956; d. Walter and Doris E. (Terrell) A. BSBA, Chgo. State U., 1978; MDiv, Gammon Theol. Sem., Atlanta, 1983. Ordained deacon United Meth. Ch., 1983, elder, 1985. Ch. sec. Grace-Calvary Ch., Chgo., 1976-78; parish sec. Ingleside-Whitfield Meth. Ch., Chgo., 1978-79; computer programmer trainee Sears, Roebuck & Co., Chgo., 1979-80; ch. sec. Gorham United Meth. Ch., Chgo., 1980; asst. pastor Cascade United Meth. Ch., Atlanta, 1980-83; assoc. min. St. Mark Ch., Chgo., 1983-86; pastor Neighborhood United Meth. Ch., Maywood, Ill., 1986-90, Ingleside-Whitfield United Meth. Ch., Chgo., 1990-97; sr. pastor Bethany of Fox Valley United Meth. Ch., Aurora, Ill., 1997—; mem. bd. ordained ministry No. Ill. Conf. Coun. on Fin. and Adminstrn.; sec. Clergy Fellowship; chairperson Black Meths. for Ch. Renewal, Chgo., 1979; mem. Acad. for Preaching of the Gen. Bd. of Discipleship of United Meth. Ch. Bd.; chairperson No. Ill. Conf. Bd. Discipleship; mem. gen. coun. on ministries United Meth. Ch., mem. coun. on Evangelism, 1995-97. Global Ministries Crusade scholar, 1981-83; Women's Div. United Meth. Ch. grantee, 1982; recipient Joseph W. Queen award Gammon Sem., 1982, James and Emma Todd award, 1983. Mem. Delta Sigma Theta. Home: 1545 Sycamore Ln Aurora IL 60504-6043 Office: 2200 Ridge Ave Aurora IL 60504-7500

ANDERSON, DAVID, Canadian government official; b. Victoria, B.C., Can., 1937; m. Sandra Anderson; children: James, Zoe. Student, Victoria Coll.; student econs. and law, U. B.C.; student Inst. Oriental Studies, U. Hong Kong. With Dept. External Affairs; M.P. for Esquimalt Saanich Ho. of Commons, Ottawa, Ont, 1968-72; founder, former chmn. spl. com. on environment pollution Ho. of Commons, —, Ont, elected leader Liberal Party B.C., 1972, M.P. for Victoria, 1993—; min. of nat. revenue Ho. of Commons, Ottawa, Ont., 1993-96; mem. Legis. Assembly for Victoria, 1972; of counsel B.C. Wildlife Fedn., 1975-78; tchr. law Sch. Pub. Adminstrn. U. Victoria, 1978-84; mem. Immigration Appeal Bd., 1984-89; spl. advisor to premier on tanker traffic Govt. of B.C., 1989; commr. Commn. Inquiry into Fraser Valley Petroleum Exploration, 1990; min. nat. revenue Govt. of Can., Ottawa, 1993-96, min. of transport, 1996-97, min. fisheries and oceans, from 1997, now min. environment; cons. Environment Can., 1975-78, 89-93. Mem. silver-medal rowing crews Rome Olympic and Chgo. Pan Am. Games. Named One of 125 Victorians Who Have Made a Difference, 1992. Mem. U. B.C. Alumni Assn. (75th Alumni of Distinction award 1990). *

ANDERSON, DAVID DANIEL, retired humanities educator, writer, editor; b. Lorain, Ohio, June 8, 1924; s. David and Nora Marie (Foster) A.; m. Patricia Ann Rittenhour, Feb. 1, 1953. B.S., Bowling Green State U., 1951, M.A., 1952; Ph.D., Mich. State U., 1960; D. Litt., Wittenberg U., 1986. From instr. to prof. dept. Am. thought and lang. to univ. disting. prof. Mich. State U., East Lansing, 1957-90; lectr. Am. Mus., Bath, Eng., 1980; editor U. Coll. Quar., 1971-80; Fulbright prof. U. Karachi, Pakistan, 1963-64; Am. del. to Internat. Fedn. Modern Langs. and Lit., 1969-93, Internat. Congress Orientalists, 1971-79, European Am. Studies Assn., 1994. Author: Sherwood Anderson, 1968 (Book Manuscript award 1961), Louis Bromfield, 1964, Critical Studies in American Literature, 1964, Sherwood Anderson's Winesburg, Ohio, 1967, Brand Whitlock, 1968, Abraham Lincoln, 1970, Suggestions for the Instructor, 1971, Robert Ingersoll, 1972, Woodrow Wilson, 1978, Ignatius Donnelly, 1980, William Jennings Bryan, 1981, Route two, Titus, Ohio, 1993, The Path in the Shadow, 1998; editor: The Black Experience, 1969, The Literary Works of Abraham Llincoln, 1970, Sunshine and Smoke: American Writers and the American Environment, 1971, (with others) The Dark and Tangled Path, 1971, Mid America, 1974, 27th edit., 2000, Sherwood Anderson: Dimensions of His Literary Art, 1976, Sherwood Anderson: The Writer at His Craft, 1979, Critical Essays on Sherwood Anderson, 1981, Michigan: A State Anthology, 1983, Myth, Memory and the American Earth: the Durability of Raintree County, 1998; editor Midwestern Miscellany, 1974—; also numerous articles, essays, short stories, poems. Served with USN, 1942-45; with AUS, 1952-53. Decorated Silver Star, Purple Heart; recipient Disting. Alumnus award Bowling Green State U., 1976, Disting. Faculty award Mich. State U., 1974, Disting. Faculty award Mich. Assn. Governing Bds., 1988, Disting Research award Mich. State U., 1988. Mem. ASA, AAUP, MLA, Popular Culture Assn., Soc. Study Midwestern Lit. (founder, exec. sec., Disting. Service award 1982), Assn. Gen. and Liberal Edn. Am. Assn. Advancement Humanities, Internat. Assn. U. Profs. English, Univ. Club. Home: 6555 Lansdown Dr Dimondale MI 48821-9428 Office: Mich State U Dept Am Thought and Lang East Lansing MI 48824

ANDERSON, DAVID FENIMORE, mathematics educator; b. Ft. Dodge, Iowa, Dec. 20, 1948; s. Duane C. and Dorothy M. (Fenimore) A.; m. Konnie Lee Fiscel, June 22, 1974; children: Sarah, Jonathan. BS, Iowa State U., 1971; PhD, U. Chgo., 1976. Asst. prof. math. U. Tenn., Knoxville, 1976-82, assoc. prof., 1982-87, prof., 1987—. Contbr. numerous articles on commutative algebra to profl. jours. Mem. Am. Math. Soc., Math. Assn. Am. Lutheran. Office: U Tenn Dept Math Ayres Hall Knoxville TN 37996

ANDERSON, DAVID GASKILL, JR., Spanish language educator; b. Tarboro, N.C., Feb. 21, 1945; s. David G. Sr. and Lucile (Gammon) A.; m. Jonetta Gentemann, Jan. 29, 1968; children: Allene Q., David III, James H., John G. AB, U. N.C., 1967; MA, Vanderbilt U., 1974, PhD, 1985. Instr. of langs. Union U., Tenn., 1975-76; from instr. Spanish to asst. prof. Ouachita Bapt. U., Ark., 1976-85; asst. prof. fgn. langs. N.E. La. U., 1985-87; asst. prof. Spanish, John Carroll U., Cleve., 1987-93, assoc. prof., 1993—, acting

chmn. dept. classical and modern langs., 1996, chmn., 1997—, George Grauel faculty fellow rsch. sabbatical, spring 1997; tchg. fellow Vanderbilt U., 1983-84, NEH summer seminar on poetry, 1990; presenter in field. Author: On Elevating the Commonplace: A Structuralist Analysis of The Odas of Pablo Neruda, 1987; contbr. articles to profl. jours. vol. ESL Peace Corps, Colombia, 1968-70. Named Outstanding Young Men of Am., 1979. Mem. Am. Assn. U. Suprs. and Coords. Fgn. Lang. Programs, Am. Assn. Tchrs. Spanish and Portuguese, Modern Lang. Assn., Cleve. Diocesan Fgn. Lang. Assn. (bd. mem. 1988-93), Cleve. Assn., Phi Beta Kappa. Democrat. Home: 2573 Dysart Rd Cleveland OH 44118-4446 Office: John Carroll Univ Spanish Dept Cleveland OH 44118

ANDERSON, DONALD THEODORE, human resources professional, consultant; b. Waltham, Mass., Sept. 15, 1932; s. Thorsten Theodore and Eveline (Edwards) A.; m. Patricia Arlene Rowe, Dec. 26, 1953 (div. Apr. 1975); children: Gregory, Synia, Jacki, Kristin, Karl; m. Sarah Elizabeth Andrews, Dec. 20, 1975; children: Susan, Sally. AA, Boston U., 1956, BSBA, 1958. Lic. ins. broker, Mass. Pvt. practice ins. broker Boston, 1958-59; prof. recruiter Raytheon Mfg., Framingham, Mass., 1960; mgr. benefits Raytheon Mfg., Portsmouth, R.I., 1960-63; pers. rep. Sylvania GT&E, Waltham, 1964-66; mgr. coll. recruiting Sylvania GT&E, Waltham and Needham, 1966-68; asst. dir. human resources Sylvania GT&E, Hillsborough, N.H., 1968-70; cons. instr. Franklin Pierce Coll., Rindge, N.H., 1970-97; dir. human resources and risk mgmt. Franklin Pierce Coll., Rindge, 1970-97; human resources cons. Andersson & Assocs., 1998—; pres. bd. dirs. Monadnock Credit Union, Keene, 1987-91; human resources cons. to higher edn., 1998—. Pres., bd. dirs. (archeology jour.) Man in the Northeast, 1972; editor-in-chief Alaskan Malamute Club of Am. Newsletter. Dir. Christian edn., Sunday sch. tchr., vestryman Episcopal Chs., Portsmouth, Chelmsford, Mass., and Peterborough, N.H., 1960-70; edn. chmn. PTA Coun., Portsmouth, 1961; chmn. awards com. Nat. Scholarship Found., Portsmouth, 1961; mem. Gov.'s Coun.-Hiring of the Handicapped, Newport, R.I., 1962; active Young Rep. Club, Peterborough, 1968; committeeman Explorer Troop-Boy Scouts Am., Portsmouth, 1963; bd. dirs. ARC, Keene, N.H., 1984-92, mem. human resources com., 1984-92; com. mem. Seatbelt Task Force, Cheshire County, N.H. Cpl. U.S. Army, 1952-54, Korea. Named Outstanding Tchr., Outstanding Educators of Am., 1975. Mem. Coll. and Univ. Pers. Assn., N.H. Coll. and Univ. Coun. Human Resource Dirs., Monadnock Pers. Assn., Alaskan Malamute Club. Am. Democrat. Episcopalian. Avocations: Alpine skiing, American Indian archeology; e-mail: aaconsult.top.monad.net. Home: 944 Mountain Rd Jaffrey NH 03452-6035 Office: Franklin Pierce Coll PO Box 60 Rindge NH 03461-0060

ANDERSON, DORIS EHLINGER, lawyer; b. Houston, Dec. 1, 1926; d. Joseph Otto and Cornelia Louise (Pagel) Ehlinger; m. Wiley Anderson, Jr. (dec.); children: Wiley Newton III, Joe E. BA, Rice U., 1946; permanent high sch. tchr. cert., U. Houston, 1948; JD, U. Tex., 1950; MLS in Museology, U. Okla. Bar: Tex. 1950, U.S. Supreme Ct. Assoc. Ehlinger & Anderson, Houston, 1950-52, ptnr., 1965—; assoc. Price, Guinn, Wheat & Veltmann, Houston, 1952-55, Wheat, Dyche & Thornton, Houston, 1955-65; life mem. Rice Assocs., Houston, 1984—; hist. lectr., Harvard Negotiation Seminar, 1992 Edn. for Ministry, U of South, 1999. Editor: Houston City of Destiny, 1980; contbr. articles to hist. pubs. Parliamentarian Harris County Flood Control Task Force, Houston, 1975—; bd. dirs. Houston Bapt. Mus Am. Architecture and Decorative Arts, 1980-90, curator costume, 1980; apptd. ambassador Inst. Texan Culture U. Tex, San Antonio; past pres. gen. San Jacinto Descendants; docent Bayou Bend Mus. Fine Arts, Houston. Recipient best interpretive exhibit award Tex. Hist. Commn., 1983, Outstanding Woman of Yr. award YWCA, Houston, 1983; named adm. Tex. Navy, 1980. Mem. ABA, UDC (pres. Jefferson Davis chpt.), Assn. Women Attys. Houston, Houston Bar Assn., Daus. Republic Tex. (Chaplain Robert E. Lee chpt., parliamentarian gen.), Am. Mus. Soc., Harris County Heritage Soc., Kappa Beta Pi (pres. Lamda alumni). Episcopalian. Home: 5556 Cranbrook Rd Houston TX 77056-1600 Office: Ehlinger & Anderson 5556 Sturbridge Dr Houston TX 77056-1623

ANDERSON, EDWARD VIRGIL, lawyer; b. San Francisco, Oct. 17, 1953; s. Virgil P and Edna Pauline (Pedersen) A.; m. Kathleen Helen Dunbar, Sept. 3, 1983; children: Elizabeth D., Hilary J. AB in Econs., Stanford U., 1975, JD, 1978. Bar: Calif. 1978. Assoc. Pillsbury Madison & Sutro, San Francisco, 1978—, ptnr., 1987-94; mng. ptnr., mem. firm mgmt. com. Skjerven Morrill MacPherson Franklin and Friel, San Jose, Calif., 1994—. Editor IP Litigator, 1995—; mem. bd. editors Antitrust Law Devel., 1983-86. Trustee Lick-Wilmerding H.S., San Francisco, 1980—, pres.; trustee Santa Clara Law Found., 1995—. Hamlin Sch. for Girls, San Francisco, 1998—. Mem. ABA, Calif. Bar Assn., San Francisco Bar Assn., Santa Clara Bar Assn. (counsel), City Club San Francisco, Stanford Golf Club, Phi Beta Kappa. Republican. Episcopal. Home: 330 Santa Clara Ave San Francisco CA 94127-2035 Office: Skjerven Morrill MacPherson Franklin and Friel 25 Metro Dr Ste 700 San Jose CA 95110-1349

ANDERSON, ELSIE MINERS, mathematics educator; b. Harare, Zimbabwe, July 4, 1931; came to U.S., 1961; d. William James and Winifred Ethel (Lowe) Miners; m. Larry Vance Anderson, Dec. 22, 1961; children: Winifred Jean Whitmore, Margaret Elizabeth Daly. BS, Rhodes U., Grahamstown, South Africa, 1951, EdD, 1952; MLS, East Tex. State U., 1966. Tchr. geography and math. Govt. Cen. African Fedn., Salisbury, 1953-61; tchr. math. Desdemona (Tex.) Ind. Sch. Dist., 1962-64; head libr. Holding Inst., Laredo, Tex., 1971-72; instr. math. Western Tex. Coll., Snyder, 1973-74, prof. math., 1974-97; exchange tchr. in geography Mill Hill, North London, Eng., 1957. Active Girl Scouts U.S., Abilene, Tex., 1972—. Recipient Theater Patron award Western Tex. Coll. Drama Dept., Snyder, 1986. Mem. Order Eastern Star. Baptist. Avocations: stamp collecting, swimming, racquetball, travel, attending drama productions. Home: PO Box 181 Rising Star TX 76471-0181

ANDERSON, ERIC SEVERIN, lawyer; b. N.Y.C., Dec. 16, 1943; s. Edward Severin and Dorothy Elvira (Ekbloom) A. BA in History summa cum laude, St. Mary's U., San Antonio, 1968; JD cum laude, Harvard U., 1971. Bar: Tex. 1971. From assoc. to ptnr. Fulbright & Jaworski, L.L.P., Houston, 1971—. Served with USAF, 1961-65. Mem. ABA, State Bar Tex., Houston Bar Assn. Democrat. Clubs: Houston Ctr., Houston City. Avocations: classical music, theater, sports. Home: 14 E Greenway Plz Unit 21-o Houston TX 77046-1406 Office: Fulbright & Jaworski LLP 1301 Mckinney St Houston TX 77010-3031

ANDERSON, ERNEST ROBERT, JR., pharmacist; b. Brockton, Mass., Sept. 21, 1953; s. Ernest Robert and June Gloria (Akerblom) A.; m. Merryle Louise Nutter, Sept. 16, 1973; children: Christopher Joseph, Betsy Heather. BS, Northeastern U., Boston, 1976, MS, 1979. Registered pharmacist. Pharmacist New Eng. Med. Ctr., Boston, 1976-81, assoc. dir. pharmacy, 1981-92; dir. pharmacy Lahey Clinic, Burlington, Mass., 1993-96; prof. Northeastern U., 1990—. Contbr. chpt. to book, articles to profl. jours. Elder Free Evang. Fellowship, Easton, Mass., 1992—, youth leader, 1988—; mission leader World Servants, Dominican Republic and Mex., 1991, 93, 95. Mem. Am. Soc. Health Systems Pharmacists, Mass. Soc. Health System Pharmacists (chair corp. sponsorship com. 1995—, Mass. Hosp. Pharmacist of Yr. 1985), Am. Pharm. Assn. Republican. Avocations: skiing, golf, basketball. Home: 489 Copeland St Brockton MA 02301-7016

ANDERSON, FRANCES SWEM, nuclear medical technologist; b. Grand Rapids, Mich., Nov. 27, 1913; d. Frank Oscar and Carrie (Strang) Swem; m. Clarence A.F. Anderson, Apr. 9, 1934; children: Robert Curtis, Clarelyn Christine (Mrs. Roger L. Schmelling), Stanley Herbert. Student, Muskegon Sch. Bus., 1959-60; cert., Muskegon Community Coll., 1964; cert. adult edn. computer course, Fruitport Cmty. Schs., 1992. Registered nuclear med. technologist Am. Registry Radiol. Technologists. X-ray file clk., film librarian Hackley Hosp., Muskegon, Mich., 1957-59, radioisotope technologist and sec., 1959-65; nuclear med. technologist Butler Meml. Hosp., Muskegon Heights, Mich., 1966-70; nuclear med. technologist Mercy Hosp., Muskegon, 1970-79, ret., 1979. Mem. Muskegon Civic A Capella choir, 1932-39; mem. Mother-Tchr. Singers, PTA, Muskegon, 1941-48, treas. 1944-48; with Muskegon Civic Opera Assn., 1950-51; office vol. Alive '88 Crusade; mem. com. for 60th H.S. Class Reunion; mem. Sr. Harvest Day Com., Muskegon County, 1995; active Forest Park Covenant Ch., mem. choir, 1953-79, 83—, choir pres. 1992, 93, choir sec. 1963-69, Sunday Sch. tchr. 1954-75, supt. Sunday Sch., 1975-78, sec., treas. 1981-86, sec. 1991, 92, 93, mem. support team, sec. 1993, chmn. master planning coun., 1982; coord. centennial com. to 1981, ch. sec. 1982-84, 87, 91, 95-96, registrar vacation Bible sch. 1988, 89, 90, 91, treas., 1995, 96; co-chmn. Jackson Hill Old Timer's Reunion, 1982, 83, 85. Mem. Am. Registry Radiologic Technologists, Soc. Nuclear Medicine (cert. nuclear medicine technologist), Omni Fitness Club (10 Yr. Mem. award). Home: 5757 Sternberg Rd Fruitport MI 49415-9740

ANDERSON, FRANCILE MARY, secondary education educator; b. Poland, Ind., Nov. 10, 1926; d. Matthew Henry and Emma Alvina (Dettinger) Worthman; m. Robert Charles Anderson, Aug. 23, 1953; children: Sally Quick, Sue Wilkinson, Robert Charles, Russell. BA, U. Mich., 1948. Tchr. Pontiac (Mich.) Sch. Dist., 1948-54; co-organizer Mich. Law Related Edn. Conf., Lansing, 1978; mem. exec. bd. North Ctrl. Assn. Commn. on Schs., Tempe, Ariz., 1996-99. Trustee North Oakland Med. Ctrs., Pontiac, 1994—; campaign chair United Way of Oakland County, 1995. Recipient Disting. Svc. award Mich. Assn. Secondary Sch. Prins., 1987; named to Mich. Edn. Hall of Fame, 1990. Mem. Oakland County Hosp. Assn. (pres.), Oakland County Bar Law Libr. Found., North Ctrl. Assn. Mich., North Oakland Med. Ctrs. Found. (pres.), Delta Kappa Gamma. Republican. Presbyterian. Home: 2570 Silverside Dr Waterford MI 48328-1760

ANDERSON, FRANCIS, media director; b. Birmingham, England, Nov. 19, 1965; s. William Robin and Marian Helen (Lurring) A.; m. Tamara Michele Hilton, Sept. 30, 1998. LLB with honors, Queen Mary Coll., London, 1987. Media planner T.M.D., London, 1988-90; acct. dir. Pattison Horswell Durden, London, 1990-96; media dir. New P.H.D., London, 1996-99, TBWA/CHIAT/DAY, N.Y.C., 1999—. Avocations: skiing, crime fiction, modern art. Home: #250 666 Greenwich St New York NY 10014 Office: TBWA/CHIAT/DAY 488 Madison Ave New York NY 10022-5702

ANDERSON, FRED RICHARD, minister; b. San Bernardino, Calif., Dec. 27, 1941; s. Elmer Duffield and Gladys Lucile (Lawlace) A.; m. Questa Lucile Donnelly, Sept. 4, 1965; children: Larra Anne, Rebecca Lucile; 1 foster child, James Gordon Cushman. BM in Voice, U. Redlands, 1963; MDiv, Princeton Theol. Sem., 1973, D in Ministry, 1981. Pastor Pompton Valley Presbyn. Ch., Pompton Plains, N.J., 1973-78; sr. pastor Pine St. Church, Harrisburg, Pa., 1978-92, Madison Ave. Presbyn. Ch., N.Y.C., 1992—; bd. dirs. Liturgical Conf., 1990-94; bd. trustees Princeton Theol. Sem., 1992—; chair edn. bd. Reformed Liturgy and Music, 1983-89. Author: Singing Psalms of Joy & Praise, 1986, The Presbyterian Hymnal, 1990; assoc. editor: Book of Common Worship, 1993; contbr. articles to profl. jours.; opera, concert singer, 1963-64. Trustee Harrisburg Hosp., 1990-92, Chilton Meml. Hosp., Pompton Plains, 1976-78; pres. Pequennock (N.J.) Sr. City Housing, 1974-78; v.p. YMCA, Harrisburg, 1987-92, v.p., 1987-92. Capt. USAF, 1964-69. Recipient Fine Arts award Bank Am., 1959. Mem. Appeal Conscience Found. (assoc.), N.Am. Acad. Liturgy, Presbyn. Assn. Musicians, Union League Club (N.Y.C.), The Pilgrims. Avocations: jogging, boating, fishing, hymntext writing, hiking the White Mountains. Office: Madison Ave Presbyn Ch 921 Madison Ave New York NY 10021-3508

ANDERSON, GEORGE HUGO, chemical engineer; b. Binghamton, N.Y., Oct. 12, 1946; s. Otto Hugo and Marie Alma (Yerkes) A.; m. Carilon D. Cain, Sept. 8, 1973; children: Michelle Lynn Anderson Wolf, Tiffany Beth, Jeffrey Scott, Matthew Christopher. BS in Biomed. Engring., Rensselaer Poly. Inst., 1968, M in Biomed. Engring., 1969; PhD of Chem. Engring., Rice U., 1977. Rsch. engr., coal liquification Exxon Rsch. & Engring., Baytown, Tex., 1977-80, sr. staff engr. synfuels, 1980-83; sect. head, planning Exxon Rsch. & Engring., Florham Pk., N.J., 1983-85; corp. tech. advisor Exxon Rsch. & Engring., Annandale, N.J., 1985-88; sect. head fuels processing devel. Exxon Rsch. & Engring., Baton Rouge, 1988-91, quality coord., 1990-91, catalyst coord., 1992—. Contbr. articles to profl. jours.; patent in field. Mem. bd. dirs. Sageglen Cmty. Assn., Houston, 1978-80; bd. mem. Parsippany (N.J.) Christian Sch., 1988. Sgt. USAF, 1970-73. Recipient 2 Internal Tech. Excellence awards Exxon Corp., 1982, Exxon Rsch. and Engring., 1993. Mem. AIChE, Sigma Xi. Baptist. Achievements include discovery of effects of shear stress on human blood platelet functions in clotting; invention of bottoms recycle process scheme for Exxon Coal Liquification process; devel. of kinetic model for coal liquification; coordination of devel. and commercialization of 6 catalysts covering reforming, fuels/lubes H/T and FCC process areas. Avocations: golf, basketball, reading, teaching Sun. sch., ch. deacon. Home: 19164 Hickory Bay Ct Baton Rouge LA 70817-1823 Office: Exxon Rsch & Devel Labs PO Box 2226 Baton Rouge LA 70821-2226

ANDERSON, GERALDINE LOUISE, medical researcher; b. Mpls., July 7, 1941; d. George M. and Viola Julia-Mary (Abel) Havrilla; m. Henry Clifford Anderson, May 21, 1966; children: Bruce Henry, Julie Lynne. BS, U. Minn., 1963. Med. technologist Swedish Hosp., Mpls., 1963-68; hematology supr. lab. Glenwood Hills Hosp., Golden Valley, Minn., 1968-70; assoc. scientist pediats. U. Minn. Hosps., Mpls., 1970-74; instr. health occupations, med. lab. asst. Suburban Hennepin County Area Vocat. Tech. Ctr., Brooklyn Park, Minn., 1974-81, 92-95, St. Paul Tech. Vocat. Inst., Brooklyn Park, 1978-81; rsch. med. technologist Miller Hosp., St. Paul, 1975-78; rsch. assoc. Children's and United Hosps., St. Paul, 1979-88; sr. lab. analyst Cascade Med. Inc., Eden Prairie, Minn., 1989-90; lab. mgr. VAMC, Mpls., 1990; tech. support scientist INCSTAR Corp., Stillwater, Minn., 1990-94; mem. network staff Clin. Design Group, Chgo., 1992-98; regulatory affairs product analysis coord. Medtronic Neurol., Mpls., 1995; quality assurance documentation coord. Lectec Corp., Minnetonka, Minn., 1995; clin. rsch. monitor Eli Lilly Rsch. Labs., Indpls., 1995-98; sr. clin. rsch. assoc. Covance, Inc., Princeton, N.J., 1998-99; sr. clin. rsch. assoc. Parexel Internat., Inc., Chgo., 1999-2000, Med. Tech. Rsch. Assn./AAI Internat., Boston, 2000—; mem. health occupations adv. com. Hennepin Tech. Ctrs., 1975-90, chairperson, 1978-79; mem. hematology slide edn. rev. bd. Am. Soc. Hematology, 1977-96; mem. flow cytometry and clin. chemistry quality control subcoms. Nat. Com. for Clin. Lab. Stds., 1988-92; cons. FCM Specialists, 1989-99, Clin. Design Group, 1992-98; mem. rev. bd. Clin. Lab. Sci., 1990-91, The Learning Laboratorian Series, 1991; contbr., presenter in Svc. Rev. in Clin. Lab. Sci., audio taped study program for ASMT, 1992. Contbr. articles to profl. jours. Mem. Med. Lab. Tech. Polit. Action Com., 1978-99; charter orgns. rep. Troop # 534 Boy Scouts Am., Viking Coun., 1988-90; resource person lab. careers Robbinsdale Sch. Dist., Minn., 1970-79; del. Crest View Home Assn., 1981—; mem. sci. and math. subcom. Minn. High Tech. Coun., 1983-88; mem. Women Scientists Spkrs. Bur., 1989-92; observer UN 4th World Conf. on Women, Beijing, 1995. Recipient svc. awards and honors Omicron Sigma. Mem. AAAS, AAUW, NAFE (Twin Cities network), Am. Med. Writers Assn., Women in Com., Inc., Assn. Clin. Rsch. Profls., Soc. Clin. Rsch. Assocs., Soc. Tech. Commn., Nat. Assn. Women Cons., Inc., Minn. Emerging Med. Orgns., Minn. Soc. Med. Tech. (sec. 1969-71), Am. Soc. Profl. and Exec. Women, Soc. Clin. Rsch. Assocs., Am. Soc. Clin. Lab. Sci. (del. to ann. meetings 1972—, chmn. hematology sci. assembly 1977-79, nomination com. 1979-81, bd. dirs. 1986-88), Twin Cities Hosp. Assn. (spkrs. bur. 1968-70), Assn. Women in Sci., World Future Soc., Minn. Med. Tech. Alumni, Am. Soc. Hematology, Internat. Soc. Analytical Cytology, Great Lakes Internat. Flow Cytometry Assn. (charter mem. 1992), Grad Women in Sci. Inc., Soc. Clin. Rsch. Assocs, Sigma Delta Epsilon (corr. sec. XI chpt. 1980-82, pres. 1982-84, nat. membership com. 1990-92, nat. nominations chair 1991-92, nat. v.p. 1992-93, nat. pres.-elect 1993-94, nat. pres. 1994-95, bd. dirs. 1996—, chmn. bd. dirs. 2000—), Alpha Mu Tau. Office: FCM Specialists 8400-33 Pl N Minneapolis MN 55427

ANDERSON, GERRY, television film producer; b. Apr. 14, 1929; m. Betty Wrightman, 1952; 2 children; m. Sylvia Thamm, 1961 (div.); 1 child; m. Mary Robins, 1981; 1 child. Prodr. (TV series) Adventures of Twizzle, 1956, Torchy the Battery Boy, 1957, Four Feather Falls, 1958, Supercar, 1959, Fireball XL5, 1961, Stingray, 1963-64, Thunderbirds, 1964-66 (Royal TV Soc. Silver medal), Captain Scarlet, 1967, Joe 90, 1968, The Secret Service, 1968, UFO, 1969-70, The Protectors, 1971-7, Space 1999, 1973-76, Terrahawks, 1982-83, Dick Spanner, 1987, Space Precinct, 1993-95, Lavender Castle, 1997, also numerous TV commls., (films) Thunderbirds are Go, 1966, Thunderbird 6, 1968, Doppelganger, 1969.

ANDERSON, GILLIAN, actress; b. Chgo., Aug. 9, 1968; d. Edward and Rosemary A.; m. Errol Clyde Klotz, Jan. 1, 1994; 1 child, Piper. BFA, DePaul U., 1990; grad., Goodman Theatre Sch., Chgo. Appeared on TV as Dana Scully in X-Files, 1993—; stage appearance in Absent Friends, Manhattan Theatre Club, 1991 (Theatre World award 1991), The Philanthropist, Along Wharf Theater, 1992; appeared in films Chicago Cab, 1995, X-Files the Movie, 1998, The Mighty, 1998, Playing By Heart, 1998, Princess Mononoke, 1999. Recipient Golden Globe awards, 1995, 97, Screen Actors' Guild awards, 1996, 97, Emmy award, 1997; nominated for Best Actress in Drama Series, 1996. Office: William Morris Agy 151 S El Camino Dr Beverly Hills CA 90212-2775

ANDERSON, GLORIA LONG, chemistry educator; b. Altheimer, Ark., Nov. 5, 1938; d. Charley and Elsie Lee (Foggie) L.; 1 child, Gerald Leavell. BS, Ark. Agr. Mech. & Normal Coll., 1958; MS, Atlanta U., 1961; PhD, U. Chgo., 1968. Instr. S.C. State Coll., Orangeburg, 1961-62, Morehouse Coll., Atlanta, 1962-64; teaching and rsch. asst. U. Chgo., 1964-68; assoc. prof., chmn. Morris Brown Coll., Atlanta, 1968-73, Callaway prof., chmn., 1973-84, acad. dean, 1984-89, United Negro Coll. Fund disting. scholar, 1989-90, Callaway prof. chemistry, 1990—; interim pres. Morris Brown Coll., 1992-93, Fuller E. Callaway prof. chemistry, 1993-99, 99—, dean sci. and tech., 1995-97, interim pres., 1998-99, Fuller E. Callaway prof. chemistry, 1999—. Contbr. articles to profl. jours. Bd. dirs. Corp. for Pub. Broadcasting, Washington, 1972-79, vice chmn. 1977-79; Pub. Broadcasting Atlanta, 1980—; mem. Pub. Telecommunications Task Force, Atlanta, 1980. Postdoctoral rsch. fellow NSF, 1969, faculty industry fellow, 1981, faculty rsch. fellow Southeastern Ctr. for Elec. Engring. Edn., 1984. Fellow Am. Inst. Chemists (cert. profl. chemist); mem. Nat. Sci. Tchrs. Assn., Am. Chem. Soc., Sigma Xi. Baptist. Home: 560 Lynn Valley Rd SW Atlanta GA 30311-2331 Office: Morris Brown Coll Dept Chemistry 643 ML King Jr Dr NW Atlanta GA 30314-4140

ANDERSON, JACK ROY, health care company executive; b. Mansfield, Ohio, Feb. 14, 1925; s. Roy L. and Katherine (Munson) A.; m. Rose-Marie J. Garcia, June 24, 1950; children—Gail Ellen, Neil Robert, Barbara Ann. B.S., Miami U., Oxford, Ohio, 1947; M.S., Columbia Bus. Sch., 1949. Acctg. mgr. Time, Inc., N.Y.C., 1950-59; asst. to controller W.R. Grace & Co., N.Y.C., 1959-62; v.p., treas. Hartford Publs., Inc., N.Y.C., 1962-65; controller McCall Corp., N.Y.C., 1965-68; v.p. Reliance Group, Inc., N.Y.C., 1968-70; pres., dir. Hosp. Affiliates Internat., Inc., Nashville, 1970-76, chmn. bd., dir., 1977-81; chmn. INA Health Care Group, Dallas, 1978-81; pres. Manor Care, Inc., Silver Spring, Md., 1981-82, Calver Corp., Dallas, 1982—; adj. faculty Owen Grad. Sch. Mgmt., 1978-79; bd. dirs. Genesis Health Ventures, Inc., Horizon Health Corp. Author: The Road to Recovery, 1976. Vis. com. Vanderbilt Owen Grad. Sch. Mgmt., 1973-77; trustee Nat. Com. for Quality Health Care, 1979-87, vice chmn., 1979-82; mem. bus. adv. coun. Miami U., 1975-78, chmn., 1978; mem. bd. overseers Hoover Instn. on War, Revolution and Peace, Stanford U.; mem. Pres.'s Cir., NAS, NAE, Inst. Medicine. Lt. (j.g.) USNR, 1943-46. Mem. Blind Brook Club (Purchase, N.Y.), Clove Valley Rod and Gun Club (LaGrangeville, NY), Desert Forest Golf Club (Carefree, Ariz.), Greenwich (Conn.) Country Club, Preston Trail Golf Club (Dallas), Reform Club (London), Stanwich Club (Conn.), Sigma Chi, Beta Alpha Psi, Beta Gamma Sigma (hon.). Office: 16475 Dallas Pky Addison TX 75001-6821

ANDERSON, JAMES DONALD, pension company executive; b. Vinton, Iowa, June 10, 1952; s. Donald Arvid and Irene Dorothea (Jones) A.; m. Patricia Rae Vaupel, Dec. 22, 1973; children: Krista Rene, Lori Jolene, Amy Marie, Betsy Ellen. BA with honors, Luther Coll., 1974; MBA, U. Iowa, 1990. CPA, Iowa. Staff acct. McGladrey & Pullen, Cedar Rapids, Iowa, 1974-77; contr. Perpetual Savs. Bank, Cedar Rapids, 1977, asst. v.p., 1978-79, v.p., 1980, sr. v.p., 1981-83, exec. v.p., 1983-84, sr. exec. v.p. fin. and planning, 1985-88, corp. sec., 1985-89, exec. v.p., 1989; dir. Perpetual Savs., Cedar Rapids, 1986-89; pres. Perpetual Diversified Svcs., Inc. subs. Perpetual Savs., Cedar Rapids, 1983-89; pres., COO BPA, Inc. (formerly Benefit Plan Administrn. Inc.), Cedar Rapids, 1990-94; pres., CEO Sci Tower Pension Specialists, Inc., Cedar Rapids, 1994—; sr. v.p., dir. Sci Fin. Group, Inc., 1995—. Deacon Cedar Valley Bible Ch., Cedar Rapids, 1977-85, elder, 1985—; chmn. sch. bd. Cedar Valley Christian Sch., 1983-87; participant Leadership for Five Seasons, Cedar Rapids, 1983; chmn. bd. Keys to Living Christian Counseling Agy., 1994—. Mem. AICPA, Iowa Inst. CPAs, CPAs in Industry Orgn. Republican. Home: 1733 Lake Terrace Rd Cedar Rapids IA 52403-9008 Office: Sci Tower Pension Specialists Inc 200 2nd Ave SE Cedar Rapids IA 52401-1298

ANDERSON, JAMES FRANCIS, lawyer; b. Glen Ridge, N.J., June 13, 1965. BA, Seton Hall U., 1987, JD, 1990. Bar: N.J. 1991, U.S. Supreme Ct. 1995. Pvt. practice Spring Lake, N.J., 1991—. Pro bono atty. Ocean-Monmouth Legal Svcs., Freehold, N.J., 1991—; mentor Manasquan (N.J.) H.S., 1994. Mem. ABA, Masons. Office: PO Box 144 Spring Lake NJ 07762-0144

ANDERSON, JAMES LINWOOD, pharmaceutical sales official; b. Bangor, Maine, June 8, 1949; s. Linwood Lamont and Helena May (Armitage) A.; m. Susan Grace Hughey, Aug. 23, 1974 (div. Aug. 1994). BS in Biology and Premedicine, U. Maine, 1971, MS in Physiology, 1972. Narcotics officer Maine State Police/Drug Enforcement Agy., 1973-74; sales rep. Wallace Labs., 1974-76, Hoechst-Roussell, Somerville, N.J., 1976-84; pharm. sales rep. I Miles (Bayer) Pharms., New Haven, 1984-90, ter. sales specialist, 1990-91, hosp. sales specialist, 1991-93, pharm. sales rep. II, 1994—. Coord. pastoral affairs Calvary Bapt. Ch., Manchester, N.H., 1976-80. Mem. USCG Aux. (flotilla comdr. New Bedford, Mass. 1992-94, divsn. capt. S.E. Mass. 1994-96, rear commodore Mass. and R.I. 1996-97, vice commodore for Maine, N.H., Mass., R.I. and part of Vt. 1998-99, dist. commodore 2000-2001), Order of DeMolay (master councilor 1965-66, state master councilor 1966-67, chevalier 1967—). Avocations: boating, gun collecting, color guard drill team. Phone: (508) 951-2014. Home: 205 Stevenson St New Bedford MA 02745-3516

ANDERSON, JAMES R., photographer, multimedia producer; b. Seattle, Feb. 13, 1969. BA, NYU, 1990; MFA, Rutgers U., 1997; PhD, U. Wash., 2000. Prs. Anderson Media Group, SEattle, 1997—. Author: Rites of Spring, 1999. Served with USMC, 1990-94. Decorated Purple Heart. Mem. Am. Soc. Media Photographers (bd. dirs. 1998—). E-mail: info@jranderson.com. Office: Anderson Media Group 117 E Louisa St Ste 413 Seattle WA 98102-3203

ANDERSON, JERRY WILLIAM, JR., technical and business consulting executive, educator; b. Stow, Mass., Jan. 14, 1926; s. Jerry William and Heda Charlotte (Petersen) A. ; m. Joan Hukill Balyeat, Sept. 13, 1947; children: Katheleen, Diane. BS in Physics, U. Cin., 1949, PhD in Econs., 1976; MBA, Xavier U., 1959. Rsch. and test project engr. Wright-Patterson AFB, Ohio, 1949-53; project engr., electronics div. AVCO Corp., Cin., 1953-70, program mgr., 1970-73; program dir. Cin. Electronics Corp., 1973-78; pres. Anderson Industries Unltd., 1978—; chmn. dept. mgmt. and mgmt. info. svcs. Xavier U., 1980-89, prof. mgmt., 1989-94, prof. emeritus, 1994—; lectr. No. Ky. U., 1977-78; tech. adviser Cin. Tech. Coll., 1971-80; co-founder, exec. v.p. Loving God "Complete Bible" Christian Ministries, 1988—. Contbr. articles on radar, lasers, infrared detection equipment, air pollution to govt. publs. and profl. jours.; author 3 books in field. Mem. Madeira (Ohio) City Planning Commn., 1962-80; founder, pres. Grassroots, Inc., 1964; active United Appeal, Heart Fund, Multiple Sclerosis Fund. With USNR, 1943-46. Named Man of Year, City of Madeira, 1964. Mem. MADD, VFW (life), Am. Mgmt. Assn., Assn. Energy Engrs. (charter), Internat. Acad. Mgmt. and Mktg., Nat. Right to Life, Assn. Cogeneration Engrs. (charter), Assn. Environ. Engrs. (charter), Am. Legion (past comdr.), Acad. Mgmt., Madeira Civic Assn. (past v.p.), Cin. Art Mus., Cin. Zoo, Colonial Williamsburg Found., Omicron Delta Epsilon. Republican. Home and Office: 7208 Sycamorehill Ln Cincinnati OH 45243-2101

ANDERSON, JEWELLE LUCILLE, musician, educator; b. Alexandria, La., Jan. 4, 1932; d. William Andrew and Ethel Dee (Hall) A. Student, Springfield Coll., 1981-82; MusB, Boston U., 1984; postgrad., Harvard U., 1995-96. Cert. music and social studies tchr., Mass. Soloist Ch. of the Redeemer Episcopal Ch., Chestnut Hill, Mass., 1964-69, St. James Episcopal Ch., Cambridge, Mass., 1970-75; kindergarten tchr. and music dir. Trinity Episcopal Ch., Boston, 1984-86; chorus music dir. Spencer for Hire, Boston, 1986; music dir. Days in the Arts summer program Boston Symphony Orch.,

Tanglewood, Mass., summer 1991, 92; chorale dir. Boston Orch. Chorale, 1996-97; music tchr. Phyllis Wheatley Middle Sch., 1996—; tchr. scholar Harvard Grad. Sch. of Edn., 1998-99; founder Jewelle Anderson Found., Inc., Boston, 1996. Vol. ARC, Boston, 1994—; bd. dirs. Mattapan Cmty. Health Ctr., Boston, 1990-92; founder, pres. Dr. William and Ethel Hall Anderson Scholarship, 1989—. Recipient Am. Music award Nat. Fedn. Music, 1970, Spl. Individual award Nat. Fedn. Music, 1969, Outstanding Contbn. to Humanity award Alexandria Civic Improvement Coun., 1967, Outstanding Achievement award Boston Tchrs. Union, 2000, Cope Plaque for Outstanding Achievement Boston Tchrs. Union, 2000. Mem. AAUW, Amnesty Internat., Black Educators Alliance of Mass., 464 Women Svc. Club (head youth group 1989—), Alpha Kappa Alpha. Democrat. Baptist. Avocations: walking on the shore, boating. Office: Jewelle Anderson Found Inc PO Box 1181 Boston MA 02103-1181

ANDERSON, JOAN BALYEAT, religion educator, minister; b. Cin., Apr. 14, 1926; d. Hal Donal and Myrtle (Skinner) Hukill Balyeat; m. Jerry William Anderson, Jr., Sept. 13, 1947: children: Katheleen, Diane. AA, Stephens Coll., 1946. Ordained Christian minister, Ohio, 1988. Christian ch. bible tchr. Cin., 1944—, Christian counselor, advisor, 1964—; founder, pres., dir., ruling elder, and pastor Loving God "Complete Bible" Christian Ministries and First Ch., Cin., 1988—; Christian Bible tchr., preacher, pastor daily and Sunday radio throughout the east and midwest, 1988—. Coord., collector Heart Fund, T.B., 1948-90; civic assn. officer, rep. edn. com. to all Madeira Schs., 1960-62; co-founder, officer Grassroots, Inc., Cin., 1962-65; mem. U.S. Rep. Senatorial Adv. Com., Washington and Cin., 1987-88; mem. Rep. Senatorial Commn., Washington and Cin., 1996-2000; mem. Cin. Art Mus., 1972—, Cin. Zoo, 1974—, Colonial Williamsburg Found., 1979—, Nat. Right to Life, 1980—, MADD, 1985—, Heritage Found., 1996—, Am. Conservative Union, 1998—, Ronald Reagan Presdl. Found., 1998—, Parents TV Coun., 1998—, Am. Prayer Network, 1998—, Am. Policy Ctr., 1998—, U.S. Justice Found., 1998—, Nat. Right to Work Legal Def. Found., 1998—, Nat. Security Ctr., 1998—, U.S. Intelligence Ctr., 1998—, Christian Action Network, 1999—, American Policy Ctr., 1999—, Citizen's United Found., 1999—, Patrick Henry Ctr., 1999—, Capitol Hist. Soc., 2000—, Am. Civil Rights Union, 2000—, Young Amercan's Found., 2000—; lifelong activist for preservation of U.S. Constitution and Bill of Rights. Mem. Blue Book of Cin. Avocations: touring America by car. Home: 7208 Sycamorehill Ln Cincinnati OH 45243-2101 Office: Loving God Complete Bible Christian Mins/1st Ch PO Box 43404 Cincinnati OH 45243-0404

ANDERSON, JOEL E., JR., university administrator; b. Newport, Ark., Jan. 20, 1942; s. Joel E. Sr. and Norris Hall Anderson; m. Ann Gaskill, Aug. 7, 1964; children: Lincoln Jay, Deverick John, Mitchell Reid. BA, Harding Coll., 1964; MA, Am. U., 1966; PhD, U. Mich., 1974. Instr. polit. sci. Harding Coll., 1966-67; from asst. to assoc. prof. U. Ark., Little Rock, 1971-81, prof., 1981—, dean grad. sch., 1977-84, vice chancellor, provost, 1984—, interim chancellor, 1993; pres. univ. assembly U. Ark., 1974-76; mem. vis. com. coll. bus. Abilene Christian U., 1994-97, chair, 1997; cons.-evaluator commn. instns. higher edn. North Ctrl. Assn. Colls. and Schs., 1994—; study dir. Plain Talk: The Future of Little Rock's Public Schools, 1997. Editor Ark. Polit. Sci. Rev., 1979-82. Charter mem. bd. trustees Kidney Found. Ark., 1975-79; mem. Pulaski County Bd. of Election Commrs., 1976-79; mem. bd. overseers Sta. KLRE-KUAR-FM, 1986-90; bd. dirs. Ark. 4-H Found., 1997—, Ark. Sci. and Tech. Authority, 1998—, Ark. Symphony Bd., 1999—. Mem. Am. Assn. State Colls. and Univs. (mem. acad. affairs resource ctr. adv. com. 1994-98), Ark. Polit. Sci. Assn. (pres. 1975), Rotary, Alpha Chi, Phi Kappa Phi. Mem. Ch. of Christ. Office: U Ark Office of the Provost 2801 S University Ave Little Rock AR 72204-1099*

ANDERSON, JOHN, Australian deputy prime minister; b. Nov. 14, 1956; s. D.A. Anderson; m. Julia Gillian Robertson, 1987; two children. Student, U. Sydney. Former farmer and grazier; MP for Gwydir NSW, Australia; dep. leader NPA; shadow min. for Primary Industry, 1993-96, min. for primary industries and energy march, from 1996; now dep. prime min. Govt. of Australia, Canberra. Mem. Nat. Party Australia. Avocations: farming, shooting, reading, photography. Office: Dept Prime Minister, Ste MG8 Parliament House, Canberra ACT 2600, Australia*

ANDERSON, SIR JOHN ANTHONY, bank executive; b. Wellington, New Zealand, Aug. 2, 1945; m. Carol M. Anderson, 1970; 3 children. Student, Christ's Coll., Victoria U., Wellington. With Deloitte Haskins & Sells, Wellington, 1962-69, Guest & Bell, Melbourne, Australia, 1969-72, South Pacific Merchant Fin. Ltd., Wellington, 1972—; CEO South Pacific Merchant Fin. Ltd., 1979—, also bd. dirs., 1979—; dep. CEO Nat. Bank New Zealand, 1988-90, CEO, bd. dirs., 1990—; chmn. New Zealand Merchant Banks Assn., 1982-90, Petroleum Corp. of New Zealand, Ltd., 1986-88, New Zealand Bankers Assn., 1992—; pres. New Zealand Bankers Inst., 1990—; bd. dirs. New Zealand Steel Ltd., 1986-87, Lloyds Merchant Bank, London, 1986-92, Lloyds Bank NZA, 1989-96, Internat. Cricket Coun., 1997—. Chmn. New Zealand Cricket Bd., 1995. Decorated knight comdr. Order Brit. Empire; recipient Commemoration medal, 1990. Fellow Inst. Chartered Accts. Avocations: rugby, cricket, golf, bridge. Home: 5 Fancourt St, Karori Wellington 5, New Zealand Office: The Nat Bank of New Zealand, 170-186 Featherston St, Wellington 6000, New Zealand

ANDERSON, KARL RICHARD, aerospace engineer, consultant; b. Vinita, Okla., Sept. 27, 1917; s. Axel Richard and Hildred Audrey (Marshall) A.; B.S., Calif. Western U., 1964, M.A., 1966; Ph.D., U.S. Internat. U., 1970; m. Jane Shigeko Hiratsuka, June 20, 1953; 1 son, Karl Richard. Engr. personnel subsystems Atlas Missile Program, Gen. Dynamics, San Diego, 1960-63; design engr. Solar divsn. Internat. Harvester, San Diego, 1964-66, sr. design engr., 1967-69, project engr., 1970-74, product safety specialist, 1975-78; aerospace engring. cons., 1979-86; cons. engring., 1979—; lectr. Am. Indian Sci. and Engring. Soc. Served to maj. USAF, 1936-60. Recipient Spl. Commendation award San Diego County Bd. Supervisors, 1985, Spl. Commendation award San Diego City Council, 1985, Spl. Commendation award City of San Diego, 1994, Grace "Peter" Sargent award San Diego City Natural Park, 1994. Registered profl. engr., Calif. Home: 5886 Scripps St San Diego CA 92122-3212

ANDERSON, KARL STEPHEN, editor; b. Chgo., Nov. 10, 1933; s. Karl William and Eleanor (Grell) a.; m. Saralee Hegland, Nov. 5, 1977; children by previous marriage: Matthew, Douglas, Eric. BS in Editl. Journalism, U. Ill., 1955. Successively advtsg. mgr., asst. to pub., then pub. Crescent Newspapers, Downers Grove, Ill., 1971-73; assoc. pub., editor Chronicle Pub. Co., St. Charles, 1973-80; assoc. pub. Chgo. Daily Law Bull., 1981-88; dir. comms., editor Ill. State Bar Assn., 1988—; past pres. Chgo. Pub. Rels. Forum. Trustee emeritus Chi Psi Edn. Trust; trustee Leo Sowerby Found.; bd. dirs. Ill. Press Found., Chgo. Legal Svcs. Found. Recipient C.V. Amenoff award No. Ill. U. Dept. Journalism, 1976, award Ill. State Bar Bd. Govs., 1987, Print Media Humanitarian award Coalition Sub Bar Assns., 1987, Robert C. Preble, Jr. award Chi Psi, 1991, Asian-Am. Bar Media Sensitivity award, 1991, Liberty Bell award DuPage County Bar Assn., 1993, Glass Ceiling Busters award Assn. Women Lawyers, 1993, Disting. Svc. award Chgo. Vol. Legal Svcs. Found., 1993, Gratitude award Lawyers Assistance Program, 1993, Outstanding Achievement in Comm. award Justinian Soc., 1994, 3rd prize Nat. Libr. Poetry, 1995, Svc. award Women's Bar Assn. Ill., 1998, Peoria County Bar Assn., 1998, Communicator of Yr. award Justinian Soc., 1999. Mem. Am. Judicature Soc. (sec. Ill. chpt.), Nat. Assn. Bar Execs., Baltic Bar Assn., Chgo. Legal Sec. Assn., Chgo. Press Vets. Assn. (bd. sec.), Ill. Press assn. (Will Loomis award 1977, 80), Kane County Bar Assn., DuPage Women Lawyers Assn., West Suburban Bar Assn., N. Suburban Bar Assn. (Pub. Svc. award 1997), Bohemian Lawyers Assn. (Liberty award 1999), No. Ill. Newspaper Assn. (past pres.), Pub. Rels. Soc. Ctrl. Ill. (Master Communicator award of achievement 1997), Soc. Profl. Journalists, Headline Club (past pres.), Nordic Law Club, Nellie Fox Soc., Chgo. Athletic Assn., Chi Psi. Home: 3180 N Lake Shore Dr Apt 14D Chicago IL 60657-4851 Office: Ill State Bar Assn 20 S Clark St Ste 900 Chicago IL 60603-1885

ANDERSON, KEITH GRAHAM, food technologist, consultant, educator; b. Kingston, Surrey, Eng., Sept. 13, 1939; s. Joseph and Catherine (Dollery) A.; m. Ann Margaret Southon, Aug. 29, 1964; 1 child, Ralph Graham. Licenciate in Biology, N.E. Surrey Coll., Ewell, Eng., 1963, M in Biology, 1971. Lab. technician Leatherhead (Surrey, Eng.) Food Rsch. Assn., 1958-62; works chemist Haywards Food Products Ltd., London, 1962-64; factory mgr., chief chemist Melbray Food Products Ltd., London, 1965-70; tech. mgr. Brooke Bond Oxo Ltd., Croydon, Surrey, Eng., 1970-75, quality control and process mgr., 1975-79, tech. svcs. mgr., 1984-89; group tech. mgr. Brooke Bond Group Plc, Croydon, 1979-84; chmn. Seasonal Products Ltd., Croydon, 1985-89; tech. mgr. regulatory affairs div. Brooke Bond Foods Ltd., Croydon, 1989-92; cons. Keith Anderson Svcs., Epsom Downs, Eng., 1993—; vis. prof. U. North London, 1997—; prin. cons. Ventress Tech. Svcs., Ltd., Cambridge, England, 1999—. Co-author: Food Industries Manual, 24th edit., 1997, Snack Foods, 1990, Vegetable Processing, 1991, Food Labelling, 2000; co-editor: Food and Drink Good Manufacturing Practice, 1987, 89, 91, Human Nutrition, 1992; series editor: Practical Approaches to Food Science and Technology, 1993; editor Food, Drinks and Drugs Industry Bull., 1993—. Bd. dirs., mem. coun. Food and Drink Fedn., London, 1991-96; trustee Inst. Food Sci. and Tech., London, 1991—, pres., 1993—. Named Personality of the Yr., Food Processing Jour., 1988. Fellow Inst. Food Sci. and Tech. (v.p. 1991—), Royal Soc. of Health; mem. European Food Law Assn., Inst. of Biology. Anglican. Avocations: motor racing, bridge, riding, boating, travel. Home and Office: 341 Reigate Rd, 341 Reigate Rd, Epsom Downs KT17 3LT, England

ANDERSON, KENNETH NORMAN, retired magazine editor, author; b. Omaha, July 10, 1921; s. Duncan McDonald and Letitia Jane (Steed) A.; m. Lois Elaine Harmon, Jan. 12, 1945; children: Eric Stephen, Randi Laine, Jani Jill, Douglas Duncan. Student, U. Omaha, 1939-41, Oreg. State Coll., 1943-44, Stanford U., 1944-45, Northwestern U. Coll. Medicine, 1945-46, U. Chgo., 1958-60. With U.S. Army Fin. Office, Nebr. and Mont., 1941-42; engring. aid U.S. Army C.E., Omaha, 1946; news editor Radio Sta. KOIL, Omaha, 1946-47; bur. mgr. Internat. News Svc., Omaha, 1947-56, Kansas City, Mo., 1947-56; spl. features editor Better Homes and Garden mag., 1956-57; assoc. editor Popular Mechanics mag., 1957-59; editor Today's Health mag., pub. by AMA, Chgo., 1959-65, Holt, Rinehart & Winston, N.Y.C., 1965-70; exec. dir. Coffee Info. Inst., N.Y.C., 1970-81; pres. Pubs. Editorial Svcs., Inc., Katonah, N.Y., 1981-90, The Editorial Guild, Inc., Katonah, N.Y., 1981-90; lectr. mag. writing New Sch. Social Research, 1959, NYU, 1960, Omaha U., 1961, Rennselaer Poly. Inst., 1964; cons. med. editor Ferguson Pub. Co., 1971-76. Author: (with others) Lawyers' Medical Cyclopedia, 1962, The Family Physician, 1963, Today's Health Guide, 1965, Pictorial Medical Guide, 1967, Field and Stream Guide to Physical Fitness, 1969, New Concise Family Medical and Health Guide, 1971, Complete Illustrated Book of Better Health, 1973, The New Complete Medical and Health Ency., 4 vols., 1977, The Sterno Guide to the Outdoors, 1977, Eagle Claw Fish Cookbook, 1978, Guide to Weight Control and Fitness, 1978, Newsweek Ency. of Family Health, 1980, Urdang Dictionary of Current Medical Terms, 1981, Pocket Guide to Coffee and Teas, 1982, Bantam Medical Dictionary, 1982, Mosby's Medical and Nursing Dictionary, 1982, Longman's Dictionary of Psychology and Psychiatry, 1983; editor: Hudson Health Newsletter, 1982—, Orphan Drugs, 1983, Gourmet Guide to Fish and Shellfish, 1984, Prentice-Hall Dictionary of Nutrition and Health, 1984, U.S. Military Operations, 1945-84, 1984, Mosby's Medical Encyclopedia, 1985, The Language of Sex, 1986, Industrial Medicine Desk Reference, 1986, New Pediatric Guide to Drugs & Vitamins, 1987, Symptoms after 40, 1987, Signet/Mosby Medical Encyclopedia, 1987, Consumer Guide Illustrated Medical Dictionary, 1988, Sex A to Z, 1989, Mosby's Medical, Nursing and Allied Health Dictionary, 4th edit., 1994, New York Public Library Desk Reference, 1989, Mosby's Pocket Dictionary of Medicine, Nursing and Allied Health, 1990, 2d edit., 1994, History of U.S. Military Operations Since World War II, 1992, History of the U.S. Marines, 1992, Internat. Menu Speller, 1993, Internat. Dictionary of Food and Nutrition, 1993, Mosby's Medical, Nursing & Allied Health Dictionary, 4th edit., 1994 (Am. Jour. Nursing Book Yr. award 1994), 5th edit., 1998; Mosby's Pocket Medical Dictionary of Medicine, Nursing and Allied Health, 2d Edition, 1994, Wordsworth Dictionary of Sex, 1994, 3d edit. 1998; contbr. Grolier, Funk & Wagnalls Encys.; adv. editor Nutrition Today, 1965-75. Home and Office: 1278 Kingswood Blvd Mountain Home AR 72653-8083

ANDERSON, KENNETH PAUL, nephrologist, administrator; b. Council Bluffs, Iowa, June 17, 1952; s. Kenneth Paul and and Kathleen Marie (Wyckoff) A.; m. Elizabeth Stephens, July 1, 1985; children: Jennifer, Cassie, Zach. BS with honors, U. Iowa, 1974; DO, Coll. Osteo. Medicine, Des Moines, 1978; MS, U. Wis., 1996; cert., Harvard U., 1993. Diplomate Am. Bd. Family Practice. Resident, chief resident Luth. Hosp.-U. Iowa, Des Moines, 1978-81, Norwalk (Conn.) Hosp.-Yale U., 1981-83; fellow in nephrology, clin. instr. U. So. Calif., L.A., 1983-85; med. dir. Mercy Hosp., Iowa Luth. Hosp., Des Moines, 1985-96; clin. instr. Coll. Osteo. Medicine, Des Moines, 1986-96; chief of staff Mercy Hosp. Med. Ctr., Des Moines, 1992-94; sec., bd. officers Iowa Luth. Hosp., Des Moines, 1989-90; chief med. officer Ptnrs. Nat. Health Plans, South Bend, Ind., 1996—; chmn., mem. ESRD Network # 12 of HCFA, Kansas City, 1984-95; pres., CEO Nephrology and Internal Medicine Specialists, Des Moines, 1985-96; med. dir. SecureCare of Iowa, Des Moines, 1992-96. Contbr. articles to profl. jours. Bd. dirs. Iowa State Bd. of Health, Des Moines, 1993-96; cons. Nat. Health Policy Adv. Team, Washington, 1989-94, Ind. Perinatal Task Force, 1997—. Fellow Am. Acad. Family Practice; mem. AMA, Am. Soc. Hypertension, Am. Coll. Physician Execs., Am. Soc. Nephrology, Iowa Osteo. Med. Assn. Democrat. Roman Catholic. Avocations: camping, blues music, fishing, biking, writing short stories. Home: 11034 Birch Lake Dr E Granger IN 46530-6013 Office: Meml Hosp and Health System 615 N Michigan St South Bend IN 46601-1033

ANDERSON, KYM, economics educator; b. Adelaide, Australia, Feb. 26, 1950; s. Max and Olive Lilian (Fuller) A.; m. Bronwyn Margaret Nankivell, Jan. 12, 1974; children: Kirsty Jane, Peta Kim, Philippa Claire. B. AG. EC., U. New Eng., Armidale, Australia, 1971; M. Ec., U. Adelaide, 1974; MA, U. Chgo., 1975; MA, PhD, Stanford U., 1977. Cert. economist. Agrl. economist S. Australia Dept. Agr., Adelaide, 1971-74; rsch. fellow dept. econs. Rsch. Sch. Pacific/Asian Studies Australian Nat. U., Canberra, 1977-83; sr. lect. dept. econs. U. Adelaide, 1984-90, prof. dept. econs., 1991—; found. dir. Centre for Internat. Econ. Studies Centre for Internat. Econ. Studies, U. Adelaide, 1989—; counselor Econ. Rsch. and Analysis Divsn. Gen. Agreement on Tariffs and Trade, Geneva, 1990-92; dispute settlement panelist World Trade Orgn., 1996-97; cons. World Bank, 1979—. Author: Political Economy of Agricultural Protection, 1986 (Tohata Meml. award 1987), Australian Protectionism, 1987, Growth, Structural Change and Economic Policy in Papua New Guinea, 1989, Changing Comparative Advantages in China, 1990, Effects of Liberalizing Trade in Farm Products, 1991, Disarray in World Food Markets, 1992; editor: New Silk Roads, 1992, The Greening of World Trade Issues, 1992, Regional Integration and the Global Trading System, 1993, Strengthening the Global Trading System, 1996. Recipient Sir John Crawford award, 1987. Fellow Acad. of Social Scis. in Australia; mem. Australian Agr. and Resource Econs. Soc. (pres. 1996-97). Mem. Uniting Ch. of Australia. Avocations: tennis, viticulture/winemaking. Home: PO Box 262, Hahndorf 5245, Australia Office: U Adelaide, Ctr Internat Econ Studies, Adelaide 5005, Australia

ANDERSON, LINDA JEAN, critical care and psychiatric nurse; b. Louisville, Ky., Mar. 28, 1956; d. James Phillip and Ellabelle Jean (Crowder) Anderson; children: Bradley, Vanessa, Frances, Joseph; m. Donald W. Goodman. BSN, U. Louisville, 1989, MSN, 2000. RN, Ky. Staff nurse Audubon Regional Med. Ctr., Louisville, 1989-90; nurse clinician Visiting Nurses Assn. Louisville, 1990-95; staff nurse Southwest Hosp., Louisville, 1990-2000; rsch. coord. electrophysiology-cardiology U. Louisville, 1993-94; staff nurse Ctr. for Behavioral Health Bapt. East Hosp., 1996-2000. Mem. alumni bd. govs. U. Louisville Sch. Nursing, 1988-97. Mem. Sigma Theta Tau. Avocations: watercolor painting, charcoal & pencil sketching, poetry, flute. Home: 2234 S Preston St Apt 2 Louisville KY 40217-1987

ANDERSON, LLOYD LEE, animal science educator; b. Nevada, Iowa, Nov. 18, 1933; s. Clarence and Carrie G. (Sampson) A.; m. Janice G. Peterson, Sept. 7, 1958 (dec. Dec. 1966); m. JaNelle R. Hall, June 15, 1970; children: Marc C., James R. Student, Simpson Coll., 1951-52, Iowa State U., 1952-53; BS in Animal Husbandry, Iowa State U., 1957, PhD in Animal Reproduction, 1961. NIH postdoctoral fellow Iowa State U., Ames, 1961-62, asst. prof., 1961-65, assoc. prof., 1965-71, prof. animal sci., 1971—, Charles F. Curtiss Disting. prof. agr., 1992—; Lalor Found. fellow Sta. Recherches Physiologie Animale, Inst. Nat. Recherche Agronomique, Jouy-en-Josas, France, 1963-64; rschr. physiology of reprodn. and cen. nervous sys.-pituitary regulation of growth for increased prodn. efficiency of farm animals: mem. reproductive biology study sect. NIH, 1984-88, NIH Reviewers Res. (NRR), 1988-92; mem. peer rev. panel animal health spl. rsch. grants on beef and dairy cattle reproductive diseases USDA, 1986-88; Honor lectr. representing Iowa State U., Mid-Am. State Univs. Assn., 1989-90; mem. sustainable agrl. panel U.S. Dept. Agr., Agrl. Rsch. Svc., Nat. Program Staff to rev. rsch. projects, 1993; mem. referees panel for sponsored rsch. Kuwait U., 1998—; mem. Janice Peterson Anderson Excellence award and scholarship Coll. of Design, Iowa State U. Mem. editl. bd. Biology Reprodn., 1968-70, 86-90, Jour. Animal Sci., 1982-87, 98—, Animal Reprodn. Sci., 1978—, Inst. for Sci. Info. Atlas of Sci., 1987-90, Domestic Animal Endocrinology, 1992-95, Endocrinology, 1993-97; contbr. articles to profl. jours. Mem. 4-H Club. With Constrn. Engrs., U.S. Army, 1953-55, Germany, Signal Corps USAR, 1955-61. Decorated Good Conduct medal, Nat. Def. Svc. medal Army of Occupation (Germany); USDA grantee, 1978—. Fellow AAAS, Am. Soc. Animal Sci. (hon. Animal Physiology and Endocrinology award 1988, Nat Pork Prodrs. Coun. Innovation award in basic rsch. 1993); mem. ACLU, NRA, VFW, Endocrine Soc., Am. Physiol. Soc., Iowa Physiol. Soc., Am. Assn. Anatomists, Soc. for Study of Reprodn., Soc. for Exptl. Biology and Medicine (mem. coun. 1980-83), Brit. Soc. for Study of Fertility, Soc. for Neurosci., Iowa Acad. Sci., Pituitary Soc., Am. Legion, Nat. Block and Bridle Club, Osborn Rsch. Club (chair 1994), Sigma Xi, Gamma Sigma Delta. Methodist. Home: 2812 Valley View Rd Ames IA 50014-4506 Office: Iowa State U Dept Animal Sci 2356 Kildee Hl Ames IA 50011-0001

ANDERSON, MARY ELIZABETH, protection services official; b. Flint, Mich., Sept. 12, 1949; d. Buford Herbert and Florence Mary (DuPrey) A. AB, U. Mich. Flint, 1976. Lic. social worker, Mich. From residence dir. to cmty. affairs dir. YWCA Greater Flint, 1977-84; dep., sgt. Genesee County Sheriff Dept., Flint, 1984-96, lt., 1996—. Mem. Criminal Justice Women of Mich. (award 1995), Planned Parenthood USA, So. Poverty Law Ctr., Hope United Meth. Ch., U. Mich. Alumni Assn. Home: 3926 Arlene Ave Flint MI 48532-5263 Office: Genesee County Sheriff Dept 1002 S Saginaw St Flint MI 48502-1410

ANDERSON, MAXWELL L., museum director; b. N.Y.C., May 1, 1956. AB, Dartmouth Coll., 1977; AM, Harvard U., 1978, PhD, 1981. Asst. curator Met. Mus., 1982-87; dir. Michael C. Carlos Mus., Atlanta, 1987-95, Art Gallery Ont., Toronto, Can., 1995-98, Whitney Mus. Am. Art, N.Y.C., 1998—; lectr. Roman art Princeton (N.J.) U., 1985; vis. prof. U. di Roma, 1987; adj. assoc. prof. Emory U., 1989—. Arranged exhbns. Treasures of the Holy Land, 1986, Roman Portraits in Context, 1988, Souls Grown Deep, 1996, Wired Mus., 1997, 2000 Biennial Exhbn. Mem. Am. Assn. Mus., Coll. Art Assn., Assn. Art Mus. Dirs. Office: Whitney Mus Am Art 945 Madison Ave New York NY 10021-2701

ANDERSON, MICHAEL STEVEN, lawyer; b. Mpls., May 25, 1954; s. Wesley James and Lorraine Kathrine (Sword) A.; m. Gail Karin Miller, June 18, 1977; children: Mark, Steven. BA magna cum laude, Cornell U., 1976; JD, Washington U., St. Louis, 1980. Bar: Wis. 1980, U.S. Dist. Ct. (ea. and we. dists.) Wis. 1980, U.S. Ct. Appeals (7th cir.) 1986, U.S. Supreme Ct. 1991. Ptnr. Axley Brynelson, Madison, Wis., 1980—; gen. counsel DEC, Internat., Inc., 1992—. Editor, author Washington U. Law Quarterly, 1979-80. Apptd. mem. local Bd. Attys. Profl. Responsibility, 1993—. Mem. Am. Corp. Counsel Assn., Lic. Exec. Soc., Order of Coif. Mem. Evangelical Free Ch. Avocation: family. E-mail: manderson@axley.com. Home: 5882 Timber Ridge Trail Madison WI 53711-5180 Office: Axley Brynelson 2 E Mifflin St Madison WI 53703-2889

ANDERSON, MICHAEL STUART, rubber company executive; b. Johannesburg, South Africa, Mar. 13, 1946; s. Nigel Iivari and Aileen Mary (Redman) A.; m. Diana Marian MacKenzie, Apr. 6, 1972; children: Catherine, Samantha, Karen. Grad, St. John's Coll., Johannesburg, 1963. Dir. Transvaal Rubber Group, Johannesburg, 1976—, mng. dir., 1980—, chmn., 1997—. Democrat. Anglican. Avocation: nature conservation. Office: PO Box 1969, Johannesburg 2000, South Africa

ANDERSON, NANCY KATHERINE, career development consultant; b. Mpls., Mpls., Apr. 17, 1948; d. Robert V. and Kathleen M. (Kanz) A.; divorced. Student, Cardinal Stritch Coll., Milw., 1966-69; BS in Psychology, George Washington U., 1979; MPA, U. Colo., 1982. Trainer, career cons. GAO, Washington, 1970-80; prin., career cons. Nancy K. Anderson & Assocs., Denver, 1980-83; mgr. mgmt. devel. Anderson Clayton Foods, Dallas, 1983-85; mgr. tng. and devel. Anchor Hocking Corp., Lancaster, Ohio, 1985-87; prin. NAW Career Assocs., Canoga Park, Calif., 1987-89; mgr. sales ops. Sebastian Internat., Woodland Hills, Calif., 1989-91; prin. Nancy K. anderson & Assocs., Woodland Hills, 1991-96; sr. performance devel. splst. Health.Net, Woodland Hills, 1996—. Contbr. articles to profl. jours. Founder ICO Brittany Found., Canoga Park, 1993—; sec.-treas., bd. dirs. Prestonwood Green Condo Assn., 1984-86; chiar women's adv. bd. to Comptroller Gen. U.S., 1977-79; mem. EEO adv. coun. GAO, 1977-78. Recipient EEO award Comptroller Gen., 1977, cert. of merit GAO, 1978, 79, others. Mem. Am. Soc. Tng. and Devel. (award 1984), Internat. Soc. Performance and Instrn. Avocations: tennis, animal advocacy, environmental advocacy. Home: 20944 Elkwood St Canoga Park CA 91304-5118 Office: 21600 Oxnard St Woodland Hills CA 91367-4976

ANDERSON, NILS, JR., former government official, retired business executive, industrial historian; b. Plainfield, N.J., Jan. 28, 1914; s. Nils and Marguerite (Stephens) A.; m. Jean Derby Ferris, July 30, 1938. Grad., Lawrenceville and Loomis Schs.; BA, Williams Coll., 1937; postgrad., Colo. Sch. Mines, George Washington U. Law Sch., Alexander Hamilton Inst. With Debevoise-Anderson Co., summers 1927-28; cadet engr. S.S. Iron Ranger Isthmian Steamship Co., summer 1930; cadet engr., chemist Koppers Co., Pitts., summers 1932-37; sales engr. Bakelite Corp., 1937-41; adv. chem. divsn., adminstr. War Prodn. Bd., 1941-45; adminstr. chief adhesives sect., govt. presiding officer Industry Adv. Com., 1942, adminstr. chief plastics br., 1944; v.p. Casein Co. Chem. divsn. Borden Co.; founder Alba S.A. Borden Co., Brazil, 1945-49; founder Casco, S.A. Borden Co., Argentina, 1945-49; pres. Debevoise-Anderson Co. Inc., 1950-60, chmn., CEO, 1965; pres. Fairfield Sales, 1950; organizer mining cos., P.R., Chile, Peru, Brazil, Angola, 1955-65, Cia Minera, Dominican Republic, C PorA, Dominican Republic; adv. chemical divsn. U.S. Dept. Agr. stockpile and shipping br., adhesive and plastic, textile, paper and pulp, plywood and furniture industry adv. coms., 1941-44; mem. 1st U.S. trade mission to Ea. Europe, 1965. Author: North American Coke Today, Chemicals, Metals and Men; contbr. tech. articles on plastics and adhesives to profl. jours. and encyclopedias. Trustee, pres. U.S. Naval War Coll. Found., 1988-89; trustee Wakeman Meml. Assn. Southport, Conn.; past pres. Sasquanaug Assn., Southport; founder, past chmn. Southport Conservancy. Mem. ASME, Coke Oven Mgrs. Assn. (England), Am. Chem. Soc., Iron and Steel Engrs. Assn., Am. Coke and Coal Chemicals Inst. (hon.), Newcomen Soc. in N. Am., Gen. Soc. Colonial Wars, Soc. of War of 1812, Pilgrim Soc., Pa. Soc., Pequot Yacht Club (Southport), Fairfield (Conn.) Country Club, Univ. Club (N.Y.C.), Links Club (N.Y.C.), Alpha Delta Phi. Republican. Episcopalian. Avocations: golf, writing.

ANDERSON, PARKER LYNN, editorial columnist, playwright; b. Wickenburg, Ariz., Apr. 19, 1964; s. Harry Milton and Darla Raejean (Hangartner) A. Mem. prodn. com. Prescott (Ariz.) Fine Arts Assn., 1993-95, 98—, adv. mem., 1987—; columnist, theatre critic The Prescott News, 1995-96; with Cath. Social Svc. of Yavapai, 1983—; mem. adv. com. The Blue Rose Theatre Co., Prescott, 1994—; guest on talk shows Sta. KUSK-TV, 1991—. Author: (plays) The Startled Cowboys, 1991, Voices From the Past, 1995, The Sleeping Toad, 1997, Virgil Earp, 1998, Until the Last Dog is Hung, 2000; freelance guest columnist and letters of comment in numerous Ariz. pubs., 1990—; pub. Roasting Roderick. Home: PO Box 1285 Prescott AZ 86302-1285

ANDERSON, PATRICIA SUE, writer; b. San Springs, Okla., July 14, 1940; d. John Monroe and Annabelle A. Degree in psychology, Okla. State U., 1963. C.E.O. Rivers Bend Lit. Agy., Cleve., 1984-99; CEO River's Bend Literary Agy., Cleveland, Okla., 1984-99. Author: Organizational Handbook, 1985, Campaign Organization, 1990, Getting Women to Participate, 1991. Democrat. Methodist. E-mail: pander86245@aol.com. Home and Office: RR 1 Box 272 Cleveland OK 74020-9723

ANDERSON, PAUL ALEXANDER, environmental scientist, biochemist; b. Glencoe, Argyll, Scotland, Mar. 27, 1953; s. James Alexander and Jean Jeffrey (Brown) A.; m. Sandra Russell, Aug. 21, 1973 (div. Mar. 1992); m. Margaret Helen Dewar, May 20, 1994. BSc in Chemistry with honors, Paisley (Scotland) Coll., 1976, PhD in Biochemistry, 1979. Biochemist DCL, Menstrie, Scotland, 1979-86, propagation mgr., 1986-92; svcs. mgr. Quest Internat., Menstrie, 1992-93, project mgr., 1993-95, environ. mgr., 1995—. E-mail: paul.anderson@questintl.com. Home: Moorgait, Kippen, Stirling FK8 3HS, Scotland Office: Quest Internat, Menstrie, Glenochil Yeast Factory, Clackmannanshire FK11 7ES, Scotland

ANDERSON, PAUL MILTON, steel company executive; b. Richland, Wash., Apr. 1, 1945; s. Paul Milton and Elfrieda (Blehm) A.; m. Kathleen Sue Kinzel, Feb. 25, 1984; children: Wendy Christine, Heather Colleen. BSME, U. Wash., 1967; MBA, Stanford U., 1969. Mgr. product planning Ford Motor Co., Dearborn, 1969-77; various positions Tex. Eastern Corp., Houston, 1977-85, v.p., 1985-87, sr. v.p., 1987-89; v.p. fin., chief fin. officer Inland Steel Industries, Chgo., 1990-91; exec. v.p. Panhandle Eastern Corp., 1991-94, pres., 1994—; pres. Panhandle Eastern Pipe Line Co., 1991—; pres., CEO Panenergy (named changed Duke Energy), Houston, 1991-97; pres., COO Duke Energy, 1997-99; CEO BHP, Inc., Melbourne, Australia, 1999—. Mem. Interstate Natural Gas Assn. Am., Inst. Gas Tech. Office: BHP Corporate Offices, 600 Bourke St, Melbourne VIC 3000, Australia

ANDERSON, PAUL SCOTT, architect; b. L.A., Oct. 28, 1958; s. Gordon John and Ruth Ellen Anderson; m. Hai Rui Wu, May 28, 1999; 1 child, Kalli Bryce. BArch, Calif. Poly. State U., 1984. Lic. arch., Calif. Sole practice La Quinta, Calif., 1991-96; prin. Shenzhen Ocean Pearl Co. Ltd./Mission Hills Group, China; program mgr. hotel architecture Walt Disney Co., Anaheim, Calif., 1998—. Mem. design rev. bd. City of La Quinta, 1991-94, mem. planning commn., 1994-96. Recipient award Desert Beautiful, Palm Desert, Calif., 1986, Award Mention Bien Ecoles D'art Americaines Fontainbleau, 1983. Mem. AIA (bd. dirs. Calif. Desert chpt. 1989-90, assoc. dir. South Calif. Coun. 1987, bd. dirs. Monterey Bay chpt. 1987). Avocations: golf, tennis, photography, painting, percussion.

ANDERSON, PETER G., mathematician; b. Bay City, Mich., Jan. 3, 1940; m. Jane Boyd; children: Scott, Julie. BS, MIT, Cambridge, Mass., 1962; PhD, MIT, 1964. Prof. Rochester Inst. Tech., N.Y., 1980-99. Mem. IEEE, Fibonacci Assn. (treas. 1998—). E-mail: anderson@cs.rit.edu. Fax: 716475-7100. Office: Rochester Inst Tech 102 Lomb Memorial Dr Rochester NY 14623-5608

ANDERSON, RAYMOND QUINTUS, diversified company executive; b. Jamestown, N.Y., Nov. 27, 1930; s. Paul N. and Cecille (Ogren) A.; m. Sondra Rumsey, June 5, 1954; children: Heidi, Kristin, Gerrit, Mitchell, Tracy, Brooks. Grad., Phillips Acad., Andover, Mass., 1949; BS in Engring., Princeton U., 1953; postgrad., Sloane Sch., MIT, MIT. With Dahlstrom Corp., Jamestown, 1957-76, exec. v.p., 1965, pres., 1968-76; founder, pres. Aarque Steel Corp., Jamestown, 1976-78, Aarque Mgmt. Corp., Jamestown, 1978-96; founder, chmn. Aarque Cos., Jamestown, 1980-96, Aarque Capital Corp., 1996—; bd. dirs. Oneida Ltd., Bus. Coun. N.Y. State, Inc., Cold Metal Products Co., Inc., Aarque Steel Group, Kardex Sys., Inc.; trustee Northwestern Mut. Life Ins. Co. Patentee in field. Chmn. Jamestown United Fund drive, 1964, 74; bd. dirs. N.Y. State Dept. Environ. Conservation; dir. Oneida, Ltd.; trustee Roger Tory Peterson Inst., Chautauqua Found. Inc.; civilian aide to Sec. of the U.S. Army; mem. adv. bd. World Econ. Forum. Served with USNR, 1954-57. Mem. Mfrs. Assn. Jamestown Area (pres. 1967-68), Empire State C. of C. (pres. 1974-76), Royal Round Table of Swedish Coun. Am., U.S. Can. Trade Coun., U.S. Dept. Commerce Ind. Sector Adv. Com., Tau Beta Pi. Republican. Episcopalian. Clubs: Moon Brook Country (Jamestown); Sportsmen's (Chautaqua, N.Y.); Union League Met. (N.Y.C.). Address: 20 W Fairmont Ave Lakewood NY 14750-0109

ANDERSON, REID BRYCE, performing company executive; b. New Westminister, B.C., Can., Apr. 1, 1949; s. Warren Nels and Phyllis Jessie Bryce (Purser) A. Student dance, Dolores Kirkwood, Burnaby, B.C., Royal Ballet Sch., 1967, 68. Dancer Stuttgart (Fed. Republic Germany) Ballet, 1969-86, prin. dancer, 1975-86, ballet master, 1982-86; artistic dir. Ballet B.C., Vancouver, 1987-89, Nat. Ballet Can., Toronto, Ont., 1989—, Stuttgart Ballet, 1996—. Choreographer numerous works for performing cos. Decorated Order of Fed. Republic Germany, 1986; recipient 1995 John Cranko prize for svc. to Art of Classical Ballet and in particular teaching, coaching and maintaining the work of the late John Cranko around the world. Office: The Stuttgart Ballet, Obere Schlossgarten 6, 70173 Stuttgart Germany

ANDERSON, REX ALBERT, accountant; b. Waikari, New Zealand, Aug. 24, 1926; s. Albert George and Isabel Mary (Jarden) A.; m. Lucy Jean Munn Anderson, Mar. 3, 1951 (div. 1976); children: Grant Stewart, Gail Jeanette; m. Beverley Yvonne Shaw Anderson, Dec. 3, 1978 (widowed Jan. 12, 1992); m. Patricia Lynn Spence Anderson, Feb. 28, 1997. BCOM, Canterbury U., Christchurch, New Zealand, 1945; MCOM, 1947. Chartered accountant, New Zealand Inst. Chartered Accts. Prin. Chartered Acct. in Pub. Practice, Christchurch, New Zealand, 1954-70; sr. ptnr. RA Anderson & Knox, Christchurch, New Zealand, 1970-72; ptnr. Price Waterhouse, Christchurch, New Zealand, 1972-93; chmn. Accting. Rsch. and Standards Bd., New Zealand Soc. Accts., 1983; pres. New Zealand Soc. Accts., 1984-85, Fedn. Asian and Pacific Accts., Manilla, 1988-89; coun. mem. Internat. Fedn. Accts., N.Y., 1985-88; commr. New Zealand Securities Commn., 1986-96. Sec. Track and Field Control Group 1974 British Commonwealth Games, Christchurch, New Zealand, 1974, New Zealand Games, Christchurch, New Zealand, 1976; mem. bd. govs. Avonside Girls H.S., Christchurch, New Zealand; chmn. Banks Ave. Sch. Com., Christchurch; chmn. fin. com. Christchurch City Mission, New Zealand, 1997—; trustee Christchurch City Mission Found.; chair cmty. adv. bd. Pegasus Med. Group. Fellow New Zealand Inst. Chartered Accts. (past pres. 1984-85), New Zealand Order of Merit, Canterbury Univ. Alumni Assn. (pres. 1998-2000). Avocations: opera, literature, rugby union football, tennis, general fitness. Home and Office: 25 Helmores Ln, Christchurch, Fendalton New Zealand

ANDERSON, RICHARD THEODORE, association executive, urban planner; b. Bklyn., Oct. 11, 1940; s. Charles Theodore and Lillian Elizabeth (Holmlin) A.; m. Anasta Frank, Oct. 3, 1970; childre; Erik Theodore, Leslie Elisabeth. AB, Rutgers U., 1962; M of Regional planning, Cornell U., 1964; postgrad., NYU, 1964-67. Pres. Regional Plan Assn., N.Y.C., 1964-92; exec. dir. The Dallas Plan, Dallas, 1993-94; pres., CEO N.Y. Bldg. Congress, N.Y.C., 1994—; pres. N.Y. Bldg. Found., N.Y.C., 1998—; vis. assoc. prof. dept. city & regional planning Pratt Inst., N.Y.C., 1974-92; chmn. Pres.' Coun. N.Y.C. Planning & Design Orgns., 1982-92. Bd. dirs. Water Resources Assn. Delaware River Basin, 1977-80, United Way, Pelham, N.Y., 1977-79; v.p., trustee Big Bros./Big Sisters, N.Y.C., 1969—, Audrey Cohen Coll., 1998—; mem. coll. adv. coun. Cornell U. Coll. Architecture, Art and Planning, 1984-94; mem. Village Planning Bd., Pelham, 1977-80; mem. Times Sq. Adv. Coun., N.Y.C., 1985-89; dir. Regional Alliance Small Contractors, 1994—; dir. ACE Mentorship Program, 1997—, Bklyn. Sports Found., 1998—; mem. Bus. Coun. N.Y. State, N.Y.C. Partnership; co-chmn. N.Y. chpt. Rebuild Am. Coalition. Recipient Ellis Island medal of honor, 1995; Vis. scholar NYU, 1992. Fellow Am. Inst. Cert. Planners; mem. Am. Planning Assn. (dir. and treas. 1978-80, pres. 1980-81, Disting. Svc. award 1985), Am. Soc. Planning Ofcls. (bd. dirs. 1977-78), N.Y. Soc. Assn. Execs., Urban Land Inst., N.Y. Acad. Scis., Met. Leadership Network, Ellis Island Medal of Hon. Soc., Rutgers Alumni Assn. (Loyal Son award 1989), N.Y.C. C. of C., Bklyn. C. of C., Empire State Transp. Alliance. Lutheran. Home: 235 Monterey Ave Pelham NY 10803-2329 Office: NY Bldg Congress 44 W 28th St New York NY 10001-4212

ANDERSON, ROBERT EDWARD, lawyer; b. Spokane, Wash., Sept. 25, 1928; s. Ewald Godried and Hazel L. A.; m. Audrey May, Nov. 29, 1947; children: Mark, Eric, Kent, Carl. B in Law, Gonzaga U., 1950, LLB, 1954, JD, 1967. Bar: Wash. 1954, U.S. Dist. Ct. (ea. dist.) Wash. 1954, U.S. Supreme Ct. 1966. Pvt. practice Spokane, 1954—. Recipient Silver Beaver award Boy Scouts Am., 1976, Lamb award Nat. Luth. Ch. Am., 1980. Mem. Kiwanis Internat. (lt. gov. 1967). Lutheran. Office: 2032 W Northwest Blvd Spokane WA 99205-3715

ANDERSON, ROBERT GEOFFREY WILLIAM, museum director; b. London, May 2, 1944; s. Herbert Patrick and Kathleen Diana (Burns) A.; m. Margaret Elizabeth Callis Lea, Mar. 31, 1973; children: William Thomas Edmund, Edward Tobias Gilbert. BA (converted to MA 1972), U. Oxford, Eng., 1967, BSc, 1968, D Philosophy, 1972; DSc (hon.), U. Edinburgh, Scotland, 1995. Asst. keeper Royal Scottish Mus., Edinburgh, Scotland, 1970-75, dir., 1984-85; asst. keeper Sci. Mus., London, 1975-80, keeper, 1980-84; dir. Nat. Mus. Scotland, Edinburgh, 1985-92, Brit. Mus., London, 1992—. Author: The Playfair Collection, 1978, (catalogue) Science in India, 1982, Science, Medicine and Dissent, 1987; editor: The Early Years of the Edinburgh Medical School, 1976, Making Instruments Count, 1993. Recipient Dexter award Am. Chem. Soc., 1986. Fellow Royal Soc. Chemistry, Soc. Antiquaries London, Soc. Antiquaries Scotland, Royal Soc. Edinburgh; mem. Internat. Union of History and Philosophy of Sci. (pres. sci. instrument comm. 1982—), Brit. Soc. History of Sci. (pres. 1988-90). Club: Athenaeum (London). Office: Brit Mus, Great Russell St, London WC1B 3DG, England

ANDERSON, ROBERT HENRY, pathology educator; b. Wellington, Salop, Eng., Apr. 4, 1942; s. Henry and Doris Amy (Callear) A.; m. Christine Ibbotson, July 9, 1966; children: Elizabeth Jane, John Robert. BSc, U. Manchester, Eng., 1963, MB, BChir, 1966, MD, 1970. Lectr. U. Manchester, 1967-72; MRC travelling fellow U. Amsterdam, 1973; sr. lectr. Nat. Heart and Lung Inst., London, 1974-77, reader, 1977-80, prof., 1980-99; prof. Inst. Child Health, U. Coll., London, 1999—; hon. cons. Brompton Hosp., London, 1974—; hon. sr. lectr. Hosp. For Sick Children, London, 1982—; hon. clin. prof. U. N.C., Chapell Hill, 1984—; hon. vis. prof. U. Liverpool, 1973—; hon. vis. prof. U. Pitts., 1984—. Author: Cardiac Anatomy, 1980, Pathology of Congenital Heart Disease, 1981, Pathology of Conduction System, 1983, Paediatric Cardiology (2 vols.) 1987; editor Internat. Jour. Cardiology, 1983-90; editor-in-chief Cardiology in the Young, 1990—; contbr. articles to profl. jours. Recipient Excerpta Media award Excerpta Medica, Amsterdam, 1977, Thomas Lewis lectr. and medal Brit. Cardiac Soc., 1978, Brit. Heart Found. prize for cardiovasc. rsch., 1984. Fellow Royal Coll. Pathologists London; mem. Brit. Cardiac Soc., Anat. Soc. U.K., Royal Soc. Medicine U.K., Pathol. Soc. U.K., Roehampton Club, Walton Heath Club, Saintsbury's Club. Socialist. Home: 60 Earlsfield Rd, Wandsworth, London SW18 3DN, England Office: Inst Child Health, 30 Guilford St, London WC1N 1EH, England

ANDERSON, ROBERT JOHN, electronic engineer; b. Birmingham, Eng., June 1, 1952; s. Alan John and Helen Audrey (Yapp) A.; m. Michèle Jacqueline Kurasch, Aug. 3, 1978; children: Poul Howard, Yan Mark. BSEE, U. Birmingham, 1973, MS in Comms. Engring., 1975. Chartered engr. Sci. officer Govt. Comms. Hdqs., Cheltenham, Eng., 1979; sr. programmer Racal Redac Ltd., Tewkesbury, Eng., 1979-82; sr. profl. and tech. officer Joint European Torus, Abingdon, Eng., 1982-87; group leader accelerator tech. group Oxford (Eng.) Instruments, 1987-98; freelance cons. radio frequency power, 1998—. Active Vol. Svcs. Overseas Royal Lao Broadcasting Corp., Pakse, Laos, 1973-74. Mem. IEE. Achievements include development of radio frequency acceleration system for world's first compact superconducting synchotron. Avocations: windsurfing, amateur radio. E-mail: bob@scilutions.com. Home and office: Trinafour Abingdon Rd, Marcham Abingdon OX13 6NU, England

ANDERSON, ROBERT MONTE, lawyer; b. Logan, Utah, Feb. 19, 1938; s. E. LeRoy and Grace (Rasmussen) A.; m. Kathleen Hansen, Aug. 12, 1966; children: Jennifer, Katrina, Alexander. AB, Columbia Coll., 1960; LLB, U. Utah, 1963. Bar: Utah 1963, U.S. Cir. Ct. Appeals (10th cir.) 1967, U.S. Supreme Ct. 1976. Assoc., shareholder, v.p. Van Cott, Bagley, Cornwall & McCarthy, Salt Lake City, 1963-82; pres., shareholder Berman & Anderson, Salt Lake City, 1982-86; v.p., shareholder Hansen & Anderson, Salt Lake City, 1986-90; pres., shareholder Anderson & Watkins, Salt Lake City, 1990-95; pres. Anderson & Smith, Salt Lake City, 1995-97; lawyer, shareholder, pres. Van Cott, Bagley Cornwall & McCarthy, Salt Lake City, 1998—; bd. dirs., mem. exec. com. Anderson Lumber Co., Ogden, Utah, 1982-2000. Trustee The Children's Ctr., Salt Lake City, 1973-77; pres. Utah Legal Svcs., Salt Lake City, 1979. Mem. ABA, Utah State Bar Assn. (cts. and judges com. 1991-99), Alta Club, Cottonwood Club, Rotary. Avocations: tennis, skiing. Office: Van Cott Bagley Cornwall & McCarthy 50 S Main St Ste 1600 Salt Lake City UT 84144-2044

ANDERSON, ROGER CLARK, biology educator; b. Wausau, Wis., Oct. 30, 1941; s. Jerome Alfred and Virginia Stella (Hoffman) A.; m. Mary Rebecca Blocher, Aug. 5, 1967; children: John Allen, Nancy Lynn. BS magna cum laude, La Crosse State Coll., 1963; MS, U. Wis., 1965, PhD, 1968. Asst. prof. So. Ill. U., Carbondale, 1968-70; arboretum dir. U. Wis., Madison, 1970-73, assoc. prof., 1970-73; assoc. prof. Cen. State U., Edmond, Okla., 1973-76; disting. prof. Ill. State U., Normal, 1976—; mem. Ill. Nature Preserves Commn., 1985-90; mem., chmn. PARKNET adv. com. Fermilab, Batavia, Ill., 1986-93. Editl. bd. Jour. Restoration Ecology, 1992; author: Environmental Biology, 1970; author: (with others) Fire in North American Tallgrass Prairie, 1990, Grasses and Grasslands Systematics and Ecology, 1982, Phenology and Seasonality Modeling, 1974; editor: (with others) Savannas, Barrens, and Rock Outcrop Plant Communities of North America, 1999; contbr. 80 articles to profl. jours. Pres. Parkland Found. Bd., McLean County, Ill., 1987—. Named McMullen lectr. Monmouth Coll., 1983. Fellow Ill. Acad. Sci.; mem. Ecol. Soc. Am., Soc. for Ecol. Restoration, Am. Bot. Soc., Kappa Delta Pi. Achievements include research on the role of fire in native grassland and savannas, on the relationships between native prairie plants and mycorrhizae fungi. E-mail: rcander@ilstu.edu. Home: 14 Mccormick Blvd Normal IL 61761-1537 Office: Ill State U Biology Dept Normal IL 61761

ANDERSON, STEPHEN JOHN, foreign service officer; b. Jeffersonville, Ind., Feb. 22, 1957; s. William Alex and Rosemary A. BA, Oberlin (Ohio) Coll., 1979; MS, MIT, Cambridge, Mass., 1983, PhD, 1987. Asst. prof. U. Wis., Madison, 1987-93; assoc. prof. Internat. U. Japan, Tokyo, 1994-97; comml. officer US & F CS, Beijing, China, 1998—; rsch. assoc. Temple U. Japan, Tokyo, 1997—; cons. USIS/Fulbright Assn., Manila, The Philippines, 1995, NHK, Tokyo, 1995-97. Author: Welfare Policy and Politics in Japan: Beyond the Developmental State, 1993 (Masayoshi Ohira Meml award, 1995); contbr. articles to profl. jours. Dir. World Wide Web Sight, Inforum Project, 1994-95; spkr. Am. C. of C. in Japan, 1994-97, Fgn. Corr. Club in Japan, Tokyo, 1995-97; mem. Internat. House of Japan, Tokyo, 1987-97. Named Oberlin Shansi rep. Oberlin Shansi Meml. Assn., 1979, Acad. Assoc. Program on U.S. -Japan Rels., Harvard U., Cambridge, 1987-88; fellow Japan Found., Tokyo, 1983; Fulbright Grad. Fellow, Japan, 1985-86. Avocations: jogging, travel. Home e-mail: sjanderson@alum.mit.edu. Office e-mail: SAnderson@es.doc.gov. Fax: 86-10 6532 3297. Office: US Embassy Beijing, # 3 Xiu Shui Bie Jie, Beijing 100600, China

ANDERSON, STEPHEN MILLS, investment broker; b. Portland, Maine, Jan. 14, 1946; s. Stuart Mills and Elaine (Crommett) A.; m. Mary Elizabeth Carter, Aug. 23, 1969; children: Melissa Carter, Hope Stuart. BA, Ohio U., 1969. Dir. admissions, dir. devel., dir. alumni affairs Gould Acad., Bethel, Maine, 1973-76; investment broker Burbank & Co., Portland, 1976-82, office mgr., 1978-82; investment broker, office mgr., v.p. A.G. Edwards & Sons, Portland, 1982—, sr. v.p., 1996—; former pres. Stroudwater Corp.; mem. dirs. coun. A.G. Edwards and Sons; chmn. adv. coun. The Capital Group, L.A. Trustee Tilton Sch.; trustee Maine Med. Ctr., 1990, bd. corporators; bd. dirs. Brighton Med. Ctr. Found., 1992-96; chmn. ann. fund Maine Med. Ctr.; mem. adv. bd. Baxter State Park. Mem. Nat. Assn. Registered Reps., Cumberland Club, Masons, Portland Country Club, Severance Lodge Club. Home: PO Box 1437 Yarmouth ME 04096-2437 Office: 2 Portland Sq Portland ME 04101-4088

ANDERSON, STUART CHARLES, pharmacy researcher; b. Birkenhead, Merseyside, Eng., Oct. 7, 1946; s. Eric Charles and Nora (Armstrong) A.; m. Christine Louise Twine, Nov. 20, 1971 (div. July 1979); 1 child, Nicholas; m. Margaret Elizabeth Goodwill, Sept. 19, 1981; children: Claire, Richard, Martin. BSc with honors, U. Manchester, Eng., 1969; diploma in pub. adminstrn., U. London, 1981, MA, 1983, PhD, 2000. Prin. pharmacist Aldey Hey Children's Hosp., Liverpool, Eng., 1974-78; chief pharmacist Westminster Hosp., London, 1978-83; dir. pharmacy svcs. St. George's Hosp., London, 1983-93; lectr. pharmacy practice Sch. Pharmacy U London, 1993-94; rsch. fellow London Sch. Hygiene and Tropical Medicine, London, 1995-96, instr. pub. health and policy, 1996—; ptnr. Thames Technician Tng., London, 1991-99. Author: A Formulary of Paediatric Preparations, 1977; editor: Alder Hey Book of Children's Doses, 2d and 3d edits., 1976, 79; mem. editl. bd. St. George's Hospital Pharmacopoeia, 10th, 11th and 12th edits., 1985, 88, 91; columnist "Anna Lytical" column in Pharmacy Mgmt., 1990—. Recipient Evans Gold medal Guild of Hosp. Pharmacists, London, 1994; ICI Travelling fellow Guild of Hosp. Pharmacists, Australia, 1986, med. fellow Coun. of Europe, Stockholm, 1991; Sonnedecker Residency fellow Am. Inst. History of Pharmacy, 1996. Mem. Royal Pharm. Soc. (Eng.), Coll. Pharmacy Practice, Soc. for Social History of Medicine (treas.), Brit. Soc. for History of Pharmacy (v.p.), Am. Inst. History of Pharmacy. Avocations: maritime history, marine painting, model boat-building. Home: 19 Den Close, Kent Beckenham BR3 6RP, England Office: London Sch Hygiene and Tropical Medicine, Keppel St, London WCIE 7HT, England

ANDERSON, STUART JAMES, neuropsychologist; b. Edinburgh, Scotland, Mar. 26, 1960; s. Denis and Agnes Nan (Brown) A. BSc, U. Natal, 1981, BSc with honors, 1982, MSc, 1984, PhD, 1997. Clin. psychologist Dept. Health, Welfare, & Population Devel., South Africa, 1985-87; lectr., rschr. U. Natal, South Africa, 1987—; cons. clin. neuropsychologist Kwa Zulu-Natal Provincial Adminstrn., South Africa, 1984-2000. Mem. Internat. Neuropsychol. Soc., Br. Psychol. Soc., South African Clin. Neuropsychology Assn. Avocations: cycling, road running, gliding. Home: PO Box 28077 Haymarket, 3200 Pietermaritzburg South Africa

ANDERSON, SUSAN ELAINE MOSSHAMER, education and organizational consultant, musician; b. Detroit, Mar. 29, 1946; d. Edgar Lee and Reta (McDonough) Mosshamer; m. Thomas Scott Anderson Jr., Nov. 1, 1975; children: Elizabeth Erin, Kirk William. MusB with honors, Mich. State U., 1967; MEd with high honors, Wayne State U., 1982. Profl. singer (mezzo), pianist and organist, 1968—, sch. choral music dir. grades 7-12, 1968-77; instrnl. designer, orgnl. devel. cons. Myers-Briggs Adminstr., Ednl. Rschr., 1982—; pres. Orgl. Strategies Ltd., Bloomfield Hills, Mich., 1995—. Collaborating author: The Challenge of Living, 1983, Death and Dying, 1996; award-winning tng. programs for Ill. Dept. Employment Security and Ford/Lincoln-Mercury Dealerships. Vol. Roeper Sch., Bloomfield Hills, 1988-95, Cranbrook Schs., Bloomfield Hills, 1993—. Mem. ASCD, Problem-Based Learning Network, Assn. Psychol. Type, Mortar Board, Phi Kappa Phi. Avocations: skiing, reading, music.

ANDERSON, THOMAS, dean, computer engineering consultant; b. Newcastle Upon Tyne, Eng., July 24, 1947; s. Frederick and May (Barrett) A.; m. Patricia Ormston, Aug. 14, 1968; children: Iain, Claire. BSc, U. Newcastle, 1968, PhD, 1972. Rsch. assoc. U. Newcastle, 1971-78; rsch. scientist NASA, Hampton, Va., 1978-79; lectr. U. Newcastle, 1979-85; rsch. engr. UCLA, 1985; prof. computing sci. U. Newcastle, 1986-92, head, computing sci., 1992-97, dean of sci., 1998—; chmn. IEEE TC on fault tolerance, 1986-87; dir. Ctr. Software Reliability, 1983—. Editor 14 books, 1979—; co-author: Fault Tolerance, 1981, 90; contbr. over 125 scientific publs. Fellow BCS. Avocations: hill walking, playing the organ. Office: U Newcastle, CSR Bedson Bldg, Newcastle NE1 7RU, England

ANDERSON, BROTHER TIMOTHY MEL, academic administrator; b. Oakland, Calif., Sept. 28, 1928. BA, St. Mary's Coll., Moraga, Calif., 1952; DLitt, St. Albert's Coll., 1976; LHD, Lewis U., 1979; DHL (hon.), U. San Francisco, 1994; D in Pedagogy (hon.), Manhattan Coll., 1994. Tchr. Sacred Heart High Sch., San Francisco, 1952-56; vice prin. La Salle High Sch., Pasadena, Calif., 1956-62; prin. San Joaquin Meml. High Sch., Fresno, Calif., 1962-64; prin., superior St Mary's High Sch., Residence Sch., Grammar Sch., Berkeley, Calif., 1964-69; pres. St. Mary's Coll. of Calif., Moraga, 1969-97; dir. spl. projects Diocese of Oakland, Calif., 1999—. Trustee St. Mary's Coll., Moraga., 1968-97. Recipient Alemany award Dominican Sch. of Theology and Philosophy, 1992, Papal Pro Ecclesia medal, 1994, Disting. Lasallian Educator award, 1997; named Alumnus of Yr., St. Mary's Coll., 1987; inductee Contra Costa County Hall of Fame, 1988, Anti-Defamation League's Torch of Liberty award, 1993; named Citizen of Yr. town of Moraga, 1994. Fellow Assn. Ind. Calif. Colls. and Univs. (sr.; exec. com. 1973—, chmn. 1988, 89); mem. Regional Assn. East Bay Colls. and Univs. (chmn. 1979-81, 90-91), Fratres Scholarum Christianarum (entered order 1947). Democrat. Roman Catholic. Lodge: Rotary Internat. Avocations: photography, woodworking, travel, drama, music. Office: Oakland Diocese 2900 Lakeshore Ave Oakland CA 94610-3614

ANDERSON, VINTON RANDOLPH, bishop; b. Somerset, Bermuda; came to U.S., 1947; m. Vivienne Louise Cholmondeley, 1952; children: Vinton Jr., Jeffrey, Carlton, Kenneth. BA, Wilberforce U., HHD (hon.), 1973; MDiv, Payne Theol. Sem., 1952; MA in Philosophy, Kans. U., 1962; postgrad., Yale U. Div. Sch.; DD (hon.), Paul Quinn Coll., Payne Theol. Sem., Temple Bible Coll., Interdenom. Theol. Sem., Eden Theol. Sem.; LHD (hon.), Morris Brown Coll., ITC Seminary, Eder Theol. Ordained to ministry A.M.E. Ch., 1952, bishop, 1972. Pastor various chs. in Kans. and Mo., 1952-72; presiding bishop A.M.E. Ch., Ala., 1972-76; presiding bishop, chief pastor A.M.E. Ch., Ohio, W.Va., Western Pa., 1976-84; dir. Office of Ecumenical Rels. and Devel. A.M.E. Ch., 1984-88, presiding bishop 5th Episcopal dist., 1988-96; presiding bishop 2nd Episcopal district A.M.E. church, Washington D.C., 19965; chmn. bd. dirs. Payne Theol. Sem., Xenia, Ohio; preacher, lectr. in Caribbean, Republic of South and West Africa, Middle East, Europe, South Pacific; del. World Meth. conf., Nairobi, Kenya, 1986; mem. exec. com. World Meth. Coun., 1981—, 1st v.p. N.Am. region; v.p. Consultation on Ch. Union; mem. Gen. Commn. Christian Unity and Interreligious Concern, United Meth. Ch.; pres. World Coun. Chs., 1991—, del. 7th assembly, moderator liaison com. of hist. black chs.; mem. governing bd., faith and order Nat. Coun. Chs.; charter mem., v.p. Congress Nat. Black Chs. Founder, editor Connector, info. publ.; editor A Syllabus for Celebrating the Bicentennial; contbr. articles to profl. jours. Mem. nat. adv. com. on the black population 1990 U.S. Census; mem. Nat. Commn. on Sch./Community Role in Improving Adolescent Health; mem. nat. adv. bd. Schomburg Ctr. for Rsch. in Black Culture; immediate past chairperson bd. trustees Wilberforce U.; chairperson bd. dirs. Payne Theol. Sem. Recipient Ann. Religion award Ebony mag., 1988, Disting. Alumni Honoree award Nat. Assn. for Equal Opportunity in Higher Edn., 1991. Home: 1134 11th St NW Washington DC 20001 Office: AME Ch 2562 Martin Luther King Jr Ave Washington DC 20020-5247*

ANDERSON, WILLIAM CARL, association executive, environmental engineer, consultant; b. Vinton, Iowa, Sept. 24, 1943; s. Ivan D. and Lois B. (Schlotterback) A.; m. Elizabeth A. Dingman, Nov. 12, 1966; children: William Carl III, Erica Dawn. BSCE, Iowa State U., 1967. Registered profl. engr., N.Y., N.J., Pa., Iowa; diplomate Am. Acad. Environ. Engrs. Dir. environ. health Cayuga County Health Dept., Auburn, N.Y., 1969-73; owner Pickard & Anderson, Auburn, 1973—; trustee Am. Acad. Environ. Engrs., Annapolis, Md., 1982-85, exec. dir., 1985—. Editor: Environmental Engineer, 1985—. Gen. chmn. Cayuga County United Way, 1982, exec. com., 1982-84, bd. dirs., 1981-84; health and safety com. Cayuga County council Boy Scouts Am., 1969-83; parish council Sacred Heart Parish, 1981-82; bd. dirs. YMCA-WEIU Cayuga County, 1982-85. Served with USNR, 1967-69. Recipient Recognition award United Way, 1982; named Honorable Conceptor, Mich. Cons. Engrs. Council, 1983. Fellow ASCE (Outstanding Service award 1981, 86); mem. Am. Water Works Assn., Air Waste Mgmt. Assn., Assn. Environ. Engring. Profs., NSPE, N.Y. Soc. Profl. Engrs., N.Y. Water Pollution Control Assn. (Lewis Van Carpenter award 1974), Water Environment Fedn. (Philip F. Morgan medal 1973), Buick Club Am. (bd. dirs. 1996—), Chi Epsilon. Republican. Roman Catholic. Office: Am Acad Environ Engrs 130 Holiday Ct Ste 100 Annapolis MD 21401-7003

ANDERSON, WILLIAM HENRY, psychobiologist, educator; b. Phila., Nov. 10, 1940; s. William Henry Schoen and Elizabeth Winifred (Laverty) A.; m. Catherine Sacchetti, Oct. 7, 1967 (dec. Sept. 1991); 1 child, Jennifer Ann Gist. B.S., MIT, 1962; M.A., U. Pa., 1967; M.D., Thomas Jefferson U., 1967; M.P.H., Harvard U., 1977. Diplomate: Am. Bd. Psychiatry and Neurology. Intern. Pa. Hosp., Phila., 1967-68; resident in psychiatry Mass.

Gen. Hosp., Boston, 1968-71, assoc. psychiatrist dept. psychiatry, 1976-97, sr. psychiatrist, 1998—, dir. postgrad. edn., 1976-81; instr. psychiatry Harvard U., Boston, 1973-75, asst. prof., 1975-81, asst. clin. prof., 1981-82, lectr., 1982—; chmn. psychiatry St. Elizabeths Hosp., Boston, 1981-92; dir. clinical svcs. Augusta Mental Health Inst.; asst. attending psychiatrist Mclean Hosp., Belmont, Mass.; Cons. Scientists' Inst. Pub. Info.; mem. Carnegie Coun. Ethics and Internat. Affairs. Contbg. editor: The New Physician, 1977-79; editorial bd. Topics in Geriatrics, 1981-87, Jour. Geriatric Psychiatry and Neurology; co-author: (with M.T. McGuire) The U.S. Healthcare Dillema, 1999. Served to lt. comdr., M.C. USNR, 1971-73. Fellow Am. Psychiat. Assn., Human Biology coun.; mem. AAAS, Am. Acad. Clin. Psychiatrists, Internat. Soc. Polit. Psychology, Coun. on Fgn. Rels. (lectr. to coms.), Med. Assn. P.R. (hon.), Mass. Med. Soc., Soc. Ethnobiology, U.S. Naval Inst., Boston Athenaeum (proprietor), Harvard Club of Boston, Union Club, Sigma Xi. Office: 34 Coolidge Hill Rd Cambridge MA 02138-5527

ANDERSON, WILLIAM ROBERT, pathologist, educator; b. Kittanning, Pa., Jan. 26, 1929; s. John Dickson and Amelia Caroline (Haferland)A.; m. Lorna McLeod, June 15, 1951 (div. 1974); children: Caroline Elizabeth Anderson Fraser, Frederick Charles; m. Carol Jane (Gorder) Tammen, Nov. 1975. BA, U. Rochester, 1951; MD, U. Pa., 1958. Asst. pathologist Mount Sinai Hosp., Mpls., 1964-67; dir. anatomic pathology Hennepin County Med. Ctr., Mpls., 1967-84, chief of pathology, 1984-95; prof. pathology U. Minn. Sch. of Medicine, Mpls., 1975—; pathology cons. Hennepin County Med. Ctr., 1997—. Contbr. numerous articles to profl. publs. Writer Habitat for Humanity, Twin Cities, 1995—; ch. coun. mem. Mt. Calvary Luth. Ch., Excelsior, Minn., 1996-99. Lt. (j.g.) USN, 1951-54. Fellow Coll. of Am. Pathologists; mem. Internat. Acad. of Pathologists, Soc. for Diagnostic Ultrastructural Pathology, Phi Beta Kappa, Sigma Xi. Lutheran. Avocations: history, travel, swimming, tennis. Home: 5725 Merry Ln Excelsior MN 55331-3310

ANDERSON, WILLIAM ROBERT, physicist; b. Moline, Ill., Nov. 7, 1950; s. Clair Howard and Mary Louise (Tingle) A.; m. Judy Ann Reber, June 16, 1983; 1 child, Jessica K. BA, Augustana Coll., 1972; PhD, Tex. A&M U., 1977. Postdoctoral assoc. Ballistic Rsch. Lab., Aberdeen Proving Ground, Md., 1977-78; rsch. physicist Chem. Systems Lab., Aberdeen Proving Ground, 1978-79, Army Rsch. Lab., Aberdeen Proving Ground, 1979—. Contbr. articles to Jour. Chem. Physics, Combustion and Flame, other sci. publs. Mem. Am. Phys. Soc., Combustion Inst., Phi Lambda Upsilon (chpt. v.p. 1974-75, pres. 1975-76). Achievements include development of detection methods for various flame molecules, study of detailed combustion chemistry of nitrogen oxides. Office: AMSRL-WM-BD Aberdeen Proving Ground MD 21005

ANDERSON-GINGOLD, ROSALIND GAYE, accountant; b. Singapore, Sept. 9, 1965; d. Ray Thomas and Margaret Elizabeth (Geach) Anderson; m. Lawrence Howard Anderson-Gingold, July 9, 1994; 1 child, Elizabeth Daisy. Diploma in Microcomputing, Canberra Inst. Technology, Australia, 1983; BComm, Australian Nat. U., 1988. Chartered acct., Australia. Rschr. Commonwealth Pub. Svc., Canberra, 1983-87; taxation cons. Arthur Andersen & Co., Sydney, 1987-90; mgr. Rost & Kitchener, Sydney, 1990-91; acctg. mgr. Time-Life Internat., London, 1991-94; sr. acct. Children's TV Workshop, N.Y., 1994-95; ind. cons. in technology N.Y., 1996-99; registered tax agt., Australia, 1991—. Mem. Australian Liberal Party, Sydney, 1999—; com. mem. Brit. Conservative Party, London, 1991-94; br. pres. Australian Young Liberals, Canberra, 1984-86; scout leader Australian Scouting Movement, Canberra, 1983-85, rover 1988-91; student rep. Faculty of Econs. and Commerce, Australian Nat. U., Canberra, 1986. Mem. Australian Soc. Chartered Accts. in Am. (exec. com. Am. Soc. Australia), Inst. Chartered Australian Accts. Avocations: music, theatre, tennis, travel, golf.

ANDERSSON, DAVID STEN, economist; b. Rossön, Sweden, July 11, 1944; s. Albert Nils and Anna Evelina (Almqvist) A.; m. Gun Brunnstedt, Feb. 18, 1978; children: Per, Ola. BS, Stockholm U., 1969; grad., Nat. Def. Acad., Stockholm, 1980; grad. health econs. of pharms., Stockholm Sch. Econs., 1996. Ofcl. Supreme Comdr.'s Staff, Stockholm, 1970-72, head divsn., 1972-78, dep. dir.-gen., 1978-83, spl. investigator, 1983-87; head divsn. Nat. Corp. Swedish Pharmacies, Stockholm, 1988-98; dir. governmental affairs AstraZeneca, Södertälje, Sweden, 1998—; Mem. commn. Ministry of Commerce, Stockholm, 1990, Ministry of Agr., Stockholm, 1990, Ministry of Fin., Stockholm, 1991-97, Ministry of Social Affairs, Stockholm, 1996-97, Ministry of Def., Stockholm, 1972-83. Lt. inf. Swedish Armed Forces, 1965-91. Author: Drugs Reimbursement, 1996, Drugs in Europe, 1998. Mem. Rotary Internat. Office: AstraZeneca Sweden Inc, Kvarnbergagatan, SE 15185 Södertälje Sweden

ANDERSSON, EDWARD WILHELM, law educator; b. Helsinki, Finland, Dec. 31, 1933; s. Herbert and Gundel (Granit) A.; m. Gunnel Ingeborg Westerlund, Dec. 7, 1957; children: Agneta, Robert, Karin. LLM, U. Helsinki, 1954, lic. law, 1955, D of Law, 1962; D of Law honoris causa, U. Stockholm, Sweden, 1984; D of Economy honoris causa, U. Gothenburg, Sweden, 1978. Asst. prof. U. Helsinki, 1958-62, prof. pub. law, 1963-98, vice rector, 1971-83, prof. emeritus, 1999—; bd. dirs. on numerous companies and founds. Contbr. articles to profl. jours. Chmn. Grankulla City Coun., 1977—, mem., 1969—; chmn., mem. several Finnish Govtl. coms. Recipient Hallbergska priset Svenska Litteratursällskapet Finland, 1963, K.J. Ståhlberg award Finnish Lawyers Union, 1995. Mem. Nordic Coun. Tax Rsch. (chmn. 1973-82), Soc. Sci. Fennica, Sci. Acad. Finland, Norwegian Acad. Sci. Svenska Folkpartiet. Avocations: walking, sailing, tennis. Home: Kavallvagen 25A, 02700 Grankulla Finland

ANDERSSON, EGIL ANDERS DANOLD, education educator; b. Lidköping, Sweden, Dec. 2, 1933; s. Ejnar Natanael and Naemi H.F. (Gustafsson) A.; m. Maria Lawenius; 1 child, Urban. BSc, Göteborg U., 1967, Lic. Philosophy, 1970, PhD, 1983, Docent, 1997. Registered psychologist, 1978. Asst. lectr. dept. psychology Göteborg U., 1965-71; rsch. psychologist Sahlgren U. Hosp., Göteborg, 1971-72; county chief edn. psychologist Mariestad, Sweden, 1972-76; rsch. grantee dept. edn. Göteborg U., 1978-79, dir. rsch., 1979—, sr. lectr., 1987-98, assoc. prof., 1998—. Author: Teacher's Conceptions of Teaching, 1983; contbr. articles to profl. jours. Platoon comdr. Royal Göta Army, 1962-63. Mem. Swedish Assn. Univ. Lectrs., Swedish Psychol. Assn., Royal Swedish Automobile Club. Avocation: genealogy. Home: Enbärsvägen 16, SE 43491 Kungsbacka Sweden Office: Göteborg U, Dept Edn Box 300, SE 40530 Göteborg Sweden

ANDERSSON, GÖRAN SVEN ARNE, museum director; b. Göteborg, Sweden, May 19, 1943; m. Ulla Andersson, June 10, 1972; children: Maria, Kerstin. PhD, U. Göteborg, 1980. Dir. Mus. Natural History, Göteborg, 1989—. Office: Mus Natural History, Box 7283, S-40235 Göteborg Sweden

ANDERSSON, HAKAN, mathematician; b. Stockholm, Apr. 13, 1964; s. Bengt and Heidi (Martykan) A.; m. Sima Bastani Andersson, July 4, 1987; children: Emanuel, Elias. BS, Stockholm U., 1987, PhD, 1994. Lectr. Stockholm U., 1987-92; mathematician Nat. Sec. Agy., 1992-95; rschr. Stockholm U., 1995-99; risk analyst Swedbank, 1999—. Contbr. articles to profl. jours. Fellow Grand Lodge Sweden. Avocations: piano, sports. Home: Odlingsvagen 1, S-170 77 Solna Sweden Office: Swedbank, Group Fin Risk Control, S-105 34 Stockholm Sweden

ANDERSSON, HELEN DEMITROUS, artist; b. Kotzebue, Alaska, Sept. 9, 1958; d. Thomas Wade Sr. and Rose (Koonook) Sours; m. Kent Gregor Andersson, June 17, 1981; children: Jason Ray, Gwendolyn Joyce Field. Student, U. Fairbanks, 1980, U. Hilo, Hawaii, 1981. Co-owner River City Billiards, Anchorage, 1981—; Exhibited works in Anchorage Mus. History and Arts Show, Stephan Fine Arts, 1984. Recipient 1st pl. Alaska Silver Anniversary Juried Arts Show; Nana Regional Corp. grantee, 1981. Avocations: painting, drawing, carving. Home: PO Box 100565 Anchorage AK 99510-0565

ANDERSSON, HELGE INGOLF, mechanical engineering educator; b. Bergen, Norway, Mar. 18, 1952; s. Carl Axel and Else (Klanderud) A.; 1 child, Lill Ann. MSc, Norwegian Inst. Tech., 1975, Dr.ing., 1982. Engr. Norwegian Electricity Bd., Oslo, Norway, 1977-78; rsch. asst. Norwegian Inst. Tech., Trondheim, Norway, 1978-83, sr. lectr., 1984-85, prof., 1985—; postdoctoral Von Karman Inst., Brussels, 1983-84; chmn. Divsn. of Applied Mechanics, 1990-99, head dept. applied mechanics thermodynamics and fluid dynamics Norwegian U. of Sci. Tech., Trondheim, Norway, 1999—; hon. prof. U. Manchester Inst. of Sci. and Technology, Manchester, U.K., 1991. Contbr. articles to profl. jours. Rsch. fellowship Royal Norwegian Coun. for Scientific and Indsl. Rsch., 1983, Sci. fellowship NATO, 1991. Mem. ASME. Office: Norwegian U of Sci/Tech, Divsn Applied Mechanics, Trondheim N-7491, Norway

ANDERSSON, KARL GUNNAR, computer company executive; b. Flen, Sweden, July 22, 1939; s. Carl Harry and Anna Katarina (Johansson) A.; m. Elsa Lena Maria Trotzig, Sept. 15, 1967; children: Marten, Carin. BBA, U. Uppsala, Sweden, 1964; MBA, U. Stockholm, 1967. Mktg. mgr. Electrolux, Stockholm, 1970-74; dep. mng. dir. Grey Advt., Stockholm, 1974-79, mng. dir., 1979-88, chmn., 1988-92; exec. v.p. Swedbank, Stockholm, 1992-98, advisor, 1998-99; v.p. corp. comms. Net Insight, Stockholm, 1999—. Fellow Calif. State Coll., Long Beach, 1961. Avocations: shooting, golfing, history. Home: Norr Malarstrand 78, IV, 11235 Stockholm Sweden Office: Net Insight, Vastberga Alle 9, S-12614 Stockholm Sweden

ANDERSSON, KARL-HUGO SVANTE, mechanical engineer, consultant; b. Stockholm, Mar. 13, 1940; arrived in Switzerland, 1993; s. Svante Wiktor and Hilma Linea (Jönsson) A.; m. Inga-Britt Gimberg, 1963 (div. 1990); children: Rickard, Martin, Lars. MS in Mech. Engrng., Royal Inst. Tech., Stockholm, 1965, degree in papermaking tech., 1967; postgrad., Advanced Mgmt. Program, Harvard U., 1989. Sales engr. ABB Fläkt, Stockholm, 1965-70; mgr. engrng. dept. ABB Fläkt, Växjö, Sweden, 1970-78, sales mgr., 1978-81, tech. dir., 1981-84; exec. v.p. ABB Fläkt, Stockholm, 1984-89; pres. ABB Fläkt, Växjö, 1989-93; v.p. engrng. ABB Power Generation, Zürich; cons., 2000—; mem. various bd. dirs. of ABB Fläkt Group within and outside Sweden, 1985—; chmn. Inmotion Mobile Software Solutions. Contbr. articles to trade jours. and conf. procs. Regular, Swedish Army, 1959-60, Linköping. Mem. Tech. Assn. Pulp and Paper Industry, VVS-Tekniska Föreningen, Air Pollution Control Assn. Lutheran. Avocations: restoring old houses, history, travel, model-building. Home and Office: Schönenwerdstrasse 1, CH-8952 Schlieren Switzerland Office: ABB Enertech AG, Brunngasse 4, CH-8401 Winterthur Switzerland

ANDERSSON, LARS GÖRAN, oral maxillofacial surgeon, researcher, educator; b. Vingaker, Sweden, Mar. 16, 1950; s. Lennart and Ulrica (Larsson) A.; m. Karin BrittMarie Elmquist, Oct. 16, 1982; children: Hedvig, Elin, Gustav. DDS, Karolinska Inst., Stockholm, 1974, PhD, 1988. Gen. dentist Stockholm County Coun., 1974-77; resident oral and maxillofacial surgery Söder Univ. Hosp., Stockholm, 1977-81, Karolinska Inst., Huddinge, 1981-82; dept. specialist Eastman Inst., Stockholm, 1981-82; cons. oral and maxillofacial surgeon Ctrl. Hosp., Västerås, 1982-87, sr. cons. oral and maxillofacial surgeon, 1988—, program dir. postgrad. specialist tng. program, 1990—, chmn. dept. oral and maxillofacial surgery, 1992—; lectr. in field; presenter seminars in field; vis. prof. U. Tenn., Knoxville, 1992, 93; vis. lectr. U. Pa., Phila., 1990, Columbia U., N.Y.C., 1994; vis. cons. oral maxillofacial surgeon Al Zahra Hosp., United Arab Emirates, 1992—. Contbr. articles to profl. jours. Mem. Swedish Assn. Oral and Maxillofacial Surgeons, Swedish Dental Soc., Scandinavian Assn. Oral and Maxillofacial Surgeons, Internat. Assn. Dental Trauma Rsch., European Assn. Oral and Maxillofacial Surgeons, Acad. of Osseointegration. Avocation: sailing. Office: Central Hosp, Dept Oral/Maxillofacial Sur, S-721 89 Västerås Sweden

ANDERSSON, LENNART N.E., chemist, researcher; b. Lönneberga, Sweden, Aug. 17, 1937; s. Karl E. and Olga W. (Karlsson) A.; m. Margareta K. Konradsson, June 8, 1974; children: Maria, Charlotta. MSc Pharm., Uppsala U., 1969. Mgr. Kabi AB, Stockholm, 1969-72, Kabivitrum AB, Stockholm, 1973-90, Kabi Pharmacia AB, Stockholm, 1991-92; chemist Kabi Pharmacia AB, Uppsala, 1992-95; chemist Pharmacia & Upjohn, Uppsala, 1995-96, cons., 1997—. Mem. Swedish Acad. Pharm. Scis. Home: Vallstanasvagen 81, SE-19570 Rosersberg Sweden

ANDERSSON, PER LENNART, computer engineer, consultant; b. Phila., Nov. 12, 1929; s. Albin Julius and Anna Maria (Johanson) A.; m. Dorothy Jeanne Leonard, June 21, 1952; children: Russell Lennart, James Albin. BSME, U. Pa., 1953. Engr., project mgr. RCA, Camden, N.J., 1953-55; mgr. engrng. and product planning UNIVAC, Phila., 1955-62; rsch. mgr. electronics ANPA Rsch. Lab., Easton, Pa., 1962-64; ind. cons. Andersson Assocs., Paoli, Pa., 1964—; v.p. Mgmt. and Tech. Inc., Corona del Mar, Calif., 1965, Scriptomatic Corp., Phila., 1984; v.p. engrng. Orca Industries, Berwyn, Pa., 1982-83; bd. dirs. Small Bus. Devel. Coun., Chester County, Pa., 1990-95. Contbg. author: Automation in Electronics and Publishing, 1965, Technological Change in Publishing and Printing, McGraw-Hill Yearbook of Science and Technology, 1970; contbr. nearly 100 articles to psofl. jours.; inventor life-saving device for divers, logic keyboard for graphic arts applications, others. Mem. troop com. Boy Scouts Am., Berwyn, 1971-76. Avocations: travel, scuba diving, computers, investing, sailing. Address: PO Box 504 Paoli PA 19301-0504

ANDERSSON, PER SUNE, geologist; b. Harnosand, Sweden, Nov. 10, 1960; s. Sune and Gudrun (Nilsson) A.; m. Andrea Filyo, Mar. 27, 1991; two children. MSc, Stockholm U., 1985, PhD, 1991. Rsch. assoc. Calif. Inst. Technology, 1991-93; sr. rschr. Lab. for Isotope Geology, Stockholm, Sweden, 1994—. Mem. Am. Geophys. Union, Geochem. Soc. Office: Swedish Mus Natural History, Lab Isotope Geology # 50007, 10405 Stockholm Sweden

ANDERSSON, SVEN-OLOF, physician; b. Jonkoping, Sweden, Aug. 24, 1943; s. Bertil and Maria (Blom) A.; m. Gunborg Ohvall, 1969; children: Erika, Helena, Kristina. MD, U. Umea, Sweden, 1971, PhD, 1995. Diplomate in Family Medicine and Psychotherapy. Asst. physician U. Hosp. of Umea, 1970-74; family practitioner County Coun. of Vasterbotten, Vannas, 1974-82, Umea, 1982—; head of primary care Healthcare Dist. of Umea, Sweden, 1979-82, 88-92; head health ctr., 1993-96; tutor for trainees in family medicine, 1981—, dir. training 1985-89; counsellor Nat. Bd. Health and Welfare, Region of Umea, 1991—, trainer, supr. med. students, 1992-97, 2000, dir. postgrad. edn. in family medicine, 1998-2000; mem. expert com. on family medicine Nat. Bd. Health and Welfare, 1999—. Editor: Power and Suffering, 1990, Time and general practice consultations, aspects of length, attendance and quality, 1995; contbr. articles to profl. jours. on consultation, family medicine, stroke, rehabilitation, and psychosomatic problems. Fellow Swedish Assn. for Gen. Practice (postdoctoral com. 1995—); mem. Swedish Med. Assn. Avocations: music, choral singing, playing double-bass in a jazz orchestra. E-mail: svenolof.anderson@telia.com. Home: Stugvagen 8, S-90355 Umea Sweden Office: Mariehem Health Ctr, Morkullevagen 9, S-90651 Umeå Sweden

ANDERSSON, THORSTEN, retired language educator; b. Stora Åby, Sweden, Feb. 23, 1929; s. Gunnar and Hanna (Carlsson) A.; m. Margarete Schmitt, July 10, 1959; children: Gudrun, Björn. PhD, Uppsala (Sweden) U., 1965. Lectr. Swedish U. Münster, Germany, 1957-60; lectr. Scandinavian langs. Uppsala U., 1965-71, prof. Scandinavian langs., 1971-94. Editor Studia Anthroponymica Scandinavica, 1983—, Namn Och Bygd, 1985—; contbr. articles to profl. jours. Mem. Kungliga Vitterhets Historie och Antikvitets Akademien, Det Kongelige Danske Videnskabernes Selskab, Det Kongelige Norske Videnskabers Selskab. Home: Grönstensvägen 32, S 75241 Uppsala Sweden Office: Sem Nordisk Namnforskning, Box 135, S 75104 Uppsala Sweden

ANDJABA, MARTIN, ambassador. Permanent rep. of Republic of Namibia UN, N.Y.C. Office: Perm Missions of Rep of Namibia 135 E 36th St New York NY 10016-3404

ANDO, HIDEYA, cell biologist, biochemistry researcher; b. Nagoya, Japan, Oct. 3, 1960; s. Kunio and Nagako (Kameyama) A.; m. Keiko Takahashi, Dec. 15, 1985; children: Maaya, Saaya. BSc, Nagoya U., 1983; PhD, Kobe (Japan) U., 1995. Rschr. SUNSTAR Inc., Osaka, Japan, 1983-95, sr. rschr., 1996—; rschr. Kobe U. Sch. Medicine, 1987-95, vis. lectr., 1997—; guest rschr. NIH, Bethesda, Md., 1997. Contbr. articles to profl. pubs. including Jour. Lipid Rsch., Jour. Investigative Dermatology, others; patentee Japan. Mem. Japanese Soc. Investigative Dermatology (councilor 1996—, Bronze award 1991), Japanese Soc. Pigment Cell Rsch. (councilor 1994—), Japanese Cosmetic Sci. Soc. Avocations: song writing, playing guitar, travel. Office: SUNSTAR Inc, 3-1 Asahi-machi, Osaka Takatsuki 569-11, Japan

ANDO, HIRONOBU, medical educator, cardiologist; b. Kobe, Japan, Nov. 23, 1940; s. Masanobu and Chieko (Masai) A.; m. Mariko Fujiwara, Nov. 17, 1968; children: Aiko, Yasuhiro, Kenji. BS, Himeji Inst. Tech., 1962; MD, Kobe Med. Coll., 1966, PhD, 1971. Diplomate in internal medicine and cardiovasc. disease Am. Bd. Internal Medicine. Intern Kobe Univ. Hosp., 1966-67, instr. medicine, 1971-72; resident in medicine U. Miss. Med. Ctr., Jackson, 1972-74, fellow in cardiology, 1974-76; asst. prof. Hyogo Coll. Medicine, Nishinomiya, Japan, 1976-86; med. cons. Japan Life Ins. Co., Osaka, 1981-95, Idemitsu Oil Co., Himeji, 1977-94; chief medicine Takatsuki (Japan) Red Cross Hosp., 1986—. Author: Electrocardiographic Manual, 1979, Radionucleid Scanning, 1981, Cardiology-Programmed Learning, 1983, 4th edit., 1996, Cardiology Review Book, 1985, Patient Management in Cardiology, 1985, Textbook of Advanced Clinical Cardiology, 1986, EKG Exercise, 1991, Cardiology Case Study, 1999. Fellow ACP, Am Coll. Cardiology, Am. Heart Assn., Am. Coll. Physicians; mem. Japanese Soc. Internal Medicine, Japanese Circulation Soc., Japan Clin. Cardiology Ednl. Soc. (trustee 1983). Buddhist. Home: 1 45 Tonoyama cho, Nishinomiya, Hyogo 662-0065, Japan Office: Takatsuki Red Cross Hosp, 1-1 Abuno Takatsuki, Osaka 569-1045, Japan

ANDO, MASANORI, chemist, researcher; b. Amagasaki, Hyogo, Japan, Aug. 31, 1962; s. Joichi and Hisako (Ueda) A.; m. Yoko Yamaguchi, Oct. 15, 1994. BS in Engrng. in Hydrocarbon Chemistry, Kyoto U., Japan, 1985, MS in Molecular Engrng., 1987, DEng in Molecular Engrng., 1990. Cert. engr. Postdoctoral fellow Sci. and Tech. Agy., Ikeda, Japan, 1990-91; rschr. Osaka Nat. Rsch. Inst., Agy. Indsl. Sci. and Tech., Ministry Internat.Trade and Industry, Ikeda, Japan, 1991-94; sr. rschr. Osaka Nat. Rsch. Inst., AIST, MITI, Ikeda, Japan, 1994—; rschr. Rsch. Devel. Corp. Japan, Ikeda, Japan, 1992-94. Contbr. articles to profl. jours. Mem. AAAS, Chem. Soc. of Japan (Young Chemist award 1996), Electrochemical Soc. of Japan. Achievements include devel. of novel optochemical sensor materials and nonlinear optical materials for future optical devices. Office: Osaka Nat Rsch Inst, Midorigaoka 1-8-31, Ikeda 563-8577, Japan

ANDO, TADAO, architect; b. Osaka, Japan, Sept. 13, 1941; m. Yumiko Kato, 1970; 1 child. Founder, dir. Tadao Ando Architect and Assocs., Osaka, 1969—. Exhbns. include Inst. for Architecture and Urban Studies, N.Y.C., 1978, Union Hungarian Architects, Budapest, 1979, Colegio Oficial de Arquitectos, Madrid, 1982, Institut Français d'Architecture, Paris, 1982, Thermen Mus., Heerlen, Netherlands, 1982, Architectuurmus., Amsterdam, 1982, Lausanne, Switzerland, 1983, Vienna and Innsbruck, Austria, 1984, others; works include Tomishima House, Osaka, 1973, Uno House, Kyoto, Japan, 1974, Tezukayama Tower Pla., Osaka, 1976, Kitano Alley, Kobe, Japan, 1977, Matsumoto House, Wakayama Prefecture, Japan, 1980, Rin's Gallery, Kobe, 1981, Bigi Atelier Bldg., Tokyo, 1982, Time's Bldg., Kyoto, 1984, Melrose Bldg., Tokyo, 1984, Festival Bldg., Okinawa Prefecture, Japan, 1984, Bigi Aobadai Bldg., Tokyo, 1985, Nakayama House, Nara Prefecture, Japan, 1985, Bigi Atelier House, Nara Prefecture, 1985, Japanese pavillion Seville's World Fair, others; author: Tadao Ando, 1981, Tadao Ando: Monographies, 1982, Tadao Ando: Buildings, Project, Writings, 1984; contbr. articles to numerous publs. Recipient Ann. Prize Arch. Inst. Japan, 1979, Japan Cultural Design prize, 1983, Alvar Aalto medal, 1985, Carlsberg Arch. prize, 1992, Pritzker Arch. Prize, 1995, Imperial Premium prize, 1996. Office: Tadeo Ando Arch & Assocs, 5-23 Toyosaki, 2-chome, Kita-ku Osaka 531-0072, Japan*

ANDO, YASUHISA, mechanical engineer; b. Yokohama, Japan, Oct. 15, 1962; s. Hiroshi and Asako (Masuda) A.; m. Atsuko Ozaki, Apr. 3, 1993; children: Koji, Masato. BS, Tokyo Inst. Tech., 1985, MS, 1987, PhD, 1997. Mech. engr. NEC Co., Tokyo, 1987-89, Mech. Engring. Lab., Tsukuba, Japan, 1989—. Contbr. articles to profl. jours. Avocations: soccer, skiing. Office: Mech Engring Lab, Namiki 1-2, Tsukuba 305-8564, Japan

ANDO, YOICHI, science educator; b. Tokyo, Apr. 10, 1939; s. Sanpei and Asano (Nishikawa) A.; m. Keiko Shikata, June 2, 1963; children: Eiichi, Tamao. PhD, Waseda U., Tokyo, 1975. Rsch. assoc. Kobe (Japan) U., 1970-79, assoc. prof., 1979-95, prof. Grad. Sch. of Sci. and Tech., 1995—, assoc. dean, councillor, 1997-99; acoustic cons. design Kirishima Internat. Concert Hall Kagoshima-Pref., Japan, 1992-95, design Tsuyama Music Cultural Hall, 1992-99; organizing com. chmn. Internat. Symposium on Music and Concert Hall Acoustice, Kirishima, 1995; organizing chmn. Internat. Workshop on New Sys. for Identification and Evaluation of Regional Environ. Noise, Kobe, 1999. Author: Concert Hall Acoustics, 1985, Architectural Acoustics, Blending Sound Sources, Sound Fields, and Listeners, 1998; co-author: Nature and Technology of Acoustic Space, 1995; co-editor: Music and Concert Hall Acoustics, 1997; editl. bd. Modern Acoustics and Signal Processing, 1993—. Recipient AIA 1995 Inst. Honor; Alexander-von-Humboldt Found. fellow, 1975. Mem. Italian Acoustical Assn. (hon.). Home: 3-6-153 Hiyodoridai, Kita Kobe 651-1123, Japan

ANDO, YUKIO, physician, biochemist, educator; b. Beppu, Japan, July 9, 1953; s. Kikuo and Etsu (Uonuma) A.; m. Eiko Nishimura, Apr. 4, 1983 (div. May 1997); children: Hisashi, Yuzuru; m. Keiko Asahara, Sept. 30, 1998. MD, Kumamoto U., Japan, 1983, DPhil, 1989. Resident Kumamoto U. Sch. Medicine, 1983-86, asst. prof., 1992—; vis. prof. Umeå (Sweden) U., 1996—; mem. primary amyloidosis rsch. Japanese Soc. Welfare, Japan, 1995—, mem. hereditary neuropathy rsch., 1998—; dir. Kumamoto Autonomic Rsch. Group, 1991—, Kumamoto U. Amyloidosis Rsch. Group, 1991—. Contbr. articles to profl. jours. Postdoctoral fellow Kumamoto U. Sch. Medicine, 1990-92. Mem. Japanese Neurol. Soc., Japanese Internal Medicine Soc., Japanese Autonomic Nervous Sys. Soc. (adv. mem. 1993—). Avocations: baseball, travel, reading, movies, writing. Home: Kyomachi 1-11-20-301, Kumamoto 860-0078, Japan Office: U Kumamoto U Hosp Int Med, 1-1-1 Honjo, Kumamoto Japan

ANDONE, IOAN IOAN, accountant, educator; b. Piatra Neamt, Moldavia, Romania, Nov. 1, 1947; s. Ioan Toader and Catinca Ioan (Vădureanu) A.; m. Maria-Adriana Ioan Andreica, July 27, 1973; children: Diana-Magdalena, Ioan-Daniel. MSc, Ctrl. Informatics Inst., Bucharest, Romania, 1972; DSc (hon.), Grad. Sch. Bus., Pitts., 1977; PhD, Al.i.Cuza U. Iasi, Romania, 1985. Acctg. diplomate; expert acct.; bus. informatics charter acct. auditor; software developer; designer info. sys. Asst. lectr. Al.i.Cuza U. Iasi, Romania, 1971-78, lectr., 1978-91, assoc. prof., 1991-95, prof., 1995—; censor Melcret Group SA, Iasi, 1992-99; chartered acct. Corp. of Experts, Bucharest, 1995-99; auditor expert, dir. projects Nat. Rsch. Coun., Bucharest, 1998—. Author: Artificial Intelligence and Expert Systems in Accounting, 1993 (V.Madgearu award 1994), Expert Systems: Principles and Applications in Business, 1995 (Romanian Acad. award 1996); co-author: Intelligent Databases in Corporate Management, 1997 (award 1998), Intelligent Systems in Management, Accounting, and Finance, 1999 (award 1999). Mem. Nat. Acctg. Assn., Scientists Assn. (Iasi br.), Acad. Sco. for Romania. Avocations: gardening, hunting, folk and country music. Home: 1 Zlataust, RO-6600 Iasi Moldavia, Romania Office: AliCuza U Iasi, 20 Copou Blvd, RO-6600 Iasi Moldavia, Romania

ANDONOPOULOS, ANDREW P., physician, researcher, educator; b. Patras, Achaia, Greece, Dec. 19, 1947; s. Panagiotis A. and Sophia (Kazanis) A.; m. Nicolitsa Georgiou, Aug. 18, 1973; children: Constantinos, Joannis. MD, Sch. Medicine, Athens, 1971; PhD, Sch. Medicine, Patras, Greece, 1982. Cert. ECFMG, 1971, physician and surgeon Mich., 1977; diplomate AM. Bd. Internal Medicine, Am. Bd. Rheumatology, Bd. Internal Medicine, Greece, Bd. Rheumatology, Greece. Med. intern, resident Wayne State U., Detroit, 1974-77, rheumatology fellow, 1977-79; sr. registrar Patras U., Agios Andreas Hosp., Patras, Greece, 1980-86; dir. rheumatology divsn. Ioannina (Greece) Gen. Hosp., 1986-88; asst. prof. medicine and rheumatology U. Patras Med. Sch., 1989-93, assoc. prof., 1993-98, prof., 1998—; chief divsn. rheumatology Patras U. Med. Sch., Greece, 1989—. Mem. editl. bd. Clinical and Experimental Rheumatology, 1988; contbr. chpts. to books, numerous articles to profl. jours. Doctor Greek War Navy, 1972-74. Recipient numerous sci. citations. Fellow ACP, Am. Coll. Rheumatology;

mem. Greek Rheumatology Soc. Avocations: philately, swimming, skiing. Office: U Patras Sch Medicine, 26500 Rio, Patras Greece

ANDOR, GYORGY, physicist; b. Budapest, Hungary, Oct. 16, 1945; s. Laszlo and Hedvig (Banhidy) A.; m. Katalin Serenyi, Sept. 4, 1971; children: Csaba, Gergely. MSc, Elte U. Budapest, 1971. Rsch. physicist Rsch. Inst. Measurements, Budapest, 1971-75, Nat. Office of Measures, Budapest, 1975-86, 88—, Nat. Bur. Standards, Gaithersburg, Md., 1986-88. Mem. Internat. Commn. Illumination (tech. com. 1989—). Avocations: games of logic and puzzles, bridge, tennis, windsurfing. Home: Rozse ut 1/A, 1125 Budapest Hungary Office: Nat Office of Measures, Pf 919, H1535 Budapest Hungary

ANDORFER, DONALD JOSEPH, university president; b. Ft. Wayne, Ind., Dec. 31, 1937; s. Joseph and Cecil J. (Minich) A.; married Dec. 26, 1960; children: Susan, Joseph, Barbara. BS in Edn., Ball State U., 1960, MA in Edn., 1965; LLD (hon.), Tiffin U., 1989. Instr. Internat. Jr. Coll. Bus., Ft. Wayne, 1960-70, dean, dir., 1971-77; controller Ind. Inst. Tech., Ft. Wayne, 1978-81, v.p. fin., 1982-85, pres., 1985—. Mem. acad. com. Luth. Hosp. Bd., 1989-93; bd. dirs. Robert Morris Coll., Chgo., 1985—; bd. dirs. Ind. Pub. Broadcasting. Mem. Ind. Colls. Ind. (bd. dirs., chmn. 1994), Nat. Assn. Ind. Colls. and Univs., Nat. Assn. Ind. Athletics (nat. coun. pres. 1991-94), Ft. Wayne C. of C., Ind. Bus. Edn. Assn. (pres. 1980-81), Future Bus. Leaders Am. (bd. dirs. Outstanding Bus. Person for Ind. award 1981), Rotary (bd. dirs., v.p. 1994, pres.-elect 1995, pres. 1996, Paul Harris fellow 1998), Summit Club (bd. dirs. 2000—), Delta Pi Epsilon. Roman Catholic. Avocations: golf, fishing, spectator sports. Home: 15423 Connors Rd Fort Wayne IN 46819-9720 Office: Ind Inst of Tech Office of the President 1600 E Washington Blvd Fort Wayne IN 46803-1228

ANDRADA, LUIS, economist; b. Rosario, Argentina, Mar. 25, 1946; s. Andrada Luis and Ada Strada. SC in Economics, Cordoba U., Cordoba, Argentina, 1971; PhD in Bus. Adminstrn., Cordoba U., 1973. Nat. pub. acct. Argentina, 1971-75; energy analyst Bocconi U., Milan, Italy, 1975-79; sr. economist Ansaldo S.P.A., Genoa, Italy, 1979-81; head econ. dept. Cesen S.P.A., Genoa, Italy, 1981—. Mem. Internat. Assn. Energy Economists, Italian Assn. Energy Economists. Office: Cesen SPA, Piazza Della Vittoria 11A/B, 16121 Genoa Italy

ANDRADE, ARMANDO, auditor, consultant; b. Ribeirão Preto, Brazil, Mar. 2, 1930; s. Mauricio and Amelia (Ferrari) A.; m. Maria Estela Pedroso Oliveira, May 1, 1952 (dec. Feb. 1996); children: Estela Maris, Viviane Elaine, Sandra Cristina, Simone; m. Maria Dizotti, Sept. 19, 1998. Prof., Mackenzie, São Paulo, 1964; acct., Faculty Unicsul, São Paulo, 1974. Cert. internal auditor, info. sys. internal auditor. Acctg. clk. Medifer Ltda., São Paulo, 1944-48; internal auditor GE, São Paulo, 1948-52; sr. internal auditor Anderson Clayton, São Paulo, 1952-56; gen. mgr. Philips Orgn., Brazil, 1956-90, Efficienta Auditoria, São Paulo, 1990—; chmn. bd. govs. Audibra-Inst. Auditor, São Paulo, 1986-98, exec. pres., 1990-92; dir. Inst. Internal Auditors-USA, Altamonte Springs, 1998-99; coord. prof. edn. Conselho Contabilidade, São Paulo, 1990—. Author: (books) Initiation in E.D.P. Auditing, 1978, Statistical Sampling Manual, 1986, Basics About Internal Auditing, 1992. Leader working group Ministry Edn., Brazil, 1997-98. Recipient Acctg. Merit medal Alvares Penteado Found., 1996. Fellow Assn. Nacional Execs. Fin. e Contabilidade, Inst. Ciência Tecn. Bahia. Avocations: reading, swimming, technical research. Home: Rua Lira Cearense 190 Ap 21, 05763450 São Paulo Brazil Office: Efficientia Auditoria Asses, Av Rouxinol 619, 04516001 São Paulo Brazil

ANDRADE, LESTER CARLOS, hospitality industry executive; b. Bombay, India, Sept. 26, 1956; s. Joaquim Jose and Nypha (Nazareth) A.; m. Thelma Virginia D'Souza, Dec. 28, 1987; 1 child, Joshua. Degree in Sci., Nat. Coll., Bombay, 1977. Dir. human resources Sheraton Hotel, Ayers Rock, Australia, 1989-91; dir. manpower devel. Shangri-La Hotel & Resorts, Beijing, China, 1991-92, regional dir. tng., 1992-93, regional dir. human resources, 1993-95; group dir. tng. Shangri-La Hotel & Resorts, Hong Kong, 1995-98, group dir. recruitment, 1998—. Fellow Australian Inst. Mgmt.; mem. Inst. Human Resources Hong Kong. Roman Catholic. Avocations: football, squash, volleyball, music. Office: Shangri-La Hotels & Resorts, 1 Tim Mei Ave, 21/F CITIC, Central Hong Kong China

ANDRADE, VIRGILLO MANUEL, administrator; b. Mexico City, Mex., May 25, 1967; s. Enrique A. and Margarita (Champion) Gonzalez. B of Bus., Northwestern U., 1991. Mgr. human resources Divertido, Mexico City, Mex., 1993; mgr. human resources La Feria, Mexico City, Mex., 1993-94, mgr. pub. rels., 1993-94; mgr. recruitment Tribunal Superior Agrasio, Mexico City, Mex., 1995-98, mgr. human resources, 1998-99; adminstrv. coord. Sira Trab. Y Prev. Social, Mexico City, Mex., 1999; v.p. Andrade Palacios, Mexico City, 1990-99; pres. VAG, S.A., Mexico City, 1998-99; v.p. human resources Inst. Svc., Mexico City, 1990-99. Mem. IAAPA. Roman Catholic. Avocations: reading, swimming, writing. Office: VAG SA De CV, Redorma 51 2 PISO, Mexico City 06700, Mexico

ANDRADE, WILLIAM THOMAS, professional golfer; b. Bristol, R.I., Jan. 25, 1964; m. Jody Andrade; children: Cameron James, Grace. BA in Sociology, Wake Forest U., 1987. Mem. Jr. World Cup Championship Team, 1981, World Amateur Championship Team, 1986, Walker Cup Championship Team, 1987; winner Kemper Open (PGA Tour), 1991, Buick Classic (PGA Tour), 1991, Bell Can. Open (PGA Tour), 1998; mem. PGA Tour Charity Team, THE TOUR Championship, 1999; co-host CVS Charity Classic, R.I., 1999. Co-organizer Billy Andrade/Brad Faxon Charities for Children, R.I. and Mass., 1991—. Office: c/o PGA Box 109601 100 Ave of Champions Palm Beach Gardens FL 33410

ANDRADE-GARDA, JOSE MANUEL, chemist; b. A Coruna, Galicia, Spain, Jan. 15, 1967; s. Manuel Andrade-Caamano and Amparo Garda-Ponte. BS, U. Santiago, Spain, 1990; MS, U. Coruna, Spain, 1994, Open U., Spain, 1994; PhD, U. A Coruna, 1995. Rschr. Ministry Edn., Spain, 1991-93; tchr. U. A. Coruna, 1993—, dir. Office for Non-Govt. Affairs, 1999—. Contbr. articles to profl. jours. Recipient 1st prize Galician-Portuguese Young Chemists, 1994, 2d prize Young Chemometrician, 1995. Mem. Spanish Assn. Chemists, Spanish Soc. Chemistry. Avocations: ship models, bird watching, classical music. E-mail: andrade@udc.es. Fax: 34-981-167065. Office: Univ A Coruna, A Zapateira s-n, E15071 A Coruna Spain

ANDRADE-PAEZ, PEDRO ENRIQUE, internist; b. San Cristobal, Venezuela, Oct. 24, 1956; s. Rafael Clemente Andrade Nino and Zaira (Paez Maya) Paez De A; m. Ana Maria Senior Aguerrevere, Nov. 19, 1983; children: Adriana, Gabriela, Cristina. MD, U. Caracas, Venezuela, 1982. Diplomate Internal Medicine. Resident Hosp. Vargas, Caracas, 1983-86, attending, 1987—; attending Centro Medico, Caracas, 1987—; emergency dir. Hosp. Vargas, Caracas, 1987-95. Mem. SVMI, ACP-ASIM. Office: Centro Medico De Caracas, Av Mariscal Sucre San Bernardino, Caracas 1010, Venezuela

ANDRAIN, CHARLES FRANKLIN, political science educator; b. Fortuna, Calif., Feb. 22, 1937; s. Milton D. and Alberta W. (Gatton) A. AB, Whittier Coll., 1959; MA, U. Calif., Berkeley, 1961, PhD, 1964. Asst. prof. dept. polit. sci. San Diego State U., 1964-67, assoc. prof., 1967-70, prof., 1970—, chmn. dept., 1972-74; rsch. assoc. Inst. Internat. Studies, U. Calif.-Berkeley, 1975-76, 78-79, 80-81, 82, 86. Author: Children and Civic Awareness, 1971, Political Life and Social Change, 2d edit., 1975, Politics and Economic Policy in Western Democracies, 1980, Foundations of Comparative Politics: A Policy Perspective, 1983, Social Policies in Western Industrial Societies, 1985, Political Change in the Third World, 1988, Comparative Political Systems, 1994, (with David E. Apter) Political Protest and Social Change, 1995, Public Health Policies and Social Inequality, 1998. Woodrow Wilson Found. fellow, 1959-60; NDEA fellow, 1960-63; Ford Found. fellow, 1968-89; NIMH fellow, 1971-72. Mem. Am. Polit. Sci. Assn., Am. Sociol. Assn., Internat. Soc. Political Psychology, Internat. Studies Assn. Office: San Diego State U Dept Polit Sci San Diego CA 92182

ANDRÁSSY, ISTVÁN, biologist, researcher; b. Szolnok, Hungary, May 5, 1927; s. István and Terézia (Szokolay) A.; m. Mariann Dsida, 1955 (marriage dissolved); children: Judith, Mariann, István; m. Etelka Nagy, 1975; 1 child, Csaba. PhD, Eötvös U., Budapest, 1950, DSc, 1956; doctorate, Acad. Scis., Budapest, 1973. Investigator Mus. of Nat. Sci., Budapest, 1950-52; rschr. U. Budapest, 1952-75, chief rschr., 1976—. Editor-in-chief Opuscula Zoologica, Budapest, 1956—, Allattani Közlemények, Budapest, 1958—; editor: Jour. Fundamental Nematology, Paris, 1978—; author: Evolution as a Basis for the Systematization of Nematodes, 1976, A Taxonomic Review of the Suborder Rhabditina, 1983, Klasse Nematoda, 1984; co-author: Parasitic Nematodes in Cultivated Plants, 1988. Fellow Internat. Co. Nematology; mem. Hungarian Biology Co. Roman Catholic. Avocations: gardening, traveling, reading. Office: Eötvö U, Eötvös U, ELTE Puskin-u 3, 1088 Budapest Hungary

ANDRE, CARL, sculptor; b. Quincy, Mass., Sept. 16, 1935; s. George Hans and Margaret Andre. Represented in public collections, Tate Gallery, London, Mus. Modern Art, N.Y.C., Rose Art Mus., Brandeis U., Columbus (Ohio) Gallery Fine Arts, Walker Art Center, Mpls., Milw. Art Center, La Jolla (Calif.) Mus. Contemporary Art, Dayton (Ohio) Art Inst., Albright-Knox Art Gallery, Buffalo, Monchengladbach Mus., Germany, Wallraf-Richartz Mus., Cologne, Haus Lange Mus., Krefeld, Germany, Kunstmus. Basel, Switzerland, Hessisches Landesmus., Darmstadt, Germany, Stedelijk Mus., Amsterdam, Van Abbe Mus., Eindhoven, Netherlands, Art Soc. Ghent, Belgium, Art Inst. Chgo., Los Angeles County Mus. Art, Musée Nat. d'Art Moderne, Paris, Carnegie Inst Mus. Art, Pitts., Musèo de Arte Moderno, Bogota, Colombia, Seattle Art Mus., High Mus. Art, Atlanta, Ohio State U. Gallery Fine Art, Bayerischen Staatsgemäldesammlungen, Munich, Kröller-Müller Mus., Otterlo, Netherlands, Detroit Inst. Arts, Guggenheim Mus., N.Y.C., City of Hartford, Conn., Mus. Boymans-van Beuningen, Rotterdam, Netherlands. also: Paula Cooper 534 W 21st St New York NY 10011-2812 also: Konrad Fischer, Platanenstr 7, Düsseldorf 40233, Germany*

ANDRE, CHARLES, physician, researcher; b. Rio de Janeiro, Brazil, Feb. 21, 1958; s. Gerard and Sarah A.; children: Pedro Minc, Laura Minc. G-rad., Fed. U. Rio de Janeiro, 1981, MSc in Neurology, 1992, PhD in Neurology, 1996. Resident in internal medicine Rio de Janeiro State U., 1982-89; ICU staff Nat. Health System, Rio de Janeiro, 1984-99, Hosp. Ctrl. do Exército, Rio de Janeiro, 1983-93; neurology staff Fed. U. Rio de Janeiro, 1985-95, prof. neurology, 1995—; med. dir. The Jorge Jaber Psychotherapy Clinic, Rio de Janeiro, 1994—. Author: (books) Stroke Manual, 1998, The Practical Guide to Neurology, 1999; contbr. more than 50 articles to profl. jours. Mem. Brazilian Acad. Neurology, Am. Stroke Assn. Avocations: Judo, scuba diving, piano, artistic drawing. Office: Rua Gen Venâancio, Flores 305/602 Leblon, 22441090 Rio de Janeiro Brazil

ANDRE, JEAN-MARIE, science educator; b. Charleroi, Belgium, Mar. 31, 1944; s. Robert Andre and Godelieve Goemans; m. Marie-Claude Roeland, May 2, 1943; children: Pascale, Damien, Vinciane, Renaud. MS, UCL, Louvain, Belgium, 1965, PhD, 1968; Doctor Honoris Causa, U. Warsaw, Poland, 1995. Rsch. fellow Belgian Nat. Sci. Found., 1968-71; docent U. Namur, Belgium, 1971-74, prof., 1974—; exec. officer U. Namur, 1991—, chmn. rsch. coun., 1993—. Author 7 sci. books; contbr. over 250 articles to sci. publs. Recipient Pierre Bruylants prize U. Louvain, 1969, Ann. award Acad. Arts and Sci., Hainaut, 1970, Louis Empain prize Univ. Found., Belgium, 1970, Triennial prize Belgian Chem. Soc., 1973, Ann. medal Internat. Acad. Quantum Molecular Sci., 1984, Francqui Found. prize, 1991; named Officer Order of King Léopold, 1990. Mem. Royal Acad. Belgium (Jean Stas prize 1969), Agathon de Potter prize 1979), Polish Chem. Soc. (hon.). Home: Rue Chapelle Lessire 12, 5020 Namur Belgium Office: U ND de la Paix, Rue de Bruxelles 61, 5000 Namur Belgium

ANDRE, JEAN-MICHEL, physical engineer; b. St. Denis, France, May 20, 1955; s. Solange André. BS, France, 1973; degree in engring., INSCIR, France, 1978; PhD, U. Pierre and Marie Curie, Paris, 1982. Phys. engr. Ctr. Nat. Rsch. Sci., France, 1982-90; x-ray optics group leader U. Pierre and Marie Curie, 1990—; cons. European Synchrotron Radiation Facility, Grenoble, France, 1994. Contbr. articles to profl. publs. Engr. French Air Force, 1978. Recipient award Matra Soc., 1979. Mem. Optical Soc. Am. (referee), Inst. Physics U.K. (referee). Avocation: biking. Office: U Pierre and Marie Curie, 11 rue Pierre & Marie Curie, 75231 Paris France

ANDRÉ, MARCEL JEAN, retired plant scientist; b. Mirebel, France, Sept. 25, 1934; s. Léon Luc and Andrée Marie (Grandvaux) A.; m. Anne Emilie Hérisson, June 25, 1962; children: Christophe, Pierre, Emmanuel. Degree in engring., U. Grenoble, France, 1958, U. Grenoble, France, 1959; cert. nuclear physics and accelerators, U. Grenoble, France, 1959. Cert. in bioengring. and rsch. in plant scis.; cert. specialist in artificial exosys. Rschr. Radio-Agronomy Inst. Basic Rsch., Cadarache, France, 1962-74; head ecophysiology lab. CEA, Cadarache, 1974-90, sci. counselor ecophysiology sect., 1990-93, sci. cons. to dir. dept. plant and microbiol. ecophysiology, 1993-96, cons. life scis. working group European Space Agy., Paris, 1986-89; cons. Celss test facility project Ames Rsch. Ctr., NASA, Calif., 1991-93; cons. Nat. Aerospace Lab., Tokyo, 1990; chmn. commn. on artificial and natural ecosys. Com. Space Rsch., 1992-96; fellow dept. plant biology Carnegie Inst. at Stanford, Calif., 1968—. Contbr. articles to sci. publs. Councilman City of Manosque, France, 1995. 2nd lt. French Mil. Res., 1962. Mem. Am. Plant Physiol. Soc., Soc. Ecophysiology (bd. dirs. 1993-96). Avocations: wood crafting, bicycling, choral singing. Home: Provence, 154 Rte de Dauphin, F04100 Manosque France

ANDRE, YVES, mathematician, pianist; b. Roanne, France, Dec. 11, 1959; s. Philippe and Andree (Romeas) A.; m. Yu Taniguchi, June 28, 1994. Lic. of Philosophy, Sorbonne, France, 1982; Diplom of Virtuosity, Schola Cantorum, Paris, 1983; Dr. Math., U. Paris 6, 1984, Habil., 1994. Rschr. in math. CNRS, Paris, 1985—. Author: G-functions and Geometry, 1989, (with F. Baldassarri) De Rham cohomology of differential modules on algebraic varieties, 2000; contbr. articles to profl. jours.; chamber music concerts, France, Germany. Humboldt stipendium A. Humboldt Stiftung, Bonn, Germany, 1989. Office: Institut de Mathematiques, Case 247, 4 Place Jussieu, 75005 Paris France

ANDREADIS, IOANNIS, engineering educator, researcher; b. Cryssoupolis, Kavala, Greece, June 1, 1960; s. Thomas and Helen (Ioannidis) A.; m. Evagelia Kontostoli, Oct. 9, 1993; 1 child, Thomas. Diploma in Engring., Elec. Engring., Xanthi, Greece, 1983; MS, Elec. Engring. & Electronics, Manchester, Eng., 1985; PhD, Instrument. & Analytical Scis., Manchester, Eng., 1989. Rschr. U. Manchester, 1984-89; prof. Tech. Inst. of Kavala, 1991-92; lectr. Democritus U. Thrace, 1992—; cons. Nestos Bldg. Co., Kavala, 1993—. Mem. editl. bd. Pattern Recognition Jour.; contbr. articles to profl. jours. With Greek Army, 1989-91. Recipient Govt. of Greece scholarships, 1978, 81, 83. Mem. IEEE, Tech. Chamber of Greece (mem. tech. edn. com. Northeastern Divsn. 1994—). Achievements include contributions to color imaging processing, especially real time indsl. applications. Avocations: swimming, football. Home: 16 Roosevelt, Cryssoupolis 64200, Greece Office: DUTH Dept of Elec Comp Engring, V Sofias, Xanthi 67100, Greece

ANDRÉANI, JACQUES, diplomat; b. Paris, Nov. 22, 1929; s. Paul and Suzanne (Hugon) A.; m. Huguette De Fonclare (div. 1981); children: Gilles, Olivia; m. Donatella Monterisi; children: Marie-Emmanuelle, Fabrice. Diploma, Inst. d'Etude Politiques, Paris, 1969, Ecole Nationale d'Administration, Paris, 1953. 2d sec. French Embassy, Washington, 1955-60; 1st sec. Moscow, 1961-64; chief Bur. Soviet Affairs Ministry Fgn. Affairs, Paris, 1964-67, chief Bur. East European and Soviet Affairs, 1967-70, dir. for Europe, 1975-79, dir. polit. affairs, 1981-84; asst. govt. rep. NATO, Brussels, 1970-72; chief French del. Conf. on Security and Corp. in Europe, Helsinki and Geneva, 1972-75; ambassador to Egypt, Cairo, 1979-81; amb. to Italy, Rome, 1984-88; chief staff French Ministry Fgn. Affairs, 1988-89; amb. to U.S. U.S., Washington, 1989-95; adviser to Min. Fgn. Affairs Paris, 1995-97; ret., 1998. Decorated comdr. Order of Merit, comdr. Legion of Honor (France). Home: 40 rue Bonaparte, 75007 Paris France Office: Ministry of Fgn Affairs, 37 quai d'Orsey, Paris France

ANDREAS, DWAYNE ORVILLE, business executive; b. Worthington, Minn., Mar. 4, 1918; s. Reuben P. and Lydia (Stoltz) A.; m. Bertha Benedict, 1938 (div.); 1 dau., Sandra Ann Andreas McMurtie; m. Dorothy Inez Snyder, Dec. 21, 1947; children: TerryLynn, Michael D. Student, Wheaton (Ill.) Coll., 1935-36; hon. degree, Barry U. V.p., dir. Honeymead Products Co., Cedar Rapids, Iowa, 1936-46; chmn. bd., chief exec. officer Honeymead Products Co. (now Nat. City Bancorp.), Mankato, Minn., 1952-72; v.p. Cargill, Inc., Mpls., 1946-52; exec. v.p. Farmers Union Grain Terminal Assn., St. Paul, 1960-66; chmn. bd., chief exec. officer Archer-Daniels-Midland Co., Decatur, Ill., 1970-97, chmn. bd., 1997-98, chmn. emeritus, 1999—; bd. dirs. Hollinger Internat. Inc.; mem. Pres.'s Gen. Adv. Commn. of Fgn. Assistance Programs, 1965-68, Pres.'s Adv. Coun. on Mgmt. Improvement, 1969-73; chmn. Pres.'s Task Force on Internat. Pvt. Enterprise. Nat. bd. dirs. Boys' Club Am.; former chmn. U.S.-USSR Trade and Econ. Coun.; former chmn. Exec. Coun. on Fgn. Diplomats; former trustee Hoover Inst. on War, Revolution and Peace; former vice chmn. Woodrow Wilson Internat. Ctr. for Scholars; former mem. Trilateral Commn.; chmn. Found. for Commemoration of the U.S. Constitution, 1986. Mem. Fgn. Policy Assn. N.Y. (dir.), Indian Creek Country Club (Miami Beach, Fla.), Blind Brook Country Club (Purchase, N.Y.), Links, Knickerbocker, Friars (N.Y.C.).

ANDREAS, STEFAN, cardiologist; b. Bremen, Germany, Dec. 11, 1961; s. Berndt and Linni (Fendt) A.; m. Kathrin Sieber, June 12, 1993; children: Marike, Moritz. MD, Free Univ. Berlin, 1988, D in Medicine, 1990; habilitation, U. Göttingen, Germany, 1997. Cardiologist Georg-August U., Göttingen, Germany, 1988—; rschr. Georg-August U., 1988—; dir. sleep lab. U. Göttingen, 1991—. Served in German Army, 1981-82. Mem. European Respiratory Soc., Deutsche Gesellschaft Schlafmedizin, Deutsche Gesellschaft Kardiologie, Deutsche Gesellschaft Pneumologie. Avocation: painting. Office: U Göttingen, Dept Cardiology, 37075 Göttingen Germany

ANDREASEN, CHARLES PETER, retired electronics executive; b. Bklyn., Mar. 18, 1930; s. Peter Kristian and Marie Paulene (Pedersen) A; m. Julia Kerekes, Nov. 27, 1952; 1 child; Jane Andreasen Della Grotta. Student, Rutgers U., 1948-49, Middlesex County Coll., 1970-71. Quality control engr. Gorn Aircraft Controls Co., Stamford, Conn., 1962-63; quality control supr. Lily-Tulip Cup Corp., Holmdel, N.J., 1963-70; corp. quality control lab. supr. Purolator Products Co., Rahway, N.J., 1970-73; mgr. quality control Scovill Mfg. Co., Waterbury, Conn., 1973-78; quality assurance mgr. All-State Legal Supply Co., Mountainside, N.J., 1979-81, Durex, Inc., Union, N.J., 1981-82; quality and reliability engr., asst. quality mgr. Triangle Microwave, Inc., East Hanover, N.J., 1982-92; ret., 1992. Mem. Bd. Edn., Edison, N.J., 1982-91; vol. Edison Twp. Domestic Violence Crisis Team, 1993-95; vol. video coord. Rutgers Coop. Ext. Svc.; vol. TV dir. Piscataway Cmty. TV Ctr. Channel 71, 1997—. Mem. Am. Soc. for Quality Control (met. section exec. bd. dirs.), Elks (audit chmn. 1970-78). Democrat. Roman Catholic. Avocations: golf, swimming, photography, model railroading, fishing. Home: 24 Burchard St Edison NJ 08837

ANDRÉASSON, GUNNAR OSBORN, consultant in sport, biomechanics and textiles; b. Göteborg, Sweden, Jan. 30, 1953; s. Gustav Osborn and Gunborg Astrid (Dagny) O.; m. Inga-Lill Theresia Rangmar, Apr. 27, 1989; children: Anna, Stina, Alexander. MS, Chalmers U. Tech., Goteborg, 1979; PhD, Chalmers U. Tech., Göteborg, 1985. Dir. studies U. Coll., Borås, Sweden, 1983-85; rsch. asst. Nordifa Ind AB, Halmstad, 1985-87, Ctr. for Biomechanics, Göteborg, 1987-93; rsch. dir. Artimplant Devel., Göteborg, 1993-95; assoc. prof. Chalmers U. Tech., Göteborg, 1995—; pres. Sport Test AB, Göteborg, 1987—; project leader Sigma Innovation, 1998—. Editor book in field; patentee and designer in field. Mem. Internat. Sport Surface Sci., Textile Inst. (chmn. Swedish session 1993). Home: Gulmaravägen 21, 43833 Landvetter Sweden Office: Sigma Innovation, Aminogatan 34, 431 53 Molndal Sweden

ANDREASSON, INGMAR JOEL, transportation scientist; b. Hassleholm, Sweden, Sept. 27, 1944; s. Arthur and Gurli (Sjogren) A.; m. Birgitta Lindgren, July 13, 1968; children: Niklas, Pontus, Henrik, Victor. MSC, Royal Inst. Technology Sweden, 1967, DSc, 1972. Pres. Volvo Transportation Sys., Sweden, 1973-88; prin. Logistik Centrum, Sweden, 1989—. Author: Simulation Methodology, 1973; contbr. articles to profl. jours. Mem. Swedish Soc. Ops. Rsch. Avocations: sailing, skiing, tennis. Home: Osbergsgatan 4A, S-42677 V Frolunda Sweden

ANDREÉ, BENGT ALOF LENNART, psychiatrist, researcher; b. Stockholm, Nov. 17, 1953; s. Dof and Inguor (Wallertun) A. BM, U. Umeå, 1977; MD, U. Linköping, 1981; PhD, Karolinska Inst., 1995—. Cert. specialist in pscyhiatry, psychotherapist. Intern Gen. Hosp., Östersund, 1981-83; resident dept. psychiatry Östersund Hosp., 1983-88, head dept. psychiatry, 1988-94, coordinating invesigator clin. drug trials dept. psychiatry, 1991-94, mem. specialist psychotherapeutic ctr. dept. psychiatry, 1992-94; head dept. psychiatry Karolinska Hosp., 1994-95, head specialist ward dept. psychiatry, 1997—. Contbr. articles to profl. publs. Mem. Swedish Med. Assn. Office: Dept Clin Neurosci Psych, Karolinska Inst, S-17176 Stockholm Sweden

ANDREELLI, FABRIZIO, physician; b. Charenton Le Pont, France, Oct. 20, 1963; s. Roberto and Anna (Desiderio) A. MD, Amiens U., France, 1996; PhD, Lyon U., France, 1999. Intern Amiens U., France, 1990-95; sr. registrar Lyon U., France, 1997—; cons. in field. Author of book; contbr. articles to profl. jours. With French Mil., 1990-91. Mem. ALFEDIAM, French Endocrine Soc. Office: E Herriot Hosp, Place D'Arsonval, 69437 Lyon France

ANDREEV, ALEKSANDR FYODOROVICH, physicist; b. Leningrad, Russia, Dec. 10, 1939; s. Fyodor and Nina Andreev; m. Tamara Turok, 1960; 1 child. DSc in Rsch. Physics, Moscow Physico-Tech. Inst., 1961. From jr. to sr. rschr. Russian Acad. Scis., 1964-79, prof., 1979—, dep. dir. Kapitza Inst. for Phys. Problems, 1984-91, dir., 1991—, v.p., 1991—; Lorentz prof. U. Leiden, 1992. Editor-in-chief Priroda, 1993—, Jour. Exptl. and Theoretical Physics, 1997—. Recipient Lomonosov prize Russian Acad. Scis., 1984, Lenin prize, 1986, Carus medal Deutschen Acad. der Naturforscher Leopoldina, Carus prize der Stadt Schweinfurt, 1987, Simon Meml. prize, 1995, Kapitza Gold medal, 1999. Office: Acad Scis Kapitza Inst, Kosygin St 2, 117334 Moscow Russia

ANDREEV, ALEXANDER VLADIMIROVICH, physicist; b. Petersburg, Russia, Oct. 14, 1949; s. Vladimir Sergeevich and Nina Ivanovna (Frolova) A.; m. Ludmila Sergeevna Semenova, Oct. 20, 1970; children: Dmitri, Pavel. Magistr, Ural State U., Ekaterinburg, Russia, 1973, PhD, 1979, habilitation, 1990. Jr. rschr. Permanent Magnets Lab., Ural U., 1973-79, sr. rschr., 1979-89, leading rschr., 1989-95; postdoctoral fellow Charles U., Prague, Czech Republic, 1981-82; rsch. fellow U. Amsterdam, Netherlands, 1990-91; vis. prof. Tokyo U., 1992-93; leading rschr. Inst. of Physics Acad. of Scis., Prague, 1995—; vis. prof. Tohoku U., Sendai, Japan, 1997-98, 2000—. Mem. editl. bd. Jour. Alloys and Compounds, 1991—; contbr. some 250 articles on magnetism to profl. jours.; holder 12 patents. E-mail: andreev@apollo.karlov.mff.cuni.cz. Home: Brdickova 1916, 15500 Prague Czech Republic Office: Charles U Dept Electronic Structures, Ke Karlovu 5, 12116 Prague Czech Republic

ANDREEV, ANATOLII VASILIEVICH, research scientist; b. Moscow, Oct. 20, 1937; s. Vasilii Aleksandrovich Andreev and Elizaveta Dmitrievna Trachuk; m. Lyudmila Petrovna Durova, Feb. 16, 1943. Student, Pedagogical Inst., 1961; Candidate Chem. Sci., 1971, D in Tech. Sci., 1999. Rsch. scientist Inst. Metallurgy, Moscow, 1963-65; sr. rsch. scientist State Inst. Rare Metals, Moscow, 1965-99, chief rsch. scientist, 1999—. Sci. editor Jour. Analytical Chemistry; contbr. articles to profl. jours. With Soviet Army, 1962-63. Fellow Coun. Applied Nuc. Physics-Russian Acad. Scis., Sci. Analytical Chemistry-Russian Acad. Scis. Achievements include 18 patents in field. Home: 1st Naprudnaiy ul 5 kv 184, 129346 Moscow Russia Office: State Inst Rare Metals, B Tolmachovsky 5, 109017 Moscow Russia

ANDREEV, IGOR VASILIEVITCH, physicist; b. Vladivostok, Russia, July 13, 1936; s. Vasily and Anna (Trofimova) A.; m. Maria Lukinitchna Kaplunenko, Dec. 3, 1965; 1 child, Denis. Degree in engring. physics, Poly. Inst. Leningrad, 1960; PhD in Physics, Lebedev Phys. Inst., Moscow, 1964, DSc, 1975. From rsch. scientist to head high-energy physics divsn. Lebedev Inst., 1964—; vis. prof. U. Marburg, Germany, 1992-93. Home: Ul Ordzhonikidze 14 24, 117071 Moscow Russia Office: PN Lebedev Phys Inst, Leninsky prospekt 53, 117924 Moscow Russia

ANDREEVA, LIDIYA NIKOLAEVNA, chemist; b. Askarovo, Russia, July 10, 1945; s. Nikolay Nikolaevich and Angelina Dmitrievna (Markova) A.; m. Felix Gergardovich Unger, July 12, 1987; children: Mariya, Alena. Diploma, Bashkirian State U., Ufa, Russia, 1968, All-Union Rsch. Inst. Pet.Ref., Moscow, 1980. Jr. rsch. scientist Bashkirian Rsch. Inst. Petroleum Processing, Ufa, 1968-86, patent specialist, 1968-86, sr. rsch. scientist, 1968-86; sr. rsch. scientist Inst. Petroleum Chemistry, Russian Acad. Sci., Tomsk, 1986—; tutor Tomsk State U., 1990; chief exec. Natural Resources Com., Tomsk, 1995-97. Author: Fundamental Aspects of the Oil Chemistry, 1995; contbr. articles to profl. jours. Avocations: traveling, skiing, nature, eastern philosophy. Home: Ul Vavilova 2 Apt 90, 634055 Tomsk Russia Office: Inst Pet Chemistry RAS, 3 Akademichesky Ave, 634021 Tomsk Russia

ANDREIC, ZELJKO, scientist; b. Zagreb, Croatia, Feb. 27, 1957; s. Valentin and Bozica (Mayer) A.; m. Jagodica Jankovic, Dec. 15, 1984; children: Amalija, Doroteja. BS, U. Zagreb, Croatia, 1980, MS, 1984, PhD, 1993. Rsch. & devel. engr. Inst. R. Boskovic, Zagreb, Croatia, 1980-89, asst., 1989-93, sr. asst., 1993-99; rsch. assoc. Inst. R. Boskovic, Zagreb, 1999—. Author: Small Observational Astronomy, 1994, Astronomy Primer, 2000. Mem. Croatian Phys. Soc., Croatian Astron. Soc. (head ednl. sect. 1994-99), Alexander von Humboldt Found., Visnjan Observatory. Roman Catholic. Avocations: astronomy, telescope making, writing. Office: Inst Rudjer Boskovic, Divn Mat Sci Bijenicka 54, 10000 Zagreb Croatia

ANDREIEV, YURA (GEORGE), electronics engineer; b. N.Y.C., June 21, 1961; s. Nikita and Maria (Tregubov) A.; 1 child, Morgan. BS in Engring. Physics, Cornell U., 1982; MS in Elec. Engring., George Washington U., 1987. Lic. pvt. pilot, FAA. Pres. Synersol Assocs., Denver, 1982-84; rsch. electronics engr. U.S. Army Night Vision and Electro-Optics Lab., Ft. Belvoir, Va., 1984-89; electronics engr. Office of Naval Intelligence, Washington, 1989-92; chief scientist radar technologies Def. Intelligence Agy., Washington, 1992-95; dir. R&D (Russia) Sci. Applications Internat. Corp., Moscow, 1995-97; dir. internat. programs Ukrainian Land and Resources Mgmt. Ctr., Kyiv, Ukraine, 1997-2000; chief scientist Environ. Rsch. Inst. of Mich., Ann Arbor, 1997-2000; security engring officer U.S. Dept. of State, Washington, 2000—; solar energy cons. Synersol Assocs., Washington, 1982—; tech. advisor On-Site Inspection Agy., Washington, 1989. Patentee in field. Block coord. Neighborhood Watch, Alexandria, Va., 1993-94. Recipient 8 spl. act awards U.S. Army, 1984-89, Letter of Commendation, U.S. Joint Chiefs of Staff, 1992. Mem. IEEE, Optical Soc. Am., Amnesty Internat. Avocations: flying, skiing. Home: 3852 Pinewood Ter Falls Church VA 22041-1215

ANDREINI, PIERANGELO, engineer, educator; b. Milan, Italy, Jan. 1, 1947; s. Augusto and Maria (Fincato) A.; m. Carla Colombo, Dec. 6, 1995. BSChE, Politecnico, Milan, 1971. Asst. prof. applied physics Politecnico, 1973-82, assoc. prof., 1982-93, prof., 1994—; gen. sec., pres. Italian Thermotech. Com., 1976-88, 88-94; rsch. leader energetic standards Nat. Rsch. Coun., Italy. Author: Certificare la Qualita, 1995, La Conduzione dei Generatori di Vapore, 1995, Riscaldamento Degli Edifici, 1995. With Italian Air Force, 1971-72. Mem. Engr. Com., Italian Heating and Cooling Assn., Italian Thermotech. Assn. (v.p. 1989-96, jour. editor 1985—), Rotary. Home: Via e de Amicis 39, 20123 Milan Italy Office: Politecnico di Milano, P Le Leonardo da Vinci 32, 20133 Milan Italy

ANDREJTSCHEFF, WENZESLAV H., physicist, researcher; b. Pleven, Bulgaria, Feb. 23, 1941; s. Haralambi V. and Vera Y. (Georgieva) A.; m. Boryana P. Stantcheva, Aug. 22, 1965. Diploma in physics, Tech. U. Dresden, 1966, PhD, 1970, DSc, 1974. Scientist Ctrl. Inst. for Nuclear Rsch. Rossendorf, Germany, 1970-75; assoc. prof. Inst. for Nuclear Rsch. and Nuclear Energy Bulgarian Acad. Scis., Sofia, 1975-83; leader nuclear spectroscopy INRNE, Sofia, 1978—, prof., 1983—; chmn. sci. coun. INRNE, 1995—; vis. nuclear physics lab. Rutgers U., 1979-80, vis. assoc. prof. physics, 1980-81; vis. prof. U. Cologne, Germany, 1996, 98; mem. sci. coun. Joint Inst. for Nuclear Rsch., Dubna, Russia, 1989—. Contbr. articles to profl. jours. including Nuclear Physics A, Physics Letters B, Phys. Rev. C., Nuclear Instruments and Methods in Phys. Rsch. A, Zeitschrift für Physik A, Jour. Physics G, Atomic Data and Nuclear Data Tables, among others. 1st lt. Bulgarian Army, 1959-61. Recipient Sci. award CINR Rossendorf, 1975, 76. Mem. Bulgarian Acad. Scis. (elect gen. assembly 1991—, Physics award 1989), Internat. Union of Pure and Applied Physics (nuclear physics commn. 1993-96), European Phys. Soc. (dir. nuclear physics confs. 1985-87), Bulgarian Physics Union. Avocation: mountain hiking. Office: Inst Nucl Rsch Nucl Energy, 72 Tzarigrad Chaussee, BG-1784 Sofia Bulgaria

ANDRENKO, ANDREY STANISLAVOVICH, radiophysicist, researcher; b. Kharkov, Ukraine, Aug. 16, 1964; s. Stanislav Dmitrievich and Nina Volodymirivna (Podchasova) A.; m. Irina Leonidivna Poddubtseva, Sept. 21, 1985 (div. Sept. 1994); children: Stanislav, Anton; m. Katerina Volodymirivna Shepelska, Sept. 16, 1994. MS in Radiophysics with honors, Kharkov State U., 1986, PhD in Radiophysics, 1992. Engr. Ukrainian Acad. Scis. Inst. Radiophysics and Electronics, Kharkov, 1986-91, rsch. scientist, 1991—; asst. prof. U. Gaziantep, Turkey, 1993-96; rsch. fellow Tokyo Inst. Tech., 1996-98; rsch. staff Info. Tech. R&D Ctr., Mitsubishi Electric Corp., Kamakura, Japan, 1998—. Contbr. articles to profl. jours. Mem. IEEE, Soviet Soc. Radio Engrs. Achievements include contributions to theory of diffraction of electromagnetic waves and antenna design. Avocations: martial arts, tennis, soccer, travel. Home: 1-8-3 202 Iwase Kamakura, Kanagawa 247-0051, Japan Office: Mitsubishi Elec/Info Tech, 5-1-1 Ofuna Kamakura City, Kanagawa 247-8501, Japan

ANDREOLETTI, LAURENT PIERRE, virologist, educator, researcher; b. Toulouse, France, June 27, 1966; s. Georges and Esperance (Zaborski) A.; m. Maryline LeGrand, June 28, 1996. PharmD, U. Toulouse, 1989; PhD in Medicine, U. Lille, France, 1994. Cert. microbiologist, pharmacist, virologist. Resident Regional and Univ. Hosp. Ctr., Lille, 1989-94, rschr., 1994-98, asst. prof., 1998—, dir. molecular biology, dept. virology, 1994—; cons., rschr. Pasteur Inst. of Lille, 1998-2000; asst. prof. U. Paris, Broussais Hosp. Contbr. articles to med. publs. Capt. Marine/French Army, 1993-94. Recipient Gold medal for rsch. in biology CHRU, 1993, Behring prize for best rsch. work in north of France, 1994. Mem. French Soc. Microbiology, European Soc. Clin. Virology, N.Y. Acad. Scis. Avocations: squash, golf. Office: Dept Virology Hosp, Broussais 96 Rue Didot, 75096 Paris Cedex 14, France

ANDREONI, PIERO MASSIMO, bank executive, consultant; b. Milan, Italy, Nov. 15, 1959; s. Paolo and Alessandra (Colombo) A.; m. Raffaella Chierichetti, June 20, 1992; children: Vittorio, Eugenio. Degree in bus. econ., U. Cattolica, Milan, Italy, 1984; MBA, U. Bocconi, Milan, Italy, 1988. Rschr. U. Cattolica, Milan, 1983-85; product mgr. Societa Assicuratrice Indsl., Milan, 1986-87; fin. instns. mgr. Riunione Adriatica di Sicurta, Milan, 1989-90; mktg. mgr. Riunione Adriatica di Sicuri, Milan, 1990-94; sr. cons. Watson Wyatt Isso, Milan, 1995-98; strategies mgr. Banca Popolare di Bari, 1999—; bd. dirs. OSC, Sudbroker Cons. Author: We Hope that the Boss Doesn't Come In, 1999; contbr. articles to profl. jours. Mem. bd. Africa Oggi, Milan, 1988-92. Sgt. Italian Mil., 1984-85. Avocations: skiing, travel, flying. Office: Banca Popolare di Bari, Via Melo 89, 70121 Bari Italy

ANDREOSE, MARIO, editor; b. Venice, Italy, Apr. 24, 1934. Editor Il Saggiatore, Milan, 1959-69; chief editor A. Mondadori Editore, Milan, 1969-78; editl. dir. Gruppo Editoriale Fabbri Bompiani Sonzogno, Milan, 1978-92, Illustrated Books, 1992-98, Bompiani Pub. House, 1999—. Office: RCS Libri SpA, Via Mecenate 91, Milan I-20138, Italy

ANDREOTTI, GIULIO, government official; b. Jan. 14, 1919; m. Livia Danese, 1941; 4 children. Grad., U. Rome, 1945; Hon. causa, Loyola U., Chgo., 1972, Sorbonne U., Paris, 1980, Copernicus U., Torun, Poland, 1984, U. Notre Dame, 1985, U. La Plata, Argentina, 1985, U. Salamanca, Spain, 1986, St. John's U., N.Y., 1986, Univ. Sci. e Tech., Beijing, 1987, Univ. Alemente d'Ocrida, Sofia, Bulgaria, 1988, Univ. Warsaw, 1989, Univ. de Gorizia, 1990. Pres. Fedn. Cath. Univs. in Italy, 1942-45; dep. to Constituent Assembly, 1945, dep. to Parliament, 1946—; under-sec. Govt. of Italy, 1947-53, minister for interior, 1954, minister of fin., 1955-58, minister of treasury, 1958-59, minister of def., 1959-66, 74-76, minister of industry and commerce, 1966-68; pres. orgn. com. Rome Olympics, 1960; chmn. Christian Dem. Parliamentary Group in Chamber of Deputies, 1968-72, chmn. fgn. affairs commn., 1973-74, 79-83; prime minister of Italy, 1972-73, 76-79, 89-92, senator, 1991—; minister of balance for econ. planning and spl. econ. interventions in South, 1973-74; minister of fgn. affairs, 1983-89; mem. European Parliament; active Interparliamentary Union, chmn. polit. affairs and disarmament com., 1981-85; mem. internat. adv. council Inst. Internat. Studies; chmn. Christian Dem. Party Directorate. Author: Concerto a Sei Voci, 1946, Pranzo di Magro per Il Cardinale, 1954, De Gasperi e Il Suo Tempo, 1965, la Sciarada di Papa Mastai, 1967, I Minibigami, 1971, Ore 13: Il Ministro deve Morire, 1975, A Ogni Morte Di Papa, 1980, Diari 1976-79, 1981, Visti da Vicino, vols. I-III, 1982, 2d edit., 1983, 3d edit., 1985 (3d vol. Premio Bancarella award 1985), De Gasperi, 1986, Onorevole, stia zitto, 1987, L'Urss Vista da Vicino, 1988, Gli Usa Visti da Vicino, 1989, Il Potere Logora...Ma è Meglio Non Perderlo, 1990, Governare Con La Crisi: dal 1944 a oggi, 1991, Onorevole, stia zitto-atto secondo, 1992, Il mistero dell'uomo grigio, 1993, Cosa Loro, 1995, De (Prima) re Publica, 1996, Operazione Via Appia, 1998, A non domanda rispondo, 1999; editor Concretezza, 1954-76, Dal 1993, dirige il mensile "30 Giorni". Office: P ZA S Lorenzo in Lucina 26, 00186 Rome Italy*

ANDREOU, DOROS, physicist, technoeconomic consultant; b. Strovolos, Cyprus, July 31, 1948; s. Andreas and Maroulla (Ppourou) A. BSc with 1st class honours, U. London, 1969, PhD, 1973. Fellow Royal Holloway Coll., U. London, 1970-78; attached scientist Culham Lab., U.K. Atomic Energy Authority, 1970-78; vis. scientist Ctr. Atomic Energy, Fontenay-aux-Rose, France, 1979-80; technoecon. cons. for devel. new energy sources, Eng., 1980-83; sci. cons. on devel. nuclear fuels D.A. Sci. Consultatations, 1983-90; sci. cons. devel. new energy sources Synergetic Resources Ltd., U.K., 1990—; sci. cons. for laser isotope separation, 1980—; technoecon. cons. for new sources in fossil fuels, 1980; adminstr. land devel. projects, Cyprus, 1990—. Contbr. numerous articles on electromagnetic theory, liquid lasers, parametric oscillators, laser designs, indsl. lasers and their applications, and laser isotope separation and nuclear fuels to sci. jours., including Nature, Jour. Physics D, Jour. Physics E., Jour. Sci. Instruments, Optics Comm., Physics Letters, Jour. Applied Physics. Achievements include patents for molecular laser isotope separation (U.S. and Eng.); research on fundamental principles of quantum mechanics. Avocations: guitar music, history and philosophy of science. Fax: 357-2-492412. Office: care Synergetic Resources, PO Box 28287, Strovolos 2092, Cyprus

ANDRES, KENNETH G., JR., lawyer; b. Trenton, N.J., Nov. 9, 1953; s. Kenneth George and Joan Margaret (Fredericks) A. BA, Swarthmore Coll., 1975; JD, Capital U., 1978. Bar: N.J. 1978, Pa. 1978, U.S. Dist. Ct. N.J. 1978, U.S. Ct. Appeals (3rd cir.) 1981, U.S. Supreme Ct. 1994; cert. civil trial atty., N.J., cert. advocate Am. Bd. Trial Advocates. Ptnr. Andres & Berger PC, Haddonfield, N.J.; adj. prof. law Mercer County C.C., 1983-89; faculty mem. Am. Trial Lawyers Assn. - N.J., 1989—. Contbr. articles to profl. publs. Mem. N.J. Supreme Ct. Dist. III ethics com., 1994-98; mem. N.J. Supreme Ct. Civil Jury Charge Com., 1996—. Named Profl. Lawyer of Yr., N.J. Commn. Professionalism in Law, 1998. Mem. ATLA, ABA, Assn. Trial Lawyers of Am.-N.J. (bd. govs. 1986-90, parliamentarian 1990-91, from asst. sec. to pres. 1990-1999, N.J. Gold Medal award 1999), Pa. State Bar Assn., N.J. State Bar Assn., Burlington County Bar Assn. (chmn. civil bench and bar com. 1992-94, trustee 1993), Mercer County Bar Assn. (trustee 1982-91). Office: Andres & Berger PC 264 Kings Hwy E Haddonfield NJ 08033-1907

ANDRESEN-GUIMARÃE, FERNANDO, diplomat, NATO official. Amb. from Portugal Algiers, Baghdad; consul-Gen. Portuguese Consulate, Luanda; counsellor Permanent Mission from Portugal UN, N.Y.C.; auditor NATO Def. Coll., Rome; pres. Interministerial Commn. on Macau; head Portuguese-Chinese Jt. Liaison Group; dir.-gen. of Devel. Aid Ministry of Fgn. Affairs, Portugal; amb. from Portugal Washington; permanent rep. of Portugal NATO and Western European Union, Brussels, 1999—. Office: NATO Hdqrs, Blvd Leopold III, 1110 Brussels Belgium

ANDRESEN-GUIMARÃES, FERNANDO, ambassador; b. Lisbon, Portugal, 1941. Degree in Econs., U. Lisbon. Sec. Embassy of Portugal, Malawi, 1970-73; first sec. Embassy of Portugal, London, 1973-76; auditor NATO Def. Coll., Rome, 1977-78; counselor UN, N.Y.C., 1978-82; consul-gen. Luanda, 1982-86; ambasssador Govt. of Portugal, Bagdad, Iraq, 1986-88, Algeirs, Algeria, 1988-91; dir. gen. devel. aid Ministry Fgn. Affairs Govt. of Portugal, 1991-92, pres. Interministerial Commn. Macau, head Portuguese-Chinese joint liaison group, 1992-95; ambassador Govt. of Portugal, Washington, 1995-99; Portuguese amb. NATO, Brussels, Belgium, 1999—. Fax: (202) 462-3726. Office: Embassy Portugal NATO Hdqtrs, Blvd Leopold 111, Brussels 1110, Belgium*

ANDRÉS-GALLEGO, JOSÉ (J.A. ANDRÉS-GALLEGO), history researcher, educator; b. Calatayud, Zaragoza, Spain, Apr. 2, 1944; s. José Andrés de Miguel and María del Carmen Gallego; m. María Jesús Urtasun, June 29, 1968; children: Inigo, Pilar, Isabel, María, Iosune, Elisa, José, Javier, Carmen, Teresa, Miguel, Pedro, Roncevalles, Edurne. PhD in History, U. Navarra, Pamplona, Spain, 1971. Prof. contemporary history U. Oviedo, Spain, 1975-77, U. Nacional de Educacion a Distancia, Madrid, 1977-83, U. Cadiz, 1983-86; rschr. Centro Estudios Históricos, Madrid, 1986—; vis. prof. U. degli Studi, Trento, Italy, 1989-90, 92-93; dir. Proyectos Históricos Mapfre, Madrid, 1993—; acad. corr. Academia Portuguesa de la Historia, Lisbon, Portugal, 1996—, Academia de Bellas Letras, Seville, Spain, 1997—; rector Cath. U. Avila, Spain, 1997-98. Author: La politica religiosa en Espana, 1889-1913, 1975, El socialismo durante la Dictadura, 1923-1930, 1977, Los Movimientos revolucionarios europeos de 1917-1921, 1979 (Premio de ensayo de la U. Sevilla 1979), Pensamiento y accion social de la Iglesia en Espana, 1984, Historia general de la gente poco importante, 1992, Quince revoluciones y algunas cosas mas, 1992, Recreacion del humanismo, 1994, Cadiz y el pan de cada dia, 1995, Los Espanoles, entre la religion y politica: el Franquismo y la democracia, 1996, Esquilache y el pan (1766), 1996, Fascismo o Estado catolico?...la Espana de Franco (1937-1941), 1997, La Iglesia en la Espana Contemporanea (1800-1999), 1999; editor: Historia General de Espana y America, 1981-92 (24 vols.), Historia de Espana (2 vols.), 1989-90, Colecciones Mapfre 1492 (245 vols.), 1992, New History, nouvelle histoire: Hacia una nueva historia, 1993, Historia De la Historiografia Espanola, 1999, Clasicos Tavera (46 cederoms) I, 1999—, Nuevas aportaciones a la historia jurídica de Iberoamérica, 2000; editor Hispania Sacra jour., 1986—; contbr. articles to profl. jours. Mem. Soc. Spanish and Portuguese History (exec com. 1992-94), Fundación Mapfre Am., Fundación Histórica Tavera. Roman Catholic. Avocations: cycling, climbing. E-mail: jandres-gallego@ceh.csic.es. Home: Fermin Caballero 56, 28034 Madrid Spain Office: Humanities Center, c/Dugue de Medinaceli 6, 28014 Madrid Spain

ANDRETTI, MARIO, race car driver; b. Montona, Italy, Feb. 28, 1940; came to U.S., 1955, naturalized, 1964; s. Alvise and Rina (Benvegnu) A.; m. Dee Ann Hoch, Nov. 25, 1961; children: Michael, Jeffrey, Barbra. Began racing career at age 19 Nazareth, Pa. Champ Car Nat. Champion, 1965, 66, 69, 84; Daytona 500 winner, 1967; three-time 12 Hrs. of Sebring winner, 1967, 70, 72; Indpls. 500 winner, 1969; three-time Indy 500 pole winner, 1966, 67, 87; USAC Nat. Dirt Track Champion, 1974; Formula One World Champion, 1978; Internat. Race of Champions titlist, 1979; Driver of the Yr., 1967, 78, 84; Driver of the Quarter Century, 1992, Driver of the Century, 1999-2000; all-time leader in Champ Car Pole Positions won (67); all-time Champ Car lap leader (7,587); all-time record holder for Champ Car Starts (407); oldest race winner in recorded Champ car history (53 years 34 days, Phoenix, 1993); only driver to win Champ Car races in four decades; had 12 Forumla One victories and captured 18 Grand Prix pole positions.

ANDREU-GARCIA, JOSE ANTONIO, territory supreme court chief justice. Chief justice Supreme Ct. of P.R. Office: Supreme Ct PR PO Box 9022392 San Juan PR 00902-2392

ANDREW, PRINCE (ALBERT CHRISTIAN EDWARD ANDREW), Duke of York, Earl of Inverness, Baron Killyleagh; b. London, Feb. 19, 1960; s. Prince Philip, Duke of Edinburgh and Queen Elizabeth II; m. Sarah Margaret Ferguson, July 23, 1986 (dissolved 1996); children: Beatrice Elizabeth Mary, Eugenie Victoria Helena. Student, Gordonstoun Sch., Scotland, Lakefield Coll. Sch., Ont., Can., Britannia Royal Naval Coll., Dartmouth, Eng. Joined Royal Navy, 1979, advanced through grades to comdr., 1999, helicopter pilot HMS Invincible South Atlantic campaign, 1982, with 702 squadron HMS Osprey, 1983, with Lynx helicopter squadron HMS Brazen, 1986, with HMS Edinburgh, 1988, flight comdr. HMS Campbeltown, 1989, comdr. HMS Cottesmore, 1993, sr. pilot 815 Squadron HMS Osprey, 1995; mem. Ministry of Defence, 1997—; colonel-in-chief Staffordshire Regiment, 1989, Royal Irish Regiment, 1992, Royal New Zealand Army Logistic Regiment, 1997, Honorary Air Commodore Royal Air Force, Lossiemouth, 1997, Queen's York Rangers, 1998. Photography exhbns. include Hamilton Gallery, 1983, Royal Albert Hall, 1986. Patron Brit. Schs. Exploring Soc., Jubilee Sailing Trust, Aycliffe Sch., SS Great Britain appeal, Fight for Sight, Brit. Deaf Assn., Commonwealth Assn. for the Deaf, Opera North, Contemporary Dance Trust. Avocations: golf, sailing, shooting. Office: Buckingham Palace, London SW1A 1AA, England

ANDREWS, ADRIENNE PAINE, psychologist; b. Phila., June 16, 1962; d. Emmons Gould and Maxine (Rupert) Paine; m. Block McDonald Andrews, July 31, 1993; children: Adrienne, Cameron. BA, U. Mass., 1984; MA, U. Kans., 1989, PhD, 1991. Assoc. dir. work group on health promotion U. Kans., Lawrence, 1991-99, assoc. rsch. prof., 1999—; program dir. Project Freedom Replication Initiative, Lawrence, 1992-97; program co-dir. Sch./Cmty. Initiative, Lawrence, 1992—; technical asst. state/regional prevention ctrs., cmty. partnerships State of Kans., 1990-98; independent cons., 1999—. Contbr. articles to profl. jours. Mem. APHA (reviewer proposals 1995—), Am. Psychol. Assn. (regional coord. divsn. 27 1996-99), Soc. Pub. Health Edn., Kans. Pub. Health Assn. Democrat. Presbyterian. Avocations: skiing, tennis, cooking, crafts. Home: 8000 W 113th Ter Overland Park KS 66210-1813

ANDREWS, ANTHONY, actor; b. London, 1948; m. Georgina Simpson; 3 children. Student, Royal Masonic Pub. Sch. Actor, 1967—; TV appearances include Doomwatch, 1972, Woodstock, 1972, Dixon of Dock Green, 1972, A Day Out, 1973, Follyfoot, 1973, Fortunes of Nigel, 1973, A War of Children, 1973, The Pallisers, 1974, QBVII, 1974, David Copperfield, 1974, The Duchess of Duke Street, Upstairs, Downstairs, 1975, London Assurance, 1976, French Without Tears, 1977, The Country Wife, 1977, Much Ado About Nothing, 1977, Danger UXB, 1978, La Ronde, Romeo and Juliet, 1979, Brideshead Revisited, 1980, Ivanhoe, 1982, The Scarlet Pimpernel, 1983, Sparkling Cyanide, 1983, A.D., 1984, Night of Paradise, The Judge's Wife, A Superstition, Burning Bridges, Z for Zachariah, The Woman He Loved, 1988, Bluegrass, 1988, Suspicion, 1986, The Hands of a Murderer, 1990, The Strange Case of Dr. Jekyll and Mr. Hyde, 1989, Columbo Goes to the Guillotine, 1989, Napoleon of Crime, 1990, (BBC TV) The Law Lord, 1991, Jewels, 1992, (BBC 2) Mothertime, 1998, David Copperfield, 1999; films include Les Adolescents, 1971, Take Me High, 1973, Mistress of Paradise, Percy's Progress, 1974, Operation Daybreak, 1975, The Holcroft Covenant, 1984, Under the Volcano, 1984, Second Victory, 1987, The Lighthorsemen, 1987, Hanna's War, 1988, Lost in Siberia, 1990, Haunted, 1995; theatre: 40 Years On, 1968, Time and the Conways, Dragon Variation, 1977, One of Us, 1986, Coming in to Land, 1987, Vertigo, 1999. Office: e/c Marmont Mgmt Ltd, 308 Regent St Langham House, London W1R 5AL, England

ANDREWS, ANTHONY HUNTER, veterinary educator, writer, consultant; b. Swindon, Wiltshire, England, Aug. 16, 1942; s. Harold Edward and Alice Winifred (Hunter) A.; m. Joan Margaret Isle, Jan. 1, 1966 (div. Oct. 1972); 1 child, Michael John; m. Celia Josephine Tucker, Oct. 21, 1972 (div. Feb. 1977); 1 child, Mark Edward Alexander. B in Vet. Medicine, U. London, 1966, PhD, 1980. Recognized specialist in cattle health and prodn. Vet. surgeon Falmouth, Cornwall, England, 1966-67, Cranleigh, Surrey, England, 1967-68, 68-70, Isle of Wight, England, 1968; Royal Smithfield Club fellow Royal Vet. Coll., U. London, 1970-73, sr. lectr. farm animal medicine, 1979-97; ind. vet. cons., 1997—; sr. vet. officer Meat & Livestock Commn., Milton Keynes, England, 1973-79; sec. Brit. Cattle Vet. Assn., 1976-79, pres., 1983-84; vet. expert Social Econ. Com. EEC, Brussels, 1989-90, House of Lords Select Com. on European Cmty., London, 1989; examiner U. London, U. Cambridge, U. Dublin, U. Edinburgh, Royal Coll. Vet. Surgeons; mem. British Pharm. Commn., 1998—; mem. Min. Agr., Fisheries and Food, Beef Assurance Adv. Panel, 1999—. Author: Calf Management and Disease Notes, 1983, The Henston Veterinary Vade Mecum edits., 1984-97, Growing Cattle Management and Disease Notes Part 1, 1985, Part 2, 1986, Outline of Clinical Diagnosis in Cattle, 1990 (Blackwell Sci.), Poisoning in Veterinary Practice, 1992; co-author, editor: Bovine Medicine, 1992 (Blackwell Sci.); editor: The Health of Dairy Cattle Blackwell Science, 2000, The Health of Dairy Cattle, 2000, The Expectant Cow, 2000, livestock editor UK Vet, 1995—; mem. editl. bd. Brit. Vet. Jour., 1988—, mem. exec. bd., 1995-98; contbr. articles to profl. jours. Recipient Bewicke award Royal Vet. Coll., 1969, Centenary prize Ctrl. Vet. Soc., 1987. Mem. Brit. Vet. Assn. (chmn. large animals com. 1983-84, chmn. sci. edn. and mktg. com. 1984-87, mem. coun. 1976-87, 90—, William Hunting award 1971), Hertfordshire and Bedfordshire Vet. Soc. (v.p. 1993-95, pres. 1995-97, sr. 1997-99), Goat Vet. Soc. (coun. mem. 1995—, vice chair 1996-97, chmn. 1998—), Vet. Assn. Arbitration and Jurisprudence (coun. mem. 1995—, vice chmn. 1997—), Farmers Club. Mem. Ch. of England. Avocations: the countryside, travel, gardening, reading, writing.

ANDREWS, BILLY FRANKLIN, pediatrician, educator; b. Graham, N.C., Sept. 22, 1932; s. Dean Franklin and Arlee (Byers) A.; m. Faye Rich, Dec. 25, 1953; children: Ann Elizabeth Feigenbaum, Billy Franklin Jr., David Ashley. Student, Brevard (N.C.) Coll., 1950, Elon Coll., 1951; BS cum laude, Wake Forest Coll., 1953; MD, Duke U., 1957; prog. Chiefs of Clinical Services, Harvard Sch. Pub. Health, 1982. Diplomate Am. Bd. Pediatrics, 1963. Commd. 2nd lt. U.S. Army, 1956, advanced through grades to maj., 1962; intern Ft. Benning (Ga.) U.S. Army Hosp., 1957-58; resident in pediat. Walter Reed Gen. Hosp., Washington, 1958-60; with mil. med. and allied scis. course Walter Reed Army Inst. Rsch., Washington, 1960-61; chief pediat. svc. Rodriguez U.S. Army Hosp., Ft. Brooke, P.R., 1961-63; chief pediat. Tropical Med. Rsch. Lab., Ft. Brooke, P.R., 1963-64; res. U.S. Army, 1964; asst. prof. pediat. U. Louisville, 1964-66, dir. newborn svcs., 1964-76, assoc. prof., 1966-68, prof., 1968—, dept. chmn. Sch. Medicine, 1969-93, chmn. emeritus, 1993—, dir. Comprehensive Health Care Ctr. for High Risk Infants and Children, 1968-98; chief of staff Kosair Children's Hosp., Louisville, 1969-93; chief-of-staff emeritus Kosair Children's Hosp., 1993—; cons. div. maternal and child health Ky. Dept. Health, 1966—; lectr. Jour. Pediatrics Found., 1972; Staley Disting. Christian scholar Mary Baldwin Coll., Washington and Lee U., Sch. Medicine of U. Va., 1990; vis. scholar in med. history and ethics Green Coll., Oxford Univ. Oxford, Eng., 1993, vis. fellow, 1998. Author: Children's Bill of Rights, 1968; editor: Small-for-Date Infants, 1970, The Newborn, Pediatric Clinics of North America, 1977, Aphorisms, Tributes and Tenets of Billy F. Andrews: In Walls, M.E., 1986, Ideals and Inspiration (F.R. Andrews), 1993, Words to Live By (F.R. Andrews), 1993, A Statement on Transplantation and Organ Donors, 1994; contbr. numerous articles to profl. publs.; inventor, poet. Pres. Kornhauser Libr., Health Scis. Ctr., 1981-82, 90-91; mem., tchr., deacon, elder United Ch. of Christ. Recipient Helen B. Fraser award Norton-Children's Hosp., 1978, Award of Recognition, XVII Internat. Congress Pediat., Manila, 1983, Wisdom award of honor, eminent fellow The Wisdom Soc., 1991, The Billy F. Andrews, M.D. Endowed Chair in Pediat., U. Louisville, 1993, Winston Churchill medal of Wisdom Soc., Eminent Churchill Fellow of Wisdom Soc., 1993, Disting. Alumnus award Wake Forest U., 1983, The Billy F. Andrews, M.D. scholarship for pediat. U. Louisville Sch. Medicine, 1986, Festschrift to Billy F. Andrews, M.D., Jour. of Perinatology, 1995. Fellow ACP, Am. Acad. Pediat., Royal Soc. Medicine (London), Internat. Biog. Assn.; mem. AMA, Am. Pediat. Soc., Am. Osler Soc. (pres. 1996-97), Am. Soc. for Bioethics and Humanities, Soc. for Pediat. Rsch., So. Soc. Pediat. Rsch. (founding), Southeastern Perinatal Soc. (founding), Nat. Assn. Children's Hosps. and Related Instns. (founding), Ky. Med. Assn. (faculty Sci. Achievement award 1971, del. 1981-82, Ednl. Achievement award 1997), Jefferson County Med. Soc., Ky. Pediat. Soc., Louisville Pediat. Soc., U. Louisville Sch. Medicine Alumni Assn. (bd. govs. 1972-75), Univ. Pediatric Found. Inc. (pres. 1982-93), Internat. Assn. Bioethics, Order of Internat. Fellowship (Cambridge), Internat. Order of Merit (Cambridge), Alpha Omega Alpha. Achievements include invention of infant oxygen hood, iontophoresis sweat induction apparatus, open infant warmer, infant blood warmer, diagnostic and treatment table with warmer and position changes,

infant transport incubator, others. Office: Kosair Charities Pediat Ctr 571 S Floyd St Ste 449 Louisville KY 40202-3830

ANDREWS, BRYANT AYLESWORTH, software company executive; b. N.Y.C., Dec. 28, 1938; s. F. Emerson and Edith Severance Andrews; m. Elisabeth Power, July 5, 1974; children: Christopher, Suzanne. BA in English, Cornell U., 1962. Engring. writer Pratt & Whitney Aircraft, East Hartford, Conn., 1962-79, supr. engring. writers, 1979-83, mgr. system devel., office automation, 1983-85; pres., co-founder Integrated Custom Software, Inc., Glastonbury, Conn., 1985—. Author: (software) System Minder, Formsprint. Chmn. Columbia Fin. Bd., 1979-87; mem., chmn. Columbia Planning and Zoning, 1971-77, Windham Regional Planning Agy., Willimantic, Conn., 1971-75. Republican. Congregationalist. Avocation: private pilot. E-mail: icsandr@ibm.net. Home: 99 Route 87 Columbia CT 06237-1023 Office: Integrated Custom Software Inc 12 National Dr Glastonbury CT 06033-1212

ANDREWS, CAROL ANN RAY, Egyptologist, researcher; b. Hitchin, Eng., Dec. 3, 1945; d. Leslie and Beatrice (McFarlane) A. BA in Classics with honors, London U., 1967, postgrad. acad. diploma in Egyptology, 1970. Curator Egyptian antiquities Brit. Mus., London, 1971-2000. Author: The Rosetta Stone, 1981, Egyptian Mummies, 1984, Ancient Egyptian Jewellery, 1990, Amulets of Ancient Egypt, 1994, Catalogue of Demotic Papyri in the British Museum, Vol. 4, 1990, among others. Mem. Egypt Exploration Soc. Avocations: opera, playing field hockey, supporting Manchester United.

ANDREWS, CHARLES ROLLAND, library administrator; b. Scranton, Pa., July 5, 1930; s. Edgar W. and Margaret (Machenry) A.; m. Harriet Williams, Dec. 27, 1954 (dec. 1985); m. Dorothy Kramer, Dec. 10, 1988. BS in Edn., Bloomsburg U., 1954; MA in English Lit., U. Okla., 1959; MS in Lib. Sci., Case Western Res. U., 1964, PhD, 1967. Head reference dept. Cleve. Pub. Library, 1966-68; head reference dept. Case Western Res. Univ. Libraries, Cleve., 1968-69, librarian Freiberger Library, 1969-72, asst. dir. pub. services, 1972-74; univ. librarian Southeastern Mass. Univ. Library, North Dartmouth, 1974-76; dean library services Hofstra U. Library, Hempstead, N.Y., 1976-96, prof. emeritus, 1997—; lectr. Hofstra U., U. Coll. Continuing Edn., 1997—. Editor: Reference Books for Small and Medium-Sized Libraries, 1973; contbr. articles, revs. to profl. jours. Bd. trustees Unitarian Universalist Congregation, Garden City, N.Y., 1998—, chair art exhibits com., 1999—. Mem. ALA, Assn. Coll. and Rsch. Librs., Archons of Colophon, L.I. Libr. Resources Coun. (chair regional automation com. 1986-92, bd. trustees 1990-94), Am. Express (sr. adv. bd. mem. 1998-99). Democrat. Avocations: calligraphy, word processing, graphics. Home and Office: 305 Hillside Ave Bellmore NY 11710-3519

ANDREWS, CHRISTOPHER JOHN, registrar in anesthesiology; b. Tamworth, Australia, Sept. 1, 1951; s. John Hayward and Hilda Olive (Reeve) A.; m. Esther Elsie Gilmore Wilson, Dec. 7, 1975 (div. 1998); children: Stephen David Christopher, Paul Anthony Brian. BE (Elec.), U. Queensland, Australia, 1970-73, MEngSc in Elec. Engring, 1976, Grad-DipCompSci, 1976, MBBS with honors, 1982, PhD in Elec. Engring., 1992. Chartered profl. engr.; registered med. practitioner; European diploma of intensive care medicine European Soc. Intensive Care Medicine. Sr. tutor in computer sci. U. Queensland, 1976-77, lectr., rsch. fellow, 1985-89; intern, sr. house officer Queensland Pub. Hosps., 1983-84, prin. house officer, registrar anesthesiology/intensive care, 1993-96; pvt. practice med. practitioner Brisbane, Australia, 1989-92; intensive care resident med. officer Wesley Hosp., Brisbane, 1988-92; med. family practitioner Indooroopilly, Australia, 1996-2000; registrar in anesthesiology Mater Hosps., Brisbane, Australia, 2000—; rschr., med. and legal cons. in elec. and lightning injuries. Assoc. editor for book revs. Australian Computer Jour., 1988-94; contbr. articles to profl. jours., chpts. to books; reviewer for jours. in field; co-editor textbook for CRC Press, Fla., U. Queensland Dept. Computer Sci. Mem. Lucian Singers, 1971-82, 84—; mem. organizing com. Nat. Royal Sch. Ch. Music Summer Sch., 1975, 94; mem. Cairns Civic Orch., 1983; musical dir., mem. com. Queensland Musical Theater, 1991-93; various musical direction positions Ignations Musical Soc., 1976—; sec. Parochial Coun. of Christ Ch. St. Lucia, 1973-74, 76-81, 84; sec. RMO Soc. Cairns Base Hosp., 1983; sec., chmn. bd. dirs. Campus Kindergarten, U. Queensland, 1990-92. Mem. IEEE (sr.), Australian Computer Soc., Instn. Radio and Elec. Engrs. (sr.), N.Y. Acad. Scis. Mem. Anglican Ch. of Australia. Avocations: amateur radio, personal computing, fine music, amateur theater, genealogy. Home and Office: Mater Hosp Dept Anaesthes, Stanley St, South Brisbane 4101, Australia

ANDREWS, DAVID CHARLES, energy and power consultant; b. London, Mar. 16, 1950; s. Alan Charles and Maisie Joy (Brien) A.; m. Janet Alison Hooker; children: Joseph James, Annabel Jane. BS in Engring. with honors, U. Cardiff, 1973. Chartered engr. Engr. Mouchel & Ptnrs., Bath, Eng., 1974-78; researcher Open Univ., Milton Keynes, Eng., 1978-82; area mgr. Ellis Tylin, London, 1982-84, Applied Energy Systems, Watford, Eng., 1984-86; mgr. sales and mktg. CHP Conversions Ltd., Llantrisant, Eng., 1986—; energy mgr. Wesser Water Plc, 1988; prin. David Andrews Assocs., Bath, 1998; mng. dir. Power Gasifiers Internat., Ltd., Silent Clean Power Ltd.; sr. cons. power project Leverton Caterpillar, Windsor, U.K., 1988—. Author: The IRG Solution, 1984, The Hidden Manager, 1985; inventor info. routing group concept. Fellow Inst. Plant Engrs.; mem. Assn. Ind. Electricity Producers (founding mem.), Instn. Diesel and Gas Turbine Engrs. (coun. 1990—), Inst. Energy (chartered engr.), Power Gasifiers Internat. (mng. dir. 1993—), British Canoe Union (chmn.). Achievements include research in domestic sterling engined co-generation for gas and electricity industry.

ANDREWS, GEORGE EYRE, mathematics educator; b. Dec. 4, 1938; s. Raymond Leslie and Rovena Pearl (Eyre) A.; m. Joy Margaret Brown, Sept. 2, 1960; children: Amy Beth, Katherine Yvonne, Derek George. BS, Oreg. State U., 1960, MA, 1960; postgrad., Cambridge (Eng.) U., 1960-61; PhD, U. Pa., 1964; Doctorate in Physics (hon.), Parma (Italy) U., 1998. Asst. prof. math. Pa. State U., University Park, 1964-67, assoc. prof. math., 1967-70, prof. math., 1970-81, Evan Pugh prof. math., 1981—, math. dept. head, 1980-82, 95-97; Hedrick lectr. Math. Assn. Am., 1980, J.S. Frame lectr., 1993; adj. prof. U. Waterloo, Ont., Can., 1982-92, regional conf. lectr., NSF-Conf. Bd. Math. Scis., 1985. Author: Number Theory, 1971, Theory of Partitions, 1976, Partitions: Yesterday and Today, 1979, q-Series, 1986, (with R. Askey and R. Roy) Special Functions, 1998; editor: Collected Papers of P.A. MacMahon, Vol. I, 1978, Vol. II, 1986, Ramanujan Revisited, 1988, The Rademacher Legacy to Mathematics, 1994, (with S. Ahlgren and K. Ono) Topics in Number Theory in Honor of B. Gordon and S. Chowla, 1999. Recipient Disting. Univ. Tchg. award Allegheny mountain sect. Math. Assn. Am., 1993, Centennial award U. Pa., 1999; Guggenheim fellow, 1982-83. Mem. Am. Acad. Arts and Scis. Avocation: piano. Home: RR 2 Box 133 Centre Hall PA 16828-9763 Office: Pa State U Dept Math 410 Mcallister Bldg University Park PA 16802-6404

ANDREWS, JOHN FRANK, editor, author, educator; b. Carlsbad, N.Mex., Nov. 2, 1942; s. Frank Randolph and Mary Lucille (Wimberley) A.; m. Vicky Roberta Anderson, Aug. 20, 1966 (div. 1983); children: Eric John, Lisa Gail; m. Janet Ann Denton, Oct. 15, 1994. AB, Princeton U., 1965; MAT, Harvard U., 1966; PhD, Vanderbilt U., 1971. Instr. English U. Tenn., Nashville, 1969-70; asst. prof. Fla. State U., Tallahassee, 1970-74, dir. grad. studies in English, 1973-74; dir. acad. programs Folger Shakespeare Library, Washington, 1974-84; chmn. Folger Inst., Washington, 1974-84; exec. editor Folger Books, Washington, 1974-84; dep. dir. div. edn. programs NEH, Washington, 1984-88; editor The Guild Shakespeare, 1988-92; pres. The Shakespeare Guild, 1992—; editor The Everyman Shakespeare, 1993—; cons. Time-Life TV, WNET/Thirteen, Corp. for Pub. Broadcasting, Pub. Broadcasting Svc., Nat. Pub. Radio, U.S. Dept. Edn., others; chmn. Nat. Adv. Panel for the Shakespeare Plays, 1979-85; core advisor The Shakespeare Hour, 1985-86; mem. adv. bd. Theatre for a New Audience, Humanities Coun. of Washington, Ctr. for Polit. and Strategic Studies, Ctr. for Renaissance and Baroque Studies, U. Md., others; cons. Shakespeare: The Globe and the World, touring exhbn., 1978-81; adminstR. program grants NEH, Andrew W. Mellon Found., Exxon Corp., Met. Life, Surdna Found., others; founder of the guild's Gielgud award for Excellence in the Dramatic Arts, 1994. Asst. editor: Shakespeare Studies, 1972-74; editor: Shakespeare Quar., 1974-85; editor-in-chief, contbr.: William Shakespeare: His World, His Work, His Influence, 1985; contbr. numerous articles to mags. and scholarly jours. Recipient rsch. awards Folger Shakespeare Libr., Fla. State U., NEH; inductee Order of the Brit. Empire, 2000. Mem. AAUP (sec. chpt. 1972-74), Modern Lang. Assn., Milton Soc. Am., Nat. Council of Tchrs. of English, Renaissance Soc. Am. (mem. council 1975-84), Internat. Shakespeare Conf., Shakespeare Assn. Am. (trustee 1979-82), The Lit. Soc. Club: Cosmos. Home and Office: 2141 Wyoming Ave NW Apt 41 Washington DC 20008-3916

ANDREWS, JOHN THOMAS, retired nuclear medicine physician, consultant; b. Brighton, Sussex, England, Mar. 20, 1927; arrived in Australia, 1959; s. John James and Amelia (Marcantonio) A.; m. Iris Mary Groves, Aug. 20, 1957; children: Peter John, Michael, Steven Thomas, David. MBBS, London U., 1955; diploma of obstetrics, Royal Coll. Ob/Gyn., England, 1958; MD, U. Melbourne, 1979. Diplomate Am. Bd. Nuclear Medicine. House surgeon, asst. dept. morbid anatomy London Hosp., 1955-57, jr. med. registrar, 1957-58; house physician Dover (Eng.) Hosp., 1955-57; med. registrar, clin. asst. in medicine Launceston (Tasmania, Australia) Hosp., 1959-61; trainee, then radiotherapist Cancer Inst. Melbourne, Australia, 1961-66; dir. nuc. medicine Royal Melbourne Hosp., 1966-92; part time physician nuc. medicine Monash Med. Ctr., Melbourne, 1992-99. Co-author: Nuclear Medicine: Clinical and Technological Bases, 1977; contbr. articles to profl. jours. Active Med. Assn. Prevention of War, 1981—. With Brit. Merchant Navy, 1943-48. Fellow Royal Australasian Coll. Physicians (Short Term Study grantee 1968), Royal Australian and New Zealand Coll. Radiologists (Baker fellow 1969); mem. Australia and New Zealand Soc. Nuc. Medicine (past chmn. accreditation bd., pres. 1979-80), Australia and New Zealand Assn. Physicians in Nuc. Medicine. Avocations: skiing, walking, music. Home: 400 New St, 3186 Brighton-Melbourne Victoria, Australia

ANDREWS, JOYCE ANN MAINES, municipal official; b. Meadville, Pa., Sept. 1, 1956; d. Jess Elmer and Viola Mae (Smith) Maines; m. Kenneth Norman Andrews, Sept. 1, 1956 (dec. Sept. 1998); children: James Kenneth, Richard Jess, Sharon Lee. Student, Randolph-East Mead High Sch., Guys Mills, Pa., 1953. Budget clk. Am. Viscose Corp., Meadville, Pa., 1953-56; sales person Stanley Home planning, expediting GE, Erie, Pa., 1956-59; sales person Stanley Home Products, Erie, 1963-65; reporter Cosmopolite Herald, Girard, Pa., 1966-68; sch. aide Garwood Elem., Fairview, Pa., 1968-69; svc. rep. Gen. Telephon Co., Girard, 1971-73; borough sec. Lake City (Pa.) Borough, 1973—, bicentennial coord., 1976; pres. Erie County Local, Erie, 1980-81. Asst. grantsperosn Sewage Treatment Plant, 1987; grantsperson N.W. Sewer Lift Sta., 1988, Keystone Dr. Improvements, 1989, N.E. Sewer Lift Sta., 1991; fundraiser Willcox Libr., Girard, 1966; blood donor coord. ARC, Girard, 1967-68, disasters coord., 1969-70. Mem. Erie County Local Govtl. Secs. Assn. (v.p. 1980-81, pres. 1982-83), Erie County Boroughs Assn. (asst. sec., treas. 1984-85), Pa. State Assn. Boroughs (voting del. 1977-87). Republican. Baptist. Avocations: grandchildren, church activities, travel, reading, making jewelry. Home: 312 Barker St Girard PA 16417-1204 Office: Lake City Borough 2350 Main St Lake City PA 16423-1509

ANDREWS, LAWRENCE WAYNE, priest, educator; b. N.Y.C., July 11, 1946; s. Thomas L. and Etta M. (Corbin) A. BA, Postdam State U., 1969; MA, Columbia U., 1972, PhD, 1976; MDiv, St. Bonaventure, 1978. Ordained priest, 1978. Tchr. Materdei Coll., 1974-86; prof. Jefferson Coll., State Law U., Canton, N.Y., 1974-2000; tchr. Lisbon, 1986-2000. Author: Nazi Propaganda, 1969. Republican. Avocations: gardening, travel. Address: 353 Hull Rd Gouverneur NY 13642-3317

ANDREWS, LINFORD LLEWELLYN, diplomat; b. Cape Town, South Africa, Apr. 3, 1969; s. Arnold Jeevanantham and Ruth Alice (Jacobs) A. BA, U. Cape Town, 1989, BA with honours, 1990; MA in Internat. Politics, U. Leicester, Eng., 1993; grad., Fgn. Svc. Inst. Pretoria, 1995. Fgn. svc. officer South African Dept. Fgn. Affairs, Pretoria, 1993—. Chair Jr. Fgn. Svc. Officers Club, Pretoria, 1995-96; youth affairs portfolio exec. com. South African-German Cultural Assn., 1995. UN Ednl. and Tng. Programme scholar, 1991. Roman Catholic. Avocations: travel, cinema, photography, walking, reading. E-Mail: saemjak@centrin.net.id, llandrews@hotmail.com. Office: South African Embassy, Lt 7, Wisma GKBI, 10210 Jakarta Indonesia

ANDREWS, MALCOLM YARDLEY, English educator; b. Talyllyn, Wales, Sept. 1, 1942; s. Francis Yardley and Marguerite Joan (West) A.; m. Mildred Randolph Pfeiffer, Aug. 7, 1967 (div. 1973); 1 child, Richard; m. Kristin Avelda Wade; children: Peter, Francis. BA, Cambridge U., 1964; postgrad. cert. in Edn., U. London, 1965, PhD, 1973. Lectr. in English U. Guelph, Can., 1966-67; lectr. in English U. London, 1969-70; prof. Victorian and visual studies U. Kent, 1971—; apptd. to chair, 1995. Author: Dickens on England and the English, 1979, The Search for the Picturesque: Landscape Aesthetics and Tourism in Britain, 1750-1800, Dickens and the Grown-up Child, 1994; editor: (anthology) The Picturesque: Sources and Documents, 1994, Landscape and Western Art, 1999. Mem. Dickens Fellowship (editor The Dickensian 1991—). Avocations: reading, performances of Dickens readings, watercolors, Haut Languedoc holidays. Office: Editor Dickensian Sch Engl, Rutherford Coll U Kent, Canterbury Kent CT2 7NX, England

ANDREWS, MELINDA WILSON, human development researcher; b. N.Y.C., Aug. 12, 1956; d. William Maurice and Natalie Maxine (Amos) Wilson; m. James Robert Andrews, Dec. 3, 1977; children: Christopher Wilson Andrews, William James Andrews. BBA in Mgmt./Mktg., Abilene (Tex.) Christian U., 1977; MS in Human Devel., U. Tex., Dallas, 1988, postgrad., 1994—. Logics adminstr. Texas Instruments, Dallas, 1977-79, contract adminstr., 1979-81, 82-83; grocery mgr., co-asst. store dir. Tom Thumb, Dallas, 1981-82; teaching asst. U. Tex. at Dallas, Richardson, Tex., 1988-91; rsch. asst. U. Tex. at Dallas, 1991—; dir. creative presch. coop., Richardson, 2000—; presenter in field. Contbr. articles to profl. jours. Mem. Richardson Symphony Orch., 1977-79, Canyon Creek Elem. PTA, 5th v.p., 1994-95, libr. rep., 1992-94; treas. exec. bd. Creative Presch. Coop., 1998-99, sec. ex. bd. 1999-2000, dir., 2000—; asst. dir. ESL Sch. Waterview Ch. Christ, 2000—; asst. dir. English as second lang. sch. Waterview Ch. of Christ. Mem. Soc. for Rsch. in Child Devel. (co-author paper-poster session 1991, 93 confs.), Southwest Soc. for Rsch. in Child Devel., Psi Chi. Mem. Ch. of Christ. Avocations: music, animals, carpentry. Home and Office: 2109 Flat Creek Dr Richardson TX 75080-2331

ANDREWS, MICHAEL WILLIAM, librarian, information specialist; b. Rome, N.Y., Mar. 22, 1948; s. Martin Joseph and Mary (Dublanica) A.; m. Karen Lynn Mauro, July 23, 1982. AB in History, Cornell U., 1970; MS in Libr. Sci., Syracuse U., 1972. Libr. govt. documents SUNY, Plattsburgh, 1971-76, L.I. U., Bklyn., 1977-79; rsch. asst. Health Info. Sharing Project, Syracuse (N.Y.) U., 1979-80; readers svcs. libr. Elizabethtown (Pa.) Coll., 1980-85; online data base libr. U. D.C., Washington, 1986-87; dir. rsch. Korn/Ferry Internat., Washington, 1987—. Editor: Proceeding of the Second Annual Government Documents Workshop, 1976. Bd. dirs. Friends Chinn Pk. Regional Libr., 1998—. Mem. Spl. Librs. Assn. Avocations: reading, photography, travel, coaching youth soccer. Home: 3825 Wagon Wheel Ln Woodbridge VA 22192-6441 Office: Korn Ferry Internat 900 19th St NW Ste 800 Washington DC 20006-2105

ANDREWS, PETER RONALD, chemist, researcher; b. Sydney, N.S.W., Australia, Feb. 12, 1943; s. Ronald Geoffrey and Helen Jane (Reading) A.; m. Heather Fleming Weir, Dec. 15, 1967; children: Jane Elizabeth, Sally Louise, Susan Helen. BSc, Melbourne (Australia) U., 1965, PhD, 1969. Postdoctoral fellow Inst Physicochem. Biology, Paris, 1970; rsch. fellow Australian Nat. U., Canberra, 1971-74, fellow, 1975-79; dean chemistry sch. Victorian Coll. Pharmacy, Melbourne, 1980-87; dean sci. sch. Bond U., Gold Coast, Australia, 1988-90; dir. Ctr. for Drug Design and Devel. U. Queensland, Brisbane, Australia, 1991—, co-dir. Inst. Molecular Sci, 2000—; CEO, IBMcom, 2000—; bd. dirs. Alchemia Pty Ltd., Cytokine Mimetics Ltd., Xenome Ltd. Mem. coun. Australian Inst. Marine Sci., Townsville, 1988-98, chmn., 1995-98. Fellow Royal Australian Chem. Inst., Australian Acad. Technol. Scis. and Engring.; mem. Asian Fedn. Medicinal Chemistry (exec. coun. 1992—, pres. 2000—). Avocations: golf, sking, scuba diving, reading. Home: St Lucia, 311 Swann Rd, Brisbane 4067 QLD, Australia Office: U Queensland, Ctr Drug Design and Devel, Brisbane 4072 QLD, Australia

ANDREWS, RALPH HERRICK, television producer; b. Chgo., Dec. 17, 1927; s. Henry Karl and Sylvia Angelica (Lorenzen Barth; m. Margaret Ann Belt, Feb. 5, 1951 (div. 1977); m. Aleksandra Vaz vel Wezykowska, June 1, 1986; children: William, Herrick, Phyllis, Patrice, Peter, James, Jakub, Matthew. Announcer, disc jockey, salesman radio stas. WSAM and WKNX, Saginaw, Mich.; page NBC, Hollywood; with Don Fedderson Prodns., Ralph Edwards Prodns.; dir. live programming Desilu; prin. Ralph Andrews Prodns.; co-founder, bd. dirs. Entertainment Industries Coun. Producer: Divorce Hearing, By the Numbers, Zoom, Show Me, You Don't Say, I'll Bet, Wedding Party, The Family Game, It Takes Two, It's Your Bet, Liars Club, The Mickie Finn Show, Celebrity Sweepstakes, 50 Grand Slam, Lingo, (movies) Silent Treatment, Skyjacked; producer, host: Lie Detector; host, writer (website) The TroubleMaker www.thetroublemaker.com. Cand. for Congress, 1972; nat. dir. edn. and tng. Rep. Nat. Com., Washington, 1972 (Presidential commendation). Republican. Roman Catholic. Avocations: skiing, flying, skating, running, sailing. Home and Office: 5021 Dantes View Dr Calabasas CA 91301-2311

ANDREWS, RICHARD ANTONY, Italian language educator; b. London, May 16, 1939; s. Cyril Dudley and Ruby Violet (Ball) A.; m. Gillian Mary Howells, Apr. 17, 1965; children: Bridget, Gregory. BA in Modern Langs. with honors, St. John's Coll., Oxford, Eng., 1962. Lectr. in Italian U. Coll., Swansea, Wales, 1963-72; sr. lectr. in Italian U. Kent, Canterbury, Eng., 1972-84; prof. Italian U. Leeds, Eng., 1984—. Author: Scripts and Scenarios: The Performance of Comedy in Renaissance Italy, 1993, A Theatre of Community Memory: Tuscan sharecropping and the Teatro Povere de Monticchiello, 1998; editor: Antonio Da Tempo: Summa artis rithimici (1332), 1977; sr. editor Italian Studies, 1990—; contbr. articles and chpts. to profl. publs. Office: U Leeds Dept of Italian, Leeds LS2 9JT, England

ANDREWS, RICHARD JOHN, education educator; b. Braintree, Essex, Eng., Apr. 1, 1953; s. John William and Sylvia (Thacker) A.; m. Dorothy Fordyce Beardshaw, Aug. 2, 1979; children: David Eric, Zoe Virginia, Grace Emily. MA, Oxford (Eng.) U., 1974; PhD, U. Hull, 1992. Tchr. in English Cedars Upper Sch., Leighton Buzzard, Bedfordshire, Eng., 1977-79, George Green's Sch., London, 1979-81, Joseph Rowntree Sch., York, Eng., 1981-83; head of English Island Sch., Hong Kong, 1983-87; edn. lectr. U. Hull, Eng., 1987-2000; prof. edn. U. York, Eng., 2000—. Author: From Rough to Best, 1982, Words 1-3, 1983, Into Poetry, 1984, Poetry Horizons, 1987, Narrative and Argument, 1989, Drafting and Editing, 1990, The Problem with Poetry, 1991, Rebirth of Rhetoric, 1992, Teaching and Learning Argument, 1995, (with Sally Mitchell) Learning To Argue in Higher Education, 2000. Recipient Urban Council Poetry prize, 1984, Double Distinction award and David Forsyth prize U. Leeds, 1977; Samuel Courtauld scholar, 1971, Baring Open scholar, 1971. Avocations: walking, music, tennis, theatre. Office: U York Sch Edn, Dept Ednl Studies, York YO10 5DD, England

ANDREWS, RICHARD VINCENT, physiologist, educator; b. Arapahoe, Nebr., Jan. 9, 1932; s. Wilber Vincent and Fern (Clawson) A.; m. Elizabeth Williams, June 1, 1954 (dec. Dec. 1994); children: Thomas, William, Robert, Catherine, James, John; m. Wyoma Upward, Oct. 18, 1997. BS, Creighton U., 1958, MS, 1959; PhD, U. Iowa, 1963. Instr. biology Creighton U., Omaha, 1958-60; instr. physiology U. Iowa, 1960-63; asst. prof. Creighton U., Omaha, 1963-65, assoc. prof., 1965-68, prof. physiology, 1968-97, asst. med. dean, 1972-75, dean grad. studies, 1975-85, dean emeritus, 1995—, prof. emeritus, 1997—; vis. prof. Naval Arctic Rsch. Lab., 1963-72, U. B.C., 1985-86, U. Tasmania, 1993-94; cons. VA, NSF, NRC, ARS; plenary speaker USSR Symposium on Environment, 1970, Internat. Soc. Biomet., 1972. Contbr. articles to profl. jours. Served with M.C. U.S. Army, 1951-54. NSF fellow, 1962-63; NSF-NIH-ONR-AINA grantee, 1963—. Fellow Explorers Club, Arctic Inst. N.Am.; mem. Am. Physiol. Soc., Am. Mammal Soc., Endocrine Soc., Soc. Exptl. Biology and Medicine, Internat. Soc. for Biometeorology, Sigma Xi.

ANDREYEV, MICHAEL DMITRIEVICH, pathologist, health center administrator; b. Khmelnitsky, Ukraine, Nov. 21, 1941; s. Dmitriy Mironovich and Anastasiya Zakharovna (Kramarenko) A.; m. Valentina Antonovna Demenchuk, May 10, 1970; 1 child, Larisa Michaylovna. Student, Med. Inst., Ternopol, Ukraine, 1966; MD, Oncology Inst., Kiev, Ukraine, 1976. From chief pathology dept. to chief pathology bur. Clinic of Khmelnitsky Region, Khmelnitsky, 1966-95; chief Ukraine Pathology Ctr., Khmelnitsky, 1995—; head pathologist Ministry Kiev, 1992-98. Author: Bronchoectatic Disease, 1992; inventor in field. Mem. N.Y. Acad. Sci. Home: Apt 107 Proskurovskaya St, Khmelnitsky 280013, Ukraine Office: Ukraine Pathology Ctr, Pilotskaya St 1, Khmelnitsky 280000, Ukraine

ANDREYEV, VLADAMIR ALEKSEYEVICH, actor, stage director; b. 1930; married; 2 children. Student, State Inst. Theatre Arts. Actor Yermolova Theatre, Moscow, 1952-70, chief dir., 1970-85, 90—; chief dir. Maly Theatre, Moscow, 1985-88; prof. State Inst. Theatre ARts Cinema, 1978—. Appeared in theatrical prodns. It's High Time!, Crazy Money, Bulgakov's Flight, I Give You Life, Love Story, Grammar of Love; prodr. plays: Last Summer in Chulimsk, The Duck Hunt, Money for Mary, The Shore, Unle Vanya, Three Sisters; appeared in some 30 films, Czech Republic, Bulgaria. Recipient Stanislavsky State prize, 1980, 93. Mem. Internat. Acad. for Life Preservation Problems. Office: Yermolova Theatre, Tverskaya 5, 103009 Moscow Russia

ANDRIANO-MOORE, RICHARD GRAF, career officer; b. Petaluma, Calif., May 25, 1932; s. Norvel Moore and Thelma Elizabeth (Cook) Koch-Andriano Atkins; m. Janice Lynn Hironaka, Jan. 10, 1976 (div. Feb. 1990); children: Erika Lynn, Stephen Albert. BA, San Jose State U., 1956; MBA, Pepperdine U., 1977; B in Metaphysical Sci., U. Metaphysics, 1993. Commd. ens. USN, 1957, advanced through grades to comdr.; 1st lt., and gunnery officer U.S.S. Jefferson Count LST1068, 1957-60; 7th grade tchr. Oasis Sch., Riverside County, Calif., 1960-63; pers. and legal officer U.S.S. Maury AGS-16, 1963-65; commdg. officer Naval & Marine Corps reserve Training Ctr., Port Arthur, Tex., 1965-68; ops. officer U.S.S. Muliphen LKA 64, 1968-69; ASW & surface program officer 11th Naval Dist., San Diego, 1970-74; commdg. officer Naval Reserve Ctr., Hunters Point, Calif., 1974-75, Army, Navy & Marine Corps Reserve Ctr., San Bruno, Calif., 1975-79; dir. of adminstrn. Nat. Com. for Employer, Washington, 1979-82; comdr., regional recruiting coord. for 10 western states, Alameda, Calif., 1982-84; chief of staff N.R. Readiness comdr., Treasure Island, Calif., 1984-85; tchr. Shoreline Unified Sch. Dist., Tomales, Calif., 1985-92, 94-2001. Editor-in-chief: California Compatriot, 1976-80. Insp. Precinct Bd., Petaluma, Calif., 1987-90; scoutmaster Boy Scouts Am., 1989-92, dist. exec., 1992-94. Decorated Defense Meritorious Svc. medal Sec. of Def., Washington, 1982; recipient Ancestral Coat of Arms of the Counts of Andriano, Wappenrolle, Austria, 1985, Rome, Italy, 1994, Disting. Alumni award San Jose State U., 1991, Scoutmaster Award of Merit Boy Scouts Am., 1992; knighted Order St. John of Jerusalem Knights Hospitaller, 1991. Mem. The Augustan Soc. Inc. (v.p., bd. dirs. 1990-93, 95-00, v.p., bd. dirs. 1990-93, 95-2000, grand chancellor Order of the Augustan Eagle 1998), Calif. Soc. SAR (state pres. 1986-87, San Francisco chpt. pres. 1976-77, Silver Good Citizenship medal 1978, Patriot medal 1985, Meritorious Svc. medal 1987, oak leaf cluster 1996), Mil. Order of Loyal Legion of U.S. (Calif. comdr. 1982-88), Naval Order U.S. Avocations: reading, hiking, biking, traveling, abstract artist. Office: 1253 Bertha Ln Santa Rosa CA 95405-7003

ANDRIANOV, DMITRY GLEBOVICH, physicist, researcher; b. Moscow, Sept. 14, 1935; s. Gleb borisovich Andrianov and Fanya Aronovna Kolodnaya; m. Zinaida Nickolaevna Petrova, Sept. 8, 1957; children: Marina, Gleb. Cert. engr.-metallurgist, Moscow Inst. Steel and Alloys, 1959; PhD in Physics, Rsch. Inst. Applied Physics, Moscow, 1965; D Physics, Moscow State U., 1984. Engr. rsch. and indsl. enterprise Sapfir, Moscow, 1959-61; sr. rsch. assoc. Inst. Rare and Metals, Giredmet, Moscow, 1965-75, head lab., 1975—, dep. chmn. dr. dissertation coun., 1985—. Contbr. over 120 articles to profl. jours. and Chem. Ency., chpt. to book; co-discoverer the property of one-electron atoms in crystal semiconductors to be deep donors. Avocations: reading classical and historical novels, museums, art exhibitions, sports. Fax: (095) 366-5362. Office: Inst Rarre Metals Giredmet, B Tolmachevsky Ln 5, 109017 Moscow Russia

ANDRIANOV, YURI NICKOLAEVICH, neurophysiologist, researcher; b. Leningrad, USSR, May 7, 1945; s. Nickolai Vasilevich and Valentina Alekseevna (Lavrickova) A.; m. Natalia Yackovlevna Savenckova, Nov. 14, 1969; children: Maria, Andrey. Student, State U., Leningrad, USSR, 1963-68; Canidate degree in biophysics, Pavlov Inst. Physiology, Leningrad, USSR, 1975, Doctoral degree in physiology, 1989. Asst. scientist Pavlov Inst. Physiology, Leningrad, USSR, 1969-72; dep. chief Lab. Physiology of Reception, 1979—; jr. scientist Pavlov Inst. Physiology, Leningrad, 1972-82, sr. scientist, 1982—; guest prof. Utrecht (The Netherlands) U., 1990. Author: Sensory Hair Cells, Synaptic Transmission, 1993; contbr. articles to profl. jours. Grantee European Sci. Found., 1990, Found. Simone et Sino del Duca, 1991-92, Orgn. for the Advance in Sci., 1993-95. Mem. Internat. Brain Rsch. Orgn., N.Y. Acad. Sci., Soc. Neurosci., Internat. Soc. Neuroethnology. E-mail: andryu@infran.ru. Office: Lab Physiology of Reception, Nab Makarova 6, 199034 Saint Petersburg Russia

ANDRIESH, ANDREI MIHAIL, physicist, researcher; b. Chisinau, Moldova, Oct. 24, 1933; s. Mihail Vasilie and Maria Petru (Grosu) A.; m. Lidia Vasilievna Climanov, Oct. 10, 1959; 1 child, Anatoly. Student, Moldora State U., 1951-56; grad., Physico-Tech. Inst., Petersburg, Russia, 1959-62; DSc, Acad. Scis., Chisinau, Moldova, 1977; D (hon.), U. Ecology, Romania, 1996, Internat. Independent U., Moldova, 1996; LHD (hon.), Adam Smith U. Am., 1997; D (hon.), U. Banat, Romania, 1998. Tchr. of physics secondary sch., Lozova, Moldova, 1956-57; asst., chair of physics Agrl. Inst., Chisinau, 1957-59; scientific collaborator Acad. Scis., Chisinau, 1962-64, learned sec., 1964-71, mem. presidium, 1978-84, gen. learned sec., 1984-89, pres., 1989—, dir. optoelectron, 1994—; chief of lab. Inst. Applied Physics, Chisinau, 1971—; prof. Engring. Acad. Russian Fedn., 1992; expert Chambre Europe des Arbitres Extrajudiciares, Rome, 1994; mem. Internationaler Hilfsfonds, Brussels, 1995. Contbr. more than 300 articles to profl. jours. Chmn. Moldova Peace Alliance, 1986—. Recipient State Prize of Moldova, 1983. Mem. Internat. Sci. Acad. Life U. (Toulouse, France), Romanian Acad. Sci., Engring. Acad. Russian Fedn., Cosmonautics Acad. (hon.), Ctrl. Eurpean Acad. Sci. and Art, European Acd. Arts, Scis. and Humanities, Internat. Sci. Acad. Life Universe Nature, Internat. Acad. Ecology and Life Protection Scis., Am.-Romanian Acad. Arts and Scis. (hon.). Achievements include 40 patents in field. Office: Acad Scis Moldova, Stefan cel Mare avn I, MD-2001 Chisinau Moldova

ANDRIEVSKI, ROSTISLAV ALEKSANDROVICH, materials scientist; b. Gorlovka, USSR, Jan. 8, 1933; s. Aleksandr Vasilievich Andrievski and Sophia Filippovna Vollerner; m. Galina Pavlovna Abramenko, Jan. 15, 1958 (div. Apr. 1968); 1 child, Elena; m. Valentina Evgenievna Polunina, July 26, 1968; 1 child, Uliana. Scientist Inst. Metallceramics, Kiev, USSR, 1958-62; head of divsn. Technol. Inst., Podolsk, USSR, 1963-76; prof. Inst. Fine Chem. Technology, Moscow, 1977-84; dep. of dir. Inst. of Physics, Franze, USSR, 1984-90; chief scientist Inst. Chem. Physics Problems, Chernogolovka, Russia, 1990—; prof. Kirghiz U., Frunze, 1984-90, Inst. Steel Alloys, Moscow, 1994-96. Co-author: (books) Principle of Powder Metallurgy, 1961 (awad of Sobolevsky 1963), Strength of Refractory Compounds, 1979, Interstitial Phases, 1977; author: (book) Powder Materials Science, 1991. Grantee Internat. Sci. Found., 1995-96, INTAS, Brussels, 1996, 98; named Outstanding Russian Scientist, Moscow, 1997. Mem. Internat. Inst. Sci. Sintering, Material Rsch. Soc. Pitts., Internat. Powder Metall. Soc. Avocations: stamps, travel, books. Home: Orechovo-Zuevski, Proezd N22 Apt 4, 109391 Moscow Russia Office: Inst Chem Physics Problems, Inst Prospect N16, 142432 Chernogolovka/Moscow Russia

ANDRIEVSKY, BORIS ROSTISLAVICH, engineering educator, researcher; b. St. Petersburg, Russia, Nov. 6, 1949; s. Rostislav Alexandrovich and Vera Vasil'evna (Golikova) A.; m. Natalia Vasil'evna Kuzina, Feb. 4, 1975; children: Valentina, Alexey. Diploma in elec. engring., Baltic State Tech. U., St. Petersburg, 1972, PhD, 1979. Rschr. Baltic State Tech. U., St. Petersburg, 1972-74, asst. prof., 1974-80, assoc. prof., 1980—; tchr. St. Petersburg Inst. Mech. Engring., 1995-99; rschr. Inst. Problems of Mech. Engring., Russian Acad. Scis., St. Petersburg, 1992—. Co-author Selected Chapters of Control Theory, 1999. Contbr. articles to profl. jours. Roman Catholic. Avocations: volleyball, drawing, philosophy. Home: Sedova St 61-54, 193171 St Petersburg Russia

ANDRIJICH, VINCENT BENEDICT, radiologist; b. Johannesburg, Gauteng, S. Africa, Oct. 18, 1958; s. Vinko Martin and Mirjana Bogda Nedelka Korunich A. MBChB, U. Pretoria, S. Africa, 1982; diploma in diving and marine medicine, Navy Med. Ctr., Simonstown, S. Africa, 1984; MD in Radiology, U. Stellenbosch, S. Africa, 1990. Diplomate Coll. of Medicine S. Africa, 1990. Intern Kalafong Hosp., Pretoria, 1983; resident Tygerberg Hosp., Capetown, S. Africa, 1986-90; pvt. practice radiologist Prinsloo, Aitken and Ptnrs., Germiston, S. Africa, 1990—; sec. So. Transvaal Radiology IPA, Johannesburg, S. Africa, 1994-95; chmn. Radnet, Johannesburg, 2000. Councillor St. Jerome's Cath. Ch., Johannesburg, 1997—. Lt. S. African Def. Force, 1984-85. Mem. Radiol. Soc. S. Africa (hon. sec., chmn. quality assurance and guidelines com. 1995—). Avocations: tennis, ecology, piano playing, reading, wine. Office: Radiol Soc S Africa, PO Box 3475, Cresta, 2118 Johannesburg South Africa

ANDRILLAT, HENRI, retired astronomy educator; b. Saint Genis Laval, France, July 18, 1925; s. Alexis and Antoinette (Tempier) A.; m. Yvette Ribelaygue, July 29, 1950. Licentiate's Degree in Math., U. Lyon, France, 1946; cert. d'etudes supérieures, U. Lyon, 1947; D in Physics, U. Paris, 1955. Astronomer Lyon Obs., 1947-60; prof. astronomy Montpellier (France) U., 1960-93; ret., 1993; cons. Consultative Com. of the Univs., Paris, 1966-69, Nat. Com. on the Nat. Ctr. Sci. Rsch., Paris, 1966-69; lectr. in field. Author: Introduction a L'Etude des Cosmologies, 1970, L'Univers sous le Regard du Temps, 1993; co-author: La Cosmologie Moderne, 1988; contbr. articles to profl. revs. Mem. Montpellier Acad. Scis. and Letters (hon. pres.). Avocations: music, Egyptology.

ANDRILLON, PIERRE JEAN, editor, journalist; b. Alger, Algeria, Dec. 2, 1942; s. Marcel Georges and Jeanne Lucie (Brunon) A.; m. Josiane Josephine Colin, Nov. 4, 1967; children: Emmanuel, Celine, Gildas, Tanguy. Editor news mag. Votre sante, Paris, 1991—; journalist Radio-Paris, 1980—. Fax: 01 4018 33 30. Office: Vous, 44 Boulevard Magenta, 75010 Paris France

ANDRISANI, PAUL J., business educator, management consultant; b. Wilmington, Del., Oct. 19, 1946; s. Paul and Mary (Tavani) A.; m. Barbara Lee Frank, Nov. 23, 1968; children: Nathan, Damian, Danielle. BS, U. Del., 1968, MBA, 1970; PhD, Ohio State U., 1973, postgrad., 1973-74. Sr. rsch. assoc. Ctr. for Human Resource Rsch. Ohio State U., Columbus, 1973-74, vis. rsch. assoc., 1979; asst. prof. Sch. Bus., Temple U., Phila., 1974-76, assoc. prof., 1977-83, prof.; dir. Bur. Econ. Rsch., Phila., 1977-78, Ctr. for Labor and Human Resource Studies, Phila.; co-dir. Ctr. for Competitive Govt., Phila., 1997—, assoc. dean, 1989-91, chmn. dept. mgmt., 1993-95; pres. Paul J. Andrisani Mgmt. Cons. Svcs., Wilmington, Del., 1974—, St. Anthony's Edn. Fund, 1986—; pres. West End Neighborhood House Social Svc. Agy., 1995-97; cons. Price Waterhouse, U.S. EEOC, UPS, U.S. Army Recruiting Command, Acme Markets, CBS, Coca-Cola, City of Tucson, City of Phila., Chevron, Chrysler, Olsten, La. Power and Light, La. Land and Exploration, PanAm, Smith Kline, Carpenter Tech., The Aerospace Corp. of Am., Boeing Co., Dynalectron Corp., Lukens Steel, Nordstrom, Phila. Police Dept., Shoney's Inc., Martin Marietta, CIGNA, Airline Pilots Assn., Prudential Ins., Traveler's Ins., Suffolk County Police Dept., Internat. Comms. Agy., N.Y. Times, U.S. Steel, Readers Digest, K-Mart, Wal-Mart, Russell Sage Found., United Food and Comml. Workers Union, Del. Econ. and Fin. Adv. Com., New Orleans Pub. Svc. Inc., Disability and Pension Rev. Com., Rockwell Internat., ARCQ, Nationwide Ins., ICI Ams., DuPont, Witco Chem., Westinghouse GTE, Inco, Gould Electronics, Chrysler, Dollar Bank, Rhone-Poulene Rorer, Ohio Edison, Delmarva Power, LaSalle Univ., govt. agys., others; lectr. Internat. Comms. Agy., Japan, Portugal, Italy, Can., Brandeis U., Pa. State U., Columbia U., William and Mary Coll., U. So. Calif., U. Pa., Nat. Employment Law Inst., San Francisco and Washington. Author: Pre-Retirement Years, vol. III, 1973, vol. IV, 1974, Career Thresholds, 1975, Work Attitudes and Labor Market Experience, 1978, Making Government Work, 2000; mem. editl. bd. Jour. Econs. and Bus., 1979-83; reviewer U. Mich. Press, Ohio State U. Press, Temple U. Press and various scholarly jours.; contbr. over 40 papers to profl. jours. and socs. Del. Temple U. Law Sch. Bd. Visitors, 1997—. With U.S. Army, 1972-73. Recipient Wilmington Man of Yr. award, 1995, West End Neighborhood House Leadership award, 1997, Prof. of the Yr. award Temple U. Chpt. Soc. for Advancement of Mgmt., 1997, awards for vol. svc., Thomas J. Reese award for cmty. svc., 2000, U. Del. Alumni Hall of Fame award, 1999; Salzburg fellow, Roosevelt Youth Policy fellow; grantee U.S. Dept. Labor, 1974-77, Nat. Commn. for Employment Policy, 1979-83, Adminstrn. on Aging, 1981-82, Social Sci. Rsch. Coun., 1982, U.S. Dept. Army, 1986, 98, Human Resource Rsch. Orgn., 1989-90, PriceWaterhouse Coopers Endowment for the Bus. of Govt., 1998-2000. Mem. Am. Econs. Assn., Indsl. Rels. Rsch. Assn., Acad. of Mgmt., U.S. Soc. Labor Economists, Strategic Mgmt. Soc. Office: Temple U Fox Sch Bus & Mgmt Speakman Hall Rm 366 Philadelphia PA 19122

ANDRITSOPOULOS, GEORGE, retired physical science educator; b. Thessaloniki, Macedonia, Greece, Dec. 12, 1935; s. John and Katerina (Drivas) A.; m. Alison Reade, Jan. 6, 1968; children: Katerina, Richard-John, Alexander. Diploma in Physics, U. Athens, 1959; PhD in Nuclear Physics, Reading U., Eng., 1965. Jr. physicist Nuclear Rsch. Ctr., Athens, 1961-62; sr. rschr. Nuclear Rsch. Ctr., 1966-72; rsch. fellow Atomic Weapon Rsch. Establishment, Aldermaston, Eng., 1962-66; prof. Physics U. Ioannina, Greece, 1972-86; prof. emeritus U. Ioannina, 1986—; dir. Ctr. for Renewable Energy, Athens, 1992—; bd. dirs. Nuclear Rsch. Ctr., 1969-72, Greek Atomic Energy Commn., 1977-81, Hellenic Army Industries, 1989-91; cons. Ministry of Def., Athens, 1992-93. Author: Introduction to Quantum Mechanices, 1986; contbr. articles to profl. jours. 2d lt. Greek Army, 1959-61. Home: 29 Chris Nezer, 16674 Glyfaola Greece Office: Ctr for Renewable Energy, 19th km Marathonos Ave, 19009 Pikermi Greece

ANDRONIKOU, ANTONIOS YIANNAGOS, Cyprus government official, tourism consultant; b. Nicosia, Cyprus, Nov. 29, 1931; s. Yiannagos and Theano (Korelli) A.; m. Klelia Avraamides June 1, 1966; children: Yiannos, Myranda. LLB, London Sch. Econs.-Polit. Sci., 1961, postgrad., 1967; postgrad., U. Mich., 1981; PhD, Pacific Western U., 1988. Dir. gen. Econ. Planning Bur., Nicosia, 1967-71; cabinet sec. Cyprus Coun. Mins., Nicosia, 1971-73; dir. gen. Cyprus Tourism Orgn., Nicosia, 1973-81, chmn., 1995—; chmn. European Travel Commn., Dublin, Ireland, 1988-91, AFM Tourism Cons., Nicosia, 1991-95; chmn. Rejollie Holdings and Investments Ltd., 1999—, Saphire Venture Capital Ltd., 1999—. Author: Tourism in Cyprus, 1986. Counsellor Municipality of Strovolos, Cyprus, 1991-95; exec. dir. Anti-Cancer Soc., 1994—. Eisenhower fellow, 1985. Fellow Brit. Inst. Mgmt.; mem. World Tourism Orgn. (chmn.), Internat. Assn. Sci. Experts in Tourism. Home and Office: 38 Archimeses St, Strovolos 2018, Cyprus

ANDRONOV, IVAN VICTOROVICH, mathematics educator, researcher; b. Leningrad, USSR, Apr. 29, 1964; s. Victor Gennadievich and Alina Ivanovna (Varlakova) A.; m. Antonina Igorevna Parovichnikova, Aug. 29, 1992; 1 child, Varvara; m. Vera Aleksandrovna Parchoutina, Apr. 30, 1999; 1 child, Nikolay. BS in Physics, Leningrad U., 1987, PhD in Math., 1991. Asst. prof. U. St. Petersburg, USSR, 1987—; rschr. U. Bordeaux, France, 1993-94; mem. organizing com. "Day on Diffrection", Internat. Ann. Seminar, 1987—; mem. St. Petersburg Organizing com. Internat. Union of Radio Sci. Symposium on Electromagnetic Theory, 1995. Contbr. articles to profl. jours. Mem. Am. Math. Soc., Ea. Europe Acoustics Assn. Avocations: tourism, chess. Home: Kv 12 18 Shirokaja Str, Saint Petersburg 189620, Russia Office: U St Petersburg Inst in Physics, Ulianovskaja 1-1, Saint Petersburg 198904, Russia

ANDRUS, JAMES BRANNON, electrical engineer; b. Ville Platte, La., Nov. 2, 1954; s. Hardy G. and Gertie F. Andrus; m. Janette Strong, May 25, 1983; 1 child, Brannon James. BSEE, La. State U., 1976. Cert. profl. engr., La. Elec. engr. City of Lafayette, La., 1977-78, substation design & ops., 1978-82, mgr. substation design, 1982-85; elec. design engr. Ctrl. La. Electric Co., Pineville, 1985-93; cons. Ville Platte, 1994; distbn. supt. Oberlin (Ohio) Mcpl. Light, 1995-96; elec. distbn. engr. Alexandria (La.) Mcpl. Electric, 1996—. Pres. Ctr. Lions Charaities, Alexandria, 1991-92. Fellow Masons; mem. La. Engring. Soc. Republican. Lutheran. Avocations: hunting, camping, outdoors, horses. Home: 8377 Huy 71 S Lecomple LA 71346 Office: City of Alexandria PO Box 71 Alexandria LA 71309-0071

ANDRUS, LORI ERIN, lawyer; b. Baton Rouge, Mar. 3, 1972; d. Vance Robert and Toni Colleen Houston Andrus. BS, Boston U., 1993; JD, Duke U., 1999. Bar: Calif., U.S. Dist. Ct. (so., cen. and no. dists.) Calif. Legis. asst. Congressman Jimmy Hayes, Washington, 1993-96; assoc. Lieff, Cabraser, Heimann & Bernstein, San Francisco, 1999—. Mem. San Francisco Bar Assn., Calif. State Bar, ATLA (lawyers com. on civil rights), ABA, ACLU. Democrat.

ANDRUSHCHENKO, ZHANNA, physicist, researcher; b. Kharpachka, Vinnitsa, Ukraine, Jan. 1, 1968; s. Mykola and Maria Andrushchenko; m. Oleg Silivra, Sept. 4, 1992. Physicst, tchr., Kiev (Ukraine) State U., 1989; PhD in Plasma Physics, Khar'kov (Ukraine) State U., 1994. Engr.-rschr. Kiev Inst. for Nuclear Rsch., 1988-94, scientist, 1994-97, sr. scientist, 1997—. Contbr. articles to sci. jours., including Physics of Plasmas, Jour. Plasma Physics. Austraian scholar Fed. Ministry for Sci. and Transport, 1994, President's scholar Pres. of Kuraine, 1997. Christian Orthodox. Fax: 0038/044/2654463. E-mail: zhanna.andrushchenko@uibk.ac.at. Office: Kiev Inst for Nuclear Rsch, Prospect Nauky 47, 03680 Kiev Ukraine

ANDRUZZI, ELLEN ADAMSON, nurse, marital and family therapist; b. Colon, Panama, Dec. 15, 1917; d. Charles and Annie Isabel (Grinder) Adamson; m. Francis Victor Andruzzi, May 28, 1941; children: Barbara F., Francis C., Judith E., Antonette T., John J. BS in pub. health nursing, Cath. U. Am., 1947, MS in Nursing, 1951. Cert. clin. specialist. Psychiat. nurse pub. health nurse Washington Health Dept., 1942-44; instr. psychiat. nursing St. Elizabeth's Hosp., Washington, 1948-57; dir. nursing Glenn Dale Hosp., Md., 1961-67; chief mental health nurse dept. human resources Govt., D.C., 1967-73; cons. NIMH,HHS, Rockville, Md., 1973-81; marital and family therapist TA Assocs., Camp Springs, Md., 1973-94; assoc. Greater Washington Inst. for Transactional Analysis, Rockville, 1975-79; instr. Charles County C.C., LaPlata, Md., 1976-78, Prince George C.C., Md., 1973-81; assoc. Ctr for Study of Human Systems, Chevy Chase, Md., 1976-94; pvt. practice psychotherapist, nurse; Chmn. plan devel. com. So. Md Health Systems Agy., Clinto, 1984-89, (sec. governing body, 1978-80), Mental Health Adv. Com. Price George County, Cheverly, Md., 1983-85; mem. Blue Ribbon Commn. on Health, Prince George's County, 1991-92; Commn. Health, Prince George's County, 1992-94, health com. and voter reporter LWV, edn. com., Manatee County, LWV Manatee County (treas. 1999-2000, bd. dirs., 1999—). Author chpts. in books. Co-capt. Price Georgians for Glendening, Prince George County, Md., 1985-86; outreach vol. Manatee Widowed Persons Svc., 1996—; rsvp vol. Oneco Elem. Sch. Recipient Disting. Nurse award St. Elizabeths Hosp., 1985, Paula Hamburer Vol. award Mental Health Assn. Md., 1985, Recognition of Svc. award Md. Nurses Assn., 1983, Prince Georgian of the Yr. award, 1994, vol. award Prince George's County, 1995. Fellow Am. Acad. Nursing, Am. Orthopsychiat. ASsn.; mem. Internat. Transactional Analysis Assn (clin.), Am. Nurses Assn., World Fedn. for Mental Health, Nat. Mental Health Assn. (v.p. 1984-87, bd. dirs. 1982-87), Mental Health Assn. Prince George County (pres. 1974-79, 87-88, Vol. of Yr. award 1993), Sigma theta Tau (Kappa chpt., Excellence in Nursing award 1984). Democrat. Roman Catholic.

ANDRZEJEWSKI, BARTLOMIEJ, physicist researcher; b. Bydgoszcz, Pomorze, Poland, June 3, 1967; s. Stefan and Maria (Niedźwiedzka) A. MSc, Adam Mickiewicz U., Poznań, Poland, 1992; PhD, Inst. Molecular Physics, Poznań, Poland, 1997. Rschr. Inst. Molecular Physics, Poznań, Poland, 1992—. Mem. Confederation of Ind. Poland, Poznań, 1990-97, mem. local authorities, 1994-96; Ind. Student Assn., 1990-92. Recipient A. Piekara award Polish Physics Soc., 1992, Award of the Head of Inst. Molecular Physics, 1992, Grant for Young Scientist, Found. for Polish Sci., 1995. Roman Catholic. Avocations: running, swimming, history, theatre, going by taxi. Home: Ziemowita 74/11, 60-063 Poznań Poland Office: Inst Molecular Physics, Smoluchowskiego 17, 60179 Poznań Poland

ANDSNES, LEIF OVE, concert pianist; b. Karmoy, Norway, Apr. 7, 1970. Student, Bergen Music Conservatory. concert pianist Oslo Philharm., Edinburgh Festival, 1989, Cleve. Orch. Philharm., Berlin Philharm., London Philharm., Chgo. Symphony, N.Y. Philharm., Boston Philharm., Kirov Orch., London Symphony Orch., Vienna Symphony Orch., L.A. Philharmonic, City of Birmingham Symphony, Brahms Piano Concerto No. 1 with CBSO and Simon Rattle, 1998; records for EMI classics, including Schumann Pianoworks and the Long Long Winter Night (a collection of Norwegian music), 1997, Haydn Piano Sonatas, 1999, Britten Piano Concerto and Shostakovich Concerto for Piano, Trumpet and Strings, 1999, Haydn Piano Concertos, 2000; recordings Virgin Classics include: Grieg: A minor and Liszt A major, Janacek: Piano Works (Deutschen Schallplaten award), Chopin: Sonatas, Nielsen Piano Works, Grieg Piano Works; maj. tours in Australia, Japan, Europe, U.S. Recipient First prize Hindemith Competition, Frankfurt-am-Main, prizewinner others, Dorothy Chandler award, L.A.; named The 1998 Gilmore Artist by Irving S. Gilmore Internat. Keyboard Festival of Kalamazoo. Home: IMG Artists Lovell House, 616 Chiswick High Rd, London London W4 2TH, England W4 5RX

ANEVSKY, SERGEY IOSIFOVICH, physicist; b. Orel, Russia, Apr. 7, 1950; s. Iosif Leontjevich and Stanislava Antonovna (Ushack) A.; m. Olga Vadimovna Aronova, Nov. 10, 1978; 1 child, Alexander Sergeevich. Degree, Inst. Electronic Engring., Moscow, 1973; PhD, All-Russian Inst. Optical and Phys. Measurements, 1985. Head of sector All-Russian Inst. Optical and Phys. Measurements, Moscow, 1986—; vice chmn. tech. com. for UV radiation, Moscow, 1995—. Contbr. articles to profl. jours. Avocation: philosophy. Home: Ivanteevskaja 3-3-35, 107150 Moscow Russia Office: All Russian Inst Optical & Phys Meas, Ozernaja 46, 119361 Moscow Russia

ANFOSSI, DOMENICO, physicist, researcher; b. Saluzzo, Italy, Apr. 11, 1945; s. Umberto and Laura (Grosso) A.; m. Ilda Giraudo, July 26, 1970; children: Laura, Alberto. PhD in Physics, U. Turin, 1969. Fellow CNR, Turin, 1970-74; 3rd level rschr., 1974-88, 2nd level rschr., 1988-91, 1st level rsch. dir., 1991—; mem. Tract Steering Com., 1988-94, Nato/CCMS on Air Pollution Model Appl., 1991—. Contbr. articles to profl. jours. Mem. Italian Phys. Soc., Royal Met. Soc., Am. Met. Soc., Italian Geophys. Soc., EURASAP. Avocations: mountain walking, skiing, theater, opera. Office: Inst Cosmogeofisica CNR, Corso Fiume 4, 10133 Torino Italy

ANG, MARCELO HUIBONHOA, JR., mechanical engineering educator; b. Manila, Luzon, Philippines, Mar. 3, 1959; s. Marcelo Ty and Rosalind (Huibonhoa) A.; m. Caroline Ngha Tecson; 1 child, Mark Adam Tecson. BS in Indsl. Mgmt. Engring. cum laude, De La Salle U., Manila, 1981, BSME, 1981; MSME, U. Hawaii, 1985; PhDEE, U. Rochester, 1988. Registered profl. mech. engr., The Philippines. Instr. De La Salle U., Manila, 1981-82; sr. tech. officer Intel Philippines Mfg. Inc., Manila, 1982-83; rsch. asst. East West Ctr., Honolulu, 1983-85; asst. prof. U. Rochester (N.Y.), 1988-89; lectr. Nat. U. Singapore, 1989-93, sr. lectr., 1993-98, assoc. prof., 1998—; vis. rsch. engr. MIT, Cambridge, Mass., 1984; cons. Brac Fabritech, Singapore, 1990—. Reviewer IEEE Tech. Jours., Proceedings, 1987—; contbr. tech. articles in robotics to profl. jours. Mem. Nat. Sci. and Tech. Bd., Singapore, 1994. Recipient outstanding paper award Singapore Indsl. Automation Assn., 1990, Awards for Excellence 2000, Most Outstanding Paper award in Indsl. Robot, 1999; rsch. scholar East-West Ctr., 1983, U. Rochester, 1985; robotics rsch. grantee Nat. U. Singapore, 1990. Mem. IEEE, Sigma Xi. Roman Catholic. Office: Nat U Singapore MPE Dept, 10 Kent Ridge Cres, Singapore 119260, Singapore

ANG, MINNI KIM-HUAI, music educator, musician; b. Kota Bahru, Malaysia, Jan. 1, 1966; d. Kok-Jee Ang and Chitralekha Gupta; m. Elok Robert Tee, May 29, 1993. BS with honors, U. Malaya, Kuala Lumpur, 1989; GBSM, Birmingham (Eng.) Conservatory, 1994; PhD, U. Putra Malaysia, Serdang, Malaysia, 1998. Cert. LTCL, ATCL. Staffworker youth & music Scripture Union, Malaysia, 1989-92; tchr. MBF Sri Garden, Kuala Lumpur, 1992-93; lectr. U. Putra Malaysia, 1995—, head music dept., 1996-99; panel Malaysian Nat. Occupational Skill Standards for Multimedia, 1999—; spkr. seminar/workshop Ministry of Edn., Malaysia, 1996, INTAN, 1996, various chs. and parach. groups, Malaysia, 1989—. TV newsreader Radio-T.V. Malaysia, Kuala Lumpur, 1989-92.; contbr. articles to profl. jours; composer; concert performer various Malaysian Orchs.; percussionist Nat. Malaysian Symphony, Kuala Lumpur, 1993. Active Luth. Ch. Malaysia, 1984-97, Borneo Inland Mission Ch., 1997—. Mem. Malaysia Mensa Soc., Percussive Arts Soc., Acoustical Soc. Am., Audio Engring. Soc. Avocations: reading, nature trips, youth work, movies. Office: U Putra Malaysia, Dept Music Faculty Hmn Ecol, 43400 UPM Serdang Selangor, Malaysia

ANG, PENG-TIAM, physician, consultant; b. Singapore, Aug. 22, 1958; s. Eng-Hee Ang and Mui-Hoi Teo; m. Siok-Lin Chua, Sept. 11, 1983; children: Yvonne, David, Daniel, Yvette. B of Medicine and Surgery, Nat. U. Singapore, 1982, M of Internal Medicine, 1986. Sr. cons., head of oncology Singapore Gen. Hosp., 1990-97; sr. cons. med. oncologist Mount Elizabeth Med. Ctr., Singapore, 1997—; dir. Nat. Corner Ctr., Singapore, 1999, Haematology and Corner Ctr., Glenagles, 1997—. Coun. mem. Breast Cancer Found., Singapore, 1998. Pres. scholarship Govt. of Singapore, 1977; Prof. Sir Gordon Arthur Ransome Gold medal Nat. U. of Singapore, 1986; recipient Nat. Sci. award Govt. of Singapore, 1996. Fellow Royal Coll. Physicians (London), ACP. Avocations: Squash, gym, computers, reading, photography. Office: Mount Elizabeth Med Ctr, 2 Mount Elizabeth #13-16, Singapore 228510, Singapore

ANG, SWEE CHAI, orthopedic surgeon, consultant; b. Penang, Malaysia, Oct. 26, 1948; d. Peng Liat Ang and Lye Hee Lee; m. Francis Khoo, Jan. 29, 1977. MBBS, U. Singapore, 1973, MS, 1976. Orthopedic splst. Royal Coll. Surgeons. Sr. registrar Royal Victoria Infirmary, Newcastle Upon Tyne, Eng., 1984-91; cons. Bishop Auckland Hosp., Eng., 1992-94; sr. cons. Newham Gen. Hosp., London, 1994-96; cons. orthopedic surgeon Royal London, 1996—; founding mem. Med. Aid for Palestinians, 1984—; cons. surgeon UN, Gaza, 1988-89, WHO, West Bank, 1989—. Author: Industrial Hand Injuries, 1976, From Beirut to Jerusalem, 1989, Field Manual in War Surgery Third World Network, 1994. Decorated Star of Palestine, Pres. Yasser Arafat of Palestine authorities, 1989; recipient Gold Medal S.E. Asia Occupl. Health Symposium, Humanitarian award Guinness, 1982. Fellow Royal Coll. Eng., Royal Coll. Surgeons, Brit. Orthopaedic Assn.; mem. Jordanian Orthopaedic Assn. (hon.), Brit. Med. Assn., Brit. Soc. for Surgery of the Hand. Presbyterian. Avocations: music, poetry. Office: MAP 33A Islington Park ST, London N1 1QB, England

ANGADI, VEERANNA BASAVANTAPPA, economist, administrator, researcher; b. Hirebommanhal, India, Apr. 8, 1944; s. Basavantappa and Parvatema (Pattanashetty) A.; m. Shanta Veeranna Ranjanagi; children: Vidya, Pramod, Basavaraj, Veena. BA, Karnatak Coll., Dharwad, India, 1965; MA, Karnatak U., Dharwad, 1967, PhD, 1976. Lectr. Arts & Sci. Coll. India, 1967-72, reader, head dept. econs., 1972-77, prin., 1977-79; rsch. officer Res. Bank India, 1979-83, asst. adviser, 1983-88, dir. Dept. Econ. Analysis, 1996—; mem. faculty Banker's Tng. Coll., India, 1991-96; vis. fellow Princeton (N.J.) U., 1988-89; rschr. in field. Contbr. articles to profl. jours. Golden Jubille scholar Res. Bank India, 1989. Avocations: classical music, TV, walking, travel. Office: Res Bank India, Shahid Bhagat Singh Rd, Mumbai 400001, India

ANGARI, KHALID BIN MUHABBAD AL-, federal official; b. 1952. PhD in Geography, U. Fla., 1981. Asst. prof. King. Saud U., 1981-83; dep. min. Ministry Mcpl. and Rural Affairs, 1983-84, min., 1990; min. Ministry Higher Edn., Riyadh, Saudi Arabia, 1991—. Office: King Faisal Hosp St, Main Ministry, Riyadh 11153, Saudi Arabia*

ANGEL, CARLOS ALBERTO, pediatric surgeon, urologist; b. Bogota, Colombia, Mar. 16, 1953; came to U.S., 1986; s. Carlos Eduardo and Margarita (De Greiff) A.; m. Claudia Malkun, Sept. 14, 1987; children: Santiago, Catalina. BS, Presbyn. Coll., Clinton, S.C., 1974; MD, Univ. del Rosario, Bogota, 1980. Resident in gen. surgery U. del Rosario, Bogota, 1983-86; fellow in pediat. surgery U. Tenn., Memphis, 1986-88, chief fellow pediat. surgery, 1988-89, fellow pediat. urology, 1990-91; fellow in pediat. oncologic surgery St. Jude's Children's Rsch. Hosp., Memphis, 1989-90; pediat. surgeon, pediat. urologist U. tex. Med. Br., Galveston, Tex., 1991—. Contbr. articles to profl. jours., chpts. to books. Active vol. colombian Red Cross Surg. Brigades, Chocó, 1985, Meta, 1986. Mem. Soc. of Critical Care Medicine, Soc. for Surgery of the Alimentary Tract, Singleton Surg. Soc. Democrat. Roman Catholic. Avocations: tennis, jogging, reading, music.

Office: Univ of Texas Med Br Rt 0353 301 University Blvd Galveston TX 77555-5302

ANGEL, HEATHER HAZEL, wildlife photographer, author; b. Fulmer, Bucks, Eng., July 21, 1941; d. Stanley Paul and Hazel Marie (Sherwood) Le Rougetel; m. Martin Vivian Angel, 1964; 1 child. BSc (hon.), Bristol U., 1962, MSc (hon.), 1965; DSc (hon.), Bath U., 1986. Spl. prof. Sch. Life and Environ. Sci., Nottingham U., 1994—. Exhbns. include The Natural History of Britain and Ireland, Sci. Mus., London, 1981, Nature in Focus, Natural History Mus., London, 1987, The Art of Wildlife Photography, Nature in Art, Gloucester, 1989, Natural Visions, touring all over the U.K., 8 vols., 3000, Kodak Calendar on The Thames 1987, Natural Visions, Nature in Arts, 2000; featured TV programs: Me and My Camera 1981, 83, Gardener's World, 1983, Nature, 1984, Nocon on Photography 1988; featured in Japanese TV documentary, filmed in U.K. and Sri Lanka, 1983; author: Nature Photography: Its Art and Techniques 1972, The Family Water Naturalist 1982, The Book of Nature Photography 1982, The Book of Close-up Photography, 1983, Heather Angel's Countryside 1983, A Camera in the Garden, 1984, A View from a Window, 1988, Nature in Focus, 1988, Landscape Photography, 1989, Animal Photography, 1991, Kew: A World of Plants 1993, Photographing the Natural World, 1994, Outdoor Photography: 101 Tips and Hints, 1997, How to Photograph Flowers, 1998, Pandas, 1998, How to Photograph Water, 1999, Natural Visions, 2000. Leader British Photographic delegation to China, 1985. Recipient Hood medal, Louis Schmidt Laureate, premier award for Biocommunications Assn., 1998. Fellow British Inst. of Profl. Photography, Royal Photographic Soc. (pres. 1984-86). Avocations: traveling to remote parts of the world of photograph wilderness areas and unusual aspects of animal behaviour. Home: Highways 6 Vicarage Hill, Farnham Surrey GU9 8HJ, England

ANGEL, JAMES JOSEPH, lawyer; b. Racine, Wis., Apr. 1, 1956; s. William J. and Dorothy P. (Potman) A.; m. Catherine Anne Cowan, Oct. 17, 1982; children: Carter Anne, Riley James, Spenser Catherine. BA, W.Va. Wesleyan Coll., 1977; JD, U. Richmond, 1979. Dep. commonwealth atty. City of Lynchburg (Va.) Commonwealth Atty. Office, 1979-84; ptnr. Smith, Angel & Falcone, P.C., Lynchburg, 1984-87; pvt. practice Lynchburg, 1987—. Chmn. Boonsboro-Peakland Neighborhood Assn., Lynchburg, 1990-99. Mem. ATLA, Va. Trial Lawyers Assn., Va. Bar Assn., Va. Coll. Criminal Def. Attys., Lynchburg Bar Assn. (past pres. criminal law sect. 1992). Avocations: golf, whitewater rafting. Office: 725 Church St Lynchburg VA 24504-1417 also: Allied Arts Bldg PO Box 1042 Lynchburg VA 24505-1042

ANGEL, MARTIN VIVIAN, biological oceanographer; b. Harrow, Middlesex, England, Apr. 14, 1937; s. Thomas Huber and Edna Laura (Pearse) A.; m. Heather Hazel Le Rougetel, Oct. 3, 1964; 1 child, Giles Philip. MA, Magdalene Coll., Cambridge, Eng., 1960; PhD, Bristol, Eng., 1965. Sr. sci. officer Nat. Inst. Oceanography, Surrey, Eng., 1965-72; prin. sci. officer Inst. Oceanographic Scis., Surrey, 1972-82, head biology, 1982-94, head Challenger Ctr. for Sea-Floor Processes, 1994-96; coun. mem. Challenger Soc. for Marine Sci., 1972-92. Editor: Progress in Oceanography, 1979—; contbr. over 130 rsch. papers to profl. publs. Active coun. WWF-UK, Godalming, Surrey, 1985—. Mem. Am. Soc. Limnology and Oceanography, Brit. Ecol. Soc. (v.p. 1990-92), Conservation Biology Soc. Avocations: photography, reading, conservation. Office: Southampton Oceanography, Empress Dock, Southampton SO14 3Z4, England

ANGEL, MICHAEL GONZALEZ, telecommunications industry executive; b. Seattle, Dec. 21, 1960; s. Jose Vincente Gonzalez and Maria (del Carmen Romero de Villa) A.; m. Leni Alcantara Alonzo, May 1, 1992; 1 child, Catherine Isabella. BS in Bus. Adminstrn. magna cum laude, Creighton U., 1981; MBA, Harvard Bus. Sch., 1983. Project mgr. Harvard Group Devel., Manchester, NH, 1984-85, sales, leasing and mktg. mgr., 1986-87, gen. mgr., 1988-90; export product line mgr. Otto GmbH and Gebr. Otto KG, Cologne, Germany, 1991-92; export sales mgr. Latin Am. Otto Industries, Inc., Charlotte, NC, 1991-95; dir. N.Am. mktg. and sales Hyundai, San Diego, 1995-96; dir. wireless sales and internet applications Digital Sound Corp., Santa Barbara, CA, 1996-97; v.p. internat. bus. devel. and sales Messer/Hoechst AG, L.A., 1998-2000; v.p. data networking technology Bell Atlantic Data Solutions Group, 2000—. Mem. Harvard Club (N.Y. and Boston). Republican. Roman Catholic. E-mail: mgangel@adnc.com or michael.g.angel@bellatlantic.com. Home: 790 Camino De La Reina San Diego CA 92108-3263 Office: Bell Atlantic Ste 2407B 1095 Avenue Of The Americas New York NY 10036-6704

ANGEL, STEVEN, musician; b. Bklyn., Aug. 2, 1953; s. Morris and Rosalyn (Sobiloff) A. Grad. H.S., L.I. Pres. Daystar Records, Santa Monica, Calif., 1991—; profl. drummer, 1960—; lectr. The Whole Life Expo, Pasadena, 1992-95, Inst. for the Advanced Studies of Human Sexuality, San Francisco; drum therapist, 1998—. Author (music and book) Angels Rejoice, 1976-80; wrote music for tv show Another World, 1987-91; wrote, recorded, produced three songs for Playboy album Music for Lovers, 1993; wrote, recorded, produced album The Erotic God, 1993; editor Unity and Difference Jour., 1994-97; began program profiled on CNN, Drumming For Your Life; featured on KNBC-TV news segments "Stop the Violence" and "Hometown Hero", KCBS "Hometown Heroes". Avocations: tennis, hiking, running. Home and Office: Daystar Records 2132 Montana Ave Apt B Santa Monica CA 90403-2017

ANGELES, RODOLFO B., elementary education educator. BS in Elem. Edn., Philippine Normal Coll., 1962, MA, 1966; PhD, U. San Francisco, 1991. Educator Binan Sch. Dist., Laguna, Philippines, 1962-69, Pasadena (Calif.) Unified Sch. Dist., 1969—; educator Pasadena City Coll., 1980—, Calif. State U., L.A., 1982; adj. faculty Nat. U., L.A., 1998. Author: (children's books) The Enchanted Bird, 1970, Fireflies in the City, 1971. Mem. NEA, Calif. Tchrs. Assn., United Tchrs. Pasadena, Phi Delta Kappa.

ANGELILLI, ROBERTA, parliament member; b. Rome, Feb. 1, 1965. Mem. European Parliament, 1999—, mem. com. citizens freedomes/rights, justice/home affairs, substitute com. culture, youth, edn., the media and sport; mem. Union for Europe of the Nations Group; mem. delegation for relations with the Mashreq countries and the Gulf. *

ANGELINI, FIORENZO CARDINAL, archbishop; b. Rome, Aug. 1, 1916. ordained priest, Roman Catholic Ch. Feb. 3, 1940, bishop (titular see of Messene) July 29, 1956. Archbishop Roman Cath. Ch., 1985—, elevated to cardinal, 1991—; pres. Curia agy. for health care workers; deacon Holy Spirit (in Sassia); Pres. Pontifical Coun. for Pastoral Assistance to Health Care Workers, 1985; elevated to Sacred College of Cardinals, 1991. Office: 00120 Vatican City State Vatican City State*

ANGELINI, GIANNI DAVIDE, surgeon, educator; b. Siena, Italy, Jan. 29, 1953; s. Marzio and Erina (Tanganelli) A.; m. Rosalind Angelini John, July 5, 1986; children: Jonathan, Timothy, Simon. Diploma in med. engring., U. Siena, Italy, 1972, MD, 1979, specialist degree in thoracic surgery, 1985; CM, U. Cardiff, Wales, 1986. Chief resident in cardiac surgery Cardiff, 1984-87; resident cardiac surgery Thorax Ctr., Rotterdam, Holland, 1988-89; sr. lectr. U. Sheffield, Eng., 1989-92; prof. cardiac surgery U. Bristol, Eng., 1992—; chmn. Bristol Heart Inst., 1995. Editor: Arterial Conducts in Nyocardial Vascularzation, 1995. Grantee Brit. Cardiac Soc., 1986, European Vascular Soc., 1989. Fellow Royal Coll. Surgeons; mem. Brit. Cardiovascular Rsch. Soc. (chmn. 1995, 96). Avocations: jazz, travel. Office: Bristol Heart Inst, BRI, Bristol BS2 8HW, England

ANGELINI, PAOLO, economist; b. Siena, Tuscany, Italy, Aug. 15, 1958; s. Ottavio and Marisa (Sabatini) A.; m. Alessandra Pennacchietti. M in Econs., Brown U., 1988, PhD in Econs., 1994. Economist Bank of Italy, Rome, 1990-96, sr. economist, 1997—; lectr. U. Rome, 1993-96, Joint Vienna Inst., 1995; cons. Internat. Monetary Fund, 1998-99. Contbr. articles to profl. jours.; assoc. editor Jour. of Banking and Fin., 1998-99. Corporal maj. Italian Army, 1985. Fulbright fellowship Fulbright Commn., 1986, Stringher fellowship Bank of Italy, 1987, Einaudi fellowship Ente L. Einaudi, 1988. Avocations: sailing, windsurfing, scuba diving. E-mail: Angelini.Paolo@insedia.interbusiness.it. Home: Via S Martino Ai Monti 22, 00184 Rome Italy Office: Bank of Italy, Via Nazionale 91, 00184 Rome Italy

ANGELL, KENNETH ANTHONY, bishop; b. Providence, Aug. 3, 1930; s. Henry L. and Mae T. (Cooney) A. AB in Philosophy, St. Mary's Sem., Balt., 1952, STB, 1954; STD (hon.), Our Lady of Providence Sem., 1975; JCD (hon.), Providence Coll., 1975. Ordained priest Roman Catholic Ch., 1956, consecrated bishop, 1974. Assoc. pastor St. Mark Ch., Jamestown, R.I., 1956; assoc. pastor Sacred Heart Ch., Pawtucket, R.I., 1956-60, St. Mary Ch., Newport, R.I., 1960-68; asst. chancellor and sec. to bishop Diocese of Providence, 1968-72, chancellor, 1972-74, aux. bishop, vicar gen., 1974-92; pastor St. John Ch., Providence, 1975-81; bishop Diocese of Burlington (Vt.), 92—. bd. dirs. Sr. Thea Bowman Black Cath. Ednl. Fund, 1995-99; trustee Wadhams Hall Seminary Coll., 1995—, Champlain Coll., 1995-98; v.p. Vt. Ecumenical Coun. & Bible Soc., 1997-99, pres., 1999—. Mem. Nat. Conf. Cath. Bishops, U.S. Cath. Conf. Office: Diocese of Burlington 351 North Ave PO Box 489 Burlington VT 05402-0489

ANGELL, LOIS LOUISE, writer, speaker, poet, comedian; b. Riceville, Iowa; d. Kenneth Edwin and Marie E. (Dynes) A.; 1 child, Jim Barrett. Student, Am. U., 1959-60, 62-63, U. Alberta, 1978. Staff dir. Justice Rehnquist U.S. Supreme Ct., 1971-80; pub. rels. dir. Better Comm. Found., Silver Spring, Md., 1984; free lance writer and performer Arlington, Va.; talk and news show guest. Performer at comedy and supper clubs, radio and TV. Recipient Spl. Achievement award U.S Dept. Justice, 1971, Outstanding Svc. to the Arts in Comm. award Capital Hill Arts Workshop, 1984. Mem. NAFE, Washington Ind. Writers, The Capitol Hill Club, Internat. Platform Assn., Capitol Hill Poetry Group, Nat. Conf. Rsch. on Women, Nat. Capitol Spkrs. Assn., Washington Conv. and Visitors Assn., World Affairs Coun., The Cato Inst. Home: 1701 N Kent St Apt 901 Arlington VA 22209-2108

ANGELL, WAYNE D., economist, banker; b. Liberal, Kans., June 28, 1930; s. Charlie Francis and Adele Thelma (Edwards) A.; children: Patrice, Wynne, Ryan, Wiley. BA, Ottawa U., 1952; MA, U. Kans., 1953, PhD, 1957. Instr. econs. U. Kans., Lawrence, 1954-56; prof. econs. Ottawa (Kans.) U., 1956-85, dean, 1969-72; pres., bd. dirs. Hume (Mo.) Bancshares, Inc., 1972-85; bd. dirs. Fed. Res. Bank, Kansas City, Mo., 1979-86, mem. bd. govs., 1986-94; chmn. com. on Fed. Res. Bank activities FRS, Washington, 1986-94; chmn. G-10 Com. on Payment and Settlement Systems, Basle, Switzerland, 1988-94; chief economist, sr. mng. dir. Bear, Stearns & Co., N.Y.C., 1994—; econ. cons. Franklin Savs. Assn., Ottawa, 1981-86; chmn. bd. dirs. 1st State Bank, Pleasanton, 1975-76. Rep. Kans. Ho. of Reps., Topeka, 1961-67; vice chmn. Rep. State Legis. Campaign Com., Topeka, 1964; chmn. Rep. Congl. Conv. 3d Dist., Overland Park, Kans., 1964. Mem. Am. Econ. Assn., Phi Beta Kappa. Republican. Baptist. Avocations: pvt. piloting, tennis, cycling. Office: Bear Stearns & Co 245 Park Ave New York NY 10167-0002

ANGELLE, PHILIPPE ALBERT, retired electrical engineer; b. Charenton-Le-Pont, France, Feb. 11, 1921; s. Marcel Frederic and Germaine Leonie (Fayard) A.; m. Françoise Marie Dubuisson, Apr. 8, 1948; children: Bernard, Frederic. Degree in engring., Ecole Centrale, Paris, 1945. Chief engr. elec. lab. Logabax, Malakoff, France, 1945-53; chief engr. tech. dept. Le Materiel Telephonique (ITT affiliate), Boulogne, France, 1953-57; chief engr. dept. prototype Compagnie Generale de Geophysique, Montrouge, France, 1957-65; tech. mgr. Societe D'Etudes, Recherches et Constructions Electroniques, Nantes, France, 1965-81, ret., 1981—. Mem. IEEE (sr.), AAAS. Avocations: amateur radio, astronomy, physics. Home: Le Haut Drezeux, 44350 Guerande France

ANGELOPOULOS, THEO, film director; b. Athens, Apr. 27, 1936; s. Spyridon and Katerina (Krassaki) A.; m. Phoebe Economopoulou, 1980; 3 children. Student, U. Athens. Film critic Athens daily Allaghi, 1965. Dir. Formix Story, 1965, Broadcast, 1968, Reconstruction, 1970 (Best Fgn. Film at Hyères Film Festival, George Sadoul award, five awards at Thessaloniki Film Festival), Days of '36, 1972 (FIPRESCI award 1973), The Travelling Players, 1974-75, The Hunters, 1976-77, Megalexandros, 1980, Athens, 1984, Voyage to Cythera, 1984, The Bee Keeper, 1986, Landscape in the Mist, 1988 (2 awards Chgo. Film Festival, Best European Film Yr. 1989), The Suspended Step of the Stork, 1991, Ulysses' Gaze, 1995 (Grand Jury prize, Cannes, 1995), Lumière et compagnie, 1995, Mia aiwniothta kai mia mera, 1998 (Golden Palm, Cannes Film Festival 1998). Recipient FIPRESCI Grand Prix, Cannes, Golden Age award, Brussels, Best Film of the Decade 1970-80, Italy, Grand Prix of the Arts and Best Film of the Yr., Japan, Best Film of the Yr., B.F.I., Interfilm award, Berlin, Best Film, Figueira da Foz Film Festival, nine awards Thessaloniki Film Festival for the Travelling Players, Golden Hugo award Chgo. Film Festival, 1978, 3 awards Venice Film Festival for Megalexandros, Best Screenplay FIPRESCI awards Cannes Film Festival, awards Venice Film Festival, Chevalier des Arts et des Lettres, France. Avocation: cultivating tomatoes. Office: BAC Films, 5 Rue Pelouze, 75008 Paris France*

ANGELOU, MAYA, writer; b. St. Louis, Apr. 4, 1928; d. Bailey and Vivian (Baxter) Johnson; 1 son, Guy Johnson. Studied dance with, Pearl Primus, N.Y.C.; hon. degrees, Smith Coll., 1975, Mills Coll., 1975, Lawrence U., 1976. Taught modern dance The Rome Opera House and Hambina Theatre, Tel Aviv; writer-in-residence U. Kans.-Lawrence, 1970; disting. vis. prof. Wake Forest U., 1974, Wichita State U., 1974, Calif. State U.-Sacramento, 1974; apptd. mem. Am. Revolution Bicentennial Council by Pres. Ford, 1975-76; 1st Reynolds prof. Am. Studies, Wake Forest U. since 1981, a lifetime appointment. Author: I Know Why the Caged Bird Sings, 1970, Just Give Me A Cool Drink of Water 'Fore I Diiie (nominated for Pulitzer Prize), 1971, Georgia, Georgia, 1972, Gather Together in My Name, 1974, Oh Pray My Wings are Gonna Fit Me Well, 1975, Singin' and Swingin' and Gettin' Merry Like Christmas, 1976, And Still I Rise, 1978, The Heart of a Woman, 1981, Shaker, Why Don't You Sing?, 1983, All God's Children Need Traveling Shoes, 1986, Now Sheba Sings the Song, 1987, I Shall Not Be Moved, 1990, On the Pulse of Morning: The Inaugural Poem, 1992, Lessons in Living, 1993, Wouldn't Take Nothing for My Journey Now, 1993, My Painted House, My Friendly Chicken, and Me, 1994, The Complete Collected Poems of Maya Angelou, 1994, Kofi and His Magic, 1996, Making Magic in the World, 1998; prodr.: Moon on a Rainbow Shawl, 1988 (by Errol John); appeared on TV in The Richard Pryor Special; author/prodr. Three Way Choice, Afro-American in the Arts (Golden Eagle award), in ltd. series Roots; appeared in revue Cabaret for Freedom and The Blacks (Obie award) with Godfrey Cambridge; adatped Ajax for Mark Taper Forum in L.A.; librettist, lyricist and composer: And Still I Rise, 1976; wrote and presented Trying to Make it Home, 1988; writer for Oprah Winfrey's Harpo Prodns.; poetry writer for film Poetic Justice, 1993; appeared in plays: Porgy and Bess, 1954-55 (Europe), 1957 (U.S.), Calypso, 1957, The Blacks, 1960, Mother Courage, 1964, Medea, Look Away, 1973; films: Roots (Emmy Nomination Best Supporting Actress), 1977, How to Make an American Quilt, 1995; contr. short stories and poems to mags.; also numerous appearances on network and local talk shows; articles, short stories, poems to Black Scholar, Chgo. Daily News, Cosmopolitan, Harper's Bazaar, Life Mag., Redbook, Sunday N.Y. Times, others. Mem. adv. bd. Women's Prison Assn.; apptd. by Dr. Martin Luther King Jr. No. Coord. Southern Christian Leadership Conf., 1959-60, apptd. by Pres. Ford to Bicentennal Commn., by Pres. Carter to Nat. Commn. on Observance of Internat. Women's Yr. Chubb fellowship award Yale U., 1970, named Woman of Yr. in Comm., 1976; Ladies Home Jour. Top 100 Most Influential Women, 1983, The Matric award, 1983, The North Carolina Award in Lit., 1987; named 1st Reynolds prof. Wake Forest U., 1981, a lifetime appointment, Woman of the Yr. Essence Mag., 1992, Disting. Woman of N.C., 1992, Horatio Alger award, 1992, Grammy award Best Spoken Word or Non-Traditional Album, 1994 (for recording of "On the Pulse of the Morning"). Mem. AFTRA, Dirs. Guild Am., Equity, Harlem Writers Guild, Am. Film Inst. (trustee), Women's Prison Assn., Horatio Alger Assn. Dist. Americans, Nat. Soc. Prevention of Cruelty to Children (Maya Angelou Ctr. opened 1992), ambassador, Unicef Internat., 1996. Office: care Dave La Camera Lordly and Dame Inc 51 Church St Boston MA 02116-5417*

ANGELOV, LYUBEN LAZAROV, epidemiologist, researcher; b. Pazardzik, Bulgaria, Dec. 17, 1934; s. Angel Iliev and Tanya Angelova (Hadzilokova) Lazarov; m. Kamenka Ivanova Chavdarova, Nov. 1963 (dec. July 1993); 1 child, Angelova Angela Lyubenova. MD, Med. U., Plovdiv, Bulgaria, 1959, PhD, 1984. Epidemiologist Ctr. for Disease Control, Dimitrongrad, Bulgaria, 1958-61; asst. Med. U., Plovdiv, 1961-63, sr. asst., 1963-73, chief asst., 1973-84, asst. prof., 1984-95; dir. Ctr. for Nasocomial Infections, Plovdiv, 1977-88; mem. expert group for lyme borreliosis WHO, 1989—, Lab. for Lyme Disease, Plovdiv, 1988—. Co-author: Nesocomial Infections, 1977, Epidemiology, 1986, 4th edit., 1994, Hospital Disinfection, 1989; contbr. articles to profl. jours. Mem. Union Bulgarian Physicians and Surgeons, Union Bulgarian Scientists. Orthodox. Home: 5 Haidushka St, 4000 Plovdiv Bulgaria

ANGELSKY, OLEG VYACHESLAVOVICH, optical engineer, educator, university dean; b. Selyatin, Ukraine, May 5, 1957; s. Vyacheslav Michailovich and Olga Maksimovna (Nechiporenko) A.; m. Svetlana Ivanovna Gorelova, Jan. 22, 1982; children: Alla, Pavel. MS, Chernivtsy U., Ukraine, 1979; postgrad., Chernivtsy U., 1983; DSc, U. Saratov, Russia, 1990; PhD, Acad. Inst., 1983. From tchr. to prof. Chernivtsy U., 1983-91, prof., 1991—, head dept., 1990—, dean faculty, 1997—. Contbr. articles to profl. jours. Grantee Internat. Sci. Found., 1993-95, Sci. Tech. Ctr. Ukraine, 1997—. Fellow Inst. Physics (Great Britain); mem. Soc. Photo-Optical Instrumentation Engrs. (chpt. bd. dirs. 1993—), Internat. Commn. Optics (chmn. chpt. 1993—), Ukrainian Optical Soc. (v.p. 1995—), European Optical Soc. (adv. com. 1995—), Russian Optical Soc. (Rozhdestvensky medal 1995). Avocations: tennis, football, reading. Office: Chernivtsy U, 2 Kotsyubinsky St, 274012 Chernivtsi Ukraine

ANGER, GOTTFRIED JOHANN, mathematician, educator; b. Radebeul, Germany, May 12, 1928; s. Louis Karl and Lina Emma (Wauer) A.; m. Brigitte Flora Philipp, Feb. 10, 1962; 1 child, Nils Gottfried. Diploma, Tech. U., Dresden, Germany, 1952, Dr. rer. nat., 1957; Dr.rer.nat. habil., U. Rostock, Germany, 1966. Asst. Tech. U., Dresden, 1952-63; researcher Inst. Pure Math., Berlin, 1963-72; prof. Martin Luther U., Halle, Germany, 1972-93; ret. Martin Luther U., Halle, 1993—. Author: Methods of Potential Theory, 1967, Inverse Problems in Differential Equations, 1990; editor: Elliptic Differential Equations, 1970, Inverse Problems, 1979, Inverse Problems: Principles and Applications in Geophysics, Technology and Medicine, 1993. Mem. Gesellschaft Angewandte Math. und Mech., Soc. Math. France, Am. Math. Soc. Home: Rathausstr 13 Whg 11/09, D-10178 Berlin Germany Office: U Halle FB Math, Universitatsplatz 10, D-06099 Halle Germany

ANGERER, PAUL, musician, educator, composer, conductor; b. Vienna, Austria, May 16, 1927; s. Otto and Elisabeth (Denk) A.; m. Anita Rosser; children: Pierre, Ursula, Veronica, Christoph. Student, Hochschule Musik Acad. and Vienna Conservatory, 1940-47. Viola player Tonhalle Zurich Orch. de la Suisse Romande, Zurich, 1948-53; viola soloist Vienna Symphony Orch., 1953-57; chef Wiener Kammer Orch., 1956-63; conductor, dir. opera Bonn, Ulm and Salzburg Theaters, Fed. Republic Germany, 1964-72; leader, conductor S.W. German Orch., 1971-81; prof. Hochschule Musik Acad., 1982-92; leader, violinist Concilium Musicum, Vienna, 1982—; permanent guest conductor Orch. Hayn, Bolzano, Italy, 1960-90; artistic dir. Hellbrunner Spiele, 1970-71. Compositions include Concert pour la Jeunesse, 1956, Die Passkontrolle (TV opera), 1958, Konzerte fur Klavier, 1962, fur Viola, 1962, Cogitatio fur 9 Instruments, 1964, Inklination der Ariadne des Monteverdi (orch. and balllet), 1967, Hotel Comedie (musical), 1970, Altoposaune, 1977, Exercitium Canonicum for 2 viols, 1980, Harfe, 1981, stage music for various theatres, film, TV; recordings include Mozart and Beethoven piano concertos, Schubert Overtures, Weihnachtslieder, Strauss Waltzes, Barockmusik, Konzerte fur Oboe und Posaune. Recipient Osterreich Staatspreis, 1956, 1st prize Salzburg Opera Competition, 1959, Kulturpreis der Stadt Wien, 1983, Nö-Kulturpreis, 1987, Nö-Preis für Mozartforschung, 1994, Nestroy-Ring der Stadt Wien, 1999. Home and Office: Esteplatz 3/26, A-1030 Vienna Austria Address: Unternalb 21, A-2070 Retz Austria

ANGERMEIER, HEINZ, history educator; b. Vilsbiburg, Germany, Apr. 11, 1924; s. Jakob and Berta A.; m. Isabel Collien, Apr. 1, 1948; children: Magnus, Jutta, Mechtild, Almut. PhD, U. Munich, 1954; Postdoctoral Lectr. Qualifications, U. Kiel, 1965. Collaborator of Historische Kommission bei der Bayer Acad. der Wissenschaften, Munich, 1954-59, scientific collaborator Historische Kommission bei der Bayer, 1959-65; pvt. lectr. U. Kiel, 1965-68; prof. of history U. Regensburg, 1968-90; leader of dept. Deutsche Reichstagsakten, Mittlere Reihe, 1974—, Deutsche Reichstagsakten, Reichsversammlungen 1556-1662, 1986—. Editor: Deutsche Reichstagsakten Mittlere Reihe Bd. V: Reichstag zu Worms 1495, 1981, Deutsche Reichstagsakten Mittlere Reihe Bd. I: Reichstag zu Frankfurt 1486, 1989, C.T. Gemeiner, Regensburgische Chronik, 1971, Säkulare Aspekte der Reformationszeit, 1983, Fortschritte in der Geschichts-Wissenschaft durch Reichstagsaktenforschung, 1988; author: Konigtum und Landfriede im deutschen Spatmittelalter, 1966, Geschichte oder Gegenwart, 1973, Die Reichsreform 1410-1555, 1985, Das Alte Reich in der deutschen Geschichte, 1991, others; contbr. articles to profl. jours. Recipient Albertus-Magnus-medal for history and sci., City of Regensburg, 1984. Mem. Historische Kommission bei der Bayerischen Akademie der Wissenschaften, Gesellschaft für Reichskammergerichtsforschung (sci. adv.), Gierkes Untersuchungen zur deutschen Staats-und Rechtsgeschichte (co-editor).

ANGERMÜLLER, RUDOLPH, music foundation executive; b. Gadderbaum/Bielefeld, Westphalia, Germany, Sept. 2, 1940. Grad. in piano, contrabass, music theory, Forsterling Conservatory Music; MA in Romance langs. and History, U. Münster, Germany, 1967; PhD, Salzburg U., Austria, 1970. Asst. instr. Musicological Inst., Salzburg (Austria) U., 1967-72, lectr., 1968-75; dir. musicology dept. Internationale Stiftung Mozarteum, Salzburg, 1982-88, sec.-gen., 1988—. Author: Sigismund Neukomm, 1977, Mozart und seine Pariser Umwelt - 1778, 1978, Figaro, 1986, Don Juan Register, 1987, Mozart: Die Opern von der Uraufführung bis heute, 1988, Vom Kaiser zum Sklaven: Personen in Mozarts Opern, 1989, Ich johannes Chrisostomus Amadeus Wolfgangus sigismundus Mozart: Eine Autobiografie, 1991, Deliciae Italiae: Mozarts Reisen in Italien, 1994, W. A. Mozart, Reisetagebuch 1819-1821, 1994, Mozart auf der Reise nach Prag, Dresden, Leipzig und Berlin, 1995, Antonio Saleiri, Die Dokumente Seines Lebens, 3 vols., 2000; contbr. articles to profl. jours., numerous programme notes; designer countless exhbns. Decorated Disting. Svc. Cross for Sci. and Art (Austria); Paul Harris fellow Rotary Internat.; recipient Mozart prize Province of Lower Austria, Mozart medallion Mozart Soc. of Vienna, Silver medallion of honor Salzburg Province, Silver Mozart medallion Internationale Stiftlung Mozarteum. Office: Internat Stiftung Mozarteum, Schwarzstrasse 26, 5020 Salzburg Austria

ANGHILERI, LEOPOLDO JOSÉ, researcher; b. Buenos Aires, Aug. 22, 1928; s. José and Maria (Orlando) A.; m. Akemi Itoh, Jan. 8, 1983; children: María Luján, Noelle, Juan Manuel. D in Chemistry, U. Buenos Aires, 1957. Rschr. Argentine Commn. Nat. Energia Atomica, Buenos Aires, 1957-60; fellow Johns Hopkins Med. Instns., Balt., 1967-69; asst. prof. U. Denver, 1969-70; rschr. German Cancer Ctr., Heidelberg, Germany, 1966-67, Tumor Rsch. Ctr., Essen, Germany, 1970-75; fellow Inst. du Radium, Paris, 1968-69; rschr. French Commissariat Energie Atomique, Paris, 1977-79, Inst. Nat. Rsch. Med., Paris, 1977-78; rsch. dir. lab. biophysics U. Nancy, France, 1980-91, ret., 1991. Editor, author: General Processes Radiotracer Localization Vol. 2, 1982, Hyperthermia in Cancer Treatment, Vol. 3, 1986, Role of Calcium in Biological Systems Vol. 5, 1982-90; contbr. 255 articles to profl. jours. Mem. Am. Chem. Soc. Home: 95 rue de Mareville, 54520 Laxou France

ANGIERSKI, BERND-RUEDIGER, process engineer, dialysis consultant; b. Magdeburg, Germany, Mar. 1, 1960; s. Adolf and Lieselotte (Kausch) A.; m. Kerstin Backhaus, Feb. 19, 1987; children: Christin, André, Anne-Marie, Alexander, Anton Quintus. Expert on chems. industries, Vocat. Coll. Fahlberg-List, Magdeburg, 1979; B in Engring., Tech. U. Dresden, Germany, 1986, grad. engr., 1986, PhD, 1990. Scientist, asst. prof. Tech. U. Dresden, 1987-90; dir. rsch. and mktg. Keradenta GmbH, Radeberg, Germany, 1990-93; mng. dir. BAMED Medizintechnik GmbH, Dresden, 1993-95, Medizintechnik Dr. Angierski, Dresden, 1996—. Author: Quality Control in Membrane Manufacture, 1986, Investigations on the Optimization, Modelling and Quality Valuation of Hollow Fibre Hemodialyzers, 1990; patentee in field of mfg. and testing of membranes and dialyzers; contbr. articles to profl. jours. Judge for comml. law, Dresden Dist. Ct., 1997—. Mem. Internat. Soc. for Artificial Organs. Office: Medizintechnik Dr Angierski, Tzschimmerstr 23, D-01309 Dresden Germany

ANGSTROM, WAYNE RAYMOND, communications executive; b. Chgo., Mar. 26, 1939; s. Raymond Harry and Dorothy Louise (Dixon) A.; m. Sandra Sue Weber, Oct. 5, 1963; children: Mark, Carl, David, Kristina. AA in Bus. Adminstrn., Chgo. City Coll., 1962; student, Northwestern U., 1963-68. Mfg. mgr. R.R. Donnelley & Sons Co., Chgo., 1962, div. dir., v.p., 1981-87; exec. v.p. Maxwell Communications Corp., St. Paul, 1987-90, Quebecor Printing Inc., Boston, 1990-91; pres., CEO, St. Ives Inc. U.S.A., 1992—; also bd. dirs. Home: 7082 Valencia Dr Boca Raton FL 33433-7404 Office: Saint Ives Inc 2025 Mckinley St Hollywood FL 33020-3139

ANGULA, HELMUT KANGULOHI, Namibian government official; b. Ontananga, Oshikoto, Namibia, Nov. 11, 1945; s. Onesmus and Adda (Thomas) A.; div. Nov. 1992; children: Adda Kaone, Vita, Priscilla, Magdalena, Monica. Cert., Nikumbi Internat. Coll., 1969; MSc in Biology, Voronezh State U., USSR, 1975. Cert. Tchr. Biology and Chemistry. Tchr. SWAPO Edn. Ctr., Nyango, Zambia, 1975-76; adminstr. SWAPO Edn. Ctr., Nyango, Zanbia, 1976-77; head of diplomatic mission SWAPO Mission, Havana, Cuba, 1977-86; head of mission SWAPO Observer Mission, UN, N.Y.C., 1986-89; deputy min. Ministry Mines and Energy, Republic of Namibia, 1990-91; min. Fisheries and Marine Resources, Republic of Namibia, 1991-95; min. of fin., 1995-96; min. Agr., Water and Rural Devel., 1997—. Author: Haimbodi Ya Haufiku 1000 Days, 1991. Activist South West Africa People's, Windhoek, 1964; youth activist Organization SWAPO, Zambia, 1966. Mem. Revival Volley Ball Club (patron), Parliamentary Football Team (capt. 1993—). Office: Embassy of Republic of Namibia 1605 New Hampshire Ave NW Washington DC 20009-2511

ANGULO, MARIO, radiology educator; b. Popayan, Colombia, Oct. 10, 1942; s. Mario Angulo and Alicia Doria; m. Ximena Mosquera, Feb. 15, 1969; children: Aurelio, Mario, Juan Andres. MD, U. Javeriana, Bogota, Colombia, 1968. Tng. in radiotherapy B.C. Cancer Agy., Vancouver, Can., 1970-73, M.D. Anderson Hosp., Houston, 1973-75; radiotherapist Nat. Inst. Cancer, Bogota, 1975-78; head oncology svc. Ctrl. Mil. Hosp., Bogota, 1978-83; head oncology svc. Santa Fe Found., Bogota, 1984-94, dir. Inst. Oncology, 1994; prof. radiotherapy U. Javeriana, 1995—. Co-author: Internal Medicine, 1984, Breast Cancer, 1988. Mem. Conservative Party. Roman Catholic. Avocations: horseback riding, swimming. Home: Diagonal 109 Apt 1-36, Bogota Colombia Office: U Javeriana, Carrera 16A No 85-92, Bogota Colombia

ANGUS, JAMES ALEXANDER, pharmacology educator; b. Sydney, NSW, Australia, Feb. 15, 1949; s. Stuart Douglas and Evelyn Simpson (Wilkie) A.; m. Helen Shirley Robinson, Dec. 28, 1971; children: Damien, Kirsten, Simon. BSc with honors in Pharmacology, U. Sydney, 1970, PhD in Pharmacology, 1974. Rsch. fellow dept. medicine Hallstrom Inst. Cardiology Royal Prince Alfred Hosp., U. Sydney, 1973, NHMRC sr. rsch. officer, 1974-75; NHMRC sr. rsch. officer Baker Med. Rsch. Inst., Prahran, Victoria, Australia, 1975-76, 80-81, NHMRC rsch. fellow, 1981-82, NHMRC sr. rsch. fellow, 1983-85, NHMRC prin. rsch. fellow, 1985, NHMRC sr. prin. rsch. fellow, 1989-93, dep. dir., 1990-92; personal chair pharmacology faculty medicine Monash U., Melbourne, Australia, 1992-93; chair pharmacology, head dept. Melbourne U., Australia, 1993—, pres. acad. bd., 2000—, pro-vice chancellor, 1999—; NHMRC C.J. Martin traveling fellow dept. pharmacology U. Coll., London, 1977, Wellcome Rsch. Labs., Beckenham, Kent, Eng., 1978, Baker Med. Rsch. Inst., 1979; chair med. rsch. grants com. NHMRC, Canberra, Australia, 1991-93; mem. nat. com. pharmacology Australian Acad. Sci., 1994—; mem. sci. program com. 15th Sci. Meeting Internat. Soc. Hypertension, 1994; mem. nat. adv. bd. Internat. Soc. Cardiovascular Pharmacotherpy, Sydney, 1996; cons. panel Microsurgery Rsch. Ctr., St. Vincent's Hosp., 1990—. Exec. editor Clin. and Exptl. Pharmacology and Physiology, 1993; editl. bd. Circulation Rsch., 1993—, Jour. Vascular Rsch., 1992-96, Endothelium, 1992—, Brit. Jour. Pharmacology, 1991-95, Jour. Cardiovascular Pharmacology, 1988—; mem. internat. adv. com. Pharmacology and Toxicology, 1993—. Bd. mem. Murdoch Inst. Birth Defects, Melbourne, 1991-97; coun. mem. Melbourne Grammar Sch., 1991-98; mem. poisons adv. com. Victorian Dept. Health & Cmty. Svcs., Melbourne, 1993-97; mem. bd. Queensland Pharm. Rsch. Inst., Griffith U., 1994—. Recipient Alfred Gottschalk medal Australian Acad. Sci., 1984; grantee Nat. Heart Found., 1979-80, 80-81, 88-89, 90-91, 91-93, NHMRC, 1982-92, Glaxo Australia and Pharmacology Lab. at Baker Inst., 1989-93, Glaxo Australia and Dept. Pharmacology, U. Melbourne, 1993-98. Fellow Australian Acad. Sci.; mem. Australian Physiol. and Pharmacol. Soc., Australian Soc. Clin. and Exptl. Pharmacology, Brit. Pharmacol. Soc., Cardiac Soc. Australia and New Zealand, High Blood Pressure Rsch. Coun. Australia, Internat. Serotonin Club, Internat. Soc. Heart Rsch. Avocations: golf, fishing, sailing. Office: U Melbourne, Dept Pharmacology, Parkville Victoria, Australia 3052

ANGUS, SIR MICHAEL RICHARDSON, chemical company executive; b. Ashford, Eng., May 5, 1930; s. William R. Angus and Doris Margaret Breach; m. Isabel Elliott, 1952; 3 children. Grad., Bristol (Eng.) U., 1951; DSc (hon.), Bristol U., 1990, Buckingham Univ., 1994; LLD (hon.), Nottingham Univ., 1996; hon. fellowship, Bristol Univ., 1998. Joined Unilever PLC, 1954, sales dir. Lever Bros. U.K., 1967-70, Co-ordinator toilet preparation products, 1970-76, Co-ordinator chemicals, 1976-80, regional dir. N.Am., 1979-84; chmn., chief exec. officer Unilever U.S., Inc., N.Y.C., 1980-84, Lever Brothers Co., N.Y.C., 1980-84; vice chair Unilever PLC, London, 1984-86, chmn., 1986-92; mktg. dir. Thibaud Gibbs, Paris, 1962-65; mng. dir. Research Bur., 1965-67; chmn. Whitbread PLC, London, 1992-2000; chmn. The Boots Co. PLC, 1994-98, dep. chmn., 1998—; dep. chmn. Brit. Airways, 1989-2000; chmn. Royal Agrl. Coll., Circencester, 1992—, Internatl. Counsellor Emeritus, Conf. Bd., Dep. Lieutenant of Gloucestershire, 1997—, Commdr. of Order of Oranje Nassau, 1992. Bd. govs. Ashridge Mgmt. Coll., 1974—, chmn. govs., 1991—; chmn. trustees Leverhulme Trust. Served with Royal Air Force, 1951-54. Mem. Netherlands-Brit. C. of C. (joint chair 1984-89). Avocations: the countryside, wines, puzzles. Address: Cerney House, North Cerney Cirencester, Gloucester GL7 7BX, England

ANGUS, ROBERT CARLYLE, JR., naturopathic physician, health administrator; b. Grand Rapids, Mich., July 23, 1946; s. Robert Carlyle Sr. and Vicki I. (Weidman) Deiters; m. Elizabeth T. Angus, May 1995; children: Tamra Ann, Robert M. BS, Donsbach U., Huntington Beach, Calif., 1985; PhD in Therapeutic Philosophy, World U., 1982. Registered cardiovascular technologist, pulmonary technologist, cardiology technologist; cert. respiratory therapist; lic. radiographer, respiratory care practitioner, Pa.; lic. hearing aid dispenser; cert. occupl. hearing conservationist; bd. cert. naturopathic physician Am. Naturopathic Med. Assn.; cert. colon hydrotherapist advanced level. Dir. cardiopulmonary St. Mary's Hosp., Grand Rapids, Mich., 1970-74; Lectr. Muskegon (Mich.) Community Coll., 1974-76; dir. respiratory therapy Hackley Hosp., 1974-76; dir. cardiovascular, cardiopulmonary Am. Internat. Hosp., Zion, Ill., 1976-78; physician's asst. Dr. William J. Mauer; dir. med. svcs., clinic adminstr. Kingsley Med. Ctr., Arlington Heights, Ill., 1978-90; dir. med. diagnostics, naturopathic physician Celebration of Health Ctr., Inc., Bluffton, Ohio, 1990—; edn. cons. Brookhaven Med. Care Facility; lectr., advisor Muskegon C.C., 1974-76; mem. Nat. Bd. Respiratory Care. Active Big Bros. Am., Muskegon, 1974-76. Mem. Nat. Bd. Cardiovascular Testing, Am. Cardiology Technologists Assn., Am. Assn. Respiratory Therapy, Am. Naturopathic Med. Assn., Nat. Soc. Cardiopulmonary Technologists, Am. Naturopathic Med. Assn., Coun. for Accreditation in Occupational Hearing Conservation, Internat. Assn. for Colon Hydrothrapy, Soc. for Noninvasive Vascular Tech., Cardiovascular Credentialing Internat. Avocations: canoeing, horses, antiques, old radios, reading.

ANGUS-LEPPAN, PETER VINCENT, consultant, educator emeritus; b. Johannesburg, Transvaal, South Africa, Sept. 4, 1930; arrived in Australia, 1962; s. Hilton and Irene Muriel (Smith) A.; m. Pamela Edith Furze, July 11, 1953; children: Heather, Gavin, Neil, Tamsin. BSc in Engring., U. Witwatersrand, Johannesburg, 1951; diploma in town planning, U. Natal, Durban, South Africa, 1958, PhD in Geodesy, 1959. Cert. land surveyor. Lectr. U. Cape Town, Cape Province, South Africa, 1953; from lectr. to sr. lectr. U. Natal, Durban, 1954-62; sr. lectr. U. NSW, Sydney, Australia, 1962-63; found. prof. U. NSW, Sydney, 1964-90; project coord. Land Titling Project, Thailand, 1985-90; cons. Pal Cons. Pty. Ltd., Coogee, NSW, Australia, 1990—; mem. Bd. Surveyors, NSW, 1966-84; chmn. nat. com. on geodesy and geophysics Acad. Sci., Australia, 1974-80, chmn. geodesy subcom., 1966-80. Editor Proceedings for First Conf. on Refraction Effects on Geodesy and Electronic Distance Measurement, 1968, Proceedings Symposium on Earth's Gravitational Field and Secular Variations in Position, 1973, (with R.S. Mather) The New South Wales Integrated Survey Grid, 1976, Progress in Thailand Land Titling Project, 1987, The Land Titling Project: Dynamics of Change; contbr. articles to profl. jours. Recipient Sr. Scientist award U.S. Acad. Sci., 1984, Cert. Achievement U.S. Dept. Army, 1971, award of Excellence for Overseas Assistance Projects Australian Govt., 1988; Rsch. fellow Can. Commonwealth F. U. N.B., 1966, Leichhardt Rsch. fellow V. Humboldt Found., 1978. Fellow Inst. Surveyors Australia (Inst. medal 1987), Explorers Club (N.Y.); mem. Australian Inst. Cartographers, Internat. Assn. Geodesy (pres. 1983-87, hon. pres. 1987—). Avocations: exploring, mountaineering. Home: 103 Beach St, Coogee NSW 2034, Australia Office: PAL Consultants Pty Ltd, PO Box 51, Coogee NSW 2034, Australia

ANGYAL, STEPHEN JOHN, chemist; b. Budapest, Hungary, Nov. 21, 1914; arrived in Australia, 1940; s. Charles and Maria (Viranyi) Engel; m. Helga Ellen Steininger, Feb. 18, 1941; children: Annette, Robert. PhD, U. Budapest, 1937; DSc, U. New South Wales, Sydney, Australia, 1967. Rsch. chemist Chinoin Pharm. Co., Budapest, 1937-39, Nicholas Propriety Ltd., Melbourne, Australia, 1941-46; lectr. U. Sydney, 1946-51; fellow Nuffield Dominion, Cambridge, U.K., 1952; assoc. prof. U. New South Wales, 1953-60, prof., 1960-79, dean Sci., 1970-79. Co-author: Conformational Analysis, 1965 (Olle prize Australia Chem. Inst. 1966); contbr. articles to profl. jours. Recipient Haworth award Chem. Soc., London, 1980, Hudson award Am. Chem. Soc., 1987. Fellow Royal Australian Chem. Inst. (H.G. Smith medal, 1958), Australian Acad. Sci.; mem. Hungarian Acad. Sci. (external). Achievements include developments in the composition and conformation of carbohydrates. Home: 304 Sailors Bay Rd, Northbridge 2063, Australia Office: Univ New South Wales, Sch Chem, Sydney 2052, Australia

ÁNGYÁN, LAJOS, physiologist; b. Böhönye, Somogy, Hungary, June 26, 1938; s. Lajos and Mária (Kalmár) A.; m. Éva Pados, Aug. 5, 1961; 1 child, Zoltán. MD, U. Pécs, Hungary, 1962; PhD, Hungarian Acad. Sci., Budapest, 1970, DSc, 1986. Cert. med. lab. examiner specialist; lic. physician. From asst. to lectr. Med. U. Pécs, 1962-95, prof., 1995—; rschr. lab. neurophysiol. faculty sci. U. Paris, 1969-70; vis. prof. sports physiology Janus Pannonius U., Pécs, 1990-98. Author: Basis of Sports Physiology, 1993, Manual of Sports Physiology, 1995, Introduction to Human Physiology, 1996, Essays in Physiology, 1997, (with L. and Z. Ányán) Arterial Blood Pressure: 100 Questions and Answers, 1999; contbr. articles to profl. jours. Named Eminant Worker Edn., Min. Health, Budapest, 1973. Mem. Hungarian Physiol. soc., Hungarian Neurosci. Soc., Internat. Brain Rsch. Orgn., European Sleep Rsch. Soc., European Brain & Behaviour Soc., European Neurosci. Assn. Avocation: gardening. Office: Med Univ Pécs Inst Physiol, Inst Kinesiology 99, 7601 Pecs Hungary

ANH, VO VAN, mathematician, researcher; b. Binh-Thuan, Vietnam, July 2, 1949; arrived in Australia, 1969; s. Lai Van and Dan Thi Vo; m. Thanh-Hai Anh, 1976; children: Nancy, Andrew. BSc with honors, U. Tasmania, Australia, 1975; PhD in Math., U. Tasmania, 1978; M in Econs., U. New Eng., Australia, 1984. Tutor U. New Eng., 1978-80; sr. rsch. officer Bur. Agrl. Econs., Australia, 1980-83; from lectr. to assoc. prof. Queensland U. Tech., Australia, 1984—; dir. Rsch. Ctr. in Statis. Sci., Queensland U. Tech., 1990-92, assoc. dir. Ctr. in Statis. Sci. and Indsl. Math., 1993—; cons. NSW Environ. Protection Authority, 1995; reviewer Math. Reviews, U.S., 1984—. Contbr. chpts. to books, articles to profl. jours. Recipient QUT award for disting. acad. svc., 1990, QUT award for outstanding contbn. in rsch. and scholarship, 1996; grantee Australian Rsch. Coun., 1995—, Hong Kong Rsch. Grants Coun., 1997—. Fellow Australian Math. Soc. (assoc. editor bull. 1987); mem. IEEE, Modelling and Simulation Soc. Australia, Am. Math. Soc., N.Y. Acad. Scis., Am. Math. Soc., Statis. Soc. of Australia. Avocations: bush walking, swimming. Office: Queensland U Tech Sch Math Scis, 2 George St, Brisbane Q 4000, Australia

ANHALT, ISTVAN, composer, writer, educator; b. Budapest, Hungary, Apr. 12, 1919; s. Arnold and Katalin (Herzfeld) A.; m. Beate Frankenberg, Jan. 1952; children: Helen, Carol.; Student, Hungarian Acad. Music, 1936-41, Nat. Conservatory Music, Paris, 1946-48; DMus (hon.), McGill U., 1982; LLD, Queen's U., 1991. Asst. condr. Hungarian Opera, 1945; from asst. to full prof. McGill U., Montreal, 1949-71, chmn. dept. theory, faculty music, 1963-69, dir. electronic music studio, 1964-71; head music dept. Queen's U., Kingston, 1971-81, prof. emeritus, 1984—; electronic music composer Electronic Music Lab., Nat. Rsch. Coun. Can., summers 1959-61; computer generation music Bell Tel. Labs., Murray Hill, N.J., summer 1961; vis. F. Slee prof. composition SUNY, Buffalo, 1969, Archive papers Nat. Libr. Canada, Ottawa. Composer Comments, Symphony No. 1, Cento, Fantasia, Foci, Symphony of Modules, Trio, Sonata for Piano, Sonata for Violin and Piano, Four Electronic Compositions, Thisness, Simulacrum, SparkskrapS, Sonance-Resonance, Doors...Shadows, La Tourangelle, 1975, Winthrop, 1983, Traces, 1995, Millennial Mall, 1999; author: Alternative Voices, 1984, Oppenheimer, 1990, A Weave of Life Lines, 1992, others. Forced laborer Hungarian Army, 1942-44. Recipient Centennial medal, 1967, Commemorative medal for 125th Anniversary, Can. Confedn., 1993, John B. Stirling medal, 1993. Mem. Can. League Composers. Address: 274 Johnson St, Kingston, ON Canada K7L 1Y4

ANICAMA GOMEZ, JOSÉ CARLOS, academic administrator; b. Lima, Peru, Nov. 4, 1949; s. José Anicama Cabrera and Susana Gomez de Anicama; m. Elena Silva Momehtriano; children: José Carlos, Sue Ellen. Lic. in psychology, UNMSM, Lima, 1976; M Salud Publica, U. Ala., 1986; MS in Psychology, UPCH, Lima, 1987, DS in Psychology, 1993. Dir. psychology sch. UPCH, 1974-90; dir. Inst. Investigative Psychology UNFV, Lima, 1991-93, dir. postgrad. faculty psychology, 1992-93, decano faculty psychology, 1993-98, rector, 1999—; cons. CEDRO, Lima, 1992-94; pres. SPAMC, Lima, 1993; nat. coord. ALAMOC, Lima, 1993-96; dir. gen. CIPMOC, Lima, 1992—. Editor: Drogas Produccion 7 Comercilizacion, 1993, Estudio Epidemiologico sobre la Violencia, 1999; editor: Drogas, Violencia 7 Ecologia, 1994, Drogas y Desarrolo Sociol-Economico, 1995. roman Catholic. Avocation: music. Office: U Nacional Fed Villareal, Av Carlos Gonzeles 285, Lima 32, Peru

ANILY, SHOSHANA, management educator. BSc, Tel-Aviv U., 1978, MA, 1983; PhD, Columbia U., 1987. Asst. prof. U. B.C., Canada, 1986-89; from lectr. to sr. lectr. Tel-Aviv U., 1989-97, assoc. prof., 1997—; vis. assoc. prof. Columbia U., N.Y.C., 1996—. Mem. editl. bd. IEE, 1994—. Recipient Oded Levin prize ORSIS, 1990. Mem. INFORMS (editl. bd. 1996—). Fax: 972-3-640-7742. E-mail: anily@post.tau.ac.il. Office: Tel Aviv U, Fac Mgmt, 69978 Tel Aviv Israel

ANINAT, EDUARDO, international banking official; b. 1948; m. Maria Teresa Sahli; six children. BA in Econs., Pontificia U. Catolica, Chile; MA in Econs., Harvard U., PhD in Econs. Former asst. prof. econs. Boston U.; prin. Aninat, Mendez y Asociados, 1981-94; fin. min. Govt. of Chile, 1994-95; chmn. bd. govs. IMF and World Bank, 1995-96, former mem. devel. com.; Latin. Am. coord. internat. tax program Harvard U., 1989; deputy mng. dir. IMF, Washington, 1999—; cons. various internat. instns. including the World Bank, Inter-Am. Devel. Bank; adv. various governments on tax policy matters; bd. dirs. various pvt. cos.; dep. mng. dir. IMF, Washington. Office: Internat Monetary Fund 700 19th St NW Washington DC 20431-0001

ANISCHENKO, GENNADY YAKOVLEVICH, physicist, researcher; b. Vologda, Russia, Oct. 23, 1937; s. Yakov Ivanovich and Polina Petrovna (Taryanik) A.; m. Rimma Nicolaevna Maramzina, July 5, 1960; children: Irina, Yaroslav. Grad. in Engring., Ural Poly. Inst., Sverdlovsk, USSR, 1961. Engr. Fed. Nuclear Ctr., Chelyabinsk, USSR, 1961-67, sr. engr., 1967-70, sr. sci. worker, 1970-85, lab. head, 1985-93, sr. sci. worker, 1993—; cons. Civil Aircraft Works, Ekaterinburg, Russia, 1990-95. Contbr. articles to profl. jours.; inventor in field; patentee in field. Chair trade-union com. of exptl. divsn. Fed. Nuclear Ctr., 1978-82. Communist. Avocations: scientific researches, Navy history. Home: Vasilieva str 14 apt 12, 456770 Snezhinsk Russia Office: Russian Inst Tech Physics, PO Box 245, 456770 Snezhinsk Russia

ANISEROWICZ, KAROL, electrical engineering educator, consultant; b. Bialystok, Poland, July 26, 1955; s. Roman and Jadwiga (Michalczuk) A.; m. Malgorzata Kosinska, Feb. 20, 1982; children: Maciej, Mateusz, Michal. MSEE, Warsaw (Poland) U. Tech., 1979; PhD, Tech. U. Szczecin, Poland, 1987. Jr. asst., then asst. Tech. U. Bialystok, 1979-87, lectr. elec. engring., 1987—, mem. dept. sci. bd., 1996—; sec. sci. bd. Ctr. Protection from Overvoltages and Electromagnetic Interferences, Bialystok, 1995—; head sect. informatics Chief Tech. Orgn., Bialystok, 1988-89; invited rschr. U. Que., Trois Rivieres, Can., 1992; cons. Polish Telecom., Warsaw, 1995-2001. Author: Computer Aided Design of Electronic Circuits, 1994; contbr. articles to sci. jours., including Quar. Polish Acad. Scis., IEEE Trans. on Industry Applications; patentee in field. Founder, mem. Solidarity, Bialystok, 1980-94. Mem. IEEE, Polish Elec. Engrs. Assn. (cert. lightning and overvoltage protection, electromagnetic compatibility, measurement tech., and software engring. expert, mem. ctrl. bd. edn. 1998—, Prof. of Best MSc Thesis in Elec. Engring. award 1998). Roman Catholic. Avocations: travel, good music, biking, watching lightning storms and his wife in the kitchen. Office: Tech U Bialystok Dept EE, Grunwaldzka 11/15, 15-893 Bialystok Poland

ANISFELD, MICHAEL H., industrial pharmacist, consultant; b. London, May 30, 1946; came to U.S., 1976; s. Arthur and Ester Anisfeld; m. Evelyn Blum (div. 1984); children: Eytan, Ginger, Elyse, Joshua, Robyn; m. Daryl A., Aug. 31, 1997. B in Pharmacy with honors, London U., 1969, M in Pharmacy, 1971; MS in Mgmt., Lake Forest Coll., 1980, MBA, 1981. Dir. quality assurance Am. Critical Care, Waukegan, Ill., 1980-82, dir. R & D, 1982-85; pres. Interpharm Consulting, Buffalo Grove, Ill., 1985—, Interpharm Press, Buffalo Grove, Ill., 1982-99; adj. prof. U. Ill. Coll. Pharmacy, Chgo., 1985—; cons. WHO, 1993——, UN Indsl. Devel. Orgn., 1990-92, UN Fund Population Activities, 1984-95. Author: (annual) International Drug GMPs, 1979—, other books; author (software) Training Tracker, 1993-99, other titles; contbr. articles to profl. jours. Capt., Med. Corps, 1970-75, Israel. Mem. Parenteral Drug Assn. (bd. dirs. 1980-82), Internat. Soc. Pharm. Engrs., Brit. Parenteral Soc., Regulatory Profls., Brit. Inst. Regulatory Affairs, Friends of Israel Def. Forces. Avocation: travel. E0-mail: anisfeld@ix.netcom.com. Office: Globepharm Consulting 313 Pine St Deerfield IL 60015-4828

ANISIMOV, OLEG ALEXANDROVITCH, climatologist, educator, researcher; b. Leningrad, Russia, Mar. 16, 1957; s. Alexander Ivanovitch and Nina Ivanovna (Zukova) A.; m. Natalia Vladimirovna Kolosova, Oct. 27, 1979; 1 child, Marina; m. Marina Arnoldovna Beloloutskaia, Jan. 31, 2000. MS, Leningrad State U., 1980; postgrad., State Hydrol. Inst., 1982-85; PhD, Inst. for Hydrometeorology, Leningrad, 1986. Engr. State Hydrological Inst., Leningrad, 1980-82, rschr., 1985-88; sr. rschr. State Hydrological Inst., St. Petersburg, 1988-95, dept. head dept. climatology, 1995—; expert on geocyrology and global change Intergovtl. Panel on Climate Change, Moscow, 1989—; exec. sec. working group VIII, USA-Russian Cooperation on Environ. Protection and Climate Change, St. Petersburg, 1993-96; cons. SUNY, Albany, 1995-96; vis. scientist U. Freiburg, Germany, 1990-92, 94; adj. prof. SUNY, Albany, 1996-99; rsch. scholar U. Del., Newark, 1998—. Co-author: Photon-Vegetation Interaction, 1991, Adapting to Climate Change: Assessments and Issues, 1995, Climate Change 1995: Impacts, Adaptation and Mitigation of Climate Change, 1996; contbr. articles to profl. jours. Grantee Alexander von Humboldt Found., Germany, 1990, 94; rsch. grantee Internat. Sci. Found., Russia-USA, 1995, USA NSF, 1996, 99, Civil Rsch. and Devel. Found., 1996. Fellow Alexander von Humboldt Club; mem. Internat. Permafrost Assn., Russian Coun. on Geocryology, Am. Geophys. Union., World Climate Rsch. Program (working group on climate change and cryosphere). Avocations: classical music, travel. E-mail: oleg@ans.usr.shi.spb.ru. Home: ap 71, 1/5 Kujbysheva St, 197046 St Petersburg Russia Office: State Hydrol Inst, 23 Second Line VO, 199053 St Petersburg Russia

ANISIMOV, SERGEI I., physicist, researcher; b. St. Petersburg, Russia, Dec. 11, 1934; s. Ivan A. Anisimov and Antonina I. Nazarova; m. Tamara I. Novikova, Aug. 8, 1957 (div. Dec. 1962); 1 child, Sergei; m. Ludmila P. Stepanova, Apr. 19, 1963; children: Anton, Ivan. BS, MS, St. Petersburg Tech. U., 1958; PhD, Inst. Physics, Minsk, Belarus, 1961; DSc, P.L. Kapitza Inst. Phys. Prob., Moscow, 1970. Sr. sci. rschr. Inst. Physics, Minsk, 1962-65; sr. sci. rschr. L.D. Landau Inst. for Theoretical Physics, Moscow, 1965-71, head lab., 1971-94, prin. sci. rschr., 1994—; prof. Moscow Inst. Physics and Tech., 1973—. Co-author: Action of High Power Radiation on Metals, 1971, Instabilities in Laser-Matter Interaction, 1995; contbr. articles to profl. jours. Recipient USSR State Prize in Sci. and Tech., USSR State Prize Com., Moscow, 1986 Alexander von Humboldt Rsch. award Alexander von Humboldt Found., Bonn, Germany, 1992; Varon Rsch. grantee Weizmann Inst. Sci., Rehovot, Israel, 1999. Mem. Russian Acad. Sci. Avocations: piano, tennis. E-mail: anisimov@itp.ac.ru. Fax: 7 095 9382077. Home: 7 Shkolny Blvd, 142432 Chernogolovka Moscow, Russia Office: LD Landau Inst Theor Physic, 2 Kosygina St, 117940 Moscow Russia

ANISIMOV, VLADIMIR NIKOLAEVICH, oncologist; b. Leningrad, Russia, Dec. 7, 1945; s. Nikolai and Maria Anisimov; m. Elena Sapozhnikova, Sept. 23, 1967; two children. MD, Pavlov Med. Inst., St. Petersburg, Russia, 1968; PhD, Petrov Rsch. Inst. Oncology, St. Petersburg, Russia, 1982, DSc, 1984. From rschr. to chief lab., prof. Petrov Rsch. Inst. Oncology, 1968—. Author: Age-related Factors in Carcinogenesis, 1985, Carcinogenesis and Aging, 1987, Evolution of Concepts in Gerontology, 1999. E-mail: aging@mail.ru.

ANISOVICH, VLADIMIR VLADISLAVOVICH, physicist, researcher; b. St Petersburg, Russia, Dec. 14, 1932; s. Luedmila Georgievna Dakhno, July 6, 1956; children: Vladislav Vladimirovich, Alexei Vladimirovich. Physicist, Leningrad U., Russia, 1956; PhD, A.F. Ioffe Inst., Leningrad, 1964; SrDr, Inst. Theoret./Exptl. Physics, Moscow, 1970. Sci. rschr. A.F. Ioffe Inst., Russia, 1956-65; sr. sci. rschr. Inst. for High Energy Physics, Russia, 1965-75; head nuclear physics divsn. St. Petersburg Nuclear Physics Inst., Russia, 1975-93, prof. physics, 1993—. Jour. editor Zeitschrift fuer Physik A, 1995-97, The European Phys. Jour., 1998—. Office: St Petersburg Nuc Phys Inst, 188350 Gatchina Russia

ANISTRATENKO, VITALIJ VJATCHESLAVOVITCH, zoologist; b. Tashkent, Uzbekistan, July 2, 1960; s. Rakkhim Muslimovitch and Galina Mikhailovna (Anistratenko) Kamilov; m. Olga Yur'evna Gribenuk, Oct. 20, 1995; 1 child, Antonina. B, Pedagogical Inst., Cherkassy, Ukraine, 1982, MS, 1984; PhD, Inst. Zollogy,, Kiev, Ukraine, 1990. Jr. rschr. Inst. Zoology, Kiev, Ukraine, 1990-91, rschr., 1991-94, sr. rschr., 1994—. Co-author: littoriniformes, Rissoiformes, 1995; contbr. articles to profl. jours. Mem. Moscow Obs. Avocations: ping-pong, swimming, Kung-fu. Home: App 98, Klavdiivska Str 36, 03164 Kiev Ukraine Office: Acad Sci Ukraine Inst Zool, B Khmelnitski Str 15, 252601 Kiev Ukraine

ANIYA, MASAMU, geographer, educator; b. Tokyo, Nov. 15, 1944; s. Masanari and Chizu (Chinen) A.; m. Mikiko Okada, Dec. 18, 1977; children: Masanori, Miho, Masahide. BA, Kyoto (Japan) U., 1967; MA, U. Ga., 1971, PhD, 1975. Rsch. assoc. U. Ga., 1976-77; from asst. prof. to assoc. prof. U. Tsukuba, Japan, 1977-97; prof. U. Tsukuba, 1997—; vis. prof. U. Ga., 1981-82; vis. scholar U. Edinburgh, Scotland, 1996. Author: (book) Fundamentals of Thematic Mapping (in Japanese), 1987, Patagonia: Glacier, Glacial Landforms, Travel, Town and People (in Japanese), 1998; co-author: (book) Analytical Techniques in Geographic Information (in Japanese), 1987. Recipient Ford Bartlett award Am. Soc. Photogrammetry, 1982. Mem. Assn. Am. Geographers, Japan Soc. Snow and Ice (councillor Western br. 1995—), Japanese Cartographic Assn. (councilor 1995-97), Am. Soc. Photogrammetry, Inst. Arctic Alpine Rsch. (interdisciplinary bd.), Internat. Mountain Soc., Assn. Japan Geographers, Japanese Geomorphological Union. Avocations: mountaineering, skiing, fishing. Office: Inst Geosci U Tsukuba, 1-1-1 Tennoudai, Tsukuba Ibaraki 305-8571, Japan

ANJANAPPA, MUNISWAM APPA, engineering educator; b. Bangalore, Karnataka, India, Nov. 19, 1951; p. Kempanna Muniswamappa and Byamma Nanjundappa; m. Nalini N. Narayana, Mar. 27, 1978; children: Ashwini, Manu Kemp. B Engring., Bangalore U., 1973; MS in Engring. Design, U. Madras, Coimbatore, India, 1975; PhD, U. Md., 1986. Design engr. Hindustan Machine Tools Ltd., Bangalore, 1976-79; instr. U. Md.,

College Park, 1981-83, Westinghouse rsch. fellow, 1984-85; asst. prof. U. Md. Baltimore County, Balt., 1986-92, assoc. prof., 1992-99, prof., 1999—, dir. grad. program mech. engring., 1997—; vis. assoc. prof. Indian Inst. Sci., Bangalore, 1994. Editor: Advances in Manufacturing Systems, 1988; contbr. chpt. to books; patentee in field. Joint sec. Vokkaligara parishat Am., 1995; sec. Kaveri Cultural Assn., Md., 1999. Recipient Tokten expert award UN Devel. Program, 1998. Mem. ASME (cert. of appreciation 1988, 89, 92, panel rep. prodn. engring. divsn. 1990-91). Avocations: reading novels, carrom indoor game, table tennis, international radio. Fax: (410) 455-1052. E-mail: anjanapp@umbc.edu. Home: 2004 Eliza Dorsey Ln Ellicott City MD 21042-1864 Office: U Md Baltimore county 1000 Hilltop Cir Baltimore MD 21250-0001

ANJARIA, SHAILENDRA J., international finance official; b. Bombay, July 17, 1946; s. Jashwantrai J. and Harvidya Anjaria; m. Nishigandha Pandit, 1972; 2 children. BS, U. Pa., 1966; MA, Yale U., 1967; MS in Econs., London Sch. Econs., 1968. Economist dept. exch. and trade rels. IMF, 1968-73; economist IMF, Geneva, 1973-75; asst. divsn. chief dept. exch. and trade rels. IMF, 1976-80, divsn. chief, 1980-86, asst. dir. and advisor dept. exch. and trade rels., 1986-88, asst. dir. North African divsn. African dept., 1988-91; dir. dept. external rels. IMF, Washington, 1991-99, sec., 1999—. Office: IMF 700 19th St NW Washington DC 20431-0001

ANKARCRONA, HENRIC TH., asset management company executive; b. Stockholm, Mar. 5, 1945; s. Sten Sison and Ebba M. (Mörner) A.; m. Anita K. Sylwan, Mar. 14, 1970; childre; Otto, Victoria. MBA, Stockholm Sch. Econs., 1968; cert. in French, U. Paris, 1969; MSc in Mgmt., Stanford U., 1979. With rsch. dept. Stockholms Enskilda Bank, 1968,, 69-70; head adminstrn. AB Vendax, Stockholm, 1971-74; with Sal @48n Reefer Svcs. AB, Stockholm, 1974-81; mng. dir. Salén Energy AB, Stockholm, 1982-87, Salénia AB, Stockholm, 1987-94; sr. cons. SMG AB of SIFO Mgmt. Group AB, Stockholm, 1994-96; mng. dir. Hinc Asset Mgmt. AB, Stockholm, 1996—; pers. asst., polit. sec. to conservative M.P., later min. commerce, Stockholm, 1969-70; mem. ctrl. bd. Stockholm City Fire Ins. Co., 1980-86, auditor, 1982-85; bd. dirs. Salénia AB and other Salén cos., Taurus Petroleum AB; mem. bd. Swedish Football Pools Svc., 1977-83; mem. Sloan adv. bd. Stanford (Calif.) U., 1982-87. Contbr. articles to newspaper. Bd. dirs. Carlsson's Sch., 1982-87, Swedish-Japanese Soc., 1983-88, Swedish House of Nobility, 1986—, Swedish Order of St. John, 1995—; mem. sponsoring com. Stanford program in humanities Stanford U., 1986—. Capt. Royal Swedish Air Force, 1963-65, 70. Mem. Assn. Fin. Cos. (auditor 1976—), New Soc. (chmn. 1998—). Mem. Moderate Party in Sweden. Avocations: opera, literature, hunting, golf. Home: Kommendorsgatan 2, 114 48 Stockholm Sweden

ANKATHIL, RAVINDRAN, cytogeneticist, cancer geneticist, educator; b. Tirur, Kerala, India, Nov. 11, 1954; s. Thampakath Sankaran Nair and Ankathil Devaky Amma; m. Kizhedath Jyothisree; children: Anjana, Ranjana. BSc, Kerala U., Trivandrum, India, 1975, MSc, 1977, PhD, 1992. Jr. rsch. fellow Regional Cancer Ctr., Trivandrum, 1979-82, sr. rsch. fellow, 1982-85, sci. officer, 1985-93, asst. prof. cancer rsch., 1993-98, assoc. prof. cancer rsch., 1998—. Contbr. numerous articles to profl. publs. Recipient Raja Ravi Sher Singh award Indian Coun. Med. Rsch., 1996; UICC Yamagiwa Yoshida Internat. Cancer Study fellow, 1999. Mem. Indian Assn. Cancer Rsch. (life), Indian Ass. Biomed. Scientists (life, Indra Vasudevan award for cancer rsch. 1993), Indian Soc. Human Genetics (life). Avocations: music, reading, gardening. Office: Regional Cancer Ctr, Med Coll Campus, 695 011 Trivandrum Kerala India

ANKER, CHARLOTTE MIRIAM, playwright, educator; b. Wilmington, Del., July 13, 1934; d. Neil Morris and Helen Sarah (Price) Lubin; m. Jerry David Anker, Apr. 12, 1959; children—Deborah, Daniel. A.B. in Sociology, Temple U., 1955; postgrad. Columbia U., 1955-56. Adminstrv. asst. Ams. for Democratic Action, Washington, 1956-57; asst. edn. dir. Internat. Union of Electric, Radio and Machine Workers AFL-CIO, Washington, 1957-60; asst. book editor World weekly newspaper, Washington, 1961-62; lectr. sociology George Washington U., Washington, 1965-71; coordinator speakers Dem. Nat. Presdl. Campaign, Washington, 1972; mng. editor Moment mag., 1987-90; editor Time-Life Books, 1990-96. Author: Last Night I Saw Andromeda, 1975 (Phila. Writer's Conf. 1st prize for children's lit. 1974); co-author: Onward Victoria (Broadway musical); (dramas) Stroke Three, 1982, Sand Castles, 1983, Third Child, 1984 (Margo Jones Playwriting award 1984, Jane Chambers Playwriting award 1985), performed off-off Broadway, 1986, at Wolsey Theater, London, 1988. Precinct vice chmn. Democratic Party, Montgomery County, Md., 1963-64, 69-70, chmn., 1986-88; dir. tutoring and enrichment program Bells Mill Elem. Sch., Montgomery County, 1969-72; mem. Wash. Commn. on the Arts and Humanities. Social Sci. Research Council fellow, 1955. Mem. Dramatists Guild, Authors Guild, Soc. Children's Book Writers, Washington Ind. Writers. Avocations: photography; art; stamp collecting.

ANKRAH-HOFFMAN, NII ADOTEY, journalist, newspaper editor, minister; b. Accra, Ghana, Aug. 16, 1956; s. Samuel Paul Kpakpo and Naomi Asantewa (Cofie) Ankrah. Diploma, Ghana Inst. Journalism, Accra, 1978; diploma, Ghana Bapt. Sem., Abuwaka-Ashanti, Afri, 1999. Journalist Ministry of Defence, Accra, Ghana, 1978; news reporter Litani mag. UN Interim Force in Lebanon, 1981-82; sr. info. asst. Ministry of Def., Ghana, 1983-90; news reporter Exodus II Mag., Liberia, 1992-93; asst. info. officer, editor Armed Forces News Ministry of Def., Ghana, 1990-94, sr. info. officer, editor, 1995-96; resigned Ministry Defence, Ghana, 1996; news reporter Amahoro (Peace) Mag. of Ghana Battalion 3, UN Assistance Mission in Rwanda, 1995; film coverage coord. Gt. Commn. Movement Ghana Staff, 1999. Editor newspaper Armed Forces News, 1991. Tchr. Christian edn. dept. Calvary Bapt. Ch., 1984, pastor, 2000. Warrant officer II Ghanan Army, 1995. Recipient Unifil Peace medal UN, 1982, ECOMOG Peace medal, 1993, UNAMIR Peace medal, 1995. Avocations: reading writing, Scrabble, Christian music. Office: PO Box C1098 Cantonments, Accra Ghana

ANKROM, CHARLES FRANKLIN, golf course architect, consultant; b. Parkersburg, W.Va., Nov. 7, 1936; s. Donsel and Elva Dale (Cale) A.; m. Alice Lynell Glass, Aug. 24, 1968; children: Steven Charles, Cheryl Lyn, Jan Ellen Lambert, Beverly Lyn Webster. Student, W.Va. U., 1955, Eli Frank Sch. Design Arts, Tampa, Fla., 1956, Indian River C.C., Stuart, Fla. Exec. dir. golf, corp. golf course architect Gen. Devel. Corp., Miami, Fla., 1964-70; exec. dir. golf, golf course architect Boise Cascade Recreation Communities Group, Palo Alto, Calif., 1970-73; pres. Charles F. Ankrom, Inc., Stuart, Fla., 1973—. Prin. works include Sabal Trace C.C., Port Charlotte, Fla., Sun 'N Lake Country Club, Sebring, Fla., Cocoa Beach Mcpl. Golf Course, Cocoa Beach City, Fla., Ft. Lauderdale (Fla.) Country Club, Boca Raton (Fla.) Mcpl. Golf Course, Woodmont Country Club, Tamarac, Fla., The Club at Emerald Hills, Hollywood, Fla., The Habitat Golf Course, Brevard County, Fla., Aquarina, Melbourne, Fla., Crane Creek C.C., Stuart, Fla., Meadowood C.C., Ft. Pierce, Fla., Indian River Planatation Resort, Jensen Beach, Fla., Metro Country Club, Dominican Republic, numerous others; over 60 planned cmtys. including Indian River Plantation Marriott Resort, Hutchinson Island, Fla., Joe's Point, Hutchinson Island, Stuart West, Martin County, Fla., Pinecrest Lakes, Jensen Beach, Crystal Lakes, Okeechobee, Fla., Panther Woods, Ft. Pierce, Crane Creek, Palm City, Fla., River Ridge, Tequesta, Fla., River Landing, Palm City. Donated design & adminstrv. svcs. for Bulldog Sportsturf Complex, Martin County (Fla.) Schs. Recipient Outstanding Achievement by Ind. in Bus. or Industry award State of Fla. Coun. on Vocat. Edn., 1992, Bus. Ptnr. award Martin County Sch. Dist., 1991. Mem. Am. Soc. Golf Course Architects (bd. dirs., various nat. coms., Presdl. citation 1993), Nat. Golf Found. Achievements include profl. svc. multi-disciplinary cons. assignments provided to clients in 28 states and 9 countries or territories, including approxiamtely 125 assignments to both the govt. and pvt. sectors, profl. orgns., coll. and univ. and the edn. industry, natl. and internat. conf. as the lectr. for seminars, including svcs. to resort ops., pvt. amenities and public ops. Office: Charles F Ankrom Inc PO Box 898 Stuart FL 34995-0898

ANKUM, JOHAN ALBERT (HANS ANKUM), Roman law and legal history educator, dean; b. Amsterdam, The Netherlands, July 23, 1930; s. Leendert Albert and Johanna Goverdina (van Kuykhof) A.; m. Johanna Catharina Houwink, Oct. 4, 1957 (div. 1970); children: Yvette Sandra, Sylvia Yolanthe, Edo Rogier; m. Pelline Johanna Van Es, Feb. 17, 1971; 1 child, Anne-Barbara Pelline. LLM, U. Amsterdam, 1953, LLD, 1962; D hon. causa, U. Aix-Marseille (France), 1985, Free U. Brussels, 1986, Ruhr U., Bochum, 1995. Lectr. Roman law and legal history U. Leiden (The Netherlands), 1960-63, prof., 1963-65, extraordinary prof. Roman law, 1965-69; asst. in Roman law U. Amsterdam, 1956-60, prof. Roman law, legal history and juridical paprology, 1965-95, dean Law Faculty, 1976-78, 89-91, vice rector, 1979, 84, 85. Contbr. numerous articles and book revs. on Roman law and legal history to profl. jours. Mem. Provincial Parliament of North Holland (The Netherlands), 1970-74. Mem. Royal Dutch Acad. Scis. (Winkler Prins award 1970). Avocations: travel, classical music, history of art. Home: Zonnebloemlaan 8, 2lll ZG Aerdenhout The Netherlands Office: U Amsterdam Law Fac Oudemanhuispourt 4-6, PO Box 1030, NL1000BA Amsterdam The Netherlands

ANMA, SO, engineer consultant; b. Hamamatsu, Shizuoka, Japan, Nov. 7, 1936; s. Yu and Chie (Matsumoto) A.; m. Fumie Kishikawa, Mar. 15, 1964; children: Ryo, Akitsu, Mizuho, Yashima. BS, Hokkaido U., Sapporo, Japan, 1959; DEng, Tokai U., Tokyo, 1987. Registered engring. geologist; profl. civil engr. Rschr. Hukada Chisitsu Inst., Tokyo, 1959-67; pres. Kisokogaku Co., Tokyo, 1967-70; exec. Kensetsu Kiso Chosa Sekkei Co., Shimizu, Japan, 1970-91; pres. Kensetsu Kiso Chosa Sekkei Co., Shimizu, 1991—; lectr. Tokai U., Shimizu, 1988—, Shizuoka (Japan) U., 2000—; bd. dirs. Shizuoka Environ. and Resources, 1989—; chapter vice chmn. Japanese Soc. of Snow and Ice, Tokyo, 1997—. Co-author: The First Ascent of Mt. Chamlang, 1965, Geology of Nepal Himalaya, 1967 (Chichibunomiya prize 1968), Patagonian Mountain Climb, 1968, Mt. Dhaulagiri-I Midwinter, 1985. Hazard reduction adviser Shizuoka Prefecture, 1984—. Recipient Chichibunomiya prize Chichibunomiya Meml. Found., Tokyo, 1968, Hokkaido prize Hokkaido Regional Govt., 1983, Asahi Sports prize Asahi Newspaper Inc., Tokyo, 1984. Mem. Internat. Geosynthetic Soc., Internat. Soc. Soil Mechanics and Found. Engring., Internat. Assn. Engring. Geology, Geol. Soc. Japan, Japanese Soc. Snow and Ice, Japanese Alpine Club (chpt. chmn. 1986-95). Avocations: mountaineering, forest watching. Office: Kensetsu Kiso Chosa Sekkei, 241-7 Kusunokishinden, Shimizu 424-0882, Japan

ANNA, ARKADJEVNA MOLDAVSKAY, anatomy educator; b. Astrakhan, Russia, Apr. 17, 1937; d. Tiosifovich Zelikson Arkadiy and Michailovna Schvartsman Faina; m. Wikolay Jefimovich Moldavskay, Nov. 4, 1967. MD. Doctor Reginal Hosp., Russia, 1961-63; aspirant of anatomy chiar Med. Inst., Astrokhan, 1963-66, asst. anatomy chair, 1966-93; prof. anatomy chair Med. Acad., 1994—. Contbr. articles to profl. jours. Grantee Med. Acad. 1999. Mem. N.Y. Acad. Sci., Nature Acad., Internat. Pers. Acad. Home: St Zvezdnaja 41/1 n 116, 414022 Astrakhan Russia Office: Med Acad, St Bakinskaja 121, 414000 Astrakhan Russia

ANNAKIN, KENNETH COOPER, film director, writer; b. Beverly, Yorkshire, England; came to U.S., 1979; s. Edward C. and Hannah J. (Gains) A.; m. Pauline Mary Carter, 1960; children: Jane, Deborah. Student, Hull U., 1934-35. Dir. The Swiss Family Robinson, 1960, A Very Important Person, 1961, The Hellions, 1961, Crooks Anonymous, 1962, The Fast Lady, 1962, The Longest Day, 1962, Those Magnificent Men in Their Flying Machines, 1965, The Battle of the Bulge, 1965, The Biggest Bundle of Them All, 1967, Those Daring Young Men in Their Jaunty Jalopies, 1969, Call of the Wild, 1972, Paper Tiger, 1974, The Fifth Musketeer, 1977, The Pirate Movie, 1982, Pippi Longstocking, 1986; screenwriter Coco Chanel, 1999, Redwing, 1999; author: So You Wanna Be a Director, 2000. Office: 9233 Swallow Dr West Hollywood CA 90069-1145

ANNAMALAI, CHITRA, computer science educator, engineer; b. Coimbatore, Tamilnadu, India, Apr. 29, 1966; d. Karuppiah and Umaiyal (Muthiah) A. BE, PSG Coll. Tech., Coimbatore, 1987, ME, 1991, PhD, 1999. Lectr. PSG Coll. Tech., Coimbatore, 1987-98, asst. prof., 1999—, coord. Impact Project, 1999—; Editor: (course material) Graphics Programming with C , 1996, Internet and Java Programming, 1997, Advanced Iowa Programming. Mem. Instn. Engrs., Computer Soc. India, Indian Soc. Tech. Edn. Avocations: reading books and magazines, internet browsing, gardening. Home: 88 PM Swamy Colony, St 2 Robertson Rd, Coimbatore 641002, India Office: PSG Coll Tech, Dept Computer Sci & Engring, Coimbatore 641001, India

ANNAMALAI, LOGANATH, research endocrinologist; b. Kuala Lumpur, Selangor, Malaysia, Sept. 29, 1950; s. Arulampalam and Kandiah (Jothippillai) A.; m. Kamalam Govindan, Aug. 28, 1985; children: Kalpana, Krithika. BSc with hons., U. Delhi, New Delhi, India, 1972; MSc, All India Inst. Med. Scis., New Delhi, India, 1977; PhD, Nat. U. Singapore, 1984. Chartered Biologist, Inst. Biology (UK). Rsch. asst. Nat. U. Singapore, 1979-81, rsch. fellow, 1981-91, sr. rsch. fellow, 1991—; cons. in reproductive endocrinology WHO, Chengdu, China, 1985; mem. organizing com., treas. 6th World Meeting on Impotence. 1993. Editor Singapore Jour. Ob-Gyn., 1995; mem. editl. adv. bd. Asia Pacific Jour. Pharmacology. Recipient WHO fellowship, Helsinki, Finland, 1990; grantee WHO, London, 1989-90. Mem. Am. Soc. Reproductive Medicine, Internat. Soc. Gynecol. Endocrinology. Avocations: badminton, soccer, music. E-Mail: obgannam@nus.edu.sg. Office: Nat U Hosp Ob-Gyn Dept, Lower Kent Ridge Rd, 119074 Singapore Singapore

ANNAN, KOFI A., diplomat; b. Ghana, 1938; married; 3 children. Grad., U. Sci. and Tech., Kumasi, Macalester Coll., St. Paul, Inst. des Hautes Etudes Internationales, Geneva, MIT. Held posts UN Econ. Commn. for Africa, Addis Ababa, Ethiopia, UN, N.Y.C., WHO, Geneva, 1962-71; adminstrv. mng. officer UN, Geneva, 1972-74; chief civilian pers. officer UN Emergency Force, Cairo, 1974; mng. dir. Ghana Tourist Devel. Co., 1974-76; dep. chief staff svcs. Office Pers. Svcs., Office of UN High Commn. for Refugees, Geneva, 1976-80, dep. dir. divsn. adminstrn., head pers. svc., 1980-83; chmn. bd. trustees UN Internat. Sch., 1987-95; dir. adminstrn. mgmt. svc., dir. budget Office Fin. Svcs. UN, N.Y.C., 1984-87, asst. sec-gen. Office Human Resources Mgmt., 1987-90, contr. Office of Programme Planning, Budget and Fin., 1990-92, asst. sec.-gen. dept. peace-keeping ops., 1992-93, under-sec.-gen. dept. peace-keeping ops., 1993-95, spl. rep. to sec.-gen. to former Yugoloavia, 1995-96, spl. envoy to NATO, 1995-96, sec. gen, 1997—. Alfred P. Sloan fellow MIT, 1971-72. Office: UN Pub Inquiries Unit Rm GA-57 UN Plz 46th St at First Ave New York NY 10017

ANNANE, DJILLALI, cardiology educator, researcher, pharmacologist; b. Terville, Moselle, France, Dec. 5, 1963; s. Abdelkader and Zoulikha (Ziane) A.; m. Frédérique Pascale Lohmann, Sept. 24, 1994. MD, U. Paris V, 1991, PhD in Pharmacology, 1996. Assoc. prof. critical care medicine Assistance Pub. Hosp. Paris, 1991-96, prof., 1996—; prof. U. Paris West, 1996—; cons. French Atomic Energy Commn., 1991—. Editor Cochrane Collaboration, 1998—; contbr. articles to med. jours., including Circulation. Grantee Merck Sharp Dohme and Chibres, 1992. Mem. AAAS, Am. Heart Assn. (M. Marcus young investigator award 1995, Leving young investigator award 1996), French Soc. Intensive Care (sci. com. 1993—), French Assn. Against Myopathies, N.Y. Acad. Scis. Avocations: Photography, history of medicine. Home: Rue Delaporte 34, 94700 Maisons-Alfort France Office: Hop R Poincare-U Paris West, Blvd R. Poincaré, 92380 Garches France

ANNAUD, JEAN-JACQUES, film director, screenwriter; b. Juvisy, France, Oct. 1, 1943; s. Pierre and Madeleine (Tripoz) A.; m. Monique Rossignol, 1970 (div. 1980); 1 child, Mathilde; m. Laurence Duval; 1 child, Louise. Student, Ecole Louis Lumière, Institut Des Hautes Etudes Cinematographiques, Paris, 1966; Lic. Lettres, The Sorbonne, Paris, 1967. Freelance film dir., screenwriter Paris, 1967—. Sreenwriter, dir.: Black and White in Color, 1976 (Oscar award Best Fgn. Film 1977), Hot head, 1978, Quest for Fire, 1981, (César award 1982), Name of the Rose, 1986 (César award 1987, Donatello award), The Bear, 1988 (César award best dir. 1988), The Lover, 1991 (Best Dir. award Japan Critics Assn., 1992); screenwriter, dir., prodr.: Wings of Courage, 1994 (in IMAX 3D), Seven Years in Tibet, 1997 (Best Fgn. Film Gilde Filmpreis, Germany, 1998); dir., prodr: Running Free, 1999, Enemy at the Gates, 2000. Decorated commandeur Ordre des Arts et Lettres; recipient Grand Prix Nat. du Cinema, prix du Cinéma de L'Académie Française, more than 100 awards for TV commercials, including Clios, Lions Cannes and Venice Festival, Art Dirs. Club. Mem. French Hollywood Cir. (pres.). Home: 9 rue Guénégaud, 75006 Paris France also: Repérage SA, 10 rue Lincoln, 75008 Paris France also: ICM 8899 Beverly Blvd Los Angeles CA 90048-2412

ANNE, PRINCESS (ELIZABETH ALICE LOUISE ANNE), Her Highness The Princess Royal; b. Aug. 15, 1950; d. Queen Elizabeth II and Prince Philip, Duke of Edinburgh; m. Capt. Mark Anthony Peter Phillips, Nov. 14, 1973 (div. 1992); children: Peter Mark Andrew, Zara Anne Elizabeth; m. Timothy Laurence, 1992. Student, Benenden Sch., Kent, Eng. Col. in Chief 14th/20th King's Hussars, Worcestershire and Sherwood Foresters Regt.; col. in chief 8th Canadian Hussars, Royal Corps of Signals, The Canadian Armed Forces Communications and Electronics Br., The Royal Australian Corps of Signals, Royal N.Z. Corps of Signals, Royal N.Z. Nursing Corps, The Grey and Simcoe Foresters Militia; Chief Comdt. W.R.N.S. Author: Riding Through My Life, 1991. Pres. Benevolent Trust; Hon. Air Commodore RAF Lyneham; Pres. Brit. Acad. Film and TV Awards, Hunters Improvement and Light Horse Breeding Soc., Save the Children Fund, Windsor Horse Trails, The Royal Sch. for Daugs. of Officers of Royal Navy and Royal Marines; Patron: numerous Brit. and worldwide orgns.; ofcl. visits throughout the world as rep. of the Crown; comdt. in Chief St. John Ambulance and Nursing Cadets, Women's Transport Service; Freeman City of London, Fishmongers Co., Middle Warden Farriers Co.; Hon. Liveryman Carmen's Co., Farriers Co.; Hon. Freeman Farmers Co., Loriners Co., Yeoman Saddlers Co.; chancellor U. London, 1981—; participant in numerous equestrian competitions including Montreal Olympics, 1976, Horse of the Year Show, Wembley and Badminton Horse Trials. Recipient Raleigh Trophy, 1971, Silver medal Individual European Three Day event, 1975, Spl. Brit. Acad. Film and TV Arts award, 1993; named Sportswoman of the Yr. Sports Writers Assn., Daily Express, World of Sport, BBC Sports Personality, 1971. Mem. RNVR Officers Assn., Brit. Equine Veterinary Assn. (Hon.), Internat. Equestrian Fedn. (pres. 1986-94). Clubs: Royal Yacht Squadron, Royal Thames Yacht, Minchinhampton Golf, others. *

ANNE, JOZEF FRANCOIS, microbiologist, educator; b. Temse, Flanders, Belgium, Sept. 2, 1944; s. Lodewijk Cyriel and Elisabeth (Meeus) A.; m. Madeleine Josephina Hayen, May 26, 1973; children: Wim, Raf, Guy. Degree in Bio-Engring., Cath. U. Leuven, Belgium, 1970, PhD, 1977. Rsch. assoc. Nat. Fund for Sci. Rsch., Leuven, 1972-76; vis. rschr. U. Nottingham, U.K., 1974-75; univ. asst. Cath. U. Leuven, 1976-78, sr. asst., 1978-82, asst. prof., 1982-89, assoc. prof., 1989-94, prof. microbiology, 1994—; vis. rschr. U. Bielefeld, Germany, 1981-82; chmn. NFWO Contact Group "General Microbiology", Belgium, 1992. Contbr. numerous articles and abstracts in jours. and books dealing in microbiology. Maj. Belgium Res., 1972. Decorated Cross of Officer of the Order of the Crown, Govt. Belgium, 1986, Cross of Officer of Order of (King) Leopold, 1991; Officer of Order of (King) Leopold, 1999. Mem. Am. Soc. Microbiology, Netherlands Soc. Microbiology (Kluyver award laureate 1978), Belgian Nat. Com. of Microbiology, Soc. Gen. Microbiology, Belgian Soc. Biochemistry and Biotech., Royal Flemish Soc. for Engrs., Royal Flemish Chem. Soc. (pres. biotech. divsn. 1992-99), Belgian Soc. Microbiology (sec. 1996—). Avocations: running, cycling, travel. Home: Wildenhoge 10, B-3020 Winksele-Herent Belgium Office: Cath U Leuven Rega Inst, Minderbroedersstraat 10, B-3000 Leuven Belgium

ANNERGREN, GORAN ERIK, chemical engineer, consultant; b. Gavle, Sweden, July 8, 1932; s. Gosta and Edith (Sundstrom) A.; m. Jane Almstrom, Apr. 2, 1960; children: Jeanette, Ingegerd, Sofie. Degree in chem. engring., Royal Inst. Tech., Stockholm, 1956. Rsch. engr. Royal Inst. Tech., Stockholm, 1956-58; rsch. engr. Billeruds AB, Saffle, Sweden, 1958-60, rsch. mgr., 1960-67, mgr., 1962-67; rsch. dir. SCA, Sundsvall, Sweden, 1967-79, sr. rsch. advisor, 1979-97; adj. prof. Royal Inst. Tech., 1983-91. Mem. SPCI (Ekman medal), TAPPI. Office: JAG Cons, Granbacken 14, SE-85634 Sundsvall Sweden

ANNERUD, CAROLYN RIEDERER, emergency physician; b. San Antonio, Nov. 17, 1953; d. Joseph Dwight and Paula Jean (Wickward) Riederer; 1 dau., Kerstin Erika. B.S. in Biology, Walla Walla Coll., 1973; M.D., Loma Linda U., 1977. Intern, White Meml. Med. Ctr., Los Angeles, 1978-79; Diplomate Am. Bd. Emergency Medicine, 1987. Barlett Meml. Hosp., Juneau, Alaska, 1980-81, Spectrum Emergency Care, Lake Havasu, Ariz., 1981; emergency physician, Juneau, Alaska, 1980-81; med. dir. Critical Air Medicine Air Ambulance Service, Emergency Physicians Med. Group, 1981—; dir. critical air medicine, San Diego, 1982-85; urgent care physician Scripps Clinic, La Jolla, Calif., 1983—; expdn. physician; travel, expdn., ship doctor Quark Expdns., TCS Expdns. to Polar Regions, remote areas Asia, Africa, South America, Siberia, 1988—; locums Marshall Islands, 1996, Hawaii; founding dir. Mater Pvt. Hosp. Ed, Townville, Australia, 1997-99; rural relief emergency doctor. Vol. Internat. Medical Corps, Zenica, Bosnia, 1996. Fellow Am. Coll. Emergency Physicians; mem. Seaview Emergency Assocs. (co-dir. 1987), Associated Emergency Physicians Group, Australasian Soc. Emergency (med. proposed team leader emergency tng. program 2000). Home: PO Box 2936, 4825 Mount Isa QLD, Australia

ANNESE, BETSY JANE, public relations executive; b. Scranton, Pa., Sept. 26, 1949; d. Frank Nicholas and Ruth Elizabeth (Pillow) A. BA in Journalism, U. S.C., 1971. Reporter The (Columbia, S.C.) State, 1971-73, The (Anderson, S.C.) Ind., 1973-74; mgr. pub. rels Bigelow Carpets, Inc., Greenville, S.C., 1974-80; from sr. pub. rels. rep. to v.p. pub. affairs R. J. Reynolds Tobacco Co., Winston-Salem, N.C., 1980-94; v.p., deputy external rels. R.J. Reynolds Internat., Winston-Salem, N.C., 1994-95; sr. v.p. internat. external rels. R.J. Reynolds Internat., Geneva, 1995-97; v.p. corp. comm. Lowe's Cos., Inc., Wilkesboro, N.C., 1999—. Bd. dirs. Family Svc., Inc., Winston-Salem, 1990—, Multiple Sclerosis Soc., Winston-Salem, 1990—, Horizons Residential Care, Inc., Winston-Salem, 1991-93, Winston-Salem Urban League, 1993—. Mem. Twin City Club (bd. dirs. 1989-93), Piedmont Club, Forsyth Country Club, Wild Dunes Beach and Racquet Club, Ad 2 Club (hon.). Office: Lowes Cos Inc 1605 Curtis Bridge Rd Wilkesboro NC 28697*

ANN-MARGRET (ANN-MARGRET OLSSON), actress, performer; b. Stockholm, Sweden, Apr. 28, 1941; came to U.S., naturalized, 1949; d. Gustav and Anna Olsson; m. Roger Smith, 1967. Student, Northwestern U. Performer radio shows, band tours; appeared with: George Burns, Las Vegas, 1961; headliner numerous appearances, Las Vegas, 1961—; made NYC debut Radio City Music Hall, 1991; actress numerous films including Pocketful of Miracles, 1961, State Fair, 1961, Bye Bye Birdie, 1962, Viva Las Vegas, 1963, The Pleasure Seekers, 1964, Kitten With a Whip, 1964, Bus Riley's Back in Town, 1964, Once A Thief, 1965, Cincinnati Kid, 1965, Stagecoach, 1966, Made in Paris, 1966, The Swinger, 1966, Murderers' Row, 1967, The Tiger and the Pussycat, 1967, R.P.M., 1970, C.C. & Company, 1971, Carnal Knowledge, 1971, Train Robbers, 1972, Outside Man, 1972, Tommy, 1975, Joseph Andrews, 1976, The Last Remake of Beau Geste, 1977, Magic, 1978, The Cheap Detective, 1978, Lookin' To Get Out, 1978, The Villain, 1979, Middle-Age Crazy, 1980, The Return of the Soldier, 1982, I Ought To Be in Pictures, 1982, Twice in a Lifetime, 1985, 52-Pick-up, 1987, A Tiger's Tale, 1988, A New Life, 1988, Something More, Newsies, 1992, Grumpy Old Men, 1993, Grumpier Old Men, 1995, Seduced by Madness, 1996, The Limey, 1999, Any Given Sunday, 1999, The Last Producer, 2000; several TV spls., 1975-76, The Last Producer, 2000; TV films Who Will Love My Children, 1983, A Streetcar Named Desire, 1984, Our Sons, 1991, Nobody's Children, 1994, Seduced by Madness: The Diane Borchardt Story, 1996, Blue Rodeo, 1996, Life of the Party: The Pamela Harriman Story, 1998, Happy Face, 1999, The 10th Kingdom, 2000, Perfect Murder, Perfect Town, 2000; mini-series The Two Mrs. Grenvilles, 1987, Alex Haley's Queen, 1993, Scarlett, 1994; TV series Four Corners, 1998; author: (with Todd Gold) Ann-Margret: My Story, 1994. Recipient 2 Acad. award nominations, 4 Emmy nominations, 5 Golden Globes. Office: William Morris Agy 151 S El Camino Dr Beverly Hills CA 90212-2775

ANNUNZIATO, EDWARD STEPHEN, investment company executive; b. N.Y.C., Nov. 2, 1955; s. Gerald Harold and Phyllis Carol (Goldberg) A.; m. Elissa J. Goodman, 1980; children: Alexandra, Nicole. BA, Brown U., Providence, 1977; J.D., Vanderbilt U., Nashville, 1980. Atty. Simpson Thacher & Bartlett, 1980-87; mng. dir. Merrill Lynch Internat., N.Y.C., 1987-93, London, 1993-2000; chmn., CEO Wit Capital Europe, London, 2000—. Office: Wit Capital Europe, 120 Old Broad St, London England

ANONGBA, PATRICK NORBERT, physicist; b. Abidjan, Cote D'Ivoire, Feb. 3, 1960; s. Guillaume and Marcelline (Kouassibie) A.; m. Maria Teresa Varela-Santos, Oct. 19, 1991; children: Tshahe, Tome, Dario. DS, EPFL, Lausanne, Switzerland, 1989. Asst. EPFL, Lausanne, Switzerland, 1985-89, U. Lausanne, 1990-92; rsch. assoc. Max-Planck Inst., Stuttgart, Germany, 1992-94; asst. prof. U. Cocody, Cote D'Ivoire, 1995-98, assoc. prof., 1998—. Contbr. articles to profl. jours. Fellow Japan Soc. Promotion Sci; mem. Swiss Phys. Soc., N.Y. Acad. Scis. Avocations: swimming, fishing, dancing. Fax: 225-440412. E-mail: anongbp@syfed.ci.refer.org. Home: GBAGBA, BP498 Bingerville Côte D'Ivoire Office: U Cocody, 22 BP582 Abidjan Côte D'Ivoire

ANOSOV, OLEG LWOVICH, bioengineer, researcher; b. Viaznici, Russia, Mar. 18, 1957; s. Lew Anosov and Mila Gorelli; m. Elena Anosova Lopuchina, Sept. 29, 1979; 1 child, Irina. Degree in radioengring., Vladimir (Russia) State U., 1980; PhD, Moscow State Pedagog. U., 1996. Rsch. engr. Vladimir State U., 1980-84; scientist Baksan Neutrino (Russia) Observatory Nuclear Rsch. Inst. RAS, 1985-92; dept. head Vladimir (Russia) Regional Cardiac Ctr., 1993—; visitor scientist Humboldt U., Berlin, 1997-99, Erlangen-Neurnberg U., Germany, 1999—. Co-author: Predictability of Complex Dynamical System, 1996. Rsch. grantee Internat. Sci. Found., 1993, 94, 95, Russian State Com. Sci. and Edn., 1996, INTAS, 1996; Alexander von Humboldt Found. rsch. fellow, 1997-99. Avocations: music, painting, travel. Home: Dompfaffstr 136, 91056 Erlangen Germany Office: Zentralinst Biomed Tech, Turnstr 5, 91054 Erlangen Germany

ANSARI, AHMAD FAROOQ, pharmacology educator; b. Hala, Sindh, Pakistan, Jan. 15, 1946; s. Allah Bux and Rahmat A.; m. Amna Ali Akbar Memon, Jan. 25, 1980; children: Saima, Waqas Ahmad. BSc with honors, U. Karachi, 1968, MSc, 1969; PhD, U. Glasgow, 1978. Postgrad. rsch. fellow U. Glasgow, 1975-78; asst. prof. U. Sindh, Jamshoro, Pakistan, 1978-84; assoc. prof. U. Sindh, 1985-90, prof., 1990—; Fulbright scholar U. Houston, 1984; vis. asst. prof. U. Houston, 1984-85; incharge biochemist Suhail Pathol. Lab., Hyderabad, 1994—. Contbr. articles to profl. publs. Mem. Bait-ul-Maal Ansari Welfare Assn., Hala, Pakistan, 1997—. Recipient scholarship Govt. of Pakistan, 1975-78. Fellow Acad. of Pharmacy; mem. Pakistan Pharmacol. Soc. (life), N.Y. Acad. Scis., Brit. Pharmacol. Soc., Med. Rsch. Soc. Pakistan, Pakistan Pharmacist Assn., Pakistan Physiol. Soc., Biochem. Soc. Pakistan, others. Avocations: reading, travel cmty. worker. Office: Dept Pharmacy, Univ Sindh, Jamshoro/Sindh Pakistan

ANSARI, BASHIR, editor; b. Amritsar, India, Sept. 18, 1932; arrived in Pakistan, 1947; s. Mian Karim and Amir (Bibi) Bakhsh. MA, Punjab U., Lahore, Pakistan, 1963. Mem. editl. bd. Tarjman-ul-Hadith, Lahore, 1975-89; chief editor Weekly Ahl-e-Hadith, Lahore, 1973-90, 1990—; dir. Ahl-e-Hadith Publs., Lahore, 1983—, Zia-Ul-Islam Acd., Lahore, 1978-86. Translator: Haj Andumra, 1978, 15 other religious books. Adv. coun. Jamiat Ahl-E-Hadith, Lahore, 1975—. Muslim. Avocation: reading. Fax: 7725525. Home: 7 Gulshanabad, Gujranwala, Punjab 52250, Pakistan Office: Markazi Jamiat Ahl-e-Hadith, 106 Ravi Rd, Lahore Punjab 54000, Pakistan

ANSARI, KARIM ULLAH, pharmacology and therapeutics educator, researcher; b. Allahabad, India, July 5, 1944; s. Hakim Ullah and Safi (Unnisa) A.; m. Sajida Karim Narvi, Mar. 1, 1970 (div.); 5 children. MBBS, M.L.N. Med. Coll., Allahabad, 1967, MD, 1972. Rsch. asst. I.C.M.R., New Delhi, India, 1968-69; intern M.L.N. Med. Coll., Allahabad, 1967-68, demonstrator, 1969-72, lectr., 1975-86, asst. prof., 1986-88, assoc. prof., 1988-93, prof., 1993—. Author: A Handbook of Experimental Pharmacology, 1978, A Handbook of Pharmacy, 1978; mem. editl. bd. Jours. I.M.A. Acad. Med. Spltys., New Delhi, 1995, Drs. Drug Reference, 1996. Hon. dir. Kidwai Charitable Hosp., Allahabad, 1974; mem. Azadi Bachao Andolan, Chatham Lines, Allahabad, 1996. Mem. Royal Soc. Health (London), N.Y. Acad. Scis., Coll. Allergy and Applied Immunology Delhi (life), Acad. Med. Spltys. (life), Indian Soc. for Clin. Pharmacology and Therapeutics (life). Avocations: social work, reading, writing, gardening. Home: D-13, GTB Nagar (Kareli), 211016 Allahabad UP, India Office: MLN Med Coll, Lowther Rd, 211001 Allahabad UP, India

ANSARI, MOHAMMED HABEEBUL HAQUE, science educator, researcher, science administrator, writer; b. Hyderabad, India, Mar. 27, 1943; s. Mohammad Saeedul and Waseema (Begum) A.; m. Mahnoor Begum Hasan, Jan. 11, 1973; 1 child, Adeel. MA, Cambridge (Eng.) U., 1968; MSc, U. Birmingham, Eng., 1965; PhD in Physics, Aligarh Muslim U., 1996. Reactor physics analyst Atomic Energy of Can. Ltd., Toronto, Can., 1965-68; physics lectr. Coll. Engring. U. Riyadh, Saudi Arabia, 1969-71; physics lectr. Christ Ch. Coll. U. Kanpur, India, 1972-74; rsch. officer in physics Aligarh Muslim U., India, 1974-98, reader in physics, 1998—. Author: Special Theory of Relativity, 1984; contbr. articles to profl. jours. including Jour. Physics and Internat. Studies in Philosophy. Recipient scholarship Nizam's Trust, Cambridge (Eng.) U., 1962-64, Govt. of Andhra Pradesh, 1956-59. Mem. Indian Philos. Congress (life), Muslim Assn. for the Advancement of Sci. Avocations: dramatics, cricket, swimming, music. Home: Ek 45 Alig Apts, Shamshad Market, Aligarh Uttar Pradesh 202002, India Office: Aligarh Muslim U, Dept Physics, Aligarh Uttar Pradesh 202002, India

ANSARI, S. M. RAZAULLAH, historian of science, former physics educator; b. Delhi, India, Apr. 4, 1932; s. S. M. Habibullah Ansari and Roshan Akhter; m. Annemarie Johannes Koch, Mar. 9, 1962 (separated); children: Nisha, Jabin, Shamim, Nusrat; m. Shaukat Nihal, Dec. 31, 1987. BSc in Physics with honours, U. Delhi, 1963, MSc in Physics, 1955; DSc, Karl-Eberhard U., Tübingen, Germany, 1966. Lectr. in physics Delhi (India) Coll., 1956-59; rsch. fellow German Coun. Rsch., Bonn, 1962-69; reader in physics Aligarh (India) Muslim U., 1970-82, prof., 1983-94, hon. prof., 1994—; prof., head dept. of History of Sci., Hamdard U., New Delhi, 1984-86; Salar Jang Meml. lectr., Salar Jang Mus., Hyderabd, India, 1996, others. Editor: Procs. Kyoto Conf., Kluwer, 2000, History Oriental Astronomy; editor Studies in History of Medicine and Sci. Jour., 1985—; contbr. over 50 articles to profl. jours. Fellow Alexander von Humboldt Found., Bonn, 1959-62; grantee Indian Nat. Sci. Acad., New Delhi, 1984-89. Mem. Internat. Astron. Union (pres. commn. for history of astronomy 1994-97), Internat. Union for History and Philosophy of Sci. (pres. commn. sci. and tech. in Islamic world 1993-97, pres. IUHPS-IAU Intern-Union commn. for history astronomy 1997—), Internat. Acad. History Sci. (Paris), Indian Soc. for History of Astronomy (pres. 1997—), Astronomical Soc. India (founder). Moslem. Avocations: stamp and coin collecting, reading. Fax: 400466. E-mail: raza.ansari@gmx.net. Home: Roshan Villa Muzammil Manzil Compound, Dodhpur Rd, Aligarh 202002, India Office: Aligarh Muslim U, care Physics Dept, Aligarh 202002, India

ANSARY, CYRUS A., investment company executive, lawyer; b. Shoraz, Oram, Nov. 20, 1933; s. A.R. and Jamali (Mostmand) A.; m. Janet C. Hodges, Aug. 1, 1970; children: Douglas, Pary Ann, Jeffrey C., Bradley C. BS, Am. U., 1955; LLB, Columbia U., 1958. Bar: Md. 1959, D.C. 1960, Va. 1961. Pvt. practice Washington, 1959-72; sr. ptnr. firm Ansary, Kirkpatrick and Rosse, 1964-72; chmn. bd. Industry Reports, Inc., Washington, 1960-72; organizer, 1st chmn. bd., pres. Woodland Nat. Bank, Alexandria, Va., 1963-67; lectr. Sch. Bus. Adminstrn., Am. U., 1967-71; chmn. bd. Fin. Dynamics Corp., Washington, 1967-72, Campbell Music Co., Washington, 1968-72, John L. Lindstrom and Assocs., Inc., Washington, 1962-86; pres. IK Investment A.G., Zurich, Switzerland, 1974-79, Investment Svcs. Internat. Co., Washington, 1973—; chmn. MACO Bancorp Md., Washington, 1988-95; dir. Washington Mut. Investors Fund. Trustee Am. U., 1968-96, chmn. bd., 1982-90; trustee Internat. Law Inst., 1976-88, Wolf Trap Found., Vienna, Va., 1977-82, Krupp Found., Essen, Germany, 1977-79, Washington Opera Soc., 1982-89; dir. Metalurgica Campo Limpo Limitada, Sao Paulo, Brazil, 1976-80, Fried Krupp GmbH, Essen, 1975-79; pres. Ansary Found., Washington, 1983—; dir. Growth Fund Washington, 1985—, Am. Funds Tax-Exempt Series I, Washington, 1986—; chmn. bd. CorPay Solutions, Inc., Washington, 1999—. With USMCR, 1959-64. Mem. Washington Soc. Investment Analysts, Economic Club of Washington, Nat. Press Club, Metropolitan Club (Washington), Chevy Chase Country Club (Bethesda), Rotary. Office: 1725 K St NW Ste 410 Washington DC 20006-1401

ANSARY, HANSON JABER, transportation and telecommunications executive; b. Tehran, Iran, May 3, 1949; arrived in Can., 1973; s. Aman-al-Allah J. and Robabeh (Naimi) A.; 1 child, Farrah R. BA in Bus., Tehran Bus. Coll., 1971; MA in Econ., Meml. U. Nfld., St. Johns, Can., 1975; MBA, Pitts. (Kans.) State U., 1976; PhD in Bus., Calif. Western U., 1982. Policy advisor Gov. Ont., Toronto, Can., 1977-78; mgr. strategic planning Domtar Inc., Montreal, Que., Can., 1978-81; mgr., planning coord. Polysar Ltd., Sarnia, Ont., 1981-83, mgr. planning and devel., 1983-84; dir. corp. devel. Ports Can., Ottawa, Ont., 1984-85, v.p. corp. svcs., 1985-88, exec. v.p., 1988-92, exec. v.p., COO, 1992-95; pres., CEO Canol Internat., Ottawa, Ont., Can., 1995-96, AmeriTest, Inc., Rock Springs, Wyo., 1996-97; COO Acosta Med. Testing Corp., Chgo., 1998—; sr. ptnr. The Maxxus Group, 1999—; bd. dirs., chmn. Electronic Data Interchange Coun. Can., Toronto, 1990; chmn. Total Electronic Commerce Svc. for Transp., 1993—. Founder, editor-in-chief quar. Portus, 1985-92. Bd. dirs. Carleton Condominium Corp., 1991-93, Can. Grain Coun., 1992—, Containerization and Intermodal Inst., 1993-94, The Van Horne Inst., 1993—. 2d lt. Armed Forces Iran, 1971-73. Fellow Chartered Inst. Transport; mem. Strategic Mgmt. Soc., Planning Forum, Am. Assn. Port Authorities (chmn. commerce com. 1993-94), Internat. Cargo Handling Coords. Assn. (internat. vice chmn. London 1992-94, chmn. 1994—, pres. Can. 1988—). Avocations: cinema, jogging. Home: 2822 186th St Apt 3N Lansing IL 60438-2945

ANSBACHER, SIDNEY FRANKLYN, lawyer; b. Jacksonville, Fla., May 28, 1961; 1 child, Benjamin Alexander. BA, U. Fla., 1981; JD, Hamline U., 1985; LLM in Agrl. Law, U. Ark., 1989. Bar: Fla., U.S. Dist. Ct. (mid. dist.) Fla., U.S. Ct. Appeals (D.C. cir.). Atty. Fla. Dept. Natural Resources, Tallahassee, 1986-87; assoc. Turner, Ford, Buckingham, Jacksonville, Fla., 1987-90; ptnr., assoc. Brant, Moore et al, Jacksonville, Fla., 1990-95; ptnr. Mahoney Adams & Criser, Jacksonville, Fla., 1995-97, Upchurch Bailey & Upchurch, St. Augustine, Fla., 1997—. Contbr. articles to profl. jours.; mng. editor Fla. Bar Environ. and Land Use CLE Manual, 1998—. Bd. dirs. Fla. Forestry Found., 1993-96. Recipient Outstanding Achievement award Fla. Wildlife Fedn., 1990. Mem. Fla. Bar Assn. (treas. environ. and land use law sect. 1998-99, sec. 1999—, bd. dirs. 1994-98, Judy Florence Outstanding Svc. award 1992, 2000), Jacksonville Bar Assn. (chair environ. and land use law sect. 1994-96). Avocations: bicycling, tennis, reading. Office: Upchurch Bailey & Upchurch PA 780 N Ponce De Leon Blvd Saint Augustine FL 32084-3519

ANSBRO, JOHN JOSEPH, philosophy educator; b. N.Y.C., Nov. 16, 1932; s. Thomas and Katherine (Reilly) A. BA, St. Joseph's Sem., Yonkers, N.Y., 1954, postgrad., 1955; MA, Fordham U., 1957, PhD, 1964. Lectr. philosophy Manhattan Coll., Riverdale, N.Y., 1958-59, instr., 1959-63, asst. prof., 1963-68, assoc. prof., 1968-79, prof., 1979-96; ret., 1996, writer, 1996—; curriculum guidance supr. of faculty counselors Sch. Arts & Scis. Manhattan Coll., 1962-73, chmn. co-curricular interdisciplinary arts program, 1962-70, chmn. com. faculty rsch. projects and grants, 1976-78, 89-92, chmn. dept. philosophy, 1977-81, chmn. sabbatical leave com., 1989-91, dir. rsch. peace studies program, 1990-91, com. faculty rsch. projects, mem. instnl. rev. bd. human subjects, task force acad. programs, liaison officer Danforth Found., others; adj. asst. prof. philos. resources for contemporary problems program Grad. Sch. Arts & Scis., Fordham U., 1975, chmn. Met. Round Table Philosophy, 1972-75; project field coord. N.Y. State Dept. Edn., 1965-67; founder, pres. Manhattan Coll. Coun. World Hunger, 1977-85. Author: Martin Luther King, Jr.: The Making of a Mind, 1982, (Mex. trans., 1985), Martin Luther King, Jr.: Nonviolent Strategies and Tactics for Social Change, 2d edit., 2000; contbr. articles and critical revs. to publs. including N.Y. Times. Fordham U. Grad. Sch. scholar in philosophy, 1956-57; Travel and Study grantee Ford Found., 1973, Summer grantee Am. Can. Co. Found., 1985, Samuel Rubin Found., 1985. Mem. AAUP, Soc. for Advancement Am. Philosophy, Am. Philos. Assn., Hegel Soc. Am., Soc. Ancient Greek Philosophy, Soren Kierkegaard Soc.

ANSCHER, BERNARD, manufacturing executive, investor, management consultant; b. Bklyn., June 9, 1922; s. Abraham and Esther (Draznin) A.; children: William, Marlene, Joseph. Student, Sch. Tech., CCNY, 1939-42; BS in Mech. Engring., NYU, 1948, MBA, 1953, postgrad., 1953-65; postgrad., Fla. Internat. U., 1997—. Cert. mfg. engr. robotics, mfg. engr. Chief metall. and fabrication devel. reactor materials br. U.S.A.E.C., N.Y.C., 1946-50; devel. mgr., gen. sales mgr. domestic sales, asst. v.p. Loewy-Hydropress, Inc., N.Y.C., 1950-55; cons., mfrs.' rep. Mercury Engring. Co., N.Y.C., 1955-65; founder, chmn. bd. dirs., pres. Nat. Molding Corp., Farmingdale, N.Y., 1965-87; pres. Anscher Mgmt. Corp. (formerly Custom Molds), Opa Locka, Fla., 1975—; founder, pres. Nat. Indsl. Robotic Controls, 1983-90; mfg. cons., 1991—; founder, instr. mktg. program in cmty. coll., N.Y.C., 1962-65; mem. industry adv. group Underwriters Labs.; mem. robotics standards com. Robot Inst.; corp. mem. Automotive Industry Action Group, 1984-87. Reviewing editor Die Design Handbook, 1954-55; polit. columnist Miami Beach Sunpost, 1991-92; contbr. articles to profl. jours.; patentee in field. Queens County committeeman Rep. Party, 1960-68; mem. Dem. Exec. Com., Dade County, Fla., 1990-92; Dem. party nominee for Congress, 18th Dist., Fla., 1990; ind. candidate Congress, 22d Dist., Fla., 1992; mem. platform com. Dem. Party Presdl. Election, 1992; treas. Temple Emanu-el, 1994-95, Lehrman Day Sch., 1994-95. With AUS, 1943-46, PTO. Recipient Spl. award Manhattan Project, 1946; cert. mfg. engr. Mem. N.Y. State Mktg. Educators (chmn. curriculum rsch. com. 1964), Soc. Mfg. Engrs., Soc. Plastics Engrs., Robotics Internat., Am. Jewish Congress (comm. law and social action, chmn. edn. com. S.E. region 1999), Pres.' Club U. Miami, NYU Alumni Assn., Stuyvesant H.S. Alumni. Office: Anscher Mgmt Corp PO Box 610157 Miami FL 33261-0157

ANSCHÜTZ, TILL RAINER, ophthalmologist; b. Halle, Germany, May 10, 1945; s. Hans-Joachim Albert and Lieselotte Therese (Russwurm) A.; m. Bärbel Inge Oetken, Aug. 19, 1977; children: Annika, Florian, Julian, Victoria. Med. examen, U. Heidelberg, 1971, approbation, 1973, Facharzt Augenheilkunde, 1977. Med. asst. U. Heidelberg, Mannheim, Germany, 1971-73, 74-77; ophthalmologist Gaggenau, Germany, 1977—; chief ophthalmology dept. Stadtklinik, Baden-Baden, Germany, 1978—; med. dir. ACL, 1997—; sec. Commn. Refractive Lasurgery, 1996—; pres. Germany Excimer-Laser Soc., Baden-Baden, 1992—. patentee in field; contbr. articles to profl. jours.; contbr. chpts. to books. City councillor, 1989-94; pres. Tennis Club, Gernsbach, Germany, 1989-93. Capt. med. corps Gemany Navy, 1973-74. Mem. Am. Acad. Ophthalmology (internat.), Am. Soc. Cataract and Refractive Surgery, German Ophthalmology Soc., Berufsverband Augenärzte, Internat. Soc. Refractive Surgery, Augen-Centrum-Laser-u. Microchirurgie, Rotary. Office: Konrad Adenauer Str 3, 76571 Gaggenau Germany

ANSEL, RENE, editor, photographer; b. Colmar, Alsace, France, Sept. 22, 1939; s. Marcel and Marie (Cariolini) A.; m. Suzanne Hill, May 31, 1969; children: Yannick, Noelle. Comml. studies, Secondary Sch., Colmar, 1957; photog. studies, Institut PhotoCinema, Colmar, 1976. Photographer Société Alsacienne d'Expansion Photographique, Ingersheim, France, 1962-68, Printery Reiff Druck, Offenburg, Germany, 1968-70, Printery Dernière Nouvelles d'Alsace, Strasbourg, France, 1970-76; editor, photographer Edira/Photo Work, Katzenthal, France, 1978—. NCO paratrooper, 1959-61. Office: Edira, 126 rue des 3 Epis, 68230 Katzenthal Alsace, France

ANSELMI, DAMIANO, physicist, researcher; b. Verona, Italy, Apr. 17, 1967; s. Mario Abramo and Angelina (Zanella) A. Degrees in physics, U. Pisa and Scuola Normale Superiore, Italy, 1990; MS in Physics, S.I.S.S.A. Trieste, 1992; PhD in Physics, U. Trieste, 1994. Rsch. asst. Harvard U., Cambridge, Mass., 1994-96; rsch. assoc. Ecole Polytechnique Palaiseau, France, 1996-98, CERN, Geneva, Switzerland, 1998—. Author: Quantum Irreversibility, 1999. Avocations: Nietzche's philosophy, philosophy of science. Office: CERN, Theory Group, CH-1211 Geneva 23, Switzerland

ANSEN, ALAN JOSEPH, retired poetry educator; b. Bklyn., Jan. 23, 1922; s. William and Bessie (Blum) A. BA, Harvard Coll., 1942; MA, Harvard U., 1942. Sec. W.H. Auden, N.Y.C., 1948-53; instr. Aegina, then Athens (Greece) Art Ctr., 1969-86. Author: (selected poems) Contact Highs, 1989; transcriber: Table Talk of W.H. Auden, 1989. Mem. PEN (Am. Ctr.). Avocation: listening to classical music. Home: 26 Timoleontos Philimonos, 11521 Athens Greece

ANSIO, KARI KALERVO, import/export company executive; b. Helsinki, Oct. 19, 1940; s. Kalervo and Hanna (Heinänen) A.; m. Sinikka Alli Järvinen, July 18, 1964; children: Marianna, Sarianna. BSc in Econs., Helsinki Sch. Econs., 1964. Sales mgr. Kaukomarkkinat Oy, Helsinki, 1964-67, dept. mgr., 1967-81, dep. dir., 1981-82, dir., 1982-87, exec. v.p., 1988-91, pres., CEO, 1991—. Mem. Finnish Assn. Watch and Jewelry Importers (chmn. 1994—), Fedn. Finnish Commerce and Trade (bd. dirs. 1994—), Finnish Japanese C. of C. (bd. dirs. 1984—), Finland-China Trade Assn. (bd. dirs. 1997—). Avocation: tennis. Office: Kaukomarkkinat Oy, Kutojantie 4, 02630 Espoo Finland

ANSLEY, SHEPARD BRYAN, lawyer; b. July 31, 1939; s. William Bonneau and Florence Jackson (Bryan) A.; m. Boyce Lineberger, May 9, 1970; children-Anna Rankin, Florence Bryan. BA, U. Ga., 1961; LLB, U. Va., 1964. Bar: Ba. 1967. Assoc. Carter & Ansley and predecessor firm Carter, Ansley, Smith & McLendon, Atlanta, 1967-73, ptnr., 1973-84, of counsel, 1984-91; bd. dirs. Prime Bancshares, Inc., Prime Bank, FSB; chmn. bd. dirs., pres. Sodamaster Co. Am.; exec. v.p. Woodridge Realty, Inc.; sr. v.p., ACA Consulting, Inc.; fin. cons. Attkisson, Carter & Akers, Inc.; bd. dirs. Jour. Pub. Law Emory U., 1961-62; bd. dirs., sec. CRM Co., LLC, L.A. County, Calif. Mem. Vestry St. Luke's Episcopal Ch., Atlanta, 1971-74; treas., mem. exec. com., bd. dirs. Alliance Theatre Co., Atlanta, 1974-85; trustee Atlanta Music Festival Assn., Inc., 1975—; v.p., bd. dirs. Atlanta Preservation Ctr. Inc., pres., 1988-90; bd. visitors Lineberger Cancer Rsch. Ctr. U. N.C. at Chapel Hill, 1987-92; pres., bd. dirs. The Study Hall at Emmaus House, Inc.; bd. dirs., The Margaret Mitchell House, Inc.; bd. govs. Ga. Pub. Policy Found., Inc., 1999—. Served to capt. U.S. Army, 1965-67. Mem. ABA, Ga. Bar Assn., Atlanta Bar Assn., Atlanta Lawyers Club, Am. Coll. Mortgage Attys., Atlanta Jr. C. of C. (bd. dirs. 1968-72), Piedmont Driving Club.

ANSTEE, JOHN HOWARD, biological studies educator, administrator; b. Neyland, U.K., Apr. 25, 1943; s. Stanley George and Anne May (Griffiths) A.; m. Angela June Young, July 18, 1966; 1 child, Quentin Mark. BSc with honors, U. Nottingham, Eng., 1965, PhD, 1968. Sr. demonstrator zoology U. Durham, Eng., 1968-71, lectr. zoology, 1971-81, sr. lectr. zoology, 1981-96, prof. zoology, 1996—; dep. dean sci. U. Durham, 1991-94, dean sci., 1994-97, pro-vice chancellor,1997—. Contbr. chpts. to books and numerous articles to profl. jours. Fellow Zool. Soc., Royal Entomol. Soc. (mem. coun. 1991-94); mem. Soc. Exptl. Biology (hon. sec. 1990-94, coun. mem. 1990—). Methodist. Avocations: cricket, sailing, rugby. Office: U Durham Sci Labs, U Durham, Old Shire Hall, Durham DH1 3HP, England

ANTAKLY, MARIE-CLAIRE, anesthesiologist, educator; b. Chyah, Lebanon, Feb. 15, 1940; d. Joseph and Marie (Letayf) Nehmé; m. Joseph Antakly, Oct. 12, 1964; children: Michel, Yara. MD, St. Joseph U., Beirut, 1964. Intern/resident U. Paris IV, 1964-67, Agregation/French U., 1972; asst. head anesthesiology dept. Hotel Hosp. Beirut, 1967-79, head anesthesiology dept., 1979-00; asst. prof. St. Joseph U., Beirut, 1973-78, prof., 1978-00. Author: I.V. Anesthetic Drugs, 1967; contbr. articles to profl. jours. Mem. ASA, IASP, ESA. Avocation: swimming. Home: 86, Ave Raymond Poincare, 75116 Paris France Office: Hotel Dieu France, Adib Ishac St, Beirut Lebanon

ANTAL, ALBERT, gynecologist, obstetrician, anesthesiologist; b. Biharkeresztes, Bihar, Hungary, July 23, 1927; s. Albert and Julianna (Venyige) A.; m. Eva Beres, 1951 (dec. 1977); children: Albert, Eva. MD, U. Szeged. Asst. U. Szeged, 1953-54; from asst. to assoc. attending physician City Hosp. Szeged, 1954-75, attending ob-gyn. physician, 1957-90, oncology cons., 1986-92, ob-gyn. cons., 1992—. Author, co-author: Series of Studies on the Treatment of Bartholin-Cysta, 1965; contbr. more than 50 articles to profl. jours. Mem. Soc. for the Advancement of Sci., European Assn. Ob-Gyns. and Anesthesiologists, N.Y. Acad. Scis., Szege Civil Club, Baross Alumni Assn. Avocations: fishing, swimming, literature, history. Home and Office: Vadasz Utca 8, 6721 Szeged Hungary

ANTALFFY, LESLIE PETER, mechanical engineer; b. Budapest, Hungary, Oct. 31, 1942; came to U.S., 1973; s. Vilmos Leslie and Margo (Simay) A.; m. Barbara Ann Clark, Jan. 19, 1970; children: Julie, Michael, Nicole. B in Mech. Engring., U. Adelaide, Australia, 1970; MBA, Sam Houston State U., 1980. Registered profl. engr., Tex.; chartered profl. engr. Instn. Engrs. Australia. Mech. engr. T. O'Connor & Sons, Adelaide, 1968-69; vessel engr. Lummus Co. Can., Toronto, 1970-71, A.G. McKee Co. Can., Toronto, 1972; sr. vessel engr. Lummus Co. Can., Toronto, 1972-73; sr. vessel engr. Fluor Daniel, Houston, 1973-75, prin. engr., 1975-80, supervising mech. engr., 1980-89, mech. engring. dir., 1989-95, sr. mech. engring. dir., 1995—, sr. tech. fellow, 1996—. Contbr. articles to profl. jours.; presenter tech. papers at internat. confs. Fellow ASME (spl. working group on high pressure vessels, task group chmn. fabrication, examination testing of ASME VIII divsn. 3, 1992—, chmn. high pressure tech.-design 1993—). Republican. Roman Catholic. Achievements include patent for coke drum unheading device for coke drums on delayed coker units; patent for an automated chute system for delayed coker units; patent for a low headroom unheading device; patent for a coke drum system with movable floor. Home: 11946 Summerdale St Houston TX 77077-3022

ANTELL, DARRICK EUGENE, plastic surgeon, educator; b. Cleve., Feb. 22, 1951; s. E. James and Wanda H. (Kociecki) A.; m. Elizabeth Ann Sobottka, July 14, 1984; children: Gillian Elizabeth, Darrick Eugene Jr., Leslie Jane, Helen Greer, Meredith James. BS in Biology, Hobart Coll., 1973; DDS, Case Western Res. U. Dental, 1978; MD, Med. Coll. of Ohio, 1982. Cert. Am. Bd. Plastic Surgery. Surgery intern Stanford (Calif.) U. Med. Ctr., 1982-83, surgery resident, 1983-85; plastic surgery resident N.Y. Hosp. Cornell, N.Y.C., 1985-87; plastic and reconstructive surgeon St. Luke's/Roosevelt, N.Y.C., 1987—; asst. clin. prof. plastic surgery Columbia U., N.Y.C., 1989—; med. dir., founder 850 Park Surg. Ctr., N.Y.C. Author: Plastic Surgery, 1991; contbr. articles to profl. jours. Trustee East Side House Settlement, N.Y.C., 1991, Hist. Soc. of the Town of Greenwich, 1999, Univ. Sch. Cleve.; trustee adv. Girl Scouts U.S.A., N.Y.C., 1991. Grantee Facial Proportions AM. Soc. for Aesthetic Plastic Surgery, 1987; recipient Pres. Citizenship award N.Y. State Med. Soc., 1992. Fellow ACS; mem. AMA, Am. Soc. Plastic and Reconstructive Surgeons, Am. Soc. Aesthetic Plastic Surgery, Am. Soc. Maxillofacial Surgeons Parliamentarian, N.Y. Regional Soc. Plastic and Reconstructive Surgeons, Internat. Soc. for Aesthetic Plastic Surgery, Internat. Acad. Dental Facial Aesthetics (founding), Am. Acad. Cosmetic Dentistry, Interplast, Lipoplasty Soc., Herbert Conway Soc., Univ. Sch. Alumni Adv. Coun., Union Club, Fishers Island Yacht Club, Cleve. Skating Club, Mill Reef Club (Antigua, W.I.). Avocations: squash, fly fishing. Office: 850 Park Ave New York NY 10021-1845

ANTES, HORST, painter, sculptor; b. Heppenheim a.d.B., Germany, Oct. 28, 1936; s. Valentin and Erika Antes; m. Dorothea Grossman, 1961; 2 children. Student, Heppenheim Coll., 1948-52. Prof. State Acad. Fine Arts, Karsruhe, Fed. Republic Germany, 1957-59, Karlsruhe, Berlin, 1984—. One man shows include Troisieme Biennale de Paris, Mus. Ulm, Stadtische Galerie Munich, 1964, Gallery Stangl Munich, 1965, 68, 72, 75, Gallery Defet, Nürnberg, 1966, 72, 88, 93, Gimpel and Hanover Gallery, Zurich and London, 1967, 70, 73, 76, 80, Lefebre Gallery, N.Y.C., 1967, 69, 72, 74, 76, 78, 80, 82, 84, 86, 23d Biennale Venice, 1966, 10th Biennale Sao Paulo, 1969, Staatliche Kunsthalle Baden-Baden, Kunsthalle Bern, Kunsthalle Bremen, Frankfurter Kunstverein, 1971-72, Badischer Kunstverein Karlsruhe, 1978, Galerie Gunzenhauser, Munich, 1979, 83, 86, 87, 93, 95, Galerie Brusberg, Hanover and Berlin, 1979, 82, 83, 88, Bruhl, Schloss Augustenburg, 1980, Galerie Valentien, Stuttgart, 1966, 70, 81, 89, Nishimura Gallery, Tokyo, 1981, 84, 90, 95, Galerie der Spiegel, Köln, 1960, 63, 65, 82, 84, 87, 93, 94, Kunsthalle Bremen, 1983, Städel Frankfurt Sprengel Mus. Hannover, 1983, Wilhelm-Hack Mus., Ludwigshafen, 1983, Gallery Krohn, Badenweiler, 1964, 67, 77, 84, 91, 94, Guggenheim Mus., N.Y., 1984, Gallery Neumann, Düsseldorf, 1985, 88, Gallery Levy, Hamburg, 1988, Freie Akademie der Kunste, Hamburg, 1988, Galerie Bernd Lutze, Friedrichshafen, 1980, 82, 88, 91, 92, Galerie der Stadt Stuttgart, 1989, Sprengel Mus., Hannover, 1989, Galerie Valentien, Stuttgart, 1989, Galerie Utermann, Dortmund, 1989, Ulmer Mus., Ulm, 1989, Kunsthalle Kiel, 1990, Galerie Lüpfert, Isernhagen, 1991, Xylon, Schwetzingen, 1992, Zeitraume, Kv. Gottingen, 1992, Galerie Huber-Nising, Frankfurt/M, 1992, 96, Palais Preysing, Munich, 1993, Haus der Kunst, Munich, 1993, Schloss Mosigkau, Dessau, 1994, Berlinische Galerie, 1994, Galerie Pels-Lensden, Berlin, 1994, Von der Heydt-Mus., Wuppertal, 1994, Burghausen, 1994, Schlop, Williagrad, 1994, K.V. friedrichshaten, 1994, Galerie Orangerie-Reinz, Köln, 1995, Prinz Max

Palais, Karlsrune, 1995, badisches Lawdesmuseum Mus. in der Majokika Manufaktur, Karlsrune, 1995, Galerie Holbein, Lindau, 1980, 87, 90, 96, Galerie Meyer-Ellinger , frankfurt, 1996, Jahrhunderthalle Howchst, Frankfurt, 1996, Kunsthalle Emden, 1996, Galleria d'Arte Narcisco Torino, 1996, Keramik Mus., Stanten, 1996, Galerie Werk Statt, Reinach, 1996, Galerie Uwe Sacksotsky, Heidelberg, 1996, Mus. tür Moderne Kunst Stiltung Wörlen, Passan, 1997; group shows include Pitts. Internat. Exhbn., 1961, 64, 70, 77; Dokumenta, Kassel, 1964, 68, 77; Europalia, Brussels, 1977; Im Namen des Volkes, Duisburg, Remscheid, Vienna, Sculptures Europeenes, Brussels, 1979; Skulptur im 20. jahrhundert, Basel Wenkenpark, 1980, Biennale Middelheim, Antwerp., Nat. Mus. Seoul, Goethe Inst., London, 1983, Nationalgalerie, Berlin, 1985, Taimei Gallery, Tokyo, 1986, Intergrafik, DDR Berlin 1987, 90, Internat. Art Show for End of World Hunger, Minn., 1987, World Hunger, N.Y., 1987, Kölner Stadt-museum, Köln, 1988, Lepold-Hoesch Mus., Duren, Aalborg, 1988, dokumenta Found., Berlin, 1988, Badischer Kunstverein, Karlsruhe, 1988, Toledo (Ohio) Mus. Art, 1988, Williams Coll. Mus. Art, Williamstown, 1989, Guggenheim Mus., N.Y., 1989, Kunstmus. Düsseldorf, 1989, Schirn Kunsthalle, Frankfurt, 1989, Ornamenta, Pforzheim, 1989, Bilderfür den Himmel-Kunstdrachen, Munich, 1989, 90, Düsseldorf, 1991, Hamburg, 1991, Berlin, 1991, Copenhagen, 1991, Torino, 1991, Rome, 1992, Sevilla, 1992, Kassel, 1993, Montreal, 1993, Sydney, 1995, Labeck, 1995, Intergrafik, Berlin, 1990, Farbe der Ferne:Blau, KV Heidelberg, 1990, Flucht, Darmstadt, 1990, Deutsche Bank, Düsseldorf, Frankfort, 1990, Zustände Deutsche Graphik nach 1960, Cappenberg, 1990, Huddersfield, 1991, Wolfsburg, 1991, 21 Biennale Sao Paulo, 1991, Staatl. Mus., Schwerin, 1992, K.H. Recklinghausen, Cowboys and Indians, 1992, Stadt Galerie, Karlsruhe, 1992, Berlinische Galerie, Berlin, k1992, Dritter Maisalon, Berlin, 1992, Galerie Brusberg, Berlin, 1992, Pfalzgalerie, Kaiserslautern, 1992, Vierter Maisalon, Berlin, 1993, Galerie Thomas, Munich, 1994, Sammlung Würth, Künzelsau, 1994, Mex. City, 1994, Passau, 1995, Buddpest, 1995, Aut Papier Kunst des 20. jahrh. aus der Deutschen Bank, Frankfurt, Berlin, Leipzig, 1995, Erzbischötliches Diözesanmuseum, Körn, 1995, Kunst in deutschland, Bonn, 1995, Internat. Print triennal, 1995, Jmpuls Sudwest Kunsthalle, Karlsruhe, 1995, Kunste des Wéstens Kunsthalle recklingnausen, 1996, Gallerie Schlichtenmaier, Gratenau, 1996, Staatsgalerie Stuttgart Magic der Zahl in der Kunst des 20. Jahrhunderts, 1997, others. Recipient UNESCO prize Biennale, Venice, 1966, Villa Romana prize, Florence, 1962, Villa Massimo prize, Rome, 1963, Hans Molfenter prize Landeshauptstadt Stuttgart, 1989, Kulturpreis des Landes Hessen, 1991, Grand Prize Fundacao Bienal de Sao Paulo for 21st Internat. Biennal of Sao Paulo. Home: Hohenbergstrasse 11, 7500 Karlsruhe Germany Office: VGBild-Kunst, Weberstrasse 61, D-53113 Bonn Germany*

ANTHONY, ANDREW JOHN, lawyer; b. Newark, Jan. 26, 1950; s. Andrew and Mary (Norton) A.; m. Raquel Perez Montoya, Sept. 29, 1990; children: Nicholas, Natalie. BA, Kean Coll., 1973; JD cum laude, U. Miami, 1976. Bar: Fla. 1977, U.S. Dist. Ct. (so. dist.) Fla. 1977. Assoc. Knight, Peters, Hoeveler, Pickle, Niemoeller & Flynn, Miami, Fla., 1977-79, Vernis & Bowling, Miami, 1979, Ligman, Martin, Shiley & McGee, Coral Gables, Fla., 1979-86; sole practice Coral Gables, 1986—. Mem. ABA, Fla. Bar Assn. Democrat. Roman Catholic. Avocations: numismatics, fishing, reading. Home: 3703 Anderson Rd Coral Gables FL 33134-7052 Office: 999 Ponce De Leon Blvd Ste 1035 Coral Gables FL 33134-3047

ANTHONY, EDWARD (TED) MASON, IV, journalist, educator; b. Pitts., Apr. 16, 1968; s. Edward Mason Anthony Jr. and Ann Louise Terbrueggen. BA in History, Pa. State U., 1990. Police reporter Harrisburg (Pa.) Patriot-News, 1990-91, state reporter, 1991-92; reporter, editor AP, Charleston, W.Va., 1992-93, Phila., 1993-94; editor, supr. internat. desk AP, N.Y.C., 1994-96, nat. corr., 1996—; lectr., presenter AP Mng. Editors, 1997-99, Nat. Writers Workshop, 1998-99. Recipient Nat. Easter Seal Soc. Equality, Dignity, Independence award, 1992. Mem. New Eng. Historic Geneal. Soc., Delta Chi (v.p. Alumni Assn. 1997—). Avocations: genealogy, poetry writing. Fax: 212-621-1567. Home: 244 W 72d St Apt 3A New York NY 10023 Office: AP 50 Rockefeller Plz New York NY 10020-1605

ANTHONY, HARRY ANTONIADES, city planner, architect, educator; b. Skyros, Greece, July 28, 1922; came to U.S., 1951, naturalized, 1954; s. Anthony G. and Maria G. (Ftoulis) Antoniades; m. Anne C. Skoufis, Sept. 23, 1950; children: Mary Anne Anthony Smith, Kathryn Harriet. B.Arch., Nat. Tech. U., Athens, Greece, 1945; student, Ecole Nat. Supérieure des Beaux Arts, Paris, 1945-46; M.City Planning, U. Paris, 1947; Docteur de l'Université, Sorbonne, Paris, 1949; Ph.D. in Arch. and Urban Planning, Columbia, 1955. Architect-planner with Constantinos A. Doxiadis, Athens, 1943-45, LeCorbusier, Paris, 1946-47, ECA, Paris, 1949-51; city planner with Maurice E.H. Rotival, N.Y.C., 1951-52; chief planner Brown & Blauvelt, N.Y.C., 1952-54; city planner, urban designer Skidmore, Owings & Merrill, N.Y.C., 1954-56; prin. planning cons. Brown Engrs. Internat., N.Y.C., 1956-60; prin. Brown & Anthony City Planners, Inc., N.Y.C., 1960-69; v.p. Doxiadis Assocs., Inc., Washington, 1971-72; mem. faculty Columbia U., 1953-72, from asst. to assoc. prof., 1956-63, prof. urban planning, 1963-72, dir. grad. div. urban planning Grad. Sch. Architecture and Planning, 1962-65; prof. urban planning Calif. State Poly. U., Pomona, 1972-83, prof. emeritus urban and regional planning, 1983—; chmn. dept. Calif. State Poly. U., 1972-76; vis. prof. urban design Tulane U., 1967-68; vis. lectr. U. Calif. at Berkeley, Stanford U., Dartmouth, San Diego State U., CUNY, U. Okla., Ohio U., Auburn U., Salk Inst. Biol. Studies, U.S. Internat. U.; lectr. urban studies and planning U. Calif., San Diego, 1980-82; scholar-in-residence U. B.C., Vancouver, 1978; planning, zoning, urban renewal and urban design cons. to several cities, U.S. and abroad; also cons. to UN, Am. Med. Bldg. Guild, corps. and pvt. firms, to govts. and univs.; planning commr., Leonia, N.J., 1958-64; master planner, cons. arch. for Ss. Constantine and Helen Greek Orthodox Ch. and Village for the Elderly, Cardiff-by-the-Sea, Calif., 1983-97 (AIA design awareness program orchid award 1997). Author, coauthor, contbr.: Four Great Makers of Modern Architecture: Gropius, Le Corbusier, Mies Van Der Rohe, Wright, Dictionary of American History, The Challenge of Squatter Settlements-With Special Reference to the Cities of Latin America, La Défense à Paris et le Quartier d'Affaires de Vancouver: Une Comparaison Urbaine, New Orleans Air Rights Study, Woodstock Growth Plan and Land Use Controls, Mt. Vernon Planning Study, Corning Area, N.Y.: Conditions and Prospects, Metairie Shore, La.: Lakefront Recreation and Comty. Devel., U.S. Navy Multiple Activity Master Plan: Norfolk Complex, Aqaba, Jordan: Future Devel., Lands of Kapua, Hawaii: Feasibility Study for Urban, Agricultural and Recreational Devel.; several master plans, city and regional planning reports, urban design plans and programs, environ. impact reports, zoning ordinances, educational videocassettes on urban planning subjects; contbr. articles to profl. jours., mags., newspapers; acad. profl. writings, awards, plans, designs and reports included in Spl. Collections Libr., U. Calif. (San Diego), 1998. Recipient Premier Grand Prix Internat. Exhbn. Housing and City Planning, Paris, 1947; William Kinne Fellows travelling fellow in planning N.Am., 1956, French Govt. fellow, 1945-47; research award Urban Center of Columbia U., 1969; named Outstanding Prof. Calif. State Poly. U., 1975; founder Met. Opera House, Lincoln Ctr. for the Performing Arts, N.Y.C. Mem. AIA (Arnold W. Brunner scholar 1958), Am. Inst. Cert. Planners (bd. examiners), Am. Planning Assn. (Disting. Svc. award 1984, San Diego Cmty. Design Awareness Program Orchid award 1997), Order of Am. Hellenic Ednl. Progressive Assn., Hellenic Cultural Soc., Internat. Land Econs. Soc. of Lambda Alpha (Richard T. Ely Disting. Educator award 1988), Univ. Calif. San Diego Faculty Club. Home: 7665 Caminito Avola La Jolla CA 92037-3956

ANTHONY, KENNY, government official. LLB, LLM, U. West Indies; PhD, U. Birmingham, Eng. Lectr., head tchg. dept. law U. West Indies; prime min. Govt. Saint Lucia, 1997—. Contbr. articles and reports to profl. jours. Office: Office Prime Min, Block C 5th Fl New Govt Bldgs, Waterfront Castries Saint Lucia*

ANTHONY, ROBERT ARMSTRONG, law educator, lawyer; b. Washington, Dec. 28, 1931; s. Emile Peter and Martha Graham (Armstrong) A.; m. Ruth Grace Barrons, Feb. 7, 1959 (div.); 1 child, Graham Barrons; m. Joan Patricia Caton, Jan 3, 1980; 1 child, Peter Christopher Caton. BA, Yale U., 1953; BA in Jurisprudence, Oxford U., 1955; JD, Stanford U., 1957. Bar: Calif. 1957, N.Y. 1971, D.C. 1972. Assoc. Pillsbury, Madison & Sutro, San Francisco, 1957-62, Kelso, Cotton & Ernst, San Francisco, 1962-64; assoc. prof. law Cornell U. Law Sch., 1964-68, prof., 1968-75, dir. internat. legal studies, 1964-74; chief counsel, later dir. Office Fgn. Direct Investments, Dept. Commerce, 1972-73; cons. Adminstrv. Conf. U.S., Washington, 1968-71; chmn. Adminstrv. Conf. U.S., 1974-79; ptnr. McKenna, Conner & Cuneo, Washington, 1979-82; sole practice Washington, 1982-83; prof. law George Mason U., Arlington, Va., 1983—; Fulbright lectr., Slovenia, 1994; lectr. Acad. Am. and Internat. Law, Southwestern Legal Found., Dallas, summers 1967-72, instr. Golden Gate U., 1961. Mem. editorial adv. bd. Jour. Law and Tech., 1986-91; contbr. articles to profl. jours. Active Pres.'s Inflation Program Regulatory Coun., 1978-79, Fairfax County (Va.) Rep. Com., 1984-86; chmn. panel U.S. Dept. Edn. Appeal Bd., 1981-83; cons., chmn. pubs. adv. bd. Internat. Law Inst., 1984—; cons. Inst. Pub. Adminstrn., Slovenia, 1994—; bd. dirs. Marin Shakespeare Festival, San Rafael, Calif., 1961-64, Nat. Ctr. for Adminstrv. Justice, 1974-79, Va. Assn. Scholars, 1990-98; commr. Sausalito (Calif.) City Planning Commn., 1962-64. Mem. ABA (coun., sec. sect. adminstrv. law and regulatory practice 1988-94), Assn. Am. Rhodes Scholars, Am. Law Inst., Stanford U. Law Soc. Washington (pres. 1982), Cosmos Club. Home: 2011 Lorraine Ave Mc Lean VA 22101-5331 Office: George Mason U Law Sch 3401 N Fairfax Dr Arlington VA 22201-4411

ANTHONY, SYLVIA, social welfare organization executive; b. Boston, Oct. 5, 1929; d. Charles and Josephine (Guastaferro) Caccamesi; children: Lyn Newbury, Edward Charles Souza Jr., Dean Souza. Student, Northeastern U., Boston, 1968-69, Lee Inst., 1966, 86-87. Lic. real estate broker, Mass. Founder, pres. Life for the Little Ones, Inc., Everett, Mass., 1987-94, Sylvia's Haven, Everett, 1994—. Recipient Arthur L. Whitaker Recognition for Outstanding Cmty. Svc. award Am. Bapt. Chs. of Mass., 1992, Recognition awards Commonwealth of Mass. State Senate, Ho. of Reps., Gov. of Mass., 1997, 99, Mass. Gov.'s Hwy Safety Bur., 1998, Mayor Dean J. Mazzarella City of Leominster, 1999. Address: PO Box 1166 Groton MA 01450-3166 Office: Sylvia's Haven PO Box 2163 Ayer MA 01432-2163

ANTHONY-BYNG, KIMBERLY ANN, social services administrator, psychotherapist; b. Winston-Salem, N.C., Mar. 9, 1961; d. Jerry Hoyle and Nancy Kate Anthony; m. Robert Hamilton Byng, Oct. 12, 1991; children: Katelyn, Weston, Kameron. AA, Lees-McRae Coll., Banner Elk, N.C., 1981; BS, Appalachian State U., 1983, MA, 1986. Lic. prof. counselor S.C. Bd. Examiners, 1991—, lic. profl. counseling supr., 1994—, lic. marriage and family therapist, 1997—. Clin. counselor Charleston County Substance Abuse Commn., Charleston, S.C., 1986-90; mental health counselor Lieber Correctional, Ridgeville, S.C., 1990-91; program mgr. Charleston County Substance Abuse Commn., 1991-95; clin. supr. Dept. Alcohol & Other Druge Abuse Svcs., Charleston, 1995—; ind. guardian ad litem, Charleston Family Ct., 1987—; ind. adoption investigator, S.C. Dept. Social Svcs., 1991-98. Support vol. Charleston Area Mother of Multiples Club, 1996—. Mem. Am. Assn. Marriage and Family Therapy (clin. mem.), Psi Chi. Avocations: reading, power walking, baking. Home: 1610 Dotterers Run Charleston SC 29414-5816

ANTHOPOULOS, LAMBROS PRODROMOS, cardiologist, educator; b. Hexaplatanos, Pella, Greece, Jan. 15, 1932; s. Prodromos P. and Sevasti K. (Petmeza) A.; m. Evripia T. Vlachea, July 23, 1967; children: Prodromos, Sevasti Telemachos. MD, U. Athens, Greece, 1956; MS, Howard U., 1966. Bd. cert. cardiology. Intern Md. Gen. Hosp., Balt., 1959-60, resident, 1960-61; resident Freedmen's Hosp., Washington, 1961-62, rsch. fellow, 1962-64; clin. asst. prof. U. Athens, Alexandra Hosp., 1964-80; assoc. prof., head dept. cardiology Red Cross Hosp., Athens, 1980-86; prof., attending cardiologist Hygeia Hosp., Athens, 1986-92; prof., head cardiologist Evangelismos, Athens, 1992—; pres. Soc. Greek Physicians Trained in the USA, 1978-79, Hellenic Angiological Soc., Athens, 1983-85, Union Med. Dirs. Athens-Pireas Hosps., 1985-88, Hellenic Cardiol. Soc., Athens, 1987-89. Author: Prevention of Non-Communicable Diseases, 1999; contbr. articles to profl. jours. Lt. Hellenic Airforce, 1957-59. Recipient Honors Achievement award The Angiological Rsch. Found., N.Y., 1965; rsch. grantee Washington Heart Assn., 1963. Fellow Am. Coll. Cardiology, European Soc. Cardiology. Fax: 772 6594 or 0294 77448. Home: 6 Ioannou Gennadiou, 115 21 Athens Greece Office: 10 Ravine St, 115 21 Athens Greece

ANTIA, H.M., astrophysicist; b. Indore, India, Nov. 6, 1955; s. M.B. and N.M. (Pavri) A. BS, Indore U., India, 1973; MS, Indian Inst. Tech., Bombay, 1975; DPhil, Bombay U., 1979. Rsch. assoc. Tata Inst. Fundamental Rsch., Bombay, India, 1979-83, fellow, 1983-89, reader, 1989-94, assoc. prof., 1994-98, prof., 1998—. Author: Numerical Methods for Scientists and Engineers, 1991; contbr. articles to profl. jours. Fellow Indian Acad. Scis.; mem. Astron. Soc. India, Internat. Astron. Union, Himalayan Club. Avocation: hiking. Office: Tata Inst Fundamental Rsch, Homi Bhabha Rd, Mumbai 400005, India

ANTICA, MARIASTEFANIA, immunologist; b. Zadar, Croatia, June 21; d. Antun and Ave Licia (Volpini) A. BSc in Biology, U. Zagreb, 1981, MSc, 1983; PhD, Ludwig Maximilian U., Munich, 1987. Postdoctoral fellow Ruder Bošković Inst., Zagreb, Croatia, 1987-90, asst. prof. molecular biology, 1994—, lab. head cellular and moecular immunology, 1998—; rsch. officer Walter and Eliza Hall Inst., Melbourne, Australia, 1990-93; sr. rsch. officer Centenary Inst. Cancer Med. Cell Biology, Sydney, Australia, 1993-94; Cert. rescue diver; vis. scientist Stemcell Lab. Mayo Cancer Ctr., Mayo Found. Med. Edn. and Rsch., Rochester, Minn., 1997. Mem. editl. bd. Croatian Med. Jour. European Molecular Biology Orgn. fellow, Heidelberg, 1990, Internat. Union Against Cancer fellow, Marseille, France, 1992; recipient Fed. award for young scientists, 1987, Nat. award Acad. Sci. and Arts for achievements in medical research, 1999, Nat. award for outstanding achievements in sci., 2000. Mem. Croatian Immunological Soc. (v.p. 1994—), Assn. Internat. Union Against Cancer, Croatian Assn. Natural Scis., Australian Soc. for Immunology. Roman Catholic. Avocations: scuba diving, tennis, skiing, wind surfing. Office: Ruder Bošković Inst, Bijenička 54, 1016 Zagreb Croatia

ANTIPENKO, YEVGENY NIKOLAEVICH, toxicologist; b. Eupatoria, Ukraine, July 25, 1923; s. Nikolai and Maria (Skovorodko) A.; m. Margarita Mihailova, July 14, 1949; two children. BA, Mil. Med. Acad., St. Petersburg, Russia, 1946, PhD, 1950. Tchr. Mil. Med. Acad., St. Petersburg, 1946-53, main investigator, 1959-69; dept. head Nuclear Firing Ground, Semipalatinsk, USSR, 1953-59; lab. head Inst. Radiology & Oncology, Kiev, Ukraine, 1969-77, Ukrainian Scientific Rsch. Ctr. Hygiene, Kiev, 1977-93; prof. Nat. Insts. Health, Kiev, 1993-96; prof., group leader Ukraine Inst. Ecohygiene & Toxicology, Kiev, 1997—. Author: Residual Phenomena of the Acute Radiation Disease, 1963; contbr. articles to profl. jours. Mem. Soc. Radiobiologists, Genetical Assn., Hygienic Assn. Achievements include being devoted to the problems repair of the chromosomes, cytogenetic effects of nonthermal intensity microwaves in mammalian and genetic consequences of environmental pollution by people. Office: Inst Ecohygiene & Toxicology, Heroiv Oborony st 6, 03022 Kiev Ukraine

ANTIPOV, YURI A., mathematician, educator; b. Szczecin, Poland, Nov. 7, 1957; arrived in Eng., 1997; s. Alexander M. Antipov and Raisa D. Antipova; m. Angela Z. Saitova, July 13, 1991; 1 child, Xenia. MSc, U. Odessa, USSR, 1979, PhD, 1983; DSc, U. Moscow, 1993. Asst. lectr. U. Odessa, 1982-84, lectr., 1984-95, prof., head dept., 1995-96; Av Humboldt fellow U. Stuttgart, Germany, 1996-97; rsch. officer U. Bath, Eng., 1997-98; lectr. U. Bath, 1999—; team leader INTAS project U. Odessa, 1994-95. Contbr. articles to profl. jours. Grantee Internat. Assn. Promotion Coop. Scientists Former Soviet Union, 1994, Av Humboldt Found., 1996, Royal Soc. London, 2000. Mem. London Math. Soc. Avocations: marathon, swimming, table tennis. Office: U Bath, Cloverton Down, Bath BA2 7AY, England

ANTOCE, GEORGIANA MAGDALENA, physician, psychiatrist; b. Vulcan, Hunedoara, Romania, Apr. 21, 1965; arrived in Australia, 1993; d. Gheorghe and Maria Ana-Antuza (Macsim) A.; m. Peter Frederick Walker, Apr. 8, 1995 (separated 1996). Med. Diploma, Med. U., Jasi, Romania, 1990. Intern Clin. Hosp. #1, Jasi, Romania, 1990-91, jr. house officer, 1991-93; jr. house officer The Prince Charles Hosp., Brisbane, Australia, 1993-94, registrar in psychiatry, 1997—, registrar in psychogeriatrics, 1998—, registrar in cmty. psychiatry, 1999; prin. house officer in psychiatry Rockhampton (Australia) Base Hosp., 1994-96; registrar in psychiatry Nambour (Australia) Gen. Hosp., 1996, Nundah Child and Adolescent MHS, Brisbane, Australia, 1996-97; registrar in cmty. psychiatry Prince Charles Hosp., 1999; sr. psychiatry registrar Belmont Pvt. Hosp., Brisbane; trainee assoc. R.A.N.Z.C.P., Australia, 1995—; participant early psychiat. intervention conf. C.I.N.P., Melbourne, Australia, 1996; clin. assoc. lectr. dept. psychiatry U. Queensland, 1997—; rschr. in field of trauma and dissociation. Author: poems; contbr. articles to profl. jours. Sub-lt. Romania, 1983-90. Mem. N.Y. Acad. Scis. Mem. Orthodox Ch. Avocations: writing, music, mountaineering, travel, photography. Office: The Prince Charles Hosp, Rode Rd, 4032 Brisbane Queensland, Australia Office: Belmont Hosp, 1220 Creek Rd, Carindale QLD, Australia

ANTOINE, FABRICE, bilingual lexicography, researcher; b. Tonnerre, France, Nov. 17, 1957; s. Julien and Ginette (Lhermitte) A.; m. Josee Benichou Antoine, July 16, 1977; Amelie, Alexandra. PhD in English, U. Paris, 1984. Tchr. of English Lycee, Boulogne-Billancourt, France, 1980-81, Poissy, France, 1981-82; Provins, France, 1982-88; sr. lectr. U. Lille 3, France, 1988-98, prof. English, 1998—; cons. editor Harrap Ltd., London, 1981-96. Author: Dictionnaires Modes D'Emploi, 1992, Dictionnaire des Mots Tronques, 2000, A Dictionary of Clipped Words, 2000; cons. editor: 11 Dictionaries, 1984-96; co-author: English in the Media, 1996; contbr. articles to profl. jours. Mem. Elextra (co-dir. 1995—). E-mail: antoine@univ-lille3.fr. Home: 23 Allee des Colverts, F-59650 Villeneuve d'Ascq France Office: Univ de Lille III, B P 149, 59653 Villeneuve d'Ascq France

ANTOINE, JACQUES, author, consultant; b. Paris, Aug. 19, 1928; s. René and Georgette (Leger) A.; m. Marie-Annette Rupied, July 11, 1952; children: Jean-Marie, Marie-Thérèse, Claire, Véronique, Dominique, Anne, Yves. Grad., de l'Ecole Polytech., 1951, ISUP, Paris, 1953; degree econ. and statistician, ENSAE, Paris, 1953. Adminstr. INSEE, Paris, 1953-58; dir. SEMA, Paris, 1958-73; mng. dir. SOFRES, Paris, 1962-73; cons. CESEM Opinion, Paris, 1973—; prof. CNAM, Paris, 1977-93; mng. dir. CESP, Paris, 1982-86; cons. Commn. des Sondages, France, 1977—; profl. stds. com. ESOMAR, Amsterdam, The Netherlands, 1995—. Author: Le sondage, outil du marketing, 1969, 81, 90, Le pouvoir et l'opinion, 1972, Valeurs de Société et stratégies des Entreprises, 1996; editor Le Sondoscope, la Revue Française des Sondages, 1980—; contbr. articles to profl. publs. Named Chevalier Légion d'honneur, 1979, Officier, 1998. Mem. Internat. Statis. Inst., Acad. des Scis. Commerciales (past pres.), Soc. Française de Statistique (past pres.), Académie de l'eau (treas. 1996—), ADETEM, ESOMAR, Assn. Française de Scis. Politiques. Avocations: piano, organ. Office: Cesem Opinion, 27 rue Taitbout, 75009 Paris France

ANTON, BARBARA, writer; b. Pocono Pines, Pa., Apr. 3, 1926; d. Walter B. and Emma Agnes (Hess) Miller; m. Albert Anton, June 23, 1949. Grad. Gemologist, Gemol. Inst. of Am., 1964. Fashion and design editor Nat. Jeweler Mag., N.Y.C., 1956-58; freelance writer novels/plays, 1956—; staff writer Writer's Guidelines and News Mag.; tchr. sr. divsn. U. South Fla./New Coll., 2000—. Contbr. articles to numerous nat. mags. including Cosmopolitan, Family Circle, Bride's Mag., Saturday Evening Post, Thema Lit. Mag., others; author plays (8 winners Fla. Studio Theatre Shorts Competition 1995-98, 91, 99, 2 Best of Last 10 Yrs., Pa. Playwrighting award and prodn. 1994, 11 Off-Broadway Prodns., Theatre Row, N.Y.C., 1996-2000, winner Lamia Ink Internat. Playwrighting Competition 1997); author: (novel) Egrets to the Flames (Top Ten/Fla. Writers Festival 1995, others); author short stories, anthologies (15 awards Writer's Digest, others). Nominated Best Of Off Broadway, Samuel French Play Festival, 1998-99; recipient First Prize Humor-Manatee Writer's Contest, 2000, Father's Hall of Fame Contest, 2000. Mem. Internat. Women's Writing Guild, Nat. Writers Assn., Dramatists Guild.

ANTON, BRUCE NORMAN, textile company executive; b. N.Y.C., Dec. 27, 1951; s. Harvey and Betty L. (Weintraub) A.; m. Laurie Sue Weinberger, Mar. 7, 1981; children: Jamie Nicole, Ashley Blair, Emily Britt. BS in Textile Engring., Phila. Coll. Textile & Sci., 1973; MBA, Fairleigh Dickinson U., 1978. Salesman Robison-Anton Textile Co., Fairview, N.J., 1973-79, v.p., 1979-88, pres., 1988—; pres. Arrow Spinning Co., Inc., 1985-89; v.p. Bloomsburg Dye Co., Inc., 1984-94, pres., 1995—; pres. R.A. Mfg., 1990—. Mem. Am. Assn. Textile Tech. Office: Robison Anton Textile Co 175 Bergen Blvd Fairview NJ 07022-1619

ANTON, FRANCIS MATTHEW, JR., software engineer; b. Cut Bank, Mont., June 4, 1966; s. Francis Matthew Anton Sr. and Mina Adeline (Paradis) Salsbery; m. Gail Lynn Tulach, May 27, 1989. BS in Pure Math., U. Chgo., 1988; PhD in Religion, ULC, Modesto, Calif., 1998. Devel. engr. Hewlett-Packard, Cupertino, Calif., 1988-89; sys. designer file sys. Transarc Corp., Pitts., 1989-90, sys. designer transaction processing, 1990-93; sr. mem. tech. staff Computer Scis. Corp., Mountain View, Calif., 1993; sr. engr. Taligent, Inc., Cupertino, 1993-96; project mgr. Apple Computer, Cupertino, 1996-97; chief arch., mgr. sys. devel. iPass Inc., Mountain View, 1997-2000; v.p. advanced tech. hereUare Commn., Inc., 2000—; contbr. IETF, 1997-2000, ETSI, 1997-2000, IEEE, 2000; spkr. in field. Republican. Roman Catholic. Avocations: sports, computers, electronics, motorcycle racing. E-mail: butch@zaphod.uchicago.edu. and butch@ipass.com. Fax: 650-237-7321. Home: 1838 Charmeran Ave San Jose CA 95124-3644 Office: iPass Inc 3800 Bridge Pkwy Redwood City CA 94065-1171

ANTON, GISELA HEDWIG, physicist, educator, researcher; b. Bullay, Germany, Mar. 27, 1955; d. Paul and Josefine (Neidhoefer) Glasmachers; m. Frank Ernst Anton, Sept. 7, 1979; children: Johannes, Christina, Matthias. Diploma, Friedrich Wilhelm U., Bonn, Germany, 1979, D in Physics, 1983. Asst. prof. physics U. Bonn, 1989-95; prof. physics U. Erlangen, Nuremberg, Germany, 1995—; rsch. fellow Accelerator Lab Saturne, Orsay, France, 1990. Recipient prize Order of Republic of Germany Pres. of Germany, 1995. Mem. Deutsche Forschungsgemeinschaft (Leibniz prize 1994). Roman Catholic. Office: U Erlangen, U Erlangen, Erwin-Rommel Str 1, D-91058 Erlangen Germany

ANTON, HANS HUBERT, history educator, researcher; b. Könen, Rhineland, Germany, Oct. 26, 1936; s. Matthias and Anna (Lutz) A.; m. Sigrun Noack, Oct. 24, 1969. Staatsexamen, U. Mainz, Germany, 1962; Dr phil, U. Bonn, Germany, 1966, Habilitation, 1970. Rsch. asst. in history U. Mainz, 1962-66; rsch. asst. in history U. Bonn, Germany, 1966-70, lectr. medieval history, 1970; prof. medieval history U. Trier, Germany, 1970—; mem. Commn. Saarländische Landesgeschichte und Volksforschung. Author: Mirrors of Kings and Ethics of Rulership in Carolingian Times, 1968, Studies in the Papal Privileges for Monasteries in the Early Middle Ages, 1975, The So-called Treatise "De Ordinando Pontifice." An Expert Opinion, 1982, Treves in the Early Middle Ages, 1987; contbr. articles to internat. hist. jours., encys. and collected edits. Mem. European Ctr. Rsch. on Monastic Congregations and Religious Orders, German Univ. Union, Union Hist. Germany, Mediaeval Acad. Ireland, Soc. for Rheinish Hist. Sci. Roman Catholic. Home: Auf den Birken 23, D-54329 Konz Germany Office: U Trier, Universitätsring, D-54286 Trier Germany

ANTON, HARVEY, textile company executive; b. N.Y.C., Nov. 10, 1923; s. Abraham J. and Byrdie (Casin) A.; student Western State Coll. Colo., 1941, Savage Sch. Edn., 1941-42; B.S., N.Y. U., 1949; m. Betty L. Weintraub, Dec. 18, 1949; children: Bruce Norman, Lynne Beth. Pres., Anton Yarn Corp. (merged with Robison Textile Co. to form Robison-Anton Textile Co. 1959), N.J., 1949-50, chmn. bd., 1989—; v.p. Arrow Spinning, Susquehanna, Pa.; adv. bd. 1st Jersey Nat. Bank; v.p. Mid-Valley Textile; sec. Bloomsburg Dye; chmn. bd. Robison-Anton Textile Co. Trustee Erza Charitable Found.; pres. Anton Found.; bd. dirs. Pascock Valley Hosp., Westwood, N.J. Served to 1st lt. AUS, 1943-46. Clubs: Masons, KP; Leonia Tennis; N.Y. Univ. Letter (N.Y.C.). Home: 41 Longview Dr Emerson NJ 07630-1507 Office: Robison Anton Textile Co 175 Bergen Blvd Fairview NJ 07022-1684

ANTON, HERMANN JOSEF, zoologist, researcher, educator; b. Düsseldorf, Germany, Jan. 25, 1922; s. Willy Ernst and Annamaria Katharina (Vossen) A.; m. Ingeliese Lehmann, Aug. 18, 1953; children: Sabine Brigitte, Gabriele Marianne, Jürgen Dieter. PhD, U. Cologne, Germany, 1953. Asst. Zool. Inst., U. Cologne, 1953-63, dozent, 1963-70, prof., 1970-87, prof. ret., 1987-97, head Isotope Lab., 1967-87, adj. prof., 1997—; leader Lab. Regeneration in Vertebrates, Cologne, 1964—; lectr. in field. Editor: Control of Cell Proliferation and Differentiation During Regeneration, 1988; contbr. articles to profl. jours. Pres. Cologne Yacht

Club, 1982-86. 2nd lt. German Army, 1945. Mem. German Zool. Soc., German Soc. Nature Rschrs. and Physicians, German Devel. Biology Soc., Internat. Assn. for Rsch. on Regeneration (hon. pres.). Roman Catholic. Avocations: civic action group for prevention of river Rhein flood, sailing, micro- and macrophotography and video production. E-mail: hjanton@uni-koeln.de. Home: Lessingstr 12, D-50996 Cologne Germany Office: U Cologne Zool Inst, Weyertal 119, D-50923 Cologne Germany

ANTON, JOAN MIHAI, engineering educator; b. Vintere, Romania, July 18, 1924; s. Mihai and Maria (Junc) A.; m. Viorica Iancu Flueras, Mar. 22, 1949; children: Hortenzia, Anton. Engr., Polytech. Sch., Timisoara, Romania, 1948; D Engring., Polytech. Inst., Timisoara, Romania, 1961, D Habil, 1972; D Hon Causa, U. Civil Engring., Bucharest, 1998, U. Politehnica, 1999. Assoc. prof. Polytech. Inst., Timisoara, Romania, 1949-62; prof. Polytech. Inst., Timizoara, Romania, 1962-90, dean faculty mechanics, 1961-63, vice-rector, 1963-66, rector, 1971-81, 89-90; prof. U. Politehnica, 1990—; dir. Tech. Rsch. Ctr., Romanian Acad., 1967-70, 96—, Rsch. Ctr. for Hydrodynamics, Cavitation and Magnetic Fluids, 1970-74, 91-96; vice-pres. Romanian Acad., Bucharest, 1974-90, interim pres., 1981-84; editor-in-chief Revue Romanian des Scis. Techniques, 1984—. Editor-in-chief: Revue Romanian des Sciences Techniques, 1984—; co-author: (book) Experimental Testing of Fluid Flow-Machines, 1959, Hydrodynamics of Bulbe Turbines and Bulbe Pump-Turbines, 1988; author: (books) Hydraulic Turbines, 1979, Cavitation, (2 vols.) 1984, 85; contbr. 240 articles to profl. jours. Recipient state prize State Coun., Romania, 1953, Aurel Vlaicu prize, Romanian Acad., 1961, Order of Scientific Merit, State Coun., 1976. Mem. Romanian Acad., Soc. Ordinami Acad. Scientific et Artium Europaea, N.Y. Acad. Scis. Greek Catholic. Avocation: classical music. Office: Tech Univ Timisoara, Bd Mihai Viteazul Nr 1, 1900 Timisoara/Timis Romania

ANTON, JOHN PETER, philosopher, educator; b. Canton, Ohio, Nov. 2, 1920; s. Peter C. and Christine (Giannopoulos) A.; m. Helen Vezos, Nov. 26, 1955; children: James, Christopher, Peter. BS, Columbia U., 1949, MA, 1950, PhD, 1954; PhD, LHD (hon.), U. Athens, 1992. Instr. Pace Coll., 1953-54; vis. lectr. U. N.Mex., 1954-55; asst. prof. U. Nebr., 1955-58; assoc. prof. Ohio Wesleyan U., 1958-62; prof. SUNY, Buffalo, 1962-67, assoc. dean grad. sch., prof., 1967-69; Fuller E. Callaway prof. Emory U., 1969-81, chmn. dept. philosophy, 1969-76; prof., provost New Coll., U. South Fla., Tampa, 1982-83, disting. prof. Greek philosophy and culture, 1983—, dir. Ctr. Greek Studies; Woods vis. prof. Mills Coll., 1981; vis. prof. Columbia U., 1966. Author: Aristotle's Theory of Contrariety, 1957, Science, Philosophy and Educational Tasks, 1966, Naturalism and Historical Understanding, 1967, Philosophical Essays, 1969, Essays in Ancient Greek Philosophy (5 vols.), 1971-92, Science and the Sciences in Plato, 1980, Critical Humanism as a Philosophy of Culture, 1981, Upward Panic: The Autobiography of Eva Palmer-Sikelianos, 1993, The Poetry and Poetics of C.P. Cavafy, 1995, Categories and Experience, 1996, Archetypal Principles and Hierarchies, 2000; co-editor (jour.) Diotima: editl. cons. Jour. History of Philosophy, 1968—, The Humanist, 1967—; mem. editl. bd. So. Jour. Philos., 1974—, Eidos, 1974—, Ancient Philosophy, 1979, Idealistic Studies, 1981, Philos. Inquiry, 1981; founding editor (jours.) Jour. of Neoplatonic Studies, 1991, Revue de Philosophie Ancienne, 1984—, Skepsis, 1997. Bd. govs. St. Lawrence Coll., 1989. With U.S. Army, 1946-47. Named Disting.scholar U. South Fla., 1985; recipient Gold medal Hon. Citizen of Samos, Greece, 1988. Mem. Am. Philos. Assn., Soc. Advancement of Am. Philosophy (founding mem.), Am. Philol. Assn., Am. Soc. Aesthetics (trustee 1973-76, 81-84), Ga. Philos. Soc. (v.p. 1972, pres. 1973), Internat. Soc. Neoplatonic Studies (chmn. exec. com., pres. 1997—), Soc. Ancient Greek Philosophy (sec., treas. 1973-81, pres. 1981-83), Modern Greek Studies Assn. (v.p. 1969—), Soc. Macedonian Studies (hon.), Acad. Athens (corr.), Internat. Assn. Greek Philos. (hon. pres. 1993), Soc. Internat. pour l'Etude de la Philosophie Mediévale, Parnassos Lit. Soc. (hon.), Phi Beta Kappa, Eta Sigma Phi, Phi Sigma Tau. Home: 10012 Oxford Chapel Dr Tampa FL 33647-2870 Office: U South Fla Dept Philosophy Tampa FL 33620

ANTON, RONALD DAVID, lawyer; b. Phila., Nov. 9, 1933; s. Emil T. Anton and Mary E. Bishara; m. Suzanne J. Winker, Aug. 19, 1976; 1 child, Ronald J. JD, U. Buffalo, 1958; LLM, U. Pa., 1959, Yale U., 1960. Bar: N.Y. 1959. Ptnr. Boniello, Anton, Conti & B., Niagara Falls, N.Y., 1960—; lectr. Univ. Buffalo (N.Y.) Law Sch., 1960-62; cons. N.Y. State Legis., Buffalo, Greater Buffalo (N.Y.) Devel. Found.; past pres. Niagara (N.Y.) County Legal Aid, 1966-68, Niagara Falls (N.Y.) Bar, 1968; past dist. gov. N.Y. State Trial Lawyers, 1984-88; moderator (tv show) The Law For You, N.Y., 1967. Author: Jesus, Saviour, 1992; contbr. articles to profl. jours. Rep. candidate N.Y. State Atty. Gen., 1990; trustee Stella Niagara Edn. Pk., Lewiston, N.Y., 1988—. Home: 175 White Tail Run Grand Island NY 14072-3223 Office: Boniello Anton Conti & B 770 Main St Niagara Falls NY 14301-1704

ANTONATOS, PANAGIOTIS (TAKIS), cardiologist; b. Athens, Greece, July 10, 1939; s. George and Zoe (Micailitsi) A.; m. Dawn Lillian Ahearne, Jan. 6, 1982; children: George, Thomas, Lucy-Katerine. MD, U. Athens, 1964, postgrad., 1972. Bd. cert. in Internal Medicine and Cardiology, Greece. Intern Naval Hosp., Greece, 1965-66; resident in medicine Mcpl. Hosp., Greece, 1967-69; resident in cardiology U. Athens, 1970-71; fellow in cardiology St. Luke's Hosp., Houston, 1973-74, Baylor U. Med. Ctr., Dallas, 1974-75; fellow in pediatric cardiology Good Samaritan Hosp., Phoenix, 1975-76; cons. Alexandra U. Hosp., Athens, 1978-86; dir., pres. A. Fleming Gen. Hosp., Athens, 1986—. Fellow Am. coll. Cardiology; mem. Hellenic Cardiol. Soc.

ANTONELLI, PIERLUIGI, pharmaceutical executive; b. Chieti, Italy, Sept. 14, 1966; s. Amerigo Antonelli and Elisabetta Di Carlo; m. Roberta Dima, Aug. 30, 1997; children: Andrea, Alessandro. Laurea in Bus. and Econs., L.U.I.S.S., Rome, 1989; MBA, Northwestern U., 1994. Owner Antonelli SpA, Chieti, 1990-92; engagement mgr. McKinsey & Co., Milan, Italy, 1994-98; dir. new initiatives Bristol Myers Squibb, Rome, 1999—. Bd. dirs. Villa Nazareth, Rome, 1994—. Noopolis scholar, 1992-94. Mem. Rotaract Club (founder). Avocations: basketball, tennis, theater, traveling. Fax: 39 06 5940156. E-mail: pierluigi.antonelli@bms.com. Office: Bristol Myers Squibb, Via V Maroso, 00142 Rome Italy

ANTONENKO, ALEXANDER NICHOLAS, researcher; b. Moldova, Russia, Feb. 20, 1954; arrived in Israel, 1997; s. Nicholas and Tatiana Ivanovna (Kushina) A.; m. Olga Grosheva, July 6, 1974; 1 child, Julia. Grad., Phys. Tech. Inst., Moscow, 1977. Rschr. Acad. Scis., Kishinev, Russia, 1977-89, Electro-Instrument Inst., Kishinev, 1989-96, AMT Ltd., Israel, 1997—. Contbr. articles to profl. jours.; inventor in field. Office: AMT Ltd, 1 Ha'atsmaut St, 40500 Eveu Yehuda Israel

ANTONI, THOMAS JOHAN, communications professional; b. Limhamn, Scania, Sweden, July 27, 1957; s. Arne Johan and Irene (Antoni) Persson; m. Annette Wanda Von Arnold, May 25, 1985; children: Anna, Carl, David, Astri, Hedvig, Gustaf. Student, Pildamm, Malmo, Sweden, 1976, U. Lund, 1980, Stella Adler Conservatory, 1981. actor Babettes Feast, 1987 (Academy award 1988). Avocations: art, hunting, music. Office: Antoni Comm, Slättåkra Gard, S-23199 Klagstorp Sweden

ANTONIADIS, IGNATIOS, physicist; b. Chios, Greece, Dec. 2, 1955; s. Efstratios and Catherine (Katoleon) A.; m. Efthymia Efthymiou, June 28, 1981; children: Alexis, Orpheus. Diploma in Math., U. Athens, 1977; DEA de Physique Theorique, U. Paris, 1978; These de 3rd Cycle, Ecole Normale Superieure, Paris, 1980; These d'Etat, Ecole Polytechnique, Paris, 1983. Attache rsch. Ctr. Nat. Rsch. Sci. (CNRS)/Ecole Polytechnique, Paris, 1982-86, charge rsch., 1986-92; dir. rsch. Ctr. Nat. Rsch. Sci. (CNRS) Ecole Polytechnique, Paris, 1992—, prof., 1997—; rsch. assoc. SLAC/Stanford U., Calif., 1983-86; staff mem. CERN, 2000—; fellow European Ctr. for Nuclear Rsch., Geneva, 1986-88; prof. Ecole Doctorale, Paris, 1994—; cons. Los Alamos (N.Mex.) Lab., 1992—; network coord. European Community, 1992—; vis. prof. UCLA, 1995-96. Recipient Scientific prize/physics Bodossaki Found., Greece, 1995; rsch. grantee CNRS/NSF, 1993, NATO, 1990. Mem. Soc. French Physics, N.Y. Acad. Scis. Office: CERN-TN, 1211 Geneve 23, Switzerland

ANTONIC, JAMES PAUL, international marketing consultant; b. Milw., Mar. 29, 1943; s. George Paul and Betti Ware (Littler) A.; m. Irene Robson, Dec. 26, 1970; 1 child, Glenn. BS in Psychology, U. Wis., 1964; MBA, Boston U., 1976. Owner JPA Supply and Warehouse Co., Milw., 1966-68; product mgr., market mgr. Delta Oil Products, Milw., 1968-74; v.p. internat. ops. Delta Oil Products, Brussels, 1974-76; pres. Internat. Market Devel. Group, Barrington, Ill., 1976-98; CEO Internat. Market Devel. Group, LLC, Ft. Myers, Fla., 1998—; bd. dirs. ASG LLC, Schaumburg, Ill.; lectr. Cast Metals Inst., Am. Mgmt. Assn., U.S. Dept. Commerce, Ga. World Congress Inst., various colls. Contbr. articles to profl. jours. With U.S. Army Combat Engrs., 1964-66. Fellow Anglo-Am. Acad.; mem. Licensing Execs. Soc., Internat. Trade Club Chgo., MIT Enterprise Forum, World Trade Assn., Japan Mgmt. Cons. Assn., Am. Foundrymen's Assn. (chair legis. task force), Oak Brook Hounds (pres.). Fax: 941-590-6061. E-mail: jamesantonic@msn.com. Home: 9111 Southmont Cv Apt 406 Fort Myers FL 33908-6298 Office: Ste 418 12730 New Brittany Blvd Fort Myers FL 33908-6632

ANTONÍN, VLADIMÍR, mycologist, researcher; b. Brno, Czechoslovakia, July 4, 1955; s. Vladimír and Anna (Špačková) A.; m. Jana Polešenská, June 30, 1978; children: Jiří, Jana. Masters, Masaryk U., Brno, 1979; PhD, Charles U., Prague, Czechoslovakia, 1991. Mycologist, rschr. Moravian Mus. Brno, 1979—. Recipient Young Rschr. award Lit. Found., Prague, 1989. Mem. Czech Sci. Soc. for Mycology (sci. sec. 1992-95, v.p. 1995—). Avocations: travel, tourism. E-mail: vantonin@mzm.cz. Office: Moravian Mus Brno, Zelny trh 6, CZ659 37 Brno Czech Republic

ANTONIO, ARTIGAS, intensive care physician, researcher; b. Barcelona, Spain, May 12, 1949; s. Artigas Vicente and Raventos Montserrat; m. Guix Roser; children: Roser, Jordi, Enric, Carlos, Joan, Marta, Sandra. Licentiat in medicine, U. Barcelona, 1973, MD, 1992, PhD, 1992, specialist in intensive care, 1982. Resident St. Paul Hosp., Barcelona, 1973-77, staff, 1977-80, clinic chief, 1980-88; chief of svc. Sabadell (Spain) Hosp., 1988—; assoc. prof. medicine Autonomous U. Barcelona, 1988-86, assoc. prof. med. physiology, 1989—; dir. emergency dept. Sabadell Hosp., 1988-93, dir. intensice care dept., 1997—; pres. 6th European Congr. Intensive Care. Editor: Adult Respiratory Distress Syndrome, 1992, The Splenclinic Circulation, 1995, Pulmonary Circulation, 1996, Acute Respiratory Failure, 1998, Circulation in Native and Artificial Kidneys, 1997, Coronary Circulation and Myocardial Ischemia, 2000. Chmn. Postgrad. Catalan Program, Barcelona, 1995, European ARDS Working Group, Grussels, 1986; mem. bd. com. European Consortium Critical Care, paris, 1995. Recipient rsch. grant Nat. Investigation Fund, 1992-96. Mem. Am. Thoracic Soc. (long-range com. 1993), Spanish Soc. Intensive Care Medicine (hon.), Catalan Soc. Intensive Care (pres. 1990-94), French Soc. Intensive Care (v.p. 1991-93), European soc. Intensive Care (founding mem.). Roman Catholic. Avocations: basketball, tennis, classical music. Office: Sabadell Hosp Intens Care, Parc Tauli s/n, 08208 Sabadell Barcel, Spain

ANTONIONI, MICHELANGELO, film director; b. Ferrara, Italy, Sept. 29, 1912; s. Carlo and Elisabetta Antonioni; m. Letizia Balboni, 1942 (div.); m. Enrica Fico, 1986. Cardent, Centro Sperimentale Cinematografia, Rome, 1942; diploma in econs., U. Bologna, Italy; D (hon.), U. Calif., Berkeley, 1993; LHD (hon.), La Sapienza U., Rome, 1993. Film critic, scriptwriter, 1936-40; with Italia libera, 1942; mem. editl. staff Cinema rev., 1942; film critic Corriere Padano, 1944-45, L'Italia Libera. Asst. dir.: Les visiteurs du soir; co-scriptwriter: Un pilota ritorna, I due foscari, Caccia tragica; dir.: (documentaries) Gente del Po (1943-47), 1947, N.U., Superstizione, L'amorosa menzogna, Cronaca di un amore, 1950, I vinte, 1952, La signora senza camelie, L'amore in città, 1953, Le amiche, 1955, Il grido, 1957, I am a camera, L'avventura, 1960 (Cannes Critics' award 1960), La notte, 1961 Silver Bear Berlin Film Festival 1961), L'Eclisse, 1962 (Cannes Internat. Film Festival Grand Prize), Il Deserto Rosso (The Red Desert), 1964 (Golden Lion 25th Venice Film Festival 1964), I tie volti, 1965, Blow-up, 1966 (Golden Palm Cannes Festival 1967, Best Dir. Nat. Soc. Film Critics), Zabriskie Point, 1970, Chung Kuo China, 1972, Professione: reporter, Il mistero di Oberwald, 1980, Identificazione di una donna, 1982 (Grand Prix Cannes 1982), Noto, mandorli, Vulcano, Stromboli, carnevale, 1992; co-dir: (with Wim Wenders) Par délà les nuages, 1994; exhbns. of pictures include Palazzo dei Diamanti, Ferrara, 1993, retrospective 25th Film Festival, Calcutta, 1994. Recipient Spl. award 35th Anniversary Cannes Film Festival, 1982, Golden Lion for entire body of work, Venice Film Festival, 1983, Maschera d'Oro for entire body of work, 1983, Prix Lumière, 1990, Cariddi d'Oro for entire body of work, Taormina, 1991, Prix Navicella, 1992, Nastro Speciale d'Argento, 1992, Felix career award, Berlin Film Festival, 1993, Nastro d'Argento career award, Rome, 1995, Acad. career award, 1995, Efebo d'Oro, 1995; named Knight Grand Cross of the Order of Merit of the Italian Republic, 1992, Comdr. Order of Arts and Letters, France, 1992, Légion d'Honneur, France, 1996. Avocations: ping-pong, tennis. Office: Via Fleming 111, 00191 Rome Italy

ANTONIOU, IOANNIS E., research scientist; b. Pireaus, Attica, Greece, Oct. 12, 1955; s. Antoniou Eusthatios I. and Maria I. Kolymbadi; m. Angelika G. Kallia, Oct. 10, 1980; children: Eusthatios, Orpheus, Rea. Degree in physics, U. Athens, Greece, 1980; PhD, U. Brussels, 1988. Rsch. fellow Ministry of Environ., Athens, 1982-83; from rsch. fellow to rschr. U. Brussels, 1983-92; sr. rschr. Internat. Solvay Inst., Brussels, 1982—, dep. dir., 1994—; vis. prof. U. Brussels, 1997—. Contbr. articles to profl. jours. Recipient De Donder prize Royal Acad., Belgium, 1991-93, Kapitza medal Russian Acad., Moscow, 1998; named prof. honoris causa Moscow U., 1998. Avocations: gymnastics, bicycling, walking. Office: Internat Solvay Inst Physic, Blvd du Triomphe CP 231, 1050 Brussels Belgium

ANTONOPOULOS, CONSTANTIN JOHN, philosophy educator; b. Athens, Greece, Sept. 24, 1945; s. John and Mary Antonopoulos; m. Chariclea Nellie Exarchou, July 30, 1970. BA in Greek and English Lit., U. Athens, 1972, BA in History and Archaeology, 1975; MPhil in Philosophy, U. Reading, Eng., 1979; PhD in Philosophy, U. Ioannina, Greece, 1984. Rsch. fellow Nat. Tech. U. of Athens, 1980-87, lectr. in philosophy, 1987-92, asst. prof., 1992-98, assoc. prof. with tenure, 1998—. Contbr. articles to profl. jours., chpts. to books. Home: Doxapatri Str 25, 11471 Athens Greece Office: Nat Tech U of Athens, Heroon Polytechniou Str 9, 15773 Athens Greece

ANTONOPOULOS, KIMON ANTONIOU, engineering educator; b. Athens, Greece, Dec. 1, 1951; s. Antonios and Irene (Diamantopoulos) A.; m. Mina Peraki, Sept. 18, 1980; children: Antonios, Yiannis. Diploma, Nat. Tech. U. Athens, 1974; MSc, U. London, 1975, diploma, 1976, PhD, 1979. Rsch. fellow Nat. Tech. U. Athens, 1980-82, lectr., 1982-87, asst. prof., 1987-92, assoc. prof., 1992-96, prof., 1996—, mem. various sci., adminstrn. and congress coms., 1987—, session chmn. internat. confs., 1987—; cons. engr., Athens, 1980-85; part-time prof. Nat. Air Force Acad., Athens, 1980-82; reviewer sci. jours., 1987—; sci. project assessor Ministry of Industry, European Union, Greece, 1987—. Author 6 books; contbr. more than 150 articles to profl. jours. Mem. ASHRAE, Internat. Solar Energy Soc., Greek Soc. Theoretical and Applied Mechanics, Internat. Assn. COMPLES, Internat. Soc. for Computational Methods in Engring., Tech. Chamber of Greece. Greek Orthodox. Avocation: music. Home: 78 Irinis St, 15341 AG Paraskevi Greece Office: Nat Tech U Athens, 9 Heroon Polytehniou, 15773 Zografou Athens, Greece

ANTONOPOULOU, CHRISTINA, psychology educator; b. Athens, Greece, July 14, 1940; d. Antonopoulos Charalambos and Anna Antonopoulou; m. Konstantine Kollaros, July 30, 1967 (div. July 1976); m. Panagiotis Moschos, May 2, 1988; children: Alexander, Xanadu. MA, New Sch. Univ., 1968, NYU, 1976; PhD, Southeastern U., 1984, NYU, 1987. Asst. Oswego Coll., N.Y., 1962-63; fgn. student advisor Queens Coll., N.Y., 1964-78; tchr. Degree Coll., Athens, 1977-82; sci. advisor Prime Min.'s Office, Athens, 1983-88; journalist TV 29, Athens, 1988-90; prof. U. Athens, 1988—, Police Acad., Athens, 1987—; sci. advisor WHO, 1989-90; advisor O.H.E., N.Y. and Greece, 1985-87. Author: (books) Educational System in Greece, 1976, Sociology of Sex Roles, 1988, Human Sexuality, 1988; contbr. rsch. articles to profl. jours. Elected mem. Coun. Europe, Athens and Strassburg, 1985. Grantee HEW, 1965, NATO, 1986. Mem. APA, Victimology Soc., Domestic Violence Inst. (pres.). Democrat Social Movement. Greek Orthodox. Avocations: theater, TV panel discussions. E-mail: cantonop@cc.uoa.gr. Home: 12 Iraklitoy St, Athens Greece Office: U Athens, 41 Acadimias St, Athens 10444, Greece

ANTONOV, IGOR NICKOLAEVICH, radiophysicist, researcher; b. Saratov, USSR, Sept. 17, 1954; s. Nickoly Ivanovich and Antonina Grigorievna (Panchenko) A.; m. Natalia Yurievna Shurigina, Oct. 8, 1977; children: Anton, Alexandra. Cert., Sch. 13, Saratov, USSR, 1972; Diploma in physics, U. Saratov, 1977. Scientific worker Poly. Inst., Saratov, USSR, 1977-81; head dept. design office, Electronics Inst. Acad. Scis., Saratov, Russia, 1981-92; asst. prof. Tech. U., Saratov, 1992—; dir. scientific-producing firm Ginfoec scientific dept. Tech. U., Saratov, Russia, 1996—. Contbr. articles to profl. jours.; patentee in field. Avocations: tourism, cooking. Home: Mezhdunarodnaya 18-17, 410052 Saratov Russia Office: U Saratov, 77 Politechnical Str, 410016 Saratov Russia

ANTONOVA, IRINA VENIAMINOVNA, physicist, researcher; b. Novosibirsk, Russia, June 26, 1957; d. Veniamin Vasilivich and Rosa Fedorovna (Teplova) Efimov; m. Vladimir Aleksandrovich Antonov, Feb. 23, 1979; children: Aleksandr, Elena. MSc, Tech. U., Novosibirsk, 1979; PhD, Inst. Semicondr. Physics, Novosibirsk, 1990. Asst. Inst. Solid State Chemistry, Novosibirsk, 1979-81; post-master Inst. Semicondr. Physics, 1981-85, sci. rschr., 1985-96, sr. rschr., 1996—. Contbg. author: Crystalline Defects, 1997; contbr. articles to sci. jours. and procs., including Physica B, NIM, Solid State Physics. Grantee Soros Found., 1992-94, Russian Found. Fundamental Rsch., 1996-97. Mem. Electrochem. Soc. Avocations: music, history. Home: Sirenevaja 37, 9, 630058 Novosibirsk Russia Office: Inst Semicondr Physics, Lavrentieva 13, 630090 Novosibirsk Russia

ANTONY, JEFF, architect; b. Trichur, India, June 8, 1956; s. Antony Francis and Treasa (Paul) Antony; m. Suby Joesph, Dec. 30, 1984; children: Kripa, Kriti. BArch, U. Kerala, India, 1977. Apprentice Johnson & Mustafa Architects, Madras, 1977-78; jr. architect Architectural Cons., India, 1979; asst. architect Anthony B. Almaida RIBA, Chartered Architects, Tanzania, East Africa, 1980-82; architect Nat. Estates & Design Co. Ltd., Tanzania, East Africa, 1982-84; architect & proprietor Atulya Architects & Assocs., Kerala, 1985—; examiner architecture course Kerala U., 1992. Editor (news bull.) Arch Window, 1996; prin. works include SOS Children's Village, Cochin, 1990 (selected South Asia Exhbn. 1991), Nav Jeevan Centre, Mumbai, 1992 (Round Table Outstanding Svc. award), Cochin Internat. Airport, Nedumbassery. Exec. mem. Papal Visit Rostrum Com., Trichur, India, 1986, Cath. Bishop House, Trichur, 1990—; bd. trustees Round Table India Charitable Cmty. Svce. Trust, Kottayam, India, 1996 (best area and nat. sec. award 1991, best chmn. award 1996). Recipient Vijayashree award Internat. Friendship Soc. India, 1992. Fellow Indian Inst. Architects, Indian Inst. Valuers; mem. Indian Inst. Architects, Indian Inst. Interior Designs, Indian Inst. Architects (Kerala chpt., exec. mem., editor), Mason (master), Rotary (Trichur Ctrl. chpt., co-convenor 1997). Roman Catholic. Avocations: music, reading, travel. Home: Dearborne Ave Rd, Trichur 680006, India Office: Atulya Architects & Assocs, IX/162 Vikas Mission Qutrs, Trichur 680 001, India

ANTONYUK, VOLODIMIR OLEKSANDROVITSH, scientific production executive; b. Kremenets, Ukraine, Apr. 18, 1955; s. Oleksandr Gerasimovits and Lydiya Yuchimivna (Simora) A.; m. Lydiya Tratsh-Lebyak; children: Lydiya, Rostislav. Degree in pharm. chemistry, State Med. Inst., Lviv, Ukraine, 1977; Cand.pharm.sci., Med. inst., Lviv, 1983. Pharm. chemist drug store, Kremenets, Ukraine, 1977-79; rschr. Med. Inst., Lviv, 1979-82, lectr., 1982-88; head sci. prodn. coop. Lectinotest, Lviv, 1988—; lectr. Med. Sch., Lviv, 1986-92; rschr. Palladin Inst. Biochem., Lviv, 1992-98. Contbr. articles to profl. jour.; patentee in field. Med. officer res. Soros grantee, 1993. Mem. Ukrainian Biochem. Soc. Avocations: gardening, mountain hiking, cooking. Home: B Chmelnitskogo Str 137/4, 290019 Lviv Ukraine Office: Sci Prodn Coop Lectinotest, Pekarska str 69, 290010 Lviv Ukraine

ANTOULAS, ATHANASIOS CONSTANTINE, mathematics educator; b. Athens, Greece, Sept. 6, 1950; came to U.S. 1982; s. Constantine A. and Mary C. (Galanou) A.; m. Silvia Stampfli, Aug. 1987. Diploma in elec. engring., Eidgenössische Tech., Zürich, Switzerland, 1975; diploma in math., Eidgenössische Tech., 1975, PhD, 1979. Engr. Rsch. Ctr. Nat. Def., Athens, 1979-80; rsch. fellow Eidgenössische Technische Hochschule, Zürich, 1981, lectr. in math. Inst. Applied Math., 1983—; prof. Rice U., Houston, 1982—; cons. Contraves Ltd., Zürich, 1984—; vis. fellow Australian Nat. U., Canberra; vis. prof. Kyoto (Japan) U., Tokyo Inst. Tech., U. Groningen. Editor-in-chief Sys. and Control Letters; mem. editl. bd. IEEE Trans. Automatic Control, Soc. Indsl. & Applied Math. Jour. Control and Optim. Linear Algebra & Applications; contbr. articles to profl. jours. Recipient Best Paper award AIAA, 1992; NSF, NASA, NATO grantee. Fellow IEEE, Japan Soc. Promotion Sci.; mem. Soc. Indsl. and Applied Math., Swiss Math. Soc., Swiss Electrotech. Soc. Mem. Eastern Orthodox Ch. E-mail: aca@rice.edu. Office: Rice U Dept Elec and Comp Eng 6100 Main St Houston TX 77005-1827

ANTOUN, ANNETTE AGNES, newspaper editor, publisher; b. Franklin, Pa., Mar. 7, 1927; d. Adrien Uriel and Charlotte Mary (McMullen) Adelman; m. Frederic George Antoun, July 19, 1947 (dec.); children: Frederic G., Gregory S., Lawrence J., Mark J. (dec.), Laureace A., Scott J., Jonathan M., Lisa A. Student, Allegheny Coll., Meadville, Pa. Founder, editor-pub. Paxton Herald, Harrisburg, Pa., 1960—; founder, owner Graphic Svcs., advt. and graphics, Harrisburg, 1972—; owner Comms. Sys. Design, 1978—; pres. Susquehanna Valley Assocs., Inc., 1978—; co-editor French Creek Patriot, cmty. newspaper, Cochranton, Pa., 1972. Mem. comms. com. Tri-County United Fund, 1973, mem. com. children's svcs., 1975-79; bd. dirs. Pa. Am. Lung Assn., 1973-98, treas., 1976, sec., 1979-80, v.p., 1980-81, treas., 1996-98; counselor to bd. Am. Lung Assn., 1989-90; bd. dirs. Harris Commn., 1975-79, Cath. Social Svc. Harrisburg, 1972-76; mem. extension planning com. YMCA, 1975-79; mem. bd. govs. Camp Curtin YMCA, 1980-85; mem. exec. bd. Lower Paxton Coalition Cmty. Groups, 1973-93; mem. comms. bd. Cath. Diocese Harrisburg, 1971-80; c. chmn. Dauphin County Ethics Com., 1979-81; chmn. bldg. com. Juvenile Detention Home, 1976-80; chmn. fund raising com. Greater Harrisburg Arts Coun., 1977-79; mem. Dauphin County bd. com. children and youth, 1982-85; vice chmn. Dauphin County Election Voting Machine Com., 1982—; mem. Tri-County Solid Waste Mgmt. Com., 1983-87; bd. dirs. Salvation Army Rehab. Svcs., 1992—, Capitol Pavilion Rehab., 1992—; mem. exec. com. spl. events United Negro Coll. Fund, 1993-98; spl. events chmn. Ctrl. Pa. UNCF, 1993-94, bd. dirs. H. John Heinz Ctr., 1994—; vice chmn. Millenium commn. City of Harrisburg, 1999—. Recipient Advocate award Paxton Area Jaycees, 1969, 73, citation Am. Legion Pa., 1971, 74, CAP, 1972, medallion Am. Legion Pa., 1972; award Am. Cancer Soc., 1969-89, March of Dimes award, 1969-89, AARP award, 1988, MADD award Hist. Preservation award, All Am. City Participation award, Nat. award Am. Lung Assn., 1992, Am. Legion REgional award, 1994, Pioneer award John Heinz Ctr., 1996, Cmty. Svc. award VFW, 1996, award for historic rehab. City Harrisburg, 1992, Cit of Harrisburg award, 1998, Gettysburg Monument Preservation award, 1998; numerous others. Mem. Am. Lung Assn. Pa. (treas. 1995-98), Internat. Platform Assn. Home: 4910 Earl Dr Harrisburg PA 17112-2123 Office: 101 Lincoln St Harrisburg PA 17112-2543

ANTOUN, ELIE, engineering executive; b. Kaduna, Nigeria, Aug. 22, 1956; d. Joseph and Olga A.; m. Mira Daboul, Dec. 27, 1980; children: Carmen, Rami. BS in Electrical Engring., U. Calif. Los Angeles, 1979, MS in Electrical Engring., 1980; MBA, Stanford U., 1989. Engr. AMI, Inc., Santa Clara, Calif., 1980-82, Xicor, Inc., Milpitas, Calif., 1982-84; engring. mgr. Xicor, Inc., Milpitas, 1984-87; dir. ops. HPL, Inc., Milpitas, 1990-92; GM Fin. LSI Logic, Tokyo, 1992-95, v.p.-gen. mgr., 1995-98; exec. v.p. consumer divsn. LSI Logic, Milpitas, 1998—. Avocations: basketball, reading, family. Fax: 408-433-6814. E-mail: elie@lsil.com. Home: 1890 Dry Creek Rd San Jose CA 95124-1005 Office: LSI Logic Corp 1551 Mccarthy Blvd Milpitas CA 95035-7451

ANTOUN, GAMAL GEORGE, agricultural researcher; b. Cairo, May 11, 1945; s. George Antoun Ibrahim and Yvon Fahmy Abd-El Malek; m. Neamat Guirguis Asaad, Jan. 11, 1976; 1 child, Mary. BSc in Agr., U. Cairo, 1965, MSc in Agr., 1972, PhD in Agr., 1978. Rsch. asst. Agrl. Rsch. Ctr., Giza, Egypt, 1966-72, asst. rschr., 1972-79, rschr., 1979-84, sr. rschr., 1984-89, chief rschr., 1989—, head agrl. microbiol. rsch., 1997—; cons. Undersec. Afforestation, Egypt, 1998—, Undersec. Soils and Water, Egypt, 1995—. Author: Foods and Nutrition, 1992. Scholar Danish Internat.

Devel. Agy., 1976, Agrl. Tech. Utilization & Transfer, U.S. AID, 1992, Nat. Agrl. Rsch. Project, U.S. AID, 1984. Mem. AAAS, Am. Soc. Microbiology. Coptic Orthodox. Avocations: reading, walking, praying, travel. Home: 5 Abd El Rahman Raqab St, 11351 Heliopolis Egypt Office: Soils Water and Environ, Rsch Inst Agrl Rsch Ctr, 12619 Giza Egypt

ANTOUN, MIKHAIL, medicinal chemistry and pharmacognosy educator; b. Khartoum, Sudan, Aug. 20, 1946; came to U.S., 1979; s. Daoud and Badia (Boulos) A.; m. Slavomira Kucerova, Sept. 14, 1973; children: Helena, David Emmanuel, Anna Maria. B in Pharm. with distinction, U. Khartoum, 1968; PhD, U. London, 1974. Asst. prof. pharm. U. Khartoum (Sudan), 1974-78, assoc. prof., 1978-81; sr. rsch. scientist Purdue U., West Lafayette, Ind., 1981-86; assoc. prof. medicinal pharmacognosy U. P.R. Sch. Pharm., San Juan, 1986-92, prof. medicinal pharmacognosy, faculty chairprof., dept. head, 1993—; vis. prof., rsch. assoc. Sch. Pharmacy & Pharm. Sci., West Lafayette, 1979-81. Contbr. articles to profl. jours. Sr. scholar U. Khartoum, 1968-69; teaching fellow U. London, 1969-73. Fellow Linnean Soc.; mem. Am. Chem. Soc., Am. Assn. Colls. Pharmacy, Am. Soc. Pharmacognosy, Sigma Xi. Avocations: piano, classical music, reading, chess, swimming.

ANTSYFEROVA, OLGA YURIEVNA, English language and literature educator; b. Ivanovo, USSR, Feb. 5, 1957; d. Yuri Andreevich and Kaleria (Alexeevna) A.; 1 child, Yuri. Student, Ivanovo State U., 1974-77; diploma with honors, Leningrad (USSR) State U., 1981; PhD, St. Petersburg (Russia) State U., 1989. Interpreter Helwan (Egypt) Iron and Steel Works, 1979-80; tchr. Beylorus State U., Minsk, USSR, 1982-84; tchr. Ivanovo State U., 1981-82, assoc. prof., sr. rsch. fellow, 1984—. Author: Tales of Henry James: From Apprenticeship toMaturity, 1998; editor: National Peculiarity of West European and American Literatures: Problem of Romanticism, 1995. Interpreter Ivanovo-Plano Sister City Orgn., 1991—. Fulbright grantee USIA, Irvine, Calif., 1999-2000, grantee, Newark, 1997; grantee RSS/Open Soc. Inst., Prague, Czech Republic, 1997-99. Mem. MLA, European Soc. for Study of English, Henry James Soc. Avocation: art, travel. E-mail: antsyf@ipn.ru. Home: Apt 5, 30/42 2nd Mezhevaya St, 153000 Ivanovo Russia Office: Ivanovo State Univ, ul Ermaka 39, 153025 Ivanovo Russia

ANTUNA DE ALAIZ, RAMIRO, diabetologist; b. Villada, Palencia, Spain, Mar. 4, 1954; s. Sabino Antuna Fernandez and Gloria de Alaiz Ruiz; m. Maria Antunia Duenas Rivera, Nov. 10, 1990; children: Maria, Ramiro. MD, Facultad de Medicine, Oviedo, 1978; Endocrinologist, Hosp. Cen. Asturias, 1984. Medical diplomate. Resident in endocrinology Hosp. Cen. Asturia, Spain, 1980-84; fellow in diabetes Jackson Meml. Hosp., Miami, 1984-85; med. dir. Clin. Diabetologia, Gijon, Spain, 1985—; diabetes cons. Hosp. Ctr. Medico Oviedo, Spain, 1985—. Contbr. articles to profl. jours. Mem. Spanish Diabetic Assn., Am. Diabetic Assn., European Assn. for Study of Diabetes (mem. psychol. aspect study group, Spain-diabetes edn. study group), Internat. Diabetes Fedn. Roman Catholic. Avocations: tennis, skiing, golf.

ANTUNES, ALEXANDER KOLSTAD, computational astrophysicist, web programmer; b. Balt., Apr. 5, 1967; s. Michael and Erica Margrethe (DiBietz) A.; m. Emma Kolstad, 1995; 1 child: Ivy Kolstad. BA, Boston U., 1989; MS, Pa. State U., 1992; postgrad., George Mason U., 1996—. Cert. systems analysis, 1987. Systems analyst Social Security Adminstrn., Balt., 1985-87; rsch. asst. Boston U., 1988-89; rsch., teaching asst. Pa. State U., 1989-92; mission scheduler Hughes STX/ISAS, Tokyo, 1992-94; XTE mission planner Hughes/STX Goddard Space Flight Ctr., Greenbelt, Md., 1994-96, Astro-E developer, 1997—; co-founder RPG Web Svcs., 1997—; speaker at annual meeting Japan Astronomical Soc., Tokyo, 1993; guest speaker elem. sch., Md., 1994—; v.p. Vantage Games, 1999—. Author: Miskatonic Univ., 1995; contbr. articles to profl. jours.; columnist Cryptych, 1992-95; editor Metagame, 1997-99; radio guest GT2K, 1999—. Convention organizer JIGG, Tokyo, 1993. Recipient Spl. Act Group award NASA, 1993, Braddock Recognition award Pa. State U., 1989-92, Senatorial scholarship U.S. Senate Office, 1985-89. Mem. Am. Astronomical Soc., Nat. Order of the Arrow (elected). Achievements include writing the Next generation of mission-independent scheduling software. Avocations: stage magic, medievalism, swimming. Home: 8302 Cypress St Laurel MD 20707-5027 Office: Goddard Space Flight Ctr Code 664 Greenbelt MD 20770

ANTUNES, DANIEL L., sales consultant, camera operator; b. Portugal, June 24, 1971; came to U.S., 1986; s. Jose A. and Judite C. Antunes. AA, Union County Coll., 1991; BA, N.J. City U., 1994. Cameraman RTP-USA TV, Newark, 1988-90, tech. dir. news, 1990-93; actor, editor NBP Prodns., Lisbon, 1993; cameraman, robotics CN8, Union, N.J., 1997—; sales rep. Bell Atlantic Mobile, Paramus, N.J., 1994—. Avocations: snow boarding, tennis, soccer, online stock trading, video productions. E-mail: dantunes@aol.com. Home: 9 Radley St Kearny NJ 07032-5915

ANTUNES, JOAO MANUEL, lawyer; b. Porto, Portugal, Mar. 14, 1958; s. Manuel and Maria de Lourdes (Lima) A.; m. Maria de Nazare Sire Mexia Alves, Sept. 18, 1993; children: Manuel Maria, Antonio Maria. B in Law, U. Catolica, Lisbon, 1986, postgrad. diploma, 1987. Legal cons. Jalles & Vasconcelos, Lisbon, 1985; legal assessor Sogrape Vinhos de Portugal, S.A., Porto, 1986—, sec., 1997—; sec. A.A. Ferreira, S.A., Porto, 1997—, Forrester & Ca, S.A., Porto, 1997—, Sogrape Investimentos, SGPS, S.A., 1997—; del. FAO, Santiago, Chile; dir. Commissao de Viticultura da Regiao dos Vinhos Verdes, Porto, 1994-96, Andovi-Associacao Nacional das Denominacoes de Origem, Porto, 1995-97; v.p. Conselho Europeu Profl. do Vinho, 1996. With Portuguese Air Force, 1987-88. Mem. Internat. Wine Law Assn. Home: Vasco da Gama, 831 Miramar, 4405-149 Arcozelo Vng Portugal Office: Sogrape Vinos de Portugal, Rua 5 de Outubro 558, 4431-852 Avintes Portugal

ANTUNES, JOSÉ VIEIRA, research scientist, educator; b. Sacavém, Lisbon, Portugal, July 14, 1954; s. Diogo José Antunes and Maria Antunes Vieira. Grad. in mech. engring., Inst. Superior Tecnico, Lisbon, Portugal, 1977; MS, Paris U., 1983, PhD, 1986. Lectr. Inst. Superior Tecnico, Lisbon, Portugal, 1978-82; asst. rschr. Lab. Nat. Engenharia e Tecnologia Insl., Sacavém, Lisbon, 1982-86; rschr. Lab. Nat. Engenharia e Tecnologia Insl., Sacavém, 1986-95; sr. rschr. Inst. Tecnologia Nuc., Sacavém, 1995—, head structural mechanics lab., 1995-96, head applied dynamics lab., 1996—; vis. rschr. CEA, Saclay, France, 1988—; invited prof. Coimbra (Portugal) U., 1992-93, ANSO, Lisbon, 1995—. Contbr. over 50 articles to profl. jours. Mem. ASME, Soc. Portuguesa Acustica, Soc. Francaise d'Acoustique. Avocations: music, photography. Office: ITN/ADL, Estrada Nacional 10, 2686 Sacavém Codex, Portugal

ANTWEILER, DENNIS FRANCIS, mechanical engineer; b. Cleve., June 16, 1949; s. Ralph Joseph and Marie Leola (Freeman) A.; m. Karen Lisa Porter, Feb. 27, 1971 (div. Feb. 2000); children: Christopher J., Brandon D., Jamie A. BSME, U. Calif. Berkeley, 1972. Mech. engr. Altare Sys., Inc., Oakland, Calif., 1973; controls and instrumentation engr. Exxon, USA Corp., Benicia, Calif., 1973-78, Hess Oil Virgin Islands Corp., St. Croix, V.I., 1978-79, Union Camp Corp., Savannah, Ga., 1979-81; mgr. ops. Stanford (Calif.) U., 1981-86; v.p. Cascade Controls, Inc., Sunnyvale, Calif., 1986—. Mem. ASME, Instrument Soc. Am. Avocation: windsurfing. Office: Cascade Controls Inc 1132 N 7th St San Jose CA 95112-4427

ANUKAM, KINGSLEY CHIDOZIE, lab administrator, pharmacologist, microbiologist; b. Port-Harecourt, Nigeria, July 31, 1966; s. Boniface Nneji and Loveth Akuba (Akezi) A. BSc in Lab. Medicine, U. Calabar, Nigeria, 1991; MSc in Pharm., U. Benin, Nigeria, 1996; M Health Planning and Mgmt., U. Benin, 2000. Mng. dir. Chidak Med. Diagnostic Lab., Benin, Nigeria, 1996—; lab. scientist Aladinma Hosp., Oweeri, Nigeria, 1993-95. Nat. Merit scholar, Nigeria, 1992; postgrad. scholar Fed. Republic Nigeria U. Benin, 1995. Mem. Am. Assn. Reproductive Health Practitioners, Am. Acad. Microbiologists, Inst. Med. Lab. Scientist Nigeria, Am. Soc. Microbiology, Nigerian Soc. Microbiology. Mem. Anglican Ch. Avocations: writing, reading, playing piano, traveling, research. Home: No 13 Umunjam Mbieri Owerri, PO Box 45, Mbieri-Owerri Imo, Nigeria Office: Chidak Med Diagnostic Lab, 200 MM Way Benin City, Benin Edo, Nigeria

ANULOV, OLEG VYACHESLAV, biochemist, researcher; b. Moscow, Nov. 20, 1969; s. Vyacheslav Iakov and Olga Tichon (Buchareva) A. MD, Moscow State Pedagogical U., 1991. Diplomate in biology and pedagogy. Rsch. scientist Inst. Molecular Genetics, Russian Acad. Scis., Moscow, 1991-93, A.N. Bach Inst. Biochemistry, Russian Acad. Scis., Moscow, 1993—. Mem. N.Y. Acad. Scis., Russian Soc. Plant Physiology. Mem. Russian Ch. of the Nazarene. Avocations: walking, bicycling, communicating via Internet. Home: Vyedenskogo 10-2-85, 117342 Moscow Russia Office: AN Bach Inst Biochemistry, Pr Leninsky 33, 117071 Moscow Russia

ANUMAKONDA, VARADA RAJULU, physicist, educator; b. Nellore, A.P., India, July 3, 1950; s. Rama Das and Subba Ratnamma (Sudha) A.; m. Urmila Devi Battina, May 18, 1979; children: A. Sunil, A. Sandeep. BSc, Venkatagiri Raja's Coll., Nellore, India, 1970; MSc, Sri Venkateswara U., Tirupati, India, 1972, PhD, 1982. Lectr. Sri Krishnadevaraya U., Anantapur, India, 1977-85; reader Sri Krishnadevaraya U., Anantapur, 1985-93, prof., 1993—; dept. head Sri Krishnadevaraya U., Anantapur, 1985-89, chmn. 1992-95. Contbr. over 80 articles to profl. jours. Active in environ. protection. Rsch. fellow Univ. Commn., New Delhi, India, 1993, Vis. fellow Indian Sci. Acad., New Delhi, 1995, India-Nepal Found. fellow, 1996, Third World Acad. Scis. South-South fellow ICTP, Trieste, Italy, 2000. Mem. Indian Soc. for Tech. Edn. (life), Ultrasonic Soc. India (life), Indian Assn. for Physics Tchrs. (life), Internat. Ctr. for Theoretical Physics. Avocations: sports, photography, music, book reading, travel. Home: Sri Krishnadevaraya U Qtrs, B 31, SV Puram AP515003, India Office: Sri Krishnadevaraya U, Dept Polymer Sci, Anantapur AP515003, India

ANUSZKIEWICZ, RICHARD JOSEPH, artist; b. Erie, Pa., May 23, 1930; s. Adam Jacob and Victoria (Jankowski) A.; m. Sarah Feeney, Nov. 26, 1960; children: Adam John, Stephanie, Christine. B.F.A., Cleve. Inst. Art, 1953; M.F.A., Yale U., 1955; B.S. in Edn., Kent State U., 1956. One-man shows at, Butler Art Inst., Youngstown, Ohio, 1955, The Contempories, N.Y.C., 1960, 61, 63, Sidney Janis Gallery, N.Y.C., 1965-67, Dartmouth Coll., 1967, Cleve. Mus. Art, 1967, Kent State U., 1968, Andrew Crispo Gallery, N.Y.C., 1975, 77, La Jolla (Calif.) Mus. Contemporary Art, 1976, Univ. Art Mus., Berkeley, Calif., 1977, Columbus (Ohio) Gallery of Fine Arts, 1977, Charles Foley Gallery, Columbus, 1982, Graham Modern, N.Y.C., 1984, Heckscher Mus., Huntington, N.Y., 1984, Schweyer-Galdo Galleries, Pontiac, Mich., 1985, Tampa (Fla.) Mus., 1986, Richard Green Gallery, N.Y.C., 1987, Galleria Sagittaria, Pordenone, Italy, 1988, Charles Foley Gallery, Columbus, 1988, Galleie Civiche D'Arte Moderna, Ferrara, Italy, 1989, Newark Mus., 1990, Maruzen Co., Ltd., Tokyo, 1990, 91, Abante Fine Art, Portland, Oreg., 1992, Ctr. fro Arts, Vero Beach, Fla., 1993, others; exhibited in group shows at, Mus. Modern Art, 1960-61, 63, 65, U. Ill., 1961, NYU, 1961, Pa. Acad. Design, 1962, Whitney Mus. Am. Art, 1962, 63-64, 70, 71, Inst. Contemporary Arts, Boston, 1962, Columbus (Ohio) Gallery Fine Arts, 1962, City Art Mus., St. Louis, 1962, Munson-Williams-Proctor Inst., Utica, N.Y., 1962, Tweed Gallery U. Minn., 1962, Silvermine (Conn.) Guild Artists, 1962, 63, Atheneum Sch., Helsinki, Finland, 1962, Mus. Modern Art, Sarasota, Fla., 1962, J.B. Speed Art Mus., Louisville, 1962, Meml. Art Gallery, Rochester, N.Y., 1962, Allentown (Pa.) Art Mus., 1963, Krannert (Ill.) Art Mus., 1963, De Cordova Mus., Lincoln, Mass., 1963, Washington Gallery Modern Art, 1963, U. Mich. Mus. Art, 1964, Sidney Janis Gallery, N.Y.C., 1964, 65, Art Inst., Chgo., 1964, 71, Tate Gallery, London, 1964, Far Gallery, 1964, Carnegie Inst., Pitts., 1964, Corcoran Gallery Art, Washington, 1965, Art Fair Cologne, Germany, 1967, Larry Aldrich Mus., Ridgefield, Conn., 1968, 71, Hopkins Center Art Galleries Dartmouth Coll., Hanover, N.H., 1969, Denver Art Mus., 1969, Va. Mus. Fine Arts, Richmond, 1970, Ind. State U., Terre Haute, 1970, Masur Modern Art, Monroe, La., 1970, Birmingham (Ala.) Mus., 1971, Whitney Mus. Am. Art, N.Y.C., 1972, Hirshhorn Mus. and Sculpture Garden, N.Y.C., 1974, Bklyn. Mus., 1977, Albright-Knox Gallery, Buffalo, 1979, Met. Mus. Art, N.Y.C., 1982, Museo de Arts Moderno, Ciudad Bolivar, Venezuela, 1984, Tel Aviv Mus., 1986, Paris-New York-Kent Gallery, Kent, Conn., 1987, Guggenheim Mus., N.Y.C., 1987-88, Marilyn Pearl Gallery, N.Y.C., 1988, James A. Michener Arts Ctr. Bucks County, Doylestown, Pa., 1988, Centre d'Art Contempora, Geneva, 1989, Provincaal Mus., Hasselt, Belgium, Ctr. d'Art en Sante Monica, Barcelona, Spain, 1989, Galleri Civiche D'Arte Moderna, 1989, Samuel P. Harn Mus. Art, Gainesville, Fla., 1990, 92, DeCordova Mus., Lincoln, Mass., 1991, Nat. Gallery Art, Washington, 1991, Cummer Gallery Art, Jacksonville, Fla., 1992, Harmon Meek Gallery, Naples, Fla., 1993, Nat. Acad. Design, Washington, 1993, N.J. State Mus., Trenton, 1994, others; represented in permanent collections, Mus. Modern Art, Whitney Mus. Am. Art, Cleve. Mus. Art, Corcoran Gallery Art, Allentown Art Mus., Albright-Knox Art Gallery, Butler Art Inst., Akron (Ohio) Art Inst., Yale Art Gallery, Chgo. Art Inst., Larry Aldrich Mus., Ridgefield, Conn., Fogg Art Mus. of Harvard U., Hirshhorn Mus. and Sculpture Garden, artist-in-residence, Dartmouth Coll., 1967, U. Wis., 1968, Cornell U., 1968, Kent State U., 1968; Contbr. articles to profl. jours. Home and Office: 76 Chestnut St Englewood NJ 07631-3045

ANUTA, MICHAEL JOSEPH, lawyer; b. Pound, Wis., Feb. 4, 1901; s. Michael Anuta and Charlotte Zudnochowsky; m. Marianne M. Strelec; children: Mary Hope Milidonis, Nancy Ellen Beauchamp, Janet Grace Dalquist, Michael John, Karl Frederick. LLB, LaSalle Extension U., 1956; LLD (hon.), Alma Coll., 1960; BS (hon.), San Vicinte De Paul, Maracaibo, Venezuela, 1965. Bar: Mich. 1929, U.S. Supreme Ct. 1932, U.S. Dist. Ct. Mich., U.S. Dist. Ct. Wis., Bar of Interstate Commerce Commn. Traffic mgr. M&M Traffic Assn., Menominee, Mich., 1938-48; pros. atty. Menominee County, Menominee, 1938-48; mcpl. judge City of Menominee, 1958-68; reserve judge Menominee, 1929—. Author: East Prussians from Russia, 1979, Ships of our Ancestors, 1983, History of Rotary Clubs in Wisconsin-Michigan, 1993, Anuta Heritage Register, 1993. Dir., v.p. Mich. Children's Aid Soc.; active Boy Scouts Am., 1945—; moderator Synod Presbyn. Ch. Mich., 1953; chmn. Menominee County Def. Council, WWII, 1953. Lt. col. CAP, Mich. Recipient Silver Beaver award Boy Scouts Am., 1945, Silver Antelope, 1967, Disting. Svc. award community svc. Radio Sta. WAGN, 1963, Disting. citation, Govt. Legislature of Mich., 1989; named Man Yr. Menominee Area C. of C., 1971. Mem. ABA, State Bar Mich., Menominee County Bar Assn., Mich. Prosecuting Attys. Assn. (pres. 1945), Menominee County Hist. Soc. (pres. 1967-74, pres. emeritus), Am. Hist. Socs. Germans from Russia (dir. 1978-81), Hist. Soc. Mich. (dir. 1972-78, award merit 1980, Charles Follow award 1983), Am. Arbitrators Assn., Panel Arbitrators Res. Mich. Judge, Rotary (gov. dist. 1963-64, pres. 1934-35), Shriners, Masons (33 degree). Republican. Avocations: pilot, amateur radio. Home and Office: # 105 1200 Northland Terrace Ln Marinette WI 54143-4193

ANWAR, CHAUDHRY MUHAMMAD, fertilizer plant administrator; b. Multan, Pakistan, June 8, 1954; s. Chaudhry Rahmat and Fazulunnisa Ali; m. Shaheen Anwar, May 7, 1982; children: Shazia, Ikram, Inam, Mehwish. BSME, U. Engring. & Tech., Lahore, Pakistan, 1976. Trainee engr. Karachi Nuclear Power Plant, Pakistan, 1977-78; mech. engr. Water & Power Devel. Authority, Multan, Pakistan, 1978-80, Ministry of Electricity & Water, Shauiba, Kuwait, 1980-90; machinery sec. D.H. Chemical, Lahore, Pakistan, 1991-93; sr. engr. Fauji Fertilizer Co. Ltd., Sadiqabad, Pakistan, 1993-96, sect. head, 1996—. Mem. ASME.

ANWAR, HABIB-OLLAH, civil engineering, consultant; b. Tehran, Iran, Mar. 21, 1927; arrived in Eng., 1960; s. Yaaghub and Afsar (Vaghar) A. Diploma in engring., U. Tehran, 1949, U. Stuttgart, Germany, 1951; D of Engring., U. Karlsruhe, Germany, 1955. Asst. prof. U. Karlsruhe, 1954-56; rsch. officer Versuchsanstalt Firma J.M. Voith, Heidenheim, Germany, 1956-59; postdoctoral rsch. fellow Imperial Coll., London, 1960, Dept. Sci. and Indsl. Rsch., Wallingford, Eng., 1961-64; sr. sci. officer Hydraulics Rsch. Sta., Wallingford, 1964-68; prin. sci. officer Hydraylics Rsch. Sta., Wallingford, 1968-86, sr. cons., 1986-89; sr. cons. UN Devel. Program, N.Y.C., 1989-90; prin. cons. Ministry of Overseas Devel., London, 1974-78; cons. to consulting engrs. Pay Kav, Tehran, 1997—. Contbr. over 50 articles to sci. publs. Mem. ASCE (reviewer 1983—), N.Y. Acad. Scis. Office: Pay Kav, Bahar shiraz Ave No 4, Tehran 15649, Iran

ANWER, JAWAD QURESHI, computer analyst; b. Lahore, Pakistan, Nov. 1, 1968; s. Javed Anwer Qureshi and Fukhanda Javed; m. Sadia Jawad, MAy 4, 1990; children: Mutahira, Moazzama, Muzzafar. BSc, MAO Coll., Lahore, 1986; MSC, Quaid-e-Azam, Islamabad, Pakistan, 1989. System analyst Lahore Stock Exch., 1990-95; CEO A. Brown & Co., Singapore, 1995-97, J.S. Computers, Lahore, Singapore, 1997—. Author: Hands on Computers, 19997. Avocations: volunteering, judo, karate, books. Home: 271-16-B1, Twp Lahore Punjab, India

ANYANWU, CHUKWUKRE, alcohol and drug abuse facility administrator; b. Ogbor-Ugiri, Nigeria, Apr. 14, 1943; came to U.S., 1963; s. Peter Ebo and Eunice Ikwuaha (Madu) A.; m. Ngozi G. Nwaike, Jan. 10, 1980; children: Okechukwu-Pat, Adaku Cathy, Ikechukwu-Uzo, Uremegbulem, Kingsley-Ugo, Ucheckukwu. BS in Biology and Chemistry, St. Joseph's Coll., 1971; MS in Biochemistry, Fairleigh Dickenson U., 1972; postgrad., Temple U., 1979; MD, Cetec U., Dominican Republic, 1981. Internationally cert. alcohol and other drug counselor. Postdoctorate Temple Hosp.; diplomatic envoy Nigeria, 1973-75; extern various hosps., Phila. area, 1977-79; obstetrician-gynecologist, cons. Lagos U. Teaching Hosp., Nigeria, 1983-84; cons. psychiatry St. Mary's Hosp., Phila., 1981-82; rsch. nuclear medicine Temple U. Hosp., Phila., 1980-81; chmn. A-B Assocs. Inc., Phila., 1970—; chief exec. officer, owner, founder A-B Assocs., Inc., Phila., 1989—; virolog rsch. A-B Assocs. Inc., Phila., 1979-82, owner, chief exec. officer, dir.; mem. staff dept. of psychiatry JFK Mental Health/Retardation, Phila., 1985-88; mem. staff dept. of drug and alcohol addiction Giuffré Med. Ctr., 1988-89; counselor in psychiatry Misericordia Hosp., Phila., 1987-88; mem. staff addiction svcs. Guiffre Med. Ctr., Phila., 1988—; founder, chief exec. officer AB Assocs. Am. Beats Addiction, Inc., Phila., 1989—; paper rev. cons. NIH, Alcohol, Drug Abuse and Mental Health Adminstrn.; mem. com. peer rev. Dept. HHS, USPHS, NIH; mem. healthy start-reduction of infant mortality Pub. Policy Phila. Dept. Pub. Health; panelist Phila. Empowerment Zone for HealthCare Providers. Author numerous poems; contbr. articles profl. jours. Senate candidate Imo State Govt., Nigeria, 1983; mem. free standing steering com, pub. policy com. and providers com. Health Start Initiative-Phila. Dept. Pub. Health, vice chmn. programs, federally funded programs for maternal infant care; Olympian athlete competing in pole vault, 1500 meters and 400 meter hurdles, Mex., 1968; bd. dirs. March of Dimes Birth Defects Found.; mem. adv. bd. Mayor's Office of Cmty. Svcs., City of Phila., 1994—; founder African Congress, 1995, CHMN.; founder State Our Family Unity, 1999; ; rep. Area D., Phila.; treas. Phila. Health Consortium; candidate for City Coun., City of Phila., 1999; candidate city coun. City of Phila., 1999. First African immigrant of 20th century to run for City Council-at-Large, Phila., 1999. Mem. AAAS, Am. Coll. Healthcare Execs., Pa. Cert. Addiction Counselors, Orgn. Nigerian Profs. USA (chmn. jud. com.), Fedn. Police Law Enforcement, Phila. Fraternal Order of Police, Interagy. Coun. Homeless. Democrat. Roman Catholic. Office: America Beats Addiction Inc PO Box 38127 Philadelphia PA 19140-0127

ANYANWU, VICTOR O(NYE), criminologist, political scientist; b. Mbano, Imo, Nigeria, Jan. 5, 1967; came to the U.S., 1987; s. George A. Aguguesi and Catherine E. Anyanwu; m. Cathryn L. Mosley, June 2, 1990 (div. May 1996); m. Assumpta C. Ohanaja, June 27, 1996; children: Emmanuel, Janice, Michelle. BS in Criminal Justice, Jackson State U., 1991, MA in Sociology, 1993, PhD in Pub. Adminstrn., 1998. Police officer Nigerian Police Force, 1982-87; rsch. analyst Jackson (Miss.) Pub. Sch. Dist., 1993-94; rsch. evaluator Jackson State U., 1994-95, rsch. cons., 1995-96; criminal justice instr. Durham (N.C.) Tech. C.C., 1998; adj. prof. N.C. Ctrl. U., Durham, 1998; computer ops. analyst Electronic Data Sys., Birmingham, Ala., 1999—; auditor, newsletter editor Nigerian Progressive Union, Jackson, 1993-98. Advisor Nigerian Peoples Party, 1994. Mem. ASPA, Conf. Minority Pub. Adminstrs., Toastmasters Club (chairperson 1994), Alpha Kappa Delta. Democrat. Avocations: soccer, swimming, reading, biking. E-mail: victor.anyanwu@bridge.bellsouth.com. Home: 922 Aspen Run Birmingham AL 35209-3018

AOKI, ERICA, intellectual property attorney; b. Sao Paulo, Brazil, Dec. 11, 1962; d. Ohiko and Luiza (Takeda) A. B in Laws, Catholic U., 1985; LLM, Seijo U., 1991, George Washington U., 1995. Fgn. atty. Hashidate Law Office, Tokyo, 1990-92; outside counsel Dorsey & Whitney, Washington, 1994-95; ptnr., head intellectual property dept. Tozzini, Freire, Teixeira & Silva, Sao Paulo, 1996—.

AOKI, HIDEO, neurosurgeon; b. Ashiya, Hyogo-Ken, Japan, Dec. 25, 1925; s. Keiju and Fuyo (Mashiyama) A.; m. Michiko Sugita, Nov. 6, 1957; children: Mioko, Hiroki. MD, Kyoto U., Japan, 1948. Lectr. Yamaguchi Med. Coll., Ube, Japan, 1954-59, asst. prof., 1959-69; dir. neurosurgery Kokura Kinen Hosp., Kitakyushu, Japan, 1969-72; prof. neurosurgery Yamaguchi U. Med. Sch., 1972-89, prof. emeritus, 1989—; adv. Tokuyama Ishikai Hosp., Japan, 1989-94, hon. dir., 1995—; dean of student office Yamaguchi University, 1987-89. Mem. Japan Neurosurgical Soc. (diplomate), Japanese Soc. Clin. Surgery, Japanese Soc. Stroke. Home: 2-22-12 Onda-Cho, Ube 755, Japan Office: Tokuyama Ishikai Hosp, 10-1 Keiman-Cho, Tokuyama 745, Japan

AOKI, HITOSHI, engineering consultant; b. Yokohama, Japan, Oct. 9, 1959; s. Atsushi and Yasue (Nanjou) A.; m. Yumiko Kogawa, Feb. 22, 1987; 1 child, Kent. BSEE, Musashi Inst. Tech., Tokyo, 1983; PhD, Tokyo Inst. Tech., Tokyo, 2000. Sys. engr. Yokogawa Hewlett-Packard Ltd., Tokyo, 1983-85, sales engr., 1985-87, mktg. engr., 1987-90; R&D engr. Hewlett-Packard Co., Santa Clara, Calif., 1990-93; mem. rsch. staff Hewlett-Packard Labs., Palo Alto, Calif., 1993-96; chief cons. Agilent Techs., Tokyo, 1996—; instr. U. Calif., Berkeley, 1994; lectr. Stanford (Calif.) U., 1995; cons. Mitsubishi Electric, Itami, 1996, Nippon Telephone Telegraph Ltd., Atsugi, 1996, Matsushita Electric, 1997, Toshiba, 1997. Author: FET Modeling, 1998; inventor in field. Mem. IEEE (sr. mem.), Inst. Electronics, Info. and Comm. Engrs., Soc. Info. Display Inc. Avocations: shopping, hiking, PC/MAC computing. E-mail: usatech@mail.at-m.or.jp. and haoki@agilent.com. Fax: 81 426-56-7825. Home: 1-29-9 Commore Shiotsu, Uenohara Kita-Tsuru-Gun 409-0126, Japan Office: Agilent Tech Japan Ltd, 9-1 Takakura-cho, Hachioji 192-8510, Japan

AOKI, ICHIRO, theoretical biophysics, systems science educator; b. Takefu, Fukui-ken, Japan, Sept. 15, 1935; s. Shoichi and Fumiko (Yamazaki) A.; m. Atsuko Ookawara, Dec. 5, 1970; children: Kyoko, Keiko. BS, Kyoto (Japan) U., 1958, MS, 1960, DSc, 1988. Assoc. prof. theoretical biophysics Osaka Med. Coll., Takatsuki, Japan, 1965-95; prof. systems sci. Shizuoka U., Hamamatsu, Japan, 1995-99. Contbr. articles to profl. jours. Grantee Yukawa Meml. Found., 1963-65, Japan Soc. for Promotion Sci., 1986-87, 88. Mem. N.Y. Acad. Scis., Internat. Soc. Ecol. Modelling (editl. bd. 1989—), Soc. Math. Biology, Internat. Assn. Ecology, Internat. Soc. for Ecol. Econs., Internat. Soc. for the Sys. Scis. Home: 10-604 Ginkakujimae-cho, Sakyo, Kyoto 606-8407, Japan

AOKI, REIKO, Japanese linguist; b. Nara City, Japan, Oct. 19, 1926; s. Shigenori and Fumi (Kanomata) A. BA, Tokyo U., 1951, PhD, 1994. Instr. Kyoritsu Women's Jr. Coll., Tokyo, 1956-59, assoc. prof., 1959-65; assoc. prof. Seikei U., Tokyo, 1965-70, prof., 1970-95, hon. prof., 1995—; lectr. Ochanomizu U., Tokyo, 1970-72, 73-82, 83-89, Tokyo U., 1982-84; committeeman Seikei U. Libr., Tokyo, 1949, 50, 53, 58, 59, 60, 61; chmn. dept. Japanese Lit. and Lang., Seikei U., 1979-82. Author: A Constructional Analysis of the Modern Japanese Particle 'Wa', 1992; compiler: A Concordance to 'Hojoki', 1965. Mem. Soc. for Study of Japanese Lang. (editor 1966-70), coun. 1976—), Soc. for Rsch. in Kunten Lang., Math. Linguistic Soc. Japan. Avocations: woodcut printing, gardening, sewing, swimming, chorus. Home: 2-8-39 Shimizugaoka Fuchu, Tokyo 1830015, Japan

AOKI, REIKO THERESE, history educator; b. Yokohama, Japan, Jan. 20, 1935; d. Izuro and Hisa (Kinosita) A. BA, U. Sacred Heart, Tokyo, 1957; MA, Georgetown U., 1963. From lectr. to assoc. prof. U. Sacred Heart, 1961-82, prof., 1983—; dean U. Sacred Heart, Tokyo, 1997—. Author: The West, The Real Feature of America, 1975, (with others) The Regions of the USA (USA Guide 2), 1992; translator (with others) The Free and the Brave (H. Graff), 1982, The Angry West (R.D. Lamm and M. McCarthy), 2000. Mem. Nat. Coun. UNESCO, 1989-96; Japanese alt. rep. to 47th and 48th sessions Gen. Assembly UN, N.Y., 1992, 93; mem. nat. coun. overseas migration Ministry Fgn. Affairs., 1993—. Mem. Japanese Assn. Univ. Women (v.p. 1986-90, pres. 1992-96), Japanese Assn. Am. Studies (mem. editl. bd. 1977-83, assoc. editor 1981-83, bd. dirs. 1977-96, mem. exec. bd. 1990-94, councillor 1996-98, auditor 1998—), Internat. Fedn. Univ. Women (v.p. 1995—). Roman Catholic.

AOKI, SUMIO, patent lawyer; b. Iizaka, Fukushima, Japan, Feb. 17, 1960; s. Yoshimitsu Tanaka and Masako Aoki; m. Masako Udagawa, Sept. 6, 1992; 1 child, Junma. BD, Osaka U., Toyonaka, Japan, 1986. Tech. advisor Osaka Patent Office, Tachikawa, Japan, 1986-89; patent atty. Sugimura Agy., Tokyo, 1989—. Mem. Internat. Assn. Protection Intellectual Property (AIPPI), Asian Patent Atty.'s Assn. (APAA). Shinto. Avocations: cooking, writing. Office: Sugimura Patent/Trademark, 2-4 Kasumigaseki 3-chome, Chiyoda-ku, Tokyo 100-0013, Japan

AOLEY, PRAKASH VITHALRAO, literature and philosophy educator; b. Nagpur, Maharashtra, India, Oct. 18, 1947; s. Vithalrao Laxmanrao Aoley and Vimal (Tara) Purankar; m. Heera Bhagade, Nov. 4, 1976. B.A., Nagpur U., 1967, M.A., 1969, Ph.D., 1981. Lectr. Rural Inst. Wardha, Maharashtra, 1969-71, Shrimati Binzani Mahila Mahavidyalaya, Nagpur, 1972—, PhD supr., 1989—. Author: Rediscovering American Studies, 1998. Pres., Nirmal Coop. Soc., Nagpur, 1982-83. Mem. Am. Studies Research Centre, Indian Assn. Am. Studies, Am. Studies Assn., Am. Centre, Emerson Soc., MLA, PEN. Hindu. Club: Vidarbha Cricket Assn. (Nagpur). Avocations: cricket, reading, meditation. Home: 2/4 Mig Flats, Med Sq, Nagpur Maharashtra 440 003, India Office: SMT Binzani M Mahavidyalaya,, Pataleshwar Rd,, Nagpur Maharashtra 440 002, India

AONO, JUN, anesthesiologist, educator; b. Matsuyama-City, Japan, Aug. 6, 1961; s. Yukio and Minako Aono; m. Rei Shingai, May 18, 1994. MD, Kochi (Japan) Med. Sch., 1987. Intern, then resident Univ. Hosp., Kochi (Japan) Med. Sch.; mem. sr. staff dept. anesthesiology Kochi Med. Sch., 1991-92, assoc. prof. anesthesiology, 1992—. Mem. Japan Soc. Anesthesiology, N.Y. Acad. Scis. Home: Katsurashima 1-10-57-1303, Kochi 783, Japan Office: Kochi Med Sch, Nankoku, Kochi 783-8505, Japan

AONO, KATSUHIRO, economist, educator; b. Matsuyama, Japan, Feb. 7, 1944; s. Kikuichi and Suzuka Aono; m. Tsuneko Miyoshi, Oct. 21, 1972; children: Mitsuhiro, Takahiro. BA, Matsuyama U., Japan, 1966; MA, Kobe U., Japan, 1968, PhD, 1988. Lectr. Coll. Econs., Matsuyama U., 1971-73, asst. prof., 1973-80, prof., 1980—, head Sponsored Rsch. Inst., 1984-89; v.p. Matsuyama Jr. Coll., 1992-94. Author: Economic Analysis of Land--Land and Economic Growth, 1984, Economic Analysis of Land Taxation, 1991, Study of a Realized Capital Gains Tax on Land, 1996. Pres. Assn. for Promotion of FAZ in Ehime; chmn. Com. for Evaluation of Pub. Investment in Ehime. Mem. Japan Econ. Policy Assn. (bd. dirs. 1997—), Assn. Urban Housing Scis. (v.p. br. 1998—). Home: 415-6 Minamikume-Cho, Matsuyama, Ehime 790-0924, Japan Office: Matsuyama U, 4-2 Bunkyo-cho, Matsuyama, Ehime 790-8578, Japan

AOTMANE, EN NACIRI, physics educator; b. Agadir, Morocco, Jan. 1, 1972; arrived in France, 1995; B in Physics, Ibnou Zohr U., Agadir, 1994, MSc in Physics, 1995; D in Matter and Materials, Metz (France) U., 1996, PhD in Physics, 1999. Engr. Metz U., 1998-99, asst. prof., 1999—. Contbr. articles to profl. jours. Avocations: football, Internet, movies. E-mail: ennacir@ipc.sciences.univ-metz.fr. Fax: 33 387315801. Office: IPEM Labo LPLI, 1 bd arago CP 87811, 57078 Metz Louraine, France

AOUIZERATE, PHILIPPE ANDRE, pharmacist; b. Paris, Nov. 13, 1965; s. Roger David and Solange Raymonde (Bogniot) A. PharmD, U. Paris V, 1996. Intern Paris Hosp., 1991-96; specialized pharmacist asst. Meaux (France) Hosp., 1996—. Contbr. articles to profl. jours. Lt. Healthcare Military Svcs., 1992-93. Mem. Assn. des Pharmaciens Hosp. d'Ile de France. Avocations: computing, sports, travel, cinema, books. Office: Ctr Hosp de Meaux Pharmacie, 6-8 rue Saint Fiacre BP-218, 77104 Meaux Cedex France

AOUN, GEORGES MICHEL, university dean; b. Beirut, Lebanon, Jan. 2, 1958; s. Michel and Eda (Raphael) A.; m. Emira Elizabeth Abilama, Oct. 18, 1980; children: Karine, Karoline, Lea. BS, U. St. Joseph, Beirut, 1978, MS, 1979, DESS, 1981; PhD, U. Paris, 1986; postgrad., London Bus. Sch., 1984. Prof. U. St. Joseph, Beirut, 1982-86, 91-94, dean, 1994—; pr. bd. dirs. Mgmt. and Advt. Agy., Beirut, 1984-86, Sofres, Beirut, 1995-98. Author: Perishable Products Distribution, 1986, Business Ethics in Middle East, 1996; editor Proche Orient Etudes en Management, 1993-98. Mem. French Mktg. Assn., Wes. Acad. Mgmt., Automobile Touring Club Lebanon. Avocations: tennis, swimming, printing, archeology. Office: Univ of St Joseph, Huvelin St Box 175 208, Beirut Lebanon

AOUN, RAGAB SALEM, physician, consultant pediatrician; b. Sabrata, Libya, June 1, 1949; s. Salem Ali and Ghalia Ahmed (Elmarghani) A.; m. Gheitheia Imhemed Muftah, Dec. 18, 1979; children: Murwa, Zeinab, Musaab, Ahmed, Muhammed, Aya, Ala. MB, B of Surgery, Garyounis Sch. Medicine, Libya, 1977. Diplomate Am. Bd. Pediat., Am. Bd. Allergy and Immunology. Resident in pediat. All Children's Hosp., St. Petersburg, Fla., 1982-85; physician in pediat. hematology-oncology Meml. Sloan-Kettering Cancer Ctr., N.Y.C., 1985-86; physician in allergy-immunology All Children's Hosp., 1986-88; lectr. Elfate Med. Sch., Tripoli, Libya, 1987-90, asst. prof., 1990-94, assoc. prof., 1994—; chief allergy unit Sabrata (Libya) Hosp., 1989—; cons. Ctr. for Transmissible Diseases, Zawia, Libya, 1991-95, Nat. Cancer Inst., Sabrata, 1995—; adminstrv. mem. Libyan Nat. Ctr. for Med. Rsch., 1998—. Fellow Am. Coll. Chest Physicians (fellowship 1992—). Islamic. Avocations: reading, gardening. Home: PO Box 176, Sabrata Libya Office: Sabrata Hosp, Sabrata Libya

AOWEI, XING, olympic athlete; b. Shandong, China, Jan. 25, 1982. Mem. men's gymnastics team China; winner gold medal in pommel horse Asian Games, 1998, winner bronze in high bar, 1998; winner team gold World Championship, 1997, 99, winner bronze in floor exercise, 1999; winner all-around, floor exercise, pommel horse Nat. Championship, 2000; winner gold medal team all-around Olympics, Sydney, Australia, 2000. Office: Chinese Gymnastics Assn, 9 Tiyuguan Rd, 100 763 Beijing China*

AOYAGI, MASARU, otolaryngologist, educator; b. Ashikaga, Japan, Jan. 3, 1946; s. Hisao and Hideko Aoyagi; m. Taeko Yaoita; 3 children. MD, Niigata U., Japan, 1970, DMs, 1986. Diplomate in medicine. Asst. physician Yamagata U., Japan, 1976, lectr., 1976-86, assoc. prof., 1986-94, prof., chmn. dept. otolaryngology, 1994-98; prof. emeritus North China Med. Coll. Coal, 1998—; asst. dir. Yamagata U. Hosp., 2000—. Mem. Japan Soc. Otolaryngology (coun.), Japan Audiol. Soc. (coun.), Japan Soc.Equilibrium Rsch. (coun.), Japan Soc. Facial Nerve Rsch. (chmn. steering com.), Japan Rhinologic Soc. (coun.), Japan Otological Soc. (coun.), Japan Laryngological Soc. (coun.), Japan Soc. Stomato-Pharyngology (coun.), Japan Soc. Immunology and Allergology in Otolaryngology (coun.), Japan Soc. for Head and Neck Surgery (coun.), Japan Soc. for Head and Neck Cancer, Japan Soc. Electroencephalography and Electromyography, Pediat. Otolaryngology Japan, Barany Soc., Internat. Evoked Response Audiometry Study Group, Yamagata Med. Assn. (dir. 2000—). Home: Sakurada-Higashi 2-4-7, Yamagata 990-23, Japan Office: Yamagata U Sch Medicine Dept Otolaryngology, Iida-Niishi 2-2-2, Yamagata 990-23, Japan

AOYAMA, HIDEYASU, medical educator; b. Dairen City, Kantoshyu, Japan, Feb. 12, 1935; s. Tetsujyuro and Tomiko (Segawa) A.; m. Sachiko Wada, May 15, 1960; children: Satoshi, Mari, Maki. MD, Okayama (Japan) U., 1959, PhD, 1964; DPH, Nat. Inst. Pub. Health, Tokyo, 1963; MPH, Johns Hopkins U., 1969. Intern, resident Okayama U. Hosp., 1961-64; assoc. prof. Okayama U. Med. Sch., 1970-80, chmn., prof., 1980—; Mem. Sci. Coun. Japan, 1994-97; chmn. Nat. Com. Cmty. Medicine, 1994-97, Nat. Com. Med. Edn., 1994-97. Author: Encyclopedia of Occupational Health and Safety, 1981, Principle and Practice of Primary Care and Family Medicine, 1994, Neurobehavioral Methods and Effects in Occupational and Environmental Health; author/editor Health Promotion and Education "Bringing Health to Life", 1996. Recipient Outstanding Internat. Grad. Awards in Pub. Health Leadership, Johns Hopkins U., 1993. Mem. Internat. Com. Occupl. Health, World Orgn. Family Doctors (counciler 1986-98), Rotary. Avocations: travel, writing. Home: 1-3-13 Ishimacho, Okayama 700-0016, Japan

APAHIDEANU, OCTAVIAN, physician, consultant; b. Resita, Banat, Romania, May 15, 1939; s. Joan and Ana A.; married, Jan. 15, 1968; 2 children. MD, U. Medicine, Timisoara, Romania, 1962, PhD, 1999. Gen. practitioner Romania, 1962-72; resident physician U. Medicine U. Hosp. # 5, Timisoara, 1975; specialist County Hosp., Amina, Romania, 1975-80; specialist in ob-gyn. County Hosp., Mocsa, Romania, 1980-81; specialist in ob-gyn. Dist. Hosp., Resita, Romania, 1981-89, sr. physician, 1989—; chief physician County Hosp., Anina, Romania, 1975-80, Bosca, Romania, 1980-81; cons. physician Dist. Hosp., Resita, 1981-89, head dept., 1989—; pres. Med. Coll. dist. Caras-Severin, 1999—. Contbr. articles to profl. jours.; lectr. in field. Mem. Caen-Calva Romania Assn., N.Y. Acad. Scis., Acad. Club Acad. Assn. Med. Interdisciplinary Studies, Timisoara Med. Assn. (bd. dirs.), Ob-Gyn. Assn. Soc. (bd. dirs.). Avocations: literature, swimming. Office: Spitalul Judetean Resita, Herculane 8, 1700 Resita Romania

APAK, M. RESAT, chemistry educator, researcher; b. Izmir, Turkey, Feb. 18, 1954; s. Hilmi Ziya and Sabiha Apak; m. Vildan Tevs, Sept. 20, 1977; 1 child, Uran. MSc in Chem. Engring., Istanbul U., 1976, PhD in Chemistry, 1982; MSc in Marine Pollution Chemistry, Liverpool (Eng.) U., 1981. Tchg. and rsch. asst. Istanbul Tech. U., 1976-78; tchg. and rsch. asst. Istanbul U., 1978-85, asst. prof., 1985-87, assoc. prof., 1987-93, prof., 1993—, acting dean Faculty of Engring., 1996-99, head chemistry dept., 1995-96, head analytical chemistry divsn., 1990—; Turkey's rep. NATO/CCMS Pilot Study, 1991-97, IUPAC, 1995-97, 2000—; environ. expert UN, 1997—. Author: Basic Analytical Chemistry, 1995, Coordination Chemistry, 1993; editor Chimica Acta Turcica, 1995—; mem. editorial bd. turkish Jour. Chemistry., 1997—; contbr. more than 110 articles to profl. jours. including Water Rsch., Talanta, Anal. Chim. Acta, JCIS, others. Mem. Nat. Com. for Solid Waste Control, Istanbul, 1988—. With Turkish Army, 1981. Fellow Brit. Coun.-UN, 1981, NATO/CCMS, 1988-96. Mem. Turkish Chem. Soc., Chem. Engrs. Turkey (bd. dirs. 1978—), Brit. Coun. Fellowship Club. Avocations: chess, philosophy of science, classical music, tree planting. E-mail: rapak@istanbul.edu.tr. Office: Istanbul U Fac Engring, Avcilar Campus, 34850 Istanbul Turkey

APANASENKO, ALEXANDER LEONIDOVICH, physicist, researcher; b. Kharkov, Ukraine, Aug. 24, 1948; s. Leonid Sergeevich and Antonina (Leontyevna) A.; m. Valentina Victorovna Tesljuk, Jan. 26, 1973 (div. Apr. 1981); 1 child, Mariya Alexandrovna; m. Tatyana Nikolayevna Kondratyeva, July 3, 1981; 1 child, Anton Alexandrovich. MS, U. Kharkov, 1971, PhD, 1983. Engr. Radioelectronic Inst., Kharkov, 1971-74; jr. rschr. U. Kharkov, 1974-77, sr. rschr. physics, 1977—; cons. in field. Contbr. articles to profl. jours.; patentee in field. Mem. Young Communist League, 1963-76. J. Soros Found. grantee, 1993. Avocations: mountaineering, skiing, dogs. Home: PO Box 1738, 76 Pobeda Ave Apt 421, 310204 Kharkov Ukraine Office: Kharkov U Lab Nuclear Spec, Svoboda Sq 4, 310077 Kharkov Ukraine

APARICIO, ANTONIO, astrophysicist; b. Granada, Spain, Feb. 13, 1960; s. Antonio and Concepcion (Juan) A.; 1 child, Hugo Antonio. BA, Instituto Padre Manjon, Granada, 1977; MD, U. Granada, 1982, PhD, 1988. Postdoctoral fellow U. Padua, Italy, 1988-90; support astronomer Instituto De Astrofisica De Canarias, La Laguna, Spain, 1990-95; prof. titular U. La Laguna, Spain, 1995—; vis. scholar Carnegie Obs., Pasadena, Calif., 1997-98. Author: (book) Arqueoastrnomia Hispanica, 1994; editor: Stellar Astrophysics for the Local Group, 1998; contbr. numerous articles to sci. jours. 2d lt. Transmisions of Spanish Army, 1983. Mem. Am. Astronomical Soc., Internat. Astronomical Union, Sociedad Española De Astromía, European Astronomical Soc., Assn. para el Avance de la Ciencia y la Technología en España. Avocations: yachting, traveling. Home: C Provincial 201, E38398 Santa Ursula Spain Office: Instituto De Astrofisica De Canarias, Via Lactea, E38200 La Laguna Spain

APARICIO, JORGE, oncologist; b. Valencia, Spain, Jan. 17, 1963; s. Aniceto Aparicio and Milagros Urtasun; m. Eva Martinez-Moragon, Apr. 30, 1991; children: Alejandro, Silvia. MD, U. Valencia, 1987. Asst. in oncology Hosp. La Fe, Valencia, 1988-91, cons. in colorectal cancer, 1992—. Editor: Bone Tumours, 1998; author: Germ Cell Tumours, 1999; contbr. articles to profl. jours. Mem. European Soc. Med. Oncology, Am. Soc. Clin. Oncology. Office: Hosp La Fe, Av Campanar 21-11, E-46009 Valencia Spain

APARICIO, NAIRO DAVID, researcher; b. Baruta, Miranda, Venezuela, Dec. 28, 1966; arrived in the U.K., 1990; s. Nelson and Yolanda Concepción (Silva) A.; m. Milagros Martínez, Sept. 19, 1998. Degree in Civil Engring. summa cum laude, U. Ctrl. Venezuela, Caracas, 1989; PhD in Applied Math., Imperial Coll. Sci., London, 1993. Lectr. U. Ctrl. Venezuela, Caracas, 1989-90; rsch. assoc. U. Cambridge, Eng., 1993-95; rsch. fellow in math. Oxford Brookes U., Eng., 1995-99; lectr. mathematics Oxford Brookes Univ., 1999—. Contbr. articles to profl. jours. Avocations: swimming, cycling, weight lifting, reading. Office: Oxford Brookes Univ, Gipsy Ln, Oxford OX3 0BP, England

APARICIO SÁNCHEZ, PEDRO, member of European parliament; b. Madrid, Oct. 4, 1942. Mem. European Parliament, Malaga, 1999—; mem. Group of the Party of European Socialists; mem. com. on culture, youth, edn., the media and sport, com. on regional policy, transport and tourism, delegation for rels. with the countries of South Asia and the South Asia Assn. for Regional Cooperation. Mem. Spanish Socialit Workers' Party. Office: Corpus Christi 11, E-29017 Malaga Spain

APASSA, CYRIL OMO-OSAGIE, clergyman, educator; b. Aba, Abbia, Nigeria, Feb. 4, 1944; s. Emmanuel Agbonfiro and Agnes (Amobo) A. BD, Urban U., 1971; diploma in edn., U. Nigeria, 1977, MEd, 1986; EdD, U. San Francisco, 1996. Ordained to ministry, Roman Cath. Ch., 1971. Tchr. govt. h.s., Nigeria, 1964, 73-77; pastor Roman Cath. chs., Nigeria, 1971-81; prin. Govt. H.S., Nigeria, 1981-90; assoc. pastor Our Lady of Lourdes Parish, Aba, Nigeria, 1990-91, Holy Angel's Parish, Arcadia, Calif., 1991, St. John Eudes Parish, Chatsworth, Calif., 1991-92, St. Theresa Little Flower Ch., Reno, 1996—; sch. counselor, chmn. disciplinary com. St. Ephrem's Secondary Sch., Owerrinta, Nigeria, 1975-79; mem. bd. govs. Mbutu Ngwa (Nigeria) Secondary Sch., 1984-89; mem. grad. coun. U. San Francisco, 1995-96. Bd. dirs. Scholz Found. and Project Restart, 1998—. Mem. ASCD, K.C. (chaplain 1991—, Svc. award 1991, 96, 99), Phi Delta Kappa. Avocations: photography, table tennis, traveling, soccer. Fax: 775-322-0196. Office: St Therese Ch of the Little Flower 875 E Plumb Ln Reno NV 89502-3507

APEL-BRUEGGEMAN, MYRNA L., entrepreneur; b. Cleve., July 19, 1942; d. Melvin Arthur and Merle Ruth (Hoffman) Rehlender; children: Timothy, Kristen, Michelle, Kim; m. Earl L. Brueggeman, May 7, 1994. BS in Edn., Kent State U., 1965, M. in Edn. Counseling, 1987. Cert. tchr., Ohio; lic. minister, Ohio. Owner, mgr. real estate investments Kent, Ohio; owner, founder IHS Counseling Ctr., Ravenna, Ohio; owner, mgr., founder IHS Home Sweet Home, Ravenna, Ohio; owner IHS Bookstore; co-owner Chapel on the Lakes; owner Stow Mobile Home Village, Southington Estates, Orchard Estates, Orchard Plaza. Mem. NAFE, Ohio Manufactured Housing Assn. (bd. dirs., pres. We. Res. chpt.), Internat. Soc. Profl. Hypnotists, Sigma Epsilon, Chi Sigma Iota.

APELT, COLIN JAMES, civil engineering educator; b. Brisbane, Queensland, Australia, Apr. 3, 1931; s. Arthur and Olive (Carter) A.; m. Margaret Mary Duffy, Aug. 13, 1960; children: Ruth, Rita, Rachel, John Clare, Thomas, Helen, Ann. B of Engring., U. Queensland, 1952; PhD, Oxford U., Eng., 1957. Profl. civil engr. Design engr. Queensland Water Resources, 1951-54; postdoctoral fellow Oxford U., 1957-58; sr. lectr. U. Queensland, 1958-64, reader in civil engring., 1965-79; rsch. assoc. MIT, Cambridge, 1966; prof. civil engring. U. Queensland, 1979—, head of civil engring. dept., 1982-94; vis. prof. Colo. State U., Ft. Collins, 1969; mem. Beach Protection Adv. Bd., Queensland, 1979-84, Queensland Govt. Hydraulics, Lab. Adv. Bd., Queensland, 1985-90, Nat. Com. Coastal and Ocean Engring., Canberra, 1981-84; sci. advisor Raine Island Corp., 1985-98. Co-author: Field Computations In Engineering And Physics, 1961; contbr. articles to profl. jours. Mem. Mater Hosp. Health Svcs. Governing Bd., Brisbane, 1987-96, chmn., 1996—; mem. Queensland State Com. of Action for World Devel., Brisbane, 1972-75; pres. Innocents Relief, Brisbane, 1962—. Recipient Univ. medal U. Queensland, 1952, Rhodes Scholarship, Rhodes Trust Oxford U., 1954, Fulbright Travel award Australian/Am. Edn. Found., MIT, Boston, 1966, Sr. Fgn. Scientist award Nat. Sci. Found., Colo., 1969. Fellow Inst. Engrs. Australia., U. Queensland Club. Avocations: bushwalking, gardening, music. Home: 40 Ivy St, Indooroopilly QLD 4068, Australia Office: Univ Queensland, Saint Lucia 4072, Australia

APERATHITIS, ELIAS ARGYRIS, research scientist, educator; b. Pireaus, Greece, Oct. 2, 1960; s. Argyris Elias and Maria (Konsta) A.; m. Vasso Flouri, June 17, 1995; children: Mareneia, Argyris. BSc in Physics, Patras U., Patra, Greece, 1983; MSc in Physics, Dundee (Scotland) U., 1984; PhD in Photovoltaics, Hull (Eng.) U., 1989. Cert. physicist. Rsch. scientist Found. Rsch. and Tech., Heraklion, Crete, Greece, 1991—; adj. prof. Crete U., Heraklion, Crete, 1992—. Contbr. articles to profl. jours. Sgt. Greek Army, 1989-91. Recipient scholarship Nat. Scholarship Found., Athens, 1983, grant Schillitzy Found., London, 1986. Avocations: amateur long distance bicycling, do-it-yourself home construction, History reading. Office: Found Rsch & Tech, PO Box 1527, Heraklion 71110, Crete

APESTEGUI, ALFREDO, fresh fruit company executive; b. San Jose, Costa Rica, Oct. 23, 1955; s. Alvaro Apestegui and Layle Barzuna; m. Olga Steinvorth, Aug. 30, 1980; children: Alfredo, Alberto, Melisa, Jose Antonio. BS, La. State U., 1980. V.p. Latin Am. diversifies products Del Monte Fresh Produce Co., San Jose, 1988—; bd. dirs. Channel 2 TV Sta., San Jose. Home: PO Box 573-1150, La Uruca Costa Rica Office: Del Monte Tropical Fruit Co, PO Box 1099-1200, San Jose Costa Rica

APESTEGUI-BARZUNA, ALVARO, biochemist; b. San Jose, Costa Rica, May 27, 1947; s. Alvaro and Layle (Barzuna) A.; m. Sylvia Gurdian, Dec. 11, 1971; children: Sylvia Maria, Laura, Karla, Gabriela, Alvaro. Lic. in Microbiology, Costa Rica U., 1971; MS, Tulane U., 1973, PhD, 1977. Researcher Hosp. Nat. Ninos, San Jose, Costa Rica, 1977-85; chmn. dept. biochemistry, v.p. acad. affairs Esc. Aut. Cienc. Med., San Jose, Costa Rica, 1978-94, pres., 1992-93; dir. Nat. Coun. Rsch. Sci. & Tech., Costa Rica, 1992—; pres. bd. dirs. Labs. Labiclin, San Jose, 1977—, BIO-TEC Internat., San Jose, 1981—; vis. prof. Univ. Costa Rica, 1994—; v.p. Panamerican Plasma Processing, San Jose, 1994—; v.p. acad. affairs U. Cienc.Med., 1999—. Author: (textbook) Biochemistry, 1979. Elections com. mem. Social Christian Party, Costa Rica, 1992-96. Orgn. Am. States scholar, 1972-74. Mem. Am. Assn. Clin. Chemistry, Costa Rican Assn. Devel. Biochemistry (founder), Rotary, Club Union. Roman Catholic. Avocations: philatelist, model building. E-mail: avapest@sol.racsa.co.cr. Office: Labs Labiclin Clinica Am, 14th Ave 0/1 St, San Jose 716-1007, Costa Rica

APETREI, CONSTANTIN, engineer; b. Zanesti, Romania, Dec. 16, 1926; s. Constantin and Olga (Ardeleanu) A.; m. Carmen Gheorghiu; children: Vladut, Pavelesco Roxana. Doctor engring., Polytech. Inst., 1953. Asst. Polytech. Inst., Timisora, Romania, 1948-54; asst. prof. Polytech. Inst., Bucharest, 1956-60, prof., 1960—; rschr. Inst. for Energy, Bucharest, 1956-75, Inst. for Elec. Machinery, Bucharest, 1975—; scientific dir. Inst. for Energy, Bucharest, 1956-75, Inst. for Elec. Machinery, 1975—, head of chair elec. machinery Poly. Inst. Bucharest, 1962-68. Contbr. articles to profl. jours. Recipient Award Traian Vuia Romanian Acad., 1974. Mem. IEEE, Cigre and Studies Com., N.Y. Acad. Sci. Home: Armeneasca NR 17, Sector 2, Bucharest Romania Office: ICPE, Bdul T Vladimirescu 45-47, 79623 Bucharest Romania

AP GWILYM, GWYNN, clergy member; b. Bangor, Gwynedd, Wales, June 23, 1950; parents William and Myfi Williams. BA, UCNW, Bangor, 1971; MA, UCNW, 1976; BA, Oxford U., 1984, MA, 1989. Lectr. Univ. Coll., Cork, Ireland, 1975-77; sec. Yr Academi Gymreig, Cardiff, Wales, 1977; curate The Church in Wales, Porthmadog, 1984-86; rector The Church in Wales, Penegoes, 1986-97, Mallwyd, 1997—; lectr. United Theol. Coll., Aberystwyth, Wales, 1987; editor Y Llan, 1989-96; mem. Welsh Bible Translation Panel, 1992. Author: Y Winllan Werdd, 1977, Gwales, 1983 (award Welsh Arts Coun. 1983), Yr Ymyl Aur, 1998; editor: Meistri A'u Crefft, 1981, Cyfres Y Meistri, 1982, Gogoneddus Arglwydd, Henffych Well, 1999. Named chaired bard Nat. Eisteddfod of Wales, Abergwaun, 1986. Mem. Gorsedd of Bards, Welsh Poetry Soc. (chmn. 1985-90). Home and Office: Y Rheithordy Mallwyd, SY20 9HJ Machynlleth Wales

APJOK, ENIKÖ, pediatrician; b. Salonta, Bihor, Romania, Mar. 12, 1966; d. Ferenc Apjok and Judit Eva Molnar. MD, U. Medicine, Tg-Mures, Romania, 1990. Physician, 2d dept. pediat. Semmelweis Med. U., Budapest, Hungary, 1992-97; med. dr. pediat. hematology-oncology dept. Semmelweis Med. U., Budapest, 1997—; data mgr. Pediatric Oncology Outreach to Hungary project, Budapest, 1992-97. Contbr. articles to med. jours. Avocation: classical music. Office: Heim Pál Children's Hosp, Budapest Hungary

APLESNIN, SERGEI STEPANOVICH, physicist; b. Karatuzkoe, Russia, May 15, 1954; s. Stepan Ivanovich and Kat Sergeevna (Manakova) A.; m. Nadya Alekseevna Pilkova, June 11, 1983; 1 child, Dimitrii. Dip.eng., Krasnoyarsk U., Russia, 1976. Jr. rschr. Inst. Physics, Krasnoyarsk, Russia, 1980-89, chief rschr., 1989—. Avocations: skiing, travel. Office: Inst Physics, 660 036 Krasnoyarsk Russia

APONTE MARTINEZ, LUIS CARDINAL, archbishop emeritus; b. Lajas, P.R., Aug. 4, 1922; s. Santiago E. Aponte and Rosa Martinez. Student, San Ildefonso Sem., San Juan, P.R., 1944, St. John's Sem., Boston, 1950; LL.D. (hon.), Fordham U., 1965. Ordained priest Roman Cath. Ch., 1950; asst. in Patillas, P.R.; pastor in Maricao, P.R., Sta. Isabel, P.R., 1953-55; sec. to bishop of Ponce, P.R., 1955-57; pastor in Aibonito, P.R., 1957-60; aux. bishop of Ponce, 1960-63, bishop, 1963-64; archbishop of San Juan, 1964—; elevated to cardinal, 1973; Chancellor Cath. U. P.R., Ponce, 1963—; pres. Puerto Rican Episcopal Conf. Served as chaplain P.R. N.G., 1957-60. Mem. Lions. Address: SER Urpanizacion 1763 Calle Fan Alejahbeo San Juan PR 00926

APOSTOLAKIS, CONSTANTINE NICOLAS, paint company executive; b. Athens, Attica, Greece, May 16, 1929; s. Nicolas Michel and Mina John (Kotopouli) A.; m. Caterina Kontomati, May 1, 1934; 1 child, Nicolas. MSc in Chemistry, Athens U. Physico-Math., 1955. Pvt. practice Perfume Mfr., Athens, Greece, 1955-60; staff quality control lab. Ethel S.A., Athens, Greece, 1960-67; tech. mgr. refrigrators GE, Athens, Greece, 1968-70; CEO, Chromoline S.A., Athens, 1971-98, cons. chemist, 1999—; cons. Viotsal S.A. Plastics co., Athens, 1960-70, Izolex S.A. Insulation co., Athens, 1970-90. Co-editor: Symposium on Paints Proceedings (6 vols.); contbr. articles to profl. jours. Mem. Masons (past grand sec. grand lodge of Greece). Mem. Greek Orthodox Ch. Home: 14 Athan Diakou, 151-22 Amarousion Attica, Greece Office: Chromoline SA, 52 Chalkokondyli, 104 32 Athens Attica, Greece

APOSTOLESCU, VLĂSTAR NESTOR, retired structural engineer; b. Cernowtzi, Ukraine, Mar. 24, 1931; s. Ion and Oltea (Nistor) A.; m. Sanda Nicoleta Pateli, Dec. 10, 1959. Degree in Civil Engring., Civil Engring. U., Bucharest, Romania, 1953. Lic. expert and verifier in civil engring. Ministry Pub. Works Romania; lic. engr. Jr. design specialist Project Bucharest, 1959; design specialist Inst. Power Design and Studies, Bucharest, 1959-77; sr. design specialist Ctr. Technol. engring. Nuclear Structures, Bucharest, 1977-89, design head nuc. power plant, 1979-95; ret., 1995; assoc. prof. nuclear structures Civil Engring. U., Bucharest, 1983-93; cons. Internat. Atomic Energy Agy., Vienna, 1991, 93, Civil Engring. Inspection, Bucharest, 1997—. Contbr. articles to profl. jours. Fellow Assn. Design Civil Engrs. Home: Boul M Kogălniceanu 47, 70603 Bucharest Romania

APOSTOLICO, ALBERTO, electrical engineer, educator; b. Salerno, Italy, Feb. 17, 1948; came to U.S., 1983; s. Gaetano Apostolico and Rosita Alfano; m. Concettina Guerra, June 17, 1985; 1 child, Rosita. Diploma, U. Salerno, 1976; D in Engring., U. Naples, 1973. Fulbright scholar Carnegie-Mellon Univ., Pitts., 1974-75; asst. prof. U. Salerno, 1975-82; assoc. prof. Purdue U., West Lafayette, Ind., 1983-90; prof. U. L'Aquila, Italy, 1987-91, U. Padova, Italy, 1992—; prof. Purdue U., 1990—. Editor: Combinatorial Algorithms on Words, 1983, Pattern Matching Algorithms, 1996; contbr. articles to profl. jours. Mem. IEEE, Assn. Computing Machinery, European Assn. Theoretical Computer Sci. E-mail: axa@cs.purdue.edu.

APOSTOLOPOULOS, VASSO, immunovaccinologist; b. Melbourne, Victoria, Australia, Feb. 19, 1970; d. Konstantinos and Hariklia (Karatas-

sou) A. BS, U. Melbourne, 1990, BS with honors, 1991, PhD, 1995; advanced cert. protein crystallography, Birkbeck Coll. and U. London, 2000. Cert. rschr. Sr. rsch. officer Austin Rsch. Inst., Melbourne, 1995-98; Nat. Health and Med. Rsch. Coun. CJ Martin rsch. fellow The Scripps Rsch. Inst., 1998—. Contbr. articles to profl. jours.; patentee in field. Hon. mayor of Amalias, Greece, 1998; hon. guest Hermes Expo, Atlantic City, 1998, N.Am. Youth Convention, Chgo., 1999; hon. mem. World Convention for Hellenes Abroad Greece, 1997, 99, Greek-Australian 2004 Athens Olympic Com., 1998. Recipient Vacation studentship Anti Cancer Coun. Victoria, 1991-92, Hellenic Distinction medal Hellenic Cmty, 1993, 97, Australian Postgrad. Rsch. award U. Melbourne, 1992-95, Travel award Lorne Cancer Conf., 1994, 95, Travel award Australian Soc. Immunology, 1994, Young Rschr. award Victorian Soc. Pathology Exptl. Medicine-Australian Soc. Med. Rsch., 1995, Victorian Young Australian of Yr. award Pacific Power Sci. and Tech. Category, 1996, Premiers Rsch. award, 1996, CRC For Vaccine Tech. award, 1996, Honor Achievement Athens Olympic Com., 1999, Sci. Achievements award U. Patras, Greece, 2000; named Young Australian of Yr., Ea. Energy Sci. and Tech., 1997, Young Achiever of Yr., 1997, Brigadier Gen. of the Phoenix Battallion, Greece Independence Day, 1997, Honor from His All Holiness Ecumenical Patriarch Bartholomew, 1997, Cross of Andrew the Apostle from Archbishop Stylianos of Australia, 1998, Zeus Honor, Greece, 1998, Olympia award, 1998, medal on internat. day for women Ataloso Filadelfos, 1999, 2000; Ian Potter Found. Travelling fellow, 1998; named one of 30 most successful women in Australia under 30, Cosmopolitan mag., 1997, Most Significant Greek Abroad, Spl. Issue in Time and Odysee mag., 1997, Arcadian of Yr., U.S., 1999. Mem. Australian Soc. Med. Rsch. (youth rschr. award 1994), Australian Soc. Immunology (postgrad. internat. travel prize 1995), Am. Assn. Immunologists, Med. Assn. Amalias (hon.), Med. Assn. So. Greece (hon.), Pan-Arcadian Fedn. Am. (hon.), Thessalonikan Assn. (hon.), EEAMA League Greeks from Egypt and Middle East (hon.), Planetary Soc., N.Y. Acad. Sci., Rotary Club of Amalias (hon.). Avocations: reading physics archaeology and astronomy, world coin and banknote collecting, playing basketball, volleyball, tennis. Office: Austin Rsch Inst, Austin Rsch Inst, Studley Rd, Heidelberg 3084, Australia

APOSTOLOV, ANTON ATANASSOV, physicist, researcher; b. Sofia, Bulgaria, May 30, 1951; s. Atanas Apostolov and Lilia Kostova (Grancharova) Domuschiev; m. Tatjana Marinova Georgieva (div. July 1985); 1 child, Alexandra Antonova. MS, Sofia U., 1974, PhD in Polymer Chemistry, 1993. Physicist Inst. Phys. Chemistry, Sofia U., 1976-83, rsch. assoc. Inst. for Protection Metals, 1983-84, rsch. assoc. Inst. for Computing Technique, 1984-85, rsch. assoc. Lab. on Structure and Properties of Polymers, 1985-98, rsch. scholar Lab. on Structure and Properties of Polymers, 1998—. Contbr. articles to internat. polymer jours., including Jour. Macromolecular Sci., Internat. Jour. Polymeric Materials, Coll. Polymer Sci., Macromolecules, Jour. Applied Polymer Sci. Avocations: jazz, movies, books. Home: 116 Geo Milev Str, Bl 57 Apt 42, 1574 Sofia Bulgaria Office: Sofia U Dept Chemistry, 1 J Bourchier Blvd, 1126 Sofia Bulgaria

APPATOV, SEMEN JOSIFOVICH, historian; b. Pervomaisk, Ukraine, Jan. 24, 1930; s. Josif and Hanna (Goichman) A.; m. Ninel Michailovna Mazur, Apr. 4, 1956; two children. PhD, Inst. Internat. Rels., 1966; DSc, Russia Acad. Scis., 1980. Tchr., lectr. high sch., Odessa, Ukraine, 1952-58; dir., lectr. State Courses Fgn. Lang., Odessa, 1958-66; from asst. prof. to prof., chmn. dept. internat. rels. Odessa U., Ukraine, 1966-99, ret., 1999. Author: USA and Europe, 1979, Analysis of American Historiography, 1984, The USA Middle East Policy in American Historiography, 1986; editor, author: American Foreign Policy Mentality in the 1980s, 1992, Ukraine and European Security, 1999.

APPEL, ALBERT M., lawyer; b. N.Y.C., May 26, 1945; s. Morris and Belle (Kaplan) A.; m. Irena Uhl, June 10, 1979; 1 child, Elliott. BS in Econs., U. Pa., 1966; JD, NYU, 1969. Bar: N.Y. 1969, U.S. Dist. Ct. (so. and ea. dists.) N.Y. 1971, U.S. Ct. Appeals (2d cir.) 1974, U.S. Ct. Appeals (4th cir.) 1979. Assoc. Spear and Hill, N.Y.C., 1969-75; assoc. Webster & Sheffield, N.Y.C., 1976-80, ptnr., 1981-91; spl. counsel Stroock & Stroock & Lavan LLP, N.Y.C., 1991-97, ptnr., 1998—. Mem. ABA, Am. Health Lawyers Assn., N.Y. State Bar Assn., Assn. of Bar of City of N.Y., Beta Alpha Psi. Home: 670 W End Ave New York NY 10025-7313 Office: Stroock & Stroock & Lavan LLP 180 Maiden Ln New York NY 10038-4925

APPEL, ANTOINETTE RUTH, neuropsychologist; b. N.Y.C., Mar. 31, 1943; d. Leon S. and Augusta (Marienberg) A. B.A., U. Vt., 1964; M.A., Mt. Holyoke Coll., 1965; postgrad., Yeshiva U., 1965-66, Hofstra U., 1966; Ph.D., CUNY, 1972. Diplomate Am. Bd. Profl. Neuropsychology, Am. Bd. Forensic Examiners, Am. Bd. Forensic Medicine, Am. Bd. Psychol. Splty. Forensic Neuropsychology). Instr. C.W. Post Coll., Greenvale, N.Y., 1968-69; lectr., instr. Queens Coll., Flushing, N.Y., 1970-71; fellow in neurology, instr. ophthalmology Mt. Sinai Sch. Medicine, N.Y.C., 1971-74; adj. asst. prof. St. Francis Coll., Bklyn., 1974; asst. prof. dept. psychology So. Ill. U. Sch. Medicine, Carbondale, 1974-76; USPHS intern Conn. Valley Hosp., Middletown, Conn., 1976-77; asst. prof., asst. project coordinator dept. psychiatry Nat. Alcohol Research Ctr., U. Conn. Health Ctr., Farmington, 1977-79; neuropsychologist, asst. prof. program in medicine Brown U., Providence, 1979-82; adj. asst. prof. psychology U. R.I., Kingston and Providence, 1979-83; pvt. practice psychology, 1981-83; dir. Neuropsychol. Assessment and Treatment Ctr., Ctr. for Neuropsychology Services, Ft. Lauderdale, 1983-90, So. Inst. Forensic Neuropsychology, 1990-97; adj. faculty Nova Southwestern U., 1997—; cons. Narco Bio-systems, 1974-75; cons. to commr. mental health State of Conn., 1978-79; invited spkr. NATO Neuropsychology Congress, 1980, Internat. Coun. Psychology, 1980, 22 Internat. Congress Psychology, 1980. Bd. dirs. Sojourner House, 1979-80, Combined Hosp. Alcoholism Program, 1978, Hartford Interval House, 1978. Served with WAC, 1963. CUNY fellow, 1972; recipient Hartford Salute award, 1979; USPHS tng. fellow, 1966-67, NIMH predoctoral fellow 1967-70. Fellow Am. Coll. Forensic Examiners; mem. APA (mem. exec. bd.), Assn. Women in Psychology (mem. steering com.), Eastern Psychol. Assn. (chmn. 1980 conv.), Conn. Psychol. Assn. (coun. 1978-79), R.I. Psychol. Assn., N.Y. Acad. Scis., Sigma Xi, Psi Chi. Home: 8714 NW 82nd St Tamarac FL 33321-1612 Office: 1200 N University Dr Plantation FL 33322-4724

APPEL, HELMUT, nuclear physicist; b. Munich, July 23, 1929; m. Kristin Keilhack, 1935; 3 children. Student, Inst. Tech. Munich, 1954, U. Erlangen, Fed. Republic Germany, 1958, U. Mainz. Rschr. AERE, Harwell, Eng., UCLA, U. Johannesburg, South Africa, U. Karlsruhe, Germany, 1961—. Contbr. nuclear physics articles to profl. jours. Mem. German Physics Soc., Royal Soc. South Africa (fgn. assoc.). Office: U Karlsruhe, U Karlsruhe, Postfach 3640, D 76021 Karlsruhe Germany

APPEL, LAWRENCE JOHN, physician, educator; b. Holyoke, Mass., Oct. 8, 1955; s. John F. and Irma G. Appel; m. Jean Marie Ricketts; children: Christopher, Laura, Katherine. AB, Dartmouth Coll., 1977; MD, NYU, 1981; MPH, Johns Hopkins U., 1989. Intern, resident to chief resident Balt. City Hosp., 1981-85; assoc. prof. Johns Hopkins U. Sch. Medicine, Balt. Contbr. articles to profl. jours. Office: Johns Hopkins U Welch Ctr 2024 E Monument St Baltimore MD 21287-0007

APPEL, MARSHA CEIL, association executive; b. N.Y.C., Dec. 3, 1953; d. Albert and Stella Joy (Glaser) A.; m. Mark D. Marcellus, Sept. 10, 1978; children: Sam, Jill. BA, SUNY, Albany, 1974; MSLS, Syracuse U., 1975. Info. specialist Am. Assn. Advt. Agys., N.Y.C., 1976-79, mgr. member info. svc., 1979-89, v.p., 1989-97, sr. v.p., 1997—. Author: Illustration Index IV, 1980, Illustration Index V, 1984, Illustration Index VI, 1988, Illustration Index VII, 1993, Illustration Index VIII, 1998; editor What's New in Advertising and Marketing, 1978-80; mem. adv. bd., contbr. Ency. Advt., 1999. Mem. Spl. Librs. Assn. (chmn. advt. and mktg. div. 1982-83). Office: Am Assn Advt Agys 405 Lexington Ave New York NY 10174-0002

APPENROTH, KLAUS JÜRGEN, plant physiologist, researcher; b. Eisenach, Germany, Nov. 19, 1948; s. Jochen and Gunda (Raddau) A.; m. Dorothea Ruda, Feb. 3, 1973; children: Judith, Clemens. Diploma in chemistry, U. Jena, Germany, 1972, PhD, 1978, Habilitation, 1991. Asst. Carl Zeiss Co., Jena, 1978; sci. co-worker U. Jena, 1979-93, privatdozent, 1993—. Contbr. more than 60 articles to profl. jours. including Photochemistry and Photobiology, Planta, and Physiologica Plantarum. Mem. Deutsch Botanische Gesellschaft, European Soc. for Photobiology, Am. Soc. for Photobiology. Roman Catholic. Avocations: walking, bicycling. Office: U Jena Inst Plant Physiolog, Dornburger Strasse 159, D-07743 Jena Germany

APPENZELLER, IMMO JULIUS, astronomy educator; b. Urach, Germany, May 13, 1940; s. Julius and Else (Knödler) A.; m. Gisela Dudek, July 17, 1970; children: Guido, Bastian, Sören. D of Natural Scis., U. Göttingen, Germany, 1966. Rsch. assoc. U. Chgo., 1966-67; staff scientist, ausserplanmassiger prof. U. Göttingen, 1967-75; prof. astronomy U. Heidelberg, Germany, 1975—; dir. State Observatory Heidelberg-Königstuhl, 1975—. Co-author: Star Formation, 1980; co-author, editor: Evolution of Galaxies, 1989; editor: Circumstellar Matter, 1987, Cosmology, 1985. Mem. Astron. Soc., Internat. Astron. Union (asst. gen. sec. 1991-94, gen. sec. 1994-97), Max-Planck Soc. (external mem.). Office: Landessternwarte, D-69117 Heidelberg Germany

APPIAH, JAMES PETER KING, writer; b. Baman, Kumasi, Ghana, Feb. 16, 1951; arrived in Italy, 1984; s. James Peter Kwadwo Appiah and Abenaa Akyiaa; m. Angela Mabel Asare, Jan. 1, 1977; 1 child, Esther Vergea. BA in Literary Studies, Pacific Western U., 1990; diploma in journalism/story writing, ICS, Scranton, 1993. Ordained to ministry Bishop Universal Ministries, 1980. Libr. asst. Ghana Libr. Bd., Accra, 1973-76; dir. Adonten Lit. Works, Kumasi, 1976-95; pub., writer Appiah Esthermat Comm. Ltd., 1995—; cons., bd. dirs. Success in Bus. with Christ, 1996—. Author, editor, pub.: Prayer—The Key to a Triumphant Christian Living, 1992, Overcomers in the Blood, 1995, (poetry) The Lord of Praise, 1988; author: The Meaning of Pentecost, 1995; co-author: (poetry anthologies) Poetry '72, 1972, Words of Praise, Vol. II, 1986, The American Poetry Anthology, Vol. VI, No. I, 1986, The Poetry of Life: A Treasury of Moments, 1987, Within Us All, 1995, The Day I Found God, 1995, A Richer Life, 1995, The 1996 Christian Poetry Companion, 1996, Ode to the Dead (Dedicated to the Princess of the People), 1998; also articles, poems (Cert. of Contbn. award BBC Network Africe, 1985, Italy Mondello Poetry award Mondello Tourist Ctr. 1987). Nat. coord. Morris Cerullo World Evangelism, Italy, 1995—; pres., founder Followers of Christ Internat. Ch., 1974—; interim coord. United Christian Assn. Chs., Italy, 1996—; mem. Ghana Young Pioneers, Kumasi, 1962; religious leader Ghana Youth Club, Kumasi, 1978-79. Honored City of Palermo, Italy, 1988. Mem. Ghana Assn. Writers (asst. gen. sec. 1971-72), United Christian Assn. (gen. sec. 1977-84), Christian Writers Forum (bd. dirs. 1996—), United Christian Assn. Italy (interim coord. 1996-97). Avocations: reading, sports, gospel music, drawing. Home: Via San Giovanni Bosco #126, 41100 Modena Italy

APPLE, DAINA DRAVNIEKS, government agency official; b. Kuldiga, Latvia, July 6, 1944; came to U.S., 1951; d. Albins Dravnieks and Alina A. (Bergs) Zelmenis; divorced; 1 child, Almira Moronne; m. Martin A. Apple, Sept. 2, 1986. BSc, U. Calif., Berkeley, 1977, MA, 1980. Economist USDA Pacific S.W. Rsch., Berkeley, 1976-85; mgr. regional land use appeals USDA Forest Svc., San Francisco, 1986-88, program analysis officer, engring., 1988-90; asst. regulatory officer USDA Forest Svc., 1990-95, strategic planner nat. forest sys. resources program, 1995-98; policy analyst US Forest Svc., 1998—. Author: Public Involvement in the Forest Service-Methodologies, 1977, Public Involvement, Selected Abstracts for Natural Resource Managers, 1979, The Management of Policy and Direction in the Forest Service, 1982, An Analysis of the Forest Service Human Resource Management Program, 1984, Organization Design-Abstracts for Natural Resources Users, 1986, Social and Legal Force Changing the Management of National Forests, 1996, Water and the Forest Service, 2000, The Forest as a Learning Organization, 2000; contbg. editor Jour. Women in Natural Resources, 1987—. Fellow Phi Beta Kappa Soc.; mem. AAAS, ESA, AWIS, Am. Water Resources Assn., Am. Forestry Assn., Soc. Am. Foresters (chair nat. capital chpt.), Assn. Am. Geographers, Am. Latvian Assn. (bd. dirs. 1995-97), Phi Beta Kappa Assns. (nat. sec. 1985-88, pres. No. Calif. 1982-84), Commonwealth Club of Calif., Exchange Club of Capitol Hill, Women of Washington, Sigma Xi. Avocations: organization and political theory, ballroom dancing, tennis, film. Office: USDA Forest Svc Policy Analysis Staff PO Box 96090 Washington DC 20090-6090

APPLE, MARTIN ALLEN, scientific federation executive, educator; b. Duluth, Minn., Sept. 17, 1938; m. M. Daina; children: Deborah Dawn, Pamela Ruth, Nathan, Rebeccah Lynn. AB, ALA, U. Minn., 1959, MSc, 1962; PhD, U. Calif., 1968. Chmn. Multidisciplinary Drug Rsch. Group U. Calif., San Francisco, 1974-78; pres. Escagen-IPRI, San Carlos, Calif., 1978-81; with EAN-Tech., Inc., Daly City, Calif., 1982-84, chmn. bd., 1983-84; with Adytum Internat., Mountain View, Calif., 1982-90, CEO, 1983-90; CEO LEADERS, Washington, 1989—; pres., Coun. Sci. Soc. Presidents, Washington, 1993—; CEO Sci. Watch, Inc., 1996-98; with Hon. Doug Walgren co-chair Leadership Network, 1995-97; adj. prof. U. Calif., San Francisco, 1982-84; cons. SRI Internat. Dept. Edn., EPA, NIH, NSF, The Network, Hughes-GM, Nat. Cancer Inst., AAAS, Nat. Sci. Tchrs. Assn., others; adj. rsch. prof. George Mason U., Fairfax, Va., 1991-92; vis. scholar Nat. Humanities Ctr., 1990-91; nat. project mgr. NSTA Scope Sequence and Coordination Project, 1991-92; bd. dirs. Am. Med. Progress Ednl. Found.; bd. dirs. ACCTION, Inc., chmn. trustees, 1995-96; expert advisor Dept. of Edn., 1996—. Author: (with F. Myers) Review Medical Pharmacology, 1976; (with M. Fink) Immune RNA in Neoplasia, 1976; (with F. Becker et al) Cancer: A Comprehensive Treatise, 1977; (with M. Keenberg et al) Investing in Biotechnology, 1981; (with F. Ahmad et al) From Genes to Proteins: Horizons in Biotechnology, 1983; (with J. Kureczka) Status of Biotechnology, 1987; (with M. Baum) Business Advantage, 1987 (winner Excellence award Software Pubs. Assn. 1987), (with R. Yager) Translating and Using Research for Improving Teacher Education in Science and Mathematics, 1998; mem. editl. bd. Computers in Medicine. Mem. Calif. Coun. Indsl. Innovation, 1982; chmn. bd. visitors U. Md./UMBI, 1999—. Recipient citation East West Ctr. Bd. of Govs., 1988, Leadership citation Coun. Sci. Soc. Pres., 1995. Fellow Am. Coll. Clin. Pharmacology, Am. Inst. Chemists; mem. Assn. Venture Founders (bd. govs. 1982-83), East-West Ctr. Assn. (trustee 1982-88, vice chmn. 1983-85), Profl. Software Programmers Assn., Leaders of Tomorrow (chmn. 1987-88), Commonwealth Club Calif., Phi Beta Kappa Assocs. (Disting. Svc. award 1984, 85), Phi Beta Kappa, Sigma Xi (bd. dirs., chmn. long-range strategic planning com. 1988-92). Office: Coun Sci Soc Presidents PO Box 33999 Washington DC 20033-0999

APPLEBY, STUART, professional golfer; b. Cohuna, Australia, May 1, 1971. Amateur winner Queensland Open, 1991; winner Victorian title, 1991; profl. golfer, 1992—; 2d pl. Bay Hill Invitational; runner-up Sprint Internat.; winner Victorian PGA Championship, 1994, S.Australia PGA Championship, 1994, Nedlands Masters Classic, 1994, Nedlands Tassie Classic, 1994, Nike Sonoma County Open, 1995, Nike Monterey Open, 1995, Honda Classic, 1997, Kemper Open, 1998, Coolum Classic, 1998, Shell Houston Open, 1999; mem. nat. team Dunhill Cup, 1997, 98, The Pres. Cup, 1998; mem. PGA Tour charity team The Players Championship, 1999; finished in top 25 NEC World Series of Golf, 1998. Named 1st Q-Sch. grad. to earn more than $1 million the following year. Avocations: action sports, motor racing. Office: Ste 1300 One Erie View Plaza Cleveland OH 44114-1715*

APPLEGATE, KARL EDWIN, lawyer; b. Cicero, Ind., July 21, 1923; s. Karl Raymond and Gladys Mae (Worley) A.; m. Elizabeth Ann Dilts, June 10, 1944; children—Eric Edwin, Raymond Alan, Robert Dale, Beth Ann. B.S., Ind. U., 1946, J.D., 1948. Bar: Ind. 1949, Fed. Ct. (7th cir.); U.S. Supreme Ct., 1968, U.S. Tax Ct., 1983. U.S. commr. So. Dist. Ind., 1953-58, cert. family and civil mediator, Ind. Fla., 1992; dep. prosecutor Monroe County, Ind., 1959; mcpl. judge, Bloomington, Ind., 1960-63; mem. Ind. Ho. of Reps., 1965-66; U.S. atty. So. Dist. Ind., 1967-70; sr. ptnr. Applegate Law Offices, Bloomington, 1970-92, sr. mem., 1991-93; sr. mem. Applegate, McDonald, Koch & Arnold, Bloomington, 1993—, now Applegate McDonald & Koch PC. legal cons. Ind. Masonic Home, Franklin, 1981-82. Trustee 1st United Methodist Ch., 1962-65. Served to staff sgt. AUS, 1941-44, ETO. Decorated Purple Heart. Named Outstanding Young Man of Bloomington, Jaycees, 1956, recipient Disting. Service award U.S. Jr. C. of C., 1956, Good Govt. award, 1961. Mem. Fed. Bar Assn., Ind. Bar Assn. (co-chair com. assistance to lawyers program 1990-94), Monroe County Bar Assn., ABA, Tri-County Bar Assn., Alpha Kappa Psi. Democrat. Clubs: Kiwanis, Elks, Masons. Home: 509 S Swain Ave Bloomington IN 47401-5129 Office: Applegate McDonald & Koch PO Box 1030 Bloomington IN 47402-1030

APPLETON, RODNEY LEWIS CLAUDE, economist, publisher, consultant; b. San Fernando, Trinidad, Trinidad and Tobago, Mar. 18, 1931; s. Claude Lennox Vivian and Mildred Gladys (Benn) A.; m. Patricia Irene Carter, May 30, 1955; adopted children: Candice, Elizabeth. BSc in Econ., Money and Banking, U. London, 1963; diploma in Nat. Resources Devel., U. Cambridge, Eng., 1973. Pub. assistance officer Dept. Social Assistance Govt. of Trinidad and Tobago, 1950-54, coop. officer grade 2 Dept. Coop. Devel., 1954-60, economist Ministry of Fin., 1963-66, economist Ministry of Labour, 1966-68, from economist to sr. economist Ministry of Petroleum and Mines, 1968-82, sr. energy analyst Ministry of Energy, 1982-88; mng. dir., editor, author Carib-Latin Energy Cons., Port of Spain, Trinidad, 1989—; petroleum cons. Petro Cons., Geneva, 1978—; petroleum attaché Embassy of Trinidad and Tobago, Washington; rep. Trinidad internat. confs., 1971—. Mem. Lions Club (sec. 1977-81), Masons (Alexandra Lodge). Presbyterian. Avocations: playing piano, organ. Office: Carib-Latin Energy Cons Ltd, PO Box 3074 St James PO, Port of Spain Trinidad and Tobago

APPLEWHITE, THOMAS HOOD, retired chemist; b. Imperial, Calif., Dec. 30, 1924; s. Thomas and Lottie Lea (McCamy) A.; m. Harriet Mary Kaplan, June 3, 1945; children—Pamela Applewhite Burke, Thomas Ted. A.A., Pasadena City Coll., 1951; B.S., Calif. Inst. Tech., 1953, Ph.D., 1957. Research chemist Dow Chem. Co., Pittsburg, Calif., 1956-59, Western Regional Research Lab., U.S. Dept. Agr., Albany, Calif., 1959-63; investigation leader Western Regional Research Lab., U.S. Dept. Agr., 1963-67; research dir. PVO Internat., Richmond, Calif., 1967-69; mgr. edible oil products Kraft Inc., Glenview, Ill., 1969-78; dir. research services Kraft Inc., 1978-87, retired; mem. sci. adv. panel United Soybean Bd., 1993—. Assoc. editor Jour. Am. Oil Chemists Soc., 1967-85, editor, 1985-91; editor Bailey Indsl. Oil & Fat Products, 1985, INFORM, 1990-93. Served with USN, 1942-45, ETO, CBI. NSF fellow, 1955-56; recipient Service award Nat. Assn. Margarine Mfrs., 1980; Merit award Kraft, 1982. Mem. Am. Oil Chemists Soc. (bd. gov. 1975-82, pres. 1977-78; A.E. Bailey award 1982, A. Richard Baldwin Disting. Svc. award, 1991, hon. mem. 1994, Disting. fellow, 1998, United Soybean bd. meritorious award, 1999), Am. Chem. Soc., Inst. Food Technologists, Sigma Xi. Republican. Presbyterian. Office: 1032 Verbena Dr Austin TX 78750-1402

APPOLINARIO, FABIO, psychologist, researcher; b. São Paulo, Brazil, Apr. 27, 1965; s. Duirio and Arlete (Branco) A.; m. Lilian Domingues Graziano, June 24, 1993; children: Juliana, Lucas. BBA, FASP, São Paulo, 1986; B.Psychology, USJT, São Paulo, 1994; MS in Psychology, U. São Paulo, 1997, postgrad., 1997—. Lic. psychologist, bus. adminstr., systems engr. CEO Tempus, São Paulo, 1994—; rschr. U. São Paulo, 1996—; assoc. prof. U. Mogi das Cruzes, 1997—, clin. coord., 1998—; assoc. prof. UNIBAN, São Paulo, 1998—; asst. prof. UNIP, Campinas, 1998-99; cons. Artes Médicas, Porto Alegre, brazil, 1997—, MBA, São Paulo, 1996-97; dir. Ass. Bras. Ter. Cognitivas, São Paulo, 1997-98, Clinica da Villa, São Paulo, 1995—. Author: Psicoterapia e Constantivisno, 1998; contbr. articles to profl. jours. Mem. APA, SBP, SPSP. Avocations: reading, electronics, computer programming. Office: UMC/Av Dr Candido Xavier, de Almeida 200, 08780911 Mogi das Cruzes Brazil

APPUKUTTAN, PADINJARADATH SANKUNNY, biochemist, researcher; b. Aluva, Kerala, India, Sept. 3, 1952; s. Velu Sankunny and Narayanan Chandramathy; m. Pazhat Sivasankaran Snehalatha, Nov. 2, 1957; children: Ajay, Ashok. MS, U. Kerala, 1974; PhD, U. Madras, India, 1982. Rsch. fellow Christian Med. Coll. Hosp., Vellore, India, 1975-76, Indian Inst. Chem. Biology, Calcutta, 1976-79; from asst. prof. to assoc. prof. Sree Chitra Thirunal Inst. for Med. Sci. and Tech., Trivandrum, India, 1979-87, additional prof., 1991—; postdoctoral fellow Uniformed Svcs. U. of Health Scis., Bethesda, Md., 1987-88. Patentee in field. Recipient Vasvik Indsl. Rsch. award Vividhlakshi Audyogik Samsodhan Vikaskendra, Bombay, 1979. Mem. Soc. Biol. Chemists. Office: Sree Chitra Tirunal Inst for Med Sci and Tech, 695011, Trivandrum Kerala, India

APREA, JOSE LUIS, process engineer; b. La Plata, Argentina, Apr. 25, 1956; s. Francisco and Elena Mercedes (Gomez) A. BS in Chem. Engring., U. Tech., La Plata, 1980. From fuels and water lab. technician to process engr. Yacimientos Petroliferos Fiscales, La Plata, 1974-83; process engring. head Atomic Energy Commn., Neuquen, Argentina, 1983-93; chief engring. Atomic Energy Commn., Arroyito, Argentina, 1993—; rsch. dir. bioleaching group U. Nat. del Comahue, Neuquen, 1993-97; prof. unit ops. U. Nat., Neuquen, 1990—; heavy water tech. expert Internat. Atomic Energy Agy., Vienna, Austria, 1996—; heavy water process cons. Atomic Energy Commn., Neuquen, 1995—, hydrogen damage working group, 1993-96; nat. sec. ISO TC/197 for Inst. Argentine Standardization, Buenos Aires, 1997—. Editor: Hidrogeno, 1998. Sec. Heavy Water Plant Club, Plottier, Argentina, 1985-94; co-founder Heavy Wat er Plant Club Libr., Arroyito, 1985. Named Outstanding Participant, Atomic Energy Commn., 1990. Mem. AAAS, N.Y. Acad. Sci. Avocations: photography, skiing, travel, tennis. Fax: 54 (299) 4480 713. Home: House # 40 CNEA, 8316 Plottier Argentina Office: Heavy Water Plant, CC 805, 8300 Neuquen Argentina

AP REES, ELFAN DYFED, publisher, editor; b. Oxford, Eng., Nov. 27, 1941; s. Brian Oyfed and Isobel (Cutler) R.; m. Linda Cook, Jan. 14, 1964 (dec. 1987); 1 child, Claire. Student pub. schs., Weston-s-Mare Somerset, 1952-59. Tech. pub. asst. Westland Helicopters, Weston-s-Mare Somerset, 1959-64; mng. dir. Avia Press Assocs., 1965—; pub. editor Helicopter Internat., Weston-s-Mare Somerset, 1977—, Helidata, 1980—; dir. Helicopters Unltd., 1982—. Author: Jane's World Military Helicopters; tech. editor Ency. Rotocraft; contbr. articles to profl. jours. Councilor North Somerset Dist. Coun., Eng., 1978—; chmn. The Helicopter Mus., 1976—. Mil. svc., 1961-65. Churchill fellow FAI Rotorcraft Com., 1992. Fellow Inst. Sales and Mktg. (pres. (hon.)); mem. Royal Aero. Soc., Helicopter Club of Gt. Britain (v.p.). Office: Avia Press Assocs, 75 Elm Tree Rd, Locking, Weston-S-Mare Somerset BS24 8EL, England

APSITIS, ROMANS, judge, court official; b. 1939. Grad., U. Latvia Faculty Law, 1963; student, Moscow State U. Faculty Law, 1972, U. Tartu, 1987; JD, 1993. Investigation officer Procurator's Office, Riga, 1962-63; assoc. prof. U. Latvia Faculty Law; head. editl. staff of philosophy and law Editl. Office of Encyc., 1976-80; dep. Supreme Coun., 1990-93, mem. Legal Commn., 1990-93; mem. Saeima, 1993-94, 95-96, mem. Legal Commn., 1993-94, 95-96; parlimentary sec. Ministry of Justice, Govt. of Latvia, Riga, 1993-94, min. justice, 1994-95; dep. chmn. Constl. Ct., Riga. Recipient Order of Three Stars, 2000. Office: Constnl Ct Rep Latvia, 1 Alunana St, Riga LV-1010, Latvia

APTE, VEENA AJAY, management consultant; b. Dharwar, Karnataka, India, June 21, 1959; d. Madhav Ramchandra and Charulata (Madhav) Pusalkar; m. Ajay Dattatraya Apte, May 24, 1981; 1 child, Renuka. BSc in Home Sci., 1978; BEd, U. Karnataka, 1981; MA, U. Poona, 1983, PhD, 1987. Prof. Fergusson Coll., Pune, India, 1983-85; rschr. Nat. Inst. Bank Mgmt., Pune, 1987-88; faculty Tata Mgmt. Tng. Ctr., Pune, 1989—; internat. cons. Sandvik AB, Sweden/Asia Pacific, 1997; vis. prof. Groupe Essec, Cergy-Pontoise, France, 1992-93; condr. workshops in stress mgmt. Contbr. articles to profl. jours. Univ. Grants Commn. grantee, 1984-86; Rotary Found. fellow, 1989. Mem. APA, Indian Psychiat. Soc., Poona Psychol. Assn. Avocations: reading, cooking, counseling. Home: 134/4/17 Ashok Nagar, Pune 411 007, India Office: tata Mgmt Tng Ctr, 1 Mangaldas Rd, Pune 411 001, India

APTED, MICHAEL DAVID, film director; b. London, Feb. 10, 1941. BA, Downing Coll., Cambridge, Eng., 1963. Dir.: (films) Triple Echo, 1972, Stardust, 1974, The Squeeze, 1976, Agatha, 1977, Coalminer's Daughter, 1980 (DGA nominee), Continental Divide, 1981, Gorky Park, 1983, Kipperbang, 1983 (Brit. Acad. TV and Film award nominee), Firstborn, 1984, Critical Condition, 1986, Gorillas in the Mist, 1988, Class Action, 1990, Thunderheart, 1991, Blink, 1993, Nell, 1994, Extreme Measures, 1996, Always Outnumbered, 1998, The World Is Not Enough, 1999, Enigma, 2000; (play) Strawberry Fields, 1978 (BAFTA, Emmy award); (documentaries) 14 UP, 21 UP (Internat. Emmy), 28 UP (Brit. Acad. award, Internat. Emmy), 1985, Bring On the Night, 1984 (Emmy, Grammy awards),

The Long Way Home, 1989, Incident at Oglala, 1991, 35 UP, 1992 (BAFTA award), Moving the Mountain, 1993 (IDA award), Inspirations, 1997, 42 Up, 1998, Me & Isaac Newton, 1999; (Brit. TV) Slattery's Mounted Foot, 1970 (Brit. Critics Best Play), The Mosedale Horshoe, 1971 (Brit. Critics Best Play), Another Sunday and Sweet F.A., 1972 (Brit. Critics Best Play), Follyfoot, 1972 (Best Children's Svcs.), Kisses at Fifty (Brit. Critics Best Play, SFTA Best Dir.), The Collection (Internat. Emmy), others.

APTEKMANN, GUENTHER See **YOELI, PINHAS**

APTOWITZER, WILLI ZEEV, insurance executive; b. Austria, Apr. 13, 1918; s. Adolph George Moses Aaron and Regina Ryfka (Weber-Cirer) A.; m. Margit Manzi Stern, Sept. 22, 1944. Student, Handelsakademie and Hochschule, 1938; D of Bus. Adminstrn. (hon.), 1989, Chartered Inst. Ins., London, 1941-44, 1989. Co-founder NIO Group cos., 1949; mng. dir. Nat. Ins. Office Ltd., 1955-67, chmn. group, 1967—; mem. Lloyd's Underwriters, London, 1976-96; dir. Haifa Econ. Corp., Sci. Based Industry Corp., Haifa, 1975-94, mem. Israel Ins. Coun., 1979-82, mem. adv. com. to supr. ins., 1990-97, Internat. Union Marine Ins., 1984—, mem. Cargo Loss Prevention Com., 1984-89. Chmn. Aptowitzer Found. for Haifa; founding trustee Haifa Found.; chmn. fin. com., trustee, bd. govs. Haifa U., chmn. control com. 1998-96, hon. fellow, 1998, trustee, bd. dirs. Tel Aviv Mus. of Art, 1996, hon. fellow 1997; bd. dirs. Haifa Mus.; chmn. fund raising com., founding mem., past chmn. Gan Hayeled; mem. Comm. of the Israel Mgmt. Ctr., 1996. Served to lt. col. Res. Israel Def. Forces, 1948—. Hon. citizen City of Haifa, 1988—; recipient diploma of honor Internat. inst. Cmty. svc.; Cert. of Merit DIB, London. Mem. Chamber Commerce and Industry, various bi-country leagues, Maccabi Sports Assn. (past dep. chmn.), Internat. Ins. Soc. (bd. govs. and electoral coll. 1983—), Masons, Rotary (past pres. Carmel, cert. of merit 1980).

APUD, JOSE ANTONIO, psychiatrist, psychopharmacologist, educator; b. San Miguel de Tucuman, Argentina, May 25, 1948; came to U.S., 1987; s. Jose and Emelin (Chagra) A.; m. Graciela Varela, Jan. 25, 1979; children: Maria Macarena, Jose Sebastian. MD, U. Tucuman, 1975; degree in pharmacology, U. Milan, 1980, degree in exptl. endocrinology, 1983; PhD, U. Buenos Aires, 1985. Diplomate Am. Bd. Psychiatry and Neurology. Investigator CONICET, Buenos Aires, 1985—; prof. pharmacology U. Buenos Aires, 1985-93; psychiatrist in residence St. Elizabeth's Hosp., Nat. Inst. of Mental Health, Washington, 1991-95; clin. assoc. neuropsychiatry br. Nat. Inst. of Mental Health, Washington, 1995-98; faculty psychiatry residency tng. program Commn. on Mental Health Svcs., Washington, 1998—; dir. psychopharmacology divsn. St. Elizabeths Hosp.-Commn. on Mental Health Svcs., Washington, 1998—; cons. Farmitalia Carlo Erba Labs, Milan, 1979-83; vis. prof. pharmacology Georgetown U., Washington, 1987-91; mem. editorial bd. Endocrinologia Clinica y Metabolism, 1982—, Neuroendocrinologia Latinoamericana, 1982—; instr. dept. psychiatry George Washington U., 1995-98, prof. psychiatry, 1998—. Contbr. numerous articles to profl. jours. Fellow Nat. Atomic Energy Commn., 1976, Dept. Endocrinology French Hosp., 1978, Inst. Pharmacology U. Milan, 1978-84, sr. staff fellow St. Elizabeth's Hosp. NIMH, 1994-98; recipient Cediquifa award in pharmacology, 1992, Upjohn award NIMH, 1993. Mem. AMA, Am. Psychiat. Assn. (sci. com. 1993-95, Burroughs Wellcome award 1993), Am. Soc. Clin. Psychopharmacology, Washington Psychiat. Soc., Italian Soc. Neurosci., Italian Soc. Pharmacology, Soc. for Neurosci., Sociedad Argentina de Farmacologia Exptl., Internat. Soc. Psychoneuroendocrinology, Internat. Soc. Neuroendocrinology, Argentina Soc. Biology and Nuclear Medicine, Serotonin Club. Roman Catholic. Achievements include identification of Gabaergic system in rats; study of the mechanism of action of psychotropic drugs; studies on schizophrenia and tardive dyskinesia; identification of an endogenous ligand for the serotonin-2 receptor in the rat brain. Avocations: reading, music, travel to foreign countries. Office: Psychopharmacology Divsn/Dept Psych St Elizabeth's Hosp 2700 ML King Jr Ave SE Washington DC 20032-2601

APURON, ANTHONY SABLAN, archbishop; b. Agana, Guam, Nov. 1, 1945; s. Manuel Taijito and Ana Santos (Sablan) P. BA, St. Anthony Coll., 1969; MDiv, Maryknoll Sem., 1972, M Theology, 1973; MA in Liturgy, Notre Dame U., 1974; LHD, U. Guam, 1998. Ordained priest Roman Catholic ch., 1972, ordained bishop, 1984, installed archbishop, 1986. Chmn. Diocesan Liturgical Commn., Agana, 1974-86; vice chmn. Chamorro Lang. Commn., Agana, 1984-86; aux. bishop Archdiocese of Agana, 1984-85, archbishop, 1986—; chmn. Interfaith Vols. Caregivers, Agana, 1984—; mem. Civilian Adv. com., Agana, 1986—; pres. Cath. Bishops' Conf. of Pacific, 1990-96; v.p. Cath. Bishops' Conf. of Oceania, 1990-98; permanent mem. Post-Synod of Bishops of Oceania, 1998—. Author: A Structural Analysis of the Content of Myth in the Thought of Mircea Eliade, 1973. Chmn. Cath. Ednl. Radio. Named Most Outstanding Young Man, Jaycees of Guam, 1984. Avocations: jogging, walking, swimming. Office: Archbishop's Office 196B Cuesta San Ramon Hagatna GU 96910-4334

AQAZADEH-KHOI, QOLAM REZA, Iranian government official; b. 1948. Min. petroleum Govt. of Iran, Teheran, Iran, 1985-98, v.p. atomic energy, 1998—. Office: Office of Pres, Palestine Crossrd/Pastor Av, Tehran Iran*

AQRAWI, ADNAN A. M., sedimentologist, geologist; b. Aqra, Ninava, Iraq, Apr. 28, 1958; s. A. Razak Mohammed and Safya M. Babakir; m. Ibtisam A. Wahab Ibrahim, Dec. 29, 1982; children: Lara, Ahmed, Abdul-Razzaq. BSc in Geology, U. Baghdad, Iraq, 1980, MSc in Geology, 1984; PhD in Sedimentology, U. London, 1993; diploma in sedimentary geology, Imperial Coll., London, 1994. Rschr. in marine sedimentology Marine Sci. Ctr., Basrah (Iraq) U., 1984-90; clay mineralogist U. London Imperial Coll., 1990-93; head geo-archaeology rsch. unit U. Baghdad, 1993-95; sr. sedimentologist Petronas Rsch. & Sci. Svc., Kuala Lumpur, Malaysia, 1995-97; geology advisor Smedvig Techs. AS (now Roxar ASA), Stavanger, Norway, 1997-99; sr. cons. PetroSediment Consultancy (PSC), Stavanger, Norway, 2000—; project cons. So. Petroleum Co., Basrah, 1984-87; project cons. for reservoir devel. Iraqi Ministry Oil, Baghdad, 1987-89, environ. sedimentologist hydrocarbon pollution rsch. team, 1987-90. Contbr. articles to internat. geol. jours. With Anti-Tank Missile Divsn. and Iraq Marines, 1980-81, 84, Iraq-Iran War. Scholar Brit. Coun., 1990-93. Mem. AAPG, IAS, SPE, NPF. Avocations: reading, music, travel. Office: PetroSediment Consultancy, Skipsbygger Knudsens Vie 10, 4085 Hundvåg Stavanger Norway

AQUILECCHIA, GIOVANNI, Italian studies educator; b. Nettuno, Rome, Italy, Nov. 28, 1923; s. Vincenzo and Maria Letizia (Filibeck) A.; m. Costantina Maria Bacchetta, May 7, 1951 (div. July 1973); children: Adolfo, Vincent Maria, Maria Letizia; m. Catherine Mary Posford, Apr. 24, 1992. Dottore in Lettere, U. Rome, 1946, Perfezionamento Filologia Moderna, 1948, Libero Docente, 1958—; MA (hon.), U. Manchester, Eng., 1965. Lectr. in Italian Univ. Coll., London, 1953-59, reader, 1959-61; prof. Italian lang. and lit. U. Manchester, 1961-70; prof. Italian Bedford Coll. U. London, 1970-85, prof. Italian, Royal Holloway Coll., 1985-89, prof. emeritus, 1990—; rsch. fellow Univ. Coll., London, 1984-97, hon. prof. Italian, 1998—; vis. prof. Victoria U., Melbourne, Australia, 1983, U. Naples, Italy, 1990; pres. Internat. Ctr. for Bruno Studies, Naples, 1996—. Author: Giordano Bruno, 1971, Schede di Italianistica, 1976, Le Opere Italiane Di G. Bruno, 1991, 2d edit., 2000, French transl., 2000, Schede Bruniane, 1993, Nuove Schede di Italianistica, 1994, G. Bruno nel suo tempo, 2000, Bibliographie des Publications (1946-2000), 2000. Mem. Univ. and Local Com. for Peace, Rome, 1948-49. Boursier du Govt. Français, Paris, 1949-50; Brit. Coun. scholar, London, 1950-51; Serena medal British Acad., 1996. Fellow Arcadia Accademia Letteraria; mem. Soc. for Renaissance Studies, Internat. Assn. for Study of Italian Lang. and Lit., Modern Humanities Rsch. Assn. Avocations: swimming, sailing, classical guitar. Office: Univ Coll, Gower St, London WC1E 6BT, England

AQUINO, ALFREDO FERNANDEZ, academic administrator; b. Calasiao, The Philippines, Jan. 12, 1940; s. Ramon Escaño and Benita (Fernandez) A.; m. Corazon Jovellanos, Sept. 6, 1964; children: Fernand, Ruth, Josephine, Naomi. BS in Indsl. Art., Philippine Coll. Arts & Trades, 1960; MA in Indsl. Edn., Tech. U. of The Philippines, 1972, DEd in Indsl. Edn. Mgmt., 1984. Cert. tchr., supt., The Philippines. Elem. sch. prin. Dept. Edn., Culture and Sports, Pangasinan, The Philippines, 1964-76; chmn. dept. So. Ilocos Poly. State Coll., Lallnion, The Philippines, 1976-83; dean Coll. Edn. U. Southeastern Philippines, Davao, 1983-85; chief divsn. R&D and tech. svcs. Bur. Tech. Vocat. Edn., Dept. Edn., Culture and Sports, Manila, 1985-97; vice grad. sch. Pangasinen State U., Lingayen, The Philippines, 1987-88, dean grad. sch., 1988-90, v.p. adminstrn. rsch. and extension, 1990—, exec. dir. open univ. sys., 1992—; field test dir. SEAMEO-INNOTECH, Quezon City, The Philippines, 1988—. Editor jours., handbook and bull. in field. Pres. Univ. Found., Pangasinan, 1999. Study grantee ILO, 1985, Colombo Plan, 1996, PASUC, 1970, 80-82. Mem. Phi Delta Kappa. Avocation: painting.

AQUINO, CORAZON COJUANGCO, former president of Republic of The Philippines; b. Manila, Jan. 25, 1933; d. Jose Cojuangco Sr. and Demetria Sumulong; m. Benigno S. Aquino Jr., Oct. 11, 1954 (dec. 1983); children: Maria Elena, Aurora Corazon, Benigno S. III, Victoria Elisa, Kristina Bernadette. BA, Coll. Mt. St. Vincent, N.Y., 1953, LHD, 1984; LHD, Ateneo de Manila U., Quezon City, Philippines, 1986, Xavier U., Cagayan de Oro City, Philippines, 1986; postgrad., Coll. of Law, Far Ea. U., Philippines; HHD, Stonehill Coll., Philippines, 1984; LLD, U. Philippines, 1986; LLD (honoris causa), Boston U., 1986, Fordham U., 1986, Waseda U., Tokyo, 1986, Far Eastern U., Metro Manila, 1987, U. Santo Tomas, Metro Manila, 1987. Pres. Republic of Philippines, 1986-92; mem. United Nationalist Dem. Orgn., 1985—. Founder, chairperson Benigno S. Aquino Jr. Found., 1983—. Decorated Orden del Libertador San Martin Pres. of Argentina, 1986, Ordine al Merito dela Republica Italiana, 1988; recipient Outstanding Asian Achievement award Ill. Minority Women's Caucus, 1986, Elizabeth Seton medal Mount Saint Vincent Coll., 1986, St. Ignatius medal Boston Coll., 1986, Berkelye medal U. Calif., 1986, Eleanor Roosevelt Human Rights award, 1986, Mother Teresa award So. Calif. Filipino-Am. Jaycees, 1987, Martin Luther King Jr. Nonviolent Peace prize Martin Luther King Jr. Ctr. for Nonviolent Social Change, 1987, Golden Medallion award Soc. Family of Man, 1987, UN Silver medal, 1987, Magnificat award Maryknoll Coll. Found., 1987, Liberal Internat. prize for Freedom, Can., 1987, Nishan-i-Pakistan award, 1988, Oper. Calif. Human Achievement award Oper. Calif., Inc., 1988, William Fulbright prize for internat. peace, 1996; named Woman of Yr. Cath. Ednl. Assn. of Philippines, 1984, Woman of Distinction Soroptimist Internat., 1986, Woman of Yr. Time Mag., 1986, Woman of Yr. Japan Broadcasting Corp., 1987. mem. bd. advisors for Metrobank Foundation; co-pres., Forum of Democratic Leaders; mem. bd. dirs., Sanyo Electric Co., Ltd. Office: 25 Times St, Quezon City The Philippines Office: Benigno S Aquino Jr Found, 119 De La Rosa Legazpi Village, Makati Metro Manila The Philippines*

ARABAS, JAN MARY, artist, art educator; b. Buffalo, June 6, 1958; d. Paul F. and Barbara M. (Skorupa) A.; divorced; 1 child, Theodore Aaron. BA cum laude, SUNY, Binghamton, 1979; diploma, Sch. Mus. Fine Arts, Boston, 1983. Program dir. Cmty. Art Ctr., Cambridge, Mass., 1985-87, Jamaica Plains (Mass.) Multi-Cultural Arts Ctr., 1987-89; dir. Hand Press Workshop, Somerville, Mass., 1987—; instr. art Middlesex C.C., Bedford, Mass., 1992—, Decordova Mus. Sch. Art, Lincoln, Mass., 1993—, Arnold Arboretum of Harvard U., Boston, 1997—; prof. art North Shore C.C., Lynn, Mass., 1996—; bd. mem. Graphic Design Adv. Bd., Lynn, 1999—; artist in residene Mass. Cultural Coun., Boston, 1983-92. Artist: Basic Printmaking Techniques, 1992; contbg. editor Exhibition of Works on Paper, 1997; one-person shows include Roberson Ctr. for Arts, 1988, Lionheart Gallery, 1994, Middlesex C.C., 1995, Bricksbottom Gallery, 2000; exhibited in group shows at Brickbotton Gallery, 1990, 92, 94, 95, 97, 98, Boston Ctr. for Arts, 1990, Fitchburg Art Mus., 1990, Mills Gallery, Boston Ctr. for Arts, 1991, Somerville Mus., 1994, Nesto Gallery, Milton Acad., 1994, Warno Maris Gallery, Westfield State Coll., 1995, Lionheart Gallery, 1995, Habitat, 1996, Chapel Gallery, Newton Art Ctr., 1996, New Eng. BioLabs., 1997, Berkshire Mus., 1997, Aidekman Ctr., Tufts U., 1997, Grossman Gallery, Sch. Mus. Fine Arts, 1997, 98, Boston Pub. Libr., 1998, Higgins Art Gallery, Cape Cod C.C., 1998, Hobson Gallery, 1999, Laura Knott Art Gallery, Bradford Coll., 1999, Boston Pub. Libr., 2000, Rau U., Johannesburg, South Africa, 2000, WGBH, Boston, 2000, others; represented in permanent collections at Midtown Payson Galleries, N.Y.C. and Boca Raton, Fla., K&T Lionheart Gallery, Boston, The Drawing Ctr., N.Y.C., Boston Pub. Libr., Bank of Boston; also pvt. collections. Recipient award in fine arts SUNY Found., 1979, Juror's awards Boston Printmakers Nat., 1986, 87, support grant Somerville Arts Coun., 1990, project grant Mass. Cultural Coun., 1994, project grant Somerville Art Coun., 1996, grants North Shore C.C., 1997-98, Middlesex C.C., 1997-98, C.C. Humanities Assn., 1999; Artists Found. fellow in printmaking, 1987, Nat. Endowment for Arts/New Eng. Found. for Arts fellowship in printmaking, 1990. Mem. Boston Printmakers Soc. (juror awards 1985, 86, 87), C.C. Humanities Assn., Appalacian Mountain Club (instr.), Cmty. Boating Inc. (instr.), Brickbottom Artists Assn. (bd. mem. 1986—). Avocations: skiing, sailing. E-Mail: jarabas@quik.com. Home: 1 Fitchburg St Apt C205 Somerville MA 02143-2127

ARABATZIS, THEODORE, science history educator; b. Thessaloniki, Greece, May 14, 1965; s. Anestis and Styliani Arabatzis. MSc, Aristotle U. Thessaloniki, Greece, 1988; MA, Princeton U., 1990, PhD, 1995. Lectr. in history and philosophy sci. U. Athens, Greece, 1996—. Contbr. articles to profl. jours. With Greek Army, 1995-96. Stanley J. Seeger fellow Princeton U., 1988-89; fellow Princeton U., 1989-93; Rsch. grantee U. Athens, 1996-97; Dibner fellow MIT, 2000—. Mem. Philosophy Sci. Assn., History Sci. Soc. Avocations: basketball, weightlifting, climbing, swimming. Home: 70 Tzavella St, GR154 51 Athens Greece Office: U Athens, 37 Panepistimiopolis, GR15771 Athens Greece

ARABCZYK, WALERIAN, chemistry editor, researcher; b. Poznikowszczyzna, Poland, June 8, 1944; s. Henryk and Maria (Wieckowicz) A.; m. Jozefa Krasnodebska, Sept. 6, 1969; children: Wojciech, Anna. MSc, Tech. U., Szczecin, Poland, 1969; Dr, Tech. U., Dresden, Germany, 1978, Dr habil, 1987. Asst. Tech. U., Szczecin, 1969-78, prof. asst., 1978-88, prof., 1988—; cons. chem. factory Pulawy, 1992—. Contbr. articles to profl. jours.; patentee in field. Recipient award Minister of Edn. of Poland, 1992, 94, 96, 97. Office: Tech U Szczecin, Pulaskiego 10, 70322 Szczecin Poland

ARAC, JONATHAN, English language educator; b. N.Y.C., Apr. 4, 1945; s. Benjamin and Evelyn (Charm) A. AB, Harvard U., 1957, MA, 1968, PhD, 1974. Jr. fellow Soc. Fellows Harvard U., Cambridge, Mass., 1970-73; asst. prof. English Princeton U., 1973-79; assoc. prof. U. Ill., Chgo., 1979-85, prof., 1985-86; prof. grad. program lit. Duke U., 1986-87; prof. English and comparative lit. Columbia U., 1987-90; prof. English U. Pitts., 1989-2000, Mellon prof. English, 2000—; assoc. dir. Inst. for Humanities, 1983-84; Drue Heinz vis. acad. Oxford U., 2000; Avalon disting. vis. prof. humanities Northwestern U., 2000. Author: Commissioned Spirits, 1979, Critical Genealogies, 1987, Huckleberry Finn as Idol and Target, 1997; editor: The Yale Critics: Deconstruction in America, 1983, Postmodernism and Politics, 1986, After Foucault, 1988, Consequences of Theory, 1990, Macropolitics of 19th Century Literature, 1991; contbr. to Cambridge History of American Literature, Vol. 2, 1995; mem. editl. bd. Comparative Lit., 1989—, Am. Lit., 2000—; asst. editor: Boundary 2: Jour. Postmodern Lit. and Culture, 1979—. Am. Coun. Learned Socs. fellow, 1978-79, NEH fellow, 1986-87, 94-95. Mem. MLA (mem. publs. com. 1997-2000), Soc. Critical Exch. (bd. dirs. 1983-90), English Inst. (mem. supervisory com. 1985-88, chmn. 1987-88), PMLA (mem. adv. com. 1990-94). Office: U Pitts Dept English 526 CL Pittsburgh PA 15260-0001

ARAGA, SHIGERU, internist, neurologist; b. Maizuru, Kyoto, Japan, Nov. 12, 1954; s. Hachiro and Chizue A.; m. Mayu Hamada, May 10; three children. MD, Tottori U., Yonago, Japan, 1979, PhD, 1985. Diplomate of Neurologist, Diplomate of Internal Medicine, Diplomate of Rehabilitation. Sr. resident Shimane Ctrl. Hosp., Izumo, Japan, 1984-87; rsch. assoc. Tottori U, Yonago, Japan, 1987-89, asst. prof., 1989-96, assoc. prof., 1996—; vis. asst. prof. U. Ala., Birmingham, 1991-93. Home: 1131 Abe Yonago, Yonago city 683-0846, Japan Office: Tottori U Divsn Neurology, 36-1 Nishimachi, Yonago 683-8504, Japan

ARAGONA, GIANCARLO, political organization executive; b. Messina, Italy, Nov. 14, 1942; married; 2 children. Degree in law, U. Messina, 1964. With diplomatic svc. Govt. of Italy, 1969-74; consul Italian Consulate, Friburg, 1974-77; counsellor Italian Embassy, Lagos, Nigeria, 1977-80, London, 1984-87; with Directorate Gen. for Polit. Affairs/Dept. for Devel. Coop., 1980-84; dep. chief of mission Italian Permanent Mission to NATO, Brussels, 1987-92; diplomatic advisor to minister of def. Italian Govt., 1992-94, dep. chief of cabinet of fgn. minister, 1994-95, chief of cabinet of fgn. minister, 1995-96; sec. gen. Orgn. for Security and Cooperation in Europe, Vienna, Austria, 1996—. Office: OSCE, Kärntner Ring 5-7, 1010 Vienna Austria*

ARAI, ASAO, mathematician, mathematical physicist, educator; b. Chichibu, Saitama, Japan, Jan. 10, 1954; s. Aijiro and Nobu (Kakizakai) A.; m. Sayoko Anada, Dec. 26, 1981; 1 child, Tomoko. BSc, Chiba (Japan) U., 1976; MSc, U. Tokyo, 1979; DSc, Gakushuin U., Tokyo, 1986. Asst. prof. Tokyo Inst. Tech., 1980-86; lectr. Hokkaido U., Sapporo, Japan, 1986-92; assoc. prof. Hokkaido U., Sapporo, 1992-94, prof., 1995—; vis. scientist, Eidgenössische Technische Hochschule, Zurich, Switzerland, 1983-84, Max-Planck Inst., Munich, Germany, 1984, Bielefeld (Germany) U., 1984-85, invited prof. Institut de Recherche Mathématique Avancée, U. Louis Pasteur, Strasbourg, France, 1994. Author: (books in Japanese) Quantum Field Theory and Statistical Mechanics, 1988, Hilbert Space and Quantum Mechanics, 1997, Mathematical Structures of Quantum Mechanics, 1999, Fock Spaces and Quantum Fields, 2000; also articles in profl. jours. Mem. Internat. Assn. Math. Physics, Math. Soc. Japan. Office: Hokkaido U, Dept Math, Hokkaido Sopporo 060-0810, Japan

ARAI, TAMIO, mechanical engineering educator; b. Tokyo; m. Masayo Arai; children: Kazuaki, Junko. BEng., U. Tokyo, 1970, MEng, 1972, PhDEng, 1977. Lectr. U. Tokyo, 1977-78, assoc. prof., 1979-87, prof., 1987—; vis. rschr. Edinburgh U., 1979-81. Author, editor: Distributed Autonomous Robotic Systems, 1994, Distributed Autonomous Robotic Systems 2, 1996; contbr. articles to profl. jours. Mem. Japan Soc. for Precision Engrng. (v.p. 1998—), Japan Assn. for Automation Advancement (pres. 1988—), CIRP. Avocations: traveling, gourmet, net surfing. Office: Dept Precision Engrng, 7-3-1 Hongo Bunkyo-ku, Tokyo 113-8656, Japan

ARAI, TOSHIHIKO, retired microbiology and immunology educator; b. Niigata, Japan, Sept. 12, 1937; s. Hachiro Sisido and Kazue Arai; m. Hatsue Aoki, Dec. 1, 1963; children: Masako, Tomoko, Kazuhiko. MD, Keio U., Tokyo, 1962; PhD, Keio U., 1968. Instr. dept. microbiology Keio U. Sch. Medicine, 1967-73, asst. prof., 1973-85, assoc. prof., 1985; prof. microbiology and immunology Meiji Coll. Pharmacy, Tokyo, 1985-97; ret., 1997; rsch. assoc. U. Tex., Dallas, 1970-72; lectr. Ochanomizu U. Sch. Sci., Tokyo, 1978-79, Chiba (Japan) U. Sch. Medicine, 1978-82, Josai Dental U., Sakedo, Japan, 1978-87, Aoyama Gakuin U., Tokyo, 1988—; cons. Kitasato Inst., Tokyo, 1981-84. Author 15 books; contbr. over 200 articles to sci. and comml. jours. Mem. Japan Soc. Bacteriology, Japan Soc. Chemotherapy (bd. dirs.), Japan Antibiotic Rsch. Assn. (bd. dirs.), Am. Soc. Microbiology, N.Y. Acad. Scis. Zen Buddhist. E-mail: ya5-1-23@mxm.mesh.ne.jp. Home: 5-1-23 Yatsu, Narashino, Chiba 275-0026, Japan Office: Kaiyu Clinic, #205 Spur, 3-3-6 Saginomiya, Narashino Tokyo 165-0032, Japan

ARAI, TOSHIRO, veterinarian, educator; b. Kawagoe City, Saitama, Japan, July 4, 1955; s. Hideo and Kazuko (Okada) A.; m. Hisako Torii, July 4, 1985; children: Mayumi, Yuta. BS, Nippon Vet. and Animal Sci. U., Tokyo, 1981, MS, 1983, PhD, 1986. Asst. prof. Nippon Vet. and Animal Sci. U., Tokyo, 1986-90, lectr., 1991-96, assoc. prof., 1996—; postdoctoral rsch. fellow U. Mich., Ann Arbor, 1989-90. Contbr. articles to profl. jours. Grantee for sci. rsch. Ministry Edn. Sci., Sports and Culture Japan, 1991, 97-99. Mem. Japanese Soc. Animal Biochemistry (councilor 1993-98). Avocations: soccer, journey. Home: 603 5-7-25 Koremasa, Fuchu Tokyo 183-0014, Japan Office: Nippon Vet & Animal Sci U, 1-7-1 Kyonancho, Musashino Tokyo 180-8602, Japan

ARAI, YUMIKO, public health physician, researcher; b. Tokyo, Jan. 30, 1964; d. Juro and Yuko A. MD, Tohoku U., Sendai, Japan, 1989, PhD, 1996; MPH, U. Edinburgh, Scotland, 1991; MA in Health Svcs., Leeds (Eng.) U., 1992. Intern Keio U. Med. Sch., Japan, 1989-90; rsch. fellow, registrar Barnet Health Authority, London, 1993-94; asst. prof. Tokyo U., 1994-95, Tohoku U. Med. Sch., 1995-97; head rsch. unit Nat. Inst. Longevity Scis., Nagoya, Japan, 1998—; cons. Inst. Health Econ. and Policy, Tokyo, 1996—, Japanese Orgn. Quality Assurance on Health Care, Tokyo, 1997—, principal investigator for carers' burden proj., Ministry, 1999. Contbr. chpts. to books, also papers. Recipient Spl. awards for Young Scientists, Ministry of Edn., Tokyo, 1994; Rotary scholar, 1989; rsch. grantee Ministry Health and Welfare, Tokyo, 1997—. Mem. Soc. Social Medicine, Japanese Pub. Health Assn. Avocations: hill walking, star gazing, classical music. Office: Rsch Unit Nursing Psychol, Nat Inst Longevity Scis, Obu-shi Aichi 474-8522, Japan

ARAI-ABRAMSON, LUCY, artist; b. Tokyo, Mar. 3, 1956; came to U.S., 1956; d. Lucian Ford Robinson and Masuko Arai; m. William John Abramson, Dec. 31, 1975. Student, Ea. Mich. U., 1974-75; BFA cum laude, U. S.C., 1979; MFA, U. Mich., 1983, grad. cert. of mus. practices, 1986. Copy editor U. Mich. Microfilms, Ann Arbor, 1979-80; mus. shop asst. mgr. U. Mich. Mus. of Art, 1983, membership coord., 1984; asst. curator Cranbrook Art Acad./Mus., Bloomfield Hills, Mich., 1985-86; cons. archives and exhbns., 1987—, freelance instr., 1987—, artist/designer, 1987—; with U.S. State Dept. Arts in Embassies Program, Bandar Seri Begawan, 2000—; archive cons. Wente Bros. Winery, Livermore, Calif., 1989-92; Japanese stitching instr. nat. quilting orgs., 1989—; lectr./panelist Am. Acad. Religion, San Francisco, 1997; lectr. Holy Name Coll., Oakland, Calif., 1998. Designer/contbr.: (artist biography/slidebooks) Of Our Own Voice: Asian American Women Artists, 1996, 98; designer: (one of a kind garments) Kasuri Dyeworks, 1994—; author: (monograph) Mirrors of the Soul, 1992, Sashiko: Innovations & Refinement of a Japanese Stitchery Technique, 1994. Vol. instr. Hawes and Jack London Schs., Redwood City and Antioch, Calif., 1992, 93, 94, 95; vol. arranger Calif. wildflower exhbn., Oakland, Calif., 1995, 96, 97, 98; garden designer/vol. coord. Dearborn (Mich.) Hist. Mus., 1997; vol. instr. Sansei Legacy Project, Alameda, Calif., 1991; mem. art embassies program U.S. State Dept., Brunei, 2000—. Work judged Best in Show U. S.C., 1979; recipient grad. fellowship U. Mich., 1980, 81, 82, 83, art scholarship U. Mich. Sch. Art, 1980, 81, 82, 83, curatorial internship grant Cranbrook Acad. Art/Mus., 1984-85. Mem. Coll. Art Assn., Asian Am. Women Artists Assn. Avocations: hiking, Calif. wildflowers, camping, travel, reading. Fax: (925) 737-7666. Office: PO Box 683 Oakley CA 94561-0683

ARAIN, GHULAM SHABIR, chemist; b. Deh Totah, Sindh, Pakistan, June 27, 1960; arrived in Scotland, 1992; s. Abdul Aziz Arain and Nawab Bibi; m. Mumtaz Fazal, Mar. 20, 1990; children: Sara Shabir, Fatima Shabir, Samra Shabir. BSc in Chemistry with honors, U. Sind, Pakistan, 1982, MSc in Organic Chemistry, 1983; postgrad. diploma in prodn.-ops. mgmt., Inst. Mgmt. Scis., Karachi, Pakistan, 1988; cert. in comm. skills in English, Cambridge (Eng.) U., 1992; MSc in Pharmaceutical Analysis, U. Strathclyde, Glasgow, Scotland, 1996; postgrad. in higher mgmt. skills, Glasgow Caledonian U., 1997—. Registered mfg. chemist; registered profl. mfg. mgr. Inst. of Mfg. U.K. Analytical chemist Nat. Nabiqasim Pharm. Industry, Karachi, 1985-88; supervisory pharmacist Abbott Labs. (Pakistan) Ltd., Karachi, 1988-92; quality control chemist Meri-Mate Ltd., softdrink mfrs., Dundee, Scotland, 1993; rsch. chemist, rschr. in synthetic organic chemistry U. St. Andrews, Scotland, 1994; quality assurance analytical chemist L.R.C. Products (Pharms.) Ltd., Dundee, 1994; chemist tchr. labs. Perth Coll., U. Highlands and Islands, Perth, Scotland, 1994-95; analytical svcs. mgr. Fleet Labs. (a D.D.D. Co.), Watford, Eng., 1997-2000; mgr. R&D project U. Oxford, 1999; analytical scientist Abbott MediSense UK Ltd., Oxfordshire, Eng., 2000—; mem. bus. and tech. edn. coun. dept. analytical chemistry Greenwich U., London, 1998; gov., chmn. premises, health and safety com. Chater Sch., Watford, U.K. Author: Safety in Science Laboratories, 1995, Bioavailability of Atenolol in Vitro Dissolution, 1996, Fast Atom Bombardment Mass Spectrometry (FAB-MS) as an Analytical Tool, 1996, Higher Management and Quality Assurance (A Guide for Managers), 1997, Current Good Manufacturing Practice, 1998, Management Development: A Guide for Managers, 1999, HPLC Method Development-General Philosophy, Computer Optimization of High Performance Liquid Chromatic Separations in Pharmaceutical Analysis, Generic Medicines and Dissolution, Testing (Jour. Acad. Multi-Skills), 2000, The Rule of Clean Rooms in Sterile Manufacture and Sterility Testing, 2000. Fellow Inst. Mgmt., Inst. Sci. Tech., Inst. Mfg. (Pres.'s and Founder's Edn. award 1998); mem. Am. Chem.

Soc., Royal Soc. Chemistry, Chromatographic Soc., Inst. for Supervision and Mgmt., N.Y. Acad. Scis., Inst. Quality Assurance (mem. com. separation sci. and tech. group 1998-99, 99—), Soc. for Chem. Industry. Avocations: playing squash and tennis, reading, socializing, photography. E-mail: gshabir@dddltd.co.uk. Home: 50 Durban Rd #1, Watford WD1 7DR, England Office: Abbott MediSense UK Ltd, Abingdon, Watford Oxfordshire OX1Y 1TR, England

ARAIZ, JOSEPH MICHAEL, securities company executive; b. Mexico City, Mex., Feb. 2, 1961; came to U.S., 1965; s. Francisco and Myra Hilda (Kagan) A.; m. Sandra Ramirez, May 25, 1990. BA, Brandeis U., 1983. Corp. bond trader Cowen & Co., Inc., 1983-85; exec. v.p. Gruntal & Co. Inc., 1985-88; exec. v.p., prin. M.J. Whitman & Co. Inc., N.Y.C., 1988-97, bd. dirs., 1989—; sr. exec. v.p. Whitman Security Corp., 1987-97; exec. v.p. M.J. Whitman Sr. Debt Corp., 1988—; dir. Whitman Investments; sr. exec. v.p. Whitman Structured Fin. Group; sr. mng. dir. Ladenburg and Thalmann, 1997-98; sr. exec. v.p., mng. dir. Imperial Capital, N.Y.C., 1998—, also bd. dirs.; pres.mgr. Further Lane Asset Mgmt., 2000—; pres., CEO Osprey Group Asset Mgmt., East Hampton, N.Y., 2000—. Mem. Nat. Trust for Historic Preservation. Mem. Am. Fine Arts Soc., Guggenheim Mus., Whitney Mus., Internat. Platform Assn., B'nai Brith. Office: Imperial Capital 280 Park Ave Fl 39W New York NY 10017-1216 Address: 295 Central Park W Apt 15G New York NY 10024-3056

ARAIZA, FRANCISCO (JOSÉ FRANCISCO ARAIZA ANDRADE), opera singer; b. Mexico City, Oct. 4, 1950; s. José and Guadalupe (Andrade) A.; m. Vivian Jaffray, Sept. 30, 1977 (div. 1995); children: José Riccardo, Maria del Carmen Cecilia; m. Ethery Inasaridse, children: Abessalom Rodrigo, Laura Imeda. Grad. in Bus. Adminstrn., U. Mexico City, 1972; grad., Nat. Sch. Music, Mexico City, 1974, Nat. Conservatory, Mexico City, 1974, Musikhochschule, Munich, 1975. Tenor roles (lyric repertory as well as dramatic parts till Wagner's Lohengrin in 1990) include performances in opera hos. Zurich, Munich, Vienna, Rome, Hamburg, Berlin, Milan, London, Parma, Florence, Venice, Barcelona, Madrid, Tokyo, Mexico City, Chgo., San Francisco, N.Y.C.; performed at Salzburg Festival, Bayreuth Festival; numerous recordings include works by Mozart, Rossini, Beethoven, Donizetti, Offenbach, Schubert, Verdi, Puccini, Gounod, Massenet, Weber and others; also six solo albums including opera arias, lieder, popular songs. Recipient Orphée d'Or, 1984, Deutscher Schallplattenpreis, 1984, Otello d'Oro performer prize, 1995, Golden Merkur best performance award, 1996, Mozart medal of Mex., 1991; named Kammersänger of Vienna State Opera, 1988. Address: c/o Elene Tschaidse, Opern-und Konzertagentur Tal 15, 80331 Munich Germany

ARAJ, GEORGE FARAH, clinical microbiologist, consultant; b. Beit Jala, Bethlehem, Palestine, Oct. 25, 1947; arrived in Lebanon, 1991; s. Farah S. and Helaneh S. Araj; m. Suad G. Musleh, Aug. 3, 1975; children: Farah, Faris, Tanya. BSc, Am. U. Beirut, 1971, MSc, 1973, PhD, 1976. Diplomate Am. Bd. Med. Microbiology. Instr. Sch. Medicine Am. U. Beirut, 1976-77; fellow, rsch. assoc. med. ctrs. Ohio, Va., Tex., 1977-81; asst. prof., head clin. microbiology faculty medicine Kuwait U., Kuwait City, 1982-85, assoc. prof., head clin. microbiology faculty medicine, 1985-90; assoc. prof., dir. clin. microbiology Sch. Medicine Am. U. Beirut and Med. Ctr., 1991-95, prof., dir. clin. microbiology Sch. Medicine, 1995—; head, cons. Mubarak Al Kubeer U. Hosp., Kuwait City, 1982-90. Contbr. numerous rsch. articles to med. jours. Fellow Am. Acad. Microbiology; mem. Am. Soc. for Microbiology. Fax: 961-1-744-464. E-mail: garaj@aub.edu.lb. Home and Office: Am U Beirut Med Ctr, PO Box 113-6044, Beirut Lebanon

ARAKAWA, HIDEO, biophysics researcher and educator; b. Tokyo, May 1, 1961; s. Masao and Saeko (Oota) A.; m. Yusa Takami, Sept. 4, 1993; 1 child, Rina. BS, U. Tokyo, 1984, MS, 1986, DSc, 1989. Technician Tokyo Inst. Tech. Yokohama, Kanagawaa, 1989-90, asst. prof. biophysics, 1990—. Contbr. articles to profl. jours. JSPS fellow, 1989. Office: Tokyo Inst Tech, 4259 Nagatsuta Midori-ku, Yokohama 226-8501, Japan

ARAKAWA, YOSHIZO, business educator; b. Yasu, Shiga, Japan, Sept. 6, 1934; s. Isaburo and Kimi (Hattori) A.; m. Toshiko Mitsui, Oct. 9, 1965; children: Jumpei, Tatsuro, Tomoko. MA in Econs., Kyoto (Japan) U., 1958. Exec. v.p. Daiwa Bank Trust Co., N.Y.C., 1981-84, pres., CEO, 1984-86; dir. and chief economist Daiwa Bank, Osaka, 1986-91; mng. dir. Daiwa Rsch. Inst., Inc., Osaka, 1991-94, sr. mng. dir., 1994-95; prof. Ritsumeikan U., Shiga, Japan, 1995-2000, Ritsumeikan Asia Pacific U., Oita, Japan, 2000—. Co-author: Japan's Monetary Policy, 1992, Function and Role of Japanese Financial Institutions, 1995. Buddhist. Avocations: golf, walking. Home: Rm No 1008 Seaside Shonin 2, 10-Kumi Shoningahama, Beppu City, Oita 874-0023, Japan Office: Ritsumeikan Asia Pacific U, 1-1 Jumonjibaru, Beppu City, Oita 874-8577, Japan

ARAKGUI, JEAN AZIZ, retired obstetrician, gynecologist, consultant; b. Cairo, Apr. 23, 1931; s. Aziz Hanna Arakgui and Josephine Warda; m. Nelly Henein Gannagé, Feb. 5, 1961 (dec. 1988); children: Farid, Gelan. MB, BCh, Cairo U., 1958; LM, Rotunda Hosp., Dublin, Ireland, 1962; diploma in obstetrics, Royal Coll. Physicians Ireland, 1962. Diplomate Am. Bd. Ob-Gyn, 1976. Intern Union Hosp., Fall River, Mass., 1965-66; resident Beth Israel Hosp., Boston, 1966-69; ob-gyn. cons., Ft. Lauderdale, Fla., 1970-77, Riyadh, Saudi Arabia, 1985-93; cons. King Faisal Specialist Hosp., Riyadh, 1977-85, 93—; ob-gyn. cons., Cairo, 1993-96; ret., 1996. Fellow ACOG. Mem. Republican Party. Roman Catholic. Avocations: photography, reading, light physical exercise. Home: 9 Omar Ibnel Khattab, 11351 Heliopolis Cairo, Egypt

ARAKI, KENJI, mechanical engineering educator; b. Yokohama, Japan, Oct. 12, 1934; s. Tamakichi and Maki (Akiya) A.; m. Kaneko Uchida, Feb. 14, 1965; children: Takashi, Maki, Hiromi. BS in Engring., Yokohama (Japan) Nat. U., 1958; PhD in Engring., U. Tokyo, 1970. Lectr. engring. U. Tokyo, 1966-70; invited prof. engring. Nat. Tsing Hua U., Taiwan, 1975; prof. mech. engring. Saitama U., Urawa, Japan, 1984-00; invited prof. mech. engring. Tohoku (Japan) U., 1992-93; head doctorate course prodn. sci. majors Saitama U., 1994-96, head Info. Processing Ctr., 1995-97, prof. emeritus, 2000—; chmn. paper com. 3d JHPS Internat. Symposium on Fluid Power, Japan, 1994-96, chmn. exec. com. FLUCOME'97 Internat. Conf., Japan, 1996-97. Editor: Procs. 3d JHPS Internat. Symposium on Fluid Power, 1996; contbr. articles to sci. jours. (Best Paper awards 1984, 96, 98). Mem. Japan-China Sci. and Tech. Exch. Assn., Japan-Italy Sci. and Tech. Coop. Project, Japan Hydraulics and Pneumatics Soc. (dir. 1984-90, 92-94). Avocations: fishing, motorboating, travel, camping. Home and Office: 1-805-4 Kushihiki, Omiya, Saitama 331-0051, Japan

ARAKI, TAKAHARU, editor, mineralogist, crystallographer, consultant; b. Kyoto, Japan, Dec. 22, 1929; came to U.S., 1965; s. Shiro and Kiyo (Ohmori) A.; m. Motoko Yoshizawa, Nov. 23, 1958 (dec. Apr. 1993); m. Marlene A. Baughman, Jan. 31, 2000. MS, Kyoto U., Japan, 1957, DSc, 1961. Rsch. assoc. Kyoto U., Japan, 1960-62; sr. chemist Tekkosha Corp., Mitaka, Tokyo, Japan, 1962-65, 68-70; rsch. fellow U. Minn., Mpls., 1965-67, 70-71; sr. rsch. scientist U. Chgo., 1971-82; sr. rsch. assoc., cons. McGill U., Montreal, Can., 1983-85; sr. assoc. editor Chem. Abstracts Svc., Columbus, Ohio, 1985-94; pvt. contractor Chem. Abstracts Svc., 1995-99. Contbr. articles to profl. jours. Named for mineral arakiite. Fellow Mineral. Soc Am.; mem. Am. Ceramic Soc., Am. Chem. Soc., Am. Crystallographic Assn. Home and Office: 4612 182nd Pl SW Lynnwood WA 98037-4625

ARAKI, TORU, French and comparative literature educator; b. Sapporo, Hokkaido, Japan, Jan. 16, 1931; s. Sugao and Chiaki (Sasaki) A.; m. Noriko Takahashi, Mar. 30, 1959; children: Tomoko, Natsumi, Thoshiko. BA, Tokyo U., 1957, MA, 1959. Lectr. French and comparative lit. Shizouka (Japan) U., 1959-62; lectr. French and comparative lit. Internat. Christian U., Tokyo, 1966-67, asst. prof., 1968-69, assoc. prof., 1970-77, prof., 1978-96; lectr. Ecole Langues Orientales, Paris, 1964-68, Inst. Langues Orientales, Paris, 1974-75, Montreal (Que., Can.) U., 1988, Ecoles Hautes Etudes, Paris, 1993, 95. Author: La Sérénité et la Plénitude de la chose, 1974, Dans un Monde où l'écho est Perdu, 1982, Roland Barthes et le Japon, 1989, Le Japonais, langue de clôture, 1989; Le Statut du Sujet et La logique du lieu en Japonais, 1997, Le Post-Modernisme Chez Karatani Kojin, 1997, La Logique du Rieu et le japonais, 2000. Mem. Soc. Japanese de Langue et Lit., Soc. Japanese de Sémiologie. Roman Catholic. Avocations: Japanese chess, gardening. E-Mail: toruarak@pluto.dti.ne.jp. Home: Midori cho 120 3 2 201, Hachioji 193, Japan

ARAMAKI, KUNITSUGU, chemist, educator; b. Tokyo, Feb. 21, 1932; s. Kunishige and Kiyoko (Kizu) A.; m. Midori Mori, Nov. 18, 1964; children: Kaori, Kunio. BA, Keio U., 1953, MS, 1955, PhD, 1966. From asst. to prof. Keio U., Tokyo, 1955-97, prof. emeritus, 1997—; rsch. fellow U. Tex., Austin, 1966-68. Contbr. articles to profl. jours. Mem. Chem. Soc. Japan, Electrochem. Soc. Japan, Electrochem. Soc. N.J. Buddhist. Avocations: swimming, golf. Home: 2-23-26 Okusawa Setagaya-ku, Tokyo 158-0083, Japan Office: Keio U Fac Sci and Tech, 3-14-1 Hiyoshi, Kohokuku Yokohama 223-8522, Japan

ARAMATA, SHIGEO, university administrator; b. Sapporo, Japan, Nov. 11, 1934; s. Misao and Takako (Kawamura) A.; m. Kazuko Yoshinaka, Sept. 13, 1966; children: Yusuke, Shigeki, Miyo. B in Econs., Hokkaido U., 1957, M in Econs., 1959, D in Econs., 1971. Lectr. Hokkaigkuen U., Sapporo, Japan, 1965-66, assoc. prof., 1966-67; instr. Hokkaido U., Sapporo, Japan, 1963-65, assoc. prof., 1967-77, prof., 1977-96; dean faculty econs. Hokkaido U., 1990-91; pres. Kushiro (Japan) Pub. U. Econs., 1996—. Author: The Theory of Wage Labour, 1968, History of Labour Policy in Tsarist Russia, 1971, Advanced Theory of Wage Labour, 1978. Mem. Hokkaido Minimum Wage Bd., 1988—; chair Hokkaido Social Ins. Medicine Conf., 1993—. Mem. Assn. Study Social Policy, Assn. Soviet and East European Studies, Rotary Internat. (Youth Exch. Program Dist. 1999—). Fax: 81-154-37-3287. Home: Miyanomori 1-10, Sapporo, Hokkaido 064-0951, Japan Office: Kushiro Pub U Econs, 4-1-1 Ashino, Kushiro 085-8585, Japan

ARAMBEL, PHYLLIS ANN, elementary education educator; b. Hays, Kans., Aug. 12, 1952; d. Melvin Joseph and Barbara Ann (Bennett) Eichman; m. Joseph John Arambel, Apr. 7, 1984; children: Jeremy Sage, Spenser Miles, Alexander Joseph. BEd, U. No. Colo., 1974; postgrad. Cert. elem. tchr., Colo., Wyo. Primary tchr. Queensland (Australia) Dept. Edn., 1974-76; 1st grade tchr. Gertrude Burns Elem. Sch., Newcastle, Wyo., 1976-77; western U.S. ednl. cons. Rand McNally, San Francisco, 1977-78; K-2 Mountain Sch. tchr. Poudre R-1 Dist., Ft. Collins, Colo., 1978-79; constrn. supr. CAR-MEL, Inc., Pierre, S.D., 1979-80; 3rd grade tchr. Sweetwater County Sch. Dist. #1, Rock Springs, Wyo., 1980-87; ret., 1987; pres./founder The Children's Discovery Found., Rock Springs, 1991—, sec., 1991-93, fundraising chairperson, 1991—, pres., 1996-2000, dir., 1997-2000); pres./founder Westridge Sch. PTO, Rock Springs, 1996-97; founder Westridge Hist. Soc., 1998—. Tiger Cub Group coach Boys Scouts Am., Rock Springs, 1996-97; soccer team parent, 1992-97, asst. registration commr., 1996-99, newsletter editor and pub., 1996—, coach, 1997—; wolf den leader Cub Scouts, Rock Springs, 1997-98, bear leader, 1998-99, webelos leader, 1999-2000. Mem. Overland Sch. Hist. Soc. (founder 2000), Girl Scouts U.S. (life), Phi Sigma Iota (life). Avocations: travel, gardening, photography, camping. Home: 904 Bonners Way Rock Springs WY 82901-4362

ARANA, MARIE, editor, writer; b. Lima, Peru, Sept. 15, 1949; came to U.S., 1959; d. Jorge Enrique and Marie Elverine (Clapp) Arana; children: Hilary Walsh, Adam Williamson Ward; m. Wendell B. Ward Jr., Dec. 18, 1972 (d. Dec. 1998); m. Jonathan Yardley, Mar. 21, 1999. BA in Russian Lang. & Lit., Northwestern U., Evanston, Ill., 1971; cert. scholarship Mandarin lang., Yale U. in China, Hong Kong, 1976; MA in Linguistics, Brit. U. Hong Kong, 1977. Lectr. linguistics Brit. U. Hong Kong, 1978-79; sr. editor Harcourt Brace Jovanovich, Pubs., N.Y.C. and Washington, 1980-89; v.p., sr. editor Simon & Schuster Pubs., N.Y.C. and Washington, 1989-92; writer, editor Washington Post, 1992-99, Book World editor-in-chief, 1999—; bd. mem., dir. Ctr. Policy Rsch., Washington, 1994-99. Editor: Studies in Bilingualism, 1978. Recipient award for excellence in editing ABA, 1985, Christopher award for excellence in editing, 1986. Mem. Nat. Assn. Hispanic Journalists (bd. dirs. 1996-99), Nat. Book Critics Cir. (bd. dirs. 1996-2000). Office: Washington Post 1150 15th St NW Washington DC 20071-0002

ARANGO, JORGE SANIN, architect; b. Bogota, Colombia, Nov. 29, 1916; s. Fernando Arango and Maria Sanin A.; m. Elizabeth Leighton, 1944; 1 child, Peter; m. Judith Brooks Wolpert, Dec. 14, 1951; children: Richard, Virginia; m. Penelope Corey, Aug. 18, 1976. Student, Universidad Catolica de Chile Sch. Architecture, 1935-42, Harvard Grad. Sch. Design, 1942-43. Head archtl. firm Arango & Murtra, Bogota, 1946-59; prof. architecture and urban design Nat. U., Bogota, 1945-47; vis. prof. Sch. Architecture U. Calif., Berkeley, 1956, 58; Pub. bldgs. dir. Colombia, 1948-49; pres. Colombian Soc. Architects, 1946-51, Colegio Engrs. and Architects of Colombia, 1955. Co-author basic plan for devel. by Lecorbusier Bogota, 1948; Author: (with L. Martinez) Architecture in Colombia, 1951, The Urbanization of the Earth, 1970, Segunda Edad Media, 1994; mem. Bd. Contbrs. Miami Herald. Recipient Excellence in Design awards Miami and Fla. chpts. AIA, 1967. Mem. AIA (mem. emeritus). Achievements include being invited to U.S. by State Dept. and Mus. Modern Art, N.Y.C. Home: 5153 SW 71st Pl Miami FL 33155-5640

ARANGUREN, ARTHUR, chemical engineer; b. Madrid, Spain, July 21, 1960; s. Arturo Aranguren and Lola Cotallo; m. Marleen Perez, May 21, 1999. Degree in engring., Ingeniero Qummico Sarria, Barcelona, 1984. Engr. Itecsa, Barcelona, 1986-88; acct. mgr. Equipos Informaticos Sun, Barcelona, 1988-89, Unisys, Barcelona, 1989-90; CEO Sysisgsa, Barcelona, 1990-93, Sgrin, Madrid, 1993-95, Deneb, Barcelona, 1995—.

ARANGUREN, QUEREJETA MARI JOSE, economics educator, researcher; b. Azpeitia, Guipuzcoa, Spain, July 6, 1969; d. Aranguren Obriozola Diego and Querejeta Garmendia Tomasa; m. Oyarazabal Gorostegu Jesus Maria, Mar. 22, 1997. Grad. in econs. and bus. adminstrn., Deusto U., San Sebastian, Spain, 1992, PhD in Econs., 1997. Instr. econs. Deusto U., 1992—, studies mgr., 1998—, tutor, 1994. Author: Creacion de Empresas, 1998; contbr. articles to profl. jours., including Small Bus. Econs., Economia Industrial. Ptnr. dir.'s coun. Sarea Found. (Caritas), Renteria, Spain, 1999. Grantee Sasakawa Found., 1993-94, HEC, 1994-95, Karlos Santamaria, 1999—. Office: Deusto U (ESTE), Mundaiz 50, 20012 San Sebastian Giputcoa, Spain

ARANOVICH, GREGORY, research scientist; b. Ordzonikidze, USSR, July 11, 1952; came to U.S., 1994; s. Lev Aranovich and Sofia Tiomkina; m. Tatyana Brodskaya, June 16, 1990; 1 child, Valeriya. BS, Inst. Elec. Engring., Moscow, 1975; PhD, Moscow Inst. Steel and Alloys, 1981; DS, Moscow State U., 1992. Engr. Inst. Earth Physics, Moscow, 1975-78; rschr. Inst. Steel and Alloys, 1978-81; sr. rschr. Inst. Chromatography, Moscow, 1981-89; leading rschr. Moscow State U., 1989-94; prin. rsch. scientist in phys. chemistry Johns Hopkins U., Balt., 1994—. Contbr. 120 articles to profl. jours. E-mail: aranovich@jhu.edu. Home: 56 Taverngreen Ct Baltimore MD 21209-5304 Office: Johns Hopkins U Dept Chem Engring 3400 N Charles St Baltimore MD 21218-2680

ARANT, EUGENE WESLEY, lawyer; b. North Powder, Oreg., Dec. 21, 1920; s. Ernest Elbert and Wanda (Haller) A.; m. Juanita Clark Flowers, Mar. 15, 1953; children: Thomas W., Kenneth E., Richard W. B.S. in Elec. Engring, Oreg. State U., 1943; J.D., U. So. Calif., 1949. Bar: Calif. 1950. Mem. engring. faculty U. So. Calif., 1947-51; practiced in Los Angeles, 1950-51; patent atty. Hughes Aircraft Co., Culver City, Calif., 1953-56; pvt. practice, L.A., 1957-97, Ventura, Calif., 1997—. Author articles. Mem. La Mirada (Calif.) City Council, 1958-60; trustee Beverly Hills Presbyn. Ch., 1976-78. Served with AUS, 1943-46, 51-53. Mem. ABA, Am. Intellectual Property Law Assn., State Bar Calif., Ala. State Bar, Santa Barbara Rotary, Univ. Club Santa Barbara. Democrat. Home: 15711 W Telegraph Rd Spc G89 Santa Paula CA 93060-4095 Office: 674 County Square Dr Ste 205 Ventura CA 93003-9023

ARANUI-FAED, JULIA ANNE, consultant psychiatrist; b. Blenheim, New Zealand, Jan. 8, 1945; d. John Colin and Anne Edith (Norman) Baird; m. James Matheson Faed, Aug. 16, 1969 (div. Oct. 1993); children: Mark John, Luke James; m. Whetu Ote-Ata Aranui, Jan. 1, 1994. B in Med. Sci., Otago U., Dunedin, New Zealand, 1968, MB ChB, 1969, DPM, 1973, diploma in child psychiatry, 1982; DHA, Massey U., Palmerston, New Zealand, 1985. House surgeon Dunedin Hosp., 1970-71; registrar in psychol. medicine U. Otago, Dunedin, 1972-73; med. officer Cherry Farm Hosp., Dunedin, 1974-78; cons. psychiatrist Northside Clinic, Syndey, Australia, 1978-79; registrar Child Psychiatry Svcs., West Lothian, Edinburgh, Scotland, 1979-81; cons. psychiatrist Otago Hosp. Bd., Dunedin, 1981-84, 89-93, dir. forensic svcs., 1981-88; sr. lectr. in psychol. medicine Otago Med. Sch., Dunedin, 1984-93; med. supt. Cherry Farm Hosp., Dunedin, 1984-88; cons. psychiatrist Star of the Morning Ltd., Wanganui, 1993—. Psychiat. adviser two biogs. by Lynley Hood; contbr. articles to profl. jours. Trustee Downie Stewart Found., Dunedin, 1984-94, Patients, Prisoners and Aid Found., Dunedin, 1990-94, Arts Access AoteaRoa, 1995-99; chmn. trustee Creative Arts Trust, Dunedin, 1986-94; med. adviser La Leche League, 1978-90, Schizophrenia Fellowship New Zealand, 1986—. Fellow Royal Australian and New Zealand Coll. Psychiatrists; mem. APA, AAAS, N.Y. acad. Scis., Internat. Hosps. Fedn., Inst. Australasia Psychiatrists New Zealand, Inc. Avocations: computer studies, creative writing, art, photography, music. E-mail: julia@juliannasong.com. Home: PO Box 46015, Home Bay 5151, Australia Office: Star of the Morning Ltd, 62 Bedford Ave PO Box 4044, Wanganui New Zealand

ARARAT, NISAN, writer, lecturer, educator; b. Tchechenovska, Poland, Sept. 12, 1933; arrived in Israel, 1935; s. Itzchak and Sara Araten; m. Rachel Kratz, Oct. 5, 1956; children: Shavit, Galit, Amit, Ariel. BA, Hebrew U., Jerusalem, 1957, MA, 1958; PhD, Yeshivah U., N.Y.C., 1971. Prin. Be'er Sheva (Israel) H.S., 1958-63; tchr. Hebrew U., 1964-68; lectr. Bar-Ilan U., Ramat-Gan, Israel, 1972-73, Technion U., Haifa, Israel, 1974—, Jew's Coll., London, 1995-96. Author: Israel's Sacrificial Rite, 1985, Truth and Grace in the Bible, 1993, Drama in the Bible, 1997. Lt. Israeli Army, 1952-55. Recipient Kaniel prize Haifa Municipality, 1997. Avocations: swimming, traveling. Home: 6 Eilat St, 32298 Haifa Israel Office: Technion U, City of Technion, 32000 Haifa Israel

ARASKOG, RAND VINCENT, former diversified telecommunications multinational company executive; b. Fergus Falls, Minn., Oct. 30, 1931; s. Randolph Victor and Hilfred Mathilda A.; m. Jessie Marie Gustafson, July 29, 1956; children: William Roy, Julie Kay, Kathleen Melinda. BSME, U.S. Mil. Acad., 1953; postgrad., Harvard U., 1953-54; LHD (hon.), Hofstra U., 1990. With Def. Dept., Washington, 1954-59, Spl. asst. to dir., 1958-59; dir. mktg. aero. div. Honeywell, Inc., Mpls., 1960-66; v.p. ITT Corp., 1971-76; exec. v.p. ITT Aerospace, Electronics, Components and Energy Group, Nutley, N.J., 1976-79; pres., CEO ITT Corp., N.Y.C., 1979-80, chmn. bd., CEO, chmn. exec. and policy coms., 1980-98; chmn., pres., CEO ITT Holdings Inc., N.Y.C., 1995-98; bd. dirs. ITT Industries, 1980—; bd. dirs. ITT Corp., Hartford Ins., Dayton-Hudson Corp., Shell Oil Corp., Dow Jones and Co., N.Y. Stock Exchange, Fed. Res. Bank of N.Y.; mem. Nat. Security Telecommunications Adv. Com., 1983—. Author: ITT Wars, 1989; contbr. articles to jours. including Reader's Digest, The New York Times. Mem. Bus. Coun., Trilateral Commn., Competitiveness Policy Coun.; bd. advisors N.Y. Zool. Soc.; mem. Rockefellow U. Coun. Served with U.S. Army, 1954-56. Decorated Officer of Nat. Order of Legion of Honor (France), Order of Merit of the Republic of Italy in the level of grand officer. Mem. The Bus. Coun., Aerospace Industries Assn. (bd. govs.), Air Force Assn. (mem. exec. coun.), Econ. Cub (chmn.), Bus. Roundtable, Coun. Fgn. Rels., Competitiveness Policy Coun., Trilateral Commn., Bus.-Higher Edn. Forum, West Point Soc. N.Y., N.Y.C. Partnership (bd. dirs.), Links Club, River Club, Meadow Club, Knickerbocker Club, Coun. U.S.-Italy (co-chmn.). Episcopalian. Office: ITT Industries Inc 4 W Red Oak Ln White Plains NY 10604-3520*

ARASTEH, KAVOUSS, communications specialist, consultant; b. Teheran, Iran, July 1, 1944; s. Mohammad Soroush and Khadijeh Peyhani; m. Shokouh Asgarian, Mar. 21, 1953; children: Siavosh, Yasmine. BS, U. Teheran (Iran), 1964; MS, Essex (Eng.) U., 1975. Head planning dept. Ministry Info. and Broadcasting, Teheran, Iran, 1967-71; head internat. short wave planning dept. Radio and T.V. Orgn., Teheran, Iran, 1971-78, head dir. internat. tech. affairs, 1978-85; head notification sect. of space svcs. dept. Internat. Frequency Registration Bd./ITU, Geneva, 1985-90; head space notifications and plans divsn. Radio Comms. Bur./ITU, 1990—. Home: 9A Plateau de Frontenex, 1208 Geneva Switzerland Office: ITU Notifications & Plans, Room V107 Place des Nations, CH-1211 Geneva 20, Switzerland

ARATA, KAZUSHI, chemist; b. Hokkaido, Japan, Sept. 8, 1940; s. Sadajiroh and Chiyo (Maeguchi) A.; m. Hiroko Saitoh, Nov. 22, 1973; 1 child, Masato. BS, Hokkaido U., Sapporo, Japan, 1965, MS, 1967, DSc, 1978; MS, Ohio State U., 1970. Assoc. prof. Hokkaido U. Edn., Hakodate, Japan, 1971-82; full prof. Hokkaido U. Edn., Hakodate, 1983—. Inventor in field. Fellow Royal Soc. Chemistry, Chem. Soc. Japan, Catalysis Soc. Japan, Japan Petroleum Inst., Am. Chem. Soc. Home: Suginami-cho 5-5, Hakodate Hokkaido 040-0004, Japan Office: Hokkaido U Edn, Hachiman-cho 1-2, Hakodate Hokkaido 040-8567, Japan

ARATOW-KULAKSIZ, KAYAN, clinical psychologist; b. Kearny, N.J., Jan. 9, 1966; d. Henry Joseph Sr. and Catherine Ann Zukowsky (Harding) A.; m. Niyazi Kulaksiz; 1 child, Alexander Hasancan. BA, U. Richmond, 1988; MA, The Cath. Univ. of Am., 1990; PhD, Friedrich-Wilhelms-U. Bonn, 1996, cert. clin. psychotherapist in cognitive-behavioral therapy, 1998. Clin. psychologist Dr. von Ehrenwall'sche Klinik, Ahrweiler, Germany, 1994—. Author: (book) Intercultural Comparison of the Pain Perception and Coping Strategies of Turkish and German Polyarthritis Patients, 1996. Mem. Amnesty Internat., 1994—. Recipient scholarship Friedrich-Naumann-Stiftung, Königswinter, Germany, 1991-94. Mem. APA, Internat. Assn. for Cross-Cultural Psychology, Arbeitskreis Ausländische Psychologen/Berufsverband Deutscher Psychologen. Avocations: bike riding, travel, violin, jogging. Home: Am Turmhof 3, 53175 Bonn Germany Office: Dr von Ehrenwall'sche Klinik, Walporzheimer Strasse 2, 53474 Ahrweiler Germany

ARAU, JAIME E., electronics educator; b. Veracruz, Mex., Apr. 11, 1960; cons. in field.; s. Jaime Arau and Dulce M. Roffiel; m. Maria G. Ruiz; children: Guillermo, Luis A. BSc, I.T. Minatitlán, Mex., 1982; PhD, U. Polit. Madrid, 1991. Rschr. Elec. Rsch. Inst., Cuernavaca, Mex., 1982-92, leader power electronics group, 1993-94; pres. electronics acad. CENIDET, Cuernavaca, 1995-97, head electronics dept., 1997—, dir. indsl. partnership program, 1998. Editor: IEEE International Power Electronics Conference, 1992, 93, 96; inventor electronic ballast for fluorescent lamp. Recipient Excellence in Edn. award Govt. of Morelos, 1999. Mem. IEEE (sr., Disting. Engr. sect. Morelos 1995), IEEE-PELS (chpt. devel. chair 1999, L.Am. liaison 1997-98), Mex. Acad. Scis., Mex. Acad. Rsch. in Elec. Engring. Avocations: reading, chess, basketball, soccer. Office: Cenidet, PO Box 5-164, Cuernavaca Morelos 62050, Mexico

ARAÜJO, JACKSON VICTOR, veterinary educator; b. Teófilo Oroni, Brazil, Apr. 15, 1962; s. Manuel Alves and Maria DaGlória Peruhype Araüjo; s. Simone Silva Reis, Dec. 12, 1992; children: Jacqueline, Victor. D in Vet., UFMG, Belo Horizonte, Brazil, 1985, MSc, 1989, PhD, 1996. Vet. tchr. UFV, Viçosa, Brazil, 1989—; mem. com. rsch. UFV, 1996—. Contbr. articles to profl. jours. Tenant Brazilian Army, 1986-87. Mem. Sch. of Vet. Parasitology from Brazil. Avocations: running, volleyball, soccer, peteca. Office: Dept Veterinaria, UFV, 36570000 Vicosa Brazil

ARAUJO, ROCIVAL LYRIO DE, physiologist, researcher; b. Juiz de Fora, Brazil, July 21, 1941; s. Augusto Romão de and Odette Lyrio de Araujo; m. Dione Maria Alves de Avila, Dec. 18, 1964 (div. 1978); children: Alessandra, Rocival Jr., Carlos Alberto; m. Iris Gonçalves Mendes de Araujo, Nov. 16, 1993; children: Cecilia, Luana. MD, Fed. U. Minas Gerais Med. Sch., Belo Horizonte, Brazil, 1965, Master, 1975. Med. Diplomate. Prof. physiology Fed. U. Minas Gerais, Belo Horizonte, Brazil, 1965-91, rschr., 1965-91, chmn. dept., 1975-78; chmn. dept. Med. Sch. Faculty Ciencias Medicas, Belo Horizonte, Brazil, 1976-87; nat. dir. program of food complementation control Spl. Sec. of Cmty. Action/Presidence, Brasilia, Brazil, 1986-90; nat. dir. program food complementation Brazilian Social Assistance Legion, Brasilia, Brazil, 1990-92; prof. physiology med. sch. Faculty Ciencias Medicas Minas Gerais, Belo Horizonte, Brazil, 1975—; MD MD Hosp. de São João de Deus, Santa Luzia, Brazil, 1990—; dir. Emergency Hosp., Santa Luzia, Brazil, 1992-94. Editor: Physiology, 1970, Brazilians Nutritional Status, 1989, 93. Home: Rua Bonfim 160, 33010220 Santa Luzia Brazil Office: Rua Direita 767, 33010000 Santa Luzia Brazil

ARAÚJO SALES, EUGÊNIO DE, archbishop; b. Acari, Brazil, Nov. 8, 1920; s. Celso Dantas and D. Josefa de Araujo Sales. Student, Seminary Fortaleza, Ceará, 1940-43. Ordained priest Roman Cath. Ch., 1943. Bishop, 1954; apostolic adminstr. See of São Salvador de Bahia, 1954-68; archbishop Sã Sebastião do Rio de Janeiro, 1971—; consecrated cardinal, 1969. Avocation: reading. Office: Palacio Sao Joaquin, Rua de Gloria 446 CP 1362, 20241-150 Rio de Janeiro Brazil*

ARAV, MARC, corrosionist; b. Paris, Feb. 18, 1946; s. Robert Arav and Colette Beziel; m. Claire Maubert; children: Marion, Juliette. Corrosion protection expert. Chmn. EPF, France, 1976-90; tech. dir. Bemaex, France, 1976-90; chmn. Uniser, France, 1983-87; dir. Static Maintenance, France, 1977-78, DAG, France, 1989-90; corrosion specialiste TML, U.K., 1990-94; chmn. EMTS, France, 1995—; assoc. prof. U. Toulon, France; assessor Conciliating Commn. of Custom Expertise. Sgt. French artillery, 1968-69. Mem. European Fedn. of Corrosion, Nace, Qualiprope. Roman Catholic. Achievements include electro static painting devels./antigraffiti patents, Devinet Software and various maintenance manuals. Office: EMTS, 655 chemin de la Blaque, 13090 Aix-en-Provence France

ARAVANOPOULOS, FILIPPOS A., forest geneticist, breeder, researcher, educator; b. Mytilene, Lesvos, Greece, June 6, 1963; s. Argyris F. and Alcyone P. (Synodi) A.; m. Georgia N. Paliouris, Sept. 2, 1995; children: Alcyone, Argirios-Alexandros. BS, Aristotle U., Thessaloniki, Greece, 1986; PhD, U. Toronto, Ont., Can., 1992. Registered profl. forest scientist. Lectr. forest genetics/tree breeding Aristotle U., Thessaloniki, 1995-99, asst. prof. forest genetics/tree breeding, 1999—; rsch./tchg. asst. U. Toronto, 1988-91, rsch. assoc., 1992; vis. scientist Swedish U. Agrl. Sci., Uppsala, 1991; rsch. assoc. Mediterranean Agronomy Inst., Chania, Greece, 1994; asst. to operating agt. Internat. Energy Agy. B.A. Task 8, Toronto, 1992. Author: Principle of Research Methodology for Natural Resource Sciences, 1994, Genetics of Forest Tree Resistance to Environmental Pollution, 1997; contbr. numerous articles to profl. jours. Mem. cultural com. Greek Students Assn., U. Toronto, 1987-90, pres. Forestry Grad. Students Union, 1988-90, rep., 1989-91. Sgt. The Hellenic Army, 1993. Recipient Ednl. award Scarborough (Can.) Bd. Edn., 1990; U. Toronto Spl. fellow, 1987-92, scholar, 1984-92, E.E. Jonson Postgrad. scholar, 1989-91, Intra-Faculty Rsch. assistantship, 1988-91, Ont. Govt. scholar, 1991-92; rsch. grantee Natural Scis. and Engring. Rsch. Coun. Can., Ont. Ministry of Natural Resources, Internat. Energy Agy.-Bioenergy Agreement, European Union, Greek Secretariat for Rsch. and Tech. Mem. Internat. Union of Forest Rsch. Orgns. (dep. chmn. working party WP2.02.13 1996—), Hellenic Soc. for Protection of Nature, Geotech. Chamber of Greece, Can. Soc. for Plant Molecular Biology, Poplar Coun. of Can., Am. Genetics Assn., Hellenic Forest Sci. Soc. (sec. general 1999—), Hellenic Sci. Soc. for Plant Genetics and Breeding. Avocations: mountain climbing, skiing, karate-DO, photography, chess. Office: Aristotle U Dept Forestry, PO Box 238, 54006 Thessaloniki Greece

ARAVINDAN, PALANISAMY, mechanical engineer, educator; b. Pamban, Tamil Nadu, India, Feb. 10, 1942; parents: Muthurakku Palanisamy and Palanisamy Thayammal; m. Aravindan Vasanthaveni, May 17, 1970; children: Vanitha A., Aravind Karthikeyan. B of Mech. Engring., Madras (India) U., 1964, MSc in Engring., 1966, PhD, 1977. Sr. rsch. asst. Gas Turbine Def., Bangalore, India, 1964-65; lectr. Peelamedu Sama Govindasamy Coll. Tech., Coimbatore, India, 1967-74, asst. prof., 1974-82, prof. engring., 1982-92, prof., head dept. engring., 1992-97; prin. Regional Engring. Coll., Tirruchirappalli, India, 1997—; cons. PSG Indsl. Inst., Coimbatore, India, 1972-96; project coord. Min. of Sci. and Tech., India, 1987-96; faculty advisor SAE Collegiate Chpt., India, 1994-96; dir. edn. tech. PSG Tech., India, 1995-97. Contbr. articles to profl. jours. Recipient award All India Mfg. Tech., Design and Rsch., 1992; fellow UNESCO, 1983. Fellow Inst. Electronics India (chmn. 1994-96), Indian Instn. Indsl. Engring. (chmn. 1994-97); mem. ASME. Achievements include work on the optimal design of gear cutters, alumina coating for tools, dynamic scheduling of flexible manufacturing systems, strategic quality management, team engineering and world class management. Fax: 91-431-500056, 500133. E-mail: arvind@rect.ernet.in. Home: Prin Quarters, Regional Engring Coll Tamil Nadu, Tiruchirappalli 620 015, India Office: Regional Engring Coll, TN Tiruchirappalli 620 015, India

ARAVOSSIS, KONSTANTIN G., mechanical engineer; b. Athens, Greece, Sept. 28, 1963; s. George and Eugenia (Floca) A. MSc in Engring., RWTH Aachen, Germany, 1986; MSc in Mgmt. Sci., diploma, Imperial Coll., London, 1987; PhD in Engring. and Ops. Rsch., Nat. Tech. U. Athens, 1991. Trainee engring. Krupp Industrietechnik, Essen, Germany, 1985-86; mgr. engring. Kepa S.A., Athens, 1987-89; rsch. asst. Nat. Tech. U. Athens, 1987-94; owner, gen. mgr. Arvis and Co., Athens, 1994—; lectr. bus. policy U. Thessaly, 1997—; tech. cons. KEKA S.A., Athens, 1991, Nat. Ctr. Pub. Mgmt. Edn., Athens, 1994. Contbr. articles to profl. jours. Founder, bd. dirs. Aachen Datt, 1985. With Greek Army, 1989-90. Fellow Imperial Coll. Alumni Assn. (sec. 1994); mem. Assn. German Engrs., Tech. Chamber of Greece (tech. cons.), Imperial Coll. MBA Assn. (pres. 1994—), City Guilds Coll. Assn., Assn. MBAs, Filothei Tennis Club (team player 1980). Avocations: tennis, sailing, reading specialized literature, skiing. Office: Arvis & Co, Sissini 35, 11528 Athens Greece

ARBER, SARA LYNNE, sociology educator, researcher; b. Chingford, Essex, Eng., Mar. 19, 1949; d. George and Kathleen Arber; m. Geoffrey H. Herrington, Aug. 28, 1979; children: Andrea, Sian, David. BSc in Sociology, London Sch. Econs., 1972; MS in Med. Sociology, U. London, 1973; PhD, U. Surrey, Guildford, Eng., 1991. Lectr. sociology U. Surrey, 1974-86, sr. lectr., 1986-94, prof., 1994—. Author: Gender and Later Life, 1991, also 6 others; contbr. over 100 articles to profl. jours. Mem. S.W. Surrey Dist. Health Authority, 1981-89; mem. social affairs com. Econ. and Social Rsch. Coun., 1984-87. Mem. Brit. Sociol. Assn. (treas. 1988-90, pres. 1999—), Royal Statis. Soc., Brit. Soc. Gerontology, Social Policy Assn. Office: U Surrey, U Surrey, Dept Sociology, Guildford GU2 5XH, England

ARBER, WERNER, microbiologist; b. Gränichen, Switzerland, June 3, 1929; married; 2 children. Ed., Aargau (Switzerland) Gymnasium, Eidgenössische Technische Hochschule, Zurich. Asst. Lab. Biophysics, U. Geneva, 1953-58, docent, then extraordinary prof. molecular genetics, 1962-70; research assoc. dept. microbiology U. So. Calif., 1958-59; vis. investigator dept. molecular biology U. Calif., Berkeley, 1970-71; prof. microbiology U. Basel (Switzerland), 1971-96, rector, 1986-88. Co-recipient Nobel prize for physiology or medicine, 1978. Mem. Nat. Acad. Scis. (fgn. assoc.), Internat. Coun. Sci. (pres. 1996-99). Office: Biozentrum der Universität, 70 Klingelbergstrasse, CH-4056 Basel Switzerland

ARBOGAST, GORDON WADE, systems engineer, executive, educator, consultant; b. Charleston, S.C., May 24, 1942; s. Valentine and Teresa Louise Arbogast; m. Dorothy Sheryl Blackwell, Mar. 5, 1966; children: Annette Marie, Christina Theresa, Valentine Scott. BS, U.S. Mil. Acad., 1963; MSEE, MSIM, Ga. Inst. Tech., 1971; PhD, Clemson U., 1986. Commd. 2d lt. U.S. Army, 1963, advanced through grades to col., 1983, ret., 1990; head, assoc. prof. dept. engring. U.S. Mil. Acad., 1986-89; assoc. dir. engring. and tech. Def. Comm. Agy., 1989-90; v.p. sys. tech. Pacific Bell, San Ramon, Calif., 1990-93; prof. Jacksonville (Fla.) U., 1994—; prin. scientist Contel, Chantilly, Va., 1990; instr., cons. Learning Tree Internat., Reston, Va., 1994—. Contbr. articles to profl. jours. Lector, eucharistic min. Cursillo Cath. Ch., 1988—. Decorated Legion of Merit, Bronze Star, Air medal, Def. Superior Svc. meda. Mem. Inst. Indsl. Engrs. (sr.), Armed Forces Comm.-Electronics Assn. (pres. West Point chpt. 1987-89), West Point Soc. of North Fla. (pres. 1998—). Achievements include initiating systems engineering at U.S. Military Academy and major work in transforming Defense Communications Agency to Defense Information Systems Agency. Home: 4572 Oak Bay Dr W Jacksonville FL 32277-1016 Office: Jacksonville U Davis Coll Bus 2800 University Blvd N Jacksonville FL 32211-3394

ARBOLEYA, CARLOS JOAQUIN, lawyer, broker; b. Havana, Cuba, Aug. 16, 1958; came to U.S., 1960; s. Carlos Jose and Marta Aurora (Quintana) A. ABA, Miami Dade C.C., 1977; BBA in Fin., U. Miami, 1980, MBA in Fin., 1981, JD, 1987. Bar: Fla. 1989, U.S. Ct. Appeals (D.C. cir.) 1990. From teller to br. mgr. Barnett Bank South Fla. N.A., North Miami Beach, 1975-84; realtor, assoc. Cervera Real Estate, 1980—; pres. Owner's Box Promotions, 1993-95; owner Carlos J. Arboleya, Jr., P.A., Coconut Grove, 1988—; adv. bd. Exec. Nat. Bank, 1994—, Linda Ray Infant Ctr., 1990—; bd. dirs. Pvt. Industry Coun. Jobs for Miami; Hispanic adv. com. U. Miami Sports Mktg., 1992-95. Bd. dirs. Greater Miami Tennis Found., 1995, U. Miami Ear Inst., 1993; vice chma. planning adv. bd. City of Miami, 1993-95, 98-99, chmn. 1995-98, chmn. code enforcement bd., 1990-91, vice chmn. 1989-90; asst. scoutmaster Boy Scouts Am.; participant joint civilian orientation conf. U.S. Dept. Def., 1995; pres. Cocogrove Illas Condominium Assn., 1998—; trustee United Way, Miami-Dade, 2000—. Mem. ABA, Nat. Soc. Hispanic MBAs, Nat. Eagle Scout Assn., Cuban Am. Bar Assn., Builders Assn. South Fla., Am. Title Ins. Co., Attys. Title Ins. Fund, Inc., Fla. Bar Assn., Latin Bus. Assn., Latin Builders Assn., Hispanic Law Students Assn., Coral Gables C. of C., Greater Miami C. of C. (sports coun., chmn., homestead motorsports complex com., 1994-97, co-chmn. existing events com., 1992-94), Leadership Miami (exec. com. 1990-93, task force 1984-88, Coconut Grove Jaycees, Phi Delta Phi, Delta Sigma Pi (Outstanding Alumni award 1982). Republican. Roman Catholic. Office: Carlos J Arboleya Jr PA 2550 S Dixie Hwy Coconut Grove FL 33133-3137

ARBONA, ANTONIO, physicist, educator; b. Esporles, Baleares, Spain, July 30, 1972; s. Pedro Arbona and Maria Nadal. Degree in Theoretical Physics, U. Barcelona, Spain, 1995; Masters Degree, U. of the Balearic Islands, Palma de Mallorca, 1996, postgrad., 1997. Asst. in computer rm. dept. computer support U. of the Balearic Islands, Palma de Mallorca, 1996, asst. prof. dept. physics, 1999—. Contbr. chpt. to book and articles to profl. jours. Rsch. grantee Balearic Islands Govt., 1998-99. Avocations: Taekwondo, swimming, hiking, anthropology. E-mail: arbona@aei-potsdam.mpg.de and vdfsaan4@clust.uib.es. Fax: 34 971 173426. Home: Blanes 21, E-07015 Portals Nous Baleares, Spain Office: Balearic Islands U-Physics, Crta de Valldemossa km 7 5, E-07071 Baleares Spain

ARBOUR, LOUISE, judge; b. Montreal, Que., Can., Feb. 10, 1947. BA, Regina Assumpta, Montreal, 1967; LLB, U. Montreal, 1970. Chief prosecutor apptd. by UN Security Coun. Internat. War Crime Tribunals for Rwanda and Yugoslavia, The Hague, The Netherlands, 1996—; appelate supreme ct. judge Can., 1999—. Office: Supreme Ct Can, 301 Wellington St, Ottawa, ON Canada K1A 0J1 Address: 130 Queen St, West Toronto, ON Canada M5H 2N5

ARBUCKLE, JULIE ANN, lawyer; b. Chgo., Aug. 19, 1972; d. William and Katherine Roberts; m. Justin Arbuckle, Nov. 6, 1999. BA in English, BA in French, U. Calif., Berkeley, 1994; JD, UCLA, 1997. Bar: L.A. 1997. Assoc. Christensen, Miller, Fink, Jacobs, Glaser, Weil & Shapiro, L.A., 1997-99, Seyfarth, Shaw, Fairweather & Geraldson, San Francisco, 1999—. Editor UCLA Law Rev., 1997. Mem. ABA, Calif. State Bar, Queen's Bench. Avocations: masters swimming, running, cooking, wine tasting. Office: Seyfarth Shaw Et Al 101 California St Fl 29 San Francisco CA 94111-5802

ARBUZOV, VALERII IVANOVICH, physicist, researcher; b. Nikitino, Russia, July 1, 1949; s. Ivan Fedorovich Arbuzov and Fedos'ya Ivanovna (Trushnikova) Arbuzova; m. Irina Il'inichna Kichina, Jan. 23, 1972; children: Inna, Karina. MS in Engring., Physics, Ural State Tech. U., Sverdlovsk, USSR, 1973; PhD, Vavilov State Optical Inst., Leningrad, USSR, 1983; DS, Vavilov State Optical Inst., St. Petersburg, Russia, 1997. Postgrad. rschr. Vavilov State Optical Inst., Leningrad, 1973-75, jr. rschr., 1975-87, sr. rschr., 1987-98, lead rschr., 1998-99, lab. head, 1999—; assoc. prof. State Inst. Precise Mechanics & Optics (Tech. U.), St. Petersburg, 1994-98, prof., 1998—; prof. Acad. Civil Aviation, St. Petersburg, 1998—; invited prof. Friedrich Schiller Univ., Jena, Germany, 1995, 96, 97; vis. rschr. Friedrich-Alexander U., Erlangen, Germany, 1999, 2000. Adv. editl. bd. Jour. Non-Cryst Solids, Gainesville, 1991—; sci. editor, editl. bd. Jour. Glass Phys. Chemistry, St. Petersburg, 1990—; contbr. articles to profl. jours. Co-pres. scientist com. Vavilov State Optical Inst., St. Petersburg, 1994—. Rsch. grantee Internat. Sci. Found., U.S.A., 1993-94, joint rsch. grantee Internat. Sci. Found. Russian Govt., 1994-95. St. Petersburg Scientist Union. Avocations: classical music, literature, travel, walking, picking berries and mushrooms. Office: Vavilov State Optical Inst, 36/1 Babushkin St, 193171 Saint Petersburg Russia

ARCACHE, JEAN, publishing executive; b. Alexandria, Egypt, June 4, 1953; s. Raymond and Nicole (Gimel) A.; m. Isabelle Turries, Aug. 5, 1983; children: Guillame, Gautier, Grégoire, Justine. MBA, Inst. d'Adminstr. Enterprises, France, 1971. Sales mgr. Partir Travel, Paris, 1977-80; mng. dir. assoc. BREA Publishing, Paris, 1981-84; devel. mgr. Chene Pub., Paris, 1984-89; editl. dir. Hachette Pub., Paris, 1990-95; gen. mgr. Hachette Pratique Pub., Paris, 1995—, Marabour Pub., Paris, 1995—. Author: Businessman Practical Guide to Middle East, 1980; editor: French Vineyard Recipes, 1996. With French Marines, 1980-81. Avocations: skiing, scuba diving, tennis, golf, cave exploration. Home: 8 Pl A Max, 75009 Paris France Office: Hachette Pub, 43 Quai de Grenelle, 75015 Paris France

ARCASOY, MUFIT MAZHAR, physician, pediatrician; b. Urfa, Turkey, Jan. 1, 1931; s. Suphi Mehmet and Naciye Ongen A.; m. Fatos Halide Yerdel, Jan. 8, 1963; children: Murat, Selim. MD, 1st Univ. Med. Sch., Istanbul, Turkey, 1954; Pediatrician, Univ. Pa., 1958; Pediatric Cardiologist, U. Wash., 1960, PhD in Molecular Biology, 1967. Specialist in pediatrics and pediatric cardiology. Assoc. prof. Ege U. Med. Sch., Izmir, Turkey, 1970-74, prof., 1974—. Editor med. books in field; contbr. numerous articles to profl. jours.; contbr. chpts. to books in field. Mem. Turkish Nat. Pediatric Assn. (pres. 1999), Pediatric Cardiology Turkish (pres. 1998), others. Office: Mimar Sinan Cad/No 24/3, Kahramanlar, Izmir 35280, Turkey

ARCE, A. ANTHONY, psychiatrist; b. San Juan, P.R., June 13, 1923; s. Angel and Juana (Baez) A.; m. Malvene Balkind, Oct. 7, 1971; children—Alan I. Scheer, Judith Ann Scheer, Michael Anthony Arce. B.S., Washington and Jefferson Coll., 1942; M.D., Temple U., 1946. Diplomate: Am. Bd. Psychiatry and Neurology; certified in adminstrv. psychiatry. Intern Mercy Hosp., Bay City, Mich. and; Frankford Hosp., Phila., 1946-47; dir. Aguadilla (P.R.) Dist. Hosp., 1947-48; chief health officer Utuado, P.R., 1950-51; physician U.S. Mil. Acad., West Point, N.Y., 1951-52; med. officer Pa. R.R., 1952-53; practice medicine Yonkers, N.Y., 1953-59; resident psychiatrist Payne Whitney Clinic, N.Y.C., 1959-62; assoc. dir. psychiatry Grasslands Hosp., Valhalla, N.Y., 1962-67; dir. psychiatry Lincoln Hall Sch., Lincolndale, N.Y., 1967-68; dir. Bur. Aftercare Services N.Y. State Dept. Mental Hygiene, 1968-71; dir. Manhattan Psychiat. Center, Ward's Island, N.Y., 1971-76, Hahnemann Community Mental Health and Mental Retardation Center, Phila., 1976-84; pvt. practice medicine specializing in psychiatry, 1962—; prof. psychiatry, dep. chmn. dept. mental health svcs. Hahnemann U., 1976-85, prof., chmn., 1985-87, prof., dir. amb. svcs., 1987-91; prof., dep. chmn. dept. psychiatry Med. Coll., U. Pa., Phila., 1991-96; chmn. dept. behavioral medicine Girard Med. Ctr., Phila., 1996—. Mem. president's council N.Y. U. Sch. Social Work, 1963-66; bd. dirs. P.R. Family Inst., N.Y.C., 1970-72. Served with AUS, 1943-46, 48-50. Mem. Am. Coll. Mental Health Adminstrs., Am. Coll. Psychiatrists, Am. Psychiat. Assn. (chmn. task force continuing care), Phila. Psychiat. Soc., Am. Assn. Psychiat. Adminstrs. (treas., pres.). Home: 1416 Academy Ln Elkins Park PA 19027-2515 Office: Girard Med Ctr 2ADC 8th St & Girard Ave Philadelphia PA 19122-9999

ARCEO, THELMA LLAVE, energy specialist; b. Manila, Philippines, Apr. 19, 1956; d. Paulino Marasigan and Nellie (Llave) A. BS in Biology, U. Philippines, 1978; MS in Energy Mgmt., N.Y. Inst. Tech., 1987; postgrad., U. Pa., 1990—. Cert. asbestos investigator. Rsch. analyst Philippine Nat. Oil Co., Quezon City, Philippines, 1983-84; asst. dir. East Manhattan Sch., N.Y.C., 1985-87; energy specialist/dir. N.Y. Urban Coalition Housing Group, N.Y.C., 1987-93; dir. technical svcs. Cmty. Environ. Ctr., Inc., Long Island City, N.Y., 1994-98, sr. mgr., dir. tech. svcs., 1998—; cons. Conserve, Inc., N.Y.C., 1991-92, Con Edison Consumer Edn., N.Y.C. Contbr. articles to profl. jours. Bd. trustee East Manhattan Sch. Mem. AAAS, Assn. of Energy Engrs., Illuminating Engring. Soc. Achievements include rsch. on comml. biogas digester designs, use of Sargassum substrate for biogas prodn., residential energy engring. and mgmt., comml. energy audits, residential environ. studies. Home: 98-50 67th Ave Forest Hills NY 11374-4965 Office: Cmty Environ Ctr Inc 43-10 11 St Long Island City NY 11101

ARCHAKOV, ALEXANDER IVANOVICH, biochemist, researcher; b. Kashin, Russia, Jan. 10, 1940; s. Ivan Ivanovich and Elizaveta Isakovna (Polonskaya) A.; m. Svetlana Grigorevna Leskova, Dec. 4, 1963; 1 child, Archakova Tatyana Alexandrovna. Student, Moscow Medical Inst., 1962, Moscow Medical Inst., 1965; PhD, Moscow Medical Inst., 1966, D in biological scis., 1972. Rsch., teaching asst. Moscow Medical Inst., 1966-69, lectr. in biochemistry, 1969-70, head of lab. of enzymology and bioenergetics, 1970-79, prof. in biochemistry, 1975—, head of biochemistry dept., 1979—; dir. Inst. of Biological and Medical Chemistry, Moscow, 1989—; organizer of 7th Internat. Conf., 1991; mem. orgn. com. 10th Internat. Conf., 1997; lectr. at nat. and internat. congresses. Author: Peroxidization of Lipids in Biomembranes, 1972, Microsomal Oxidation, 1975, Oxygenases of BIological Membranes, 1983, Cholesterosis, 1983, Cholesterosis: Membrane Cholesterol, Theoretical and Clinical Aspects, 1984, Cytochrome P 450 and Active Oxygen, 1990; editor: Phosphatidylcholine: Effects on Cell Membranes and Transport of Cholesterol, 1989, Problems in Medical Chemistry, 1996—. Deputy chmn. medical-biological problems Min. of Sci., Russia; mem. Internat. Scientific Coun. on Biophysics and Biochemistry of Cytochrome; com. mem. Internat. Biochemists Union. Recipient Bach prize of Acad. of Scis. of USSR, 1982, State Prize of USSR, 1985, State Prize of Russian Federation, 1989; recipient numerous grants. Mem. Biochemical Soc. of Russia, Biochemical Soc. Great Britain, Internat. Adv. Com. Cytochrome P450, Russian Acad. of Medical Scis., N.Y. Acad. of Scis. Avocation: football. Home: Ostrovityanova 30/2/33, 117321 Moscow Russia Office: Inst of Biomedical Chemistr, 10 Pogodinskaya str, 119832 Moscow Russia

ARCHAMBAULT, GEORGE FRANCIS, editor, pharmaceutical consultant; b. Springfield, Mass., Apr. 29, 1909; s. George Charles and Catherine V. (Mayette) A.; m. Lillian Herbert, Sept. 3, 1934; children: Joan Anne Archambault Rubis, Lillian Kathleen Archambault Matan, Patricia Gay Archambault Kachik, Frances Helen Archambault Parks, George Francis, William Herbert. Ph.G., Mass. Coll. Pharmacy, 1931, Ph.C., 1933, Pharm.D. (hon.), 1960; J.D., Northeastern U., 1941; D.Sc. (hon.), Phila. Coll. Pharmacy, 1951; LL.D. (hon.), Temple U., 1961. Bar: Mass. 1942, U.S. Supreme Ct. 1976, D.C. 1980; Registered pharmacist in Mass., 1932. Mem. faculty Mass. Coll. Pharmacy, 1933-45, lectr. pharmacy and bus. adminstrn., 1933-47; practiced in Belmont, Mass. and Washington, 1945-47; dir. profl. relations in New Eng. states Liggett Drug Co., 1945-47; commd. pharmacist officer USPHS, 1947-67, pharmacist dir., 1952; chief pharmacy br., div. hosps. Bur. Med. Services, 1947-65; also pharmacy liasion officer Office Surgeon Gen. USPHS, 1960-67, medicare pharmacy planning cons. div. med. care adminstrn., 1965-67; dean, prof. pharmacy adminstrn. Coll. Pharmacy, U. Fla., Gainesville, 1967; editor Hosp. Formulary Jour., 1967-79; Washington editor Drug Intelligence and Clin. Pharmacy Jour., from 1979; cons. on pharmacy and instnl. and other drug distbn. systems, 1967—; cons. United Mine Workers Am. Health and Retirement Fund, 1971-76, Am. Soc. Cons. Pharmacists, 1972—, Hill-Burton program USPHS, 1969-79; mem. revision com. U.S. Pharmacopeia, 1950-60, trustee, 1960-75, USPHS del., mem.-at-large, 1975, cons. to exec. dir., 1976—, mem. subcoms. on external and internal preparations; hon. mem., 1980—; mem. faculty Inst. Hosp. Law of Am. Hosp. Assn., 1954-69; mem. joint com. Am. Soc. Hosp. Pharmacists and Am. Hosp. Assn., 1955-68; pharm. cons. Catholic Hosp. Assn., 1950—; pharmacy cons. profl. exam. service Am. Pub. Health Assn., 1949-59; adv. pub. health service pharmacy and prescription trend, div. prices and cost of living Bur. Labor Statistics, 1955-67; mem. nat. adv. com. Law-Medicine Research Inst., Boston U., 1960-65; lectr. law hosp. pharmacy and drugs including investigational drugs; Samuel Melendy Meml. lectr. U. Minn. Coll. Pharmacy, 1962. Author numerous articles, chpts. in books. Recipient Harvey A. Whitney Hosp. Pharmacy award Am. Soc. Hosp. Pharmacists, 1956; Andrew Craigie award Assn. Mil. Surgeons, 1962; certificate of appreciation Cath. Hosp. Assn., 1956; certificate of appreciation Kappa Psi Pharm. Frat, 1962; certificate of appreciation U.S. Naval Sch. Hosp. Adminstrn., 1964; Disting. Service medal USPHS, 1965; Remington medal Am. Pharm. Assn., 1969; Disting. Alumni award Mass. Coll. Pharmacy, 1976; Disting. Alumni award Northeastern U. Sch. Law, 1980; named Man of Year Am. Druggist, 1966; George Archambault ann. award established in his honor by Am. Soc. Cons. Pharmacists, 1972; Pres.'s award Am. Soc. Pharmacy Law, 1982. Life mem. Am. Pharm. Assn. (chmn. council 1959-60, com. publs. 1958-59, pres. Washington chpt. 1950, nat. pres. 1962-63); fellow AAAS (v.p. 1958, mem. council from 1959), Am. Pub. Health Assn., Am. Soc. Hosp. Pharmacists (hon. charter, pres. 1954-55); mem. Commd. Officers Assn. USPHS (chmn. exec. com. 1961-62), Mass. Soc. Hosp. Pharmacists (founder, hon.), La. Socs. Hosp. Pharmacists (hon.), Nat. Health Lawyers Assn., Am. Soc. Law and Medicine, Am. Soc. Hosp. Attys., Am. Med. Writers Assn., Fed. Bar Assn., D.C. Bar Assn., Nat. Press Club, Am. Soc. Pharmacy Law, Nat. Assn. Uniformed Services, Ret. Officers Assn., Kappa Psi, Rho Chi.

ARCHAMPONG, EMMANUEL QUAYE, surgery educator, university dean, consultant; b. Accra, Ghana, Oct. 12, 1933; s. Emmanuel Quarmine and Mary Naayi (Abbey) A.; m. Catherine Awula Ata Knnotey-Ashulu, July 27, 1968; children: Eliz, Ruth, David, Timothy, Emmanuel. BSc in Spl. Anatomy with honours, Univ. Coll. London, 1958; MB, BS with honours and distinction, Univ. Coll. Hosp., London, 1961; MS, U. London, 1974. Rsch. fellow, sr. lectr. Univ. Coll. Hosp. Med. Sch., 1970-71; lectr. surgery U. Ghana Med. Sch., Accra, 1967-70, sr. lectr., 1972-76, assoc. prof., 1976-78, prof., 1978-96, emeritus prof., 1996—, dean, 1984—; chmn. sectional com. Ministry Sci. and Tech., Ghana, 1985—; WHO cons. to Coll. Medicine and Allied Health Scis./Connaught Hosp., Freetown, Sierra Leone, 1994-99. Editor: Principles and Practice of Surgery, 1986, 2d edit., 1994; editor-in-chief West African Jour. Medicine, 1992. Commonwealth med. fellow, 1970-71, Commonwealth sr. fellow, London and Leeds, 1993, Commonwealth devel. fellow, Freetown, Sierra Leone, 1993-94. Fellow Royal Coll. Surgeons (Eng.), Royal Coll. Surgeons (Edinburgh), Internat. Coll. Surgeons, Ghana Acad. Arts and Scis., Assn. Surgeons Gt. Britain and Ireland; mem. Ghana Med. Assn. (editor 1973-80), West African Coll. Surgeons (v.p. 1992-97, pres. 1997-99), West African Soc. Gastroenterology (pres. 1989-93). Methodist. Avocations: music, gardening, table tennis, travel.

ARCHDEACON, SARAJANE, writer, photographer; b. Phila., Mar. 5, 1925; d. Spencer and Frances Bernadette A. Student, UCLA, 1949-56. vis. artist Malgache Acad., Madagascar, 1963-64. Writer, photographer Parade, So. Rhodesia, 1962-63, Westways, 1964, Transition, Uganda, 1964, Plexus, France, Italy, 1967-68, Avant Garde, 1969, London Times, 1969, Abu Dhabi Times, 1972-75, Mid. E. Sketch, Beirut, 1972-74, Shukan Asahi Weekly, Tokyo, 1974; one-woman shows include Paa Ya Paa Gallery, Nairobi, Kenya, 1967, Soc. Francaise de Photographie, Paris, 1968, archives Bibliotheque Nat., 1968, Expo 70, Japan, 1970, Debonair, India, 1978-87; translator: Bhagwan Ram's Aughar Vani; spl. collections 42nd St. Libr., N.Y.C., 1994, The Sun, N.C., 1993-99. Gray lady Red Cross, 1950; leader Campfire Girls, Bel Air, Calif., 1960.

ARCHER, BRIAN HARRISON, economics educator, consultant; b. Liverpool, U.K., July 31, 1934; s. Arthur Cecil and Elizabeth (Summerscales) A. BA, U. Cambridge, U.K., 1958; MA, 1963; BS in Econ., U. London, 1962; PhD, U. Wales, U.K., 1972. Dir. Inst. Econ. Rsch., U. Wales, 1972-77; sr. lectr. Adran Econ. U. Wales, 1969-77; head of dept., prof. U. Surrey, U.K., 1978-88; pro vice chancellor, 1987-94, prof. emeritus, 1994—. Contbr. over 100 articles to academic jours. Lt. British Army, 1953-55. Avocations: cricket, rugby, hockey, conjuring. Home: 3 The Cedars Milford, Godalming GU8 5DH, England Office: DOMS Stag Hill, Univ Surrey, Surrey GU2 5XH, England

ARCHER, JOHN ERNEST, psychology educator; b. Windsor, Berkshire, Eng., Aug. 2, 1944; s. James Thomas and Jessie Moorfield (Stubbings) A.; m. Rita Evelyn Gibbons, Aug. 25, 1973 (div. July 1981); m. Dieuwertje Anna Francesca Proud, Feb. 21, 1986. BSc with honors, U. Wales, Aberystwyth, 1965; PhD, U. Bristol, 1970. Rsch. fellow U. Sussex, Brighton, Eng., 1969-75; lectr. Lancashire Polytechnic (now U. Ctrl. Lancashire), Preston, Eng., 1975-87; prin. lectr. Lancashire Poly. (name now U. Ctrl. Lancashire), Preston, Eng., 1987-92, prof., 1992—. Author: The Behavioral Biology of Aggression, 1988; (with Barbara lloyd) Sex and Gender, 1982, 2nd edit. 1986, The Nature of Grief, 1999; editor: Male Violence, 1994; mem. editl. bd. Animal Behavior, 1981-84, British Jour. of Social Psychology, 1987—, Aggressive Behavior, 1997—. Simon Indsl. and Profl. fellow U. Manchester, 1991-92. Fellow Brit. Psychol. Soc.; mem. Human Behavior and Evolution Soc., Internat. Soc. for Rsch. on Agression (pres.-elect), Assn. for Study

Animal Behavior (coun. 1980-83), Amnesty Internat., Friends of Earth. Mem. Labour Party. Avocations: running, movies, watching cricket, rock music, theatre. Office: U Ctrl Lancashire, Dept Psychology, Preston PR12HE, England

ARCHER, JOHN WILLIAM, electrical engineer; b. Sydney, Australia, Jan. 29, 1950; s. Robert William and Dorothy Jean (Holzhauser) A.; m. Joan Elizabeth Gregory, Jan. 27, 1973; children: Michael John Gregory Archer, Paul William Gregory Archer. BSc, Sydney U., 1971, BEE, 1973, PhD, 1978. Sr. electronics engr. Nat. Radio Astronomy Obs., Socorro, N.Mex., 1977-79, Charlottesville, Va., 1979-84; chief rsch. scientist Telecomm. and Indsl. Physics Commonwealth Sci. and Indsl. Rsch. Orgn., Sydney, 1984—; mem. editorial bd. Wiley's Microwave & Optical Tech. Letters, N.Y.C., 1988—. Contbr. chpts. to books, articles to profl. jours.; patentee in field. Fellow IEEE (editorial bd. Transactions on Microwave Theory and Techniques 1990—). Avocations: fishing, golf, tennis, bicycling. Office: CSIRO Telecomm Indsl Physic, PO Box 76, Epping NSW 1710, Australia

ARCHER, JONATHAN ROBBINS, biomedical researcher; b. Boston, May 2, 1955; s. Robert Raymond and Nancy Miller Archer; m. Carolyn Lee Gray, July 3, 1999. BS, U. Mass. Student trainee JAX Lab., Bar Harbor, Maine, 1976-77; rsch. asst. JAX Lab., Bar Harbor, 1977-80, profl. asst., 1980-2000, database specialist, 2000—. Contbr. articles to profl. jours. Mem. Bar Harbor Folk Dancers (folkdance tchr. 1997—). Quaker. Avocations: gardening, dancing, sailing, international band, alternative energy projects. E-mail: jra@jax.org. Office: The Jackson Lab 600 Main St Bar Harbor ME 04609-1500 also: Hc 60 Box 173 Gouldsboro ME 04607

ARCHER, RICHARD EARL, product designer, alternative energy design consultant; b. Springfield, Ill., Aug. 24, 1945; s. Earl Wiley and Era Marie (Fentress) A.; m. Elizabeth Lou Lutz, Aug. 9, 1969 (dec.); children: Jeremy Richard, William Earl. BA in Design, So. Ill. U., Carbondale, 1970; MS, Gov.'s State U., 1979. Instr. design So. Ill. U., 1971-79, coord. design program, 1979-80, asst. prof. comprehensive planning and design, 1980-00; ret., 2000; dir. Applied Alternatives; mem. Nat. Alcohol Fuels Commn., 1980; chmn. Carbondale Energy Futures task force, 1980-81; mem. Ill. Legislature Alternative Energy Commn., 1981-83; mem. adv. panel U.S. Congl. Office Tech. Assessment, 1982; cons., tchr. problem solving class U.S. Army War Coll., 1988—. Editor: Ill. Solar Resource Adv. Coun. Grants Newsletter, 1979-81; contbr. articles to profl. jours.; originator Great Cardboard Boat Regatta. chmn. bd. Innovative Problem Solving Found., 1990—. Recipient Outstanding Tchr. Yr. award Coll. Human Resources, So. Ill. U., 1979; U.S. Dept. Energy grantee, 1979-81, U.S. Dept. Labor grantee, 1978-79, Ill. Dept. Energy grantee, 1980-81; named Outstanding Tchr. of Yr., Sch. Art, 1985. Mem. Solar Lobby (dir. 1978-80). Home: 1 Unicorn Hill Rd De Soto IL 62924-3313

ARCHIBALD, FRED JOHN, newspaper executive; b. Sept. 10, 1922; s. Fred Irwin and Edna Esther (Olson) A. BS, U.S. Mil. Acad., 1945. Commd. 2d lt. U.S. Army, 1945, advanced through grades to capt., 1951; served various assignments U.S. Army, U.S., Philippines, Japan; resigned U.S. Army, 1955; mng. editor Frederick (Md.) News-Post, 1956-78, assoc. pub., 1978-85; gen. mgr., editor News-Post News Svc., Frederick, 1985-87; lectr. journalism and pub. relations, various instns., 1947—; cattle breeder Armadale Farms, Frederick, 1964—. Decorated Bronze Star. Mem. Airedale Terrier Club Am. (treas. 1959-61), Md. Hereford Assn. (pres. 1979-81), Mil. Order Carabao, Am. Legion, Nat. Press Club, Army and Navy Club, Georgetown Club, Overseas Press Club, Sigma Delta Chi, Sigma Alpha Epsilon. Democrat. Episcopalian. Avocations: theatrical productions, experimentl gardening, art collecting, press and garden photography. Home: Armadale Farms PO Box 74 Frederick MD 21705-0074 Office: Frederick News-Post PO Box 578 Frederick MD 21705-0578

ARCHIBALD, JAMES KENWAY, lawyer; b. Mass., Mar. 29, 1949; s. John Lawrence and Jean (Kenway) A.; m. Joanne Mary Ricciuti, Aug. 16, 1975; children: Kathryn, John. BA, Johns Hopkins U., 1971; JD, U. Md., 1975. Bar: Md. 1975, D.C. 1985, U.S. Dist. Ct. Md. 1976, U.S. Ct. Appeals (4th cir.) 1978, U.S. Supreme Ct. 1979, U.S. Ct. Appeals (9th cir.) 1984, Maine 1998. Assoc. Venable, Baetjer and Howard, Balt., 1975-83, ptnr., 1983—. Co-author: Pleading Causes of Action in Maryland, 1990, Model Witness Examinations, 1997. Chmn. bd. trustees Md. State Colls. and Us., 1984-86; trustee Johns Hopkins U., 1997—; bd. dirs. Roland Park Country Sch., Inc., Balt., 1989-94; pres. Homeland Assn., Inc., Balt., 1990. Recipient Disting. Svc. award Litigation Sect. Md. State Bar, Md., 1981. Mem. ABA (litigation sect., co-chair com. 1987—), Internat. Assn. Def. Counsel, Def. Rsch. Inst. (Exceptional Performance award 1989, Md. state chair 1989-93), Md. Assn. Def. Trial Counsel (pres. 1988-89), Johns Hopkins Alumni Coun. (v.p. 1996-98, pres. 1998—), Johns Hopkins Second Decade Soc. (nat. chair 1989-91), Am. Law Inst. Home: 13037 Jerome Jay Dr Cockeysville MD 21030-1523 Office: Venable Baetjer & Howard 1800 Mercantile Bank Bldg 2 Hopkins Plz Ste 2100 Baltimore MD 21201-2982

ARCHIBEQUE, CHARLENE PAULLIN, music educator; b. Mt. Sterling, Ohio, July 15, 1935; d. Howard Samuel and Roberta Mae (Miller) Paullin; 1 child, Melissa. BME, U. Mich., 1957; MA, San Diego State Coll., 1965; DMA, U. Colo., 1969. Tchr. San Diego Unified Sch. Dist., 1957-69; dir. San Jose (Calif.) State U. Choraliers, 1970—; cons., guest lectr. many univs.; conductor choirs in 42 states and Can. Contbr. articles to profl. jours. Dir. chorus San Jose Symphony, 1970-2000, bd. dirs. 1993—. Named Woman of Vision Career Ctr., Disting. Alumni U. Colo., 1986, Woman of Achievement in Arts San Jose Mercury News and Women's Fund, 1998; recipient Pen award, 1996, numerous others. Mem. Am. Choral Dirs. Assn. (state pres. 1971-73, nat. chair 1973-75), Music Educators Nat. Conf., Internat. Choral Fedn. Avocations: travel, reading, cooking, entertaining. Home: 11511 Summit Wood Rd Los Altos Hills CA 94022-4512 Office: Sch of Music and Dance San Jose State U 1 Washington Sq San Jose CA 95112-3613

ARCHWICHAI, LAA, geologist; b. Mukdahan, Thailand, May 7, 1956; s. Boonme and Sao (Phatatoom) A.; m. Dontree Hongsomdee, Dec. 31, 1980; children: Sasithorn, Suriyachack, Phin Phong. BSc, Khon Kaen (Thailand) U., 1980; MSc, Imperial Coll. Sci., Tech., and Medicine, London, 1983; diploma, Imperial Coll, London, 1983. Lectr. engring. geology Khon Kaen U., 1980-87, asst. prof. engring. geology, 1987—; head. dept. geotech. Khon Kaen U., 1986-90; assoc. dean planning devel. faculty tech., 1990—. Mem. editl. bd. Proceedings Conf. Geology Mineral Resources Devel. N.E., Thailand. Am. Field Svc. award, 1975; Royal Thai Govt. scholar, 1976-80, 92-95, British Coun. Open scholar, 1982-83; decorated companion 2nd class Most Exalted Order of the White Elephant, 1985, knight comdr. 2nd class, 1995, comdr. Most Noble Order of the Crown of Thailand, 1987, knight comdr., 1990. Mem. Geol. Soc. Thailand, Internat. Assn. Engring. Geology. Home: Khon Kaen U, Srithan 123/645 Soi 8, MOO 16 Khon Kaen 40002, Thailand Office: Dept Geotech Faculty Tech, Khon Kaen U, Khon Kaen 40002, Thailand

ARCOS, CRESENCIO S., ambassador; b. San Antonio, Nov. 10, 1943; m. Patricia Cordova; 2 children. BA, U. Tex., 1966; MA, Johns Hopkins U., 1973. Various pub. and cultural affairs positions Leningrad, USSR, Sao Paulo, Brazil; consulate gen. Leningrad, Russia; various pub. and cultural affairs positions Am. Embassy, Lisbon, Portugal, from 1973; counselor pub. affairs Am. Embassy, Tegucigalpa, Honduras, 1980-85; dep. dir. Nicaraguan Humanitarian Assistance Office, U.S. Dept. State, Washington, 1985-86, dep. coord. Latin Am. and Caribbean pub. diplomacy, 1986-87, dep. asst. sec. state for Cen. Am., 1988-89; coord. pub. diplomacy White House Office Communications and Planning, Washington, 1987-88; amb. to Honduras, 1990-93; sr. dep. asst. Sec. State for Internat. Narcotics and Crime, 1993-95; v.p. AT&T Latin Am., Coral Gables, Fla., Latin Am., 1995—; mem. adv. group UN Drug Control Program Commn.; lectr. U. Calif. Irvine Regents, 1998—; mem. White House Pres.'s Fgn. Intelligence Adv. Bd., 1999—. Mem. Hispanic Coun. on Internat. Rels., Washington; bd. dirs. Caribbean-Latin Am. Action, Coun. of the Americas, N.Y.C.; adv. com. Fla. Internat. Univ. Latin Am. Carribean Ctr.; bd. visitors Zamorano Agr. Sch., Honduras; dir. United Negro Coll. Fund Inst. Internat. Pub. Policy. Recipient awards USIA, Superior Honor awards State Dept.; named to Orden de Morazan, Honduras; U. Calif. Regents' fellow, 1998-99. Mem. Coun. Fgn. Rels., Am. Fgn. Svc. Assn., Coun. of the Ams. (bd. dirs.). Office: 2333 Ponce De Leon Blvd Coral Gables FL 33134-5422

ARCOT, RANGARAJ GOVINDRAJ, retired physician; b. Vellore, Chennai, India, Mar. 12, 1917; s. Govindraj and Lokanayaki (Masilamani) A.; m. Amita Chaudhury, Aug. 11, 1966. MB BS, Madras Med. Coll., 1941; diploma in pub. health, Osmania U., 1960. Med. officer, col. Indian Army, 1941-66; field rep. UNICEF, Delhi, India, 1967-69; sr. med. officer WHO, Afghanistan, 1969-77; sr. health coord. UNHCR, Thailand, 1979-83; med. officer ICM, Hong Kong, 1984, Malaysia, 1986; regional sr. med. adviser ICM, Malaysia,, Taiwan, The Philippines, 1987-90; cons. WHO, Saudi Arabia, The Gulf countries, 1978, Somalia, 1979, Ethiopia, 1986; county health planner Mgmt. for Scis., Malawi, 1985; cons. UNICEF, Nigeria, 1986. Contbr. articles to profl. jours. Recipient numerous awards. Avocations: reading, travel, learning new languages, computers.

ARDAL, BJORN, pediatrician; b. Reykjavik, Iceland, Jan. 24, 1942; s. Ingi Ardal and Helga Bjornsdottir; m. Kolbrun Saemundsdottir, June 7, 1966; children: Sigridur Thora, Helga Gudny, Kolbrun Birna. Candidate Medicine and Surgery, U. Iceland, Reykjavik, 1970; postgrad., U. Conn., 1972-74, McGill U., Montreal, Can., 1974-76. Bd. cert. in pediats., allergy and clin. immunology. Intern U. Iceland, Reykjavik, 1970-71; dist. dr. Isarjordur, Iceland, 1971-72; intern U. Conn., Hartford, 1972-73, resident, 1973-74; resident McGill U., Montreal, 1974-76, fellow, 1976-77; specialist in pediats. U. Iceland, Reykjavik, 1977—. Mem. Am. Assn. Asthma, Allergy and Immunology (corr.); mem. Icelandic Assn. Allergy and Immunology (chmn. 1994-99). Avocations: tree planting, tennis, skiing, sailing. Home: Holtasel 46, 109 Reykjavik Iceland Office: Leknastodin Uppsolum, Kringlan 8-12, 103 Reykjavik Iceland

ARDALAN, NADER, architect; b. Tehran, Iran, Mar. 9, 1938; s. Abbas Gholi and Faranguis Davar Ardalan; m. Laleh Bakhtiar, 1962 (div. 1976); 3 children; m. Shahla Ganji, 1977; 1 child. Student, Carnegie-Mellon U., Harvard U. Designer S.O.M., 1962-64; chief arch. Nat. Iranian Oil Co., 1964-66; design ptnr. Aziz Farmanfarmaian & Assocs., 1966-72; mng. dir. Mandala Collaborative, Tehran and Boston, 1972-79; prof. of design Faculty Fine Arts Tehran U., 1972-79; pres. Nader Ardalan Assocs., 1979-92; prin. Jung/Brannen Assocs. Inc., Boston, 1983—; mng. prin. Jung/Brannen Assocs. Inc., Abu Dhabi, 1992; sr. v.p. KEO Internat. Cons., 1994—; vis. prof. Harvard U. Grad. Sch. Design, 1977-78, 81-83, Yale U., 1977, MIT, 1980; mem. Aga Khan Award Steering Com., 1976-80, King Fahd Award, 1987. Author: Sense of Unity, 1972, Habitat Bill of Rights, 1976, Pardisan, Environmental Park, 1976, Blessed Jerusalem, 1985; contbr. articles to profl. jours. Recipient Design awards. Avocations: study of sacred architecture, photography, swimming, hunting. Office: KEO Internat Cons, PO Box 3679, Safat 13037, Kuwait

ARDASH, GARIN, mechanical engineer; b. Detroit, July 14, 1963; s. Berge and Lucy Alice (Souldourian) A. BSME, U. Mich., 1986, MME, 1988. Grad. rsch. asst. U. Mich. Coll. Engring., Ann Arbor, 1986-87, Los Alamos (N.Mex.) Nat. Lab., 1987; analysis engr. Naval Reactors Facility, Idaho Falls, Idaho, 1989-92, rsch./analysis engr. materials tech. dept., 1992-94; sr. rsch./analysis engr. materials tech. dept. Bettis Atomic Power Lab. Bechtel Bettis Inc., West Mifflin, Pa., 1994—. U. Mich. Coll. Engring. fellow, 1986-87; State Mich. Coop. scholar, 1982-83. Mem. ASTM, AAAS, ASME, Nat. Assn. Corrosion Engrs., Internat. Legion Intelligence, Mensa, Pitts. South Soccer Assn. Avocations: soccer, photography, skiing, chess. Home: 700 Penn Center Blvd #202 Pittsburgh PA 15235-5912 Office: Bettis Atomic Power Lab Materials Tech M/S O5N/MT PO Box 79 West Mifflin PA 15122-0079

ARDELEAN, IOAN, microbiologist, researcher; b. Arad, Romania, Mar. 10, 1957; s. Ioan and Victoria (Bulgăr) Ardelean; m. Emilia Cornelia Axente, Mar. 11, 1989; children: Ioana, Maria-Alexandra, Ana-Valentina. Grad., Faculty Biology, Bucharest, Romania, 1981, MS, 1982, PhD, 1997. Biologist diplomate. Coll. tchr. Hârsova, Romania, 1982-84; jr. scientist Inst. Biology, Bucharest, 1984-90, scientist, 1990-95, sr. scientist, 1995-98, sr. scientist II, 1998—; sec. Commn. Biology-Ministry Sci. and Tech., Bucharest, 1995-98. Co-author: Research in Photosynthesis, 1992, Cyanobacterial Nitrogen Metabolism and Environmental Biotechnology, 1997; contbr. articles to sci. jours. Exec. dir. Civil Protection, Inst. Biology, Bucharest, 1990-94. Mem. Internat. Soc. Photosynthesis Rsch., Romanian Biol. Soc. Avocations: jogging, gardening, making wine, cinema. Home: Aleea Zorelelor, nr 1 Bl 43 ScA ap 62, 77514 Bucharest Romania Office: Inst Biology, Spl Independ 296 POB 56-53, 79651 Bucharest Romania

ARDEN, DONALD S(EYMOUR), bishop; b. Bournemouth, Hampshire, Eng., Apr. 12, 1916; s. Stanley and Winifred (Morland) A.; m. Jane Grace Riddle, Sept. 29, 1962; children: Bazil, Christopher. Student, St. Peter's Coll., Adelaide, Australia, 1926-33; BA with honors, Leeds (Eng.) U., 1934-37; postgrad., Coll. of the Resurrection, Mirfield, 1937-39. Ordained deacon Anglican Ch., 1939, ordained priest, 1940. Asst. priest St. Catherine's, New Cross, London, 1939-40, Potten End, Herts, Eng., 1941-43; chaplain Ashridge Hosp., Herts, 1941-43; asst. priest African Mission, Pretoria, South Africa, 1944-51; dir. Usuthu Mission, Swaziland, 1951-61; bishop Nyasaland, Malawi, 1961-81; archbishop Ctrl. Africa, 1971-80; asst. bishop Diocese of London, 1981—; priest in charge St. Margaret's Uxbridge, London, 1981-86; vol. asst. priest St. Alban's, North Harrow, Eng., 1986—. Author: Out of Africa Something New, 1976; editor: Youth's Job in the Parish, 1939. Named Canon of Zululand and Swaziland, 1959, Comdr. of Brit. Empire, 1981. Mem. Concern Universal (trustee 1994—), Mines Adv. Group (patron), Mozambique-Angola Anglican Assn. (trustee 1989—), Malawi Assn. for Christian Support (patron 1994—), Nchima Trust (patron). Avocations: photography, walking. Fax: 020 8868 8013. E-mail: djarden@compuserve.com. Home and Office: 6 Frobisher Close, Pinner, Middlesex HA5 1NN, England

ARDEN, JOHN, playwright; b. Barnsley, Eng., Oct. 26, 1930; s. Charles Alwyn and Annie Elizabeth (Layland) A.; m. Margaretta Ruth D'Arcy, 1957; 5 children. BA, Sedbergh Sch., King's Coll., Cambridge, 1953; Diploma, Edinburgh Coll. Art, 1955. Fellow in playwriting Bristol (Eng.) U., 1959-60; vis. lectr. politics and drama NYU, 1967; Regent's lectr. U. Calif., Davis, 1973; writer in residence U. New England, Australia, 1975; co-founder Corrandulla Arts Club, 1971, Galway Theatre Workshop, 1975. Plays: All Fall Down, 1955, The Life of Man, 1956, The Waters of Babylon, 1957, Live Like Pigs, 1958, Sergeant Musgrave's Dance, 1959, Soldier, Soldier, 1960, Wet Fish, 1962, The Workhouse Donkey, 1963, Ironhand, 1963, Armstrong's Last Goodnight, 1964, Left Handed Liberty, 1965, Pearl, 1977, To Put it Frankly, 1979, The Ingenious Gentleman, 1980, Garland for a Hoar Head, 1982, The Old Man Sleeps Alone, 19982, The Little Novels of Wilkie Collins, 1998, Woe Alas the Fatal Cashbox, 1999, (with Margaretta D'Arcy) The Business of Good Government, 1960, The Happy Haven, 1960, Ars Longa Vita Brevis, 1964, Friday's Hiding, 1966, The Royal Pardon, 1966, Muggins is a Martyr, 1968, The Hero Rises Up, 1968, The Ballygombeen Bequest, 1972, The Island of the Mighty, 1972, Keep These People Moving, 1972, The Non-Stop Connolly Show, 1975, Vandaleur's Folly, 1978, The Little Gray Home in the West, 1978, The Making of Muswell Hill, 1979, The Manchester Enthusiasts, 1984, Whose is the Kingdom?, 1988, A Suburban Suicide, 1994; TV documentary (with Margaretta d'Arcy): Profile of Sean O'Casey, 1973; essays: (with Margaretta D'Arcy) To Present the Pretence, 1977, (with Margaretta D'Arcy) Awkward Corners, 1988; novels (U.S. title: Vox Pop) Silence Among the Weapons, 1982, Books of Bale, 1988, Cogs Tyrannic, 1991, Jack Juggler and the Emperor's Whore, 1995. Office: care Casarotto Ramsay Ltd, 60-66 Wardour St, London W1V 3HP, England

ARDUINO, PEDRO, engineering educator; b. Córdoba, Argentina, Sept. 12, 1963; came to the U.S., 1990; s. Héctor Augusto and Susana Ferrer Arduino; m. Carolina Rosso Arduino; children: Lucia, Sofia Arduino. Degree in civil engring., U. Nat. Córdoba, 1988; MS, U. P.R., 1993; PhD in Civil Engring., Ga. Inst. Tech., 1996. Rsch. asst., instr. U. Nat. Córdoba, 1988-90; rsch. asst. U. P.R., Mayagüez, 1990-93, lab. instr., 1990-92; rsch. asst., tchg. asst. Ga. Inst. Tech., Atlanta, 1993-96; asst. prof. U. Wash., Seattle, 1997—. Contbr. articles to profl. jours. Roman Catholic. Avocations: tennis, soccer. Office: U Wash PO Box 352700 Seattle WA 98195-2700

ÅREDAL, ÅKE, management consultant; b. Luleå, Norrbotten, Sweden, Mar. 8, 1942; s. John Anders Andersson and Margoth Justina (Sundqvist) Å.; m. Barbro Britt-Louise Lanner, Nov. 25, 1967; children: Johan, Marie Louise, Charlotte. PhD, U. Stockholm, 1989. Sec. edn., regional sec. Union Fin. Sector Employees, Stockholm, 1968-69; mgr. Aktieinvest, Stockholm, 1969-72; mgmt. cons. Conatus AB, Stockholm, 1972—; pres., CEO SkyCab AB, Stockholm, 1993—; chmn. bd. Conatus AB, Stockholm, 1995—; rschr. Scandinavian philoshopher, metascientist and psychoanalyst Carl Lesche, Stockholm, 1975-93; inventor/dir. The Lesche-archive, Sweden, 1996—. Author: Invisible Social Control: A Hermeneutical Study of Social Control in the Swedish Dental Administration, 1989; contbr. articles to profl. jours. Bertil Wennborg Found. grantee, 1998, 99, 2000. Avocations: philosophy, mythology, oil painting, Idla gymnastics. Fax: 46 8 6677710. E-mail: skycab@telia.com. Home: Narvavägen 21, S-11460 Stockholm Sweden

AREF, AMJAD JALAL-EDDIN, structural engineer, educator; b. Turmos Aya, Palestine, July 31, 1963; came to U.S., 1989; s. Jalal Eddin Aret and Marium Sadeg Hamed; m. Farizah Farid Asmar, Nov. 11, 1984; children: Jalal, Renad, Maryam, Noor, Juman. BS in Civil Engring., Birzeit U., West Bank, Palestine, 1987; MS in Civil Engring., N.J. Inst. Tech., 1991; PhD in Civil Engring., U. Ill., 1997. Asst. prof. State U. N.Y., Buffalo, 1997—. E-mail: aaref@eng.buffalo.edu. Office: State Univ NY Civil Engring Dept 235 Ketter Hall Buffalo NY 14260-4300

AREFIEVA, ELENA, management consultant; b. Moscow, Mar. 21, 1950; d. Boris and Margarita (Korobova) Klutchevitch; m. Igor Arefiev, Mar. 4, 1978 (dec. 1992); 1 child, Arseny. Diploma, Moscow State U., 1973, PhD in Econs., 1977. Jr., sr. researcher, head of sect. Inst. for Oriental Studies Acad. of Sci., Moscow, 1976-86; sr. researcher Inst. World Econ. and Internat. Rels., Moscow, 1986-91; dir. mgmt. cons. Ctr. for Fgn. Investment and Privatization, Moscow, 1992-94; cons., rep. in Moscow Edison Gas S.p.A., Milan, 1994—; vis. scholar Overseas Devel. Coun., Washington, 1990, Internat. Ctr. for Devel. Policy, Washington, 1991, Overseas Devel. Inst., London, 1991; cons. OECD, Paris, 1991, U.S. AID, Moscow, 1993. Author: Developing Countries of Asia in World Industrial Structure, 1989, (with W.D. Bowles) Proposals for Joint U.S.-USSR Cooperation with Developing Countries, 1990; contbr. chpts. to books, articles to profl. jours. and newspapers. Home: Sokolnichesky val d 24/3/5, 107113 Moscow Russia Office: Edison Gas care Tecnimont, 32a Leninsky prosp, 117334 Moscow Russia

AREFJEV, ALEXANDRE SERGEYEVICH, engineering educator, researcher; b. Voronesch, Russia, Mar. 20, 1940; s. Sergey Ivanovich and Maria Efimovna (Charey) A.; m. Tatiana Anatolievna, June 27, 1975. Student, Radioengring. Inst., Ryazan, Russia, 1962; diploma (hon.), Radioengring. Inst., Ryazan, 1962; postgrad., Electroengring. Inst., Leningrad, Russia, 1963-66; student, Conservatory Leningrad, 1963-68. Sr. lectr. Radioengring. Inst., Ryazan, 1970-72, assoc. prof. Indsl. Electronics Dept., 1972-77, head Indsl. Electronics Dept., 1977-93, prof. Indsl. Electronics Dept., 1993-94; dean faculty Electronics and Radioengring. Acad., Ryazan, 1994—. Lt. Regime, Russian Army, 1968-69. Mem. N.Y. Acad. Scis. Home: Vessennaya St 21-6, 390026 Ryazan Russia Office: Radioengring Acad, Gagarin St 59-1, 391000 Ryazan Russia

AREGHEORE, EROAROME MARTIN, agricultural science educator, researcher; b. Ozoro, Delta, Nigeria, Nov. 26, 1955; s. Egovie Ctr and Dora Ejobornake (Uguh) A.; m. Okwei Felicia Omo-Erigbe, Aug. 1. 1992; children: Onowhoakpo Marion, Emleakpobino Andreas. BS in Agr., U. Tenn., 1979; MSc in Dairy Prodn., U. Ibadan, Oyo, Nigeria, 1982, PhD in Animal Nutrition, 1985. Rsch. asst. Cocoa Rsch. Inst. of Nigeria, Ibadan, Oyo, 1974-77; mem. Nat. Youth Svc. Corps, Lagos, Oyo, Nigeria, 1980-81; lectr. Coll. Edn., Warri, Bendel, Nigeria, 1981-90; vis. animal scientist U. Zambia, Lusaka, Nigeria, 1990-91; reader, dir. Coll. of Edn., Warri, Delta, Nigeria, 1993-95; livestock cons. Delta Agrl. Devel. Programs, Ibusa, Delta, 1992-95. Contbr. articles to profl. jours. including: Animal Feed Sci. & Tech., Veterinary and Human Toxicology, Small Ruminant Rsch. (Provost prize 1991); editor-in-chief Warri Jour. Sci. and Tech. Pres. Progressives Club, Warri, 1993. Recipient scholarship Bendel State Govt., U. Tenn., Knoxville, 1977; postgrad. scholarship Fed. Govt. Nigeria, Ibadan, 1982-84, Letter of Commendation, Coll. of Edn., 1989; guest scientist Alexander von Humboldt Rsch. fellow U. Hohenheim, 1996-97. Mem. AAAS (internat. mem.), N.Y. Acad. Sci. (internat. mem.), Sci Tchr. Assn. of Nigeria. Roman Catholic. Achievements include: pioneer research on the nutritional requirements of pregnant Gwembe Valley goats-Zambia. Avocations: travel, lawn tennis, photography. Office: U South Pacific Coll of Edn, Dept Argl Sci Sch of Agrl Animal Sci, Apia Delta, Western Samoa

ARENA, ALEJANDRO PABLO, mechanical engineer, educator; b. Godoy Cruz, Mendoza, Argentina, Feb. 12, 1963; arrived in Italy, 1993; s. Hercules Paulino and Dolores Haydee (Granados) A.; m. Estela Adrana Di Lorenzo, Aug. 26, 1994; children: Marco Francesco, Florencia. B in Engring., U. Tech., Mendoza, 1992; PhD, Poly. Torino, Turin, Italy, 1997. Postdoctoral fellow Italian Min. Fgn. Affairs, Turin, 1993-96, Poly. Torino, Turin, 1997-98, Argentinian Nat. Coun. Sci. & Tech. Rsch., Mendoza, Argentina, 1998—; dir. energy environ. and sustainable devel. rsch. group Tech. U. Agentina. Author: Viscous Friction of Fluids on Ducts, 1997; editor: Rational Use of Energey in Thermal Power Plants; contbr. articles to profl. jours. dir. energy environment and sustainable devel. rsch. group Tech U. Argentina (Rooth award for contbns. in rsch. field, 1999). Doctoral fellow Italian Ministry Fgn. Affairs, 1983-90, postdoctoral fellow Poly. Turin, 1997-98; recipient Outstanding Grad. award for dedication and contbns. to sci. knowledge Nat. Tech. U., 1999. Fellow Internat. Solar Energy Soc., Italian Thermotech. Assn.; mem. Internat. Study Group for Water and Energy Systems. Avocations: mountain climbing, skiing, mountain biking, music, reading. E-mail: aparena@lab.cricyt.edu.ar. Home: 25 de Mayo 636, 5500 Mendoza Argentina

ARENBERGER, PETR, dermatologist; b. Prague, Czech Republic, Dec. 4, 1958; s. Miloslav and Marie (Pavlickova) A. MD, Charles U., 1984, PhD, 1991, DSc, 1994. Physician Univ. Hosp., Prague, Czech Republic, 1984-88; asst. prof. Charles U., Prague, 1988-89; rsch. fellow LMU Univ., Munich, Germany, 1989-91; prof. Charles U., 1991—; vis. researcher Psoriasis Rsch. Inst., Palo Alto, Calif., 1992-93; cons. Staticon Clin. Rsch. Orgn., Munich, 1994—. Author: Practical Dermatology, 1991, Dermatology for Nurses, 1992, Repetitorium of Dermatology, 1994, Tests in Dermatology, 1994, Dermatology News, 1997, Dermatotherapy, 1998, Dermatological Therapy, 1998. Mem. European Soc. Dermatol. Rsch., German Dermatol. Soc. (hon. corr. mem.). Home: Cimicka 84, 18200 Prague Czech Republic Office: Charles U Dept Dermatology, Srobarova 50, 10034 Prague Czech Republic

ARENDT, JOSEPHINE, biochemist; b. Newark, U.K., Feb. 13, 1941; d. Harry and Margaret (Clark) Wragg; m. John Harry Arendt; children: Rachel, Robert, Paul. BSc, London U., 1962, PhD, 1966. Rsch. asst. Inst. of Obstetrics and Gyn., London, 1962-65; rsch. asst. U. Geneva, Switzerland, 1966-70, maitre asst., 1970-77; rsch. fellow U. Surrey, Guilford, U.K., 1977-81, sr. lectr., 1981-84, reader, 1984-89, prof., 1989—; cons. in field; bd. dirs. 2 cos. Author: Melatonin and the Mammalian Pineal Gland, 1994; contbr. over 250 articles to profl. publs. Mem. European Pineal Soc. (pres. 1990-93). Avocations: cooking, gardening, riding. Office: Sch of Biol Scis, Univ of Surrey, Guildford GUZ 5XH, England

ARENHÖVEL, HARTMUTH, physicist; b. Münster, Germany, Dec. 24, 1938; s. Wilhelm and Gertrude (Michel) A.; m. Mariana Lozanova; children: Sibylle, Anna. MS in Physics, U. Freiburg, Germany, 1964; PhD in Physics, U. Frankfurt, Germany, 1965. Asst. U. Frankfurt, 1965-67; postdoctoral asst. Nat. Bur. Stds., Washington, 1967-68; asst. U. Frankfurt, 1968-69; rsch. assoc. MPI Chemistry, Mainz, Germany, 1969-72; prof. physics U. Mainz, 1972—. Mem. Am. Phys. Soc., German Phys. Soc. Office: U Mainz Inst Kernphysik, JJ Becher-weg 45, D-55099 Mainz Germany

ARENSON, STANLEY, property manager; b. Krugersdorp, Gauteng, South Africa, May 8, 1945; s. Robert Chonne and Becky (Tapnack) A.; m. Carol Shirley Entin, Dec. 26, 1967; children: Hayley, Ryan, Gary. Chartered Acct., U. Witwatersrand, Johannesburg, South Africa, 1967. Sole practitioneer S. Arenson & Co., Rondfontein, South Africa, 1967-84; property broker Richard Ellis, Johannesburg, 1984-88; dir. R.M.B.T. Property Svcs., Johannesburg, 1988-96; mng. dir. C.B. Richard Ellis, Johannesburg, 1996—. Chmn. Victory Park Hebrew Congregation, Johannesburg.

Mem. Comml. and Indsl. Brokers Assn. Jewish. Office: CB Richard Ellis, PO Box 650555, Benmore 2010, South Africa

ARETOVA, MARIANA BORISOVA, publishing executive; b. Jakoruda, Bulgaria, Nov. 16, 1955; d. Boris Georgiev and Tsveta Ivanova (Drincolova) Grukova; m. Nikolai Aretov, Jan. 8, 1980; children: Dobrin, Alexander. Grad., Coll. Econs., Blagoevrad, 1975. Acct. BN Bank, Yakoruda, Bulgaria, 1976-80, Glavproect, Sofia, Bulgaria, 1980-90, A. Panov Pub. House, Sofia, 1990-92, Kralica Mab Pub. House, Sofia. Author: Quick, Tasty, Appetizing, 1993, Light Pastry with Cream, 1994, The Joys of Christmas and Christmas Eve: Folk Customs, Dishes Traditional and New, 1994, How to Receive Guests at Buffet Supper, 1995, Homemade Pickled Vegetables: 138 Tried-out Recipes, 1995, Tasty and Crispy Pastry, 1996, Easter Surprises: Easter Cake and Holiday Dishes, 1997, Complete Cookery Book, 1997, culinary Bible, 2000. Mem. Assn. Pub. Bulgaria. Home: Ap 21, Mladost 1 Bl 29 A Bx 2, 1750 Sofia Bulgaria Office: Kralica Mab Pub House, 3 Gerlovo St, 1504 Sofia Bulgaria

AREY, WILLIAM GRIFFIN, JR., former government official; b. Shelby, N.C., Feb. 18, 1918; s. William Griffin and Catherine (Roberts) A.; m. Louise Turner Craft, Mar. 7, 1942 (dec. 1988); children: William Griffin III, John G. C.; m. Jean Getman, July 13, 1991. AB, U. N.C., Chapel Hill, 1939. Pub., editor Cleveland Times Pub. Co., Shelby, 1941-48; pub. affairs officer U.S. Dept. State, Bogota, Colombia, 1948-51, Panama, Republic of Panama, 1951-53; pub. rels. officer Panama Canal Co., Balboa Heights, C.Z., 1954-62; with U.S. Travel Svc., U.S. Dept. Commerce, Washington, 1963-76, dir. travel promotion, 1963-67, dep. dir., 1967-70, exec. officer, 1970-73, exec. dir., 1973-76; asst. exec. v.p. Nat. Trust Hist. Preservation, 1976-81, corp. sec., 1981-83, ret., 1987. 1st lt. USAAC, 1942-45. Recipient Silver medal Commerce Dept., 1973. Mem. Pub. Rels. Soc. Am., Internat. Union Ofcl. Travel Orgns. (v.p.), pacific Area Travel Assn. (dir.), Sigma Nu, Nat. Press Club, Cosmos, Rotary. Methodist. Home: Wintergreen Resort RR 1 Box 563 Roseland VA 22967-9204 also: Four Seasons Resort Estates, Box 656, Charlestown Nevis Island, Leeward Islands

ARFE, GIANPAOLO, philosopher, physicist; b. Sondrio, Lombardia, Italy, Jan. 7, 1942; s. Ferdinando and Adriana (Ponzano) A. Degree in Law, U. Genova, Italy, 1967, degree in Philosophy, 1987. State pensioner. Contbr. articles to profl. jours. Recipient Sys. Rsch. Found. award 1990. Mem. AAAS, N.Y. Acad. Scis.

ARGAMAN, YERACHMIEL, engineering educator; b. Haifa, Israel, Apr. 21, 1937; s. Shalom and Bella (Wendlinger) A.; m. Chaya Stern, Aug. 8, 1960; children: Ohad, Neta, Vered. BSc cum laude, Technion, Haifa, 1961, MSc, 1964; PhD, U. Calif., Berkeley, 1968. Sr. lectr. Technion, 1968-76, assoc. prof., 1976-86, prof., 1986—, Millstone/St. Louis chair environ. engring., 1994, dean civil engring. dept., 2000—; tech. dir. Aware Eckehfelder Inc., Nashville, 1973-75, 80-82, 88-89, 95-96; adj. prof. Vanderbilt U., Nashville, 1988-89. Contbr. articles to profl. jours. Mem. Israel Soc. Ecology and Environ. Quality Scis. (hon.). Office: Technion, Israel Inst Tech, 32000 Haifa Israel

ARGANDOÑA, ANTONIO, economics educator; b. Barcelona, Spain, Jan. 4, 1943; s. Vicente Argandoña and Generosa Ramiz. Licenciate in Econs., U. Barcelona, 1964, D in Econs., 1969. Rsch. ast. U. Navarre, Barcelona, 1963-65, lectr., 1965-78, prof., chair econ. and ethics IESE, 1978—, vice dean for faculty, 1987-91, sec. gen., 1991—; asst. prof. U. Barcelona, 1969-77, prof., 1975-77, 82-89; prof. U. Malaga, Spain, 1977-79. Author: La Teoria Monetaria Moderna, 1972-82; co-author: People in Corporations, 1990, Macroeconomia Avanzada I, 1996; editor: The Ethical Dimension of Financial Institutions and Markets, 1995, Macroeconomia Avanzada, vol. 2, 1997, Una historia del desempleo en España, 1999. Mem. European Bus. Ethics Network (treas. 1993-96), Mont Pelerin Soc., Am. Econ. Assn, Royal Acad. Econ. and Fin. Office: U Navarre IESE, Av Pearson 21, 08034 Barcelona Spain

ARGANOZA, MARIA TERESA, research scientist; b. Detroit, June 2, 1965; d. Fred and Elenea (Uberas) A. BS in Biol. Scis., West Visayas State U., Iloilo, Philippines, 1985; BS in Biology, Marygrove Coll., Detroit, 1988; MS in Biochemistry, Wayne State U., 1994; cert. continuing med. edn., Rush-Presbyn.-St. Luke's; postgrad., Mich. State U. Libr. assoc. reader svcs. Marygrove Coll., Detroit, 1986-88; rsch. fellow Wayne State U., Detroit, summer 1988, grad. rsch. asst., 1988-89, rsch. asst., 1989-94, rsch. assoc., 1994—. Contbr. articles to profl. jours.; editl. asst. Hi-Lites, 1981-83. Mem. Kabataang Barangay, Philippines, 1981-82. Mem. AAAS, Am. Assn. Microbiology (edn. outreach cons. 1994—), Met. Detroit Internat. Inst. Achievements include hetero karyon incompatibility mutants in neurospora crassa, hybrid mitochondrial plasmids in neurospora crassa, alternative treatments for candida infections, assistance in cloning and characterization of fungal amphotericin B resistance gene. Avocations: reading, biking, hiking, roller blading, singing, painting. Office: Wayne State U Divsn Inf Diseases or Biochemistry 540 E Canfield St Detroit MI 48201-1928

ARGENTINI, ALESSANDRO, engineer; b. Pise, Toscana, Italy, July 23, 1948; arrived in The Netherlands, 1981; s. Piero and Irma (Sbrana) A.; m. Lucia Chini, Oct. 26, 1975; children: Ranieri, Caterina. Diploma Aeronaut. Engring., Pisa U., 1974. Asst. Instituto de Macchine (Fluidics), Pisa U., 1974; cons. on artificial kidney and heart valves Pisu U., 1977-78; R & D profl. O.T.O. Melara, La Spezia, Italy, 1975-81; cons., 1984-86; patent examiner European Patent Office, The Hague, The Netherlands, 1981-84, 86—; cons. on digital mil. sys. testing equipment O.T.O. Melara, 1985; cons. on maintenance Air Traffic Control, 1986. Mem. AAAS, Planetary Soc. Achievements include patents in the field of fluidic system for carburation control in lower power range and deceleration of I.C. engines. Avocations: scuba diving, shooting, sailing, reading. Home: DR HS Mooklaan 29, Rijswijk 2286 BA, The Netherlands Office: European Patent Office, Patentlaan 2, Rijswijk 2288EE, The Netherlands

ARGERICH, MARTHA, pianist; b. Buenos Aires, June 5, 1941. Studied with, V. Scaramuzzo, Friedrich Gulda, Nikita Magaloff, Madeleine Lipatti, Arturo Genedetto Michaelangeli. Debut in Buenos Aires, 1949; London debut, 1964; soloist with internat. leading orchs. Recipient 1st prize Busoni Contest, Geneva internat. Music Competition, 1957, Internat. Chopin Competition, Warsaw, 1965. Address: c/o J T Agence Artistique, 15 Ave Montaigne, 75008 Paris France

ARGHIR, GEORGE, metallurgical engineering educator, researcher; b. Brosteni, Vrancea, Romania, June 9, 1937; s. Barbu and Ana (Caloianu) A.; m. Maria Popazov, Apr. 9, 1962. Diploma in engring., Tech. U., Cluj-Napoca, Romania, 1961; diploma in physics, U. Cluj-Napoca, 1971, U. Bucharest, Romania, 1987; PhD, U. Notre Dame, 1977. Design engr., asst. chief metallurgist Mech. Works, Cugir, Alba, Romania, 1961-66; design engr. Tehnofrig, Cluj-Napoca, 1966-68; sci. rschr. Romanian Acad., Cluj-Napoca, 1968-78; sr. sci. rschr. Tech. U., 1978-79, asst. prof. dept. materials sci. tech., 1979-90, assoc. prof., 1990-91, prof., 1991—. Author: Crystallography, 1982 (Vermeil medal 1989), Crystallographic Characterization by X-ray Diffraction of Metals and Their Alloys, 1993, Thermodynamics of Solid, 2000, others; editor Procs. Romanian Internat. Conf. on Materials, 1994, on Power Metallurgy, 1996, on Materials, 1998, Powder Metallurgy, 2000, others; also articles; inventor thermal engine. Capt. Romanian Army, 1960-61. Mem. Am. Soc. for Metals, Am. Powder Metall. Inst., N.Y. Acad. Scis., Romanian Assn. Engrs., Romanian Powder Metallurgy Assn., Inst. of Materials (U.K.), Lausanne Universal Acad., Sigma Xi. Eastern Christian Orthodox. Avocations: air modeling, stamp collecting. Fax: 40 64 414036. Home: Detunata Str 17, 3400 Cluj-Napoca 9, Romania Office: Tech U, Muncii Ave 103-105, 3400 Cluj-Napoca 14, Romania

ARGIRIOU, ATHANASSIOS A., physicist, researcher; b. Athens, Attiki, Greece, Dec. 27, 1960; s. Achilleus A. Argiriou and Vassiliki-Adelaide C. Drossou; m. Elena G. Bonti, July 25, 1983; children: Dimitra-Adelaide, Achilleus-Alexios. Diploma in physics, U. Patras, Greece, 1983; DEA, Nat. Poly. Inst. Grenoble, France, 1984; PhD, U. Provence, Marseilles, France, 1987. Rsch. assoc. U. Athens, 1992-95; rschr. rank D, Nat. Observatory Athens, 1995-98, rschr. rand C, 1998—, coord. rsch. projects, 1995—. Author: Natural Cooling Techniques, 1994, Passive Cooling in Buildings, 1996, Daylight Techniques in Buildings, 1997; contbr. numerous articles to various sci. jours. Sgt. Hellenic Air Force,1988-89, Athens. Mem. Hellenic Meteolog. Soc., Internat. Solar Energy Soc., ASHRAE. Christian Orthodox. Avocations: theater, cinema, music, literature. E-mail: thanos@astro.noa.gr. Office: Nat Observatory Athens, I Metaxa & V Pavlou, GR152 36 Palaia Pendeli Attiki, Greece

ARGIROVA, RADKA MLADENOVA, virologist; b. Kovachevetz, Bulgaria, Nov. 4, 1944; d. Mladen Dimitrov and Nikolina Stanoeva (Tanetovich) A. MD, Sofia, Bulgaria, 1969; PhD, Ivanovski Inst. Virology, Moscow, 1973. Rschr. Ctr. Oncology, Sofia, Bulgaria, 1974-82, Inst. for Tumor Biology, Freiburg, Germany, 1980-81; sr. rschr. Inst. Gen. Comparative Pathology, Sofia, Bulgaria, 1982-87; chief Nat. AIDS Ref. Lab., Sofia, Bulgaria, 1987-98, chief lab. for retroviruses, 1998—; mem. Task Force of Global Mgmt. Com., Global Prog. AIDS, 1993-95, 95-97; prof. in virology, 1997; program coord. bd. UNAIDS, 1995-97. Contbr. chpts. to books, articles to profl. jours. Participant Mission on AIDS planning for Salvation Army, Manilla, The Phillipines, 1994, Brazzaville, Congo, 1996; Dep. Minister Health, Sofia, Bulgaria, 1995-97. Mem. NYAS. Office: Nat Retrovirus Ref Lab, 44 A Stoletov Str, 1233 Sofia Bulgaria

ARGLEBE, CHRISTIAN, retired biochemist; b. Neisse, Silesia, Germany, Feb. 17, 1935; s. Alfred and Caecilie (Bartsch) A.; m. Annerose Buschmueller, June 16, 1966. Diploma in agr., U. Leipzig, Germany, 1957; Dr.sc.agr., Georg-August-U., Goettingen, Germany, 1966. Postdoctoral fellow Roswell Park Meml. Inst., Buffalo, 1966-67; postdoctoral fellow dept. horticulture U. Wis., Madison, 1967-68; rsch. scientist Max-Planck Inst. fur Exptl. Medizin, Goettingen, 1969-70; rsch. scientist biochem. lab. ear, nose and throat dept. U. Goettingen, 1971-2000, head biochem. lab. ENT dept., 1971-2000, akademischer rat, 1979-2000, akademischer oberrat, 1990-2000; ret., 2000; Contbr. over 60 articles to profl. jours. and books. Recipient Ernst Preuss prize Ernst Preuss Found., 1989. Mem. AAAS, N.Y. Acad. Scis. Avocations: music, botany, film history, English literature, oenology. Home: Am Soelenborn 10, D-37085 Göttingen Germany

ARGONZ, RAQUEL, mechanical engineer, researcher; b. Mar Del Plata, Buenos Aires, Argentina, Jan. 7, 1959; arrived in Brazil, 1994.; d. Eduardo and Azucena Agustina (Etchegaray) A. Diploma in Mech. Engring., Nat. U. Mar Del Plata, 1986; MSME, Unicamp, Campinas, Brazil, 1996. Rschr. Unicamp, Campinas, 1994-99. Office: Unicamp/Fem/Dema, CP 6122, 13081970 Campinas Brazil

ARGYLE, JOHN MICHAEL, psychology educator, researcher; b. Nottingham, Eng., Aug. 11, 1925; s. George Edgar and Phyllis (Hawkins-Ambler) A.; m. Sonia Kemp, June 24, 1949 (dec. 1999); children: Miranda, Nicholas, Rosalind, Ophelia. BA, Cambridge (Eng.) U., 1950, MA, 1952; MA, Oxford (Eng.) U., 1952, DSc, 1979; DLitt, Adelaide (Australia) U., 1982; DSc in Psychology (hon.), U. Brussels, 1982. Lectr. social psychology Oxford U., 1952-69, reader, 1969—, acting head dept. exptl. psychology, 1978-80, fellow Wolfson Coll., 1965; emeritus prof. psychology Oxford Brooker U., 1992—; fellow Ctr. for Advanced Study in Behavioral Scis., 1958-59; vis. prof. U. Mich., U. Del., SUNY, Buffalo, U. B.C., U. Adelaide, Jerusalem U., U. Ghana, U. Leuven, U. Bologna, U. York, U. Nev., U. Kans., U. New South Wales, U. Hawaii, Flinders, Del.; lectr. in field; participant in confs. Author 16 books, including: Bodily Communication, 1975, 88; (with M. Cook) Gaze and Mutual Gaze, 1976; (with P. Trower and B. Bryant) Social Skills and Mental Health, 1978; (with P. Trower) Person-to-Person, 1979; (with A. Furnham and J.A. Graham) Social Situations, 1981; (with M. Henderson) The Anatomy of Relationships, 1985, Psychology of Happiness, 1987, The Psychology of Leisure, 1996, Psychology and Religion, 2000, (with A. Furnham) The Psychology of Money, 1998; editor 6 books; mem. editl. bds., cons. editor jours.; contbr. numerous articles to profl. jours. Served as flying officer RAF, 1943-47. Grantee Dept. Sci. and Indsl. Rsch., 1956-58, Med. Rsch. Coun., 1959-63, Social Sci. Rsch. Coun., 1964-67, 67-70, 70-75, 75-80, 80-85, 85-87, Oxford Regional Hosp. Bd., 1968-76. Fellow Brit. Psychol. Soc. (coun., chmn. social psychology sect. 1964-67, 72-74); mem. European Assn. for Social Psychology. Anglican. Avocations: travel, Scottish country dancing. Home: 309 Woodstock Rd., Oxford OX2 7NY England

ARHAR, FRANCE, banker. Gov. Bank of Slovenia. Office: Bank of Slovenia, 1505 Ljubljana, Slovenska Slovenia

ARIAN, EYAL, applied mathematician; b. Rehovoth, Israel, July 23, 1962; came to the U.S., 1993; s. Asher and Shoshana Arian; m. Einat Arian, Sept. 21, 1992; children: Morelle, Yuval. BS in Physics and Math., Hebrew U., Jerusalem, 1987; MS in Physics, Tel Aviv U., 1990; PhD in Applied Math., Weizmann Inst., Rehovoth, 1994. Staff scientist Inst. Computer Applications in Sci. and Engring., NASA, Hampton, Va., 1994-99; asst. prof. dept. math. Ohio U., Athens, 1999—. E-mail: arian@math.ohiou.edu.

ARIARAJAH, WESLEY SEEVARATNAM, clergyman, church administrator; b. Jaffna, Sri Lanka, Dec. 2, 1941; s. Ponniah David and Grace Annalukshimi (Sinnappu) S.; m. Christine Shyamala Chinniah, Dec. 7, 1953; children: Sudharshini, Niroshini, Anushini. BSc, Madras Christian Coll., India, 1963; BD, United Theol. Coll., Bangalore, India, 1966; ThM, Princeton (N.J.) Seminary, 1972; M. Phil., U. London, 1974, PhD, 1987. Ordained to ministry Methodist Ch. Minister Meth. Ch. of Sri Lanka, Jaffna, 1966-68; lectr. Theol. Coll. Lanka, Pilimatalawa, Sri Lanka, 1969-71; chmn. North and East Dist. Meth. Ch., Jaffna, 1974-81; program staff WCC program on Dialogue with People of Living Faiths, Geneva, 1981-83; dir. World Council Chs. program on Dialogue with People of Living Faiths, Geneva, 1983-91; dep. gen. sec. World Coun. Chs., Geneva, 1991=97; prof. Drew U., Madison, N.J., 1997—. Author: Dialogue, 1980, The Bible and People of Other Faiths, 1986, Hindus and Christians: A Century of Protestant Ecumenical Thought, Currents of Encounter Series, Vol. 5, 1991, Did I Betray the Gospel-The Letters of Paul and the Place of Women, Risk Series, 1996, Not Without My Neighbor-Issues in Interfaith Dialogue, W.C.C., 1998; contbr. articles to profl. jours. Home: Grand Saconnex, 5 chemin de Taverney, CH-1218 Geneva Switzerland Office: Drew U Sch Theology 36 Madison Ave Madison NJ 07940*

ARIAS, INOCENCÍO F., diplomat; b. Albox, Spain, Apr. 20, 1940; married; 3 children. Degree in law, U. Complutense, Madrid. Mem. Spanish Diplomatic Svc., 1967—; dir. Diplomatic Info. Office Spain Fgn. Ministry, 1980-82, 85-88, 1996-97, undersec., 1988-91, state sec. internat. cooperation and Iberamerican affairs, 1991-93; permanent rep. of Spain UN, 1997—; mem. session European Coun., NATO summit, 1997.; mem. conf. on environ. and devel. UN, 1992; participant 4 Iberoamerican summits, Mid. East summit, Madrid, 1991. Contbr. articles to profl. publs. Gen. dir. Real Madrid Soccer Club, 1993, 95. Office: UN 345 E 46th St Fl 9 New York NY 10017-3004

ARIAS-PÉREZ, ROBERTO, lawyer; b. Bogota, Colombia, Dec. 15, 1923; s. Enrique and Cecilia (Perez) Arias; m. Gloria Nieto, July 18, 1946. BA, Coll. Mayor del Rosario, Bogota, 1940; LLD, U. Coll. Mayor del Rosario, Bogota, 1946; diploma, Faculty of Droit, Paris, 1950, PhD, 1951; diploma, Internat. Law Acad., The Hague, 1952. Consul Uruguay, 1946-48; fgn. officer Colombia, 1946-48; mayor City of Girardot, Colombia, 1948-49; Latin Am. dir. World Fedn. UN Assns., Geneva, Paris, 1951-56; dir. Colsubsidio, Bogota, 1958-84, hon. pres., 1984—; pres. U. Coll. Mayor de Nuestra Senora del Rosario, Bogota, 1986-90; pres. lega commn. Internat. Social Security Assn., Geneva, 1973, pres. family allowances com., 1978-80; internat. law prof. various univs. Author: Social Security Human Dimension, 1994; contbr. articles to profl. jours. Bd. dirs. Found. Valenzuela, Bogota, 1980—; bd. dirs. Soc. Mejoras, Bogota, 1980-95, v.p., 1990-95. Decorated Cruz de Boyaca (Colombia), Order del Sol (Peru), Order des Arts et des Letters (France). Mem. Soc. por Colombia (bd. dirs. 1990—), Los Lacartos Club (pres. 1996-99). Roman Catholic. Home: Calle 120 A N:6226 PH 901, Bogota Colombia Office: Calle 120-A #6260, Bogota Colombia

ARIAS SANCHEZ, OSCAR, former president of Costa Rica; b. Sept. 13, 1940. Law and econs., U. Costa Rica, 1967; M in Polit. Sci., U. Essex, Eng., 1974. Prof. U. Costa Rica, 1969-72; minister nat. planning Republic of Costa Rica, 1972-77; rep. Legis. Assembly, Costa Rica, 1978-82; pres. Republic of Costa Rica, 1986-90; internat. sec. Nat. Liberation Party, 1975, gen. sec., 1979-81, v.p. bd. dirs. Cen. Bank of Costa Rica, 1970-72, dir., 1972-77; bd. dirs. Tech. Inst., Costa Rica, 1974-77; mem. Nat. Coun. Univ. Rectors, 1974-77; bd. dirs. Internat. U. Exch. Fund, Switzerland, 1976; mem. internat. adv. coun. Inst. Internat. Studies; participant numerous profl. confs. and seminars throughout the world. Author: Grupos De Presión En Costa Rica, 1970 (Essay's Nat. Award, 1971), Quién Gobierna En Costa Rica, 1976. Latin American Democracy, Independence and Society 1977, Roads for Costa Rica's Development, 1977, New Ways for Costa Rican Development, 1980. Mem. adv. coun. Stockholm Internat. Peace Rsch. Inst., The Inn at The Carter Ctr., Internat. Press Svc., UNCED, Internat. Peace Acad., The Interaction Coun., The Commn. on Global Govts., Inst. Internat. Studies Stanford U. Recipient Nobel Peace prize, 1987, Martin Luther King Peace prize, 1987, Prince of Asturias award, 1988, Co-recipient Liberty medal Phila., 1991. Office: Arias Found Peace & Human Progress, Apdo 8-6410-1000, San Jose Costa Rica

ARIE, THOMAS HARRY DAVID, psychiatry educator; b. Prague, Aug. 9, 1933; m. Eleanor Arie; three children. MA, Oxford (Eng.) U., BM, BCh. Cons. psychiatrist Goodmayes Hosp., London, 1969-77, Nottingham (Eng.) Health Authority, 1977-95; prof., head dept. health care of elderly U. Nottingham, 1977-95, prof. emeritus, 1995—; vis. prof., lectr. in field. Decorated Comdr. of the Order of the Brit. Empire, 1995. Fellow Royal Coll. Psychiatrists (former v.p.), Royal Coll. Physicians; mem. World Psychiat. Assn. (chmn. geriatric psychiatry sect.). Office: Queen's Med Ctr Med Sch, Dept Health Care of Elderly, Nottingham NG7 2UH, England

ARIENS, KARLA RAE, library director; b. Tremonton, Utah, July 3, 1966; d. Paul Elias and Lorna May Adams; m. Thaddeus William Ariens, Mar. 17, 1988; childre: Talia Louise, Tori May, Terese Claire. BS in Elem. Edn., Utah State U., 1988. Tchr. asst. Children's Home, Logan, Utah, 1988-89; music specialist Hilltop Sch., Logan, Utah, 1988-89; chpt. I aide Adams Elem. Sch., Logan, Utah, 1989-90; gifted/talented specialist Cache County Sch. Dist., Logan, Utah, 1989-90; libr. dir. Brookville (Ind.) Town-Twp. Libr., 1991—. Sec. Franklin County Cmty. Network Com., Brookville, 1995. Mem. LDS Ch. Avocations: music, cooking, reading, piano, singing. E-mail: kariens@cnz.com. Office: Brookville Town-Twp Libnr 919 Main St Brookville IN 47012-1429

ARIESAN, CLAUDIU, philologist, researcher; b. Timisoara, Timis, Romania, June 1, 1963; s. Ioan Ariesan and Valeria Ileana Tomoiagă. Bachelor's, We. U., Timisoara, Romania, 1987, PhD, 1998. Instr. Univ., Timisoara, 1990-92, jr. lectr., 1992-96, sr. lectr., 1996—. Author: Hermeneuthics of the Sympathetic Humour, 1999; editor: (book collection) Logos, Cum Patribus, 1993-99; contbr. articles to profl. jours. Mem. Internat. Assn. Patristic Studies (assoc.), N.Am. Patristics Soc., Classical Studies Soc. (Romania). Roman Catholic. Avocations: foreign languages, sports, translations, music. Home: str Bucuresti 34, sc B ap 16, 1900 Timisoara Timis, Romania Office: U de Vest Facultatea de Lit, str V Pârvan 4, 1900 Timisoara Timis, Romania

ARIF, MUSTAFA KAMAL, electrical engineer; b. Jhalokathi, Bangladesh, Jan. 1, 1965; arrived in Can., 1999; s. M. Golam and Shamsun (Nahar) Mostafa; m. Rokeya Begum, Sept. 29, 1989; children: Suchinta, Mustafa Moin. BS in Engring., BUET, Dhaka, Bangladesh, 1988. Hardware engr. Datec, Dhaka, 1988-89; asst. engr. Minipilo Electric, Chittagong, Bangladesh, 1989-90; from sr. engr. to factory mgr. Rahimafrooz, Dhaka, 1991-98; battery cons. Micro Electronics, Dhaka, 1999—. Mem. IEEE, Instn. Engrs. Bangladesh, BCS. Islam. Avocations: reading, TV, travel. Home: Nandan Apt 2, 6/1 S Kallanpur, Dhaka 1207, Bangladesh

ARIFFIN, YOHAN, political scientist, researcher; b. Kuala Lumpur, Malaysia, Feb. 27, 1965; s. Muda and Lotti Tina (Banholzer) A. BA, U. Lausanne, Switzerland, 1988, MPhil, 1992; postgrad., U. Inst. of Devel., Geneva, 1989. Rsch. scholar dept. internat. rels. London Sch. Econs., 1994, vis. fellow Devel. Studies Inst., 1994-95; asst. Sch. Social and Polit. Scis. U. Lausanne, 1988-93, premier asst., 1993-98; rschr. Swiss Natl. Sci. Fund, 1998—; rschr. Swiss Nat. Sci. Fund, 1998; vis. rsch. fellow Inst. d'Etudes Politiques, Paris, 1998, 2000. Contbr. articles to profl. jours. Vis. fellow Victoria and Albert Mus., London, 1999. Mem. N.Y. Acad. Scis. Office: U Lausanne Faculty SSP Inst Polit Internat, IEPI BFSH 2, 1015 Lausanne Switzerland

ARIMA, AKITO, academic administrator; b. Osaka, Japan, Sept. 13, 1930; s. Jyoji and Kazuko Arima; m. Hiroko Aota, Mar. 16, 1957; children: Yoshihito, Akiko. BS, U. Tokyo, 1953, DSc, 1958; DSc (hon.), Glasgow (Scotland) U., 1984; DrS (hon.), Drexel U., 1992. Dir. computer ctr. U. Tokyo, 1981-85, dean faculty of sci., 1985-87, v.p., 1987-89, pres., 1989-93; pres. Inst. of Phys. and Chem. Rsch., Riken, Japan, 1993-98; mem. Ho. of Councilors, Tokyo, 1998—; min. edn. Japanese Govt., Tokyo, 1998-99, min. for sci. and tech., 1999, min. edn., 1999—. Author: The Interacting Boson Model, 1987; contbr. articles to profl. publs. Recipient prize Nishina Found., 1978, award Humboldt Found., 1987, Grosse Verdienstkreuz award German Govt., 1991, award of Comdr. in Order of Orange Nassau, Her Majesty Queen Beatrix of the Netherlands, 1991, Tom W. Bonner prize Nuclear Physics Am. Physical Soc., 1993. Mem. Phys. Soc. Japan (pres. 1981-82), Haijin Assn. (prize 1988), Japan Writers' Assn., Japan Pen Club. Avocations: reading, painting. Home: Sangenjaya 2-23-6, Setagaya-ku, Tokyo 154-0024, Japan Office: 2-1-1 Nagata-cho RM 223, Sangiin-Kaikan Chiyoda-ku, Tokyo 100-8962, Japan

ARIMA, EITOKU, surgeon, hospital administrator; b. Kanoya City, Japan, Feb. 20, 1933; s. Tohemon and Ura (Kawabata) Tsurudome; adoptive s. Yuhjiro and Yasuko (Mesaki) Arima; m. Naoko Yamaguchi Arima, May 19, 1964; children: Jun-ichi, Yukie, Masae. BM, Kagoshima (Japan) U., 1958, DMS, 1964. Registered anesthetist, Japan, 1964. Intern Nat. Sagamihara Hosp., Kanagawa, Japan, 1958-59; resident Kagoshima U. Hosp. Surgery, 1959-64; asst. in anesthesiology Kyushu U. Hosp. Anesthesiology, Fukuoka, Japan, 1964-65; rsch. fellow dept. surgery UCLA Sch. Medicine, 1971-73; asst. Kagoshima U. Hosp., 1966-74, lectr. 2d dept. surgery, 1974-80, lectr. dept. pediatric surgery, 1980-98, ret., 1998-2000; dir. Heim Berg Geriatric Health Svcs. Facility, Mizusawa, Japan, 1998-2000; vice dir. Miki Hosp., Keiaikai Inc. Med., Iwate, Japan, 1998-2000; vis. prof. sect. electron microscopy, histology, embryology and gastroenterol. surgery First Mil. Med. Coll. PLA, Guangzhou, China, 1995—; vis. prof. surgery Jinzhou (China) Med. Coll., 1997—; lectr., surg. cons. Chinese Med. Assn., Beijing, 1984—, Electron Micros. Assn., 21 cities, China, 1984—; lectr. U. Sao Paulo (Brazil) Postgrad. Sch., 1996—; UNIFE, Sao Paulo, U. Fed. Sao Paulo Postgrad. Sch., 1997—; com. mem. for diagnostic criteria Japanese Study Group on Pancreaticobiliary Maljunction, Tokyo, 1983—; local chmn. 9th Japanese Symposium on Scanning Electron Microscopy for Biomedicine, Ibusuki, Japan, 1980. Author: Guide Book on Pediatric Surgery for Citizens, 1969; co-author 16 books on surgery; contbr. articles to med. jours., including Jour. Pediatric Surg., Jour. Trace and Microprobe Techniques; editl. cons. Japanese Jour. Pediatric Surgery, 1977—; med. columnist Kagoshima Shinpo, 1969. Rescue physician, trainer Judo Assn. So. Calif., L.A., 1971-73; rescue physician 5,000 kilometer Rally Raid Mongol Ulaanbaatar and others, 1995; condr. seminar on resuscitation, Kanoya City, 1989. Fellow Japan Surg. Soc. (diplomate), Japanese Soc. Pediatric Surgeons (diplomate, spl. mem.), Japanese Soc. Gastroent. Surgeons (diplomate, spl. mem.), Japanese Soc. Hepato-biliary-pancreatic Surgery (spl. mem.), Japanese Soc. of Pediatric Surgeons; mem. Pacific Assn. Pediatric Surgeons (sr.), Haraldria Soc. Order of Peace Universal, Brit. Assn. Pediat. Surgeons, Orgn. Mondiale de Gastroenterologie. Avocations: mountain climbing, touring, fishing, judo (5th Dan), golf. Home: 6-33-19 Murasakibaru, Kagoshima 890-0082, Japan Office: Miki Hosp, Maesawa-Cho Iwate 029-4201, Japan

ARIMOTO, AKIRA, education educator; b. Hiroshima, Japan, Oct. 26, 1941; s. Setsumi and Miyako (Nishikawa) A.; m. Masako Masukawa, May 8, 1971; children: Akiko, Jun, Yu. BA, Hiroshima U., 1964, MA, 1966, PhD, 1985. Rsch. assoc. edn. Hiroshima U., 1969-71; lectr. edn. Osaka (Japan) U. Edn., 1971-75, assoc. prof. edn., 1975-84, prof. edn., 1983-88; prof. edn., Rsch. Inst. Higher Edn. Hiroshima U., 1988—; chmn. dept. edn. Osaka U. Edn., 1986-87; dir. Rsch. Inst. Higher Edn., 1993-99; adj. prof. edn., Kyoto (Japan) U., 1981-84, 92-93, Nagoya (Japan) U., 1994-95. Author: Sociology

of Academics, 1981, Study of Sociology of Science in R.K. Merton, 1987, Study on Centers of Learning, 1994, Comparative Study on Academic Profession, 1996; editor Japanese Ednl. Sociology, 1994-98. Mem. Japanese Univ. Accreditation Assn., Tokyo, 1995—; mem. ad hoc com. Univ. Chartering Coun., Ministry Edn., Tokyo, 1988-94, supr. com. univ. supervision, 1997—; mem. steering com. Six-Nation Edn. Project, U. Pa., 1995—. Nitobe Social Scis. fellow, Internat. Ho. Japan, Tokyo, 1976-78; 21st Century Culture and Acad. Sci. grantee Kigawada Found., Tokyo, 1986-88. Mem. Japanese Assn. Rsch. Inst. Higher Edn. (pres. 1996—), Japanese Assn. Ednl. Sociology (trustee 1994—), Japanese Assn. Rsch. in Higher Edn. (trustee, sec. gen. 1997—). Avocations: music, reading. Fax: 0824-22-7104. Home: 4-30-11 Takaya Takamigaoka, 739-2115 Higashi, Hiroshima Japan Office: Rsch Inst Higher Edn, 2-2-1 Kagamiyama, Hiroshima 739-8115, Japan

ARIMOTO, SUGURU, engineering educator; b. Hiroshima, Japan, Aug. 3, 1936; s. Yoshimi and Fusako (Yoshida) A.; m. Noriko Takashita, Mar. 15, 1965; children: Hisashi, Itaru. BS, Kyoto U., 1959; D in Engring., U. Tokyo, 1967. Engr. Oki Elec. Industry Ltd., Tokyo, 1959-62; assoc. prof. Osaka U., 1968-73, prof., 1973-88; rsch. asst. U. Tokyo, 1962-67, lectr., 1967-68, prof., 1988-97; prof. Ritsumeikan U., Kusatsu, Japan, 1997—. Contbr. articles to profl. jours. Recipient Sawaragi award Inst. Sys., Control, and Info. Engring., 1989. Fellow IEEE (IT Soc. Best Paper award 1974, Nat. medal with purple ribbon 2000, The Third Millennium Meml. medal 2000); mem. Robotics Soc. Japan (v.. 1993-995, pres. 1995-97, Best Paper award 1994), Soc. Instrument Control Engrs. (Best Paper award 1968, 76, 87). Avocations: go, Japanese chess. Office: Ritsumeikan U, 2-11-5 Ishiyamadera, Ohtsu 520-0861, Japan

ARINGAZIN, ASCAR KANAPIEVICH, physicist, researcher; b. Alma-Ata, Kazakhstan, Oct. 6, 1961; s. Kanapia Mubarakovich and Dina Ibraevna (Ashigalieva) A.; m. Roza Zhastlekovna Balsarina, 1998, one child: Ansar. MS, Moscow State U., 1985, PhD, 1988; Doctor of Scis., Degree in Phys. and Mathematics, 1998. Rschr. Karaganda (Kazakhstan) State U., 1988-89, lectr., 1989-90, asst. prof., 1990-91, head dept. theoretical physics, 1991-97, prin. investigator, 1992-93, dir. Inst. Fundamental Rsch., 1997—; prof. theoretical physics Inst. Basic Rsch., Palm Harbor, Fla., 1992—. Editor Hadronic Jour., 1990—, Hadronic Jour. Supplement, 1990—; contbr. articles to sci. jours. Mem. Am. Biog. Inst. Rsch. Assn. (dep. gov.), Internat. Ctr. Theoretical Physics, Internat. Order Fellowship, N.Y. Acad. Scis. Avocations: table tennis, chess, computer games, music. Home: 15-40 Abdirov St, 470055 Karaganda Kazakhstan Office: Karaganda State U, Dept Theoretical Physics, 470074 Karaganda Kazakhstan

ARINZE, FRANCIS CARDINAL, archbishop; b. Eziowelle, Anambra, Nigeria, Nov. 1, 1932; s. Joseph Nwankwu and Bernadette (Ekwoanya) A. BD, Urban U., Rome, 1957, MDiv, 1959, DD, 1960; diploma in edn., U. London, 1964; DLitt (hon.), U. Nigeria, Nsukka, 1986; PhD (hon.), Cath. U. Am., 1998; DD (hon.), Wake Forest U., 1999. Ordained priest Roman Cath. Ch., 1958. Lectr. in philosophy, logic Bigard Meml. Sem., Enugu, Nigeria, 1961-62; ednl. sec. Cath. Ch. Ea. Nigeria, Enugu, 1962-65; aux. bishop of Onitsha Nigeria, 1965-67, archbishop of Onitsha, 1967-85; pres. Cath. Bishops Conf. Nigeria, Lagos, 1979-84, Pontifical Coun. for Inter-religious Dialogue, Vatican City, 1984—; created cardinal Vatican City, 1985—. Author: Sacrifice in Ibo Religion, 1980, Answering God's Call, 1982, Living Our Faith, 1983, Alone with God, 1987, Church in Dialogue, 1990. Patron Soc. for Promotion of Ibo Language and Culture, Onitsha, 1979; v.p. Africa United Bible Socs., Stuttgart, Fed. Republic Germany, 1980. Roman Catholic. Avocation: lawn tennis. Office: Pontifical Coun Inter-religious Dialogue, Via Dell' Erba 1, 00120 Vatican City Vatican City

ARIOLI, RICHARD, consulting company executive; b. Basel, Switzerland, Feb. 28, 1935; s. Richard A. and Hanna M. (Kaspar) A.; m. Rosemarie Spiller, Sept. 3, 1962; children: Katharina S., Matthias, Dominik R. Diploma in engring., Swiss Fed. Inst. Tech., Zurich, 1959; postgrad., U. Washington, 1956-57. Registered land surveyor. Rsch. land use mgr. SFIT, Zurich, 1960-61; ofcl. land surveyor Chur and Basel, Switzerland, 1962-67; prof. dept. surveying FHBB, Muttenz, Switzerland, 1964-68; head dept. city planning Schneider Ingenieure AG, Chur, 1969-82, CEO, 1983—. Contbr. articles to profl. jours. Lt. col. arty. Swiss Army, until 1991. Mem. Swiss Soc. Engrs. and Architects (bd. dirs. 1977-90), FKV-SIA (bd. dirs. Office: Schneider Ingenieure AG, Rossbodenst 15, CH 7000 Chur Switzerland

ARISALYA, HARISH CHANDRA, missionary, administrator; b. Serango, Orissa, India, Aug. 26, 1963; s. Padma Charan and Luisma (Pani) A.; m. Stella Amin, May 13, 1993; children: Namrata, Kalyan. BA with honors and distinction, SKCG Coll., Orissa, 1979; MA, Berhampur U., India, 1983; LLB, Balasore Law Coll., 1999; MA in Leadership, Mgmt., Briercrest Biblical Seminar-O.M. India, Canada, 2000. Cert. tchr. Distbn. promoter Bible Soc., India, 1986-91; assoc. Operation Mobilisation India, 1991-92, state dir., 1993-94; coord. Operation Mobilisation India, Balasore, 1995—; tchr. Operation Mobilisation India, 1984-86; preacher chs., India, 1987-94; spkr. in field. Evangelical Bapt. Avocations: gardening, games, traveling, analysis, research. Home: Box 12 Tech Sch Compound, 756001 Balasore Orissa, India

ARISS, DAVID WILLIAM, SR., real estate developer, consultant; b. Toronto, Ont., Can., Nov. 29, 1939; s. William H. and Joyce Ethel (Oddy) A.; m. Lillie Ariss, Jan. 26, 1962 (div. 1989); m. Debra Ann Nocciolo, Nov. 17, 1990 (div. 1998); children: Katherine Joyce, David William Jr., Dylan William. BA, Claremont Men's Coll., 1961. Lic. real estate broker. Real estate broker Coldwell Banker, Torrance, Calif., 1971-75; v.p. The Lusk Co., Irvine, Calif., 1975-77; pres. DAL Devel. Co., Corona, Calif., 1977-84; mng. dir. Calif. Commerce Ctr. at Ontario, Ontario, Calif., 1984—. Chmn. Inland Empire Econ. Coun., Ontario, Calif., 1991-92; pres., adv. com. Chaffey Coll., Ontario, 1989; apptd. Calif. World Trade Commn., 1993, 95, 97. Maj. USMC, 1961-70, Vietnam. Decorated Silver Star, Disting. Flying Cross, two Purple Hearts, numerous Air medals. Mem. Urban Land Inst., Nat. Assn. Fgn. Trade Zone, Nat. Assn. Indsl. and Office Parks. Republican. Avocations: skiing, music, reading. Office: PIB Realty Advisors 1050 Ontario Mills Dr Ste B Ontario CA 91764-5245

ARISTODEMOU, LOUCAS ELIAS, industrial engineer, manufacturing company executive; b. Paphos, Cyprus, Oct. 17, 1946; s. Elias and Eleni (Alexandrou) A.; m. Mary Heraclides, Dec. 28, 1975; children: Eliagne L., Constantinos L. MSc in Engring., Poly. Inst. Bucharest, Romania, 1972, PhD in Indsl. Mgmt., 1977. Asst. prof. Poly. Inst., Bucharest, 1976-77; gen. mgr. Couvas Bros. Ltd., Limassol, Cyprus, 1977-78, Nemitsas Industries Ltd., Limassol, 1978-80, Metalco (Heaters) Ltd., Nicosia, Cyprus, 1980-99, A. Hajivassilou Ltd., Nicosia, 1999-2000; cons. Commonwealth Secretariat, London, 1983-87; adv. com. industry and tech. Govt. of Nicosia, 1990—; mem. Cyprus Standards Orgn., Nicosia, 1991-2000; mem. syllabus com. Higher Tech. Inst., Nicosia, 1986-99; assoc. judge Cyprus Labor Ct., Nicosia, 1988-2000; bd. dirs. Cyprus Employers and Industrialists Fedn., Nicosia, 1992. Editor, co-author Ency. of Math., 1975; co-author: Informatic and Activity Analysis of Enterprises, 1976; chief editor Tech. Word, 1990-97; contbr. to tech. publs. Mem. Cyprus Profl. Engrs. Assn. (pres. 1992-96), Cyprus Tech. and Sci. Chamber (gen. sec. 1992-96), Cyprus Consumer Assn. (pres. 1998-2000), Am. Mgmt. Assn., Internat. Solar Energy Soc., European Fedn. of Nat. Engrs. Assns. (pres. nat. monitoring com. 1995—). Home: 3 Doridos St, CY-2023 Nicosia Cyprus Office: PO Box 28564, CY-2080 Nicosia Cyprus

ARISTODIMOU, CHRISTOFOROS **See CHRYSOSTOMOS**

ARISTOV, YURII IVANOVICH, chemist; b. Bikhov, USSR, Sept. 23, 1953; s. Ivan Fedorovich and Anastasia Yakovlevna (Maksimova) A. BA in Chem. Physics, Phys.-Tech. Inst., Moscow, 1975, MS in Chem. Physics, 1977; PhD in Chemistry, Inst. of Catalysis, Novosibirsk, USSR. Engr. Inst. of Catalysis, Novosibirsk, 1977-82; sr. rschr. Boreskov Inst. of Catalysis, Novosibirsk, 1986-97; head of lab. Boreskov Inst. of catalysis, Novosibirsk, 1997—. Contbr. articles to profl. jours., reviewer in field. Rsch. grantee Internat. Sci. Found., N.Y., 1994-95, linkage grantee NATO, Brussels, 1997-98, fellowship grantee NATO/CNR, Brussels, 1994, rsch. grantee RFBR, Moscow, 1997-2001; recipient Gold medal 27th Internat. Salon of Inventions, Geneve, 1999. Mem. Russian Chem. Soc. Office: Boreskov Inst Catalysis, Pr.Lavrentieva 5, Novosibirsk 630 090, Russia

ARITA, TATSUO, economist, educator; b. Tokyo, Mar. 25, 1928; s. Taiji Cho (Yamazaki) A.; m. Kumiko Shigeta, May 6, 1962; 1 child, Miho. B in Econs., Waseda U., 1950, DSc, 1986. From assoc. prof. to prof. Meijo U., Nagoya, Japan, 1975—; counselor Meijor U., Nagoya, 1985-91, dean faculty of commerce, 1989-91, chmn. grad. sch. commerce, 1989-91, dir. placement office, 1993-97; mem. coun. on big retail shops Min. Internat. Trade & Industry, Tokyo, 1994—. Author: Public Policy of Small Business in Postwar Japan, 1990, Study of Small Business—History, Theory, Policy, 1997. Mem. Japan Econ. Policy Assn. (trustee 1983—), Japan Assn. Small Business Studies (vice chmn. 1992-95, mng. trustee 1995—). Avocations: music, tennis. Home: 704 Miyukiyama, 468-0075 Nagoya Aichi, Japan Office: Meijo U Faculty Econs, 1-501 Shiogamaguchi Tenpaku, 468-8502 Nagoya Aichi, Japan

ARITOME, TERUCHICA, physician; b. Kaseda, Japan, Sept. 5, 1930; s. Sigehiko and Enko (Kuroki) A.; m. Etuko Morita. MD, Gikeikai U., Tokyo, 1955. Rschr. Kyushu U., Fukuaha, Japan, 1956, 59-70; asst. Tottori U., Yanago, Japan, 1956-59; mem. hosp. staff Okemoodei Hosp., Kwachi, Japan, 1970-90; dir. Meigaian Clinic, Masiko, Japan, 1992-99; cons. in field. Author: Anti-self Anxiety and Psychiatric Diseases, Self-existance and Psychiatric Diseases; inventor in field. Mem. Japanese Psychiat. Assn., Japanese Psychosomatic Medicine, N.Y. Scientific Assn. Avocations: reading, music. Office: Meijaian Clinic, 2583-1 OOsawa, Masiko machi 321-4104, Japan

ARKA, IDA BAGUS, veterinary public health educator; b. Bangli, Bali, Indonesia, Apr. 27, 1937; s. Ida Bagus Meru and Anak Agung Made Oka; m. Made Adi Sumiati, Dec. 4, 1964; children: Ida Bagus Pramana Suaryasa, Ida Bagus Dwija Ariwinangun, Ida Ayu Diah Trisnadewi. DVM in Vet. Sci., Bogor Agrl. U., Indonesia, 1961; grad. diploma in food tech., U. New South Wales, Sydney, Australia, 1973; PhD in Animal Sci., Padjadjiran U., Bandung, Indonesia, 1984. Student asst. Faculty Vet. Sci., Bogor, 1958-61; vet. Dept. Agr., Balikpadan, Indonesia, 1961-63; lectr. Dept. Edn. and Culture, Denpasar, Indonesia, 1963—; dean faculty vet. sci. Dept. Edn. and Culture, Denpasar, 1978-80. Author: Veterinary Public Health, 1985, Meat Science and Technology, 1994. Mem. Bogor Student Cmty., 1956-61, Australian Inst. Food Sci. and Tech., Sydney, 1973. Recipient Karya Satya award Pres. Republic of Indonesia, Jakarta, 1993. Mem. Indonesian Vet. Assn. Hindu. Avocations: tennis, traveling, sports, photography. E-mail: ibarka@dps.centrim.nes.id. Home: Jalanir Ida Bagus Oka 1, Denpasar 80114, Indonesia Office: Udayana Univ, Jalan Sudirman Sanglah, Denpasar 80114, Indonesia

ARKADIEV, VLADIMIR ALEXANDROVICH, physicist; b. Moscow, Jan. 31, 1953; s. Alexandr Ivanovich and Zinaida Ivanovna (Samoylova) A.; m. Natalia Dmitrievna Rozhkova, Aug. 21, 1975; 1 child, Elena. Diploma in physics, Moscow State U., 1976; PhD, V.A. Steklov Math. Inst., Moscow, 1984. Rschr. Moscow High Tech. Sch., 1979-84, I.V. Kurchatov Inst. Atomic Energy, Moscow, 1984-94, Inst. Gerätebau GmbH, Berlin, 1994—. Contbr. articles to profl. jours.; lectr. in field. Mem. Internat. Soc. for Optical Engring. (mem. program com. 1996). Achievements include the extension of inverse scattering transform method to singular solutions of nonlinear equations, designing and manufacturing x-ray capillary systems, combining x-ray capillary optics with conventional ones. Office: Inst Gerätebau GmbH, Rudower Chaussee 29-31, 12489 Berlin Germany

ARKHIPCHUK, VICTOR VLADIMIROVICH, scientist; b. Budapest, Hungary, Oct. 12, 1958; s. Vladimir Ivanovich and Larisa Evgenievna Arkhipchuk; m. Mariya Vasilievna Malinovskaya, July 15, 1993. Grad., Kiev (Ukraine) U., 1981; PhD, Inst. Plant Physiol./Genetics, Kiev, 1988; D of Biol. Scis., Inst. Animal Breeding/Genetics, Kiev, 1995. Cert. biologist-geneticist. Lab. asst. Kiev U., 1975-76; sr. lab. asst. Inst. Botany, Kiev, 1981-83; scientist Inst. Hydrobiology, Kiev, 1986-91, sr. scientist, 1991—. Contbr. papers to profl. jours.; patentee in field. Mem. Bulgarian Union Scientists (hon.), N.Y. Acad. Scis. Avocations: reading, computer, sports. Fax: 380 44 418 22 32. E-mail: ecos@inhydro.kiev.ua. Home: Semashko 12 Fl 16, Kiev 252142, Ukraine Office: Inst Hydrobiology, Geroyev Stalingrade Ave 12, Kiev 254210, Ukraine

ARKOSSY, OTTO, nephrologist; b. Esztergom, Hungary, Jan. 27, 1965; s. Otto and Katalin (Oszthеimer) A; children: Mate, Zsofia. MD, Budapest Med. Sch., 1989. Asst. physician St. Margit Hosp., Budapest, 1989-94, registrar, 1994-96; rsch. fellow Royal Postgrad. Med. Sch., London, 1993; specialist in internal medicine, nephrology Postgrad. Med. Sch., Budapest, 1996—; vice med. dir. Fresenius Nephrology Ctr., Miskolc, Hungary, 1998-99; med. dir. Fresenius Dialysis Ctr. St. Margit Hosp., Budapest, Hungary, 1999—; cons. Medimark Ltd., Budapest, 1996-. Lt. Budapest Mil., 1990-91. Mem. Internat. Soc. Nephrology, Internat. Apheresis Soc., European Soc. Artificial Organs, European Dialysis and Transplant Assn./European Renal Assn., Vascular Access Soc., Internat. Soc. for Apheresis. E-mail: arkossy@mail.elender.hu. Office: FMC Dialysis Ctr, Becsi ut 132 POB 144, H-1032 Budapest Hungary

ARKWRIGHT, PAUL CHRISTOPHER, English language services company executive; b. Blackpool, Lancashire, England, May 19, 1969; arrived in Hong Kong, 1994; s. Christopher Brian and Kathleen Susan (Schofield) A.; m. Lily Chan. BSc honors in Ecology, U. E. Anglia, Norwich, England, 1991. Rsch. asst. U. E. Anglia, 1991, Brit. Sugar Plc, England, 1991-93; sr. technician SGS, Hong Kong, 1995-96; rsch. asst. Chinese U. Hong Kong, 1996-97; dir. Excel Lang. Consultancy, Hong Kong, 1997—. Avocation: training civil servants in mgmt. and leadership skills. Office: Excel Language Consultancy, 901 Fu Lee Comml Bldg 14-20, Jordan Kowloon HongKong, China

ARLACCHI, PINO, protective services official; b. Gioa Tauro Marina, Feb. 21, 1951. Degree in Sociology, U. Trento, 1973. Expert criminologist, 1984-86; v.p. Italian Parliamentary Commn. on Organized Crime, 1987-91; cons. Bicameral Parliamentary Inquiry Commn., 1991, v.p., 1996; prof. U. Calabria; dep. Dem. Party of the Left; mem. Justice Commn.; Senator Dem. Party of the Left, 1996-97; dir. Office Drug Control and Crime Prevention UN, 1997—; vis. prof. Columbia U., N.Y.C. Contbr. articles to profl. jours. Named Hon. Pres. Giovanni Falcone Found. Office: UN Internat Drug Control Program, Vienna Internat Ctr POB 500, 1400 Vienna Austria*

ARLEEVSKY, IGOR PETR, cardiologist; b. Gorodok, Belarus, Oct. 13, 1931; s. Pezets David and Rebecca Lazar (Massarskaya) A.; m. Phaina Israel Mazgolina; children: Marina, Julia. Postgrad., Kazan State Med. Acad., 1962-65, PhD in Medicine, 1985. Physician State Hosp. Leninogorski, 1954-62; asst. Kazan (Russia) State Med. Acad., 1965-75; docent State Med. Acad. of Kazan, 1975-86, prof., 1986—. Contbr. articles to sci. and profl. jours. Mem. Tatarstan Cardiol. Soc. (chmn.). Home: 1/38-75, Latyshskikch Strelkov, 420089 Kazan Russia Office: Kazan State Med Acad, Moostitary St 11, 420012 Kazan Russia

ARLEN, MICHAEL J., writer; b. London, Dec. 9, 1930; s. Michael and Atlanta (Mercati) A.; m. Ann Warner, 1957 (div. 1971); children—Jennifer, Caroline, Elizabeth, Sally; m. Alice Albright Hoge, 1972; stepchildren—Alicia, James Patrick, Robert Hoge. Grad., St. Paul's Sch., Concord, N.H., 1948, Harvard U., 1952; LLD (hon.), Colby Coll., 1984. Reporter Life mag., 1952-56; contbr., TV critic The New Yorker mag., 1957-82; juror Columbia U.-Dupont awards for broadcast journalism, 1969-72, 78-80; faculty Bread Loaf Writers Conf., 1980; bd. dirs. Nat. Arts Journalism Program. Author: Living-Room War, 1969, Exiles, 1970, An American Verdict, 1973, Passage to Ararat, 1975, The View from Highway 1, 1976, Thirty Seconds, 1980, The Camera Age, 1981, Say Goodbye to Sam, 1984. Recipient award for television criticism Screen Dirs. Guild, 1968; Nat. Book award for contemporary affairs, 1976; Le Prix Brémond, 1976. Mem. Authors Guild (exec. coun.), PEN Am. Ctr., Knickerbocker Club, Century Assn., Harvard Club of N.Y.

ARLINGHAUS, SANDRA JUDITH LACH, mathematical geographer, educator; b. Elmira, N.Y., Apr. 18, 1943; d. Donald Frederick and Alma Elizabeth (Satorius) Lach; m. William Charles Arlinghaus, Sept. 3, 1966; 1 child, William Edward. AB in Math., Vassar Coll., 1964; postgrad., U. Chgo., 1964-66, U. Toronto, Ont., Can., 1966-67, Wayne State U., 1968-70; MA in Geography, Wayne State U., 1976; PhD in Geography, U. Mich., 1977. Vis. instr. math. U. Ill., Chgo., 1966; vis. asst. prof. geography Ohio State U., Columbus, 1977-78, lectr. math., 1978-79; lectr. math. Loyola U., Chgo., 1979-81, asst. prof. math., 1981-82; lectr. math. and geography U. Mich., Dearborn and Ann Arbor, 1982-83; founding dir. Inst. Math. Geography, Ann Arbor, 1985—; pres. Arlinghaus Enterprises, Ann Arbor, 1998—; guest lectr. U. Chgo., 1979, 87, 2000, U. Calif., 1979, Syracuse U., 1991, U. No. Iowa, 1991; guest lectr. U. Mich., Ann Arbor, 1983, 90-93, adj. prof. math. geography, population-environ. dynamics Sch. Natural Resources and Environ., 1994—, adj. prof. Coll. Architecture and Urban Planning, 1997; cons. Transp. Rsch. Inst., Coll. Architecture, 1985-86, Coll. Edn., 1992, Cmty. Sys. Found., 1993—; prodr. Ann Arbor Cmty. Access TV, 1988-90; dir. spatial analysis divsn. Cmty. Systems Found., 1996—, dir. fellowship tng. divsn., 1996—, dir. mapping, 1997—; co-founder Arlinghaus Enterprises, 1997. Author: Down the Mail Tubes: The Pressured Postal Era, 1853-1984, Essays on Mathematical Geography, 1986, Essays on Mathematical Geography-II, 1987, An Atlas of Steiner Networks, 1989, Essays on Mathematical Georgraphy-III, 1991; co-author: Population-Environment Dynamics, Sectors in Transition, 1992 and later editions through 1998, Mathematical Geography and Global Art, 1986, Environmental Effects on Bus Durability, 1990, Fractals in Geography, 1993; founder, editor, co-author Solstice, 1990—, Image Interactive Atlases, Image Game Series, Image Discussion Papers, Internat. Soc. Spatial Scis., 1995—; author, editor-in-chief Practical Handbook of Curve Fitting, 1994; co-author, editor-in-chief Practical Handbook of Digital Mapping: Terms and Concepts, 1994; editor-in-chief Practical Handbook of Spatial Stats., 1995; editor internat. monograph series; reviewer Mathematical Reviews, 1992—; contbr. articles, book reviews to profl. jours. in field of geography, psychology, math., biology, history, philately. Planning commr. City of Ann Arbor, 1995—, sec., 1997—; bd. dirs., mem. chmn. Bromley Homeowners Assn., Ann Arbor, 1989-93, pres., 1990-93, 95-96; co-vice chair citizens adv. com. North East Area Master Plan Revision, 1999—; bd. dirs. World Jr. Bridge Championships, Ann Arbor, 1990-91; bd. dirs. Dolfins Inc., 1993-96; artist Math. Awareness Week, Lawrence Tech. U., 1988; mem. bd. trustees Cmty. Sys. Found., 1995—; co-vice chair citizens adv. com. NE Ann Arbor master plan revision, 1999—. Recipient Cmty. Svc. award City of Ann Arbor, 1999. Fellow Am. Geog. Soc. (rep. search com. for curator of collection in Golda Meir Libr. U. Wis.-Milw. Libr. 1993-94); mem. AAAS, Am. Math. Soc., Math. Assn. Am., Assn. Am. Geographers, Internat. Soc. Spatial Scis. (founder), N.Y. Acad. Scis., Engring. Soc. Detroit, Regional Sci. Assn. Achievements include discovery of exact fractal characterization of the geometry of central place theory and its electronic interpretation; alignment of earth marking sculptures to solstices and equinoxes in Minnesota, Washington, Alaska, New Brunswick, Canada, and USSR; creator of one of world's first refereed electronic journals; creator of applications of chaos theory in geography and population environment dynamics, maps for major international projects for Syria and Pakistan. Office: U Mich Sch Natural Resources Ann Arbor MI 48109

ARLT, THILO, chemist, mineralogist; b. Munich, Bavaria, Germany, Sept. 4, 1967; s. Günter and Josefa (Sever) A. Diploma in chemistry, U. Munich, 1994; PhD, U. Bern, 1998. Rschr. Tech. U., Munich, 1994-95, Mineralog. Inst., Bern, Switzerland, 1995-98, Bayr Geoinstitut, U. Bayreuth, Germany, 1998-99, Wella AG, Darmstadt, Germany, 2000—. Contbr. articles to profl. jours. including Am. Mineralogist, European Jour. Mineralogy, Physics and Chemistry of Minerals, and Mineralogical Mag., Mineralogy and Petrology, Physics Review B. Avocations: mining archaeology, history, mountaineering. Office: Cosmital SA (Wella), Route de Césalles 21, CH-1723 Marly Switzerland

ARLYUK, BORIS JLICH, aluminum technological consulting, company executive; b. St. Petersburg, Russia, Jan. 8, 1937; s. Ilija and Margarita (Minskaja) A.; m. Tamara Ivanova, May 4, 1940; children: Sergei, Dmitri. Grad., St. Petersburg Mining Inst., 1959, MS (hon.), 1968; DS (hon.), VAMI Inst., 1988. Rschr. VAMI Inst., St. Petersburg, 1959-88, head lab., 1988-95; mng. dir. Alumconsult Ltd., St. Petersburg, 1995—. Author: Sintering Process in Alumina Production, 1970, Leaching of Sinter in Alumina Technology, 1979, Complex Processing of Alkali-Aluminum Containing Raw Materials, 1994; contbr. numerous articles to profl. jours. Mem. N.Y. Acad. Scis. E-mail: arlyuk@online.ru. Home: 2 Shkiperski protok apt. 42, 199106 Saint Petersburg Russia

ARMAND, GEORGES JULES, physicist, consultant; b. Paris, June 12, 1929; s. Roger Emile and Raymonde (Despratx) A.; m. Nicole Grangier, May 17, 1952; children: Martine, Brigitte, Phillipe, Pascal, Véronique. Degree in engring., U. Arts et Métiers, Paris, 1951; DSc in Physics, U. Paris, 1951; PhD, U. Paris Sud, Orsay, France, 1976. Engr. Commissareat Energie Atomique, Saclay, France, 1951-62, rschr. in physics, 1962-89, cons., 1989-99. Contbr. articles to sci. jours. Mem. French Phys. Soc., Assn. Culture Sci. Roman Catholic. Home: 42 bis Bd de Mondétour, 91400 Orsay France

ARMAND, JEAN PIERRE, oncologist; b. Constantine, Algeria, Oct. 14, 1943; s. Louis and Simone (Sicard) A.; m. Liya Ju; children: Xuan, Marie Anne. MD, U. Paul Sabathia, Toulouse, 1973. Resident Ctr. Claudius Regaud, Toulouse, 1968-73; with Mil. Med. Svc., Katmandu, Nepal, 1968-70; head of svc. Inst. d'Regaud, Toulouse, France, 1978-85; head of svc. Inst. Gustave Roussy, Villejuif, France, 1985-96, head dept. med. oncology, 1996-2000; exec. medical dir. Fed. European Cancer Societies, 2000—. Author: Handbook of Chemotherapy in Clinic. Mem. European Soc. Med. Oncology (pres. 1992-94), French Cancer Soc. (pres. elect. sec. 1999—). E-mail: armand@igr.fr. Office: Inst Gustave Roussy, 39 Rue Camille Desmouline, 94805 Villejuif France

ARMAN GELENBE, DENIZ, concert pianist; b. Ankara, Turkey, Oct. 8, 1944; came to U.S., 1962; d. Abdul Kerim and Ayse Mediha (Raif) A.; m. Erol Gelenbe, June 8, 1968; 1 child, Pamir Emre. Student, Eastman Sch. Music, 1962-64; MusB, Juilliard, 1967, MusM, 1968; postgrad., U. Mich., 1970-71. Founder, artistic dir., prof. piano Paris U., 1979-90; founder, artistic dir. Arman Ensemble, N.C., 1994—, Arman Ensemble, Arman Trio, Paris, 1994—; vis. assoc. prof. piano U. Ctrl. Fla., Orlando, 1998—. Recitals in Carnegie Weill Hall, N.Y., Salle Gaveau, Paris, Nat. Gallery Art, Washington, Tonhalle, Zurich, Wigmore Hall, London, Concerts de Midi, Liege; soloist for Ensemble Orchestral Paris, Tokyo, Istanbul, Ankara Philharm., Spain, Philippines, N.C. Triangle Symphony; performance (CD's) with Haydn Quartet, 1994, 2000, Arman Ensemble, 1996. Emerging Artist grantee, Durham, N.C., 1984. Mem. Chamber Music Am. Avocations: painting, reading, walking. Home: 100 Detmar Dr Winter Park FL 32789-3901

ARMANI, GIORGIO, fashion designer; b. Piacenza, Emilia Romagna, Italy, July 11, 1934. Student, U. Bologna, Italy; D (hon.), Royal Coll. Art, London, 1991. Fashion coord. La Rinascente, Milan, 1957-64; designer, product developer Cerutti Co., Milan, 1964-70; freelance designer Milan, 1970; co-founder Giorgio Armani SpA, Milan, 1975—. Served with Italian Army, 1953-54. Recipient Neiman Marcus award, 1979, Cutty Sark award, 1980, 81, 84, 86, 87, men's style award GQ mag., 1981, Nanstyle award for best designer in the world, 1982, Ambrogino D'Oro award municipality of Milan, 1982, gold medal municipality of Piacenza, 1983, internat. designer award Coun. Fashion Designers Am., 1983, L'Occhio D'Oro award 1984, 86, 87, 88, 94, L'Occhiolino D'Oro award 1986, 87, Grand Ufficiale Dell'Ordine al Merito Della Repubblica govt. Italy, 1986, Gran Cavaliere govt. Italy, 1987, Lifetime Achievement award Coun. Fashion Designers Am., 1988, Cristobal Balenciaga award Madrid, 1988, Media Key award Armani Perfume commercial directed by Martin Scorsese, 1988, Fiorino d'Oro, Florence, for promoting "Made in Italy", 1992, Woolmark award Best Intern. Menswear Collection, 1992, Woolmark award as Best Indsl. Designer N.Y., 1989, Senken award Senken Newspaper, Japan, 1989, Publicità E Successo award for Armani Jeans Comml., 1989, award People Ethical Treatment Animals, 1990, Aguja de Oro award for best internat. designer Madrid, 1993, Telva Triunfador award for best designer of yr. Madrid, 1993; named Most Influential Designer Outside Am. Coun. Fashion Designers Am., 1983, First Designer Laureate of The Cutty Sark, 1985, 87. Office: Giorgio Armani Corp 114 5th Ave Fl 17 New York NY 10011-5607 also: Via Borgonuovo 11, 20121 Milan Italy also: Giorgio Armani Corp 650 Fifth Ave New York NY 10019-6108*

ARMANNSSON, HALLDOR, geochemist, researcher; b. Reykjavik, Iceland, Oct. 3, 1942; s. Armann Halldorsson and Sigrun Gudbrandsdottir; m. Margret Skuladottir, June 29, 1968; children: Armann, Thorbjorg, Sigrun Mjoll. BS, U. Coll. North Wales, 1964; PhD, U. Southampton, 1979. Chemist Indsl. Rsch. and Devel. Inst., Reykjavik, 1967-72; hydrogeochemist Orkustofnun, Reykjavik, 1977-85, 87—; resident geochemist expert UN-DTCD, Nairobi, 1985-87; part-time lectr. U. Iceland, Reykjavik, 1982-84, 1997-2000; geochemist cons. UN-DDSMS, Kampala, Uganda, 1993; lectr. UN Geothermal Progam, Reykjavik, 1982-85, 88—; vis. prof. U. Oreg., 1995; hon. prof. East China Geol. Inst., Jiangxi Province, 1999. Assoc. editor Applied Geochemistry, 1992—, Water-Rock Interaction, 1995; mem. editl. bd. Geothermics, 1996—; editor: Geochemistry of the Earth's Surface, 1999; contbr. articles to profl. jours. Fellow NATO, 1972. Fellow Sci. Soc. Iceland (selection com. 1997-); mem. Assn. Chartered Engrs. Iceland (organizer 9th NASTEC 1981-83), Internat. Assn. Geochemistry & Cosmochemistry (exec. com. WRI group 1986—, sec.-gen. WRI-5 1986), Geosci. Soc. Iceland. Lutheran. Avocation: contract bridge. Home: Fellsmuli 10, IS-108 Reykjavik Iceland Office: Orkustofnun, Grensavegur 9, IS-108 Reykjavik Iceland

ARMATO, UBALDO, anatomist, cell biologist, researcher, educator; b. Trieste, Italy, Apr. 30, 1943; s. Giuseppe and Rosalba (Pace) A.; m. Maria Grazia Cimmino, Aug. 20, 1970 (dec. Oct. 1993); children: Andrea, Federico; m. Ilaria Dal Pra, Oct. 24, 1998. Diploma Classical Letters, Liceo R. Franchetti, Venice, Italy, 1961; Degree (hons.) in Medicine and Surgery, U. Padua, Italy, 1967, Diploma in Hematology, 1969, Diploma (hons.) in Internal Medicine, 1975. Rsch. assoc. U. Padua, 1969-71, rsch. assoc. with tenure, 1971-80, assoc. prof. human anatomy, 1980-86; guest worker Can. Nat. Rsch. Coun., Ottawa, Ont., 1980, 96; prof. histology and embryology U. Verona, Italy, 1986—, dir. Tissue Culture Lab., 1986—, prof. exptl. oncology Sch. Dermatology, 1991—; cons. Regione Veneto Ctr. for Treatment and Prevention of Burns Injuries, 1989—. Contbr. chpts. to books, articles to sci. jours. Pres. funding com. U. Verona, 1989-96, mem. Atheneum's Com., 1990-93; mem. Atheneum's Linguistic Ctr. Directorate, 1994—, tech. com., 1995—. Recipient Sci. Productivity award U. Padua, 1971-73, Millipore Sci. Edn. award Millipore Ltd., Verona, 1987. Mem. Tissue Culture Assn., Am. Soc. Cell Biology, Italian Anatomical Soc. (T.L. Colonnello award 1976), European Tissue Repair Soc. Avocations: swimming, jogging, cross-country skiing, reading, Anglo-Saxon literary and historic authors. Home: 40 Via Linate, 36100 Caldogno Vicenza Italy Office: U Verona Dept Biomed Surg Scis, 8 Strada le Grazie, 37134 Verona Italy

ARMATRADING, JOAN, singer, songwriter; b. St. Kitts, West Indian Islands, Dec. 9, 1950. Albums include Whatever's for Us, 1972, Back to the Night, 1974, Joan Armatrading, 1976, Show Some Emotion, 1977, To the Limit, 1978, Steppin' Out, 1979, Me Myself I, 1980, How Cruel, 1980, Walk Under Ladders, 1981, The Key, 1983, Track Record, 1983, Secret Secrets, 1985, Sleight of Hand, 1986, The Shouting Stage, 1988, Hearts & Flowers, 1990, The Very Best Of, 1991, Square The Circle, What's inside, 1994, Lullabies, 1998, The Messenger, A Tribute Song to Nelson Mandela, 2000. Fax: 0181 992 6593.

ARMBRUSTER, KLAUS, electronic media artist, educator; b. Tübingen, Germany, Nov. 29, 1942; s. Heinrich and Hildegard (Grau) A.; s. Ruth Bussmann; 1 child, Philipp. Painter Germany, 1962-72; author, dir., TV editor NDR, Hamburg, Germany, 1972-82; univ. prof. film and audiovisual comm. U. Polytechnics, Essen, Germany, 1983—; artistic dir., mng. dir. Interartes, Essen, 1994—. Dir. video prodns. including Die Spieldose, 1993, Ruhrwerk, 1998. Recipient Youth Prize of Art, 1968. Office: Interartes Filmprodn GmbH, Gelsenkirchener Str 181, D-45309 Essen Germany

ARMEFTIS, COSTAS CHRISTOU, English educator; b. Episkopi, Cyprus, Aug. 21, 1950; s. Christos Demetriou and Kalliopi Georgiou (Eracleous) A.; m. Georgia Themistokleous Frangou, Nov. 7, 1987; children: Chryssothemis, Despina. BA, U. Athens, 1978. English tchr. Sch. of English, Greece, 1980-84, Cyprus, 1984-92; English tchr. Pub. Schs., Cyprus, 1992—; dir. State Inst. for Further Edn. in Yeroskipou Paphos, Cyprus, 2000. Author: I'll Call the Infinity to Stop, 1973, Vertiginous Inertia, 1993. Mem. Paphos Literary Soc., Internat. Assn. of Tchrs. of English as a Foreign Language. Avocations: reading, painting, fishing.

ARMENTANO, RICARDO LUIS, biomedical engineering researcher; b. Paysandu, Uruguay, Aug. 3, 1957; s. Luis Alberto and Olga (Feijoo) A.; m. Marina Cocchi, Jan. 7, 1983; children: Pablo, Matilde. BS, Justo Jose de Urquiza Coll., Concepción del Uruguay, Argentina, 1977; grad. in elec. engring., Nat. Tech. U., Buenos Aires, 1984; PhD, U. Buenos Aires, 1994, Paris VII Univ., 1999. Biomed. engr. Favaloro Found., Buenos Aires, 1982-84, jr. rschr. tchg. dept., 1984-94, sr. rschr., 1994—; invited rschr. unit 28, INSERM, Paris, 1986-88, 90-91, 93-94, 95-96, 97-98, 99-2000, unit 263, 1989; assoc. prof. electronics dept., Nat. Tech. U., Favaloro Univ., Buenos Aires U., 1992—, chmn. M Biomed. Engring. program, 1993—; sr. rschr. 5th degree U. Republica, Montevideo, Uruguay, 1993—; pres. Coun. for Rsch. and Devel. Favaloro U. Editor: Biomecanica Arterial, 1994, Hipertension Limitrofe, 1994, sistemas y Señales, 1997; contbr. articles to Circulation Rsch., Am. Jour. Physiology. Recipient Rosalia F. de Garfunkel award Nat. Acad. Medicine, 1988, 94, Nuevas Ingenierias award Centro Argentino de Ingenieros. Mem. Argentinian Soc. of Bioengring. (past pres.). Avocations: literature, music, football, swimming. E-mail: armen@favaloro.edu.ar. Office: Favaloro Found, Favaloro Univ, Solis 453, 1078 Buenos Aires Argentina

ARMENTROUT, FREDERICK SHERMAN, publisher, editor; b. Chgo., Feb. 23, 1946; s. Frederick and Irene (Cottini) A.; m. Rodelia Rubis DeLizo, May 30, 1993; children: Lena, Philippa, Irene. BA, CUNY, 1971; postgrad., CCNY, 1976-77. Mng. editor Staten Island Register, N.Y.C., 1971-73; gen. mgr. Star Reporter Publ. Co., Bklyn., 1974-75; adj. prof. creative writing Staten Island Coll., 1975-76; rsch. assoc. Coun. Econ. Priorities, N.Y.C., 1976-77; exec. editor mag. Petroleum News Southeast Asia Publ. Ltd., Hong Kong, 1977-78; festival editor Urban Coun. Hong Kong, 1978-79; dir. publs. Andamans East Internat. Ltd., 1979-86; editor Orientations mag. Pacific Mags., Ltd., 1979-80; dep. editor inflight mag. Hong Kong Publ. Co., 1980-82; editor mags. Emphasis Hong Kong Ltd., 1982-86; editor Pacific mag. Pacific Publs. Ltd., 1980-86; publs. mgr. Am. C. of C., Hong Kong, 1986—. Avocations: photography, reading, blues and classical music, Spanish guitar.

ARMFIELD, DIANA MAXWELL, artist, educator; b. Ringwood, Eng., June 11, 1920; d. Joseph Harold Armfield and Gertrude Mary Uttley; m. Bernard Dunstan, 1949; 3 children. Student, Slade Sch. Art, Ctrl. Sch. Arts and Crafts, London. Tchr. Byam Shaw Sch. Art, 1959-89; artist in residence, Perth, Australia, 1985, Jackson, Wyo., 1989. One-woman shows include Browse & Darby, London, 1979-2000, also in U.S., Australia, The Netherlands; author: (books) Mitchell Beazley Pocket Guide to Painting in Oils, Mitchell Beazley Pocket Guide to Drawing, The Art of Diana Armfield (Julian Halsby). Commr. HRH Prince of Wales, Reuters, Contemporary Art Soc. Wales Natural Trust. Mem. New English Art Club, Royal W. of Eng. Acad., Royal Cambrian Acad., Pastel Soc. (hon.), Royal Acad. Arts, Royal Watercolor Soc. Avocations: music, gardening. Address: 10 High Park Rd Kew, Richmond Surry TW9 4BH, England

ARMIGER, GENE GIBBON, telecommunications executive, consultant; b. Balt., Oct. 17, 1931; s. Edward Gibbon and Irene Juliet (Peppler) A.; m. Cynthia Clare Carroll, Feb. 14, 1954 (div. 1971); children: Karen Lee, Scott Andrew; m. Dorothy Sue Looney, Feb. 17, 1979. Archtl. student, U. Md., 1951-52, Md. Inst., 1956-58. Cert. lic. capt. USCG. Project engr. Cook Electric Co., Chgo., 1958-62, U.S. Underseas Cable Corp., Washington, 1962; gen. mgr. sales/mktg. Superior Cable Corp., Hickory, N.C., 1963-74; dir. sales/mktg. No. Telecom Inc., Nashville, 1974-76, Porta Systems Inc., Syosset, N.Y., 1976-78; founder/chief exec. officer Armiger & Assocs. Inc., Ft. Worth, Tex., 1978-86; v.p. Richard Thomas & Assocs., Chgo., 1986-88, Suttle Armiger Telecom, Hector, Minn., 1988-90; cons. Telecom. Cons., Ft. Worth, 1990—; mem. FCC Telecom Industry Ad-hoc com. Washington, 1979-87. Contbr. articles to profl. jours. Bd. dirs. Telecommunications Industry Assocs., Washington, 1985-87. Sgt. U.S. Army, 1951-61, Korea. Mem. Am. Mgmt. Assn., U.S. Power Squadron, USCG Aux., Tel. Pioneer Assn., Ind. Tel. Pioneer Assn. (v.p. 1968-69), Va. Yacht Club, Petroleum Club, Ridglea Country Club, Shriners. Republican. Episcopalian. Avocations: deep water sailing, golf, tennis, snow skiing, hunting. Home: 5330 Collinwood Ave Fort Worth TX 76107-3634

ARMISTEAD, KATHERINE KELLY (MRS. THOMAS B. ARMISTEAD, III), interior designer, travel consultant, civic worker; b. Pitts., Apr. 14, 1926; d. Joseph Anthony and Katherine Arnold (Manning) Kelly; grad. Finch Jr. Coll., 1946; m. Thomas Boyd Armistead, III, Nov. 29, 1952; children: Katherine Kelly (Mrs. W. Michael Roark), Thomas Boyd IV. Editor news Sta. WOR, N.Y.C., 1946-51; with Dumont TV, 1951-52; editor Social Service Rev., L.A., 1956-57; interior designer, L.A., 1963—; travel cons. Gilner Internat. Travels, Beverly Hills, Calif., 1980—. Editorial bd. Previews Mag., 1984-87. Pres. Jrs. Social Svc., L.A., 1962-64; nat. chpt. chmn. Associated Alumnae of Sacred Heart, 1960-66; pres. Las Floristas, 1967-68; pres. L.A. Orphanage Guild, 1969-70; coord. Jr. Mannequin Assisteens, Assistance League So. Calif., 1971-72; pres. docent coun. L.A. County Mus. Art, 1976-77, pres. decorative arts coun., 1977-80, chmn. Am. Antiques Conf., 1979-81, mem. costume coun., mem. past pres.' coun., 1981—, mem. capital gifts campaign com.; bd. dirs. L.A. Orphanage Guild, 1970—; Cert. travel cons. Recipient Eve award Assistance League So. Calif. Mem. Am. Soc. Travel Agts., Inst. Cert. Travel Agts. (cert.), Lady Comdr. with star Equestrian Order of the Holy Sepulchre of Jerusalem. Republican. Roman Catholic. Clubs: Birnam Wood Golf (Santa Barbara, Calif.), Bel Air Garden.

ARMITAGE, JOHN VERNON, academic administrator; b. Settle, England, May 21, 1932; s. Horace and Evelyn Newlyn (Hauton) A.; m. Sarah Catherine Clay, Dec. 21, 1963; children: Jonathan Mark, Nicholas Richard. BS, U. Coll. London, 1953; postgrad., Cuddesdon Coll., 1955-56, PhD, 1956. Asst. master Pontefract (England) High Sch., 1956-58, Shrewsbury (England) Sch., 1958-59; lectr. math. U. Durham (England), 1959-67; sr. lectr. math. King's Coll., London, 1967-70; prof. math. U. Nottingham (England), 1970-75; prin. Coll. Higher Edn., Coll. St. Hild & St. Bede, Durham, 1975-79; prin. U. Durham, Coll. St. Hild & St. Bede, 1979-97, hon. sr. fellow math., 1997—; dean colls. U. Durham, 1988-93. Author: Companion to Advanced Mathematics, 1969; editor: Jounies Arthmetic, 1981. Fellow Royal Astronomical Soc., Inst. Math.; mem. Am. Math. Soc. Mem. Ch. of England. Avocations: railways, history, theology, cricket. Home: 7 Potters Close, DH1 3UB Durham England Office: U Durham Dept Math Scis, South Rd, DH1 3LE Durham England

ARMITAGE, KENNETH, sculptor; b. Leeds, Eng., July 18, 1916; married, 1940;. Student, Leeds Coll. of Art, 1934-38, Slade Sch.; Hon. Dr., Royal Coll. Art, 1969, Royal Acad. Arts, London, 1994. Tchr. of sculpture Bath (Eng.) Acad. of Art, 1947-56; Gregory fellow Leeds U., 1953; Brit. Coun. visitor in sculpture, Venezuela, 1963-64; guest artist City of Berlin, 1967-69. One-man shows, London, 1952, 57, 62, 65, N.Y., 1954, 56, 58, 62, Whitechapel Art Gallery, London, 1959, Sala Mendoza, Caracas, Venezuela, 1982, Jeremy Clerk Gallery, London, 2000, touring exhbn. Tokyo, Osana and Nagoya, Japan, 1978; represented in permanent collection at Venice biennale, 1958; group exhbns. include Seoul (Korea) Olympics, 1988, World Expo., Brisbane, Australia, 1988, numerous others; commd. sculpture at New Brit. Embassy, Brasilia, Brazil, 1985. Decorated comdr. Brit. Empire; recipient David Bright prize Venice Biennale, 1958. Address: Tate Gallery, Millibank, London SW1P 4RG, England

ARMITAGE-WOODWARD, FIONA LOUISE, educator, researcher in social sciences; b. Nairobi, Kenya, Oct. 24, 1940; d. Alfred Colin and Anne (Laycock) Maher; m. Michael Stockdale Armitage, Jan. 18, 1964 (div. 1985); children: Rachel Lynne, Julian Paul, Zoe Ellen; m. Julian Woodward, Aug. 14, 1993; stepchildren: Oliver, Lorna. BA in History with honours, London U. (UCRN), Harare, Zimbabwe, 1963; BSc in Sociology with honours, London U., 1972; MLitt, Aberdeen (Scotland) U., 1976; postgrad. diploma, Surrey (Eng.) U., 1986. Cert. tchr. Social worker in child care Birmingham (Eng.) Corp., 1964; social worker Nat. Coun. Social Svc., Edinburgh, Scotland, 1965; lectr., tutor, rschr., vol: Swaziland, 1968-74; lectr. Surrey County Coun., Redhill, Eng., 1980-87; cmty. edn. officer Open U., West Surrey, Eng., 1986-87; rschr. Oxfam, Oxford, Eng., 1990-93; rschr., educator Oxford, 1993—; mem. steering com. Oxford Conf. Ednl. Reform, Internat. Jour. Ed., Oxford, 1990, 92, Group for Anthropology in Policy and Practice, London, 1982-94, vol. rschr. in milk powder use World Food Programme, Mbabane, Swaziland, 1971. Editor Focus on Swaziland, 1991-94, Britain-Zimbabwe Soc. Newsletter, 1988-91; contbr. articles to profl. jours. Fellow Royal Anthrop. Inst., 1985. Mem. Britain Zimbabwe Soc. (sec. 1988-91), Swaziland Soc. (editor 1991-94), Anthropology in Action (sec. 1993), Tropical Agr. Assn. Avocations: music, art, environmental and intercultural associations. Home: 24 Jackson Rd, Oxford OX2 7TR, England

ARMOGATHE, JEAN-ROBERT, clergyman, educator; b. Marseilles, France, July 6, 1947; s. Jean-Marie and Marie-Christine (Vetault) A. Degree in religious scis., Ecole Pratique Hautes Etudes, 1970; Docteur es-lettres, Paris, 1998; PhD, Sorbonne U., Paris, 1972; diploma in patristic theology, Patristicum, Rome, 1976. Prof. Ecole des Hautes Etudes, Sorbonne, 1972—; vis. fellow Trinity Coll., Oxford (Eng.) U., 1983-84, All Souls Coll., 1985-86; vis. prof. U. Toronto, Can., 1994-95, Superior Inst., Bossuet, 1992—; mem. Comitato Dottorato Filosofia, U. La Sapienza, Rome, 1996—, Comitato dei Garanti, Rome, 1997—; pastor St. Pierre de Chaillot, Paris, 1985-90, St. Germain des Pres, Paris, 1990-92; chaplain Ecole Normale Superieure, 1981—; lent spkr. Notre Dame de Paris, 1998-2000. Author: Paul ou L'Impossible Unite, 1980 (Grand Prix Catholique de Lit. 1980); editor: Le Grand Siecle et la Bible, 1989 (Prix Inst. de France 1989). Decorated Officer Palmes Academiques, Arts et Lettres. Fellow Internat. Acad. for the History of Sci., Accademia S. Carlo; mem. Leibniz-Gesellschaft Hannover, Soc. d'Etude du XVII Siecle (pres. 1997—), Centre d'Etudes Cartesiennes Sorbonne. Home: Rue Guynemer 6, 75006 Paris France Office: EPHE Scis Religieuses, Sorbonne 45 Rue des Ecoles, 75005 Paris France

ARMOUR, JAMES LOTT, lawyer; b. Jackson, Tenn., May 19, 1938; s. Quintin and Frances (Breeden) A.; m. Nancy Stokes Johnson, Mar. 17, 1962; 1 son, John Lawson. BA, Vanderbilt U., 1961, LLB, 1964; LLM, So. Meth. U., 1967. Bar: Tenn. 1964, Tex. 1965, U.S. Supreme Ct. 1967, N.Y. 1969, Okla. 1972. Assoc. firm Turner Rodgers Winn Scurlock & Terry, Dallas, 1965-67; internat. atty. Mobil Corp., N.Y.C. and London, 1967-71, Phillips Petroleum Co., Bartlesville, Okla., 1971-74; asst. gen. counsel Conoco, Inc., Stamford, Conn., 1974-83; ptnr. firm Locke Liddell & Sapp LLP, Dallas, 1984—. Mem. adv. bd. oil and gas SW Legal Found., chair, 1996-99; mem. Dallas Com. on Fgn. Rels.; former mem. alumni bd. Vanderbilt Law Sch. Mem. ABA, Assn. of Bar of City of N.Y., State Bar Tex., Dallas Bar Assn., Petroleum Club, Phi Delta Phi, Kappa Sigma. Episcopalian. Home: 4541 Belfort Pl Dallas TX 75205-3618 Office: Locke Liddell & Sapp LLP 2200 Ross Ave Ste 2200 Dallas TX 75201-6776

ARMOUR, PETER JAMES, humanities educator; b. Fleetwood, Eng., Nov. 19, 1940; s. James and Anne Mary (Monaghan) A. BA with honors, U. Manchester, 1966; PhD, U. Leicester, 1980. Lectr. Italian U. Sheffield (England), 1966-72, U. Leicester (England), 1972-79, Bedford Coll., U. London, 1979-84, U. Coll. London, 1984-89; prof. Italian Royal Holloway, U. London, 1989—; vis. sr. lectr. U. Western Australia, Perth, 1973; assoc. dir. Inst. Romance Studies, London, 1991-92, 94-99; vis. prof. U. Melbourne, 1987, U. Va., 1995, 98. Author: The Door of Purgatory, 1983, Dante's Griffin and the History of the World, 1989; contbr. articles to profl. jours. Personal grantee Brit. Acad., 1983, 94. Fellow Royal Soc. Arts; mem. Soc. Italian Studies, Dante Soc. Am. (life), Soc. Dantesca Italiana, Modern Humanities Rsch. Assn., Middlesex County Cricket Club. Avocations: reading, opera, travel, cricket. Office: Royal Holloway U London, Egham Hill, Surrey TW20 0EX, England

ARMSON, FREDERICK SIMON ARDEN, company executive, not-for-profit organization; b. Yoxall, U.K., Sept. 11, 1948; s. Frank Gerald Arden and Margaret Fenella (Newton) A.; m. Marion Albinia Hamilton-Russell, Feb. 8, 1975; children: Meriel, Patrick, Katie. MS in Mental Health, London U., 1997. Cert. health svc. adminstr. Asst. pers. officer North Birmingham (U.K.) Hosps., 1972-73; pers. officer Salop Area Health Authority, Shrewsbury, U.K., 1974-75; sr. pers. officer Dudley (U.K.) Area Health Authority, 1975-77; asst. area pers. officer Oxfordshire (U.K.) Health Authority, 1977-82; dep. dist. adminstr. Milton Keynes Health Authority, U.K., 1982-84; asst. gen. sec. The Samaritans, Slough, U.K., 1984-89, CEO, 1989—. Fellow Royal Soc. Arts Companion, Inst. of Mgmt. Mem. Ch. of Eng. Avocations: wood-turning, music, cross-country cycling, sailing. Home: Broad Oak Hurley, Maidenhead Berkshire SL6 5LW, England Office: The Samaritans, 10 The Grove, Slough SL1 1QP, England

ARMSTRONG, ALFREDA JUANITA, real estate executive; b. Phila., July 31, 1939; d. Col. Alfred and Lillie Mae (Watt) Dunn; m. Nathaniel C. Armstrong, Feb. 5, 1960 (dec. 1981); children: Nathaniel Jr., Rita, Clarence, Armstrong. Student, Pa. State U., 1974-79; Union Labor/Mgmt. Mediator, Internat. Corres. Sch., 1992. Lic. judge profl. boxing sport; cert. in police investigative sci. Adminstrv. sec. Sch. Dist. Phila., 1970-85; exec. officer, founder LeaseScore Inc., Phila., 1985—; exec. officer, founder Matter As Fact, Phila. County, 1992; mediator labor union mgmt. Corr. sec. Dem. Women Phila., 1980-81; mem. Phila. Mayor's Commn. for Women; exec. officer, founder Baby Safe Haven, Inc., 1991; founder Women's Watch, Inc., 1995. Mem. Apt. Owners Assn., Phila. Credit Bur. Assn., Phila. Fedn. of Tchr. Retirees. Office: LeaseScore Inc PO Box 5 Donalds SC 29638-0005

ARMSTRONG, BILLIE BERT, retired highway contractor; b. Roswell, N.Mex., Apr. 18, 1920; s. Gayle G. and Murphy (Shannon) A.; m. Betty-Ellen Wilcox, Aug. 16, 1941; children: Billie B. Jr., Judith C., Robert G., Riley A. Student, N.Mex. Mil. Inst., 1935-39, Washington & Lee U., 1939-41. Mng. ptnr. Armstrong & Armstrong Ltd., Roswell, 1950—, G.G. Armstrong & Son, Ltd., Roswell, 1950—; chmn. bd. dirs. Sunwest Nat. Bank of Roswell, 1967-84; pres. Assoc. Gen. Contractors Am., Washington, 1966-67, Assoc. Contractors N.Mex., Santa Fe, 1952-53, 63; bd. dirs. Southwestern Pub. Svc. Co., Sunwest Fin. Svcs., Inc. Pres. Conquistador Coun. Boy Scouts Am., Roswell, 1981-82, bd. regents N.Mex. Mil. Inst., Roswell, 1960-62. Major U.S. Army, 1942-45. Named Citizen of Yr. Realtors N.Mex., 1969, Roswell, 1968, Jaycees, 1964; recognized for svc. to mankind Sertoma, 1966. Mem. Masons, Shriners, Jesters. Methodist. Avocation: golf. Home: 2801 N Kentucky Ave Apt 134 Roswell NM 88201-5878 Office: Armstrong & Armstrong Ltd PO Box 1873 Roswell NM 88202-1873

ARMSTRONG, BRUCE IRVING, mechanical engineer; b. Montebello, Calif., July 28, 1957; s. John William and Kathryn Winifred (Stevenson) A. AA in Engring., Mt. San Antonio Coll., Walnut, Calif., 1979; BSME, Calif. State U., Fresno, 1985. Mech. engr. Naval Warfare Assessment Sta. USN, Corona, Calif., 1985—; participant in fastener hearings Gen. Acctg. Office, Washington, 1991; advisor thread tech. U.S. Dept. Commerce, Washington, 1992; advisor USN Gen. Coun., Washington, 1993. Mem. ASME (mem. B1.2 screw thread std. com. 1992—, B1.15 screw thread std. com. 1992—), Lambda Chi Alpha. Republican. Presbyterian. Avocations: backpacking, mountain climbing, reading American history, travel to historic sites. Home: 3157 Florinda St Pomona CA 91767-1013

ARMSTRONG, C. MICHAEL, communications company executive; b. Detroit, Oct. 18, 1938; s. Charles H. and Zora Jean (Brooks) A.; m. Anne Gossett, June 17, 1961; children: Linda, Julie, Kristy. BS in Bus. Econs, Miami U., Oxford, Ohio, 1961; grad., Dartmouth Inst., 1976; LLD (hon.), Pepperdine U., 1997, Loyola Marymount U., 1998. With IBM Corp., 1961-92, dir. systems mgmt. mktg. div., White Plains, N.Y., 1975-76, v.p. market ops. East, 1976-78, pres. data processing divsn., 1978-80, v.p., asst. group exec. plans and controls, data processing product group, 1980-83, v.p., group exec., 1983-84, sr. v.p., group exec., 1984-92; also pres. IBM Corp., Europe, Paris, until 1988; pres., dir. gen. World Trade Europe/Middle East/Africa IBM Corp., 1987-89, chmn. World Trade Corp., 1989-92; chmn., CEO Hughes Aircraft Co., L.A., 1992-93, GM Hughes Electronics (now Hughes Electronics Corp.), 1993—, AT&T, Basking Ridge, N.J., 1997—; Mem. GM Pres. Coun.; bd. dirs. Travelers Corp., Hartford, Conn., The Times-Mirror-Co., L.A.. Citigroup; mem. supervisory bd. Thyssen-Bornemisza Group; chmn. Pres.'s Export Coun., The White House, 1994—. Trustee Johns Hopkins U., chmn. adv. bd. Johns Hopkins Med. Sch.; mem., CEO bd. of adv. U. So. Calif. Bus. Sch.; mem. bus. adv. coun. Miami U.; mem. Coun. on Fgn. Rels., Nat. Security Telecomm. Adv. Com., Def. Policy Adv. Com. on Trade (DPACT); adv. bd. Yale Sch. Mgmt.; vice-chmn. World Affairs Coun., L.A.; chmn. Sabriya's Castle of Fun Found.; bd. trustees Carnegie Hall. Mem. Calif. Bus. Roundtable. Office: AT&T Corp Corp Hdqs 295 N Maple Ave Basking Ridge NJ 07920-1025

ARMSTRONG, CHRISTOPHER JOHN, information scientist; b. Hove, Sussex, U.K., June 13, 1947; s. John Ernest and Brenda Ethel Clara (Barnett) A.; m. Katherine Marcus (dec.); children: Benjamin Iwan, Daniel Owen, Joel Ioan. B in Librarianship, U. Wales, 1978. Rsch. officer Coll. Librarianship Wales, Aberystwyth, 1978-87; dir. Info. Automation Ltd., Aberystwyth, 1987—; mgr. Ctr. Info. Quality Mgmt., Aberystwyth, 1993—; cons. Brit. Coun., Jakarta, Indonesia, 1990-93; vice-chair U.K. Online User Group, 1995—. Co-author: (with R.J. Hartley) Key Guide to Online and CD-Rom Database Searching, 1997; editor: Manual of Online Search Strategies, 1988, 2d edit., 1992, CD-Rom Products: The Evaluating Guide, 1990-93, Staying Legal: a guide to issues and practice for users and publishers of electronic resources, 1999. Fellow Instn. Analysts and Programmers, Inst. Info. Scientists. Avocations: walking, badminton, table tennis, gardening Bonsai. Office: Information Automation Ltd, Penbryn Bronant, Aberystwyth SY23 4TJ, Wales

ARMSTRONG, DAVID MILLAR, physiology educator, academic administrator; b. Workington, Cumbria, Eng., May 25, 1941; s. James and Jeannie Alexandra (Millar) A.; m. Lucinda Russell Kennedy, Aug. 12, 1964; children: Katharine Anne, James Graham. BA, Oxford (Eng.) U., 1963, BSc, 1965; PhD, Australian Nat. U., 1967. Lectr. in physiology U. Bristol, Eng., 1968-78, reader, 1978-84, prof., 1984—, dept. chair, 1990-95; bd. dirs. neurosci. U.K. Med. Rsch. Coun., 1987-91. Editor: LocoMotor Neural Mechanisms in Arthropods and Vertebrates, 1991; mem. editorial bd. Jour. of Physiology, 1979-86. Med. Rsch. Coun. grantee, Wellcome Trust grantee, Action Rsch. grantee, Royal Soc. grantee. Mem. Physiol. Soc., Marine Biol. Assn., European Neuroscis. Assn., Brain Rsch. Assn. Mem. Labour Party. Office: U Bristol Dept Physiology, University Walk, Bristol BS 8 1TD, England

ARMSTRONG, EDWARD BRADFORD, JR., oral and maxillofacial surgeon, educator, naval officer; b. Teaneck, N.J., Sept. 24, 1928; s. Edward Bradford and Ruth Elizabeth (Fippinger) A.; AB, U. Pa., 1950; DDS, N.Y.U., 1954; m. Dusanka Vladimirovna Jakovljevic, Nov. 5, 1960; children: Edward Bradford, III, James B., Hugh B. Commd. lt. j.g. U.S. Navy, 1954, advanced through grades to capt. 1971; intern oral surgery Roosevelt Hosp., N.Y.C., 1958, assoc. attending oral surgery, 1959—, attending oral surgeon out-patient dept., 1959—, chmn., moderator Oral Surgery Staff Confs., 1963-70; resident Carle Hosp., Urbana, Ill., 1959; assoc. attending oral surgeon Flower and Fifth Ave. hosps., N.Y.C., 1960-78; asst. attending oral surgeon Hackensack (N.J.) Hosp., 1963-65; adminstrv. officer Naval Res. Dental Co. 3-2, 1965-68, exec. officer, 1968-71, comdg. officer, 1971-73; comdt.'s rep. 3d Naval Dist., Naval Acad., 1972-78, 3d Naval Dist for Dentistry, 1973-75, group staff officer for dentistry and medicine, 1973-75, Ready Res. Unit 502, 1975-77, VTU 0207, 1977-79, ret., 1979; assoc. clin. prof. oral surgery N.Y. Med. Coll., 1963-93; adj. assoc. clin. prof. oral surgery Columbia U. Sch. Dentistry, 1973-89; chmn. bd. E. & R. Armstrong, Inc., Albany, N.Y., 1966-77; pres. Edward B. Armstrong, P.C., N.Y.C., 1979-90; dir. Songtime, Inc., Boston; dir., mem. exec. com. PGP Internat. Corps, Inc. Bd. dirs., trustee Christian Mission Farms of Paraguay, Inc., 1974-84; pres., trustee Central Bible Chapel, Palisades Park, N.J.; area rep., ann. giving U. Pa., 1960-68; Blue and Gold officer Naval Acad. Admissions Com.; sec. bd. dirs., trustee Boys' Club of N.Y. Health Svcs., Inc. Diplomate Am. Bd. Oral Surgery. Fellow N.Y. Acad. Dentistry (sec., dir., pres. 1979-80), Am., Internat. Colls. Dentists (life), Am. Coll. Oral and Maxillofacial Surgeons (founding), Am. Dental Soc. Anesthesiology (hon. life); mem. ADA (life, 1st dist. life), Am. Assn. Oral and Maxillofacial Surgeons (life, N.J. rep. Ho. of Dels. 1963-65), N.Y. Soc. Oral Surgeons (life, chmn. audit and budget com. 1972-79), First Dist. Dental Soc. (life), N.Y. Dental Soc., Bklyn. Dental Soc., Yokosuka Dental Soc. (hon.), Assn. Mil. Surgeons U.S., Mil. Order World Wars, Naval Res. Assn. (life), Union League (chmn. art com. 1973-76, bd. govs. 1974-77, 82-84, v.p. 1977-80, 85-88), Met. Club (bd. gov. 1992-96, 98—), N.Y.C., U. Pa. Club, U. Pa. Club of Met. N.J. (dir. 1982—), Acacia, Xi Psi Phi, Psi Omega (hon.), Delta Sigma Delta. Mem. Plymouth Brethren Ch. Home: 110 Broad Ave Leonia NJ 07605-2003

ARMSTRONG, HART REID, minister, editor, publisher; b. St. Louis, May 11, 1912; s. Hart Champlin and Zora Lillian (Reid) A.; m. Iona Rhoda Mehl, Feb. 21, 1932; 1 son, Hart Reed. Grad, Life Bible Coll., 1931; AB, Christian Temples U., 1936; LittD, Geneve Theol. Coll., 1967; DD (hon.), Ctrl. Sch. Religion, Surrey, Eng., 1972; ThM, Ctrl. Christian Coll., 1968, ThD, 1970; PhD in Religion, Berean Christian Coll., 1980. Ordained to ministry Assembly of God, 1933. Pastor Assembly of God, 1932-34; dean Bible Standard Coll., Eugene, Oreg., 1935-40; missionary Indonesia, 1941-42; editor Open Bible Pubs., Des Moines, 1944-46, Gospel Pub. House, Springfield, Mo., 1947-53, Gospel Light Pubs., Glendale, Calif., 1954; crusade adminstr. Oral Roberts Assn., Tulsa, 1955-62; exec. dir. Assembly Homes, Inc., Glenwood, Minn., 1963-66; pres. Defenders Christian Faith, Kansas City, Mo., 1967-80; founder, pres., editor Christian Comm., Inc., Wichita, Kans., 1981—; editor Devotional Letter Monthly. Author: To Those Who Are Left, 1950, You Should Know, 1951, The Rebel, 1967, The Beast, 1967, How Do I Pray, 1968, All Things for Life, 1969, What Will Happen to the United States, 1969, Impossible Events of Bible Prophecy, 1979, All You Need to Know About Bible Prophecy, 1980, Thoughts at Three Score and Ten, 1981, The A-B-C of Last Day Events, 1982, The World that Then Was, How Great Thou Art!, The Gospel of John--A Commentary, 1983, The True Site of the Temple of Solomon, The Holy Jerusalem, UFOs--Art They For Real, Petra--The Mysterious City, 1984, The Seven Churches of Revelation, Verses from the Heart, Katherine Beard--A Life Poured Out, 1985, Let Them Speak to You, The Primary Movers (3 sects.), Where is the Art of the Covenant?, The Sacred Festivals of the Lord, 1989, Commentary on the Book of Revelation (vols. I-IV), 1992, Why Not?-Biography of Dr. Frank Lindquest, Glory to Come!, 1993, The Olivet Discourse, The Last Seven on Earth, The Story of God, 1994, When Is the Rapture? I Found the Ark, The Last Great Day of God Almighty, 1995, The Miracle Voyage of the Ghost Shop, Visions Yet Future in the Book of Daniel, 1996, The Rebel and the Beast, 1998, Redemption! So Great Salvation, 1999. Fellow London Royal Soc. Arts; mem. Nat. Sunday Sch. Assn., Pope County Hist. Soc., Rotary (past charter pres. Glenwood), Sigma Delta Chi. Home: 6436 N Hillside St Wichita KS 67219-1805 Office: 6450 N Hillside St Wichita KS 67219-1805

ARMSTRONG, JOHN DENNIS, retired hotel facility executive, consultant; b. Bradford, Yorkshire, England, Oct. 16, 1928; s. Gilbert and Beatrice (Baldwin) A.; m. Joan Mary Cadoux, July 27, 1957; children: John Mark, Bridget Ruth, Vanessa Jill, Caroline Margaret. MA, Univ. Coll., Oxford, England, 1952. Technical acct. Powers-Samas, Leeds, England, 1954-59; mgmt. cons. Urwick, Orr & Ptnrs., London, 1959-63; acct. Finance Dept. Unilever Ltd., London, 1963-65, comml. officer Rsch. Divsn., 1965-69; chief acct. Joseph Crosfield & Sons, Ltd., Warrington, 1969-76; group fin. controller North West Farmers, Nantwich, Cheshire, England, 1977; sr. leisure adv. 3i PLC, London, 1978-88; dir. Gough Hotels Ltd., Edmunds, 1988—, Source Two Ltd., London, 1988-90; chmn. Parkbands Nursing Home, Redditch, 1994-95, Menzies Hotels Ltd., Belper, Derbyshire, 1995—. Mem. Solihull Health Authority, 1988-90. Mem. Church of England. Avocations: mountaineering, music, books.

ARMSTRONG, KEITH BERNARD, engineering consultant; b. Ashford, Eng., Sept. 8, 1931; s. George Roland and Doris Maud (Weatherley) A.; m. Dulcie Marina Sampson, Mar. 31, 1956; children: Bernard Paul, Gillian Ruth, Derek George Andrew. H.N.C., Kingston (Eng.) Poly., 1952; MSc, City U., London, 1978, PhD, 1990. Aviation apprentice Vickers-Armstrongs Ltd., Weybridge, Eng., 1948-52, design draughtsman, 1952-55; sr. draughtsman Vickers-Armstrongs (Aircraft) Ltd., Weybridge, 1958-60; exptl. officer Nat. Phys. Lab., Teddington, Eng., 1960-67; devel. engr. Brit. Airways, Heathrow, London, 1967-77, sr. devel. engr., 1977-88, prin. devel. engr., 1988-91; cons., 1991—; chmn. Internat. Air Transport Assn. Composite Repair Task Force, Montreal, Can., 1988-91. Youth leader Meth. Ch., Ashford, Middlesex, Eng., 1952-55, Ashford Common, Middlesex, Eng., 1961-64. Flying officer RAF, 1955-58. Fellow Plastics and Rubber Inst., Instn. Mech. Engrs., Royal Aero Soc.; mem. Soc. Automotive Engrs. Avocations: flying, family history. Home: 20 Homewaters Ave, Sunbury on Thames TW16 6NS, England

ARMSTRONG, LLOYD, JR., university official, physics educator; b. Austin, Tex., May 19, 1940; s. Lloyd and Beatrice (Jackson) A.; m. Judith Glantz, July 9, 1965; 1 son, Wade Matthew. BS in Physics, MIT, 1962; PhD in Physics, U. Calif., Berkeley, 1966. Postdoctoral physicist Lawrence Berkeley (Calif.) Lab., 1965-66, cons., 1976; sr. physicist Westinghouse Research Labs., Pitts., 1967-68, cons., 1968-70; research asso. Johns Hopkins U., 1968-69, asst. prof. physics, 1969-73, assoc. prof., 1973-77, prof., 1977-93, chmn. dept. physics and astronomy, 1985-87, dean Sch. Arts and Scis., 1987-93; provost, sr. v.p. for acad. affairs U. So. Calif., L.A., 1993—, prof. physics, 1993—; assoc. rsch. scientist Nat. Ctr. Sci. Rsch. (CNRS), Orsay, France, 1972-73; vis. fellow Joint Inst. Lab. Astrophysics, Boulder, Colo., 1978-79; program officer NSF, 1981-83, mem. adv. com. for physics, 1985-87, mem. visitors com. physics divsn., 1991; chmn. com. atomic and molecular scis. NAS/NRC, 1985-88, mem. bd. physics and astronomy, 1989-96; mem. adv. bd. Inst. for Theoretical Physics, Santa Barbara, 1992-96, chmn., 1994-95, Inst. Theoretical Atomic and Molecular Physics, Cambridge, Mass., 1994-97, Rochester Theory Ctr. for Optical Sci. and Enging., 1996—, chmn., 1997—; bd. dirs. So. Calif. Econ. Partnership, 1994—, Calif. Coun. on Sci. and Tech., 1994—, Pacific Coun. on Internat. Policy, 1996—. Author: Theory of Hyperfine Structure of Free Atoms, 1971; contbr. articles to profl. jours. NSF grantee, 1972-90; Dept. Energy grantee, 1975-82. Fellow Am. Phys. Soc. Office: U So Calif Office Provost University Park Los Angeles CA 90089-0001

ARMSTRONG, NEIL, health and exercise sciences educator; b. Ashington, Eng., Jan. 24, 1949; s. Thomas and Mary (Jacques) A.; m. Dorothy Bland, Sept. 14, 1968; children: Tom, Sarah. BEd, Loughborough, Eng., 1971, MS, 1972; PhD, Exeter, Eng., 1989. Chartered biologist. Tchr. Coll. Sch., Loughborough, Eng., 1972-74; head dept. Burleigh Coll., Loughborough, Eng., 1974-78; sr. lectr., head divsn. Coll. of Higher Edn./Polytechnic, Liverpool, Eng., 1978-84; lectr., sr. lectr. U. Exeter, Eng., 1984-91, reader, 1991-93, prof., 1993—; dir. Coronary Prevention in Children Project, Eng., 1985—, Children's Health and Exercise Rsch. Ctr., Eng., 1987—; chair Rsch. Assessment Exercise Subject Panel, Univs. Funding Coun., Eng., 1992, 96. Author: Young People and Physical Activity, 1997; editor: New Directions in Physical Education, Vol. 1, 1990, Vol. 2, 1992, Vol. 3, 1995, Issues in Physical Education, 1991; editor Brit. Jour. Phys. Edn. Rsch. Supplement, 1988-95, European Jour. Phys. Edn., 1995—; contbr. over 350 rsch. and profl. papers to profl. jours. Broadcaster BBC/Ind. TV/Radio, U.K., 1987—; vice-chair South Western Regional Coun. for Sport, Eng., 1990-95; chair Sports Devel. Com., S.W. Eng., 1992-95. Prince Philip Fellows lectr. Phys. Edn. Assn., 1989, A.D. Munrow lectr. Brit. U. Phys. Edn. Assn., 1991, Northcott lectr. Northcott Med. Found., 1994. Fellow Phys. Edn. Assn. (pres. 1992-95), Royal Soc. Health, Inst. Biology, Am. Coll. Sports Medicine, Royal Soc. of Arts, European Coll. Sports Sci., Am. Acad. Kinesiology and Phys. Edn., Brit. Assn. Sports Scis. (chmn. 1989-91); mem. N.Am. Soc. Pediat. Exercise Medicine. Avocations: sport, reading, music, theatre, family. Office: U Exeter, Heavitree Rd, Exeter EX1 2LU, England

ARMSTRONG, NEIL A., former astronaut; b. Wapakoneta, Ohio, Aug. 5, 1930; s. Stephen A.; children: Eric, Mark. B.S. In Aero. Engring., Purdue U., 1955; M.S. in Aero. Engring., U. So. Calif. With Lewis Flight Propulsion Lab., NACA, 1955; then aero. research pilot for NACA (later NASA, High Speed Flight Sta.), Edwards, Calif.; astronaut Manned Spacecraft Center, NASA, Houston, 1962-70; command pilot Gemini 8; comdr. Apollo 11; dep. assoc. adminstr. for aeros. Office Advanced Research and Tech., Hdqrs. NASA, Washington, 1970-71; prof. aerospace engring. U. Cin., 1971-79; chmn. AIL Sys., Inc., 1989-2000, EDO Corp., 2000—. Mem. Pres.'s Commn. on Space Shuttle, 1986, Nat. Commn. on Space, 1985-86. Served as naval aviator USN, 1949-52, Korea. Recipient numerous awards, including Octave Chanute award Inst. Aero. Scis., 1962, Presdl. Medal for Freedom, 1969, Exceptional Service medal NASA, Hubbard Gold medal Nat. Geog. Soc., 1970, Kitty Hawk Meml. award, 1969, Pere Marquette medal, 1969, Arthur S. Fleming award, 1970, Congl. Space Medal of Honor, Explorers Club medal. Fellow AIAA (hon., Astronautics award 1966), Internat. Astronautical Fedn. (hon.), Soc. Exptl. Test Pilots; mem. Nat. Acad. Engring.

ARMSTRONG, OTIS PRICE, chemical engineer, environmental engineer; b. Hot Springs, Ark., Mar. 16, 1955; s. Otis Price and Jacqueline Rachael A. Student, U. Ark., 1973-75, U. Tex., 1975-77; BS in Civil Engring., U. Colo., 1984. Lic. profl. engr., Colo. Rsch. engr. Great Western Sugar Co., Loveland, Colo., 1978-79; process engr. Great Western Sugar Co., Denver, 1979-80; pvt. engring. cons. Denver, 1980-84; process engr. Stone & Webster Inc., Denver, 1984-86; engr. Ball Assocs., Denver, 1986-87; design engr. Chevron/RJ Roberts, Rangely, Colo., 1987; ops. engr. Saudi Aramco Uthmaniyah Gas Plant/Process Unit, Uthmaniyah, Saudi Arabia, 1987-91, Saudi Aramco Abqaiq Plant Ops. Engring/NGL Unit, Saudi Arabia, 1991-94; projects engr. Saudi Aramco Abqaiq Plant Ops. Engring./Projects Unit, Saudi Arabia, 1994-97; proprietor Armstrong Lighting & Supply Co., 1997—; engring. asst. Ctr. for Energy Studies, U. Tex., Austin, 1976-77, Texas Instruments, Austin, 1977; sales engr. Environ. Enterprises, Little Rock, 1977-78; del. to PRC with citizen amb. program del. on chemistry and process engrs., 1995; owner Armstrong's Lighting and Elec. Supply, Little Rock, 1998. Contbr. articles to profl. jours. Pres. LRCHS Chess Club, Little Rock, 1973, U. Ark. Chess Club, Little Rock, 1975; statistician Ark. Chess Assn., Little Rock, 1974; advisor Jr. Achievement, Denver, 1986. With Civil Air Patrol, 1967-69. Recipient Outstanding Youth award Outstanding Young Men of Am. Found., 1987. Mem. AIChE, Soc. Petroleum Engrs., Toastmasters. Republican. Presbyterian. Avocations: chess, skiing, bicycling, history, economics. Office: Armstrong's Lighting Ste 38 7123 I-30 Little Rock AR 72209

ARMSTRONG, PATRICK HAMILTON, geography educator; b. Leeds, Yorkshire, Eng., Oct. 10, 1941; s. Edward Allworthy and Eunice Joan (Uttley) A.; m. Moyra Elizabeth Jane Irvine, Aug. 8, 1964; children: Timothy, Alexander. BSc with hons., U. Durham, Eng., 1963, MA, 1966; PhD, Coll. Arts and Tech., Cambridge, Eng., 1970; diploma in edn., U. Durham, Eng., 1964. Lectr. in geography Cambridge Coll. Arts and Tech., 1964-75; sr. lectr. in geography U. Western Australia, Nedlands, W.A., 1975—; dept. head geography U. Western Australia, 1980-82; vis. fellow Open U., Eng., 1982, Durham U., 1993; vis. assoc. Darwin Coll., Cambridge U., 1989, So. Conn. State U., New Haven, 1988; dep. chief examiner Internat. Baccalaureate, 1996-2000, chief examiner, 2000—. Author: 20 books including: The Changing Landscape, 1975, Ecology and Ecosystems, 1986, Reading Australian Maps, 1987, Darwin's Desolate Islands: A Naturalist in the Falklands, 1992, The English parson-naturalist: a companionship between science and religion, 2000; contbr. numerous articles to profl. and sci. jours. Mem. British Ecol. Soc., Geog. Assn., Inst. Australian Geographers, Inst. British Geographers. Anglican. Avocations: photography, exploring old churches, collecting books, golf. Office: U Western Australia, Dept Geography, Nedlands 6907 WA, Australia

ARMSTRONG, PETER, radiologist; b. London, Aug. 31, 1940; s. Alexander and Ada (Lapidas) A.; m. Carole Jennifer Gray, July 22, 1967; children: Damon (dec. 1972), Natasha, Jethro. MB BS, London U., 1962. Registrar in radiology Middlesex Hosp., London, 1964-66, sr. registrar in radiology, 1966-68; sr. registrar in radiology Guy's Hosp., London, 1968-70; cons. radiologist King's Coll. Hosp., London, 1970-77; prof. radiology U. Va., 1977-89; prof. radiology St. Bartholomew's Hosp., London, 1989—, clin. dir., 1990-96. Author: (textbooks) Imaging of Diseases of the Chest, 1989, 3d edit., 2000, Diagnostic Imaging, 1989, 4th edit., 2000; editor: Critical Problems in Diagnostic Radiology, 1999; editor-in-chief Clinical Radiology, 1990-94. Fellow Royal Coll. Radiologists (warden 1994-98, pres. 1998—). Office: St Bartholomew's Hosp, Acad Dept Radiology, London EC1A 7BE, England

ARMSTRONG, PETER MINSHULL, lawyer; b. Ndola, Zambia, Aug. 4, 1949; s. Colin Minshull and Barbara (Coe) A.; m. Susan Margaret Armstrong, July 5, 1986 (div. July 1990). BA, U. Cape Town, South Africa, 1970; LLM, U. Coll. London, 1973. Bar: high ct. Eng. and Wales, 1982. Adminstr. officer Brit. Standards Instn., London, 1974-77; legal asst. Morgan, Finnegan, Pine, Foley & Lee, N.Y.C., 1977-78; ptnr. Bartletts de Reya, London, 1985-89; ptnr., head entertainment divsn. Mishcon de Reya, London, 1989-95; ptnr. Theodore Goddard, London, 1995—; bd. dirs. Brit. Film Commn., London; chmn. entertainment law com. Internat. Bar Assn., London, 1995-99. Contbr. articles to profl. jours. Fellow Royal Commonwealth Soc.; mem. Royal TV Soc. Avocations: the arts, travel. Office: Theodore Goddard, 150 Aldersgate St, London EC1A 4EJ, England

ARMSTRONG, ROBERT TEMPLE (LORD ARMSTRONG OF ILMINSTER), science administrator; b. Oxford, Eng., Mar. 30, 1927; s. Sir Thomas Henry Wait and Lady Hester Muriel (Draper) A.; m. Serena Mary Benedicta Chance, July 25, 1953 (div. 1985; dec. 1994); children: Jane Orlanda, Teresa Brigid; m. Patricia Carlow, Sept. 6, 1985. Grad. with 2d class honours, Oxford U., 1947, 49; LLD (hon.), U. Hull, Eng., 1994. With Her Majesty's Treasury, London, 1950-70; prin. pvt. sec. to prime minister, London, 1970-75; dep. under sec. of state Home Office, London, 1975-77, permanent under sec. of state, 1977-79; sec. of cabinet, London, 1979-87; head Home Civil Svc., London, 1981-87; chmn. Biotech. Investments Ltd., Guernsey, Channel Islands, 1989-2000, 3i Biosci. Investment Trust plc, 2000—; chmn. Forensic Investigative Assocs. plc, 1997—; non-exec. dir. BAT Industries plc, NM Rothschild and Sons Ltd., RTZ Corp. plc, IAM Gold Ltd.; chmn. Bristol and West Bldg. Soc., 1993-97. Chmn. bd. trustees Victoria and Albert Mus., 1988-98. Decorated knight grand cross Order of Bath, comdr. Royal Victorian Order; life peerage, 1988. Mem. Brooks's, Garrick. Anglican. Avocation: music. Office: Sixth Fl Forum House, 15-18 Line St, London EC3M 7AP, England

ARMSTRONG, ROBERT WILLIAM, marketing educator; b. Warren, Ohio, Nov. 17, 1953; arrived in Australia, 1988; s. Robert D. and Melba Ailene (Warner) A.; m. Michelle Diane Vincent, May 22, 1992. BS, Kent State U., 1976, MBA, 1985, PhD, 1988. Supr. Copperweld Steel, Warren, 1976-78; mgr. Standard Steel, Burnham, Pa., 1979-83; asst. dir. Kent State U., Ohio, 1984-88; prof. Murdoch U., Perth, Australia, 1988—; bd. dirs. Diamond Ridge Winner, Australia. Contbr. articles to profl. jours. Mem. Am. Mktg. Assn. Avocations: guitarist, fisherman, philosopher. Office: Murdoch U, South St, Murdoch 6150, Australia

ARMSTRONG, SHEILA ANN, classical vocalist; b. Eng., Aug. 13, 1942; d. William and Janet Armstrong; m. David E. Cooper, 1980. Student, Royal Acad. Music.; MA (hon.), U. Newcastle; DMus, U. Durham. Appeared in opera prodns. at Glyndebourne, Scottish Nat. Opera, Sadlers Wells, English Nat. Opera North, Royal Opera House, Covent Garden; recitals with maj. orchestras; numerous recordings. Mem. Kathleen Ferrier Soc. (pres., Kathleen Ferrier Meml. award, trustee K.F. Meml. scholarship), Royal Philharm. Soc. (com. mem.). Avocations: collecting keys, interior design, flower arranging, sewing, gardening. Address: Harvesters, Tilford Rd, Hindhead Surrey GU26 6SQ, England

ARMSTRONG, THOMAS NEWTON, III, art and garden specialist; b. Portsmouth, Va., July 30, 1932; s. Thomas Newton, Jr. and Mary Saunders (Tabb) A.; m. Virginia Whitney Brewster, May 18, 1963; children: Thomas Newton IV, Whitney, Eliot, Amory. Student, Cornell U., 1950-54, Art Students League, summer 1953, Inst. Fine Arts, NYU, 1965-67. Personnel coordinator, asst. to chmn. bd. Stone & Webster, Inc., N.Y.C., 1957-65; curator, assoc. dir. Colonial Williamsburg-Abby Aldrich Rockefeller Folk Art Collection, Williamsburg, Va., 1967-71; dir. Pa. Acad. Fine Arts, Phila., 1971-73; dir. Whitney Mus. Am. Art, 1974-90, dir. emeritus, 1990—; dir. Andy Warhol Mus., Pitts., 1993-95; dir., pres. The Garden Conservancy; mem. selection com. Luce Scholars Program, Henry Luce Found., Inc.; dir. Nat. Bldg. Mus., 1999—; cons. Sothebys. Trustee Exhbns. Internat., 1999—.

ARMSTRONG-JONES, EARL ANTONY (ANTONY CHARLES ROBERT ARMSTRONG-JONES, EARL OF SNOWDON), photographer; b. London, Mar. 7, 1930; s. Ronald Owen Lloyd Armstrong-Jones and Anne, Countess of Rosse; m. Princess Margaret, 1960 (div. 1978); 2 children; m. Lucy Lindsay-Hogg, 1979; 1 child. Ed., Eton Coll., Jesus Coll., Cambridge, Eng.; D (hon.), Bradford U., 1989; LLD (hon.), Bath. U., 1989; DLitt (hon.), U. Portsmouth, 1993. Cons. Coun. Indsl. Design, 1962-87; provost Royal Coll. Art, 1996—; editl. adviser Design mag.; artistic adviser The Sunday Times, Sunday Times Publs. Ltd., London, 1962-90, The Telegraph Mag., 1990-95, Brighton-Bradford-Bath Exhbn., 1989; constable Caernarvan Castle, 1963—; mem. Civic Trust for Wales, Contemporary Art Soc. for Wales, Welsh Theatre Co.; v.p. Univ. Bristol Photographic Soc.; v.p. Price on Wales adv. group on disability. Author: London, 1958, Assignments, 1972, Inchcape Review, 1977, Pride of the Shires, 1979, Personal View, 1979, Tasmania Essay, 1981, Sittings, 1983, Stills, 1987; (with S. Sitwell) Malta, 1958, (with John Russel and Bryan Robertson) Private View, 1965, (with Derek Hart) A View of Venice, 1972, Israel: A First View, 1986, (with Lord Tony Pandy) My Wales, 1986, (with A. Ferguson and T. Mowl) The Sack of Bath, 1973, Serependity, 1989, Public Appearances, 1991, Wild Flowers, 1995, Snowdon on Stage, 1997, Wild Fruit, 1997; TV documentaries Don't Count the Candles, 1968 (2 Emmy awards), Love of a Kind, 1970, Born To Be Small, 1971, Happy Being Happy, 1973, Mary Kingsley, 1975, Burke and Wills, 1975, Peter, Tina and Steve, 1977, Snowdon on Camera, 1981; photog. exhbns. include Photocall, London, 1958, Snowdon on Stage Nat. Theatre, 1997, London Sight Unseen, 1999, Snowdon A Retrospective, 2000; photog. assignments in London, Cologne, Brussels, U.S., Can., Japan, Australia, Denmark, France, The Netherlands. Mem. council Nat. Fund for Research for the Crippled Child; founder Snowdon award Scheme for Disabled Students, 1980; pres. (Eng.) Internat. Yr. of Disabled People; chmn. Snowdon Report on Integrating the Disabled, 1981; patron Nat. Youth Theatre, Metropolitan Union of YMCA's, British Water Ski Fedn., British Theatre Mus., Welsh Nat. Rowing Club, Circle of Guide Dog Owners, Snowdon Council; designed Snowdon Aviary, London Zoo, 1965, Chairmobile, 1972, (with Jeremy Fry) The Squirrel, 1989. Decorated 1st Earl, UK, 1961; recipient Cert. of Merit, Art Dirs. Club of N.Y., 1969, Soc. of Publication Designers, 1970, Wilson Hicks Cert. of Merit for Photocommunication, 1971; Soc. of Publication Designers' Award of Excellence, 1973; Design and Arts Dirs. award, 1978; Royal Photographic Soc. Hood award, 1979; Silver Progress medal RPS, 1985. Fellow Inst. British Photographers, Soc. Indsl. Artists and Designers, Royal Coll. Art (sr.), Inst. Brit. Photographers (hon.), Royal Photographic Soc., Royal Soc. Arts, Manchester Coll. Art and Design; mem. Faculty Royal Designers for Industry, Council Royal Court Theatre, North Wales Soc. Architects (hon.), South Wales Inst. Architects (hon.). Home: 22 Launceston Pl, London W8 5RL, England

ARMSTRONG-LAW, MARGARET, school administrator; b. Fargo, N.D., Jan. 21, 1931; d. Theron L. and Besse Ross Armstrong; m. Robert Harold Law, Sept. 6, 1952 (div. Oct. 1964); children: William Robert, Anne Elizabeth Law Buckingham, Amy Catherine Law Burman. BS in English, N.D. State U., 1952, MS Secondary Sch. Adminstrn., 1974; postgrad., UCLA, Moorhead State U., 1984, Mich. State U., 1985; Cert., Harvard Prin.'s Sch., London, 1986. Cert. tchr., ednl. adminstr.; speaker in field. Tchr. English Kamehameha Schs., Honolulu, 1967-68; tchr. English North High Sch., Fargo, N.D., 1968-74, asst. prin., 1974-78; secondary head Taipei Am. Sch., Taiwan, 1978-87, Vienna Internat. Sch., Austria, 1987-90; dir. Internat. Sch. Amsterdam, The Netherlands, 1990-97; internat. ednl. cons., 1998—; bd. dirs. European Coun. Internat. Schs., London, 1991-96, chair bd. dirs., 1994-96, prof. devel. com.; mem. No. European Coun. Internat. Schs., head coun., 1991-97. Author: (booklet, film) Future: The Quality of Life, 1975; contbr. articles to profl. jours. Mem. adv. bd. Coll. Arts, Humanities and Social Scis. N.D. State U., 1998—; chmn. Bd. Christian Edn. Plymouth Congl. Ch., Fargo, 1998-99, mem. coun., 1998-99, mem., vice chair women's fellowship bd., 1999; active World Peace Com. in The Netherlands, 1997-98; pres. Fargo-Moorhead Opera Bd., 1999—. Recipient Bd. Dirs. award for Extraordinary Svcs. European Coun. Internat. Schs., Promotion of Internat. Edn. award, 1996; named hon. mem. for disting. svcs., European Coun. Internat. Schs., 1997; scholarship named in her honor by bd. govs. Internat. Sch. Amsterdam, 1997—. Mem. Assn. Advancement of Internat. Edn., Am. Assn. Sch. Adminstrs., Am. Women's Club/Amsterdam, Am. C. of C., Rotary (bd. dirs. 1993-94, program chair 1993-94, v.p. 1994-96, pres. 1995-96/Amsterdam), World Future Soc., World Peace Com. (The Hague, Netherlands), De Amsterdamschekring Club, Phi Kappa Phi. Democrat. Congregational. Avocations: Chinese brush painting, music listening, reading, tennis, interior decorating.

ARNALA, ILKKA OLAVI, orthopaedic surgeon; b. Helsinki, Finland, Apr. 7, 1952; s. Kauko Olavi and Irma Annikki (Kaatonen) A.; m. Merja Anneli Paukkonen, July 31, 1976; children: Tuomas, Meri. MD, U. Kuopio, Finland, 1977, PhD, 1983, specialist in surgery, 1988, specialist in orthopaedic surgery, 1995. Gen. practitioner Suolahti, Suonenjoki, 1977-83; resident in surgery U. Kuopio, 1983-88; postdoctoral fellow U. Ky., Lexington, 1985-86, 91-92; asst. prof. U. Kuopio, 1988-93; sr. cons. in surgery Kuopio U. Hosp., 1993-96; head of dept. surgery Hyvinkaa (Finland) Hosp., 1996-99; head dept. orthop. surgery Hameenlinna (Finland) Ctrl. Hosp., 2000—; cons. Mehiläinen Hosp., Helsinki, 1996—. Editor: Annales Chirurgiae et Gynecologiae, 1988. Mem. Finnish Bone Soc. (founder mem., v.p. 1995-97), Finnish Osteoporosis Soc. (founder mem.), Am. Soc. Bone and Mineral Rsch., North Savo Med. Soc. (pres. 1995-97), Old Tablers Suomi Finland. Avocations: traveling, skiing, golf. Home: Kauksaarentie 24, 13800 Katinala Finland Office: Hameenlinna Central Hosp, Sairaalankatu 1, 13530 Hameenlinna Finland

ARNAUDOV, ATANAS DIMOV, veterinarian; b. Plovdiv, Bulgaria, Nov. 2, 1961; s. Dimo Janev and Dora (Argirova) Rogochlieva A.; m. Krassimira Kuneva Stoeva, Sept. 10, 1986; 1 child, Teodora Atanassova. MS, Higher Inst. Zootech. Vet., Stara, Zagora, 1986; PhD, Agrl. Acad., Sofia, 1998. Vet. State Vet. Svc., Tchernozem, Bulgaria, 1986-87; rsch. assoc. Regional Vet. Rsch. Inst., Plovdiv, Bulgaria, 1988—. Author: Proceedings of 10th European Symposium on Waterfowl, 1995; co-editor: 60 Years Regional Veterinary Research Institute Plovdiv, 1996; contbr. articles to profl. jours. Sgt. Ministry of Def., 1979-81. Mem. Union Scientists in Bulgaria, Internat. Transfer Factor Soc. Avocations: soccer fan, jazz, evergreen music, history, postcard collecting, swimming. Home: PR Slavejkov 8, 4000 Plovdiv Bulgaria Office: Regional Vet Rsch Inst, Nezavissimost Boul 111, 4006 Plovdiv Bulgaria

ARNAULT, BERNARD JEAN, trade company executive; b. Roubaix, France, Mar. 5, 1949; s. Jean and Marie Jo (Savinel) A.; children: Delphine, Antoine, Alexandre, Frederic, Jean. Diploma, Ecole Poly. Paris, 1971. With Ferret Savinel S.A., Roubaix, 1972—, gen. mgr., 1976—, pres., 1983—; CEO LVMH (Louis Vuitton Moet Hennessy), Paris; pres. Financière Agache, 1984, Christian Dior, 1984; chmn., CEO LVMH Moet Hennessey Louis Vuitton, 1989—; pres. LVMH Luxury Goods Group, 1989—, chair, 1992—; pres. bd. dirs. Montaigne, 1997—. Decorated Chevalier Order Nat. Merit, Chevalier de la Legion d'Honneur. Mem. Polo Interallie Club. Avocations: tennis, piano. Office: LVMH Moet Hennessy Louis Vuitton, 30 Ave Hoche, F-75008 Paris France

ARNBJÖRNSSON, EINAR ÓLAFUR, pediatric surgeon; b. Reykjavik, Iceland, Aug. 27, 1950; s. Arnbjörn Olafsson and Fjõla Einarsdõttir; m. Runa Kerstin Jonasson, Aug. 16, 1980; children: Sven Arnbjörn Einarsson, Einar Mikael Einarsson. MD, U. Iceland, Reykjavik, 1975, grad. cert., 1975; PhD, U. Lund, Sweden, 1983. Intern U. Hosp., Reykjavik, 1975-76; sr. registrar Gen. Hosp., Karlskrona, Sweden, 1976-77; resident U. Hosp., Lund, 1977-80, sr. registrar, 1980-81, cons., 1981—; assoc. prof. U. Lund, 1985. Home: Drevkarlsgränden 15, S-22652 Lund Sweden Office: Univ Hosp, S-22185 Lund Sweden

ARNDT, DIANNE JOY, artist, photographer; b. Springfield, Mass., Dec. 20, 1939; d. Samuel Vincent and Carrie Lillian Annino; m. Joseph Vincent Bower, June 16, 1979 (dec.); 1 child by previous marriage, Christabelle Nita Arndt. Student, Art Students League, 1965-71; BFA with honors in Painting, Pratt Inst., 1974; postgrad., Columbia U., 1979-86; MFA, Hunter Coll., 1981. Photojournalist; photo cons. to mags. and bus., N.Y.C., 1978—; artist, filmmaker, 1962—. One-woman shows include Modernage, N.Y., 1992, 96, 99-2000, others; group show sinclude Islip Art Mus., L.I., N.Y., 1999, White Walls Conceptual Art Jour., Chgo., 2000, numerous others; exhbns. include Am. Cultural Ctr., U.S., New Delhi and Bombay, 1987, Bathurst Arms Installation, Eng., 1987, Camden Arts, London, 1987, Nat. Inst. Archtl. Edn., 1988, Phillip Morris Traveling Photo Exhibit, 1988, Centennial Libr. Gallery, Isca Graphics, Edmonton, Alta., Can., 1988, Nat. Inst. Archtl. Edn., 1988, N.Y. Sci. & Tech. Gallery, N.Y., USSR, 1989, Mercer Gallery, 1989, Circolo Pickwick, Alessandria, Italy, 1989, Balt. Mus. Industry, 1992, Aaron Davis Hall, 1992, N.Y. City Coll., Alijira Gallery, Newark, 1994, UN, 1994, Phila. Art Alliance, Phila., 1995, Columbia U., 1995, Severoceske Mus., Liberec, Bohemia, 1996, Naproskovo Mus., Prague,

1996, Modern Age, N.Y.C., 1996, Lever House, N.Y.C., 1996, St. Marks/ Bowery, N.Y.C., 1997, Eighth Floor Gallery, N.Y.C., 1997, Velan Gallery, Torino, Italy, 1998, Islip Art Mus., 1998, 99, Bound for Glory, N.Y., 1999-2000, In Frame, Chgo., 2000; represented in permanent collections Archives Can. Postal Mus., Ottawa, Jean Brown Archives, Mass., Franklin Furnace, N.Y., Nat. Inst. Design and Lalit Kala Akademi, Ne WDelhi, Printed Masser, N.Y., Tate Gallery, London; films include Mullenium, N.Y., 1985, A.I.R., N.Y., 1978, Women's Interart Ctr., N.Y., 1976, Artists Space, N.Y., 1975. Mem. Am. Soc. Media Photographers, Am. Soc. Picture Profls., Artists Talk on Art (bd. dirs.), Profl. Women Photographers, Working Press Nation.

ARNDT, HEINZ WOLFGANG, economics educator; b. Breslau, Germany, Feb. 26, 1915; s. Fritz Georg and Julia (Heimann) A.; m. Ruth Strohsahl, July 12, 1941; children: Christopher, Nicholas, Bettina. BA, Oxford U., 1936, BLitt, 1938, MA, 1940. Asst. lectr. U. Manchester, Eng., 1943-46; sr. lectr. U. Sydney, Australia, 1946-50; prof. econs. Australian Nat. U., Canberra, 1951-80, prof. emeritus, vis. fellow, 1981—; vis. prof. U. S.C., 1954, Indian Statis. Inst., Indian Planning Commn., 1958-59, rsch. div. UN Econ. Commn. for Europe, Geneva, 1960-61; cons. UN Conf. on Trade and Devel., Geneva, 1966, 67; field work, Indonesia, 1964-83; cons. UNIDO, 1983, 84, 85, Asian Devel. Bank, 1984-90. Author: The Economic Lessons of the Nineteen-Thirties, 1944, rev. edit., 1993, The Australian Trading Banks, 1957, 5th edit., 1977, A Small Rich Industrial Country: Studies in Australian Development, Trade and Aid, 1968, The Rise and Fall of Economic Growth: A Study in Contemporary Thought, 1978, 1984, The Indonesian Economy--Collected Papers, 1983, A Course Through Life: Memoirs of an Australian Economist, 1985, Asian Diaries, 1987, Economic Development: The History of an Idea, 1987, (in Indonesian) Indonesia's Economic Development: As Seen by a Neighbour, 1991, Fifty Years of Development Studies, 1993, Essays in International Economics, 1944-94, 1996, Essays in Domestic Macroeconomics 1949-1999, 2000, Essays in Biography: Australian Economists, 2000; mem. editorial bd. Econ. Record, 1955-75, Internat. Devel. Rev., 1970-78, Quadrant, 1977-80; editor Bull. Indonesian Econ. Studies, 1965-82, Asian Pacific Econ. Lit., 1987—. External examiner in econs. Univs. Malaysia and Singapore, 1968-70, Singapore, 1976-80; mem. governing coun. UN Asian Inst. for Econ. Devel. and Planning, Bangkok, 1969-75; mem. expert group on World Employment Conf., Internat. Labour Office, 1975; mem. expert group on econ. devel. planning UN Econ. and Social Commn. for Asia and Pacific, Bangkok, 1975, 77; dep. dir. country studies div. OECD, Paris, 1972; com. Australia-Japan Rsch. Ctr., Australian Nat. U., 1972—. Mem. Econ. Soc. Australia and New Zealand (pres. 1957-59), Social Sci. Rsch. Coun. Australia (hon. sec. 1957-59), Acad. Social Scis. Australia (fellow 1959-77), Australian Assn. for Cultural Freedom (pres. 1977-86). Avocations: chess, music. Home: 14 Hopetoun Cir, Deakin, Canberra 2600, Australia Office: Australian Nat U, Canberra 0200, Australia

ARNELL, RICHARD ANTHONY SAYER, composer, conductor; b. London, Sept. 15, 1917; s. Richard Sayer Arnell and Helène Marie Scherf; m. Joan Heycock, 1992; 3 children from previous marriage. Student, Hall Sch., U. Coll. Sch., Royal Coll. Music. Music cons. BBC N.Am. Svc., 1943-46; lectr. Trinity Coll. Music, London, 1948-87, Royal Ballet Sch., 1958-59; music dir., bd. dirs. London Internat. Film Sch., 1975-89; music dir. Ram Filming Ltd., 1980-85; dir. A plus A Ltd., 1984-89; Fulbright vis. exch. lectr. Bowdoin Coll., Maine, 1967-68; prof. Hofstra U., N.Y., 1969-71. Editor: The Composer, 1961-64; compositions include (opera) Love in Transit, 1953, Moonflowers, 1958, (film scores) The Land, 1941, The Third Secret, 1963, The Visit, 1964, The Man Outside, 1966, Topsail Schooner, 1966, Bequest for a Village, 1969, Second Best, 1972, Stained Glass, 1973, Wires Over the Border, 1974, Black panther, 1977, Antagonist, 1980, Dilemma, 1981, Toulouse Lautrec, 1984, Light of the World, 1988; other works include Symphonic Portrait, Lord Byron, for Sir Thomas Beecham, 1953, Landscapes and Figures, 1956, (puppet operatta) Petrified Princess, 1959, Robert Flaherty, Impression for Radio Eireann, 1960, Musica Pacifica, 1963, Festival Flourish, 1965, Overture, Food of Love, 1968, My Ladye Greene Sleeves, 1968, (ballets) Punch and the Child, 1948, Harlequin in April, 1951, The Angels, 1962, others; also 6 symphonies, 2 violin concertos, harpsichord concerto, 2 piano concertos, 6 string quartets, 2 quintets, works for string orch., wind ensembles, brass ensembles, song cycles and electronic music. Chair Friends of London Internat. Film Sch., 1982-87, v.p., 1987—; chair jr. dept. Friends of Trinity Coll. of Music, 1986-87, v.p., 1987—. Recipient Composer of Yr. award Music Tchrs.' Assn., 1966, Merit award Tadcaster Town Coun., 1991. Mem. Composers Guild of Great Britain (chair 1974-75, 77-79, v.p. 1992—), Saxmundham Music and Arts (pres. 1996—), Tadcaster Civic Soc. Music and Arts (chair 1988-91). Avocations: cooking, travel. Address: Benhall Lodge, Benhall Suffolk 1P17 1JD, England

ARNETT, DEBRA JEAN, lawyer; b. Horton, Kans., July 15, 1956; d. Ralph E. and Margaret J. (Parry) A.; 1 child, Taylor Margaret Arnett. BSW, U. Kans., 1979, JD, 1982. Bar: Kans. 1982, U.S. Dist. Ct. Kans. 1982, U.S. Ct. Appeals (10th cir.) 1985. Atty., dir. McDonald, Tinker, Skaer, Quinn & Herrington, P.A., Wichita, Kans., 1982-91; judge pro tem State of Kans. 6th Judicial Dist., Miami County, 1993—; dir. Hartley, Nicholson, Hartley & Arnett, P.A., Paola, Kans., 1991-99; Law Offices of Debra J. Arnett, Paola, Kans., 1999—; adj. assoc. prof. law Wichita State U., 1984-90. Rsch. asst. (book) Jurisdiction in Civil Actions, 1983. Vol., bd. dirs. Christmas in Oct., Miami County, Kans., sec. 1992—; bd. dirs., sec. Paola Free Libr. Found., 1992—, Lakemary Ctr., 1999—. Recipient Justice Lloyd Kagey Leadership award U. Kans. Sch. Law, 1982, Robert C. Foulston & George Siefkin prize for excellence in appellate advocacy, 1981; mem. Nat. Moot Ct. Team, U. Kans. Sch. Law, 1981; invited Hague (The Netherlands) Treaty Roundtable on Internat. Adoptions, U.S. State Dept., 1993. Mem. ABA (litigation, family law, and ins. practice sects.), Nat. Assn. Women Bus. Owners (sec. Wichita chpt. 1988-89, v.p. 1989-90, pres. 1990-91), Def. Rsch. Inst., Kans. Bar Assn. (sec. litigation sect. 1991-92, pres.-elect 1992-93, pres. 1993-94), Kans. Assn. Def. Counsel (bd. govs. 1983—), Miami County Bar Assn. (treas. 1995—), Wichita Bar Assn., Jenny Mitchell Kellogg Circle (bd. dirs. 1995—), Rotary (Paola chpt.). Office: 1 W Shawnee PO Box 211 Paola KS 66071-0211

ARNETT, FOSTER DEAVER, lawyer; b. Knoxville, Tenn., Nov. 28, 1920; s. Foster Greenwood and Edna (Deaver) A.; m. Jean Medlin, Mar. 3, 1951; children: Melissa Lee Arnett Campbell, Foster Jr. BA, U. Tenn., 1946; LLB, U. Va., 1948. Bar: Va. 1948, Tenn. 1948, U.S. Dist. Ct. (ea. dist.) Tenn. 1949, U.S. Ct. Appeals (6th cir.) 1954, U.S. Supreme Ct. 1958, U.S. Dist. Ct. (ea. dist.) Ky. 1978, U.S. Dist. Ct. (mid. dist.) Tenn. 1983, U.S. Dist. Ct. (ea. and we. dists.) Va. 1990. In practice Knoxville, 1948—; ptnr. Arnett, Draper & Hagood (and predecessors), 1954—; mem. Nat. Conf. Commrs. on Uniform State Laws, 1980-83; life mem. U.S. Ct. Appeals (6th cir.) Jud. Conf. Contbr. articles to profl. jours. Pres. Knox Children's Found., 1959-61, 75-76, East Tenn. Hearing and Speech Ctr., 1963-65, Knoxville Teen Ctr., 1969-71, Knoxville News-Sentinel Charities Inc., 1985—; v.p. Ft. Loudon Assn., 1972-75; del. Rep. Nat. Conv., 1964; bd. dirs., exec. com. Tenn. Mil. Inst., 1973-75; formerly active ARC, Am. Cancer Soc., United Fund. With AUS, 1942-46, PTO; to lt. col. USAR, ret. Decorated Silver Star, Bronze Star, Purple Heart. Fellow Am. Coll. Trial Lawyers (former chair legal ethics com., mem. atty.-client relationship com., mem. other coms.), Internat. Acad. Trial Lawyers (trustee Acad. Found. 1984-91, dean 1988-89, pres. 1992-93, mem. Found. Bd. 1983-92), Internat. Soc. Barristers, Am. Bar Found. (life), Tenn. Bar Found. (charter); mem. ATLA, ABA (mem. standing coms. on unauthorized practice of law and assn. comm., aviation and space law, state cert. legal specialist), Am. Bd. Trial Advs. (adv., charter, 1st pres. Tenn. chpt. 1985-86), Am. Inns of Ct. (charter, master of the bench emeritus Hamilton S. Burnett chpt.), Southea. Legal Found. (legal adv. bd.), Tenn. Bar Assn. (pres. 1968-69), Knoxville Bar Assn. (pres. 1959-60, Govs. award 1989), Internat. Assn. Def. Counsel (sec.-treas. 1981-84), S.E. Def. Counsel Assn. (v.p. 1966), Am. Acad. Hosp. Attys. of Am. Hosp. Assn. (charter), Tenn. Hosp. Assn., Am. Soc. Law, Medicine and Ethics, Fedn. Ins. and Corp. Counsel, Def. Rsch. Inst. (charter), U.S. Supreme Ct. Hist. Soc. (founder), Tenn. Supreme Ct. Hist. Soc. (founder), Federalist Soc., SAR, Scribes, U. Tenn. Nat. Alumni Assn. (pres. 1961-62, chmn. nat. ann. giving program 1961-63), Scabbard and Blade, Scarrabbean, Torchbearer, U. Va. Law Sch. Alumni Assn. (pres. 1991-93, nat. chmn. appeals Law Sch. Found. 1986-88), Raven Soc., 511th Parachute Infantry Regiment Assn., Civitan Club, Farmington Country Club, Charlottesville, Va.), Cherokee Country Club, LeConte Club, Univ. Club (hon.), Men's Cotillion (bd. dirs. 1960-61, 63-64, 66-68, trustee 1962—), Appalachian Club (pres. 1974-76), 511th Parachute Infantry Regiment Assn., Phi Gamma Delta, Phi Delta Phi (hon.), Omicron Delta Kappa (hon.). Presbyterian. Home: 4636 Alta Vista Way Knoxville TN 37919-7605 Office: Arnett Draper & Hagood Ste 2300 First Tennessee Plaza Knoxville TN 37929-2300

ARNETT, PETER, journalist; b. New Zealand, 1934; div.; 2 children. With Assoc. Press in various capacities AP, 1960—; war corr. Vietnam, 1962-75; White Horse corr. AP, 1970's; global corr. CNN (Cable News Network), Atlanta, Ga., 1981-99; eyewitness corr. Persian Gulf War. CNN, 1991; chief fgn. corr. ForeignTV.com, N.Y.C., 1998—; Has covered 17 wars for various news orgn. Author: Live From the Battlefield: 35 Years Inside the World's War Zones, 1994. Avocations: collecting art, books, gourmet cooking. Office: ForeignTV.com Inc 120 5th Ave New York NY 10011 also: ForeignTV.com Inc 162 5th Ave Ste 105A New York NY 10010-5902*

ARNIS, EFSTATHIOS CONSTANTINOS, mechanical engineer; b. Thermon, Hellas, Apr. 14, 1931; s. Constantinos Efstathios and Joanna Andrew (Pachnis) A. Student, U. Athens, Hellas, 1950-51, 61-70; cert. in mech. engrng. design, Technol. Sch. Benos-Palmer, Athens, 1972. Pvt. practice designer in mech. engrng., 1952-94, ret., 1994; specialist in sci. field of energization of isolated phys. sys. Contbr. articles to profl. jours.; patentee in field of centrifugal space navigation. Mem. AIAA, AAAS, Hellenic Astron. Soc. (expert sec. 1992—), Planetary Soc., N.Y. Acad. Scis. (theoretician physicist). Avocations: astronomical obersvations, UFO investigator, Alpine climbing. Home: 10 Gortynos St, Hellas 112 54 Athens Greece Office: Hellenic Astron Soc, 14 Voulis St, Hellas 105 63 Athens Greece

ARNKRAUT, JOE, legal administrator, writer; b. Newark, Jan. 3, 1960; s. Sam F. and Jill E. Arnkraut. BS in Fin., UCLA, 1990. Legal adminstr. Santa Monica, Calif., 1990—, writing cons., trainer, 1990—. Demorat. Roman Catholic. Avocations: freelance writing, skydiving, spelunking, cross-country and super marathon races. Fax: 310-559-6617. Office: 2272 Colorado Blvd # 1228 Los Angeles CA 90041-1143

ARNOLD, CRAIG ANTHONY (TONY ARNOLD), law educator; b. Montreal, Que., Can., May 22, 1965; came to U.S., 1968; s. Lloyd Edison and Shirley Ann (Gossett) A.; m. Donna Jean Higdon, June 17, 2000. BA with highest distinction, U. Kans., 1987; JD with distinction, Stanford U., 1990. Bar: Mo. 1990, U.S. Ct. Appeals (10th cir.) 1990, Tex. 1992, U.S. Dist. Ct. (we. dist.) Tex. 1992, U.S. Ct. Appeals (5th cir.) 1993. Law clk. to James K. Logan, U.S. Ct. Appeals for 10th Cir., Olathe, Kans., 1990-91; assoc. Matthews & Branscomb, P.C., San Antonio, 1991-95; vis. prof. U. P.R. Sch. of Law, 1995; tchg. fellow Stanford Law Sch., 1995-96; asst. prof. Law Sch. Chapman U., 1996-99, assoc. prof., 1999—; dir. Ctr. for Land Resources, 1999—; adj. faculty Trinity U., 1995. Exec. editor Stanford Law and Policy Rev., 1988-90; contbr. articles to legal jours. Organizer, chmn. Jefferson Bicentennial Meeting on Constn., Lawrence, Kans., 1987; mem. Willie Velasquez Book Fund Com., San Antonio, 1992; ordained deacon First Presbyn. Ch., San Antonio, 1994-95, worship leader, 1994-95, strategic planning com., 1994-95, leader classes and Bible studies, 1992-95; co-leader, participant Mission trips to Mex. and Kenya; bd. dirs. Good Samaritan Ctr.; bd. dirs. Fedn. Ecumènica Fe y Accion, San Antonio, 1992-95, Lawyers Com. for Civil Rights Immigrant and Refugee Rights Project, 1993-95; adv. bd. careers in law program North Orange County Regional Occupl. Program, 1998-99; adv. bd. Raymond Nichols League of Former Student Leaders, U. Kans., 1999—; commr. City of Anaheim Planning Commn., 1999—; worship com. Trinity United Presbyn. Ch., 1999—. Recipient Time Mag. Achievement award; Harry S Truman scholar Truman Scholarship Found., 1985; Rosemary Ginn fellow Mortar Board Nat. Found., 1987; Hagman conf. scholar UCLA Land Use Law and Planning Conf. Mem. ABA, State Bar Tex. (Pro Bono Coll.), Phi Beta Kappa. Avocations: hiking, running, horseback riding.

ARNOLD, DESMOND CLAUDE, financial executive; b. Eshowe, South Africa, Mar. 18, 1940; s. Edward Reginald and Giovanna Juliette (Charlotte) A.; m. Christine Julia Bailey, July 3, 1965. Grad. H.S. Fin. mgr. Barlow's Tractor Divsn., 1973-77; asst. group acctg. mgr. Barlow Rand Ltd., 1978-80, group fin. and acctg. mgr., 1980-84; fin. dir. bldg. materials steel & paint fin. dir. Barlow Rand Industries, 1984-89; fin. dir. Rand Mines Ltd., 1989-91, Barlow Rand Industries Ltd., 1992-93, Barlow Ltd., Sandton, South Africa, 1993—; mem. Acctg. Practices Bd., 1976—. Mem. Internat. Fedn. Accts. (mgmt. acctg. com. 1992-95), Pub. Accts. and Auditors Bd. (exec. com. 1989-91), East, Ctrl. and So. African Fedn. Accts. (pres. 1997-98), South African Inst. Chartered Accts. (hon. life mem., past pres.), Tvl. Soc. Chartered Accts. (past pres.), Royal Johannesburg Golf Club (past pres.), Johanesburg Country Club. Avocations: golf, squash, tennis, fishing. Office: Barlow Ltd, PO Box 782248, Sandton 2146, South Africa*

ARNOLD, HARRY JOHN PHILIP, science administrator, writer, astronomy photographer; b. Oct. 3, 1932; s. George and Dorothy (Prior) A.; m. Audrey Cox, Apr. 1957; 1 child, Helen. BA, Wadham Coll., Oxford, Eng., 1954, MA, 1972; diploma, Comm., Advt. and Mktg. Ednl. Found., 1974. Feature writer, then fgn. news editor and Soviet affairs corr. The Fin. Times, London, 1956-60; editor FBI Review, 1960-62, Pulse, 1963-65; exec. sec. Gen. Practitioners' Assn., 1963-65; pub. rels. adviser, asst. to mng. dir. Kodak Ltd., London, 1966-74; mng. dir. Space Frontiers Ltd., 1974-2000; tech. cons., photo libr., lectr. in field of space flight, astronomy and photography. Author: Aid for Developing Countries, 1961, Aid for Development, 1966, Photographer of the World, 1969, Another World (The Photography of H.G. Ponting), 1975, Photographic Pioneer and Man of Science (Biography William Henry Fox Talbot), 1977 (Disting. Achievement award Photog. Hist. Soc. N.Y. 1978), Images from Space, 1979, Night Sky Photography, 1988, Man in Space: An Illustrated History of Spaceflight, 1993, Astrophotography: An Introduction, 1995, (with Doherty and Moore) The Photographic Star Atlas, 1997, Eclipse '99, 1999; writer BBC TV documentary of life and work of Ponting, 1979; contbr. articles to profl. jours. With Army Intelligence Corps, 1954-56. Fellow Royal Astron. Soc., Brit. Interplanetary Soc., Remote Sensing Soc.; mem. Mensa, Inst. Advanced Motorists. Home and Office: Sol Invictus, 30 Fifth Ave, Havant Hampshire PO9 2PL, England

ARNOLD, HEINZ, academic administrator; b. Bad Endbach, Germany, Mar. 5, 1953; s. Fritz and Ilse (Rentzsch) A.; m. Karin Grebe, Oct. 29, 1992; 1 child, Konstantin. Grad., U. Marburg, Germany, 1979; D Social Scis., U. Kassel, Germany, 1988. Documentist Info-Ctr. Social Scis., Bonn, Germany, 1984-89; dir. Euro-Bus. Coll., Trier, Germany, 1990-99, European Vocat. Inst., Bitburg, Germany, 1999—; lectr. U. Kassel, 1990-99, U. Trier, 1990-99. Author: Sociological theories in Social Geography, 1988, Regional Disparities in Europe, 1995, Societies—Spaces—Geographies, 1997; contbr. articles to profl. publs. Mem. Gewerkschaft Erziehung und Wissenschaft, Trier-Forum.

ARNOLD, HEINZ LUDWIG, editor; b. Essen, Nordrhein, Germany, Mar. 29, 1940; s. Heinz and Elisabeth (Weinreich) A.; m. Christiane Freudenstein, Dec. 6, 1985; 1 child, Hannah. Prof. Georg-August U., Göttingen, 1995. Editor Text & Kritik, 1963——, Kritisches Lexikon zur Deutschsprachingen Gegenwartsliteratur, 1978—, Kritisches Lexikon zur Fremdsprachigen Gegenwartsliteratur, 1983—, Die deutsche Literatur seit 1945, 1995-2000. Mem. P.E.N.-Ctr. Germany, Deutsche Akademie Sprache und Rertung, Amnesty Internat. Office: Text Kritik, Tuckermannweg 10, D-37085 Göttingen Germany

ARNOLD, J(AMES) BARTO, III, marine archaeologist; b. San Antonio, Jan. 9, 1950; s. J. Barto Jr. and Wilnora (Barton) A.; m. Aurora Irene Foreman, Aug. 28, 1970; children: Kathryn, Julia, Jessica. BA cum laude, U. Tex., 1971, MA, 1973. Rsch. asst. Tex. Archeol. Rsch. Lab. U. Tex., Austin, 1970-72; asst. state marine archaeologist Tex. Antiquities Com., Austin, 1972-75; state marine archaeologist Tex. Hist. Com., Austin, 1975-97; dir. Tex. ops. Inst. of Nautical Archaeology, Tex. A&M U., College Station, 1997—; cons. NOAA, 1977-91, Nat. Trust Hist. Preservation, Washington, 1979-90, Congl. Office Tech. Assessment, Washington, 1986; mem. Md. Gov.'s Adv. Com. on Marine Archaeology, Annapolis, 1987-90; mem. history area com. nat. park sys. adv. bd. U.S. Dept. Interior, 1994-95; dir. La Salle Shipwreck Project, 1995-96, Confederate Blockade-Runner Denbigh Shipwreck Project, 1997—. Co-author: Nautical Archaeology of Padre Island, 1978, Documentary Sources for the Wreck of the New Spain Fleet of 1554, 1979 (Presidio La Bahaia 1979), others; Plenum series editor Underwater Archaeology, 1995—; contbr. articles to profl. jours. Recipient Achievement award for Hist. Preservation Dept. Interior, 1980. Mem. Soc. Profl. Archaeologists (cert.; sec.-treas. 1987-89, Spl. Achievement award 1990), Soc. Hist. Archaeology (pres. 1993), Tex. Archeol. Soc., Archaeol. Inst. Am., Explorers Club, Phi Beta Kappa. Methodist. Avocations: stamp collecting, science fiction. E-mail: barnold@tamu.edu. Office: Tex A&M U Inst Nautical Archaeology PO Drawer HG College Station TX 77841-5137

ARNOLD, JAY, retired engineering executive, educator; b. Balt., Jan. 1, 1936; s. Otto Joseph and Margaret (Flannery) A.; m. Harriet Mary Metzbower, July 4, 1959; children: Kelly Marie Arnold Wood, Philip Driscoll Arnold, Michael Flannery Arnold. BS, Loyola Coll., Balt., 1965; MBA, Loyola Coll., Potomac, Md., 1977; postgrad., George Washington U., 1980-81, Berlitz Inst., Washington, 1987-90, U. So. Fla., 1994-95. With real times sys. IBM, Kingston, N.Y., 1962-65, Washington, 1962-65; software and systems engrng. positions including mgt. NASA's Manned Space Program IBM, Houston, 1965-68; with FAA's Air Traffic Control, Atlantic City, 1968-73, FSD Advanced Tech., Bethesda, Md., 1973-78; vis. IBM prof. Morgan State U., Balt., 1978-79; planner of automation strategy Fed. Systems div. IBM, Gaithersburg, Md., 1979-81; sr. mgr. systems design depts. USAF Data Systems Modernization Fed. Systems div. IBM, Gaithersburg, 1981-83, sr. mgr. systems design depts. FAA Advanced Automation System, 1983-87; dir. network mgmt. and control Comsat Systems div. Communications Satellite Corp., Clarksburg, Md., 1987-88, sr. dir. Deutsche Fermelde Satellite program, 1988-90, sr. dir. MOSCOM program, 1990, sr. dir. engrng. advanced systems, 1991-94; program dir. computer tech. St. Petersburg (Fla.) Jr. Coll., 1993-97; speaker, instr. and lectr. in field; tchr., entrepreneurial acad. Greater St. Petersburg C. of C., 1996-98. Caregiver Frederick County Hospice, 1984-87; club leader Frederick County 4-H, 1975-80; pres./v.p. Frederick County Sheep Breeders Assn., 1983-84; chmn. bd. govs. Am. Bouviers Des Flandres Club, 1981-82; mem. St. Peter's Ch. Parish Coun., 1991-92; active Suncoast Tiger Bay, 1994-98, Leadership St. Pete Alumni, 1995—, Leadership Tampa Bay Alumni, 1997—. With USAF, 1958-62, Korea, 1960-61. Recipient Parenting awards Future Farmers of Am., 1978-80, Award for Advancement of Human Rights UN Assn., 1984; named Alumni of Yr. Mt. St. Joseph Coll. H.S., 1989. Mem. Am. Assn. for Retired Persons, St. Petersburg Yacht Club, Vinoy Golf Club, St. Petersburg Sail and Power Squadron, Kiwanis Club St. Petersburg (Outstanding Chmn. 1997-98), St. Petersburg Cmty. Alliance. Roman Catholic. Avocations: farming, golf, personal computing, boating. Home: 62 Glengary Dr Delaware OH 43015-7610

ARNOLD, JOHN EDWARD, marketing executive, consultant, financial planner; b. Champaign, Ill., June 26, 1936; s. Earnest Stanford and Vaneta (Ratcliff) A.; m. Teresa Ann Burris, Apr. 11, 1981; children: Mark John, Robert A. BA in Psychology, U. Tulsa, 1960; MBA, U. Ill., 1963; MSCE, Park Coll., 1992; PhD, Pacific Western U., 2000. Asst. prof., asst. dean students Park Coll., Parkville, Mo., 1963-66; sales rep. S.R.A. (IBM), Chgo., 1966-71; dir. mktg. Evans Learning Co., Denver, 1971-73; mgr. mktg. devel. DeNoier Geppert, Chgo., 1973-76; v.p. mktg. Edn. Cons., Inc., Ballwin, Mo., 1976—; asst. dean students Park Coll., 1963-66. Vice pres. Young Reps., Kansas City, Mo., 1963. Mem. Phi Beta Kappa, Psi Chi (pres. 1959). Home: 6701 Christopher Dr Saint Louis MO 63129-4910

ARNOLD, KEITH, banker. Gov. Ctrl. Bank Belize. Office: Ctrl Bank Belize, POB 852, Belize City Belize*

ARNOLD, LEONARD JOSEPH, construction executive; b. San Diego, Mar. 17, 1947; s. William W. and Thelma C. (Cook) A.; m. Judy Lynn Keeton, Aug. 30, 1969; children: Alyssa Noelle, Lorienne Eve. BS in Constrn. Mgmt., Colo. State U., 1970. V.p. G. E. Johnson Constrn., Colorado Springs, Colo., 1970-76; pres. Wyoming Johnson Inc., Casper, 1976-79; v.p. Hensel Phelps Constrn. Co., Greeley, Colo., 1979-88, Phelps, Inc., 1988-89, Hensel Phelps Constrn. Co., Greeley, Colo., 1990-94; pres. Rainbow Lake Investments, 1994—. Chmn. Weld County Econ. Devel., Greeley, 1986-88. Mem. Urban Land Inst., Associated Gen. Contractors Am., Soc. Am. Mil. Engrs., U.S. Space Found., Colo. Assn. Sch. Bds., Sigma Lambda Chi. Republican. Avocations: fishing, classic car collection, auto racing, outdoors activities. Home: 527 Hickory Dr Lyons CO 80540-8031 Office: Rainbow Lake Investments LLC 1600 Wapiti Cir Unit 24 Estes Park CO 80517-5410

ARNOLD, MITYLENE B., special education educator, consultant; b. Waco, Tex., Feb. 13, 1946; d. John Edward and Frances (Judd) Boykin; children: Susan, Edward. BS, Baylor U., 1969; MEd, U. Ga., 1981, EdD, 1984. Cert. tchr., Tex., Ga., Miss. Classroom tchr. Austin (Tex.) Ind. Sch. Dist., 1969-75, Morgan County Schs., Madison, Ga., 1976-81; project dir. univ. affiliated program U. Ga., Athens, 1984-89; asst. prof. spl. edn. U. Miss., Oxford, 1989-95, assoc. prof., 1995—; coord. Miss. Interagy. Coordinating Coun. for Infants and Toddlers; pres. Found. for Disability Resources, Inc., Oxford, 1993—; bd. dirs. Lift, Inc. Author: Supported Employment for Persons with Developmental Disabilities, 1993; mem. editl. bds. Autism and Other Devel. Disabilities, Career Devel. for Exceptional Individuals. Mem. Coun. for Exceptional Children, Assn. for Supported Employment, Assn. for Mental Retardation. Republican. Episcopalian. Avocations: reading, travel. Home: 708 Park Dr Oxford MS 38655-2417 Office: U Miss 139 Education University MS 38677

ARNOLD, PATRICK JULES ANTOINE, bridge company executive; b. Evrehailles, bas, Belgium, Dec. 20, 1956; s. Victor and Margherita (Blasutig) A. Rep. Sybetra SA, Belgium, 1977-81; analyst John Deere Internat. Ltd., 1981-85; adminstr. Falcon Bridge Internat. Ltd., Brussels, 1985-92; audiovisual adminstr. Initiative Media Brussels, 1992—. E-mail: parnold@initiative.be. Office: Initiative Media Brussels, Place des Maieurs 2, 1150 Brussels Belgium

ARNOLD, RINEE' STEPHEN, petroleum engineer; b. Dallas, July 22, 1951; s. Jesse Daniel and Betty Ruth (Rougeau) A.; m. Betty Lou Waggoner Arnold, July 31, 1976; children: Joshua Heath, Heather Dawn. BS in Petroleum Engrng., Hamilton U., 1992, MS in Petroleum Engrng., 1998. Supr. Otis Engrng. Corp., Lake Charles, La., 1973-79; v.p. Pressure Control Inc., Longview, Tex., 1979-81; dist. mgr. Schlumberger, Lake Charles, 1981-91; v.p. Slickline Electronics Inc., New Iberia, La., 1991-97; field svc. mgr., electronics/explosives Stric-Lan Cos. Corp., Lafayette, La., 1997-99; sr. field support engr. Micro-Smart Systems, Inc., Houston, 1999—; mem. La. State Police Explosive Adv. Coun., Baton Rouge, 1996—; instr., explosive safety course, Houston, 1996—. Contbr. articles to profl. jours. With USMC, 1970-73. Mem. Soc. Petroleum Engrs., Internat. Soc. Explosive Engrs. Avocations: martial arts, boating, flying, motorcycling. Fax: 713-433-2443. E-mail: micro-smart@yahoo.com. Home: 3581 Hwy 383 Kinder LA 70648-5004 Office: Micro Smart Systems Inc 5355 Anderson Rd Houston TX 77053-2137

ARNOLD, ROBERT WILLIAM, nonprofit corporation executive; b. Denver, May 27, 1950; s. Clyde Lawrence and Nadyne Skeen Arnold; m. Kaaren S. Anderson, June 23, 1978; 1 child, Michael Lawrence. BA, U. Colo., Boulder, 1972; MPA, U. Colo., Denver, 1987. Exec. dir. Boulder County Enterprises, 1974-88; assoc. exec. dir. Devel. Distbrs. Resource Ctr., Lakewood, Colo., 1989-00; past pres. Colo. Found. Dentistry, Denver, 1990-99; pres. Jefferson County Pvt. Industry Coun., Golden, 1989-99, Colo. Rehab. Enterprises, Denver, 1982. Mem. Nat. Assn. Pub. Adminstrn., Rotary. Avocations: gardening, golf, cooking, reading, Scouts. E-mail: barnold@ddrcc.com. Home: 1706 3d Ave Longmont CO 80501 Office: DDRC # 300 11177 W 8th Ave Ste 300 Lakewood CO 80215-5520

ARNOLD, RONALD HENRI, nonprofit organization executive, consultant; b. Houston, Aug. 8, 1937; s. John Andrew and Carrie Virginia (Henri) A.; m. Phoebe Anne Trogdon, Oct. 12, 1963 (dec. Feb. 1974); 1 child, Andrea; m. Janet Ann Parkhurst, Aug. 8, 1974; stepchildren: Andrea Wright, Rosalyn Wright. Tech. publ. Boeing Co., Seattle, 1961-71; cons. Northwoods Studio, Bellevue, Wash., 1971—; exec. v.p. Ctr. for Def. of Free Enterprise, Bellevue, 1984—; advisor Nat. Fed. Lands Conf., 1988-92. Author: James Watt and the Environment, 1981, Ecology Wars, 1987, The

Grand Prairie Years, 1987, (with Alan Gottlieb) Trashing the Economy, 1993, Politically Correct Environment, 1996, Ecoterror, 1997, Battered Communities, 1998, Undue Influence, 1999, Power to Hurt, 2000; editor: Stealing the National Parks, 1987; contbg. editor Logging Mgmt. mag., 1978-81, Western Conservation Jour., 1974-81. Recipient Editorial Achievement award Am. Bus. Press, 1981. Mem. AFTRA, Forest History Soc. Republican. Avocation: music. Home: 12605 NE 2nd St Bellevue WA 98005-3206

ARNOLD, ROSLYN MARY, educator, education consultant; b. Sydney, NSW, Australia, Jan. 25, 1945; d. John Clarence and Margaret Joan (McDonald) A.; 1 child, Louisa M. BA, U. Sydney, 1966, MA, 1977, MEd, 1984, PhD, 1987. From lectr. to sr. lectr. U. Sydney, 1974-94, assoc. prof. literacy devel., head of dept., 1995—, pro-dean, 1997; coun. mem. Loreto Normanhurst; chair contemporary English exam. com. Bd. of Studies, NSW, 1997; dir. 3d Internat. English Conf., Sydney. Author: (books) Writing Development—Magic in the Brain, 1991, Mirror the Wind, 1997; author, editor: (book) Timely Voices, 1983, The New Intelligence, 2000; contbr. articles to profl. jours. Mem. Nat. Assn. Drama in Edn. (mem. editl. bd. 1994—), Nat. Coun. Tchrs. English (mem. editl. adv. panel U.S. jour. English edn.), Australian Assn. for Rsch. in Edn. 1993—). Avocations: writing, gardening, traveling, music. Home: 5/322 Edgecliff Rd, 2025 Woollahra 2025, Australia Office: U Sydney, 2006 Sydney NSW, Australia

ARNOLD, WALTER KONRAD, physicist; b. Wangen in Allgau, Germany, Dec. 29, 1943; s. Eugen and Agathe (Prinz) A.; m. Ingeborg Maria Eberlein, Mar. 14, 1986. Diploma in physics, Tech. U., Munich, Germany, 1970, PhD, 1974. Scientific asst. Tech. U., Munich, 1972-73; rschr. Max-Planck Inst. for Solid State Physics, Stuttgart, Germany, 1973-76, 77-79; IBM vis. scientist IBM Rsch. Ctr., N.Y., 1976-77; rschr. BBC and CIC Rsch. Ctr., Dättwil, Switzerland, 1979-80; group leader Fraunhofer Inst., Saarbrücken, 1980-91, dept. head, 1991—, hon. prof., 1998—. Contbr. articles to prof. jours. Mem. IEEE, European Phys. Soc., Germany Phys. Soc., German Soc. for Non Destructive Testing, German Soc. Acoustics. Roman Catholic. Avocation: mountaineering. Office: Fraunhofer Soc, Bldg 37 University, 66041 Saarbrucken Germany

ARNOLD, WILLIAM EDWIN, health advocate, consultant; b. Charleston, S.C., Aug. 13, 1938; s. Edwin Gustaf and Sara Louise (Hitchcock) A. BA, Yale U., 1960. Pres. Dixon & Rippel, Inc., Saugerties, N.Y., 1965-70; v.p. Taj Enterprises Ltd., 1965-67, Bellern Rsch. Corp.; pres. Dixon & Rippel divsn., Saugerties, 1970-75; v.p. H & G Industries, Inc.; pres. World Brushworks, Inc., 1982-84; v.p. CFO Optimax III, Inc., N.Y.C., 1983-84; mng. dir. Brush Trading, Ltd., 1983-87; pres. Chestnut Holdings Ltd., 1985-91, Computerworx, Inc., Washington, 2000—; part-time mng. dir. Cassi Properties, 1984—; pres. Swan Holding Ltd., 1985-88. Bd. dirs. ARCS, 1991-92; chair Dutchess County AIDS Consortium, 1989-95; chmn. Dutchess County HIV Health Svcs. Planning Coun., 1995-96; bd. dirs. Multi County Cmty. Devel. Corp., 1990-96, ARCS Cmty. Educator, 1989-91; pres. Hudson AIDS Cmty. Progress, Inc., 1987-94; exec. dir. Title II Nat. AIDS Coalition, 1994-95; CEO Title II Cmty. AIDS Nat. Network, Washington, 1995—; chair working group AIDS Drug Assistance Program, Washington, 1995—; pres. Cordts Mansion, Inc., Kingston, N.Y., 1999—. 1st lt. U.S. Army, 1961-63. Mem. Res. Officers Assn., Yale Club Washington. Home: 1755 Seaton Pl NW Washington DC 20009-2625 Office: 1775 T St NW Washington DC 20009-7124

ARNOLD, WILLIAM MCCAULEY, lawyer; b. Waco, Tex., May 3, 1947; s. Watson Caulfield and Mary Rebecca (Maxwell) A.; m. Karen Axtell, May 17, 1980; children: Margaret McCauley, William Axtell. BA, Duke U., 1969; JD, U. Tex., 1972. Bar: Tex. 1973, Va. 1975, D.C. 1977, Md. 1983, U.S. Dist. Ct. (ea. dist.) Va. 1975, U.S. Ct. Appeals (4th cir.) 1977, U.S. Ct. Claims 1977, U.S. Supreme Ct. 1978. Spl. atty. U.S. Dept. Justice, Newark, 1973-75; asst. county atty. County of Fairfax, Va., 1975-78; ptnr. Cowles, Rinaldi & Arnold, Ltd., Fairfax, 1978-95; ptnr. McCandlish & Lillard, Fairfax, 1995—; instr. No. Va. Community Coll., Alexandria. Pres. Clifton Betterment Assn., Va., 1979-81; chmn. Clifton Planning Commn., 1980-85; mem. Clifton Town Council, 1985—; bd. dirs. Clifton Gentlemen's Social Club, 1981-84. Mem. ABA, Va. State Bar Assn., Fairfax County Bar Assn., Va. Trial Lawyers Assn., Am. Arbitration Assn. (arbitrator), Associated Builders and Contractors (counsel to bd. dirs.). Office: McCandlish & Lillard PC 11350 Random Hills Rd Ste 500 Fairfax VA 22030-6044

ARNOLD, WILLIAM PARSONS, JR., retired internist; b. Waterbury, Conn., May 10, 1922; s. William Parsons and Dorothy Amanda (Granniss) A.; m. Mildred Opal Beleu, Oct. 27, 1948; children: Susan Emerson Arnold Brainerd, Jane Elizabeth Arnold Pittari. BS, Yale U., 1943; MD, Columbia U., 1946. Diplomate Am. Bd. Med. Examiners. Intern St. Luke's Hosp., N.Y.C., 1946-47, resident in medicine, 1949-51, chief resident in medicine, 1951-52; pvt. practice Middlebury, Conn., 1952-89; attending physician medicine Waterbury (Conn.) Hosp., 1952-89; assoc. attending physician St. Mary's Hosp., Waterbury, 1952-89; dir. health Middlebury (Conn.) Dept. Health, 1954—; sch. physician Region 15 Elem. Schs., Middlebury, 1955-92; asst. med. examiner Conn. State M-E Office, Middlebury, 1956-84; surgeon Middlebury Vol. Fire Dept. and Middlebury Police Dept., 1964—. Capt. U.S. Army Med. Corps, 1947-49, ETO. Recipient John N. Lewis Founders award Waterbury Vis. Nurse Assn., 1988. Mem. AMA, ACP, Conn. State Med. Soc., New Haven County Med. Assn., Waterbury Med. Assn. Republican. Congregational. Avocations: western riding, rodeos. Home: 142 White Deer Rock Rd Middlebury CT 06762-1314

ARNOLD, WILLIAM THOMAS, software developer, chemist; b. N.Y.C., Oct. 6, 1948; s. Herbert S. and Miriam Arnold. BS in Chemistry, Carnegie-Mellon U., 1970; MS in Chemistry, Fla. State U., 1976; postgrad. in enology, U. Calif., Davis, 1977-78. Winemaker Smothers Winery, Santa Cruz, Calif., 1978-85; consulting enologist Stag's Leap Wine Cellars, Napa, Calif., 1985-87; winemaker, gen. mgr. Domaine Laurier Vineyard, Forestville, Calif., 1987-88; sr. chemist U.S. Treasury Dept., San Francisco, 1990-97; prin. William Arnold Consulting, Walnut Creek, Calif., 1997—, Investorspreadsheet.com, 1999—; lectr., U. Calif., Santa Cruz, 1998; instr., Fed. Law Enforcement Tng. Ctr., Glynco, Ga., 1992-93; prin. Investorspreadsheet.com, 1999—; instr. computer sci. U. Calif., Berkeley, 2000—. Author: (computer programs) Standard Curve Pro & Chemical Databases, 1997—, Technicell 80 Stock-Market Program, 1999; contbr. articles to profl. jours. Sgt., USAF, 1971-74, Washington. Recipient Gold medal for comml. cabernet sauvignon, Sonoma (Calif.) Harvest Fair, 1982, Gold medal for comml. gewurztraminer, L.A. County Fair, 1981. Mem. Assn. Ofcl. Analytical Chemists Internat. (pres. Pacific region 1997-98), Am. Soc. Enology and Viticulture (mem. tech. projects com. 1992-97). Fax: 510-938-7280. Office: W Arnold Consulting 1240 Walker Ave Apt 209 Walnut Creek CA 94596-4829

ARNOLD HUBERT, NANCY KAY, writer; b. Kalamazoo, Mich., May 9, 1951; d. Byron Lyle and Ada (Doorlag) Arnold; m. Louis Scott Hubert, May 5, 1989. BFA in Painting, Western Mich. U., 1983, postgrad., 1985-86. Writer Advanced Systems & Designs, Inc., Farmington Hills, Mich., 1987-89; pres., owner TechWrite, Kalamazoo, 1989—. Author: (poetry) Tetragonal Pyramids, 1982; exhibited in group shows, Kalamazoo, 1983, Western Mich. U., 1982, 85. Mem. AAUW, NAFE, Kalamazoo County C. of C., Humane Farming Assn. Am. People for Ethical Treatment of Animals. Libertarian. Avocations: bike riding, reading, piano, singing, cross-country skiing. Office: PO Box 481 Oshtemo MI 49077-0481

ARNOLDS, EEF JOHANNES MARIA, mycology educator, nature conservationist; b. Doorn, Utrecht, The Netherlands, Aug. 14, 1948; s. Alphonsus L.M. and Margaretha M. (Ariëns) A.; m. Birgitta M.J.T. Driessen, Feb. 2, 1995. MSc, State U., Utrecht, 1974, PhD, 1981. Rsch. asst. State U., Leiden, The Netherlands, 1974; rsch. asst. Agrl. U., Wageningen, The Netherlands, 1975-76, asst. prof. mycology, 1977—; dir. Biol. Sta. Agrl. U., Wijster, The Netherlands, 1990-98; postdoctoral fellow Cornell U., Ithaca, N.Y., 1986. Author: Ecology and Coenology of Macrofungi in Grasslands, Vol. 1, 1981, Vol. 2, 1982, Handbook of Vegetation Science, Vol. 19, 1992; editor: The Changing Mycoflora of The Netherlands, 1985, (with Th.W. Kuyper and M.E. Noordeloos) Survey of Macromycetes in The Netherlands, 1995. Mem. Netherlands Mycol. Soc. (pres. 1993-98), European Coun. for Conservation Fungi (pres. 1985-92). Avocations: painting, gardening, regression therapist. Office: Wageningen U, Soil Biol Group Box 8005, 6700 EC Wageningen The Netherlands

ARNOLDSSON, JONAS PETER, mining company executive; b. Karlstad, Varmland, Sweden, Feb. 27, 1971. MBA, Lund (Sweden) U., 1997. Market analyst Boliden, Sweden and Can., 1997—. With Swedish Air Force, 1992. Home: Blekholmsterassen 3, 11164 Stockholm Sweden Office: Boliden, Gaulegatan 22, 11164 Stockholm Sweden

ARNON, ARIE, economist; b. Amsterdam, Holland, June 1, 1947; arrived in Israel, 1948; s. Jacob and Louis (Asher) A.; m. Ruth Butler; children: Inbal, Adam. BSc, Hebrew U., Jerusalem, 1971, MA, 1975, PhD, 1980. Lectr. Ben Gurion U., Beer-Sheva, Israel, 1983-89; sr. lectr. Ben Gurion U., Beer-Shera, Israel, 1989-97, assoc. prof., 1998—, chair dept. econs., 1999—; sr. economist rsch. dept. Bank of Israel, Jerusalem, 1990-98. Author: Thomas Tooke: Pioneer of Monetary Theory, 1991, The Palestinian Economy: Between Imposed Integration and Voluntary Separation, 1997. Active leading forum Peace Now, 1990-97; chmn. Committment to Pace and Social Justice. Office: Ben Garion U, PO Box 653 Dept Econ, 84105 Beer-Sheva Israel

ARNOTT, ERIC JOHN, ophthalmologist; b. Sunningdale, Berkshire, Eng., June 12, 1929; s. Robert and Cynthia Emita Amelia (James) A.; m. Veronica Mary Langue, Nov. 19, 1960; children: Stephen John, Tatiana Amelia, Robert Lauriston John. BA, Trinity Coll., Dublin, 1953, M.B., B.Ch., BAO, 1954; DO, U. London, 1955. Houseman Royal Victoria Eye & Ear Hosp. and Adelaide Hosp., Dublin, 1953-54; resident surg. officer Moorfields Eye Hosp., London, 1959-60; sr. registrar U. Coll. Hosp., London, 1961-63; cons. ophthalmologist surgeon Royal Eye Hosp., London, 1965-74, Charing Cross Hosp., London, 1971-94; med. dir. Fyodorov Arnott Apple Internat. Eye Inst., Gibraltar, 1998—; faculty U. London, 1966—, Royal Coll. Opthalmologists, London, 1966—; vis. prof. Devi Amilya U., Indore India, 1998; hon. vis. prof. Devi Amilya U. Indore, India; ophthalmic dir. Fyodorov Arnott Apple Internat. Eye Inst. Co-author: Extracapsular Cataract Surgery, 1983; author: (with others) Emergency Surgery, Intraocular Lens Implantation, Current Perspectives in Ophthalmology, A Color Atlas of Lens Implantation; contbr. articles to profl. jours.; developer, inventor totally encircling loop intraocular lens for implantation into the capsular bag of the eye after surgery, diamond tipped spear headed surgical knife; pioneer in small incisional cataract surgery, excimer laser, lasik, retinal detachment and glaucoma surgery; patentee in field. Founder, chmn. The Arnott Trust, The Great London Treasure Hunt. Fellow Royal Coll. Surgeons, Royal Coll. Ophthalmologists, Am. Acad. Ophthalmologists; mem. Internat. Assn. Ocular Surgeons (past pres.), Chelsea Clin. Soc. (past pres.), Order of St. John, Outpatient Ophthalmic Surgery Soc., London Med. Soc., Royal Soc. Medicine, European Phaco & Laser Soc. (pres. 1986-92), Kildare St. Club (Dublin), RAC, The Garrick Club (London). Home: Trottsford Farm Headley, Nr Bordon, Hampshire England GU358TF

ARNOTT, GEOFFREY DALE, academic administrator; b. Hamilton, Australia, Aug. 26, 1948; s. George Henry Gordon and Elsie Elizabeth (Ball) A.; m. Sandra Faye Baird, Nov. 16, 1974; children: Andrew, Adrian, Richelle. BEC, Monash U., Melbourne, Australia, 1970, BED, 1973; diploma in Bus. Adminstrn., Swinburne U. Tech, Melbourne, Australia, 1975. Tchr. Dept. Edn., Victoria, Australia, 1970-74; tchr. Swinburne U. Tech., 1974-87, head dept., 1987-93, dep. head sch., 1993—. Author: The Micro Economy, 1984, The Macro Economy, 1985, Understanding Politics Through Newspapers, 1988, Understanding U.C.E. Economics, 1990, The Micro Economy: A Business Economics Aproach, 1992, The Macro Economy: A Business Economics Approach, 1993. Avocations: gardening, agriculture, hiking, running. Office: Swinburne U Tech Social Scis & Arts Sch, TAFE Divsn 142 High St, Prahran Victoria 3181, Australia

ARNOTT, WILLIAM GEOFFREY, Greek educator; b. Bury, England, Sept. 17, 1930; s. Bertie and Edith May (Smith) A.; m. Vera Hodson, Aug. 20, 1955; children: Ann Rosemary, Alison Susan, Hilary Julia. BA, Cambridge U., England, 1952, MA, 1956, PhD, 1960. Asst. lectr. Bedford Coll., London, 1955-59; asst. dir. exams. Civil Svc. Commn., London, 1959-60; asst. lectr. U. Hull, 1960-61; lectr. U. Newcastle-Upon-Tyne, 1961-66, sr. lectr., 1966-67; prof. Greek U. Leeds, 1968-91, U. Bologna, Italy, 1998; Princeton Inst. Advanced Study, 1973; vis. fgn. scholar U. B.C., Can., 1982; vis. prof. U. Wellington, N.Z., 1982, U. Alexandria, Egypt, 1983, U. Queensland, Australia, 1987. Author: Menander, Plautus, Terence, 1975, Alexis: The Fragments, 1996, Loeb Edition of Menander, I, 1979, II, 1996, III, 2000. Gov. St. Peter's Sch., York, England, 1971-83. Fellow Italian Soc. Study Classical Antiquity, Gonville and Caius Coll., Cambridge, 1987. Fellow Brit. Acad.; mem. Birdwatchers Club (pres. 1981-84). Avocations: ornithology, lecturing, travel, photography. Office: The Univ Sch Classics Leeds, U Leeds, Leeds LS2 9JT, England

ARNOULD, HENRI-LAURENT, publishing executive; b. Banyuls, France, Oct. 27, 1940; s. Francis and Dauder A.; m. Claude Arnould, Mar. 19, 1968; children: Corinne, Franck. Grad. in Oenologist, Ecole Nationale, Superieure Agronomique, Montpellier U., 1966. Fabrication engr. Pernod, Paris, 1967-73; dir. Coop. Buzet, France, 1973-76; dir. tech. unite prodn. Soc. Vins de France, Lyon, 1976-92; dir. gen. Bourgogne Publ., Macon, France, 1992—, Saq. Action Qualitè, Lyon, 1994—. Editor: Revue des Oenologues, 1982, Collection Avenir Oenologie, 1984. Pres. Coucours Chardonnay du Moude, 1994; dir. festival Internat. Oenovideo, 1993; dir. gen. Oeno-Plurimedia, 1996. Mem. Lions Club. Home and Office: Maisons des Vianerons du, Chateau de Chaintre, 71570 Chaintre France

ARNOULD, MARCEL LEOPOLD, science educator; b. Ittre, Brabant, Belgium, Apr. 14, 1943; s. Rene and Lambertine Lacroix; m. Monique Theodora Syoen, Oct. 28, 1967. M in Physical Scis., Free U., Brussels, 1966, DSc, 1971. Grantee CNRS Inst. Astrophysique, Paris, 1970; sr. rsch. asst. Belgian Found. Sci. Rsch., Brussels, 1971-76; rschr. U. Ill., Urbana-Champaign, 1975-76; rsch. assoc. Belgian Found. Sci. Rsch., Brussels, 1976-94; prof. Free U., Brussels, 1994—; head Astrophysique Inst. Free U., Brussels, 1983—; expert physics panel European Commn., Brussels, 1994—; mem. peer review com. CERN, Geneva, 1992-96; mem. selection com. Royal Belgium Observatory, Brussels, 1997—; vice chmn. Belgian Nat. Com. Astronomy, 1999. Co-editor: Tours Symposium on Nuclear Physics III, 1998; contbr. articles to profl. jours. Recipient Fulbright Hays Rsch. scholarship, 1975-76; fellow Alexander Von Humboldt, 1977-79; medal Paris Astrophysics Inst., 1989. Mem. Internat. Astronomical Union. Office: Inst Astronomy U Brussels, CP 226 Campus Plaine, B-1050 Brussels Belgium

ARNS, PAULO EVARISTO CARDINAL, archbishop emeritus; b. Criciuma, Brazil, Sept. 14, 1921; s. Gabriel and Helena (Steiner) A. Ed., U. Parana, Sorbonne, 1952; LLD (hon.), U. Notre Dame (Ind.), 1977, Siena Coll., Albany, N.Y., 1981, Fordham U., N.Y.C., 1981, Seton Hall U., South Orange, N.J., 1982, U. Münster, Fed. Republic of Germany, 1983, St. Francis Xavier U., Antigonish, Can., 1986, U. Dubuque, 1988, U. S. Francisco, São Paulo, 1989, Piracicaba, SP, 1990; LHD (hon.), Manhattanville Coll., 1991; LLD (hon.), U.S.C. Jesus Bauru, Sao Paulo, 1992, Nimegen, Holland, 1993, Goiânia, 1998, Extremo sul Catarinense, 1998, U. Fed. do Acre, 1998, U. Cath. Minas Gerais, 1999, U. Fed. do Párana, 1999, Pontificia Fac. Teologia Assunção, São Paulo, 1999, U. Fed. Viçosa, Minas Gerais, 1999. Ordained priest Roman Cath. Ch., 1945. Prof. patrology and didatics Cath. U. Petropolis, pastor, 1956-66; aux. bishop of São Paulo, 1966-70, archbishop of São Paulo, 1970-98, archbishop emeritus of São Paulo, 1998—; created cardinal of São Paulo, 1973; chancellor Pontifical Cath. U., São Paulo, 1970-98. Author 48 books. Recipient Nansen medal for def. of human rights in Latin Am., U.N., 1985, Niwano Peace prize, 1994. Office: Av Higienópolis 890, 01238000 São Paulo SP, Brazil

ARNTSEN, ARNT PETER, engineer, consultant; b. Hvaler, Norway, Oct. 23, 1921; s. Arnt Peter and Helene Oleane (Helgesen) A.; m. Margot Petra Nilsen, Oct. 24, 1953; children: Tom David, Carol Ann, John Frederick. Registered profl. engr., Mass. Engr., Westinghouse Research Center, Pitts., 1962-64; sr. engrng. scientist RCA Corp., Burlington, Mass., 1964-89; cons., 1989-96, ret., 1996. Patentee in field. Home and Office: 9 Lincoln Ave Manchester MA 01944-1119

ARNTZEN, HELMUT, literature educator; b. Duisburg, North Rhine-Westphalia, Germany, Jan. 10, 1931; s. Otto and Elisabeth Gertrude (Kröck) A.; m. Regina Gabriele Martha Pienkny, Mar. 23, 1965; 1 child, Viola. PhD, U. Cologne, Fed. Republic of Germany, 1957, diploma in libr. scis., 1958. Sci. asst. Free U. Berlin, 1959-67, lectr., 1967-68; prof. German lang. and lit., dir. Inst. German Lang. and Lit. Westphalian Wilhelms-U. Münster, Fed. Republic of Germany, 1968—, dean Sch. German Lang. and Lit., 1976-77; lectr. Sch. Theology, Berlin, 1961-62; vis. prof. Ain Shams U., Cairo and Heliopolis, Egypt, 1982, Hebrew U. Jerusalem, 1994-95; A. Azhar U., Cairo, 1990; Max Kade Disting. vis. prof. U. Kans., Lawrence, 1987. Author 15 books; editor 6 books; contbr. articles to profl. jours. Recipient Robert Musil medal City of Klagenfurt, Austria, 1983. Mem. Internat. Union German Lang. and Lit., Internat. PEN. Club: Ambassador (Münster). Home: Am Schlosspark 21, D 48308 Senden Germany Office: Westphalian Wilhelms-U Munster, Domplatz 10-22, D48143 Muenster Germany

ARNU, THOMAS JOSEPH, surgeon; b. Voelklingen, Saar, Germany, Oct. 22, 1960; s. Joseph Jules and Gisèle Mary (Senzig) A.; m. Sabina Rybak, Apr. 19, 1990. MBBCh, U. Saar, Homburg, Germany, 1986, MD, 1989. Bd. cert. neurosurgery, sports medicine, orthopaedic surgery, rheumatology, chiropractic. Resident U. Heidelberg, Germany, 1986-90, U. Clinics Homburg, Germany, 1990-93; pvt. surgeon dept. spinal surgery St. Johannis Hosp., Landstuhl, Germany, 1993-97; 1st surgeon dept. orthopedics Puttlingen/Saar, 1997-2000; chief in svc. Orthopaedic Svc., Enkenbach-Alsenborn, 2000—; cons. Court of Social Affairs Rheinpfalz County, Mainz, Speyer, Germany, 1990—; club physician Am. Football Club Kaiserslautern (Germany) Warriors, 1990—; cons. dept. orthopedics St. Johannis Hosp., Landstuhl, 1993—; lectr. in field. Contbr. articles to profl. jours. Mem. Deutsche Gesellschaft für Sports Medicine. Avocations: music, biking, football. Office: Orthopedic Svc, Hauptstrasse 22, 67677 Enkenbach-Alsenborn Germany

AROM, SIMHA, ethnomusicologist. Docteur es-Lettres, U. Sorbonne, Paris, 1985. Head music div. Kol Israel Israel Broadcasting Office, Jerusalem, 1980-82; ethnomusicologist CNRS, Paris. Author: African Polyphony and Polyrhytm, 1991; recorder: Grece. Hommage a Tsitsanis.Buzuki, 1984 (recipient Grand Prix du Disque, 1985); Anthologie de la Musique des Pygmees Aka (Album) (recipient Grand prix du Disque, 1978), 1978. Recipient Medaille d'Argent, Centre National de la Recherche Scientifique, 1984. Mem. Internat. Council for Traditional Music, Internat. Musicologidal Soc., Société Francaise de Musicologie. Office: Lacito CNRS, 7 rue Guy Moquet Bat 23, 94800 Villejuif France 75014

ARON, PETER ARTHUR, charitable foundation executive, private investor; b. Memphis, May 26, 1946; s. Jack R. and Jane (Baerwald) A.; m. Erika Maria Kostron, Mar. 11, 1972; children: Heather Jane, Holly Frances. BA, Tulane U., 1969. Asst. v.p. J. Aron & Co., Inc., N.Y.C., 1965-83; v.p., treas. Lafayette Enterprises, Inc., N.Y.C., 1983—; pres. Ridgefield, Inc., Thibodaux, La., 1998—; pres., exec. dir. J. Aron Charitable Found., N.Y.C., 1974—; dir. William B. Reily Co., New Orleans, 1993—; dir., sec. J. Aron & Co., Inc., New Orleans, 1988—; trustee FTI Funds, Pitts., 1995—. Editor: Aspiration and Perseverance, 1984. Chmn. bd. trustees South Street Seaport Mus., N.Y.C., 1987-99; chmn. bd. dirs. Avon (Conn.) Old Farms Sch., 1992—; trustee Lenox Hill Hosp., N.Y.C., 1975—; vice chmn. Tulane U., New Orleans, 1981-96; hon. life trustee The Asia Soc., N.Y., 1997—; trustee Village of Kings Point, N.Y., 1999—. 1st lt., U.S. Army, 1970-71, Vietnam. Decorated Bronze Star; recipient Pub. Svc. award Nat. Neurofibromatosis Found., N.Y.C., 1994, Disting. Trustee award United Hosp. Found., N.Y.C., 1995, Tulane U. Disting. Alumnus award, 2000; named Man of Yr., Cystic Fibrosis Found., 1998. Mem. Asia Soc. Galleries Friends (past chmn.), Conferie Chevalier du Tastevin New Orleans. Avocations: yachting, Asian art, scuba diving.

ARON, ROBERTO, lawyer, writer, educator; b. Mendoza, Argentina, Nov. 1, 1915; s. David and Catalina (Trostanetzky) A.; m. Catalina Berstein, May 1, 1940 (dec. Oct. 1965); children: Jaim, Sylvia, Daniel; m. Eva Coriat, Dec. 14, 1968; stepchildren: Sonia, Aileen (twins). BA in Law, U. Chile, 1943; LLM in Internat. Law, NYU, 1977, LLM in Corp. Law, 1979, M in Hebrew and Judaic Studies, 1995. Bar: Israel 1960. Sr. ptnr. Aron and Cia, Santiago, Chile, 1943-57, Arón, Tamir and Arón, Tel Aviv, 1960—; adj. tchr. NYU, 1983; lectr. Tel Aviv U., 1985—, bd. govs., 1982; vis. prof. faculty of law U. Chile, 1991; bd. dirs. Otzar Itiashvut Hayeudim Bank, Tel Aviv; mem. Israeli del. to UN, 1975; participant Oxford Trial Advocacy Program. Co-author: How To Prepare Witnesses for Trial, 1985, Trial Communications Skills, 1986, Cross-Examination and Impeachment of Witnesses, 1989. Mem. Nat. Inst. Trial Advocacy (participant workshops on teaching trial advocacy Harvard Law Sch.), Advocates Assn., Assn. Trial Lawyers Am. Avocations: golf, pipe collecting. Home: 985 5th Ave Apt 12A New York NY 10021-0142 Office: Paradise and Alberts 630 3rd Ave Rm 1701 New York NY 10017-6762 also: Arón and Stern, 7 ABA Hillel St, Ramat Gan 52522, Israel

ARONIN, ALEXANDER SEMENOVICH, physics researcher; b. Moscow, June 20, 1952; s. Semen Borisovich and Valentina Pavlovna (Artyuhina) A.; m. Galina Evgenievna Abrosimova, Nov. 26, 1982. Engr., Moscow Steel and Alloy Inst., 1975, PhD, 1982. Probation rsch. assoc. Inst. of Solid State Physics, Chernogolvke, Russia, 1975-89, sr. scientist, 1989—; asst. prof. Moscow Steel and Alloy Inst., Technol. Univ., Moscow, 1989-97. Contbr. articles to profl. jours. Office: Inst of Solid State Physics, RAS, 142432 Chernogolovka Russia

ARONOFF, CRAIG ELLIS, management educator, consultant; b. Atlanta, May 18, 1951; s. Marvin Charles and Patricia (Sabin) A.; children: Lara Lorena, Emily Rose. BS in Journalism, Northwestern U., 1971; MA, U. Pa., 1974; PhD, U. Tex., 1975. Asst. prof. mgmt. Ga. State U., Atlanta, 1975-79, assoc. prof., 1979-83; prof. mgmt. Kennesaw State U., Marietta, Ga., 1983—, Dinos disting. chair pvt. enterprise, 1983—, chmn. dept. mgmt., 1984-86; dir. Family Enterprise Ctr., 1987—, eminent scholar, 1999—; chmn. Cobb Transit Adv. Bd., Marietta, 1988-90; exec. dir. Bus. Owner Resources, Marietta, 1989—; CEO Family Bus. Comm., Inc., 1989—, Family Bus. Cons. Group, Inc. 1994—. Co-author: Public Relations: The Profession and the Practice, 4th edit., 1996, Family Business Leadership Series, 13 vols., 1992—; co-editor: The Future of Private Enterprise, 3 vols., 1982-84; also author, co-author, editor other books, 1979—; contbg. editor, columnist Family Bus. Planning, Nation's Bus. mag., 1990-99; mem. editl. bd. Jour. Pvt. Enterprise Edn., 1986—, Family Bus. Rev., 1992—; exec. editor Family Bus. Advisor, 1991—. Commr. Marietta Bd. Zoning and Planning, 1987-90; bd. dirs. Temple Kol Emeth, Marietta, 1989-92; mem. Leadership Cobb, 1986-87; co-pres. West Side Elem. Sch. PTA, 1992-93. Recipient Leavey award Freedoms Found., 1987, Outstanding Educator award Nat. Fedn. Ind. Bus. Found., 1989, Disting. Leadership award Leadership Cobb, 1988. Mem. Assn. Pvt. Enterprise Educators (pres. 1978-79, bd. dirs. 1977-91, Kent-Aronoff award 1988), Family Bus. Forum (founder, bd. dirs. 1987—), Family Firm Inst. (bd. dirs. 1989-94, sec., treas. 1990-92, pres. 1992-94, Richard Beckhard award 1997), Southeastern Legal Found. (bd. dirs. 1990-97), Ga. Coun. Econ. Edn. (trustee 1983—), Cobb C. of C. (vice chmn. 1986, 91-93), Progressive Club (pres. 1976-77), Kiwanis (pres. Marietta chpt. 1990, Outstanding Kiwanian award 1989). Home: 2061 E Side Dr NE Marietta GA 30062-6426 Office: Kennesaw State U 1000 Chastain Rd NW Kennesaw GA 30144-5591

ARONOVICH, ILYA, fraternity president, small business owner; b. Leningrad, USSR, June 18, 1972; s. Yakov I. and Marina Aronovich. BA, Rutgers U., 1995; postgrad., Fordham U., 1998—. Dir. eastbound ocean traffic Unitrans-P.R.A. Co., Inc., Fair Lawn, N.J., 1995-96; v.p. new product devel. and fin. IBK Corp., East Brunswick, N.J., 1996-97; pres., owner Cyweb Inc., East Brunswick, 1998—; nat. pres. Lambda Sigma Upsilon Frat., Hoboken, N.J., 1998—; rsch. asst., dir. death penalty project Fordham U. Sch. Law, N.Y.C., 1999-2000; summer assoc. Gibney, Anthony & Flaherty, LLP, N.Y.C., 2000. Assoc. editor Fordham Fin., Securities and Tax Law Forum, 1999-2000; editor-in-chief Fordham Jour. Corp. and Fin. Law, 2000—. Jewish. Avocations: world travel, playing classical piano, dancing mambo and salsa, developing websites. Fax: 212-636-6204. E-mail: iaronovich@lsu79.org. Office: Lambda Sigma Upsilon Frat PO Box 645 Hoboken NJ 07030-0645

ARONOW, EDWARD, psychologist, educator; b. Dec. 22, 1945; s. Hyman and Gertrude (Bakst) A.; m. Anna Aronow; children: David, Rebecca. BA in Psychology, CUNY, 1967; MA in Psychology, Fordham U., 1969, PhD in Clin. Psychology, 1973. Psychology trainee VA, N.Y.C., 1968-72; prof. psychology Montclair (N.J.) State U., 1972—; sr. clin. psychologist St. Vincent's Hosp., N.Y.C., 1972-79; clin. psychologist Verona, N.J., 1974—. Author: Rorschach Content Interpretation, 1976, A Rorschach Introduction: Content and perceptual Approaches, 1982, The Rorschach Technique, 1994. Fellow Am. Bd. of Assessment Psychology; mem. APA, Ea. Psychol. Assn., N.J. Psychol. Assn., Soc. Personality Assessment. Office: 69 Forest Ave Verona NJ 07044-1217

ARONOW, WILBERT SOLOMON, physician, educator; b. N.Y.C., Oct. 30, 1931; s. Simon and Bella (Safrin) A.; m. Ina Gloria Brody, Sept. 20, 1958; children—Michael Steven, Janice Susan. BS, Queens Coll., 1953; MD, Harvard U., 1957. Diplomate Am. Bd. Internal Medicine. Intern Michael Reese Hosp. and Med. Ctr., Chgo., 1957-58, resident, 1958-61; practice medicine specializing in internal medicine and cardiology; cardiologist, chief Noninvasive Cardiovascular Lab., Long Beach (Calif.) VA Hosp., 1964-72, chief cardiovascular diseases, 1973-82, asst. chief medicine for rsch., 1975-80; asso. prof. medicine U. Calif., Irvine, 1972-75, prof. medicine, 1975-82, prof. cmty. and environ. medicine, 1975-82, prof. pharmacology and therapeutics, 1976-82, vice chief cardiovascular div., chief cardiovascular research, 1974-82; prof. medicine, chief cardiovascular rsch. Creighton U., Omaha, 1982-84; vis. prof. U. Tex. Southwestern Med. Sch., Dallas, 1976, U. Man., 1979, U. Toronto, 1979, Tex. Tech U. Sch. Medicine, Lubbock, 1983, U. Medicine and Dentistry of N.J.-Rutgers Med. Sch., 1983; vis. prof. geriatrics U. Rochester Sch. Medicine, 1999; cons. cardiology Orange County Med. Center, 1968-82; staff cardiology service St. Joseph Hosp., Omaha, 1982-84; cons. FDA, 1970-77, mem. ad hoc sci. ad. coms., 1970-72, mem. cardiovascular and renal advisory com., 1973-76; cons. U. Calif. Project Clear Air, 1970, Calif. Air Resources Bd., 1973, 78, 80, EPA, 1973, 78, 79, 80, 81, 82, 83, dept. drugs AMA, 1974, 78, 81, 93, NIH, 1976, 80, W. Ger. Dept. Health, 1978, U.S. Dept. Justice Law Enforcement Assistance Adminstrn., 1978, NHLBI, 1979, FTC, 1980, 81, Dept. Health and Environ. Scis., State of Mont., 1980, Nat. Ctr. Health Stats., 1981; cons. and chmn. spl. rev. com. Nat. Cancer Inst., 1980; cons. and mem. subcom. on smoking Am. Heart Assn., 1980-83; med. dir. Hebrew Hosp. Home, 1984—; cons. in medicine Albert Einstein Coll. Medicine, 1990—, State of N.Y. Dept. of Health Office of Pub. Health, 1986, 93, 94; adj. prof. geriatrics and adult devel. Mt. Sinai Sch. Medicine, 1992—. Mem. editorial bd. Jour. Pharmacology and Exptl. Therapeutics, guest field editor, 1981; editorial bd.: Am. Jour. Cardiology, 1980-82, Jour. Circulation, 1980-83, E R Reports, 1981-84, Physician's Drug Alert, 1982—, Jour. Cardiovascular and Pulmonary Technique, 1983-86, Clin. Pharmacology and Therapeutics, 1977-83, Jour. ACC, 1982-83, Drugs and Aging, 1990—, Am. Jour. Noninvasive Cardiology, 1986-95, Jour. Cardiovascular Diagnosis and Procedures, 1992—, Jour. Noninvasive Cardiology, 1996—, Preventive Cardiology, 1998—, Jour. Am. Med. Dirs. Assn., 1999—, Caring for the Ages, 1999—, Jour. Gerontology: Med. Scis., 2000—; contbr. to research publs. Served to capt., M.C. AUS, 1961-63. Fellow A.C.P., Am. Geriatrics Soc., Am. Coll. Cardiology, Am. Coll. Chest Physicians (vice-chmn. coronary disease sect. 1978-79, gov. So. Calif. 1977-83, chmn. coronary disease sect. 1979-81, vice chmn. gov.'s council, mem. exec. council 1979-81, chmn. forum on cardiovascular disease 1980-81, sec. council on govs. 1981-82), Council Clin. Cardiology of Am. Heart Assn., Coun. on Geriatric Cardiology (chmn. program com. 1993—, bd. dirs. 1994—); mem. Am. Soc. Clin. Pharmacology and Therapeutics (chmn. cardiovascular and pulmonary diseases sect. 1973-74, 1975-77), Am. Fedn. Clin. Research, Assn. VA Cardiologists (pres. 1975-77), Long Beach Heart Assn. (dir. 1972-75), Orange County Heart Assn. (dir. 1979-81), Phi Beta Kappa. Jewish. Home: 23 Pebbleway Rd New Rochelle NY 10804-3914 Office: Hebrew Hosp Home 801 Co Op City Blvd Bronx NY 10475-1603

ARONS, KARL ERIK, museum administrator; b. Riga, Latvia, Aug. 25, 1933; s. Janis and Marta (Abolkalns) A. Physician, Latvian Med. Acad., Riga, 1957; D Med, Latvian U., 1966; historian, Latvian U., Riga, 1973; D honoris causa, Latvian Acad. Scis., 1998. Lectr., docent Latvian Med. Acad., Riga, 1959—; dir. P. Stradin Mus. of History of Medicine, Riga, 1960—, Inst. of History of Medicine, Riga, 1991-99. Editor: Latvian Medical Dictionare, Riga, 1965-85, Acta Medico-Historica Rigensia, 1965—. Recipient Pagel medal, 1985. Mem. European Assn. of Mus. of History of Med. Scis. (mem. coun. 1985), Fraternitas Metropolitana Riga. Latvian Orthodox. Avocations: traveling, music. Office: P Stradin Mus of History of Medicine, Antonijas 1, LV-1360 Riga Latvia

ARONSON, EDGAR DAVID, venture capitalist; b. N.Y.C., June 17, 1934; s. Aaron Solomon and Ida Claire (Minevitch) A.; m. Nancy Carol Pforzheimer, Dec. 23, 1956; children: Edgar David, Alison C., Edith S., Peter Borrah. A.B., Harvard U., 1956, M.B.A., 1962. Successively trainee, asst. cashier, v.p. 1st Nat. Bank of Chgo., 1962-67; v.p. Republic Nat. Bank of N.Y., 1968; trainee Salomon Bros., N.Y.C., 1968-69; ltd. partner Salomon Bros., 1970, v.p., 1971-72, gen. partner, 1972-79; mng. dir. Salomon Bros. Internat. Ltd., London, 1971-76; chmn. bd. Dillon, Read Internat., 1979-81; pres. EDACO, Inc., 1981—; bd. dirs. APL N.V., Curacao, Petrogas Ltd., Hong Kong, MidAmEnergy Holdings Pte., Inc., Omaha, H.L. Oakes & Co., Inc., Panama, Hertford Internat., N.V., Curacao. Author: (with others) New Old World, 1962, Response to Change, 1963. Trustee Lesley Coll., Cambridge, Mass., 1981-84, South St. Seaport Mus., N.Y., Marine Mil. Acad., Harlingen, Tex.; bd. dirs. Carl and Lily Pforzheimer Found., N.Y.C. 1st lt. USMCR, 1956-60, maj. FMF ret. res. Mem. Marine Corps Res. Officers Assn., 1st Marine Divsn. Assn., The Cruising Assn. (U.K.), Mensa, N.Y. Yacht Club, Bass Harbor Yacht Club (Maine), Harvard Club N.Y.C., Royal Cork Yacht Club, Eire, The Brook (N.Y.C.), Annabel's (London). Office: EDACO Inc 551 Fifth Ave Rm 512 New York NY 10176-0599

ARONSON, JAN, artist, educator; b. New Orleans, Dec. 19, 1949; d. Bernard J. and Merle (Wiener) A.; m. Edgar Miles Bronfman Sr., Sept. 2, 1993. BA, U. New Orleans, 1971; MFA, Pratt Inst., 1973. Instr. New Orleans Mus. Art, 1973-74, Dillard U., New Orleans, 1974-76; asst. prof. Ethan Allen C.C., Manchester, Vt., 1978-81; instr. So. Vermont Art Ctr., Manchester, 1978-81, Stratton (Vt.) Mtn. Sch., 1981; artist N.Y.C., 1986—; adj. faculty Pratt Manhattan Ctr., N.Y.C., 1988, 89; asst. prof. Ethan Allen C.C., Manchester, 1977-81; tutor external degree program Johnson (Vt.) State Coll., 1976-85; creator, tchr. art program Pub. Sch. 198, Manhattan, N.Y., 1992-94. One-woman exhbns. include Bienville Gallery, New Orleans, 1976, Henri Gallery, Washington, 1978, Park McCullough House, No. Bennington, Vt., 1979, Weston Playhouse Art Gallery, Weston, Vt., 1979, Green Mtn. Coll., Poultney, Vt., 1979, So. Vt. Art Ctr., Manchester, 1979, U. New Orleans, 1980, 85, Christine Price Gallery, Castleton, Vt., 1981, McKissick Mus., Columbus, S.C., Helio Galleries, N.Y.C., 1988, Stuart Kingston, Wilmington, Dela., 1991, Anne Reed Gallery, Ketchum, Idaho, 1994, 95, 99, Winston Wachter Fine Art, N.Y.C., 1996, 98, Hahn Gallery, Phila., 1997, Thomas J. Walsh Art Gallery, Fairfield, Conn., 1999; group exhbns. at San Diego Watercolor Soc., 1980, Moonbrook Gallery, Rutland, Vt., 1981, Phyllis Needleman Gallery, Chgo., 1982, Brattleboro (Vt.) Mus., 1982, AVA Gallery, Hanover, N.H., 1983, Stratton (vt.) Arts Festival, 1981, 82, 83, 84, 85, Helio Galleries, 1988, Art Unlimited Gallery, Key West, Fla., 1989, Anne Reed Gallery, 1992, 93, 95, 96, 97, 99, Hollis Taggart Galllery, N.Y.C., 1994, Boise Art Mus., 1994, Renee Fotouhi Gallery, N.Y.C., 1995, Marguerite Oestreicher Gallery, New Orleans, 1993, Winston Wachter Fine Art, 1997, 98, 99, 00, Gallery 54, N.Y.C., 1997, Central Fine Arts, N.Y.C., 1998, Discovery Mus., Bridgeport, Conn., 2000; represented in permanent collections at Fairfield U., Estee Lauder, New Orleans Mus. Art, Eiteljorg Mus. Western and Indian Art, U.N. Watch of the World Jewish Congress, U.S. Mission, Vt. Coun. Arts, Isidore Newman Sch. Vt. Country Store Art Collection, and pvt. collections; contbr. articles to mags. Bd. dirs. Skowhegan Sch., N.Y.C.; bd. vistors U. New Orleans; nat. adv. panel Contemporary Art Ctr., New Orleans. Grantee Vt. Coun. Arts, 1981-82. Mem. Nat. Assn. Women Artists, Artists Equity. Jewish. Avocations: swimming, tennis, cycling, hiking, reading.

ARONSON, JEFFREY KENNETH, pharmacologist; b. Glasgow, UK, Aug. 31, 1947; s. Samuel and Sybil (Solomon) A.; m. Renée Elaine Wellins, Aug. 20, 1973; children: Simon, Natalie. B Medicine, B Surgery, U. Glasgow, 1970; DPhil, U. Oxford, 1977, MA, 1984. Clin. lectr. U. Oxford (England), 1980-84, clin. reader, 1984—; cons. physician Oxfordshire Health Authority, 1990—; vis. prof. U. Ceará, Brazil, 1991. Author: An Account of the Foxglove and Its Medical Uses, 1785-1985, 1985; co-author: The Oxford Textbook of Clinical Pharmacology and Drug Therapy, 2d edit., 1992, ABC of Monitoring Drug Therapy, 1994; author papers on ion transport and cardiac glycosides; editor: Side Effects of Drugs Annuals, 1991—; mng. editor European Jour. Clin. Pharmacology, 1985-93, reviews editor, 1994—. Recipient Paul Martini prize, 1980; fellow Green Coll., Oxford, 1985—. Fellow Royal Coll. Physicians; mem. Assn. Physicians of Gt. Britain and Ireland, Brit. Pharmacol. Soc. Avocations: reading, writing, arithmetic, cinema, cricket. Office: Radcliffe Infirmary, Dept Clin Pharmacology, Oxford OX2 6HE, England

ARONSON, KRISTIN JANINA, philosopher, educator; b. Norwalk, Conn., Sept. 28, 1945; d. Herbert Leon and Janina (Urbanowicz) A. BA, Ohio State U., Columbus, 1967; MA, Ohio State U., 1971, PhD, 1983. Instr. philosophy U. Conn., Waterbury, 1973-74; lectr. philosophy/speech Middlesex C.C., Middletown, Conn., 1974-91; asst. prof. philosophy U. Hartford, Conn., 1988, Ctrl. Conn. State U., New Britain, 1989-91, We. Conn. State U., Danbury, 1993—; adj. prof. philosophy Cen. Conn. State U., 1976-93, St. Joseph Coll., Hartford, 1988; nat. poetry contest judge Conn. Poetry Soc., 1991, 98, Milford Arts Coun., 1998, Chem. Injury Info. Network, 1999. Author: To Eat Flesh They Are Willing: Are Their Spirits Weak? Vegetarians Who Return to Meat, 1996; guest editor: Conn. River Rev., 1999, assoc. editor, 1991-92; contbr. poetry to literary jours.; playwright: Pointed Questions, 1978, The Butterfly Net, 1980, Bending the Bow, 1985; actress in various roles, 1973-93. Recipient Ohio Grant for Humanities, 1978, Perpetual Pendulum award Clockwork Repertory Theater, 1991, rsch. grant Conn. State U./AAUP, 1998, others. Mem. Ecol. Health Orgn. (bd. dirs.), Conn. Poetry Soc., N.Am. Vegetarian Soc., Phi Beta Kappa. Avocations: backpacking, canoeing, mountain climbing. Office: Dept Philosophy/Humanistic We Conn State U/181 White S Danbury CT 06810

ARONSON, MARC, artist; b. Seattle, June 26, 1948; s. Leonard and Marian (August) A.; m. Sue Elizabeth Steiner, June 28, 1971; 1 child, Elliot. BA, Western Wash. U., Bellingham, 1971; MA, NYU, 1989, postgrad., 1989—. Exhibited in group shows Seattle Art Mus. Pavilion, 1971, Warren Benedek Gallery, N.Y.C., 1974, U. Denver Sch. Art, 1975, Orgn. Ind. Artists Fed. Courthouse, Bklyn., 1977, Aldrich Mus. Contemporary Art, Ridgefield, Conn., 1978, Foster White Gallery, Seattle, 1980, Rensselaer Poly. Inst., Troy, N.Y., 1980, Sci. Mus. Tokyo, 1985, Embellishment of Statue of Liberty Barneys N.Y., 1986, Island Introductions Galveston (Tex.) Arts Ctr., 1990, Art of N.E. USA Silvermine Guild Arts Ctr., New Canaan, Conn., 1991, Nat. Midyear Exhbn. Butler Inst. Am. Art, Youngstown, Ohio, 1991, Am. 500 Centro Cultural Recoleta, Buenos Aires, 1992, The Emerging Collector, N.Y.C., 1992, Art of Northeast USA Silvermine Guild Arts Ctr., New Canaan, Conn., 1993, Butler Inst. Am. Art, Youngstown, Ohio, 1994, Washington Sq. East Galleries, N.Y.C., 1995, Art of Northeast USA Silvermine Guild Arts Ctr., New Canaan, Conn., 1996., Nat. Competition Finalists' Exhibition Provincetown Art Assn. and Museum, 1998, S.I. (N.Y.) Biennial Juried Art Exhibition, 1998, Art of N.E. Silermine Guild Arts Ctr., New Canaan, Conn., 1999, Provincetown (Mass.) Art Assn. and Mus., 2000, represented in permanent collection Time Warner Inc. Nat. Endowment for Arts fellow, 1976, N.Y. Found. Arts fellow, 1980. Mem. Kappa Delta Pi. Jewish. Avocation: racquetball.

ARONSON, NORMAN LEONARD, publishing executive, consultant; b. Washington, June 7, 1924; s. Herman and Bertha Martha (Miller) A.; m. Marcia Ross Rosey, Mar. 29, 1952 (dec. Nov., 1989); children: Susan Elizabeth Aronson Baratta, John Michael. BS in Bus. and Pub. Adminstrn., Georgetown U., 1947, JD, 1949. V.p. Esquire Mag., N.Y.C., 1951-75; publisher Univ. Comms., Rahway, N.J., 1975-76; advt. dir. Signature Mag., N.Y.C., 1976-82; pres. Best Publs. Inc., N.Y.C., 1982-86; CEO Musculoskeletal Transplant Found., Little Silver, N.J., 1986-88; editor, publisher "Q" Physicians Guide to Quality, Princeton, N.J., 1988—; entrepreneur, investor founder, pres. The Kings Ct. Restaurants, Princeton, N.J., Charlottesville, Va., Bostons Restaurant, Trenton, N.J., 1977-80; pres. The Svc. News Stands, Pentagon Bldg., Washington, 1965-75; cons. Universal Press Syndicate, Kansas City, Mo., 1988-89, Target Mktg., Kansas City, 1988—. Publisher The Book of Bests, 1983-84. Lt. j.g. US Navy, 1942-46 PTO. Recipient Lone Sailor award, U.S. Navy, Washington, 1990. Mem. The Nassau Club, Univ. Club (N.Y.). Avocations: wine, cooking.

ARORA, SHYAM SUNDER, biomedical engineering and physics educator, researcher; b. Amritsar, Punjab, India, Dec. 16, 1947; s. Harnam Dass and Kaushalya Devi Arora; m. Manju Narula, Sept. 12, 1978; 1 child, Sachin. BS, D.A.V. Coll., Amritsar, 1967; B of Electronics Engring., Indian Inst. Sci., 1970; MSc in Biomechanics, U. Surrey, U.K., 1975; PhD, U. Sheffield, U.K., 1978. Sr. sci. asst. Ctrl. Sci. Instruments Orgn., Chandigarh, India, 1970-71, scientist "A", 1971-73, scientist "B", 1973-81; asst. prof. Postgrad. Inst. Med. Edn. and Rsch., Chandigarh, India, 1981-85, assoc. prof., 1986—. Recipient Commonwealth scholarship, U.K., 1974-75, fellowship Med. Rsch. Coun., U.K., 1975-78, fellowship Colombo Plan, U.K., 1993-94, Disting. Standing Rsch. Bd. Adv. Am. Biog. Inst., N.C., 1999. Mem. Assn. Med. Physics India (life). Avocations: walking, gardening. Office: Postgrad Inst Med Edn and, Rsch Dept Biophysics, 160012 Chandigarh India

ARORA, VIPIN, laboratory administrator; b. Mhow, India, Oct. 1, 1956; s. Chaman Lal and Kamla Devi Arora; m. Meena Chawla, NOv. 27, 1986; children: Suruchi, Charu. BS, U. Indore, India, 1976, MB BChir, 1982; MD in Pathology, M.S. U., Baroda, India, 1986. Sr. resident Med. Coll., Baroda, 1986; tutor Med. Coll., Surat, India, 1986; pathologist class 1 New-Civil Hosp., Bharuch, India, 1986-88; pathologist Al-Obaid Clinics, Al-Aksa, Saudi Arabia, 1988-95; lab. dir. Sceco Hdqs. Health Svcs., Dammam, Saudi Arabia, 1995—; tutor Med. Coll., Surat, 1980-86; cons. New Civil Hosp., Bharuch, 1986-88, Al-Obaid Clinics, Al-Amsa, 1988-95. Mem. Melian Assn. Pathologists. Avocations: reading books, hiking, trekking, driving, watching TV. Office: Sceco Hdqs, PO Box 5190, 31422 Dammam Saudi Arabia

AROUCA MARQUES DOS SANTOS, LUIZ FREDERICO, economics educator, civil engineering consultant; b. Lisbon, Portugal, July 29, 1934; s. Francisco M.G.M. Santos and Maria A.A.Assis; m. Maria Isabel Jose de Mello, Dec. 22, 1957 (div. 1983); children: Maria Leonor, Maria Mafalda; m. Maria Helena Lampreia, Feb. 9, 1984 (div. 1995); children: Frederico, Diana. MSc in Civil Engring with merit, U. Lisbon, 1957, MSc in Econs. with merit and honors, 1967; diploma in engring., U. Delft (The Netherlands), 1958; diploma in politics with merit, U. Paris, 1970; PhD in Econs., U. London, 1977. Exec. Previdente Group Cos., Lisbon, 1958-72; sr. exec. Portuguese Fin. Group Cos., Lisbon, 1972-74; cons. engring. and bus. Lisbon, Paris, London, 1974—; sr. exec. Sapec Group Cos. Brussels, Lisbon, 1976-82; asst. prof. econs., lectr. Tech. U. Lisbon, 1967-74; prof. econs. Livre U. Lisbon, 1979-85; prof. econs., vice rector Aut. U., Lisbon, 1986-90, rector, 1990-92, prof. econs., 1992-96, rector, 1996—. Author numerous books; editor The Political Economy Culture, Jour. Liberdade, 1974—. Gen. sec. Portuguese Group Liberal Internat., 1974—. With Portuguese Army, 1958-61. Mem. Ordem Engrs., Ordem Economists, Nat. Ctr. Scientific Rsch. (CNRS), Am. Econ. Assn., Assn. Comparative Econ. Studies, Portuguese Human Rights Assn. (pres. 1978—), Amnesty Internat. Liberal Internat., Circulo Eca de Queiroz, Gremio Literario (Lisbon), Savile Club (London), Cercle Interallie (Paris). Fax: 351 1 859 23 11. E-mail: uni@uni.pt. Office: 17 Rua Padre Antonio Vieira, 1070-195 Lisbon Portugal and: Univ Independente, Av Marechal Gomes da Costa, 1800-255 Lisbon Portugal

ARP, HALTON CHRISTIAN, astronomer; b. N.Y.C., Mar. 21, 1927; s. August C. and Anita C. (Cryst) A.; m. Susanna Bixby Dakin, 1970 (div. 1982); children: Kristana, Alissa, Andrice; m. Marie-Helene DeMoulin, Jan. 19, 1984; 1 child, Delphine. AB, Harvard Coll., 1949; PhD, Calif. Inst. Tech., 1953. Astronomer Carnegie Instn. of Washington, D.C., 1957-85, Max Planck Inst. for Astrophysics, Munich, Germany, 1985—. Author: Atlas of Peculiar Galaxies, 1966, Quasars, Redshifts & Controversies, 1987, Seeing Red: Redshifts, Cosmology and Academic Science, Cat Southern Pec Galaxies, 1987. Mem. Cong. Racial Equality, Pasadena, 1965; chmn. Fedn. Am. Scientists L.A. chpt., 1970-73. With USN, 1945-46. Recipient Newcomb-Cleveland prize AAAS, 1960, medal Coll. de France, Paris, 1984, Alexander Humboldt Sr. Sci. award 1985. Mem. Internat. Astron. Union (working group chmn. 1988-92), Am. Astron. Soc. (past councilor, Helen Warner prize 1958), Astron. Soc. Pacific (pres. 1980-83). Office: Max Planck Inst for Astro, Karl Schwarzschild St 1, 85740 Munich 8046, Germany

ARPI, MAGNUS HARALD, greeting card company executive; b. Koping, Sweden, July 26, 1960; s. Tord and Solveig Emy (Christiansson) A.; m. Rosemarie Johanny, June 6, 1992; 1 child, Jannike. BSc in Math and Business Adminstrn., U. Karlstad, 1985. Mng. dir. Pictura Ltd, Hailsham, England, 1987-91; from mng. dir. to group dir. The Pictura Group, Karlstad, Sweden, 1991—.

ARPINO, MARIO, NATO official; b. Tarvisio, July 20, 1937. Grad., Air Force Acad., 1960. Commd. 2d lt. Italian Armed Forces, 1960, advanced through grades to lt. gen., 1994, pilot, then flight comdr., 1960-67, officer, comdg. ops., 1967-73, comdr. electronic warfare squadron, 1973-74, various appointments with air staff planning/ops. br., 1974-76, chief of flight divsn., then comdg. officer Tactical Transp., 1977-79, chief of ops. office, then chief of plans office Air Staff, 1979-82, dep. Air Staff Plans/Ops. br., 1982-86, chief of fin. and gen. planning br., Italian Def. Gen. Staff, 1986, comdt. Air Force Acad., then dep. comdr. 2d air region, 1987-89, Italian Air Force rep., chie of Italian Air Force Liaison, 1990-91, dep. chief of staff Italian Air Force, 1991-94, comdr. in chief 1st Air Region, 1994-95, chief of staff Italian Air Force, 1995-99; now chief of Italian Def. Staff, 1999—. Decorated Knight Mil. Order of Italy, Kight of Grand Cross of Merit of Italian Republic, Legion of Honor or France, Legion of Merit of U.S., numerous others. Office: Def Gen Staff Palazzo Capra, Via xx Settembre 11, 00100 Rome Italy also: NATO Hdqrs, Blvd Leopold III, 1110 Brussels Belgium*

ARQUIT, NORA HARRIS, music educator; b. Brushton, N.Y., June 30, 1923; d. Samuel Elton George and Esther Cecelia (Gillen) Harris; m. Gordon James Arquit, Nov. 12, 1948; children: Christine Elaine Arquit, Kevin James Arquit, Candace Susan Arquit-Martel. BS in Music Edn., Ithaca Coll., 1945, MS, 1962; postgrad., St. Lawrence U., 1946-47, 74, Cornell U., 1970-71, N.Y. State Coll., Potsdam, 1973. Music dir., band dir., tchr. N.Y. and N.J. State Schs., 1945-77; guest conductor U.S. Air Force Band, Washington, U.S. Navy Band, Washington, various massed bands in U.S.A., Canada, Europe; dir., coord. St. Lawrence County ann. High Sch. Band Day, 1973-2000. Author: Before My Own Time and Since, 1978, From Hamlet to Cold Harbor, 1989, Our Lyon Line, 1993, The History of the New York State, Society of the National Society of the Daughters of the American Colonists, 1994. Mem. AAUW, Internat. Assn. U. Women, Summit N.J. Club, Am. School Band Dirs. Assn. (past state and nat. chmn.), Dist. Bandmaster Am. award, North Am. Band Dirs. Coordinating Coun. (past pres.), N.Y. State United Retired Tchrs., Delta Omicron Internat. Music Fraternity, Ithaca Music Club (past pres.), Nat. Soc. of Magna Charta Dames, Plantagenet Soc., Colonial Order of The Crown (Order of Charlemagne), Nat. Soc. Sons and Daus. of the Pilgrims, Nat. Soc. U.S. Daughters 1812 (past pres.), Nat. Soc. Daughters of Founders & Patriots of Am. (past pres.), Nat. Soc. Sons and Daughters of Colonial Wars, Nat. Soc. New England Women, De Schilpen Soc. (Holland), Daughters of Union Vets., N.Y. Ct. Assts. of Nat. Soc. Women Descendents of Ancient and Honorable Artillery Co. (past state officer), Nat. Soc. Daughters of Am. Revolution (hon. regent Cayuga chpt., past state chmn.), The State Officers Club, Denison Soc., Nat. Soc. Daughters of Am. Colonists (hon. N.Y. state regent, state genealogical chmn.), Colonial Dames of Seventeenth Century (Atlantic Coast chmn. 2000—, nat. com. chmn. 2000—), Colonial Daughters of Seventeenth Century (pres.). Avocations: writing, photography, research. Home: 130 Christopher Cir Ithaca NY 14850-1702

ARRABAL, FERNANDO, writer; b. Melilla, Spain, Aug. 11, 1932; m. Luce Moreau; children: Samuel, Lélia. Author: (novels) Baal Babylone, 1959, The Burial of Sardine, 1982, Fêtes et Rites de la Confusion, 1965, The Tower Struck by Lightning (Prix Nadal 1983), The compass Stone, The Red Madonna, La Fille de King Kong, L'Extravagante Croisade d'un castrat Amoureux, El Mono, Ceremonia por un teniente abandonado, Le Funambule De Dieu, 1998, Porté Disparu, 2000, Levitación, 2000, Sex and Boost Behind Bars, 2000; (poetry) La Pierre de la folie, 1963, 100 Sonnets, 1966, Liberté Couleur De Femme, 1993, Arrabalesques, 1994, Humbles Paradis 1986; numerous plays include: the Architect and the Emperor of Assyria, And They Put Handcuffs on the Flowers, Garden of Delights, Fando and Lis, The Automobile Graveyard, Guernica, The Grand Ceremonial; (essays) The Panic, the New York of Arrabal, Letter to General Franco, Fischer, 1973, Echecs et Mythe, Letter fo Fidel Castro, 1984, Chroniques d'Echecs de l'Express, 1986, Greco, 1991, Goya-Dali, 1992, Genios y Figuras, 1993, La dudosa luz del Dia, 1994, Un esclave nommé Cervantès, 1996; writer and dir. films: Viva la Muerte, J'irai comme un cheval fou, L'arbre de Guernica, Le Cimetière des Voitures, Odyssey of the Pacific, Adieu Babylone, Jorge Luis Borges. Founder Panique movement with Topor and Jodorowsky, polit. prisoner, Spain, 1997. Recipient award Ford Found., 1959, Grand Prix du Théâtre, 1967, Grand Prix Humour Noir, 1968, Lugnë Poe, 1965, Obie award, 1976, Superdotado, 1942, Worlds Theater prize, 1984, Medalla de Oro de Bellas Artes, Spain, 1989, Officier Ordre des Arts et des Lettres, Paris, 1994, Prix de Théâtre de L'Académie Française, 1993, Premio Internacional de Novela Nabokov, 1994, Grand prix La Société des Gens de Lettres, 1996, Grand Prix de la Ville d'Antibes, 1997, medal Ctr. French Civilization and Culture, N.Y.U., 1997, Premio Europa di Poesia Alessandro Manzoni, 1999, Premio Mariano De Cavia, 1998, Prix De La Francophonie, 1998, Satrape du Collège de Pataphysique, 2000, premio ENINCI Cine y Literatura, 2000, others. E-mail: arrabalfernando@csi.com.

ARREBOLA-ARANDA, MARIA LEONOR, research scientist; b. Malaga, Andalucia, Spain, Feb. 27, 1964; arrived in The Netherlands, 1993; d. Pedro Arrebola-Larrubia and Leonor Aranda-Aguilera; m. Arie Cornelis Hoek, June 27, 1996; children: Ari Leon, Leo Ariel. B in Langs., U. Granada, 1984, MSc in Pharmacy, 1987, PhD in Pharmacy, 1992; postgrad., U. Leiden, The Netherlands, 1993-98. Contbr. chpts. to books, articles to sci. jours. Fellow Junta de Andalucia, U. Granada, 1989-93, U. Granada, U. Leiden, 1993-95, European Union, U. Leiden, 1996-98. Roman Catholic. Avocation: photography. Home: Klipperwerf 18, 2317 DZ Leiden The Netherlands Office: Leiden U Gorlaeus Labs, PO Box 9502 Einsteinweg 55, 2300 RA Leiden The Netherlands

ARREGUIN-CORTES, FELIPE, hydraulics engineer, researcher, educator; b. Mexico City, Mex., May 26, 1948; s. Juan Arreguin and Julia Cortes; children: Felipe, Luz. Degree in civil engring., UNAM, Mexico City, 1977, MS in Engring., 1979, PhD in Engring., 1985. Prof. U. Nacional Autonoma de MExico, Mexico City, 1976—; office head Secretaria de Asentamientos Humanos y Obras Publicas, Mexico City, 1978-79; tech. dir. Tecnologia Avanzade en General, Sociedad Anonima, Mexico City, 1984-89; area dir. Inst. Mex. Tech., Cuernavaca, 1989—; cons. UN, Quito, Ecuador, 1979, Panam. de Proyecto, Mexico City, 1979; prof. U. Autonoma de Queretaro, Queretaro, 1982-86. Editor: Efficient Water Use, 1994; author: Dams, 1987, Mathematics Methods, 1990; editor Internat. Jour. Water Resources Devel., 1994. Recipient Nat. Rschr. award Edn. Ministry, 1998. Mem. Am. Water Works Assn., Hydraulics Mex. Assn. (Enzo Levi award 1996). Home: Privada de la Cabana No 30, Col Chapultepec, 62450 Cuernavaca Morelos, Mexico Office: Mex Inst Water Tech, Paseo Cuauhnahuac No 8532, 62550 Jiutepec Morelos, Mexico

ARRHENIUS, SARA ANNA, critic, writer; b. Stockholm, Sept. 19, 1961; d. Erik and Birgit Arrhenius; m. Peter Hagdahl. BA in Arts and Humanities, Stockholm U., 1986; Degree in Journalism, Poppius U., Stockholm, 1987. Art critic, arts editor Aftonbladet, Stockholm, 1989-98; editor Index Mag., Stockholm, 1991-98; art critic Dagens Nyheter, Stockholm, 1998—; editor Wa: The Nordic Art Rev., Stockholm, 1999—. Author: (with Cecilia Sjöholm) Ensam och Pervers, 1995, (atlas) En Riktig kvinna, 1999; contbr. essays and articles to Swedish and internat. cultural mags. and anthologies. Rotary scholar Rotary Internat., 1991; travel grantee Swedish Inst., 1996, work grantee Svenska Författarfonden, 1996. Mem. Internat. Assn. Art Critics. Office: Index, PO Box 151, 104 65 S Stockholm Sweden

ARRIAGA, EDGAR AUGUSTO, chemistry educator; b. Guatemala City, Oct. 22, 1962; s. Edgar A. Arriaga and Maria Teresa Aguilar. BSc in Chemistry, U. Del Valle, Guatemala, 1985; PhD in Chemistry, Dalhousie U., Halifax, N.S., Can., 1990. Mgr. quality control Colortec, S.A., Guatemala, 1985, prodn. mgr., 1986; mem. temporary faculty U. del Valle, Guatemala, 1985; tchg. asst. Dalhousie U., Halifax, 1986-90; postdoctoral assoc. U.

Kans. Med. Ctr., Kansas City, 1990-92, U. Alta., Edmonton, Can., 1992-94; rsch. assoc. U. Alta., Edmonton, 1994-98; asst. prof. U. Minn., Mpls., 1998—. Fraternity advisor Beta chpt. Alpha Chi Sigma, Mpls., 1999—. Grantee Rsch. Corp., 1999, Minn. Microtech. Lab., U. Minn., Mpls., 1999. Avocations: sea kayaking, jazz dancing. Office: Dept Chemistry U Minn 207 Pleasant St SE Minneapolis MN 55455-0431

ARRIGO, ROBIN JEAN SEMPEY, piano educator, accompanist; b. Miami, Fla., Jan. 11, 1962; d. Edward James and Jean (Packman) Sempey; m. John Joseph Arrigo, July 23, 1988; children: Alyssa, Angela, Amanda. MusB in Piano Performance, Fla. State U., 1984, M Music Edn., 1987; D of Musical Arts in Accompanying and Chamber Music, U. Miami, 1998. Tchr. piano South Dade Sr. H.S., Homestead, Fla., 1987-88, Camden Mid. Sch., Kingsland, Ga., 1988-89; pvt. tchr. piano, Fernandina Beach, Fla., 1989-92; artist-in-residence Dreyfoos Sch. Arts, West Palm Beach, Fla., 1993-95; adj. prof. piano Palm Beach Atlantic Coll., West Palm Beach, 1995—; accompanist Fla. Philharm. Chorus, Ft. Lauderdale, 1996, Fla. Grand Opera, Miami, 1996; judge Pathfinder Scholarship Competition, West Palm Beach, 1999. Co-editor: The Mendelssohns: Their Music in History, 1999; featured soloist WXEL's Ovation South Fla. Mem. Music Tchrs. Nat. Assn., Am. Coll. Musicians. Avocations: painting, raising her children. E-mail: robinja@aol.com.

ARRIGONE, JORGE LUIS, architect, housing and development consultant; b. Buenos Aires, Jan. 1, 1930; arrived in S. Africa, 1975; s. Baltasar Carlos and Maria Angela Daglio A.; m. Helga Mariana Peralta, Feb. 16, 1962; 1 child, Jorge Carlos. Degree in architecture, Nat. U., Buenos Aires, 1955; Specialist on Social Housing, InterAm. Housing/Planning Ctr., Bogota, Colombia, 1958. Various positions as tech. adviser/housing expert Inst. de Vivienda de Maracaibo, Venezuela, 1959; low-income housing expert UN Devel. Programme, Dar es Salaam, Tanzania, 1963-67; tech. adviser to Sec. of State for Housing, Ministry of Social Welfare, Buenos Aires, 1968-70; low-income housing expert UN Devel. Programme, Lima, Peru, 1970-72, Mbabane, Swaziland, 1973-75; sr. chief rsch. officer Coun. for Sci. and Indsl. Rsch., Pretoria, South Africa, 1975-90; urban policy analyst Devel. Bank of So. Africa, Midrand, South Africa, 1990-96; housing and devel. cons. J.L. Arrigone & Assocs., Pretoria, 1996—; dir. Cope Affordable Housing, Johannesburg, South Africa, 1994-97; project mgmt. cons. UN Devel. Programme, Georgetown, Guyana, 1981; low-income housing cons. UN Ctr. for Human Settlements, Nairobi, Kenya, 1980; rural housing expert Orgn. Am. States, Quito, 1969. Contbr. numerous articles to profl. jours. Recipient Riley Schachat award for Bldg. Technology Rsch., Johannesburg, 1983. Mem. Soc. Cen. Arquitectos, Buenos Aires. Avocations: reading, photography, theater, gardening. Home: 105 Republic St, 0184 Silverton/Pretoria South Africa Office: JL Arrigone & Assocs, PO Box 13694/Hatfield 0028, Pretoria South Africa

ARRIGONI, ENRICO, physicist; b. Treviso, Veneto, Italy, Jan. 28, 1966; s. Giannantonio and Mariateresa (Piazza) A.; m. Babette Bechtold, June 1, 1996; 1 child, Giulio. MS in Physics, U./Scuola Normale Superiore, Pisa, Italy, 1989, PhD in Physics, 1993; habilitation in theoretical physics, U. Wuerzburg, 2000. Rschr., European fellow U. Wuerzburg, Germany, 1995-98, scientific asst., 1998—; guest scientist Max Planck Inst., Stuttgart-Dresden, 1994-95. Contbr. articles to profl. jours. Mem. Civil Svc. Caritas, Italy, 1992-93. Mem. Club Alpino Italiano, Associazione Guide e Scout Cattolici Italiani. Avocations: Alpinism, cycling, jogging. Office: U Wuerzburg Inst Theoret, Physik Am Hubland, Würzburg Bayern 97074, Germany

ARRINGTON, HARRIET ANN HORNE, historian, biographer, researcher, writer; b. Salt Lake City, June 22, 1924; d. Lyman Merrill and Myrtle (Swainston) Horne; m. Frederick C. Sorensen, Dec. 22, 1943 (div. Dec. 1954); children: Annette S. Rogers, Frederick Christian, Heidi S. Swinton; m. Gordon B. Moody, July 26, 1958 (div. Aug. 1963); 1 child, Stephen Horne; m. Leonard James Arrington, Nov. 19, 1983. BS in Edn., U. Utah, 1957. Cert. tchr., Utah, Ga. Supr. surg. secs. Latter-day Sts. Hosp., Salt Lake City, 1954-58; tchr. Salt Lake City Schs., 1957-58, Glynn County Schs., Brunswick, Ga., 1958-59, 60—; from med. sec. to office mgr. Dr. Horne, Salt Lake City, 1962-83; tchr. Carden Sch., Salt Lake City, 1973-74, women's history rschr., biographer; mem. Utah Women's Legis. Coun.; co-establisher Arrington Archives, Utah State U.; speaker hist. and women's confs. Author: Heritage of Faith, 1988, (essay) Worth Their Salt, 1997, Nearly Everything Imaginable: The Everyday Life of Utah's Mormon Pioneers, 1999; contbr. chpts. to books and articles to profl. jours., biog. and encys. Dist. chmn. Utah Rep. Com., 1972-76; mem. art com. Salt Lake City Bd. Edn.; chmn. art exhibit Senator Orrin Hatch's ann. Utah Women's Conf., 1987; past pres. L.D.S. Women's Relief Soc., Twin Falls, cultural refinement and/or spiritual living tchr.; chmn. Utah Women Artists' Exhbns., AAUW, Utah divsn., 1986-87, Springville Mus. of Art; bd. dirs. Annigton Archives Bd. Dirs. Nominated Pres. Ronald Reagan's Vol. Action award Utah Women Artists' Exhbn., 1987; recipient resolution of appreciation Utah Arts Coun., 1989. Mem. AAUW (Utah state cultural refinement chmn., cert. of appreciation 1988), DAR (regent 1998-2000, Princess Timpanogos Utah Chpt., Utah State DAR bd. historian 2000-02, Friends of Humanities, Arts, Scis. and Social Sci. award 1995), Old Main Soc. Utah State U., Classics Club, Chi Omega, Xi Alpha (past pres. alumni chpt.). Avocations: art, writing, gourmet cooking, needle point. Home and Office: 2236 S 2200 E Salt Lake City UT 84109-1135

ARRINGTON, MICHAEL BROWNE, travel management company executive; b. Chgo., Mar. 24, 1943; s. W. Russell and Ruth Marian (Browne) A.; m. DeEtta Jane Watson, Dec. 15, 1966 (div. 1969); m. Trudi Jeanne Robertson, Dec. 4, 1971 (div. 1992); children: Jennifer Lorraine, Patrick Browne. AA, Kendall Coll., Evanston, Ill.; BA in Polit. Sci., U. Ill. Adminstrv. asst. to Senate Majority Leader State of Ill., Springfield, 1966-67; dir. pub. affairs Union League Club of Chgo., 1967-68; exec. dir. South Loop Improvement Orgn., Chgo., 1968-69; pres., chief exec. officer The Arrington Found., Chgo., 1979—, Arrington Travel Ctr., Inc., Chgo., 1969-99, Recon Mgmt Svcs., Evanston, Ill., 1999—; bd. dirs. Better Bus. Bur., Chgo.; mem. Nat. White House Conf. Travel and Tourism, Preferred Hotels and Resorts Worldwide Travel Agt. Adv. Bd., Disting. Entrepreneurship Bd., U. Ill., Chgo. Bd. dirs. Robert R. McCormick Chgo. Boys & Girls Club, 1982—, Friends of Prentice Hosp., Chgo., 1986—; mem. chancellor's adv. bd. U. Ill., Chgo. Cpl. USMC, 1962-64. Named to Outstanding Young Men of Am., The Outstanding Ams. Found., 1970, Who's Who in Chgo. Bus., Crain's Chgo. Bus. mag., 1989-99, finalist Entrepreneur of Yr. 1989, 90; recipient Excellence in Phys. Fitness award USMC, 1962, Man of Yr. Ill. Vietnam Vets. Leadership Program, 1993, Significant Contbn. to Dental Health award Ill. Dental Health Soc., 1967; inducted into Hall of Fame Nat. Assn. Trade and Tech. Schs., 1988, Entrepreneurship Hall of Fame, Chgo., 1994. Mem. World Pres.'s Orgn., Econ. Club of Chgo., Chgo. Club, Union League, Westmoreland Country Club, 100 Club Cook County, Chgo. Pres.'s Orgn., Chief Execs. Orgn. Republican. Episcopalian. Avocations: golf, boating, skiing, scuba diving. Office: Recon Mgmt Svcs Inc 929 Edgemere Ct Evanston IL 60202-1428

ARRIOLA-ISAIS, CARLOS, obstetrician-gynecologist, educator; b. La Paz, BajaCalSur, Mex., July 22, 1958; s. Carlos Arriola-Sepulveda and Maria Teresa Isais-Famania; m. Ana Luisa Palacios-Llera, Apr. 21, 1989; children: Carlos Arriola-Palacios, Ana Grecia Arriola-Palacios. MD, Autonoma U. Guadalajara, Mex., 1981. Intern Salvatierra Gen. Hosp., La Paz, 1981; chief ob-gyn divsn., 1999—; social svc. ISSSTE Gen. Hosp., La Paz, 1982-83, rotating resident, 1984-85; resident in ob-gyn. ISSSTE Gen. Hosp., Mexico City, 1985-88; obstetrician, gynecologist Soc. Security of Mex. Labor Union, La Paz, 1985—; chief resident ISSSTE Gen. Hosp.; prof. Nat. Autonoma U. Mex., Mexico City, 1998; svc. chief ob-gyn. Salvatierra Gen. Hosp., La Paz, 1999—. Supporter San Diego Opera. Fellow Mex. Ob-gyn. Coun., Ob-gyn. Mex. Fedn., Baja Calif. Ob-gyn. Assn. Avocations: scuba-diving, water-skiing, playing guitar, judo, target shooting. Home: Madero 935, 23000 La Paz BajaCalS, Mexico Office: Albanez 1400, Bravo y Meliton, 23000 La Paz Mexico

ARRONS-LANE, MARION JEAN, artist, educator; b. N.Y.C., July 8, 1928; d. Herman Arrons and Anita Gordon; m. Sidney Lane, Dec. 26, 1953 (div. Dec. 1988); children: Spencer G. Lane, George D. Lane. Student, Pratt Inst., Bklyn. Mus. Art Sch.; BA in Art Edn., William Paterson U., 1976; MFA, Rutgers U., 1978; postgrad., Pratt Inst., Bklyn. Mus. Art Sch. adj. prof. Bergen C.C., Paramus, N.J., 1979-85; part-time tchr., therapist Manhattan Psychol. Ctr., N.Y.C., 1986— acting curator Bergen County Mus., Paramus, 190-71. One-woman and group exhbns. include Bklyn. Mus., 1958 (award), Montclair Mus., 1960, 65 (awards), Jersey City Mus., 1965, 66, State Mus., Trenton, N.J., 1968, 70, Bergen County Mus., 1972, Nat. Assn. Women Artists Annual, 1973, Kraushaar Gallery, N.Y., 1974, Rockland County Ctr. for Arts, 1975, Pleaides Gallery, N.Y., 1976, 78, 98, Rutgers U. Newark, Paul Robeson Ctr., 1980, Rutgers U., New Brunswick, 1982, Edward Williams Coll., N.J., 1980, 82, 99, Women's Caucus for Art, N.Y., 1982, Hunterdon Art Ctr., N.J., 1983, City Without Walls Gallery, N.J., 1983, 84, Noyes Mus., N.J., 1984, Newark Mus., 1961, 64, 85, Glassboro State Coll., 1985, Jersey State Coll., 1985, Ramapo Coll., N.J., 1985, Fair Lawn Libr., N.J., 1986, Pavillion Gallery Meml. Hosp., 1986, Women's Caucus for Art, NYU Grad. Sch., 1986, Monmouth Mus., N.J., 1988, William Carlos Williams Ctr. for Arts, 1990, William Paterson Coll. N.J., 1992, 94, Kerygma Gallery, 1993, Fourteen Sculptors Gallery, N.Y., 1995, 96, Kerygma Gallery, N.J., 1995, Nabisco Corp. Hdqrs., N.J., 1995, Westbeth Gallery, N.Y., 1996, West Beth Gallery, 2000, La Mama La Galeria, N.Y., 1996, Broomest Gallery, N.Y., 1996, numerous others; represented in permanent collections at Bloomfield Coll., Bergen County Mus., also many corp. and pvt. collections. Fellow N.J. State Coun. on Arts, 1983, 88, Edward Albee Found., 1983; Robert Florsheim Art Fund grantee, 1999. Avocations: photography, hiking, ballet. Home: 55 Bethune St # D351 New York NY 10014-2010

ARROTT, ELIZABETH, journalist; b. Detroit, Oct. 1, 1960; d. Anthony Schuyler and Patricia Graham Arrott; m. Rafael Alexeevich Ekimyan, Sept. 16, 1995; children: Alexei Rafaelevich Ekimyan, Elizabeth Rafaelevna Ekimyan, Catherine Rafaelevna Ekimyan. AB, Harvard U., 1983. Moscow corr. Voice of Am., Moscow, 1993-97; anchor NewsNow Voice of Am., Washington, 1998—. Mem. Ch. LDS. Home: 5026 Reno Rd NW Washington DC 20008-2951 Office: Voice of Am 330 Independence Ave SW Washington DC 20547-0003

ARROW, KENNETH JOSEPH, economist, educator; b. N.Y.C., Aug. 23, 1921; s. Harry I. and Lillian (Greenberg) A.; m. Selma Schweitzer, Aug. 31, 1947; children: David Michael, Andrew. BS in Social Sci., CCNY, 1940; MA, Columbia U., 1941, PhD, 1951, DSc (hon.), 1973; LLD (hon.), U. Chgo., 1967, CUNY, 1972, Hebrew U. Jerusalem, 1975, U. Pa., 1976, Washington U., St. Louis, 1989, Harvard U., 1999; D. Social and Econ. Scis. (hon.), U. Vienna, Austria, 1971; LLD (hon.), Ben-Gurion U. of the Negev, 1992; D. Social Scis. (hon.), Yale, 1974; D (hon.), Université René Descartes, Paris, 1974, U. Aix-Marseille III, 1985, U. Cattolica del Sacro Cuore, Milan, Italy, 1994, U. Uppsala, 1995, U. Buenos Aires, 1999, U. Cyprus, 2000; Dr.Pol., U. Helsinki, 1976; MA (hon.), Harvard U., 1968; DLitt, Cambridge U., Eng., 1985; LLD (hon.), Harvard U., 1999. Rsch. assoc. Cowles Commn. for Research in Econs., 1947-49; asst. prof. econs. U. Chgo., 1948-49; acting asst. prof. econs. and stats. Stanford, 1949-50, assoc. prof., 1950-53, prof. econs., stats. and ops. rsch., 1953-68; prof. econs. Harvard, 1968-74, James Bryant Conant univ. prof., 1974-79; exec. head dept. econs. Stanford U., 1954-56, acting exec. head dept., 1962-63, Joan Kenney prof. econs. and prof. ops. rsch., 1979-91, prof. emeritus, 1991—; economist Coun. Econ. Advisers, U.S. Govt., 1962; cons. RAND Corp.; Fulbright prof. U. Siena, 1995; vis. fellow All Souls Coll., Oxford, 1996. Author: Social Choice and Individual Values, 1951, Essays in the Theory of Risk Bearing, 1971, The Limits of Organization, 1974, Collected Papers, Vols. I-VI, 1983-85; co-author: Mathematical Studies in Inventory and Production, 1958, Studies in Linear and Nonlinear Programming, 1958, Time Series Analysis of Interindustry Demands, 1959, Public Investment, The Rate of Return and Optimal Fiscal Policy, 1971, General Competitive Analysis, 1971, Studies in Resource Allocation Processes, 1977, Social Choice and Multicriterion Decision Making, 1985. Served as capt. AUS, 1942-46. Recipient Alfred Nobel Meml. prize in econ. scis. Swedish Acad. Scis., 1972, Kempé de Feriet medal, 1998, medal U. Paris, 1998; Social Sci. Rsch. fellow, 1952; fellow Ctr. for Advanced Study in the Behavioral Scis., 1956-57, Churchill Coll., Cambridge, Eng., 1963-64, 70, 73, 86; Guggenheim fellow, 1972-73. Fellow AAAS (chmn. sect. K. 1983), Am. Acad. Arts and Scis. (v.p. 1979-81, 91-93), Econometric Soc. (v.p. 1955, pres. 1956), Am. Statis. Assn., Inst. Math. Stats., Am. Econ. Assn. (exec. com. 1967-69, pres. 1973, John Bates Clark medal 1957), Internat. Soc. Inventory Rsch. (pres. 1983-90); mem. NAS (mem. coun. 1990-93), Inst. Medicine (sr.), Internat. Econs. Assn. (pres. 1983-86), Am. Philos. Soc., Inst. Mgmt. Scis. (pres. 1963, chmn. coun. 1964, 1973 Von Neumann prize 1986), Finnish Acad. Scis. (fgn. hon.), Brit. Acad. (corr.), Western Econ. Assn. (pres. 1980-81), Soc. Social Choice and Welfare (pres. 1991-93), Pontifical Acad. Social Scis., Game Theory Soc. Fax: 650-725-5702. E-mail: arrow@leland.stanford.edu. Office: Stanford U Dept Econs Stanford CA 94305-6072

ARROWSMITH, JOSEPH BERNARD, writer; b. Auckland, New Zealand, Dec. 9, 1916; arrived in Australia, 1928; s. Bernard and Clarice Warner (Bain) A.; m. Veda Joyce Dowling, Aug. 6, 1946; children: Philip, Martin, Paul. apptd. 1st acct. gen. treas. Colony of North Borneo, 1946. Author: The Science of Consciousness, 1992; contbr. over 135 articles to profl. jours. With Australian Army, 1939-45. Avocations: mountain climbing. Home: 56 Pohlman St, Southport Q4215, Australia

ARROYAVE, CARLOS ENRIQUE, engineering educator, researcher; b. Yarumal, Colombia, Apr. 2, 1954; s. Abraham and Mabel Posada A.; m. Maria Fabiola Henao, Dec. 27, 1979; children: Daniel Enrique, Juan David. BMetE, U. Antioquia, Medellin, Colombia, 1979; MSc Metall. Engring. and Materials Sci., Fed. U. Rio De Janeiro, Brazil, 1988; DSc in Chem. Scis., Complutense U. Madrid, 1995. Cert. profl. engr. Prof. dept. metall. engring. U. Antioquia, 1979-91, prof. emeritus, 1991—, chmn. dept., 1983-86, dir. Engring. Faculty Rsch. Ctr., 1990-92; ptnr., advisor Materials Svcs. and Tech., Medellin, 1991-92; coord. nat. program Colciencias, Bogota, 1989-90; coord. doctoral programs in engring. S&T Ctr. of Antioquia, Medellin, 1999-2000. Mem. Colombian Assn. Corrosion and Protection (pres. 1997—), Metall. Engrs. Assn. U. Antioquia (treas. 1981-82, pres. 1982-83, Disting. prof. 1991). Avocations: photography, music, scientific literature. Fax: 57-4-2119028. E-mail: carroyav@udea.edu.co. Office: U Antioquia, PO Box 1226, Medellin Antioq, Colombia

ARROYO, RODNEY LEE, city planning and transportation executive; b. Miami, Fla., Dec. 31, 1958; s. Julian Avelino and Marilyn (Marsh) A.; m. Leslie Ponessa; children: Nicholas Julian, Anthony Eugene. BA cum laude, U. South Fla., 1980; M in city planning, Ga. Inst. Tech., 1982. Asst. dir. South Fla. Regional Planning Coun., Hollywood, Fla., 1982-86; sr. assoc. Barton Aschman Assocs., Inc., Southfield, Mich., 1986-89; v.p. Birchler Arroyo Assoc., Inc., Southfield, 1989—; founder and editor, Planning Mich. Magazine, 1988-91. Contbr. articles to profl. jours. Recipient Outstanding Planning Project award Mich. Soc. Planning Ofcls. and Mich. chpt. Am. Planning Assn., 1997, 98. Mem. Inst. Transp. Engrs. (sub. com. mem. 1986—), Am. Planning Assn. (Mich. exec. com. 1989-91, award for excellence in small town and rural planning Small Town & Rural Planning Divsn. 1998), Am. Inst. Cert. Planners. Avocations: golfing, running, geneaology, photography. Office: Birchler Arroyo Assocs Inc 20245 W 12 Mile Rd Ste 200 Southfield MI 48076-6407

ARROYO MARROQUIN, ROMÁRICO, federal official; b. Tulancingo, Hildago, Mex., Dec. 13, 1942; married. BA in Civil Engring., Nat. Autonomous U.; MA in Sci., Stanford U. Chief analysis Ctr. Calculation, Sec. Hydraulic Resources, 1966; asst. dir. Nat. Tourism Fund, 1973-76, dir., 1976-77; adv. to undersec. Min. Housing Pub. Credit, 1977-78; undersec. basic industry Sec. Mines, Inter-State Industry, 1982-87; dir. gen. United Shipyards, 1987-91; dep. dir. gen. Hydraulic, Urban and Indsl. Infrastructure, 1991-94; undersec. Agr. and Livestock, 1995-98; sec. Agr., Livestock and Rural Develop., 1998—. Office: Secretaria de Agricultura, Insurgentes Sur 476, Col Roma Sur, Piso 06760, Mexico*

ARSALI, MOHAMMAD, engineering consultant, realtor; b. Kerman, Iran, Oct. 4, 1955; s. Abbas and Khanoum (Mehrabi) A.; m. Afsoon Iranpour Arsali, Sept. 14, 1985; children: Arash, Aryan, Armin. BSEE, U. Ala., Birmingham, 1980, MSEE, 1981; PhD, Fla. Atlantic U., Boca Raton, 1998. Cert. profl. engr., Ala., Ga., Fla. Prin. engr. Ga. Power Co., Atlanta, 1981-87; project mgr. Fla. Power & Light, Miami, 1987-95; sr. project cons. Southern Engring., Atlanta, 1995-96; exec. cons. Energy Encounter, Palm Beach, Fla., 1996—; adv. Epri, Egeas Com., San Francisco, 1985-92, Dept. Energy, Washington, 1991-95. Author: Climate Challenge Action Plan Between Fla. Power & Light & Dept. Energy, 1995; editor: Climate Challenge Option Book, 1995; contbr. articles to profl. jours. High sch. adv. Jr. Achievement Programs, Atlanta, 1982-87. Recipient Outstanding Work, The Edison Electric Insts., Washington, 1994. E-mail: arsali@yahoo.com. Fax: (561) 740-1319. Home: 3 Harbour Dr N Ocean Ridge FL 33435-6212

ARSEBÜK, GÜVEN, anthropoarchaeologist, educator; b. Istanbul, Turkey, July 2, 1936; s. Emin and Ulviye A.; m. Sevinç Birsen, July 20, 1962; children: Emir, Zeynep. BA, Robert Coll., Istanbul, 1958; MA, U. Istanbul, 1962, PhD, 1969; MA, U. Chgo., 1974. Asst. prof. human evolution and prehistory U. Istanbul, 1970-81, assoc. prof. sect. of pre-history Faculty of Letters, 1981-88, prof. sect. of pre-history Faculty of Letters, 1988—; rsch. assoc. U. Chgo., 1986. Author: Insan ve Evrim, 1990, 2d edit., 1997; editor: Light on Top of the Black Hill, 1998; contbr. articles to profl. jours. 2d lt. Turkish ground forces, 1964-65. Mem. Am. Rsch. Inst. (pres. 2000—), Turkey, German Archeol. Inst., Turkish Inst. Archeol., Turkish Touring Club. Home: Feneryolu Sok 45, 81040 Istanbul KZL Turkey Office: U Istanbul Facutly Letters, Sect of Pre-History, 34459 Istanbul Turkey

ARSENAULT, SAMANTHA, Olympic athlete; b. Peabody, Mass., Oct. 11, 1981. Recipient Gold medal 4 x 200-meter freestyle (team) Sydney Olympics, 2000; 2d pl. 200-meter freestyle U.S. spring nats., 1999, 3d pl. 100-meter and 200-meter freestyle U.S. summer nats., 1999. Office: USA Swimming 1 Olympic Plz Colorado Springs CO 80909-5746*

ARSENE, MELANIA-LILIANA, biochemist, researcher; b. Bucharest, Romania, Dec. 11, 1956; d. Stefan and Silvia (Dumitriu) A. BSc, U. Bucharest, 1979, MSc, 1980, PhD, 1998. Biochem. diplomate. Biochemist Drugs Factory, Bucharest, 1980-83, Biosynthesis Factory, Calafat, Romania, 1983; biochemist Chem. and Biochem. Energetics Inst., Bucharest, 1983-88, rschr., 1988-90; sr. rschr. III Chem. Rsch. Inst., Bucharest, 1990-95, sr. rschr. II, 1995—; assoc. asst. U. Poly., Bucharest, 1986-90, U. Bucharest, 1990-93. Contbr. articles to profl. jours.; patentee in field. Mem. Romanian Biol. Soc., Romanian Biotech. Engring. Soc., N.Y. Acad. Scis. Eastern Orthodox. Home: Cozla nr 8 Bl A 7/Apt 49, 74636 Bucharest Romania Office: ICECHIM-Dept Biotech, Spl Independentei 202, 77208 Bucharest Romania

ARSENYAN, TATIANA ISHKHANOVNA, physicist, researcher; b. Moscow, June 27, 1938; s. Ishkhan Arsen'evich and Natalia (Kabanova) A.; m. Alexander Alexandrovich Semenov, Jan. 27, 1962. Diploma, Moscow State U., 1961, PhD, 1967; DSc in Physics and Math., Tomsk (Russia) State U., 1990. Rsch. asst. Moscow State U., 1961-62, scientific rschr., 1962-86, scientist, 1986-90, sr. scientist, 1990-95, head scientist, 1995—; lectr.; cons. engring. insts., 1966—. Editor: Statistical Methods in Experimental Physics and Technics, 1969; contbr. more than 120 articles to profl. jours. Grantee Russian Found. for Basic Researches, Moscow, 1994-95, Russian Min. of Edn., 1995-96. Mem. IEEE. Avocations: arts, poetry, history, foreign languages. E-mail address: arsenit@fluct.phys.msu.su. Fax: (095) 932-8820. Office: Moscow State U, Vorob'evy gory, 119899 Moscow Russia

ARSHADY, REZA, chemistry educator, research director, author; b. Kashan, Central, Ctrl. Iran; arrived in England, 1972; s. Farajjollah Arshady and Khanom Rashidi. BS, U. Tchrs., Tehran, 1970; PhD, U. Liverpool, Eng., 1976. Chartered chemist. Faculty U. Tabriz, Iran, 1970-80, head indsl./polymer sect., 1976-78; Wolfson rsch. fellow Imperial Coll., Sci. Tech. Med. U., London, 1981-83; prof., head chemistry dept. Coll. Scis. (U. Teachers), Kashan, 1984-98; dir. sci. and tech. Citus Ltd., Kashan, 1998—; sr. fellow Imperial Coll. Sci. Tech. Med. U. London; MRC Cambridge, Eng., U. Lund, Sweden, U. Padova, Italy, Tech. U., Munich, Germany; cons./adviser pvt. and pub. orgns. Europe, Iran, U.S., 1983—; chemistry editor Culture and Vision, Tehran, 1985; field of rsch. specialty polymers for chem. industry, engring., biotech., medicine. Editor: Functional Polymers for Emerging Technologies, Microspheres, microcapsules and Liposomes (multi-volume series); mem. editorial bd. Trends in Polymer Sci.; editor-in-chief Citus Books, 1998—; contbr. over 140 articles to profl. jours. With Iranian Army, 1964-65. Fellow Royal soc. Chemistry; mem. AAAS (internat.), Am. Chem. Soc., N.Y. Acad. Scis., Culture and Vision Soc. (sr.), European Peptide soc., Soc. of Authors. Avocations: history and philosophy of sci., sci. and tech. in soc. Office: Dept Chemistry, Citus Ltd, 176 Franciscan Rd, London SW17 8HH, England

ARSHI, GURCHARAN SINGH, academic facility administrator; b. Patiala, India, Feb. 11, 1944; s. Singh Jaswant and Kaur Adarsh A.; m. Jagdish Kaur, Oct. 16, 1966; children: Parvinder, Rajinder, Harpreet. BA, U. Delhi, 1963, MA, 1965, PhD, 1973. Lectr. Deshbandhu Coll., Delhi, India, 1965-76; assoc. dir. corr. courses Punjabi U., Patiala, 1976-78, reader, then prof., 1978—; head dept., dean langs. faculty, dir. planning and monitoring Punjabi U., 1986—. Recipient awards for lit. criticism Punjabi Govt., 1975, 95, 95; recipient Kartar Singh Dhaliwal meml. award, 1997. Avocations: music, cinematography. Home: A-4 Punjabi Univ Campus, 147002 Patiala Punjab, India

ARSLAN, LEVENT MUSTAFA, engineering educator, consultant; b. Besni, Adiyaman, Turkey, Sept. 2, 1968; s. Abdülkadir and Ayse Sidika (Aytekin) A. BS, Bogazigi U., Istanbul, Turkey, 1991; MS, Duke U., 1993, PhD, 1996. Rsch. asst. Duke U., Durham, 1991-96; rsch. engr. Tex. Instruments, Dallas, 1994-96; mem. tech. staff Entropic Rsch., Washington, 1996-98; assoc. prof. Bogazigi U., 1998—; cons. Deutsch-Hill Assn., 1999—, Sakhr Software, 1998—; project mgr. Turkcell, Turkey, 1999—. Patentee in field; contbr. articles to profl. jours. Mem. IEEE. Avocations: playing violin, painting, tennis, soccer, volleyball.

ARSOV, YANKO BOYANOV, institute director; b. Pazardjik, Bulgaria, June 12, 1934; s. Boyan Arsov and Efrossina (Ivanchova) Yanev; m. Hristodoli Nedialkova Dikova, Apr. 5, 1958; children: Boyan Yankov, Nedyalko Yankov. Engr. Metallurgist, U. Chemistry & Chem. Tech., Sofia, Bulgaria, 1958; PhD, High Inst. Steels & Alloys, Moscow, 1964, DSc, 1975. Registered engr. Head steel prodn. shop Rwy. Works, Sofia, 1958-60; rsch. assoc. Ctrl. Rsch. Engring. Inst., Sofia, 1960-64; sr. specialist State Com. Sci. & Tech. Progress, Sofia, 1964-66; dep. dir. Inst. Metal Sci., Bulgarian Acad. Sci., Sofia, 1966-89, dir., 1989—, prof., 1991; mem. Higher Certifying Commn., Sofia, 1995—; mem. Nat. Coun. Engring. Progress, Sofia, 1997. Author: Steel Castings, 1974, Metal Technology, 1981, Casting Properties of Alloys, 1984; chief editor Jour. Tech. Ideas, 1992—. Recipient gold medal Inst. Metal Sci., Bulgarian Govt., 1968, award for devel. gas counter pressure method Inst. Metal Sci., 1991. Mem. Soc. Am. Engrs., Am. Soc. Materials, Am. Foundrimen Soc., Bulgarian Acad. Sci. (corr., dep. chmn. gen. assembly 1989—). Avocations: wood carving, mushroom gathering, alpine tourism, photography. Home: 34 Edisson Str, 1111 Sofia Bulgaria Office: Inst Metal Sci, 67 Shipchensky Prohod Str, 1574 Sofia Bulgaria

ARST, HELGI, geophysicist; b. Tallinn, Estonia, Dec. 23, 1931; d. Juhan and Linda (Kaevalt) Ardve; m. Georg Egon Arst, July 18, 1975. BS, U. Tartu, 1955, PhD, 1962, DSc, 1991. Rschr. Inst. Physics & Astronomy, Tartu, Estonia, 1960-63; sr. rschr. Inst. Astrophysics and Atmospheric Physics, Tôravere, Estonia, 1963-75, Inst. Thermophysics and Electrophysics, Tallinn, Estonia, 1975-90; sect. head Inst. Ecology & Marine Rsch., Tallinn, 1990-92; sr. rschr. Estonian Marine Inst., Tallinn, 1992—; supervisor PhD students U. Tartu, 1993—. Author: Optical Remote Sensing in Oceanology, 1990; contbr. articles to profl. jours. Mem. Nat. Geog. Soc. Home: Gonsiori St 24-17, 10128 Tallinn Estonia Office: Estonian Marine Inst, Paldiski Rd 1, 10137 Tallinn Estonia

ARTÉMIADIS, NICOLAS K., educator; b. Constantinople, Greece, May 17, 1917; citizen U.S. and Greece; s. Kyriacos A. and Despina N.(Docmedjoglou) A.; m. Zafiria Pyrlidis, Aug. 14, 1964. MA U. Thessaloniki, Greece, 1939; diplôme d'Etudes Supérieures en Analyse Supérieure, Sorbonne, Paris, 1954; diplôme d'Etudes Supérieures en Algèbre et Théorie des Nombres, Sorbonne, 1956, doctorat ès Sciences Mathématiques with high honors, doctorat d'Etat, 1957. Tchr. secondary edn. Greece, 1941-42, 48-51; asst. prof. U. Wis., Milw., 1958-60, assoc. prof., 1961-66; grantee Math.

Rsch. Ctr., 1959-61; prof. U. Thessaloniki, Greece, 1960-61, So. Ill. U., Carbondale, 1966-77; prof., dean sch. math. and physics U. Patras, Greece, 1975—; prof. emeritus U. Patras, 1984—; Greek rep. Internat. Congresses, 1976, 78; invited speaker various univs. U.S. and Europe; mem. Greek Nat. Math. Com. Author: Real Analysis, 1976; 3 textbooks in Real Analysis, Functional Analysis Complex Analysis, History of Mathematics; reviewer Zentralblatt für Mathematik; contbr. rsch. papers to profl. publs., U.S. and Europe. Served to 1st lt. Greek Army, 1940-41. Decorated medal for excellent acts; recipient Stavropoulos prize Greek Embassy, Paris, 1957; French govt. fellow, 1951-58. Mem. Acad. Athens (pres. Greek nat. com. for math., v.p. 1999, pres. 2000), Acad. Tiberina, Am. Math. Soc., Math. Assn. Am., AAUP, Greek Math. Soc. (pres.), Sigma Xi, AHEPA, N.Y. Acad. Scis. Greek Orthodox. Home: 169 Megalou Alexandrou St, Thrakomakedones 13676, Greece

ARTHUR, THOMAS HAHN, theater educator, director; b. Chgo., 1937; s. Maxwell Arthur and Josephine Edith (Hahn) A.; m. Carolyn Ruth Dry (div. 1967); 1 child, Michael Dry; m. Ellen Mary Sharkey, Mar. 28, 1968 (div. 1976); children: Adam Stephen, Benjamin Douglas; m. Kathleen Alden Giles, Dec. 28, 1976; 1 child, Robert Kenneth. BS, Northwestern U., 1959; MA, Ind. U., 1969, PhD, 1973. Promotion dir. Graphic Arts Buyer Mag., Chgo., 1960-63; publicity supr., actor Court Theatre, U. Chgo., 1963, 64; teaching asst. Ind. U., Bloomington, 1965-68; co-founder, dir., publicity mgr. Ind. Summer Repertoire Theatre, Ind. U., Bloomington, 1966; asst. prof. theater Ill. State U., Normal, 1969-73; adj. lectr. theater history Ill. Wesleyan U., Bloomington, 1972-73; prof. theater, head dept. theatre and dance James Madison U., Harrisonburg, Va., 1973-94; dir. Sch. Theatre and Dance, 1994-95; artistic dir. The Dinner Theatre, James Madison U., 1977, 82, 85, 88, 91, 92, 93; radio interviewer BBC, 1981, 84; acad. specialist USIA, South Africa and Finland, 1989, Hungary, 1994; cons. USIA, Naples, Italy, 1996; individual lectr. Am. Theatre, U. East Anglia, Richmond, Eng., Brit. Inst. Florence, Italy, 1990, Internat. Fedn. Theatre Rsch., Tel Aviv, 1996, Dhaka, Bangladesh, 1997, Ahmedabad, India, 1997, Ankara, Turkey, 1997, Nicosia, Cyprus, 2000; program evaluator Nat. Assn. Schs. Theatre, 1990—; guest dir., actor Sweet Briar Coll., Amherst, Va., 1972-73. Author: See You at the Movies: The Autobiography of Melvyn Douglas, 1986; contbg. editor Dramatics mag., 1979-84; contbr. interviews, articles, revs. and poetry to various mags. and jours.; dir. TV vignettes for NEH grant, 1979-80; prodr. Am. Coll. Theatre Festival prodn. Sizwi Bansi is Dead, Kennedy Ctr., Washington, 1992; dir. Am. Coll. Theatre Festival prodn. Carriage, Kennedy Ctr., 1998; dir. Shakespeare Festival, Williamsburg, Va., 1998; dir. Tex. Shakespeare Festival, 1999, Harrow Prodns., Va., 2000. Mem. Gov.'s Commn for 200th Aniv. of Constn., Richmond, 1983-84. NDEA fellow in Am. studies, 1965-68; grantee So. Ednl. Communications Assn., 1980. Mem. Va. Writers Club, Am. Studies Assn., Assn. Theatre in Higher Edn., Comm. Assn. Am., Soc. Theatre Rsch., Nat. Assn. Schs. of Theatre (chmn. com. on nominations 1995, chmn. com. on ethics 1996—), Internat. Fedn. Theatre Rsch., Southeastern Theater Conf., Va. Theatre Assn. (v.p. 1983-84, chair theatre divsn. 1991-95). Avocations: reading, travel. Home: 298 Campbell St Harrisonburg VA 22801-4014 Office: James Madison U Dept Theatre And Dance Harrisonburg VA 22807-0001

ARTIGUES, JEAN MARIE, ophthalmologist; b. Narbon, France, Aug. 22, 1934; s. Francois and Genevieve (Caillassou) A.; m. Daniele Richard, June 11, 1957 (div. 1965); 1 child, Philppe; m. Chantal Tondreau, Nov. 9, 1967; 1 child, Alexandre. MD, U. Paris, 1961. Externe various hosps., Paris, 1955-61; interne in ophthalmology Hopital des 15/20, Paris, 1959-63; practice medicine specializing in ophthalmology Bayonne, France, 1963—. Served to lt. M.C. French Army, 1961-63. Mem. Societe Francaise Ophthalmologie, Societe Francaise Photocoagulation. Club: Vet. Car (St. Jean de Luz, France). Avocations: classic cars, wind surfing, skiing, pelote basque. Home: Pessenia, 64200 Arcangues France Office: Ctr Med Chirurgical Ophthalmologie, 3 place du Reduit, 64100 Bayonne France

ARTIK, SUZAN, immunologist; b. Herborn, Germany, Mar. 12; d. Naci and Hella (Uhde) A. Postgrad., U. Düsseldorf, Germany, 1997; MD, Harvard U., 1997. Rschr. in immunology Med. Inst. Environ. Hygiene, Dusseldorf, Germany, 1997-99, resident in dermatology, 1999—. Avocations: playing tennis, photography, travel, art. Office: Dept Dermatology, Moorenstrasse 5, 10225 Dusseldorf Germany

ARTISYUK, VLADIMIR VASILYEVICH, nuclear engineer; b. Axakovo, Russia, May 24, 1962; s. Vasiliy Samoilovich and Antonina Petrovna (Osechkova) A.; m. Elena Yurievna Kirushina, Aug. 6, 1988; 1 child, Anna. PhD, Obinsk Inst. Nuclear Power, Russia, 1991; Dr.Engring., Tokyo Inst. Tech., 1997. Asst. prof. Obninsk Inst. Nuclear Power Engring., 1991-92, assoc. prof., 1992-99; asst. prof. Tokyo Inst. Tech., 1999—. Avocation: Russian and Japanese poetry. Home: Aoba-ku, 2-46-643 Fujipaoka, Yokohama-shi Japan Office: Tokyo Inst Tech Rsch Lab, 2-12-1 O-Okayama Mepuro-ku, Tokyo 52, Japan

ARTNER, GUENTHER, investment banker, financial analyst; b. Mistelbach, Austria, Jan. 5, 1973; s. Johann and Elfriede (Stangl) A. M, U. Econs. and Bus. Adminstrn., Vienna, Austria, 1996. CFA. Securities analyst Schoeller Bank, Vienna, 1994-95; corp. fin. analyst CAIB Investment Bank, Vienna, 1995-97, sr. analyst, 1997-98, assoc., 1998-2000; sector equity analyst ERSTE Bank, Vienna, 2000—. Avocations: tennis, dancing, personal investments, reading. Fax: 43-1-53100-3016. Home: Bahnzeile 16, 2130 Mistelbach Austria Office: ERSTE Bank AG, Boersegasse 14, 1010 Vienna Austria

ARTOIS, TOM JOZEF, biology educator; b. Turnhout, Belgium, Jan. 28, 1972; s. Kamiel Stefaan Karel Artois and Rita Van Tiggelen; m. Nele Lea Maria Spelmans, Aug. 21, 1999. Student biology, Limburgs U. Centrum, Diepenbeek, 1993; Licentiate Biology, U. Ghent, 1995. Asst. Limburgs U. Centrum, 1995—. Mem. Royal Belgian Zool. Soc., Internat. Assn. Meiobenthologists. Avocation: bird watching. Office: Limburgs U Centrum Dept SBG, Universitaire Campus Gebouw D, 3590 Diepenbeek Limburg, Belgium

ARTS, FRANK, investment manager; b. Antwerp, Belgium, Aug. 13, 1943; s. Jozef aand Mania (Dekkers) A.; married, Dec. 28, 1968; 5 children. Finance, Ufsia, Antwerp, 1967. Banker Bank Financia, Belgium, 1967-69, Paribas Bank, Belgium, 1969-82; investment mgr. Janssen Pharmaceutica N.V., Beerse, Belgium, 1982—; bd. dirs. Fortin B. Belgium, Fortales N.V. Belgium, Certimmo N.V. Belgium. Contbr. articles to profl. jours. Home: Vosholle i 36, 2930 Braasschoot B Belgium Office: Janssen Pahramaceutica NV, 30 Turnhoutseweg, B 2340 Beerse Belgium

ARTS, THEO ALBERT, chemicals production manager; b. Aalst, Belgium, Jan. 2, 1942; s. Pieter Frans Arts and Marie Fieremans; m. Marie-Yvonne Goegebeur, Feb. 29, 1988; m. Helena Van Dorpe, Mar. 15, 1967 (dec. Aug. 1986); children: Jan, Hilde, Peter. Garden technician, St.-Barbara Inst., Wetteren, Belgium, 1960; indsl. engr. chemistry, St.-Lieven, Ghent, Belgium, 1964; civil engr. chemistry, Cath. U. Leuven, Belgium, 1967. Cert. chem. engr. Plant mgr. BASF, Antwerp, Belgium, 1969-80, divsn. dir., 1980-96, audit coord., 1996-2000. Contbr. sci. articles to profl. jours. Mem. Internat. Assn. Bryologists, Royal Belgian Bot. Soc. (Crépin prize), Brit. Bryol. Soc., others. Avocations: gardening, traveling, reading. E-mail: theo.arts@worldonline.be. Home: Kerklei 56, B-2960 St.-Job-in-'t-Goor Belgium

ARTURSSON, KARIN INGEGERD, microbiologist; b. Tidaholm, Skaraborg, Sweden, Aug. 13, 1960; d. Bengt Gunnar Ingemar and Elsa Ingegerd Irene (Gustafsson) Höjer; m. Per Artur Sven Artursson, June 3, 1989; children: Sara, Björn. MS in Vet. Medicine, Swedish U. Agrl. Scis., 1984, PhD in Vet. Immunology, 1993. Pvt. practice Sweden, 1985-86; lab. vet., head of dept., mem. sci. coun. Nat. Vet. Inst., Uppsala, 1993—. Recipient Best PhD Thesis award Swedish U. Agrl. Scis./Royal Swedish Acad. Agr. and Forestry, 1995. Mem. Swedish Soc. Med. Microbiology, Scandinavian Soc. for Immunology, Brit. Equine Vet. Assn., European Soc. Emerging Infections, Am. Soc. Rickettsiology.

ARTZ, JOHN CURTIS, lawyer; b. Columbus, Ohio, Mar. 4, 1946; s. Curtis Price and Kathryn Lucille (Risley) A.; m. Nancy Eileen Jones, Apr. 5, 1969; children: John Curtis Jr., Alexander Hardie, Kathryn Cullen. BA disting. mil. grad., Allegheny Coll., 1968; JD magna cum laude, U. S.C., 1976. Bar: Pa. 1976, U.S. Dist. Ct. (we. dist.) Pa. 1976, U.S. Ct. Appeals (3d and 6th cirs.) 1996, U.S. Supreme Ct. 1980. From assoc. to ptnr. Eckert Seamans Cherin & Mellott, Pitts., 1976-94; shareholder, dir. Polito & Smock, P.C., Pitts., 1994—; adj. asst. prof. Grad. Sch. Pub. Health U. Pitts., 1988-92; part-time instr. Robert Morris Coll., Pitts., 1998—; seminar and workshop presenter Nat. Safety Coun., Western Pa. Safety Coun., Pa. Bar Inst., Allegheny County Bar Assn., Pitts. Human Resources Assn., Butler County Pers. Assn., Constrn. Fin. Mgmt. Assn., Pa. Inst. CPAs, Western Pa. Cmty. Accts. Notes editor U. S.C. Law Rev., 1975-76; contbr. articles to profl. jours. Dir. Jr. Achievement S.W. Pa., Pitts., 1994—, vice-chair adminstrn., 1998—. Capt. USAF, 1968-73. Recipient Bronze Leadership award Jr. Achievement S.W. Pa., 1993. Fellow Allegheny County Bar Found.; mem. ABA (com. on occupl. safety and health law 1981—), Soc. for Human Resource Mgmt., Pa. Bar Assn. (com. on legal ethics and profl. responsibility 1987-94), Pitts. Human Resources Assn. (treas. 1997, sr. profl. human resources 1998—), Omicron Delta Kappa. Office: Polito & Smock PC 444 Liberty Ave Ste 400 Pittsburgh PA 15222-1237

ARTZT, EDWIN LEWIS, consumer products company executive; b. N.Y.C., Apr. 15, 1930; s. William and Ida A.; m. Ruth Nadine Martin, May 12, 1950; children: Wendy Anne, Karen Susan, William M., Laura Grace, Elizabeth Louise. BS, U. Oreg., 1951. Account exec. Glasser Gailey Advt. Agy., L.A., 1952-53; with Procter & Gamble Co., Cin., 1953-95, brand mgr. advt. dept., 1955-58, assoc. brand promotion mgr., 1958-60, brand promotion mgr., 1960, 62-65, copy mgr., 1960-62, mgr. advt. dept. paper products div., 1965-68, mgr. food products divsn., 1968-69, v.p. food products divsn., 1969-70, v.p., acting mgr. coffee div., 1970, v.p., group exec., 1970-75, bd. dirs., 1972-75, 80-95, exec. v.p. then vice chmn. internat. ops., 1980-89; group v.p. European ops. Procter & Gamble Co., Europe, Belgium, 1975-80; pres. Procter & Gamble Internat., 1984-89, chmn., chief exec. officer, 1995-99; bd. dir. GTE Corp., Delta Air Lines, Am. Express Co., Spalding Holdings Corp., Barilla G.e R.F.lli S.p.A., Italy, Am. Inst. for Contemporary German Studies, Am. Enterprise Inst. for Public Policy Rsch. Bd.; mem. Internat. Adv. Bd. Babson Coll. Internat. councilor Ctr. for Strategic and Internat. Studies, Washington; mem. Coun. on Fgn. Rels., The Jackson Hole Land Trust; bd. trustees Cin. Inst. of Fine Arts; mem. exec. com. The Business Coun.; past chmn. residential div. United Appeal; past chmn. Public Library Capital Funds campaign; past dist. chmn. Capital Fund Raising dr. Boy Scouts Am., past leadership tng. chmn.; past chmn. advt. com. Sch. Tax Levy, County Govt. Issue; past trustee Kansas City Philharmonic, Nutrition Found., Boys' Clubs Greater Cin.; past bd. dirs. Kansas City Lyric Theater; past bd. govs. Kansas City Art Inst. Recipient Martin Luther King, Jr. Salute to Greatness award, 1995, Leadership Conf. on Civil Rights Private Sector Leadership award, 1995; inducted to Nat. Sales Hall of Fame, 1995, Advt. Hall of Fame, 1996. Mem. Am. C. of C. Belgium (v.p.), Conf. Bd. Europe (adv. council), Internat. C. of C. (exec. com. U.S. council), Nat. Fgn. Trade Council, Queen City Club, Commercial Club, Camargo Club, Teton Pines Club. Clubs: Queen City (Cin.), Cin. Country (Cin.), Comml. (Cin.). Office: Procter & Gamble Co 1 Procter And Gamble Plz Cincinnati OH 45202-3393*

ARUGA, NATSUKI, history educator; b. Tokyo, July 15, 1944; d. Toshimi Hirasawa and Toyo (Wada) Hirasawa; m. Tsutomu Aruga, June 18, 1968; children: Mika, Kentaka. BA, Ochanomizu Women's U., Tokyo, 1968; MA, U. Tokyo, 1970, U. Calif., Berkeley, 1973; PhD, Stanford U., 1996. Rsch. assoc. U. Tokyo, 1978-80; lectr. Saitama U., Urawa, Japan, 1980-82, assoc. prof., 1982-86, prof. sociology and history, 1986—. Author: A Social History of American Feminism, 1988 (Yamakawa Kikue award 1988, Japan-U.S. Friendship Commn. award 1989). Mem. Coun. on Policies for Women, Urawa, Japan, 1992—. Nitobe fellow Internat. House of Japan, 1981-83; grantee Am. Coun. Learned Socs., 1990-91. Mem. Japanese Assn. Am. Studies (exec. bd. dirs. 1992—). Avocation: singing. Home: 1-13-3 Matsunoki, Suginami-ku, Tokyo 166-0014, Japan Office: Saitama U, 255 Shimo-Okubo, Urawa Japan

ARUJ, ESTRELLA, fashion designer, artist; b. Cordoba, Argentina, Oct. 23, 1934; came to U.S., 1963; d. Alberto and Regina (Gaguine) A.; m. Moises Aruj, Apr. 5, 1952; children: Hector Ricardo, Alberto Silvio. Degree in fashion design, Fashion Inst. Tech., 1968, degree in buying and merchandising, 1970. Designer Herman Gowns Pvt. Collection, N.Y.C., 1963-64; fashion coord. Bonwit Teller, Westchester, N.Y., 1964-68; head designer, master patternmaker Aaron Kahmi-Kamhi Group, N.Y.C., 1968-87, Dorothea of Palm Beach, Fla., 1993-94; costume designer, prodr. Fla., 1990—, Duncan Theatro, 1995. One-woman shows at Carimor Gallery, N.Y., 1985; exhitibed in group shows at Argentinean Consulate, N.Y.C., 1985, Jewells Fine Art Gallery, N.J., 1985, 86, Art in Public Places Program, Palm Beach, 1990, 92, Palm Beach C.C., 1991, Kravis Ctr., Palm Beach, 1995, Spanish Latin Am. Mus. Art, Miami, 1997, Find Art Galleria, Ft. Lauderdale, Fla., 1998, Jewish Mus., Aventura, Fla., 1999, Cornell U. Art Gallery, Ithaca, N.Y., 1999, Armory Arts Mus., 1999. Tchr. art to underprivileged children, Palm Beach County. Mem. Argentina Arts Orgn. (pres. 1995-96, exec. dir. bd. 1995—), Palm Beach Cultural Coun. of Arts, Orgn. Cultural Argentina (head, bd. dirs. 1992—), Ctr. for Creative Edn. (exec. com. 1994—), Nat. Women's Art Mus. (Washington), Met. Mus. (N.Y.), Sephardi Fedn. (Palm Beach), World Jewish Congress, Argentina Fla. C. of C., Spanish Am. C. of C. Jewish. Avocations: painting, swimming, reading, volunteer work, travel. Office: Argentina Arts Orgn 7752 Forestay Dr Lake Worth FL 33467-7820

ARUMUGAM, MURUGESAN, electrical engineering educator; b. Nandimangalam, Tamilnadu, India, June 10, 1943; s. R. Murugesan and M. Thaili Ammal; m. A. Santha, June 7, 1973; children: A. Kavitha, A. Senthilvasan. B of Engring. with honors, U. Madras, 1966, MSc in Engring., 1968; PhD, India Inst. Tech., Kanpur, 1971. Lectr. Coll. Engring. Guundy, Madras, India, 1971-72; asst. prof. elec. engring. Regional Engring. Coll., Tiruchcirapalli, Tamilnadu, 1972-79, prof., 1979—, dean, 1996—; prin. Regional Engring. Coll., Tiruchirapalli, 2000—. Author: Electric Circuit Theory, 1979; contbr. articles to profl. jours. Mem. IEEE. Hindu. Avocations: reading, chess, table tennis. Office: Regional Engring Coll, Tiruchirapalli 620 015, Tamilnadu, India

ARUNACHALAM, VISWANATHAN, educator, researcher; b. Mullipet, Arni, India, July 29, 1969; s. A.M. and Samundeeswari Viswanathan; m. Nirmala Shanmugam, July 15, 1998. MSc, Anna U., Madras, India, 1992; PhD, Indian Inst. Tech., Madras, 1996. Rsch. fellow Tel Aviv (Israel) U., 1996-97; asst. prof. U. Los Andes, Bogota, Colombia, 1997—. Indian InNst. Tech. sr. rsch. fellow, 1994.91. Mem. Soc. Mathematical Biology, Soc. Indsl. and Applied Math. Avocations: sports, sciences, reading. E-mail: aviswana@uniandes.edu.co. Home: Ave 39 No 8-91 Apt 1101, Bogota Colombia Office: U Los Andes, Dept Math, Bogota Colombia

ARUNANONDCHAI, SURAT, construction and trading company executive; b. Bangkok, Sept. 28, 1956; s. Kebrati Young and Malee (Champreeda) A.; m. Vanida Yingyongpaiboon, May 10, 1982; children: Vinai, Visanu, Visit, Vithan. BBA, Bangkok, 1977; MBA, Dartmouth Coll., PhD, 1980. Mng. dir. Siam Crops Co., Bangkok, 1980-89, Siam Am. Trading, Bangkok, 1982—, Siam Sino Tech. Co., Bangkok, 1985—; cons., dir. Unique Place Co., Bangkok, 1990-93. Inventor in field. Coord. Chartered Bus., Bangkok, 1985. Lt. Thailand Army, 1971-73. Recipient Mgmt. award Thailand Mgmt., 1990, Writing award Fgn. and Thai Granting, 1993. Mem. N.Y. Acad. Sci., Nat. Geog. Soc. Buddhist. Avocations: writing, collecting stamps, tennis, swimming. Home: 991-6-7 Bantadtona Rd, Bangkok Thailand 10330 Office: Siam Am Trading, 286 6-7 Surawonose Rd, Bangkok Thailand

ARUNDALE, C. JEAN, psychotherapist; b. Detroit Lakes, Minn., Sept. 21, 1938; d. E.G. and Doris (Cutler) Prohaska; m. Dwight Arundale, Aug. 15, 1960 (div. 1982). BA in Math and Philosophy, U. Colo., 1960; BS in Psychology, U. London, 1980; PhD in Psychology, U. Coll. London, 1993. Lic. psychotherapist, Brit. Assn. Psychotherapists. With Atkinson Morley's Hosp., London, 1974-76; pvt. practice of psychoanalytic psychotherapy London, 1977—; psychotherapist and supr. Guy's Hosp., London, 1976—; tchg. and tng. Brit. Assn. of Psychotherapists, London, 1980—, various other orgns., 1980—. Editor Brit. Jour. Psychotherapy, 1993—, contbr. editls., 1993—; contbr. articles to profl. jours. Mem. BCP, APP, BAP, IGA. Avocations: tennis, classical music, walking, theatre, films. Home: 11 Albert Pl, W8 5PD London England Office: Guys Hosp-York Clin, 47 Weston St, SE1 3RR London England

ARUNDELL, VICTOR CHARLES, accountant, international business consultant; b. Greenwich, London, Eng., July 15, 1931; s. William Hewitt and Constance (Hook) A.; m. Margaret Howe, June 6, 1961 (dec.); children—Deborah, Caroline, Sally, Jill, Zoe. Student Roan, Greenwich, 1942-47. Controller Chgo. Pneumatic Tool Co., N.Y.C., 1967-72; group controller, dir. Siebe PLC, Windsor, Eng., 1972-78; group coordinator Parinter, S.A., Paris, 1978-84; dir. Comasec Ltd., Durban, South Africa, 1980-84; mng. dir. Dipco Ltd., Slough, Eng., 1979-85; mng. dir. Cosmo Internat. Ltd., London, Honolulu, L.A., 1991—, Melody Ltd., London, 1993-96; gov. Edward Betham CE Sch., 1996—; dir. Earls Court YMCA, 1997—. Leader opposition Fulham Borough Council, London, 1960-63; chmn. Barons Ct. Young Conservatives, London, 1959-63. Served with RAF, 1954-56. Fellow Inst. Chartered Acct. Eng. and Wales, Inst. of Dirs., London. Conservative. Anglican. Club: Wimereux Golf (France). Home and Office: 164 Ealing Rd, Brentford Middlesex TW8 9PX, England also: 3 Barrio Triana, La Garnatilla, Motril, Granada Spain

ARUTYUNOV, ARAM VLADIMIROVICH, mathematician, educator, researcher; b. Tbilisi, USSR, Oct. 6, 1956; s. Vladimir Ishuevich Arutyunov and Amalia Aramovna Sarkisian; m. Natalia Yurievna Sedova Chernikova; children: Mardgan, Andranick. MSc, Moscow State U., 1978, PhD in Math., 1981; DSc, USSR Acad. Scis., Moscow, 1988. Assoc. prof. math. Friendship of Nations U. Russia, Moscow, 1982-89, prof. math., 1989—, chair dept. differential equations, 1997—; prof. math. Moscow State U., 1993—. Author: Extremum Conditions, 1997; contbr. articles to profl. jours. Grantee ISF, 1995, Russian Fedn. Basic Rsch., 1994-98. Mem. Moscow Math. Soc. Home: Lomonosovksy prospect 18, Apt 396, 117296 Moscow Russia Office: Peoples Friendship U Russia, Micklucho-Macklay St, 6, 117198 Moscow Russia

ARUWA, ABDULKAREEM AYIKOYE, magistrate, consultant; b. Idah, Kogi State, Nigeria, Oct. 9, 1962; s. Omale Gabriel and Ajifa Jameela (Ayikoye) A.; m. Nafisat Aladi Hussain, Nov. 16, 1991; children: Mansour, Naseer, Aisha, Hameedat. LLB in Common Law, U. Maiduguri, Nigeria, 1989, LLB in Sharia, 1989; degree of barrister at law, Nigerian Law Sch., Lagos, 1990. Adminstrv. officer Fed. Poly., Idah, 1981-86; pvt. practice Owerri, Nigeria, 1990-91; lectr. in law Fed. Poly., Idah, 1991-92; chief magistrate Kogi State Judiciary, Lokoja, Nigeria, 1992—; cons., Kogi State, 1995—. Author: (books) Fasting in Perspective, 1983, Sharia Application: Benue State as a Case Study, 1989, Confluence Blues, 2000, (play) Experience of Brother Maruf in Adversity, 1984. Exec. sec. Coun. of Ulama, Kogi State, 1998—; co-founder Women Devel. Ctr., Idah, 1991, Kogi State Coun. of Ulama, Lokoja, 1998; founder Nurul Islam Nursery/Primary Sch., 1992. Mem. Nigerian Bar Assn., Magistrates Assn. of Nigeria (gen. sec. 1999—), Muslim Corpers Assn. of Nigeria (grand patron 1999—). Moslem. Avocations: reading, news, table tennis, lawn tennis, swimming. Office: Kogi State Judiciary, 2 Nuj St Opposite Police Hdqrs, PMB 1040 Lokoja Nigeria

ARVAI, ERNEST STEPHEN, consulting executive; b. Detroit, Sept. 9, 1950; s. Ernest and Maria Magdolna (Horvath) A.; m. Mary Ann Hughes, Oct. 11, 1980; 1 child, Marc Alexander. BS in Indsl. Engring. with high distinction, U. Mich., Dearborn, 1971; MS in Indsl. Adminstrn., Carnegie Mellon U., 1974. CPA, N.H. Rsch. asst. Hwy. Safety Rsch. Inst., Ann Arbor, Mich., 1970-73; sr. cons. Arthur Andersen & Co., Detroit, 1974-77; dir. N.Am. mgmt. cons. Arthur D. Little Inc., Cambridge, Mass., 1978-90; v.p., mng. dir. tech. mgmt. Battelle Meml. Inst., Columbus, Ohio, 1990-91; pres., CEO Arvai Group, Inc., Windham, N.H., 1991—; bd. advisors Cislunar Corp., Madison, Conn., 19925; bd. dirs. Giro, Inc. Author newsletter The Expert Network, 1994; contbr. articles to profl. jours. Bd. dirs., coord. Windham Baseball League, 1993. Mem. AICPA, N.H. Inst. CPAs, Internat. Order Characters, Wings Club. Republican. Avocations: aviation, skiing, golf. Home: 16 Telo Rd Windham NH 03087-1151 Office: Arvai Group Inc PO Box 468 Windham NH 03087-0468

ARVANI, AZITA, technology company executive; b. Tehran, Iran; came to U.S., 1978; d. Mohammad and Alieh Z. Arvani. BS in Math. and Computer Sci. magna cum laude, UCLA, 1983; MS in Computer Sci., U. So. Calif., 1986; MS in Mgmt., Stanford U., 1999. Project mgr. electronics divsn. Xerox, El Segundo, Calif., 1983-90; mgr. systems software Xerox, El Segundo, 1991-93; asst. to sr. v.p. of R & D Xerox, Stamford, Conn., 1994-96; dir. corp. strategy Xerox, Stamford, 1996-98; v.p. mktg., consulting Altimum.com, Milpitas, Calif., 1999; dir. bus. strategy Xerox/Content Guard, Palo Alto, Calif., 1999-2000; v.p. bus. devel. and strategy ActivSky, Redwood City, Calif., 2000—; moderator, host, spkr. Internat. Angel Investors, 1999-2000. Named Best Spkr., Toastmasters, 1992-93. Avocations: exercise, dance, alternative health, fashion, hiking. Office: ActivSky 730 Bair Island Rd Apt 101 Redwood City CA 94063-5525

ARVANITAKIS, CONSTANTINE S., gastroenterologist; b. Thessaloniki, Greece, Nov. 9, 1939; s. Spyros and Terpsithea A.; m. Sanda Nousia, June 3, 1967; 1 child, Marianna. Diploma, Anatolia Coll, 1958; MD, U. Thessaloniki, 1965, postgrad., 1976. Diplomate Am. Bd. Internal Medicine, Am. Bd. Gastroenterology. House physician Nat. Health Service, Eng., 1967-70; resident, fellow U. Wis., Madison, 1970-73; asst. prof. medicine U. Kans., Kansas City, 1973-77, assoc. prof., 1977-79; clin. assoc. prof. U. Kans., 1979—; assoc. prof. medicine U. Thessaloniki, 1979-96; prof. medicine, 1996; dir. gastrointestinal unit, first dept. medicine U. Thessaloniki, AHEPA Gen. Hosp., 1980-97, chmn. fourth dept. medicine U. Thessaloniki, Hippocration Gen. Hosp., 1997—. Author: Drug Treatment of Gastrointestinal Disease, 1976; chmn. editl. bd. Hellenic Jour. Gastroenterology Internat., 1993-96, Hepatogastroenterology, Internat. Jour. Pancreatology, Arch. Hepatogastroenterology Gut, 1992-99; editor: Helleniki Iatriki,1993-98, Gastroenterology Intern, World Jour. Gastroenterology; contbr. 150 papers on gastroenterology and internal medicine. NIH grantee, Bethesda, Md., 1978-80. Fellow ACP, Royal Coll. Physicians (London); mem. Am. Gastroenterology Assn., Hellenic Soc. Gastroenterology (bd. dirs. 1987-88, pres. 1996), Cen. Soc. Clin. Rsch., Am. Physiol. Assn., Internat. Assn. Pacreat (mem. gov. bd. 1988-92), Gastroent. Rsch. Group, Am. Pancreatic Assn., Assn. Nat. European Mediterr Gastroenterology (pres. 1992-97), United European Gastroenterology Fedn. Coun. (chmn. 1998), ERASMUS (coord. European course transfer sys. program, pres. 1st unit Europe Gastroent. Week Athens 1992), Hellenic Soc. of Gastroenterology (pres. 1996), European Pancreatic Club (pres. 1997-98, chmn. organizing com. XXX meeting 1998). Christian Orthodox. Home: PO Box 322, 57001 Thermi Greece Office: U Thessaloniki 4 Dept Med, Hippocration Gen Hosp, 54006 Thessaloniki Greece

ARVANITIS, AGNI VLAVIANOS, biologist; b. Athens, Mar. 9, 1936; came to U.S., 1953; d. George and Maria (Rudolph) Vlavianos; m. Athanasios Arvanitis. BA, Columbia U., 1957; MS, NYU, 1961; PhD, U. Athens, 1978. Pres., founder Biopolitics Internat. Orgn., Athens, 1985—; tchr. Am. Community Schs., Athens, U. Md./overseas br., Friends Seminary, N.Y.C.; researcher Univ. Athens, Univ. Paris-Orsay, Am. Mus. of Natural History, N.Y.C. Author numerous publs. including Biopolitics - The Bio-Environment Vols. 1-7, 1988-99 (various fgn. translations), Biopolitics - The Bio-Environment/Bio-Culture in the Next Millennium, 1994, Biopolitics-Business Strategy for the Bio-Environment, Vols. 1-4, others, (poetry books), Agni Vlavianos-Arvanitis: Reflections, 1980, Roots, 1981, Oscillations, 1982; numerous other tech. publs. Vice-pres. UNESCO Man and Biosphere, Internatl. Bioethics Soc., Hellenic nat. com.; co-founder/trustee Internat. Univ. for Experiential Edn.; commr. The Global Commn. to Fund the UN; bd. trustees Uganda Nat. Found. Rsch. & Devel. Named to Foremost Women of the Twentieth Century, 1994; recipient Abdi Ipekci Peace and Friendship prize, 1993; nominee Nobel Prize for Peace, 1995, 97, 98, 99; recipient Peace Through Tourism award World Assn. of Travel Agents. Mem. Alliance for Environmental Edn. (bd. dirs.), United Nations Assn. of Sri Lanka (hon. pres./life), Pontificial Acad. for Life, Adv. Bd. Jour. of Cleaner Prodn., Hon. Prof., St. Petersburg State Univ., Hon. PhD, Mendeleyev Univ., Moscow. Avocations: swimming, music. Office: Biopolitics Internat Orgn, 10 Tim Vassour, 115 21 Athens Greece

ARVERS, PHILIPPE, physician, researcher; b. Paris, Aug. 2, 1956; s. Georges and Colette (Zimet) A.; m. Odile Rabourdin, July 5, 1980; 3 children. Methodology in Statistics, Ctr. d'Etudes Statistiques Appliques a la Medecine, Paris, 1983, Clin. Biol. Rsch., 1985, Epidemiology, 1986; DEA, Genie Biologique et Med., Lyon and Grenoble, France, 1988; MD (hon.), U. Alexis Carriere, Bordeaux, France, 1980; PhD (hon.), U. Claude Bernard, Lyon, France, 1998. Gen. practitioner Ecole de Def. Nucleaire Biol. Chimique de l'Armee de Terre, Grenoble, France, 1981-87, 34 RG, Epernay, France, 1987-89; rsch. asst. Ctr. de Recherches due Svc. de Santé des Armeés, Grenoble, 1989-95, rsch. splst. mil. medicine, 1995—, médecin en chef, 1997; cons. Diection Regionale des Affaires Sanitaires et Sociales, Rhône-Alps, Lyon, 1998-99, French Min. Youth and Sport, Paris, 1999—. Author: L'Alcool a chiffres ouverts, 1997; contbr. articles to profl. jours. Decorated chavalier Order Nat. Mèrite, 1996. Avocations: church organ. Home: 2 rue Vicat, 38000 Grenoble France Office: CRSSA, BP 87, 38702 La Tronche France

ARYA, MAHENDRA PAL SINGH, agronomist; b. Buland Shahr, India, Dec. 18, 1954; s. Tara Singh and Narayani Devi (Singh) A.; m. Omvati Singh, Feb. 21, 1976; children: Omendra Arya, Yidyotma, Yatendra Arya. BS in Agr., Raja Balwant Singh Coll., Bichpuri, Agra, India, 1973, MS in Agr., 1976; MPhil, Inst. Advanced Studies, Meerut, 1977, PhD in Agr., 1981. Rsch. assoc. G.B. Pant U. Agr. and Tech., Pantnagar, India, 1979-81, jr. rsch. officer, 1983-86, sr. rsch. officer, 1986-99; prin. scientist agronomy Nat. Rsch. Ctr. Women in Agriculture, Bhubaneswar, India, 1999—; sr. tech. asst. Directorate Rice Devel., Patna, India, 1981-83; dept. head agronomy sect. G.B. Pant U. Agr. and Tech., Ranichauri, 1983-99, seed sci. and tech., Ranichauri, 1997-99. Contbr. articles to profl. jours. Mem. Indian Soc. Agronomy (life mem.), Indian Soc. Weed Sci. (life mem.), Bhartiya Krishi Anusandhan Samiti (patron mem.), Indian Soc. Agrl. Scis. Mem. Arya Samaj, Bhubaneswar. Avocations: religious songs, badminton. Office: Nat Rsch Ctr Women Agricult, 1199 Jagamara PO Khandagiri, Bhubaneswar 751 030, India

ARYA, MOHAMMAD JAVAD, pathologist; b. Estahban, Fars, Iran, Sept. 6, 1966; s. Mohammad Ali Arya and Fatemeh Mosen. MD in Pathology, Shiraz U., Iran, 1995. With dept. pathology Yazd (Iran) U. Med. Scis., 1995—, head dept. pathology, 1995—. Office: Rahnemoon Hosp, Farokhi St PO Box 89165-918, 89138 Yazd Iran

ARYA, ROSHAN LAL, agricultural researcher; b. Etawah, India, Mar. 3, 1964; s. Ram Swarup and Vidya A.; m. Indira, May 10, 1979; children: Renu, Sonam, Anupriya, Rohit. BS in Agrl., Chandra Shekhar Azad U. Agr. & Tech., Kanpur, India, 1981; MS in Agronomy, Indian Agrl. Rsch. Inst., New Delhi, 1986; PhD in Agronomy, Indian Agrl. Rsch. Inst., 1989. Scientist Nat. Acad. Agrl. Rsch. and Mgmt., Hyderabad, 1989, Cen. Rsch. Inst. for Dryland Agr., Hyderabad, 1990; sr. scientist Indian Grassland and Fodder Rsch. Inst., Jhansi, 1990-99, Indian Inst. Pulses Rsch., Kanpur, 1999—. Recipient fellowship, IARI, New Delhi, 1984-89. Mem. (life) Indian Soc. Agronomy, Indian Soc. Dryland Agrl., Indian Soc. Range Mgmt. Avocations: computers, badminton, music.

ARYAN, KISHAN CHAND, artist, art historian; b. Amritsar, Punjab, India, Aug. 11, 1919; s. Harnam Das and Thakar (Devi) Malhotra; m. Kamla Vati Kapur, Mar. 1943; 5 children. Chmn., dir. Home Folk Art, Gurgaon, India, 1986; establisher mus. Home of Folk Art, Gurgaon, Haryana, 1986. Author 23 books including Rekha, 4 edits., 1948-52, Simplified Applied Art, 1952, 96, Folk Bronzes of India, 1973, 91, Punjab Paintings, 1975, Punjab Murals, 1977, Hanuman in Art, 1975, 94, Practical Guide to Lettering, 1976, 96, How to Draw Birds and Animals, 1978, 96, Little Goddesses (Martikas), 1980, Basis of Decorative Element in Indian Art, 1981, Cultural Heritage of Punjab, 1983, Rural Art of the Western Himalaya, 1985, References, Symbols and Evolution of Devanagari Script, 1989, 96, Unknown Pahari Wall Paintings in North India, 1991, Sadhana Kala Yatra, 1998, The Aryans: History of Vedic Period, 1998; one-person shows include Indian Acad. Fine Arts, Amritsar, 1939, Delhi Silpi Chakra, Delhi, 1950, Modern Sch., Delhi, 1955, Freemasons Hall, Delhi, 1956, Graham's Studio, Malabar Hill, Bombay, 1957, Delhi Blue Art Pottery, Delhi, 1958, Indian Embassy, Afghanistan, 1958, Indian Club, Baghdad, 1958, Residence of Late Dr. Pritpal Singh of WHO, Beirut, 1958, Kumar Gallery, New Delhi, 1959, 60, Punjab U., Chandigarh, 1963, Kumar Gallery, New Delhi, 1963, Lalit Kala Galleries, New Delhi, 1966, All India Fine Arts and Crafts Soc., New Delhi, 1966, All India Fine Arts and Crafts Soc., New Delhi, 1984, Govt. Mus. and Art Gallery, Chandigarh, 1991. Recipient silver medal Indian Acad. Fine Arts, Amritsar, 1953, gold medal, 1957, nat. award Lalitkala Akademi, New Delhi, 1964, bronze plaque from Japan, Vet. artist's award and cash prize A.I.F.A.C.S., New Delhi, 1984, Kala Vibhushan cash prize and silver plate A.I.F.A.C.S., New Delhi, 1991. Avocations: collecting Indian folk, tribal and neglected art. Home: 2009 Sector 4 Urban Estate, Gurgaon Maryana 122001, India Office: Rekha Prakashan, 16 Darya Ganj, New Delhi 110002, India

ARYKOV, ANATOLY ALEXANDROVICH, physicist; b. Guryev, Russia, Aug. 16, 1948; s. Alexandr Vasilyevich Arykov and Galina Ivanovna Polyakova; m. Antonina Yakovlevna Lopatkina, June 15, 1949; children: Arykov Andrey, Arykov Dmitrii. MS, Gorky State U., 1973, Candidate in Physics and Maths., 1981. Cert. radiophysicist. Sr. asst. Polar Geophys. Inst./Kola Sci. Ctr., Apatity, Russia, 1973-75, scientific rschr., 1975-84, sr. rschr., 1984-87, head of lab., 1987-92, leading rschr., 1992—; assoc. prof. physics Kola Br. of Leningrad Mining Inst., Kirousk, Russia, 1992-95; assoc. prof. in math. Kola Br. of Petrozavodsky State U., Apatity, 1995-96, chief dept. of applied math., 1996—. Contbr. articles to profl. jours. Avocations: truck farming, hiking. Home: 22 Zinovyeva St Apt 45, 184200 Apatity Russia Office: Polar Geophys Inst, 184200 Apatity Russia

ARZI, YOHANAN, industrial engineer, educator; b. Tel-Aviv, Isreal, June 29, 1954; married; 2 children. BSc, Technion-Israel Inst., Haifa, 1979, MSc in Indsl. Engring., 1983, DSc in Indsl. Engring., 1991. Adj. sr. lectr. Technion-Israel Inst., Haifa, 1979-89; sr. lectr. Branda Coll. Tech., 1988—; lectr. Tel-Aviv (Israel) U., 1991-2000; head indsl. engring. dept. ORT Braude Coll., Karmiel, Israel, 2000—; cons. Haifa Chems. Ltd., 1981, Haifa Municipality, 1986. Author: (with Maital and Roll) Inter-Plant Productivity Comparison, 1983, (with Roll) A Guide to control of Production Productivity in the Plant, 1985; contbr. articles to profl. jours. Miriam and Aaron Gutwirth scholar Technion, 1981, 1986, Efter scholar Technion, 1982; grantee The Fleischman Fund Tel-Aviv U., 1995, 1996, Ministry of Defense, 1996. Mem. Internat. Found. Prodn. Rsch., Inst. Indsl. Eng. (edtl. bd., 1996—), Inst. Operation Rsch. Mgmt. Scis., Tel-Aviv U. (computer com., tchg. com., spl. curriculum com., deptal. curriculum com.). E-mail: arazi y@inter.net.il. Fax: 972-4-9901989. Office: ORT Braude Coll, Dept Indsl Engring PO Box 78, Karmiel 20101, Israel

ASADA, KANJI, orthopedic surgeon, physician; b. Hirakata City, Osaka, Japan, May 1, 1941; s. Masami and Toshiko Asada; m. Kazuko Asada; children: Junko, Taku. MD, Osaka City U. Med. Sch., 1967, PhD, 1975. Clin. physician Nat. Hosp., Osaka, 1976-78; asst. teaching staff dept. orthopedic surgery Osaka City U. Med. Sch., 1978-86, lectr., 1986-93, assoc. prof., 1993-94; dir. Asada Orthopaedic Clinic, Osaka, 1994—. Editor, author: Biomechanical Orthopaedics, 1993; contbr. articles to Laser Therapy, Hip Surgery, others. Mem. Soc. Internat. de Chirurgie Orthopédique et de Traumatologie, Internat. Laser Therapy Assn., Rotary. Buddhist. Avocations: collecting classic cameras, tea ceremony, wine tasting, chinaware collecting, photography. Office: Todacho 3-47 101, 573-0045 Hirakata Osaka, Japan

ASADA, TOSHI, seismologist, educator; b. Tokyo, Dec. 15, 1919; s. Shunsuke and Sumi (Asakura) A.; m. Teruko Uchida, Nov. 29, 1955; children: Takashi, Satoshi, Yuko. BS, U. Tokyo, 1944, DSc, 1958. Rsch. asst. U. Tokyo, 1944-55, mem. faculty, 1955—, prof. seismology, 1966-80, prof. emeritus, 1980—; prof. geophysics Inst. R&D Tokai U., 1980-92, prof. emeritus, 1993—; chmn. coordinating com. for earthquake prediction Geog. Survey Inst., 1980-90; chmn. earthquake assessment com. Japan Meteorol. Agy., 1980-90; chmn. Geodesy coun. Ministry of Edn., Sci. & culture, 1986-94. Author papers on microearthquakes, explosion seismology, ocean bottom seismometers, earthquake prediction. Recipeint medal with purple ribbon, 1984, The Order of the Sacred Treasure with gold and silver star, 1990; sr. fellow Carnegie Instn., Washington, 1960-61. Mem. Seismol. Soc. Japan, Am. Geophys. Union. Home: 3-13-17 101 Shimo-ochiai, Shinjuku-ku, Tokyo 161-0033, Japan Office: Rsch Inst Sci/Tech Tokai U, 1117 Kitakaname, Hiratsuka 259-12 Kanagawa-ken, Japan

ASADI, ROBERT SAMIR, high school principal; b. Salt Lake City, Dec. 21, 1953; s. Abdul-Aziz and Wilma (Craig) A.; m. Karen Lee Schenk, June 16, 1990; children: Scott, Ryan. BS, U. Wyo., 1986; MEd, No. Ariz. U., 1994. Cert. tchr. and adminstr. Tchr., coach Cactus H.S., Glendale, Ariz., 1986-89, Holbrook (Ariz.) H.S., 1989-91; tchr., adminstrv. asst., coach Agua Fria Union H.S. South, Avondale, Ariz., 1991-94; prin. Agua Fria Union H.S.-North, Goodyear, Ariz., 1994-98, Millennium H.S., 1998—. Mem. West Valley Fine Arts Coun., Avondale, 1995-96, Leadership West II, Avondale, 1995-96; bd. dirs. Leadership West, 2000—. Mem. ASCD, Tri City West C. of C., Ariz. Sch. Adminstrs., Nat. Assn. of Secondary Sch. Prins. Avocations: computers, golf, backpacking, spectator sports. Home: 9139 W Evans Dr Peoria AZ 85381-3784 Office: Millennium HS 14802 W Wigwam Blvd Goodyear AZ 85338

ASADOV, EDUARD ARKADEVICH, poet; b. Merv, Turkmen, U.S.S.R., Sept. 7, 1923; s. Arkady and Lidya A.; m. Galina Asadova, 1961; 1 child. Student, Gorky Literary Inst., Moscow, Gorky Inst. World Lit. Author: Again into the Line, 1948, Bright Roads, 1951, Snowy Evening, 1956, I Love You Forever, 1965, Be Happy, Dreamers, 1966, I Fight, I Believe, I Love, 1983, The Highest Duty, 1986, Collected Works, 3 vols., 1987-88, Letter from the Battle Front, 1993, Never Surrender, People, 1997, others. With Red Army, 1941. Avocations: music, especially gypsy songs, books, collecting funny names of streets and people. Address: Astrakhansky per 5, Apt 78, Moscow 129010, Russia

ASAHINA, TAKASHI, conductor; b. Tokyo, July 9, 1908; s. Kaichi Watanabe; m. Machiko Asahina, 1940; 2 children. LLB, Kyoto Imperial U., 1931, BA, 1937. Permanent condr., gen. dir. Osaka Philharmonic Orch., 1947—; condr. 35 overseas tours, 1953-96; chair panel judging Tokyo Internat. Music Competition for Conducting, 1976. Condr. Berlin Philharmonic, Sinfonieorchester des Norddeutscher Rundfunks Hamburg, numerous others; recordings include complete symphonies of Beethoven, Bruckner, Brahms, Wagner's Ring des Nibelungen. Recipient Officer's Cross for sci. and art, Austria. Mem. Nippon Condrs. Assn. (pres.). Avocations: reading, sports. Fax: 06-6656-7714. Home: 4-4-3 Shinoharakita-machi, Nada-ku, Kobe 657-0068, Japan Office: Osaka Philharm 1-1-44, Kishinosato-Nishinari-ku, Osaka 557-0041, Japan

ASAI-SATO, CAROL YUKI, lawyer; b. Osaka, Japan, Oct. 22, 1951; came to U.S., 1953; d. Michael and Sumiko (Kamei) Asai; 1 child, Ryan Makoto Sato. BA cum laude, U. Hawaii, 1972; JD, Willamette Coll. Law, 1975. Bar: Hawaii 1975. Assoc. firm Ashford & Wriston, Honolulu, 1975-79; counsel Bank of New Eng., Boston, 1979-81; assoc. counsel Alexander & Baldwin, Honolulu, 1981-83, sr. counsel, 1984-88; of counsel Rush, Moore, Craven, Sutton, Morry, Beh, 1988-89, ptnr., 1989-97; ptnr. Alston Hunt Floyd & Ing, 1997—. Willamette Coll. Law Bd. Trustees scholar, 1972-73. Mem. ABA, Hawaii Bar Assn., Hawaii Women Lawyers, Phi Beta Kappa, Phi Kappa Phi. Democrat. Office: Alston Hunt Floyd & Ing Pacific Tower 18th Fl 1001 Bishop St Ste 1800 Honolulu HI 96813-3689

ASAMOAH, JOSEPH KWASI, chemical engineer, energy and the environment consultant; b. Essikadu, Ghana, Sept. 2, 1951; arrived in South Africa, 1986; s. Kwasi Damey and Abenaa Serebour; m. Comfort Asamoah nee Duah, Aug. 18, 1984; children: Kwame, Kwaku, Amma. BSChemE with honors, Kwame Nkrumah U. Sci. & Tech., Kumasi, Ghana, 1976; MBA, Heriot-Watt U., Edinburgh, Scotland, 1993. Devel. engr. Firestone Ghana Ltd., Bonsa, 1977-80; process engr. Tarkwa (Ghana) Goldfields, 1980-82; sr. chemist Cocoa Products Factory, Takoradi, Ghana, 1982-86; tutor Ngcongolo Sr. Secondary Sch., Nqamakwe, South Africa, 1986-90; project mgr. Transkei Mining Corp., Umtata, South Africa, 1990-94; chief energy specialist Dept. Minerals and Energy, Pretoria, South Africa, 1995-98; dir. Omega Sci. Rsch., Johannesburg, South Africa, 1999, EnerWise Africa, Pretoria, 1999—; cons. Danced, Pretoria, Sanea (WEC), Johannesburg. Co-author: (books) A Concise Ordinary Level Chemistry, 1986, Joint Implementation: Carbon Colonies or Business Opportunities?, 1995. Recipient Thomas Kuhn's medal Internat. Acad. Scis. and Internat. Union of Air Pollution and Environ. Protection Assns., 1998. Mem. South African Inst. Chem. Engrs., Nat. Assn. for Clean Air, Internat. ad hoc Working Group on the Clean Devel. Mechanism, South African Nat. Energy Assn. Avocations: football, music, tennis, surfing the Internet. Fax: 27 12 997 0674. E-mail: joasa@mweb.co.za. Office: EnerWise Africa, PO Box 101847, Pretoria Moreleta Plaza 0167, South Africa

ASAMOAH, OBED YAO, Ghanaian government official; b. Likpe Bala, Ghana, Feb. 6, 1936; s. William Kofi and Monica Akosua A.; m. Yvonne Marguerite Asamoah, Feb. 1, 1964; children: Yolanda Afua, Keli Komla, Senanu Yao. Grad., U. London, LLB with honors, 1960; LLM, Columbia U., 1963, JD, 1967. Bar: Middle Temple 1960, Ghana 1960. Practiced law Ghana, 1960-61, 65—; rsch. asst. Carnegie Endowment for Internat. Peace, N.Y.C., 1964, 65; asst. dir. Dag Hammarskjold Seminar in Internat. Law, The Hague, The Netherlands, 1964, 65; lectr. law U. Ghana, Legon, 1965-69; chmn. bd. Ghana Films Industries, Inc., Ghana Bauxite Co.; mem. Constituent Assembly, M.P., 1969-72; gen.-sec. United Nat. Conv., 1979, All Peoples Party, 1981; sec. fgn. affairs Govt. of Ghana, 1982-97, min. justice, atty. gen., 1993—. Author: The Legal Significance of the Declarations of the General Assembly of the United Nations, 1967; contbr. articles to law jours. Mem. Ghana Bar Assn. Presbyterian. Avocations: reading, farming. Office: PO Box M 60, Accra Ghana also: Min Justice, Office of Minister, Accra Ghana*

ASANO, HIROYUKI, cosmetic company researcher; b. Toyohashi City, Japan, Feb. 23, 1962; s. Takayuki Asai and Hiroko Asano; m. Yoshiko Wakamatsu, Apr. 30, 1988; children: Asano Masahiro, Asano Akiko. DSc, Sci. U. Tokyo, 1991. Tchr. Aichi Pref., Toyohashi, Japan, 1984-85; asst. of lab. sci. U. Tokyo, 1991-93; rschr. Nippon Menard Cosmetic Co. Ltd., Nagoya, Japan, 1993—. Author: (with others) Mixed Surfactant Systems, 1993, Structure-Performance Relationships in Surfactants, 1997; contbr. articles to profl. jours. Mem. Am. Chem. Soc., Chem. Soc. of Japan, Oil Chem. Soc. of Japan. Avocation: fishing. Home: 9-9 Aza-Goh Yamada-cho, Toyohashi 441-8101, Japan Office: Nippon Menard Cosmetic Co, 2-7 Torimi-cho Nishi-ku, Nagoya 451-0071, Japan

ASANO, HITOSHI, engineering educator; b. Tagami, Japan, July 11, 1953; s. Shinji and Kazue (Susa) A.; m. Ikuko Sekiguchi, Oct. 8, 1982; children: Shiho, Kazuki. B in Engring., Tokyo U. Agriculture & Tech., 1977; M in Engring., Tokyo Inst. Tech., 1979. With Niigata Engring. Co. Ltd., Tokyo, 1979-81; asst. Nagaoka (Japan) U. Tech., 1982-92; assoc. prof. Nagaoka Jr. Coll., 1992-94, Niigata U. Mgmt., Kamo, Japan, 1994-98; prof. Niigata U. Mgmt., Kamo, Japan, 1998—. Mem. Niigata Info. Network Assn. (chmn. 1994-98), Nagaoka Japan Germany Assn. (trustee 1996—); Kamo Gyosei Gakuen (trustee 1998—). Office: Niigata U Mgmt, Kibogaoka 2909-2, Kamo 959-1321, Japan

ASANO, KEIKO, psychology educator; b. Toyokawa, Aichi, Japan, June 14, 1949; d. Sanji Ishiguro and Akiko (Kamiya) I.; m. Kiyoshi Asano, July 30, 1977. B Edn., Nagoya U., Japan, 1972; M Edn., Nagoya U., 1974. Asst. Chukyo Women's U., Obu, Japan, 1975-77, instr., 1977-84, asst. prof., 1984-99; prof., 1999—. Co-author: (books) Social Attitude of Adolescence, 1989, Life-cycle Psychology for Woman, 1994; contbr.: Handbook of Adolescent Psychology, 1988; editor/author: Psychology of Classroom Teaching, 1991. Mem. Japanese Psychol. Assn. Office: Chukyo Womens Univ, 55 Nadakayama Yokone-cho, 474-0011 Obu Aichi, Japan

ASANO, MAKISHIGE, medical educator; b. Gunma, Japan, Aug. 1, 1928; s. Harusuke and Shima (Amagawa) A.; m. Tetsuko Sakai, Nov. 23, 1957. MB, Tokyo Med. and Dental U., 1955, MD, 1962. Med. diplomate. Researcher Nat. Inst. of Pub. Health, Japan, 1956-66, head of sect., 1966-81, dir. of dept., 1981-90, hon. rschr., 1990—; prof. emeritus, 1998—; prof. Tokyo Med. and Dental U., 1990-94, dean Sch. Allied Health Scis., 1993-94; prof. Japan Women's U., Tokyo, 1994-97; chmn. Promotion Com. for Health City Tokyo, 1999—. Author: Circulatory Physiology, 1976, Health Science of Smoking, 1985; editor Microcirculation Ann., 1985—. Study Abroad grantee WHO, 1968. Fellow Internat. Coll. Angiology; mem. Internat. Soc. Biorheology, Internat. Union Angiology, European Soc. Microcirculation, N.Y. Acad. Scis. Avocations: fishing, playing piano, reading. Home: Tamagawa-heim 2-1002, 2-24-10 Shimomaruko, Ota-ku Tokyo 146-0092, Japan Office: Nat Inst Pub Health, 4-6-1 Shirokanedai Minato-ku, Tokyo 108-8638, Japan

ASANO, SHIRO, nuclear engineer; b. Tamano, Okayama, Japan, Feb. 27, 1963; s. Kazuo Miyoko Asano; m. Miyuki Shimotsu; children: Masayo, Norihito. B, Kyoto (Japan) U., 1986, M, 1988. Rschr. R&D Ctr. Toshiba Corp. Ltd., Kawasaki, Japan, 1988-97, specialist Power & Indsl. Sys. R&D Ctr., 1998—. Mem. Phys. Soc. Japan, Japan Soc. Plasma Sci. and Nuc. Fusion Rsch. Avocations: gliding, playing piano. Office: Toshiba Corp Ltd, 4-1 Ukishima-cho, Kawasaki 210 0862, Japan

ASANTE-WIAFE, ISAAC, farming director; b. Accra, Israel, Dec. 14, 1970; s. Ernest and Hellena Abena (Ofosua) A.; m. Ellen Akrasi, July 6, 1996. GCE, Inst. Adult Edn., Accra, Ghana, 1994. Mng. dir. Iclen Farms, Accra, Ghana, Israel, 1995—; regional organizer New Patriotic Party, 1992. New Patriotic Party. Presbn. Avocations: reading, sports, news.

ASAO, TETSURO, biology educator; b. Kesennuma, Miyagi, Japan, Apr. 3, 1940; parents: Jiro and Hideko (Takahashi) A. MA in Sci., Tokyo U., 1967, PhD in Sci., 1970. Cert. tchr. sr. h.s. Asst. Tokyo Kyoiku U., 1972-75; lectr. St. Marianna U., Kawasaki, Japan, 1975-79; asst. prof. St. Marianna U., 1979-82, prof., 1982—; rschr. in embryology. Author: Relationship Among Character, Name and Blood Type, 1983, Illustrated Modern Biology, 1990, Japanese Mentality and the Education of Japan, 1999; inventor in field. Mem. Zool. Soc. Japan, Japanese Soc. Devel. Biologists, Japanese Biochem. Soc. Avocations: playing chess, Japanese chess. Home: 2-31-1 Kitasenzoku Ohta, Tokyo 145-0062, Japan Office: St Marianna U Dept Biology, 2-16-1 Sugao Miyamae, Kawasaki 216, Japan

ASAOKA, HISATOSHI, chemist, educator; b. Niigata-Ken, Japan, Mar. 5, 1932; s. Masatoshi and Iyo (Sudoh) A.; m. Makiko Saitoh, Apr. 30, 1967; children: Toshihiro, Mayumi. BS, Niigata (Japan) U., 1954, MD, 1963. Asst. sch. of medicine Niigata U., 1954-62, lectr. faculty of sci., 1962-64, assoc. prof. gen. edn., 1964-72, prof. gen. edn., 1972-94, hon. prof., 1994. Contbr. articles to profl. jours.; research in new inorganic compounds named Bolite-compound. Mem. Chem. Soc. Japan. Avocations: fishing, reading, composing haiku. Fax: 81-25-267-8240. Home: Hamauracho 2-46-9, Niigata-Shi 951-8151, Japan

ASARI, EIKICHI, information sciences educator, researcher; b. Fonto, Karafuto, Japan, Feb. 10, 1929; s. Shoukichi and Kiku (Kotaki) A.; m. Satsuko Yamada, June 13, 1959; 1 child, Kimie. Grad., Military Scis. and Tech. Acad. Imperial Army of Japan, 1945; 1st class radio engr. (hon.), Ministry Telecom. of Japan, 1952; attended, Hokkaido U., Sapporo, Japan, 1959-61, Polytech. Nippon Telegraph and Pub. Corp., Tokyo, 1964. Radio engr. Nippon Telegraph and Tel. Pub. Corp., Sapporo, 1951-64, mem. mgmt. staff, 1964-69; assoc. prof. Tokai U., Sapporo, 1969-88, Hokkaido Tokai U., Sapporo, 1988-92; prof. info. scis. Hokkaido Coll. Arts and Scis., Ebets, 1993-97; part-time lectr. info. scis. Nat. Otaru U. Commerce, 1970-97, Sapporo Polytech. of Nippon Telegraph and Telephone Pub. Corp., Hokkaido, 1970-85, Rakuno Gakuen U., Ebets, 1997-99. Editor, author: Encyclopedia of Operations Research, 1974-75, Encyclopedia of hokkaido,1979-81; contbr. articles to profl. publs.; inventor complete solution and applications of renewal theory, 1967, microwave propagation in precipitation, 1974, theory of countermeasures for cold damage of rice cultivation in subpolar climate dists., 1973-77, weather forecast method by meteorological noises, 1989, ski resort radiosys., 1989-90 (govt. prize 1992). Commr. com. distbn. in Hokkaido, Ministry Transp., 1975-76; chmn. com. optimization of rice cultivation in Hokkaido, Hokkaido Govt., 1977-78; chmn. com. establish planning Hokkaido teleport Hokkaido Inst. Future Advancement, 1985-86; chmn. com. ski resort radio systems Ministry Post and Telecom., 1989-90, detection of clear air turbulences, 1999. Technical corp. telecom. Imperial Army Japan, 1945-46. Recipient award of merit of cold dist. devel. Civil Assns. Dist. Devel., Hokkaido, 1991, award of merit for radio sci. devel. Hokkaido br. Ministry Post and Telecom., 1992, fellow Operations Rsch. Soc. of Japan, 1995. Mem. IEEE, N.Y. Acad. Scis., Hokkauido/Mass. Soc., The Planetary Soc., Ops. Rsch. Soc. Japan (councilor 1970-92), Inst. Electronics and Communication Engrs. Japan, Cold Dists. Agrl. Sci. Soc. Ministry Agriculture, Forest and Fishery of Japan. Avocations: travel, photography, mysteries and science fiction, history of wars research. Home and Office: Shinkawa 2-Jo 2-chome, Kita-ku Sapporo 001-0922, Japan

ASARO, V. FRANK, lawyer; b. San Diego, July 28, 1935; s. Frank B. and Josephine (Quinci) A.; m. Barbara A. Mansfield, Aug. 16, 1958 (div. Mar., 1988); children: Dean, Valerie, Stephanie, Audrey. BA, San Diego State U., 1957; postgrad., Loyola U., L.A., 1957-60; JD, LLB, Southwestern U., L.A., 1961. Bar: Calif. 1962; U.S. Dist. Ct. (so. dist.) Calif. 1962, U.S. Dist. Ct. Ala. 1990; U.S. Ct. Appeals (9th cir.) 1965, U.S. Ct. Appeals (6th cir.) 1983. Clk. to the Hon. Justice Coughlin Calif. Dist. Ct. Appeal (4th dist.), San Diego, 1961-62; assoc. atty. Jenkins & Perry, San Diego, 1962-65, partner, 1965-70; partner Gant & Asaro, San Diego, 1970-80; sr. partner Asaro, Gattis & Sullivan, San Diego, 1980-82, Asaro & Long, San Diego, 1982-85, V Frank Asaro and Assocs., San Diego, 1985—; judge pro-tem San Diego Superior Ct., 1975—; arbitrator, San Diego Superior Ct., 1975, 1997; lectr. Practicing Law Inst. Author: Balance Between Order and Chaos, 1988, A Primal Wisdom, 1997; contbr. columnist Dicta County Bar Journal, 1965-70. Chairman Harborview Redevelopment Com., San Diego, 1975-85; mem. County Airport relocation SANPAT Com., San Diego County, 1970-75, City Center Planning Com., San Diego, 1986-90. Recipient citation for pub. svc., Mayor San Diego, 1989. Mem. Calif. State Bar Assn. (del.), San Diego County Bar Assn., Rotary Club (program chair 1996—, pres. 1998—), Barristers Club San Diego (dir.). Achievements include patent for avalanche rescue markers. Avocations: writing, music, philosophy. Office: V Frank Asaro and Assocs 4370 La Jolla Village Dr San Diego CA 92122-1249

ASBURY, STEPHEN WALTER, environment and safety consultant; b. Burton upon Trent, England, Oct. 21, 1965; s. Alan and Betty Lillian Asbury. MBA with distinction, De Montfort U., Eng., 1995, PhD, 1996. Diplomate in Environ. and Ops. Mgmt. Prodn. contr. John Carr, Eng., 1982-89; mgr. safety/quality J.B. Kind, Eng., 1989-91; mgr. safety/environment BTR, Eng., 1991-95; mgr. safety and environ. sys. GKN Sankey Ltd., Eng., 1995-97; sr. loss control cons. Hazard Mgmt. Ltd., Middlesex, Eng., 1997-99; cons. Corp. Risk Sys. Ltd., Burton upon Trent, Eng., 1999—; presenter confs. in field. Chmn. Burton and Dist. Occupl. Health and Safety Group, Staffs, Eng., 1989-95. Named Safety Profl. of Yr. (engring.) Royal Soc. for Prevention of Accidents, 1995. Fellow Inst. Occup. Safety and Health (registered safety practitioner, CPD com. 1990—, PA com. 1998—); mem. Inst. Mgmt. (chmn. 1995-97), Inst. Environ. Mgmt. and Assessment, Ergonomics Soc. Avocations: scuba diving, theater. Home: The Cedar Cottage, Hall Grounds, Rolleston on Dove DE13 9BS, England Office: Corp Risk Sys Ltd, Clay House 5 Horninglow St, Burton upon Trent DE14 1NG, England

ASCARD, JOHAN, agricultural researcher; b. Malmoe, Sweden, Oct. 3, 1959; m. Ingrid Alberts; children: Ellen, Martin. MS in Horticulture, Swedish U. Agrl. Scis., 1985, D in Agr., 1995. Postdoctoral fellow Cornell U., Ithaca, N.Y., 1994; sr. rschr. Dept. Agrl. Engring., Alnarp, Sweden, 1995-97; lectr. vegetable prodn. Dept. Horticulture, Alnarp, 1996, sr. rsch. officer vegetable prodn., 1997—; mem. sci. com. and session chmn. 4th Internat. Conf. on Non-Chem. Weed Control, Dijon, France, 1993, European Weed Rsch. Soc. 11th Symposium, Basel, Switzerland, 1999. Contbr. articles to profl. mags.; lectr. in field; referee for weed rsch., 1994—. Recipient scholarship Sweden Am. Found., 1994; Golden Kernel prize Land Mag., 1993. Mem. Internat. Soc. Horticultural Scis., European Weed Rsch. Soc., Scandinavian Assn. Agrl. Scis. Office: Swedish U Agrl Scis, PO Box 44, S-23053 Alnarp Sweden

ASCH, LEOPOLD, medical educator; b. Schiltigheim, France, Dec. 14, 1926; s. Arthur and Jeanne (Guthmann) A.; m. Gitta Goldberg, Mar. 22, 1961; children: Laurence, Pierre Henri. MS, U. Strasbourg, 1952, MD,

1956, agregation of medicine, 1966. Prof. medicine U. Strasbourg, France, 1966-95; prof. emeritus U. Strasbourg, 1995—; chief dept. rheumatology Univ. Hosp., Strasbourg, 1977-92, cons. 1992-95. Contbr. numerous articles to profl. jours. Recipient Laureate award French Acad. Medicine, 1990. Mem. French Assn. Against Rheumatic Diseases (pres. Alsace region 1975-78), Soc. of Rheumatology of NE France (pres. 1984-87). Avocation: history of art. Home: 8 rue de l'Observatoire, 67000 Strasbourg France Office: Hosp Hautepierre, Serv Rhumatologie, 67098 Strasbourg France

ASCHER, JAMES JOHN, pharmaceutical executive; b. Kansas City, Mo., Oct. 2, 1928; s. Bordner Fredrick and Helen (Barron) A.; m. Mary Ellen Robitsch, Feb. 27, 1954; children: Jill Denise, James John, Christopher Bordner. Student, Bergen Jr. Coll., 1947-48, U. Kans., 1946-47, 49-51. Rep. B.F. Ascher & Co., Inc., Memphis, 1954-55; asst. to pres. B.F. Ascher & Co., Inc., Kansas City, Mo., 1956-57, v.p., 1958-64, pres., 1965—. Bd. dirs. Childrens Cardiac Ctr., 1964-70, pres., 1968-70; mem. cen. governing bd. Children's Mercy Hosp., 1968-80; bd. dirs. Jr. Achievement of Middle Am., 1970-90, pres., 1973-76, chmn., 1979-81; edn. chmn. Young Pres.'s Orgn. 6th Internat. Univ. for Pres., Athens, 1975. 1st. lt. inf., U.S. Army, 1951-53, Korea. Decorated Bronze Star, Combat Infantryman's Badge. Mem. VFW, Am. Mgmt. Assn. (pres.'s assn.), Lenexa City C. of C., Drug, Chem. and Allied Trades Assn., World Pres.'s Orgn., Consumer Health Care Products Assn., Chief Execs. Orgn., Midwest Healthcare Mktg. Assn., Lotos Club, N.Y. Athletic Club, Kansas City Club, Mercury Club, Indian Hills Country Club, Delta Chi. Home: 6706 Glenwood St Shawnee Mission KS 66204-1451 Office: 15501 W 109th St Lenexa KS 66219-1307

ASCHERMAN, STANFORD WARREN, surgeon; b. Chgo., Aug. 18, 1926; s. Elmer N. and Irma G. (Kapper) A. AB, Stanford U., 1947; BS, U. Ill., 1948, MD, 1950. Lic. physician N.Y., Ill., Calif., Australia. Intern Cook County Hosp., Chgo.; resident in surgery Bellevue Hosp., N.Y.C., Mt. Sinai Hosp., Bronx (N.Y.) Mcpl. Hosp.; pvt. practice San Francisco, 1959—; endowed chair in elec. engring. Stanford U., 1978, endowed prof. in molecular genetics, 1997. Contbr. articles to profl. jours. Mem. Hadassah Med. Devel., N.S.W. Med. Bd., 1970—. Fellow ACS, Am. Trauma Soc., Nat. Bd. Med. Examiners, Am. Med. Writers Assn., Pan-Am Med. Soc., Internat. Coll. Surgeons, Am. Coll. Legal Medicine; mem. AAAS (life), Pan Pacific Surg. Assn., Australian Med. Assn., Commonwealth Club, Press Club, World Trade Club. Democrat. ADDRESS: 1177 California St Apt 724 San Francisco CA 94108-2221

ASCHERMANN, MICHAEL, cardiologist, researcher; b. Prague, Nov. 21, 1944; s. Emil and Ludmila (Kalvodova) A.; m. Alexandra Flieglova, Feb. 18, 1969; children: Ondrej, Marek. MD, Charles U., 1969, PhD, 1988, DrSc, 1997. Physician, mem. faculty Univ. Hosp., Prague, 1970-76, asst. prof., 1976-91, assoc. prof., 1991—, dir. cardiovasc. lab., divsn. cardiology, 1991—, prof., 1998—; prof. medicine, head dept. internal medicine Charles U., Prague, 1999—; cons. Dist. Hosp., Ostrava, Czech Republic, 1997—. Author: Coronary Angioplasty, 1995, Unstable Angina, 1998; contbr. articles to profl. jours. Maj. Army of Czech Republic, 1969-70. Mem. Internat. Soc. Andreas Gruentzig, European Soc. Cardiology, Czech Soc. Cardiology. Avocation: competitive orienteering running. Home: Svermova 475, 25210 Mnisek pod Brdy Czech Republic Office: Univ Hosp Dept Internal Med, U nemocnice 1, 128-08 Prague Czech Republic

ASCHOFF, ALFRED WALTER, neurosurgeon; b. Bavaria, Germany, Sept. 15, 1946; s. Friedrich and Elisabeth (Georg) A.; m. Barbara Greven, Nov. 3, 1976; children: Ursula, Johanna. Degree, U. Erlangen, Germany, 1974, MD, 1981, Habilitation, 1995. Resident dept. anesthetics U. Erlangen, 1975-77, resident dept. neurosurgery, 1977-83; resident dept. neurosurgery U. Heidelberg, Germany, 1983-86, sr. neurosurgeon, 1986—; mem. DIN Feinmechanik, Pforzheim, 1991—; del. com. for hydrocephalus valves ISO, 1991—. Mem. editl. bd. Critical Revs. in Neurosurgery, 1992—; contbr. articles to profl. publs. With German Army Med. Svc., 1976-77. Recipient Robert Pudenz award of distinction for excellence in physiology CFS, Santa Barbara, Calif., 1991. Fellow Deutsche Gesellschaft Neurosurgery; mem. Soc. Rsch. into Hydrocephalus and Spina Bifida Eng., Soc. Pediatric Neurosurgery. Office: U Heidelberg, Im Neuenheimer Feld 400, 69120 Heidelberg Germany

ASCHOFF, GERD, journalist; b. Norden, Germany, Feb. 11, 1956; s. Guenther and Gisela (Dressler) A.; m. Astrid Kretzer, Dec. 30, 1982. Diploma of social affairs, U. Gottingen, 1983. Freelance journalist various orgns., 1977-92; spokesman Ministry of Econs. and Transport, State of Lower Saxony, 1991-92; journalist Goettinger/Eichsfelder Tageblatt, 1992-93; editor Briefmarken Spiegel, Goettingen, Germany, 1993—, Briefmarken Post, Goettingen, Germany. Mem. Ry. Rides Assn. Pro Bahn (chmn. 1985—). Avocations: collecting stamps, railways. E-mail: philabms@aol.com. Home: Kurt-Schumacher-Weg 16a, D-37075 Goettingen Germany Office: Briefmarken Spiegel, PO Box 3042, 37020 Gottingen Germany

ASCHOFF, LAWRENCE MICHAEL (MICK ASCHOFF), computer information scientist; b. N.Y.C., Feb. 14, 1950; s. Edward William and Marie Louise (Marshall) A. BA in Art History, U. Fla., 1971; MBA in Fin., NYU, 1984, advanced profl. cert. in computer applications and info. systems, 1988. Sales rep. VIP Fabrics, N.Y.C., 1978-81; asst. to v.p. mktg. RAM Data, N.Y.C., 1981-82; sales agt. Equitable Life Assurance Soc., N.Y.C., 1982; programmer/analyst Drexel Burnham Lambert, N.Y.C., 1984-86, sr. programmer/analyst, 1986-88, project leader, 1988-89, project mgr., asst. v.p., 1989-90; mgr. project mgmt. competency ctr., nat. consumer svcs. strategic tech. Chase Manhattan Bank (formerly Chem. Bank), N.Y.C., 1990-91, officer, 1991-2000; dir. architecture and innovation program office AXA Global I.T. Orgn., N.Y.C., 2000—; treas. Saunders Owners of Queens, Ltd., 1989-91, pres., 1991—. Clin. assoc. Suicide and Crisis Prevention Ctr., Gainesville, Fla., 1972; treas. Saunders Owners of Queens, Ltd., 1989-91, pres. 1991—; mem. pres.'s coun. U. Fla., 1992—; vol. fundraiser Walk Am. program March of Dimes. Mem. Mensa, Phi Beta Kappa (sec. L.I. Alumni Assn. 1985-87, pres. 1987-93), Alpha Lambda Delta. Democrat. Avocations: travel, fitness, history, amusement parks, arts & sciences. Office: AXA Global IT Orgn 30 Rockefeller Plz Fl 20 New York NY 10112-2099

ASCHWANDEN, FELIX, licensing company executive; b. Lugano, Switzerland, Feb. 22, 1942; s. Alois and Margrit (Kuettel) A.; divorced; children: Corinne, Philipp. Elec. Engr., Swiss Fed. Inst. Tech., Zurich, 1967. Lic. engr. Test engr. STR, Zurich, 1967-68; design engr. Philips, Zurich, 1968-70, Redifusion, Zurich, 1970-71, Zellweger, Uster, Switzerland, 1971-73; design engr. Labs. RCA, Zurich, 1973-82, group leader, 1982-90, head digital TV, 1990—. Patentee in field. Lt. Swiss Army, 1962-96. Recipient Chester Sall award Consumer Electronics Soc., 1997. Mem. IEEE (mem. tech. program com. 1992-97, svc. award 1997). Avocations: skiing, hiking, travel. Home: 29 Alpenstrasse, 8800 Thalwil Switzerland Office: Labs TMM Ltd, 569 Badenerstrasse, 8048 Zurich Switzerland

ASCOTT, TERENCE, broadcast executive; b. Bromley, Kent, Eng., Oct. 2, 1947; s. George T. and Margarate Elizabeth (Bright) A.; m. Jacqueline Ann Doble, Oct. 14, 1972; children: Gavin Wasiim, Jonathan Rafik, Mona Theresa. BSc in Civil Engring. with 1st class hon, Middlesex (U.K.) U., 1972. Founder, pub. Christian Lit. Agy., Eng., 1969-73; lit. prodn. coord. Operation Mobilization, Beirut, Lebanon, 1973-75; prodn. cons. Living Bibles Internat., Beirut, 1974-77; founding dir. Middle East Media, Beirut, 1975-78; internat. dir. Middle East Media, Nicosia, Cyprus, 1979-95; CEO SAT-7, Nicosia, 1996—; founder, sec. Arabic Lit. Conv., Larnaca, Cyprus, 1986-95, Arabic Broadcasting Conv., Larnaca, 1989-95. Editor: The Cooperative Strategy Group Report on the Christian Presence in the Middle East, 1993; pub. Huwawa Hiya mag., 1977-93; exec. prodr.: (TV series) The Real Story, 1995. Dep. chmn. Human Rights Orgn. (MEC), 1992-96. Mem. Am. Inst. Graphic Arts, world Assn. for Christian Comm., Internat. Christian Media Commn., Evang. Alliance (UK). Avocations: photography, watercolor painting. Office: SAT-7 Media Svcs, PO Box 26760, CY 1647 Nicosia Cyprus

ASEER, GHULAM NABI, business executive; b. Sohawa, Punjab, Pakistan, Feb. 2, 1940; s. Dhanpat Rai and Kaniz Fatima A.; children from previous marriage: Tabassam, Shabana. MS, Punjab U., 1963; Shorthand degree, Danton Shorthand Sch., Delhi, India, 1959. Civilian clk. Army Sch. of Adminstrn., Kuldana-Murre Hills, 1958-59; stenographer Mangla Dam Project, Wapda, Mangla, 1960-62; asst. devel. officer Ideal Life Ins. Co., Karachi, 1963-64; prodn. officer Adamjee Ins. Co., Ltd., Lahore, 1965-66; proprietor Aseer Sohawy Corp., Lahore, Pakistan, 1968—. Muslim League. Clubs: Am. Library, Brit. Library. Avocation: reading. Office: Aseer Sohway Corp, GPO Box 1752, Lahore Punjab 54000, Pakistan

ASENOV, ASEN MIHAYLOV, science educator; b. Sofia, Bulgaria, Jan. 30, 1954; s. Mihail Asenov and Ivanka Iordanova (Gendova) M.; m. Darinka Stefanova Kernova, Nov. 4, 1979; children: Mihaela, Plamen. MSc in Physics, Sofia U., 1979; PhD, Bugaria Acad. Scis., Sofia, 1989. Sr. rschr. Inst. Microelectronics, Sofia, 1979-91; prof. Glasgow U., 1991—; head dept. electronics & elect. engring. Glasgow U., 2000—; vis. prof. U. Munich, 1989-90. Contbr. articles to profl. jours. Mem. IEEE, Inst. Elec. Engrs., Union Bulgarian Scientists. Home: 33 Chesterfield Ct, Glasgow G12 0BW, Scotland Office: Glasgow U, Electronics & Elec Engring, Glasgow 612 8LT, Scotland

ASERO, RICCARDO SALVATORE, physician; b. Milan, Italy, Feb. 27, 1956; s. Biagio and Vanna (Carnevali) A.; m. Luisa Faravelli, July 4, 1987. MD, U. Milan, 1982, Specialist in Allergy/Clin. Immunology, 1985. Postdoctoral fellowship Allergy and Clin. Immunology U. Milan, 1982-85; head Allergy Unit Ospedale Caduti Bollatesi, Bollate, Milan, 1990—; cons. allergist Pirelli Spa, Milan, 1988—; editl. staff: The Lancet, 1983-96. Contbr. articles to profl. jours. Mem. WWF, Italy, 1990—; vol. rschr. Allergy and Clin. Immunology Sch., U. Milan, 1985-88. Recipient scholarship Allergy and Clin. Immunology Sch., U. Milan, 1988-89. Mem. Italian Soc. of Allergy and Clin. Immunology, European Acad. Allergology and Clin. Immunology. Avocations: sports, music. Office: Ospedale Caduti Bollatesi, Via Piave 20, 20021 Bollate Milan, Italy

ASGRIMSSON, HALLDOR, Icelandic government official; b. Iceland, 1947; m. Sigurjona Sigurdardottir; 3 daus. Grad., Coop. Comml. Coll., 1965; post-grad., comml. colls. in Bergen and Copenhagen, 1971-73. Chartered acct., Iceland, 1970. Lectr. auditing and acctg. U. Iceland, 1973-75; M.P. representing Eastern parts of Iceland Icelandic Parliament, 1974-78, 79—; minister of fisheries Govt. of Iceland, 1983-91, min. justice and ecclesiastical affairs, 1989-91; chmn. bd. dirs. Cen. Bank of Iceland, 1981-83; Icelandic mem. Nordic Coun., 1977-78, 79-83, chmn. del., 1982-83; vice chmn. Progressive Party, 1981-94, chmn., 1994—; min. Nordic Coop., 1985-87, 95-99, min. fgn. & external trade, 1995—. Office: Ministry of Foreign Affairs, Raudararstigur 25, 150 Reykjavik Iceland

ASH, BRIAN MAXWELL, barrister; b. London, Jan. 31, 1941; s. Carl and Irene (Atkinson) A.; m. Barbara Anne Maxwell, Mar. 27, 1971; children: Cavan Michael, Kathleen Anne, Michael Phineas. BA, Oxford (Eng.) U., 1964. Bar: Gray's Inn, 1975, Queen's Counsel, 1990. TV producer BBC-TV, London, 1967-70, reporter, presenter, 1970-73; pvt. practice London, 1975—; sec. Local Govt. Planning & Environ. Bar Assn., 1990-92. Mem. Royal Norwich Golf Club, Royal Mid-Surrey Golf Club. Avocations: golf, skiing, sailing, music. Office: Grays Inn, 4/5 Grays Inn Sq, London WC1R 5AY, England

ASH, DOROTHY MATTHEWS, civic worker; b. Dresden, Germany, Nov. 10, 1918; came to U.S., 1924; d. Kurt Horst and Ana (Sekes) Matthesius; m. Harry A. Ash, Apr. 13, 1941 (dec. June 1981); children: Fredrick Curtis, Dorothea Ash Linklater. Dancer, 1933-40; treas. Inheritance Abstractors Inc., Chgo., 1949-70; reporter Miami (Fla.) Sun Post, 1983; reporter, columnist Social Mag., Miami, 1984—; chmn. Miss Universe Pageant, 1983-85; cruise chmn. Miami U., 1984, mem. Pres.'s Club, 1983. Pres. Big Bros. and Big Sisters, 1982-83; founding mem. World Sch. of Arts, 1985—; founding Notable Douglas Gardens 1988: Pres.'s Club U. of Miami, 1989; founding and bd. mem. Cancer Link Rsch., 1990; mem. Bd. Animal Welfare; active Project: Newborn, Am. Cancer Soc., March of Dimes, chmn. quest for the best, 1988-92, winner gourmet gala, 1988, leading lady 1998; active Children's Resource, Erase Diabetes, founding and bd. mem. 1990, Cerebral Palsy Found., Theatre Arts League, Linda Ray Infant Ctr., Miami City Ballet, Am. Ballet; bd. dirs. Greater Miami Opera, 1975—, Leading Ladies, Inc. 1997; pub. rels. vol. Miami Heart Inst., 1988—; com. mem. Miami Beach (Fla.) Beautification Program, 1984; mem. bd. Miami Mayor's Ad Hoc Com., 1984; mem. com. Challenger Seven Meml., 1988; active Cousteau Soc.; numerous others. Named Woman of Yr., Big Bros. and Big Sisters, Miami, 1981, Best Dressed, Am. Cancer Soc., 1981, Outstanding Humanitarian and Civic Leader, Mayor City of Miami, 1985, Woman of the Yr., Project: New Born, 1985, Miss Charity, Biscayne Bay Hosp., 1986, Queen of Hearts, Miami Children's Hosp., 1988, Leading Lady, March of Dimes, 1998; recipient Shining Star award Bon Secours Hosp., 1993, Patron Recognition award Mia Heart Rsch. Inst., 1993, Goddess of Love award Villa Maria Hosp., 1995, Shining Angel award Villa Maria Hosp., 2000. Mem. Miami Internat. Press Club. Avocations: reading, writing, painting. Home: 10245 Collins Ave Bal Harbour FL 33154-1407 also (summer): 330 W Diversey Pkwy Chicago IL 60657-6231

ASH, MAJOR MCKINLEY, JR., dentist, educator; b. Bellaire, Mich., Apr. 7, 1921; s. Major McKinley Sr. and Helen Marguerite (Early) A.; m. Fayola Foltz, Sept. 2, 1947; children: George McKinley, Carolyn Marguerite, Jeffrey LeRoy, Thomas Edward. BS, Mich. State U., 1947; DDS, Emory U., 1951; MS, U. Mich., 1954; Doctoris Medicine Honoris Causa, U. Bern, 1975. Instr. sch. dentistry Emory U., Atlanta, 1952-53; instr. U. Mich., Ann Arbor, 1953-56, asst. prof., 1956-59, assoc. prof., 1959-62, prof., 1962—, chmn. dept. occlusion, sch. dentistry, 1962-89, dir. stomatognathic physiology lab., sch. dentistry, 1969-89, dir. TMJ/oral facial pain clinic, sch. dentistry, 1983-89, Marcus L. Ward prof. dentistry, 1984-89, prof. emeritus, rsch. scientist emeritus, 1989—; cons. N.E. Regional Dental Bd., 1988-92; vis. prof. U. Bern, 1989, U. Tex., San Antonio, 1990-98; pres. Basic Sci. Bd., State of Mich., 1962-74; cons. over the counter drugs FDA, Washington, 1985-89. Author, co-author 69 textbooks, 1958—; editor 4 books; contbr. over 186 articles to profl. jours. Served to tech. sgt. Signal Corps, U.S. Army, 1942-45, ETO. Nat. Inst. Dental Research grantee, 1962-85. Fellow Am. Coll. Dentists, Internat. Coll. Dentists, European Soc. Craniomandibular Disorders, European Soc. Oral Physiology; mem. AAAS, Am. Dental Assn. (cons. coun. on dental therapeutics 1982—, cons. coun. sci. affairs 1995—), N.Y. Acad. Scis., Washtenaw Dist. Dental Soc. (pres. 1963-64), Phi Kappa Phi. Presbyterian. Avocations: photography, bird watching. Office: U of Mich Sch of Dentistry Ann Arbor MI 48109

ASH, MITCHELL GRAHAM, history educator; b. Mineola, N.Y., Sept. 26, 1948; s. Warren Howard and Carol Ann (Loeb) A.; m. Christiane Hartnack, Jan. 2, 1989. BA, Amherst Coll., 1970; AM, Harvard U., 1973, PhD, 1982; postgrad., Free U. Berlin, 1977-82. Rsch. assoc. Psychol. Inst., U. Mainz, Germany, 1982-84; asst. prof. history U. Iowa, Iowa City, 1984-89, assoc. prof., 1989-96, prof., 1996-97; prof. history U. Vienna, Austria, 1997—; vis. prof. U. Goettingen, Germany, 1992, U. Vienna, Austria, 1993; mem. editorial bd. Isis, Madison, Wis., 1991-94. Psychologie und Geschichte, Heidelberg, Germany, 1990—, Jour. of History of Behavioral Scis., N.Y., 1997—, History of Psychology, Washngton, 1997—. Author: Gestalt Psychology in German Culture 1890-1967, 1995; editor: (with W.R. Woodward) The Problematic Science: Psychology in Nineteenth-Century Thought, 1982, (with U. Geuter) Geschichte der deutschen Psychologie im 20. Jahrhundert, 1985, (with Woodward) Psychology in Twentieth-Century Thought and Society, 1987, (with A. Soellner) Forced Migration and Scientific Change, 1996, German Univs. Past and Future, 1997, Mythos Humboldt-Vergangenheit und Sukunft der deutschen universitaeten, 19992; gen. editor Cambridge Studies in the History of Psychology,1988—; contbr. chpts. to books., articles to profl. jours. Bd. dirs. Iowa City Fgn. Rels. Coun., 1990-94; mem. adv. bd. Iowa City Sci. Ctr., 1992-97. Fulbright fellow, 1978-80, German Rsch. coun. postdoctoral fellow, 1982-84, NSF rsch. fellow, 1986-87, 95-97, Inst. Advanced Study Berlin fellow, 1990-91; U. Iowa Faculty scholar, 1992-95. Mem. History of Sci. Soc., Am. Hist. Assn., Brit. Soc. History of Sci., Gesellschaft fuer Wissenschaftengeschichte (governing bd. 1996—, v.p. 1999—), Internat. Soc. for History of Social and Behavioral Scis., Internat. Soc. for History of Psychoanalysis, Forum for History of Human Sci. (steering com. 1991-92, chair 1992-96). Democrat. Jewish. Avocation: singing lieder and opera. Office: U Vienna Dept History, Dr Karl-Lueger-Ring 1, A-1010 Vienna Austria

ASHARIF, MOHAMMAD REZA, electrical engineer, educator; b. Tehran, Iran, Dec. 15, 1951; s. Reza Asharif and Zarangiz Naghshgar; m. Maryam Zavieh, May 27, 1982; children: Faramarz, Elika. BSc in Elec. Engring., U. Tehran, 1973, MSc in Elec. Engring., 1974; Dsc in Elec. Engring., U. Tokyo, 1981. Chief engr. Nat. Iran Radio & TV, Tabriz, Rezaeih, 1974-77; assoc., prof. tech. edn. Iran Islamic Rep. Broadcast Faculty, Tehran, 1981-85; sr. rschr. Fujitsu Labs. Co., Kawasaki, Japan, 1985-92; assoc. prof. Tehran U., 1992-97; prof. dept. info. engring. U. Ryukyus, Okinawa, Japan, 1997—; Author: VLSI Signal Processing, 1990; contbr. articles to profl. jours. Mem. IEEE (sr.), Computer Engring. Soc. Iran. Moslem. Avocations: swimming, karate. Home: Shimashi 253 7-502, 901-2213, Ginowan Okinawa, Japan Office: U Ryukyus Fac Engring, 1-sen baru, 903-0213 Nishihara Okinawa, Japan

ASHAUER, GUENTER, banker; b. Frankfurt, am Main, Germany, June 22, 1934; s. Heinrich and Lina (Reisser) A.; m. Ursula Allendorff, Mar. 29, 1961; children: Ulrike, Annette, Michael. Diploma Handelslehrer, U. Frankfurt, Germany, 1960; diploma in bus. adminstrn., U. Frankfurt, 1961, PhD, 1965. With Effectenbank/Hessische Landesbank, Frankfurt, 1953-56; referendar Rheinland-Pfalz, Mainz, Germany, 1961-63; dep. mgr. Hessische Sparkassenschule, Frankfurt, 1963-69; mgr. Lehrinstitut, Bonn, Germany, 1969-70; prof. Pädagogische Hochschule, Köln, Germany, 1970-73; gen. mgr. German Savs. Banks Acad., Bonn, 1973-97; hon. prof. U. Cologne, 1973—. Author: Grundwissen Wirtschaft, 12 edits., 1973-94, Von der Ersparungscasse zur Sparkassen-Finanzgruppe, 1991, Grundwissen Bankwirtschaft, 1998. Mem. Rotary Internat. (pres. 1978-79). Office: Deutsche Sparkassen-Akademie, U Cologne Gronewaldstr 2, 50931 Cologne Germany

ASHBERY, JOHN LAWRENCE, language educator, poet, playwright; b. Rochester, N.Y., July 28, 1927; s. Chester Frederick and Helen (Lawrence) A. Grad., Deerfield Acad., 1945; B.A., Harvard U., 1949; M.A., Columbia U., 1951; postgrad., NYU, 1957-58; D.Litt. (hon.), Southampton Coll. of L.I.U., 1979. Copywriter Oxford U. Press, N.Y.C., 1951-54; copywriter McGraw Hill Book Co., N.Y.C., 1954-55; art critic European edit. N.Y. Herald Tribune, Paris, 1960-65; Paris corr. Art News, 1964-65; exec. editor Art News, N.Y.C., 1966-72; prof. English Bklyn. Coll., 1974-90, Disting. prof., 1980-90, Disting. emeritus prof., 1990; Charles P. Stevenson prof. langs. and lit. Bard Coll., 1990—; editor quar. rev. Art and Lit., Paris, 1963-66; art critic Art Internat., Lugano, Switzerland, 1961-64; editor Locus Solus, Lans-en-Vercors, France, 1960-62; poetry editor Partisan Rev., 1976-80; art critic New York Mag., 1978-80, Newsweek, 1980-85; Charles Eliot Norton prof. poetry Harvard U., 1989-90; conducted spl. rsch. on life and work of Raymound Roussel. Author: (poems) Turandot and Other Poems, 1953, Some Trees, 1956, 70, 78, The Poems, 1960, The Tennis Court Oath, 1962, Rivers and Mountains, 1966, 77, Selected Poems, 1967, Three Madrigals, 1968, Sunrise in Suburbia, 1968, Fragment, 1969, The Double Dream of Spring, 1970, 76, The New Spirit, 1970, Three Poems, 1972, 77, The Vermont Notebook, 1975, Self-Portrait in a Convex Mirror, 1975, 76, 77, Houseboat Days, 1977, As We Know, 1979, Shadow Train, 1981, 82, A Wave, 1984, Selected Poems, 1985, 86, 87, April Galleons, 1987, 88, Flow Chart, 1991, 92, Hotel Lautréamont, 1992, And the Stars Were Shining, 1994, Can You Hear, Bird, 1995, Wakefulness, 1998; (plays) The Heroes, 1952, The Compromise, 1956, The Philosopher, 1963; author: (novel) (with James Schuyler) A Nest of Ninnies, 1969, 76, 87; works represented in numerous anthologies, including Reported Sightings: Art Chronicles, 1957-87, 89, 90; also author numerous articles art criticism, chronicles, translations; contbr. verse to lit. periodicals; verse set to music. Recipient Yale Series of Younger Poets prize, 1956, Harriet Monroe Poetry award Poetry Mag., 1963, 75, Union League Civic and Arts Found. prize, 1966, Nat. Inst. Arts and Letters award, 1969, Shelley award Poetry Soc. Am., 1973; guest of honor Poetry Day Modern Poetry Assn., 1974; Pulitzer prize, 1976; Nat. Book award, 1976; Nat. Book Critics Circle award Harvard U., 1976; poetry award English-Speaking Union, 1979; Mayor's award N.Y.C., 1983; Charles Flint Kellogg award Bard Coll., 1983; Jerome J. Shestack poetry award Am. Poetry Rev., 1984, Bollingen prize in poetry Yale U. Library, 1985, Lenore Marshall poetry prize the Nation, 1985, Common Wealth award in lit. MLA, 1986, Creative Arts award Brandeis U., 1989, Ruth Lilly Poetry prize Poetry Mag. and Modern Poetry Assn. and Am. Coun. for Arts, 1992, Robert Frost medal Poetry Soc. of Am., 1995, Grand Prize Biennales Intnernat. Poetry, Belgium, 1996; named Phi Beta Kappa Poet Harvard U., 1979, Literary Lion, N.Y. Pub. Libr., 1984, Poet of Yr. Pasadena City Coll., 1984; Fulbright scholar U. Montpellier, France, 1955-56; Fulbright scholar Paris, France, 1956-57; Poets' Found. grantee, 1960, 64; Ingram Merrill Found. grantee, 1962, 72; Guggenheim fellow, 1967, 73; Rockefeller Found. grantee, 1979-80, Wallace Stevens Fellow Yale U., 1985; McArthur Found. Fellow, 1985-90. Fellow Acad. Am. Poets; mem. Am. Acad. and Inst. Arts and Letters (Gold Medal 1997), Acad. Am. Poets (chancellor 1988—), Am. Acad. Arts and Scis. Office: c/o George Borchardt Inc 136 E 57th St New York NY 10022-2707 Address: Dept Langs and Lit Bard Coll PO Box 5000 Annandale NY 12504-5000

ASHBOLT, ALFRED ANTHONY, hotel executive; b. Tamworth, Eng., June 11, 1944; s. Alfred and Marion (Lothian) A.; m. Gaynor Wensley New, Oct. 11, 1967 (div. June 1977); children: Tony John, Vanessa Gay; m. Jennifer May Roberts, June 8, 1980; children: Andrew Anthony, Laura Melanie, Lucinda Meg. Grad., Tamworth High Sch., Eng., 1960. Cert. hotel adminstr. Mgmt. trainee Belfry Hotel, Sutton Coldfield, Eng., 1960-65; mgr. Living Room Theatre Restaurant, Brisbane, Australia, 1966-68; sr. hotel mgr. Roberts Group of Hotels, Brisbane, Australia, 1968-76; gen. mgr. Contacio Hotel, Perth, Australia, 1976-77, Palm Lake Hotel, Melbourne, Australia, 1977-78; gen. mgr. Noahs Hotel, Melbourne, Australia, 1978-82, Christchurch, New Zealand, 1982-84; gen. mgr. Ramada Hotels, Surfers Paradise, Queensland, 1984-86, Furama Hotels Internat., Bunbury, Australia, 1986-91; owner, propr. Memories of the Bond Store, 1991—; v.p. Catering Inst. Australia, 1993-95; chmn. Tourism Tng. Devel., Australia, 1984-86, Tourism Devel. Com., 1988-91, S.W. Devel. Authority, 1987-88, Bunbury Tourist Bur., 1988-90; v.p. Catering Inst., 1994. Councillor City of Bunbury, 1988-91; bd. dirs. S.W. Devel. Commn., 1994. Fellow Catering Inst. of Australia, Soc. Sr. Execs., Australian Inst. Mgmt., Australian Mktg. Inst.; mem. Les Toque Blanches, Hospitality Mgmt. Guild. Avocations: dragonboat racing, motorcycling, canoeing. Home: 9 Upper Esplanade, Bunbury 6230, Australia Office: SW Coll Tafe Hospitality Tourism & Retail, Robertson Dr, Bunbury 6230, Australia

ASHBROOK, KATE JESSIE, charitable organization director; b. London, Feb. 1, 1955; d. John Benjamin and Margaret (Balfour) A. BSc with honors, Exeter (Eng.) U. Gen. sec. Open Spaces Soc., Eng., 1984—. Editor Open Space mag., 1984—. Mem. Ramblers' Assn. (chmn. 1995-98, EC mem. 1982—), Dartmoor Preservation Assn. (pres. 1995—), Coun. for Nat. Parks (vice-chmn. 1998—), Countryside Agy. (bd. dirs. 1999—). Office: Open Spaces, 25A Bell St, Henley-on-Thames RG9 2BA, England

ASHBURTON, LORD See BARING, JOHN FRANCIS HARCOURT

ASHBY, LINDSEY GORDON, railroad transportation executive; b. Pittsburg, PA, Dec. 7, 1933; s. James Lindsey and Nina Gordon (Johnson) A.; m. Rosa Lee Frost, Dec. 27, 1961; 1 child, Leah. BS in Petroleum Engr., La. State U., 1956; MS in Basic Sci., U. Colo., 1967. Gas engr. Peoples Gas Light & Coke, Chicago, IL, 1956-58, Pub. Svc. Co. Colo., Denver, 1960-63; petroleum engr. Marathon Oil Co., Littleton, Colo., 1963-85; pres. Georgetown (Colo.) Loop R.R., 1973—, Canon City & Royal George R.R., 1998—; v.p. Tourist Rwy. Assn., N.Y.C., 1989-97, pres. 1997—; v.p. Colo. R.R. Mus., Golden, 1996-99. Democrat. Avocations: railroads, jeeping, photography, computers. Office: Georgetown Loop RR Inc PO Box 217 Georgetown CO 80444-0217

ASHBY, ROBERT EDWARD, biotechnologist; b. London, Apr. 22, 1948; s. Edward Walter and Lilian Rose (Shearer) A.; m. Annette Ashby, Aug. 29, 1969; children: Zoe Anne, Jodie Susan, Robin James Edward. BSc, U. Birmingham, 1969; MSc, Univ. Coll. Wales, 1975. Rsch. asst. U. Leeds, 1972-75; exptl. officer U. Kent, 1975-81; rsch. officer Cranfield Inst. Tech., 1981-83, sr. rsch. officer, 1983—; gen. mgr. biotech. Cranfield U., 1985—; sec. Cranfield Diagnostics Ltd., 1994—; advisor Cabinet Office OST and CVCP, London, 1994-95. Contbr. articles to profl. jours. Mem. Assn. Univ. Tchrs. (pres. Cranfield chpt. 1992—), Soc. for Applied Bacteriology, Soc. for Gen. Microbiology, Brit. Assn. of Rsch. Quality Assurance, Inst. Biology.

Avocations: gardening, water coloring. Office: Cranfield U, Biotech Ctr, Silsoe Beds MK45 4DT, England

ASHCOM, JOHN M., sales executive, general management executive; b. Pitts., Apr. 7, 1945; s. John M. and Mary Grace (Herron) A. BSBA, Youngstown (Ohio) State U., 1969. Mgr. comm. Rockwell Internat., Pitts., 1972-77; dir. comm. Litton Industries, N.Y.C., 1977-78; dir. mktg. and comm. Republic Steel-LTV, Canton, Ohio, 1979-86; gen. mgr. Hanel Storage Systems, Pitts., 1986-92; sr. assoc. Green Assocs., Pitts., 1992-93; v.p. mktg. ACCU-Sort Systems, Inc., Telford, Pa., 1993-94; owner JM Assoc., Quakertown, Pa., 1994—; divsn. mgr. TherMax divsn. Kooltronic Inc., Hopewell, N.J., 1994-96; nat. sales mgr. Versa Conveyor-Tompkins Industries, Columbus, Ohio, 1996-98; prin. JM Assocs., 1998-2000; cons., 1999—. Editor: Republic Profiler mag., 1979-84, Water Journal mag., 1972-78, Gas Line mag, 1972-78. Mem. Soc. Mfg. Engrs., Material Handling Inst., Am. Mgmt. Assn., Bus./Profl. Advertisers. Republican. Club: Clan Donald, Pitts. Avocations: golfing, reading, biking. Home: 2045 Clover Mill Rd Quakertown PA 18951-2142

ASHCROFT, PHILIP GILES, retired legal consultant; b. Stourbridge, Worcesters, England, Nov. 15, 1926; s. Edmund Samuel and Constance Ruth (Giles) A.; m. Kathleen Margaret Senior, Apr. 27, 1968 (div. 1983); 1 child, Richard Edmund; m. Valerie May Smith, Sept. 14, 1985. LLB, Durham U., 1950. Solicitor of the Supreme Ct. Eng. 1951. Asst. Treasury Solicitors Dept., London, 1955-60; sr. asst. Ministry of Power Legal Dept., London, 1961-67; asst. legal adviser Land Commn., Newcastle, Eng., 1967-71; asst. treasury solicitor Treasury Solicitor's Dept., London, 1971-72; under sec. Dept. Trade & Industry, London, 1973; legal advisor Dept. of Energy, London, 1974-80; dep. solicitor The Post Office, London, 1980-81; solicitor Brit. Telecom, London, 1981-87; cons. Bldg. Socs. Commn., London, 1987-96. Signalman Royal Signals, 1944-48. Mem. The Law Soc. Mem. United Reformed Ch. Avocations: music, literature. Home: 24A Rudds Ln Haddenham, Aylesbury Bucks, England HP178JP

ASHDOWN, JEREMY JOHN DURHAM, political party official; b. New Delhi, Feb. 27, 1941; s. John and Lois A.; m. Jane Courtney; children: Kate, Simon. Grad., Bedford Sch. Commd. 2nd lt. Royal Marines, 1959, advanced through grades to capt., 1969, resigned, 1971; 1st sec. U.K. Mission to UN, Geneva, 1971-76; withcomml. mgr.'s dept. Westlands Group (Normalair Garrett) Morlands' Yeovil, 1976-78; mgr. Morlands Ltd., 1978-81; with Dorset County Coun. Youth Svc., 1982-83; M.P. Ho. of Commons, London, 1983—; leader Liberal Democrats, 1988-99; appointed privy councillor, 1989—; Liberal candidate for Yeovil, 1976; apptd. spokesman on trade and industry affairs Liberal, 1983-86; spokesman on edn. and sci. Liberal/SDP Alliance,1987-88; spokesman on No. Ireland Social and Liberal Dems., 1988-91. Author: Citizen's Britain, 1989, Beyond Westminster, 1994. Mem. Nat. Liberal Club. Office: House of Commons, London SW1A 0AA, England

ASHDOWN, MARIE MATRANGA (MRS. CECIL SPANTON ASHDOWN, JR.), writer, lecturer; b. Mobile, Ala.; d. Dominic and Ave (Mallon) Matranga; m. Cecil Spanton Ashdown Jr., Feb. 8, 1958; children: Cecil Spanton III, Charles Coster; children by previous marriage: John Stephen Gartman, Vivian Marie Gartman. Student, Maryville Coll. Sacred Heart; student, Springhill Coll. Feature artist, women's program dir. daily program Sta. WALA, WALA-TV, Mobile; v.p., dir. Met. Opera Guild, N.Y.C., opera instr. in-svc. program, 1970-80; opera instr. in-svc. program Marymont Coll., N.Y.C., 1979-85; exec. dir. Musicians Emergency Fund, Inc., N.Y.C., 1985—; mem. internat. adv. coun. Van Cliburn Found., 1998—; cons. No. Ill. U. Coll. of Visual and Performing Arts, 1985—; lectr. in field. Author: Opera Collectables, 1979, contbr. articles to profl. jours. Internat. cons. Van Cliburn Found. Recipient Extraordinary Service award March of Dimes, 1958, Medal of Appreciation award Harvard Bus. Sch. Club N.Y.C., Cert. Appreciation, Kiwanis Internat., Arts Excellence award N.J. State Opera, Ciparío award. Mem. AAUW, Nat. Inst. Social Scis., Com. for U.S.-China Rels. Avocations: collecting art, antique ceramics and porcelains, bookbinding. Home: 25 Sutton Pl S Apt 16K New York NY 10022-2456 Office: Musicians Emergency Fund Inc PO Box 1256 New York NY 10150-1256

ASHEK, ULLAH MOHAMMED, apparel executive; b. Nabinagar, Bangladesh, Oct. 10, 1963; s. Abdul and Mahmuda (Begum) H.; m. Nazma Akter. BA, U. Dhaka, Bangladesh, 1982. Correspondent Natun Bangla, Bangladesh, 1980-84, BNA, Dhaka, 1984-87; sr. correspondent TNN, Tokyo, 1988-92; CEO Trade Exchange Media Svcs., Japan/Bangladesh, 1992—; dir. Fancy Fashion Sweaters, Ltd., Bangladesh, 1997—; founder TEMS Found., Japan, 1992—; dir. WARBE, Bangladesh, 1997-99, Human Resources Devel. Orgn., Bangladesh, 1996—; mem. Bangogandhu Coun., 1990—. Pres. Bangladesh Student Assn.; mem. Nat. Geographic Soc., 1996—. Fellow Angel Bankers Capital; mem. Internat. Airliine Passengers Assn. Bangladesh Awamelige. Avocations: music, travel. Home: 6-B 3/9 Mirpur, 1216 Dhaka Bangladesh Office: Fancy Fashion Sweaters Ltd, 169/A W Dolaipar, 1204 Dhaka Bangladesh

ASHENBERG, JOSHUA, aerospace engineer; b. Rehovot, Israel, May 7, 1953; m. Alena Ashenberg; 1 child, Orr. BS, Israel Inst. Tech., 1979, MS, 1981; MS, U. Tex., Austin, 1989, PhD, 1993. Rsch. engr. Israel Armament Authority, Haifa, 1981-88; lectr. Israel Inst. Tech., Haifa, 1994-95; scientist, cons. Harvard Smithsonian Ctr. Astrophysics, Cambridge, Mass., 1995-97; scientific software developer Smithsonian Astrophys. Obs., Cambridge, Mass., 1997—. Contbr. articles to profl. jours. Mem. AIAA. Avocations: soaring, sailing, wind surfing. Office: Smithsonian Astrophys Obs 60 Garden St # MS81 Cambridge MA 02138-1516

ASHER, DUFFEY ANN, lawyer; b. Juneau, Alaska, Nov. 25, 1959; d. John O'Hair and Jane (Fitzgerald) A. Diploma, Leningrad State U., USSR, 1980; student, London Sch. Econs., 1980-81; BA, Wellesley Coll., 1982; JD, Harvard U., 1986. Bar: N.Y. 1987. Asst. fgn. affairs advisor Office Rep. Edward Heath, M.P., M.B.E., London, 1980-81, 82-83; summer assoc. Baker & McKenzie, Chgo., summer 1984; assoc. Shearman & Sterling, N.Y.C., 1986-88, London, 1988-90; sr. transactor Citibank Shipping Bank, S.A., Greece, 1990-96; prin. Asher Consulting, 1996—. Thomas J. Watson fellow, 1982. Home: D Poliorkitou 122, Thrakomakedones, Athens Greece

ASHER, JANE, actor, writer, business owner; b. Apr. 5, 1946; m. Gerald Scarfe; 3 children. Proprietor Jane Asher Party Cakes Shop and Sugarcraft, 1990—; designer, cons. Sainsbury's Cakes, 1992-99; spokesperson, cons. McVities (now Heinz Frozen Foods), 1993—; designer Dakenhaus Jane Asher Raye. Appeared in films, including Greengage Summer, Masque of the Red Death, Alfie, Deep End, Henry the Eighth and His Six Wives, Success is the Best Revenge, Dreamchild, Paris By Night; appearances (TV) Walter, Murder Most Horrid, 1991, Brideshead Revisited, Wish Me Luck, Closing Numbers, 1994, The Choir, 1995, (plays) Henceforward..., 1989, School for Scandal, 1990, Making It Better, 1992, The Shallow End, 1997, Things We Do for Love, 1998, House and Garden, 2000; author: The Moppy Stories, 1987, Keep Your Baby Safe, 1988, Calendar of Cakes, 1989, Eats for Treats, 1990, Time to Play, 1993, Jane Asher's Book of Cake Decorating Ideas, 1993, The Longing, 1996, The Question, 1998. Mem. Nat. Autistic Soc. (pres.). Avocations: reading, crosswords. Address: care London Mgmt, 24 Noel St, London W1V 3RB, England also: 24 Cale St, London SW3 3QU, England

ASHER, KATHLEEN MAY, communications educator; b. Vassar, Mich., Aug. 19, 1932; d. Thomas Henry and Jessie (Smith) Pierce; m. Donald William Asher, July 17, 1957; children: David Kevin, Diane Kerri. BS, Ctrl. Mich. U., 1956, MA, 1967. Cert. fundraiser Williamsburg Devel. Inst., cert. QTH trainer. Tchr. speech and theater Standish (Mich.) Pub. Schs., 1956-58, Vassar (Mich.) Pub. Schs., 1959-67; prof. speech, adminstr. Mott C.C., Flint, Mich., 1967-89; assoc. prof. speech Palm Beach C.C., Lake Worth, Fla., 1990—, fundraiser, 1991-95; faculty polit. action chairperson Palm Beach C.C., Lake Worth, 1996-97; cons. in speech, Flint, Mich., 1973-89; cons. quality total mgmt. Pres. Homeowner Assn., Lake Worth, 1993-95; chairperson Tuscola County Dem. Com., 1975-85; del., whip Dem. Conv. and Rules Com., 1976; del. Fla. Dem. Conv., 1999; mem. Vassar Zoning Bd.; officer City Coun. Mem. United Faculty Palm Beach C.C. (chpt. pres.), Fla. Tchg. Profession, NEA, Nat. Collegiate Hons. Coun. (collegiate 1991-95), Mich. Women's Studies Assn. (pres. 1974-75), C.C. Humanities Assn., Phi Theta Kappa (leadership prof.). Presbyterian. Avocations: percussionist, reading, golf, bowling, biking. Home: 4713 Rainbow Dr Lake Worth FL 33463-3610 Office: Palm Beach CC 4200 Congress Ave Lake Worth FL 33461-4705

ASHER, RONALD E., linguist, educator; b. Gringley-on-the-Hill, Eng., July 23, 1926; s. Ernest and Doris (Hurst) A.; m. Chin Asher; children: David, Michael. BA, U. London, 1950, cert. in the phonetics French, 1951, PhD, 1955; DLitt, U. Edinburgh, Scotland, 1992. Lectr. Sch. Oriental and African Studies, U. London, 1953-65; sr. lectr. in linguistics U. Edinburgh, 1965-70, reader in linguistics, 1970-77, prof. linguistics, 1977-93, head dept. linguistics, 1976-80, 83-86, assoc. dir. Ctr. for Speech Tech. Rsch., 1984-85, assoc. dean faculty arts, 1985-86, dean faculty arts, 1986-89, vice-prin., 1990-93, curator of patronage, 1991-93, dir. Ctr. for Speech Tech. Rsch., 1994, hon. fellow Faculty Arts, 1993—; vis. asst. prof. Tamil, U. Chgo., 1961-62; vis. prof. linguistics U. Ill., Champaign-Urbana, 1967; Dr. R.P. Sethu Pillai Silver Jubilee Endowment lectr. U. Madras, India, 1968; vis. prof. Tamil and Malayalam, Mich. State U., 1968; vis. prof. linguistics U. Minn., 1969; chaire des professeurs étrangers Coll. de France, Paris, 1970; Subrahmaniya Bharati fellow Tamil U., Thanjavur, India, 1984; vis. prof. linguistics and internat. comm. Internat. Christian U., Tokyo, 1994-95; Vaikom Muhammed Basheer chair Mahatma Gandhi U., Kottayam, Kerala, India, 1995-96. Author: Some Landmarks in the History of Tamil Prose, 1973, Tamil, 1982, Malayala bhasa-sahitya pathanannal, 1989, National Myths in Renaissance France: Francus, Samothes and the Druids, 1993, Malayalam, 1997, Bashir: malayalattinre sargavismayam, 1999; editor: (with R. Radhakrishnan) A Tamil Prose Reader: Selections from Contemporary Tamil Prose with Notes and Glossary, 1971, (with E.J.A. Henderson) Towards a History of Phonetics, 1981, (with C. Moseley) Atlas of the World's Languages, 1994, (with E.F.K. Koerner) Concise History of the Language Sciences: From the Sumerians to the Cognitivists, 1995; editor-in-chief: The Encyclopedia of Language and Linguistics, 10 vols., 1994, Bashir: Svatantrya samara kathakal, 1998; translator: Me Grandad 'ad an Elephant!: Three Stories of Muslim Life in South India, 1980, Scavenger's Son, 1993. Fellow Royal Asiatic Soc., London, 1964, gold medal Kerala Sahitya Akademi, Trichur, India, 1983, Royal Soc. Edinburgh, 1991; recipient medal Coll. de France, Paris, 1970. Mem. Internat. Assn. Tamil Rsch. (pres. 1981-89), Philol. Soc. (coun. mem. 1980-85, 89-94, 96—), Gen. Counc., Tamil Sahitya Acad., 2000—; Linguistic Soc. India, Dravidian Linguistics Assn. Office: Univ Edinburgh, George Sq, Edinburgh EH8 9LL, Scotland

ASHFORD, CLINTON RUTLEDGE, judge; b. Honolulu, Mar. 23, 1925; s. Huron Kanoelani and Lillian Radcliffe (Cooke) A.; m. Joan Beverly Schumm, Aug. 24, 1951; children: Marguerite, Frank, Bruce, James. B.A., U. Calif.-Berkeley, 1945; J.D., U. Mich., 1950. Bar: Hawaii 1950, U.S. Supreme Ct. 1967, Republic of Marshall Islands 1985. Ptnr. Lee & Ashford, Honolulu, 1951-53; dep. atty. gen. Hawaii, 1953-55; ptnr. Ashford & Wriston, Honolulu, 1955-89, of counsel, 1990—; chief justice Supreme Ct., Republic of Marshall Islands, 1989-96. Bd. dirs. Child and Family Svc., Honolulu, 1967-73, pres., 1971; bd. dirs. Health and Cmty. Svcs. Coun., 1973-75, Mediation Ctr. of the Pacific, 1999—, Aloha United Way, 1975-81, exec. com., 1977-79; bd. dirs. Hawaii Justice Found., 1994-99, pres., 1996. With USNR, 1943-46, res., 1950-64, ret. lt. comdr. Fellow Am. Bar Found., Am. Coll. Trust and Estate Counsel, Am. Coll. Real Estate Lawyers, Am. Coll. Trial Lawyers, Am. Acad. Appellate Lawyers, Coll. Law Office Mgmt.; mem. ABA (bd. govs. 1979-82, exec. com. 1981-82), Hawaii Bar Assn. (pres. 1972), Am. Law Inst., Am. Judicature Soc. (bd. dirs. 1981-86, chpt. bd. dirs. 1998—), Internat. Acad. Estate and Trust Law, Order of Coif, Lambda Alpha (Aloha chpt.). Avocations: amateur radio operator, blue water sailor. Email: cashford@awlaw.com. Home: 45-628 Halekou Pl Kaneohe HI 96744-5203 Office: Ashford & Wriston PO Box 131 1099 Alakea St Fl 14 Honolulu HI 96813-4500

ASHFORD, NIGEL JOHN GLADWELL, political scientist, educator; b. Bristol, Eng., Feb. 12, 1952; s. Peter Kenneth and Patricia Ann (Gladwell) A. BA with honours, Exeter (Eng.) U., 1973; MA, Warwick U., Coventry, Eng., 1975, PhD, 1983. Exec. dir. European Dem. Students, London, 1976-78; lectr. Paisley (Scotland) U., 1979-83, Strathclyde U., Glasgow, 1983-84; lectr. Staffordshire U., Stoke-on-Kent, Eng., 1984-93, prin. lectr., 1993—. Author: U.S. Politics Today, 1999; editor: A Dictionary of Conservative and Libertarian Thought, 1991, Public Policy and the Impact of the New Right, 1993; contbg. author: Britain and the EC, 1992, Contemporary American Politics, 1995, Republican Take-over of Congress, 1998, American Politics: 2000 and Beyond, 2000. Mem. coun. Atlantic Com. of the U.K., London, 1992—. Recipient Internat. Fisher Trust prize, 1992; Fulbright scholar, 1973; Marguerite Eyer Wilbur fellow, Santa Barbara, Calif., 1986, Jean Monnet fellow European Integration, 1997—, vis. fellwo Social Philosophy and Policy Ctr., 2000; Bradley rsch. scholar, 1989-90. Mem. Am. Politics Group (chmn. 1986-87), Polit. Studies Assn. U.K. (treas. 1988-89). Avocations: walking, visiting historic sites, dancing. Home: 77 Paris Ave, Newcastle-under-Lyme ST5 2QX, England Office: Staffordshire U, College Rd, Stoke-on-Trent ST4 2DE, England

ASHHURST, ANNA WAYNE, foreign language educator; b. Phila., Jan. 5, 1933; d. Astley Paston Cooper and Anne Pauline (Campbell) Ashhurst; m. Ronald G. Gerber, July 22, 1978. AB, Vassar Coll., 1954; MA, Middlebury Coll., 1956; PhD, U. Pitts., 1967. English tchr. Internat. Inst. Spain, Madrid, 1954-56; asst. prof. Juniata Coll., Huntingdon, Pa., 1961-63; asst. prof. Spanish dept. Franklin and Marshall Coll., Lancaster, Pa., 1968-74, acting chmn. Spanish dept., 1972, convenor, fgn. lang. council, 1972-74; assoc. prof. dept. modern fgn. langs. U. Mo., St. Louis, 1974-78. Author: La literatura hispano-americana en la crítica española, 1980. Mem. Welcome Wagon of Lancaster, Pa., 1968-70, 71-74. Fulbright-Hays grantee, Colombia, S.Am., summer 1963; Ford Humanities fellow, summer 1970; Mellon fellow, 1970-71. Mem. AAUW (pres. Ferguson-Florissant br. 1989-91, 95-98, chmn. St. Louis area interbranch coun. 1992-94, chair environ. task force Mo. 1992-95, local arrangements chair for Mo. state conv. 1997, Woman of Distiction award 1998), Internat. Inst. in Spain, Instituto Internacional de Literatura Iberoamericana, Am. Assn. Tchrs. Spanish and Portuguese. Home: 2105 Barcelona Dr Florissant MO 63033-2805

ASHIHARA, YOSHINOBU, architect, educator; b. Tokyo, July 7, 1918; s. Nobuyuki and Kikuko (Futita) A.; m. Hatsuko Takahashi, Dec. 24, 1944; children: Yukiko, Taro. BArch, U. Tokyo, 1942; MArch, Harvard U., 1953; D of Engrng. in Architecture, U. Tokyo, 1961. Prin. Yoshinobu Ashihara Architect & Assocs., Tokyo, 1956—; prof. architecture U. Tokyo, 1970-79, Musashino Art U., Tokyo, 1979-89; prof. emeritus U. Tokyo and Musashino Art U., Tokyo, 1989—; archtl. councillor Nat. Diet Library, Tokyo. Designer numerous bldgs. including: Chuo-Koron Bldg. (Archtl. Inst. Japan award 1960), Komazawa Olympic Gymnasium (Archtl. Inst. Japan Spl. award 1965), Sony Bldg. 1966, Japanese Pavilion, Expo'67 (Min. of Edn. award of Arts 1968), Nat. Mus. Japanese History, 1980, Tokyo Met. Art Space, 1990. Mem. adv. com. on grant aid Ministry Fgn. Affairs, Tokyo; mem. coun. Nat. Mus. Modern Arts, Tokyo. Decorated Order Commendatore (Italy), Order of Culture, 1998; recipient Golden Triangle award Nat. Soc. Interior Designers, 1970, Person of Cultural Merits award, 1991. Fellow Am. Inst. Architects (hon.), Royal Australian Inst. Architects (hon.); mem. Archtl. Inst. Japan (hon., pres. 1985-87), Japan Art Acad., Rotary.

ASHKAR, ABRAHAM CHARBEL SERAPHIM, medical products executive; b. Dick-el-Mehdi, Lebanon, July 2, 1934; arrived in Ghana, 1934; s. Charbel Boutros Seraphim and Anissa Saraphin (Chebib) A.; m. May Ibrahim Zeynoun, Feb. 28, 1960; children: Naaman Abraham Seraphin, Nadim Abraham Seraphim. Grad. high sch., Beirut. Mgr. wholesale/retail C.B. Seraphin & Sons, Accra, Ghana, 1958-60, mng. dir., 1960-65; deputy mng. dir. Seraphin Textiles Ltd., Accra, Ghana, 1966-69, mng. dir., 1970-73; deputy chmn. Seraphin Surg. Ltd., Accra, Ghana, 1985—; dir., chmn. Akramang Farms Ltd., Accra, 1983, Akramang Food Processing Ltd., Accra, 1993; mem. adv. bd., dept. chmn. Cedar House Sec. Sch., Accra, 1979-93, St. Marouns Ch. Com., Accra, 1984-94. Life mem. Chana Red Cross, Accra, 1979—; mem. Ghana Soc. PRevention Tuberculosis, Accra, 1988. Mem. Lebanon House, Scottish Lodge (past master, dist. grand jr. warden), mem. Ghana Nat. Steering Group of Indsl. Radiation Processing of the Ghana Atomic Energy. Maronite. Avocations: body building, football, golf, swimming, classical music. Office: Seraphin Surg Ltd, Ring Rd Indsl Area N, 7189 Accra North, Ghana

ASHKENAZY, VLADIMIR DAVIDOVICH, concert pianist, conductor; b. Gorky, USSR, July 6, 1937; s. David and Evstolia (Plotnova) A.; m. Thorunn Johannsdottir, Feb. 25, 1961; children—Vladimir Stefan, Nadia Liza, Dimitri Thor, Sonia Edda, Alexandra Inga. Student, Cen. Music Sch., Moscow, Moscow Conservatory; studies with, Sumbatyan, Lev Oborin. Condr., music dir. Royal Philharm. Orch., London, 1987-95; prin. guest conductor Cleve. Orch., 1987-94; music dir. Deutsches Symphonie Orchester (formerly Radio Symphony Orch.), Berlin, 1989-99; music. dir. Czech Philharm. Orch., 1998—. London debut, London Symphony Orch. under George Hurst, later solo recital, Festival Hall, 1963, recs., concerts throughout world. Music dir. Czech Philharm. Orch., Prague, 1998. Recipient 2d prize Internat. Chopin Competition, Warsaw, 1955, Gold medal Queen Elizabeth Internat. Piano Competition, Brussels, 1956, Grammy awards 1973, 78, 81, 85, 87; co-recipient Tchaikovsky Piano Competition award, Moscow, 1962. Office: care Harrison/Parrott Ltd, 12 Penzance Pl, London W11 4PA, England

ASHKIN, RAJASPERI MALIAPEN, marketing executive; b. Penang, Malaysia, Mar. 1, 1956; came to U.S., 1984; d. Maliapen A.M.N. (Annasamy) and Jayaletchemi (Chelliah) M.; m. Ronald Evan Ashkin, Nov. 25, 1984; 1 child, Jacqueline Ariel. BS in Forestry, U. Canterbury, 1978, DBA, 1979. Mktg. asst. Forest Rsch. Inst., Rotorua, Nw Zealand, 1978-79; mktg. officer Consulate Gen. India, Sydney, Australia, 1980-81; nat. mktg. coord. Estee Lauder Ltd., Sydney, 1981-84; assoc. buyer Brown Store Group, Terre Haute, Ind., 1984-85; mktg. mgr. A.T.C. Time Inc., Terre Haute, Ind., 1985-87; v.p. New Concepts Inc., Terre Haute, Ind., 1987-90; chief exec. officer, mng. dir. Excelsior Corp., Terre Haute, Ind., 1990—, also bd. dirs.; mktg. & advt. cons. in field; organizer Christmas Food Drive Salvation Army, Terre Haute, 1985-86; vol. reader Vigo County Pub. Libr. Literacy Program, 1989—. Mktg. com. Leadership Terre Haute, 1986-87; TV moderator Valley Point of View, Terre Haute, 1986—; bd. dirs. YWCA, Terre Haute, 1986—; internat. rels. chairperson Altrusa Club, Terre Haute, 1985-87; cake bake chairperson, on site rep. Century Club, YWCA, 1986; cmty. vol. Am. Embassy, Sarajevo, 1999; vol. Internat. Women's Club, Sarajevo, 1999. Recipient Letter of Commendation Ralph Davidson Time Inc., 1986, Nat. System Mktg. award A.T.C. Time Inc., 1986, Grand Prize HBO Summer Sales Campaign, 1986, Letter of Commendation Disney Channel, 1986, Outstanding Creative Contbrn. award, 1987, Tempo TV award, 1987; named to Scholastic Honor Soc. Pamarista Ind. State U., 1989, Literacy Grante Internat. Network for Women, 2000 Notable Am. Women Hall of Fame, A.B.I., 1990, Woman of Yr., A.B.I., 1990, Internat. Leaders in Achievement, IBC, 1990. Mem. NAFE, India Assn. Terre Haute, United Hebrew Congregation Terre Haute, Country Club of Terre Haute, M.V.P. Club Larry Bird, Altrusa Club of Terre Haute, YWCA, Leadership Terre Haute. Avocations: travel, gardening, music, fine arts, skiing.

ASHLEY, LYNN, educator, consultant, administrator; b. Rock Island, Ill., Nov. 18, 1920; d. Francis Ford and Cleo Marguerite (Monahan) Haynes; m. Edward Messenger Ashley, Aug. 16, 1946; children: Edward Jr., Ann Rice, Rebecca Pocisk, William. BS in Social Psychology, Union Inst., Cin., 1978; MEd., U. Cin., 1979, EdD, 1985. Clk. Lumberman's Mutual Casualty Co., Chgo., 1940-41; account asst. Quaker Oats Co., Chgo., 1941-43; riveter Douglas Aircraft Co., Chgo., 1943-44; organizer, dir. Forest Park Youth Ctr., Forest Park, Ohio, 1967-73; staffing coord. Presbytery of Cin., 1973-78; grad. teaching asst. U. Cin., 1978-84; pres. Nat. Corrective Tng. Inst., Cin., 1979—; adj. faculty, mem. undergrad. studies bd. Union Inst., 1986—; cons. Hamilton County Probation Dept., Warren County Juvenile Ct., 1987—; field rep. Women in Mil. Svc. for Am.; trainer, cons. Allen County Juvenile Ct., W.O.R.T.H. Ctr. Councilwoman City of Forest Park, 1981-85, organizer cmty. rels. coun., 1983; mem. Cin.-Harare, Zimbabwe Sister Cities Assn., 1989—; mem. Ohio Gov.'s Adv. Com. on Women Vets., 1993—. With WAC, 1944-46. Recipient in Recognition award Forest Park City Coun., 1985, In Appreciation award Union Inst., 1987, Recognition award AMVETS, U. Cin., 1993, award Commonwealth of Ky., 1989; inducted into Ohio Vets. Hall of Fame, 1999. Mem. Am. Corrections Assn., Nat. Assn. Corrective Tng. Affiliates (pres. 1987—), Women's Army Corp Vet. Assn., Assn. Family and Conciliatiion Cts., Am. Probation and Parole Assn. Avocations: photography, foreign travel, computers, camping, fishing. Office: Nat Corrective Tng Inst 811 Hanson Dr Forest Park OH 45240-1921

ASHLEY, MICHAEL MATTHEW, radiologist; b. Basrah, Iraq, July 7, 1945; s. Jason and Makia (Smith) A.; m. Carole Anne Edlington, Nov. 11, 1958. MD, U. Baghdad, 1968. Registrar St. Bartholomew's Hosp., London, 1984; rsch. lectr. Guys & St. Thomas Hosp., London, 1985; sr. registrar Middlesex Hosp., London, 1986; asst. med. dir. Compton Hospice, Wolmerhampton, England, 1988; med. dir., cons. St. Rocco's Hospice, Warrington, England, 1992—. Mem. Assn. Palliative Medicine, Royal Coll. Radiologists, Br. Med. Assn. Avocations: writing, reading, horseback riding, bird watching, exploring the countryside.

ASHLEY, PERRY JONATHAN, journalism educator; b. West Lebanon, Ind., May 1, 1928; s. Terrell Garner and Viola Ethel (Whitmer) A.; m. Lita Grey Cochran, Nov. 29, 1952; children: Jonathan Edward, Richard Douglas. AB in Journalism, U. Ky., 1956, MA in Polit. Sci., 1966; PhD in Journalism, So. Ill. U., 1968. Instr. Sch. Journalism U. Ky., Lexington, 1956-65; teaching assoc. Sch. Journalism So. Ill. U., Carbondale, 1965-67; prof. Coll. Journalism and Mass Comm. U. S.C., Columbia, 1967-93, interim dean Coll. Journalism, 1985-86, assoc. dean, 1986-92, disting. prof. emeritus, 1993—; dir. Ky. Scholastic Press Assn., U. Ky., 1956-65; dir. media rsch. Coll. Journalism, U. S.C., 1970-90; dir. S.C. Scholastic Press Assn., U. S.C., 1971-74; cons.on audience analysis S.C. Ednl. TV System, 1969-72. Editor: Newspaper Publishing in South Carolina, 1980, American Newspaper Journalists, 1873-1900, 1983, American Newspaper Journalists, 1901-1925, 1984, American Newspaper Journalists, 1926-1950, 1984, American Newspaper Journalists, 1690-1872, 1985, American Newspaper Publishers, 1951-1990, 1993. Mem. Gov.'s Safety Coun., Commonwealth of Ky.; mem. East Richland Pub. Svc. Commn., Columbia, 1972-79, chmn., 1973-77; trustee Richland County Sch. Dist. 2, Columbia, 1981-87, chmn., 1985. Cpl. U.S. Army, 1950-52, Germany. Named Nation's Outstanding Yearbook Adviser Nat. Coun. Coll. Publs. Advisers, 1964. Mem. Am. Journalism Historians Assn. (program chmn., bd. dirs. 1988-91), Assn. Edn. in Journalism and Mass Comm., Soc. Profl. Journalists (Disting. Campus Chpt. Adviser 1982), Alpha Delta Sigma, Kappa Tau Alpha, Alpha Epsilon Rho, Phi Alpha Theta, Psi Sigma Alpha, Omicron Delta Kappa. Independent. Presbyterian. Avocations: miniaturist, travel, reading, amateur photography, gardening, backyard birdwatching. Home: 3747 Greenleaf Rd Columbia SC 29206-3362

ASHMAN, ADRIAN FREDERICK, humanities educator; b. Sydney, NSW, Australia, May 29, 1948; s. William Frederick and Mary Aileen (Pattinson) A. BA, U. NSW, 1974; MEd, U. Alberta, Can., 1976; PhD, U. Alberta, 1978; MA, Queensland U. Tech., 1999. Lectr. U. Newcastle, Newcastle, Australia, 1978-83; sr. lectr. U. Newcastle, 1984-86, U. Queensland, Brisbane, Australia, 1987-92; assoc. prof. U. Queensland, 1993-96, prof., 1997—, dir. Fred & Eleanor Schonell Spl. Edn. Rsch. Ctr., 1994—; cons. psychologist U. Queensland, 1987—, U. Newcastle, 1978-86. Editor: Jour. Cognitive Edn., 1994-98, Internat. Jour. Disability, Devel. and Edn., 1989-94; author/editor: (textbook) Educating Children with Special Education Needs, 1990, 2d edit., 1994, 3rd edit., 1998. Councillor Intellectually Disabled Citizens' Coun. of Queensland, Brisbane, 1996—; pres. Australian Soc. for the Study of Intellectual Disability, 1990-92; mem. Adv. Coun. on Spl. Edn. Needs, Brisbane, 1994-95. Recipient Disting. Svc. award Australian Soc. for the Study of Intellectual Disability, 1994, Commonwealth U. scholarship Queensland U. Tech., 1997, Queen Elizabeth scholarship U. Alberta, 1977-78. Fellow APA, Internat. Assn. for the Scientific Study of Intellectual Disability, Internat. Assn. for Cognitive Edn. Avocations: bicycling, running, reading, photography, art. Office: Schonell Spl Edn Ctr, U Queensland, Brisbane QLD 4072, Australia

ASHMEAD, ALLEZ MORRILL, speech, hearing, and language pathologist, orofacial myologist, consultant; b. Provo, Utah, Dec. 18, 1916; d. Laban Rupert and Zella May (Miller) M.; m. Harvey H. Ashmead, 1940; children: Harve DeWayne, Sheryl Mae Harames, Zeltha Janeel Henderson, Emma Allez Broadfoot. BS, Utah State U., 1938; MS summa cum laude, U. Utah,

1952, PhD summa cum laude, 1970; postgrad., Idaho State U., Oreg. State Coll., U. Denver, U. Utah, Brigham Young U., Utah State U., U. Washington, U. No. Colo. Cert. secondary edn., remedial reading, spl. edn., learning disabilities; cert. ASHA clin. competence speech pathology and audiology; profl. cert. in orofacial myology. Tchr. pub. schs. Utah, Idaho, 1938-43; speech and hearing pathologist Bushnell Hosp., Brigham City, Utah, 1943-45; sr. speech correctionist Utah State Dept. Health, Salt Lake City, 1945-52; dir. speech and hearing dept. Davis County Sch. Dist., Farmington, Utah, 1952-65; clin., field supr. U. Utah, Salt Lake City, 1965-70, 75-78; speech pathologist Box Elder Sch. Dist., Brigham City, 1970-75, 78-84; teaching specialist Brigham Young U., Provo, 1970-73; speech pathologist Primary Children's Med. Ctr., Salt Lake City, 1975-77; pvt. practice speech pathology and orofacial myology, 1970-88; del. USSR Profl. Speech Pathology seminar, 1984, 86; participant numerous internat. seminars. Author: Physical Facilities for Handicapped Children, 1957, A Guide for Training Public School Speech and Hearing Clinicians, 1965, A Guide for Public School Speech Hearing Programs, 1959, Impact of Orofacial Myofunctional Treatment on Orthodontic Correction, 1982, Meeting Needs of Handicapped Children, 1975, Relationship of Trace Minerals to Disease, 1972, Macro and Trace Minerals in Human Metabolism, 1971, Electromotive Potential Differences Between Stutterers and Non-stutterers, 1970, Learning Disability, An Educational Adventure, 1969, New Horizons in Special Education, 1969, Developing Speech and Language in the Exceptional Child, 1961, Parent Teacher Guidance in Primary Stuttering, 1951, numerous others; contbr. research articles to profl. jours. Student Placement chair Am. Field Service, Kaysville, Utah, 1962-66; ednl. del. Women's State Legis. Council, Salt Lake City, 1958-70; chairwoman fund raising Utah Symphony Orch., Salt Lake City, 1970-71; sec., treas. Utah chpt. U.S. Council for Exceptional Children, 1958-62, membership com. chair, 1962-66, program com. chair, 1966-68. Recipient Scholarship award for Higher Edn. U. Utah, Salt Lake City, 1969; Phi Kappa Phi scholar, Delta Kappa Gamma scholar, 1968; rsch. grantee Utah Dept. Edn., 1962. Mem. NEA, Utah Ednl. Assn., Am. Speech, Lang. Hearing Assn. (life, continuing edn. com. 1985, Ace award for Continuing Edn. 1984), Western Speech Assn., Internat. Assn. Orofacial Myology (life, bd. examiners, Sci. Contribution award 1982), Utah Speech, Hearing and Lang. Assn. (life, sec., treas. 1956-60), AAUW (Utah state bd. chair status of women 1959-62, Kaysville br. 1957-60, bd. dirs. Kaysville-Davis br. 1987-92, chair internat. rels. 1987-91, chair cultural interests Kaysville-Davis br. 1991-92), Delta Kappa Gamma (state scholarship award 1968, del. Woman's State Legis. Coun. 1958-70, profl. affairs chair 1963-67, tchr. of yr. award 1978), AAUW (bd. dirs. internat. rels. Kaysvile-Davis br., 1988-91), Daus. Utah Pioneers (parliamentarian Kaysville 1980-92, historian 1974-80, lesson leader 1992-95, capt. 1996-98), Soroptimists (charter, bd. dirs. 1954-56, pres. Davis County chpt. 1965-69, Rocky Mountain regional bd. dirs. 1965-70, cmty. svc. award 1968, pub. svc. award 1970), Sigma Alpha Eta, Theta Alpha Phi, Psi Chi, Zeta Phi Eta, Phi Kappa Phi. Republican. Mem. LDS Ch. Avocations: international travel, reading, boating, sports, fine and performing arts. Home: 719 E Center St Kaysville UT 84037-2138

ASHMEAD, HARVE DEWAYNE, nutritionist, executive, educator; b. Brigham City, Utah, June 6, 1944; s. Harvey Harold and Allez (Morrill) A.; m. Eugele Baird, June 24, 1966; children: Stephen, Jilane, Brett, Angelique, Heidi. BS, Weber State U., 1969; PhD, Pacific Inst., 1970; PhD magna cum laude, Donsbach U., 1981. Cert. nutritional cons. With Ch. Jesus Christ of Latter Day Saints, Paris, 1963-66; v.p. Albion Labs., Ogden, Utah, 1966-71, exec. v.p., Clearfield, Utah, 1971-82, pres., 1982—, also bd. dirs.; pres. Albion Internat.; adj. prof. Weber State U., also nat. adv. coun. U. Utah; former advisor Weber County Sch. Dist.; bd. dirs. Albion Internat., Zions Bank, Albion Labs., Inc., Unilabco, Inc., Albion Nutrition SARL, Albion Europe; guest lectr. Adv. Fruit Heights City (Utah); pres. PTA. Fellow Am. Coll. Nutrition; mem. Am. Soc. Animal Sci., Am. Assn. Nutrition and Dietary Cons., Internat. Acad. Nutritional Cons., Am. Assn. Nutritional Cons., Am. Acad. Applied Health Sci., AAAS, Am. Biographical Inst. (bd. govs.), Clearfield C. of C. (bd. dirs.), Delta Sigma Pi. Mormon. Author: Chelated Mineral Nutrition, 1981, Mineral Absorption Mechanisms, 1981, Chelated Mineral Nutrition in Plants, Animals and Man, 1982, A New Era in Plant Nutrition, 1982, Intestinal Absorption of Metal Ions and Chelates, 1985, Foliar Feeding of Plants with Amino Acid Chelates, 1986, In Search of a Rainbow, 1988; Conversations on Chelation and Mineral Nutrition, 1989, The Roles of Amino Acid Creates in Animal Nutrition, 1993; contbr. numerous articles to profl. jours. Office: Albion Labs 101 N Main St Clearfield UT 84015-2243

ASHMORE, JONATHAN FELIX, biophysicist, researcher; b. Oxford, Eng., Apr. 16, 1948; s. Peter Eric and Rosalie Sylvia (Crutchley) A.; m. Sonia Elizabeth Newby Ashmore; children: Joseph, Lucia. BS, U. Sussex, Eng., 1968; PhD, U. London, 1971; MS, U. Coll., London, 1974. Vis. scientist Internat. Ctr. for Theoretical Physics, Treste, Italy, 1971; rschr. UCL, London, 1974-77; lectr. U. Sussex, Brighton, U.K.; rschr. UCSF, San Francisco, 1977-80; lectr., reader, prof. U. Bristol, U.K., 1983-96; prof. biophysics UCL, London, 1996—; Nuffield biol. scholar, London, 1972-74; Fulbright scholar UCSF, 1977-80. Contbr. articles to profl. jours. Scientific adv. Defeating Deafness, London, 1993—; mem. MRC Bd., London, 1997—. Fellow Royal Sóc., London, 1996. Mem. Physiol. Soc., Assn. for Rsch. in Otolaryngology. Avocation: travel, reading. E-mail: j.ashmore@ucl.ac.uk. Office: Dept Physiology, University Coll of London, London WCIE6BT, United Kingdom

ASHOKKUMAR, MATHUPANDIAN, chemistry educator, researcher; b. Madurai, Tamil Nadu, India, May 3, 1961; s. S. Muthupandian and Pandiammal (Venkatachalam) M.; m. Indra Chinnasamy, Feb. 1990; 1 child, Srikkumar. BS, Madurai U., 1982, MS, 1984; PhD, U. Madras (India), 1989. Lectr. U. Melbourne (Australia), 1995—. Contbr. articles to profl. jours. Maxwell fellow French Acad. Scis., U. Paris, Orsay and Ecole Polytechnique at Palaiseau, 1990-92, fellow Japan Soc. Promotion Sci., 1994, Toyko Inst. Tech. Office: U Melbourne, Sch Chemistry, Parkville Vic 3010, Australia

ASHOUR, NABIH IBRAHIM, agriculturalist; b. Cairo, Egypt, Feb. 12, 1937; s. Ibrahim Ashour and Anaiat Azia; m. Adlia Hafez Sharaf-El Din, Mar. 9, 1967; children: Magdi, Gehan, Shaemaa. BSc, Cairo U., 1958; PhD, Acad. Scientific Rsch., Moscow, 1964. Asst. lectr. Zagazig U., Egypt, 1958-60; from rschr. to prof. Nat. Rsch. Ctr., Cairo, 1965-94, v.p., 1994—. Editor: Agricultural Development of North Sinai, 1997; contbr. articles to profl. jours. Avocations: swimming, tennis. Office: Nat Rsch Ctr, El-Tahrir St, Dokki Cairo Egypt

ASHRAF, BASHIR KOYILOTRA MOHAMMED, sales executive; b. Kannur, Kerala, India, Apr. 30, 1965; s. Mohammed Koyilotra Mohammed Bashir and Aysha B.; m. Naseema, Dec. 17, 1989; children: Dana, Amaan. BS in Botany, Sir Sayed Coll. Thaliparamba, Kerala, 1988; SSLC, Islamic Coll., 1981-82. Mgr. Video Recording Ctr., Kozhikob, Kerala, 1988-89, Muscat Rsch., Buraimi, 1990-92; PRO/aviation supr. Fallon Tours, Rasalkhama, United Arab Emirates, 1992-94, Time Travel, Ras, United Arab Emirates, 1995-98; sales exec. Fujaira Air Craft, United Arab Emirates, 1998-99; cargo mgr. Fujaira Air Craft, 1999—. Avocations: table tennis, cricket, football, sports. Office: Fujaira Air Craft Charterin, PO Box 4984/ Northern Emirat, Fujaira United Arab Emirates

ASHRAF, CHAUDHRI MUHAMMAD, chemist, researcher, consultant; b. Sheikhupura, Punjab, Pakistan, Dec. 14, 1940; s. Chaudhri Rehmat Ali and Bibi Fazal; m. Zahida Parveen, Sept. 6, 1966; 2 children. BSc, Punjab U., Lahore, Pakistan, 1961, MSc in Chemistry, 1964; PhD in Chemistry, Queen's U., Belfast, No. Ireland, 1971. Lectr. Inst. Chemistry, Punjab U., 1971-75; sr. lectr. chemistry dept. Makerere U., Kampala, Uganda, 1975-81; sr. lectr., assoc. prof., head chemistry dept. U. Jos, Nigeria, 1981-85; rsch. chemist, tech. asst. Pakistan Coun. Sci. and Indsl. Rsch., Lahore, 1964-68, prin. sci. officer, 1985-97, chief sci. officer, 1997-99, head applied chemistry rsch. ctr., 1999—; cons. to various industries, Pakistan and fgn. countries, 1971—. Co-author: Unique Organic Chemistry for Intermediate Students, A Key to Intermediate Chemistry for First Year, Concise Organic Chemistry, Part I; contbg. author: Herbal Drugs of Controversial Identity; contbr. over 100 articles to sci. jours., including Jour. Chem. Soc., Can. Jour. Chemistry, Australian Jour. Chemistry, Analyst, Jour. Praktische Chemie, Internat. Jour. Chem. Kinetics, Indian Jour. Chemistry, Jour. Organic Chemistry, Bull. Chem. Soc. Belgium, Kenya Jour. Sci. and Tech., Indian Jour. Chem. Edn., Jour. U. Kuwait, Egyptian Jour. Chemistry, Nigerian Jour. Biotech, Arab Gulf Jour. Sci. Rsch., Arabian Jour. Sci. and Engring., Jour. Ethanopharmacology, Pakistan Jour. Sci. and Indsl. Rsch., Sci. Rsch., Jour. Chem. Soc. Pakistan, Hamdard Medicus, Jour. Pakistan Coun. for Sci. and Tech., also Sci. mag., Pakistan Times. Sec. Red Cross Soc., Tehsil Sheikhupura, 1953-55. Govt. scholar Lahore Bd., 1959. Fellow Pakistan Inst. Chemists (chartered chemist), Royal Soc. Chemistry (U.K.) (Pakistan rep. 1993, cons. forum 1999—, rsch. grantee 1992), Chem. Soc. Pakistan, Punjab U. Acad. Staff Assn. (joint sec. 1973-74). Achievements include processes for white and brown factice, flavor enhancer and preservative for mango juice, soluble blue, tackiness remover for photopolymer and flexo printing, stencil ink, plywood and woodwork adhesive, casein-based adhesive, modified rosin sizer, stamp pad ink, lead ferrocyanide, controlled smoulder, ultraphonic conductivity gel, preservative wood borer, zinc stearate, fire retardant formulation, asphalt sheet, special shoe adhesive, special disk for enhancing pliability of textile fiber, process for zinc sulphate from commercial zinc waste, deodorization of petroleum product, hydrogen peroxide stabilizer for textile industry, wooden glue, modification of commercial paraffin wax for match industry, lead thiocynate. Avocations: social welfare, writing articles, general education, creating scientific awareness. Home: 37 Sikander Block, Allama Iqbal Town, Lahore 54570, Pakistan Office: PCSIR Labs Complex, Ferozepur Rd, Lahore 54600, Pakistan

ASHRAF, MOHAMMAD, management scientist, educator; b. Jhang, Pakistan, Jan. 1, 1950; s. Chaudhry Mohammad Din and Batool Begum; m. Neelam Ashraf; children: Najia, Nabeel, Nauman. M in Commerce, Punjab U., 1971. Mgmt. acct. Sadiqabad Textile Mills Ltd., Pakistan, 1971-74; accts. officer Syed Industries Ltd., Pakistan, 1975-76; dep. mgr. accts. Pak Saudi Fertilizer, Pakistan, 1977-81; chief acct. Holland Beton Group, Qatar, 1982-84; sr. adminstr., treas. Lahore Univ. Mgmt. Scis., Pakistan, 1985-94, gen. mgr. fin. & adminstrn., 1994—; trustee Lahore Sch. Econs.; sec. bd. govs. Nat. Mgmt. Found., Lahore. Author: Governance of Industrial Clusters, Economics of Privately Managed Higher Education, Commercialization of Institutional Services, Development of Innovative Programmes. Mem. Lahore Chamber Commerce & Industry, Nat. Econs. Found. (bd. govs.), N.Y. Acad. Scis., Lahore Garrison Golf & Country Club, Cosmopolitan Club. Avocations: reading, gardening. Home: House 4 Lahore Univ Mgmt, Opp Sect U LCCHS Lahore Can, 554792 Lahore Punjab, Pakistan

ASHRAF, MUHAMMAD SOHAIL, travel and tourism consultant; b. Karachi, Sindh, Pakistan, July 25, 1964; s. Shaikh Muhammad and Nargis Mohammad (Yacoob) A. BA, Karachi U., 1989, MA, 1992, postgrad., 1993. Tour operator Super Travels, Karachi, 1983-84; passanger sales asst. Pakistan Internat. Airlines, Karachi, 1985-84, sales exec., 1985-87; reservation agt. SBy, Abudhabi, United Arab Emirates, 1988-90; reservation officer, group cons. Gerry's Internat., Karachi, 1991-94; RTO, travel cons. Matchless, Karachi, 1994—; cons. Comprehensive Computer's Resources, N.Y.C., 1989. Editor We and Nature, 1992 (univ. appreciation award 1993), Passion for Love and Belief, 1996 (Rememberance award 1997. Fellow Karachi U., 1992-94. Mem. Greenpeace (Peace and Love aaward 1994). Avocations: reading, writing, poetry, charity, awareness to people for bringing peace and love in this universe. Home: Adj Civic Ctr, Apt H-19 Karim Plaza, Karachi 75300, Pakistan

ASHTON, DAVID HUNGERFORD, botanist, researcher; b. Melbourne, Australia, July 6, 1927; s. Frank Hungerford and Louisa Julia (Cox) A. BSc, Melbourne U., 1949, PhD, 1957. Sr. demonstrator Melbourne U. Dept. Botany, 1953-57, from lectr. to reader, 1960-89, assoc., 1990-2000, assoc. prof., 1999; rsch. fellow La Trobe U. Dept. Botany, 1993-98. Contbr. articles to profl. jours. Mem. Ecol. Soc. Australia (v.p. 1977-79), Royal Soc. Victoria. Mem. Ch. of Eng. Avocations: classical piano, landscape oil painting. Home: 92 Warrigal Rd, Melbourne 3127, Australia Office: Melbourne U, Dept Botany, Parkville 3052, Australia also: La Trobe U, Dept Botany, Bundora 3082, Australia

ASHTON, MICHAEL JOHN, magazine editor; b. Coventry, Eng., Nov. 14, 1945; s. Albert Fletcher and Hannah Elizabeth (Padbury) A.; m. Jane Vivian Frances Carswell, Aug. 23, 1969; children: Stephen John, Paul Timothy, Jeremy Michael, Lucy Jane. Diploma in Architecture, Leicester (Eng.) Poly., 1970. Registered architect, U.K. Planning and design dir. Corby Dist. Coun., Northants, Eng., 1975-85; editor Christadelphian Mag. Pub. Co., Birmingham, Eng., 1985—, editor monthly mag. The Christadelphian, 1986—. Author: The Exiles Return, 1992, Tabernacle Study Guide, 1989, Miracles, Wonders and Signs, 1995. Christadelphian. Office: The Christadelphian, 404 Shaftmoor Ln, Birmingham B28 8SZ, England

ASHTON, SIMON MARK, food products executive; b. Oldham, Lancashire, England, Oct. 24, 1960; s. John and Evelyn (Dyson) A.; m. Alison Margaret Hall, Apr. 29, 1989. BSc in Physics with hons., Salford U., 1982; MBA, diploma in Mktg., Cranfield U., 1988. Cons. Spicer & Pegler, Manchester, Eng., 1982-87; sr. cons. Courtaulds PLC, Derby, Eng., 1987-89; comml. dir. CTAP, Manchester, 1989-91; CEO Teknit, Nottingham, Eng., 1991-96, Weavestyle, Silsden, Eng., 1995-96; mng. dir. Armitage & Rhodes Ltd., Dewsbury, Eng., 1996-98; CEO Pritchitt Foods, Kent, Eng., 1999—. Mem. Inst. Chartered Accts. in England & Wales.

ASHVIL-BIBI, SIGALIT, musician, artist; b. Kutaissi, Georgia, Apr. 28, 1952; came to U.S., 1983; BA, Acad. Music, Tbillissi, USSR, 1973; studied with Mordechai-Misha Dzanashvili, 1973-83; cert., N.Y. Acad. Art, 1993. Mem. staff Mus. Beit Ha'Omamin, Jerusalem, Mus. Yad Le Banim, Hulon, Israel, Yeshiva U. Mus., N.Y.C., The White House, Washington. One-man shows include The White House, Washington, 1981, 96, Queens "Y", N.Y., 1996, 97, 98, 99, 00, Chassidic Art Inst., Bklyn., 2000; exhibited in group shows at Bklyn. Mus., 1989, Yeshiva U. Mus., Manhattan, N.Y., 1991-92. Recipient Gold Medal award 6th Internat. Festival Between Musicians, USSR, 1968. Mem. Asn Israeli Artists (bd. dirs. 1979), Am. Artist Profl. League, Judaic Art. Home and Studio: 11001 62nd Dr Apt 2C Forest Hills NY 11375-1201

ASHWIN, PETER BRIAN, mathematics researcher; b. Uppingham, Eng., Nov. 2, 1965; s. Clive Frederick and Elisabeth Jane (Bowle) A.; m. Angela Andrea Kelber, Aug. 22, 1992; children: Julian, Melanie. MA, U. Cambridge, Eng., 1987, Cert. Advanced Study in Math., 1988; PhD, U. Warwick, Coventry, Eng., 1991. Rschr. U. Marburg, Germany, 1991-92, U. Warwick, Coventry, 1992-95, Inst. Non Linéar de Nice, Nice, France, 1995-96; lectr. U. Surrey, 1996-99, reader, 1999—. Mem. Am. Math. Soc., London Math. Soc.

ASHWORTH, BRENT FERRIN, lawyer; b. Albany, Calif., Jan. 8, 1949; s. Dell Shepherd and Bette Jean (Brailsford) A.; m. Charlene Mills, Dec. 16, 1970; children: Amy, John, Matthew, Samuel (dec.), Adam, David, Emily, Luke, Benjamin. BA, Brigham Young U., 1972; JD, U. Utah, 1975. Bar: Utah 1977. Asst. county atty. Carbon County, Price, Utah, 1975-76; assoc. atty. Frandsen & Keller, Price, Utah, 1976-77; v.p. legal affairs, sec., gen. counsel Nature's Sunshine Products, Provo, Utah, 1977—. Bd. dirs., gen. counsel Carbon County Nursing Home, Price, Utah, 1976-77; mem. Provo Landmarks Commn., 1997—, co-chair sesquicentennial com., 1998-99; chmn. Utah County Cancer Crusade Com., 1981-83; chmn. Provo LCOC Arts subcom., 1998-99; city councilman Payson City, Utah, 1980-82, mem. planning commn., 1980-82, mayor pro tem, 1982; bd. dirs. ARC, Utah County chpt., 1988-94, Springville Mus. Art, 1998—, Celebration of Health Found., 1999—; pres. Deseret Village Spani Fork, Utah, 1988-90; gen. counsel Brigham Young Acad. Found., 1995—; co-chair sesquecentennial com. Provo Utah, 1998-99. Mem. ABA, SAR (pres. Utah County chpt. 1989-90, state chpts. 1st v.p. 1990-91, state soc. pres. 1991-92, chancellor 1992-94), ATLA, Southeastern Utah Bar Assn. (sec. 1977), Utah State Bar, Am. Corp. Counsel Assn. (sec. Intermountain chpt. 1990-91), Emily Dickinson Soc. Utah (pres. 1995-97), Sons Utah Pioneers, Kiwanis Club (v.p. 1995-96, pres. 1997-98), Phi Kappa Phi, Phi Eta Sigma. Home: 1377 Cambridge Ct Provo UT 84604-4178 Office: Natures Sunshine Products 1655 N Main St Spanish Fork UT 84660-1010

ASIEDU, THOMAS KOFI, political scientist; b. Tema, Ghana, Nov. 7, 1963; s. Michael Kodwo Asiedu and Mary Daiki Osabutey; m. Joycelyn Yawovi Tay, Aug. 28, 1992. BA with honors, U. Ghana, Legon, 1993. Cert. ins. counsellor. Pres. Young Christian Students, Koforidua, Ghana, 1985-86, Legion of Mary, Kofordva, Ghana, 1988-89; v.p. Polit. Sci. Students Assn., Legon, Ghana, 1992-93; counsellor United Ghana Life Ins. Co., Tema, 1995—. Mem. editorial bd. Youth mag., 1994—; contbr. articles to profl. jours. Tchr. Ghana Edn. Svc., Dunkwa-On-Offin, 1989-90; rsch. officer Ghana Broadcasting Corp., 1993-94; v.p. Tema-Battor Deanery Cath. Youth Coun. Mem. Catholic Orgn. for Social and Religious Advancement (pres.), Young Profl. Bus. Assn. Execs., Knights of Marshall. Roman Catholic. Avocations: soccer, reading, music, visitation, hiking. Home: PO Box 18, Tema Ghana Office: Millicom Ghana Ltd PMB TUC, Barnes Rd, Accra Ghana

ASIKAINEN, ILMARI, neurology specialist; b. Somero, Finland, Apr. 5, 1941; d. Antti and Helmi (Kojo) A.; m. Ulla Paavilainen, July 18, 1970; children: Laura, Klaus, Anna. MD, U. Bern, 1969; specialist in neurology, U. Helsinki, 1979, D in Med. Sci., 2000. Ward physician in charge Mikkeli Ctrl. Hosp., Finland, 1970-72; gen. practitioner Lahti, Finland, 1972-75; asst. physician in neurology Helsinki U. Ctrl. Hosp., Finland, 1975-78; specialist in neurology Kotka Ctrl. Hosp., Finland, 1979-80, Kauniala Hosp., Finland, 1980—; pvt. practice Helsinki, 1978—. Contbr. articles to profl. jours. Mem. AAAS, Finnish Med. Assn. Helsinki, Finnish Fedn. of Neurology. Avocations: gardening, traveling, conditioning. Home: Vanha Turuntie 36, 02700 Kauniainen Finland Office: Kauniala Hosp, Kylpylantie 19, 02700 Kauniainen Finland

ASIRIFI, MARY MAGDALENE, publisher, author, consultant; b. Kumasi, Ashanti, Ghana, Aug. 12, 1948; d. Samuel Kwasi and Rose (Arthur) Asamoah; m. Aburam Asirifi (dec. Dec. 1992); children: Wendy, Alberta, Darlene, Mavice, Priscilla. BA Adminstrn., Howard Payne Coll., 1973. Audit clerk Liverpool Victoria Assurance, Ltd., London, 1975-77; gen. mgr. Goodbooks Pub. Co., Accra, Ghana, 1978-90; mng. dir. All Goodbooks Pub. Co., Accra, 1993—; agent PPS Export, Johannesburgh, South Africa, 1996-97, Std. Carton Enterprises Printing, Ltd., Mauritius, 1997-98. Author, editor: Kindergarten Mathematics, 1993; author, pub. My Sum Book, 1A, 1993; author, editor, pub. Asirifi English Workbooks 1-4, 1997, The Basket of New Skins, Baba the Naughty Boy, Suku and Esi, The Pingting Family, Granny and Her Three Granddaughters, The Funny Grey Eggs. Bd. dirs., chmn. Home For the Homeless, 1997. Recipient Pub. of Yr. award Ghana Book Devel. Coun., 1996. Mem. Ghana Book Pubs. Assn. (treas. 1996-98, mem. coun. 1996—, v.p. 1998—). Avocations: travelling, reading, table tennis, pools, sightseeing. Office: All Goodbooks Ltd, PO Box AN 10416, Accra-North Ghana

ASKA, WARABÉ, artist, writer; b. Kagawa, Japan, Feb. 3, 1944; arrived in Can., 1979; s. Satoru and Miyoko (Fujimoto) Masuda; m. Keiko Inouye, Oct. 17, 1979; children: Yohyoh, Mari, Kohta. Student, Takamatsu Technol. Sch., Kagawa, 1963. Founder, pres. Ad House, Tokyo, 1964-78; apptd. jury Gov.-Gen.'s Lit. Awards, 1993. One-man shows include Konohana Gallery, Tokyo, 1972, Mitsukoshi Gallery, Takamatsu, 1973, 95, 99, Osaka, 2000, Sapporo, 2000, Madden Gallery, London, 1975, 82, Tokai Gallery, Nagoya, Japan, 1978, Gustafsson Gallery, Toronto, 1982, Shayne Gallery, Montreal, 1984, Colborn Lodge, Toronto, 1984, Art Emporium, Vancouver, 1986, Royal Can. Acad. Arts, 1991, Isetan Art Gallery, Tokyo, 1995, Art Gallery Fushimi, Nagoya, 1995, Onada Pub. Libr., Yamaguchi, 1995, Maruzen Art Gallery, Tokyo, 1995, Art Gallery Mississauga, 1996, UNICEF Exhbn. Gallery, N.Y., 1998, Living Arts Ctr., Mississanga, Hokkoku Shinbun Hall, Kanazawa, 1999, Heartful TakeFu, Fukui, Japan, 2000, Nagoya Pub. Aquarium, 2000, Daimaru Mus., Tokyo, 2000, Tsuruya Gallery, Kumamoto, 2000, Artspot Matsudo, Seitoku U. Matsudo, Kariya City Art Mus., Aichi, 2000; group exhibits include UNESCO Exhbn., Tokyo, 1966, Market Gallery, Toronto, 1983, Biennale of Graphic Design, Brno, 1984, 88, 92, 96, Soc. Graphic Designers Can., 1985, Internat. Book Design Exhbn., Leipzig, 1985, 89, Biennale of Illustrations Exhbn., Bratislava, 1985, 87, 91, Biennale of Illustration, Barcelona, 1986, 92, Illustrators Exhbn., Bologna, 1986, 92, Vancouver Art Gallery, 1988, Glendon Coll., Toronto, 1989, Can. at Bologna, 1990, Internat. Biennal, Belgrade, Yugoslavia, 1992, Tehran Internat. Biennale Illustrations, Iran, 1993; represented in pub. collections Imperial Family Japan, Hino Motors Co. Ltd., Tokyo, Corp. of the Coll. of the City of Toronto, Osborn Coll., Toronto Pub. Libr., NTT Docomo, Shikoku; author: Discovering Japan in Eighty Days, 1973, A Midsummer Night's Dream, 1976, Ma Vlast and Harry Janos, 1977, Dandelion Puffs, 19981, P-yororo O-yororo, 1982, Who Goes to the Park, 1984 (City of Toronto Book award 1985), Who Hides in the Park, 1986, Seasons, 1990 (Mr. Christie's award, Studio Mag. Gold award), Aska's Animals, 1991, Aska's Birds, 1992, Aska's Sea Creatures, 1994, (with Her Imperial Highness Princess Takamodo and UNICEF) Lulie the Iceberg, 1998, Wondeful Life-Poems for the Earth, 1999, The World of Warabé Aska, Poems for the Earth, 1999.. Shintoist. Avocations: driving, swimming. Address: 1019 Lorne Park Rd, Mississauga, ON Canada L5H 2Z9

ASKANAS-ENGEL, VALERIE, neurologist, educator, researcher; b. Poland, May 28, 1937; came to U.S., 1969, naturalized, 1975; d. Marian and Leontyne Hornik; m. W. King Engel; 1 dau., Eve Monique Kerr. MD, Warsaw Med. Sch., Poland, 1960, PhD, 1967; Doctor honoris causa, U. d'Aix-Marseille, France, 1987. Rotating intern Univ. Hosp. Warsaw Med. Sch., 1960-61, resident in neurology, 1961-64, fellow in neuromuscular diseases, 1964-65; asst. prof. neurology Warsaw Med. Sch., 1965-69; assoc. mem. Inst. Muscle Diseases, N.Y.C., 1969-73; asst. prof. NYU Med. Sch., 1973-77; sr. investigator NIH, Bethesda, Md., 1977-81; prof. neurology and pathology U. So. Calif., L.A., 1981—; co-dir. Neuromuscular Ctr. at Hosp. Good Samaritan, 1981—, Muscular Dystrophy Assn. Clinic, 1981—, The Jerry Lewis ALS Clin. and Rsch. Ctr., 1988—; v.p. 6th Internat. Congress on Neuromuscular Diseases, 1986, 7th, 1990, 8th, 1994; vis. prof. internat. congresses, Europe, S.Am., Can., Far East; hon. lectr. Royal Coll. Physicians and Surgeons, 1999. Contbr. numerous articles, chpts., abstracts to med. publs.; sr. editor: (book) Inclusion-Body Myositis and Myopathies, 1998. Recipient Dean's prize for outstanding rsch., 1967, NIH Merit award, 1999—, Gaetano Conti Gold Medal for Basic Rsch., Napoli, 1999; Premio Associazione Stampa Medica Italiana Di Giurnal ItalianaIsmo Medico, 1980; grantee NIH, 1974-77, 83—, NIH Merit award, 1999—, Muscular Dystrophy Assn., 1969-77, 81—. Fellow Am. Acad. Neurology, L.A. Acad. Medicine; mem. Soc. for Neurosci., Am. Neurol. Assn., d'Honneur de la Soc. Francaise de Neurologie, Am. Soc. Cell Biology, Am. Assn. Neuropathology, Histochem. Soc., Uruguayan Neurological Assn. (hon. mem.), L.A. County Med. Assn., Polish Neurol. Assn. (hon.). Home: 527 S Arden Blvd Los Angeles CA 90020-4737 Office: U So Calif Neuromuscular Ctr Good Samaritan Hosp 637 Lucas Ave Los Angeles CA 90017-1912

ASKEW, WILLIAM GEORGE, publisher; b. Aldershot, Hampshire, Eng., Nov. 5, 1916; s. William and Catherine (Higgins) A.; m. Audrey Brumhead, June 21, 1941 (dec. Aug. 1950); children: Ann, Adrian; m. Elizabeth Mary Seed, Apr. 16, 1952; children: Mary, Jane, Caroline, William, John. Student, Birmingham Tech. Coll., 1933-34. Chartered elec. engr. Rsch. asst. Midland Lab. Guild, Birmingham, 1933-35; supt. Hall St. Metal, Birmingham, 1935-38; editor Louis Cassier Co., London, 1938-39, Inst. Metals, London, 1946-49, Soc. Chem. Industry, London, 1949-50; publicity mgr. George Kent Ltd., Luton, Eng., 1950-58; dir. pub. IEE, London and Stevenage, Eng., 1958-77; chmn. Rsch. Studies Press, Baldock, Eng., 1977—; mng. dir. Peter Peregrinus Ltd., London, 1964-77; chmn. Unesco Adv. Group, Paris, 1968-69, Alpsp, London, 1977-78, George Godwin Ltd., London, 1977-82. Contbr. articles to profl. jours. Mem. coun. Letchworth Urban Dist. Coun., Eng., 1959-66; mem. Hertfordshire Edn. Com., 1966-80; freeman City of London, 1967; liveryman Stationers Co., London, 1967; chmn. Govs. St. Michael's Sch., Stevenage, 1969-72. Maj. Middlesex Yeomanry, 1939-46. Decorated Mil. Cross, King George VI, Alamein, Egypt, 1942, Mention in Dispatches, King George VI, Italy, 1945, Knighthood of S. Gregory the Great, Pope Paul VI, 1975. Fellow Instn. Elec. Engrs. Roman Catholic. Avocations: horse racing, chess. Home: 18 Riddell Gardens, Baldock SG7 6JZ, England Office: Rsch Studies Press Ltd 15/16, Coach House Cloisters 10 Hitchin St, Baldock 5G7 6AE, England

ASKINAS, SAMUEL WALTER, dentist, educator; b. Hartford, Conn., May 21, 1925; s. Abraham and Jennie (Smith) A.; m. Frances Roslyn Cooper, Oct. 15, 1950 (dec. Jan. 1993); m. Mae Rivkin Herman, 1996. BS in Biology, Yale U., 1945; DDS, NYU, 1949. Diplomate Am. Bd. Prosthodontics. Dental intern Phila. Gen. Hosp., 1949-50; pvt. practice Paw-

catuck, Conn., 1953-56; commd. capt. USAF, 1956, advanced through grades to col., 1970, ret., 1983; assoc. prof. sch. dental medicine Tufts U., Boston, 1983-92, chairperson dept. restorative dentistry, 1986—, prof., 1992—, exec. dean Sch. Dental Medicine, 1995—; emeritus prof. restorative dentistry, exec. dean emeritus Tufts Sch. Dental Medicine, Boston, 1997—; prof. restorative dentistry, chief divsn. restorative/cmty. dentistry Nova Southeastern U. Coll. Dental Medicine, Ft. Lauderdale, Fla., 1997. Chmn. blood drive ARC, Pawcatuck, 1956. Served to capt. USAF, 1951-53/. Decorated Legion of Merit, Commendation medal with 2 oak leaf clusters. Fellow Am. Coll. Prosthodontists, Am. Coll. Dentists, Internat. Coll. Dentists; mem. ADA, Am. Prosthodontic Soc., Springfield Occulusal Study Club (v.p. 1968-73), Leeward Prosthodontic Study Club (pres. 1978-81). Democrat. Jewish. Avocations: bicycling, music, film, reading detective fiction. Home: 6313 Crystal View Ln Boynton Beach FL 33437-4041 Office: Nova Southeastern Coll Dental Med 3200 S University Dr Fort Lauderdale FL 33328-2018

ASKOVIC, RADOMIR VELIMIRA, engineering educator; b. Mali Borak, Yugoslavia, Aug. 22, 1938; arrived in France, 1987; s. Velimir and Zivana (Ciglic) A.; m. Andjelija Malesevic, June 17, 1973; children: Marko, Veljko. Degree in engring., Faculty Mech. Engring., Belgrade, Yugoslavia, 1961; MSc, Faculty Scis., Belgrade, 1963; DSc, Faculty Scis., 1966. Asst. Faculty Mech. Engring., Belgrade, 1962-77, assoc. prof., 1977-81, prof., 1981-87; vis. prof. U. Valenciennes, France, 1987-89; prof. U. Valenciennes, 1989—; postdoc. visitor Laval U., Quebec, Can., 1966-67, vis. prof., 1969-70; vice dean Faculty Mech. Engring., Belgrade, 1979-81, dean, 1981-84, head chair fluid mechanics, 1985-87. Author: Hydraulics and Pneumatics, 1978. Mem. N.Y. Acad. Sci., French Soc. Mechanics. Achievements include research in Laminar unsteady three-dimensional boundary layer, turbulent boundary layer. Office: U Valenciennes, Le Mont Houy BP 311, 59304 Valenciennes France

ASLAM, ASHFAQ, telecommunications consultant, engineer; b. Oxford, Eng., Aug. 10, 1968; s. Mohammad and Shafkat Aslam. B. Eng with honours, Essex (Eng.) U., 1991, MSc in Telecomms. and Info. Systems, 1993, PhD in Electronics Systems Engring., 1997. With comms. divsn. Logica UK Ltd., London, 1997-99; with comms. and high tech. group Andersen Cons., Sophia Antipolis, France, 1999-2000; with network mgmt. systems Vodafone Ltd., U.K., 2000—. Mem. IEEE, IEEE Computer Soc., IEE, Engrg. (assoc.), N.Y. Acad. Scis. Office: Vodafone Ltd Astor House, Newbury Bus Park London Rd, Newbury RG14 2PZ, United Kingdom

ASLAM, TOQEER, general practice physician; b. Lahore, Punjab, Pakistan, Aug. 17, 1957; arrived in the U.K., 1962; s. Mohammed and Zahida (Naseem) A.; m. Ruby Sharif, Mar. 1989; children: Leeza, Tania. MB, BChir, Bristol (U.K.) U., 1981. Gen. medicine physician Royal Devon and Exeter (U.K.) Hosp., 1981-82; gen. surgery physician Bristol (U.K.) Royal Infirmary, 1982; accident & emergency, orthopaedics, gen. surgery physician Maidstone (U.K.) Hosp., 1982-85; ob-gyn. physician All Saints Hosp., Chatham, Kent, U.K., 1985; gen. practice trainee Rochester (Eng.) Hosp., 1985-86; clin. med. officer Medway Health Authority, Gillingham, Kent, 1986-87; prin. gen. practice Princes Park Med. Ctr., Walderslade, Kent, 1987—; pres., founder Wishing Well Charity, Maidstone, 1983-90; founder Maidstone (U.K.) Hospice, 1983; chmn., founder Medway Consortium of Non-Fundholder Gen. Practitioners, 1994-96; founder, proprietor Welcomes House Residential Care Home, 1986—, Princes Park Med. Ctr., Chatham, 1988—; founder and first chmn. The Medway and Swale Providers Forum, 1995-96. Chief election commr. Kent (U.K.) Muslim Welfare Assn., 1991-94, coord. to the justice com., 1993-94. Mem. Nat. Assn. Commissioning Gen. Practitioners. Muslim. Office: Princes Park Med Ctr, Dove Close, Walderslade Chatham ME5 7TD, England

ASLANIAN, DANIEL LAURENT, marine geologist; b. Grenoble, France, Sept. 16, 1963; s. Jean Gérard and Colette (Cerisier) A. DEA in Geoscis., Montpellier, France, 1989; PhD in Geophysics, Brest, France, 1993. Geophysicist Internat. Subsea Mapping, France, 1993-94; postdoctoral fellow U. Cambridge, England, 1995-97; geologist rschr. U. Brest, France, 1997, 99—, IFREMER, Brest, France, 1998. Contbr. articles to profl. jours. Avocations: cuisine, wine, aircraft. Office: IFREMER Brest/DRO-GM, BP 70, 29280 Plouzane France

ASLANIDES, TIMOSHENKO JOHN, poet; b. Sydney, Australia, Dec. 24, 1943; s. John Paul and Olive Emma (Browne) A.; m. Jennifer Beryl Stewart, 1978; 1 son. BA, Sydney U., 1967; BEc, Australian Nat. U., Canberra, 1976. Various positions NSW Govt. and Australian Govt. Depts., 1963-85; profl. poet Canberra, Australia, 1985—. Author: (poetry books) The Greek Connection, 1977, Passacaglia and Fugue, 1979, One Hundred Riddles, 1984, Australian Things, 1990, Australian Alphabet 1992, AnniVersaries, 1998; coauthor: (with Jennifer Stewart) travel guides Goulburn and Environs, 1983, Canberra and the ACT, 1988. Winner British Commonwealth Poetry prize, 1978, 2nd prize Australian Bicentennial Lit. awards, Sydney, 1988. Avocations: bushwalking, travel, Australian wine.

ASMUSSEN, NILS WIRENFELDT, pharmaceutical executive; b. Copenhagen, Jan. 12, 1938; s. Robert Wirenfeldt and Grethe (Abildgaard) A.; m. Marianne Bang, July 8, 1967; 1 child, Nicolai. BA, Østersøgades Gymnasium, Copenhagen, 1957; PhB, Copenhagen U., 1960; postgrad., Brunel U., Eng., 1982. Med. dir. Boehringer Ingelheim, Copenhagen, 1967-73; area med. dir. Searle, Copenhagen, 1973-79; regional med. dir. Ciba-Geigy, Copenhagen and Basel, Switzerland, 1979-83; regulatory dir. Europe Abbott, Paris, 1983-85; med. dir. Upjohn, Copenhagen, 1985-93; pres., med. dir. Wirenfeldt Asmussen, Denmark, 1993—; cons. Medi-Lab, Copenhagen, 1994—; mem. com. Medicines Industry Assn. Denmark, 1985-93. Bd. dirs. Royal Guards Soc., Copenhagen, 1963, Gentofte Med. Lab., 1970; mem. Danish Salmon Found., Copenhagen, 1997. Guardsman Danish Royal Guards, 1962-63. Fellow Royal Soc. Medicine; mem. Am. Coll. Clin. Pharmacology, Drug Info. Soc., Internat. Soc. for Pharmacoecons. and Outcomes Rsch., Royal Yacht Club. Avocations: hunting, skiing, sports fishing, yachting.

ASPE, ALBERTO GARCIA, soccer player; b. Mexico, May 11, 1967. Midfielder America (Mex.) Football Club, Puebla F.C. Office: Puebla FC, Avenida Juárez #2107, CP742000 Puebla Mexico*

ASPLUND-CARLSON, ANETTE MARIA, physician, researcher; b. Vetlanda, Smaland, Sweden, Apr. 9, 1955; d. Roland and Eivor (Nyström) Asplund; m. Lars Anders Carlson; children: Carolina, David. MD, Karolinska Inst., Stockholm, 1987, PhD, 1994. Registrar various hosps. Sweden, 1982-87, Karolinska Hosp., Stockholm, 1987-94; rschr. Karolinska Inst., Stockholm, 1989—; lectr. in field of metabolism. Contbr. articles to profl. jours. Mem. Swedish Med. Assn. Avocations: literature, gymnastics, baking bread. Office: King Gustaf X Rsch Inst, Karolinska Inst, S-17176 Stockholm Sweden

ASPÖCK, HORST, parasitologist, entomologist; b. Budweis, Bohemia, Czechoslovakia, July 21, 1939; s. Friedrich and Manka (Knapp) A.; m. Ulrike Pirklbauer, Nov. 16, 1963; 1 child, Christoph. PhD, U. Innsbruck, Austria, 1962; dozent, U. Vienna, Austria, 1970. Rsch. assoc. Inst. Hygiene, U. Vienna, 1963-70, lectr., asst. prof., 1970-77, prof., 1977—; head dept. med. parasitology Inst. Hygiene, U. Vienna, 1966. Author: Die Neuropteren Europas, 1980 (Meigen medal 1995), Die Raphidiopteren der Erde, 1991 (Meigen medal 1995); contbr. over 500 articles to profl. jours. Recipient Cultural prize Govt. of Upper Austria, 1987, award Scientific Com. of SIEEC, 1991, Prowazek medal, 1997. Mem. Austrian Soc. Tropical Medicine and Parasitology (pres. 1981-83, 95-97), Internat. Assn. Neuropterology (pres. 2000—), Austrian Entomol. Soc. (pres. 1990-93, dep. pres. 1993—), Hungarian Entomological Soc. (hon. mem.), Soc. Physicians Vienna (corr. mem), Slovak Parasitological Soc. (hon. mem., Jan Hovorka medal 1995). Roman Catholic. Avocation: music. Office: U Vienna Inst Hygiene Dept Med Parasitology, Kinderspitalgasse 15, A-1095 Vienna Austria

ASSAAD, JAMAL SAMI, physicist; b. Baalbek, Liban, Sept. 7, 1960; s. Sami and Souad A.; m. Nathalie Wagenaar, Apr. 9, 1988; children: Souad-Marie, Obayda-Julien, Imane-Victoria. BSEE, ISEN, Lille, France, 1989; PhD, U. Valenciennes, 1992, DSc, 1997. From asst. prof. to prof. U. Valenciennes, France, 1993—. Home: 20 Clos du Bel Air, 59790 Ronchin France

ASSAF, AHMED ABDEL-RAHMAN, ophthalmic surgeon, consultant, educator; b. BeitNabala, Lod, Palestine, July 19, 1947; arrived in the U.K., 1973; s. Abdel-Rahman Sulieman Assaf and Hanieh Mohamed Safi; m. Tahani Ghalib Jarrar, Aug. 5, 1982; children: Noor Dawn, Sarah. MB, BChir, Coll. Medicine, Baghdad, Iraq, 1971; diploma in ophthalmology, Royal Colls., London, 1975; MD, U. Sheffield, Eng., 1984. Sr. house officer ophthalmology St. Pauls Eye Hosp., Liverpool, Eng., 1974-75; registrar in ophthalmology Sheffield U. Hosps., 1976-78; lectr. in ophthalmology Coll. Medicine, U. Sheffield, 1978-86; cons. ophthalmologist pediat. ophthalm & strabismus Coll. Medicine, Riyadh, Saudi Arabia, 1987-93; cons. pediat. ophthalm & strabismus King Khaled Eye Hosp., Riyadh, 1988-93; cons. ophthalmologist Stoke Mandeville Hosp./Milton Keynes NHS Trust, Aylesbury, Eng., 1994—; asst. prof. ophthalmology Coll. Medicine, U. Kuwait, 1981-82, Coll. Medicine, King Saud U., Riyadh, 1987-90, assoc. prof., 1990-93; dir. residency tng. in ophthalmology King Saud U.-King Khaled Eye Hosp., Riyadh, 1990-94. Contbr. articles to profl. jours.; inventor in field. Scholar U. Baghdad, 1965-71. Fellow Royal Coll. Surgeons Edinburgh (cert. higher surg. tng. 1980), Royal Coll. Ophthalmologists London (examiner 1996—); mem. Internat. Strabismological Assn., European Strabismological Assn. Avocations: computer programming, chess, table tennis, ground tennis. Office: Stoke Mandeville Hosp, Mandeville Rd, Aylesbury HP21 8AL, England

AS-SALAAM, JAMAAL (WILLIAM LOUIS WILLIAMS, JR.), poet, film producer, writer; b. Albany, N.Y., Apr. 20, 1955; s. William Louis Williams Sr. and Helen Virginia Williams-Smith; m. Veronica Foster, June 20, 1980 (div. June 1985); children: Qwinde, Shani O.; m. Arlene Hooks (div. Sept. 1992); 1 child, Jamar Williams; m. Terisita Ann Lopez; 1 child, Mieko O. Lopez. Student, SUNY, Purchase, 1972-76, U. No. Colo., 1984-86, Nat. U., Encino, Calif., 1990-92, Calif. Arts Partnership, 1995-98. Cert. Microsoft cert. sys. engr. Ednet Career Inst., Microsoft software trainer, Microsoft cert. profl., A+ cert. computer svc. technician. Track laborer Burlington No. Railroad, 1978-85; computer specialist Denver Pub. Schs., 1980-86; Saks cons. Tom Hopkins Sales Tng., Denver, 1984-86; tech. support Telepoetics, L.A., 1988-94; computer technician L.A. County Schs., Bellflower, Calif., 1987-94; video editor Calif. Arts Comty. Ptnrs., L.A., 1994-99; rschr. Sales, Inc., Beverly Hills, Calif., 1996-97; ind. prodr. Lightland Prodns., L.A., 1999—; freelance prodr. Mile High Cable Co., Denver, 1983-86; radio announcer Sta. KUVO, Denver, 1984-85. Author: (anthology) Portraits of Life, 1997 (Editors Choice award), (chapbook) Facing East, 1995; actor: (TV shows) Naked Truth, General Hospital, also commls. and theatrical prodns.; dir., writer, prodr.: (short film) Leimert Park, 1996, (theatrical prodns.) New Age Perspective, The Muse, (video) Poetry 101; dir., writer: (theatrical prodns.) Persona Suite, Kwanzaa Adatation; dir., prodr.: (video) History Revisited. Vol. Inner City Cultural Ctr., 1989-95; founding mem. Denver Black Arts Theater Co., 1980-85; mem. Win/Win Bus. Forum, Denver, 1984; vol., mem. Telepoetics, L.A., 1994; vol. L.A. In Support of Gang Truce, 1996. Recipient Calif. Arts Comty. Project award Calif. Inst. of Arts, 1996, 98, 1st prize Upstate Photography, Albany, N.Y., 1973. Mem. Black Radical Congress. Buddhist. Avocations: reading, sports, swimming, Conga, martial arts, art restoration. E-mail: jamaal21@hotmail.com. Home and Office: PO Box 71735 Los Angeles CA 90071-0735

ASSEL, HEINRICH GEORG, theologian; b. Burgbernheim, Germany, Feb. 9, 1961; s. Heinrich and Luise (Schmidt) A.; m. Beatrix Vogler, Feb. 1, 1960; children: Katharina, Marie-Victoria. Dr. Theology, Erlangen, 1993; Dr. habil., U. Bonn., 1999. Reverend Luth. Ch., Erlangen, Germany, 1988-90; rsch. asst. U. Erlangen, 1990-96; asst. prof. U. Bonn, Germany, 1996—; prof. U. Koblenz, 1999-2000. Author: Der andere Aufbruch, 1994, Grundwissen Dogmatik, 1995; editor: Der du die Zeit in Händen hast, 1992, R. Hermann, Religions Philosophie, 1995. Office: Ecumenical Inst, An Der Schlosskirche 1, 53113 Bonn Germany

ASSEN, NIGEL ST. DENNIS, travel writer and investment consultant; b. Singapore, June 21, 1929; arrived in Eng., 1958, Germany, 1973; s. Thomas Maxwell and Hilda Doreen (Perera) A. Diploma in Bibl. and Religious Studies, London U., 1971; BA (hon.), Open U., Eng., 1985; diploma in Christian studies, Westminster Coll., Oxford, Eng., 1998. Account clk. City Coun. of Singpore, 1949-58; clerical officer London County Coun., 1958-63; accountancy asst. London Borough of Southwark, Eng., 1963-73; acct. Cigna Ins. Co. of Europe, Frankfurt, Germany, 1973-94; mng. dir. Nessa Brasil, Frankfurt, 1992—. City councillor of Fgn. Residents' Coun. of City of Frankfurt, 1991-97; mgr. Hilda Assen Benevolent Fund. Mem. Royal Overseas League (hon. corr sec. 1981—), Royal Soc. St. George, English Speaking Union, English Speaking Club of 1894 (patron 1998—). Anglican. Avocations: philately, filming, travel. Home and Office: Waldschmidt STR.63, 60316 Frankfurt M, Germany

ASSERATE, PRINCE ASFA-WOSSEN, international business consultant; b. Addis Ababa, Ethiopia, Oct. 31, 1948; s. Prince Ras Asserate Kassa and Princess Zuriash-Work Gabre-Igziabher. Student, German Elem. and Secondary Sch, Addis Ababa, Eberhard-Karl-U., Tübingen, Germany, 1968-70, Magdalene Coll., Cambridge, 1970-72; PhD in History with honors, Johann-Wolfgang-von-Goethe U., Frankfurt, 1978. With press and pub. rels. dept. Frankfurt (Germany) Internat. Fairs and Exhbns. Co., Ltd., 1978-79; free-lance journalist and lectr. Europe and U.S.A., 1979-80; dir. press and info. dept. Düsseldorf (Germany) Internat. Fairs and Exhbns. Co. Ltd., 1980-83; mng. dir., ptnr. Internat. Comm. Svcs. GmbH, Mainz, Germany, 1983-86; internat. bus. cons. Africa and Middle East, 1986—; bd. dirs. GeoPetroleum A.G., Frankfurt, Kenwete Ethiopia-Soc. for the Support of the Disabled, Addis Ababa; lectr. in field. Author: The History of Shoa (Ethiopia) 1700-1865, 1980, Ethiopia from Saba to Marx, 1982; contbr. essays and articles to profl. publs. Chmn. bd. of patrons Orbis Aethiopicus Soc. for the Preservation and Promotion of Ethiopian Culture. Mem. Coun. for Civil Liberties in Ethiopia (chmn. 1974—), Internat. Children's Aid and Rsch. Endowment (vice chmn. 1982—), Frobenius Inst. for Social Anthropology, German Journalists Fedn., German Djibouti Assn. (vice chmn. 1999—). Home: Niedenau 72, D-60325 Frankfurt Germany

ASSIMAKOPOULOS, PANAYOTIS ADAM, physics educator; b. Athens, Greece, Feb. 16, 1940; s. Adam Panayotis and Panayota (Anagnostopoulos) A.; m. Jane Ann Nisselson, Dec. 6, 1965; children: Anna Michelle, Eugenia Daphne. BA, Brandeis U., 1961; DIC, Imperial Coll., London, 1963; MSc, Rutgers U., 1967; PhD, Thomas Jefferson U., 1971. Rsch. physicist Greek Atomic Energy Commn., Athens, 1965-77; prof. U. Ioannina, Greece, 1977—, chmn. dept. physics, 1984—. Author books; contbr. numerous articles to profl. jours. Sgt. Greek Army, 1963-65. NATO grantee, CEC grantee. Greek Orthodox. Office: U Ioannina, Dept of Physics, 45332 Ioannina Greece

ASSIMITI, DANIELA, clinical biochemist, researcher; b. Braila, Romania, Oct. 26, 1962; d. Giorgio and Viorica (Pavlov) A. M of Biochemistry, U. Bucharest, Romania, 1985; Specialist in Clin. Chemistry, U. of Medicine, Bucharest, 1995. Diplomate in medicine. Tchr. Gymnasium, Intorsura Buzaului, Romania, 1985-89; clin. chemist Hosp. Intosura Buzaului, 1989-91, Hosp. Faurei, Romania, 1992-94, County Hosp., Braila, 1994—; lectr. Nursing Coll., Braila, 1991—. IAEA tng. fellow, London, 1996. Fellow Romanian Soc. Clin. Lab. Sci.; mem. Am. Assn. for Clin. Chemistry, Assn. Clin. Biochemsits U.K. Seventh-day Adventist. Avocations: knitting, travel, classical and opera music, dog breeding, psychology (psycho-endocrinology). Home: P-ta Gh Doja No 10 O p 4, 6100 Braila Romania Office: County Hosp Clin Lab, Sos Buzaului No 2, 6100 Braila Romania

ASSINI, VINCENT PAUL, financial executive; b. Newark, Dec. 1, 1950; s. Vincent A. and Jean L. (Di Pietro) A.; m. Elisabeth Schmidt, May 2, 1979. BSBA, U. Fla., 1972. CPA, N.Y. Contr. Ingersoll-Rand, Vienna, 1976-81; mgr. planning OTIS, Paris, 1982-86; dir. fin. OTIS, Munich, 1987-90; divsn. contr. J.I. Case, Paris, 1990-92; divsn. gen. mgr. Alusuisse-Lonza, Singen, Germany, 1993-96; CFO, Leica AG, St. Gallen, Switzerland, 1996-98; bd. dirs. Leica Microsys., Wetzlar, Germany, Leica Geosys., Heerbrugg, Switzerland. Mem. AICPA, Swiss Fin. Execs. Home and Office: 4321 Dewey Dr New Port Richey FL 34652-3114

ASSINK, EGBERT MARIA, psychology educator; b. Goor, Overijssel, The Netherlands, July 11, 1944; m. Gerard J. Assink and Jo Anna W. Koebrugge; m. Johanna G. Nijhof; children: Eva, Jelle. PhD, Utrecht (The Netherlands) U., 1983. Lectr. psychology Utrecht U., 1979—; Editor: Literacy Acquisition and Social Context. Mem. Soc. for Sci. Study Reading. Office: Utrecht U Psychology Dept, Heidelberglaan 2, 3584 CS Utrecht The Netherlands

ASSION, HANS-JÖRG, neurologist, psychiatrist; b. Gerolstein, Germany, Feb. 8, 1964; s. Walter Jakob and Anne Claire (Güth) A. Student, U. Cologne. Psychiatrist U. Bonn, Germany, 1990-96; neurologist St. Josef Hosp., Oberhausen, Germany, 1996-98; psychiatrist U. Bochum, Germany, 1998—. Author: Carbamazepine, 1990, Personality Disorder, 1998, 99. Mem. World Psychiat. Assn. (chmn. 1997), German Psychiat. Orgn., Soc. Biol. Psychiatry. Avocations: piano, literature. Office: Westf Zentrum Psychiat Univ, Alexandrinenstr 1, 44791 Bochum Germany

ASSIS, MOSHE, Jewish studies scholar, educator; b. Aleppo, Syria, Dec. 7, 1942; arrived in Israel, 1962; s. Shlomo and Adele (Dweck) A. BA, The Hebrew U., Jerusalem, 1966, MA, 1971, PhD, 1977. Asst., instr. Ben-Gurion U., Beersheba, Israel, 1970-75, The Hebrew U., Jerusalem, 1971-76; asst. prof. Hebrew Union Coll., Cin., 1976-79; from lectr. to assoc. prof. Tel-Aviv U., 1979—. Contbr. articles to profl. jours. Fellow Inst. Advanced Studies, 1980-81, Ctr. Judaic Studies, 1993-94. Mem. World Union Jewish Studies, Hist. Soc. Israel, Acad. Hebrew Lang. Jewish. Avocations: hiking. Office: Tel Aviv U, 69978 Tel Aviv Israel

ASSUMPCAO, FRANCISCO BAPTISTA, JR., psychiatrist, educator; b. Sao Paulo, Brazil, Sept. 7, 1951; s. Francisco Baptista and Lybia (Felice) A.; children: Tatiana, Thaís. MD, Medical Sch. FUABC, S. Andre, Brazil, 1974; M in psychology, PUC S Paulo, Sao Paulo, 1985, D in psychology, 1988. Dir. of rehabilitation ctr. APAE, Sao Paulo, 1981-88, dir. of rsch., 1989-91; dir. of psychology svc. Medical Sch. USP, Sao Paulo, 1994-96; dir. of child psychiatry svc. Fac. Med. USP, Sao Paulo, 1996—, prof. child psychiatary. Author: Psiquiatria Infantil Brasileira, 1995, Psiquiatria Da Infancia E Adolescencia, 1994, Autismo, 1996, Adolescence, 1999; contbr. articles to profl. jours. Mem. Brazilian Psychiatry Soc. (pres. child psychiatry dept. 1996-98), Child Psychiatry Soc., Latinoam. Psychiatry Assn. (sec. child psychiat. dept. 1999-2001). Avocations: music, books, comics, drawing. Fax: 55-11-5590-7125. Home: R Manoel de Nobrega 1240/81, 04001901 São Paulo Brazil Office: R Otonis 697 V Mariana, 04025002 São Paulo Brazil

ASTAKHOV, VALERY IVANOVICH, research geologist, educator; b. Voznesensk, USSR, July 19, 1939; m. Natalie N. Beiline. MS, Leningrad (USSR) U., 1961; PhD, Geol. Inst., Leningrad, 1972. Mapping geologist Hydrogeol. Expedition, Leningrad, 1961-68; rsch. scientist Inst. Remote Sensing for Geology, Leningrad, 1971—; prof. II U. Bergen, Norway, 1995—; rsch. scientist St. Petersburg (Russia) U., 1997—; Field explorer No. Russia, various expeditions, 1961—; guest lectr. various univs. and geol. surveys, Sweden, Can., U.S., Norway, 1988—; vis. prof. univ. courses on Svalbard, Norway, 1996—; organizer expeditions to Russian Arctic, Russian-Norwegian Project Palaeoenviron. and Climate History of the Russian Arctic, 1993—. Contbr. sci. articles to profl. jours. Postgrad. scholar Geol. Inst., 1968-71. Home: 12 Line 37 Apt 30, 199178 Saint Petersburg Russia Office: St Petersburg U Geol Fac, Universitetskaya 7/9, 199034 Saint Petersburg Russia

ASTAKHOVA, IRINA SERGEEVNA, chemistry educator, researcher; b. Pushkino, Russia, June 21, 1942; d. Sergey Alecseevith Anuphriev and Valentina Georgievna (Sukova) A.; m. Oleg Georgievith Epiphantsev, Nov. 27, 1969; 1 child, Irena. Diploma in engring., Moscow Inst. Tin Chem. Tech., 1966. Jr. rschr. Inst. Organic Element Compounds-Russian Acad. Scis., Moscow, 1966-69; sr. rschr. Siberian Iron and Steel Inst., Novokusnetsk, Russia, 1969-89; head X-Ray Lab., Siberian Acad. Metallurgy, Novokusnetsk, 1989—. Contbr. articles to profl. jours. Home: Kutuzov Str 14-107, 654000 Novokusnetsk Kemerovo, Russia Office: Siberian Acad Metallurgy, Kirov Str 42, 654000 Novokusnetsk Kemerovo, Russia

ASTHANA, CHANDRA BHUSHAN, research scientist; b. Bhalgalpur, Bihar, India, June 1, 1955; s. Ram Lakhan and Shakuntala Prasad; m. Salonee Verma, Dec. 23, 1982; children: Saumaya, Siddharth. B of Tech., Indian Inst. Science, Kharagpur, India, 1977; M of Engring., Indian Inst. Science, Bangalore, India, 1979, PhD, 1998. Cert. basic aircraft maintenance. Grad. engr. trainee Air India, Bombay, 1979-81, engr. III, 1981-85; scientist C Def. R & D Lab., Hyderabad, India, 1985-90; scientist D Rsch. Ctr. Imarat, Hyderabad, 1991-96, scientist E, 1996—. Editor 21st Nat. Sys. Conf. procs., 1997; contbr. rsch. articles to profl. jours. Mem. AIAA, Aero. Soc. India. Avocations: reading, swimming, badminton. E-mail: cbasthana@yahoo.com. Home: D-37/7 Lab Quars, Kanchanbagh, Hyderabad 500058, India Office: Rsch Ctr Imarat Cont Sys Lb, Vigyanakancha, Hyderabad 500069, India

ASTILLERO, CARLITO LAPAR, physician, microbiologist, consultant; b. Tangub City, Misamis Occidental, Philippines, Dec. 13, 1940; s. Esperidion Dilamag and Expectacion (Lapar) A.; m. Elena Clador Baltazar, June 19, 1966; children: Gerbylito, Aileen, Roselle, Carlito. MD, South-Western U., Cebu City, Philippines, 1968. Asst. prof. South-Western Coll. Medicine, Cebu City, 1971-76; physician Ministry of Health, Bandar Abbas, Iran, 1976-78; dir. labs. Ministry of Health, Misurata, Lybia, 1979-81; clin. microbiologist Al Mana Gen. Hosp., Al-Khobar, Saudi Arabia, 1981-83; asst. med. dir. Al-Saudi Specialist Dispensary, Riyadh, Saudi Arabia, 1984-85; dir. labs. Al-Mishari Gen. Hosp., Riyadh, 1987—. Pres. Filipino Cmty., Bandar Abbas, Iran, 1976-78, Misurata, Lybia, 1979-81, pres., chmn., Riyadh, 1991—. Recipient New Hero award Philippine Govt., 1992, Spl. Presdl. award, 1996; named Outstanding Overseas Worker Philippine Govt., 1994. Fellow Philippines Soc. Microbiology and Infectious Diseases, Am. Soc. Clin. Pathologists; mem. European Soc. Microbiology and Infectious Diseases, Knights of Rizal (chpt. comdr. 1999—). Avocations: reading, swimming, basketball, ping pong, picnicking. Office: Al-Mishari Gen Hosp, PO Box 56929, 11564 Riyadh Saudi Arabia

ASTLEY, NEIL PHILIP, book publisher; b. Portchester, Hampshire, Eng., May 12, 1953; s. Philip Thomas and Margaret Ivy (Soleman) A.; m. Julie Callan, Sept. 4,1976 (div. 1985); m. Kate Keens-Soper, Oct. 8, 1988 (div 1999). BA (hon.), U. Newcastle upon Tyne, Eng., 1978, DLitt, 1996. Editor, mng. dir. Bloodaxe Books Ltd., Newcastle upon Tyne, 1978—; bd. dirs. Password (Books) Ltd., London, 1984-87, Poetry Book Soc., London, 1986-88. Author: The Speechless Act, 1984, Darwin Survivor, 1988, Biting My Tongue, 1995; editor: Ten North-East Poets, 1980, Bossy Parrot, 1987, Poetry With An Edge, 1988, 93, Dear Next Prime Minister, 1990, Tony Harrison, 1991, Wordworks, 1992, New Blood, 1999. Recipient Eric Gregory award Soc. of Authors, 1982. Avocation: work. Office: Bloodaxe Books Ltd, Highgreen Tarset, Northumberland NE48 1RP, England

ASTOBIETA, INAKI, dental educator; b. Bilbao, Spain, Apr. 27, 1954; s. Andres and Maria Jesus (Odriozola) A.; m. Maria Aranzazu Basterrechea Astobieta, Oct. 1, 1982; 1 child, Aitor. Lic. in Medicine and Surgery, U. Basque Country, Spain, 1977, diploma in Stomatology, 1988, lic. in Pharmacy, 1993. Pathology rsch. Hosp. Santiago Apostol, Vitoria, Spain, 1979, Hosp. Ramon y Cajal, Madrid, Spain, 1980-81; orthopedics rsch. Hosp. Civil, Bilbao, Spain, 1981-83; med. practice Clinica Salcedo, Bilbao, Spain, 1983-88; dentist Clinica Ledesma, Bilbao, Spain, 1988-95; head dental edn.]ept. KFMMC, Dharan, Saudi Arabia, 1995—. Author: The Study Challenge, 1995, The Lumbar Spine Cure, 1997. Mem. Am. Pharmacy Assn. Avocations: reading, music, swimming, gymnastics. Home: KFMMC 54/402, Dhahran 31932, Saudi Arabia Office: King Fahd Mil Med Complex, Dhahran 31932, Saudi Arabia

ASTON, MICHAEL HARPER, information systems specialist; b. London, Jan. 23, 1939; s. Frederick William and Ellen (Smart) A.; m. Berwyn Payne, Apr. 13, 1968; children: Gavin, Tamsin. BSc with honors, U. Coll. London, 1960; Cert. F. Edn., Garnett Coll., 1966. Sys. Analyst Merc. and Gen. Reins. Co., London, 1960-66; chm. math. stats. computing St. Albans Tech. Coll., Hertfordshire, Eng., 1968-78; dep. dir., nat. coord. Adv. Unit for

Computer Based Edn., Hatfield, Eng., 1978—; chmn. Nat. Working Adv. Group for Computer Based Edn., 1981—; mem. Coun. Ednl. Tech., London, 1980—; info. tech. cons. in edn. UNESCO, Paris, Moscow, 1999—; cons. on IT in edn. World Bank and African Devel. Bank, 1994—; sch. inspector, 1997, quality assurance assessor in tchr. edn., 2000. Author: Parents Guide to Educational Software, 1985; contbr. articles to profl. jours. Fellow Royal Statis. Soc.; mem. Scout Assn. (internat. commr. 1994—). Mem. Ch. of Eng. Avocations: gourmet, travel, banjo playing. Office: AU Consultants, 126 Great North Rd, Hertfordshire Hatfield AL9 5JZ, England

ASTON, PETER GEORGE, music educator, composer, conductor; b. Birmingham, Eng., Oct. 5, 1938; s. George William and Elizabeth Oliver (Smith) A.; m. Elaine Veronica Neale, Aug. 13, 1960; 1 child, David Philip. ARCM, Royal Coll. of Music, London, 1958; GBSM, Birmingham (Eng.) Sch. Music, 1960; FTCL, Trinity Coll. of Music, 1961; DPhil, U. York, Eng., 1970. Lectr. in music U. York, 1964-72, sr. lectr., 1972-74; prof., head music U. East Anglia, Eng., 1974-98, profl. fellow, 1998—; musical dir. The Tudor Consort, Eng., 1958-65, English Baroque Ensemble, 1968-70; prin. condr. Aldeburgh Festival Singers, Eng., 1975-88; artistic dir. Norwich Festival of Contemporary Ch. Music, 1981—; guest condr., cons. Sacramento Area Bach Festival, 1993—, Incontri Corali Internat. Choral Festival, Alba, Italy, 1996, Schola Cantorum Gedanensis, Poland, 1999; chmn. Royal Sch. Ch. Music Norfolk Area, 1998—. Composer numerous choral and orchestral works, ch. anthems and svcs., chamber music works, opera; author: The Music of York Minster, 1972; co-author: Sound and Silence, 1970, German edit., 1972, Italian edit., 1979, Japanese edit., 1982, Music Theory in Practice, 3 vols., 1992-93; editor various compositions by 16th and 17th century composers, including The Collected Works of George Jeffreys. Fellow Curwen Inst. (hon.), Guild of Ch. Musicians (hon.), Royal Sch. Ch. Music (hon.); mem. Royal Coll. Music (hon.), Ea. Arts Assn. (chmn. music panel 1976-81), Trianon Music Group (pres. 1984-96), Norfolk Assn. for Advancement of Music (chmn. 1991-94, pres. 1994-2000), Guild Ch. Musicians (acad. bd. 1996—). Mem. Ch. of Eng. Avocations: bridge, cricket, travel, detective fiction. Office: U East Anglia, Sch of Music, Norwich NR4 7TJ, England

ASTRELIN, IGOR MIKHAILOVICH, chemical engineering and technology educator; b. Troitsk, Russia, Feb. 5, 1942; s. Mikhail Vasilievich and Elene Julievna (Blokhina) A.; m. Nina Fedorovna Chernyshova, Feb. 7, 1965; 1 child, Oleg Igorevich. Diploma in Engring./Chem. Tech., Kiev (Ukraine) Poly. U., 1964, CandSci in Engring., 1968; DSc in Engring., St. Petersburg Tech. U., Russia, 1990. Asst. Polytech. U., Kiev, 1968-71, asst. prof., 1972, asst. prof., dep. dean dept. chem. tech., 1977-82; head dept. Annaba (Algeria) U., 1973-76; head chair tech. and inorganic substances and gen. chem. te. Nat. Tech. U. Ukraine, Kiev, 1983; cns. Sci. Coun. of Ukraine, Kiev, 1990-98, Tech. Coun. of Ministry of Industry, Kiev, 1992—. Author: Progress in the Chemical Technology of the Ukraine, 1976, Theory of the Processing of the Inorganic Productions, 1992 (State award 1994); inventor. Head Coun. Higher Chem. Edn., Kiev, 1987—. Recipient Gold medal Indsl. Exhbn., Moscow, 1992; Internat. Assn. for Promotion of Cooperation with Scientists/New Ind. States of the Former Soviet Union grantee, 1995. Mem. Ukrainian Higher Sch. Acad. Scis., N.Y. Acad. Scis., European Fedn. Chem. Engring., Internat. Zeolite Assn. Christian. Avocations: sports, poetry, summer cottage, belles-lettres, cars. Home: 25 Pobeda Ave Apt 91, 252055 Kiev Ukraine Office: Nat Tech U Ukraine, 37 Pobeda Ave, 252056 Kiev Ukraine

ASTRIAB, STEVEN MICHAEL, army officer; b. Pitts., Mar. 10, 1952; s. Steven Leonard and Anna (Popivchak) A.; m. BettyLou Elaine Gimmi, Dec. 27, 1975. BA in Psychology, Washington and Jefferson Coll., 1974; MS in Manpower Planning, W.Va. U., 1976; grad., Commd. & Gen. Staff Coll., 1985. Commd. 2d lt. U.S. Army, 1974, advanced through grades to lt. col., 1992; div. social work officer 1st Cav. Div., Ft. Hood, Tex., 1976-77, med. platoon leader, then med. co. comdr. 15th med. bn., 1977-79; med. ops. officer 1st Cav. Div. Hdqs., Ft. Hood, Tex., 1979-81; chief M.C. procurement Office Army Surgeon Gen., Washington, 1982-85; chief combat medicine Office Project Mgr., Saudi Arabian Nat. Guard, Riyadh, 1985-88; pers. officer 62 Med. Group, Ft. Lewis, Wash., 1988-90; asst. chief staff for med. civil and mil. ops. 3d U.S. Army (Army Cen. Command), Riyadh, 1990-91; med. ops. officer Hdqrs. I Corps, Ft. Lewis, 1991-93; chief med. plans for S.W. Asia Hdqs. 3d U.S. Army, Atlanta, 1993-95; chief coalition integration for S.W. Asia Hdqs. 3d U.S. Army, 1995-96; chief med. plans and intelligence S.W. Asia Hdqrs. 3d U.S. Army, 1996; sr. med. and fgn. mil. sales advisor U.S. Mil. Tng. Mission for Saudi Arabia, Riyadh, 1996-98; chief of ops. Divsn., exec. officer Pacific Regional Med. Command, 1998-2000; dep. surgeon U.S. Army Pacific, 2000—; assoc. faculty Ctr. Excellence for Disaster Mgmt. and Humanitarian Assistance, 1999—. Decorated Bronze Star medal, Def. Meritorious Svc. medal, Meritorious Svc. medal (6), Joint Svc. Commendation medal, Army Commendation medal (2), Joint Meritorious Unit award, Nat. Def. Svc. medal (2), S.W. Asia Campaign medal (3), Armed Forces Expeditionary Medal, liberation of Kuwait medal (Saudi Arabia), Liberation of Kuwait medal (Kuwait). Republican. Baptist. Avocations: running, weight training, computer applications.

ASTRUC, ALEXANDRE, director, writer; b. Paris, July 13, 1923; s. Marcel Astruc and Huguette Haendel; m. Elyette Helies, 1983. Dir. (films) Le Rideau cramoisi, 1952, Les Mauvaises Rencontres, 1955, Une Vie, 1958, La Proie pour l'ombre, 1960, Education sentimentale, 1961, Evariste Galois, 1965, La Longue Marche, 1966, Flammes sur l'Adriatique, 1968, Sartre par lui-même, 1976; TV reporter Radio Luxembourg, 1969-72; film critic Paris Match, 1970-72; contbr. to Figaro-Dimanche, 1977—; author: Les Vacances, 1945, Le Serpent Jaune, 1976, Le Permissionnaire, 1982, Le Roman de Descartes, 1989, De la caméra au stylo, 1992, L'Autre versant de la colline, 1993, Evadiste Galois, 1994, Le Montreur d'ombres, 1996, Le Siècle À Vemir, 1998, La France du Coeur, 2000, also others. Decorated chevalier Légion d'honneur, officier Ordre du Mérite, comdr. des Arts et des Lettres; recipient grand prix René Clair cucineme Acad. Francaise. Avocations: mathematics, literature. Home: 168 rue de Grenelle, 75007 Paris France

ASTWOOD, SIR JAMES RUFUS, court administrator; b. Oct. 4, 1923; s. James Rufus Sr. and Mabel Winifred A.; m. Gloria Preston Norton, 1952; 3 children. Student, Berkeley Inst., Bermuda, U. Toronto, Can. Bar: London, 1956, Jamaica, 1956. Joined Jamaican Legal Svc., 1957, dep. clk. cts., 1957-58, clk. cts., 1958-63, resident magistrate, 1963-74, puisne judge, 1971, 73; stipendiary magistrate, judge grand ct. Cayman Islands, 1958-59; sr. magistrate Bermuda, 1974-76, acting dep. gov., 1977; chief justice of Bermuda, 1977-93; pres. Ct. of Appeal of Bermuda, 1995—, Ct. of Appeal of Turks and Caicos Islands, 1997—; mem. various coms., tribunals and bds. enquiry, Bermuda and Jamaica. Named Hon. Bencher, Gray's Inn Bar, 1985, Knight Bachelor, Knight Comdr. of Brit. Empire. Mem. Bermuda Sr. Golfers Soc., Mid Ocean Club. Avocations: golf, cricket, photography, reading, bridge. Fax: 1-441-236-8816.

ASWENDT, PETRA GERTRAUDE, material engineer, researcher; b. Chemnitz, Germany, Apr. 6, 1959; d. Manfred Hans and Gertraude Thea (Rech) Taubert; m. Bernd Jurgen Aswendt, Jul. 25, 1981; 1 child, Markus. Diploma engr., Bergakademie, Freiberg, Germany, 1982; PhD, Dortmund Univ., Germany, 1995. Scientist Acad. Sci., Chemnitz, 1982-91; scientist Fraunhofer Inst., Chemnitz, 1992—, laser metrology, mechs. of materials, 1998—, head micro-measurement group, 1998—. Author: Proceedings SPIE, 1990, 91, 95, 96, 97, 99; contbr. articles to profl. jours; patentee in field. Office: Fraunhofer Inst IWU, Reichenhainer Str 88, D 09126 Chemnitz Germany

ASYLMURATOVA, ALTYNAI, dancer; b. Alma-Ata, 1962; m. Konstantin Zaklinsky; 1 child. Student, Vaganova Ballet Sch., Leningrad; grad., Leningrad Choreographic Sch., 1978. With ballet co. Kirov Theatre, 1978-99; artistic dir. Vaganova Ballet Co., 1999—. Dancer with Kirov (now Mariinsky) Ballet, 1980; numerous fgn. tours Paris, 1982, U.S., 1987, Can., 1987; appeared in ballets, including Swan Lake, Legend of Love, Don Quixote, Sleeping Beauty, Boyaderka, Giselle. Address: Mariinsky Theatre, Teatralnaya pl 1, Saint Petersburg Russia

ASZÓDI, ANDRÁS, chemist; b. Budapest, Hungary, Aug. 20, 1964; s. Károly and Ágota (Bogdány) A.; m. Viktória Csordás, Dec. 31, 1994; 1 child, Anna Eszter. MSc, U. Budapest, 1988, PhD, 1991. Soros scholar Wadham Coll. U. Oxford, England, 1988-89; vis. scientist Albert-Ludwigs U., Freiburg, Germany, 1990; postdoctoral fellow Inst. Enzymology, Budapest, 1991-92; staff scientist NIMR, London, 1992-96; head of lab. Novartis Forschungsinstitut, Vienna, 1996—. Avocations: hiking, cooking, creative writing.

ATA, KHALED AHMAD, physician, medical researcher; b. Karachi, Sindh, Pakistan, Dec. 23, 1954; s. Ghulam Ahmad Ata and Nasira Sultana; m. Amatul Hai Ahmad, Mar. 29, 1981; children: Noorudin Mahmood, Nasirudin Tahir, Mohyudin Umar. MB, BChir, Nishtar Med. Coll., Multan, Pakistan, 1979; PhD, Uppsala (Sweden) U., 1999. Med. officer Fazle Omar Hosp., Rabwah, Pakistan, 1981-82, Pvt. Clinic, Rabwah, Pakistan, 1982-84, 88-91; missionary doctor Nusrar Jahan, Tanzania, 1985, Sierra Leone, 1985-88. Capt. Army Med. Corps Pakistan, 1979-81. Decorated Quaid-e-Azam medal Pakistan Army, 1981. Mem. Swedish Med. Assn. Ahmadi Muslim. Avocations: sports, traveling, books.

ATAEVA, AKSOLTAN, diplomat; b. Ashgabat, Nov. 6, 1944; m. Tchary Pirmoukhamedov, Apr. 25, 1969; children: Ainabat, Azat. Dipl. medicine, Turkmen State Med. Inst., 1968; DS (hon.), Soviet Union Sci. Rsch. Inst., 1989; assoc. (hon.), Internat. Acad. Computer Scis., Kiev, Ukraine, 1993. Staff, asst. to chief doctor Hosp. No. 1, Ashgabat, Turkmenistan, 1968-80; vice dir. Regional Health Dept., Ashgabat, 1980-85; vice min., min. Health of Turkmenistan, Ashgabat, 1985-94; min. Social Security of Turkmenistan, Ashgabat, 1994-95; now permanent rep. Turkmenistan UN, N.Y.C., 1995—; Contbr. numerous articles to profl. jours. Mem. Supreme People's Coun. Turkmenistan, 1993—. Mem. Dem. Party of Turkmenistan. Avocations: art, reading, sports. Office: Presidental Palace, 22 K Marx St, Ashkhabad 744014, Turkmenistan Office: Permanent Mission Turkmenistan UN 866 United Nations Plz Rm 424 New York NY 10017-1822*

ATAGANA, HARRISON IFEANYICHUKWU, microbiology educator, consultant, researcher; b. Obiaruku, Delta St, Nigeria, Jan. 11, 1956; s. Nicholas Igwebuike Atagana and Comfort Amlaibli Enomate; m. Favour Ogochukwu Achugbue, Dec. 31, 1978; children: Hilary, Ifelunwa, Ishioma, Chinedu. BSc with honors, U. Benin, Nigeria, 1987, MSc in Microbiology, 1991; postgrad., U. Natal, Pietermaritzburg, South Africa. Sci. tchr. Obiaruku (Nigeria) Grammar Sch., 1984; biology lectr. Coll. of Edn., Agbor, Nigeria, 1988-92; lectr. Delta State U., Abraka, Nigeria, 1993-95, Wits Technikon, Johannesburg, South Africa, 1996, U. of the North, Qwa Qwa, South Africa, 1997, Mangisuthu Technikon, Durban, South Africa, 1998—; dir. Haifyat Cons., Obiaruku, Nigeria, 1992-95; cons. Hafra Envoclean, Obiaruku, 1993-95. Contbr. articles to profl. publs. Chmn. Federated Union of Ndokwa Students, Benin, 1986; sec. Sr. Staff Assn. of Univs. and Allied Instns., Agbor-Nigria, 1989-90; mem. Obiaruku Solidarity Front, Obihruku, 1990—; coord. Bendel East Sci. Tchrs. Assn. of Nigeria, Agbor, 1988-90. With Nigerian Nat. Youth Svc. Corp., 1981-82. Mem. Am. Soc. Microbiology, British Ecol. Soc., Internat. Assn. for Water Quality, South African Soc. for Microbiology. Avocations: photography, swimming, fishing, driving. Home: 17 Visagie Rd, The Grange, Pietermaritzburg KZN 3200, South Africa Office: Dept Microbiology U Natal, P/Rag X01, Pietermaritzburg KZN 3209, South Africa

ATAMAN, OKTAR, NATO official; b. Istanbul, 1939; m. Nedret Ataman; 2 children. Grad., Turkish Mil. Acad., 1961. Commd. 2d lt. Turkish Army, 1961, advanced through grades to lt. gen., 1997, early assignments include forward observer, battery comdr., asst. Turkish mil. attaché, liaison officer with UN, 1966-68, command positions in arty. units, 1973-75, project officer ops. and plans divsn., Turkish Gen. Staff, 1975-77; instr. Turkish Army Staff Coll., 1977-80; staff officer plans and policy divsn., NATO Supreme Hdqrs. Belgium, 1980-83; sec. gen. hdqrs. staff, Turkish Land Forces Command Turkish Army, 1983-84, comdr. corps of cadets regiment, Turkish Mil. Acad., 1984-86, sr. instr., Turkish Army Staff Coll., chief of instrn., head of bd. of instrs. Army Staff Coll., chief of plans and ops., divsn. Turkish Gen. Staff, 1988-90, comdr. 14th mechanized infantry brigade, 1990-92, chief strategy and force planning divsn., Turkish Gen. Staff, 1992-95; comdr. 1st mechanized infantry divsn., 1995-97; chief of ops. Turkish Gen. Staff, 1997-98; mil. rep. of Turkey to NATO Mil. Com., Brussels, 1998—. Avocations: reading, music, water sports, travel. Office: NATO Hdqrs, Blvd Leopold III, 1110 Brussels Belgium*

ATAMAN, OROL SADRETTIN, consultancy firm executive; b. Çankaya, Ankara, Turkey, Sept. 1, 1945; s. Huseyin Kazim and Hatice Zehra (Okay) A.; m. Tevhide Hürmüz Sarsilmaz, May 11, 1971; children: Selahattin Uygar, Cemile Gizem. BArch, Mid.E. Tech. U., Ankara, 1968, MA in Regional Planning, 1970. Chief arch. Min. of Settlements, Ankara, 1969-77; gen. dir. tourism planning Min. of Tourism, Ankara, 1977-82; sr. planner Makkah Region Planning Office, Saudi Arabia, 1982-85; v.p., CEO Tech. Svcs. Bur., 1985-94; overseas bus. devel. mgr. TEPE Constrn. Ind. Inc., 1996-99; exec. mgr. New Towns Investments Inc., 1999—; instr. dept. architecture Selçuk U., Konya, Turkey, 1976-79; chm. BKP-Regional Devels. Projects Cons., Inc., Ankara, 1987-90; pres. Hill and Knowlton--Turkey Internat. Pub. Rels. Inc., Ankara, 1990-92. Editor: Metropolitan Ankara Population Survey, 1969-70 (Best Rsch. award 1971). bd. dirs. Union of Turkish Engrs. and Archs., Ankara, 1974-76. Recipient 1st mention Zonguldak Met. Area Planning Competition, 1973, 1st mention Gaziantep Urban Area Planning Competition, 1974, Best Profl. Svc., Municipality of Iskenderun, Turkey, 1987, 30 Yrs. Svc. award Ankara Chamber Archs., 1998, 30th Anniversary medal Mid.E. Tech. U., 1998. Mem. Turkish Chamber of Archs. (pres. 1980-82, sec.-gen. 1994-96), Chamber of Turkish City and Regional Planners (pres. 1973-77), Club Flipper, Horse-Riding Club. Avocations: travel, horseback riding, playing chess. Home: Turan Günes Bulvari, No 43/41, 06450 Çankaya Ankara, Turkey Office: Yeni Kentler Yatirim, Holding Cemal Nadir Sok 4/3, 06550 Çankaya Ankara, Turkey

ATAMIAN, SUSAN, nurse; b. Cambridge, Mass., Sept. 14, 1950; d. Raymond H. and Alice (Chakerian) A. BA, Simmons Coll., 1972, MS, 1995. RN, Mass.; cert. infection control. Staff nurse Mass. Gen. Hosp., Boston, 1972-74, pvt. duty nurse, 1975-76, staff nurse, 1976-77; rsch. asst. III U. Cinn. Hosp., 1980-81; rsch. study nurse Mass. Gen. Hosp., Boston, 1977-80, instr. nursing, 1982-84, sr. rsch. study nurse, 1984-87, dir. clin. rsch. nurse group, 1985-90, infection control nurse, 1988-90; infection control nurse clinician Mass. Gen. Hosp., Boston, Boston, 1990-92; staff nurse Kimberly Nurses, Orange, Calif., 1982; coord., clin. rsch., vascular surg. div. Mass. Gen. Hosp., 1992-99, individual assignments/spl. projects staff, 1999—; cons. nutrition and liver diseases, McGaw Labs., Santa Ana, Calif., 1980-81; chmn. faculty devel. libr. com. Shepard Gill Sch., Boston, 1983-84; mem. rsch. nurses forum, Mass. Gen. Hosp., 1992—. Class agt. 1972 Simmons Coll., 1972, 86-97, mem. com. alumnae fund, 1987-89, reunion com., 1990—, com. on classes, 1991-92, class of 1972 reunion fund chair, 1991-92, chmn. class of 1972 reunion fund 1996-97, v.p. Class of 1972, 1997—. Mem. ANA, Am. Nurses Found. Century Club, Soc. for Vascular Nursing, Mass. Nurses Assn., Rsch. Nurses Forum Mass. Gen. Hosp., Simmons Coll. Nursing Honor Soc., Simmons Club Boston (bd. dirs. 1988-90, 2000—, v.p. 1990-92, co-chmn. boutique 1992-94, mem. nominating com. 1994-95), Coun. Armenian Am. Nurses, Sigma Theta Tau. Mem. Armenian Apostolic Ch. Avocations: travel, reading, knitting.

ATANOV, GENNADIY ALEXEEVICH, physicist, educator; b. Donetsk, Ukraine, Sept. 1, 1939; s. Alexi Gavrilovich and Olimpiada Alexeevna Atanov; m. Liudmila Petrovna Tkalenko, Apr. 21, 1962; children: Elena, Yulia. MS, Aircraft Inst., Kharkov, Ukraine, 1963; Candidate of Scis., Hydrodynamic Inst., Kiev, Ukraine, 1969; DSc, Computing Ctr., Moscow, 1978. Engr. Machine-bldg. Plant, Petropavlovsk, Kazakhstan, 1963-66; asst. prof. State U., Donetsk, Ukraine, 1966-70, assoc. prof., 1970-80, head of dept., 1980—; rector Inst. Social Edn., Donetsk, 1997—. Author: Fundamentals of One-Dimensional Unsteady Gas Dynamics, 1979, Optimization of Modes of Hydropower Installations, 1985, Hydroimpulsive Installations for Rock Breaking, 1987, Gas Dynamics, 1992. Coord. Union of Electore, Donetsk, 1990. Internat. Sci. Fund Grantee, 1994. Mem. Internat. Soc. Water Jet Tech. (bd. dirs. 1989—), Internat. Artificial Itelligence in Edn. Soc., Nat. com. Theoretical and Appllied Mechanics of Ukraine (mem. of secretariat 1993—). Avocations: fishing, gardening. Home: 14 ul 50 let SSSR Kv 27, 83055 Donetsk Ukraine Office: Donetsk State U, 24 Universitetskaya Str, 340055 Donetsk Ukraine

ATARASHI, HIROTSUGU, cardiologist, educator; b. Fukaya-shi, Saitama, Japan, Aug. 19, 1949; s. Jonosuke and Chizuko Atarashi. MD, Nippon Med. Sch., Tokyo, 1974. Asst. prof. Nippon Med. Sch., Tokyo, 1992-97, assoc. prof., 1997—. Mem. Internat. Soc. Cardiovascular Pharmacotherapy, Am. Heart Assn. Office: Nippon Med Sch 1st Dept Int, Med Tama-Nagayama Hosp, Tokyo 206-8512, Japan

ATASSI, GHANEM, oncologist; b. Homs, Syria, Jan. 7, 1936; s. Khalil and Aicha Atassi; m. May Atassi, Apr. 4, 1950; children: Clair Soulayma, Farah. Degree in pharmacy, Free U. Brussels, 1964, M Clin. Biology, 1972, PhD in Pharm. Scis., 1976, agrégé, 1981. Dir. med. analysis lab. Kounitra (Syria) Hosp., 1965-70; asst. prof. Free U. Brussels, 1971-72, prof., 1985—, dir. exptl. chemotherapy and screening lab., 1972-90; dir. exptl. oncology divsn. Inst. Rsch. Servier, Suresnes, France, 1990-2000; strategic adv. rsch. Inst. Rsch. Servier, 2000—. Contbg. author: Advances in Oncology, 1986, Nude Mice in Oncology Research, 1992; patentee in field; contbr. numerous articles to profl. jours. Mem. Am. Assn. for Cancer Rsch., European Assn. for Cancer Rsch., Belgian Assn. for Studies on Cancer. Home: 4 Rue Josephine, 7 Rue Michel Salles, 92210 Saint Cloud France Office: IDRS, 11 Rue des Moulineaux, 92150 Suresnes France Office: Pharmacy I Free U Brussels, Pharmacy I Free U Brussels, Bd du Triomphe, 1050 Brussels Belgium

ATATÜR, MEHMET KUTSAY, hydrobiology, researcher; b. Ankara, Turkey, Feb. 15, 1947; s. Abdurrahman and Ferda (Kutsay) A.; m. Azize Nihal Ozgen, Feb. 13, 1974; children: Aynur Burcu, Refik Burak. MSc in zoology, Ege Univ., Izmir, Turkey, 1973, PhD in zoology, 1978. Asst. of zoology Ege Univ., Izmir, 1972-78, asst. prof. zoology, 1979-85, assoc. prof. zoology, 1986-94, prof. hydrobiology, 1994. Contbr. articles to profl. jours. With Marines, 1975. Mem. Nat. Geographic Soc., N.Y. Acad. Scis. Avocations: photography, mineral collection, hikes in nature. Office: Ege U, Fen Fak/Biyoloji Bol, Hidrobiyoloji A Dali, 35100 Izmir Turkey

ATAWNEH, AHMAD MAHMOUD, linguistics educator; b. Hebron, Palestine, Nov. 23, 1946; s. Mahmoud Abdul-Hadi and Ezzyah Ahmad Atawneh; m. Dawlat Shehdeh Jabari, Dec. 13, 1946; children: Hazim, Raid, Areej, Aiyette. BA in English, Damascus (Syria) U., 1972; MA in TESFL, U. Wales, 1983; ArtsD, SUNY, Stony Brook, 1991, PhD in Applied Linguistics, 1991. Chmn. dept. English Hebron U., 1985-87, 92—, Dean of Arts, 1995-99; translation cons. Suffolk County, N.Y., 1989-91; tchr. pragmatics and linguistics Arabic, UN, N.Y.C., 1991-; v.p. Acad. Afffairs, 1999—. Contbr. articles to profl. jours. Pres. Beit Kahil Charitable Soc., 1972-79; cons. Palestinian Ministry Edn. for ESL. Mem. AAAL, PATEFL (sec. 1994—), TESOL, Arab Deans of Art. Moslem. Avocations: reading, swimming. Office: Hebron U, PO Box 40, Hebron Israel

ATCHER, RANDY, musician, narrator, entertainer, retired realtor; b. Tip Top, Ky., Dec. 7, 1918; s. George Christopher and Mary Agnes (Ray) A; m. Daphne Lilian Fuller, Dec. 24, 1943 (dec. Dec. 1977); children: Randall Mark, Christopher Clay; m. Elizabeth Thorne, July 14, 1979; stepchildren: Laura, Judy, Kathy, John. Student, Western Ky. U., 1936-37. Musician, singer Sta. WHAS, Louisville, 1932-38, musician, singer, bandleader, 1947-49; musician, singer Sta. WIND, Sta. WJJD, Gary, Ind. and Chgo., 1938-41, Sta. WBBM, Chgo., 1941; musician, singer, disc jockey Sta. WKLO, Louisville, 1949; bandleader, singer, announcer, master of ceremonies Sta. WHAS Radio-TV, Louisville, 1950-70; narrator Am. Printing House, Louisville, 1970—; realtor Coldwell Banker (formerly Gibson/Pfannenschmidt Inc.), Louisville, 1970-80, Atcher-Goff Realtors, 1979-84; ret., 1984; realtor Atcher-Goff Realtors, 1980-92; recorded with Columbia Records and MGM Records. Songwriter numerous works. Chmn. Muscular Dystrophy Assn., Louisville, 1951-92; master of ceremonies, musician, singer Sta. WHAS Crusade for Children Telethon, 1953-70, 92—; active Country Music Found. and Hall of Fame, Nashville; mem. adv. bd. The Dream Factory; active Western Singing Trio High, Wide and Handsome, 1993—; commr. Meadow View Estates. Maj. AC, U.S. Army, 1942-46. Recipient numerous awards and certificates Ky. Derby Festival, Muscular Dystrophy Assn., Multiple Sclerosis, Am. Heart Assn., Cystic Fibrosis, Key to the City of Louisville, 1991. Alexander Scourby award Found. for the Blind; named Man of Yr., Firemans Assn., Louisville, 1956, Man of Yr., Police Assn., Louisville, 1957, Musician of Yr., Louisville Fedn. of Musician, 1989. Mem. Am. Fedn. Musicians, Wildwood Club (bd. dirs.). Democrat. Roman Catholic. Avocations: golf, tennis. Home: 1900 Manor House Dr Louisville KY 40220-1405

ATCHESON, SUE HART, business educator; b. Dubuque, Iowa, Apr. 12; d. Oscar Raymond and Anna (Cook) Hart; m. Walter Clark Atcheson (div.); children: Christine A. Hischar, Moffet Zoe Onofrei, Claye Williams. BBA, Mich. State U.; MBA, Calif. State Poly. U., Pomona, 1973. Cert. tchr. and adminstr. Instr. Mt. San Antonio Coll., Walnut, Calif., 1968-90; bd. dirs. faculty assn. Mt. San Antonio Coll.; mem. acad. senate Mt. San Antonio Coll.; originator vol. income tax assistance Mt. San Antonio Coll.; speaker in field; adj. lectr. in bus. mgmt. Calif. State Polytech U., Pomona, 1973-75. Author: Fractions and Equations on Your Own, 1975. Charter mem. Internat. Commn. on Monetary and Econ. Reform; panelist infrastructure funding reform, Freeport, Ill., 1989. Mem. Cmty. Concert Assn. Inland Empire (bd. dirs.), Scripps Coll. Fine Arts Found., Recyclers Club (pres. 1996).

ATCHISON, ARTHUR MARK, industrial, research and development engineer; b. Cleve., Aug. 22, 1944; s. James Edward and Zella Katherine (Beecher) A.; m. Lora Suzanne Ferlet (div.); 1 child, Tiara Lynne; m. Patricia Fay Jones, July 9, 1983; 1 child, James Edward II. AA, Cuyahoga C.C., Parma, Ohio, 1971; BS in Indsl. Mgmt., U. Akron, 1973; MS in Indsl. Engring. and Ops. Rsch., Va. Poly. Inst. and State U., 1980; PhD in Indsl. Engring., Kennedy-Western U., 1992. Supr. indsl. engring. Firestone Tire and Rubber Co., Akron, Ohio, 1973-76; divisional indsl. engr. Firestone Internat. Co., Akron, 1976-77; regional ops. engr. Reynolds Aluminum Co., Richmond, Va., 1981-82; plant engr. AMP, Inc., Harrisonburg, Va., 1982-83; supr. engring. lab. E.R. Carpenter Co., Richmond, 1977-81; mgr. corp. devel. engring. E.R. Carpenter Co., Elkhart, Ind., 1983-94; sr. tech. cons. Carpenter Co., Richmond, Va., 1994—; co. advisor Jr. Achievement, Akron, 1976. Inventor, implementer hundreds of tech. proprietary process improvements for new devels. for various cos. Vol. for emergency comms. Kodak Liberty Bike-a-thon, Richmond, 1986; vol. lic. examiner FCC; weather spotter Skywarn, 2000. With USN, 1964-70, Vietnam. Mem. Am. Inst. Indsl. Engrs. (sr.), Am. Soc. Quality Control, Amateur Radio Relay League, Richmond Amateur Telecom. Soc., Internat. Amateur Radio Soc., Greater Richmond Sailing Assn., Delta Sigma Pi (life). Republican. Episcopalian. Avocations: amateur radio, photography, coin collecting, sailing, art collecting. Office: Carpenter Co 5016 Monument Ave Richmond VA 23230-3620

ATCHISON, JOSEPH EDWARD, pulp and paper industry consultant; b. Barnum, W.Va., Dec. 25, 1914; s. Edward Washington and Frederica Catherine (Kerns) A.; m. Frances Julia Winebrinier, July 3, 1951 (dec. Apr. 1965); m. Betty Jeanne Pugh, May 30, 1968; children: Leah, Robert, Scott (dec.), Kevin (dec.). BSCE, La. State U., 1938; MS in Pulp & Paper Tech., Inst. Paper Chem., 1940, PhD in Pulp & Paper Tech., 1942. Tech. dir. John Strange Paper Co., Menasha, Wis., 1946-48; chief pulp & paper br. Marshall Plan, Washington, Paris, 1948-52; mill mgr., project dir. Portarican Paper Products, Inc., San Juan, P.R., 1952-53; v.p., sr. v.p. Parsons & Whittemore, Inc., N.Y.C., 1953-67; pres., owner Joseph E. Atchison Cons., Inc., N.Y.C., 1968-97, Atchison Cons., Inc., Sarasota, Fla., 1997—. Author: Waste Paper Recycling, 1972, Kenaf for Paper Pulp, 1976; contbr. articles to profl. jours. Lt. col. U.S. Army, 1942-46. Decorated DSM Bronze Star with oak leaf cluster; named to Paper Industry Internat. Hall of Fame, 1997; named Man of Quarter, In Paper Internat., 1999. Mem. TAPPI (Gunnar Nicholson Gold medal 1996), Internat. Soc. Sugar Cane Technologists. Presbyterian. Avocations: tennis, fitness, dancing, travel, theatre.

ATCHISON, RODNEY RAYMOND, lawyer, arbitrator; b. Hanford, Calif., Nov. 14, 1926; s. Clyde Raymond and Velma May (Watts) A.; m. Evaleen Mary McFadden, June 27, 1948; children: Cathlin Atchison, Susan Barisone, Kerry Dexter, Brian. Student, San Jose State Coll., 1946-49; JD, U. Santa Clara, 1952. Bar: Calif. 1953, U.S. Dist. Ct. (all dists.) Calif. 1953, U.S. Ct. Appeals (9th cir.) 1953, U.S. Supreme Ct. 1971. Assoc. Mullen & Filippi, Attys., San Francisco, 1953-55; dep. county counsel Santa Clara Calif.

County Counsel, San Jose, 1955-57; city atty. City of Mountain View, Calif., 1957-62, City of Santa Cruz, Calif., 1962-90; pres. Atchison, Anderson, Hurley & Barisone, Profl. Law Corp., Santa Cruz, 1980-96; of counsel Atchison Barisone & Condotti, Profl. Law Corp., Santa Cruz, 1996, Law Offices of Rodney R. Atchison, 1996—; arbitrator Am. Arbitration Assn., San Francisco, 1970—. Pres. Rotary Club Mountain View, Calif., 1961-62, Santa Cruz (Calif.) County Bar Assn., 1973. With USNR, 1944-46. Mem. ABA, Santa Cruz Rotary Club, Elks Lodge (life). Roman Catholic. Avocations: skiing, travel, golf. Office: Law Offices of Rodney R Atchison 333 Church St Santa Cruz CA 95060-3811

ATES, AHMET FEYZI, information technology specialist; b. Bursa, Turkey, Nov. 8, 1967; s. Osman Halidun and Guner (Kocal) A. BS, Yildiz U., Istanbul, Turkey, 1990; MS, Bilkent U., Ankara, Turkey, 1993, U. So. Calif., L.A., 1994. Intern IBM Turkish Ltd. Co., Istanbul, 1988; sys. adminstr. Toros Securities Inc., Bursa, 1991; tchg. asst. Ege U., Izmir, Turkey, 1994-96; software engr. Telsoft, Inc., Istanbul, 1997-98; network adminstr. So. Sea Area Command, Izmir, 1989-99; plant info. tech. infrastructure supr. Cargill Inc., Orhangazi, Bursa, Turkey, 1999—; vis. rschr. U. Aizu, Aizu-Wakamatsu City, Japan, 1994, 96. Contbr. papers to profl. jours. Grad. fellow Bilkent U., 1991; scholar Ministry Nat. Edn., 1993. Mem. IEEE Computer Soc., IEEE Comms. Soc., Assn. for Computing Machinery, Inst. Elec. and Electronic Engrs. Avocations: soccer, swimming, photography, running, traveling. Home: Kukurtulu Cad No 5/7, 16080 Bursa Turkey Office: Cargill Inc, Orhangazi, 16840 Bursa Turkey

ATES, YALIM, orthopaedic surgeon; b. Istanbul, Turkey, Nov. 16, 1963; s. Azmi Huseyin and Suna Guner (Acuner) A.; m. Yesim Tanriverdi, Nov. 21, 1987; 1 child, Emre. MD, Hacettepe U., Ankara, Turkey, 1987. Cons. orthop. Turkish Health Found., Ankara, 1992-94; tchg. staff Ministry of Health, Ankara Hosp., 1994-98, assoc. prof., 1997—; chief orthop. surgeon 2nd Orthop. Clinic, Ankara SSK Tchg. Hosp., 1998—. Dep. editor Jour. Medicine and Health, 1996-99; adv. editor Jour. Arthroscopy and Arthropsty, 1997—. Avocations: tennis, fishing. Address: Iunolihilmi Cad 98/18, Kovaklidere, Ankara 06542, Turkey

ATES, YESIM, anesthesiologist, educator; b. Ankara, Turkey, Nov. 12, 1962; d. Ismail and Gönül (Peksavas) Tanriverdi; m. Yalim Ates; 1 child, Emre. MD, Hacetteppe U., Ankara, Turkey, 1987; specialist in anesthesia, Ankara U., 1994. Govt. physician Ministry of Health, Ankara, 1987-89; resident in anesthesiology Ankara U., 1989-94, staff anesthesiologist, 1994-99, assoc. prof. anesthesiology, 1999—; rsch. fellow Ludwig-Maximillians U., Munich, 1990-91. Contbr. articles and abstracts to profl. jours. Mem. Internat. Anesthesiology Rsch. Soc., Am. Soc. Regional Anesthesiology, European Soc. Anesthesiologists. Avocations: volleyball, swimming, skiing, tennis. Home: Resit Galip Cad 80/5, 06700 Ankara Turkey Office: Ankara U Med Faculty, 1BN-I Sina Hospital, Ankara Turkey

ATHA, BERNARD PETER, town councilor, actor; b. Leeds, Eng., Aug. 27, 1928; s. Horace Michael Atha and Mary Elizabeth Quinlan. LLB with honors, Leeds U., 1949; tchr. qualification, RAF Sch. Edn., London, 1950. Barrister-at-law, Grays Inn, Eng. Profl. dancer U.K., 1952-56; councillor Leeds City Coun., 1957—; profl. film and TV actor, 1969—; vice chmn. W. Leeds Health Authority, Leeds, 1988-90, St. James Hosp., Leeds, 1990-98, Sports Coun. Lottery Bd., 1995—. Mem. Arts Coun. Gt. Britain, London, 1979-82; bd. dirs. Opera North, Leeds, 1984—, Sports Aid Found., London, 1980—; chmn. Leeds Grand Theatre, 1988—, Red Ladder Theatre Co., Leeds, 1984—, W.Y. Playhouse, Leeds, 1978—, Leeds City Varieties, U.K., 1988—; chmn. Brit. Paralympic Assn., London, 1989-97, U.K.S.A. People Mental Handicap, London, 1981—, Leeds Indsl. Coop. Soc., 1980—, Yorkshire Dance Ctr., Leeds, 1986—; pres. Internat. Sports Assn. on People with Mental Handicaps, 1993—; chmn. No. Ballet Theatre, 1995—; exec. Internat. Paralymic Com.; vice chair com. sport disabled European U.; lord mayor City of Leeds, 2000. Named to Order Brit. Empire, The Queen of Eng., 1991. Fellow Royal Soc. Arts; mem. royal Acad. Dance. Mem. Labour Party. Roman Catholic. Avocations: sports, arts. E-mail: bernard.atha@leeds.gov.uk. Home: 25 Moseley Wood Croft, Leeds LS16 7JJ, England Office: Town Hall, Leeds LS1 3AD, England

ATHANASIADIS, SPIROS, economic studies educator, consultant; b. Kalithea, Athens, Greece, Sept. 11, 1953; s. Nikolaos and Athina Athanassiadis. BS, North Adams State U., U.S., 1977; MA, SUNY, Albany, 1979, postgrad., 1979-81; postgrad., U. Bradford, 1996—. Tchg. asst. SUNY, Albany, 1978-81; advisor Greek Embassy, Washington, 1981-83; rschr. Ministry of Agr., Athens, 1983-90; dir. MTC Ltd., Athens, 1990—; asst. prof. U. La Verne, Athens, 1988—; bd. dirs. Papoulias SA, Athens; part-time instr. Cen. Tex., 1987-88, City Coll. Chgo., 1986-87, Greek productivity ctr., Athens, 1984-85. Author: Production of Legumes in Greece, 1983, Economic Analysis of Cotton Production in Greece, 1984, The Bread Market in Greece, 1984, Bioconversion An Economic Analysis, 1987, Train the Trainers, 1998, Modern Management, 1999. Officer Greek Air Force, 1981-83. Grantee European Union, 1993, 94, 96. Fellow Greek Mgmt. Assn.; mem. Greek Econ. Assn., Am. Econ. Assn. Democrat. Avocations: farming, fishing, sailing. Home: Mesinias 5 Agios Dimitrios, 17341 Athens Greece Office: U La Verne, PO Box 51105, 14510 Athens Greece

ATHANASOPOULOS, PANAGIOTIS EVANGELOS, food science educator; b. Filiatra, Peloponisos, Greece, Sept. 16, 1939; s. Evangelos and Georgia (Bitsikas) A.; m. Persa Parissos, May 22, 1994; 1 child, Evangelos. BS, U. Athens, 1963; MS, Mich. State U., East Lansing, 1975, PhD, 1977. AG engr. AG Bank of Greece, Athens, 1964-72, specialist, 1977-90; vis. prof. AG U., Athens, 1978-88; asst. prof. AG Univ., Athens, 1988-2000, assoc. prof., 2000—. Author: Thermal Operations in Food Industry, 1984, Fundamentals in Food Quality Control, 1988; co-author: Frozen Foods in Greece, 1988, Equipment for Food Industries, 1999. Mem. Agrili Local Soc. (pres. 1997—), GIFS (pres. 1997-99), IFT, IIR. Avocations: travelling, reading, philosophy. Home: Aigiou 32, 11527 Athens Greece Office: IERA ODOS 75, 11855 Athens Greece

ATHANASSIADI, KALLIOPI, cardiothoracic surgeon; b. Athens, Greece, Dec. 5, 1964; d. Angelos and Dorothea (Tournavitou) A. Deutches Abitur, German Sch. Athens, 1982; cert., Wagner Coll., S.I., N.Y., 1982; medical dr., U. Athens, 1989. Cert. cardiothoracic surgeon, Greece. Trainee in gen. surgery Gen Hosp. Pireaus, Greece, 1991-94; trainee in cardiothoracic surgery Gen. Hosp. Evangelismos, Athens, 1995-98; physician Hosp. Grosshansdorf, Hamburg, Germany, 1998; fellow thoracic surgeon Campus Hotel Dieu, Montreal, Que., Can., 1999; cardiothoracic surgeon Medizinsche Hochschule Hannover, Germany, 1999-2000, Kronidi (Greece) Health Ctr., 2000, Gen. Hosp. Piraeus, Greece, 2000; dir. sci. com. Prevention of Nuclear War of IFM SA, Vienna, 1987-90; coun. Athens U., 1988-90. Contbr. articles to profl. jours. Gen. sec. HELMSIC, Athens, 1985-88; mem. Hellenic Action Against Cancer, Athens, 1990—, Medecins du monde, Athens, 1991—; mem. sci. com. Evangelismos Gen. Hosp., 1997. Recipient Greek Oncologic Soc. award, 1993, Greek Medical Soc. award, 1996, grant Medizinsche Hochschule Hannover, 1999. Mem. European Soc. Thoracic Surgery, N.Y. Acad. Scis., Internat. Union Angiology, Soc. Advanced Trauma Life Support. Avocations: languages (speak fluently Greek, French, German, English, Swedish, Russian, Italian, Spanish), piano, reading, tennis, skiing, dancing. Home: Konstantinoupoleosstr 34 A, 15562 Holargos Athens Greece

ATHANASSIOU, ATHANASSIOS E., medical oncologist, researcher; b. Volos, Greece, May 22, 1945; s. Eustathios and Helen Athanassiou; m. Agatha Psychogios, Mar. 8, 1975; children: Eustathios, Andreas. MD, Med. Sch., Athens, Greece, 1978. House officer Med. Sch., Athens, 1973-78; registrar Greek Cancer Soc., Athens, 1978-80; hon. sr. registrar Med. Sch., London, 1980-82; sr. registrar Metaxa Cancer Hosp, Piraeus, Greece, 1982-85, dir., 1985—; cons. to hosps., Athens, 1985—; cons. Greek Oncol. Soc., Athens, 1990—; pres. Metaxa Acad. Bd., Piraeus, 1993—; advisor Nat. Drug Orgn., 1994—; founding mem., sec.-gen. Balkan Union of Oncology, 1995—. Editor: Ovarian Cancers, 1993; editor-in-chief Jour. of the Balkan Union of Oncology, 1996—; contbr. articles to profl. jours. Advisor Ministry of Health, Athens, 1986-88, 96—, pres. nat. com. oncology, 1996—. Lt. Greek Army, 1970-72. Mem. AAAS, Am. Soc. Clin. Oncology, European Soc. Med. Oncology, N.Y. Acad. Scis., Chemotherapy Found., European Assn. Cancer Rsch., Assn. Cancer Physicians (U.K.), European Orgn. Rsch. and Treatment of Cancer, Orgn. European Cancer Insts. (nat. rep.), Nat. Com. Cancer Experts of European Union, Balkan Union Oncology. Office: Metaxa Cancer Hosp, 51 Botassi, Piraeus 185 37, Greece

ATHANASSOGLOU, PANAYOTIS PANTELIS, economist; b. Athens, Greece, Aug. 18, 1948; s. Pantelis B. and Ecateriny P. (Apostolidou) A. BA, U. Piraeus, Greece, 1971; diploma in bus. adminstrn., U. Athens, 1979; MA in Econs., U. Okla., 1980; PhD in Econs., U. Sussex, Brighton, Eng., 1990. Fin. mgr. A.V.O. Ltd., Athens, 1970-71, Elieser Bros. ltd., Athens, 1973; sr. economist Bank of Greece, Athens, 1975—; mem. Com. for Promotion of Fgn. Investment in Greece, 1988-93, Com. for Encouragement of Reciprocal Promotion of Investment Between Greece and Other Countries, 1990-93; mem. Competition Com., Athens, 1988-95; mem. bd. Athens Stock Exch., 1990-96. Author: Economic Policy and the Balance of Payments, 1992; contbr. chpts. to books. Fellow State Fellowships Found. Greece, Athens, 1981; recipient award Athens Acad. Arts and Scis., 1990. Mem. Internat. Econs. Study Group, Greek Econ. Assn., Greek Mgmt. Assn., Athenian Club. Christian Orthodox. Avocations: music, collection of old cards. Office: Bank of Greece, 21 El Venizelou St, GR 10250 Athens Greece

ATHANASSOPOULOS, ANASTASSIOS ANDREAS, urologist, consultant; b. Patra, Ahaias, Greece, Feb. 23, 1957; s. Andreas George and Adamantia Anastasios (Paraskevopoulou) A.; m. Maria Alexader Tsirigouli, Aug. 24, 1980; children: Adamantia, Aikaterini, Alexia. Laurea, U. G D'Annunzio, Chieti, Italy, 1982; Doctorate, U. Patra, 1990. Cert. med. specialist in urology Greek Ministry Health. Rural physician Med. Ctr., Kilini, Greece, 1984-85; resident Hosp. Aigiou, Greece, 1985-86, Elpis Hosp., Athens, 1986-87, U. Hosp., Patra, 1987-90; clin. asst. Somerset and Taunton Hosp., Eng., 1991-92; attending urologist Univ. Hosp., Patra, 1993-99; cons. Inst. Social Welfare, Patra, 1992-99; dir. Ctr. Urodynamic Urology, Patra, 1992—; dir. urodynamic lab. Taunton and Somerset Hosp., 1992; tutor Inst. Profl. Edn., Patra, 1993; lectr. urology U. Patra, 1999—. Contbr. rsch. articles to Urologie Internat., Internat. Urogynecology Jour., Med. Rev. Hellenic Armed Forces. Med. soldier Greek Army, 1983-84. Recipient award for best oral presentation Balkan Congress Oncology, 1996. Mem. Internat. Continence Soc., European Assn. Urology, N.Y. Acad. Scis. Achievements include modification of Stamey needle suspension technique for female incontinence. Home: Papadiamadopoulou 38 St, 26225 Patra Achaia, Greece Office: Ctr for Urodynamic Urology, Vas Georgiou Sq 27, 26221 Patras Achaia, Greece

ATHANASSOPOULOS, KONSTANTIN, mathematician, educator; b. Athens, Greece, Mar. 5, 1961; s. George and Eirine (Zouganeli) A. Diplom, U. Athens, 1983, PhD, 1986. Fellow Nat. Fellowship Found., Athens, 1984-86; rsch. fellow Alexander von Humboldt Found., Berlin, 1988-90; vis. prof. U. Crete, Iraklion, Greece, 1991-93, lectr. math., 1993-97, asst. prof., 1997—. Contbr. rsch. articles to Math. Zeitschrift, Manuscripta Mathematica, Bull. London Math. Soc., others. Served with Greek Army Arty., 1987-88. Office: U Crete, Iraklion Crete, Greece 71409

ATHER, M. HAMMAD, urologist; b. Sindh, Pakistan, Feb. 17, 1966; Hussain Siddiqui and Masooda Hakim Ather; m. Tahmeena Hammad Siddiqui, Apr. 10, 1996; children: M. Faiz, M. Hasan. B Medicine B Surgery, Dow Med. Coll., Karachi, Pakistan, 1990. Cert. Pakistan Med. and Dental Coun. Resident Sindh Inst. Urology and Transplantation, Karachi, 1992-95; clin. observer Ctrl. Middlesex, London, 1995; sr. registrar Zia Uddin Med. U., Karachi, 1996; instr. Aga Khan U. Hosp., Karachi, 1996-98, sr. instr., 1998-99; asst. prof. Aga Khan U. Hosp., Karachi, 1999—; cons. Aga Khan U. Hosp. Author rsch. papers in field. Fellow Coll. Physicians and Surgeons, European Bd. Urology; mem. Pakistan Med. Assn., N.Y. Acad. Scis., European Urology Assn. Avocations: squash, reading scientific journals. Fax: 92 21 493 4294. E-mail: hammad.ather@aku.edu. Home: G-10 Block 16A, Gulistan-E-Jauhar, 74400 Karachi Sindh, Pakistan Office: Aga Khan U Hosp, Stadium Rd PO Box 3500, 74800 Karachi Sindh, Pakistan

ATHERTON, JUNE CHRISTINA, analytic psychologist, educator; b. N.Y.C.; Irish citizen; m. Alexander J. Arbuckle (div. 1963); children: Thomas, William, Nancy; m. Clarence Quinn-Berger (dec.); children: Jeffrey, Michael, Lisa; m. Harley Atherton, Feb. 26, 1999; stepchildren: Helen, James. BA in Biol. Sci., Sussex (Eng.) Tech. Coll., 1968; MA in Psychology, Southwestern U., 1972; PhD in Psychology, Brantridge U., 1992. Pvt. practice analytical psychotherapy, 1970—; dir. Jungian Sandtherapy Inst. Ireland, Dublin; vis. prof. St. U. St. Petersburg, Russia, 1993—; lectr., Russia, Estonia, Latvia. Contbr. articles to profl. jours. Mem. Labour Party, Dublin. Fellow Internat. Jungian Sandtherapy Assn. (internat. coord. 1996-97, internat. chairperson 1997-98); mem. Irish Assn. Counselling and Therapy (bd. dirs. 1985-95), United Arts Club Dublin, Lansdowne Club London, All Ireland Polo Club (Dublin chpt.). Roman Catholic. Office: Jungian Sandtherapy Inst, Ballyshane Clonmore, Clonmore Co Carlow Carlow, Ireland

ATHERTON, PHILIP GWYTHER, chemical engineer; b. Toowoomba, Queensland, Australia, Feb. 9, 1931; s. Samuel and Frances Marian (Millar) A.; m. Lynelle June Wilkins, May 3, 1954; children: Vicki Lynelle, Peter Samuel, Janine Anne. B in Applied Scis. with honors, U. Queensland, 1952, diplom in sugar tech., 1953. Sugar technologist Sugar Rsch. Inst., Mackay, Australia, 1954-55; rsch. engr. Australian Estates Co., Ayr, 1955-65; sr. mill technologist Bur. Sugar Expt. Stas., Bundaberg, Australia, 1965-71, chief mill technologist, leader agri-milling, 1971-93; mgr. cane and sugar quality Bur. Sugar Expt. Stas., Bundaberg, 1993-96, cons., 1996—; mem. faculty bd. engring. U. Queensland, 1988-90. Mem. com. Bundaberg Coll. Tech. and Further Edn., 1981—, U. Coll. Cen. Queensland, 1990—, Open Learning Ctr., Bundaberg, 1991; coun. Anglican Parish, Bundaberg, 1982-92. Fellow Instn. Engrs. (Australia, mem. emeritus, chem. coll. bd.), Royal Australian Chem. Inst., Australian Inst. Mgmt. (past br. chmn.); mem. So. Inst. Sugar Mill Engrs. (past chair), So. Inst. Sugar Chemists (past chmn.), Instn. Engrs. Local Group (founding chair), Australian Soc. Sugar Cane Technologists (hon. life, past pres.). Avocations: music, bush walking, bird watching, cabinet making. Office: 3 Thorburn St, Bundaberg 4670, Australia

ATHOTA, RAO RAMA, biochemistry educator; b. Tenali, India, Sept. 15, 1950; s. Raja Ratnam and Navomi (Mullapudi) A.; m. Padma Chilaka; children: Susmitha, Sam. BSc, Andhra U., 1971, MSc, 1973; PhD, U. Manitoba, 1989. Tech. asst. Andhra U., Visakhapatnam, India, 1973-77, lectr., 1977-90, reader, 1990—; doctoral fellow U. Manitoba, Winnipeg, Can., 1984-88, postdoctoral fellow, 1988-89; head biochemistry dept. Andhra U., Visakhapatnam, 1995-98, coord. A.U. Study Circle, 1993-94. Patentee in field. Exec. mem. OCRCD, 1990-97, sec., 1997—. Nat. Overseas scholarship Govt. of India, 1983. Mem. Indian Immunology Soc. (life, exec. mem.), Soc. of Bio. Chem. (life, sec.), Indian Acad. of Allergy (life). Baptist. Avocations: acting, training, social activites, tourism. Home: 111 Maripalem VUDA Colony, Visakhapatnam 530 003, India Office: Dept of Biochemistry, Andhra Univ, Visakhapatnam 530 003, India

ATIBA, JOSHUA OLAJIDE O., internist, pharmacologist, oncologist, educator; b. Enugu, Nigeria, July 6, 1956; s. Joseph Ojo and Abigail Olayo A.; m. Stella N. Mordi, June 26, 1981; children: April, Annamarie, Joseph. MD, U. Lagos, Nigeria, 1979; MHA, St. Mary's Coll., 1999. Diplomate Am. Bd. Internal Medicine, Am. Bd. Oncology. Rotating intern Ahmadu Bello U. Tchg. Hosp., Kaduna, Nigeria, 1979-80; resident in internal medicine Lagos U. Tchg. Hosp., 1981-83; fellow in med. oncology Cancer Control Agy., Vancouver, B.C., Can., 1988-90; fellow in clin. pharmacology Stanford U. Med. Ctr., Palo Alto, Calif., 1983-86; pvt. practice Irvine, Calif.; dir. clin. investigation U. Calif., Irvine, 1991-95; mem. U. Calif. Irvine Med. Ctr., Orange, North Bay Med. Ctr., Fairfield, Calif., Vaca Valley Hosp., Vacaville, Calif.; asst. prof. medicine, pharmacology U. Calif., Irvine. Med. dir. North Bay Hospice, Fairfield, Calif.; pres. Newport Oncology and Healthcare Found. Fellow Royal Coll. Physicians Can.; mem. ACP, AMA, Am. Fedn. for Clin. Rsch., Am. Soc. of Clin. Pharmacology and Therapeutics, Am. Soc. Clin. Oncology, Calif. Med. Assn., Solano County Med. Soc. (sec./treas., pres.-elect, pres.), Physician Peer Rev. Orgn. (dir.), KC (knight 1997). Republican. Roman Catholic. Office: North Bay Cancer Ctr 1860 Pennsylvania Ave Ste 230 Fairfield CA 94533-3550

ATILGAN, TIMUR FAIK, structural engineer; b. Adana, Turkey, July 15, 1943; came to U.S., 1972; s. Faik Ahmet and Sacide (Togman) A.; m. Gulsum Z. Kuzuoglu, Dec. 7, 1977 (div. 1980); m. Mirat Gurol, July 20, 1992. BS in Civil Engring., Aegean U., Izmir, Turkey, 1967; MS in Structural Engring., U. Md., 1979. Registered profl. engr., Va. Civil engr. NATO/Infrastructure Dept., Ankara, Turkey, 1970-72; structural engr. Bendix Field Engring., Columbia, Md., 1977-79; sr. design engr. Northrop Svcs. Inc., NASA, GSFC, Greenbelt, Md., 1979-82; sr. antenna engr. COMSAT Gen. Corp., Washington, 1982-83; sr. structural engr. OAO Corp., Greenbelt, 1983-84; engring. specialist PRC-Kentron, Inc., Hampton, Va., 1984-86; prin. engr. Fairchild Space Co., Greenbelt, 1986-91; sr. engr. Def. Systems, Inc., McLean, Va., 1991-94; sr. staff engr. Astro Space divsn. Lockheed Martin, Valley Forge, Pa., 1995-98; sr. prin. engr. Canada-France-Hawaii Telescope Corp., Kamuela, Hawaii, 1999-2000. Mem. AIAA (sr.), Turkish Architects, Engrs. and Treas. Scientists in Am., Am. Turkish Assn. (bd. dirs. Washington chpt. 1981-83). Avocations: music, reading, swimming, cinema.

ATIQUE, A. R., investment counselor, stockbroker; b. Madaripur, Bangladesh, Nov. 20, 1949; s. Fakaruddin Ahmed and Joynab Begum; m. Kamrun Nahar, Nov. 5, 1992; children: Antu, Muna, Tanvir, Diti. BA in Internat. Rels. with hons., Dhaka U., 1972, MSS, 1973, LLB, 1975. Cert. journalism Thompson Found., U.K.; bus. mgr. Iba Dhaka; security markets profl. UNDP Dhaka. Staff reporter, sub-editor Daily Ganakantha, Dhaka, 1972-75; self-employed bus. prof. Bariedhi Corp. Ltd., Dhaka; chmn., mng. dir. Capital Roots Ltd., Dhaka; dir. Corp. Securities Mgmt. Ltd., Dhaka; bd. dirs. Eagle Box and Cartoon Mfg. Co. Ltd., Dhaka; investment cons. Green Delta Ins., Dhaka; issue advisor Doel Group of Industries, Bengal Group, Dhaka, Zia Engring. Dhaka. Editor Fortnightly Share Bazar. Vice chmn. Lions Eye Hosp., Dhaka, 1993-94; sec. Bangladesh Lions Found., Dhaka, 1990-92; mem. Diabetic Assn., Dhaka, Red Crescent Soc., Dhaka, OISCA Bangladesh chpt., Islamia Eye Hosp. Mem. Bangladesh Indenting Agts. Assn. (sr. v.p. 1988-90), Nat. Press Club, Dhaka Stock Exch., Lions Club Dhaka West (dist. gov. dist. 315A2 1995-96, sec. PDG forum), Dhaka Club, Ltd., Dhammondi Recreation Club. Avocations: travel, reading, writing, music.

ATIYAH, SIR MICHAEL FRANCIS, mathematician; b. London, Apr. 22, 1929; s. Edward Selim and Jean (Levens) A.; m. Lily J. Brown, July 30, 1955; children: John, David, Robin. BA, Trinity Coll., Cambridge, 1952, PhD, 1955; DSc (hon.), Bonn, 1968, U. Durham, 1977, Trinity Coll., Dublin, 1983, U. Chgo., 1983, Cambridge (Eng.) U., 1984; others. Fellow Trinity Coll., Cambridge, 1954-58, 97—, hon. fellow, 1976-97, master, 1990-97; hon. prof. dept. math. U. Edinburgh, Scotland, 1997—; lectr., fellow Pembroke Coll., Cambridge, 1958-61, hon. fellow, 1983; Commonwealth Fund fellow Princeton, 1955-56, prof. Inst. Advanced Study, 1969-72; reader Oxford U., 1961-63, Savilian prof. geometry, fellow New Coll., 1963-69; rsch. prof., fellow St. Catherine's Coll., 1973-90, hon. fellow, 1991; dir. Isaac Newton Inst. for Math. Scis., Cambridge, Eng., 1990-96; chancellor Leicester U., 1995—; pres. Pugwash Confs. Sci. and World Affairs, 1997—. Author: K-Theory, 1966, Commutative Algebra, 1969; contbr. articles to math. jours., also collected works, 1987. Decorated knight; recipient Fields medal Internat. Congress Mathematicians, Moscow, 1966, DeMorgan medal London Math. Soc., 1980, Feltrinelli prize Accademia Nazionale dei Lincei, 1982, King Faisal Found. Internat. prize for sci., Saudi Arabia, 1987, Order of Merit, 1993. Fellow Royal Soc. (hon. 2000, pres. 1990-95, Royal medal 1969, Copley medal 1988), Royal Soc. Edinburgh (hon.), Royal Instn. (hon.), Royal Acad. Engring. (hon.), Acad. Med. Scis. (hon.), Faculty Actuaries (hon.); mem. Internat. Math. Union (exec. com. 1966-74), Math. Assn. (pres. 1981), London Math. Soc. (pres. 1975-77), Nat. Acad. Scis. U.S.A. (fgn.), Leopoldina Acad. (fgn.), Am. Acad. Arts and Scis. (fgn.), Swedish Royal Acad. (fgn.), Academie des Scis. (fgn.), Royal Irish Acad. (fgn.), Am. Philos. Soc. (fgn., Benjamin Franklin medal 1993), Third World Acad. Scis., Indian Nat. Sci. Acad. (fgn.), Chinese Acad. Sci. (hon. prof.), Ukrainian Acad. Scis. (fgn.), Venezuelan Acad. Sci., Australian Acad. Sci., Russian Acad. Sci., Georgian Acad. Sci., Order Andres Bello, Order Cedars of Lebanon. Office: James Clerk Maxwell Bldg, Dept Math/Stats Mayfield Rd, Edinburgh EH9 3JZ, Scotland

ATKARE, VILAS GULABRAO, business exeuctive, animal scientist, researcher; b. Borgaon Dori, India, Apr. 2, 1971; s. Gulabrao Tulshiramji and Ratnaprabha Gulabrao (Raut) A. BSc, Agrl. Coll., Amravati, India, 1994; MSc in Agr., Dr. P.D.K.V., Akola, INdia, 1996, PhD in Animal Husbandry/Livestock Prodn., 1999. Supr. (cotton seed oil mill) Dayal Industries, Akola, 1997—; rschr. Dayal Industry, 1997—. Contbr. articles to Indian Vet. Jour. Recipient Appreciation Letter, Supt. Horticulture Officer, Amravati, 1994, VANARI, 1996, cert. Dept. Animal Reprodn., Akola, 1996. Mem. Bhartiya Janata Party. Hindu. Avocations: gardening, reading, swimming. Home: care Vilas Tailor's, Main Rd, Mothi Umari, Akola 444 005, India Office: Dept Animal Husbandry/Dairy, Dr PDKV, Akola 444 104, India

ATKIN, EDITH, artist, poet; b. Washington, Nov. 12, 1921; d. Phillip and Sylvia Hirschel; m. Irwin Symour; children: Shron Welch, Joan Atkin Winewriter. Student, Md. Coll. Art & Design, 1973-79, Strayers Bus. Coll., Alice Kilbaum's Coll. Music. Group exbhns. at Lynn Kottler Galleries, N.Y.C., Gudowsky Gallery, Silver Spring, Md., Akademia Raymond Duncan, Paris, Ligoa Duncan, N.Y.C., Salon Surindependants, Paris; represented in numerous pvt. collections. Recipient award for creative achievement Holly Daly Herman Palm Beach Galleries, 1984. Mem. Nat. Tobacco Distbrs. Assn., Bnai Brith Women's Assn. Jewish.

ATKIN, LOUIS PHILLIP, business executive, screenwriter, media producer; b. Rochester, N.Y., Apr. 18, 1951; s. Morris and Etta (Korpeck) A.; m. Jodi Rosenshein. Student, Am. Coll. Paris, 1970-71; BA, George Washington U., 1973; MA, U. So. Calif., 1977. Asst. editor Alan Landsburg Prodns., L.A., 1977-78; pres. L. Atkins Sons Inc., Rochester, 1991—, Day for Night Prodns., Rochester, 1985—; Genesee Scrap & Tin Baling Corp., Inc.; pres. Atkin's Waste Materials, Inc., Rochester, 1990—, Tent City, 1990—, Pathways of Rochester, Inc., 1993—, Personal Pathways Inc., 1999—. Producer (with others), Jewish Community Fedn., documentary, 1982, Flights of Fancy, 1980; producer stage play Paradoxical Effects, 1987; writer, producer (play aired on Cable TV): Paradoxical Effects; writer, dir. Ceremony of Carols, 1974; scriptwriter, photographer, Posters of the First World War, 1983, exhibitor of posters, 1983. Interviewer Holocaust Com., Rochester, 1984; mem. Rochester Mus. and Sci. Ctr., 1985—, Meml. Art Gallery, GEVA Angels Repertory Contributors, 1985, Landmark Hist. Soc., Rochester, 1985, Nat. Trust for Hist. Preservation; mem. citizens' adv. com. Solid Waste for Monroe County; adv. bd. mem. Retail Rochester, 1995; bd. dirs., exec. com. Jewish Home of Rochester; bd. dirs. Jewish Cmty. Ctr. NEH grantee, 1979, LIFT grantee N.Y. State Coun. Arts, 1987. Mem. Dramtists Guild (assoc.), Young Pres.' Orgn., George Eastman Ho., U. So. Calif. Cinema Alumni Assn. Avocations: collecting World War I posters, photography, writing. Office: 80 Steel St Rochester NY 14606-2112

ATKINS, PETER WILLIAM, chemistry educator; b. Amersham, U.K., Aug. 10, 1940; s. William Henry and Ellen (Edwards) A.; m. Judith Ann Kearton, Aug. 22, 1964 (div. 1983); 1 child, Juliet Louise Tiffany; m. Susan Adele Greenfield, Mar. 30, 1991. BSc, U. Leicester, 1961, PhD, 1964; MA, U. Oxford, 1965; DSc, U. Utrecht, Netherlands, 1992. Harkness fellow UCLA, 1964-65; lectr. U. Oxford, U.K., 1965—; fellow, tutor Lincoln Coll., Oxford, 1965—, prof. chem., 1998—. Author: Molecular Quantum Mechanics, 3d edit., 1996, The Second Law, 1984, Molecules, 1987, Physical Chemistry, 6th edit., 1998, Inorganic Chemistry, 3rd edit., 1999, Quanta, 2d edit., 1991, Atoms, Electrons and Change, 1991, General Chemistry, 4th edit., 2000, The Elements of Physical Chemistry, 3d edit., 2000, Creation Revisited, 1992, The Periodic Kingdom, 1995, Concepts of Physical Chemistry, 1995, Chemical Principles, 1999. Recipient Meldola medal Chem. Soc., 1969, Nyholm medal, 1999. Office: Lincoln Coll, Oxford England OX1 3DR

ATKINS, RICHARD BART, film, television producer; b. Paterson, N.J., May 11, 1951; s. S. Stephen and Alice B. (Stein) A.; m. Joanna Pang; 1 child, David. AB in Polit. Sci., Princeton U., 1973. With Cadence Industries, N.Y.C., 1973-74; mgr. TV program devel. Benton & Bowles, N.Y.C., 1977-79, mgr. daytime programming, 1980; v.p. prodn. Telecom Entertainment,

N.Y.C., 1981-83; pres. Atkins Pictures Inc./A-Films, Florham Park, N.J., 1984—; programming and prodn. cons. Hearst Entertainment, Whittle Communications, D'Arcy Masius Benton & Bowles, King World Prodns., 1989-91, Quartier Latin, Paris, 1992, TeleVest, 1997-98. Prodr. (TV films) Murder in Coweta County, 1983, The Gift of Love: A Christmas Story, 1983, Trapped in Silence, 1986; exec. in charge prodn. About Sarah, 1998; prodr., writer (videocassette) Knowing Childbirth, 1985; prodr., writer (feature film) Forced March, 1989; producer: (feature film) Asunder, 2000; dir. (documentary) Mongolia, 1995; author: Method to the Madness: Hollywood Explained, 1975, (musical plays) Getting to Know You, 1994, 97, In the Mirror, 1995, 98, Independence, 1996. Mem. Friar's Club, Princeton Club. Jewish. Avocations: golf, computers. Home and Office: A-Films 149 Ridgedale Ave Florham Park NJ 07932-1708

ATKINS, WILLIAM AUSTIN, SR. (BILL ATKINS), former state legislator; b. Tate, Ga., Aug. 16, 1933; s. Austin and Gladys Atkins; children: Chip, Paige. BS in Pharmacy, Mercer U., 1954. Former owner Atkins Pharmacy, Smyrna, Ga.; mem. Ga. Ho. of Reps., 1982-94, mem. appropriations, regulated beverages and industry coms.; dir. Drugs and Narcotics Agy. State of Ga., 1994—; past chair Cobb County Joint House and Senate Legis. Delegation; past chmn. Ga. State Bd. Pharmacy. Leader, vocalist Bill Atkins Band. Mem. adminstrv. bd. 1st United Meth. Ch.; bd. dirs. Mercer U. Sch. Pharmacy; mem. governing bd. Brawner Hosp., 1993-96; mem. long-range planning bd. Smyrna Hosp., 1993-96. Recipient Appreciation plaque Ga. div. Am. Cancer Soc., 1991, Legislator of Yr. Friendship award Personal Care Homes of Ga., 1991, Liberty Bell award Cobb County Bar Assn., 1991, Pharmacist of Yr. in Ga. award, Phi Delta Chi, 1978, One of a Kind award Cobb Clean Commn., 1992, Meritorious Svc. award Mercer U., So. Sch. Pharmacy, 1992, others. Mem. Ga. Pharm. Assn. (award for dedication and svc. to profession of pharmacy 1986, Cmty. Svc. award 1997), Ga. Pharmacists Assn. (past bd. dirs.), Ga. Assn. Chiefs of Police, 7th Dist. Pharmacists Assn. (past pres.), Atlanta Metropol, Cobb C. of C., Moose (named Mr. Cobb County 1993). Home: 4719 Windsor Dr SW Smyrna GA 30082-4465

ATKINSON, BARBARA FRAJOLA, pathologist; b. Mpls., Oct. 19, 1942. BA, Coll. of Wooster, Ohio, 1964; MD, Thomas Jefferson U., 1974. Diplomate Am. Bd. Pathology in clin. and anatomic pathology and cytopathology; lic. physician, Pa. Intern in clin. and anatomic pathology U. Pa., Phila., 1974-75, resident, 1975-78, NIH pulmonary tng. fellow in pulmonary pathology, 1976-77, NIH rsch. fellow in pulmonary pathology, 1977-78; asst. instr. pathology dept. pathology U. Pa. Sch. Medicine, Phila., 1974-78, asst. prof. dept. pathology and lab. medicine, 1978-84, assoc. prof., 1985-87; mem. pathology grad. group U. Pa. Sch. Medicine, 1985-87; prof., chair dept. pathology and lab. medicine Med. Coll. of Pa. and Hahnemann U., Phila., 1987-94; sr. mem. Ctr. for Gerontol. Rsch. Med. Coll. Pa., Phila., 1994-96; Annenberg dean Med Coll Pa and Hahnemann Sch. Medicine MCP Hahnemann Sch. Med. Allegheny U. Health Scis., 1996-99; assoc. scientist Wistar Inst. Anatomy and Biology, 1983-87; mem. staff dept. pathology Hosp. of U. Pa., 1978-87, dir. cytopathology, 1978-87, med. program dir. Sch. Cytotech., 1978-86; chair dept. pathology and lab. medicine Med. Coll. Pa., 1987-94; dir. Delaware Valley Regional Lab. Svcs., Med. Coll. Hosps. and St. Christopher's Hosp. for Children, 1991-96; chair dept. pathology and lab. medicine Med. Coll. Pa. and Hahnemann U., 1994-96; trustee Am. Bd. Pathology, 1992-95, pres., 1998—. Mem. editl. bd. Lab. Investigation, 1988-94, Modern Pathology, 1990-94, Human Pathology, 1992-94; manuscript reviewer Cancer, Diagnostic Cytopathology, Modern Pathology, 1988-94; abstract rev. bd. U.S. and Can. Acad. Pathology, 1989-92; rev. panel Am. Soc. Clin. Pathology Abstract, 1991-96; contbr. articles to profl. jours., chpts. to books. Bd. dirs., treas. Laennec Soc. Phila., 1979-81; bd. dirs. Thyroid Soc. Phila., 1982-84; exec. com., bd. dirs. Med. Coll. Pa., 1994-96; bd. trustees Hahnemann U., 1994-96. Recipient Golden Apple Teaching award for excellent sci. teaching, 1994; grantee NIH, 1985-88, Takeda-Abbott R&D, 1989-94, NIA, 1991-94. Mem. AMA, Am. Soc. Cytology, Coll. Am. Assn. Exptl. Biologists, Am. Med. Women's Assn. (Janet M. Glasgow Meml. Scholarship 1974), Am. Soc. Clin. Pathologists (coun. on cytopathology 1989-94), Assn. Pathology Chmn. (v.p. 1992-94), Am. Assn. Cancer Rsch., Internat. Acad. Cytopathology, Phila. Pathology Soc., Pa. Assn. Pathologists, Coll. Physicians Phila., Phila. Cancer Rsch. Assn., Phila. County Med. Soc., Papanicolaou Soc. Cytopathology, Coun. of Deans of AAMC, Am. Bd. Pathology (Treasurer, 1998—).

ATKINSON, JEFF JOHN FREDERICK, law educator, lawyer, writer; b. Mpls., Nov. 12, 1948; S. Frederick Melville Atkinson and Patricia (Bauman) Atkinson Farnes; m. Janis Pressendo, Dec. 22, 1982; children: Tara, Abigail, Grant, Kelsey. BS, Northwestern U., 1974; JD summa cum laude, DePaul U., 1977. Bar: Ill. 1977, U.S. Ct. Appeals (7th cir.) 1977, U.S. Dist. Ct. (no. dist.) Ill. 1978, U.S. Supreme Ct 1982. Editor, reporter various Chgo. area newspapers and radio stas., 1967-71; assoc. Jenner & Block, Chgo., 1977-80; pvt. practice Evanston, Wilmette and Chgo., 1980—; vis. prof., instr. Loyola U. Law Sch., Chgo., 1982-91; adj. prof. DePaul U. Coll. Law, Chgo., 1991—; spl. govt. employee and pvt. sector advisor U.S. State Dept., 1997—; prof.-reporter Ill. Jud. Conf., 1989—. Author: Modern Child Custody Practice (2 vols.) 1986, 2d edit., 2000, Am. Bar Assn. Guide to Family Law; contbr. articles on criminal, family, constl. law, health law and ethics to various publs. Elected bd. v.p. Avoca Sch., 1999—. Mem. ABA (chmn. child custody com. 1983-84, 86-87, 89-92, mem. editl. bd. Family Advocate 1988-96, mem. publs. devel. bd. 1984-89, mem. task force on needs of children 1983-85, chmn. rsch. com. 1987-88, advisor to Nat. Conf. Commrs. on Uniform State Laws 1994—, Merit awards 1984, 86-94, 2000), ACLU (bd. dirs. Ill. div. 1972-74), Ill. Bar Assn., Am. Health Lawyers Assn., Northwestern U. Coll. Alumni Assn. (v.p. 1987-89). Home: 3514 Riverside Dr Wilmette IL 60091-1050

ATKINSON, MALCOLM, engineering scientist; b. Bridlington, Eng., Apr. 21, 1930; s. Frederick and Anne Laister (Fawcett) A.; m. Margaret Anne Capon, Mar. 27, 1958 (div. 1983); children: Colin, Robert, David. BSc in Engring., U. London, 1956. Lab. mechanic in physics City Univ., London, 1951-52; metallurgist Fairey Aviation, U.K., 1954-58; prin. rsch. officer British Steel, 1959-68; sr. lectr. U. Wollongong, Australia, 1969-88; dir. Atkinson Engring. Software, Australia, 1991-97; exec. com., panel convenor Brit. Deep Drawing Rsch. Group, 1962-68; cons. John Lysaght, Australia, 1969-74; assessor Australian Rsch. Coun., 1985—. Contbr. articles to profl. jours. Craftsman REME, 1948-50. Grantee U. Wollonong, Australian Rsch. Coun. Mem. Australian Inst. Metal (sec. Port Kembla br. 1972-74), Wollongong Chamber Musi Soc. (sec. 1975-85), Wollongong Fencing Club (pres. 1990—). Avocations: fencing, music, model engineer.

ATKINSON, NEIL NORMAN, mechanical engineer; b. Woburn, Mass., Oct. 18, 1952; s. Norman Joseph and Carol Gilman (Wildes) A.; m. Neringa Marija Perminas, Oct. 6, 1984; 1 child, Ariana Salome. BS in Physics, Lowell Tech. Inst., 1974; BSME, Southeastern Mass. U., 1980. Registered profl. engr., Maine, N.H., Vt., Mass., R.I., Conn., N.Y., N.J., Pa., Va., N.C., Ga. Designer Atkinson Engring. Inc., Mattapoisett, Mass., 1970-80, v.p., 1981-87, pres., 1988-91; sr. project engr. Thompson Cons. Inc., Marion, Mass., 1992—. Contbr. tech. articles to profl. publs. vol. instr. fitness YMCA, New Bedford, Mass., 1974-76; vol. instr. juggling Eistedfod Folk Festival, North Dartmouth, Mass., 1982-87. Mem. Am. Soc. for Heating, Refrigeration and Air Conditioning Engrs., Nat. Soc. Profl. Engrs. (Order of Engr. 1988), Nat. Fire Protection Assn., Construction Specifications Inst., Refrigeration Svc. Engrs. Soc. (v.p. Whaling City chpt. 1993-95, sec. 1995). Avocations: personal fitness, philosophy, juggling. Office: Thompson Cons Inc 525 Mill St Marion MA 02738-1552

ATKINSON, RICHARD CHATHAM, university president; b. Oak Park, Ill., Mar. 19, 1929; s. Herbert and Margaret (Feuerbach) A.; m. Rita Loyd, Aug. 20, 1952; 1 dau., Lynn Loyd. Ph.B., U. Chgo., 1948; Ph.D., Ind. U., 1955. Lectr. applied math. and stats. Stanford (Calif.) U., 1956-57, assoc. prof. psychology, 1961-64, prof. psychology, 1964-80; asst. prof. psychology UCLA, 1957-61; dep. dir. NSF, 1975-76, acting dir., 1976, dir., 1976-80; chancellor, prof. cognitive sci. U. Calif., San Diego, 1980-95; pres. U. Calif. Sys., 1995—. Author: (with Atkinson, Smith and Bem) Introduction to Psychology, 12th edit., 1996, Computer Assisted Instruction, 1969, An Introduction to Mathematical Learning Theory, 1965, Contemporary Developments in Mathematical Psychology, 1974, Mind and Behavior, 1980, Stevens' Handbook of Experimental Psychology, 1988. Served with AUS, 1954-56. Guggenheim fellow, 1967; fellow Ctr. for Advanced Study in Behavioral Scis., 1963; recipient Distinguished Research award Social Sci. Research Council, 1962. Fellow APA (Disting. Sci. Contbn. award 1977, Thorndike award 1980), AAAS (pres. 1989-90), Am. Psychol. Soc. (William James fellow 1985), Am. Acad. Arts and Scis.; mem. NAS, Soc. Exptl. Psychologists, Am. Philos. Soc., Nat. Acad. Edn., Inst. of Medicine, Cosmos Club (Washington), Explorer's Club (N.Y.C.). Home: 70 Rincon Rd Kensington CA 94707-1047 Office: U Calif Office Pres 1111 Franklin St Oakland CA 94607-5201

ATKINSON, ROBERT G., human development educator; b. Amityville, N.Y., Aug. 5, 1945; s. Leon B. and Helen (Waldorf) A.; m. Cynthia Deroche. BA, L.I. U., Southampton, 1967; MA, SUNY, Cooperstown, 1968, U. N.H., 1981; PhD, U. Pa., 1985. Researcher Hudson R. Sloop Restoration, Cold Spring, N.Y., 1969-71; instr. L.I. U., 1971, Oceanics Sch., 1971, Furman U., Greenville, S.C., 1974-75, U. N.H., Durham, 1980-81; teaching fellow Harvard U., Cambridge, Mass., 1981-82; clin. researcher U. Chgo., 1985-87; assoc. prof. human devel. U. So. Maine, Gorham, 1987—, dir. Ctr. for Study Lives,, 1988—, dir. Sea Program, 1995—; affiliate faculty Landegg Acad., 2000—. Author: The Gift of Stories: Practical and Spiritual Applications of Autobiography, Life Stories and Personal Mythmaking, 1995, The Life Story Interview, 1998; co-author: (with Offer, Ostrey and Howard) The Teenage World: Adolescents' Self Image in Ten Countries, 1987; editor: Songs of the Open Road: The Poetry of Folk-Rock and Journey of the Hero, 1974, Celebrating the Lives of Students, 1990; prodr. video: Gabriel Woman, Passamaquaddy Basketmakers, 1998; contbr. over 12 articles to jours. Mem. Assn. for Humanistic Psychology, Am. Society on Aging, Oral History Assn. Baha'i Faith. Office: U So Maine 400 Bailey Hall Gorham ME 04038

ATKINSON, ROWAN SEBASTIAN, actor, writer; b. Jan. 6, 1955; s. Eric and Ella A.; m. Sunetra Sastry, 1990. Stage appearances include Beyond a Joke, 1978, The Nerd, 1985, The New Revue, 1986, The Sneeze, 1988; TV appearances include Not the Nine O'Clock News, 1979-82, Blackadder, 1983, Blackadder II, 1985, Blackadder The Third, 1987, Blackadder Goes Forth, 1989, Mr. Bean, The Return of Mr. Bean, The Curse of Mr. Bean, 1990-91, Mr. Bean Goes to Town, 1991, The Trouble With Mr. Bean, 1992, Mr. Bean Rides Again, 1992, Merry Christmas Mr. Bean, 1992, Mr. Bean in Room 426, 1993, Rowan Atkinson on Location in Boston, 1993, Mind The Baby Mr. Bean, 1994, Do-It-Yourself Mr. Bean, 1994, Back to School Mr. Bean, 1994, Full Throttle, 1994, The Thin Blue Line-Series One & Two, 1995-96; films include Never Say Never Again, 1989, The Tall Guy, 1989, The Appointments of Dennis Jennings, 1989, The Witches, 1990, Hot Shots - Part Deux, 1993, Four Weddings and a Funeral, 1994, Bean, The Ultimate Disaster Movie, 1997, Blackadder Back & Forth, 1999. Avocations: motor cars, motor sports. Office: c/o PBJ Mgmt Ltd, 7 Soho St, London W1D 3DQ, England

ATLAN, HENRI, biologist, philosopher; b. Blida, Algeria, Dec. 27, 1931; s. Benjamin and Anna (Chiche) A.; m. Liliane (div. 1977); children: Mireille, Michael; m. Bela Rachel Kohn, July 7, 1977. MD, U. Paris, 1958, PhD, 1973. Prof. biophysics Med. Sch., Rouen, France, 1966-73, Univ. Hosp. Broussais-Hotel Dieu, Paris, 1973—; rsch. assoc. NASA, Moffett Field, Calif., 1966-68; vis. prof. Weizmann Inst., Rehovot, Israel, 1970-73; prof., head biophysics dept. Hadassah Univ. Hosp., Jerusalem, 1975-96, scholar in residence in philos. and ethics of biol., 1992—, dir. Human Biology Rsch. Ctr., 1992—; head biophysics & nuclear medicine Hotel Dieu Hosp., Paris, 1991-97; dir. rsch. Ecole des Hautes Etudes en Scis. Sociales (EHESS), Paris, 1995—. Author: Theory of Self-Organization and Complex Systems, 1972, 79, 82, 92, Philosophy of Knowledge based on Intercritique of Science and Myth, 1986, 91, 99, Questions of Life Between Science and Opinion, 1994; co-author: Magnetic Resonance Imaging: Basis for Interpretation, 1988; co-editor: Theories of Immune Networks, 1989; contbr. articles to profl. jours. Mem. French Nat. Ethics Com., N.Y. Acad. Sci., European Acad. Arts., Sci. and Humanities. Jewish. Avocation: Jewish studies. Office: EHESS, 54 Blvd Raspail, 75006 Paris France also: Human Biology Rsch Ctr, Hadassah Univ Hosp Ein Karem, Jerusalem Israel

ATLAS, JEFFREY A., psychologist, educator; b. N.Y.C.; m. Anne Page Tiffany. BA, U. Chgo., 1978; PhD, Columbia U., 1984. Lic. psychologist, N.Y. Adj. instr. Marymount Manhattan Coll., N.Y.C., 1980-83; adj. assoc prof. Columbia U. Tchrs. Coll., N.Y.C., 1984-95; assoc. clin. prof. psychiatry Albert Einstein Coll. Medicine, Bronx, N.Y., 1994—; assoc. psychologist Bronx Children's Psychiat. Ctr., 1988—; affil. clin. prof. St. John's U., Queens, N.Y., 1993-94; adj. assoc. prof. SUNY, Purchase, 1994; mem. trauma policy project work group N.Y. State Office Mental Health, Albany, 1996-98. Contbr. numerous articles to profl. publs., including Psychol. Reports, New Ideas in Psychology; editor spl. issue Psychiat. Quarterly, 1994. Univ. scholar U. Chgo., 1973. Mem. N.Y. State Psychol. Assn. (disaster crisis response mem. 1992), Phi Beta Kappa, Sigma Xi, Kappa Delta Pi. Avocations: producing videos, ceramics, guitar, skiing, architectural design. Office: Bronx Childrens Hosp Albert Einstein Coll Med 1000 Waters Pl Bronx NY 10461-2701

ATLAS, SCOTT WILLIAM, radiologist; b. Chgo., July 5, 1955; m. Janice M. Rossi; children: Joseph, Ben. BS in Biology, U. Ill., 1977; MD, U. Chgo., 1981. Diplomate Am. Bd. Radiology. Resident, chief resident in radiology Northwestern U. Med. Ctr., Chgo., 1982-85; fellow in neuroradiology Hosp. U. Pa., Phila., 1985-87; asst. prof. radiology U. Calif., San Francisco, 1987-88; from asst. prof. to assoc. prof. radiology Hosp. U. Pa., Phila., 1988-95; chief neuroradiology, prof. radiology Oreg. Health Scis. Ctr., N.Y.C., 1995-96, Mt. Sinai Sch. Medicine, Portland, 1996-98, Stanford (Calif.) U. Sch. Medicine, 1998—; mem. adv. bd. GE Med. Systems. Editor: MRI of the Brain and Spine, 1991, 2d edit., 1996. Mem. Am. Soc. Neuroradiology, Am. Coll. Radiology. Office: Stanford U Med Ctr 300 Pasteur Dr Rm S047 Stanford CA 94305-5105

ATLASS, THEODORE BRUCE, lawyer, educator; b. Chgo., June 2, 1951; s. Ralph Louis Atlass and Opal Jeanne Collins. BSBA, U. Denver, 1972; JD, DePaul U., 1975; LLM, U. Miami, Coral Gables, Fla., 1976. Bar: Colo. 1975, U.S. Tax Ct. 1976, U.S. Supreme Ct. 1982. Shareholder Theodore B. Atlass, P.C., Denver, 1976-83, Atlass Profl. Corp., Denver, 1986—; ptnr. Welborn, Dufford, Brown & Tooley, Denver, 1983-85; lectr. Colo. Soc. CPAs, 1977—, Coll. Law U. Denver, 1976—. Chmn. Advanced Estate Planning Symposium U. Denver, 1982—; bd. dirs. St. Joseph Hosp. Found., Denver, 1982-97, Colo. Ballet, Denver, 1985-92. Fellow Am. Coll. Tax Counsel, Am. Coll. Trust & Estate Counsel (Colo. state chair 1996—; fiduciary income tax com. chair 1997-2000); mem. Denver Estate Planning Coun. (pres. 1991-92), Denver Tax Assn. (pres. 1985), Centennial Estate Planning Coun. (pres. 1993-94). Republican. Presbyterian. Office: Atlass Profl Corp Ste 100 3665 Cherry Creek North Dr Denver CO 80209-3712

ATLAY, ROBERT DAVID, gynecologist, administrator; b. Liverpool, Eng., June 26, 1936; s. Robert Henry and Sarah (Griffiths) A.; m. Jean Cole, Feb. 11, 1967; children: Josephine Sarah, Victoria Jane. MB ChB, U. Liverpool, 1960. Clin. lectr. dept. ob.-gyn. U. Liverpool, 1970—; chmn. bd. faculty medicine U. Liverpool, Liverpool, 1995-96; med. dir. Liverpool Ob-Gyn. Trust, 1990-99; examiner in ob-gyn. for med. degrees at univs. Liverpool, Manchester, Glasgow, Birmingham, Cambridge, London, W.I., Amman, Jordan; postgrad. examiner Royal Australian Coll. Ob-Gyn.; mem. Eng. Nat. Bd. for Nursing, Midwifery and Health Vis., 1988-93; mem. nat. transplant panel Dept. Health, London, 1983—, mem. maternity svc. adv. com., 1982-85. Contbr. chpts. to books, articles to profl. jours. Mem. bd. govs. Wirral Grammar Sch., Merseyside, 1992-2000. Fellow Royal Coll. Ob-gyn. (hon. sec. Royal Coll. 1980-87, chmn. continuing med. edn. com. 1992-95, chmn. European com. 1995-98, postgrad. examiner), Royal Australian Coll. and Royal Coll. Ob-Gyn. (Lockyer traveling fellow 1977); mem. Brit. Med. Assn. (various coms.), Waterloo Rugby Football Club (pres. 1981-83), Liverpool Artists Club (pres. 1998-99). Avocations: rugby football, golf, traditional jazz, European travel. Home: 27 Merrilocks Rd, Blundellsands, Liverpool L23 6UL, England Office: Liverpool Women's Hosp, Crown St, Liverpool England

ATLEE, JOHN LIGHT, physician; b. Lancaster, Pa., Feb. 22, 1941; s. John Light Jr. and Ann (Stevens) A.; m. Barbara Sheaffer, June 20, 1964 (dec. Apr. 14, 1967); m. Barbara Sanford, Feb. 3, 1968; children: Sarah Sanford, John Light. BA, Franklin & Marshall Coll., 1963; MD, Temple U., 1967, MS in Pharmacology, 1971. Diplomate Am. Bd. Anesthesiology. Intern Germantown Hosp., Phila., 1967-68; resident in anesthesiology Temple U. Hosp., Phila., 1968-70; postdoctoral rsch. fellow pharmacology Temple U. Grad. Sch. Medicine, 1970-71; staff anesthesiologist U.S. Naval Hosp, Bethesda, Md., 1971-73; asst. prof. anesthesiology U. Wis., Madison, 1973-78, assoc. prof. anesthesiology, 1978-85, prof. anesthesiology, 1985-88; prof. anesthesiology Med. Coll. Wis., Milw., 1988—; mem. editl. bd., referee, cons. peer rev. jours. Anesthesia & Analgesia, Am. Jour. of Physiology, Anesthesiology, Med. and Biol. Engring. and Computing, Jour. of Cardiothoracic and Vascular Anesthesia; chmn., CEO Cardiac Control Techs.; cons. Medtronic Inc., Neurex, Mallinckrodt, Wyeth-Ayerst Labs. Author: Perioperative Cardiac Arrhythmias, 1985, 2d edit., 1990, Arrhythmias and Pacemakers, 1996; editor: Perioperative Management of Pacemaker Patients, 1992, Complications in Anesthesia, 1999; contbr. articles to profl. jours.; patentee in field. Lt. comdr. USN, 1971-73. NIH grantee, 1978—. Fellow Am. Coll. Cardiology and Anesthesiology; mem. Am. Soc. Anesthesiologists, Assn. Univ. Anesthesiologists, N.Am. Soc. Pacing and Electrophysiology, Am. Soc. Exptl. Pharmacology and Therapeutics, Soc. Register Assn., Sigma Xi. Republican. Episcopalian. Achievements include development of a new transesophageal stimulation and recording technology for use in anesthesiology, cardiology, emergency medicine and intensive care. Home: N71w29436 Tamron Ln Hartland WI 53029-9249 Office: Froedert Meml Luth Hosp E Med Coll Wis 9200 W Wisconsin Ave Milwaukee WI 53226-3522

ATLURI, VIJAYALAKSHMI, computer science educator; b. Vijayawada, India, May 31, 1956; came to U.S., 1990; d. Venkteswara Rao and Sesharatnam Atluri; m. Jayadev Vellanki, July 2, 1978; children: Priyathama, Raghava. B Tech., Jawaharlal Nehru Tech. U., Kakinada, India, 1977; M in Tech., Indian Inst. Tech., Kharagpwr, India, 1979; PhD, George Mason U., 1994. Lectr. Nagarjuna U., India, 1980-82, 83-85, asst. prof., 1985-90; lectr. Andhara U., India, 1982-83; rsch. asst. George Mason U., Fairfax, Va., 1990-94; asst. prof. Rutgers U., Newark, N.J., 1994—. Author: Multilevel Secure Transaction Processing, 1999; contbr. articles to profl. jours. Recipient Career award NSF, 1996, Rsch. award Rutgers U., 1999; grantee Nat. Security Agency, 1996. Mem. IEEE Computer Soc., Assn. Computing Machinery, Internat. Fedn. for Info. Processing. E-mail: atluri@andromeda.rutgers.edu. Office: Rutgers Univ 180 University Ave Newark NJ 07102-1897

ATMOYUWONO, SISWADI, language institute director; b. Madiun, East Java, Indonesia, July 4, 1936; s. Hamzah and Aisiah (Ilham) A.; m. Suprihati Hardjosoetomo, Sept. 29, 1963; children: Nugrahani Widyasih, Dwikarti Widyastuti, Sigit Pinardi Widodo. BSc in Tchr. Tng., Bahasa Inggeris, Banjarmasin, Indonesia, 1961; grad., Tchr. Tng., Cirebon/Bandung, 1985; Doktorandus, U. Gunung Jati, 1985. Cert. translator. Tchr. Agrl. Vocat. Sch., Banjarmasin, 1956-63; dir. Agrl. Mechanization Project, Pontianak/Salatiga, Indonesia, 1964-75; tchr. English LIA Lang. Inst./LIA Found., Jakarta, Indonesia, 1975-82, dept. head, mgr., 1982-91, dep. dir., 1991-93, dir., 1993-96; chmn. Sub-consortium of English Directorate of Mass Edn., Ministry Edn., Jakarta, 1987—. Joint book writer: General English Basic 1-4, Intermediate 1-4, Advanced 1-4, 1994-96; scriptwriter A/AV prodn. book programs, free programs, exposure programs; Javanese puppeteer Javanese Shadow Play. Chmn. Employee's Coops., Jakarta, 1990-96; chmn. bd. commrs. P.T. Siwibakti Darma; dir., founder P.T. Cipta Wiyata Sarana Producing Teaching Aids. Recipient Tut Wuri Handayani award Internat. Mgmt. Indonesia Enterprise, Jakarta, 1996. Mem. Bali Permai, Serasi Self-Defence Club. Home: Kav Polri D-XII/1136, Jelambar, Jakarta 11460, Indonesia Office: LIA Lang Inst/LIA Found, Jalan Pramuka Kav 30, Jakarta 13120, Indonesia

ATREJA, PREM PARKASH, dairy scientist, researcher, educator; b. Panipat, India, Apr. 2, 1949; s. Bhoja Ram and Chanderawal Bai (Sukhija) A.; m. Chanchal Kumari Nagpal, Apr. 13, 1980; 1 child, Deepak. MSc in Dairying, Nat. Dairy Rsch. Inst., Karnal, India, 1972; spl. student, dairy sci., U. Wis., 1976; diploma, Royal Agr. & Vet. U., Copenhagan, 1982; PhD in Animal Nutrition, Nat. Dairy Rsch. Inst., 1983. Jr. scientist Nat. Dairy Rsch. Inst., 1977-83, sr. scientist, 1983-86, 1986—; internat. course coord., Nat. Dairy Rsch. Inst., 1994-95. Inventor in field. Food & Agrl. Orgn. fellow, 1975-76; Danida fellow Govt. Denmark, 1982. Mem. Animal Nutrition Soc. India (life), Indian Dairy Assn. (life). Hindu. Avocations: spirituality, light music, social work, painting, singing. Home: 131 Sector 14 Urban Estate, Karnal 132001, India Office: National Dairy Rsch Inst, Karnal, Haryana 132001, India

ATSADA, CHAIYANAM, diplomat. Rep. to UN Govt. of Thailand, N.Y.C., 1997—. Office: Permanent Mission Thailand to UN 351 E 52nd St New York NY 10022-6302

ATSARKIN, VADIM ALEKSANDROVICH, physicist, educator; b. Moscow, June 13, 1936; s. ALeksandr Nikolaevich and Adelaide Solomonovna (Posvyanskaya) A.; m. Viktorova Irina Ivanovna; 1 child, Natalia. Grad., Moscow State Univ., 1959; cand. of sci., Inst. Radio Engring. & Elec., 1965; D of sci., IRE RAS, Moscow, 1971. Jr. scientist IRE RAS, Moscow, 1959-72, sr. scientist, 1972-86, head of lab., 1986—; prof. physics IRERAS, Moscow, 1989—, Tech. U. Radio Engring., Elec. & Automatics, 1991—; chmn. Moscow Seminar on Magnetic Resonance, 1981—, chmn. program com. Russian Sch. Magnetic Resonance, 1981—. Author: Dynamic Polarization of Nuclei in Non-Conducting Solids, 1980; contbr. numerous articles to profl. jours. Recipient rsch. grants. Mem. Internat. EPR Soc., Ampere Group (com. European sci. 1998—). Avocation: poetry. Home: 23 Baykalskaya Str Apt 36, 107207 Moscow Russia Office: Inst Radio Engring & Elec, 11 Mokhovaya Str, 103907 Moscow Russia

ATTA, ELSAYED KHALIL, agriculture educator; b. Roseta, Behaira, Egypt, Apr. 26, 1947; s. Khalil Ibrahim and Fekra Abd Elazíz (Elgamil) A.; m. Sanaa Abd Elhamid Batisha, Aug. 2, 1977; children: Aymen, Alaa, Ahmed, Omnia. BSc in Agriculture, Alexandria U. Egypt, 1966, MSc in Agriculture, 1971, PhD in Agriculture, 1977. Asst. rschr. Skha Rsch. Ctr., Kafer Elshieku, Egypt, 1967-71; asst. rschr. Alexandria Salinity Lab., 1971-77, rschr., 1977; lectr. agriculture Suez Canal U., Ismailia, Egypt, 1977-82, assoc. prof., 1982-87, prof., 1987—; cons. Environ. Rsch. Ctr., Ismailia, 1990—. Office: Suez Canal U, Faculty of Agriculture, Ismailia 41522, Egypt

ATTALI, BERNARD, bank executive; b. Algiers, Nov. 1, 1943; s. Simon Attali and Fernande Abecassis; m. Hélène Scebat, 1974; 1 child. Student, Faculty of Law, Paris, Inst. d'Etudes Politech., Paris, Ecole Nat. d'Admin. Auditor Cour des Comptes, 1968; adviser, 1974; on secondment Comm. Gen. du Plan d'Equipement et Productivity, 1972-74; del. Aménagement du Terr. Action Regionale, Datar, 1974-80; fin. dir. Soc. Club Mediterranean, 1980-81; pres. regional com. EEC, 1981-84; pres. Groupe des Assurances Nationales, Gan, 1984-86, Banque pour l'Industrie Française, 1984-86, Euroberlin, 1988; chmn. supervisory bd. Banque Arjil, Paris, 1993—; vice chmn. global investment banking Deutsche Bank, Frankfurt, Germany, 1999—; pres. Union de transports aériens, 1990, Assn. des Transporteurs Aériens Européens, 1991, Adminstrn. Aérospatiale, 1989—, Air Inter, 1990—; chief adviser revenue ct. Ordre Nat. du Mérite. Author: Les Guerres du Ciel, 1994. Chevalier Legion d'honneur. Office: Deutsche Bank AG, Taunusanlage 12, 60262 Frankfurt Germany*

ATTARIAN, HOUSHANG, rheumatologist; b. Tehran, Iran, May 16, 1944; s. Ismail and Khavar Attarian; m. Dania Avak Babayan, Mar. 15, 1978; children: Rodgoon, Roxanne. MD, Melli U., Tehran, 1974. Intern Tehran U., 1981; rheumatologist Shariati Hosp., Tehran, 1981-84; rheumatologist in pvt. practice Tehran, 1984—; cons. rheumatologist Foolad Nat. Ctr., Tehran, 1996-98. Mem. Rheumatology Soc. Avocation: tennis. E-mail: rodgoon@hotmail.com. Home: 6th Apt No 10 3d West Mehr, Mirzapor Ave Shariati St, Tehran 19336, Iran Office: 24 Shahid Hosseini Ave, Pvt Clinic Sepaah St, Tehran 16199, Iran

ATTEBURY, WILLIAM HUGH, construction company executive; b. Amarillo, Tex., Jan. 8, 1929; s. Arnold Gentry and Lula Vivian (Dunn) A.; m. Joyce B. Kallin, June 7, 1951; children: Julie Anne, William Arnold, Nancy Ellen, Elizabeth Grace, Edward Anton. BA, Okla. U., 1951. V.p. Attebury Elevators, Inc., Amarillo, 1954—; pres. Bison Devel. Co., 1960—,

A & S Steel Bldgs. Inc., Houston, 1962-69; CEO, U.S. I. A&S, 1969-72, El Poso Oil Co., Amarillo, 1969—, Bison Chem. Co., Port Neches, Tex., 1969-74; ptnr. Tex. Beef Prodrs. Group, 1978—; bd. dirs. Western Data, Inc., 1st Nat. Bank Am. Mem. adv. bd. Salvation Army, 1973-77; mem. bd. mgrs. Amarillo Hosp. Dist., 1978-79; bd. dirs. Amarillo Children's Home, 1978-82, Village of Hope, 1972-74; chmn. bd. dirs. Harrington Cancer Ctr.; elder Westminster Presbyn. Ch., 1970—. Served with USNR, 1951-54, Korea. Mem. Panhandle Prodrs. and Royalty Owners, Tex. Cattle Feeders Assn. (bd. dirs. 1981-83, 90-94), Nat. Cattleman's Assn. (bd. dirs. 1990-94), Amarillo Club, Amarillo Country Club. Home: 3202 S Lipscomb St Amarillo TX 79109-3536 Office: PO Box 7446 Amarillo TX 79114-7446

ATTENBOROUGH, KEITH, physics educator; b. Nottingham, Eng., Jan. 21, 1944; s. Frank Henry and Beatrice Joyce (Houghton-Evans) A.; m. Jean Cossar Bain, Dec. 9, 1977; children: David Balfour, Lindsay Dunlop. BS in Physics with honors, Univ. Coll., London, 1965; PhD, U. Leeds, 1969. Chartered engr. Rsch. asst. Univ. Coll. Sch. Architecture, London, 1968-69; rsch. fellow U. Liverpool, Eng., 1969-70; lectr. Open U., Milton Keynes, Eng., 1970-76, sr. lectr., 1976-86, reader in acoustics, 1986-92, prof. acoustics, 1992-99; prof., head Sch. Engring. U. Hull, 1999—; vis. prof. U. Miss., 1982—, U. Leuven, Belgium, 1982-91; chief examiner Inst. Acoustics Dipl., 1997—. Editor-in-chief Applied Acoustics Jour., Acta Acustica; contbr. articles to profl. jours. Fellow Inst. Acoustics, Acoustical Soc. Am. Avocations: flute, choral singing, walking. Home: 9 Crofters Dr, Cottingham HU16 4SD, England Office: Hull U Sch Engring, Hull HU6 7RX, England

ATTENBOROUGH, BARON RICHARD SAMUEL, actor, producer, director, goodwill ambassador; b. Cambridge, England, Aug. 29, 1923; s. Frederick Attenborough; m. Sheila Beryl Grant Sim; 3 children. Leverhulme scholar to Royal Acad. Dramatic Art, 1941 (Bancroft Medal); DLitt (hon.), U. Leicester, 1970, U. Kent, 1981, U. Sussex, 1987; DCL (hon.), U. Newcastle, 1974; LLD (hon.), Dickinson Coll., 1983; DLit (hon.), Am. Internat. U., 1994; DLitt (hon.), Cape Town, 2000. Fleming Meml. lectr. R.T.S., 1989; Cameron Mackintosh vis. prof. of theatre Oxford U., 1996; pro-chancellor U. Sussex, 1970-98, chancellor 1998—. First stage appearance as Richard Miller in Ah, Wilderness, Intimate Theatre, Palmers Green, 1941; Ralph Berger in Awake and Sing, Arts (West End debut), 1942; The Little Foxes, Piccadilly, 1942; Brighton Rock, Garrick, 1943. Joined RAF 1943; seconded to RAF Film Unit for Journey Together, 1944; demobilised, 1946. Returned to stage in The Way Back (Home of the Brave), Westminster, 1949; To Dorothy a Son, Savoy, 1950, Garrick, 1951; Sweet Madness, Vaudeville, 1952; The Mousetrap, Ambassadors, 1952-54; Double Image, Savoy, 1956-57, St. James's, 1957; The Rape of the Belt, Piccadilly, 1957-58; film appearances: In Which We Serve (screen debut), 1942; School for Secrets, The Man Within, Dancing With Crime, Brighton Rock, London Belongs to Me, The Guinea Pig, The Lost People, Boys in Brown, Morning Departure, Hell is Sold Out, The Magic Box, Gift Horse, Father's Doing Fine, Eight O'Clock Walk, The Ship That Died of Shame, Private's Progress, The Baby and the Battleship, Brothers in Law, The Scamp, Dunkirk, The Man Upstairs, Sea of Sand, Danger Within, I'm All Right Jack, Jet Storm, SOS Pacific; The Angry Silence (also co-prod.), 1959; The League of Gentlemen, 1960; Only Two Can Play, All Night Long, 1961; The Dock Brief, The Great Escape, 1962; Seance On a Wet Afternoon (also prod., Best Actor, San Sebastian Film Festival and Brit. Film Acad.), The Third Secret, 1963; Guns at Batasi (Best Actor, Brit. Film Acad.), 1964; The Flight of the Phoenix, 1965; The Sand Pebbles (Hollywood Golden Globe), 1966; Dr. Dolittle (Hollywood Golden Globe), The Bliss of Mrs. Blossom, 1967; Only When I Larf, 1968; The Last Grenade, A Severed Head, David Copperfield, Loot, 1969; 10 Rillington Place, 1970; And Then There Were None, Rosebud, Brannigan, Conduct Unbecoming, 1974; The Chess Players, 1977; The Human Factor, 1979, Jurassic Park, 1992, Miracle on 34th St., 1994, The Lost World, 1996, Elizabeth, 1997; producer: Whistle Down the Wind, 1961; The L-Shaped Room, 1962; producer, dir.: Oh! What a Lovely War (16 Internat. Awards including Hollywood Golden Globe and BAFTA UN Award), 1968; dir.: Young Winston (Hollywood Golden Globe), 1972; A Bridge Too Far (Evening News Best Drama Award), 1976; Magic, 1978; producer, dir.: Gandhi (8 Oscars, 5 Brit. Acad. TV and Film Artists Awards, 5 Hollywood Golden Globes, Dirs.' Guild of Am. Award for Outstanding Directorial Achievement), 1980-81, Cry Freedom (Berlinale Kamera, BFI award tech. achievement), 1987, Chaplin, 1992, Shadowlands, 1992 (Alexander Korda award for outstanding Brit. film of yr., BAFTA), In Love and War, 1997, Grey Owl, 1998; publications: In Search of Gandhi, 1982, Richard Attenborough's A Chorus Line (with Diana Carter), 1986, Cry Freedom, A Pictorial Record, 1987; actor: Light Keeps Me Company (Europe), 2000, TheRailway Children, 2000 (TV), Joseph and the Amazing Technicolor Dreamcoat, 2000. Goodwill amb. UNICEF, 1987—; mem. Brit. Actors' Equity Assoc. Council, 1949-73, Cinematograph Films Council, 1967-73, Arts Council of Great Britain, 1970-73; formed Beaver Films with Bryan Forbes, 1959, Allied Film Makers, 1960; dir. Chelsea Football Club, 1969-82, life v.p., 1993—; dir. Young Vic, 1974-84; chmn. The Actor's Charitable Trust, 1956-88, pres., 1988—; chmn. European Script Fund, 1988-96, hon. pres., 1996—, Combined Theatrical Charities Appeals Council, 1964-88, pres., 1988—; chmn. Brit. Acad. TV and Film Artists (v.p. from 1971-94, chmn. trustees, 1970—), 1969-70, Royal Acad. Dramatic Art, mem. council 1963—, chmn., 1972—, Capital Radio, 1972-92, life pres., 1992—, Help a London Child, 1975—; trustee King George V Fund for Actors and Actresses, 1973—; chmn. U.K. Trustees Waterford-Kamhlaba Sch., Swaziland (gov. 1987—), 1976—, Duke of York's Theatre, 1979-92, Brit. Film Inst., 1981-92, Goldcrest Films & TV, 1982-87, Com. of Inquiry into the Arts and Disabled People, 1983-85, Channel Four TV (dep. chmn. 1980-86), 1987-92, Brit. Screen Adv. Council, 1987—; Gov. Nat. Film Sch., 1970-81, 96, hon. pres. 96; pres. Muscular Dystrophy Group of Great Britain (v.p. 1962-71), 1971-96, hon. pres. 1996—; pres. The Gandhi Found., 1983—, Brighton Festival, 1984-95, Brit. Film Yr., 1984-86; trustee Tate Gallery, 1976-82, 94-96, Tate Found., 1986—, Found. Sport and Arts, 1991—; pres. Arts for Health, 1989—, Gardner Centre Arts, Sussex U., 1990—; gov. Motability, 1977—; patron Kingsley Hall Community Ctr., 1982—; R.A. Centre Disability & Arts, Leicester, 1990—. Decorated Commander Brit. Empire, 1967, Knighted 1976; recipient Evening Std. Film award, 40 yrs. svc. to Brit. Cinema, 1983, Praemium Imperiale award, 1998, Martin Luther King Jr. Peace Prize, 1983, Padma Bhushan, India, 1983, award of merit for humanitarianism in film making, European Film awards, 1988, Shakespeare prize Outstanding Contbn. European culture, 1992; named Commandeur, Ordre des Arts et des Lettres, France, 1985; Chevalier, Order de la Legion d'Honneur, France, 1988; named Freeman of City of Leicester, 1990; named fellow Kings Coll. London, 1993; named Baron, Life Peer of Long Borough of Richmond upon Thames, 1993; recipient hon. fellowship U. Wales, Bangor, 1997, Manchester Poly., 1994, Kings Coll., 1993. Fellow BAFTA, Brit. Film Inst.; mem. Garrick Club, Beefsteak Club. Avocations: collecting paintings and sculpture, listening to music, watching football. Home: Old Friars, Richmond Green Surrey, England Office: Richard Attenborough Prodns, Beaver Lodge, Richmond Surrey TW9 1NQ, England*

ATTETKOV, ALEXANDER VLADIMIROVICH, mathematics educator, researcher; b. Moscow, Nov. 13, 1955; s. Vladimir Nikolaevich and Nadezhda Potapovna (Skonkina) A.; m. Ludmila Nikolaevna Vlasova, Oct. 31, 1980. Diploma in engring. with honors, Moscow State Tech. U., 1979, D of Tech. Scis., 1985. Rschr. Moscow State Tech. U., 1979-89, chief dept. spl. mech. engring., 1989-93, reader dept. applied maths., 1993—; expert Russian Sci. Rsch. State Inst. Patent Expertise, Moscow, 1988-91. Contbr. articles to profl. jours. Grantee Internat. Sci. Found., 1993, Russian Found. Basic Rsch., 1994-95, 96—. Avocations: basketball, detective novels. Home: Octiassrskaya 42-84, 127018 Moscow Russia Office: Moscow State Tech U Dept Applied, Math 2 Baumanskaya 5, 107005 Moscow Russia

ATTEYA, AHMAD MAMDOUH, judge. Chief justice Supreme Ct. Egypt, Cairo. Office: Ministry Justice, Midan Lazoughi, Nasr City, Cairo Egypt*

ATTI, ROBERTA MARIA, nutritionist, chef, educator; b. Bologna, Italy, May 24, 1956; came to U.S., 1983; d. Luciano Atti and Maria Rubini; children: Henry David, Nicoletta. Student, Manfredi Sch. Travel and Lang., Bologna, Italy, 1969-74, Kushi Inst., 1980, 84; EMT, Northeastern U., 1984; grad., Natural Gourmet Cookery Sch., 1992, Hippocrates Health Inst., 1995. Health educator, cooking instr. Chefs' tng. program Nat. Gourmet Inst. Food and Health, N.Y.C., 1991-99; nutritionist, whole foods educator Wellness Ctr., N.Y.C., 1997—; nutrition asst. Child Life program Gay Men's Health Crisis, N.Y.C., 1994-95; cons., chef Balducci's, N.Y.C., 1993; health educator, cooking instr. Earth Literacy program Genesis Organic and Farm and Learning Ctr., Blairstown, 1991-93; lectr. in field; guest Kaleidoscipe for Tomorrow TV program, Fairfax, Va.; mem. adv. bd. Whole Foods project Food and Hunger Hotline; cooking demonstratoor for TV program Living with Aids, 1992, others. Author: Nutrition, Immunity and Spiritual Growth, 1991.

ATTIPOE, BLOOMFIELD CROSBY, agricultural engineer; b. Nsawam, Ghana, Jan. 24, 1956; s. Garnett Crosby and Josephine Akua (Djan) A.; m. June Dzidedi Abla Fummey, Jan. 1998; children: Ralph, Ronald, Ruby, Rosemond. BSc in Agrl. Engring., U. Sci. and Tech., Ghana, 1979; MSc in Irrigation Engring., U. Southampton, Eng., 1984. Engr. Weija Irrigation Co., Ghana, 1979-84, dir. engring., 1985-89, acting mng. dir., 1989-92; mng. dir. Perd Consult Ltd., Tema, Ghana, 1992—. Mem. Ghana Inst. Engrs., Ghana Inst. Mgmt., Ghana Inst. Engrs. (sr. mem.), Ghana Assn. of Cons. (coun. mem. 1993—), Scripture Union, Ghana Fellowship of Evangelical Students (assoc. mem.). Avocations: meeting people, sports. Office: Perd Consult Ltd, PO Box C02408, Tema Ghana

ATTIYATE-SCHWARZENBACH, YVONNE HÉLÈNE, linguistics publishing executive, retired; b. Ghent, Belgium, Feb. 25, 1930; d. Edwin Julius and Helene Hedwig (Jung) Schwarzenbach; m. A.M. Attiyate, Nov. 25, 1950 (div. 1999). Diploma, U. Geneva, 1950. Asst. editor Swiss Electrotech. Assn., Zürich, 1958-62; European editor Iron Age Internat., Chilton Co., Radnor, Pa., 1962-71; editor-in-chief Internat. Product Design, Chilton Co., 1971-77, Food Engring. Internat., Chilton Co., 1977-79, Kunststoffe-Plastics, Vogt-Schild Solothurn, Switzerland, 1979-83; chief exec. Compulex, Zürich, 1983—, now ret.; cons. Siemens, Munich, 1988-90, Engring. Info., N.Y., 1991-93. Author, pub.: NC Lexicon, 1971, 77, 89; co-author (reference) Dictionary of Microelectronics and Microcomputer Technology, 1984, 92, Robot Guide. Mem. IEEE, Swiss Tech. Press Assn. Avocation: chess. Home: Ferdinand Hodler Str 46, 8049 Zürich Switzerland

ATTOH-OKINE, NII O., civil and environmental engineering educator; b. Accra, Ghana, Oct. 10, 1958; came to U.S., 1990; s. Richard Attoh-Okine and Georgina Quaynor; children: Nii Attoh, Naa Djama. MS in Civil Engring., Rostov (Russia) Inst., 1986; PhD, U. Kans., 1992. Lectr. engring. U. Sci. and Tech., Kumasi, Ghana, 1987-89; instr. soil mechanics U. Kans., Lawrence, 1990-91, rsch. assoc., 1992, rsch. engr., 1993; project engr. Mng. Tech. Inc., Overland Park, Kans., 1993; rsch. assoc., adj. prof. civil engring. Fla. Internat. U., Miami, 1993-94, sr. rsch. assoc., 1994, adj. prof., sr. rsch. assoc., 1995, asst. prof. civil and environ. engring., 1995-99; asst. prof. civil and environ. engring. U. Del., Newark, 1999—; organizer, chmn. 2d Internat. Workshop on Artificial Intelligence and Math. Mehods in Pavement and Geomch. Systems, Newark, 2000, 1st Internat. Workshop, Miami, 1998; organizer, invited spkr., various seminars and confs.; external examiner U. Miami, 1994; reviewer various jours., forums and confs.; mem. Dade County Brownfield Task Force, 1996—; mem. Transp. Rsch. Bd. Contbr. numerous articles and papers to profl. jours. and internat. conf. procs., chpts. to books. Mem. ASCE, IEEE (assoc.), Ghana Instn. Engrs. (asst. hon. sec. no. sector 1987-90), Phi Beta Delta. Office: U Del Dept Civil & Environ Engrg 137 Dupont Hall Newark DE 19716

ATTOLINI, GIANCARLO, tax lawyer, accountant; b. Reggio Emilia, Italy, Sept. 25, 1961; s. Giancarlo Attolini and Franca Franchi. D of Econs. and Bus., U. Modena, Italy, 1988. Cons. in econs. of waste disposal various cos., Italy, 1985-89; v.p. bd. dirs. Laget SRL, Reggio Emilia, 1988-92; founding ptnr. Attolini Spaggiari & Assocs., Reggio Emilia, 1994—; pres. bd. trustees Ordine Dottori Commercialist di Reggio Emilia, 2000—. Co-author: Separate Collection of Exhausted Batteries, 1985; editor: Plastics & Waste, 1987. Founder, treas. Assn. Insieme Per Il Teatro, 1997—. Recipient Environment Protection award World Wildlife Fund, 1986. Mem. Unione Giovani Dottori Commercialisti di Reggio Emilia (v.p. 1994-97, pres. 1998—), Unione Nazionale Giovani Dottori Commercialisti (mem. nat. coun. 1998—), Associazione Azionisti Cassa di Risparmio di Reggio Emilia (pres. 1996—), Consiglio Nazionale Dottori Commercialisti (continuing profl. edn. com. 1999—). Avocations: sailing, swimming, jogging. Office: Attolini Spaggiari & Assoc, Via Che Guevara 2, I-42100 Reggio Emilia Italy

ATUCHIN, VICTOR VALERIEVICH, physicist, researcher; b. Prokopievsk, Russia, Aug. 16, 1957; s. Valery Mihailovich and Maria Grigorievna (Eremetova) A.; m. Nina Valentinovna Fedotova, Oct. 30, 1979; children: Marina, Ann, Nikita. MSc, Tomsk (Russia) State U., 1979; PhD, Inst. Semiconductor Physics, Novosibirsk, Russia, 1993. Engr. Inst. Atmosphere Optics, Tomsk, 1980, Novosibirsk State U., 1980-83; sr. rsch. physicist Inst. Semiconductor Physics, Novosibirsk, 1983—. Contbr. articles to profl. jours. and conf. procs. Greek Orthodox. Avocations: gardening, travel. Home: Equatornaya, 10, apt. 45, 630060 Novosibirsk Russia Office: Inst Semiconductor Physics, Pr. Lavrenteva 13, 630090 Novosibirsk Russia

ATWOOD, JAMES R., lawyer; b. White Plains, N.Y., Feb. 21, 1944; s. Bernard D. and Joyce Rose A.; m. Wendy Fisler, Aug. 22, 1981 (div. July 1993); children: Christopher Charles, Carl Fisler. BA, Yale U., 1966; JD, Stanford U., 1969. Bar: Calif. 1969, D.C. 1970. Law clk. to judge U.S. Ct. Appeals, L.A., 1969-70; law clk. to Chief Justice Warren Burger U.S. Supreme Ct., 1970-71; mem. Covington & Burling, Washington, 1971-78, ptnr., 1977-78, 81—; dep. asst. sec. for transp. affairs U.S. Dept. State, Washington, 1978-79, dep. legal adviser, 1979-80; acting prof. Law Sch. Stanford U., 1980. Author: (with Kingman Brewster) Antitrust and American Business Abroad, 2nd edit, 1981. Mem. bd. visitors Law Sch. Stanford U., 1995-97. Mem. ABA, Am. Soc. Internat. Law, D.C. Bar Assn. Home: 8020 Greentree Rd Bethesda MD 20817-1304 Office: Covington & Burling PO Box 7566 1201 Pennsylvania Ave NW Washington DC 20044-7566

ATWOOD, MARGARET ELEANOR, writer; b. Ottawa, Ont., Can., Nov. 18, 1939; d. Carl Edmund and Margaret Dorothy (Killam) A. BA, U. Toronto, 1961; AM, Radcliffe Coll., 1962; postgrad., Harvard U., 1962-63, 65-67; LittD (hon.), Trent U., 1973, Concordia U., 1980, Smith Coll., Northampton, Mass., 1982, U. Toronto, 1983, U. Waterloo, 1985, U. Guelph, 1985, Mt. Holyoke Coll., 1985, Victoria Coll., 1987, Univ. de Montréal, 1991, McMaster U., 1996; LLD (hon.), Queen's U., 1974. Lectr. in English U. B.C., 1964-65, Sir George Williams U., 1967-68, U. Alta., 1969-70; asst. prof. English York U., Toronto, 1971-72; writer-in-residence U. Toronto, 1972-73, U. Ala., Tuscaloosa, 1985; Berg Chair NYU, 1986; writer-in-residence Macquarie U., Australia, 1987, Trinity U., San Antonio, 1989. Author: (poetry) Double Persephone, 1961, The Circle Game, 1967, The Animals in That Country, 1968, The Journals of Susanna Moodie, 1970, Procedures for Underground, 1970, Power Politics, 1973, Poems for Voices, 1970, You Are Happy, 1975, Selected Poems, 1976 (Am. edit. 1978), Selected Poems, 1966-84, 1990, Margaret Atwood Poems, 1965-75, 1991, Two-Headed Poems, 1978, True Stories, 1981, Interlunar, 1984, Selected Poems II: Poems Selected and New, 1976-1986, 1986, Morning in the Burned House, 1995; (novels) The Edible Woman, 1969 (Am. edit. 1970), Surfacing, 1972, (Am. edit. 1973), Lady Oracle, 1976, Life Before Man, 1979, Bodily Harm, 1981, The Handmaid's Tale, 1985, Cat's Eye, 1988 (City Toronto Book award 1989, Coles Book of the Yr. 1989, Can. Booksellers Assn. Author of the Yr., 1989, Book of the Yr. award Found. for Advancement of Can. Letters, Periodical Marketers Can., 1989, Torgi Talking Book award 1989), The Robber Bride, 1993 (award for Fiction Can. Authors Assn., 1993, Trillium award for Excellence in Ont. Writing 1993, Regional Commonwealth Lit. award), Alias Grace, 1996 (Giller Prize 1996, Medal of Honor for Literature, Nat. Arts Club 1997), The Blind Assassin, 2000; (short stories) Dancing Girls, 1977, Bluebeard's Egg, 1983, Murder in the Dark, 1983, Wilderness Tips, 1991 (Trillium award 1992, Book of the Yr. award Periodical Marketers of Can., 1992), Good Bones, 1992; (juvenile) Up in the Tree, 1978, Anna'a Pet, 1980, For the Birds, 1990, Princess Prunella & the Purple Peanut, 1995; (non-fiction) Survival: A Thematic Guide to Canadian Literature, 1972, Second Words: Selected Critical Prose, 1982, Strange Things: The Malevolent North in Canadian Literature, 1995;. Recipient E.J. Pratt medal, 1961, Pres.'s medal U. Western Ont., 1965, YWCA Women of Distinction award, Gov. Gen.'s award, 1966, 1st pl. Centennial Commn. Poetry Competition, 1967, Union Poetry prize Chicago, 1969, Bess Hoskins prize of Poetry Chicago, 1974, City of Toronto Book award, 1977, Can. Booksellers Assn. award, 1977, award for short fiction Periodical Distbr. Can., 1977, St. Lawrence award for Fiction, 1978, Radcliffe Grad. medal, 1980, Molson award, 1981, Internat. Writer's prize Welsh Arts Council, 1982, Book of Yr. award Periodical Distbrs. of Can. and Found. for Advancement Can. Letters, 1983, Los Angeles Times Fiction award, 1986, Gov. Gen.'s Lit. award, 1986, Ida Nudel Humanitarian award, 1986, Toronto Arts award, 1986, Arthur C. Clarke award for Best Sci. Fiction, 1987, shortlisted for Ritz Hemingway prize, Paris, 1987, Commonwealth Lit. Prize regional award, 1987, 94, Silver medal for Best Article of Yr. Council for Advancement and Support of Edn., 1987, Nat. Mag. award 1st prize, 1988, Sunday Times award for literary excellence, YWCA Women of Distinction award 1988, Centennial medal Harvard U., 1990, John Hughes prize Welsh Devel. Bd., 1992, Commemorative medal 125th Anniversary of Can. Confedn., 1992, Trillium award for excellence in Ont. writing, 1995; Guggenheim fellow, 1981; decorated companion Order of Can., 1981, Order of Ont., 1990; named Woman of Yr. Ms. Mag., 1986, Humanist of Yr., 1987, Chevalier de l'Ordre des Arts et des Lettres, 1994. Fellow Royal Soc. of Can., Am. Acad. Arts and Scis. (fgn. hon. lit. mem. 1988). Address: care Oxford U Press, 70 Wynford Dr, Don Mills, ON Canada M3C 1J9

ATWOOD, MARY SANFORD, writer; b. Mt. Pleasant, Mich., Jan. 27, 1935; d. Burton Jay and Lillian Belle (Sampson) Sanford; B.S., U. Miami, 1957; m. John C. Atwood, III, Mar. 23, 1957. Author: A Taste of India, 1969. Mem. San Francisco/N. Peninsula Opera Action, Hillsborough-Burlingame Newcomers, Suicide Prevention and Crisis Center, DeYoung Art Mus., Internat. Hospitality Center, Peninsula Symphony, San Francisco Art Mus., World Affairs Council, Mills Hosp. Assos. Mem. AAUW, Suicide Prevention Aux. Republican. Club: St. Francis Yacht. Office: 40 Knightwood Ln Hillsborough CA 94010-6132

ATWOOD, RAYMOND PERCIVAL, JR., lawyer; b. Ossining, N.Y., June 25, 1952; s. Raymond Percival and Berniece Lucille (Beach) A.; m. Theresa Carol Goeken, Aug. 13, 1977; children: Shannon, Heather, Sarah, Raymond III, Jennifer. BS cum laude, U. Nebr., 1972, JD, 1974; cert. Trial Advocacy, Hastings Coll. Law U. Calif., San Francisco, 1978; Advanced Trial Advocacy, Harvard U. Law Sch., 1988. Bar: Nebr. 1975, U.S. Dist. Ct. Nebr. 1975, U.S. Bankruptcy Ct. 1975, Mo. 1978, U.S. Ct. Appeals (8th cir.) 1979. Agy. legal counsel Nebr. Workmen's Compensation Ct., Lincoln, 1975-77; staff counsel Hartford Ins. Co., Kansas City, Mo., 1977-78; ptnr. McCord, Janssen & Atwood, Lincoln, 1978-80, Healey, Wieland, Kluender, Atwood, Geier & Bartle, Lincoln, 1980—; educator Lincoln Sch. Commerce, Nebr., 1978-81; bd. dirs. legal studies Lincoln Sch. Commerce, Nebr., 1979-81; educator U. Nebr. Coll. Law, Lincoln, 1982—; legal seminar lectr., 1976—. Contbr. articles to profl. jours. Organizer United Way, Lincoln, 1975-77; campaign chmn. Larson for Legislature, Lincoln, 1984. Mem. ABA, Nebr. Order Barristers, Nebr. Trial Lawyers Assn., Assn. Trial Lawyers Am., Nebr. State Bar, Delta Theta Phi. Unitarian. Office: Healey Atwood Geier & Bartle PO Box 83104 1141 H St Lincoln NE 68508-3256

AU, BAK LING, publisher; b. Hong Kong, May 13, 1928; m. Lam Man Ling; children: Alex, Anita, Allen, Augustus, Angela. Self-taught. Founder, owner, chmn., CEO Ling Kee Group, Hong Kong, Shanghai, London, N.Y.C., 1943, Ling Kee Group of Cos., Hong Kong, Shanghai, London, N.Y.C., 1949, Bak Ling Group, Hong Kong, 1970—, Unicorn Group, Hong Kong and London, 1982—; chmn., CEO Century Cir., Vancouver, B.C., Can., 1990, Beautiworld Group, 1991—, Blaussen Group, 1992, NCR Group, 1994. Pres. Hong Kong Fedn. Youth Group, 1977—; dir. Tung Wah Group of Hosps., 1965-66. Fellow Coll. Tchrs. Eng. (charter); mem. Hong Kong Ednl Pubrs. Assn. (founder, pres. 1975-79, 83-85), Hong Kong Booksellers and Stationers Assn. (chmn. 1960), Rotary, Oriental Ceramics Soc. Address: Bak Ling Ent Ltd Unicorn Trade Ctr 11th Fl, 127-131 Des Voeux Rd C, Hong Kong Hong Kong

AU, OTTO YUM-TO, plastic surgeon, educator; b. Hong Kong, Dec. 1, 1925; s. Lum and Hor Kun (Tse) A.; m. Pauline Lau, Apr. 24, 1953; children: Anthony, Victor, Karen. MD, Jefferson Med. Coll., 1957. Diplomate Am. Bd. Plastic Surgery. Intern Hosp. Good Samaritan, L.A., 1957-58, surg. resident, 1958-61; plastic surgery resident St. Joseph Hosp., Ann Arbor, Mich., 1961-63; cons. plastic surgery Hong Kong Ctrl. Hosp., 1964—, Canossa Hosp., Hong Kong, 1964-97, Hong Kong Sanitorium & Hosp., 1999—; clin. prof. plastic surgery Chinese U., Hong Kong, 1997—. Mem. Hong Kong Acad. Medicine, Hong Kong Soc. Plastic Surgery (pres. 1967-68), Brit. Med. Assn. (Hong Kong br. pres. 1969-70), Oriental Soc. of Aesthetic Plastic Surgery (pres. 1999—). Avocations: swimming, bridge, horse racing. Office: 407 New World Tower, Hong Kong Hong Kong

AU, PETER CHAK TONG, chemist, educator; b. Yuen Long, Hong Kong, May 26, 1953; s. Chun Pong and Lai Mui (Wan) A.; m. Sophia Liu, June 2, 1979; children: Zaneta, Lemuel. BSc, U. Liverpool, 1977; PhD, U. Bradford, 1981. Postdoctoral rschr. Univ. Coll., Cardiff, Wales, 1980-86; from assoc. prof. to prof. Xiamen U., China, 1986-90; from lectr. to prof. Hong Kong Bapt. U., 1990—; vis. scholar Free U. Berlin, 1985. Fellow Royal Soc. Chemistry, Ctr. for Surface Analysis & Rsch.; mem. Hong Kong Scholars Soc. Avocation: Taoism. Office: Hong Kong Bapt U, Dept Chemistry, Kowloon Hong Kong China

AU, TSIEN-MING, electrical engineer; b. Hong Kong, China, Nov. 14, 1965; child of Sum Au and Lau Ying Wong. BSEE, Chinese U. Hong Kong, 1989, MPhil, 1992; PhD, City U. Hong Kong, 1995. Chartered engr. Postdoctoral fellow elec. engring. dept. Nat. U. Singapore, 1996, sr. rsch. engr., mem. tech. staff Ctr. Wireless Comm., 1996-98; prin. engr. Comm. Def. Elecs. Transp. Techs. Pte Ltd., Singapore, 1998—. Recipient Japan Microwave prize Asia-Pacific Microwave Conf., 1994. Mem. IEEE, Inst. Elec. Engrs. Avocations: classical music, Chinese tea, Tai-chi, photography. Fax: 65-2732073. Home: #05-00 Permai Ct, 524 Kg Bahru Rd, Singapore 099455, Singapore Office: CET Techs Pte Ltd, 100 Jurong E St 21, Singapore 609602, Singapore

AUBERT, ANDRE ERNEST, biophysicist, educator, biology researcher; b. Antwerp, Belgium, Apr. 16, 1943; s. Virgile Irenee and Irene (Kniepigl) A. Lic.Phys., Katholieke Univ. Leuven, Belgium, 1965, DrSc, 1973. Asst. Catholic U Leuven, 1965-78, lectr., 1978-85, prof. exptl. cardiology, 1985—; organizer over 30 nat. and internat. sci. confs. Editor: Biomaterials, 1983, Pacemaker Leads, 1984, 91, Euro-Pace '93, 1993, Cardiac Pacing and Electrophysiology: A Bridge to the 21st Century, 1994, Cardio-Omni, 1995; inventor in field. Cpl. Belgian Mil., 1970-71. Recipient IBM Travel award Nat. Sci. Found., Brussels, 1979; named laureate Ministry of Edn., Brussels, 1978; fellow Sci. Rsch. Orgn. for Industry and Agriculture, 1965. Fellow European Soc. Non-Invasive Cardiology (sec. 1980—); mem. Biol. Engring. Soc. (London), Flemish Soc. Bioengring. (bd. dirs.), Hungarian Soc. Cardiology (hon.). Avocations: sailing, tennis, skiing, horseback riding, history. Office: U Z Gasthuisberg 0-N, Herestraat 49, Leuven 3000, Belgium

AUBERTIN, MADELINE KATHERINE, retired nursing educator, medical/surgical nurse, mental health services professional; b. Detroit, May 16, 1930. BS in Nursing Edn., Mercy Coll., 1951; MEd, Wayne State Coll., 1995. RN, Mich. Staff nurse Vets. Hosp., Dearborn, Mich., 1951-58; staff nurse, nursing educator St. John's Hosp., St. Louis, 1960-64; staff nurse U. Mich., Ann Arbor, 1965-66; instr., staff nurse Harper Hosp., Detroit; insvc. dir., nursing instr. Holy Cross Hosp., Detroit, 1966-68; insvc. instr., dir. Grace Hosp., Detroit, 1968-72; nursing instr. Wayne County Community Coll., Detroit, 1972-96; ret., 1996. Mem. ARC, Detroit, 1962-92, Am. Heart Assn., Southfield, Mich., 1962-92, Assn. for Learning Disabilities, Farmington, Mich., 1972-92, Nat. League of Nursing, Detroit, 1962-92. Democrat. Roman Catholic. Avocations: singing, church choir, sewing, reading. Home: 9576 Winston Redford MI 48239-1660

AUBERY, STEPHEN ROYSTON EDMUND, film producer; b. Kingston Upon Hull, Yorkshire, Eng., July 4, 1951; came to U.S., 1964; s. Gerald Royston and Doreen (Stevens) A.; m. Rose Marie Marks, Feb. 23, 1973 (div. Dec. 1991); children: Suzanne Marie, Julia Dawn, Wendy Lynn, Katrina Rose; m. Tamara Phizacklea, Oct. 4, 1994 (div. Apr. 2000). Student, U. Utah, 1968-70, Brigham Young U., 1974-75. Sound dept. mgr. Brigham Young U. Motion Picture Studio, Provo, Utah, 1972-76; film prodr., ptnr. Linton Prodns., Salt Lake City, 1976-79; prodr., gen. ptnr. Seven Star Pictures, Salt Lake City, 1979-82; news editor KUTV Inc., Salt Lake City, 1982-84; film prodr., mgr. LDS Audiovisual, Salt Lake City, 1984-94; film prodr., owner Encore Prodns., Salt Lake City, 1995-96; film prodr. Mountain Prodns., Inc., Draper, Utah, 1997-99, Mark Phillips Philms & Telephision,

L.A., 1999-2000; film prodr., mgr. flixnpix.com, L.A., 2000—; film prodr. Challenger Schs., Salt Lake City, 1994-95; film dept. instr. U. Utah, Salt Lake City, Brigham Young U., Provo. Co-author, prodr., cinematographer (screenplay, book, feature motion picture) Knocking at Heaven's Door, 1980; film prodr. (internat. film) Temple Open House, 1992 (Telly award 1993); film prodr., dir. (ednl. film) Phonics Fun, 1993 (two Telly awards 1994); prodr., dir. (motivational film) From Thoughts to Things, 1997 (Telly Communicator award 1997), dir. photography, editor, Undercover Stings, Learning Channel, 1999, The Jer-Z Games, Disney Channel, 2000, K-9 Cops-The Learning Channel, 2000, Bridges to Freedom, 2000; author, contbg. editor Super 8 Filmaker Mag., 1975-80. Bd. dirs. World Firefighters Assistance League, Salt Lake City. Mem. Internat. TV Assn., Soc. Motion Picture and TV Engrs. (presenter tech. paper L.A. conv. 1974-80, cert. presentation 1995). Avocations: vocal performing, playing guitar, computers, manager of Tapestry top 40 soft rock dance band 1980-97. E-mail: steve@flixnpix.com and aubery@earthlink.net. Fax: 323-655-5490. Office: flixnpix.com 2037 Latham St Simi Valley CA 93065-1116

AUBIER, MICHEL, medical educator; b. Paris, Dec. 10, 1947; s. Paul and Florette (Norand) A.; m. Isabelle Sylvie Piekarski, Jan. 23, 1975; children: Benjamin, Maud. MD, U. Paris VII, 1977. Intern Hosp. de Paris, 1974-78; rsch. fellow McGill U., Montreal, 1978-80; head pulmonary unit Hosp. Bichat, Paris, 1988—; rsch. dir. Inst. Nat. de la Santé et Recherche Medicole, Paris, 1984—; asst. prof. medicine Hosp. Beaujon, Paris, 1980-87; prof. medicine U. Paris VII, 1988. Contbr. articles to profl. jours. Mem. European Respiratory Soc., Am. Lung Assn.

AUBRY, CECILE (ANNE-JOSÉ BERNARD), writer; b. Paris, Aug. 3, 1928; d. Lucien Bénard and Marguerite Candelier; m. Prince Brahim el Glaoui, 1951 (div.); 1 child. Student, Lycée Victor Duruy, Paris. Author TV scripts and series, including Poly, Belle et Sébastien Parmi les Hommes, Sébastien et la Mary Morgane, Le Jeune Fabre, others; author 3 novels, 1974-85; author numerous children's books; appearances in films, including Manon, 1948, The Black Rose, 1950, Barbe Bleue, 1951. Named Officier des Arts et des Lettres. Address: Le Moulin Bleu, 6 Chemin du Moulin Bleu, 91410 Saint-Cyr-sous Dourdan, France

AUBRY, MARTINE, government official; b. Paris, Aug. 8, 1950; married; 1 child. Diploma, Inst. Polit. Studies, Paris, 1972, Nat. Sch. Adminstrn., Paris, 1975. Sr. civic servant Ministry Labor, 1975-79; legal asst. Conseil d'Etat, 1980-81; asst. dir. Ministry Labor, 1981-83, dir. labor rels., 1984-87; legal advisor Conseil d'Etat, 1987; asst. gen. mgt. Pechiney, 1989-91; min. Ministry Labor, Employment & Vocat. Tng., 1991-93; chmn. Action Against Exclusive Found., 1993—; v.p. Lille Urban Cmty., France, 1995; 1st deputy mayor Lille, France, 1995; min. Ministry Employment & Sodilarity, Paris, 1998—. Office: Ministry Employment, 127 rue de Genelle, 75700 Paris France*

AUBRY, SERGE JEAN, theoretical physicist, researcher; b. Valenton, France, Jan. 11, 1945; s. Roger and Marcelle (Geniez) A.; m. Jacqueline Aufrère, 1973 (div. 1985); children: Olivia, Sébastien; m. Maryvonne LeMoine, May 30, 1987; children: Benjamin, Floriane. Student, Ecole Polytechnique, Paris, 1965-67; DEA in Solid State Physics, Orsay, France, 1968; PhD, U. Paris, 1975. Physicist CNRS, France, 1969-84, CEA, France, 1984—; cons. CNET, France, 1985-93. Contbr. more than 130 articles to sci. jours. including Physica D., Physics Rev. B, Jour. Physics of Condensed Matter, Europhysics Letters, Phys. Rev. B and E, Phys. Rev. Letters, Jour. Statis. Physics, Jour. Physique Nonlinearity, European Jour. Phys. B. Recipient Bronze medal CNRS, 1977, Langevin prize SFP, 1983, Silver medal CNRS, 1984; Ulam fellow, 1992. Office: Lab Léon Brillouin, CE Saclay, 91191 Gif-sur-Yvette France

AUBY, JEAN-BERNARD, law educator, consultant; b. Phnom-Penh, Cambodia, Apr. 12, 1950; s. Jean-Marie and Genevieve (Archambault) A.; m. Christine Clus; 1 child, Antoine. Law Doctorate, U. Bordeaux, France. Prof. U. Rennes, France, 1983-87; prof. U. Paris XII, France, 1987-94, law sch. dean, 1989-93; prof. U. Paris II, 1994—; cons. in field. Author: Droit de L'Urbanisme et de la Construction, 5th edit., 1998; editor: Juris. Classeur Administratif. Office: 19 Blvd Henri IV, 75004 Paris France

AUCAR, GUSTAVO ADOLFO, physics educator, researcher; b. Resistencia, Chaco, Argentina, Nov. 12, 1956; s. Felipe Carlos and Dina Marta (Barbetti) A.; m. Carmen Susana Mourazos, Aug. 10, 1985; children: Francisco J., I. Agustin, M. Emilia, M. Gabriela, M. Cielo, Juan I., M. Esperanza. Lic. in phys. sci., U. Northeastern, Corrientes, Argentina, 1983; D Phys. Sci., U. Buenos Aires, 1991. Postdoctoral fellow Natural Sci. Rsch. Coun. Denmark, Odense, 1992-94; fellow Nat. Rsch. Coun. Argentina, Corrientes, 1985-91; mem. Sci. Rsch. Coun. Argentina, Corrientes, 1995—; dir. atomic and molecular physics group U. Northeastern, Argentina, 1988—, adj. prof. Exact and Natural Sci. Faculty,, 1991—; vis. prof. U. Alicante, 1995, U. Odense, 1996, 97, U. Modena, 1999; dir. Mercosur Summer Inst. on Molecular Physics, 1999, 2000. Contbr. articles to Jour. Molecular Structure, Jour. Magnetic Resonance, Internat. Jour. Quantum Chemistry, Chem. Physics Letters, Phys. Rev. Rsch. grantee ANTORCHAS Found., 1992, 96, Conicet, 2000. Fellow Internat. Soc. Theoretical Chem. Physicists; mem. Argentinian Soc. Physicists. Roman Catholic. Avocations: music, basketball, fishing, aeronautical models. Home: JA Roca 2159, 3500 Resistencia Chaco, Argentina Office: U Northeastern Exact Sci Faculty, Campus U Av Libertad, 5500 Corrientes Argentina

AUCELLA, LAURENCE FRANK, counseling administrator, educator; b. Waterbury, Conn., July 24, 1959; s. Louis Joseph and Julia Janet A. BA, Anna Maria Coll., Paxton, Mass., 1982; MEd, Boston Coll., 1984; EdD, U. Bridgeport (Conn.), 1997. Lic. profl. counselor/gifted sch. counselor. Counselor Morris Found., Waterbury, 1984-86; adj. faculty Tunxis C.C., Farmington, Conn., 1991, So. Conn. State U., New Haven, 1992-96, Albertus Magnus Coll., New Haven, 1998—, Mattatuck C.C., Waterbury, 1985-90; disability specialist Western Conn. State U., Danbury, 1997—; ednl. counselor Waterbury Adult Edn., 1986—; Mem. Ctr. for Blood Rsch., Boston, 1999—. Contbr. articles to profl. jours. Moderator (election official) City of Waterbury, 1995—; city coord. United Way, 1988 (Cmty. Spirit Award 1988); pres. La Casa Bienvenida, Waterbury, 1987—. Recipient Impact 99 Blessing Award Hispanic chs. of Waterbury, 1999, Riverfront Preservation Award Riverfront Preservation Soc., Rock Hill, Conn., 1999; named an Outstanding Young Man of Am. Jaycees, 1985-88. Mem. Am. Counseling Assn., Am. Statis. Assn., Am. Advance of Sci., Conn. Counseling Assn., Kiwanis (treas. 1991-94, Treas. award 1994), Phi Delta Kappa. Republican. Roman Catholic. Avocations: collecting books, history books, books on U.S. presidents, immigration. Home: 90 Oakleaf Dr Waterbury CT 06708-3633 Office: Waterbury Adult Edn 28 E Clay St Waterbury CT 06706-1216

AUCH, SUSAN, retired speed skater; b. Winnipeg, Can., Mar. 1, 1966. Student, U. Calgary. Mem. Can. Nat. Women's Speed Skating Team, 1986-98; ret. Recipient Silver medal women's speed skating 500 meters, Olympic Games, Nagano, Japan, 1998, Brure Kidd award 27th Can. Sports Award, 2000. Avocations: downhill skiing, horseback riding. Office: Can Assn Adv Women & Sport, 1600 James Naismith Dr, Glouscester, ON Canada K1B-5N4*

AUCHINCLOSS, LOUIS STANTON, writer; b. Lawrence, N.Y., Sept. 27, 1917; s. Joseph Howland and Priscilla (Stanton) A.; m. Adele Lawrence, Sept. 1957; children: John, Blake, Andrew. Student, Yale U., 1939; LLB, U. Va., 1941; LittD, NYU, 1974, Pace U., 1979, U. of the South, 1986. Bar: N.Y. bar 1941. Assoc. Sullivan & Cromwell, 1941-51; assoc. Hawkins, Delafield & Wood, N.Y.C., 1954-58, ptnr., 1958-86. Author: The Indifferent Children, 1947, The Injustice Collectors, 1950, Sybil, 1952, A Law for the Lion, 1953, The Romantic Egoists, 1954, The Great World and Timothy Colt, 1956, Venus in Sparta, 1958, Pursuit of the Prodigal, 1959, The House of Five Talents, 1960, Reflections of a Jacobite, 1961, Portrait in Brownstone, 1962, Powers of Attorney, 1963, The Rector of Justin, 1964, Pioneers and Caretakers, 1965, The Embezzler, 1966, Tales of Manhattan, 1967, A World of Profit, 1968, Motiveless Malignity, 1969, Second Chance, 1970, Edith Wharton, 1971, I Came As a Thief, Richelieu, 1972, The Partners, A Writer's Capital, 1974, Reading Henry James, 1975, The Winthrop Covenant, 1976, The Dark Lady, 1977, The Country Cousin, 1978, Persons of Consequence, 1979, Life, Law and Letters, 1979, The House of the Prophet, 1980, The Cat and the King, 1981, Watchfires, 1982, Exit Lady Masham, 1983, The Book Class, 1984, Honorable Men, 1985, Diary of a Yuppie, 1986, Skinny Island, 1987, The Golden Calves, 1988, Fellow Passengers, 1989, The Vanderbilt Era, 1989, The Lady of Situations, 1991, False Gods, 1992, Three Lives, 1993, Tales of Yesteryear, 1994, The Style's The Man, 1994, Collected Stories, 1994, The Education of Oscar Fairfax, 1995, The Man Behind the Book, 1996, LA Gloire, 1996, The Atonement, 1997. Trustee emeritus Josiah Macy, Jr., Found.; chmn. Mus. City of N.Y. Lt. USNR, 1941-45. Mem. AAAL (pres. emeritus), Assn. Bar City N.Y., Century Assn. Episcopalian. Home: 1111 Park Ave New York NY 10128-1234

AUCHMUTY, GILES, applied mathematics educator; b. Dublin, Ireland, June 1, 1945; s. James J. and Margaret (Walters) A. BSc, Australian Nat. U., Canberra, 1966; MS, U. Chgo., 1968, PhD, 1970. Rsch. instr. SUNY, Stony Brook, 1970-72; from asst. prof. to assoc. prof. Ind. U., Bloomington, 1972-81; prof. U. Houston, 1982—; vis. mem. Inst. for Advanced Study, Princeton, N.J., 1989; vis. prof. U. Leipzig, 1996, U. Sydney, 1997. Editor publs. in applied math. for Am. Math. Soc., 1987-90; mng. editor Houston Jour. Math., 1993-96, editor, 1996—; editor Electronic Problems Section SIAM Review, 1999—; contbr. more than 50 articles to profl. jours. Fellow Brit. Sci. Rsch. Coun., 1975-76; rsch. grantee NSF, 1971—; recipient rsch. award Robert A. Welch Found., 1984-90. Office: U Houston Dept Math Houston TX 77204-0001

AUCUTT, RONALD DAVID, lawyer; b. St. Paul, Dec. 28, 1945; s. Howard Lewis and Eleanor May (Malcolm) A.; m. Grace Diane Kok, Apr. 3, 1976; children: David Gerard, James Andrew. BA, U. Minn., 1967, JD, 1975. Bar: Minn. 1975, D.C. 1976, Va. 1978, Tex. 1999, U.S. Supreme Ct. 1978, U.S. Tax Ct. 1980, U.S. Dist. Ct. D.C. 1980, U.S. Ct. Appeals (D.C. cir.) 1980, U.S. Ct. of Claims 1980, U.S. Claims Ct. 1982, U.S. Ct. Appeals (fed. cir.) 1982, U.S. Dist. Ct. (ea. dist.) Va. 1986, U.S. Ct. Appeals (4th cir.) 1986. Assoc. Miller & Chevalier, Chartered, Washington, 1975-81, ptnr., 1982-98; ptnr. McGuire, Woods L.L.P., McLean, Va., 1998—; mem. bd. advisors IRS Practice Alert, N.Y.C., 1987-93; adj. prof. Sch. Law U. Va., 1998—; mem. adv. com. Philip E. Heckerling Inst. on Estate Planning U. Miami, 1999—. Mem. bd. advisors Jour. Taxation Exempt Orgns., 1989—, Bus. Entities, N.Y.C.; mem. editl. bd. Estate Planning, N.Y.C., 1993—, mem. adv. bd. Tax Mgmt. Estates, Gifts, and Trusts Jour., 1999—; editl. adv. bd. Judges and Lawyers Bus. Valuation Update, Portland, Oreg., 1999—; contbr. articles to profl. publs. Sec.-treas. Miller and Chevalier Charitable Found., Washington, 1980-82, pres., 1993-97; bd. dirs. Evang. Free Ch. Am., Mpls., 1986-92, vice moderator, chmn. bd. dirs., 1993-95, moderator, 1995-97; bd. dirs. Coun. for Ct. Excellence, Washington, 1993-99, Advocates Internat., Fairfax, Va., 1997—, vice chmn. 1999—; Orgn. Security and Coop. in Europe internat. observer Bulgarian Parliamentary election, 1997; mem. adv. bd. Trinity Law Sch., Santa Ana, Calif., 1998—; bd. visitors U. Minn. Law Sch., 1998—; bd. regents Trinity Internat. U., Deerfield, Ill., 2000—. Lt. USN, 1970-73. Fellow Am. Bar Found., Am. Coll. Tax Counsel, Am. Coll. Trust and Estate Counsel (bd. regents 1996—, chmn. bus. planning com. 1997-2000, sec. 1999-2000, treas. 2000—). Mem. ABA (chair taxation sect., com. on estate and gift taxes 1986-88, vice chmn. com. on govt. submissions 1989-91, chmn. 1991-93, coun. 1993-97, liaison to sect. real property, probate and trust law 1990—, vice chair com. ops. 1998-2000), Internat. Acad. Estate and Trust Law (exec. coun. 2000—, academician), Christian Legal Soc., Met. Club Washington, Univ. Minn. Law Alumni Assn. (bd. dirs. 1998—). E-mail: raucutt@mcguirewoods.com. Home: 3417 Silver Maple Pl Falls Church VA 22042-3545 Office: McGuireWoods LLP 1750 Tysons Blvd Ste 1800 Mc Lean VA 22102-4231

AUDENINO, ALBERTO LUIGI, engineering educator; b. Moncalieri, Turin, Italy, Feb. 2, 1962; s. Carlo and Luciana (Gherzi) A.; m. Elisabetta Maria Zanetti, Dec. 7, 1996. MS in Engring., Poly., Torino, 1987, PhD in Machine Design, 1992. Lab. tech. Tech. U., Torino, 1991-94; lectr. Tech. U., Turin, Italy, 1994-98; prof. machine design U. Catania (Italy), 1998—. Author: Metodi Sperimentali Per La Progettazione, 1997; contbr. articles to profl. jours. Town counsellor Trofarello City, Torino, Italy, 1992-96. Served with Italian Army, 1988-89. Roman Catholic. Avocations: piano, classic car restoration, choral singing, photography. Home: S Vito Revigliasco 364/6, 10133 Turin Italy Office: Poly di Turin Dept Mech, Duca Degli Abruzzi 24, 10129 Turin Italy also: Dept Indsl/Mech Engring, Andres Done 6, 95125 Catania Italy

AUDET, CHARLES, mathematician, educator; b. Loretteville, Que., Can., May 8, 1969; came to U.S., 1998; s. Pierre and Christiane (Fisette) A.; m. Annie Angers; 1 child, Francois Xavier. BSc, U. Ottawa, Ont., Can., 1992; PhD, Ecole Polytechnique, Montreal, 1998. Linear programming analyst Ultramar Can., Montreal, 1996-97; rsch. prof. GERAD, Montreal, 1998; instr. math. Rice U., Houston, 1998—. Contbr. chpt. to book, articles to profl. jours. Recipient prize for excellence Inst. of Math. Scis., Montreal, 1995-96; Nat. Scis. and Engring. Rsch. Coun. Can. grantee, 1992-93, 93-96, 98—. Avocations: cycling, rock climbing, travel, reading. E-mail: charlesa@caam.rice.edu. Office: Rice U 6100 Main St CAAM MS 134 Houston TX 77005

AUDI, PIERRE RAYMOND, artistic director; b. Beirut, Sept. 11, 1957; arrived in U.K., 1975; s. Raymond and Andrée (Fattal) A. Grad., Lycée Français, Beirut; MA, Oxford U., 1978. Artistic dir. De Nederlandse Opera, Amsterdam; founding artistic dir. Almeida Theatre & Festival, London, 1979-89; artistic dir. De Nederlandse Opera, Amsterdam, 1988—; dir. operas Almeida Theatre & Festival, De Nederlandse Opera, also festivals in Spain, France, U.S., U.K. Dir. Il Ritorno d'Ulisse in Patria, 1990-91, 92-93, Die glückliche Hand, 1990-91, 95, Gassir, 1990-91, 92-93, Il Combattimento di Tancredi e Clorinda, 1990-91, 92-93, Mitridate, Re di Ponto, 1991-92, Snatched by the Gods, 1991-92, Broken Strings, 1991-92, La Bohème, 1992-93, Punch and Judy, 1992-93, l'Incoronazione di Poppea, 1993-94, Il Re Pastore, 1993-94, Noach, 1993-94, Ertwartung, 1995, Von heute auf morgen, 1995, L'Orfeo, 1995, 96, Die Zauberflöte, 1995, Timon of Athens, 1995, Measure for Measure, 1996, Venus and Adonis, 1997, Der Ring des Nibelungen, 1997—. Recipient Leslee Boosey Award for Outstanding Contbn. to British Mus. Life from Performing Rights Soc. U.K. & Royal Philharm. Soc. U.K., 1990. Office: De Nederlandse Opera, Waterlooplein 22, 1011 PG Amsterdam The Netherlands*

AUDINOS, RÉMY HENRI GEORGES, science educator; b. Clamart, Seine, France; s. Emile and Lucie (Authie) A.; m. Suzanne Vulin, Dec. 23, 1965; children: Sophie, Florence, Pierre-Laurent. Bachelier, Lycée Pierre de Fermat, Toulouse, 1952; Lic. es Scis., Faculty of Scis., Toulouse, 1955; degree in chem. engring., Chem. Engring. Inst., Toulouse, 1957; DSc, U. Paul Sabatier, Toulouse, 1972. Engr. Nat. Ctr. Sci. Rsch., Toulouse, 1957-58; asst. prof. Faculty of Scis., Toulouse, 1959-69; assoc. prof. U. Paul Sabatier, Toulouse, 1969-84, prof., 1985-89; prof. Inst. Nat. Poly., Toulouse, 1989—, ret.; rep. UN-Econ. Commn. Europe, Geneva, Switzerland, 1987, 95; expert European Comty., Brussels, 1988-91. Author: Artificial Membranes, 1983; editor: (dictionary) Technical Terms of Membrane Processes, 1986; holder 3 patents in field. Recipient 1st prize Ministry of Environment, Toulouse, 1987; decorated chevalier Ordre Nat. du Mérite, Paris, 1988. Mem. Indian Membrane Soc., French Nat. Assn. Drs. in Sci., French Filtration Soc., N.Y. Acad. Scis., French Membrane Club. Home: 72 chemin Basso Cambo, 31 100 Toulouse France

AUDOUARD, CHRISTIAN, judge. 1st. pres. Cour d'Appel de Forte-de-France, Martinique. Office: Morne Tartenson, Ave St John Perse BP 634, 97200 Fort-de-France Martinique*

AUDREN, CHRISTOPHE (CHRIS AUDREN), composer, musician; b. Quimperlé, France, Mar. 30, 1968; s. Joseph and Henriette (Tanguy) A.; m. Nolawit Beyene Kassa, Sept. 28, 1996. Diploma in computer sci., Inst. Univ. Tech., Nantes, France, 1990. Comml. rep. northwest France IML, 1992-95; comml. rep. String Music Import, 1996-97, Roland, France, 1998—. Composer, performer: Full Moon Insomnia, 1995, Nevenoe, 1996, Music for Carabossa, 1998; composer, performer, prodr.: Opus 1, 1995. Mem. French Copyright Soc. Avocation: travel. Home: 4 rue de la Biquenée, 44240 La Chapelle sur Erdr France

AUDREN, JEAN THIERRY, executive; b. Paris, Mar. 1, 1951. Degree in elec. engring., ENSEEC, Caen, France, 1974. Project engr. SFIM, Massy, France, 1975-87, mgr. rsch. & devel., 1987-92, mgr. bus. devel., 1992-99, indsl. property mgr., 1998-99; peodn. line mgr. SAGEM, Nauterre, France, 2000—. Inventor/patentee in field. Mem. Assn. Armement Terrestre, Soc. French Optics. Avocation: sailing. Home: 5 rue des ecoles, 78470 Saint Remy Chevreuse France Office: SAGEM, 61 rue Salvador Allende, 92751 Nanterre France

AUE, WALTER PAUL, chemist, senior researcher chemical disarmament; b. Winterthur, Zurich, Switzerland, Mar. 12, 1950; s. George K. and Emilie (Heiz) A.; m. Esther Lampart, Apr. 5, 1975 (div. Nov. 1995); children: Martin, Daniel. Diploma, Fed. Inst. Tech., Zurich, Switzerland, 1973, PhD, 1979; lectr., U. Berne, Switzerland, 1987. Postdoctoral fellow MIT, Cambridge, Mass., 1980-82; group head U. Basel, Switzerland, 1982-86, U. Berne, Switzerland, 1986-89, Def. Procurement Agy., Switzerland, 1989-91; sr. staff A.C. Lab., Spiez, Switzerland, 1991—. Patentee: method for recording spin resonance spectra, 1982; contbr. numerous articles to profl. jours. including Jour. of Chem. Physics, Jour. Magnetic Resonance, Biochemistry. 1st lt. Nuclear Biol. Chem. Protection, 1986—. Mem. NBC Officers Assn. (treas. 1998—), Model Airplane Assn. (sec. 1993—), Swiss Alpine Club. Avocations: mountaineering, swimming, model airplanes, piano. Office: AC Laboratorium, Ruettistr 11, CH-3702 Hondrich BE, Switzerland

AUEL, JEAN MARIE, writer; b. Chgo., Feb. 18, 1936; d. Neil Solomon and Martha Amelia (Wirtanen) Untinen; m. Ray Bernard Auel, Mar. 19, 1954; children: RaeAnn Marie, Karen Jean, Lenore Jerica, Kendall Poul, Marshall Philip. MBA, U. Portland, 1976, LittD (hon.), 1984; HHD (hon.), U. Maine, 1986; LHD (hon.), Mt. Vernon Coll., 1986; HHD (hon.), Pacific U., 1995. Office and tech. positions, then tech. writer, credit mgr. Tektronix, Inc., Beaverton, Oreg., 1964-76. Author: The Clan of the Cave Bear, 1980 (Friends of Lit. award 1980, finalist Best First Novel Nat. Book Awards 1980), The Valley of Horses, 1982, The Mammoth Hunters, 1985, The Plains of Passage, 1990 (Waldo award Waldenbooks 1990, Persie award WIN/WIN 1990). Bd. dirs. Oreg. Mus. Sci. and Industry, 1993-96; hon. campaign chair Oreg. Coun. for Humanities, 1991; speaker, fund raiser various charitable and ednl. orgns. Recipient Excellence in Writing award Pacific N.W. Booksellers Assn., 1980, award Scandinavian Kaleidoscope of Art and Life, 1982, Bronze Sculpture award Publieksprijs voor het Nederlandse Boek, 1990, Silver Trowel award Sacramento Archeol. Soc., 1990, contbn. award Dept. Interior/Soc. for Am. Archaeology, 1990, Nat. Zoo award, Centennial medal Smithsonian Instn., 1990, Golden Plate award Am. Acad. Achievement, 1986. Mem. PEN, Authors Guild, Willamette Writers (life), Oreg. Writers Colony (charter mem.), Internat. Women's Forum (bd. dirs. 1985-93), Mensa (hon. v.p. 1990—). Avocation: travel. Office: Jean V Naggar Lit Agy Ste 1 E 217 E 75th St New York NY 10021-2902

AUER, IGNAZ OSCAR, gastroenterologist, rheumatologist; b. Weiden, Germany, June 9, 1942; s. Franz Seraph and Gertraud (Goetz) A.; m. Erltraud Schulze, Dec. 30, 1967 (dec. 1994); children: Katja, Patrick. MD, U. Munich, 1967; prof. medicine, U. Würzberg, Germany, 1982. Postdoctoral fellow SUNY, Buffalo, 1970-73; lectr. U. Würzburg, 1978-82, prof. medicine, 1982-88; chmn. dept. medicine Juliusspital, Würzburg, 1988—. Contbr. over 200 articles on gastroenterology, rheumatology, and clin. immunology to profl. jours. Mem. Gastroenterol. Assn. Bavaria (pres. 1993), Am. Gastroenterol. Assn., Deutsche Gesellschaft für Verdauungs-U. Stoffwechsel Krankheiten, Deutsche Gesellschaft für Rheumatologie e.V. Home: Wilhelm-Hoegnerstr 19, D-97230 Estenfeld Germany Office: Juliusspital Dept Medicine, Juliuspromenade 19, D-97070 Würzburg Germany

AUERBACH, ANITA L., clinical psychologist; b. Flushing, N.Y., Dec. 23, 1946; d. Ben and Gussie (Zuckerman) Weiss; B.A. cum laude, SUNY, Buffalo, 1968, M.A., 1970; Ph.D. (N.Y. State Regents fellow 1970-72), George Washington U., 1977; m. Steven Miles Auerbach, May 25, 1969. Chief research youth crime control project D.C. Dept. Corrections, 1970-74; intern clin. psychology No. Va. Tng. Center, Fairfax, 1974-75, staff psychologist, then chief psychol. services, 1975-79; pvt. practice clin. psychology, dir. Commonwealth Psychol. Assocs., Mc Lean, Va., 1979—; lectr. Washington Tech. Inst., 1972-74, George Mason U., 1978—; cons. in field. Adv. bd. family edn. project Joseph P. Kennedy, Jr. Found., 1977-79; mem. regional appeals bd. No. Va. Public Sch. System, 1977-79. Recipient N.Y. State Scholar Incentive award, 1969; diplomate Am. Bd. Med. Psychotherapists, Internat. Acad. Behavioral Medicine. Mem. Am. Psychol. Assn., Am. Soc. Clin. Hypnosis (approved cons.), Va. Acad. Clin. Psychologists, Va. Psychol. Assn., No. Va. Soc. Clin. Psychologists, Washington Soc. Study Clin. Hypnosis, Psi Chi, Alpha Lambda Delta. Author articles in field. Office: 1479 Chain Bridge Rd Mc Lean VA 22101-5730

AUERBACH, FRANK, artist; b. Berlin, Apr. 29, 1931; s. Max and Charlotte Auerbach; m. Julia Wolstenholme, 1958; 1 child. Student, St. Martin's Sch. Art, London, Royal Coll. Art. One man shows: Beaux-Arts Gallery, London, 1956, 59, 61, 62, 63, Marlborough Fine Art, London, 1965, 67, 71, 74, 83, 87, 90, 97, Marlborough Gallery Inc., N.Y.C., 1969, 82, 94, 98, Villiers Art Gallery, Sydney, 1972, U. Essex, Colchester, 1973, Galleria Bergamini, Milan, 1973, Marlborough, Zurich, 1976, Anthony d'Offay, London, 1978, Retrospective Exhbn., Arts Coun., Hayward Gallery, London, Fruit Market Gallery, Edinburgh, 1978, Bernard Jacobson, N.Y.C., 1979, Brit. Pavilion Venice Biennale, 1986, Kunstverein, Hamburg, 1986, Folkwang Mus., Essen, 1987, Centro De Arte Reina Sofia, Madrid, 1987, Rijksmus. Vincent Van Gogh, Amsterdam, 1989, Marlborough Graphics, 1990, Yale Ctr. Brit. Art, New Haven, 1991, Nat. Gallery, London, 1995, Campbell-Thiebaud Gallery, San Francisco, 1995, Rex Irwin, Sydney, 1996, Charlottenborg, Copenhagen, 2000; group shows include: Tooths Gallery, London, 1958, 71, Carnegie Internat. Exhbn., Pitts., 1958, 61, Dunn Internat. Exhbn., London, 1963, Gulbenkian Exhbn., London, 1964, Peter Stuyvesant Found. Collection, London, 1967, L.A. County Mus., 1975, European Painting in the Seventies, U.S.A., 1976, New Spirit in Painting, R.A., London, 1981, Westkunst, Cologne, 1981, Eight Figurative Painters, Yale Ctr. Brit. Art, 1981, Tate Gallery, London, 1984, Gallery Western Australia, Perth, 1985, R.A., London, 1987, Kunstnernes Hus, Olso, 1987, Manchester City Art Gallery, 1991, Israel Mus., Jerusalem, 1992-93, A Sch. London, Asrup Fearnley Mus. Moderne Kunst, Oslo, 1994, Scottish Nat. Gallery Modern Art, Edinburgh, 1995-96, L'Ecole de Londres, Found. Dina Vierny-Musée Maillol, Paris; works in pub. collections in U.K., Australia, Brazil, U.S.A., Mex., Israel. Recipient Sivler medal for painting Royal Coll. Art; joint winner Golden Lion prize Venice Biennale, 1986. Office: care Marlborough Fine Art, 6 Albemarle St, London W1X 4BY, England

AUERBACH, JONATHAN LOUIS, securities trader; b. Phila., Nov. 25, 1942; s. Joseph and Judith (Evans) A.; m. Ann Gardner Luce, Nov. 10, 1989; children: Gabrielle, Jake, Nicholas, Patrick (dec.), Alexander. BA, Yale Coll., 1964. Asst. v.p. Bache & Co., N.Y.C., 1966-71; v.p. F.S. Smithers & Co., N.Y.C., 1971-73; sr. v.p. Atlantic Capital Corp., N.Y.C., 1973-80, Dillon Read & Co. Inc., N.Y.C., 1980-84; mng. dir. Dillon Read Ltd., London, 1984-86, J.L. Auerbach & Co., London, 1986-88; chmn. Cresvale, Internat. Inc., N.Y.C., 1988-92, Auerbach Grayson & Co. Inc., 1992—. Producer: (film) Vortex, 1983. Bd. dirs. Shakespeare Globe, N.Y.C., 1989—, Russia Privitization Fund. Mem. Downtown Assn., Nat. Assn. Securities Dealers (dist. 12 com. 1989-92, dist. 10 vice chmn. 1992).

AUERBACH, JOSEPH, lawyer, educator, retired; b. Franklin, N.H., Dec. 3, 1916; s. Jacob and Besse Mae (Reamer) A.; m. Judith Evans, Nov. 10, 1941; children: Jonathan L., Hope B. Pym. AB, Harvard U., 1938, LLB, 1941. Bar: N.H. 1941, Mass. 1952, U.S. Ct. Appeals (1st, 2d, 3d, 5th, 7th and D.C. cirs.), U.S. Supreme Ct. 1948. Atty. SEC, Washington and Phila., 1941-43, prin. atty., 1946-49; fgn. service staff officer U.S. Dept. State, Dusseldorf, W. Ger., 1950-52; ptnr. Sullivan & Worcester, Boston, 1952-82, counsel, 1982—; lectr. Boston U. Law Sch., 1975-76; lectr. Harvard Bus. Sch., Boston, 1980-82, prof., 1982-83, Class of 1957 prof., 1983-87, prof. emeritus, 1987—; prof. Harvard Extension Sch., 1988, 91-95; bd. dirs. Nat. Benefit Life Ins. Co., N.Y.C. Author: (with S.L. Hayes, III), Investment Banking and Diligence, 1986, Underwriting Regulation and Shelf Registration Phenomenon in Wall Street and Regulation, 1987, also chpt. to book, papers and articles in field. Trustee Mass. Eye and Ear Infirmary, Boston, 1981—, chmn. devel. com., 1985-88, chmn. nominating com., 1993-94; mem. adv. bd., former chmn. devel. com. Am. Repertory Theatre, Cambridge,

Mass., 1985—; bd. dirs., past pres. Friends of Boston U. Librs., 1972—; past v.p., bd. dirs. Shakespeare Globe Ctr., N.A., 1983-90; overseer New Eng. Conservatory of Music, 1992-98, mem. fin. com.; bd. dirs. English Speaking Union, Boston, 1995-98; chair 1938 Harvard Pres. Assn.; active Harvard Coll. Fund, Harvard Law Sch. Fund. Decorated Army Commendation medal; recipient Disting. Svc. award Harvard Bus. Sch., 1996, Disting. Teaching award 1993, Exemplary Svc. award Harvard Extension Sch., 1995. Mem. ABA, Mass. Bar Assn., Boston Bar Assn., Harvard Mus. Assn., St. Botolph Club, Harvard Club N.Y.C., Shop Club, Downtown Club. Home: 300 Boylston St Apt 512 Boston MA 02116-3923 Office: Sullivan & Worcester 1 Post Office Sq Ste 2300 Boston MA 02109-2129 also: Harvard Bus Sch Cumnock Hall Rm 300 Boston MA 02163

AUERBACH, PAUL IRA, lawyer; b. N.Y.C., Dec. 30, 1932; s. Joseph and Fannie (Steingard) A.; children: Stuart Andrew, Beth Royce. LLB, Bklyn. Law Sch., 1954; CLU, Am. Coll., 1980, ChFC, 1982. Bar: N.Y. 1955, Fla. 1991, U.S. Dist. Ct. (so. and ea. dists.) N.Y., U.S. Dist Ct. (so. dist.) Fla. 1991. Trial counsel Cosmopolitan Mutual Ins. Corp., N.Y.C., 1955-57, Hertz Corp., N.Y.C., 1957-59; ptnr. Brent, Phillips, Auerbach & Dranoff, Rockland, N.Y., 1959-63; prin. Paul I. Auerbach, Atty. at Law, N.Y.C. and Bronx, 1963-97, Palm Beach Gardens, Fla., 1990—. Founder Young Dem. Com., Bronx, 1955-60; committeeman Rep. Com., South Orangeton, N.Y., 1970-76. Mem. ABA, KP, N.Y. Bar Assn., N.Y. Criminal Bar Assn., Bronx Bar Assn. (chmn. criminal law com. 1990-91), Nat. Assn. Criminal Def. Lawyers, Internat. Assn. Fin. Planners, Rotary (chmn. drug prevention 1970-74), Palm Beach County Bar Assn. (pres.), North Palm Beach Bar Assn., Nat. Acad. Elder Law Attys., Sunrise W. Palm Beach Rotary Club, Masons. Avocations: tennis, gourmet food, golf. Home: 11215 Curry Dr Palm Bch Gdns FL 33418-3510

AUEWARAKUL, CHIRAYU, medical educator; b. Bangkok, Jan. 2, 1964; d. Suchinda and Yupha (Sukcharoen) Udomsakdi; m. Prasert Auewarakul, Mar. 14, 1996; children: Bhumipak, Bhirapat. MD with 1st class honors, Siriraj Hosp., Bangkok, 1988; PhD in Pathology, U. B.C., Vancouver, Can., 1992. Diplomate Am. Bd. Internal Medicine, Am. Bd. Hematology. Resident in internal medicine Duke U. Med. Ctr., 1992-95; postdoctoral fellow Terry Fox Lab. B.C. Cancer Agy., Vancouver, 1988-92; fellow in hematology-oncology Brigham and Women's Hosp., Boston, 1995-97; rsch. fellow Harvard Inst. Medicine, Boston, 1996-97; hematology-oncology fellow Harvard Med. Sch., Boston, 1995-97; mem. Chulabhorn Bone Marrow Transplant Ctr. Siriraj Hosp., Bangkok, 1997—, instr. faculty medicine, 1997—. Recipient Terry Fox Physician-Scientist Fellowship award Nat. Cancer Inst. Can., 1990, Can. Rsch. Soc. Fellowship award, 1990, Am. Soc. Hematology Travel award, 1990; Siriraj grantee for R&D, 1992-95. Mem. AMA, ACP, Mass. Med. Soc., N.Y. Acad. Sci. Avocations: tennis, traveling. Home: Soi Chaophaya Hosp, 826/264 Pinklow River Pkvw, Bangkok 10700, Thailand Office: Siriraj Hosp Fac Medicine, Dept Med Div Hematology, Bangkok 10700, Thailand

AUFFERMANN, GUDRUN, chemist, researcher; b. Duisburg, Germany, Sept. 4, 1957; d. Wilhelm Hugo and Gisela Anna (Becker) A. Diploma, Technische Hochschule Aachen, Germany, 1984, PhD, 1987, postgrad., 1987-90. Asst. Technische Hochschule Aachen, 1990-96; scientist Max Planck Inst., Stuttart, Germany, 1996-98, Max Planck Inst. for Chem. Physics Solid Matter, Dresden, Germany, 1998—. Mem. German Soc. Chemistry, N.Y. Acad. Scis. Avocations: skiing, theatre, tennis, piano. Office: Max Planck Inst Chem-Phys, Nöthnitzer Str 40, 01187 Dresden Germany

AUFFERMANN, WOLFGANG FRIEDRICH WILHELM, radiologist, neuroradiologist; b. Duisburg, Germany, Oct. 28, 1956; s. Wilhelm and Gisela A.; m. Annette Margarete Klöpper, Sept. 1, 1989; children: Paul Bernhard, Rose Charlotte, Luise Karoline. Student, U. Münster, Germany, 1975-76, U. Düsseldorf, Germany, 1976-77; BA, U. Bochum, Germany, 1978; MD, U. Aachen, Germany, 1982. Resident U. Cologne, Germany, 1982-83, U. Aachen, 1983-86, U. Münster, 1988-90; rsch. fellow U. Calif., San Francisco, 1986-88; asst. Free U. Berlin, 1990-92; assoc. U. Bochum, 1993—; pvt. practice, Hamburg, Germany, 1993—; fellow U. Leiden, Netherlands, 1983, U. Chgo., 1984; cons. BYK Gulden, Konstanz, Germany, 1985-86, NYCOMED Co., Oslo and Germany, 1991-93, Schering, Berlin, 1993. Author: Magnetic Resonance Imaging of the Body, 1987, 3d edit., 1993; editor: Radiology for Students, 1986, 2d edit., 1993, Endocrine Imaging, 1993, 2d edit., 1994; also over 100 articles. Grantee German Rsch. Soc., 1986-88, 89 Mem. Radiol. Soc. N.Am., Soc. Magnetic Resonance, Am. Roentgen Ray Soc., German Roentgen Ray Soc., Am. Heart Assn. (award 1987), European Soc. Magnetic Resonance. Avocations: piano, tennis, sailing, skiing. Office: Pvt Clinic Radiology, Alte Holstenstrasse 16, 21031 Hamburg Germany

AUGER, PIERRE, marketing director; b. Bouake, Côte d'Ivoire, Feb. 20, 1964; s. Paul Auger and Marie Menard; m. Sonsoles Caro; 1 child, Ines. DES in Comerce and Adminstrn., Ecole Sup. de Commerce Pau, 1987; MBA, Cath. Inst. Bus. Adminstrn., Madrid, 1987. Sales supr. Citroën, Paris, 1987-88, mktg. asst., 1988; promotion asst. Citroën, Madrid, 1988-89; trade promotion mgr. Gillette, Madrid, 1989-90, brand group mgr., 1990-94; mktg. dir. CIC (Universal/Paramount/Dreamworks), Madrid, 1994—. Avocations: cinema, golf, windsurfing. Office: CIC, Albacete 5-3, 28027 Madrid Spain

AUGOUSTIDES, JOHN GEORGE THEMISTOCLES, cardiothoracic anesthesiologist, educator; b. Cape Town, South Africa, May 31, 1967; came to U.S., 1994; s. Themistocles Alexander and Marina (Yamoyany) A. MB CHB, U. Cape Town, 1990. Diplomate Am. Bd. Anesthesiology; cert. in perioperative echocardiography. Residency in family practice Cape Town, Pt. Elizabeth, South Africa, 1991-94; resident in internal medicine Grad. Hosp., Phila., 1994-95; resident in anesthesia U. Pa., Phila., 1995-98, cardiothoracic anesthesia fellow, 1998-99, clin. asst. prof., 1999—. Author: (book chpts.) Echocardiography Atlas, 1999, (CD-Rom chpt.) Cardiothoracic Anesthesia, 1999. Recipient Anesthesiology medal S. African Soc. Anesthetists. Mem. Am. Soc. Anesthesiologists, Soc. Cardiovascular Anesthesiologists, Hellenic Med. Soc. of Greater Phila. (founding, treas. 1997, 98). Greek Orthodox. Avocation: film, impressionist art, swimming, tennis, theology. E-mail: yiandoc@hotmail.com. Office: Dept Anesthesia Penn Tower 3400 Spruce St Philadelphia PA 19104

AUGSTEIN, RUDOLF, publisher; b. Nov. 5, 1923. D.H.C., Bath U., 1983, U. Wuppertal, 1987, Moscow State Inst. Internat. Rels., 1999; Senator (hon.), U. Hamburg, 1988. Publisher Der Spiegel (weekly), Hamburg, 1947—; under arrest (for alleged polit. offence), 1962-63. Author: Spiegelungen, 1964; Konrad Adenauer, 1964, Preussens Friedrich und die Deutschen, 1968, Jesus Menschensohn, 1972. Elected Bundestag, 1972, resigned, 1973. Served to lt. German Army, World War II. Named Hon. citizen Hamburg, 1994; recipient Commander's Cross of the Order of Merit of the Federal Republic of Germany, 1997, Ludwig-Börne-award, 2000. Mem. German PEN. Office: Der Spiegel, Brandstwiete 19, D-20457 Hamburg Germany

AUGUST, JUNE, artist, educator; b. Warren, Ohio, Jan. 28, 1957; d. Fred Homec and Maria Susan (Grunbaum) Homec; children: Trillium Hinton. BFA, Syracuse (N.Y.) U., 1979; postgrad., U. N.H., 1979-88; MFA, Tufts U., 1996. Art tchr. Stratham (N.H.) Sch., 1983-2000; lectr. in field. Artist: Target III, Biennial Portland Mus., 1998, Red Banners, Museo d'Art Conte, Brazil, 1999, Target II, Gallery, Cologne, Germany, 1998, others; one-woman shows include O'Farrell Gallery, Brunswick, Maine, 1999, Fondazione Adolph Carmine, Florence, Italy, 1999, others; exhibited in group shows at Museo d'Art Moderna, Rio de Janeiro, Brazil, 1999, Norsk Internat. Print Triennale, Fredrikstad, Norway, 1999, German Internat. Grafik Triennal, Frechen, Germany, 1999, O Mio Dolce Ardor-Ableben, Orangerie Köln Gallery, Cologne, 2000, Westbrook Coll., Maine, 2000, others; works represented at Galerie Michele Broutta, Paris, O'Farrell Gallery, Brunswick; work collected at Royal Mus. of Fine Arts, Antwerp, Belgium, Boston Pub. Libr., Singapore, Malaysia, Belgium, others. Active fundraiser Aids Action Com., Boston, 1994-99; contbr. December Sale scholarship, Boston, 1991-99; artist Polit. Art. vs. War, U.S. and Europe, 1992-99. Recipient Frans Masereel Flemish Min. of Culture, Kasterlee, Belgium, 1995-99, Fulbright Fund Alt. to France, 1992, to Japan, 1997, Cite Internat. des Arts award French Min. of Culture, Paris, 1991-99, award Finnish Union of Artists, Turku, 1993, 95, award CAGE, Cin., 1995, others. Achievements include work in sculpture, installation, painting and printmaking with internat. shows and awards. Avocations: voice lessons, opera arias, film. Home: PO Box 160 North Hampton NH 03862-0160

AUGUSTE LE BRETON, (MONTFORT), author; b. Lesneven (Finistere) France, Feb. 18, 1913; s. Eugene and Rosalie (Gorel) M.; m. Marguerite Lecacheur, Aug. 29, 1964; 1 child, Maryvonne. Served with French Forces, 1940-44. Decorated Croix de Guerre with stars au titre de la Resistance. Mem. Société des Auteurs, Compositeurs, Editeurs de Musique, Société Auteurs, Compositeurs, Dramatiques. Author: Du Rififi Chez les Hommes, 1954; Les Hauts Murs (Roman autobiographique), 1954; La Loi des Rues (Roman autobiographique), 1955; Razzia sur la Chnouf, 1954; Le Rouge est mis, 1954; La serie des Rififi á Frarers le monde 11 vols. dont Rififi á New York, 1961; Les Jeunes Voyons, 1965, Brigade Anti-Gangs, 1965, Le clan des Siciliens, 1966; Les Mag's, 1967, Le Tueur a la Lune, 1971, Les Pégriots, 1973, Mr. Crab, 1992, 94; (poems) Du Vent, 1968; Malfrats and Co., 1970; Les Bourlingueurs, 1972; Rouges Étaient les Emeraudes, 1971; Monsieur Rififi (biography), 1974; Aventures sous les Tropiques, 1977; La mome Piaf, 1980; Série Brigade Anti-Gang de 36 vols., Fortif's, 1982; 2 sous D'Amour (biography), 1986, Dictionnaire réactualisé d'Argot, 1986, Du Rebecca chez les Aristos, 1991, Ils ont dansé le Rififi (memories), 1991, 95, le Bedeau (Roman noir); others. Address: 12 rue Pasteur, 78110 Le Vesinet France

AUGUSTI, GIULIANO, structural engineering educator, consultant; b. Naples, Italy, Feb. 13, 1935; s. Massimo and Jole (De Bernardo) A.; m. Gabriella Tocco, Aug. 11, 1962; 1 child, Mario. Grad. in civil engring., U. Naples, 1958; PhD in Engring., Cambridge (Eng.) U., 1964, DSc, 1999; D in Engring (hon.), Ruhr U., Bochum, Germany, 1997. Asst. prof. U. Naples, 1959-69, lectr., 1969-70; lectr. U. Palermo, Sicily, Italy, 1970-71; lectr. U. Florence, Italy, 1971-72, prof., 1973-85, dean engring., 1982-85; assoc. prof. U. Cagliari, Sardinia, Italy, 1972-73; prof. structural engring. U. Rome La Sapienza, 1985—; mem. Inter-univ. Rsch. Ctr. Bldg. Aerodynamics and Wind Engring., Florence, 1987-98, dir., 1992-98, hon. pres., 1998—; mem. several coms. for structural and bldg codes, Italy and Europe; mem. Nat. com. for Enging., Rome, 1989-94; chmn. com. for univ. internat. rels. Ministry Univ. and Sci. Rsch., 1990-93; Italian Acad. rep. Com. of CEE Erasmus Program, 1991-94; mem. Min. Com. for Internat. U. Coop., 1998-2000; chmn. WG2 of European Thematic Network Higher Engring. Edn. for Europe, 1996-99, promoter Activity 2, Enhancing Engring. Edn. for Europe, 2000-2003. Co-author: Probabilistic Methods in Structural Engineering, 1984; contbr. over 200 articles on structural mechanics and engring. and engring. edn. to profl. jours. Fellow European Soc. Engring. Edn. Sefi (pres. 1987-88, bd. dirs. 1980-92); mem. Italian Assn. Earthquake Engring. (v.p. 1986-90, 98—), Italian Assn. Theoretical and Applied Mechanics (editor Internat. Jour. "Meccanica" 1990-98, bd. dirs. 1998—), Internat. Assn. Wind Engring. (pres. 1989-99), Order Rome Engrs., Russian Acad. for Arch. and Constrn. Scis. (fgn. mem.). Fax: 39-06-488-4852. E-mail: gaugusti@uniroma1.it; augusti@scilla.ing.uniroma1.it. Home: Via Treviso 15, 00161 Rome Italy Office: U Rome La Sapienza Fac Eng, Via Eudossiana 18, 00184 Rome Italy

AUGUSTIN, MARC DOMINIQUE, communications company executive; b. Suresnes, France, Feb. 8, 1959; s. Bernard Andre and Annette Berthe Augustin. Diploma ISG, Inst. Supérieur de Gestion, Paris, 1981; MBA, NYU, 1986. Assoc. CITROEN S.A., Neuilly, France, 1981-84; sr. cons., asst. mgr. banking and ins. dept. EUREQUIP S.A., Nanterce, France, 1986-95; mng. internat. devel. IBM Global Svcs., 1996-99; founder, mng. dir. Abacus Telecom SA, Paris, 1999—. NYU scholar, N.Y.C., 1985. Mem. Yachting Club, Club de Bernières S/Mer, Am. C. of C. Paris. Avocations: hobie cat, golf. Home: 19 Rue de Marnes, Sèvres, Haute de Seine, 92380 Garches Franch Office: EUREQUIP SA, 5 Esplanade Charles de Gaulle, 92733 Nanterce Cedex France

AUGUSTINE, JEROME SAMUEL, merchant banker; b. Racine, Wis., May 7, 1928; s. Lester Samuel and Pearl (Hilker) A.; m. Camilla Sewell, Feb. 7, 1953; children: Theodore Samuel Purnell, Julia Sewell Augustine Marshall, Elizabeth Stroebel Augustine Burgoyne. AB cum laude, Harvard U., MBA, 1952. Cons. Scudder, Stevens & Clark, Boston, 1952-56; founder, treas., dir. Vencap, Inc., Boston, 1956-58; treas., dir. Consumer Products, Inc., Boston, 1956-58; founder, treas., dir. Microsonics, Inc., Hingham, Mass., 1956-58; treas., dir. Capitol Mgmt. Corp., Boston, 1956-58; cons. Kidder, Peabody & Co., Boston, 1958-64; pres. Cosmos Am. Corp., N.Y.C., 1964-66; founder, pres., dir. Cosmos Securities Corp., 1965-70, Cosmos (Bahamian) Ltd., Nassau, 1964-70; mng. dir. J. Samuel Augustine & Co., Ltd., Toronto, Ont., Can., 1966—; 1st v.p. Van Alstyne, Noel & Co., N.Y.C., 1973-74; v.p. Wright Investors' Svc., Bridgeport, 1974-87, sr. v.p., 1987-92; pres. Kredietbank (Belgium) Global Asset Mgmt., Stamford, 1992-94; bd. dirs. Chicken Soup, Plus, Inc. Trustee Low-Heywood Sch.; trustee The Augustine Family Charitable Trust. Named to Washington Hall of Fame, 1986. Mem. Boston Fin. Rsch. Assocs. (gov. 1960-64, v.p. 1963-64), New Eng. Amateur Rowing Assn. (past pres.), Union Boat Club, Harvard Club, Noroton Yacht Club, Royal Canadian Yacht Club, Ox Ridge Hunt Club, Calif. Polo Club, Royal Ascot Polo Club, East India Club (London). Anglican. Fax: 206-374-6442. E-mail: augustco@concord.net. Office: Ste F24, 122 St Patrick St, Toronto, ON Canada M5T 2X8

AUGUSTINE, JIM HENRY, history educator, baseball coach; b. Litchfield, Ill., Apr. 9, 1942; s. Henry (Hank) and Margariete (Kreuter) A.; children: Amy, Jamie, Driscoll Henry. BA, So. Ill. U., 1967. Social studies chmn. Livingston (Ill.) High Sch., 1963-99, tchr., coach, 1969-93; mem. sec. of state police force, investigator Springfield (Ill.) Office, 1963-69. Precinct committeeman Dem. Orgn., Olive Twp., 1970—; twp. trustee Olive Twp., 1990—; mem. Madison County bd., 1998, Livingston Vol. Fire Dept. Mem. NRA (life), Nat. Slovak Soc., Laborers Union, KC (Staunton), Lions (Livingston-Williamson). Democrat. Roman Catholic. Home: PO Box 11 Livingston IL 62058-0011 Office: Livingston High Sch SAR 3A US Rt 66 Livingston IL 62058

AUGUSTINE, NORMAN RALPH, organization executive, educator; b. Denver, July 27, 1935; s. Ralph Harvey and Freda Irene (Immenga) A.; m. Margareta Engman, Jan. 20, 1962; children: Gregory Eugen, René Irene. BSE magna cum laude, Princeton U., 1957, MSE, 1959; DEng (hon.), Rensselaer Poly. Inst., 1988; DSc (hon.), U. Colo., 1989; ED (hon.), Western Md. Coll., 1990; DEng (hon.), U. Md., 1992; D Aerospace Mgmt. (hon.), Embry Riddle U., 1992; DEng (hon.), Stevens Inst., 1993; HHD (hon.), Wheeling Jesuit Coll., 1994; DSc (hon.), SUNY, 1994; DEng (hon.), U. Ctrl. Fla., 1995, Worcester Polytech., 1996; LHD (hon.), U. Denver, 1996, Georgetown U., 1997, Trinity Coll., 1997; DEng (hon.), U. Ariz., 1997; LLD (hon.), Duke U., 1997; DEng (hon.), Milw. Sch. Engring., 1998. Rsch. asst. Princeton U., 1957-58; program mgr., chief engr. Douglas Aircraft Co., Inc., Santa Monica, Calif., 1958-65; asst. dir. def. rsch. and engring. U.S. Govt., Office of Sec. Def., Washington, 1965-70; v.p. advanced systems Missiles and Space Co., LTV Aerospace Corp., Dallas, 1970-73; asst. sec. army The Pentagon, Washington, 1973-75; undersec. army The Pentagon, 1975-77; v.p. ops. Martin Marietta Aerospace Corp., Bethesda, Md., 1977-82; pres. Martin Marietta Denver Aerospace Co., 1982-85, sr. v.p. info. systems, 1985, from pres., COO to chmn., CEO, 1986-95, also bd. dirs.; pres. Lockheed Martin Corp., Bethesda, 1995-96, pres., CEO, 1996-97; lectr. (rank of prof.) Princeton U., 1997—; chair American Red Cross, Washington, 1999—; bd. dirs. Phillips Petroleum Co., Procter & Gamble Co., New Am. Schs. Devel. Corp.; cons. office Sec. of Def., 1971—, Exec. Office Pres., 1971-73, Dept. Army, Dept. Air Force, Dept. Navy, FAA, Dept. Energy, Dept. Transp.; mem. USAF Sci. Adv. Bd.; chmn. Def. Sci. Bd., Exel Comm., 1997—; mem. NATO Group Experts on Air Def., 1966-70, NASA Rsch. and Tech. Adv. Coun., 1973-75, chmn. Space Sys. and Tech. Adv. Bd., 1985-89; mem. Chief of Naval Ops. Exec. Bd., 1989-92; chmn. def. policy adv. com. on trade, 1988-91, 93—; lectr. Princeton U., 1997—. Author: Augustine's Laws; coauthor: The Defense Revolution, 1990, Augustine's Travels, 1997; mem. adv. bd. Jour. Def. Rsch., 1970—; assoc. editor Def. Systems Mgmt. Rev., 1977-82; mem. editorial bd. Astronautics and Aerospace. Trustee Johns Hopkins U., Princeton U., MIT; mem. bd. govs. Colonial Williamsburg, 1996—; chmn. White House/NASA Adv. Com. on Future of U.S. Space Program, 1991, Nat. Security Telecomm. Adv. Com., U.S. Antarctic Program Rev. Com., 1996-97; nat. program evaluation com., coun. v.p. Boy Scouts Am., pres., 1993—; chmn. ARC; mem. Pres.'s Com. of Advisors on Sci. and Tech. Recipient Meritorious Svc. medal Dept. Def., 1979, 5 Disting. Civilian Svc. medals Dept. Def., Nat. Engring. award Am. Assn. Engring. Socs., 1991, Am. Acad. Achievement Golden Plate award, 1995, James Madison medal Princeton U., 1995, Blumenthal award Johns Hopkins U. Sch. Engring., 1996, Gold Eagle award Soc. Am. Mil. Engrs. Acad. of Fellows, 1996, Ralph Coates Roe medal ASME, 1996, M. Eugene Merchant Mfg. medal, 1997, Nat. Medal of Technology, 1997; named Personality of Yr., Flight Internat. Aerospace, 1996. Fellow IEEE (Founders' award 1996), AIAA (hon., bd. dirs. 1978-85, pres. 1983-84, Goddard medal 1988), Am. Astron. Soc., Am. Helicopter Soc. (dir. 1974-75), Royal Aero. Soc.; mem. NAE (chmn. 1994—, Arthur M. Bueche award 1991), Am. Acad. Arts and Scis., Internat. Acad. Astronautics, Assn. U.S. Army (pres. 1980-84, chmn. 1990—, George C. Marshall medal), Nat. Security Indsl. Assn. (Forrestal medal 1988), Indsl. Coll. Armed Forces (Eisenhower award 1990), Armed Forces Comm. and Electronics Assn. (Sarnoff medal 1990), Nat. Space Club (Goddard Trophy 1991), Rotary (Nat. Space Trophy 1992), Planetary Soc. (bd. dirs.), Phi Beta Kappa, Sigma Xi, Tau Beta Pi. Presbyterian. Office: Lockheed Martin Corp 6801 Rockledge Dr Bethesda MD 20817-1877 also: Amer Red Cross Nat Hdqs Bldg 17th & D St NW Washington DC 20006

AUGUSTITHIS, STYLIANOS-SAVVAS, publisher; b. Addis Abeba, Ethiopia, Feb. 2, 1931; s. Panagiotis and Maria (Germeni) A. BSc, U. Durham, U.K., 1953; Dr.rer.nat., U. Hamburg, Germany, 1956. Dir., organizer Prospectors Tng. Ctr., Ethiopia, 1957-67; prof. mineralogy and petrography Nat. Tech. U., Athens, 1967-84; dir. Theophrastus Pubs., Athens, 1984—; hon. prof. China U. Geoscis., Beijing, 1996; bd. dirs. Lab. of Textural Analysis, Pagrati, Greece, Theophrastus Pubs. Author (atlas) Atlas of Textural Patterns of Granties, Gneisses and Assoc. Rock Types, 1973, Atlas of the Textural Patterns of Basic and Ultrabasic Rocks and their Genetic Significance, 1979. Pres. Internat. Commn. for the Study of Bauxites, Alumina and Aluminium, 1978-82; councillor Internat. Assn. Genesis of the Ore Deposits, 1966-68. Named Hon. Academician by Academia Internat. (Vebrano Holy), named Academician by Acad. Internat. de Lucete (Paris). Fellow Russian Acad. Nat. Sci. (fgn.); mem. Croatian Acad. Zagreb (corr.), N.Y. Acad., Order Internat. Fellowship, Croatian Acad. Scis. & Arts (corr.). Home: 33 J Theologou, 157 73 Zographou Greece Office: Lab of Textural Analysis, 89 Hymettou, Pagrati Greece

AUGUSTI-TOCCO, GABRIELLA, developmental biology educator; b. Naples, Italy, Aug. 25, 1935; d. Donato Tocco and Filomena D'Argenio; m. Giuliano Augusti, Aug. 11, 1962; 1 child, Mario. Degree laurea in medicine, U. Napoli, Naples, 1960. Post-doctoral fellow King's Coll., London, 1962-63, Brandeis U., Waltham, Mass., 1968-69; rschr. Nat. Rsch. Coun., Naples, Italy, 1964-78, Florence, Italy, 1978-80; full prof. U. Napoli, Naples, 1980-84, U. La Sapienza, Rome, 1984—; dir. dept cellular and devel. biology U. La Sapienza, 1989-94; part-time lectr. U. di Napoli, Naples, 1975-78. Contbr. articles to profl. jours. Mem. Internat. Soc. Neuro-Chemistry, Internat. Soc. Devel. Neuroscis., European Molecular Biology Orgn. Home: Via Treviso 15, 00161 Rome Italy Office: U La Sapienza Dept Cell and Devel Biolog, Piazzale A Moro 5, 00185 Rome Italy

AUGUSTO, WALTER RUIZ, chemist, researcher; b. Piura, Peru, Aug. 4, 1950; s. Jose Cabredo Augusto and Elena Ruiz; m. Marta Marquezan, July 19, 1980; children: Tassia Alicia, Walter. Master, I.N.A.N.F., Piura, 1966; Doctor, LaMolina, Lima, Peru, 1974. Pesquisador IIA, Lima, 1972-79; prof. titular Furg, Rio Grande, Brazil, 1979—, supt. pesquisa, 1989-91, tutor-pet, 1991—, coordendor-pos grad., 1995-97, proprietor, 1998—; cons. Capes, Brazil, 1989—, SBCTA, Brazil, 1995—, Fapergs, Brazil, 1991—. Editor Vector. Mem. AOAC. Home: Rua Cap Aristides, Garnier 185, 96216100 Rio Grande Brazil Office: Furg, Av Alfredo Huch 475, CP 474 Rio Grande Brazil

AUH, YANG JOHN, librarian, educational administrator; b. Chulla Namdo, Korea, Mar. 18, 1934; came to U.S., 1962, naturalized, 1971; s. Sam Hyuck and So Yae (Suh) A.; m. Karen Kyung-ja Kim, Mar. 11, 1969; 1 child, Alice Kim. BA, Chung-ang U., 1957; MA in LS, Western Mich. U., 1964; Cert. in Libr. Adminstrn. Devel., U. Md., 1973; Cert. in Advanced Librarianship, Columbia U., 1975; Cert. in Mgmt., Clarkson U., 1978; MBA, St. John's U., 1979; postgrad., NYU, 1996, Oxford (Eng.) U., 1997. Asst. libr. Korean Nat. Libr., Seoul, 1957; tech. svcs. libr. Korean Mil. Acad. Libr., Seoul, 1958-61; asst. libr. Branch County Libr., Coldwater, Mich., 1964; head union catalog L.I. U. Librs., Greenvale, N.Y., 1965-68; head catalog dept., tech. svcs. coord. Wagner Coll. Libr., S.I., N.Y., 1968-71, libr. dir., 1972-84, dir. Libr. and Learning Resources Ctr., 1984-2000; dir. Internat. Exch. program Wagner Coll., S.I., N.Y., 2000—; pres. Highland Realty Mgmt., 1984—; evaluator, Commn. Higher Edn., Middle States Assn. Colls. and Schs., 1984; trustee Am. Friends of Chung-ang U., 1979—; rsch. bd. advisors, dep. gov. Am. Biographical Inst., Inc., Raleigh, N.C., 1998—; mem. adv. coun. Internat. Biographical Ctr., Cambridge, Eng., 1999—. HEW fellow, 1973, 78. Mem. ALA, N.Y. State Libr. Assn., Korean Libr. Assn., N.Y. Librs. Club, Omicron Delta Kappa (chpt. admintrv. mem. 1995). Office: Wagner Coll Horrmann Libr One Campus Rd Staten Island NY 10301-4428

AUKUTSIONEK, SERGEJ PAVLOVICH, economist, researcher; b. Moscow, Dec. 9, 1948; s. Pavel and Raia Aukutsionek; m. Nina Zhukova; children: Vladimir Zhukov, Oleg Zhukov. Master's degree, Moscow State U., 1971; Doctorate, Inst. World Economy & Internat. Rels., Moscow, 1974. Cert. in math. methods of econ. analysis. Jr. rschr. Inst. World Economy and Internat. Rels., Moscow, 1974-75, rschr., 1975-81, sr. rschr., 1981-91, chief rschr., 1992-95, head of rsch. group on transitional econ. crisis, 1992—; head Ctr. Rsch. Transition Econ., Moscow, 1995—; prof. Moscow State U., 1989—. Author: (books) Contemporary Western Theories and Models of Business Cycle, 1984, The Discussion on the Theory of Business Cycle, 1990, Theory of Transition to the Market Economy, 1993, 2d edit., 1995, Empirira of Transition to the Market Economy, 1998; co-founder, editor: (bull.) Russian Econ. Barometer, 1992—. Grantee Soros Found., 1996, Ford Found., 1997. Mem. Ctr. for Internat. Rsch. on Econ. Tendency Surveys. Office: Inst World Econ Intern Rels, 23 Profsoyuznaia St, 117859 Moscow Russia

AULD, ROBIN ERNEST, judge; b. Sunbury on Thames, U.K., July 19, 1937; s. Ernest and Adelaide Mary (Mackie) A.; m. Catherine Eleanor Mary Pritchard, June 8, 1963; children: Catherine Rohan, Timothy Rawdon. LLB, King's Coll., London, 1958, PhD, 1963. Barrister-at-law, 1959; Queen's Counsel, 1975-87; Bar: N.Y. 1984. Barrister The Temple, London, 1959-87; High Ct. judge Queen's Bench Divsn., London, 1987-95; Lord Justice of Appeal London, 1995—; sr. presiding judge for Eng. and Wales, 1995-98; recorder of Crown Ct., London, 1977-87; legal assessor to Gen. Med. Coun., 1982-87; chmn. criminal com. Jud. Studies Bd., 1989-91; presiding judge We. Cir., 1991-94; conducted criminal cts. revs., Eng. and Wales, 1999-2000. Decorated Knight, The Queen of Eng., 1987; apptd. privy counsellor to the Queen, 1995. Fellow King's Coll. London; mem. Worshipful Co. Woolmen, Athenaeum Club. Office: Royal Cts Justice, Strand, WC2A 2LL London England

AULEYTNER, JULIAN JAN, physicist; b. Studzianki, Poland, Feb. 13, 1922; s. Kazimierz and Wanda (Zakrzewska) A.; m. Jolanta Lepszy. MSc, Univ. Warsaw, 1952, DSc, 1959. With Inst. Exptl. Physics Warsaw U., 1954-61; assoc. prof. Inst. Physics Polish Acad. Sci., 1954-67, extra ordinary prof. Inst. Physics, 1967-74, prof. in ordinary Inst. Physics, 1974—. Contbr. 220 articles to profl. jours.; inventor in field. Mem. Polish Phys. Soc., European Phys. Soc., Polish Soc. Synchroton Radiation, Polish CoDATA Nat. Com. Roman Catholic. Home: Krasinskiego 28/19, 01-769 Warsaw Poland Office: Inst Physics Polish Acad Sci, Al Lotnikow 32/46, 02-668 Warsaw Poland

AULIN, ARVID YRJÖ, mathematician, physicist; b. Oulu, Finland, Aug. 7, 1929; s. K. Arvi E. and Jenny (Päkkilä) A.;m. Pirkko Anneli Aulin-Ahmavaara, May 26, 1970. MA, U. Helsinki, Finland, 1950, PhD, 1954. Research fellow Nordic Inst. for Theoretical Atom Physics, Copenhagen, 1957-59; researcher Atomic Energy Commn., Helsinki, 1960-61; lectr. theoretical physics U. Helsinki, 1962-63, acting prof. philosophy, 1968-70; prof. theoretical physics U. Turku, Finland, 1963-67; research prof. Acad. Finland, Helsinki, 1971-74; prof. math. and methodology U. Tampere, Finland, 1974—; cons. The Finnish State Broadcasting Co., Helsinki, 1968-70.

Author: Information, 1969, 2d edit., 1970, 3d edit., 1975, Cybnernetic Methodology, 1969, 2d edit., 1970, The Cybernetic Laws of Social Progress, 1982, Essays on This Time, 1987, Foundations of Mathematical System Dynamics, 1989, The Impact of Science on Economic Growth and Its Cycles, 1998, Taboos of the Welfare State, 1998; contbr. numerous sci. papers; essayist Kanava mag., Helsinki, 1982— (WSOY literary prize 1987). Fellow Finnish Acad. Sci. and Letters. Avocations: classical music, jazz, tennis. Home: Oulunkylantori 2 C 16, 00640 Helsinki Finland

AULITZKY, HERBERT, climatologist, educator, forester; b. Innsbruck, Tyrol, Austria, Feb. 25, 1922; s. Karl and Ida (Demetz) A.; m. Franziska Wolf, Aug. 9, 1947; children: Helmut, Wolfgang, Herbert, Walter, Elisabeth. B in Engring., U. Agrl., Vienna, Austria, 1948; D, U. Bodenkultur, Vienna, Austria, 1950. Forest engr. Austrian Svc. Torrent and Avalanche Control, Innsbruck, 1949-53, chief of county, 1963-71; chief of country Austrian Svc. Torrent and Avalanche Control, Linz, 1971-72; rsch. engr., group leader Forest Rsch. Inst., Innsbruck, 1953-62; prof. U. Bodenkultur, Vienna, 1972-90; lectr. bioclimatology U. Bodenkultur, Vienna, 1967—; cons. Austrian Parliament Forestry, Environ. Control, Torrent and River Control, Vienna, 1974-92. Author: Endangered Alpine Regions and Disaster Prevention Measures, 1974, Bioklimatische Grundlagen einer standortsgemässen Bewertschaftung des subalpinen Arven-Lärchenwaldes, 1982, Das Forsttechnische System der Wildbachverbauung. Lt. German Army Res., 1940-45. Recipient Verdienstkreuz Tyrol-Country, Govt. Tyrol, 1971, Grosses Silbernes Ehren Zeichen Verdienste, Fed. Rep. Austria, 1983, Österreichisches Ehrenzeichen f. Wissenchaft, Pres. Rep. Austria, 1992. Mem. European Acad. Scis. and Arts, Soc. Torrent Control Engrs. Austria (hon.), Soc. Torrent Control China (hon.), Assn. Italy Idronomia, Rsch. Soc. Disaster Prevention (hon.). Roman Catholic. Avocations: fine arts, history, philosophy. Home: Schmalzgasse 10/4, A-6020 Tulfes Austria Office: U Agrl, Peter Jordanstr 82, A 1190 Vienna Austria

AULSEBROOK, WILLIAM ALEXANDER, dental surgeon, consultant, researcher; b. Johannesburg, South Africa, Feb. 21, 1935; s. William and Willemina Elizabeth (Verhoef) A. B Dental Surgery, U. Witwatersrand, Johannesburg, 1958, PhD, 1993; Diploma in Computing, Natal Tng. Ctr., 1961. Pvt. practice dental surgery, London, 1959-60, Johannesburg, 1961-79; sr. lectr., head facial prosthetics U. Durban-Westville, 1982-89; head comms. dept. health svcs. and welfare Ho. of Dels., Durban, 1990-92; cons. and rschr. in craniofacial identification, Durban, 1993—; clin. lectr. U. Witwatersrand, 1961-70; prosthetic cons. Westworth Hosp., Durban, 1982-90; external examiner U. Pretoria, South Africa; lectr., cons. in Visual Basic computer lang., Fairfield, N.J., 1997—; hon. cons. in forensic odontology and craniofacial identification, forensic medicine. Author: (booklet) Peten Amen: The Priest of Akhmim, 1997; contbg. author: Encyclopedia of Forensic Science, 1998; contbr. articles to profl. jours. Mem. South African Dental Assn., South African Med. and Dental Coun. Home and Office: 502 Yarningdale, 199 Marine Parade, Durban 4001, South Africa

AULT, JEFFREY MICHAEL, investment banker; b. Norfolk, Va., Jan. 20, 1947; s. Frank Willis and Helen Blake (Hamner) A.; 1 child, Jeffrey Franklin. BS, U. Calif., San Diego, 1974; postgrad., U. San Diego, 1975-84, Word of Faith Bible Inst., Dallas. Ordained to ministry Fedn. Gen. Assemblies Internat., 1988. Dir. nat. bus. devel. Mayflower, San Diego, 1970-75; dir. new accounts Aero-Mayflower Transit Co., Alexandria, Va., 1976-78; v.p. Mchts. Mgmt. Co., Washington, 1976-78; v.p. mktg. Stevens Van Lines, various states, 1978-80; exec. v.p. Fla. Am. Van Lines Inc., Tampa, 1980-84; pres. Victory World Trade Corp., Washington, 1984-85; chmn., CEO Maranatha Van Lines, Inc., Tampa, 1984-90; exec. dir. Maranatha Vision Ministries Inc., Tampa, Swords Into Plowshares, France, Russia, Vietnam, U.S.; pres. Ea. Star Trading Co., Minsk, Belarus; pres. JRW Corp., S.A., Santiago, Tampa, Seattle, Moscow, Bangkok, Mpls., Buenos Aires, Miami, Zurich; v.p., sr. ptnr. Noord Prince Mchts. Bank, Curacao; sr. ptnr. Geneses Group, Mpls.; trustee Gold-Lyon Trust, The Bear Trust, Vaduz, Leichtenstein. Mem. U.S. Senate Trust, Hillsborough County Republican Party; sustaining mem. Rep. Nat. Com. Sgt. USMC, 1966-72, Vietnam. Mem. DAV, Aircraft Owners and Pilots Assn., U. Calif. at San Diego Alumni Assn., First U.S. Marine Div. Assn., USMC Combat Corrs. Assn., Mensa. Home: PO Box 811 18026 Lindawoods St Odessa FL 33556-4713 Office: JRW Corp SA PO Box 391 Tampa FL 33601-0391 also: Samarkandsky Bulvar 15/1, Flat 142, Moscow Russia

AULT, PHILLIP HALLIDAY, author, editor; b. Maywood, Ill., Apr. 26, 1914; s. Frank W. and Bernda (Halliday) A.; m. Karoline Byberg, June 5, 1943 (dec. Jan. 1990); children: Frank, Ingrid, Bruce; m. Jane Born, May 1, 1993. AB, DePauw U., 1935. Reporter LaGrange (Ill.) Citizen, 1935-37; corr. editor UPI, Chgo., N.Y.C., Iceland, North Africa, London, 1938-48; bur. chief UPI, London, 1944-45; asst. mng. editor, dir. editorial page Times-Mirror Co., L.A., 1948; editorial page editor L.A. Mirror-News, 1948-57; exec. editor Associated Desert Newspapers, 1958-68; assoc. editor South Bend (Ind.) Tribune, 1968-79, cons. editor, 1979—. Author: This Is the Desert, 1959, News Around the Clock, 1960, How to Live in California, 1961, Home Book of Western Humor, 1967, Wonders of the Mosquito World, 1970, These Are The Great Lakes, 1972, Wires West, 1974, All Aboard, 1976, By the Seat of Their Pants, 1978, Whistles Round the Bend, 1982; co-author: Springboard to Berlin, 1943, Reporting and Writing the News, 1983, Introduction to Mass Communications, 1960, Public Relations: Strategies and Tactics, 1986, Essentials of Public Relations, 2000; editor: Santa Maria Historical Photo Album, 1987. Named to Ind. Journalism Hall of Fame, 1998. Mem. Am. Soc. Newspaper Editors, Assn. Edn. in Journalism, Western Writers Am. (Spur award 1977), Sigma Nu. Home: 21408 157th Dr Sun City West AZ 85375-6626

AULTMAN, WILLIAM ROBERT, career officer; b. Ft. Benning, Ga., July 15, 1953; s. William Wilmer and Kazuko Suzie (Sano) A.; m. Barbara Ellen Tison, Dec. 22, 1979; children: Sara Alexandra, Nicholas Christian. BS in Engring, U.S. Military Acad., 1975; MSSM, USC, 1987; MS in Strategic Intelligence, Joint Mil. Intelligence Coll., 1994; diploma, U.S. Army War Coll., 1996. Commd. 2d lt. U.S. Army, 1975, advanced through grades to col., 1998; platoon leader, bn. S-2 intelligence officer 3rd infantry div. U.S. Army, Aschaffenburg, Fed. Republic Germany, 1975-78; tactical reconnaissance officer 82nd Airborne Div., Ft. Bragg, N.C., 1980-81; co. commdr. 1st Mil. Intelligence Battalion, Ft. Bragg, 1981-82; ops. officer Ft. Shafter, HI, 1982-85; plans officer Defense Intelligence Agy., Washington, 1985-88; chief intelligence collection mgmt. Combined Field Army, Camp Red Cloud, Korea, 1988-89; chief ADP applications Intelligence Ctr. Pacific, Camp Smith, Hawaii, 1989-91; VII Corps G2 staff Operation Desert Storm, Persian Gulf, 1991; chief logistics mgmt. Joint Intelligence Ctr., Pacific, Pearl Harbor, Hawaii, 1992-93; chief project mgmt. U.S. Army Info. Systems Command Pentagon, Washington, 1993-95; project officer TAADS-R U.S. Army, Ft. Belvoir, Va., 1995-97; dep. for Army electronic warfare programs OUSD (A&T)/S&TS/EW Pentagon, Washington, 1997-2000; comdr. U.S. Army Rsch., Devel. & Standardization Group, London, 1997-2000. Mem. NRA, Ret. Officers Assn., Assn. Grads. U.S. Mil. Acad., Va. Shooting Sports Assn., Army War Coll. Alumni Assn., Assn. Old Crows, Def. Sys. Mgmt. Alumni Assn. Baptist. Avocations: travel, reading, Japanese swords, beaches. Office: OUSD (A&T)/S&TS/EW Psc 802 Box 15 FPO AE 09499-0015

AUMOEUALOGO, SOLI SALANOA, public defender; b. Faga'alu, Am. Samoa, May 25, 1939; s. Salanoa S.P. and Faa'alo (Lepogafaiga) A.; m. Fialupe Fiaui, Dec. 7, 1964 (div.); children: Freda Anoni, Robin Peteroni, Sofia Leilani. BS, Okla. Christian Co., Oklahoma City, 1964; JD, Calif. Western Sch. Law, San Diego, 1973. Bar: Am. Samoa 1973. Asst. atty. gen. Dept. Legal Affairs, Pago Pago, Am. Samoa, 1973-77; dir. Pub. Defender's Office, Govt. Am. Samoa, Pago Pago, 1978-95; senator Am. Samoa Legislature, 1995-97, asst. legis. counsel, 1997—; chmn. Am. Samoa Devel. Corp., 1989-92. Chmn. Immigration Bd., 1973-77, Parole Bd., 1973-77, House Rules Com. Legislature, 1966-68; mem. Criminal Justice Adv., 1973-86; candidate for Rep. U.S. Congress, 1986, 88. Mem. Am. Samoa Bar Assn. (pres. 1987-88), Calif. Western Alumni Assn. (pres. 1985-87). Avocations: lawn tennis, fishing. Home: PO Box 4437 Pago Pago AS 96799-4437 Office: Salanoa S Aumoeualogo Law Office Solis Profl Bldg PO Box 5589 Pago Pago AS 96799-5589

AUNG-KHIN, CHERIE, antique dealer, designer, owner; b. Sittwe, Arakan, Burma, May 21, 1949; d. Tha and Hla (Khin) A.; m. Sonny Aung-Khin (div.). MA, Rangoon Arts & Scis. U., Rangoon, Burma, 1972. Sec. Reading & Bates, Rangoon, Burma, 1972-73; office mgr. Mitsui Oil, Rangoon, Burma, 1974-76; personal asst. Philippines, Rangoon, Burma, 1976-78; office mgr. Marut Burrag Law Office, Bangkok, Thailand, 1978-80, Elephant Shop, Bangkok, Thailand, 1980-81; owner, designer Elephant House Co. Ltd., Bangkok, Thailand, 1981—; CEO Sun Myanmar, Bangkok, Thailand, 1992—, River View Co. Ltd., Bangkok, Thailand, 1995—, Green Elephant Co. Ltd., Bangkok, Thailand, 1995—, Elephant House, Burma, Bangkok, 1996—; pres., designer Internat. Co. Ltd., Naarden, Holland. Avocations: reading, music, ballet, design. Office: 286/69-71 Soi Pattana, Suriwong Rd, 10500 Bangkok Thailand

AUNG SAN SUU KYI, human rights activist, writer; b. Yangon, Myanmar, June 19, 1945; d. Bogyoke Aung San and Khin Kyi; m. Michael Aris, 1972; children: Alexander, Kim. Student, Lady Sri Ram Coll., India, Delhi U., India; BA, Oxford (Eng.) U., 1967; postgrad., U. Kyoto, Japan, London (Eng.) U. Former tchr., rsch. asst. Eng.; formerly with UN, N.Y.C.; former rsch. officer on UN affairs Office of Fgn. Ministry; founder, sec.-gen. Nat. League Democracy, 1988-95, gen. sec., 1995—; mem. Nat. League for Democracy; under house arrest, 1989-95. Author essays including Freedom from Fear, 1988, Burma and India: Some Aspects of Intellectual Life under Colonialism, 1990, Towards a Trus Refuge, 1993. Recipient Thorolf Rafto Meml. prize for Human Rights, 1990, Sakharov prize for Freedom of Thought, 1991, Nobel Peace prize, 1991, Simon Bolivar Prize, 1992. Address: Burma Fund, 97-B W Shwegondine St, Bahan Tp Yangon Myanmar*

AURADA, KLAUS D., physical geography educator; b. Teplice-Sanov, Germany, May 15, 1941; s. Robert and Anna (Lienert) A.; divorced; 1 child, Susanne. Diploma, Martin Luther U., Germany, 1964, DSc, 1969. Geograph. diplomate. Engr. of hydrology Water Mgmt. Bur., Halle, Germany, 1964-67, chief hydrologist, 1967-69, head rsch. dept., 1969-77; scientific sec. Geographical Soc. of GDR, Leipzig, Germany, 1977-81; asst. prof. U. Halle, 1981-83; prof. U. Greifswald, Germany, 1983; directorships Water Coun. South, Halle, 1975-77, 81-83; vice rector of maths. and natural sciences, U. Greifswald, 1988-90; head dept. geography, U. Greifswald, 1994-98. Co-editor: (book) Umweltforschung, 1984; editor: Strukturen and Prozesse in der Geofraphie, 1987, Geographie-Okonomie-Okologie, 1989; editor: (jour.) Vorträge des 10. Deutschsprachigen Kolloquiums fur Theorie und Quantitative Methoden in der Geographie, 1994; contbr. articles to profl. jours. Mem. Geographic Soc. of Finland. Office: Ernst-Moritz-Arndt-U Inst Geography, Ludwig Jahn StraBe 16, D-17489 Greifswald Germany

AURAN, PER GUNNAR, research scientist; b. Soknedal, Norway, Nov. 3, 1968; s. Per Agnar and Grethe Johanne (Tysko) A. Msc, Norwegian Inst. Tech., Trondheim, 1991, Dr.Ing., 1996. Sci. asst. Norwegian Inst. Tech., 1992-96; rsch. scientist PFI, Trondheim, Norway, 1996-2000, FAST Search and Transfer ASA, Trondheim, 2000—. Contbr. articles to profl. jours. Assoc. mem. Smithsonian Inst. Mem. IEEE, SPIE, Assn. of Computing Machinery (mem. Internat. Orgn. Standardization and European Com. Standardization coms.), Norske Sivilingeniorens Forening, Internat. Fedn. Automatic Control, Internat. Assn. Pattern Recognition, Inc., The Planetary Soc., Scandinavian Standardization Orgn. Avocations: backpacking, fishing. Office: FAST Search & Transfer ASA, Sverresgate 15 PO Box 4452 Hosps Loekkan, N-7418 Trondheim Norway

AURDI, DANIELLE, foreign diplomat; b. Clermont-Ferrand, France, Feb. 29, 1944. Mem. European Parliament, 1999—, mem. com. on agr. and rural devel., substitute com. fgn. affairs, human rights, common security, substitute com. on women's rights and equal opportunities; vice-chair Group of the Greens/European Free Alliance; mem. delegation to the EU-Czech Republic Joint Parliamentary Com. *

AURELL, MATTIAS NILS, nephrology educator; b. Mangskog, Sweden, Aug. 5, 1934; s. Tage and Kathrine (Zimmer) A.; m. Elisabeth G. Sterner, Feb. 26, 1960; children: Erik, Olof. MD, U. Göteborg, Sweden, 1963, PhD, 1969. Cert. in internal medicine, nephrology, clin. physiology. Intern Sahlgrenska U. Hosp., Göteborg, 1963-65; rsch. fellow in medicine U. Göteborg Med. Sch., 1965-69, sr. rsch. fellow, 1969-72, cons. dept. nephrology, 1972-82, prof., 1982-99, dir. med. dept., 1986-89; hon. pres. Med. Students' Union, Göteborg, 1985-99. Contbr. over 300 articles on hypertension, kidney physiology and renin-angiotensin sys. to med. jours. Bd. dirs. Found. for Care of Elderly, Göteborg, 1988—, Bot. Garden, Göteborg, 1995—. Mem. Internat. Soc. Nephrology, Internat. Soc. Hypertension, Rotary. Mem. Conservative Party. Lutheran. Home: Prästgårdsgatan 56, S-41271 Göteborg Sweden Office: Sahlgrenska U Hosp, Dept Nephrology, S-413 45 Göteborg Sweden

AURIACOMBE, MARC, psychiatrist, educator, researcher; b. May 5, 1959; s. Pierre-Robert and Monique (Croisile) A.; m. Sophie Bergeaud, Oct. 10, 1989; children: Claire, Clemence. MD, U. Bordeaux, France, 1985, cert. in psychiatry, 1990. Resident Univ. Hosp., Bordeaux, 1985-90; fellow U. Pa., Phila., 1990-92; chef de clinique U. Bordeaux, 1992-97, practitioner Hosp. Universitaire, 1997—; adj. asst. prof. U. Pa., 1993—. Fax: 33-556-5635-15. E-mail: marc.auriacombe@labopsy.u-bordeaux2.fr. Office: U Bordeaux Ctr Carreire, 121 Rue De La Béchade, 33076 Bordeaux France

AURNER, ROBERT RAY, II, oil company, auto diagnostic, restaurant franchise and company development executive; b. Madison, Wis., Mar. 24, 1927; s. Robert Ray and Kathryn (Dayton) A.; m. Phyllis Barrett, 1951 (div. 1966); children: Sheryl, Roxanne, Kathryn, Suzanne, Robert III; m. Deborah Marion Lucas, Jan. 31, 1976 (div. 1999); children: William Lucas, Christopher Ray. AA, Monterey Peninsula Coll., 1949; BA, Calif. State U., Fresno, 1950; postgrad., U. Calif. Berkeley, Duquesne U. Lic. in real estate, Calif., Pa., N.Y.; registered investment advisor. Announcer Radio Sta. WSUI, Iowa City, 1946-48; featured celebrity Cowboy Bob, William Randolph Hearst Radio Sta. WISN-CBS, Milw., 1951-52; sr. sales supr. Shell Oil Co., San Francisco, 1952-60; dir. ctrl. Calif. coast real estate devel. Gulf Oil Corp., 1960-67; dir. Midwest ops. Sunray DX Oil Co. (merger Sunoco), Tulsa, 1967-72; mgr. site devel. franchising Milex Auto Diagnostic Franchise, Inc., Plymouth Meeting, Pa., 1972-74; mgr. real estate store devel. Pitts. divsn. Atlantic & Pacific Tea Co. Supermarkets, 1974-77; real estate adminstr. store devel. N.E. U.S. region Steak and Ale Restaurant divsn. Pillsbury Cos., Dallas, 1977-80; real estate mgr. N.Y. and Phila. regions Burger King Corp. divsn. Pillsbury Cos., 1980-87; real estate mgr. Ky. Fried Chicken divsn. Pepsico, Inc. (formerly owned by Heublein) and Pizza Hut divsn. Pepsico, Inc., Metro and SMSA, N.Y.C., 1987-89; nat. dir. real estate and franchising, resturant devel. Nathan's Famous Coney Island Hot Dog Restaurants, Inc., N.Y.C., 1989-90; chmn. bd. dirs., pres., CEO Bristlecone Trading and Devel., Inc., Carmel, Calif.; pres., CEO Aurner and Assocs. Resource Devel. & Project Mgrs. (Robert Aurner Assocs.), Carmel, 1987—, chmn. bd. dirs., 1990—; tower devel. mgr. So. N.J. Nextel Wireless Telecom. Corp., N.J., 1994-95; founder Trader Bob, Inc., Carson City, Nev., 1997. Staff officer Flotilla 64, C.G. Aux., Coast Guard Sta., Monterey, Calif., 1999—. With USNR, 1944-46, PTO. Named to Hon. Order Ky. Col., Gov. of Ky., Commodore in Okla. Navy Gov. of Okla. Mem. USS Yellowstone Assn. (USNR), U. Iowa and Calif. State U. Fraternity, Carmel Valley C. of C. (sec. bd. dirs. 1999—), Buccaneer Club (past pres. N.Y. and Conn.), Elks, Monterey Rotary, Monterey Peninsula Yacht Club, Sigma Alpha Epsilon. Republican. Episcopalian. Avocations: golf, precious metals conniseuer, Civil War buff. Fax: 831-626-3747. Office: Aurner & Assocs PO Box 222135 Carmel CA 93922-2135 also: Bristlecone Trading & Devel 3855 Via Nona Marie Carmel CA 93923-8614 also: Trader Bob Inc 251 Jeanell Dr Ste 3 Carson City NV 89703-2129

AURSNES, IVAR ANDREAS, clinical pharmacologist; b. Namsos, Norway, Oct. 16, 1939; s. Ivar and Ingebjorg Anna A.; m. Inger Lise Jacobsen, Apr. 18, 1967; children: Andreas, Ragnhild, Knut Øyvind. MD, U. Oslo, Norway, 1964, PhD, 1975. Cert. medicine. Intern Drammen Hosp., Norway, 1965; registrar Aker Hosp., Oslo, 1968-70; rsch. fellow U. Oslo, 1971-74, assoc. prof., 1987-93, prof., 1994, chmn, dept. pharmacotherapeutics, 1991—; sr. registrar, cons. Aker Hosp., Oslo, 1975-84; sr. registrar Ullevel Hosp., Oslo, 1985-86; cons. Norwegian Sports Medicine Inst., Oslo, 1987—. Co-author: Drugs Affecting Lipid Metabolism, 1996; contbr. articles to profl. jours. Lt. Norwegian Mil., 1966-67. Mem. Norsk Selskap Farmakologi og Toksikologi (bd. dirs. 1998—, chmn. 1999—), Forskerforbundet (bd. dirs. 1991-95). Avocations: music, dancing, bridge, gardening. Fax: 47-22119013. E-mail: i.a.aursnes@ioks.uio.no. Home: Nils Collett Vogts vei 30, N-0765 Oslo Norway Office: U Oslo, 1065 Blindern, N-0316 Oslo Norway

AUSLANDER, KELLY BOYCE, financial planner; b. Utica, N.Y., Dec. 7, 1948; d. Howard Douglas and Marjorie Claire (Ackerman) Kelly; m. Thaddeus Boyce, June 27, 1970 (div. 1983); children: Matthew, Dylan, Devin, Ryan; m. Paul H. Auslander, Aug. 4, 1984. Student, St. Lawrence U., 1966-68; BA, Vassar Coll., 1971; MS, SUNY, New Paltz, 1979. CFP. Fin. cons. Hudson Valley Mgmt. Group, Poughkeepsie, N.Y., 1981-83, Merrill Lynch, Poughkeepsie, N.Y., 1983-87; pres. Am. Fin. Advisors, Poughkeepsie, N.Y., 1987—. Contbr. articles to profl. jours. Co-founder All Women in Bus., Ltd., Poughkeepsie, 1982-86; treas., v.p., bd. dirs. YWCA, Poughkeepsie, 1986-88. Named Woman of Yr. All Women in Bus., Ltd., 1984. Mem. Internat. Assn. Fin. Planners (pres. Mid-Hudson chpt. 1990), Internat. Bd. CFPs. Episcopalian. Avocations: golf, conservation. Office: Am Fin Advisors Inc 187 Church St Poughkeepsie NY 12601-4114

AUSLENDER, MARK, research scientist; b. Sverdlovsk, Ural, Soviet Union, Apr. 12, 1950; arrived in Israel, 1991; s. Yehuda Auslender and Adela Anixt; m. Svetlana Gimpel, June 1, 1976; children: Sophia, Eliah. MSc in Physics, Ural State U., Sverdlovsk, USSR, 1972; PhD, Inst. Met. Phys., USSR Acad. Sci., Sverdlovsk, 1977. Physics diplomate. Jr. rschr. AC.SCI.USSR, Sverdlovsk, 1975-83, sr. rschr., 1983-90; rschr. Ben-Gurion U., Beer-Sheva, Israel, 1991—; lectr. Ben-Gurion U., Beer-Sheva, 1992—. Contbr. 75 articles to profl. jours. Grantee Israel Ministry Sci., 1991-93, Israeli Academia, 1999; honoree Israel Ministry Sci., 1994. Mem. Israel Phys. Soc., Optical Soc. Am.

AUSLOOS, MARCEL RAYMOND, physics educator and researcher; b. Charleroi, Belgium, Oct. 19, 1943; s. Raymond Hubert and Leonie Elvire (Demarthe) A.; m. Paulette Clippe, Feb. 8, 1975; children: Cyril, Floriane. Engr., U. Liege, Belgium, 1967; MSc, Brown U., 1970; PhD, Temple U., 1973. Vis. prof. Free U. Berlin, 1972-73; 1st asst. U. Liege, 1986-90, maitre de conf., 1979—, chef de travaux, 1990—; expert Communaute Francaise de Belgique, Brussels, 1988—. Editor: Magnetic Phase Transitions; contbr. numerous articles to profl. jours. Fulbright-Hays travel grantee, 1967; Temple U. fellow, 1970-72; Brit. Coun. grantee, 1983; Acad. of Scis. grant, Brussels, 1976, 81, 83. Mem. Internat. Union Pure and Applied Physics (mem. commn. on low temperature physics), Kiwanis (pres. 1991-92). Office: U Liege, Supras Inst de Physique B5, Liege B-4000, Belgium

AUSMEES, ANDRUS, physicist; b. Narva, Estonia, Oct. 16, 1960; s. Heimar and Alla A.; m. Nora Martin, July 9, 1981; children: Kaarel, Kristiina. BS, U. Tartu, Estonia, 1984, PhD, 1991. Engr. Inst. Physics, U. Tartu, Estonia, 1984-85, jr. rsch. assoc., 1985-87; postgrad. Inst. Physics, U. Tartu, 1987-90, rsch. assoc., 1991-95; rsch. assoc. dept. physics Uppsala U., Sweden, 1996-99. Contbr. articles to profl. jours. Mem. Estonian Physical Soc., Users Orgn. Swedish Nat. Synchrotron Radiation. Avocations: literature, music. Office: Dept Physics, Laggerhyddsv 1 Box 530, Uppsala SE-75121, Sweden

AUSSEIL, JEAN, government official; b. Vincennes, France, Apr. 30, 1925; s. Jean Achille Ausseil and Francine Bonnet; m. Catherine Hine, Aug. 19, 1940; children: Sarah, David. Student, Ecole France D'Outre Mer, Paris, 1946-48. Counsellor technique Cabinet du Premier Minister, Paris, 1968-69; consul gen. Ministry Fgn. Affairs, Tanger Maroc, France, 1969-75; French ambassador to Montevideo, Uruguay, 1975-78, Addis Abeba, Ethiopia, 1978-80; dir. African affairs Paris, 1981-85; minister of state Principality of Monaco, 1985-91; amb. of Monaco to Spain Madrid, 1991—. Avocation: golf. Home: Camino Viejo 9 La Moraleja, 28109 Madrid Spain Office: Villanueva 12, 28001 Madrid Spain

AUSSEL, JEAN-PAUL, aluminum company official; b. Cahors, Lot, France, July 24, 1956; s. Jean-Louis and Jacqueline-Simone (Deforge) A.; m. Veronique Malosse; 1 child, Florence. Ingenieur Civil des Mines degree, Paris Sch. of Mines, 1979. Potline mgr. Aluminium-Pechiney Lannemezan-Works, Lannemezan, France, 1981-83, prodn. mgr., 1983-85; reduction mgr. Aluminium-Pechiney Prodn. Rsch., St. Jean-de-Maurienne, France, 1985-86; start-up project mgr. Aluminium-Pechiney with Hydro-Aluminium, Karmoy, Norway, 1986-87; plant process mgr. Alusaf Hillside Smelter, Richards Bay, South Africa, 1994-97; tech. licensing project mgr., sr. tech. tng. expert Aluminium-Pechiney, Voreppe, France, 1988-93; mission leader in South Africa Aluminum-Pechiney, Voreppe, France, 1994-97; purchasing gen. mgr. Aluminium Pechiney, Voreppe, France, 1998-99, opers. v.p., 1999—. Lt. French Navy, 1979-80, res. 1999—. Decorated chevalier Nat. Order of Merit (France). Home: Chemin des Gros Bois, La Buisse 38500, France Office: Aluminium Pechiney, BP 7, 38340 Voreppe France

AUSSURE, PIERRE, executive recruiter; b. Saint-Mande, France, June 9, 1952; s. Roger and Odette (Rangè) A.; m. Anna Tepli, Oct. 18, 1986; children: Marc, Alexandra. Grad. summa cum laude, Inst. d'Etudes Politiques, Paris, 1973; LLM, U. Paris, 1975, PhD in Econs., 1976; MBA, Inst. Superieur des Affaires, 1978, Stanford U., 1978. Spl. advisor to French Embassy, Eng., 1978-80; product mktg. mgr. Tex. Instruments, France, 1980-82; European mktg., mgr. Tex. Instruments Europe, 1983-84; asst. to exec., v.p. CEP-Comm., 1984-86, internat. devel. mgr., 1986-88; cons. Tasa Internat. (now TMP Worldwide Exec. Search), 1989-92, mng. ptnr., 1997—; asst. prof. Inst. d'Etudes Politiques Paris, 1980-87, prof., 1988-94; pub. Objectif Export, 1989—. Mem. Conseiller du Commerce Exterieur de la France. Office: TMP Worldwide Exec Search, TMP Worldwide Exec Search, 42 Ave Montaigne, 75008 Paris France

AUSTELL, EDWARD CALLAWAY, banker; b. Spartanburg, S.C., Aug. 9, 1937; s. Edward and Frances Roberta (Glenn) A.; m. Louise Arnold Zimmerman, May 14, 1966; children: Frances Barrett, Elizabeth Callaway. A.B., Davidson Coll., 1959; M.B.A., U.N.C., 1960; postgrad., Nat. Trust Sch. Northwestern U., 1968. Vice pres. trust dept. First Nat. Bank S.C., 1964-71; sr. v.p. trust dept. Ga. R.R. Bank & Trust Co., Augusta, 1971-83; sr. v.p. Wachovia Bank, N.A., Winston-Salem, NC, 1983—. Served with AUS, 1960-62. Mem. N.C. Soc. Fin. Analysts, Ga. Bankers Assn. (past pres. trust div.), Beta Theta Pi. Presbyterian (elder). Home: 1241 Kent Place Ln Winston Salem NC 27104-1140 Office: Wachovia Bank NA PO Box 3099 Winston Salem NC 27150-0001

AUSTEN, W(ILLIAM) GERALD, surgeon, educator; b. Akron, Ohio, Jan. 20, 1930; s. Karl A. and Bertl (Jehle) A.; m. Patricia Ramsdell, Jan. 28, 1961; children: Karl Ramsdell, William Gerald, Jr., Christopher Marshall, Elizabeth Patricia. BS, MIT, 1951; MD, Harvard U., 1955; HHD (hon.), U. Akron, 1980; DSc (hon.), U. Athens, Greece, 1981, U. Mass., 1985, Northeastern Ohio U. Coll. Medicine, 1996. Diplomate Am. Bd. Surgery, Am. Bd. Thoracic Surgery. Intern, then resident surgery Mass. Gen. Hosp., Boston, 1955-61, chief surg. cardiovascular rsch. unit, 1963-69, chief surgery, 1969-97, surgeon-in-chief, 1989-97, surgeon-in-chief emeritus, 1997—; surgeon clinic surgery Nat. Heart Inst., 1961-62; pres. Mass. Gen. Physicians Orgn., Boston, 1994-98, CEO, 1998-99, chmn., 1999—; assoc. in surgery Harvard Med. Sch., 1963-65, assoc. prof. surgery, 1965-66, prof. surgery, 1966-74, Edward D. Churchill prof. surgery, 1974—; mem. residency review com. surgery Accreditation Coun. Grad. Med. Edn., 1988-93. Author, editor med. textbooks; contbr. articles to profl. jours. Mem. corp. MIT, 1972—, life mem. corp., 1982—, mem. exec. com. corp., 1986-98; trustee John S. and James L. Knight Found., 1986—, vice chmn., 1991-96, chmn., 1996—; bd. dirs. Found. Biomed. Rsch., 1988—; trustee Mass. Eye and Ear Infirmary, 1991—, Ptnrs. HealthCare System Inc., 1994-97, Gen. Hosp. Mass. Gen. Hosp., 1997-99, Dana Farber/Ptnrs. Cancer Care Inc., 1999—; hon. trustee Mass. Gen. Hosp., 1999—. Markle scholar, 1963-68. Fellow AAAS, Royal Coll. Surgeons Eng. (hon.), Am. Acad. Arts & Scis.; mem. NAS Inst. Medicine, Am. Heart Assn. (pres. 1977-78), Am. Surg. Assn. (sec. 1979-84, pres. 1985-86), Am. Assn. Thoracic Surgery (v.p. 1987-88, pres. 1988-89), Am. Bd. Surgery (mem. bd. 1969-74, sr. 1974—), Am. Bd. Thoracic Surgery (bd. dirs. 1984-90), ACS (regent 1982-91, chmn. bd. regents 1989-91, pres. 1992-93), Assn. Acad. Surgery (pres. 1970), Soc. Univ. Surgeons (sec. 1967-70, pres. 1972-73), New Eng. Cardiovascular Soc. (pres. 1972-73), Mass. Heart Assn. (pres. 1972). Home: 330 Beacon St Apt C66

Boston MA 02116-1190 Office: Mass Gen Hosp BUL 3 Boston MA 02114-2696

AUSTERMANN, CHRISTOPHER BRENT, English language educator; b. Rolla, Mo., Nov. 5, 1971; s. Charles Ross and Dorothy Karen (Matlock) Austermann. BS in Mgmt. Info. Sys., Maryville U., 1994. Tchr. English and Internatl. Studies Shiunji-(Japan) Bd. Edn., 1994-98; liaison Sister City Relationship, Shiunji, Japan and St. James, 1998—; translator Cultural Liaison Nagano Olympics, Nagano, Japan, 1998—. Counselor AM. Field Svc., U.S., 1989-94, Japan, 1994—. Mem. Japan Assn. Lang. Tchrs. (publicity chair 1997-98). Home: 99 Yoneko, Shiunji Niigata 957-0225, Japan Office: Shiunji-machi Bd Edn, 2361 Inarioka, Shiunji Niigata 957-0204, Japan

AUSTIN, COLIN FRANÇOIS LLOYD, Greek language educator; b. Melbourne, Australia, July 26, 1941; arrived in U.K., 1947; s. Lloyd James and Jeanne Françoise Guérin A.; m. Mishtu Mazumdar, June 28, 1967; children: Teesta, Topun. MA, Jesus Coll., Cambridge U., Eng., 1965; DPhil, Christ Church Coll., Oxford U., Eng., 1965. Asst. lectr. The Univ., Cambridge, 1969-73, lectr., 1973-88, reader, 1988-98, prof. Greek, 1998—; fellow Trinity Hall, Cambridge, 1965—, wine steward, 1973—, praelector, 1988—. Author: Nova Fragmenta Euripidea, 1968, Menandri Aspis et Samia, 2 vols., 1969-70, Comicorum Graecorum Fragmenta, 1973; co-author: Poetae Comici Graeci, 8 vols., 1983—. Mem. Cambridge Philo. Soc. Avocations: wine tasting, cycling, philately. Home: 7 Park Terr, Cambridge CB1 1JH, England Office: Trinity Hall, Cambridge CB2 1TJ, England

AUSTIN, DANIEL WILLIAM, lawyer; b. Springfield, Ill., Feb. 24, 1949; s. Daniel D. and Ruth A. (Ahrenkiel) A.; m. Lois Ann Austin, June 12, 1971; 1 child, Elizabeth Ann. BA, Millikin U., 1971; JD, Washington U., 1974. Bar: Ill. 1974, U.S. Dist. Ct. (cen. dist.) Ill. 1979, U.S. Ct. Appeals (7th cir.) 1980, U.S. Supreme Ct. 1980, U.S. Tax Ct. 1986. Assoc. Miley & Meyer, Taylorville, Ill., 1974-78; ptnr. Miley, Meyer & Austin, Taylorville, 1978-81; prin. Meyer, Austin & Romano P.C., Taylorville, 1981—. Pres. United Fund, Taylorville, 1980, Christian County YMCA, Taylorville, 1983-85, St. Vincent Meml. Hosp. Found., 1998—. Named one of Outstanding Young Men Am., 1985, Outstanding Citizen of City of Taylorville, 1993. Mem. ABA, Ill. Bar Assn., Christian County Bar Assn., Order of Barristers. Democrat. Presbyterian. Club: Taylorville Country (pres. 1985). Lodge: Sertoma (Taylorville pres. 1976). Avocations: golf, photography. Home: 14 Westhaven Ct Taylorville IL 62568-9064 Office: Meyer Austin & Romano PC 210 S Washington St Taylorville IL 62568-2245

AUSTIN, FRED, consultant mechanical engineer; b. Vienna, Austria, Apr. 3, 1936; s. Mathias and Frieda (Sonnenschein) A.; m. Myrna Lee Bogner, June 16, 1957; children: Martin, Howard. B in Mech. Engring., Cooper Union, 1957; M in Mech. Engring., NYU, 1960, PhD in Mech. Engring., 1968. Registered profl. engr., N.Y. Engr. Control Instrument Co., Bklyn., 1957-58, Sperry Gyroscope Co., Great Neck, N.Y., 1958-62; sr. staff scientist Northrop Grumman Corp., Bethpage, N.Y., 1962-98; pvt. practice cons. engr., 1999—. Contbr. articles to AIAA Jour., Jour. Am. Helicopter Soc., Jour. Guidance, Control & Dynamics, Jour. Spacecraft & Rockets. Recipient New Tech. award NASA, 1982, Rotorcraft Air-to-Air Combat award U.S. Army Aviation Sys. Command, 1990. Mem. ASME, Sigma Xi. Achievements include adaptive wing patent; devel. optimum method to load structures in static and fatigue tests, method to automatically pilot aircraft in dog fights, methods to control and simulate spinning elastic satellites, methods to improve finite element models by using test data. Home and Office: 5 Zinnia Ct Commack NY 11725-3616

AUSTIN, JAMES GROVER, JR., theologian, pastor, telecommunications manager; b. Phila., May 12, 1951; s. James G., Sr. and Florence (Hendon) A.; m. Valerie Gills, June 9, 1989; children: Asanti, Tyshan; 1 step-child, Angela. AA, L.A. City Coll., 1976; BA in Theology, Christian Bible Coll. Seminary, 1992, MA in Exegetical Theology, 1993, PhD, 1994; grad. summer program in theology, Oxford U., 1997, 98; D in Ministry, Grad. Theol. Found., 1998. Cryptologist U.S. Navy, 1971-89; chief secure comm. svcs. br. U.S. Coast Guard, Alexandria, Va., 1993—; educator D.C. Bible Inst., 1997—. Mem. Chief of Police Adv. Coun., Fairfax, Va., 1995—. Mem. ASCD, Am. Assn. Christian Counselors, Assn., Am. Soc. Christian Therapist (cert. Christian marriage family therapist, cert. pastoral addictions counselor, cert. domestic abuse counselor), Evang. Tng. Assn., Christian Soc. for the Healing of Dissociative Disorders, World Pastoral Care Ctr. Baptist. Home: 4384 Stepney Dr Gainesville VA 20155-1246

AUSTIN, JOHN DELONG, judge; b. Cambridge, N.Y., May 31, 1935; s. John DeLong and Mabel Cowles (Bascom) A.; m. Marcia Kay Behan, Aug. 15, 1969 (dec.); children: John DeLong, Susan Behan. AB, Dartmouth Coll., 1957; postgrad., u. Minn., 1959; JD, Albany Law Sch., 1969. Bar: N.Y. 1970. Editl. dir. Glens Falls (N.Y.) Times, 1960-66; sole practice Glens Falls, 1970-79; law asst. Warren County Judge and Surrogate, 1975-79, N.Y. State Supreme Ct., 1980-84; judge Warren County Family Ct., N.Y., 1984-99, Warren County Ct. and Surrogate's Ct., 1999—; Instr. Adirondack Comm. Coll., Glens Falls. Editor New Eng. Hist. and Geneal. Register, 1970-73; contbr. hist. and geneal. articles to various periodicals. Councilman Town of Queensbury, N.Y., 1969-71, supr., 1972-74; budget officer Warren County, N.Y., 1974; mem. N.Y. State Local Govt. Records Adv. Coun. With U.S. Army, 1958-60. Recipient Adminstrv. Law prize Albany Law Sch., 1969. Fellow Am. Soc. Genealogists; mem. N.Y. State Bar Assn., Warren County Bar Assn., Mohican Grange, Elks. Republican. Office: Warren County Mcpl Ctr Lake George NY 12845

AUSTIN, JOHN NORMAN, classics educator; b. Anshun, Kweichow, China, May 20, 1937; s. John Alfred and Lillian Maud (Reeks) A. B.A., U. Toronto, Ont. Can., 1958; M.A., U. Calif.-Berkeley, 1959, Ph.D., 1965. Vis. lectr. Yale U., New Haven, 1971; asst. prof., then assoc. prof. UCLA, 1966-76; Aurelio prof. Greek Boston U., 1976-78; prof., chmn. dept. classics U. Mass., Amherst, 1978-80; prof. classics U. Ariz., Tucson, 1980—, acting dean humanities, 1987-88, head, dept. classics, 1995—; vis. prof. Leeds U., 1999. Author: Archery at the Dark of the Moon, 1975, Meaning and Being in Myth, 1990, Helen of Troy and Her Shameless Phantom, 1994; editor: (with others) The Works of John Dryden, vol. III; sr. editor Calif. Studies Classical Antiquity, vols. VI and VII. Jr. fellow Ctr. for Hellenic Studies, 1968-69, J.S. Guggenheim Found. fellow, 1974-75. Mem. Am. Philol. Assn. (bd. dirs. 1983-86). Episcopalian. Home: 2939 E 3rd St Tucson AZ 85716-4122 Office: U Ariz Dept Classics PO Box 210067 Tucson AZ 85721-0067

AUSTIN, MARGARET SCHILT See DUCZYNSKI, MARGARET SCHILT

AUSTIN, MICHAEL CHARLES, insurance company executive; b. Syracuse, N.Y., Dec. 7, 1955; s. Harold Ernest and Helen (Sanderson) A.; m. Patricia Farrell, Aug. 12, 1978; 1 child, Bryan Michael. AA in Liberal Arts, Mohawk Valley Community Coll., 1974; BA in English, SUNY, Oswego, 1976. Dir. pub. rels. United Way of Greater Utica, N.Y., 1976-79; asst. mgr. advt. and pub. relations Utica Nat. Ins. Group, 1979-81, asst. dir. corp. communications, 1981-89, dir. corp. communications, 1989—; v.p. Utica (N.Y.) Mut. Ins. Co., 1997; adj. faculty Mohawk Valley Community Coll., Utica, 1982. Contbr. articles to profl. jours. Bd. dirs. United Cerebral Palsy Found., Utica, 1987—, pres., 1992-95, 98-99; pres. bd. trustees Mohawk Valley C.C. Found., 1990-95; chmn. Mohawk Valley Stop-DWI, Utica, 1994-99; Mohawk Valley Coun. on Alcoholism, Utica, 1987-93, United Way, Utica, 1982. Recipient Alumni Merit award Mohawk Valley C.C., 1989, Honor Roll award SUNY Alumni, 1996, STOP-DWI Cmty. Svc. award 1997; named Outstanding New Yorker Jaycees, 1994. Mem. Ins. Consumer Affairs Exch., Ins. Mktg. Comm. Assn., Utica C. of C. (bd. dirs. 1998—), Mohawk Valley Advt. Club (pres. 1989-90, dir. 1982-93, awards excellence, Ad Person of Yr. 1992, 95), Syracuse Ad Club, MV Ad Club, Profl. Ins. Comm. Am. Roman Catholic. Avocations: photography, comic book collecting, autograph collecting. Office: Utica Nat Ins Group 180 Genesee St Utica NY 13502-4324

AUSTIN-KELLEY, PATRICIA DAVIS, publishing executive; b. Lynn, Mass.; d. Lorne C. and Margaret M. (Baker) Davis; m. Robert E. Kelley; children: Campbell, Taylor Emily, Loren. BA, Tufts U., 1965; MEd, Salem (Mass.) Coll., 1971; cert. advanced study, Harvard U., 1977. Editorial asst. Saturday Rev., N.Y.C., 1965-67; grant writer Malden (Mass.) Pub. Schs., 1977-85; cons. Austin Assocs., Wenham, Mass., 1985-91; project dir. North Shore C.C., Danvers, Mass., 1991-93; project leader The Network, Andover, Mass., 1993-95; pres., publ. Wright Stuff Press Ariz., Phoenix, 1996—; mem. edn. policies com. Tufts U., Medford, Mass., 1978-82; cons. R.I. Dept. Edn., Providence, 1994-95, Frank Lloyd Wright Found., Scottsdale, Ariz., 1997; mem. faculty Ariz. State U., 1998-99; dir. devel. Freedoms Found., Valley Forge, Pa., 1999—. Author: (children's books) Cher Locke: The Case of the Missing Cockatiels, 1996, Cher Locke: The Dragon's Tale, 1997. Bd. dirs. Ariz. Ctr. for the Book, 1998-99. Mem. Bryn Mawr Newcomers Club (bd. dirs.). Avocations: piano, children. Office: Wright Stuff Press Ariz 917 Merion Square Rd Gladwyne PA 19035-1509

AUSTIN-THORN, CYNTHIA KAY, religious organization administrator, poet; b. Dallas, Feb. 24; d. Kenneth Yoshito and Anita E. Fujii; m. George Edward Austin, Dec. 20, 1978 (dec. July 1990); 1 child, Christopher Robin; m. Kenneth Wayne Thorn, July 3, 1994 (dec. Aug. 1999). AAS, El Centro Coll., Dallas, 1987. Sr. accounts payable clk. Plymouth/Poco Shops, N.Y.C.; mgr. Funky Things, Huntington Beach, Calif.; with select inventory mgmt. office Joske's Dept. Store, Dallas; sec., receptionist George E. Austin Piano Tech., Dallas; owner, writer, design creator Son of Dust Creations, Dallas; active The Road to Damascus Ministries, Dallas. Contbg. poet: (anthologies) A Muse to Follow, 1996 (Editor's Choice award 1996), A Tapestry of Thoughts, 1996 (Editor's Choice award 1996), (cassettes) The Sound of Poetry, 1996, 97 (named 1 of 10 best poets 1996, 97), Searching for Soft Voices, 1997. Mem. choir 1st Family Ch., Dallas, 1996-97, 99, 2000. Recipient cert. of achievement 1st Family Ch., 1996. Republican. Avocations: creative writing, song writing, singing in church plays, intercessory prayer, ministering to others. Home and Office: Son of Dust Creations 10404 Lone Tree Ln Apt D Dallas TX 75218-3003

AUSTRIACO, NICANOR PIER GIORGIO, clergy member, researcher; b. Manila, The Phillipines, Nov. 1, 1968; s. Nicanor Camacho and Lilia Robles A. BSE in Bioengring. summa cum laude, U. Pa., 1989; PhD in Biology, MIT, 1996. Joined Order Preachers (Dominicans). Fellow Ludwig Inst. for Cancer Rsch. U. Coll. London, 1996-97; seminarian Dominican House of Studies, Washington, 1997—. Contbr. articles to profl. jours. Fellow Internat. Human Frontier Sci. Program, 1996-97, Howard Hughes Med. Inst., Bethesda, 1990-95; recipient Best Article award Nat. Assn. Engring. Coll. Mags., 1997. Roman Catholic. Home and Office: Dominican House of Studies 487 Michigan Ave NE Washington DC 20017-1584

AUSTRIAN, ROBERT, physician, educator; b. Balt., Apr. 12, 1916; s. Charles Robert and Florence (Hochschild) A.; m. Babette Friedmann Bernstein, Dec. 29, 1963; stepchildren: Jill Bernstein, Toni Bernstein. AB, Johns Hopkins U., 1937, MD, 1941; DSc honoris causa, Hahnemann Med. Coll., 1980, Phila. Coll. Pharmacy and Sci., 1981, U. Pa., 1987, SUNY, 1996. Diplomate: Am. Bd. Internal Medicine. House officer Johns Hopkins Hosp., 1941-50, asst. dir. med. out-patient dept., 1951-52; assoc. prof. medicine, then prof. medicine SUNY Coll. Medicine, 1952-62; John Herr Musser prof., chmn. rsch. medicine U. Pa. Sch. Medicine, 1962-86, prof. emeritus, chmn. emeritus, 1986—; attending physician Hosp. U. Pa.; Tyndale vis. lectr. and prof. Coll. Medicine U. Utah, 1964; spl. research on infectious diseases, bacterial genetics; mem. Meningococcal Infections Commn., 1964-72, Commn. on Acute Respiratory Disease, 1965-72, Commn. Streptococcal and Staphylococcal Diseases, 1970-72, Armed Forces Epidemiol. Bd.; cons. surg. gen. U.S. Army Research and Devel. Command, 1966-69; mem. subcom. streptococcus and pneumococcus Internat. Com. Bacteriol. Nomenclature; mem. allergy and immunology study sect. Nat. Inst. Allergy and Infectious Diseases, 1965-69, mem. bd. sci. counselors, 1967-70, chmn., 1969-70; mem. WHO Expert adv. panel Acute Bacterial diseases, 1979—. Mem. editl. bd.: Jour. Bacteriology 1964-69, Am. Rev. Respiratory Diseases, 1963-66, Bacteriol. Rev., 1967-71, Jour. Infectious Diseases, 1969-74, Antimicrobial Agents and Chemotherapy, 1972-86, Infection and Immunity, 1973-81, Revs. of Infectious Diseases, 1979-89, Vaccine, 1983—; guest editor: Drugs and Aging, 1999. Trustee Johns Hopkins U., 1963-69. Served to capt. M.C. AUS, 1943-45. Recipient U.S. Typhus Commn. medal, 1947; Albert Lasker Clin. Med. Research award, 1978; Phila. award, 1979; Willard O. Thompson award Am. Geriatric Soc., 1981, Lifetime Sci. award Inst. Advanced Studies in Immunology and Aging, 1997, Pasteur Merieux MSD award 1st Internat. Symposium on Pneumococci and Pneumococcal Diseases, 1998. Fellow ACP (master, James D. Bruce Meml. award 1979), N.Y. Acad. Scis., Am. Acad. Microbiology, AAAS (chmn. sect. on med. scis. 1975); mem. Assn. Am. Physicians, Am. Soc. Clin. Investigation, Am. Clin. and Climatol. Assn. (pres. 1984), Am. Soc. Microbiology (v.p. N.Y. br. 1961-62), Am. Philos. Soc., Nat. Acad. Scis., Soc. Exptl. Biology and Medicine, Harvey Soc., Am. Fedn. Clin. Rsch., Inst. Medicine (sr.), Balt. Med. Soc., Am. Assn. Immunologists, N.Y. Acad. Medicine (sec. sect. microbiology 1961-62), Phila. County Med. Soc. (Strittmatter award 1979), Coll. Physicians Phila. (Meritorious Svc. award 1980, pres.-elect 1986, pres. 1988-89, Disting. Svc. medal 1997), Interurban Clin. Club (pres. 1970), Infectious Disease Soc. Am. (pres. 1971, Maxwell Finland lecture award 1974, Bristol award 1986), Johns Hopkins Soc. Scholars, Phi Beta Kappa, Sigma Xi, Alpha Omega Alpha, Omicron Delta Kappa. Club: 14 W. Hamilton Street (Balt.). Achievements include demonstration of the continuing importance of lobar pneumonia as a cause of death despite treatment with antibiotics and of the efficacy of polyvalent pneumococcal vaccine in preventing such illness, leading to its relincensure. Office: U Pa Sch Medicine Dept Rsch Medicine 552 Johnson Pavilion Philadelphia PA 19104-6088

AUSTVIK, OLE GUNNAR, educator. Cand.oecon, U. Oslo, 1980; MPA, Harvard U., 1989. Statistician Oslo, 1981-85, Norwegian Inst. Internat. Affairs, Oslo, 1985-91; prof. Lillehammer (Norway) Coll., 1991—; adj. prof. Norwegian Sch. Mgmt., 1989-99. Fax: 47 612 77252. Home: Kaldor, Øyer N 2636, Norway Office: Lillehammer Coll, Lillehammer N2601, Norway

AUTEUIL, DANIEL, actor; b. Algeria, 1950; 1 child. Appeared in plays Le Garçon d'Appartement, 1980; films include Let's Make a Dirty Movie, 1975, Act of Aggression, 1975, La Nuit de Saint Germain des Prés, 1976, Rape of Love, 1976, Monsieur Papa, 1977, Les Héros n'ont pas froid aux oreilles, 1978, Bête mais discipliné, 1979, An Adventure for Two, 1979, Les Sous-doués, 1980, Clara and the Swell Guys, 1980, La Banquière, 1980, Les Sous-doués en vacances, 1981, Men Prefer Fat Girls, 1981, Que les gros salaires lèvent le doigt!!!, 1982, Pour 100 briques t'as plus rien, 1982, T'empêches tout le monde de dormir, 1982, L'Indic, 1983, Les Fauves, 1983, P'tit con, 1984, The Syringe, 1984, Dame vom Palast Hotel, 1985, Love on the Quiet, 1985, The Journalist, 1986, Ugolin, 1986, Manon of the Spring, 1986 (Best actor award Cannes), A Few Days with Me, 1988, Mama, There's a Man in Your Bed, 1989, The Elegant Criminal, 1990, My Life is Hell, 1991, A Heart of Stone, 1992, My Favorite Season, 1993, Queen Margot, 1994, The Separation, 1994, A French Woman, 1995, Pereira Declares, 1996, The Eighth Day, 1996, The Child of the Night, 1996, Death In Therapy, 1996, On Guard, 1997, An Interesting State, 1999, La Fille sur le pont, 1999, The Lost Son, 1999, Mauvaise passe, 1999, La Veuve de Saint-Pierre, 2000, Sade, 2000; (TV series) Les Fargeot, 1974. Office: care Artmedia, 20 Avenue Rap, 75007 Paris France*

AUTRUM, HANSJOCHEM OTTO, zoology educator; b. Bromberg, Posen, Germany, Feb. 6, 1907; s. Autrum Otto and Goerges (Olga) A.; m. Ilse geb Bredow, Oct. 11, 1935; 1 child, Swantje. PhD, U. Berlin, 1931; D (hon.), U. Frankfurt (Germany), 1963, U. Göttingen (Germany), 1987, U. Regensburg (Germany), 1989, U. Würzburg, 1994. Asst. prof. U. Berlin, 1935-45, U. Göttingen, 1945-52; prof., head dept. U. Würzburg, Germany, 1952-58, U. Munich, 1958-75. Editor: Handbook Sensory Physiology, 1972; editor Jour. Comparative Physiology, 1970-95. Recipient Disting. Orde of Merit with Star, Fed. Republic of Germany, 1977, Order pour le mérite, Fed. Republic of Germany, 1977. Mem. Bavarian Acad. Sci., German Acad. Leopoldina. Home: Maximilianstrasse 46, 80538 Munich Germany

AUVENSHINE, WILLIAM ROBERT, academic administrator; b. Waco, Tex., June 21, 1937; s. E.H. and Corinne (Clark) A.; m. Anna Banks, Dec. 21, 1963; children: Karen, Lee. AA, Arlington State Jr. Coll., 1957; BS, Tex. Christian U., 1959; MS, West Tex. State U., 1967; EdD, U. No. Colo., 1973. Tchr. music Chico (Tex.) Pub. Schs., 1957-60, Ranger (Tex.) Pub. Schs., 1960-64; mgr., part-owner Megert Music Co., Amarillo, Tex., 1964-70; counselor Loveland (Colo.) Pub. Schs., 1970-72; dean Ranger Jr. Coll., 1972-84; pres. Hill Coll., Hillsboro, Tex., 1984—. Mem. Heritage League, Hillsboro, 1984—; chmn. State Task Force on C.C. Annexation, 1993; chmn. bd. dirs. Eastland County Tax Appraisal Dist., 1979-84; mem. Indsl. Com., Cleburne, 1984—, Hillsboro, 1984—; mem. First United Meth. Ch., Hillsboro; mem. gen. bd. discipleship com. that rewrote Book of Worship for Meth. Ch.; past lay leader Ctrl. Tex. Conf., leader del. to gen. conf.; bd. dirs. Nat. Jr. Coll. Atletic Assn., 1993—, Harris Meth. Hosp. Sys., 1997—. Recipient Disting. Alumni award West Tex. State U., Canyon, 1983, Jefferson Davis award United Daus. of Confederacy, 1991; named Man of Yr., Ranger C. of C., 1963. Mem. Tex. Jr. Coll. Assn. (pres. 1991-92), Tex. Pub. Community Jr. Coll. Assn. (sec., treas. 1985-90), Tex. Assn. for C.C. Chief Student Affairs Adminstrs. (pres. 1982-83), Tex. C.C. Ins. Consortium (pres. 1992—), Hillsboro C. of C., Lions (dist. gov. 1977-78, Internat. Press award 1983, Lion of Yr. award Ranger chpt. 1975, Citizen of Yr. award Hillsboro chpt. 1986), Sons of Confederate Vets. (past comdr. 1988-90), Sons of Union Vets. of Civil War (chaplain), Masons (32d degree), Shriners, Hillsboro Country Club (pres. 1993-95), Phi Delta Kappa. Avocations: golf, restoring antique cars, reading. Home: 1107 E Walnut St Hillsboro TX 76645-2637 Office: Hill Coll 111 Lamar Dr Hillsboro TX 76645-2712

AUVINEN, JUHA YRJO, researcher, administrator; b. Helsinki, May 21, 1963; s. Raimo Yrjo and Anna-Liisa A.; m. Katri Irmeli Hietanen, Sept. 4, 1993; children: Hille Inari, Inka Loviisa. M Social Scis., U. Helsinki, 1990, Lic. Social Scis., 1994; PhD, U. Sussex, 1996; Docent Internat. Politics (hon.), U. Helsinki, 1999. Jr. asst. prof., rschr. U. Helsinki, 1990-92; rschr. Acad. of Finland, Brighton, U.K., Helsinki, 1993-95; prof. internat. rels. U. Lapland, Rovaniemi, Finland, 1996-97; mem. cabinet adminstr. European Commn., Brussels, 1997—; project dir. U. Helsinki, 1996; cons. Mins. for Fgn. Affairs, Helsinki, 1996-97. Mem. editl. bd. Kosmopolis jour., 1995-97, Jour. of Peace Rsch., 1998; contbg. author books in field; contbr. articles to profl. jours. Docen U. Helsinki, 1999—. Recipient Tieto Finland award for best info. book, 1999; rsch. grantee Acad. Finland, 1992-94, Govt. of U.K., Brighton, 1993-94. Mem. Internat. Polit. Sci. Assn. (rsch. com. 1995—). Avocations: soccer, lead vocal in a dancing orchestra, travel.

AUWARTER, BRIAN WILLIAM, sculptor; b. Greene, N.Y., Mar. 22, 1950; s. Frederick Alvin and Mildred Louise (Hill) A.; m. Kathryn Maureen Hendrick, Aug. 16, 1972 (div. Apr. 1999); children: Tyler, Tessa. BS in Edn., SUNY, Buffalo, 1974. Tchr. Ballston Spa (N.Y.) Schs., 1974—; owner Design Mill, 1999—; design dir. AdROC, Gansevoort, N.Y., 1998—. Exhibited in group shows at Schenectady (N.Y.) Mus., 1981, 98, Munson-Williams-Proctor Mus. Art, Utica, N.Y., 1982, 88, Rice Gallery, Albany (N.Y.) Inst. History and Art, 1984, 89, 95, 98, Corp. Woods, Albany, 1986, Burlington County Coll., Pemberton, N.J., 1989-91, Hyde Mus. Art, Glens Falls, N.Y., 1981, 87, 90, Contemporary Artist Ctr. Gallery, North Adams, Mass., 1994, Center Galleries, Albany, 1999, Nat. Historic Trust at Chesterwood, Stockbridge, Mass., 1983, 90, 95.

AU YONG, TING KUN, nuclear medicine physician; b. Hong Kong, Nov. 20, 1963; p. Leung Au Yong and Sui Keng Foo; m. Sau Yee Cho, Jan. 12, 1992; children: Long Wai, Wai Him, Kai Wai. B Medicine B Surgery, U. Hong Kong, 1987; MSc in Nuclear Medicine, U. London, 1994. Med. officer Queen Elizabeth Hosp., Hong Kong, 1989-93, sr. med. officer, 1995-97, 97-99; hon. registrar Guy's Hosp., London, 1993-94; hon. asst. prof. UCLA, 1997. Author, editor: Manual in Nuclear Medicine, 1997; contbr. articles to profl. jours. Fellow Hong Kong Coll. Radiologists, Hong Kong Acad. Medicine; mem. Hong Kong Soc. Nuclear Medicine (pres. 1999—), Hong Kong Soc. Clin. Position Emission Tomography (hon. treas. 1995-99), Soc. Nuclear Medicine, European Assn. Nuclear Medicine. Avocations: tennis, music, hiking. Home: Block A 9C, 5 Ho Man Tin Hill Rd, Kowloon Hong Kong Office: Queen Elizabeth Hosp, Dept Nuclear Medicine, Kowloon Hong Kong

AUZEL, FRANÇOIS-EMILE, physicist, educator; b. Roanne, Loire, France, July 5, 1938; s. Georges and Renée (Lesuisse) A.; m. Odile Leprince, Mar. 28, 1963; children: Pierre-Louis, Jérôme, Jean-Baptiste, Anne-Sophie. Degree in engring., Inst. Supérieur d'Electronique, Paris, 1961; lic. in scis., U. Paris, 1962, PhD, 1968. Rsch. engr. Ctr. Nat. d'Etudes des Telecomm., Paris, 1961-69, group leader, 1969-84, dept. head, 1984-94, expert for direction, 1995-98; head electronic lab. Ecole Ctr. des Arts et Mfs., Paris, 1974-84, chef de travaux, 1971-99; prof. U. d'Orsay, France, 1992-99; cons. OSRAM Co., Munich, 1991-94; vis. prof. U. Pernambuco, Recife, Brazil, 1982, 84, 86, 97; prof., lectr. Ettore Majorana Internat. Sch., Erice, Italy, 1977—; mem. internat. com. Internat. Conf. on Luminescence, 1981—. Contbr. articles to profl. jours.; local editor for France, Jour. of Luminescence, 1981—, European Phys. Jour., 1998—; patentee in field. Nominated mem. Com. Nat. de la Recherche, Paris, 1995-98. Served with French Navy, 1963-65. Decorated Order Palmes Académiques, 1997; recipient Winter-Klein prize French Acad. for Scis., Paris, 1989, Foucault prize French Soc. Physics, 1973. Roman Catholic. Avocations: horology, Chinese language. Office: GOTR UPR 211 CNRS, 1 pl A Briand, 92195 Meudon France

AVAKOFF, JOSEPH CARNEGIE, medical and legal consultant; b. Fairbanks, Alaska, July 15, 1936; s. Harry B. and Margaret (Adams) A.; m. Teddy I. Law, May 7, 1966; children: Caroline, Joey, John. AA, U. Calif., Berkeley, 1956, AB, 1957; MD, U. Calif., San Francisco, 1961; JD, Santa Clara U., 1985. Bar: Calif. 1987; diplomate Am. Bd. Surgery, Am. Bd. Plastic Surgery. Physicist U.S. Naval Radiol. Def. Lab., San Francisco, 1957, 59; intern So. Pacific Gen. Hosp., San Francisco, 1961-62; resident in surgery Kaiser Found. Hosp., San Francisco, 1962-66; resident in plastic surgery U. Tex. Sch. Medicine, San Antonio, 1970-72; pvt. practice specializing in surgery Sacramento, 1966-70; pvt. practice specializing in plastic surgery Los Gatos and San Jose, Calif., 1972-94; cons. to med. and legal professions, 1994—; clin. instr. surgery U. Calif. Sch. Medicine, Davis, 1967-70; chief dept. surgery Mission Oaks Hosp., Los Gatos, 1988-90; chief divsn. plastic surgery Good Samaritan Hosp., San Jose, 1989-91; expert med. reviewer Med. Bd. Calif., 1995—; spl. cons. Calif. Dept. Corps., 1997—; presenter numerous med. orgns. Contbr. numerous articles to med. jours. Mem. San Jose Adv. Commn. on Health, 1975-82; bd. govs. San Jose YMCA, 1977-80. Mem. AMA, Calif. Med. Assn., Santa Clara County Bar Assn., Santa Clara County Med. Assn., Union Am. Physicians and Dentists, Phi Beta Kappa, Phi Eta Sigma. Republican. Presbyterian. Avocations: music, photography, computer programming. Home: 6832 Rockview Ct San Jose CA 95120-5607

AVASTHI, AJIT KUMAR, psychiatrist, educator; b. Srinagar, India, Aug. 12, 1954; s. Hans Raj and Shanta (Modi) A.; m. Vishiv Kirti Sharma, Dec. 6, 1982; children: Avijit, Avinit. MB BChir, Govt. Med. Coll., Jammu, India, 1977; MD in Psychiatry, Postgrad. Inst. Med. Ed./Rsch., Chandigarh, India, 1981. Lectr. Arab Med. U., Benghazi, Libya, 1984-86; sr. resident Postgrad. Inst. Med. Edn. and Rsch., Chandigarh, 1982-84, from asst. prof. to assoc. prof., 1987-97, additional prof., 1997—; guest lectr. sci. and profl. meetings; presenter papers at nat. and internat. sci. meetings; organizing sec., joint organizing sec. various nat. and internat. med. confs. Editor: (books) Schizophrenia: The Indian Scene, 1997, Management of Depression, 1997, Anxiety Disorders, 1997, also 8 book chpts.; contbr. numerous rsch. articles to med. jours.; assoc. editor: Indian Jour. Social Psychiatry, 1988-94; mem. editl. bd.: Indian Jour. Psychiatry, 1999—, Archives of Indian Psychiatry, 1999—, Jour. Mental Health and Human Behavior, 1996—. Fellow Indian Psychiat. Soc. (life, pres. North Zone 1998-99, Maxfatia award 1989, PPA-I award 1990, 99, Dr. A.K. Kala award 1997, Dr. G.C. Boral award 1997), Indian Assn. Social Psychiatry (life). Office: Postgrad Inst Med Ed/Rsch, Dept Psychiatry, Chandigarh India

AVEDON, RICHARD, photographer; b. N.Y.C., May 15, 1923; s. Jack and Anna (Polonsky) A.; m. Dorcas Nowell, 1944; m. Evelyn Franklin, Jan. 29, 1951; 1 child, John. Student, Columbia U., 1941-42; studied with Alexey Brodovitch, Design Lab. New Sch. for Social Rsch., N.Y.C., 1944-50; DSc (hon.), Royal Coll. Art, London, 1989, Parsons Sch. Design, N.Y.C., 1994, Kenyon Coll. Staff photographer Jr. Bazaar, 1945-47, Harper's Bazaar, 1945-65; photographer French collections, 1947-84; staff photographer, editor Theatre Arts, 1952-53; staff photographer Vogue mag., 1966-90; first staff photographer The New Yorker, 1992—; Visual cons. for film: Funny Face, Paramount Studios, 1957; conducted master class in photog. (with Marvin Israel), Avedon studio, 1967. Author: (comments by Truman

Capote) Observations, 1959, (text by James Baldwin) Nothing Personal, 1964, (intro. by Harold Rosenberg) Portraits, 1976, (essay by Harold Brodkey) Avedon Photographs, 1947-1977, 1978, In the American West, 1985; author spl. bicentennial edit. Rolling Stone mag. The Family, 1976; editor: Diary of a Century (photographs by Jacques Henri Lartigue), 1970, (with Doon Arbus) Alice in Wonderland: The Forming of a Company, The Making of a Play, 1973, An Autobiography, 1993, (essays by Jane Livingston, Adam Gophik) Evidence: 1944-94, 1994; photographs in permanent collections: Smithsonian Instn., Met. Mus. Art, N.Y.C., Mus. Modern Art, N.Y.C., Amon Carter Mus., Fort Worth, San Francisco Mus. Modern Art, Mus. Fine Arts, Houston, Victoria and Albert Mus., London, Nat. Portrait Gallery, Washington, Nat. Portrait Gallery, London, Ctr. for Creative Photography U. Ariz., Tucson, Kunstaus Zurich, Switzerland, Kunstaus, Basel, Switzerland, Andreas Reinhart Found., Winterthur, Switzerland; one-man retrospective exhbn. Smithsonian Instn., Washington, 1962, Mpls. Inst. Arts, 1970, Univ. Art Mus., Berkeley, Calif., 1980, Whitney Mus. Am. Art, 1994; one-man shows: Mus. Modern Art, 1974, Marlborough Gallery, 1975, Met. Mus. Art, N.Y.C., 1978, Amon Carter Mus., 1985, Corcoran Gallery of Art, Washington, DC, San Francisco Mus. Modern Art, Art Inst. Chgo., Phoenix Art Mus., Inst. Contemporary Art, Boston, The High Museum, Atlanta, 1985, Installation Brandenburg Gate, Carnegie Mus. of Art, Pitts., 1991; group shows include: Mus. Modern Art, 1955, Met. Mus. Art, 1959, 60, 63, 67, Musée Réattu, Arles, France, 1965, N.Y. World's Fair, 1965-66, Fogg Art Mus., Cambridge, Mass., 1967, Mus. Modern Art, N.Y.C., 1964, 65, 69, Expo '70, Osaka, Japan, 1970, Whitney Mus. Am. Art, 1974, Corcoran Gallery Art, Washington, 1985, Nat. Gallery Art, Washington, 1989; photographed civil rights movement in the South, 1963, anti-war movement across U.S., 1969, Vietnam, 1971, Am. Working Class, 1978-84. With USMC, 1942-44. Recipient highest achievement medal awards Art Dirs. Show, 1950—; voted one of world's ten greatest photographers Popular Photography, 1958; citation of dedication to fashion photography Pratt Inst., 1976; Nat. Mag. award Visual Excellence, 1976; Pres.'s fellow RISD, 1978; Chancellor's citation U. Calif., Berkeley, 1980; named to Hall of Fame Art Dirs. Club, 1982; Photographer of Yr., Am. Soc. Mag. Photographers, 1985; Best Photog. Book of Yr. award Maine Photog. Workshop, 1985; Dir. of Yr., Adweek mag., 1985; Comml. Dir. of Yr. award of excellence Eastman Kodak, 1985; Lifetime Achievement award Coun. Fashion Designers Am., 1989.; Internat. Photography prize Erna and Victor Hasselblad Found., 1991; Master of Photography award Internat. Ctr. Photography, 1993, Prix Nadar Bibliotheque Nationale, 1994, Humanitarian award Mental Health Assn., N.Y.C., 1996, Lifetime Achievement award Columbia U. Grad. Sch. of Journalism, 2000. Office: The New Yorker care Elizabeth Biondi 407 E 75th St New York NY 10021-3102

AVEN, TERJE, risk and safety educator; b. Stavanger, Norway, June 6, 1956; s. Einar and Anna (Ness) A.; m. Anne-Grethe Lundberg, Aug. 11, 1979; children: Filip, Sofie. Cand.real, U. Oslo, 1980, PhD, 1984. Asst. prof. U. Oslo, 1980-84, prof. II (adj. prof.) of reliability and risk analysis, 1990—; rsch. fellow U. Calif., Berkeley, 1984; assoc. prof. stats./risk analysis Stavanger (Norway) Univ. Coll., 1984-86, 90-92, prof. II (adj. prof.) risk analysis, 1988-90, prof. risk analysis, 1992—, assoc. dean faculty sci. and tech., 1992-93, dean, 1994-96; reliability and risk analyst Statoil, 1986-90; prof. II (adj. prof.) reliability engring./safety mgmt. Norwegian U. Sci. and Tech., Trondheim, 1990-95; prin. cons. Det Norske Veritas, 1990-95, rsch. fellow, London, 1995; prin. cons. Rogaland Rsch., 1984—. Author: Stochastic Models in Reliability, 1999, Reliabilty and Risk Analysis, 1992, 2d edit., 1998, Views on Safety Management Norwegian Continental Shelf, 1994; mem. editl. bd. Reliability Engring. and Sys. Safety, 1995—. Recipient Safety award Safety Com. Norway, 1996. Mem. Norwegian Assn. for Reliability and Risk Analysis (bd. dirs. 1994—), Norwegian Acad. Technol. Scis. Office: Stavanger Univ Coll, PO Box 2557 Ullandhaug, 4091 Stavanger Norway

AVENARIUS, STEFAN MICHAEL, pediatrician; b. Magdeburg, Germany, Dec. 18, 1957; s. Ferdinand Bretschneider and Hanna Bromann; m. Gesine Avenarius, July 12, 1980. MD, Otto-von-Guericke U., Magdeburg, Germany, 1990. Resident Hosp., Burg, Germany, 1985-89; asst. prof. neonatology Med. Faculty-Sch. Medicine Otto-von-Guericke U., Magdeburg, Germany, 1993-94, cons. neonatologist, 1995—; cons. in field. Contbr. articles to profl. jours. Capt. German Mil., 1976-79. Fellow Med. Faculty-Sch. Medicine Otto-von-Guericke U., 1990-92. Mem. German So. Pediatrics, Neonatology & Pediatric Intensive Care, Profl. Fedn. German Pediatricians. Avocations: scuba diving, tennis. Office: Ctr Pediatrics, Wiener St, 39112 Magdeburg Germany

AVENDAÑO-REYES, LEONEL, science educator, researcher; b. Mexico City, July 13, 1962; s. Manuel Avendaño-Sumano and Aurora Reyes-Vózquez; m. Edith Pérez-Lagunas, May 11, 1991; children: Leonel, Edith. BS, U. Autónoma Baia Calif., Mexicali, Mexico, 1984; MS, U. Nat. Autónoma Mexico, 1989; PhD, Miss. State U., 1999. Assoc. prof. U. Nat. Autónoma Mexico, 1986-88; assoc. prof. U. Autónoma Baia Calif., Mexicali, 1989-92, prof., 1992—. Contbr. articles to profl. jours.; patentee in field. Mem. Am. Dairy Sci. (assoc.), Assn. Mexicana Producción Animal, Sigma Xi. Roman Catholic. Avocations: basketball, softball, tennis. Home: Cataratas de Iguazú 1793, Fracc Santa Mónica Mexicali Baja Calif 21339, Mexico Office: U Autónoma Baja Calif PO Box 2483 Calexico CA 92232-2483

AVENHAUS, RUDOLF, physics educator, research scientist; b. Zwickau, Sachsen, Germany, Aug. 6, 1938; s. Wilhelm and Marianne (Wehnert) A.; m. Ingeborg Abb, Dec. 30, 1964; children: Wolfgang, Silke. Diploma, U. Munich, 1964; PhD, U. Karlsruhe, 1967; Habilitation, U. Mannheim, 1975. Asst. prof. U. Karlsruhe, 1964-67, U. Geneva, 1967-68; rsch. scholar Nuclear Rsch. Ctr., Karlsruhe, 1968-73, 75-80, Internat. Inst. for Applied Sys. Analysis, Laxenburg, 1973-75; prof. Armed Forces U., Neubiberg, 1980—, faculty dean, 1989-90, v.p., 1993-94, acting pres., 1993-94. Author: Material Accountancy, 1978, Safeguards Systems Analysis, 1986, (with M. Canty) Compliance Quantified, 1996; contbr. articles to profl. jours. Elected coun. mem. German Assn. for Friedens and Konfliktforschung, 1976-83. Recipient Oce van der Grinten prize for Sci. Work on Environ. Problems, 1980. Mem. Kerntechnische Assn., German Statis. Assn., German Assn. for Math. U. Op Rsch. Avocations: classical music, hiking, skiing. Home: Mozartring 17A, D-85598 Baldham Bavaria, Germany Office: U der Bundeswehr Munchen, Werner-Heisenberg-weg 39, D-85577 Neubiberg Bayern, Germany

AVERBACH, MARGARA, literature educator, translator; b. Buenos Aires, July 31, 1957; d. Salomón and Berta Averbach; m. Odino Ciai, Apr. 12, 1985; children: Dante Nahuel, Tamara Painé, Selva Aimé. Diploma in philosophy and letters, U. Buenos Aires, 1981, DLitt, 1988. cert. lit. and tech. transl. Inst. Nacional Enseñanza Superio en Lenguas Vivas "J.R. Fernandez," 1978; prof. in lit. U. Buenos Aires. Ayudante de primera Am. lit. faculty philosophy and letters U. Buenos Aires, 1984-87, jefa de trabajos practicos Am. lit. fac. philos. and letters, 1987-92, 93-99; prof. literary transl. I and II Inst. Nacional de Enseñanza Superior en Lenguas Vivas, Buenos Aires, 1992-99; prof. Am. lit. seminars faculty philosophy and letters U. Buenos Aires, 1994-99; lit. critic Clarín Newspaper, Buenos Aires, 1986-99. Author: (books) Blue Giraffe, Green Rhinoceros, 1992 (1st prize 1992), Stories of Upwards and Downwards, 1993, Panadero en la ciudad, 1995 (Premio Cuadro de Honor Tucuman 1995), Lonely and Its Shadow, 1998, The Explorers, 2000; transl. 48 novels. Mem. bd. editors Taller, Assn. Polmtica Cultura y Sociedad, Buenos Aires, 1997-99; bd. dirs. Contexto, Revista do Dept. de Lenguas e Letras Mestrado de Letras: Lit. Brasiliera, U. Vitoria, Brazil, 1997-99; bd. dirs. transit cir. Revista de la Assn. Brasiliera de Estudos Americanos, 1998-99; bd. editors De Sur a Norte, Perspectivas Americanas sobre los Estados Unidos, Centro Regional de Estudios Sobre los EEUU, Buenos Aires, 1994-99. Recipient 2d prize essay on Saul Bellow, Inst. de Intercambio Cultural y Cientifico entre Israel y Argentina, 1987, prize in contest Te cuento tus derechos, Educando para la Libertad, Amnesty Internat., 1995; rsch. grantee CONICET, 1983-85, USIS grantee Summer Inst., U. Calif., Santa Barbara, 1997.

AVERBOUKH, ELENA, systems engineer, consultant; b. Kharkov, Ukraine, Jan. 8, 1957; arrived in Germany, 1993; d. Abram and Olga (Osherova) A.; m. Mikhail Gouzman, Oct. 1, 1980 (div. Jan. 1995); 1 child, Asja. Diploma in systems engring. with honors, Tech. U. Twer, Russia, 1978; diploma in math., State U. Twer, Russia, 1982; D in Engring., Tech. U. Twer, 1983; habilitation in tech. cybernetics, Moscow Power Inst. (Tech. U.), 1992; habilitation in quality control systems, U. Kassel, Germany, 1996. Rschr. Tech. U. Twer, 1978-83, sr. rschr., 1983-86; head lab. GERS AG, Twer, 1986-91; assoc. prof. systems engring. State U. Twer, 1986-91; dir. INCOLAB Ltd., Twer, 1991-93; sr. rschr., assoc. prof. U. Kassel, 1993—; nominated expert in TC122 CEN, Deutsche Institut für Normung e. V., Berlin, 1996—; assoc. prof. quality control systems U. Kassel, 1996—. Editor: Information and System Aspects in Modelling, 1986, Automatisation of Chemical-Technical Processes, 1987. Recipient Silver medal All Union Exhbn. of Nat. Econ. Achievements, USSR, 1984; recipient rsch. award Japanese Govt., Tokyo, 1995. Mem. IEEE, Internat. Fedn. Automatic Control, Internat. Ergonomics Assn. Achievements include 9 patents, one of which, Technology for Optimising the Color of Electrovacuum Glasses, is impelemented in as technical standard from 1985 until the present day in Russia; invention (co-author) of a system for stabilisation of quality of electrovacuum glasses and a method for interpretation of geophysical data. Office: LUSI-Centre, Mönchebergstr 31, D-34125 Kassel Germany

AVEROFF, IOANNIS, member European Parliament; b. Athens, Greece, Dec. 29, 1944. Mem. European Parliament, Brussels; mem. com. on budgets, com. on agr. and rural devel., mem. substitute del. to European Bulgaria Joint Parliamentary Com. and Romania Joint Parliamentary Com. Mem. Group of European People's Party (Christian Dems.) and European Dems. Mem. New Democracy Party. *

AVERSA, DOLORES SEJDA, educational administrator; b. Phila., Mar. 26, 1932; d. Martin Benjamin and Mary Elizabeth (Esposito) Sejda; m. Zefferino A. Aversa, May 3, 1958; children: Dolores Elizabeth, Jeffrey Martin, Linda Maria. BA, Chestnut Hill Coll., 1953. Owner Personal Rep. & Pub. Rels., Phila., 1965-68; ednl. cons. Franklin Sch. Sci. and Arts, Phila., 1968-72; pres., owner, dir. Martin Sch. Bus., Inc., Phila., 1972—; file reader, cons. for ct. reporting and travel tng. Southwestern Pub. Co., 1990; mem. ednl. planning com. Ravenhill Acad., Phila., 1975-76. Active Phila. Mus. Art, Phila. Drama Guild. Mem. Nat. Bus. Edn. Assn., Pa. Bus. Edn. Assn., Am. Bus. Law Assn., Pa. Sch. Counselors Assn., Am.-Italy Soc., Phila. Hist. Soc., World Affairs Coun. Phila., Hist. Soc. Pa., Phila. Orch., Am. Soc. Travel Agts. (sch. divsn., nat. educators com., sec. Del. chpt., edn. chmn., PAC chmn. 1997-98, 98-99, 99-2000, 2000-2001), Chestnut Hill Coll. Alumnae Assn. (sec. class '53), Lower Bucks County C. of C. Roman Catholic. Home: 2111 Locust St Philadelphia PA 19103-4802 Office: 2417 Welsh Rd Philadelphia PA 19114-2213

AVERY, BIRTHE MARGIT, embryologist, educator, researcher; b. Lemvig, Denmark, Apr. 13, 1941; d. Freddy Kermit and Marta (Olsen) Christensen; m. John Scales Avery, Oct. 28, 1976; children: Anne, Julie Marion, James Emil. MD, U. Copenhagen, 1977, ednl. cert. fgn. grads. (Am. degree), 1977; PhD in Embryology, Royal Vet. and Agrl. U., Copenhagen, 1991. Staff in neurosurgery, orthopedic surgery, cardiology various hosps., Copenhagen, 1977-81; rsch. scientist in immunology Royal Vet. and Agrl. U., 1981-82, rsch. scientist in reproductive biology, 1982-94, assoc. prof. reproductive biology, 1994—; guest prof. Cornell U., Ithaca, N.Y., 1984, U. Estate São Paulo, Jaboticabal, Brazil, 1993, U. Wis., Madison, 1996; invited spkr. numerous nat. and internat. scientific confs. Co-author: Recent Advances in Cellular and Molecular Aspects of Angiotensin Receptors, 1996, Reproduction and Animal Breeding, Advances and Strategies, 1995; contbr. numerous articles to internat. scientific jours; rschr. in in vitro fertilization (Hede Nielsen prize 1987). Recipient grants State Agrl. and Vet. Rsch. Coun., Copenhagen, 1982, 85, 91, Carlsberg Found., Copenhagen, 1984. Mem. European Embryo Transfer Assn., Soc. Study of Fertility, Internat. Embryo Transfer Soc., Danish Soc. Reprodn. and Fetal Devel. Lutheran. Avocations: literature, music, philosophy, religion. Home: Snebaerhaven 42, DK-2620 Albertslund Denmark Office: Royal Vet U Dept Reprodn, Dyrlaegevej 68, DK-1870 Frederiksberg C, Denmark

AVERY, JOHN SCALES, chemistry educator; b. Beirut, Lebanon, May 26, 1933; parents U.S. citizens; s. Bennett Franklin and Margaret Ann (Scales) A.; m. Inger Anne Margit Granath, 1960 (div. 1972); children: Helen, Jens, Cecilia; m. Birthe Margit Christensen, Oct., 28, 1976; children: Anne, Julie, James. BSc in Physics, MIT, 1954; MSc in Physics, U. Chgo., 1955; PhD in Theoretical Chemistry, U. London, 1965; D.I.C., Imperial Coll. Sci. & Tech., London, 1965. Physicist Nat. Bur. Standards, Washington, 1951-59 summers; vis. rsch. scholar Cambridge (Eng.) U., 1957-58; tchg. asst. U. Chgo., 1959-61; temporary lectr. Edinburgh (Scotland) U., 1961-62; lectr. Imperial Coll., U. London, 1963-73; assoc. prof. U. Copenhagen, Denmark, 1973; tech. expert WHO European Regional Office, 1988-95; contact person for Denmark Pugwash Confs. on Sci. and World Affairs, 1990—. Author: (books) The Quantum Theory of Atoms, Molecules and Photons, 1972, Spanish translation, 1975, Creation and Annihilation Operators, 1976, Hyperspherical Harmonics, 1989, Science and Society, 1995, Progress, Poverty, Population, 1997, Hyperspherical Harmonics and Generalized Sturmians, 1999; editor: (books) Membrane Structure and Mechanisms of Bilogical Energy Transduction, 1973, Local Density Approximations, 1983, New Methods in Quantum Theory, 1995; founder, mng. editor Jour. Bioenergetics and Biomembranes, 1969-80; contbr. numerous sci. articles to profl. jours. Co-recipient (with other Pugwash Conf. mems.) Nobel Peace Prize, 1995; named fellow Royal Soc. European Programme, 1968-70. Mem. Danish Acad. Scis. and Letters (fgn. mem.), Royal Instn. Great Britain, Sigma Xi. Avocations: painting, music, cycling. Home: Snebaerhaven 42, DK-2620 Albertslund Denmark Office: U Copenhagen Chem Inst, Universitetsparken 5, DK-2100 Copenhagen Denmark

AVERY, JULIA CATHERINE, science administrator; b. Berkeley, U.K., May 26, 1970; d. Norman William and Anne (Rowntree) A.; m. Justin Chinks Bharucha, July 31, 1999. BSc in Biochemistry with honors, U. London, 1991, PhD in Cell Physiology, 1996. Postdoctoral rsch. fellow Yale U., New Haven, 1996-97, Max Planck Inst. for Biophys. Chemistry, Göttingen, Germany, 1997-98; sci. editor Elsevier Sci., London, 1998-2000; scientific programme officer The Wellcome Trust, London, 2000—. Contbr. articles to profl. jours., chpt. to book. Fellow Max Planck Soc., 1996-98; Med. Rsch. Coun. studentship, London, 1991-96. Mem. Royal Coll. Sci. (assoc.). Mem. Ch. of England. Avocations: swimming, walking, aerobics. Home: 18 Finland St, London SE16 7TP, England Office: The Wellcome Trust, 183 Euston Rd, London NW1 2BE, England

AVERY, ROBERT NEWELL, sculptor; b. May 22, 1940; s. Robert Newell and Margaret (Andrews) A.; m. Karen Lissol, Aug. 27, 1963 (div. 1978); 1 child, Robert Walter; m. Amanda Fair Jones, May 5, 1979; 1 child, Melinda Hopkins. BFA, Calif. Coll. Arts and Crafts, Oakland, 1962; postgrad., Coll. of San Mateo, Calif., 1969-70, Coll. of Redwoods, 1975-76. Freelance comml. artist Mendocino, Calif., 1971-75; exec. dir. Mendocino Art Ctr., Inc., 1975-79; proprietor Missing Link Prodns., Mendocino, 1979-93; mng. dir. Mezzanine Gallery at Daly's, Ft. Bragg, Calif., 1986-87, 91-93; exec. dir. Staunton/Augusta Art Ctr., Staunton, Va., 1995-96; proprietor Avery Studio Gallery, Staunton, 1996—; art dir. The Mendocino Rev., 1983-91; judge Sonoma County Fair, Santa Rosa, Calif., 1977; auctioneer many arts/ednl./polit. events; art dir. The Mendocino Rev. #3, 1975; disc jockey Radio Sta. KMFB-FM, Mendocino, 1971-73, KJAZ-FM, Berkeley, Calif., 1960-61; lead player (play) The Great American Desert, 1975, Candida, 1977, Mousetrap, 1978, Rain, 1979, The Real Inspector Hound, 1984; prodr.: Twin Peaks (stage play), 1985; host interviewer: Art View, 1987-89, The Now and Then Show, 1985-91; prodr., programmer radio show: Odd Bob Comedy Show, KZYX-FM, 1989-90. Contbr. articles, photographs, illustrations to profl. jours.; columnist The Mendocino Daily Planet, 1972-73, The Mendocino Beacon, 1975-79, The New Settler Interview, 1986, Mendocino Grapevine, 1977-82; illustrator: The House that Jack Built; one man shows include Winona Gallery, Mendocino, 1990, Stock Exch. Deli, Waynesboro, Va., 1995, Augusta County Libr., Fishersville, Va., 1996; group shows include Mendocino Art Ctr., 1986, 1990, 91-93, Mayhew Wildlife Gallery, Mendocino, 1986-93, Mezzanine Gallery, Ft. Bragg, 1986-88, Caspar Studios Gallery, 1990, Shenandoah Valley Art Ctr., Waynesboro, Va., 1994-95, Beverley St. Studio Sch., Staunton, Va., 1995, Jordan Gallery, Charlottesville, Va., 1995, Lynchburg Fine Arts Ctr., 1995, Augusta Art Ctr., 1997, others;. Master of ceremonies 4th of July Parade, Mendocino, 1976-93; judge Bodega Bay Fisherman's Festival Ann. Arts Show, 1976; chmn. art acquisition com. Augusta Hosp. Corp., 1997; mem. founding bd. Mendocino Performing Arts Co., Inc.; past pres. Mendocino Cmty. Land Trust, Inc.; trustee Mendocino Unified Sch. Dist., 1973-77, pres., 1977; past dir. Mendocino Bus. and Profl. Coun.; mem. citizen's adv. coun. Coll. of the Redwoods, 1979-80; mem. exec. com. Calif. Arts Coun., Rural Arts Svcs., 1978-79; trustee Mendocino Art Ctr., Inc., 1980-85, chmn. citizen's adv. com., 1991, hon. life mem. Recipient numerous sculpture awards various art assns. Mem. Assn. of Sci. Fiction Artists, Internat. Sculpture Commn. Home and Office: 4855 Morris Mill Rd Swoope VA 24479-2323

AVERY, STEPHEN NEAL, playwright, author; b. Hot Springs, Ark., Mar. 20, 1955; s. Leo A. Avery and Dedette Carol (Miles) Andree; m. Kathleen Annette Twin, Sept. 7, 1979. Free-lance reporter Hot Springs Sentinel-Record and New Era, 1970-73. Author: Hungry: 3 Plays, 1991, Because, 1991, Insidious, 1992, Burning Bridges, 1999. With USN, 1973-77. Mem. Dramatists Guild Inc., Authors League of Am., Theatre Comms. Group. Avocations: museum and gallery exhbns.

AVER'YANOV, ANDREY A., plant physiologist; b. Moscow, Mar. 18, 1947. MS, Moscow State U., 1970, PhD, 1975, DS in Biology, 1995. Rsch. fellow Moscow State U., 1974-80; sr. investigator Rsch. Inst. of Phytopathology, 1980-89, leading scientific rschr., 1989—. Contbr. articles to profl. jours. Rsch. grantee Russian Acad. of Sci., 1996, 98, 99, Ctr. Internal des Etudiants et Stagiares, Nat. Inst. Agronomical Rsch., Dijon, France, 1996. Mem. Am. Phytopathol. Soc. Avocation: travel. Office: Rsch Inst Phytopathology, P/O B Vyazemy, 143050 Moscow region Russia

AVIDOR, ARIE, publisher; b. Roman, Romania, Sept. 10, 1932; arrived in Israel, 1951; s. Eliezer and Ety (Katz) Hascalovici; m. Liliane Weil, Jan. 1, 1959; children: Daniel, Anat, Lyat. Diploma in econ. and internat. rels., The Hebrew U., Jerusalem, 1957. Amb. State of Israel, Bolivia, 1981-84; pres. Grupo Editorial Aurora, Tel-Aviv, 1984—; bd. dirs. Instituto Cultural Israel Ibero Am., Jerusalem. Editor (Spanish weekly) Aurora, Israel, 1963-84, (mag.) Israel & Middle East. Hon. consul Bolivia, Tel Aviv, 1997. Recipient Condor de los Andes Bolivian Govt., 1984. Mem. Rotary Internat. (gov. 1991-92; Paul Harris fellow 1991). Home: Hacarmel 24, 47230 Ramat-Hasharon Israel Office: Grupo Editorial Aurora, Hanatziv 30, 61180 Tel Aviv Israel

AVIERINOS, CHRISTIAN YVES, cardiologist; b. Marseille, France, Jan. 15, 1945; s. Jean Christian and Georgette (Caravas) A.; m. Elisabeth Madeleine Martin, July 12, 1967; children: Jean-Francois, Cecile. BS, U. Marseille, 1961, MD, 1973. Pres. Syndicate of Cardiologists, Provence, 1985-99, Union of Cardiologists, France, 1999—; pres. Cardiologist Assoc., Provence, 1988—. Lt. French navy, 1968-69. Mem. Nat. Coll. French Cardiologists (pres. 1991-94, exec. sec. 1995—), Coll. Cardiologists, Lions. Roman Catholic. Avocations: tennis, opera. Office: 4 Ave Delphes, 13006 Marseille Provence, France

AVILA, CARLOS ALBERTO, physics researcher, inventor; b. May 7, 1950; s. Manuel Antonio Avila and Natalia Rivera; m. Gladys Esther Rivera, Feb. 9, 1973; children: Carlos Jr., Rolando, Elias, David. Grad. personal mechanography, Royal Comml. Coll., Arecibo, P.R., 1977; grad. computer programming, Electronic Coll., San Juan, P.R., 1979; BAW in Chemistry and Gen. Sci., Inter Am. U., P.R., 1988; MA in Sci. Edn., NYU, 1992. Tchr. of sci. Dept. Edn., P.R., 1976-86, tchr. chemistry lab., 1992-93; rschr. physics dept. U. Puerto Rico, 1993—; Spanish cmty. svcs. staff Dept. Edn., Penns Grove, N.J., 1982-83; substitute tchr. Dept. Edn., Meml. H.S., 1983-84. Songwriter Man Should Understand. With U.S. Army, 1991-92. Mem. Nat. Sci. Assn. Achievements include inventor of Thermoelectric battery and power plant using the same; developer of Avila's Singunification Theory. Avocations: reading science and technology books and magazines, music. Home and Office: PO Box 14 Angeles PR 00611-0014 also: 40150 Friar Tuck Trl Zephyrhills FL 33540-7702

AVILA, RENE ARNOLD, city official; b. Loma Linda, Calif., Aug. 29, 1960; s. Ruben Arnold and Elizabeth Avila; m. Peggy Lee Deciest, Sept. 1, 1987; children: Jason, Jacob, Amina, Janeen, Rene. Supervising bldg. inspector Jurisdiction of Colton, Calif., 1987-96; plans examiner/sr. inspector Jurisdiction of Ontario, Calif., 1996—. Vol. Dem. Party, Inland Impire, 1996—. Mem. ICBO (chpt. pres. 1998-2000). Roman Catholic. Avocations: guitar and music, politics, biking, history. Office: City of Ontario 303 E B St Ontario CA 91764-4196

AVILES, ALICE ALERS, psychologist; b. N.Y.C; d. Jose Oscar and Pauline (Irizarry) Alers; m. Jose A. Aviles, Aug. 13, 1954 (div. Oct. 1981); children: Jeffrey (dec.), Brian, Gregory; m. Clifford M. Goldman, June 29, 1997. BS magna cum laude, SUNY, Oswego, 1955; MA, Queens Coll., 1978; PhD, Yeshiva U., 1984; postdoctoral diploma in psychoanalysis and psychotherapy, Adelphi U., 1991. Lic. psychologist, N.Y. Tchr. elem. schs. Spring Valley, N.Y., 1955, Erlangen (Fed. Republic Germany) Am. Sch., 1955-56; tchr. elem. schs. Uniondale, N.Y., 1956, Freeport, N.Y., 1957-58, Island Park, N.Y., 1973-75; psychology clk. Fifth Ave. Ctr. for Counseling and Psychotherapy, N.Y.C., 1978-80; psychology intern St. Vincent's Hosp. and Med. Ctr., N.Y.C., 1980-81; psychologist Kingsboro Psychiat. Ctr., Bklyn., 1981-84; psychologist to assoc. psychologist South Beach Psychiat. Ctr., Bklyn., 1984-86; pvt. practice Valley Stream, N.Y., 1985—; from staff psychologist to sr. psychologist Luth. Med. Ctr., Bklyn., 1986-95; cons. Beach Terrace Care Ctr., Long Beach, N.Y., 1995-97; mem. adv. com. Hispanic Counseling Ctr. of Family Svc. Assn. of Nassau County, Hempstead, N.Y., 1978-80; cons. Nassau County Extended Care Ctr., Hempstead, 1997-99, Resort Nursing Home, Far Rockaway, N.Y., 1998-2000, Woodmere (N.Y.) Rehab. and Health Care Ctr., 1999—. Ford found. grad. fellow, 1978-81. Mem. APA, N.Y. State Psychol. Assn., Nassau County Psychol. Assn. (mem. pvt. practice com. 1992-93), Adelphi Soc. Psychoanalysis and Psychotherapy. Office: 10 Valley Ln E North Woodmere NY 11581-3629

AVILES PEREA, MARIA ANTONIA, member of European parliament; b. Murcia, Spain, June 28, 1944. Mem. European Parliament, Brussels, 1999—; mem. Group of European People's Party (Christian Democrats) and European Democrats; mem. com. on employment and social affairs, com. on women's rights and equal opportunities, delegation for rels. with the Palestinian Legis. Coun., delegation to the European Econ. Area Joint Parliamentary Com. Mem. People's Party. Office: Parlamento Europeo, Rue Wiertz ASP 11E209, B-1047 Bruxelles Belgium*

AVINASH, KHARE, physicist, researcher; b. Satna, India, July 23, 1957; s. Maharaj Bahadur and Savitri (Beohar) K.; m. Varsha Shrivastav, June 15, 1982; children: Ojasvi, Megha. BSc, Delhi U., 1975; MSc in Physics, A.P.S. U., Rewa, India, 1977; PhD in Plasma Physics, Gujrat U., Ahmedabad, 1983. Rsch. assoc. Phys. Rsch. Lab., Ahmedabad, 1984-86; scientist Culham Lab., Oxford, Eng., 1986-87, Joint European Torus, Culham, Oxford, Eng., 1987-89; fellow Inst. for Plasma Rsch., Bhat, 1989-92, assoc. prof., 1992—. Mem. editl. bd. Indian Jour. Physics, 1997—; contbr. over 100 articles to profl. jours. Recipient Young Scientist award Homi Bhabha Fellow Coun., 1993; associateship Internat. Ctr. Theoretical Physics (Italy), 1995. Mem. Plasma Sci. Soc. of India. Avocations: classical music, physical exercise, martial arts, football. Home: A-201 Manila Twr, Satellite, Ahmedabad 380054, India Office: Inst For Plasma Rsch, Bhat Gandhinagar 382428, India

AVISSAR, NELLY EMANUELLA, biochemist, researcher; b. Peta Tikua, Israel, June 23, 1943; came to U.S., 1985; d. Jacob M. and Rachel Fajnholc; m. Sasson Avissar, Feb. 21, 1974; children: Uri, Ruth, Michael. BS, Hebrew U., Jerusalem, 1967; MS, Hebrew U., 1969; PhD, Tel Aviv U., 1980. Head red blood cell unit Beilinson Med. Ctr., Peta Tikua, 1968-85; scientist U. Rochester (N.Y.) Med. Ctr., 1985-96, asst. prof., 1996—. Contbr. articles to sci. jours. Sgt. Israeli Army, 1960-62. Mem. Am. Soc. Exptl. Biology, Am. Gastroent. Soc., Am. Thoracic Soc., N.Y. Acad. Sci., Am. Soc. for Nutritional Sci. Office: U Rochester Med Ctr Dept Surgery 601 Elmwood Ave Rochester NY 14642-0001

AVKSENTYUK, BORIS PETROVICH, physicist, researcher; b. Kharkov, Ukraine, July 16, 1941; s. Peter Grigorievich and Alexandra Ivanovna (Shumilova) A. MS in Physics, Novosibirsk (Russia) State U., 1964; PhD in Thermal Physics, Russian Acad. Scis., Novosibirsk, 1973. Intern Kutateladze Inst. Thermophysics, Sibirian Br., Novosibirsk, 1965-66, jr. rschr.,

1966-77, sr. rschr., 1977-86, lead rschr., 1986-98, chief rschr., 1998—. Contbr. articles to profl. jours. Avocations: classical music, sports. Home: Zolotodolinskaj 7 Apt 60, 630090 Novosibirsk Russia Office: Kutateladze Inst Thermophys, pr Lavrenteva 1, 630090 Novosibirsk Russia

AVRAAMIDES, LYSANDROS MICHAEL, researcher; b. Nicosia, Cyprus, May 3, 1939; s. Michael and Elli Michael (Epiphanidou) A.; m. Maria Lysandrou, Feb. 2, 1962; children: Linos, Corinna. MA in Polit. Behaviour, U. Essex, Colchester, Eng., 1983. With Cyprus Broadcasting Corp., Nicosia, 1957-95, prin. programs officer, 1983-95; rsch. fellow R&D Ctr.-Intercollege, Nicosia, 1995—. Author: (vols. of poetry) Semioseis, 1991, Parallaghes, 1993, Proschedia, 1995. Avocations: playing violin, composing music. Home: 131 Odysseas Elytis St, 2546 Dhali Cyprus Office: R&D Ctr Intercollege, 46 Makedonitissa Ave, 1700 Nicosia Cyprus

AVRAAMIDOU, MARIA LYSANDROU, television director; b. Kyrenia, Cyprus, Apr. 21, 1939; d. John and Theodora John Christou; m. Lysandros Michael Avraamides; children: Linos, Corinna. Grad., Pancyprian Gymnasium, Nicosia, Cyprus, 1957; cert., Thomson Found. TV Coll., 1969. With Cyprus Broadcasting Corp., Nicosia, 1958-97, sr. programs officer, 1990-97; pvt. practice Nicosia, 1997—. Author: (plays) The Beautiful Tale of Rosa, 1984 (1st prize Cyprus Nat. Theater 1984), Harsh Angel, 1985 (1st prize Cyprus Nat. Theater 1986), The Primeval Cry, 1988 (1st prize Cyprus Nat. Theater 1988), The Summer of Our Love, 1990 (1st prize Cyprus Nat. Theater 1990), This Distracted Globe, 1992 (2d prize Cyprus Nat. Theater 1992), (novels) Letter to My Lonely Brother, 1987, Oh, The Beautiful Sundays, 1994, (short stories) The Last Separation, 1979. Greek Orthodox. Home: 131 Odysseas Elytis St, 2546 Dhali Cyprus

AVRAM, MORRELL M., nephrologist, educator, consultant; b. N.Y.C., Nov. 11, 1929; m. Maria G. Kunzle; children: Rella Marie, Marc Robert, Eric Michael, Mathew Mendel, David Keith. BS, L.I. U., 1951, DS (hon.), 1988; MD, U. Geneva, 1959. Intern L.I. Coll. Hosp., Bklyn., 1959-60, chief resident, 1962-63, fellow in nephrology, 1963-64, chief hemodialysis lab., 1964—, first dir. renal clinic, 1966—, first chief div. nephrology, 1970—, chief renal clin. rsch. lab., 1987—; clin. prof. SUNY, Bklyn., 1979—; cons. in field; cons. Southampton Hosp., Univ. Hosp., SUNY, Cath. Med. Ctr.—Bklyn./Queens; vis. physician Kings County Med. Ctr., N.Y.C., 1964—; founder, dir. The Bklyn. Kidney Ctr., 1971—; vis. prof. numerous univs. including U. Conn., U. Ariz., SUNY, Johns Hopkins U., Harvard U., UCLA, univs. in Beijing, Rio de Janeiro, Tel Aviv, Cairo; speaker in field. Author: Parathyroid Hormone in Kidney Disease, 1980, Prevention of Kidney Disease and Long-Term Survival, 1982, Protenuria, 1985; (with C. Giordano) Ambulatory Peritoneal Dialysis, 1990; contbg. author numerous books; mem. editorial bd. Nephron, 1978—, Clin. Nephrology, 1981—, Dialysis and Transplantation, 1980—, Jour. Geriatric Nephrology and Urology, 1990—, Internat. Jour. Artificial Organs, 1978—, Internat. Jour. Pediatric Nephrology, 1980, Jour. Diabetic Complications, 1987, Hypertension, 1975-77, Urology Times, 1974-84; reviewer various publs.; contbr. numerous articles to profl. jours. Chmn. med. adv. bd. Nat. Kidney Found. N.Y./N.J., Inc., 1982-87, med. adv. bd. mem. 1999; founding mem. Am. Soc. Hypertension, 1986—; bd. dirs., exec. com. World Affairs Coun., 1989—; bd. mem. St. Luke's Roosevelt Hosp. Ctr., L.I. Coll. Hosp., Pianofest; co-chmn. bd. dirs. World Affairs Coun., Southampton, N.Y.; active numerous community and svc. orgns. With U.S. Army, 1951-53, Korea. Clin. rsch. tng. fellow L.I. Coll. Hosp., 1968—, Nat. Kidney Found. fellow L.I. Coll. Hosp., 1969—; recipient Lester Hoenig award Nat. Kidney Found., 1984. Fellow ACP; mem. AMA, AAAS, Am. Soc. Nephrology, Am. Soc. for Internal Organs (editor Transactions XXXIII 1987), Internat. Soc. Nephrology, Internat. Soc. Artificial Internal Organs, Bklyn. Acad. Medicine, Am. Anthropol. Soc., N.Y. Acad. Scis., N.Y. Soc. Nephrology (pres. 1977-78), Renal Network N.Y. (pres. 1978-79). Home: 115 Remsen St Brooklyn NY 11201-4212 Office: LI Coll Hosp Div Nephrology Atlantic Ave Brooklyn NY 11201-5526

AVRETT, ROZ (ROSALIND CASE), writer, advertising creative director; b. Upper Montclair, N.J., Apr. 19, 1933; d. William Lyon and Doris Edna (Clift) Case; m. William Thomas Reynolds, Feb. 20, 1960 (div. 1968); 1 child, Gerald William Thomas; m. John Glenn Avrett, Dec. 31, 1972. BA in Creative Writing, Chatham Coll., 1951-55. Copy trainee Young & Rubicam, Inc., N.Y.C., 1955-56; copy writer Hicks & Greist, Inc., N.Y.C., 1958-61; sr. copy writer Dancer-Fitzgerald-Sample, N.Y.C., 1961-63; creative supr. The Marschalk Co., N.Y.C., 1963-68; assoc. creative dir. BBDO Internat., N.Y.C., 1968-78; author N.Y.C., 1978—; advt. lectr. Sch. of Visual Arts, 1970, 71. Author: My Turn, 1983, 72nd and Rodeo, 1983; author short stories. Patron Met. Opera. Recipient Leadership award Am. Biog. Inst., Raleigh, N.C. Mem. PEN, Author's Guild, People for Ethical Treatment of Animals, Met. Opera Club, River Club. Republican. Episcopalian. Avocations: animal rights, opera.

AVVAKUMOV, EVGENII GRIGORIEVICH, chemist, researcher; b. Kirov, Russia, Dec. 26, 1934; s. Grigorii Mikhailovich and Aleksandra Nikolaevna (Synczova) A.; m. Irina Vladimirovna Nikolaeva, Mar. 29, 1959; children: Aleksandr Evgenievich, Sergey Evgenievich. Chemist, State U. Leningrad, Russia, 1957; DSc in Chemistry with hons., Inst. Inorganic Chemistry, Siberian Br. Russian Acad. Sci Novosibirsk, 1965, PhD in Chemistry with hons., 1987; prof., Higher Certification Commn., Russia, 1996. Jr. sci. collaborator Inst. Inorganic Chemistry Siberian Br. Russian Acad. Scis., Novosibirsk, Russia, 1958-68; oldest sci. collaborator Inst. Chem. Kinetics and Combustion Siberian Br. Russian Acad. Scis., Novosibirsk, 1968-75; oldest sci. collaborator Inst. Solid State Chemistry Siberian Br. Russian Acad. Scis, Novosibirsk, 1975-88; head mechanochem. reactions lab. Inst. Solid State Chemistry and Mechanochemistry, Siberian br. Russian Acad. Scis., Novosibirsk, 1988—. Author: Monography: Mechanical Methods of Activation of Chemical Processes, 1979, 2d rev. edit., 1986, Monography: Cordierite-Perspective Ceramic Material, 1999; editor: Mechanochemical Synthesis in Inorganic Chemistry, 1991; contbr. 172 articles to profl. jours.; 41 inventions in field mechano chemical synthesis of inorganic and ceramic materials. Recipient State prize of Russia in sci. and technique, Moscow, 1993, Govt. reward-medal for labour achievments, Moscow, 1975; grantee Russian Found., Moscow, 1995, 97. Mem. All Russian D.J. Mendeleev Chem. Soc. Avocation: gardening. Home: Morskoi Prospect 40 Apart 3, 630090 Novosibirsk Siberia, Russia Office: Inst Sld St & Mechano Chem, ul Kutateladze 18, 630128 Novosibirsk Russia

AWAD, JAMAL MASOUD, trading company executive; b. Alras, Palestine, Oct. 20, 1948; s. Masoud Said and Bahieh (Abdel Hafez) A.; m. Hanan Amin Swais, Sept. 5, 1978; 5 children. BCom in Accountancy and Adminstrn., Damascus U., 1971. Acct. Al Sdairawi Hosp., Kuwait, 1972-74; accounts in charge Spltys. Co., Dubai, United Arab Emirates, 1974-75; sr. acct. Ministry of Finance, Abu Dhabi, United Arab Emirates, 1975-79; finance mgr. Salam Studio, Abu Dhabi, 1979-81; dep. mng. dir. Grand Stores, Emirates, 1981—; cons. Safestway, Dubai, 1986—, Emdico, Jeddah, Saudi Arabia, 1991—, Grand Stores, Amman, Jordan, 1986—. Office: Grand Stores, Al-Garhoud, Dubai PB 2144, United Arab Emirates

AWAD, MAHMOUD MOHAMED, cardiologist, consultant; b. Zagazig, Egypt, Dec. 26, 1954; s. Mohamed Ahmed and Zeinab Ali (Khater) A.; m. Susan Ezzel-Din Hilmi, Aug. 2, 1984; children: Bahgat, Carmen. MB BCh, Zagazig Faculty Medicine, 1980; MS in Cardiology, Cairo Faculty Medicine, 1985. Intern Zagazig Gen. Hosp., 1981-82, sr. resident in cardiology, 1984-87; resident in cardiology Gen. Mil. Hosp., Cairo, 1982-84; rsch. assoc. U. Ala., Birmingham, 1987-90; asst. cons. King Faisal Specialist Hosp. and Rsch. Ctr., Riyadh, Saudi Arabia, 1990-93; pvt. practice Zagazig, 1993-94; cons. Ministry of Health, Cairo, 1994-96; rsch. fellow U. Rome Tor Vergata, 1997; asst. cons. King Faisal Specialist Hosp. and Rsch. Ctr., 1997—. Contbr. articles to profl. jours. 1st lt. Med. Corps, Egyptian Army, 1982-84. U.S. AID scholar, Birmingham, Ala., 1987; Italian Nat. Coun. Rsch. scholar, 1997. Fellow Am. Coll. Cardiology (assoc.); mem. Internat. Soc. Cardiovascular Ultrasound. Avocations: music, travel, reading, sports. Home: 2 Al-Moudir St, Manshiat Abaza, 44511 Zagazig Egypt Office: King Faisal Splst Hosp, PO Box 3354, Riyadh 11211, Saudi Arabia

AWADALLAH, OSAMA GHAZI ZEIN, public relations executive, consultant; b. Jeddah, Saudi Arabia, Feb. 23, 1968; p. Ghazi Zein Awadallah and Fawziah Khalil Kuwaiti; m. Tahani Mohammad Tahlawi, Jan. 2, 1994; children: Shahad, Shadi, Mushal. Bachelor's, King Abud Al Aziz U., Jeddah, 1994; Master's, U. Miami, 1999. Fgn. info. officer Saudi Fgn. Info., Jeddah, 1994—; pres. Mid. East Media Ctr., Jeddah, Saudi Arabia; counselor Internat. Advt. Agy., Cairo, 1991, Media Internat. Agy., Cyprus, 1994. V.p. Human Relief Org., Cyprus, 1992. Mem. Journalism Edn. Assn., Soc. Profl. Assn., Investigative Reporters Assn., Soc. Profl. Journalists. Avocations: tennis, soccer, golf. Office: Mid East Media, PO Box 2221, Jeddah 21451, Saudi Arabia

AWAD EL KARIM, RIHAB ABDEL MAGID, immunologist; b. Elobied, Sudan, Sept. 24, 1964; d. Abdel Magid and Nadia Kamil (Ghandour) Awadaluah; m. Ibrahim Abdelkareim Bedri, Dec. 5, 1990; 1 child, Mohammed Bedri. MBBS, Faculty of Medicine, Khartoum, Sudan, 1989; PhD in Immunology, Karolinska Inst., Stockholm, 1999. Intern Ministry of Health, Khartoum, 1990-91; med. officer Atbara (Sudan) Hosp., 1991-93; med. practitioner Shaab Hosp., Khartoum, 1993, Omdurman (Sudan) Hosp., 1994; registrar Dept. Pathology, Khartoum, 1995; postdoctoral fellow Karolinska Inst., 1999—; Contbr. articles to Jour. Human Antibody, Infection and Immunity, others. Mem. Brit. Soc. for Immunology, Scandinavian Soc. for Immunology, N.Y. Acad. Sci. Avocations: reading, swimming, listening to music. Office: Linkoping U Hosp/Clin Immun, care Jan Ernerudh, 58185 Liknöping Sweden

AWADI, SHARIFA IBRAHIM, systems analyst; b. Muharraq, Bahrain, Apr. 4, 1957; parents Ibrahin Ismail Awadi and Shaikha Mubarak Nass; m. Khalid Hassan Dossari, Jan. 19, 1984. BA in Econs., Dammamm Secondary Sch., 1979. Sys. analyst Expec Network Op., Dhahran, 1995—. Avocation: reading. E-mail: sharifaawadi@hotmail.com. Office: Expec Network Op, Dhahran 31311, Saudi Arabia

AWAJI, MITSUHIRO, physicist, researcher; b. Himeji, Hyogo, Japan, Mar. 31, 1965; s. Kouhei and Hiromi (Harada) A. BSc, Okayama (Japan) U. Sci., 1987, MSc, 1989, PhD, 1992. Fellow Japan Soc. Promotion of Sci., Okayama, Japan, 1991-93; postdoctoral fellow dept. materials, vis. fellow St. Cross Coll., Oxford U., Eng., 1993-95; fellow ctr. of excellence Nat. Rsch. Inst. for Metals, Tsukuba, Japan, 1995-97; lectr. Rsch. Ctr. for Ultra-High Voltage Electron Microscopy Osaka U., 1997-98; rschr. Japan Synchrotron Radiation Rsch. Inst., Harima, 1998—. Contbr. articles to profl. jours. Recipient Nishina prize Okayama-Nishina Found., Okayama, 1992; Japan Soc. for the Promotion of Sci. fellow for rsch. abroad, 1993-95. Fellow The Royal Microscopical Soc.; mem. Phys. Soc. Japan, Japanese Soc. for Synchrotron Radiation Rsch. Avocations: yachting, watercolors, tea ceremony, swimming, horseback riding. Home: Mukudani 712 Hayashita, Himeji Hyogo 679-4211, Japan Office: Japan Synchrotron Radiation Rsch Inst, Kouto 1-1-1, Mikazuki Sayo-gun Hyogo 679-5198, Japan

AWAN, IFTIKHAR AHMAD, corporate marketing manager; b. PEshawar, Pakistan, May 14, 1950; s. Wazir Mohammad and Anjuman Ara (Daud) Khan; m. Raffat Abbas Kiyani. B of Commerce, Commerce Coll., Peshawar, Pakistan, 1972; BS, Punjab U., Lahore, Pakistan, 1974. Rsch. officer Nat. Bank Pakistan, Peshawar, 1972-77; adminstrn. mgr. Al-Mashrik Constrn. Co., Jubail, Saudi Arabia, 1977-79; supr. tech. dept. Hoshan Co., Al-Khobar, Saudi Arabia, 1979-80, sales supr., 1981-85. Sec. gen. NAt. Bank Pakistan Employees Union, Peshawar, 1973-76. Islam. Avocations: reading, music, swimming,walking, travel. Home: PO Box 59270, Riyadh Saudi Arabia Office: Hoshanco, Olaya, 11525 Riyadh Saudi Arabia

AWASTHI, VIDYA NIDHI, accounting educator; b. Jhansi, India, July 8, 1955. BSc, Meerut (India) U., 1974, MA, 1976; MBA, Calif. State U., Fresno, 1984; PhD, U. Wash., 1988. CPA, Wash., cert. mgmt. acct., cert. in fin. mgmt. Bank officer State Bank of India, Kanpur, 1976-82; tchg. assoc. U. Wash., Seattle, 1984-88; asst. prof. Santa Clara (Calif.) U., 1988-96, Seattle U., 1996-99; assoc. prof. Seattle U., 1999—. Contbr. articles to profl. jours. Mem. Am. Acctg. Assn., Inst. Mgmt. Accts., Mensa. Office: Seattle U 900 Broadway Seattle WA 98122-4340

AWAYA, NOBUYOSHI, electronics engineer, materials researcher; b. Tokyo, Apr. 26, 1956; s. Toshinobu and Haruko (Kondoh) A.; m. Ryoko Yamashita. BS, Waseda U., Tokyo, 1979; MS, Waseda U., 1981, PhD, 1996. Rsch. engr. NTT Elec. Comm. Labs., Tokyo, 1981-89; sr. rsch. engr. NTT Sys. Electronics Labs., Atsugi, Japan, 1989-98; gen. mgr. Sharp Co. IC Group, Fukayama, Japan, 1998—; session chmn. advanced metallization for ULSI, Murray Hill, N.J., 1991, Electrochem. Soc. Mtg., San Antonio, 1996; mem. com. Japanese Semicondr. Loadmap; mem. program IITC. Co-author: Surface Reaction Process for ULSI Fabrications, 1994; contbr. over 70 articles to profl. jours., confs.; patentee in field; editor Current Status of Cuinterconnection for ULSI Application. Mem. IEEE, Electro Chem. Soc., Material Rsch. Soc., Japan Soc. Applied Physics, Inst. Electronics, Info. and Comm. Engrs. Avocations: skiing, sports. Home: 1-13-10 Higashi Fukatsu, Fukuyama Hiroshima 721-0974, Japan

AWBI, HAZIM BASHIR, engineering educator; b. Mosul, Nineva, Iraq, Jan. 21, 1945; arrived in U.K., 1962; s. Bashir Yakoub Awbi and Najiba Issa Mahfooth; m. Janette Heeps (div. Dec. 1995); children: Chantal, Anita, Amanda; m. Janet Ashak, Nov. 1997; 1 child, Nadine. BS, U. Manchester, 1967, MS, 1969; PhD, Nottingham Trent U., 1974. Chartered engr. Asst. lectr. U. Technology, Baghdad, 1969-71, lectr., 1975-81; engr. Engring. Scis. Data Unit Internat., London, 1974-75; sect. head Bldg. Svcs. Rsch. and Info. Assn., Bracknell, Eng., 1981-83; lectr. Napier U., Edinburgh, 1983-90; sr. lectr. U. Reading, Eng., 1990—; dir. World Renewable Energy Network, Reading, 1994—; chmn. Internat. Conf. RoomVent 2000. Author: (book) Ventilation of Buildings, 1991; mem. editl. bd. Renewable Energy Jour., 1995—; contbr. articles to profl. jours. Hon. prof. Chongqing Jianzhu U., China, 1994. Mem. ASHRAE, Instn. Mech. Engrs., Chartered Instn. Bldg. Svcs. Engrs. Roman Catholic. Office: Univ Reading, Whiteknights, RG6 6AW Reading Berkshire, England

AWDRY, CHRISTOPHER VERE, author; b. July 2, 1940; s. Wilbert Vere and Margaret Emily (Wale) A. Student, St. Chad's Sch., Lichfield, Worksop Coll. Writings include: Really Useful Engines, 1983, James and the Diesel Engines, 1984, Great Little Engines, 1985, More About Thomas the Tank Engine, 1986, Gordon, the High-speed Engine, 1987, Percy and the Postman: Sticker Book, 1988, Thomas and the Evil Diesel, 1988, Thomas and the Lost Cat: Sticker Book, 1988, Thomas and the Missing Christmas Tree, 1988, Toby, Trucks and Trouble, 1988, Henry Pulls the Express Train, 1989, James and the Rescue Train, 1989, Meet Thomas the Tank Engine and His Friends, 1989, Thomas and the Twins, 1989, Thomas's Book of Colors, 1989, Thomas's Big Book of Games and Puzzles, 1989, Thomas and the Good Train, 1989, Thomas Gets Tricked and Other Stories, 1989, Thomas the Tank Engine and the Great Race, 1989, Thomas the Tank Engine's Noisy Trip, 1989, Trouble for Thomas and Other Stories, 1989, Up and Down with Percy, 1989, Thomas the Tank Engine's ABC's, 1990, Breakfast Time for Thomas, 1990, Jock the New Engine, 1990, Catch Me, Catch Me!, 1990, Happy Birthday, Thomas!, 1990, Henry and the Elephant, Encyclopedia of British Railway Companies, 1990, Thomas Visits a Farm, 1991, Thomas and the Great Railway Show, 1991, Thomas and the Station Cat, 1991, Henry Goes to the Hospital, 1991, Thomas's Big Book of Words, 1992, Thomas and the Tiger, 1992, Thomas and the Hurricane, 1992, Thomas and the Dinosaur, 1992, Tell the Time with Thomas, 1992, Percy and the Kite, 1992, Brunel's Broad Gauge Railway, 1992, Thomas Goes to the Seaside, 1993, Thomas and the Pony Show, 1993, Over the Summit: How Britain's Railways Crossed the High Hills, 1993, Learn with Thomas, 1993, Henry and the Ghost Train, 1993, Henry and the Express, 1993, Wilbert the Forest Engine, 1994, Thomas the Tank Engine Press-out Model Book, 1994, Thomas the Tank Engine European Words Book, 1994, Thomas Catches a Thief: Mini Pop-ups, 1994, Thomas and the Scrambled Eggs: Mini Pop-ups, 1994, Thomas and the Prize Pig, 1994, Percy and the Scarf: Mini Pop-ups, 1994, Percy and the Night Train, 1994, James and the Signal, Mini Pop-ups, 1994, James and the Fat Controller, 1994, Edward and the Bear, 1994, Chuff, Chuff, Here Comes Thomas: A Single Sound Book, 1994, Thomas's Big Busy Book, 1994, The Fat Controller's Engines, 1995, Thomas and the Helicopter Rescue, 1995, Thomas's Amazing Pop-up Train Set Book, 1995, Thomas the Tank Engine Easy-to-Read Treasury, 1995, Awdry's Steam Railways, 1995, New Little Engine, 1996, Thomas Goes to School, 1996, Railways Galore, 1996, The Chips Express, 1996, Is That You Thomas?, 1996. Mem. Soc. Authors, Railway and Canal Hist. Soc., Railway and Corr. Travel Soc. Mem. Ch. of Eng. Home: The Old Sratian House, Oundle, Peterborough PE8 5LA, England

AWODIYA, MUYIWA PETER, theater educator, researcher, arts administrator; b. Ilesha, Osun, Nigeria, Aug. 14, 1947; s. James Esan and Maryann Ibilola (Kupoluyi) A.; m. Carol Alero Akapa, Apr. 2, 1983; children: Aanu, Folasade, Feyisayo. Diploma in theater arts, U. Ibadan, Nigeria, 1976; MFA in Theater, U. Ga., 1979. Producer Radio Nigeria, Abeokuta, 1970-74, Nigerian TV Authority, Lagos, 1974-77; theater arts sr. lectr. U. Benin, Benin City, 1987-89, head dept., 1989-95; gen. mgr. The Musical Soc. of Nigeria, 1995-96; cons. Osun State Coun. for Arts and Culture, Osogbo, 1992; dir. Awadol Theater Troupe, Benin City, 1990. Author: Interpretive Essays on Femi Osofisan, 1994, Critical Perspective on Femi Osofisan I, 1994; editor: Excursions in Drama, 1993. Rsch. grantee Kola Abiola Found., 1992. Mem. Assn. Nigerian Authors, Soc. Nigerian Theater Artists, Assn. Nigerian TV Producers. Avocations: reading, writing, traveling, music, walking. Office: U Benin, Dept Theater Arts, Benin City Nigeria

AWOFESO, NIYI, public health physician; b. Lagos, Nigeria, July 2, 1964; s. Deji and Remi (Oduleye) A. BS, U. Ife, 1984, MBBS, 1987; MPH, U. New South Wales, 1996, PhD, 1997—; MBA, Ahmadu Bello U., 1997. Med. officer-in-charge Zaria Leprosy Hosp., Nigeria, 1990-91; acting dir. Nat. TB/Leprosy Tng. Ctr., Nigeria, 1991-93; sr. med. officer-in-charge Kaduna State TB/Leprosy Control Project, Zaria, 1991-95; pub. health cons. UNICEF, Kaduna, 1996—; pub. health officer New South Wales Corrections Health Svc., 1998—. Contbr. articles to profl. jours. Dean's scholar U. New South Wales, 2000. Mem. Nigerian Med. Assn. Avocations: traveling, soccer. Address: U NSW, Sch Health Svcs Mgmt Faculty Medicine, Sydney 2052, Australia

AWOONOR, KOFI NYIDEVU, diplomat, English literature educator; b. Mar. 13, 1935; s. Kowiwo and Atsu A.; ed. U. Ghana, Univ. Coll. London, SUNY; Ph.D., married; 5 children. Research fellow Inst. African Studies; mng. dir. Film Corp.; asst. prof. comparative lit. program, prof., chmn. SUNY, Stony Brook; now chmn. dept. English, U. Cape Coast, Ghana, also dean Faculty Arts; sec.-gen. Action Congress Party, Ghana; ambassador to Brazil, 1984-90; amb. to UN, 1990-94; perm. rep. to UN, 1990-99; vis. prof. U. Tex., Austin, New Sch. Social Research, N.Y.C.; adj. prof. U. Fla., Gainesville; detained in Ghana for allegedly harbouring leader of coup, 1975, on trial, 1976, sentenced 1 year imprisonment, 1976, pardoned, 1976. Longmans fellow; Fairfield fellow; recipient Gurrey prize for poetry, 1979, Nat. Book Council award for poetry, 1979. Author: (poetry) Rediscovery, 1964; Messages, 1970; Night of My Blood, 1971; House by the Sea, 1978; (prose) This Earth My Brother, 1971; Guardians of the Sacred Word, 1973; Ride Me Memory, 1973; Breast of the Earth, 1974; Where Is the Mississippi Panorama, 1974; Fire in the Valley: Folktales of the Ewes, 1980; (novel) Alien corn, 1974; (poems) Until the Morning After, The Ghana Revolution, 1990, Comes the Voyage At Last, 1991, Africa, The Marginalized Continent, 1995. Office: Palace, PO Box 1627, Osu Accra Ghana*

AWUA, PAUL KWAME, food products executive, biochemist; b. Akimaboabo, Eastern Region, Ghana, Dec. 25, 1941; s. Kenneth Andrew Mensali and Alice Adjoa Amanimaa; m. Grace Vivian Appiah, Jan. 1, 1970; children: Justus A., Evelyn P., Emelia A., Stella A., Emmanuel A., Esther O. BS in Biochemistry with honors, U. Sci. and Tech., Kumasi, Ghana, 1967; MS in Food Sci. and Microbiology, U. Strathclyde, Glasgow, Scotland, 1978; Higher Nat. Cert. in Mgmt. Studies, Glasgow Coll. Tech., 1978; Cert. in Agri-Bus. Mgmt. Programming, Santa Clara U., 1995. Mgmt. trainee Tokoradi (Ghana) factory Cocoa Processing Co. Ltd., 1967-69, prodn. technologist Tokoradi factory, 1969-72, chief chemist Tokoradi factory, 1972-79, gen. mgr. Tema (Ghana)factory, 1979-83, mng. dir., 1991—; also bd. dirs.; gen. mgr. Tema Food Complex Corp., 1983-89; tech. advisor Nat. Com. Codes Alimentarius Commn., Accra, Ghana, 1982-83. Contbr. articles tor profl. jours. Chmn. PTA S.O.S. Prep. Sch., Tema, Ghana, 1983-88; patron Okyeman Kuo, Tema, 1992-98; asst. regional leader Pentecost Men's Fellowship Greater Accra region b Ch. of Pentecost Internat., chmn. Tema north dist. marriage counseling com. Recipient 10th Golden Europe award for quality Trade Leaders Club of Madrid, 1996, 8 gold medals Monde Selection Competition of Brussels, 1997, 2nd Nat. Corp. Citizen award Ghana Govt., Accra, 1997; named Mktg. Man of Yr. Chartered Inst. Mktg., Ghana, 1997. Mem. Internat. Assn. Mission (pres. 1994-98), Sci. Soc. Ghana, Biochem. Soc. Ghana, Inst. Mktg., Inst. Food Sci. and Tech. Avocations: football, athletics, Christian activities, reading. Home: PO Box 1002, Greater Accra Region Tema Ghana Office: Cocoa Processing Co Ltd, Heavy Industrial Area, Pvt Mail Bag Tema, Ghana

AXCELL, DOUGLAS NORMAN, business consultant, minister; b. Southend-on-Sea, Essex, Eng., Jan. 13, 1934; s. Frank Norman and Evelyn Ida (Giles) A.; m. Nora Ellen Tree, Aug. 3, 1957 (div. 1972); children: Ruth Ellen, Joy Evelyn; m. Janita Dianne Lines, June 21, 1980. BDiv with honours, Knightsbridge U., Denmark, 1992; Bus. Mgmt. Diploma, Ford Mktg. Inst. Cert. road transport engr., transport adminstr. Apprentice Malcolm Motors, Leigh-on-Sea, Eng., 1949-55; technician RAF, U.K., Gibraltar, Africa, 1955-57; foreman Abbott Motors, Leigh-on-Sea, Eng., 1957-66; svc. mgr. Harpurs of Letchworth, Eng., 1966-69; depot mgr. Charles King, Bedford, Eng., 1969-73; group svc. mgr. Welch & Co., Bristol, Eng., 1973-75; gen. mgr. Mohsin Haider Darwish, Sultanate of Oman, 1975-88; cons. on Arab bus. affairs, 1988—; minster Javea Internatl. Baptist Ch., Javea, Spain. Deacon, Ferndale Bapt. Ch., Southend-on-Sea, 1957; lay asst. pastor Westcliff Free Ch., Westcliff-on-Sea, 1961; lay pastor Rochford (Eng.) Bapt. Ch., 1964; itinerant preacher Bunyan Ch. Soc., Bedford, 1967-72; chorister and gospel singer, 1957—. Mem. Inst. Road Transport Engrs., Inst. Transport Adminstrn. Avocations: singing, European history, theology, photography, target shooting. E-mail: dangard@beeb.net. Home: Charis 3 Shelley Close, Sandilands, Sutton on Sea, Lincolnshire LN12 2HD, England

AXEL, BERNARD, finance executive; b. Bklyn., May 23, 1946; s. Joseph and Irene (Rosen) A.; m. Tobie Reznik, Sept. 3, 1995. BS, U. Ala., 1967; grad., Am. Inst. Banking, 1970. Asst. cashier, comptroller Nat. Bank of Commerce (formerly Am. Nat. Bank), Birmingham, Ala., 1967-72; supr. internat. travel Travel Anywhere, Birmingham, 1972; acctg. and purchasing agt. U.S. Dept. Justice, Texarkana, Tex., 1972-74; mgr. Styslinger Realty, Birmingham, 1974-75; pres. Christian's Inc., Birmingham, 1975-92, Christian's Tutwiler, Inc., Birmingham, 1992-98; mgr. Tucker Cos., Tuscaloosa, Ala., 1998—; v.p. Tucker Fin. Co., Tucker Title Co., Tuscaloosa, 1998—; gourmet chef Top of Morning show Sta. WVTM-T-V, Birmingham, 1991—, Good Day Ala. WBRC-TV, Birmingham, 1996—. Contbr. recipes to mags. Judge March of Dimes Gourmet Gala, Birmingham, 1986, Miss Ala.-U.S.A. Pageant, 1990, 91, Miss Teen Ala., 1992; mem. gov.'s staff State of Ala., Montgomery, 1968-70, mem. lt. gov.'s staff, 1980-84; bd. dirs. Temple Beth El, 1969-72; mem. adv. bd. U. Ala. Sch. Restaurant Hospitality Mgmt., 1989—, chmn. adv. bd., 1992—. Awarded Key to City of Birmingham, Ala., 1991. Mem. Nat. Restaurant Assn. (cert. foodsvc. mgmt. profl., mem. adv. bd. polit. action com. 1987-98, state chmn. 1993-98, bd. dirs. 1996-98), Am. Culinary Fedn. (bd. dirs. Birmingham chpt., medal 1986, Appreciation award 1991), Ala. Restaurant and Food Svc. Assn. (bd. dirs. 1983-98, pres. 1990-92, trustee self-ins. fund 1994-96, Restaurateur of Yr. 1992, Polit. Eagle award 1994), Birmingham-Jefferson County Restaurant Assn. (bd. dirs. 1981-83, 89-98, Restaurant Operator of Yr. 1995), Birmingham-Jefferson Restaurant Assn. (pres. 1995), Chaine des Rotisseurs (L'Order Mondial des Gourmets Degustateurs 1989, coord. culinaire south ctrl. 1996-97), Les Disciples d'Auguste Escoffier Assn. Gastronomique, Commanderie des Cordon Bleus France. Republican. Avocations: travel, cooking. Home: 1716 Dauphine Dr Tuscaloosa AL 35406-3070 Office: Tucker Cos 3302 Mcfarland Blvd E Tuscaloosa AL 35405-2424

AXEL, DOROTHEA ILSE, pharmacologist; b. Stuttgart, Germany, Oct. 28, 1964; d. Gerhard and Ute (Amos) A.; m. Wolf-Kristian Siegel, Sept. 11, 1998. D of Pharm., PhD, U. Tuebingen, Germany, 1993. Chief cell culture lab. in cardiology Tuebingen, Germany, 1993-99. Contbr. articles to profl. jours. Mem. European Soc. Cardiology (mem. scientific com.). Avocations: dancing, travel, sports, music. Office: U Tuebingen Med Clinic, Olfried-Mueller St 10, D-72076 Tuebingen Germany

AXELROD, GLEN SCOTT, publishing company executive; b. Newark, Nov. 4, 1953; s. Alan Robert and Janet Lee Axelrod; m. Jennifer Anderson, June 24, 1979; children: Jason Aaron, Daniel Jay. BA in Biology, Rutgers U., 1975; MSc in Zoology/Ichthyology, Rhodes U., Grahamstown, South Africa, 1978. Asst. to pres., sr. editor TFH Pubs., Inc., Neptune City, N.J., 1979-81; asst. to prin. Six Star Cablevision Group, Englewood, N.J., 1981-82; exec. v.p. Breckenridge Devel. Corp., Wayne, N.J., 1985-92; pres., CEO Design Svcs., Riverdale, N.J., 1992-95; pres. GJA Prodn. Corp., Mahwah, N.J., 1982—; exec. v.p. TFH Pubs., Inc., Neptune City, 1996-97, pres., CEO, 1997—; bd. dirs. TFH Pubs., Inc. Exec. editor zool. mags.; patentee in field; contbr. articles to profl. jours. Trustee, treas. Deerhaven Assn., Mahwah, 1990-97. Fellow The Zool. Soc. London (sci.), Masons. Achievements include taxonomic description of new Pisces species. Avocations: skiing, diving, hiking, aquarium hobbyist, writing. Office: TFH Publications Inc One TFH Plz 3d & Union Neptune City NJ 07753

AXELROD, JULIUS, pharmacologist, biochemist; b. N.Y.C., May 30, 1912; s. Isadore and Molly (Leichtling) A.; m. Sally Taub, Aug. 30, 1938; children: Paul Mark, Alfred Nathan. BS, CCNY, 1933; MA, NYU, 1941, DSc (hon.), 1971; PhD, George Washington U., 1955, LLD (hon.), 1971; DSc (hon.), U. Chgo., 1965, Med. Coll. Wis., 1971, Med. Coll. Pa., 1974, U. Pa., 1986, Hahnemann U., 1987; LLD (hon.), CCNY, 1972; D honoris causa, U. Panama, 1972, U. Paris (Sud), 1982, Ripon Coll, 1984, Tel Aviv U., 1984; DSC (hon., McGill U., Montreal, 1989. Chemist Lab. Indsl. Hygiene, 1935-46; research assoc. 3d N.Y. U. research divsn. Goldwater Meml. Hosp., 1946-49; assoc. chemist sect. chem. pharmacology Nat. Heart Inst., NIH, 1949-50, chemist, 1950-53, sr. chemist, 1953-55; acting chief sect. pharmacology Lab. Clin. Sci. NIMH, 1955, chief sect. pharmacology, 1955-84; guest worker Lab. Cell Biology NIMH, 1984—; scientist emeritus NIH, 1996; Otto Loewi meml. lectr. N.Y. U., 1963; Karl E. Paschkis meml. lectr. Phila. Endocine Soc., 1966; NIH lectr., 1967; Nathanson meml. lectr. U. So. Calif., 1968; James Parkinson lectr. Columbia U., 1971; Wartenberg lectr. Am. Acad. Neurology, 1971; Arnold D. Welch lectr. Yale U., 1971; Harold Carpenter Hodge distinguished lectr. toxicology U. Rochester, 1971; Bennett lectr. Am. Neurol. Assn., 1971; Harvey lectr., 1971; Mayer lectr. Mass. Inst. Tech., 1971; distinguished prof. sci. George Washington U., 1972; Salmon lectr. N.Y. Acad. Medicine, 1972; Eli Lilly lectr., 1972; Mike Hogg lectr. U. Tex., 1972; Fred Schueler lectr. Tulane U., 1972; numerous other hon. lectures; vis. scholar Herbert Lehman Coll. City U. N.Y., 1973; professorial lectr. George Washington U., 1959—; panelist U.S. Bd. Civil Service Examiners, 1958-67; mem. research adv. com. United Cerebral Palsy Assn., 1966-69; mem. psychopharmacology study sect. NIMH, 1970-74; mem. Internat. Brain Research Orgn.; mem. research adv. com. Nat. Found.; vis. com. Brookhaven Nat. Lab., 1972-76; bd. overseers Jackson Lab., 1974-88. Mem. editorial bd. Jour. Pharmacology and Exptl. Therapeutics, 1956-72, Jour. Medicinal Chemistry, 1962-67, Circulation Research, 1963-71, Currents in Modern Biology, 1966-72; mem. editorial adv. bd. Communication in Behavioral Biology, 1967-73, Jour. Neurobiology, 1968-77, Jour. Neurochemistry, 1969-77, Jour. Neurovisceral Relation, 1969, Rassegna di Neurologia Vegetativa, 1969—, Internat. Jour. Psychobiology, 1970-75; hon. cons. editor Life Scis, 1961-69; co-author: The Pineal, 1968; contbr. papers in biochem. actions and metabolism of drugs, hormones, action of pineal gland, enzymes, neurochem. transmission to profl. jours. Recipient Meritorious Rsch. award Assn. Rsch. Nervous and Mental Diseases, 1965; Gairdner award disting. rsch., 1967; Nobel prize in med. physiology, 1970; Alumni Disting. Achievement award George Washington U., 1968; Superior Service award HEW, 1968; Disting. Svc. award, 1970; Claude Bernard professorship and medal U. Montreal, 1969; Disting. Svc. award Modern Medicine mag., 1970; Albert Einstein award Yeshiva U., 1971; medal Rudolf Virchow Med. Soc., 1971; Myrtle Wreath award Hadassah, 1972; Leibniz medal Acad. Sci. East Germany, 1984; Salmon medal N.Y. Acad. Medicine, Bristol-Myers award for disting. rsch. in neurosci., 1989, Thudicum medal Brit. Biochem. Soc. (lectr.), 1989, Gerard medal Soc. Neuroscience, 1991. Felow AAAS, Am. Acad. Arts and Scis., Am. Soc. Neuropsychopharmacology; mem. German Pharmacol. Soc. (corr.), Am. Chem. Soc., Am. Soc. Pharmacology and Exptl. Therapeutics (Torald Sollmann award 1973), Nat. Acad. Scis., Am. Neurol. Assn. (hon.), Royal Soc. London (fgn.), Inst. Medicine (sr.), Am. Philos. Soc., Deutsche Academie Naturfoucher (East Germany), Am. Psychopathol. Assn. (hon.), Sigma Xi. Home: 10401 Grosvenor Pl Rockville MD 20852-4646 Office: NIH Dept Health Edn & Welfare 9000 Rockville Pike Rm 3a-15 Bethesda MD 20892-0003

AXELROD, NORMAN N(ATHAN), technical planning and technology application consultant; b. N.Y.C., Aug. 26, 1934; s. Louis E. and Sadie (Katz) A.; m. Victoria Ann Grant, Mar. 21, 1975; children: Lauren Grant, Brian George. AB, Cornell U., 1954; postgrad., U. Paris, France, 1958; PhD in Optics and Physics, U. Rochester, 1959. Aerospace scientist NASA, Goddard Space Flight Ctr., Washington, 1959-60; rsch. fellow U. London, 1960-61; asst. prof. U. Del., 1961-65; mem. tech. staff Bell Labs., Murray Hill, N.J., 1965-72; prin. Axelrod Assocs., N.Y.C., 1972—; bd. dirs. World Resources Devel. Corp., Input-Output Tech., Inc.; mem. adv. bd. Del. Dept. Edn., 1963-64; participant vis. scientist program Am. inst. Physics, 1963-64; cons. Met. Mus. Art, N.Y.C., 1969-72; advisor to White House, 1969-70, French Ministry Nat. Def. and War, 1971, Am. Consumer Products, Inc., Bausch & Lomb, Calor plc, Compuscan, Corning, CPC, Delco, Finnegan, Henderson et al, GE, Honeywell, IBM, ITT, Internat. FiberCom, Konishiroku, Johnson & Johnson, Labatt, Lear Siegler, Medtronic, Recognition Equipment Inc., Perkin-Elmer, Sharp, Proctor & Gamble, Sensar, Teradyne, Timken Co., Unilever Rsch., Wall St. Jour., Wheatland Tube, Woodgrain Millwork; guest cons. Marine Biol. Lab., Woods Hole, Mass., 1993—. Editor: Optical Properties of Dielectric Films, 1968; book reviewer, cons. John Wiley & Sons, 1965-68, Rheinhold-Van Nostrand, 1968-70, Pergamon Press, 1969-70; contbr. articles to profl. jours. Patentee in field. Boldt scholar; recipient Fortune 500 Corp. award for tech. contbn., 1990; grantee NATO, NSF, Office of Naval Rsch. Fellow AAAS; mem. IEEE, Am. Phys. Soc., Am. Optical Soc., Soc. Mfg. Engrs. (cert. by stature as CMfgE in machine vision), Del. Acad. Sci., N.Y. Acad. Sci., Electrochem. Soc., Sigma Xi, Sigma Pi Sigma, Pi Mu Epsilon. E-mail: naxelrod@axelrodassociates.com. Home: 445 E 86th St New York NY 10028-6433 Office: Norman Axelrod Assocs 121 W 27th St Ste 601 New York NY 10001-6207

AXELSEN, NILS HOLGER, biochemistry educator, administrator; b. Skanderborg, Denmark, Jan. 8, 1942; s. Holger and Inge-Lise Weincke (Laybourn) A.; m. Elisabeth Marianne Bock, Jan. 26, 1942. MD, U. Copenhagen, 1969, DSc, 1976. Rsch. asst. protein lab. U. Copenhagen, 1969-72, assoc. prof. protein lab., 1972-78; head dept. treponematoses Statens Serum Inst., Denmark, 1978-85; head dept. infection-immunology Statens Serum Inst., Denmark, 1989-95, head dept. clin. biochem., 1995—; med. dir. Statens Seruminstitut, Copenhagen, 1985-88, dir. div. biotech., 1990-95; bd. dirs. Fonden Til Laegevidenskabens Fremme, Denmark; chmn. bd. genetic engring. group ATV Inst., Denmark, 1988-91. Editor A Manual of Quantitative Immunoelectrophoresis, 1973, Quantitative Immunoelectrophoresis, New Developments and Applications, 1975, Carcinembryonic Proteins, 1977, Handbook of Immunoprecipitation In Gel Techniques, 1983, Scientific Misconduct and Good Scientific Practice, 1992. Mem. Danish Govt. Biotech. Com., Denmark, 1987-90; bd. dirs. Lundbeck Found., Copenhagen, 1987—; bd. dirs. Chr. Hansen Holding Ltd., Denmark, 1996—, mem. expert panel biol. stand WHO, 1986-90. Mem. Danish Soc. Immunology and Allegology (pres. 1980-84), Danish Com. Sci. Dishonesty, 1992—, Nordic Com. Bioethics, 1994—. Home: 20 Tonysvej, DK-2900 Charlottenlund Denmark Office: Statens Seruminstitut, 5 Artillerivej, DK-2300 Copenhagen Denmark

AXELSON, JOSEPH ALLEN, professional athletics executive, publisher; b. Peoria, Dec. 25, 1927; s. Joseph Victor Axelson and Florence (Ealen) Massey; m. Malcolm Rae Smith, Oct. 7, 1950 (dec.); children: David Allen, Mark Stephen, Linda Rae. B.S., Northwestern U., 1949. Sports info. dir. Ga. So. U., Statesboro, 1957-60, Nat. Assn. Intercollegiate Athletics, Kansas City, Mo., 1961-62; tournament dir. Bowling Proprs. Assn. Am., Park Ridge, Ill., 1963-64; asst. exec. sec. Nat. Assn. Intercollegiate Athletics, Kansas City, Mo., 1964-68; exec. v.p., gen. mgr. Cin. Royals Profl. Basketball Team, Cin., 1969-72; mgr. Cin. Gardens, 1970-72; pres., gen. mgr. Kansas City Kings Profl. Basketball Team, Kansas City, Mo., 1972-79, 82-85; pres., gen. mgr. Sacramento Kings Profl. Basketball Team, 1985-88, exec. v.p., 1988-90; pres. Arco Arena, Sacramento, 1985-88; exec. v.p. Sacramento Sports Assn., Arco Sports Complex, 1988-90, Profl. Team Publs., Inc., Stamford, Conn., 1991-92; pub. Between The Vines Newsletter, 1993—; exec. v.p. ops. NBA, N.Y.C., 1979-82, chmn. competition and rules com., 1975-79; trustee Naismith Basketball Hall of Fame; co-host The Sports Page, Sta. KFMB-AM, San Diego, 1994-97. Author: Basketball Basics, 1987. Mem. Emil Verban Meml. Soc., Washington. Capt. Signal Corps. AUS, 1949-54. Named Nat. Basketball Exec. of Yr. The Sporting News, St. Louis, 1973, Sportsman of Yr., Rockne Club, Kansas City, 1975; recipient Annual Dirs. award Downtown, Inc., Kansas City, Mo., 1979, Nat. Assn. Intercollegiate Athletics Frank Cramer Nat. Svc. award, 1983, Man of Yr. award Sacramento (Calif.) C. of C., 1986, Sacramento Bus. Cmty. award, 1986; named to Ga. So. U. Sports Hall of Fame, 1990. Mem. Am. Philatelic Soc., Phi Kappa Psi. Republican. Presbyterian. Office: 1112 1st St Ste 410 Coronado CA 92118-1407

AXELSON, MAGNUS E.G., medical educator, researcher; b. Täby, Upland, Sweden, May 11, 1949; s. Otto Axel and Britt Elisabeth (Svensson) A.; m. Lena Margareta Nilsson, Apr. 30, 1973; children: Niklas, Peter, Malin. PhD, Karolinska Inst., Stockholm, 1976; MD, Karolinska Inst., 1982. Med. diplomate. Sr. lectr. chemistry I Karolinska Inst., Stockholm, 1970-76, asst. prof. chemistry I, 1977-80, assoc. prof., 1980, prof. clin. chemistry, 2000; resident in clin. chemistry Karolinska Hosp., Stockholm, 1982-84, asst. cons. clin. chemistry, 1985-92, asst. head dept. clin. chemistry, 1992-98, head dept. clin. chemistry, 1998—. Contbr. over 100 articles to profl. jours.; patentee in field. Grantee Swedish Med. Rsch. Coun., 1986—. Avocations: tennis, golf, travel. Office: Karolinska Hosp, Dept Clin Chemistry, 171 76 Stockholm Sweden

AXELSSON, GUDJON, prosthetic dentist, educator; b. Stokksevri, Iceland, Oct. 21, 1935; s. Axel Svanberg and Gudbjörg Jona (Bjarnadottir) Thordarson; m. Soveig Gudmundsdottir; children: Kristrun, Gudbjörg, Unnur, Johanna. Degree in odontology, U. Iceland, 1960. Prof. U. Iceland, Reykjavik, Iceland, 1973-99. Contbr. many articles to profl. jours. Mem. Icelandic Dental Soc., Scandinavian Soc. for Prosthetic Dentistry, European Prosthodontic Assn., Internat. Coll. Prosthodontists, Acad. Osseointegration. Avocation: fishing. Home: Ystaseli 35, 109 Reykjavik Iceland 109 Office: U Iceland, Vatnasmyrarvegi 16, 101 Reykjavik Iceland

AXELSSON, SUNE ROLF JAKOB, scientist; b. Härlunda, Sweden, June 24, 1940; s. Axel Julius and Elsa Ottilia (Algotsson) Johansson; m. Birgitta Ulla Forsberg, July 17, 1965; children Jan, Jakob. MS, Chalmers U. Tech., Sweden, 1965; licentiate in elec. engring., Royal Inst. Tech., Stockholm, 1970, PhD, 1975, docent in applied electronics, 1976. Sys. engr. Saab, Linköping, Sweden, 1965-85, specialist, 1985-93, chief scientist sensor theory, 1993—; adj. prof. remote sensing Linköping Univ., 1983-95; adj. rsch. mgr. Nat. Inst. Def., Linköping, 1990—. Contbr. sci. articles to internat. jours. on frequency modulated radar, synthetic aperture radar, radar altimetry, and the modelling of microwave backscattering and thermal heat flow of ground; patentee in field; author poetry and short stories. Mem. IEEE, Nat. Com. Radio Sci. (adj.).

AXELSSON, UNO TORE, retired hematologist; b. Karlstad, Sweden, Dec. 22, 1927; s. Gunnar E. and Svea C. (Boström) A. MD, Uppsala (Sweden) U., 1954. Registrar Gen. Hosp., Malmö, Sweden, 1960-63, sr. registrar, 1963-73; cons. State Bd. Health, Sweden, 1963-64, Gen. Hosp., Karlstad, Sweden, 1973-92. Contbr. articles to profl. jours. Mem. SHT. Avocations: opera music, gardening. Home: Granlidsv 69, Karlstad Sweden 65351

AXENTE, LIVIU MIRCEA, business consultant; b. Bucharest, Romania, June 6, 1966; s. Aurelian and Maria (Vatra) A. Cert. internat. financier, U. of the Ams., 1995; degree in freelance press photography, Freelance Photogs. Orgn., Lewisville, N.C., 1996; grad., Alexander Hamilton Inst., 1998. Cert. Profl. Cons., Cons. Inst. Freelance journalist Bucharest, 1982-89; country rep. Sipa Press Paris, Bucharest, 1990-95; dir. Global Network Corp., Wilmington, Del., 1997—; pres. Atlantis Internet Svcs. Corp., Wilmington, Del., 1999—. Contbr. photos to numerous mags. Sgt. Romanian Army, 1985-86. Recipient Spl. Excelence prize Nat. Daily Last Word, 1994. Mem. Internat. Sport Press Assn., Internat. Freelance Photographers Orgn., Assoc. mem., Assn. of Cert. Fraud Examiners Region, Natl. Geographic Soc., The Highlander Club, The Oxford Club. Avocations: fishing, travel, reading, writing. Office: 3422 Old Capitol Trl Wilmington DE 19808-6124

AXFORD, ROY ARTHUR, nuclear engineering educator; b. Detroit, Aug. 26, 1928; s. Morgan and Charlotte (Donaldson) A.; m. Anne-Sofie Langfeldt Rasmussen, Apr. 1, 1954; children: Roy Arthur, Elizabeth Carole, Trevor Craig Charles. B.A., Williams Coll., 1952; B.S., Mass. Inst. Tech., 1952, M.S., 1955, Sc.D., 1958. Supr. theoretical physics group Atomics Internat., Canoga Park, Calif., 1958-60; assoc. prof. nuclear engring. Tex. A&M, 1960-62, prof., 1962-63; assoc. prof. nuclear engring. Northwestern U., 1963-66; assoc. prof. U. Ill., Urbana, 1966-68, prof., 1968—; cons. Los Alamos Nat. Lab., 1963—. Vice-chmn. Mass. Inst. Tech. Alumni Fund Drive, 1970-72, chmn., 1973-75; sustaining fellow MIT, 1984. Recipient cert. of recognition for excellence in undergrad. teaching U. Ill., 1979, 81; Everitt award for teaching excellence, 1985. Mem. ASME, Am. Nuclear Soc. (Excellence in Undergrad. Teaching award 1990, 95, 97, 99, Disting. faculty Alpha Nu Sigma 1991), SAR (sec.-treas. Piankeshaw chpt. 1975-81, v.p. chpt. 1982-3, pres. chpt. 1984-86), Kiwanis (charter life patron fellow 1992), Sigma Xi, Tau Beta Pi, Phi Kappa Phi. Home: 2017 S Cottage Grove Ave Urbana IL 61801-6353

AXLER, OLIVIER LOUIS, critical care physician, researcher, consultant; b. Falaise, France, Aug. 9, 1956; s. Jean-François Albert and Jane Jacqueline (Chretien) A. MD (silver medal), U. Pitié-Salpétrière, Paris, 1986; MS, U. Paris V, 1990, PhD with honors, 1997. Cert. in cardiovasc. diseases, Paris, 1989, in critical care medicine, Paris, 1991, in pulmonary medicine, Paris, 1991, in echocardiography, Paris XII, 1990-91. Ancien interne Hopitaux de Paris, Paris, 1984-89, ancien chef de clinique-asst., 1989-91; critical care physician Hop. Henry Dunant-French Red Cross, Paris, 1991-92; clin. and rsch. fellow, critical care Vancouver, B.C., Can., 1993-94; head critical care unit Clinique La Francilienne, Pontault-Combault, France, 1994-97; co-dir. critical care and emergency medicine dept. Antoine Beclere Hosp. Assistance Pub., Hosp. Paris, Univ. Paris, 1997—. Contbr. articles to internat. med. jours. Mem. com. Paris Hops. Residents Union, 1984-88. Recipient rsch. grants Am. Hosp. Paris and GE, Vancouver, 1993, 94, Paris Hosps. Rsch. Found., 1989, 90. Fell. Coll. of Chest Phys.(FCCP); mem. Soc. de Reanimation de Langue Française, French Cardiology Soc. (echocardiography section), European Soc. of Intensive Care Medicine. Avocations: funboard, downhill skiing, snowboarding, jogging, mountain biking. Home: 10 Allee Prof Ducros, 98800 Noumea New Caledonia Office: Hosp Antoine Béclère, 157 rue de la Porte Trivaux, F-92141 Clamart France

AXSATER, SVEN BERTIL, engineering educator; b. Stockholm, May 16, 1941; s. Gunnar S. and Ingegerd D. (Noren) A.; m. Birgitta M. Wangberg, Feb. 20, 1965; children: Annika Axsater Blume, Fredrik, Anneli. MSc in Engring., Royal Inst. Tech., Stockholm, 1965, Tekn lic, 1967; Docent, Linkoping (Sweden) Inst. Tech., 1977. Prof. engring. Linkoping Inst. Tech., 1972-85, Lulea (Sweden) Inst. Tech., 1985-93, Lund (Sweden) U., 1993—. Author 6 books; contbr. over 100 articles to profl. jours. Mem. Royal Swedish Acad. Engring. Scis., Internat. Soc. Inventory Rsch. (pres. 1996-98). Fax: 46 46 2224619. E-mail: sven.axsater@ie.lth.se. Office: Lund U, Box 118, SE221 00 Lund Sweden

AXTELL, CLAYTON MORGAN, JR., lawyer; b. Deposit, N.Y., Aug. 4, 1916; s. Clayton Morgan and Olive Aurora (Vosburgh) A.; m. Margaret Williamson RitchieApr. 24, 1943; children: Margaret R. Axtell Stevenson, Clayton Morgan III, Karen R. Axtell Arnold, Susan R. Axtell. AB, Cornell U., 1937, JD, 1940. Bar: N.Y. 1940, U.S. Dist. Ct. (no. dist.) N.Y. 1941, U.S. Supreme Ct. 1964. Assoc. Hinman, Howard & Kattell, Binghamton, N.Y., 1940-48; ptnr. Hinman, Howard & Kattell, Binghamton, 1948—; former mem. adv. bd. First-City Nat. Bank, Binghamton; bd. dirs. Farmers Nat. Bank, Deposit, N.Y., First City Nat. Bank, Binghamton. Pres. N.Y. State Sch. Bd. Attys., Albany, 1962-63, Broome County Bar Assn., Binghamton, 1967-68, Conrad and Virginia Klee Found.; mem. N.Y. State Rep. Com., Binghamton, 1988-93. 1st lt. US Army, 1942-46 ETO. Decorated Bronze Star U.S. Army, 1945, Croix de Guerre, Govt. of France, 1945; recipient Disting Svc. award U.S. Jr. C. of C., 1942; named Young Man of Yr. Binghamton Jr. C. of C., 1949. Mem. ABA, N.Y. State Bar Assn., Hillcrest -Port Dick Kiwanis (past pres.), Binghamton Club. Republican. Lutheran. Home: 1338 Chenango St Binghamton NY 13901-1539 Office: Hinman Howard & Kattell 80 Exchange St Ste 700 Binghamton NY 13901-3490

AXTON, MARIE, English language lecturer; b. Lima, Ohio, June 25, 1937; came to Eng., 1959; d. Charles Edwin and Kathryn (Kunkel) Horine; m. Richard Patrick Axton, Apr. 7, 1962; children: John Myles, Lucy Margaret. BA in History and Literature, Radcliff Coll., 1959; BA in English, Cambridge U., Eng., 1961; PhD, Cambridge U., 1966. Research fellow Girton Coll., Cambridge, 1963-65; lectr. in Eng. Cambridge U., 1984-99; archivist La Seigneurie, Sark, C.I., 1981—; proctor U. Cambridge, 1979-80; councillor Council of the Senate U. Cambridge, England, 1980-84; chmn. U. Theatre Syndicate, Cambridge, 1983-99. Author: The Queen's Two Bodies, 1977. Rsch. fellow Girton Coll., 1963-65, Newnham Coll. Cambridge U., 1976-82; grantee British Acad., 1982-84. Mem. Cambridge Bibliog. Soc., Bibliog. Soc. (U.K.), Cambridge Guild of Spinners and Weavers, Royal Hist. Soc. (Whitfield Prize). Avocation: flute and chamber music. Address: English Faculty, 9 West Rd, Cambridge CB3 9DP, England

AXWORTHY, LLOYD, Canadian government official; b. North Battleford, Sask., Can., Dec. 21, 1939; s. Norman Joseph and Gwen Jane A.; m. Denise Ommanney, Aug. 3, 1984; 1 child, Stephen. BA, U. Winnipeg; MA, Princeton U., PhD. Min. employment and immigration Canada, 1980-83, min. responsible for status of women, 1980-81, min. transp., 1983-84; critic on internat. trade Official Opposition, 1984-88; critic Liberal Caucus Com. on External Affairs and Nat. Defense, 1988—; vice chmn. Standing com. on External Affairs and Internat. Trade, 1991—; dir. U. Rsch. Inst, assoc. prof.; min. human resources devel., western econ. diversification Canada, 1993-96; min. fgn. affairs Canadian Govt., Ottawa, 1996—; elected to various positions. Office: House of Commons, Rm 418-N Centre Block, Ottawa, ON Canada K1A 0A6

AY, KARL-LUDWIG, historian, editor; b. Reichenbach, Saxony, Germany, Nov. 22, 1940; s. Kurt and Käthe (Gerlach) A.; m. Margrit Heinisch, Aug. 28, 1968; 1 child, Judith. DPhil, U. Munich, 1967. Rschr. Bayerische Akademie der Wissenschaften, Munich, 1968—. Editors' editor Complete Edition of Max Weber's Works; author monographs, documentation volumes, contbr. articles to profl. jours. Fellow Japanese Soc. for Promotion of Sci.; mem. AAAS, Com. Social and Econ. History. Office: Bayer Akad Wissenschaften, Marstallplatz 8, D-80539 Munich Germany

AYABE, SIDNEY K., lawyer; b. Honolulu, June 15, 1945; s. Yoshio and Betty S. Ayabe; m. Gloria Doo, June 7, 1977; children: Lisa, Sara, Marie. BA, Lawrence U., Appleton, Wis., 1967; JD, U. Iowa, 1970. Dep. atty. gen. State Atty. Gen.'s Office, Honolulu, 1970-72; ptnr. Ayabe Chong Nishimoto Sia & Nakamura, Honolulu, 1972—. Dir. Mediation Ctr. of the Pacific, Honolulu, 1997—. recipient Cert. of Appreciation for contbn. in real estate Hawaii Real Estate Commn., 1987, Spl. Bd. Recognition award Neighborhood Justice Ctr., 1998. Fellow Am. Coll. Trial Lawyers (Appreciation for Outstanding Leadership as chair of Hawaii state com. 1995); mem. ABA, Am. Bd. Trial Advocates (assoc.), Hawaii State Bar Assn. (pres.), Internat. Assn. Def. Counsel, Hawaii Def. Lawyers Assn. (v.p. 1989—). Home: 1745 Nalulu Pl Honolulu HI 96821-1338 Office: Ayabe Chong Nishimoto et al #2500 Pauahi 1001 Bishop St Ste 2500 Honolulu HI 96813-3590

AYACHE, JEANNE GILBERTE, materials scientist, electron microscopist; b. Alger, Algeria, Oct. 12, 1951; arrived in France, 1962; d. Marcel Abraham and Paule Aziza (Sportich) Ayache. PhD, U. Orsay, France, 1978; Doctorat d'Etat es Scis., U. Orléans, France, 1987. Cert. in sci. rsch. Technician U. Orsay, France, 1974-77, Nat. Ctr. Sci. Rsch., Orléans, France, 1977-88; engr. Nat. Ctr. Sci. Rsch., Paris, 1988-90, rsch., 1990—. Mem. SFu Paris, EMRS Strasbourg, France. Avocations: country mountains, piano music, literature, rock climbing. Email: ayache@csnsm.in2P3.f2. Home: Paris Hauts de Séine, 2 Pl Henri Barbusse, 92350 Plessis Robinson France Office: Nat Ctr Sci Rsch CSNSM, U. d'Orsay Bahiment 108, 91405 Orsay Campus, France

AYACHE, NICHOLAS JÉRÔME, research scientist; b. Paris, Nov. 1, 1958; s. Henri and Simonne (Lemeunier) A.; m. Isabelle Françoise Quere, Sept. 8, 1990; children: Justine Jeanne Simonne, Eliot Henri Roger, Thaïs Joséphine Anna Léonie. Degree in engring., Sch. of Mines, France, 1980; MS, UCLA, 1981; PhD, U. Paris XI, 1983, D d'Etat, 1988. Rschr. Nat. Rsch. Inst. for Computer Science & Automatic Control, Paris, 1981-88, rsch. dir., 1988-92; rsch. dir. Nat. Inst. Informatics and Automation Rsch. (INRIA), Sophia-Antipolis, France, 1992—; assoc. prof. Ecole Ctrl., Paris, 1986—, U. Paris-Orsay, 1988—; cons. MATRA, Paris, 1988—, Focus-Med., France, 1992—; co-founder Noesis, 1985. Author: Artificial Vision for Mobile Robots, 1991; editor: Computer Vision, Virtual Reality, Robotics in Medicine, 1995; co-editor-in-chief, founder Med. Image Analysis jour., 1996. Recipient Recognition award ECVNet, Vienna, Austria, 1996. Achievements include U.S. patents for Geometric Tomography, Extraction of Crest lines in volumetric images. Office: INRIA, 2004 Rt des Lucioles, 06902 Sophia Antipolis France

AYAD, JOSEPH MAGDY, psychologist; b. Cairo, Egypt, May 21, 1926; s. Fahim Gayed and Victoria Gabour (El-Masri) A.; came to U.S., 1949, naturalized, 1961; B.A. in Social Scis., Am. U., Cairo, 1946; M.A. in Clin. Psychology (Univ. scholar), Stanford U., 1952; Ph.D. in Clin. Psychology (Univ. scholar), U. Denver, 1956; m. Widad Fareed Bishai, May 29, 1954; children—Fareed Merritt, Victor Maher, Michael Joseph, Mona Elaine. Translator Hoover Inst. War and Peace, Stanford U., 1950-51; asst. to chief psychologist Colo. Psychopathic Hosp., 1952-54; cons. Child Guidance Clinic, State Dept. Pub. Welfare, Denver, 1953-56; cons. psychologist Dept. Pub. Welfare, State of Tex., 1957-72; cons. psychologist Dept. Insts., Social and Rehab. Svc., State of Okla., 1960-72, N.Mex. Dept. Pub. Welfare, 1960-72; lectr. Fitzsimmons Army Hosp., Denver, 1953-54; vis. psychologist State Dept. Pub. Welfare, Child Guidance Clinic, Pueblo, Colo., 1953-54; staff psychologist Cons. Psychol. Svc., Denver, 1956-57, High Plains Neurol. Ctr., Amarillo, Tex., 1957—; pres. JMA Cattle Co., Amarillo, 1973—; v.p., treas. Filigon Inc., Amarillo, 1962-75, pres., 1976—. Mem. profl. adv. bd. Amarillo Mental Health Assn., 1968-69. Mem. Amarillo Child Welfare Bd., 1961-63; area chmn. U. Denver Fund Raising Campaign, 1963; mem. profl. adv. bd. St. Paul's Meth. Ch. Sch. for Children with Learning Disabilities, Amarillo, 1969-70. Recipient Grad. Sr. award in Philosophy Am. U. at Cairo, 1946. Mem. Am. Psychol. Soc., Am. Psychol. Assn., Internat. Assn. Applied Psychology, Am. Assn. Marriage and Family Therapists, Potter-Randall County (Tex.) Psychol. Soc. (pres. 1974), Tex. Psychol. Assn., Calif. Psychol. Assn. Presbyn. Club: Amarillo Country. Contbr. articles to profl. jours. Home: 4239 Erik Ave Amarillo TX 79106-6008 Office: High Plains Neurological Ctr 2301 W 7th Ave Amarillo TX 79106-6601

AYADI, OLUSEGUN FELIX, finance educator; b. Erinje, Ondo, Nigeria, Mar. 7, 1956; came to the U.S., 1987; s. Thompson Morayo and Dorcas Metele Ayadi; m. Morenike Elizabeth Oyinsulu, Dec. 26, 1986; children: Olufemi, Olukemi, Olusegun Jr. BS in Banking and Fin., U. Lagos, Nigeria, 1980; MS in Fin., U. Lagos, 1983; PhD in Fin., U. Miss., 1991. Lectr. U. Lagos, 1980-87; asst. prof. Lemoyne-Owen Coll., Memphis, 1991-92; asst. prof. Savannah (Ga.) State U., 1992-94, acting dean, 1993; assoc. prof. Fayetteville (N.C.) State U., 1994-97, prof. fin., 1997—; assoc. grad. faculty Ga. So. U., Statesboro, 1992-94. Author: Modern Commerce in West Africa, 1995; guest editor Managerial Fin., 1996-98; contbr. numerous articles to profl. jours. Cons. Jr. Achievement, Savannah, 1992-94, Cumberland County Planning Com., Fayetteville, 1996-97; adv. bd. mem. Savannah Youth Entrepreneur, 1993-94; spkr. C. of C., Savannah, 1992, Cumberland County Schs., Fayetteville, 1995, 98. Recipient Positive Image award Pee Dee Newspaper Group, Greenville, S.C., 1996; named Tchr. of Yr., Sch. Bus. and Econs., Fayetteville State U., 1998-99; Nissan fellow in fin. Nissan Corp./Ednl. Testing Svc./Historically Black Colls. and Univs., Chgo., 1994. Mem. Am. Fin. Assn., Am. Acad. Econs. and Fin., Assn. for Global Bus., Fin. Mgmt. Assn., Ea. Fin. Assn., Nat. Assn. African Am. Studies (N.C. state chair 1995-99). Avocations: reading, tennis, fishing, traveling, watching television. E-mail: fayadi@sbe1.uncfsu.edu. Office: Fayetteville State Univ 1200 Murchison Rd Fayetteville NC 28301-4298

AYALA-RAMIREZ, VICTOR, engineering educator, researcher; b. Salamanca, Guanajuato, Mexico, July 14, 1966; s. J. Belem Ayala and Es-

peranza Ramirez; m. Martha-Laura Alfaro-Tellez, Apr. 22, 1995; children: Victor, Eric-Daniel. BS in Electronics Engring., U. Guanajuato, Salamanca, Mexico, 1988, M in Electronics Engring., 1994. Bench test engr. Nissan Mexicana, Cuernavaca, Mexico, 1989-91; software devel. engr. Ingenieria Aplicada Guanajuato S.A., Salamanca, 1992-93; rschr. U. Guanajuato, Salamanca, 1993-99; assoc. rschr. LAAS-CNRS, Toulouse, France, 1996—; dept. head electronics engring. U. Guanajuato, Salamanca, 1995-96. Contbr. articles to profl. confs. Grantee Consejo Nat. Ciencia Tecnologia, Mexico City, 1996. Mem. IEEE, Soc. Photo-Optical Instrumentation Engrs. Avocations: chess, science fiction books, mathematical recreations, soccer. Office: LAAS-CNRS, 7 Av du Col Roche, 31077 Toulouse France

AYANO, KATSUTOSHI, management educator; b. Hitoyoshi, Japan, Mar. 3, 1949; s. Tokuichi and Asako Ayano; m. Chieko Yoshimitsu, Jan. 25, 1976; children: Masatoshi, Mitsuhiro, Hidenori, Yumi. BA in Mgmt. Engring., U. Electro-Communications, Japan, 1974; MA in Econs., Tsukuba (Japan) U., 1978; PhD, SUNY, Syracuse, 1982. Instr. Union of Japanese Scientists and Engrs., Tokyo, 1975-79, counselor, 1982-86; assoc. prof. Tokai U., Hiratsuka, Japan, 1986-93, prof., 1993—. Author: Current Waste Problems, 1985, Quality Management for Non-technical Students, 1998; contbr. articles to profl. jours. Mem. Japanese Soc. Quality Control, Am. Soc. Quality Control, Inst. Environ. Scis. (sr.), Am. Mgmt. Assn., Soc. Strategic Planning, World Future Soc., Am. Biog. Inst. Rsch. Assn. (lifetime dep. gov.), Internat. Biog. Centre (life dep. dir. gen., Deming Prize com.). Home: 2985-13 Hon-machida, Machida, Tokyo 194-0032, Japan Office: Tokai U, 1117 Kitakaname, Hiratsuka 259-1292, Japan

AYAS, KAREN, management consultant, educator; b. Istanbul, Turkey, Aug. 23, 1962; Immigrated to Israel, The Netherlands, U.S.; d. Max Ayas; m. Didier Sabag, Aug. 21, 1985 (div. Aug. 1993); 1 child, Lior; m. Atilla Habip, Apr. 24, 1997. BSc, Technion, Israel, 1985, MSc, 1988; PhD, Erasmus U., The Netherlands, 1997. Asst. rschr. Technion, Israel, 1985-88; dep. human resource dir. Rambam Med. Ctr., Israel, 1988-90; human resource dir. Wolfson Med. Ctr., Israel, 1990-92; fellow rschr. Rotterdam Sch. Mgmt., 1992-96; sr. cons. Bus. Mgmt. Group, The Netherlands, 1996-97; asst. prof. Erasmus U., Rotterdam, 1997; prin. Ripples Inst., 1998. Author: (book) Design for Learning for Innovation, 1997; author, editor: (book) Organisational Learning, 1996; assoc. editor Reflections: The Soc. for Orgnl. Learning Jour.; contbr. chpts. to books in field, numerous articles to profl. jours. Basketball coach NAA. Avocations: swimming, jazz dancing, classical music, theater, basketball. Home and Office: 80 High Rock Ter Chestnut Hill MA 02467-2654

AYBAR, FEHMI, architect, real estate developer; b. Istanbul, Turkey, Dec. 10, 1945; s. Saim Mustafa and Nermin Fatma (Ekmekci) A.; m. Leyla Ocel, Aug. 3, 1973; 1 child, Simla. Degree in architecture, Zafer Art Sch., Ankara, Turkey, 1971; M, McLean Art Sch., London, 1972. Project mgr. Isbank, Istanbul, 1971-77; CEO Bahgesehir, Istanbul, 1977-83, Vinylex, Istanbul, 1983—; cons. Akkok, Istanbul, 1983-90, shopping mall, Istanbul, 1990, real estate, Istanbul, 1985; art dir. advt., Istanbul, 1975-85; real estate cons., Istanbul, 2000. Served with Turkish mil., 1983. Mem. Internat. Assn. Lions Clubs, Lions Internat. Club Found. Avocations: philosophy, cinema. Home and Office: Ahmet Ceudet Pasa Sok, Polat Camlik A/13, 81110 Istanbul Turkey

AYBAY, AYDIN, law educator, university dean; b. Istanbul, Turkey, June 4, 1929; s. Raci and Mujgan (Sagnak) A.; m. Burcin Gultepe; children: Elif, Erdem. DSc, Istanbul U., 1958. From asst. law faculty to asst. dean polit. scis. faculty U. Istanbul, 1953-96; dean law faculty Maltepe U., 1997—; chmn. Nazim Hikmet Found., 1993—; cons. T. Ticaret Bank, 1983—. Mem. Istanbul Bar Assn. Home: Selamicesme Tugrul So 1, Istanbul Turkey Office: Aybay & Aybay Law Offices, Siraselviler 87, Taksim Turkey

AYCKBOURN, SIR ALAN, playwright; b. Hampstead, London, Eng., Apr. 12, 1939; s. Horace and Irene Maude (Worley) A.; m. Christine Helen Roland, May 9, 1959 (div. 1997); children: Steven Paul, Philip Nicholas; m. Heather Stoney, Sept. 19, 1997. Ed., Haileybury; DLitt (hon.), U. Hull, 1981, U. Keele, 1987, U. Leeds, 1987, U. York, 1992, U. Bradford, 1994, U. Cardiff, 1995, Open U., 1998. Stage mgr., actor Stephen Joseph Theatre, Scarborough, Eng., 1957-59, writer, dir., 1959-61; writer, artistic dir. Stephen Joseph Theatre, Scarborough, 1970—; founder mem., actor, writer, dir. Victoria Theatre, Stoke-on-Trent, Eng., 1961-64; radio drama prodr. BBC, Leeds, Yorkshire, Eng., 1964-70; vis. playwright, dir. Nat. Theatre, London, 1977, 80, 86-88; prof. contemporary theater St. Catherine's Coll., Oxford, Eng., 1992. Author: (plays) The Square Cat, 1959, Love After All, 1959, Dad's Tale, 1960, Standing Room Only, 1961, Xmas vs. Mastermind, 1962, Mr. Whatnot, 1963, The Sparrow, 1967, Relatively Speaking, 1967, How the Other Half Loves, 1969, Family Circles, 1970, Ernie's Incredible Illucinations, 1970, Time and Time Again, 1971, Absurd Person Singular, 1972 (London Evening Standard Best Comedy award 1973), Mother Figure, 1973, The Norman Conquests, 1973 (London Evening Standard Best Comedy award 1974, Plays and Players Best Comedy award 1974), Absent Friends, 1974, Confusions, 1974, Bedroom Farce, 1975, Just Between Ourselves, 1976 (London Evening Standard Best Comedy award 1977), Ten Times Table, 1977, Joking Apart, 1978, Sisterly Feelings, 1979, Taking Steps, 1979, Season's Greetings, 1980, Way Upstream, 1981, Intimate Exchanges, 1982, It Could Be Any One Of Us, 1983, The Westwoods, 1984, A Chorus of Disapproval, 1984 (London Evening Standard Best Comedy of Yr. award 1985, Olivier Best Play award 1985, Drama award 1985, Plays and Players Best Comedy award 1985), Woman in Mind, 1985, A Small Family Business, 1987 (London Evening Standard Best Comedy award 1987), Henceforward..., 1988 (London Evening Standard Best Comedy award 1989), Man of the Moment, 1990 (London Evening Standard Best Comedy award 1990), The Revengers' Comedies, 1991, Time of My Life, 1992, Communicating Doors, 1994 (Best West End Play award Writers' Guild of Great Britain 1996), Haunting Julia, 1994, Things We Do For Love, 1997 (Lloyds Pvt. Banking Playwright of the Year award 1997), 1997, Comic Potential, 1998, adaptation Ostrovsky's The Forest, 1998, House Garden, 1999, Virtual Reality, 2000, also children's plays including Mr. A's Amazing Maze Plays, 1988, Invisible Friends, 1989, This Is Where We Came In, 1990, The Musical Jigsaw Play, 1994, The Champion of Paribanou, 1996, Gizmo, 1998, The Boy Who Fell Into A Book, 1998, Callisto # 7, 1999, Whenever, 2000, (musicals) Men on Women on Men, 1978, Suburban Strains, 1980, Me, Myself and I, 1981, Making Tracks, 1981, Dreams From a Summer House, 1992, A Word From Our Sponsor, 1995, (with Andrew Lloyd Webber) By Jeeves, 1996, Whenever, 2000; dir. numerous plays, including A View From The Bridge, 1987 (Plays and Players Dir. of Yr. award 1987). Apptd. Comdr. of Brit. Empire, knighted, 1997; named Playwright of Yr. by Variety Club of Great Britain, 1974. Mem. Garrick Club. Avocations: music, reading, cricket, films. Address: Casarotto Ramsay & Assocs, Nat House 60-66 Wardour St, London W1V 4ND, England also: Stephen Joseph Theatre, Westborough, Scarborough YO11 1JW, England

AYDIN, MURAT, dentist; b. Mersin, Turkey, Nov. 29, 1958; s. Ethem Ibrahim and Naciye (Ünlüatli) A.; m. Nilgün Birsen Erdoğan, June 7, 1985; children: Oğuz, Onur. MD in Dentistry, Dentistry Faculty Istanbul, Turkey, 1980; PhD in Microbiology, Çukurova U., Adana, Turkey, 1997. Rschr. Med. Faculty, Adana, 1993-98; spkr., lectr. in field. Author: Oral Bacteriology, 2000, Bacterial Identification by Computer, 2000; co-author: Endodontics, 1999; contbr. articles to profl. jours. Mem. AIDS Prevention Soc., Anaerobe Working Group, N.Y. Acad. Scis. Avocations: computer sciences, chess. E-mail: M-aydin@usa.net. Home: Kurtulus mh 19 sk 48/1, 01120 Adana Seyhan, Turkey Office: Dental Clinic, Kurtulus mh 10 sk 22/7, 01129 Adana Turkey

AYE, KYI, bank executive; b. Yangon, Myanmar, Nov. 2, 1933; s. U Ba Aye and Daw Mya Thin; m. Daw Khin Khin Swe, May 30, 1964; children: Kyaw San Oo, Tin Tun Win, Min Thein, Swe Zin Win. B in Commerce, U. Yangon, Myanmar, 1956, LLB, 1958; diploma in world banking and fin., Colo. U., Inst. Econs., 1988. Registered acct., Myanmar. Gov. Ctrl. Bank of Myanmar, Yangon; bd. sec. Ava Bank Ltd., Yangon, 1959-63; dep. mgr. Peoples' Bank # 15/16, Yangon, 1963-68; acct. Ctrl. Bank of Myanmar, Yangon, 1969-80, sr. acct., 1981-86, dep. chief acct., 1986-87, chief acct., 1987-89, exec. dir., 1989-91, gov., 1992—; mng. dir. Myanma Econ. Bank, Yangon, 1991-92. Office: Ctrl Bank Myanmar, 24-26 Sule Pagoda Rd POB184, Yangon Myanmar*

AYE, LU, mechanical engineering educator, researcher; b. Rangoon, Insein, Burma, Oct. 9, 1957; s. Maung and Tin (Nu) Galay; m. Khin Swe Lwin, May 20, 1988; 1 child, Htun-Htun Lu. BE in Mech. Engring., Rangoon Inst. Tech., 1979; M in Engring. Sci., U. Melbourne, Australia, 1990; PhD in Mech. and Mfg. Engring., U. Melbourne, 1995. Instr. engring. Rangoon Inst. Tech., 1980-82, asst. lectr., 1982-90; lectr. Yangon (Myanmar, Burma) Inst. Tech., 1990-95; rsch. fellow advanced engring. ctr. mfg. U. Melbourne, 1995-98, lectr. dept. civil & environ. engring., 1999—. U. Melbourne scholar, 1990, Dept. Employment Edn. and Tng. Overseas Postgrad. Rsch. scholar, Australia, 1990. Mem. ASME (assoc.), Australian Inst. Refrigeration, Air Conditioning and Heating, Internat. Inst. Refrigeration, Australian Computer Soc. Inst. Engrs. Avocations: reading, judo, swimming, cycling. Home: 4/315 Flemington Rd, Melbourne VIC 3051, Australia Office: U Melbourne Dept Mech & Mfg Engring, Kernot Rd, Melbourne VIC 3052, Australia

AYE, NU NU, pharmacologist, researcher; b. Athoke, Myanmar, Apr. 22, 1961; arrived in Japan, 1994; s. U-Tin Aye and Daw-Yin Sein. MBBS, Inst. of Medicine II, Yangon, Mayanmar, 1986; postgrad., Yamanashi Med. U., Tamaho, Japan, 1996—. Demonstrator anatomy dept. Inst. of Medicine II, 1989-93; demonstrator pharmacology dept. Inst. of Medicine I, 1993—. Contbr. articles to European Jour. Pharmacology, Cardiovascular Jour. Pharmacology, Toxicology and Applied Pharmacology, Brit. Jour. Pharmacology, others. Japanese Ministry Edn. scholar, 1994—. Mem. Japanese Pharmacol. Soc. in Kyoto, Myanmar Med. Assn. Avocations: tennis, reading. Office: Inst Med I Dept Pharmacolog, Lanmadaw Township, Yangon Myanmar

AYGUN, A. DENIZMEN, medical educator; b. Istanbul, Turkey, Nov. 20, 1954; s. A. Omer Aygun and Melek Tanrikut; m. D. Tulay Ozdemir, Aug. 3, 1983; children: Berk, Mert. Faculty medicine, Istanbul (Turkey) U., 1973-79; Doctorate, Vakif Gureba Hosp., Istanbul, 1987. Asst. prof. Firat U., Elazig, Turkey, 1991-96; assoc. prof., clin. chief dept. pediat. Firat U., Elazig, 1996—. Fellow Turkey Milli Pediatri Dernegi Elazig Subesi, Tenis Ihtisas Kluba. Home: Firat Univ, Rektorluk Lojmanlari R3 D8, 23119 Elazig Turkey Office: Firat Univ, Firat Tip Merkezi, 23119 Elazig Turkey

AYGUN, ILHAMI, electronics engineer; b. Aksaray, Turkey, Nov. 10, 1958; s. Muammer and Mualla (Kestek) A.; m. Nevcan Ozkan, Sept. 6, 1986; children: Ece, Bars-Denis. BS in Electronics, Mid. East Tech. U., Ankara, Turkey, 1981, MS in Electronics Engring., 1984. expert on satellite comm. U. Southampton, 1991. Engr. Turkish PTT, Ankara, 1981-82, chief engr., 1982-84, dir. SATCOM ctr., 1984-90; dir. satellite program Aerospatiale, Cannes, France, 1990—; dir. gen., CEO EURASIASAT Internat. Satellite Operator-Monaco, 1996—; cons. Teuchos, Paris, 1991—. Mem. IEEE, Assn. for Computing Machinery, N.Y. Acad. Scis., AAAS, The Planetary Soc. Avocations: golf, football, swimming. Home: 86 Boulevard Du Midi, Cannes 06150, France Office: Eurasiasat, 2 rue Lugernetta, MC 98000 Monaco Monaco

AYLING, DEREK JOHN, training executive; b. Dewsbury, England, Oct. 10, 1944; s. Ronald John and Dorothy Ida (Groves) A.; m. Alison Joy Rushworth, July 11, 1987; children: Simeon John, Benjamin James, Timothy Paul, Zoey Lauren. BS, Loughboroug U., 1967; MBA, City U., London, 1982. Stress engr. Wstland Helicopters Ltd., Munich, 1963-69; sales engr. Ramsey Corp., Richmond, Ont., Can., 1969-70; mktg. mgr. W.C. Youngman Ltd., Crawley, England, 1970-73; export mgr. Stone-Platt-Houchin Ltd., Ashford, England, 1973-77; franchise advisor Comml. Devices Partnership, London, 1977-81; ptnr. Comml. Devices, Winchester, England, 1981-89; tng. mgr. British Telecom, London, 1989-94; sr. ptnr. Comml. Devices, Buckingham, England, 1994—; dir. Ture-Up Ltd., Bracknell, England, 1987-89. Author: Enter the Hippo, 1995; contbr. articles to profl. jours. Sch. gov. Aylesbury Vale Edn. Office, 1994—. Fellow Inst. Mgmt. Cons., Inst. Personnel & Devel. Avocations: banjo, cycling, public speaking. Office: Comml Devices/Hippotrain, 18 Falconwood Close, Fordingbridge Hants 5P6 1TB, England

AYLING, JOHN VERNON, advertising executive; b. Fulmer, Eng., Apr. 18, 1944; s. Stanley Harradine and Phyllis Evelyn (Jenkins) A.; m. Marilyn Whinray Lee Hargreaves, Apr. 6, 1982; 1 child, Caroline Jane. BA in Geography with honors, U. Exeter, Eng., 1965. Media asst. Masius Wynne-Williams, London, 1965-66; media planner S.H. Benson, London, 1966-68; media mgr. Garland-Compton, London, 1968-71; media dir. The Kirkwood Co., London, 1971-78; prin. John Ayling & Assocs., London, 1978—; founder AMI/AMCO. Contbr. articles to profl. jours. Trustee, coun. mem. Lord's Taverners Charities, London. Office: 27 Soho Sq, London W1, England

AYLING, LAURENCE JOHN, scientist, consultant; b. Watford, Hertshire, Eng., July 27, 1939; s. John Edward and Enid Margaret (Fryer) A.; m. Sheila Mary Crichton, June 1966 (div. 1980); children: Clive Laurence, Bruce Crichton, Duncan John; m. Elsa Stacy Dace. MA in Mech. Scis., Cambridge (Eng.) U., 1963; DMS with distinction, St. Helens U., Lancashire, Eng., 1965. Grad. trainee Shell Internat., Cambridge, 1958-61; Far East sr. planning Shell Internat., London, 1969-72; project mgr. Shell UK Stanlow Refinery, Cheshire, Eng., 1961-69; planning mgr. Seal Ltd., London, 1972-74; constrn. mgr. Mobil North Sea, London, 1974-77; founder, chmn. Maris Internat., London, 1977—. Contbr. articles to Jour. Royal Engrs. (Best Paper of Yr. award 1989); inventor seabed protection structure, seabed drilling rig, continous circulation drilling coupler. Lt. col. Brit. Royal Engrs., 1984-94. Decorated Territorial Decoration with two bars. Fellow Inst Petroleum, Instn. Mech. Engrs. (chartered), Soc. Petroleum Engrs., Instn. Royal Engrs. (publs. com. 1990-93), Soc. for Underwater Tech. (publs. com. 1985—), Brit. Inst. Mgmt. Mem. Liberal Democrat Party. Avocations: inventing, spiritual healing, musical instruments, skiing, talking and listening.

AYLMER, GERALD EDWARD, historian, educator; b. near Ludlow, Shropshire, Eng., Apr. 30, 1926; s. Edward and Gladwys Phoebe (Evans) A.; m. Ursula Adelaide Nixon, Aug. 6, 1955; children: Thomas Bartholomew, Emma Clare. BA in Modern History with honors, U. Oxford, 1950, DPhil, 1955. Asst. lectr. dept. history U. Manchester, Eng., 1954-57, lectr., 1957-62; prof. head dept. history U. York, Eng., 1963-78; master St. Peter's Coll. U. Oxford, Eng., 1978-91; vis. mem. Inst. Advanced Study, Princeton U., N.J., 1975. Author: The King's Servants, 1961, 2nd edit., 1974, The Struggle for the Constitution, 1963, 2nd edit., 1975, A Short History of 17th Century England, 1963, 2nd edit., 1975, The State's Servants, 1973; editor: The Levellers in the English Revolution, 1975, (with R. Cant) A History of York Minster, 1977, Rebellion or Revolution? England 1640-1660, 1986, 87. Served with Royal Navy, 1944-47. Fellow Brit. Acad.; mem. Royal Hist. Soc. (hon. v.p., pres. 1984-88, chmn. Royal Commn. on Hist. Manuscripts 1989-94). Home: The Old Captains, Hereford Rd, Ledbury HR8 2PX, England also: 18 Albert St, Oxford OX2 6AZ, England

AYLMORE, LANCE ARTHUR GRAHAM, soil science educator; b. Three Springs, Australia, Jan. 5, 1933; s. Cyril Lindly and Doreen Marika (Seels) A.; m. Karen Ruth Hender, Aug. 17, 1963; children: Mark Graham, Anthony James. BSc in Physics with honors, U. Adelaide, Australia, 1955, PhD, 1960. Postdoctoral rsch. fellow dept. chemistry Columbia U., N.Y.C., 1960-61, Imperial Coll., London, 1961-63; lectr., sr. lectr. U. Western Australia, Perth, 1963-78, assoc. prof., 1978-89, head dept. soil sci., 1979-83, prof. soil sci., 1990—; vis. prof. dept. chemistry Pa. State U., 1969-70, Bristol (U.K.) U., 1976-77; vis. prof. dept. land, air and water resources, U. Calif., Davis, 1983-84. Contbr. over 160 articles to profl. jours. Fellow Royal Australian Chem. Inst.; mem. Soil Sci. Soc. Australia (J.A. Prescott medal 1995), Internat. Soc. Soil Sci., Soil Sci. Soc. Am. Avocations: reading, woodworking, music, travel. Office: U Western Australia, Dept Soil Sci, Nedlands 6009 WA, Australia

AYMERICH, JOSE GROS, oncologist; b. Zaragoza, Spain, Sept. 21, 1952; s. Jose Gros Zubiaga and Concepcion Aymerich Alix. B, Colegio del Salvador, Zaragoza, 1969; Lic. Medicine, U. Autonoma Madrid, 1976. Resident Fundacion Jimenez Diaz, Madrid, 1978-81; emergency physician Social Security, Alcala de Henares, Spain, 1983-84; primary care physician Social Security, Madrid, Spain, 1989-92, Madrid, 1992—; clin. rsch. coord. Upjohn, Madrid, 1984-88. Lt. Spanish Air Force, 1976-78. Mem. European Soc. Med. Oncology, Spanish Soc. Med. Oncology, N.Y. Acad. Scis. Roman Catholic. Avocations: mechanics, aviation, music. Home: Jazmin-76, E-28033 Madrid Spain

AYOUB, ADHAM MOHAMED, ophthalmology educator; b. Cairo, Mar. 7, 1970; s. Mohamed Ibrahim Ayoub and Sanaa Mahmoud Hathout. Gen. cert. edn., U. London, 1986; MBBch, Cairo U., 1992, MSc in Ophthalmology, 1996. Cert. ophthalmic medicine and surgery. Resident ophthalmology Cairo U., 1994-97, asst. lectr. ophthalmology, 1997—; visitor Johns Hopkins U., 1998. Mem. Egyptian Ophthalmol. Soc. (life), Egyptian Soc. Cataract and Corneal Diseases. Achievements include patent describing a new design of intraocular lenses. Avocation: computers. E-mail: Ayoub@link.com.eg. Fax: 202 2821624. Home: 4 Osman Towers, Kourniche Maadi Maadi, Egypt Office: Kasr El Aini Hosps, Manial Tchg Hosp, Cairo Egypt

AYOZIE, DANIEL OGECHUKWU, marketing educator; b. Port Harcourt, Rivers, Nigeria, Nov. 28, 1964; s. Nathaniel Amadi and Victoria Mgbechikwere Ayozie; m. Ayozie Victoria Uche, June 3, 2000. Sch. cert., cert. of edn., Meth. Coll., Abia, Nigeria, 1981; higher sch. cert., Fed. Sch. Arts and Sci., Aba, Nigeria, 1983; higher nat. diploma, nat. diploma, Fed. Poly., Ilaro, Ogun, Nigeria, 1990; postgrad. diploma, Nigerian Inst. Journalism, Ikeja, 1993-94; MBA, Ogun State U., Ago-Iwoye, 1995-97. Cert. mktg. lectr. Sales clk. Danayo Inc. Comms., Umuahia, Abia, 1981; sales/accounts clk. Aristoplast Co. Lagos, Nigeria, 1987-88; lectr. Army Day Secondary Sch. N.Y.S.C., Sokoto, Nigeria, 1990-91; mktg. mgr. Danayo Inc. Comms. Co., Umuahia, 1991-92; lectr. I Fed. Poly., Ilaro, 1992—; head of dept., lectr. Ondo State Poly. Satellite Town Lagos Study Ctr., 1997-98; coord. mktg. U. Benin Jukev Study Ctr., Lagos, 1997—; mktg. cons., examiner Cert. Inst. Mktg. Nigeria, Lagos, 1997—; advt. cons., rep. Advt. Practioners Coun. Nigeria, Lagos, 1998—; vis. lectr. U. Ado Ekiti Abeokuta Study Ctr., Nigeria, 1999—; part-time lectr. mktg. Fed. U. Tech. Akure-Lagos Study Ctr., Nigeria, 2000. Author, editor: (textbook) Marketing Principles and Practice, 1996 (CIMN Fellow award 1999); author: (textbook) Successful Advertising, The Only Advertising Textbook for You, 1997 (Chartered Marketer award 1998). Dep. nat. pres. Fed. Poly. Ilaro Nat. Alumni Assn., 1992—; pres. Alumni Assn. Ogun State, 1993—; gen. sec. Students Union Govt., Fed. Poly., Ilaro, 1988-89, editor, gen. sec. Poly. Press Club, 1987-89. Fellow Cert. Inst. Mktg. of Nigeria; mem. Advt. Practitioners Coun. Nigeria (First Prize in Tenth Yr. Anniversary contest 1999), Chartered Inst. Mktg. London (chartered and registered marketer 1998). Avocations: philanthropy, philately, reading novels, traveling, country music. E-mail: ayozie@ikeja.nipost.com.ng. Office: Fed Poly Dept Mktg, PO Box 652, Ilaro Ogun, Nigeria

AYRAPETYAN, SINERIK NERSES, biophysicist; b. Nagorno, Karabagh Republic, May 28, 1941; s. Nerses Ayrapet and Varia (Poghosyan) Dadayan; m. Naira Artashes Babayan, Aug. 28, 1967; children: Haik, Gayane. PhD, Ukrainian Acad. Sci., 1970, DSc, 1980. Researcher Inst. Physiology, Yerevan, Armenia, 1969-71; assoc. prof. Yerevan State U., 1971-73; from sr. researcher to head membranol. lab. Inst. Exptl. Biology, Yerevan, 1973-89; from head biophys. dept. to head biophysics ctr. Nat. Acad. Scis., Yerevan, 1989—; pres. Life Sci. Internat. Higher Edn. Sch.; chmn. life scis. UNESCO. Author: Transmembrane Ionic Transport & Ionic Radiation, 1990; editor: Metabolic Regulation of Membrane Function, 1990, Biological Effects of Electric Magnetic Fields, Vols. 1 and 2, 1994; co-editor: (with V. Apkarian) Pain Mechanisms and Management, 1998. Mem. All-Union Membranol. Rsch. Coun., Armenian Biophysical Soc. (pres.). Home: Vahram Papazyan St 16B # 35, 375012 Yerevan Armenia Office: Biophysics Ctr NAS, Hasratyan str 7, 375014 Yerevan Armenia

AYRES, JANICE RUTH, social service executive; b. Idaho Falls, Idaho, Jan. 23, 1930; d. Low Ray and Frances Mae (Salem) Mason; m. Thomas Woodrow Ayres, Nov. 27, 1953 (dec. 1966); 1 child, Thomas Woodrow Jr. (dec.). MBA, U. So. Calif., 1952, M in Mass Comms., 1953. Asst. mktg. dir. Disneyland, Inc., Anaheim, Calif., 1954-59; gen. mgr. Tamasha Town & Country Club, Anaheim, Calif., 1959-65; dir. mktg. Am. Heart Assn., Santa Ana, Calif., 1966-69; state exec. dir. Nev. Assn. Mental Health, Las Vegas, 1969-71; exec. dir. Clark Co. Easter Seal Treatment Ctr., Las Vegas, 1971-73; mktg. dir., fin devel. officer So. Nev. Drug Abuse Coun., Las Vegas, 1973-74; exec. dir. Nev. Assn. Retarded Citizens, Las Vegas, 1974-75; assoc., cons. Don Luke & Assocs., Phoenix, 1976-77; program dir. Inter-Tribal Coun. Nev., Reno, 1977-79; exec. dir. Ret. Sr. Vol. Program, Carson City, Nev., 1979—; chair sr. citizen summit State of Nev., 1996; presenter in field. Bd. suprs. Carson City, Nev., 1992—; commr. Carson City Parks and Recreation, 1993—; obligation bond com., legis. chair Carson City; bd. dirs. Nev. Dept. Transp., 1993; active No. Corp. for Nat. and Cmty. Svc. by Gov., 1994, V&TRR Commn., 1993, chair, 1995, vice-chair, chair pub. rels. com., bd. dirs. Hist. V&TRR Bd., chair PR Cmty./V&TRR Commn., vice-chair Carson City Gen. Obligation Bond Commn., Nev. Home Health Assn.; appointed liaison Carson City Sr. Citizens Bd., 1995; chair summit Rural Nev. Sr. Citizens, Carson City; pres. No. Nev. R.R. Found., 1996—; chair Tri-Co-R.R. Commn., 1995; chair Gov.'s Nev. Commn. for Corp. in Nat. and Cmty. Svc., 1997—, pres. 1998., Carson City Pub. Transp. Commn., 1998—, Carson City Commn. for Clean Groundwater Act, 1998—; chairperson Celebrate Svc. Conf., Americore, 2000. Named Woman of Distinction, Soroptimist Club, 1988, Outstanding Dir. of Excellence, Gov. State of Nev., 1989, Outstanding Dir., Vol. Action Ctr., J.C. Penney Co., Outstanding Nev. Women's Role Model Nev. A.G., 1996; recipient Gold award Western Fairs Assn., 2000; invitee to White House for outstanding contbns. to Am. Mem. AAUW, Am. Mgmt. Assn. (bd. dirs.), Am. Mktg. Assn. (bd. dirs. 1999—), Internat. Platform Assn., Pub. Rels. Soc. Am. (chpt. pres., Silver Spike award 1996), Women Radio and TV, Nat. Soc. Fund Raising Execs., Nev. Fair and Rodeo Assn. (pres.), Nev. Assn. Transit Svcs. (bd. dirs., legis. chmn.), Nev. Women's Polit. Caucus, Nat. Women's Polit. Caucus, Am. Soc. Assn. Execs., No. Nev. Railroad found. (pres. 1996). Home: 1762 Montelena Ct Carson City NV 89703-8376 Office: Ret Sr Vol Program 501 E Caroline St Carson City NV 89701-4054

AYRES, JONATHAN GEOFFREY, respiratory medicine educator, physician, research; b. Potters Bar, Hertfordshire, Eng., Feb. 14, 1950. BSc, London U., 1971; MBBS, Guys Hosp., 1974; MD, U. London, 1984. Tng. Guys Hosp., London U., Brompton Hosp., Birmingham Heartlands Hosp., Birmingham U.; prof. respiratory medicine U. Warwick, Birmingham Heartlands Hosp., West Midlands, West Midlands, Eng. Contbr. papers to profl. pubIs. Fellow Royal Coll. Physicians; mem. Brit. Thoracic Soc., Group Respiratory Soc. , Internat. Epidemiological Assn., Am. Thoracic Soc. Avocations: pencil sketching, water color painting, cricket. Office: Birmingham Heartlands Hosp, Dept Resp Med Bordesley Green E, Birmingham B9 5SS, England

AYRES, MARY ELLEN, government official; b. Spokane, Wash., June 23, 1924; d. Frank H. and Marion (Kellogg) A. Student, U. Wash., 1942-43; B.A., Stanford U., 1946; postgrad., Am. U., 1960. With Henry von Morpurgo, Advt., 1946-47; reporter Wenatchee Daily World, Wash., 1947-50, Washington Post, 1951-52; with U.S. Fgn. Service, Dept. State, 1950-51; mem. editorial staff Changing Times, 1952-61; editor Family Guide, Kiplinger Washington Editors, 1958-61, Bur. Labor Stats., Manpower Adminstrn., U.S. Dept. Labor, 1962-67; pub. info. specialist Bur. Indian Affairs, U.S. Dept. Interior, 1967-75; writer-editor Bur. Labor Stats., 1975—; tchr. newsletter class Dept. Agriculture Grad. Sch., 1975-89, editing style and technique class, 1987-89; past treas. Govt. Info. Orgn. Mem. publicity com. Nat. Capitol YWCA, 1982-83; dir. Wenatchee High Sch. Scholarship Found., 1988—. Mem. Nat. Assn. Govt. Communicators (founding treas., dir. 1975-80, 89-91, chmn. Blue Pencil Contest 1987, nat. capital chpt. treas. 1989), Nat. Press Club (Washington), Washington Athletic Club, Am. News Women's Club, Am. Econ. Assn., Stanford U. Alumnae Assn., Kappa Kappa Gamma. Episcopalian. Home: 2400 Virginia Ave NW Apt C802 Washington DC 20037-2657 Office: Bur Labor Stats 2 Massachusetts Ave NE Washington DC 20212-0022

AYRES, RAYMOND MAURICE, mechanical engineer; b. Leicester, Eng., Aug. 25, 1945; s. Maurice Harold and Kathleen Mary (Young) A.; m. Claire Pidgeon, Dec. 16, 1979. BSc, Nottingham (Eng.) U., 1967; MSc, London U., 1969; PhD, Leicester (Eng.) U., 1979. cert. chartered engineer. Student apprentice A.A. Jones-Shipman Ltd., Leicester, 1964-69; devel. engr. Rolls-Royce Ltd., Derby, Eng., 1969-71; rsch. fellow U. Leicester, 1971-75; devel. engr. London Borough of Hammersmith, 1975-79; cons. Systems Designers Ltd., Camberley, Eng., 1979-90; tech. dir. Silicon Valley Systems Ltd.,

Camberley, Eng., 1990—; founder Silicon Valley Group plc, 1992—; mng. dir. Mass Cons. Ltd., St. Neots, Cambridgeshire, 1993—; dir. Grove House Investments, Ltd., St. Neots, Cambridgeshire, 1995—; dir. Eayre & Smith Ltd., Derby, 1975—. Freeman City of Leicester, 1966—. Mem. AIAA, Inst. Mech. Engrs., Brit. Inst. Mgmt., Coun. Engring. Instns., Chartered Engrs. Achievements include development of parachute aerodynamic theory; world authority on the tuning theory and dynamic structural analysis of bells rung for change-ringing; consultation in application of computers to command and control for air defence and air traffic control applications; integrated logistical support of large high technology systems; development of response measurement system for automated testing of electronic warfare suite for European fighter aircraft; development of guidance control lab for Egypt and commercial call center software systems. Home: 239 Upper Chobham Rd, GU15 1HB Camberley Surrey, England Office: Silicon Valley Group PLC, High St Sandhurst, GU17 8DY Camberley Surrey, England

AYTAÇ, GÜRSEL, foreign language educator; b. Eskisehir, Turkey, Aug. 27, 1940; d. Ibrahim Necip Metiner and Nazmiye Aygünoldu Aytaç; m. Kemal Aytaç, Sept. 4, 1963; 1 child, Bedrettin. Student, Ankara (Turkey) U., 1962, Ankara (Turkey) U., 1966, Ankara (Turkey) U., 1970. Prof. Ankara U., 1975—. Author: Die Glückseligkeit in Wielands Geschichte des Agathon, 1971, Çağdas Türk Romanlari üzerine Incelemeler, 1990, Romanci Yönüyle Heinrich Böll, 1996, Karsilastirmali Edebiyat Bilimi, 1997, othrs. Recipient Literary Translation prize Austrian Cultural Ministry, 1992. Mem. Internat. Verein der Germanistik, Turkish Pen Club, Edebiyatçilar Birliği. Home: Halit Ziya Sok 20/5, 06540 Ankara Turkey Office: Dil Ve Tarih-Cografya Fak, Ankara Univ, Sihhiye Ankara Turkey

AYUB, YACUB, financial consultant; b. Bombay, India, May 14, 1944; s. Ayub and Aziza Abbas; children: Murtaza, Marzia. MBA, U. Karachi, Pakistan, 1966. CPC, CFP. Rep. officer United Bank of Pakistan, Tehran, 1966-73; calling officer Bank Credit and Commerce Internat. (Iran Arab Bank), Tehran, 1974-78; audit officer Bank Credit and Commerce Internat., London, 1978-79; mgr. br. ops. Bank Credit and Commerce Internat., Panama City, Panama, 1979-83; mgr. mktg. and bus. devel. Bank Credit and Commerce Internat., N.Y.C., 1983-88; fin. cons. Investment & Mgmt. Cons. Inc., Holmdel, N.J., 1988—. Fellow Life Underwriters Tng. Coun. Republican. Home: 38 Bayberry Dr Holmdel NJ 07733-1040

AYUS, JUAN CARLOS, nephrologist; b. Buenos Aires, Argentina, Feb. 25, 1941; came to U.S., 1973; s. Jose and Matilde A.; m. Linda Maria Giudici; children: Sebastian, Mariana. BS, Nat. Coll., 1959; MD, U. Buenos Aires, 1967. Diplomate Am. Bd. Internal Medicine, Am. Bd. Nephrology. Resident in internal medicine U. Buenos Aires, 1968-71, fellow in nephrology, 1971-72; resident in internal medicine U. Mass., Worcester, 1973-74, U. Minn., Mpls., 1974-75; fellow in nephrology U. Calif., San Francisco, 1975-77; chief renal svc. Ben-Taub Regional hosp., Houston, 1977-84; from assoc. prof. to prof. medicine Baylor Coll. Medicine, Houston, 1984—. Fellow Am. Coll. Physicians; mem. Lat. Am. Soc. Nephrology (sec.-treas. 1993-96,v.p. 1996-99), Argentine Soc. Critical Care (founder). Home: 1967 Haddon St Houston TX 77019-5762

AYUSO, OSCAR MIGUEL, manufacturer's representatives company executive; b. Belize, Belize, Oct. 17, 1928; s. Lucilo Prospero and Sara (Muñoz) A.; m. Simona Josefina Medero, June 22, 1957; children: Oscar Miguel Jr., Ester Josefina. Student high sch., Belize. Clk., cashier Royal Bank Can., Belize, 1946-51; asst. acct. Royal Bank Can., Caracas, Venezuela, 1952-59; head loan and discount dept. Banco Nat. Descuento, Caracas, 1960-61; head payroll sect. Am. Embassy, Caracas, 1964-66; ptnr. G. Ayuso & Son, Belize, 1961, 66-82; pres. G. Ayuso & Son Ltd., Belize, 1982—. Roman Catholic. Avocations: exercise, playing dominos, sports, good music, reading foreign political news. Home and Office: 2 Daly St, Belize Belize

AYUSO GONZALEZ, MARIA DEL PILAR, member of European parliament; b. Badajoz, Spain, June 16, 1942. Mem. European Parliament, Madrid, 1999—; mem. Group of the European People's Party (Christian Democrats) and European Democrats; mem. com. on environ., pub. health and consumer policy, com. on agr. and rural devel., com. on industry, external trade, rsch. and energy, delegation to the EU-Romania Joint Parliamentary Com., EU-Czech Republic Joint Parliamentary Com. Mem. People's Party. Office: Plaza Reyes Magos 4, E-28007 Madrid Spain*

AZAD, ABUL KASHEM MOHAMMOD, engineer; b. Dhaka, Bangladesh, Jan. 1, 1959; s. Monazzir Ali and Meherunnessa Khanam; m. Sabira Azad, Sept. 9, 1988; 1 child, Tanjiv. BS, U. Dhaka, 1984, MS, 1987; PhD, U. Sheffield, Eng., 1994. Asst. engr. Atomic Energy Ctr., Bangladesh, 1978-81, 85-87, jr. engr., 1982-84; lectr. U. Dhaka, 1987-88; rsch. fellow U. Portsmouth, Eng., 1996—. Recipient Chancellor's award U. Dhaka, 1986; rsch. fellow U. Sheffield; Commonwealth scholar, England, 1988-94. Mem. IEEE, IEE (assoc.), ISA (sr.). Avocation: travel. Office: U Portsmouth Dept EE, Anglesea Rd, Portsmouth PO1 3DJ, England

AZAD, NIRMAL SINGH, economics educator; b. Ransinke-Mira Punjab, India, Mar. 4, 1948; s. Kartar Singh Goraya and Parkash Kaur Randhawa; m. Balbir Kaur Brar, June 15, 1975; children: Rajan Singh, Puneet Kaur. BA (hons.), Khalsa Coll., Amritsar, India, 1968; MA in econs., Panjab Univ., Chandigarh, India, 1970; diploma in nat. econ. planning, Cen. Sch. Planning & Statistic, Warsaw, Poland, 1980; PhD in econs., Punjabi Univ., Patiala, India, 1981. Lectr. econ. dept. Punjab and Punjabi Univ., 1970-83; reader econ. dept. Punjabi Univ., 1983-88, prof. econ. dept., 1988—, senator senate com., 1989-91, head econ. dept., 1991-94, chmn. bd. econs., 1991-94; mem. fin. com. Punjabi Univ., 1991-92, mem. acad. coun., 1989-94, chmn. adminstrv. com. dept. econs., 1991-94, mem. coll. mgmt. com., 1989—. Author: Capitalism and Small Peasantry, 1990, Political Economy of Development, 1995; editor: The Punjab Economy, 1983, Jour. of Social Sciences, 1992-95; contbr. articles to profl. jours. Sec. Punjab Students Union, 1965-67, convenor Progressive Thinkers' Forum, 1973-80, organising sec. Punjab Socialist Coun., 1980-87; convenor Punjab Thinkers' Forum, 1992—. Recipient rsch. scholarship Univ. Grants Commn., 1977-78, Polish Govt. scholarship Gov. of Poland, 1979-80, Indo-French Cultural Exchange Programme Univ. Grants, 1983-84. Mem. Indian Soc. Labour Econs. (life), Indian Soc. Agrl. Econ., Indian Sch. Social Scis. (assoc.). Avocations: reading literary works, reading and writing poetry, walking, talking. Home: 230 Urban Estate I, 147002 Patiala India Office: Punjabi Univ Dept Econ, 147002 Patiala India

AZAR, RAZA, chemicals executive; b. Lahore, Punjab, Pakistan, Jan. 5, 1971; s. Saghir Azar and Azra (Obaidullah) Saghir; m. Mahwish Shaikh, Nov. 16, 1996; 1 child, Zara. BSChemE, UET, Lahore, 1994. Mgmt. trainee ICI Pakistan Ltd., Lahore, 1994-95; shift mgr. ICI Pakistan Ltd., Khewra, Pakistan, 1995-97; plant mgr. ICI Pakistan Ltd., Khewra, 1997—; trainee Brunner Mond Ltd., Eng., 1999. Mem. Winnington Club (sports sec. 1997-98, social sec. 1998—). Avocations: badminton, tennis, swimming. Home: St 134 House 169-N, Defence Society, Lahore Punjab, Pakistan Office: ICI Pakistan Ltd, Soda Ash Business, Khewra Jhelum, Pakistan

AZARI, ZITOUNI, engineering educator; b. Casablanca, Morocco, Nov. 19, 1951; arrived in France, 1974; s. Mohamed and Aicha (Sabri) A.; m. Marie Huckert, Dec. 21, 1986; children: Sarah, Jihane. Engring. diploma, France, 1980, postgrad., 1981; D in Mech., Acad. Metznawy, France, 1985. Jacataire Metz Min. Scis., 1983-85, asst., 1985-87; lectr. High Inst. Scis., France, 1988-98; prof., rsch. dir. Amiens U., France, 1998—; dir. Rsch. Team Divsn., France, 1986-99. Contbr. articles to profl. jours. Mem. Sci. Franco-Moroccan Assn., Congress Mechs. Morocco, European Structural Integrity Soc.. Home: 5/11 Rue de la Caserne, 57000 Metz France Office: Fac Sci Metz Lab Fiabilite, Ile du Saulay, 57000 Metz France

AZCARATE, ISMAEL NORBERTO, physicist; b. Saladillo, Argentina, Mar. 27, 1944; s. Ismael and Ilda (Lucangioli) A.; m. Haydee Beatriz Badano, Jan. 17, 1975. BSc, Nat. Coll. Saladillo, Argentina, 1961; MSc in Physics, Nat. U. La Plata, 1968, PhD, 1988. From fellow to asst. researcher IAFE, Buenos Aires, 1974-80; from asst. researcher to ind. researcher Inst. Argentino de Radio Astronomia, Villa Elisa, 1980—. Mem. Internat. Astronomical Union, Argentine Astronomical Assn., N.Y. Acad. Scis. (com. on human rights of scientists), Am. Astronomical Soc. Home: Calle 2 #1532 Dto C, 1900 La Plata Argentina Office: Inst Argentino de Radio Astronomia, Casilla de Correo #5, 1894 Villa Elisa Argentina

AZCÁRRAGA, JOSÉ ADOLFO DE, theoretical physics educator; b. Valencia, Spain, Oct. 12, 1941; s. Adolfo and Amparo (Feliu) de A. Lic. Ciencias Físicas, Madrid U., 1962; PhD in Physics, Barcelona U., 1968. Assoc. prof. Barcelona U., Spain, 1968-73; prof. Salamanca U., Spain, 1974-77, Valencia U., Spain, 1978—; vis. scholar Cambridge U., U.K., 1969-71, Oxford U., U.K., 1975-76; vis. prof. Cambridge U., U.K., 1988-89, 96-97; jour. referee. Editor: Conference Proceedings "Topics in Quantum Field Theory", 1977, Conference Proceedings "Supersymmetry and Supergravity", 1984; author: Lie Groups, Lie Algebras, Cohomology and Some Applications in Physics, 1995. Mem. Spanish Phys. Soc., Am. Phys. Soc., European Phys. Soc., Math. and Phys. Soc. Office: U Valencia Dept Theor Physics, Faculty of Physics, 46100-Burjasot Valencia Spain

AZEGAMI, HIDEYUKI, mechanical engineer, educator; b. Nagano, Japan, Sept. 1, 1956; s. Tadao and Yoshiko Azegami; m. Yoshiko Shirahata, Nov. 23, 1982; children: Emi, Akira. BEng, Yamanashi (Japan) U., 1979; MEng, U. Tokyo, 1982, DEng, 1985. Rsch. assoc. U. Tokyo, 1985; rsch. assoc. Toyohashi (Japan) U. Tech., 1986-89, lectr., 1989-91, assoc. prof., 1991—; vis. scholar U. Mich., Ann Arbor, 1991-92; guest assoc. prof. U. Tokyo, 1998—. Contbr. articles to profl. jours. Mem. Japan Soc. Mech. Engrs. (Young Engrs. award 1989). Home: 5-104 2-1 Higashiura, Kitayama-cho, 441-8105 Toyohashi Aichi, Japan Office: Dept Mech Engr Toyohashi U, 1-1 Hibarigaoka Tempaku-cho, 441-8580 Toyohashi Aichi, Japan

AZEVEDO, JOAO LUIS TOSTE, academic education educator; b. Azores, Portugal, Jan. 22, 1963; s. Manuel Luis and Maria Conceicao (Toste) A.; m. Ana Margarida Canais, Sept. 17, 1989; children: Inês, Pedro. Student, Instituto Superior Tecnico, Lisbon, Portugal, 1986. Rsch. asst. Instituto Superior Tecnico, Lisbon, 1986-94, auxiliary prof., 1994—. Contbr. 14 articles to profl. jours. Home: Av Fernando Namora 34-7D, 1600 Lisbon Portugal Office: Instituto Superior Tecnico, Av Rovisco Pais, 1049-007 Lisbon Codex 1096, Portugal

AZEVEDO, JOÃO ROBERTO DUFF, neurosurgeon; b. São Paulo, Brazil, Aug. 25, 1945; s. Aroldo Azevedo and Maria Gertrudes Duff; m. Heloisa Carveiro Mello, June 19, 1972; 1 child, Gabriela. MD, U. Santa Casa São Paulo, 1971. Neurosurgeon São Paulo, 1972—; staff neurosurgeon State Hosp., São Paulo, 1978-94; rschr. U. São Paulo, 1998. Author: Ficar Joven Leva Tempo, 1998; contbr. articles to profl. jours. Mem. Brazilian Neurosurgery Soc. Avocations: swimming, jazz. Office: R Benedito Larin 167, 04532040 São Paulo Brazil

AZIMI, DARIUSH, physicist, researcher, educator; b. Tehran, Iran, June 12, 1944; arrived in Can., 1992; s. Ali Azimi and Behjat Gharib; m. Mahshid Lotfi, June 27, 1980; 1 child, Navid. BSc, U. Tehran, 1966, MSc, 1968; MSc, U. London, 1974, PhD, 1976. European charted physicist. Instr. Nuclear Ctr., Tehran, 1966-69, Reactor Ctr., Ascot, England, 1975-76; asst. prof. U. Tehran, 1976-85; rsch. fellow ENEA-DISP, Rome, 1985-89; scientific officer PSI, Villigen, Switzerland, 1989-92; rschr. Can. Com. for UN Programs on Environ. and Devel., Ottawa, Can., 1994-97; cons. MI.EL, Milan, Italy, 1990, IDRC, Ottawa, 1995; rschr. GSC, Ottawa, 1994. Contbr. over 70 articles to profl. jours.; assoc. editor Internat. Jour. Atmospheric Environment, 1992; editl. bd. mem. Internat. Jour. Indoor and Built Environment, 1994. Named Alien of Extraordinary Ability, U.S. Dept. Justice, 1994. Fellow British Inst. Physics, British Inst. Nuclear Engrs.; mem. Am. Nuclear Soc. Avocations: reading, music, movies, home improvement. Fax: (714) 832-8231. E-mail: dazimi@hotmail.com. Office: BuyMedicals 2852 Walnut Ave Ste H1 Tustin CA 92780-7061

AZIMIOARA, MIHAI DUMITRU, chemistry researcher; b. Bucharest, Romania, Oct. 27, 1965; came to U.S., 1984; s. Corneliu and Ioana Azimioara; m. Mirona Lungu, June 29, 1996; 1 child, Stefan George. BS in Chemistry, Calif. Inst. Tech., 1989; MA in Organic Chemistry, Harvard U., 1992. Rsch. assoc. Biogen, Inc., Cambridge, Mass., 1996; sr. rsch. assoc. ARIAD, Inc., Cambridge, 1996-98; rsch. assoc. Tanabe Rsch. Labs., USA, Inc., San Diego, 1998-2000, Arena Pharms., San Diego, 2000—. Co-editor: Reagents for Organic Synthesis, vol. 17, 1994; contbr. articles to profl. jours. Wasserman Undergrad. scholar Calif. Inst. Tech., Pasadena, 1988, 89. Mem. Am. Chem. Soc. Republican. Avocations: world and European history, music, reading, computers. E-mail: mazimio1@san.rr.com and mazimioara@arenapharm.com. Fax: 858-453-7210. Home: 7693 Palmilla Dr Apt 2221 San Diego CA 92122-5086 Office: Arena Pharms Inc 6166 Nancy Ridge Dr San Diego CA 92121-3223

AZIMOV, YAKHYE, prime minister. Prime min. Republic of Tajikistan; economy & foreign rels. minister Republic of Tajikstan. Office: Ministry of Economics & Foreign Rels, PR Rudaki 42, Dushanbe Tajikistan*

AZINGER, PAUL, professional golfer; b. Holyoke, Mass., Jan. 6, 1960; m. Toni Azinger; 2 children. Student, Broward Jr. Coll., Fla., Fla. State U. Profl. golfer PGA, 1982—; mem. Ryder Cup Team, 1989, 91, 93, World Cup Team, 1989, President's Cup Team (co-capt.), 1994. Winner Phoenix Open, 1987, Las Vegas Invitational, 1987, Canon Greater Hartford Open, 1987, 89, Bay Hill Classic, 1988, Tournament of Champions, 1990, AT&T Nat. Pro-Am, 1991, Tour Championship, 1992, Meml. Tournament, 1993, PGA Championship, 1993, New England Classic, 1993, Sony Open in Hawaii, 2000; named PGA Tour Player of Yr., 1987. Office: PGA Tour 112 Tpc Blvd Ponte Vedra Beach FL 32082-3077

AZIZ, AASMA, family physician; b. Gujrat, Punjab, Pakistan, Apr. 24, 1965; d. Abdul and Atiya (Nasreen) A.; m. Ijaz Ali Malik, Oct. 5, 1989; 1 child, Fatima Malik. Student, F.G. Coll. for Women, Rawalpindi, India, 1983; MB BChir, Rawalpindi Med. Coll., 1989. Diplomate Am. Bd. Family Practice. Family physician Shif Internat. Hosp., Islamabad, Pakistan, 1999—; mem. tchg. faculty Shifa Coll. Medicine, Islamabad, 1999. Pres. Patients Welfare Aux., Shifa Internat. Hosp., Islamabad, 1999. Home: 8/56 Valley Rd Westridge I, Rawalpindi Pakistan

AZIZ, CROWN PRINCE ABDULLAH BIN ABDUL, crown prince of Arabia, military official; b. Riyadh, Saudi Arabia, 1924; s. King Abdul Aziz. Apptd. comdr. Nat. Guard, Saudi Arabia, 1963—; apptd. 2d deputy premier Saudi Arabia, 1975—. Avocations: reading, visiting the desert. Address: The Royal Palace, Riyadh Saudi Arabia*

AZIZ, LUTFUL, anaesthesiologist; b. Dhaka, Bangladesh, Feb. 20, 1962; s. Abdul Barek and Lutfun (Nahar) Bhuiah; m. Tayyeda Nasir, Apr. 26, 1987; children: Sheahan, Kiyoshi, Kyoko. MBBS, Dhaka Med. Coll., 1985; PhD, Okayama U. Med. Sch., Okayama, Japan, 1995; FCPS, Bangladesh Coll. Physicians, 1997. Resident Dhaka Med. Coll., Bangladesh, 1985-89; anaesthesiologist Okayama U. Med. Sch., Japan, 1990-95; cons. Bangladesh Med. U., Dhaka, 1995—. Contbr. articles to profl. jours. Recipient scholarship Govt. Bangladesh, 1986-89, 97-99; fellowship Govt. Japan, 1990-95; grantee N.H.S., Bangladesh, 1999. Avocations: games, study, travel. Home: 137/E Jahanara Gardens, Green Rd, 1215 Dhaka Bangladesh

AZIZ, SAJID, electronics engineer, consultant; b. Lahore, Pakistan, Oct. 21, 1951; s. Rahman and Rashida (Khanum) A.; m. Sohaila Khanum Aziz, Nov. 26, 1978; children: Haris, Kashif, Saba. BS in Elec. Engring., U. Engring. & Tech., Lahore, Pakistan, 1975; MEE, McGill U., Montreal, Can., 1978. Engr. II Engrs. Internat., Lahore, Pakistan, 1975-76; asst. engr. Karachi (Pakistan) Power Plant, 1976-80; sr. engr. Fuel Plant, Chashma, Pakistan, 1981-83; sr. engr., prin. engr. head elec. divsn. Minerals Ctr., Lahore, Pakistan, 1983-95; dir. technical Arden Engring. & Automation Ltd., Lahore, Pakistan, 1995—; control system testing Karachi (Pakistan) Power Plant, 1978-80; elec. support Fuel Plant Chashma, Pakistan, 1981-83; tech. mgmt. Minerals Ctr., Lahore, Pakistan, 1983-95; dir. tech. Arden Engring. & Automation Ltd., Lahore,, Pakistan, 1995—. Author: (poems) Ravi, 1969; author, poet: Pencoma, 1971-72 (best article 1974). Recipient Honorarium Fed. Govt., Chashma, 1982. Mem. IEEE (sr., chmn. profl. activities com. 1998, adv. Pakistan sect. by-laws), Pakistan Engring. Coun., Lahore Gymkhana Club. Muslim. Avocations: tennis, reading. writing, chess.

AZIZ, SAMIR MOHAMED FOUAD, obstetrician-gynecologist, educator, consultant; b. Cairo, Egypt, Mar. 26, 1957; came to U.S., 1997; s. Mohamed Fouad Khalaf and Naiema Ahmed (Siam) Aziz; m. Iman Abdel Rahman Ismail, July 30, 1985; children: Reham, Dina, Ahmed. MB, BChir, Al-Azhar Faculty of Medicine, Cairo, 1982, MSc in Ob-Gyn., 1985, MD in Ob-Gyn., 1992; ob-gyn. tng., Royal Coll. Ob-Gyn., Leeds, U.K., 1993. Intern Al-Azhar U., Cairo, 1983-84; resident in ob-gyn. Al-Azhar Hosp., Cairo, 1985-87, asst. lectr. ob-gyn., 1987-93, lectr. ob-gyn., 1993-98; resident in surgery Suez Mil. Hosp., 1984-85, asst. prof. ob-gyn, 1998; fellow ob-gyn M.D. Anderson Cancer Ctr., Houston, 1998; asst. prof. ob-gyn. Al-Azhar U., 1998—; chmn. ob-gyn Al-obid Hosp., Saudi Arabia, 1999—, Al-Azhar Faculty Medicine, Cairo, Egypt, 2000. Mem. editl. bd. obgyn.net, 1999—; reviewer The Lancet. Nat. assessor UNICEF, Cairo, 1996. Mem. Internat. Gynecol. Cancer Soc., Egyptian Soc. for Breast Feeding, Egyptian Soc. for Mother and Child Health, World Oncology Network. Home: 10 Shazly St El-Naam, Helmiat El Zeitoun, Cairo Egypt Office: Al-Hussein U Hosp, Dept Ob-Gyn El Darasa, Cairo Egypt also: 10 Shazly St El Naam, Helmiat El Zeiton, Cairo Egypt

AZIZ, SHAGUFTA, psychologist, educator, researcher; b. Bahawalpur, Punjab, Pakistan, Jan. 15, 1965; s. Abdul and Saeeda (Akhter) A.; m. Ghulam Murtaza, July 20, 1997. BA, Islamia U., Bahawalpur, 1985; MSc in Applied Psychology, U. Punjab, Lahore, Pakistan, 1988; MPhil in Psychology, Quaid-I-Azam U., Islamabad, Pakistan, 1992; postgrad., U. Surrey, Eng., 1999—. Cert. psychologist. Rschr. Ministry Edn., Lahore, 1988; hon. lectr. Govt. Degree Coll., Bahawalpur, 1989; rsch. asst. U. Grants Commn., Islamabad, 1991-92; project in charge Nat. Inst. Psychology, Islamabad, 1992-95, lectr., 1992—; rsch. fellow Pakistan Psychol. Found. UNICEF, Islamabad, 1994-95; counseling svcs. Lahore H.S., 1988; vis. lectr. Nat. Inst. Handicapped, Islamabad, 1993-97; with counseling and psychometric svcs. divsn. Kashmir Edn. Found., Azad Kashmir, Pakistan, 1996-97. Consulting editor Pakistan Psychol. Abstracts, 1993—; editor NIPsychology Newsletter, 1993-97; evaluator National Book Coun., 1994-96, Univ. Grants Commn., 1994-96; contbr. articles to profl. jours. Mem. Women Welfare Soc., 1994—. Mem. APA Internat. Affliate, Pakistan Psychol. Assn. (life), Pakistan Psychol. Found. (founder), Afro-Asian Psychol. Assn. Avocations: touring, music, literature, sports, movies. Office: U Surrey, Psychology Dept, Guildford Surrey GU2 5XH, England

AZIZ, SHAUKAT, minister of finance. Banker Citibank; min. fin. Pakistan, 1999—. Office: Ministry of Fin, Pakistan Secretariat Blk Q, Islamabad Pakistan*

AZIZOGLU, MERAL, engineering educator; b. Ankara, Turkey, Dec. 2, 1965. BS, Middle East Tech. U., Ankara, 1986, MS, 1989, PhD, 1994. Rsch. asst. Middle East Tech. U., Ankara, 1986-94; vis. scholar U. Wis., Madison, 1994-95; postdoctoral assoc. Columbia U., N.Y.C., 1995-96, adj. asst. prof., 1996; asst. prof. Middle East Tech. U., 1996-97, assoc. prof., 1997—. Contbr. articles to profl. jours. Recipient award for MS Thesis, 1988, for PhD Thesis, 1994; Tubitak postdoctoral scholar, 1995. Office: Middle East Tech U, 06531 Ankara Turkey

AZNAR, JOSÉ MARÍA, Prime Minister of Spain, political organization official; b. Madrid, 1953. Student, U. Complutense, Madrid. Former tax inspector; joined Rioja br. Alianza Popular, 1978; dep. sec.-gen., mem. Cortes, 1982; premier Castilla y León Autonomous Region, 1987; pres. Partido Popular (formerly Alianza Popular), 1990—; opposition leader Govt. of Spain, Madrid, 1990-96, Prime Min., 1996—, President of Govt., 1996—. Author: Libertad y Solidaridad, 1991, La Segunda Transición, 1994, La España en la que Yo Creo, 1995. Office: Partido Popular, Génova 13, 28004 Madrid Spain also: Office of the Pres, Complejo de la Moncloa, 28071 Madrid Spain

AZNAVOUR, CHARLES (VARENAGH AZNAVOURIAN), singer, actor; b. May 22, 1924. s. Micha Aznaourian; m. Micheline Rugel, Mar. 16, 1946; m. Evelyne Plessis, Oxt. 28, 1955; m. Ulla Thorsel, Jan. 11, 1967; children: Katia, Mesha, Nicolai, Patricia, Patrick (dec.). Ed., Ecole Centrale de T.S.F., Centre de Spectacle, Paris. With Jean Dasté Co., 1941. Pierre Roche in Les facheux and Arlequin, 1944. Performed numerous song recitals in Europe and U.S.A., Films include: La Tets Contre les Murs, 1959; Ne Tirez pas sur le Pianiste, 1960; Un Taxi pour Trobrouk, Le Testament d' Orphée, Le Diable et les dix Commandments, Houte-Infidélité, 1964; La Métamorphose des Cloportes, 1965; Paris au mois d'Aout, 1966; Le Facteur s' en Va-t-en Guerre, 1966; Le Diable par le Queue, 1968; Candy, 1969; Les Intrus, 1973; Sky Riders, 1976; Fodies Gourgeoises, 1976; Dix Petits Négres, 1976; the Twist, 1976; The Tin Drum, 1979. Composer, singer numerous songs. Composer operetta: Monsiuer Carnaval, 1965. Decorated chevalier des Arts et des Lettres. Address: c/o Levon Sayan, 9 Chemin de Plonjon, 1207 Geneva Switzerland

AZODI, DJAHANGIR, engineer; b. Teheran, Iran, Aug. 16, 1937; s. Mohammed and Turan Azodi; m. Helga Roth, Dec. 20, 1968; 1 child, Sasan. Diploma in mech. engring., Tech. U., Darmstadt, Fed. Republic Germany, 1968. Stress analyst Allgemeine Elektrizitäts Gesellschaft (AEG), Frankfurt, Fed. Republic Germany, 1968-73; sr. scientist, official adviser fracture mechanics Gesellschaft für Reaktorsicherheit, Cologne, Fed. Republic Germany, 1973—. Office: Gesellschaft für Reaktorsicherheit, Schwertnergasse 1, 50667 Cologne Germany

AZOULAY, ANDRE D., government official; b. Essaouira, Morocco, Apr. 17, 1941; s. Salomon and Laetitia (Oinounou) A.; m. Katia E. Brami, Sept. 1, 1966; children: Judith, Sabrina, Audrey. Grad., H.S. Journalism, Paris, 1962. Exec. v.p. Paribas, Paris, 1968-91; counselor His Majesty The King of Morocco, Rabat, 1991—; dir. Ctrl. Bank Morocco. Bd. dirs. Al Akhawayn U., Ifrane, Morocco, 1994—; founder, chmn. Identity and Dialogue, Paris, 1974; co-pres. Jud. Ctr. for Peace in Mid. East., Tel Aviv, 1986—, Peres Ctr. for Peace, Tel Aviv, 1998; mem. Moroccan Royal Acad. 1998—. Decorated Legion d'Honneur (France); officer Ordre du Trône (Morocco). Jewish. Home: Villa Darna, Temara Morocco Office: Royal Cabinet, Rabat Morocco

AZPIROZ, FERNANDO, physician, researcher; b. San Sebastian, Spain, May 19, 1954; s. Ramon Azpiroz and Josefina Vidaur; m. Alicia Maria Franch, Feb. 27, 1993; children: Josefina, Carlos, Alicia. BS, German Sch., San Sebastian, 1970; MD, U. Valladolid, Spain, 1977; PhD, U. Complutense, Madrid, 1986. Resident Hosp. Clinico U., Madrid, 1978-82; rsch. fellow Mayo Clinic, Rochester, Minn., 1982-85; instr. Mayo Med. Sch., Rochester, 1985; rsch. assoc. Hosp. Vall d'Hebron, Barcelona, Spain, 1986, chief gut rsch. unit, 1987—; prof. surgery Autonomous U., Barcelona, 1990—; Benjamin Meaker vis. prof. U. Bristol, U.K., 1992; mem. Multinat. Working Team on Functional Gut Disorders, 1997—; advisor Internat. Found. for Functional Gastrointestinal Diseases, 1997—. Mem. editl. bd. Revista Española de Enfermedades Digestivas, Spain, 1995&, Am. Jour. Physiology, 1997—; inventor computerized tensostat; contbr. articles to profl. jours. Fulbright scholar, 1982; recipient Kendall award for meritorious rsch. Mayo Alumni Assn., 1986, Almirall prize, 1986, Fourth Janssen Rsch. award Internat. Motility Soc., 1999. Mem. European Motility Soc., Royal Gastroenterol. Soc. Belgium (hon.), Spanish Soc. Gastrointestinal Motility (pres.). Avocations: music, painting. Office: Hosp Gen Vall d'Hebron, Digestive Sys Rsch Unit, 08035 Barcelona Spain

AZUMA, TAKAMITSU, architect, educator; b. Osaka, Japan, Sept. 20, 1933; s. Yoshimatsu and Yoshiko (Ikeda) A.; m. Setsuko Nakaoka, Mar. 17, 1957; 1 child, Rie. BArch, Osaka U., 1957, DArch, D. of Engring, 1985. Designer, Ministry of Postal Svcs., Osaka, 1957-60; chief designer Junzo Sakakura Architect & Assocs., Osaka, 1960-63; chief designer Junzo Sakakura Architect and Assocs., Tokyo, 1963-67; prin. Takamitsu Azuma Architect & Assocs., Tokyo, 1967-85; instr. Tokyo U. Art and Design, 1976-78, Tokyo Denki U., 1980-82, Tokyo U., 1983-85; instr. Osaka U., 1981-85, prof., 1985-97, emeritus prof., Osaka U., 1997—; instr. Osaka Art U., 1985-87; architect Azuma Architects & Assocs., 1985—; vis. prof. Sch. Architecture Washington U., St. Louis, 1989; prof. Chiba Inst. Tech., 1997—. Recipient Diplomatic Design prize Kinki Br. of Archtl. Inst. Japan Competition, 1957. Author: Reevaluation of the Residence, 1971, On the Japanese Architectural Space, 1981, Takamitsu Azuma-Contemporary Japanese Architects Series (4), 1982, Philosophy of Living in the City, 1983, Device from Architecture, 1986, Space Analysis of Urban Residence, 1986, 100

Chpt. for Children's Place, 1987, White Book about Tower House, 1987, Cities and Urban Residences, 1998. Mem. Archtl. Inst. Japan (Archtl. Design prize 1995), Japan Inst. Archs. Home: 3-39-4 Jingumae, Shibuya-ku, Tokyo 150-0001, Japan Office: 3-6-1 Minami-Aoyama Minato-ku, Tokyo 107-0062, Japan

AZZATO, LOUIS ENRICO, manufacturing company executive; b. N.Y.C., Oct. 8, 1930; s. John A. and Margaret (Ronca) A.; m. Margaret Jean McCarthy, June 25, 1955; children: Jean Bernadette and Patricia Bernadette (twins), John Kevin, Maureen Ann. BSChemE cum laude, CCNY, 1952. Process/project engr. Foster Wheeler Energy Corp., Clinton, N.J., 1952-63, project mgr., 1963-67, sr. v.p., group exec., 1978-80, also bd. dirs.; exec. v.p. equipment div. ops. Foster Wheeler Energy Corp., 1980-81; pres., CEO Foster Wheeler Corp., Clinton, N.J., 1981-88; also chmn. bd. dirs. Foster Wheeler Corp, Clinton, N.J.; v.p., mgr. process plants and fired hired heater activities Foster Wheeler Italiana, Milan, 1967-74; chmn., chief exec. officer, pres. Foster Wheeler Corp., Clinton, N.J., 1988-94; ret., 1994; chmn., CEO Glitsch, Inc., Dallas, 1974-78; bd. dirs. several subs. cos. Foster Wheeler Corp. Patentee catalytic cracking. Roman Catholic. Avocations: golfing, swimming, jogging. Home: 22 Lord William Penn Dr Morristown NJ 07960-3216

AZZOPARDI, MARC ANTOINE, astrophysicist, scientist; b. Philippeville, Algeria, Oct. 28, 1940; s. Antoine Philippe and Marie Madeleine (Grech) A.; divorced; children: Pauline, Mathilde, Marceau; m. Alexandra L. Giorla, June 30, 1994; children: Anne-Sophie, Mary. Lic. es sci., Algeria and Marseilles U., France, 1963; DSc, Toulouse U., France, 1981. Astronomy aide U. Toulouse, 1964-81, adj. astronomer, 1981-83; adj. astronomer U. Marseilles, France, 1983-87, astronomer 2d class, 1987-92, astronomer 1st class, 1992—; astronomer in charge European South Obs. Sta., Zeekoegat, South Africa, 1964; vis. scholar U. Tex., Austin, 1982-83; mem. sci. adv. coun. Can.-France-Hawaii Telescope Co., Hawaii, 1984-87, vis. scientist, 1994-96; sci. assoc. European So. Obs., Garching, Germany, 1983-87, mem. users com., 1988-91, chmn., 1990-91, guest prof., 1992-93, panel mem. observing program com., 1996-97. Contbr. articles to profl. jours. Recipient NSF-Ctr. Nat. Sci. Rsch. award, 1982-83. Mem. Soc. French Specialists in Astronomy, Am. Astron. Soc., European Astron. Soc. Roman Catholic. Office: Observatoire de Marseilles, 2 place le Verrier, F-13248 Marseille Cedex 4, France

BA, DINH XUAN, mathematics educator; b. Vinh, Vietnam, Mar. 26, 1935; s. Dinh xuan Khoa and Tran thi Hue Chat; m. Doan Thi Tuyet Nga, July 29, 1961; children: Hoai Giang, Hong Ky. B of Math., Hanoi U., Vietnam, 1963; Assoc. Prof. of Math., Hanoi Polytech U., Vietnam, 1991. Rschr. Hanoi Polytech U., Vietnam, 1959-61, lectr. math., 1962-82; scientific trainee Polytech Inst., Grenoble, France, 1983-84; lectr. Hanoi Polytech U., 1985-87, dean faculty, 1988-92; pres. Secoin Co., Ltd., Hanoi, 1989—; vis. prof. UNDP, Hanoi, 1986; v.p. VAIP, Hanoi, 1988-92; dir. IT Tng. Ctr. of Hanoi Polytech U., 1989-93. Author: Introduction of Nomogram, 1964, Mathematical Statistics, 1972, Optimal Control in Manufacturing, 1982, Multicriteria Optimization, 1983, Membership Function of Fuzzy Set, 1984, Introduction of Informatics, 1986. Mem. admintrv. bd. Internat. Fedn. Assns. of Elderly, Paris, 1992—; mng. dir. Environ. Engring. Ctr. Vietnam, 1993—. Fellow Barons BWW; mem. Vietnam Assn. Econ. Sci., Vietnam Assn. Constrn. Avocations: table-tennis, travel. Office: Secoin Co Ltd, Secoin Co Ltd Rm 9-12 3d Fl, Cho Hom Pho Hue, Hanoi Vietnam

BAAG, CZANGO, geophysics educator; b. Daegu, Republic of Korea, Nov. 8, 1934; arrived in U.S. 1967; became U.S. citizen; reclaimed Korean citizenship to teach at Kangwon Nat. U., 1990.; s. Yunmog and Seonyi (Jeong) B.; m. Bokhee Bae, Nov. 13, 1961; children: Dongho, Namho. BS, Seoul (Republic of Korea) Nat. U., 1959; MA, Washington U., St. Louis, 1968; PhD, U. Tex. at Dallas, 1973. Exploration geophysicist Exxon, Houston, 1974-82; sr. geophys. advisor Mobil Exploration and Prodn. Svcs., Inc., Dallas, 1982-86; rschr. Hawaii Inst. Geophysics, U. Hawaii, Manoa, 1988-89; prof. geophysics Kangwon Nat. U., Chuncheon, Republic of Korea, 1990-2000; v.p. Korean Nat. Com. for IUGG, 1993-95; pres., 1995—; mem. faculty disciplinary com., Kangwon Nat. U.,1993-95; bd. dirs. Korean Soc. Petroleum Geology, 1992-95; pres. Korean-Am. Scientists and Engrs. Assn. Southwestern chpt., Houston, 1978. Contbr. articles to profl. jours. Pres. Geumho Village Condominium Assn., Chuncheon, 1992-93, 96-98; v.p. Korean Cath. Ch. Coun., Houston, 1976-80; auditor Korean-Am. Assn., Houston, 1982. Recipient Wheeler fellowship Washington U., 1967-68, Soc. of Exploration Geophysicists scholarships, Tula, Okla., 1969-72. Mem. Am. Geophys. Union, Soc. Exploration Geophysicists, Assn. to Hire Univ. Profs. on Merits (pres. 1996—), Sigma Xi. Roman Catholic. Avocations: golf, go-game, travel. Home: 721-2 Seogsa-Dong, Daewoo Apt 103-602, Chuncheon 936-180, Republic of Korea

BAAKLINI, WALID ANTOINE, physician, educator; b. Beirut, June 25, 1968; came to U.S., 1993; s. Antoine Elias Baaklini and Siham Jamil Azoury. BS in Biology, Am. U. Beirut, 1989, MD, 1993. Intern in internal medicine Bklyn. Hosp. Ctr., 1993-94; resident in internal medicine Baylor Coll. Medicine, Houston, 1994-96, fellow in pulmonary/critical care medicine, 1996-99, asst. prof., 1999-2000; asst. prof. Houston VA Med. Ctr., 1999-2000. Fax: 713-794-7295. Home: 7200 Almeda Rd Apt 615 Houston TX 77054-2149 Office: Houston VA Med Ctr 2002 Holcombe Blvd # 111 Houston TX 77030-4211

BAALE, JOHN OLALERE, pharmacist; b. Osi, Kawara, Nigeria, Oct. 23, 1959; s. Samuel Alabi and Felicia Osegbongan Baale; m. Margaret Moradeke Famiwo, Apr. 27, 1985; children: Ifelere, Ifedamola. BPharm, Ahmadu Bello U., Zaria, Nigeria, 1981; MBA, U Lagos, Nigeria, 1984; PGDHE, U. Standrens, 1995. Group product mgr. Przer, Nigeria, 1989-90, mktg. mgr., 1990-96; dir. mktg. and strategic planning Pfizer, Nigeria, 1996-97, acting country mgr., 1997, dir. mktg. and sales, 1998; pharm. divsn. dir. Pfizer, Lagos, Nigeria, 1999—; cons. CMD, Lagos, 1991—, IES, Lagos, 1992—, Jedidah, Lagos, 1999—, Restral, Lagos, 1999—. Contbr. articles to profl. jours. Chmn. Pharm. Bus. Group, Nigeria, 1995—; exec. mem. PSN, Nigeria, 1994-95; exec. mem., Full Gospel Businessmen's Fellowship Internat., Nigeria, 1993—. Fellow NAPF, Pharm. Soc. Nigeria (Merit award 1997), Lagos C. of C. and Industry (dep. chmn. pharm. group 1996—), Ikoyi Club. Avocations: reading, traveling, writing, singing, golf. Office: Pfizer Regional Office, Afribank St PMB 80081, Victoria Island Nigeria

BAALES, MICHAEL, archaeologist; b. Gerolstein, Germany, Nov. 3, 1963; s. Peter and Annemarie (Annasenzl) B.; m. Sabine Kerstin Gayck, Oct. 25, 1996. Magister Artium, U. Cologne, Germany, 1990, D in Natural Scis., 1992. Rschr. Forschungsbereich Altsteinzeit Roman-Germanic Central Mus. Mainz, Neuwied-Monrepos, Germany, 1990—; excavation leader Ctr. Paleolithic Rsch. of Roman-Germanic Cen. Mus. Mainz, Neuwied-Monrepos, 1993—. Author: Ecology and Hunting-Economy of the Ahrensburgian Reindeer Hunters in the Uplands, 1996; contbr. articles to profl. publs. With German mil., 1982-83. Grantee Prince Max of Wied Found., 1990-92, Roman-Germanic Cen Mus Mainz, 1993, German Rsch. Coun., Bonn, 1994-00. Mem. German Soc. of Pre- and Protohistory, Friends of the Antiquity Soc. (Bonn). Roman Catholic. Office: Roman-Germanic Cen Mus, Schloss Monrepos, 56567 Neuwied-Monrepos Germany

BAALI, ABDALLAH, diplomat. Rep. to UN Govt. of Algeria, 1996—. Office: Permanent Mission Algeria to UN 326 E 48th St New York NY 10017-1747*

BAARS, FRANCISCUS JACOBUS, geologist; b. Vanderbijlpark, South Africa, Jan. 17, 1965; s. Willibrordus and Jannetje (den Bakker) B.; m. Lydia Maria Lobato, Apr. 30, 1993; 1 child, Laura. BSc, U. Cape Town, 1986, MSc, 1990, postgrad. Geologist De Beers-Sopemi, Brasilia, Brazil, 1990-93, Projeto Espinhaço, Belo Horizonte, Brazil, 1993; sr. rsch. geologist Docegeo-CVRD, Belo Horizonte, 1993-99; founder, CEO Roots Rock Ltd.; cons. in geology Mineral Resources Database Systems and Translation, 1999—. Mem. Am. Geophys. Union, Soc. Econ. Geologists, Brazilian Soc. for the Progress of Sci., South African Geol. Soc., Brazilian Geol. Soc., Brazilian Soc. Geochemistry, South African Bot. Soc., Planetary Soc., Internat. Assn. Gondwana Rsch. Office: Aven Afonso Pena 4343/402, Mangabeiras, 30130008 Belo Horizonte MG, Brazil

BAASAN, RAGCHAA, diplomat; b. Ulaanbaatar, Mongolia, Nov. 19, 1943; d. Tumer and Demberel (Tsendsuren) Ragchaa; m. Jamsran Gendendaram, Sept. 1967; children: Enhbat, Enhtsetseg, Enhtuvshin. Diploma, Moscow Inst. Fgn. Langs. Asst. officer Ministry of External Rels., Ulaanbaatar, 1967-69; diplomat Mongolian Embassy in India, New Delhi, 1969-74; attache Ministry of External Rels./Asian Dept., Ulaanbaatar, 1974-78, 2d sec., 1981-83; 2d sec. Mongolian Embassy, Kabul, Afghanistan, 1978-81, Embassy Mongolia, New Delhi, 1983-88; 1st sec., counsellor Ministry External Rels., Ulaanbaatar, 1988-97; 1st sec., polit. Embassy Mongolia, Washington, 1997—. Decorated Polar Star Order (Mongolia); recipient Honor of Svc. award Govt. of Mongolia, 1991/. Buddhist. Avocations: reading, analysing, knitting, cooking. E-mail: Baasan@aol.com. Home: XI Region SA Apt 26, Ulaanbaatar Mongolia Office: Embassy of Mongolia 2833 M St NW Washington DC 20007-3712

BABA, HISAMICHI, surgeon, health facility administrator; b. Kumamoto, Japan, Nov. 23, 1935; m. Junko Yosida Baba, Apr. 11, 1964; children: Yuko, Shoko, Masayuki. MD, Nagasaki (Japan) Sch. Medicine, 1962, PhD, 1968. Cert. cardiovascular surgeon. Clin. fellow Nagasaki U., 1967-70; cardiovascular surgeon Nagasaki Chuo Nat. Hosp., Japan, 1971-74; rsch. fellow Sinai Hosp., Detroit, 1974-75; chief surgeon Nagasaki Chuo Nat. Hosp., Japan, 1976-88; v.p. Nagasaki Chuo Nat. Hosp., 1989-96; hosp. dir. Saga Nat. Hosp., Japan, 1997—. Contbr. articles to profl. jours. Med. cooperator JICA, Kenya, East Africa, 1968-69; mem. rsch. com. Nat. Cir. Ctr., Osaka, Japan, 1993-94. Recipient Clin. Rsch. of Cong. Heart Disease award, 1990-92, Clin. Rsch. of Peripheral Cir., 1994-96, Clin. Rsch. of Transf. Medicine, 1987-97, Min. of Pub. Welfare. Mem. Japanese Assn. Thoracic Surgery, Japanese Assn. Transf. Medicine, Internat. Soc. Cardiovascular Surgery. Avocations: baseball, golf. Office: Saga Nat Hosp, 1-20-1 Hinode, Saga 849-0923, Japan

BABA, ISAMU, construction company executive; b. Oita, Japan, June 13, 1923; s. Gunroku and Kimiko Baba; m. Fumiko Takita, Nov. 3, 1948; children: Shiro, Kyoko Kojima. B in Engring., Osaka (Japan) U., 1945; PhD, Waseda U., Japan, 1990. Cert. architect, cons. engr., value specialist. Mgr. R & D Fujita Corp., Tokyo, 1965-75, dir., 1975-85, exec. v.p., 1985-90, sr. exec. v.p., 1990-94, exec. adviser, 1994—. Author: The Method of Value Engineering in the Construction Industry, 1975, Basics of Construction Value Engineering, 1983, Application of Construction Value Engineering, 1983, Illustration of the Method of Keeping Costs Down in the Construction Industry, 1984, The Study of Development and Application of Value Engineering For Construction Site Management, 1990, Terminos Practicos de Ingenieria Civil y Arquitectura, 1993. Chmn. bd. trustees Tottori Women's Coll., Japan, 1991—, exec. adviser, 1999—. Recipient Presdl. Citation Soc. Am. Value Engrs., 1981, Soc. award Associated Gen. Contractors of Japan, 1985, Presdl. Citation Archtl. Inst. Japan, 1992, 4th Order of Merit with the Rising Sun, 1998. Mem. Internat. Coun. Bldg. Rsch., Studies and Documentation, Soc. Japanese Value Engrs. (trustee, Best Paper prize 1973, Promotional Achievment award 1984, Presdl. Citation 1990), Soc. Korean Value Engrs. (adviser), Archtl. Inst. Japan, Japanese Value Engring. (Soc. award 1990), Soc. Japanese Value Specialis (pres.). Avocation: noh (Japanese classic art). Home: 2-29-21 Irima-cho, Chofu Tokyo 182, Japan Office: Fujita Corp, 4-6-15 Sendagaya, Shibuya-ku, Tokyo 151, Japan

BABA, JUNICHIRO, glass artist; b. Kanagawa, Yokohama, Japan, Feb. 19, 1964; s. Yuji and Emiko Baba. BFA, Dokkyo U., Saitama, Japan, 1987; postgrad., Tokyo Glas Art Inst., 1991; MFA, Rochester (N.Y.) Inst. Tech., 1996. Resident artist Creative Glass Ctr. of Am., Millville, N.J., 1996, Penland (N.C.) Sch. of Crafts, 1997-2000; instr. Takinami Glass Factory, Tokyo, 1993. Solo exhbns. include: "Glass and Textile," Tokyo, 1992, Blue Art Design, Tampa, Fla., 1999, Earville (N.Y.) Opera House, 1999, Gallery W.D.O., Charlotte, N.C., 2000, Apparatian Ctr. for Crafts, Smithville, Tenn., 2000; exhibited in group shows at Tokyo Glass Art Exhbn., 1990, GHG's Mill Gallery, Guilford, Conn., 1996, CAA's Gallery A., Cooperstown, N.Y., 1996, Gloucester County Coll., N.J., 1996, Tucson Mus. Art, 1997, Chappell Gallery, Boston, 1997, 99, Bevier Gallery, Rochester, 1998, Penland Gallery, 1998, 99, Wheaton Village, Millville, N.J., 1999, Navy Pier, Chgo., 1999, Gallery W.D.O., Charlotte, 1999, Heller Gallery, N.Y.C., 2000, Blue Spiral 1, Asheville, N.C., 2000; works in permanent collections at Creative Glass Ctr. of Am., Millville, N.J., Wallace Libr. at Rochester Inst. Tech., Anzen Co., Ltd., Aichi pref., Japan, Tokyo Glass Art Inst.; contbr. articles to profl. jours. Recipient Purchase Award prize Rochester Inst. Tech., 1996; Creative Glass Ctr. of Am. Artist's fellow, 1996; Rochester Inst. Tech. scholar, 1994, 95. Home: Minato-ku, 5-2-18-1111 Mita, Tokyo 108, Japan Office: 5-2-18-1111 Mita, Minato-ku, Tokyo 108, Japan

BABA, MARIETTA LYNN, business anthropologist; b. Flint, Mich., Nov. 9, 1949; d. David and Lillian (Joseph) Baba; m. David Smokler, Feb. 14, 1977 (div. 1982); 1 child, Alexia Nicole Baba Smokler. BA with highest distinction, Wayne State U., 1971, MA in Anthropology, 1973, PhD in Phys. Anthropology, 1975; MBA, Mich. State U., 1994. Asst. prof. sci. and tech. Wayne State U., Detroit, 1975-80, assoc. prof. anthropology, 1980-88, prof., 1988—, spl. asst. to pres., 1980-82, econ. devel. officer, 1982-83, asst. provost, 1983-85, assoc. provost, 1985-89, dir. internat. programs, interim assoc. dean Grad. Sch., 1988-89, assoc. dean Grad. Sch., 1989-90, acting chair dept. anthropology, 1990-92, chair dept. anthropology, 1996—; program dir. transformations to quality orgns., dir. social, behav., and econ. scis. NSF, 1994-96; founder, corp. officer Applied Rsch. Teams, Mich., Inc., Detroit, Intelligent Techs., Inc., Detroit; evolution rschr. Wayne State U., 1975-82; cons. GM Rsch. Labs., 1988-92, Electronic Data Sys., 1990-93, McKinsey Global Inst., 1991; rsch. contractor GM/EDS, 1990-94; lectr. nat. and internat. symposia, profl. confs. Adv. for editor orgnl. anthropology: American Anthropologist, 1990-93; issued letters patent for method to map joint ventures and maps produced thereby; contbr. numerous papers and abstracts to tech. jours.; patentee in field. Bd. dirs. City-Univ. Consortium, Detroit, 1980-83; v.p. Neighborhood Svc. Orgn., Detroit, 1980-85; mem. State Rsch. Fund Feasibility Rev. Panel, 1982-94; mem. adv. panel on tech. innovation and U.S. trade U.S. Congl. Office Tech. Assessment, 1990-91, mem. panel on electronic enterprise, 1993-94; active Leadership Detroit Class IV, 1982-83; dir. Mich. Tech. Coun. (S.E. divsn.), 1984-85. With USAF, SBIR, 1992-94. Job Partnership Tng. Act grantee, 1981-90, NSF grantee, 1982, 84-85, 99-01. Fellow Am. Anthrop. Assn. (bd. dirs. 1986-88, exec. com. 1986-88, del. to Internat. Union Anthrop. and Ethnol. Sci. 1990-94, chair global commn. anthropology 1993-98), Nat. Assn. Practice Anthropology (pres. 1986-88), Soc. Applied Anthropology, Phi Beta Kappa, Sigma Xi (Morton Fried award 1991), Beta Gamma Sigma. Office: Wayne State U 137 Manoogian Hall Detroit MI 48202

BABAEVA, ANNA GEORGIEVNA, cytologist, researcher; b. Tbilisi, Georgia, USSR, Apr. 15, 1929; d. Georgii Cristoforovich and Flora Vasil'evna (Salinova) B.; m. Evgenii Alexeevich Zotikov, Feb. 23, 1954; 1 child, Andrey Evgenievich. Student, The 2d Moscow State Med. Inst., 1947-53; cand. Med. Scis., U. Moscow, 1957, D in Med. Scis., 1971, prof. in Embryology, Histology, 1985. Postgrad. student Inst. Exptl. Biology, Moscow, 1953-56, rschr., 1956-64, sr. rschr., 1964-69; sr. rschr. Inst. Med. Genetics, Moscow, 1969-71; sr. rschr. Inst. Human Morphology, Moscow, 1971-79, head of lab., 1979—; mem. sci. coun. Moscow State U., 1977—. Author: (books) Immunological Mechanisms of the Reparative Processes Regulation, 1972 (Premium Moscow Soc. Naturalists 1975), Structure, Function and Adaptive Growth of the Salivary Glands, 1979 (Ministry of Higher Edn. prize 1980), Regeneration and the System of Immunogenesis, 1985, (Premium Moscow Soc. Naturalists 1987), Immunology of the Processes of the Adaptive Growth, Proliferation and Their Transgression, 1987. Recipient Discovery diploma USSR State Com. for Discovery, 1981, Russian Assn. for Discovery, 1996, 2000; stipend Russian Fund of Fundamental Investigations, 1994—. Mem. Moscow Soc. Naturalists, Marcus Singer Soc. Regeneration and Devel. Avocations: literature, art, history. Office: Inst Human Morphology, Tsurupa Str 3, 117418 Moscow Russia

BABAILOV, SERGUEY PAVLOVITCH, chemist; b. Pervomayskii, Chita, Russia, Apr. 8, 1960; s. Pavel Alexandrovitch Babailov and Nelli Ivanovna Bogatirova Anedchenko; m. Svetlana Alexandrovna Syutkina; 2 children: Vasilina, Anna. Diploma, Physico-Math. Sch., Novosibirsk, Russia, 1977, Novosibirsk State U., 1982. Rschr., probationer Inst. of Inorganic Chemistry, Novosibirsk, 1982-84, engr., 1984-85, jr. rsch. collaborator, 1985-91, rsch. assoc., 1991-92, sr. rsch. assoc., 1992—; chmn. Siberian Young Specialists Sch., Novosibirsk, 1990—; referee Jour. of Structural Chemistry, Novosibirsk, 1991-96, 98—. Contbr. articles to profl. jours. Grantee Internat. Sci. Found., 1992, 94; project awardee Russian Found. for Basic Rsch., 1994, 96, 98, 2000, project awardee Novosibirsk Regional Adminstrn., 1998. Avocations: collecting postage stamps, tourism, bicycling. Home: Russkaya 25-147, 630058 Novosibirsk Russia Office: Inst Inorganic Chemistry, SB RAS pr Lavrentyev 3, 630090 Novosibirsk Russia

BABAN, SERWAN MUHAMMAD JIHAD, geoscientist, educator; b. Kirkuk, Kurdistan, Iraq, Apr. 23, 1958; s. Muhammad Jihad and Dura (Salah Al Deen) B.; m. Judith Anne Beaumont, Jan. 1, 1964; children: Shereen, Zana. BSc, Univ. Baghdad, 1980, MSc, 1983; PhD, Univ. East Anglia, Norwich, U.K., 1991. Geophysicist, mgr. asst. Iraqi Nat. Oil Co., Baghdad, 1985-86; rsch. assoc. Univ. East Anglia, Norwich, 1991-92; lectr. in geography Coventry Univ., Coventry, U.K., 1992-93, sr. lectr. in geography, 1993-2000; prof. surveying & land info. U. West Indies, Trinidad, 2000—; cons. Environ. Agy., U.K., 1996-98; dir. CIS and Remote Sensing Rsch. Group, 1994—; lectr. Iraq, Morocco, Tunisia, Jordan, Malaysia. Contbr. numerous articles to profl. jours.; chpts. to books. Recipient rsch. grants, 1996-98. Fellow Royal Geographic Soc.; mem. British Remote Sensing Soc., Inst. Assn. of Hydrological Scis., British Geological Soc. Avocations: volleyball. Office: U West Indies, Dept Surveying & Land Info, Saint Augustine Trinidad, West Indies

BABANI, FATBARDHA, biophysics researcher; b. Tirana, Albania, May 19, 1951; d. Hasan and Vlona Durresi Lame; m. Frederik Babani; children: Jola, Ergin. Diploma in Physics, Tirana U., 1975, DS, 1986. Rschr. Faculty of Natural Scis., Tirana, Albania, 1975-77; rschr. Biol. Rsch. Inst., Tirana, Albania, 1978-86, scientific rschr., dept. biochemistry/biophysics, 1986—; lectr. physics and biophysics, Tirana U., 1984-97. Author: Biophysics, 1997; inventor in field. Grantee PNUD, France, 1989, DAAD, Germany, 1993, 97, DFG, Germany, 1998. Mem. Albanian Biochem. and Biophys. Soc. (v.p. 1995—), Balkan Bioscis. Assn. (mem. com. 1996—), Internat. Soc. Photosynthesis. Avocations: computers, lit. Home: Nikollatupe str, Tirana Albania Office: Biol Rsch Inst, Tirana Albania

BABANIN, ALEXANDER VLADIMIROVITCH, physical oceanographer, researcher; b. Zhdanov, Stalino, Soviet Union, Apr. 1, 1960; immigrated to Australia, 1996.; s. Vladimir Andreevitch and Vera Nikolaevna (Kamardina) B. Master, Moscow State Univ., Soviet Union, 1983; PhD, Marine Hydrophys. Inst., Soviet Union, 1990. Cert. physics, physical oceanography. Eng. MHI, Sebastopol, Soviet Union, 1983-85, jr. scientist, 1985-90, rsch. asst., 1990-94; sr. scientist Marine Hydrophys. Inst., Sebastopol, Ukraine, 1994-96; vis. fell. Univ. New South Wales, Sydney, Australia, 1996-97; rsch. asst. Defense Force Acad., Canberra, Australia, 1997—. Author numerous scientific papers in field. Recipient personal fellshp., Pres. Ukraine, 1994. Orthodox Christian. Avocations: world history, weight lifting. Office: Australian Defense Force Acad, Sch of Civil Engrg Northcott Dr, 2600 Canberra ACT, Australia

BABAO, DONNA MARIE, community health and psychiatric nurse, educator; b. St. Louis, May 6, 1945; d. Wilbert C. and Cecelia (Hogan) Bremer; widowed; 1 child, Tonya J. Diploma, Henry Ford Hosp. Sch. Nursing, Detroit, 1966; BSN, Calif. State U., Sacramento, 1978, MS in Nursing, 1990; MA in Edn., Calif. State U., Chico, 1985. Cert. pub. health nurse; master tchr. cert.; cert. clin. use of interactive guided imagery. Staff nurse U. Calif. Med. Ctr., San Francisco, 1968-72; staff and charge CCU nurse Children's Hosp. of San Francisco, 1972-78; pub. health nurse Sutter-Yuba Health Dept., Yuba City, Calif., 1979-81; prof. nursing Yuba Coll., Marysville, Calif., 1981—; psychiat. charge nurse Sunridge Hosp., Yuba City, 1994-96; mem. exam. item writing panel NCLEX-RN, 1998. Writer health column, 1986-90; chpt. to textbooks; reviewer nursing textbooks and jour. articles; contbr. articles to profl. jours. 1st lt. Nurse Corps, U.S. Army, 1966-68. Mem. Nat. League Nursing, Calif. Tchrs. Assn., Vietnam Vets. Am., Am. Holistic Nurses Assn. Office: Yuba Coll Dept Nursing 2088 N Beale Rd Marysville CA 95901-7605

BABAYEVSKY, PETER GORDEEVICH, educational administrator; b. Erkin-Yurt, USSR, Oct. 2, 1939; s. Gordei Petrovich and Anastasia Grigorievna (Grudieva) B.; m. Nataliya Yakovlevna Livshina, Dec. 31, 1962; children: Irina, Pavel. Engr., Inst. Tech., Moscow, 1962; Candidate Sci., Mendeleev Inst., Moscow, 1968; DSc, Lomonosov Inst. Chem. Tech., Moscow, 1984. Plant engr. Light Equipment Plant, Likhoslavl, Russia, 1962-63; rsch. engr. Russian State U. Tech., Moscow, 1963-67, asst. prof., 1967-71, assoc. prof., 1971-84, prof., 1984-87, head dept., 1987—, vice rector, 1992—, hon. prof., 1999; dep. chmn. sci. coun. Ministry Sci. and Engring., Moscow, 1986-91; head dept. continuing edn. Ministry Aircraft Industry, Moscow, 1983-91; dep. chmn. Coun. Higher Edn., Ministry Edn., Moscow, 1992—; v.p. RAS, Moscow, 1991—; cons. RSc Energia, Korolev, Russia, 1986—; vis. rschr. MIT/Princeton U., 1971-72; prof. Tsiolkovsky Inst. Aviation, Moscow, 1986. Author, editor: Polymer Materials, 1980 (Premium of Ministry Higher Edn. 1980); author: Toughness of Polymer Composites, 1991; patentee in field. Grantee Intas, Eu, Brussels, 1994-96; recipient state medal Pres of Russian Fedn., 1997. Mem. Russian Acad. Spacemanship, N.Y. Acad. Avocations: books, travel, garden activities. Home: 46 Apt 3 Dostoevskogo St, 103030 Moscow Russia Office: Russian State U, 3 Orshanskaya St, 121552 Moscow Russia

BABB, GLENN ROBIN WARE, South African diplomat; b. Johannesburg, South Africa, June 4, 1943; s. Eric Ware and Ora Constance (Loverock) B.; m. Brenda Anne Bedborough; 3 children. BA, Stellenbosch U., South Africa, 1964; MA, Oxford (Eng.) U., 1966; LLB, U. South Africa, Pretoria, 1971. Adv. Supreme Ct. South Africa. 2d sec. South African Embassy, Paris, 1969-72, counsellor, 1975-78; counsellor South African Embassy, Rome, 1978-80; tng. dir. Dept. Fgn. Affairs, Pretoria, 1972-75, dir. Africa div., 1980-85; amb. to Can., Ottawa, Ont., 1985-87; dep. dir.-gen. Dept. Fgn. Affairs, Pretoria, 1987-89; amb. to Italy, Rome, 1991-95; amb. to Albania, 1992-95, high commr. to Malta,, 1993-95, amb. to Republic of San Marino,, 1994-95; M.P., Parliament of South Africa, Cape Town, 1989-91; permanent rep. FAO, 1993-95; chmn. Agip Lubricants (Pty) Ltd., 1995-98; bd. dirs. VELO Pty Ltd. Author: Training for the Foreign Service, 1984; contbr. articles and book criticism to mags. and newspapers. Chmn. Felix Trust, Johannesburg, 1990—; trustee John Locke Trust, Johannesburg, 1991—, Arthur Child Army Award Trust, Pretoria, 1991—; adminstr. Testaccio Non-Cath. Cemetery, Rome, 1992-95; bd. dirs. Cape Town Philarm. Orchestra, 1997-2000; mem. com. Kalk Bay and St. James Residents' Assn., 1998-2000—; hon. consul-gen. Turkey for Western, No. and Ea. Cape, 1998—. Decorated chevalier Order of Merit (Italy), chevalier Order of St. Agatha (San Marino); recipient Pericles prize, 1995, Brianza prize, 1995. Mem. Burckardt Inst. (hon.), Italian C. of C. for So. Africa (hon.), Italo-South African C. of C. (hon. pres. 1991-95, dep. chmn. 1999—), Kalk Bay and St. James Bus. Assn. (chmn. 1999). Avocations: collecting maps, windsurfing. Home and Office: 16 St James Rd, St James Cape Town 7945, South Africa

BABBEL, DAVID FREDERICK, finance and insurance educator; b. Salt Lake City, Apr. 12, 1949; s. Frederick William and June (Andrew) B.; m. Mary Jane Benson, Aug. 27, 1975; children: Tara Nicole, Elise Kiera, Karisa Rose, Tyson Frederick. BA, Brigham Young U., 1973; MBA, U. Fla., 1975, PhD, 1978; MA (hon.), U. Pa., 1986. Prof. of fin. U. Calif., Berkeley, 1978-85; prof. fin. and ins. U. Pa. Wharton Sch., Phila., 1985—; v.p. Goldman, Sachs & Co., N.Y.C., 1987; pres. A/L Tech. Bryn Mawr, Pa.; cons. IBM, Morgan Guaranty, MMC, World Bank, Bell Atlantic, Morrison-Knudson, Goldman Sachs, Aetna, G.E. Capital, Met Life, 1978—. Author 6 books on fin. and ins.; contbr. 85 articles to profl. jours. Fulbright fellow, 1976-77. Republican. Mormon. Office: Wharton Sch U Pa 303 Colonial Penn Ctr Philadelphia PA 19104

BABBITT, BRUCE EDWARD, federal official; b. June 27, 1938; m. Hattie Coons; children—Christopher, T.J. BS magna cum laude, U. Notre Dame; MS, U. Newcastle, Eng., 1962; LL.B., Harvard U., 1965. Bar: Ariz. 1965. Assoc. Brown and Bain, Phoenix, 1965-74; atty. gen. State of Ariz., Phoenix, 1975-78; gov. State of Ariz., 1978-87; ptnr. Steptoe & Johnson, Phoenix; sec. U.S. Dept. Interior, Washington, 1993—; mem. President's Commn. on Accident at Three Mile Island, 1979-80; chmn. Nuclear Safety Oversight Com., 1980-81, Western Govs.' Policy Office, 1982; mem. Adv. Commn. on

Intergovtl. Relations, 1980-84; chmn. task force on fed. budget deficit Roosevelt Ctr. for Am. Policy Studies, 1984; chmn. Nat. Groundwater Policy Forum, 1984—. Author: Color and Light: The Southwest Canvases of Louis Akin, 1973, Grand Canyon: An Anthology, 1978. Trustee Dougherty Found.; candidate for Dem. Party nomination for Pres. of U.S. Recipient Thomas Jefferson award Nat. Wildlife Fedn., 1981, spl. conservation award Nat. Wildlife Fedn., 1983. Mem. Nat. Govs. Assn. (chmn. subcom. on water resources), Democratic Govs. Assn. (chmn. 1985). Democrat. Office: US Dept Interior Office of Secretary 1849 C St NW Washington DC 20240-0001

BABBITT, MILTON BYRON, composer; b. Phila., May 10, 1916; s. Albert E. and Sara (Potamkin) B.; m. Sylvia Miller, Dec. 27, 1939; 1 dau., Betty Ann. AB, NYU, 1935; MFA, Princeton U., 1942; MusD, Middlebury Coll., 1968, NYU, 1968, Swarthmore Coll., 1969, New Eng. Conservatory, 1972, U. Glasgow, 1980; DFA (hon.), Northwestern U., 1988; DHL, Brandeis U., 1991; MusD, Princeton U., 1991, PhD, 1992; MusD, U. Rochester, 1997. Music faculty Princeton U., 1938-84, math. faculty, 1943-45, bicentennial preceptor, 1953-56, William Shubael Conant prof. music, 1966-84, prof. emeritus, 1984—; faculty Salzburg Seminar in Am. Studies, 1952, Princeton Seminar in Advanced Musical Studies; dir. Columbia-Princeton Electronic Music Center; composition faculty Juilliard Sch.; faculty Internationale Ferienkurse, Darmstadt, 1964; Fromm Found. vis. prof. Harvard U., 1988. Author: The Function of Set Structure in the Twelve Tone System, 1946, Words About Music, 1987, also articles in mus. jours.; composer: Music for the Mass, 1940, String Trio, 1941, Three Compositions for Piano, 1947, Composition for Four Instruments, 1948, Composition for Twelve Instruments, 1948, Composition for Viola and Piano, 1950, Woodwind Quartet, 1953, String Quartet No. 2, 1954, All Set, 1957, Composition for Synthesizer, 1961, Vision and Prayer, 1961, Ensembles, 1964, Philomel, 1964, Relata I, 1965, Relata II, 1968, String Quartets 3 & 4, 1970-71, Occasional Variations, 1971, Tableaux, 1972, Arie da Capo, 1973, Reflections, 1975, Concerti, 1976, Solo Requiem, 1977, Images, 1979, Paraphrases, 1979, Dual, 1980, Ars Combinatoria, 1981, The Head of the Bed, 1981, String Quartet No. 5, 1982, Melismata, 1982, Canonical Form, 1983, Piano Concerto, 1986, Transfigured Notes, 1986, The Joy of More Sextets, 1986, Whirled Series, 1987, Beaten Paths, 1988, Glosses, 1988, Consortini, 1989, Emblems, 1989, Soli e Duettini, 1989, Play It Again, Sam, 1989, Envoi, 1990, Preludes, Interludes and Postlude, 1991, Septet, But Equal, 1992, Counterparts, 1992, String Quartet No. 6, 1993, Piano Quartet, 1995, Clarinet Quintet, 1996, Piaqno Concerto No. 2, 1998. Recipient Joseph A. Bearns prize, 1942, N.Y. Music Critic's citation, 1949, 64, Nat. Inst. Arts and Letters award, 1959, gold medal Brandeis U., 1970, Pulitzer Prize citation, 1982, George Peabody medal, 1983, Madison medal 1986, Gov.'s Achievement award 1987, Music award Miss. Inst. Arts and Letters, 1988, gold medal in music Am. Inst. Arts and Letters, 1988, award Schoenburg Inst., 1988, William Schuman award, 1992, Musical Am.'s Composer of Yr., 1996; John Simon Guggenheim fellow, 1960-61, MacArthur fellow, 1986—; named to Am. Classical Music Hall of Fame, 1999. Mem. Internat. Soc. Contemporary Music (pres. 1951-52, del. 1952 Festival), League of Composers, AAAL (Gold medal), Am. Acad. Arts and Scis., Am. Inst. Physics, Arnold Schoenberg Inst. (hon.), Phi Beta Kappa. Home: 222 Western Way Princeton NJ 08540-5306

BABCOCK, CATHERINE EVANS, artist, educator; b. Rydal, Pa., Feb. 23, 1924; d. William Wayne and Marion (Watters) Babcock; m. Douglas Paul Torre, May 28, 1977; 2 stepchildren. Diploma, Sarah Lawrence Coll., 1942; BFA, Temple U., 1944, MFA, 1948. Tchr. Rudolf Steiner Sch., 1949; tchr. jr. high sch. Stratford, Conn., 1959-63; tchr. elem. art Locust Valley Primary and Elem. Sch., 1963-68; instr. Darien Cmty. Ctr., 1975-81; art tchr. Rowayton (Conn.) Arts Ctr., 1979—, also bd. mem.; rec. sec. Portrait painter; artist to Sea Svcs. (USCG and USN); equestrian artist Fairfield Hunt Club Show's Benefit Horse Show, 1993; watercolor tchr. Darien Cmty. Assn., 1993-94. Illustrator: Atheneum, 1968 (libr. award), Cutaneous Cryosurgery (Douglas Torre), 1978, rev., 1979; translator: Undertown (Finn Havrevold), 1968; painter, mural for Babcock Surg. Wards, Temple U. Hosp., Phila., 1944; designer display Cryosurgery of Skin Cancer, Dalls, 1979 (Gold award); author: Biography in American References, 1989, (poem) Vikings Habitat, The National Library of Poetry, River of Dreams, 1994, Poetic Voices of America, 1995, Best Pastels, 1996, Chips and Chirps of Verses, 1998; exhbns. include internat. miniature shows Fine Arts Club, Washington, 1984, New Canaan Soc. for the Arts, 1988, 93, Grand Nat. Salmagundi Club, St. Petersburg Mus., Fla., Degas Pastel Soc., New Orleans, 1990-95, Mus. of Art, New Orleans, 1990; participant various art shows, also permanent collctions USN, dept. dermatology N.Y. Hosp., 1997, UN, 1997; exhibited at N.Y. State Univ. Club, 2000; painting accepted for COGAP 2000 Art (Coast Guard). Recipient awards including 10 USCG awards, Am. Acad. Dermatology Art Shows, 2 award Rowayton Arts Ctr., 1993-94, Best Poems award Nat. Libr. Poetry, 1996, Amherst Soc. award, Sparrowgrass Soc. award, cert. appreciation USCG, 1971-82, Naval Sta. of N.Y., 1981, 1st prize Rowayton Art Ctr., 2000; named to Alexander Hamilton U.S. Custom Ho., 2000. Mem. Internat. Soc. Poets (lifetime, Merit award 1997, medal 1997), Met. Portrait Inst., Conn. Pastel Soc., Pastel Soc. Am. (cert. of merit), USCG Art Program (ofcl. artist), COGAP artist, 1999. Congregationalist. Home and Office: 122 Rowayton Ave Norwalk CT 06853-1409

BABEL, DIETRICH, chemistry educator; b. Bonn, Germany, July 28, 1930. Diploma in chemistry, U. Tûebingen, 1958, Dr. of Natural Scis., 1961, habilitation, 1962-68; postdoctoral, Tech. U., Munich, 1961-62. Head inorganic structural chemistry dept. U. Tûebingen, 1969-71; prof. chemistry Fachbereich Chemie, U. Marburg, 1971—, dean, 1977-78, 86-87. Contbr. numerous articles to profl. jours., 1959—. Mem. Gesellschaft Deutscher Chemiker. Office: Fachbereich Chemie Philipps U, Hans-Meerwein-Strasse, 35043 Marburg Germany

BABER, WILBUR H., JR., lawyer; b. Shelby, N.C., Dec. 18, 1926; s. Wilbur H. and Martha Corinne (Allen) B.; BA, Emory U., 1949; postgrad. U. N.C., 1949-50, U. Houston, 1951-52; JD, Loyola U., New Orleans, 1965. Bar: La. 1965, Tex. 1966. Sole practice, Hallettsville, Tex., 1966—. Trustee Raymond Dickson Found. Served with U.S. Army. Mem. ABA, ASCE, La. Bar Assn., Tex. Bar Assn., La. Engring. Soc., Tex. Surveyors Assn. Methodist. Lodge: Rotary. Office: PO Box 294 Hallettsville TX 77964-0294

BABICH, ALEXANDER, metallurgy researcher, educator, consultant; b. Donetsk, Ukraine, Nov. 12, 1952; s. Ilya and Rebecca (Pinnes) B.; m. Eugenia Goldstein, Nov. 25, 1975; 1 child Yuri. Student Metallurgy Engring., Polytech. Inst., Donetsk, Ukraine, 1974, PhD in Tech., 1984. Cert. in Metallurgy. Furnace worker Steel Plant, Donetsk, Ukraine, 1974-75, foreman, 1975-76; engr. Polytech. Inst., Donetsk, Ukraine, 1976-83, rsch. worker, 1983-85, assoc. prof., 1985-96; rschr. Nat. Ctr. Metallurg. Investigations, Madrid, Spain, 1997-98; rsch. worker Aachen U. Tech. Inst. Ferrous Metallurgy, 1998—; leader of R&D projects, 1987-96, sec. methodical commn. for tng. of metallurg. students, 1988-93, mem. selection com. for univ. entrants, leading of postgrads., 1990-95, Donetsk (Ukraine) State U. Tech.; cons. of steel corp. C&I Planos, Gijon, Spain, 1996. Author: Intensifying Pulverized Coal Use in Blast Furnace Operation, 1993; patentee: Verfahren zur Erhöhung des Verbrennungsgrades und der Verbrennungsgeschwindigkeit von Einblaskohlen, 1992; contbr. some 100 publs. in field; patentee in field. Grant: Min. Edn. and Sci., Spain, 1995. Avocations: photography, travel. Fax: (49-241) 88 88 368. E-mail: babich@iechk.rwth-aachen.de. Home: Hauptstr 78 Whg 13, 52060 Aachen Germany Office: Inst für Eisenhüttenkunde, RWTH, D-52056 Aachen Germany

BABIDGE, MARK HANSFORD, investment company executive, consultant; b. Adelaide, Australia, Feb. 27, 1947; s. Jack Hansford and Emmilene Hélène (Macick) B.; m. Merilyn Joy Longmore, Dec. 29, 1970; children: Kate Hélène, Sally Marie. R.D. Agr., Agrl. Coll. Roseworthy, Australia, 1967, R.D. Oenology, 1969; grad. diploma in bus. adminstrn., South Australian Inst. Tech., Adelaide, 1973. Dir. Castlemaine Tooheys Group Devel., Sydney, Australia, 1978-82; gen. mgr. Allied Vintners, Melbourne, Australia, 1982-85; exec. acquisition and investment Bond Corp., (Global), 1985-88; chmn. Compania de Telefonos de Chile S.A., Santiago, 1988-90; CEO's rep. Western Australia, gen. mgr. Telecom, Perth, Australia, 1991-94; dir. Minyango Resources NL, Perth, Australia, 1996-97; mng. dir. Sumich Group, Perth, Australia, 1997-98; prin. MMKS Pty. Ltd., 1985—; mng. dir. Oberon Perth, Jilin, China, 1994; gen. mgr. Robowash, Perth, 1985; winemaker, Coonawarra Cabernet Sauvignon, 1972 (Bristol Internat. Wine Show Double Gold seal, worldwide category, 1978); dir. Southern Wine Corp., 1998—, Stoneham Estate, 1999—, Sumich Group, 1997-98. Bd. mem. Commonwealth Colls. Advanced Edn., Canberra, Australia, 1969-75; coun. mem. Australian Wine and Brandy Prodr.'s Assn., Adelaide, 1978-85; coun. mem. Australian Olympic Fundraising Com., Perth, 1990-94; mem. Oz Concert Com. Ethnic & Arts, Perth, 1991-94. Recipient alumni award Stanford (Calif.) U., 1983, Australian Writers and Art Dirs. award, Sydney, 1982; fellow Australian Inst. Mgmt., 1992—. Fellow Australian Inst. Mgmt.; mem. Am. Soc. Enology and Viticulture (profl.), Australian Soc. Oenology and Viticulture (founder, pres. 1980-85), Rolls-Royce Owners' Club Australia (historian, various coms., 1983—), Sir Henry Royce Found. (Western Australia del. 1996—). Church of England. Avocations: vintage Rolls-Royce cars, wine. Office: 802 Canning Hyw, Applecross WA 6153, Australia

BABILAS, WOLFGANG JOHANNES, romance language educator; b. Ratibor, Silesia, Germany, Sept. 19, 1929; s. Franz and Else (Prox) B.; m. Lydia Antonia Hiller, Aug. 19, 1960. PhD in Romance Langs., U. Münster, Germany, 1957. Sci. asst. U. Münster, 1957-66, privat docent, 1965-66, assoc. prof., 1966-71, prof., chmn. romance philology, 1971-94, prof. emeritus, 1994—; head dept. Romance and Slavic Philology, U. Münster, 1970-71, 80-81, dir. Inst. of Romance Philology, 1971-94/. Author: (books) Das Frankreichbild in P. Claudels Personnalité de la France, 1958, Tradition und Interpretation, 1961, Die Sermoni Subalpini, 1968; editor: Heinrich Lausberg Zum Gedenken, 1995; contbr. articles tor profl. jours.; website author Louis Aragon Online (www.uni-muenster.de/Romanistils/Aragon). Decorated Officer in Order of Palmes Académiques, Govt. of France, 1994. Avocation: photography. E-mail: babiles@uni-muenster.de. Office: Romanisches Seminar der WWU, Bispinghof 3A, D48143 Münster Germany

BABITSKY, VLADIMIR ILYICH, mechanical engineering researcher, consultant, educator; b. Gomel, USSR, Apr. 4, 1938; s. Ilya and Maria (Graus) B.; m. Eleonora Lublina, June 14, 1968; 1 child, Ilya. Diploma with distinction in Mech. Engr., Moscow U. of Tech., 1960; PhD in Theory of Machines & Mechanisms, USSR Acad. of Scis., 1964, DSc in Machine Dynamics, 1972. Engr. Inst. Machine Studies, USSR Acad. Scis., Moscow, 1960-61, rsch. assoc., 1961-67, sr. rsch. assoc., 1967-87, originator and head lab., 1987-91; cons. in industry Munich, Germany, 1992—; prof. Loughborough (Eng.) U., 1995—; guest prof. Inst. B. of Mechanics, Munich Tech. U., 1990; supervisor undergrad., grad. and PhD students, 1964-91; prof. Moscow Tech. U., 1989-91. Author: Theory of Vibro-Impact Systems, 1978, (with V.L. Krupenin) Oscillations in Strongly Nonlinear Systems, 1985, Theory of Vibro-Impact Systems and Applications, 1998, (with V.K. Astashev and M.Z. Kolovsky) Dynamics and Control of Machines, 2000; reviewer Mech. Revs., Mechanics of Solids, Machine Science, Machine Manufacture and Reliability, Jour. Sound and Vibration; co-editor Springer series Foundations of Engineering Mechanics; ; contbr. articles to handbooks and profl. jours.; patentee in field. Mem. IFAC, EUROMECH. Office: Dept Mech Engring, Loughborough U, Loughborough Leicestershire LE11 3TU, England

BABITZKE, THERESA ANGELINE, health facility administrator; b. Madison, Ill., Dec. 19, 1925; d. Victor Joseph and Angela (Ziolkowski) Sobolewski; m. Douglas Christ Babitzke, May 2, 1953; children: Charlotte, Mary Ann, Rose Marie, Helen. Student, Quincy Coll., 1943; diploma, St. John's Sch. Nursing Edn., Springfield, Ill., 1949; student, U. Ill., Chgo., 1970; BA, St. Francis Coll., 1973; MA in Geronology summa cum laude, Sangamon State U., 1982. Co-founder, admin. dir. Mayslake Village, Oakbrook, Ill., 1962, St. Paschal's Infirmary, Oakbrook, 1962; night supr. Godair Home, Hinsdale, Ill., 1958-72; DON King Bruwaert House, Hinsdale, 1973-76; head nurse Mt. Sinai Hosp., Chgo., 1976-82; DON Rosary Hill Home, Justice, Ill., 1989—. Election judge Rep. Com. DuPage County, 1953-98; mem. adv. bd. Gower Grade Sch., 1973-76; mem. adv. com. Burr Ridge Marriot Brighton Gardens Assisted Living, 1996—. Named Ill. Nurse of Yr. of the Midwest, 1981, Catholic Woman of Yr. 1962, St. Mary's Ch., Joliet, Ill. Mem. Downers Grove and Suburban Nurses Club (pres. Downers Grove chpt.), U. of Ill. Gerontology, Forty and Eight, Premier Nurse Ill., Am. Legion Aux., Sigma Phi Omega (Eta chpt. U. Ill.). Roman Catholic. Avocations: travel, bicycling, doll collecting, reading.

BABORSKI, ANDRZEJ JOZEF, economist; b. Piekary, Poland, Mar. 14, 1936; s. Otomar and Krystyna (Wodzinowska) Baborski; m. Bozena Baborska; two children. MSc, Tech. U. Wroclaw, 1959, PhD, 1970, DSc, 1980. Asst. Tech. U. Wroclaw, Poland, 1960-70; asst. prof. Econ. U. Wroclaw, 1970-80, assoc. prof., 1980-89; vis. prof. Calif. State U., Northridge, 1985-86; prof., rector Econ. U., 1990-99. Author: Elements of Economics Cybernetics, 1977, 2d edit., 1983; author, editor: Effective Management and AI, 1991. E-mail: baborski@manager.ac.wroc.pl. Home: Pilnikarska 32, 53-206 Wrocław Poland

BABOURINA, OLGA, biologist, researcher; b. Baku, Azerbaijan, Russia, Sept. 24, 1959; d. Kouzma Babourin and Lioudmila Nikolenko; m. Konstantin Voltchanskii, Aug. 12, 1991; 1 child, Tanya. PhD, Acad. Sci. USSR, Moscow, 1990. Rsch. scientist Inst. Plant Physiology, Moscow, 1982-94; exptl. scientist CSIRO, Adelaide, Australia, 1995-96; sr. rsch. assoc. U. Tasmania, Hobart, Australia, 1997—. Contbr. articles to profl. jours. Office: U Tasmania Sch Math & Phy, GPO Box 252 21, Hobart TAS 7001, Australia

BABSON, IRVING K., publishing company executive; b. Tel Aviv, Apr. 15, 1936; came to U.S., 1940; s. Matthew and Miriam B.; m. Laurie Sher; children: Stacey B., Mia L., Christopher. BBA, CCNY, 1957; postgrad. NATO seminars, Harvard U., 1965. Dir. Tribune/Fox Cos., 1987-90; chmn. BMT Publs., Inc., Tulsa, 1989-91, Convenience Store News, U.S. Distbn. Jour., Gaming Bus. Mag., Smokeshop Mag., N.Y.C., Jour. Petroleum Mktg., N.Y.C.; mng. ptnr. Babson Capital Ventures, J.V., 1995—, Holdsworth Investments Inc., Belize, 1995—; ptnr. Mag. Devel. Fund, Babson Family Investment, J.V., N.Y.C., Babson Capital, 1988. With AUS, 1956-57. Mem. Nat. Assn. Corp. Dirs. Club: Friars. Home: 19707 Turnberry Way Aventura FL 33180-2566

BABUŠ, VLADIMIR, epidemiologist, educator; b. Mali Raven, Croatia, June 24, 1932; s. Marko and Marija (Busija) B.; m. Branka Markušić, Dec. 8, 1961. MD, U. Zagreb, Croatia, 1962; DPH, A. Stampar Sch. Pub. Health, Zagreb, 1971; MS, U. Zagreb, 1975, DSc, 1983. Gen. practitioner Health Sta., Orehovec, Croatia, 1962-65; chief preventive svcs. Health Ctr., Ivanić-Grad, 1965-69; epidemiologist Inst. Pub. Health Croatia, Zagreb, 1969-79; lectr. Med. Sch., U. Zagreb, 1979-93, asst. prof., 1993—. Editor: (book) Epidemiology, 1987, 3d edit., 1997; contbr. articles to profl. jours. Home: Kraljevec 16, 10000 Zagreb Croatia Office: A Stampar Sch Pub Health, Rockefellerova 4, 10000 Zagreb Croatia

BACALL, LAUREN, actress; b. N.Y.C., Sept. 16, 1924; m. Humphrey Bogart, May 21, 1945 (dec. 1957); children: Stephen, Leslie; m. Jason Robards, July, 1961 (div.); 1 son, Sam. Student pub. schs., Am. Acad. Dramatic Art. Actress in Broadway plays Franklin Street, 1942, Goodbye Charlie, 1959; motion picture actress, 1944—, film appearances include To Have and Have Not, 1945, Confidential Agent, 1945, The Big Sleep, 1946, Dark Passage, 1947, Key Largo, 1948, Young Man With a Horn, 1949, Bright Leaf, 1950, How To Marry a Millionaire, 1953, Woman's World, 1954, The Cobweb, 1955, Blood Alley, 1955, Written on the Wind, 1956, Designing Woman, 1957, The Gift of Love, 1958, Flame Over India, 1959, Shock Treatment, 1964, Sex and the Single Girl, 1965, Harper, 1966, Murder on the Orient Express, 1974, The Shootist, 1976, Health, 1980, The Fan, 1981, Tree of Hands, 1987, Appointment With Death, 1987, Mr. North, 1988, Misery, 1990, A Star for Two, 1991, All I Want for Christmas, 1991, Ready to Wear (Prêt-à-Porter), 1994, My Fellow Americans, 1996, The Mirror Has Two Faces, 1996, The Line King: Al Hirschfield, 1996, Le Jour et la Nuit, 1997, Diamonds, 1999; appeared in Broadway play Cactus Flower, 1966-68, Applause, 1969-71 (Sarah Siddons award 1975); also road co., 1971-72, London co., 1972-73 (Tony award for best actress in a musical 1970); Broadway play Woman of the Year, 1981 (Tony award for best actress in a musical 1981, Sarah Siddons award 1983), Sweet Bird of Youth, 1983 (London, 1985, Australia, 1986, L.A., 1987); TV spl. The Paris Collections, 1968, Applause, 1973, A Commercial Break (Happy Endings), 1975; TV movies: Perfect Gentlemen, 1978, Dinner at Eight, 1989, The Portrait, 1992, A Foreign Field, 1993, From the Mixed Up Files of Mrs. Basil E. Frankweiler, 1995; author: Lauren Bacall By Myself, 1978, Lauren Bacall Now, 1994. Recipient Am. Acad. Dramatic Arts award for achievement, 1963, Standard award London Evening, 1973, Nat. Book award, 1979; decorated comdr. Order of Arts and Letters (France), 1995. Office: care Johnnie Planco William Morris Agy 1325 Avenue Of The Americas New York NY 10019-6026

BACANLI, HASAN, educational psychologist; b. Denizli, Turkey, Apr. 8, 1961; s. Salih and Ayse (Duzsoz) B.; m. Feride Erdogan, Oct. 11, 1986; 1 child, Salih Safa. BA, Ankara U., Turkey, 1982, MA, 1984, PhD, 1990. Psychol. counselor Guidance & Rsch. Ctr., Mardin, Turkey, 1985-86; rsch. asst. Selcuk U., Konya, Turkey, 1986-92; asst. prof. Gazi U., Ankara, Turkey, 1992-96, assoc. prof., 1996—; vice head dept. edn. Gazi U., 1992-96. Author: Self in Social Interactions, 1997, Educational Psychology, 1999, Social Skills Training, 1999, Affective Education, 1999; contbr. articles to profl. jours. Vis. scholar Ohio State U., Columbus, 1994. Mem. APA, Turkish Psychologists Assn., Turkish Psychol. Counseling & Guidance Assn., Internat. Coun. Psychologists, Internat. Assn. Cross-Cultural Psychology, Asian Assn. Social Psychology, Internat. Assn. Applied Psychology. Avocation: culture and self. Home: Senlik Mah Gurkan, Sok Nr 56/4, 06310 Ankara Turkey Office: G U Gazi Faculty Edn, 06500 Ankara Turkey

BACCHUS, ROBBY AHMAD, metabolic physician. MB, Nat. U., Ireland, 1963; PhD, London U., 1972. Dir. pathology and lab. svcs. Armed Forces Hosp. Ministry Def. and Aviation, Saudi Arabia, 1980-94; dir. WHO Regional Collaborating Ctr. External Quality Assessment, 1980-94; regional advisor posgrad. edn. in pathology Royal Coll. Pathologists, Saudi Arabia, 1985-94; overseas advisor postgrad. edn. in pathology Royal Coll. Pathologists, 1994—; chmn.-secretariat for pathology in developing countries World Assn. Pathology and Lab. Medicine, 1997—. Fellow Royal Coll. Pathologists, Royal Coll. Physicians Ireland, Royal Soc. Medicine; mem. Brit. Med. Assn., Assn. Clin. Biochemists, Savage Club. Islam. Avocations: gardening, theater, music, opera, foreign travel. Office: 2 Carlton House Terr, London SW1Y 5AF, England

BACH, CHRISTIAN FRIIS, economics educator; b. Copenhagen, Apr. 29, 1966; s. Erik and Ellen Birgitte (Nielsen) B.; m. Karin Ursula Dahlerup, Mar. 2, 1991; children: Anna Cecilie, Sofie Louise, Asker. MSc in Agronomy, Royal Danish Agrl. U., 1992, PhD in Internat. Econs., 1996. Spl. assignment The World Bank, Washington, 1995; researcher Danish Inst. Agrl. and Fisheries Econs., Copenhagen, 1996; asst. prof. Inst. Econs. U. Copenhagen, 1996-2000; assoc. prof. econs. Royal Danish Agrl. U., Frederiksberg, 2000—; cons. Australian Dept. Arts, Sports, Environment and Territories, 1993, Danish Fgn. Affairs Ministry, 1994, Internat. Trade Divsn. of World Bank, 1996-97; instr. global trade analysis project Purdue U., West Lafayette, Ind., 1996-97; chmn. Danish Assn. for Internat. Cooperation, 1997. Contbr. articles to profl. jours. Office: Royal Danish Agrl U, Rolighedsveg 23, DK-1958 Frederiksberg C, Denmark

BACH, CHRISTIAN MICHAEL, orthopedic surgeon; b. Vienna, Austria, Dec. 18, 1968; s. Wolfgang and Dagmar Bach. MD, U. Vienna, 1994, diploma sports medicine, 1998; diploma chirotherapy, 2000. Surgeon Krankenhaus Barmherzige Schwestern, Vienna, 1995-96; traumatologist Unfallkrankenhaus Meidling, Vienna, 1996; neurologist Rehabilitationszentrum Weisser Hof, Vienna, 1996; internal medicine physician KH Eggenburg, 1997; orthopedic surgeon U. Innsbruck, Austria, 1997—; cons. Erasmus U., Rotterdam, The Netherlands, 1993, Semmelweis U., Budapest, Hungary, 1994; sports medicine physician Judo Orgn., Austria, 1995—; mem. Dept. Orthopedics. Contbr. articles to profl. jours. Mem. Austrian Soc. for Orthopedics, Orthopedic Surgery. Roman Catholic. Avocations: mountain biking, squash, power training. Office: U Innsbruck Dept Ortho Surg, Anichstr 35, 6020 Innsbruck Austria

BACH, HEINZ JÜRGEN, physician, researcher; b. Solingen, Germany, Dec. 1, 1946; s. Heinz and Ruth (Kern) B. Med. diplomate. Dir. Clin. Cancer Rsch., Solingen, Germany, 1988—. Mem. Deutsche Krebsgesellschaft, Metastasis Soc. Home: Siemenstr 35, 42697 Solingen Germany

BACH, THOMAS HANDFORD, lawyer, investor; b. Vineland, N.J., Dec. 25, 1928; s. Albert Ludwig and Edith May (Handford) B. A.B., Rutgers U., 1950; LL.B., Harvard U., 1956. Bar: N.Y. State bar 1957. Asso. firm Hawkins, Delafield & Wood, N.Y.C., 1956-61, Reed, Hoyt, Washburn & McCarthy, N.Y.C., 1961-62; ptnr. Bach & Condren, N.Y.C., 1963-71, Bach & McAuliffe, N.Y.C., 1971-79, Stroock & Stroock & Lavan, N.Y.C., 1979-88, Sullivan & Donovan, N.Y.C., 1989—; co-counsel N.Y. State Senate Housing and Urban Devel. Com., 1971; fiscal cons. N.Y.C. Fin. Adminstrn., 1967-70; asst. counsel State Fin. Com., N.Y. State Constl. Conv. of, 1967; del. U.S./Japan Bilateral Session, 1988, Moscow Conf. on Law and Bilateral Econ. Rels., 1990; spkr. Practicing Law Inst., Mcpl. Bond Workshop, N.Y., 1995-97. Contbr. articles to profl. jours.; co-author: A Guide to Certificates of Participation, 1991, the Handbook of Municipal Bonds, 1994. Mem. N.Y. State Commn. to Study Constl. Tax Limitations, 1974-75; chmn. subcom. Pub. Securities Assn.; dir. Citizens Union of N.Y. Served with U.S. Army, 1951-53, 1st lt. U.S. Army, 1952-53, Japan. Mem. Am. Bar Assn., N.Y. State Bar Assn. (internat. law. sect.), Assn. of Bar of City of N.Y., N.J. Bar Assn., N.Y. Mcpl. Analysts Group (chmn. 1973-74), Mcpl. Forum of N.Y., Tax Collectors and Treas. Assn. of N.J., Market Technicians Assn., Internat. Fin. Svcs. Vol. Corps. Episcopalian. Home: 4 E 89th St New York NY 10128-0636 also: 615 W Oak Rd Vineland NJ 08360-2262 Office: Sullivan & Donovan 415 Madison Ave New York NY 10017-1111

BACH, THOMAS JÖRG ANTON, plant biochemist; b. Bad Peterstal, Germany, Feb. 1, 1948; arrived in France, 1991; s. Anton Franz Josef and Lieselotte Anna Maria Theresia (Zölle) B.; m. Irmtraud Riemensperger, June 4, 1976; children: Tilmann Marc Anton, Annelen Dorothea Gisela. Degree in chemistry and biology, U. Karlsruhe, Germany, 1975, PhD, 1981, Habilitation in Plant Biochemistry, 1989. NATO fellow U. Cin. and USDA, Berkeley, Calif., 1982-83; rsch. asst. U. Karlsruhe, 1975-80, rsch. assoc., 1980-82, rsch. asst. prof., 1983-89, assoc. prof., 1990-91; prof. U. Strasbourg I, France, 1991—; ad hoc referee jour. series, Europe and U.S.A., 1984—; referee grant proposals USDA, NIH, others, 1986—. Co-editor INFORM, Am. Oil Chem. Soc., 1990—; co-editor Progress in Lipid Rsch., 1994—; contbr. articles and revs. to profl. publs. Grantee German Sci. Found., Bonn, 1986-92, NATO, Brussels, 1988-95, Nat. Ctr. Sci. Rsch., France, 1991—. Mem. Am. Soc. Plant Physiology, German Botany Assn., Fedn. European Soc. Plant Physiology, German Assn. Biochemistry and Molecular Biology, German Biol. Soc., German Univ. Assn. Avocations: classical music/violin and viola, science, history, politics. Office: CNRS-IBMP, 28 Rue Goethe, F-67083 Strasbourg France

BACHARACH, WALTER ZWI, historian; b. Hanau, Hessen, Germany, Sept. 7, 1928; s. Moritz and Erna Berta (Strauss) B.; m. Hannah Weiss, Dec., 1949; children: Menachem, Malka, Eran. BA, Tel-Aviv U., 1961, PhD, 1975; MA, Hebrew U., 1963. D. of Humanities, Contemporary History. Head dept. gen. history Bar-Ilan U., Israel, 1982-85, 88-90, prof. dept. gen. history., 1991—, prof. emeritus, 1997—, head Inst. Holocaust Rsch., 1992; bd. dirs. Leo Baeck Inst., Jerusalem, 1995—; incumbent S. Braun Chair for the History of Jews in Prussia, 1994-97; mem. internat. bd. Yad-Washem, Jerusalem, 1979—, participant project for History of hte Holocaust, 1988—. Author: Modern Antisemitism, 1979, Ideologies in the Twentieth Century, 1980, Racism-The Tool of Politics-From Monism Towards Nazism, 1984, Anti-Jewish Prejudices in German-Catholic Sermons, 1993. Mem. internat. academic adv. bd. Simon Wiesenthal Ctr., L.A., 1984—. Recipient awards Wurzweiler Found. Leo Baeck Inst., 1976, Israeli Acad. Scis., 1980, Meml. Found., 1993. Home: Bloch St 32, 64161 Tel Aviv Israel Office: Bar-Ilan U, Dept Gen History, 52900 Ramat Gan Israel

BACHELDER, JOSEPH ELMER, III, lawyer; b. Fulton, Mo., Nov. 13, 1932; s. Joseph Elmer and Frances Evelyn (Gray) B.; m. Louise Este Mason, June 12, 1955; children: Louise Stewart Bachelder Alcock, Christina Cathryn Bachelder Dufresne, Hilary Houston. BA magna cum laude, Yale U., 1955; LLB, Harvard U., 1958. Bar: N.Y. 1959. Assoc. Mudge, Rose, Guthrie & Alexander, N.Y.C., 1958-67, McKinsey and Co., Inc., N.Y.C., 1967-69; ptnr. Satterlee and Stephens, N.Y.C., 1969-72, Leboeuf, Lamb, Lieby & MacRae,

N.Y.C., 1972-80; founder, sr. ptnr. Law Offices Joseph E. Bachelder, N.Y.C., 1980—; chmn. The Bachelder Group, Inc., 1989—; pub. The Bachelder CEO Bull., 1990—; lectr. NYU Ann. Inst. on Fed. Taxation, 1972-74, Practicing Law Inst., 1977-80, 2000, Am. Law Inst., 1980, 97, 98, The Conf. Bd., 1986. Co-author, editor: Employee Stock Ownership Plans, 1979; columnist N.Y. Law Jour. 1977—; speaker Academia Symposia Stanford Law Sch., 1999, 2000, Northwestern U. , Kellogg Sch. Bus., 1999, U. Del., 2000. Mem. Princeton Twp. (N.J.) Zoning Bd., 1981-82; trustee Concord (Mass.) Acad., 1986-92. Fellow Am. Coll. Tax Counsel; mem. ABA, N.Y. State Bar Assn., Assn. of Bar of N.Y.C. Republican. Congregationalist. Clubs: The Down Town Assn. (N.Y.), Yale Club N.Y.; Bedens Brook (Princeton), Nassau (Princeton); Siasconset Casino (Nantucket, Mass.). Home: 226 Constitution Dr Princeton NJ 08540-6712 Office: 780 3rd Ave New York NY 10017-2024

BACHELDER, ROBERT STEPHEN, minister; b. Middletown, N.Y., Nov. 2, 1951; s. Stephen and Dorothy Esther (Gunderson) B.; m. Beverly June Brandt, Sept. 17, 1977; children: Stephen, Elizabeth. AB, Dartmouth Coll., 1973; MDiv, Yale U., 1978. Ordained to ministry United Ch. of Christ, 1978. Money markets trader R.I. Hosp. Trust Nat. Bank, Providence, 1973-75; pastor United Ref. Ch., Pangbourne, Eng., 1978-79; min. 1st Congl. Ch., Shrewsbury, Mass., 1980-84; min. for mission and svc. Worcester (Mass.) Area Mission Soc., 1984—; advisor to religious congregations for charitable giving. Author: Mystery and Miracle, 1983, Between Dying and Birth, 1983; contbr. chpts. to books, articles to profl. jours. Bd. dirs. Mass. Coun. of Chs., 1991-93, Worcester Interfaith, 1992-94, Worcester County Ecumenical Coun., 1992-96, Mass. Conv. Congl. Mins., 1983-85, Ctrl. Assn. Mass. Conf., United Ch. of Christ, 1983—, Worcester Coop. Coun., 1985-89, Accord: The Ctr. for Human Rels., 1991-93, Corx, Inc., 1993—, Martin Luther King Jr. Bus. Empowerment Ctr., 1993-99 (chair Bus. Advisory Coun. 1999—), WCHR Securities, Inc., 1993—, Mass. Congl. Fund, 1999—, New Am. Cmty. Forum, 1995-97, Pakachoag Cmty. Music Sch., 1996-98, Congl. Christian Hist. Soc., 1997—, Worcester Pastoral Counseling Ctr., 1998-2000, Greater Worcester Cmty. Found. Exec. Com., 1998—, Colony Retirement Homes, 1998—, Worcester Area Campus Ministry, 1998—, Jeremiah's Hospice, 2000—, United Way of Ctrl. Mass., 2000—; pres. Habitat Worcester, 1984-86, Worcester Cmty. Loan Fund, 1986-90, Worcester Com. on Homelessness and Housing, 1988-91, Worcester Cmty. Housing Resources, 1993-95; mem. City Mgr.'s Housing Task Force, 1990-92; v.p. Worcester Housing Partnership, 1991-93; distbn. com. mem. Fed. Emergency Mgmt. Agy., Ctrl. Mass., 1984-86, Housing Ind. Fund, 1989-92, Greater Worcester Cmty. Found., 1994—, chair, 1998—; v.p. Higgins Armory Mus., 1994-97, pres., 1997-99, chmn. Planned Giving 2000—; v.p. New Horizons Ret. Homes, 1992-97; chair Worcester Housing Summit,1990-91; mem. adv. com. Clara Barton Birthplace Mus., 1996-99; cmty. trustee United Way of Ctrl. Mass., 1995-98, 2000—; incorporator Protestant Youth Ctr., 1995-98; co-founder Greater Worcester Interreligious Legis. Network, 1985, Worcester AIDS Housing Task Force, 1993; co-founder, chair The Neighborhood Forum, 1996-99; mem. steerng com. Main South Credit Union, 1997-99; founder Neighborhood Leaders Fund, 1996. Recipient award Pernet Family Svc., 1993, Outstanding Charitable Svc. award United Ch. of Christ, 1995, Nipmuc Women's Health Coalition award, 1999. Mem. St. Wulstan Soc., United Ch. of Christ Ministers' Fellowship (pres. 1982-83), Dartmouth Club of Ctrl. Mass. (pres. 1991-93), Yale Club (N.Y.C.). Home: PO Box 67 North Oxford MA 01537-0067 Office: Worcester Area Mission Soc 128 Central St Auburn MA 01501-2820

BACHELET, DOMINIQUE MARIE, ecologist, researcher; b. Arras, France, July 16, 1957; came to U.S., 1979; d. Paul and Bernadette (Boubet) B.; m. Steven Wondzell, Nov. 23, 1988. Diplome D' Etudes Approfondies in Plant Ecology, Orsay, Paris, 1979; PhD, Colo. State U., 1983. Postdoctoral assoc. dept. soil sci. U. Calif., Riverside, 1984-86; rsch. specialist N.Mex. State U., Las Cruces, 1986-88; rsch. scientist Mantech Environ. Tech., Inc.-US EPA Environ. Lab., Corvallis, Oreg., 1988-94; vis. scientist in Toulouse CNRS, France, 1994-95; asst. prof. U. N.H., Durham, 1995-96; asst. prof., dept. bioresource engrng. Oreg. State U., Corvallis, 1989-99, assoc. prof., 1999—. Co-editor Validation of Flow and Transport Models Procs.; contbr. articles in ecol. modelling, tree physiology, photochemistry to profl. publs. Mem. Internat. Soc. Ecol. Modelling, Internat. Assn. Landscape Ecology, Ecol. Soc. Am., Am. Soc. Agronomy. Home: 2905 Hampton Dr SW Tumwater WA 98512-6257 Office: FSL 3200 SW Jefferson Way Corvallis OR 97331-8550

BACHER, ADELBERT, biochemist, educator. PhD, Tuebingen U., 1969, MD, 1974. Prof. Tech. U. Munich, Germany, 1992—. Office: Inst Organic Chemistry & Biochem, Lichtenberg str 4, D-85747 Garching Germany

BACHI, RUTH KOLODNY, broadcaster; b. Haifa, Israel, Oct. 27, 1939; d. Moses and Malka (Fisz) Kolodny; children: Ora, Avishai, Tamar, Noa. BA, Hebrew U., 1963, MA, 1967. From sr. documentary reporter to dir. tng. ctr. Israel Broadcasting Auth., 1969-89; sr. editor The Voice of Israel Kol Isreal, 1989—. Author: Russian Roulette, 1992, To begin in the beginning; Teddy Kollek-a biography by friends; The Josephine File; Olga. Recipient Givton prize for spl. journalistic achievement Israel Broadcasting Authority, 1979, ZIV prize, 1981, Sadeh prize Israel Def. Forces, 1993, Wizo prize for creative woman writer Women Zionist Orgn., 1997, Bnei Brit prize for outstanding broadcaster, 1997, Ze'ev prize Israeli Ministry Edn., 1998, Prime Min. prize for writers, 1999.

BACHIASHVILI, ISOLDE, philologist, translator; b. Tbilisi, Georgia, Mar. 12, 1930; d. Archil Bachiashvili and Nina Jikuradze; m. Nodar Tsikoridze; children: Nana Tsikoridze, Shalva Tsikoridze. Diploma, Tbilisi State U., 1953; postgrad., Tbilisi Inst. Fgn. Langs., 1961; Cert., Tbilisi, 1971. Exec. Youth Orgns. of Georgia, Tbilisi, 1953-60; prof. French lit. and lang. Tbilisi State U., 1961—; dean faculty of West European Langs. and Lit., 1973-85, chmn. sci. coun. faculty West European Langs. and Lit., 1973-85, mem. sci. coun., 1965-85. Author: Manuel de Français for Students of the Chemical Faculty, 1969, Foreword and Commentary, 1969, The Theatre of Jean Anui, 1972, Training Appliance of French for Students, 1983, (brochures) The Programme of the Special Course "French Theatre of the XX Century", 1985, The Programme for Students of the Romance Philology "The History, Theory and Praktik of the Artistically Translation, 1986, 94; translator: (from French to Georgian) Antigone (Jean Anui), Medea (Jean Anui). Mem. Methodical Coun. Ministry Higher Edn. Georgia, 1973-85. Recipient Ivane Javakhishvili medal, 1968, 85. Avocations: theatre, travelling. Home: Apt 87, Al Qazbeg Ave 29 II Bldg, 380077 Tbilisi Georgia Office: Tbilisi State U, Il Chavchavadze Ave 1, 380028 Tbilisi Georgia

BACHILLER, RAFAEL, astronomer; b. Madrid, Spain, Feb. 24, 1957; s. Jose and Maria (Garcia) B.; m. Adoracion Perea, Feb. 3, 1986; children: Diana, Irene. MD, U. Madrid, 1986. Fellow Grenoble (France) U., 1981-85; guest prof. U. Joseph Fourier, France, 1991-99; staff astronomer Nat. Observatory Spain, 1986—; mem. Spanish Nat. Commn. for Astronomy, 1994—, Commn. Internat. Astronomy Union, Radio Astronomy Frequencies; mem. ALMA scientific com., 2000—, first co-investigator, 1999—. Contbr. articles to profl. jours. Mem. European Astron. Soc., Internatl Astron. Union, Spanish Royal Soc. Physics. Office: Observatorio Astron Nat, Apartado 1143, E-28800 Alcala De Henares Spain

BACHMAIR, BEN, media science educator; b. Germany, Sept. 6, 1943. Degree in edn., U. Munich; D in Pedagogy, Psychology, Physiology, U. Erlangen, Germany. Prof. pedagogy and media edn. U. Gesamthochschule, Kassel, Germany, 1978—; vis. prof. U. Klagenfurt, Germany, U. Florence, Italy; rsch. fellow Inst. Edn. U. London; head media rsch. Deutsches Jugendinstitut, Munich. Co-editor: Media Communications in Everyday Life, 1990, TV Kids, 1993, Höllen-Inszenierung Wrestling, 1996, Fernsehkultur, 1996, Fernsehen zum Thema Machen, 1997, Cosa fa la TV ai Bambini?, 1997. Home: Alpenstrasse 47, 86159 Augsburg Germany Office: U Gesamthochschule, Nora-Platiel Str 1, 34109 Kassel Germany

BACHMAN, JERALD GRAYBILL, psychologist, researcher; b. Harrisburg, Pa., Oct. 20, 1936; s. Jacob Clarence and Harriet Mathias Bachman; m. Virginia Ludy, Nov. 28, 1957; children: Terri Lynne Dyer, Steven Jerald, Jon Andrew. AB, Lebanon Valley Coll., 1958; MA, U. Pa., 1961, PhD, 1962. Rsch. asst. U. Pa., Phila., 1958-59, asst. instr., 1959-62; study dir. U. Mich., Survey Rsch. Ctr., Inst. for Social Rsch., Ann Arbor, 1962-67, sr. study dir., 1967-72, program dir., sr. rsch. scientist, 1972-98, disting. sr. rsch. scientist, 1998—; mem. nat. adv. panel Nat. Ctr. for Ednl. Stats., Washington, 1982—; mem. com. on mil. performance NAS, Washington, 1983-89, mem. com. on youth population and mil. recruitment, 1999—. Author: (book series) Youth in Transition, 1967-78, The All-Volunteer Force, 1977, Smoking, Drinking, and Drug Use in Young Adulthood, 1997; cons. editor Am. Jour. Sociology, 1983-85; contbr. chpts. to books and articles to profl. jours. NSF fellow, Washington, 1959, 60, 62. Mem. Am. Assn. for Pub. Opinion Rsch., Soc. for Psychol. Study Social Issues, Inter-Univ. Seminar on Armed Forces and Soc. Avocations: sailing, cross-country skiing, house renovation, hiking, traveling. E-mail: jbachman@umich.edu. Office: Inst for Social Rsch Univ Mich 426 Thompson St Ann Arbor MI 48104-2321

BACHMAN, JOHN REED, sales management motivator; b. Cleve., June 6, 1921; s. Reed Ernst Bachman and Ann Augusta Schantz; m. Rosemary Jamison (div. Feb. 1973); m. Charelene Ross, Mar. 29, 1973; children: Nancy Claire, Jamison Reed. BA, U. Mich., 1942. Airline pilot, capt. TACA, San Jose, Calif., Modern Air, Miami, Fla.; salesman Brown & Bigelow, St. Paul; sales mgmt. staff Brown & Bigelow, San Diego, Chgo.; sales tng. dir. Brown & Bigelow, St. Paul, v.p. nat. accounts program. Lt. USN, 1942-45. Mem. LaGorce C.C. (bd. mem. 1975-76), Indian Creek C.C. Republican. Avocations: golfing, playing bridge, gin and rummy. Home: 10245 Collins Ave Apt 11E Bal Harbour FL 33154-1418

BACHMANN, BILL, photographer; b. Pa., Mar. 4, 1946; s. Ernest Edward and Helen May (Himler) B. BS, Roberts Wesleyan Coll., Rochester, N.Y., 1967; MBA, SUNY, Brockport, 1971; postgrad., U. London, U. Calif., Berkeley, Rochester Inst. Tech., U. Pitts., Ft. Lauderdale Art Inst. Freelance comml. and advt. photographer Miami, N.Y.C., Orlando, 1972—; worked in over 100 countries worldwide; instr. photography Triangle Inst., 1992, S.E. Ctr. for Creative Arts, Daytona, 1990—; dir. TV commls. and co. videos; vis. instr. photography at several colls. and univs.; guest numerous TV programs, 1978—; lectr. in field, 1980—. Prin. works include Miami Herald, 1978-80, Fla. Tourism, 1982—, Sheraton Hotels, 1982—, Gen. Mills Restaurants, 1983—, Olive Garden, 1986—, Marriott Hotels, 1992—, Bahamas Tourism, Radisson Hotels, 1986—, Grosvenor Hotels, 1988—, Revlon, 1991—, Harris Corp., 1993—, Sea Escape Cruises, 1988—, Century Club, 2000—, Regent China Tours, 1999—, Burger King, 1988—, Caribbean Travel & Life, 1990—, Fuji, 1990—, Nickelodeon, 1989—, Merv Griffin's Paradise Island, Bahamas, 1990—, Kodak Films, 1976—, McDonalds, 1987—, Stern Mag., 1987—, Regal Boats, 1990—, Renaissance Cruises, 1996—, Universal Studios, 1990—, Citibank VISA, 1990—, Delta Airlines, 1991—, Am. Showcase, 1991—, Creative Black Book, 1994—, PepsiCo, 1994—, Saga Holidays, 2000—, Hilton Hotels Internat., 1992—, NuSkin, 1995—, Pizza Hut, 1996—, Grey Poupon, 1995—, Home Depot, 1996—, Whale Cay, 1997—, People Mag., 1998—, Pitcom, 1999, Saga Holidays, 1999—, Regent China Tours, 1999—; dir. TV commls. and videos, 1987—; author: Clicking the Shutter is the Easy Part, 1988, Introspective World, 1996, Welcome Back Berlin, 1990, Bali-Paradise in Indonesia, 1994, Shooting Figure Studies, 1990, Kathmandu, A Jewel Discovered, 1996, One Dream Too Many, 1989, Images of Women, 1997, Treasures of the Caribbean, 1992, China's Greatest Resource, It's Diverse People, 1997, Orlando-The City Beautiful, 1998; photographer 295-Day Kodak World Photo Tour, 1992-95, Photo Pro Mag., 1991—; photgraphed over 700 mag. covers. Bd. dirs. Big Bros.; active Vols. in Action, 1989—. Named Photographer of Yr. Fla. Peoples Choice Awards, 1987, Photographer of Yr. Asia, 1993; recipient Addy awards, 1976—. Mem. One Club (bd. dirs. 1988—), Sales and Mktg. Execs. (bd. dirs., officer), Am. Soc. Media Photographers N.Y., Orlando C. of C. (pres.' club 1983—), Cen. Fla. Photographers Assn. (v.p., bd. dirs. 1983—), Fla. Motion Pictures and TV Guild, Heathrow Club (social dir. 1986—), Rotary. Republican. Methodist. Avocations: snow skiing, tennis, golf, writing. Home and Office: PO Box 950833 Lake Mary FL 32795-0833

BACHMANN, GREGOR, surgeon; b. Aachen, Germany. Degree, U. Koeln, 1992. JHO in surgery QEH, Gateshead, U.K., 1993, Freeman Hosp., Newcastle, U.K., 1994, Stracathro Hosp., Brechin, U.K., 1993-94; SHO in Surgery ARI, Aberdeen, U.K., 1994; asst. UNI-HNO, Cologne, Germany, 1994—. Contbr. articles to profl. jours. Office: Univ Cologne, Hals Nasen Ohren Klin, 50931 Cologne Germany

BACHMANN, MICHAEL, theologian, educator; b. Minden, Westfalen, Germany; s. Wilhelm and Asta (von Winterfeldt) B.; m. Ursula Henning, 1969. ThD, U. Münster, 1978; habilitation, U. Basel, 1990. Asst. U. Münster, 1975-77; lectr. Pädagogische Hochschule, Freiburg, Germany, 1980-95; prof. theology U. Siegen, Germany, 1995—. Mem. Soc. for the Study of the New Testament, Wissenschaftliche Gesellschaft für Theologie. Office: U Siegen, Adolf-Reichwein-Str 2, D 57068 Siegen NRhnWstf, Germany

BACHMANN, PETER KLAUS, chemist; b. Annweiler, Fed. Republic Germany, Sept. 28, 1950; s. Edmund and Ottilie (Heilig) B.; m. Ute Linz, Oct. 20, 1986. MSc, Tech. U., Darmstadt, Fed. Republic Germany, 1975, PhD, 1980. Researcher Philips Rsch. Labs., Aachen, Fed. Republic Germany, 1980-86; vis. scientist Materials Rsch. Lab., Pa. State U., University Park, 1986-88; researcher Philips Rsch. Labs., Aachen, 1988-91, sr. scientist, 1991—. Assoc. editor Diamond and Related Materials, 1991—; organizer of Diamond Films conf. series, 1990—; editor 7 diamond-related books; contbr. articles to profl. jours. Recipient German Ceramics Soc. Sigri-Great Lakes Carbon Promotional award, 1992. Mem. Bunsengesellschaft for Phys. Chemistry, Optical Soc. Am., Materials Rsch. Soc. Avocations: windsurfing, photography, biographical books. Home: Glueck-Auf-Strasse 22, D-52146 Wuerselen Germany Office: Philips Rsch Labs, Weisshausstrasse, D 52021 Aachen Germany

BACHNER, BARBARA LAVERDIERE, artist; b. Waterville, Maine, Sept. 14, 1934; d. Thaddeus Eugene and Bernadette Arthemise (Vashon) LaVerdiere; m. Robert Lawrence Bachner, Mar. 22, 1959; 1 child, Suzanne Jouvé. BA in Fine Arts magna cum laude, NYU, 1968; student, Nat. Acad. Sch. Design, 1975-78, Art Students League, 1977-80, 82-84; MFA in Studio Art, Johnson State Coll., 1999. lectr. Woodstock Sch. of Art 1994, Ulster County Art Assn., 1992; tchr. Woodstock Sch. Art, 1999, 2000. Solo shows include Kleinert Arts Ctr., Woodstock, N.Y., 1992, TAI Gallery, N.Y.C., 1994, 98, Pen and Brush, N.Y.C., 1995, 99, Fletcher Gallery, Woodstock, N.Y., 1995, Woodstock Artists Assn., 1997, Julian Scott Meml. Gallery, Johnson State Coll., Johnson, Vt., 1999, West Chelsea Artwalk, NY, 1997—; juried and invitational shows include Pastel Soc. Am., N.Y.C., 1978, 80, Five Towns Juried Show, Woodmere, N.Y., 1983, Woodstock Artists Assn., 1989— (exhbn. com. 1991-94, 98—, dir. 1992-95, trustee 1995—), Springfield (Mo.) Art Mus., 1990, U. Tex., Tyler, 1991, Gallery Korea, N.Y.C., 1993, CUNY, Bayside, 1994, Nat. Arts Club, N.Y.C., 1984, 95, Nat. Assn. Women Artists, 1996, 99, Krasdale Corp. Galleries, White Plains, N.Y., 1995-96, Harper Collins, N.Y.C., 1996, SUNY, New Paltz, 1996, The Art Studio, Bearsville, NY, 1997, Cork Gallery, Lincoln Ctr., N.Y.C., 1998, N.Y. State Mus., Albany, 1998, Dist. Coun. 37, N.Y.C., 1999, Orensanz Found., N.Y.C., 1999, Schoharie County Art Assn., Cobbleskill, N.Y., 1999, Interfaith Ctr., N.Y.C., 1999, Biennale Internat. Dell'Arte Contemporanea, Florence, Italy, 1999, Los Angeles Printmaking Soc., No. Hollywood, Ca., 1999, 2000, Dutchess County Art Assn., Nat. Print Show, Barrett House, Poughkeepsie, N.Y., 1994, Elements 2000 Ernest Rubenstein Gallery, N.Y.C., 2000, Florence New York Orensanz Found., N.Y.C., 2000, It's About Time Barrett Art Ctr., Poughkeepsie, N.Y., 2000, Utopia/Dystopia Kleinert Art Ctr./Byrdcliffe outdoor invitational, Woodstock, NY, 2000; group shows include Artists of Ulster County, Kingston, N.Y., 1989, Woodstock (N.Y.) Artists Assn. Mems. Show, 1989—, Pen & Brush, N.Y.C., 1990—, SUNY, New Paltz, 1992, A.I.R. Gallery, N.Y.C., 1992, Woodstock Sch. Art, 1994—, Nat. Assn. Women Artists, 1996—; corp. and permanent collections include Texaco Corp., Houston, Printmaking Workshop, N.Y.C., Kaatsbaan Internat. Dance Ctr., Tivoli, N.Y., Four Seasons Hotel Corp., Las Vegas, Nev., Nat. Assn. Women Artists, numerous pvt. collections; author: Behind Closed Eyes, 1999; subject of articles. Mem. Nat. Assn. Women Artists (rec. sec. 1999—, Medal of Honor 1998, Elizabeth Stanton Blake meml. award 1998), Women's Caucus Art, Coll. Art Assn., N.Y. Artists Equity Assn., Pen & Brush (co-chair graphics divsn. 1994-98, Solo Show award 1993, 96), Woodstock Artists Assn. (svc. in the arts dir. 1992-95, trustee 1995—, exhbn. com. 1998—, Dan Gottschalk award 1991, Breth-Borkmann award 1995, mem. exhbn. com. 1998—), Ulster Arts Alliance, Art Students League (life; Concours award 1978, 81, 84, Merit scholar 1979, 83), L.A. Printmaking Soc. Avocations: music, theatre, travel. Home: 25 Sutton Pl S Apt 19N New York NY 10022-2455

BACHNER, JOHN PHILIP, business consultant; b. Boston, Nov. 8, 1944; s. Barnard and Bertha (Bellar) B.; m. Marcia L. Davis, Aug. 7, 1966 (div.); children: Barnard David (dec. 1991), Lissa Suzanne; m. Patricia B. Gartenhaus, June 14, 1997. AB, Harvard U., 1966. Screenplay writer Screen Presentations Inc., Washington, 1967-68; account exec. Hoffman Assocs. Inc., Silver Spring, Md., 1968-71; pres. Bachner Communications INc., Silver Spring, 1971—; pres. Bachner Mgmt. Systems, 1973—; exec. v.p. Cons. Engrs. Coun. of Met. Washington, Silver Spring, 1971-96, Property Mgmt. Assn., Silver Spring, 1973-96, Washington Area Coun. Engrng. Labs., Silver Spring, 1975-93; exec. v.p. ASFE/Profl. Firms Practicing in the Geoscis., 1973—; pres., chmn. bd. Constrn. Industry Tech. Inc., Silver Spring, 1973—; pres. Most for the Lease, 1982—; v.p. Bachner R.E., 1985-97; exec. v.p. Mid-Atlantic Coun. of Shopping Ctr. Mgrs., 1986-93; exec. v.p. Inst. Profl. Practice, Silver Spring, 1988-94, Coll. Property Mgmt. Found., Silver Spirng, 1988-96; pres. Cons. Engrs., Ednl. Found. Inc., 1990; exec. dir. Profl. Liability Agts. Network Inc., 1991-98, Mid-Atlantic Cancer Rsch. Found., Silver Spring, 1992-95, Internat. Found. Advancement of Thrombosis and Hematosis Rsch. Inc., Silver Spring, 1992-98, Calif. R.E. Inspection Assn., 1993-98, Metro Washington Heat Pump Assn., 1994-99; pres. Bus. Art and Graphics, 1993-97. Author: Marketing and Promotion for Design Professionals, 1977, Guide to Practical Property Management, 1991, Practice Management for Design Professionals, 1991, ASFE Contract Reference Guide, 3d edit., 1996, 3.1 edit., 1998, ECS Contract Reference Guide, 1997, 2nd edit., 1999, RA&MCO Contract Reference Guide, 1997; writer 25 motion picture screenplays; contbr. numerous articles to profl. publs., popular mags.; author contract reference guides, 1996-2000. Home: 9206 Sterling Montague Dr Great Falls VA 22066-4002

BACHOR, EDGAR, otolaryngologist, researcher; b. Bueckeburg, Germany, Oct. 13, 1963. MD, Med. Sch., Hannover, Germany, 1990. Resident in otolaryngology Staedtisches Klinikum, Fulda, Germany, 1990-91, U. Regensburg, Germany, 1992-95; faculty staff dept. otolaryngology U. Essen, Germany, 1995-99; attending physician dept. otolaryngology U. Ulm, Germany, 1999—. Mem. Assn. Otolaryngology, German Soc. Otorhinolaryngology, Head and Neck Surgery, The Schuknecht Soc. (Boston). Office: U Ulm Dept Otolaryngology, Pritt Witz Str 43, 89075 Ulm Germany

BACHSTEIN, HARRY SAMUEL, lawyer, educator, author, publisher, genealogist; b. Oakland, Calif., Aug. 6, 1943; s. Elizabeth (Rodenhouse) B.; children: Harry S. III, David Jason, Jesse Remington. BS in Bus. Adminstrn., No. Ariz. U., 1966; JD with honors, U. Ariz., 1969. Bar: Ariz. 1969, U.S. Supreme Ct. 1973, U.S. Ct. Customs and Patent Appeals, U.S. Dist. Ct. Ariz., U.S. Ct. Appeals (9th cir.), U.S. Bankruptcy Ct. Spl. investigator ethics com. Pinal County Bar Assn., 1971; juvenile ct. referee Ariz. Superior Ct., 1972-76; mem. med. liability rev. panel Superior Ct., 1981, mem. domestic rules rules com., 1988; CEO, Polaris Publ. Group Inc.; lawyer arbitrator Better Bus. Tucson; mem. U.S. Presdl. Task Force, 1981-88; mem. faculty Pima Coll., 1982-83. Author: Who's Who in Scuba Diving, 1993, Guerilla Divorce For Men, 1995, Bachsteins in America, 1997, Trails of Our Fathers, 1999; editor: Ariz. Law Rev., 1967-69; columnist Vigo County (Ind.) Voice, Oil Patch newspaper, Houston; contbg. writer Underwater USA, Fitness Plus, Vigo (Ind.) Examiner, Jackson (Tex.) Oil Patch. Mem. Devel. Authority for Tucson's Expansion, 1970-76. Mem. State Bar Ariz. (sec., exec. coun. young lawyers' sect. 1972-73), ABA (Ariz. rep. com. on div. law and procedures 1976), Pima County Bar Assn. (grievance com. 1978-86, spl. investigator for ethics com. 1971), Profl. Assn. of Diving Instrs. (dive master), Profl. Diving Instrs. Corp. (cert. open water scuba instr. 1988), Nat. Assn. Scuba Educators (cert. instr.), Internat. Diving Educators Assn. (cert. instr.), Explosub (cert. instr.), Nat. Com. on Diving Instructional Standards and Safety, Recreational Scuba Tng. Coun., Am. Nat. Standards Inst., Confdn. Mondiale des Activites SubaquatiSques de Paris (cert. instr.), Delta Chi (sec., pledgemaster 1961-65), Optimist Internat. Club (state gov. Ariz. 1976, lt. gov. 1972-73, pres. 1971-72, Outstanding Gov. and Disting. Gov. 1976), Masons, Shriners. Avocations: hunting, deep sea diving, genealogy. Office: PO Box 85477 Tucson AZ 85754-5477

BACK, LLOYD H., mechanical engineer, researcher; b. San Francisco, Feb. 13, 1933; s. Uno and Elna (Norgard) B.; m. Carol Peterson, Dec. 17, 1955; children: Martin, Carla, Debra. BS, U. Calif., Berkeley, 1959, PhD, 1962. Supr. fluid dynamic, reactive processes and biomed. rsch. Jet Propulsion Lab./Calif. Inst. Tech., Pasadena, 1962-92; clin. asst. prof. medicine U. So. Calif., 1974-92; cons. in field, 1992—; vol. faculty mem. Sch. Medicine, U. So. Calif., L.A., 1992—. Author book chpt. Sgt. U.S. Army, 1953-55, Korea. Recipient Exceptional Svc. award NASA, 1979. Fellow ASME (life; chmn. heat transfer divsn., tech. editor jour., Heat Transfer Divsn. Disting. Svc. award 1987, 50th Anniversary award 1988), AIAA (assoc.; assoc. editor jour.). Achievements include contributions to the understanding of fundamental aspects of fluid mechanics and heat transfer in rocket propulsion, fluid dynamics of blood flow through diseased arteries, and in other experimental and analytical investigations of laminar and turbulent flows. Avocations: travel, fishing, hiking. Home: 16 Rushingwind Irvine CA 92614-7409

BACK, MICHAEL WAYNE, lawyer; b. Gary, Ind., Oct. 27, 1949; s. Virlan and Eunice Inez (Dooley) B.; m. Deborah Lynn Martinez, Oct. 1, 1988; children: Michael Christiaan, Amelia Michelle, Mark W., Hillary E. BS, Purdue U., 1976; postgrad., John Marshall Law Sch., 1979; 1979. Bar: Ind. 1979, U.S. Dist. Ct. (no. and so. dists.) Ind. 1979. Pvt. practice (atty.) Crown Point, Ind., 1979-87; hearing officer Lake County Circuit Ct., Crown Pl., 1980-87; pvt. practice Lake County Circuit Ct., 1987—. Sargeant USAF, 1969-71. Ind. State Bar Assn., Lake County Bar Assn. (bd. dirs. 1996—), Fed. Bar (bd. govs.), Ind. Trial Lawyers Assn. (bd. govs. 1996—). Democrat. Roman Catholic. Club: Innsbrook Country, Merrillville (sec. 1986-87, bd. dirs. 1985-93, pres. 1991-93). Avocations: golf, tennis. Office: Lake County Circuit Ct 1 Professional Ctr Ste 204 Crown Point IN 46307-1882

BACK, TORBIORN GUNNAR ALBIN, lawyer; b. Mariestad, Sweden, Oct. 21, 1935; s. Gunnar and Inga Maj (Svensson) B.; m. Aslog Karin, Aug. 6, 1972. Grad., U. Stockholm, 1962. Atty. Advokaterna Back AB, Vasteras, Sweden, 1967—. Capt. Swedish Army, 1958-75. Mem. Swedish Bar Assn., Rotary (pres. 1986-87). Home: S-TA Ursulas VAG 39, 722 18 Vasteras Sweden Office: Advokaterna Back AB, Box 523, 721 09 Vasteras Sweden

BÄCKER, ANNIKA E., dentist, researcher; b. Lindesberg, Sweden, Sept. 19, 1965; d. Bernt and Ulla Bäcker; 1 child, Eric Björkner. DDS, Göteborg (Sweden) U., 1991, PhD, 1999. Dentist, rschr. faculty odontology U. Göteborg U., 1991-92, 99—. Avocation: karate. Office: Dept Endodontics, Box 450, SE40530 Göteborg Sweden

BACKER, CARL L., pediatric cardiac surgeon, educator; b. Mpls., Apr. 29, 1955; s. Gordon L. and Arlene I. Backer; m. Julia Ford Backer, May 1, 1992; children: Charlotte, Annabelle. BA with honors, Northwestern U., Evanston, Ill., 1976; MD, Mayo Med. Sch., 1980. Diplomate Am. Bd. Surgery, Am. Bd. Thoracic Surgery. Asst. prof. surgery Northwestern U., Chgo., 1988-96, assoc. prof. surgery, 1996-99, prof. surgery, 2000—; attending cardiovascular surgeon Children's Meml. Hosp., Chgo., 1988—. Editor: Arterial Switch, 1991, Coarctation, 1993, Pediatric Cardiac Surgery, 1994. Named to Wausau (Wis.) Hall of Fame, Wausau Sch. Dist., 1994; recipient Physician's Recognition award AMA, 1997. Fellow ACS, Am. Coll. Cardiology, Am. Assn. Thoracic Surgery, Soc. Thoracic Surgeons, Drs.' Mayo Soc., Internat. Soc. Heart and Lung Transplantation, Phi Beta Kappa. Avocations: skiing, sailing, tennis, golf. Office: Children's Surg Found 2300 N Childrens Plz Chicago IL 60614-3363

BACKER, MATTHEW DE BRACEY, musician, educator; b. New Orleans; s. Jolly De Bracey and Jacqueline (Newman) B.; m. Elisa Margaret Richards, Jan. 5, 1994; 1 child, Lucas De Bracey. Student, Hampshire Coll., Amherst, Mass., 1978-79, Berklee Coll. Music, Boston, 1979-80; BA with honors, U. Warwick, Eng., 1983; student, Hampshire Coll., Amherst, Mass. Guitar and bass player; session musician, recorded and/or performed live and/or on TV with Sinead O'Connor, Cher, Montserrat Caballe, Aimee Mann, Swing Out Sister, The Dog's Breakfast, The Beautiful South, Steve Earle, Kate St. John, Elton John, Shirley Bassey, Michael Ball, Edward Ball, Daniel Cartier,

Daniel Lanois, Joe Cocker, Julian Lennon, Sarah Jane Morris, Suzanne Rhatigan, Tony Ferrino, Bob Geldof. Avocations: reading, tennis, oenology, owl stretching, travel.

BACKER, WILLIAM EARNEST, food products executive; b. Fulton, Mo., Dec. 3, 1922; s. William Earnest and Ida Lorraine (Smith) B.; m. Marjorie Jean Keller, Dec. 25, 1943; children: W. Dale, Vicki Lynn McDaniel, Carolyn Sue Cave. BA in Chemistry, Westminster Coll., 1943; postgrad., Wayne U., 1954. Chemistry lab. technician Delco Remy, Muncie, Ind., 1943-44; gen. mgr. Backer Potato Chip Co., Fulton, Mo., 1946-50, pres., chief exec. officer, 1957-88, chmn. of bd., 1988—; regional sales exec. A.P. Green Refractories, Mexico, Mo., 1950-51; salesman A.P. Green Refractories, Detroit, 1951-53; test engr. Ford Motor Co., Dearborn, Mich., 1953-57. Patentee M39-20mm Cannon components, package machine components, socket holder (also a socket wrench sorter having Braille for the blind). Pres. Fulton C. of C., 1977, also bd. dirs., chmn. planning and zoning; v.p. adminstrn./product sales Great Rivers coun. Boy Scouts Am., Columbia, Mo., 1980-92, also current trustee; chmn. bldg. and grounds Westminster Coll., Fulton, 1990-91; chmn. nominating com. Children's Hosp., Columbia; established Fulton Visitor Ctr./Collector Vehicle Mus., 1996; founding bd. dirs. The Carpenter's Kids, 1999. Recipient Resolution, donation for bldg., Callaway County Commrs., Fulton, 1989, Disting. Eagle Scout award Nat. Eagle Scout Assn., 1995, Disting. Eagle Scout award Mo. Ho. of Reps., 1996, Excellence in Cmty. Svc. award Daughters of the Am. Revolution, 2000; named Disting. Indsl. Developer, Fulton Rotary, 1994. Mem. Kiwanis Internat. (lt. gov. Mo./Ark. divsns 1987-88), Fulton Kiwanis (pres. 1968, Kiwanian of Yr. 1984, 94). Republican. Presbyterian. Avocation: collector of vintage automobiles. Home: PO Box 128 Fulton MO 65251-0128 Office: Backer Potato Chip Co One Industrial Rd Fulton MO 65251

BACKHOUSE, SUE, art curator, writer, publisher; b. Hobart, Tasmania, Australia, Mar. 23, 1955; d. Leonard Lukin and Margaret Elsie (Kelty) B.; m. Stephen Harris, Jan. 2, 1978; children: Briony, Nickolas. BA in Visual Arts, U. Tasmania, Hobart, 1978. Tchr. Tamanian Edn. Dept., Hobart, 1977-78; lectr. Sch. of Art, Hobart, 1978-79; asst. curator Tasmanian Mus. and Art Gallery, Hobart, 1981-83; art cons. Hobart, 1983-87; registrar, curator Tasmanian Mus. and Art Gallery, Hobart, 1989—; mng. dir. Pandani Press, Hobart. Author: (books) Tasmanian Artists of the Twentieth Century, 1988, (with J. B. Kirkpatrick) Native Trees of Tasmania, 6 edits.; pub. various books on natural history and art. Grantee Australian Visual Arts Bd., 1979; fellow Tasmanian Arts Adv. Bd., 1982. Mem. Australian Mus. Assn., Australian Registrars Com. Avocations: art history research, botanical illustration, bush walking. Office: Tasmanian Mus & Art Gallery, 19 Davey St, Hobart TAS 7000, Australia

BACKMAN, MELVIN ABRAHAM, English educator; b. Lynn, Mass., Feb. 12, 1919; s. David A. Backman and Sophie Berman; m. Dorothy Weisman, Dec. 23, 1946 (dec. Oct. 1962); children: Sherril Jo Backman Aaron, Maren Ruth (dec.); m. Lisbeth-Anne Niesz, June 27, 1971. BS, Bridgewater Tchrs. Coll., 1941; MA, Columbia Tchrs. Coll., 1947; PhD, Columbia U., 1960. Instr. English Richmond (Va.) Profl. Inst., 1948-51; prof. humanities Clarkson Coll. Tech., Potsdam, N.Y., 1953-67; prof. English C.W. Post Coll., L.I. U., Brookville, N.Y., 1967-89, prof. emeritus, 1989—. Author: Faulkner: The Major Years, 1966, (French translation) William Faulkner, 1968; contbg. author: Hemingway and His Critics, 1961, The Stoic Strain in American Literature, 1979. Staff sgt. USAAC, 1943-46, China, Burma, India. Avocations: reading, gardening. Home: 11 Northfield Rd Glen Cove NY 11542-1717

BÅCKSTRÖM, URBAN, banker; b. Sollefteå, May 25, 1954; s. Sven-Ake Båckström and Maj-Britt Filipsson; m. Ewa Hintze, 1978; 2 children. G-rad., Stockholm U., Stockholm Sch. Econs. Rsch. asst. Inst. for Internat. Econ. Studies, Stockholm, 1978-80; 1st sec. internat. dept. Ministry of Fgn. Affairs, 1980-82; chief economist Moderate Party, 1982-83, 86-89; under-sec. of state Ministry of Fin., 1991-93; gov., chmn. exec. bd. Sveriges Riksbank; pres. chmn. Bank Internat. Settlements; bd. dirs. Bank for Internat. Settlements. Office: Sveriges Riksbank, S-103 37, Stockholm Sweden

BACKUS, IRENA DOROTA, history educator, researcher; b. Warsaw, Poland, Apr. 10, 1950; Immigrated to Great Britain, 1961, resident in Switzerland since 1977.; m. Guy Colin Backus, Apr. 7, 1973. BA with honors, Oxford U., Great Britain, 1972, MA with honors, 1976, DPhil, 1976; D Theol. Hab., Bern, Switzerland, 1988. Rsch. asst. Royal Commn. on Historical Manuscripts, London, 1975-77; maitre asst. U. Geneva, Switzerland, 1977-83, maitre d'enseignement et de recherche, 1983-91, prof. titulaire, 1991—; pvt. dozent U. Bern, Switzerland, 1988—; vis. prof. U. Lausanne, Switzerland, 1990-91, Ecole Pratique des H. Etudes, Paris, 1996; com. mem. Revue des Etudes Augustiniennes, Paris, 1994—, Renaissance & Reformation Review, London, 1996—, Zwingliverein, Zurich, 1989—, Oxford Studies in Hist. Theology, 1997—. Author: Lectures Humanistes de Basile de Cesaree, 1991, La Patristique et les Guerres de Religion en France, 1993, Le Miracle de Laon, 1994, Das Prinzip sola scriptura und die Kirchenvater in den Disputationen von Baden und Bern, 1997; editor: Martini Buceri Enarratio in Evangelium Iohannis, 1988, The Reception of the Church Fathers in the West, 1997, Reformation Readings of the Apocalypse, 2000; (series) Kluwer Studies in Early Modern Religious Reforms, 1999—. Recipient scholarship Leverhulme Fund., 1974, British Acad. Exchange award Briish Acad. FNRS, 1986, 95. Office: U. Geneva, 3 Place de l'Universite, CH-1211 Geneva Switzerland

BACON, A. SMOKI, television host; b. Brookline, Mass., Jan. 29, 1928; d. Alfred Leon and Ruth Dorothy (Burns) Ginepra; m. Edwin Conant Bacon, May 11, 1957 (dec. July 1974); children: Brooks Conant, Hilary Conant; m. Richard Francis Concannon, Oct. 13, 1979. Student, Art Inst. Boston, 1947; grad., Jackson Von Ladau Sch. Design, Boston, 1951. Pub. rels. cons. Boston, 1968—; pres. Bacon-Concannon Assocs., Boston, 1979-95; dir. craftsmobiles Summerthing Program, Boston, 1968-73; dir. exhibits Citifair, Boston, 1974; dir. Victorian exhibits Bicentennial Boston 200, 1975, dir. spl. events, 1976; cons. spl. events. Inst. Contemporary Art, 1977-78, Boston Tea Party Ship, 1978-79; fundraiser Mass. Assn. Mental Health, 1979; dir. promotions Met. Ctr., 1979; coord. grand finale celebration Boston Jubilee 350, 1979-80; coord. Elliot Norton Awards, 1983; pub. rels. Dyansen Gallery, Boston, 1987-88, French Speaking League, 1987; cons. spl. events Jordan Marsh, 1987; fundraiser, pub. rels. Boston Philharmonic, 1988; coord. 30th anniversary celebration Charles Playhouse, 1988; fundraiser Elliot Norton Awards, 1989; coord. benefit New Eng. Premiere of film Glory Afro-Am. Mus., 1990; pub. rels. cons. Boston Chamber Music Soc., 1990; pub. rels. Paul Sorota Gallery of Fine Arts, 1990-91; fundraising cons. Internat. Inst., 1991; pub. rels., fundraiser Brookline H.S. Sesquicentennial Celebration, 1992-93; co-host radio show Celebrity Time, 1980—; co-host TV show On the Town; guest lectr. Boston U. Sch. Pub. Rels., 1979, ARC, 1987, Radcliffe Coll. 4'0'Clock Forums, 1989, publicity club Boston, ARC, YMCA, Boston U. Sch. Pub. Rels., Mass Polit. Women's Conf., Women's Italian Club, Brookline Rotary, Harvard Coll. Rotary Club; contbg. editor Design Times Mag. Social calendar editor Boston Tab Newspaper, 1987-90; contbg. editor Design Times Mag.; columnist BeaconHill News. Candidate Dem. State Rep., Mass., 1980; Bastille Day chmn. French Libr. Boston, 1994—; local adv. com. Nat. Trust for Historic Preservation; bd. dirs. Boston Lit. Hour; host parents com. Harvard Coll.; bd. dirs. Mugar Libr., Spl. Collections, 1994—; vis. com. Mus. Fine Arts, Egyptian Dept., 1994—; bd. trustees Boston Arts Festival, 1960-63; bd. dirs., treas. Samaritans, Boston, 1974-84; art auction chairperson WGBH-Pub. Radio-TV, Boston, 1969-70; bd. dirs. Urban League Ea. Mass., Boston, 1975-85, Elders Living at Home Program, Boston City Hosp. Kids Fund ; former mem. numerous civic coms. Recipient Woman of Great Achievement award Cambridge Young Women's Assn., 1991, appreciation award The Samaritans, 1991, Leadership award friends of the Pub. Garden, 1975; Named One of Boston's 100 Female Leaders, Boston Mag., 1980, One of the Boston Area Schs. Notable Grad. List, 1994; Guest of Honor, Womens' City Club Ann. Dinner Dance, 1979; Honored Those who Help Keep Boston's Non-Profit Agencies Alive Horizons for Youth, 1972, Charitable and Civic Endeavo Boston Italian Women's Club, 1995; Donated personal ofcl. documents Women's Time Capsule Schlesinger Libr. Radcliffe Coll., 1981. Mem. Am. Assn. U. Women, Harvard Club Boston, Women's City Club. Democrat. Avocation: artistics graphics. Home: 94 Beacon St Apt 1 Boston MA 02108-3329 Office: Bacon Concannon Assocs 94 Beacon St Boston MA 02108-3329

BACON, ANDREW KENNETH, anesthetist; b. Warwickshire, Eng.; arrived in Australia, 1971.; s. Aidan H. Bacon; 4 children. MB BS, St. Bartholemew's Hosp., London, 1966. Specialist in anaesthetics. Sr. house officer, registrar, dept. anaesthetics Salisbury (Eng.) Group Hosps., 1968-69; registrar, sr. registrar, tutor in anaesthetics Bristol (Eng.) Hosps. and U. Bristol, 1970-71; cons. in anaesthetics Dandenong (Australia) Hosp., 1971—, cons. in intensive care, 1972-83, dir. anaesthetics, 1981-88; chief med. coord. State Emergency Response Plan, Victoria, Australia, 1995—; dir. anaesthetics Surgicentre, Dandenong, 1982—; med. dir. Met. Ambulance Svc., Melbourne, 1992—; occasional lectr. Australian Counter Disaster Coll., Macedon, Victoria, 1984—; area med. coord. State Disaster (Emergency) Response Plan, 1981-95; vis. lectr. Ambulance Officer Tng. Ctr., Melbourne, 1975—; clin. tchr. faculty medicine Monash U., 1981—; del. Australian Day Surgery Coun. Contbr. articles to profl. jours. Fellow Faculty Anaesthetists Royal Coll. Surgeons Eng., Faculty Anaesthetists Royal Australasian Coll. Surgeons, Royal Coll. Anaesthetists Eng., Australia and New Zealand Coll. Anaesthetists; mem. Australian Soc. Anaesthetists, Assn. Anaesthetists U.K., Assn. Anaesthetists Gt. Britain and Ireland, Internat. Anaesthesia Rsch. Soc., Australian Med. Assn. Roman Catholic. Office: PO Box 259, Berwick 3806, Australia

BACON, JENNIFER HELEN, civil servant; b. Birmingham, Eng., Apr. 16, 1945; d. Lionel James and Joyce (Chapman) B. BA with honors, New Hall, Cambridge, Eng., 1967. Various positions London, 1967-77; prin. pvt. sec. Sec. of State for Employment, London, 1977-78; contr. govt. tng. ctrs. Manpower Svcs. Commn., London, 1978-80; dir. adult tng. Manpower Svcs. Commn., Sheffield, Eng., 1982-86; head machinery of govt. mgmt. pers. Cabinet Office, London, 1981-82; under-sec. sch. curriculum and assessment Dept. Edn. and Sci., London, 1986-89; prin. fin. officer Employment Dept., London, 1989-91, dir. resources and strategy, 1991-92; dep. dir. gen. Health and Safety Exec., London, 1992-95, dir. gen., 1995—; vis. fellow Nuffield Coll., Oxford, Eng., 1989-97; hon. fellow New Hall Cambridge, 1997; mem. Adv. Com. Degree Adwarding Powers, 1997; bd. dirs. Sheffield Devel. Corp., 1992-95. Decorated companion Order of Bath. Avocations: travel, classical music/opera, walking. Office: Health and Safety Exec, 2 Southwark Bridge, London SE1 9HS, England

BACON, PAUL ANTHONY, rheumatology educator, consultant; b. London, May 3, 1938; s. Francis William and Phyllis Bacon; m. Jean Mary Leech; children: Sarah, Alison, Lucy; children from previous marriage: Emma, Timothy. BA, Cambridge (Eng.) U., 1959, MBBCh, 1962. Rsch. registrar Kennedy Inst., London, 1965-67; sr. registrar St. Bartholomew's Hosp., London, 1967-71; rsch. fellow UCLA, 1971; cons. physician Royal Nat. Hosp. Rheumatic Disease, Bath, Eng., 1972-81; hon. sr. lectr. U. Bath., 1972-81; prof. rheumatology Med. Sch. Birmingham, Eng., 1981—; vis. rsch. fellow NIH, 1987-88; vis. prof., U. Amsterdam, 1994—, U. Melbourne, Australia, 1997—; lectr. confs. Contbr. numerous articles about vasculitis to med. jours. Fellow Royal Coll. Physicians; mem. Brit. Soc. Rheumatology (former coun. mem., former chmn. edn. com.), Brit. Soc. Immunology, Am. Rheumatism Assn. (overseas mem.). Office: Dept Rheumatology, Birmingham U, Birmingham B15 2TT, England

BACOW, LAWRENCE SELDON, academic administrator, environmental educator; b. Detroit, Aug. 24, 1951; s. Mitchell Leon and Ruth Wertheim Bacow; m. Adele Fleet, June 1, 1975; children: Jay, Kenneth. SB, MIT, 1972; JD, M in Pub. Policy, Harvard U., 1976, PhD, 1978. Bar: Mass. 1978. Asst. prof. law and environ. policy MIT, Cambridge, 1977-84, assoc. prof. law and environ. policy, 1984-90, dir. Ctr. for Real Estate, 1990-92, prof. law and environ. policy, 1992-97, Lee and Geraldine Martin prof. environ. studies, 1997—, chmn. faculty, 1995-97, chancellor, 1998—; vis. assoc. prof. law Hebrew U., Jerusalem, 1981-82; rsch. assoc. Harvard Law Sch., Cambridge, 1982-88; vis. prof. Politecnico di Torino, Italy, 1990, U. Bari, Italy, 1991, Gabriela Mistral U., Santiago, Chile, 1992, 93, 94, 95, 97, Faculty Econs.-U. Amsterdam, The Netherlands, 1993-94; rsch. fellow The Tinbergen Inst., Amsterdam, 1993-94. Author: Bargaining for Job Safety and Health, 1980; co-author: (with M. O'Hare and D. Sanderson) Facility Siting and Public Opposition, 1982, (with L. Susskind and M. Wheeler) Resolving Environmental Regulatory Disputes, 1983, (with M. Wheeler) Environmental Dispute Resolution, 1984. Mem. presdl. transition team Occupl. Safety and Health Adminstrn., 1977; mem. socio-econ. subcom. NAS Com. on Surface Mining and Reclamation, 1978-79; advisor Mass. Spl. Legis. Commn. on Hazardous Water, 1980; gubernatorial appointee Mass. Hazardous Waste Facility Site Safety Coun., 1980-83; Town Meeting mem., Arlington, Mass., 1981-83; advisor Israel Environ. Protection Svc., 1981-83; chair citizens adv. com. Mass. Water Resources Authority, 1989; exec. com. One Thousand Friends Mass., 1989-95; advisor Cross Israel Hwy. Commn., 1994-95; dir. MIT Hillel, Cambridge, 1995-98, Jewish Cmty. Housing for the Elderly, Brighton, Mass., 1995—; trustee Hebrew Coll., Brookline, Mass., 1999—, Wheaton Coll., Norton, Mass., 1999—. Recipient William S. Ballard award Am. Soc. Real Estate, 1991; adminstrn. fellow Harvard U., 1972-76, post-doctoral fellow Ford Found., 1977; Legal scholar Ctr. for Pub. Resources, 1985. Mem. Mass. Bar Assn., Phi Beta Kappa. Jewish. Avocations: sailing, skiing, running. E-mail: bacow@mit.edu. Office: MIT 77 Massachusetts Ave Cambridge MA 02139-4307

BACZYK, KAZIMIERZ MARIAN, medicine educator; b. Kozmin, Poland, Mar. 1, 1926; s. Stanislaw and Elzbieta (Polrolniczak) B.; m. Maria Teresa Frankiewicz, July 2, 1949 (wid. Dec. 1996); children: Alice, Karola. Phys., Acad. of Medicine, Poznan, 1952, MD, 1960, Assoc. Prof., 1966; Prof Medicine, U. Med. Sci., Poznan, 1984. Medical diplomate. Asst. tutor Acad. of Medicine, Poznan, 1950-60, tutor, 1960-66, asst. prof., 1966-84; prof. medicine U. Med. Sci., Poznan, 1984-96; dep. rector Acad. Medicine, Poznan; organizer applied math. in medicine courses, 1961-66; coun. mem. Nefrologia i Dializoterapia Polska, 1998—. Mem. adv. coun. Min. of Health and Social Welfare, Warsaw, 1979-88; mem. nephrology coun. Gdansk, 1985—. Maj. RKU Poznan, 1976. Recipient award for Young Scientists, Min. of Health, 1953, Disting. medal Nat. Kidney Found., Washington, 1990. Mem. Polish Soc. of Nephrology (pres. 1986-89), Polish Assn. Nephrology (pres. 1998—), N.Y. Acad. of Scis., Polish Renal Assn. (pres. 1997—), Poznan Found. of Dialysis (pres. adv. coun. 1991—). Avocations: gen. history, math. Office: Dept Nephrology, 49 Przybyszewskiego, 60-355 Poznan Poland

BADAL, JOSÉ IGNACIO, geophysics educator; b. Murcia, Spain, July 30, 1945; s. José Badal and Encarnación Nicolás; m. Carmen Soriano, June 26, 1972; 1 child, Alejandro. BS in Physics with honors, U. Zaragoza, Spain, 1968; PhD in Physics, U. Zaragoza, 1976. Asst. prof. U. Zaragoza, 1971-76, assoc. prof., 1976-77, 78-79, sr. lectr., 1979-84, prof., 1985—, head seismology group, 1990—; dir. rsch. projects, 1987—; project officer, project coord., U.E.; referee Nat. Agy. for Sci. Evaluation, Madrid, 1995—; rsch. scientist Geophys. Obs. of Toledo, Nat. Geog. Inst., Spain, 1987-88; dep. dir. Nat. Geog. Inst., Spain, 1996; v.p. exec. coun. European-Mediterranean Seismol. Ctr.; mem. joint sci. commn. Air Force Tech. Applications Ctr. U.S. and Nat. Geog. Inst. Spain; mem. coun. Internat. Seismol. Ctr. Mem. planning bd. Consejo Seguridad Nuc. España, com. d'orientation sci. Ctr. Euro-Mediterranéen d'Evaluation et de Prevention du Risque Sismique, Com. Estatal Coordianción. Fellow French Govt., Geophys. Lab., U. Grenoble, France, 1977-78. Mem. Am. Geophys. Union, Seismol. Soc. of Am., European Geophys. Soc., Europeam Seismol. Commn. (titular). Avocations: classic music, jazz music, reading, hist. novel. Fax: 34 976 761140. E-mail: badal@posta.unizar.es. Office: U. Zaragoza Faculty Scis, Bldg B, Pedro Cerbuna 12, 50009 Zaragoza Spain

BADALAMENTI, ANTHONY, financial planner; b. St. Louis, Apr. 1, 1940; s. Sebastino and Grace (Orlando) B.; 1 child, Annette Marie. BS in Acctg., Washington U., 1970. CPA, Mo.; registered investment advisor. Staff acct. Fischer & Fischer, CPAs, St. Louis, 1959-63; acct. McDonnell Aircraft Corp., St. Louis, 1963-65; asst. chief acct. Dempsey Tegler, Inc., St. Louis, 1965-66; contr. Cummins Mo. Diesel, Inc., St. Louis, 1966-67; sr. acct. Elmer Fox & Co., CPAs, St. Louis, 1967-71; pvt. practice St. Louis, 1972-94; fin. planner Asset Builders Fin. Planners, St. Louis, 1995—; tchr. Meramec C.C., St. Louis, 1973-75. Mem. Mo. Soc. CPAs, Crestwood-Sunset Hills C. of C. (pres. 1980-81, Bus. Profl. Month award 1986, 91), Rotary (pres. Crestwood-Sunset Hills chpt. 1982-83). Republican. Roman Catholic. Avocations: basketball, softball, dancing. Home: 1865 Locks Mill Dr Fenton MO 63026-2662 Office: 4400 S Lindbergh Blvd Ste 3 Saint Louis MO 63127-1603

BADALAMENTI, FRED LEOPOLDO, artist, educator; b. Long Island City, N.Y., June 25, 1935; s. Leopoldo and Concetta (Vitale) B.; m. Barbara J. Frankenfield, June 14, 1959; children: Katherine, Alexander, Frederick. Student, Pratt Inst., 1953-55, U. Alaska, 1957-58; BS, SUNY, New Paltz, 1961; MFA, Bklyn. Coll., 1967. Art tchr. Newburgh (N.Y.) Pub. Schs., 1960-63, Deer Park (N.Y.) High Sch., 1963-65; prof. emeritus Bklyn. Coll., 1967-92; vis. prof. art, lectr. SUNY, Stony Brook, 1977-78, 80, 81, 83; dep. chmn. for studio art Bklyn. Coll., 1990-92, dep. chmn. for grad. art, 1972-89; dir. First St. Gallery, N.Y.C., 1978; adj. faculty art dept. Bklyn. Coll., 1992-93, Stony Brook U., 1993-99. One man shows include Suffolk Community Coll., 1971, First Street Gallery, 1973, 76, 80, 89, Nassau County Mus. of Fine Arts, 1987, St. Joseph's Coll., 1987, The Alfred Van Loen Gallery, South Huntington, N.Y., 1998; exhibited paintings and drawings of representational art in N.Y.C. and L.I., 1967—. With USAF, 1955-59. Bklyn. Coll. grad. fellow, 1965-67. Mem. Coll. Art Assn., AAUP. Avocations: travel, tennis, gardening. Home: 182 Lower Sheep Pasture Rd East Setauket NY 11733-1826

BADANIAN, SHALIKO HOVAKIM, chemistry researcher, educator; b. Akhalkalak, Georgia, Oct. 24, 1932; s. Hovakim Sahak and Bersabe Hovhannes (Manoukian) B.; m. Susan Ghazar Vardapetian, Nov. 29, 1959; 1 child, Narine. MS in Chemistry, Yerevan (Armenia) State U., 1956, PhD in Chemistry, 1961, DSc, 1971, Prof., 1972. Rschr. inst. organic chemistry Armenian Nat. Acad. Sci., Yerevan, 1956-58, head lab., 1968-88, head inst., 1988—; academician, 1996; rschr. Oxford (Eng.) U., 1967, U. Paris, 1976, Max-Plank Inst. Medicine, Heidelberg, Germany, 1978; adj. prof. South Ill. U., Carbondale, Ill., 1980. Contbr. over 350 articles to profl. jours. Rsch. grantee Internat. Sci. Found., 1994. Fellow Armenian Nat. Acad. Sci. Home: Apt 18 47/1 Furmanov St, Yerevan Armenia Office: Nat Acad Sci Inst Org Chem, 167 a Zak Kanakertsi St, Yerevan Armenia

BADARY, OSAMA AHMED, pharmacologist, educator; b. Cairo, Egypt, Mar. 8, 1961; s. Ahmed Mohamed Badary and Faika Mahmoud Khater; m. Mona Kamal Darwish, Dec. 12, 1995; 1 child, Marwan. B, Cairo U., 1983; biochemist, Al-Azhar U., 1985, MS, 1988; PhD, Al-Azhar U., U. Ga., 1991. Demonstrator, lectr., asst. prof. Al-Azhar U., Cairo, 1984-90, 91-96; rsch. assoc. U. Ga., Athens, 1990-91; assoc. prof. King Saud U., Riyadh, Saudi Arabia, 1996-98, Ain Shams U., Cairo, 1998—. Contbr. articles to profl. jours. Grantee USA/AID, 1990. Mem. Internat. Fedn. Clin. Chemistry, Egyptian Soc. Pharmacology, Egyptian Soc. Clin. Chemistry. Home: 26th July St Bldg 2, El-Mohandeseen Cairo, Egypt Office: Dept Pharmacology and Toxicology, Fac Pharm, Al-Azhar U, Nasr City Cairo Egypt

BADAWI, MOHAMED EL SAYED MOHAMMED, engineering manager; b. Suez, Egypt, Feb. 27, 1950; s. El Sayed Mohamed B.; m. Eslah Abd El Ghafar Rashed; children: Iman, Ahmed, Mahmoud. BS in Chem. Engring., Alexandria U., Egypt, 1974, postgrad., 1975. Process engr. Alexandria Petroleum Co., 1974-78; project chem. engr. Braun Egypt Engring. Co., 1978-80; chem. engr. leader ENPPI, Cairo, 1980-84, sr. lead chem. engr., 1984-89, deputy mgr. chem. engring. dept., 1989-93, project mgr., 1993-96, engring. mgr., 1996—; engr. or mgr. on over 38 projects in fields of petroleum and petrochem. industries, gas processing, oil and gas prodn. (onshore and off-shore) and offsites and utilities prodn. and distbn., know-how and process lic. selection, techno-econ. feasibility studies. Office: ENPPI, 1A Ahmed Elzomor, 11361 Cairo Egypt

BADDELEY, ALAN DAVID, psychologist; b. Leeds, Eng., Mar. 23, 1934; s. Donald and Nellie (Hansen) Baddeley; m. Hilary Ann White; children: Roland, Gavin, Barty. BA in Psychology with honors, U. Coll., London, 1956; MA in Psychology, Princeton U., 1957; PhD, Cambridge (Eng.) U., 1963. Scientist Med. Research Council Applied Psychology Unit, Cambridge, 1958-67, dir., 1974-95; prof. dept. psychology U. Bristol, 1995—; lectr. then reader in psychology U. Sussex, Eng., 1967-72; prof. dept. psychology U. Stirling, Scotland, 1972-74. Author: The Psychology of Memory, 1976, Your Memory: A User's Guide, 1982, Working Memory, 1986, Human Memory Theory and Practice, 1990, Essentials of Human Memory, 1999. Decorated comdr. Brit. Empire; Chuchill Coll. fellow, 1987-95. Fellow Royal Soc.; mem. European Acad., Brit. Psychol. Soc., Exptl. Psychology Soc., Psychonomic Soc., European Soc. for Cognitive Psychology, Am. Acad. Arts and Scis. Office: U Bristol Dept Psychology, 8 Woodland Rd, Bristol B58 1TN, England

BADDERS, REBECCA SUSANNE, military officer, educator, writer; b. Knoxville, Tenn., Jan. 6, 1962; d. John Albert and Tamara Elizabeth (Day) B. BA in Edn., U. Fla., 1984; MA in Edn., U. South Fla., Tampa and St. Petersburg, 1997. Cert. profl. tchr., Fla. Commd. ensign USN, 1984, advanced through grades to lt. commdr., 1995; oceanographic watch officer Naval Facility Brawdy, Wales, 1984-86; oceanographic officer anti-submarine warfare Comdr. Undersea Surveillance, Norfolk, Va., 1986-90; dept. head Readiness Tng. Facility, Dam Neck, Va., 1990-93; tchr. Pinellas County Schs., Largo, Fla., 1994-97; commanding officer Naval Weapon Sta., Charleston, S.C., 1995-97; exec. officer Naval Res. Ctr., Kearny, N.J., 1997-99, Earle, N.J., 1999—; faculty rep. Pinellas County Tchrs. Assn., Largo, 1994-97. Author: Maddy and the Peek-A-Boo Moon, 1995. V.p., bd. dirs. Pilot Club Internat., Mid-Pinellas, Fla., 1993-99. Recipient Navy Achievement medal, 1990, 93, 96. Mem. Naval Res. Assn., Res. Officers Assn., Navy League of U.S., Coun. for Exceptional Children, U. Fla. Alumni Assn., LHS Alumni Assn., Internat. Order of Rainbow (worthy advisor, pres. 1975-82), Scabbard and Blade, Kappa Delta Pi. Republican. Episcopalian. Avocations: travel, computers, reading, gourmet cooking, arts. E-mail: rbadders@aol.com. Office: Naval Res Ctr Earle 201 Hwy 34 S Bldg C-3 Colts Neck NJ 07722-1902

BADDILEY, SIR JAMES, biochemist; b. Manchester, England, May 15, 1918; s. James and Ivy Logan (Cato) B.; m. Hazel Mary Townsend, Sept. 20, 1944; 1 child, Christopher James. BSC in Chemistry, U. Manchester, 1941, MSc, 1942, PhD, 1944, DSc, 1954; DSc (hon.), Heriot-Watt U., Bath U.; ScD, U. Cambridge, 1986. Staff dept. biochemistry Lister Inst. Preventive Medicine, London, 1949-54; Rockefeller traveling fellow Harvard U. Med. Sch., 1954; prof. organic chemistry U. Newcastle upon Tyne (formerly U. Durham), 1955-77, prof. chem. microbiology, 1977-83, dir. microbiology chemistry rsch. lab., head Sch. Chemistry, 1968-78; sci. and engring. rsch. coun. sr. fellow U. Cambridge, 1981-84; adb. bd. Brit. Nat. Com. Biochemistry, 1961-66, govt. grant bd. Royal Soc., 1962-66, coun., 1977-79, mem. coun. and coms. sci. and engring. rsch. coun., 1979-81; adv. com. CIBA and CIBA-GEIGY fellowships, 1966-88; Karl Folkers lectr., vis. prof. U. Ill., 1962. Knighted 1977; recipient Meldola medal Royal Inst. Chemistry, 1947; Sir Clement Toyds meml. scholar U. Manchester, 1942, Beyer fellow, 1943-44; Imperial Chem. Industries fellow U. Cambridge, 1945-49, Swedish Med. Rsch. Coun. at Wenner-Grens Inst., Stockholm, 1947-49; fellow Pembroke Coll., Cambridge U. Fellow Royal Soc. (Leeuwenhoek lectr. 1967, Davy medal 1974), Royal Soc. Edinburgh, Royal Soc. Chemistry (past meml. coun., Corday-Morgan medal and prize 1952, Tilden lectr. 1959, Pedler lectr. 1978); mem. Biochem. Soc. (com. 1964), Soc. Gen. Microbiology (coun. 1973-75), Am. Soc. Biochemistry and Molecular Biology (hon.). E-mail: james@baddiley.fsnet.co.uk. Office: U Cambridge Dept Biochemistry, Tennis Court Rd, Cambridge CB2 1QW, England also: c/o Royal Soc, 6 Carlton House Terr, London SW1Y 5AG, England

BADDOUR, ANNE BRIDGE, pilot; b. Royal Oak, Mich.; d. William George and Esther Rose (Pfiester) Bridge; m. Raymond F. Baddour, Sept. 25, 1954; children: Cynthia Anne, Frederick Raymond, Jean Bridge. Student, Detroit Bus. Sch., 1948-50; BA, Pine Manor Coll. Stewardess Eastern Airlines, Boston, 1952-54; instr. aero. Powers Sch., Boston, 1958; co-pilot, flight attendant Raytheon Co., Bedford, Mass., 1958-63; flight dispatcher, ferry Pilot Comerford Flight Sch., Bedford, 1974-76; adminstrv. asst., ferry pilot Jenney Beachcraft, Bedford, 1976; mgr., pilot Balt. Airways, Inc., Bedford, 1976-77; rsch. pilot Lincoln Lab. Flight Test Facility MIT, Lexington, 1977-97; aviation cons., corp. pilot Energy Resources, Inc., Cambridge, Mass., 1974-84; holder World Class speed records for single-engine aircraft; Boston to Goose Bay, Labrador, 1985, Boston to Reykjavik, Iceland, 1985, Por-

tland, Maine to Goose Bay, 1985, Portland to Reykjavik, 1985, Goose Bay to Reykjavik, 1985; records for twin-engine aircraft: Sept Isles to Goose Bay, 1988, Mont Joli to Goose Bay, 1988, Presque Isle to Goose Bay, 1988, Millinocket to Goose Bay, 1988, Bedford to Goose Bay, 1988, Goose Bay to Narssassrag, Greenland, 1988, Narssassrag to Klevelevic, Iceland, 1988, Narssassrag to Reykjavik, 1988, Bedford to Narssassrag, 1988, Millinochet to Narssassrag, 1988, Presque Isle to Narssassrag, 1988, Bedford to St. John, 1991, Bedford to Charlottetown, 1991, Charlottetown to Kennebunk, 1991, Charlottetown to Portsmouth, 1991, Muncton to Bedford, 1991, St. John to Kennebunk, 1991, St. John to Bedford, 1991. Bd. dirs. Cambridge Opera, 1977-79; mem. campaign coun. Mus. Transp., Boston; mem. coun. assocs. French Libr. in Boston; commr. Commonwealth of Mass., Mass. Aero. Commn., 1979-83; chmn. regional adv. coun. FAA, 1984-88; trustee bd. adminstrn. Amelia Earhart Birthplace Mus., 1992-93; trustee Daniel Webster Coll., Nashua, N.H., 1995—; v.p., trustee Friends of the Libr. Spl. Collections Boston U., 1997—; bd. dirs. Smithsonian Nat. Air & Space Mus., 1998—. Winner trophy Phila. Transcontinental Air Race, 1954, New Eng. Air Race, 1957, Clifford B. Harmon trophy Internat. Aviatrix, 1988; recipient Spl. Recognition award FAA, 1990; honoree Internat. Aviation Forest of Friendship, Atchison, Kans., 1991; named Pilot of the Year, New Eng. sect. Internat. Women Pilots Orgn./The Ninety-Nines, Inc., 1992. Mem. DAR, Fedn. Aeronautique Internat., Nat. Aero. Assn., Ninety-Nines (New Eng. Safety trophy 1986), Aero Club New Eng. (v.p. 1978-80, dir. 1978—), Aircraft Owners Pilots Assn., Nat. Pilots Assn., U.S. Sea Plane Pilots Assn., Assn. Women Transcontinental Air Race, Bostonian Soc., English Speaking Union, Soc. Exptl. Test Pilots, Friends of Switzerland, French Ctr. Libr., Belmont Hill Club, St. Botolph Club, Chilton Club, Boston Women's Travel Club, Harvard Travellers Club, Fairchild Tropical Garden Club. Republican. Episcopalian.

BADDOUR, FREDERICK RAYMOND, environmental consultant company executive; b. Boston, Feb. 21, 1957; s. Raymond Frederick and Anne Marie Baddour; m. Annette M. Casuso, Oct. 15, 1983; 1 child, Frederick R.G. BS in Geology, Syracuse U., 1980; MS in Marine Geology and Geophysics, U. Miami, 1983. Lic. site profl., Mass.; profl. geologist, Fla., N.C., S.C. Geologist Ea. Rsch. Group, Boston, 1984-86, Camp Dresser & McKee, Boston, 1986-88; dir. consulting svcs. Enviropact, Inc., Miami, 1988-92; pres. CRB Geol. and Environ. Svcs., Inc., Coral Gables, Fla., 1992—. E-mail: fbaddoul@crbgeo.net. Fax: 305-567-2853. Home: 6490 SW 122nd St Miami FL 33156-5549 Office: CRB Geol & Environ Svcs Inc 4573 Ponce De Leon Blvd Coral Gables FL 33146-1832

BADELL YTURRIAGA, MARIANA, chemical engineer; b. Havana, Cuba, Apr. 7, 1948; d. Eduardo and Rufina G. (Yturriaga) B.; m. Carlos Ernesto Roque Otero, Dec. 13, 1968 (div. 1976); 1 child, Vivianne Roque Badell; m. Rafael Peláez González, Feb. 20, 1981. Chem. engr., Polytech. U., 1971; MS, Polytech. U.-McMaster U., 1977; PhD, Mendeleiev Chem. Tech. Inst. 1983. Prodn. mgr. Opotherapic Plant, Havana, 1972-73, Vaccine and Hemoderivates Ctr., Havana, 1975-76; head computer-aided engring. dept. State Com. for Econ. Cooperation, Cuba, 1976-78, project developer chem. and pharm. industry, 1980-88; rschr., head engring. dept. Ctr. of Pharm. Chemistry, Havana, 1988-92; designer, tech. and automation Insulin Plant, Havana, 1992-93; prodn. lab. asst. Chewing Gum Factory Fleer Espanola, Barcelona, Spain, 1995; rsch. prof. U. Politech. Cataluña, Barcelona, 1995—; Referee Internat. Jour. of Prodn. Econs.; cons. in field. Contbr. numerous articles to profl. jours. Named Best Rschr. Ctr. of Pharm. Chemistry, 1990. Mem. Prodn. and Ops. Mgmt. Soc., Union de Ingenieros y Arquitectos de Cuba. Roman Catholic. Avocations: beach sports, swimming, photography, music, good films. Home: Onze de Setembre 15-17Ent 2, 08860 Castelldefels Spain Office: U Poltecnia Chem Engr Dept, Diagonal 647 ETSEIB DEQ, 08028 Barcelona Spain

BADEN HELLARD, RONALD, management consultant, arbitrator; b. London, Jan. 30, 1927; s. Ernest Baden and Alice May (Banks) Hellard; m. Kathleen Peggy Fiddes, Dec. 16, 1950 (wid. 1998); children: Sally, Diana Jaqueline. Dip. Arch., FRIBA, FCIARB, FAQMCI, FIM. Acting sec. Chartered Inst. Arbitrators, 1972-73; founding ptnr. Polycon-Architects and Mgmt. Cons., London, 1955-88; chief exec. TQM/Polycon, London, 1988-90; chmn. Polycon Cons., London, 1990—; chief exec. Polycon 3A's, 1996—; dir. TQM/Minosegzervezesi, Budapest, Hungary. Author: Management in Architectural Practice, 1964, Managing Change, 1971, Training for Change, 1972, Managing Construction Conflict, 1987, Total Quality in Construction Projects, 1993, Project Partnering in Principle and Practice, 1995; contbr. articles to profl. pubs. Capt. staff duties, Brit. mil. 1945-48, Mid. East. Fellow Royal Inst. Brit. Architects (pres. London soc. 1967-69), Chartered Inst. of Arbitrators (mem. coun. 1970-84), Brit. Inst. Mgmt. (chmn. so. region 1959-64), Brit. Quality Found. (chmn. steering group of cons. 1994-98). Avocations: badminton, tennis, travel. Office: Polycon Group of Cons, 97 Vanbrugh Park, London SE3 7AL, England

BADER, HERMANN JOSEPH, pharmacologist, educator; b. Furtwangen, Germany, Nov. 23, 1927; s. Joseph Bernhard and Martha (Müllegger) B.; m. Gertraude Haack, May 1, 1958; children: Sylvia, Andreas, Raoul, Maureen, Gregor, Oliver, Niklas, Matthias, Dominik. MD, U. Munich, 1955. Rsch. assoc. dept. physiology U. Munich, 1954-56, intern dept. medicine, 1956-57, German Sci. Found. scholar, 1957-58; instr. dept. physiology Vanderbilt U., Nashville, 1959-60, asst. prof., 1960, 63-66; instr. U. Munich, Germany, 1960-61; asst. prof. dept. physiology U. Wurzburg, Germany, 1961-63; assoc. prof. dept. pharmacology and toxicology U. Miss. Sch. Medicine, Jackson, 1966-70, prof., 1970-72; prof., head dept. pharmacology and toxicology U. Ulm, Germany, 1972-96, emeritus prof., 1996—; dir. minority admission U. Ulm, 1969-72, dean sch. medicine, 1974-75, 79-83. With German Infantry, 1944-45, prisoner of war, U.S.A., 1945-46. Mem. Am. Soc. Pharmacology and Exptl. Therapeutics, German Soc. Pharmacology and Toxicology, Biophys. Soc. U.S.A., German Biophys. Soc., German Biol. Chemistry soc., German Phys. Soc. Roman Catholic. Home: Neue Welt 6, 89269 Voehringen-Illerberg Germany

BADESCU, MIHAIL VIOREL, thermal engineering educator, researcher; b. Bughea de Jos, Arges, Romania, Sept. 24, 1953; s. Mihai and Eugenia (Malancioiu) B.; m. Jenica Basu, Dec. 2, 1978; children: Alina Mihaela, Gabriel Alexandru. BS, Dr. Petru Groza Coll., Bucharest, Romania, 1972; MSc, Polytech. Inst., Bucharest, Romania, 1977; PhD, Polytech. U., Bucharest, Romania, 1993; diplomate, World Engish Inst., Ann Arbor, Mich., 1995. Insp. engr. Enterprise for Artificial Fibres Viscofil, Bucharest, Romania, 1978-82; rschr. Polytech. Inst., Bucharest, Romania, 1982-90; asst. prof. Polytech. U., Bucharest, Romania, 1990-93, lectr., 1993-99, assoc. prof., 1999—; vis. fellow U. Southampton, Eng., 1995, vis. acad. 1997, 99; vis. prof. U. Copenhagen, 1999, U. Chemnitz, Germany, 1999; peer reviewer Internat. Sci. Found., N.Y.C., 1996—; editl. policy cons. Kluwer Acad. Pubs., Dordrecht, The Netherlands, 1996—. Author: The Physics of Selenium and Tellurium, 1979 (Romanian Acad. prize for physics 1981), Recent Advances in Finite-Time Thermodynamics, 1999, Thermodynamic Optimization of Complex Energy Systems, 1999; also articles in Jour. Physics, Jour. Solar Energy, Jour. Applied Physics. Recipient award for energetics Romanian Inst. Energetics, Bucharest, 1985; grantee: European Commn., Brussels, 1992; named to Atlas of Experts, World Energy Found., Paris, 1998. Mem. Internat. Solar Energy Soc., European Astron. Soc., Internat. Radiation Physics Soc. Avocation: sports. Home: Sos Pantelimon 89, Blvd 404-405 ap 63, Bucharest Romania Office: Polytech U of Bucharest, Spl Independentei 313, 79590 Bucharest Romania

BADGER, RONALD KAY, lawyer; b. Horton, Jabs., Aug. 24, 1933; s. Clarence E. and Josephine L. (Rick) B.; m. Janet L. Horner, Feb. 16, 1963; children: Hellen J. Badger Haag, Ronald K. Jr., Laura J. Badger Davis. BS in Bus., U. Kans., 1958, BS in Law, 1961, JD, 1968. Bar: Kans. 1961, U.S. Dist. Ct. Kans. 1961, U.S. Ct. Appeals (10th cir.) 1973, U.S. Supreme Ct. 1982, U.S. Ct. Claims 1990. Law clk. to Judge Arthur J. Stanley, US. Dist. for Kans., Kansas City, 1961-62; spl. asst. to U.S. atty. for dist. of Kans., Dept. Justice, Topeka, 1962-64; assoc. Foulston & Siefkin, Wichita, Kans., 1964-66; atty. in contract adminstrn. Boeing Co., Wichita, 1966-68; pvt. practice, Wichita, 1968—. Bd. dirs. Kans. Bar Jour., 1966-82; contbr. articles to legal jours. Bd. dirs. Wichita Symphony Soc., 1970—. Mem. FBA (pres. Kans. chpt. 1978-80), Kans. Bar Assn., Wichita Bar Assn., Wichita Estate Planning Coun. (sec. 1996-97, pres. 1997-98) Lions (pres. Wichita

1984-85), Christian Legal Soc. Republican. Methodist. Office: 343 N Market St Ste 200 Wichita KS 67202-2009

BADGER, WILLIAM ALDON, JR., business executive; b. Balt., July 19, 1955; s. William Aldon Sr. and Carol Badger; m. Kathi Badger, June 24, 1978 (div. Aug. 1985); m. Patricia Colleen Badger, Oct. 11, 1986; 1 child, Hilary Shea. BS, Towson U., 1976. Cert. econ. developer. Sr. bus. rep. Md. Dept. Bus. Econ. Devel., Balt., 1977-94; pres., CEO Anne Arundel Econ. Devel. Corp., Annapolis, Md., 1995—. V.p. Harbor Valley Homeowners Assn., Brooken Park, Md.; bd. mem. No. Anne Arundel County Chamber, Glen Burnie, Md., Internat. Devel. Coun., Linthicum, Md. Mem. Am. Econ. Devel. Coun. (assoc.), Indsl. Devel. Rsch. Coun. (assoc.). Republican. Avocations: golf, running, tennis. E-mail: bbadger@aaedc.org. Home: 5631 Harbor Valley Dr Baltimore MD 21225-2967 Office: Anne Arundel Econ Devel Corp 2660 Riva Rd Ste 200 Annapolis MD 21401-7305

BADGLEY, JOHN ROY, architect; b. Huntington, W. Va., July 10, 1922; s. Roy Joseph and Fannie Myrtle (Limbaugh) B.; m. Janice Atwell, July 10, 1975; 1 son, Adam; children by previous marriage: Dan, Lisa, Holly, Marcus, Michael. AB, Occidental Coll., 1943; MArch, Harvard, 1949; postgrad., Centro Internazionale, Vincenza, Italy, 1959. Pvt. practice, San Luis Obispo, Calif., 1952-65; chief architect, planner Crocker Land Co., San Francisco, 1965-80; v.p. Cushman & Wakefield Inc., San Francisco, 1980-84; pvt. practice, San Rafael, Calif., 1984—; tchr. Calif. State U. at San Luis Obispo, 1952-65; bd. dirs. Ft. Mason Ctr., Angel Island Assn. Served with USCGR, 1942-54. Mem. AIA, Am. Arbitration Assn., Golden Gate Wine Soc. Home and Office: 1356 Idylberry Rd San Rafael CA 94903-1074 .

BADHAM, LINDA FRANCES, Welsh government official; b. Malta, May 26, 1950; (parents Brit. citizens); d. Gordon James and Mary Audrey (Puleston) Elson; m. Paul Brian Leslie Badham, Aug. 9, 1969; 1 child, Dominic Gordon Leslie. BSc with 1st class honours, U. Birmingham, Eng., 1971; cert. in edn., U. Birmingham, 1972; PhD, U. Wales, Lampeter, 1981. Tchr. Edgbason H.S. for Girls, Birmingham, 1972-73, Lampeter Secondary Sch., 1974-78; tchr.r, head VI form Aberaeron (Wales) Comprehensive Sch., 1982-87; TVEI coord. Dyfed (Wales) Local Edn. Authority, 1988-90; dir. whole curriculum Curriculum Coun. for Wales, Cardiff, 1991-94; asst. chief exec. Curriculum and Assessment Authority for Wales, Cardiff, 1994-97, Qualifications, Curriculum & Assessment Auth. Wales, Cardiff, 1997—; tutor, counsellor for MA in edn. Open U. Wales, 1991-95. Co-author: Immortality or Extinction?, 1982, Evaluation in Schools, 1992; co-editor, author: Death and Immortality in the Religion of the World, 1987; contbr. articles to profl. jours. Mem. Ch. in Wales. Avocations: singing, tennis, walking, swimming, concerts. Office: Qualif Curriculum-Assess, Auth for Wales, Womanby St, Cardiff CF10 9SX, Wales

BADILLO, VICTOR MANUEL, agronomist, educator; b. La Guaira, Venezuela, Oct. 15, 1920; s. Victor M. and Rosa Elvira (Franceri) B.; m. Nelly M. Blanco, Oct. 10, 1964; children: Enrique, Fernando, Nelly Mercedez, Hector, Sergio. Agronomist, Ctrl. U. of Venezuela, Caracas, 1948. Sch. dir. faculty of agronomy U. Ctrl. Venezuela, Caracas, 1949, dean faculty of agronomy, 1949-51, assoc. prof. dept. botany, 1951-53, titular prof. faculty of agronomy, 1953-76, active emeritus prof. faculty of agronomy, 1976—. Editor: Caricaceae, Segundo Esquema, 1993; author: Enumeracion de las Compuestas de Venezuela, 1994, Clave de la Familias de Plantas Superiores de Venezuela, 1951, 6 edits.; contbr. articles to profl. jours. Mem. Natural Sci. Soc., Prof's Assn. U. Ctrl. Venezuela. Avocations: reading, collection of plant's, botanical's explorations, botanical nomenclature. Office: U Ctrl Venezuela, Fac Agronomia Apartado 4579, Maracay 2101, Venezuela

BADING, HILMAR, molecular neurobiologist; b. Berlin, Nov. 3, 1958; s. Horst and Gisela (Heinze) B.; two children: Mila, Ruben. MD, U. Heidelberg, 1984. Rschr. Max Planck Inst. for Molecular Genetics, Berlin, 1985-89, Harvard Med. Sch., Boston, 1989-92, MRC Lab. of Molecular Biology, Cambridge, Eng., 1993—; mem. neurosci. panel Wellcome Trust; mem. editl. adv. bd. Jour. Molecular Neurosci. Contbr. articles to profl. jours. Grantee Deutsche Forschungs Gesellschaft, European Cmty., Epilepsy Rsch. Found. Mem. Am. Soc. for Neurosci. Office: MRC Lab of Molecular Biol, Hills Rd, Cambridge CB2 2QH, England

BADINSKI, NIKOLAI I., composer, pedagogue, violinist; b. Sofia, Bulgaria, Dec. 19, 1937. Student, Acad. Music, Bulgaria, 1956-61; masterclass attencance, Acad. Arts, East Berlin, 19967-70, Acad. Musicale Siena, Italy, 1976, 76. Composer, dozent, soloist, concert master; guest prof. Univs. Stockholm and Copenhagen; lectr. in field. Over 130 compositions, including ballets, 3 symphonies, 4 violin concertos, concerto for viola and orch., concerto for harpsicord, concerto for piano and piano orch., Reflexions of Wisdom for soloists, choir and orch., 7 Memorial Stones in Memoriam of the Holocaust Victimes, requiem for string orch., The Intoxicated Bat for orch., Decipio-Cycle, chamber music, electroacoustic music; numerous performances and broadcasts of his works worldwide, including several records, numerous CDs. Recipient first place prize 28th Internat. Competition for Composition, Violli, Italy, 1977, Internat. Stockhausen Competition for Composers, Italy, 1978, 29th Internat. Competition for Composers, Italy, 1978, Internat. Trieste prize for symphonic music, 1979, Prix de Rome, 1979, Prix de Paris, 1982. Mem. European Acad. Arts, Scis. and Humanities, Internat. Soc. Contemporary Music, German Composers Union, Internat. Haendel Soc., Richard Wagner Union. Home: Fröaufstrasse 3, 12161 Berlin Germany

BADIU, CORIN VIRGIL P., endocrinologist, educator; b. Bucharest, Romania, Mar. 6, 1964; s. Petru Silviu T. and Iulia T. (Badicel) B.; m. Liliana Trusca, Nov. 29, 1985; 1 child, Ruxandra Gabriela. Grad. in biochemistry, Sava Nat. Coll., Bucharest, 1983; MD, U. Bucharest, 1989. Physician Emergency Hosp., Bucharest, 1989-91; tng. in endocrinology, then endocrinologist C.I. Parhon Inst., Bucharest, 1991—; asst. prof. endocrinology Davila U., Bucharest, 1994-99, assoc. prof. endocrinology, 1999—. Author: Lecture Notes on Endocrinology, 1994, Textbook of Endocrinology, 1997; contbr. articles to med. jours., including Cell Tissue Rsch. Sgt. Romanian Army, 1981-82. Fellow Internat. Soc. Psychoneuroendocrinology; mem. Romanian Psychoneuroendocrine Soc. (treas. 1993—), N.Y. Acad. Scis. Avocations: classical music, electronic engineering, informatics. E-mail: rpnes@sunu.rnc.ro. Home: Ctim Aricescu Str 21 Ap 3, Bucharest Romania Office: Inst Endocrinology, Bd Aviatorilor 34-36, 71279 Bucharest Romania

BADLEY, WILLIAM J., education program director, English language educator. BA, U. Iowa, 1967; MDiv, So. Bapt. Theol. Sem., 1971; DA, Middle Tenn. State U., 1993. English/social studies tchr./substitute Louisville Pub. Schs., 1974-77; English instr. U. Louisville, 1976-78, Concordia Coll., Moorhead, Minn., 1978-79; English adj. Tenn. State U., Nashville, 1981-85; English adj. Middle Tenn. State U. Murfreesboro, 1981-85, devel. studies English instr., 1985—, dir. gen. studies, 1998—; ex-officio mem. gen. studies com. Middle Tenn. State U. Murfreesboro, 1998—, mem. dean's coun., 1998—. Contbr. articles to profl. jours. Mem. AAUP, Am. Assn. for Higher Edn., Coun. for Adminstrn. Gen. Studies (pres.-elect), Murfreesboro C. of C., Phi Kappa Phi. E-mail: wbadley@mtsu.edu. Office: Middle Tenn State Univ PO Box 78 Murfreesboro TN 37132-0001

BADLISHAH, ABDUL HALIM MU'ADZAM SHAH, Sultan of Kedah; b. Alor Star, Kedah, Malaysia, Nov. 28, 1927; s. Sultan Badlishah of Kadeh; m. Tunku Hajjah Bahiyah, Mar. 1956; 3 children. Grad., Sultan Abdul Hamid Coll., Alor, 1949; diploma social sci. and pub. adminstrn., Oxford (Eng.) U., 1955; D. Polit. Sci. (hon.), Thammasat U., Bangkok, Thailand. With Dist. Office, then Treasury Alor State, 1955—; raja muda of Kedah, 1949-57, regent, 1957-58; sultan State of Kedah, 1958—; dep. king, then king Conf. of Rulers, 1965-75; col.-in-chief Royal Malay Regt., 1975. Decorated D.K., 1964, D.K.M., 1971, D.M.N., 1959, D.U.K., 1958, S.P.M.K., 1964, D.K., 1969, D.K. (Pehang), 1970, 1st class Order Rising Sun (Japan), 1970, Bitang Maha Putera, Klas Satu (Indonesia), 1970, hon. knight grand cross Order Bath (U.K.), 1972, assoc. knight Order St. John, 1972, Order Ramnata (Thailand), 1973. Avocations: gold, billiards, photography, tennis. Office: c/o Press Attache Malaysian Embassy 2401 Massachusetts Ave NW Washington DC 20008-2851*

BADMAN, JOHN, III, real estate developer, architect; b. Kansas City, Mo., July 11, 1944; s. John II and Barbara (Smith) B.; m. Katherine Ballantine, May 12, 1984; children: Lindsay Cathryn, Barbara Smith, John IV. BA, Yale U., 1966, MArch, 1969, postgrad., 1969-70, M in Environmental Design, 1971. Registered architect, Conn.; real estate broker, Conn. Gen. mgr. S.J. Willy, Architects, New Haven, Conn., 1971-73; v.p. Schumacher & Forelle, Great Neck, N.Y., 1973-77, exec. v.p., 1986-87; dir. planning and devel. Dravo Engrs., N.Y.C., 1977-81; sr. v.p. Parsons, Brinckerhoff, Quade & Douglas, N.Y.C., 1981-86, also bd. dirs.; chmn., chief exec. officer Ballantine and Badman, Inc., Real Estate Developers, Greenwich, Conn., 1986—; sr. v.p. H.W. Lochner, Planners and Engrs., 1991—; chmn. Conf. of Patriotic and Hist. Socs., N.Y.C., 1993—. Mem. Lacrosse all-Am. Team U.S. Intercollegiate Lacrosse Assn., 1966. Mem. AIA, Soc. Colonial Wars (coun. 1987—, chmn. exec. com. 1996—, gov. 1996—), The Pilgrims of the U.S., Colonial Order of the Acorn (chancellor 1997—), Baronial Order of the Magna Charta, Jamestown Soc., Nat. Coun. Archtl. Registration Bds. (cert.), New Eng. Soc. N.Y., Round Hill Assn., Mayflower Soc., Plymouth Com., Yale Club (N.Y.C.), Greenwich Country Club, Greenwich Polo Players Club, Adirondack League Club (Old Forge, N.Y.). Republican. Episcopalian. Home: 20 Mackenzie Gln Greenwich CT 06830-3421

BADR, AHMED ZAKI, engineering educator; b. Tanta, Gharbia, Egypt, Jan. 1, 1956; s. Zaki B.; m. Nayera Moftah, June 22, 1985; children: Yasmine, Nesma. BSEE, Ain Shams U., Cairo, 1978, MSEE, 1982, PhD, 1986. From asst. to asst. prof. Ain Shams U., Cairo, 1978-92, assoc. prof. computer and sys. engring. dept., 1992-98, prof., 1998—; cons. and rschr. in field. Recipient Disting. Rsch. award Ain Shams U., 1995. Mem. IEEE (sr. mem.). Office: Faculty Engring, Abassia 1 Elsarayat St, 11517 Cairo Egypt

BADRAN, ABDULKARIM, biomedical engineer; b. Damascus, Syria, Jan. 3, 1960; s. Omer and Amina Badran; m. Roba Al-Abbasi, Apr. 10, 1987; children: Abdul Allah, Dian, Abdul Rahman, Dania. B of Engring., U. Damascus, 1983, diploma computer sci., 1985; MS, PhD, U. Strathclyde, Glasgow, 1990; PGCE, U. Corby, 1995. Cert. quality assurance. Comml. cons. Damascus, 1982-84; lectr. in electronics U. Damascus, 1984-86; computer advisor U. Strathclyde, 1986-90; postdoctoral rschr. Glasgow, 1990-96; lectr. in computing London, 1996—; cons. Nat. Hosp., London, 1986-90; translator Strathclyde Interpreting, 1987-96; tchr. English/Arabic, 1986-95. Contbr. articles to profl. jours. including Jour. of Biomed. Engring., Magnetic Resonance Imaging, Radar and Remote Sensing, English for Engineers. Mem. IEE (Cert. of Merit 1995), Translation Inst. of Linguists, Ednl. Inst. for Scotland, Dept. for Edn. and Employment. Achievements include optimum teaching for secondary school children. Office: Coulsdon Coll, Placehouse Ln Old Coulsdon, Surrey CR5 1YA, England

BADREK-AMOUDI, HASSAN SAID, pediatrician; b. Hadramaut, Dec. 15, 1937; s. Said Hassan Badrek-Amoudi; married; four children. MB BCh, U. Wales, 1964; D of Tropical Medicine and Health, Liverpool Sch. Tropical Med., 1965; Diploma in Child Health, Royal Colls., London, 1972; Diploma in Tropical Child Health, U. Liverpool, 1971. Resident in medicine Royal Guent Hosp., Wales, 1964-65; resident in pediatrics Queen Elizabeth Hosp., Aden, 1966-67, Alder Hey Children's Hosp., Liverpool, Eng., 1970-71; specialist Infectious Diseases Hosp., Jeddah, Saudi Arabia, 1967-69; pediatrician Lebanese Hosp., Jeddah, 1972-79; pediatrician, med. dir. Bugshan Gen. Hosp., Jeddah, 1980-87; pediatrician Dr. Hassan Badrek Clinics, Jeddah, 1988—; cons. pediatrician Al Salama Hosp., Jeddah, 1991-93. Founding ptnr., dir. planning and mgmt. Bugshan Gen. Hosp., 1976-87. Fellow Royal Soc. Tropical Medicine and Hygiene (local sec. 1985—), Am. Acad. Pediatrics, Internat. Soc. Tropical Pediatrics (standing com.); mem. Brit. Med. Assn., Internat. Pediatrics Assn., Consultative Coun. Saudi Pediatric Assn. Muslim. Avocations: reading, photography, swimming, travel. Office: Dr Hassan Badrek Clinics, PO Box 1845, Jeddah 21441, Saudi Arabia

BADURA, CARL WERNER, information systems specialist; b. N.Y.C., Oct. 23, 1937; s. Carl Ottomar and Herta Helene (Goetze) B.; m. Christina Elizabeth Schrot, June 12, 1960; children: Carolyn, Carl H., Christopher, Curt. AAS in Elec. Engring., Westchester Community Coll., Valhalla, N.Y., 1963; student, NYU, 1963-64. Registered profl. engr., N.Y. Jr. elec. engr. Otis Elevator Co., N.Y.C., 1956-67; sr. programmer analyst Orange & Rockland Utilities, Spring Valley, N.Y., 1967-69; sr. systems engr. RCA Computer Div., N.Y.C., 1969-71; programming mgr. Nestle Co., Inc., White Plains, N.Y., 1971-78; data processing mgr. Columbus Line, Inc., N.Y.C., 1978-85; dir. info. svcs. Maryknoll (N.Y.) Fathers & Bros., 1985-93; ind. bus. cons. Watkinsville, Ga., 1993—. Spoke chmn. Jaycees, New City, N.Y., 1969; com. chmn. Boy Scouts Am., Congers, N.Y., 1975-77, scoutmaster, 1978-79; fin. sec. South Hudson Tres Dias, Peekskill, N.Y. Mem. Am. Mgmt. Assn., Data Processing Mgmt. Assn. Avocations: little leagues, golf, tennis, bowling. Address: 1060 Creek Bridge Dr Watkinsville GA 30677-4906

BAE, HYUNG, economist; b. Pusan, Korea; s. Joon and Pilja (Kim) B.; m. Chong Ok Kim, Jan. 29, 1989; children: Hyunji, Hyungkwon. BA, Sungkyunkwan U., Seoul, Korea, 1981; MA, U. Wis., 1984, PhD, 1985. Asst. prof. Dongguk U., Seoul, 1987-90, assoc. prof., 1990-95, prof., 1995—. Editor Jour. Korean Econometric Soc.; contbr. articles to profl. jours. Mem. Korean Econ. Assn. (Chongram Acad. award 1992). Office: Dongguk U Dept Econs, 3-26 Pil-Dong Chung-ku, Seoul 100-715, Republic of Korea

BAE, SUNG NAM, cable television company executive; b. Seoul, Republic of Korea, Nov. 1, 1944; s. Hyung-Jin and Yu-Sil (Lim) B.; children: Sung-Hyun, So-Hyun. Grad., Kyunghee U., Seoul, 1966, Korea U.; grad. Sch. Bus. Adminstrn., Yonsei U.; grad. London Bus. Sch., Brit. Coun.; hon. degree of polit. sci., Moscow U., Almati, Kazakhstan; hon. degree, Chong Ha U., China, 1999. Rep. pres. Hanil Prodn. Co., Seoul, 1968-89; pres. Hanil Prodn. Co., 1989—; chmn. Youngsan Cable TV, Inc.; pres. Yongsan Cable TV Inc., Seoul, 1973—. Pres. adv. coun. Dem. Peaceful Unification; chmn. Yongsan Dist. Consultative Coun. Adv. Coun. on Dem. and Peaceful Unification; mem. Sch. Violence Prevention Com., Yong San Ku; mem. Yong San-Ku Inhabitants Disting. Svc. Judge Com.; bd. dirs. Yong San Cultural Ctr.; chmn. pub. rels. sect. establishment com. Baek Bum Memory Hall; founding mem. Millennium Dem. Party; mem. consulting com. Yongsan Tax Office. Recipient Am. CLIO award (4th), 1974-85, Japan Advt. award (5th), 1975-84, Korea Broadcasting Advertisement award (2nd), 1984-85, citation from pres., commendation from Pres. Millennium Dem. Party; named hon. amb. State Ark., hon. amb. and hon. citizen Little Rock, Ark., hon. amb. and hon. citizen North Little Rock, Ark., hon. amb. Am. Taekwando Assn. Mem. Korea Advt. Assn. (bd. dirs. 1985), Korea Nonfiction and Comml. Film Prodrs. Assn. (chmn. 1985-89), Film Policy Adv. Com. (com. mem. 1986), Korea Cable TV Assn. (auditor), Korean Callgrapher Assn. (mem. consulting com.), Korea-New Zealand Culture Assn., Alumni Assn. Korea U. (bd. dirs.), Assn. of Korean Life-Long Edn. and Welfare Promotion (dir.), Korean-Am. Friendship Coun., Alumni Assn. Yonsei U. (bd. dirs.), KAIST Alumni Assn. (v.p.), Seoul Fgn. Correspondents Club, Yong San ku residents merit judge com., Korea Press Club, Rotary, Horse Riding Assn. (pres. 1989), Choongchungnam-Do. Avocations: golf, sea fishing. Office: Hanil Prodn Co Ltd Yongsan Cable TV Inc CHU Bldg, 244-9 Huam-dong Yongsan ku, Seoul Republic of Korea

BAE, YOUNG CHAN, chemical engineering educator; b. Taegu, Korea, Jan. 7, 1958; s. Bong Soo Bae and Hae Jung Park; m. Mikyung Joo, Dec. 23, 1987; children: Jang-ho, Joo-ho. BS, Hanyang U., Seoul, Korea, 1981; MS, Wayne State U., 1984, PhD, 1989; postgrad., U. Calif., Berkeley, 1989-91. Group leader Soane Techs., Inc., Hayward, Calif., 1991-94; asst. prof. Hanyang U., Seoul, 1994-97, assoc. prof., 1998—; dir. planning divsn. Grad. Sch. Advanced Material and Chem. engring., Hanyang U., Seoul, 1995—, dir. planning divsn. BK21 project, 1999; dir. Feasibility Evaluation Supporting Ctr., Seoul, 1998—. Evaluation com. mem. Ministry Edn. Korea, Seoul, 1999; WTA technomart adv. bd. Daejeon (Korea) City, 1999. Mem. Korean Phys. Soc. Achievements include 5 patents in field. Home: 508 Poongnap-Dong Songpa-ku, Seoul Korea Office: Hanyang U Divsn Chem Engr, 17 Hangdang-dong Sungdongku, Seoul 133-791, Korea

BAEHR, JUERGEN, geographer; b. Kassel, Germany, Oct. 31, 1940; s. Bruno and Marie (Goedecke) B.; m. Gudrun Patzke; 1 child, Ulrike. PhD, U. Marburg/Lahn, Fed. Republic Germany, 1967; Habilitation, U. Bonn, Fed. Republic Germany, 1973. Privatdozent U. Bonn, 1973-75; prof. U.

Mannheim, Fed. Republic Germany, 1975-77; full prof. U. Kiel, Fed. Republic Germany, 1977—; prorector U. Kiel, 1999—. Author: Chile, 1979, Bevoelkerungsgeographie, 1983; editor: Schleswig-Holstein, 1987, Die lateinamerikanische Grosstadt, 1995. Office: U Kiel, Olshausenstrasse 40, 24098 Kiel Federal Republic of Germany

BAEHR, RUDOLF, philologist; b. Bamberg, Fed. Republic Germany, Jan. 6, 1922; s. Georg and Barbara (Goertler) B.; m. Gabriele Seemeier, June 30, 1950; children: Christoph, Susanne. Abitur, Humanistisches Gymnasium, Bamberg, Fed. Republic of Germany, 1940; PhD, Univ., Munich, 1952, pvt. docent, 1954; PhD (hon.), Univ., Reims, France, 1973. Asst. prof. Univ., Munich, 1952-63; prof. Univ., Salzburg, Austria, 1964—. Author: Spanische Verslehre, 1962 (Gebhardt award 1963), Französische Verslehre, 1970; editor: Romanische Übungstexte, 1969—; contbr. articles to profl. jours. Decorated Grosses Silbernes Ehrenzeichen (Austria); Officier Légion d'Honneur (France); Officier Palmes académiques (France); Österreichisches Ehrenkreuz für Wissenschaft und Kunst I. Klasse (Austria); Ufficiale Ord. Merito (Italy); Officier Ordre Merite (Luxembourg); recipient Festschrift Internat. colleagues Göppingen, 1981, Internat. colleagues Tübingen, 1987. Mem. Deutsche Dante-Gesellschaft, Internat. Arthurian Soc., Österreichische Akademie der Wissenschaften. Roman Catholic. Office: Institut für Romanistik, Akademiestrasse 24, A-5020 Salzburg Austria

BAEK, WON-PIL, nuclear engineer, researcher, educator; b. Kochang, Korea, May 5, 1961; s. Byong-Jong and Jung-Hyo (Moon) B.; m. Pil-Soun Kwak, Jan. 10, 1988; children: Young-min, Young-joon. BS, Seoul Nat. U., 1982; MS, Korea Adv. Inst. Sci. and Tech, Seoul, 1984; PhD in Nuclear Engring., Korea Adv. Inst. Sci. and Tech, Taejon, 1991. Asst. sect. chief Korea Heavy Industries & Constrn. Co., Ltd., Changwon, Korea, 1984-87; postdoctoral fellow Korea Advanced Inst. Sci. and Tech., Taejon, 1991-92, sr. rschr., 1994—; vis. scientist Atomic Energy Can. Ltd., Chalk River, 1993; adj. assoc. prof. Chosun U., Kwangju, Korea, 1995—; Co-author: Critical Heat Flux, 1997, Nuclear Safety, 1998; contbr. articles to profl. jours.; patentee large passive pressurized water reactor, 1997. Mem. Korean Nuclear Soc., N.Y. Acad. Scis. Roman Catholic. Avocations: singing, table tennis. Home: 305-1503Expo Apt, Chonmin-dong, Yusong-Gu, Taejon 305-390, Korea Office: Korea Adv Inst Sci and Tech, 373-1 Kusong-dong, Yusong-gu, Taejon 305-701, Korea

BAENA, GUILLERMINA MARIA EUGENIA, communications educator, political consultant; b. Mexico City, June 25, 1947; d. Luis Baena and María Luisa (Fernández) Paz; m. Sergio Montero, June 8, 1981; children: Patricia, Alethia, Sergio Jonathan. Lic. in info. sci., Nat. U. Autonoma Mex., Mexico City, 1971, D in L.Am. Studies, 1981, MPA, 1984. Planification chief Nat. U. Autonoma Mex., 1982-84, chief radio programation, 1985-86, sci. comm. coord., 1990-94, educator polit. sci., cons., 1995-97; nat. investigator I Nat. Coun. Sci. and Tech., Mex., 1995—; cons. Burson Marsteller, Mex., 1997—, Pub. Internat., Mex., 1997—. Author seventeen books, including: Scientific Discourse Method, 1998, Political Credibility and Marketing Mix, 1998, Journalistic Discourse, 1999, Quality and Higher Education, 1999. Recipient Educative Excellence diploma Nat. and Acad. Inst. Ednl. Capacitation and Actualization, Mex., 1996, 3d Place Fimpes prize, 1998. Mem. N.Y. Acad. Scis., Assn. Comm. Rschrs., Apoyo Profl. en Comm. (pres. 1984), Coun. Nat. de Radiofusion Mex. (pres. 1990). Avocations: listening to radio, painting, writing books. Home: Colonia Portales, Rumania 509 Bis, 03300 Mexico City Mexico

BAER, ANNE, consultant; b. Fontenay-aux-Roses, France, June 11, 1967; d. Arnold and Colette (Veil) B.; m. Dan Golan, May 18, 1988 (div. July 1991); Yohann Dumas. BA in Polit. Scis., Hebrew U., Jerusalem, 1989; MA in Devel. and Coop., Sorbonne U., Paris, 1993; postgrad., ENGREF, 2000—. comm. officer for word water vision UNESCO, 1998-99. Adminstr., officer, consular Israeli Embassy, Kinshasa, Zaire, 1989-91; project officer for the Mediterranean Internat. Rsch. Ctr. on Devel. and Socio-Econ. Change, Paris, 1996-97; cons. UNESCO, Paris, 1993—; sci. advisor for the Euro-Mediterranean Conf. on Craft, French Craft Chamber, Paris, 1996-97. Co-author: Conjoncture, 1996-97; contbr. articles to profl. jours. Mem. French com. against Modern Slavery, 1997—. Mem. Aries Internat. Rsch. Agy. for Environment and Socs. (founding mem.). Office: UNESCO 6BP106, 1 rue Miollis, 75732 Paris Cedex 15, France

BAER, JOHN METZ, entrepreneur; b. Md., June 30, 1908; s. Adam Daniel and Leah Bertie (Metz) B.; m. Joan Cushwa, Oct. 16, 1976; children: John Metz, Deborah Ann. BS, Goshen Coll., 1932. Food distgn. cons.; pres. Profl. Arts Assocs. Inc., Greencastle (Pa.) Ice and Cold Storage Inc., Baer Packing Corp., Greencastle; Nat. Frozen Foods Assn. ofcl. rep. to 1st Internat. Foods Conf., Paris, 1950; participant numerous internat. food confs. Pres. Washington County Hosp., Hagerstown, 1958-60, Washington County Bd. Edn., 1962-68; bd. dirs. Am. Heart Assn. of Md.; trustee Hagerstown Jr. Coll.; chmn. United Way of Washington County; hon. mem. Greater Hagerstown Club; chmn. Hagerstown Parking Authority; bd. dirs. Md. Symphony Orch. Mem. Produce Mktg. Assn. (past pres.), Fountainhead Country Club, Assembly of Hagerstown, Rotary. Republican. Methodist. Home: 13217 Hillandale Rd Hagerstown MD 21742-2647 Office: 5 Public Sq Hagerstown MD 21740-5528

BAER, MICHAEL ALAN, political scientist, educator; b. Atlanta, Feb. 4, 1943; s. Kurt Arthur and Beulah (Mendelson) B.; m. Charlotte Glazer, Aug. 16, 1964; children: Daniel Noach, Naomi Aviva. BA, Emory U., 1964; MA, U. Oreg., 1966, PhD, 1968. Rsch. asst. Center Advanced Study Ednl. Adminstrn., U. Oreg., 1964-68; faculty U. Ky., Lexington, 1968-90, prof. polit. sci. and pub. adminstrn., 1980-90, chmn. dept. polit. sci., 1977-81, dean Coll. Arts and Scis., 1981-90; polit. analyst WAVE-TV, Louisville; prof. polit. sci. Northeastern U., Boston, 1990-2000, provost, sr. v.p. acad. affairs, 1990-98; sr. v.p. for programs and analysis, dir. Ctr. for Policy Analysis, Am. Coun. on Edn., Washington, 1998—. Co-author: Lobbying: Influence and Interaction in American State Legislatures, 1969; co-editor: Political Science in America, 1991; mem. editorial bd.: State and Local Govt. Rev, 1977-81; contbr. articles to profl. jours. Bd. dirs. Ctrl. Ky. Civil Liberties Union, 1973-77, Congragation Ohavay Zion, Lexington, 1976-78, Ctrl. Ky. Jewish Assn., 1970-74, 79-84, pres. 1973-74, Bluegrass chpt. NCCJ, 1980-81, Coun. Colls. Arts and Scis., 1983-89, pres. 1988, Jamaica Pond Assn., 1992-97; rec. sec. Bluegrass chpt. Ky. Assn. Gifted Edn., 1983-85; mem. Mayor's com. to establish Lexington Children's Mus., 1988-90, bd. dirs., 1990; mem. coun. Inter Univ. Consortium for Polit. and Social Rsch., U. Mich, 1988-94, chmn. 1990-92. Leverhulme fellow, 1974-75. Mem. Am. Polit. Sci. Assn. (endowed programs com. 1993-94, 95-98), Midwest Polit. Sci. Assn. (exec. coun. 1980-83), Brit. Politics Group (exec. coun. 1978-80), So. Polit. Sci. Assn. (chmn. nominating com. 1993-94, 96), Ky. Conf. Polit. Sci., Nat. Assn. Univ. and Land Grant Colls. (commn. on arts and scis. 1986-90, chmn. 1990). Home: 4103 38th St NW Washington DC 20016-2217 Office: Am Coun on Edn 1 Dupont Cir NW Washington DC 20036-1110

BAER, OLAF, vocalist; b. Dresden, Germany, Dec. 19, 1957; s. Ernst Edwin Baer and Dora Anneliese Pfennig; m. Carola Tantz, 1993. Student Music Sch., Carl Maria von Weber, Dresden. Mem. Dresden Kreuzchores, 1967-76. Brit. début at Wigmore Hall, 1983, Am. début in Bach's St. Matthew Passion with Chgo. Symphony Orch., 1987; prin. baritone Dresden State Opera, 1983-91; recital and concert tours in all maj. cities Europe, Australia, U.S., Japan. Named winner inaugural Walther Gruner Lieder Competition, 1983; recipient Robert-Schumann-Preis der Stadt Zwickau, 1998. Avocations: music, poetry, literature, painting. Address: Steglichstrasse 6, 01324 Dresden Germany

BAER, WILLIAM HAROLD, business executive; b. Eatontown, N.J., Dec. 6, 1947; s. Irving and Martha Ann (Ruddy) B. BSBA, Waynesburg Coll., 1971. Pres. Baldinos, Inc., Fayetteville, N.C., 1976—, Rondout Country Club, Ltd., Accord, N.Y., 1979-81, W.H.B. Cons., Accord, N.Y., 1979-85, Baldinos Giant Jersey Subs., Inc., Hinesville, Ga., 1982—; with Baldinos Mgmt. Group, Ltd., Augusta, Ga., 1987—; pres. Baldinos of Atlanta, 1991; pres. Leisure Life Inc., Tinton Falls, N.J., 1980-87, Baldinos of Savannah, 1989—, Pro Active Enterprises, Inc., Savannah, Ga., 1986-89, bd. dirs., 1989; bd. dirs. Triumph Steel, Inc., Birmingham, Ala., 1992, vice chmn. Chmn. campaign March of Dimes, Liberty County, 1986-87; dir. Coastal Ga. March of Dimes, Savannah, 1986-92; mem. Forward Atlanta, 1992—, Atlanta Sports Coun., 1992—. 1st lt. USMC, 1971-75. Recipient Navy Achievement medal. Mem. Hinesville-Liberty County, Ga. C. of C. (bd. dirs. 1989-91), Atlanta C. of C., Coastal Racquet Club (pres. 1986-87, treas.-sec. Hinesville chpt. 1987—), Ga. Hospitality Travel Assn. (bd. dirs. 1999—). Home: 708 Robinson Farms Dr Marietta GA 30068-3277 Office: 760 Elaine St Hinesville GA 31313-4825

BAERGA-VAQUER, RAFAEL ANTONIO, insurance agent; b. Ponce, P.R., Oct. 16, 1948; s. Rafael Baerga and Isabel Vaquer; m. Carmen Ortiz-Abreu, Dec. 27, 1969; children: Abel, Amanda, Luis, Vanesa, Maria-Victoria. BA in Econs., U. P.R., 1969. Registered rep., CLU, ChFC. Instr. econs. CUNY-Lehman Coll., N.Y.C., 1970-74; life ins. agt. Equitable Life Assurance Soc. of U.S., Ponce and San Juan, P.R., 1977—; dist. mgr. Equitable Life Assurance Soc. of U.S., Ponce, 1979-82, San Juan, 1982-93. Mem. Fondo de Mejoramiento, 1986—. Mem. Am. Soc. CLU & ChFC (pres. 1993-94).

BAERISWYL-ROUILLER, IRÈNE ANDRÉE, psychologist, speech pathologist; b. Glarus, Switzerland, Dec. 3, 1948; d. Lucien C. and Hermine (Thomann) Rouiller; m. Franz J. Baeriswyl, Oct. 6, 1973; children: Nicolas, Nathalie. Speech pathologist, U. Freiburg, Switzerland, 1980; MA in Spl. Edn. and Psychology, U. Freiburg, 1987. Grad. sch. tchr. various pub. schs., Freiburg, 1968-78; speech pathologist U. Hosp., Bern, Switzerland, 1980-81; speech pathologist U. Freiburg, 1981-83, sci. position in autism, 1987-91; dir. early intervention Les Buissonnets, Freiburg, 1991-99; pvt. practice psychology and speech pathology, 1999—; cons. Swiss Assn. Parents Autistic Children, 1987-91; pres. bd. dirs. Child Care Ctr. Freiburg, 1983-93; bd. dirs. Found. for Treatment of Children with Psychiat. Problems, 1995—, pres., 1999—. Author: Die Situation Autistische Menschen, 1991, les Personnes Autistes Prise en Charge et Perspectives, 1991. active Parliament of the Canton of Freiburg, 1976-86, City Parliament of Freiburg, 1986—, pres., 1997-98; active Social Dem. Party Switzerland. Mem. Internat. Soc. for the Study in Behavioral Devel. Avocations: reading, writing, skiing, music. Home: Heiterastrasse 48, 1700 Freiburg Switzerland

BAERLECKEN, MARTA, literature educator; b. Dusseldorf, Germany, Mar. 3, 1909; d. Albert and Elizabeth (Heubler) Hechtle; Dr. phil., univs. Bonn, Berlin, Cologne, 1937; m. Wilhelm Baerlecken; children—Stefan, Michael. Univ. lectr., developer Dutch studies programs U. Cologne, 1937-61, U. Aix la Chapelle, 1966-74, U. Berlin, 1975-77, public schs. North Rhine, 1971-74. Pres., German Dutch Assn. Germany, 1953-63; bd. dirs. German group Internat. Fedn. Univ. Women, 1952-58; bd. dirs. found. Europe German sect., 1985—; German European Counsel; mem. 8th Commn. Status of Women, UN, 1954; bd. dirs. European Movement for Germany, 1995—; mem. Commn. of Women. Mem. Internat. Assn. Dutch Studies, Internat. Assn. German Studies, Steuben Schurtz Assn., German-Dutch Assn. Author: Walter v.d. Vogelweide, 1937; The Flemish Literature, 1942; Modern Literature in the Netherlands, 1968; Lyric Poetry of the Netherlands, 1974, Cyriel Verschaeve - a myth in Germany?, 1994. Roman Catholic. Home: 117a Rheinallee, 40545 Düsseldorf Germany

BAERMANN, FRANK, mathematician, scientist; b. Gladbeck, Germany, Sept. 22, 1960; s. Heinz and Liesel B.; m. Carmen Schmidt. MA in Math., Düsseldorf (Germany) U., 1986, PhD in Physics, 1989. Head artificial intelligence group Bayer AG, Leverkusen, Germany, 1989-95; prof. math. and informatics Gelsenkirchen (Germany) U. for Applied Scis., 1995—. Contbr. articles to profl. jours. Mem. Internat. Neural Network Soc., European Neural Network Soc. Home: Graudenzer Str 5, 40599 Duesseldorf Germany Office: FH Gelsenkirchen, FB Physikalische Technik, Neidenburger Str 43, 45877 Gelsenkirchen Germany

BAERNS, MANFRED G.O., chemistry educator, science administrator; b. Berlin, July 23, 1934; m. Barbara Beckmann. MS in Chemistry, U. Hannover, Germany, 1959, PhD in Chem. Reaction Engring. & Tech., 1961, Habilitation and Venia legendi, 1970. Postdoctoral fellow Argonne (Ill.) Nat. Lab., 1962-64; sr. sci. engr. Inst. Tech. Chemistry U. Hannover, 1965-69; head chem. R & D Krupp Chem. Engring. Divsn., Essen, Germany, 1969-74; prof. chem. reaction engring. and tech., chair, head lab. Ruhr U., Bochum, Germany, 1974-95, dean faculty, 1978-79, 90-91, mem. senate, 1987-89; sci. dir. Inst. Applied Chemistry Berlin-Adlershof e.V., 1995—; mem., chmn. various working parties Deutsche Gesellschaft für Chemische Technik und Biotechnologie e.V.; cons., referee Deutsche Foschungsgemeinschaft, Norwegian Rsch. Coun., various petrochemical and chem. industries; hon. prof. Humboldt U., Berlin, 1996, Tech. U., Berlin, 1996. Author, editor: Chemical Reaction Engineering, Vol. 1, 1992, 96; co-editor: Bases of Chemical Processes, Vol. 3, 1996, Unit Operations, Vol. 2, 1996; contbr. over 240 articles to profl. jours. Recipient Dechema Titannium medal for scientific achievements. Mem. Am. Chem. Soc., German Chem. Soc. Achievements include numerous patents in chemical process development. Office: Inst Applied Chem Berlin-Adlershof eV, Rudower Chaussee 5, D-12484 Berlin Germany

BAERTEN, JEAN, history educator; b. Tongeren, Limburg, Belgium, May 13, 1936; s. Piere Baerten and Juliette Devignat; m. Ida Ilegems, July 13, 1963 (dec.); 1 child, Aldo; m. Joaquina Suárez Lopez, July 2, 1994. B, Royal Atheneum, Tongeren, 1951, Royal Atheneum, Brussels, 1952; D of History, U. Libre Brussels, 1961. Aspirant Nat. Found. Sci. Rsch., Brussels, 1957-59; tchr. Royal Atheneum, Koekelberg, Belgium, 1959-62; archivist Gen. Archives, Brussels, 1962-69; prof. Free U. Brussels, 1966-96; dir. redaction Rev. Belge de Philologie et d'Histoire, Brussels, 1957-87. Author: Het Graafschap Loon, 1969 (Mantelius award 1970), Du Statère à l'European Currency Unit, 1983, Harde Vlaamse koppen: de boeren van Voeren.Van de middeleeuwen tot 1962, 1995, Voeren 1921-95: De Belgische democratie op drift, 1997, Van zilverling tot euro.De Geschiedenis van het geld, 1999, Unions et unifications monetaires en Europe depuis la Grece antique jusqu'a l'euro, 1999. Avocations: piano, swimming, walking. Home: Mezenlaan 11, St-Genesius-Rode Belgium 1640

BAERWALD, JOHN EDWARD, traffic and transportation engineer, educator; b. Milw., Nov. 2, 1925; s. Albert J. and Margaret M. (Brandt) B.; m. Elaine S. Eichstaedt, Apr. 3, 1948 (dec.); children: Thomas J., James K., Barbara Baerwald Bowman; m. Donna D. Granger, May 24, 1975. Student, Valparaiso U., 1943, 46-48; BSCE, Purdue U., 1949, MSCE, 1950, PhDCE, 1956. Registered profl. engr., Calif., Ill., Ind. Rsch. asst. Purdue U., 1949-50, rsch. assoc., instr. hwy. engring., 1950-52, rsch. engr., instr. hwy. engring., 1952-55; asst. prof. traffic engring. U. Ill., Urbana-Champaign, 1955-57, assoc. prof. traffic engring., 1957-60, prof. traffic engring., 1960-69, prof. transp. and traffic engring., 1969-83, univ. traffic engr., 1957-63, dir. Hwy. Traffic Safety Ctr., 1961-83, prof. emeritus, 1983—; staff assoc. Police Tng. Inst., 1969-91; cons. traffic engr., 1952—; pres. John E. Baerwald P.C., Santa Fe, N.Mex., 1982—; chmn. Champaign Parking and Traffic Commn., Ill., 1960-69; liaison mem. staff subcom. Ill. Gov.'s Ofcl. Traffic Safety Coordination Com., 1962-69, mem. subcom. hwy. safety program deficiencies, 1970-72; mem. Champaign-Urbana Urbanized Area Transp. Study, 1963-83, tech. adviser to policy com., 1963-75, chmn. policy com., 1977-83; mem. Ill. Sec. State Adv. Com. Vehicle Registration and Titling Matters, 1973-74; trustee Champaign-Urbana Mass Transit Dist., 1973-83, chmn., 1975-83; mem. tech. adv. com. Ill. Transp. Study Commn., 1977-81. Editor: Traffic Engineering Handbook 3rd edit., 1965; sr. editor: Transportation and Traffic Engineering Handbook 1st edit., 1976; contbr. over 100 articles and papers to profl. jours. With AUS, 1943-46. Recipient Pub. Svc. award Ill. Sec. State, 1976, past. pres. award Ill. Sec. Inst. of Transp. Engrs., 1983. Fellow ASCE, Inst. Transp. Engrs. (internat. pres. 1970, dir. 1964-65, 67-71, internat. coun. 1977-83, dir. Ill. sect. 1963-64, exec. com. expert witness coun. 1986-90, vice-chmn. 1988, chmn. 1989, exec. com. transp. safety coun. 1992-95, vice chmn. 1993, chmn. 1994, other offices and coms., Past Pres.' award 1953, Theodore M. Matson Meml. award for outstanding contbns. to the traffic engring. profession 1988, Burton W. Marsh Disting. Svc. award 1996); mem. Transp. Rsch. Bd. (divsn. B coun. 1974-83, other offices and coms.), Pan Am. Hwy. Congress (best tech. paper award 1963, 67), Santa Fe Host Lions Club (pres. 1994-95, Melvin Jones Internat. fellow 1997), Am. Legion, Masons, Sigma Xi, Chi Epsilon. Lutheran. Home: 35 Shilo Rd Santa Fe NM 87505-7004 Office: 1221 S Saint Francis Dr Ste C Santa Fe NM 87505-4036

BAERWALD, SUSAN GRAD, television broadcasting company executive producer; b. Long Branch, N.J., June 18, 1944; d. Bernard John and Marian Grad; m. Paul Baerwald, July 1, 1969; children: Joshua, Samuel. Degre des Arts and Lettres, Sorbonne, Paris, 1965; BA, Sarah Lawrence Coll., 1966. Script analyst United Artists, L.A., 1978-80; v.p. devel. Gordon/Eisner Prodns., L.A., 1980-81; mgr. mini-series and novels for TV, NBC, Burbank, Calif., 1981-82, dir. mini-series and novels for TV, 1982, v.p. mini-series and novels for TV, 1982-89; exec. producer NBC Prodns., 1989-95, Savoy Pictures TV, 1995-96, Citadel Entertainment, 1996-97. Producer TV mini-series: Blind Faith, 1990, Lucky Chances (Jackie Collins), 1990, One Spl. Victory, 1991, Cruel Doubt, 1993, A Time to Heal, 1994, Inflammable, 1995. Bd. dirs. The Paper Bag Players, N.Y.C., 1974—; vol. L.A. Children's Mus., 1978-80; mem. awards com. Scott Newman Found., 1982-84; bd. dirs. L.A. Goal, 1996—. Recipient Vol. Incentive award NBC, 1983. Mem. ATAS (bd. govs. 1993-97, nat. awards chmn. 1997-98), Am. Film Inst., Hollywood Radio and TV Soc.*

BAETZ REUTERGÅRDH, LARS BERTIL, educator, consultant; b. Vaxholm, Sweden, Sept. 2, 1948; s. Stig Olof Bertil and Mary Madeleine (Baetz) Reutergerdh; m. Karin Britt Boquist, July 1971 (div. Apr. 1992); children: Joakim, David; m. Somsri Panukchoklarb, Aug. 27, 1994; 1 child, Ernst. BSc, Stockholm U., 1971, MSc, 1973, PhD, 1988; prof., Vietnam Nat. U., Hanoi, 1996. Cert. environ. engring. Royal Swedish Inst. Tech. Tchr. natural scis. Stockholm, 1971-73; chief exec. mgr. Product Control Leander & Fri Ltd., Solna, Sweden, 1973-75; sr. rschr. Stockholm U., 1975-79; with Swedish EPA, Solna, 1979-88; chief tech. advisor UNESCO, Indonesia, 1988-89; team leader World Bank, Indonesia, 1990; prof. Asian Inst. Tech., Pathumthani, Thailand, 1991-96, Gifu (Japan) U., 1997-2000; fellow Internat. Union for Pure and Applied Chemistry, Research Triangle Park; advisor Internat. Coun. for the Exploration of the Sea, Copenhagen; cons. FAO, Manila, Philippines, 1979. Contbr. articles to profl. jours. Advisor IAEA, FAO, UNEP, WHO, Rome, 1984; expert European Commn., Brussels, 1982-91, Oslo Paris Commn., 1984, 86, 88, Asian Devel. Bank, Indonesia, 1994, UNEP, Estoril, Portugal, 1996; UN Food and Agrl. Orgn. Mem. Internat. Soc. for Environ. Biotechnology (exec. bd. mem. 1994—), Internat. Assn. for Impact Assessment, Swedish Assn. Graduated Engrs. Avocations: sailing, skiing. E-mail: ecochemica@usa.net. and lars@green.gifu-u.ac.jp. Fax: 81 58 293 2062. Home: Yunite Inoue 404, Oritate 840-1, Gifu-shi 501-1132, Japan Office: Gifu Univ, 1-1 Yanagido, Gifu-shi 501-1193, Japan

BAEUERLE, DIETER WILLY, applied physics educator; b. Chemnitz, Germany, May 2, 1940; arrived in Austria, 1978; s. Karl Wilhelm and Liselotte Bäuerle; children: Anne, Christoph. PhD in Physics, U. Stuttgart, Germany, 1969; habilitation, U. Aachen, Germany, 1973. Max-Kade-Found. fellow Lab. of Atomic and Solid State Physics, Ithaca, N.Y., 1969-70; rsch. assoc. Cornell, N.Y., 1970-71; rsch. fellow Physics Rsch. Labs., Aachen, 1971-75; prof. exptl. physics U. Osnabrück, Germany, 1975-78; prof. applied physics Johannes-Kepler U. Linz, Austria, 1978—; rsch. scientist Max-Planck-Inst. for Festkörperforschung, Stuttgart, 1972-73; coun. mem. European Phys. Soc., 1979-83, mem. com. on semiconductor and insulators sect., 1980-86; mem. European com. Materials Rsch. Soc., 1983-87; mem. sci. com. CNRS, Paris, 1987-91. Author: Chemical Processing with Lasers, 1986, Laser Processing and Chemistry, 1996, 3rd edit., 2000; co-editor Applied Physics A, 1986—, LaserOpto, 1995—; contbr. articles to profl. jours.; patentee in field. Recipient Adolf-Schärf award for sci., 1984. Fellow Christian Doppler Soc. (sr.); mem. Austrian Phys. Soc., German Phys. Soc., Soc. German Scientists and Doctors, N.Y. Acad. Scis. Home: Oberklammerstrasse 47, A-4203 Altenberg Austria Office: Johannes Kepler Univ, Altenbergerstrasse 69, A-4040 Linz Austria

BAEV, STANISLAV, surgeon, consultant, researcher; b. Sadovetz, Bulgaria, Dec. 11, 1932; s. Bayo Stoynov and Nadezda Ivanova (Neicheva) B.; m. Sasha Loukova Vlassakova, Sept. 30, 1956 (div. Feb. 1975); children: Boyan, Mina; m. Dimitrina Yordanova Andonova, July 6, 1975; 1 child, Angelina. MD, Higher Med. Inst., Sofia, Bulgaria, 1957. Jr. surgeon Surg. Unit, Aitos, Bulgaria, 1957-60; jr. surgeon II Med. Acad., Sofia, 1960-63, asst. surgeon I/jr., sr. surgeon/chief surgeon, 1963-76; assoc. prof. susrgery, chmn. surgical dept. Pleven Med. Faculty, Sofia, 1976-84; prof. surgery, chmn. II surg. dept. Med. Acad., Sofia, 1986-90; dir. Nat. Inst. Surgery, Sofia, 1986-90; rep. cons. surgery, Min. Health, Sofia, 1986-95; dep. dir. Nat. Inst. Surgery, Sofia, 1984-86. Author, editor: Surgery of the Liver; Abdominal Surery; General Surgery; Surgical Diseases, 2 vols.; Manual of Surgery, 4 vols.; Application of Lazers in Surgery; contbr. chpt. to book, over 300 articles to profl. publs., over 50 to fgn. mags.; mem. editl. bd. Lyon Chirurgical. Recipient Hon. diploma Internat. Red Cross, South Yemen, Aden, 1968, Hon. badge Bulgarian Med. Union, Sofia, 1996, Golden Order of Labor, Bulgarian Acad. Scis., 1980. Fellow World Assn. Hepato-Pancreato-Billiary Surgery; mem. Internat. Coll. Surgeons (v.p. 1990-96), Eurosurgery (standing com., Paris, 1992-97), Lyon Surg. Soc. (fgn. corr.), Cuban Surg. Soc. (hon.), Greek Surg. Soc. (hon.). Eastern Orthodox. Avocations: classical music, chess, travel. Home: Zona B5 Bl 16 Vhod K, Sofia Bulgaria Office: Alexanders Hosp Dept Surg, 1 Georgi Sofiiski Str, 1431 Sofia Bulgaria

BAEY, LIAN PECK, manufacturing executive; b. Singapore, July 13, 1931; s. Kim Swee and Huat Tee (Seow) B.; m. Daisy Tan, May 27, 1956; children: Barbara, Henry, Deborah, Charles. Diploma in bus. mgmt., Met. Coll., Albans, Eng., 1958; DSc, The Open Internat. U., 1990. Sales exec. Baey Kim Swee and Co., Singapore, 1948-51, exec. dir., 1951-77, exec. chmn., 1977—; exec. chmn. Am. Internat. Industries (Pte.) Ltd., Singapore, 1966—; bd. dirs., chmn. Am. Internat. Industries, Ltd., Moscow, AII-Beijing Metals (PTE) Ltd.; bd. dirs. Copper Slag Industries (M) Sdn Bhd; chmn. AII Group Cos.; exec. chmn. Gaspower Coenergy Sys. Gmbh, Germany, Gaspower Coenergy Sys. Pte Ltd., Singapore; chmn. supervisory bd. Maschinenbau Halberstadt GmbH, Germany. Chmn. Singapore Metrication Bd., 1971-81, NTUC Welcome Consumers Coop. Ltd., 1973-82, Singapore Corp. Rehab. Enterprises, 1975-87; chmn. com. Treatment and Rehab. Drug Addicts, 1977-79, chmn. adv. com., 1979-88; pres. Singapore Anti-Narcotics Assn., 1977-96; pres. Internat. Fedn. Non-Govtl. Orgns. Against Drug Abuse, 1983-84, 90-91, roving amb., 1993—; mem. Coun. Advisors, 1983—; dir. IFNGO Found., 1992—; chmn. Nat. St. John Coun. of Singapore, chmn. 1992—, bd. trustees 1992—; mem. consortium internat. NGOs on primary prevention substance abuse WHO, Geneva, 1996—; dep. registrar Registry of Marriages; active Singapore Housing and Devel. Bd., 1969-78, East-West Ctr. Assn., 1987—, mem. Nat. Coun. Against Drug Abuse, 1995-96; 1st vice chmn. Asia Pacific NGO Com. for Prevention Drug and Substane Abuse, Bangkok, 1996—. Decorated Order of St. John (Eng.); named Justice of Peace Govt. Singapore, 1979; recipient Plaque of Honor, The Nat. Coun. on Social Welfare of Thailand, 1984, Friends of Labor medal Trade Union Congress, 1974; Pub. Svc. Star, Govt. of Singapore, 1974, Pub.Svc. Star (bar), 1996; Internat. award of Honor Internat. Narcotic Enforcement Officers Assn., 1993, SANA gold medal of honor, Singapore, 1996. Mem. Tanglin Club, Pyramid Club, Singapore Island Country Club, Sentosa Golf Club, Keppel Golf Club, Masons. Buddhist. Home: 39 Gilstead Rd, 309083 Singapore Singapore Office: Am Internat Industries Ltd, 20 Jalan Buroh, 619477 Singapore Singapore

BAEZ, JOAN CHANDOS, folk singer; b. S.I., N.Y., Jan. 9, 1941; d. Albert V. and Joan (Bridge) B.; m. David Victor Harris, Mar. 1968 (div. 1973); 1 son, Gabriel Earl. Appeared in coffeehouses, Gate of Horn, Chgo., 1958, Ballad Room, Club 47, 1958-68, Newport (R.I.) Folk Festival, 1959-69, 85, 87, 90, 92, 93, 95, extended tours to colls. and concert halls, 1960s, appeared Town Hall and Carnegie Hall, 1962, 67, 68, U.S. tours, 1970—, concert tours in Japan, 1966, 82, Europe, 1970-73, 80, 83-84, 87-90, 93—, Australia, 1985; rec. artist for Vanguard Records, 1960-72, A&M, 1973-76, Portrait Records, 1977-80, Gold Castle Records, 1986-89, Virgin Records, 1990-93, Grapevine Label Records (UK), 1995—, Guardian Records, 1995—, European record albums, 1981, 83, award 8 gold albums, 1 gold single; albums include Gone From Danger, 1997, Rare, Live & Classic (box set), 1993; author: Joan Baez Songbook, 1964, (biography) Daybreak, 1968, (with David Harris) Coming Out, 1971, And a Voice to Sing With, 1987, (songbook) An Then I Wrote, 1979. Extensive TV appearances and speaking tours U.S. and Can. for anti-militarism, 1967-68; visit to Dem. Republic of Vietnam, 1972, visit to war torn Bosnia-Herzegovina, 1993; founder, v.p. Inst. for Study Nonviolence (now Resource Ctr. for Nonviolence, Santa Cruz, Calif.), Palo Alto, Calif., 1965; mem. nat. adv. coun. Amnesty In-

ternat., 1974-92; founder, pres. Humanitas/Internat. Human Rights Com., 1979-92; condr. fact-finding mission to refugee camps, S.E. Asia, Oct. 1979; began refusing payment of war taxes, 1964; arrested for civil disobedience opposing draft, Oct., Dec., 1967. Office: Diamonds & Rust Prodns PO Box 1026 Menlo Park CA 94026-1026

BAEZ, JOANNE MARIE, school psychologist; b. Chgo., June 4, 1962; d. Rafael Marino and Maria Ana (Lopez) B. BA, Bradley U., Peoria, Ill., 1984; MS, Northwestern State U., Natchitoches, La., 1991; PsyD, Ctrl. Mich. U., 1997. Sch. psychologist Milw. Pub. Schs., 1992—; mem. Hispanic women's adv. coun. Alverno Coll., Milw., 1992—. Mem. Hispanic Women's Adv. Coun., Alverno Coll., Milw., 1992—. Mem. Nat. Assn. Sch. Psychologists, 1986—, Psychologists Assn. of Milw. Pub. Schs. (sec. 1996—). Roman Catholic. Home: 3720A S 88th St Milwaukee WI 53228-1736 Office: Milw Pub Schs Div Spl Svcs Ctr Psychol Svcs 6620 W Capitol Dr Milwaukee WI 53216-2040

BAEZ, JULIO A., lawyer; b. Santo Domingo, Dominican Republic, July 6, 1954; came to U.S. 1962; s. Julio A. and Maria Carmela (Fland) B. BA, SUNY, Stony Brook, 1976; JD, U. Aix-Marseille III, France, 1978, LLM, 1979; postgrad., various. Law intern, Office of Legal Affairs UN, N.Y.C., 1979-80; escort interpreter U.S. Dept. State, Washington, 1980; law cons., Ctr. for Transnat. Corps. UN, N.Y.C., 1980-81, legal officer, Office of Legal Affairs, 1981-85, 88-92; legal officer, Food and Agrl. Orgn., Office Legal Counsel UN, Rome, 1985-87; asst. sec., Former Yugoslavia War Crimes Commn. UN, Geneva, 1992-94; asst to. ind. jurist, Western Sahara Referendum UN, 1994-96; legal officer, Divsn. Ocean Affairs and Law of the Sea, Office of Legal Affairs UN, N.Y.C., 1994-96; legal officer, Internat. Trade Law Br., Office of Legal Affairs UN, Vienna, 1996-99; legal officer, Divsn. Ocean Affairs, Law of the Sea, Office of Legal Affairs UN, N.Y.C., 1999—. Pro bono counselor Tenants' Union of the West Side, N.Y.C., 1980-85. Mem. Madrid Bar, New York State Bar Assn. Democrat. Roman Catholic. E-mail: baez1@un.org. Home: 41 Jane St New York NY 10014-5127 Office: United Nations Secretariat Office of Legal Affairs DC2-464 New York NY 10017

BAFAQEEH, SAMEER ALI, otorhinolaryngologist, educator, consultant; b. Al-Madina, Saudi Arabia, Apr. 2, 1956; s. Ali Abdul Rahman Bafaqeeh and Wedad Abdullah Taha; m. Fawziyah Mohammed Al-Kandri, Aug. 14, 1982; children: Ahmmad, Mohammed, Alia, Maryam, Fatema. MBBS, Cairo U., 1980. Rotating intern Cairo U. Hosps., 1981-82; resident otorhinolaryngology U. Georg August, Göttingen, Germany, 1985-89; facharzt Halse Nasen Ohren Göttingen U., 1989; sr. house officer in otorhinolaryngology King Saud U. King Abdul Aziz U. Hosp., Riyadh, Saudi Arabia, 1982-85, sr. registrar ear, nose and throat dept., 1989-91, asst. prof., 1989-95, assoc. prof., 1995—, cons., 1992; mem. Nat. CPR Com., 1991—, Prevention and Treatment Passive Smoking Com., 1992—; mem. organizing com. Asian-Pacific Com. on Deafness, 1992—; participant numerous confs. and congresses; ear, nose, and throat cons.; participant most facial plastic and endoscopic paranasal sinus surgery courses in U.S. and Europe, 1989—; hmn. organizing com. facial plastic surgery symposium King Saud U., 1996; spkr. in field; overseas invited spkr., co-chmn. World Symposium on cosmetic surgery, Manila, The Philippines. Contbr. articles to Internat. Jour. Pediatric Otorhinolaryngology, Annals Saudi Medicine, Med. Jour. Cairo U. Faculty Medicine, Pakistan Jour. Otorhinolaryngology, Am. Jour. Rhinology, Otorhinolaryngol Nova, Zeitschrift für Geriatrie, Am. Jour. Otolaryngologu, Annals of Otology, Rhinology and Laryngology, Immunobiology of Otorhinolaryngology, Annals of Otology, Rhinology and Laryngology, The Can. Jour. Plastic Surgery, Brit. Jour. Plastic Surgery, Plastic Reconstructive Surgery, Indian Jour. Otolaaryngology, also others. Mem. AAAS, European Rhinologic Soc., Am. Acad. Facial Plastic and Reconstructive Surgery, Am. Acad. Otolaryngology - Head and Neck Surgery Found., Inc., Am. Rhinologic Soc., Soc. for Minimally Invasive Therapy, Saudi Soc. E.N.T. Diseases and Head and Neck Surgery, German Soc. E.N.T. Diseases and Head and Neck Surgery. Office: King Saud U, ENT Dept PO Box 245, Riyadh 11411, Saudi Arabia

BAG, ORHAN OZLEM, economist; b. Iskenderun, Turkey, Feb. 6, 1967; s. Arif Yasar and Ulku Bag. Degree in econs. and indsl. rels., U. Ankara, Turkey, 1989. Stock exchange cons. for pvt. investments Ankara, 1989-91; exec. coord. Alami Trading Co., Ankara, 1991-92; asst. gen. mgr. Gensys Software, Ankara, 1992-94; mgr. of seminar dept. congress T&T Tourism and Travel, Ankara, 1992-95; gen. mgr. Issos Enterprises, Ankara, 1996—. Sgt. Turkish Army, 1991. Faculty of Polit. Sci. grantee U. Ankara, 1989. Mem. Ankara C. of C., Tema Environment and Nature Found. Avocations: travel, music, collecting antiques, sports. Office: Issos Enterprises, Cinnah St 44/6 Cankaya, Ankara 06680, Turkey

BAGABANDI, NATSAGIIN, President of Mongolia; b. Zavkhan, Mongolian People's Republic, Apr. 22, 1950; s. Mendiin Natsag and Rashjamtsyn Dogoo; m. Azadsurenguin Oyunbileg, Mar. 5, 1970; children: Bagabandiin Bayarma, Bagabandiin Batbayar. Cert., Tech. Coll., Leningrad, Russia, 1972; diploma in Food Tech., Inst. Food Tech., Odessa, Russia, 1980; diploma in Social Scis., Acad. Social Scis., Moscow, 1987. From mechanic to engr. Food Factory, Mongolian People's Republic, 1972-75; chief dept. Mongolian People's Revolutionary Party Com., Ctrl. Province, 1980-84; advisor, lect. ctrl. com. Mongolian People's Revolutionary Party Com., Ulaanbaatar, 1987-90, from sec. to dep. chmn., 1990-92; M.P., chmn., speaker Mongolian State Gt. Hural Parliament, Ulaanbaatar, from 1992; pres., comdr. in chief armed forces, chief nat. security Mongolia, 1997—; mem. conf. Ruling Mongolian People's Revolutionary Party; chmn. exec. coun. Mongolian Parliamentarian Group, Ulaanbaatar, 1992—, ACH/Ulaanbaatar, 1992-96. Avocations: collecting feature books, theatre, amateur sports, national wrestling. Office: State Palace, Ulaanbaatar Mongolia

BAGAEV, VITALY ARKADEVITCH, physiologist, researcher; b. Kiev, Ukraine, USSR, Sept. 13, 1947; s. Arkady Vasilevitch and Aleksandra Andreevna (Pinzhura) B.; m. Tatiana Rostislavovna Veresova, Apr. 15, 1971; 1 child, Andrey. Diploma, State U., Voronezh, USSR, 1970; PhD, Pavlov Inst. Physiology, St. Petersburg, 1976, DSc, 1996. Jr. researcher Pavlov Inst. Physiology, St. Petersburg, 1975-83, sr. researcher, 1983-87, actual scientific sec., 1983-86, dep. dir. rsch., 1986-90, head lab., 1987—. Author: (with N. Beller et al) Cortical Regulation of Visceral Functions, 1980, (with A. Kurygin et al) Motor Function of Gut, 1994, (with A. Nozdrachev and S. Panteleev) Vago-vagal Reflectory Arc, 1997; contbr. more than 40 articles to profl. jours. Grantee Internat. Sci. Found., 1994, Russian Found. of Basic Research, 2000; re ipient state stipend for scientists Moscow, 2000. Mem. Russian Physiol. Soc., Internat. Brain Rsch. Orgn. Office: Pavlov Inst Physiology, nab Makarova 6, 199034 Saint Petersburg Russia

BAGAJEWICZ, MIGUEL, engineering educator; b. Rosario, Argentina, Sept. 16, 1951; s. Roscislaw and Maria (Korabinski) B.; m. Patricia Iris Lara. Chemical engr., Universidad Nat. del Litoral, Santa Fe, Argentina, 1977; MS, Calif. Inst. Tech., PhD. Assoc. prof. U. Okla., Norman, 1995—; sr. devel. engr. Simulation Sci., Brea, Calif., 1993-95; rsch. assoc. U. Calif. Los Angeles, 1989-93; assoc. prof. Universidad Nacional del Litoral, Santa Fe, Argentina, 1980-89; dir. Ctr. Engring. Optimization, U. Okla. Author: (book) Design and Upgrade of Process Plant Instrumentation, 2000; contbr. articles to profl. jours. Fax: 405-325-5813. E-mail: bagajewicz@ou.edu. Office: CEMS U Okla 100 E Boyd St Rm T335 Norman OK 73019-1028

BAGARIA, GAIL FARRELL, lawyer; b. Detroit, Oct. 6, 1942; d. Vincent Benjamin and Inez Elizabeth (Coffey) Farrell; m. William James Bagaria, Nov. 28, 1964; children: Bridget Ann, William James, Benjamin George. BA, U. Detroit, 1964; JD, Cath. U. Am., 1980. Bar: Md. 1980, U.S. Dist. Ct. Md., 1982. Cons. Miller & Webster, Clinton, Md., 1980-82; pvt. practice Bowie, Md., 1982—. Prince George's County adv. com. on Aging, 1998—. Mem. Prince George's Women's Lawyers Caucus (sec. 1984, pres. 1986, treas. 1997), Md. State Bar Assn., Women's Bar Assn. Md., Prince George's County Bar Assn., Soroptimist Internat. (Bowie-Crofton chpt., pres. 1988-89, 93-94), Greater Bowie C. of C. (bd. dirs. 1995-97, 99-2000, sec. 1997-98, 98-99, Outstanding Bus. Person 1997). Democrat. Roman Catholic. Office: PO Box 759 Bowie MD 20718-0759

BAGBY, JOSEPH RIGSBY, financial investor; b. Banner Elk, N.C., Aug. 23, 1935; s. Wesley Marion and Ila Paunee (Rigsby) B.; m. Martha Green, Jan. 1, 1965; 1 child, Meredith Elaine. Student, Fla. State U., 1955; BBA, U. Miami, 1959; MCR, Inst. Corp. Real Estate, West Palm Beach, Fla., 1977. Employee and supr. Miami Herald Pub. Co., 1953-63; rsch. and sales asst. Oscar Dolly Assocs., Miami, 1961-63; sales, appraising and property mgr. Jack Thomas Realty, Miami, 1963-65; dir. corp. real estate Burger King Corp., Miami, 1965-70; founder, pres. Internat. Assn. Corp. Real Estate Execs., Coral Gables, Fla., 1969-88; chmn. bd. trustees Nat. Assn. Corp. Real Estate Execs., Coral Gables, Fla., 1973-88, bd. dirs., 1971—; pres., founder Property Resources Corp. and 14 other investment cos., Miami and Palm Beach, 1970—; founder merger and acquisition investment co., 1997; mem. businessman's adv. com. U.S. Postal Svc., Washington, 1984-88. Author: Real Estate Financing Desk Book, 1975, rev. edits. 1977, 81, Real Estate Directory, 1975. Pres. interfraternity coun. U. Miami (co-editor campus newspaper); mem., chmn. fin. com. St. Edward's Cath. Ch., Palm Beach, Fla., 1985-93. With U.S. Army, 1959-61. Named to Hall of Fame, Nat. Assn. Corp. Real Estate Execs., 1991. Mem. Nat. Assn. Location Analysts and Negotiators (founder), Progress Club of Miami (co-founder), Optimist (founding mem. Miami Downtown club), Rotary (Harris fellow), Interfaith Cotillian (co-founder), Sigma Chi (past pres.), Alpha Kappa Psi. Democrat. Avocations: swimming, tennis. Home: 125 Brazilian Ave Palm Beach FL 33480-4221 Office: Property Resources Corp PO Box 3149 Palm Beach FL 33480-1349

BAGBY, MARTHA L. GREEN, real estate holding company executive, novelist, publisher; b. West Palm Beach, Fla., June 17, 1937; d. Hampton and Louise (Lambert) Green; m. Joseph R. Bagby, 1966; 1 child, Meredith E. AA, Palm Beach Jr. Coll., 1957; AB, U. Miami, 1959; MA, Pa. State U., 1964. Tchr. journalism, English, Palm Beach County, 1959-62; instr. journalism Pa. State U., 1962-63; city editor, writer Palm Beach News & Life, 1963-64; editor Alfred Hitchcock Mag., Riviera Beach, Fla., 1964; editor, supr. editorial services, pub. relations employee newspaper Nat. Airlines, Inc., Miami, Fla., 1965-73; corp. sec., chmn. bd. Property Resources Co., Palm Beach, Fla., 1971—; Ill. franchisee Burger King Corp.; founder Internat. Health Awareness Assn.; lectr. journalism, Dade, Palm Beach counties; instr. Barry Coll., Miami; pub. The Bagby's Health Digest, 1985—. Author: Stranglehold, 1977, The Complete Real Estate Dictionary, 1992, The Real Estate Financing Deskbook, 1979-90; (with others) The Complete Real Estate Book. Mem. exec. bd. Childbirth and Parent Edn. Assn., Miami. Mem. Fla. Pub. Relations Assn., S. Fla. Indsl. Chmn. Internat. Council Indsl. Editors, Airline Editors Conf. (chmn.), Air Transport Assn. Am., Women in Communications (pres.), Internat. Assn. Corp. Real Estate Execs. (founder, trustee, exec. editor, dir. life); founder Internat. Health Awareness Assn. Office: 125 Brazilian Ave Palm Beach FL 33480-4221

BAGBY, WILLIAM RARDIN, lawyer; b. Grayson, Ky., Feb. 19, 1910; s. John Albert and Nano A. (Rardin) B.; m. Mary Carpenter, Sept. 3, 1939; 1 child, John Robert; m. Elizabeth Hinkel, Nov. 22, 1975. AB, Cornell U., 1933; JD, U. Mich., 1936; postgrad., Northwestern U., 1946-47. Bar: Ky. 1937, Ohio 1952, U.S. Tax Ct. 1948, U.S. Supreme Ct. 1950, U.S. Ct. Appeals (6th cir.) 1952. Pvt. practice Grayson, 1937-43; atty., judge City of Grayson, 1939-43; counsel Treasury Dept., Chgo., Cleve. and Cin., 1946-54; pvt. practice Lexington, Ky., 1954—; prof. U. Ky., 1956-57; gen. counsel Headley-Whitney Mus., 1974-84; mem. Bd. of Adjustment, Lexington-Urban County City Govt., 1965-98, chmn., 1980-98. Trustee Bagby Found. Musical Arts, N.Y.C., 1963-74; trustee, gen. counsel McDowell Cancer Found., 1979-91, pres., 1988-91. Lt. USN, 1943-46. Mem. ABA (hon. life), Am. Judicature Soc., Ky. Bar Assn. (hon. life), Fayette County Bar Assn., Lexington Club, U. Ky. Faculty Club, Rotary. Democrat. Home: 228 Market St Lexington KY 40507-1030 Office: 1107 1st National Bldg Lexington KY 40507

BAGCHI, GOPA, communication educator; b. Varanasi, India, Apr. 15, 1957; s. P.K. and Santwana Bagchi; m. Shahid Ali; 1 child, Shashwat Azad. MA, Banaras Hindu U., India, 1982, M in Journalism, 1987; PhD, Guru Ghasidas U., Bilaspur, India, 1988—. Field supr., editor WHO/ICMR Project, Banaras Hindu U., 1987-88; lectr., head journalism and mass comm. Guru Ghasidas U., Bilaspur, India, 1988—; editor publ. unit WHO/ICMR project Banaras Hindu U. Contbr. articles to profl. jours. Avocations: reading, music. Office: Head Dept Journalism, Guru Ghasidas Univ, Bilaspur MP, India

BAGCHI, GURU DAS, botanist, researcher; b. Varanasi, UP, India, Oct. 5, 1953; s. Binoy Krishna Bagchi and Ram Dasi Roy; m. Falguni Mukherji; 1 child, Saurabh. BSc, Lucknow (India) U., 1973, MSc, 1975, PhD in Botany and Pharmacognosy, 1981. Rsch. scholar dept. botany Lucknow U., 1976-80; from sr. sci. asst. III to scientist IV Ctrl. Inst. Medicinal and Aromatic Plants, Lucknow, 1980-94, scientist IV (3), 1994—. Contbr. chpts. to books, also over 40 articles to sci. publs. Sr. rsch. fellow CSIR, New Delhi, 1979. Avocation: trekking. Home: 25/27 Indira Nagar, Lucknow 226016UP, India Office: Ctrl Inst Med Aroma Plants, Lucknow 226015UP, India

BAGCHI, SUVENDRA NATH, microbiologist, educator, researcher; b. Calcutta, Nov. 12, 1959; s. Sourendra Nath and Kanika (Sanyal) B.; m. Divya Mishra, June 28, 1988; 1 child. BS, Motilal Vigyan Mahavidyalay, Bhopal, India, 1978, MS, 1980; PhD, Sch. Life Sci., Hyderabad, India, 1985. Rsch. fellow U. Hyderabad, 1980-84; lectr. in microbiology U. Jabalpur, India, 1984-89, 96-95; assoc. prof. microbiology U. Ajmer, India, 1995-96; reader microbiology U. Jabalpur, 1997—; postdoctoral fellow Tex. A&M U., Bryan, 1986, Bayreuth (Germany) U., 1988-89, Konstanz (Germany), 1989-90; incharge head U. Ajmer, 1995-96. Contbr. 38 articles to scientific jours. Recipient Alexander von Humboldt Found. award, Bonn, Germany, 1988, Fulbright award Coun. Internat. Exch. of Scholars, Washington, 1986, Young Scientist award Indian Nat. Sci. Acad., 1991, Sci. and Engring. Resource Coun. vis. award Dept. Sci. and Tech., Delhi, India, 1994. Fellow Indian Botanical Soc.; mem. Soc. Biol. Chemistry. Avocations: music, painting, cricket. Home: Pachpedi, B-1 Uttarayan Enclave, MP Jabalpur 482 001, India Office: R D Univ, Dept Biological Sci, MP Jabalpur 482 001, India

BAGDASARIAN, HENRY, information systems auditor; b. July 23, 1963; came to the U.S., 1989; s. Michael Bagdasarian and Armenohi Eskandari; m. Eileen Bagdasarian, May 23, 1998. AA, Malcolm X Coll., 1991; BS in Acctg., U. Ill., Chgo., 1993. Cert. info. sys. auditor, cert. fin. svcs. auditor. Internal auditor Household Internat., Chgo., 1994-95; ops. acctg. mgr. Household Credit Svcs., Salinas, Calif., 1995-96; elec. data processing auditor Pacific Stock Exch., San Francisco, 1996-97; sr. info. sys. auditor Universal Studies, Universal City, Calif., 1997-98; info. sys. audito supr. The Walt Disney Co., Burbank, Calif., 1998-2000; info. tech. mgr. Fox Entertainment Group, Northridge, Calif., 2000—. Contbr., supporter Coalition to Preserve Mount Davidson, San Francisco, 1997. Mem. Info. Sys. Audit and Ctrl. Assn. (cert.), Nat. Assn. Fin. Svcs. Auditors (cert.), Info. Sys. Security Assn., Inst. Internal Auditors. Avocations: stock research and investments, swimming, table tennis, creative business ideas, writing. E-mail: henryb@fox.com. Home: 19672 Yosemite Cir Northridge CA 91326-4119

BAGDY, GYORGY, pharmacologist, researcher; b. Budapest, Hungary, July 31, 1955; s. Gyorgy and Maria (Lukacs) B.; m. Katalin Szemeredi, June 1, 1976; children: Judit, Gyorgy. Diploma in Pharmacy, Semmelweis U. Medicine, Budapest, 1979; PhD in Pharmacy and Pharmacology, Semmelweis U. Medicine, 1981; cert. in Pharmacology, Postgrad. Med. U., Budapest, 1983; cert. vis. fellowship program, NIH, Bethesda, Md., 1989; DSc, Hungarian Acad. Scis., Budapest, 1998. Pharmaceutical-pharmacol. diplomate. Rsch. fellow Psychopharmacology Nat. Inst. Nervous and Mental Diseases, Budapest, 1979-85; vis. fellow Clin. Neuropharmacology NIH, Bethesda, 1986-89, vis. assoc. Clin. Neuroendocrinology, 1989-90; rsch. assoc. Nat. Inst. Psychiatry and Neurology, Budapest, 1991-92; chief Lab. Exptl. Medicine Nat. Inst. Psychiatry and Neurology, 1992-93, chief Lab. Neurochemistry and Exptl. Medicine, 1994—; rsch. cons. Clin. Neuropharmacology NIH, 1989-90; cons. Psychopharmacology Nat. Inst. Psychiatry and Neurology, 1991—; program cons. PhD program of Semmelweis U. Medicine and I. Haynal Med. U., 1995—; sec. Scientific and Ednl. Bd., Nat. Inst. Psychiatry and Neurology, 1994—. Author: (book chpt.) Pharmacology of Depression in Depression by M. Arato, 1994, Methods in Neuroendocrinology, 1998; contbr. numerous articles to profl.jours., 9 book chpts. Recipient various rsch. grants, 1990-2000. Mem. European Soc. for Neurochemistry, Internat. Soc. of Psychoneuroendocrinology, Serotonin Club, European Neuroendocrine Assn., Hungarian Coll. Neuropsychopharmacology (organizer), Internat. Soc. Neuroendocrinology. Avocations: sports, music, travel. Office: Nat Inst Psychiatry and Neurology, Lab Neurochem Exp Med, Huvosvolgyi ut 116, 1021 Budapest Hungary

BAGGE, SVERRE HÅKON, history educator; b. Bergen, Norway; s. Sverre H. and Gunvor (Bagge) Olsen; m. Guromette Skrove, June 9, 1968; children: Jon, Elin, Otto. Candidate in Philosophy, U. Bergen, 1970, PhD, 1980. Asst. U. Bergen, 1970-73, lectr., 1973-74, sr. lectr., 1974-91, prof., 1991—. Author: The Political Thought of The King's Mirror, 1987, Society and Politics in Snorri Sturluson's Heimskringla, 1991, From Gang Leader to the Lord's Anointed, 1996. Home: Granlia 27, N-5104 Eidsvag Norway Office: U Bergen Dept History, Sydnesplass 7, N-5007 Bergen Norway

BAGGIO, DINO, soccer player; b. Italy, July 24, 1971. Midfielder Parma Italy Football Club. Address: Viale Partigiani d italia, 1 Parma, Parma Italy*

BAGGIO, ROBERTO, professional soccer player; b. Caldogno, Italy, Feb. 18, 1967. Forward Vicenza Football Club, Italy, Fiorentina Football Club, Italy, Juventus Football Club, Italy; winner Italian Cup, 1993, UEFA Cup, 1993, Seria A, 1995; forward AC Milan, Italy; winner Seria Championship, 1996; forward Bologna Football Club, Italy, 1997-98, Inter, Italy, 1998—. Named European Footballer of Yr., 1993, World Footballer of Yr., 1993. Office: Avenue Alfred Maës, BP 236, 62304 Lens Cedex Italy*

BAGGS, SYDNEY ALLISON, architect, educator, environmental impact consultant; b. Sydney, NSW, Australia, July 15, 1930; s. Sydney Staples and Emily Hilda (Hare) B.; m. Joan Constance Mendham, Feb. 2, 1952; children: David Warwick, Allison Joan, Kate Louise. Diploma in arch., Sydney Tech. Coll., 1952; BArch, U. NSW, 1968, grad. diploma in landscape design, 1970, MArch, 1975, PhD in Arch. and Sci., 1982, grad. diploma in bldg. biology/ecology, 1994. Chartered architect, environ. arch. scientist, landscape architect. Archtl. draftsman, architect J.W. Roberts & Assocs., Sydney, 1949-53, assoc., 1953-60; ptnr. Roberts & Baggs Pty. Ltd., Sydney, 1960-75; sr. lectr. U. NSW, Sydney, 1975-86; joint mng. dir. Eca Space Design Pty. Ltd., Sydney, 1984—; dir. The P.E.O.p.l. Group, Sydney, 1989—; co-organizer 1st Internat. Conf. on Energy Efficient Bldgs. with Earth Shelter Protection, 1983, editor Australian procs.; invited lectr. Kirghizian Inst. USSR Acad. Scis., 1985; lectr. Royal Soc. NSW, Sydney, 1993, organizer Summer Sch. Cities of the Future, 1994. Author 6 books; contbr. over 60 publs. to profl. jours. in Europe, Eng., USSR, China, Thailand, Japan, U.S., and Australia; prin. author, illustrator: Australian Earth-Covered Building, 1985, revised 2d edit., 1991, The Healthy House, 1996; regular contbr. (mag.) Nature & Health; former editor-in-chief (jour.) Geotecture. Co-recipient with NSW Govt. Arch. and D.W. Baggs Bradford CSR Energy Conquest Design merit award Brewarrina Aboriginal Cultural Mus., NSW, 1992-93, Top Home awards Housing Industry Assn., 1989-93. Fellow Royal Soc. Arts (London), Rsch. Soc. Centenary Inst. Cancer Medicine and Cell Biology, Royal Australian Inst. Architects (Blackett award 1990), Internat. Biog. Ctr. (Cambridge, Eng.), Am. Biol. Inst. Rsch. Assn. (dep. gov 1994-98); mem. Bldg. Biology and Ecology Inst. New Zealand, Australian Coll. Nutritional and Environ. Medicine (assoc.), Environic Foundational Internat. (Notre Dame U., mem. internat. bd. advisors), Internat. Design for Extreme Environments Assn. (founding mem.), Nat. Environ. Law Assn., Royal Soc. NSW, Environment Inst. Australia, Geotecture Internat. Assn. (founder, founding pres.), Australian Soc. Authors, Royal Brit. Inst. Architects. Avocations: hiking, reading, travel, swimming. Office: Eca Space Design Pty Ltd, PO Box 876, NSW Newport Beach 2106, Australia

BAGHAEI-YAZDI, NAMDAR, microbiologist; b. Tehran, Iran, Dec. 12, 1959; arrived in Eng., 1979; parents Mohammad Baghaei-Yazdi and Parvin Shahmolki-Baghaei. BSc (hon.), Kings Coll., London, 1986; PhD, Imperial Coll., London, 1992. Indsl. trainee Brit. Gas, London, 1984-85; rsch. asst. Imperial Coll., London, 1986-90, 91-94; rsch. cons. U.K. Atomic Energy Authority, Harwell, 1990-91; asst. mgr. Agrol Ltd., Guildford, U.K., 1994—; rsch. cons. U.K.A.E.A., 1990-91, Imperial Coll., 1994—. Author rsch. papers in field (Cereal prize 1993). Recipient Prix Céréalier, Céréaliers de France, 1993. Mem. Soc. Chem. Industry, Soc. for Gen. Microbiology, Biochem. Soc., Inst. Biology (chartered biologist). Islam. Avocations: music, sports, current affairs, Persian literature, cats. Office: Agrol Ltd Agrol House, Woodbridge Meadows, Guildford Surrey GU1 1BA, England

BAGHERWAL, RAJENDRA KUMAR, veterinarian, researcher; b. Bhanpura, India, July 18, 1959; s. Bardi Chand and Shanta (Joshi) B.; m. Shobha Telang, June 6, 1987 (div.); children: Ruchi, Jaya. B Vet. Sci. and Animal Health, Vet. Coll., Mhow, India, 1983, M Vet. Sci. and Animal Health, 1985; PhD, D.A.V.U., Indore, India, 1994. Asst. vet. surgeon Vet. Dept., Bhopal, India, 1987-88; asst. prof. vet. medicine Vet. Coll., Mhow, India, 1988—; cons. Ahilya Mata Goshala, India, 1995—. Co-author: Advances in Veterinary Science; contbr. articles to profl. jours. Served with Indian mil., 1994—. Recipient Young Scientist award M.P. Coun. Sci. and Tech., 1991, Appreciation award Indian Soc. Vet. Medicine, 1993. Mem. Indian Assn. Advanced Vet. Rsch. (joint sec. 1997—, award 1998), Rotary Club (sec. 1998-99). Rashtriya Syayam Sewak Sangh. Avocations: horseback riding, table tennis, reading, social activities. Home: Vet Coll, 453446 Mhow, Madhya Pradesh India Office: Vet Coll Mhow, Campus Rasalpura, 453446 Mhow, Madhya Pradesh India

BAGHERZADE, IRADJ A., publisher; b. Vienna, Austria, Dec. 27, 1942; s. A.M. and M. (Elhamy) B.; m. Shahnaz Hakimzadeh, Mar. 15, 1981; children: Tara, Nezam. BA, Oxford (Eng.) U., 1965, MA, 1966. Asst. editor Time-Life, N.Y., 1966-69; dep. mgr. Time-Life Internat., Amsterdam, The Netherlands, 1969-71, regional mgr., 1971-72; mng. dir. Time-Life Books, London, 1972-75; pres. Danesheh Now Pub. Co., Tehran, Iran, 1975-79; editor I.B. Tauris, London, 1983—, also chmn. bd. dirs.; freelance cons., 1979-83; bd. dirs. Triana Films, London. Fellow Brit. Soc. for Mid. East Studies; mem. Reform Club. Avocations: Islamic art, whitewater rafting. Office: I B Tauris Co Ltd, Victoria Ho, Bloomsbury Sq, London WC1B 4DZ, England

BAGLA, PALLAVA, journalist, photographer; b. Kanpur, UP, India, Oct. 30, 1962; s. Sita Ram and Sharad Bagla; m. Subhadra Menon, Nov. 24, 1988; children: Nayantara, Avishkar. BSc with honors, U. Delhi, India, 1984, MSc, 1986. Cert. in T.V. journalism. Jr. rsch. fellow Indian Inst. of Sci., Bangalore, 1986-87; rsch. assoc. Indian Inst. Pub. Administrn., New Delhi, 1987-89; India photographer Corbis Images (formerly Westlight Internat.), L.A., 1990—; India corr. Science, New Delhi, 1997—; news prodr. T.V. Today, New Delhi, 1997; asst. editor Science Reporter, New Delhi, 1990-95; cons. World Wide Fund for Nature, New Delhi, 1989, The World Bank, 2000; anchor Doordarshan, New Delhi, 1999; spl. contbr. The Indian Express, New Delhi, 1998—. Photographer: Buddhism, 1999, Trees of the Indian Sub-Continent, 2000; editor: Ravaged Forests & Soiled Seas, 1989; contbr. over 300 articles and 1500 photographs to Nature, Nat. Geographic, Sci., BBC Wildlife, The Economist, FrontLine, others. Recipient Wildlife Essay Writing award BBC, London, 1993; sci. writing fellow Marine Biol. Labs., Woods Hole, Mass., 1994. Mem. Indian Sci. Writers Assn., Soc. Nature Photographers Delhi. Hindu. Avocations: travel, gardening, reading, wildlife watching. E-mail: pbagla@vsnl.com. Home and Office: Mayur Vihar Phase I, 72 Samachar Apts, Delhi 110 091, India

BAGLEY, EUGENY ANANIEVICH, research scientist; b. Kiev, Ukraine, Mar. 27, 1939; s. Ananiy Mihailovich Bagley and Anastasiy Ivanovna Chayka; m. Nelly Mihailovna Dzuba, Nov. 5, 1968; children: Kondratenko Helen, Kryvenko Nataly. MD, A.A. Bogomolec Med. U., Kiev, 1962; Candidate Med. Sci., Chem. Physics Inst., Moscow, 1968; D in Med. Sci., Inst. Problem Oncology, Kiev, 1984. Sci. rschr. Inst. Problem Oncology, Kiev, 1968-71, sci. sec., 1971-77, sr. sci. rschr., 1977-84; head lab. Inst. Ecogigiene and Toxicology, Kiev, 1985—. Author: (with E.P. Sidorik, M.Y. Danko) Biochemiluminescence of Cell and Tumour Process, 1989; contbr. articles to profl. jours. Expert hygienic com. Komitet of Gigienic Reglamentation, 1995—. Recipient Bogomoletz prize Nat. Ukraine Acad., 1991. Avocations: art, literature, sports. Home: 5 Tobolsky per, 03039 Kiev Ukraine Office: LI Medved Inst Ekogigiene, Geroev Oboroni 6, 03022 Kiev Ukraine

BAGLEY, HUGHES ANDERSON, retail executive, consultant; b. St. Louis, Dec. 13, 1924; s. William Jefferson and Ivy B. (Wells) B.; m. Marilyn Ann Blattner, May 5, 1945; children: Hughes A. Jr., Herbert F., Brett J., Mary Rebecca, Melissa Ann, Ellen E., Heidi M. BSBA, Wash. U., 1948. Beef mktg. exec. Royal Packing Co., St. Louis, 1949-56; merchandiser Kroger Co. Cin., St. Louis, Charleston, W.Va., 1956-58, Chgo., 1958-65, Columbus, Ohio, 1965-67; pres. Tradewell Supermarkets, Seattle, 1967-68; v.p. Bohack Corp., Bklyn., 1968-70; asst. pres. First Nat. Stores, Somerville, Mass., 1968-71; v.p. mktg. Iowa Beef Processors, Dakota City, Nebr., 1971-75, Spencer (Iowa) Foods, 1975-78; exec. v.p. Dubuque Packaging Co., 1978-79; ind. cons., 1979-84; dir. meat and deli Super-Valu Cub Foods Divsn., Stillwater, Minn., 1985-87; COO Cub Foods, Atlanta, 1987-88; ind. cons. Xtra Divsn., 1988-89, Seaboard Farms, 1990, Beef Specialists of Iowa, Hartley, 1992, Ukrop Super Markets, Richmond, Va., 1993, Grupo Ganadero Indsl., Costa Rica, 1993, Berliner & Marx, Plume de Veau Veal, South Bend, Ind., 1997, Packerland, Green Bay, Wis., 1996; mem. Chgo. Mercantile Exch., 1971. Republican. Avocations: reading, studying industry trends, marketing. Home and Office: Hereford Trading Corp Consulting 22632 Grenoble Ave Sioux City IA 51108

BAGLEY, THOMAS STEVEN, private equity investor; b. Chgo., Oct. 25, 1952; s. James A. and Corinne M. (Catania) B.; m. Christine A. Elliott; 1 child, Derek Elliott Bagley. BA in Econs. cum laude, North Park Coll., Chgo., 1974; MBA in Fin., DePaul U., 1977. Mgr. contr. divsn. Continental Ill. Nat. Bank, Chgo., 1975-78, officer Cleve. Office, 1978-81, asst v.p. Corr. Banking, 1981, v.p. mgr. Ill. & Wisc., 1981-84; v.p. area mgr. of Midwest Area of Leveraged Capital Group Citicorp North Am., Inc., Chgo., 1984-88; founder, mng. gen. ptnr. Pfingsten Ptnrs., Deerfield, Ill., 1989—; founder, gen. ptnr. Chgo. Assocs. Internat., 1988-89; bd. dirs. Woodall Pub. Group, Inc., Hallcrest, Inc., Huebcore Comm., Inc., Am. Acad. Suppliers, Inc., Park Foods, L.P., Barjan Products, L.P., Norcraft Cos. LLC, Pfingsten Pub. LLC, Four Wheel Drive Hardware LLC. Blum Glover scholar, 1973-74. Mem. Union League Club of Chgo., Conway Farms Golf Club, Geneva Nat. Golf Club, Execs. Club Chgo., Econs. Club Chgo., Delta Mu Delta. Republican. Lutheran. Home: 1155 Ashlawn Dr Lake Forest IL 60045-1504 Office: Pfingsten Ptnrs Corporate 500 Centre 520 Lake Cook Rd Ste 375 Deerfield IL 60015-5632

BAGLEY, WILLIAM EVAN, application technology specialist; b. Marfa, Tex., Jan. 28, 1949; s. Cleon Lester Jr. and Alice Lucille (McKinney) B.; m. Cynthia Gail Keener, June 23, 1952; children: William Lester, Evan Blake, Jason Lee, Keri Lynn. BS in Entomology, Tex. A&M U., 1971. Extension entomologist Tex. Agrl. Extension Svc., Pecos, Tex., 1972-75; dir. R&D Stull Chem., San Antonio, 1975-87; product mgr. Wilbur Ellis Co., Fresno, Calif., 1987—. Mem. devel. coun. Tex. A&M U. Coll. of Agriculture. Mem. ASTM, Nat. Roadside Vegetation Mgmt. Assn., Nat. Agrl. Aviation Assn., Inst. of Liquid Atomization and Spray Systems, Am. Soc. of Agrl. Engrs., Entomological Soc. of Am., Southwestern Entomology Soc., Nat. Coalition Drift Minimization. Avocations: karate (3rd degree black belt), refereeing, Tae Kwon Do, racing pigeons. Home and Office: 6307 Ridge Pass San Antonio TX 78233-3935

BAGLOW, DAVID RICHARD, marine facility administrator; b. Manchester, Eng., May 14, 1939; s. Wilfrid Charles and Edith (May) B. Cert. heat engines/gas industry supply; cert. comms. engr. Engr. indsl. gas supply M.W. Gas Bd., Manchester, 1958-62; comms. engr. Cable & Wireless Ltd., various locations, 1962-74; asst. mgr. The Moorings Ltd., Tortola, British Virgin Islands, 1974-75; mgr., v.p. W.I. Yacht Charter, Tortola, 1975-78; gen. mgr., v.p. Navy Cay Marine Ctr., Tortola, 1978-80; ops. mgr. South Pacific Yacht Charter, Tonga, Tahiti, Logan, Utah, 1980-85; base mgr., rschr. The Moorings Ltd., Tortola, Tonga, Grenada, Bahamas, 1985-94; ops. mgr., co-dir. The Moorings Australasia Pty./Ltd., Sydney/Whitsunday Islands, Australia, 1994—. Author: Cruising Guide to Isles Sous le Vent and Tahiti, Vava'u Islands of Tonga, Tonga Guide, 1980, Tahiti Guide, 1982. Avocations: yachting, music, yacht engineering research, reading nonfiction, travel. Home and Office: Ocean View PO Box 6454 Ocean View HI 96737-6454

BAGNARD, WILLIAM W., company executive; b. Santa Monica, Calif., Jan. 22, 1960; s. William L. and Jaqueline Bishop Bagnard; m. Tamara Leah Pearlstein, Sept. 12, 1987; children: Alexa, Matt, Marielle. BA in Psychology, U. So. Calif., L.A., 1981, MBA, 1984, MS, 1984. Paralegal asst. Bateman Eichler, Hill Richards, Inc., L.A., 1981-82; fin. cons. Merrill Lynch, L.A., 1984-88; v.p. Am. Funds Distbrs., inc., L.A., 1988—. Mem. Bel Air Bay Club, L.A. Country Club, Kappa Beta Phi. Republican. Episcopalian. Avocations: volleyball, motorcycling, music, travel. E-mail: wwb@capgroup.com. Fax: 310-454-1854. Office: Am Funds Distbrs Inc 50th Fl 333 S Hope St Fl 50 Los Angeles CA 90071-1406

BAGNEID, ALI ABDALLA, physics educator; b. El-Giza, Dec. 18, 1954; s. Abdalla Salem Bagneid and M. S. Bazaraa; m. Hanan Salah El-Din Sayed Ahmed, Jan. 26, 1993; children: Hesham, Seif. BSc, Cairo U., 1976; MS, U. Pitts., 1980; PhD, Purdue U., 1988. Demonstrator, asst. lectr. Cairo U., El-Giza, Egypt, 1976-88; tchg. and rsch. asst. Purdue U. and U. Pitts., 1979-88; asst. prof., then assoc. prof. physics Umm Al-Qura U., Makkah, Saudi Arabia, 1988—. Contbr. articles to sci. and profl. jours. David Ross Summer fellow, purdue U., 1983-88; recipient cert. of merit Cairo U., 1977. Mem. Am. Phys. Soc. Home: PO Box 6438, Makkah Saudi Arabia Office: Umm Al-Qura U, Dept Physics, Makkah Saudi Arabia

BAGOLAN, PIETRO, surgeon, consultant; b. Rome, Mar. 5, 1954; s. Paolo and Elvira Giustina (Granzotto Basso) B.; m. Marta Corvini, May 4, 1981; children: Sara, Jacob, Paolo. MD, Sapienza U., Rome, 1978. Med. diplomate gen. surgery and pediat. surgery. Resident surgery Sapienza U., Rome, 1983; resident pediat. surgery Tor Verata U., Rome, 1988; lectr. Sapienza U., Rome, 1979-81; asst. Bambino Gen. Hosp., Rome, 1981-90, cons., 1990-97, chief, 1997—; cons. Artemisia Prenatal Ctr., Rome, 1987—, Fatebenetratelli Hosp., Rome, 1989—, S. Eugenio Hosp., Rome, 1992—; prof. Ob-Gyn. Spl. Sch., 1998—. Mem. British Assn. Pediat. Surgery, Italian Soc. Pediat. Surgery, French Soc. Pediat. Surgery. Roman Catholic. Office: Bambino Gesu Hosp, Pizza Sonofrio 4, 00165 Rome Lazio, Italy

BAGSHAW, MALCOLM A., radiation oncologist, educator; b. Adrian, Mich., 1925. BA, Wesleyan U., 1946; MD, Yale U., 1950. Diplomate Am. Bd. Radiology. Surg. intern Grace-New Haven Hosp., 1950-51, resident in surg. pathology, 1951-52; resident in radiology U. Mich., 1953-56, clin. instr. radiology, 1955-56; instr. Stanford U., Palo Alto, Calif., 1956-59, asst. prof., 1959-62, assoc. prof., 1962-69, prof., 1969-92, Henry S. Kaplan-Harry Lebeson prof. emeritus, 1992—, dir. div. radiation therapy, 1960-92, chmn. radiology dept., 1972-86, chmn. radiation oncology dept., 1986-92; resident etranger Inst. Gustave-Roussy, France, 1962-63; cons. radiation therapy VA Hosp., Palo Alto, Calif., 1960-92. Recipient Medal of Honor, Am. Cancer Soc., 1984, Gold Medal award Am. Soc. for Therapeutic Radiology and Oncology, Disting. Alumnus award Wesleyan U., 1996, Charles P. Kettering Gold medal Gen. Motors Co., 1996. Mem. AMA, Radiological Soc. of N.Am. (Gold Medal 1999). Office: Stanford U Med Ctr 300 Pasteur Dr Palo Alto CA 94305

BAGSHAWE, KENNETH DAWSON, oncologist; b. Marple, Eng., Aug. 17, 1925; s. Harry and Gladys (Dawson) B.; m. Ann Alice Kelly, Dec. 26 (Div. Jan. 1977): children: Janita Marie, James Adrian; m. Sylvia Dorothy Corben, Jan. 29, 1977 (dec. Jan. 1996); m. Surinder Kanta Sharma, July 20, 1998. Student, London Sch. Econs., 1942-43; MB, BS, St. Mary's Hosp. Med. Sch., London, 1952, John Hopkins Hosp., 1956; MD, Charing Cross Hosp. Med. Sch., London, 1961. Fellow Royal Coll. Physicians of London. Sr. registrar St. Mary's Hosp. Med. Sch., 1956-60; sr. lectr. Charing Cross Hosp. and Med. Sch., 1961-63, cons. physician, 1963—, prof. med. oncology, 1975-90, prof. emeritus, 1990-2000; bd. dirs. Kemble Instrument Co., Eng.; chmn. scientific com. Cancer Rsch. Campaign, Eng., 1983-88, exec. com., 1988-90; mem. Gen. Motors Cancer Awards Assembly, 1985-89. Author: Choriocarcinoma, 1969; contbr. 300 articles to profl. jours.; editorial bd. several cancer rsch. jours.; inventor and patentee in field. Lt. Royal Navy, 1943-46. Decorated comdr. Order of Brit. Empire, 1990. Fellow Royal Coll. Ob-Gyn, Royal Coll. Radiology, Royal Soc., Royal Soc. Medicine (pres. oncology section 1974-75), British Assn. Cancer Rsch. (pres. 1989-94), Assn. Cancer Physicians (pres. 1985-94), Athenaeum. Home: 115 George St, London WIH T5A, England Office: Charing Cross Hosp, Dept Med Oncology, London W6 8RF, England

BAGUINON, NESTOR TALAMAYAN, ecology educator; b. Gattaran, Cagayan, The Philippines, May 17, 1950; s. Francisco Acantilado Baguinon and Vicenta Talamayan; m. Agnes-Nemesia Capupus, Apr. 4, 1983; children: Franz-Lorenz, Gmelina-Maria, John-Matthew. BS, U. Philippines, Los Baños, 1977, MS, 1981, PhD, 1997. Rsch. asst. U. Philippines, Los Baños, 1977-78; grad. asst. U. Philippines, Los Baños, 1978-81, rsch. assoc., 1981-82, instr., 1982-90, asst. prof., 1990-97, assoc. prof., 1997—; biodiversity conservation cons. World Wildlife Fund-Biodiversity Conservation, The Philippines, 1995-96; vegetation specialist Maunsell-Western Mining Corp., The Philippines, 1996-99; tech. cons. Bechtel-Ogden Pacific Mfg. Resources Quezon Power Plant, The Philippines, 1997-98; team leader Wellspring Mgmt. Corp.-Global Cement, Inc., The Philippines, 1998-99. Author: "Established Coupled Agro-Forest Ecosytems" in Spirit of Enterprise (Rolex awards 1993). Ecologist for environ. risk assessement Diocese of Tagbilaran, Bohol, The Philippines, 1995; vol. ecologist Social Action Ctr., Diocese of Boac, Marinduque, The Philippines, 1997; team leader Environ. Legal Assistance Ctr. Española, Palawan, The Philippines, 1997. Recipient Cert. of Achievement, S.E. Asia Mins. Edn. Orgn., Regional Ctr. Grad. Study and Rsch. in Agriculture, The Philippines, 1997; scholar Peace Happiness Prosperity, Singapore and Tokyo, 1994. Mem. AAAS, U. Philippines Beta Sigma (grand counselor Los Baños chpt. 1999), Phi Sigma, Gamma Sigma Delta. Avocations: basketball, chess, cycling. Home: 5B Apt Tindalo St, CFNR-UP at Los Baños Coll, Laguna The Philippines Office: Dept Forest Biol Scis, UP at Los Baños Coll, Laguna The Philippines

BAGWILL, JOHN WILLIAMS, retired pension fund company executive; b. Seattle, Aug. 9, 1930; s. John Williams and Amy (Munday) B.; m. Emily Bend Sedgwick, Dec. 28, 1953; children: John Williams III, David Sedgwick, Elizabeth Bagwill Komjathy. BA, Hamilton Coll., 1952; MBA, Harvard U., 1958. CFP. Asst. to pres. George O. Muir, Inc., N.Y.C., 1961-64; v.p. Fin. Instns. Retirement Fund, White Plains, N.Y., 1964-85, exec. v.p., 1985-87, pres., 1987-94; ret., 1994; gov. Newport (R.I.) Health Care Corp., 1997. Bd. dirs. Town Club New Castle, Chappaqua, N.Y., 1975-79, pres., 1978-79; alumni coun. Hamilton Coll., 1977-82, pres., 1980-82; trustee, treas. Newport Art Mus., 1997—. Mem. Newport Reading Rm. Episcopalian.

BAHAA AL-DIN, HUSSEIN KAMAL, Egyptian government official, pediatrician; b. Charkieh, Egypt, 1932; married; 1 child. BA in Medicine, U. Cairo, PhD in Pediatry, 1959. Prof., head pediatrics dept. Cairo U.; pres. Egyptian Assn. Pediatry; mem. permanent coun. World Pediatrics Union; cultural councilor Egyptian Embassy in Germany; Min. of Edn. Govt. of Egypt, 1991—. Office: Ministry of Natural Education, Sharia el-Falaky, Bab al-Louki Cairo, Egypt*

BAHADUR, ARUNA, material scientist; b. Punjab, India, May 11, 1945; d. Parmeshwar Dayal and Indira Mathur; m. Satyendra Bahadur, May 6, 1968; children: Sona Mahavni, Rajat. BSc with honors, Delhi U., 1966, MSc, 1968; PhD, Patna U., 1992. Sr. asst. dir., scientist A Nat. Metallurgical Lab., Jamshedpur, India, 1976-81, scientist B, 1981-86, scientist C, 1986-91, scientist E1, 1991-94, scientist EII, 1994—; vis. faculty Regional Inst. of Tech., Jamshedpur, India; cons. in industry; spkr. in field; prin. organizer tech. seminars. Contbr. rsch. papers to profl. jours. Merit scholarship Delhi U., 1965-68. Fellow Indian Inst. of Metals (life fellow, former chairperson Jamshedpur chpt.); mem. N.Y. Acad. Scis., Material Rsch. Soc. India, Indian Soc. for Non-Destructive Testing. Avocations: swimming, walking, reading, socializing, TV watching. Office: Nat Metallurgical Lab, PO Burma Mines, Jamshedpur 831007, India

BAHBAH, BISHARA ASSAD, editor; b. Jerusalem, Apr. 10, 1958; came to U.S., 1976; s. Assad R. and Filomene H. Bahbah; m. Heather Del Parsons, Sept. 24, 1983; children: Leila Jean, As'ad Victor, Jubran Ronald, Remzi Robert. BA, Brigham Young U., 1979; MA, Harvard U., 1981, PhD, 1983. Editor-in-chief Al-Fajr Newspaper, Jerusalem, 1983-84; dir. United Palestinian Appeal, Washington, 1985-87; pres., chmn., CEO Internat. Mktg. and Fund Raising Assocs., Inc., Woodbridge, Va., 1987—; editor-in-chief The Return Mag., Washington, 1988-90; exec. com. mem. Ctr. Policy Analysis on Palestine, Washington, 1990-96; assoc. dir. Middle East Inst., Kennedy Sch., Harvard U., 1992-96; pres., CEO TV Devel. Ptnrs., Inc., N.Y.C., 1997; regional rep. Middle East and Africa RSL COM and RSL Studios, N.Y.C., 1997-98; pres., CEO BHB Enterprises, Woodbridge, Va., 1998—, Holy Land Enterprises, Woodbridge, 1999—; vis. prof. Brigham Young U., Provo, Utah, 1985, adj. prof. polit. sci., 1985-90; sr. fellow Kennedy Sch. Govt. Harvard U., 1996-98. Author: Israel and Latin America--The Military Connection, 1986; mem. adv. bd. Internat. Ency. Comm., 1984—. Chmn., bd. dirs. Palestine Children's Relief Fund, U.S.A.; bd. dirs. Givat Haviva, U.S.A., Palestine Consultancy Group, Jerusalem: mem. Nat. Policy Coun., Arab Am. Inst., Washington; mem. Palestinian Del. to the Multi-Lateral Peace Talks on Arms Control and Regional Security, 1991—. Mem. Nat. Soc. Fund Raising Execs., Direct Mktg. Assn. Washington.

BAHGAT, ALAAELDIN ABDELHAMIED, physicist, educator, researcher; b. Alexandria, Egypt, Aug. 2, 1949; s. Abdelhamied and Hekmat Ibrahiem (Fahmy) B.; m. Maha Mohammad Mohiieldin, May 19, 1977; children: Wael, Omar, Roba. BSc, Al-Azhar U., Cairo, 1970, MSc, 1973, PhD, 1975. Instr. Al-Azhar U., 1971-76, asst. prof., 1976-82, assoc. prof., 1982-87, prof. physics, 1987—, dir. solid state physics lab., 1987—; postdoctoral rschr. U. Tex., Austin, 1977, Tex. Tech. U., Lubbock, 1978-79; prof. Sanaa U., Yemen, 1988-90; cons. Nuclear Rsch. Ctr., Inshaas, 1980-82, Gen. Authority for Fish Resources Devels., 1984, Ministry of Industry, Cairo, 1991, Mobil Oil of Egypt, Cairo, 1992-94, Nat. Inst. Laser Enhanced Rsch., Giza, 1995, Mubarak City for Scientific Rsch. and Tech. Applications, 1999. Co-editor Arabic impression Time Life Books 21st Century Encyclopedia of Sci. and Tech., 1997; contbr. 107 articles to profl. jours. and newspapers. Recipient Postdoctoral grant Min. Higher Edn., Cairo, 1977, Mutual Edn. and Cultural Exchg. award U. Tex. Austin, 1977, R.A. Welch Found. award Tex. Tech. U., 1978, award DAAD German Acad. Exchg. Svc., Bonn, Germany, 1984, ICTP Internat. Ctr. for Theoretical Physics grant, Trieste, Italy, 1986, 88, Yarmouk U. grant, 1989; Inst. Physics/Chinese Acad. Sci. grant, 1990, Nat. prize of advanced sci. tech. Egyptian Acad. Sci. Rsch. and Tech., 1999. Mem. Internat. Disordered-Sys. Assocs. Soc. (life), Am. Phys. Soc., Egyptian Corrosion Soc., Egyptian Soc. Solids and Applications. Avocations: electronics, photography. E-mail: alaabahgat@hotmail.com. Office: Al-Azhar U Faculty Sci Dept Physics, Nasr City, 11884 Cairo Egypt

BAHILL, A. TERRY, systems engineering educator; b. Washington, Pa., Jan. 31, 1946; m. Karen Bahill, July 31, 1971; children: Alex, Zach. BSEE, U. Ariz., 1967; MSEE, San Jose State U., 1970; PhD, U. Calif., Berkeley, 1975. Registered profl. elec. engr., Calif., Pa. Asst. and assoc. prof. biomed. engr. Carnegie Mellon U., Pitts., 1976-84; asst. prof., then assoc. prof. neurology Med. Sch. U. Pitts., 1977-84; prof. sys. engr. U. Ariz., Tucson, 1984—; pres. Bahill Intelligent Computer Systems, 1986—. Author: Bioengineering: Biomedical, Medical and Clinical Engineering, 1981, Keep Your Eye on the Ball: The Science and Folklore of Baseball, 1990, Verifying and Validating Personal Computer-Based Expert Systems, 1991, Linear Systems Theory, 1992, 2d edit., 1998, Engineering Modeling and Design, 1992, Metrics and Case Studies for Evaluating Engineering Designs, 1997, Keep Your Eye on the Ball: Curve Balls, Knuckle Balls and Baseball Falacies, 2000; contbr. articles to profl. jours. Patentee in field. Lt. USN, 1967-71. Fellow IEEE (v.p. 1980-87), Internat. Coun. Sys. Engring. Roman Catholic. Office: Sys & Ind Engring Univ Ariz Tucson AZ 85721-0001

BAHIRI, SIMCHA, economist; b. N.Y.C., Aug. 24, 1927; arrived in Israel, 1950; s. Juda and Sarah (Rosenbaum) Breitbart; m. Anita Hudaly, Oct. 4, 1954 (div. Oct. 1978) children: Amos, Gidon, Kim; m. Doreen Belle Mirvish, Jan. 25, 1979;. B Enging., Liverpool (Eng.) Coll. Tech., 1956; MSc, U. Birmingham, Eng., 1967, PhD, 1970. Recipient cert. Ford Found., 1966, Parapsychology Found., 1984, Armand Hammer Peace Found., 1985; chartered engr. Cons. Matmatica, Princeton, N.J., 1969-71; sr. lectr. Tel Aviv U., 1971-75, sr. rschr. Interdisciplinary Forecasting Ctr., 1980-85, dir. Bahiri Peace Econs., 1986—; mng. dir. Icarus Health Aids, Netanya, Israel, 1971-75; vis. prof. Rensselaer Poly. Inst., Troy, N.Y., 1979-80; forecasting cons. Nat. Cement Co., Tel Aviv, 1972-79; cons. Econ. Coop. Found., Tel Aviv, 1992-95; program specialist Instn. Adminstrn., Enugu, Nigeria, 1963-66. Author: Peaceful Separation or Enforced Unity, 1984; co-author: Peace Pays, 1993; contbr. articles to profl. jours. Activist Amnesty Internat., 1989—; co-chair Israel/Palestine Ctr. for Rsch. and Info., Bethlehem and Jerusalem, 1992—; founding bd. dirs. Palestine Israel Jour., Jerusalem, 1994—; trustee Internat. Ctr. for Peace in the Mid. East, Tel Aviv, 1984-97. With USN, 1945-46. Mem. Man, Nature and Law, Assn. Civil rights in Israel. Social Democrat. Jewish. Avocations: maps, swimming, hiking, theater, music. Home and Office: 28 Hovevei Zion St, Tel Aviv 63346, Israel

BAHK, JAE-HYON, anesthesiologist educator; b. Seoul, S. Korea, Feb. 19, 1964; s. Chae-Nam and Heung-Sook (Song) B.; m. Junghye Ra, Apr. 25, 1992; children: Jun-Beom, Jenny. BA, Seoul Nat. U., 1987, MS, 1995, PhD, 1997. Bd. cert. anesthesiologist. Intern Seoul Nat. U. Hosp., 1987-88, resident, 1988-91, military doctor, 1991-94; attending physician Samsung Med. Cen., Seoul, 1994-96; instr. Seoul Nat. U., 1996-99, asst. prof., 1999—; vis. scholar, U. Calif. L.A., 1998-2000. Contbr. articles to profl. jours. Office: Dept Anes, Seoul Nat U Hosp 28, YongonDong ChongnoGu 110-744, Korea

BAHL, HORST, biologist, researcher; b. Beelitz, Potsdam, Germany, Dec. 23, 1953; s. Kurt and Margarete (Neumann) B.; m. Ellen Burmeister, Aug. 19, 1982; 1 child, Nele. Diplom, U. Hamburg, 1987. Scientist, editor Fed. Rsch. Centre of Fisheries, Hamburg, 1993—; cons. Senate, Berlin, 1989-90. Editor Informationen fuer die Fischwirtschaft, 1993-98, Info. Mgmt. Fed. Rsch. Ctr. of Fisheries, 1999—.

BAHL, SAROJ MEHTA, nutritionist, educator; b. New Delhi, India, Apr. 4, 1946; came to U.S., 1972; d. L.D. and G.D. Mehta; m. Vishwa Mittar Bahl; children: Rahul, Ragini. BS in Home Sci., Delhi U., 1965, MS in Nutrition, 1967, PhD in Nutrition, 1973. Lectr. Lady Irwin Coll., New Delhi, 1970-71; instr. U. N.D., Grand Forks, 1972-74; rsch. assoc. U. Tex. Med. Sch., Houston, 1976-78; asst. prof. U. Tex. Sch. Allied Health, Houston, 1979-87, assoc. prof., 1987—; program dir. Peace Corps, Houston, 1984. Author: Nutritional Management of the AIDS Patient; contbr. articles to profl. jours. Den leader Boy Scouts Am., Houston, 1983; mem. ednl. com. March of Dimes, Houston, 1986—; mem. exec. bd. Indo-Am. Charity Found. of Houston, 1995-98. Recipient several awards for tchg. excellence including John P. McGovern award, 1992, 95; named Outstanding Dietetic Educator Tex. Tex. Dietetic Assn., 1995; nominated for U.S. Prof. of Yr., 1993, 94. Mem. Am. Inst. Life Threatening Illness (assoc.), Soc. Nutrition Edn. (editor newsletter), Minority Faculty Assn. (pres. 1996-97), Vivekananda Vedanta Soc. (pres. 1993—). Avocations: painting, music, reading. Office: U Tex Dental Sch 6516 John Freeman St Rm B-37 Houston TX 77030-3402

BAHLMAN, DAVID ARTHUR, cultural society administrator; b. Mishawaka, Ind., July 6, 1945; s. Henry Louis and Hanna (Haugen) B. BA, Ohio State U., 1967, MA, 1970. Exec. Lincoln Ctr., Inc., N.Y.C., 1981-83; assoc. dir. pub. rels. N.Y. Philharmonic, N.Y.C., 1983-85; exec. dir. Soc. of Archtl. Historians, Phila., 1985-93, Found. for San Francisco Arch. Heritage, 1993-99, Landmarks Pres. Coun. Ill., 1999—. Active Landmarks Preservation Coun. Ill. Mem. Mozart Soc. of Phila. (pres. 1981-93), Phila. Historic Preservation Corp. (bd. dirs. 1989-93), Charlotte Cushman Club (Phila.). Presbyterian. Office: 53 W Jackson Blvd Ste 752 Chicago IL 60604-3610 Address: 329 N Mayflower Rd Lake Forest IL 60045-2323

BAHNASSI, AFIF, art history and architecture educator; b. Damascus, Syria, Apr. 17, 1928; s. Ahmed Rafik and Mekieh (el Oushe) B.; m. Maysoun Jazairi; children: Ayad, Anas, Yola, Kinan, Omar. Lic. in Law, Damascus U., 1949; diploma in History of Art, Ecole de Louvre, Paris, 1961; D of Modern Art, Sorbonne, 1964; State Doctorate; PhD in Philosophy, Sorbonne U., Paris, 1978. Dir. dept. fine art Damascus Ministry of Culture, 1960-71, gen. dir. antiquities and museums, 1971-89. Author 55 books and dictionaries. Recipient 12 medals, 1st prize in Islamic Archt., 1991; named Comdr. of Order of Arts and Letters, Syria, Germany, France, Italy, Bulgaria, Poland, Denmark, Belgium, Yemen. Mem. Assn. Fine Art (pres.), Union Arab Writers. Avocations: running, painting, sculpture, poetry. Fax: 3319368. Office: 4 Gazzi St, Rawda Damascus Syria

BAHR, JANE MARIE, writer, retired English educator. BS in English, U. Wis., River Falls, 1971; MST in English, U. Wis., Whitewater, 1978. English tchr. Whitewater (Wis.) H.S., 1973-82, Eau Claire (Wis.) Meml. H.S., 1985, Glenwood City H.S., summers 1990-91; freelance writer Wis. Regional Writers' Assn., 1985—, Wis. Fellowship of Poets, 1981—, Wis. Arts Bd. Grant, 1998. WRWA Soar scholar Sch. of Arts, U. Wis., Madison, 1999.

BAHRS, OTTOMAR, medical sociologist; b. Hamburg, Germany, Nov. 27, 1951; s. Hans Ottomar Adolf and Marie Anne Auguste (Hillermann) B.; 1 child, Katharina. Abitur, U. Hamburg, 1970. Diplomate of social scis. Rsch. asst. dept. med. sociology U. Göttingen, Germany, 1978-88, rsch. asst. dept. gen. medicine, 1988-90; rsch. asst., project leader dept. gen. medicine U. Hannover, Germany, 1992-96; rsch. fellow, project leader dept. med. psychology U. Göttingen, Germany, 1996—; bd. dirs. Acad. for Patient-Centered Medicine, Ritterhude, Germany. Author: (with J. Wilhelm) Rehabilitierung beginnt Zuhause, 1989, (videotape) Ärztliche Qualitätszirkel, 1993; editor: (with F. M. Gerlach and J. Szecsenyi) Ärztliche Qualitätszirkel, 1994, (with W. Fischer-Rosenthal and J. Szecsenyi) Vom Ablichten zum Im-Bilde-Sein, 1996. Mem. Soc. on Promoting Comm. in Medicine (mng. dir. 1990—), European Task Force on Patient Evaluation of Gen. Practice, European Task Force on Dr.-Patient Comm., German Soc. Gen. Medicine, League Against Epilepsy. Avocations: crime novels, sports. Home: Beethovenstr 11a, 37085 Göttingen Germany Office: Humboldtallee 38, 37073 Göttingen Germany

BAI, BIN, physicist; b. Kunming, China, July 24, 1964; came to U.S., 1990; s. Huanxin Bai and Peili Tang; m. Ying Shen, Dec. 21, 1990. BS, Nanjing (China) U., 1985, MS, 1988; PhD, Washington State U., 1997. Rsch. assoc. Inst. Acoustics, Academia Sinica, Beijing, 1988-90; rsch. asst. Washington State U., Pullman, 1991-97; test engr. Micron Electronics, Inc., Nampa, Idaho, 1997—; panel organizer Internat. Test Conf., Atlantic City, N.J., 1999. Mem. AAAS, IEEE Computer Soc. (test and technology tech. coun.), Am. Phys. Soc., N.Y. Acad. Scis. E-mail: bai@micron.net. Home: 5210 N Joe Robbie Ave Boise ID 83713-1254

BAI, CHARLES XIAOSHU, finance company executive; b. Chengdu, Sichuan, China, May 31, 1961; arrived in Can., 1990; s. Lianshen and Zhenfu (Shu) B.; m. Ying Chen. B of Econ. (hon.), Chengau (China) U., 1983; MBA, IMD, Laussane, Switzerland, 1989. Sr. staff Tax Bur. Chengdu Municipality, 1983-84; economist Sichuan Provincial Commn. Econ. Reform, Chengdu, 1984-88; assoc. Richardson Greenfield Can. Ltd., Toronto, 1993-95; assoc. dir. Deutsche Morgan Grenfell, Hong Kong, 1995-97; fin. dir. Ogden Energy Asia Pacific Ltd., Hong Kong, 1997—; cons. Bex Internat., Toronto, 1990-91, R.B.C. Dominion Securities, Toronto, 1991-92. Contbr. articles to profl. jours. Mem. Mainland Overseas Chinese Profl. Assn. (founding mem.), Can. Securities Inst. Avocations: water color, reading, history, biographies, classic music.

BAI, GILL-HAN, mycobacteriologist, veterinarian; b. Kangsu-Ku, Pusan, Republic of Korea, May 2, 1947; s. Chong-Jin Bai and Bok-Soo Huh; m. Ok-Kyu Park, Feb. 4, 1979; children: Jae-Yun, Jae-Hyun. DVM, U. Seoul, Republic of Korea, 1975; MPH, Seoul Nat. U., Seoul, 1977, PhD, 1989. Rschr. Kyunggi (Korea) Provincial Govt., Korea, 1976-78; lab. chief Korean Inst. Tuberculosis, Seoul, 1979-98, dep. dir., 1998—; vis. fellow NIH, Bethesda, Md., 1990-92; temporary adviser WHO, Geneva, 1995—. Contbr. articles to profl. jours. Team couple Worldwide Marriage Encounter, Seoul, 1988—. Sgt. Korean Army, 1970-73. Grantee Ministry Sci. and Tech., Seoul, 1998, 99, Ministry Health and Welfare, Seoul, 1999. Mem. Korean Soc. for Microbiology (councilor 1997—). Roman Catholic. Avocations: reading books, listening to music, mountain climbing. E-mail: baigh@knta.or.kr. Fax: 82 2 573 1914. Home: Parktown 129-805, Soonae-dong Pundang-gu, Sungnam Kyunggi 463-020, Republic of Korea Office: Korean Inst Tuberculosis, 14 Woomyun-dong Socho-gu, Seoul 137-140, Republic of Korea

BAI, HSUNLING, environmental engineering educator; b. Taichung, Taiwan, June 25, 1963; d. Wen-Chien Bai and Jian-Lian Hsu; m. Chung-Sying Lu; children: Rebecca Lu, Chia-Yi Lu. B, Nat. Cheng-Kung U., Tainan, Taiwan, 1985; M, U. Cin., 1989, PhD, 1992. Rsch. asst. Nat. Taiwan U., Taipei, 1985-87; assoc. prof. Nat. Chiao-Tung U., Hsinchu, Taiwan, 1992-98, prof., 1998—. Contbr. articles to jours. in field. Mem. com. Appeal and Hearing Bds. Environ. Affairs, Miao-Li, Taiwan, 1994—, Found. of Air Pollution, Environ. Protection Agy., Taipei, 1995-98. Rsch. grantee Nat. Sci. Coun., Taiwan, 1993-2000, Environ. Protection Agy., Taiwan, 1994, 96, Adminstrn. of Sci. Bd. Indsl. Pk., Hsinchu, 1994—. Mem. Air and Waste Mgmt. Assn. (treas. Taiwan sect. 1994-99), Chinese Assn. Aerosol Rsch., Chinese Inst. Environ. Engring. (com. 1995—), Chinese Assn. Environ. Engring. (Best Paper award 1997, 99). Avocations: hiking, piano, reading. Office: Inst Environ Engring, 75 Po-Ai St, Hsinchu 30039, Taiwan

BAI, JUN, medical researcher; b. Tianjin, China, May 3, 1966; arrived in Australia, 1992; s. Zhi Y. Z. Bai and Jing Gui Liu; m. Melinda G. F. Han, June 9, 1993; 1 child, Adrian. MB, Tianjin Med. U., 1988; MPH, U. Sydney, Australia, 1996. Rsch. asst. U. Sydney, 1995-96; rsch. officer Liverpool Hosp., Sydney, 1996-98, data mgr., 1998—. Contbr. articles to profl. jours. E-mail: junbai@accsoft.com.au and jun.bai@swsahs.nsw.gov.au. Fax: 61-2-98285672.

BAI, YONG, engineering executive, educator; b. Jiang Xi, China, May 30, 1963; arrived in Norway, 1991; s. J. Bai and M. Liu; m. Hua Peng, Aug. 26, 1986; children: Lihua, Carl Junhua. PhD in Engring., Hiroshima (Japan) U., 1989. Rschr. CRC Rsch. Ctr., Osaka, Japan, 1989-90; postdoctoral fellow Danish Tech. U., Copenhagen, 1990-91, Norwegian Tech. U., Trondheim, 1991-92; sr. engr. Det Norske Veritas, Oslo, 1992-96; postdoctoral fellow U. Calif., Berkeley, 1994; mgr. advanced engring. JP Kenny, Stavanger, Norway, 1996-99; prof. U. Stavanger, 1997—. Contbr. articles to jours. in field. Named Best Grad. in Naval Architecture, China State Edn. Com., Beijing, 1982; fellow Norwegian Rsch. Coun., Oslo, 1991. Mem. Internat. Soc. Offshore and Polar Engrs. (com., chair), Internat. Conf. Offshore Mechanics and Arctic Engring. (com., chair, recipient best paper award), Internat. Congress Ship and Offshore Structures. Avocations: jogging, table tennis. Home: 3415 Hackberry Ct Spring TX 77388-2712 Office: Am Bureau of Shipping 16855 Northchase Dr Houston TX 77060-6006 also: U Stavanger, Ullandhaug, 4091 Stavanger Norway

BAIBICH, MARIO NORBERTO, physicist; b. Buenos Aires, Argentina, Sept. 24, 1949; s. Paulo and Sara (Krasiuk) B.; m. Ione Maluf, Feb. 21, 1974 (div. Feb. 1990); children: Roberto Maluf, Andre Maluf. BSc in Physics, U. Fed. de Rio Grande do Sul, Porto Alegre, Brazil, 1972; MSc in Physics, McGill U., Montreal, Que., Can., 1979, PhD in Physics, 1982. Tchr. Colegio Israelita Brasileiro, Porto Alegre, 1970-72; tchr. U. Fed. do Rio Grande do Sul, Porto Alegre, 1975, assoc. prof., 1982—; tchg. asst. McGill U., Montreal, 1975-81; mem. internat. sci. bd. Internat. Ctr. for Solid State Physics, Brasilia, 1996—. Achievements include discovering giant magneto resistance (GMR) in 1988. Avocation: cooking. Office: UFRGS/Av Bento Goncalves, 9500-CP 15051, 91501970 Porto Alegre Brazil

BAICAN, ROMAN HORATIU, physicist, project engineer; b. Blaj, Romania, Feb. 23, 1940; came to Fed. Republic of Germany, 1982; s. Virgil Vasile and Elvira (Muresan) B.; m. Branda Bogdan, Jan. 19, 1974; children: Bianca, Livia, Elvira. BS, U. Cluj, Romania, 1962, MS in Physics (hon.), 1962, PhD in Physics, 1972. Asst. U. Cluj, 1963-69; rschr. Ctrl. Inst. Physics, Bucharest, Romania, 1969-79, Inst. Isotope and Molecular Tech., Cluj, 1979-82, U. Frankfurt, Germany, 1982-83; project engr. Std. Elektrik Lorenz, Germany, 1983-87, Adam Opel AG, Rüsselsheim, Germany, 1987—. Author: Solid State Maser, 1976, Microwave Oscill. and Amplifiers with Semiconductor Devices, 1979, Microwave Integrated Circuits, 1996, (with Dan Necsulescu) Applied Virtual Instruments, 1999; patentee in field; contbr. over 60 articles to profl. jours. Recipient Prize for physics Romanian Acad., 1978. Mem. IEEE (sr.), N.Y. Acad. Scis. Roman Catholic. Avocations: travel, skiing, bicycling, reading. Home: Goerdelerstrasse 70, Offenbach Main 63071, Germany Office: Adam Opel AG, Bahnhofstrasse 1, Russelsheim 65423, Germany

BAICHOROV, ALEKSANDR MUKHTAROVITCH, diplomat; b. Grodno, Belarus, Oct. 4, 1948; s. Mukhtar E. and Valentina P. (Belayeva) B.; m. Larissa Ivanovna Valko, July 7, 1973; children: Artem, Anasstassia. MA in Polit. Sociology, Belarus State U., Minsk, 1971, PhD in Polit. Sci., 1974; DSc in Polit. Sci., Belarus Acad. Scis., Minsk, 1986; cert. professorship highest qualificat., Commn. Ministry of Edn., Moscow, 1988. Polit. affairs officer UN Secretariat, N.Y.C., 1980-87; chmn. of dept. Inst. Politology and Social Adminstrn., Minsk, 1987-91, Belarus State U., Minsk, 1991-93; head internat. security and disarmament dept. MFA, Minsk, 1993-96; mem. OSCE mission to Georgia Tbilisi, 1996; dep. head mission of Belarus to EU Brussels, 1996—, dep. head Belarus mission to NATO, 1998—; dir. Ctr. for Strategic Studies and Internat. Rels., Minsk, 1991-93; chief rep. Belarus to 1st Comm. of UNGA, N.Y.C., 1993, 94, Prep. Commn. of OPCW, The Hague, 1993-97, JCIC (START Treaty), Geneva, 1993-96; dep. head Belarus Del. to OSCE Forum for Security Coop., Vienna, 1993-96. Author: (books) The USA in the 1970s: Social Problems and Contradictions, 1979, From the "Beat" Generation to Counter-Culture, 1982, Neo-colonialism and International Terrorism, 1985 (Award of State Com. on Publs. 1986), Introduction in Political Science, 1991, (book chpt.) The Future Role of Russia in Europe and in the World, 1997, others. Mem. Belarus Assn. Politologists, Internat. Club St. Anne. Avocations: tennis, swimming, theater, chamber music.

BAIER, AUGUSTO CARLOS, plant researcher; b. Bagé, Rio Grande do Sul, Brazil, May 10, 1941; s. Karl Fabian and Johanna (Bossard) B.; m. Selma Mielke; children: Luciane Mielke, Auro Augusto. Bel. Agronomy, E.A Eliseu Maciel, Pelotas, Brazil, 1968; D in Agr., Tech. U., Munich, 1972. Wheat breeder EMBRAPA/CNPT, Passo Fundo, Brazil, 1972-77; triticale breeder EMBRAPA/CNPT, Passo Fundo, 1977—, coordinator nat. triticale research program, 1981—, lupin breeder, 1982-91; coord., organizer Nat. Wheat Rsch. Ctr., Brazil, 1974, head, 1995; organizer 2d Internat. Triticale Symposium, 1990; vis. scientist U. Mo., Columbia, 1993-94. Author: As Lavouras de Inverno I and II, 1988, Centeio, 1994, (book chpt.) Hibridacao em Triticale, 1999, Melhoramento do Triticale, 1999; co-author: Triticale cultivo e aproveitamento, 1994; contbr. articles to profl. jours. Recipient Medalha Marechal Hermes award Ministro do Exército, Bagé, 1960. Mem. Am. Soc. Agronomy, Soc. Brasileira P/Prog. da Ciência, Soc. Brasileira de Genética, Internat. Tritacale Assn. (pres. 1986-90), Coun. for Agrl. Sci. and Tech. Club: Passo Fundo (pres. 1982-83), Loj. Luz do Planalto (ven. master 1986-87). Lutheran. Avocation: gardening. Home: R Independencia 2245, 99010-041 Passo Fundo RS, Brazil Office: Nat Wheat Rsch Ctr, Cx Postal 451, 99001-970 Passo Fundo RS, Brazil

BAIER, PAUL WALTER, electrical engineering educator; b. Backnang, Germany, June 10, 1938; s. Paul and Marta (Sannwald) B.; m. Anna-Lena Nystroem, May 22, 1970; children: Paul Christian, Martin Henrik. Diploma in Engring., Tech. U., Munich, Germany, 1963, DEng, 1965, Dr. ing. habil., 1969. Rsch. asst. Tech. U., Munich, Germany, 1963-69, privat dozent, 1969-70; project leader, chief of lab. Siemens, Munich, Germany, 1970-73; full prof. U. Kaiserslautern, Germany, 1973—; cons. in field. Co-author: Advances in Electronics and Electron Physics, 1980, Störunterdrückende Funkübertragungstechnik, 1984; guest editor IEEE-Jour. Selected Areas in Comm.; editor Wireless Personal Comm., Internat. Jour. Wireless Info. Networks, 1993—; contbr. articles to profl. jours.; patentee in field. Recipient Innovation award Mannesmann Mobile Radio Found., 1999, VDE Ring of Honours, 2000. Fellow IEEE, Internat. Union Radio Sci., Info. Tech. Soc. within German Assn. Elec. Engrs. Avocations: sailing, skiing. Office: U Kaiserslautern, Dept Elec Engring, PO Box 3049, D-67653 Kaiserslautern Germany

BAIG, ABDUL SATTAR, physician, researcher; b. Faisalabad, Punjab, Pakistan, Jan. 22, 1970; s. Abdul Ghani and Haneefan Bibi; m. Naveeda Gul, Apr. 23, 1997; children: M. Talha Ali (dec.), Abdul Wahhab. Secondary Sch. Cert., Govt. Iqbal H.S., Faisalabad, Pakistan, 1987; Cert. in Tchg., Lylpur Alementary Coll., Faisalabad, Pakistan, 1990; First Exam in Sci., Govt. Coll. Samman Abad, Faisalabad, Pakistan, 1991; diploma in Homeo. Med. Sys., Al-Sehat Homoo. Med. Coll., Faisalabad, Pakistan, 1993. Organizer Baig Corr. Club, Faisalabad, 1988-96; physician WE Offer Internat., Faisalabad, 1996—, Baig Clinic and Pub. Health Ctr., Faisalabad, 1992—; organizer Rehman Nursery Sch., Faisalabad, 1995—. Muslim. Avocations: penfriendship, bank notes, coins, magazine collections. Home: Ch No 202 RB Bhaiwala, Manan Wala Rd, Hajwairy Town Faisal Abad PH NO 786072, Pakistan Office: We Offer Internat, PO Box No 988, 38000 Faisalabad Punjab Pakistan

BAIG, HASIB TAHIR, aeronautical engineer, consultant; b. Lahore, Punjab, Pakistan, Oct. 8, 1960; s. Mirza Tahir and Razia Tahir (Majeed) B.; m. Raheela Hasib, Dec. 24, 1984; children: Zeeshan Hasib, Zahra Hasib, Iza Hasib. B in Aero. Engring., Pakistan Air Force Coll. Aero., Karachi, 1982; BS, Air War Coll., Karachi, 1997; MBA, Bus. and Commerce, Peshawar, Pakistan, 1999; MS in Structures (hon.), Nanching Aircraft Mfg. Co., Nanchang, China, 1989. Design engr. Nanchang Aircraft Mfg. Company, China, 1987-89; sr. engr. Pakistan Air Force, 1989-91, dy dir., 1991-93, squadron comdr., 1997-99, head tng., 1999—; design engr. AMF, Kamra, Pakistan, 1993-97; dy chief engr. PAC, Kamra, Pakistan, 1993-95, Aircraft Mfg. Factory, Kamra, 1995-97. Recipient commendation Base Comdr., Peshawar, 1999. Mem. Pakistan Engring. Coun. Avocations: music, reading, tennis. E-Mail: hrzi@brain.net.pk. Home: D 2 55 The Mall, Peshawar Pakistan

BAIG, MIRZA MUJEEB, controller; b. Warangal, India, Oct. 20, 1955; s. Mirza Habiburrahman and Durdana Begum Baig; m. Sameena Kareem Baig, Apr. 25, 1982; 1 child, Mirza-Shiraz. B of Commerce, Arts and Sci. Coll., Warangal, 1975; MBA, Osmania U., Hyderabad, 1977. Procurement & contracts contr. Saudi Bros. Comml. Co., Jeddah, Saudi Arabia, 1978—; advisor PMCG, Jeddah, 1980; cons. Westech, Jeddah, 1989. Dir. NRI Forum, Jeddah, 1990; advisor Siva, Jeddah, 1993. Mem. Country Club. Avocations: visiting places, reading. Fax: 00966-2-6718319. E-mail: mirza@saudibrothers.com. Home: Prince Fahad, Jeddah 21432, Saudi Arabia Office: Saudi Bros Comml Co, Al Kayal Alrawda Dist, Jeddah 21432, Saudi Arabia

BAIG, MUNAWAR WAHEED, international trade executive, consultant; b. Lahore, Punjab, Pakistan, Sept. 30, 1952; s. Abdul Waheed and Shamim (Akhtar) B.; m. Yasmin Munawar, Aug. 2, 1978; children: Shavana, Mirza Kamran. BA, Forman Christian Coll., Lahore, 1973. Cert. pilot, Lahore Flying Club. Mgr. sales and ops. Pakistan Gen. Aviation Ltd., Lahore, 1977-78; flight oper. officer Lahore Flying Club, 1978-79; dir. mktg. and sales Flyers Internat. Aviation Specialists and Cons., Lahore, 1979-81; sales and mtkg. cons. Al-Mussallam Trading Est., Jeddah, Saudi Arabia, 1983-84; v.p. Tex. Gulf Iberia Navigation Co., Tulsa, 1981-84; dir. ops. for Asia and Mid. East regions World Trade Svcs. Inc., Tulsa, 1981-84; dir. devel. Akburn & Co. (Pvt.) Ltd., Lahore, 1985-90; dir. ops. Falcon Bus. Concepts (Pvt.) Ltd., Lahore, 1990; dir. pub. rels. Progressive Svcs. (Pvt.) Ltd., Lahore, 1989; mktg. cons. N.E. Air Svcs. Def. Contractors of U.S.A., Norwell, Mass., 1991; fin. cons., fund mgr. Prestige Assocs., Inc. (with Nationsbank of N.C., U.S.A.), 1994; dir. ops. RTV Recreational TV Network Group Inc., Dubai, United Arab Emirates, 1995; cons. for Pakistan and Mid. East Specialized Svcs. Internat. Ltd., Fla., 1995-96; CEO Glitterati Trade Group Inc., Lahore, 1987—, Triangle Resources Holding Co., 1998—; dir. fgn. affairs Jamia-Al-Farooq Al-Islamia, Rahimyar Khan, Pakistan, 1996; dir. ops. Londin INd. Hosp., London's Referral Office in Lahore, Med. Remedy Svcs., 1999—. Editor: (magazine) Fortnightly Indsl. Affairs, 1990, Soaring, 1971. Mem. All Pakistan Students Welfare Fedn., Lahore, 1969; marshal Friends Club, Lahore, 1972. Recipient award Internat. Civil Aviation Orgn., Can., 1975, ABC Gliding Instrs. award Soaring Soc. Am., 1972. Muslim. Avocations: flying, traveling, reading, social services, tennis. Home and Office: Glitterati Trade Group Inc, 124/D Gulberg-2, Lahore 54660, Pakistan

BAIG, TAQI M., electrical engineer; b. Kathmandu, Nepal, Oct. 25, 1966; arrived in Saudi Arabia, 1998.; s. Muzaffar M. Baig and Meher Nigar Khan; m. Mahvish Farooqui, Dec. 23, 1994; 1 child, Imran. BSEE, Rensselaer Poly. Inst., 1991; MS in Elec. and Computer Engring., U. Rochester, 1996. Design engr. IBM, East Fishkill, N.Y., 1988-89; sys. engr. Xerox, Rochester, N.Y., 1991-94; mem. tech. staff AT&T Bell Labs., Holmdel, N.J., 1995-98, Lucent Techs., Holmdel, 1998—. Vol. Highlan Hosp., Rochester, N.Y., 1995-96. Mem. IEEE. Republican. Islam. Achievements include research on flow control in ATM networks; designer internet design for STC. Avocations: reading, computer networks, sports. E-mail: baig@lucent.com. Fax: 96612398669.

BAIK, SEUNG-CHUL, metallurgist, researcher; b. Seoul, Korea, Apr. 27, 1966; s. Ki-Jong and Kyung-Suk (Lee) B.; m. Dae-Young Kim, Mar. 30, 1966; children: Jong-Hyun, Jong-Min. B in Engring., Seoul Nat. U., 1989, M in Engring., 1991, PhD in Engring., 1995. Rschr. Tech. Rsch. Labs.-Pohang Iron and Steel Co., Pohang, Korea, 1995—. Contbr. articles to profl. jours. including Jour. Materials Processing Tech., Scripta Metallurgica et Materialia, Internat. Jour. Mech. Sci., and Jour. Korean Instn. Metals and Materials. 2d lt. South Korean Army, 1991-92. Recipient Tech. award for young rschrs. Korean Inst. Metals and Materials, 1999, Material Microstructure Photography award, 1999. Mem. Iron/Steel Inst. Japan. Avocations: tennis, soccer, traveling with family, classical music, movies. Office: POSCO Sheet Products & Proc, PO Box 36 1 Koedong-dong, Pohang Kyungbuk 790-785, South Korea

BAIK, YOUNG-JOON, research scientist; b. Seoul, Korea, Jan. 22, 1959; s. Chunsuk Baik and Kwang-Hee Kim; m. Kyoung Suk Bae, June 8, 1985; children: Seung-Joo, Ji-Woo. BS, Seoul Nat. U., 1981; MS, Korea Advanced Inst. Sci. and Tech., Seoul, 1983, PhD, 1986. Sr. rsch. scientist Korea Inst. Sci. and Tech., 1986-94, prin. rsch. scientist, 1995—; vis. scholar Pa. State U., State College, 1991-92. Contbr. articles to profl. jours.; patentee in field. Mem. Materials Rsch. Soc., Internal Microelectronics and Packaging Soc., Electrochem. Soc. Avocations: golf, tennis, hiking, travel. Office: Korea Inst Sci and Tech, PO Box 131 Cheongryang, Seoul 130-650, Korea

BAIKOV, KONSTANTIN STANISLAVOVICH, biologist, researcher; b. Novosibirsk, Russia, Apr. 9, 1965; s. Stanislav Ivanovich and Svetlana Borisovna (Sudakova) B.; m. Elena Valentinovna Mikhailova, Feb. 23, 1985; 1 child, Ivan Konstantinovich. Diploma, State U. Moscow, 1987; PhD, Ctrl. Siberian Bot. Garden, Novosibirsk, 1993. Probationer Ctrl. Siberian Bot. Garden, Novosibirsk, 1987-88, jr. sci. worker, 1988-93, sci. worker, 1993-96, sr. sci. worker, 1996—. Grantee Internat. Sci. Found., 1994, 95, Russian Found. Fundamental Investigations, 1995, 98, 99, Siberian br. Russian Acad. Scis., 1998, 2000. Mem. Russian Bot. Soc., Moscow Soc. Naturalists. Avocations: cactus collecting, phylogeny modeling. Home: Rubinovaya Str 3 Apt 54, 630055 Novosibirsk Russia Office: Ctrl Siberian Bot Garden, Zolotodolinskaya Str 101, 630090 Novosibirsk Russia

BAIKOV, YURII MIKHAILOVICH, physical chemist, researcher; b. Pskov, Russia, Sept. 9, 1933; s. Mikhail Grigorievich and Adina Augustovna (Mazul) B.; m. Lioudmila Grigorievna Khodakova, July 26, 1958; 1 child, Mikhail. Student, Polytech. U., St. Petersburg, 1952-58; PhD, Ioffe Physico-Tech. Inst., St. Petersburg, 1971. Researcher Ioffe Physico-Tech. Inst., St. Petersburg, 1958-82, sr. researcher, 1982—, head lab., 1997—. Contbr. articles to profl. jours. Recipient award Internat. Sci. Found., 1994, 95, German Svc. of Sci. Exch., 1993, 95, Russian Found. Basic Rsch., 1998, 99, 2000, Intas, 2000. Mem. N.Y. Acad. Sci., Electrochem. Soc., Inc. Avocations: history of science, sports, skiing. Home: Gavrskaja h 11 apt 192, 194017 Saint Petersburg Russia Office: Ioffe Physico-Tech Inst, Polyteknicheskaja 26, 194021 Saint Petersburg Russia

BAIL, CHRISTOPH, lawyer, policy advisor; b. Rummelsburg, Germany, Dec. 26, 1944; s. Fritz Joachim Bail and Hedda (Overbeck) Leberzammer; m. Angelika Susanne Huber, May 17, 1985. Law degree, U. Munich, 1969; M of European Integration, Coll. Europe, Bruge, Belgium, 1975; LLM, Harvard U., 1975. Rschr. U. Munich, 1972-75; lawyer Strobl and Killius and Vorbrugg, Munich, 1976; adminstr. competition dept. EC Commn., Brussels, 1976-81, prin. adminstr. legal svc., 1981-85; legal advisor del. EC Commn., Geneva, 1985-91, advisor forward studies unit, 1991-95, head unit global environment DGXI, 1995-98, head unit environment & devel. DG ENV, 1998—. Contbr. articles to profl. jours. Chmn. SPD Group, Brussels, 1980-83, mem. bd., 1978-80. Office: EC Commn, 200 Rue de la Loi, 1049 Brussels Belgium

BAILEY, (THOMAS) ALAN, marketing and public relations consultant; b. Sunderland, Eng., Oct. 28, 1928; s. Thomas Dobson and Violet Vera (Walker) B.; m. Mary Baldock, Aug. 7, 1950 (dec. Oct. 1995); 1 child, Paul Kimball. Asst. clk. Brentwood UDC, Eng., 1950-62; undersec Royal Instn. Chartered Surveyors, London, 1962-69; chief exec. World of Property Housing Trust, London, 1969-79, Andrews Group, London, 1979-84; chmn. City and West Clubs Ltd., London, 1971—, Focus Group (now ABS Comms.), London, 1971—; chmn. Alastor Ltd., London, 1986—; bd. dirs. Asset Corp., Ltd., London; chmn. Merchant Internat. Group, London, 1995-98; vis. lectr. Coll. of Estate Mgmt., U. Reading, Eng., 1980-90. Author: The Little Bedside Property Book, 1986, How to Be a Property Developer, 1988, 2d edit. 1991, How to Be an Estate Agent, 1991, All Write!, 1993, revised 2000, Placemakers Humour, 1998, Sex For Surveyors, 2000; columnist The Times, Guardian, Illustrated London News, Director, Estates Gazette, Property Week, others. Bd. dirs. Internat. Shakespeare Globe Ctr., London, 1981-90; trustee Help the Aged, Action Aid, other charitable orgns., London, 1979-84; trustee Cyril Wood Meml. Trust, London, 1980-91. Capt. Intelligence Corps, Brit. Army, 1946-64. Mem. Chartered Inst. Journalists, Inst. Pub. Rels., Chartered Inst. Mktg., Comms. Advt. and Mktg. Found., Spl. Forces Club, Wig and Pen Club. Avocations: drawing, painting, writing. Home: 7 Bradbrook House, Studio Pl, London SW1X 8EL, England Office: ABS Comms, 14 Kinnerton Pl S, London SW1X 8EH, England

BAILEY, CECIL DEWITT, aerospace engineer, educator; b. Zama, Miss., Oct. 25, 1921; s. James Dewitt and Matha Eugenia (Roberts) B.; m. Myrtis Irene Taylor, Sept. 8, 1942; children: Marilyn, Beverly. B.S., Miss. State U., 1951; M.S., Purdue U., 1954, Ph.D., 1962. Commd. 2d lt. USAF, 1944, advanced through grades to lt. col., 1965, pilot, 1944-56, sr. pilot, 1956-60, command pilot, 1960-67, asst. prof. Air Force Inst. Tech., 1954-58, assoc. prof., 1965-67, ret., 1967; assoc. prof. aero. and astronautical engring. Ohio State U., Columbus, 1967-69; prof. Ohio State U., 1970-85, prof. emeritus, 1985—; dir. USAF-Am. Soc. Engring. Edn. summer faculty research program Wright-Patterson AFB, Ohio, 1976-78. Contbr. numerous articles to profl. jours. Mem. Soc. Exptl. Stress Analysis, Am. Soc. Engring. Edn., Am. Acad. Mechanics, Res. Officers (life), Ret. Officers Assn. (life), Am. Legion (life), Sigma Xi, Sigma Gamma Tau. Club: USAF Officers. Achievements include research into a unified theory of mechanics, dynamics and the calculus of variations, the general energy equation. Demonstrated in 1975, for the first time in the history of applied mathematics, direct analytical solutions (i.e., solutions obtained without the mathematical theory of differential equations) to the time dependent problems of the motion of matter in time and space. A significant application, recently demonstrated in papers by Oz and Adiguzal, results in the elimination of the coupled non-linear "Riccati" differential equations from the mathematics of control calculations. Home and Office: 4176 Ashmore Rd Columbus OH 43220-4683

BAILEY, CHARLES-JAMES NICE, linguistics educator; b. Middlesborough, Ky., May 2, 1926; s. Charles Wise and Mary Elizabeth (Nice) B. AB in Classical Philology highest honors, Harvard U., 1950, MTh, 1955; DMin, Vanderbilt U., 1963; AM, U. Chgo., 1966, PhD, 1969. Mem. feculty dept. linguistics U. Hawaii, Manoa, 1968-71, Georgetown U., 1971-73; prof. Technische U. Berlin, 1974-91, univ. prof. emeritus, 1991—; vis. prof. U. Mich., Ann Arbor, 1973, U. Witwatersrand, Johannesburg, 1976, U. Brunei, Darussalam, 1990; Forcheimer prof. U. Jerusalem, 1986; propr. Orchid Land Publs.; hon. col. Staff Gov. of Ky. Fellow Netherlands Inst. Advanced Study (life), Internat. Soc. Phonetic Scis.; mem. AAAS, Linguistic Soc. Am. (life), European Acad. Scis., Arts and Letters (corr.), N.Y. Acad. Scis., Soc. Linguistica Europaea, Am. Dialect Soc. (life), Internat. Palm Soc.

BAILEY, CLIFFORD JAMES, diabetes research educator; b. Bishop's Stortford, Eng., Mar. 30, 1949; s. Harry Clifford Bailey and Camille Deane; m. Caroline Day, June 7, 1984; children: Andrew Vincent, David James. BS with honors, Sheffield (Eng.) U., 1970; PhD, Aston U., Eng., 1973. Lectr. Aston U., 1973-87, sr. lectr., head of diabetes rsch., 1987—; cons. to pharm. industry; reviewer for maj. internat. jours. and grant-awarding bodies. Editor: New Antidiabetic Drugs, 1990; contbr. more than 250 sci. and med. papers and revs. to profl. publs.; mem. editl. bd. Brit. Jour. Pharmacology, Diabetes, Obesity and Metabolism. Fellow Royal Coll. Pathologists London, Royal Coll. Physicians Edinburgh; mem. European Assn. for Study of Diabetes, Soc. for Endocrinology U.K. (com. mem. 1991-94), Brit. Diabetic Assn. (sci. sec. 1991-94), Brit. Pharmacol. Soc. Achievements include research on pathogenesis and treatment of diabetes mellitus, especially antidiabetic drugs. Office: Aston U, Aston Triangle, Birmingham B4 7ET, England

BAILEY, COLIN BARRY, curator; b. London, Oct. 20, 1955; arrived in Can., 1995; came to U.S., 2000; s. Max and Hilda (Feldman) B.; life ptnr. Alan P. Wintermute. BA, Brasenose Coll., Oxford, Eng., 1978; diploma in history of art, U. Paris IV, Sorbonne, 1982-83; MA, Oxford U., 1982, PhD, 1985. Asst. curator European painting and sculpture The Phila. Mus. Art, 1985-89; curator European painting and sculpture Kimbell Art Mus., Ft. Worth, 1989-90, sr. curator, 1990-94; chief curator Nat. Gallery Can., Ottawa, Ont., 1995-98; dep. dir., chief curator Nat. Gallery Can., Ottawa, 1999-2000; chief curator The Frick Collection, N.Y.C., 2000—; vis. prof. U. Pa., 1988; vis. prof. dept. art Bryn Mawr Coll., 1989. Author: The First Painters of the King, 1985, The Loves of the Gods: Mythological Painting from Watteau to David, 1992, Renoir's Portraits, 1997, Jean-BaptisteGreuze, The Laudress, 2000; co-author: Masterpieces of Impressionism & Post-Impressionism, 1989; mem. editl. bd. The Oxford Art Jour., 1982-84. Clark fellow Sterling and Francine Clark Art Inst., Williamstown, 1999; recipient Vasari award Dallas Mus. Art, 1993, Chevalier de l'ordre des arts et des lettres, French Govt.; Paul Mellon sr. vis. fellow Ctr. Advanced Studies Visual Arts, Nat. Gallery Art, Washington, 1994. Avocations: running, tennis, piano, opera. Home: 419 E 57th St New York NY 10022-3060 Office: The Frick Collection 1 E 7th Ave New York NY 10021

BAILEY, DELTON O., investment management executive; b. Bklyn., July 14, 1930; s. Delton B. and Marie Bailey; m. Cindy Bailey, July 7, 1970. PhD, U. S.C., 1981. CFP. Owner Bailey & Assocs., Columbia, S.C., 1981—. With USAF, 1947-77. Mem. IAFP (pres.). Office: Bailey and Assocs 1136 Washington St Ste 602 Columbia SC 29201-3253

BAILEY, DEREK, musician; b. Sheffield, Yorkshire, Eng., Jan. 29, 1930; s. George Edward and Lily (Wing) B.; m. Joan Burns, May 5, 1964 (div. 1980); 1 child, Simon. Solo guitarist, accompanist various clubs, theatres, halls, radio, TV, Eng., 1952-65; soloist worldwide, 1965—; bd. dirs. Incus Records, London (founder 1970), Compatible Records, London; founder Company Ensemble of improvisational musicians, Eng., 1976. Recorded more than 100 albums on various labels; author: Improvisation: Its Nature and Practice in Music, 1980 (translated into German, French, Italian , Japanese, Swedish and Spanish), 2d rev. edit., 1993; writer and narrator TV series on improvisation, 1992. Nominated for Grammy award Nat. Acad. Recording Arts and Scis., 1982. Avocation: cricket. Home and Office: INCUS Records & Pub Ltd, 14 Downs Rd, London E5 8DS, England

BAILEY, DONALD WILLIAM, lawyer; b. St. Albans, Eng., Sept. 7, 1947; s. Jack Henry and Isabel Marye (George) B.; m. Wendy Iris Adams; children: Andrew, Peter, Rebecca. BA with Honors, Oxford U., 1968. Asst. solicitor Stephenson Harwood, London, 1972-74; solicitor Balham Law Ctr., London, 1974-79, Edward Coningsby, Croydon, Eng., 1979-81; ptnr. Templeton Bailey, London, 1981-90; prin. London, 1990—. Chair Southwark Children's Found., 1995—. Mem. Law Soc. Mem. Labour Party. Mem. Ch. of Eng. Avocations: gardening, swimming, theater art.

BAILEY, DONOVAN, Olympic athlete; b. Manchester, Jamaica, Dec. 16, 1967; 1 child, Adrienna. Diploma in bus. adminstrn., Sheridan Coll. Recipient Silver medal in 100 and 200 meters, Pan Am Trials, 1991, in 400 meter relay, Pan Am Games, 1991, in 100 meters, Harry Jerome Classic, 1991, Gold medal in 100 meters, 1996, Bronze medal in 200 meters, Can. Nat. Indoor Championship, 1992, Meeting der Spitzenklasse, Lindau, Germany, 1993, Silver medal in 100 meters, Rendez-Vous MontrCal, 1993, in 200 meters, Can. Nat. Championships, 1993, Bronze medal in 100 meters, 1993, Silver medal in 100 meters, Jeux de la Francophonie, Paris, 1994, Gold medal in 4x100 meter relay, Commonwealth Games, 1994, Silver medal,

Comunidad de Madrid, 1995, Lausanne Grand Prix Meeting, 1995, Bronze medal, Gateshead Games, 1995, Gold medal, Mutual Games, 1995, Internat. Quelle Fest in Narnberg, 1995, Ill. State Championships, 1995, in 4x100 meter relay, World Outdoor Championships, Giteborg, Sweden, 1995, Bronze medal in 100 meters, Atlanta Grand Prix, 1996, Gold medal in 100 meters, Brazil Grand Prix, 1996, Can. Olympic Trials, 1996, in 4x100 meter relay, 1996, Olympic Games, Atlanta, 1996; winner World's Fastest Man Race, 1997, 2d pace World Championships, Athens, 1997. Office: c/o Flynn Sports MGmt, 606-1185 Eglinton Ave E, Toronto, ON Canada M3C 3C6

BAILEY, EXINE MARGARET ANDERSON, soprano, educator; b. Cottonwood, Minn., Jan. 4, 1922; d. Joseph Leonard and Exine Pearl (Robertson) Anderson; m. Arthur Albert Bailey, May 5, 1956. B.S., U. Minn., 1944; M.A., Columbia U., 1945; profl. diploma, 1951. Instr. Columbia U., 1947-51; faculty U. Oreg., Eugene, 1951—, prof. voice, 1966-87, coordinator voice instrn., 1969-87, prof. emeritus, 1987—; faculty dir. Salzburg, Austria, summer 1968, Europe, summer 1976; vis. prof., head vocal instrn. Columbia U., summers 1952, 59; condr. master classes for singers, developer summer program study for h.s. solo singers, U. Oreg. Sch. Music, 1988—, mem. planning com. 1998-99 MTNA Nat. Convention. Profl. singer, N.Y.C.; appearances with NBC, ABC symphonies; solo artist appearing with Portland and Eugene (Oreg.) Symphonies, other groups in Wash., Calif., Mont., Idaho, also in concert; contbr. articles, book revs. to various mags. Del. fine arts program to Ea. Europe, People to People Internat. Mission to Russia for 1990. Recipient Young Artist award N.Y.C. Singing Tchrs., 1945, Music Fedn. Club (N.Y.C.) hon. award, 1951; Kathryn Long scholar Met. Opera, 1945. Mem. Nat. Assn. Tchrs. Singing (lt. gov. 1968-72), Oreg. Music Tchrs. Assn (pres. 1974-76), Music Tchrs. Nat. Assn. (nat. voice chmn. high sch. activities 1970-74, nat. chmn. voice 1973-75, 81-85, NW chmn. collegiate activities and artists competition 1978-80, editorial com. Am. Music Tchr. jour. 1987-89), AAUP, Internat. Platform Assn., Kappa Delta Pi, Sigma Alpha Iota, Pi Kappa Lambda. Home: 17 Westbrook Way Eugene OR 97405-2074 Office: U Oreg Sch Music Eugene OR 97403

BAILEY, GEORGE THEODORE, writer, liaison officer; b. Chgo., Nov. 28, 1919; s. George Theodore and Ila Ruth (Jacobson) B.; m. Beate Ross, Oct. 25, 1949, 1 child, Ariane Eliza. BA, Columbia U., 1943, Magdalen Coll., Oxford, Eng., 1949; MA, Magdalen Coll., Oxford, Eng., 1949; LittD (hon.), U. Tampa, 1986. Resettlement officer U.S. Army Intelligence Collection Ctr., Oberursel, Germany, 1950-51; liaison officer Provost Marshal, Berlin, 1951-54, Dept. of Army, Washington, 1954-56; reporter Ullstein Verlag, Berlin, 1956-57; writer, editor The Reporter Mag., N.Y.C., 1957-68; dir. Radio Liberty, Munich, 1982-85; TV panelist Nord West Deutscher Rundfunk, Bayrischer Rundfunk, Oesterreichischer Rundfunk, Cologne, Germany, Munich, Vienna, Austria, 1957—; cons. La Pensée Russe, Paris, 1975—, Radio Liberty, Munich, 1985; lectr. Munich, Heidelberg, 1990—. Author: Germans, The Biography of an Obsession, 1972, 2d rev. edit., Munich, 1991, Armageddon in Prime Time, 1984, Galileo's Children, 1990 (Booklist Editors' Choice, 1990), Battleground Berlin, CIA vs KGB in the Cold War (with David Murphy and Sergei Kondrashev), 1977. Fund raiser Assn. of Friends of Kontinent, Paris, 1974-82, Andrei Sakharov Inst., Paris, 1978-84. 1st lt. Mil. Intelligence, 1943-46, ETO. Recipient Best Mag. Reporting of Foreign Affairs award Overseas Press Club, 1959; fellow Russian Am. Coun. of Learned Socs., Washington, 1942; establishment of George Bailey Collection at Mugar Meml. Libr., Boston U., 1969. Mem. Overseas Press Club of Am. Avocations: languages (particularly Hungarian), travel, sauntering, sonneteering. Home: Ambergerstrasse 21, 81679 Munich Bavaria, Germany

BAILEY, HOWARD ROLAND, retired power company executive; b. Booz, Wis., May 19, 1916; s. Howard Lee and Grace Edith (Carley) B.; m. Hazel Orella Berg, Oct. 20, 1937; children: DiAnna Rebecca, Mary Lynn, Lydia Lee. BSEE, Internat. Corres. Sch., Scranton, Pa., 1942; Degree in Elec. Metering Engring., Ft. Wayne (Ind.) Corres. Sch., 1951; student, Rochester (Minn.) Coll., 1954, U. Minn., 1964, U. Wis., River Falls, 1972. Meter reader, lineman No. States Power, Zumbrota, Minn., 1937-41; asst. divsn. engr. No. States Power, Fairbau, Minn., 1941-44; maint. transmission linesman No. States Power, Zumbrota, 1945-51, dist. rep., 1951-78; weather observer U.S. Weather Bur., Zumbrota, 1951-78. Columnist Rochester Post Bull., Bottom Line, 1984-93, Zumbrota News; author: Bailey's Folly, 1989. Pres. Indsl. Devel., Zumbrota, 1958, Hiawatha Pioneer Trail Coun., 1966; chmn. Emergency Housing, Praire Island Reservation, 1966, Goodhue County Draft Bd., Red Wing, Minn., 1968, Gov. Al Quie Trail Ride, Nerstrand, Minn., 1975; mem. Citizen's Action Coun., Zumbrota; sec. S.E. Minn. Devel., Rochester, 1968; dist. chmn. rep. Party, red Wing, 1975; councilman, acting mayor City of Zumbrota, 1976-84; bd. dirs. Recreation, Convervation Devel., Zumbrota, 1977. With USN, 1944-45. Named WCCO Good Neighbor, 1967; recipient Selective Svc. award Pres. Lyndon B. Johnson, 1968, Vista award Great Lakes Region Cert. of Appreciation, 1968, Cert. of Achievement, Pres. Gerald Ford, 1976. Lutheran. Avocations: quarter horses, reading, landscaping, home improvement. Home: 15 Mill St Zumbrota MN 55992-1239

BAILEY, JAMES CURTIS, college administrator; b. Cullman, Ala., Nov. 7, 1936; s. James C. and Chiquita M. Bailey; m. Ann Meyers Bailey, Dec. 26, 1960; children: Gina Bailey McKell, Bethany Bailey Pappas. BA, Athens State Coll., 1959; MA, U. Ala., Birmingham, 1971, AA cert., 1975; EdD, Nova U., 1981. Tchr. Fairview High Sch., Cullman, 1960-69; tchr. Wallace State Coll., Hanceville, Ala., 1969-71, pres., 1971—, athletic dir., 1990—; chmn. of the bd. Regions Bank, Cullman, 1976—. Adv. bd. Athens (Ala.) State Coll., 1983—; pres., mem. Cullman County Indsl. Devel. Bd., Cullman, 1981—; mem. found. bd. Cullman County Park and Recreation, Cullman, 1989—; mem. Cullman Regional Med. Ctr. Found. Bd., 1993—; mem. Cullman Cmty. Health Coalition Com., 1996—; bd. trustees Ala. Bus. and Profl. Women's Found., 1993-97; mem. Johnsons' Crossing Water System Bd., 1985—. Recipient CEO Leadership award Community Coll. Leadership Program, U. Tex., Austin, 1989. Mem. Ala. Jr./Tech. Coll. Presidents Assn. (com. mem. 1971—), Ala. Bankers Assn., Cullman County C. of C. (past pres. 1980-81, v.p. 1979-80, bus. & industry com. 1986-87). Democrat. Lutheran. Avocations: basketball, baseball, gardening, spectator sports. Office: George C Wallace State Coll c/o William E Simpson-Libr 801 Main St NW Hanceville AL 35077-5462*

BAILEY, LARRY ALAN, mechanical engineer; b. Knoxville, Tenn., May 2, 1962; s. Gerald Henry and Shirley Louise (Stapleton) B.; m. Mary Kay Logan, Jan. 29, 1964; children: Erin C., Micheal E., Matthew C., Logan M. BS in Mech. Engring., U. Tenn., 1986; MBA, East Tenn. State U., 1993. Registered profl. engr., Tenn. Prodn. engr. TRW Steering and Suspension Divsn., Rogersville, Tenn., 1986-88; project engr. TRW Automotive Divsn., Rogersville, 1988-89; advanced mech. design engr. Holston Def. Corp., Kingsport, Tenn., 1989-93; advanced mech. engr. Eastman Chem. Co., Kingsport, 1993-96, sr. purchasing engr., 1996—. Founding mem. United We Stand Am., Tenn., 1993. Mem. ASME (assoc.), Eastman Profl. Devel. Club, Pi Tau Sigma, Phi Sigma Kappa (pres. 1982). Baptist. Avocations: computers, gardening, hunting, traveling, skiing. Home: 1040 Stagshaw Ln Kingsport TN 37660-1077 Office: Eastman Chem Co PO Box 511 Kingsport TN 37662-5000

BAILEY, MICHAEL STEWART, political science educator; b. Langdale, Ala., July 10, 1959; s. Arthur Lee Bailey and Mary Louise (Mathes) Battle. BA in Journalism and Econs., Clark Atlanta U., 1981; MA in Journalism, Ohio State U., 1982, MA in Black Studies, 1983, MA in Polit. Sci., 1987, PhD, 1990. Asst. prof. polit. sci. U. Ill., Chgo., 1988-90, W.Va. U., Morgantown, 1990-91, U. Mo., St. Louis, 1991-92; prof. polit. sci. Clark Atlanta U., 1992—; dir. Ctr. for Polit. Rsch. and Analysis, Atlanta, 1996—. Author: The Black Mayoral Agenda, 1998; contbr. entries Ency. Minority Politics, 1998. Chair issues com. The Atlanta Black Agenda, Inc., 1996—; vol. Ctrl. Fulton Sr. Svcs., Atlanta, 1995—. Mem. Nat. Conf. Black Polit. Scientists, Am. Polit. Sci. Assn., Midwest Polit. Sci. Assn., Alpha Phi Alpha, Alpha Kappa Mu. Democrat. Avocation: violin. Home: 3197 Hazelwood Dr SW Atlanta GA 30311-3033 Office: Clark Atlanta U 316 Knowles Hall 223 James P Brawley Dr SW Atlanta GA 30314-4358

BAILEY, MICHAEL WALLACE, aerospace engineer; b. Shelby, Miss., Sept. 24, 1968; s. Wallace Bryant and Flossie Mae (Cobb) B. BS in Aerospace Engring. summa cum laude, Miss. State U., 1990. Sr. specialist engr. Internat. space sta. program Boeing Co., Huntsville, Ala., 1990-97; sr. specialist engr. express rack program Internat. Space Sta., Boeing Co., Huntsville, Ala., 1998-99, sr. specialist engr. propulsion module program, 1999—. Mem. AIAA, Tau Beta Pi, Phi Kappa Phi. Baptist. Avocations: motorcycling, car restoration, racing.

BAILEY, NORMAN ALISHAN, economist; b. Chgo., May 22, 1931; s. Percival and Yevnige (Bashian) B.; m. Lorraine Baillargeon, Sept. 1, 1962 (div. Feb. 1966); m. Suzin Robbins, July 8, 1966 (dec. Oct. 1997); children: Stacy, Anthony, Samara, Gabrielle. AB, Oberlin (Ohio) Coll., 1953; M of Internat. Affairs, Columbia U., 1955, PhD, 1962; LLD (hon.), Hanyang U., Seoul, Korea, 1983. Economist Mobil Oil Co., N.Y.C., 1960-62; prof. CUNY, Queens, 1962-83; pres. Bailey, Tondu, Warwick & Co., N.Y.C., 1962-75; spl. asst. to Pres. Reagan The White House, Washington, 1981-83; pvt. practice Washington, 1984—. Author 8 books; contbr. numerous articles to profl. jours. Cons. Rep. Campaign, N.Y., Washington, 1980, 84, 88, 92, 00. With U.S. Army, 1956-58. Named Knight of the Order of Our Lady of the Conception of Vila Vicosa, 1988. Mem. The Univ. Club (Washington), Columbia Club of N.Y., Phi Beta Kappa. Avocations: swimming, boating, writing. Office: Norman A Bailey Inc 1311 Dolley Madison Blvd Ste 2A Mc Lean VA 22101-3925

BAILEY, PETER HAMILTON, lawyer, educator; b. Melbourne, Australia, Sept. 3, 1927; s. Kenneth Hamilton and Yseult Editha Olga (Donnison) B.; m. Leila May Giles, Dec. 10, 1955 (dec. Oct. 1999); children: Julian, Timothy, Simon, Joanna. MA, Oxford (England) U., 1953; LLM, Melbourne U., 1954. Barrister High Ct. Australia. Asst. sec. Dept. Treas., Canberra, Australia, 1962-65; 1st asst. sec. Dept. Prime Min., 1965-72; dep. sec. dept. Prime Min. and Cabinet Canberra, 1972-74; mem. Royal Commn. on Australian Govt. Adminstrn., Canberra, 1974-76; dep. chmn., CEO Human Rights Commn., Canberra, 1981-86; vis. fellow faculty of law Australian Nat. U., Canberra, 1987-98; adj. prof. Australian Nat. U., 1999—. Author: Bringing Human Rights to Life, 1993, Human Rights: Australia in an International Context, 1990; contbg. author: Halsbury's Laws of Australia, 1998; co-editor, contbr. The Laws of Australia, 1996; contbr. chpts. to books and articles to profl. jours. Pres. Canberra Marriage Guidance Coun., 1968-72, 89-90, v.p., 1990-96; pres. Nat. Marriage Guidance Coun., 1970-71. Decorated mem. Order Brit. Empire, mem. Order of Australia; Rhodes scholar, 1950. Mem. Internat. Commn. Jurists (pres. Canberra br. 1996—), Commonwealth Club. Mem. Anglican Ch. Avocations: music, gardening, squash, motorcycling. E-mail: Peter.Bailey@anu.edu.au. Home: 12/14 Currie Crescent, Kingston ACT 2604, Australia Office: Faculty of Law, Canberra 0200, Australia

BAILEY, PHILIP SIGMON, JR., university official, chemistry educator; b. Charlottesville, Va., Mar. 17, 1943; s. Philip Sigmon Bailey and Marie Jeanette (Schultz) Hatch; m. Christina Anne Wahl; children: Karl, Jennifer, Kristen, Michael. Student, Am. U., Cairo, 1961; BS in Chemistry, U. Tex., 1964; PhD, Purdue U., 1969. Asst. prof. chemistry Calif. Poly. State U., San Luis Obispo, 1969-73, prof., assoc. dean, 1973-83, prof. chemistry, dean Coll. Sci. and Math., 1983-89, v.p. acad. affairs, sr. v.p., 1989-90, dean, 1990—. Author: (lab texts) Experimental Chemistry for Contemporary Times, 1975, Organic Chemistry, 1978, (textbook) Organic Chemistry, 1978, 6th edit., 2000. Mem. Am. Chem. Soc., Alpha Chi Sigma. Home: 1628 Royal Way San Luis Obispo CA 93405-6334 Office: Calif Poly State U Coll Sci And Math San Luis Obispo CA 93407

BAILEY, RHONDA RENICK, administrative assistant; b. New Albany, Miss., Apr. 11, 1966; d. Grady Lee Renick and Mary Alice Rooker; m. Moody Eldridge Bailey, Sept. 30, 1988 (div. Oct. 1995). A in Applied Sci., N.E. Miss. Jr. Coll., 1986. Notary pub., Miss. Exec. sec. Byhalia (Miss.) Health Care, 1992-96; adminstrv. asst. Marshall County Indsl. Devel., Holly Springs, Miss., 1996—. Chmn. Pilot Club Polit. Rally, Holly Springs, 1999, Barbecue Festival, Holly Springs, 1990-95, Christmas Parade, Holly Springs, 1991-98, 99, pres.-elect, 2000—; bd. dirs. Marshall County Leadership Program, 1996-99; mem. Com. on Schs. to Careers, 2000—. Mem. Am. Econ. Devel. Coun., Miss. Econ. Devel. Coun. Democrat. Baptist. Avocations: reading, crafts, sewing. E-mail: mcida@dixie-net.com. Office: Marshall County Indsl Devel PO Box 128 Holly Springs MS 38635-0128

BAILEY, RITA MARIA, investment advisor, psychologist; b. Frankfurt, Germany; came to U.S., 1957; d. Ludwig and Gertrude (Cierniak) Fleischmann; m. William W. Bailey, Feb. 17, 1974; children: Anne Christine, Cynthia Patricia. BS in Psychology, Austin Peay U., 1975, MA in Psychology, 1977, postgrad., 1977-79. Cert. counselor, Tenn. Editor U.S. Army Spl. Warfare Inst., Ft. Bragg, N.C., 1967-74, edn. officer, 1979-82; edn. officer Augsburg (Germany) Cmty. Ctr., 1982-85; pvt. practice counseling Leavenworth, Kans., 1985-90; pvt. practice investments, 1990—; sr. investment advisor pvt. orgns., Washington, 1991—. Author: Extroversion and Introversion, 1978, Special Warfare Training Plan, 1981; author, editor tng. manual Foreign Small Arms, 1982. Dir. Energy Conservation Campaign, Clarksville, 1976; founder, dir. Women's Support Ctr., Leavenworth, 1986. Mem. Nat. Assn. Investors, Alpha Mu Gamma. Roman Catholic. Avocations: long distance swimming, gardening, German poetry.

BAILEY, WILLIAM WADDELL, writer, communications executive; b. Gordonsville, Va.; s. George W. and Phyllis K. (Kennon) B.; m. Rita Maria Fleischmann, Feb. 17, 1974. BA in Psychology, U. Miss., 1973; MA in Internat. Rels., U. So. Calif., 1985; disting. grad., Command and Gen. Staff Coll., 1987. Cert. software engr. Commd. 2d lt. U.S. Army, 1973, advanced through grades to lt. col.; officer U.S. Army, Ft. Bragg, N.C., 1973-82; software mgr. U.S. Govt., Augsburg, Germany, 1982-85; modernization mgr. U.S. Govt., Leavenworth, Kans., 1985-90; divsn. chief U.S. Govt., Arlington, Va., 1990-92, spl. exec., 1992-93; sr. advisor to pvt. orgns. Washington, 1993-97; pres. Writer's Ink, Fayetteville, N.C., 1997—; resident artist Urban Arts Prgm., 1998, Arts and Tech., 1999; cons. Sierra Cybernetics, Yorba Linda, Calif., 1993—. Author, editor: 2004 Future Architecture, 1987, Modernization Plan, 1989; author: Desert Storm Lessons Learned, 1991; contbr. articles, stories and poems to mags. and jours. Mem. fundraising com. Hist. Mus., Fayetteville, 1981; mem. Arts Coun., 1996—. Decorated Legion of Merit. Avocations: astronomy, fencing.

BAILHACHE, SIR PHILIP MARTIN, judge; b. Jersey, Channel Islands, Feb. 28, 1946; s. Lester Vivian and Nanette Ross (Ferguson) B.; m. Christine Anne Bate, July 21, 1967 (div. 1981); children: Robert, Rebecca, Catherine, John; m. Linda Le Vavasseur Dit Durell, June 2, 1984; children: Alice, Edward. MA with honours in Jurisprudence, Oxford (Eng.) U., 1967. Barrister Middle Temple, London, 1968; adv. Royal Ct. Jersey 1969; created Queen's counsel, 1989. Pvt. practice as advocate, Jersey, 1969-74; dep. States of Jersey, 1972-74; solicitor gen. for Jersey, 1975-85, atty. gen. for Jersey, 1986-93; dep. bailiff Govt. of Jersey, 1994, bailiff and chief justice, 1995—. Editor Jersey Law Rev. Chmn. Jersey Arts Coun., 1987-89. Named hon. fellow Pembroke Coll., Oxford (Eng.) U., 1995; Knight Bachelor, 1996. Mem. Middle Temple, Reform Club (London). Avocations: music, gardening, wine, golf. Office: Govt of Jersey, States Bldg, Saint Helier Jersey JE1 1DD, Channel Islands

BAILLET, GILLES PIERRE, orthodontist; b. Paris, Dec. 6, 1948; s. Lucien Pierre and Madeleine Alphonsine (Champoix) B.; m. Daniele Luce Floch, Dec. 6, 1980; 1 child, Victoire. DS, Paris U., Paris, 1974; MS, Nantes U., Nantes, 1980; diploma in Orthodontist, Paris U., Paris, 1978; diploma in oral dental survey, Montpellier U., Montpeller, 1992. Cons. Helio-Marin Ctr., Roscoff, 1978-83; clin. asst. Gen. Hosp., Morlaix, 1980-82; asst. prof. Dental U., Brest, 1980-82, prof. orthodontic dept., 1982-86; assoc. prof. Gen. Hosp., 1988-91; pvt. practice Morlaix, 1977—. Contbr. articles to profl. jours. Mem. ADA, Am. Assn. Orthodontist, European Orthodontic Soc., Coll. European Orthodontist. Avocation: motorcycle biker. Office: 8 Ter Place Du Powliet, 29600 Morlaix France

BAILLIE STRONG, STUART, computer software consultant; b. Alexandria, Egypt, Aug. 25, 1943; s. William and Guertrude Margaret (Wood) B.S.; m. Patricia Mary Marjoribanks, Sept. 15, 1970; children: Alastair, Jonathan. BSChemE with Honors, Edinburgh (Scotland) U., 1965; lic. applied econs., U. Louvain, Leuven, Belgium, 1970; MBA, U. Chgo., 1973. Chem. engr. Amoco Corp. Rsch. and Devel., Whiting, Ind., 1965-69; systems analyst ICI Holland B.V., Rotterdam, The Netherlands, 1970-73; project mgr. ICI Europa Ltd., Brussels, 1973-78; sr. sales rep. Ethyl S.A. ICD, Brussels, 1978-81, mktg. product mgr., 1981-85, market devel. mgr., 1987-89, regional sales mgr., 1989-90, dir. sales, 1990-91, strategic sourcing mgr., 1991-93; phosphazene devel. mgr. Ethyl Corp., Baton Rouge, La., 1985-86, mktg. product mgr., 1986-87; supply mgr. Albemarle S.A., Brussels, 1993-95; computer software project leader Albemarle PPC S.A., Thann, France, 1995-98; software cons., 1998—; mng. dir. Strategic Bus. Systems Consulting BVBA. Contbr. articles to profl. publs. Active St. Andrews Ch.; parent's rep. European Sch. 1, Brussels. Mem. U. Chgo. Alumni Assn. (pres. Brussels chpt. 1981-83, main bd. mem. 1993—), Cercle Gaulois Artistic and Lit. Soc. Presbyterian. Avocations: genealogy, skiing, swimming, tennis. Office: SBS Consulting, Veeweidestraat 29, B-3040 Huldenberg Belgium

BAILLOU, JEAN, surgeon; b. Pons, France, July 17, 1924; s. Raymond and Marie (Enard) B.; m. Janine Fillon, Nov. 15, 1947 (div. 1969); children: Catherine, Martine, Philippe; m. Francoise Boyrie, Jan. 30, 1970; 1 child, Marie. Student, U. Bordeaux, 1944-45; degree in medicine, U. Paris, 1955. Med. diplomate, Paris. Intern Seine and Marne Hosps., Fontainebleau, 1950-55; surgeon Clinic Maubourguet, France, 1956-60, Clinic and Hosp., Bagneres de Bigorre, France, 1961—; prof. human anatomy, Lyceum Bagneres de Bigorre, 1965-73. Co-author: First Aid in Mountain, 1970; contbr. articles to med. publs. Mem. Orthopedic Surg. Soc., French Mountain Fedn. (mem. med. bd. 1967—), Lions, Grande Loge de France. Roman Catholic. Avocations: photography, film making. Home: La Casita, 65200 Trebons France Office: Centre Hosp Gen, Gambetta St, 65200 Bagneres de Bigorre France

BAILY, RICHARD, artist, music composer; b. L.A., Feb. 16, 1953; s. Jack Hyman Baily and Sheila Goroshnik. BFA, Calif. Inst. of Arts, 1977. Animator Robert Abel & Assocs., Hollywood, Calif., 1977-82, computer animator, 1982-86; freelance computer animator L.A., 1986-92; owner, animator Image Savant, Hollywood, 1992—. Animator: (TV comml.) Sexy Robot, 1985 (Clio award 1985), other projects. Bd. govs. Otis Art Inst., 2000—. Mem. Mus. Contemporary Art (dirs.' forum 1998—). Avocations: composing music, painting. E-mail: baily@netcom.com.

BAIMAKOVA, OLGA ARKADYEVNA, physicist, educator; b. Ufa, Russia, Oct. 8, 1970; d. Arkadiy Leonidovich and Alexandra Petrovna (Vershinina) B.; m. Andrey Valentinovich Baimakov, Aug. 17, 1990 (div. Feb. 1991); m. Andrey Valeryevich Denisov, July 4, 1998. Physicist, Bashkir State U., Ufa, Russia, 1994; Doctor of Physics, Bashkir State U., 1997. Lab. asst. Bashkir State U., Ufa, Russia, 1988-91; engr. Bashkir State U., Ufa, 1991-94; postgrad. Bashkir State U., 1994-97, tchr., 1997-99. Contbr. articles to profl. jours. Avocations: reading, travel, sewing, knitting, sports. Office: Bashkir State U, 50 year USSR St 34, 450001 Ufa Russia

BAIN, LOWELL SHERMAN, automotive company executive; b. Chgo., May 10, 1931; s. Gorman LeRoy and Nova Ellen (Ewing) B.; m. Edith Joy Burgan, Dec. 26, 1951 (div. 1982); children: Carron, Cindy, Christy, Jeffrey, Cathy, Cheryl Rene; m. Linda Lou Huffman, Mar. 22, 1985; 1 child, Matthew. BS, Ind. U., 1973; MBA, U. Ark., 1982. Ordained to ministry Christian Ch., 1952, Meth. Ch., 1974. With Copper dept. Ford Meter Box, Wabash, Ind., 1953-56; quality assurance mgr. Ex-cello (Textron) Corp., Elwood, Ind., 1956-69; quality control mgr. Gen. Corp. Automotive, Wabash, 1969-74; quality control mgr. Gen. Corp. Automotive, Batesville, Ark., 1974-77, prodn. mgr., 1977-79; plant mgr. Gen. Corp. Automotive, Ft. Smith, Ark., 1980-82, Marion, Ind., 1983-84, Batesville, 1984-88; gen. mgr. Gen. Corp. Automotive, Shelbyville, Ind., 1988-91, Wabash, Ind., 1991-94; dir. ops. Bailey Mfg. Corp., Seabrook, N.H., 1994-95; gen. mgr. Std. Products, Lexington, Ky., Gaylord, Mich., 1995-98; plant mgr. Plastech Engineered Products, Wauseon, Ohio, 1998—; minister Christian Ch., Hubbard Springs, St. Charles, Longhollow and Mt. Olive, Va., 1950-53, Curtisville, Ind., 1953-63, Atlanta, Ind., 1963-73; assoc. minister United Meth. Ch., Batesville, 1974-79. Patentee (pending) for electromotive propulsion of automobiles. Chmn. Boy Scouts, Omega Christian Ch., Atlanta, Ind., 1970; chmn. Red Cross Independence County, Batesville, 1977-80; mem. bus. adv. coun. Ark. Coll., Batesville, 1980-88. Mem. Soc. Mech. Engrs. Republican. Christian and United Methodist. Avocations: bicycling, trophy hunting, fishing, writing, singing, golf. Home: 412 W Lutz Rd Archbold OH 43502-1190 Office: Plastech Co 535 Lindfoot Rd Wauseon OH 43567

BAIN, NEVILLE CLIFFORD, company executive, consultant; b. Dunedin, New Zealand, July 14, 1940; s. Charles Alexander and Gertrude Mae B.; children: Susan Mary, Peter John; m. Anne Patricia Kemp, Sept. 18, 1987; 1 child, (stepdaughter) Kristina. B in Acctg., Otago U., 1962, B in Econs., 1963, M in Commerce with honors, 1968, LLD, 1993. Acct. Inland Revenue, U.K., 1956-59; acct. Price Waterhouse, Dunedin, U.K., 1959-62; cost acct. Cadbury Schweppes PLC, 1962-67, fin. dir., 1968-72, fin. and export dir., 1973-75; group chief exec. Cadbury Schweppes PLC, South Africa, 1975-80; group strategic planning dir., main bd. dir. Cadbury Schweppes PLC, U.K., 1981-83, mend. dir. U.K. confectionery, 1983-86, mng. dir., worldwide confectionary, 1986-90, dept. group chief exec., 1990-97; group chief exec. Coats Viyella PLC, London, 1993-97; chmn. Hogg Robinson PLC, Farnborough, Eng., 1997—, The Post Office, London, 1998—, SHL Group Plc, 1998—; bd. dirs. Gartmore Split Capital Investment Trust, Gartmore Scotland Investment Trust, Scottish & Newcastle Plc. Author: Successful Management, 1995; co-author: (with D. Band) Winning Ways through Corporate Governance, 1996, (with B. Mabey) The People Advantage, 1999. Mem. Inst. Dirs. (coun., chair audit com.), Nat. Coun. Econ. and Social Rsch. (gov.), Coun. for Excellence in Mgmt. and Leadership. Avocations: reading, sports, business education, music. E-mail: neville.bain@postoffice.co.uk. Office: The Post Office, 148 Old St, London EC1V 9HQ, England

BAIN, WILLIAM DAVID, electronics systems technician, writer; b. Flint, Mich., Sept. 3, 1958; s. William David and Frances Geraldine B. Student Jordan Coll., 1984-85. Theater mgr. asst. Northwest Theater, Flint, 1975-81, Commonwealth Theater, Denver, 1981-82; theater mgr., promotions asst. Towne Cinemas, Flushing, Mich., 1987-91; pvt. practice Flint, 1991—. Author: Oasis, 1995, Inspirational Collection, 1997, Tear Drops Fall Like Rain, 1997, Romantic Collection, 1997, Verses From The Heart, 1999. Mem. Comms. com. Democratic Party, 1994-98; delegate Democratic Party, 1996-98; elected exec. bd. trustees UAW, 1999—. Mem. The Acad. Poets, United Automobile, Aerospace, Agrl. Implement Workers. Avocations: writing, nature photography, gardening, cookouts, political advocate for people. E-mail: Author58@yahoo.com. Home and Office: PO Box 310475 Flint MI 48531-0475

BAINBRIDGE, BERYL, author; b. Nov. 21, 1934; d. Richard and Winifred (Baines) Bainbridge; m. Austin Davies, 1954 (div.); 3 children. Student, Merchant Taylor's Sch., Liverpool, Arts Ednl. Schs., Tring. Author of plays: Tiptoe Through the Tulips, 1976, The Warriors Return, 1977, It's a Lovely Day Tomorrow, 1977, Journal of Bridget Hitler, 1981, Somewhere More Central (TV), 1981, Evensong (TV), 1986; author books: A Weekend with Claude, 1967, Another Part of the Wood, 1968, Harriet Said..., 1972, The Dressmaker, 1973 (film 1989), The Bottle Factory Outing (Guardian Fiction award), 1974, Sweet William, 1975, A Quiet Life, 1976, Injury Time (Whitbread award), 1977, Young Adolf, 1978, Winter Garden, 1980, Watson's Apology, 1984, Mum and Mrs. Armitage, 1985, Forever England, 1986, An Awfully Big Adventure, 1995; (film) Filthy Lucre, 1986, The Birthday Boys, 1991, Every Man for Himself, 1996 (Whitbread award 1996), Master Georgie, 1998 (James Tate Black, W.N. Smith award, Commonwealth Eurasian prize).

BAINES, PETER GEORGE, meteorologist, researcher; b. Melbourne, Australia, May 23, 1941; s. George Henry and Sybil Ethel (Stewart) B.; m. Gail Sylvia Coote, Jul. 23, 1969, (div. 1989); children: Jonathan Piers, Marcus Quentin. BA (hons.), Melbourne Univ., 1964, BS, 1965; D of philosophy, Cambridge Univ., 1969. Experimental officer Aeronautical Rsch. Labs., Melbourne, 1964-66; rsch. assoc. Mass. Inst. Tech., Cambridge, Mass., 1969-71; fellowship in marine sci. CSIRO, Melbourne, 1971-73; sr. rsch. scientist CSIRO Atmospheric Rsch., Melbourne, 1973-77, prin. rsch. scientist, 1977-88, sr. prin. rsch. scientist, 1988-98, chief rsch. scientist, 1998—; mem. editl. bd. Dynamics of Atmospheres & Ocean, 1983—, Australian Meteorological Mag., 1981-89, 91-98; cons. European Ctr. for

Medium Range Weather Forecasts, 1991. Author: Topographic Effects in Stratified Flows, 1995; contbr. articles to profl. jours. Recipient Queen's fellowship in marine scis. Commonwealth of Australia, 1971-73. Fellow Royal Meteorological Soc.; mem. Australian Met. & Oceans Soc. (pres. 1988-90, Priestley medal 1998), Am. Geophysical Union, Internat. Commn. for Dynamical Meteorology. Avocations: tennis, history, music, the arts. Office: CSIRO Divsn Atmospheric Rsch, 107-121 Station St, 3195 Aspendale Australia

BAINOTTI, ALBERTO EMILIO, microbiologist; b. Rafaela, Argentina, Nov. 27, 1960; s. Emilio Bainotti and Virginia Forni. Grad. cum laude, Nat. U. Litoral, Santa Fe, Argentina, 1985; M in Engring., Inst. Agrochem. and Food Tech., Valencia, Spain, 1995; DSc in Biochemistry Engring., U. Hiroshima, 1998. Rschr. dept. bioengring. Nat. U. Litoral, Santa Fe, 1985-92; rsch. prof. dept. molecular biotech. Hiroshima U., 1998—. Mem. N.Y. Acad. Sci., Soc. Fermentation & Bioengring. Japan, Argentinian Assn. Microbiology.

BAINTNER, KÁROLY, animal physiologist, educator; b. Budapest, Hungary, Sept. 26, 1938. DVM, U. Vet. Medicine, Budapest, Hungary, 1962. Rsch. Rsch. Ctr. for Animal Breeding and Nutrition, Herceghalom, Hungary; prof. microbiology dept. physiology Pannon U. Agr., Kaposvár, Hungary, 1992—. Author: (monograph) Intestinal Absorption of Macromolecules and Immune Transmission from Mother to Young, 1986; (book) How to Write a Scientific Paper, 1982. Home: Dózsa Gy-ut 64, 1076 Budapest Hungary

BAINTON, DONALD J., diversified manufacturing company executive; b. N.Y.C., May 3, 1931; s. William Lewis and Mildred J. (Dunne) B.; m. Aileen M. Demoulins, July 10, 1954; children—Kathryn C., Stephen L., Elizabeth A., William D. BA, Columbia U., 1952, postgrad., 1960. With The Continental Group, Inc., 1954-83, gen. mgr. prodn. planning, 1967-68, gen. mgr. mfg. Eastern divsn., 1968-73, gen. mgr. Pacific divsn., 1973-74, gen. mgr. Eastern divsn., 1974-75; v.p., gen. mgr. ops. U.S. Metal, 1975-76; exec. v.p., gen. mgr. CCC-USA, 1976-78, corp. exec. v.p., pres. diversified ops., 1978-79; pres. Continental Can Co., 1979-81; pres. Continental Packaging, 1981-83, exec. v.p., operating officer parent co., bd. dirs., 1979-83; chmn., CEO, dir. Viatech Inc., Syosset, N.Y., 1983-92; chmn., CEO Continental Can Co., Inc., Boca Raton, Fla., 1992-99; chmn., CEO, dir. Continental Container Corp., Sunrise, Fla., 1999—; bd. dirs. Viatech Inds., LLC. Bd. dirs. Columbia Coll. With USN, 1952-54, Korea. Mem. Inst. Applied Econs. (dir.), Milbrook Country Club (Greenwich, Conn.), Winged Foot Club (Mamaroneck, N.Y.), Union League Club (N.Y.C.), Royal Palm Yacht and Country Club (Boca Raton, Fla.). Republican. Roman Catholic. Office: Continental Container Corp 5001 N Hiatus Rd Sunrise FL 33351-8018

BAINTON, J(OHN) JOSEPH, lawyer; b. Long Branch, N.J., May 21, 1947; s. Robert L. and Elizabeth (Dowling) B.; 1 child, John Joseph Jr. BA, Kenyon Coll., 1969; JD, Rutgers U., Newark, 1973. Bar: N.Y. 1973. Assoc. Burke & Burke, N.Y.C., 1972-76; ptnr. Reboul, MacMurray, Hewitt, Maynard & Kristol, N.Y.C., 1976-89, Shea & Gould, N.Y.C., 1989-90, Whitman & Ransom, N.Y.C., 1991-92, Ross & Hardies, N.Y.C., 1993-98, Bainton McCarthy & Siegel, LLC, N.Y.C., 1998—. Contbr. articles to legal jours. Mediator Mandatory Mediation Program So. Dist. N.Y. Mem. U.S. Trademark Assn. (editor 1976), Internat. Anticounterfeiting Coalition (bd. dirs. 1986-92), Products Liability Adv. Coun., Nat. Inst. Trial Advocacy (faculty). Avocation: yacht racing. Office: Bainton McCarthy & Siegel LLC 130 E 35th St New York NY 10016-3815 also: 400 Main St Stamford CT 06901-3004

BAIR, WILLIAM ALOIS, engineer; b. Bklyn., Aug. 13, 1931; s. Henry Auchu and Anna Margaret (Zidar) B.; m. Patricia Anne Doyle, July 23, 1955; children: William A. Jr., Joseph M. Student, Pa. State U., 1949-51; BS in Engring., U.S. Naval Acad., 1955; BS in Civil Engring., Rensselaer Poly. Inst., 1958; MS in Nuclear Engring., U. Calif., 1966; grad. advanced mgmt. program, Wharton Sch., 1987. Registered profl. engr., N.Y., N.J., Pa., Conn., Md., Del., Va., S.C., Ga., D.C. Commd. ensign USN, 1955, advanced through grades to comdr., 1969; with USN Civil Engr. Corps, 1957-77; ret. USN, 1977; project mgr. Raytheon Engrs. and Constructors Inc., Princeton, N.Y., 1977-85, 88-96; dir. program planning and devel. Ebasco Svcs. Inc., N.Y.C., 1985-88; pres. Bair Engring. Cons., 1996—; appointed mem. spl. 3 man NATO tech. com. to evaluate effectiveness of European Airfield Phys. Protection Program to counter damage from attack by Warsaw Pact Nations, 1972. Author: Helium 3 Neutron Spectrometer, 1966; contbr. articles to profl. jours. Scoutmaster Boy Scouts Am., Rockville, Md., 1969-70; coun. mem. European br., Casteau, Belgium, 1971-75. Decorated Legion of Merit, Bronze Star with V, Joint Svc. Commendation medal, Vietnamese Cross of Gallantry, Vietnamese Medal of Honor 1st class. Fellow ASCE; mem. VFW, Am. Nuclear Soc., Soc. Am. Mil. Engrs., Am. Legion. Republican. Roman Catholic. Achievements include research and development of innovative process/procedures for decontamination and demolition of radioactive structures. Home and Office: Bair Engring Cons 21 Lorrie Ln Princeton Junction NJ 08550-5112

BAIR, YUEIH JIN, civil engineer; b. Taipei, Taiwan, Aug. 9, 1958. Diploma, Inst. Tech., Kao Hsiung, Taiwan, 1978; B, Nat. Chino Tung U., Taiwan, 1985; M, Nat. Taiwan U., 1988. Engr. Taiwan, 1981-82, 1985-86, geologist, 1989-90, design engr., 1990-95, jobsite mgr. construction, 1995—; tchr. Bldg. Bureau, Taiwan, 1996. Mem. Chinese Taiwan Tunnelling Assn. (outstanding tunnelling engr. award). Home: 15-1 177 Alley, 30 Lane Yuung Jir Rd, Taipei Taiwan

BAIRAMOV, BAHISH HALILOGLU, physicist; b. Marneuli, Republic of Georgia, June 1, 1944; s. Halil B. and Tarlala Kerimova; m. Leili Ramazanova, Feb. 7, 1983; children: Farid, Goolie. BS, MS, State Tech. U. Leningrad, 1969; PhD, U. Tartu, 1972; DSc, A.F. Ioffe Physico-Tech. Inst., 1991. Jr. rsch. scientist Ioffe Inst., Leningrad, Russia, 1972-75; sr. rsch. Scientist Ioffe Inst., St. Petersburg, Russia, 1975-91; rsch. fellow, prof. A.F. Ioffe Physico-Tech. Inst., St. Petersburg, 1991—; rsch. fellow Cavendish Lab., U. Cambridge, Eng., 1993-94; vis. scientist Zentralinstitut fur Festkurperphysik und Werkstofforschung, Dresden, Germany, 1976-77, Zentralinstitut fur Electronen Physik, Berlin, 1990, Wihuri Phys. Lab. U. Turku, 1980, U. Oulu, 1983, Helsinki U. Tech., Espoo, Finland, 1985, Fachbereich Physik der Bergakademie, Freiberg, Germany, 1984, 90, U. Ill., Urbana, 1986-87, 90, Max-Planck Inst., Stuttgart, Germany, 1990, Tech. U. Munchen, 1990, Paul-Drude Inst. U. Braunschweig, Germany, 1995; vis. prof. U. Cin., 1992, U. Bilkent, Ankara, Turkey, 1992-93, 95, 96, Tech. U. Bergakademie, Freiberg, 1996, N.C. State U. Ctr. Intelligent Design and Mfg. Electronics, 1998, Va. Commonwealth U., Richmond, 1999. Contbr. chpt. in book, articles to profl. jours. Home: 33 M Torez Av K 108, 194223 Saint Petersburg Russia Office: AF Ioffe Physico-Tech Inst, Polytekhnicheskaya ul 26, 194021 Saint Petersburg Russia

BAIRD, ABIGAIL ALICIA, psychologist; b. Springfield, Mass., Oct. 21, 1969; d. Donald Graham Baird and Maureen Coralie Murphy. BA, Vassar Coll., 1991; MA, Boston U., 1995, Harvard U., 1999. Spl. edn. tchr. U. Sydney, Australia, 1989-90; rsch. asst. NIMH, Bethesda, Md., 1991-94; asst. psychomatrician Boston U. Med. Sch., 1994-95; rsch. asst. McLean Hosp., Belmont, Mass., 1995-97; asst. investigator McLean Hosp., Belmont, 1997-99; tchg. fellow Harvard U., Cambridge, Mass., 1999; sophomore tutor Harvard U., Cambridge, 1999—; spkr. Internat. Neuropsychol. Soc., Orlando, Fla., 1997. Inst. scholar Health Emotions Symposium, Madison, Wis., 1998, 99; Undergrad. Rsch. Summer Inst. fellow Vassar Coll., 1989. Mem. APA, Am. Psychol. Soc. Avocations: photography, elephants, scuba. E-mail: baird@wjh.harvard.edu. Office: Harvard U William James Hall #1145 33 Kirkland St Cambridge MA 02138-2044

BAIRD, CHARLES BRUCE, lawyer, consultant; b. DeLand, Fla., Apr. 18, 1935; s. James Turner and Ethelyn Isabelle (Williams) B.; m. Barbara Ann Fabian, June 6, 1959 (div. Dec. 1979); children: C. Bruce Jr., Robert Arthur, Bryan James; m. Byung-Ran Cho, May 23, 1982; children: Merah-Iris, Haerah Violet. BSME, U. Miami, 1958; postgrad., UCLA, 1962-64; MBA, Calif. State U., 1966; JD, Am. U., 1971. Bar: Va. 1971, U.S. Dist. Ct. (ea. dist.) Va. 1971, D.C. 1973, U.S. Dist. Ct. D.C. 1973, U.S. Ct. Appeals (4th cir.) 1974, U.S. Supreme Ct. 1975. Rsch. engr. Naval Ordnance Lab., Corona, Calif., 1961-67; aerospace engr. Naval Air Systems Command, Washington, 1967-69; cons. engr. Bird Engring. Rsch. Assts., Vienna, Va., 1969-71; prof. Def. Systems Mgmt. Coll., Ft. Belvoir, Va., 1982; spl. asst. for policy compliance USIA Voice of Am., Washington, 1983-84; cons. Booz, Allen & Hamilton, Inc., Bethesda, 1975-82, IBM, Bethesda, Md., 1984, Logistics Mgmt. Inst., McLean, Va., 1986-98, TelcoExchange.com, 1998-99; adj. prof. Fla. Inst. Tech., 1988. Contbr. articles to profl. jours.; inventor computer-based comm. systems for the gravely handicapped. Bd. govs. Sch. Engring. U. Miami, 1957; trustee Galilee United Meth. Ch., Arlington, Va., 1983-87. Mem. ATLA, Internat. Soc., Fed. Comm. Bar Assn., United We Stand Am. (founding mem.), Sigma Alpha Epsilon. Home and Office: 5396 Gainsborough Dr Fairfax VA 22032-2744

BAIRD, GREGORY ROSS, university program director, theater educator; b. Lapeer, Mich., Feb. 13, 1961; s. Ronald Edwin Baird and Marjorie Ruth Weston. Student, North Ctrl. Mich. Coll., Petoskey; degree in speech/theater edn., Ctrl. Mich. U., Mt. Pleasant, 1992. Cert. secondary edn. speech/theater tchr., Mich. Performing arts dir. Camp Sloane, Lakeville, Conn., 1989-91, 93-96; hall dir. Interlochen (Mich.) Ctr. for the Arts, 1994-96; residence life/student activities dir., theater educator North Ctrl. Mich. Coll., Petoskey, 1996—; dir. lecture series North Ctrl. Mich. Coll., 1996—, mem. hall coun., 1996—, guest lectr., 1996—, advisor student senate, 1996—. Author: (plays) Mime, Music & Mayhem, 1989, Mime, Music & an Evening of Imagination, 1994, Mime, Music & an Encore for the Audience, 1996. Bd. dirs. Friends North, Traverse City, Mich., 1993-95. Excellence scholar Ryan White Youth Conf., 1997-99. Avocations: swimming, travel, directing theater, public speaking, acting. E-mail: gbair@ncmc.cc.mi.us. Home: 1525 Howard St Petoskey MI 49770-8717 Office: North Ctrl Mich Coll 1515 Howard St Petoskey MI 49770-8717

BAIRD, IAIN STEWART, federal agency executive; b. N.Y.C., Apr. 7, 1945; s. Thomas Baird and Helen Ronald Purdie; m. Virginia Ann Matheny, May 31, 1970; children: Sara Jeanne, Michael Iain. BA, Johns Hopkins U., 1968, MA, 1972; diploma, Nat. Def. U., Washington, 1982. Policy analyst U.S. Dept. Commerce, Washington, 1972-79, dir. priorities and allocations divsn., 1979-85, dir. individual validated licensing divsn., 1985-88, dir. office of export licensing, 1988-93, dep. asst. sec. for export adminstrn., 1993—; vis. scholar George Washington U., Ashburn, Va., 1998. Author: (novels) Alligator Point, 1998, Dog Island, 1999. Founding mem., vice-chmn. Loudoun Ballet Co., 1990-95. Sgt. mil. intelligence U.S. Army, 1969-72. Avocations: writing, fishing, traveling. Fax: (202) 482 3911. E-mail: ibaird@bxa.doc.gov. Home: 21507 Oatlands Rd Aldie VA 20105-1703 Office: 14th And Constitution Rm 3886C Washington DC 20230-0001

BAIRD, JAMES L., utility executive; b. Chestnut Hill, Pa., Apr. 21, 1947; s. James William and Sara (Freas) B.; m. Debra Morris Baird, Nov. 16, 1986; children: Brittany, Arielle. BSEE, Pa. State U., 1969; MBA in Fin., U. Pa., 1978. Registered profl. engr., Pa. Mgr. constrn. Honeywell, Phila., 1969-76; mgr. energy systems group Williard, Inc., Phila., 1976-80; mgr. sales and mktg. Delaware Valley York, Phila., 1980-87; dir. worldwide controls group York (Pa.) Internat., 1987-2000; CEO comml. group Washington Gas, Washington, 2000—; instr. Pa. State U., Ogontz, 1981-85, Pa. Gov.'s Energy Commn., Phila., 1983-87. Contbr. articles to mag.; inventor super pak. With U.S. Army, 1969-72. Senatorial scholar Pa. State U., 1965-69. Mem. Assn. Energy Engrs. (instr. 1983-86, speaker 1985), U. Pa. Wharton Sch. Alumni Assn. (bd. dirs. 1979-87). Republican. Avocations: sailing, skiing, golf, remodeling. Home: 14 Brian Daniel Ct Reisterstown MD 21136-4635 Office: Washington Gas 6801 Industrial Rd Springfield VA 22151-4206

BAIRD, JULIAN THOMPSON, JR., art dealer; b. Harlingen, Tex., Jan. 28, 1938; s. Julian Thompson and Faye Devilbiss Baird; m. Carol Friedell Baird (div. 1985); m. Elaine Fraser Baird, Jan. 9, 1986. AB magna cum laude, Harvard U., 1960, PhD, 1968; BA, Oxford (Eng.) U., 1962, MA, 1967. Assoc. prof. Boston U., 1967-80; pres. Baird Enterprises d/b/a Tree's Place, Orleans, Mass., 1981—; lectr. Cape Mus. Fine Art, Old Lyme Acad. Art, St. Botolph Club, Boston, others. Contbr. articles to profl. jours. Mem. Orleans Charter Commn., 1989-90; pres. Orleans Bd. of Trade, 1983-84, Orleans Taxpayers Assn., 1985-87; fine wine charity auctioneer Cape Mus. Fine Arts, 1994-96. Recipient Spl. Distinction award Boston U. Alumni Assn., 1990. Mem. St. Botolph Club, Oxford and Cambridge Soc. Avocations: collecting art, wine and books, boating, gardening, computers, investing. Home: 4 Mayflower Cir PO Box 666 Orleans MA 02653-0666 Office: Tree's Place 62 Route 6A Orleans MA 02653-2411

BAIRD, MALCOLM DAVID, company executive; b. Melbourne, Australia, July 6, 1948; s. Ron and Jessie Baird; m. Elizabeth Ruth Reynolds, Dec. 8, 1949; children: Danielle, Nicole. B in econs., Monash Univ., Melbourne, Australia, 1969. Chief acct. Australian Eagle Ins. Co. Ltd., Melbourne, 1976-84, asst. gen. mgr. corp. fin. & group svcs., 1984, gen. mgr. corp. fin. & group svcs., 1984-86; divsn. dir. internat. fin. Eagle Star Ins. Co. Ltd., London, 1987-90; exec. dir. Australian Eagle Ins. Co. Ltd., Melbourne, 1991-92; gen. mgr. Australian Aviation Underwriting Pool Pty. Ltd., Melbourne, 1992—. Rep. Australian Olympian Track & Field, 1972, Commonwealth Games Track & Field, 1970. Office: Australian Aviation Underwriting Pool Pty Ltd, 15 Queen St, Melbourne 3000, Australia

BAIRD, MURRAY PHILIP, barrister, solicitor; b. Melbourne, Victoria, Australia, Apr. 16, 1954; s. Brian and Margaret Allen (Gass) B.; m. Rosemary Frances Evans, Feb. 4, 1978; children: Cameron, Stuart, Fiona. BA, Monash U., Melbourne, Australia, 1975, LLB, 1977. Sr. ptnr. Moores Legal, Melbourne, 1980—; v.p. Insight for Living Inc., Melbourne, 1990—. Mem. Box Hill C. of C. (v.p. 1986-88), Rotary Club of Box Hill Ctrl. (pres. 1993-94). Avocations: reading, sailing, skiing, cricket. Home: 3 Acacia Ave, Blackburn 3130, Australia Office: Moores Legal, 9 Prospect St, Box Hill 3128, Australia

BAIRD, ROBERT WILLIAM, microbiologist, infectious diseases physician; b. Melbourne, Victoria, Australia, Oct. 18, 1957; s. Cameron William and Lorna Isabel (Murfitt) B.; m. Linda Mary Patricia Rendall, Jan. 30, 1982; children: Lauren Kate, Andrew William, Lachlan James. HSC, Scotch Coll., Melbourne, 1974; MBBS, Melbourne U., 1980. FRACP, FRCPA. Resident Royal Metro Hosp., Melbourne, 1981-82; registrar Repatriation Hosp., Melbourne, 1983-85; registrar Fairfield Hosp., Melbourne, 1986-87, dep. dir. microbiology, 1990-93; fellow U. Tenn., Memphis, 1988-89; cons. Melbourne Pathology, 1991—; cons. Repatriation Hosp., 1992—. Mem. ASD/ASM, AASM. Avocation: beekeeping. Office: Cabrine Hosp Pathology, 105 Victoria Parade, Collingwood Victoria 3066, Australia

BAIRD, ROGER NEALE, surgeon; b. Edinburgh, Scotland, Dec. 24, 1941; s. John Allan and Margaret Edith (Shand) B.; m. Affra Mary Varcoe-Cocks, Oct. 12, 1968; children: Susan Catherine, Richard Douglas. BSc with honors, Edinburgh U., 1963, B of Surgery, 1966, ChM, 1977. House surgeon Royal Infirmary, Edinburgh, 1966-67, research scholar dept. clin. surgery, 1967-69, registrar, 1969-72; lectr. surgery Bristol (Eng.) U., 1973-77, sr. lectr., 1977-95, clin. reader, 1995—, Long Fox lectr., 1981; cons. surgeon Royal Infirmary, Bristol, 1977—; med. dir. United Bristol Healthcare Trust, 1996-99; special trustee United Bristol Hosps., 1999—. Author books on vascular surgery; contbr. articles to med. jours. Fulbright scholar Harvard U. Med. Sch., Boston, 1975-76. Fellow Royal Coll. Surgeons (Eng.) (examiner 1981-86, Hunterian prof. 1980, Kinmonth lectr. 1984), Royal Coll. Surgeons (Edinburgh) (Learmonth lectr. 1980); mem. Intercollegiate Bd. in Gen. Surgery (examiner 1991-98), Univ. of Hong Kong (examiner in surgery 1998), Vascular Surg. Soc. Gt. Britain and Ireland (pres.-elect), Assn. Surgeons Gt. Britain and Ireland (hon. treas. 1985-90), European Soc. Vascular Surgery (dir., trustee), Internat. Cardiovascular Soc. (Brit. nat. del. 1982-90, Justin Miller lectr. Australasian chpt. 1997, hon. mem. 1997—), Soc. Vascular Surgery (fgn. corr. 1993—), Bristol Medico-Chirurgical Soc. (pres. 1994-95), Vas. Soc. So. Africa (corr. mem.). Club: Clifton (Bristol) Army and Navy (London). Avocations: travel, skiing. Home: 23 Old Sneed Park, Bristol BS9 1RG, England Office: Royal Infirmary, Bristol BS2 8HW, England

BAIRD, RONALD A., sculptor; b. Toronto, Ont., Can., Mar. 29, 1940; s. Cyril and Nellie (Arnott) B.; m. Lynda M. Hunt, Aug. 4, 1977; children: Emory, Zachary, Melissa, Patrick Jessie. Assoc. degree, Ontario Coll. Art, 1964. sculptor in residence U. Toronto, 1965-66, Seneca Coll., 1970; ectr. U. Toronto Sch. Arch. Prin. works included at Casa Loma, Toronto, Sci. North, Sudbury, Ont., Uxbridge, Ont., Barrie, Ont., Horseshoe Valley, Ont., St. John's ch., Oakville, Ch. of the Good Shepherd, Scarborough, Rivera Park, Lindsay, Ont., Philco-Ford, Markham, Ont., Lyndhurst Hosp., Toronto, Bell Can., Scarborough, Ont., Manhattan, N.Y., Waterfront, Sarnia, Ont., Valhalla Inn, Markham, West Park Hosp., Toronto, Seller's Residence, Toronto, Beth Sholom Synagogue, Toronto, St. Peter's HOsp., Hamilton, Ont., 1992, Cardinal Carter Chapel, Interasia Trading Co., N.Y.C., Oakville Centennial Meml. Hosp., Gerome Markson Arch., Cabbagetown, Toronto, Can. Forces Base, Kingston, Ont. Mus. for Telecom. Tech., Flemingdon Recreation Ctr., Mel Lastman Sq., City North York, Credit Valley Hosp., Princess Margaret Hosp., Londonberry, North Ireland, Hockley Valley, Ont., Lakeridge Health Crop., Oshawa, Ont., Toronto Parks Dept., many others. Avocations: skiing, sailing, kayaking. Address: RR #3, Stouffville, ON Canada L4A 7X4

BAIRLEIN, FRANZ XAVER, ornithologist, zoologist; b. Oberndorf, Germany, Dec. 7, 1952; s. Franz Xaver and Marianne (Friedl) B.; m. Brigitte Bayer; children: Michaela, Christian. Degree in biology, U. Konstanz, 1977, PhD, 1980. Postdoctoral fellow Max-Planck-Inst. Ethology, Germany, 1980-82; from rsch. asst. to asst. prof. zoology, Heisenberg fellow U. Koeln, Germany, 1982-90; dir. Inst. fuer Vogelforschung, Wilhelmshaven, Germany, 1990—; sr. prof. zoology U. Oldenburg, Germany; mem. contact group Conservation of Wild Birds, Commn. European Cmtys., 1984-85; officer Coun. for Study of Coastal Area of Northwest Germany. Author: Atlas of Bird Migration, Vol. III, 1995, Ecology of Birds, 1996; editl. bd. Oecologia, Zoology, Ringing & Migration, Vogelwarte, Vogelwelt; contbr. articles to profl. jours. Recipient Heinz Meier Leibnitz prize Min. Edn. & Sci., 1985; editor-in-chief Jour. for Ornithologie, 1998—. Mem. German Ornithol. Soc. (chmn. rsch. coun. 1988-97, prize 1991), European Union for Bird Ringing (exec. bd. 1992—), European Sci. Found. (chmn. network on bird migration 1993-96, chmn. sci. programme on optimality in bird migration 2000), German Zool. Soc., German Soc. Ecology, German Soc. Tropical Ecology, Br. Trust Ornithology, Br. Ornithol. Union, Am. Ornithol. Union, Cooper Ornithol. Soc., Wilson Ornithol. Soc., Swiss Soc. Ornithology, Rotary, N.Y. Acad. of Sci. Avocations: traveling, back-packing, gardening. Office: Inst. Vogelforschung, An der Vogelwarte 21, 26386 Wilhelmshaven Germany

BAIRSTOW, FRANCES KANEVSKY, labor arbitrator, mediator, educator; b. Racine, Wis., Feb. 19, 1920; d. William and Minnie (DuBow) Kanevsky; m. Irving P. Kaufman, Nov. 14, 1942 (div. 1949); m. David Steele Bairstow, Dec. 17, 1954; children: Dale Owen, David Anthony. Student U. Wis., 1937-42; BS, U. Louisville, 1949; student Oxford U. (Eng.), 1953-54; postgrad. McGill U., Montreal, Que., 1958-59. Rsch. economist U.S. Senate Labor-Mgmt. Subcom., Washington, 1950-51; labor edn. specialist U. P.R., San Juan, 1951-52; chief wage data unit WSB, Washington, 1952-53; labor rsch. economist Canadian Pacific Ry. Co., Montreal, 1956-58; asst. dir. indsl. rels. ctr. McGill U., 1960-66, assoc. dir., 1966-71, dir., 1971-85, lectr., indsl. rels. dept. econs., 1960-72, asst. prof. faculty mgmt., 1972-74, assoc. prof. faculty mgmt., 1974-83, prof., 1983-85; lectr. Stetson Law Sch., Fla. spl. master Fla. Pub. Employees Rels. Commn., 1985-97; dep. commr. essential svcs. Province of Que., 1976-81; mediator So. Bell Telephone, 1985—, AT&T and Comm. Workers Am., 1986—; cons. on collective bargaining arbitrator to OECD, Paris, 1979; cons. Nat. Film Bd. of Can., 1965-69; arbitrator Que. Consultative Coun. Panel of Arbitrators, 1968-83, Ministry Labour and Manpower, 1971-83, United Airlines and Assn. Flight Attendants, 1990-95, Am. Airlines and Transport Workers Union, 1997-98, State U. System of Fla., 1990-97; FDA, 1996-98, Social Security Adminstrn., 1996-97, Am. Airlines, 1997—; arbitrator Tampa Gen. Hosp., 1996—, mediator Canadian Public Svc. Staff Rels. Bd., 1973-85; contbg. columnist Montreal Star, 1971-85. Chmn. Nat. Inquiry Commn. Wider-Based Collective Bargaining, 1978. Fulbright fellow, 1953-54. Mem. Canadian Indsl. Rels. Rsch. Inst. (exec. bd. 1965-68), Indsl. Rels. Rsch. Assn. Am. (mem. exec. bd. 1965-68, chmn. nominating com. 1977), Nat. Acad. Arbitrators (bd. govs. 1977-80, program chmn. 1982-83, v.p. 1986-88, nat. coord. 1987-90), Ctrl. Fla. Indsl. Rels. Rsch. Assn. (pres. 1999). Home and Office: 1430 Gulf Blvd Apt 507 Clearwater FL 33767-2856

BAIRSTOW, RICHARD RAYMOND, retired lawyer; b. Waukegan, Ill., Sept. 26, 1917; s. Fred Raymond and Mildred (Wright) B.; m. Mary Kelley, Aug. 8, 1942 (dec. June 19, 1979); children: Kathleen Bairstow Young, Suzanne Bairstow Hicks, Mary Bairstow Neely; m. Agnes Macaitis Caldwell, July 22, 1980 (dec. July 22, 1995). AB, U. Ill., 1939, JD, 1947; postgrad., George Washington U., 1939-41. Bar: Ill. 1947, U.S. Dist. Ct. (no. dist.) Ill. 1964, U.S. Ct. Mil. Appeals 1963, U.S. SUpreme Ct. 1963. Assoc. Hall, Meyer & Carey, Waukegan, 1947-49; asst. state's atty. Lake County, Waukegan, 1949-53; ptnr. McClory & Bairstow, Waukegan, 1953-60, McClory, Bairstow, Lonchar & Nordigan, Waukegan, 1960-66; prin. Richard R. Bairstow & Assocs., Waukegan, 1966-98; ret., 1998; dist. atty. Fox Lake Fire Protection Dist., Ingleside, Ill., 1948-98; adminstrv. law judge Ill. Dept. Revenue, Chgo., 1953-87. Bd. dirs. ARC, Lake County, 1947-73; mem., pres. Salvation Army, Waukegan, 1954-66; bd. dirs. Lake County Family YMCA, 1990-91. Col. AUS, 1941-46, ETO, USAR, 1946-71, ret. U.S. Army Command and Gen. Staff Coll., 1965. Mem. ABA, Ill. Lake County Bar Assn., Assn. U.S. Army, The Ret. Officers Assn., Am. Legion, Glen Flora Country Club, Waukegan City Club, Elks, Delta Tau Delta, Phi Alpha Delta. Republican. Episcopalian. Home: 2122 Ash St Waukegan IL 60087-5033

BAIS, ASHOK SINGH, shoe company executive; b. Khamgaon, India, May 22, 1950; s. Arjun Singh and Vimal (Gaharwar) B.; m. Meena Sengar, Dec. 6, 1975; children: Aditi, Akanksha. B of Mech. Engring., Madhav Engring. Coll., Gwalior, India, 1971. Asst. mgr. Bata India Ltd., Patna, India, 1971-79; prodn. mgr. Tata Exports Ltd., Dewas, India, 1979-83; gen. mgr. Pond's (India), Madras, 1983-92, bus. mgr. leather, 1992-94; chmn., nat. exec. for leather Unilever India, Madras, 1993-94; tech. dir. (India) Ecoletsko, Denmark, Madras, 1994-97; mng. dir. TFL Leather Technique Pvt. Ltd., Chennai, India, 1997—; mem. exec. com. Pond's (India), Madras, 1992-94; bd. dirs. Shoecad Pvt. Ltd., Madras. Sec. PTA, St. Joseph of Cluny Sch., Pondicherry, 1991-93, pres., 1999—. Mem. Indian Shoe Fedn. (mem. expert com. panel for shoe components 1992-93), Confedn. Indian Industry (mem. regional com. for consumer forum 1993—), Nat. Inst. Quality and Reliability. Avocations: reading, cricket, tennis, snooker. Home: #4 19th Cross St Avvainagar, 605008 Pondicherry India Office: Ashiana No 4, 19th Cross St, Avvainagar, Pondicherry India 605008

BAITSAR, ROMAN IVANOVYCH, physics educator, researcher; b. Lviv, Ukraine, July 20, 1947; s. Ivan Pavlovych and Teodora Teodorivna (Kardan) B.; m. Hanna Stepanivna Posatska, Aug., 1972; children: Ulana, Anastasija. Diploma in electronic engring., Lviv Poly. Inst., 1975; PhD in Tech., Leningrad Sci. Inst. Metrol., Russia, 1986; sr. scientific rschr., Lviv Poly. Inst., 1988, DSc in Tech., 1995. Engr. Lviv Poly. Inst., 1973-79, sr. scientific rschr., 1979-90, chief of lab., 1991-92, chief of dept., 1992-97; assoc. prof. physics State U. Lviv Poly., 1997-2000, prof., 2000—; cons. postdoctoral rsch. work State U. Lviv Poly., 1975—. Contbr. articles to profl. jours.; patentee in field. Mem. Ukrainian Phys. Soc. Avocations: bicycling, travel. Office: State U Lviv Poly, St Bandery str 12, 76946UA Lviv Ukraine

BAJAJ, SATINDER KHURANA, academic administrator, educator; b. Malakwal, India, Sept. 25, 1939; s. Sampuran Singh and Jaswant Kaur Khurana; m. Yashpal Singh, Aug. 22, 1965. BSc, Delhi U., India, 1960, MSc, 1962; PhD, Mich. State U., 1969. Lectr. Lady Irwin Coll., New Delhi, 1962-65, dir., 1991—; rsch. assoc. Mich. State U., East Lansing, 1966-69; post doctorate fellow U. Heidelberg, Germany, 1970-72, U. Nottingham, Eng., 1972-73; prof., dean Punjab Agrl. U., India, 1973-83; joint dir. Nat. Inst. Child Devel., New Delhi, 1983-88; head dept. home sci. U. Delhi, 1992—; cons. Unicef, Thimpu, Bhutan, 1988. Author: (poetry) Summer Sun, 1976. Recipient Mahila Shiromani award, New Delhi, 1992, Outstanding Alumna award Mich. State U., 1996. Fellow Nat. Acad. Agrl. Scis.; mem. Nutrition Soc., Indian Ecological Soc. Home: H458 New Rajinder Nagar, New Delhi 110060, India

BAJAR, VICTORIA RAQUEL, computer scientist, educator; b. Buenos Aires, July 6, 1942; d. Salomon and Estrella (Simsolo) B.; m. Juan Manuel Navarro, Feb. 11, 1971; 1 child, Rebeca. Lic. in math., U. Buenos Aires, 1964; diploma in info. scis., U. Mex., 1966; M in Computer Scis., U. Grenoble, France, 1969, D in Computer Scis., 1973. From asst. to attached

prof. U. Buenos Aires, 1961-66; attached prof. U. Nat. Autonomous Mex., 1967-68; asst. U. Grenoble, 1968-73; prof. U. Buenos Aires, 1973-74; rschr. Cinvestav-Ipn, Mexico City, 1974-78; founder computing ctr., acad. depts. and curricula and gen. dir. computing divsn. Inst. Tech. Autonomo Mex., 1979-94; dir. summer computing sch. Found. Arturo Rosenblueth, 1993-94; pres. seminar Nat. Computing Congress, 1994; informatics sch. dean and informatics cons. of pres. Intercontinental U., 1995-97; gen. mgr. Mader Centro and ind. cons., 1997—. Author: Operating System RSX-11M, 1980, Pascal, 1982, Faculty Management at University, 1998; co-author: Computing Curricula, 1989; author curricula design at various schs.; contbr. articles to profl. jours. Mem. IEEE, Assn. for Computing Machinery, Assn. for Computing Execs., Assn. of Software Developers, Acad. Computing Mex., French Assn. Info. Sci. and Tech., Assn. Computing Univ. Schs. (v.p. 1986-88, pres. 1988-90), Assn. Engring. Schs. Avocation: piano. Office: Insurgentes Sur 4303, Col Sta Ursula Xitla-Tlalpan, 14420 Mexico City Mexico

BAJCSAY, ANDRAS, radiation and clinical oncologist; b. Budapest, Hungary, Oct. 2, 1960; s. Pal and Margit (Szaplonczay) B.; m. Eva Haraszti; children: Marton, Mate, Julia, Kinga, Zsofia. Diplomate, Semmelweis U. Medicine, Budapest, 1987. Cons. dept. radiotherapy Nat. Inst. Oncology, Budapest, Hungary, 1987—. Mem. European Soc. Therapeutic Radiology and Oncology, Hungarian Oncological, Radiological, Pulmonological, Radiotherapeutic, and Ophthalmologic. Soc. Roman Catholic. Avocations: music, swimming, basketball. E-mail: bajcsay@oncol.hu. Office: Nat Inst Oncology, Rath Gyorgy u 7-9, 114/Pf21 Budapest Hungary

BAJETTA, CARLO MARIA, literary scholar, educator, translator; b. Milan, Lombardy, Italy, Aug. 17, 1966; s. Piero Bajetta and Anna Maria Rancilio; m. Jana Balážová. BA, Cath. U., Milan, 1992, PhD, 1997. Tchr. English S. Paolo Hosp. Nursing Sch., Milan, 1992-93; lectr. Inst. European Studies, Milan, 1996—; univ. lectr. Cath. U., Milan, 1996—, Brescia, Italy, 1996—; cons., translator Signorelli Pub. Inc., Milan, 1994-95, Vita e Pensiero, Milan, 1995—. Author: Sir Walter Ralegh poeta di corte elisabettiano, 1998, Some Notes on Printing and Publishing in Renaissance Venice, 2000, Whole Volumes in Folio, 2000; contbg. author: Dictionary of National Biography; contbr. articles to profl. jours. Scholar London/Cambridge Bibliog. Soc., 1995. Roman Catholic. Avocations: music, computing, skiing. E-mail: bajetta@mi.unicatt.it. Office: Cath Univ, Largo Gemelli 1, 20123 Milan Italy

BAJKOVA, ANISA TALGATOVNA, radio astronomy imaging and digital signal processing researcher; b. Yamakai Village, Russia, Apr. 1, 1953; d. Talgat Minnislamovitch and Amina Abulkhaerovna (Zainetdinova) B.; m. Vadim Vadimovitch Bobylev, June 8, 1994. Masters with honors, Aviation Inst., Ufa, Russia, 1975, Bashkirian State U., Ufa, Russia, 1981; Candidate of Sci., Electrotech. Inst. Comm., Leningrad, Russia, 1984; DSc, Inst. Applied Astronomy Russian Acad. Sci., St. Petersburg, Russia, 1995. Engr. Design Office Kabel Comm., Ufa, 1975-85; jr. sci. rschr. Spl. Astrophys. Obs. Russian Acad. Sci., Leningrad, 1985-88, sci. rschr. Inst. Applied Astronomy, 1988-89; sci. sec. Inst. Applied Astronomy Russian Acad. Sci., St. Petersburg, 1989-94, dep. head lab. Inst. Applied Astronomy, 1994-95, leading sci. rschr. Inst. Applied Astronomy, 1995—; head imaging group Inst. Applied Astronomy Russian Acad. Sci., 1988—, mem. acad. bd., 1989—, sci. sec. dissertation bd., 1991—, mem. editl. bd., 1996—. Contbr. articles to books and profl. jours. Mem. Union of Scientists, St. Petersburg, 1990—. Recipient grant Russian Found. Basic Researches, 1993-95, Am. Astron. Soc., 1994. Mem. Astron. Union Moscow State U., Internat. Union Radio Sci. (corr. 1994-96), European Astronomical Soc. Avocations: theatre, painting, ping-pong, tourism, fishing. Home: 35 9 Turbinnaya ul, 198099 St Petersburg Russia Office: Inst Applied Astronomy, 8 Zhdanovskaya ul, 197110 St Petersburg Russia

BAJO, MOMODOU CLARK, banker. Gov. Ctrl. Bank The Gambia, Banjul. Office: Ctrl Bank The Gambia, 12 Buckle St, Banjul The Gambia*

BAJOGHLI, AMIR A., physician; b. Isfahan, Iran; s. Mehdi and Zary B. MD, Medical Coll. Va., 1994. Diplomate Am. Bd. Dermatology and Internal Medicine. Resident Dept. Dermatology Boston Univ., 1992—; regional dir. William & Mary Alumni Admissions Com., Boston, 1999. Contbr. articles to profl. jours. CPR instr. Am. Red Cross, Williamburg, Va., 1988-90. Mem. Am. Acad. Dermatology, AMA, Mass. Medical Soc. Avocations: sailing, skiing. E-mail:bajoghli@bu.edu. Office: Boston Univ 609 Albany St Boston MA 02118-2515

BAJREKTAREVIĆ, ANIS H., former vice-consul to Germany, legal consultant, researcher; b. Sarajevo, Bosnia-Herzegovina, Mar. 31, 1964; s. Hakija M. and Sabiha I. (Škrijelj) B.; m. Sofia B. Vidaković, June 22, 1993; 1 child, Mak. BA in Law, Sarajevo Sch. Laws, 1988; MA, Ctrl. European U., Budapest, 1999. Bar: Belgrade, Fed. Ministry Justice, 1990; high specialization from Diplomatic Acad. Vienna, Austria, 1993; cert. in arbitration and mediation, Vienna Ctrl. European Initiative Project on Comm. Law (European Bank Reconstruction and Devel.-London, Internat. Devel. Law Inst.-Rome), 1995, cert. in privatization and fgn. investment, 1996. Lawyer Lubović Law Office, Inc., Sarajevo, 1989-90, lic. lawyer, 1990-92; lic. lawyer Bajrektarević's Law Office, Sarajevo, 1993-94; II sec. and vice-counsul to Germany Fgn. Ministry, Sarajevo, 1992-93; practitioner Austrian Higher Ct., Vienna, 1994-95; rsch. fellow Bruno Kreisky Found., Vienna, 1995—; chmn. of the Court of Honor Assn. Bosnian Judges, Pub. Prosecutors and Licensed Lawyers in diaspora, Vienna, 1994-99; legal officer Internat. Ctr. Migration Policy Devel.-Vienna, Austria, 1996—; legal expert ABA/Ctrl. East European Law Initiative, 1996—; cons. European Union Adminstrn. for Bosnia, Brussels, 1994-95, Johns Hopkins-SAIS, Washington, 1993-95; legal advisor Malaysian Trade Chamber, Kuala Lumpur, 1996-97; OZS Europa dept. polit. advisor Karl Renner Inst., 1997—. Editor internat. affairs Bosnian youth Weekly NASI DANI, Sarajevo, 1984-87; prodr., dir. ind. film and theatre prodns., 1986-92; exec. dir. ind. TV, 1991—. Recipient personal grant Austrian Fgn. Ministry, 1992. Mem. Young Lawyers Assn. Bosnia (pres. 1990-96), Bosnian Bar Assn. (mem. governing body 1990-96). Bosniak (Bosnian Muslim). Avocations: bicycling, skiing, tennis. Home: 10 Angeligasse 83/7/5, A-1100 Vienna Austria Office: 4 Möllwaldplatz 4/3, A-1040 Wieu Austria

BAJUSZ, SÁNDOR, chemistry educator; b. Magyaróvár, Hungary, Aug. 24, 1931; s. Sändor and Sändorné (Frühwirth) B.; m. Sändorné Kosztolányi, June 12, 1954; 1 child, Judit Bajusz. PhD, Eötvös U., 1968; DSc, Hungarian Acad. Scis., 1980. Educator Kölcsey F. Secondary Sch., Körmend, Hungary, 1954-55; rsch. Inst. for Drug Rsch., Budapest, 1955-64, sr. rschr., 1964-71, head of dept., 1971—; vis. prof. Tulane U. Sch. Medicine, New Orleans, 1985-88. Patentee in field. Mem. European Peptide Soc. (nat. rep. 1991-98), Am. Peptide Soc. Avocation: history. Office: Inst for Drug Rsch, Berlini u 47-49 PO Box 82, H-1325 Budapest Hungary

BAK, FLEMMING, automotive importing company executive; b. Copenhagen, Dec. 20, 1963. BS in Econs. and Bus. Adminstrn., Aarhus (Denmark) Bus. Sch., 1985, MS in Econs. and Bus. Adminstrn., 1988. Product mgr. Toyota Danmark A/S, Copenhagen, 1990-93, mgr. advt. and pub. rels., 1993-95, mgr. pub. rels., 1995-97, gen. mgr. sales and mtkg., 1997-98, dir. sales and mktg., 1998-99, pres., 1999—. Mem. Danish Automobile Importers Assn. (bd. dirs. 1999—). Office: Toyota Danmark A/S, Dynamovej 10, DK-2730 Herlev Denmark

BAKÁCS, TIBOR, oncologist, immunologist, researcher; b. Budapest, Hungary, Dec. 28, 1946; s. Tibor Bakács and Erzsébet Polgár; m. Éva Marton, Mar. 24, 1973; children: Tamás, Éva. MD, Semmelweis U., Budapest, 1971; PhD, Hungarian Acad. Scis., Budapest, 1978, DSc, 1986. Clinician Heim Pál Children's Hosp., Budapest, 1971-73; rschr. Nat. Inst. Vaccines, Budapest, 1973-75; rsch. fellow, dept. tumor biology Karolinska Inst., Stockholm, 1975-77; head lab. immunology Nat. Inst. Oncology, Budapest, 1977-82; rsch. fellow, dept. immunology Paterson Lab., Manchester, Eng., 1982-83; head dept. immunology Nat. Inst. Oncology, Budapest, 1983-99; v.p. rsch. United Cancer Rsch. Inst., Alexandria, Va.; with Alfréd Rényi Math. Inst., Hungarian Acad. Scis., Budapest; vis. prof. exptl. immunology br. Nat. Cancer Inst., NIH, Bethesda, Md., 1993-94. Mem. N.Y. Acad. Scis. Home: Mikó utca 3, 1012 Budapest Hungary Office: Alfred Rényi Math Inst, Realtanoda utca 13-15, 1053 Budapest Hungary

BAKARDJIAN, HOVAGIM BEDROS, brain function researcher; b. Russe, Bulgaria, June 12, 1961; arrived in Japan, 1993; s. Bedros Hovagim and Mari Sarkis Bakardjian. Student, Sofia (Bulgaria) Inst. Tech., 1982-83, Jena (Germany) Inst. Physiol., 1986-87; BSc, MSc, Ilmenau (Germany) Tech. U., 1988. Cert. biomed. engr. Rsch. fellow Inst. Biomed. Engring. Sofia Med. U., 1988-92; rsch. fellow Graz (Austria) U. Tech., 1992-93, Hokkaido U., Sapporo, Japan, 1994-97, Nat. Inst. Biosci. and Human Tech., Tsukuba, Ibaraki, Japan, 1997—. Contbr. articles to profl. jours. With Bulgarian Army, 1980-82. Austrian Govt. fellow for sci., 1992-93, Japanese Govt. fellow for sci., 1994-97. Mem. IEEE Engring. in Medicine and Biology Soc., Internat. Fedn. for Med. and Biol. Engring., Internat. Fedn. for Pattern Recognition, Soc. for Neurosci., Chaos Group. Avocations: traveling, psychology, inter-cultural philosophy, numismatics. Fax: 81 298 61 6662. E-mail: hova@nibh.go.jp. Office: Nat Inst Biosci/Human Tech, 1-1 Higashi, 305-8566 Tsukuba Ibaraki, Japan

BAKARI, MUHAMMAD, dermatologist; b. Tanga, Tanzania, Nov. 18, 1960; s. Kambi Bakari and Rehema Muhammad; m. Salim Mwanahamisi, Nov. 19, 1989; children: Rahma, Kailat, Arafa, Bakari. MD, U. D'Salaam, 1988, M in Medicine, 1993. Tutor MATC, Tanga, Tanzania, 1988-90; resident MMC, D'Salaam, Tanzania, 1990-93; physician MMC, D'Salaam, 1993—; lectr. U. D'Salaam, 1994—; dermatology trainee Hosp. Dublin, Ireland, 1993-94. Mem. MAT. Islamic. Avocation: football. Home: PO Box 5440, Dar es Salaam Tanzania Office: Muhimbili Med Ctr, PO Box 65066, Dar es Salaam Tanzania

BAKER, ANITA DIANE, lawyer; b. Atlanta, Sept. 4, 1955; d. Byron Garnett and Anita (Swanson) B.; m. Thomas Johnstone Robison III, Sept. 26, 1995. BA summa cum laude, Oglethorpe U., 1977; JD with distinction, Emory U., 1980. Bar: Ga. 1980. Assoc. Hansell & Post, Atlanta, 1980-88, Kitchens, Kelley, Gaynes, Huprich & Shmerling, 1989-90; asst. gen. counsel NationsBank Corp., 1991-97; v.p., gen. counsel Adaris Corp., 1997-99; pvt. practice Atlanta, 1999—. Mem. Ga. Bar Assn., Atlanta Bar Assn., Ga. Assn. Women Lawyers, Atlanta Hist. Soc., Concourse Athletic Club, Ga. Alliance of Private Clubs, Pace Acad. Alumni Assn., Oglethorpe U. Alumni Assn., Stormy Petrel Bar Assn., Order of Coif, Phi Alpha Delta, Phi Alpha Theta, Alpha Chi, Omicron Delta Kappa. Office: 1827 Powers Ferry Rd SE Bldg 5 Atlanta GA 30339-5692

BAKER, BRUCE EDWARD, orthopedic surgeon, consultant; b. Oswego, N.Y., Mar. 22, 1937; s. Elbert J. and Reatha (Hartranft) B.; m. Patricia Therese Gormel, Aug. 19, 1961; children: Brett, Clayton, Sean, Reatha. BSME, Syracuse U., 1959; MD, SUNY-Syracuse, 1965. Intern State U. Iowa, Iowa City, 1965-66, asst. resident, 1966-67; resident orthopaedics SUNY-Upstate Med. Ctr., Syracuse, 1969-72, NIH orthopaedic rsch. fellow, 1972-73, asst. prof. orthopaedic surgery, 1973-79, assoc. prof., 1979-86, prof., 1986-89; dir. univ. sports medicine svc. divsn. dept. orthopaedic surgery 1980-89; team physician, dir. sports medicine athletic dept., Syracuse U., 1973-93, orthopaedic cons. Student Health Ctr., 1973-93, staff SUNY Hosp., Syracuse, 1973-89, Syracuse VA Hosp., 1973-89, A.C. Silverman Pub. Health Hosp., 1973-77, Crouse-Irving Meml. Hosp., 1973—; cons. in field. Contbr. numerous articles to profl. jours. Capt. USAF, 1967-69. Recipient AMA Physicians Recognition award, 1978, Bronze medal award Am. Roentgen Ray Soc., 1980, Gold medal award Sound Slide Prodn. Conditioning, 1977; Syracuse U. scholar, 1955; N.Y. State Regents scholar, 1955-59; USPHS grantee, 1973-74; Hendricks Research fund grantee, 1973-75; NIH grantee, 1974-76, 76-77. Fellow ACS, Am. Acad. Orthop. Surgeons; mem. AMA, Med. Soc. State N.Y., Onondaga County Med. Soc., Orthop. Rsch. Soc., Am. Coll. Sports Medicine, N.Y. Soc. Orthop. Surgeons, Royal Soc. Medicine, Internat. Soc. Arthroscopy, Knee Surgery and Orthop. Sports Medicine, Am. Orthop. Soc. Sports Medicine, European Soc. Sports Trauma, Knee Surgery and Arthroscopy, Arthroscopy Assn. N. Am. Office: 600 E Genesee St Ste 117 Syracuse NY 13202-3108

BAKER, BRUCE JAY, lawyer; b. Chgo., June 18, 1954; s. Kenneth and Beverly (Gould) B. Student, U. Leeds, Eng., 1974-75; BS, U. Ill., 1976; JD, Washington U., 1979. Bar: Ill. 1979, U.S. Dist. Ct. (no. dist.) Ill. 1984. Asst. atty. gen. antitrust divsn. State of Ill., Chgo., 1979-83; assoc. Mass, Miller & Josephson Ltd., Chgo., 1983-86; sr. counsel Discover Card Services Inc., Riverwoods, Ill., 1986-89; sr. legis. counsel Dean Witter Fin. Svcs. Group, Riverwoods, 1989-91; gen. counsel Ill. Commr. Banks and Trust Cos., Chgo., 1991-94; ptnr. Schiff Hardin & Waite, Chgo., 1994-99, of counsel, 1999—; sr. v.p., gen. counsel Ill. Bankers Assn., 1999—. Contbr. articles to profl. jours. Registered lobbyist Ill. Legislature, Springfield, 1985-91, 94—. Named Ill. State scholar, 1972. Mem. ABA (antitrust com., banking com., chmn. state banking law devels. task force 1998—), Ill. State Bar Assn. (comml. banking and bankruptcy sect.), Chgo. Bar Assn. (fin. insts. com.), Ill. Bankers Assn. (legis. counsel 1985-86, gen. counsel 1994—, Disting. Bank Counsel award 1991, 97). Office: Ill Bankers Assn 111 W Jackson Blvd Ste 910 Chicago IL 60604-3502 also: Schiff Hardin & Waite 7200 Sears Tower Chicago IL 60606

BAKER, CHARLES DEWITT, research and development company executive; b. Dayton, Ohio, Jan. 5, 1932; s. Donald James and Lillian Mae (Pund) B.; m. June Thordis Tandberg, June 25, 1954; children: Charles, Robert, Thomas, Michael. AA in Elec. Engring., Long Beach City Coll., 1953; ed., Boston U., 1954, Pacific Coast U., 1963, U. Utah, 1980. Registered profl. mfg. engr., Calif. Chemist Shell Oil, Torrance, Calif., 1957-60; materials and process engr. Northrop Corp., Hawthorne, Calif., 1960-63; packaging engr. Jet Propulsion Lab., Pasadena, Calif., 1963-71; med. design engr. Utah Biomed. Test Lab., Salt Lake City, 1971-78, sect. mgr., 1978-83; v.p. Tech. Rsch. Assocs., Salt Lake City, 1983-88, pres., 1988—; pres. Thordis Corp., 1980—. Contbr. articles to profl jours.; 20 patents in field. Chmn. bd. dirs. Care Holder Group, 1996—; mem. cmty. adv. com. Heart and Lung Inst., spl. study sect rev. NIH, Tech. Transfer Forum, U. Utah, 1984. Recipient Cost Reduction award NASA, 1969, New Tech. award, 1969, 71, 75. Mem. ASME, Soc. Mfg. Engrs., Utah Mfg. Assn., Acad. of Tech., Entrepreneurs and Innovators. Republican. Avocations: teaching, reading, car rebuilding.

BAKER, CHARLES ROGER, sales executive; b. Muskogee, Okla., Feb. 12, 1947; s. Roger Leon Baker and Gracie Wilma whisenant; m. Wilma Kay Carpenter; children: Charmane, Amber, Sybil Ann, Charles Jr. AA, Tulsa Jr. Coll., 1970; BA, U. Okla., 1971. Dist. mgr. Frigidaire Co., Dublin, Ohio, 1988-97; pvt. practice sales Marshall, Ark., 1997—. Mem. Mason (web master Muskogee 1985, web master Marshall 1999-00). Office: HC 79 Box 209 Marshall AR 72650-9720

BAKER, DAVID ARTHUR, small business owner, manufacturer; b. Cranston, R.I., Jan. 5, 1941; s. Andrew Harris and Phyllis Evelyn (Partridge) B.; m. Anne Marie Perron, July 14, 1959; children: Susan Marie, Pamela Phyllis. Diploma, Brit. Inst. Homeopathy, Middlesex, Eng., 1995, DHM, 1996. With Supreme Coat Co., Worcester, Mass., 1960-74; owner D.A. Baker Mfg. Co., Auburn, Mass., 1975—, Eagle's Nest Video Prodns., Auburn, 1985—; bd. dirs. Royal Arts Found. of Belcourt Castle, Newport, R.I. Producer (ednl. video) Popular Amazons, 1986, Macaws, 1987, Cockatoos, 1988, Parrot Keeping, 1989, and others. Treas. Boston Soc. Aviculture, 1983-85; co-founder, bd. dirs. Exotic Cage Bird Soc., 1986-88; mem. Plaza Club, Worcester, 1985-91; res. dep. sheriff Worcester County. Recipient Outstanding Svc. award Boston Soc. Aviculture, 1984, Exotic Cage Bird Soc. New Eng., 1985, Cert. of Merit, Les Comité des Vins de France, 1982; named Knight Order of St. John, 1999. Fellow Brit. Inst. Homeopathy; mem. Homeopathic Acad. Naturopathic Physicians, Internat. Platform Soc., Internat. Soc. Food and Wine, Nat. Trust Hist. Preservation, Boston Soc. Aviculture (treas. 1983-85), Prservation Soc. Newport County, Exotic Cage Bird Soc. (co-founder, bd. dirs. 1986-88), Friends Ballroom Dancing, Friends of the Royal Arts Found. (v.p.), Rolls Royce Owners Club, Daimler and Lanchester Club, Club Maxine's, Health Scis. Inst., Leicester Bus. Assn. (v.p.), Knight Cottage Assn. (pres.), St. Andrew Soc. of R.I. Republican. Avocations: art and antiques collector, shooting, boating, aviculturist. Home: Knight Cottage Bellevue Ave Newport RI 02840 Office: Eagles Nest Villa 196 Leicester St Auburn MA 01501-1406

BAKER, DAVID ERIC DALE, physicist, consultant; b. Melbourne, Victoria, Australia, May 28, 1960; s. Lawrence Andrew and Aileen (Fauckner) B.; m. Kerry Leigh Lanagan, Dec. 28, 1996; 1 child, David Rehard Martyn. BS with honors, Australian Nat. U., Canberra, 1983; MS with honors, Macquaire U., Sydney, Australia, 1990. Diploma Med. Ultrasound. Physicis Lairdynamics, Gold Coast, Australia, 1985-92; ultrasonographer W.A. Vascular Diagnostic, Perth, Australia, 1992-94, Kings Coll. Hosp., London, 1994, Charing Cross Hosp., London, 1994-95; physicist Laserdyne P/L, Gold Coast, 1995—; tech. dir. Jet Tech Surg., Perth, 1992-96. Contbr. articles to profl. jours.; patent for high pressure pulses infusion pump, 1993. Avocations: salt water aquarium, aviculture, motorcycling. Home: 4 Mingaletta Dr, Ashmore Queensland 4214, Australia

BAKER, DEBORAH JANE, epidemiology and health services researcher; b. London, Sept. 23, 1949; s. Arthur John and Elsie Eleanor (Hobbs) Taylor; m. Matthew Peter Baker, Aug. 28, 1974; children: Zoe, Hannah, James. BSc in Psychology, Brunel U., Uxbridge, Eng., 1973; PhD in Social Psychology, Bath (Eng.) U., 1986. Chartered psychologist. Rsch. officer U. Bath, 1987-91; lectr. health psychology U. Bath., 1993-95; rsch. fellow in social medicine U. Bristol, Eng., 1991-92; sr. rsch. fellow in child health Bristol (Eng.) U., 1995-98; sr. rsch. fellow in epidemiology Nat. Primary Care R&D Centre, U. Manchester, Eng., 1998—; vis. fellow divsn. child health Bristol U., 1998—. Editor: (with S. Skevington) The Social Identity of Women, 1989; author monographs; contbr. numerous articles to profl. jours. Fellow Brit. Psychol. Soc. (assoc.). Avocations: badminton, reading, Manchester United Football Club. Office: Natl Primary Care R&D Fl 5, Williamson Bldg/Oxford Rd, Manchester M13 9PL, England

BAKER, DENNIS R., bank officer; b. Poplar Bluff, Mo., Jan. 12, 1960; s. Glen Eugene and Martha (Arl) B.; m. Anita Marie, Aug. 8, 1981; children: Kurt, Kelsey. BS in Agrl., U. Mo., Columiba, 1982; MBA, Drury Coll., Springfield, Mo., 1993. Br. mgr. Farm Credit Svcs., Houston, Mo., 1982-85; v.p./loan officer The Bank of Houston, Houston, 1985-92, Comerce Bank, Cassville, Mo., 1992—. Treas. Optimist Club, Houston, Mo., 1988-91. Mem. Rotary Club (pres. 1997-98, dist. constn./bylaws com. 1999-2000). Avocations: scuba diving, hunting, travel. Office: Commerce Bank 715 Main St Cassville MO 65625-1421

BAKER, ELLEN, management educator, researcher; b. Birkenau, Germany, Feb. 14, 1939; d. Max and Rena (Loeb) Baer; m. Earl Baker, May 29, 1962; children: Richard, Arnold. BA, NYU, 1960; BSc, U. London, 1964, PhD, 1967. Asst. prof. psychology Pratt Inst., N.Y., 1967-69; assoc. prof. psychology Kean Coll., N.J., 1970-73; lectr. in psychology New South Wales Inst. of Tech., Australia, 1974-83; sr. lectr. in mgmt. U. Tech., Sydney, 1984-90, dep. head mgmt., 1991-92, hon. assoc., 1994—, rsch. assoc., 1998-2000; vis. rsch. fellow Inst. for the Future, Menlo Park, Calif., 1993; project fellow Warren Ctr. for Advanced Engring., U. Sydney, 1983-85; vis. scholar info. sys. dept. London Bus. Sch., 1990; program chair Computer Support for Groups Conf., Sydney, 1988; rschr. global household tech. adoption project Inst. Future, Menlo Park, Calif., 1997-98. Author: (with others) Psychology at Work, 1985, 2d edit., 1990., Teleconferencing and Beyond, 1984; contbr. articles to profl. jours. Rsch. grant Australian Rsch. Coun., 1994, Faculty of Bus., U. Tech., 1995, Australian Rsch. Coun., 2000. Mem. APA, Australian Computer Soc. (state chmn. nat. office automation com. 1987-91, founder office sys. group 1989), Assn. for Info. Sys., Academy Mgmt., Phi Beta Kappa. Avocations: travel, theatre, walking. Office: Univ Tech Sydney Sch Mgmt, Broadway, Sydney NSW 2007, Australia

BAKER, F. M., psychiatry educator; b. N.Y.C., Sept. 15, 1942. BA, Hunter Coll., 1964; MA, NYU, 1967; MD, U. Rochester, 1975; MPH, Johns Hopkins U., 1985. Diplomate Am. Bd. Psychiatry and Neurology; added qualifications in geriatric psychiatry. Intern Greenwich (Conn.) Hosp.Assn., 1975-76; resident in psychiatry Yale U. Sch. Medicine, New Haven, 1976-79, asst. prof. dept. psychiatry, 1979-84; liason psychiatrist Primary Care Ctr. Yale-New Haven Hosp., 1979-81, asst. dir. psychiat. cons. liason svc., dir. psychiat. emergency svc., 1979-82, liason psychiatrist geriatric assessment unit, 1981-84, med. dir. rape crisis team, 1981-82; cons. psychiatrist Gaylord Rehab. Hosp., Wallingford, Conn., 1979-82, Golden Manor Nursing Home, New Haven, 1980-81; assoc. ward chief Hill-West Haven div. Conn. Mental Health Ctr., 1982-83, ward chief 5th fl. in-patient div., 1983-84; med. staff fellow USPHS, NINCDS, NIH, 1984-87; assoc. prof. dept. psychiatry U. Tex. Health Sci. Ctr., San Antonio, 1987-90; chief geriatric psychiatry program Audie L. Murphy Meml. Vets. Hosp., 1987-90; assoc. prof. Inst. for Psychiatry and Human Behavior U. Md., Balt., 1990-95, prof. Inst. for Psychiatry and Human Behavior, 1995-96; prof. dept. psychiatry Ind. U. Sch. of Medicine, Indpls., 1996-98; prof. dept. psychiatry, dir. rsch. John A. Burns Sch. Medicine, Honolulu, 1998-2000; med. dir. Lower Shore Clinic, Salisbury, Md., 2000—; prof. Inst. for Psychiatry and Human Behavior, 2000—; asst. prof. part-time dept. psychiatry Johns Hopkins U. Sch. Medicine, Balt., 1985-87; adj. researcher biometry and field studies br. Nat. Inst. Neurologic Disorders and Stroke NIH, Bethesda, 1987-89; vis. scientist dept. health scis. rsch. The Mayo Clinic, Rochester, Minn., 1987-90; vis. and cons. scientist mental disorders of the aging rsch. br. NIMH, Rockville, Md., 1989-92; cons. scientist geriatric div. Nat. Inst. Aging, NIH, Rockville, 1990-92. Author: (with others) Evaluation of the Consumer Health Training and Education Program, 1973, Manual of Psychiatric Peer Review, 2d edit., 1981, (with others), An Overview of Legal Issues in Geriatric Psychiatry, 1986, Dementing Illness in African American Populations, 1991; contbr. articles to profl. jours. Mem. psychogeriatric adv. bd. cen. office VA, Washington, 1990-94. Fellow Am. Psychiat. Assn. (chmn. task force on forensic issues in geriatric psychiatry 1982-86, vice chmn. coun. on aging 1984-89, mem. com. on ethnic elders 89-95, mem. selection adv. com. for APA/NIMH fellowship 1988-91); mem. Am. Assn. for Geriatric Psychiatry (bd. mem. 1988-91, chmn., ethnic elder com. 1989-92, treas. elect 1992-95), Black Psychiatrists Am. (rep. Nat. Conf. on Manpower and Recruitment 1980, ant. sec., asst. editor Bottom Line Newsletter 1980-82, assoc. editor 1982-84, editor 1987-89, nat. treas. 1984, 86, exec. com. 1987-89), Tex. Soc. Psychiat. Physicians, Nat. Coun. Negro Women, Boston Soc. for Gerontologic Psychiatry, Inc., Conn. Psychiat. Soc. (com. on women 1979-81, program com. 1980-81, ins. com. 1979-84), Gerontol. Soc. Am., Am. Geriatric Soc., Internat. Psychogeriatric Assn., Psychiat. Physicians (chair sci. program ann. meeting 1989), Md. Psychiat. Soc. (geriatric psychiatry com. 1990-96, editorial com. 1991-96, continuing edn. com. 1991-92).

BAKER, GREGORY RICHARD, mathematician; b. Johannesburg, Transvaal, Republic South Africa, Nov. 9, 1947; came to U.S., 1972; s. Mervyn Colin and Valerie Rita (Deary) B.; m. Joanne Broker, Nov. 5, 1971 (div. Apr. 1978); 1 child, Kim; m. MaryEllen Asgeirsson, Oct. 7, 1979; 1 child, Kathryn Anne. BS, U. Natal, Durban, Republic South Africa, 1970, MS, 1973; PhD, Calif. Inst. Tech., 1977. Rsch. fellow Calif. Inst. Tech., Pasadena, 1976-77; instr. MIT, Cambridge, 1977-79, asst. prof., 1979-81; assoc. prof. U. Ariz., Tucson, 1981-86; rsch. math. Exxon Rsch. and Engring. Co., Annondale, N.J., 1986-88; eminent scholar Ohio State U., Columbus, 1988—; cons. Cambridge Hydrodynamics Inc., Princeton, N.J., 1976-86, Inst. for Computer Applications in Sci. and Engring., NASA-Langley, 1980-81; mem. applied math. rev. panel for Dept. Energy, 1993; mem. NSF Small Bus. Innovation Rsch. Rev. Panel, 1993; mem. NSF/NRC Convocation on Sci., Math., Engring. and Tech. Edn., 1995, NSF Review Panel on Fluid Mechanics, 1997, 98. Contbr. articles to profl. jours. including Physics of Fluids, Jour. Fluid Mechanics. Recipient Presdl. Young Investigator award, NSF, 1984. Mem. Soc. Indsl. and Applied Math., Am. Physics Soc. Achievements include development of reliable numerical methods for studies of evolution of free-surfaces in incompressible fluid flow. Office: Ohio State Univ Math Dept Columbus OH 43210

BAKER, HARRISON SCOTT, computer consultant; b. Marion, Ohio, Mar. 12, 1950; s. Stanley Wallace and Starling (Dixon) B. BA, BS, Fla. State U., 1972, 80; MBA, Embry-Riddle Aeronaut. U., 1986. A&P rating, FAA; cert. product specialist, Microsoft; cert. computing technology, Computing Technology Industry Assn.; radiotelephone lic. with radar enforcement FCC. Mgr. Vincent Auto Parts, Inc., Marathon, Fla., 1972-78; maintenance supr. Ea. Air Lines, Inc., Miami, 1980-92; computer cons. Upper Sandusky, Ohio, 1992—. Author: Index to the Muster Rolls of PA in War of 1812, 1995, Early Settlers of Wyandot County, 1995; indexer: Obituaries in Upper Sandusky newspapers 1868-1911, 1994, Obituaries in Upper Sandusky newspapers 1912-1937, 1996, Obituaries in Upper Sandusky newspaper 1938-1958, 1997, Obituaries in Upper Sandusky newspapers 1959-1979, 1997, Journal of William Kennedy Beall, 1999. trustee Wyandot County Geneaol. Soc., 1995—. Mem. SAR (pres. Hancock chpt. 1995-96), IEEE Computer Soc., Assn. Computing Machinery, Soc. War of 1812 (Ohio pres. 1996-99),

Sons of Union Vets. (camp sec. 1994-98, Dept. of Ohio signals officer 1999—). Avocations: electronics, genealogy. Home: PO Box 411 Upper Sandusky OH 43351-0411

BAKER, IAN HELSTRIP, university official; b. Johannesburg, South Africa, Nov. 26, 1927; s. Henry Hubert and Mary Clare B.; m. Susan Anne Lock, June 23, 1956; children: Edward Ian (dec.), Robert William, Joanna Susan. Ed., St. Peter's Sch., York, St. Edmund Hall, Oxford. Commd. lt. Royal Arty., 1948, transfered to Royal Tank Regt., 1955, advanced through grades to maj. gen., 1978; comdg. officer 1st Royal Tank Regt., 1967-70; comdr. 7th Armored Brigade, 1972-74; brig. gen. staff hdqrs. U.K. Land Forces, 1975-77, asst. chief gen. staff, 1978-80, gen. officer comdg. N.E. dist., 1980-82; sec., head adminstrn. Univ. Coll. London, 1982-91. Mem. Order of Brit. Empire, 1965 (comdr. 1977). Address: Owen's Farm Hook, Hampshire England

BAKER, J. A., II, executive management advisor and consultant, monetary architect, financial engineer; b. N.Y.C., Dec. 12, 1944; s. Leonard Ernest and Miriam Violet (Roché) B. Postgrad. in fin. svcs. mgmt., The Am. Coll., 1994—. ChFC, CLU, fin. planning advisor, assoc. registered investment advisor, property/casualty/liability field underwriter, comml. and personal lines; cert. instr., Monitor continuing and profl. edn.; cert. in advanced mgmt. Cons. mgr. Life Ins., N.Y.C., 1964-79; supr. Physician's Planning Group, Atty.'s Planning Svc., Bus. Planning Svcs., Profl. Svc. Corp., N.Y.C., 1979-81; CEO J A L B Enterprises, East Garden City, N.Y., 1980—; monitor N.Y. State continuing edn. program, 1996—, instr. continuing profl. edn. program, 1996—, licensing courses, 1996—. Bd. dirs. Medic Alert, Nassau County, N.Y., 1985-87; rep. The Living Bank; nominated mem.: Citizen Ambassador Program Internat. Fellow Life Underwriters Coun.; mem. Nat. Assn. Life Underwriters (emeritus mem., pres. Cortland chpt. 1974-75, legis. chair 1972-74, v.p. pub. info. Nassau County 1980-87, instr. Bklyn. 1987-90, Queens 1991-92), Am. Automobile Assn., Am. Coun. Ind. Life Underwriters, Soc. Fin. Svc. Profls., N.Y.C. Life Underwriters Assn., Profl. Ins. Agts. Fraternal Order of Police, N.Y. Civil Svc. Ret. Employee Assn., Gen. Agts. Mgrs. Assn. Internat. (charter mem. Falls Church chpt.), United Assn. of Entrepreneurs, N.Y. Jaycees (past dir.), Sovereign Mil. Order of Malta (pilgrim 1999), Am. Assn. Office: J A L B Enterprises Dept 2053 630 Old Country Rd East Garden City NY 11531-2053

BAKER, DAME JANET, vocalist; b. Hatfield, Yorks, Eng., Aug. 21, 1933; d. Robert Abbott and May Baker; m. James Keith Shelley, 1957. Student, York Coll. for Girls, Eng.; DMus (hon.), Birmingham, 1968, Leicester, 1974, London, 1974, Hull, 1975, Oxford, 1975, Leeds, 1980, Cambridge, 1984, Lancaster, 1983, York, 1984. Pres. London Sinfonia, 1986—; chancellor U. York, 1991—. Author: Full Circle, 1982. Trustee Found. Sport and Arts, 1991—; mem. Opera Bd. Royal Opera House, Convent Garden, 1994-97. Recipient Kathleen Ferrier Meml. prize, 1956, Queen's prize, 1959, Shakespeare prize F.v.S. Found. Hamburg, Grand prix French Nat. Acad. Lyric Recordings, 1975, Leonie Sonning prize Denmark, 1979, Gold medal Royal Philharmonic Soc., 1990; named Comdr. Ordre des arts et des lettres; Hon. fellow St. Anne's Coll., Oxford, 1975; hon. fellow Downing Coll., Cambridge, 1985. Avocation: reading. Address: care Transart UK Ltd, 8 Bristol Gardens, London W9 2JG, England

BAKER, JEFFREY CHARLES, telecommunications executive; b. Springfield, Ohio, Feb. 23, 1952; s. Robert Jones and Elizabeth (Hunt) B.; m. Linnea Liane Strehlow, May 14, 1977 (div. Mar. 1985); m. Maryanne Elise Lubresky, Mar. 24, 1986 (div. 1999); children: Megan Elisabeth, Kelle Marie. BFA in Comms., U. Cin., 1976. Acct. exec., sta. mgr. Continental Cablevision, Springfield, 1976-78; spl. projects mgr. Tele-Communications, Inc., Middletown, Ohio, 1978; dir. mktg. Viacom Inc., Dayton, Ohio, 1978-80, gen. mgr., 1980-82; gen. mgr. Viacom Inc., Everett, Wash., 1982-86, v.p., bus. & mktg. ops., 1986; v.p., gen. mgr. Viacom Inc., Tacoma, Wash., 1986-90; pres. Sound Comms., Inc., Sky Comms., Inc., Bellevue, Wash., 1991-; v.p., gen. mgr. Supershuttle, Phoenix, 1994-95; v.p. S.W. region Cornell Bokelmann, Phoenix, 1995-97; pres. ICS of Ariz., Phoenix, 1997—; mem. bd. dirs. Wash. State Cable Comms. Assn., Seattle, 1985-90; mem. Women in Cable, Seattle, 1984-90; com. chair Ohio Cable TV Assn., Columbus, Ohio, 1976-80. Republican. Presbyterian. Avocations: collecting vintage American-made electric guitars from 1950's and 60's. Home: 10417 E Texas Sage Ln Scottsdale AZ 85259-8522 Office: Gainey Ranch Town Ctr Ste 300 7702 E Doubletree Ranch Rd Scottsdale AZ 85258-2132

BAKER, JERRY HERBERT, executive search consultant; b. Concord, N.C., Aug. 16, 1946; s. Herbert Junius and Doylen Walsh (Lowe) B.; m. Cassandra Jo Martin, June 28, 1969; children: Josephine D., Martin M. BA, Wake Forest U., 1968; MDiv, Harvard U., 1971. Min. Congl. Ch., N.J. and Fla., 1971-73; human resources specialist Am. Thread Co., Stamford, Conn., 1974; exec. recruiter Miller Brewing Co., Milw., 1974-76; exec. search cons. B.F. & E., Atlanta, 1976-79, MSL Internat., Atlanta, 1979-83; ptnr. Lamalie Assocs, Inc., Atlanta, 1983-91, Baker & Parker Inc., Atlanta, 1991—. Trustee Wake Forest U., Winston-Salem, N.C., 1997—; bd. visitors Harvard Div. Sch., 1997—. Mem. Assn. Exec. Search Cons. (sec.-treas. 1986-91), Harvard Divinity Sch. Alumni Assn. (pres. 1995-97). Republican. Home: 375 Dogwood Trl SE Marietta GA 30067-4643 Office: Baker & Parker Inc 5 Concourse Pkwy NE Ste 2440 Atlanta GA 30328-6111

BAKER, JOHN HAMILTON, legal historian, educator; b. Sheffield, Yorks., Eng., Apr. 10, 1944; s. Kenneth Lee Vincent and Marjorie (Bagshaw) B.; m. Veronica Margaret Lloyd, Apr. 20, 1968; children: Alys Katharine, Anstice Elizabeth. LLB, Univ. Coll. London, 1965, PhD, 1968; LLD, U. Cambridge, 1984; LLD (hon.), U. Chgo., 1992. Barrister, 1966; Queen's Counsel, 1996. Asst. lectr. law Univ. Coll. London, 1965-67, lectr. law, 1967-71; libr. Squire Law Libr. U. Cambridge, 1971-73, lectr. law, 1973-83, reader in English legal history, 1983-88, prof. English legal history, 1988—. Author: Introduction to English Legal History, 1971, 3d edit., 1990, The Reports of Sir John Spelman, 1978, The Legal Profession and the Common Law, 1986, Readings and Moots at the Inns of Court, 1990, others; contbr. articles to profl. jours. Recipient Ames medal Harvard U., 1985; named Hon. Bencher, Inner Temple, 1988; U. Coll. London fellow, 1991, St. Catharine's Coll./Cambridge U. fellow, 1971—. Fellow Royal Hist. Soc., Brit. Acad.; mem. Selden Soc. (lit. dir. 1981—). Office: Cambridge U St Catharines Coll, Trumpington St, Cambridge CB2 1RL, England

BAKER, JOSEPHINE L. REDENIUS (MRS. MILTON G. BAKER), minister, civic leader, retired career officer, former public relations company executive; b. Oceanville, N.J., Aug. 31, 1920; d. Jacob and Josephine (Palmer) Redenius. Student, Columbia U., 1948-49, L.I. U., 1957-58, George Washington U., 1947-48; grad., U.S. Army Indsl. Coll., 1962; MA in Journalism, Am. U., 1963; LHD, Temple U., 1964; MA in Religious Studies, St. Charles Sem., 1981; MDiv., Eastern Baptist Theol. Sem., 1984; D Ministry, Ea. Bapt. Theol. Sem., 1990. Ordained Deacon Episcopal Ch., 1987. Enlisted as pvt. WAAC, 1943; advanced through grades to lt. col. U.S. Army, 1963; col. Pa. N.G., 1967; intelligence officer atomic installations throughout U.S. and Can., 1943-53; asst. office chief of staff Army Forces Far East, Japan, 1953-56; pub. info. officer Office Chief of Info., Washington, 1958-61; chief Women's Army Corps recruiting U.S. Army, 1962-66, U.S. Army Command info liaison officer, 1966-67, ret., 1967; dir. pub. rels. and devel. Valley Forge Mil. Acad. and Coll., Wayne, Pa., 1967-71, bd. trustees, 1970-79, 93—, chair pers. and benefits, 1993-99; pres. St. Cornelius the Centurian Chapel Valley Forge Mil. Acad. and Jr. Coll., Wayne, Pa., 1976—, life pres., 1997; pres. Potential Inc., Ardmore, Pa., 1979-83, Intercounty Trading Co., Inc., Surfside, Fla., 1976-80; with missionary Women to Women Fedn. Mission to No. China, 1993. Deacon All Souls' Episcopal Ch., Miami Beach, Fla., 1987-93; bd. dirs. Valley Forge Freedom Valley dist. Girl Scouts Am., Republican Women of Pa., Opera Guild of Miami; dir. St. Anne's Home for Women, Phila.; v.p. Episcopal Ch. Women, Diocese of Pa., 1982-84; pres. Episcopal Women, Diocese of S.E. Fla., 1990-93, mem. exec. bd., 1990-93; bd. dirs. Duncan Conf. Ctr, 1990-93, Delray Beach, Fla.; dr. of ministry All Saints Episcopal Ch., Norristown, Pa., 1993-97. Decorated Legion of Merit, Pa. Meritorious Service medal; U.S. Army Commendation medal with oak leaf cluster; recipient Order Golden Sword Valley Forge Mil. Acad., 1986, Martha Washington medal S.R., 1990; named Outstanding Alumnus Am. U., 1969. Mem. AAUW, Pub. Rels. Soc. Am., Am. Personnel and Guidance Assn., Am. Coll. Personnel Assn., Nat. Vocat. Guidance Assn., Am. Sch. Counselors Assn., Pa. Med. Missionary Soc. (dir. 1983-89), Am. Legion Aux., Ret. Officers Assn. (v.p. Valley Forge chpt. 1993—), Assn. U.S. Army (Anthony J. Drexel Biddle medal 1968), Army-Navy Union, Assn. Measurement and Evaluation in Guidance, Am. Legion, La Boutique Des Hult Chapeaux et Quarante Femmes, Emergency Aid of Pa., Women in Communications, Soc. of St. Francis (3d order), Ret. Officers Assn. (dist. v.p., 1993—), Mil. Order World Wars, Miami Heart Inst. Aux., Miami Heart Instl. Rev. Bd., Surf Club, Bald Peak Colony Club, Miami Beach Women's Club, Miami Beach Garden Club (chaplain), St. David's Golf Club, Acorn Club.

BAKER, LYNN R., health facility administrator; b. Dubai, United Arab Emirates, Apr. 2, 1969; d. Ahmled Abdulrahiu and Serena Monica (Mandody) B. BA in Bus., Ajman U., United Arab Emirates, 1990; BS in Economics, U. Am., Panama, 1997; MA in Internat. Bus., Am. U. Dubai, 1998. Architect DUTCO, Dubai, United Arab Emirates, 1982-84; sales exec. Poster Flags, Chiswick, U.K., 1986-87; acct. Gen. Med. Ctr., Dubai, 1989, adminstrv. officer, 1990, adminstrv. mgr., 1992, clin. mgr., 1995—; group dir. Group Aneres, Dubai, 1999—; freelance social psychol., Dubai, 1989-92; strategic mktg. adv., Gen. Med. Ctr., 1993-98; freelance mktg. cons., 1995-99. Contbr. articles to periodical. Avocations: horseback riding, swimming, sowash, reading. Phone: 0097142684994.

BAKER, MARK ALLEN, author, historian, consultant, graphologist; b. Binghamton, N.Y., Mar. 27, 1957; s. Ford William and Marilyn A. (Allen) B.; divorced; children: Aaron Anthony, Elizabeth Margaret, Rebecca Jeanne. BA, SUNY, Oswego, 1979. Computer operator Gen. Electric Corp., Liverpool, N.Y., 1980-81, tng. specialist, 1981-82; art dir. Genigraphics Corp., Liverpool, 1982-83, mgr. market research, 1983-85, exec. asst. to pres. and chief exec. officer, 1985-86, corp. bus. planner, 1986-90; pvt. rschr., 1986—; historian Internat. Boxing Hall Fame; appeared in numerous pubs. such as USA Today and also on TV, incluidng VH-1. Author: Baseball Autograph Handbook, I and II, 1990, Team Baseballs, All Sport Autograph Guide, 1994, Complete Guide to Boxing Collectibles, 1995, Auto Racing, 1995, Collector's Guide to Celebrity Autographs, 1996, Rock and Roll Memorabilia, 1997, The Standard Guide to Collecting Autographs, 1999, Advanced Autograph Collecting, 1999, Collector's Guide to Celebrity Autographs, 2000; contbr. articles to profl. jours. Lifetime donor mem. Baseball Hall Fame, Historian Internat. Boxing Hall of Fame. Mem. Am. Mgmt. Assn. (pres. 1985—), Assn. Computer Mfrs. (pres. 1985—), Assn. Med. Illustrators (corp. rep., pres. 1986—), Am. Assn. Individual Investors (pres. 1987—), Siggraph (pres. 1985—), Manuscript Soc. Avocations: forensic document analysis, literature, finance. Address: 166 Ridings Way Lancaster PA 17601-1730

BAKER, MARTI A(NN), human resources consultant; b. Indpls., Nov. 6, 1953; d. Donald A. and Georgia Ann (Pitcher) B.; 1 child, Courtney Jo Allison. BSN, Ind. U., 1976, JD, 1988. Staff nurse, charge nurse various hosps., Ind., 1976-92; clin. instr. nursing Ivy Tech. State Coll., Bloomington, Ind., 1980, Evansville (Ind.) Sch. Practical Nursing, 1982; atty. Price & Shula, Indpls., 1989-90; chief nurse cons. Ind. State Dept. Health, Indpls., 1992-95, program dir. info. dispute resolution Office Legal Affairs, 1995-97; benefits mgr. employee benefit divsn. State Personnel Dept., State of Ind., 1997-98; asst. dir. divsn. organiational devel. Family & Social Svcs. Adminstrn., State of Ind., 1998-99; human resources cons. Cmty. Hosps. Indpls., 1999—. Vol. Marion County Dem. Election, Perry Twp., 1992-99. Mem. Exec. Women in Health Care, Ind. Dem. Club, Alpha Chi Omega. Roman Catholic. Avocations: aviculture, camping, gardening, gourmet cooking, raising domestic livestock. E-mail: mabaker@commhospindy.org. Home: 3725 E Thompson Rd Indianapolis IN 46237-1537 Office: Cmty Hosps Indpls 1500 N Ritter Ave Indianapolis IN 46219-3027

BAKER, MARTIN WILLIAM, management consultant; b. Kingston, Surrey, Eng., Aug. 22, 1950; s. William French and Kathleen Audrey (Richards) B.; m. Elaine Rosemary France, July 27, 1973; children: Alexander Martin, Clare Jane. BS, Holloway, London, 1973; PhD, Rutherford, Kent, Eng., 1980. Chartered engr., chartered mathematician. Engr. Brit. Post Office, London, 1968-73; exec. engr. Brit. Telecom., London, 1973-78; comms. cons. CAP Ltd., London, 1978-82; dir. tech. UNICOM, London, 1982-85; prin. cons. York Devel. and Rsch., Reigate, Eng., 1985—; prin. cons. Planning and Strategy Ltd., Reigate, 1988-96, also bd. dirs.; mng. dir. York Devel. and Rsch. Ltd., Reigate, 1985—; lectr. on money mgmt., computers in tech. analysis, risk and trading. Author: Expanding the Scope of Technical Analysis, 1988; contbr. series of articles to profl. publs. Named Brain of Kent, Mensa Competition, 1975. Mem. Inst. Math. and Its Applications (assoc.), Soc. Tech. Analysts, Brit. Computer Soc., Malden and Dist. Soc. Model Engrs. (dir.). Office: York Devel & Rsch, 22 Belmont Rd, Surrey Reigate RH2 7EE, England

BAKER, MARY EVELYN, former church librarian, retired academic librarian; b. Columbus, Ohio, May 8, 1912; d. Abram Jackson and Martha Maria (Dailey) Shoemaker; m. Richard Heinley Baker, Sept. 18, 1937 (dec.); children: Richard Shoemaker, David Guy. BA, Ohio State U., 1934; BS in Libr. Sci., Western Res. U., Cleve., 1935. Mem. staff libr. Ohio State U., Columbus, 1935-37, 38-44, 1955-74, part-time libr., 1955-66, adminstrv. asst., 1958, serial cataloger, 1958-67, asst. reviser, sr. cataloger, 1967-68, head serial div. catalog dept., 1968-71, head catalog dept., 1971-74; libr. com. First Congl. Ch., Columbus, 1941-97, libr. co-chmn., 1962-65, 74-75, libr. chmn., 1976-97; past mem. ALA, sec. serials sect., resources and tech. div., 1970-73. Den mother Boy Scouts Am., Columbus, 1953-58; libr. co-chmn. Friendship Village, Dublin, Ohio, 1981-97, chmn., 1997—. Mem. Ohioana Libr. Assn. (past chmn. various coms., life mem.), PEO (telephone chmn. chpt. V 1987—), DAR (Indians com.), Ohio State Univ. Women's Club (past pres.), Agrl. Circle (past pres.), Franklin Co-Ret. Tchrs. Assn. (life mem.), Ohio Ret. Tchrs. Assn. (life mem.), Ohio State Alumni Assn. (life mem.), Polar Bear Alumni Assn. Columbus North H.S. (life), Alumni Assn. Univ. Sch. (life), Ohio State U. Retirees Assn. (life, bridge chmn. 1984—), Ohio Hist. Soc., Worthington Hist. Soc., Columbus Hist. Soc., Ch. Women United of Columbus and Franklin County, Columbus Mus. art, Columbus Zoo, Gypsies Travel Club, Motts Mil. Mus. (charter), Phi Mu (various offices including pres. active and alumni chpts.). Republican. Home: 6000 Riverside Dr Apt 233A Dublin OH 43017-1494

BAKER, MONA, translator, educator; b. Cairo, Sept. 20, 1953; arrived in Eng.; d. Saeed Ahmed El Hilali and Aziza Mustapha Hegazi; m. Mohammed Khalid, 1975 (div. 1977); m. Kenneth John Baker, Aug. 21, 1979. BA in English, Comparative Lit., Am. Univ., Cairo, 1976; MA in Spl. Applications of Linguistics, U. Birmingham, Eng., 1987. Freelance translator Eng., 1980-86; freelance editor COBUILD, Birmingham, Eng., 1988-92; projects mgr. COBUILD, Birmingham, 1992-93; hon. rsch. assoc. UMIST, Eng., 1994-95, reader in translation studies, 1995-2000, prof. translation studies, 2000—; lectr. U. Birmingham, 1988-92; chmn. edn. tng. Inst. Translation Interpreting, Eng., 1992-94; vis. prof. Middlesex U., London, 1995-97; cons. U. Sheffield, Eng., 1996—; mem. translation com. Arts Coun. Eng., 1996-99. Author: In Other Words, 1992, 6th edit., 1999; editor: Text and Technology, 1993, The Translator, 1995—, Routledge Encyclopedia of Translation Studies, 1998. Mem. British Comparative Lit. Assn. (exec. com. 1996-97), British Ctr. Literary Translation (adv. panel 1995-96), Internat. Fedn. Translators (rep. com. translator tng. and qualifications 1993-96). Avocations: research, reading literature in translation, travel. Home: 2 Maple Rd West, Manchester M23 9HH, England Office: UMIST Ctr for Translation, Dept Lang Engring PO Box 88, Manchester M60 1QD, England

BAKER, PETER, veterinary surgeon; b. Montreal, Que., Can.; s. Bruce Earle and Saxe Claire Baker; m. Elizabeth Baker; children: Carrie, Alison, William, Robert. Address: PO Box 92031, Norwood 2117, South Africa

BAKER, PETER ALAN, professional golfer; b. Shifnal, Eng., Oct. 7, 1967; s. Alan and Joan (Price) B.; m. Helen Yardley, Oct. 6, 1990; children: Georgina, Grace. Grad. high sch., Wolverhampton, Eng. Turned profl., 1986; mem. PGA European Tour; Winner Benson & Hedges Internat. Open, 1988, UAP Under 25s Championship, 1990, Dunhill Brit. Masters, 1993, Scandinavian Masters, 1993, Perrier Paris European 4-Ball, 1994; mem. Ryder Cup Team, 1993, Dunhill Cup Team, 1993, 98 (capt.), Eng. World Cup Team. Named Rookie of Yr., 1987. Avocations: music, cars, sports, Wolves Football Club. Office: c/o IMG (UK) Ltd, Pier House, Strand on Green, London W4 3NN, England

BAKER, REBECCA LOUISE, musician, music educator, consultant; b. Covina, Calif., Apr. 12, 1951; d. Allan Herman and Hazel Margaret (Maki) Flaten; m. Jerry Wayne Baker, Dec. 22, 1972; children: Jared Wesley, Rachelle LaDawn, Shannon Faith. Grad. high sch., Park River, N.D.; student, Trinity Bible Inst., 1968-69. Sec. Agrl. Stblzn. & Conservation Svc. Office, Park River, N.D., 1969; pianist, singer Paul Clark Singers & Vic Coburn Evangelistic Assn., Portland, Oreg., 1969-72; musician, singer Restoration Ministries Evangelistic Assn., Richland, Wash., 1972-80; musician, pvt. instr. Calvary Temple Ch., Shawnee, Okla., 1980-81; organist, choirmaster St. Francis Episcopal Ch., Tyler, 1984-87; co-founder, owner Psalmist Sch. of Music & Recording Studio, Whitehouse, 1983—; pianist/entertainer Willowbrook Country Club, Tyler, Tex., 1991—; pianist, vocalist Mario's Italian Restaurant, Tyler, 1994—; pianist Garner Ted Armstrong, Tyler, 1986—; pianist, dir. Children's Choir, Calvary Bapt. Ch., Tyler, 1987—; pianist, entertainer Ramada Hotel, Tyler, 1988-90; pianist Whitehouse (Tex.) Sch. Dist. choirs, 1988—; accompanist Tyler Area Children's Chorale, 1988-90, Univ. Interscholastic League; pvt. instr. keyboard and vocal. Composer: Religious Songs (12 on albums), 1979; pianist, arranger, prodr., rec. artist 6 albums; editor, arranger: Texas Women's Aglow Songbook, 1987; editor Shekinah Glory mag., 1989—; developer improvisational piano course; star, prodr. weekly, nationally syndicated mus. religious programs for TV, 1995, 96, Proclaim His Glory, 1997—; played for receptions honoring Gov. George Bush, Tex. Senator Phil Gramm and Congressman John Bryant. Performer, spkr. many charitable, civic and religious orgns., Tex. and U.S. including AAUW, Kiwanis Clubs; co-founder Psalmist Mins. Internat., 1988—; founder, pres. Christian Music Tchr.'s Assn., 1991; worship leader Mayor's Prayer Breakfast, Tyler, 1994. Mem. Women's Aglow Fellowship (music dir., spkr., performer at retreats and tng. seminars). Republican. Full Gospel. Avocations: travel, reading, interior decorating, collecting. Home and Office: Psalmist Music & Recording PO Box 961 Whitehouse TX 75791-0961

BAKER, RICHARD SOUTHWORTH, lawyer; b. Lansing, Mich., Dec. 18, 1929; s. Paul Julius and Florence (Schmid) B.; m. Kathleen E. Yull, 1956 (dec. 1964); m. Marina J. Vidoli, 1965 (div. 1989); children: Garrick Richard, Lydia Joy; m. Barbara J. Walker, 1997. Student, DePauw U., 1947-49; A.B. cum laude, Harvard, 1951; J.D., U. Mich., 1954. Bar: Ohio 1957, U.S. Dist. Ct. (no. dist.) Ohio 1958, U.S. Tax Ct. 1960, U.S. Supreme Ct. 1971, U.S. Ct. Appeals (6th cir.) 1972. Since practiced in Toledo; mem. firm Fuller & Henry, and predecessors, 1956-91; pvt. practice Toledo, 1991—; Chmn. nat. com. region IV Mich. Law Sch. Fund, 1967-69, mem.-at-large, 1970-85. Bd. dirs. Asso. Harvard Alumni, 1970-73; mem. Epworth Assembly, Ludington, Mich.. Served with AUS, 1954-56. Fellow Am. Coll. Trial Lawyers; mem. ABA, Ohio Bar Assn., Toledo Bar Assn., Lawyer-Pilots Bar Assn., Toledo Club, Harvard Club (pres. Toledo chpt. 1968-77), Capital Club, Phi Delta Theta, Phi Delta Phi. Office: 2819 Falmouth Rd Toledo OH 43615-2215

BAKER, RONALD PHILLIP, service company executive; b. Kansas City, Mo., Feb. 15, 1942; s. Harry and Ruth Sarah (Bornstein) B.; m. Marilyn Gitterman, Dec. 27, 1964 (div. Dec. 1993); children: Kevin, Corey; m. Dierdre Christensen, May 8, 1994. Student, U. Okla., 1960-63; BA in Sociology and Govt., U. Mo., Kansas City, 1965, postgrad., 1965. Acct. rep. Am. House and Window Cleaning Co., Kansas City, 1965-69; dist. ops. mgr. Am. Bldg. Services, Kansas City, 1969-72; pres. BG Maintenance Mgmt., Kansas City, 1972-86; chmn. bd. dirs. BGM Industries, Kansas City, 1987—; bd. dirs. Flo Harris Supporting Found., V.p. Jewish Community Ctr., Kansas City, 1985-88, pres., 1989-90; pres. Jewish Vocat. Svcs., Kansas City, 1979-81; bd. dirs. Beth Shalom Synagogue, Kansas City, 1985-89, Jewish Community Ctrs. Assn., 1989-93, exec. com., 1990-91; co-chmn. Jewish Fedn. Greater Kansas City, 1986-92, v.p., 1992-93; bd. dirs. Jewish Community Found. Greater Kansas City, 1991-94, strategic planning com., 1997. Mem. Bldg. Svc. Contractors Assn. Internat. (bd. dirs., chmn. seminars, conv. speaker, pres. club 1981-93, mem. edn. com. 1981-90, chmn. edn. com. 1989—, info. ctrl. com. 1985-93, chmn. ann. conv. 1988, exec. com. 1988—, treas. 1989, v.p. 1990-92, pres. 1994, chmn. fin. com. 1990, mem. exec. com., chair strategic planning task force 1989-90, chmn., CEO seminar com. 1997-99, strategic planning com. 1996—, govt. affairs com. 1996—), Bldg. Owners and Mgrs. Assn. Kansas City, Jewish Fedn. Kansas City (v.p. 1986-87, 91-93, co-chmn. fin. resources planning com., Young Leadership award 1981), Menninger Found. (pres. Topeka chpt. 1986—), Hallbrook Country Club, Sigma Alpha Mu, Delta Sigma Pi. Republican. Avocations: water sports, boating, snow skiing, running, reading. Office: BGM Industries 1225 E 18th St Kansas City MO 64108-1605

BAKER, RUTH HOLMES, retired secondary education educator; b. Tewksbury, Mass., July 8, 1922; d. William Angus and Anna Martha (Lynch) MacIntyre; m. William Otis Baker; children: Leigh Holmes Flannery, Bruce William, Christopher Doty, Douglas MacIntyre, Deborah Woodbury Black. BA, Tufts U., 1944; postgrad., U. Wyo., 1944-45, Union Theol. Sch., 1947-48, Columbia U., 1947-48. Cert. water safety instr. Instr. swimming ARC, Manchester-by-the-Sea, Mass., 1937-54, Wenham, Mass., 1954—; tchr., athletic dir. Shore Country Day Sch., Beverly, Mass., 1960-71, Gov. Dummer Acad., Byfield, Mass., 1972-79; tchr., coach Manchester-by-the-Sea H.S., Mass., 1980-83; bookstore and snack bar mgr. Pingree Sch., Hamilton, Mass., 1984—. Republican. Episcopalian. Home: 40 Cherry St Wenham MA 01984-1313

BAKER, TIMOTHY DANFORTH, physician, educator; b. Balt., July 4, 1925; s. Frank and Alice Elizabeth (Chandler) B.; m. Susan Lowell Pardee, June 23, 1951; children: Timothy, David, Susan. BA, Johns Hopkins U., 1948, MPH, 1954; MD, U. Md., 1952. Intern U. Md. Hosp., Balt., 1952-53; resident pub. health N.Y. State Dept. Pub. Health, N.Y.C., 1953-56; health officer Syracuse, N.Y., 1958-59; asst. and acting chief health USAID, India, 1956-58; assoc. prof. Johns Hopkins U. Sch. Pub. Health, Balt., 1959-67, asst. dean, 1959-77, prof. internat. health, health svcs. adminstrn., and environ. health, 1967—, pres. faculty gen. assembly, 1987—; dir. Hubert H. Humphrey scholars program Johns Hopkins U. Sch. Pub. Health, 1987—; v.p., dir. Univ. Assocs., 1973-77; vis. prof. epidemiology U. Minn., 1976; dir. Intermed., 1982—; cons. health planning, med. edn., Brazil, Burma, India, Indonesia, Taiwan, Saudi Arabia, Kuwait, Ukraine, Viet Nam, Yunnan, China, Armenia, Md., Calif., D.C.; external examiner U. Singapore. Author: Health Manpower in a Developing Economy, Assessment of Health Status and Needs, International Health Perspectives; contbr. articles to profl. publs. First vice chmn. Balt. com. Republican party; del., nominating com. Republican party; bd. dirs., treas. Pan Am. Health Edn. Found. Served with USAF, 1943-45; USPHS, 1956-58. Recipient Disting. Grad. award Balt. Polytechnic Inst. Fellow AAAS (govs. commn. on minority health, task force on violence); mem. Am. Pub. Health Assn. (chmn. epidemiology sect., internat. health sect., Lifetime Achievement award 1994), Md. Med. Soc. (chmn. health manpower com., ho. of dels.), Md. Pub. Health Assn. (pres.), Balt. Med. Soc. (chmn. med. care com.), Omicron Delta Kappa, Delta Omega. Republican. Home: 4705 Keswick Rd Baltimore MD 21210-2322 Office: Johns Hopkins U Sch Hygiene 615 N Wolfe St Baltimore MD 21205-2103

BAKER, TIMOTHY HOLLAND, physician, echocardiographer; b. Bridgwater, Eng., May 22, 1948; s. John Charles and Doreen Margaret (Bagnall) B.; m. Diana Cecilia Clegg, Nov. 24, 1973; children: Joanna Clare, Philippa Helen. B. in Medicine, Royal Free Hosp., London, 1972. Sr. house officer Orsett Hosp., Eng., 1973-75; Northampton Hosp., Eng., 1975-76; sr. prin. Congleton, Eng., 1976—; dir. Dept. Echocardiography, Macclesfield Hosp., Eng., 1984—. Recipient Handcock prize Royal Coll. Surgeons, Eng., 1972. Avocations: fishing, shooting. Home: Marton, Old School House School Ln, Macclesfield Cheshire SK11 9HD, England Office: Readesmoor Med Group, 29/31 West St, Congleton Cheshire CW12 1JP, England

BAKER, VINCENT LAMONT, professional basketball player; b. Lake Wales, Fla., Nov. 23, 1971. Grad., Hartford U., 1993. Player Milw. Bucks, 1993-97, Seattle Supersonics, 1997—. Named to NBA All-Rookie First Team, 1994, All-NBA Third Team, 1996-97, All-NBA Second Team, 1997-98, NBA All Star, 1995-97. Avocation: singing. Office: c/o Seattle Supersonics 190 Queen Anne Ave N Ste 200 Seattle WA 98109-4926

BAKER, WALTER WRAY, JR., lawyer; b. Raleigh, N.C., July 27, 1942; s. Walter Wray and Maggie Lee (Holland) B.; m. Jane Marlyn Green, June 14, 1964; children: Susan, Valerie, Walter. AA, Campbell Coll., 1962; AB, U.

N.C., 1964, JD, 1966. Bar: N.C. 1966, U.S. Dist. Ct. (ea. and mid. dists.) N.C., U.S. Supreme Ct. 1974. Rsch. asst. to chief justice N.C. State Supreme Ct., Raleigh, 1966-67; pvt. practice High Point, 1967-94; ptnr. Baker & Boyan, PLLC, High Point, 1994—; writer, lectr. continuing legal edn. personal injury & ethics; adj. prof. trial advocacy Wake Forest Sch. Law. Mem. N.C. Acad. Trial Lawyers (pres. 1985-86), High Point Bar Assn. (pres. 1985), N.C. State Bar (councillor 18th jud. dist.), Am. Bd. Trial Advocates, Joseph Br. Inn of Ct., Million Dollar Advocates Forum. Democrat. Mem. Wesleyan Ch. Office: Baker & Boyan PLLC 820 N Elm St High Point NC 27262-3920

BAKHAREV, BORIS VASILIEVITCH, radiophysicist, researcher; b. Baku, Azerbaijan, USSR, Aug. 28, 1946; s. Vasiliy Vasilievitch and Fanny Vladimirovna (Konevskaya) B.; m. Ludmila Petrovna Khyazeva, Mar. 14, 1968; children: Olga, Vladimir. BS in Radiophysics, Gorki State U., 1970. Probationer Inst. Cell Biophysics Russian Acad. Scis., Moscow, 1970-71, sr. labr. asst., 1971-72, engr., 1972-78, sr. engr., 1978-80, jr. rsch. worker, 1980-91, rsch. worker, 1991-98, sr. rsch. worker, 1998—. Author: Statistical Compuer Programs, 1989. Home: Microdist G-19-44, 142290 Pushchino Moscow, Russia Office: Russian Acad Scis, Inst Cell Biophysics, 142290 Pushchino Moscow, Russia

BAKHCHADJYAN, ROBERT, physical chemist, researcher; b. Gumry, Armenia, Feb. 27, 1957; arrived in France, 1995; s. Harutyun and Sima (Keshishyan) B.; m. Isabelle Chakiryan, Sept. 8, 1984; children: Harutyun, Anush. Degree in chemistry, Yerevan State U., 1979; DSc, Inst. Chem. Physics, Moscow, 1986, French Inst. Sci. Tech. Rsch., Paris, 1996. Jr. sci. rschr. Inst. Chem. Physics NAS of Armenia, Yerevan, 1979-81, sci. rschr. Inst. Chem. Physics, 1981-89, sr. sci. rschr. Inst. Chem. Physics, 1989-95; rschr., chemist CNRS Nat. Higher Sch. Synthesis, Processes, Chem. Engring., Aix-Marseilles, 1996—. Contbr. more than 45 articles to profl. jours. including Reports of Acad. Scis., Archivum Combustionis, and Internat. Jour. Chem. Kinetics; patentee in field. Grantee Internat. Sci. Found., U.S., 1994, Cmty. of Commons of Marseilles Province Met., France, 1997; postdoctoral fellow CNRS, 1996-98. Mem. Armenian Apostolic Ch. Avocations: chess, art, history of sciences. Office: CNRS UMR 6516 ENSSPICAM, Ave Escadrille Normandie-Niemen, 13397 Marseille Cedex 13, France

BAKHEIT, ABDEL MAGID, physician, medical educator, consultant; b. Kassala, Sudan, Nov. 23, 1949; m. Margaret Hamilton Thomson, 1994. DM with 1st class honors, LVOV, USSR, 1975; MSc, U. London, 1983; PhD, U. Glasgow (Scotland), 1990, MD, 1993. Diplomate European Bd. Phys. Medicine and Rehab. House physician Kassala (Sudan) Hosp., 1975-76; med. officer Medani Hosp., Sudan, 1976-80; sr. house physician, registrar Eng., 1982-87; sr. lectr. in rehab. medicine U. Southampton (Eng.), 1990-97; lectr. in neurology U. Glasgow, 1987-90; prof. U. Plymouth, Eng., 1997—; cons. physician Plymouth Cmty. Hosps. Trust, Eng., 1997—. Contbr. over 50 articles to profl. jours. Mem. Brit. Soc. Rehab. Medicine (Phillip Nichols prize 1993). Office: Beauchamp Ctr, Mount Gould Hosp, Plymouth PL4 7QD, England

BAKHSHIEV, NIKOLAY GRIGORIEVICH, adult education educator, researcher; b. Moscow, USSR, Jan. 31, 1930; s. Grigoriy Alexandrovich and Nadezhda Sergeevna (Kharitonova) B.; m. Galina Fedorovna Dmitrieva, Jan. 26, 1952 (dec. Sept. 1997); 1 child, Galina. Degree in Secondary Edn., Sch. 45, Leningrad, USSR, 1948; degree in Higher Edn. (hon.), Leningrad Inst. Precise Mechanics and Optics, 1954. Registered profl. engr. Rschr. State Optical Inst., Leningrad, USSR, 1954-61, sr. rschr., 1961-78, lab. chief, 1978-87, chief rschr., 1987—; lab. chief Leningrad State U., USSR, 1963-88; prof. Leningrad State U., 1988—; sci. coun., Leningrad State U., 1964-2000, State Optical Inst., 1968-2000; editl. bd. Jour. Flourescence, Balt., 1990-96, Jour. Optical Tech., St. Petersburg, USSR, 1990—. Author: Spectroscopy of Molecular Interactions, 1972, Introduction to Molecular Spectroscopy, 1974, 87; editor, co-author: Solvatochromism: Problems and Methods, 1989, Spectrochemistry of Intra- and Intermolecular Interactions, 1975, 6th rev. edit., 1995. Named Soros Prof., Soros Found., 1994; Internat. Sci. Found. grantee, 1994-95, Russian Found. Basic Rschs. grantee, 1993,96; recipient Scientific Works award St. Peterburg State U., 2000. Mem. Russian Acad. Natural Scis., Russian Optical Mem., Ho. Sci. Avocation: numismatics. E-mail: root@univ.chem.lgu.spb.su. Home: 31 Zheleznovodskaya St Apt 32, 199155 St Petersburg Russia Office: St Petersburg State U, 2 Univ pr Petrodvoretz, 198904 St Petersburg Russia

BAKHTEREV, VLADIMIR VASSILIEVICH, geophysicist, researcher; b. Asbest, Russia, Jan. 3, 1936; s. Vassiliy Ignatievich and Anna Yakovlevna (Fedorova) B.; m. Aleonora Petrovna Astafieva; children: Dmitry, Boris. Cert. mining engr., geophysicist, Sverdlovsk Mining Inst., Ekaterinburg, Russia, 1961; D of Geol. and Minerol. Scis., Russia Acad. Scis., Ekaterinburg, Russia, 1971; PhD in Tech. Scis., Russia Acad. Scis., Moscow, 1991. Engr., geophysicist Inst. Geophysics-Urals Br. Russian Acad. Scis., Ekaterinburg, 1961-63, jr. sci. rschr., 1963-75, sr. sci. rschr., 1975-85, maj. sci. rschr., 1985—. Contbr. over 100 articles to sci. jours.; inventor in field. Grantee Russian Found. Basic Rsch., 1996-97, 99—. E-mail: bakh@etel.ru. Home: 161 Bazhov str apt 214, 620055 Ekaterinburg Russia Office: Inst Geophy Urals Br RAS, 100 Amundsen str, 620219 Ekaterinburg Russia

BAKHTIN, VICTOR IVANOVICH, mathematics educator; b. Voronezh, Russia, Sept. 15, 1961; s. Ivan Alexeyevich and Antonina Andreyevna (Diomina) B. M in Math., Moscow State U., 1978-83, PhD in Math., 1987. Prof. math. Belarusian State U., Minsk, 1989—. Lt. Soviet Army, Moscow, 1987-89. Grantee Am. Math. Soc, 1993, 94, Internat. Sci. Found., 1993, Russian Acad. Natural Scis., 1994. Office: Belarusian State U Dept Physics, Fr Scoriny 4, 220 050 Minsk Belarus

BAKIRTZIS, CHARALAMBOS, archaeologist; b. Thessaloniki, Greece, Apr. 8, 1943; s. Nikolaos and Olga (Fezou) B.; m. Demetra Papanikola, Aug. 20, 1945; children: Nikolaos, Olga-Maria. BA, U. Thessaloniki, 1967, MA in Byzantine Archaeology, 1973, PhD, 1984. Curator Byzantine antiquities Ctrl. and Western Macedonia, Greece, 1973-76; prof. Byzantine archaeology U. Thessaloniki, Greece, 1988-98; ephoros Byzantine antiquities E. Macedonia and Thrace, Greece, 1976-97; ephoros Byzantine Antiquities Thessaloniki, 1997—; vis. scholar U. Ill., Urbana, 1984-85; dir. Greek archaeol. expedition to Cyprus, 1991—; mem. Com. Protection Holy Mount Athos, 1990-92, 94—, Ctrl. Archaeol. Com., 1999—. Author: Byzantina Tsoukalolagena, 1989, Archaeologikai Meletai, 1993, Miracula S. Demetrii, 1997; co-author: Philippi at the Time of Paul and After his Death, Contemporary Art and Archaeology Exposition Synaxis, 1995, Synaxis Maroneias, 1994. Fellow Archaeol. Soc. Athens, Christian Archaeol. Soc.; mem. Soc. Des Hommes Des Lettres Thessaloniki (com. mem.). Home: Philippou 47, 546 31 Thessaloniki Greece

BAKIS, HENRY GERALD HUBERT, geographer, sociologist, communications educator; b. Bône, Algeria, Nov. 29, 1949; arrived in France, 1962; m. Chantal Mamou, 1978; children: Jacques, Elisabeth, Elie. D in Humanities, U. Paris I, 1983; D in Geography, U. Paris VIII, 1974, M in Sociology, 1974. Monitor U. Paris VIII, 1971-73; chargé de cours U. I.U.T., St. Denis, France, 1974-75; journalist Editions Test, Paris, 1976; rschr. France Câble and Radio, Paris, 1976-78, France Telecom., CNET, Issy-les-Moulineaux, France, 1978-95; prof. U. Montpellier (France) III, 1995—; head rsch. U. Paris IV-Sorbonne, 1991-96; expert Obs. Télécomm. dans. la Ville, Paris, 1991-95; expert Plan Urbain, 1986. Author: Les réseaux et leurs enjeux sociaux, 1993, Géopolitique de l'information, 1987, Entreprise, espace, telecommunication, 1988; editor Communication Geography Newsletter, 1985-95, Netcom-Networks and Communication Studies, 1987—; issue editor Internat. Polit. Sci. Rev., July 1995. Chmn. Internat. Geog. Union Commn. on Networks and Telecomm. Geography, 1992—. Served with French Army, 1975-76. E-mail: henry.bakis@univ-montp3.fr. Office: U Montpellier III, BP 5043 Rte de Mende, F-34032 Montpellier Cedex 1, France

BAKKER, JAMES WESSEL, insurance company executive; b. Jakarta, Indonesia, May 11, 1930; arrived in Australia, 1951; s. Cornelis Christian and Elfrieda Stephanie (Bertsch) B.; m. Shirley May Murray, Nov. 19, 1960; children: Robert, Victoria. Mgr. Eagle Ins., Australia, 1960-64; mng. dir. Ind. Ins. Brokers, Australia, 1964-83; CEO Sedgwick Internat., 1983-86; mng. dir. Jammay Group, Australia, 1986—. Fellow Australian Inst. Mgmt.; mem. Nat. Ins. Brokers Assn. Australia (founding dir.), Australian Ins. Inst. (assoc.), Chartered Ins. inst. London (assoc., life mem.), Lions (charter pres. Brisbane Ctrl. chpt.), Australia Netherlands C. of C. Inc. (life mem., founding pres.). Avocations: croquet, bridge, chess.

BAKLANOV, GRIGORIY YAKOVLEVICH, writer; b. Voronezh, Russia, Sept. 11, 1923; s. Jakov Friedman and Ida Kantor; m. Elga Sergeeva, 1953; 2 children. Student, Gorky Inst. Lit., Moscow. Editor-in-chief Znamya, 1986-93. Author: In Snegiri, 1954, Nine Days, 1958, The Foothold, 1959, The Dead Are Not Ashamed, 1961, July 41, 1964, Friends, 1975, Forever Nineteen, 1980, The Youngest of the Brothers, 1981, Our Man, 1990, Time to Gather Stones, 1989, Once it was the Month of May, 1990, The Moment Between the Past and the Future, 1990, Come through the Narrow Gates, 1993, Short Stories, 1994, Kondratiy, 1995, Short Stories, 1996, And then the Marauders Come, 1996, My General, 1999, Life Awarded Twice, 1999. Soldier to lt. of artillery, 3rd Ukranian Front, 1941-45. Recipient U.S.S.R. State prize, 1982, Russian Fedn. State prize, 1998. Avocation: gardening. Fax: 334-6136. Address: Lomonosovsky Prospekt 19, Apt 82, 117311 Moscow Russia

BAKONYI, IMRE, physicist; b. Va'l, Fejér Megye, Hungary, Mar. 27, 1948; s. Imre and Maria (Bakonyi) Nagy; m. Judit Marianna Moser, Feb. 15, 1975; children: Zsuzsanna, Borba'la. Diploma, Eötvös U., Budapest, Hungary, 1972, PhD, 1976. Sci. rsch. fellow Ctrl. Rsch. Inst. Physics, Budapest, 1976-91; sr. rsch. scientist Rsch. Inst. Solid State Physics, Budapest, 1992—, dept. head, 1995—; vis. rsch. fellow U. Pasteur, Strasbourg, France, 1981, Max Planck Inst., Stuttgart, Germany, 1990-91; Humboldt fellow U. Munich, Germany, 1985-86; Brit. Coun. Sci. fellow U. Bristol, 1999. Contbr. more than 100 articles to profl. jours.; co-editor conf. procs. Mem. Eötvös Phys. Soc. (Z. Gyulai award 1989), European Phys. Soc., Materials Rsch. Soc. E-mail: bakonyi@power.szfki.kfki.hu. Office: Hungarian Acad Sci, Rs Inst, Solid St Physics, PO Box 49, H-1525 Budapest Hungary

BAKOPOULOS, EMMANOUIL, member European Parliament; b. Thessaloniki, Greece, Oct. 3, 1942. Mem. European Parliament, Brussels; mem. com. on regional policy, transport and tourism, com. on environ. pub. health and consumer policy, mem. substitute dels. to European Union-Estonia Joint Parliamentary Com. and Hungary Joint Parliamentary Com. mem. Bur., Condfed. Group of European United Left/Nordic Green Left. Office: Vouli ton Ellinon, Bureau DIKKI, Syntagma, Athens Greece*

BAKOS, GEORGE CHRIS, engineering educator, consultant; b. Georganades, Trikala, Greece, Apr. 18, 1965; s. Chris and Maria (Michael) B. BS, MS, Democritus U., Xanthi, Greece, 1988; PhD, U. Liverpool (Eng.), 1991; Tech. Diploma, Mil. Sch., Pirgos, Greece, 1992. Researcher Univs. Rsch. Reactor, Risley, Eng., 1988-90, U. Liverpool, 1988-91; lectr. U. Thrace, Xanthi, Greece, 1993-98; asst. prof. U. Thrace, Xanthi, 1998—; cons. Seners Ltd., Athens, 1998—; guest scientist NIST, Md., 1997, Chiba U., Tokyo, 1997. Contbr. articles to profl. jours. Tech. splst. Tech. Br., 1992-93. Rsch. grantee Soc. EIE, 1996-97, DAAD, 1996, Ministry Edn., Russia, 1997; recipient Matsumae Internat. award, 1997, Fulbright Sr. award, 1997. Mem. A.S.H.R.A.E., I.E.E., I.S.E.S. Avocations: music, chess, golf, volleyball, travel. Office: Democritus U Thrace, VAS Sofias (PROKAT), 67 100 Xanthi Thrace, Greece

BAKOS, JÓZSEF, chemist, researcher; b. Budapest, Hungary, Oct. 22, 1960; s. József Béla and Józsefné (Ladányi) B.; m. Mária Krázel, Dec. 30, 1988; 1 child, Gergely. MSc in Chemistry, Eötvös L. U., Budapest, 1985. Rschr. Nat. Rsch. Inst. for Radiobiology and Radiohygiene, Budapest, 1985—. Contbr. articles to sci. publ. Mem. EBEA. Office: Nat Rsch Inst Radiobiol/Hyg, Anna u 5, H-1775 Budapest Hungary

BAKOS, LUCIO, dermatologist, educator; b. Zadar, Croatia, Nov. 18, 1942; arrived in Brazil, 1951; s. Antonio and Nevenka (Kraljev) B.; m. Margaret Marchiori, Nov. 30, 1968; children: Renato, Mauricio. Physician, Faculty Medicine, Porto Alegre, Brazil, 1966, dermatologist, 1968; MD, Fed. U., Rio de Janeiro, 1984, PhD, 1990. vis. scholar Cambridge (Eng.) U., 1972; vis. rsch. fellow London Sch. Hygiene and Tropical Medicine, 1989. Physician Sec. of Health, Porto Alegre, 1968—; asst. prof. Faculty Medicine, Porto Alegre, 1969-84, assoc. prof., 1984-90, full prof., 1991—; head svc. of dermatology Hosp. de Clinicas, Porto Alegre, 1981—, founder, head residency in dermatology, 1982—. Contbr. articles to profl. jours. Fellow Am. Acad. Dermatology, Brazilian Soc. Dermatology (1st prize rsch. in dermatology 1995, 2nd prize rsch. in dermatology 1996), Internat. Soc. Dermatology, Brazilian Group Melanomas (founder). Avocation: yachting. Home: N S Aparecida 71, 91920690 Porto Alegre Brazil Office: Hosp de Clinicas, Ramiro Barcelos 2350, Porto Alegre Brazil

BAKOSS, STEPHEN LEWIS, civil engineering educator; b. Szombathely, Hungary, Mar. 7, 1938; s. Anthony Steven and Maria (Vlasits) B.; m. Eleonora Irene Heltay, Feb. 10, 1961; children: Jo-Ann Nicole, Richard Heltay. B of Engring., U. Sydney, Australia, 1961; M of Engring. Sci., U. NSW, Australia, 1969; MS, U. Calif., Davis, 1975; PhD, U. NSW, Australia, 1985. Constrn. engr. NSW Pub. Svc., Australia, 1960-65; cons. engr. Willing and Partners, Sydney, Australia, 1966; design engr. Dept. of Main Rds., NSW, Australia, 1967-69; lectr. NSW Inst. Tech., Sydney, Australia, 1969-74; sr. lectr., prof. U. Tech., Sydney, Australia, 1975-88, head Sch. of Civil Engring., 1988-93, alternate dean Faculty of Engring., 1990-94, prof., 1989—; dir. Ctr. for Local Govt. Edn. and Rsch., 1990-94; dir. Ctr. for Built Infrastructure Rsch., 1999—. Contbr. numerous publs. on structural mechanics to profl. jours. Internat. fellow Hungarian Acad. Engring., 1993; hon. mem. of senate Tech. U., Budapest, Hungary. Fellow Instn. of Engrs. Australia; mem. Internat. Assn. Bridge and Structural Engrs. Avocations: tennis, bridge, theatre, travel, wine. E-mail: steve.baskoss@uts.edu.au. Home: 1 Calool Rd, Beecroft 2119, Australia Office: U Technology Sydney, CBIR, Broadway 2007, Australia

BAK-ROMANISZYN, LEOKADIA, gastroenterology, educator, pediatrician; b. Mielec, Poland, Apr. 14, 1957; d. Michal and Janina (Kozioł) Bak; m. Mirosław Stanislaw Romaniszyn, Oct. 17, 1992. MD, Med. U., Łódź, Poland, 1982, 1st degree in pediatrics, 1986, 2d degree in pediatrics, 1992; PhD, Mil. Med. U., Łódź, 1996, 3d degree in gastroenterology, 1998. Jr. asst. dept. pediatrics Hosp. TB and Pulmonary, Łódź, 1982-83; asst. Inst. Mother's and Children's Diseases, Łódź, 1983-88; lectr., rschr. assoc. Polish Mother's Meml. Hosp., Łódź, 1988-89; sr. lectr., rsch. assoc. Mil. Med. U., Inst. Polish Mother's Meml. Hosp., 1989-96, asst. prof. dept. pediatrics, 1996—. Contbr. articles and abstracts to profl. publs. Grantee Polish. Sci. Found., 1992-95, Environ. Protection Fund for Province of Łódź, 1995-98, 99-2000, Polish Acad. Scis., 2000—; recipient 1st award sci. com. 25 Congress of Polish Pediat. Sci., 1997. Mem. Polish Pediat. Soc., Polish Gastroenterologic Soc. (1st award sci. com. VI congress 1994, 97), N.Y. Acad. Scis. Avocations: embroidery, travel. Home: Chelmonskiego 12, Apt 17, 93-139 Łódź Poland Office: Mil Med U Inst Polish Meml, Rzgowska Str 281, 93-338 Łódź Poland

BAKSHI, SANDHYA ARUN, anesthesiologist, consultant; b. Amravati, India, Dec. 15, 1958; s. Prabhaker Ganesh Sargaonkar and Padma Prabhkar (Chincholikar) S.; m. Arun Purushottam Bakshi, July 5, 1983; children: Shreyas, Priyanka. MBBS, Govt. Med. Coll., Nagpur, India, 1980, diploma in Anesthesiology, 1983, MD in Anesthesiology, 1985; diploma in Info. Tech., Pune, India, 1999. Resident G.M.C., Nagpur, India, 1981-82; resident G.M.C., Ambajogai, India, 1983-85, lectr. in anesthesiology, 1986, sr. lectr. in anesthesiology, 1994—; postgrad. tchr. Marathwada U., Aurangabad, India, 1984; officer in charge of libr., Dept. Anesthesiology, Ambajogai, India, 1993—. Author: Indian Journal of Anaesthesia, 1990, 94, Tropical Doctor, 1999; editor: Anaesthesia News Bulletin, 1997, 98. Med. camps Lions Club, Latur, India, 1988; advisor Ladies Club, Ambajogai, India, 1999. Recipient Spl. prize Best Paper, Indian Soc. of Care, Bombay, India, 2995, 1dt prize for Best Paper, Indian Soc. Anaesthetist, India, 1998. Mem. Indian SOc. Anaesthetist, Med. Tchrs. Assn. Avocations: reading. singing, listening to music, table tennis, travel. Home phone: 02446-47769. Office phone: 02446-47060. Home: No P-6-4 Medical, Ambajogai 431517, India Office: Dept Anaesthesiology, Govt Rural Medical College, Ambajogai 431517, India

BAKSHT, FEDOR GRIGORIY, physicist; b. St. Petersburg, Russia, Oct. 19, 1935; s. Grigoriy Arkadiy and Angelica Fedor (Lerman) B.; m. Galina Boris Artsyhovskaya, June 27, 1969. Engr./Physicist, Electrotech. U., St. Petersburg, 1957; Cand. Phys.-Math. Scis., Ioffe Inst., 1966, D Phys.-Math. Scis., 1971. Sci. rschr. Ioffe Inst., St. Petersburg, 1957-77, sr. sci. rschr., 1977-86, leading sci. rschr., 1986-95, prin. sci. rschr., 1995-99, head lab., 1999—; mem. sci. coun. dept. plasma physics, atomic physics and astrophysics, Ioffe Inst., 1989—, mem. sci. coun. for award of sci. degrees on plasmaphysics, gasdynamics and math., 1993—. Co-author: Thermionic Converters and Low-Temperature Plasma, 1973 (Russian), 1978 (English), Mathematical Modelling of the Processes in Low-Voltage Plasma-Beam Discharge, 1990; contbr. articles to profl. jours. Grantee Russian Found. Fund. Rsch., 1994-95, Internat. Sci. Found., 1994-95, 1995, Internat. Assn./Brussels, 1995-97. Mem. N.Y. Acad. Scis. Office: Ioffe Phys-Tech Inst, 26 Polytechnicheskaya, 194021 Saint Petersburg Russia

BAKULE, LUBOMÍR, researcher, educator; b. Prague, Czechoslovakia, Sept. 19, 1946; s. Václav and Věra (Roubíčková) B.; m. Blažena Hradilova, Dec. 18, 1976; children: Martin, Dana. MS, Czech Tech. U., Prague, 1969; PhD, Acad. Scis., Prague, 1974. Cert. control engring. Rsch. asst. Acad. Scis., Prague, 1973-74, rschr., 1974-79, sr. rschr., 1979-88, dir. rsch., 1988—; cons. Power Rsch. Inst., Prague, 1976, Water Rsch. Mgmt. Inst., Prague, 1985-89; vis. prof. Tech. U. Catalonia, Barcelona, 1991-94, U. of the Basque Country, Bilbao, Spain, 1995-96. Editor: 2nd Formator Symposium, 1975, 3rd Formator Symposium, 1979, 4th Formator Symposium, 1983; contbr. articles to profl. jours. Grantee Acad. Finland, Helsinki, 1977, Acad. Scis., Berlin, 1984, DFG, Bonn, 1988, NSF, Washington, 1990, Spanish Govt., Madrid, 1991-92, Generalitat, Barcelona, 1992-94, Basque Govt., Vitoria, Spain, 1995-96 Acad. Scis., Prague, 1993-95, 98—. Mem. Internat. Fedn. Automatic Control (tech. com. large scale systems), Czech Soc. for Cybernetics and Informatics. Avocations: tourism, swimming. E-mail: bakule@utia.cas.cz. Fax: 420-2-688 4903. Office: Inst Info Theory Automation, Pod vodarenskou vezi 4, 182 08 Prague 8, Czech Republic

BAL, ANUPAM DEEP SINGH, information technology engineer; b. Patiala, Punjab, India, Sept. 12, 1970; s. Sant Singh and Adarsh Kaur Bal. B Computer Engring., Amravati U., Maharashtra, India, 1993; postgrad. in computer sci., Newcastle (Australia) U., 1996; M of Engring., U. Tech. Sydney, Australia, 1996. Cert. Inst. Engrs. Australia. Tech. specialist Icom Solutions Pty. Ltd., Sydney, 1997; info. tech. engr. Sunbeam Corp. Ltd., Campsie, Australia, 1997—; cons. Icom Solutions Pty. Ltd., 1998—. Mem. AAAS, IEEE, N.Y. Acad. Scis., Assn. Computing Machinery. Jat Sikh. Avocations: American literature, running, weight training, golf. Office: Sunbeam Corp Ltd MIS Dept, Wade St, Campsie NSW 2194, Australia

BAL, PARAM AJEET SINGH, broadcasting executive; b. Singapore, June 2, 1936; s. Tara Singh and Gurcharan Kaur (Thakar) B.; m. Naresh Kaur Phoolka, Jan. 14, 1966; children: Parvesh Kaur, Brindha Kaur, Ratanesh Kaur. BA, U. Malaya, Singapore, 1959, BA in History with honors, 1960; MA in Econs. with honors, Australian Nat. U., 1963. Temporary grad. tchr. Ministry of Edn., Singapore, 1960-61; adminstrv. officer Singapore Adminstrv. Svc., 1963-70, asst. sec., prin. asst. sec., 1970-77, dep. sec., 1977-82; asst. gen. mgr. Singapore Broadcasting Corp., 1982-94; sr. v.p. TV Corp. of Singapore, 1994-96; dir. Singapore Broadcasting Authority, 1997-98; dep. sec.-gen. Asian Media Info. Comm. Ctr., 1998-99; chmn. Media Rsch. Pte Ltd., Singapore, 1989-97; dir. Asian Mass Comm. Rsch. and Info. Ctr., Singapore, 1995—. Mem. com. Singapore Sikh Adv. Bd., 1975-80; mem. Ulu Pandan Citizens Consultative Com., Singapore, 1992; mem. Coun. of Elders, Singapore, 1992—; mem. com. Centre Sikh Gurdwara Bd., Singapore, 1995-99. Served with Singapore Mil., 1952070, 2d lt. People's Def. Force, 1966-70. Recipient Pub. Adminstrn. medal Singapore Govt., 1969; Commonwealth scholar Australian Govt., 1961. Sikhism. Avocations: sports (golf and sailing), community service. Home: 31 Greenleaf Rd, 279332 Singapore Singapore

BALA, OVIDIU EUGEN, surgeon; b. Sibiu, Romania, Apr. 22, 1966; s. Mircea George and Brandusa Zina Bala. MD, U. Med./Pharm. I. Hatieganu, Cluj, Romania, 1991. Cert. surgeon Romanian Health Ministry. Physician County Hosp., Cluj, 1991-92; resident in gen. surgery Surg. Clinic III, Cluj, 1992-95, surgeon, 1995—; sr. lectr. U. Medicine and Pharmacy I. Hatieganu, Cluj, 1995—; instr. Tng. Ctr. for Laparoscopic Surgery, Cluj, 1995—; cons. surgeon Surg. Clin. III, Cluj, 1999—; spkr. in field. Contbr. chpts. to books. Mem. Romanian Soc. Laparoscopic Surgery and Stapling (treas.), Romanian Soc. Hepato-Bilio-Pancreatic Surgery, Internat. Coll. Surgeons, European Digestive Surgery Soc., N.Y. Acad. Scis., Internat. Soc. Surgery. Orthodox Christian. Avocations: music (classical, jazz, progressive), travel, museums, basketball, computers. E-mail: obala@personal.ro or ovi@medscape.com. Office: Surg Clinic III, Croitorilor 19-21, Cluj Romania

BALABAN, MILOSLAV ALEXANDROVICH, scientist, educator; b. Odessa, Ukraine, USSR, June 7, 1927; s. Alexandre Pavlovich Balaban and Klavdia Konstantinovna Gus.; m. Anna Andreevna Nikitina, May 5, 1949; children: Andrew, Pavel, Olga. Diploma in tchg., Pedinstitute, Gorky, USSR, 1949; PhD, Linguistic U., Moscow, 1962. Secondary sch. tcur. USSR, 1949-56; chair dept. Pedagogical Inst., Paporogyo, Ukraine, 1959-66; docent Pedagogical Inst., Orekhovo-Zuevo, USSR, 1967-77; sr. scientist Moscow State U., 1978—. Author: English for Technical Schools, 1957, Linguistic Data in Automata, 1985, Park-School, 1992, (with Tamas Gergely) Human Mind: Its Development, Use and Abuse, 1994. With Soviet Air Force, 1944-45. Home: ul Textilnaya 21 kv 55, 142611 Orekhovo-Zuevo Moscow, Russia Office: Moscow State U Computer Ctr, Vorobyevy Gory, 119899 Moscow Russia

BALABAN, MURAT OMER, food science educator; b. Ankara, Turkey, Feb. 5, 1952; came to U.S., 1977; s. Faruk Mehmet and Selma (Fetgeri) B.; m. Canan Bayezit, Aug. 10, 1977; 1 child, Denis Tan. BChemE, Mid. East Tech. U., 1976; PhD in Food Sci. & Tech., U. Wash., 1984. Ind. software cons., 1984-85; postdoctoral rsch. assoc. food sci. dept. Rutgers U., New Brunswick, N.J., 1985-86; asst. prof. food processing & engring. U. Fla., Gainesville, 1986-91; assoc. prof. food processing & engring. U. Fla., 1991-97, prof., 1997—; mem. scientific adv. bd. FMC Corp., 1991—; ops. analysis group Singleton Seafood, Tampa, Fla. Assoc. editor Jour. Aquatic Food Product Tech., 1997-99; editl. bd. Food Tech. in Turkey. Recipient Food Engrng. award and medal Food Process Engring. Inst., 1998, U. Fla. Productivity award, 1999; Fulbright scholar, 1995. Mem. Nat. Assn. Colls. & Tchrs. Agr., Inst. Food Technologists (exec. com. food engring. group 1989-92, ann. program com., exec. com. seafood divsn. 1995-99), Am. Soc. Agrl. Engrs., Inst. Thermal Processing Specialists, Tropical and Subtropical Fisheries Soc. (exec. com. 1994-99), Gamma Sigma Delta. Home: 4008 NW 122nd St Gainesville FL 32606-3631 Office: U Fla FSHN 359 Gainesville FL 32611

BALACHANDRAN, AMMU, lawyer; b. Madras, India; d. Ouseph and Philomena (Thomas) Joseph; m. Krishnamurthy Balachandran, Apr. 9, 1967. BSc, U. Madras, 1959, MSc in Marine Zoology, 1963; LLB, U. Kerala (India), 1976. Legal advisor Nicco Cables Ltd., Madras, 1984—, Shipping Corp., Bombay, 1986—, Union Bank India, Madras, 1988—, State Bank Mysore, Madras, 1989—; counsel for ctrl. govt. at Madras Govt. of India, New Delhi, 1993-96; legal advisor Reliance Industries Ltd., Ahemedabad, India, 1996; visitor U.S. Info. Agy. Bur. Edn. Cultural Affairs, Washington, 1985. Contbr. articles to profl. legal jours. Mem. Joint Action Coun. for Women, Madras, 1990—, Madras Legal Aid Bd., 1990—; v.p. City Civic Welfare Fedn., Madras, 1992-93; legal advisor T. Nadu Slum Dwellers Fedn., Madras, 1995—. Fellow Indian Coun. Arbitration; mem. Women Lawyers Assn. (pres. 1989-91), Assn. Social Health (v.p. 1995—), Assn. Constnl. Empowerment (pres., founder 1996). Avocations: writing legal articles, painting, reading, German and French language study. Home and Office: Falcon, 13 Dr Muniappa Rd, Madras 600010, India

BALACHANDRAN, CHIDHAMBARAM, veterinary pathologist, educator; b. Mannargudi, Tamil Nadu, India, July 28, 1957; parents Ramalingam Chidhambaram and Chidhambaram Pushpavalli; m. Balachandran Suseela, Apr. 7, 1982. B in Vet. Sci., Madras Vet. Coll., Chennai, India, 1980; M in Vet. Sci., Madras Vet. Coll., 1984. Asst. prof. Tamil Nadu Vet. and Animal Scis. U., Chennai, 1980-88, assoc. prof., 1988-96, prof., 1996—. Contbr. articles to profl. jours. Mem. Indian Assn. Vet. Pathologists (life),

Indian Poultry Sci. Assn. (life), Tamil Nadu Vet. Coun. (life). Home: 10 Ranga Nagar III St, Kilkattalai 600117, India Office: Tamil Nadu Vet & Animal Scis U, Centralised Clin Lab Madras Vet Coll, Chennai 600007, India

BALACHANDRAN, KRISHNAN, mathematician, researcher, educator; b. Muthugapatty, India, Mar. 25, 1956; s. Krishnan Kolanda Gounder and Chinnammal Krishnan; m. Poongodi Balachandran, Sept. 7, 1989; 1 child, Parithi. BSc in Math., U. Madras, India, 1976, MSc in Math., 1978; BEd in Methods of Tchg. Math., U. Mysore, India, 1979; MPhil in Applied Math., U. Madras, 1980, PhD in Control Theory, 1985. Jr. rsch. fellow Bharathiar U., Coimbatore, India, 1981-83, sr. rsch. fellow, 1983-85, postdoctoral fellow, 1985; lectr. Govt. Arts Coll., Namakkal, India, 1985-86, Madras U., 1986-88; reader Bharathiar U., 1988-94, prof. math., 1994—; vis. fellow U. Tenn., Chattanooga, 1993; vis. scientist Internat. Ctr. for Theoretical Physics, Trieste, Italy, 1987, 90; vis. prof. Sophia U., Tokyo, 1998; vis. rsch. prof. Pusan Nat. U., South Korea, 1999. Contbr. over 150 articles to profl. jours. Fulbright fellow, Washington, 1996, Chandna Math. award, 1999. Mem. Am. Math. Soc., Indian Math. Soc. (life), Indian Sci. Congress Assn. (life). Avocation: reading. Fax: 91-422-422387. E-mail: kbc@bharathi-ernet.in. Office: Bharathiar U, Dept Math, Coimbatore 641 046, India

BALACHANDRAN, SWAMINATHAN, industrial engineering educator; b. Coimbatore, India, Nov. 6, 1946; s. Ardhanari Swaminathan and Karunambal (Chettiar) B.; m. Lalitha Kathiresan, Dec. 1, 1976; children: Jay Shankar, Dave Kumar. BME, U. Madras, India, 1968; M in Aerospace Engring., Ind. Inst. Sci., 1970; PhD in Indsl. Engring., Va. Poly. Inst. and State U., 1984. Grad. rsch. asst. Va. Poly. Inst. and State U., Blacksburg, 1974-76, instr. indsl. engring., 1976-80, asst. prof., 1980-85; assoc. prof. U. Wis., Platteville, 1985-88; prof. Va. Poly. Inst. and State U., Platteville, 1986—, prof. indsl. engring., 1988—; chmn. indsl. engring. U. Wis., Platteville, 1986-94; program evaluator Accreditation Bd. for Engring. and Tech.; cons. in field; expert witness in product liability cases. Reviewer profl. jours. NSF grantee, 1988. Mem. Inst. Indsl. Engring. (sr.), Soc. Mfg. Engrs., Am. Soc. Engr. Edn., Am. Soc. Quality Control (sr.), Am. Prodn. and Inventory Control Soc., Human Factors and Ergonomics Soc., Inst. Ops. Rsch. and Mgmt. Studies, Phi Kappa Phi, Alpha Pi Mu. Hindu. Avocations: collecting stamps, playing tennis, swimming, playing table tennis. Home: 270 Flower Ct Platteville WI 53818-1914 Office: U Wis Dept Mech Indsl Engring Indsl Engring Program 1 University Plz Platteville WI 53818-3001

BALACHANDRAN, WAMADEVA, electronics systems educator, consultant; b. Inuvil, Jaffna, Sri Lanka, July 19, 1946; arrived in Eng., 1974.; s. Selliah and Ratnambikai (Vairamuttu) Wamadeva; m. Helen Rose Watson, Sept. 25, 1978; children: Bavani-Sarah, Ashley Amaran, Sophie Preya. BSc, U. Sri Lanka, Colombo, 1971; MSc, U. Bradford, Eng., 1975, PhD, 1979. Demonstrator, tutor U. Sri Lanka, 1971; contract tchr. Ministry of Edn., Freetown, Sierra Leone, 1971-74; part-time demonstrator U. Sierra Leone, Freetown, 1972-74; rsch. asst. Water Rsch. Ctr., Stevenage, Eng., 1975-78, sci. officer, 1978; rsch. fellow U. Southampton, Eng., 1979-83; lectr. in electronics U. Surrey, Guildford, Eng., 1984-91, sr. lectr., 1991-93, reader in electrostatic sys., 1993-95, prof. electronic syss., 1995—, head dept. systems engring., 1999—; cons. via sole trader co. GEST, Guildford, 1992—; cons. in field for 19 cos., U.K., Europe, and U.S., 1980-91; internat. pres. ILASS, 1997—; chmn. Stahi Elec. Group, IUP, London, 1993-99; organizer several internat. confs. Mem. editl. bd. Internat. Jour. Atomisation and Sprays, 1989—, Particle Sci. and Tech., 1993—; contbr. more than 200 articles to profl. jours. Mem. PTA com. Onslow First County Sch., Guildford, 1990-93. Rsch. grantee numerous industries and research coun., 1980—. Fellow Inst. Elec. Engrs. U.K. (chartered), Inst. Physics (chmn. static electrificatin com. 1993—, chartered physicist, Inst. Measurement and Control U.K., Royal Soc. Arts; mem. IEEE (sr., electrostatics process com.), Electrostatic Soc. Europe (coord.), Internat. Coun. Liquid Atomisation and Sprays (pres.). Achievements include 8 patent applications for ultrasonic flow measurement, electrostatic spray head, electostatic atomiser for drug inhalation, electrostatic deposition PVDF sensor, optical sensors, and personal navigation system. Avocations: swimming, cooking, sports for fitness, reading. Office: Brunel Univ, Uxbridge Middlesex UB8 3PH, England

BALADÃO, ANA, artist, educator; b. Rio Grande, Brazil, Oct. 4, 1947; d. Jorge Alberto Miller and Ondina Porciuncula de Oliveira; divorced; children: Paula, Luciano, Eduardo. Student, Cath. U. Rio Grande do Sul, Brazil, 1975, 90; diploma, U. Nancy, France, 1968; postgrad. in Linguistics, Porto Alegre, Brazil, 1990. Tchr. French Porto Alegre pub. schs., 1969-94; artist, painter, 1980—; tchr., owner art sch., Porto Alegre, 1995—; program coord. IR-MANO, Porto Alegre, 1995-99; ofcl. translator, Porto Alegre, 1976—; invited artist Am. Studies Ctr., Swansea, U.K., 1992. One woman show at Embassy of Brazil/Holland, 1990, Cery Richards Gallery, U. Wales, Swansea, 1992, Espacio Miró, Porto Alegre, 1996, Judy Saslow Gallery, Chgo., 1997, Arte e Fato Gallery, Porto Alegre, 1999; exhibited in group shows at Marion Coll. Arts, Indpls., 1992, Santiago de Compostela, Spain, 2000. Grantee Marion Coll., Indpls., 1992, Vt. Studio Ctr., 1997. Mem. Ptnrs. of Americas (artist-in-residence 1992, vol. 1991—, program coord. 1995-99, Very Spl. Art Coord. for Rio Grande do Sul). Avocations: music, books, movies, caring for abandoned animals, plants. Office: Ana Baladão Atelier, Rua João Bastian 129, 91330270 Porto Alegre RS, Brazil

BALADI, ANDRÉ, international financier; b. Heliopolis, Egypt, Mar. 11, 1934; Swiss citizen.; s. Albert and Laura-Elena (Ventura) B.; m. Adrienne-Sylvia Barben, 1959; children: Viviane, Sibyl, Alex. Student, English Sch., Jesuit Coll., French Lycée, Cairo, 1939-52; grad., Geneva U., Switzerland; postgrad., Brit. Inst. Mgmt., London, IMD Harvard U. Bus. Sch., Switzerland, Mgmt. Ctr. Europe, Brussels. Freelance journalist Geneva, 1955-57; internat. exec. Nestlé Co., Europe, Asia and U.S., 1958-72; corp. devel. dir. Lesieur, Paris, 1973-74; exec. v.p., bd. dirs. Interfinexa, Co. Internat. pour le Dével., Geneva, 1974-77; dir. Soc. Gen. de Surveillance, Geneva, 1977-79; founder Baladi & Co. Internat. Devel. Group, Geneva, 1980—; chmn. Genevas Internat. Dispute Resolution Orgn.; hon. participant Coun. Instnl. Investors, Washington; internat. adv. bd. ParisBourse. Chmn. Assn. pur l'Arbitrage Internat. en matière de Commerce et d'Industrie. Mem. Assn. for Corp. Growth, Internat. Corp. Govenance Network (co-founder, co-chmn. London chpt.), Corp. Governance Forum of the Ctr. for European Policy Studies (Brussels), Assn. Swiss Fin. Analysts, Am. Internat. Club, Internat. Fin. Mgmt. Assn. (Geneva), Cercle de l'Union Interalliée (Paris), La Nautique Yacht Club (Geneva), Met. Club (N.Y.C.). Office: Baladi & Assocs, 3 rue Robert de Traz POB 141, CH-1211 Geneva 12, Switzerland

BALADI, ROLAND, artist; b. Cairo, July 12, 1942; s. Albert and Laura Elena (Ventura) B.; m. Catherine Chatiliez, 1972 (div. 1980); 1 child, Antonin; m. Dominque Castagnet, 1998; children: Marie, Pierre. Grad. plastic arts, audio-visual comm., Folkwanghochschule Gestaltung, Germany, 1970. Art dir. SNIP Advt. Agy., Paris, 1970-71; founder Internat. Selected Ideas and Sys., Paris, 1971-74; prof. U. Nancy, France, 1974-76; insp. French Nat. Bd. Arch. and Plastic Arts, 1974—; prof. U. Bourges, 1984, UCLA, summer 1978; rschr. artistic application sci. and tech. Exhibited in Mus. Modern Art, Paris, 1971, Annick Le Moine Art Gallery, Paris, 1974, La Defense Art Gallery, Paris, 1976, Pompidou-Beaubourg Ctr., Paris, 1977, Mus. Modern Art, N.Y.C., 1978, Galleria del Naviglio, Milan, 1979, O.K. Harris Gallery, N.Y.C., 1981, 83, 85, O.K. Harris West, Scottsdale, Ariz., 1982, Sculpture Tricentennial, Phila., 1982, Taft Mus., Cin., 1983, O.K. Harris Artists, Palm Beach, 1985, Modern Stone Age Gallery, N.Y.C., 1990, Pascal Paradis Gallery, Nice, France, 1992, Galerie du Trèsor, Clermont Ferrand, France, 1994, 98-99; prin. works include French Nat. Electricity Corp., 1971, Ephemeral Graffiti Wall, 1973, Kinoplan at French Indsl. Exhbn. China, Peking, 1974, Solar Low Relief, 1975, Les Halles, 1978, The Marble Cadillac Project, 1986; patentee artistic applications computer scis. Fellow MIT Ctr. for Advanced Visual Studies. E-mail: roland.baladi@wanadoo.fr. Home and Studio: 13 rue St Sauveur, 58 Av Nationale, 18340 Levet France

BALADI, VIVIANE, mathematician; b. Tour de Peilz, Vaud, Switzerland, May 23, 1963; d. André and Adrienne Sylvia (Barben) B. MSc in Math. and Computer Sci., U. Geneva, 1986, PhD in Math., 1989. Fellow IBM Rsch., Yorktown Heights, N.Y., 1990-91; head of rsch. CNRS, Lyons, France, 1990—; asst. prof. math. Eidgenossische Technische Hochschule Zurich, Switzerland, 1993-95; maître d'ens. et rsch. U. Geneva, 1995—. Author: Positive Transfer Operators and Decay of Correlations, 2000; contbr. articles to Jour. of Statis. Physics, Comms. in Math. Physics, Nonlinearity, Ergodic Theory and Dynamical Sys., Invent. Math., Jour. Math. Pures et Applications. Mem. Am. Math. Soc., Soc. Math. Suisse, Soc. Math. de France, Femmes et Maths. Office: Topologie et Dynamique CNRS UMR 8628, Bat 425/430 Univ de Paris-Sud, F 91405 Orsay Cedex, France

BALADJAY, MARIBLE GUERRERO, diplomat; b. San Fernando La Union, Philippines, May 23, 1970; d. Rogelio Ventura and Mary (Guerrero) B. BS in Edn., DMMMSU, Philippines, 1990. Diplomat Fgn. Affairs, Philippines, 1992—; passport processor Fgn. Affairs, Manila, 1992-95, sec., 1995-96; consular asst. Philippine Embassy, Stockholm, 1996-98, records and property officer, 1996—. Sec. YMCA, 1992-94. Mem. Ch. of Christ. Avocations: swimming, cooking, reading novels and books, bowling, travel. Home: Varmfronstgatan 4, 128 34 Skarpnack Sweden

BALAGUROV, BORIS YAKOVLEVICH, theoretical physicist, researcher; b. Vytegra, Russia, Aug. 23, 1941; s. Yakov Alekseevich and Mariya Vasilievna (Feklistova) B.; m. Natalya Anatolievna Khlopotunova, May 27, 1967; children: Fedor, Anna. BSc in Physics, Moscow Physics and Tech. Inst., Dolgoproudnaya, Russia, 1965, MSc in Physics of Low Temperature, 1967; PhD in Theoretical and Math. Physics, Landau Inst. Theoretical Physics, Chernogolovka, Russia, 1972. Engr., jr. rschr. Kurchatov Inst. Atomic Energy, Moscow, 1969-74; sr. rschr. Moscow Phys. Engring. Inst., 1975-78, Inst. of Power Supply, Moscow, 1978-92, Semenov Inst. Chem. Physics, Moscow, 1992-96; head scientist Emanual Inst. Bio-chem. Physics, Moscow, 1996—. Contbr. articles to profl. jours. Grantee Internat. Sci. and Tech. Ctr., Moscow, 1995-97, Russian Fund Basic Rsch., Moscow, 1995-97. Home: Apt 97, Priorova St 2a, 125299 Moscow Russia Office: Inst Biochem Physics, Kosygina St 4 Block 11, 117334 Moscow Russia

BALAKIRSKY, VLADIMIR BORIS, mathematician, educator; b. St. Petersburg, Russia, Oct. 2, 1957; s. Boris Balakirsky and Tatiana Mikhaleva; m. Mouravieva Maria. MA, Leningrad Aircraft Inst., 1980, D in Engring., 1987. Engr. LOMO, St. Petersburg, 1980-90, Lenpromstroiproekt, St. Petersburg, 1991, Pargolovsky Zavod, St. Petersburg, 1992-93; rschr. U. Lund, Sweden, 1993-94, U. Bielefeld, Germany, 1995-98, U. Eindhoven, The Netherlands, 1999—; cons. Confident, St. Petersburg, 1994—. Mem. IEEE. Home: Grazhdansky Prosp 104-4-21, 195267 Saint Petersburg Russia Office: U Eindhoven Elec Engr Dept, EH 11 33 PO Box 513, 5600 MB Eindhoven The Netherlands

BALAKRISHNAN, ARCOT RAMACHANDRAN, engineering educator, researcher; b. Chennai, Tamil Nadu, India, Oct. 3, 1950; s. Arcot and Susila (Krishnaswahy) R.; m. Aniat Venugopal, Aug. 31, 1977; children: Shalini, Kritanjali. B.Tech., U. Madras, Chennai, India, 1972; MA, U. Waterloo, Ont., Can., 1974, PhD, 1977. Rch. engr. Waterloo (Can.) Rsch. Inst., 1976-78; tech. mgr. Arbitech Polymerics (P) Ltd., Chennai, 1978-88; asst. prof. chem. engring. Indian Inst. Tech., Madras, 1988-92, assoc. prof. chem. engring., 1992-95, prof., 1995—. Co-editor: Heat and Mass Transfer, 1991, Advances in Chemical Engineering, 1996; contbr. over 75 articles to profl. jours. Mem. Indian Inst. Chem. Engrs. Home: 15 Rajarathuam St, Chennai 600 010, India Office: Indian Inst Tech Madras, Dept Chem Engring, Chennai 600 036, India

BALAN, VLADIMIR, adult education educator; b. Suceava, Romania, Oct. 2, 1958; s. Dumitru I. and Galina S. (Kostina) B.; m. Aurelia Gabriela Anghelin, June 4, 1983; children: Diana, Alexandru. BS, U. Bucharest, Romania, 1982, MS, 1983; PhD, U. Iassy, Romania, 1993. Mathematician Inst. Computer Tech. & Info., Bucharest, Romania, 1983-86, scientific rschr., 1986-90, prin. rschr. III, 1990; asst. Politehnica U. Bucharest, Romania, 1990-95, prof., 1995—. Co-author: Problems in Mathematical Analysis, 1981, Physical Principles of Differential Geometry, 1999. Mem. Am. Math. Soc., Balkan Soc. Geometers, Tensor Soc. Japan, European Math. Soc. Avocations: classical music, collecting stamps. Home: Str Timisoara 27 bl H Apt19, RO-77312 Bucharest Romania Office: Politech U Bucharest, Str Splaiul Independentei 313, RO-77206 Bucharest Romania

BALANDA, KEVIN PETER, statistician; b. Brisbane, Queensland, Australia, Oct. 17, 1955; s. John Patrick and Joan Delphia (Setterfield) B. BSc in Math. with honors, U. Queensland, Australia, 1977, PhD in Math., 1982, MSc in Statistics, 1986. Sr. tutor U. Queensland, Brisbane, Australia, 1983-86, lectr., 1987, statistician, 1991—; epidemiologist Queensland Health, Brisbane, 1988-90; assoc. dir. Wesley Rsch. Inst., Brisbane, 1995; head statistics sect. Ctr. Health Promotion & Cancer Prevention Rsch., Brisbane, 1995—; cons. Queensland Health, 1991-95. Contbr. articles to profl. jours. Mem. Statistical Soc. Australia, Pub. Health Assn. (exec. Brisbane chpt. 1995—). Home: 93 Jean St, Q-4051 Grange Queensland, Australia Office: U Queensland Med Sch, Herston Rd, Q 4006 Herston Queensland, Australia

BALANDIN, DMITRY VLADIMIROVICH, mathematician, researcher; b. Gorky, Russia, July 31, 1957; s. Vladimir Vasiljevich and Zoya Konstantinovna (Anikina) B.; m. Maria Alexandrovna Gushina, Dec. 21, 1984; 1 child, Konstantin. MS, Gorky State U., 1979; PhD, Inst. Problems in Mechanics, Moscow, 1990; DSc, Moscow State U., 1998. Engr. Rsch. Inst. for Applied Math. and Cybernetics, Gorky, 1979-85, rschr., 1986-89, sr. rschr., 1990-92; head rsch. sector Rsch. Inst. for Applied Math. and Cybernetics, Nizhni Novgorod, 1993—; vis. rschr. U. Va., Charlottesville, 1997; assoc. prof. Nizhni Novgorod State U., 1996-98; mem. sci. coun. Rsch. Inst. for Applied Math. and Cybernetics, 1992-97. Contbr. articles to profl. jours.; mem. editl. bd. Jour. News of Nizhni Novgorod State U., 1994-98. Grantee Russian Found. Fundamental Rsch., Moscow, 1993, Internat. Sci. Found., Moscow, 1995, NATO Sci. Program and Coop. Ptnrs. Program, Brussels, 1997. Avocation: ping-pong. Office: Rsch Inst Applied Math & Cybernetics, 10 Uljanov St, 603005 Nizhni Novgorod Russia

BALANESCU, SERBAN MIHAI, cardiologist; b. Constanta, Romania, Nov. 7, 1962; s. Vasile Valeriu and Elena (Preda) V.; m. Andra Rodica Dumbrava, July 2, 1988; 1 child, Dinu Valentin. MD, Carol Davila U. Medicine, Bucharest, Romania, 1988, PhD, 2000. Resident Grivita Clin. Hosp., Bucharest, 1988-90; registrar Univ. Hosp., Bucharest, 1990-94, sr. registrar, 1994-95, cons. in cardiology, 1997—; vis. registrar Centre Hospitalier Universitaire, Toulouse, France, 1995; hon. vis. registrar Southampton (Eng.) Gen. Hosp., 1996-97; mem. med. bd. Soros Found. for an Open Soc., Bucharest, 1994-95; sec. cardiology commn. Ministry of Health, Bucharest, 1997. Co-author: Textbook of Internal Medicine, 1997, Recent Progress in Cardiology, 1998, Medical Disorders During Pregnancy, 1999. Lt. Romanian Army, 1981-82. Mem. Romanian Soc. Cardiology, European Soc. Cardiology (tng. fellow 1996-97). Russian Orthodox. Avocations: computer science, tennis, reading, classical music. Office: U Hosp Bucharest, 159 Splaiul Independentei, 79800 Bucharest Sector 5, Romania

BALARAM, THAYANUR SHIVRAM, editor-in-chief; b. North Paravoor, Kerala, India, May 15, 1938; s. P. Shirvam Nair and Thankamma T. Shivram; m. Menon Vasanthi, Sept. 10, 1966; children: Menon, Balraj, Balram. BA in Econs., Union Christian Coll., Alwaye, India, 1959. Journalist Times of India, Mumbai, 1961-82, Arab News, Jeddah, Saudi Arabia, 1982-93; editor Assignments Abroad Times, Mumbai, 1994—. Recipient Order of Merit for Mgmt., ICME, 1997. Fellow Spl. Exec. Magistrate's Soc. (life, Gold medal 1998), Mgmt. Studies Promotion Inst. Home: 1/A Margaret House, S M Rd, Wadala Mumbai 400 037, India Office: Assignments Abroad Times, 102 Vinayak Siddhi DK Sandu, Marg Chembur Mumbai 400 071, India

BALAREW, CHRISTO CHRISTOV, chemist, educator; b. Sofia, Bulgaria, June 23, 1934; s. Christo Zankov and Vasilka Ivanova (Popova) B.; divorced; 1 child, Boriana. Diploma, U. St. Cl. Okhridski, Sofia, 1957; PhD, Bergakademie, Freiberg, Germany, 1969; Dr. habil, Bulgarian Acad. Scis., Sofia, 1983. Chemistry tchr. Chr. Botev Sch., Sofia, 1957-59; chemist Bulgarian Acad. Scis., 1959-67, sr. scientist, 1973-88, prof. chemistry, 1988—; assoc. prof. Tech. U. Burgas, Bulgaria, 1967-73, dir. inorganic chemistry dept., 1967-73; dir. inorganic salts lab. Bulgarian Acad. Scis., 1989—, mem. bd. mgrs., 1994-96, vice min. edn., sci. and tech., 1997. Capt. Bultarian army. res., 1957-89. Alexander von Humboldt Found. fellow, 1976; recieint Contbn. to Sci. Progress award Nat. Com. Sci. and Tech., 1969, Distinction medal Bulgarian Acad. Scis., 1976, U. Valladolid, Spain, 1992, N.S. Kurnakov medal Russian Acad. Scis., 1990. Mem. Internat. Union Pure and Applied Chemistry (assoc. mem. commn. 1991), Bulgarian Nat. Oceanographic Com. (pres. 1993—). Mem. Union of Dem. Forces. Eastern Orthodox. Avocations: sports, travel. Home: Bul Patriarch Eftimi 32, 1000 Sofia Bulgaria Office: Inst Gen & Inorganic Chem, Acad G Bonchev Str Bl 11, 1040 Sofia Bulgaria

BALASCHEVICH, LEONID, ophthalmologist; b. Rogachev, Gomel, Belorussia, Feb. 6, 1937; s. Josef Balashevich and Lubov Kalmanovich; m. Bella German, 1959 (div. 1974); children: Svetlana, Robert; m. Angelina Bezic, Feb. 4, 1986; 1 child, Oleg. Degree in surgery, Mil. Med. Acad., Leningrad, USSR, 1960, degree in ophthalmology, 1969; Candidate Med. Sci., U. Leningrad, 1974; D Med. Sci., U. St. Petersburg, Russia, 1996. Mil. surgeon USSR Navy, Petropavlovisk-Kamchatski, 1960-65, ophthalmologist, 1965-67; resident Mil. Med. Acad., Leningrad, 1967-69; head eye dept. Navy Hosp., Severodvinsk, USSR, 1969-71; rschr. Mil. Med. Acad., Leningrad, USSR, 1971-73, lectr., 1973-87; dep. dir. Eye Microsurgery Complex, St. Petersburg, 1987-94, dir., 1994—; chief dept. ophthalmology Med. Acad. Postgrad. Edn., St. Petersburg, 1996—. Author: Light Injuries of the Eye, 1986; inventor laser ophtalmocoagulator, diode laser ophthalmocoagulator (1st prize Health World Orgn. 1997). Col. Soviet Navy, 1960-86. Mem. Marine Assembly St. Petersburg. Russian Orthodox. Avocations: photography, collecting old cameras. Office: Eye Microsurgery, Yaroslav Gashec Str 21, 192283 Saint Petersburg Russia

BALASSA, SANDOR, composer; b. Budapest, Jan. 20, 1935; s. János Balassa and Eszter Bora; m. Marianna Orosz, 1994; 2 children. Student, Budapest Conservatory; diploma, Music Acad. Budapest, 1965. Music dir. Hungarian Radio, 1964-80; tchr. instrumentation Music Acad. Budapest, 1981. Compositions include (vocal) Legenda, 1967, Antinomia, 1968, Requiem for Lajos Kassák, 1969, Cantata Y, 1970, Motetta, 1973, Tresses, 1979, Kyrie, 1981, The Third Planet, 1986, Chant of Orphans, 1995, Capriccio, 1996, Spring Song, Autumn Song, 1997, others; (operas) The Man Outside, 1976, Karl and Anna, 1992; (instrumentals) Dimensioni, 1966, Quartetto per percussioni, 1969, Xenia, 1970, Tabulae, 1972, The Last Shepherd, 1978, Quintet for Brass, 1979, The Flowers of Hajta, 1984, Sonatina for harp, 1993, Sonatina for Piano, 1996, Preludes and Fantasia for Organ, 1996, others; (orchestral) Lupercalia, 1971, Iris, 1972, Chant of Glarus, 1978, The Island of Everlasting Youth, 1979, Calls and Cries, 1980, A Daydreamer's Diary, 1983, Three Phantasies, 1984, Little Grape and Little Fish, 1987, Fairy Ilona, 1992, Prince Csaba, 1993, Bolcske Concerto, 1993, Mucsai Dances, 1994, Sons of the Sun, 1995, Four Portraits, 1996, Number 301 Parcel, 1997, Pecs Concerto, 1998, Hungarian Coronation Music, 1998, Hun's Valley, 1999; (chamber music) Little Girland-trio for flute, violin and harp, 1994, John's Day music for violin, 1994, String Quartet, 1995, Nyirbator's bells for brass, 1996, Duets for flute and harp, 1998, Pastoral and rondo for violin and horn, 1998; (pieces for chorus) Woodcutter for male choir, 1998, Moongesang and Sun anthem for male choir, 1998, Winter cantata for children chorus and string orchestra, 1999, Christmas legend for female choir, 1999. Recipient Erkel prize, 1972, Critics' prize Hungarian Radio, 1972, 74, Listeners' prize Hungarian Radio, 1976, Distinction for Best Work of Yr., Paris Internat. Tribune of Composers, 1972, Kossuth prize, 1983, Bartók-Pásztory prize, 1988, 99; named Merited Artist Hungarian People's Republic, 1978. Avocation: nature. Address: str 18 Sümegvár, 1118 Budapest Hungary

BALASSANIAN, JEAN-MARIE FRANÇOIS HAÏG, astronomer; b. Ézanville, Val-d'Oise, France, Sept. 8, 1935; s. Léon and Zevarth Takouhi (Ketenedjian) B. Degree, Lycée Jaccard, Lausanne, Switzerland, 1956. Author: Fables et Contes Divers, 1979, Dialogues sur des Questions Modernes, I, 1983, II, 1992. Mem. Astron. Soc. France, French Assn. Astronomy, Planetary Soc., Club de Freschines (pres. 1995-96). Gregorian. Avocations: literature, painting, writing, photography, reading.

BALASUBRAMANYA, RUDRAPATNA HIRIYANNAIAH, microbiologist, researcher; b. Rudrapatna, Karnataka, India, May 3, 1948; s. Hanyal Seetaramashastry Hiriyannaiah and Hanyal Hiriyannaiah Sharadamma; m. Rudrapatna Balasubramanya Sarojini, Aug. 5, 1975; 2 children. BSc in Agr., Agr. Coll., Bangalore, India, 1969, MSc in Agrl. Microbiology, 1972, PhD in Agrl. Microbiology, 1978. Rsch. asst. U. Agrl. Sci., Bangalore, 1971-76; scientist S-1 Cen. Inst. for Rsch. on Cotton Tech., Mumbai, India, 1976-86, sr. scientist, 1986-97, prin. scientist, head, 1997—. Patentee in field. Recipient Best Rsch. Worker award Punjabrao Krishni Vidyapeeth, 1989. Fellow Textile Assn. India; mem. Assn. Microbiologists of India (life), Indian Soc. for Cotton Improvement (life), Indian Fibre Soc. (life), Assn. Food Scientists and Technologists, Indian Soc. of Mushroom (life), Indian Pulp and Paper Tech. Assn., Bur. Indian Stds., N.Y. Acad. Scis. Home: 10 Sarini Sector 16A Vashi, 400703 Vashi Navi Mumbai Thane, India Office: Cen Inst Rsch Cotton Tech, Adenwala Rd Matunga, 400019 Mumbai India

BALAYA, PALANI, physicist; b. Pondicherry, India, June 20, 1963; s. Palani Krishnan and Muniammal Palani; m. Thamizhselvi Balaya, Aug. 23, 1993; children: Gautham, Monika. BS, Anna Gov. Arts Coll., Karaikal, India, 1983; MS, Annamalai U., Chidambaram, India, 1985; MPhil, U. Hyderabad, India, 1986, PhD, 1993. Rsch. assoc. Indian Inst. Sci., Bangalore, India, 1994-96; scientist Inter U. Consortium Dept. Atomic Energy Facilities, Mumbai, India, 1996—. Contbr. articles to profl. jours. Jr. rsch. fellow Dept. Sci. and Tech., New Delhi, 1987, Sr. Rsch. fellow Coun. Sci. and Indsl. Rsch., New Delhi, 1991. Avocations: teaching yoga asanas. Home: Anushakti Nagar, 109 Akash Ganga, Mumbai 400 094, India Office: Inter U Cons DAE Facilities, R5 Shed SSPD, Mumbai 400 085, India

BALÁZS, ANDRÁS, biophysicist, consultant; b. Budapest, Hungary, Nov. 15, 1949; s. Béla and Márta (Szinkovich) B.; m. Mária Majoros, Aug. 25, 1972; 1 child, Zoltán. Diploma, Eötvös L. U., Budapest, 1974, MSc, 1976; PhD, Acad. Scis., Budapest, 1992. Rsch. assoc. Eötvös L. U., Budapest, 1977-82, rsch. worker, 1982-95; cons. biophysics dept. biol. physics Loránd Eötvös U., Budapest, 1995—. Contbr. articles to profl. jours. Mem. European Cell Biology Orgn., Union Hungarian Chemists, Hungarian Biol. Assn. Home: Bartók Béla u 6, H-2049 Diósd Hungary Office: Eötvös L U/ Biol Phys, 1117 Pázmany Sétány 1, Budapest Hungary

BALBI, KENNETH EMILIO, environmental lead specialist, researcher; b. N.Y.C., Apr. 13, 1963; s. George Emilio and Blanca Amelia (Fonseca) B.; m. Julie Ann Lopez, Feb. 19, 1989; children: Danielle Elizabeth, Joshua Emilio. MD, U. Ctrl. del Este, Dominican Republic, 1985; BS, SUNY, Albany, 1989. Rsch. assoc. Montefiore Med. Ctr., N.Y.C., 1988-94; govtl. case cons. SCITEC Corp., Kennewick, Wash., 1994-95; dir. tng. and profl. svcs. U.S. Lead, Oyster Bay, N.Y., 1995-97; v.p., co-founder ANDO Internat., Bklyn., 1995—; dir. franchise ops. PRO-TECT Franchising Inc., Oyster Bay, N.Y., 1996-97; v.p. rsch. & design AIA Environ. Corp., Astoria, N.Y., 1997-99. Contbr. articles to profl. jours. Mem. St. Michael's Hispanic Assn., Flushing, N.Y., 1991—, Cuban-Am. Assocs., Flushing, 1988—, Alliance to End Childhood Lead Poisoning, Washington, 1992—. Mem. AAAS, ASTM, Nat. Assn. Lead Inspectors, Nat. Lead Abatement Coun., Interam. Coll. Physicans and Surgeons, N.Y. Acad. Sci., United Internat. Med. Grads., Am. Indsl. Hygiene Assn., Steel Structure Painting Coun. Roman Catholic. Home: 24015B Oak Park Dr Douglaston NY 11362-2608 Office: ANDO Internat 861 Manhattan Ave Brooklyn NY 11222-2585

BALBO, SANDRINE HÉLÈNE, computer scientist; b. Talence, Gironde, France, Mar. 16, 1966; arrived in Australia, 1994; d. Edmond Maurice and Geneviève (Chanaud) B. B Computer Sci., U. Aix en Provence (France), 1986, M Operating Systems, U. Grenoble (France), 1989, DEA in Computer Sci., 1990, PhD in Computer Sci., 1994. Tutor in computer sci. U. Grenoble, 1990-93; sr. tchg. fellow Bond U., Gold Coast, Australia, 1993-95; rsch. scientist Commonwealth Sci. Indsl. Rsch. Orgn. divsn. Math. Info. Sci., Sydney, 1995—. Editor Queensland Symposium on Human-Computer Interaction, 1995; contbr. articles to profl. jours. and confs. Région Rhônes Alpes scholar, 1990-94. Mem. Computer-Human Interaction Spl. Interest Group. Avocations: scuba diving, sky diving, traveling, yoga. Office: Commonwealth Sci Indsl Rsch, Orgn, Locked Bag 17, North Ryde NSW 1670, Australia

BALBOLOV, ENTSHO CHRISTOV, chemistry educator, researcher; b. Bourgas, Bulgaria, July 23, 1946; s. Christo Ivanov and Tonka Entsheva (Grozdeva) B.; m. KrasiMetodieva Ruseva, Apr. 20, 1975; children: Antoaneta, Methodi. MSc, Higher Inst. Chem. Tech., Bourgas, 1970, PhD in Chem. Engring., 1980. Shift engr. Petrochem. Works, Bourgas, 1972-73; asst. prof. chemistry Higher Inst. Chem. Tech., 1973-88, assoc. prof. chemistry, 1988—; head dept. organic synthesis, Higher Inst. Chem. Tech., 1992-96. Co-author: Transition Metal Catalysis, 1989. Mem. Bulgarian Catalysis Soc. Democrat. Christian. Avocations: fishing, climbing. E-mail: balvolov@btu.bg. Home: Compl Izgrev bl 38 entr 4, 8008 Bourgas Bulgaria Office: Prof Dr As Zlatarov U, 1, Prof Yakimov Str, 8010 Bourgas Bulgaria

BALCELLS, SANTIAGO GORINA, architect; b. Barcelona, Spain, Oct. 3, 1913; s. Eduardo Buigas and Eugenia Sanz (Gorina) B.; m. Mercedes Batlle Canela, Oct. 28, 1942 (dec. Dec. 1964); children: M. Eugenia, José Luis, M. Victoria, Isabel, Fernando, Marta, Jorge, M. Cristina. BS, Colegio P.P., Barcelona, 1929; Dr. Arch., Escuela Superior Architectura, Barcelona, 1961. Lic. architect. Pvt. practice Barcelona, 1940—; architect Forense, Barcelona, 1992—. Contbr. articles to profl. jours.; editor, dir. tech. rev. constrn. prices Bull. Econs. in Constrn. Ensign, Engrs. Corps, Spanish Mil., 1936-40. Recipient Extraordinary award U. Barcelona, 1943. Mem. Colegio Oficial Arquitectos de Cataluna (past pres., mem. commn., Hon. Mention in the contest of projects). Mem. Popular Party. Roman Catholic. Avocations: skiing, tennis, swimming. Home: Emancipacion 28-4, 08022 Barcelona Spain Office: Emancipacion 28-1, 08022 Barcelona Spain

BALCEROWICZ, LESZEK, economics educator; b. Lipno, Poland, Jan. 19, 1947; s. Waclaw and Barbara B.; married; 3 children. DEcon., Ctrl. Sch. Planning and Econs. (now Warsaw Sch. Econs.), Warsaw; PhD, Ctrl. Sch. Planning and Econs. (now Warsaw Sch. Econs.); MBA, St. John's U., N.Y.C.; hon. degree, U. Aix-en-Provence, 1993, U. Sussex, 1994, De Paul U., Chgo., 1996, U. Szczecin, U. torun, Staffordshire U., Dundee U., 1998. Mem. staff Warsaw Sch. Econs., 1970—, dir. chair internat. comparative studies, 1993—; mem. staff Inst. Internat. Econ. Rels., 1970-80; dep. prime min., min. of fin., pres. econ. com., dep. chair Coun. Ministers, 1989-91, 97—; chair Freedom Union, 1995—. Contbr. over 100 articles to profl. jours. Chair Ctr. for Social and Econ. Rsch., Sarsaw. Recipient award Min. of Sci., Higher Edn. and Tech., 1978, 80, 81, Ludwig Erhard prize, 1992. Mem. Polish Assn. Econs., Polish Assn. Sociologists, European Econ. Assn. Avocations: history, sports. Office: Freedom U, Marszalkowska Str 77/79, 00 683 Warsaw Poland

BALCHIN, ANTHONY ARTHUR, physicist, research consultant; b. Guildford, Surrey, Eng., June 20, 1932; s. Arthur William and Emma Frances (Ward) B.; m. Hilary Margaret Bowley, July 27, 1957; children: Andrew Timothy, Patrick Christopher, Jeremy James Philip. BS, Queen Mary Coll., London, 1953; MS, Birkbeck Coll., London, 1960, PhD, 1968. Chartered physicist. Rsch. scientist Birmingham Steel Assn., Sheffield, Eng., 1953-54; crystallographer GE, London, 1957-60; sr. lectr. U. Brighton, Eng., 1962-89; cons. Brighton, 1990—; vis. prof. Sardar Patel U., India, 1984; gen. cert. of edn. examiner Univs. of Oxford and Cambridge, 1973-86; counselor The Open Univ., Brighton, 1969-83. Contbr. rsch. articles to profl. jours. Divsn. sec. Sussex Assn. Change Ringers, Brighton, 1992-94; chmn. The Hassocks Chorus, Sussex, 1991-94. Served as flying officer RAF, 1954-57. Rsch. grantee The Royal Soc., London, 1978, Sci. and Engring. Rsch. Coun., 1981, 84. Fellow Inst. Physics Gt. Britain; mem. Brit. Crystallographic Assn., Brit. Assn. for Crystal Growth. Mem. Ch. of Eng. Avocations: choral singing, change ringing on church bells, calligraphy. Home and Office: 23 Wilmington Close, Hassocks West Sussex BN6 8QB, England

BALCI, SEVIN M., pediatrician, medical geneticist; b. Ankara, Turkey, Dec. 23, 1938; s. Fuat and Naciye Balci. MD, Med. Faculty, Ankara, 1962; specialist in pediat., Hacettepe U., Ankara, 1966. Assoc. prof. pediat. Hacettepe U., Ankara, 1972-78, prof. pediat., 1978—. Mem. European Soc. Human Genetics. Avocations: photography, travel. Home: Kibris Sok 1718, 06690 Ankara Turkey Office: Hacettepe U, Dept Clinical Genetics, 06100 Ankara Turkey

BALČIŪNIENE, MILDA LEONARDA, physicist, researcher; b. Marijampole, Lithuania, Oct. 15, 1943; d. Leonas and Adele (Sirutyte) Adomynas; m. Stanislovas Algimantas Balčiunas, Aug. 26, 1972; 1 child, Neringa. M in Tech., Poly. Inst., Kaunas, Lithuania, 1967; PhD, Inst. Physics, Lithuania, 1993. Engr. Inst. Physics, Vilnius, Lithuania, 1967-71; jr. sci. rschr. Inst. Physics, Vilnius, 1972-86, sr. sci. rschr., 1987—. Contbr. articles to profl. jours. Roman Catholic. Home: Laisves 43-57, 232050 Vilnius Lithuania Office: Inst Physics, Savanoriu 231, 232028 Vilnius Lithuania

BALCOU, YVES, retired physicist, educator; b. Penvenan, Britanny, France, June 18, 1931; s. Jean and Marguerite (Allanet) B.; m. Nelly Guyomard, Mar. 25, 1961; children: Jean-Pierre, Philippe. Licence in Maths. and Physics, U. Rennes, France, 1955; Agregation Scis. Physiques, Paris, 1956; D, U. Rennes, France, 1970. Sch. master physics and chemistry Pontivy (France) Sr. High Sch., 1956-60; asst. prof. U. Rennes, 1960-93. Contbr. articles to Jour. Chimie Physique, Mikrochimica Acta, Bull. Soc. Sci. Bretagne, Rapid Comms. in Mass Spectrometry. Mem. IEEE, AAAS, European Sci. Orgn., French Phys. Soc. (ednl. com. 1970-80), French Chem. Soc., Soc. des Electriciens et Electroniciens. Achievements include rsch. in exptl. study of solid polysubstituted benzines, enhanced Fourier analysis of complex temporal transients, application to various spectrometries and vibration analysis. Home: 18 Rue La Fontaine, F 35700 Rennes Britanny, France

BALD, EDWARD, chemistry educator, researcher; b. Brzeziny, Poland, Feb. 16, 1941; s. Mieczyslaw and Janina (Loba) B.; m. Jadwiga Kowalkiewicz, Oct. 3, 1947; 1 child, Lukasz. MS, U. Lodz, Poland, 1964, DSc, 1971. Asst. U. Lodz, 1964-71, asst. prof., 1971-90, assoc. prof., 1990—; postdoctoral fellow U. Tokyo, 1974-76; vis. prof. U. Ottawa, Can., 1981-83. Contbr. over 50 articles to profl. jours. Mem. Polish Chem. Soc. Avocations: gardening, cycling, sightseeing. Home: Paprotnia 6, 96-140 Brzeziny Lodz Poland Office: Univ Lodz, Pomorska 163, 90-236 Lodz Poland

BALDACCINI, NATALE EMILIO, ethology educator, researcher; b. Camaiore, Italy, Apr. 3, 1944; s. Alvaro Baldaccini and Anna Maria Lombardi; m. Patrizia Maria Lunardini, Aug. 14, 1971; children: Emanuele, Paolo Emilio. PhD, U. Pisa, Italy, 1969. Asst. prof. U. Pisa, 1970-80; prof. U. Parma, Italy, 1981-91, U. Pisa, 1992—; dir. Inst. Zoology, Parma, 1987-90, Dept. Ethology, Ecology, Evolution, Pisa, 1994—. Author: Il Colombo Viaggiatore, 1986, Etologia, 1992, Zoologia, 1994, Anatomia Comparata, 1996. Mem. Italian Soc. Ethology (pres. 1989-95), Unione Zoologica Italiana (sec. 1995-99). Office: Dept Ethology Ecol Evol, Via Volta 6, 56100 Pisa Italy

BALDARI, MARCO, physician; b. Rome, Italy, Aug. 9, 1957; m. Lorella Brignoli; 1 child, Lorenzo. MD, U. Verona, Italy, 1984; Specialist in Physiotherapy, U. Pavia, Italy, 1989; Specialist in Infectious Disease, U. Siena, Italy, 1994; Diploma in Tropical Medicine and Hygiene, U. Liverpool, Eng., 1994. Asst. physician Pub. Health Office, Bergamo, Italy, 1987-91; med. dir. Pub. Health Office, Grosseto, Italy, 1991-99, Infectious Disease Unit, Grosseto, 1999—. Contbr. articles to Epidemiol. Bull. Active Red Cross, Grosseto, 1998. Mem. Order of Medicine of Grosseto. Avocations: sports, camping. Office: U O Malattie Intaltive, Osp di Grosseto, Via Senese, 58100 Grosseto Italy

BALDASSANO, VINCENT J., artist; b. Staten Island, N.Y., Apr. 27, 1943; s. Vincent F. and Antonette Baldassano; m. Carole Ann Baldassano; children: Alexandre, Francesca. BA, Wagner Coll., 1964; MFA, U. Oreg., 1966. Asst. prof. fine arts Niagara County C.C., Sanborn, N.Y., 1966-74; ptnr., pres. A.J. Murray & Co., Inc., N.Y.C., 1974-83; owner, pres. Artpak Transport Ltd., N.Y.C., 1983-90; owner, dir. Sta. Gallery, Katonah, N.Y., 1990-96; mng. dir. No. Westchester Ctr. for Arts, Mt. Kisco, N.Y., 1996; gallery dir. Silvermine Art Ctr., New Canaan, Ct., 1997-2000. One-man exhbns. include J. Fields Gallery, N.Y.C., 1981, U. Wis., Superior, 1983, Jean Lumbard Fine Arts, N.Y.C., 1983, Marie Pellicone Gallery, South Hampton, N.Y., 1984, Jakob Kunsthandlung, Basel, Switzerland, 1986, Nardin Fine Arts, Cross River, N.Y., Zimmerman-Saturn Gallery, Nashville, 1987, Anna Howard Gallery, Washington Depot, Conn., 1993, Gallery at the Courtyard, Katonah, N.Y., 1994, The Schoolhouse, Croton Falls, N.Y., Hammond Mus., 1996, Stamford (Conn.) Mus., 1997, Greenwich (Conn.) Academy, 1999, Inner Space Gallery, Mpls., 1999, others; group exhbns. include Deutsche Amerikanisches Inst., Regensburg, Germany, 1988, Olaf Clausen Gallery, N.Y.C., 1990, Butler Art Inst., Youngstown, Ohio, 1990, Noel Fine Arts, Bronxville, N.Y., 1994, No. Westchester Ctr. Arts, 1994, Carriage Barn Space, New Canaan, 1995, Gallery at the Courtyard, 1996, Housatonic Mus. Art, Bridgeport, Conn., 1995, 98, Soho 20 Invitational, N.Y.C., 1996, Vt. Coll. Art, Montpelier, 1996, Broome St. Gallery Invitational, N.Y.C., 1999, Mus. Cagnes sur Mer, France, 1998, Savannah (Ga.) Coll. Art & Design, 1997, Silvermine Galleries, 1999, The Silo, New Milford, Conn., 1998, Alan Stone Gallery, N.Y.C., 1977-81, 99, 2000, others; represented in pub. collections Savannah Coll. Art & Design, Burchfield Penney Mus., Housatonic Mus. Art, Hammond Mus., U. Oreg., Wagner Coll., Sacred Heart U., Westchester C.C., Norwalk C.C. Trustee Hammond Mus., North Salem, N.Y., 1998. Grantee N.Y. State Coun. Arts, 1975, 71, 99, Va. Ctr. Creative Arts, 1978; SUNY Painting fellow, 1969, 70, 71, 73. Mem. Silvermine Guild (artist mem.), N.Y. Artist Equity (artist mem.).

BALDASSINI, PIER GIORGIO, ski resort executive; b. Sarzana, Italy, June 23, 1943; m. Ilse Wenger. Cert. qualified acct. Tech. & Comml. Inst. Mng. dir. Tourism Co., Lignano, 1965-78, Azienda Promoz Tur. (tourist office), Tarvisio, 1978-80, Lignano Pineta SpA and Marina Uno Co., 1980-84; cons. Valtur/Camporosso due SpA, Milan, 1984-90, Promotur Spa, Udine, 1990-95; mng. dir. Tarvisio 2006 Spa, 1995—. Contbr. articles to profl. jours. Coun. City Lignano, 1985-90; v.p. Tourism Bd., Lignano, 1983-90; councillor Coun. Italian Cities, 1985-92, Regional Coun. Tourism Friuli-V.G., 1984-89, City of Lignano, 1985-90. Mem. Italian Journalist Assn., Assn. Dirs. Ski Resorts, Rotary, Panathlon. Avocations: tennis, skiing. Office: Tarvisio 2006 Spa, PBO 103, 33018 Tarvisio Italy

BALDI, ALFONSO, pathologist; b. Salerno, Italy, Feb. 22, 1968; s. Feliciano Baldi and Amalia Rinaldi; m. Nicoletta Onori, May 15, 1999. Diploma in medicine, U. Federico II, Naples, Italy, 1992. Resident in pathology U. Federico II, Naples, 1992-96; prof. molecular pathology Second U., Naples, 1998—; postdoctoral fellow Temple U., Phila., 1993-94, Thomas Jefferson U., Phila., 1994-96, U. Navarra, Pamplona, 1997; rschr., tutor U. Campus Biomedico, Rome, 1997—; chief. Lab. Molecular Diagnostic Centro Diagnostico, Rome, 1998—; rschr. Regina Elena Cancer Inst., Rome, 2000—. Mem. AAAS, Soc. Neurosci., N.Y. Acad. Scis. Roman Catholic. Achievements include patent for Human Retinoblastoma-Related Genomic DNA and Methods for Detecting Mutations Therein; discovery of Retinablastoma-related gene; involvement of Simian Virus 40 in the pathogenesis of human mesothelioma; prognostic role of the CDK-Inhibitor P27 in lung cancer; characterization of a new in vivo model of neuronal apoptosis. Avocation: collecting ancient paintings. E-mail: baldi@ifo.it. Office: Regina Elena Cancer Inst, Via delle Messi D'oro #156, 00158 Rome Italy

BALDI, STÉPHANE, education researcher, sociologist; b. Paris, Jan. 31, 1969; s. Georges and Marie-Claude (Gardan) B. BA, U. Mass., 1992; MA, U. Conn., 1993; PhD, Ohio State U., 1997. Cons. NRC, Washington, 1997; rsch. analyst Am. Insts. Rsch., Washington, 1997-99, sr. rsch. analyst, 1999; adminstr. Orgn. Econ. Coop. and Devel., Paris, 1999-2000; sr. rsch. analyst Am. Insts. Rsch., 2000—; reviewer Am. Sociol. Review, Work and Occupation, Ednl. Evaluation and Policy Analysis, Sociol. Forum. Author: The American Sociologist, 1994, 97, Scientrometrics, 1995, The Sociological Quarterly, 1995, Work and Occupations, 1997, American Sociological Review, 1998, International Education Indicators, 2000; contbr. articles to profl. jours. Recipient rsch. grant NSF, 1996; Fgn. Lang. Area Studies fellow U.S. Dept. Edn., 1995. Mem. Am. Sociol. Assn., Am. Ednl. Rsch. Assn. E-mail: sbaldi@air.org. Office: Am Insts for Rsch 1000 Thomas Jefferson St NW Washington DC 20007-3835

BÁLDI, TAMÁS, geology educator, researcher; b. Szombathely, Vas County, Hungary, Aug. 24, 1935; s. Imre Báldi-Becht and Ilona Király Báldi-Becht; m. Mária Beke, Dec. 26, 1958; children: Éva, András, Kati. Diploma in geology, Hungary, 1958; D in Paleontology, Eötvös Loránd U. Sci., Hungary, 1961; PhD in Geoscis., Hungarian Acad. Scis., 1968. Asst. Eötvös Lóránd U., Budapest, 1958, prof., 1966—; museologist dept. geology paleontology Mus. Natural Sci., Budapest, 1959-66; head dept. geology Eötvös U., Budapest, 1971-94. Author: Mollusc Fauna of the Hungarian Upper Oligocene, 1973 (Miksa Hantken medal), A történeti földtan alapjai, 1978 (Niveau Prize of Editor 1978), Mid-Tertiary Stratigraphy and Paleogeographic, 1986; editor Chronostratigraphie und Neostratotypen. Office: ELTE TTK Földtani, Tanszék Muzeum krt 4/A, 1088 Budapest Hungary

BALDINI, EDOARDO, surgeon; b. Piacenza, Italy, Dec. 22, 1962; s. Giovanni and Anna (Capra) B.; m. Paola Pareti, June 26, 1999. MD, U. Parma, 1987, postgrad. in gen. surgery, 1992; diplome, U. Laparoscopic Surgery, Nice, France, 1994; diplome etude approfondies, U. Paris XI, 1999. Physician Mil. Hosp., Piacenza, Italy, 1988; physician Civil Hosp., Guastalla, Italy, 1990-91, Aosta, Italy, 1991; surgeon Ctrl. Hosp. Univ., Nice, France, 1991-2000, Civil Hosp., Piacenza, Italy, 2000—. Achievements include research in hepatobiliary surgery, liver transplantation, laparoscopic surgery. Home: Via Campesio 3, 29100 Piacenza Italy

BALDINI, STEFANO, long distance runner; b. Italy, May 25, 1971. Winner World half-marathon, Palma de Mallorca, 1996, 2nd place award London Marathon, 1997, Italian record, 1997, 6th place award, 2000, Italian record in half-marathon, Rome, 1997, 3rd place award N.Y.C. Marathon, 1997, 1st place award Rome Marathon, 1998, European Marathon, Budapest, 1998, Italian record in half-marathon, Malmoe, 2000; finalist 10,000 meter race World Championships, 1995, 97, Summer Olympics, 1996. Address: 17 rue Princesse Florestine, BP 358 Monte Carlo 98007, Monaco

BALDINO, JOSE CARLOS OLIVEIRA, communications executive; b. Lisbon, Portugal, July 14, 1961; s. Luis Jose Dos Santos and Suzete Martins (Oliveira) B.; m. Maria Manuela L.O. Costa, Oct. 22, 1988; 1 child, Jose Miguel. Law, Lisbon U., Portugal, 1987. Cons. Supreme Ct., Lisbon, Portugal, 1981-88; editl. adv. Texto Editora, Lisbon, 1988-90, editor and mktg. dir., 1990-98; gen. mgr. SAPO/PT Multimedia Internet Portal, Lisbon, 1998—; bd. dirs. Zip.Net, Brasil. Author: (book) Economic Laws, 1990. Office: Saber E Lazer SA, Av 5 de Outubro 206 - 2, 1050-065 Lisbon Portugal

BALDONADO, CELESTE BULAN, obstetrician/gynecologist, consultant; b. Manila, Feb. 24, 1965; d. Julio and Antonina (Bulan) B. BS in Basic Med. Sci., U. The Philippines, Manila, 1984, MD, 1989; PhD, U. Navarre (Spain), 1996. Resident ob-gyn. Clinica U., Pamplona, Spain, 1990-93, sr. sonographer dept. ob-gyn., 1993-95; rsch. fellow dept. genetics U. Navarre, 1995-96; head surg. specialties Niger (Nigeria) Found. Hosp., 1996—. Contbr. articles to profl. jours. Fundación Empresa U. rsch. grantee, Pamplona, Spain, 1992-95. Mem. Ednl. Cooperation Soc., Med. and Dental Coun. Nigeria, Frequence Plus. Roman Catholic. Avocations: travel, Spanish-English translating, gardening, piano. E-mail: nfh@alpha.linkserve.com.ng. Home: Ind Layout, 11 Igboeze St PO Box 2459, Enugu Nigeria Office: Niger Found Hosp Ind Layout, 22 Alvan Ikoku St PO 4206, Enugu Nigeria

BALDONI, ROBERTO, computer science educator; b. Rome, Feb. 1, 1965; s. Guido and Anna Mastacchi; m. Dora Evangelista, Feb. 26, 1994; 1 child, Edoardo. Laurea in Computer Engring., U. Rome La Sapienza, 1990, PhD in Computer Sci., 1993. Cert. in engring. Rschr. IRISA, France, 1994-95; vis. prof. Cornell U., Ithaca, N.Y., 1996; asst. prof. U. Rome La Sapienza, 1996-98, prof., 1998—. Avocations: soccer, painting. Fax: 390685300849. E-mail: baldoni@dis.uniroma1.it. Office: Dept Info and Systems, Via Salaria 113, 00198 Rome Italy

BALDRACHI, RYAN MICHAEL, psychologist; b. Bartlesville, Okla., Mar. 15, 1973; s. Michael and Susan (Black) B. BA in Psychology cum laude, U. Ark., 1998; postgrad., Ohio U., 1999—. Crisis line vol. N.W. Ark. crisis Intervention Ctr., Springdale, 1996-99; supported employment specialist Lifestyles Inc., Fayetteville, Ark., 1997-98; rsch. asst. Personality Assessment and Psychotherapy rsch. Lab., U. Ark., Fayetteville, 1996—, Psychotherapy rsch. Lab., Ohio U., Athens, 1999—. Sandra Lawson Taylor fellow Ohio U., 1999, Silo Adv. Coun. Undergrad. rsch. fellow, 1997, W.J. richards Meml. awardee, U. Ark., 1997. Mem. ACLU, Internat. Rsch. Soc., Soc. for Personality Assessment. Avocations: electronic music production, photography, film making. Office: Ohio Univ Dept Psychology 200 Porter Hall Athens OH 45701

BALDWIN, ALLEN ADAIL, lawyer, writer; b. St. Augustine, Fla., July 15, 1939; s. Larrie Paul and Bertha Mae (Capallia) B. BA, Brigham Young U., 1969; JD, So. U., Baton Rouge, 1975. Bar: Fla. 1975. Tchr. Putnam County Sch. Bd., Palatka, Fla., 1969-71; pvt. practice Palatka, 1975—. Author: Tricks to Make the Angels Weep, 1986, Call It Not Heaven, 1991, Redeem Us From Virtue, 1992. Mem. Latter-day Saints Ch. Avocations: reading, swimming, hiking. Office: 308 Saint Johns Ave Palatka FL 32177-4723

BALDWIN, BETTY JO, computer specialist; b. Fresno, Calif., May 28, 1925; d. Charles Monroe and Irma Blanche (Law) Inks; m. Barrett Stone Baldwin Jr. (dec. 1998); two daughters. AB, U. Calif., Berkeley, 1945. With NASA Ames Rsch. Ctr., Moffett Field, Calif., 1951-53, math tech. 14' Wind Tunnel, 1954-55, math analyst 14' Wind Tunnel, 1956-63, supr. math analyst structural dynamics, 1963-68, supervisory computer programmer structural dynamics, 1968-71, computer programmer theoretical studies, 1971-82, adminstrv. specialist astrophys. experiments, 1982-85, computer specialist, resource mgr. astrophysics br., 1985—; v.p. B&B Baldwin Farms, Bakersfield, Calif., 1978-98. Mem. IEEE, Assn. for Computing Machinery, Am. Geophys. Union, Am. Bus. Womens Assn. (pres., v.p. 1967, one of Top 10 Women of Yr. 1971). Presbyterian. Avocations: reading, bridge, hiking. Office: NASA Ames Rsch Ctr Mail Stop 245-6 Moffett Field CA 94035-1000

BALDWIN, CYNTHIA ANN, industrial hygienist; b. Fort Sill, Okla., Sept. 18, 1951; d. Arthur Roy Baldwin and Dolores Mae Hill. BS in Biology, Met. State Coll., Denver, 1973; MS in Environ. Health, Colo. State U., 1981. Cert. in comprehensive practice indsl. hygiene Am. Bd. Indsl. Hygiene, 1988. Clk. typist admissions and records Colo. State U., Ft. Collins, 1974-75, student coordinator, office supr. dept. microbiology, 1975-80, grad. research asst. dept. microbiology, 1980-81; indsl. hygienist Consultation div. Iowa Bur. Labor, Des Moines, 1981-84; dir. occupational health Amana (Iowa) Refrigeration, Inc., 1984-93, mgr. environ. health and safety, 1993-95; sr. project mgr. Beling Cons., Moline, Ill., 1995-97; sr. indsl. hygienist Pointer Environ. Inc., Davenport, Iowa, 1997—; mem. adv. council U. Iowa Inst. Agrl. Medicine and Occupational Health, Iowa City, 1986-90. Diplomate Am. Acad. Indsl. Hygiene; mem. Am. Indsl. Hygiene Assn. (pres. Iowa-Ill. sect. 1987-88), Am. Foundrymen's Assn., Quad-City Engring. & Sci. Coun. (pres.). Avocations: dance, needlework. Office: Pointer Environ Inc 6305 Silvercreek Dr Davenport IA 52806-1651

BALDWIN, DOROTHY LEILA, secondary school educator; b. Irvington, N.J., Feb. 28, 1948; d. Daniel Thomas and Lillian Frances (Wainright) B. BA, Kean Coll., Union, N.J., 1969, MA in Edn. and Humanities, 1971; EdD in Adminstrn. and Supervision, Seton Hall U., 1987, cert. reading specialist, 1979, cert. bus. adminstr., 1985. Tchr., reading coord. St. Paul Apostle Sch. Irvington, 1969-74; tchr. Summit (N.J.) Jr. High Sch., 1975-79; social studies coord. K-9, chmn. dept. 7-9 Summit Pub. schs., 1979-87; social studies supr. Livingston (N.J.) Pub. Schs., 1987; prin. Point Road Sch, Little Silver, N.J., 1987-89; dir. gifted edn. K-12 Clifton, N.J., 1989-90; prin. Sch. Two, Clifton, N.J., 1989-90, Deerfield Sch., Mountainside, 1990-92, Eisenhower Sch., Bridgewater-Raritan, N.J., 1992—; adj. prof. Montclair (N.J.) State Coll.; tchr. adult and community schs.; cons. in field; workshop coord. Author books; contbr. articles to profl. jours. PTA scholar, 1965. Mem. ASCD, Nat. Assn. Elem. Sch. Prins., Nat. Coun. Social Studies, Am. Assn. Sch. Adminstrs., N.J. Assn. Elem. Sch. Prins., N.J. Prins. Ctr., Somerset County Assn. Elem. Sch. Prins., Phi Delta Kappa, Kappa Delta Pi. Home: 737 River Rd Chatham NJ 07928-1136 Office: Eisenhower Sch Bridgewater NJ 08807

BALDWIN, GEORGE KOEHLER, retired retail executive; b. Cedar Rapids, Iowa, Nov. 17, 1919; s. Nathan and Ada Lillian (Koehler) B. BBA, State U. Iowa, 1942. From office mgr. to mgr. Wapsie Valley Creamery, Cedar Rapids, Iowa, 1946-60; treas., head payroll, accounts payable, sales audit dept. Armstrong's Inc., Cedar Rapids, 1960-87; also bd. dirs., treas. Armstrong's of Dubuque, Iowa, 1982-87; ret., 1987; mem. adv. coun. Firstar Club, Firstar Bank, Cedar Rapids. Composed and copyrighted for band Kinnick Stadium band march, 1992. Mem. Cedar Rapids Performing Arts Commn.; bd. dirs., pres. Cedar Rapids Cmty. Concert Assn.; pres. State U. of Iowa Concert Band, 1941-42; sec., treas., asst. conductor El Kahir Shrine Band of Cedar Rapids; bd. dirs. Cedar Rapids Stamp Club, 1997-2000; chmn. adminstrv. bd. Trinity United Meth. Ch., 1987-92, head usher and staff parish rels. com. chmn.; apptd. by mayor to Cedar Rapids Mcpl. Band Commn., 1994, vice chmn. 1998—; organist Paramount and Iowa theaters, Cedar Rapids. With U.S. Army, 1942-46, ETO. Decorated Bronze Star medal; named hon. Ky. Col.; George K. Baldwin day proclamation in his honor, Mayor of Cedar Rapids, Apr. 16, 1987. Mem. VFW, Cedar Rapids Consumer Credit Assn. (pres. 1968-69), Am. Theatre Organ Soc. (bd. dirs., treas. Cedar Rapids chpt.), Am. Legion, Rotary, Masons, Shriners (past pres. uniformed units), Rotary Svc. Club (chmn. fellowship com., sgt. of arms), State U. Iowa Pres.'s Club. Methodist. Home: 1017 F Ave NW Cedar Rapids IA 52405-2724

BALDWIN, GORDON BREWSTER, law educator, lawyer; b. Binghamton, N.Y., Sept. 3, 1929; s. Schuyler Forbes and Doris Ambeline (Hawkins) B.; m. Helen Louise Hochgraf, Feb., 1958; children: Schuyler, Mary Page. LLB, Cornell U., 1953; BA, Haverford Coll., 1950. Bar: N.Y. 1953, Wis. 1965. Pvt. practice Rochester and Rome, N.Y., 1953-57; prof. law U. Wis., Madison, 1957-99, Evjue-Bascom prof. law, 1991-99; emeritus prof. U. Wis., Masidon, 1999—; assoc. dean law U. Wis., Madison, 1968-70; dir. officer edn. U. Wis., 1972-99; of counsel Murphy & Desmond, S.C., Madison, Wis., 1986-95; chmn. internat. law U.S. Naval War Coll., 1963-64; Fulbright prof., Cairo, 1966-67, Tehran, Iran, 1970-71; lectr. State Dept., Cyprus, 1967, 1969, 1971; counselor internat. law U.S. Dept. State, Washington, 1975-76, cons., 1976-77; vis. prof. Chuo U., Tokyo, 1984, Giessen U., Fed. Republic Germany, 1987, 92, Thommasat U., Thailand, 1997; cons. U.S. Naval War Coll., 1961-65; chmn. screening com. on law Fulbright Program, 1974; mem. constl. law com. Multi-State Bar Exam, 1972-82; chmn. State Pub. Def. Bd., 1980-83, Wis. Elections Bd., 1991-96; cons., rep. Marshall Island Constn. Conv., 1990. Mem. Wis. Bd. Elections, 1991-95, Wis. Land Coun., 1998—, Wis. State Ethics Bd., 2000—. Ford Found. fellow, 1962-63. Fellow Am. Bar Found.; mem. AAUP (nat. coun. 1975-78, pres. Wis. conf. 1986-87), Bar Assn. (vice chmn. sect. on individual rights 1973-75), Fulbright Alumni Assn. (dir. 1979-82), Am. Law Inst., Order of Coif, Madison Club, Madison Lit. Club (pres. 1985-86), Univ. Club, Rotary (pres. Madison 1980, dist. gov. 1999-00), Phi Beta Kappa. Home: 3958 Plymouth Cir Madison WI 53705-5212 Office: U Wis 975 Bascom Mall Sch Law Madison WI 53706-1399

BALDWIN, JEFFREY NATHAN, pharmacy educator; b. Sidney, N.Y., Dec. 20, 1947; s. Reverdy Ernest and Helen Elizabeth (Humphrey) B.; m. Suzanne Marie Smith, Dec. 27, 1969; children: Paul Kevin, Gregory Michael. AS, Jamestown C.C., 1967; BS in Pharmacy summa cum laude, SUNY, Buffalo, 1970; DPharm, U. Ky., 1973. Lic. pharmacist, Ky., Nebr. Resident in pharmacy U. Ky.-A.B. Chandler Med. Ctr., Lexington, 1970-73; pharmacy faculty U. Nebr. Med. Ctr. Coll. Pharmacy, Omaha, 1973—; med. faculty U. Nebr. Med. Ctr., Coll. Medicine, Omaha, 1977—; pres., cofounder Nebr. Coun. for Continuing Pharm. Edn., Inc., Omaha, 1980-82. Author: (chpts.) Points of Light: A Guide for Assisting Chemically Dependent Health Professional Students, 1996; sect. editor: Applied Therapeutics: The Clinical Use of Drugs, 1995; author 15 chpts. to books and over 20 articles to profl. jours. Chmn. Nebr. Pharmacist Recovery Network, Lincoln, Nebr., 1988—; chair tng. com. Mid Am. Coun., Boy Scouts, Omaha, 1997-98, scout leader, 1983—; counselor Camp CoHoLo, Gretna, Nebr., 1985-98, 2000. Recipient Leadership award McKesson, 1995. Fellow Am. Pharm. Assn. (Merit award 1995), Am. Soc. Health-Sys. Pharmacists (chair pediatric pharmacy spl. interest group 1977-78), Am. Assn. Colls. Pharmacy (chair substance abuse spl. interest group 1988-97, chair pharmacy practice sect. 1998-99), Nebr. Pharmacists Assn. (pres.-elect 1994-95, pres.

1995-96, chmn. bd. 1996-97, NARD Leadership award 1995). Avocations: travel, bicycling, backpacking, camping, whitewater rafting. Office: 982135 Nebr Med Ctr Omaha NE 68198-0001

BALDWIN, JOHN CHARLES, surgeon, researcher; b. Ft. Worth. BA summa cum laude, Harvard U., 1971; MD, Stanford U., 1975; MA Privatim (hon.), Yale U., 1989. Diplomate Am. Bd. Internal Medicine, Am. Bd. Surgery, Am. Bd. Thoracic Surgery. Fellow in medicine Harvard Med. Sch., Boston, 1975-77; fellow in surgery, resident in surgery Mass. Gen. Hosp., 1977-81; resident in cardiothoracic surgery Stanford (Calif.) U., 1981-82, chief resident cardiothoracic surgery, 1983, asst. prof., 1984-87; dir. heart-lung transplantation transplant rsch. lab. Stanford U., 1986-87; prof. surgery and chief cardiothoracic surgery Yale U., New Haven, 1988-94; cardiothoracic-surgeon-in chief Yale-New Haven Hosp.; DeBakey/Bard prof., chmn. Baylor Coll. Medicine, Houston, 1994-98; sr. attending physician, chief surg. svcs. Meth. Hosp., Houston, 1994-98; sr. attending physician, surgeon in chief Ben Taub Gen. Hosp., Houston, 1994; dean med. sch., v.p. health affairs Dartmouth Coll., 1998—; bd. dirs. United Network Organ Sharing, 1984-87; mem. clin. rsch. com. ad hoc rsch. grant rev. Cystic Fibrosis Found.; trustee New Eng. Organ Bank, 1988; mem. solid organ transplant com. Blue Cross & Blue Shield of Conn., 1990-94; mem. sci. adv. bd. Alexion Pharms., Inc., 1991-94; bd. dirs. Baylor Coll. Medicine Health-care, Inc.; mem. adv. bd. Donate Life Found.; mem. exec. faculty Baylor Coll. of Medicine, pres.'s coun.; bd. dirs. New England chpt. Transplant Recipients Internat. Orgn., 1992-94. Co-editor: Thoracic Surgery, Oxford Textbook of Surgery, 1989—; assoc. editor Jour. Applied Cardiology, 1985-92; editorial bd. Jour. Thoracic and Cardiovascular Surgery, 1990-97, Transplantation, 1990—, Transplantation Sci., 1992-95, Andromeda Interactive Ltd., The Cardiovasc. System Interactive Teaching Program, 1993—; contbr. numerous articles and book chpts. in field. Mem. Harvard Club Schs. Com., Harvard Coll. Fund, Harvard U. Undergrad. Admissions Interview Com.; fellow Timothy Dwight Coll. Yale U., Yale U. Art Gallery Assocs.; mem. appointments and promotions com. Sch. Medicine, Yale U., 1991-94, bd. dirs. Neighborhood Music Sch. New Haven., 1989-92; bd. overseers Harvard U., 1995—; bd. permanent officers Yale U., 1988-94. John Harvard scholar, 1969, 70, Wendell scholar Harvard U., 1969, Rhodes scholar Oxford U., 1971, Alumni scholar Stanford Sch. Medicine, 1974 ; medalist Gothenburg (Sweden) Thoracic Soc., 1985; recipient Medaille de la Ville de Bordeaux French Thoracic Soc., 1987, travelling lectureship, 1988, Master Tchr. award Cardiovascular Revs. & Reports, 1990; travelling fellow Australia and New Zealand chpt., ACS, 1989; traveling lectureship, 1989. Fellow ACP, ACS, Royal Coll. Surgeons (Eng., traveling lectr. 1989), Am. Coll. Angiology, Am. Coll. Cardiology (mem. transplantation com. 1991-94, Am. task force cardiac donor procurement Bethesda Conf. 1992), Am. Coll. Surgeons (bd. govs. 1993-97), Am. Coll. Chest Physicians, Mass. Med. Soc.; mem. AMA, AAAS, Am. Assn. Thoracic Surgery (mem. com. grad. edn. thoracic surgery 1992-97, chmn. Evarts A. Graham Meml. Traveling Fellowship com. 1993-99), Am. Soc. Transplant Surgeons (com. on heart transplantation 1986-89, adv. com. in issues 1989—, chmn. subcom. on heart transplantation, physician payment reform commn. 1989-92), Nat. Heart, Lung and Blood Inst. (cons. divsn. extramural affairs rev. br. 1990—), Assn. Acad. Surgery, Am. Physiol. Soc., Am. Heart Assn. (mem. rsch. grant peer rev. subcom 1984-87, coun. circulation, cert. of appreciation for outstanding svc. 1986), Am. Surg. Assn., Am. Thoracic Soc., Am. Soc. Artificial Internal Organs, Am. Soc. Extracorporeal Tech., Am. Assn. Lab. Animal Sci., Am. Organ Transplant Assn., Am. Venous Forum, Internat. Soc. Heart and Lung Transplantation (chmn. program com. 1988), Internat. Assn. Cardiac Biol. Implants, Internat. Fedn. Surg. Colls., Internat. Soc. Cardiovasc. Surgery, Internat. Soc. Cardio-Thoracic Surgeons (pres. 1999), Internat. Soc. for Heart Rsch. (mem. Am. sect.), Internat. Soc. for Artificial Organs, Mediterranean Assn. for Cardiology and Cardiac Surgery, New Century Soc., Thoracic Surgery Found. for Rsch. and Edn., Norman E. Shumway Surg. Soc., New Eng. Surg. Soc., Pan Am. Med. Assn. (coun. on organ transplantation), North Am. Soc. Pacing and Electrophysiology, Societe Internat. de Chirurgie, Royal Soc. Medicine, Soc. Univ. Surgeons, Thoracic Surgery Dirs. Assn. (chmn. curriculum com. transplantation 1993-94), Transplantation Soc., Assn. Alumni of Magdalen Coll. Oxford U., Assn. Rhodes Scholars, Acad. Surg. Rsch., Assn. Surg. Edn., Assn. Program Dirs. in Surgery, Conn. Thoracic Soc., Harris County Med. Soc., Calif. Med. Assn., Calif. Thoracic Soc., Calif. Thoracic Soc. Respiratory Care Assembly, No. Calif. Cystic Fibrosis Found., So. Calif. Transplant Soc., Conn. Med. Soc., Conn. Soc. Am. Bd. Surgeons, Mass. Med. Soc., N.Y. Soc. Thoracic Surgery, Harvard Med. Alumni Assn. (assoc.), Soc. Crit. Care Medicine, Soc. Thoracic Surgeons, Southeastern Surg. Congress, Southern Surg. Assn., Southwestern Surg. Congress, Tex. Surg. Soc., Halsted Soc., Houston Surg. Soc. Soc. for Organ Sharing, San Francisco Surg. Soc., Santa Clara Med. Soc., Stanford Med. Alumni Assn., Stanford Club Conn., Harvard Clubs San Francisco, Peninsula, N.Y.C., So. Conn., Houston, Boston, Mory's Assn., New Haven Lawn Club, Inner Quad Stanford U., The Hasty Pudding Club - Inst. 1770, Quinnipiack Club, Forum World Affairs, Ambs. Roundtable, Oxford Soc., Phi Beta Kappa, others. Office: Dartmouth Coll Dartmouth Med Sch Office Dean 1 Rope Ferry Rd Hanover NH 03755-1404

BALDWIN, MARK ALAN, communications consultant, writer; b. Sheboygan, Wis., June 13, 1958; s. Robert Franklin and Lucille Bertha (Karsteadt) B. BA, U. Wis., La Crosse, 1980. Pub./client rels. specialist Cap-Rock-Walworth, Janesville, Wis., 1981-82; energy advisor Madison (Wis.) Gas & Electric, 1982-85; devel. specialist WHA-TV, Madison, 1985-89; devel. assoc., editor San Francisco AIDS Found., 1989-92; dir. found. rels. Sierra Club Legal Def. Fund, San Francisco, 1992-94; devel. dir. Marin Cons. Corps, San Rafael, Calif., 1995-96; dir. comms. Merritt Cmty. Capital Corp., Oakland, Calif., 1996—; pub. rels. cons. Bay Area Cmty. Svcs., Oakland, 1997—; fundraising cons. Brothertown Indian Nation, Woodruff, Wis., 1980—. Author: (brochure) Winds of Change, 1987. Home: 1935 Clay St Apt 102 San Francisco CA 94109-3432 Office: Merritt Cmty Capital Corp 1736 Franklin St Ste 600 Oakland CA 94612-3423

BALDWIN, PETER ALAN CHARLES, broadcasting consultant; b. London, Feb. 19, 1927; s. Alec and Anne (Dance) B.; m. Judith Elizabeth Mace, Oct. 1953 (div. 1982); m. Gail Johnston Roberts, Sept. 16, 1982. Apprentice Army Tech. Sch., 1942; dep. dir. radio Ind. Broadcasting Authority, London, 1979-87, dir. radio, 1987-90; chief exec. Radio Authority, London, 1990-95. Vice chmn. Eyeless Trust; trustee Com. Svc. Vols. Maj. gen. Royal Signals, 1942-80. Decorated Comdr. Brit. Empire. Fellow Radio Acad., Royal Soc. Arts; mem. D'Oyly Carte Opera Co. (trustee), Army and Navy Club, Marylebone Cricket Club. Anglican. Avocations: cricket, music, theat.r, golf.

BALDWIN, RALPH BELKNAP, retired manufacturing company executive, astronomer; b. Grand Rapids, Mich., June 6, 1912; s. Melvin D. and Julie (Belknap) B.; m. Louis Virginia Johnston, Aug. 3, 1940; children: Melvin Dana II, Pamela, Bruce Belknap. B.S., U. Mich., 1934, M.S., 1935, PhD, 1937, LLD (hon.), 1975; ScD (hon.), Grand Valley State U., 1989, Aquinas Coll., 1999. Asst. dept. astronomy U. Mich., 1935-36, U. Pa., 1937-38; instr. dept. astronomy Northwestern U., 1938-42; lectr. Adler Planetarium, Chgo., 1940-42; sr. physicist Applied Physics Lab. Johns Hopkins, Silver Spring, Md., 1942-46; cons. Johns Hopkins, East Grand Rapids, Mich., 1946-47; acting supt. schs. East Grand Rapids, 1947; prodn. mgr. Oliver Machinery Co., Grand Rapids, 1947-56; dir. Oliver Machinery Co., 1948-87, successively personnel dir., prodn. mgr., sec., 1949-56, v.p., 1956-70, pres., 1970-84, chmn. bd., 1984-87; Chmn. bd. Internat. Woodworking Machinery and Furniture Supply Fair-U.S.A., 1969-70, 77-78. Author: The Face of the Moon, 1949, The Measure of the Moon, 1963, The Moon—A Fundamental Survey, 1966, The Deadly Fuze: Secret Weapon of World War II, 1980, They Never Knew What Hit Them, 1999; contbr. articles to profl. jours. Recipient Presdl. Cert. of Merit, 1947, U.S. Naval Bur. Ordnance award, 1945, U.S. Army Chief of Ordnance award, 1945, Disting. Alumnus award U. Mich., 1967, Woodworking and Furniture Digest award Forest Products Rsch. Soc., 1973, J. Lawrence Smith medal Nat. Acad. Scis., 1979, G.K. Gilbert award Geol. Soc. Am., 1986, Disting. Alumni award Ctrl. H.S., Grand Rapids, Mich., 1997. Fellow AAAS, Am. Geophys. Union, Meteoritical Soc. (Leonard medal 1986, Barringer medal 2000), Am. Acad. Arts and Scis.; mem. Am. Astron. Soc., Royal Astron. Soc. Can. (hon.), Grand Rapids Mus. Assn., NAM (dir. 1963-64), Employers Assn. Grand Rapids (pres. 1960-64), Woodworking Machinery Mfrs. Assn. (pres. 1964-68). Home: 4401 Gulf Shore Blvd N Apt 702 Naples FL 34103-3451

BALDWIN, SHERYL DENISE, chemist, writer, editor; b. Va., Apr. 13, 1948; d. William Jacob and Josephine (Rife) B. BS in Chemistry with high honors, Va. Commonwealth U., 1975, PhD in Phys. Chemistry, 1979. Asst. prof. chemistry U. Richmond, Va., 1980-82; quality control, supr. support Hercules, Inc., Hopewell, Va., 1982-83, rsch. chemist, 1983-86; rsch. sci. R & D Philip Morris, Richmond, 1986-90, sr. rsch. sci., 1991-96, sect. leader, paper devel., 1990-94; mgr. bus. devel. Am. Chem. Soc. Industry Rels., Washington, 1996—; cons. Bear Island Paper Co., Doswell, Va., 1980-82, Alexandria Pub. Svcs., 1993-95, Environ. Friendly Packaging, Richmond, 1994-96. Editor: Plastics, Rubber and Paper Recycling: A Pragmatic Approach, 1995; contbr. articles to profl. jours. including U.S.-China Rev. Bd. dirs. Sister Cities program Richmond-Zheng Zhou, China, 1994—; del. Environ. Tech. Del. to China, 1994; mem. City of Richmond Com., 1986-94. Recipient Star award Va. Commonwealth U. Alumni, 1997. Mem. Am. Chem. Soc. (mem. cellulose and paper divsn., mem. exec. com. 1991-95, Judge Anselme Payen awad 1992-94, indsl. liaison chair 1992-93, mem. exec. coun. Va. sect. 1982—, chmn. 1992. alt. councilor 1994—, councilor 1998—, Disting. Svc. award Va. sect. 1996), U.S.-China People's Friendship Assn. (bd. dirs. 1995-97), Friendship Through Sci. and Tech. (coord. 1997—), Mensa, Sigma Xi (assoc.), Phi Kappa Phi, Kappa Sigma Rho. Achievements include eight patents on novel cigarette papers and cigarettes. Office: Am Chem Soc Industry Rels 1155 16th St NW Washington DC 20036-4800

BALE, RETO JOSEF, physician; b. Eschen, Liechtenstein, Feb. 23, 1969; s. Heinrich Bale and Maria Elisabeth Marxer B.; m. Simone Binder. MD, U. Innsbruck, Austria, 1995. Med. diplomate. Tutor Inst. Histology U. Innsbruck, 1989-90, tutor Inst. Anatomy, 1992-95, resident, 1995-96; resident dept. surgery U. Clin., Innsbruck, 1996-97, resident dept. radiology, 1997—. Inventor Vogele-Bale-Hohner targeting device, image guiding surgery system; contbr. articles to profl. jours. and books. Recipient Best Poster awards various confs. in field, 1997. Avocations: skiing. E-mail: reto.baleguibk.ac.at. Office: Radiology Dept I, Anichstr 35, 6020 Innsbruck Austria

BALEANU, DUMITRU, physicist, researcher; b. Slivilesti, Gorj, Romania, Dec. 4, 1964; s. Iancu and Elisaveta (Olaru) B.; m. Mihaela Cristina Iliescu, Sept. 24, 1986; children: Alexandra Daniela. PhD, Inst. Atomic Physics, Bucharest, 1996. Physicist Inst. Nuclear Reactors, Pitesti, Romania, 1989-90; physicist Inst. of Gravity and Space Scis., Bucharest, 1990-95, prin. scientist, 1995-98; prin. scientist rschr. JINR-BLTF, Dubna, Russia, 1998-99; lectr. math. and computer scis. Cankaya U., Ankara, Turkey, 2000—. Contbr. articles to profl. jours. Pres. Found. "The Chanche of the Future, 1995-96. NATO grantee, Mid. East Tech. U., Ankara, 1999. Mem. European Phys. Soc., Russian Gravitational Soc., Turkish Phys. Soc., Kiwanis. Avocations: literature, music. Home: Soseaua Pantelimon #86, Bl 409 A sc 2 et 8 ap 80, Bucharest Romania

BALEK, VLADIMIR, materials scientist, educator, nuclear chemist; b. Kvášňovice, Czech Republic, Mar. 16, 1940; s. Edouard and Božena (Sádlová) B.; m. Karla Cyrusová; 1 child, Denisa. MSc, Tech. Univ., Prague, Czech Republic, 1961; DSc in Materials Sci, Tech. Univ., 1988; PhD in Chemistry, Moscow State U., 1967. Asst. prof. Charles U., Prague, 1961-64, 68-72; head dept solid state rsch. Nuclear Rsch. Inst., Řež, Czech Republic, 1973-79; sr. staff mem., rsch. project mgr. Nuclear Rsch. Inst., Řež, 1987—; mem. sci. directorate Ministry Edn., Prague, 1979-87. chmn. Soc. Thermal Analysis, Prague, 1967; assoc. prof. Charles Univ., Prague, 1984—; translator, interpretor Russian, French, German, English, Spanish. Author, co-author 5 books and 15 inventions; editor Proceedings of Thermal Analysis Meetings, 1985, 91; mem. editl. bd. Thermochim. Acta, 1972-91; regional editor Jour. Thermal Analysis, 1991—; contbr. over 200 articles to profl. jours. Fellow Moscow State U., 1964-67; recipient Czech Sci. and Tech. award, 1985, German Soc. Thermal Analysis award, 1988, N.Am. Thermal Analysis Soc. award, 1990. Mem. Internat. Confederation Thermal Analysis and Calorimetry (councillor 1982-90). Avocations: travel, photography. Office: Nuclear Rsch Inst, CZ25068 Řež u Prahy Czech Republic

BALEN, ADAM HENRY, obstetrician, gynecologist; b. London, Apr. 30, 1960; m. Frances G. Hunt; children: Toby, Cara. MB, BChir, St. Bartholomews Med. Sch., London, 1983; MD, U. London, 1995. Jr. ob-gyn. Queen Charlottes Hosp., 1983-90, St. Marys Hosp., 1983-90; fellow Hallam Med. Ctr., London, 1990-93; subspecialty sr. registrar reproductive medicine John Radcliffe Hosp., Oxford, Eng., 1994-96; cons., subspecialist in reproductive medicine Leeds (Eng.) Gen. Infirmary, 1997—. Co-author: (with H. Jacobs) Infertility in Practice; contbr. articles to profl. jours. Rsch. fellow The Middlesex Hosp., 1990-93. Fellow Royal Coll. Ob-Gyn.; mem. British Fertility Soc. (treas.) Am. Soc. Reproductive Medicine.

BALEPIN, VLADIMIR VLADIMIROVICH, aerospace propulsion scientist; b. Vilnius, Lithuania, USSR; s. Vladimir Mikhailovich and Regina Ivanovna (Boyarunas) B.; m. Tatiana Vladimirovna Sosounova, Apr. 25, 1979; 1 child, Ivan Balepin. BS in Aerospace Propulsion Engring., Moscow Aviation Inst., 1976, MS in Aerospace Propulsion Engring., 1979; PhD in Aerospace Propulsion Engring., Ctrl. Inst. Aviation Motors, 1986. Rsch. engr. to sr. engr. Ctrl. Inst. for Aviation Motors, Moscow, 1979-85, rschr. to sr. rschr., 1985-90, head of rsch. group, 1990-93; vis. rschr. Nat. Aerospace Lab., Kakuda, Japan, 1993-94; vis. prof. Inst. for Space and Astronautical Sci., Sagamihara, Japan, 1994-95; cons. Techspace Aero Co., Milmort, Belgium, 1996-97; sr. rschr. Ctrl. Inst. for Aviation Motors, 1997; staff scientist MSE Tech. Applications, Inc., Butte, Mont, 1997—; lectr. Moscow Aviation Inst., Moscow, 1986-92; cons. Marubeni Corp., Tokyo, 1996; lectr. Internat. Space U., Strasbourg, France, 1996. Contbr. articles to profl. jours. including SAE Transactions, Jour. of Aerospace, Progress in Astronautics and Aeronautics, others; patentee in field. Recipient Arch. T. Colwell merit award Soc. Automotive Engrs., 1996; Sci. and Tech. Agy. of Japan fellow, 1992. Mem. AIAA (sr., Pacific N.W. sect. def. and space engring. tech. achievement award 1999). Achievements include research in the field of concepts of combined propulsion cycles for single-stage to orbit vehicles, development of the precooled airbreathing cycles including a potentientially revolutionary earth-to-orbit propulsion cycle known as KLIN and ATREX engine subject to firing test, study of the air separation technology based on the vortex tube. Office: MSE Tech Applications Inc PO Box 4078 200 Technology Way Butte MT 59702

BALESTRINI, ARISTÓBULO ENRIQUE, cardiologist; b. Córdoba, Argentina, Apr. 18, 1941; s. Aristóbulo Melchor and Isabel Haydée (van Cauwelaert) B. B., Santo Tomás/Monserrat, Córdoba, 1959; MD, Univ. Nacional, Córdoba, 1966. Resident, med. intern Centro de Educacion Medica e Investigaciones Clinicas, Buenos Aires, 1967-68; resident cardiology Hosp. Italiano Buenos Aires, 1969-71; chief of residents Hosp. Durand, Buenos Aires, 1972; staff cardiology dept. Hosp. Posadas, Buenos Aires, 1973-88; assoc. prof. U. Buenos Aires, 1975—, dir. univ. career specialist cardiology, 1995—; chief pacemaker ctr. Policlinico Bancario, Buenos Aires, 1976-81; chief cardiology dept. Hosp. Posadas, Buenos Aires, 1988—; dir. annual course echocardiology and cardiac doppler Hosp. Posadas, 1988—; bd. dirs. Centro Medico Cardiovasc-CARDIOS, Buenos Aires, 1982—. pres. adminstrn. Coun. Fundación Dr. William Harvey. Mem. Soc. Argentina Cardiologia (prize 1970, 95, 97), Soc. Argentina Estimulacion Cardiaca, Consejo Argentina Cardiologia Clinica-Soc. Argentina Cardiol. Home: Juan Maria Gutierrez 2751, 5o A, 1425 Buenos Aires Argentina Office: CARDIOS Centro Medico CV, Mansilla 2450 PB A, 1121 Buenos Aires Argentina

BALFOUR, ALAN HAROLD, clinical research scientist; b. Birkenhead, Eng., Aug. 18, 1946; s. Harold and Ann (Pringle) B.; divorced; children: Charlotte Brie, Justin Daniel. BTech. in Applied Biology with honors, U. Bradford, 1969; MTech in Applied Immunology, Brunel U., 1972; PhD, U. Liverpool, 1976. Rsch. microbiologist Express Dairy Co., London, 1969-70; tech. officer Clin. Rsch. Ctr., London, 1970-73; rsch. asst. dept. medicine U. Liverpool, Eng., 1973-76; cons. clin. scientist, head of dept. Regional Pub. Health Lab., Leeds, Eng., 1976-94; hon. rsch. fellow U. Leeds, 1994—; cons. in immunodiagnostics and complementary therapies, Leeds, 1994—; cons. Northumbria Biols. Ltd., Cramlington, Northumberland, Eng., 1982-91, Mercia Diagnostics, Guilford, Surrey, Eng., 1982-86, Amersham (Eng.) Internat., 1988-92, E-Y Labs. Inc., San Mateo, Calif., 1990-95, HD-Health Dimensions, Leeds, Eng., 1994—. Author: (book chpt.) Elisa in the Clinical Laboratory, 1990; contbr. sci. papers to profl. jours. Equipment grantee Med. Rsch. Coun., 1981. Mem. Inst. Biology (cert. biologist and clin. scientist), Brit. Soc. for Immunology (local organizer 1972-90), The Dr./Healer Netwo rk. Achievements include research in serodiagnostic work, particularly in toxoplasma infections. Avocations: hypnosis, Reiki healing master, massage, mind/body interactions in relation to health, disease and human potential. Home: 314 Broadway Horsforth, Leeds LS18 4QU, England

BALFOUR, CHARLES GEORGE YULE, stock exchange executive; b. São Paulo, Brazil, Apr. 23, 1951; s. Eustace Arther Goschen and Anne Balfour; m. Reichgräfin Svea Maria VonGoëss, Sept. 19, 1987; children: Eleanor Cecily Isabelle, George Eustace Charles. Student, Eton Coll., England. With Hoare Govett & Co., 1970-73, Hill Samuel & Co. Ltd., 1973-76, Dillon Read Overseas Corp, 1976-79; exec. dir. Banque Paribas, 1972-92; sr. v.p., managing dir. The NASDAQ Stock Mkt., London, 1992—; sr. mng. dir. Nesdeq Stock Market, 2000—. Mem. Queen's Bodyguard for Scotland, Royal Co. Archers. Office: The Nasdaq Stock Market, Durrant House 8/13 Chiswell St, London EC1Y 4XY, England

BALFOUR, JOHN MANNING, lawyer; b. Calcutta, India, Oct. 2, 1952; parents Brit. citizens; s. James Richard and Eunice Barbara (Manning) B. MA, Oxford (Eng.) U., 1975. Solicitor, Supreme Ct. of Eng. Asst. solicitor Frere Cholmeley, London, 1979-86; ptnr. Frere Cholmeley Bischoff, London, 1986-97, Beaumont and Son, London, 1997—. Author: European Community Air Law, 1995; contbg. editor: Forms and Precedents: Carriage, 1988, Shawcross and Beaumont: Air Law, 1996; joint editor: European Air Law Association Papers, 1991-95. Fellow Chartered Inst. Transport; mem. Royal Aero. Soc. (past chmn. air law group), European Air Law Assn. (sec.). Office: Beaumont and Son, Lloyds Chambs 1 Portsoken, London E1 8AW, England

BALGIMBAYEV, NURLAN, former Kazakhstan prime minister; b. Guriev (now Atyrau), Kazakhstan, Nov. 20, 1947. Degree in mining engring., Kazak Poly. Inst., 1973; postgrad., U. Mass., Boston, 1992-93. From asst. driller to chief engr. state-run oil cos., Kazakhstan, 1964-86; dep. head chief dept. oil extraction Ministry of Oil and Gas Industry of USSR, Moscow, 1986-92; minister of oil and gas industry Govt. of Kazakhstan, 1994-97; prime minister Republic of Kazakhstan, from 1997; chmn. Kazakhoil Nat. Oil & Gas Co., Kazakhstan. Office: Kazakhoil Nat Oil & Gas Co, ul Bogenbai Batyr 142, Almaty Kazakhstan*

BALI, VISHAL, health services administrator; b. New Delhi, Jan. 8, 1967; s. S.K. and Neelam B.; m. Tanya Gupta, Feb. 24, 1995. BS, Mithibai Coll., Bombay, 1989; MBA, Sydenham Inst. Mgmt. Studies, Bombay, 1991. Product exec. Wockhardt Hosp. and Heart Inst., Bangalore, India, 1992-94, product mgr., 1994-96, ctr. mgr., 1996-99, gen. mgr., 1999—. Recipient Pres.'s award for Promoting Med. Edn., Med. Edn. and Rsch. Trust, 1994. Mem. Sydenham Mgmt. Assn. (gen. sec. 1990), Confedn. Indian Industry, Indo-Am. C. of C. Avocations: reading, collecting ties, music. Fax: +91 080 2281149. E-mail: whhi@vsnl.com. Office: Wockhardt Hosp Heart Inst, 14 Cunningham rd, KRN Bangalore 560052, India

BALIAN, ROGER, physicist; b. Lyon, France, Jan. 18, 1933; s. Noubar and Nevarte (Avedissian) B.; m. Lauris Denise Semerdjian, July 20, 1957; children: Katia, Pierre, Jacques. Degree in Physics, 1st ranked, Ecole Polytechnique, Paris, 1955. Rsch. physicist Phys. Theory Svc. Atomic Energy Commn., Saclay, France, 1956—, head Phys. Theory Svc., 1979-87; prof. physics Ecole Polytechnique, Paris, 1972-98; dir. Summer Sch. of Physics, Les Houches, France, 1972-80. Author: From Microphysics to Macrophysics: Methods and Applications of Statistical Physics, 2 vols., 1991, 92; editor: Series of Proc. of the Les Houches Summer Sch., 1967, 72-80; editor-in-chief Europhysics Letters, 1992-95; contbr. over 120 articles to profl. jours. Mem. Royal Soc. Sci. (Uppsala, Sweden), French Acad. Scis. (Henri Poincaré prize 1954, Rivet-Lamb prize 1954, des Laboratoires prize 1972), French Phys. Soc. (pres. 1997-99, Langevin prize 1966, Jean Ricard prize 1977). Achievements include research in theoretical physics. Office: CEA/Saclay, Physics Theory Service, 91191 Gif-sur-Yvette Cedex, France

BALIGA, PANKAJ MADHAV, marketing executive; b. Mumbai, India, Oct. 18, 1946; s. Madhau Ramchandra and Heera Madhua Baliga; m. Neelima Kuukarni, Nov. 5, 1971; children: Amrish, Girish. BCE, Regional Engring. Coll., Durgapur, India, 1968; MBA, IIM, Ahmedabad, India, 1970. Mktg. mgr. CIDCO, Mumbai, 1970-78; v.p. mktg. The Taj Group of Hotels, Mumbai, 1978—; bd. dirs. Asia Pacific Hotels, Ltd., India, Taj Karnataka Hotels and Resorts Ltd., India, Apex Hotel Mgmt. Svcs., Ltd., Singapore; alt. del. Hotel Del Annopurna. Ford Found. scholar, 1974; Spurs fellow MIT, 1975. Mem. Rotary Internat., Bombay Gymkurna. Avocations: cricket, football, hockey, music. Office: The Taj Group Hotels, Mandlik House Mandlik Rd, Colaba Mumbai 400001, India

BALIK, ISMAIL, medical educator; b. Afyon, Turkey, Feb. 13, 1960; s. Mustafa and Emine Balik; m. Ozlem Gunaydin, Nov. 25, 1990; 1 child, Burak. Med. diploma, U. Bursa, 1983. Gen. practitioner Pub. Health Ctr., Afyon, 1983-85; fellow infectious diseases dept. Ankara (Turkey) U. Med. Faculty, 1985-89, asst. prof. infectious diseases dept., 1989-91, assoc. prof. infectious diseases dept., 1991-96, prof. infectious diseases dept., 1996—; rsch. assoc. Milan U. Med. Faculty, 1988-89; vis. prof. lab. cellular physiology and immunology Rockefeller U., N.Y.C., 1999; mem. antimicrobial drug approval com. Ministry of Health, 1989—, advisor adv. com., 1989—. Author: (Web site) Turkish Infection Web Site, 1998; asst. editor 2 med. jours., 1994—; mem. editl. bd 11 med. jours. Mem. Nat. AIDS Com., Ankara, 1990-93. Recipient Roche Viral Hepatitis award of Turkey, 1996. Mem. Internat. Soc. for Infectious Diseases, European Soc. Clin. Microbiology and Infectious Diseases, Turkish Soc. Clin. Microbiology and Infectious Diseases, Turkish Soc. Microbiology, Turkish Viral Hepatitis Soc. (bd. dirs. 1994—), Ankara Soc. AIDS (bd. dirs. 1994—). Avocations: Internet, traveling. Fax: 90(312)324 0328. E-mail: baliki@infeksiyon.org. Office: Ankara U Med Faculty, Ibni Sina Hastanesi, Ankara 06100, Turkey

BÁLINT, ANDOR, agricultural studies educator emeritus; b. Tiszavárkony, Szolnok, Hungary, May 21, 1920; s. Ödön Büchler and Margit Ungár; m. Anna Hesslein, Mar. 29, 1949; children: Vera, Ferenc. Student, U. Tech. and Econ. Scis., 1939-46; Candidate Agrl. Scis., Hungarian Acad. Scis., Budapest, 1952, D of Biol. Scis., 1969; PhD (hon.), U. Agrl. Scis., Gödöllő, Hungary, 1993. Ofcl. City Adminstrn., Kiskunfélegyháza, 1945-46; rschr. Inst. Genetics and Plant Breeding, Budapest, 1947-50; head dept. biology Agrl. U., Budapest, 1950-54; vice rector U. Agrl. Scis., 1953-55, head dept. plant breeding, 1954-85, dean faculty agr., 1957-60, 69-72, prof. emeritus, 1996—. Author: Genetics and Evolution, 1964, 4th rev. edit., 1977, Plant Breeding, 1966, 2d rev. edit., 1976. Recipient Fleischmann plaque Ministry Agr., 1986, Prize Acad. Scis., Laureatus Acad. 1998. Avocations: psychology, reading novels. Home: Bimbó út 168/a, H-1026 Budapest Hungary Office: Sz State U, Páter Károly út. 1, 2103 Gödöllő Hungary

BALINT, GABOR ALEXANDER, pharmacologist; b. Szeged, Csongrad, Hungary, Jan. 7, 1936; s. Julius Alexander and Mary Margaret (Sandor) B.; m. Magdalen Fogarasi, July 16, 1960; children: Erica, Andras. MD summa cum laude, Szeged U., 1960; PhD in Medicine, Makerere Med. Sch., Kampala, Uganda, 1974; DSc in Medicine, Hungarian Acad. Scis., Budapest, 1987. Cert.. radioisotope technique in medicine, med. physiology; diplomate clin. pharmacology, clin. pathology. Lectr. dept. pharmacology Szeged U. Med. Sch., 1960-69, reader, 1st dept. medicine, 1975-88; sr. lectr. József Attila Unive, Szeged, 1969-70; 1st sr. lectr. dept. physiology Makerere Med. Sch., Kampala, Uganda, 1970-74; prof., head dept. pharmacology Addis Ababa U., 1988-90; assoc. prof., head Lab. Clin. Pharmacology, New Clinics Albert Szent-Györgyi Med. U., Szeged, 1990-98, prof., head lab. clinic pharmacology, 1998—; sr. cons. specialist Szeged Out-Patients' Hosp., 1963-78; sr. cons. specialist medicine Armed Forces Hosp., Dhahran, Saudi Arabia, 1991; WHO expert, 1991—. Contbr. articles to profl. jours., chpts. to books. Lt. col. Hungarian Armed Forces, 1991, 96. Recipient Commemorative medal Pres. of Republic, 1996, In the Service of Peace and Freedom medal NATO/IFOR, 1996. Mem. N.Y. Acad. Scis., Hungarian Pharmacological Soc., Royal Soc. Medicine (Overseas fellow 1995), Hungarian Physiol. Soc., Hungarian Soc. Gastroenterology, Internat. Brain Rsch. Orgn., Internat. Soc. Xenobiotics, European Brain and Behavioral Soc., Ro-

tary. Roman Catholic. Fax: 36-(62)-545-973. E-mail: balint@nepsy.szote.u-szeged.hu. Home: Szentharomsag u.17, H-6722 Szeged Hungary Office: Albert Szent Gyorgyi Med U, New Clinics PO Box 427, H-6701 Szeged Hungary

BÁLINT, GÉZA PETER, clinical rheumatologist, physiotherapy educator; b. Budapest, Hungary, Nov. 8, 1935; s. Géza and Gézáné (Tax Terézia) B.; m. Elvira Hatos, Sept. 12, 1956; children: Géza, Péter, Bertalan. MD, Semmelweiss Med. U., Budapest, 1960; DSc, Hungarian Acad. Scis., Budapest, 1995. Specialization rheumatology & physiotherapy, 1964. Registrar Nat. Inst. Rheumatology, Budapest, 1968-71; cons. rheumatology Inst. Rheumatology, Budapest, 1971-72; rsch. fellow Ctr. Rheumatic Diseases, Glasgow, Scotland, 1977-78; head physiotherapy dept. Inst. Rheumatology, Budapest, 1976-87; head physician Chair Rheumatology Postgrad. Med. U., Budapest, 1972-76, reader physiotherapy, 1987-91; dir. Nat. Inst. Rheumatology & Physiotherapy, Budapest, 1991—; prof. physiotherapy Imre Haynal U. Health Sci., Budapest, 1996—; vis. prof. McMaster U., Hamilton, Can., 1985; inventor in field. Author: Occupational Rheumatic Diseases, 1989, Rheumatology, State of the Art, 1992, Clinical Examination of the Musculoskeletal System, 1996. Recipient Bayer prize EULAR com., Wiesbaden, Germany, 1979, Excellent Physician award Minister Welfare, Budapest, 1991, Markusovszky prize Orvosi Hetilap, Budapest, 1991. Mem. Brit. Soc. for Rheumatology, Coll. Rheumatologists (pres. 1991), Purkinje Soc. (hon.). Avocations: poetry, history, touring, travel. Home: Palanta u 19, H-1025 Budapest Hungary Office: Nat Inst Rheumatology, Frankel Leo u 17/19, H-1027 Budapest Hungary

BALIS, JENNIFER LYNN, computer technology educator; b. Hamlin, W.Va., Nov. 23, 1946; m. James Pearsall; 1 child, Theodore Berndt. AA, Del Mar Coll., 1987; BA, U. Tex., 1989; BS, So. Ill. U., 1992. Peer counselor U. Tex., Edinburg, 1989-90; tchr. Mission (Tex.) Ind. Sch. Dist., 1990; instr. San Diego Job Corps, 1992-95; placement specialist St. Louis Job Corps Ctr., 1997-98; instr. computer tech. Kaskaskia Coll., Centralia, Ill., 1997—; coord. Kaskaskia Coll. Vandalia Ctr., Vandalia, Ill., 2000—; coord. Vandalia Ctr., Kaskaskia Coll., 1999—; owner Mulberry Grove Mercantile. First responder Mulberry Grove (Ill.) Fire Dept., 1999—; chmn., sec. Mulberry Grove Zoning Bd. Appeals, 1999—. With USNR, 1984—. Mem. Psi Chi (pres. 1989-90). Republican. Roman Catholic. Avocations: folk medicine, mineral collector, archery.

BALK, ALFRED WILLIAM, journalist; b. Oskaloosa, Iowa, July 24, 1930; s. Leslie William and Clara Irene (Buell) B.; m. Phyllis Lorraine Munter, June 7, 1952; children: Laraine M., Diane M. Student, Augustana Coll., Rock Island, Ill., 1948-49; BS, Northwestern U., 1952, MS, 1953. Reporter Rock Island Argus, 1946-50; newswriter-producer WBBM (CBS), Chgo., 1952-53; reporter Chgo. Sun-Times, 1956; mag. writer, pub. relations J. Walter Thompson Co., Chgo., 1957-58; freelance writer nat. mags., including spl. writer Saturday Evening Post, 1958-66; feature editor Saturday Rev., 1966-68, editor at large, 1968-69; vis. scholar Russell Sage Found., 1968-69; lectr. journalism, editor Columbia Journalism Rev., 1969-73; editor World Press Rev., 1974, editor-pub., 1975-84, editorial dir., 1985-86, editorial cons., contbg. editor, 1986-94; mng. editor IEEE Spectrum, N.Y.C., 1989-91; assoc. prof. Syracuse U., 1991-94; freelance writer, cons. Syracuse, 1994—; cons., rapporteur 20th Century Fund Task Force on Nat. News Coun., 1971-72, Ford Found., Markle Found.; mem. faculty Bread Loaf Writers Conf., Middlebury, Vt., 1971; exec. sec. N.Y. Gov.'s Com. on Employment Minority Groups in News Media, 1968-69; mem. adv. com. World Press Inst., 1984-96. Author: The Free List: Property Without Taxes, 1970, A Free and Responsive Press, 1973, The Myth of American Eclipse: The New Global Age, 1990, Movie Palace Masterpiece: Saving Syracuse's Loew's State/Landmark Theatre, 1998; co-editor: Our Troubled Press, 1971. Bd. dirs. Landmark Theatre Found., 1996-99. Mem. Am. Soc. Mag. Editors (exec. coun. 1977-83), Am. Soc. Journalists and Authors (pres. 1967), Soc. Profl. Journalists, Overseas Press Club (gov. 1978-79), Century Assn. Home: 13225 Michigan Ave Huntley IL 60142-7480

BALKA, SIGMUND RONELL, lawyer; b. Phila., Aug. 1, 1935; s. I. Edwin and Jane (Chernicoff) B.; m. Elinor Bernstein, May 29, 1966. AB, Williams Coll., 1956; JD, Harvard U., 1959. Bar: Pa. and D.C. 1961, N.Y. 1969, U.S. Supreme Ct. 1966. Sr. atty. Lilco, Mineola, N.Y., 1969-70; v.p., gen. counsel Brown Boveri Corp., North Brunswick, N.J., 1970-75; asst. gen. counsel Power Authority State N.Y., N.Y.C., 1975-80; gen. counsel Krasdale Foods, Inc., N.Y.C., 1980—; pres. Graphic Arts Coun. N.Y., 1980—. Chmn. Hunts Point Environ. Protection Coun., N.Y.C., 1980—; chmn. law com. N.Y.C. Community Bd. 6, Queens, 1980-88, chmn. econ. devel. com., 1988-99; chmn. Soc. for a Better Bronx, 1985—; bd. dirs. Bronx Arts Coun., 1981—, Greater N.Y. Met. Food Coun., 1986—; bd. dirs. Jewish Repertory Theatre, 1987—, co-chmn., 2000—; chmn. Bronx Borough Pres.'s Adv. Com. on Resource Recovery, 1988-90; chair fellows, mem. vis. com. Williams Coll. Mus. of Art, 1996-99. Fellow Am. Bar Found.; mem. ABA (co-chmn. pro bono project corp. law dept. 1986-88, chmn. 1988-90, com. of corp. gen. counsel 1974—, planning chmn. 1994-96, membership chmn. 1996-98, pro bono chair 2000—), Am. Corp. Counsel Assn. (bd. dirs. Met. N.Y. chpt. 1987—, bd. dirs. Found. 1992-99), Assn. Bar City N.Y. Office: Krasdale Foods Inc 400 Food Center Dr Bronx NY 10474-7098

BALKO, GEORGE ANTHONY, III, lawyer, educator; b. Bklyn., June 22, 1955; s. George Anthony Jr. and Settimia (Palumbo) B. AB, Yale U., 1977; JD, U. Calif., San Francisco, 1986. Bar: Mass. 1986, U.S. Dist. Ct. Mass. 1987, U.S. Dist. Ct. Conn. 1999, U.S. Ct. Appeals (1st cir.) 1987, D.C 1990. Assoc. Swartz & Swartz, Boston, 1986-87, Bowditch & Dewey, Worcester, Mass., 1987-95; ptnr. Bowditch & Dewey, Worcester, 1996—; adj. prof. Anna Maria Coll., Paxton, Mass., 1988-2000, mem. paralegal studies adv. bd., 1988-95. Author: Risk Management for Nursing Homes: A Primer In Long-Term Care Adminstration Handbook, 1993, Ambulatory Care and the Law: Lien Claims Where None Exist As of Right, 1995; legal columnist Jour. of Workers Compensation, 1996-99. Mem. Rice Sch. PTA, Holden, Mass., 1989-93; bd. health Town of Holden, 1995-99, chmn. 1996-99; moderator, 1999—; pres., bd. dirs. Elm Park Ctr. for Early Childhood Edn., 1994-96, mem. 1993-97. Recipient Am. Jurisprudence award for Ins. Law Lawyers Coop. Pub. Co. and Bancroft Whitney Co., 1985. Roman Catholic. Avocations: history, travel, tennis. Home: 4 Chestnut Hill Rd Holden MA 01520-1603 Office: Bowditch & Dewey 311 Main St Worcester MA 01608-1552

BALL, DAVID JOHN, librarian; b. Rowley Regis, United Kingdom, Aug. 8, 1950; m. Margaret MacLean, Apr. 21, 1977; 1 child, Helen. BA with honors, Keble Coll., Oxford, Eng., 1972; diploma in librarianship, Coll. of Librarianship, Aberystwyth, Wales, 1977; MLitt, U. Strathclyde, Glasgow, Scotland, 1985. Sub-libr. U. Strathclyde, Glasgow, Scotland, 1979-88; info. mgr. Glasgow Herald & Evening Times, 1988-93; libr. Bournemouth (Eng.) U., 1994—; convenor librs. project group So. Univs. Purchasing Consortium, Reading, Eng., 1996—. Author: Thomas Mann's Recantation of Faust: Doktor Faustus in the Context of Mann's Relationship to Goethe, 1986. Mem. Inst. Mgmt., Inst. Info. Scientists. Fax: 01202-595475. E-mail: dball@bournemouth.ac.uk. Office: Bournemouth Univ, Fern Barrow, Poole BH12 5BB, England

BALL, DAVID TERRY, university chaplain, academic administrator; b. Cin., Aug. 15, 1960; s. John Terry and Ellen (Graham) B.; m. Kim Keethler, Mar. 15, 1997; children: Anna Marie Cooper, Vincent Terry Cooper, John Terry Ball. BA, Ohio Wesleyan U., 1982; MDiv, Boston U., 1986; JD, U. Calif., Berkeley, 1991; PhD, Grad. Theol. Union, Berkeley, 1998. Bar: Calif. 1991. Assoc. Farella, Braun & Martel, San Francisco, 1991-94; pastor First United Meth., Wapakoneta, Ohio, 1995-96; dir. religious life and svc.-learning Denison U., Granville, Ohio, 1996—; mem. faculty Nat. Svc. Leadership Inst., San Francisco, 1999—; adj. faculty Meth. Theol. Sch., Delaware, Ohio, 1999—; regional trainer Learn and Serve Exch., Washington, 1999—; mem. exec. com. Ohio Campus Compact, Granville, 1997—. Contbr. articles to profl. jours. including The Christian Century, The Nat. Law Jour., Novum Testamentum. Founder Interfaith Legal Svcs., Columbus, Ohio, 1999; bd. dirs. Family Health Svc., Newark, Ohio, 1997—, Licking County Housing Coaltion, Newark, 1997—; mem. Granville Ministerium, 1996—. Paul Harris fellow Rotary Internat., 1983-84; grantee Denison U., 1998; Martin Luther King Jr. grantee Corp. for Nat. Svc., Washington, 1997. Mem. Nat. Assn. Coll. and Univs. Chaplains, Am. Acad. Religion, State Bar Calif. Democrat. Baptist. Avocation: golf. Home: 231 Broadway W Granville OH 43023-1119 Office: Denison U PO Box M Granville OH 43023-0810

BALL, SIR (ROBERT) JAMES, economics educator; b. London, July 15, 1933; s. Arnold James Hector B.; m. Patricia Mary Hart Davies, 1954 (div. 1970); children: Charles, Stephanie, Deborah, Joanna; m. Lindsay Jackson Wonnacott, 1970; 1 stepson, Nigel. BA, Oxford U., 1957, MA, 1960; PhD, U. Pa., 1973; DSc (hon.), U. Aston, Birmingham, Eng., 1987. Rsch. officer, statistics Oxford U., 1957-58; IBM fellow U. Pa., 1958-60; lectr. U. Manchester (Eng.), 1960; sr. lectr. London Bus. Sch., 1963-65, gov., 1969-84, dep. prin., 1971-72, prin., 1972-84, prof. econs., 1965-97, prof. emeritus, 1997—, fellow, 1998; bd. dirs. Royal Bank Can., chmn. Royal Bank Can. Holding (UK) Ltd., 1995-98; bd. dirs. IBM U.K. Pensions Trust Ltd.; chmn. Legal and Gen. Group plc., 1980-94; econ. advisor Touche Ross & Co., 1984-95. Author: Econometric Model of U.K., 1961, Inflation and the Theory of Money, 1964; editor: Inflation, 1969, The International Linkage of National Economic Models, 1972, Money and Employment, 1982, (with M. Albert) Toward European Economic Recovery in the 1980s (Report to European Parliament), 1984, The Economics of Wealth Creation, 1992, The World Economy: Trends and Prospects for the Next Decade, 1994, The British Economy at the Crossroads, 1998; contbr. articles to profl. jours. Served with RAF, 1952-54. Mem. Foulkes Found., The Economist, Royal Automobile (Pall Mall). Avocations: gardening, chess. Office: London Bus Sch, Sussex Pl Regents Pk, London NW1 4SA, England

BALL, JAMES, communications executive, consultant; b. Chgo., Jan. 24, 1963; m. Sept. 13, 1997; 1 child, Isabel. BA in Pschology, Ind. U., 1985. Nat. accounts mgr. MFS Telecom, Chgo., 1994-97; dir. Epoch Internet, Chgo., 1997-98; regional v.p. Level 3 Comm., Denver, 1998-99; pres. Mpower Comm., Chgo., 1999—; scout coms. Elmhurst, Ill., 1991—. Dir. MBCA, Chgo., 1995—. Avocations: music, reading, wine, mentoring. E-mail: jball@mpower.com. Office: Mpower Communications 1460 Renaissance Dr Park Ridge IL 60068-1331

BALL, JOSEPH ANTHONY, mathematician; b. Washington, June 4, 1947; s. William Howard and Angela Marie (Hosinski) B.; m. Amelia Yoshie Sullivan, Mar. 20, 1982. BS, Georgetown U., 1969; PhD, U. Va., 1973. Asst. prof. Va. Polytech Inst. and State U., Blacksburg, 1973-78; assoc. prof. Va. Tech. U., Blacksburg, 1978-82, prof., 1982—. Co-author: Interpolation of Rational Matrix Functions, 1990; contbr. numerous articles to profl. jours. Office: Dept Math Va Polytech Inst /State U Blacksburg VA 24061

BALL, KENNETH JAMES, independent financial advisor; b. Birmingham, Eng., Apr. 19, 1935; s. James Thomas and Jessie May (Barsby) B.; m. Iris May Brindley, July 6, 1957 (div. 1988); 1 child, Susan Elisabeth; m. Anita Jeniferre Elson, Jan. 31, 1998. Proprietor K.J. Ball Fin. Svcs., Bromsgrove, Eng., 1966—; chmn., mng. dir. Midlands Fin. Group, Bromsgrove, 1985-95; with Appeals Tribunal Fin. Intermediaries, Mgrs. and Brokers Regulatory Assn., 1988—, H.M. Treasury Fin. Svcs. Act Tribunal U.K., 1994—, Personal Investment Authority Membership and Disciplinary Appeals Tribunal U.K., 1996—, Securities and Futures Authority Membership and Disciplinary Appeals Tribunal, 1997—. Fellow Inst. of Co. Accts., Inst. of Mgmt.; mem. Life Ins. Assn. Anglican. Avocations: business, dinner parties, travel, Mensa, languages.

BALL, PHILIP CHARLES, writer; b. Newport, U.K., Oct. 30, 1962; s. David and Jennifer (Porter) B. BA in Chemistry, Oxford (U.K.) U., 1983; PhD in Physics, U. Bristol, U.K., 1988. Editor Nature Mag., London, 1988-99. Author: Designing the Molecular World, 1994, Made to Measure, 1997, The Self-Made Tapestry, 1998, H2O: A Biography of Water, 1999. Avocations: musician, physical-theatre performer, travel. Office: Nature, 4-6 Crinan St, London N1 9XW, England

BALL, SAMUEL, educational administrator, psychologist; b. Sydney, NSW, Australia, Jan. 9, 1933; s. Joseph Patrick and Sarine (Jacobs) B.; divorced; children: Catherine, John, Pamela, David; m. Marita Joan MacMahon, Sept. 29, 1979; children: Rachel, Simone. Tchg. cert., Balmain Tchrs. Coll., Australia, 1951; BA in Ednl. Psychology with honors, U. Sydney, 1956, MEd with honors, 1961; PhD in Ednl. Psychology, U. Iowa, 1964. Prof. of psychology and edn. Tchrs. Coll., Columbia U., N.Y.C., 1964-78; sr. rsch. psychologist Ednl. Testing Svc., Princeton, N.J., 1968-78; prof. of edn. U. Sydney, 1978-84, pro vice chancellor, 1991-93; CEO Bd. of Studies, Victoria, Australia, 1993—; founding mem. bd. govs. U. Western Sydney, Australia, 1988-91; chmn. acad. bd., fellow of senate U. Sydney, 1988-91; dir. of rsch. Sesame Street, U.S., 1968-72. Author: (books) Encyclopedia of Educational Evaluation, 1975, Motivation in Education, 1977, The Profession and Practice of Program Evaluation, 1978; editor: Jour. of Ednl. Psychology, 1978-84. Chair NSW Childrens Week Com., Sydney, 1982-86. Recipient Alexander von Humboldt medal NSW Radiography Assn., 1985. Fellow APA (chmn. coun. of edn. 1983-84); mem. Australian Assn. for Rsch. in Edn., Am. Edn. Rsch. Assn. Avocations: tennis, reading, family. Home: 12 Atkinson Close, Windsor VIC 3181, Australia Office: Bd of Studies, 15 Pelham St, Carlton VIC 3053, Australia

BALL, WILLIAM LEE (ATLEY FALL), sportswriter; b. Dover, N.J., May 18, 1946; s. Frederick J. and Mary Elizabeth (Decker) B.; m. Gail Williams, Mar. 9, 1979. Grad., N.Y. Acad. Theatrical Arts, 1964; AS, La Salle Ext. U., 1978. Mem. staff West Coast Lit. Assocs., Aptos, Calif., 1993-95, Aardvark Lit. Agy., Amherst, N.Y., 1997-98; free lance writer Linden, N.J., 1998—. Contbr. over 65 articles to mags., including Ea. Outdoors, The Fisherman. Mem. Internat. Platform Assn., Authors Guild. Republican. Baptist. Avocations: fishing, photography. Home: 542 Springfield Rd Linden NJ 07036-5131

BALL, WILLIAM PAUL, physicist, engineer; b. San Diego, Nov. 16, 1913; s. John and Mary (Kajla) B.; m. Edith Lucile March, June 28, 1941 (dec. 1976); children: Lura Irene Ball Raplee, Roy Ernest. AB, UCLA, 1940; PhD, U. Calif., Berkeley, 1952. Registered profl. engr. Calif. Projectionist, sound technician studios and theatres in Los Angeles, 1932-41; tchr. high sch. Montebello, Calif., 1941-42; instr. math. and physics Santa Ana (Calif.) Army Air Base, 1942-43; physicist U. Calif. Radiation Lab., Berkeley and Livermore, 1943-58; mem. tech. staff Ramo-Wooldridge Corp., Los Angeles, 1958-59; sr. scientist Hughes Aircraft Co., Culver City, Calif., 1959-64; sr. staff engr. TRW-Def. Systems Group, Redondo Beach, Calif., 1964-83, Hughes Aircraft Co., 1983-86; cons. Redondo Beach, 1986—. Contbr. articles to profl. jours.; patentee in field. Bd. dirs. So. Dist. Los Angeles chpt. ARC, 1979-86. Recipient Manhattan Project award for contbn. to 1st atomic bomb, 1945. Mem. AAAS, Am. Phys. Soc., Am. Nuclear Soc., N.Y. Acad. Scis., Torrance (Calif.) Area C. of C. (bd. dirs. 1978-84), Sigma Xi. Home and Office: 209 Via El Toro Redondo Beach CA 90277-6561

BALLANTINE, JOHN TILDEN, lawyer; b. Louisville, Feb. 26, 1931; s. Thomas Austin and Anna Marie (Pfeiffer) B.; m. Mary January Strode, May 15, 1954 (div. 1964); children: John T. Jr., William Clayton, Douglas C.; m. Beverley Jo Hackley, Dec. 8, 1967; 1 child, Susan Marie. BA with high distinction, U. Ky., 1952; JD, Harvard U., 1957. Bar: Ky. 1957, U.S. Ct. Appeals (6th cir.) 1958, U.S. Supreme Ct. 1982. Law clk. to presiding judge U.S. Dist Ct. (we. dist.) Ky., 1957-58; assoc. then ptnr. Ogden Newell & Welch PLLC, Louisville, 1958—; mem. civil rules com. Ky. Supreme Ct., 1988-96. Bd. dirs. Family and Children Agy., Louisville, 1965-75, pres., 1971-74; bd. dirs. Our Lady of Peace Hosp., Louisville, 1968-73, 88—, chmn., 1968-69, 91-93; bd. dirs. Met. United Way, Louisville, 1975-81; mem. Hist. Landmarks and Preservation Dists. Commn., Louisville, 1976-88; bd. dirs. Ky. Derby Festival, Louisville, 1975-81, v.p., 1975. 1st lt. USAF, 1952-54. Recipient Outstanding Young Man in Field of Law award Louisville Jaycees, 1966. Fellow Am. Coll. Trial Lawyers; mem. ABA, Ky. Bar Assn. (bd. govs. 1996—, ho. of dels. 1985-86, chmn. 1989-90, clients' security fund 1993-96, Ky. evidence rules rev. commn. 1995—), Louisville Bar Assn. (bd. dirs. 1969-71, 88, 89, 92, 93, 96—, pres. 1970, profl. responsibility com. 1988-93, past chmn. physician-atty. com.), U.S. 6th Cir. Ct. Appeals Jud. Conf. (life), Am. Bd. Trial Advs., Fed. Ins. and Corp. Counsel, Ky. Def. Counsel (pres. 1981-82), Louis D. Brandeis Am. Inn of Ct. (pres. 1997-98), Ky. Character and Fitness Com., Pendennis Club, The Law Club, Lawyers Club, Jefferson Club, Phi Beta Kappa. Office: Ogden Newell & Welch PLLC 1700 Citizens Plaza 500 W Jefferson St Ste 1700 Louisville KY 40202-2874

BALLARD, JOSEPH RAYMOND, nurse anesthesist; b. Washington, Aug. 16, 1953; s. Joseph Oscar and Melba Jean Ballard; m. Rita Ann Ballard, Aug. 4, 1973; children: Brandi, Tiffany. AS, Angelina Jr. Coll., Lufkin, Tex.; cert. RN anethesist, Charity Hosp. Sch. Anesthesia, New Orleans. Mem. Jacksonville (Tex.) City Coun., 1989-84. Mem. Am. Assn. Nurse Anesthetists, Masons, Shriners. Republican. Baptist. Avocations: golf, hunting. Home: 1900 Meadowhill Dr Jacksonville TX 75766-5234

BALLARD, LOUIS WAYNE, composer; b. Miami, Okla., July 8, 1931; s. Charles Guthrie and Leona Mae (Quapaw) B.; m. Ruth Sands, Dec. 6, 1965; children by previous marriage: Louis Anthony, Anne Marie, Charles Christopher. B.Mus. and Music Edn., U. Tulsa, 1954; M.Mus., 1962; D.Mus. (hon.), Coll. Santa Fe, 1973. Dir. vocal and instrumental music Nelagoney (Okla.) Public Sch., 1954-56; dir. vocal music Webster High Sch., Tulsa, 1956-58; pvt. music tchr., 1959-62; music dir. Inst. Am. Indian Arts, Santa Fe, 1962-65; dir. performing arts Inst. Am. Indian Arts, 1965-69; nat. dir. music edn. curriculum and rev. Bur. Indian Affairs, Washington, 1969-79; lectr., clinician, 1960—; pres. First Am. Indian Films, Inc., 1969—; disting. vis. prof. music Wm Jewell Coll., Liberty, Mo., 2000—. Composer, Santa Fe, 1979—; guest composer West German Music Festival, Saarbrü, 1986, Musik im 20 Jahrhundert, Ariz. State U., 1992, U. Ill. at Champagne, 1992, Ea. Music Festival, Greensboro, N.C., 1994, 95, 96; gala concert Carnegie Hall, 1992; full concert in Beethoven Chamber Music Hall, Bonn (first Am. composer), 1989; (ballet) Koshare, 1964, The Four Moons, 1967, Maid of the Mist and the Thunderbeings, 1991; (orchl. music) Fantasay Aborigine, Nos. I, II, III, IV, V; (chamber music) Rhapsody for Four Bassoons, Incident at Wounded Knee, Desert Trilogy, Ritmo Indio, Katcina Dances for cello-piano suite; (choral cantatas) The Gods Will Hear, Portrait of Will Rogers, Thus Spake Abraham; (oratorio) Dialogue Differentia text in Latin, Lakota-Sioux, English, Live On, Heart of My Nation (choral cantate with native Am. dialect), Manitoo, Gitche Manitoo (Am. Indian Doxology); (band works) Nighthawk Keetowa; (percussion) Cecega Ayuwipi, Music for the Earth and the Sky; (guitar) Quetzalcoatl's Coattails, 1992, The Lonely Sentinel, 1993, The Fire Moon (string quartet), A City of Silver, A City of Fire, A City of Light (piano concert pieces), numerous others.; commd. writer Lila Wallace Reader's Digest Arts Ptnrs./Meet the Composer, 1991; commd. writer (opera) Ministry Lower Saxony (Germany), 1993-94; author: The American Indian Sings, Book 1, 1970, Book 2, 1991, American Indian Chants for the Classroom, Oklahoma Indian Chants for the Classroom, also articles. Recipient 1st Marion Nevins MacDowell award chamber music, 1969, Nat. Indian Achievement award, 1972, Catlin Peace Pipe award Nat. Indian Lore Assn., 1976, ASCAP award, 1966-88, Lifetime Music Achievement award First Americans in Arts, 1997; F.B. Parriott grad. fellow, 1969; grantee Ford Found., 1970; grantee Nat. Endowment Arts, 1967, 69, 76, 79; commd. by Martha B. Rockefeller Found., 1969, Am. Composers Orch., 1982, commd. by Ministry Lower Saxony for Opera in Norden Gymnasium, West Germany, 1994. Mem. ASCAP, Music Educators Nat. Conf. (chmn. minority concerns com. for N.Mex. 1976), Am. Symphony Orch. League, Internat. Soc. for Polyaesthetic Music Edn. and Performance (lectr.), Phi Beta Kappa (alumni mem. Beta chpt. Okla. 1999). Lodge: Masons, Scottish Rite (32d degree). Office: PO Box 2072 Santa Fe NM 87504-2072

BALLARD, MARION SCATTERGOOD, software development professional; b. Montclair, N.J., Dec. 19, 1939; d. Alfred G. and Helen F. (Galey) Scattergood; m. Frederic L. Ballard Jr., Dec. 20, 1974; children: William, Robert; 1 stepchild, Anne A. Ballard. BA, Smith Coll., 1961; MA, U. Pa., 1963; MBA, American Univ., 1990. Lectr. Temple U., Phila.; mathematician UNIVAC, Blue Bell, Pa.; v.p. FINPAC Corp., Narberth, Pa.; pres. DataPlus, Inc, Washington. Chmn. bd. Sandy Spring Friends Sch., Washington Area Women's Found.; sec. bd. Sidwell Friends Sch. Mem. Nat. Assn. Women Bus. Owners, Phi Beta Kappa, Sigma Xi.

BALLARD, ROBERT CLIFFORD, automation engineer, failure analysis consultant; b. Norton AFB, Calif., Apr. 29, 1952; m. Donna Regi, July 2, 1983; children: Jody, Kristine, Candy, Valerie. Student in engrng. tech., Southern Tech. Inst., Marietta, Ga., 1983; assoc. in aerospace engrng., Air Force C.C., Maxwell AFB, Ala., 1986; BSEE, Thomas Edison State Coll., 1996. Avionics F 4 Phantom maintenance specialist USAF, 1971-80; aircraft modification engr. Dynalectron Corp., Dallas, 1980-81; environ. test engr. Loral Electronic Systems, Atlanta, 1981-83; prodn. supr. Sys. Instruments Rsch., Atlanta, 1983-85; calibration engr. Rockwell Internat., Duluth, Ga., 1985-89; prototype engr. Nordson Corp., Norcross, Ga., 1989-91; owner Intelligent Engring., Norcross, Ga., 1983—; fire/arson investigator Assn. Cons. Engrs., Atlanta, 1989—. Design engr. 1 Mil Bar Code Reader, 1992, Automated Monorail Train Maintenance Facility, 1995. Staff sgt., USAF, 1971-80, Vietnam. Served Ga. Air Nat. Guard, 1983-86. Recipient Achievement award for computer design to assist persons with disabilities, Johns Hopkins U., Balt., 1991. Mem. IEEE, Internat. Assn. Arson Investigators, Ga. Fire Investigators Assn., Ala. Assn. Arson Investigators. Office: Intelligent Engring 1108 Hillcrest Ct Norcross GA 30093-4606

BALLDIN, ULF INGEMAR, medical researcher; b. Malmö, Sweden, Apr. 5, 1939; came to U.S., 1992; s. Anton and Ebba T. (Engholm) B.; m. Susanne Ploman, June 29, 1974; children: Carl H., B. Christian, Fredrik J. BA, U. Lund, Sweden, 1959, MD, 1967, PhD, 1973; D (hon.), State Scientific Rsch. Inst., Moscow, 1995. Lic. physician, Sweden. Instr. physiology U. Lund, Sweden, 1964-67, rsch. physician, 1968-73; resident U. Hosp., Lund, Sweden, 1974; acting assoc. prof. U. Lund, 1975; rsch. flight surgeon Nat. Defense Rsch., Linköping, Sweden, 1976; sr. rsch. med. officer Nat. Defense Rsch. Establishment, Stockholm, 1977-86; rsch. dir. Nat. Def. Rsch. Establishment, Stockholm, 1987-99; dir. Inst. Aviation Medicine Nat. Def. Rsch. Establishment, Sweden, 1987-92; cons. in aerospace medicine, 1999—; adj. prof., head dept. aerospace medicine Karolinska Inst. Med. Sch., Stockholm, 1982-91; liaison scientist Brooks AFB, USAF, San Antonio, 1992-98; clin. asst. prof. U. Tex. Med. Br., Galveston, 1997—. Co-author: (chpt.) Textbook of Military Medicine, 2000; contbr. articles to profl. jours. Surgeon Lt. comdr. Swedish Air Force, 1976-99. Fellow Aerospace Med. Assn. (v.p., coun. mem.); mem. Royal Swedish Acad. War Scis., Internat. Acad. Aviation and Space Medicine (dir. 1993-97, 2d v.p. 1997-99, 1st v.p. 1999—). Achievements include improving inert gas elimination for decreasing risk of decompression sickness in divers and during extravehicular space activity, improved G-tolerance in fighter pilots with balanced pressure breathing during G and extended coverage anti-G suit. Avocations: flying, sailing, diving, music, jogging. Home: 14227 Parkhurst St San Antonio TX 78232-4733 Office: USAF Rsch Lab AFRL/HEP 2504 Gillingham Dr Ste 25 Brooks AFB TX 78235-5102

BALLE, ANNEMARIE SCHACK, editor; b. Copenhagen, Feb. 8, 1950; Mogens and Grete (Moller) B.; m. Jorgen Christian Jensen, Oct. 25, 1975; children: Michael, Charlotte. Degree in philosophy, Aarhus U., 1970. Editor Folkevirke, Denmark, 1981—, Danskvvs, Denmark, 1985—; chmn. Folkevirke H.S. Author: Dotremont and his logogrammes, 1976, Dotremont, 1979, Mogens Balle, 1981, The Christmas Tales of Anders and Rikke, 1983, Snus' Wonderful Day Out, 1985, Ghana A Country on Its Way Forward, 1987. Home and Office: Evanstoneyej 2 3rd Fl, 2900 Hellerup Denmark Address: Folkevirke, Niels Hemmingsens Gade 10 3, DK-1153 Copenhagen Denmark*

BALLÉ, MICHAEL ANDRÉ, management consultant, writer; b. Paris, Oct. 10, 1965; s. Freddy Jean-Jacques and Catherine Jacqueline (Zwobada) B. Deug Physique et Math. Appliques, Poitiers U., France, 1985; Diplome Ecole Superieure Commerce, Paris, 1991; Diplome D'Etudes Approfondies, La Sorbonne Paris IV, 1996. Mgmt. cons. Coopers & Lybrand, London, 1991-92; dir. B & A Conseil, Paris, 1992—; vis. prof. Higher Sch. Commerce, Troyes, France, 1995-97, Internat. Inst. Commerce and Distbn., 1997—, INSEEC, 1999—; sr. editor L'Harmattan Eds., 1996—; collection dir. Dynamiques d'enterprises, 1996—. Author: L'eveil, 1996, Vox Dei, 1996, 4 books on mgmt. Mem. UCPA (skipper 1994—). Avocations: sailing, riding, medieval history and art. Home: 19 Rue St Nicolas, 28170 St Maixme, Hauterive France Office: B&A Conseil, 45 bd de Montmorency, 75016 Paris France

BALLEARI, ENRICO, internist, rheumatologist, educator, researcher; b. Genoa, Italy, June 8, 1957; s. Luigi and Piera (Cuneo) B.; m. Anna Maria Allegro, June 7, 1987; children: Giulia, Federico. MD, U. Genoa, 1982. Postdoctoral fellow in rheumatology U. Genoa, 1983-86, asst. prof. dept. internal medicine, 1987—. Mem. Italian Soc. Rheumatology, Italian Soc. Exptl. Hematology. Avocation: gardening. Office: U Genoa Dept Internal Med, Viale Benedetto XV No 6, 16132 Genoa Italy

BALLER, DETLEV, physician, cardiologist, physiologist, researcher; b. Celle, Germany, Oct. 28, 1951; s. Gerhard and Irmgard (Schuch) B.; m. Brigitte Diestel, May 16, 1987; 1 child, Sven-Eric. MD summa cum laude, U. Göttingen, Germany, 1979. Assoc. prof. in physiology, 1983, assoc. prof. cardiology, 1992; assoc. prof. internal medicine Heart Ctr. North Rhine Westfalia, Bad Oeynhausen, Germany, 1990, coord. cons. physician nuclear-cardiac activities and interventional cardiology, 1993—. Contbr. articles to profl. jours. Mem. Martin Luther Ch. Avocations: photography (awards). Office: Heart Ctr N Rhine Westfalia, Georgstr 11, 32545 Bad Oeynhausen Germany

BALLESTER OLMOS, VICENTE-JUAN, automobile manufacturing company executive; b. Valencia, Spain, Dec. 27, 1948; s. José Ballester Anguis and Maria Nieves Olmos Soriano; m. Maria Asunción Miquel Muñoz, Sept. 16, 1977; children: Laura, Blanca, Daniel. B Superior, San José Coll., Valencia, 1967; minor degree in computer programming, U. Valencia, 1973. With Ford España, S.A., Valencia, 1976—, mgr. ins., benefits and pensions, 1983—; rep. Mut. UFO Network, Inc., Seguin, Tex., 1985—; v.p., rsch. dir. Fundación Anomalía, Santander, Spain, 1996—. Author: A Catalogue of 200 Type-I UFO Events in Spain and Portugal, 1976, Ovnis: El Fenómeno aterrizaje, 1978, 3d edit., 1984, Investigación Ovni, 1984, Expedientes Insólitos, 1995; co-author: Los Ovnis y la Ciencia, 1981, 2d edit., 1989, Enciclopedia de los Encuentros Cercanos con Ovnis, 1987; editor-in-chief Upiar Rsch. in Progress, 1983-85; mem. editl. bd. European Jour. UFO and Abduction Studies, 1999—; contbr. articles to profl. jours. Recipient Alvin H. Lawson award Fund for UFO Rsch., Washington, 1983, grantee, 1982. Fax: 34-96-1792600. E-mail: ballester-olmos@yahoo.es. Address: Apartado de Correos 12140, 46080 Valencia Spain Office: Ford España SA AO/AT-2, Poligono Industrial, 46440 Almussafes Valencia, Spain

BALLESTEROS, JUVENTINO RAY, JR., minister; b. L.A., June 27, 1953; s. Juventino Ray and Esther Marie (Mendoza) B.; m. Rebecca Ann Williamson, Dec. 30, 1978. BA, Birmingham South Coll., 1977; MA, Presbyn. Sch. Christian Edn., 1979; D Ministry, Union Theol. Sem., 1982. Intern minister Crystal Cathedral, Garden Grove, Calif., 1978, Philippi Presbyn. Ch., Raeford, N.C., 1980-81; assoc. minister 1st Presbyn. Ch., Fayetteville, N.C., 1982-84, Orlando, Fla., 1984-92; pastor, Christian Edn. Crystal Cathedral, Garden Grove, Calif., 1992—; chmn. Div. Edn., Fayetteville, 1982-84, Nat. Tchr. Edn. Program, Fayetteville 1983-84. Bd. dirs. Cumberland County Clean Community Council, Fayetteville, 1982-84, Nat. Tchr. Ednl. Program, Durham, N.C.; bd. advisors Jr. League, Fayetteville, 1983-84; v.p. Spouse Abuse Inc., Orlando, 1984-86; bd. trustees Union Theol. Sem./Presbyn. Sch. Christian Edn., 1996—. Mem. Religious Educators Assn., Assn. Presbyn. Ch. Educators. Republican. Avocation: all sports. Office: Crystal Cathedral 12141 Lewis St Garden Grove CA 92840-4699

BALLESTEROS, PAULA M., nurse; b. Jonesport, Me., Oct. 18, 1950; d. Paul Frederick and Janice Madeline (Beal) Mitchell; m. Ernesto Gascon Ballesteros, Apr. 4, 1981; children: Christopher, Jonathan. BS in Profl. Arts, St. Joseph's Coll., 1984; BSN, Husson/Ea. Me. Med. Ctr. Baccalaureate Sch. Nursing, 1994. Cert. Nursing Administrn. Patient care mgr. Ea. Me. Med. Ctr., Bangor, 1974—, bd. trustees, 1993-95; chairperson adv. bd. Ea. Maine Tech. Coll., Bangor, Me., 1993-94; pres. Me. Coun. Nurse Mgrs., 1991-93, Ea. Me. Med. Ctr. auxiliary, Bangor, Me., 1993-95. Contbr. articles to profl. jours. Mem. St. Joseph Hosp. Auxiliary. Mem. Am. Orgn. Nurse Execs., Penobscot Med. Soc. Auxiliary, Me. Assn. Hosp. Auxiliaries (pres. 1994—). Democrat. Protestant. Avocations: skiing, tennis, reading. Home: 78 Packard Dr Bangor ME 04401-2531 Office: Ea Maine Med Ctr 489 State St Bangor ME 04401-6616

BALLESTEROS, SEVERIANO, professional golfer; b. Pedrena, Spain, Apr. 9, 1957; s. Baldomero and Carmen (Sota) B.; m. Carmen Botin O'Shea; children: Javier, Miguel, Carmen. Chmn. Fairway, S.A., Madrid, 1981; main victories include Under 25 Nat. Championship, Vizcaya Open, 1974, Under 25 Nat. Championship, 1975, Profl. Championship Catalonia, Profl. Championship Tenerife, Dutch Open, Lancome Trophy, Donald Swaelens Meml., World Cup, 1976, French Open, Braun Internat., UniRoyal Internat., Swiss Open, Japanese Open, Dunlop-Phoenix (Japan), Otago Charity (New Zealand), World Cup, 1977, Kenia Open, Under 25 Nat. Open Championship, Greensboro Open, Martini Internat., German Open, Scandinavian Open, Swiss Open, 1978, Lada English Golf Classic, Brit. Open, El Prat Open (Spain), 1979, Masters, 1980, 83, Madrid Open, Martini Internat., Dutch Open, 1980, Scandinavian Open, Spanish Open, Suntory World Match Play, Australian PGA Championship, Dunlop-Phoenix, 1981, San Remo Masters, Madrid Open, French Open, Suntory World Match Play, 1982, M.H.T. Westchester Classic, Irish Open, Lancome Trophy, Sun City Challenge, Sun Alliance Championship, 1983, Brit. Open, 1984, 88, Suntory WMP, Sun City Challenge, 1984, USF&G Classic, World Match Play Championship, Irish Open, French Open, Sanyo Open, Spanish Open, Ryder Cup (mem. winning team), 1985, Dunhill Brit. Masters, Carrolls Irish Open, Johnnie Walker Montecarlo Open, Peugeot French Open, KLM Dutch Open, Lancome Trophy, 1986, Suze Open, APG Larios, Ryder Cup winning team, 1987, A.P.G. Larios, Mallorca Open de Baleares, Westchester Classic Scandinavian Enterprise Open, German Open, Lancome Trophee British Open, Visa Taiheiyo Club Masters, 1988, Epson Gran Prix, Cepsa Madrid Open, Swiss Open/Ebel European Masters, Ryder Cup (tied), 1989, Open Baleares, 1990, Volvo PGA Championship, Dunhill Brit. Masters, Chunichi Crowns, Toyota World Match Play, 1991, Turespaña Open de Baleares, Dubai Desert Classic, 1992, Benson and Hedges Internat. Open Mercedes (German) Masters, 1994, Tornoi Perrier, Peugeot Spanish Open, Five Tours Andersen Consulting, Ryder Cup, Campeonato Espana Profesionales, 1995, Ryder Cup, 1997, Seve Ballesteros Trophy, 2000; Capt. European Ryder Cup Team, 1997. Recipient Prince of Asturias award, 1989, Olympic Order, 1998. Roman Catholic. Office: Fairway SA, Pasaje de Pena 2-4, 39008 Santander Spain also: PGA 100 Ave of the Champions Palm Beach Gardens FL 33410 Address: Dep Tecnico S Ballesteros, Pasaje de Pena 2, 39008 Santander Spain*

BALLINGALL, PATRICK CHANDLER GORDON, retired solicitor; b. Devonport, Eng., Dec. 5, 1926; s. David Charles Gordon and Rosa Beatrice (Chandler) B.; m. Mary Hamilton Mackie, May 10, 1952; children: Anne Helen Ballingall Lever, James Gordon Mackie. MA, Cambridge (Eng.) U., 1950. Ptnr. Barwell, Blakiston & Ballingall, Seaford, Eng., 1958-89. Chmn. Lewes Constituency Conservative Assn., Eng., 1978-81, East Sussex Conservative European Constituency Council, Eng., 1984-88. Decorated mem. Order of Brit. Empire. Mem. Sussex Law Soc. (pres. 1974-75). Home: 4 Chyngton Gardens Seaford, East Sussex BN25 3RP, England

BALLOU, JEFFREY PIERRE, producer; b. Pitts., Aug. 2, 1967; s. Kasib Rashid and Geneva (Williams) B. BA in Journalism and African American Studies, Pa. State U., 1990; MA in Journalism and Pub. Policy, Am. Un., 1992; grad., Howard U., 1992. Hearst news prodr. fellow-in-residence Sta. WCVB-TV, Boston, 1990-91; freelance newswriter WTTG-TV, Washington, 1992; assignment editor C-SPAN, Washington, 1992; freelance corr. Sta. WAMU-FM, Washington, 1990-92; asst. editor Sta. WTOP-AM, Washington, 1992-93; asst. prodr. Nat. Pub. Radio, Washington, 1990-93; White House prodr. CONUS Comm., Washington, 1993-95; prodr., 1995-99, White House prodr., 1996-99; planning editor WTTG-TV (Fox TV), Washington, 1999—; commencement spkr. Pa. State U., McKeesport, 1999. Author selected op-ed columns and feature stories. Named One of Outstanding Young Men of Am., 1989, 99. Mem. AFTRA, Nat. Press Club, Radio and TV News Dirs. Assn. (mem. diversity task force), Soc. Profl. Journalists (bd. dirs. D.C. chpt. 1993-95, Taishoff Broadcast fellow 1994), Nat. Assn. Black Journalists, Washington Assn. Black Journalists (v.p. 1993, pres. 1994), Capital Press Club, Pa. State Alumni Assn. Coll. Comm. (bd. dirs. 1993-95), Pa. State U. Alumni Coun. (bd. dirs. 1993-96), Nat. INROADS Alumni Assn., White House Corrs. Assn., Radio and TV Corrs. Assn., Nat. Eagle Scout Assn., Alpha Phi Alpha, Free and Accepted Masons (Prince Hall affiliation). Baptist. Avocations: reading, dancing, writing, community service, travel. Home: 1011 Independence Ave SE Washington DC 20003-3921 Office: WTTG/Fox TV 5151 Wisconsin Ave NW Washington DC 20016-4124

BALLWEG, RUTH MILLIGAN, physician assistant, educator; b. Feb. 29, 1944. BS in Sociology, So. Oregon State Coll., 1969; grad. MEDEX N.W. physician asst. program, U. Wash., Seattle, 1978, MPH, 1997. Lic. State Bd. Med. Examiners, Oregon, Wash.; cert. Nat. Commn. on Cert. of Physician Assts. Dir. physician asst. program MEDEX Northwest, U. Wash. Sch. Med., 1985—; mem. Nat. Adv. Bd. Nat. Health Svc. Corps, 1994-96; commr. PEW Commn. on the Health Professions, 1997-99. Co-Editor: Physician Assistant: A Guide to Clinical Practice, 1994, 2d edit., 1999; mem. editl. bd. Clinician Reviews, 1996, Physician Assistant, 1989-90, 96—; contbr. articles to profl. jours. Primary Care Health Policy fellow, Bureau Health Professions, 1992; recipient Disting. Svc. award Nat. Indian Health Bd., 1987, Lifetime Achievement award MEDEX Alumni Assn., 1997. Mem. Assn. Physician Asst. Programs (pres. elect 1989-90, pres. 1990-91, 91-92, chair external rels. com. 1991—, co-dir. new program devel. project, bd. mem.-at-large 1993-95, UPJOHN Presidential award 1991), Am. Acad. Physician Assts., Wash. Acad. Physician Assts. (bd. mem. 1984-86, v.p. 1986-88, chair health policy coun. 1993—, pres.-elect 1998-99, pres. 1994-95, Special Recognition award, 1988). Office: MEDEX NW UWMC Roosevelt 4245 Roosevelt Way NE Seattle WA 98105-6008

BALLY, LAURENT MARIE JOSEPH, software engineering company executive; b. Fort-de-France, Martinique, France, Dec. 23, 1943; s. Raoul and Therese (de Gentile) B.; m. Iris Kirstaetter, Oct. 8, 1971; 1 child, Laetitia. Diploma in engring., Inst. Superieur d'Electronique, Paris, 1966. Systems analyst NCR Corp., London, 1966-67; systems engr. Siemens A.G., Karlsruhe, Fed. Republic Germany, 1968-71; tech. mgr. Sesa-Deutschland GmbH, Frankfurt, Fed. Republic Germany, 1971-78; head of dept. Siemens A.G., Munich, 1979-84; head of div. Sesa S.A., Paris, 1984-88; dep. gen. mgr. Cap Sesa Tertiaire, Paris, 1989-92; gen. mgr. Cap Sesa Telecom, Paris, 1992-95, Cap Gemini Telecom France, Paris, 1996—. Contbr. articles to profl. jours. Office: Gap Gemini Telecom France, Tour Europlaza, 92927 La Defense CEDEX, France

BALLY, PETER, hotel executive; b. Linz, Austria, 1937; s. Peter and Anne Marie (von Pirquet) B.; children by previous marriage: children: Hubert, Blanca, Cristina. Student, Gourdonstoun Sch., Scotland, 1954-57, Cambridge U., Eng., 1956. Asst. mgr. Palace Hotel, Madrid, 1961-62, Hotel Ritz, Madrid, 1962-63; reception mgr. Dochester Hotel, London, 1964-65; mng. dir. Park Hotel, Vitznau, Switzerland, 1968—; pres. Tourist Bd. Vitznau, 1973—, Central Swiss Fin. Bd. Tourime, 1977—; trustee Ecole Hotelière Lausanne, 1974-87; mem. Coun. of Djibouti, Africa. Served to capt., inf., 1968. Mem. Central Swiss Hotel Assn. (pres. 1974-81), Relais et Chateaux Switzerland (pres. 1978-87), Rotary. Roman Catholic. Home and Office: Park Hotel Vitznau, CH-6354 Vitznau Switzerland

BALME, LOUIS, electrical engineering educator; b. Grenoble, France, Aug. 23, 1951; s. André Joseph Marcel and Marie Louise Andrée (Meunier) B.; m. Evelyne Germaine Coeur, Apr. 7, 1973; children: David, Julien, Matthieu. Master, Institut d'Etudes Politiques, Grenoble, 1972; PhD in Electronics, Institut Nat. Polytechnique, Grenoble, 1976. Prof. Institut Nat. Polytechnique, Grenoble, 1972—, dir. master degree in equality of computers, 1989—, responsible for PCB testing rsch. activity TIM3 Lab., 1984—; pres., founder SYMAG Computers, Grenoble, 1979-84. Contbr. articles to sci. publs. Mem. IEEE. Roman Catholic. Office: Institut Nat Poly, 46 Ave Felix Viallet, 38031 Grenoble France

BALMENT, RICHARD JOHN, physiology educator, researcher; b. Barnstaple, Eng., Apr. 6, 1951; s. Charles Henry and Kathlyn Mary (Yeo) B.; m. Janet Antrich, Aug. 2, 1975; children: Jennifer Helen, Martin Kimberley. BSc in Zoology with honors, U. Sheffield, Eng., 1972, PhD in Physiology, 1975, DSc in Comparative Physiology, 1997. vis. lectr. U. Zimbabwe, Harare, 1983-84; sr. Ciba Geigy fellow, U. Nice, France, 1987; vis. assoc. prof., Kitasato Med. Sch., Japan, 1991. Fellow U. Sheffield, 1975-77; lectr. Manchester (Eng.) U., 1977-89, sr. lectr., reader, 1989-93, prof. zoology, 1994—, chmn. grad. sch., 1995; dean Internat. and Grad. Edn., 1998—; vis. lectr. U. Zimbabwe, Harare, 1983-84; sr. Ciba Geigy fellow, U. Nice, France, 1987; vis. assoc. prof., Kitasato Med. Sch., Japan, 1991. Editor: New Insights into Vertebrate Kidney Function, 1993; contbr. over 90 aritcles to profl. jours. Traveling fellow Japanese Soc. Promotion Sci., Tokyo, 1996-97; recipient Rsch. grant U.K. Rsch. Coun., 1985-97. Mem. Soc. Endocrinology, London (coun. mem. 1991-95), Physiol. Soc., Soc. Exptl. Biology (com. mem. 1989). Mem. Church of England. Avocation: bonsai. Office: U Manchester Sch Biol Scis, G 38 Stopford Bldg, Manchester M13 9PT, England

BALMUTH, BERNARD ALLEN, retired film editor; b. Youngstown, Ohio, May 19, 1918; s. Joseph and Sadie (Stein) B.; m. Rosa June Bergman, Mar. 2, 1952; children: Mary Susan, Sharon Nancy. BA in English, UCLA, 1942. Postal clk. U.S. Postal Svc., L.A., 1946-55; asst. and apprentice film editor, film editor L.A., 1955-90; ret., 1990; instr. film editing dept. of the arts UCLA Extension, 1979-99 (cert. of appreciation); film editing cons. Am. Film Inst., L.A., 1982-92. Author: The Language of the Cutting Room, 1979, Introduction to Film Editing, 1989. Initiator petition STOP Save TV Original Programming and Stop Excessive Reruns, 1971-75. Sgt. U.S. Army, 1942-45. Recipient Honor Cert. for Contribution Acad. TV Arts and Scis., 1974, Emmy nomination Best Editing, 1982. Mem. Am. Cinema Editors (life, bd. dirs. 1982-85, 97-99, sec. 1985-87, v.p. 1987-91, chmn. spl. awards com. 1988-99, hon. historian 1993—), Hollywood Entertainment Labor Coun. (rep. for Editors Guild 1972—), Stage Soc. (bd. dirs., sec. 1949-54). Democrat. Jewish. Avocations: cinema, theatre, dancing, cinema books, tennis. Address: care Rosallen Publs PO Box 927 North Hollywood CA 91603-0927

BALNAVE, DERICK, agricultural studies educator; b. Lisburn, Ireland, June 17, 1941; arrived in Australia, 1977; s. David and Doris (Pollen) B.; m. Maureen Dawson, Aug. 2, 1968; children: Christopher David, Nikola Robyn. BSc, Queen's U., Belfast, Ireland, 1963; PhD, Queen's U., 1966, DSc, 1983. Sci. officer Dept. Agr., No. Ireland, 1966-69, sr. sci. officer, 1969-73, prin. sci. officer, 1973-77; lectr. Queen's U., Belfast, 1967-75, sr. lectr., 1975-77, reader, 1977; sr. lectr. U. Sydney, Australia, 1978-81, assoc. prof., 1981—; adj. prof. N.C. State U., 1995—; mem. working party Agrl. Rsch. Coun., Eng., 1970-75; expert advisor Agrl. Med. Rsch. Coun., Eng., 1974; rsch. dir. poultry rsch. found. U. Sydney, 1978—; chair organizing com. Australian Poultry Sci. Symposium, 1988—. Contbr. over 140 articles to profl. jours. Fellow Royal Soc. Chemistry.; mem. Poultry Sci. Assn. Inc., N.Y. Acad. Sci., World's Poultry Sci. Assn. (Australian Poultry award 1998). Office: U Sydney, Werombi Rd, Camden 2570, Australia

BALNAVES, CHARLES, petroleum engineer; b. Acton, Eng., June 26, 1952; arrived in Australia, 1956; s. Francis John and Joyce Elvira (Weiland) B.; m. Tanya Standish, May 3, 1975; children: James, Michael. BA in Applied Math., U. Canberra, Australia, 1972. Asst. scientist BHP Steel divsn. Broken Hill Pty., Wollongong, Australia, 1973-77; jr. petrophysicist BHP Petroleum, Perth, Australia, 1977-79; reservoir engr. BHP Petroleum, Perth, 1979-81; sr. reservoir engr. BHP Petroleum, Melbourne, Australia, 1982-86; reservoir engring. mgr. BHP Petroleum, Melbourne, 1986-89; engring. mgr. BHP Petroleum, Houston, 1990-94; global leader petroleum engring. BHP Petroleum, Melbourne, 1995—; advisor Ctr. for Petroleum Engring. in N.S.W., Sydney, 1996—; advisor Ctr. for Oil and Gas, U. We. Australia, 1997—. Contbr. articles to profl. jours. Mem. Soc. Petroleum Engrs. (chair Victoria/Tasmania 1987-88, 96-98), Soc. Profl. Well Log Analysts, Soc. Core Analysts. Roman Catholic. Avocations: reading, woodworking, model house construction, aerobics. Office: BHP Petroleum, 120 Collins St, Melbourne 3000, Australia

BALOCCO-MOUNEYRAC, CATHERINE NADINE, biologist, researcher, educator; b. Orleans, France, July 19, 1964; d. Joseph Charles and Marie-Louise Suzanne (Ghio) Balocco; m. Bernard Jean Mouneyrac; children: Laureen, Rupluarelle. PhD in Physiology, U. Lyon (France) I, 1993. With UCO, Angers, France, 1992—; dir. adjoint IRFA/UCO, Angers, 1998—. Contbr. articles to profl. jours. Mem. Union des Oceanographes de France, N.Y. Acad. Scis. Avocations: surfing, scuba diving. Home: 61 Grand Rue, 49610 Juigne Sur Loire France Office: Univ Cath de l Ouest, 3 Pl A Leroy, 49008 Angers France

BALOCO, RICHARD, investment executive; b. Plainfield, N.J., Aug. 22, 1970; s. Ricardo and Muriel Baloco. BA in Econs., Seton Hall U., 1998. Lic. NASD Series 7 and 63. Customer rels. Sears, Cranford, N.J., 1990-93; accounts receivable Chem Lawn, South Plainfield, N.J., 1993-94; comml. collector Garden State Bus. Machines, Springfield, N.J., 1994-95; customer rels. staff United Nat. Bank, Bridgewater, N.J., 1995-96; sales rep. King Teleservices, South Plainfield, N.J., 1996-98; investment exec. Gibraltar Securities, Floraham Park, N.J., 1998—. Avocation: reading. Home: 52 Craig Pl N Plainfield NJ 07060-4752 Office: Gibraltar Securities 25 Hanover Rd Ste 2 Florham Park NJ 07932-1407

BALODIS, VILNIS, pulpwood technologist, consultant; b. Riga, Latvia, June 30, 1927; s. Andrejs Adolfs and Sofia (Rosenfeld) B.; m. Dorothy Elizabeth Ryan, Oct. 1955. BSc, U. Queensland, Brisbane, 1960, MSc, 1966; DSc, U. Melbourne, 1989. Mem. clerical and tech. staff Forestry Commn. of NSW, Sydney, 1948-55; timber technologist Queensland Forest Svc., Brisbane, 1955-62; scientist CSIRO Australia, Melbourne, 1962-86, sr. prin. rsch. scientist, 1988-92, hon. rsch. scientist, 1992—; vis. rsch. fellow Forest Sch., U. Melbourne, 1986-87, sr. assoc., 1986—; officer in charge pulp and paper physics CSIRO Forest Products, Melbourne, 1968-72; pulping and pulpwood assessment program, Melbourne, 1976-86; leader CSIRO-Chinese Acad. Forestry, Melbourne, Nanjing, 1988-92. Contbr. articles to profl. jours. including Jour. Inst. Wood Sci., Jour. Exptl. Botany, Appita, among others. Recipient Hon. Rsch. fellow CSIRO, 1992—. Fellow Australian Inst. Physics, Inst. Wood Sci.; mem. TAPPI, APPITA. Avocations: photography, family genealogy, tropical industrial wood plantations, siddha yoga. E-mail: V.Balodis@ffp.csiro.au. Office: CSIRO Forestry-Forest Prods, Bayview Ave, Clayton VIC 3168, Australia

BALOGH, FERENC, urologist; b. Sajoszentpeter, Borsod, Hungary, Jan. 29, 1916; s. Louis and Lidia (Farkas) B.; m. Elisabeth Koppany, Aug. 24, 1944; children: Lidia, Melinda. MD, Pazmany U. Medicine, 1941. Asst. Pathol. Inst., Budapest, Hungary, 1938-42; asst., lectr. Urol. Clinic, Budapest, 1942-63; prof. Urol. Clinic, Pecs, Hungary, 1963-74; prof. Urol. Clinic, Budapest, 1974-86, urologist, 1986; ret., 1986. Author: Pathology and Clinic of Kidney Tumors, 1960; co-author: Cancer of the Prostate, 1965, Nephrology, 1980; author 13 sci. books and co-authored 12 books; contbr. more than 483 articles to profl. jours. Pres. Soc. Hungarian Urologists, 1972-85, Illye's Commemorative medal, 1984. Mem. European Assn. Urology (founder), Internat. Assn. Urology, Urol. Soc. Germany (corr.), Levay Club (pres. 1986—). Avocation: reading. Home: Pusztaszeri 42/A, H-1025 Budapest Hungary Office: Urological Clinic, Ulloi 78/B, H 1082 Budapest Hungary

BALOGH, SANDOR, historian; b. Pereszleny, Slovakia, July 31, 1926; s. Istvan and Batovsky Maria B.; m. Ratkoci Maria, July 28, 1972; children: Erno, Sandor. Diploma, Eotvos Lorand U., Budapest, Hungary, 1951, U. Econs., Budapest, Hungary, 1951, Acad. Hungarian Workers Party, Budapest, Hungary, 1952; PhD, Lomonoszov U., Moscow, 1958; D of Hist. Scis., Budapest, 1973. Aspirant candidate Lomonoszov U., Moscow, 1954-58; sr. lectr. Eotvos Lorand U., Budapest, Hungary, 1964-68, prof., 1968-88; dir. Inst. Polit. History, Budapest, Hungary, 1988-91. Author: Parliamentary and Parties' Struggles in Hungary Between 1945-1947, 1975 (Acad. award 1976), The History of Hungary After the Second World War 1944-1980, 1986, Foreign Policy of Hungary Between 1945-1950, 1988, Reparations and What is Behind It 1945-1949, 1998. Chmn. Hungarian Hist. Soc., Budapest, 1986-91, Nat. Conciliation Com. Hungarian Socialist Party, Budapest, 1989-94, Polit. Hist. Fund., Budapest, 1991—. Lt. Hungarian Army, 1952-81. Office: Polit Alapitvany, Alkotmany u 2, 1054 Budapest Hungary

BALOYANNIS, STAVROS JOANNIS, neurologist, educator, researcher; b. Thessaloniki, Macedonia, Greece, Aug. 24, 1944; s. Joannis K. and Maria (Stefanidou) B.; m. Heleni G. Bozini, 1965; children: Joannis, Maria, Georgia, Angeliki. MD, Aristotelian U., Thessaloniki, 1968, PhD, 1975, Docent, 1980; MSc in Theology, Thessaloniki, Thessaloniki, 1979. Postdoctoral fellow London U., Nat. Hosp., Inst. Neurology, 1974-75, U. Catholique de Louvain, Belgium, 1975-76; fellow in neuropathology U. Pa., Phila., 1977-78; docent Aristotelian U., Thessaloniki, 1980-83, asst. prof., 1983-87, assoc. prof., 1987-2000, head 1st dept. neurology, 1992—, dir. lab. of neuropathology, 1993, prof., 2000—; vis. prof. Tufts U., Boston, 1986, Democretian U., Alexandroupolis, Greece, 1989-90, Sch. Philosophy, Aristotelian U., Thessoloniki, 1993—. Author: Clinical Neuropathology, vols. I-III, 1984-88, Diseases of the Muscles, 1991, Neurology, Vols. I, II, Pastoral Psychiatry, 1986, Psychology, Via Psychology, 1984, Andreas Vesalius on the Human Brain, 1995, The Role of Calcium in the Life and Death of the Nerve Cell, 1995, The Receptors of Existatroy Amino Acids, 1996, Introduction to Neurosciences, 1996, Neurology, Vol. 1, 1996, From Ardzean Vesalien to Santiago Ramon y Cajil, 2000; mem. editl. bd. 7 sci. jours. of neurology, neuropathology and immunology; contbr. more than 450 papers on neurology, neuropathology, and electron microscopy to profl. publs. 2nd lt. Greek Air Force, 1968-72. Recipient Gold medal of St. Demetrius, Orthodox Ch., Thessaloniki, 1984, Gold medal of St. Paul, 1988, Gold medal of Holy Theotokos, 1989, 91, Gold medal Greek Red Cross, 1994, Gold medal of St. Cyrillus and Methodius, Gold medal St. Gregorius, Thessaloniki, 1997. Fellow Royal Soc. Medicine (London); mem. Internat. Brain Rsch. Assn., Collegium Orl, Am. Assn. Neuropathology, Internat. Soc. Neuropathology, European Neuropathol. Soc. (founding mem.), Hellenic Neuropathol. Soc. (pres. 1986-97), N.Y. Acad. Scis., European Soc. Psychogeriats. Orthodox Ch. Avocations: philosophy, painting, poetry, classical music, linguistics-glossology. Home: Angelaki 5, Thessaloniki Greece 54621 Office: Aristotelian Univ 1st Dept Neurology, Neuropathol & Exptl Neurol, Thessaloniki 54006, Greece

BALSAMELLO, JOSEPH VINCENT, information services manager; b. Bronx, N.Y., Feb. 8, 1956; s. Joseph and Marie (Fariello) B.; m. Carmela Totaro, Aug. 22, 1981; children: Nicholas, Sarah, Alyssa, Jenna, Stephen (dec.). BA in Psychology, William Paterson Coll., 1980. Inside salesperson Gen. Sportcraft Co. Ltd., Bergenfield, N.J., 1978-84, MIS mgr., 1984-88; sr. programmer, analyst UPS, Mahwah, N.J., 1988-93, MIS project leader, 1993—; bus. adv. coun. CPI Bus. Schs., Paramus, N.J., 1986-89. Coord. St. Mary's Ch., Pt. Jervis, N.Y., 1990-91; vol. Expectant/New Father Resource, Mothers of Supertwins, 1998—. Roman Catholic. Avocations: reading, music, theater, hiking, swimming.

BALSAMO, SIMONETTA MARIA, computer scientist, educator; b. Modena, Italy, Mar. 22, 1958; d. Carlo and Jetie (Van Hehert) B.; m. Antonio Del Vecchio, Mar. 9, 1985. Laurea in Computer Sci., U. Pisa, Italy, 1981. Cons. U. Pisa, Italy, 1981-83, assoc. rschr. info. dept., 1984-88; vis. scientist T.J. Watson IBM Rsch. Lab., Yorktown Heights, N.Y., 1985-86; assoc. prof. dept. math. U. Modena, Italy, 1989-91; assoc. prof. dept. info. U. Pisa, Italy, 1992-93; prof. faculty of sci. U. Udine, Italy, 1994-99; prof. faculty sci. U. Venice, 1999—. Contbr. numerous articles to profl. jours. and chpts. to books. Pres. Circolo Pisano della Soc. di Danta, Pisa. Mem. IEEE, Assn. Computer Machinery, Italian Soc. Computer Simulation. Avocations: music, dance, reading, historical dances. Office: U Venice Info Dept, Via Torino 155, Mestre Venezia Italy

BALSIGER, HANS RUDOLF, physics educator; b. Bern, Switzerland, Sept. 12, 1937; s. Rudolf and Marie (Feucht) B.; m. Trudi Steiner, Aug. 14, 1964; children: Christoph, Barbara. MS in Physics, U. Bern, 1964, PhD, 1967. Postdoctoral fellow dept. space sci. Rice U., Houston, 1968-70; lectr. U. Bern, 1970-79, asst. prof., 1979-84, assoc. prof., 1984-90, prof. physics, 1990—, dir. Physikalisches Inst., 1993—; chmn. solar sys. working group European Space Agy., Paris, 1986-87, chmn. space sci. adv. com., 1987-90, lunar study steering group, 1990-91, chmn. sci. program com., 1996-99; chmn. Kommission für Weltraumforschung, Swiss Acad. Scis., Bern, 1987-98; mem. Eidg. Kommission für Weltraumfragen, 1989—, Akademische Kommission, U. Bern, 1991—; Forschungsrat Swiss Nat. Sci. Found., 1993—. Contbr. over 160 articles to profl. jours. With Swiss Army, 1960-

92. Recipient Cortaillod prize U. Neuchâtel, Switzerland, 1981. Mem. Internat. Acad. Astronautics, Acad. Sci. Artium Europaea, Acad. Europaea. Office: Univ Bern Dept Physics, Sidlerstrasse 5, 3012 Bern Switzerland

BALSLEV-CLAUSEN, PETER, theologian, clergyman, educator; b. Vejlby, Jutland, Denmark, Feb. 15, 1943; s. Thorkild Balslev and Ruth (Jessen) Clausen; m. Elsebet Bjerrum, Aug. 6, 1971; children: Jacob Peter, Andreas Peter, Anne Sofie, Katrine. ThM, U. Copenhagen, 1969, PhD, 1989. Vicar Ch. of Denmark, Hellerup, 1971—; dean Ch. of Denmark, Gentofte, 1996—; assoc. prof. U. Copenhagen, 1981—; rsch. fellow Inst. of Ch. History, Copenhagen, 1991-93. Author: The Feathered Word on N.F.S. Grundtvigs Hymnody, 1991, The Hymnwriter B .S. Ingemann, 1989, Motives and Structures of the Hymnody of N.F.S. Grundtvig, 1989; editor: Danish Bull. of Hymnology, 1985—; Biblical Hymns and Songs, 1988, Songs from Denmark, 1988. Rep. Den Danske Praesteforening, 1985-96; pres. The Ch. Sch. Svc., Gentofte, 1991—. Chaplain Royal Danish Navy, 1979—. Mem. Grundtvig Soc. (pres. 1990—), Hymn Soc. (pres. 1996—), B.S. Ingemann Soc. (com. mem. 1992—), Official Danish Hymn Com. (sec. 1991—, mem. 1997—), Nordic Inst. Hymnology (com. mem. 1996—). Mem. Liberal Party. Lutheran. Fax: 011-45-39624509. E-mail: pbc@km.dk. Home: Ahlmanns Alle 14, DK-2900 Hellerup Denmark Office: Hellerup Sognegaard, Margrethevej 7 B, DK-2900 Hellerup Denmark

BALT, CHRISTINE ANN, family nurse practitioner; b. Gary, Ind., July 24, 1962; d. Casimir and Barbara Ann (Sohaney) B. AAS in Nursing, Purdue U., 1982; BSN, Ind. U., Indpls., 1986, MSW, 1992; MS in Primary Care Nursing, Ind. Wesleyan U., Marion, 1996. RN, Ind.; cert. family nurse practitioner; AIDS cert. RN. Staff nurse St. Catherine Hosp., East Chicago, Ind., 1983-84, Riley Hosp. for Children, Indpls., 1983-84, St. Francis Hosp., Beech Grove, Ind., 1984-85; pvt. duty nurse St. Vincent Stress Ctr., Indpls., 1985-86; staff nurse St. Joseph Hosp., Chgo., 1986-87, VA Med. Ctr., Indpls., 1987-96; family nurse practitioner St. Francis Med. Group, Indpls., 1996-98; nurse practitioner divsn. infectious diseases Ind. U. Dept. Medicine, Indpls., 1999—; mem. adv. bd. Midwest AIDS Tng. and Edn. Ctr., Indpls., 1998—. Chair Marion County HIV/AIDS Coalition, Indpls., 1993; bd. dirs. Friends of Walther Cancer Rsch. Ctr., Indpls., 1990-91. Mem. Assn. Nurses in AIDS Care (chair nat. membership and pub. rels. com. 1998-99, bd. dirs. - dir. at large 1999—), Ind. State Nurses Assn., Sigma Theta Tau. Avocations: music, cross stitch, golf. Office: Ind U Dept Medicine Wishard Meml Hosp 1001 W 10th St Ste 430 Indianapolis IN 46202-2859

BALTAKIS, PAUL ANTANAS, bishop; b. Troškunai, Panevezys, Lithuania, Jan. 1, 1925; s. Juozas and Apolonia (Lauzikaite) B. PhD, Franciscan Sem., Rekem, Belgium, 1949; ThD, Franciscan Sem., St. Truidem, Belgium, 1955. Assoc. pastor Roman Cath. Parish of Resurrection, Toronto, Ont., Can., 1953-69; councilman Lithuanian Franciscan Vicariate, Kennebunkport, Maine, 1967-79, provincial superior, 1979-84; Roman Cath. bishop Lithuanian Catholics, Bklyn., 1984—. Spiritual adviser Lithuanian Boy Scouts Assn., Bklyn., 1964-84, Lithuanian Vets., Bklyn., 1970-79. Recipient For the Merits award Lithuanian Boy Scouts Assn., 1988, For the Merits award Lithuanian Vets., 1977, Ellis Island Medal of Honor, 1993, Merits award Lithanian Republic, 1994. Mem. Knights of Lithuania (hon.), Nat. Conf. Bishops & U.S. Cath. Conf. Home and Office: 361 Highland Blvd Brooklyn NY 11207-1910

BALTAS, ALEXANDROS, member European Parliament; b. Greece, Mar. 17, 1939. Mem. European Parliament, Brussels; mem. com. on industry, external trade, rsch. and energy, com. on agr. and rural devel., vice chmn. substitute del. to European Union-Bulgaria Joint Parliamentary Com., mem. substitute del. to European Union-Hungary Joint Parliamentary Com. Mem. Group of Party of European Socialists. Mem. Panhellenic Socialist Movement. Office: European Parliament, Rue Wiertz 13G165, B-1047 Brussels Belgium*

BALTAS, MICHEL, chemist, researcher; b. Athens, Feb. 27, 1959; s. Ioannis and Ismini (Leontaridou) B.; m. Virginie Sallion, Dec. 27, 1986; 1 child, Alexandra. Maitrise, U. Toulouse, France, 1980, DEA, 1981, PhD, 1984; PhD, U. Toulouse, France, 1987. Tchg. asst. U. Toulouse, 1981-84; rschr. Roussel-UCLAF, 1984-86; postdoctoral rschr. U. Toulouse, 1987-88; rschr. CNRS, 1986—; postdoctoral rschr. ETH, Zurich, 1996-97; mem. Sci. Consul, U. Toulouse, 1992—, Sci. Exam. Commn., 1998—. Mem. Franco-Hellenic Assn. Toulouse (v.p. 1996—). Avocations: chess, history, swimming, tennis. Home: 2 Impasse Paul Eluard #10, 31320 Castauet-Tolosay France Office: U Toulouse 3 ESA CNRS 5068, 118 Rt Narbonne, 31062 Toulouse 4, France

BALTAZAR, ROMULO FLORES, cardiologist; b. Naga, Camarines Sur, Philippines, Oct. 15, 1941; came to U.S., 1970; s.Melecio Perez and Socorro (Flores) B.; m. Ophelia Zarzuela, June 6, 1970; children: Maria Cristina, Romulo Jr. BA, U. Philippines, 1961, MD, 1966. Intern U. Philippines, Philippine Gen. Hosp., 1965-66; resident medicine Philippine Gen. Hosp., 1966-69, chief resident medicine, 1969-70; instr. medicine U. Philippines, 1969-70; resident medicine Sinai Hosp., Balt., 1970-71, resident cardiology, 1971-73, assoc. cardiology, 1975-87, dir. non-invasive cardiology, 1987—; resident pediatric cardiology Johns Hopkins Hosp., Balt., 1971-72; fellow cardiology Maimonides Med. Ctr., N.Y.C., 1973-75; instr. medicine Johns Hopkins U. Sch. Medicine, Balt., 1977-87, asst. prof. medicine, 1987—; reviewer Archives of Internal Medicine, 1991—, JAMA, 1988. Contbr. articles to med. jours. Fellow Am. Coll. Cardiology; mem. Assn. Philippine Physicians (pres. 195-97). Roman Catholic. Avocations: listening to popular music, playing chess, reading, travel, photography. Office: Sinai Hosp Balt Div Cardiology Baltimore MD 21215

BALTER, FRANCES SUNSTEIN, civic worker; b. Pitts.; d. Elias and Gertrude Susntein; m. James Stone Balter, May 15, 1948; children: Katherine (Mrs. Ross Anthony), Julia Frances, Constance Cantor, Daniel Elias. Student, Sarah Lawrence Coll., 1939-41, New Sch. Social Rsch., 1941-43; cert. Inst. Arts Adminstrn., Harvard U., 1973. Adminstrv. asst., assoc. prodr. Ednl. TV Sta. WQED-TV, Pitts., 1963-67; prodr., mng. dir. Freedom Readers, 1964-67; co-founder, incorporator, sec. bd. dirs. Pitts. Coun. Arts, 1967-70; cultural cons. Mayor's Office Dir. Office Cultural Affairs, Pitts., 1968; initiator Three Rivers Arts Festival 1960; co-dir. Ohio and Miss. River Valley Art Festival, 1961-62; mem. Pa. Coun. Arts, 1972-78; co-founder Pioneer Crafts Coun., Mill Run, Pa., 1972; exec. dir. Poetry on the Buses, 1974—. Bd. dirs. Coun. for Arts MIT, 1985-93, Palm Beach Festival, 1987-89. Named Woman of Yr. Art Post-Gazette, 1969. Mem. Assn. Couns. on Arts, Nat. Soc. Arts and Leteters.

BALTIMORE, DAVID, university president, microbiologist, educator; b. N.Y.C., Mar. 7, 1938; s. Richard I. and Gertrude (Lipschitz) B.; m. Alice S. Huang, Oct. 5, 1968; 1 dau., Teak. BA with high honors in Chemistry, Swarthmore Coll., 1960; postgrad., MIT, 1960-61; PhD, Rockefeller U., 1964. Research assoc. Salk Inst. Biol. Studies, La Jolla, Calif., 1965-68; assoc. prof. microbiology MIT, Cambridge, 1968-72, prof. biology, 1972-95; Ivan R. Cottrell prof. molecular biology and immunology MIT, 1994-97; inst. prof. MIT, Cambridge, 1995-97, Am. Cancer Soc. prof. microbiology, 1973-83, 94-97, dir. Whitehead Inst. Biomed. Rsch., 1982-90; pres. Rockefeller U., N.Y.C., 1990-91, prof., 1990-94; pres. Calif. Inst. Tech., Pasadena, 1997—. Mem. editorial bd. Jour. Molecular Biology, 1971-73, Jour. Virology, 1969-90, Sci., 1986-98, New Eng. Jour. Medicine, 1989-94. Bd. govs. Weizmann Inst. Sci., Israel; bd. dirs. Life Sci. Rsch. Found.; co-chmn. Commn. on a Nat. Strategy of AIDS; ad hoc program adv. com. on complex genome, NIH; mem. office AIDS rsch. adv. coun. NIH, chair vaccine adv. com., 1997—. Recipient Gustav Stern award in virology, 1970; Warren Triennial prize Mass. Gen. Hosp., 1971; Eli Lilly and Co. award in microbiology and immunology, 1971; Nat. Acad. Scis. U.S. Steel award in molecular biology, 1974; Gairdner Found. ann. award, 1974; Nobel prize in physiology or medicine, 1975, Nat. medal of sci., 1999. Fellow AAAS, Am. Med. Writers Assn. (hon.), Am. Acad. Microbiology; mem. NAS, Am. Acad. Arts and Scis., Inst. Medicine, Am. Philos. Soc., Pontifical Acad. Scis., Royal Soc. (Eng.) (fgn.), French Acad. Scis. (fgn. assoc.). Office: Calif Inst Tech 1200 E California Blvd Pasadena CA 91125-0001

BALTKAJS, JANIS, pharmacology educator; b. Riga, Latvia, July 12, 1935; s. Janis and Zelma (Srogus) B.; m. Sarmite Abolina; children: Daina, Maris. Diploma, Riga (Latvia) Med. Inst., 1960, MD, 1965; MD habilitation, Latvia Acad. Medicine, Riga, Latvia, 1993. Asst. Riga (Latvia) Med. Inst., 1966-67, sr. lectr., 1967-72, vice-dean, 1969-88, asst. prof., 1972-94; prof. pharmacology Latvia Acad. Medicine, 1994—. Co-author: (book) Drug Interactions, 1991; inventor of a device for the registration of animal motor activity, 1965. Home: Salaspils iela 12-5-90, LV 1057 Riga Latvia Office: Latvia Acad Medicine, Dzirciema 16, LV1007 Riga Latvia

BALTZ, RICHARD ARTHUR, chemical engineer; b. Red Bud, Ill., Aug. 1, 1959; s. Arthur A. and Arlou M. (McDonald) B. BSChemE, U. Mo., Rolla, 1981. Process design engr. corp. engring. dept. Monsanto, St. Louis, 1981-83; process engr. Nitro Plant Monsanto, Nitro, W.Va., 1983-89; process engring. specialist W.G. Krummrich Plant Monsanto, Sauget, Ill., 1989-97; process engring. specialist W.G. Krummrich Plant, Solutia, Inc., Sauget, Ill., 1997—. Mem. AIChE. Roman Catholic. Home: Apt J 3749 Huntington Valley Dr Saint Louis MO 63129-2267 Office: Solutia Inc 500 Monsanto Ave East Saint Louis IL 62206-1137

BALUEV, ANATOLII VICTOROVICH, chemist, consultant, researcher; b. Chita Region, USSR, Mar. 19, 1949; s. Victor Alekseevich Baluev and Zoia Grigorievna Necrasova Golubkova; m. Anna Valentinovna Smirnova, Oct. 22, 1972 (div. Feb. 1989); 1 child Maxim Anatolievich Baluev. Diploma, Leningrad U., USSR, 1966, PhD, 1975. Jr. scientist V. G. Khlopin Radium Inst., Leningrad, 1974-81, sr. scientist, 1981-90, leading rschr., 1990—; cons. St. Petersburg State U., 1973-98. Contbr. articles to profl. jours. Capt. Russian Army Res., 1971—. Recipient Honor award Soros Fund, 1993, 94; grantee All Union State Program Superconductivity, 1991-92. Mem. Trade Union, N.Y. Acad. Scis. Avocations: hobbies, history, vocal music. Home: Flat 20, St. J. Duclo, 8, Bd. 2, 194223 Saint Petersburg Russia Office: V G Khlopin Radium Inst, 2d Murinsky Av., 28, 194021 Saint Petersburg Russia

BALUEV, BORIS PETROVICH, historian, journalist; b. Veretchagino, Perm, Russia, May 12, 1930; s. Peotr Feoktistorich and Taisia Mercurjevna (Nezhdanova) B.; divorced; 1 child, Grigory (dec.). PhD in History, Moscow State U., 1954, postgrad., 1957-60. Exec. sec. Newspaper, Armavir, 1954-57; asst. prof. Moscow State U., 1960-71; prof. Acad. of Social Sci., 1971-79; head of chair Acad. of the Ministry of Internal Affairs, Moscow, 1979-85; leading rschr. Inst. of Russian History, Russian Acad. of Scis., Moscow, 1985—. Author: Political Reaction in the 1880's of the XIX Century and Russian Journalism, 1971, Lenin and the Bourgeois Press, 1983, Liberal Narodnichestoo at the Turn of XX Century, 1996, Debates over the Destiny of Russia, 1999. Grantee Russian State Humanitarian Fund, 1998. Mem. Commn. Historic Sci. of Russia. Home: App 184, 20/9 Profsojuznaja St, 117292 Moscow Russia

BALYBIN, EUGENI SERGEEVICH, nuclear medicine physician, immunophysiologist; b. Verkhnespasskoye Village, Tambov, Russia, Nov. 26, 1941; s. Sergei Alexeyevich and Matrena Vasilyevna (Stromova) B.; m. Vera Borisovna Markelova, Nov. 17, 1962; children: Victor, Nell, Zhanna. Med. diploma, Med. Acad., Astrakhan, Russia, 1965; grad. in med. radiology, Russian Med. U., Moscow, 1972, MD, 1973. Head therapy dept. Dist. Hosp., Volchki, Russia, 1965-67; med. chief Divsnl. Hosp., Shpykulovo, Russia, 1967-68; asst. Med. Acad., 1972-74; jr. sci. worker, lab. founder Leprosy Rsch. Inst., Astrakhan, 1974-78, sr. sci. worker, 1978—, head Med. Radiology Lab., 1978—. Contbr. articles to med. jours., including Internat. Jour. Leprosy, Problems of Tb, Jour. Neuropathology and Psychiatrics. Recipient honor mark USSR Health Ministry, Moscow, 1982, hon. diploma from gov., Astrakhan, 1996, medal for svcs. to motherland Pres. of Russia, Moscow, 1998. Mem. All-Russian Soc. Neuroimmunology (chmn. regional divsn. 1996), N.Y. Acad. Scis. Avocations: books on yoga, religious and occult literature, cycling, swimming, singing. Office: Leprosy Rsch Inst, Ostrowsky Passage 3, 414057 Astrakhan Russia

BALZ, FRANK JOSEPH, trade association executive, researcher; b. Wilkes-Barre, Pa., July 26, 1950; s. Joseph William and Ann (Pendergast) B.; m. Carole Cangiano, Dec. 18, 1976; children: Joanna, Alison. BA in Govt., King's Coll., 1972; MA in Polit. Sci., George Washington U., 1975, M in Philosophy, 1989. Loan officer U.S. SBA, Wilkes-Barre, 1972-73; program adminstr. Close UP Found., Washington, 1975-77; v.p. for rsch. and policy analysis Nat. Assn. Ind. Colls. and Univs., Washington, 1978—. Mem. nominating com. Montgomery Coll. Bd. Trustees, Rockville, Md., 1988-91; judge U.S.A. Today All Acad. Team, Arlington, Va., 1987—; bd. dirs. Adoption Svc. Info. Agy., Washington, 1990-95; mem. faculty devel. programs selection com. United Negro Coll. Fund, Fairfax, Va., 1995—; mem. selection com. AFL-CIO Union Privilege Scholarship Program, Washington, 1993—. Democrat. Home: 14201 Shoreham Dr Silver Spring MD 20905-4479 Office: Nat Assn Ind Colls & Univs 1025 Connecticut Ave NW Ste 700 Washington DC 20036-5409

BALZAR, DAVOR, physicist; b. Zagreb, Croatia, June 10, 1957; s. Franjo and Viktorija (Hraste) B. PhD in Physics, U. Zagreb, 1993. Scientific asst. U. Zagreb, 1981-90; rsch. asst. prof. Ruder Boskovic Inst., Zagreb, 1993-95; physicist NIST, Boulder, Colo., 1995—; lectr. U. Col., Boulder, 1998—; vis. scientist NIST, Boulder, 1990-93.; referee Am. Inst. Physics, Ridge, N.Y., 1998—, Internat. Union of Crystallography, Chester, Eng., 1993—, Mineral. Soc. Am., Washington, 1998—, Minerals, Metals and Materials Soc., Warrendale, Pa., 1992—; mem. com. powder diffraction Internat. Union Crystallography, 1999—. Mem. com. European Powder Diffraction Conf., 1998, conf. program com. mem., Budapest, 1998, mem. Spl. Interest Group on Powder Diffraction European Crystallographic Assn., 1999—. Mem. Am. Materials Rsch. Soc., Am. Crystallographic Assn., Neutron Scattering Soc. of Am. Achievements include devel. of a method to obtain the info. on strains and structure defects from diffraction-line broadening; method to determine elastic strain from diffraction data; improved modeling of diffraction-line broadening. Avocations: basketball, film and theater, travel, photography. E-mail: balzar@nist.gov. Office: NIST Divsn 853 325 Broadway St Boulder CO 80305-3337

BALZAROTTI, ADALBERTO, physicist, educator; b. Como, Italy, Mar. 23, 1939; s. Pasquale and Maria (Tommasi) B.; m. Maria Luisa Malandri, Nov. 21, 1964; children: Luca, Fabio, Marco. Laurea in Physics, U. Pavia, Italy, 1961. Rsch. asst. U. Messina, Italy, 1962-66, prof. physics, 1976-77; asst. prof. U. Rome, 1966-76; prof. physics, dean Faculty Sci. U. L'Aquila, Italy, 1977-80; prof. physics U. Rome I and II, 1981—; dir. dept. physics U. Rome II, 1985-88. Mem. editl. bd. Internat. Jour. Condensed Matter Rsch.; contbr. numerous articles to profl. jours. Mem. Italian Phys. Soc., Am. Phys. Soc., Italian Crystallographic Soc., European Phys. Soc., European and Italian Synchtrotron Radiation Soc. Office: U Rome Tor Vergata Dept Physics, Ricerca Scientifica 1, Rome 00133, Italy

BALZER, BERND ROBERT, German literature educator; b. Berlin, Germany, Jan. 2, 1942; s. Robert Karl and Gertrud Ellen (Schlennstedt) B.; m. Helga Damrath, Dec. 22, 1967. PhD, Freie U., Berlin. Asst. Freie U., Berlin, 1967-71, asst. prof., 1971-77, prof., 1977—; vis. prof. U. Wis., Madison, 1978, Peking U., China, 1982. Author: Bürgerliche Reformationspropaganda, 1972, Borchert, 1985, Hochhuth, 1986, Böll, 1988, 90, 97; editor Heinrich Bölls Werke, 1978. Home: Krusauer Str 121A, D 12305 Berlin Germany Office: Freie U Berlin FB Philosophie u Geisteswiss, Habelschwerdter Allee 45, D 14195 Berlin Germany

BALZER, LESLIE ALFRED, investment manager; b. Sydney, NSW, Australia, Oct. 17, 1944; s. Leslie Christian and Beryl Lester (Burton) B.; m. Jannette Elaine Mulcahy, Feb. 3, 1968; children: Richard Leslie, Heidi Jane. BE with honors I, U. NSW, 1968, BSc, 1969; PhD, U. Cambridge, Eng., 1974; grad. diploma, Securities Inst. Australia, Sydney, 1990. Chartered mathematician, U.K.; chartered in various positions, Australia. Chmn. mfg. and mgmt. group U. Tech., Sydney, 1976-83; mgr. advanced tech. ctr. NSW Dept. Indsl. Devel., Sydney, 1983-85; dean of engring. Royal Melbourne Inst. Tech., 1985-86; exec. Pring Dean & Coy, Sydney, 1986-89; prin. William M. Mercer, Sydney, 1989-90; investment mgr. Lend Lease Corp., Sydney, 1991-2000; sr. portfolio mgr. State Street Global Advisors, Sydney, 2000—; pres. Q-Group (Australia), Sydney, 1996-97; sec. NSW Computer Industry Adv. Coun., Sydney, 1983-85; dir. ASX Settlement & Transfer Corp. Contbr. articles to profl. jours. Fellow Instn. Engrs. Australia, Inst. Math. and Its Applications (U.K.), Australian Inst. Co. Dirs., Australian Inst. Mgmt. (assoc.), Securities Inst. Australia. Avocations: gym, skiing, running. Home: PO Box 785, Pymble NSW 2073, Australia Office: State St Global Advisors, L44 Gateway 1 Macquarie Pl, Sydney NSW 2000, Australia

BALZER, WOLFGANG, educator; b. Darmstadt, Hessen, Germany, Dec. 26, 1947; s. Hans and Ella (Meyer) B.; m. Phillio Marcou, Sept. 12, 1979. Diploma in math., U. Munich, 1975, doctor, 1978, Dr.phil.habil, 1983. Asst. prof. U. Osnabrück, Germany, 1976-77; asst. prof. U. Munich, 1978-83, prof., 1984—. Author: Soziale Institutionen, 1993, Theorie and Messung, 1985; co-author: An Architectonic for Science, 1987, Models for Genetics, 1997. Lt. German Army, 1967-68. Recipient Rsch. award in Humanities Acad. of Finland, 1995; rsch. grant NIAS, 1982-83. Mem. Assn. for Found. Sci. (exec. bd.). Avocation: farming. Home: Adelheidstr 36, Munich D-80796, Germany Office: U Munich, Ludwigstr 31, D-80539 Munich Germany

BAMANA, YOUNOUSSA, government official of Mayotte. Pres. gen. coun. Govt. of Mayotte, Mamoudzou, 1977—. Mem. Mouvement Populaire Mahorais (leader). Office: Conseil Général, BP 101, 97600 Mamoudzou Mayotte*

BAMBERG, ELMAR, biochemistry educator; b. Salzburg, Austria, July 20, 1942; s. Josef and Maria (Mertlik) B.; m. Edeltraud Schaffraneck; children: Wolfgang, Maria, Johannes. Dr.med.vet., Vet. U. Vienna, 1969, Dr.med.vet. (hon.), 1989. Asst. prof. Vet. U. Vienna Dept. Biochemistry, 1969-76, assoc. prof., 1976-81, head dept., 1981—; rector Vet. U. Vienna, 1991-95; dir. L. Boltzmann Inst. Vet. Endocrinology, 1977—. Avocations: skiing, biking, swimming, hiking. Office: Vet Med U, Veterinaerplatz 1, 1210 Vienna Austria

BAMEUL, FRANCK, entomologist; b. Cherbourg, France, Dec. 9, 1965; s. Pierre and Marie-Jose (Penverne) B.; m. Gaetane Gaute, Dec. 7, 1997. MSc, U. Bordeaux, 1993, MD, 1995. Intern CHR de Bordeaux, France, 1994-95, asst. in parasitology lab, 1995-97; gen. practice physician Bordeaux, 1997—; cons. Water Beetle Specialist Group, Gent, Belgium, 1992—; mem. (cons. specialist) sci. coun. Nature in Aquitaine, Bordeaux, 1995—. Mem. Fr. Soc. Entomol., Coleopterists Soc., Soc. Systematic Biologists, Balfour-Browne Club. Home: Mahela B 132, 2 Ter Rue de Bethmann, F-33000 Bordeaux France

BAMMÉ, ARNO, social science educator; b. Maehr, Schoenberg, Germany, May 28, 1944; arrived in Austria, 1985; s. Helmut and Emma (Strycek) B. Diploma, Free U., Berlin, 1973, 76; PhD, Tech. U., Berlin, 1983. Asst. prof. U. Berlin, 1978-83, U. Hamburg, Germany, 1983-84; univ. prof. U. Klagenfurt, Austria, 1985—. Author: ...sub specie machinae, 1994, Wissenschaft und Belletristik, 2000. (with E. Holling) Alltagswirklichkeit des Berufsschullehrers, 1982, Maschinen-Menschen..., 1983, Berufliche Sozialisation, 1983. Mem. German Sociol. Assn., Deutsche Gesellschaft Erziehungswissenschaft.

BAMVUGINYUMVIRA, FREDERIC, federal official. 1st v.p. Govt. of Burundi. Office: Office of Vice President, Bujumbura Burundi*

BAN, GÁBOR, physicist, researcher; b. Mezökövesd, Hungary, May 30, 1954; arrived in Italy, 1990; s. Gáspár and Gáspárné (Margit) B.; m. Éva Tóth Gombos, July 11, 1981; children: Fanni, Zsófia. MSc in Physics, Kossuth Lajos U. Arts and Sci., Debrecen, Hungary, 1978. Rschr. CSEPEL Metalworks, Budapest, Hungary, 1978-87; libr. Rsch. Inst. Hungarian Aluminum Industry, Budapest, 1987-88, rschr., 1989-90; cons. Ctr. Sviluppo Materiali, Rome, 1990-92; sr. rschr. Ctr. Sviluppo Materiali, Terni, Italy, 1992—; cons. United Nation's Indsl. Devel. Orgn., 1988-89. Contbr. articles to profl. jours. Mem. First Liberal Labour Union Hungarian Scientists, 1989. Lt. Hungary Army, 1972-73. Named Rschr. of Yr., Hungarian Acad. Scis., Budapest, 1984. Achievements include patent for laster treatment of electrotechnical steel production. Avocations: books, sports, travel.

BAN, TSUNENOBU, education educator; b. Fukui-ken, Japan, Feb. 27, 1950; s. Tetsugyu and Sumie (Washimi) B.; m. Kyoko Yoso, Mar. 4, 1979; children: Hidenori, Masanobu, Takeshi. BA, Hiroshima U., Japan, 1974, MA, 1976, EdD, 1979. Rschr. Nat. Inst. Ednl. Rsch., Tokyo, 1979-80; ofcl. Min. Edn. Japan, Tokyo, 1980-83; assoc. expert Unesco Inst. for Edn., Hamburg, Germany, 1983-84; assoc. prof. Naruto (Japan) U. Edn., 1984-98, prof., 1998—; rep. mem. of Japan Internat. Consortium for Understanding and Promotion of Values Edn., 1997—; mem. Edn. Coun. Tokushima, Japan, 1998—. Editor: Moral Education in the World and Japan, 1999. Coord., organizer Internat. Forum on Youth, 1999. Recipient rsch. grant Cultural and Acad. Found. for 21st Century, 1984, rsch. grant Uehiro Found. on Ethics and Edn., 1998. Mem. Comparative and Internat. Edn. Soc., Japan Soc. for Child Study (editor 1997—). Avocation: tennis. Fax: 011-81-88-687-7252. Home: 61-1 Nakasu Nakakirai, Matsushige-cho, Tokushima-ken 771-0212, Japan Office: Naruto U Edn, Takashima Naruto cho, Naruto City 772-8502, Japan

BÁN, ZSÓFIA, literature educator, researcher; b. Rio de Janeiro, Sept. 23, 1957; s. Laszlo and Eva (Bolgar) B. MA, Eotvos Lorand U. of Budapest, Hungary, 1981; PhD, Eötvös Lorand U., Budapest, Hungary, 1997. Cert. English, French and lit. tchr., Hungary. Asst. dir. Mafilm (Hungarian Film Co.), Budapest, 1981-84; freelance writer and translator Budapest, 1984-85, 88; Am. lit. educator Eötvös Loránd, Budapest, 1988—. Contbr. articles to profl. jours. Hungarian Ministry of Cultural Affairs rsch. fellow, 1987-88; Hungarian Acad. of Scis. Rsch. scholar, 1985-88, Fulbright scholar Rutgers U., 1992-93. Jewish. Home: Hollan EU 49, 1136 Budapest Hungary Office: Eötvös Lorand U, Ajtósi Dürer Sor 19, 1146 Budapest Hungary

BANA, AJEET, cardiac surgeon, consultant; b. Meerut, UP, India, June 1, 1965; s. Udai Veer Singh and Jagdish (Kaur) Bana; m. Mona Goth, Dec. 29, 1991; 1 child, Avtansh. MBBS with honors, Lala Lajpat Rai Meml. Med. Coll., Meerut, 1989, M of Sugery, 1993; M of Cardiothoracic Surgery, Delhi (India) U., 1996. Resident in gen. surgery SVBP Hosp., Meerut, 1990-93; sr. resident in cardiothoracic surgery All India Inst. Med. Scis., Delhi, 1993; sr. resident in cardiothoracic surgery G.B. Pant Hosp., Delhi, 1994-96, registrar in cardiothoracic surgery, 1996-97; cardiac surgeon Nat. Heart Inst., Delhi, 1997-98; cons., cardiac surgeon Sir Ganga Ram Hosp., Delhi, 1998—. Contbr. articles to med. jours., including Indian Heart Jour., Internat. Jour. Cardiology, others. Mem. Subharti Sewa, Meerut, 1989-93, Earthquake Relief Med. Team, 1991, Pulse Polio Immunization, Delhi, 1997. Mem. Indian Med. Assn., Indian Assn. Thoracic and Cardiovascular Surgeons. Avocations: badminton, squash, music, mountaineering, driving. Home: E 108 Mayur Vihar Phase II, Delhi 110091, India Office: Dept Cardiac Surgery, Sir Ganga Ram Hosp, RajinNag New Delhi 110060, India

BANA, DHIREMDRA SINGH, physician; b. Chitauli, India, July 1, 1941; came to U.S., 1965; s. Baljit Singh and Vidya Wati Rana; m. Cora C. Bana, Jan. 15, 1973. MB BS, All India Inst. Med. Scis., New Delhi, 1964. Diplomate Am. Bd. Internal Medicine, Am. Bd. Nephrology. Rotating intern Queens Gen. Hosp., N.Y., 1965; house physician Whipps Cross Hosp., London, 1966; resident Lemuel Shattuck Hosp., Boston, 1966-67; resident VA Hosp., Boston, 1967-68, clin. fellow in nephrology, 1968-69; rsch. fellow in nephrology Univ. Hosp., Boston U. Sch. Medicine, 1969-70; med. specialist Safdarjang Hosp., New Delhi, 1970-71; physician Bangor (Maine) State Hosp., 1971-73; dir. Rsch. Divsn. Headache Rsch. Found./The Faulkner Hosp., Boston, 1973-88; mem. John R. Graham Headache Ctr./ The Faulkner Hosp., Boston, 1990—; dir. John R. Graham Headache Ctr. Faulkner Hosp., Boston, 1997—; pvt. practice internal medicine Boston, 1973—; cons. in nephrology Lemuel Shattuck Hosp., Boston, 1973-77. Author: (with others) Evaluation and Treatment of Chronic Pain; contbr. articles to profl. jours. including Headache, Am. Heart Jour. Fellow ACP; mem. Am. Soc. Nephrology, Internat. Soc. Nephrology, Am. Soc. Echocardiology, Am. Headache Soc. Office: John R Graham Headache Ctr 1153 Centre St Boston MA 02130-3446

BANACH, ART JOHN, graphic artist; b. Chgo., May 22, 1931; s. Vincent and Anna (Zajac) B. Grad. Art. Inst. of Chgo., 1955; pupil painting studies Mrs. Melin, Chgo.; m. Loretta A. Nolan, Oct. 15, 1966; children: Heather Anne, Lynnea Joan. Owner, dir. Art J. Banach Studios, 1949—, cartoon syndicate for newspapers, house organs and advt. functions, 1954—, owner

and operater advt. agy., 1954-56, feature news and picture syndicate, distbn. U.S. and fgn. countries. Dir. Speculators S Fund. Recipient award 1st Easter Seal contest Ill. Assn. Crippled, Inc., 1949. Chgo. Pub. Sch. Art Soc. Scholar. Mem. Artist's Guild Chgo., Am Mgmt. Assn., Chgo. Assn. of Commerce and Industry, Chgo. Federated Advt. Club, Am. Mktg. Assn., Internat. Platform Assn., Chgo. Advt. Club, Chgo. Soc. Communicating Arts, Am. Ctr. For Design, Chgo. Calligraphy Collective, Columbia Yacht Club, Advt. Execs. Club, Art Dirs. Club (Chgo.). Home: 1076 Leahy Cir East Des Plaines IL 60016-6050

BANAFAA, OMAR SALEH, consultant obstetrician and gynecologist; b. Aden, Yemen, Feb. 12, 1944; s. Saleh Abdulla and Noor (Mohammad) B.; m. Sharifa Alawiya Ghurbani. MB ChB, St. Andrews U., Scotland, 1969; DTM&H, Liverpool Sch. Trop. Medicine, Eng., 1972. Sr. house officer Yorkshire Health Bd., Bradford, Eng., 1969-74, Kirklees Health Authority, Huddersfield, Eng., 1974-76; registrar Lothian Health Bd., Edinburgh, Scotland, 1976-79, Glasgow Health Authority, 1979-81, Lanarkshire Health Authority, Airdrie and Bellshill, 1981-82; cons., head dept. ob-gyn. Al-Mana Gen. Hosp., Al-Khobar, Saudi Arabia, 1982—. Fellow Royal Coll. Ob-Gyn.; mem. European Soc. Human Reproduction & Embryology, Faculty Family Planning London. Islamic. Avocations: economics, music, poetry. Home: Al-Mana Gen Hosp, PO Box 1364, Al-Khobar 31952, Saudi Arabia

BANAS, SUZANNE, middle school educator; b. Miami, Fla., Mar. 28, 1959; d. Frank and Norma (Eliscu) B. BA in Sci., U. Miami, 1981, MS in Edn., 1986; PhD, Union Inst., 1994. Cert. tchr. sci., Fla.; nat. bd. cert. tchr. early adolescence generalist Nat. Bd. Profl. Tchg. Stds. Tchr. Dade County Pub. Schs., Miami, 1988—; curriculum writer Gender Equity Network, Miami, 1993-97, Arise Found., Miami, 1995-97; tchr., chairperson dept. sci., team leader Cutler Ridge Mid. Sch., Miami, 1990—; adj. prof. Fla. Internat. U., Miami, 1996—; advisor Acad. for Instrnl. Leadership, Miami, 1994-96, Annenberg Challenge Grant, Miami, 1995-96; cons. Urban Sys. Initiative, 1995-98; Internet tchr. trainer/mentor, 1998—. Recipient Fla. Explores! award Fla. State U./TDRA, 1993, Tchyr. of Yr. award Cutler Ridge Mid. Sch., 1996. Mem. Dade County Sci. Tchrs. Assn. (pres. 1994—), Fla. Assn. Sci. Tchrs. (bd. dirs. 1998—), Nat. Sci. Tchrs. Assn. Office: Cutler Ridge Mid Sch 19400 Gulfstream Rd Miami FL 33157-8658

BANASIK, KAZIMIERZ, hydrologist, hydraulic engineer, educator; b. Wielki Garc, Gdansk, Poland, May 26, 1950; s. Stanislaw and Natalia (Cabaj) B.; m. Elżbieta Macjon, Sept. 4, 1955; children: Jerzy, Natalia, Aleksander. MS in Engring., Warsaw (Poland) Agrl. U., 1975, PhD, 1983, DSc, 1995. Lectr., rsch. engr. Warsaw Agrl. U., 1975-84, asst. prof., 1984-98, assoc. prof., 1999—; prof. Coll. Environ. Protection, Radom, Poland, 1995—; vis. assoc. prof. U. Ill. Urbana-Champaign, 1997-98. Recipient Gold medal Ministry of Environ. Protection and Forestry, Warsaw, 1996. Mem. Internat. Assn. Hydrological Scis., Internat. Assn. Hydraulic Rsch., Am. Geophys. Union. Home: Malcuzynskiego 5 m 26, 02-793 Warsaw Poland Office: Warsaw Agrl U-SGGW, ul Nowoursynowska 166, 02-787 Warsaw Poland

BANASZAK, GRZEGORZ MARIAN, mathematician, educator; b. Gostyń, Poland, Feb. 10, 1958; s. Leon and Wanda Teresa (Skowronek) B.; m. Beata Magdalena Chwarścianek, Oct. 12, 1996. MS, Adam Mickiewicz, Poznań, Poland, 1982; PhD, Ohio State U., 1990. Rsch. and tng. staff Szczecin (Poland) U., 1982-86; grad. tchg. assoc. Ohio State U., Columbus, 1986-90, vis. lectr., 1990-91; postdoctoral fellow for advanced study McMaster U., Hamilton, Ont., Can., 1991-93; asst. prof. Szczecin (Poland) U., 1993-94; asst. prof. Adam Mickiewicz U., Poznań, 1994-98, assoc. prof., 1998—. Editor: Algebraic K-Theory, 1996. Recipient Waclaw Sierpiński award Polish Math. Soc., Toruń, Poland, 1995; Komitet Badan Naukowych grantee Polish Com. for Sci. Rsch., 1994-96, 96—. Roman Catholic. Office: Adam Mickiewicz U, Ul Matejki 48/49, 60769 Poznan Poland

BANASZKIEWICZ, MAREK WŁADYSŁAW, physicist; b. Poznán, Poland, Dec. 1, 1950; s. Aleksander and Marcelina (Kowalska) B.; m. Magdalena Teresa Pieni—żek, Sept. 30, 1975 (dec. June 2000); children: Adam, Filip. MSc, Warsaw (Poland) U., 1973, PhD, 1982, habilitation, 1999. mem. Polish Com. Space and Satellite Rsch., 1999—. Rsch. scientist Space Rsch. Ctr., Warsaw, 1976—. Contbr. articles to profl. jours. Recipient Group Achievement award for Cassini Mission, 1998. Mem. Polish Astronautical Soc. (pres. 1996—), Cospar, European Astron. Soc., European Geophys. Soc., Internat. Space Sci. Inst. (mem. sci. coun.). Home: Hirszfelda 18/6, 02-776 Warsaw Poland Office: Space Rsch Ctr, Bartycka 18A, 00-716 Warsaw Poland

BANATVALA, JANGU, virology educator, consultant, researcher; b. London, Jan. 7, 1934; s. Edal and Ratti (Shrof) B.; m. Roshan Mugaseth, Aug. 15, 1959; children: Nicholas, Jonathan, Christopher, Emma (dec.). BA, Cambridge (Eng.) U., 1955, MA, 1958; MB, BChir, London Hosp. Medicine, 1959, MD, 1964, diploma in child health, 1961, diploma in pub. health, 1961. House officer London Hosp., 1958-59; sr. house officer, pediatrician Gen. Hosp., Kettering, Eng., 1959-60; rsch. fellow dept. pathology Cambridge U., 1961-64; postdoctoral fellow Yale U., New Haven, 1964-65; sr. lectr., reader, then prof. clin. virology United Med. and Dental Sch. St. Thomas Hosp., London, 1965-99; emeritus prof. Gugs, King, and St. Thomas Sch. Medicine, 1999—; mem. senate, various coms. U. London, 1988—; chair adv. group hepatitis Dept. Health, London, 1990-98; asst. registrar, 1984-85, registrar, 1985-87, v.p., 1987-90, coun. mem. and exec., 1993-96; examiner in pathology U. London, U. Cambridge, Eng., U. West Indies, U. Riyadh. Co-editor: Principal Practice of Clinical Virology, 1987, 4th edit., 2000; editor: Viral Infections of the Heart, 1993; contbr. articles to profl. jours. Freeman City of London. Named Comdr. Brit. Empire. Fellow Royal Soc. Medicine, Royal Soc. Hygiene and Tropical Medicine, Royal Coll. Physicians, Royal Coll. Pathologists; mem. Pub. Health Lab. Svc. Bd. (UK). Avocations: antiques, cricket, lawn tennis, opera. Home: Church End, Henham, Bishop's Stortford CM22 6AN, England

BANBURY, FRITH (FREDERICK HAROLD BANBURY), theater director, actor; b. Plymouth, May 4, 1912; s. Rear Admiral Frederick Arthur Frith Banbury and Winifred Fink. Student, Oxford U., Royal Acad. Dramatic Art. Appeared in plays and films, 1933-47; dir. (plays) Dark Summer, 1947, The Holly and the Ivy, 1950, Waters of the Moon, 1951, The Deep Blue Sea, 1951, Morosco, 1952, A Question of Fact, 1953, Marching Song, 1954, Love's Labours Lost, 1954, The Diary of Anne Frank, 1956, A Dead Secret, 1957, Flowering Cherry, 1957, A Touch of the Sun, 1958, The Ring of Truth, 1959, The Tiger and the Horse, 1960, The Wings of the Dove, 1963, The Right Honourable Gentleman, 1965, Howards End, 1967, Dear Octopus, 1967, Enter a Free Man, 1968, My Darling Daisy, 1970, The Winslow Boy, 1970, Captain Brassbound's Conversion, 1971, Reunion in Vienna, 1972, The Day After the Fair, 1972, In U.S.A., 1973, Glasstown, 1973, Ardèle, 1975, Family Matter, 1976, On Approval, 1977, Motherdear, 1980, Dear Liar, 1982, The Aspern Papers, 1984, The Corn is Green, 1985, The Admirable Crichton, 1988, Screamers, 1989, The Gin Game, 1999, numerous others in N.Y.C., Paris, Tel Aviv, Toronto, Hong Kong, Johannesburg, Nairobi, Sydney, Melbourne. Avocation: playing piano. Address: 18 Park Saint James, Prince Albert Rd, London NW8 7LE, England

BANCE, ALAN FREDERICK, German studies educator; b. London, Mar. 7, 1939; s. Frederick and Agnes Mary (Wilson) B.; m. Sandra Davis, Aug. 31, 1964; children: Georgia, Miriam. BA, Univ. Coll. London, 1961; PhD, U. Cambridge (Eng.), 1968. Lektor U. Graz (Austria), 1964-65; lectr. U. Strathclyde, Glasgow, Scotland, 1965-67; lektor U. Cologne (Fed. Republic Germany), 1972-73; lectr. U. St. Andrews (Scotland), 1967-81, sr. lectr., 1981; prof., head of dept. U. Keele (Eng.), 1981-84, U. Southampton (Eng.), 1984—. Editor Germanic sect. Modern Lang. Rev., 1988-94; author: Theodor Fontane: The Major Novels, 1982, The German Novel '45-'60, 1980; editor: Weimar Germany: Writers and Politics, 1982, Ö. v. Horvath 50 Years On, 1988, Theodor Fontane: The London Symposium, 1995, The Legacy of the British Occupation in Germany, 1997; contbr. numerous articles to profl. jours. Mem. Conf. Univ. Tchrs. German in Gt. Britain and Ireland (pres. 1994-96), Modern Humanities Rsch. Assn. (hon. life). Home: 8 Oakmount Ave Highfield, Southampton SO17 1DR, England Office: U Southampton, German Studies, Highfield, Southampton SO17 1BJ, England

BANCEWICZ, MALGORZATA MAGDALENA, physicist, educator; b. Szczecin, Poland, Sept. 22, 1953; d. Jerzy Dymala and Barbara Maria Rakowska; m. Tadeusz Bancewicz, Apr. 25, 1975; 1 child, Iga Maria. MSc, Adam Mickiewicz U., Poznań, Poland, 1977; PhD, Nicolas Copernicus U., Toruń, Poland, 1990. Tech. asst. Poznań U. Tech., 1977-84, asst., 1984-91, adj. prof., 1991—. Contbr. articles to profl. jours. Avocations: history. Home: Wichrowe Wzgorze 27/47, 61 677 Poznan Poland Office: Inst Physics Poznań U, Piotrowo 3, 60 965 Poznan Poland

BANCIU, AXENTE CONSTANTIN, chemist; b. Bucharest, Romania, Oct. 13, 1938; s. Axente Sever and Clara Flora (Filip) B.; m. Banciu Elsa Christa Witschel, July 15, 1965 (dec. Apr. 1995); 1 child, Banciu Radu. MSc, Tech. U., Dresden, Germany, 1963; PhD, Poly. Inst., Bucharest, 1974. Chem. diplomate. Chemist Chem. Pharm. Rsch. Inst., Bucharest, 1963-67; chemist Inst. Chem. Physics, Romanian Acad., Bucharest, 1967-70, sci. rschr., 1970-78, prin. sci. rschr., 1978—. Reviewer Rev. Roumaine Chim, 1975—; contbr. articles to profl. jours.; patentee in field. Fellow Romanian Chem. Soc.; mem. N.Y. Acad. Scis. Christian Orthodox. Avocations: history and geography of world, history of arts. Home: Bl D-24 Apt 36, Str Izvorul Trotusului Nr 1, RO-75395 Bucharest Romania Office: Inst Chem Physics, Spl Independentei 202, RO-77208 Bucharest Romania

BANCROFT, ANNE (MRS. MEL BROOKS), actress; b. N.Y.C., Sept. 17, 1931; d. Michael and Mildred (DiNapoli) Italiano; m. Mel Brooks, 1964; 1 son. Broadway stage appearances include Two for the Seesaw, 1957 (Tony award 1957), The Miracle Worker, 1959-60 (Tony award 1960), Devils, 1977, Golda, 1977-78, Duet for One, 1981; stage appearances include Mystery of the Rose Bouquet, 1989; motion pictures include Treasure of the Golden Condor, 1952, Don't Bother to Knock, 1952, Tonight We Sing, 1953, The Kid from Left Field, 1953, Demetrius and the Gladiators, 1954, Gorilla at Large, 1954, The Raid, 1954, A Life in the Balance, 1954, The Brass Ring, 1954, Naked Street, 1955, New York Confidential, 1955, The Last Frontier, 1955, Girl in the Black Stockings, 1957, Restless Breed, 1957, The Pumpkin Eater, 1964, Seven Women, 1966, Slender Thread, 1966, The Graduate, 1967, Young Winston, 1972, The Prisoner of 2nd Avenue, 1975, The Hindenburg, 1975, Lipstick, 1976, Silent Movie, 1976, The Turning Point, 1977, Fatso, 1979, The Elephant Man, 1980, To Be or Not to Be, 1983, Garbo Talks, 1984, Agnes of God, 1985, 'Night, Mother, 1986, 84 Charing Cross Road (Brit. Acad. award 1987), Torch Song Trilogy, 1988, Bert Rigby You're a Fool, 1989, Honeymoon in Vegas, 1992, Love Potion #9, 1992, Point of No Return, 1993, Mr. Jones, 1993, Malice, 1993, How to Make an American Quilt, 1995, Home for the Holidays, 1995, Dracula, Dead and Loving It, 1995, GI Jane, 1997, Critical Care, 1997, Great Expectations, 1998, Antz, 1998, Mark Twain's America in 3D, 1998, Up at the Villa, 1999, Deep in My Heart, 1999; TV appearances include Kraft Music Hall, Jesus of Nazareth, 1977, Marco Polo, 1982, Broadway Bound, 1992, Mrs. Cage, PBS, 1992, Oldest Living Confederate Widow Tells All, 1994, The Homecoming, 1996, Sunchasers, 1997,AFI's 100 years ... 100 Movies, 1998, Deep in My Heart, 1999, A Salute to Dustin Hoffman, 1999; dir., writer, star: (TV spl.) Annie-The Woman in the Life of Men, 1970 (Emmy award 1970). Recipient Acad. award for performance in The Miracle Worker, 1962, Best Actress award Cannes Internat. Film Festival for performance in Pumpkin Eater, 1964, Lifetime Achievement in Comedy award Am. Comedy Awards, 1996. Address: c/o The Culver Studios 9336 Washington Blvd Culver City CA 90232-2628

BANCROFT, PAUL, III, investment company executive; b. N.Y.C., Feb. 27, 1930; s. Paul and Rita (Manning) B.; m. Monica M. Devine, Jan. 2, 1977; children by previous marriage: Bradford, Kimberly, Stephen, Gregory. BA, Yale U., 1951; postgrad., Georgetown Fgn. Svc. Inst., 1952. Account exec. Merrill Lynch Pierce Fenner & Smith, N.Y.C., 1956-57; assoc. corp. fin. dept. F. Eberstadt & Co., N.Y.C., 1957-62; ptnr. Draper, Gaither & Anderson, Palo Alto, Calif., 1962-67; with Bessemer Securities Corp., N.Y.C., 1967-92; ind. venture capitalist N.Y.C., 1992—; v.p. Venture Capital Investments, 1967-74, sr. v.p. securities investments, 1974-76, pres., CEO, dir., 1976-87; cons. Bessemer Securities Corp., 1988-92; bd. dirs. Unova, Inc.; founder, past pres. and chmn. Nat. Venture Capital Assn. 1st lt. USAF 1952-56,. Mem. Yale Club, Pacific Union Club, Bohemian Club. Home and Office: PO Box 6639 Snowmass Village CO 81615-6639

BANDA, RICHARD ALLEN, chief justice; b. Nkhata Bay, Malawi, Nov. 20, 1937; s. Duncan Stewart and Matilda Mwase Banda; m. Dorothy Mhango, Jan. 1960 (div. 1982); children: Stanley, Etta, Ian, Susan; m. Joyce Hilda Mtila, Jan. 23, 1983; children: Kambe, Njaliwe. Grad. in Law, Inns Ct. Sch. Law, London, 1966. Legal aid advocate Malawi Ministry Justice, Blantyre, 1966-67, with traditional ct. com., 1967-68, state advocate, 1968-69; min. justice Malawi Ministry Justice, Lilongwe, 1974-76; sr. resident magistrate Malawi Judiciary, Blantyre, 1969-70, chief resident magistrate, 1980, judge high ct., supreme ct. appeal, 1980-92, chief justice, 1992—; dir. pub. prosecutions A.G. Chambers, Zomba, Malawi, 1970-72; min. Malawi Min. Local Govt., Lilongwe, 1974-76, Min. Parliamentary Affairs, Lilongwe, 1975-76. 1st Malawian apptd. sr. counsel after independence, Pres. Malawi, 1972. Mem. Olympic and Commonwealth Games Assn. Malawi (chmn. 1986—), Footbal Assn. Malawi (chmn. 1988-92). Avocations: golf, soccer, law tennis, athletics. Home: SS 109 Kabula Hill, Blantyre Malawi Office: High Court of Malawi, PO Box 30244, Chichiri Blantyre Malawi*

BANDAR, PRINCE BIN SULTAN BIN ABD AL-AZIZ AL SAUD, Saudi Arabian ambassador to U.S.; b. Taif, Saudi Arabia, Mar. 2, 1949; s. Prince Sultan ibn Abdulaziz al-Saud; m. Princess Haifa bint Faisal ibn Abdulazia al-Saud; children—Lulua, Rema, Khalid, Faisal. B.A., Brit. Royal Air Force Acad., Cranwell, Eng., 1969; Grad., Advanced Fighter and Instr. Pilot Program, USAF, 1979; M.A., Johns Hopkins U., 1980. Fighter pilot Royal Saudi Air Force, Dhahran Air Base, Khamis Mushayt Air Base, Taif Air Base, 1969-82, comdr. 7th Royal Saudi Air Force Squadron, 1976-79, comdr. Peace Hawk Project, Dhahran, 1976-79; in charge spl. AWACS Saudi Arabian Liaison Mission to U.S., 1981; mem. Saudi Arabia Mil. Mission to U.S., def. and mil. attache, 1982-83; mem. Saudi Del. to UN Gen. Assembly, 1983; Saudi Arabian ambassador to U.S., 1983—. Served to col. Royal Saudi Air Force. Decorated Flying Hawk medal; King Abdulaziz Sash, for work in attaining Lebanese ceasefire, King Fahd, 1983. Muslim. Home: Fgn Ministry Saudi Arabia, Riyadh Saudi Arabia Office: Royal Embassy of Saudi Arabia 601 New Hampshire Ave NW Washington DC 20037-2405*

BANDARANAYAKE, RAJA CHRISTIE, anatomist, educator; b. Kandy, Sri Lanka, Apr. 4, 1935; arrived in Australia, 1976; s. Don Hendrick and Phoebe Ukkumenike (Ratnayake) B.; m. Chandrani Henrietta Paranavitane, Aug. 12, 1964; children: Rohan, Ruveni, Roshini. MBBS, U. Ceylon, 1959; PhD, U. London, 1967; MSEd, U. So. Calif., 1973. Med. officer Dept. Health, Colombo, Ceylon, 1959-60; demonstrator in anatomy U. Ceylon, Colombo, 1960-62; lectr. anatomy U. Sri Lanka, Peradeniya, 1962-76; lectr. med. edn. U. New South Wales, Sydney, Australia, 1976-92; assoc. prof. U. New South Wales, Sydney, 1992-97; prof. anatomy Arabian Gulf U., Manama, Bahrain, 1997—; cons. WHO, 1974—, World Bank, India, 1994—, Australian Med. Coun., 1989-96. Co-author: Multiple Choice Questions in Basic, 1991, 2d edit., 1997; contbr. chpts in books and articles to profl. jours. Fellow Royal Australian Coll. Surgeons (bd. examiners 1992-96); mem. Australian and New Zealand Assn. for Med. Edn. (pres. 1993-95, Fred Katz Meml. medal for achievements 1991), Assn. for Med. Edn. We. Pacific Region (exec.). Avocations: collecting rare books and manuscripts, history, tennis, snooker. Home: 20 Strickland St Rose Bay, NSW Sydney 2029, Australia

BANDARCHI-CHAMKHALEH, BIZHAN, physician; b. Tehran, Mar. 8, 1965; s. Nasser Bandarchi-C. and Batool Fassihi-Langroudi. Cert. English Lang., Nat. Inst. English Lang., Tehran, 1980; Diploma, Alborz H.S. (formerly Am., Coll. of Iran), 1982; Medical Diploma, Shaheed Beheshti U. (formerly, Nat. U. of Iran) Tehran, 1992. Cert. Ednl. Commn. for Fgn. Med. Grads. Pathology resident Shaheed Modarres Hosp., Tehran, 1990-91, U. Fla. Health Sci. Ctr., Jacksonville, 1997-2000, Mass. Gen. Hosp./Harvard Med. Sch., Boston, 2000—; physician-in-charge Mil. Base Clinic, Tehran, 1992-94, Ministry of Health, Qeshm, Iran, 1994-95; gen. practitioner Tehran, 1993-97; rsch. asst. Iran Pezeshk Clinic, Tehran, 1993-96; poster presenter in field. Translator: (book) Clinical Neurology, 1993 (1st prize Med. Students Authorship Competition/Iran 1996); editor: (book, Farsi translation) Physiology of Special Senses, 1985, others; contbr. articles and abstracts to med. jours. including Breast Jour., Modern Pathology. Higher supr. in polio eradicating program, Ministry of Health in cooperation with WHO, Hormozgan, Iran, 1995. 1st lt. Iranian mil., 1992-94. Mem. AMA, U.S. and Can. Acad. Pathology, N.Y. Acad. Scis., Med. Ethics Coun. of Iran, Am. Soc. Clin. Pathologists, Coll. Am. Pathologists. Home: 10 Summer St Apt 1006S Malden MA 02148-3945 Office: Mass Gen Hosp Dept Pathology Warren Bldg 55 Fruit St Boston MA 02114-2622

BANDEMER, HANS WALTER, mathematics educator; b. Halle, Germany, Apr. 1, 1932; s. Konrad L.A. and Martha M. (Teichmann) B.; m. Elfrida M. Bischoff, Aug. 20, 1955; 1 child, Ulrike M. Diploma math., Halle U., Germany, 1958; PhD of natural scis., Freiberg Mining Acad., Germany, 1961; habilitation, Freiberg Mining Acad., 1965. From asst. to assoc. prof. Freiberg Mining Acad., Germany, 1958-69, prof., 1969-97, prof. emeritus, 1997—. Author: Optimal Experimental Design, 1974, Fuzzy Data Analysis, Fuzzy Set Theory, 1985-95, Reasonable Computing, 1997; author, editor: (handbook) Optimal Experimental Design, 1977, 80. Office: Tu Bergakademie Freiberg, Cotta Str 2, D-09596 Freiberg Germany

BANDER, EDWARD JULIUS, law librarian emeritus, lawyer; b. Boston, Aug. 10, 1923; s. Abraham and Ida (Lendman) B. BA, Boston U., 1949, LLB, 1951; MLS, Simmons Coll., 1955. Bar: Mass. 1951. Asst. reference libr. Harvard U., Cambridge, Mass., 1954-55; libr. U.S. Ct. Appeals (1st cir.), Boston, 1955-60; asst. libr., asst. prof. NYU, N.Y.C., 1960-70, assoc. prof., curator, assoc. libr., 1970-78; prof., libr. Suffolk U. Law Sch., Boston, 1978-90, libr., prof. emeritus, 1991—. Author: Mr. Dooley and the Choice of Law, 1963, Mr. Dooley and Mr. Dunne, 1981, Justice Holmes Ex Cathedra, 1966, 91, Searching the Law, 1986, Shakespeare on Lawyers and the Law, 1998; co-editor bi-monthly rev. law books, 1990—. Served with USN, 1942-46. Recipient Dean Frederick A. McDermott award Suffolk U. Student Bar Assn., 1980. Mem. Assn. Am. Law Schs., New Eng. Law Libr. Democrat. Jewish. Office: 50 Church St Concord MA 01742-3050

BANDERAS, ANTONIO, actor; b. Malaga, Spain, Aug. 10, 1960. Films include: Labyrinth of Passion, 1982, Y del sefuro...llbranos señor!, 1983, El Caso Almeria, 1983, The Stilts, 1984, La corte de Faraon, 1985, Requiem por un campesino espanol, 1985, The Puzzle, 1986, 27 Hours, 1986, Matador, 1986, Delirios de amor, 1986, The Way They Were, 1987, Law of Desire, 1987, The Pleasure of Killing, 1988, Baton Rouge, 1988, Women on the Verge of a Nervous Breakdown, 1988, Going South Shopping, 1988, Si que dicen que cai, 1989, The White Dove, 1989, Tie Me Up! Tie Me Down!, 1990, Against the Wind, 1990, New Land, 1991, Woman in the Rain, 1991, Madonna: Truth or Dare, 1991, Borges Tales, Part I, 1991, The Mambo Kings, 1992, Shoot!, 1993, Outrage, 1993, Philadelphia, 1993, The House of the Spirits, 1993, Of Love and Shadows, 1994, Interview With the Vampire, 1994, Never Talk to Strangers, 1995, Miami Rhapsody, 1995, Four Rooms, 1995, Desperado, 1995, Assassins, 1995, Two Much, 1996, Evita, 1996, The Mask of Zorro, 1997, Crazy in Alabama, 1998, The 13th Warrior, 1999, Play it to the Bone, 1999, Dancing in the Dark, 2000, The Body, 2000; dir. Crazy in Alabama, 1999, Malaga Burning, 2000; prodr. White River Kid, 1999, Forever Lulu, 2000. Office: care CAA 9830 Wilshire Blvd Beverly Hills CA 90212-1804 also: Agents Assocs/Guy Bonnet, 201 Rue du fauborg, Saint Honore Paris 75008, France

BANDGAR, BABASAHEB PANDURANG, chemist, educator, researcher; b. Nazare, India, May 26, 1955; s. Pandurang Nivratti and Chandrabhaga Pandurang (Bandgar) B.; m. Sonali Babasaheb Bandgar, May 10, 1977; children: Sunita, Sunil. BSc in Chemistry, Shivaji U., Kolhapur, India, 1976, MSc in Organic Chemistry, 1979, MPhil, 1985; PhD, Vienna (Austria) U., 1991. Jr. lectr. Tech. Inst., Baramati, India, 1979-80; lectr. Rao Bahadur Narayanrao Borawake Coll., Shrirampur, India, 1980-87, sr. lectr., 1987-95, reader, 1995-97; prof., head chemistry dept. Swami Ramanand Teerth Marathwada Univ., Vishnupuzi, Nanded, India, 1997—; cons. rschr. Nanded U., 1997—. Fellow Indian Coun. Chemists (life, young scientist 1995); mem. Indian Sci. Congress, Molecular Diversity Preservation Internat. Hindu. Avocations: coin collecting, chemicals collecting, friendship letters, working on farm, body building. Home: Ankdhal Post Chinake, 413709 Sangola-Dist-Solapur India Office: SRTM Univ, Sch Chem Scis P Box 87, Nanded Vishnupuri 431602, India

BANDLER, VIVICA AINA FANNY, theater director; b. Helsingfors, Finland, Feb. 5, 1917; d. Erik von Frenckell and Ester-Margaret Lindberg; m. Kurt Bandler, 1943 (div. 1963). BA, U. Helsinki. artistic dir. Tampere Internat. Theatre Festival, Finland, 1989-95; pres. bd. Swedish Theatre Union/Swedish Internat. Theatre Inst., 1978-92, mem. exec. com., 1981-86, mem. drama com., 1990-92; pres. Theatre Acad. Sweden, Stockholm, 1992-99; patron Hangö Festival, Finland, 1996-97. Dir. Swedish Theatre, Helsingfors, 1948; head theatre sect. Helsinki's 400th anniversary, 1950; founded Peasants' Theatre Group, 1951; mgr., prin. dir. Lilla Teatern, Helsingfors, 1955-67; mgr., dir. Oslo Nye Teater, Norway, 1967-69; head Stockholm City Theatre, Sweden, 1969-80; artistic dir. Tampere Internat. Theatre Festival, Finland, 1989-95; dir. Eri dance theatre, Finland, 1989—; co-author: Addressee Unknown, 1992; author numerous dramatisations of novels, film scripts, musicals; contbr. articles to profl. publs. With armed forces, 1939-40, 41-43. Recipient Golden Boot Daily Newspaper Dagens Nyheter, Sweden, medal City of Stockholm, medal Swedish Parliament in Finland, August award Swedish Dramatists' Assn., Letterstedt Found. medal for Nordic coop., Thalia award Swedish Actor's Assn., Finland prize, Memory medal of war, 1939-40; named Comdr. Finnish Lion, Pro Finlandis, Finland, Comdr. No. Star Sweden. Mem. Swedish Author's Assn. Finland (hon.), Union Theatre Dirs. Address: Villagatan 1 B, SF-00150 Helsinki Finland

BANDO, MASAYASU, biochemist, researcher; b. Tokushima, Japan, Mar. 27, 1947; s. Kinosuke and Chiyoko (Moritomo) B.; m. Akiko Kaneda, Apr. 25, 1981; children: Asuka, Chihiro. B in Engring., Tokyo Inst. Tech., 1969, MSc, 1971; PhD, Juntendo U., Tokyo, 1980. Rsch. assoc. dept. ophthalmology Juntendo U. Sch. Medicine, Tokyo, 1971—; instr. Tokai U. Sch. Medicine, Isehara, Japan, 1980-86; asst. prof. Tokai U. Sch. Medicine, 1986-90, assoc. prof., 1990—; rsch. assoc. dept. chemistry Ga. Inst. Tech., Atlanta, 1981-83, rsch. cons., 1988; rsch. cons. dept. ophthalmology Keio U. Sch. Medicine, Tokyo, 1985-90; cons. Eye Rsch. Inst. Cataract Found., Tokyo, 1996—. Contbr. articles to profl. jours. Rsch. grantee Japanese Ministry Edn., Sci. and Culture, 1981, 94, 98-99, Eye Rsch. Inst. Cataract Found., 1988, 89. Mem. Japanese Biochem. Soc., Japanese Ophthal. Soc., N.Y. Acad. Scis. Office: Dept Ophthalmology, Tokai U Sch Medicine, Isehara 259-1193, Japan

BANDOUVAS, EMMANUEL JEAN, surgeon, educator; b. Heraclion, Crete, Greece, Aug. 21, 1929; s. Jean George Bandouvas and Maria Constantine Anagnostakis. Doctorate, Athens U., 1978. Cert. gen. surgeon, oncologist. Pvt. practice Athens, 1955-70; registrar Anticancer Inst. Athens, St. Savas Hosp., 1979-87; spl. asst. Breast Clinic of Royal Marsden Hosp., London, 1979-80; collaborator Exptl. Ctr. Nude-Mice, London, 1979-80; asst. prof. surgery Athens U., 1989—; asst. prof. Med. Sch. Athens, 1989; cons. Breast Cancer Clinic, St. Savas Hosp., 1987, Oncol. Clinic of Gen. State Hosp., 1988, 2d Surg. Clinic of Helena Venizelou Hosp., 1989; v.p. Olympic Idea Organism, 1995, Ancient Hellenic Spirit Orgn., 1989; spkr. in field. Author: Methods of Surgical Treatment of Breast Cancer in First Surgical Clinic of Athens University, 1973; contbr. articles to profl. jours. Coun. mem., v.p. Pancrete Union, Athens. Recipient Cert. of Gratitude (2), Greek Govt., 1941-45. Mem. Olympic Idea Orgn. (v.p.), Ancient Greece Spirit (v.p.), Disting. Athens Club Cakled Athinaiki. Home: 28 Menelaou Loundemi St, 15121 Pefki Athens Greece Office: Med Office, 12 Licavittou St, 10672 Athens Greece

BANDOW, DOUGLAS LEIGHTON, editor, columnist, policy consultant; b. Washington, Apr. 15, 1957; s. Donald E. and Donna J. (Losh) B. A.A., Okaloosa-Walton Jr. Coll., Niceville, Fla., 1974; B.S. in Econs., Fla. State U., 1976; J.D., Stanford U., 1979. Bar: Calif. 1979 D.C. 1984. Sr. policy analyst Reagan for Pres. Com., Los Angeles, 1979-80, Arlington, Va., 1980; sr. policy analyst Office of Pres. Elect, Washington, 1980-81; spl. asst. to the Pres. for policy devel. White House, Washington, 1981-82; editor Inquiry Mag., Washington, 1982-84; sr. fellow Cato Inst., Washington, 1984—; nat. syndicated columnist Copley News Svc., San Diego, 1983—. Author: Unquestioned Allegiance, 1986, Beyond Good Intentions: A Biblical View of Politics, 1988, Human Resources and Defense Manpower, 1989, The Politics

of Plunder: Misgovernment in Washington, 1990, The Politics of Envy: Statism as Theology, 1994, Tripwire: Korea and U.S. Foreign Policy in a Changed World, 1996; editor: U.S. Aid to the Developing World, 1985, Protecting the Environment, 1986; co-editor: The U.S.-South Korean Alliance, 1992, Perpetuating Poverty, 1994; contbr. articles to periodicals. Recipient Freedom Leadership award Freedoms Found., Valley Forge, Pa., 1977; recipient cert. for polit. and journalistic activities Freedoms Found., Valley Forge, Pa., 1979; named Man of Yr. N.Y. State Coll. Reps., 1982; recipient Nat. Young Am. award Boy Scouts Am., 1977. Mem. Calif. Bar Assn., ABA, D.C. Bar Assn., Washington Ind. Writers. Office: Cato Inst 1000 Massachusetts Ave NW Washington DC 20001-5400

BANDT, PAUL DOUGLAS, physician; b. Milbank, S.D., June 22, 1938; s. Lester Herman and Edna Louella (Sogn) B.; m. Mary King, Aug. 26, 1962 (div. Feb. 1974); children: Douglas, Peggy; m. Inara Irene Von Rostas, Apr. 1, 1974; 1 child, Jennifer. BS in Edn. with distinction, U. Minn., 1960, BS in Medicine, 1966, D in Medicine, 1966. Diplomate Am. Bd. Diagnostic Radiology, Am. Bd. Nuclear Medicine. Intern U.S. Pub. Health Svc., San Francisco, 1966-68; physician U.S. Pub. Health Svc., Las Vegas, 1968-69; resident Stanford U., Palo Alto, Calif., 1969-72; pres., physician Desert Radiologists, Las Vegas, 1972—; vice chief med. staff Desert Springs Hosp., Las Vegas, chmn. dept. radiology; past chief of staff U. Med. Ctr. So. Nev., Las Vegas. Contbr. articles on diagnostic radiology to profl. jours. With USPHS, 1966-69. Recipient Nev. Physician Yr. award, 1998. Mem. Am. Coll. Radiology, Am. Coll. Nuclear Medicine, Clark Med. Soc., Nev. State Med. Soc. Avocations: skiing, scuba diving, photography. Office: Desert Radiologists 2020 Palomino Ln Las Vegas NV 89106-4812

BANDYOPADHYAY, MANAS, environmental engineer; b. Calcutta, India, Jan. 18, 1942; s. Mriganka and Malaya (Chattopadhyay) B.; m. Swapna Mukhopadhyay, July 26, 1969; children: Lopamudra, Tania. BCE, Jadavpur U., Calcutta, 1963; ME, Calcutta U., 1966; PhD in Engring., Jadavpur U., 1975. Asst. engr. Govt. W. Bengal, India, 1963-72, exec. engr., 1972-84; superintending engr. Govt. W. Bengal, 1985; prof. Indian Inst. Tech., Kharagpur, 1985—, head dept. civil engring., 1999—; cons. Tata Iron and Steel Co., 1992—, Govt. W. Bengal, 1994-97; mem. acad. coun. Indian Sch. Mines, Dhanbad, 1997—. Contbr. articles to profl. jours. Recipient Gold medal, Jadavpur U., 1963. Fellow Institution of Engrs.; mem. Institution Pub. Health, Indian Assn. Environ. Mgmt. Avocations: basketball, volleyball, painting, music. Office: Dept Civil Engring, Indian Inst Tech, 721302 Kharagpur 721302, India

BANDYOPADHYAY, RAM SHYAMAL, molecular biologist, researcher; b. West Bengal, India, Feb. 6, 1952; came to U.S., 1983; s. Ram Sekhar and Geeta Bandyopadhyay; m. Sabita Bandyopadhyay, Feb. 26, 1982. PhD, U. Calcutta, West Bengal, 1982. Postdoctoral fellow U. Fla., Gainesville, 1983-87; rsch. assoc. Tufts U., Boston, 1987-92, Boston U., 1992—. Author: Cell Biochemistry and Biophycis, 1999. Mem. AAAS, Am. Chem. Soc. Avocations: painting, music, sports. Office: Boston U Sch of Medicine 80 E Concord St Boston MA 02118-2307

BANEGAS, ESTEVAN BROWN, environmental biotechnology executive; b. Hatch, N.Mex., May 10, 1941; s. Estevan Vera Banegas and Josephine (Brown) Crew; m. Amanda Martin, Sept. 5, 1970. BS, N.Mex. U., 1964; MBA, Wake Forest U., 1978. Sales mgr. agr. divsn. Ciba-Geigy Corp., San Juan, P.R., 1968-73; mktg. mgr. agr. divsn. Ciba-Geigy Corp., Greensboro, N.C., 1974-80; dir. corp. planning Ciba-Geigy Corp., Ardsley, N.Y., 1980-81; dir. product mgmt. agr. divsn. Ciba-Geigy Corp., Greensboro, 1981-83, dir. strategic planning agr. divsn., 1983-85; pres. joint venture Union Carbide Corp. and DNA Plant Tech. Agri-Diagnostics Assocs., Cinnaminson, N.J., 1985-92, also bd. dirs.; pres. Techshare, Inc, Greensboro, 1992—; pres., CEO Dominion BioScis., Inc., Blacksburg, Va., 1993—, also bd. dirs.; sci. bd. The Egg Factory, Ronake, Va., 1998—, spkr. mktg. biotech. products Agbio Conf., 1989; vis. faculty joint ventures and strategic partnering Internation Rsch. Inst., 1992; bd. advisors U. Minn., St. Paul, 1985-88, N.Mex. State U. Hispanic Leadership Project, 1993-96, Radford Coll. for Global Studies, 1994; bd. dirs. Va. Tech. Intellectual Properties, Inc., 1994—; mem. agrl. devel. bd. Ohio State U., Columbus, 1987-93; mem. Coun. Entrepreneural Devel., spkr., 1995; spkr on biopesticides BioIndustry Conf., 1997. Capt. USMC, 1964-67, Vietnam. Decorated Cross of Gallantry with silver star (South Vietnam). Mem. Am. Chem. Soc. (speaker mktg. strategies 1988), Biotech. Industry Orgn. (spkr. 1997), Coun. for Entrepreneurial Devel. Republican. Roman Catholic. Avocations: golf, gardening, hiking, church activities. Office: Techshare Inc 3558 Old Onslow Rd Greensboro NC 27407-7826

BANERJEE, AMITAVA, English educator; b. Delhi, India, Aug. 16, 1936; s. Bhubaneshwar and Protiva (Ganguly) B.; m. Jacqueline Patricia Brown, Aug. 7, 1970; children: Nigel, Robin. BA with honors, U. Delhi, 1956, MA, 1958; MA, U. Wis., 1965; PhD, U. Leicester, England, 1970. Lectr. English Delhi Coll., U. Delhi, 1958-64; lectr. English U. Wis., Whitewater, 1965-66, U. Cape Coast, Ghana, 1970-72; assoc. prof. English U. Poona, India, 1972-75; lectr. English U. Birmingham, England, 1976-77; sr. mem. St. Edmund's Coll., U. Cambridge, England, 1977-79; prof. English Kobe Coll., Nishinomiya, Japan, 1979—; acting head dept. English, U. Poona, India, 1972-73, chair bd. studies, 1972-73; mem. rsch. inst. Kobe Coll, Japan, 1986-88. Author: Spirit Above Wars, 1976; Editor: Modern English Poetry, 1985, D.H. Lawrence's Poetry, 1989; editor Kobe Coll. Studies, 1986-88. Fulbright-Smith-Mundt scholar U.S. State Dept., 1964-66; recipient rsch. award Sir Ernest Cassel Trust, England, 1969, Christopher Meml., England, 1975-76. Mem. Modern Lang. Assn. Am., Japan English Lit. Soc., Japan Am. Lit. Soc., Soc. Authors, Cambridge Soc. Home: 4 156 Okadayama, Nishinomiya 662, Japan Office: Kobe Coll, 4 1 Okadayama, Nishinomiya 662, Japan Also: Walton -on-Thames, 53 Mayfield Close, Surrey KT12 5PR, England

BANERJEE, ANJAN KUMAR, surgeon; b. Northampton, Eng., Sept. 12, 1962; s. Arup Kumar and Aleya Banerjee; m. Alison Clare Parberry, Apr. 29, 1995. MB, BS with honours and distinction, U. London, 1985, MSc with distinction, MS, 1991; MD, U. Nottingham, Eng., 1996. House officer St. Thomas's Hosp., London, 1985-86, Manchester (Eng.) Royal Infirmary, 1985-86; sr. house officer Hammersmith Hosp. and Med. Rsch. Coun. Clin. Rsch. Ctr., London, 1986-89; hon. lectr., med. rsch. coun., tng. fellow in surgery Kings Coll. Hosp., London, 1989-91; registrar in surgery Nottingham Hosps., 1992-93; sr. registrar Sheffield (Eng.) Hosps., 1994-96, St Mark's Hosp., London, 1996; cons. gen. and colorectal surgeon Royal Halifax (Eng.) Infirmary, 1996—; sr. clin. lectr. surgery Leeds U. Med. Sch., 1996—; Hunterian prof. Royal Coll. Surgeons Eng. Contbr. over 75 articles on surg. gastroenterology to med. jours., including Recent Advances in Surgery, Current Practice in Surgery, Gastroenterology, Digestive Diseases Sci., Am. Jour. Gastroenterology, Annals Surgery. Beaney and Musgrove scholars St. Thomas's Hosp., 1982-84; British Jour. of Surgery travel fellow U. Paris, 1995. Fellow Royal Coll. Surgeons (Ronald Raven/Barbers award 1998-99), Assn. Coloproctology, Assn. Surgeons, Assn. of Endoscopic Surgeons of Great Britain and Ireland, Royal Coll. Physicians (London and Edinburgh); mem. Brit. Soc. Gastroenterology, Surg. Rsch. Soc., Biochem. Soc., Inst. Biology, Am. Soc. Colon and Rectal Surgeons. Avocations: theatre, cricket, travel, good food. Home: Hopewell House Leeds Rd, Lightcliffe, Halifax HX3 8SD, England Office: Royal Halifax Infirmary, Free School Ln, Halifax HX1 2YP, England

BANERJEE, ARUP KUMAR, landscaping and agro-chemical consultant; b. Allahabad, India, June 23, 1936; s. Kshetradas and Gouri (Kshetradas) B.; m. Juliana Edeltraud, Feb. 11, 1966; 1 child, Nandita. BS in Agronomy, Am. Agr. Inst., Allahabad, India, 1954; MSc in Agrl. Chemistry, U. Allahabad, 1956, PhD in Soil Sci., 1959; D Agr. in Plant Nutrition, U. Giessen, Fed. Republic Germany, 1965. Sci. officer Coun. Sci. and Indsl. Rsch., Govt. of India, 1960-62; German acad. exchange scholar U. Giessen, 1963-65; market rsch. officer agr. div. Fabwerke Hoechst, Fed. Republic Germany, 1965-66; agrl. advisor Hoechst, India, 1966-68; market devel. officer agr. div. BASF, Fed. Republic Germany, 1968-69; div. mgr. agr. BASF, India, 1969-82; mgr. Agrl. Devel. and Supply Co., Dubai, United Arab Republics, 1982-84; bd. dirs. Agri-Energy Roundtable, Inc., Washington, 1982—; mem. Indian agts. com. Nitrex/Complex, Zurich, Switzerland; mem. Indo-German Agr. Project, West Bengal, India; bd. dirs. Chemicolor, Bombay. Mem. Brit. Inst. Mgmt., Phytopath. Soc. India (life), Entomol. Soc. India (life), Nat. Orgn. Profl. Execs. (life), Mktg. Mgmt. Alumni Assn. (pres. Bombay). Home and Office: Lenzhahner Weg 5, Niedernhausen, 65527 Taunus Germany

BANERJEE, ASHIS, physician; b. Calcutta, India, Oct. 19, 1954; arrived in Eng., 1982; s. Gopal Chandra and Aruna (Chakrabarty) B. MBBS, Madras (India) U., 1978, MS in Gen. Surgery, 1981. Intern Christian Med. Coll. Hosp., Vellore, India, 1977-78; resident Christian Med. Coll. Hosp., Vellore, 1978-81; surg. rsch. fellow Kothari Ctr. Gastroenterology, Calcutta Med. Rsch. Inst., 1981-82; sr. house officer in accident and emergency Basildon (Eng.) Hosp., 1982; sr. house officer in orthop. surgery Ipswich (Eng.) Hosp., 1983-84; sr. house officer in neurosurgery Newcastle Gen. Hosp., Newcastle upon Tyne, Eng., 1984; sr. house officer in plastic surgery Addenbrooke's Hosp., Cambridge, Eng., 1984-86; sr. house officer in plastic and hand surgery Wexham Park Hosp., Berkshire, Eng., 1986-87; registrar, sr. registrar in accident and emergency Ctrl. Middlesex Hosp., London, 1987; sr. house officer in accident and emergency Wexham Park Hosp., Slough and Heatherwood Hosp., Ascot, 1988; registrar in accident and emergency Manor Hosp., Walsall, 1988-90; sr. registrar in accident and emergency East Birmingham (Eng.) and Dudley Rd. Hosps., 1991-94; cons. in accident and emergency Whittington Hosp. NHS Trust, London, 1994—; cons. Kent and Canterbury (Eng.) Hosp., Oldchurch Hosp., Romford, Harold Wood Hosp., Brentwood, 1991; mem. N. Thames Specialty Tng. Com. Accident Emergency; hon. sr. lectr. dept. surgery U. Coll. Med. Sch., London; presenter in field. Contbr. articles to profl. jours. Freedom City of London. Fellow Royal Coll. Surgeons, Faculty of Accident Emergency Medicine; mem. British Med. Assn., British Assn. Accident Emergency Medicine, British Assn. Sport Medicine, Mastermind Club (semifinalist 1991). Avocations: walking, guitar, reading, traveling, history. Office: A&E Dept Whittington Hosp, Highgate Hill, London N19 5NF, England

BANERJEE, BASU DEV, biochemist, educator; b. Howrah, India, June 14, 1957; s. Badal Krishna and Geeta (Ghatak) B.; m. Rita Banerjee, Dec. 4, 1984; 1 child, Annesha. BSc in Chemistry with hons., Aligarh (India) Muslim U., 1977, MSc in Biochemistry, 1979, MPhil in Biochemistry, 1981, PhD in Biochemistry, 1984. Rsch. fellow dept. biochemistry Nat. Inst. Communicable Diseases, Delhi, India, 1980-85; asst. rsch. officer Nat. Inst. Communicable Diseases, Delhi, 1985, rsch. scientist, prin. investigator, 1985-87, sr. rsch. officer, co-investigator, 1987; asst. prof. dept. biochemistry All India Inst. Hygiene Pub. Health, Calcutta, 1988-92; reader dept. biochemistry U.C.M.S., U. Delhi, 1992—; bd. dirs. Nat. Accreditation Bd. Testing Calibration Lab.; tech. com. ctrl. pollution control bd. Min. Environ. Forest, Govt. India; visitor Inst. Hygiene, Heinrich-Heine U., Dusseldorf, Germany, 1998; vis. scientist dept. pub. health Albert Szent-Gyorgyi U. Med. Sch., Szeged, Hungary, 1999; presenter in field. Editor Jour. Basic Applied Biomedicine; contbr. over 60 articles to profl. jours. CSIR fellow, 1980, 4th FAOB, Singapore Biochem. Soc./Indian Nat. Sci. Assn. fellow, 1986, fellow Internat. Union Toxicology, 9th Internat. Congress of Toxicology, Paris, 1998; grantee Dept. Sci. Tech., 1985, 1987, 2000, Indian Coun. Med. R sch., 1995, 2000; Univ. Grant Commn., 1995. Mem. Indian Immunology Soc. (life), Indian Toxicol. Soc. (life), Soc. for Biol. Chemists, Soc. for Atherosclerosis Rsch. Hindu. Avocations: writing, reading. drama, badminton. Home: Mayur Vihar Phase I Extn, 503 Bl II Plot 16 Kirti Apt, Delhi 110091, India Office: Dept Biochemistry U Coll, GTB Hosp Shahdara, U Delhi, Delhi 110095, India

BANERJEE, BIMAL, artist, educator; b. Calcutta, India, Sept. 4, 1939; naturalized, 1978; s. Dashurathee and Madhabilata B. Baccalaureate with 1st class honors, Indian Coll. Art, Calcutta, 1960; student, Coll. Art, New Delhi, 1965-67, Atelier 17, Paris, 1967-69, Ecole des Beaux-Arts, Paris, 1967-70, Pratt Inst., N.Y.C., 1969-72; studies with H.W. Jensen, NYU, 1976; Ed.M., M.A., Columbia U., 1978, Ed.D., 1988. Lectr. NAD, N.Y.C., 1969, Bloomfield (N.J.) Coll., 1980-81; lectr. Parsons Sch. Design/New Sch., N.Y.C, 1979, faculty, 1983-88; art therapist St. John's Episc. Hosp., Queens, N.Y., 1981-83; tchr., art cons. N.Y.C. Pub. Schs., 1984—; art tchr. Cath. High Sch., N.Y.C., 1987; lectr. Columbia U. Tchrs. Coll., N.Y.C., 1988—; guest lectr. Tchrs. Coll., Columbia U., 1984. Multi-media performance artist shows include Parsons Sch. Design/New Sch., 1986, Columbia U., 1978, 79, 84, Hofstra U., 1979, Just Above Midtown Gallery, N.Y.C., 1977, 78, Bertha Urdang Gallery, N.Y.C., 1976, Fremar Gallery, L.I., N.Y., 1974, Galerie du Haut Pave, Paris, 1968-69, Mcpl. Galeria, Levanto, Italy, 1968, Kumar Gallery, New Delhi, 1970, Arts & Prints Gallery, Calcutta, 1963, 64, Art Heritage Gallery, New Delhi, 1990, Chitrakoot Gallery, Calcutta, 1990, Bertha Urdang Gallery, N.Y.C., 1991, Chemould Gallery, Calcutta, 1993, Cite Internationale des Arts, Paris, 1994, 99, numerous others; internat. biennials in Paris, Tokyo, Rejika, Miami, Hawaii, Bradford, Eng., Biella, Ibiza, Triennale-India, Berlin Triennale, Joan Miro Drawing prize, Barcelona, Ljubljana, others; exhibited in 28 one-man shows, U.S., Europe and India; introduced new media Fumage and Carbontransfer; represented in permanent collections Mus. Modern Art, Paris, Mus. Modern Art, Barcelona, Spain, Mus. Fine Arts, Boston, Mus. Art, Iowa City, Mus. Modern Art de la Ville de Paris, Mus. Internat. of Electrography Art, Cuenca, Spain, Ctr. National d'Art Contemporain, Paris, Ministry Cultural Affairs, France, Neil Saek Gallery, Johannesburg, South Africa, Nat. Gallery Modern Art, New Delhi, Nat. Acad. Art, New Delhi, Essex Libr., London, The Pallas Gallery, London, Bibliothèque Nat., Paris, Honolulu Acad. Art, Rockefeller Bros. Found., N.Y.C., N.Y. Pub. Libr. Art Collection, N.Y.C., Bklyn. Mus., others; represented in pub. collections Mus. Modern Art, Paris, Mus. Modern Art, Barcelona, Mus. Fine Arts, Boston, Mus. Art, Iowa City, Mus. Modern Art de la Ville de Paris, Mus. Internat. Electrography Art, Cuenca, Spain, Centre National d'Art Contemporain, Paris, Min. Cultural Affairs, France, Neil Sack Gallery, Johannesburg, Nat. Gallery Modern Art, New Delhi, Nat. Acad. Art, New Delhi, Essex Libr., London, Pallas Gallery, London, Bibliotechque Nationale, Paris, Honolulu Acad. Art, Rockefeller Bros. Fund, N.Y.C., N.Y. Pub. Libr., N.Y.C., Radford U. Mus., Va., Bklyn. Mus. Inst. Arts and Scis., Radford U. Mus., Bklyn. Mus., others; contbr. articles, poetry, short stories, children's lit. to profl. jours. Recipient awards Hawaii Biennial, 1971, 73, 79, Arthur Kaplan award, 1978, award Painters and Sculptors Soc., 1972, Culturelle Internat. award, Paris, 1968, Nat. award Nat. Art Acad., India, 1967, 70, State Acad. award Bengal State, and Punjab State, 1967, Statue of Victory world cultural prize Nat. Ctr. Study and Rsch., Salsomiggiore, Italy, 1984, also others; grantee Govt. of India, 1965-67, Govt. of France, 1967-70, Adolph and Esther Gottlieb Found., 1989; Nat. scholar Indian Govt., French Govt. Mem. Mus. Modern Art, Found. for Community of Artists of N.Y.C., Coll. Art Assn. of Am., Print Club Philadelphia, World Print Council, Smithsonian Instn., Ancient Art—Paris. Home: Loft 2C 106 Ridge St New York NY 10002-2554 Office: Bertha Urdang Gallery 23 E 74th St New York NY 10021-2617

BANERJEE, JYOTI PRASAD, electronics educator; b. Calcutta, W. Bengal, India, Feb. 8, 1947; s. Sital Chandra and Subadani (Banerjee) B.; m. Sukla Chaudhuri, Jan. 21, 1979; children: Suranjana, Atindra Mohan. BS with honors, U. Calcutta, 1967, MS, 1970, PhD in Tech., 1986. Lectr. in physics S.S. Coll., Howrah, West Bengal, India, 1971-79, 84-86; tchr., fellow U. Calcutta, 1980-84, sr. scientist, 1986-89, reader, 1989—, prof. Inst. Radiophysics and Electronics, 1998—; course dir. Acad. Staff Coll., U. Calcutta, 1994; mem. expert com. All India Coun. Tech. Edn. Contbr. about 100 articles to profl. jours. Recipient grant Univ. Grants Commn., New Delhi, 1980; Nat. Merit scholar, India, 1962; Vis. fellow Indian Nat. Sci. Acad. Fellow IETE (hon. sec.); mem. Indian Physics Assn., Soc. of EMI & EMC. Avocations: singing, mountaineering, cycling. Home: Keota Garbagan, 712104 West Bengal India Office: Univ Calcutta, 92 Acharya Prafulla Chandra, 700 009 Calcutta India

BANERJEE, JYOTIRMOY, science educator, researcher; b. Calcutta, India, Nov. 2, 1946; s. Sailesh Chandra and Dipti (Bhattacharya) B.; m. Deb Shyamali, June 28, 1974; 1 child, Arjun. BA with honors, St. Xavier's Coll., Calcutta, 1966; MA, Jadavpur U., Calcutta, 1968, PHD, 1976. Rsch. fellow Jadavpur U., 1969-70, lectr. internat. rels., 1970-83, reader internat. rels., 1983-90, prof. internat. rels., 1991—, dept. head, 1985—; guest prof. Calcutta U., 1983-84; lectr. in Higher Svcs. Ctr., Jadavpur U., annually 1972—; Rockefeller Found. Social Sci. Rsch. Coun. fellow, U. Calif., Berkeley, 1988—, sr. Fulbright fellow, 1993-94; presenter in field. Author: India in Soviet Global Strategy, 1977, GDR and Detente, 1981, Strategic Studies, 1998; contbr. articles to India and fgn. jours. Organizer cultural events Netaji Bhawan, 1985; mem. Indian Life Saving Soc. Fulbright scholar, 1974-75, 85-86, 93-94; Univ. Grants Commn. grantee, 1977; Alexander Von Humboldt fellow, 1970-80, 86, 91, 98. Mem. Ghandi Peace Found., Inst. Defence Studies & Analyses, Netaji Rsch. Bur., Am. Univ. Ctr., Goethe Inst. Calcutta (scholar 1968, organizer cultural events 1983), St. Xavier's Coll. Alumni Assn. (editor, organizer cultural events 1985), Humboldt Club. Hindu. Avocations: reading, foreign languages, western music, travel. Home: 26/H Gariahat Rd,, Calcutta, 700 029 India Office: Dept Internat Relations, Jadavpur Univ, Calcutta, 700, 032, India

BANERJEE, PRABIR, nuclear physicist; b. Calcutta, India, June 14, 1962; s. Noni Gopal and Dipti (Chatterjee) B.; m. Saswati Mukhopadhyay, Dec. 6, 1996; 1 child, Shrabasti. MSc, Calcutta U., 1985, PhD, 1996. Jr. rsch. fellow Saha Inst. Nuclear Physics, Calcutta, 1987-88, sr. rsch. fellow, 1988-96; postdoctoral rsch. fellow U. Surrey, Guildford, Eng., 1996-98; rsch. assoc. Saha Inst. Nuclear Physics, 1998—. Contbr. articles to profl. jours. Recipient Rank Eleven, Coun. Sci. and Indsl. Rsch., New Delhi, 1989. Mem. Indian Physics Assn. (life). Avocations: reading books, playing chess, sky watching, wandering, listening to songs and music. Office: Saha Inst Nuclear Physics, 1/AF Bidhan Nagar, Calcutta 700064, India

BANERJEE, RAMENDRA NATH, hematologist, consultant; b. Burdwan, Bengal, India, Jan. 1, 1926; s. Bhupendra Nath and Sudakshina Banerjee; m. Usha Mukherjee, Dec. 10, 1953; 1 child, Sharmistha. MBBS, Carmichael Med. Coll., Calcutta, India, 1949; MD in Medicine, K.G. Med. Coll., Lucknow, India, 1954; PhD in Medicine, Middlesex Med. Sch. and Hosp., London, 1962. Sr. resident medicine Carmichael Med. Coll., Calcutta, 1950-51; R.L. Basu rsch. fellow Calcutta Sch. Tropical Medicine, 1951-52; lectr. pathology M.G.M. Med. Coll., Indore, India, 1952-53; med. specialist Indian Armed Forces, 1953-58; def. scientist, head dept. nuclear medicine Inst. Nuclear Medicine and Allied Sci., Delhi, 1958-68; chief cons., head dept. medicine, hematol. and nuclear med. Safderjung Hosp. & Univ. Coll. Medicine, Delhi, 1968-83; dir. cons. Meml. Med. Ctr., Delhi, 1983—; prof., head dept. medicine U. Coll. Medicine, Delhi, 1972-82; vis. scientist Internat. Atomic Energy Agy. (Vienna) USSR, Am. Cancer Soc., N.Y.C. Contbr. articles to profl. jours. Lt. col. M.C. Indian Army, 1953-68. Recipient Nuffield fellowship, London, 1960-62. Fellow Acad. Med. Specialists, Coll. Chest Physicians, Internat. Coll. Angiology, Indian Coll. Physicians; mem. Indian Med. Assn. (founder, pres. 1978). Avocations: literature, poetry, dramatics. Office: Memorial Med Ctr, A-6 Chittaranjan Park, New Delhi 220019, India

BANERJEE, SANJAY, geoscientist; b. New Delhi, 1965; came to U.S., 1991; s. Mrinal Kanti and Neelima (Ghoshal) Banerjee. BS with honors, U. Calcutta, India, 1987; MScTech., Indian Sch. Mines, Dhanbad, 1991; PhD in Geology, U. Okla., 1997. Staff geoscientist TRW/BDM Petroleum Techs., Bartlesville, Okla., 1997—. Rsch. grantee Geol. Soc. Am., Boulder, Colo., 1994, 95, Am. Assn. Petroleum Geologists, Tulsa, 1994. Mem. Am. Assn. Petroleum Geologists (peer reviewer sci. papers 1997—), Geol. Soc. Am., Am. Geophys. Union, Soc. Sedimentry Geology. Achievements include establishment of a relationship beween magnetite-hosted chemical remagnetization in organic-rich and burial diagenesis/maturation of these rocks; palemagnetic components need to be evaluated not only in terms of their direction as in the current practice, but also their unblocking temperature ranges. Office: TRW/BDM Petroleum Techs Hwys 60 and 123 Bartlesville OK 74005

BANERJEE, SRILEKHA, science educator; b. Allahabad, India, May 12, 1946; d. Narendra Nath and Gouri (Banerjee) Mukerjee; m. Rabindra Nath Banerjee, Dec. 5, 1965; children: Manisha, Bhaskar. MSc, Allahabad (India) U., 1967; MPhil, Calcutta (India) U., 1976, PhD in Sci., 1982; MS in Informatics, Vrije Univ., Brussels, 1989. Tchr. Higher Secondary Sch., Calcutta, 1968-75; sys. analyst Bus. Efficiency Svcs., Calcutta, 1982-85; vis. fellow SN Bose Nat. for Basic Scis., Calcutta, 1990-92, sci. officer, 1992-94, fellow, 1994-98, reader, 1998—. Contbr. rsch. articles to profl. jours. Avocations: gardening, reading, needlework. Office: SN Bose Nat Ctr Basic Scis, Blk JD Sector III Salt Lake, 700091 Calcutta India

BANETH, GAD, veterinarian; b. Jerusalem, Aug. 20, 1959; s. Hillel and Sheila (Sosnovik) B.; m. Anat Zuck, June 6, 1983; children: Tal, Zohar, Carmel. BS, Hebrew U., Rehovot, Israel, 1986, DVM, 1990, PhD, 2000. Intern Hebrew U., Rehovot, 1990-91, resident in vet. medicine, 1991-94, lectr., 1995-97, head dept. small animal medicine, 1997-2000; postdoctoral fellow N.C. State U., 1994-95. Contbr. articles to profl. jours. Rsch. grantee Israeli Ministry Health, 1996, USAID, 1998, Israeli Ministry Environ., 1996; Lady Davis fellow, 1994. Mem. Israel Vet. Med. Assn. (rsch. instn. vets. sect. head 1995-98), Am. Soc. for Rickettsiology and Rickettsial Diseases, Israel Soc. for Parasitology, Am. Soc. for Tropical Med. and Hygiene, Israel Soc. for Parasitology. Jewish. Home: Kibbutz Tzora, 99803 Shimshon Israel Office: Hebrew Univ, PO Box 12, 76100 Rehovot Israel

BANFALVI, GASPAR, biochemist, researcher; b. Nemesnadudvar, Hungary, Oct. 8, 1943; s. Karoly and Ilona (Tokobi) B.; m. Gyongyi Maria Kelemen, Sept. 11, 1971; children: Judith, George. MS in Pharmacy, Med. U. Szeged, Hungary, 1968, PhD, 1972; Cand. Sci., Med. U. Budapest, Hungary, 1981, DSc, 1989, D.Med.Habil., 1994; D.Habil., U. Sci., Szeged, 1994. Lic. pharmacist, specialist of pharmacology and toxicology. Asst. prof. Med. U. Szeged, 1970-72; staff scientist Drug Rsch. Inst., Budapest, 1972-74; assoc. prof. Med. U. Budapest, 1974-2000; prof. U. Debrecen, 2000—; rsch. fellow Harvard Med. Sch., Boston, 1981-82, vis. scientist, 1983-84, vis. lectr., 1987-88, vis. prof., Cambridge, Mass., 1994; staff fellow Boston Biomed. Rsch. Inst., 1980-82, rsch. fellow, 1983-84, vis. scientist, 1987-88, Fulbright fellow, 1994; rsch. faculty U. Sci. Szeged, 1991-96; vis. prof. Weizman Inst., Rehovot, 1998-99. Author: Molecular Biology, 1995; contbr. articles to profl. jours.; inventor in field; editl. bd. Biokemia. Pres. Trade Union of Hungarian Med. Univs., Budapest, 1993. Soros fellow Leiden U., Holland, 1988; ORISE/ORAU fellow, 1996, Szecheny fellow, 1997—. Mem. World Hungarian Med. Acad. Avocations: building molecular models, book reviews. Home: 8 Wesselenyi, 1075 Budapest Hungary Office: Dept Animal Physiol, 1 Egyetem ter, 4010 Debrecen Hungary

BANG, GISLE, pathologist, researcher; b. Lillehammer, Norway, Mar. 25, 1927; s. Asbjörn and Signe (Klevdahl) B.; m. Arna Helene Tösdal, May 29, 1954; children: Anne Katrine, Sturla. DDS, U. Oslo, 1951, MD, 1961; PhD, U. Bergen, Norway, 1974. Rsch. physiologist USAF, Fairbanks, Alaska, 1955-57; rsch. fellow Harvard U. Sch. Dental Medicine, Boston, 1957; rsch. fellow Sch. Dentistry, Oslo, 1958-59, Bergen, 1962-65, 67-72; postdoctoral scholar Bone Rsch. Lab. UCLA, 1965-66; prof. dept. oral pathology U. Bergen, 1972—, sr. resident dept. pathology, 1973—, chief attending physician, 1983—; vis. pathologist dept. oral pathology Ind. U., Indpls., 1966. Contbr. sci. articles to profl. jours. Recipient med. award NYCO, 1958, Norsk Tannvern award, 1959, Dr. Voss Forensic med. award, 1970, Cert. of Merit, Am. Acad. Dental Medicine, 1960, Prof. Bergersen Found.'s prize for achievement in med. and dental rsch., 1996. Mem. Scandinavian Soc. Oral Pathology and Medicine (pres.), Norwegian Soc. Forensic Odontology (pres.), Norwegian Dental Assn., Internat. Soc. Forensic Odontostomatology, European Soc. Pathology, Internat. Assn. Oral Pathology, Internat. Assn. Dentistry, Scandinavian Soc. Forensic Odontology. Avocations: sports, hunting, fishing, outdoor life. Office: Haukeland Univ Hosp, Dept Oral Pathology, 5021 Bergen Norway

BANG, HU ER, nuclear scientist, educator; b. Shanghai, Aug. 26, 1940. Degree, Tsinghua (China) U., 1964. Asst. rschr. China Inst. for Radiation Protection, Taiyuan, 1964-88, assoc. rschr., vice prof., 1988-90, rsch. fellow, prof., 1990, dir. dept., 1991-98; part-time prof. Fudan U., Shanghai, 1998—, Tongji U., Shanghai, 1999—; guest scientist Karlsruhe (Germany) Nuc. Rsch. Ctr., 1986-87; dir. Specialist Com. for Clean Product, Taiyuan, 1999—; mem. Specialist Com. for Nuc. Environ., NEPA, Beijing, 1991—; mem. Specialist Com. for Nuc. Accident Emergency, Emergency Office Guangdong Province, 1995—; mem. Specialist Com. for Nuc. Accident Emergency, Chinese Nat. Nuc. Corp., 1995-99. Author: Atmospheric Diffusion and Its Environment Impact Assessment for Nuclear Power Plant, 1999; chief editor: Technology and Methodology of Environment Risk Assessment, 1999. Named Outstanding Young and Middle-age Specialist, Chinese Nat. Nuc. Corp., 1994. Mem. Chinese Assn. for Environ. Assn. (exec. dep. pres. 1998—), Chinese Assn. for Atmospheric Environ. (dep. pres. 1998—). Avocations: table tennis, TV, reading novels. Office: China Inst Radiation Protec, Xuefu St, Taiyuan Shanxi 030006, China

BANG, MOON-SUK, medical educator; b. Seoul, Republic of Korea, June 2, 1961; s. Il-Young and Myung-Sun (Seo) B.; m. Hyn-Mi Yang, June 19, 1991; children: Young-Oh, Soo-Oh. MD, Seoul Nat. U., 1986, MS, 1994, PhD, 1996. Intern Seoul Nat. U. Hosp., 1986-87, resident, 1990-94, fellow, 1994-95, instr., 1995-97; asst. prof. Seoul Nat. U. Coll. Medicine, 1997—. Contbr. articles to profl. jours. Lt. Army of Republic of Korea, 1987-90. Mem. Assn. Acad. Physiatrists (Athena award for outstanding paper presentation 1998), Internat. Med. Soc. of Paraplegia, Korean Acad. Rehab. Medicine (sec. gen. 1995-97). Avocations: skiing, swimming. E-mail: msbang@medicine.snu.ac.kr. Office: Rehab Medicine Seoul Nat U, 28 Yeongun-dong, Chongno-gu, Seoul 110-744, Republic of Korea

BANG, RAMESHWAR LAL, physician; b. Napasar, India, July 21, 1941; s. Mohan Lal and Gawarja Devi (Jhanwar) B.; m. Sarla Maheshwari, Nov. 23, 1976; children: Pratik Kumar, Prerna. Resident Med. Coll. Hosps., Kanpur, India, 1967-68; resident various hosps., Eng., 1969-71, 72-74, sr. resident, 1975-81; asst. prof., cons. plastic surgeon Faculty Medicine, Kuwait, 1981-94, assoc. prof., cons. plastic surgeon, 1995—. Contbr. articles to profl. jours. Mem. British Assn. Plastics Surgeons (assoc.), Am. Cleft Palate Cranio Facial Assn., Assn. Plastic Surgeons India, Internat. Soc. Burn Injuries. Hindu. Avocations: music, reading, photography, cricket, travel. Office: Kuwait U Faculty Medicine, PO Box 24923, Safat 13110, Kuwait

BANGALORE, SRINIVAS, computer engineering researcher; b. Hyderabad, India, May 13, 1969; s. Ranganna and Narmada Ranganna Bangalore; m. Purnima Vasireddi, Aug. 8, 1998. B Engring., Osmania U., Hyderabad, Andhra Pradesh, 1989; M Tech., Indian Inst. Tech., Kanpur, Uttar Pradesh, 1991; PhD, U. Pa., 1997. Rsch. asst. U. Pa., Phila., 1991-97, postdoctoral fellow, 1997; mem. sr. tech. staff AT&T Rsch. Labs., Florham Park, N.J., 1997—. Contbg. author: Symbolic, Connectionist and Statistical Approachs to Learning for Natural Language Processing, 1996; contbr. articles to sci. jours. Recipient Morris and Dorothy Rubinoff award U. Pa., 1998; rsch. fellow Inst. for Rsch. in Cognitive Sci., 1994. Mem. Assn. for Computational Linguistics (jour. and conf. reviewer 1997—). Fax: 973-360-7111. E-mail: srini@research.att.com. Office: AT&T Rsch Labs 180 Park Ave Bldg 103 Florham Park NJ 07932-1004

BANGASH, HUMAYUN KHAN, securities company executive; b. Kohat, Pakistan, Dec. 16, 1940; s. Naqshbank Khan and Sardar Begum Bangash; m. Shahina Humayun Ashraf, Nov. 20, 1966; children: Haroon Khan, Maliha Humayun Gilani, Obaid Khan, Zebunnisa Humayun, Haider Khan. BA, Pakistan Mil. Acad., Kakul, 1961; MSc, Quaid-E-Azam U., Islamabad, 1980; grad., Army Staff Coll., 1970, Army War Coll., 1977, Nat. Def. Coll., 1980. Commandant Infantry Sch., Quetta, 1989-90; inspector gen. Frontier Corps, Peshawar, 1990-91; adjutant gen. Pakistan Army, Rawalpindi, 1991-93; corp. comdr. Pakistan Army, Lahore, 1993-96; amb. Pakistan Embassy, Ankara, Turkey, 1996-99; exec. dir. 1st Capital Securities, Lahore, 1999—; staff officer HQ Centro, Ankara, 1975-77. Lt. gen. Pakistan Army, 1961-96. Recipient Tamgha-Basalat award Govt. Pakistan, 1981, Hilal-I-Imtiaz award Govt. Pakistan, 1992. Mem. Pakistan Rifle Assn. (pres. 1993-96), Garrison Golf Club (patron 1993-96), Def. Housing Soc. Club (patron 1993-96). Avocations: golf, reading, swimming. Home: 3 Askari Villas Sarwar Rd, Lahore Pakistan Office: 1st Capital Securities Corp, 103-C/II Gulberg-III, Lahore Pakistan

BANGASH, MOHAMMAD YUSAF HASSAN, structural engineering educator; b. Hangu, Pakistan, Jan. 4, 1930; arrived in Eng., 1962; s. M. Rahim and Margalala Bangash; m. Aiman Sarah Bangash, Jan. 3, 1967; children: Shaharyar T., Techmiryar, Fehmin S., Arsham, Shafaeen N. BS, U. Peshawar, Pakistan, 1953, B of Civil Engring., 1957; MS, Carnegie Inst. Tech., 1963; PhD, London U., 1979, DSc, 1989. Chartered civil, structural, nuclear engr., Eng. Structural engr. U.S. Corps of Engrs., Karian, Pakistan, 1953-55; sr. lectr. U. Peshawar, 1957-60; civil engr. Swindeller Dresseler, Pitts., 1961-62; structural engr. Alan Grant & Ptnrs., London, 1962-64; sr. structural engr. Kaiser Engrs., Inc., Twickenham, Eng., 1965-66; sr. engr. Taylor Woodrow Constrn., Southall, Middlesex, Eng., 1966-67; group engr. Atomics, Sutton, Surrey, Eng., 1967-69; lectr., sr. lectr. U. Greenich, London, 1969-83; reader, prof. Middlesex U., London, 1984-91; group tech. dir. Ward & Cole Cons., St. Margarets, Eng., 1991—; chief cons. A&Z Ptnrs., Illford, Essex, Eng., 1992—; cons. in field. Author: Concrete and Concrete Structures--Numerical Modelling and Applications, 1989, 2d edit., 2000, Impact and Explosions, 1992, Structural Details in Concrete, 1992; Structural Detail in Steel, 2000, Prototype Building Structures, 1999, Prototype Bridge Structures, 1999, Spatial Structures, 2000; contbr. more than 90 rsch. papers to profl. publs. Gov. Nat. Muslim Ednl. Coun., Union of Muslim Orgns., U.K., Ireland, London, 1992—; chmn. Muslim Ednl. Coun., London, 1981-92. Fullbright fellow, 1960. Fellow ASCE, Instn. Civil Engrs. U.K., Instn. Structural Engrs. U.K., Instn. Nuclear Engring. (U.K.), Brit. Nuclear Energy Soc. Mem. Conservative Party. Avocations: driving, wildlife, protection of environment, football, photography. Office: Ward & Cole Cons, Ward & Cole Cons, 1 Old Lodge Pl, Saint Margarets England

BANGASSER, RONALD PAUL, physician; b. Freeport, Ill., Jan. 25, 1950; s. Paul Francis and Florence (Ihm) B.; m. Susan Marie Andretta, June 19, 1971; children: Debra, Sandi. BA, Northwestern U., Chgo., 1971; MD, Chgo. Med. Sch., 1975. Physician Valley Family Med., Yucaipa, Calif., 1978-93; physician Beaver Med. Group, Redlands, 1993—, med. dir., 1997—; med. dir. San Bernardino Found. for Med. Care, 1984-89, Redlands Med. Group, Redlands, Calif., 1986-92, Calif. Found. for Med. Care, San Francisco, 1991-94, Beaver Med., Redlands, 1997—; legis. com. mem. CMA, San Francisco, 1991-95, LOPAC, San Bernardino, 1992-99, Leg Affairs Commn., San Francisco, 1994—; bd. dirs. CAL PAC, San Francisco, 1990-96. Bd. dirs. Blue Shield of Calif., 1998—. Mem. AMA (Calif. del. chair 1995-99), Calif. Med. Assn. (bd. dirs. 1995—, vice spkr. 1999—, exec. com. 1999—). Republican. Roman Catholic. Avocations: scuba diving, skiing, swimming, hiking. Home: 12724 Valley View Ln Redlands CA 92373-7632 Office: Beaver Med Group 2424 Cajon St Redlands CA 92373-5202

BANGHA, MARTIN WULTOFF, demographer; b. Jinkfin-Kom, Cameroon, Mar. 3, 1966; s. Joseph Bangha Yong and Cecilia Ninying Chongwain Bangha. BSc with honors, U. Yaounde, Cameroon, 1988; MA, U. Ghana, 1990, MPhil, 1992. Tchg. asst. U. Ghana, Legon, 1991-92; rsch. cons. Pan African Assn. Anthropologists/ICASSRT, Yaounde, 1993-94; rsch. assoc. Demographic Tng. and Rsch. Inst. U. Yaounde, 1994-97; rsch. officer, asst. coord. Small Grants Programme/Union for African Population Studies, Dakar, Senegal, 1997-2000, interim coord., 2000—; sec. internat. organizing com. Population Conf., Durban, 1998-99; editl. asst. Union for African Population Studies Publs., Dakar, 1997-2000; mem. sci. com. SGP/Union for African Population Studies, Dakar, 1997-2000; coord. conf. activities Union for African Population Studies, Durban, 1998-2000. Contbr. articles to profl. jours. Mem. Cameroon Nat. Assn. Family Welfar, Yaounde, 1994-97. UN fellow African Futures Forum Inc., 1989-92. Mem. Social Sci. and Medicine Africa Network, Coun. for Devel. Social Sci. Rsch. in Africa. Baptist. Avocations: travel, sightseeing, swimming. Home: SICAP Baobab, Dakar Senegal Office: UAPS/UEPA Rond-Pont Mermoz Km, 7.5 Ave Cheikh Anta Diop, BP 21007 Dakar-Ponty Dakar, Senegal

BANGSUND, EDWARD LEE, former aerospace company executive, consultant; b. Two Harbors, Minn., July 16, 1935; s. Ilo Henry and Hildur Margaret (Holter) B.; m. Caryl Ann Billingsley, Oct. 10, 1956; children: Julie Ann, Trina Lee, John Kirk, Edward Eric. BME, U. Wash., 1959. With Boeing Co., 1956-71; engr. Apollo program Boeing Co., Cape Kennedy, Fla., 1967-69, Houston, 1969-71; mgr. space vehicle design Space Systems div. Boeing Aerospace, Seattle, 1971-76, mgr. Inertial Upper Stage Futures, 1976-85, mgr. space transp., 1985-87, dir. strategic planning, 1987-90, dir. space mktg., 1990-95; pres., CEO BCA Enterprises, 1995—; cons. engring. Orbital Techs. Corp., 1995—. Contbr. articles to profl. publs.; patentee in field. Pres. Springbrook Parents Adv. Com., 1972-75; chmn. Citizens Budget Rev. Com., 1973-75, 76-78, Citizens Facility Planning Com., 1977-78, Citizens for Kent (Wash.) Schs. Levy, 1974, 76; bd. dirs. Kent Youth Ctr., 1980-83; pres. Kent Sch. Bd., 1978-84. Named to Apollo-Saturn Roll of Honor, NASA, 1969; recipient Golden Acorn award Wash. Congress PTA, 1977, Vol. of Yr. award Kent Sch. Dist., 1977, 78. Fellow AIAA (assoc., mem. space systems tech. com. 1985-87, dep. dir. region VI 1986-89, chmn. space transp. tech. com. 1987-90, pub. policy com. 1989-94); mem. Internat. Acad. Astronautics, Internat. Astronautical Fedn. (chmn. space transp. exec. com. 1991-94), Nat. Space Found., Aerospace Industries Assn. (mem. space com. 1987-94, chmn. 1990-94), Space Bus. Roundtable (pres. Seattle chpt., bd. dirs. 1988-95), Boeing Mgmt. Assn. (vice chmn. 1990-91, chmn. 1993-94). Republican. Lutheran. Home and Office: 13611 SE 251st St Kent WA 98042-6631

BANHAM, JOHN, communications executive; b. Aug. 22, 1940; s. Terence Middlecott and Belinda Joan Banham; m. Frances Barbara Molyneux Favell, 1965; 3 children. BA, Cambridge U., 1962, hon. fellow, 1989; LLD (hon.), U. Bath, 1987; DSc (hon.), Loughborough U., 1989, U. Exeter, 1993, U. Strathclyde, 1995. Asst. prin. Her Majesty's Fgn. Svc., 1962-64; dir. mktg. wallcoverings divsn. Reed Internat., 1965-69; assoc. McKinsey & Co., 1969-75, prin., 1975-80, dir., 1980-83, contr., mem. audit commn., 1983-87; dir. gen. CBI, 1987-92; chmn. Westcountry TV Ltd., 1992-96; chmn. bd. dirs. Kingfisher PLC, London, 1996—; chmn. Labatt Breweries of Europe, 1992-95; bd. dirs. Nat. Westminster Bank, Nat. Power, John Labatt, Merchants Trust. Author: Future of the British Car Industry, 1975, Realizing the Promise of a National Health Service, 1977, The Anatomy of Change: Blueprint for a New Era, 1994, numerous reports for Audit Commn. on edn., housing, social svcs. and local govt. fin., 1984-87, for Confedn. Brit. Industry on Brit. economy, skills, transport, infrastructure urban regeneration and mfg. Chmn. Local Govt. Commn. for Eng., 1992-95; mem. Brit. Overseas Trade Bd., 1989-92; bd. dirs. Bus. in the Cmty., 1989-92; mem. coun. Policy Studies Inst., 1986-92, Forum for Mgmt. Edn. and Devel., 1988-93, Brit. Exec. Svc. Overseas, 1991-92; mem. coun. of mgmt. People's Dispensary for Sick Animals, 1982-93; mem. governing body London Bus. Sch., 1987-92; mng. trustee Nuffield Found., 1988—; hon. treas. Cancer Rsch. Campaign, 1991—. Named Knight Brit. Empire, 1992. Avocations: walking, gardening, music. Office: Kingfisher PLC, 119 Marylebone Rd NW House, London NW1 5PX, England*

BANIC, STANKO ANDREJ, microbiologist, educator; b. Brezje by Krsko, Slovenia, Nov. 22, 1913; s. Andrej Mihael and Marija (Lekse) B.; m. Sonja Ivana Sovdat, Aug. 11, 1951; children: Andrej, Borut, Igor. MD, U. Beograd, Yugoslavia, 1938; postgrad., Inst. Microbiology, Ljubljana, Slovenia, 1950, DSc, 1970. Med. diplomate. Physician Gen. Hosp., Murska Sobota, Slovenia, 1939-41, Maribor, Slovenia, 1941-46; asst. Inst. of Microbiology/Med. Faculty, Ljubljana, 1946-51, sr. lectr., 1951-59, extraordinary prof., 1969-72, ordinary prof., 1972-82, dir., 1961-82, rschr., 1982—; Author: New findings on allergy in infectious diseases, 1946, Repetitorium of Microbiology for the students of Stomatology, V edit., 1981; editor: Microbiological Dictionary, 1994, Latin Proverbs, 1996. Recipient Medal for Work with Golden Wreath (Yugoslavia), Kidric award U. Ljubljana, 1982; WHO fellow State Serum Inst., Copenhagen, 1954, others. Mem. Slovenian Med. Soc., Slovenian Microbiology Soc., Slovenian Allergology and Immunology Soc. Roman Catholic. Avocation: chess. Home: Trubarjeva 61, 1000 Ljubljana Slovenia Office: Inst Microbiology/Immunology, Zaloska 4, 1105 Ljubljana Slovenia

BANIOTOPOULOS, CHARALAMBOS, civil engineer, educator; b. Thessaloniki, Greece, Apr. 18, 1958; s. Constantinos and Christina (Sakellariou) B.; m. Anastasia Bontzidou, Dec. 28, 1988; children: Christina, Pantelis. Diploma in civil engring., Aristotle U., Thessaloniki, 1981, PhD in Civil Engring., 1985. Registered profl. civil engr. Tech. Chamber of Greece. Rsch. assoc. Aristotle U., 1981-88; Alexander von Humboldt rsch. fellow Tech. U., Aachen, Germany, 1987-88; lectr. Aristotle U., Thessaloniki, 1988-91, asst. prof., 1991-96; rsch. fellow Joint Rsch. Ctr. European Union, Ispra, Italy, 1993-94; assoc. prof. civil engring. Aristotle U., 1996-2000, prof., 2000—; cons. Xenos Ltd., 1981-96. Contbr. over 50 articles to profl. jours. European rsch. fellow European Commn., 1993-94. Mem. ASCE, Internat. Soc. Computational Mechanics, Greek Soc. for Rsch. in Metal Structures, Gesellschaft für Angewandte Mathematik und Mechanik, Tech. C. ofGreece, Greek Assn. for Computational Mechanics, Internat. Soc. for the Interaction Between Mathematics and Mechanics. E-mail: ccb@civil.auth.gr. Home: Makedonomahou Stogianni 7, 55236 Thessaloniki Greece Office: Inst Steel Structures, Aristotle U, 54006 Thessaloniki Greece

BANISTER, ARTHUR JAMES, chemistry educator; b. Cheadle Hulme, Cheshire, Eng., Dec. 22, 1932; s. John and Annie (Berry) B.; m. Judith Anne Scott, Aug. 26, 1961; children: John, Paul, James, Catherine. BSc, U. Bristol, Eng., 1954, PhD, 1957, DSc, 1988. Chartered chemist. Asst. lectr. Queen Elizabeth Coll., U. London, 1957-61; rsch. fellow U. Newcastle upon Tyne, Eng., 1961-63; lectr. in chemistry U. Durham, Durham City, Eng., 1964-80, sr. lectr. chemistry, 1980-89, reader in chemistry, 1989-96; emeritus reader in chemistry, 1997—; mem. inorganic chemistry subcom. Sci. and Engring. Rsch. Coun., 1983-86. Contbr. chpts. to books and articles to profl. jours. Chmn. Waddington St. Ctr. Ltd., Durham City, 1981—. Dithiadiazolyl radical ions and their metal complexes grantee Engring. and Phys. Scis. Rsch. Coun., Swindon, 1993-96. Fellow Royal Soc. Chemistry (Main Group Element Chemistry Silver Medal award 1991). Mem. United Reformed Church (elder). Avocations: music, pottery, country walking. Home: 16 The Peth, Durham DH1 4PZ, England Office: U Durham Dept Chemistry, South Road, Durham DH1 3LE, England

BANKA, BALDEO PRASAD, steel producing company executive; b. Calcutta, India, June 2, 1948; arrived in Indonesia, 1981; s. Shyam Sunder and Phool Devi Banka; m. Manju Devi Agarwal, July 9, 1973; 1 child, Puja. B. Commerce, Calcutta U., 1967, M. Commerce, 1969, B. Law, 1970. Asst. Sahujain Svcs. Ltd., India, 1965-73; asst. gen. mgr. Jay Engring. Works Ltd., India, 1973-81; mng. dir., CEO, Pt Ispat Indo, Indonesia, 1981—. Recipient Internat. Best Exec. award Asean Programma Cons., Indonesia, 1996. Mem. West Bengal Bar Coun. Office: Pt Ispat Indo Sepanjang, Sidoarjo, PO Box 1083, Surabaya Indonesia

BANKER, JOE DAN, naval officer, educator; b. Fort Worth, Nov. 15, 1956; s. Harry Wilson and Dorothy Faye (Elders) B.; m. Nancy Armour, Apr. 2, 1983; 1 child, Ashley Faye. BA in Psychology, U. Tex., 1979; MA in Nat. Security Affairs, U.S. Naval War Coll., Newport, R.I., 1996. Commd. ensign USN, 1980, advanced through grades to comdr., 1995; 3rd lt. USS St. Louis, San Diego, 1979-80; navigator USS Point Defiance, San Diego, 1980-82; weapons officer USS Truxtan, San Diego, 1982-84; sci. instr. Surface Warfare Sch., San Diego, 1984-86; combat systems officer USS Taylor, Charleston, S.C., 1986-88; ops. officer Destroyer Squadron Four, Charleston, 1988-90; flag sec., comdg. officer Mine Warfare Command, Corpus Christi, Tex., 1991-94; exec. officer USS Klakring, Charleston, 1994-96; prof. U.S. Naval War Coll., Newport, R.I., 1996-2000; naval sci. instr. NJROTC Lee County H.S., Leesburg, Ga., 2000—. Decorated Navy Meritorious Svc. medal; recipient medal NATO, 1995. Mem. VFW, Surface Navy Assn. (sec.-treas. 1986—), NRA. Episcopalian. Avocations: model rockets, exercise, bike riding. E-Mail: bankerjo@lee.k12.ga.us. Home: 275 Smithville Rd N Leesburg GA 31763-3912 Office: Naval Sci Dept US Naval War Coll One Trojan Way Leesburg GA 31763

BANKL, HANS CHRISTIAN, physician, researcher; b. Vienna, Mar. 14, 1968; s. Hans and Christa Bankl; m. Patricia Pfeffer, Aug. 30, 1997. MD, U. Vienna, 1992. Postdoctoral rsch. fellow dept. internal medicine/hematology U. Vienna, 1992-94, resident Inst. Lab. Medicine/Immunology, 1994-95, resident dept. clin. pathology, 1995—; part-time lectr. U. Applied Arts, Vienna, 1996—. Author: Klinische Pathologie, 1996, Pathologisch-Morphologische Diagnostik, 1999. Mem. Austrian Soc. Pathology. Avocations: arts, linguistics, tennis. Office: U Vienna Dept Clin Pathology, Wahringer Gurtel 18-20, A-1090 Vienna Austria

BANKOV, BANKO PETKOV, civil engineer, educator; b. Lovetch, Bulgaria, July 2, 1936; s. Petko Minkov and Rada Minkova (Duleva) B.; m. Evdokia Dobreva Ruskova, Mar. 7, 1965; children: Petko, Dobri. Degree in civil engring., U. Arch. Civil Engring., Sofia, Bulgaria, 1960; DSc, U. Arch. Civil Engring., 1975. Practioner engr. State Factory Bldg. Corp., Plovdiv, Bulgaria, 1960-62, Burgas, Bulgaria, 1962-64; from asst. prof. to prof. U. Arch. Civil Engring., Sofia, 1964-91, prof., 1991—, vice dean civil engring., 1990-94, dean, 1995-99; scientist Ctr. Technique Indsl. Constrn. Metallique, Paris, 1974-75; mem. Civil Engring. Scientific Coun., Sofia, 1990—, Bulgarian Nat. Com. Theoretical Applied Mechanics, Sofia, 1995—. Co-author: From the Cave to the Skyscraper, 1976 (Min. Edn. award 1976), Investigation of Civil Engineering Structures by the Finite Element Method, 1989, The Finite Element Method in the Structural Mecanics, 1996. Cons. Ctrl. House Bulgarian Students, Sofia, 1988-94. Recipient Merit medal Presidium Nat. Assembly, 1961, 63, Nat. Com. Celebration 1300 Anniversary Bulgarian State, 1981. Mem. Union Bulgarian Scientists, Union Bulgarian Writers (cons., award 1980, 82, 88, 99). Avocations: fiction, dramaturgy, swimming, tennis. Home: Dejan Belichki blok 1 ap 36, 1404 Sofia Bulgaria Office: U Arch Civil, Blvd Hristo Smirnenski 1, 1421 Sofia Bulgaria

BANKS, ALLAN RICHARD, artist, art historian, researcher; b. Dearborn, Mich., Feb. 15, 1948; s. Henry Selman and Lillian Margaret (Radovic) B.; children: Christine Marie, Aaron Richard; m. Holly Hope Tumblin, Jan. 1997. Ind. pvt. study, Soc. Arts and Crafts, Detroit, 1966-69; student, Atelier Lack, Inc., Mpls., 1970-73, R.H. Ives Gammell Studio, Williamstown, Mass., 1976. Artist, with studio in Newburg, N.Y., 1979-81, Huron, Ohio, 1981-87; portrait artist, with studio in Spring Hill, Fla., 1987-93; dir. Atelier of Plein Air, Safety Harbor, Fla., 1993—; lectr./demonstrator Portraits South, Inc., Raleigh, N.C., 1993, Atelier LeSueur, Mpls., 1995. Exhibited in group shows Sotheby's, N.Y.C., 1997, Guild of Boston Artists, 1996, 20th Century Exhbn., Amarillo Tex.-Springville, Utah, 1982, Butler Inst. Am. Art, Vixseboxse Art Galleries, Cleve., Salmagundi Club, Amarillo (Tex.) Art Ctr., Maryhill Mus. Art, Goldendale, Wash., Historic East-West Russia Exhibit, 1996, others; represented in collections at Wadsworth Athenaeum, Newark Art Mus., Montclair (N.J.) Mus., Hamilton Fish Meml. Libr., Nat. Portrait Gallery/Smithsonian. Trustee Mus. Natural History, Safety Harbor, 1995—; mem. Downtown Bus. Assn., Inc., Safety Harbor, 1994—. Elizabeth T. Greenshields Found. fellow, Montreal, 1972, 73; John and Anna Stacey Found. grantee, N.Mex., 1979, Ohio Arts Coun. grantee. Mem. Am. Soc. Portrait Artists (vice chmn. 2000—), Am. Soc. Classical Realism (pres. 1997—), Met. Mus. Art, Appleton Mus. Art (Ocala, Fla.), Salmagundi Club, New Am. Acad. Ard. Lutheran. Avocations: travel, museums. Home: PO Box 233 Safety Harbor FL 34695-0233

BANKS, ERIC KENDALL, lawyer; b. St. Louis, Aug. 21, 1955; s. Willie James Banks Jr. and Grace (Kendall) Palmer; children: Brittany Renee, Bryson Kendall. BSBA, U. Mo., St. Louis, 1977; JD, U. Mo., Columbia, 1980. Bar: Mo. 1980, Ill. 1988, U.S. Dist. Ct. (we. dist.) Mo. 1980, U.S. Dist. Ct. (ea. dist.) Mo. 1984, U.S. Ct. Appeals (8th cir.) 1984, U.S. Ct. Appeals (D.C. cir.) 1988, U.S. Tax Ct. 1988, U.S. Supreme Ct. 1996. Asst. gen. counsel Mo. Pub. Svc. Commn., Jefferson City, 1980-84; asst. atty. Office Circuit Atty., St. Louis, 1984-87; pvt. practice, St. Louis, 1987-91, Clayton, Mo., 1991-92; corp. counsel Siegel-Robert, St. Louis, 1992-97; city counselor City of St. Louis, 1997-99; ptnr. Thompson, Coburn, 1999—, Thompson Coburn, St. Louis, 1999—; adj. prof. civil law St. Louis U. Law Sch., 1987-92, Washington U. Sch. law, 1991; sec. bd. dirs. Black Leadership Tng. Program, St. Louis, 1975-77. Sec. bd. dirs. Wesley House Assn.; bd. trustees Mo. U. Law Sch. Found. St. Louis Met. Leadership Program fellow, 1975-77. Mem. ABA (labor and employment com.), Nat. Bar Assn., Bar Assn. Met. St. Louis, Mo. Bar Assn. (adminstrv. law com., com. counsel), Mound City Bar Assn., Bar Assn. Met. St. Louis. Lutheran. Club: Toastmasters Internat. (adminstrv. v.p. 1983, William Tellman award 1982). Avocations: karate, reading, photography, public speaking, community work. Fax: (314) 552-7256. E-mail: ebanks@thompsoncoburn.com. Home: 2755 Russell Blvd Saint Louis MO 63104-2137 Office: Thompson Coburn One Firstar Plz Saint Louis MO 63101

BANKS, JOHN ROBERT, JR., lawyer; b. Balt., Mar. 15, 1958; s. John Robert and Ida Carol (Cromer) B. BA, Coll. William and Mary, Williamsburg, Va., 1980; JD, U. Houston, 1983. Bar: Tex. 1983, U.S. Dist. Ct. (so. dist.) Tex. 1983; cert. bus. bankruptcy law Tex. Bd. Legal Specialization. Assoc. Levin & Kasner, P.C. fka Levin, Roth & Kasner, P.C., Houston, 1983-96; pvt. practice Houston, 1997; ptnr. Mason, Coplen & Banks, LLP, Houston, 1998-99; shareholder Mason, Coplen, Shuchart, Hutchins & Banks, P.C., Houston, 2000—. Dir. Cmty. Assn. Inst. Greater Houston, 1995-97, chmn. amb.'s subcom., 1995-97, chmn. legal com., 1995, vice chmn. legal com., 1994, chmn. mem. svc. com., 1998; mem. adminstrv. bd. Chapelwood United Meth. Ch., 1997—, trustee, 1998—. Mem. Am. Bar Assn. Republican. Avocation: stamp collecting. Telecopier: (713) 785-8651. E-mail: johnbanksjr@msn.com. Office: Mason Coplen Shuchart Hutchins & Banks PC Attys at Law 7500 San Felipe St Ste 700 Houston TX 77063-1709

BANKS, LAURIE JEAN, communications company owner, consultant; b. Fort Fairfield, Maine, Nov. 17, 1956; d. Harvey H. and Emily R. (Hagerman) Banks; 1 child, Morgan Allen. BS, U. Maine, 1978. News photographer, reporter WLBZ-TV, Bangor, Maine, 1979-81; promotion dir. WCBB-TV, Lewiston, Maine, 1981-83; broadcast dir. Chellis, Conwell & Gale, Portland, Maine, 1983-86; mktg. dir. Linda Lee Advt., Portland, 1986-89; mktg. dir., owner Perry Banks Kemp (formerly known as Perry & Banks, Inc.), Portland, 1989—; prof. U. So. Maine Bus. Sch., Portland, 1995; lectr. in field. Bd. dirs. Big Brother/Big Sister, Portland, 1996—, Males Prevent/Pregnancy, Portland, 1987-89, 75 State St., Portland, 1983, Found. 51, 1999—. Mem. Am. Assn. Advt. Agys., Portland Ad Club (pres. 1994-95, Broderson awards 1979-96). Avocations: collecting antiques, photography. Office: Perry Banks Kemp 15 Franklin Arterial Portland ME 04101-5009

BANKS, MELANIE ANNE, nutritionist, biochemist, educator, dietitian; b. McKeesport, Pa., Oct. 27, 1956; d. Raymond Joseph and Emma Dea (Thomas) B. BA in Music, U. Pitts., 1976, BS in Biochemistry, 1977; MS in Chemistry, Duquesne U., 1980; PhD in Nutritional Biochemistry, W.Va. U., 1986. Cert. nutrition specialist; registered dietitian. Clin. rsch. technician Children's Hosp., Pitts., 1979-82; rsch. asst. W.Va. U., Morgantown, 1982-86; rsch. assoc. dept. Pathology U. Pitts., Pitts., 1986-87; rsch. assoc. divsn. respiratory diseases Nat. Inst. of Occupl. Safety and Health, Morgantown, 1987-89; rsch. assoc. dept. food sci. and human nutrition U. Fla., Gainesville, 1989-91; instr. divsn. health sci. Santa Fe C.C., Gainesville, 1989-92; rsch. chemist divsn. food chem. Am. Bacteriol. and Chem. Rsch. Corp., Gainesville, 1991-92; rsch. chemist lipid nutrition lab. USDA, Beltsville, Md., 1992-94; instr. biology Prince George's C.C., Largo, Md., 1993-94; asst. prof. biochemistry Lecom, Erie, Pa., 1994-96; instr. biology and chemistry Notre Dame Coll., South Euclid, Ohio, 1996-97; clin. dietitian Sarah A. Reed Retirement Ctr., Erie, 1998-99; comty. nutritionist Family Health Coun., Erie, 1998—; instr. nutrition Jamestown (N.Y.) C.C., 1998-99; asst. prof. nutrician and dietetics Youngstown State U., 1999-2000; dietetic intern Cleve. Clinic Found., 1996-98; nutrition cons., owner Lake Erie Med. Nutrition Therapy, Erie, 1999—. Capt. M.S.C., USAR, 1990-96. Postdoctoral fellow NRC, 1986, USDA, 1992. Fellow Am. Coll. Nutrition; mem. Am. Chem. Soc., Am. Inst. Nutrition, Am. Dietetic Assn., Sigma Xi. Avocation: musician. Home: 3122 Peach St Erie PA 16508-2734

BANKS, MONICA, sculptor; b. N.Y.C., Mar. 29, 1959; d. Stanley and Rela (Heuberg) Banks; m. Philip A. Schultz, Jan. 28, 1995; children: Elias Banks Schultz, August Rawley Schultz. AB, Vassar Coll., 1981; student, Domus Acad., Milan, 1985. Graphic designer Milton Glaser Inc., N.Y.C., 1982-87, Monica Banks Inc., N.Y.C., 1987-95. One-woman shows include Univ. Gallery, U. Mass., Amherst, 1991, Lizan Tops Gallery, East Hampton, N.Y.; exhbn. of resin and fabric sculpture Barneys N.Y., 1989; steel rod Horse sculpture in Binghamton (N.Y.) Visitor Ctr., 1996, Faces Times Square: 18 ton steel bar 160 ft. long sculpture, N.Y.C., 1996. Recipient Excellence in Design award Art Commn. City of N.Y., 1996. Mem. Internat. Sculpture Ctr. Home: 88 Osborne Ln East Hampton NY 11937-2207

BANKS, O'DREAN EDYTHE, publishing company executive; b. Joliet, Ill., Feb. 10, 1951; d. Ecoma Sr. and Bobbie Lee Banks; divorced; children: Ronald Eugene, Jamie Andre, Ny'kia Rashan, Cartelas Jovaz. Cert. of completion, U. Wis., 1978, Atlanta Area Tech., 1980. Adminstrv. asst. Argonne Nat. Lab., Lemont, Ill., 1969-78, Coca-Cola Co., Atlanta, 1978-85; CEO, owner J & O's Fashions, Atlanta, 1982-88; adminstrv. asst. B & E Jackson & Assocs., Atlanta, 1988-91; owner, CEO Tot's Childcare & Learning Ctr., College Park, Ga., 1991—; engring. and archtl. specifications profl. Rosser Internat., Atlanta, 1993-98; owner, CEO O'ron Jaki Pub., College Park, 1998—; cons. Income Tax Prep, College Park, 1991—; cons., trainer Computer Tech., College Park, 1991—. Author, pub.: (novel) Devastating Rumors, 1998 (Editor's Choice award 1998); contbr. poetry to anthologies (Editor's Choice award 1997). Mem. Save the Children, Atlanta, 1991—; poll tender Dem. Party, Lockport, Ill., 1969-74; census taker Bur. of Census, Joliet. Mem. Atlanta Assn. Black Journalists. Baptist. Avocations:

writing, family activities, traveling, publishing, swimming. Office: O'Ron Jaki Pub PO Box 862 Red Oak GA 30272-0862

BANKS, RELA, sculptor; b. Yaroslav, Poland, Oct. 8, 1933; came to U.S., 1947; d. Jacob and Freida (Weintraub) Heuberg; m. Stanley Frederic Banks, Aug. 9, 1953; children: Andrew Howard, J. Monica, Gary Mitchell. Student, Mus. Modern Art, 1957, Art Students League, N.Y.C. and Woodstock, N.Y., 1958-61, Summit (N.J.) Art Ctr., 1966-75. Chmn. nat. juried exhibit Summit Art Ctr., 1976, mem. adminstrv. com., 1977-79, chmn. standing com. spl. events, trustee; mem. exec. com. Phoenix Gallery, N.Y.C., 1983; chmn. membership com. Stone Sculpture Soc. N.Y., 1980-82. One-woman shows include Robins Art Gallery, South Orange, N.J., 1973, Montclair (N.J.) Coll., 1974, Caldwell (N.J.) Coll., 1974, 83, Summit Art Ctr., 1976, Newark Acad., Livingston, N.J., 1976, Douglas Coll., New Brunswick, N.J., 1978, First Women's Bank, N.Y.C., 1979, Phoenix Gallery, 1979, 81, 83, Morris Mus. Arts and Scis., Morristown, N.J., 1983, Ann Leonard Gallery, Woodstock, 1983, NECCA Mus., Bklyn., Conn., 1985, Schiller-Wapner Galleries, N.Y.C., 1985, 87, Ann Norton Sculpture Galleries, West Palm Beach, Fla., 1987, David Gary Ltd, Millburn, N.J., 1988; exhibited in group shows at Phoenix Gallery, 1979, 83, Morris Mus. Art, 1979, 83, Invitational Woodstock Artists Assn., 1980, 84, Eilaine Benson Gallery, Bridgehampton, N.Y., 1980, Searles Art Ctr., Great Barrington, Mass., 1980, Nabisco Art Gallery, 1981, Summit Art Ctr., 1981, First Womens Bank, 1981, Fairleigh Dickinson U., Madison, N.J., 1983, NYU Grad. Sch. Bus., 1983, AT&T Gallery, Basking Ridge, N.J., 1984, Shering Plough Gallery, N.J., 1984, New Orleans Mus. Art, 1986, Gallery Contemporary Art at U. Colorado Springs, Colo., 1986, Schiller-Wapner Galleries, 1986, Lever House, N.Y.C., 1986, Aldrich Mus. Contemporary Art, Ridgefield, Conn., 1986, Okla. Art Ctr., Oklahoma City, 1987, "After Henry Moore", Emily Lowe Mus., Hofstra U., Hempstead, N.Y., 1988, group exhibition , Poland; represented in permanent collections New Orleans Mus. Art, Everson Mus., Syracuse, N.Y., Morris Mus. Sci. and Art, Okla. Art Ctr., Vassar Coll. Gallery, Poughkeepsie, N.Y., Millburn (N.J.) Pub. Library, Minn. Mus. Art, Mpls., Woodstock Hist. Soc., Fordham U., Lincoln Ctr., N.Y.C., Aldrich Mus. Contemporary Art, Warsaw Mus., Poland, various pvt. and corp. collections. Mem. Woodstock Artists Assn. Office: Rela Banks Studio Mink Hollow Rd Woodstock NY 12498

BANKS, ROBERT J., bishop; b. Winthrop, Mass., Feb. 26, 1928; s. Robert Joseph and Rita Katherine (Sullivan) B. AB, St. John's Sem., Brighton, Mass., 1949; STL, Gregorian U., Rome, 1953; JCD, Lateran U., Rome, 1957. Ordained priest Roman Cath. Ch., 1952, ordained titular bishop of Taraqua, 1985. Prof. canon law St. John Sem., Brighton, Mass., 1959-71, acad. dean, 1967-71; rector St. John's Sem., 1971-81; vicar gen. Boston Archdiocese, 1984; aux. bishop Boston, 1985-90; bishop Diocese of Green Bay, Wis., 1990—. Office: Diocese of Green Bay PO Box 23825 Green Bay WI 54305-3825

BANKS, ROBERT LEE, publisher, author, jazz guitarist, composer, arranger; b. Buckingham County, Va., July 11, 1952. Student, Bronx C.C., 1970-71, L.I. U., 1994-96. Lic. real estate broker, N.Y. Broker/pres. Premier Nat. Realty, Jamaica, N.Y.; tchr. music Beacon Sch. program Jr. H.S. 8, Jamaica, 1993—; pres. Total Package Pub. Co., Jamaica, 1997—, Creative Artists, Ltd., Jamaica, 2000—, Artists Choice, Ltd., Jamaica, 2000—; former tchr. Henry Street Settlement Music Sch., 1976-87. Author: (autobiography) Against All Odds, 1993-97, The Art of Expressions are in the Progressions, volumes 1 & 2, Chord Melodies for the Innovative Guitarist, vols. 1, 2, 3, The Virtuoso Pianist, volume 1; guitarist, performed with Bobbie Humphrey, Gattertail Jackson, Stanley Turrentine, Delores Carr, Sherells, Charlie Rouse Quartet, bands of Dizzy Gillespie, Frank Foster and Ray Abams; TV appearances include Positively Black, Like It Is, CBS cable show; performed at Avery Fischer Hall, Lincoln Ctr., N.Y.C., Felt Forum, Manhattan Ctr., Mikell's, Munk's After Dark, Ariz.'s Tempi, Baker's Keyboard Lounge, Chgo., Just Jazz, Phila., Astrodome Stadium, Houston, Blues Alley, Washington, WRVR concert series with Bobbie Humphrey; performer jazz festivals of Kool and Newport, coll. concerts featuring Banks Brothers and Robert Banks Sextet; discography includes Sophisticated Funk (with Brother Jack McDuff) and Breezin', Funk Power, Moving World, Fight For What Is Right, and Approaching Storm (with Creative Funk). Recipient various honors and awards; scholar United Fedn. Tchrs. Fax: 718-323-7764. Home and Office: Total Package Pub Co PO Box 200009 S Ozone Park NY 11420-0009

BANKS, SANDY B., accountant; b. Salt Lake City, June 17, 1959; d. Vaughn R. and Patricia T. Brierley; m. Darin J. Banks; children: Daniel, Stacy, Michelle, Eric, Jared, Becky. BS in Acctg. cum laude, U. Utah, 1981, M Profl. Accountancy, 1982. CPA, Utah. Tax preparer Stayner & Co., P.C., Salt Lake City, 1982-90, tax mgr., owner, 1990—. Bd. mem. Salt Lake Estate Coun., 1999—, dir., 1995—. Mem. AICPA. Avocations: golf, camping, hiking. E-mail: sbanks@stayner.com. Office: Stayner & Co PC 455 S 300 E Ste 300 Salt Lake City UT 84111-3234

BANKS, WILLIAM MCKERRELL, mechanical engineer, educator; b. Dreghorn, Ayrshire, Scotland, Mar. 28, 1943; s. William and Jeannie Love (McKerrell) B.; m. Martha Ruthven Hair, Sept. 23, 1966; children: Sinclair, Kenneth, Kerrell. BSc, Strathclyde U., 1965, MSc, 1966, PhD, 1977. Student apprentice Glacier Metal Co., Ltd., Ayrshire, 1961-65; sr. rsch. engr. G & J Weir, Ltd., Glasgow, Scotland, 1966-70; from lectr. to prof. mech. engring. U. Strathclyde, Glasgow, 1970—, dir. Ctr. for Advanced Structural Materials; dir. Scottish Polymer Tech. Network, 1998—. Editor Materials: Design and Applications. Fellow Instn. Mech. Engrs. (coun., James Clayton rsch. prize 1977, Donald Julius Groen prize 1994, 150th Anniversary gold medal 1998), Inst. Materials (coun.), Royal Soc. Encouragement Arts, Mfrs. and Commerce. Avocations: reading, family activities, Bible teaching. Home: 19 Dunure Dr Hamilton, ML3 9EY Glasgow Scotland Office: U Strathclyde Dept Mech Engring, 75 Montrose St, Glasgow G1 1XJ, Scotland

BANNACH, BURKHARDT, medical physicist; b. Essen, Germany, Oct. 18, 1953; m. Oct. 18, 1984. Diploma in physics, U. Bochum, Germany, 1984. Physicist Hosp., Duisburg, Germany, 1985; med. physicist Univ. Hosp., Duesseldorf, Germany, 1985-89, sr. physicist, 1989—; cons. physicist Johanniter Hosp., Duisburg, 1987-90; cons. Deutsche Industrie Norm, Germany, 1995-96. Research in total body irradiation in radiotherapy, conformal radiotherapy, stereotactic radiosurgery and radiotherapy. Mem. European Soc. for Therapeutic Radiology and Oncology, Deutsche Gesellschaft für Medizinische Physik e.V., Deutsche Gesellschaft für Radioonkologie e.V., Deutsche Physikalische Gesellschaft. Office: Heinr Heine U Duesseldorf, Moorenstrasse 5, D 40225 Düsseldorf Germany

BANNELIER, FLORENCE ANNE, financial analyst; b. Paris, Apr. 12, 1959; d. Pierre Joseph and Denise (Germaine Liebgott) Picard; m. Pierre Louis Bannelier, Sept. 14, 1984; children: Alice, Juliette, Heloise. LLB, U. Paris II, 1980; grad., Scis.-Po, Paris, 1982; LLM, U. Paris II, 1983. Fund mgr. Credit Comml. de France Bank, Paris, 1985-88, AXA Ins. Co., Paris, 1988-89; dir., v.p. NSM, Paris, 1990-96; internat fin. analyst, v.p. ABN-AMRO France, Banque de Neuflize, Schlumberger et Mallet, Paris, 1997—. Mem. Soc. Française des Analstes Financiers, Assn. des Gerants et Analystes de Marches Européens. Roman Catholic. Avocations: windsurfing, bridge, home architecture. Home: 5 rue Auber, 78110 Le Vesinet France Office: Banque de Neuflize, 40 rue de Courcelles, 75008 Paris France

BANNER, DAVID IAN, lawyer; b. Bellshill, Scotland, Apr. 14, 1936; s. John David and Georgina Stewart (Johnston) B.; m. Mary Elizabeth Rourke, June 18, 1975; children: Peta C.S., Clare M.S. B of Law, U. Glasgow, 1956. Navigator Royal Air Force, 1956-58; asst. solicitor Neill Clerk & Murray, Greenock, Scotland, 1959-62; ptnr. Neill Clerk & Murray, Greenock, 1966—; asst. solicitor Wilkinson & Grist, Hong Kong, 1962-66; dir. Neill Clerk Group PLC, London, 1994-99. Chmn. Sir Gabriel Wood's Mariners' Home, Greenock, 1982—, Greenock Dist. Scout Coun., 1989-98; hon. pres. Greenock Dist. Scout Coun., 1999—. Mem. Law Soc. Scotland, David Lloyd Clubs. Episcopalian. Avocations: tennis, curling, bridge, scouting. Home: 33 The Esplanade, Greenock PA16 7RY, Scotland Office: Neill Clerk & Murray, 3 Ardgowan Sq, Greenock PA16 8NW, Scotland

BANNERT-DROOFF, ANDREA, marketing professional; b. Berlin, June 7, 1965; d. Hans-Ulrich and Annemarie Bannert; m. Stephan Georg Drooff, May 7, 1997. Cert., Sorbonne Paris U., 1985; diploma in bus. mgmt., U. Tech., Berlin, 1990. Project control Magnetic Transit of Am. (subsidiary of AEG), L.A., 1988-89; sci. colleague Tech. Transfer, Berlin, 1990-92; pers. cons. of the gen. mgr. lic. svcs. Berlin 2000 Olympia GmbH, Berlin 2000 Mktg. GmbH, 1992-93; sales promotion mgr. Berlin Tourismus Mktg. GmbH, 1994-98; dir. TV and merchandising Kiddinx Media AG, 1999—; bd. dirs. European Fedn. Conf. Towns, 1996-98. Avocations: tennis, jogging, hockey, culture. E-mail: bannert@kiddinx.de Fex: 49(0)30-68 972 125. Home: Wangenheimstrasse 31, 14193 Berlin Germany Office: Kiddinx Media AG, Lahnstrasse 21, 12055 Berlin Germany

BANNISTER, CANDIDA CLEVE, business analyst; b. Lincoln, Nebr., Mar. 3, 1957; d. Robert L. and Miwako Cleve; m. Jermoe Bannister II. BA, UCLA, 1980. Info. sys. mgr. UCLA, 1980-97; sr. sys. analyst Franklin (Tenn.) Am. Life, 1997-99; info. sys. mgr. Micro Diagnostics Inc., Nashville, 1999-2000; with CNA Life Ins., Nashville, 2000—. Mem. NAFE, Augustan Soc. (bd. dirs. 1994—, v.p. elec. info. sys. 1999—). E-mail: ccbannister@home.com.

BANNISTER, GORDON CAMPBELL, orthopaedic surgeon; b. Nuneaton, England, May 5, 1950; s. Ralph Victor and Phyllis Elizabeth (Crabbe) B.; m. Josephine, Oct. 21, 1946; 1 child, Miles. Grad., Oakham Sch., Rutland, Eng., 1968; MBChB (hons. in pharmacology), U. Birmingham (Eng.) Med. Sch., 1974; MChOrth, U. Liverpool, Eng., 1983; MD, U. Bristol (Eng.), 1994. ECFMG, 1975, Fellow Royal Coll. Surgeons Eng., 1979, Fellow Royal Coll. Surgeons Edinburgh, 1979, in orthopedics, 1985. House physician Gen. Hosp., Birmingham, Eng., 1974-75; house surgeon Dudley Rd. Hosp., Birmingham, Eng., 1975; casulty officer/anatomy demonstrator, dept. human morphology Nottingham (Eng.) Gen. Hosp., 1975-76, orthopaedic sr. house officer, 1976; resident III, orthopaedics U. B.C., Vancouver, Can., 1977; rotating surg. registrar United Birmingham Hosps., 1977-79; neurosurg. registrar Midland Ctr. for Neurosurgery and Neurology, Eng., 1979-80; locum sr. house officer Birmingham Accident Hosp., 1980; registrar orthopaedic and trauma surgery Bristol (Eng.) Royal Infirmary and Winford Hosps., 1980-82, lectr. in orthopaedic and trauma surgery, 1982-87; cons. sr. lectr. orthopaedic and trauma surgery Southmead and Winford Orthopaedic Hosps., Bristol, 1987-92, cons. orthopaedic/trauma surgery, adult joint replacement, 1992—, hon. sr. lectr. orthopaedics, 1992—; presenter numerous scientific socs. and confs., 1981—. Contbr. numerous articles to internat. med. jours.; mem. editl. bd. Jour. Bone and Joint Surgery, 1995-99, Hip Internat., 1993—, Sarthoplasty, 2000—; referee Jour. Antimicrobial Chemotherapy, Clin. Orthopaedics and Related Rsch., Jour. Bone and Joint Surgery, Brit. Med. Jour., Brit. Jour. Surgery. Recipient numerous rsch. grants; recipient Hampson Meml. prize South West Orthopaedic Club, 1987. Fellow Brit. Orthopaedic Assn. (Robert Jones Gold medal 1994); mem. Brit. Shoulder and Elbow Soc. (founder), European Hip Soc. (sec. gen.). Avocations: tennis, bridge. Home: 19 Cranbrook Rd, Bristol BS6 7BL, England

BANNISTER, MICHAEL KEITH, materials engineer, researcher; b. Sydney, NSW, Australia, June 26, 1963; s. Michael John and Barbara Bannister; m. Ruth Denholm Neilson, Jan. 4, 1992; children: Lachlan, Emma. BS with honors, Monash U., Melbourne, Victoria, Australia, 1985, B of Engring. with honors, 1987; PhD in Engring., U. Cambridge, Eng., 1990. Exptl. scientist Commonwealth Sci. Indsl. Rsch. Orgn. (CSIRO), Melbourne, 1990-91; rsch. engr. U. Calif., Santa Barbara, 1991-92, Coop. Rsch. Ctr.-Advanced Composite Structures, Melbourne, 1992-94; sr. rsch. engr. Coop. Rsch. Ctr. (CRC)-Aerospace Structures, Melbourne, 1994-99, program coord., 1999—; affiliated rschr. Royal Melbourne Inst. Tech., Melbourne, 1997-99; treas. 11th Internat. Conf. on Composite Materials, Melbourne, 1996-98; keynote lectr. 6th Internat. Conf. on Automated Composites, 1999. Author: (book chpt.) Resin Transfer Moulding for Aerospace Structures, 1998; contbr. papers to profl. jours. Professorial fellow Royal Melbourne Inst. Tech., 1999; Packer scholar Cambridge Commonwealth Trust, 1987. Mem. Australian Composite Structures Soc. (nat. coun. 1998—, sec. Melbourne chpt. 1996-98, pres. Melbourne chpt. 1998—). Avocations: hiking, swimming, wine. Fax: 61 3 9646 0583. E-mail: mbcrcas@ozemail.com.au. Office: CRC-ACS, 506 Lorimer St, Victoria Melbourne 3207, Australia

BANNISTER, SIR ROGER GILBERT, neurologist, college administrator; b. London, Mar. 23, 1929; s. Ralph and Alice Bannister; m. Moyra Elver Jacobsson; 4 children. BA with honors in Physiology, Merton Coll., Oxford U., 1950; MSc, St. Mary's Hosp., 1952; MB BCh, Oxford U., 1954, DM, 1963; LLD, U. Liverpool, 1972; DLitt (hon.), U. Sheffield, 1978; numerous other hon. degrees. Hon. cons. neurologist Nat. Hosp. for Neurology and Neurosurgery, London, St. Mary's Hosp., London; v.p. St. Mary's Hosp. Med. Sch., 1985-88; master Pembroke Coll., Oxford, 1985-93; gov. Nat. Hosp. Neurology and Neurosurgery, 1994-96; hon. cons. neurologist Oxford Regional and Dist. Health Authority, 1985-95; chmn. St. Mary's Hosp. Med. Sch. Devel. Trust, 1998—. Author: First Four Minutes, 1955; editor: Brain and Bannister's Clinical Neurology, 7th edit., 1992; Autonomic Failure, 4th edit. (with C.J. Mathias), 1999; contbr. numerous articles to med. jours. Brit. Mile Champion, 1951, 53, 54; world record one mile, 1st mile run in under 4 minutes, 1954; recipient Hans-Heinrich Siegbert prize, 1977. Fellow Royal Coll. Physicians; mem. Royal Coll. Surgeons, Oxford U. Athletic Club (pres. 1948), Athenaeum. Office: 21 Bardwell Rd, Oxford OX2 6SU, England

BANNO, HISAO, ceramist; b. Tokai, Aichi, Japan, Mar. 24, 1935; s. Takeo Achiwa and Masa Banno; m. Hiroko Narita, Apr. 18, 1961; children: Toshiki, Yasuyuki. BS, Nagoya (Japan) U., 1957. Engr. prod. tech. dept. NGK Spark Plug Co. Ltd., Nagoya, 1957-61, scientist R&D lab., 1961-77, mgr. R&D lab., 1977-83, dir. R&D lab., 1983-89, mng. dir. R&D lab. piezoelectric ceramic divsn. and patent dept., 1989-91, sr. mng. dir., head R&D lab. and patent dept., 1991-95, exec. tech. advisor, 1995-98, corp. tech. advisor, 1998—; organizer numerous meetings and symposia. Author, editor: New Ceramics, 1984; editor, co-author: Ceramics for Automotive Components, 1987, assoc. editor: Journal of the Ceramic Soc. of Japan, 1996-97, editor-in-chief, 1997-98; co-author: Encyclopedia of Physical Science and Technology 1989 Yearbook, 1989, Encyclopedia of Advanced Materials, 1994. Recipient Richard M. Fulrath award U. Calif., Berkeley, 1980. Fellow Am. Ceramic Soc., Acad. of Ceramics (academician; mem. adv. bd. for sci. 1997-2000, mem. Forum 2000 com. 1998-00); mem. Ceramic Soc. of Japan (trustee 1989-91, 93-98, chmn. electronic divsn. 1989-91, chmn. Tokai br. 1995-96, Tech. award 1986), Tokai Chem. Industry Assn. (award 1973), Marine Acoustics Soc. Japan (paper award 1996), Japan Fulrath Meml. Soc. (vice-chmn. 1989—), Electro-Chem. Soc. Japan (vice chmn. chem. sensors divsn. 1993-95), Japanese Soc. Electronic Ceramics and Their Processing (v.p. 1995-97, pres. 1997—), Internat. Con. on Electronic Components and Materials (mem. program com. 1989-95), Internat. Con. on Ceramic Microstructure (mem. adv. com. 1996), IEEE Ultrasonics, Ferroelectrics, and Frequency Control Soc. (mem. ferroelectric com. 1995-98), N.Y. Acad. Scis., Japan Fine Ceramics Assn. (trustee 1993-95, chmn. pub. info. com. 1993-95, chmn. functional ceramics divsn. 1995-97), Japan Electronic Materials Mfrs. Assn. (chm. div. of ceramic substrates for integrated circuits 1993-97), New Ceramics Forum/Japan (trustee 1993-99, mem. editl. com. 1997-99), Asian Meeting on Ferroelectricity (mem. organizing com. 1995—), Central Japan Aerospace Tech. Center (trustee 1993-95), Development Engring. Soc. of Japan (trustee 1993-95), Central Japan Electronics Show Assn. (trustee 1985-97), Nagoya C. of C. & Industry (steering com. of ceramic divsn. 1990-97), Assn. Synthetic Mineral Sci. and Tech. Japan (v.p. 1994—). Buddhist. Avocations: reading, music, golf, travel. Home: 136 Nakayashiki Araomachi, Tokai Aichi 476-0003, Japan Office: NGK Spark Plug Co Ltd, 14-18 Takatsuji-cho Mizuho, Nagoya 467-8525, Japan

BANNO, KAREN L., executive assistant; b. Chgo., Aug. 25, 1957; d. Anthony J. and Margaret M. Banno; m. Dennis R. Phillips, Aug. 18, 1979 (div. Mar. 1980). BS, Ill. State U., Normal, 1984. Nurse's aide Brokaw Hosp., Normal, Ill., 1976-77; sec. Ill. State U., Normal, 1978-84; exec. asst. Am. Coll. Ob-gyn., Washington, 1985-93, Hereiu Welfare Pension, Naperville, Ill., 1995-98, Freeman White, Inc., Charlotte, N.C., 1998—. Democrat. Avocations: Reiki master, amateur historian, amateur sociologist. E-mail: omega@rhtc.net and kbanno@freemanwhite.com. Office: Freeman White Inc 8001 Arrowridge Blvd Charlotte NC 28273-5665

BANNO, SUSUMU, chemist; b. Nagoya, Aichi, Japan, May 24, 1969; s. Hiroshi and Takako (Terada) B. M.Applied Chemistry, Osaka U., Suita, Japan, 1995. Cert. class A hazardous materials engr. Min. of Home Affairs, 1998. Chemist Hitachi Ltd., Ome, Japan, 1995—. Contbr. articles to profl. jours. Avocations: Ainu culture, ethnology, badminton, soccer, skiing. Office: Hitachi Ltd/Htg & Lighting, Shinmachi 6-16-2, Ome 198-8611, Japan

BANNOCK, GRAHAM BERTRAM, economist; b. London, July 10, 1932; s. Eric Burton and Winifred (Sargent) B.; m. Francoise Marcelle Vranckx, Feb. 26, 1971; 1 child, Laurent. BSc, London Sch. Econs., 1955. Market analyst Ford Motor Co., Dagenham, Eng., 1955-56; rschr. Thomas & Baldwins, London, 1957-58; mgr. market rsch. Rover Co., Solihull, Eng., 1958-60, chief econ. and market rsch., 1962-67; sr. adminstr. OECD, Paris, 1960-62; mgr. advanced programmes Ford of Europe, London, 1968-69; dir. rsch. Com. of Inquiry on Small Firms, 1970-71; mng. dir. Economists Adv. Group Ltd., London, 1971-81, The Economist Intelligence Unit, London, 1981-84; chmn. Graham Bannock & Ptnrs. Ltd., London, 1985—; bd. dirs. Ctrl. Banking Publs., Ltd. Author: The Juggernauts, 1971, Taxation in the European Community, 1990, (with R.E. Baxter Evan Davis) The Penguin Dictionary of Economics, 1972, (with Sir Alan Peacock) Corporate Takeovers and the Public Interest, 1991, (with William Manser) International Dictionary of Finance. Mem. adv. coun. Inst. Econ. Affairs, 1990—. Sgt. Royal Army, 1950-52. Mem. Royal Auto Mobile Club, Royal Econ. Soc. Avocations: karate, the arts. Office: Bannock Cons Ltd, 47 Marylebone Ln, London W1M 6LD, England

BANSAK, STEPHEN A., JR., investment banker, financial consultant; b. Bridgeport, Conn., Sept. 19, 1939; s. Stephen A. and Genevieve Bansak; m. Susan Jean Dizon, July 20, 1984; children: Cynthia A., Thomas S., Stephen A. III, Kirk C. BS, Yale U., 1961; MBA, U. Pa., 1968. With Kidder, Peabody & Co., Inc., N.Y.C., 1968-89, v.p., 1971-75, co-mgr. dept. corpl fin., 1975-84; vice chmn. Kidder, PEabody Internat., N.Y.C., 1984—; bd. dirs. Kidder Peabody P.R., KP Realty Advisers; sr. cons. Concord Internat. Ptnrs., 1990—, bentley Assocs., 1990-92; vice chmn. Myers, Craig, Vallone, Francois, Inc., 1992-93; sr. advisor Universal Tech. inst., 1995-97, Motay Electronics, Inc., 1993-97, Buenavenjura Filamor Echuas (Manila), 1991-94; vis. lectr. Wharton Grad. Sch., U. Pa., 1989; bd. dirs. Filbrin, Inc., Lighthouse Ptnrs., Troy Bioscis., Inc.; bd. dirs., vice chmn. Computerized Med. Sys., Inc.; mem. adv. bd. Global Health Care Ptnrs. (DLJ Mcht. Banking); adv. com. Manschot Opportunity Fund. Past trustee, v.p. Rumson (N.J.) Country Day Sch. Lt. USN, 1962-66, Vietnam. Mem. Philippine-Am. C. of C. (bd. dirs.), U.S.-Asia inst. (past bd. dirs.), India House (past pres. Broad St. Club), Navesink Country Club, Yale Club N.Y.C., Troon Golf and Country Club, Securities Industry Assn. (chmn. corp. fin. com., rule 415 com.), Am. Stock Exch. (ofcl.).

BANSAL, VISHAL, chemical engineer; b. Agra, India, Apr. 29, 1970; came to U.S., 1992; s. R.K. and M.D. B. BS, Indian Inst. Tech., Bombay, 1992; PhD, U. Okla., 1997. Rsch. engr. DuPont, Richmond, Va., 1997-99, sr. rsch. engr., 1999—. Contbr. articles to profl. jours. Mem. AIChE, Tech. Assn. Paper and Pulp Industry, Am. Chem. Soc. Avocations: astrophysics, psychology, photography, Freud, racquetball. E-mail: vishal.bansal@usa.dupont.com. Office: DuPont Nonwovens 5401 Jeff Davis Hwy Richmond VA 23234-2257

BANSAL, YASH PAL, physician; b. Moga, Panjab, India, Nov. 30, 1948; s. Des Raj and Dwarki Devi Aggarwal; m. Sneh Lata Aggarwal, May 11, 1974; children: Sonia, Neetu. B Medicine B Surgery, Dayanand Med. Coll., India, 1972; DGO, U. Vienna, Austria, 1983, FGO, 1983. Med. officer Govt. of Panjab, India, 1973-75, Govt. of Kenya, 1975-82; registrar Pumwani Maternity Hosp., Nairobi, Kenya, 1984-87; cons. Jamaa Maternity Hosp., Nairobi, 1987-93, Mater Hosp., Nairobi, 1993—; mem. Internat. Avd. Bd. 23d Congress on Pathology of Pregnancy, U. Miss. Sch. Medicine, 1991; cons. M.P. Shah Hosp., Nairobi, 1995—, Aga Khan Hosp., Nairobi, 1995—, Guru Nanak Hosp., Nairobi, 1987—, Westlands Cottage Hosp., Nairobi, 1995—. Contbr. articles to profl. jours. Organizer Free Med. Camps, Arya Samaj Nairobi, 1996—. Fellow Internat. Coll. Surgeons; mem. Am. Med. Soc. Vienna (life), Family Planning Assn. Kenya, Orgn. Gestosis (hon. life), Oxford Club. Arya Samaj. Avocations: bridge, badminton, swimming, reading, palmistry. Home: Mogotio Rd, Nairobi Kenya Office: Mater Hosp, Indsl Area, Nairobi Kenya

BANSINATH, MYLARRAO, pharmacologist, educator; b. Mudigere, India, Sept. 4, 1950; came to U.S., 1985; s. Mylari G. and Nagarathnamma T. Rao; m. Sabitha M.K. Bansinath, Jan. 27, 1989; children: Bina B., Bindu B. BSc, U. Mysore, Karnataka, India, 1970; MSc, Kasturba Med. Coll., Manipal, India, 1974; PhD, Inst. Med. Edn. & Rsch., Chandigarh, India, 1984. Lectr. Kasturba Med. Coll., 1975-79, M.S.R. Med. Coll., Bangalore, India, 1983-84; rsch. assoc. U. Ill., Chgo., 1985-86; rsch. asst. prof. NYU Med. Ctr., N.Y.C., 1986—; external examiner for PhD, Gujarat U., Mangalore and Madras U. Contbr. articles to Jour. Pharmacology, Jour. Pharmacology Toxicology methods, Jour. Neurochemistry, Neurchem. Rsch., Neurosci., Gen. Pharmacology; contbr. chpts. to books. Inst. Med. Edn. and Rsch. scholar, 1979-83; fellow J.J. Hosp. Bombay, 1981, Indian Coun. Med. Rsch., 1981. Mem. Am. Soc. Pharmacology and Exptl. Therapeutics, Indian Pharmacol. Soc. (life), Assn. Physiologists and Pharmacologists India (life), N.Y. Acad. Scis. Achievements include resarch in defining the pharmacological and biochemical properties of opiate and excitatory amino acid receptor sytbypes, effect of nitric oxide and cocaine in regulation of glial and neuronal cell proliferation. Home: 26 Shawn Ct New Brunswick NJ 08902-5009 Office: NYU Med Ctr Anesthesia 550 1st Ave New York NY 10016-6402

BANSKALIEVA, VENETA BORISSOVA, chemist, educator; b. Gotze Deltchev, Bulgaria, Dec. 1, 1941; d. Boris Michailov and Raina Georgieva (Liaskova) B.; m. Gospodin Dobrev, Mar. 12, 1967. BA, Sofia U., Bulgaria, 1966; PhD, Agricultural Acad., Sofia, 1977. Rschr. Inst. Animal Sci., Kostinbrod, Bulgaria, 1966—; assoc. prof. Inst. Animal Sci., Kostinbrod, 1981—. Contbr. articles to profl. jours. Mem. Forum Bulgarka, Sofia, 1998. Mem. Nat. Coun. Animal Sci. (sec.), Union Scientists in Bulgaria. Avocations: reading, writing. Office: Inst Animal Science, 2232 Kostinbrod Bulgaria

BANTEKAS, DEMETRIOS, electrical engineer, researcher, educator; b. Volos, Greece, Apr. 21, 1966; s. Vasilios and Despina (Gerovasili) B. Diploma in Elec. Engring., Democritos U., Xanthi, Greece, 1990; PhD, 1994. Tech. mgr. Hartix S.A., Xanthi, 1990-92, Xanthi Cables S.A., Xanthi, 1993-94, Blioumis S.A., Xanthi, 1994—; prof. elec. engring. Technol.-Ednl. Inst. Kavala, Greece, 1995—; gen. mgr. Invest-Business Consultand, Xanthi, Greece, 1996-97. Contbr. articles to profl. jours. Non-commissioned officer, Technical Armed Forces, 1993-94, Xanthi. Mem. N.Y. Acad. Scis., U. Strathclyde-Development Office, Technical C. of C. Christian Orthodox. Avocations: football. swimming. Home: Ipeirou 30, 67100 Xanthi Greece Office: Invest-Consultand Co, Ipeirou 30, 67100 Xanthi Greece

BANTELMANN, KURT C., author; b. Berlin, Germany, May 5, 1925. MA, Mainz U., 1951. Internat. trade exec. Germany; founder, owner Import Agys., Venezuela; founder, CEO of chalk plant Venezuela; founder, dir. Bus. Acad., Venezuela; founder, CEO Internat. Translation Agy., Germany; dir. of mgmt. cons. Dusseldorf, Germany, 1996; ethics and globalisation cons. for govt. pub. and pvt. orgns. Author: Cosmosofy: The Religious-Political Revolution at the Turning Point of the 21st Century. Active in human rights issues; anti-militarist since 1945. Mem. German Translators' Assn. Avocations: philosophies of religion and law, modern langs. Office: Franklinstr 35, D-40479 Düsseldorf Germany

BANTRY, BRYAN, entrepreneur, producer, director; b. Jacksonville, Fla., Oct. 12, 1956. Owner, operator dog-walking svc., 1969-73; photographer's agt. Patrick Demarchelier, 1973—; owner Bryan Bantry Hair-Makeup Agy., N.Y.C., 1973—, Bryan Bantry Celebrity Model Mgmt., N.Y.C., 1992—; chmn., chief exec. officer Royal Atlantic Airways, N.Y.C., 1987—. Co-prodr. (Broadway plays) You Can't Take it With You, 1983, Aren't We All, 1985, (off-Broadway plays) Greater Tuna, 1982, Hey Ma...Kaye Ballard, 1984; creator TV pilot Man's Best Friend, 1983; prodr. (feature documentary) The Cream Will Rise: The Sophie B. Hawkins Story, 1998, (feature film) Ladies Who Do, 2001; theatre prodr. (Broadway musical) Street Corner

Symphony, 1997-98; prodr., co-dir. feature short film Eventual Wife, 1999. Chmn. Batoto Yetu inner-city youth program, N.Y.C., 1992—; bd. dirs. The Trevor Project, L.A. Mem. League of Am. Theatres and Prodrs.

BANTZIS, CONSTANTINE, pharmaceutical company executive; b. Patras, Greece, Nov. 25, 1951; s. Panayiotis and Aphrodite (Corfiatis) B.; m. Fani Pavlopoulou, Dec. 13, 1987; children: Antigone, Panayiotis. BSc, McGill U., Montreal, Que., Can., 1976, diploma in mgmt., 1977, MBA, 1978. Brand mgr. Cooper Labs., Montreal, 1978-79; rsch. dir. Hugh-Owens, Montreal, 1979-81; planning mgr. Ranx-Xerox, Athens, Greece, 1981-84; product mgr. Ciba-Geigy, Athens, 1984-86; mktg. dir. Bristol Myers Squibb, Athens, 1986-90; gen. mgr. Parke-Davis sect. Warner-Lambert, Athens, 1990-98, UCB Pharma A.E., 1998—. Pres. Hellenic Soc. of McGill U., 1975. Mem. Hellenic Mgmt. Inst. Home: 57 Agnoston Martyron St, 171 23 Nea Smyrni Athens Greece Office: VCB Pharyx AE, Voulisigurenis 580, 16452 Argiroupolis Greece

BANYAR, JOZSEF, economist; b. Asuanyraro, Hungary, Apr. 11, 1961; s. Jozsef and Jozsefne (Karoly) B. Diploma, Budapest U. of Economics, 1985, Doctorate, 1996. Prof. asst. dept. microeconomics Budapest U. Economics, 1985-89; head section State Insurance Co., Budapest, 1990-91; actuary Nationale-Nederlanden, Budapest, Hungary, 1991-93; mng. dir. OTP-Garancia Insurance Co., Budapest, 1993-96; dir. ABN-AMRO Insurance Co., Budapest, 1996-99; 1st asst. to prof. Budapest U. Economics/Insurance E&R Ctr., Budapest, 1999—. Author: (book) Bisics of Life Insurance, 1994, Basics of Insurance Mathematics, 1995, Life Insurance, 1997. Avocations: reading, music, running, tennis, horseback riding. Home: Tompa u 8, 1094 Budapest Hundary Office: BUE Insurance, Ksngues Kalman Inst, 1087 Budapest Hungary

BÁNYÁSZ, CSILLA, electrical engineer; b. Ujpest, Hungary, Feb. 10, 1946; d. István and Jolán (Horváth) B.; m. László Keviczky, July 3, 1970; children: Zoltán, Tamás. MSc, Tech. U., 1969; PhD, Hungarian Acad. of Scis., 1976. Rschr. Computer and Automation Inst., Budapest, 1969—. Contbr. articles to profl. jours. Recipient Frigyes Csaki medal Scientific Soc. for Measurement and Automation, 1994, Krusper medal, 1996. Mem. IEEE (sr.), Hungarian Acad. of Engring. Scis., N.Y. Acad. Scis. Avocations: reading, music, gardening. Office: Inst of Hungarian Acad Scis, Kende U 13-17, H-1111 Budapest Hungary

BANYASZ, TAMAS, physiology educator, researcher; b. Sajoszentpeter, Borsod, Hungary, Mar. 15, 1960; s. Vince Banyasz and Maria Darago; m. Erzsebet Papp, Aug. 6, 1988; children: Emese, Tamas. MD, U. Med. Sch. Debrecen, Hungary, 1984, PhD, 1996. Asst. lectr. dept. physiology U. Med. Sch. Debrecen, 1984-96, asst. prof., 1996—. Office: U Debrecen Med/Hlth Sci Ctr, PO Box 22, 4012 Debrecen Hungary

BÁNZER SUÁREZ, HUGO, president; b. Concepción, Bolivia, May 10, 1926. Degree, Army Mil. Sch., La Paz, Bolivia, Mil. Sch. Argentine Republic, Buenos Aires, Sch. Arms Instrn., Sch. of High Command of Bolivian Army, Armored Sch. of U.S.A., Sch. of Nat. Superior Studies of Bolivia. Mil. prof., chief high command, dep. comdr. divsn.; chief intelligence dept. Bolivian Army, comdr. mil. sch.; comdr.-in-chief Armed Forces of Bolivia; mil. attaché Embassy of Bolivia to U.S.; minister of edn. Govt. Bolivia, 1964-66; pres. Republic of Bolivia, 1971-78, 97—; amb. of Bolivia Argentine Republic, 1978-97. Founder, chmn. Nat. Dem. Action Party, Bolivia, 1979—, presdl. cand., 1980, 85, 89, 93, 97; pres. Polit. Coun. Patriotic Alliance, 1989. Recipient Gold medal Mayor's Office of Sucre, Bolivia, Gold medal Ret. Magistery, merit excellence medal, Guerrilleros Lanza medal, El Cóndor de los Andes award Govt. Bolivia, Army Mil. Merit medal, U.S.; decorated Govts. Argentina, Brazil, Colombia, Ecuador, Panama, Paraguay, Peru, Uruguay, Venezuela. Office: Palacio de Gobierno, Plz Murillo, La Paz Bolivia*

BANZHAF, WOLFGANG, computer science educator; b. Stuttgart, Germany, Sept. 17, 1955; s. Dieter and Ruth (Besserer) B.; married; three children. Diploma in physics, U. Munich, 1982; PhD in Physics, U. Karlsruhe, Germany, 1985. Rsch. asst. U. Stuttgart, 1985-89; vis. rschr. Ctrl. Rsch. Lab. Mitsubishi Electric, Amagasaki, Japan, 1989-92; sr. vis. rschr. Mitsubishi Electric, Cambridge, Mass., 1992-93; prof. computer sci. U. Dortmund, Germany, 1993—; vis. scholar Internat. Computer Sci. Inst., Berkeley, Calif., 1997, U. New South Wales, Australia, 1999; bd. dirs. Register Machine Learning, Inc., Informatik Centrum Dortmund. Author: Genetic Programming-An Introduction, 1998; editor: Evolution and Biocomputation, 1995, EURO GP '98, 1998, FOGA 6, 1998, Proceedings Genetic Programming Conference, 1998, 1st Internat. GECCO Conf., 1999, 3rd Euro GP '2000; patentee in field; editor in chief Jour. Genetic Programming and Evolvable Machines. Roman Catholic. Office: LS XI FB Informatik, U Dortmund, 44221 Dortmund Germany

BAO, KATHERINE SUNG, pediatric cardiologist; b. Soochou, Kiangsu, China, Sept. 7, 1920; came to U.S., 1953; d. Yung H. Bao and Ming King; m. William S. Ting, May 2, 1948; children: Gordon K., Albert C. MD, Nat. Ctrl. Univ. Med. Coll., Nanking, China, 1944. Diplomate Am. Bd. Pediatrics. Intern Mercer Hosp., Trenton, N.J., 1953; resident Children's Meml. Hosp. Northwestern U., Chgo., 1954-57; fellow in pediatric cardiology Children's Hosp. L.A., Calif., 1957-59; attending cardiologist Children's Hosp. L.A., Calif., 1960—; chief pediatric cardiology City of Hope Med. Ctr., Duarte, Calif., 1965-68; chief heart bd. L.A. Unified Sch. Dist. and PTA Specialty Health Clinics, L.A., 1968—; attending pediatrician, cardiologist Hollywood Presbyn. Med. Ctr., L.A., 1970—, UCLA, L.A., 1973—; vis. pediatric cardiologist to univs. in Taipei Nat. Sci. Coun., Republic of China, 1983; pres.'s appointee Pres.'s Com. on Nat. Medal of Sci., 1983-85; adv. com. on health and med. care svcs. Dept. Health Svcs., Calif., 1988-90; pres. Chinese Physicians Soc. of So. Calif., 1969; speaker in field. Active Rep. Eagle, Rep. Presdl. Task Force, Rep. Presdl. Round Table. Rsch. Fellow Cardiologist, NIH, 1960-63; recipient Physician of Yr., Hon. Svc. award Calif. Congress of PTA, Inc., 1984, U.S. Rep. Senatorial Medal of Freedom, 1994. Fellow Am. Acad. Pediatrics; mem. AMA, AAAS, World Med. Assn., Calif. Med. Assn., L.A. County Med. Assn., Am. Heart Assn., Internat. Cir. of L.A. World Affairs Coun., N.Y. Acad. Scis., Hollywood Acad. Medicine (pres. 1995), Scripps Clinic La Jolla (coun.). Office: PO Box 10456 Beverly Hills CA 90213-3456

BAO, YIWANG, engineering researcher; b. Nanchan, Jiangxi, China, Apr. 28, 1957; s. Zhiyuan Bao and Chun-er Ding; m. Li Sun; 1 child, Mingxi. B, Wuhan (China) U. Tech., 1982, M, 1985; D, China Bldg. Materials Acad., Beijing, 1990. Lectr. Wuhan U. Grad. Sch., Beijing, 1985-88; rsch. engr. China Bldg. Materials Acad., Beijing, 1989-95, prof., rschr., 1997—; postdoctoral rschr. Jülich (Germany) Rsch. Ctr., 1995-97. Author: Numerical Method for Thin Shells, 1986, Characterization of Mechanical Properties for Brittle Materials and Ceramics, 1996, Handbook of Advanced Ceramics, 1995; contbr. over 70 articles to profl. publs. Recipient 2d prize for sci. and tech. Ministry of Bldg. Materials, Beijing, 1993, 96, 1st prize for sci. and tech., 1994, 2d prize for sci. progress China Sci. Com., Beijing, 1995. Mem. Materials Rsch. Soc. China, A.v. Humboldt Club. Avocations: chess, fishing, stamp collecting, cooking. Office: China Bldg Materials Acad, Guanzhuang, Beijing 100024, China

BAO, ZHUOJUN, software engineer; b. Huhhot (Inner Mongolia), China, Jan. 19, 1961; s. Nimaaoser Bao and Yulan Zhou; m. Xiaomei Wang, Nov. 21, 1997; 1 child, Kaixi-Kathy. B Engring., Nanjing (China) U. Sci. & Tech, 1982; diploma in engring., U. Karlsruhe, Germany, 1990, PhD in Engring., 2000. Asst. Nanjing U. Sci. and Tech., 1982-86; sci. rschr. U. Karlsruhe, 1990-96; product devel. engr. SDRC, Munich, 1996—; rschr. in field. Author: Computer Aided Collision Detection on the Basis of a B-rep/Polytree/CSG Hybrid Model, 2000; contbr. articles to profl. jours. Mem. Soc. German Engrs. Avocations: classical music, sports, biographic literature. Office: SDRC Product Devel, Richard-Reitzner-Allee 4, 85540 Munich Germany

BAPTISTA, LUIZ OLAVO, lawyer, educator; b. Itu, Brazil, July 24, 1938; s. Luiz and Irma (Quagliato) B.; m. Marta Rossetti, Mar. 27, 1967; 1 child, Humberto Rossetti Baptista. LLB, Cath. U. São Paolo, Brazil, 1964; postgrad., U. São Paolo, 1970-71, Parkes Sch. Internat. Law, summer 1973; LLD, Paris U., 1975. Ct. clk. Tribunal de Alçada de São Paulo, 1958-64; ptnr. L.O. Baptista, Assocs., São Paolo, 1964; prof. law Fundação Getulio Vargas, São Paulo, 1977-80, Cath. U. Sã Paulo, 1976-80; prof. law U. São Paulo, 1994—, head internat. law dept., 1994-98; vis. prof. Mich. State U., 1979-80, Paris U., 1997-99, Paris I U., 1999—; cons. Ctr. Transnat. Corps.-UN, Angola, Niger, 1983-87; fgn. cons. Unidroit, Rome, 1977—; mem. Permanent Ct. Arbitration, The Hague; arbiter Mercosul. Author: Commercial Laws of the World, Brazil Chapter, 1989, 96, Les Joint Ventures das les Relations Internationales, 2d edit., 1996, Contratos Internacionais, 1994, Arbitragem Comercial e Internacional, 1989. Sec. to min. edn. Govt. of Brazil, 1963; mem. bd. elections City of São Paolo, 1970-73. Recipient Anchieta medal City of São Paolo, 1980; named great officer Order of Rio Branco, Ministry of Fgn. Rels., 1991. Mem. Am. Soc. Internat. Law, Internat. ABA, Internat. Arbitration Ct., World Assn. Lawyers, Soc. Legal Comparée, São Paolo Lawyer Assn. E-mail: lob@baptista.com.br. Office: LO Baptista Assocs, 1294 Ave Paulista 8th Fl, 01310915 São Paulo Brazil

BAPTISTA, WILSON, JR., management consultant, educator, management simulation developer; b. Belo Horizonte, Minas Gerais, Brazil, June 21, 1945; s. Wilson Baptista and Hortensia (Teixeira de Lima) B.; m. Ana Maria Lopes da Silva Nunes, Feb. 8, 1971; children: Manuel and Pedro Nunes Baptista (twins). BSc in Acctg., Pontifícia Universidade Católica Minas Gerais, Belo Horizonte, Brazil, 1978, BSc in Econs., Bus. Adminstrn., 1979; cert. in bus. adminstrn., Conselho regional Admistracão Minas Gerais, 1981. Computer programmer various cos., Belo Horizonte, 1969-72; systems analyst Grupo Banco Co. Industries M.G., Belo Horizonte, 1972-74; systems analyst, project team leader Engedata S.A., Belo Horizonte, 1974-75; EDP mgr., project cons. RR Projetos e Consultoria Ltda., Belo Horizonte, 1975-78, Leme Engenharia, Belo Horizonte, 1979-82; planning and info. sys. asst. to CEO Companhia Indsl. Belo Horizonte, 1982-90; mng. ptnr., dir. tech. Soluções Empresariais Consultoria e Negócios, Belo Horizonte, 1990—; mng. ptnr. Futuro Consultoria, Belo Horizonte, 2000—; cons. Instituto Recursos Hidraulicos y Electrificación, Panama City, Panama, 1993, 94, Administración Nacional Electricidad, Paraguay, 1994, 95; tech. coordinator info. program Postgrad. Studies Ctr., Faculty Adminstrn. Champagnat, Belo Horizonte, 1983; planning and coordination supt. dir. state of sec. justice Minas Gerais, Belo Horizonte, 1991, 92; mem. info. sys. and automation com. Associação Comercial Minas Gerais, Belo Horizonte, 1988, 90, bus. coun. svcs. sector, 1991; mem. adv. bd. Ctr. Managerial Devel. and Bus. Simulation Coll. Bus. Adminstrn. Ga. So. U., 1997—. Author: An Introduction to Cobol, 1972; co-author (mgmt. simulation software) SIMINDUS, 1993, SIMSERVI, 1996, SIMNET, 1997, SIMMALL, 1997, SIMNERGY, 1997, SIMCARD, 1998, SIMMULT, 1998, SIMDIST, 1999, SIMSORV, 1999, SIMAGRO, 1999, SIMFREE, 2000. Mem. Soc. Brazilian Planners (bd. dirs.), Assn. Brazilian Adminstrs., Assn. Comercial de Minas Gerais (commn. for the mfg. industry 1989—, commn. for info. processing and automation 1988—), Soc. Computer Simulation Internat., Assn. Bus. Simulation and Exptl. Lng., Internat. Simulation and Gaming Assn., Instituto Estratégia e Prospectiva (founding mem.), Sociedade brasileira Planejamento Empresarial (reg. dir. 1987, 88, 93, 95), World Assn. Case Method Rsch. and Application, charter mem. and fellow World Assn. Bus. Simulation and Active Learning. Roman Catholic. Club: Mineiro dos Cacadores. Avocations: photography, cycling, target shooting. Home: Rua Pium i 312 #303 A, 30310 080 Belo Horizonte Minas Gerais, Brazil Office: Soluções Empresariais Consultoria, Rua Tomé de Souza 860/707, 30140 131 Belo Horizonte Minas Gerais, Brazil

BAPTISTE-AHMED, LINDA, social services professional; b. New Orleans, Sept. 11, 1951; d. Adrian J., Sr. and Helen Tillis; m. El Khair E. Ahmed, Oct. 17, 1993; children: Dionne, Michha. BS, Calif. State U., Sacramento, 1985, MS, 1987; PhD, Okla. State U., 1991. Assoc. clin. social worker. Family builder's specialist Edwin Fair Cmty. Mental Health Clinic, Ponca City, Okla., 1988-91; asst. coord. Okla. State U. Clearing House for Rehab. Tng. Materials, Stillwater, 1987-88; exec. dir./adminstr. Kair In-Home Social Svcs., Inc., Oakland, Calif., 1994—; case mgr. Alameda County Behavioral Care Agy., Oakland, 1995—; cons. Kair In-Home Social Svcs., Inc., Oakland, 1994—; social worker Kids of the Kingdom, Sacramento, 1992-95; presenter in field. Grad. student intern Payne County Commr. Office, Stillwater, 1989-90, Congressman Ronald V. Dellums, Oakland, 1986-87; activist Niagara Movement, Oakland, 1986. Mem. Lions, Omega Phi. Democrat. Muslim. Avocation: reading. Office: Alameda County Behav Hlth 10700 Macarthur Blvd Ste 15 Oakland CA 94605-5260

BAQI, MUHAMMAD ABDUL, education educator; b. Comilla, Chittagong, Bangladesh, Jan. 1, 1953; s. Muhammad Abdul Hamid and Ayesha Begum; m. Jahanara Begum, Jan. 1, 1968; children: Fatima Uddin Muhammad Muslah. SSC, Dhampti Alia, Comilla, Bangladesh, 1968, Kamil, 1970; HSC, Jogonath Coll., Dhaka, Bangladesh, 1972; BA with honors, Dhaka U., 1974, MA, 1975, PhD, 1993. Lectr. Mirpur Girls Coll., Dhaka, 1978-81; lectr. Dhaka U., 1981-86, asst. prof., 1989-92, assoc. prof., 1992-99, prof., 1999—; house tutor and provost Salimullah Hall, Dhaka, 1984-95; libr.-in-charge Islamic studies Dhaka U., 1983-88. Contbr. articles to profl. jours. Recipient Nurun Nesa Biddh Bindini award Dhaka U., 1974. Mem. Asiatic Soc. of Bengal, Bangladesh Itihas Parisad, Bangladesh Islamic Studies Assn. Muslim. Avocations: singing, travel, stamp collecting. Office: Islamic Studies Dept, Dhaka Univ, Dhaka Bangladesh

BAQUER, NAJMA ZAHEER, biochemistry, educator; b. Ajmer, Rajasthan, India, Aug. 11, 1940; d. Sajjad and Razia Sajjad (Dilshad) Zaheer; m. Ali Baquer, Mar. 1, 1968; one child. BSc, Muslim U., Aligarh, India, 1960; MSc, Lucknow (India) U., 1962, PhD, 1966, DSc, 1996. Sr. rsch. fellow Lucknow U., 1966-67; rsch. assoc. Middlesex Hosp., London, 1968-75; assoc. prof. Jawaharlal Nehru U., New Delhi, 1975-84, prof., 1984—, dean Sch. Life Scis., 1995-97. Contbr. articles to profl. jours. Homi Bhabha fellow, Bombay, 1980-82. Fellow Royal Acad. Pharmacy Spain; mem. Internat. Soc. Neurochem., Biochem. Soc., Internat. Diabetes Fedn., Soc. Biol. Chemists India (life), Assn. Clin. Biochemists (life), Nat. Acad. Scis. (Allahabad). Islam. Avocations: reading modern writers, music, cooking, theatre, television. Fax: (011) 616-5886. E-mail: nzbaquer@hotmail.com. Office: Sch Life Sci, Jawaharlal Nehru U, New Delhi 110067, India

BAQUERO-PARRA, RAFAEL, physicist, researcher; b. Santa Fe de Bogota, Colombia, Oct. 7, 1940; s. Rafael Baquero-Herrera and Graciela (Parra) B.; m. Llibuse Salaquardova, Feb. 26, 1965; children: Rafael, Alexander. MSc, CINVESTAV, Mexico City, 1970, PhD in Physics, 1976. Asst. prof. U. Puebla, Mex., 1973-78, assoc. prof., 1979-81, prof. physics, 1982-90; prof. physics Ctr. Rsch. and Advanced Studies, 1990—, acad. coord., 1994-96. Recipient Disting. Scientist award Mare of Puebla, 1991, Disting. Citizen award Municipality of Puebla, 1990, City of Puebla medal, 1990. Mem. Mex. Phys. Soc. (v.p. 1992-94). Avocations: music, painting, literature. Office: CINESTAV Dept Physics, Ave IPN 2508, 07300 Mexico City Mexico

BARA, BRUNO GIUSEPPE, psychology educator; b. Milan, Feb. 28, 1949; s. Adone Bara and Grazia Pirrone; m. Marcella Pellicanò, Apr. 23, 1983; children: Giulio, Simona, Elena. MD, U. Milan, 1973, PhD in Psychology, 1976. Assoc. prof. psychology U. Milan, 1977-85; prof. U. Florence, Italy, 1986-90; prof. psychology of comm. U. Torino, Italy, 1991—, dir. Ctr. Cognitive Sci., 1993—, dir. Sch. Cognitive Psychotherapy, 1994—; vis. rschr. Applied Psychology Unit-Med. Rsch. Coun., Cambridge, U.K., 1985-95; sr. rschr. U. Calif., Berkeley, 1997—. Author: Cognitive Science, 1995; editor: Computational Models of Natural Language Processing, 1984, Handbook of Cognitive Psychotherapy, 1996. Lt. Italian mil., 1975-76. Grantee European Sci. Found., 1979, 80. Mem. European Soc. Cognitive Psychology, Internat. Pragmatics Assn., Cognitive Sci. Soc. Avocations: poker, opera. Home: 13 Via del Caravaggio, 20144 Milan Italy Office: Ctr Cognitive Sci, 3 Via Lagrange, 10123 Torino Italy

BARABÁS, MIKLÓS, physicist, researcher; b. Budapest, Hungary, Apr. 3, 1953; s. István and Éva (Friedländer) B. MS, U. Roland Eötvös, Budapest, 1977, Dr. Univ., 1987, PhD, 1995. Asst. rschr. Computer and Automation Inst., Hungarian Acad. Scis., Budapest, 1977-79, rschr., 1979-93; rschr. Tech. U., Budapest, 1983-90, cons., 1990-97; examiner Hungarian Patent Office, Budapest, 1997—; lectr. Tech. U., Budapest. Contbr. articles to profl. jours. including Optical Comm., Applied Optics, others. Mem. SPIE, Optical Soc. Am., Eötvös Phys. Soc. Home: Ponty u 14, H 1011 Budapest Hungary Office: Hungarian Patent Office, Garibaldi U 2, H-1054 Budapest Hungary

BARABASH, ALEXANDER STEPANOVICH, physicist; b. Dalnii, China, 1952; s. Stepan Grigorievich and Polina Stepanovna Barabash; m. Tamara Alexandrovna Mironova, Apr. 2, 1950; children: Nataliya, Anastasiya. M in Engring. and Physics, Moscow Phys. Inst., 1975, D in Physics and Math., 1983. Engr. Inst. Nuc. Rsch., Moscow, 1975-76, rschr., 1977-85; rschr. Inst. Theoretical and Exptl. Physics, Moscow, 1986-91, leading rschr., 1991-97, head of lab., 1997—. Author: Liquid Ionization Detectors, 1993; contbr. articles to profl. jours. Recipient Silver medal for scientific rsch., Moscow, 1978. Avocation: sports. Home: Troitsk, 142092 Moscow Russia Office: Inst Theor and Exptl Phys, B Cheremushkinskaya 25, 117259 Moscow Russia

BARAC, BOSKO ANTUN, neurologist, educator; b. Zagreb, Croatia, Sept. 11, 1930; s. Antun Mate and Nevenka Mihovil Barac; m. Dragica B. Sokacic, Sept. 21, 1963; children: Iva, Ana, Mirna. MD, U. Zagreb, 1956, Dr. Med. Sc., 1965. Neuropsychiatrist Hosp. Vinogradska Str., Zagreb, 1959-62; clin. asst. dept. neurology Med. Faculty U. Zagreb, 1965-68, asst. prof. neurology, 1968-75, leader postgrad. study in neurology, 1972-84, assoc. prof., 1975-77, prof., 1977-95, founder, 1st head neurol. ICU, 1970-79, chief neurology, 1979-87; prof. neurology, head dept. neurology Osijek U. Sch. Medicine, 1995—; organizer symposia on cerebrovascular disease, 1971, 74, 79, 85, 89; trustee Internat. Neuropsychiat. Symposia, Pula, Croatia, 1974—, sec.-gen. 1985—; v.p. Assembly for Sci. Work Croatia, Zagreb, 1982, pres., 1985-87; chmn. rsch. group on orgn. of neurology World Fedn. Neurology, 1985—, mem. rsch. group on neurology edn. Author: Neurology, 1978, 79, Fundamentals of Neurology, 1979, Neurology, 1989, 2d rev. edit., 1992; editor: Neurology in Developing Countries, 1991; pres. editorial bd. Neurologija, Zagreb; contbr. over 250 articles to profl. jours. Dep. Parliament Croatia, 1978-82. Fellow Intensive Care Soc. of Brit. Med. Assn.; mem. Assn. Neurology and Psychiatry Yugoslavia (sec. gen. 1965-68), Yugoslav Neurol. Assn. (trustee 1984-91), Croatian Neurol. Soc. (pres. 1979-88), Soc. E.E.G. and Clin. Neurophysiology Croatia (pres. 1972-81), Croatian Med. Acad. Zagreb, N.Y. Acad. Scis., Am. Acad. Neurology (hon. corr.), Am. Neurol. Assn., World Fedn. Neurology (Yugoslav del. 1984-91), World Fedn. Neurology (mem. rsch. coun.), South-East European Soc. for Neurology and Psychiatry, Rsch. Group for Orgn. and Delivery of Neurol. Svcs. Office: University Hospital Neurology, J Huttlera 4, 31.000 Osijek Croatia

BARACHEVSKY, VALERY ALEXANDER, physicist researcher; b. Emezk, Russia, Dec. 17, 1937; s. Alexander Michail and Augusta Ivanov (Udal'stova) B.; m. Ludmila Gavriil Ioiyleva, Nov. 1, 1959; 1 child, Kuzina Nataly. MD, St. Petersburg (Russia) U., 1960, PhD, 1965. Rsch. scientist Dye Inst., Moscow, 1963-67, head lab., 1967-69, head dept., 1969-89; rsch. scientist Inst. Chem. Physics Russian Acad. Scis., Moscow, 1989-96; rsch. scientist Photochemistry Ctr. of Russian Acad. Scis., Moscow, 1997—. Author: (book) Photochromism and Its Application, 1977; editor: (book) Nonsilver and Unusual Media for Holography, 1978, New Recording Media for Holography, 1982, Properties of Light-Sensitive Materials and Their Applications in Holography, 1987; author: (book) Polymers in Optics: Physics, Chemistry and Application, 1996; assoc. editor: Scientific and Applied Photography; editor: Optical Memory and Neural Networks; contbr. articles to profl. jours. Mem. Russian Sci. Coun. on Holography, Sci. Coun. on Optical Memory, Sci. Coun. on Recording of Optical Info., Internat. Soc. Optical Engring., Soc. Imaging Sci. and Tech. Avocations: recreational activities with dogs. Fax: (095) 936-12-55. E-mail: barva@photonics.ru. Home: 13/19-1-12 Gorodetskaya Str, 111672 Moscow Russia Office: Russian Acad Scis, 7a Novatorov Str, 117421 Moscow Russia

BARACZKA, KRISZTINA, neurologist; b. Budapest, Hungary, Sept. 20, 1949; d. Istvan and Eva (Kosztolanyi) B.; m. Laszlo Szegedy, Apr. 3, 1981. MD, I Med. U., Moscow, 1975; PhD, Hungarian Acad. Scis., 1994. Diplomate in neurology, psychiatry and labor medicine. Asst. prof. Clinic of Psychiatry, Budapest, 1975-79, rschr., 1980-89; rsch. pharmacologist Med. U., Vienna, 1979; cons. neurologist II Clinic of Internal Medicine, Budapest, 1989—; chief dept. neuroimmunology Nat. Inst. Rheumatology, Budapest, 1991—. Contbr. articles to profl. jours. Mem. Hungarian Soc. Neurology, Hungarian Soc. Rheumatology, N.Y. Acad. Scis. E-mail: apiutacsi@ruol.liu. Office: Nat Inst Rheumatism/Physiology, Frankel Leo ut 38-40, H-1525 Budapest Hungary

BARAD, MIRYAM, quality assurance and management professional; b. Bucharest, Romania; arrived in Israel, 1950; d. Morris and Leah (Grunberg) Weinberg; 1 child, Liat. BSc in Chem. Engring., Technion, Haifa, Israel, MSc in Indsl. and Mgmt. Engring., DSc in Indsl. and Mgmt. Engring., 1970. Plant engr. Vulcan Battery Works, Haifa; asst. instr. Technion, Haifa; lectr. Ben Gurion U., Beer Sheba, Israel; sr. lectr. Tel Aviv U., 1979-87, head indsl. engring. dept., 1987-91, 2000—, assoc. prof., 1996—; vis. assoc. prof. U. Iowa, Iowa City, 1984-85, U. Sci. and Tech. China, Hefei, 1991-92, U. NSW, Sydney, Australia, 1992-94; vis. rsch. scholar Purdue U., West Lafayette, Ind., 1994. Contbr. articles to profl. jours. Mem. Ops. Rsch. Soc. Am., Inst. Indsl. Engrs., Internat. Found. Prodn. Rsch. (internat. coun. mem.), N.Y. Acad. Scis. Avocations: hiking, swimming, classical music, jazz. Office: Tel Aviv U, Dept Indsl Engring, Tel Aviv Israel

BA-RADHWAN, ABDULRAHMAN BIN AL-SHEIK ABDULLAH, government official; b. Makkah, Saudi Arabia, Nov. 11, 1951; s. Al-Sheik Abdullah bin Mohammed and Rugaya bint Al-Sheik Abdulrahman (Ba-Harath) Ba-R.; m. Anita Kathleen Heaton, June 3, 1981; 1 child, Sara. BS in Econs., Southeastern Okla. State U., 1985, MS in Tech., 1990. Analyst, programmer King Khalid Nat. Guard Hosp., Jeddah, 1982-83; sr. data contr. Royal Commn./Arabian Bechtel Co., Al-Jubail, 1986-88; assets control section mgr. Royal Commn./Jubail Project, Al-Jubail, 1990—. Avocations: reading, computers, tennis, nature enthusiast.

BARAHONA DE BRITO, ALEXANDRA, political scientist; b. Lisbon, Portugal, Nov. 1, 1965; d. Carlos Barahona de Brito and Helen Terry (Browne) Geary. BA, Manchester U., 1988; MPhil, Oxford U., 1990, DPhil, 1993. Asst. rschr. Coun. Hemispheric Affairs, Washington, 1986; rschr. Leverhulme Found. Project, Buenos Aires, 1993; rschr., program coord. Inst. Strategic & Internat. Studies, Lisbon, 1993-96; rschr. Inst. European-Latin Am. Rels., Madrid, 1996-98; vis. fellow Princeton (N.J.) U., 1999—; cons. European Parliament, Brussels, 1998-99,. Author: Human Rights and Democratization in Latin America, 1997; editor: Transitional Truth and Justice, 2000; editor Open Integration newsletter, 1996-99; editl. bd. Jour. Interam. Studies & World Affairs, 1998—, Politica Internacional, 1998—; contbr. articles to profl. jours. Avocations: sports, travel, creative writing, film, painting.

BARAK, AHARON, judicial administrator; b. Lithuania, 1936; married; 4 children. ML, Hebrew U. Jerusalem, 1958, PhD, 1963. Assoc. prof. law Hebrew U. Jerusalem, 1968, appt. prof. Sch. Law, 1972, appt. dean faculty law, 1974; with UN Commn. Internat. Trade Law, 1970-72; atty. gen. Govt. of Israel, Jerusalem, 1975-78, appt. justice supreme ct., 1978, appt. dep. pres. supreme ct., 1993, pres. Supreme Ct., 1995—; lectr. Sch. Law NYU, 1970-72; adj. prof. Sch. Law Hebrew U. Jerusalem, 1978-94. Recipient Kaplan prize for excellence in sci. and rsch., 1973. Mem. Israeli Acad. Scis. Office: Supreme Ct Israel, Shaarei Mishpat St Kiryat, Ben Gurion Jerusalem 91950, Israel

BARAK, AZY, psychologist, educator; b. Petach-Tikva, Israel, Apr. 15, 1947. BA, Tel-Aviv U., 1971, MA, 1973; PhD, Ohio State U., 1976. Lic. expert psychologist, Israel. Prof. Tel-Aviv U., 1976-94, U. Western Ont., London, Can., 1993-97; prof. psychology U. Haifa, Israel, 1997—. E-mail: azy@construct.haifa.ac.il. Office: U Haifa, Mount Carmel, Haifa Israel 31905

BARAK, EHUD, prime minister of Israel; b. Kibbutz Mishmar-Hasharon, Israel, Feb. 12, 1942; m. Nava Barak; 3 daus. BSc in Physics and Math., Hebrew U., Jerusalem, 1968; MSc in Econ.-Engring. Sys., Stanford (Calif.) U., 1978. Rose through ranks to lt. gen., chief gen. staff Israel Def. Forces, 1959-94, head gen. qtrs., 1982, comdr. ctrl. command, 1986, dep. chief gen. staff, 1987, chief gen. staff, 1991; ret., 1995; min. interior Govt. of Israel,

1995, min. fgn. affairs, 1995-96; chmn. Israeli Labor Party, 1997—; prime minister of Israel, 1999—, min. def.; served in 6 Days and Yom Kippur wars; various command roles, including comdr. Tank Comdr.'s Course, 1974, comdr. Batallion Comdr.'s Course, 1980; head gen. staff planning dept., 1982-83; dir. mil. intelligence, Israeli Def. Forces, 1983-86; comdr. Cent. Command, 1986-87; dep. chief gen. staff, 1987-91. Decorated Itur Mofet medal for disting. and outstanding svc. and action award, additional citations, Israeli Def. Forces. Avocations: playing piano, singing. Office: Office of Prime Minister, 3 Kaplan St, Hakirya Kiryat Ben-Gurion 91919, Israel

BARAKAT, ELHAJ ELHUSSIEN, electrical engineer; b. Khartoum, Sudan, Jan. 1, 1942; s. Elhussien Mohmed and Amna Abdulah (Ahmed) B.; m. Samia Abdul Rahman Mohmed; 4 children. BSc with honors, Lanchester Poly., Rugby, U.K., 1972; MSc, U. Manchester, Eng., 1975; PhD, Brunel U., London, 1978. Lectr. Khartoum Poly., 1967-68; rsch. fellow Brunel U., London, 1976-78; design engr. Riyadh Elec. Co., Saudi Arabia, 1980-82; sr. engr. Saudi Consol. Elec. Co., Riyadh, 1983-94, sr. expert, 1994—. Contbr. articles to profl. jours. Recipient Best Applied Rsch. award GCC-Cigre, State of Qatar, 1992. Avocations: tennis, car racing, football. Home: PO Box 1429, Khartoum Sudan Office: SCECo(C), PO Box 57, Riyadh 11411, Saudi Arabia

BARAKAT, KHALED JAMIL, chemist, researcher; b. Jerusalem, Aug. 15, 1957; came to U.S., 1982; s. Jamil Ali and Fatmeh Hamdan B.; m. Nimeh Atweh, Jan. 2, 1994; children: Worood, Warrad, Sabrina. BS, Jordan U., Amman, 1981; MS, Fairleigh Dickinson U., 1985; PhD, Stevens Inst. Tech., 1992. Scientist Merck & Co. Inc., Rahway, N.J., 1991—. Patentee in field. Home: 188 29th St Brooklyn NY 11232-1704

BARAKAT, MAHMOUD FOAD, nuclear, radiation, chemistry educator, researcher; b. Cairo, Sept. 28, 1936; s. Foad Ahmed Barakat and Fatma Mahmoud Ibrahim; m. Mervat Mohamed El-Baroudy; children: Manal, Wael. BSc in Chem. Scis., Cairo U., 1956; PhD in Radio and Nuclear Chemistry, Moscow State U., 1963. Rsch. asst. Faculty of Scis. Alexandria U., Egypt, 1957-58; asst. prof. nuclear chemistry Atomic Energy Authority, Cairo, 1963-70, assoc. prof., 1963-70, prof., 1977—; vis. prof. Alexandria U., Tanta U., Ain Shams U., Helwan U., Egypt, 1977-88; dir. Midddle Ea. Reg. Radioisotope Ctr., Cairo, 1986-90; chmn. Nat. Ctr. Nuclear Safety and Radiation Ctrl., Cairo, 1990-93; dir. gen. Arab Atomic Energy Agy., League of Arab States, Tunis, Tunisia, 1993-2001. Recipient chem. scis. state prize Acad. Sci. Rsch. and Tech., Cairo, 1970, scis. and arts decoration 1st degree Egypt, 1972. Mem. Internat. Catomic Soc., Nat. Geog. Soc. Avocations: geography, electronics, classical music, swimming. Office: Arab Atomic Energy Agy, PO Box 402, 1004 El Manzah Tunis Tunisia Home: 11 Mohamed Shafit St, Heliopolis, Cairo Egypt

BARAK-EREZ, DAPHNE, law educator; b. Boston, Jan. 2, 1965; arrived in Israel, 1966; d. Elazar Berkman and Judith (Toporek) Barak; m. Chen Erez, Sept. 19, 1991; children: Eran, Yuval. LLB summa cum laude, Tel Aviv U., 1987, LLM summa cum laude, 1989, JSD, 1992. Bar: Israel. Lectr. Law Sch. Tel Aviv U., 1992-97, sr. lectr., 1997—, dep. commr. disciplinary matters, 1996-2000; dep. dean Tel Aviv U. Law Sch., 2000—; vis. rschr. Harvard Law Sch., 1993-94; chair Coun. Adminstrv. Tribunals, Ministry of Justice, Israel, 1998-2000; commr. disciplinary matters, 2000—; dir. Minerva Ctr. Human Rights, 2000—, vice dean, 2000—. Author: Contractual Liability of Public Authorities, 1990, Constitutional Torts, 1993; editor: A Jewish and Democratic State, 1996, First Judgments, 1999; contbr. articles to profl. jours. Maj. Israeli Def. Forces, 1989-90. Colton fellow Tel Aviv U., 1990-91. Mem. Israel Bar Assn., Law and Soc. Assn., Internat. Assn. Constitutional Law, Israel Soc. Pub. Law. Jewish. Home: 36 Harav Amiel St, 62263 Tel Aviv Israel Office: Tel Aviv U, Law Sch, Tel Aviv Israel

BARAKET, EDMUND S., JR., general contractor, contracting consultant; b. N.Y.C., Oct. 10, 1947; s. Edmund S. and Agnes B.; AA Lehigh County C.C., 1970; BA Pa. State U., 1974; m. Maryann; children: Christopher, Melissa, Joseph, Susan. Insp. metall. layout Bethlehem Steel Corp., 1967-69, mem. research and devel. staff, 1970-73; owner, mgr. Baraket Constrn. Co., Allentown, Pa., 1973—. Recipient award for restoration of early colonial family residences Keystone Publs., 1978. Mem. Gen. Contractors Assn. Lehigh Valley, Concrete Contractors Assn., Am. Soc. Concrete Constrn. Office: Ed Baraket Gen Contractors 1322 Tweed Ave Allentown PA 18103-4265

BARAKZAI, MYHAMMED NAEEM, engineering executive; b. Mirpurkhas, Pakistan, Aug. 19, 1951; s. Abdul Ghaffar and Gulshan Ara (Begum) B.; m. Rehana Naeem Noor Barabzai, May 21, 1981; children: Parisa Naeem, Umer, Nida, Gulshan Ara, Mohammad Azam. BE in Mechanical Engrng., U. Sindh, Pakistan, 1974. Section officer Irrigation and Power Dept., Karachi, Pakistan, 1977-81; exec. engr. Guddu mech. divsn. Irrigation and Power Dept., Sukkur, Pakistan, 1981-89; exec. engr. Irrigation and Power Dept., Khairpur, Pakistan, 1989-93, Sakrand, Pakistan, 1993-98; exec. engr. Hala Tubewell divsn. Irrigation and Power Dept., Hyderabad, Pakistan, 1999—. Mem. Hyderabad Gymkhana. Avocations: reading technical books, watching TV, construction work. Home: No 296, Doctors Colony Hirabad, Hyderabad Pakistan Office: Irrigation & Power Dept, Govt of Pakistan, Sindh, Sindh Karachi Pakistan

BARALE, VITTORIO, oceanographer, researcher; b. Vercelli, Italy, Jan. 17, 1954; s. Ettore and Enide (Picco) B.; m. Marilena Denti Barale, Sept. 16, 1979; children: Andrea, Luca. MS in Oceanography, U. Calif., San Diego, 1982, PhD in Oceanography, 1986. Rsch. fellow U. Statale di Milano, Milan, Italy, 1978-79; rsch asst. Scripps Inst. Oceanography, San Diego, 1979-86; sci. cons. pvt. practice, Milan, Italy, 1986-90; sr. scientist Joint Rsch. Ctr. of European Commn., Ispra, Italy, 1990—; vis. scientist Mass. Inst. Tech., Boston, 1984, NASA, Goddard Space Flight Ctr., Washington, 1985. Author: Mare, 1990; editor: Ocean Colour: Theory and Applications in a Decade of CZCS, 1993; contbr. articles to profl. jours. Mem. Am. Geophys. Union, Commn. Internat. Scientific Mediterranean Exploration, TETHYS Rsch. Inst., Europe Conservation. Roman Catholic. Avocations: popular science, farming, horse riding. E-mail: vittorio.barale@jrc.it. Fax: 39 0332 789034. Office: Joint Rsch Ctr Europe Commn, Via Enrico Fermi 1, 21020 Ispra Italy

BARAN, ENRIQUE JOSÉ, inorganic chemist; b. Olavarria, B.A., Argentina, July 10, 1940; s. José and Anna (Windisch) B.; m. Claudia Antonia Marcon, Jan. 26, 1973; children: Gabriela Patricia, Verónica. Lic. en Quimica, Nat. U. La Plata, Argentina, 1964, D in Chemistry, 1967. Asst. Nat. U. La Plata, 1960-67, adj. prof., 1970-80, assoc. prof., 1980, prof. inorganic chemistry, 1981—; investigador superior Nat. Rsch. Coun., 1993; cons. in field. Author: Química Bio-Inorgánica, 1984, 95; contbr. over 500 articles to profl. jours. Recipient Konex de Platino award Konex Found., 1993, H.J. Schumacher award Nat. Acad. Scis., 1993; Alexander V. Humboldt Found. fellow, 1968-70, 74, TWAS awrd in chemistry, 1996. Mem. Chem. Soc. Argentina, Argentina Soc. Phys. Chem. Rsch. (founder), Internat. Assn. Bioinorganic Scientists, Nat. Acad. Scis. (Argentina), Third World Acad. Sci. Roman Catholic. Office: Nat U La Plata Fac Ciencias, Calle 47 Esq 115, 1900 La Plata Argentina

BARAN, LUBOMIR WLODZIMIERZ, engineering educator; b. Zniatyn, Poland, Sept. 27, 1937; s. Teodor and Maria (Bazarko) B.; m. Maria Gabryela Jankowska, Sept. 27, 1970; children: Anna, Miroslawa. MS, Warsaw Tech. U., 1961, PhD, 1966, Dr. habil., 1972. Asst. faculty of geodesy Olsztyn (Poland) U., 1960-66, asst. prof., 1966-68, assoc. prof., 1968-76, prof., 1976—; dean faculty of geodesy Olsztyn U. Agriculture and Technology, 1969-75, 78-81, 92-99, vice rector, 1981-84, rector, 1984-87. Author: The Use of Least Squares Method, 1971, A Theoretical Basis of Geodetic Data Processing, 1983, 2d edit., 1999; co-author: Adjustment Computations, 1980, The Levelling, 1993. Fellow Internat. Assn. of Geodesy; mem. European Geophys. Soc., Polish Acad. Scis., Polish Astron. Soc., Am. Geophys. Union. Home: Kromera 1/6, 10-169 Olsztyn Poland Office: Inst Geodesy OU, Oczapowski 1, 10-957 Olsztyn Poland

BARAN, PERVER KORÇA, urban planner, educator, researcher; b. Struga, Yugoslavia, May 18, 1958; came to U.S., 1996; d. Mücahit and Belkis Korça; m. Mesut Baran, 1997. BArch., U. Kiril I Methodij, Skopje, Macedonia, 1981; M of Urban Planning, Istanbul Tech. U., 1984, PhD in Urban Planning, 1989. Rschr., tchg. asst. in urban planning Istanbul Tech. U., 1984-91, asst. prof. urban planning, 1991-93, assoc. prof., 1993-98; rsch. assoc. N.C. State U., Raleigh, 1997-99, vis. rsch. assoc. prof., 1999—; cons. Altinok Inc., Istanbul, 1996; vis. scholar N.C. State U., 1996-97, U. Mich., Ann Arbor, 1990. Contbr. articles to profl. jours. Mem. exec. com., treas. Taskisla Ednl. and Cultural Assn., Istanbul, 1994-96. Recipient 26th July awrd Frank Harcourt-Munning Fund, London, 1981, Chancellor Honor award U. Kiril I Methodij, 1983, 84, 89; Istanbul Tech. U. fellow, 1990; Sci. and Tech. Rsch. Coun. Turkey grantee, 1992, 94. Mem. Tourism Rsch. Info. Network, Environ. Design Rsch. Assn. Avocations: photography, hiking, travel. E-mail: kperver@unity.ncsu.edu. Office: NC State U PO Box 7106 Raleigh NC 27695-0001

BARANANO-MARTINEZ, ANA MARIA, management educator; b. Madrid, Feb. 17, 1965; d. Federico Baranano Cristobal and Encarnacion Martinez Brieva. PhD in Mgmt., U. Autonoma de Madrid, 1994. Rschr. Inst. Sociology of New Technologies, Madrid, 1989-94; tutor of tng. activities Autonomous U., Madrid, 1993-94; lectr., rschr. Open U., Lisbon, Portugal, 1995-97, Instituto Superior de Gestao, Lisbon, 1997—. Contbr. articles to profl. jours. Grantee Spanish Programme for R&D, Spain, 1991-94. E-mail: abaranano@isg.pt. Office: Instituto Superior Gestao, Rua Vitorino Nemesio 5, 1750 Lisbon Portugal

BARANDUN, JUERG, physician; b. Zurich, Switzerland, Feb. 8, 1958; s. Johannes and Vittoria Barandun; m. Benedicta Gahlinger, May 23, 1958; children: Flavia, Romina, Manuela. MD, U. Zurich, 1982. Intern Limmattal-Spital; resident Kant. Spital Luzern; asst. med. dir. Clinic of Altitude, Montana, Switzerland, 1989-90; asst. med. dir., fellow Clinic of Altitude, Wald, Switzerland, 1990-92; fellow pulmonary divsn. Mt. Sinai Hosp., Miami Beach, Fla., 1992; chief physician, specialist in pulmonary medicine, med. dir. Clinic of Altitude, Davos-Clavadel, Switzerland, 1993-98; head Ctr. Lung Diseases Clinic Hirslanden, Zurich, Switzerland, 1998—. Contbr. articles to med. jours. 1st lt. Swiss mil., 1988—. Fellow, mem. many Swiss profl. orgns.; mem. Am. Thoracic Soc. Office: Lungenzentrum Hirslanden, CH-8008 Zurich Switzerland

BARANIDHARAN, SETHURAMAN, research scientist; b. India, Oct. 7, 1964. PhD, Indian Inst. Sci., Bangalore, 1990. Postdoctoral fellow Indian Inst. Sci., 1991-93, Purdue U., West Lafayette, Ind., 1994-96; rsch. scientist Purdue U., West Lafayette, 1999—; postdoctoral rsch. investigator J. David Gladstone Insts., U. Calif., San Francisco, 1997-98. Contbr. 22 articles to profl. jours. Mem. sci. coun. Am. Heart Assn. Recipient award AHA, 1997. Mem. Am. Crystallographic Assn. (award), The Protein Soc., Am. Inst. Physics, AAAS, Am. Chem. Soc., Fedn. Am. Soc. Exptl. Biology. Fax: 765-496-1189. E-mail: barani@deft.cc.purdue.edu. Office: Purdue U B-407 Lilly Hall of Life Scis Lafayette IN 47907

BARANOV, ANDREY OLEGOVICH, chemist, researcher; b. Moscow, July 15, 1958; s. Oleg Nikolaevich and Zoya Sergeevna (Kuvshinova) B. Cert. engr. chemist, Moscow Inst. Chem. Tech., 1981; PhD in Chem. Scis., Russian Acad. Scis., Moscow, 1990. Cert. engring. Engr. Inst. Chem. Physics, Russian Acad. Scis., Moscow, 1981-83, jr. rsch. worker, 1983-89, rsch. worker, 1989—. Co-author: Preparing and Properties of Ion- and Electron- Exchange Fibers, 1984; contbr. articles to sci. jours., including Jour. Applied Polymer Sci., Chem. Revs., others. Recipient 2d place award for Young Scientists, Rsch. Inst. Phys. Chemistry V.L. Karpov, Moscow, 1986; rsch. grantee Mockvich automobile factory, Moscow, 1991, 93, Russian Found. Basic Rsch., Moscow, 1995. Avocations: reading, philately, computer software, Internet.

BARANOV, PAVEL SERGEEVICH, research scientist; b. Kursk, Russia, Sept. 2, 1928; s. Sergei Fedorovich and Lidia Pavlovna (Lebedeva) B.; m. Roza Hamidovna Muchamedieva, Oct. 21, 1955; 1 child, Sergei. Diploma in physics with honors, Irkutsk State U., Russia, 1951; PhD in Physics, Lebedev Phys. Inst., Moscow, 1955, Doctorate, 1974. Cert. physicist. Rsch. scientist Lebedev Phys. Inst., Moscow, 1955-61, sr. rsch. scientist, 1961—; chief nuclear investigation High Energy Lab., Lebedev Phys. Inst., 1986-95. Contbr. articles to profl. jours. Recipient Medal for Distinction in Labor, USSR Supreme Soviet, 1970, 850th Anniversary of Moscow award, 1997; grantee Internat. Assn. for Promotion of Cooperation with Scientists of Ind. New States of Former Soviet Union-93, 1995, Russian Found. for Basic Rsch., 1995, Russian Found. for Basic Rsch.-Deutsche Forschungsgemeinschaft, 1996. Avocations: bicycling and foot trips, chess. Office: Lebedev Phys Inst, Leninski Prospect 53, 117924 Moscow Russia

BARANOV, SERGUEI PAVLOVITCH, physicist, researcher; b. Moscow, Nov. 19, 1956; s. Pavel Sergeyevitch and Roza Khamidovna (Moukhamedieva) B. Diploma in physics, Moscow State U., 1979; PhD, P.N. Lebedev Phys. Inst., Moscow, 1989. Rsch. scientist Russian Acad. Scis., P.N. Lebedev Physics Inst., Moscow, 1979—. Contbr. articles to profl. jours. Grantee Soros Sci. Found., 1994, Russian Found. for Basic Rsch., 1995, Deutsches Forschungs Gemeinschaft, 1998. Home: 21 Mosfilm 2d St Apt #52, 119285 Moscow Russia Office: Russian Acad Sci Lebedev Physics Inst, Leninsky prospect 53, 117924 Moscow Russia

BARANOV, VLADIMIR BORISOVICH, physicist, educator; b. Moscow, Sept. 16, 1934; s. Boris Ivanovich and Lyudmila Veniaminovna (Dobrovinskaya) B.; m. Irena Zdzislavovna Zaradzinskaya, July 13, 1931; children: Yuliya, Igor. Degree, Moscow State U., 1957, postgrad., 1957-61; degree in music edn., Music Coll., Moscow, 1952. Engr. Inst. Thermal Processes, Moscow, 1959-66; sr. sci. rschr. Inst. Space Rschs.-Russian Acad. Scis., Moscow, 1966-72, head Gasdynamics and Magnetohydrodynamics Lab., 1972-86, head Phys. Gasdynamics Lab., Inst for Problems in Mechanics, 1987—; asst. prof. Moscow State U., 1966-76, prof., 1976—. Author: Hydrodynamic Theory of Space Plasma, 1977, (Chapligin's prize Russian Acad. Scis. 1982), Hydro-aerodynamics and Gasdynamics, 1987; mem. editl. bd. Jour. of Fluid Mechanics, 1980—. Named Order of Znak Pochyeta, Govt. of Russia, 1972; sci. grantee Soros Found., 1995, Soros prof., 1995-2000. Avocations: classic music, playing violin, chess, soccer. E-mail: baranov@ipmnet.ru. Office: Inst Problems Mechanics RAS, Prospect Vernadskogo 101, 117526 Moscow Russia

BARANOVICH, DIANA LEA, music educator; b. New Orleans, Nov. 1, 1961; d. Walter Horace and Margaret (Rothman) B.; m. Robert Charles Shoup, June 12, 1982; children: Nadia Lea, Raymond Christopher. MusB, Loyola U., 1983, MEd, 1986; Dalcroze cert., Carnegie-Mellon U., 1993; postgrad., U. Houston, 1990-93. Cert. tchr. music, dance, drama, English, h.s. counselor, Tex. Tchr. music St. Tammany Schs., Slidell, La., 1983-84, Lynn Oaks Sch., Braithwaite, La., 1984-86; choir dir. Fort Bend Pub. Sch., Houston, 1990-93; tchr., cons. music and dance New Orleans, 1996—; prof. music edn. Normal U. Beijing, China, 1995-97; cons., trainer tchrs. music and dance Kinderland Learning Ctr., Singapore, 1996—; vol. tchr. dance, movement and Chinese studies Alice Harte Elem. Sch., New Orleans, 1996—; pvt. tchr. piano and movement, 1996—; tchr. tap dancing and choreography New Orleans Dance Acad., 1997—. Contbr. articles to profl. jours. Sponsor St. Joseph's Indian Sch., Childreach, Food for the Poor. Mem. Music Tchrs. Nat. Assn., Music for People, Dalcroze Soc. Am. (patron). Avocations: theater, ethnic dancing, creative writing, composing children's music, piano. Home: 2531 Binz St Houston TX 77004-7565

BARANOWSKI, ANDREW PAUL, anesthetist; b. Pwllheli, Wales, June 18, 1959; s. Vincent and Sheila (Bodington) B.; m. Judith Maria Hearn, July 24, 1982; children: Natasha Maria, Paul Jan. BSc in Pathology and Med. Sci. with hons, U. London, 1980, B Medicine B Surgery, 1983, MD, 1993. Rsch. fellow St. Thomas Hosp., U.K., 1989-91; sr. registrar various hosps., U.K., 1991-96; cons. U. Coll. London Hosps., 1994—, hon. sr. lectr., 1994—; dir. pain mgmt. King Edward VII Hosp. for Officers, 1995—; hon. cons. St. John's & Elizabeth's Hosp., 1994—. Author: The Consequences of Peripheral Nerve Injury and Regeneration for the Expression of the Neuro Peptides, 1993; contbr. articles to profl. jours. Recipient Frances and Augustus Newman Found. award, 1995; MRC rsch. fellow, 1989; Assn. Anaesthetists rsch. grantee, 1990. Fellow Royal Coll. Anaesthetists; Mem. Internat. Assn. for Study of Paul (mem. subgroup 1998—), Royal Soc. Medicine. Office: U Coll London Hosps, Queen Sq, London WC1N 3BG, England

BARANOWSKI, PAUL JOSEPH, instrumentation technician; b. Norwich, Conn., July 29, 1950; s. Joseph Baranowski Jr. and Margaret Olive (Croteau) Momut; m. S. Rose Bottom, Sept. 3, 1977; 1 child, Bettyann Pellerin. AS in Indsl. Electronics, Thames Valley State Coll., 1982; cert., Inst. Nuclear Power Ops., 1992. Cert. control technician Nat. Acad. Nuclear Tng. Welder Gen. Dynamics Elec. Boat, Groton, Conn., 1973-74; automotive technician Goodyear, Norwich, 1974-75, Mallon Chevrolet, Norwich, 1975-77; maintainence mechanic Wyre Wynd, Jewett City, Conn., 1977-79; engring. technician Victor Elec. Wire & Cable, Westerly, R.I., 1982-84; instrumentation and controls technician, mech. tech. various nuclear facilities, 1984-90; instrumentation and controls technician Calvert Cliffs Nuclear Power Plant Balt. Gas & Elec. Co., Lusby, Md., 1990-96; instrumentation technician Spirol Internat. Corp., Danielson, Conn., 1996-98; sr. I.E.C. technician Exeter Energy Ltd. Partnership, Sterling, Conn., 1998—. With USN, 1968-73. Mem. Am. Legion. Democrat. Avocations: fishing, collecting old bottles, antiques, gardening. Home: 3 Center St Plainfield CT 06374-1203

BÁRÁNY, PETER FRANZ, nephrologist; b. Stockholm, Oct. 26, 1955; s. Franz Rudolf and Margareta Ruth Ingrid (Nyland) B.; m. Åsa Gunilla Wallje, May 3, 1986; children: Elsa, Aina. Grad. Med. Faculty, Karolinska Inst., Stockholm, 1983, Dr. Med. Sci., 1993. Lic. physician, Sweden. Resident in nephrology dept. renal medicine Huddinge U. Hosp., Stockholm, 1987-94, specialist in nephrology, 1994-99; sr. physician in nephrology Huddinge U. Hosp., 1999—. Contbr. articles to profl. jours. Mem. Swedish Soc. Nephrology, European Dialysis and Transplantation Assn., Internat. Soc. Nephrology, Internat. Soc. for Peritoneal Dialysis, Am. Soc. Nephrology (corr.). Office: Huddinge Univ Hosp, Dept Renal Medicine, S-14186 Stockholm Sweden

BARAR, KIRAN VIJAY, pharmacology educator; b. Jaipur, Rajasthan, India, Mar. 3, 1957; d. Munnalal and Bhagvati Devi (Mehta) Jain; m. Rajnish Vijay Barar, Apr. 11, 1988; two children. BSc in Biology, U. Rajasthan, Jaipur, 1976, MSc in Medicine/Pharmacology, 1980; PhD in Medicine/Pharmacology, U. Rajasthan, 1993; postgrad., Postgrad. Inst. Med. Edn./Rsch, Chandigarh, India, 1998, 99. Sr. demonstrator pharmacology Sawai Man Singh Med. Coll. Dept. Med. and Health, Govt. Rajasthan, Jaipur, 1982-91, sr. demonstrator pharmacology Jawahar Lal Nehru Med. Coll., 1991-94, asst. prof. pharmacology Jawahar Lal Nehru Med. Coll., 1994-1999, assoc. prof. pharmacology Ravindra Nath Tagore Med. Coll., 2000—; hon. prof. Albert Schweitzer Internat. U.; presenter in field. Editor Current Med. Jour., 1999—; columnist Jour. North Zone, 1999—; contbr. 30 articles to profl. jours. Mem. Indian Pharmacol. Soc. (life). Avocations: playing with children, solving puzzles, playing word games, cooking, traveling. E-mail: kiranvb@usa.net. Home: Campus Ajmer, 12 Jawahar Lal Nehru Hospital, 305001 Rajasthan India Office: Dept Pharmacology, Ravindra Nath Med Coll, 313001 Udaipur Rajasthan, India

BARASH, JEFFREY ANDREW, philosopher, educator; b. Chgo., Dec. 13, 1949; s. Bernard and Dorothy Barash; m. Silvana Condemi. BA, Stanford U., 1971; MA, U. Chgo., 1973, PhD, 1982; Habil., U. Paris X, 1993. Instr. U. Chgo., 1981-82; Mellon fellow Columbia U., N.Y.C., 1983-85; Humboldt fellow U. Bielefeld, Germany, 1985-87; prof. philosophy U. Paris XII, 1988-89; fellow European U. Inst., Florence, Italy, 1987-88; prof. philosophy U. Amiens, France, 1989—; dir. dept. philosophy U. Amiens, 1992—. Author: Heidegger et son siecle, 1995, Martin Heidegger and the Problem of Historical Meaning, 1988; contbr. articles to profl. jours. Recipient Marc Perry Galler prize U. Chgo., 1982. Mem. French Philosophy Soc., Soc. of Fellows of Columbia U. Office: U Picardie Fac Phil & Scis, Jules Verne Chemin du Thil, F-80025 Amiens Cedex 1, France

BARATAY, CLAUDE RAYMOND JOSEPH, consultant, educator; b. Lugrin, France, Feb. 27, 1952; s. Raymond Henri and Henriette Anne-Marie (Pralong) B.; m. Christiane Michele Vesin, Oct. 5, 1974; children: Sylvie, Olivier, Emeline. Engr., CNAM, Paris, 1979. Ops. mgr. BULL, Grenoble, France, 1972-80; MIS engr. Thomson, Grenoble, 1980-87; telecoms. mgr. SGS-Thomson, Grenoble, 1988-92; ind. cons. Grenoble, 1993-95; cons. in telecoms Devotech, Paris, 1995-96; assoc. cons. Menway Cons., Grenoble, 1996—; tchr., advisor E.F.R.E.I., Villejuif, France, 1994-99. Contbr. articles to profl. jours. Mem. ADIRA (pres. for telecoms. 1994-99), Telecom Mgrs. Assn. Avocation: guitar. Office: Menway Cons, 25 Rue Pierre Semard, 38000 Grenoble France

BARÁTOSSY, KATALIN, banker, economist; b. Budapest, Hungary, Aug. 12, 1944; d. Nándor and Nándorné (Albert) Visi; m. György Barátossy, May 13, 1967; 1 child, Noémi. Economist, U. Econs., Budapest, Hungary, 1966. Referent Hungarian Investment Bank, Budapest, 1966-86, chief referent, 1969-71; mgr. State Devel. Bank, Budapest, 1972-85; mng. dir. Nat. Savings Bank, 1986-96; sr. mng. dir. Nat. Savings and Comml. Bank, 1996-97, Hungarian Credit Bank, Budapest, 1996-97; asst. sec. state Min. Fin., 1998-2000, dep. state sec., 2000—. Avocations: sport, music. Office: Ministry of Finance, József nádor ter 2-h, H-1051 Budapest Hungary

BARATTA, GIOVANNI BATTISTA, astronomer; b. Priverno, Italy, Dec. 8, 1942; s. Domenico Baratta and Zinfarosa Lattanzi; children: Luciana, Annalisa. Degree in physics, U. La Sapienza, Rome, 1967. Rschr. Nat. Rsch. Coun., Rome, 1968-70; astronomer Osservatorio Astronomico, Rome, 1970—. Syndicalist, CISL, Rome, 1980—. Recipient tng. grant Edinburgh, Scotland, 1972-74. Mem. Internat. Astron. Union. Avocations: ethology, ecology, medicine, biology, psychology. E-mail: baratta@oarhp1.rm.astro.it. Office: Osservatorio Astronomico, Via Parco Mellini 84, I-00136 Rome Italy

BARAYUGA, PETRONIO JACOSALEM, college executive; b. Nueva Ecija, The Philippines, May 31, 1946; s. Domingo Alamon and Eusebia Jacosalem Barayuga; m. Luz Lucena Lapena, Mar. 26, 1969; children: Rodney Alden, Rhondee Ian, Liezl Ann. AB, BSE, Mountain View Coll., The Philippines, 1969; MA, Northeastern Coll., 1980; PhD, Pacific Western U., 1998. Cert. Tchr.'s Bd. Asst. prin. No. Luzon Acad., The Philippines, 1969-71; prin. Tirad View Acad., The Philippines, 1971-76, N.E. Luzon Acad., The Philippines, 1976-84; pres. Mountain Provinces Mission, The Philippines, 1984-86; field sec. No. Luzon Mission, The Philippines, 1986-88; prin. No. Luzon Acad., The Philippines, 1988-90; pres. No. Luzon Adventist Coll., The Philippines, 1990—; dir. Assn. Christian Schs. and Colls., 1988-98, BOT Adventist U. Philippines, 1990—; bd. sec. BOT NLAC, 1990—; bd. dirs. EXCOM No. Luzon Mission. Author: (books) A Guide to Board Members, 1996; contbr. articles to mags. and publs. Named Outstanding Achiever, Municipality of Sisen, 2000. Mem. ACSC (v.p. 1990-91, sec. 1991-92), ESAP (pres. 1990—), ASAP (pres. 1990—, Rotary (pres. 2000), Toastmasters Club (pres. 1998). Seventh-day Adventist. Avocations: swimming, tennis, badminton, shooting. Home: Artache Sisen, Pangsinan The Philippines Office: No Luzon Adventist Coll, Artaches Sisen, Pangasinan The Philippines

BARBA, EUGENIO, theater director; b. Brindisi, Italy, Oct. 29, 1936; s. Emanuele Barba and Vera Gaeta; m. Judith Patricia Howard Jones, 1965; 2 children. Student, U. Oslo; Dr. h.c., U. Aarhus, 1988, U. Ayacucho, 1998, U. Bologna, 1998; Reconnaissance de merite scientifique, Montreal U. Founder, dir. Odin Teatret, 1964—, Internat. Sch. Theatre Anthropology, 1979—; Bd. advisers Internat. Com. Théâtre des Nations, 1975-80, Internat. Assn. Performing Arts Semiotics, 1981-85; adviser Danish Ministry of Culture, 1981-82; UNESCO adviser Ctr. de Estudios Teatrales, Museo de Arte Moderno, Bogotá, 1983; adviser Ctr. Theatre Exchanges, Rio de Janeiro, 1987—; lectr. in field. Author: In Search of a Lost Theatre, 1965, The Floating Islands, 1978, Beyond the Floating Islands, 1985, The Dilated Body, 1985, The Secret Art of the Performer, 1990, The Paper Canoe, 1992, Theatre--Solitude, craft, revolt, 1996, Land of Ashes and Diamonds, 1998, others; contbg. editor TDR New Theatre Quar. Recipient Danish Acad. award, 1980, Mex. Theatre Critics' prize, 1984, Diego Fabbri prize, 1986, Pirandello Internat. prize, 1996, Sonning prize, 2000. Mem. Internat. Assn. Comparative Lit. Address: Nordisk Teaterlaboratorium, Odin Teatret Box 1283, 7500 Holstebro Denmark

BARBA, HARRY, author, educator, publisher; b. Bristol, Conn., June 17, 1922; s. Michael Hovanessian and Sultone (Mnatsignanian) B.; m. Roberta Ashburn Riley, 1955 (div. 1963); 1 child, Gregory Robert; m. Marian An-

drea Homelson, Oct. 29, 1965. AB, Bates Coll., 1944; MA, Harvard U., 1951; MFA, U. Iowa, 1960, PhD with honors, 1963; postgrad., NYU, 1955-56, Boston U., 1950-51, NYU, 1955-56, CCNY, 1956-57, Columbia U., 1957-58, U. Middlebury, 1945. Stringer, feature writer Bristol (Conn.) Press, 1944-45; file clk. supr. new departure GM Corp., 1944-45; instr. English and writing Wilkes Coll. 1947, U. Conn., Hartford, 1947-49; tchr. English Seward Park H.S., N.Y.C., 1955-59; instr. U. Iowa, 1959-63; asst. prof. Skidmore Coll., 1963-68; prof. English, dir. writing Marshall U., Huntington, W.Va., 1968-70, title I writing arts dir., 1969-70; comml. and pub. svcs. radio-TV interviewee, reader, lectr., 1961—; prof. English, dir. writing Marshall U., Huntington, W.Va., 1968-70; Title I Writing Arts dir. W.Va., 1969-70; vis. prof., Fulbright grantee, vis. Am. specialist Damascus U., 1963-64; disting. vis. lectr. contemporary lit., cons. SUNY, Albany, 1977-78; reader, lectr. USIS Libr., Damascus, Syria, 1963-64; innovator, dir., devel. writers confs. for creative growth in several nat., regional and urban contexts, 1964—; dir. The Workshop Under the Sky, 1968—; pres., pub., exec. dir. Harian Creative Books, Ballston Spa, N.Y., 1967—; cons. Bantam Books, Random House, 1967, 69-70, Nat. Found. for Arts, Nat. Found. for Humanities, U.S. Dept. Edn., N.Y. State Coun. Arts, N.Y. State Edn. Dept., Poets & Writers, Inc., Harvard U., others. Author: For the Grape Season, 1960, 3 By Harry Barba, 1967 3 X 3, 1969, The Case for Socially Functional Education, Art and Culture, 1970-74, One of A Kind, (The Many Faces and Voices of America), 1976, The Day the World Went Sane, 1979, series What's Cooking in Congress? A Congressional Smorgasbord of Recipes, 1979, 83 (compiled and co-editor with Marian Barba), 1983; Gospel According to Everyman, 1981, Round Trip to Byzantium, 1985 (Pulitzer prize nominee 1985), When the Deep Purple Falls, a Story (PEN Syndicated Fiction award 1985), Mona Lisa Smiles (co-published with Princeton U. Press), 1993. Founder, dir. Skidmore Coll. Writers and Educators Conf., 1967, Adirondack-Metroland Writers and Educators Conf., 1967—. Recipient cert. of merit Dictionary Internat. Biography, 1974, Internat. Man of Yr. award Cambridge (Eng.) Internat. Biographical Ctr., 1996-97; grad. fellow U. Iowa, 1961-62, Yaddo residence fellow, 1950, Macdowell Colony residence fellow, 1970, World's Hall of Fame in Lit., 1997—, Guggenheim fellow, 1989-90; Skidmore rsch. grantee, 1965-68, N.Y. State coun. Arts grantee, 1971, U. Benedeum grantee, 1969; established Harian Creative awards for fiction, poetry, essays, mus. compositions, photography and graphic arts, 1973. Mem. MLA, Coll. English Assn., Authors Guild, Writers Union PEN, Com. Small Press Editors and Pubs., Harvard Grad. Soc. Advanced Study and Rsch., Harvard Alumni Assn., Harvard Club La. N.Y. (dir. 1975-79). Home and Office: 47 Hyde Blvd Ballston Spa NY 12020-1607

BARBA, VENTURA, lawyer; b. Barcelona, Spain, Sept. 13, 1971; s. Buenaventura and Isabel (De Villalonga) B. B Constl. Law cum laude, U. Barcelona, 1992, B in Civil Law cum laude, 1993; postgrad., U. Pompeu Fabra, Barcelona, 1993; JD, U. Barcelona, 1994; LLM in Cultural Indsl. Mgmt., U. Complutense, Madrid, 1997. Lawyer Sociedad Gen. de Autores y Editores, Barcelona, 1994; tchr. asst. U. Uruguay, Montevideo, 1994; legal dept. The Arenan Group, L.A., 1995; solicitor Enrich & Amat Advocats, Barcelona, 1995-98, Tods Murray WS, Edinburgh, 1996; legal and bus. affairs mgr. BMG, Madrid, Spain, 1998—; legal dir. Yahoo! Spain, 2000—; tchr. asst. pvt. internat. law Internat. U. Catalonia, Barcelona, 19996-98; in-house counsel Festival de Otono, Madrid, 1995; counsel Copyrait, Barcelona, 1996-98. Recipient grant Fgn. Affairs Ministry Spain, 1994. Avocations: motion pictures, music, sports, reading. E-Mail: ventura@es.yahoo-inc.com. Office: Yahoo! Spain, Maria de Molina, 40, 4oB, 28006 Madrid Spain

BARBADIMOS, ARIS N., physician; b. Levadia, Greece, Sept. 12, 1956; U.S. citizen; s. Nicholas A. Barbadimos and Arghiro I. Babalouka; m. Tina A. Bousa, June 1, 1984; 1 child, Niki. Phys. therapy diploma, U. Rome; M in Rehab., L.I. U.; MD, Am. U. Caribbean. Fellow sports medicine U. London; med. dir. South Bronx Med. Complex; asst. clin. prof. Albert Einstein U. Contbr. articles to profl. jours. Fellow Am. Acad. Phys. Medicine and Rehab.; mem. AMA, Am. Acad. Cardiovasc. and Pulmonary Rehab. Greek Orthodox. Avocations: soccer, jogging. Home: 89 Berrian Rd Stamford CT 06905-2412

BARBALHO MARTINS, FERNANDO, lawyer; b. Porto Alegre, Brazil, Mar. 20, 1977; s. Belmar Meira Martins and Elisabete Santiago Barbalho. LLB, U. Estácio De Sa, Rio de Janeiro, 1994. Trainee Pub. Atty.'s Office, Rio de Janeiro, 1992, Escritório de Advocacia Dr. Balbino, Rio de Janeiro, 1992-93, H. Barata Neto Advogados, Rio de Janeiro, 1993-95; assoc. Köhler, Janequine & Mourão, Rio de Janeiro, 1995-97; legal adviser Itapemirim Transportes Aéreos S/A, Rio de Janeiro, 1997-98; legal counselor AGA S/A, Rio de Janeiro, 1998—, Fed. U. Rio de Janeiro, 1998; asst. legal counselor Personal Office of Mayor, City of Rio de Janeiro, 1997; sr. prtnr. Janequine & Barbalho Advogados, 1998—. Editor A Aspiração, 1989. 2d reginal sec. young group Liberal Party, Rio de Janeiro, 1990; vol. spkr. Rio 2004 Olympic Bid Com., Rio de Janeiro, 1997; lectr. economy, politics, and social actualities Curso Volotão Prep. Sch., 1999. Mem. Rio de Janeiro Bar Assn., Club Aeros. Avocations: sports marketing research, fencing. Home: Rua Conde de Bonfim 568/303, 20520055 Rio de Janeiro Brazil Office: Janequine & Barbalho Advogados, Av Nilo Pçauha 1z-Stes 413/415, Rio de Janeiro Brazil

BARBANTI, PAOLO, management consultant, educator; b. Milan, Mar. 22, 1956; s. Emilio and Carla (Ravini) B. MS in Biology, U. Milan, 1980, PhD in Toxicology, 1984; MBA, SDA Bocconi, Milan, 1990. Cert. biologist. Rschr. Nat. Cancer Inst., Milan, 1981-84, Recordati SpA, Milan, 1985; rschr. Sch. Medicine U. Brescia, Italy, 1986-88; mgr. nat. biotech. program Nat. Rsch. Coun., Milan, 1988-90; mgmt. cons. Thinktank srl, Milan, 1991-96, Pivot/Cross Border, Milan, 1997—; vis. scientist NIH, Bethesda, 1988; mgmt. cons. Value Ptnrs., Milan, 1995; lectr. Scuola Normale Superiore Studi S. Anna, Pisa, Italy, 1993—; SDA Bocconi, Milan, 1995—; Sch. Pharmacy, U. Milan, 1996—; Advanced Biotech. Ctr., Genoa, Italy, 1994-95; bd. dirs. nat. biotech program CNR, 1998—; prof. U. Bologna (Italy) Sch. Biotech., 2000—. Contbr. chpts. to books, articles to jours. Fellow Nat. Cancer Inst., 1982, Associazione Italiana Ricerca Cancro, 1983; recipient fellowship Fondazione Marco Senepa, 1989. Fellow Italian Fedn. Immunol. Socs., Gruppo di Cooperazione Immunologia, MBA Alumni SDA Bocconi (bd. dirs. 1991—); mem. Ordine Nazionale Biologi, Italian Assn. Pharm. Mktg., Soc. Pharm. Scis. Roman Catholic. Avocations: skiing, trekking, motorcycling, reading. Home: Via Placido Riccardi 19, 20132 Milan Italy

BARBANTI, SERGIO, diplomat; b. Milan, Italy, Aug. 28, 1957; came to U.S., 1994; s. Bruno and Francesca (Boga) B. LLB magna cum laude, Rome U., 1977-85. Cert. lawyer, Rome. Atty., 1985-86; dep. head Africa Desk, Gen. Directorate Econ. Affairs Ministry Fgn. Affairs, Rome, 1987-90; head Italian Delegation Paris Club, 1988-90; dep. chief mission Embassy of Italy, Harare, Zimbabwe, 1990-94; counselor, dep. head Press and Info. Office Embassy of Italy, Washington, 1994-98; dep. head NATO, 1998—; rep. gen. directorate polit. affairs Ministry Fgn. Affairs, Rome, 1998—; rep. Italian Govt. Orgn. Am. States, Washington, 1995-98. Mem. Harare Club, Cosmos Club. Roman Catholic. Avocations: poetry, literature, philosophy. Home: via Sardegna 29, 00187 Rome Italy Office: Ministry Fgn Affairs, Piazza Farnesina 1, 00100 Rome Italy also: Embassy of Italy 1601 Fuller St NW Washington DC 20009-5601

BARBARA, JOHN A.J., microbiologist; b. Cairo, Egypt, Apr. 2, 1946; parent British citizens; s. Francis and Theresia (Micallef) B.; m. Gillian Barnes, Aug. 2, 1968; children: Claire, David. BA, Cambridge U., 1968, MA, 1969; MSc, Birmingham U., 1969; PhD, Reading U., 1972. Demonstrator Reading U., U.K., 1969-72; lectr. Reading U., 1972-74; head microbiology No. London Blood Ctr., 1974-96; lead microbiologist London, 1996-2000; prin. Nat. Transfusion Microbiology Labs., 2000—; cons. Nat. Blood Authority, England, 1993—;. Author: Microbiology in Blood Transfusion, 1983; contbr. articles to profl. jours. Fellow Inst. Biology, Royal Coll. Pathologists; mem. Br. Blood Transfusion Soc. (pres. 1995-97), Internat. Soc. Blood Transfusion (v.p. 2000—), Am. Assn. Blood Banks, Assn. Clin. Microbiologists. Avocations: gardening, reading, recreational cycling. Office: No London Blood Transfusion Nat Blood Svc, Colindale Ave, London NW9 5BG, England

BARBARAO, ANNA, molecular geneticist; b. Messina, Italy, Oct. 16, 1970; d. Aldo Barbaro and Maria Grazia Casella. Biology degree, U. Messina,

---

1992; specialization in applied genetics, U. Rome "La Sapienza", 1996, specialization in criminalistic scis., 1998. State exam. for biologist profession and consequent certification. Forensic molecular geneticist, chief of dept. Office Med. and Forensic Investigations, Reggio Calabria, Italy, 1992—. Contbr. sci. articles to profl. jours. Mem. Internat. Assn. for Identification, Nat. Order Biology, Italian Soc. Criminalistics, N.Y. Acad. Scis. Avocations: world travel, dance, dogs. Office: Office Med/Forensic Invest, Via Nicolo da Reggio 4, 89128 Reggio Calabria Italy

BARBARO, GIUSEPPE, physician; b. Rome, Aug. 22, 1958; s. Vincenzo and Rosetta (Pandolfo) B. MD, U. La Sapienza, Rome, 1983, postgrad., 1988-92. Postdoctoral fellow U. La Sapienza, Rome, 1983-88, asst. cardiologist, rschr. dept. emergency medicine, 1991—; postdoctoral fellow cardiology U. Tor Vergata, Rome, 1988-92; cons. in field. Co-author: Cardiology in AIDS, 2000; mem. editl. bd. AIDS News, 1990-93; book reviewer European Jour. Emergency Medicine, 1996—; contbr. articles to nat. and internat. jours. and chpts. to textbooks. Lt. Italian mil., 1985-86. Recipient Farmitalia award for electrocardiography, 1990. Fellow Am. Coll. Chest Physicians, Royal Soc. Medicine; mem. AAAS, Italian Soc. Internal Medicine, Italian Soc. Cardiology, Italian Soc. Gastroenterology, Italian Soc. Infectious Diseases, Internat. Soc. Infectious Diseases, European Soc. Internal Medicine, European Soc. Emergency Medicine, Am. Heart Assn. (coun. clin. cardiology), Internat. Fedn. AIDS Socs., N.Y. Acad. Scis., KM. Avocations: informatics, cinema, theatre. Home: Viale Anicio Gallo # 63, 00174 Rome Italy

BARBAS, MARIO PANAGIOTIS, marketing professional; b. Thessaloniki, Greece, Sept. 3, 1967; s. Nicuolaos and Dorothy Barbas. BA in Econs. with honors, Manchester (Eng.) Met. U., 1990; MBA, Nottingham (Eng.) U., 1991; postgrad., U. Pavia, Italy, 1988-90. Mgmt. trainee Hellenic Bottling Co./Coke Greece, 1993-94; area sales mgr. HBC-Coca Cola, Greece, 1994-95; sr. brand mgr. Ferrero Western Europe, Luxembourg, 1995-98; market mgr. Ferrero Luxembourg, 1998; mktg. mgr. Britvic Internat., Eng., 1998—. Served with Greek Armed Forces, 1991-93. Avocations: music composition, financial interests. Home: 18 Belgrave Ct, Wellesley Rd, Chiswick W4 4LG, England

BARBASHOV, BORIS MIKHAILOVICH, physicist, researcher, educator; b. Moscow, Apr. 26, 1930; s. Mikhael Pavlovich and Anna Ivanovna Barbashov; m. Svetlana Vasil'evna Verem'eva (div. 1982); children: Elena, Mikhael. PhD, State U., Moscow, 1962. Jr. rschr. Joint Inst. Nuclear Rsch., Dubna, Russia, 1954-58, sr. rschr., 1958-68, leading rschr., 1968-82, prof., 1982—; lectr. Moscow State U., 1964-79. Author: The Model of Relativistic String in Hadron Physics, 1990; contbr. numerous articles to profl. jours. Recipient Hon. medal Russian Atomic Energy Commn., 1998; Russian Found. for Fundamental Rsch. grantee, 1996-98. Mem. Russian Phys. Soc. E-mail: barbash@thsun1.jinr.ru. Home: Moskovskaya 2, 141980 Dubna Russia Office: Joint Inst Nuclear Rsch, Joliot-Curie 6 Bogoliubov Labor Theor Ph, 141980 Dubna Russia

BARBE, YVES, association administrator, consultant; b. Le Begude de Mazenc, Drome, France, Mar. 15, 1961; s. Andre and Elise (Latard) B.; m. Christine Lintant, Apr. 17, 1987; children: Jeremy, Timothee. Degree in engring., Tech. Inst. Nat. Sch. Food Industry Process, Nantes, France, 1984; postgrad., Tech. Inst. - Chateau Gombert, Marseille, 1987. Tchr. Lycee Agricole, Perpignan, 1984-86; engr. Ducros (Spices), Carpentras, 1987-89; dir. Indsl. Laundry, Montpellier, 1989-93, Messidor, Vienne, 1993-97, Foyer Protestant, Castres, 1997—; dir. Social Ctr. Children, Social Ctr. Loner, Driving Sch., Profl. Tng. Ctr. dir. Crusade Christian Lit., cons. Mem. Gedeons. Fax: 011-33-5-63-53-82-35. E-mail: FoyerProte@aol.com. Home: 16 Rue Pierre Paul Sirven, 81100 Castres France Office: 7 Rue Pasteur Hubac, 81100 Castres France

BARBEE, GARY CLIFTON, environmental scientist, consultant; b. San Rafael, Calif., July 17, 1957; s. Alfred Clifton and Beverly Carol B. BS, Tex. A&M U., 1979, MS, 1983; MPH, U. Tex. Sch. Pub. Health, Houston, 2000. Cert. profl. soil scientist Am. Registry Cert. Profls. in Agronomy, Crops and Soils. Rsch. assoc. Tex. A&M U., College Station, 1983-86; risk assessment mgr. K.W. Brown & Assocs., Inc., College Station, Tex., 1988-90, Fugro Environ., Inc., Houston, 1990-95; sr. scientist Applied Earth Scis., Inc., Houston, 1996-98; sr. environ. scientist The WCM Group, Inc., Humble, Tex., 1998-00. Contbr. articles to profl. jours., including Bull. Environ. Contamination & Toxicology, Environ. & Molecular Mutagenesis, Hazardous Waste & Hazardous Materials, Soil Sci., others; contbr.: Basic Environmental Toxicology, 1994. Eagle Scout, Boy Scouts Am., Annandale, Va., 1971; missionary, Living Stream Ministry, Taipei, Taiwan, 1986-87, St. Petersburg, Russia, 1992-93. Mem. Internat. Soc. Exposure Analysis, Nat. Ground Water Assn., Gamma Sigma Delta. Avocations: foreign languages, photography, rollerblading.

BARBEE, GEORGE E. L., financial services and business executive; b. Washington, Jan. 26, 1943; s. H. Randolph and Grace Lunt (Davenport) B.; m. Molly Morse Johnson, May 21, 1977; children: Gregory, John, Scott, Jefferson. AB, Brown U., 1965; MBA, U. Va., 1967. Fin. analyst W. R. Grace & Co., N.Y.C., 1968; product mgr. Wilkinson Sword Inc., Mountainside, N.J., 1968-70; mgr. new products Noxell divsn. Procter & Gamble, Balt., 1970-74; sr. mktg. exec. Gillette Corp., Boston, 1974-79; co-founder, exec. dir. Consumer Fin. Inst., Newton, Mass., 1979-86; prtnr., exec. dir. personal fin. svcs. PricewaterhouseCoopers LLP, Waltham, Mass., 1986-91; ptnr., exec. dir. client svcs. nat. office PricewaterhouseCoopers LLP, N.Y.C., 1991-92; ptnr. Worldwide Client Svc., 1992—; dir. Victory Van Internat., Washington; TV commentator fin. and bus. news NBC, CNN, PBS, ABC, CBS, 1981—. Author fin. and bus. articles. Republican. also: Price Waterhouse Coopers LLP 160 Federal St Fl 9 Boston MA 02110-1700

BARBEE, VICTOR, ballet dancer; b. Raleigh, N.C., June 21, 1954; s. Joseph Edward and Ruth Evelyn (Wilder) B. Student, N.C. Sch. of Arts, 1968-70, Sch. of Am. Ballet, 1970-75; Student, Leningrad-Kirov Ballet Sch., Leningrad. Former dancer Jacob's Pillow, N.C. Drama Theatre, The Eglevsky Ballet Co., The Villella Ballet Co., The Tulsa Civic Ballet, The Los Angeles Ballet Co.; dancer Am. Ballet Theatre, N.Y.C., 1975-79, soloist, 1979-83, prin. dancer, 1983—; artistic asst., 1995—; artistic asst. Am. Ballet Theatre, 1995. Created roles in Natalia Makarova's La Bayadere, in Mikhail Baryshnikov's Don Quixote and Cinderella, other repertory includes Bach Partita, Bouree Fantastique, Concerto, The Informer, Gaité Parisienne, Giselle, Graduation Ball, Great Galloping Gottsschalk, The Leaves Are Fading, Miss Julie, Les Noces, Pillar of Fire, Push Comes to Shove, others; appeared on Broadway in Woman of the Year, 1983, Song and Dance, 1986; film appearances include The Turning Point, 1978, Dancers, 1987; appeared in TV series Hart to Hart, 1983, Laverne and Shirley, 1983. Office: care Am Ballet Theatre 890 Broadway New York NY 10003*

BARBEOSCH, WILLIAM PETER, banker, lawyer; b. N.Y.C., Nov. 25, 1954; s. Peter Joseph and Marie Delores (Slesiona) B.; m. Marta B. Varela, Sept. 6, 1986. AB magna cum laude, Brown U., 1976; JD, Columbia U., 1979; MBA, Yale U., 1989. Bar: N.Y. 1980, U.S. Tax Ct. 1985. Atty. Casey, Lane and Mittendorf (and successor firms), N.Y.C., 1979-86, Milbank, Tweed, Hadley and McCloy, N.Y.C., 1986-87; mgmt. assoc. Swiss Bank Corp., N.Y.C., 1989-90; v.p. The Chase Global Pvt. Bank, N.Y.C., 1990-99; mng. dir. The Chase Manhattan Pvt. Bank, N.Y.C., 1999—; practice head Wealth Transfer and Succession Planning Group, 2000—; bd. advisors The Chase Jour., 1997—. Mem. N.Y. State Bar Assn., Assn. of the Bar of City of N.Y., Brown U. Club N.Y., Stone House Club, Yale Club (N.Y.C.), Phi Kappa Psi (sec. R.I. Alpha chpt. 1974-75). Republican. Roman Catholic. Avocations: swimming, history, politics. Home: 545 W 111th St Apt 7E New York NY 10025-1965 Office: The Chase Manhattan Bank 1211 Ave of the Americas New York NY 10036-8890

BARBER, ANN MCDONALD, physician; b. Washington, Jan. 14, 1951; d. Charles Finch and Lois Helen (LaCroix) B. MS in Math., BS in Math., Stanford U., 1974; MD, Northwestern U., Chgo., 1981. Diplomate Am. Bd. Internal Medicine. Mathematician NIH, Bethesda, Md., 1974-76; program analyst engr. II Mass. Gen. Hosp., Boston, 1976-77; resident in internal medicine Northwestern U. Med. Ctr., Chgo., 1981-84; med. staff fellow NIH, Bethesda, 1984-87; sr. staff fellow Nat. Cancer Inst., Bethesda, 1987-91; computer scientist DOE, 1991-92; attending physician Providence Hosp.,

---

Washington, 1992-96; v.p. investments Reliance Group Holdings, N.Y.C., 1996—; peer reviewer Annuals Of Internal Medicine, ACP, Phila. 1986-96; cons. Inst. for New Generation Computer Tech., Tokyo, 1991. Contbr. articles to profl. jours. Vol. Zacchaeus Free Med. Clinic, Washington, 1990-96. Recipient Physician's Recognition award AMA. Fellow ACP; mem. AAAS, Am. Med. Info. Assn. Office: Reliance Group Holdings FDR 8106 New York NY 10150-8106

BARBER, ANTHONY JOHN, geology educator, geological researcher; b. London, Sept. 10, 1929; s. Cyril and Irene Constance (Crisp) B.; m. Brenda Josephine Bayly, Dec. 28, 1958; children: Steven, Jayne, Nicholas. BS with honors, Chelsea Coll., 1956; PhD, Imperial Coll., 1969, D.I.C., 1969. Asst. lectr. Chelsea Coll., London, 1959-64, lectr., 1964-76, sr. lectr., 1976-83, reader, 1983-85; reader Royal Holloway & Bedford New Coll., London, 1985-94; cons. tech. com. for coordination offshore prospecting UN, Bangkok, Thailand, 1978-79; project mgr. Univ. London Consortium for Geol. Research Southeast Asia, London, 1982-94. Author: (with others) Geology and Tectonics Studies in East Asian Tectonics and Resources, 1980, Geology and Tectonics Studies in East Asian Tectonics and Resources, 1981; editor: Jour. Proceedings of the Geologists and Eastern Indonesia, 1981; editor: Jour. Proceedings of the Geologists Assn., 1972-78; assoc. editor: Jour. of Structural Geology, 1978-84, Jour. S.E. Asian Earth Scis., 1989-96; deputy editor-in-chief Jour. Asian Earth Scis., 1997—. Fellow Geol. Soc. (mem. coun. 1979-82); mem. Geologists Assn. (mem. coun. 1972-81). Avocations: travel, music, stamp collecting. Office: Royal Holloway/Bedford Coll, Geology Dept, Egham Surrey TW20 0EX, England

BARBER, BENJAMIN R., director, educator. Cert., London Sch. Econ. & Polit. Sci, 1959; BA with honors, Grinnell Coll., 1960; MA, Harvard U., 1963, PhD, 1967. With Ecole des hautes etudes en sci. sociol., 1990-91, Princeton U., 1991; prof. polit. sci. Rutgers U. Walt Whitman Ctr. for Culture and Politics of Democracy, New Brunswick, N.J., 1969—; cons. White House Millennial Com., Corp. for Nat. Svc., U.S. Info. Agency, NEH, UNESCO, European parliament, Swedish parliamentary commn., Mission 2000 (French commn.), various polit. and civic leaders including Pres. Bill Clinton, V.p. Al Gore, Senator Bill Bradley, Germany Pres. Roman Herzog. Author: Marriage Voices, 1981, Strong Democracy, 1984, Jihad vs. McWorld, 1995 (recent internat. best seller), The Struggle for Democracy, 1988, A Place for Us, 1998; founding editor, editor-in-chief Political Theory; contbrs. articles to Harper's Mag., N.Y. Times, The Atlantic, The Nation, Le Nouvel Observateur, Die Zeit, and numerous others in U.S. and Europe; co-scriptwriter The Struggle for Democracy, Greek Fire (U.K.), The American Promise, and other ednl. documentaries; (theater) Kaspar.

BARBER, CHARLES EDWARD, newspaper executive, journalist; b. Miami, Fla., Oct. 30, 1939; s. James Plemon and Margaret Katherine (Grimes) B. m. Judith Margaret Tuck, May 28, 1960; children: Janet Lynn Wood, Christopher Edward. AA, Santa Fe Community Coll., 1971. Prodn. mgr. dept. student publs. U. Fla., Gainesville, 1966-68, ops. mgr., 1968-70, asst. dir., 1970-72, dir. div. publs., 1974; prodn. mgr. State Univ. System Press, Gainesville, 1975-76; pres., gen. mgr. Campus Communications, Inc., Gainesville, 1976—; pres. The Herald Pub. Co., Inc., 1990—, Tuck Barber & Assocs., 1995—; pub. The High Springs Herald, 1990—; dir. Campus Press; cons. in field. Co-author: (with Judy Barber) screenplay This Small Island, 1989; adv. editor Fla. Quar., 1973-74; contbr. articles to profl. jours. Mem. 1989; adv. coun. Stephen Foster Elem. Sch., Gainesville, 1976-77, Santa Fe H.S., 1991, Spring Hill Mid. Sch., 1992; mem. Friends of Five, 1975-77, Friends of Libr., 1975-77; mem. Fla. Newspaper Oral History Project, 1996—; chmn. book com. Fla. State Prison, 1973-85, 89-94; bd. dirs. Gainesville H.S. Band Boosters, 1978-79, 83-84, treas., 1984; key communicator Alachua County Sch. Bd., 1980-91; spl. registered dep. sheriff Alachua County Sheriff's Dept., 1979-92; mem. gifted students boosters Howard Bishop Mid. Sch., 1980-82; dir. Howard Bishop Band Boosters, 1980-82; mem. pres.'s coun. U. Fla., 1978—; mem. Leadership Gainesville, 1979, Leadership Fla., 1997; mem. steering com. Fla. Alliance for Better Campaigns; mem. Fla. Correct Ct. Com. for 2000 Census; pack com. chmn. Cub Scouts Am., 1977-78; dir. The Prevention Partnership, 1992-94, Fla. podrome State Theatre, 1992-95. With USCGR, 1957-65. Recipient Nat. 1st pl. for Editl. Writing Hearst Found., 1965, Svc. award Santa Fe C.C., 1982, Cert. of Appreciation Big Bros. and Big Sisters of Gainesville, 1984, Vols. for Internat. Student Affairs, 1986, 88, 89, 90, Fla. Track Club, 1988, U. Fla. Divsn. Housing, 1990, 91, Addy award Gainesville Advt. Fedn., 1986, 87; named to Ind. Fla. Alligator Hall of Fame, 1996. Mem. Am. Collegiate Network (adv. com. 1989-91), Am. Advt. Fedn., 1978-88, Nat. Press Club, Assn. for Edn. in Journalism and Mass Communication, Coll. Newspaper Bus. and Advt. Mgrs. (bd. dirs. 1980-81), Fla. Scholastic Press Assn. (newspaper judge 1981-85), Fla. Newspaper Advt. and Mktg. Execs. (chmn. edn. com. 1984-87), Fla. Press Club, Fla. Press Assn. (bd. dirs. 1992—), v.p. 1997, pres. 1998, chmn. bd. dirs., chmn. continuing edn. com. 1992—, award for weekly newspaper advt. 1993, 1st pl. award for editl. writing 1994, 1st pl. award for newspaper promotion 1992, 1st pl. award weekly newspaper advt. 1994, Best of Show award weekly newspaper advt. 1994, 1st pl. award weekly newspaper promotion 1995, 1st pl. award for weekly newspaper cmty. svc., 1995, 3rd pl. award weekly newspaper advt. 1996, 3d pl. weekly newspaper promotion 1997, award of appreciation 1999), Fla. Bus. Leadership Network, Foresight Inst., Journalism Adv. Coun., U. Fla. Coll. Journalism and Comm., Gainesville Advt. Fedn. (bd. dirs. 1979-80), Internat. Newspaper Fin. Execs., Internat. Newspaper Mktg. Assn., Coll. Media Advisers, Nat. Newspaper Assn. (H.M. for weekly newspaper promotion, 1996), Newspaper Assn. Am., New Media Fedn., Soc. of News Design, So. Univ. Newspapers (bd. dirs. 1980-89), High Springs Hist. Soc., First Amendment Found. (trustee), Alachua C of C, Gainesville Area C. of C., High Springs C. of C., Alligator Alumni Assn. (bd. dirs. 1980—, named C., Mr. Alligator 1986, Hall of Fame, 1996), U. Fla. Nat. Alumni Assn., Soc. Profl. Journalists (treas. No. Fla. chpt. 1972-75, 86-91, pres.'s club 1994-95), Substance Abuse Prevention Partnership (coun. 1992-95), Leadership Gainesville Alumni Assn., Red Herring Club, Rotary (sustaining, sec. 1993-94), The Heritage Club, Alpha Phi Gamma. Office: Campus Comm Inc PO Box 14257 Gainesville FL 32604-2257

BARBER, CHARLES LAURENCE, retired educator; b. Brentwood, Essex, Eng., Apr. 20, 1915; s. Charles Henry and Agnes Maud (Pitts) B.; m. Barbara Best, July 27, 1943; children: Elizabeth, Karin Judith, Charles Nicolas, John Andrew. BA in English, U. Cambridge, 1937, MA in English, 1941; filosofie licenciat in English, U. Gothenburg, 1956, PhD in English, 1957. Sch. tchr. Wandsworth Sch., London, 1938-47; lectr. U. Gothenburg, Sweden, 1947-56; asst. lectr. U. Belfast, Northern Ireland, 1956-59; lectr. U. Leeds, Eng., 1959-62, sr. lectr., 1962-69, reader, 1969-80, chmn. sch. of English, 1978-80. Author: The Idea of Honour in the English Drama, 1591-1700, The Story ofLanguage, 1964, Linguistic Change in Present-Day English, 1964, Early Modern English, 1976, The Story of English, 1978, York Notes: Shakespeare "As You Like It", 1981, York Notes: Shakespeare "Richard III", 1981, Poetry in English: An Introduction, 1983, The Theme of Honour's Tongue: A Study of Social Attitudes in the English Drama from Shakespeare to Dryden, 1985.. Macmillan Master Guides: Richard II by William Shakespeare, 1987, The English Language: A Historical Introduction, 1993; editor: Hamlet, 1964, A Trick to Catch the Old One, 1968, Women Beware Women, 1969, A Chaste Maid in Cheapside, 1969. Hon. sec. Leeds Theatre Trust, 1980-91. Flight lt. Royal Air Force, 1940-46. Recipient Charles Oldham Shakespeare prize U. Cambridge, 1936, Storey-Miller prize for Ednl. Theory U. London, 1938. Avocations: music, theatre, fell-walking. Home: 7 North Parade, Leeds LS16 5AY, England

BARBER, DAVID JOHN, physics educator; b. London, Feb. 14, 1935; s. George William and Amelia Sarah (Harris) B.; m. Vivien Joan Hayward, June 25, 1958 (div. 1974); children: Peter David (dec.), Douglas George, Rosalind Claire, Alison Sarah; m. Jill Elizabeth Edith Sanderson, Oct. 17, 1975; 1 child, Alastair Francis David. BSc in Physics, U. Bristol (Eng.), 1956, PhD in Physics, 1960. Investigator Alcan Internat., Banbury, Eng., 1959-62; scientist Nat. Bur. Standards, Washington, 1962-65; lectr. U. Essex, Colchester, Eng., 1965-78, prof. physics, 1979-96, prof. emeritus, 1997—, pro-vice chancellor, 1981-85; prof. physics Hong Kong U. Sci. and Tech., 1991-96; vis. prof. Pa. State U., State College, 1979-80, U. Calif., Berkeley, 1984, 89, 95, Technische Hochschule, Darmstadt, Germany, 1986, Cranfield U., 1996—, Greenwich U., 1997—. Co-author: An Introduction to the Properties of Condensed Matter, 1989; editor: Deformation Processes in Minerals, Ceramics and Rocks, 1990; contbr. articles to profl. jours. Gov. Felsted (Eng.) Sch., 1985-88. Recipient medal Electron Microscopy Soc.

Am., 1964, prize Am. Ceramic Soc., 1965, prize Royal Microscopic Soc., 1978. Fellow Inst. of Physics, Inst. of Materials; mem. Mineralogical Soc. (v.p.), Materials Rsch. Soc. Avocations: carpentry, sailing, walking, music. Office: U Essex, Dept Physics, Colchester CO4 3SQ, England

BARBER, EARL EUGENE, consulting firm executive; b. Dayton, Ohio, Dec. 8, 1939; s. Earl Garnet and Mary Helen (Brown) B.; m. Sandra Kay Reese, Mar. 11, 1960; children: Steven, Amy, Dana. BS, Ball State U., 1963; MDiv., Asbury Theol. Sem., Wilmore, Ky., 1977. Tchr. Muncie (Ind.) Community Schs, 1963-65; exec. mem. Gen. Motors, Muncie, 1965-73; pres. Barber Electric, Wilmore, 1973-77; sr. pastor Calvary Temple, Plainview, Tex., 1977-79; exec. Borg Warner Corp., Muncie, 1979-84; chief ops. officer Barber Cons. Resources, Muncie, 1984—. Author: Statistical Process Control for the Worker, 1985, Statistical Process Control: The Basic Tools, 1986, Team Leader Training, 1989, Problem Solving, 1992, 96, Understanding SPC for Short Production Runs, 1990, Total Quality Management, 1991, Team Building, 1992, Problem Solving, 1994, Time Management, 1995. Mem Mayor's Task Force, Muncie 1980. Mem. Am. Soc. Quality Control (Ptnrs. award for quality 1989, sustaining mem.), Delaware County Ministerial Assn., Epsilon Pi Tau. Republican. Methodist. Avocations: writing, music, boating. Office: Barber Cons Resources Inc 5509 N Sollars Dr Muncie IN 47304-6028

BARBER, EDWARD BRUCE, medical products executive; b. Chgo., Mar. 11, 1937; s. Edward Vanrennsaler and Alice (Reinertsen) B.; m. Louise Joy Griebler, May 23, 1964. BS, Lake Forst (Ill.) Coll., 1957; MBA, U. Chgo., 1958. Market rsch. cons. Container Corp. of Am., Chgo., 1959-61; pres. Christiansen & Barber Assoc. Ltd., Chgo., 1961—; chmn., CEO Odyssey Travel Ltd., Chgo., 1974—; founder, chmn. M.E. Team, Inc., South Plainfield, N.J., 1980—, also bd. dirs.; pres. Colts Necks Farms, Inc. 1990—; cons. Lab. Supply Co., Louisville, 1990—, Graham-Field Surg., Inc., Hauppage, N.Y., 1990—; ptnr. Wynne Med./Statco Med., 1996—, Sci. Supply Co., Schiller Park, Ill., 1990—; bd. dirs. Golden Eagle Travel, Huntington Beach, Calif. Mem. Internat. Assn. of Travel Agys., Health Industries Distbr. Assn., Masons. Republican. Lutheran. Avocations: travel, coin collector. Office: Christiansen Barber Assocs Ltd Ste 310 6800 W Raven St Chicago IL 60631-2528

BARBER, ELAINE, social worker, psychotherapist; b. Boston, May 17, 1964; d. T.X. and Catherine B. BA, Bard Coll., 1986; MSW, Boston U., 1990. Lic. social worker, Md., D.C. Social worker Nat. Rehab. Hosp., Washington, 1991-96, Stoddard Home, Washington, 1997-98; case coord. Sibley Hosp., Washington, 1998—; counselor Nat. Prebyn. Ch. Counseling Ctr., Washington, 1999. Speaker in field. Recipient Iddings Bell prize Bard Coll., N.Y., 1989. Mem. NASW. Avocation: silent film history.

BARBER, JAMES, biochemist, educator; b. Hatfield, Hert., U.K., July 16, 1940; s. Stanley William George and Sophia (Ford) B.; m. Marilyn Jane Emily Barber, Aug. 15, 1965; children: Neil James, Julie Anne. BSc, U. Wales, Swansea, 1964; MSc, U. East Anglia, Norwich, 1965, PhD, 1967; PhD (hon.), U. Stockholm, 1992. Unilever fellow U. Leiden, Netherlands, 1967-68; lectr. Imperial Coll., U. London, 1968-72, reader, 1972-79, prof. plant physiology, 1979-89, Ernst Chain prof. biochemistry, 1989—, dean Royal Coll. of Sci., 1989-91, head dept. biochemistry, 1989-99; mem. U.K. exec. com. Weizmann Inst. Found., London, 1991—. Contbr. over 500 articles to profl. jours.; editor of 11 vols.: Topics in Photosynthesis, others. Selby fellow Australian Acad. Scis. Fellow Royal Soc. Chemistry; mem. Academiae Europaeae, Coun. of the World Innovation Found. Achievements include research on understanding of the molecular processes of photosynthesis, especially the reactions of photosystem II and dynamics of the thylakoid membrane. Office: London U, Imperial Coll Biochem Dept, London SW7, England

BARBER, PIERRE YVES, engineering executive; b. Oran, Algeria, France, May 21, 1942; s. Jacques and Yvonne (Guerin) B.; m. Nicole Delhoume, Apr. 20, 1965; children: François, Carole. Engring. degree, Sch. Mechanics and Aeros., Poitiers, France, 1964, MS, 1964. Rsch. engr. French AEC, Paris, 1964-73; start-up engr. Gen. Atomics, Ft. S'Vrain, 1973-74; design engr. Technicatome, Paris, 1974-78; sales engr. Cogema, Paris, 1978-80; safety engr. Inst. Protection, Paris, 1980-86; internat. Ministry Industry, Paris, 1986-91; dir. internat. Andra, Paris, 1991—. Mem. Am. Nuclear Soc., French Nuclear Soc.

BARBER, RICHARD WILLIAM, publishing executive; b. Dunmow, Essex, Eng., Oct. 30, 1941; s. Geoffrey Osborn and Daphne (Drew) B.; m. Helen Rosemary Tolson, May 7, 1970; children: Humphrey Thomas, Elaine Mary. BA, Cambridge (Eng.) U., 1963, PhD, 1982. Editor G. Bell & Sons, London, 1968-72; mng. dir. Boydell & Brewer, Woodbridge, Eng., 1972—; chmn. Boydell & Brewer Inc., Rochester, N.Y., 1987—. Author: The Knight and Chivalry, 1970, rev. edit., 1996 (Somerset Maugham prize 1970), Edward Prince of Wales & Aquitaine, 1976, King Arthur, 1984, Penguin Guid to Medieval Europe, 1984, 20 other books. Fellow Royal Soc. Lit., Soc. Antiquaries, Royal Hist. Soc.

BARBER, SALVADOR, food company executive; b. Valencia, Spain, Jan. 8, 1933; s. Salvador and Josefa (Perez) B.; m. Carmen Benedito; children: Carmen, Berta, Salvador. PhD, Faculty of Scis., Valencia, 1960. Rsch. assoc. Inst. Agroquimica y Tecnologia de Alimentos, Valencia, 1961-71, prof. cereals chemistry and technology, 1965-86, prof. food biochemistry, 1966-85, prof. rsch., 1971-74, chief cereals lab., 1974-76, 79-85, dir., 1976-79; dir. Espanola de I&D, S.A., Moncada Valencia, Spain, 1985—; prof. Indian Inst. Technology Ford Found., Kharajpur, 1976; rice cons. FAo, Alexandria, Egypt, 1978, UNIDO, S.E. Asia, 1980; cons. Commn. European Cmtys., Brussels, 1988, 90. Co-author: Rice, Chemistry and Technology, 1972, Rice, Production and Utilization, 1980, Rice Bran, An Under Utilized Raw Material, 1985; patentee treated rice. Lt. Spanish Navy, 1956. Recipient Franco prize Nat. Rsch. Coun., 1968, Certs. of Appreciation Govt. of U.S., 1964, 69; IA A prize, Gold medal SIAL, 1968. Mem. Internat. Union Food Sci. and Technology (mem. exec. com. 1974-82), European Confedn. Chemistry Socs. (del. Spain 1980-86), UN Univ. (instnl. coord. 1983-86), Union Food Sci. and Technology of Spain (pres. 1984-90), Assn. Food Scientists and Technologists of Valencia (founder), Nat. Coll. Chemists Spain. Avocations: gardening, reading. Office: Espanola de I&D SA, c/215-209 Poligono Virgen Dolores, 46113 Moncada Valencia Spain

BARBERA, AUGUSTO ANTONIO, law educator, former member of parliament; b. Aidone, Italy, June 25, 1938; s. Giovanni and Alessandra (Locatelli) B.; m. Maria Montemagno, Dec. 16, 1970; children: Alessandro, Teresa. Degree, U. of Catania Laurea, Giurisprudenz, Italy, 1960; postgrad., U. Heidelberg, Fed. Republic Germany, 1967. Prof. various colls., Catania, Ferrara, Bologna; prof. constnl. law U. Bologna, Italy; M.P. Govt. of Italy, 1976-94. Contbr. articles to profl. jours. Democratic Party of the Left. Roman Catholic. Home: 29 IV Raibolini, 40069, Zolapredosa Bologna Italy Office: 22 Zamboni St, 40126 Bologna Italy

BARBERA, JOSE EDUARDO, international trade professional; b. Cordoba, Argentina, Aug. 8, 1950; came to U.S., 1988; s. Antonio and Petrona (Moreno) B. Lic. Bus. Adminstrn., U. Cordoba, Argentina, 1979; MBA, U. Wis., 1984; postgrad., U. Cordoba, 1985—. CPA, Argentina. Gen. mgr. Bertolina S.A., Cordoba, 1972-82; advisor Govt. of Cordoba, 1985-87; undersec. Ministry of Fgn. Trade, Cordoba, 1987—; dir. Cordoba Trade Ctr., N.Y.C., 1989—; prof. U. Cordoba, 1982-90, Cath. U., Cordoba, 1984-85, U. Rio IV, Argentina, 1984; U.S. rep. Banco de la Prov. de Cordoba in N.Y., 1987. Mem. Am. Soc., Argentine Am. C. of C. Avocations: hiking, tennis, camping. Office: Cordoba Trade Ctr 52 E End Ave # 7A New York NY 10028-7954

BARBEY, ADÉLAÏDE, publisher; b. Vallorcine, France, Aug. 21, 1948; 1 child, Alice Gissinger-Barbey. Attachée de direction Inst. Études Politiques, Paris, 1971-74; chargée de mission French Ministry Culture, Paris, 1974-79; exec. editor Hatier, Paris, 1979-82; pub. Hachette Littérature Générale, Paris, 1982-95, mng. dir. TF1 Édits., 1996.

BARBEY, GEORGES SIMON, chemical company executive; b. Nancy, Lorraine, France, Dec. 23, 1960; s. Jean and Françoise (Charoy) B. Lic Oec HSG, Hochschule St Gallen, Switzerland, 1985. Chief fin. officer BASF-Chile S.A., Santiago de Chile, 1990-94; v.p. fin. BASF-Quimica Columbiana SA, Bogota, 1994-97; chief acct. Elenac Group, Oberhausbergen, France, 1997—; dir. BASF-Peruana S.A., Lima, Peru, BASF Ecuatoriana S.A., Quito, BASF-Quimica Colombiana S.A., Bogota, 1997, TAQSA, Tarragona, Spain, 1999—. Roman Catholic. Avocations: skiing, golf, history, arts, music. Office: Elenac SA, 8 Rue Parc, 67000 Oberhausbergen France

BARBIERI, BRUNO, pharmaceutic quality assurance professional; b. Norrköping, Östergötland, Sweden, Oct. 1, 1965; s. Aldo and Stina-Britt Ingegärd (Larsson) B.; m. Heléne Beatrice Enghardt, Oct. 10, 1998; 1 child, Fabian Marchs. BSc in Chemistry, Linhöping U., Sweden, 1990; PhD in Exptl. Pathology, Karolinska Inst., Stockholm, 1997. Tchr. Norrköping, 1990; rsch. engr. Huddinge U. Hosp., Stockholm, 1990-93, rsch. chemist, 1993-96; tech. mgr. Vitamex, Norrköping, 1997; head quality assurance and regulatory affairs Numico/Vitamex, Norrköping, 1997—; expert/advisor Englet, Huskvarna, Sweden, 1994-96; solicitor Academician Union Karolinska Inst., Stockholm, 1994-96. Author: (with others) Current Topics in Microbiology and Immunology, 1997; contbr. articles to profl. publs. Lt. Protection Against ABC-Weapon, 1986-87. Mem. Internat. Co Q10 Assn. Avocations: Alfa Romeo car and club, fishing, saxophone. Home: Robert Almströmsg 3, 11336 Stockholm Uppland, Sweden Office: Vitamex/Numico, Bergslagsg 9, 60116 Norrköping Sweden

BARBIERI, RENATO, retired chemistry educator; b. Padova, Italy, Mar. 24, 1930; s. Giovanni and Carla (Bressan) B.; m. Anna Maria Reffo, Aug. 4, 1958 (dec. 1983); children: Lorenza, Giovanna, Adriana; m. Maria Teresa Musmeci, July 4, 1984; 1 child, Giovanni. Doctor of Chemistry, U. Padua, Italy, 1956. Asst. tchr. chem. disciplines U. Padua, 1956-65; rschr. H.C. Orsted Inst., Copenhagen, 1963-64, Rutgers U., New Brunswick, N.J., 1970, U. Uppsala, Sweden, 1970; prof. gen. and inorganic chemistry U. Palermo, Italy, 1965-2000, head Inst. Gen. Chemistry, 1965-76; ret., 2000; dean, coun. chem. U. Palermo, 1981-86; coord. PhD, 1981-96. Contbr. articles to profl. jours. Mem. Italian Chem. Soc., Chem. Soc. London, Am. Chem. Soc., N.Y. Acad. Scis. Achievements include rsch. on the interaction of organotin compounds with biol. molecules, the antitumor activity of organotin compounds, 119 Sn Mossbauer Spectroscopy. Home: Piazza San Marino 2, 90146 Palermo Italy Office: Parco O'orleans II, Viale delle Scienze, 90128 Palermo Italy

BARBIERI, SERGIO, neurologist; b. Clusone, Lombardy, Italy, Nov. 28, 1954; s. Luigi Domenico and Angela Antonia (Poletti) B.; m. Giovanna Pinardi; children: Beatrice, Giacomo. MD, U. Milan, 1979, PhD in Neurol. Scis., 1989. Rsch. fellow in electromyography Mayo Sch. Medicine, Rochester, Minn., 1982; resident neurology U. Milan, 1983; asst. neurology dept. Ospedale Maggiore di Milano, Milan, 1987-89, head clin. neurophysiology lab., 1989—, head neurohabilitation dept., 1989—; cons. Istituto Ortopedico Galeazzi, Milan, 1982-96, Citta' di Milano, 1987—, Italian Got. Commn. for Seveso, 1982-84; prof. Sch. Neurology, U. Milan, 1988—. Contbr. articles to profl. jours., chpts. to books. Sec. Confederazione Italiana Medici Ospedalieri, 1997. Grantee Unione Italiana Lotta Alla Distrofia Muscolare, Milan, 1981, Centro Dino Ferrari, Milan, 1983. Mem. Am. Acad. Electrodiagnostic Medicine, European Neurol. Soc. Avocations: books, music, movies. Home: Viale Bligny 54, 20136 Milan Italy Office: Ospedale Maggiore di Milan, Via F Sforza 35, 20122 Milan Italy

BARBOSA, RUBENS ANTONIO, Brazilian ambassador; b. Sao Paulo, June 13, 1938; s. Jose Orlando and Lice (Farina) B.; m. Maria Ignez Correa da Costa, June 13, 1969; children: Joao Bernardo, Mariana. BA in Law, U. Sao Paulo; BA in Diplomacy, Brazil's Fgn. Svc. Acad.; MA in Latin Am. Politics, London Sch. Econs./Polit. Sci. 3rd sec. Brazil's Ministry of Fgn. Rels., Brasilia, Brazil and London, 1962-66; 2d sec. Brazilian Embassy, London, 1966-73, counselor, 1976-79, min., 1979-84; chief of staff to min. of fgn. rels., 1985-86; undersec. gen. for multilateral and spl. polit. affairs Ministry of Fgn. Rels., 1986-87; sec. for internat. affairs Brazilian Fin. Ministry, 1987-88; Brazilian amb. Latin Am. Integration Assn., 1988-91, pres. com. of reps., 1991-92; undersec. gen. for trade, regional integration/econ. affairs Ministry of Fgn. Rels., 1991-93, v.p. permanent com. on fgn. trade, 1992-93; Brazilian amb. to the Ct. of St. James London, 1994-99; Brazilian amb. to the U.S., 1999—; Brazilian govt. coord. Mercosul Issues, 1991-93; exec. sec. com. on trade with East European Countries, 1976-83. Author: American Latina em Perspectiva: a Integraçao Regional da Retórica à Realidade, 1991, Panorama visto de Londres, 1998. Mem. Assn. of Cofee Producing Countries (pres. 1994-99). Office: Brazilian Embassy 3006 Massachusetts Ave NW Washington DC 20008-3699

BARBOTKO, ALEXANDER IVANOVITCH, gerontologist; b. Kemerovo, Russia, June 2, 1955; s. Ivan Mikhailovitch and Maria Alekseievna (Glazirina) B. BA, Sch. 8, Kemerovo, Russia, 1972; Diploma in Gerontology, Med. Inst., Kemerovo, Russia, 1977; Diploma technician-electrician, Technikal Sch., Kemerovo, Russia, 1985. Economist Factory Karbolit, Kemerovo, Russia, 1975-80; gerontologist pvt. practice, Russia, France, 1977-99; press photographer freelance, Russia, France, 1977-99. Fellow The Writers Bureau; mem. Home of Writers, European Circle of Bus. Home: BT 508 RCD, 56 BLD Michel Montaigne, 95200 Sarcelles France

BARBOUR, BLAIR ALLEN, electro-optical engineer, researcher; b. Huntington, W.Va., Aug. 12, 1962; s. James Alfred and Carolyn Louise (Meadows) B.; m. Susan Lynne Bird, June 30, 1984; children: Amanda Nicole, Jenna Elyse, Brett Allen, Scott Adam. BS of Engring. Physics, Marshall U., 1984; MS in Electro-Optics, U. Dayton, 1986. Registered profl. engr., Ala. Lab. mgr. Fillite USA Inc., Huntington, 1980-84; rsch. physicist UDRI, Dayton, Ohio, 1984-86; sr. optical engr. The Boeing Co., Huntsville, 1986-92; divsn. dir. Nichols Rsch. Corp., Huntsville, 1992—; pres. Photon-X, Inc., Huntsville, 1999—; founder Sport-X, Inc., 1999—; founder Sport-X, Inc., 1999—; bd. dirs., gov. U. Ala., Huntsville, 1992—, mem. optical alliance, 1992—; divsn. dir. Nichols Rsch. Corp., Huntsville, 1992—; optical cons. The Boeing Co., Huntsville, 1988-94; bd. dirs., chmn. AVMC. Contbr. articles to profl. jours. Sunday sch. tchr. 1st Bapt. Ch., Huntsville, 1988-92; youth softball coach Westco League, Madison, Ala., 1992—; youth soccer coach Nat. Youth Soccer Orgn., Madison, Ala., 1993-94; boys youth leader Royal Ambs.-FBC, Huntsville, 1993—. Mem. Soc. Photo-Instrumentation Engrs., Optical Soc. Am., Sigma Xi. Achievements include patent for ice monitoring and detection system; patent pending for spatial phase sensor, for achromatic waveplate, for phase measuring RF/MMW sensor; development of revolutionary spatial phase measurement technology that will change and improve standard amplitude measurement sensor, wave measurement sensor, system for receiving and enhancing electromagnetic radiation input signals; rsch. in noninvasive glucose monitor. E-mail: barb5609@aol.com. Office: Photon X Inc MS 913 102A Wynn Dr NW Huntsville AL 35805-1957

BARBOUR, CLAUDE MARIE, minister; b. Brussels, Oct. 2, 1935; came to U.S., 1969; Diploma d'État d'Infirmières, École d'Infirmières, Paris, 1956; diploma d'Études Religieuses, Faculté Libre de Théolog, Paris, 1958; MST, N.Y. Theol. Sem., 1970; DST, Garrett Evang. Theol. Sem., 1973. Ordained to ministry Presbyn. Ch., 1974. Youth counselor Young Women's Christian Assn., Geneva, 1959-61, Edinburgh, 1965-67; missionary Paris Evang. Missionary Soc., So. Africa, 1962-64; deaconess Ch. of Scotland, Edinburgh, 1967-69; from asst. to assoc. pastor First United Presbyn. Ch., Gary, Ind., 1974-80; from asst. to assoc. prof. Cath. Theol. Union, Chgo., 1976-86, prof., 1986—; prof. McCormick Theol. Sem., Chgo., 1990-96; founder, dir. Shalom Ministries and Community, Chgo., 1975—; parish assoc. First Presbyn. Ch., Evanston, Ill., 1983—. World Coun. Chs. scholar, Geneva, 1969, United Presbyn. Ch. Commn. on Ecumenical Mission and Rels., N.Y., 1972; recipient Laskey award United Meth. Ch. Womens Div. the Bd. Global Ministries, N.Y., 1972, Civic award Ind. Women's Coun., 1976, Challenge of Peace award Chgo. Ctr. for Peace Studies, 1991, Martin P. Wolf O.F.M. award Justice, Peace and Integrity of Creation Coun. of the English-Speaking Conf. of the Order of Friars Minor, 1996. Mem. AAUW, Internat. Assn. for Mission Studies, Nat. Assn. Presbyn. Clergywomen, Am. Soc. Missiology, Assn. Prof. Mission, Midwest Fellowship Prof. Mission, Assn. Presbyn. in Cross-Cultural Mission. Home: 1649 E 50th St Apt 21A Chicago IL 60615-6110 Office: Catholic Theological Union 5401 S Cornell Ave Chicago IL 60615-5664

BARBOUR, ROBERT ANGUS, retired academic educator; b. Gawler, Australia, July 29, 1931; s. Robert and Ruth (Macloy) B.; m. Ruth Calvert Murrell, May 19, 1956; children: Simon John Alexander, Angela Helen, Timothy David Andrew, Rachel Elizabeth. B of Medicine/B of Surgery, U. Adelaide, 1955, MD, 1962. Intern Royal Adelaide Hosp., 1955; lectr. U. Adelaide, 1956-61, sr. lectr., 1961-94, dept. head, 1979-93, assoc. dean, 1991-94; ret., 1994; mem. adv. com. in podiatry U. South Australia, Adelaide, 1963-94, chmn., 1976-94. Author: (with others) The Biology of Marsupials, 1977; contbr. articles to profl. jours. Mem. Saint Andrews Sch. Coun., Walkerville, South Australia, 1982-88, dep. chmn., 1984-87. Mem. Anatomical soc. of Great Britain and Ireland, Anatomical Soc. of Australia and New Zealand. Mem. Anglican Ch. Avocations: gardening, lawn bowls. Home: 504 Kensington Rd, Wattle Park 5066 South Australia, Australia

BARBOZA, ANGEL ALBERTO, aerodynamics engineer; b. Guadalajara, Jal, Mexico, Oct. 17, 1968; came to U.S., 1978; s. Juan C. and Mary C. (Gonzales) B. Student, San Bernardino Valley Coll., 1990-92; BS in aerodyns., Calif. Poly U., 1992-96; MS in Aerospace Engring., U. Wash., 2000. Aerodyns. engr. Boeing Comml. Airplane Group, Seattle, 1996—. Mem. AIAA, Boewg Soaring Club. Avocations: Tae Kwon Do Black Belt. Office: Boeing Comml Airplane Group PO Box 3707 Seattle WA 98124-2207

BARBOZA, ANTHONY, photographer, artist; b. New Bedford, Mass., May 10, 1944; s. Anthony Canto and Lillian (Barros) B.; m. Laura Carrington, June 15, 1985; children: Danica Chizu-Alita, Alexio Kyoshi-Tuari, Lien Orianna; children by previous marriage: Leticia, Laryssa. Grad. high sch., New Bedford. Lectr. Internat. Ctr. Photography, 1975, 83, Mass. State Coun. of Arts, 1982, Columbia Coll. Photography, Chgo., 1983, Oberlin (Ohio) Coll., 1984, Ohio U., Athens, 1986, Mus. Sch. Fine Arts, Boston, 1989, Lowell (Mass.) U., 1989, Rochester (N.Y.) Inst. Tech., 1991; freelance photographer for advt. campaigns including Clairol, Hanes, Coca-Cola, Pepsi-Cola, United Negro Coll. Fund., Burger King, Soft Sheen Products, Kodak, McDonalds, Anheiser Busch, AT&T, Coors, Universal Pictures, Spike Lee Prodns., numerous others; panelist, judge Mass. State Coun. of Arts, 1978, Nat. Endowment Arts, 1981. Solo exhbns. include Pensacola (Fla.) Art Mus., 1966, Jacksonville (Fla.) Art Mus., 1969, Light Impressions Gallery, Rochester, N.Y., 1973, Friends Gallery of N.Y., 1974, Studio Mus. Harlem, N.Y.C., 1982; group shows include Addison Gallery Am. Arts, Andover, Mass., 1971, Mus. Modern Art, N.Y.C., 1978, Photokina, Germany, 1982, 84, City of Munich, 1985, Washington Project for Arts, 1989; in permanent collections Mus. Modern Art, N.Y.C., Newark Art Mus., U. Ghana, U. Mex., others; contbr. to books A Day in the Life of Hollywood, 1992, Color of Fashion, 1992, Songs of My People, 1992, The African Americans, 1993, A Day in the Life of Israel, 1994. Grantee N.Y. State Coun. of Arts, 1974, 76, Nat. Endowment Arts, 1980. Avocations: painting, writing, gardening, design, literature. Home: 915 Gloucester Ct Westbury NY 11590-5301 Studio: 13 Laight St Apt 17 New York NY 10013-2119

BARBU, VIOREL P., mathematician, educator; b. Deleni, Vaslui, Romania, June 14, 1941; s. Panaite and Anelia (Tugulea) B.; m. Margareta Galateanu, Aug. 28, 1965; children: Tudor, Catalina. PhD, U. Iasi, Romania, 1969; D Honoris Causa, U. Nebr., 1993. Prof. U. A. I. Cuza, Iasi, 1964—, pres., 1981-89; vis. prof. U. Rome, 1976; prof. U. Cin., 1990-91, Ohio U., Athens, 1993-95. Author: Nonlinear Semigroups, 1976, Optimal Control, 1984. Mem. Am. Math. Soc., Romanian Acad. (prize 1972). Home: SF Teodor 1, 6600 Iasi Romania Office: Univ Al I Cuza, Blvd Carol 11, 6600 Iasi Romania

BARBULESCU, SORIN ADRIAN, electronic engineer, researcher; b. Bucharest, Romania, Oct. 13, 1959; arrived in Australia, 1991; s. Iordan Petre and Maria Luiza (Demiriam) B. m. Antoaneta Miclos, July 15, 1982; 1 child, Oana-Cristina. MSc, Polytech. U., Bucharest, Romania, 1984; PhD, U. South Australia, Adelaide, 1996, Grad. Cert. in Mgmt., 1999. Electronic engr. Inst. De Cercetari Electronice, Bucharest, Romania, 1984-87, sr. sci. rschr., 1988-90; rsch. engr. Inst. for Telecomm. Rsch., Adelaide, Australia, 1992-95; rsch. assoc. Inst. for Telecomm. Rsch., Adelaide, 1995-96, rsch. fellow, 1996-99; Contbr. articles to profl. jours.; presented papers at sci. confs. E-mail: adrian.barbulescu@unisa.edu.au. Office: Inst for Telecomm Rsch, U South Australia, Mawson Lakees SA 5095, Australia

BARBUSINSKI, KRZYSZTOF, environmental engineering educator, researcher; b. Kalisz, Poland, June 24, 1958; s. Jozef and Jadwiga (Wojnicz) B.; m. Katarzyna Migier, Dec. 27, 1986; 1 child, Agnieszka. MSc, Silesian Tech. U., 1983, PhD in Tech. Scis., 1992. Asst. Silesian Tech. U., Gliwice, Poland, 1983-90, sr. asst., 1990-93, asst. prof., 1993—; asst. prof. Cen. Mining Inst., Katowice, Poland, 1996—; cons. Inst. of Ecology of Indsl. Areas, Katowice, 1995-96, Cen. Mining Inst., 1995-96; supr. rsch. project Chem. Works of Kedzierzyn, Poland, 1996-99, Chem. Works of Organika-Azot, Jaworzno, Poland, 1997-98, State Com. for Sci. Rsch., Poland, 1997-98; chmn. organizing and sci. com. All-Poland Conf.-Advances and Problems of Industrial Wastewater Treatment, 1998; cons. Hydrosan, Gliwice, Poland, 1998-99; lectr. H.S. Economy and Adminstrn., 1999—. Author: Lexicon of Environmental Biotechnology, 1993, 99; co-author: The Chosen Problems of Environment Protection, 2000; patentee in field; contbr. articles to sci. and profl. jours. Mem. Nat. Geographic Soc., Soc. Chem. and Ecological Engring. (Poland), 1999. E-mail: krzybar@zeus.polsl.gliwice.pl. Office: Silesian Tech U, Konarskiego 18, 44-101 Gliwice Poland

BARCA, GEORGE GINO, winery executive, financial investor; b. Sacramento, Jan. 28, 1937; s. Joseph and Annie (Muschetto) B.; m. Maria Sclafani, Nov. 19, 1960; children: Anna, Joseph, Gina and Nina (twins). AA, Grant Jr. Coll.; student, LaSalle U., 1963. With United Vintners, U.S.A., St. Helena, Napa Valley, Calif., 1960—; chmn., pres. Barcamerica U.S.A., Barcamerica Internat. U.S.A., Barca Wine Cellars, Calif. Wine Cellars, U.S.A., Calif. Grape Growers, U.S.A., Calif. Vintage Wines, U.S.A., Am. Vintners, U.S.A., Barca Investment Trust, U.S.A. Named Best Producer of Sales and Fin. Investments, United Vintners, U.S.A. Mem. KC. Roman Catholic. Achievements include development of wine trademarks and brands.

BARCA-SALOM, FRANCESC XAVIER, science and technology educator, researcher; b. Tarragona, Catalunya, Spain, Mar. 29, 1954; s. Nicolas and Berta (Salom) Barca; m. Gloria Fontova-Hugas, Apr. 17, 1984; 1 child, Aina. Grad. in Indsl. Engring., U. Poly., Catalunya, 1977; D of Econs., U. Sci. Socials, Grenoble, France, 1978; M of History of Scis., U. Autonoma, Barcelona, Spain, 1995. Tchr. math. Generalitat Catalunya, Barcelona, 1979—; assoc. prof. history of scis. and tech. U. Poly., Catalunya, 1987—. Author: El Dic Flotant I Deposant Del Port De Barcelona, 1993, (chpt.) Ciencia I Tecnica Als Paisos Catalans. Una Aproximacio Biografica, 1995; mem. editl. com. Quaderns D'Hist. Enginyeria, 1996. Named Internat. scholar Soc. History Tech., 1999—. Mem. Catalan Soc. History Sci. and Tech. (sec. 1991-98). E-mail: barca@ma1.upc.es. Home: Roger De Flor 289, 1, 08025 Barcelona Spain Office: Univ Poly Catalunya, Diagonal 647 History Tech, 08028 Barcelona Spain

BARCELÓ MEZQUITA, JOSÉ LUIS, political scientist; b. Madrid, July 15, 1963; s. José Luis Barceló Fdez de la Mora and María Luisa Mezquita Uría; m. María Pilar Vicente Martínez, Apr. 26, 1994; 1 child, Gonzalo. Lic. faculty polit. sci., U. Complutense, Madrid, 1993, D Inst. de Europa Oriental, 1996. With social tech. staff Spanish Red Cross, Madrid, 1989-90, regional dir., 1990-92; dir., editor El Mundo Financiero, Madrid, 1991-96; rschr. Inst. de Europa Oriental U. Complutense, Madrid, 1995-96. Author: (dictionary) Summa Colombina, 1989, (book) Guia Verde, 1986, (poetry) Trazas Crepusculares, 1988; editor-in-chief: Portavoz de la Economia, Madrid, 1982, 85; editor: El Mundo Financiero, Madrid, 1985-91, (monthly mag.) ADDA-Madrid, 1991-94. Pres. Green Party in Spain; founder Union Centrista, 1993, Consejo de la Juventud de Madrid, 1985-87; sec. Solidaridad-Derechos Humanos, Madrid, 1986-89; local dir. Spanish Red Cross, Galapagar, Spain, 1985-91; del. Assn. Iberoam. de Periodistas Especializados y Técnicos, Madrid, 1987-90; dir. Acualidad Turistica, Madrid, 1988-92, Assn. Defensa Derechos Animals, Madrid, 1991-94; councilor Mcpl. Govt. Galapagar, Madrid, 1999; founder Toro Verde, 1999. Recipient Silver medal Spanish Red Cross, 1988. Mem. Spanish Assn. Writers and Artists, Internat. Assn. Writers, European Philatelic Soc. Mem. Green Party-Centrist Union. Avocations: philately, numismatics, painting, reading and writing, swimming. E-mail: mundofinanciero@nauta.es. Fax:

34-1-5773376. Home: Calle Hermosilla 93, E-28001 Madrid Spain Office: El Mundo Financiero, PO Box 6119, E-28080 Madrid Spain

BARCELOS, EDUARDO DORNELES, space company executive; b. Porto Alegre, Brazil, Oct. 14, 1962; s. Ely Melo and Maria de Lourdes (Dorneles) B.; m. Maria Paula De Castro Chaves, Jan. 16, 1988; children: Daniel, Natalia. MPhil, U. São Paulo, 1991, PhD, 1997. Rschr. Mus. Astronomy, Rio de Janeiro, 1991-92, Nat. Coun. Rsch., Brasilia, Brazil, 1992-93; with Cabinet's Chief Ho. of Reps., Brasilia, Brazil, 1993-94; advisor Brazilian Space Agy., Brasilia, Brazil, 1995, coord., 1997—, dir., 1996-97; history prof. UPIS, Brasilia, Brazil, 1999—; assoc. rschr. Ministry of Sci. and Tech., Brasilia, 1998—; cons. in field. Contbr. articles to profl. jours. Mem. The Planetary Soc., Brazilian Soc. History Sci., Brazilian Astronomy Club. Avocations: cycling, volleyball. Office: Brazilian Space Agy, SBM Q 02ED Eng Paulo Mauric, 70040905 Brasilia Brazil

BARCHARD, JOHN HARLEY, timber importing company executive; b. Hessle, England, Aug. 22, 1927; s. William and Gladys (Bright) B.; m. Marguerite Warburton, June 7, 1975. Grad., Hymers Coll. From works dir. to chmn. Barchard Ltd., Hull, England, 1948—.

BARCK, KARLHEINZ RUDOLF, university administrator; b. Quedlinburg, Germany, Nov. 28, 1934; s. Rudolf and Margarete Frida (Schuetze) B.; m. Simone Henriette Eichel, Mar. 23, 1967; children: Maximilian, Catharina, Henriette. BA, Gutsmuths-Olerrealschule, Quedlinburg, 1953; Diplomphiloloqe, Humboldt U., 1958; Dr.Phil., Rostock U., 1965; Dr.sci., Acad. Sci. of Berlin, 1984. Asst. Humboldt U., 1959-61; asst. prof. Rostock U., 1961-64; rsch. dir. Acad. Sci. Berlin, 1966-90, Centre for Lit. Studies, Berlin, 1991—; assoc. prof. U. Montreal, 1994—. Editor: Góngora, 1968, Rimbaud, 1972, French Surrealism, 1986; co-editor: Aisthesis Perspectives of An Other Esthetics; chief editor: Historical Dictionary of Esthetic Categories, 7 vols., 2000. Recipient Werner-Krauss medal Acad. Sci. Berlin, 1986, Encomienda de la Orden de Isabel la Católica, Spanish King, 1993. Mem. German Soc. Aesthetics (advising mem. 1992-98). Avocation: jazz. Home: Grosse Hamburger Str 31, 10115 Berlin Germany Office: Zentrum fur Literaturforsch, Jaegerstrasse 10/11, 10117 Berlin Germany

BARCLAY, ALAN NEIL, immunologist, researcher; b. Wantage, Eng., Mar. 12, 1950; s. Frank Rodney and Betty Cowie (Watson) B.; m. Ella Geraldine Quinn, July 10, 1975; children: Mark Robert, Alison Tanum, Luke Stuart. BA, Oxford (Eng.) U., 1973, DPhil, 1976. Rsch. fellow U. Goteborg, Sweden, 1976-78; rsch. scientist Med. Rsch. Coun., Oxford, 1978—, spl. appointment, 1994; prof. molecular immunology Med. Rsch. Coun., 1998; dir. Everest Biotech Ltd., 1999—; acad. advisor Oxford U. Bioinformatics Ctr., 1993-99. Co-author: The Leucocyte Antigens Factsbook, 1993, 97; contbr. approximately 100 articles to scientific jours.; mem. editl. bd. (scientific jour.) Immunogenetics, 1997. Mem. Brit. Soc. Immunology, Biochem. Soc., Scandinavian Soc. Immunology (hon.). Avocations: music, writing novels and children's stories, literature, travel. Office: Sir Wm Dunn Sch Pathology, U Oxford Oxford OX1 3RE, England

BARCLAY, THOMAS LAIRD, plastic surgeon; b. Huddersfield, Yorkshire, Eng., Mar. 26, 1925; s. William and Mary Frances B.; m. Isabel Mary Raffan, Sept. 19, 1953; childen: William, Philippa. M.B.,Ch.B., Edinburgh U., Scotland, 1947; Ch.M., Edinburgh U., 1970. House surgeon Royal Infirmary, Edinburgh, 1947-48; sr. registrar in plastic surgery Mt. Vernon Hosp., Northwood, Eng., 1955-60; cons. plastic surgeon Bradford Hosps., Yorkshire, Eng., 1960-85; hon. cons. plastic surgeon Bradford Hosps., 1985—. Author: Burns and Their Treatment, 1962, 3rd edit. 1986; editor: Operative Surgery, 1987; contbr. articles to profl. jours. Maj. Royal Army Emergency Res., 1962-68. Fellow Royal Coll. Surgeons of Edinburgh, Royal Coll. Surgeons of Eng.; mem. Brit. Assn. Plastic Surgeons (coun. mem. 1968-70, 79-81, v.p. 1982, pres. 1983). Avocations: golf. Home: 3 Taverngate Hawksworth, Guiseley England LS208NX Office: Yorkshire Clinic, Bradford Rd, Bingley England BD161TW

BARCOS, LUIS OSVALDO, veterinarian; b. Colón, Argentina, Apr. 3, 1957; s. Juan Carlos and Angela Matilde (Bianchimano) B.; m. Maria del Carmen Cepeda, Aug. 7, 1981; children: Maria Eugenia, Juan Ignacio, Agustín. DVM. Livestock mgr. Dirección Remonta y Veterinaria, Buenos Aires, 1980-92; exec. sec. CABIA, Buenos Aires, 1983-85; gen. vet. advisor San Sebastian S.A., Buenos Aires, 1990-96; tech. dir. SANOFI, Buenos Aires, 1993-96; pres. Nat. Agrifood Health and quality Svc., Buenos Aires, 1997—; reprodn. advisor Rhonemerieux, Buenos Aires, 1995-96; dir. Argentine Artificial Insemination Chamber, 1993-96; CABIA rep. SRA, 1995-96. Author: Fiebre Aftosa, Analisis Cualitativo de Riesgo, 1997, BSE Risk Factors in Argentina, 1998, Scrapie, Risk Factors in Argentina, 1998. Roman Catholic. Avocations: tennis, hiking. Home: Soler 4280, Buenos Aires Argentina Office: SENASA, Paseo Colón 367, 1063 Buenos Aires Argentina

BARCYS, JONAS, publishing executive; b. Uta, Varena Dist., Lithuania, Oct. 19, 1933; s. Stasys and Vanda (Barciene) B.; m. Ramute Gumbinaite Barciene, Oct. 25, 1958 (div. Mar. 1977); children: Gintautas, Audrone. Master's degree in Lithuanian Lang., Vilnius Pedagogical Inst., 1957. Tchr. Ežerelis Secondary Sch., 1957-58, dir., 1958-59; head Kaunas Ednl. Dept., 1959-63; dir. Kaunas Secondary Sch. No. 8, 1963-66; inspector Kaunas Ednl. Dept., 1966-68; editor-in-chief Kaunas Šviesa Pubs., 1968-80, dir., 1980—. Author 3 chrestomatical readers of Lithuanian lang. for secondary schs.; translator books from Russian lang. for secondary sch. Avocation: gardening. Office: Sviesa Pubs, Vytauto 25, 3000 Kaunas Lithuania

BARCZA, SZABOLCS, astrophysicist, educator; b. Budapest, Hungary, Jan. 28, 1944; s. Gedeon and Erzsèbet (Ba'nyai) B.; m. Anna Maria Szuromi, 1976; six children. MS, L. Eötvös U., Budapest, 1967, PhD, 1969. Asst. Konkoly Obs., Budapest, 1967, rsch. fellow, 1970, sr. rsch. fellow, 1981; asst. prof. astrophysics L. Eötvös U., Budapest, 1984—. Author: The Life of Stars, 1979; contbr. articles to profl. jours. Office: Konkoly Obs, H-1525 Budapest Pf 67, Hungary

BARCZAK, ANDRZEJ STANISŁAW, statistician, researcher; b. Ruda Śu, Silesia, Poland, Feb. 4, 1939; s. Stanisław and Jadwiga (Wyrębska) B.; m. Mirosława Marczyk, June 28, 1969; children: Stanisław, Aleksandra. MBA, Acad. of Econs., Katowice, Poland, 1962; Dr., Acad. Econs., Katowice, Poland, 1968, Dr.Habil., 1976. Asst. Acad. Econs., Katowice, 1962-68, asst. prof., 1968-72, assoc. prof., 1972-85, full prof. stats. and econometrics, 1985—, dean, 1984-87, vice rector, 1981-84; pres. bd. Feuix, Katowice, 1995—; cons. Vojevodship, Katowice, 1993—. Author: Macromodels, 1968 (Ministry of Edn. award 1969), Econometric Models, 1971 (Ministry of Edn. award 1971); editor Statis. Revue, 1993—. Moderator Voivodship Office, Katowice, 1992—. Recipient Award of Nat. Edn., Ministry of Edn., Warsaw, 1982, Polonia Restituta award, Pres. Poland, 1986. Fellow Polish Acad. Scis.,; mem. Polish Assn. Stats., Rotary (pres. 1991-92). Roman Catholic. Avocations: climbing, fencing, music. Home: Kotlarza 9D m4, 40-139 Katowice Silesia, Poland Office: Academy of Economics, Academy of Economics, Bogucicka 12, 40-226 Katowice Silesia, Poland also: Jagiellonian U Fac Mgmt, Golebie 24, Krakow 31-007, Poland

BARCZYK, GRZEGORZ RAFAL, hydrogeology researcher, educator; b. Warsaw, Poland, Oct. 23, 1959; s. Wieslaw and Ewa (Popiel) B.; m. Agata Obrocka, Oct. 9, 1983 (div. 1995); 1 child, Michalina. MSc Faculty of Geology, U. Warsaw, 1983, PhD, 1994. Specialist of hydrogeology Inst. Balneology, Warsaw, 1983-85; asst. Inst. Hydrogeology and Environ. Geology, U. Warsaw, 1985-95, sr. asst. rschr., 1995—; tchr. geography and computer sci., elem. sch., Warsaw, 1990—. Author, editor: Polish Bibliography of Geology of Tatra Mountains, 1990; contbr. articles to sci. publs. Mem. Polish Soc. Geologists. Avocations: mountain touring, history of World War II, history of Middle Ages, plastic modeling, Irish culture and music. E-mail: gb59@geo.uw.edu.pl. Office: Warsaw U Inst Hydrogeol EG, Zwirki i Wigury 93, 02-089 Warsaw Poland

BARD, ALLEN JOSEPH, chemist, educator; b. Dec. 18, 1933; m. Fran; children: Eddie, Sara. BSc in Chemistry summa cum laude, CCNY, 1955; MA in Chemistry, Harvard U., 1956, PhD in Chemistry, 1958. Instr. chemistry The U. Tex., Austin, 1958-60, asst. prof., 1960-62, assoc. prof., 1962-67, prof., 1967—, Jack S. Josey Professorship Energy Studies, 1980-82, Norman Hackerman Prof. Chemistry, 1982-85, Hackerman-Welch Regents Chair Chemistry, 1985—; lectr. numerous univs., 1969-96; mem. U.S. nat. com. Internat. Union Pure and Applied Chemistry-Nat. Rsch. Coun., 1983—, chair, 1988-89, bd. energy and environ. sys., 1983-86, 93—, bd. chem. scis. tech., 1982-87, co-chair, 1985-87, nat. materials adv. bd. com. on electrochem. aspects of energy conservation and prodn., 1985, com. on chem. scis. and ad hoc panel on DOE rsch., 1980-84, NAS, NRC liaison com. on high temp. sci. and tech., 1984; pres. Internat. Union Pure and Applied Chemistry, 1991-93; mem. adv. bd. Dept. Energy and Energy Rsch., panel on Cold Fusion, 1989; chem. adv. com. NSF, 1981-84; mem. external adv. com. Beckman Inst., 1989—; bd. govs. Weizmann Inst., 1995—, sci. & acad. adv. com., 1995—. Author: Chemical Equilibrium, 1966, Integrated Chemical Systems, 1994; co-author: Electrochemical Methods, 1980; editor Electroanalytical Chemistry, 19 vols., 1966—, Encyclopedia of the Electrochemistry of the Elements, 16 vols., 1973—, (with others) Standard Potentials in Aqueous Solution; mem. editl. and adv. bds. Jour. Am. Chem. Soc., editor-in-chief, 1982—; mem. editl. bd. Electrochimica Acta, divsn. editor, 1978-80; mem. editl. and adv. bds. Dictionary of Modern Sci. and Tech., 1989—, Ency. of Sci. Instrumentation, 1990—, Ency. of Phys. Sci. and Tech., 1984—, Ency. of Sci. and Tech., 1992—, Analytical Letters, 1967—, Analytical Scis., 1985—, Catalysis Letters, 1988—, Chem. Instrumentation, 1967-77, Chem. Physics Letters, 1992—, Critical Revs. in Analytical Chemistry, 1985-91, Jour. Photoacoustics, 1982-84, New Jour. Chemistry, 1978-93, Jour. Supercritical Fluids, 1988—, Organic Thin Films and Surfaces, 1991—, Heterogeneous Chemistry Revs., 1993—, Accounts of Chem. Rsch., 1993—, Russian Chem. Bull., 1995—; contbr. over 600 articles to profl. jours. Recipient Outstanding Achievement in Fields of Analytical Chemistry award Eastern Analytical Symposium, 1990, Townsend Harris medal City Coll. N.Y., 1989, Edward Mack award Ohio State U., 1989, Math. and Phys. Scis. award N.Y. Acad. Scis., 1986, Docteur Honoris Causa award U. de Paris-VII, 1986, Bruno Breyer Meml. award Royal Australian Chem. Inst., 1984, Scientific Achievement award City Coll. N.Y., 1983, Sherman Mills Fairchild scholar Calif. Inst. Tech., 1977, Ward Medal in Chemistry, 1955, Luigi Galvani medal Societa Chimica Italiana, 1992, Sigillum Magnum di Bologna, 1996. Fellow Electrochem. Soc. (Olin-Palladium medal 1987, Henry Linford award 1986, Carl Wagner Meml. award 1981); mem. AAAS (coun. del. 1992-95, chair-elect chemistry sect. 1996), Am. Chem. Soc. (G.M. Kosolapoff award 1992, Oesper award Cin. sect. 1989, Analytical Chemistry award 1988, Willard Gibbs award Chgo. sect. 1987, Fisher award in Analytical Chemistry 1984, Harrison Howe award Rochester sect. 1980), Nat. Acad. Scis. (chmn. chemistry sect. 1996-99, award in chem. scis. 1998), Am. Acad. Arts and Scis. (award 1990), Internat. Soc. Electrochemists (Linus Pauling award 1998), Am. Philos. Soc., Assn. Harvard Chemists, Sigma Xi. Achievements include research involving application of electrochemical methods to study of chemical problems and include investigations in electroanalytical chemistry, electron spin resonance, electro-organic chemistry, high resolution electrochemistry, electrogenerated chemiluminescence and photoelectrochemistry. Office: U Tex Lab Electrochem Dept Chemistry Austin TX 78712

BARD, DAVID ROY, medical researcher; b. London, Aug. 23, 1946; m. Sarah Judith Yarrow Eccles, Aug. 21, 1982; children: Deborah, Jonathan. BSc, U. Bath, U.K., 1969; MSc, U. Surrey, U.K., 1970, PhD, 1974. Postdoctoral rschr. Strangeways Rsch. Lab., Cambridge, Eng., 1973-79; sr. scientist Strangeways Rsch. Lab., Cambridge, 1979-92, head cancer rsch. group, 1992—; vis. prof. Teikyo U., Sagamiko, Japan, 1989; com. mem. Cancer Rsch. Campaign, Targeting Trials Group, London, 1992—; med. rsch. adviser Nat. Lottery Charities Bd., 1998-99. Editorial bd.: Drug Delivery Jour., 1993—; inventor in field; contbr. articles to profl. jours. Elected mem. South Cambridgeshire Dist. Coun., Cambridge, 1987—, chmn. fin. com., 1993—; chmn. Icknield County Primary Sch. Govs., Cambridge, 1997—. Recipient rsch. grants Cancer Rsch. Campaign, 1986, 89, 92, CRC Tech., 1991. Mem. Biochem. Soc., Soc. for Endocrinology, N.Y. Acad. Sci. Office: Strangeways Rsch Lab, 2 Worts Causeway, Cambridge CB1 4RN, England

BARDAK, YAVUZ KAMIL, ophthalmologist; b. Malkara, Turkey, May 27, 1966; s. Ibrahim and Aysen (Savkli) B.; m. Handan Hatun Kirca, Mar. 16, 1994; children: Emre, Eren. MD, Haceteppe U., 1990. Rsch. asst. Ankara U., Turkey, 1991-95; ophthalmologist Kulchahamon State Hosp., Ankara, 1995-96; fellow in ophthalmology Nijmegan U. Inst. Ophthalmology, The Netherlands, 1996-97; asst. prof. ophthalmology Suleyman Demirel U. Med. Sch., Isparta, Turkey, 1997—. Avocations: reading, sport, traveling. Home: Istiklal Mah 1115 Sok 14/2, 32300 Isparta Turkey Office: Suleyman Demirel U, Med Sch Ophthalmology Dept, 32040 Isparta Turkey

BARDAN, VIRGIL, geophysicist; b. Strehaia, Romania, Nov. 4, 1939; s. Ion and Aurelia (Briceag) B.; m. Alina Mihai, Aug. 15, 1948; 1 child, Monica. MSEE, Polytech U., Bucharest, Romania, 1961; MS in Math., Bucharest U., 1970, PhD in Math., 1977; PhD in Data Processing, Polytech U., 1992. Sr. geophysicist Prospectiuni S.A., Bucharest, Romania, 1961—; assoc. prof. Polytech. U., Bucharest, Romania, 1970-83, Bucharest U., 1991—; cons. Western Geophys., London, 1997—. Contbr. articles to profl. jours. 2d lt. Romanian Mil., 1961-62. Mem. EAEG, Romanian Soc. Geophysics. Avocations: tennis, chess, literature, arts, sports. Home: Str Iani Buzoiani 3 Bl 16, Sc 1 Apt 30, 78223 Bucharest Romania Office: Prospectiuni S A, Str Coralilor 20, 78449 Bucharest Romania

BARDEN, KENNETH E., lawyer; b. Nov. 21, 1955; s. Lloyd C. and Beverly A. (Coverdale) B. BA in Polit. Sci. cum laude, U. Indpls., 1977; JD, Ind. U., 1981; postgrad., Harvard U., 1983, Yale U., 1999. Bar: Ind. 1981, U.S. Dist. Ct. (so. dist.) Ind. 1981, U.S. Tax Ct. 1983, U.S. Ct. Mil. Appeals 1983, U.S. Ct. Appeals (6th and 7th cirs.) 1983, U.S. Ct. Internat. Trade 1983, U.S. Ct. Claims Ohio 1990, Rep. of Palau, 1998. Pub. defender Marion County Mcpl. Ct., Indpls., 1981; law clk. U.S. Dist. Ct., Indpls., 1981-84; city atty., corp. counsel dept. law City of Richmond, Ind., 1984-89; chief gen. counsel dept. law City of Dayton, 1989-98; asst. atty. gen. Ministry Adminstrn. Republic of Palau, 1998—; adj. prof. bus. law and gen. law Marion County Superior Ct., Indpls., 1981; adj. prof. law Ind. Ctrl. U., Indpls., 1983; adj. prof. bus. law, ethics and labor rels. The Union Inst., 1995-98; legal counsel Richmond Greater Progress Com., 1987-89. Contbr. articles to profl. jours. Nat. v.p. Coll. Dems. of Am., 1979-82; ward chmn. Marion County Dems., 1977-81; precinct committeeman Wayne County Dems., 1985-89, treas. 2nd dist., 1986-89; delto NATO European Youth Leadership Conf., 1980; co-founder Hubert H. Humphrey Tng. Inst. for Campaign Politics, 1980; treas. Perry Twp. Dem. Club, 1980-83; alt. del. Dem. Nat. Conv., 1980; del. White House forum on Domestic and Econ. Policy, 1975; del. Youth Conf. on Nat. Security and the Atlantic Alliance , Mt. Vernon Coll., Washington, 1976, Am. Coun. Young Polit. Leaders Fgn. Policy Conf., 1987; mem. U.S. Youth Coun. under Pres. Carter, 1980, Ind. Gov.'s Cmty. Corrections Com., 1973-75, adv. coun. Friends of the Battered, 1985-88, pers. policies forum Bur. Nat. Affairs, 1985-88, Dem. Leadership Coun., 1987—, Am. Coun. of Young Polit. Leaders, 1986—; legal counsel Richmond Greater Progress Com., 1987-89; founding mem., bd. dirs. Richmond (Ind.) Cmty. Devel. Corp., 1987-89. Recipient Youth in Govt. award Optimist Club, 1972; named one of Outstanding Young Men in Am., 1986. Mem. ABA (com. on industry regulation, Young lawyers divsn. labor law com., urban, state and local govt. sect., vice chair Town Hall com. 1985-87, chair 1987-91, vice chair citizenship edn. com. 1987-88, 87-94, victims com. sect. of criminal justice 1985—, lawyers and arts com., chair Arson Law Project 1993-94, contbr. editor Arson Law Reporter), Fed. Bar Assn., Fed. Energy Bar Assn. (legis. and regulatory devel. com. 1989), Wayne County Bar Assn., Bur. Nat. Affairs Pers. Policies Forum, Am. Soc. Pub. Adminstrs., Ohio Mcpl. Lawyers Assn., Ind. Mcpl. Lawyers Assn., Ohio State Bar Assn., Ind. State Bar Assn., Indpls. Bar Assn. (ethics com. 1986-89), Ind. Assn. Cities and Towns, Ind. Coun. on World Affairs, Nat. League of Cities, Athenaeum Club (Indpls.), World Trade of Ind. Club, Kiwanis, Phi Alpha Delta, Epsilon Sigma Alpha, Alpha Phi Omega. E-mail: kbarden@palaunet.com. address: PO Box 1858, 96940 Koror Republic of Palau

BARDIN, BORIS VASILJEVITCH, electrical engineer; b. Bazhetsk, Tverskaya, Russia, Sept. 10, 1941; s. Vasily Ivanovitch and Anna Vasiljevna (Kuznetsova) B.; m. Tatjana Alexandrovna Kljavina, Sept. 22, 1978; 1 child, Maria. BS, Inst. Elec. Comm., St. Petersburg, Russia, 1964; PhD in Tech. Sci., Inst. Granit, St. Petersburg, 1976. Instr. Inst. Granit, St. Petersburg, 1964-76, rschr., 1976-82; rsch. scientist Inst. Analytic Instrument Making, Russian Acad. Sci., St. Petersburg, 1983—. Contbr. articles to profl. jours. Recipient grant RFBR, Russia, 1993, 96. Avocations: mountaineering, mountain skiing, historical literature, classical music. Home: Turcu St, h. 23, c.1 ap 17, 192241 Saint Petersburg Russia Office: Inst Analy Instr Making RAS, Rizhskii pr, h.26, 198103 Saint Petersburg Russia

BARDODEJ, ZDENEK, toxicologist, educator; b. Holesov, Czech Republic, May 20, 1924; s. Alfons and Marie (Jadrnickova) B.; m. Eva Zelena, Mar. 11, 1961; 1 child, Otakar. Degree in chem. engring., Chem. U., Praha, Czech Republic, 1949; RNDr in Chemistry and Biology, Masaryk U., Brno, Czech Republic, 1950, PhMr in Pharmacy, 1953; PhD, Charles U., Praha, 1963, DSc, 1981. Asst. prof. indsl. hygiene Masaryk U., Brno, 1951-53; prof. indsl. health Charles U., Praha, 1953-70, prof. chief med. chemistry, 1970-91, prof. chief dept. med. chemistry and toxicology, 1991-94, prof., chief dept. toxicology Postgrad. Sch. Med. & Pharm., 1994-98; rsch. worker Mil. Acad. Medicine, Hradec Kralove, 1998—; vis. prof. indsl. medicine Eberhard Karls U., Tubingen, 1967-68; mem. sci. bd. Inst. Toxicology, Pardubice, 1970-76; chmn. com. on MACS and carcinogens, Praha, 1972—; chief Nat. Lab. for Biol. Monitoring, Praha, 1974-92; expert task groups WHO, Internat. Labor Office, Moscow, 1971, Helsinki, 1982, Tbilisi, 1983, Copenhagen, 1985, Teheran, 1986; cons. Nat. Health Svc., Czech Republic, 1953—. Author: Introduction to Chemical Toxicology, 1991, 2d edit., 1994, 3d edit., 1999; co-author: (with B. Svestka) Occupational Medicine, 1978 (award 1980), (with A. Berlin, A.H. Wolff and Y. Hasegawa)The Use of Biological Specimens for the Assessment of Human Exposure to Environmental Pollutants, 1979, (with A. David, V. Sedivec, S. Skramovsky, and J. Teisinger) Exposure Tests in Industrial Toxicology, 1980, (with B. Holmstedt, R. Lauwerys, M. Mercier, and M. Roberfroid) Mechanisms of Toxicity and Hazard Evaluation, 1980; editor: (20 vols. proceedings) Czech Chem. Soc. Divsn. Toxicology, 1966—; contbr. more than 135 articles to profl. jours. 2d lt. Med. Corps, 1954-56. Recipient prize Sci. Bd. Czech Ministry of Health, 1969. Fellow Czech Chem. Soc. (pres. divsn. toxicology 1984—); mem. Czech Med. Soc. (hon., J.E. Purkynje medal 1989), Czech Lit. Found. (prize 1986). Roman Catholic. Avocations: international relations, literature, tourism. Home: Jablonova 2/2891, 10600 Praha 10, Czech Republic

BARDOS, RICHARD PAUL, environmental scientist, educator; b. Coventry, Eng., Oct. 4, 1961; s. Eric Imre and Florence (Passmore) B. BSc, U. Southampton, Eng.; PhD, U. Reading, 1987. Chartered biologist. Prin. scientific officer/mgr. Contaminated Land Bus. Ctr. Warren Spring Lab., Eng., 1987-93; head Waste and Soil Treatment Divsn. CRBE, Nottingham Trent U., Eng., 1994-96; mng. dir. R3 Environ. Tech. Ltd., 1997—; vis. prof. U. Nottingham, 1999—. Author: (book) The Complete Guide to Garden Composting, 1994; editor: Nicole News jour., 1996—. Mem. Soc. Gen. Microbiology, Inst. Wastes Mgmt., British Soc. Soil Sci. E-mail: paul@r3environmental.co.uk. Office: R3 Environ Tech Ltd, PO Box 58, SG12 9UJ Ware SG12 OYY, England

BARDOT, BRIGITTE, actress; b. Paris, Sept. 28, 1934; d. Louis and Ann Marie (Mucel) B.; m. Roger Vadim, Dec. 12, 1952 (div.); m. Jacques Charrier, June 19, 1959 (div.); 1 child, Nicolas; m. Gunther Sachs, July 14, 1966 (div.). Ed. Paris Conservatory. Films include: Act of Love, 1954, Doctor at Sea, 1955, The Light Across the Street, 1955, Helen of Troy, 1955, And God Created Woman, 1956, Heaven Fell That Night, 1957, Une Parisienne, 1957, En Cas de Malheur, 1957, Please Mr. Balzac, 1957, The Devil is a Woman, 1958, Mam'zelle Pigalle, 1958, Babette Goes to War, 1959, Please Not Now, 1961, The Truth, 1961, Vie Privee, 1961, Love on a Pillow, 1962, Contempt, 1964, Dear Brigitte, 1965, Viva Maria, 1965, Musculin Feminin, 1967, Two Weeks in September, 1967, Shalako, 1968, The Novices, 1970, The Legend of Frenchy King, 1972, Don Juan, 1973, L'Histoire Tres Bonne et Tres Joyeuse de Colinot Trousse-Chemise, 1973. Decorated d'Honneur, 1985, Sorriso del grande tentator, 1975. Office: Found Brigitte Bardot, 45 rue Vineuse, 75116 Paris France*

BARENBOIM, DANIEL, conductor, pianist; b. Buenos Aires, Nov. 15, 1942; s. Enrique and Aida (Schuster) B.; m. Jacqueline DuPre, June 15, 1967 (dec.); m. Elena Bashkirova, Nov. 28, 1988; 2 children. Student, Mozarteum, Salzburg, Austria, Accademia Chigiana, Siena, Italy; grad., Santa Cecilia Acad., Rome, 1956. Music dir. Chgo. Symphony Orch., 1991—. Debut with Israel Philharm. Orch., 1953, Royal Philharm. Orch., Eng., 1953, debut as pianist, Carnegie Hall, N.Y.C., 1957, Berlin Philharm. Orch., 1963, N.Y. Philharm. Orch., 1964, 1st U.S. solo recital, N.Y.C., 1958, as pianist performed in N.Am., South Am., Europe, Soviet Union, Australia, New Zealand, Near East; condr., 1962—, conducted English Chamber Orch., London Symphony Orch., Israel Philharm. Orch., N.Y. Philharm. Orch., Phila. Symphony, Boston Symphony, Chgo. Symphony Orch., others; mus. dir., Orchestre de Paris, 1975-89, Chgo. Symphony Orch., 1991—, Staatsoper Berlin, 1992—; artistic adviser, Israel Festival, 1971-74, over 100 recordings as pianist and condr.; debut as pianist at age 7, Buenos Aires. Recipient Beethoven medal, 1958; Harriet Cohen Paderewski Centenary prize, 1963, Legion of Honor, France, 1987. Office: 29 rue de la Coulouvreniere, 1204 Geneva Switzerland also: Chgo Symphony Orch c/o Synneve Carlino 220 S Michigan Ave Chicago IL 60604-2596

BÄRENZUNG, ERIC, digital TV software company executive; b. Antony, France, Nov. 11, 1962. Degree in engring., E.N.S.I.E.G., Grenoble, France, 1987. Software engr. Dassault, Paris, 1988-91, IBEX Computing, Archamps, France, 1991-93; mgr. Cam Svcs., Annemasse, France, 1993-95; Asia mgr. Syselog, Paris & Shanghai, 1995-98; China CIO Carrefour China, Beijing, 1998-99; program mgr. Lysis SA, Lausanne, Switzerland, 1999—. Lt. French Air Force, 1987-88. Office: Ly:is SA, 8 cotes de Montbenon, CH-1003 Lausanne Switzerland

BARER, ARNOLD, medical educator; b. Kiev, Ukraine, Sept. 26, 1927; s. Semion and Zinaida (Pikovskaya) B.; m. Natalia Agapova, Dec. 10, 1951 (dec. Dec. 1971); m. Larisa Lilia, June 1, 1974; 1 child, Ekaterina. Physician, Med. Inst. Moscow, 1951, MD (hon.), 1958, PhD (hon.), 1965. Med. officer Russian Air Force, 1951-58; chief physiologic lab. Russian Air Force Ctrl. Hosp., 1958-60; chief aerospace medicine dept. Zvezda Co., Moscow, 1960—; EVA med. support group leader Mission Control Ctr., Koroliev, Russia, 1965—; mem. coun. space medicine Ministry Health, Koroliev, 1966—, mem. sci. coun. Inst. Biol. and Med. Problems, Moscow, 1966—. Author: Guide in Physiology. Physiology of Thermoregulation, 1984; editl. bd. mem. Space Biology & Medicine Jour., 1974—; inventor in field; contbr. articles to profl. jours. Recipient State prize Russian Govt., 1978. Mem. Internat. Astronautic Acad., Internat. Acad. Scis. of Nature and Soc., Russian Cosmonautic Acad., N.Y. Acad. Scis. Home: 184-2 Prospect Mira Apt 299, 129301 Moscow Russia Office: RD&PE Zvezda, 39 Gogol St, 140070 Moscow Tomilino, Russia

BARES, JAN, physicist. MS in Physics, Charles U., Prague, 1961, PhD in Physics, 1965. Postdoctoral fellow Soviet Acad. Scis., St. Petersburg, Russia, 1965, Poly. of Milan, 1968-70, Rensselaer Poly. Inst., 1970-72; sr. scientist Xerox corp., Webster, N.Y., 1972-98; scientist Eastman Kodak Co., Rochester, N.Y., 1998-99; sr. rsch. scientist Nexpress Solutions LLC, Rochester, 1999—. Co-author: Experiments in Polymer Science, 1973; contbr. articles to profl. jours.; 35 patents in field. Mem. Am. Phys. Soc., N.Y. Acad. Scis., Soc. Imaging Sci. and Tech. (sr.).

BARES, LUDEK FRANCIS, neurologist, consultant; b. Mlada Boleslav, Czech Republic, July 5, 1929; s. Francis and Ludmila (Kulhava) B.; m. Edith Kurzova, Dec. 4, 1954; children: Jindrich, Vilem. BA, Pekar Gymn. Coll., 1948; MD, Charles U., Prague, 1953, PhD in Med. Scis., 1984. Diplomate in neurology. Demonstrator, scientist Charles U. Sch. Medicine, 1951-52; resident, attending, vice head Regional Hosp., Carlsbad, 1953-57; head dept. Dist. Hosp., Rumburk, 1958-64, Prague-East, 1965-89; rsch. group leader Czech Acad. Scis., Prague, 1989-91; cons. dept. surgery Med. Sch., Prague, 1965-68, Dist. Hosp., Brandys, 1992—; sworn expert High Ct. of Justice, Prague, 1967—. Author: Cranio-vertebral Junction's Syndromes, 1990; coauthor film; patentee. Fellow Royal Soc. of Medicine (London); mem. Am. Acad. Neurology (hon.), N.Y. Acad. Scis., Czech Neuroradiol. Soc. Roman Catholic. Avocations: Baroque, Gothic. Home: Vestecká 1037, Stara Boleslav Czech Republic

BARFOD, JØRGEN HENRIK PAGH, editor; b. Copenhagen, Mar. 2, 1918; s. Halfdan and Helga (Pagh) B.; m. Sigrun Sams, Apr. 27, 1947; children: Halfdan, Gunner, Troels. Grad., U. Copenhagen, 1947. Historian Danish Naval Ministry, 1947-54; high sch. tchr. Lyngby, Denmark, 1954-79; censor U. Copenhagen, Arhus and Odense, 1969-88; curator Mus. Fight for Freedom of Denmark, 1971-88. Author: Denmark-Norways Merchant Navy 1648-1699, 1967, Hell Has Many Names, 1969, A Center in the Periphery, Bornholm During the War, 1976, Niels Juel, a Danish Admiral of the 17th Century, 1977, Christian IV the Nyboder, 1983, The Birth of the Royal Danish Navy 1414-1533, 1990, The Barfod Saga, 1992, Christian 3.s Royal Navy, 1533-1588, 1996, Niels Juels Navy, 1660-1720, 1997, Fight for the Navy, 1999. Active Danish Resistance Movement, 1940-44. Decorated Order of Zastava, Ridder of Dannebrog Order. Mem. Friends of Freedom Mus. (hon.), Family Assn. Barfod (pres. 1952—), Gestapo Prisoners (pres. 1963-74), Assn. Danish Maritime History (pres. 1974-95). Home: Ved Fortunen 10A, 2800 Lyngby Denmark

BARFOOT, JOAN, writer, journalist; b. Owen Sound, Can., May 17, 1946. BA, U. We. Ont. Reporter, religion editor Windsor Star, 1967-69; feature and news writer Mirror Publs., Toronto, Can., 1969-73, Toronto Sunday Sun, 1973-75; with London Free Press, 1976-79, 80-94; tchr. journalism and creative writing Sch. Journalism, U. We. Ont., 1987—; Can. del. First Internat. Feminist Book Fair and Festival, U.K., 1983; judge Gov.-Gen.;s award for English Lang. Can. Fiction, 1995, Trillium Lit. award, 1996. Author: Abra, 1978, Dancing in the Dark, 1982, Duet for Three, 1985, Family News, 1989, Plain Jane, 1992, Charlotte and Claudia Keeping in Touch, 1994, Some Things About Flying, 1997, Getting Over Edgar, 1999. Recipient First Novel award Books in Can., 1978, Marian Engel award, 1992. Mem. Writer's Union of Can., PEN Can. Address: 286 Cheapside St, London, ON Canada N6A 2A2

BARFORD, BRIDGET CAROLINE, solicitor; b. Crowborough, E. Sussex, Eng., June 7, 1962; d. Thomas Rowland and Mary Nicholette Barford. LLB, U. Wales, 1984. Solicitor, ptnr. Max Barford & Co., Tunbridge Wells, Eng., 1987—. Mem. Duty Solicitor Law Soc. Office: Max Barford & Co, 16 Mt Pleasand Rd, Tunbridge Wells TN1 1QU, England

BARFORD, NORMAN CHARLES, retired physics researcher, educator; b. London, Jan. 17, 1921; s. Alfred George and Alma May (Davis) B.; m. Enid Alice, Feb. 22, 1947; children: Alison Jane, Roger, Sarah Christabel. BSc, London U., 1940; MA in Math., Cambridge (Eng.) U., 1947. Rsch. engr. E.M.I. Ltd., Hayes, Eng., 1942-45; lectr., reader Imperial Coll., London, 1947-81; secondment as prof., head of dept. U. of Cape Coast, Ghana, 1962; cons. EMI Ltd., Hayes, 1945-65; sci. advisor F.H. Biddle Ltd., London, 1947-86. Author: Experimental Measurements, 1967, 85, Mechanics, 1973. Named for Best TV Paper of Yr., Inst. Elec. Engrs., London, 1958. Avocations: foreign travel, theatre, classical music. Office: Imperial Coll Physics Dept, Prince Consort Rd, London SW7 2AZ, England

BARGACH, SAAD, oil industry executive; b. Rabat, Morocco, Mar. 21, 1958; arrived in England, 1995, Egypt, 1998; s. Abdelfattah and El Batoul (Alaoui) B.; m. Kenza Guedira, Sept. 3, 1990; children: Salma, Youssef. BS, MS in Elec. Engring., U. M.V.-E.M.I., Rabat, 1981. Mgr. field svcs. Schlumberger, Quito, Ecuador, 1986-87; recruiting mgr.-Africa-Mediterranean Schlumberger, Milan, 1987-88; divsn. mgr. North Africa Schlumberger, Paris, 1988-92; dir. pers. South East Asia unit Schlumberger WL/TG, Jakarta, Indonesia, 1992-93; mgr. new product devel. Schlumberger-Anadrill, Houston, 1993-94; v.p., gen. mgr. Schlumberger-Anadrill, London, 1995-98, Schlunberger Logelco, Inc., Cairo, 1998-99; pres. Anadill div. Schlunger Oilfield Svcs., Houston, 1999—; asst. prof. U. M.V.-E.M.I., 1981-83. Inventor in field. Recipient Engring. Innovation award 1983. Mem. Soc. Petroleum Engrs., Internat. Measurement While Drilling Soc., Soc. Petrophysics and Well Logging Analysis. Avocations: football, art, golf, antiques. Home: 300 Schlumberger Dr Bldg 1 Sugar Land TX 77478-3155 Office: Schlumberger Logelco Inc, PO Box 790, 79011728 Cairo Egypt

BARGER, KATHLEEN CARSON, lawyer; b. Tacoma, Apr. 15, 1948; d. Ralph Anthony and Bertaleigh (Pyle) C.; m. James V. Barger, Aug. 31, 1968 (div. Aug. 1985); children: Julia L., Jonathan C. BA, Duquesne U., 1968; MA, U. Pitts., 1972; JD, U. N.C., 1976. Bar: N.C. 1976, U.S. Dist. Ct. (mid. dist.) N.C. 1976, U.S. Ct. Appeals 1988. Atty. Western Electric, Greensboro, N.C., 1976-80; atty. AT&T, Basking Ridge, N.J., 1980-84, Washington, 1984-89; atty., ptnr. Thompson & Mitchell, Washington, 1989-92; ptnr. Wickwire Gavin, P.C., Vienna, Va., 1992—; lectr. Fed. Publs., Washington, 1988—, mem. adv. bd., 1988—; mem. adv. bd. BNA-Fed. Contracts Report, Washington, 1990—. Mem. ABA (coun. pub. contract sect. 1989—, chmn. acctg., cost & pricing com. 1986—). Roman Catholic. Avocation: Irish history. Home: 905 St Stephens Rd Alexandria VA 22304-1724 Office: Wickwire Gavin PC 8100 Boone Blvd Ste 700 Vienna VA 22182-7732

BARI, MOHAMMED ABDUL, civil engineer; b. Kushtia, Bangladesh, Jan. 1, 1958; arrived in Australia, 1988; s. Tofazzel Hossain and Motia Begum; m. Nahid Sharmin, May 11, 1990; 1 child, Ishraq Shadman. BSCE, Bangladesh U. Engring. & Tech., Dhaka, 1983; M in Engring., Asian Inst. Tech., Bangkok, 1987. Design engr. Rahman & Assocs., Dhaka, 1983-84, Bangladesh Water Devel. Bd., Dhaka, 1984-86; exptl. scientist Commonwealth Sci. and Indsl. Rsch. Orgn., Perth, Australia, 1988-89; engr. Water Authority of Western Australia, Perth, 1989-95; sr. engr. Water and Rivers Commn., Perth, 1995—. Contbr. articles to profl. jours. Mem. Instn. Engrs. of Australia, Assn. Profl. Engrs. and Scientists (Australia), Asian Inst. Tech. Alumni Assn. (life). Mem. Australian Labour Party. Moslem. Avocations: photography, swimming, jogging, collecting art, gardening. Home: 30 Larkspur Ln, Ballajura Perth WA6066, Australia Office: Water and Rivers Commn, Hyatt Ctre 3 Plain St, East Perth WA 6004, Australia

BARIC, JOSIP, academic administrator; b. Split, Croatia, Oct. 22, 1958; s. Tomislav and Katica (Pavisic) B.; m. FrankaKacic, Sept. 14, 1991; 1 child, Ljupka. Dipl.iur, Pravni Fakultet, Croatia, 1982. Atty. VSF, Split, Croatia, 1983-93; with Splitska Ftz, Split, Croatia, 1993-95; adminstr. High Sch. Medicine, Split, Croatia, 1995—. Co-author: Old Picture of Town Split, 1996. Roman Catholic. Avocations: philately, collecting old picture postcards. Office: High Sch Medicine, Soltanska 2, HR21000 Split Croatia

BARIE, PHILIP STEVEN, surgeon, educator; b. Buffalo, Aug. 18, 1953; s. Kenneth George and Eleanor Lucille (Davis) B.; m. Elaine Catherine Dash, May 31, 1981; children: Catherine, Steven, Alexandra. AB cum laude, MD, Boston U., 1977. Diplomate and surgical critical care cert. Am. Bd. Surgery. Jr. resident in surgery N.Y. Hosp.-Cornell Med. Ctr., N.Y.C., 1977-79; fellow in surgery and physiology Albany (N.Y.) Med. Coll., 1979-81; sr. resident in surgery N.Y. Hosp.-Cornell Med. Ctr., 1981-83, adminstrv. chief resident surgery, 1983-84; asst. prof. surgery Cornell U. Med. Coll., N.Y.C., 1984-89, assoc. prof., 1989—, chief divsn. trauma and critical care dept. surgery, 1998—; attending surgeon, dir. surg ICU, N.Y. Hosp., N.Y.C., 1984—; cons. in surgery Cath. Med. Ctr., N.Y.C., 1985—; chmn. inst. rev. bd. Med. Coll. Cornell U., N.Y.C., 1988-92; cons. specialist, mem. med. control bd. Health Ins. Plan Greater N.Y., 1990-98; cons. in critical care therapeutics U.S. Pharmacopeial Conv., 1991—; mem. med. adv. bd. N.Y. Blood Ctr., 1999—. Editor-in-chief Surg. Infections; mem. editl. bd.: Surg. Infections: Index and Revs., 1993-99, Shock, 1996—, Contemporary Surgery, 1996—, Air Med. Jour., 1997—, Jour. of Surg. Outcomes, 1997-2000, Jour. of Trauma, 1998—, Critical Care Medicine, 1998—, New Horizons, 1998—, Pediatric Critical Care Medicine, 2000—; co-editor: Surgical Intensive Care, 1993 (Best New Book in Med Scis. Assn. Am. Pubs. 1994); contbr. articles to profl. jours. Fellow ACS, Am. Coll. Critical Care Medicine, Am. Surg. Assn.; mem. N.Y. Acad. Medicine (sec. surg. sect. 1991-92), N.Y. Surg. Soc. (coun. mem.-at-large 1995-2000), Soc. Critical Care Medicine (sec.-treas. surg. sect. 1995-96, chair-elect surg. sect. 1996-97, mem. coun. 1997—, chair surg. sect. 1997-98), Am. Thoracic Soc., Am. Assn. for Surgery of Trauma (Peter C. Canizaro award 1992), Internat. Surg. Soc., Am. Physiol. Soc., Soc. Univ. Surgeons, N.Y. State Soc. Surgeons (bd. dirs. 1992—, sec. 1995-97, pres.-elect 1997-99, pres. 1999—), N.Y. Acad. Scis., Surg. Infection Soc. (mem. coun. 1994-97, treas. 1998—), Soc. Civil War Surgeons, Assn. for Acad. Surgery, Shock Soc., Ea. Assn. for Surgery of Trauma (bd. dirs. 1996-99), Am. Med. Writers Assn., Halsted Soc., Surg. Infection Soc. Found. (trustee 1998—, treas. 1998—), Critical Care Medicine Edn. and Rsch. Found. (trustee 2000—). Office: NY Hosp-Cornell Med Ctr Dept Surgery 525 E 68th St Dept Surgery New York NY 10021-4885

BARIL, MAURICE, career officer; b. Saint-Albert de Warwick, Que., Can., Sept. 22, 1943; m. Huguette Desjardins; children: François, Hélène. Student, U. Ottawa, 1961-64; cert., Officer Tng. Corps, 1964, École Supérieure de Guerre, Paris, 1977. Commd. 2nd lt. Royal 22nd Regiment, 1963, advanced through ranks to lt. gen., 1977; with 1st Commando Airborne Rgt., Valcartier and Edmonton, Can., 1968-71; comdr. tng. co. Recruit Sch.; ops. officer, adjutant 3d Bn., Valcartier, Can., and Cyprus; comdr. 2d Bn., La Citadelle, Québec, 1980; comdt. Inf. Sch. Comd. Forces, Command and Staff Coll. Command and Staff Coll., 1984; dep. commdt. Can. Forces Command and Staff Coll., 1985; dir. land ops., tng., and resources, dir. inf. Nat. Def. Hdqs., Ottawa, Can., 1986, dir. gen. land doctrine ops., 1989; mil. advisor UN Dept. Peacekeeping Ops., 1992; comdr. Land Force Que. Area, Montréal, 1995, Land Force Command, 1995-97; chief of def. Govt. of Canada, 1997—. Avocations: ultralight flying, fishing, hunting. Office: Chief Def Staff Nat Def Hdqs, 101 Colonel By Dr, Ottawa, ON Canada K1A 0K2

BARILLARI, PAOLO, surgeon, researcher; b. Rome, June 25, 1960; s. Franco and Angela (Grossi) B.; m. Alessandra Cerasi, Dec. 7, 1984; children: Claudia, Angelica. MD cum laude, U. Rome, 1984. Med. diplomate. Resident surgery U. La Sapienza, Rome, 1989; asst. U. Rome, La Sapienza, 1987-97, dirigent, 1997—. Author: New Trends in Surgical Oncology, 1994, Il Cancro Del Retto, 1995, Manuale di Chirurgia, 1997. Fellow Soc. Italiana Chirurgia, N.Y. Acad., Am. Soc. Devel. Scis. Avocation: art collecting. Home: u della Camilluccia 589/C, 00135 Rome Italy Office: U Rome La Sapienza, Dept Surgery, 00168 Rome Italy

BARING, JOHN FRANCIS HARCOURT (LORD ASHBURTON), retired banker; b. Nov. 2, 1928; s. 6th Baron Ashburton and Doris Mary Thérèse Harcourt; m. Susan Mary Renwick, 1955 (dissolved 1984); 4 children; m. Sarah Crewe, 1987. MA, Oxford (Eng.) U., 1989. Lord Warden of Stannaries, Duchy of Cornwall, 1990-94. Dir. Baring Bros. & Co. Ltd., 1955-89, chmn., 1974-89; dep. chmn. Royal Ins. Co. Ltd., 1975-82, dir., 1964-82; chmn. Outwich Investment Trust Ltd., 1968-86, Baring Stratton Investment Trust, 1986-98; dir. Dunlop Holdings Ltd., 1981-84; chmn. Bank of Eng., 1983-91, Jaguar, 1989-91; dir. British Petroleum Co. PLC, 1982-95, chmn., 1992-95; chmn. Barings PLC, 1985-89, non-exec. dir., 1989-94; chmn. Accepting Houses Com., 1977-81, chmn. com. fin. for industry NEDC, 1980-86; mem. British Transp. Docks Bd., 1966-71, pres. com. CBI, 1976-79; mem. exec. com. NACF, 1989-99; hon. fellow Hertford Coll., Oxford, 1976. High steward Winchester Cathedral; trustee Winchester Cathedral Trust, 1989—, chmn., 1993—; trustee Rhodes Trust, 1970-99, chmn., 1987-99; trustee Nat. Gallery, 1981-87, Southampton U. Devel. Trust, 1986-96, chmn., 1989-96; trustee, hon. treas. Police Found., 1989—, DL Hants, 1994—. Decorated Knight Bachelor, knight Order of the Garter, knight comdr. Royal Victorian Order (Brit.); Eton Coll. fellow, 1982-97, Hon. fellow Trinity Coll., 1989. Mem. British Bankers' Assn. (v.p. 1977-81), Overseas Bankers' Club (pres. 1977-78).

BARINSKY, IGOR FELIX, virologist, researcher; b. Kiev, Ukraine, Feb. 14, 1937; s. Felix Gregor Barinsky and Julia Victor Solovjova; m. Larisa Konstantin Artjukh, May 5, 1966; 1 child, Konstantin. D, 1st Med. Inst., Moscow, 1960; PhD, D of Med. Sci., Acad. Med. Sci., Moscow, 1963. Jr. sci. worker Acad. Med. Sci., Moscow, 1960-68, sr. sci. worker, 1968-74, head of lab., 1975—. Author 7 books; contbr. over 350 articles to jours. in field.; mem. editl. bd. Jour. Problems of Virology, 1994-97; patentee in field. Recipient award Govt. USSR, 1984. Mem. Acad. Natural Scis., N.Y. Acad. Scis., Pharmacopy Com. Avocation: tennis. Home: 9-9 Koneva Str, 123060 Moscow Russia Office: D I Ivanovsky Inst Virology, Gamaleya Str 16, 123098 Moscow Russia

BARISH, LAWRENCE STEPHEN, nonpartisan legislative staff administrator; b. Bklyn., Nov. 30, 1945; s. Louis C. and Anna (Sanders) B.; m. Sharon Lee Shapiro, July 2, 1967; 1 child, Lauren. BS in Polit. sci., U. Wis.-Madison, Wis., 1967; MA in Govt., U. Ariz., 1970. Legis. analyst Legis. Reference Bur., Madison, Wis., 1971-87, dir. of reference and info. svcs., 1987—; chmn. rsch., comm. staff sec. Nat. Conf. State Legislatures, Denver, 1995-97; redistricting cons. Wis. Legis. and Local Govt. units, 1980—. Editor State Almanac, 1987—; contbr. articles to profl. jours. Home: 1429 W Skyline Dr Madison WI 53705-1134 Office: Wis Legis Reference Bur 100 N Hamilton St Madison WI 53703-4118

BARIŠIĆ, NINA, pediatrician, neurologist, educator; b. Zagreb, Croatia, Feb. 11, 1957; d. Emil and Nada Barišić. MD, Med. Faculty, Zagreb, Croatia, 1980; pediatrician, child neurologist, Zagreb Med. Sch., 1988; PhD, Med. Faculty, Zagreb, 1990. Cert. med. dr., consulting child neurologist, asst. prof. pediats. Med. dr. Primary Health Care, Zagreb, 1980-84; pediat. resident dept. pediats. Zagreb Med. Sch., 1984-88, pediatrician, specialist, child neurologist dept. pediats., 1988—, child neurologist, cons., assoc. prof. pediats., 1997—; child neurologist, neurophysiologist EMG/EEG, cons. Dept. Pediats., Zagreb, 1989—, pediat. clin. pharmacologist, 1990—. Contbr. sci. articles to profl. jours. Mem. exec. com. Childcare Assn. during war in Croatia, Zagreb, 1991-95; mem. Women Intellectuals Assn., Zagreb, 1995—. Recipient Honor award Croatia Med. Assembly, 1999; grantee Am. Austrian Found., 1999. Mem. Croatian Child Neurology Soc. (exec. bd. 1988), Am. Soc. Child Neurology (Bernard D'Souza award 1995), European Pediat. Neurology Soc. (U.K.), Croatia Clin. Pharmacology Soc. Fax: 385 1 2421-894. E-mail: nbarisic@rebro.mef.hr. Office: Zagreb Med Sch Dept Pediats, Kišpatićeva 12, Zagreb 10000, Croatia

BARK, THEO J., banker; b. Leiden, The Netherlands, Feb. 6, 1945; s. Willem and An M. (Koopman) B.; m. Antoinette H.M. Bark Van Cleef, May 13, 1971; children: Willem, Anne, Marie Claire. Degree in Bus. Adminstrn., The Hague, 1968. With ABN Bank, Leiden, 1962-66; trainee internat. ABN Bank, Amsterdam, 1969; asst. mgr. ABN Bank, Tokyo, 1970-74, asst. regional mgr., 1975; asst. regional mgr. ABN Bank, Hong Kong, 1976-77; gen. mgr. ABN Bank, Seoul, 1978-81; gen. mgr. ABN Bank, Bahrain, 1982, reg. mgr. Mid. East, 1983; reg. mgr. Europe ABN-AMRO Bank, Amsterdam, 1989-97; pres., CEO ABN-AMRO Bank, Canada, 1997—; chmn. Dutch-Kazakstan Trade Coun., The Hague, Holland, Russian-Dutch Trade Coun., 1992-97, Bulgarian-Dutch Trade Coun.; hon. consel The Netherlands, Bahrain, 1982-84. 1st lt. Infantry, The Netherlands, 1966-68.

BARKANOV, EVGENY, engineering educator; b. Riga, Latvia, Jan. 8, 1964; s. Nikolaj and Lubov (Liberova) B. Dipl.Ing. 1st class, Riga Poly. Inst., 1986; Dr.Sc.Ing., Riga Tech. U., 1993. Engr. Riga Poly. Inst., 1986-88, postgrad fellow, 1988-91; rschr. Riga Tech. U., 1991—, sr. lectr., 1997—. Contbr. articles to profl. jours. Recipient Gold medal Min. of Edn., 1981. Mem. Internat. Assn. for Computational Mechanics. Orthodox. Avocations: swimming, volleyball, football, travel, reading. Home: Ieriku St 60-131, LV-1084 Riga Latvia Office: Riga Tech Univ, Kalku St 1, LV-1658 Riga Latvia

BARKAT, ABUL, economics educator, researcher; b. Kushtia, Bangladesh, Sept. 27, 1954; s. Abul Quasem and Nurun Nahar; m. Shahida Akhter, Dec. 25, 1985; children: Aroni, Anokhi, Abonti. Degree, Kushtia Govt. Coll., 1973; MSc in Econs., Acad. of Econs., Moscow, 1978, PhD in Devel. Econs., 1982. Vis. fellow Bangladesh Inst. Devel. Studies, Dhaka, 1982-84; lectr. dept. econs. Dhaka U., 1984-89, asst. prof., 1989-84, assoc. prof., 1994—, prof., 2000—; chief advisor Human Devel. Rsch. Ctr., Dhaka, 1989-93, head, 1993—; cons. UN Population Fund, Dhaka, 1994, 96, 97; rsch. team leader World Bank/UN Devel. Program/Rockefeller Found., 1990—; fellow U. N.C., Chapel Hill, 1997. Prin. author: Transforming Human Deprivation into Human Development, 1995 (Bridge of Light award 1996), Political Economy of the Vested Property Act, 1997 (award Assn. for Land Reform 1997), Family Planning Unmet Need in Bangladesh, 1997 (award The Future Group 1997); prin. editor: Population and Development Issues in Bangladesh, 1997 (award Ministry of Health 1997). Mem. mng. coms. 5 primary schs. for the poor, Kushtia, 1994—; mem. exec. bd. Assn. for Land Reform and Devel., Dhaka, 1995-97; mem. nat. com. Human Rights of Religious Minorities, Bangladesh, 1995—; mem. sono-diagnostic Arsenic Environment Initiative, Kushtia, 1996—; mem. Nat. Population Coun., Govt. Bangladesh, 1996, mem. nat. population policy com., 1997; adv. chair regional program com. Internat. Planned Parenthood Fedn., London, 1995—. Mem. Am. Pub. Health Assn., Bangladesh Econ. Assn. Avocations: music, writing articles on current socio-economic problems, providing funding support to rural primary schools in Bangladesh. Home: N Fuller Rd 48/J, Dhaka U R/A, Dhaka Bangladesh Office: Dept Econs, U Dhaka, Dhaka 1000, Bangladesh

BARKAT GOURAD HAMADOU, prime minister of Djibouti. Former mem. French Senate; former minister of health; prime minister of Djibouti, 1978—, minister of ports, 1978-87, minister planning and land devel., 1987; mem. Reassemblement Populaire pour le Progrès. Address: Office of the Prime Minister, PO BOX 2086, Djibouti Djibouti*

BARKEN, BERNARD ALLEN, lawyer; b. St. Louis, July 20, 1924; s. Gottlieb and Hattie E. (Rubin) B.; m. Jocelyn Moss Kopman, Sept. 1, 1948; children: Thomas L., Dale Susan. JD, Washington U., 1947. Bar: Mo. 1947, U.S. Dist. Ct. (ea. dist.) Mo. 1947, U.S. Ct. Appeals (8th cir.) 1954, U.S. Tax Ct. 1966, U.S. Ct. Appeals 2nd cir.) 1985, U.S. Supreme Ct. 1984. Sole practice St. Louis, 1947-80; ptnr. Shifrin & Treiman, St. Louis, 1980-88; pres. Bernard A. Barken, St. Louis, 1988-91; ptnr. Barken & Bakewell L.L.P., St. Louis, 1991—. With USAAF, 1943-44. Mem. ABA, Bar Assn. Met. St. Louis (v.p. 1958, chmn. young lawyers 1953). Avocations: piano, tennis, gardening. Home: 30 Vouga Ln Saint Louis MO 63131-2628 Office: Barken & Bakewell LLP 500 N Broadway Ste 2000 Saint Louis MO 63102-2130

BARKER, BARBARA ANN, ophthalmologist; b. Paterson, N.J., Nov. 10, 1943; d. Earle Louis and Dorothy Louise (Williamson) Barker; m. Joel Ira Papernik, July 28, 1972. BA magna cum laude, Conn. Coll., 1965; BS, Yale U., 1967; MA, Rutgers Med. Sch., 1974; MD, Mt. Sinai Sch. Medicine, 1976. Diplomate Am. Bd. Ophthalmology. Intern Beth Israel Med. Ctr., 1977; resident Mt. Sinai Sch. Medicine/Beth Israel Med. Ctr., 1980, fellow in glaucoma, 1980-81, fellow cornea, refractive surgery, 1981-82, now mem. staff; rsch. technician The Rockefeller U., N.Y.C., 1965-66; tchr. Riverdale Country Sch., N.Y.C., 1967-68; rsch. asst. Sloan Kettering Inst., N.Y.C., 1969-72; asst. clin. prof. Mt. Sinai Sch. Medicine, N.Y.C., 1982—; pvt. practice medicine specializing in ophthalmology, N.Y.C., 1983—; mem. staff N.Y. Eye and Ear Hosp., Beth Israel/St. Luke's/Roosevelt Hosp. Recipient Resident Paper award Beth Israel Med. Ctr., 1989, Honor award Am. Acad. Ophthalmology, 1995; Beth Israel Rsch. grantee, 1983, NSF grantee 1966. Fellow ACS, N.Y. Acad. Medicine; mem. AMA, Am. Med. Women's Assn., Women's Med. Soc. N.Y.C., N.Y. County Md. Assn., Phi Beta Kappa. Home and Office: 11 E 86th St New York NY 10028-0501

BARKER, CHRISTOPHER DAVID, audiologist, researcher; b. Vancouver, B.C., Can., July 10, 1956; arrived in Australia, 1970; s. Peter Howard and Dorothy Lesley (Horscroft) B.; m. Francina Sara Kater, Dec. 17, 1983; children: Duncan, Joanna. BA with honours, U. Melbourne, Australia, 1978, postgrad., 1979; MA with honours, Macquarie U., Sydney, Australia, 2000. Cert. in clin. competence in audiology, small bus. mgmt., group instrnl. skills. Pediatric audiologist Nat. Acoustic Labs., Brisbane, Australia, 1985-88; mgr. Hearing Ctr., Nat. Acoustic Labs., Maroochydore, Australia, 1988-94; adult specialist audiologist Australian Hearing, Maroochydore, 1994-98, clin. adviser, 1998-99; audiology rschr. and developer Australian Hearing/Nat. Acoustic Labs., Maroochydore, 1999—; lectr. Inst. Otolaryngology, Beijing, 1997. Contbr. articles to Ear and Hearing. Mem. Audiological Soc. Australia. Avocations: reading, cycle touring, triathlons. Office: Australian Hearing NAL, 61 The Esplanade, Maroochydore Qld 4558, Australia

BARKER, CLIVE, artist, screenwriter, director, producer, writer; b. Liverpool, Eng., 1952; s. Len and Joan B. Student, U. Liverpool, Eng. Author: (plays) Incarnations (Frankenstein in Love, History of the Devil, Colossus), Forms of Heaven (Paradise Street, Subtle Bodies, Crazyface); (short story collection) Books of Blood I-VI (books IV, V, and VI released in U.S. as The Inhuman Condition, 1986, In the Flesh, 1986, Cabal); (novels) The Damnation Game, 1985, Weaveworld, 1987, Cabal, 1988, The Great and Secret Show, 1989, Imajica, 1991, The Thief of Always, 1992, Everville, 1994, Sacrament, 1996, A-Z of Horror, 1997, Galilee, 1998, The Essential Clive Barker, 1999; prodr. Hellraiser II: Hellbound, 1990, Candyman, 1992, Hellraiser III: Hell on Earth, 1992, Candyman II: Farewell to the Flesh, 1995, Hellraiser: Bloodline, 1996, Gods & Monsters, 1997, (Fox TV) Spirits and Shadows, 1997; (writer and dir. screenplays) Hellraiser, 1987, Nightbreed, 1990, Lord of Illusions, 1995, Art Exhibition, 1998.

BARKER, CLYDE FREDERICK, surgeon, educator; b. Salt Lake City, Aug. 16, 1932; s. Frederick George and Jennetta Elizabeth (Stephens) B.; m. Dorothy Joan Bieler, Aug. 11, 1956; children: Frederick George II, John Randolph, William Stephens, Elizabeth Dell. BA, Cornell U., 1954, MD, 1958. Diplomate Am. Bd. Surgery. Intern Hosp. U. Pa., Phila., 1958-59, resident in surgery, 1959-64, fellow in vascular surgery, 1964-65; fellow in med. genetics U. Pa. Sch. Medicine, Phila., 1965-66, assoc. in surgery, 1964-68, assoc. in med. genetics, 1966-72; attending surgeon Hosp. U. Pa., Phila., 1966—; chief div. transplantation U. Pa. Sch. Medicine, Phila., 1966—, asst. prof. surgery, 1968-69, assoc. prof. surgery, 1969-73, prof. surgery, 1973—, J. William White prof. surg. research, 1978-82, chief div. vascular surgery, 1982—, Guthrie prof. surgery, 1982—, John Rhea Barton prof. surgery, 1983—, chmn. dept. surgery, 1983—; chief surgery Hosp. U. Pa., Phila., 1983—; dir. Harrison Dept. Surgery research U. Pa., Phila., 1983—; mem. immunobiology study sect. NIH; chmn. clin. practices U. Pa., 1987-89. Mem. editl. bd. Jour. Transplantation, 1977—, Clin. Transplantation, 1988—, Jour. Surg. Rsch., 1979-85, Jour. Diabetes, 1981-86, Archives of Surgery, 1987—, Transplantation Procs., 1990—, Surgery, 1991-95, Cell Transplantation, 1991—, Postgrad. Gen. Surgery, 1991-95, Jour. ACS, 1994—, Annals of Surgery, 1995—; contbr. articles to profl. jours. and textbooks. Markle Found. Scholar, 1968-74; NIH grantee, 1974—; recipient Merit award NIH, 1987-95. Fellow AOA, NAS (Inst. Medicine), ACS (com. Forum on Fundamental Surg. Problems 1983-88, vice chmn. 1987-88, bd. govs. 1994—, pres. Phila. chpt. 1991-92), Coll. Physicians Phila., Royal Coll. Surgeons Eng. (hon.), Royal Coll. Surgeons Ireland (hon.); mem. AMA, Royal Coll. Surgeons of Ireland (hon.), Assn. Acad. Surgery, Am. Diabetes Assn., Am. Soc. Artificial Internal Organs, Am. Fedn. Clin. Rsch., Juvenile Diabetes Found., Soc. Univ. Surgeons, Am. Surg. Assn. (recorder 1991-96, pres. 1996-97), Soc. Clin. Surgery (chmn. membership 1984-85), Halsted Soc. (chmn. membership 1984-85, v.p. 1985-86, pres. 1986-87), Surg. Biology Club II, Soc. Vascular Surgery, Internat. Cardiovascular Soc., Internat. Surg. Group (treas. 1988-94, pres. 1994-95), Internat. Soc. Surgery (v.p. U.S. chpt. 1995-97, pres. 1997—), Transplantation Soc. (councilman 1978-84, 94—), Am. Soc. Transplant Surgeons (chmn. membership 1980-81, treas. 1988-91, pres. 1992-93), Am. Acad. Arts and Scis., Assn. Am. Physicians, Phila. Acad. Surgery (program chmn. 1984-86, v.p. 1986-88, pres. 1988-89), Greater Del. Valley Soc. Transplant Surgeons (pres. 1978-80), Am. Philos. Soc. Home: 3 Coopertown Rd Haverford PA 19041-1012 Office: Hosp Univ Pa Dept Surgery 3400 Spruce St Philadelphia PA 19104-4206

BARKER, DAVID JAMES, medical researcher; b. London, June 29, 1938; s. Hugh and Joye Francis (Higgs) B.; m. Angela Beatrice Coddington, Apr. 30, 1960 (dec. Apr. 1980); children: Peter, Mary, Simon, John, Ruth; m. Janet Elizabeth Franklin, Mar. 14, 1983; children: Toby, Francesca, Rebecca. BSc, U. London, 1959, MBBS, 1962; PhD, U. Birmingham, Eng., 1966; MD, U. London, 1973. Rsch. fellow U. Birmingham, 1963-66, clin. lectr., 1966-69; lectr. U. Makerere, Uganda, 1969-72; sr. lectr. U. Southampton, Eng., 1972-79, prof., 1979—, dir. Med. Rsch. Coun. unit, 1984—; cons. physician Royal South Hants Hosp., 1972—. Author: Practical Epidemiology, 1973, Epidemiology in Medical Practice, 1976, Mothers, Babies and Health in Later Life, 1994; editor: Fetal and Infant Origins of Adult Disease, 1992. Recipient Gold medal Royal Soc., London, 1994. Fellow Royal Soc., Royal Coll. Physicians London, Royal Coll. Obstetricians (hon.). Mem. Ch. of England. Avocations: writing, drawing, fishing, golf. Home: Manor Farm, East Dean, Salisbury SP5 1HB, England Office: Gen Hosp, MRC Unit, Southampton S016 6YD, England

BARKER, DOUGLAS ALAN, lawyer; b. Martinsville, Va., Oct. 25, 1957; s. Cecil Ray and Virginia Adeline (Bryant) B.; m. Daphne A. Burns; children: Daryn Ruth, Dylan Victoria. BS, Va. Tech., 1981; MBA, The Citadel, 1988;

JD cum laude, Pepperdine U., 1993. Bar: Calif. 1993, U.S. Dist. Ct. (ctrl. dist.) Calif. 1993, S.C. 1996, U.S. Dist. Ct. S.C. 1996. Assoc. Haight, Brown & Bonesteel, Santa Monica, Calif., 1993-96, Young Clement Rivers & Tisdale, Charleston, S.C., 1996-97; pvt. practice Charleston, S.C., 1997—. Lt. comdr. USN, 1981-87. Decorated Expeditionary medal USN, Beirut, Lebanon, 1983. Mem. ABA, L.A. Bar Assn., Charleston County Bar Assn., Assn. Bus. Trial Lawyers, L.A. JD/MBA Assn., Phi Delta Phi (magister 1992-93). Avocation: military history. Home: 1253 Sam Snead Dr Mount Pleasant SC 29466-6923 Office: 171 Church St Ste 160 Charleston SC 29401-3137

BARKER, GEOFFREY RONALD, physician, consultant, surgeon; b. Birmingham, Eng., Apr. 4, 1943; s. Ronald James and Edith Gertrude (Fisher) B.; m. Jane McEwen Trushell, Nov. 12, 1978 (div. Apr. 1994); children: Simon Geoffrey, Matthew Ronald. BDS, London U., 1969, BSc in Physiology 1st class honors, 1966, B Medicine B Surgery, 1973; MSc, Manchester (Eng.) U., 1985. Certificate in aviation medicine. House physician, surgeon Guys Hosp., Hereford Hosp., 1973-74; splst. med. practitioner Alderney & Guernsey, 1974-78; lectr. in oral surgery Birmingham (Eng.) U., 1978-81; lectr., sr. lectr. cons. in oral surgery, medicine Manchester (Eng.) U., 1981-87; prof. oral surgery, medicine, pathology Welsh Nat. Sch. Medicine, 1987-91; med. dir. ASTRA Pharmaceuticals, Herts., Eng., 1991-97; cons., oral physician, surgeon Royal Free Hosp., 1997—; pvt. practice, ptnr. Deer Park Med. Ctr., West Witney, Oxford, Eng., 1997—; cons. oral surgeon Royal Army Med. Corp., 1982-94; internat. head med. affairs and drug safelty Actellon Ltd., Allschwill, Switzerland, 1999. Contbr. numerous articles to profl. jours. Commanding officer Royal Army Med. Corps, 1991-94, lt. col. 1993-94. Territorial decoration Royal Army Med. Corps., 1994. Fellow Royal Coll. Surgeons Great Britain and No. Ireland, Royal Coll. Physicians Great Britain and No. Ireland, Royal Coll. Dental Surgeons Great Britain and No. Ireland. Avocations: walking, photography, golf. Home: Höhenstrasse 24, Riehen CH 4125, Switzerland

BARKER, JAMES STUART FLINTON, biologist, researcher; b. Ayr, Australia, July 6, 1931; s. Harold Onslow and Lilian Vance (Stuart) B.; m. Maureen Elizabeth Ferguson, Apr. 30, 1955; children: Penelope Helen, Michael Stuart (dec.), John Flinton, Elizabeth Megan. B in Agrl. Sci. with honors, U. Queensland, Brisbane, Australia, 1955; PhD, U. Sydney, Australia, 1962. Asst. husbandry officer Dept Agrl. and Stock, Brisbane, 1954-56; lectr. animal genetics U. Sydney, 1956-61, sr. lectr. animal genetics, 1962-65, assoc. prof. animal genetics, 1965-79; prof. animal sci. U. New Eng., Armidale, Australia, 1979-93, ARC sr. rsch. fellow, 1993-98; prof. emeritus, 1998—. Joint editor 6 sci. books; contbr. over 200 articles to profl. jours. Fellow Australian Acad. Technol. Scis. and Engring., Assn. for the Adv. of Animal Breeding and Genetics; mem. Australian Assn. Animal Breeding and Genetics (pres. 1979-81), Genetics Soc. Australia (pres. 1981-82), Soc. Advancement Breeding Rsch. in Asia and Oceania (v.p. 1989-93, pres. 1994-97). Office: U New Eng, Dept Animal Sci, Armidale NSW 2351, Australia

BARKER, MARTHA SMITH, retired mental health nurse; b. Columbia, S.C., Mar. 30, 1935; d. Lonnie Edward and Virginia Fairey (Faulkner) Smith; 1 child, Michele de Calverhall. Diploma, Columbia Hosp., 1957; BS in Nursing with honors, Med. U. S.C., 1980; M in Nursing, U. S.C., 1988. Instr. Med. U. S.C. Sch. Nursing, Charleston, 1960-67; assoc. prof./dir. practical nurse program & ADN program Med. U. S.C. Coll. Allied Health Scis., Charleston, 1967-85; dir. nursing edn., staff devel. S.C. Dept. Mental Health, Columbia, 1985-93; retired, 1993, con. in psychiat. nursing issues, 1993—. Home: 1905 Haile St Camden SC 29020-3017

BARKER, MICHAEL DAVID, design engineer; b. Hertford, England, Sept. 29, 1926; s. Noel Ernest and Mary (Detrolio) B.; m. Irene Mabel Marsh, Sept. 12, 1959 (dec.); m. Linda Joy Brentnall, Nov. 5, 1990. Student corr. coll., Cambridge (Eng.) U., 1948. Engring. apprentice D. Wickham & Co. Ltd., Ware, Hertforshire, Eng., 1943-45, 48-51, draughtsman, 1951-61, design engr., 1961—. Patentee 5 indsl. pumps, 2 braking devices. Served to cpl. Royal Signal Corps, 1945-48, MTO. Decorated Palestine Service medal with clasp. Avocation: amateur archtl. activities. Home: Woodlands Hunsdonbury, Hunsdon near Ware, Hertfordshire SG12 8PW, England

BARKER, PAT, writer; b. Thornaby-on-Tees, Eng., May 8, 1943; married; 2 children. Student, London Sch. Econ. Author: Union Street, 1982, Blow Your House Down, 1984, The Century's Daughter, 1986 (retitled Liza's England, 1996), The Man Who Wasn't There, 1989 (trilogy WWI novels) Regeneration, 1991, The Eye in the Door, 1993, The Ghost Road, 1995 (Booker prize for fiction 1995), Another World, 1998. Decorated Comdr. Brit. Empire, 2000; recipient Fawcett prize, 1983, Guardian prize for fiction, 1993. Address: Gillon Aitken Assocs, 29 Fernshaw Rd, London SW10 0TG, England

BARKER, PHILIP GEORGE, computer science educator, researcher, author, chemist, engineer; b. Pontypool, Wales, Apr. 21, 1944; s. Joshua and Ada Maud (Bruntly) B.; m. Jennifer Wright, Oct. 5, 1970 (div. 1983); m. Alix Grabham, Oct. 25, 1989; children: Hannah Rachel, Stephanie Lauren. B.Sc. in Chemistry, U. Wales, 1965, Ph.D., 1968. Chartered engr., registered chemist, U.K. SRC research fellow U. Wales, Swansea, 1968-70; computer cons. BHC Chems., Port Talbot, Wales, 1970-71; lectr. computer sci. Teesside Poly., Middlesbrough, Eng., 1971-73, prin. lectr. computer sci., 1979-87, reader applied computing and info. technology, 1987-91, prof. applied computing, 1991—; lectr. computing U. Durham (Eng.), 1973-79; dir. Programming Language One Ltd., Milton Keynes, Eng., 1976-82, Interactive Systems Research Group, Middlesbrough, Eng., 1978—; founder, mem. North of Eng. HCI Rsch. Consortium. Author: Computers in Analytical Chemistry, 1983 (Russian edit. 1987), Introducing Computer Assisted Learning, 1985, Author Languages for CAL, 1987, Multi-media Computer Assisted Learning, 1989, Basic Principles of Human-Computer Interface Design, 1989, Electronic Books, 1991, Exploring Hypermedia, 1993; editorial bds. Engineering Applications of Artificial Intelligence, 1987, Jour. Artificial Intelligence in Edn., 1989, Jour. of Information Sci. and Technology, 1990, Jour. Ednl. Multimedia and Hypemedia, 1991, Interactive Multi-media, 1990, Internat. Jour. Human-Computer Studies, 1993; assoc. editor Assn. of Learning Tech. Jour.; contbr. numerous tech. articles to profl. publs. Recipient Ayling prize Univ. Coll. Swansea, 1965. Fellow Brit. Computer Soc. (sec. 1976-79), Royal Soc. Chemistry; mem. Assn. Computing Machinery, IEEE, Long Distance Walkers Assn. Clubs: Stockton Rambling, IVC. Home: 35 Stokesley Rd Marton, Middlesbrough Cleveland TS7 8DT, England Office: U Teesside Sch Computing & Math, Borough Rd, Middlesbrough Cleveland TS1 3BA, England

BARKER, VIRGINIA LEE, nursing educator. Diploma, Ind. U. Sch. Nursing, 1952, BS, 1955, MS, 1961, EdD, 1969. Dean sch. nursing, prof. Alfred (N.Y.) U., 1969-78; prof., dean nursing U. Louisville, 1978-81; dean Mary Black Sch. Nursing, prof. U. S.C., Spartanburg, 1981-90; dean prof. studies, prof. nursing SUNY, Plattsburg, 1990-98; cons. N.Y. Regents Coll. Nursing Program, 1972-91; project dir. federally funded telenursing project for rural upstate N.Y., 1993-98; dir. project to develop virtual reality simulations for edn. physicians, nurses, allied health pers., 1995—. Contbr. articles to profl. jours. Mem. ARC. Recipient N.Y. State Nurses Assn. Soc. Disting. Practitioners Grants. Mem. ANA, N.Y. Nurses Assn. (pres.), Nat. League for Nursing (com. mem.), S.C. League for Nursing, Am. Assn. Higher Edn., AAUW, Ind. U. Sch. Nursing Alumni Assn. (pres.), S.C. Deans and Dirs. Nursing Fedn. (chair), Sigma Theta Tau, Phi Kappa Phi, Kappa Delta Pi.

BARKES, GEOFFREY ROGERSON, electrical distributor; b. Durham, Eng., July 24, 1927; s. Wilfred and Kathleen Herbert (Ranken) B.; divorced; children: Alexandra, Sarah, William; m. May 16, 1981. BA, U. Oxford, Eng., 1949, MA, 1952. Dir. Short Bros., Sunderland, Eng., 1953-63, Brit. Elec. & Mfg. Co. Ltd., Newcastle on Tyne, Eng., 1963-92; ret., exec. dir. Brit. Elec. & Mfg. Co. Ltd., Newcastle on Tyne, 1992—. Served as maj. Brit. cavalry, 1947-49. Mem. Inst. Dirs. (chmn. no. counties 1984-90). Anglican. Club: No. Countries (Newcastle on Tyne). Avocations: shooting, fishing. Home: The Manor House, Kirkheaton, Newcastle on Tyne NE19 2DQ, England

BARKHAN, RONNIE CECIL, psychotherapist; b. Johannesburg, Gauting, South Africa, Oct. 25, 1916; m. Kitty Marshak, 1961 (dec. June 1969); m. Lilian Goldberg, July 31, 1980 (dec. Jan. 1998). PhD in Psychology, London Coll. Applied Sci., 1965; PhD, Nat. U. Toronto, 1967. Asst. gen. mgr. OK Bazaars Ltd., Johannesburg, 1944-46; chmn., mng. dir. Barkhan Pty. Ltd., Johannesburg, 1946-71; pvt. practice hypnotherapy and psychotherapy Johannesburg, 1971—; dep. dir. gen. Internat. Biog. Ctr., Cambridge, Eng., 1997. Coun. Johannesburg C. of C., 1952-68, chmn., founder export sect., 1956-57; officer in charge, reservist Hillbrow Johannesburg South African Police, 1965-74. with African Air Force, 1940-44; commr. of oaths Dept. Justice, South Africa, 1984. Fellow Am. Assn. Profl. Hypnotherapists; mem. Chartered Soc. Psychiatric Practitioners, Springbok Legion (founding), South Africa Legion (life), South African Jewish Ex Svc. League (life), South African Air Forc Assn. (life), Sandringham Gardens (life). Avocations: bowls, philately. Home and Office: 102 Roslin St Sydenham, Johannesburg 2192, South Africa

BARKHASH, VLADIMIR ALEXANDROVICH, chemical engineer; b. Moscow, Sept. 27, 1933; s. Alexandr Pavlovich and Revekka Yakovlevna (Elkina) B.; m. Dina Vladimirovna Korchagina, Nov. 29, 1973; 1 child, Andrey. Chem. engr., Chem. Tech. Inst., Moscow, 1956. Asst. Chem. Tech. Inst., 1959-63; sr. scientific worker Inst. Organic Chemistry, Novosibirsk, Russia, 1963-89, head of lab., 1989—. Author: Modern Problems in Chemistry of Carbonium Ions, 1975, Topics in Current Chemistry, 1984, Nonclassical Carbocations, 1984. Recipient Lenin prize, Moscow, 1990. Avocation: travel. Home: Zolotodolinkaya, 630090 Novosibirsk Russia Office: Novosibirsk Inst Org Chem, Lavrentiava 9, 630090 Novosibirsk Russia

BARKHOFF, MARTIN KRISTIAN TOBIAS, retired editor; b. Wattenscheid, Germany, May 8, 1951; arrived in Switzerland, 1982; s. Wilhelm-Ernst and Otti (Grave) B.; m. Ruth Keil, Mar. 27, 1975. Ass.Jr., Freie Universität, Berlin, 1980. Admitted to Germany bar, 1980. Pvt. practice law Berlin, 1980-82; asst. Das Goetheanum, Dornach, Switzerland, 1982-83, editor, 1984-95; ret., 1995; dir. Law Confs. of Sch. Spiritual Sci., Goetheanum, 1982-96; mem. Konferenz der Anthroposophischen Gesellschaft in Deutschland, 1982-96. Author: Zur S%6ulenweisheit, Dornach, 1992. Address: Düppelstr 4, D-14163 Berlin Germany

BARKLEY, CHARLES WADE, retired professional basketball player; b. Leeds, Ala., Feb. 20, 1963. Student, Auburn U., 1981-84. mem. U.S. Olympic Basketball Team, 1992. With Phila. 76ers, 1984-92, Phoenix Suns, 1992-96, Houston Rockets, 1996-2000; ret., 2000; mem. U.S. Olympic team, 1992, 1996. Author: (with Roy S. Johnson) Outrageous! The Fine Life and Flagrant Good Times of Basketball's Irresistible Force, 1992; film appearances include: Forget Paris, 1995. Recipient NBA All-Star Game Most Valuable Player award, 1991, Schick Pivotal Player award, 1986-88, NBA Most Valuable Player Award, 1993, IMB award, 1986-88; named to NBA All-Star team, 1988-93. Named to All-Rooki Team, 1985. Holds single game records for most offensive rebounds in one quarter-11, and most offensive rebounds in one half-13, 1987. Office: Houston Rockets Two Greenway Plz Ste 400 Houston TX 77046-3865

BARKLEY, WILLIAM DONALD, museum administrator; b. New Westminster, B.C., Can., Apr. 4, 1941; s. Donald MacMillan and Ethel Margaret (Mines) B.; m. Helen Gayle Alanson, Aug. 29, 1964; children: Warren Vincent, Colleen Michelle. BS, U. B.C., 1964, MA, 1971. Cert. tchr. Can. Tchr. Salmon Arm (B.C.) Sr. Secondary Sch., 1965-68; wildlife biologist Wye Marsh Wildlife Ctr., Midland, Ont., Can., 1968-72; chief interpretation Can. Wildlife Svc., Ottawa, Ont., 1972-77; asst. dir. B.C. Provincial Mus., Victoria, 1977-84; CEO Royal BC Mus., Victoria, 1984—; advisor cultural resource mgmt. program U. Victoria, 1985—; lectr. univs. Contbr. articles to Nat. History Interpretation mag., 1965—. Bd. dirs. Tourism Victoria, 1985—. Recipient Disting. Svc. award Interpretation Can., Ottawa, 1983, Can. 125 award for svc. to mus. cmty. Fellow Can. Mus. Assn.; mem. Can. Mus. Assn. (pres. 1987-89), B.C. Mus. Assn., Internat. Coun. of Mus.-Can., Can. Pks. and Wilderness Soc., Can. Nature Fedn., Victoria A.M. Tourism Svcs. Assn. (treas.). Mem. United Ch. Can. Avocations: design and production stained glass, backpacking, skiing, wind surfing, numismatics. Office: Royal BC Mus, 675 Belleville St, Victoria, BC Canada V8V 1X4

BARKMAN, JON ALBERT, lawyer; b. Somerset, Pa., Oct. 8, 1947; s. Blair Albert and Billie (Dietz) B.; m. Annette E. Shaulis, Dec. 1, 1983. BA, Washington and Jefferson U., 1969; JD, Duquesne U., 1975. Bar: Pa. 1975, U.S. Dist. Ct. (we. dist.) Pa. 1975, U.S. Supreme Ct. 1984, U.S. Ct. Appeals (3rd cir.) 1989. Mem. claims dept. Liberty Mut. Ins. Co., Pitts., 1969-71; dist. justice Commonwealth of Pa., Somerset, 1973-93; pvt. practice Somerset, 1975—; pres. Barkman Realty, Inc., Somerset County Settlement and Abstract Co. Inc. Advisor Com. Against Sexual Assault, Somerset, Pa., 1984; Pa. del. Nat. Spl. Ct. Judges Conv., Honolulu, 1989, Atlanta, 1991. Paul Harris fellow, 1989. Mem. ABA, ATLA, Pa. Trial Lawyers Assn., Somerset County Bar Assn. (pres. 1990—), Allegheny County Bar Assn., Elks, Rotary. Republican. Methodist. Home: 388 High St Somerset PA 15501-1301 Office: 116 N Center Ave Somerset PA 15501-2027

BARKO, GYORGY, chemical and mechanical engineer; b. Debrecen, Hungary, July 22, 1969; s. Gyula and Erzsebet (Toronyai) B. BSc, U. Veszprém, 1990, MSc, 1992, PhD, 1997. Assoc. prof. U. Veszprém, 1997—, dir. Chem. Sensor Lab. dept. earth and environ. sci., 1997—. Mem. Orgn. Mech. Engrs., mem. Hungarian Chem. Soc. Avocation: computer games. Home: Hajo 12, 4024 Debrecen Hungary Office: U Veszprém, Egyetem 10 PO Box 158, 8201 Veszprém Hungary

BARKOVA, NATALIA ALEXANDROVNA, educator; b. Leningrad, Russia, July 18, 1945; d. Alexander Alexeevich Azovtsev and Vera Ignatjevna (Ukraintseva) Azovtseva; m. Alexej Vasiljevich Barkov, Nov. 20, 1965; 1 child, Marianna. Engr. in electronmech., Leningrad Shipbuilding Inst., Leningrad, 1969, PhD, 1979. Engr. Scientific Rsch. Inst., Leningrad, 1969-72; researcher Rsch. Lab. Naval Elec., Leningrad, 1975-80; sr. researcher Leningrad Shipbuilding Inst., Leningrad, 1980-83, assoc. prof., 1983-92; assoc. prof. St. Petersburg State Marine Tech. Univ., St. Petersburg, 1992—; Scientific sec. rsch. work dept. Leningrad Shipbuilding Inst., 1980-92; scientific dir. Vibrotechnique, Inc., 1990-92, VibroAcoustical Systems & Tech. Inc., 1992—. Author: The Vibration and Vibroacoustics of the Electrical Equipment on Ships, 1986, (with Barkov A.V.) Rotating Machines Monitoring and Diagnostics by Vibration, 2000; contbr. articles to profl. jours.; patentee in field. Mem. N.Y. Acad. Sci. Avocations: psychology, sailing. Office: St Peterburg Marine Tech, Lotsmanskaya Str 3, 190008 Saint Petersburg Russia

BARKSDALE-LADD, MARY ALICE, education educator; b. Roanoke, Va., Feb. 12, 1954; d. Byrd H. and Mary Anne (St. Clair) Barksdale; m. Frank L. Ladd, July 28, 1990. BA in Elem. Edn., Clemson U., 1976, MEd in Reading Edn., 1979; EdD in Curriculum and Instrn., Va. Tech., 1988. Tchr. Greenville (S.C.) Schs., 1976-81, Bedford (Va.) County Schs., 1981-83; grad. asst. Va. Tech., Blacksburg, 1983-88; prof. W.Va. U., Morgantown, 1988-94, U. South Fla., Tampa, 1994—; presenter in field. Co-editor Jour. Computing in Childhood Edn., 1995-97; contbr. articles to profl. jours.; reviewer publs. in field. Fulbright scholar 1995. Mem. Internat. Reading Assn. (Albert J. Harris award 1995), Fla. Reading Assn., Nat. Reading Conf., Coll. Reading Assn., Ea. Ednl. Rsch. Assn., Fulbright Assn., Phi Delta Kappa. Office: Childhood/Lang Arts/Reading Dept 4202 E Fowler Ave Tampa FL 33620-8000

BARKWORTH, PETER WYNN, actor, writer; b. Margate, Kent, Eng., Jan. 14, 1929; s. Walter W. and Irene M. B. Student, Royal Acad. Dramatic Art. Appeared in plays, including Roar Like a Dove, 1957-60, The School for Scandal, 1962, Crown Matrimonial, 1972, Donkey's Years, 1976, Can You Hear Me at the Back?, 1979-80, A Coat of Varnish, 1982, Siegfried Sassoon, 1987, Hidden Laughter, 1990-91, The Winslow Boy, 1994; TV appearances include The Power Game, 1966, Manhunt, 1969, Winston Churchill: The Wilderness Years, 1975, Telford's Change, 1978, Late Starter, 1984, The Price, 1984; films include Where Eagles Dare, 1968, Mr. Smith, Escape From the Dark, Champions, 1983, Wilde, 1997; author: About Acting, 1980, First Houses, 1983, More About Acting, 1984, The Complete About Acting, 1991, For All Occasions, 1997. Recipient Best Actor award Brit. Acad. Film and TV Arts, 1974, 77, Best Actor award Royal TV Soc., 1977, Best Actor award Writer's Guild, 1977. Avocations: walking, gardening, looking at paintings. Address: 47 Flask Walk, London NW3 1HH, England also: 26 Marlborough Ct, Earls Ave Folkestone, Kent CT20 2PN, England

BARLETTA, ANTONIO, physicist; b. Siena, Italy, Aug. 12, 1963; s. Luigi and Iris (Lorenzetti) B.; m. Cinzia Ercoles, Dec. 4, 1988; children: Enrico, Marco. Degree in physics, U. Bologna, 1987. From asst. prof. to assoc. prof. U. Bologna, Italy, 1990—; lectr. U. Parma, Italy, 1994. Reviewer of internat. Scientific jours. Contbr. articles to profl. jours. Recipient Outstanding Reviewer of ASME Jour. of Heat Transfer, 1999. Mem. ASME, Unione Italiana di Termofluidodinamica, Associazione, Termotecnica Italiana. Roman Catholic. Avocations: music, novels, movies. Office: U Bologna DIENCA, Viale Risorgimento 2, I-40136 Bologna Italy

BARLETTA, ELISABETTA, mathematician, researcher; b. Florence, Italy, Jan. 10, 1957; d. Ottavio and Lorenza (Nannucci) B.; m. Sorin Dragomir, Nov. 12, 1994. Grad. in math., U. Florence, 1979. Prof. a contratto U. Ancona, Italy, 1984-86; math. rschr. U. Basilicata, Potenza, Italy, 1986—. Contbr. articles on complex variables and differential geometry to profl. jours., including Revue Roumaine Mathematiques Pures et Appliquées, Bollettino Unione Matematica Italiana, Ind. U. Math. Jour., Complex Variables, Annali Di Mat. Pura e Appl., Le Matematiche, Note Matematica, Rendiconti Circolo Matematico Palermo, Kodai Math. Jour., Rendiconti Matematica, Comm. in Partial Differential Equations, Abhandlungen Mathematischen Sem. U. Hamburg, Atti Seminario Mat. Fis. U. Mod. Sci. Mem. Unione Matematica Italiana, Gruppo Nazionale per le Strutture Algebriche e Geometriche e loro Applicazioni of Consiglio Nazionale delle Ricerche, N.Y. Acad. Scis. Home: Via Roma 219, 85050 Tito Potenza, Italy Office: U Basilicata Dept Math, Via Nazario Sauro 85, 85100 Potenza Italy

BARLETTA CALDARERA, GIACOMO, lawyer; b. Catania, Sicily, Italy, July 29, 1925; s. Giuseppe Barletta and Anna Caldarera; m. Christiane De Blauwe, Oct. 22, 1942; children: Anna-Sophie, Giuseppe, Guglielmo, Lorenzo. Diploma in Law, U. Catania, 1945. Solicitor Bar, Italy, 1947-61; barrister Supreme Ct., Italy, 1961—, Internat. EEC; arbitrator Internat. Chambre Maritime, Monaco-Montecarlo, 1974—; ins. lawyer Maritime West, Eng.; asst. prof. criminal and procedure law, 1945-47; founder, v.p. Internat. Ctr. of Sociol. Penal and Penitentiary Rsch. and Studies Messina, 1972—; gen. sec. F.F. Internat. Assn. of Penal Law, 1973-75; dir. seminars Coun. of Europe ane expert EEC Drugs Problem, 1982-92; cons. UN, Geneva, others. Contbr. articles to profl. jours., monographs. Nat. councillor Young Groups of Democrazia Cristiana, 1950-51; mng. dir. Democrazia Cristiana, Catania, 1945-55; pres. Found. Ardizzone Gioeni, Catania, 1995—, others. Named Cavaliere Repubblica, Italy, 1960, Ivory Coast, 1972. Mem. Law Soc., Internat. Law Assn. Helsinky. Avocation: football. Office: Studio Assoc Barletta Cald, Via Milo N 9/11, 95125 Catania Sicily Italy

BARLEY, VICTOR LAURENCE, oncologist; b. Stoke-on-Trent, Worcesters, Eng., June 16, 1941; s. George Alec and Evelyn Mary (Gocher) B.; m. Janet Purcell, Jan. 25, 1969 (div. Apr. 1989); children: Peter Andrew, Elizabeth Mary, Madeline Anne, Christine Diana; m. Anthea Margaret David, Dec. 3, 1999. MA, M.B.B.Ch., U. Cambridge, Eng., 1966; DPhil, Oxford (Eng.) U., 1972. Univ. demonstrator anatomy dept. U. Oxford, 1968-69, rsch. fellow Nuffield dept. ob-gyn., 1969-72; registrar Churchill Hosp., Oxford, 1972-74, sr. registrar, 1974-78; cons. clin. oncologist Bristol (Eng.) Oncology Ctr., 1978-88, clin. dir., 1988-96, chmn. hosp. med. com., 1997-99; Macmillan lead clinician Avon & Somerset Cancer Svcs., 1997-99; deputy editor British Journal Radiology, 1999—. Joint editor/author: MIMS Handbook of Oncology, 1998. Trustee L.H. Gray Trust, Brit. Inst. Radiology, London, 1985-90. Lalor Found. fellow, 1970-72. Fellow Royal Coll. Surgeons (Edinburgh), Royal Coll. Radiologists (faculty bd. 1997—); mem. Brit. Inst. Radiology (coun. mem. 1996-99). Conservative Party. Ch. of Eng. Avocations: classical music, walking. Home: 11 Barrow Court Mews, Barrow Gurney BS48 3RW, England Office: Bristol Oncology Centre, Horfield Rd, Bristol BS2 8ED, England

BARLIK, MARCIN, geodesist, educator; b. Bydgoszcz, Poland, Nov. 11, 1944; s. Bolesław Jan and Władysława Małgorzata (Baranowska) B.; m. Teresa Urszula Katna, Apr. 29, 1972; children: Tomasz, Agnieszka. MSc, Warsaw (Poland) U. Tech., 1968, PhD, 1976; DScT, Warsaw U. Tech., 1986, prof. ScT, 1995. Sci. worker Warsaw U. Tech., 1968-76, assoc. prof., 1980-96, prof., 1996—, dep. dean Faculty of Geodesy and Cartography, 1990-96, vice-dir. Inst. Geodesy and Geod. Astr., 1986-90, 96—; asst. prof. U. Baghdad, Iraq, 1977-79; cons. l'Inst. Nat. Cartographique, Alger, Algerie, 1986; prof. Mil. Tech. Acad., Warsaw, 1987—. Author: Introduction to Dynamical Geodesy, 1976 (award of mil. svc. 1977), Introduction to the Theory of The Figure of the Earth, 1994 (award of the Rector of Warsaw U. Tech. 1996), Gravimetric Determinations in Geodesy, 1997. Recipient Gold Cross of Merit, Pres. of Poland, Warsaw, 1991. Mem. European Geophys. Soc., Soc. Polish Surveyors (pres. 1995-97), Polish Acad. Scis. (sec. Com. of Geodesy sect. of geodynamic 1991—, sec. geodetic networks 1991—, sect. navigation 1993—). Avocations: science fiction literature, belletristic, motorization. Fax: 48-22-621-00-52. E-mail: barlik@gik.pw.edu.pl. Home: Iberyjska Str No 4/65, 02-764 Warsaw Poland Office: Warsaw Univ Tech, Politechniki Sq No 1, 00-661 Warsaw Poland

BARLING, GERALD EDWARD, lawyer; b. Preston, Eng., Sept. 18, 1949; s. Banks Hubert and Barbara Margarita (Myerscough) B.; m. Myriam Frances Ponsford, July 2, 1983; children: Sophie, Bryony, Isobel. MA in Law, New Coll., Oxford, Eng., 1972. Bar: 1972. Barrister, pvt. practice, 1972-91, Queen's Counsel, 1991—; asst. recorder, Eng., 1989-93, recorder, 1993—; chmn. Bar European Group, 1994-96; lectr. in law New Coll., 1972-77. Editor: Practitioners' Handbook of EC Law, 1998. Recipient Peel Found. Travel scholarship, 1968. Roman Catholic. Avocations: tennis, trees, fishing.

BARLOW, AUGUST RALPH, JR., minister; b. Sewickley, Pa., Oct. 9, 1934; s. August Ralph and Kathryn Viola (Adams) B.; m. Elizabeth Evone Anderson, Aug. 27, 1960; children: Paul Martin, Andrew Ralph, Ann Kathryn. BA, Haverford Coll., 1956; BD, Yale U., 1959, STM, 1964. Ordained to ministry Meth. Ch., 1959. Pastor Fox Chapel Meth. Ch., Pitts., 1959-60, Butler St. Meth. Ch., Pitts., 1961-62, Lawrenceville Cmty. Ch., Pitts., 1962-63; intern Cleve. Inner City Protestant Parish, 1960-61; from tchg. min. to pastor Beneficent Congl. Ch., Providence, 1964-97, pastor emeritus, 1997—; bd. govs. Beneficent House, 1970-97, Beneficent Commons Housing, Providence, sr. min., devel. team, 1991-95; bd. dirs. Pastoral Counseling Ctr., Greater Providence, v.p., 1984-86, pres., 1995-97; pres. Steere House, Providence, 1983-86, past bd. dirs.; bd. dirs. Home Health Svcs. of R.I., 1986-93, chmn. ch. in soc. com., 1985-86; mem. R.I. Conf., United Ch. of Christ, 1964—, mem. com. on ministry, 1981-83, past bd. dirs.; mem. urban divsn. R.I. Coun. Chs., 1979-82. Editor-in-chief: (jour.) Expanding Horizons, 1996—; contbr. articles to Christian Century, editorials, commentaries to Providence Jour.-Bull., The East Bay Window, Expanding Horizons, Religious Broadcasting Sta. WEAN, 1964-87. Adv. coun. Providence Pub. Libr., 1968-71; bd. dirs. Mouthpiece Coffee House, Providence, 1969-75, pres., 1974-75; bd. dirs. Citizens United Renewal Enterprises, 1972-77; alumni class agt. for scholarship funds Haverford Coll. and Yale U. Div. Sch., 1979-95; active R.I. Hosp. Corp., 1980-95. Rsch. fellow Yale U. Div. Sch., 1979; recipient Alumnal Bd. award Yale U. Div. Sch., 1997. Mem. Providence Intown Chs. Assn., Mins. Assn. R.I. Conf. United Ch. of Christ, Dodeka Symposium, Rotary (trustee Rotary Charities Found. 1977-82, Paul Harris fellow), Beneficent Order of Spike, Phi Beta Kappa. Democrat. Home and Office: 103 Angell Rd Lincoln RI 02865-4710

BARLOW, DAVID JOHN HARDING, psychiatrist; b. Bulawayo, Rhodesia, Feb. 26, 1928; arrived in Eng., 1955, Australia, 1966; s. Murrell Harding and Isabel Florence (Norvall) B.; m. Deidre Imogen Landless, Sept. 26, 1953; children: Jennifer Hamilton, Kenneth Barlow, Karyn Barlow, Gillian Coon. MB BCh, Witwatersrand U., Johannesburg, South Africa, 1951; DPM, Royal Colls., Eng., 1963; BA, Latrobe U., Australia, 1978. Diplomate in psychol. medicine. Psychiatrist supt. Hobson Park Hosp., Traralgon, Australia, 1966-67; dep. chmn. Mental Health Authority, Victoria, Australia, 1967-69; psychiatrist supt. Larundel Hosp., Melbourne,

Australia, 1969-74, 78-87; dir. Mental Retardation Svcs., Victoria, 1975-78; mem. Mental Health Rev. Bd., Victoria, 1987—; mem. Victorial Psychol. Coun., 1969-74; sr. assoc. dept. psychiatry U. Melbourne, 1970-74, 79-87; clin. dean Larundel Clin. Sch., Monash U., 1978-84; hon. sr. lectr. dept. psychol. medicine Monash U., 1984-87. Mem. Commn. of Inquiry into Oakley Hosp., Auckland, New Zealand, 1971. Fellow Royal Australian and New Zealand Coll. Psychiatrists, Royal Australian Coll. Med. Adminstrs.; mem. Royal Coll. Psychiatrists. Avocations: reading, music, genealogy. Home: 11 Thornton St, 3095 Eltham Victoria, Australia

BARLOW, F(RANK) JOHN, mechanical contracting company executive; b. Milw., July 12, 1914; s. Ernest A. and Alice E. (Norton) B.; m. Dorothy M. Marx, Oct. 13, 1935; children: Joyce D., Bonnie M., Joan C., Grace M., Jacqueline S., Wendy J., Terri L., Alice M. BS in Mech. Engring., U. Wis., 1937; DSc (hon.), 1994. Engr. Buffalo Forge Co., 1937-40; sales engr. Buffalo Forge Co., Chgo., 1940-42; plant engr. A.O. Smith Corp., Milw., 1942-44; chief mech. engr. Western Condensing Co., Appleton, Wis., 1944-46, profl. mgr., 1946-53; owner Azco, Inc., Appleton, Wis., 1953—, pres., 1959-80, chmn. bd., 1959—; chmn. bd. Azco Group Ltd., 1982—; pres. Sanco, Ltd., Appleton, 1959—, Baldwin Barlow Corp., Appleton, 1965-83, The Downey Co., Milw.; pres. Ave. Dept. Inc., Appleton, Inc.; treas. Winagamie Corp., 1965-88; bd. dirs. Beta Color Inc., First Nat. Bank Appleton; dir., mem. exec. com. Air Wis., 1965-92; chmn. bd. dirs. Transpace Carriers, 1986-88. County chmn. March of Dimes, 1957—, state co-chmn., 1958; industry chmn. com. fund dir., 1968-69; bd. dirs. Nat. Cert. Pipe Welding Bur., Cmty. Found., 1986—, Beth Color Inc., 1991—, Bergstrom-Mahler Mus., 1993-95 (also pres. 1995); trustee Azco Employees Profit Sharing Trust, Wis. Acad. Scis., Arts & Letters, 1988—; pres. Appleton Devel. Coun., 1983-86; mem. adv. bd. Mich. Tech. U. Seaman Mus., 1995. Recipient Industry award Wis. Soc. Profl. Engrs., 1967, Cert. Commendation Gov. Tommy Thompson, 1998, Disting. Svc. award Curtis J. Tompkins, 2000. Mem. CAP, ASCE, Mech. Contractors Assn. Am. (nat. dir., pres. 1974-75, disting. service award 1982), Mech. Contractors Assn. Wis. (pres.), Wis. Soc. Profl. Engrs. (chpt. pres. 1968—), Am. Soc. Heating, Refrigerations and Airconditioning Engrs., Appleton C. of C., Flying Engrs., Nat. Soc. Profl. Engrs. Clubs: Butte Des Morts Golf (dir., pres. 1961, 62). Lodges: Masons, Shriners, Rotary, Elks (past exalted ruler). Home: 2703 Fox Run Appleton WI 54914-8727 Address: PO Box 177 Appleton WI 54912-0177

BARLOW, MATTHEW BLAISE JOSEPH, merchant banker; b. Carlisle, Eng., Jan. 30, 1935; s. John Barlow and Elsie (Butler) Corner-Barlow; m. Mary Alice Jenkins, Aug. 15, 1964; 1 child, Mark Gerard. BA, Ealing Coll.; BSc, U. Petroleum and Minerals Dharan, Saudi Arabia, 1978; BS, U. Oriental Africa Studies, Lagos, Nigeria, 1981; MSc, Aston U., Birmingham, Eng., 1986. FBIM, FAAI. Dep. mng. dir. fin. and adminstrn. Nat. Bank of Nigeria, Lagos, 1979-82; project mgr. Chemsult, Sacramento, Calif., and Johannesburg, Republic of South Africa, 1978-91; loss leaders rep. Arabian Oil, Saudi Arabia, 1977-97; from asst. supt. to supt. Complant Internat., Saudi Arabia, 1989—; assoc. asst. Life Ins. Pension Svc., Gloucester, Eng., 1979—; gen. mgr. Western Exec., Cheltenham, Eng., 1986—; acct. marine aviation Tops, Gloucester, 1988—; tech. mgr. Wescott Freight, Gloucestershire, 1990—; chartered act. PES Middlesborough, Lucern, Switzerland and Dhahran, Boston, 1977-97. With U.K. mil., 1953-55. Fellow Inst. Acctg., Inst. Cost and Mgmt. Acctg., Am. Inst. Cost and Consulting Engrs., British Inst. Mgmt., Royal Inst. British Architects, Inst. Internat. Accts.; mem. N.Y. Acad. Scis. Home: 10 Vectis Close Tudor Park Estates, Lincoln Hills Rd, Ross on Wye Herefordshire HR9 5LR, England also: Savoi Arabea Social Inv PO Box 500 Biggs CA 95917-0500

BARLOW, WILLIAM PUSEY, JR., accountant; b. Oakland, Calif., Feb. 11, 1934; s. William P. and Muriel (Block) B. Student, Calif. Inst. Tech., 1952-54; AB in Econs., U. Calif., Berkeley, 1956. CPA, Calif. Acct. Barlow, Davis & Wood, San Francisco, 1960-72, ptnr., 1964-72; ptnr. J.K. Lasser & Co., 1972-77, Touche Ross & Co., San Francisco, 1977-78; self employed acct., 1978-89; ptnr. Barlow & Hughan, 1990—. Co-author: Collectible Books: Some New Paths, 1979, The Grolier Club, 1884-1984, 1984; editor: Book Catalogues: Their Varieties and Uses, 2d edit., 1986, Officially Sealed Notes, 1996—; contbr. articles to profl. jours. Fellow Gleeson Libr. Assocs., 1969, pres., 1971-74; mem. coun. Friends Bancroft Libr., 1971-98, chmn., 1974-79; bd. dirs. Oakland Ballet, 1982-99, pres., 1986-89, chmn., 1995-98. Recipient Sir Thomas More medal Gleeson Libr. Assocs., 1989; named to Water Ski Hall of Fame, 1993. Mem. Am. Water Ski Assn. (bd. dirs., regional chmn. 1959-63, pres. 1963-66, chmn. bd. 1966-69, 77-79, hon. v.p. 1969—), Internat. Water Ski Fedn. (exec. bd. 1961-71, 75-78), Bibliog. Soc. Am. (coun. 1986-92, pres. 1992-96), Grolier Club (N.Y.C.), Roxburghe Club (San Francisco), Book Club of Calif. (bd. dirs. 1963-76, pres. 1968-69, treas. 1971-83). Home: 1474 Hampel St Oakland CA 94602-1346 Office: 1182 Market St Ste 400 San Francisco CA 94102-4922

BARLOW-STEWART, KRISTINE KAY, public health service officer; b. Sydney, NSW, Australia, Nov. 6, 1949; d. John Robert Barlow and Sheila Winifred (Neville) Davidson; m. Robert Neil Stewart, Aug. 14, 1976; children: Laura Elizabeth, Claire Suzanne. BS, U. Sydney, 1971; PhD, U. NSW, 1979. Cert. genetic counselor. Rschr. Commonwealth Scientific and Indsl. Rsch. Org., Sydney, 1971-72; tchr. London, 1973-74; lectr. dept. genetics U. Sydney, 1978-80, post-doctoral fellow Sch. Pub. Health, 1981-86; policy analyst NSW Dept. Health, Sydney, 1986-89; dir. NSW Genetics Edn. Program, Sydney, 1989—; chair NSW Birth Defects Com., 1989—. Editor: (periodical) Directory of Genetics Svcs., Support Groups and Info. for Australia and New Zealand; author chpt. Towards an Informed Choice in Handbook of Prenatal Diagnosis, 1995; contbr. articles to profl. jours. Mem. Human Genetics Soc. of Australasia, Assn. of Genetic Support of Australasia (Found. pres. 1988-91), Nat. Assn. Genetic Counsellors. Avocations: reading, golf, gardening, bushwalking. Office: NSW Genetics Edn Program, Royal North Shore Hosp, Saint Leonards NSW 2065, Australia

BARLYBAEV, ADIGAM AGZAMOVICH, economist, educator; b. Baymak, Russia, Aug. 30, 1958; s. Agzam Ramazanovich Barlybaev and Fatima Valeevna Adigamova; m. Firuza Biktimirovna Harrasova, Apr. 30, 1983; children: Azamat, Ural. Diploma as lectr. polit. economy, Rostov U., Rostov-on-Done, Russia, 1981; PhD in Econ. Sci., Moscow Regional Pedagogic Inst, 1990. Instr. dept. polit. economy Ufa (Russia) Aviation Inst., 1981-84; instr. Sterlitamak (Russia) State Pedagogical Inst., 1984-87, asst. prof. dept. polit. economy and sociology, 1990-94; asst. prof. dept. polit. economy and fin. Sibay (Russia) Inst. BSU, 1994-96, head dept. econ. and fin., 1996-98, dep. rector edn. br., 1998-99. Co-author: Problems of Transition of Russian Economy to Market Relations, 1996, Economy of Bashkortostan, 1998. Avocations: water travel, bee-keeping, gardening. Home: Chaykovsky, 32-19, 453640 Sibay Bashkort, Russia Office: Sibay Inst BSU, Mayakovsky, 5, 453640 Sibay Bashkort, Russia

BARMORE, FRANK EDWARD, physics educator; b. Manhattan, Kans., June 20, 1938; s. Mark Alfred and Elizabeth (Jenkins) B.; m. Irene Elizabeth Wilcox, Jan. 21, 1967; children—Nathaniel, Christopher. B.S. with honors, Wash. State U., 1960; M.S., U. Wis.-Madison, 1963, Ph.D., 1973. Asst. prof. natural sci. Milton Coll., Wis., 1970-73; asst. prof. physics Middle East Tech. U., Ankara, Turkey, 1974-76; research assoc. physics U. Calgary, Alta., Can., 1976-77; project scientist Ctr. for Research in Exptl. Space Sci. York U., Toronto, Ont., Can., 1977-78; lectr. physics U. Wis.-La Crosse, 1978-83, asst. prof. 1983-86, assoc. prof. 1986— . Contbr. articles to profl. publs. Mem. AAAS, Am. Geophys. Union, Am. Assn. Physics Tchrs., Optical Soc. Am., Soc. Archtl. Historians, Sigma Xi, Phi Beta Kappa. Home: 2025 State St La Crosse WI 54601-3735 Office: U Wis Physics Dept Cowley Hall La Crosse WI 54601

BARNA, NICU, university administrator, advertising agent; b. TG Ocna, Bacau, Romania, July 6, 1961; s. Neculah and Luta (Avadahi) B.; m. Liliana Larion, Aug. 18, 1990 (div. 1995); 1 child, Capriana; m. Despina Magazin, 1997; 1 child, Andreea. Student, U GH Aachi, Iasi, Romania, 1991. Supt. Practizahul, Bacau, Romania, 1991; rschr. Ambro SA, Suceava, Romania, 1991-92; mktg. exec. Ambro SA, Suceava, 1992-94, import and export exec., 1994-96, export exec., 1996-2000; sec. Stefan Lupascu U., Suceava, 2000—; pres./mgr. Spatial Impex SRL Svc., 1999; mgr./founder Barna NICU Libr., 1999. Mem. Alliance for Romania party, 1999. Mem. IMC, Brit. Airways, SAS. Mem. Christian Orthodox Ch. Avocations: travel, reading. Fax: 30 517654; e-mail: spatial@suceava.iiruc.ro. Home: Lt Mircea Damaschin 7, RO-5800 Suceava Romania Office: Stefan Lupascu U, PO Box 8-35 Calea Uhirii 15, RO-5800 Suceava Romania

BARNA, PETER B., physicist; b. Tata, Hungary, July 18, 1928; s. Louis and Theresa (Hereghi) B.; m. Eva Puskas, May 13, 1974; children: Daniel, Gabriel. MS, Eotvos Lorand U., 1950; PhD, Hungarian Acad. Sci., 1964, DSc, 1999. Prof.'s asst. dept. physics Eotvos Lorand U., Budapest, 1949-59; dept. head Rsch. Inst. for Optics, Budapest, 1959-61, Rsch. Inst. Tech. Physics Hungarian Acad. Sci., Budapest, 1961—; dir. internat. workshop on thin films I Internat. Ctr. for Theoretical Physics, Trieste, Italy, 1994, internat. workshop on thin films II, 1996, internat. workshop on thin films III, 1999; dir. NATO ARW on Protective Coatings, Portimao, Portugal, 1996; chmn. 17th Internat. Conf. on Amorphous Semiconductors, Budapest, 1997; rep. gen. assembly Hungarian Acad. Sci., 1994-98; chmn. Sci. Coun. Ctr. Electron Microscopy, Halle/S, 1978-80; sec. thin film divsn. IUVSTA, Brussels, 1979-89; titular prof. Kossuth Lajos u., Debrecen, 1992—; mem. adv. bd. rsch. insts. Hungarian Acad. Scis., 1995-98. Mem. internat. adv. bd. Romanian Reports in Physics, 1994—, Acta Physica Solvaca, 1993—; author: Vacuum Physics, 1959; guest editor: VACUUM Selected Procs. IVC-11, 1990; mem. editl. bd. Thin Solid Films, 1988—. Recipient Small Cross Order Hungarian Republic, 1992, Prize of Physics Hungarian Acad. Scis., 1994, Gold Medal of Physics and Chemistry Slovak Acad. Scis., 1995, Miculescu prize Romanian Acad. Sci., 1974. Mem. Hungarian Eotvos Phys. Soc. (sect. chair 1978-85, hon. chair 1985, Selenyi medal 1966), Hungarian Electronmicroscopy Soc. (bd. dirs. 1988-94). Mem. Hungarian Reformed Ch. Home: Serleg u 6, H-1118 Budapest Hungary Office: Rsch Inst Tech Physics, Konkoly Trege u 29-33, H-1121 Budapest Hungary

BARNABY, CHARLES FRANK, writer; b. Andover, Eng., Sept. 27, 1927; s. Charles Hector and Lilian (Sainsbury) B.; m. Wendy Elizabeth Field, Dec. 19, 1972; children: Sophie Elizabeth, Benjamin Frank. BSc, U. London, 1948, MSc, 1951, PhD, 1960; DSc (hon.), Free U., Amsterdam, 1981, Southampton U., 1995. Scientist Atomic Weapons Rsch. Establishment, Aldermaston, Eng., 1957; physicist U. Coll., London, 1957-67; exec. sec. Pugwash Confs. on Sci. and World Affairs, London, 1967-70; dir. Stockholm Internat. Peace Rsch. Inst., 1971-81; prof. Free U., Amsterdam, 1982-86; chmn. Just Def., 1986—; co-chmn. World Disarmament Campaign, 1986—; cons. Oxford Rsch. Group, 1998—. Author: Prospects for Peace, 1984, The Automated Battlefield, 1986, Star Wars Brought Down to Earth, 1986, The Invisible Bomb, 1989, The Gaia Peace Atlas, 1989, The Role and Control of Weapons in the 1990s, 1992, How Nuclear Weapons Spread, 1993, Instruments of Terror, 1997. Home: Brandreth Station Rd, Chilbolton, Stockbridge SO2O 6AW, England

BARNABY, DARYL JOHN, business and systems consultant; b. Colchester, Essex, Eng., Apr. 4, 1956; s. Gerald Alexander James Barnaby and Jean Doreen (Hodges) Lane; m. Judith Amanda Hannah, July 22, 1978 (div. Aug. 1990); m. Julie Sharon Clark, Apr. 27, 1991 (div. Aug. 1994); m. Jayne Elizabeth Poundall, May 25, 1996. Computer trainee The Boots Co., Nottingham, Eng., 1977-78, programmer trainee, 1978-79, programmer, 1979; programmer analyst Gamma Software Contracts Ltd., Nottingham, 1979-80, Scicon Consultancy Internat., Nottingham, 1980-82; fin. systems analyst Time Utilising Bus. Systems Ltd., Leicester, Eng., 1982-83; systems cons. Zeda Computer Systems Ltd., Nottingham, 1983-88; projects mgr. Zeda Info. Mgmt. Cons. Ltd., Nottingham, 1988-90; sr. bus. cons. Zeda Ltd., Nottingham, 1990-92; assoc. Perot Sys. Europe Ltd., Nottingham, 1992-2000; info. head profession English Nature, Peterborough, 2000—. Mem. British Computer Soc. Avocations: rugby, home brewing, science fiction, music, gardening. Home: Ridge Cottage Main Rd, Elton, Nottinghamshire NG13 9LB, England Office: Engl Nature, Northminster, House, Northminster, Peterborough PE1 1UA, England

BARNARD, ANNA MARION, county official; b. Magnolia, Ark., Oct. 30, 1953; d. Harvey Wesley and Virginia Sue (Herring) Callicott; m. Robert Richard Edington, Aug. 5, 1972 (dec. Oct. 1974); m. Rickie Lynn Barnard, May 15, 1976; children: Melanie Lynn, Hilary Anne, Matthew Ryan. Student, So. State Coll., 1975-76. Cert. treas., Ark. Teller, ins. clk. Peoples Bank, Waldo, Ark., 1971-74; teller collections, sec. to pres. First Nat. Bank, Magnolia, Ark., 1976-80; acct., bookkeeper Hamlin & Nolte Water Wells, Taylor, Ark., 1987-95; adminstrv. asst. Columbia County, Magnolia, Ark., 1995-96, county treas., 1997—. Mem. com. Leadership Magnolia, 1998-99; bd. dir.s, treas. Bussey/Sharman Fire Dist., Taylor, Ark., 1996—; mem. South Ark. Women's Network, Magnolia, 1997-98, Magnolia Econ. Devel. Corp., 1999—. Mem. Ark. County Treas. Assn. Baptist. Avocations: church pianist, singing, reading, cooking, cross-stiching. Office: Columbia County Treas 101 S Court Sq Magnolia AR 71753-3511

BARNARD, CHARLES EDUARD, environmental lawyer; b. Johannesburg, South Africa, Oct. 28, 1943; s. Jan Paul and Phillippina Elizabeth (Marx) B.; m. Helena Christiana Steyn, Apr. 30, 1968; children: Helena Christiana, Phillippa Elizabeth. B of Commerce, U. Stellenbosch, South Africa, 1965, LLB, 1967. Law lectr. U. South Africa, Pretoria, 1968; prosecutor Dept. Justice, Vryheid & Cape Town, South Africa, 1972-74; sr. state advocate Dept. Justice, Pretoria, 1974; mem. Pretoria Bar, 1975-92; pvt. practice environ. law Pretoria, 1992—; owner, dir. Brickmaking Co., Vryheid, 1969-72; dir. Helios Power Ltd., Pretoria, 1989-93; mng. dir. PV Lights Ltd., Pretoria, 1990—; cons. and lectr. in environ. law. Bd. dirs. Coun. for the Environment, Pretoria, 1992-95; active Environ. Justice Networking Forum, 1994—. Mem. Solar Energy Soc. South Africa (chmn. 1994-96), Internat. Solar Energy Soc. (bd. dirs. 1995-98). Avocations: hiking, reading, music. Home and Office: 127 Marais St, 0181 Pretoria South Africa

BARNARD, GEORGE SMITH, lawyer, former federal agency official; b. Opelika, Ala.; s. George Smith and Caroline Elizabeth (Dowdell) B.; m. Muriel Elaine Outlaw, July 26, 1945; children: Elizabeth Elaine Barnard Crutcher, Charles Dowling, Beverly Laura Barnard Parker, Andrew Carey. BA, U. Ala., 1948, LLB, 1950. Bar: Fla. 1978, Ala. 1950, U.S. Tax Ct. 1950, U.S. Dist. Ct. Ala. 1950, U.S. Dist. Ct. Fla. 1978, U.S. Dist. Ct. (so. dist. trial bar) Fla. 1995, U.S. Supreme Ct. 1965, U.S. Ct. Claims 1979, U.S. Ct. Appeals (Fed. cir.) 1984, U.S. Ct. Appeals (11th cir.) 1985. Pvt. practice Opelika, 1950-51; with IRS, 1951-78; attache, revenue service rep. Sao Paulo Brazil, S.Am. and Lesser Antilles, 1965-71, Mexico City, Bermuda Is., Bahamas, Panama, Major Antilles, C.Am., 1971-77; ptnr. Barnard, P.A., Miami, Fla., 1978-87; of counsel Barnard, P.A., 1987-91; lectr. taxation U. Ala., 1958-60. Pres. Rocky Ridge Vol. Fire Dept., 1956-58, Rocky Ridge Civic Club, 1959, Ala. chpt. Nat. Assn. Internal Revenue Employees, 1962; commr. Rocky Ridge Civic Water Works, 1960-62; bd. dirs. S.E.Pompano Homeowners Assn., 1996-99. With USAAF, 1942-46. Recipient Albert Gallatin award U.S. Treasury Dept., 1978; named Hon. Citizen of Tex., 1979, Hon. Admiral in Tex. Navy, 1979. Mem. Fgn. Svc. Retirees Assn. of Fla. (advisor/dir. for S.E. Fla. 1987-98, dir. emeritus 1998—, original incumbent historian 1998—), Kappa Sigma. Republican. Home: 671 SW 6th St Apt 912 Pompano Beach FL 33060-7739 Office: Charles D Barnard PA 3940 N Andrews Ave Fort Lauderdale FL 33309-5240

BARNARD, JOHN MICHAEL, educator; b. Folkestone, England, Feb. 13, 1936; s. John Claude and Dora Grace (Epps) B.; m. Katherine Jane Duckham, July 18, 1961 (div. 1975); children: Josephine, Clio, Jason; m. Hermione Lee, Mar. 22, 1991. BA with honors, Oxford U., England, 1959, BLITT, 1964, MA, 1964. Rsch. asst. Yale U., New Haven, Conn., 1961-64; lectr. U. Leeds, Sch. English, England, 1965-78, prof., 1978—; vis. lectr. U. Calif., Santa Barbara, 1964-65. Author: John Keats, 1987; co-author: The Early Seventeenth York Century Book Trade and John Foster's Inventory of 1616, 1994; editor: Pope: The Critical Heritage, 1973, John Keats: The Complete Poems, 1973, Selected Poems, 1988. Rsch. fellow William Clark Meml. Libr., 1965, 84, Huntington Libr., L.A., 1984. Mem. Johnson Club. Avocation: walking. Office: U Leeds, Sch English, Leeds LS2 9JT, England

BARNARD, KURT, retail trend/consumer spending forecaster, publisher; b. Hamburg, Germany, Apr. 16, 1927; s. León and Senta (Künstlinger) Barnard-Jeserski; m. Wendy Holly Love, Dec. 9, 1979; 1 child, Lance Jonathan. Student, NYU, 1948, N.Y. State U., 1953; grad., New Sch. for Social Research, 1957. N.Y. corr. European and Japanese bus. publs., 1957-60; dir. Latin Am., Far Eastern pub. relations Anglo-Affiliated Corp., N.Y.C., 1955-60; mktg. dir. Am. Research Merchandising Inst., Chgo., 1960-67; exec. dir. Internat. Mass Retail Assn., N.Y.C., 1967-69; exec. v.p. Internat. Mass Retailing Assn., N.Y.C., 1969-74, pres., 1974-76; exec. dir. Fedn. Apparel Mfrs., N.Y.C., 1976-86; launched Barnard's Retail Cons. Group and Barnard's Retail Mktg. Report, 1984; launched Barnard's Retail Cons. Group and Barnard's Retail Mktg. Report, 1984 (now Barnard's Retail Trend Report); cons. on wage-price freeze to dir. U.S. Office Emergency Preparedness, 1971-72; condr. retailing seminars in Europe, U.S.; frequent forecaster and commentator on retailing and consumer spending issues on TV, Radio, including McNeil-Lehrer Newshour, CBS Evening News, NBC's Today Show, ABC's Good Morning Am. show, CNN, CNBC, Wall Street Journal Radio; organizer Nat. Loss Prevention Coun., 1972, Store Thieves and Their Impact, A Study, 1973; named mem. U.S. Govt. Industry Sector Adv. Com., 1978; mem. U.S. Govt. Exporters Adv. Com., 1979; chmn. bd. N.Y. Internat. Fashion Fair, 1980; leader nat. campaign against fair trade laws. Author: Cargo of Death, 1966, An Untapped Source of Store Profits, 1974, Picture of a Tragedy, 1974, How Chains Succeed With Non-Foods, 1974, Can Supermarkets Capture Non-Food Sales?, 1974, In Retailing: Future Shock is Now, 1975, Guidelines to Effective Marketing Strategies for Self-Service Retailers, 1975; co-author: Mass Merchandisers Guide to Sales and Expense Reporting, 1969, Marketing: Key to Retail Prosperity, 1985; contbr. articles to mags. and profl. jours. Recipient Disting. Service award U.S.O., 1965, Am. Soc. Assn. Execs. award, 1965; commd. Ky. col., 1975; DuPont Co. grantee, 1971-75. Mem. Nat. Assn. Bus. Economists, Mus. Modern Art. Office: 17 Kenneth Rd Montclair NJ 07043-2541

BARNARD, PHILIP DONALD, market research company executive; b. Antrim, No. Ireland, Aug. 15, 1941; s. Donald and Rosina Alice (Swain) B.; m. Jean Iris Miller-Crispe, May 5, 1964; children: Ian Karl, Scott Donald. BA in Natural Scis., Cambridge U., Eng., 1963, MA, 1967. Trainee exec. Unilever, London, 1964-73; internat. mktg. dir. Rsch. Internat., Rotterdam, The Netherlands, 1973-77; dir. Rsch. Internat., London, 1977-84; chmn. Rsch. Internat., Hamburg, Germany, 1984-86; chmn, CEO, Rsch. Internat., London, 1986-89, N.Y.C., 1989-91; dir. RI East Africa Ltd, Kenya, 1977—, Seced/RI France, Paris, 1991—, JMRB, Tokyo, 1995—, chmn., CEO, Rsch. Internat. Group, London, 1991-95; chmn., CEO, Kantar Group, London, 1995—; bd. trustees Mktg. Sci. Instn., 1989—. Contbr. articles to profl. jours., chpts. to books. State scholar Brit. Govt., 1960. Fellow Inst. Dirs., Market Rsch. Soc.; mem. United Oxford & Cambridge Univ. Club, Am. Mktg. Assn. Avocations: reading, natural history, skiing, history. Home: Maidens Green Farm, Windsor SL4 4SR, England Office: Rsch Interat Group, The Kantar Group, 4 Grosvenor Pl, London SW1X 7HF, England

BARNARD, ROBERT C., lawyer; b. 1913; s. Robert C. and Elsie (Francis) B.; m. Helen Hurd, Dec. 25, 1939; children—Robert Christopher, Mary Anne. BA, Reed Coll., 1935; postgrad. Columbia U. Law Sch. 1935-36; BA, Oxford (Eng.) U., 1938, BCL (Rhodes scholar), 1939, MA, 1951. Bar: Wash., 1940, D.C., 1947, U.S. Sup. Ct., 1943. Chief app. sect. antitrust div., chief legal adv. Office of Asst. Solicitor Gen., Dept. Justice, Washington, 1939-47; assoc. Cleary, Gottlieb, Steen & Hamilton, Washington, 1947-49, in charge Paris office, 1949-52, Washington, after 1952, sr. ptnr., 1961-84, of counsel, 1984—. Recipient Internat. Achievement award Internat. Soc. for Regulatory Toxicology and Pharmacology, 1995. Mem. ABA, Am. Indsl. Health Coun. (sci. advisor), Fed. Bar Assn., D.C. Bar Assn., Washington Bar Assn. Contbr. articles to profl. jours. Home: 5409 Dorset Ave Chevy Chase MD 20815-6627 Office: 2000 Pennsylvania Ave NW Washington DC 20006-1812

BARNARD, ROLLIN DWIGHT, retired financial executive; b. Denver, Apr. 14, 1922; s. George Cooper and Emma (Riggs) B.; m. Patricia Reynolds Bierkamp, Sept. 15, 1943; children: Michael Dana, Rebecca Susan (Mrs. Paul C. Wulfestieg), Laurie Beth (Mrs. Kenneth J. Kostelecky). BA, Pomona Coll., 1943. Clk. Morey Merc. Co., Denver, 1937-40; ptnr. George C. Barnard & Co., Denver, 1946-47; v.p. Foster & Barnard, Inc., 1947-53; instr. Denver U., 1949-53; dir. real estate U.S. P.O. Dept., Washington, 1953-55, dep. asst. postmaster gen., bur. facilities, 1955-59, asst. postmaster gen., 1959-61; pres., dir. Midland Fed. Savs. & Loan Assn., Denver, 1962-84; vice-chmn. Bank Western Fed. Savs. Bank, 1984-87; vice-chmn., pres. Western Capital Investment Corp., 1985-87. Mayor City of Greenwood Village, Colo., 1989-93, chmn. Planning and Zoning Commn., 1969-73, mem. coun., 1975-77; pres. Denver Area coun. Boy Scouts Am., 1970-71, mem. exec. bd., 1962-73; mem. adv. bd. Denver Area coun. Boy Scouts Am., 1973—; bd. dirs. Downtown Denver Improvement Assn., pres., 1965; bd. dirs. Bethesda Found., Inc., 1973-82, Children's Hosp., 1979-84, treas., 1983-84; bd. dirs. Children's Health Corp., Inc., 1982-93; trustee Mile High United Fund, 1969-72, Denver Symphony Assn., 1973-74; bd. dirs. Colo. Coun. Econ. Edn., 1971-80, chmn. 1971-76; trustee, v.p., treas. Morris Animal Found., 1969-81, pres., chmn. 1974-78, trustee emeritus, 1981—; trustee Denver Zool. Found., 1994—, exec. vice-chmn., 1996-2000, vice-chmn., 2000—; mem. acquisitions com. Friends Found. Denver Pub. Libr., 1994—; dir. Wings over the Rockies Air & Space Mus. Found., 1998—. Named one of Ten Outstanding Young Men in Am., U.S. Jaycees, 1955, 57; recipient Disting. Svc. award Postmaster Gen. U.S., 1960; Silver Beaver award Boy Scouts Am., 1969; named Outstanding Citizen of Yr., Sertoma, 1982, Colo. Citizen of Yr., Colo. Assn. Realtors, 1982, Citizen of West, Nat. Western Stockshow, 1994. Mem. Greater Denver C. of C. (pres. 1966-67), U.S. League Savs. Instns. (bd. dirs. 1972-77, vice-chmn. 1979-80, chmn. 1980-81, mem. nat. legis. com., exec. com. 1974-77), Savs. League Colo. (exec. com. 1969-73, pres. 1971-72), Colo. Assn. Commerce and Industry (dir. 1971-76), Fellowship Christian Athletes (Denver area dir. 1963-76), Western Stock Show Assn. (dir. 1971—, exec. com. 1982-94, 1st v.p. 1985-94), Mountain and Plains Appaloosa Horse Club (pres. 1970-71), Roundup Riders of the Rockies (bd. dirs. 1979-2000, dir. emeritus 2000—, treas. 1980-87, v.p. 1987-89, pres.-elect 1989-91, pres. 1991-93). Republican. Presbyterian. Home: Surrey Ridge Estates 9902 N Heather Dr Castle Rock CO 80104-9133

BARNARD, TIMOTHY CHARLES, managing director; b. Wheathampstead, Eng., Apr. 19, 1964; s. Brian and Jean Eleanor May (Wilkinson) B.; m. Julia Ann Stannard, Oct. 19, 1991; children: Oliver Ian, Sophia Charlotte. St. Georges, Harpenden, Hartfordshire, Eng., 1976-81. Mng. dir. Techmate Ltd., Hertfordshire, Eng., 1981—. Mem. Milton Keynes Waterski Club (hon. sec. 1994-96). Avocations: golf, waterskiing, motorsports, snowboarding. Office: Techmate Ltd, 10 Bridgeturn Ave, Milton Keynes MK12 SQL, England

BARNES, BEN BLAIR, computer company executive, electrical engineer; b. Gadsden, Ala., Mar. 7, 1935; s. Newton Eldridge Jr. and Sarah Aileen (Roach) B.; m. Pat Harris, June 3, 1956 (div. 1989); 1 child, Douglas Harris; m. Elba Crowe Clarke, Feb. 25, 1991. BEE, Ala. Poly. Inst., 1956; MSEE, U. Ala., 1962; PhD, Auburn U., 1965. Registered profl. engr., Ala., Tenn. Instrument engr. E.I. du Pont de Nemours & Co., Aiken, S.C., 1957-59; computer engr. NASA Marshall Space Flight Ctr., Huntsville, Ala., 1959-63; mem. faculty elec. engring. dept. Va. Poly. Inst. and State U., Blacksburg, 1965-66; dept. mgr. Computer Scis. Corp., Huntsville, 1966-67; asst. dean engring. U. Tenn., Knoxville, 1967-70; dir. Computer Ctr. Auburn (Ala.) U., 1970-80; head computer sci. Calif. State Coll. Stanislaus, Turlock, 1981; prin. Ben Barnes & Assocs., Auburn, 1981-87; chief exec. officer Ala. Supercomputer Authority, Huntsville, 1987-98; v.p. SilverTech Assocs., Dadeville, Ala., 1998—. 2d lt. U.S. Army, 1956-57. Mem. IEEE, Assn. for Computing Machinery. Home: 13 Eagle Peak Cir Dadeville AL 36853-5625 Office: SilverTech Assocs 1622 Sandstone Ct Montgomery AL 36117-1704

BARNES, DIANA MARION, biochemist, consultant; b. Sandy, Eng., Mar. 16, 1937; d. Barrie and Marion Alice (Jordan) Campbell; m. Nicholas Martin Barnes, Feb. 23, 1963; children: Katherine Emma, Matthew John. BSc, U. London, 1958; PhD, Postgrad. Med. Sch., 1963, D.Sc., 1998. Rsch. scientist RPMS, London, 1958-64; biochemist Christie Hosp., Manchester, Eng., 1974-82, head clin. endocrinology, 1982-86; rsch. biochemist clin. oncology unit Imperial Cancer Rsch. Fund Guy's Hosp., London, 1987-90, cons. biochemist, 1990-97, head breast pathology group, 1997—. Mem. British Breast Group, British Assn. Cancer Rsch., Am. Assn. Cancer Rsch. Home: Cornbrash House, Kirtlington OX5 3HF, England Office: Hedley Atkins/ICRF, Guys Hosp Breast Path Lab, London SE1 9RT, England

BARNES, GARY JOHN, psychiatrist; b. Brisbane, Queensland, Australia, Feb. 24, 1938; s. Louis Gabriel and Muriel Eileen (Bourke) B.; m. Joanna Lamb, Oct. 18, 1969; children: Sarah, Edward. MB BChir, U. Queensland, 1962. Registrar Kings Coll. Hosp., London, 1970-71; lectr. London U., 1972; cons. psychiatrist Claybury Hosp., London, 1973, Oxford Mental Health Ctr., Ont., Can., 1973-74, Royal Prince Alfred Hosp., Sydney, Australia, 1982—; pvt. practice Sydney, 1975—; mem. ethics com. Ramsay Hosp., Australia, 1994—. Contbr. articles to profl. jours. Mem. Amnesty Internat. Fellow Royal Australian and New Zealand Coll. Psychiatry (bd. continuing edn. 1976-83, convenor NSW br. sci. program 1976-84, mem. psychopharmacology com. 1989-94); mem. Royal Coll. Psychiatrists, Australian Med. Assn. Avocation: gardening. E-mail: gjbrns@telstra.com. Office: 7a Ashburner St Manly, Sydney 2095 NSW, Australia

BARNES, GRAHAM, psychotherapist, educator, consultant; b. Creswell, N.C., Oct. 24, 1936; arrived in Sweden, 1983; naturalized, 1996; s. Will Mitchell and Wilma (Norman) B.; m. Ethel Dale McBride, Aug. 8, 1959 (div. Sept. 1978); children: Christopher David, James McBride; registered domestic ptnr.: Stephanos Giotas. BA, Roanoke Bible Coll., 1959; MA, Abilene Christian U., 1964; STB, Harvard U., 1967. Lic. psychotherapist; cert. group psychotherapist; cert. marital family therapist. Founder, dir. Fellowship for Racial and Econ. Equality, Lynchburg, Va., 1969-73; founder, pres., faculty S.E. Inst., Chapel Hill, N.C., 1973-78; lectr., supr. Psychotherapy Insts. & Univs. in 12 European Countries, 1979-88; head sch. for cybernetics of psychotherapy, dept. psychiatry U. Zagreb, Croatia, 1990-97; chmn. Inform AB, Stockholm, Sweden, 1991-99, The Barnes Ctr., Stockholm, Sweden, 2000—; instr. Roanoke Bible Coll., 1961-62; adj. lectr. dept. psychiatry U. N.C., Chapel Hill, 1973-78; lectr. Sch. Pub. Health, U. N.C., 1976; field faculty Goddard Coll., 1975-77; cons. Norwegian Sport Fedn., Oslo, 1979-83, Corp. Strategic Planning Team, Pharmacia AB, Uppsala, Sweden, 1981-83, Hydro Aluminum A/S, Oslo, 1984-96, Swedbank, Stockholm, 1995—, IRIS Devel. Ctr., Stockholm, 1991—; vis. lectr. dept. psychiatry U. Zagreb, 1990—; adv. bd. Parsons-FEIN Tng. Inst. for Psychotherapy and Hypnosis, N.Y., 1998—; bd. dirs. KLUAB, Stockholm; assoc. cons. Network AB, Stockholm; advisor Found. 2020, Zagreb, 1999—. Author: Justice, Love and Wisdom Linking Psychotherapy to Second-Order Cybernetics, 1994; editor: Transactional Analysis After Eric Berne, 1977; mem. editl. bd. Transactional Analysis Jour., 1997-99, Hypnos-Swedish and European Jour. Hypnosis, 2000—; contbr. over 30 articles to profl. jours. Mem. adv. com. City of Lynchburg, 1971-73; mem. human rels. task force Lynchburg Pub. Schs., 1971-73; mem. John Lynch Soc., Lynchburg, 1971-73; bd. dirs. Orange County Mental Health Assn., 1974-78; life mem. Disciples of Christ Hist. Soc. Irwin-Sweeney-Miller Found. grantee, Columbus, Ind., 1969, 70, 71, Lilly Endowment, Inc. grantee, Indpls., 1973. Mem. AAAS, Am. Group Psychotherapy Assn. (clin. mem.), Internat. Transactional Analysis Assn. (v.p. 1976-77, bd. trustees 1973-77, 82-84, tchg. mem. 1972—), Am. Soc. for Cybernetics, Swedish Soc. Clin. and Exptl. Hypnosis (dep. bd. mem. 2000—), Latin Am. Assn. Transactional Analysis (hon.). Office: The Barnes Ctr, Box 17, SE-101 20 Stockholm Sweden Home: Drottninggatan 73C, SE-111 36 Stockholm Sweden

BARNES, HOWARD ANTHONY, rheologist, engineer, educator; b. Abergavenny, Wales, Apr. 8, 1944; s. Elijah and Doris (Liddy) B.; m. Pauline Sandra Brind, Dec. 2, 1967; children: Timothy, Andrew, Stephen. BSc, U. Aberystwyth, Wales, 1965, PhD, 1970, DSc, 1994. Chartered engr., 1995. Scientist Unilever Rsch., Port Sunlight, Eng., 1970-87, sr. scientist, 1987-00, prin. scientist, 2000—; vis. prof. Liverpool U., 1990—, Aberystwyth, 1990—. Co-author: Introduction to Rheology, 1989; contbr. over 60 articles to profl. jours. and sci. confs. Decorated Officer of the Order of the Brit. Empire, Queen Elizabeth II, 1997; recipient RSC award Royal Soc. Chemistry, London, 1984, Hanson medal, Instn. Chem. Engrs., 1993. Fellow Instn. Chem. Engrs., Inst. Materials, Royal Acad. Engring.; mem. Brit. Soc. Rheology (pres. 1994-96). Mem. Christian Brethren Ch. Avocations: writing, preaching. Office: Unilever Rsch, Port Sunlight, Merseyside L63 3JW, England

BARNES, JAMES NEIL, lawyer; b. Tulsa, June 28, 1944; s. William Harvey and Mildred E. (Norsworthy) B.; children: Deborah, Sociana; m. Anne E. Fuhrman, Dec. 18, 1992. BA, Northwestern U., 1966; JD, U. Mich., 1970. Bar: U.S. Dist. Ct. D.C. 1971, U.S. Ct. Appeals (D.C. cir.) 1973, U.S. Supreme Ct. 1977. Law clk. to judge U.S. Dist. Ct D.C., Washington, 1970-71; staff atty. Ctr. for Law and Social Policy, Washington, 1971-72, 77-81, co-dir., 1980-81; staff atty. Pub. Def. Svc., Washington, 1972-74; assoc. Hudson & Co., Port Vila, New Hebrides Islands, 1974-75; cons. Coun. for Pub. Interest Law, Washington, 1975-76; assoc. Wilmer, Cutler and Pickering, Washington, 1976-77; founder, dir. Antarctica Project, Washington, 1981-93; gen. counsel Antarctic and So. Ocean Coalition, Sydney, Australia, 1981—; East coast dir. Threshold Internat. Ctr. for Environ. Renewal, Washington, 1981-87; sr. atty. Environ. Policy Inst. and Friends of Earth, Washington, 1987-94, head internat. dept. Friends of the Earth, 1990-94; counselor Les Amis de La Terre-France and Friends of the Earth Internat., 1994—; CEE Bankwatch Network, Cracow, Poland, 1995—. Author: Let's Save Antarctica, 1982, Bankrolling Successes: A Portfolio of Sustainable Projects, 1988, 2d edit., 1995, Russian Roulette: Nuclear Power Reactors in Eastern Europe and Former Soviet Union, 1992-93, Promises, Promises: A Review of G-7 Economic Summit Declarations on Environment and Development, 1994; contbr. articles to profl. jours.; prodr.: (video) Antarctica: Soul of the Blue Planet; editor ECO, 1978—. UN rep. Greenpeace Internat., 1983-85, bd. dirs., 1984-85; active State Dept. Adv. Com. on Law of the Sea, 1977-82, pub. adv. com. on Antarctica, 1978-92; mem. commn. on law and policy Internat. Union for Conservation of Nature and Natural Resources, 1980—; pres. Meridian Hill Studios Coop., 1987-90, treas., 1991-94. Recipient Golden Ark award His Royal Highness Prince Bernhard, 1998; named Internat. Environmentalist of Yr., Nat. Wildlife Fedn., 1991. Mem. Internat. Coun. Environ. Lawyers. Avocations: photography, guitar and harmonica, cycling. Home: Rue Edouard Dupuy, 24140 Villamblard Dordogne, France

BARNES, JOHN ALFRED, city official; b. Sunderland, Eng., Apr. 29, 1930; s. John Joseph and Margaret Carr (Glenwright) B.; m. Ivy May Walker; children: Shirley May Barnes, Jennifer Ann Barnes. BS, U. Durham, 1952, MA, 1957, MEd, 1958. Head of geography dept. Grangefield Grammar Sch., Stockton on Tees, 1953-57; asst. edn. officer Edn. Dept., Barnsley County Borough, 1957-61; dep. dir. edn. Edn. Dept., City of Wakefield, 1961-63, dir. edn., 1963-68; chief edn. officer Edn. Dept., City of Salford, 1968-84; dir. gen. City and Guilds of London Inst., London, 1984-93; sec. U.K. Skills, 1990-93; chmn. Sir Isaac Pitman Ltd., London, 1990-93; treas. Nat. Found. for Ednl. Rsch., U.K., 1979-84. Contbr. articles to profl. jours. Mem. County Coun., Buckinghamshire, 1993-97; trustee City Parochial Found. and Trust for London, 1993—. With RAF, 1948-49. Decorated comdr. Brit. Empire. Fellow Royal Soc. of Arts, City and Guilds of London Inst. (hon.), Inst. of Tng. and Devel. (hon.), Coll. of Preceptors (hon.), Chartered Inst. of Pers. and Devel. (hon. companion). Methodist. Avocations: educational activities, charitable works, travel world wide. Home and Office: 37 Woodfield Park, Amersham HP6 5QH, England

BARNES, JOHN GILBERT PRESSLIE, computer language designer; b. London, Aug. 19, 1937; s. Gilbert Arthur and Edith Helen (Pressle) B.; m. Barbara Winifred Juffkins, Sept. 8, 1962; children: Janet Elizabeth, Helen Jane. BA in Math., Cambridge U., 1961, MA, 1964. Mathematician Imperial Chem. Industries, Reading, Eng., 1961-68, sect. mgr., 1969-75; cons. Imperial Chem. Industries, Slough, Eng., 1975-78; vis. fellow U. Edinburgh (Scotland), 1968-69; dir. lang. research S P L Internat., Abingdon, Eng., 1978-84; tech. dir. Systems Designers, Camberley, Eng., 1984-85; mng. dir. Alsys Ltd., Henley, Eng., 1985-91; owner John Barnes Informatics, 1985; cons. Dept. Industry, London, 1976-78; indsl. fellow Wolfson Coll., Oxford, Eng., 1979-81; vis. prof. Imperial Coll., London, 1982-84; mem. bd. ADA, Washington, 1986-87, pres. ADA-Europe, 1991—. Author: RTL/2 Design and Philosophy, 1976, Programming in ADA, 1982, 3d edit., 1996, High Integrity ADA, 1997, ADA 95 Rationale, 1995; editor: ADA in Use, 1985; contbr. articles to software to profl. publs. Fellow Brit. Computer Soc. (chartered engr.). Home: 11 Albert Rd, Caversham, Reading RG4 7AN, England

BARNES, KIRSTEN JENNIFER, management consultant, sport psychologist; b. London, Mar. 26, 1968; came to Canada, 1969.; d. Michael Paul and Gerildine Anna B. BA in Human Performance, U. Victoria, Victoria, Canada, 1993; PhD in Sport Psychology, U. Bristol, Eng., 1997. Venue and media operations asst. Canada Summer Games, Kamloops, 1993; rsch. asst. U. Bristol (England), 1993-96; with Ln. 4 Mgmt. Group, Berkshire, Eng., 1997—; mem. Nat. Rowing Team, Ottawa, Canada, 1987-92. Recipient two Gold medals Internat. Olympic Com., Barcelona, Spain, 1992; two World Rowing Championship Gold medals Internat. Fed. Soc. d'Aviron, Vienna, 1991; Gold medal Pan-Am. Games, Indpls., 1987.

BARNES, LARRY GLEN, journalist, editor, educator; b. Louisville, July 10, 1947; s. Roy Glen and Phyllis Jane (Dunn) B.; m. Susan Gayle Morrow, Dec. 27, 1969 (dec. July, 1973); 1 child, Brian; m. Mary Frances Meiman, July 14, 1979. Student, Murray State U., 1965-68, 71-73, Def. Info. Sch., 1968. Journalist, editor various locations Dept. of the Army, 1968-71; staff writer Louisville Courier-Jour., 1972-75, Lexington (Ky.) Herald-Leader, 1975; mng. editor Corydon (Ind.) Harrison County Press, 1976-77; assoc. editor Ky. Sports World, Louisville, 1977-81; editor Publs. Divsn., Ft. Knox, Ky., 1981-82, Inside the Turret, Ft. Knox, 1982—. Editor Army Newspaper, 1984, 86, 91, 93, 96, 98, (named Army's Dean of Newspaper editors 2000), DOD Newspaper, 1986. With U.S. Army, 1968-71. Recipient Naismith citation Atlanta Tipoff Club, 1981, Journalist award Dept. Army, Washington, 1986, 1st pl. commentary writing Tng. & Doctrine Command, Ft. Monroe, Va., 1985, 87, 88, 89, 90, Thomas Jefferson award Dept. Def., Washington, 1982, 86; named Editor of Yr., Army Tng & Doctrine Command, 1982. Mem. Soc. Profl. Journalists, Am. Fedn. Govt. Employees. Democrat. Baptist. Avocations: photography, watching movies, collecting, 45 r.p.m. records, reading. Home: 2220 Manchester Rd Louisville KY 40205-3044 Office: Pub Affairs Office PO Box 995 Fort Knox KY 40121-0995

BARNES, MARYLOU RIDDLEBERGER, retired academic administrator, educator; b. Bridgewater, Va., Feb. 27, 1930; d. Hensel Dorsey Riddleberger and Ruby Elizabeth Heltzel; children: Tenley Elizabeth, Rachel Patricia. BS, Madison Coll., 1952; MS, Med. Coll. Va., 1957; MA, James Madison U., 1968; EdD, W. Va. U., 1975; DSc (hon.), U. Indpls., 1993. From staff phys. therapist to dir. clin. edn. Woodrow Wilson Rehab. Ctr., Fishersville, Va., 1958-64, dir clin. edn., 1964-67; chief phys. therapy Rockingham Meml. Hosp., Harrisonburg, Va., 1958-59; prof., dir., chair dept. phys. therapy W. Va. U., Morgantown, W. Va., 1968-79; from prof., chair dept. phys. therapy to prof. emeritus Ga. State U., Atlanta, 1979-95, prof. emeritus, 1995—; adv. bd. Perry Inst., Strafford, Pa., 1993-95; co-chair program com. Joint Am.-Can. Phys. Therapy Annual Conf. Author: Patient at Home, 1972, Neurophysiological Basis of Physical Therapy Care, vol. I, 1973, vol. II, 1977, Physical Therapy, 1989, Motor Control and Motor Learning in Rehabilitation, 1993; contbr. articles to profl. jours. Vol. Centennial Olympic Games, Atlanta, 1996, Goodwill Industries Book Ctr., Atlanta, 1999. Mem. Am. Phys. Therapy Assn. (nat. survey pool for accreditation of schs. 1974-95, pres. neurology sect. 1985-87, task force on profl. devel. 1994, chair continuing edn. bd. 1994-95, Mary McMillan Lectr. award 1992, Catherine Worthingham fellow 1994, leadership in edn. award 1995, svc. to neurology sect. award 1998, Lucy Blair Svc. award 1998). Presbyn. Avocations: amateur archaeologist, travel, reading, tree climbers of Am. Home: 3127 W Roxboro Rd NE Atlanta GA 30324-2541 Office: Dept Phys Therapy Ga State Univ Atlanta GA 30303

BARNES, MICHAEL PATRICK, language educator; b. London, June 28, 1940; s. William Edward Clement and Gladys Constance (Hooper) B.; m. Kirsten Heiberg Røer, Aug. 8, 1970; children: Catherine, Anne Helen, William Michael, Kirsten Emily. BA, U. Coll., London, 1963, MA, 1966. Asst. lectr. U. Coll. London, 1964-67, lectr., 1967-75, reader, 1975-83, prof., 1983—; instr. lang. U. Oslo Internat. Summer Sch., Norway, 1974-96. Author: Old Scandinavian Texts, 1968, Draumkvaedet An Edition and Study, 1974, the Runic Inscriptions of Maeshowe Orkney, 1994, The Norn Language of Orkney and Shetland, 1998, A New Introduction to Old Norse, I: Grammar, 1999; co-author: The Runic Inscriptions of Viking Age Dublin, 1997; translator: The Birds, 1968; editor jour. Saga-Book, 1970-84, Nowele, 1989—. Mem. Viking Soc. No. Rsch., Gustav Adolfs Akademien, Det Norske Videnskaps-Acad. Mem. Liberal Ch. Eng. Avocations: badminton, walking disused railways. Home: 93 Longland Dr, London N20 8HN, England Office: U Coll London, Gower St, Dept Scandinavian Studies, London WC1E 6BT, England

BARNES, NICHOLAS MARK, medical researcher and lecturer; b. Peterborough, Eng., Oct. 17, 1963; s. John Thomas Guy and Pauline Ruby (Parrish) B. BSc with honors, U. Leicester, Eng., 1985; PhD, U. Bradford, Eng., 1988. Rsch. fellow U. Bradford, 1988-90, sr. rsch. fellow, 1990-96; lectr. The Med. Sch., U. Birmingham, Eng., 1996—, sr. lectr. dept. pharmacology, 1996—; mem. adv. bd. Med. Rsch. Coun., U.K.; INSERM expert, France. Exec. editor Neuropharmacology. Mem. Soc. for Neurosci., Brit. Pharmacol. Soc. (Bowman prize lectureship 1995), Serotonin Club. Office: U Birmingham Med Sch, Dept Pharmacology, Birmingham B15 2TJ, England

BARNES, PATRICIA ANN, art educator; b. San Antonio, Sept. 26, 1942; d. John Homer and Dorothy Bernice (Foster) Sanders; m. Henry Franklin Snodgrass, Oct. 31, 1960 (div. 1966); children: William Franklin, George Huston II, John Charles Joseph; m. Joseph LeRoy Barnes Jr., Aug. 18, 1969; children: Shana Lynn, Janna Lee, Joseph Leroy III. AAS, Bee County Coll., 1986; BFA, Corpus Christi State U., 1988; MA, Tex. A&M U., 1990. Art tchr. J.T.P.A. Summer Youth Program, Beeville, Tex., 1990; adj. art tchr. St. Philips Coll., San Antonio, 1991-93; art tchr. Runge (Tex.) Ind. Sch. Dist., 1993-96; art tchr., chmn. fine arts Skidmore (Tex.)-Tynan Ind. Sch. Dist., 1996—, chmn. fine arts, 2000—; owner Patty's Pyrographics, Three Rivers, Tex., 1995—; Delphi forum mgr. Poly's Clay Castle, 1999—; Upward Bound art tchr. Coastal Bend Coll., Beeville, Tex., 1999; rep. Polyform Products, 1999—. Mem. Nat. Art Edn. Assn., Nat. Polymer Clay Guild (charter mem., pres. 1999—), Tex. Art Edn. Assn. (presenter convs. 1997-99, Region 5 rep. 2000—), Coastal Bend Art Edn. Assn., South Tex. Polymer Clay Guild (charter). Avocations: glass fusing, polymer clay art, reading, fishing, sewing. Home: RR 1 Box 497 Three Rivers TX 78071-9711 Office: Skidmore-Tynan Ind Sch Dist PO Box 409 Skidmore TX 78389-0409

BARNES, PETER, lawyer; b. Cambridge, Mass., Apr. 13, 1940; s. C. Tracy Barnes and Janet (White) Lawrence; children: K. Tracy, John E.; m. Jan Adair. BA magna cum laude, Yale U., 1962; LLB cum laude, Harvard U., 1965. Bar: D.C. 1966, Md. 1984. Assoc. Leva, Hawes, Symington, Martin & Oppenheimer, Washington, 1965-71, ptnr., 1972-83; ptnr. Venable, Baetjer & Howard, Balt., 1983-86; mem., shareholder Swidler & Berlin, Chtd., Washington, 1987-98; ptnr. Swidler Berlin Shereff Friedman, LLP, Washington, 1998-99, counsel, 1999—; bd. dirs. Walker & Dunlop, Inc., Washington. Mem. The Met. Club, The Elkridge Club. Home: 4 Deep Run Ct Cockeysville MD 21030-1600 Office: Swidler Berlin Shereff Friedman LLP 3000 K St NW Ste 300 Washington DC 20007-5116

BARNES, PETER JOHN, thoracic medicine educator, consultant, physician; b. Birmingham, Eng., Oct. 29, 1946; s. John and Eileen Gertrude (Thurman) B.; m. Olivia Mary Harvard-Watts, Sept. 11, 1976; children: Adam John Harvard, Toby Samuel Harvard, Julian Peter Harvard. MA, Cambridge (Eng.) U., 1973; DM, Oxford (Eng.) U., 1982, DSc, 1987. Registrar Univ. Coll. Hosp., London, 1975-78; Med. Rsch. Coun. rsch. fellow Royal Postgrad. Med. Sch., London, 1978-79, sr. lectr., 1983-85; sr. registrar Hammersmith Hosp., London, 1979-83, cons. physician, 1983-85; prof. clin. pharmacology Cardiothoracic Inst., London, 1985-87; prof. thoracic medicine Nat. Heart and Lung Inst., U. London, 1987—; cons. physician Royal Brampton Hosp., London, 1985—; chmn. respiratory sci. Imperial Coll., London, 1997—. Editor: Asthma, 1989, also 30 books; contbr. more than 700 articles on lung pharmacology and asthma to med. jours. Fellow Royal Coll. Physicians, Acad. Med. Sci. (mem. coun. 1998); mem. Brit. Thoracic Soc. (coun. 1990), Am. Thoracic Soc., Physiol. Soc., Brit. Pharmacology Soc. Avocations: travel, gardening. Office: Nat Heart and Lung Inst, Dovehouse St, London SW3 6LY, England

BARNES, PHILLIP ROBERT JOHN, neurologist; b. Sheerness, Kent, Eng., July 31, 1961; s. Alan John and June Sylvia (O'Keefe) B.; m. Elizabeth Anne Niblett, July 5, 1986; children: Benjamin, Alexander. BSc, U. London, 1981, PhD, 1985; BMBCh, U. Oxford, Eng., 1987. Neuromuscular fellow U. Oxford, 1991-93; sr. registrar neurology U. Hosp., Nottingham, Eng., 1993-94; cons. neurologist Kings Coll. Hosp., London, 1995—. EP Abraham fellow Green Coll., Oxford, 1993. Fellow Royal Coll. Physicians; mem. Assn. British Neurologists, World Muscle Soc., South of Eng. Neurosci. Assn. (hon. sec. 1996-98). Office: Neurology Kings Coll Hosp, Denmark Hill, London SE5 9RS, England

BARNES, RAYMOND D., optometrist; b. Oakland, Calif., Mar. 24, 1934; s. Wilbur Clayton and Helen Agnes B.; m. Elinor Louise Barnes, Nov. 1, 1953 (div. Aug. 1, 1979); children: Steven David, Lorri Michelle Bordeaux, Kristine Ellen Roberts; m. Elizabeth Moen Alton, Dec. 27, 1980. BA, U. Calif., 1958; PhD, U. Calif., Davis, 1966; D Optometry, New Eng. Coll. of Optometry, Boston, 1982. Pvt. practice Shelburne, Vt., 1982—. Home: 3934 Highbridge Rd Fairfax VT 05454 Office: Shelburne Eyeworks 2989 Shelburne Rd Shelburne VT 05482-6833

BARNES, RICHARD CHARLES, psychiatrist, consultant; b. Oldham, Eng., Dec. 4, 1965; s. Clarence Charles and Kathleen (Mellor) B.; m. Carol Robinson; 1 child, Jack. MB, B of Surgery, Liverpool (Eng.) Med. Sch., 1989. Trainee psychiatrist Liverpool Tng. Sci., 1990-94; psychiatrist Liverpool Rotation, 1994-97; cons. psychiatrist Ormskirk (Eng.) Dist. Gen. Hosp., 1997—; team dr. St. Helens (Eng.) Rugby League Club, 1994—. Contbr. articles to profl. jours. Mem. Royal Coll. Psychiatrists London, Liverpool Psychiat. Soc. (hon. sec. 1994-96), Rugby League Med. Assn. Office: Ormskirk and Dist Gen Hosp, Wigan Rd, Ormskirk W Lancashire L39 2AZ, England

BARNES, SALLY ANDERSON, human resources consultant, organization effectiveness and employee involvement facilitator; b. Sioux City, Iowa, Feb. 9, 1955; d. William David and Betty Ruth (Smith) Anderson; m. Barney B. Barnes, Oct. 22, 1986. BS in Journalism, U. Houston, 1979. Asst. tng. specialist U. Tex., Austin, 1975-77; client coord. Bus. Internat. Corp., NY, Houston, 1978-79; employment counselor John L. Cloud Placement Svc., Houston, 1979; sr. employment recruiter Tex. Commerce Bank, Houston, 1979-81; dir., pers. officer Post Oak Bank, Houston, 1981-82; pers. rep. Austin divsn. Lockheed Corp., 1982-90, TQM/employee involvement facilitator, 1991-94, mgr. Career Transition Ctr., 1994-95; pres., CEO The Right People, Inc., 1995—; exec. dir. Lockheed's Bucks of the Month Club, 1983-84; dir. Lockheed Employee Recreation Assn., 1982-84; bd. dirs. Lockheed Lone Stars Assn. Mem. Nat. Employee Recreation Assn., Nat. Mgmt. Assn. Republican. Methodist. Avocations: sailing, cooking, reading. Home: 3611 Black Mesa Holw Austin TX 78739-7534

BARNES, SANDRA HENLEY, publishing company executive; b. Seymour, Ind., Jan. 15, 1943; d. Ray C. and Barbara (Cockerham) Henley; m. Ronald D. Barnes, Sept. 3, 1961; children: Laura Winkler, Barrett and Garrett (twins). Student, Ind. State U., 1962-63. Asst. sales mgr. Marquis Who's Who, Indpls., 1973-79, sales, svc. mgr., 1979-82, mktg. ops. mgr., 1982-84; mktg. mgr. Marquis Who's Who, Chgo., 1984-86; dir. mktg. Marquis Who's Who, Wilmette, Ill., 1986-87; v.p. mktg. Macmillan Directory Div., Wilmette, 1987-88; group v.p. product mgmt. Marquis Who's Who, Wilmette, 1988-89; pres. Marquis Who's Who, 1989-92; v.p. Reed Reference Pub., New Providence, N.J., 1992-96; v.p., fulfillment Reed Elsevier-New Providence, 1996-97, LEXIS-NEXIS, Dayton, Ohio, 1997-98, Lexis Law Pub., Charlottesville, Va., 1997-98, Congrl. Info. Svc., Bethesda, Md., 1997-98; sr. v.p. Ednl. Comms., Inc., Lake Forest, Ill., 1998—. Republican. Avocation: reading. Office: Ednl Comm Inc 721 N Mckinley Rd Lake Forest IL 60045-1849

BARNES, WILLIAM ANDERSON, real estate investment executive; b. Cin., Mar. 11, 1944; s. Frederick Walter and Catherine Gardner (Bowden) B.; m. Sara Winkler, Dec. 13, 1980; children: Tucker, Charlie, Hanne. BA, Yale U., 1966; MBA, Harvard U., 1970; postgrad. in Internat. Econs., Inst. D'Etudes Politiques, Paris, 1993. Adminstrv. asst. to pres. Boise Cascade Corp., Palo Alto, Calif., 1970-71; project gen. mgr. Boise Cascade Corp., Incline Village, Nev., 1971-73; sr. devel. dir. The Rouse Co., Columbia, Md., 1973-76; exec. dir. Pa. Ave. Devel. Corp., Washington, 1977-82; mng. dir. Edward Plant Co., San Francisco, 1982-87; pres. Broadacre Pacific Corp., San Francisco, 1987-92; pres. Barnes and Co., San Francisco, 1992—, CEO, 1998—; CEO, Stapleton Devel. Corp., Denver, 1996-98; guest lectr. Harvard Bus. Sch., Cambridge, Mass.; faculty mem. Profl. Devel. Sem.; dist. coun. exec. com. Urban Land Inst.; lectr. Smithsonian Instn., U. San Francisco, mem. adv. coun.; chair Am. Russian Tech. Assn. Trustee Navy Meml. Found., Brichard Properties Trust, S.H. Children's Svcs., Inc., Columbia Interfaith Housing Corp., 1974-76; mem. U.S./USSR Trade Mission, 1975, Bay Area Coun. Housing Action Task Force, 1983-85, Mill Valley City Gen. Plan Com.; treas. Yale U. Class of 1966. U.S. White House fellow, Washington, 1976, German Marshall Fund fellow, 1979; recipient Presdl. Design award, 1988. Office: Barnes and Co Ste 860 One Embarcadero Ctr San Francisco CA 94111

BARNES, WILLIAM DAVID, non-profit charities consultant, publisher; b. Gary, Ind., July 14, 1938; s. Frank J. and Marie M. (Jasorka) B.; m. Suzanne Frost Barnes, June 10, 1961 (div. June 1977); children: Adam Frost, Eric Earl; m. Ellen M. Vager, Dec. 30, 1997. BA in Edn., Ariz. State U., 1960; Cert., Northwestern U., Chgo., 1965. Asst. editor The Arizonian Newspaper, Scottsdale, 1960-61; asst. v.p. First Security Bank, Mesa, Ariz., 1962-65; dir. mktg., v.p. Great Western Bank, Phoenix, 1966-67; dir. alumni fund Ariz. State U., Tempe, 1967-71; pres., sr. editor Barnes Assocs., Inc., Phoenix, Sacramento and Modesto, Calif., 1971—. Author: How to Build Your Development Program, 1973, More on How to Build Your Development Program, 1974, Fund Raiser's Planning and Budgeting Guide, 1976. V.p. United Way, Mesa, 1962; Ariz. bus. chmn. Com. to Re-elect Pres., 1972; cons. to 68 local, state and nat. polit. campaigns, 1960-84 (62 victories); chair pub. rels. com. Ariz. Bankers Assn., 1968. Recipient Nat. 1st pl. award in mktg. Chrysler Corp. Young and Rubicam, 1974, Silver Triange award Am. Advt. Assn., 1977, Exec. Leaders Inst. award Lilly Endowment/Nat. Soc. Fund Raising Execs., 1990, Man of Yr. award for vol. work Rainbow Acres Ranches for Developmentally Challenged, 1982. Mem. Nat. Soc. Fund Raising Execs. (cert., nat. bd. dirs. 1975-78, One of 25 Authors Worldwide Contributing Most to Profession 1985, Outstanding Fund Raising Exec. No. Calif. 1987). Roman Catholic. Avocations: tennis, gardening. Office: Barnes Assocs Inc 909 15th St Ste 9 Modesto CA 95354-1130

BARNES DE CASTRO, FRANCISCO JOSE, academic administrator. Degree in Chemistry, Nat. Autonomous U. of Mex.; MS, U. Calif., Berkeley, PhD in Chem. Engring.; Dr.h.c., Astrophys./Optical/Elec.Inst, 1998. Rector U. Nat. Autonoma Mex., dir. chemistry faculty, gen. sec., prof. chemistry and dean; condr. various seminars and continuing edn. courses; tech. cons. various pvt. instns.; bd. dirs. Rsch. Ctr. and Advanced Studies; mem. internat. adv. bd. Nat. Rsch. Inst. of Dept. Energy, U.S.A.; mem. Pub. Joint Adv. Com. on Environ. Coop. of N.Am. Contbr. articles to profl. jours.; patentee in field; co-author: Engineering Processes. Tech. sec. Mexican Petrochem. Commn., Secretariat of Energy, Mines and Semi-State Industry; gen. mgr. Mexican Oil Inst. Recipient Nat. Chemistry award Andrés Manuel del Rio in tchg. Chem. Soc. Mex., 1994, Profl. Excellence award Mexican Fedn. Chemistry Profls., 1995. Office: Ciudad U, Del Coyoacan 04510, Mexico*

BARNETT, ANTHONY HOWARD, internist, medical educator; b. Leeds, Yorkshire, Eng., May 29, 1951; s. Geoffrey and Beulah (Statman) B.; m. Catherine Elizabeth O'Donnell, Nov. 11, 1975; children—Clare, Sarah, James, Anna, Jonathan, Robert. B.Sc. with 1st class honors, King's Coll., London, 1972, M.B.B.S., 1975; M.D., U. London, 1981. Sr. research fellow Med. Research Council, 1979-81; sr. registrar endocrinology/diabetes, Christchurch, N.Z., 1981-82; sr. registrar medicine/diabetes, Southampton, 1982-83; sr. lectr., hon. cons. physician medicine/diabetes U. Birmingham, Eng., 1983—, prof. medicine, 1992—; adviser subjects related to diabetes mellitu Eng., 198 3—. Author: Immungenetics of Insulin Dependent Diabetes, 1987; contbr. articles to profl. jours. Research grantee Med. Research Council, Wellcome Trust, Juvenile Diabetes Found. Internat., Lilly Industries U.K., Brit. Diabetic Assn., Nordisk Found., Pfizer, U. Birmingham, 1983—. Fellow Royal Coll. Physicians; mem. Med. Research Soc., Brit. Diabetic Assn., European Diabetic Assn. Avocations: reading, family, walk-

ing. Office: Birmingham Heartlands Hosp Dept Medicine, Bordesley Green E, Birmingham B9 5SS, England

BARNETT, BENJAMIN LEWIS, JR., retired physician; b. Woodruff, S.C., July 22, 1926; s. Benjamin Lewis and Mattie Bernice (Skinner) B.; m. Annalyne Louise Hall, Oct. 25, 1958; children: Benjamin Lewis III, Jane Kristen. BS, Furman U., 1946, LLD, 1978; MD, Med. U. S.C., 1949. Diplomate Am. Bd. Family Practice (mem. exam. bd. 1975-81, dir. 1976-81, exec. com. 1979-81, pres. 1980-81). Intern Protestant Episcopal Hosp., Phila., 1949-50; pvt. practice Woodruff, 1950-70; assoc. prof. family practice Med. U. S.C., Charleston, 1970-74; prof. family practice Med. U. S.C., 1974-77, asst. dir. family practice residency program, 1970-75, chief undergrad. curriculum, 1970-77, vice-chmn. dept. family practice, 1973-77, asst. dean for student affairs, 1975-77; clin. staff Med. U. Hosp., Charleston County Hosp., 1970-77; Walter M. Seward prof. U. Va. Med. Sch., 1977-2000, chmn. dept. family medicine, 1977-96, baccalaureate, prof. emeritus, 1986, 00, faculty senate, 1988-92, 1988-92, 86-2000, prof. emeritus, 2000—; family medicine physician-in-chief U. Va. Med. Center Hosp., 1977-96; admissions com. U. Va. Med. Sch., 1997-99; Stoneburner lectr. Med. Coll. Va., 1975; Daniel Drake lectr. U. Cin., 1976; Robert P. Walton lectr. Med. U. S.C., 1978; Goodlark prof. U. Tenn., 1979; Roy J. Gerard lectr. Mich. State U., 1992; vis. scholar U. Mich. Med. Sch., 1984; vis. lectr. Med. Coll. of Ga., 1982; vis. prof. Case Western Res. Sch. Medicine, 1984, U. Vt., 1988, U. N.Mex., 1991, U. S.C. Sch. Medicine, 1999; Mack Lipkin vis. prof. U. Oreg., 1987, U. Utah, 1989; Donald J. Welter Meml. lectr. Med. Coll. Wis., 1989; Frederick Lytel Meml. lectr., Abington, Pa., 1989; Bradford Strock lectr. Harrisburg (Pa.) Gen. Hosp., 1989; 7th Leland Blanchard Meml. lectr. Soc. Tchrs. Family Medicine ann. meeting, Nashville, 1985; health officer, Town of Woodruff, 1950-54; keynote speaker Assn. Depts. Family Medicine, Clearwater, Fla., 1991; commencement speaker U. Va. Med. Sch., 1992, 97; Grand Prof. Rounds St. Margaret's Hosp., Pitts., 1993; Julian Keith lectr. Bowman Gray Sch. Medicine, 1993; keynote speaker leadership conf. Fla. Med. Assn., Ponta Vedra, 1994, AHEC conf. S.C. Family Practice, Myrtle Beach, 1994; B. Leslie Huffman lectr. Med. Coll. of Ohio, Toledo, 1994; grad. speaker McLennan County Med. Edn. and Rsch. Found., Waco, Tex., 1995; Inaugural Buck Crockett lectr., Roanoke, Va., 2000; founder's prof. U. Okla. Health Scis. Ctr., Tulsa, 2000; Harlan Thomas Meml. lectr.; lectr. and cons. in field. Author: Between the Lines (Reflections of a Physician), 1989; editor: S.C. Family Physician, 1973-74; contbr. articles to med. jours. and chpts. to textbooks. Mem. Spartanburg County Bd. Edn., 1968-70, sec. 1969-70; trustee Bethea Bapt. Home for Aged, Darlington, S.C., 1972-73; mem. bd. trustees Furman U., 1994-99. Named Citizen of Year Woodmen of World, 1968; recipient Golden Apple award for clin. teaching Student AMA, 1973; Thomas W. Johnson award Am. Acad. Family Physicians, 1976, Disting. Alumnus award Med. U. S.C., 1993; endowed Barnett Professorship in Family Medicine established U. Va. Bd. Visitors, 1997; Thomas Jefferson award U. Va., 1997. Mem. AMA (mem. residency rev. com. for family practice 1974-79), Va., Albemarle County med. socs., Soc. Tchrs. Family Medicine (v.p. 1974, sec.-treas. 1975, dir. 1981-85, cert. of excellence 1983, F. Marian Bishop award 1996), Am. Acad. Family Physicians, S.C. Acad. Family Physicians (v.p. 1973, pres. 1975-76), Spartanburg County Med. Soc. (v.p. 1968), Am. Philatelic Soc., Coun. Acad. Socs., Furman U. Alumni Assn. (dir. 1972-77), U. Va. Raven Soc., Alpha Omega Alpha (faculty councilor, vis. prof. U. S.C. Sch. Medicine 1999), Alpha Kappa Kappa (pres. 1948), Kappa Alpha (v.p. 1944). Baptist (deacon, chmn. bd.). Home: 4734 Talleybrook Dr NW Kennesaw GA 30152-5484

BARNETT, CHARLES THOMAS, retired secondary education educator; b. Finleyville, Pa., June 19, 1929; s. Charles Joseph and Barbara Louise (Kuchinic) B.; m. Shirley Lorraine Casey, Jan. 10, 1976. BS, U. Dayton, 1950; MS, U. Pitts., 1956. Cert. in secondary edn. Tchr. Chaminade, Mineola, N.Y., 1950-56, Colegio San Jose, P.R., 1956-58, St. Patrick's, Asaba, Nigeria, 1959-61, Holy Ghost Coll., Kenya, 1961-63, Nkhatta Bay, Malawi, 1964-65, Moeller, Cin., 1965-68, St. Paul's Coll., Victoria, Australia, 1968-76, St. Kevin's Coll., Victoria, 1976-88. Mem. ch. coms., Melbourne, 1968—. Mem. Marine Rsch. Group, Bird Observers Club. Roman Catholic. Avocations: tennis, classical music, opera, ballet. Home: 55 Vincent St, 3146 Glen Iris Victoria, Australia

BARNETT, CRAWFORD FANNIN, JR., internist, educator, cardiologist, travel medicine specialist; b. Atlanta, May 11, 1938; s. Crawford Fannin and Penelope Hollinshead (Brown) B.; m. Elizabeth McCarthy Hale, June 6, 1964; children: Crawford Fannin III, Robert Hale. Student Taft Sch., 1953-56, U. Minn., 1957; AB magna cum laude, Yale U., 1960; postgrad. (Davison scholar) Oxford (Eng.) U., 1963; MD (Trent scholar), Duke, 1964. Intern internal medicine Duke U. Med. Center, Durham, N.C., 1964-65, resident, 1965; resident internal medicine Wilmington (Del.) Med. Ctr., 1965-66; dir. Tenn. Heart Disease Control Program, Nashville, 1966-68; pvt. practice medicine specializing in internal medicine and travel medicine, Atlanta, 1968—; dir. Travel Immunization Ctr., Atlanta; mem. staff Crawford Long, Northside, Grady Meml., West Paces, North Fulton, hosps. (all Atlanta); mem. teaching staff Vanderbilt Med. Ctr., Nashville, 1966-68, Crawford Long Meml. Hosp., 1969—; clin. instr. internal medicine, dept. medicine Emory U. Med. Sch., Atlanta, 1969—. Bd. govs. Doctors Meml. Hosp., 1971-80; bd. dirs. Atlanta Speech Sch., 1976-80, 92—, Historic Oakland Cemetery, 1976-86, So. Turf Nurseries, 1977-92, Tech Industries, 1978-92; bd. dirs. Am. Chestnut Found., 1990, bd. trustees Mary Brown Found. of Atlanta, 1998—. Served as surgeon USPHS, 1966-68. Fellow Am. Geog. Soc., Royal Soc. of Tropical Medicine and Hygiene, Royal Geog. Soc., Royal Soc. Medicine, Explorers Club (life, N.Y.C.); mem. Am. Soc. Tropical Medicine and Hygiene, Am. Fedn. Clin. Rsch., Coun. Clin. Cardiology, AMA, Ga. Med. Assn., Atlanta Med. Assn., Am. Heart Assn., Ga. Heart Assn., Am. Soc. Internal Medicine, Am. Coll. Physicians, Ga. Soc. Internal Medicine, Am. Assn. History Medicine, Ga. Hist. Soc., Atlanta Hist. Soc. (bd. govs. 1976-84), Ga. Trust for Hist. Preservation, Nat. Trust Hist. Preservation, Internat. Hippocratic Found. Soc. (Greece), Faculty of History of Medicine and Pharmacy Worshipful Soc. Apothecaries of London, Atlanta Com. on Fgn. Relations (chmn. exec. com. 1972-88), So. Council Internat. and Public Affairs, Newcomen Soc., Atlanta Clin. Soc., Wilderness Med. Soc., Internat. Soc. Travel Medicine (founding), Travelers Century Club, Circumnavigators Club, South Am. Explorers Club, Victorian Soc. Am. (bd. advisers Atlanta chpt. 1971-86), Mensa, Gridiron, Piedmont Driving Club, Yale Club (dir. 1970-74), Nine O'Clocks Club, Pan Am. Doctors Club, Phi Beta Kappa. Episcopalian. Contbr. articles to profl. publs. Home: 2739 Ramsgate Ct NW Atlanta GA 30305-2817 Office: 3250 Howell Mill Rd NW Ste 205 Atlanta GA 30327-4108

BARNETT, DAVID PHILIP, funeral administrator, horticulturist; b. Jacksonville, N.C., Nov. 18, 1956; s. Frederick D. and Janet (Holdridge) B.; m. Eileen Nickerson, Aug. 19, 1978; children: Jake, Marie. BS, U. Conn., 1978; MS, U. Calif., Davis, 1983, PhD, 1987. Collections crew leader The Morton Arboretum, Lisle, Ill., 1978-81; asst. dir. Planting Fields Arboretum, Oyster Bay, N.Y., 1986-93; dir. horticulture Mt. Auburn Cemetery, Cambridge, Mass., 1993-99, dir. ops. and horticulture, 1999—. Asst. scoutmaster Boy Scouts Am., Boxborough, Mass., 1996—. Mem. Am. Assn. Botanical Gardens & Artoreta (bd. dirs. 1995-98, chmn. N.Am. plant collections consortium 1998—, bd. dirs. 1995-98), Worcester County Horticultural Soc. (chmn. Cary award plant selection com. 1995—), Internat. Dendrology Soc., Internat. Soc. Arboriculture, N.Y. Hortus Club (v.p. 1990-93), Horticultural Club Boston (chair program com. 1996-00). Avocations: running marathons, hockey, camping, hiking, gardening. Office: Mt Auburn Cemetery 580 Mount Auburn St Cambridge MA 02138-5529

BARNETT, DAVID RICHARD, illustrator, designer; b. Leicester, England, Sept. 18, 1931; s. Thomas Samuel and Annie (Needham) B.; m. Jean Winifred Gatton, March 23, 1957; children: Robert, Christine, Edward. Student, Coll. of Art, Leicester, 1947-49. Apprentice, designer, visualizer to Frank Gayton Advt. Ltd., Leicester, England, 1950-77; freelance illustrator Leicester, 1977—; illustrator various curriculum's and major pub. and advt. agys. in Europe and U.S. Illustrator: Wild White Stallion, 1977, My First Prayer Book, 1977. Recipient award Design Council, London, 1987. Mem. Granville Tennis Club, Oadby Club. Anglican. Home and Office: 41 Hidcote Rd, Oadby Leicester LE2 5PG, England

BARNETT, ERIC OLIVER, foundation administrator; b. Feb. 13, 1929; s. Eric Everard and Maude Emily Louise (Oliver) B.; m. Louise Francesca Lindenberg, Feb. 13, 1950 (dec. Jan. 1984); m. Vivienne Goodwin, Mar. 13, 1986. Student, U. Cape Town, South Africa, 1950-52, U. South Africa, 1950-54, U. Natal, Durban, South Africa, 1955-57, Univ. Coll., London, 1957-63. Lectr. in psychology U. Natal, 1956; hon. vice chmn. Arthur Barnett Found., 1963-71, hon. chmn., 1971—. Hon. chmn. Rural Ecology and Resources Com., Southern Africa, 1978—; founder, hon. chmn. Com. for Basic Tech., 1984-96, African Epidemiology Study, 1988—; hon. chmn. Eric Barnett Found., 1997—; other philanthropic and charitable coms. Avocations: human ethology, sci. history, music, painting, salmon fishing. Home and Office: Kirkhill Castle, Colmonell, Ayrshire Scotland

BARNETT, GENE HENRY, neurosurgeon; b. Phila., Feb. 2, 1955; s. Edgar Tryon and Anne Shirley (Wenner) B.; m. Kathleen Marie Seng, May 9, 1984 (div. Sept. 1990); 1 child, Alexander; m. Cathy Ann Sila, Dec. 9, 1990; children: Austin, Addison. BA summa cum laude, Case Western Res. U., 1976, MD, 1980. Intern Cleve. Clinic Found., 1980-81, neurosurgery resident, 1981-86, staff neurosurgery, 1987—, co-dir. residency program, 1992-95, vice chmn. dept. neurosurgery, 1993—, program dir. dept. neurosurgery, 1995—, dir. Brain Tumor Ctr., 1995—, dir. Gamma Knife Ctr., 1997—; hon. registrar U. Edinburgh, Scotland, 1985; fellow Harvard Med. Sch., Mass. Gen. Hosp., 1986-87; cons. in field. Editor: Image Guided Neurosurgery: Clinical Applications of Surgical Navigation Systems, 1998; contbr. over 100 articles to profl. jours., 26 chpts. to books. Grantee Epilesy Found. Am., 1979, NINDS, 1995; clin. and rsch. fellow Harvard Med. Sch., Mass. Gen. Hosp., Boston, 1986-87. Office: Cleve Clinic Found 580 9500 Euclid Ave Cleveland OH 44195-0001

BARNETT, HAROLD, writer; b. June 4, 1964. Student, John J. Coll. Criminal Justice. Correctio officer Dept. of Correction, East Elmhurst, N.Y., 1990—. Author: The Mohawk Has Spoken, 1998. Mailing Address: PO Box 8274 Long Island City NY 11101-8274

BARNETT, JOHN HENRY, judge; b. Ballarat, Victoria, Australia, May 19, 1943; s. Thomas Henry and Joyce Evelyn (Brown) B.; m. Nanette Janice Berry, Nov. 21, 1970; children: Sarah Jane, Mimi Emma Louise. LLB, U. Melbourne. Pvt. practice Melbourne, 1971-90; judge County Ct., Victoria, 1990—. Mem. ethics com. Donor Tissue Bank Victoria, 1992—; dep. chmn. Youth Parole Bd., Victoria, 1991—. Mem. Victorian Inst. Forensic Medicine (mem. coun. 1985—), Richmond Football Club (Victoria). Avocations: reading, travel. Office: County Ct, 223 William St, Victoria Melbourne 3002, Australia

BARNETT, MARILYN, advertising agency executive; b. Detroit; d. Henry and Kate (Boesky) Schiff; children: Rhona, Ken. BA, Wayne State U. Founder, part-owner, pres. Mars Advt. Co., Southfield, Mich. Bd. dirs. Mich. Strategic Fund; apptd. to Mich. bi-lateral trade team with Germany. Named Outstanding Retail Woman of Yr., Outstanding Retail Mktg. Exec., Bd. Dirs. Oaklakd U., Mich.'s Top 25 Women Bus. Owner's List, Entrepreneur of Yr., Oakland Exec. of Yr. Mem. AFTRA (dir.), SAG, Exec. Women Am., Am. Women in Radio & TV (Top Agy. Mgmt. award, Outstanding Woman of Yr.), Internat. Women Forum, Com. of 200, Women's Econ. Club (Ad Woman of Yr.), Adcraft. Office: MARS Advt 23999 Northwestern Hwy Southfield MI 48075-2528 also: MARS Advt Co 6671 W Sunset Blvd Ste 1591 Los Angeles CA 90028-7170

BARNETT, MARILYN DOAN, secondary education business educator; b. Trafalgar, Ind., Jan. 14, 1934; d. Roscoe James and Nellie Margaret (Betts) Doan; m. Joe A. Barnett, Mar. 23, 1952; 1 child, Michael Shayne. BS, Ball State U., 1965, MA, 1972. Cert. bus. tchr., Ind. Vocat. bus. tchr. John H. Hinds Area Vocat. Sch., Elwood, Ind., 1966-72; bus. tchr. Elwood Community High Sch., 1973-91, chair bus. dept., 1979-89; sponsor Future Bus. Leaders Am., Elwood, 1973-91. Mem. YMCA; vol. Meals on Wheels, Elwood. Mem. NEA, Ind. State Tchrs. Assn., Ind. Bus. Edn. Assn., Elwood Classroom Tchrs. Assn., Delta Kappa Gamma, Pi Omega Pi, Delta Pi Epsilon. Mem. Disciples of Christ Ch. Avocations: travel, piano. Home: 9416 N Meadowlark Ln Elwood IN 46036-8844

BARNETT, MICHAEL, sports agent, business manager; b. Olds, Alta., Can., Oct. 9, 1948; came to U.S., 1988; s. Terence R. and Mary M. Barnett; m. Dalyce M. Giordano, Apr. 2, 1988; children: Jesse, Joey, Justin, Janie, Jenna. Student, St. Lawrence U., 1968-70; BS in Health and Phys. Edn., U. Calgary, 1973. Registered agent Nat. Hockey League Players Assn., Sports Lawyers Assn. Profl. hockey player, 1973-75; founder, CEO Corpsport Internat.; agent, bus. mgr. Wayne Gretzky, 1981—; internat. v.p. Internat. Mgmt. Group; gen. mgr. Ninety-Nine All Stars; pres. Internat. Mgmt. Group Hockey, 1990. Active H.E.L.P., L.A. Named one of Top 100 Most Powerful in Sports, The Sporting News, 1994, 95, 96, 98, 99, One of Twelve Most Powerful in Hockey, Hockey News, 1995. Mem. U.S.A. Hockey, U.S. Golf Assn. Avocations: golfing, running. Home: PO Box 50 Lake Arrowhead CA 92352-0050 Office: PO Box 565 Ste 01-270 28200 Hwy 189 Lake Arrowhead CA 92352

BARNETT, URSULA ANNEMARIE, literary agent; b. Maribor, Slovenia, Apr. 25, 1924; arrived in South Africa, 1935, England, 1989; d. Felix and Else (Rosenblum) Gross; m. Hyman Barnett (dec. Jan. 1986); children: Shelley, Adrienne, Lionel, Michael. BA, Rhodes U., South Africa, 1944; MA, U. Cape Town, South Africa, 1945; MS in Journalism, Columbia U., 1948; PhD in Literature, U. Cape Town, 1971. Asst. Internat. Press Agy., South Africa, 1946-60, dir., mng. editor, 1961-88, dir., London rep., 1989—; lectr. U. Cape Town, 1984; bus. mgr. ENglish Alive, South Africa, 1985-88; com. mem. South AFrican Coun. English Edn., 1985-88. Author: Ezekiel Mphahlele, A Vision of Order. Chair Women's Movement Peace, South Africa, 1987-88; area treas. Anti-Apartheid Movement, Britain, 1992-94; mem. African Nat. Congress, 1991-96. Jewish. Avocations: reading, plays, films, concerts, walking, swimming. Home: 4 Shoreham Rd, Upper Beeding West Sussex BN44 3TN, England Office: 17 Fairmount Rd Brixton, London SW2 2BJ, England

BARNEVIK, PERCY NILS, electrical company executive; b. Simrishamn, Sweden, Feb. 13, 1941; s. Einar and Anna Barnevik; m. Aina Orvarsson, 1963; 3 children. MBA, Gothenburg Sch. Econs., Sweden, 1964; postgrad., Stanford U., 1965-66; TechnDr honoris causa, U. Linkoping, Sweden, 1989; Econ. Dr. honoris causa, U. Gothenburg, Sweden, 1991; JD (hon.), Babson Coll., 1995; Sci. Dr. honoris causa, Cranfield U., 1998; D (hon.), U. Manches, 1999. With The Johnson Group, Sweden, 1966-69; with Sandvik AB, Sandviken, Sweden, 1969-80, group controller, 1969-75; pres. U.S. affiliate, 1975-79; exec. v.p. Sandvik, Sweden, 1979-80; pres., chief exec. officer ASEA, 1980-87; chmn. Sandvik AB, 1983—; pres., CEO Asea Brown Boveri Ltd., 1988-96, chmn., CEO, 1996-97; chmn. Investor AB, Sweden, 1997—, ABB Ltd., 1997—, AstraZeneca PLC, U.K., 1999—; bd. dirs. GM, Detroit. Office: ABB Ltd, PO Box 8131, CH-8050 Zurich Switzerland also: Investor AB, S-10332 Stockholm Sweden

BARNEY, AUSTIN DUNHAM, II, estate planner; b. Hartford, Conn., Apr. 27, 1945; s. Philip Cushman and Elizabeth Cole (Freeman) B.; m. Susan C. Rumney, Aug. 26, 1976 (div. Mar. 1998); children: Austin C. D. III, Amanda Brandegee. BA in Polit. Sci., Yale U., 1967; MPA, Syracuse U., 1969. Lic. real estate broker, Conn., N.Y., Mass.; lic. life/health ins., securities, Conn. Mgmt. asst. U. Hartford, Conn., 1967-68; jr./sr. planner Hartford Police Dept., 1969-70; sr. planner Commn. on City Plan City of Hartford, 1970; sr. adminstrv. analyst fin. dept. City of Hartford Budget and Rsch. Divsn., 1970-71, prin. adminstrv. analyst fin. dept., 1971-72; dir. land use policy planning State of Conn., Dept. Environ. Protection, 1972-73; exec. dir. Environ. Ctrs. Inc., 1973-75; pvt. practice cons., 1975-76; dir. natural resources mgmt. and community design Westledge Ctr. for Edn., 1976-78; sr. cons. corp. citizenship Cigna Corp. (Conn. Gen. Ins. Corp.), 1979-82; dir. contbns. and civic affairs Cigna Corp., Conn. Gen. Ins. Corp., 1982-84; pres., founder Farmvest, Inc., 1984—; prin. Bus. Planning Assocs., 1991-96; pres. Life Legacy Advisors, LLC, Avon, Conn., 1996—; dir. Spiritus Wines, Inc., Aid to Artesans; ptnr. Folly Farm Assocs., 1983-90; pres. Folly Farm, Inc., 1983-90. Zoning commr. Town of Simsbury, Conn., 1976—, sec., 1993—; del. People's Republic China, Yale-China Assn., fall 1979, 80; corporator Hartford Pub. Libr., 1981—; corporator The Ctr. Families and Children, 1996—; bd. dirs., exec. com. Riverfront Recapture, Inc., 1981-90; bd. trustees Hartford Art Sch., 1969—, pres. 1984-86, 96—; bd. dirs. Conn. Trust for Hist. Preservation, 1982-85, The Nature Conservancy, treas. 1986-89, vice-chmn., 1989—, Oak Leaf award, 1995; bd. dirs. U. Conn. Found., 1988-92, Ensign-Bickford Found., 1987-93, v.p., 1989-93; bd. dirs. Ea. States Expo.; chmn. Conn. trustees 1993—; elector Wadsworth Atheneum, 1983—; bd. dirs., chmn. fin. com. Conn. Earth Day 20, Inc., 1990; regent U. Hartford, 1980-86, 90—. Recipient Oak Leaf award Nature Conservancy, 1995. Mem. Nat. Assn. Life Underwriters, Am. Assn. Life Underwriters, Conn. Assn. Life Underwriters, Hartford Assn. Life Underwriters, Conn. Life Leaders.

BARNEY, CHRISTINE J., artist; b. Bath, N.Y., Sept. 9, 1952; d. Willis H. and Elsa P. (Heney) B. BA, Goddard Coll., 1975; MA, NYU, 1988. Proprietor, designer, craftsperson Laurel Mountain Glass, Bosswell, Pa., 1975-83; tchg./tech. asst. Alfred (N.Y.) U., 1983-85; freelance designer Seguso Arte Vetro, Murano, Venice, Italy, 1985-87; lectr. in field; guest artist Artpark, Lewiston, N.Y., summers 1992, 94; vis. artist Tyler Sch. Art, Phila., 1993, Ohio State U., 1992; artist-in-residence Golden Glass Studio and Sch., Cin., 1991-92. Solo shows include Kavesh Gallery, Sun Valley, Ketchun, Idaho, 1991, Christy/Taylor Gallery, Boca Raton, Fla., 1990, 91, 92, Vespermann Gallery, Atlanta, 1994, Portia Gallery, Chgo., 1997; exhibited in group shows at Traver-Sutton Gallery, Seattle, 1982, So. Alleghenies Mus. Art, Loretto, Pa., 1983, Querini Stampaglia Gallery, Venice, 1984, U. di Architettura de Venezia, enice, 1985, 80 Washington Sq. East Galleries, N.Y.C., 1988, Spaso House, Am. Embassy, Moscow, 1988-89, Grohe Gallery, Boston, 1989, Newark Mus., 1989, Sotheby's Internat. Glass Auction, N.Y.C., 1990, N.J. Ctr. for Visual Arts, 1990, Morris Mus., Morristown, N.J., 1991, Mus. Am. Glass, Millville, N.J., 1993, Gallery at Wheaton Village, Millville, 1994, Grohe Gallery, 1995, South Shore Art Ctr., Cohasset, Mass., 1996; works in collections at Corning Mus. Glass, Mus. Am. Glass, Millville, N.J., Tropicana Products, Inc., Bradenton, Fla., Centeon Pharm., King of Prussia, Pa.; contbr. articles to profl. jours. Creator Arts in Achievement awards Middlesex County Cultural and Heritage Commn., 1990-94, Artpark award, 1993. Commd. Carnegie Inst. prize, 1981; Creative Glass Ctr. of Am. fellow, 1988, 96, N.J. State Coun. on the Arts fellow, 1989-90. Avocation: dance. Home: 432 Monmouth St Jersey City NJ 07302-2326

BARNHART, LARRY LEROY, transportation executive; b. Hagerstown, Md., Feb. 23, 1947; s. Leroy Grant and Helen Mildred B. Student, U. Tenn., 1968; A in Traffic and Transp. Mgmt., Humboldt Inst., 1966. Cert. pilot, single and multi engine rated. Sr. transp. splst. ICI Ams., Wilmington, Del., 1974-81; sr. transp. splst. Hercules, Wilmington, 1981-84, mgr. import transp., 1984-90, sr. transp. splst., 1990—, acting mgr. corp. flight dept., 1996-97. Sgt. USAF, 1966-70. Mem. Chem. Mfrs. Assn. Avocations: flying.

BARNHILL, GREGORY HURD, investment banker; b. Balt., Feb. 20, 1953; s. Robert Bell and Margaret Katherine (Hurd) B. Student, Inst. d'Etudes Europèenes, 1974, Banque Nat. de Paris, 1974; BA in Econs., Brown U., 1975; postgrad., Inst. Fin., N.Y.C., 1975. Lic. N.Y. Stock Exchange/Nat. Assn. Securities Dealers. Internat. investment banking mng. dir. Deutsche Bank Alex Brown, Investment Bankers, Balt., 1975—; bd. dirs. Agora Press, BTAB-Cook Overseas Ltd., BTAB-Stark Ltd. Partnership/AB-Stark Overseas Ltd., Captel-Nat. Cap. Telesvcs., L.L.C., View Tech., SportingAuction, Inc., NASA/Goddard Space Flight Ctr. Balt. Incubator; chmn. bd. Ocean Race Chesapeake. Mem. adv. bd. Inst. d'Etudes Europèenes; affiliate Balt. Mus. Art, Walters Art Gallery; chmn. fundraising com. Balt. Arts Festival, 1980-84; bd. dirs. Palm Beach Maritime Mus., 1990—, Balt. Heritage Inc., 1981-83, Md. Ballet, 1982-83, Nat. Taxpayers Union Found., 1984—, The Netherlands-Am. Amity Trust, Inc., 1993—, Balt. Columbus 500, 1987—; bd. dirs. Md. Art Place, 1982-90, pres. 1982-86, pres. bd. trustees, 1985-86; co-chmn. Businesspeople for Mayor Schaefer's Re-election, 1982-83; mem. fin. com. Congresswoman Helen Delich Bentley; mem. Balt. Operation Sail (chmn. fin. com., bd. dirs. 1987—, pres. 1988-93), hon. mem. Christopher Columbus Quincentennary Commn., 1989—; mem. Nat. Rep. Fin. Com., 1991—; vice chmn. bd. dirs. Greater Balt. Med. Ctr., 1992—; trustee Md. Internat. Ctr. Md., 1993—; mem. bd. govs. Faberge Arts Found., 1992—; mem. 2000 com. Walters Art Gallery, 1978—; nat. vice-chmn. The Pres.'s Dinner, 1989—; mem. mayor's adv. com. internat. affairs, 1988—; mem. gov's bus. com. for Md.-St. Petersburg, 1993—; bd. trustees St. Paul's Sch., 2000—. Mem. Bond Club Md., Balt. Hist. Soc. (trustee), Md. Hist. Soc. (trustee 1992—, co-chmn. MHS 150 1993—), Md. Soc. Preservation of Antiquities (dir. 1981-83), Mcpl. Arts Soc. (trustee 1985—, dir. 1981—), Md. Acad. Scis. (bd. dirs), Brown U. Club of Md. (pres. 1976-81), McDonogh Sch. Alumni Assn. (dir. 1976—), Nature Conservancy (bd. dirs. 1987—), Maryland Club (bd. govs., treas. exec. com, bd. dirs. 1995), Newport Reading Room Club, Greenspring Valley Hunt Club, Sigma Chi. Republican. Fax: 410-895-3153. E-mail: gregory.barnhill@db.com. Home: 10801 Stevenson Rd Stevenson MD 21153-0679 Office: Deutsche Banc Alex Brown MS 1-15-3 1 South St Baltimore MD 21202-3298

BARNHILL, JOHN HERSCHEL, government administrator; b. Walnut Ridge, Ark., Mar. 2, 1947; s. Herschel and Ada (Rasdon) B.; m. Barbara Leah Clayton, July 19, 1980 (div. 1995); 1 child, William Bryant. AA, Del Mar Coll., Corpus Christi, Tex., 1974; BA, Corpus Christi State U., 1976; MA, Okla. State U., 1978, PhD, 1981. Teaching asst. Okla. State U., Dept. History, Stillwater, 1977-81; dep. dir. 45th Inf. div. Mus., Oklahoma City, 1981-82; videotape archivist Okla. Dept. Libr., Oklahoma City, 1982-84; historian Engring. Installation div. Tinker AFB, Oklahoma City, 1984-85; program analyst 1985th Comm. Computer Systems Group, 1985-93, DISA WE4, 1993—; referee Ark. Hist. Quar., 1991. Author: From Surplus to Substitution, 1983; contbr. articles to profl. jours., encyclopedias, book revs. Mem. City Charter Commn., 1991, city planning commr. 1993-98. With USAF, 1966-70. Recipient Disting. Alumnus award Corpus Christi State U., 1984, excellence awards Air Force Orgn., 1985, 87, 89, 91, 93, Beacon of Freedom, 1991, Federal Employee Point of Light, 1991. Mem. Phi Kappa Phi. Avocations: reading, personal computers, fiction writing.

BARNHILL, LARRY JARRETT, JR., neuropsychiatrist; b. Greenville, N.C., Aug. 12, 1949; s. Larry Jarret and Evelyn Roberson Barnhill; m. Robin Lynn Paschel, Mar. 22, 1975; children: Sarah Kathleen, Larry Jarrett III. BA, U. N.C., 1971; MD, Wake Forest U., 1975. Asst. prof. E. Carolina U., Greenville, 1979-80, 81-83; asst. prof. Wake Forest U., Winston-Salem, N.C., 1980-81, clin. asst. prof., 1983-87; asst. clin. prof. U. N.C., Chapel Hill, 1987-95, assoc. prof., 1995—; dir. child adolescent treatment units Charter Hosp., Winston-Salem, 1983-87; cons. Caswell Conte, Kinston, N.C., 1987-00, Dorothea Dix Hosp., Raleigh, N.C., 1992-00, Murdoch Ctr., Butner, N.C., 1999-2000. Fellow Am. Psychiatris Assn., Am. Acad. Child Psychiatry; mem. N.C. Coun. Child & Adolescent Psychiatry (pres. 1995-97), N.C. Psychiatric Assn. (v.p. 2000), N.C. Tourrette's Assn. (med. advisor 1989-00). Avocations: music, paleontology. Office: U NC CB # 7160 Dept Psychiatry Chapel Hill NC 27599-7160

BARNHURST, CHRISTINE LOUISE, broadcast executive; b. Salt Lake City, Sept. 3, 1949; d. Joseph Samuel and Luana Jean (Jackson) B. BS, U. Utah, 1971. From account exec. to mktg. specialist Bonneville Internat. Corp. KSL TV, Salt Lake City, 1972-84; mgr. corp. media funding U. Utah, Salt Lake City, 1985-86; dir. advt. Larry H. Miller Group, Salt Lake City, 1986-89; dir. mktg. and promotion Sta. KXIV TV Am. TV of Utah, Salt Lake City, 1989-92; gen. sales, mktg. and promotion mgr. Sta. KJZZ TV Larry H. Miller Comms., Salt Lake City, 1993-96; owner, developer Cruisin' Cards, 1997—; cons., dir. Cause Mktg. KSL-TV, 1997—; freelance producer of corp. sales and tng. videos, TV documentary. Bd. dirs., telethon producer March of Dimes; bd. dirs. YWCA, Relief Soc. LDS Ch. Gen. Bd.; mem. Salt Lake Conv. Bur. Recipient Nat. Print Ad award Athena, 1990, Walt Disney Top Mktg. and Promotion award, 1992, INTV Indy award, 1991, BPME Gold/Silver/Bronze awards, 1989-93, Telly awards, 1992, 93, 94, 95, 96, Gold/Silver/Bronze Addy award Utah Advt. Fedn., Emmy award, 1992, 94, March of Dimes Recognition Svc. award, 1982. Mem. Am. Mktg. Assn. (exec. mem.), Promax.

BARNICH, MICHEL, finance marketing advisor; b. Brussels, May 13, 1943; arrived in France, 1973; s. George-Auguste and Anne (Evely) B.; m. Marina Della Riva, Oct. 13, 1973; children: Laetitia, Graziella. Grad., St. Louis U., Brussels, 1964. CPA, France. Account exec. Benton & Bowles for Procter & Gamble, Brussels, 1968-70; product mgr. Unilever, Brussels, 1970-72; mktg. mgr. L'Oreal, Paris, 1973-75; mktg. and sales dir. Scholl France,

Paris, 1976-80; chief exec. Rothmans France, Paris, 1981-82; sec.-gen. European Fin. Mktg. and Mgmt. Assn., Paris, 1982—. Decorated chevalier de l'Ordre de la Couronne (Belgium). Mem. of Circle De L'Union Interalliee Paris.

BARNSLEY, LESLIE, rheumatologist, educator; b. Newcastle, Tyne, Eng., Oct. 4, 1959; arrived in Australia, 1975.; s. Stewart and Jean Margaret (Lewars) B.; m. Maxine Phillipa Smith, Dec. 4, 1982; children: Lara, Nadia. MB with honors, U. Newcastle, Australia, 1982; Grad. Diploma in Epidemiology, U. Newcastle, 1991, PhD, 1993. Resident med. officer Prince of Wales Hosp., Sydney, Australia, 1983-84; med. registrar Royal Newcastle Hosp., Newcastle, Australia, 1985-90; doctoral rsch. scholar cervical spine rsch. unit Univ. Newcastle, 1991-93; attending physician and rheumatologist Gosford (Australia) Hosp., 1994; staff specialist in rheumatology Concord Hosp., Sydney, 1994—; sr. lectr. in rheumatology U. Sydney, 1994; state councillor Australasian Rheumatology Assn., Sydney, 1995; expert reviewer Painclinic Jour. Club Jour., N.Y.C., 1995. Author chpt. in textbook, 1995; contbr. articles to profl. jours. Recipient Rsch. scholarship Motor Accidents Authority of NSW, Sydney, 1991, Gold Std. in Rheumatology award Pfizer, 1992. Fellow Royal Australasian Coll. Physicians. Avocations: tennis, swimming, surfing, bushwalking. Office: Concord Hosp, Hosp Rd Concord, Sydney NSW 2139, Australia

BAROCCI, SERGIO, immunogeneticist, biologist, researcher; b. Genoa, Liguria, Italy, Mar. 16, 1947; s. Virgilio and Orsola (Froso) B.; m. Alba Virgillo; 1 child, Federico. Chemist Diplomate, Tech. Inst., Genoa, 1969; Biologist, U. Genoa, 1975; Biochemist, U. Pavia (Italy), 1981; Pathologist, U. Genoa, 1985. Asst. researcher in immunology unit San Martino Hosp., Genoa, 1976-89, biologist assoc. in immunology unit, 1989—; regional coord. biologist program, 1990-94; prof. biochemistry Sch. Technicians Regional Sch., Genoa, 1985-96; prof. clin. pathology U. Genoa, 1997—. Author: Manuale Corso Teorico-Pratico su "Metodologie Innovative e Lore Impiego In Campo Diagnostico", 1993; contbr. articles to profl. jours. Trade unionist Trade Union U.I.L. of Health, Genoa, 1998. Health under officer Mil. in Navy, 1969-71. Mem. A.S.H.I., Internat. Soc. Organ Transplantation, E.F.I. Roman Catholic. Avocations: football, tennis. Home: Via Aurelio Robino 87, 16142 Genoa Liguria, Italy Office: S Martino Hosp Det Transpla, Largo R Benzi 10, 16132 Genoa Liguria, Italy

BAROLDI, GIORGIO CESARE, cardiovascular pathology educator; b. Rapallo, Genoa, Italy, Nov. 10, 1924; s. Ferruccio and Cesara (Torelli) B.; m. Fiorella Monzino, Aug. 8, 1956; children: Luca Andrea, Roberto, Orsina. MD, U. Milan, 1949, PhD in Pathology, 1959. Resident in pathology and anatomy U. Milan, 1949-51, asst. prof. pathology and anatomy, 1953-57, from assoc. prof. to prof. pathology and anatomy, 1957-82, chmn. cardiovascular pathology, 1982-96, prof. emeritus, 1996—; dir. Inst. Clin. Pathology Nat. Rsch. Coun., Milan, 1985—; mem. vis. staff Armed Forces Inst. Pathology, Washingotn, 1964-80; vis. prof. cardiology U. Omaha, 1974-80; vis. prof. pathology U. Toronto, Can., 1967—; cons. com. cardiology-cardiac surgery Ministry of Health, Rome, 1990—. Author: Coronary Circulation in Normal Pathologic Heart, 1967 (AHA award 1968), (with others) Coronary Diseases, 1991, Sudden Death in Ischemic Heart Disease, 1995; editor: Cardiomyopathies, 1989; contbr. articles to profl. jours. Lt. physician, Italian mil., 1951-53. Recipient Hektoen Silver medal Am. Heart Assn., 1964, Silver award Am. Soc. Clin. Pathology, 1965; 2000 Disting. Achievement award Soc. Cardiovascular Pathology; NIH rsch. fellow, 1962-64. Fellow Am. Coll. Cardiology, European Soc. Cardiology; mem. Brit. Soc. Cardiology (corr. mem.), Soc. Cardiovascular Pathology (councillor 1991-94, 2000 Disting. Achievement award), Italian Cardiovascular Pathologist Group (chmn. 1989—). Roman Catholic. Avocation: farming. E-mail: ifenig@tin.it. Office: Inst Fisiologia Clinica CNR, Centro de Gasperis Ospedale, 20162 Milan 20162, Italy

BAROLI, PAOLO, bank executive; s. Rinaldo and Maria Gabriella (Zecca) B. Student, U. Bocconi, Milan, 1992; M in Banking, CEFOR, Milan, 1995. Teller Credito Valtellinese-Verano, 1993-96; mktg. profl. Gruppo Credito Valtellinese-Sondrio, 1995, rschr., 1996—; rep. Istituto Centrale Delle Banche Popolari Italiane, Brussels, 1999—. Office: ICBPI, rue de l'industrie 60, 1040 Brussels Belgium

BARON, CHARLES HILLEL, lawyer, educator; b. Phila., Aug. 18, 1936; s. Samuel A. and Rose (Bailinky) B.; m. Irma Elaine Frankel, June 15, 1958 (dec. 1985); children: Jessica Susan, Ira Benjamin, David Hume; m. Dianne M. Quartarone, Sept. 9, 1988; 1 child, Samuel Guy. AB in Philosophy with honors, U. Pa., 1958, PhD in Philosophy, 1972; LLB, Harvard U., 1961. Bar: Pa. bar 1967, U.S. Supreme Ct. bar 1970, Mass. bar 1972. Asst. prof. law U. Pa., 1965-66; assoc. firm Blank Rome Klaus & Comisky, Phila., 1966-68; chief law reform, consumer's adv. Community Legal Svcs., Inc., Phila., 1968-70; assoc. prof. law Boston Coll., 1970-74, prof., 1974—, assoc. dean, 1972-74; exec. dir. Resource Ctr. Consumers Legal Svcs., 1975-77. Author: (with M. Saks) The Use, Nonuse, and Misuse of Applied Social Research, 1980, Droit Constitutionnel et Bioéthique: L'Expérience Americaine, 1997; contbr. articles to profl. jours. Chmn. Cheltenham Twp. (Pa.) Dem. Party, 1966-68; mem. Mass. Health Facilities Appeals Bd., 1974-75; chmn. Mass. Gov.'s Adv. Com. on Prepaid Legal Svcs., 1978-86; bd. dirs. CEPA Found.; mem. bd. overseers Mass. Supreme Jud. Ct. Hist. Soc., 1999—. Recipient various community awards; U. Pa. fellow, 1961-63. Mem. ABA, Am. Assn. Law Schs., Soc. Am. Law Tchrs., Am. Soc. Law and Medicine (bd. editors Am. Jour. Law and Medicine 1978—, bd. dirs.), Civil Liberties Union Mass. (bd. dirs., pres. 1989-91, trustee Mass. Civil Liberties Found.), ACLU. Jewish. Home: 60 Grove Hill Ave Newton MA 02460-2335 Office: Boston Coll Law Sch 885 Centre St Newton MA 02459-1148

BARON, DENNIS E., English language educator; b. N.Y.C., May 9, 1944; s. R.C. Roy and Sylvia (Mayer) Baron; m. Iryce White, Oct. 21, 1979; children: Cordelia, Rachel, Jonathan. AB, Brandeis U., 1965; MA, Columbia U., 1968; PhD, U. Mich., 1971. Cert. tchr. English, N.Y., Mass. Tchr. English Francis Lewis High Sch., N.Y.C., 1966-68, Wayland (Mass.) High Sch., 1968-69; asst. prof. English Ea. Ill. U., Charleston, Ill., 1971-73, CCNY, N.Y.C., 1973-74; asst. prof. English/linguistics U. Ill., Urbana, 1975-81, assoc. prof. English/linguistics, 1981-84, prof. English/linguistics, 1984—; head English dept. U. Ill., Urbana, France, 1997—. Author: (books) Grammar and Good Taste, 1982, Grammar and Gender, 1986, Declining Grammar, 1989, The English-Only Question, 1990, Guide to Home Language Repair, 1994. Fulbright fellow CIES, France, 1978-79, fellow Ctr. for Advanced Study, U. Ill., 1984-85, program for study of cultural values and ethics, U. Ill., 1992, NEH, 1989. Mem. MLA, Am. Dialect Soc. (editor monograph series 1984-93), Nat. Coun. Tchrs. English (mem. commn. on lang. 1984-87), Linguistic Soc. Am. (mem. com. on lang. and the schs. 1992—), Coun. Writing Program Adminstrs., Conf. on Coll. Composition and Comm. Avocations: reading, writing, art. E-mail: debaron@vivc.edu. Office: Univ Ill Dept English 608 S Wright St Urbana IL 61801-3630

BARON, FRANKLIN ANDREW MERRIFIELD, Dominican government official; b. Portsmouth, Dominica, 1923; attended Portsmouth Govt. Sch., Dominica Grammar Sch., St. Mary's Acad. Became mgr. A.A. Baron and Co., import/export, gen. mdse. and groceries firm, 1939, became partner, 1945; mem. Roseau Town Council, 1945-49; mem. Dominica Legislature, from 1954; minister of trade and prodn. Commonwealth of Dominica, 1956-60, chief minister and minister of fin., 1960-61; amb. to U.S., 1982-86; permanent rep. of Dominica to UN, N.Y.C., 1982-95; permanent rep. to OAS, Washington, 1982-95; proprietor Paramount Printers Ltd., 1992—; pub. Chronicle, 1996—; mem. local policy adv. bd. Barclays Bank Internat.; mem. bd. mgmt. Dominica Banana Growers' Assn., 1945-75; mem. Boundaries Commn., 1978-90, Electoral Commn., 1979-90; chmn. Dominica Library Com., 1983-89; chmn. bd. dirs. Dominica Electricity Services, 1983-91; mem. Indsl. Devel. Corp. Dominica, 1984-89; high commr. to U.K., 1986-92; chmn. Nat. Comml. Bank, 1986-90 ; dir. New Chronicle Printery, chmn. Club: Rotary (pres. Dominica, 1976-77, also rep. from Dominica to internat. convs.). Office: PO Box 57, 14 Cork St, Roseau Dominica also: Syb Bar Aerie, Champs Fleurs, Eggleston Dominica

BARON, GINO VICTOR, chemical engineering educator; b. Roeselare, Belgium, Oct. 26, 1948; s. Marcel J. Baron and Francine Calmeyn; m. Anne C. Lauwers, July 26, 1971; children: Ilan, Eline. Degree in chem. engring., Vrije U. Brussels, 1971; DSc in Engring., Technion, Haifa, Israel, 1976. Cert. chem. engr. Instr. chem. engring. Technion, 1972-74; Asst. Vrije U. Brussels, 1971-72, asst., 1974-81, lectr., 1981-89, prof., 1989—. Contbr. articles to profl. jours.; inventor, patentee in field. Recipient I. Akerman award NSF, 1983. Fellow Royal Flemish Inst. Engrs. Avocations: running, tennis, gardening. Home: Bleuckeveldlaan 34, B 3080 Tervuren Belgium Office: Vrije Universiteit Brussels Dept CHIS, Pleinlaan 2, B1050 Brussels Belgium

BARON, JEAN-CLAUDE, neuroscientist, researcher; b. Tunis, Tunisia, Mar. 25, 1949; s. Marcel and Reine Yolaine (Bonan) B.; m. Annik Irene Arnette de la Charlonny, Mar. 2, 1974; three children. MD, U. Paris, 1976, cert. in neurology, 1980. Resident in medicine Univ. Hosp. Paris, 1974-79; fellow Harvard U. Sch. Medicine, Boston, 1976-77; sr. registrar med. physics U. Paris, 1979-82, sr. registrar neurology, 1982-86; dir. rsch. INSERM, Caen, France, 1986—, dir. neurosci. unit, 1989—; sci. dir. Cyceron PET Ctr., Caen, France, 1988—; assoc. cons. neurology Univ. Hosp., Caen, 1986—. Editor: The Ischemic Penumbra, 1986, The Dopamine System Studied by Pet, 1991, Positron Emission Tomography, Handbook of Neuropsychology, 1995. Mem. Soc. Française Neurovasculaire, European Fed. Neurol. Socs. (chmn. neuroimaging task force 1995-97, neuroimaging scientist panel 1997—), Am. Neurol. Assn., French Soc. Neurology, European Stroke Coun. Avocations: guitar, jogging, skiing. Home: 135 rue Basse, 14000 Caen France Office: INSERM U320, Cyceron BP 5229, 14074 Caen France

BAR-ON, RAPHAEL RAYMOND, tourism consultant; b. London, Dec. 4, 1927; s. Edward and Dolly (Silman) Baron; m. Jocheved Johanna Lurie, May 25, 1952 (dec. 1977); two children. BA, Trinity Coll., Cambridge, U.K., 1947, MA, 1951; PhD in Applied Econs., Cambridge, 1975. Asst. prin. Gen. Register Office, London, 1950-51; dir. rsch. divsn. Israel Productivity Inst., Jerusalem, 1951-54; statistician Shell-Mex & BP, London, 1954-55; dir. planning and devel. Ctrl. Bur. Statistics, Jerusalem, 1956-72; dir. rsch. and statistics Min. Tourism, Jerusalem, 1972-91; tourism & econ. cons. Israel, 1992—; prin. advisor Union of Local Authorities in Israel. Fellow Tourism Soc. (U.K.); mem. Internat. Statis. Inst., B'nai B'rith. Home: 28 Ha-Mitnachlim St, Ramat Hasharon 47203, Israel

BARON, SIMSON, mathematics educator emeritus; b. Tartu, Estonia, Apr. 20, 1929; arrived in Israel, 1979; s. Avraham-David and Ethel (Antin) B.; m. Zeitchik Tamar; children: David, Hene, Leah. MA, Tartu U., 1956, PhD, 1959. Watch-maker Govt. Alator, Chuwash, 1942-45, Govt. Tartu, Estonia, 1945-53; tchr. math. High Sch., Tartu, Estonia, 1953-57; lectr. Tartu U., 1957-59, sr. lectr., 1959-61, asst. prof., 1961-63, assoc. prof., 1963-79; assoc. prof. Bar-Ilan U., Ramat Gan, Israel, 1980-84, prof., 1984-97, prof. emeritus, 1997—; reviewer in field. Author: Introduction to the Theory of Summability of Series, 2d edit., 1977, also others; editor-in-chief Acta Commentationes, U. Tartuensis, Math. and Mechanics, 1958-79; contbr. over 80 articles to profl. jours. Mem. Am. Math. Soc., Israel Math. Union. Jewish. Home: Pesah Hevroni 116 Apt 33, 96633 Jerusalem Israel Office: Bar-Ilan U, Dept Math and Computer Sci, 52900 Ramat Gan Israel

BARON, THEODORE, public relations executive; b. Harbin, Manchuria, China, Aug. 20, 1928; came to U.S., 1946; s. Solomon and Bella (Gelesny) B.; m. Irene Cunnington, Oct. 23, 1958; children: Susan Elaine, Michael. BA, U. Calif., Berkeley, 1950; LLB, NYU, 1957. Bar: N.Y. 1958. Newspaper reporter The Record, Coalinga, Calif., 1950-51; writer, editor Associated Press, San Francisco, 1951-52; writer, acct. exec. N.Y.C. Pub. Rels. firms, N.Y.C., 1952-58; pres. Ted Baron Inc., N.Y.C., 1958-98; ret., 1998. Contbr. articles to profl. jours. and consumer mags. Fellow Pub. Rels. Soc. Am. (pres. N.Y. 1990-91); mem. Far Eastern Soc., Salty Flyrodders N.Y., Princeton Club. Home and Office: 2300 Lindenmere Dr Merrick NY 11566-4312

BARON COHEN, GERALD, accountant, writer; b. London, July 13, 1932; s. Morris and Miriam (Nicholsby) B-C.; m. Daniella Naomi Weiser, June 12, 1962; children: Jonathan Amnon, Erran Boaz, Sacha Noam. BA, U. Wales, 1951. Chartered acct. Prin. Baron-Cohen & Co., London, 1961—; dir. House of Baron Group of Cos., Eng., 1967—. Founding editor Mosaic Nat. Mag. for Youth, 1960-64; dep. editor New Middle East, (internat. monthly), 1968-70. Past pres. First Lodge of Eng. Bnai B'rith; v.p. Bnai B'rith Hillel Found., London; trustee Oxford Jewish Comty. Ctr.; chmn. Bamah-Forum for Jewish Dialogue. Home and Office: 760 Finchley Rd, London NW11 7TH, England

BARON CRESPO, ENRIQUE, member European parliament; b. Madrid, Mar. 27, 1944. Min. transport, tourism and comms. Spain, 1982-85; mem. European Parliament, Brussels, 1986—, pres., 1989-92, chmn. com. on fgn. affairs and security, 1992-94; chmn. Group of the Party of European Socialists; mem. com. on constnl. affairs, budgets, delegation for rels. with Japan. Mem. Spanish Socialist Workers' Party. Office: Parlamento Europeo, Rue Wiertz ASP 6H 263, B-1047 Bruxelles Belgium also: Oficina del Parlamento Euro, Paseo de la Castellana 46, E-28046 Madrid Spain

BARONE, ROSE MARIE PACE, writer, retired educator, entertainer; b. Buffalo, Apr. 26, 1920; d. Dominic and Jennie (Zagara) Pace; m. John Barone, Aug. 23, 1947. BA, U. Buffalo, 1943; MS, U. So. Cal., 1950; cert. advanced study, Fairfield (Conn.) U., 1963. Tchr. Angola (N.Y.) High Sch., 1943-46, Puente (Calif.) High Sch., 1946-47, Jefferson High Sch., Lafayette, Ind., 1947-50; dir. Warren Inst., Bridgeport, Conn., 1951-53; instr. U. Bridgeport, 1953-54; tchr. bus. subjects Bassick H.S., Bridgeport, 1954-74, Harding H.S., Bridgeport, 1974-80; instr. Fairfield U., Conn., 1969; freelance writer, 1980—; chair State Poetry Festival, 1987. Founder Pet Rescue; chmn. comty. affairs com. Area Coun. Cath. Women, 1988-90, sec., 1990-91, chmn. family affairs com., 1991, v.p., 1992-93; chmn. comty. affairs Ch. Women United, 1992—, state area chmn., 1995-97, state UN chair, 1997—. Pace-Barone Minority yearly scholar Fairfield U., Auerbach Found. scholar, 1956; recipient Playwriting prize Conn. Federated Women's Clubs, 1955, 1st prize for poetry, 1985, Short Story award Federated Women Conn., 1987, 88, 90, Citizen award Bridgeport Dental Assn., 1982, State/Town Hero award, 1986, Anniversary medal and marble statuette Fairfield U., Cmty. Care Successful Aging award, 1992, Salute to Women award YWCA, 1993, Woman of Substance award, 1994, Woman Distinction Girl Scout award, 1998, craft and flower awards, State Arts award, 2000. mem. NEA, AAUW (treas. 1957-58, named gift grant 1989, cultural and poetry chair 1992—, rec. sec. 1992-93, internat. rels. 1993-94, v.p. program 1995-97, contest chair 1995—, Conf. of Women award 1997), Am. Assn. Ret. People (v.p. 1987-88, pres. 1988-89, 94-95, instr. 55 Alive, cmty. affairs chair 1990-94, 95—), Owl (sec. 1987-89, pres. 1989-90), Nat. League Am. PEN Women (Bridgeport historian 1966-84, state historian 1983—, treas. br. 1985-88, state pres. 1986-88, state lit. chair 1988—, br. membership chair 1990, Nat. Historian award 1976, 88), Fairfield Area Poets (founder, pres. 1990—, editor 5 vols. Conn. poets), UN Assn. USA (pres. Bridgeport 1964-66, 68-70, v.p. 1988—, chmn. area UN Days 1960—, pres. Conn. 1971—, state chmn. UNICEF to 1984, area UNICEF Ctr. 1984—, state historian 1984—), Conn. Bus. Tchrs., Bridgeport Edn. Assn. (sec. 1966-68), VFW (aux. 1989—), Am. Legion (aux. contest chair 1989—, historian 1993-95, Aux. Nat. Cmty. Svc. award 1993), Fairfield Arts Coun., Fairfield Philatelic Soc. (sec. 1971-78, founder advisor Philatelic Jrs. 1972-80), Fairfield U. Women's Club (founder, pres. 1950, 74—, v.p. 1973-74), Southport Women's Club (garden dept. sec. 1981-85, chmn. 1985-87), John & Rose Marie Barone Resource Ctr. St. Vincent's Coll., Pi Omega Pi. Home: 1283 Round Hill Rd Fairfield CT 06430-7329

BARON NOTHOMB, SIMON PIERRE, civil servant, educator; b. Habay, Luxembourg, Belgium, July 4, 1933; s. Pierre and Ghislaine (Montens D'Oosterwyck) Baron N.; m. Dominique D'Aspremont Lynden Maillen, May 30, 1960; children: Philippe, Pierre, Eva. Diploma, Inst. des Etudes Politiques, Paris, 1960; BA, U. Louvain, Belgium, 1964; MA, U. Paris VIII, 1993. UN observer in Palestine UNTSO, 1955-57; advisor Belgian ministry of Fgn. Trade and Tech. Assistance, 1962-65; dir. then dir. gen. Catholic U. Louvain, 1965-72, 83-92; dep. dir. UN Inst. Rsch. and Tng., Geneva, 1972-75; dep. sec. gen. Agy. for Cultural and Tech. Coop., 1976-82; founder, sec. gen. Coimbra Group, Brussels, 1985—; sec. gen. Econ and Social Com of European Cmtys., Brussels, 1992-96, European Throughout the the World, 1996—. Author: Arab Near East, 1959; contbr. articles to profl. jorus. Lt. col. Belgium Mil., 1953-90. Avocations: chess, paragliding. Office: Found Universitaire, 11 Rue d'Egmont, 1000 Brussels Belgium

BARR, GEOFFREY SAMUEL, head and neck surgeon, research administrator; b. Liverpool, Eng., Nov. 1, 1952; s. Samuel James and Edith Patricia (Sowersby) B.; m. Rowena Mary Bickerton, May 5, 1984; children: James, Richard, Helena. MB, B of Surgery, Dundee U., Scotland, 1977, M of Surgery, 1990. Rsch. fellow U. Dundee, 1988-89; head and neck surgeon U. Birmingham, Eng., 1989-93; head and neck surgeon, cons. Gwynedd Hosp., Wales, 1993—; health svc. computing advisor Nat. Health Svc., Wales, 1995—. Author: Assessment of Nasal Function, 1989; contbr. over 50 articles to profl. jours. Fellow Royal Coll. Surgeons Edinburgh, Royal Soc. Mecicine; mem. Brit. Assn. Otolaryngologists Head and Neck Surgeons, Brit. Assn. Head and Neck Oncologists, Oricle Soc. (hon. life), Schofield Statis. Soc. (hon. archivist). Mem. Ch. of Wales. Avocations: painting, drawing, piano. Office: Gwynedd Hosp, Perhosgarnedd, LL57 2PW Bangor Wales

BARR, JAMES HOUSTON, III, lawyer; b. Louisville, Nov. 2, 1941; s. James Houston Jr. and Elizabeth Hamilton (Pope) B.; m. Sarah Jane Todd, Apr. 16, 1970 (div.); 1 child, Lynn Jamison, m. Cindy Ann Jeffries, May 31, 1997; one child, Worden Washington. Student, U. Va., 1960-63, U. Tenn., 1963-64; BSL, JD, U. Louisville, 1966. Bar: Ky. 1966, U.S. Ct. Appeals (6th cir.) 1969, U.S. Supreme Ct. 1971, U.S. Ct. Mil. Appeals 1978. Law clk. Ky. Ct. Appeals, Frankfort, 1966-67; asst. atty. gen. Ky. Frankfort, 1967-71, 79-82; asst. U.S. atty. U.S. Dept. Justice, Louisville, 1971-79, 83—; 1st asst. U.S. Atty., 1978-79; asst. dist. counsel U.S. Army C.E., Louisville, 1982-83. Lt. comdr. USNR, 1967-81, lt. col. USAR, 1981-91. Mem. FBA (pres. Louisville chpt. 1975-76, Younger Fed. Lawyer award 1975), Ky. Bar Assn., Louisville Bar Assn., Soc. Colonial Wars, SAR, Washington Family Soc., Pendennis Club, Louisville Boat Club, Filson Club, Delta Upsilon. Republican. Episcopalian. Home: 100 Westwind Rd Louisville KY 40207-1520 Office: US Atty 510 W Broadway Ste 1000 Louisville KY 40202-2281

BARR, JOHN BALDWIN, chemist, research scientist; b. Niagara Falls, N.Y., Nov. 8, 1932; s. Lorne Haworth and Myra (Baldwin) B.; m. Patricia Jane Kromer, Sept. 18, 1954; children: Mark Kromer, John Robert, Kathryn Jean, Karen Patricia. BA, U. Buffalo, 1954; MS, U. Mich., 1956; PhD, Pa. State U., 1961. Rsch. chemist Corning Glass Works (N.Y.), 1961-62; sr. rsch. chemist Union Carbide Corp., Parma, Ohio, 1962-71; rsch. scientist Union Carbide Corp., Parma, 1971-82, sr. rsch. scientist, 1982-86; sr. rsch. scientist Amoco Performance Products, Parma, 1986-90, Alpharetta, Ga., 1990-91; assoc. rsch. scientist Amoco Performance Products, Alpharetta, 1991-95; cons. Rsch. Opportunities, Inc., Torrance, Calif., 1996—. Contbr. articles to profl. jours.; patentee in field. Shell Oil Co. fellow, 1959. Mem. Am. Chem. Soc., Am. Carbon Soc., N.Am. Thermal Analysis Soc., Sigma Xi, Phi Lambda Upsilon. Republican. Episcopalian.

BARR, JOHN MONTE, lawyer; b. Mt. Clemens, Mich., Jan. 1, 1935; s. Merle James and Wilhelmina Marie (Monte) B.; student Mexico City Coll., 1955; BA, Mich. State U., 1956; JD, U. Mich., 1959; m. Marlene Joy Bielenberg, Dec. 17, 1954; children: John Monte, Karl Alexander, Elizabeth Marie. Admitted to Mich. bar, 1959, since practiced in Ypsilanti; mem. Ellis B. Freatman, Jr., 1959-61; ptnr., chief trial atty. Freatman, Barr, Anhut & Moir and predecessor firm, 1961-63; pres. Barr, Anhut, Assoc. PC, 1963-94; pres. Barr, Anhut & Assocs., 1994—; city atty. City of Ypsilanti, 1981. Lectr. bus. law Eastern Mich. U., 1968-70. Pres., Ypsilanti Family Service, 1967; mem. Ypsilanti Public Housing Com., 1980-84; sr. adviser Explorer law post Portage Trail council Boy Scouts Am., 1969-71, commr. Potawatomi dist., 1973-74, commr. Washtenong dist., 1974-75, dist. committeeman, 1984, wolverine coun. v.p., 1992, v.p. Great Saulk Trail coun., 1995—; bd. dirs. Mich. Mcpl. League Legal Def. Fund., pres. 1989-90. Served with AUS, 1959-60. Recipient Silver Beaver award Boy Scouts Am., 1992, Mich. Mcpl. League award of Merit Mcpl. League Legal Def., 1992. Mem. State Bar Mich. (grievance bd. hearing panel 1969-97, state rep. assembly 1977-82, bd. commrs. 1993—), Am., Ypsilanti, Washtenaw County (pres. 1975-76, Profl. and Civility award 1998) Bar Assns., Washtenaw County Trial Lawyers Assns., Mich. Mcpl. Attys. Assn. (pres. 1989-90, MAMA dist. mcpl. atty. award, 1993), U.S. (instr. piloting, seamanship, sail), Ann Arbor (comdr. 1972-73) power squadrons. Lutheran. Club: Washtenaw Country. Contbr. articles to boating mags. Home: 1200 Whittier Rd Ypsilanti MI 48197-2152 Office: 105 Pearl St Ypsilanti MI 48197-2611

BARR, JON-HENRY, lawyer; b. Livingston, N.J., Sept. 1, 1970; s. Gary and Susan Barr. BA, Lehigh U., 1992; JD, Seton Hall U., 1995. Bar: N.J. 1996, D.C. 1998, U.S. Dist. Ct. N.J. 1996, U.S. Ct. Appeals (3d cir.) 1997. Jud. law clk. Superior Ct. N.J., Freehold, N.J., 1995-96; assoc. Law Offices of Robert Blackman, Edison, N.J., 1996-98; ptnr. Barr & Canada, LLC, Clark, N.J., 1998—. Sec. Union Middlesex REACT, Woodbridge, N.J., 1989—; councilman Twp. of Clark, N.J., 1993-94; mem. Clark Rep. Civic Assn., 1996—. Named one of Outstanding Young Men of Am., 1998. Mem. ABA, N.J. State Bar Assn., Union County Bar Assn. Jewish. Avocations: politics, travel. Home: 69 Fairview Rd Clark NJ 07066-2904 Office: Barr and Canada LLC 21 Brant Ave Clark NJ 07066-1512

BARR, LESTER, surgeon; b. Glasgow, Scotland, June 28, 1954; s. John & Tina (Kaars) B.; m. Nicola Beth Worrall, July 5, 1986; children: Amy, Katy, Molly. BSc, U. St. Andrews, 1975; MB ChB, U. Manchester, 1978, ChM, 1986. Chmn. Northwest Breast Group, 1994—. Author: Pocketbook of Oncology, 1997.; contbr. papers on breat cancer, soft tissue tumors and sarcoma. Fellow Royal Coll. Surgeons England. Office: The Nightingale Ctr, Withington Hosp Nell Ln, M20 2LR Manchester England

BARR, MARK DAVID, food products executive; b. East London, Cape Province, South Africa, Feb. 8, 1955; arrived in Australia, 1989; s. Cyril Saul and Genenda (Lazarus) B.; m. Elana Radomsky, Feb. 12, 1989; children: Jared, Cayli. B.Com., U. Cape Town (South Africa), BA, BA in Econs. with honors. Mng. dir. Dolce Vita (Pty) Ltd., South Africa, 1982-84; bus. mgr. personal care Kimberly Clark, South Africa, 1984-89; mktg. mgr. Frito Lay, Australia, 1989-91, comml. dir., 1993-96; mktg. dir. Pepsi, Australia, 1991-93; mng. dir. Uncle Toby's, Australia, 1996—. Cpl. South Africa, 1973. Mem. Northside Monash Soccer. Jewish. Avocations: soccer, gardening, travel.

BARR, MICHAEL CHARLES, financial consultant; b. White Plains, N.Y., Nov. 2, 1947; s. Charles Yerger and Joan Tames (Biggar) B.; m. Helen June Rumsey, Mar. 17, 1973. Student, Washington and Lee U.; BA summa cum laude, Rutgers Coll., 1969; JD, Columbia U., 1972, MBA, 1980. Bar: N.J. 1976, N.Y. 1978, U.S. Supreme Ct. 1976. Assoc. McCarter & English, Newark, 1976-77, Conboy, Hewitt, O'Brien & Boardman, N.Y.C., 1977-78; investment banker Kidder, Peabody & Co., Inc., N.Y.C., 1980-82; v.p. Mfrs. Hanover Trust Co., N.Y.C., 1982-90, A-L Assocs., N.Y.C., 1990-92; corp. sec., dir. H. Rivkin & Co., Inc., N.Y.C., 1992-93; securities analyst Standard & Poor's Corp., N.Y.C., 1993-98; Russian securities specialist H. Rivkin & Co., Inc., N.Y.C., 1998-99; emerging markets specialist HP Capital Mkts. Group, N.Y.C., 1999-2000; fin. cons. AXA Advisors, Inc., N.Y.C., 2000—; guest commentator on Russia, CNN, 1998-2000. Adv. bd. Washington and Lee Alumni Coll., 1996-98. Lt. USN, 1972-76. Recipient Loyal Son award Rutgers Alumni Assn., 1976. Mem. U.S. Polo Assn., Phi Beta Kappa.

BARR, ROSEANNE See ROSEANNE

BARR, SPENCER, opto-electronic engineer; b. Portsmouth, Eng., Nov. 13, 1965; s. Donald George and Jean Barr. B in Engring., U. Bradford, 1988; MSc, King's Coll., 1996. Chartered elec. engr. Engr. Plessey Avionics, Havant, U.K., 1988-92; sr. engr. GEC-Plessey Avionics, Havant, U.K., 1992-93; prin. engr. GEC-Marconi Radar and Def. Systems, Portsmouth, U.K., 1993-98; sr. R&D engr. Snell & Wilcox, Petersfield, Eng., 1998—. Mem. Instn. Elec. Engrs. Achievements include inventor of thermally stabilized optical devices. Office: Durford Mill, Petersfield Hants GU31 5AZ, England

BARR, WILLIAM ROBERT, industrial engineer, consultant; b. Detroit, Oct. 25, 1947; s. Robert Webb and Marion (Squire) B.; m. Diane Gayle Buddemeier, June 25, 1988 (dec.). BSIE, U. Mich., 1970, MSIE, 1974; MBA, Western Mich. U., 1977. Registered profl. engr., Mich. Indsl. engr. Upjohn Co., Kalamazoo, 1974-82; program mgr. Kellogg Co., Battle Creek, Mich., 1982-91; pres. William Barr Assoc. Inc., Augusta, 1991—; instr. Western Mich. U., Kalamazoo, 1980-92. Contbr. articles to profl. jours. Active ordinance com. Ross Twp., Mich., 1987, chmn. road improvement

com., 1989, active zoning bd., 1995-99. With U.S. Army, 1972-73. Mem. NSPE, Inst. Indsl. Engrs. (chpt. officer 1995—), Indsl. and Ops. Engring. Acad. U. Mich., Alpha Pi Mu, Tau Beta Pi. Achievements include the development of computer model for the analysis of capacity in production facilities. Avocations: backpacking, tennis, cross-country skiing. Office: William Barr Assoc Inc PO Box 507 Augusta MI 49012-0507

BARRAD, CATHERINE MARIE, lawyer; b. Moscow, Idaho, Dec. 12, 1953; d. Richard Gary and Hazel Mae (Hollon) Morrison; m. Mark William Barrad, Dec. 29, 1974 (div. June 1997); children: Joshua, Samuel, Rachel. Student, Saddleback Coll., 1971-72, UCLA, 1972-73, U. Calif., Irvine, 1973-74, Calif. State U., Long Beach, 1976-77; BS in Law, JD, Western State U., 1980. Bar: Calif. 1980, Hawaii 1993. Pvt. practice Law Offices of Catherine M. Barrad, Long Beach, 1980-93, Maui, 1993—; arbitrator court annexed arbitration program 2d Cir. Ct. Hawaii, 1993—. Del. Coun. Jewish Fedns., Long Beach, 1990, bd. dirs., 1983-93; del. Jewish Community Rels. Coun., 1987-92; cubmaster Pack 111 Boy Scouts Am., Long Beach, 1989-93; v.p. Jewish Arts and Edn. Coun. Maui, 1994-97. Recipient Neuberger Young Leadership award Jewish Fedn. Long Beach, 1990, Chai Vol. award Jewish Community Ctr., Long Beach, 1990. Mem. Women Lawyers of Long Beach (sec. 1981-82, pres. 1982-83), Hawaii State Bar Assn, Maui County Bar Assn., Aloha House (bd. dirs. 1995-97), Rotary Maui Upcountry (pres. 1994-96, bd. dirs. 1994-97). Democrat. Jewish. Fax: 808-573-0853. Office: PO Box 1591 Makawao HI 96768-1591

BARRAGRY, THOMAS BERNARD, veterinary pharmacology and therapeutics educator; b. Dublin, Ireland, Aug. 16, 1948; s. Thomas Patrick and Bella (McCarthy) B.; m. Maeve Philomena Gilligan; children: Ruth Ann, Miriam Elizabeth. MVB, Univ. Coll., Dublin, 1971, MSc, 1974, PhD, 1981. Sr. lectr. Univ. Coll., Dublin, 1971—; expert on panel E.M.E.A.; mem. Irish Medicines Bd.; mem. com. for med. products European Union; mem. Internat. Equine Doping Adv. Bd. Author: Veterinary Drug Therapy, 1995; contbr. chpts. to vet. books, articles to sci. jours.; peer reviewer for internat. vet. jours. Mem. Royal Coll. Vet. Surgeons, European Coll. Vet. Pharmacology and Toxicology (diplomate/specialist), Irish Vet. Assn. Avocations: classical music, European history, German history. Office: U Coll Dublin Fac Vet Med, Shelbourne Rd, Ballsbridge Dublin 4, Ireland

BARRAL, SUSANA G., artist, small business owner; b. Havana, Cuba, May 15, 1959; m. Antonio J. Barral, July 14, 1978. AA, Miami Dade C.C., 1982; BFA, Fla. Internat. U., 1985. Sec., treas. A. B. Installations, Inc., Hialeah, Fla., 1985—. One-woman shows include Infinite Possibilities Gallery, Hollywood, Fla., 1996, I've Been Framed Gallery, Miami, 1996, Mus. New Arts, Ft. Lauderdale, Fla., 1996, 97, Art and Culture Ctr., Hollywood, Fla., 1998. Mem. Vivas Las Artes, Broward Art Guild, Hollywood Art Guild. Republican. Roman Catholic. Avocations: bicycling, book collecting, reading. E-mail: Sgbarral@aol.com. Office: 7417 W 30th Ct Hialeah FL 33018-5207

BARRANCO, GREGORY CROFFORD, lobbyist; b. Balt., July 14, 1965; s. Charles F. and Mary Seely (Klair) B.; m. Allison Brewster Porter, June 20, 1998;. BS, James Madison U., 1988. Legis. analyst Health Ins. Assn. Am., Washington, 1994-97; asst. v.p. govt. rels. Nat. Coun. Cmty. Behavioral Healthcare, Rockville, Md., 1997-99; dir. govt. rels. Am. Coll. Occupl. Environ. Medicine, Washington, 1999—. Mem. Am. Soc. Assn. Execs. Roman Catholic. Avocations: sailing, swimming, carpentry. Fax: 202-466-7517. E-mail: gcbarranco@aol.org. Home: 124 6th St SE Washington DC 20003-1132 Office: Am Coll Occupl Environ Medicine 1990 M St NW Ste 340 Washington DC 20036-3422

BARRATT, BARBARA INGEBORG PATRICIA, entomologist, research scientist, researcher; b. High Wycombe, Eng., Nov. 3, 1948; arrived in New Zealand, 1977; d. Jack and Ingeborg Jenny Gertrude (Chmielewski) Bowden; m. Andrew Barratt, Aug. 26, 1972 (div. 1994). BSc in Zoology with honors, U. Durham, Eng., 1972, PhD, 1975. Zoology tutor U. Durham, 1975-76, rsch. asst., 1976-77; Nat. Rsch. Adv. Coun. postdoctoral fellow Ministry Agr. and Fisheries, Mosgiel, New Zealand, 1978-81; scientist MAF, Mosgiel, New Zealand, 1981-88, USDA-Pa. State U., State College, 1988; sr. scientist, programme leader Ag Rsch., Mosgiel, 1989—. Author: Grassrub and Porina: A Guide to Management and Control, 1990; author 4 book chpts.; contbr. more than 70 articles to profl. jours. Mem. Otago Conservation Bd., Dunedin, 1984-93. Mem. New Zealand Entomol. Soc. (pres. 1991-93), New Zealand Inst. Agrl. Sci. Avocations: conservation, sports, wine, photography. Office: Ag Research, Invermay Agr Ctr PB 50034, Mosgiel New Zealand

BARRATT, DONNA LEE, elementary school educator; b. Westwood, N.J., Nov. 23, 1965; d. Robert Roy B. and Arlene Rose (Solar) Landwehr. BA in English Edn. cum laude, Trenton St. Coll., 1988; MA in Edn., Georgian Ct. Coll., 1998; supervisory cert., 1999, instrnl. tech. cert., 2000. Cert. tchr. English, N.J., Pa., elem. tchr., N.J. Tchr. English St. Mary H.S., South Amboy, N.J., 1989-92; mid. sch. lang. arts tchr. Joyce Kilmer Sch., Milltown, N.J., 1992-94; lang. arts tchr. Manalapan-Englishtown (N.J.) Mid. Sch., 1994—; Presenter inservice writing workshop Manalapan-Englishtown Bd. Edn., Manalapan, N.J., 1997; presenter interdisciplinary instr. N.J. ASCD state conf., East Windsor, N.J., 1999, N.J. Ednl. Assn. Good Ideas Forum, 2000. Recipient Outstanding Ednl. Program award N.J. ASCD, 1998. Mem. Nat. Coun. Tchrs. English, Kappa Delta Pi Edn. Honor Soc.. Roman Catholic. Avocations: reading, music, bike riding, hiking. Office: Manalapan Englishtown Middle Sch 155 Millhurst Rd Manalapan NJ 07726-4002

BARRATT, ERIC GEORGE, accountant; b. Stokenchurch, England, Apr. 15, 1938; s. Frank Ronald and Winifred Mary (Hayward) B. Chartered acct. Ptnr. Tansley Witt & Co., London, 1966-79, Arthur Andersen & Co., London, 1979-82; sr. ptnr. MacIntyre & Co., London, 1982-2000; dir. Automotive Products P.L.C., Leamington, 1977-86, Montague Boston Investment Trust P.L.C., London, 1982-85, Milton Keynes Devel. Corp., 1980-85; chmn. MacIntyre Strater Internat. Ltd., 1990—, Ely Pl. Holdings Ltd. Chmn. Stokenchurch Parish Council, 1975-86; vice-chmn. buckinghamshire County Council, Aylesbury, 1981-85; dir. Commn. for New Towns, 1986-90; tras. Oriel Coll., Oxford, 1986, St. Augustine's Found., Canterbury; bd. trustees Alzheimer's Rsch. Trust. Fellow Inst. Chartered Accts. Conservative. Anglican. Clubs: Atheneaum, Carlton, City of London (London). Home: Stockfield, Stokenchurch HP14 3SX, England Office: MacIntyre & Co, Oriel Coll, Oxford OX1 4EW, England

BARRÉ, RÉMI ABDON ANDRÉ, science agency administrator, economist; b. Boulogne-Sur-Seine, Hauts-De-Seine, France, Apr. 7, 1948; s. Jacques and Françoise (Lozac'hmeur) B.; m. Marie-Danièle Fichet, Apr. 30, 1977; children: Julien, Pierre, Flora. Student, École Nationale Supérieure Des Mines De Nancy, U. N.C., Ecole des Hautes Etuces; diploma in Civil Engring., MA in Regional Planning, PhD in Econ. Teaching asst. U. N.C., Chapel Hill, 1974-75; asst. Resources Planning Assocs., 1975-77; dir. Groupe d'Etudes Ressources Planification Aménagement, 1977-81; agent to min. of rsch. and tech., 1983-86; lectr., rschr. dept. econ. and mgmt. Conservatoire Nat. Des Arts et Métiers, 1982-89; dir. Observatoire Des Scis. et Des Techniques, Paris, 1990—; assoc. prof. Conservatoire Nat. Des Arts er Métiers, 1997—. Decorated chevalier de l'Ordre Nat. du Mérite. Avocation: water colors. Home: 8 rue Guy de la Brosse, 75005 Paris France Office: Observatoire Des Sci et des Tech, 93 rue de Vaugirard, 75006 Paris France

BARREAU, HERVE ALBERT, philosopher; b. Le Mans, France, Apr. 27, 1929; s. Rene Albert and Simone (Lemire) B.; m. Marianne Horstel, Dec. 28, 1965. Lic. in philosophy, Le Saulchoir, Paris, 1953, U. Strasbourg, France, 1957; agregation philosophie, U. Paris, 1959. Prof. enseignement secondaire Oran, Lille, France, 1959-62; asst. enseignement superieur Strasbourg, 1962-66; charge de recherche Centre National de la Recherche Scientifique, Paris, 1966-81; maitre de recherche Strasbourg, 1981-85, directeur de recherche, 1985—, mem. elu, 1971-80; sec. scientifique de la sect. 45, 1975-80; dir. de l'UPR 265, Strasbourg, 1983-94. Author: Aristote et l'analyse du Savoir, 1972, L'Epistemologie (Coll. que sais-je?), 1990, Le Temps, 1996; editor: L'Explication dans les sciences de la vie, 1983, Le Meme et l'Autre, 1986, Theories biologiques Ethique et Experimentation en Medecine, 1988, La Mathematique non-standard, 1989, Le Cerveau et l'Esprit, 1992, Jean Louis Destouches Physicien et Philosophe, 1909-80,94. Sec. Congres du peuple europeen, Turin, 1958. Served with French Army, 1951-52. Fellow Soc. Francaise d'Histoire des Scis. (v.p. 1984-88), Internat. Soc. for the Study of Time, Acad. Internat. Philosophy of Scis., Acad. of Alsace (v.p. 1996-99). Avocations: marching, gardening. Fax: 33-03-88-61-77-74. E-mail: hbarreau@cybercable.fr.

BARRECA, CHRISTOPHER ANTHONY, lawyer; b. Pittsfield, Mass., Sept. 15, 1928; s. Christopher Joseph and Jennie (Cannici) B.; m. Alice Hazlehurst, Sept. 5, 1953. AA, Boston U., 1950, JD, 1953; LLM, Northwestern U., 1968. Bar: Mass. 1954, Ky. 1969, U.S. Dist. Ct. Ky. 1970, U.S. Dist. Ct. Mass. 1995, U.S. Ct. Appeals (6th cir.) 1970, Conn. 1988. With Gen. Electric Co., Fairfield, Conn., 1953-93, labor arbitration and litigation counsel, 1971-80, sr. labor and employment law counsel, 1980-93; ptnr., office chair, sr. counsel Paul, Hastings, Janolsky & Walker LLP, Stamford, Conn., 1993-99, sr. counsel, 1999—; mem. arbitration services adv. com. Fed Mediation and Conciliation Service, 1973—; adj. prof. U. Louisville, 1970-71, U. Bridgeport (Conn.) Sch. of Law, 1986-90; selectman Weston, 1997-00. Co-author, editor: Labor Arbitrator Development, 1983, A Practical Guide for Advocates, 1990; contbr. articles to profl. jours. Chmn. Weston (Conn.) Bd. Edn., 1977-82; trustee, vice chair exec. com., chmn. com. legal affairs Boston U., 1977—. Served with AUS, 1946-47. Mem. ABA (chmn. labor and employment law sect. com. labor arbitration advocacy, elected to governing council of labor and employment law sect. 1986—, chair 1996-97), Boston U. Sch. Law Alumni Assn. (Silver Shingle award 1982), Aspetuck Valley Country Club (Weston, pres. 1995-96). Home: 6 Aspetuck Hill Ln Weston CT 06883-2601 Office: Paul Hastings Janolsky & Walker LLP 1055 Washington Blvd Stamford CT 06901-2216

BARREDO, RITA M., auditor; b. Torrington, Conn., June 24, 1953; d. Avelino and Josephine (DiNoia) B. BA, U. Conn., 1975; BS, Post Coll., 1981; MS in Acctg., U. Hartford, 1984, MBA, 1990. CPA, Conn.; cert. info. sys. auditor, cert. internal auditor; cert. mgmt. acct.; diplomate Am. Bd. Forensic Accts., Am. Bd. Forensic Examiners. Timekeeper Timex Corp., Waterbury, Conn., 1976-85; auditor Def. Contract Audit Agy., Lowell, Mass., 1985—. Mem. AICPA, Am. Coll. Forensic Examiners, Am. Womens Soc. CPAs, Conn. Soc. CPA (continuing profl. edn. com. 1989-95, 97— social and recreation com. 1996-97), Inst. Mgmt. Accts. (sec. Waterbury chpt. 1994—), Inst. Internal Auditors, Info. Sys. Audit and Control Assn. Home: 130 Dawes Ave Torrington CT 06790-3627 Office: Def Contract Audit Agy 400 Main St East Hartford CT 06108-0968

BARREN, BRUCE WILLARD, merchant banker; b. Olean, N.Y., Jan. 28, 1942; s. James Lee and Marion Frances (Willard) B.; children: James Lee, Christina Roseanne. Student, The Hun Sch. of Princeton, 1959; BS, Babson Coll., 1962; MS, Bucknell U., 1963; grad. cert., Harvard U., 1967, Cambridge U., England, 1968. CPA, Pa., FCA, Eng. Sr. cons. Price Waterhouse, N.Y., 1963-67; v.p. Walston & Co., Inc., N.Y., 1967-70; sr. v.p. Delafield Childs, Inc., N.Y., 1970-71; chmn. The EMCO/Hanover Group Ltd., L.A., 1971—; sr. v.p. Goodway, Inc., 1972-73; pres. Park West Med. Group, Inc., 1980-81; CEO First Pacific Bank, 1984-85; exec. editor The Mgmt. Gazette, 1988-98; chmn., mem. exec. adv. com. Vitafort Internat. Corp., L.A., 1996-97; vice-chmn. Four Winds Enterprises Inc., San Diego 1985-87, F.W. Myers & Co., Rouses Point, N.Y., 1990-91; vice chmn., CEO Hydro-Mill Co., Chatsworth, Calif., 1996-98; bd. dirs. various U.S. and internat. cos., 1978-95; author, instr. CPA, CPE courses, Tex., Calif. and N.Y.; U.S. rep. Transatlantic Bio-scis. Fund, London, 1988-91; instr. loan documentation and valuation procedures Sanwa Bank, 1995-96; CEO, dir. Potomac Worldwide, 1998-2000; lectr. UCLA Exec. MBA Program, 1988—, U. S.C. Grad. Sch., Pepperdine Exec. MBA Program. Whittier Sch. Law, Chapman U. Sch. Law. Contbr. over 100 articles to profl. jours. including CFO, Contr. Alert, KPMG Banking Insider. Recipient Disting. Svc. awards Calif. State Senate and State Assembly, Office of the Gov., Office of State Treas., Counties of L.A. and Orange, Calif., San Diego, City of L.A., Congl. Tribute, U.S. Senate, 1986, 2000, U.S. Ho. of Reps., 1988, 89, Mayor L.A., 1987, 90-91, Office of U.S. V.p., 2000; named to Athletic Hall of Fame, HUN/Princeton, 1999. Mem. Am. Mgmt. Assn. (author, instr. 1991-92). Roman Catholic. Avocation: writing. Home: 12118 W Sunset Blvd Apt D Los Angeles CA 90049-4144 Office: The EMCO/Hanover Group Inc, Standbrook House 2-5 Old Bond St, London W1H 3TB, England

BARRENECHEA, RICARDO MIGUEL, civil engineer; b. Buenos Aires, Argentina, Aug. 23, 1961; s. Juan Carlos and Elena Luisa (Graziani) B.; m. Dinorah M. Carnielli Barrenechea, Nov. 28, 1987; children: Catalina, Tomas, Manuela, Felipe, Juana. MS in Civil Engring., U. Catolica, 1986; PhD in Telecommunications, 1990. Technical mgr. Sys. Para Ingenigria, Buenos Aires, Argentina, 1985—; cons. Portland Content Assn., Buenos Aires, Argentina, 1990-93. Contbr. articles to profl. jours. Avocations: computers, photography. Office: Sistemas Para Ingenieria, San Martin 1143, 1004 Buenos Aires Argentina

BARRERE, CLEM ADOLPH, business brokerage company executive; b. Bradford, Pa., Jan. 5, 1939; s. Clem A. and Ruth Eleanore (Brauner) B.; m. Jamie Elizabeth Newton, Aug. 30, 1969; 1 child, John Coleman Barrere. B Engring., Yale U., 1960; PhD in Chem. Engring., Rice U., 1965; postgrad., Emory U., 1975. Registered profl. engr., Tex., Okla.; bd. cert. broker; cert. bus. intermediary. Group leader rsch. dept. Conoco, Inc., Ponca City, Okla., 1965-69; dir. gas engring. Conoco, Inc., Houston, 1969-72, dir. gas ops., 1972-77, mgr. loss control, 1977-81; mgr. Dupont-Transp. Svc., Houston, 1981-87, Dupont-Safety and Environ., Houston, 1987-89; pres. Barrere & Co. Ventures, Houston, 1989—; dir. Barrere & Co. Realtors, Houston, 1978—. Contbr. articles to profl. jours.; 7 patents in field. Mem. Mus. Fine Arts, Houston, Zool. Soc., Houston, Mus. Natural Sci., Houston, 1970-96. Recipient Citations for Svc., Am. Petroleum Inst., 1988, Gas Processors Assn., 1989; NSF rsch. grantee, 1963-65. Fellow Internat. Bus. Brokers Assn. (dir. 1998—); mem. Tex. Bus. Brokers Assn., Houston Gas Processors Assn. (pres. 1981-82), Tex. Rolls-Royce Assn. (dir. 1987-96, Spl. award 1991), Houston Gun Collectors (pres. 1964), Houston Area Realtors, Petroleum Club, Lakeside Country Club, Phi Lambda Upsilon. Republican. Methodist. Avocations: car restorations, travel, sailing, genealogy. E-mail: clembarrer@aol.com. Office: Barrere & Co Ventures 5652 Doliver Dr Houston TX 77056-2322

BARRERE, JAMIE NEWTON, real estate executive; b. Russellville, Ark., June 7, 1946; d. James Edward Jr. and Martha (Spillers) Newton; m. Clement Adolph Barrere Jr., Aug. 30, 1969; 1 child, John Coleman. BA in Math., U. Ark., 1968; graduate, Realtor Inst., 1984. Cert. real estate brokerage mgr.; grad. Realtor Inst.; accredited relocation coord. Asst. programmer, analyst Conoco, Ponca City, Okla., 1968-69; programmer, analyst Bonner & Moore Assocs., Houston, 1969-70; tchr. math. Lamar Consol. H.S., Rosenberg, Tex., 1970-72; assoc. broker Betty James, Realtors, Houston, 1972-78; pres. Barrere & Co., Realtors, Houston, 1978-96, Barrere Relocation Svcs. affiliate Heritage Tex. Properties, Houston, 1996—; mem. adv. bd. Western Bank-Westheimer, Houston, 1986; mem. Employee Relocation Coun. Mem. Harris County Heritage Soc., Houston, 1970—, Houston Jr. Forum, 1980—, Am. Heart Assn. Guild, Houston Zool. Soc.; guild mem. Mus. Fine Arts, Houston, 1978—, Covenant House; trustee St. Luke's United Meth. Ch.; bd. dirs., children's dept. vol. bd. dirs. Moores Sch. Music Soc. U. Houston, 1992—; life mem. Tex. Real Estate Polit. Action Com.; former cub scout leader Boy Scouts Am. Mem. Nat. Assn. Realtors (mem. Equal Opportunity Com. 1985), Tex. Assn. Realtors (bd. dirs. 1989-98, mem. Multiple Listing Svc. com. 1985-90), Houston Assn. Realtors (bd. dirs. 1986-89, 93-95, v.p. 1993, mem. and chmn. various coms.), Houston C. of C. (amb. 1986), DAR, U. Ark. Alumnae Assn. (life, v.p. Houston chpt. 1985-88), RELO Internat. Relocation Network, Lakeside Country Club, Petroleum Club, Tanglewood Garden Club (bd. dirs. 1973-86, 93-95), Delta Delta Delta (past pres. Houston alumnea). Avocations: swimming, travel, music, geneology, historical preservation. Office: Barrere & Co 4295 San Felipe St Ste 300 Houston TX 77027-2915

BARRETO, BRUNO, film director and producer; b. Rio de Janeiro, Mar. 16, 1955; s. Luis Carlos and Lucy Barreto; m. Amy Irving; 1 son. Dir., prodr., writer: (films) Tati, A Garota, 1973, Dona Flor e Seus Dois Maridos, 1978, Amor bandido, 1979, O Beijo No Asfalto, 1981, Gabriela, 1983, Além Da Paixao, 1985, Romance de Empregada, 1987, A Show of Force, 1990, The Heart of Justice, 1992, Carried Away, 1996, O Que É Isso, Companheiro?, 1997, One Tough Cop, 1998, Bossa Nova, 1999. Office: Rua Visconde De Caravelas, 28 Bota Fogos, Rio de Janeiro Brazil also: 3000 Olympic Blvd Ste 2325 Santa Monica CA 90404-5073*

BARRETT, ANDREW WILLIAM, oral pathologist, educator; b. London, Jan. 22, 1961; s. Geoffrey William and Thelma Dorothy (Anderson) B.; m. Virginia Jane Kingsmill, Oct. 7, 1995. BDS, Royal Dental Hosp., London, 1984; MSc, London Hosp., 1987; PhD, U. Newcastle-Upon-Tyne, 1993. Lic. Gen. Dental Coun. House surgeon Guy's Dental Hosp., London, 1985, St. George's Hosp., London, 1985-86; demonstrator U. Newcastle-Upon-Tyne Dental Sch., 1987-91; registrar U. Bristol Dental Hosp., 1991-93; lectr. Eastman Dental Inst. for Oral Health Care Scis., U. London, 1993-98, sr. lectr., 1998—. Co-author: Lucas' Tumors of the Oral, 1998, Clinical Oral Sciences, 1998, Color Atlas of Oral Disease, 3d edit., 2000. Recipient awards Oral and Dental Rsch. Trust, 1990, Royal Coll. Surgeons Edinburgh, 1995, Wellcome, 1997. Fellow Royal Coll. Surgeons Edinburgh; mem. Royal Coll. Pathologists, Internat. Assn. Oral Pathologists, Brit. Assn. Oral and Maxillofacial Pathology (coun. mem. 1995-98), Brit. Soc. Oral Medicine, Brit. Soc. Dental Rsch. Avocations: cricket, real ale, writing. E-mail: A.Barrett@eastman.ucl.ac.uk. Home: 10 Portland Sq, London E1W 2QR, United Kingdom Office: Eastman Dental Inst, 256 Grays Inn Rd, London WC1X 8LD, England

BARRETT, CRAIG R., computer company executive; b. 1939. Assoc. prof. Stanford U., 1965-74; with Intel Corp., Chandler, Ariz., 1974—, v.p. components tech. and mfg. group, sr. v.p., gen. mgr. components tech. and mfg. group, exec. v.p., mgr. components tech., now pres., COO. Office: Intel Corp 5000 W Chandler Blvd Chandler AZ 85226-3699

BARRETT, DONALD STEELE, classicist, educator; b. Adelaide, Australia, Sept. 25, 1929; s. John Frederick and Kathleen (Steele) B.; m. Karen Fong, July 9, 1976; children: Jane, Clare. BA with honors, U. Queensland, Brisbane, Australia, 1950, MA, 1953; tchg. cert., Kelvin Grove Tchrs. Tng. Coll., Brisbane, 1950. Registered elem. and secondary sch. tchr., Queensland. Secondary sch. tchr. Dept. Edn., Brisbane, 1951-59; lectr. classics and ancient history U. Queensland, Brisbane, 1960-65, sr. lectr. classics and ancient history, 1966-72, reader in classics and ancient history, 1973-94, dean faculty arts, 1983-94, hon. rsch. cons. classics and ancient history, 1994—; part-time tchr. Latin Brisbane Grammar Sch., 1996—; coord. ancient history studies Brisbane campus U. New Eng., 2000—; mem. senate U. Queensland, 1990-94, mem. acad. bd. standing com., 1992-93; mem. coun. U. So. Queensland, Toowoomba, Australia, 1991-92. Author: Previews and Reruns, 1977, Greek and Roman Coins, 1982; co-author: Threshold of Time, 1977, A Map History of the Ancient World, 1985; contbr. over 65 articles to profl. jours. Inst. Classical Studies grantee U. London, 1966. Mem. U. Queensland Staff and Grads. Club, U. Queensland Acad. Staff Assn. (hon. life mem.; sec. 1972-94), Assn. for Tertiary Edn. Mgmt. (hon. mem.). Avocations: classical music, running, surfing, cooking, collecting reference books. Home: 3 Jenkinson St, Brisbane QLD 4068, Australia Office: Dept Classics Ancient History, U Queensland, Indooroopilly Brisbane QLD 4072, Australia

BARRETT, ELIZABETH ANN MANHART, nursing educator, psychotherapist, consultant; b. Hume, Ill., July 11, 1934; d. Francis J. and Grace C. (Manhart) Fridy; children: Joseph B., Jeffrey F., Paula G. Brown, Pamela M. Temple, Scott D. BSN summa cum laude, U. Evansville, 1970, MA, 1973, MSN, 1976; grad., Gestalt Assocs. Psychotherapy, 1982; PhD in Nursing, NYU, 1983; grad., Am. Inst. for Mental Imagery, 1995. From instr. to asst. prof. nursing U. Evansville, Ind., 1970-76; staff nurse Welborn Bapt. Hosp., Evansville, 1975-76, Bellevue Psychiat. Hosp., N.Y.C., 1976-79; clin. tchr. CUNY, 1977-82; asst. prof. Adelphi U., 1979-80; group practice Nurse Healers, 1979-82; pvt. practice psychotherapy, 1980—; nurse rschr. Mt. Sinai Med. Ctr., N.Y.C., 1982-86, asst. dir. nursing, 1983-86; assoc. prof. Hunter Coll., N.Y.C., 1986-89, prof., 1994—, dir. grad. studies, 1989-92, coord. Ctr. for Nursing Rsch., 1993—; cons. Internat. Soc. Univ. Nurses; cochair adv. com. Martha E. Rogers Ctr. for Study of Nursing Svc., 1994-96; com. mem. Regional Health Planning Coun., Evansville, 1974-77. Mem. editl. bd. Alt. Therapies in Health and Medicine, 1995—. Recipient Disting. Nursing Alumnus award NYU, 1994, Disting. Nurse Rschr. award Found. N.Y. State Nurses Assn., 1995. Fellow Am. Acad. Nursing; mem. ANA (cert. psychiat.-mental health), NOW, Nat. League Nursing, Ea. Nursing Rsch. Assn. (charter), Ea. Nursing Rsch. Soc., Soc. Rogerian Scholars (cofounder, 1st pres. 1988-90), Phi Kappa Phi, Sigma Theta Tau (Upsilon chpt. pres. 1986-88), Alpha Tau Delta, Sigma Xi. Home: 415 E 85th St Apt 9E New York NY 10028-6358 Office: Hunter Coll 425 E 25th St New York NY 10010-2547

BARRETT, JALMA See BOERSMA, JUNE ELAINE

BARRETT, JAMES EDWARD, JR., management consultant; b. Lowell, Mass., Dec. 9, 1929; s. James E. and Margaret A. (Holland) B.; m. Dorothy G. Walle; children: James Edward III, Dorothy Anne, william H., M. Stephen. BA, Harvard U., 1951; postgrad., Air Command and Staff Coll., 1953. Asst. prof. Harvard U., 1955-58; sys. analyst, mgr. Raytheon Co., 1958-62; mktg. mgr. Kepner-Tregoe, Inc., Princeton, N.J., 1963-65; mgr., dir. K-T Europe, 1966-67; pres. AAI, 1967-68, Cresheim Co., Inc., Phila., 1968—; chmn. Cresheim, Ltd. (U.K.), 1979-95, Cresheim do Brasil, Sao Paulo, 1980-99. bd. dirs. Swansea Press, Inc. 1986-95. Author: Managing Your Distributors; columnist Family Bus. mag., 1994—; contbr. numerous articles to profl. jours. Pres. Wyndmoor (Pa.) Cmty. Assn., 1977-79; dir. Alzheimer's Assn. Southeastern Pa., 1995—, v.p., 1996-99. Capt. USAF, 1951-55. Mem. Am. Assn. Small Rsch. Cos. (pres. Phila. chpt. 1977-80), Inst. Mgmt. Cons. (v.p. chpt. 1977-81, nat. dir. 1981-87, nat. v.p. 1983-86), Harvard Club (N.Y.C., Phila.), Adcesno Inst. (chmn. 1999). Home: 8315 Flourtown Ave Wyndmoor PA 19038-7924 Office: Cresheim Management Cons PO Box 27785 Philadelphia PA 19118-0785

BARRETT, JANINE LOUISE, veterinarian; b. Camden, N.S.W., Australia, Oct. 10, 1966; d. Stephen Hugh and Susan Marcelle (White) Scarlett; m. George Mark Brownlee, Oct. 11, 1997. B of Vet. Sci., U. Sydney, 1989; M of Vet. Sci., U. Queensland, Australia, 1998, postgrad., 1998—. Pvt. practice Sydney, 1990-92, London, 1993-94; vet. pathology intern U. Queensland, Australia, 1995-97. Mem. Australian Coll. Veterinary Scientists. Avocations: scuba diving, skiing. Office: The Univ Queensland, 4072 Brisbane Australia

BARRETT, JOHN CHARLES ALLANSON, minister; b. King's Lynn, Norfolk, Eng., June 8, 1943; s. Leonard W. A. and Marjorie J. (Hares) B.; m. Sally Elisabeth Hatley, Aug. 12, 1967; children: James, Rachel. BA in Econs. with honors, U. Newcastle Upon Tyne, Eng., 1965; BA in Theol. with honors, Fitzwilliam Coll., Cambridge, Eng., 1967, MA, 1969; DD, Fla. So., 1992. Ordained to ministry Meth. Ch., 1970. Chaplain, lectr. Westminster Coll., Oxford, Eng., 1968-69; asst. tutor Wesley Coll., Bristol, Eng., 1969-71; pastor Werrington Meth. Ch., Stoke on Trent, Eng., 1971-73; chaplain, head of religious studies Kingswood Sch., Bath, Eng., 1973-83; headmaster Kent Coll., Pembury, Eng., 1983-90; leadmaster The Leys Sch., Cambridge, Eng., 1990—; trustee Epworth Old Rectory, 1986—. Author: Family Worship, 1982, Methodist Education in Britian, 1989, co-author: A New Collection of Prayers, 1983, From Roots for Fulfillment, 2000; contbr. articles to profl. jours. Mem. World Meth. Coun. (exec. com. 1981—, sec. British com. 1986-97, chmn. edn. com. 1991—, chmn. Brit. com. 1999—), Rotary. Home and Office: The Leys Sch, Cambridge CB2 2AD, England

BARRETT, KATHERINE, writer, multimedia producer; b. N.Y.C., May 24, 1954; d. Herbert and Betty (Palash) B.; m. Richard H. Greene, Feb. 21, 1982; children: Benjamin, Sandra. BS in Journalism, Northwestern U., 1976. Reporter Comml. Appeal, Memphis, 1976-78; assoc. editor, sr. writer, sr. editor Ladies' Home Jour., N.Y.C., 1980-84, contbg. editor, 1984-98; freelance writer, columnist numerous publs., 1984—; prodr. Walt Disney Family Edn. Found., San Francisco, 1996—; spl. project editor Governing mag., Washington, 1997—; spkr. on state and city mgmt., 1992—; mem. adv. bd. Govtl. Acctg. Stds. Bd., Norwalk, Conn., 1996—, Urban Inst., Washington, 1996-99; curator Walt Disney Family Mus. web site. Author: The Man Behind the Magic, 1991, Frankly, My Dear, 1996; co-prodr. (CD-ROM) Walt Disney: An Intimate History, 1998; contbr. numerous articles to Redbook, Reader's Digest, Glamour, Ladies Home Jour., Fin. World, also others. Recipient award for excellence N.Y. Soc. CPA's, 1991, Children's

Choice award Internat. Reading Assn., 1992, Washington Monthly Journalism award, 1999.

BARRETT, MICHAEL JOHN, engineer; b. Eastbourne, Sussex, Eng., May 20, 1938; s. William George and Nellie Florence Barrett; m. Brenda Ann Barrett, July 16, 1972; children: Hilary, Rachel. Grad., Great Malvern, Nottingham. Chartered engr., Eng. Engr. Plessey Telecoms., Nottingham; design mgr. Assoc. Engring., Ltd., Rugby; prodn. mgr. GSiLumonics, Rugby, 1974-83, design office mgr., 1983-85, svc. mgr., 1985-94, stds. and compliance mgr., 1994—, safety officer, 1980—; U.K. expert on laser safety. Mem. Coun. Engring. Instns., Inst. Elec. Engrs., Inst. Quality Assurance. Avocations: breeder and exhibitor of world class Persian longhair cats. Home: Green Spinney, Gibbet Ln, Shawell Leicestershire LE17 6BT, England Office: GSiLumonics, Cosford Ln, Rugby CV21 1QN, England

BARRETT, PETER STEPHEN, management educator; b. London, Nov. 16, 1957; s. Edward George and Barbara Emily (Farrow) B.; m. Lucinda Clare Fowler, Nov. 22, 1980; children: Oliver, Camilla, Raphaella, Clementine. MS in Constrn. Mgmt., Brunel U., London, 1984; PhD, South Bank U., London, 1989. Surveyor King and Chasemore, Oxford, Eng., 1976-82, Buckell and Ballard, Oxford, 1982-84, Hunter and Ptnrs., London, 1984-85; sr. lectr. South Bank Poly., London, 1985-88; from lectr. to sr. lectr. Salford U., Manchester, Eng., 1988-92, prof., 1992—, chmn. dept. surveying, 1993-96, dir. rsch. ctr., 1993-99, dean faculty bus. and informatics, 1999—; mem. coun. Constrn. Rsch. and Innovation Strategy Panel, London, 1995-98. Author: Profitable Practice Management, 1992, Facilities Management, 1995, Better Construction Briefing, 1999; contbr. papers and articles to profl. jours. Fellow Royal Instn. Chartered Surveyors (profl. assoc., chmn. rsch. com. 1992-98, mem. gen. coun. 1990-95). Avocations: calligraphy, walking, badminton. Office: U Salford, Rsch Ctr Built/Human Envirn, Salford M5 4WT, England

BARRETT, ROBERT DAVID, engineering executive; b. Chgo., June 7, 1919; s. Julius and Lena Miriam (Lasky) B.; m. Phyllis Paul, July 22, 1945 (div.); children: Ira, Fred, Ellie, Judy, Jeff. BSME, Ill. Inst. Tech., 1941, MSME, 1944. Registered profl. engr., Ill. Design analyst Internat. Harvester, Chgo., 1941-46, design analysis engr., 1946-55; chief engr. chassis sect. Internat. Harvester, Hinsdale, Ill., 1955-60, chief engr. power train, 1960-63, chief engr. advanced engring., 1963-78; pres. Energy Efficiency Sys., Northlake, Ill., 1980—; v.p. Cmty. Mktg., Inc.; exec. v.p. engring. and fin. NEEDS Corp.; bd. dirs. Inventor's Choice. Contbr. articles to profl. publs. Mem. Dist. 209 H.S. Bd., 1971-77; mem. adv. coun. Ret. Sr. and Vol. Program, River Grove, Ill., 1983—; mem. coun. Suburban Area Agy. on Aging, Oak Park, Ill., 1994—; bd. dirs. Citizens for Med. Freedom. Charter mem. Inventure Place, Nat. Inventors Hall of Fame, Akron, Ohio. Mem. ASME, Soc. Automotive Engrs., Pi Tau Sigma, Tau Beta Pi. Achievements include 12 patents related to farm equipment, patent for clasp for aid to handicapped, patent on high performance extend range electrical cars, trucks and buses, patent on mower that can selectively cut weeds only or weeds and grass; research on a mechanical non-pharmaceutical, non-vacine test and cure for HIV and other viruses including the common cold. Avocations: gardening, carpentry, music, reading. Home: 401 W Lake St Northlake IL 60164-2401

BARRETT, ROBERT JAMES, III, investment banker; b. Bangor, Maine, July 23, 1944; s. Robert James and Catherine Pauline (Rogan) B.; m. Susan Hopkins Vander Poel, July 26, 1975 (div.); children: Robert James IV, Graham Halsted; m. Catherine M. Tankoos, Apr. 22, 1995. B.A. cum laude, Georgetown U., 1966; J.D., Columbia U., 1969; M.B.A. with honors, Harvard U., 1971. Bar: N.Y., 1969, Maine 1970. Assoc. Morgan Stanley, N.Y.C., 1971-76; sr. v.p. E.F. Hutton & Co. Inc., N.Y.C., 1976-83; dir. Prudential-Bache Securities, N.Y.C., 1983-90; ptnr. Barrett & Whitman., N.Y.C., 1991-92; sr. fin. cons. Merrill Lynch, 1992-95; pres. R.J. Barrett, Inc., 1998—. Trustee Husson Coll., Bangor, 1989-96, U. Maine, R.J. Barratt, Beatrix J. Farrand Fund, Landscape Hort. Mem. Bar Harbor Inst. (pres.), Union Club (N.Y.C.), Kebo Golf Club (Bar Harbor, Maine), Everglades Club (Palm Beach, Fla.), Phi Beta Kappa, Phi Alpha Theta. Republican. Roman Catholic. Avocations: tennis, squash, hunting, fishing, golf. Home: 340 Royal Poinciana Way Ste 341 Palm Beach FL 33480-4067

BARRETT, SCOTT ALEXANDER, environmental economics educator, consultant; b. Boston, Oct. 23, 1957; s. Bruce William and Nita (Frangoulis) B.; m. Gail Elaine Gunn, May 19, 1984; children: Jackson, Kira. BS summa cum laude, U. Mass., 1979; MA, U. B.C., Vancouver, Can., 1983; PhD, London Sch. Econs., 1989. Rsch. economist U.S. EPA, Washington, 1979; economist Data Resources, Inc., Lexington, Mass., 1980-82; sr. economist Nat. Econ. Rsch. Assocs., N.Y.C., 1983-85; rsch. dir. Ctr. Soc. and Econ. Rsch. on Global Environ., London, 1991—; assoc. prof. econs. London Bus. Sch., 1988-99; prof. environ. econs. and internat. polit. economy Johns Hopkins U., 1999—; cons. Internat. Union Conservation of Nature and Natural Resources, Gland, Switzerland, 1987-89, commn. of European communities, Brussels, 1991—, Orgn. Econ. Co-operation and Devel., Paris, 1990—, Washington, 1993—; lead author intergovtl. panel on climate change. Recipient dissertation prize Resources for the Future, Washington, 1990, Erik Kempe prize, 1996; overseas rsch. scholar London Sch. Econs., 1986-88; Am. Friends of the London Sch. Econs. scholar, 1985-86. Office: Johns Hopkins Univ Paul H Nitze Sch Adv Intern Studies/1619 Massachusetts Washington DC 20036

BARRETT, STANLEY, veterinarian; b. Murwillumbah, Australia, May 15, 1933; s. Sidney and Mary (Jackson) B.; m. Marjorie Hughes, May 11, 1959; children: Paul, Helen. BVSc, Liverpool (Eng.) U., 1957, MVSc, 1961. Rsch. asst. Liverpool Sch., 1957-60; lectr. dept. parasitology U. Queensland, 1960-63; asst. Dept. of Primary Industries, 1963-64; pvt. practice Brisbane, Australia, 1964-90; prin. pig farm, 1990-97. Mem. Rotary (internat. dir. 1964—). Mem. Ch. of Christ. Avocations: gardening, painting, reading. Home and office: 7 Hill St, Jimboomba Qld 4280, Australia

BARRICHELLO, RUBENS, race car driver; b. São Paulo, May 23, 1972; m. Silvana Barrichello. Race car driver Stewart GP, 1989—, Formula 1 (Ferrari), Brazil, 1999—. 5-time karting champion, Brazil, 1981-88; 6-time winner Lotus Euroseries, 1990, champion Brit. Formula 3, 1991, 3d pl. Formula 3000, 1992; named Best Amateur Driver of Yr., Brazilian Olympic Com., São Paulo City Best Driver, São Paulo Mcpl. Sec. of Sports; winner German Grand Prix at Houckenheimring, 2000. Office: Ferrari SpA, via Ascari 55-57, I-41053 Maranello Italy*

BARRIE, CHRISTOPHER ALEXANDER, military officer; b. Sydney, NSW, Australia, May 29, 1945; s. Alexander William and Dorothy Clare (Crystal) B.; m. Maxine Metaxia Cassidy, Jan. 26, 1992. BA, Deakin U., Australia, 1983, MBA, 1996. Advanced navigation course Royal Navy. Internat. fellow Nat. Def. U., Washington, 1986-87; force devel. planning staff hdqs. Australian Def. Force, 1987-89; def. attache New Delhi, India, 1989-91; comdg. officer HMAS Watson Royal Australian Navy, Australia, 1991-92, dep. maritime comdr. Australia, 1992-95, dep. chief naval staff, 1995-97; vice chief def. force Royal Australian Navy, 1997—, chief def. force, adm., 1998—. Decorated officer Order of Australia. Fellow Australian Inst. Mgmt.; mem. Australian Naval Inst. (pres. 1995-96), United Svcs. Inst. of ACT (dep. pres. 1996-98). Avocations: skiing, golf, opera, war gaming, piano. Office: Dept of Def, R1-5B-CDF Suite, 2600 Canberra ACT, Australia

BARRIE, THOMAS, architecture educator, architect, writer; b. Quincy, Mass., Apr. 10, 1955; s. Carl Ephramson and Eleanor Colwell B.; m. Lisa Grele, Nov. 7, 1987; children: Ian Harris, Simon Colwell. BA in English, U. N.C., 1978; MArch, Va. Poly. Inst. and State U., 1981; MPhil in Archtl. History-Theory, U. Manchester, Eng. Registered architect, Mass., Mich. Tchg. asst. Va. Poly. Inst. and State U., 1979-81; with Archtl. Resources Cambridge Inc., 1980, Huygens and DiMella Inc., Boston, 1981-83, Payette Assocs., Inc., Boston, 1983-87; owner Thomas Barrie Architects, Boston, 1987-90, Royal Oak, Mich., 1993—; vis. lectr. Manchester Met. U., Eng., 1990-91, U. Manchester, Eng., 1991-92; assoc. prof. Lawrence Tech. U., 1993—; coord. The Detroit Studio, Lawrence Tech. U., 1999—, co-coord. Jr. Yr. Integrated Design Studios, 1994—; adj. prof. Roger Williams U., 1987-90, 93; co-dir. Oasis Studio Inc., Boston, 1988-90, dir. lecture series, 1984-87; juror Syracuse U. Thesis Superjury, 1999; guest lectr. Wayne State U., 1997, U. Detroit Mercy, 1997; guest critic U. Man., Can., 1997, U. Ill. Urbana-Champaign, 1997, U. Ark., 1997, Manchester Met. U., U.K., 1994, 97, MIT, 1987-90, RISD, 1990, Wentworth Inst. Tech., 1990, Boston Archtl. Ctr., 1989-90; plenary spkr. U. Cin., 1997; presenter numerous conf. papers, lecture series. Author: Spiritual Path-Sacred Place: Myth, Ritual, and Meaning in Architecture, 1996, Community Visions of Royal Oak: Re-building the American Small City, 1997, The Orchard Lake Community Project: A Handbook for Community Input and Neighborhood Revitalization, 1998, numerous book reviews; founding editor Touchstone mag., 1984-86; pub. numerous newspaper and mag. articles. Mem. housing concerns com. Old South Ch., Boston, 1989-90. Rsch. fellow Lawrence Tech. U., 1999, vis. rsch. fellow U. Manchester, 1993; grantee Boston Found. for Architecture, 1987, Boston Arts Lottery Coun., 1988-89, 89, Lawrence Tech. U., 1994, City of Royal Oak, Mich., 1996, City of Pontiac, Mich., 1998, City of Hamtramck, Mich., 1999, Northern Area Assn., Detroit, 1999; recipient Merit award Vietnam Vets. Meml. Competition, 1981, City of Royal Oak, 1996, 1st prize Russel Hill Rogers Art Competition, 1981. Mem. AIA, NCARB (cert.), ACSA (dir. east ctrl. region 1998—, faculty councilor 1996-98, nominations com., pubs. com. architecture in society com., session co-chair, moderator annual meeting 2000), Downtown Royal Oak Assn., Greater Royal Oak C. of C. Home: 922 N Washington Ave Royal Oak MI 48067-1740 Office: 21000 W 10 Mile Rd Southfield MI 48075-1051

BARRINGER, J. MICHAEL, electrical engineer; b. Salisbury, N.C., Aug. 14, 1957; s. John Henry and Betty Jean Barringer; m. Susan Coley Barringer, Apr. 11, 1998; children: Ryan Wade Coley, Adam Chase Coley. BSEE, N.C. State U., 1980. Registered profl. engr., Md. Jr. engr. Duke Power Co., Winston-Salem, N.C., 1981-82; asst. dist. engr. Duke Power Co., Winston-Salem, 1982-84, supr. spl. projects, 1984-85, supr. dist. svcs., 1985-88, distbn. engr., 1988-90; distbn. designer Aide, Inc., Greenville, S.C., 1990-91; distbn. engr. So. Md. Electric Coop., Inc., Hughesville, Md., 1993-94; supr. distbn. engring. So. Md. Electric Coop., Inc., Hughesville, 1994—. Office: SMECO 15035 Burnt Store Rd Hughesville MD 20637

BARRINGTON-WARD, FRANCIS MILES, accountant; b. Oxford, U.K., July 9, 1956; s. Frank and Heather Beatrice (Warmington) B-W.; m. Deborah Johnson, Oct. 12, 1991; 1 child, Simon Alexander. BA, Oxford Polytech., 1980. Market rsch. assoc. DAf TRucks GB Ltd., Marlow, U.K., 1977-79; acct. Queensland United Food, Brisbane, Australia, 1981-82; group acct. Computeracc Pty. Ltd., Brisbane, 1982-84; mgmt. acct. Rsch. Machines Ltd., Oxford, 1986-87; group fin. controller Lowe & Oliver Ltd., Oxford, 1987-91; mgmt. cons. to internat. computer distbrs. and mfrs. Barrington-Ward Assocs., Oxford, 1991-97, Minerva Trading Ltd., Oxford, 1997—. Fellow Australian Soc. CPAs (assoc.). Avocations: sailing, swimming, skiing, reading, chess.

BARRIO, FRANCISCO JAVIER DELGADO, Spanish supreme court justice. Justice, pres. Supreme Ct. of Spain. Office: Trib Sup/Palacio Justice, Plaza de la villa de Paris, 28004 Madrid Spain*

BARRIO, JOSÉ MARÍA, philosophy educator, researcher; b. Madrid, July 13, 1960; s. Ricardo Barrio and Maria Luisa Maestre. Lic. philosophy, Complutense U. Madrid, 1984, DPhil, 1987. Tchr. ethics, philosophy secondary schs., Madrid, 1984-88; assoc. prof. ethics edn. Complutense U. Madrid, 1988-94, prof. philosophy, anthropology edn., 1994—; postdoctoral fellow rschr. U. Munster, Germany, 1991-92; vis. prof. U. Piura, Peru, 1996, U. La Sabana, Colombia, 1998. Author: Positivism and Violence, 1997, Value Education, 1997, Moral and Democracy, 1997, Elements of Pedagogical Anthropology, 1998, 2d edit., 2000, The Limits of Freedom, 1999; contbr. articles to profl. jours. Roman Catholic. Avocation: classical music (Bach). Office: U Complutense Dept Edn, Paseo de las Moreras S/N, 28040 Madrid Spain

BARRIOS, MARCELO BERNARDO, health and medical products executive; b. Buenos Aires, Oct. 31, 1968; s. Marcelo Fortunato Barrios and Elsa Marina Parajon. BA in Econs., U. del Salvador, Buenos Aires, 1991, prof. econs., 1992; MBA, Empresariales Inst. Studies, Buenos Aires, 1994; postgrad., U. Buenos Aires, 1995; PhD in Geography, U. del Salvador, Buenos Aires, 1998. Cons. Barrios Soc. Anonima, Buenos Aires, 1986-87; external cons. Solagamic S.A., Buenos Aires, 1987, jr. economist, 1987-89, sr. economist, 1989-91, dir., 1991-95, v.p., 1995—; ptnr. Farmacia San Carlos S.C.S., Buenos Aires, 1987-96, Magistral S.C.S., Buenos Aires, 1987-96, Belgrant S.C.C., Buenos Aires, 1987-96; adj. prof. U. del Salvador, 1992—; prof. Cath. U. Argentina, 1995—. co-author: La Argentina Contemporanea, 1995, Anales Asociacion Argentina de Economia Politica, 1995. Vis. faculty scholar Ind. U., Bloomington, 1994; vis. scholar Stanford (Calif.) U., 1995. Mem. Am. Econ. Assn., Western Econ. Assn. Internat., Fedn. Argentina Consejo Profls. de Ciencias Econs. (rschr.). Avocations: diving, fishing, sailing. Office: Solagamic SA, Moreno 900, 1091 Buenos Aires Argentina

BARRISKILL, MAUDANNE KIDD, primary school educator; b. Balt., Apr. 2, 1932; d. John Graydon and Maudine (Adams) Kidd; m. Peter Herbert Barriskill, Nov. 30, 1957; children: John, Michael. BA, So. Meth. U., 1954; student early childhood edn., Old Dominion U., 1970; student, Katharine Gibbs Sch., N.Y.C., 1954-55, Juilliard Sch. Music, N.Y.C., 1948-50. Exec. sec., copywriter trainee J. Walter Thompson Advt. Agy., N.Y.C., 1955-59; founder Maude Barry Interior Design, Virginia Beach, 1970-73; founder, dir. The Home Sch., Virginia Beach, 1975—; tchr. Ea. Shore Chapel Presch., Virginia Beach, 1970-75, Montessori Child Devel. Ctr., Virginia Beach. Author children's books and workbooks. Tchr. Sunday sch. Home: 4721 Newgate Ct Virginia Beach VA 23455-4033

BARRITT, KEITH ASHLEY, lawyer; b. Cedar Rapids, Iowa, Apr. 7, 1961; s. Paul Franklin and Joyce Anita (Hill) B.; m. Margarita Cuadra, Aug. 15, 1987; children: Alexander Ashley, David Franklin. BA with distinction, U. Va., 1983, JD, 1989. Bar: Va. 1989, D.C. 1991. Legis. aide to Congress John P. Murtha, U.S. Ho. of Reps., Washington, 1983-86; atty. Mintz, Levin, Cohn, Ferris, Glovsky & Popeo, Washington, 1989-93, Fish & Richardson, Washington, 1993—. Contbr. articles to law jours., including Intellectual Property Today, Legal Times, Nat. Law Jour., Radio Comm. Report. Sec. Collingwood-on-Potomac Citizens Assn., Alexandria, Va., 1999, pres., 2000—. Mem. Internat. Trademark Assn. E-mail: barritt@fr.com. Office: Fish & Richardson 601 13th St NW Ste 901S Washington DC 20005-3824

BARRON, JEFFREY LAWRENCE, chemist, consultant, educator; b. Cape Town, South Africa, Aug. 2, 1942; arrived in Eng., 1985; s. Aubrey and Avis (Harris) B.; m. Janet Neicia Phillips, Dec. 6, 1970; children; Jonathan, Lisa, Ann. BSc, Rhodes (South Africa) U., 1963; MSc, Stellenbosch (South Africa) U., 1965; MB, BChir, Cape Town U., 1973, M in Medicine, 1978. Cert. chem. pathology. Sr. lectr. U. Cape Town; cons. chem. pathologist St. Helier Hosp., U.K.; hon. sr. lectr. St. Georges Hosp. Med. Sch., U.K.; dir. South West Thames Regional Infant Screening; chmn. South Thames Specialist Tng. Com. for Chem. Pathology, 1997—. Contbr. articles to profl. jours. Fellow Royal Coll. Pathologists; mem. Assn. Clin. Pathologists (so. br. chmn. 1998—), Brit. Med. Assn. (br. chmn. 1998—). Office: Dept Chem Path & Metabolism, St Helier Hosp, Carshalton SM5 1AA, United Kingdom

BARRON, PAUL DOUGLAS, film producer; b. Toronto, Dec. 26, 1949; arrived in Australia, 1972; s. Alex E. and Nina M. (Burrows) B.; m. Marina Medigovich, Nov. 3, 1984; children: Aleksia Helen, Nikolas Stefan, Kristian James, Valentina Marina. BA with honors, Queens U., Ont., 1972. Community arts officer Fed. Pub. Service, Canberra, Australian Capital Territories, 1973-75; dir. Frevideo, Fremantle, Western Australia, 1975-76, Film and TV Inst. of Western Australia, Fremantle, 1976-81; mng. dir. Barron Entertainment Ltd., Perth, Western Australia, 1981—. Producer: (feature films) Shame, Windrider, Bush Christmas, Father, Fran, blackfellas; (mini-series) A Waltz Through the Hills; (documentary) First Impressions; (telefeatures) Tudawali, Natural Justice, Singapore Sling; exec. prodr. (features) I Own the Racecourse, Father; (documentaries) Long Time No See, Ronnie, River of Giants, Anyone Can Be a Genius, Reflections of Myself; (TV series) Tracks of Glory, Clowing Around, Clowing Around II, Ship to Shore, Ship to Shore II, Ship to Shore III, Kicking Around, Haydaze, A Waltz Through the Hills, The Gift, Fast Tracks I, Fast Tracks II, Driven Crazy, Chuck Finn, Tiger, Tiger; co-producer, exec. producer: (feature) Bush Christmas; producer, exec. producer: (TV series) Kicking Around, Haydaze; co-exec. prodr. (TV series) Misery Guys. Mem. Screen Producers Assn. Australia. Office: Barron Entertainment Ltd, 45 York St, Subiaco 6008, Australia

BARRON, PEGGY PENNISI, management consultant; b. Chgo., Jan. 27, 1958; d. Louis Legendre and Jane Harriet (Peters) Pennisi; m. Stan Barron, May 3, 1986; children: Brian Alexander, Christine Deanna. BS with honors, U. Ill., Chgo., 1979. Data processing mgr. Oasis Aviation, Inc., L.A., 1980-87; pres. Millennium Enterprises, L.A., Calif., 1987—. Author: Broken Bloodlines, 1997, The Big Daddy, 1999. Mem. NAFE, Phi Beta Kappa, Phi Kappa Phi. Avocations: scuba diving, sky diving, cooking and travel.

BARRON, SUSAN, clinical psychologist; b. Chgo., May 13, 1940; d. Earl and Trixie (Chernoff) B.; m. Eugene Pratt, Jan. 18, 1975 (div. 1983). BBA, CCNY, 1960, MA, 1963; PhD, CUNY, 1973. Lic. psychologist; diplomate Am. Bd. Psychol. Specialties; cert. alcohol and related substance abuse APA Coll. Profl. Psychology. Intern psychologist Bellevue Psychiat. Hosp., N.Y.C., 1964-65, psychologist, 1966-67; thcg. fellow CUNY, 1965-66; staff psychologist Lighthouse, N.Y. Assn. for the Blind, N.Y.C., 1968-71, sr. clin. psychologist, 1971-74; dir. psychol. counseling svcs. Peninsula Ctr. for the Blind, Palo Alto, Calif., 1974-75; cons. psychologist N.Y. State Commn. for Blind and Visually Handicapped, N.Y.C., 1975-78, 86—; dir. psychol. svcs. Thoms Rehab. Hosp., Asheville, N.C., 1978-79; state coord. psychol. svcs. N.Y. State Office Vocat. Rehab., Albany, 1979-85; founder, dir. Family Support Program ICU N.Y. Infirmary-Beekman Downtown Hosp., N.Y.C., 1982-84; cons. clin. psychologist N.Y. Hosp. Cornell U. Med. Ctr., 1987—; pvt. practice, 1987—; behavioral scientist diabetes control/complications trial NIH Cornell U. Med. Ctr., N.Y.C., 1987—; cons. clin. psychologist Joslin Ctr. for Diabetes St. Luke's-Roosevelt Hosp. Ctr./Columbia U. Phys. and Surg., N.Y.C., 1994-95; cons. clin. psychologist Joslin Ctr. Diabetes, St. Lukes-Roosevelt Hosp. Ctr., U. Hosp. of Columbia U. Coll. of Physicians and Surgeons, N.Y.C., 1994-95, Health Psychology Assocs., Calif., 1997—, N.Y.C., 1997—; mem. Nat. Human Svcs. Adv. Bd.-Retinitis Pigmentosa Found., Balt., 1975-82; cons. Del. State Commn. for Blind, 1975-78, Am. Found. Blind, 1974-82, Calif. Dept. Rehab., 1974-82, Hawaii State Svcs. Blind, 1974-82, Ariz. State Svcs. Blind, 1974-82, Nev. State Svcs. Blind, 1974-82; spkr. Nat. Multiple Disabilities Conf., 1982, NAS, 1981; mem. adv. bd. doctoral psychology internship program Rusk Inst. of Rehab. Medicine, NYU Med. Ctr., 1979-84; behavioral scientist Diabetes Control and Complications Trial NIH-Cornell U. Med. Ctr., 1987—; mem. mended hearts NYU Med. Ctr., Cardiac Prevention and Rehab. Ctr. Contbr. articles to profl. jours. Recipient Leadership award Alumni Assn. CCNY, 1960, 62, Rsch. award Retinal Dystrophy Soc., Australia, 1975, Charles H. Best medal for disting. svc. Am. Diabetes Assn., 1994. Fellow Am. Coll. Advanced Practice Psychologists (bd. cert.), Am. Orthopsychiat. Assn. (life); mem. APA, AAAS, Am. Coll. Forensic Examiners, Calif. State Psychol. Assn., N.Y. Acad. Scis., Mended Hearts. Office: 347 5th Ave Rm 603 New York NY 10016-5010

BARRON, THOMAS HUGH KENNETH, retired physics educator; b. Kew, Surrey, Eng., July 27, 1926; s. Thomas Bertram and Florence Nightingale (Kingston) B.; m. Gillian Mary Sherrard, July 11, 1956; children: Thomas Keith, William Hugh, James Richard, Ruth Margaret. Student, Epsom Coll., Surrey, 1939-44; MA, D. Philosophy, Oxford U., Eng., 1955. Postdoctoral fellow Nat. Rsch. Coun. Can., Ottawa, Ont., 1955-57, asst. rsch. officer, 1957-58; lectr. chemistry U. Bristol (Eng.), 1958-68, reader in theoretical chemistry, 1968-77, head honours sch. chem. physics, 1976-88, reader in chem. physics, 1977-91; prin. rsch. officer Commonwealth Scientific and Indsl. Rsch. Orgn., Sydney, Australia, 1975-76. Co-author: (with G.K. White) Heat Capacity and Thermal Expansion at Low Temperatures, 1999; contbr. articles to profl. jours. With Brit. Royal Navy, 1944-47. Mem. Inst. of Physics; mem. Am. Phys. Soc. Anglican. Avocations: reading, walking, music. Office: U Bristol Sch Chemistry, Cantock's Close, Bristol BS8 1TS, England

BARROS, RICARDO CARVALHO, nuclear engineering educator; b. Rio de Janeiro, Apr. 23, 1957; s. Alipio Firmo and Delma (Carvalho) B. BS in Physics, U. Estado Rio de Janeiro, 1981, MSc in Nuclear Engring., 1985; MSc in Math., U. Mich., 1989, PhD in Nuclear Engring., 1990. Assoc. prof. COPPE U. Fed. U. Rio de Janeiro, 1991, full prof. nuclear engring. Inst. Politech., 1994—, rsch. group leader, 1997—; assoc. rschr. IEN/CNEN, Rio de Janeiro, 1991. Contbr. articles to profl. jours. Mem. Am. Nuclear Soc. (math and computation divsn.), Brazilian Assn. Nuclear Engring. Avocation: accordion. Office: Inst Polit/UERJ, Rua Alberto Rangel S/N, 28601970 Nova Friburgo Brazil

BARROW, LOGIE, history educator; b. London, May 10, 1945; arrived in Germany, 1980; s. Derek Waller and Nina Thornber (Bradley) B.; m. Barbara Ilse Brandt Dabrowski, June 23, 1990. BA in History, U. Cambridge, Eng., 1966; PhD in History, U. London, 1975. Lectr. liberal studies Poly., Kingston, Thames, Eng., 1967-77; lectr. English studies U. East Anglia, Norwich, Eng., 1977-80; prof. U. Bremen, Germany, 1980—. Author: Independent Spirits: Spiritualism and British Plebeians, 1986; joint author: (with Ian Bullock) Democracy and the British Labour Movement 1880-1914, 1996. Avocations: European and Indian classical music, mountain and cliff walking. Office: U Bremen, 28359 Bremen Germany

BARROW, PAUL CHRISTOPHER, toxicologist; b. Melton Mowbray, Leics, Eng., Jan. 20, 1959; arrived in France, 1989; s. Paul Anthony and Julie (Dobson) B.; m. Monique Chan Kwong, Dec. 4, 1983; children: Vanessa, Jade. BSc with honors, N.E. London Polytech., Eng., 1983. Registered toxicologist, Europe. Rsch. technician U. Nottingham, Eng., 1977-80; sci. officer Beecham Pharms., Harlow, Eng., 1980-84; study dir. Life Sci. Rsch., Rome, Italy, 1986-89, Hazleton France, Lyon, 1989-91; dept. head Pharmakon Europe, Lyon, France, 1991-95; dir. Chrysalis, Lyon, 1996—; lectr. faculty of pharmacy U. Lyon, 1990—, Vet. Sch. Toulouse, France, 1991—, U. Paris, S., 1994—, Conservatoire Nat. A.M., Lyon, 1996—, Med. Sch. Lyon, 1997—; presenter in field. Author: Technical Procedures in Reproductive Toxicology, 1990. Mem. Inst. Biology (chartered biologist), Am. Teratology Soc., European Teratology Soc. Avocation: mountain cycling. Office: Phoenix, Les Oncins BP 118, 69593 L'Arbresle Cedex, France

BARROW, THOMAS DAVIES, oil and mining company executive; b. San Antonio, Dec. 27, 1924; s. Leonidas Theodore and Laura Editha (Thomson) B.; m. Janice Meredith Hood, Sept. 16, 1950; children: Theodore Hood, Kenneth Thomson, Barbara Loyd, Elizabeth Ann. BS, U. Tex., 1945, MA, 1948; PhD, Stanford U., 1953; grad. advanced mgmt. program, Harvard U., 1963. With Humble Oil & Refining Co., 1951-72; regional exploration mgr. Humble Oil & Refining Co., New Orleans, 1962-64, sr. v.p., 1967-70, pres., 1970-72, also bd. dirs.; exec. v.p. Esso Exploration, Inc., 1964-65; sr. v.p. Exxon Corp., N.Y.C., 1972-78; chmn., CEO Kennecott Corp., Stamford, Conn., 1978-81; vice chmn. Standard Oil Co., 1981-85; investment cons. Houston, 1985-89; chmn. GX Tech., Houston, 1990—; pres. Thomson-Barrow, 1989—; sr. chmn., bd. dir. GeoQuest Internat. Holdings, Inc., Houston, 1990-97; pres. Tecolotita, Inc., 1991—, T-BAR-X, Houston, 1995—; chmn. bd. dirs. GPS Tech. Corp., Houston, 1986-98, Tobin Internat., 1998—; mem. commn. on natural resources NRC, 1973-78, commn. on phys. sci., math. and natural resources, 1984-87, bd. on earth scis., 1982-84; trustee Woods Hole Oceanographic Instn., 20th Century Fund-Task Force on U.S. Energy Policy; chmn. bd. dirs. Petroleum Info./Dwights, 1994-97. Pres. Houston Grand Opera, 1985-87, chmn., 1987-91; trustee Am. Mus. Natural History, 1972-82, Stanford U., 1980-90, Tex. Med. Ctr., 1983—, Geol. Soc. Am. Found., 1982-87; trustee Baylor Coll. Medicine, 1984—, vice chmn bd. trustees, 1991-99. Served to ensign USNR, 1943-46. Recipient Disting. Achievement award Offshore Tech. Conf., 1973, Disting. Engring. Grad. award U. Tex., 1970, Disting. Alumnus, 1982, Disting. Geology Grad., 1985, Disting. Natural Sci. Grad., 1990; named Chief Exec. of Yr. in Mining Industry, Fin. World, 1979. Fellow N.Y. Acad. Scis.; mem. Nat. Acad. Engring., Am. Mining Congress (bd. dirs. 1979-85, vice chmn. 1983-85), Am. Assn. Petroleum Geologists, Geol. Soc. Am., Internat. Copper Research Assn. (bd. dirs. 1979-85), Nat. Ocean Industry Assn. (bd. dirs. 1982-85), AAAS, Am. Soc. Oceanography (pres. 1970-71), Am. Geophys. Union, Am. Petroleum Inst., Am. Geog. Soc., Houston Country Club, The Hills Club, Petroleum Club, River Oaks Country Club, Houston

Club, Sigma Xi, Tau Beta Pi, Sigma Gamma Epsilon, Phi Eta Sigma, Alpha Tau Omega. Episcopalian. Office: 5847 San Felipe St Ste 3830 Houston TX 77057-3008

BARRY, ALIOU HAMADY, chemist, researcher; b. Tethiane, Kaedi, Mauritania, May 4, 1964; arrived in Tunisia, 1990; s. Abdoul Bocar and Aissé (Mbodeiry) B.; m. Djeinaba Samba, Aug. 21, 1992; 1 child, Fatimeta Aliou. Student, U. Nouakchott, Mauritania, 1987-90; PhD, U. Tunis II, 1996. Vis. prof. chemistry U. Nouakchott, Mauritania, 1997—; tchr. U. Dakar, Senegal, 1998—. Contbr. articles to profl. jours. Jour. Solid State Chemistry and Acta Crystallographica, Zeitschrift für anorgannische und allgemeine chemie. E-mail: barry@univ nkc.mr. Office: U Nouakchott Fac Scis/Tech, BP 5026, Nouakchott Mauritania

BARRY, BERNARD ANTHONY, management consultant; b. Cardiff, Wales, Dec. 19, 1935; s. Gerald and Eileen Mary (Thompson) B.; m. Angela Margaret McGlade. Diploma in Social Scis., Univ. Coll., Swansea, 1958; MS, Univ. Coll., Cardiff, 1965; PhD in Social Scis., Loughborough U. of Tech., 1972. Chartered psychologist; assoc. fellow Brit. Psychol. Soc. Rsch. officer Ashridge Mgmt. Coll., 1965-68, asst. dir. of rsch., 1968-70, dir. of rsch., 1970-81; prof. bus. admintrn., dir. advanced mgmt. education U. Melbourne, 1981-84; prof. orgn. behaviour Cranfield Sch. mgmt., 1984-89; computations prof. of mgmt. Monash U., Melbourne, 1989—, dir. Grad. Sch. Mgmt., 1990-94, chmn. dept. mgmt., 1992-95; bd. dirs. Yarra Internat., 1995—. Mem. Soc. Sr. Execs. (nat. pres. 1991-95), Chartered Inst. Pers. and Devel. (companion). Office: Faculty of Bus and Econs, Monash Univ, 3168 Melbourne Australia

BARRY, BRIAN WILLIAM, pharmaceutical technology educator; b. Liverpool, U.K., Apr. 20, 1939; s. William and Jean (Manson) B.; m. Betty Boothby, Mar. 26, 1966; 1 child, Simon. BSc, U. Manchester, Eng., 1960; DSc, U. Manchester, 1981; PhD, U. London, 1967. Cmty. and indsl. pharmacist Boots the Chemist, U.K., 1960-62; asst. lectr. U. London, 1962-66, lectr., 1966-67; sr. lectr. pharm. tech. U. Portsmouth, U.K., 1967-70; reader in pharmacy U. Portsmouth, 1970-77; prof. pharm. tech. U. Bradford, U.K., 1977—; dean natural and applied scis. U. Bradford, 1991-94; vis. scientist Syntex Rsch., Palo Alto, Calif., 1974. Author: Dermatological Formulations: Percutaneous Absorption, 1983; contbr. articles to profl. jours. Fellow Royal Pharm. Soc. Gt. Britain (Brit. Pharm. Conf. Sci. award 1973), Royal Soc. Chemistry, Am. Assn. Pharm. Scientists; mem. Royal Inst. Chemistry (assoc.), Pharm. Soc. Avocations: fell walking, reading, computers. Office: Univ Bradford, Sch Pharmacy, Bradford BD7 1DP, United Kingdom

BARRY, HERBERT, III, psychologist; b. N.Y.C., June 2, 1930; s. Herbert and Lucy Manning (Brown) B. BA, Harvard U., 1952; MS, Yale U., 1953, PhD, 1957. USPHS-NIMH rsch. fellow Yale U., 1957-59, asst. prof. psychology, 1960-61; asst. prof. psychology U. Conn., Storrs, 1961-63; rsch. assoc. prof. pharmacology U. Pitts. Sch. Pharmacy, 1963-70, prof., 1970-87; prof. pharmacology and physiology U. Pitts. Sch. Dental Medicine, 1987-94; prof. pharm. scis. U. Pitts. Sch. Pharmacy, 1995—; mem. alcohol rsch. rev. com. Nat. Inst. Alcohol Abuse and Alcoholism, 1972-76; mem. soci-obehavioral subcom. AIDS rsch. rev. com. Nat. Inst. Drug Abuse, 1988-89. Author: (with H. Wallgren) Actions of Alcohol, 1970, (with A. Schlegel) Adolescence; An Anthropological Inquiry, 1991; field editor Psychopharmacology, 1974-91; contbr. articles to profl. jours. Mem. Allegheny County Dem. Com., 1984—; bd. dirs. Schalkenbach Found., 1997—; trustee Ctr. for the Study of Econs., 1988—. Recipient NIMH Research Scientist Devel. award, 1967-77. Fellow AAAS, Am. Psychol. Assn. (coun. reps. 1975-76, pres. divsn. psychopharmacology 1980-81), Am. Assn. Pharm. Scientists; mem. Am. Soc. Pharm. Exptl. Therapeutics, Psychonomic Soc., Am. Coll. Neuropsychopharmacology, Phi Beta Kappa, Sigma Xi. Unitarian Universalist. Home: 552 N Neville St Apt 83 Pittsburgh PA 15213-2830 Office: U Pitts 512 Salk Hall Pittsburgh PA 15261-1905

BARRY, JAMES ALBERT, JR., financial planner; b. Arlington, Mass., Sept. 27, 1935; s. James Albert and Irene Madlin Barry; m. Rosemarie Barry, Dec. 5, 1954; children: Rose Barry Wood, Irene Barry Leicht, James M. Assoc., U.S. Armed Forces Inst., 1956; student, Bentley Coll., 1957-59; BBA, Burdett Coll., 1960; CFP, Coll. Fin. Planning, 1974. Sr. v.p. Putnam Mgmt. Group, Boston, 1968-75; chmn. bd. dirs. Barry Fin. Group, Boca Raton, Fla., 1975—. Host TV programs (Fox and America One TV) Talk About Money, 1986—, (PBS) Jim Barry's Fin. Success, 1983—; author: Financial Freedom: A Positive Strategy for Putting Your Money to Work, 1982, 2d edit., 1993; contbr. articles to profl. jours.; interviewed for various publs., TV programs. Trustee Coll. for Fin. Planning, Denver, 1975-78; mem. Fla. Atlantic U. Found., Boca Raton, 1979, sen. adv. for CFP curriculum, 1984-85; mem. Greater Boca Raton Estate Planning Coun., 1989—; bd. dirs. Highland Beach (Fla.) Libr. Found., 1996—; mem. exec. adv. bd. Am. Heart Assn., Ft. Lauderdale, Fla., 1997—; ptnr. level mem. Garnet Soc./WXEL Pub. TV, Boynton Teach, Fla., 1997—; creative svcs. coord. Zachariah Family Heart Run, Ft. Lauderdale, 1998—; mem. Boca Raton Hist. Soc., 1996—; corp. ptnr. mem. Kravis Ctr. for Performing Arts, West Palm Beach, Fla., 1997—; Fla. State fin. vice chmn. Bob Dole Presdl. Campaign, Ft. Lauderdale, 1995-96; disting. mem. Nat. Rep. Senatorial Com., Ft. Lauderdale, 1989, Rep. Senatorial Inner Cir., Ft. Lauderdale, 1989. Sgt. U.S. Army, 1953-56. Mem. Fin. Planning Assn., Nat. Assn. Life Underwriters, Million Dollar Round Table. Office: Barry Fin Group 40 SE 5th St Ste 600 Boca Raton FL 33432-5507

BARRY, JAMES P(OTVIN), writer, editor; b. Alton, Ill., Oct. 23, 1918; s. Paul Augustine and Elder (Potvin) B.; m. Anne Elizabeth Jackson, Apr. 16, 1966. BA cum laude, Ohio State U., 1940. Commd. 2d. lt. Arty. U.S. Army, 1940, advanced through grades to col., served ETO, 1944-46; adviser to Turkish Army, 1951-53; detailed Army Gen. Staff, Washington, 1953-56; ret., 1966; adminstr. Capital U., Columbus, Ohio, 1967-71; freelance writer, editor Columbus, 1971-77; dir. Ohioana Library Assn., 1977-88; editor Ohioana Quar., 1977-88; sr. editor Inland Seas, 1984—; photographer, documentary and book illustrator, 1968—. Author: Georgian Bay: The Sixth Great Lake, 1968, 3rd edit., 1995, The Battle of Lake Erie, 1970, Bloody Kansas, 1972, The Noble Experiment, 1972, The Fate of the Lakes, 1972, The Louisiana Purchase, 1973, Henry Ford and Mass Production, 1973, Ships of the Great Lakes, 1973 (Dolphin Book Club selection), Ships of the Great Lakes, rev. edit., 1996, The Berlin Olympics, 1975, The Great Lakes: A First Book, 1976, Wrecks and Rescues of the Great Lakes, 1981 (Dolphin Book Club selection), Georgian Bay: An Illustrated History, 1992, Old Forts of the Great Lakes, 1994, also booklet on Lake Erie for Ohio EPA, 1980; contbr. articles to mags. and jours.; over 300 photographs accepted for permanent collection Inst. Gt. Lakes Rsch. Recipient award Am. Soc. State and Local History, 1974, Nonfiction History award Soc. Midland Authors, 1982; named Gt. Lakes Historian of Yr., Marine Hist. Soc. Detroit, 1995. Mem. Internat. Assn. Gt. Lakes Rsch., Assn. Gt. Lakes Maritime History, Can. Nautical Rsch. Soc., Gt. Lakes Hist. Soc., Marine Hist. Soc., Ohio Hist. Soc., World Ship Soc., Royal Can. Yacht Club, Columbus Country Club, Capital Club, Phi Beta Kappa. Home: 353 Fairway Blvd Columbus OH 43213-2507

BARRY, JERARD MICHAEL, principal research scientist, educator; b. Sydney, Australia, Aug. 24, 1942; s. James and Alma Beatrice (Hunt) B.; m. Enda Jacqueline Barry; children: Tara Dale, Clodagh Jacqueline. BSc, U. NSW, 1966, BA, 1982; MSc, Sydney U., 1975; PhD, Wollongong U., 1982. Tchr. NSW Dept. Edn., 1962-66; rsch. scientist Australian Nuclear Sci. and Tech. Orgn., Sydney, 1967-72; sr. rsch. scientist Australian AEC, Sydney, 1975-84, prin. rsch. scientist, 1984—; vis. prof. U. Tenn., Knoxville, 1986; vis. scientist Oak Ridge Nat. Lab., Tenn., 1986. Author monograph Introduction to Pascal, 1984; contbr. nuclear sci. and engring. articles to profl. jours. Organizer, lectr. Summer Sch. on Sci. for high sch. students, Sydney, 1972-82; dir. 2d Australian Supercomputer Conf.; dir. St. John Bosco Wind Ensemble, Engadine. Mem. Soc. Indsl. and Applied Math., Australian Math. Soc. (chmn. com. computational math. group 1990-91), Lucas Height Sci. Soc. (treas. 1978-81, Sci. medal 1983), NATO Advanced Study Inst. Signal Processing-Linear Algebra and Parallel Algorithms. Roman Catholic. Avocations: music, walking. Home: 7 Geelong Rd, Engadine New South Wales 2233, Australia Office: Australian Nuclear Sci & Tech, Orgn Pvt Mail Bag 1, Menai New South Wales 2234, Australia

BARRY, MICHAEL JAMES, ecotoxicologist, educator; b. Melbourne, Australia, Feb. 19, 1958; s. James Hardman and Edith Elizabeth (Fletcher) B. BS with honors, Monash U., Melbourne, Australia, 1981, PhD, 1991. Rsch. asst. dept. zoology Hebrew U. Jerusalem, Israel, 1984-85; rsch. fellow Key Ctr. for Applied and Nutritional Toxicology RMIT/U. Melbourne, 1992-97; vis. scientist Max Planck Inst. Limnology, Ploen, Germany, 1998; sr. rsch. fellow Sch. Life Sci. & Technology Victoria U., 1998—. Contbr. articles to Ecotoxicology and Environ. Safety, Australasian Jour. Ecotoxicology, Aquatic Toxicology, Freshwater Biology. Advocate, So. Citizen Advocacy, Melbourne, 1992—; vol. recreation worker Spastic Soc. Victoria, Melbourne, 1987-92; vol. visitor Do Care, Melbourne, 1987-92. Mem. Australasian Soc. Ecotoxicology, Australian Soc. for Limnology. Avocations: traditional yoga, painting. Office: Sch Life Scis Tech Victria U, St Albans Campus Po Box 14428, 8001 Melbourne Australia

BARRY, PAULA JEAN, artist; b. Elmhurst, Ill., June 20, 1962; d. Jon David and Grace Elizabeth (Bergendorff) Schneider; m. Daniel James Barry, July 18, 1980; children: Dustin Michael, Eric Jon, Danielle Marie. Basic Art Certificate, Art Instrn. Schs., 1993. Works published in Illustrator mag., 1994, The Drawing Board, 1995; art piece displayed, Mpls., 1993. Tchr. Hearts at Home home sch., Manteca, Calif., 1991-93; contbr. Moore Found. home sch., 1991—. Mem. Smithsonian Inst. (assoc.), 700 Club. Avocations: working with leather, jewelry making, horseback riding, studying philosophy, singing.

BARRY, QUINTIN, solicitor; b. Worthing, Sussex, Eng., Mar. 7, 1936; s. Garrett Wright and Elizabeth (Ash) B.; m. Anne Willcox, 1959 (div. 1974); children: Sarah, Josephine, John.; m. Diana Claire, Sept. 11, 1975; stepchildren: Clara, Katherine, Oliver. BA, Open U., Eng., 1984. Articled clk. Johnson, Mileham & Scatliff, Brighton, 1953-58; asst. solicitor Cronin & Son, Brighton, 1959-60; asst. solicitor Mileham Scatliff & Allen, Brighton, 1960-62, pntr., 1962-70; pntr. Donne Mileham & Haddock, Brighton, 1970-97; Chmn. So. Radio Plc, Eng., 1993—, South Downs Health NHS Trust, Brighton, 1997—. Chmn. Indsl. Tribunal, London, 1994; parliamentary candidate, Sussex. Named Dep. Lt., East Sussex, 1991. Mem. Law Soc., Sussex Law Soc., Legal Aid Practitioners Group (life pres.). Avocation: history. Office: Donne Mileham & Haddock, 42 Frederick Pl, Brighton BN1 1AT, England

BARRY, RICHARD FRANCIS, retired life insurance company executive; b. N.Y.C., Aug. 28, 1917; s. Thomas Francis and Gertrude Mary (Spillane) B.; m. Irene Patricia Schulties, July 24, 1948. B.B.A., St. John's U., Bklyn., 1948; J.D., Fordham U., 1953. Bar: N.Y. 1954. With Met. Life Ins. Co., N.Y.C., 1937-82; v.p., office of pres., then v.p. human resources Met. Life Ins. Co., 1979-80, sr. v.p. human resources, 1980-81, sr. v.p. office of chmn., 1981-82, ret. 1982; mem. faculty St. John's U., 1955-60. Bd. dirs. Urban Acad. for Mgmt., Inc., 1979-82, Met. Life Found., 1981-82; sec. Nat. Assn. Drug Abuse Problems, N.Y.C., 1979-82; mem. Coop. Edn. Commn. N.Y.C., 1979-82. Served with AUS, 1943-45. Mem. Adminstrv. Mgmt. Soc. (pres. N.Y.C. chpt. 1972-73), Life Office Mgmt. Assn., Bar Assn. State N.Y., N.Y. C. of C. and Industry. Republican. Roman Catholic. Home: 237 Berry Hill Rd Syosset NY 11791-2105

BARRY, ROBERT HUGH, banker; b. Sydney, NSW, Australia, Feb. 16, 1947; s. Hugh Collis and Mary Gordon (Matters) B.; children: Nicholas, Kate, Andrew. B of Commerce, U. New S. Wales, Australia, 1969. Fellow Cert. Practicing Accts., Securities Inst. Australia. Staff Spry Walker & Co. Australia, Sydney, 1965-66; mktg. mgr. Overseas Containers Australia, Ltd., Sydney, 1969-70; investment mgr. Wm. Brandts & Sons, Ltd., London, 1971-72; fixed interest adviser A.C. Goode & Co, Sydney, 1973-76; co-founder Dominguez & Barry Group, Sydney, 1976-83; prin., CEO Dominguez Barry Samuel Montagu Ltd., Sydney, 1983-87; head capital mkts. Midland Montagu Ltd., London, 1987-90; dir. Samuel Montagu Ltd., London, 1987-90, SBC Warburg Australia (formerly SBC Dominguez Barry Ltd.), Sydney, 1990-99; exec. dir. Australian Wheat Bd., 1999—; bd. dep. chmn. Australian Wheat Bd., Melbourne, 1999; exec. dir. Unireach Ltd., 1999; Sugar Australia Phytel New Zealand Sugar Co., Ltd., 1998; exec. dir. Warbury Dillan Read, 1997; exec. dir. Generon Hydro Nadery Ltd., 2000. Vice-chmn. St. Luke's Hosp. Complex, 1993—; dep. chmn. Queen's Trust Australia, Melbourne, 1993—; bd. dirs. Univ. New S. Wales Found., 1993—. Mem. Australian Club, Royal Sydney Golf Club, Cabbage Tree Club. Avocations: tennis, skiing, surfing, farming. Office: SBC Warburg Australia Ltd, Lev 25 Gov Phillip Tower 1, Sydney NSW 2025, Australia

BARRY, WILLIAM PETER, international trade consultant, chemical specialist; b. Melbourne, Victoria, Australia, June 30, 1931; s. William Peter and Mary Magdalene Barry; m. Valda Marjorie Trezise, Jan. 23, 1954; children: Mark, Christine Patricia. B of Commerce, U. Melbourne, 1963. Clk. Dept. Repatriation, Melbourne, 1953-59; pers. advisor Dept. Labor and Nat. Svc., Melbourne, 1959-61; investigation officer Dept. Trade, Melbourne, 1961-64; trade commr. Dept. Trade, Canberra, Australia, 1964-80; exec. dir. Australian Chem. Spec. Mfrs. Assn., Melbourne, 1980-93; cons., 1993—. Fellow Australian Soc. Assn. Execs. (chmn. 1990-91), Australasian Fleet Mgrs. Assn. (sec. 1995—), Australian Chem. Spec. Mfrs. Assn. (life). Roman Catholic. Avocations: golf, reading, international relations. Home and Office: 1/53 Ferguson St, MacLeod 3085, Australia

BARSALONA, FRANK SAMUEL, theatrical agent; b. S.I., N.Y., Mar. 31, 1938; s. Peter and Mary (Rotunno) B.; m. June Harris, Sept. 1, 1966; 1 dau., Nicole. BA, Wagner Coll., S.I., 1958; postgrad., Herbert Berghof Sch., N.Y.C., 1959-60. Agt. Gen. Artists Corp., N.Y.C., 1960-64; founder, since pres. Premier Talent Agy., N.Y.C., 1964—; co-founder, pres. Phila. Fury, 1977-80; lectr., moderator music industry; founding ptnr. Precision Media Corp., 1984-97. Bd. govs., trustee Rock & Roll Hall of Fame Mus., Cleve. Recipient numerous awards Billboard Publs., cover subject spl. issue, 1984; named to Performance Mag. Hall of Fame, 1988. Mem. Mus. Am. Folk Art. (internat. adv. bd.). Office: Premier Talent Agy 17 E 76th St New York NY 10021-1720

BARSAMIAN, J(OHN) ALBERT, lawyer, judge, educator, criminologist, arbitrator; b. Troy, N.Y., May 1, 1934; s. John and Virginia (Tachdjian) B.;m. Alice Missirilan, Apr. 21, 1963; children: Bonnie, Tamara. BS in Psychology with honors, Union Coll., 1956; JD, 1968; LLB, Albany Law Sch., 1959; postgrad., SUNY, Albany, 1964, Nat. Jud. Coll., 1997. Bar: N.Y. 1961, U.S. Dist. Ct. (no. dist.) N.Y. 1961, U.S. Supreme Ct. 1967; fire tng. cert. N.Y. State Exec. Dept. Pvt. practice, 1961—; dir. criminal sci., chmn. dept. Russell Sage Coll., 1970-88, assoc. prof. criminal sci., 1977-82, prof., 1982-87, prof. emeritus, 1987—; lectr. office local govt. divsn. criminal justice svcs. State N.Y., 1964-72, N.Y. State Police Acad., 1970; judge adminstrv. law N.Y. State Pub. Employment Rels. Bd., 1996—; faculty pub. affairs and policy pub. svc. tng. program Nelson A. Rockefeller Coll., 1986-91, Sch. Labor Rels. Extension divsn. Cornell U., 1986; gaming cons. Gov.'s Office Indian Rels., N.Y., 1991-92; spl. counsel Office of Police Chief, Cohoes, N.Y., 1986-92, to city mgr., Troy, N.Y., 1993; counsel Watervliet Police Assn., 1967-74, Cohoes Police Assn., 1967-74, Colonie Police Assn., 1977-80, Troy Police Command Officers Assn., 1981-85, North Greenbush Police Assn., 1985-90, Office of the Police Chief, Syracuse, N.Y., 1985-90, Fire Dept. Union, Albany, N.Y., 1986, Schenectady Fire Fighters Union, 1992-95; gen. counsel Internat. Narcotic Enforcement Officers Assn., 1982-84, Troy Uniformed Firefighters Assn., 1977-97; spl. investigator Rensselaer County Dist. Atty., 1959-61; mem. law guardian panel N.Y. State Family Ct., 1967-77; mem. mediation panel N.Y. State Pub. Employment Rels. Bd., 1968-73. Founder, chmn. dept. police sci. Hudson Valley C.C., 1961-69; mem. adv. bd. History Ctr. Skidmore Coll., 1993—; bd. dirs. Rensselaer County ARC, 1966-70; memm. alumni coun. Union Coll., 1981-86; mem. parish coun. St. Peter Armenian Ch., Watervliet, N.Y., 1979-83, chmn., 1981-83, vice chmn., 1984; evaluator office of non-collegiate programs N.Y. State Dept. Edn., 1985—; hon. dep. sheriff St. Mary Parish (La.). Tarzian scholar Union Coll., 1952-56, Porter scholar, 1954-56, Saxton scholar, 1956-59; decorated chevalier, knight comdr. Sovereign Order of Cyprus; recipient Police Sci. Students' award Hudson Valley C.C., 1968, award for meritorious svc. to law enforcement Law Enforcement Officers Soc., 1969, Archbishop's cert. merit Armenian Ch. Am., 1973, Lawyers Coop. Pub. Co. prize in criminal law, 1957. Mem. ATLA, ABA (com. on police selection and tng. 1967-69, mem. Rensselaer county criminal justice coord. coun., 1976-78), N.Y. Bar Assn. (chmn. com. on police 1970-72, trial lawyers sect. com. cont. legal edn. 1977-97, subcom. on adminstrv. law judges 2000), Nat. Assn. Adminstrv. Law Judges, Am. Arbitration Assn. (Svc. award 1983), Acad. Criminal Justice Scis., Am. Assn. Criminology, Union Coll. Alumni Assn. (Silver medal 1956), Les Amis d'Escoffier Soc., Masonic Vet. Assn. Troy (life), N.Y. State Trial Lawyers Assn., N.Y. State Assn. Adminstrv. Law Judges (bd. dirs. 1999—), N.Y. Vet. Police Assn. (life, hon., counsel), Royal Order of Jesters, Shriners, Rose Croix (most wise master Delta chpt. 1986), Phi Delta Theta, Alpha Phi Sigma, Lambda Epsilon Chi. Home and Office: 5 Sage Hill Ln Albany NY 12204-1315

BARSAN, ROBERT BLAKE, dentist; b. Akron, Ohio, Apr. 7, 1948; s. Emil O. and Letitia (Dobrin) B.; m. Cheryl Lee Adams, Dec. 16, 1972; children: Erin Lee, Kathleen Letitia. BS, U. Cin., 1970, DDS, Ohio State U., 1974. Resident U. Chgo., 1976; gen. practice dentistry Cuyahoga Falls, Ohio, 1976—. Contbr. editor Modern Dental mag., 1984-89. Bd. dirs. Akron Civil Theatre, 1996—. Fellow Acad. Gen. Dentistry; mem. ADA (chmn. CPR 1984-90), Am. Endodontic Soc., Akron Gnathological Soc. (pres. 1986), Am. Acad. Cosmetic Dentistry, Fedn. Dentaire Internat., Canton Akron Cleve. Orthodontic Study Club (pres. 1994-98). Home: 3084 Silver Lake Blvd Silver Lake OH 44224-3033 Office: 330 Stow Ave Cuyahoga Falls OH 44221-2516

BAR-SEVER, ZVI, physician; b. Cfar-Saba, Israel, May 6, 1958; s. Ze'ev and Rina Bar-S.; m. Michal Rapaport, June 4, 1991; children: Einat, Jonathan, Tamar. MD, Tel-Aviv U., 1987. Chief resident Beilinson Med. Ctr., Petach Tikva, 1991-92, resident in pediats., 1987-92; resident in nuclear medicine Harvard U., Boston, 1993-95, chief resident, 1995-96; fellow in pediat. nuclear medicine Children's Hosp., Boston, 1995-96; staff physician nuclear medicine Rabin Med. Ctr., Petach Tikva, 1996—. Capt. Israeli Med. Corps. E-mail: barsev@idsn.net.il. Office: Rabin Med Ctr/Dept Nucl Med, 1 Danmark St, 49100 Petach Tikva Israel

BARSHEFSKY, CHARLENE, diplomat. BA with honors, U. Wis.; JD, Catholic U. Ptnr. Steptoe & Johnson, Washington, 1975-93; dep. U.S. trade rep. Exec. Office of the Pres. of the U.S., Washington, 1993-96, U.S. trade rep., 1996-97, 1997—. Office: Exec Office of the President US Trade Rep 600 17th St NW Washington DC 20508-0001

BARSOE, CLAUS, marketing executive; b. Brorup, Denmark, Aug. 24, 1949; s. Eduard and Else (Petersen) B.; m. Else Bayer, July 26, 1975; children: Casper, Thomas. MSc, Bus. Sch., Aarhus, Denmark, 1974. Mktg. cons. P/P/Ptnrs., Aarhus, 1974-77; internat. mktg. mgr. Alfa-Laval, Denmark, 1977-85; pres., CEO Busak & Shamban, Crissier, Switzerland, 1985—. Avocations: tennis, skiing, books. Office: Busak & Shamban, Rte Sous-Riette 29, 1023 Crissier Switzerland

BARSOME, MICHAEL YASSA, pulmonarist, consultant; b. El-Faoum, Egypt, Mar. 7, 1959; s. Yassa Gargas and Amera Youkb (Abelsead) B.; m. Mervet Sabhy Khozame, Aug. 14, 1959; children: Mireue, Mina. MB BCh, Faculty of Medicine, 1982; MSc, Ain Sharus U., 1988. Registrar in chest disease Mil. Chest Hosp., 1984-88, specialist of chest physician, 1988-94, cons. of chest disease, 1994—; supr. intensive care unit Misr Internat. Hosp., 1988—; cons. chest disease Good Shepherd Hosp., 1994—. Home: 62 Sheehabe, Giza Egypt Office: Clinic Privet, Mina El-Sereg, Cairo Egypt

BARSON, ANTHONY JAMES, perinatal pathologist, educator; b. Timperley, Cheshire, Eng., Oct. 19, 1936; s. William and Lily (Goulden) B.; m. Beryl Jones, Apr. 2, 1962; children: Andrew William, Jonathan Anthony. MB, ChB, U. Manchester, Eng., 1960; MD, U. Manchester, 1965. Diplomate in child health Royal Coll. Physicians and Surgeons London. Resident in pathology Hosp. for Sick Children, Toronto, Ont., Can., 1967-68; rsch. asst. dept. zoology U. Toronto, 1968-69; asst. lectr. dept. anatomy U. Manchester, 1964-66, lectr. pathology, 1969-71, sr. lectr., 1971-94, reader, 1994-99; med. dir. N.W. Perinatal Survey Unit, Manchester, 1990-99; chmn. Regional Working Party on Perinatal Medicine, 1992—; mem. pathology working group U.K. Dept. Health, 1993—; N.W. regional coord. for CESDI, 1993-99; participant Confidential Inquiry into Stillbirths and Deaths in Infancy. Editor: Laboratory Investigation of Fetal Disease, 1981, Fetal and Neonatal Pathology, 1982; contbr. articles to med. jours. Recipient Casey Holter Meml. prize Assn. for Rsch. into Spinal Bifida and Hydrocephalus, 1967; grantee Wellcome Trust, 1969, N.W. Regional Health Authority, 1993. Fellow Royal Coll. Pathologists, Royal Coll. Pediatrics and Child Health; mem. Paediatric Pathology Soc., Brit. Paediatric Pathology Assn., Brit. Paediatric Assn. Avocations: walking, ornithology. Office: St Mary's Hosp, Hathersage Rd, Manchester M13 0JH, England

BÁRTA, JOSEF, metallurgist, research scientist; b. Ostrava, Czechoslovakia, Oct. 4, 1948; s. František and Antonie (Kotalová) B.; m. Hana Sykorová, Nov. 12, 1983; 1 child, Lucie. Grad. in Engring., Tech. U. Ostrava, Czechoslovakia, 1974, PhD, 1992. Rschr. Steelworks and Wire Mfr., Bohumin, Czechoslovakia, 1974-76; rsch. scientist Vitkovice, Ostrava, Czech Republic, 1976-94; expert in material sci. Moravsko-Slezska Armaturka, Dolni Benešov, Czech Republic, 1994—; lectr. Tech. U. Ostrava, 1986-92; project mgr. European Cmty., Brussels, 1993-94. Contbr. numerous articles to profl. jours. Mem. ASTM, Am. Soc. Metals, Assn. Corrosion Engrs., European Fedn. Corrosion. Avocations: skiing, windsurfing, hiking, literature, music. Office: MSA as, Hlucinska 41, 74722 Dolni Benesov Czech Republic

BARTÁK, JAROSLAV VLADIMÍR, cardiologist, clinic administrator; b. Prague, Czech Republic, Sept. 3, 1958; s. Jaroslav and Božena B.; m. Eva Bartáková. MD, Charles U., Prague, 1983, specialization in internal medicine, 1987, specialization in angiology, cardiology, 1991. Asst. prof. Charles U., 1984-87; internist Tchg. Hosp. Charles U., 1987-88; head dept. internal medicine Měš County Hosp., Prague East, 1989-90, head dept. internal medicine and angiology, 1990-96; pres., CEO, Modřany Pvt. Clin., Prague, 1997—. Editor: Internat. Jour. Angiology; contbr. over 200 articles to med. jours. Recipient over 20 awards from med. congresses and angiology socs. Mem. Lions (charter pres. 1990, sec. 1991-98, pres. 1999—). Mem. Christian Dem. Union. Roman Catholic. Avocations: history, travel.

BARTCHY, S(TUART) SCOTT, history educator, researcher; b. Canton, Ohio, Nov. 9, 1936; s. Jacques Robert Bartchy and Dorothy Elizabeth Engle; m. Diane Walker, June 13, 1956 (div. Jan. 1988); children: Beth, Christopher; m. Nancy L. Breuer, Nov. 19, 1988. BA cum laude, Milligan Coll., 1958; MDiv, Harvard U., 1963, PhD, 1971. Dir. Inst. zur Erforschung des Urchristentums, Tuebingen, Germany, 1971-74, 77-79; prof. Bibl. studies Emmanuel Sch. Religion, Johnson City, Tenn., 1974-77; resident New Testament scholar Westwood Christian Found., L.A., 1979-87; assoc. prof. history dept. UCLA, 1988-96, prof. Christian origins and history of religion, 1996—, dir. Ctr. for the Study of Religion, 1997—; cons. Arts and Entertainment Network, 1996-97; undergrad. coun. Acad. Senate UCLA, 1998—; external examiner grad. programs Fuller Theol. Sem., Pasadena, Calif., 1998; lectr. in field. Author: First Century Slavery and Corinthians, 1973, 85; assoc. editor Religion, 1996—; contbr. chpts. to books and articles to profl. jours. Recipient Hebrew Scholar's award Indpls. Hebrew Congregation, 1960, Thomas Evans award U. Religious Conf., L.A., 1999. Fellow The Context Group; mem. Am. Acad. Religion (pres. 1998-99), Soc. Bibl. Lit. (nat. com. chair 1997—), Cath. Bibl. Assn., Inst. for Bibl. Rsch., Studiorum Novi Testamentum Socs. Avocations: jazz piano improvising, competitive running. E-mail: bartchy@history.ucla.edu. Office: UCLA Dept History PO Box 951743 Los Angeles CA 90095-1743

BARTEE, JAMES WILLIAM, psychologist; b. Helena, Mont., Aug. 16, 1947; arrived in Israel, 1991; s. James Matthew and Mary Virginia (Jones) Bartee; m. Julie Kay Pascoe, Sept. 19, 1982; children: Jordan, Chase. BA, U. Wash., 1969, 70, MEd, 1980, PhD, 1983. Lic. psychologist, Oreg.; cert. elem. tchr., secondary sch. tchr. Sch. counselor Pub. Sch., Moss Rock, Oreg., 1976-80; clin. psychologist Mental Health Svcs., Everett, Wash., 1984-85; dir. counseling svcs. Pacific U., Forest Grove, Oreg., 1986-92; cons. psychologist Baha'i World Ctr., Haifa, Israel, 1992—; assoc. prof. psychology Pacific U., Forest Grove, 1985-92; med. expert Office Hearings and Appeals, Social Security, Portland, Oreg., 1986-92; cons. Tuality Cmty. Hosp., Hillsboro, Oreg., Forest Grove Cmty. Hosp., 1988-92. Contbg. editor, book reviewer Brooks/Cole, Wm C. Brown, Houghton Mifflin.

Avocations: oboe, linguistics, computers. Office: Bahai World Ctr, PO Box 155, 31001 Haifa Israel

BARTEK, GORDON LUKE, radiologist; b. Valparaiso, Nebr., Dec. 27, 1925; s. Luke Victor and Sylvia (Buner) B.; m. Ruth Evelyn Rowley, Sept. 10, 1949; children: John, David, James. BSc, U. Nebr., 1948, MD, 1949. Diplomate Am. Bd. Radiology. Intern Bishop Clarksen Hosp., Omaha, 1949-50; resident in medicine Henry Ford Hosp., Detroit, 1952-53, resident in radiology, 1953-56; staff radiologist Ferguson Hosp., Grand Rapids, Mich., 1956-76, Holland City Hosp., Mich., 1956-76, Logan Hosp., Utah, 1976-78, St. Lawrence Hosp., Lansing, Mich., 1978-97, Spectrum Health, Grand Rapids, 1997—; asst. clin. prof. dept. radiology Mich. State Univ. Coll. Medicine, 1977-93, asst. prof. radiology, 1993-97; organizer Care Choices HMO, Lansing, 1983, bd. dirs., 1983-93. Served to lt. USN, 1949-52. Fellow Am. Coll. Radiology (councilor 1972-76, emeritus); mem. Mich. Radiology Practice Assn. (bd. dirs. 1984-97, chmn. western Mich. sect. 1970-71), Peninsular Club, Terravita Country Club. Republican. Roman Catholic. Avocations: flying, photography, skiing, snorkeling. Home and Office: 1350 Briarcliff Dr SE Grand Rapids MI 49546-9679

BARTELDS, J.L.M. (HANS), finance company executive. CEO Fortis, Brussels, 1996—; chmn. exec. bd.; co-chmn. Fortis and Fortis (NL); mng. dir. Fortis (B); chmn. Fortis Ins. Office: Fortis, Rue Royale 20, 1000 Brussels Belgium*

BARTELS, HANS-JOCHEN, mathematician, educator, actuary; b. Göttingen, Germany, Apr. 9, 1948; s. Theophil and Elisabeth (Ross) B.; m. Sabine Kleinschmidt, Apr. 7, 1978; children: Johannes, Cora, Benjamin. Diplom. Mathematiker, U. Göttingen, 1970, DrRerNat, 1974, Habil., 1979. Asst. prof. U. Göttingen, 1973-83, privat-dozent, 1979-85, apl. prof., 1985-90; mgr. Gothaer Lebensversicherung a.G., Göttingen, 1984-90, chief actuary, 1986-93; prof. Fachhochschule Ulm, Germany, 1990-91, U. Mannheim, Germany, 1991—; cons. actuary Gothaer Lebensversicherung A.G., 1990—. Contbr. rsch. articles to profl. jours. Mem. Deutsche Mathematiker Vereinigung, Deutsche Gesellschaft für Versicherungsmathematik, Deutsche Aktuat vereinigung, Deutsche Gesellschaft für Finanzwirtschaft, Deutsche Verein für Versicherungswissenschaft. Lutheran. Avocation: hiking. Home: Wintergasse 17, D 69469 Weinheim Germany Office: U Mannheim, A5, D 68131 Mannheim Germany

BARTELS, JOACHIM CONRAD, marketing and publishing corporation executive; b. Ueberlingen, Germany, Dec. 3, 1938; came to U.S., 1966, naturalized, 1975; s. Conrad Heinrich and Charlotte (Simmendinger) B.; m. Beryl Garner, Mar. 6, 1965; children: Rachael M.J., Andreas H. Diploma in mech. engring., Coll. F. Trade and Industry, Giengen, Fed. Republic Germany; diploma in bus. adminstrn., Comml. Coll., Giengen, Fed. Republic Germany; grad. mgmt. program, Wharton Sch., U. Pa., 1973. Gen. mgr. No Nail Boxes Ltd., Ettelbruck, Luxemburg, 1963-66; sales mgr. N.Am. No Nail Boxes Ltd., Chester U.K. and Barrington N.J., 1967-68; v.p. Metal Edge Industries, Barrington, 1969-71; mgr. research and devel. Directory div. The Reuben H. Donnelley Corp., Phila., 1972-73; gen. mgr. Donnelley Mktg., Ettlingen, Fed. Republic Germany, 1974-76; v.p., regional mgr. Dun and Bradstreet Internat., Frankfurt, Fed. Republic Germany, 1977-79; v.p. Dun and Bradstreet Internat., N.Y.C., 1980-82, sr. v.p., 1983-85; sr. v.p. bus. mktg. divsn. The Dun and Bradstreet Corp., Wilton, Conn., 1986-87; sr. v.p. global bus. devel. The Dun and Bradstreet Corp., Murray Hill, N.J., 1987—; exec. editor, creator D&B publ. China: Opportunity and Risk; monthly contbr. The Exporter, a US-based trade mag.; vis. fellow DePaul U. Bus. Sch., Chgo. Pub. Am. C. of C. in Germany, Frankfurt, 1978-80. bd. dirs. Information Industry Assn., 1994-98. Mem. Rotary. Avocation: flying. Home: 239 Palmer Ct Ridgewood NJ 07450-2316 Office: Dun & Bradstreet 1 Diamond Hill Rd Murray Hill NJ 07974-1218

BARTELS, SIEGFRIED HANS MURRAY, educator; b. Riesenburg, Germany, Jan. 28, 1930; s. Hermann-Friedrich and Helene Bartels (Siegfried) B.; m. Hildegard Benz, July 26, 1974. Promotion, Goethe U., 1972. Teaching asst. Fb. Sozial-u.Kulturw., FH Darmstadt, Germany, 1973-75; assoc. prof. social, com. and cultural scis. Fb. Sozial-u.Kulturw., FH Darmstadt, 1975-79, prof., 1979-95. Stadtrat seit Stadt Rödermark, 1997. Home: Wingertstrabe 12 A, D-63322 Rödermark Germany Office: Fachhochscule Darmstadt, Haardtring 100, D-64295 Darmstadt Germany

BARTELSKI, LESLAW, writer; b. Warsaw, Poland, Sept. 8, 1920; s. Zygmunt and Zofia Ulanowska; m. Maria Zembrzuska, 1947; 2 children. Student, U. Warsaw. Mem. Art and Nation, 1942-44; co-editor Nowiny Literackie, 1947-48, Nowa Kultura, 1953-63, Kultura, 1963-72; vis. prof. U. Warsaw, 1970-71, 77-78. Author: Ludzie zza rzeki, 1951, Wodorosty, 1964, Mickiewicz na wschodzie, 1966, Dialog z cieniem, 1968, Niedziela bez dzwonów, 1973, Rajski ogród, 1978, others. Mem. Presidium Gen. Coun., Union Fighters for Freedom and Democracy, 1969-79, dep. pres., 1979-90; v.p. Warsaw City Coun., 1973-80. Recipient Petrzak prize, 1969, 85, Warsaw prize, 1969, Prize Min. Culture and Art, 1977, award Pres. of Warsaw, 1990, Reymont's prize, 1998, Comdrs. Cross, Order of Polonia Restituta, Order of Banner of Labour, Order of Cyril and Methodius Bulgaria, Cross of Valour, Warsaw Insurgent Cross, Partisan's Cross. Mem. PEN, Polish Writers Assn. (chair Warsaw br. 1972-78, dep. pres. 1989-2000, hon. pres. 2000—), Janusz Korczak Internat. Assn. (bd. dirs.). Avocations: history of WWII, sports. Address: ul Joliot Curie 17 m1, 02-646 Warsaw Poland

BARTENEV, GEORGII MIKHAILOVICH, physicist, physicochemist, researcher; b. Gulkevichi, Russia, Jan. 12, 1915; s. Michail and Maria (Semunina) B.; m. Maria Geraskyna, May 1939 (div. Nov. 1956); m. Cheslava Lemaeva, May 27, 1958; 1 child, Alla. Diploma, Moscow State U., 1939, PhD, 1943; DSc, Moscow Mendeleev Chem.-Tech. Inst., 1948. Metal worker Machine Constrn. Plant, Krasnodar, Russia, 1931-33; asst. dept. physics Moscow State U., 1943-45; chief phys. lab. Rsch. Inst. Rubber, Moscow, 1946-55; chief dept. solid state physics, dir. lab. polymer physics Moscow Lenin Tchr. Tng. U., 1950-72; chief lab. Inst. Phys. Chemistry, Russian Acad. Scis., Moscow, 1972-90, sr. scientist, 1991—; mem. Sci. Attestation Commn. of USSR, Moscow, 1960-82. Author: The Structure and Mechanical Properties of Inorganic Glasses, 1967, Relaxation Properties of Polymers, 1992, Strength and Fracture Mechanism of Polymers, 1984, Superstrong and High-Strong Inorganic Glasses, 1974; mem. adv. editl. bd. Advances in Material Rsch., 1965-71, Jour. Non-Crystall. Solids, 1968-88, Jour. Materials Sci. and Engring., 1965-80; mem. editl. bd. Jour. Plaste u. Kautschuk, 1960-93; contbr. 20 monographs and over 1000 articles to profl. jours.; hon. inventor in field. Mem. Com. on Polymeric Materials USSR, Moscow, 1975. Named Honored Scientist of Russian Fedn., 1966; recipient Hon. Cert., All-Union Bd. of Sci. and Tech. Socs. of USSR, 1965, 67, 70, 80, Silver Honored medal Gesellschaft Kammer der Technik, Berlin, 1985. Mem. Russian Acad. Scis. (reviewer Inst. Sci. and Tech. Info. 1970—, mem. sci. coun. on colloid chemistry and phys.-chem. mechanics 1965—), Mendeleev Chem. Soc. USSR (dept. physics of polymers 1960-85). Home: Flat 135, Cherniakhovskogo Str 5, 125319 Moscow Russia Office: Inst Phys Chemistry, Russian Acad Sci, Leninskii prospect 31, 117915 Moscow Russia

BARTENSTEIN, MARTIN, government official; b. Graz, Austria, June 3, 1953. D of Chemistry, Graz U., 1978. Fed. chmn. Austrian Union Young Industrialists, 1988; deputy regional chmn. Styrian OVP; elected MP, 1991; state sec. Ministry Pub. Economy & Transport, 1994-95; min. Ministry Environ. Affairs, 1995-97, Ministry Environ. & Family Affairs, Vienna, Austria, 1997-2000, Ministry Econ. Efforts and Solutions, Vienna, Austria, 2000—. Office: Fed Min Environ & Family, Stubenwug 1, A-1010 Vienna Austria

BARTER, STEPHEN LESLIE, chartered surveyor, real estate investment banker; b. Hampton Court, Middlesex, Eng., Mar. 4, 1957; s. Leslie Francis and Joyce Winifred (Davis) B.; m. Alyson Jane Greenbury, June 23, 1984; children: Olivia Marguerite Louise, Hannah Bryony Elizabeth. BA, Gonville & Caius Coll., Cambridge, 1978, MA, 1982. Grad. surveyor Property Svcs. Agy., London, 1978-79; with Insignia Richard Ellis, London, 1979-2000; assoc. ptnr. Richard Ellis, London, 1984, ptnr., 1987, equity ptnr., 1993; founder dir. Richard Ellis Fin. Svcs. Ltd., London, 1984-90; head cons. group, 1990-2000; head European real estate Babcock & Brown, London, 2000—; non-exec. dir. Ministry of Def. Estates Agy., 1997—; chmn. Pvt. Fin. Panel Property Adv. Group, 1996-97; property advisor to U.K. Govt. on privitization of Brit. Rwys., 1993-97, pub.-pvt. partnership for London Underground, 198-2000; advisor to U.K. govt. on winning bidder on maj. property partnership transactions, including Dept. Social Security, Inland Revenue/HM Custons & Excise, London Ground; mem. Joint Royal Instn. of Chartered Surveyors/Confedn. of Brit. Industry Task Force Rev. of the UK Planning System, 1992, Property Forum Brit. Industry Confedn., 1993—, Bank of Eng. Property Forum, 1993—. Editor, co-author: Real Estate Finance, 1988; co-author: Property Securitisation, 1995; co-creator Property Income Certificates (PINCS), 1986. Gov. London Inst., 1998—; mem. adv. coun. London Symphony Orch., 1997—; bd. dirs. City Arts Trust, 1992-97, chmn., 1995-97; mem. coun. Girls' Day Sch. Trust, 1996-99, mem. property com., 1994-99; mem. Corp. London Common Coun., 2000—. Recipient Freedom of the City of London award, 1998. Fellow Royal Instn. Chartered Surveyors, Royal Soc. Arts. Mem. Ch. of Eng. Avocations: opera, choral singing, family. Office: Babcock & Brown, 1 Fleet Pl, Berkeley Sq London EC4M 7NR, England

BARTFELD, FERNANDE, retired French literature educator; b. Skierniewice, Poland, Mar. 14, 1931; arrived in Israel, 1953; d. Herzmeyer and Ryvka (Goldfarb) Jakoubovitch; divorced. BA, U. Sorbonne, France, 1952, PhD, 1965. From asst. lectr. to sr. lectr. Hebrew U., Jerusalem, 1965-82, fellow prof., 1982-92, prof., 1992-97, prof. emeritus, 1999—. Author: L'Effet tragique. Essai sur le tragique dans l'oeuvre de Camus, 1988; contbr. chpts. to books and articles to jours. Home: 17 Nili St, 92548 Jerusalem Israel Office: Hebrew U, Mt Scopus Campus, 91905 Jerusalem Israel

BARTH, ANDREAS, chemist; b. Wuppertal, Germany, Feb. 22, 1953; s. Werner and Helga (Birkendahl) B. Diploma in chemistry, U. Bonn, Germany, 1978; PhD in Theoretical Chemistry, U. Heidelberg, Germany, 1983. Sci. asst. U. Heidelberg, 1984; software developer Fachinformationszentrum, Germany, 1984-87, project mgr., 1987-88, head R & D, 1988-91, dir. devel., 1991—; cons. Govt. of Germany, Bonn, 1993—. Author: Datenbanken in den Naturwissenschaften, 1992; editor: Codata, 1993—; contbr. articles to profl. publs. Mem. Assn. for Computing Machinery, Assn. for Info. Avocations: reading, photography, travel, computers. Home: Blumenstrasse 2, D-76297 Stutensee Germany Office: Fachinformationszentrum, PO Box 2465, D-76012 Karlsruhe Germany

BARTH, FRIEDRICH GÜNTHER, zoology neurobiology scientist; b. Munich, Germany, Apr. 18, 1940; s. Hans and Marianne (Staudenmeyer) B.; m. Ortrun Eberbach Barth, 1967; children: Natalie, Raphael. PhD, U. Munich, Germany, 1967. Asst. prof. U. Munich, Germany, 1968-71, assoc. prof., 1971-73; prof. U. Frankfurt, Germany, 1974-87, U. Vienna, Austria, 1987—. Author: Biologie einer Begegnung, 1982, Insects and Flowers, 1985; editor-in-chief Jour. Comparative Physiol. A; editor: Neurobiology of Arachnids, 1985; contbr. articles to profl. jours. Mem. European Academy, Austrian Acad. Scis.. Bavarian Acad. Scis., Deutsche Akademia der Naturforscher Leopoldina. Office: U Vienna Institut für Zoologie, Althanstr 14, A-1090 Vienna Austria

BARTH, JOHN SIMMONS, writer, educator; b. Cambridge, Md., May 27, 1930; s. John Jacob and Georgia (Simmons) B.; m. Harriette Anne Strickland, Jan. 11, 1950 (div. 1969); children: Christine Anne, John Strickland, Daniel Stephen; m. Shelly I. Rosenberg, Dec. 27, 1970. BA, Johns Hopkins U., 1951, MA, 1952; LittD (hon.), Univ. Md., 1969. Instr. English Pa. State U., 1953-56, asst. prof. English, 1957-60, assoc. prof. English, 1960-65; prof. English SUNY, Buffalo, 1965-73; prof. creative writing Johns Hopkins U., Balt., 1973-91, prof. emeritus creative writing, 1991—. Author: The Floating Opera, 1956 (Nat. Book award nomination 1956), The End of the Road, 1958, The Sot-Weed Factor, 1960, Giles Goat-Boy, 1966, Lost in the Funhouse, 1968 (Nat. Book award nomination 1968), Chimera, 1972 (Nat. Book award 1973), Letters, 1979, Sabbatical: A Romance, 1982, The Literature of Exhaustion, and The Literature of Replenishment, 1982, The Friday Book: Essays and Other Nonfiction, 1984, Don't Count on It: A Note on the Number of the 1001 Nights, 1984, The Tidewater Tales: A Novel, 1987, The Last Voyage of Somebody the Sailor, 1991, Once Upon a Time: A Floating Opera, 1994, Further Fridays: Essays, Lectures, and Other Non-fiction, 1984-94, 1995, On with the Story, 1996. Recipient Brandeis Univ. Creative Arts award, 1965, F. Scott Fitzgerald award, 1997, PEN/Malamud award, 1998, Lifetime Achievement award Lannan Found., 1998, Lifetime Achievement in Letters award Enoch Pratt Soc., 1999; Rockefeller Found. grantee, 1965-66, Nat. Inst. Arts and Letters grantee, 1966. Mem. AAAL, Am. Acad. Arts and Scis. Office: Writing Seminars Johns Hopkins U Baltimore MD 21218

BARTH, THOMAS ROLF, energy executive; b. Zurich, Apr. 13, 1953; s. Edmund Heinrich and Yvonne Paula (Cornu) B.; m. Franziska Burki, July 5, 1966. MBA, Ecole Des Roches, 1974. Sales mgr. Ed Barth Verpackungs Maschinen & Verpackungs Materialien, Kilchberg, Switzerland, 1977-79; project mgr. Gen. Diener GmbH, Jebel Ali, United Arab Emirates, 1979-80; sales mgr. NICO Internat., Dubai, United Arab Emirates, 1980-88; deputy gen. mgr. NICO/MSG, Abu Dhabi, United Arab Emirates, 1988-90; comml. mgr. Deutsche Babcock, Abu Dhabi, United Arab Emirates, 1990-94, resident mgr., 1994-98, area mgr. Gulf, 1999; CEO Babcock Borsig Gulf, 1999—. Mem. Golf Club Abu Dhabi, Marina Club Abu Dhabi. Roman Catholic. Avocations: yachting, diving, skiing, fishing, music. Office: Deutsche Babcock Energie, PO Box 46698, Abu Dhabi United Arab Emirates

BARTH, TOMISLAV, biochemist, researcher, educator; b. Roztoky, Czech Republic, Aug. 22, 1938; s. Josef and Anna (Růžicková) B.; m. Jana Kaiferová, Jan. 28, 1964. BSc, Charles Univ., Prague, 1963, MSc, 1968; PhD, Acad. Scis., Prague, 1966, DSc, 1987. Tech. Rsch. Inst. of Antib., Roztoky, 1956-58; doctoral fellow Inst. Organic Chemistry Biochemistry, Prague, 1963-66, researcher, 1966-77, head of rsch., 1977-89, head of dept., 1989-95, deputy of the dir., 1990-92; head of division Prague Inst. of Advanced Studies, 1991; researcher Inst. Animal Physiol Genetic, Prague, 1993. Contbr. over 350 articles to profl. jours.; patents in field. Mem. Czech Soc. Biochemistry and Molecular Biology, Czech Biotechnology Soc., European Peptide Soc., Am. Peptide Soc., European Aouatic Soc., Sigma Xi. Home: P O Box 16, 25263 Roztoky Czech Republic Office: Inst Organic Chemistry & Biochem, AS Czech Rep, 16610 Prague 6 Czech Republic

BARTHA, DANIELA C., music educator; b. Erding, Germany, Sept. 7, 1967; d. Manfred and Monika B. BMus in Piano Performance, U. Denver, 1992; MMus in Piano Performance, U. Kansas City, 1994; postgrad., U. Cin. Teaching asst. U. Cin., 1996-99; instr. music Muskingum Coll., New Concord, Ohio, 1999-2000; lectr. of music U. N.Mex., Albuquerque, 2000—. Contbr. articles to profl. pubs. Music Activity grantee U. Denver, 1988-92; recipient Non Resident Chancellor's award U. Kansas City, 1992-94; grad. scholarship U. Cin., 1994-96. Avocation: pets. E-mail: dcbartha@yahoo.com. Office: U NMex Albuquerque NM 87111

BARTHEL, GÜNTER, Germany; b. Erfurt, Thuringia, Mar. 17, 1941; s. Gerhard Richard Arnold and Hildegard (Funke) B.; m. Helga Henriette Seidel, Jan. 20, 1962; children: Birgit, Dirk. MA, Karl Marx U., Leipzig, German Dem. Republic, 1963, PhD, 1966, DrSci, 1970; postgrad., Ain Shams U., Cairo, 1967-68. Assoc. prof. Leipzig U., 1971-75, prof., 1975-96, dep. dir. dept. African and Middle Eastern studies, 1970-75; chmn. Sci. Adv. Coun. for Asian, African and Latin Am. Studies, Berlin, 1975-81; vice chmn. Central Coun. for Asian, African and Latin Am. Studies, Leipzig, 1982-86, chmn., 1987-89; vis. scholar U. Tex., Austin, 1982, Harvard U., Cambridge, 1982. Author, editor 28 books, more than 160 articles and numerous revs. in field of North African and Middle Eastern studies. Recipient Nationalpreis German Dem. Republic Coun. of State, 1983. Mem. Nat. Com. Asian, African and Latin Am. Scis., Société Egyptienne d'Economie Politique de Statistique et de Legislation (corr.).

BARTHEL, HENNER LUTZ, speech communication scholar; b. Halle, Germany, Apr. 23, 1947; s. Johannes and Jutta (Wolff) B.; m. Gisela Mundt, Aug. 3, 1981. Student, Martin Luther U., Halle-Wittenberg, 1967-71, Pushkin Inst., Moscow, 1980-81. Scholar U. Leipzig, 1971-76, Humboldt U., Berlin, 1976-94; prof., chmn. U. Koblenz-Landau, Germany, 1994—. With German Army, 1973-75. Mem. Nat. Comm. Assn., German Assn. for Sprechwissenschaft and Sprecherziehung, Assn. for Angewandte Sprachwissenschaft. Avocations: visiting cultural interest locations. E-mail: barthel@uni-landau.de. Office: Univ Koblenz-Landau Abt Landau, Sprechwiss Marktstr 46, 76829 Landau Germany

BARTHEL, JOSEF M.G., chemistry educator; b. Zerf, Germany, Mar. 9, 1929; s. Johann and Antonia Theresa (Heinen) B.; m. Margaretha Schneider. Lic.es.Sc., U. Saarbrucken, 1952, Dipl.math., 1953, Dr.rer.nat., 1956, Dr.habil., 1959; doctor honoris causa, U. Paris VII, 1997. Dozent chemistry dept. U. Saarbrucken (Germany), 1961-69, prof. chemistry dept., 1969-71; prof., head Inst. Phys. Chemistry U. Regensburg (Germany), 1971-97, dean faculty chemistry and pharmacy, 1974-77, v.p., 1979-82, prof. emeritus, 1997—; vis. prof. dept. organic phys. chemistry U. Paris, 1966-84. Author: Electrolyte Data Collection, 12 vols., 1992-99, Thermometric Titrations, 1975, Ionen in nichbwassrigen Losungen, 1976, (with P. Turg and M. Chemla) Transport, Relaxation and Kinetic Processes, 1992, (with H. Krienke and W. Kunz) Physical Chemistry of Electrolytes, 1997; contbr. 280 chpts. to books and articles to profl. jours.; editor-in-chief Jour. Molecular Liquids. Recipient Kurnakov medal Russian Acad. Sci., 1997; corr. mem. Acad. Peloritana, Messina, Italy, 1993, European Acad. Sci., Paris, 1998. Mem. Physikalische Chemie, Dechema, Gesellschaft Deutscher Chemiker. Home: Eichendorffstrasse 1, 93138 Lappersdorf Germany Office: U Regensburg, Inst Phys Chemistry, 93040 Regensburg Germany

BARTHELEMY, JEAN-PAUL FRANCOIS, orthopedic surgeon; b. Uzerche, Correze, France, Sept. 13, 1947; s. Maurice Barthelemy and Suzanne Croizet; m. Marie-Christine Bourgeais; children: Laurent, Olivier, Julien, Manon. BA, Coll. Gregoire, Tours, France, 1966; MD, Inst. Medicine Tours, 1976. Intern Tours Hosp., 1972-76, resident in plastic surgery, 1972, gen. surgery, 1972-74, resident in gen. surgery, 1972-74, fellow in orthopedic surgery, 1974-76, asst. in orthopedic surgery, 1976-78; orthopedic surgeon Clin. des Dames Blanches, Tours, 1976-86, Clinic St. Gatien, Tours, 1986—. Contbr. articles to profl. publs. Mem. French Coll. Orthopedic Surgeons, French Assn. Orthopedic and Trauma Surgery, European Soc. Knee Surgery and Arthroscopy, French Arthroscopic Soc., Am. Coll. Sport Medicine, Am. Soc. Sports Medicine, Herodicus Soc., SICOT. Roman Catholic. Home: La Martiniere, 37230 Fondettes France Office: Clinic St Gatien, 8 Place de la Cathedrale, 37000 Tours France

BARTHÉLEMY, LUC, geographer and researcher; b. Marseille, France, Apr. 28, 1948; s. Jean and Regine (Carron) B.; m. Anne-Marie Lethève, Dec. 18, 1971; children: Pierre, Emmanuel, Louis-Joseph, Matthieu. MS, U. Paris X, Nanterre, France, 1971, PhD in Geography, 1976. Engr. U. Paris X, Nanterre, 1971-97; co-dir. Centre de Géographie Physique Henri Elhaï, Nanterre-Cedex, 1981-97; maitre de conf. U. Jean Moulin, Lyon; co-organizer sci. trips and internat. colloquiums and confs. Editor 12 sci. books; contbr. articles to profl. jours. Mem. Comité National Français de Géographie (sec. Commn. de la Montagne 1988-98). Avocations: sailing, walking. Home: 256 rue Vendome, F-69003 Lyon France Office: CNRS-UMR 5600 U Jean Moulin, 18 rue Chevreul, F-69362 Lyon Cedex 07, France

BARTHELET, YVES, anesthesiologist, intensive care physician; b. Paris, Oct. 31, 1966; s. Alain and Marie Noelle (Aumont) B.; m. Sarah Varenne; children: Cyril, Gael. MD, Montpellier U., 1997, DES, 1997. Mpcl. resident CHU Montpellier, 1991-97, physician, 1997—; physician Hopital el Marrouf, Comoros Islands, 1993-94; cons. allergy-anesthesia CHU Montepellier, 1997—. Aspirant Tech. Cooperation, 1993-94. Avocations: trecking, climbing, diving. Office: Hopital Lapeyronie, CHU Montpellier, F 34295 Montpellier CEDEX 5, France

BARTHELMAS, NED KELTON, investment and commercial real estate developer; b. Circleville, Ohio, Oct. 22, 1927; s. Arthur and Mary Bernice (Riffel) B.; m. Marjorie Jane Livezey, May 23, 1953; children: Brooke Ann, Richard Thomas. B.S. in Bus. Adminstrn., Ohio State U., 1950. Stockbroker Ohio Co., Columbus, 1953-58; pres. First Columbus Securities Corp., 1958—; pres., dir. Ohio Fin. Corp., Columbus, 1960—; pres. Thwirs, Inc., Columbus, 1986—; trustee, chmn. Am. Guardian Fin., Republic Fin.; bd. dirs. Nat. Foods, Midwest Capital Corp., Capital Equity Corp., Midwest Nat. Corp., 1st Columbus Realty Corp., Dublin Nat. Corp. (all Columbus). Served with Adj. Gen.'s Dept., AUS, 1944-47. Mem. Nat. Assn. Securities Dealers (past vice chmn. dist. bd. govs.), Investment Bankers Assn. Am. (exec. com. 1973), Investment Dealers Ohio (sec., treas. 1956-72, pres. 1973), Nat. Stock Traders Assn., Young Pres.'s Orgn. (pres. 1971), World Bus. Coun., Columbus Pres.'s Assn., Nat. Investment Bankers (pres. 1973), Internat. Real Estate Inst., Columbus Jr. C. of C. (pres. 1956), Ohio C. of C. (trustee 1957-58), World's Pres.'s Assn. (Exec. Hall of Fame award 1993), Columbus Area C. of C. (dir. 1956, named an Outstanding Young Man of Columbus 1962), Newcomen Soc., Coun. for Ethics in Econs., Coun. of Orgn. of Am. States, Wisdom Hall of Fame, Internat. Soc. Financiers, Oxford Club, Execs. Club, Pres.' Club (Ohio State U.), Internat. Platform Assn., Stock and Bond Club (past pres.), named top 25 corp. Dirs. (1984-90), Columbus Club, Scioto Country Club, Crystal Downs Country Club, Ohio State U. Faculty Club, Kiwanis (legion of honor 1992), Am. Legion, Admirals Club, Alpha Kappa Psi, Phi Delta Theta (Golden Legion award). Office: 1241 Dublin Rd Columbus OH 43215-7000

BARTHES-LABROUSSE, MARIE-GENEVIEVE, surface scientist, researcher; b. Saint Clair du Rhone, France, Sept. 11, 1953; d. Andre and Marie-Louise (Canac) Barthès; m. Michel Labrousse; children: Sylvie, Claire, Agnès. MSc, U. Paris, 1975, D of Metallurgy, 1978, D es Sci., 1981. Rsch. attaché CNRS, Paris, 1979-81; in charge of rsch. CNRS, Paris and Vitry, France, 1981-92; dir. rsch. CNRS, Vitry, 1992—. Contbr. articles to profl. jours. Recipient Bronze medal CNRS, 1981, prix de chimie-physique French Chem. Soc., 1986. Mem. Soc. Francaise du Vide (sec.-gen. 1995-97, pres. elect 1997-99, pres. 1999—), Internat. Union for Vacuum Sci. Technique and Applications (sci. sec. 1996-98, pres. elect 1998—). Home: 29 bd Henri Ruel, 94120 Fontenay-sous-Bois France Office: CNRS-CECM, 15 rue Georges Urbain, 94407 Vitry Cedex, France

BARTHEZ, FABIEN, professional soccer player; b. Lavelanet, France, June 28, 1971. Goalkeeper Toulouse Football Club, France, 1986-92, Marseille Football Club, France, 1992-95; winner champion league title European Champions Club Cup, 1993; goalkeeper Monaco Football Club, France, 1995—; winner French League Title, 1997; goalkeeper French Nat. Team, 1998—, Manchester (Eng.) United. Office: Manchester United FC, Sir Matt Busby Way, Old Trafford Manchester M16 0RA, England*

BARTHLEY, ROLSTON LUSHINGTON, insurance company executive; b. All Saints, Antigua, West Indies, Oct. 22, 1942; s. Adolphus and Doris Barthley; m. Zona Iotha Carr, June 9, 1966; children: Zorol, Carol-Jean, Ian, Vincere, Bruce, Sonia. D of Bus. Adminstrn. (hon.), Hawthorne U., 1997. Diploma in ins. mgmt. Salesman First Fedn. Life, Antigua, West Indies, 1966-69, staff mgr., 1969-71, dist. mgr., 1971-76; gen. mgr. State Ins. Corp., Antigua, West Indies, 1977—; dir., treas. Nat. Devel. Found., Antigua, 1990—. Treas. Antigua Netball Assn., 1986; mem. Diocese of Northeastern Caribbean and Aruba, Antigua, 1984—. Mem. Inst. Assn. Caribbean (dir. 1986—), Rotary Club Antigua (pres. 1987-88, Paul Harris fellow 1987), St. Johns Masons (treas. 1990—). Anglican. Avocations: reading, swimming, cricket. Home: Matthews Rd, All Saints Antigua and Barbuda Office: State Ins Corp, Redcliffe St, Saint John's Antigua and Barbuda

BARTHOLD, THOMAS A., economist; b. St. Louis, Nov. 23, 1953; s. Carl H. and Nancy D. Barthold; m. Laurie Richmond; children: Faye Ellen, Ross Owen. BA in Math. and Econs., Northwestern U., 1975, MS in Math., 1975; MA in Econs., Harvard U., 1978, PhD in Econs., 1980. Asst. prof. econs. Dartmouth Coll., Hanover, N.H., 1980-87; staff economist Joint Com. on Taxation, U.S. Congress, Washington, 1987-95, sr. economist, 1995—. Contbr. articles to profl. jours. Treas. Argyle Village Homeowners' Assn., Silver Spring, 1990-98. Mem. Am. Econs. Assn., Nat. Tax Assn., Phi Beta Kappa. Office: Joint Com on Taxation 1015 Longworth Hob Washington DC 20515-0001

BARTHOLOMAI, ALAN, retired museum director; b. Boonah, Queensland, Australia, Dec. 31, 1938; m. Patricia Sheehy; 1 child, Leigh. BSc, U. Queensland, 1961, MSc, 1969; PhD, U. Queensland, 1, 1972. Curator ge-

ology Queensland Mus., Brisbane, Australia, 1961-66; rsch. curator geology Queensland Mus., 1966-69, dir., 1969-99. Mem. Royal Soc. Queensland, World Fund for Nature (Australia). Home: 7 Woodlands Ave, Camira Australia QLD4300 Office: Queensland Mus, PO Box 3300, South Brisbane QLD, Australia 4101

BARTHOLOMAY, WILLIAM C., insurance brokerage company executive, professional baseball team executive; b. Evanston, Ill., Aug. 11, 1928; s. Henry C. and Virginia (Graves) B.; m. Sara Taylor, 1950, (div. 1964); children: Virginia, William T., Jamie, Elizabeth, Sara; m. Gail Dillingham, May 1968 (div. Apr. 1980). Student, Oberlin Coll., 1946-49, Northwestern U., 1949-50; BA, Lake Forest Coll., 1955. Ptnr. Bartholomay & Clarkson, Chgo., 1951-63; v.p. Alexander & Alexander, Chgo., 1963-65; pres. Olson & Bartholomay, Chgo. and Atlanta, 1965-69; sr. v.p. Frank B. Hall & Co. Inc., N.Y.C. and Chgo., 1969-72, exec. v.p., 1972-73, pres., 1973-74, vice chmn., 1974-90; chmn. bd., dir. Atlanta Braves, 1966—; pvt. practice cons. Chgo., 1990-91; pres. Near North Nat. Group, 1991—; vice chmn. Turner Broadcasting System, Inc., Atlanta; bd. dirs. WMS Industries Inc., Chgo., Midway Games, Inc., Exec. Coun. Maj. League Baseball, Maj. League Baseball Players Pension Plan. Commr. Chgo. Park Dist., 1980—, Chgo. Pub. Bldg. Commn., 1989—; bd. dirs. Chgo. Maternity Ctr., Lincoln Park Zool. Soc.; trustee Adler Planetarium, Mus. Sci. and Industry, Roosevelt U., Chgo., Ill. Inst. of Tech.; former trustee Lake Forest (Ill.) Coll., Ogelthorpe Coll., Atlanta, Marymount Manhattan Coll., N.Y. With USNR, 1951-54. Mem. Chief Execs. Orgn., World Pres.'s Orgn., Chgo. Pres.'s Orgn., Nat. Assn. CLU, Chgo. Assn. CLU, Chgo. Club, Racquet Club, Saddle and Cycle Club, Econ. Club, Onwentsia Club, Shoreacres Club (Lake Forest), Brook Club, Links Club, Racquet & Tennis Club, Doubles Club (N.Y.C.), Piedmont Driving Club, Atlanta Country Club, Peachtree Golf Club, Commerce Club. Episcopalian. Home: 180 E Pearson St Chicago IL 60611-2130 Office: Near North Nat Group 875 N Michigan Ave Ste 2000 Chicago IL 60611-1954 also: Atlanta Braves PO Box 4064 Atlanta GA 30302-4064

BARTHOLOMEW, DAVID JOHN, statistics educator; b. Oakley, Eng., Aug. 6, 1931; s. Albert and Joyce (Payne) B.; m. Marian Elsie Lake, 1955; children: Ruth Elizabeth, Ann Christine. BSc, Univ. Coll., London, 1953; PhD, Univ. Coll., 1955. Scientist Nat. Coal Bd., London, 1955-57; lectr. U. Keele, Eng., 1957-60, U. Coll. Wales, Aberystwyth, Eng., 1960-67; prof. U. Kent, Canterbury, Eng., 1967-73; prof. stats. London Sch. Econs., 1973-96; pro-dir. London Sch. Econs., 1989-91; vis. prof. Harvard U., Cambridge, Mass., 1964-65, U. Calif.-Berkeley, 1969, U. Melbourne, Australia, 1977, 86, Inst. for Advanced Study, U. Ind., 1987; vis. scientist Bell Telephone Labs., Holmdel, N.J., 1973. Author: Stochastic Models for Social Processes, 1967, Statistical Techniques for Manpower Planning, 1979, God of Chance, 1984, Latent Variable Models and Factor Analysis, 1987, 2d edit. (with M. Knott), 1999, Uncertain Belief, 1996, The Statistical Approach to Social Measurement, 1996, others; contbr. articles to profl. jours. Fellow Royal Statis. Soc. (sec. 1976-82, recipient Guy medal in bronze 1971, treas. 1989-93, pres. 1993-95), Brit. Acad., Inst. Math. Stats.; mem. Internat. Statis. Inst., Manpower Soc. (hon. v.p. 1986). Methodist. Avocations: gardening, steam railways, theology. Office: London Sch Econs, Houghton St, London WC2A 2AE, England

BARTHOLOMEW, MICHAEL ANTHONY, telecommunications industry executive, journalist; b. London, Jan. 10, 1951; s. Robert Bartholomew and Diana Rachel (Ornadel) Frank; m. Veronique Patricia Devis, June 20, 1986; 1 child, Oliver. BS in Journalism, Northwestern U., 1972, MS in Journalism, 1973. News reporter AP, Hartford, Conn., 1973-75; news corr. Radio Free Europe/Radio Liberty, Washington, 1975-81; bur. chief Radio Free Europe/Radio Liberty, Brussels, 1981-85; pres. Bart Info. and Monitoring Svcs., Brussels, 1985-94; dir. Motion Picture Assn., Brussels, 1994-98; la Biennale di Venezia Dept. of Cinema, Venice, 1999-2000; dir. European Public Telecom. Network Operator's Assn., Brussels, 2000—; v.p. Internat. Press Assn., Brussels, 1989-92. Author: Essays On Managing, 1990 (Book of the Month 1990); contbr. to newsletter EU Brief, 1988—; columnist Wall St. Jour. newspaper, 1990-94. Century mem. Boy Scouts Am., Brussels, 1994, 95. Grantee European Commn., Brussels, 1993. Mem. European Inst., Ctr. for European Policy Studies, Cercle Royal Gaulois Artistique and Litteraire (elected), The Am. Club. Avocations: biking, golf, skiing. Office: Euro Pub Telecom Network Operators Assn, 33 Blvd Bischoffsheim 33, Brussels 1000, Belgium

BARTHOLOMEW, SHIRLEY KATHLEEN, municipal official; b. Marysville, Wash., Jan. 26, 1924; d. Clarence E. and Mary (Hall) B. Grad. high sch., Marysville, 1943. Sec. Everett (Wash.) Broadcasting Corp. Inc., 1960-77, 1st Pacific Broadcasting, Everett, 1977-80; news dir. Sta. KRKO, Everett, 1943-80. Mem. coun. COunty of Snohomish, Everett, 1980-89, chmn., 1987-88; mem. Marysville City Coun., 1994—. Named to Edward R. Morrow Broadcast Hall of Fame, 1980; recipient Mng. Editors Citation AP, 1958-73. Republican. Avocations: opera, symphony. Office: City of Marysville 4822 Grove St Marysville WA 98270-4456

BARTHOVÁ, JANA KAIFEROVÁ, biochemist, educator; b. Prague, Czechoslovakia, Jan. 8, 1941; d. Jan and Otilie (Obalilová) K.; m. Tomislav Barth, Jan. 28, 1964. BSc, Charles U., Prague, 1963, MSc, 1967, PhD, 1969. Researcher faculty of sci. Charles U., Prague, 1966-90, assoc. prof., 1990—. Co-author 11 biochemistry textbooks; contbr. articles to profl. jours.; patentee in field. Mem. Czech Soc. Biochemistry and Molecular Biology (com. mem. 1994), European Peptide Soc., N.Y. Acad. Sci. Home: Masarykova 884, Roztoky 252 63, Czech Republic Office: Charles Univ Dept Biochem, Albertov 2030, 128 40 Prague 2 128 40, Czech Republic

BARTKIW, ROMAN, artist; b. Montreal, Que., Can., Mar. 8, 1935; s. Ivan and Annastasia Bartkiw; 4 children. Assoc., Ont. Coll. Art, 1960; student, Sheridan Sch. Design, Mississauga, 1969, Alfred U., 1970, 74-75. Owner, operator pottery studio, Toronto, Markdale, Ont., Can., 1961-71, glass blowing studio, Combermere, Ont., 1975-77, pottery studio, N.S., Can., 1981; pottery tchr. pvt. studio, Toronto, 1961-62, No. Coll. Inst., Toronto, 1962; head ceramics Ont. Coll. Art, 1968-69; instr. ceramics and glass blowing Georgian Coll. Applied arts, 1971-74; founder arts and crafts program Chesterfield Inlet, N.W.T., Can., 1978; instr. various summer and night courses; resident mastercraftsman potter St. Clair Coll., Chatham, Ont.; demonstrator, panel mem. Internat. Glass Symposium, Denmark, 1976; presenter pottery workshop Cambrian Coll., 1977; craft cons. Upper Clements Park, 1988; head master craftsman, glass blower and presser Upper Clements Park, N.S., 1989, 90. One-man ceramic exhibits include Can. Guild Crafts Gallery, Toronto, 1964, Can. Guild Potters, 1967, Wells Gallery, Ottawa, 1985, Dresden Gallery, Halifax, 1985; one-man glass exhibits include Wells Gallery, Ottawa, 1976, Thomas Gallery, Winnipeg, 1976, Alice Peck Gallery, Hamilton, 1976; group exhibits Umea and Gothenburg Mus., Sweden, Denmark and Finland, 1974-76, Masters Exhbn., Toronto, 1976; represented in permanent collections Royal Ont. Mus., Umea and Gothenburg Mus., Mus. Decorative Arts, Copenhagen, N.S. Dept. Culture and Recreation, Cultural Ctr. Japan, Massey Coll., Industry Min. Coll., Seagram Coll. Recipient Design award in ceramics Can. Guild Crafts, 1965, Carling Festival Arts award, Toronto, 1969, Can. Coun. award, 1969, Marriott award for hand blown glass, 1977; J.S. McClean scholar Ont. Coll. Art, 1960, Can. Scandinavian Found. traveling scholar, 1974; travel grantee Can. Scandinavian Found., 1974, Can. Guild Crafts, 1975; grantee Can. Coun., 1973, Ont. Arts Coun., 1979, Dept. Culture grantee N.S. Province Govt., Internat. Art Glass Mus., Ebeltoft, Denmark, 1986. Mem. Royal Can. Acad. Arts, Visual Arts Ont., N.S. Designer's Craftsman, Can. Crafts Coun., Ont. Crafts Coun., Can. Ceramic Soc., Ont. Potters Assn., Ont. Arts Coun. Address: 11227 Hwy 1 RR 1, Wolfville, NS Canada B0P 1X0

BARTKO, GYÖRGY JENŐ, psychiatrist; b. Budapest, Hungary, May 10, 1947; s. György and Erzsèbet (Paxy) B.; m. Ilona Herczeg, July 28, 1990; 1 child, Anna Lilla. MD, Semmelweis U. Medicine, Budapest, 1973; PhD, Hungarian Acad. Scis., Budapest, 1996; MSc in Health Adminstrn., Haynal Imre U. Hlth Scis., Budapest, 1998. Clin. psychiatrist Nat. Inst. Nervous Mental Disorders, Budapest, 1979-90; dept. head Jahn Ferenc South Pest Hosp., Budapest, 1992-93, dep. med. dir., 1993—; mng. dir. Medic-CNS Ltd., Budapest, 1997—; expert on quality assurance, 2000—. Editor Psychiatria Hungarica, 1994—; contbr. articles to profl. jours. Pres. Pszichoinnova Found., Budapest, 1999—. Mt. Sinai Sch. Medicine fellow, N.Y., 1990-92, DAAD fellow, Munich, Germany, 1988. Mem. European Coll. Neuropsycho Pharmacology, Hungarian Coll. Neuropsychopharmacology, Assn. Hungarian Psychiatrists. Office: Medic-CNS Kft, Zöldlomb u 46 Fszt 1, 1025 Budapest Hungary

BARTLETT, ARTHUR EUGENE, franchise executive; b. Glens Falls, N.Y., Nov. 26, 1933; s. Raymond Ernest and Thelma (Williams) B.; m. Collette R. Bartlett, Jan. 9, 1955; 1 dau., Stacy Lynn. Sales mgr. Forest E. Olson, Inc., 1960-64; co-founder, v.p. Four Star Realty, Inc., Santa Ana, Calif., 1964-71, v.p., sec., 1964-71; founder, pres. Comps, Inc., Tustin, Calif., 1971-81; co-founder, chmn. of bd., pres., CEO Century 21 Real Estate Corp., Tustin, 1980—; pres. Larwin Sq. LLC Shopping Ctr, Tustin, Calif., 1979—. Chmn. bd. United Western Med. Ctrs., 1981-87. Named to Internat. Franchise Assn. Hall of Fame, 1987. Mem. Internat. Franchise Assn. (v.p., bd. dirs. 1975-80). Lodge: Masons. Office: 275 Centennial Way Ste 209 Tustin CA 92780-3709

BARTLETT, CHERYL ANN, public health service administrator; b. Norwich, Conn., June 28, 1954; d. William Jr. and Frances (Fredette) B.; m. Rogers Washburn Cabot Jr., June 5, 1982 (div. July 1995); m. Bruce Templin Miller, Sept. 10, 1995. ASN, Quinnipiac Coll., 1979; student healthcare adminstrn., Stonehill Coll. Cert. Infection Control, dialysis nursing, HIV/AIDS nursing. Nursing supr. Nantucket (Mass.) Cottage Hosp., 1981-95, dir. nursing, 1995, dir. clin. svcs., 1995-97; public health officer Public Health Assocs. of Nantucket, Southeastern, Mass., 1989—; exec. dir. Nantucket AIDS Network, 1989—; spkr. in field. Bd. dirs. Nantucket Housing Authority Properties Inc., Nantucket, 1997—; apptd. pres. Cmty. Action Com., Cape Cod and Islands, 1993—; selectman Town of Nantucket, 1993-96, county commr., 1993-96, chmn. Nantucket Bd. Health, 1992-94; mem. Coun. for Health and Human Svcs., 1990-93, chmn., 96—, chmn., 1998-99; pres. bd. dirs. Family and Children's Svc. Recipient Cmty. Recognition award AIDS Action Com. of Mass., 1996, Outstanding Cmty. Health Program, U.S. Dept. of Health and Human Svcs., 1993, Outstanding Citizens award Nantucket Rotary Club, 1992, Recognition for Dedication and Commitment for the Care of AIDS Patients, Mass. State Senate, 1991, Mass. House of Reps., 1991. Mem. ANA, Assn. of Nurses in AIDS Care (govt. rels. com. 1997, chmn. govt. rels. com. 1999), Assn. of Infection Control Practitioners (nominating com. 1991-92, bd. dirs.), Mass. Nurses Assn., Alpha Sigma Lambda. Avocations: reading, gourmet cooking, 3rd world travel, public health volunteer work. E-mail: cbartlett@nanet.org. Home: PO Box 1248 Nantucket MA 02554-1248 Office: Nantucket AIDS Network 35 Old South Rd Nantucket MA 02554-2895

BARTLETT, JAMES WILSON, III, lawyer; b. Pasadena, Calif., Mar. 21, 1946; s. James Wilson Jr. and Helen (Archbold) B.; m. Jane Edmunds Graves; children: Matthew Archbold, Polly Graves. BA, Washington & Lee U., 1968; JD, Vanderbilt U., 1975. Bar: Md. 1975, U.S. Dist. Ct. Md. 1975, U.S. Dist. Ct. (no. dist.) Ohio, 1992, U.S. Ct. Claims 1984, U.S. Ct. Appeals (4th cir.) 1976, U.S. Ct. Appeals (6th cir.) 1992, U.S. Supreme Ct. 1995. Assoc. Semmes, Bowen & Semmes, Balt., 1975-85; pvt. practice Balt., 1985-86; ptnr. Kroll & Tract, Balt., 1986-87; ptnr. Wilson, Elser, Moskowitz, Edelman & Dicker, Balt., 1987-98, mng. ptnr., 1998—; permanent mem. jud. conf. 4th Cir. Assoc. editor: Am. Maritime Cases, 1997—; contbr. articles to profl. jours. Chmn. law firm campaign United Fund, Balt., 1979; bd. dirs. Roland Park Civic League, 1987-90. 1st lt. U.S. Army, 1969-71. Mem. ABA (chmn. admiralty and maritime litigation com. litigation sect. 1997-99, vice chmn. 1985-88, chmn. admiralty and maritime law com. tort and ins. practice sect. 1990-91, vice chmn. 1992-95), Md. Bar Assn., Balt. City Bar Assn., Maritime Law Assn. U.S. (proctor, bd. dirs. 1998—, chair practice and proc. com. 2000—), Def. Rsch. Inst., Md. Assn. Def. Trial Counsel, Assn. Average Adjusters (Eng.), Assn. Average Adjusters U.S., Am. Boat and Yacht Coun., St. Andrews Soc., Md. Club, Propeller Club U.S. (gov. Balt. chpt. 1984-87, 97—, v.p. 1987-88, exec. v.p. 1988-89, pres. 1989-90, nat. regional v.p. 1991-92, nat. 3d v.p. 1995-96). Republican. Presbyterian. Home: 307 Edgevale Rd Baltimore MD 21210-1913 Office: Wilson Elser Moskowitz Edelman & Ducker 400 E Pratt St Fl 7 Baltimore MD 21202-3116

BARTLETT, MAURICE STEVENSON, statistician, biomathematician; b. London, June 18, 1910; s. William Stevenson and Eva (White) B.; m. Sheila Rosemary Chapman, Sept. 11, 1957; 1 child, Penelope. BS, U. London, 1931, DSc, 1937; BA, Queens' Coll., Cambridge, Eng., 1932; DSc (hon.), U. Chgo., 1966, U. Hull, Eng., 1976. Asst. lectr. stats. U. Coll., London, 1933-34, prof. stats., 1960-67; statistician Imperial Chem. Industries, Ltd., London, 1934-38; lectr. math. U. Cambridge, 1938-47; on nat. svc. Min. Supply, Eng., 1939-46; prof. math. stats. U. Manchester, Eng., 1947-60; prof. biomath. U. Oxford, Eng., 1967-75, prof. emeritus, 1975—. Author: (book) Introduction to Stochastic Processes, 1955, Stochastic Population Models in Ecology and Epidemiology, 1960, Essays in Probabiity and Statistics, 1962, Probability, Statistics and Time, 1975, The Statistical Analysis of Spatial Pattern, 1976, Selected Papers, 3 vols., 1989. Recipient Rayleigh prize U. Cambridge, 1933, Weldon prize and medal U. Oxford, 1971. Fellow Royal Soc. London (Coun. 1965-67), Royal Statis. Soc. (pres. 1966-67, Guy silver medal 1952, Guy gold medal 1969), Manchester Statis. Soc. (hon., pres. 1959-60); mem. Internat. Statis. Inst. (hon.), Biometric Soc. (Brit. region pres. 1965-66), U.S. Nat. Acad. Sci. (fgn. assoc.). Home: Overcliff 4 Trefusis Terr, Exmouth EX8 2AX, England

BARTLETT, MICHAEL JOHN, swimming pool company executive; b. Bristol, Eng., July 5, 1934; s. Robert Raymond and Anne Gwendoline (Williams) B.; m. Jacqueline Susan; children: Christopher, John, Julia, Trudi Jane Fiona. Student, St. Davids Coll., 1950. Sales dir. R.R. Bartlett & Sons Ltd., Bristol, 1950—. Author: (with others) Towards a Perfect Pool, 1982. Served with Royal Air Force, 1952-55. Mem. Inst. Swimming Pool Engrs., Swimming Pool and Allied Trades Assn. (pres. 1984-85, various coms., rep. 1975-85), Royal Soc. Health, Spata Golf Soc. Ch. of Eng. Avocations: gardening, walking, golfing, reading, computer programming. Office: Robert R Bartlett & Sons Ltd, Millbrook Rd Stover Trad Estate, Bristol BS17 5PB, England

BARTLETT, THOMAS FOSTER, international management consultant; b. Oklahoma City, Nov. 28, 1918; s. Martin Johnson and Clara Nell (Mattingly) B. BS, Harvard U., 1943, MBA, 1948; cert., Sorbonne, Paris, 1987, Oxford (Eng.) U., 1988, Cambridge (Eng.) U., England, 1989, U. Salamanca, 1993, U. Genoa, 1994; grad., US Command and Gen. Staff Coll, Ft. Leavenworth, Kans., 1945. Asst. to pres. Am. Express Co., N.Y.C., 1948-50; export promotion specialist Dept. of State, Paris; mem. U.S. Mission to NATO Dept. Def., London and Paris; econ. cons. Am. Embassy, Rome, 1950-55; exec. asst. to pres. for internat. devel. Kaiser Industries, Oakland, Calif., 1955-56; mktg. specialist Bigelow-Sanford Inc., N.Y.C., 1957-59; pres. Internat. Mgmt. Cons. Thomas F. Bartlett & Assocs., N.Y.C., 1959—; cons. for UN, U.S. and fgn. govts. corps., other orgns. Capt. U.S. Army, 1943-46, maj. USAF Res. Mem. Am. Soc. Profl. Cons., Am. Mgmt. Assn., Am. Mktg. Assn., Harvard Club. Avocations: travel, photography, lecturing. Office: Thomas F Bartlett & Assoc 330 E 52nd St New York NY 10022-6718

BARTLEY, ROBERT LEROY, newspaper editor; b. Marshall, Minn., Oct. 12, 1937; s. Theodore French and Iva Mae (Radach) B.; m. Edith Jean Lillie, Dec. 29, 1960; children: Edith Elizabeth, Susan Lillie, Katherine French. BS, Iowa State U., 1959; MS, U. Wis., 1962; LLD, Macalester Coll., 1982, Babson Coll., 1987; HHD, Adelphi U., 1992. Reporter Grinnell (Iowa) Herald-Register, 1959-60; staff reporter Wall Street Jour., Chgo., 1962-63, Phila., 1963-64; editorial writer Wall Street Jour., N.Y.C., 1964-70, Washington, 1970-71; editor editorial page Wall Street Jour., N.Y.C., 1972-78; editor Wall Street Jour., 1979—, v.p., 1983—. Author: The Seven Fat Years, 1992. Trustee emeritus Mayo Found. Served to 2d lt. USAR, 1960. Recipient Overseas Press Club citation, 1977, Gerald Loeb award, 1979, Pulitzer prize for editorial writing, 1980. Mem. Am. Soc. Newspaper Editors, Soc. Profl. Journalists, Nat. Conf. Editl. Writers, Am. Polit. Sci. Assn., Coun. on Fgn. Rels., Heights Casino Club. Office: The Wall Street Jour 200 Liberty St New York NY 10281-1003

BARTNICKA, KALINA HANNA, history of education educator, researcher; b. Warsaw, Poland, July 3, 1937; d. Alfred Konstanty and Helena (Kaim) Wojnarski; m. Andrzej Piotr Bartnicki, Dec. 17, 1956; 1 child, Sławomir. MA in History of Fine Arts, Warsaw U., 1959, MA in History, 1961, D in Humanities (History Edn.), 1970; habilitation, Polish Acad. Scis., Warsaw, 1980. Grad. asst. Inst. History of Scis. Polish Acad. Scis., Warsaw, 1963-71, adj. lectr., 1971-80, assoc. prof., 1980-92, prof., 1992—; prof. pedagogical dept. Warsaw U., 1989—; chair history of edn. pedagogical dept. Pultusk (Poland) Sch. of Humanities, 1994—. Author: (books) Polish Fine Arts Schools at the Turn of the 18th Century (1764-1831), 1970, The Patriotic Education in Schools of the Commission for National Education, 1973, The Educational Activities of Jan Sniadecki, 1980 (Spl. prize Polish Acad. Scis. 1981); editor: Archiwum Dziejów OŚwiaty, Warsaw,; co-author, editor Kwartalnik Pedagogiczny, 1994— (prize Pedagogical dept. Warsaw U. 1997), co-editor: Rozprawy z Dziejów OŚwiaty, Warsaw, 1975—. Co-recipient prize The Rector of Yaquellonian U., 1985. Mem. Polish Acad. Scis. (com. history of scis and tech.), Internat. Standing Conf. for History of Edn. Roman Catholic. Avocations: tourism, fairy-tales, folk music. Home: Skloby 5, 01-473 Warsaw Poland Office: Inst Hist of Scis, Lil Nowyswiat 72, 00330 Warsaw Poland

BARTNICKI, KAREN JO, social services administrator; b. Beverly, Mass., May 2, 1958; d. Edward W. and Ruth B. Bartnicki. BA in Sociology, Regis Coll., 1980; MA in Psychology, Calif. State U., Sacramento, 1997. Cert. Coun. on Social Work Edn., Meeting Planners Internat. Activities dir. Redwood Villa Retirement Residence, Mountain View, Calif., 1989-90; dir. social svcs., admissions and mktg. Southpark Cmty. Hosp., Sacramento, 1990-91, Gold Country Health Ctr., Placerville, Calif., 1991-92; social worker, social work cons. Vital Care Am., Gardena, Calif., 1993-94, Mediplex, Lowell, Mass., 1994-95; adminstr. John Bertram House Assisted Living, Salem, Mass., 1995-96; event cons. Interface Found., Newton, Mass., 1997; mgr. social svcs. Vencor Hosp., Boston-North Shore, Peabody, Mass., 1998-99; exec. dir. Valley Terrace, Terrace Cmtys., Hartford, Vt., 1999-2000; mem. adv. bd. City of Santa Clara-Silicon Valley 1986 Conv., Santa Clara, Calif., 1986; exec. dir. Meetings Plus, Fremont, Calif., 1986-89; program cons., event planner Computer Faire Inc./The Interface Group, Needham, Mass., 1984-86; program mgr., conf. dir. CW Comms., Inc., Framingham, Mass., 1981-84; mem. adv. bd. West Coast Computer Faire, San Francisco, 1987, 88. Author: (book) An Exploration of Life Experiences, Personality Traits and Sleep Habits in Relation to Dream Recall and Dream Content, 1997; prodr., author: (videotape) Microcomputer Application Spotlight: Desktop Publishing, 1987. Mem. Inst. Noetic Scis., Assn. Rsch. and Enlightenment, Am. Soc. Psychical Rschrs., Assn. for Study of Dreams, Psi Chi, Pi Gamma Mu. Avocations: sleep and dream research, philosophy and religion, poetry, creative writing, outdoor recreation. Address: PO Box 142 Beverly MA 01915-0003

BARTNOFF, JUDITH, judge; b. Boston, Apr. 14, 1949; d. Shepard and Irene F. (Tennenbaum) B.; m. Eugene F. Sofer, Sept. 10, 1978; 1 child, Nelson Bartnoff Sofer. BA magna cum laude, Radcliffe Coll., 1971; JD (Harlan Fiske Stone scholar), Columbia U., 1974; LLM, Georgetown U., 1975. Bar: D.C. 1975, U.S. Dist. Ct. D.C. 1975, U.S. Ct. Appeals (D.C. cir.) 1980, U.S. Ct. Appeals (fed. cir.) 1985, U.S. Ct. Appeals (11th cir.) 1988, U.S. Ct. Appeals (3d cir.) 1989, U.S. Claims Ct. 1991. Fellow Inst. Pub. Interest Representation, Georgetown Law Ctr., Washington, 1974-75; staff atty. Council Pub. Interest Law, Washington, 1975-77; spl. asst. to asst. atty. gen. criminal div. Dept. Justice, Washington, 1977-78; assoc. dep. atty. gen. Dept. Justice, 1978-80; spl. asst. U.S. atty. Office of U.S. Atty., Washington, 1980-81, asst. U.S. atty., 1982-85; assoc. firm Patton, Boggs & Blow, 1985-87, ptnr., 1988-94, assoc. ind. counsel, 1993-94; assoc. judge Superior Ct. of D.C., Washington, 1994—; mediator U.S. Dist. Ct. D.C., 1991-94; mem. com. on pro se litigation U.S Dist. Ct., 1991-94. Mem. D.C. Bar Task Force on Children at Risk, 1997-98. Fellow Am. Bar Found.; mem. Nat. Assn. Women Judges, D.C. Bar, Women's Bar Assn. Office: 500 Indiana Ave NW Washington DC 20001-2131

BARTO, BRADLEY EDWARD, small business owner, educator; b. N.Y.C., Nov. 25, 1956; s. Kenneth William and Edna Ruth (Dalton) B.; m. Cheryl Annette Pray, Nov. 28, 1987; 1 child, David Bradley. B Engring., N.Y. Maritime Coll., 1982; M Gen. Adminstrn., U. Md., 1989; postgrad., U. Sarasota. Sr. engr. Advanced Tech., Inc., McLean, Va., 1982-85, Arinc Rsch., Inc., Annapolis, Md., 1985-87; pres., owner B Square Computing, Inc., Riva, Md., 1987—; pres. BCD Enterprises, Riva, Md., 1995—; prof. U. Md., College Park, 1990—, portfolio reviewer Excel program, 1995—. Inventor Chocks, 1995. Republican. Lutheran. Avocations: gofl, baseball, tennis, writing children's books. Home: 905 Malvern Hill Dr Davidsonville MD 21035-1242 Office: B Square Computing PO Box 606 Riva MD 21140-0606

BARTOL, ERNEST THOMAS, lawyer; b. Mineola, N.Y., Feb. 2, 1946; s. Frank Henry and Mary Ann (Kretlein) B.; m. Christine Ann Pillis; children: Jacqueline Marie, Aimee Elizabeth, Suzanne Melissa. BS in Acctg., Fordham U., 1967; JD, Villanova U., 1970. Bar: N.Y. 1971, U.S. Dist. Ct. (ea. and so. dists.) N.Y. 1973, U.S. Ct. Appeals (2d cir.) 1975, U.S. Supreme Ct. 1974. Staff acct. Pustorino, Puglisi, Behan & Co., N.Y.C., 1965-70; tax specialist Arthur Young & Co., Phila., 1970; acct. Arthur Andersen & Co., N.Y.C., 1970-71; assoc. Gehrig, Ritter, Coffey et al, Hempstead, N.Y., 1971-78; founder, sr. ptnr. Murphy, Bartol & O'Brien, LLP, Mineola, N.Y., 1978—; bd. dirs. numerous cos.; counsel to senator N.Y. State Senate, Garden City, 1985-90. Exec. leader Nassau County Rep. Com., Westbury, N.Y., 1978—, Oyster Bay Rep. Com., 1978—; sec., mem. parish coun. and spl. sch. com. St. Edward Roman Catn. Ch., Syosset, N.Y., 1978-80; mem. exec. com. United Cerebral Palsy Assn. Nassau County, 1978—, chmn. forget-me-not ball, 1987-92; pres., founder cmty. adv. coun. Syosset Cmty. Hosp., 1987-92; bd. dirs. L.I. Children's Mus., 1996-99; bd. trustees NY Inst. Tech., 1997-99. Named Man of Yr., United Cerebral Palsy Assn. Nassau County, 1993. Mem. ABA, N.Y. State Bar Assn. (trusts and estates law com. 1983—, lectr. on estate topics), Nassau County Bar Assn. (estates and trusts law com. 1975—), profl. ethics com. 1980-86, 89-93), Criminal Cts. Bar Assn., Nassau Lawyers Assn. L.I. (bd. dirs. 1977—, chmn. 1992-93, rec. sec. 1993-94, corr. sec. 1994-95, 1st v.p. 1995-97, pres. 1997-98), Fed. Bar Coun., N.Y. State Trial Lawyers Assn., Cath. Lawyers Guild Diocese Rockville Centre, Chaminade H.S. Alumni Assn. (class rep. 1971, class dir. 1971-72, 1st v.p. 1972-74, pres. 1974-76), Rotary (sec.-treas. Syosset club 1980-90), Alpha Kappa Psi. Roman Catholic. Avocations: racquetball, tennis, fishing, softball, stamp collecting. E-mail: mbolegal@aol.com. Office: Murphy Bartol & O'Brien LLP 22 Jericho Tpke Ste 103 Mineola NY 11501-2976

BARTOLI, CECILIA, soprano; b. Italy, 1967; d. Pietro Angelo and Silvana B. Attended, Academia de Santa Cecilia. Recording artist Decca/London, 1986—. Stage debut, Verona, 1987; appearances include La Scala, Met. Opera, Opéra Bastille, Carnegie Hall, Berlin, Nantes, Warsaw, Naples, Zürich, Orch. Hall, Chgo.; albums: Rossini Recitals, Mozart Arias, Rossini Heroines; #1 album If You Love Me (33 weeks Billboard charts, Grammy nomination, Best Classical album, 1994), 1992, Mozart Portraits, 1995, An Italian Songbook, 1997, Vivaldi album, 1999. Named Musical America's Vocalist of Yr., 1993; recipient Grammy award Best Classical Vocal, 1994. Office: c/o Edgar Vincent 157 W 57th St Ste 502 New York NY 10019-2210

BARTOLI, ETTORE, medical educator; b. Piacenza, Italy, Feb. 10, 1938; s. Italo Bartoli and Anna Giuditta Ruggeri; m. Sonia Rossi Compostella, Oct. 10, 1979; children: Laura, Eleonora. MD, Med. U. Parma, 1962. Intern, resident, fellow U. Torino, Italy, 1962-69; fellow CNR, San Francisco, 1969-71; asst. rschr. U. Calif. San Francisco, 1971-73; resident U. Tex. San Antonio, 1974-75; asst., prof. U. Sassari, Italy, 1975-89; prof. U. Udine, Italy, 1989-99, U. Novara, 1999—. Author, editor: Yearbook of Nephrology, 1995; contbr. articles to profl. jours. Mem. EDTA, Internat. Soc. Nephrology, Italian Soc. Internal Medicine. Office: U Novara Dept Sci Medicine, Via Solaroli 17, 28100 Novara Italy

BARTOLI, IVAN RENZO, scientific marketing service executive; b. Novellara, Re, Italy, Sept. 5, 1950; s. Alberto Ildebrando and Zuma Luciana (Bo) B.; m. Claudia Francesca Barbieri, June 5, 1974; children: Fulvia, Federica. BSc, MD, U. Milan, 1977. Product mgr. Roche, Milan, 1980-82; sales mgr. Abbott Labs., Rome, 1982-84; bus. mgr. Kontron, Milan, 1984-86; gen. mgr. Am. Hosp. Supply, Milan, 1986-87, Kaneka, Milan, 1987-90; pres. Sci. Mktg. Svc., Milan, 1990—. Inventor: menopause test, 1995; contbr. articles to profl. jours. Trade union rep., Milan, 1971-76; pres. Ednl. Activities, Merate, Italy, 1990-92. Mem. Ferrari Owner's Club, Horse Jumping Club.

Avocations: Ferrari car driver, horse rider. Home: Via Statale 11/P, 23807 Merate Italy Office: Sci Mktg Svc, Vis S Maria Valle 7, 20123 Milan Italy

BARTOLIC, JURAJ, microwave electronics educator; b. Zagreb, Croatia, May 22, 1948; s. Juraj and Ana (Pernar) B.; m. Nevenka Leskovar, July 14, 1973; 1 child, Nina. Diploma in Engring., U. Zagreb, 1971, MS, 1975, PhD, 1982. Constructor RIZ, Zagreb, 1972-74; rsch. asst. U. Zagreb, 1974-83, asst. prof., 1983-93, assoc. prof., 1993-96, prof., 1996—. Author: Mixing and Mixers, 1995. Recipient Award Skolska Knjiga, 1996. Mem. IEEE, Korema Zagreb, Elmar Zadar. Home: Ribnjak 32, HR-10000 Zagreb Croatia Office: Faculty Elec Engring, Unska 3, HR-10000 Zagreb Croatia

BARTOLOTTI, JOSSIF PETER See CARRINGTON, J(OE) P(ETER)

BARTON, ALLAN DOUGLAS, retired university executive; b. Melbourne, Australia, Mar. 3, 1933; s. Ralph Thomas and Emily (Whiteside) B.; m. Valerie Sheila Bunn, Nov. 6, 1964 (div. 1981); children: Belinda Anne, Amanda Kim. Cert. acct., Australia. Tutor Melbourne U., 1954-56; rsch. student Cambridge U., Eng., 1956-59; lectr. econs. to reader Adelaide U., South Australia, 1959-66; prof. acctg. Macquarie U., Sydney, N.S.W., 1967-74; prof. acctg. Australian Nat. U., Canberra, 1975—, treas., 1984—. Author: Anatomy of Accounting, 1975, 78, 84, (monograph) Objectives and Basic Concepts of Accounting, 1982; editor: Readings in Advanced Accounting Theory, 1980, 82, 84. Fellow Royal Econ. Soc., Australian Soc. Accts. (pres. A.C.T. divsn. 1983-84); mem. Acctg. Assn. Australia and N.Z. (pres. 1968), Am. Acctg. Assn., Am. Econ. Assn. Presbyterian.

BARTON, DIANE PATRICIA, parasitologist; b. Sydney, May 18, 1966; d. Francis Charles and Mary Therese (Donnelly) B. BS, U. Queensland, 1986, BS with honors, 1987; PhD, James Cook U., 1995. Rsch. asst. dept. parasitology U. Queensland, Brisbane, Australia, 1988; tutor James Cook U., Townsville, Australia, 1989-92, assoc. lectr., 1992-97, lectr., 1998—; rschr. CSIRO Toad Project, Venezuela, 1994. Contbr. articles to profl. jours. Rsch. grantee CSIRO, 1994, James Cook U., 1994. Mem. Australian Soc. Parasitology, Wildlife Disease Soc., Soc. Study Amphibians and Reptiles. Avocation: rugby. Office: James Cook U Dept Zoology, Townsville 4811, Australia

BARTON, EVERARD NATHANIEL, medical educator, consultant nephrologist; b. Scarborough, Tobago, Jan. 29, 1948; arrived in Jamaica, 1989; s. Daniel Marcus Barton and Cislyn Priscilla (Chapman) Romeo; m. Joycelyn Anderson, Oct. 18, 1995. BSc with honors, U. W.I., Trinidad and Tobago, 1974; MBBS, U. Ibadan, Nigeria, 1980; DM in Internal Medicine, U. W.I., Kingston, Jamaica, 1992. Med. cert. Nigeria, 1980, Trinidad & Tobago, 1983, Jamaica, 1989. Intern Univ. Coll. Hosp., Ibadan, 1980-81; med. officer Osogbo (Nigeria) State Hosp., 1981-83; sr. ho. officer Port-of-Spain (Trinidad) Hosp., 1983-89; resident Univ. Hosp. of W.I., Kingston, Jamaica, 1989-92, cons. physician, 1992—; lectr. U. W.I., 1992-93, Commonwealth rsch. fellow in nephrology Nottingham (Eng.) City Hosp. renal unit, 1993-94, lectr. dept. medicine U. W.I., 1994-95, sr. lectr., 1996—; mem. various coms., Univ. Hosp. W.I., mem. splty. bd. in medicine, 1995—. Editor-in-chief West Indian Med. Jour., 1999—; contbr. articles to profl. med. jours. Resource person Ch. of God 7th Day, Kingston, 1995—; welfare and edn. mem. Renal Support Found., Kingston, 1994—; exec. mem. Kidney Found., Kingston, 1993—; mem. resource pers. Lupus Found., Kingston, 1995—; del. People to People Internat., South Africa, 1996, Egypt, 1998. Recipient Cert., People to People Amb. Programs, 1998; ACP fellow, 1997; Renal Care grantee Renal Support Found., 1997; nephrology fellow Commonwealth Med. Fellowship, Eng., 1993. Mem. AAAS, N.Y. Acad. Scis., Internat. Soc. Nephrology. Mem. Ch. of England. Avocations: writing poetry, chess, swimming, community work. Office: U of WI, Dept Medicine, Mona Kingston 6, Jamaica

BARTON, GABOR JOZSEF, clinical scientist; b. Pecs, Hungary, Oct. 19, 1968; s. Jozsef and Jozsefne Eva (Gerenday) B.; m. Szilvia Rippl, Sept. 25, 1993; 1 child, Bence. MD, Med. U. Pecs, Hungary, 1993. Rsch. assoc. Liverpool John Moores U., England, 1995-96, lectr. sports sci., 1996; gait analyst Alder Hey Children's Hosp., Liverpool, 1996—. Co-author: (chpt.) A Fizioterapia Elmelete es Gyakorlata, 1995; contbr. articles to profl. jours. Avocations: information technologies, travel, sports. Office: Alder Hey Childrens Hosp, Eaton Rd, Liverpool L12 2AP, England

BARTON, JOHN BERNARD ADIE, drama director and dramatic adaptor; b. London, Nov. 26, 1928; s. Sir Harold Montague and Joyce (Wale) B.; m. Anne Righter. Ed., Kings Coll., Cambridge, Eng. Asst. dir. Royal Shakespeare Co., London, 1959-64; assoc. dir., 1964-91, advisory dir., 1991—; co-dir. Royal Shakespeare Co. at Stratford, 1968-74. works include The Tming of the Shrew, 1960, The Hollow Crown, 1961, The Art of Seduction, 1962, The War of the Roses, 1963-64, Henry IV, Parts I and II, 1964-66, Henry V, 1964-66, Love's Labour's Lost, 1967, 78, Coriolanus, 1967, 89, All's Well That Ends Well, 1967, Julius Caesar, 1968, Troilus and Cressida, 1968, 76, Twelfth Night, 1969, When Thou Art King, 1969, Measure for Measure, 1970, The Tempest, 1970, Richard II, 1971, 73, Othello, 1971, Dr. Faustus, 1974, King John, 1974, Cymbeline, 1974, Perkin Warbeck, 1975, Much Ado About Nothing, 1976, The Winter's Tale, 1976, A Midsummer Night's Dream, 1977, Pillars of the Community, 1977, The Way of the World, 1978, The Merchant of Venice, 1978, 81, The Greeks, 1979, Hamlet, 1980, Titus Andronicus, 1981, Two Gentlemen of Verona, 1981, La Ronde, 1982, Life's a Dream, 1983, The Devils, 1986, Three Sisters, 1988, Peer Gynt, 1994, Cain, 1995; dir.: The School for Scandal, Haymarket, 1983, Duke of York's, 1983, The Vikings at Helgeland, Den Nationale Scene, Bergen, 1983, Peer Gynt, Oslo, 1990, 91, Measure for Measure, Oslo, 1991, As You Like It, Oslo, 1991, Workshops, N.Y., 1996, 97; writer, presenter: Playing Shakespeare, LWT, 1982, Channel 4, 1984; narrator: Morte d'Arthur, BBC2, 1990; author: The Hollow Crown, 1962, 2nd edit., 1971, The Wars of the Roses, 1970, The Greeks, 1981. Office: 14 De Walden Ct, 85 New Cavendish St, London W1M 7RA, England*

BARTON, JOHN MURRAY, artist, lecturer; b. N.Y.C., Feb. 8, 1921; s. Boris and Lena (Sirota) Silver; m. Irene Zevon, Dec. 15, 1945 (div. 1958); 1 child, Leonard Steven; m. Hilda, Jan. 21, 1966; 1 child, Erika Jane. Fine Art degree, Art Students League, 1936, 45; student, Tschacbasov Sch. Creative Art, 1955. Cert. Appraisal Studies in Fine and Decorative Arts, NYU, 1996. Pres. John Barton Assos., Inc., N.Y.C., 1966-85, J.M.B. Pub. Ltd., N.Y.C., 1968-85, Multiple Reprodns. Inc., N.Y.C., 1968-85; appraiser 19th and 20th century prints. One-man shows include Fantasy Gallery, Washington, Hudson Guild, N.Y., Highgate Gallery, N.J., Glassboro State Coll., N.J., Swain Art Gallery, N.J., Fromuth Gallery, Pa., J. Walter Thompson, N.Y.; executed murals Pub. Sch. 41, N.Y., Mid. Sch. 141, N.Y., Carolina State Bank, S.C., U.S. Rubber Co.; represented in collections in Bibliotheque Nathionale, Paris, Bklyn. Mus., Met. Mus., N.Y., Butler Mus., Ohio, Fort Worth Art Ctr., Tex., Haifa Mus. of Modern Art, Israel, N.Y. Pub. Libr., Newark Pub. Libr., Phila. Mus. Art, Phila., Yale U. Mus., New Haven, N.C. Coll., Durham, U. N.C., Greensboro, Libr. Cong., Washington. Home: 45 Christopher St New York NY 10014-3533 Studio: 92 Grove St New York NY 10014-3548

BARTON, JÓZSEF, retired physician, dentist; b. Villány, Baranya, Hungary, July 31, 1937; s. József and Mária (Herr) B.; m. Éva Gerenday, Apr. 24, 1968; children: József Gábor, Balázs. MD, Med. U., Pécs, Hungary, 1961, DD, 1965; Sports Physiology Diploma, OTKI, Budapest, Hungary, 1979. Surgeon City Hosp., Komló, Hungary, 1961-62; dentist Stomatology Clinic, Pécs, Hungary, 1962-65; sports dr. Janus Pannonius U., Pécs, 1965-86; biomechanists U. Phys. Edn., Budapest, Hungary, 1986-93; vice dir. Faculty Health Scis. Med. U. Pécs, Zalaegerszeg, Hungary, 1993-97; ret., 1998. Author: (textbook) Biomechanics, 1984; contbr. articles to profl. jours. Scholar TEMPUS, 1991, TEMPUS-PHARE, 1997, Soros Found., 1997. Mem. Hungarian Sports Medicine Soc. Avocations: travel, swimming, skiing, photography. Home: Siklósi 80, 7632 Pécs Baranya, Hungary

BARTON, NICHOLAS JAMES, surgeon, educator; b. Ruislip, Middlesex, Eng., May 28, 1935; s. Ronald Cecil Nicholson and Mary Carty (Farrell) B.; m. Margaret Anne Joyce Rowe, Aug. 13, 1960; children: Neil, Katherine, Jane, Clare, David. MA, Cambridge U., 1956; MBBCh, Middlesex Hosp. Med. Sch., 1960. House surgeon, casualty officer Middlesex Hosp., London, 1959-60, 62; demonstrator U. Newcastle-Upon-Tyne, Eng., 1962-63; sr. house officer orthopaedics Addenbrooke's Hosp., Cambridge, Eng., 1964-66; fellow Harkness Found., 1967-68; registrar Robert Jones and Agnes Hunt Ortho. Hosp., Oswestry, Eng., 1966-67, 68-71; cons. orthopaedic surgeon Nottingham (Eng.) Univ. Hosp., 1971-95; clin. tchr. Nottingham U., 1971-95. Author: The Lost Rivers of London, 1962; editor: Fractures of the Hand and Wrist, 1988, The Upper Limb and Hand, 1999. Fellow Royal Coll. Surgeons Eng., Brit. Ortho. Assn.; mem. Brit. Soc. for Surgery of Hand (hon., pres. 1989), Am. Soc. for Surgery of Hand (corr.), Brazilian Soc. for Surgery of Hand (hon.), South African Soc. for Surgery of Hand (hon.), Hong Kong Soc. for Surgery of Hand (hon.). Avocations: reading, walking, cricket.

BARTON, NICK, rock mechanics and tunneling engineer; b. Leamington, Eng., Aug. 10, 1944; s. John Ryland and Phyl (Fox) B.; children: David, Andrew, Laurence, Karsten. BSc with honours, King's Coll., London, 1966; PhD in Rock Mechanics, Imperial Coll., London, 1971. Sr. engr. Norwegian Geotech. Inst., Oslo, 1971-80; sr staff cons. Terratek Inc., Salt Lake City, 1980-83, mgr. geomechanics, 1983-84; div. dir. Norwegian Geotech. Ins., Oslo, 1984-89, tech. advisor, 1989-99; prin. Nick Barton & Assocs., 2000—; adj. prof. U. Utah, Salt Lake City, 1983-84, U. Luleá, Sweden, 1986-90, U. São Paulo, Brazil, 1997—; prin. investigator for rock mechanics NEA/OECD Internat. Stripa Project, Sweden, 1986-92; geotech. cons. UK Nirex Ltd., Sellafield Nuclear waste repository project, 1990-96; cavern engring. cons. Hong Kong Geotech. Control Office, 1989-91, Atomic Energy of Can., Ltd., 1983, Norwegian Petroleum Directorate Ekofisk Res. Subs., 1985-86, Mingtan Pumped Hydro Project, Sinotech, Taiwan, 1987-90, UN Devel. Project, India, 1988, Gjovik Olympic Cavern, Norway, 1990-91, Shimizu Tunnel, Tomei II Hwy., Japan Fuji Rsch. Inst. Corp., 1995-97, Dul Hasti TBM Tunnel, Kashmir for Statkraft, 1997-98, Pont Ventoux TBM Tunnel, Nocon, Italy, 1997-99; gen. internat. cons. NGI, Oslo, 2000—; cons. Yucca Mountain Nev. nuclear waste repository for Morrison Knudsen/TRW, 2000; mem. expert panel for Oslo Tunnel, for Fjellingen, 1987-88, Carmel Tunnels; Haifa for Netivey Carme, 1994-95; Strategic Sewage Tunnels, Hong Kong for Mottconnell, 1994—, Hallandsås Tunnels, Sweden for Kraftbyggarna, 1993-94. Author book on TBM tunnelling, 2000; contbr. over 190 articles to tech. jours., conf. procs. Recipient award U.S. Nat. Com. Rock Mechanics, 1975, E.B. Burwell Jr. Meml. award Geol. Soc. Am., 1978, Lauritz Bjerrum Meml. lecture, Oslo, 1985, Manuel Rocha Meml. lecture, Lisbon, 1987. Mem. Internat. Soc. for Rock Mechanics (com. for rock joints, com. for scale effects in rock masses, com. for failure mechanisms in underground openings 1988-92, coord. internat. working party recommendations for quantitative description of discontinuities in rock masses 1977-78). Achievements include development of principal international method of characterizing rock masses for designing tunnel and rock cavern support (Q-system, Barton, Lien and Lunde 1974); co-development of Barton-Bandis joint constitutive model for computer modelling of rock mass response to excavation, 1981; co-development of NMT Concept, Norwegian Method of Tunnelling, 1992; development of Q-TBM method for machine-bored tunnels, 1999, TBM tunnelling in jointed and faulted rock, 2000.

BARTON, NOEL, accountant; b. London, July 8, 1930; s. Arnold and Margaret Edna (Pearson) B.; m. Christine Wyatt Amos, Oct. 13, 1951; children: Paula Margaret Munro, Diane Elizabeth Kendall, Sandra Lynne Painter. Student, Kings Sch., Canterbury, Kent, Eng., 1944-47. Chartered acct. Ptnr. Peat, Marwick, Mitchell, Salisbury, Rhodesia, 1954-66; co. sec. The Zambia Sugar Co., Ltd., Lusaka, Zambia, 1966-69; asst. to chief acct. Tate & Lyle, Ltd., London, 1969-70; ptnr. Pannell, Kerr, Forster, Brit. Virgin Islands, 1970-83; sr. ptnr. Peat, Marwick, Mitchell (now KPMG Peat Marwick), Brit. Virgin Islands, 1983-89; chmn. Havelet Trust Co., Tortola, Brit. Virgin Islands, 1989-00. Contbg. author: Spitz Tax Havens Ency., 1975, Practical International Tax Planning, 1995. Fellow Inst. Chartered Accts. in Eng. and Wales; mem. Rotary, Sussex County Cricket Club (life), Internat. Tax Planning Assn. Mem. Ch. of Eng. Avocations: sports, travel, philately. Fax: (284-49) 45471.

BARTON, PAUL B., artist, sculptor; b. Worcester, Mass., Oct. 2, 1946; s. Walter E. Barton and Elsa Benson; m. Lorraine Barton-Haas, July 1, 1967; 1 child, Hannah C. BFA, Boston U., 1980. Journeyman carpenter Brotherhood Carpenters & Joiners, 1972-80; artist, 1980—. Prin. works include pub. sculpture Beulah Cmty. Ctr., 1997. Mem. Beulah (Colo.) Water Works Dist., 1997-99. Recipient Silver medal Boston U. Alumni, 1980. Mem. Internat. Sculpture Ctr., Nat. Sculpture Soc., Colorado Springs Art Guild, Pueblo Art Guild. Mem. Soc. of Friends. Avocations: fly fishing, fly tying, fly rod building. Home and Office: PO Box 176 Beulah CO 81023-0176

BARTON, PAUL J., lawyer; b. Price, Utah, Sept. 24, 1946; s. John O. and Mae L. Barton; m. Elaine L. York, Oct. 12, 1974 (div. Sept. 1997); children: Susan, John, James. BA in Econs., Brigham Young U., 1970; JD, U. Utah, 1973; LLM in Taxation, Washington U., 1974. Pvt. practice Salt Lake City, 1973—, real estate broker, 1979—; investment advisor Washington, and Utah, 1988—. Contbr. articles to profl. jours. With U.S. Army, 1969. Scholar Hinckley Inst., 1971, John A. Widtsoe Meml. scholar, 1972-73. Mem. Internat. Assn. Fin. Planners, Estate Planning Coun., Utah State Bar Assn. (probate and tax sect. 1974-2000, unauthorized practice law sect. 1994-99, advt. com. 1994-99). Mem. Ch. Jesus Christ Latter Day Sts. Avocations: basketball, hunting. Office: 345 E 400 S Ste 201 Salt Lake City UT 84111-2971

BARTON, SARAH MURIEL, lawyer; b. London, Mar. 23, 1958; d. Russell William Andrew Charles and Katherine Grizel (Maitland-Makgill-Crichton) B.; children: Daniel Russell Bernard, Caroline Sarah Katherine. BA, U. Toronto, Ont., Can., 1978; JD, Union U., Albany, 1981; LLM in Admiralty, Tulane U., 1982. Bar: N.Y. 1982, La. 1983, U.S. Dist. Ct. (ea. dist.) La. 1983, N.J. 1985, U.S. Dist. Ct. (we. dist.) La. 1985, U.S. Dist. Ct. (so. dist.) N.Y., U.S. Ct. Appeals (5th cir.) 1986. Assoc. Law Offices Frederick Gisevius, New Orleans, 1982-83, James Hanemann and Assocs., New Orleans, 1983-85; assoc. counsel Am. Bur. Shipping, N.Y.C. and London, 1985-96; gen. counsel ABS Group of Cos., Inc., Houston, 1997—, v.p., 1998—; spkr. Maritime Cyprus Legal Forum, 1993, Nat. Inst. and Royal Inst. Naval Archs., London, 1994. Mem. Am. Corp. Counsel Assn., Maritime Law Assn. (proctor). Home: 5100 San Felipe St Apt 57 Houston TX 77056-3600 Office: ABS Group of Cos Inc 16855 Northchase Dr Houston TX 77060-6006

BARTOS, ANDRES ESTEBAN, physician, educator; b. La Paz, Bolivia, May 31, 1946; s. Jorge B. and Susana Miklos; m. Luisa Margarita Amory; children: Jorge Luis, Jose Oscar, Andres Alegandro. MS, U. Lousanne, Switzerland, 1972. Pres. Bolivian Pediatric Assn., 1983-87; dir. maternal & child health Min. Health, Bolivia, 1986-88; pediatrician pvt. practice, Bolivia, 1979—; prof. pediatrics U. San Andres, Bolivia, 1991—; chief dept. pediatrics Hosp. Oberero No. 1, Bolivia, 1998—. Editor: Peistz de la Sociedad Bolivia de Pediatric, 1991-95. Fellow AAAP; mem. ALAPE. Avocations: acting, piano. Home: PO Box 3-12400, La Paz Bolivia

BARTOŠ, PAVEL, phytopathologist, geneticist, researcher; b. Pilsen, Czechoslovakia, Mar. 30, 1930; s. František and Marie (Votavová) B.; m. Zdenka Kořínková, Feb. 5, 1958; children: Hana, Pavel. Diploma Engring., Tech. U. Agr., Prague, 1954; PhD, Czechoslovak Acad. Agrl. Scis., Prague, 1962; DSc, Czechoslovak Acad. Scis., Prague, 1985. Asst. Rsch. Inst. Crop Prodn., Prague, 1953-66; leading scientist, 1969—; postdoctoral fellow Can. Nat. Rsch. Coun. Rsch. Sta., Can. Dept. Agr., Winnipeg, 1966-68; lectr. postgrad. courses U. Agr., Prague; mem. Cereal Rusts Found., 1980-92; mem. cooperation in field sci. and tech. rsch. 817-European Commn., 1995—. Co-author: Wheat, 1970, Genetics of Crops, 1987, General Plant Pathology, 1989, Resistance of Crop Plants against Fungi, 1997; contbr. articles to profl. jours.; mem. editl. bd. Plant Protection Sci., 1980—, Cereal Rsch. Comm., 1985—, Jour. Applied Genetics, 1995—; patent for seed treatment chem. Recipient award for sci. papers Czech Found. for Lit., 1986; grantee FAO, Rome, 1971, Volkswagen Stiftung, 1993-94. Mem. Eucarpia, Czech Acad. Agr., Czech Phytophathol. Soc., Czech Scientific Soc. Mycology, Carolinum. Avocations: hiking. Office: Rsch Inst Crop Prodn, Drnovská 507, 161 06 Prague Czech Republic

BARTOSCH, THORSTEN, electrotechnical engineer, researcher; b. Erlangen, Germany, Feb. 28, 1966; s. Eckehart and Isolde (Rose) B. Diploma in engring., U. Erlangen-Nuremberg, 1993, Dr in Telecomm., 2000. Rschr. Inst. Hochfrequenztechnik U. Erlangen-Nurenberg, 1993-94, rschr. Inst. Telecomm., 1994-98; sys. engr. Giesecke & Derrient GmbH, Gmunol, Germany, 1998-99; engr. automotive devel. Steyr-Daimler-Puch AG, Graz, Austria, 1999—. Contbr. articles to profl. jours. Active Tibet Initiative Deutschland. Office: Steyr-Daimler-Puch AG, Liebenauer Hauptstrasse 317, 8041 Graz Austria

BARTOSCHEWITZ, RAINER, chemist; b. Gifhorn, Germany, May 27, 1955; s. Kurt and Lieselotte (Käding) B.; m. Claudia Laatsch, June 16, 1983; children: Sven, Kira. Diploma in engring., U. Lübeck, Germany, 1980. With Volkswagen AG, Wolfsburg, Germany, 1980—. Contbr. articles to jours. in field. Mem. Meteoritical Soc., N.Y. Acad. Scis., Mineralogy and Geology Soc. Avocations: meteorite research and collecting, mineralogy. E-mail: bartoschewitz.metorite-lab@t-online.de.

BARTOSEK, KAREL, historian, writer; b. Skutec, Czech Republic, June 30, 1930; s. Karel Bartosek and Frantiska Stepankova; m. Suzanne, 1959; 3 children. Student, Charles U., Prague. Rsch. asst. Inst. History Czechoslovak Acad. Scis., 1960-69; rschr. Inst. d'Histoire du Temps Présent, CNRS, 1983-96. Author: Les Aveux des Archives, 1996; co-author: Le Livre noir du Communisme, crimes, terreur, répressions, 1997, Directeur de la revue La Nouvelles Alternatibe, 1986—. Avocations: swimming, skiing. Address: 6 rue du Moulin de la, Pointe, 75013 Paris France

BARTOSIK, ARTUR STANISLAW, scientist, educator; b. Pinczow, Poland, Dec. 30, 1953; s. Stanislaw and Janina (Szalapska) B.; m. Ewa Maria Rybak, Feb. 22, 1986; children: Filip, Julia. MS, Tech. U., Wroclaw, Poland, 1977; PhD, Tech. U., Kielce, Poland, 1989. Constructor Tech. U., Kielce, Poland, 1983-89, asst. prof., 1989—; dir. Continuing Edn. Ctr., Kiele, 1994—; cons. Polish Assn. Blind, Warsaw, 1993—. Contbr. articles to profl. jours.; inventor in field. Postdoctoral fellow U. Saskatchewan, Can., 1990-91. Mem. Polish Acad. Scis. (fluid mechanics sect.), World User Assn. Applied Computational Fluid Dynamics. Avocations: tennis, classical music, cycling. Home: Samsonow 51, 26-050 Samsonon Poland Office: Tech U, Al 1000-Lecia 7, 25-314 Kielce Poland

BARTOSZEWICZ, ANDRZEJ PAWEL, engineering educator, researcher; b. Lodz, Poland, Aug. 24, 1962; s. Jerzy and Maria (Zgliczynska) B. MSc, Tech. U. Lodz, 1987, PhD, 1993. Cert. engr. Fulbright vis. scholar Purdue U., West Lafayette, Ind., 1991-92; rsch. assoc. U. Leicester, Eng., 1995-96; rsch. assoc. Tech. U. Lodz, 1987-94, lectr., 1994—. Contbr. articles to profl. jours. Avocation: skiing. Office: Tech U Lodz, 18/22 Stefanowskiego St, 90-924 Lodz Poland

BARTOSZEWSKI, WLADYSLAW, Polish government official. Min. fgn. affairs Govt. of Poland, Warsaw. Office: Ministry of Fgn Affairs, Aleje 1 Szucha 23, 00-580 Warsaw Poland*

BARTOW, BARBARA JENÉ, university program administrator; b. Buffalo, June 26, 1950; d. Nicholas Michael Bojack and Lillian Lenore Bennett; m. Michael Hartzell Bartow; children: Barbara Simmons, Edward Michael Hagen. AA in Journalism, Miami Dade Jr. Coll., 1970; M. in Non-fiction Writing, USAF Air U., 1975, M. Adminstrn. Auto. mechanic Amoco, Miami, Fla., 1969-70; cargo dispatcher McKinley Transport Worldwide, Ont., Can., 1970-72; office adminstr. Modernage Furniture, Miami, 1972-74; social svc. rep. Vets. Adminstrn. and DAV and Am. Legion, 1976—; commdr. DAV and Am. Legion, 1985-86; deputy chief of staff DAV, 1986. Contbr. poetry to World of Poetry, Internat. Soc. Poets, Internat. Libr. of Poetry, Libr. of Congress, 1990—. Active crisis intervention CASA, Fla., 1984-86; foster parent DCFS, Ill.; Dem. polit. activist, Ill., Fla., N.Y., Pa., 1976—. Sgt USAF, 1974-82. Recipient citation of merit DAV, Fla., 1985. Roman Catholic. Avocations: writing, social work, wheelchair racing. Home: 1515 Lantern Ln Joliet IL 60433-2910

BARTRAM, RALPH HERBERT, physicist; b. N.Y.C., Aug. 16, 1929; s. Herbert L. and Grace L. Bartram; m. Ellen Anderson Devlin, Oct. 9, 1953; children: Ellen Ruth, Robert Arthur. Student, Northwestern U., 1948-49; BA cum laude, NYU, 1953, MS, 1956, PhD, 1960. Engr. Sylvania Electric Products Inc., Kew Gardens, N.Y., 1953-56; advanced rsch. physicist Gen. Telephone & Electronics Labs., Inc., Bayside, N.Y., 1956-61, cons., 1961-85; mem. faculty U. Conn., Storrs, 1961—, prof. physics, 1971-92, dept. head, 1986-92, prof. emeritus, 1992—; rsch. assoc. Atomic Energy Rsch. Establishment, Harwell, Eng., 1967-68; vis. prof. U. Oxford, Eng., 1978; sr. vis. fellow U. Strathclyde, Scotland, 1993; cons. U.S. Army, 1966-71, Am. Optical Co., 1966-78, Brookhaven Nat. Lab., 1971-85, Timex Corp., 1981-82, Polaroid Corp., 1987-88, Boston U., 1993-99, ALEM Assocs., 1996-99. Author: (with J.-M. Spaeth and J.R. Niklas) Structural Analysis of Point Defects in Solids, 1992, (with B. Henderson) Crystal-Field Engineering of Solid-State Laser Materials, 2000; contbr. articles on physics to profl. jours.; patentee microwave devices. Served with USN, 1946-48. Grantee U.S. AEC, 1963-69, U.S. Army Rsch. Office, 1971-78, 82-92, NSF, 1974-77, 83-91, NATO, 1985-90. Fellow Am. Phys. Soc.; mem. Optical Soc. Am., AAUP, Conn. Acad. Sci. Engring., Phi Beta Kappa, Sigma Xi, Phi Kappa Phi, Sigma Pi Sigma, Phi Eta Sigma. Home: 67 Independence Dr Mansfield Center CT 06250-1541 Office: U Conn Dept Physics Storrs Mansfield CT 06269-0001

BARTSCH, CHRISTIAN REINHARD, biochemist; b. Görlitz, Saxonia, Germany, Sept. 6, 1951; s. Werner Oskar and Ruth (Lehmann) B.; m. Hella Änne Trompelt, Mar. 26, 1981; 1 child, Angelika. BSc in Chemistry, U. Bonn, Fed. Republic Germany, 1974; MSc in Biochemistry, U. Tübingen, Fed. Republic Germany, 1985, PhD in Biochemistry, 1988; student in Neurochemistry, 2000. Rsch. chemist All-India Inst. Med. Scis., New Delhi, India, 1975-80; rsch. biochemist dept. gynecology U. Tübingen, 1989—. Contbr. articles to profl. publs. Studienstiftung d. Deutschen Volkes scholar, 1985-88. Mem. German Endocrine Soc., European Pineal Soc., Internat. Chronobiol. Soc., European Chronobiol. Soc., N.Y. Acad. Sci. Avocations: music, aikido, family. Office: U Tübingen Ctr Rsch Med, Ob Dem Himmelriech 7, D-72074 Tübingen Germany

BARTSCH, HELMUT, toxicologist, oncologist, educator; b. Endersdorf, Germany, Oct. 23, 1940; s. Wilhelm and Paula (Adam) B.; m. Gudrun Beutel, July 26, 1968; children: Eva, Friedemann, Stefani, Sebastian. BSc, MSc, U. Heidelberg, Germany, 1965, PhD, 1968; habilitation, Med. Sch., Hannover, Germany, 1979. Rsch. assoc. German Cancer Rsch. Ctr., Heidelberg, 1968-70, divsn. head, 1993—; postdoctoral fellow U. Wis., Madison, 1970-73; scientist WHO, Internat. Agy. Rsch. on Cancer, Lyon, France, 1973-80; unit chief WHO, IARC, Lyon, 1980-93; prof. U. Heidelberg, 1993—. Editor: (books) Host Factors in Human Carcinogenesis, 1982, Role of Cyclic Nucleic Acid Adducts in Carcinogenesis and Mutagenesis, 1986, The Relevance of Nitroso Compounds in Human Cancer: Exposure and Mechanisms, 1987, Methods for Detecting DNA Damaging Agents in Humans: Applications in Cancer Epidemiology and Prevention, 1988, Exocyclic DNA adducts in mutagenesis and Carcinogenesis, 1999. Recipient Rsch. award French Acad. Scis., Paris, 1990, French Acad. Medicine, Paris, 1990. Mem. Am. Assn. Cancer Rsch., European Assn. Cancer Rsch. Avocations: violin, viola, chamber music. Office: German Cancer Rsch Ctr, Im Neuenheimer Feld 280, D-69120 Heidelberg Germany

BARTSOCAS, CHRISTOS SPYROS, physician, educator; b. June 20, 1937; s. Spyros and Dora (Papaioannou) B.; m. Anna N. Petridou, Nov. 10, 1965; children: Spyros Nicholas, Nicholas Alexander. MD, U. Athens, 1960, DMS, 1963. Resident in pediats. Ag. Sofia Children's Hosp., Athens, 1963-64, attending pediatrician, 1968-73; resident in pediats. Yale-New Haven Hosp., 1964-66; clin. and rsch. fellow in pediat. endocrinology and metab. Mass. Gen. Hosp., Boston, 1966-68; tchg. asst. Yale U., New Haven, 1964-65, instr., 1965-66; rsch. fellow Harvard U., Cambridge, Mass., 1966-68; from assoc. prof. to prof. pediats. Athens U., 1974—. Author: Mycenaean Medicine, 1964, Management of Genetic Disorders, 1979, Progress in Dermatoglyphic Research, 1982, Skeletal Dysplasias, 1982, Endocrine Genetics and Genetics of Growth, 1985, Genetics of Neuromuscular Disorders, 1989, Genetics of Kidney Disorders, 1989, Genetics of

Hematological Disorders, 1991, Dysmorphology and Genetics of Cardiovascular Disorders, 1994, Genetic Counseling, 1998; contbr. articles to profl. jours. Pres. Juvenile Diabetes Found. Hellas. With Hellenic Navy, 1960-63. Fellow Am. Acad. Pediats., Am. Coll. Med. Genetics; mem. Soc. Pediat. Rsch., European Soc. Pediat. Rsch., European Soc. Human Genetics (pres. 1990), Hellenic Diabetes Assn. (pres. 1992). Greek Orthodox. Home: 47 Vasilissis Sofias Ave, GR-10676 Athens Greece Office: P&A Kyriakou Children's Hosp, PO Box 17177, GR-10024 Athens Greece

BARTUNEK, JIRI, agriculture educator; b. Velke Mezirici, Czech Republic, Feb. 21, 1933; s. Jan and Marie (Jaskova) B.; m. Pavla Cabova Bartunkova, July 27, 1962; 2 children. Degree in forest engring., U. Agr., Brno, Czech Republic, 1957, DSc, 1991. Dist. forester Forest Enterprise Velke Mezirici, Czech Republic, 1957-63; tchr. U. Agr., Brno, Czech Republic, 1964—; edtl. bd. Lesnictvi Forestry, 1990-97. Author: Forestry Economics, 1987; co-author: Management of Forestry and Economics, 1993; mem. editl. bd. Lesnictvi Forestry, 1990-97. Mem. Internat. Union of Forestry Rsch. Orgns. Avocation: music. Home: Alesova 47, 61300 Brno Czech Republic Office: Mendel U of Agr and Forestry, Zemedelska 3, 61300 Brno Czech Republic

BARTUNKOVA, JIRINA, immunologist; b. Prague, Czech Republic, Feb. 5, 1958; d. Josef and Jirina Zumr; children: Lenka, Jana. MD, Charles U., Prague, Czech Republic, 1983, PhD, 1989. Assoc. Charles U., Prague, Czech Republic, 1989-95; asst. prof., head Inst. Immunology, Prague, Czech Republic, 1995—. Contbr. articles to profl. jours. Rsch. grantee Czech Ministry Health, 1995—; fellow Hosp. Necker, Paris, 1991, WHO, Switzerland, 1994, Germany, 1995. Mem. Czech Soc. Immunology, European Soc. Immunodeficiences, Soc. Leukocyte Biology, Clin. Immunology Soc. Avocation: piano. Office: Inst Immunology, Uvalu 84, 15006 Prague Czech Republic

BARTZOKAS, ARISTIDES, meteorologist, climatologist; b. Rethymnon, Crete, Greece, Aug. 23, 1956; s. Nicholas and Sophia (Karoubali) B.; m. Katerina Nassika, June 25, 1961; children: Sophia-Athina, Efthalia-Erato. BSc in Physics, Thessaloniki (Greece) U., 1979; MSc in Meteorology-Climatology, Birmingham (Eng.) U., 1981; PhD in Meteorology-Climatology, Ioannina (Greece) U., 1989. Lab. asst. dept. physics Ioannina U., 1982-85, 87-90, lectr. dept. physics, 1990-95, asst. prof., 1995—. Author: (with D.A. Metaxas) Introduction to Dynamic Meteorology, 1992, (with B.D. Katsoulis and D.A. Metaxas) A Course in Meteorology, 1996; contbr. articles to sci. jours. Mem. Greek Meterol. Soc., Royal Meteorol. Soc., Union Greek Physicists, Ioannina Lions Club. Avocations: fishing, accordion, stamps, climbing. Office: Univ Ioannina Dept Physics, Lab Meteorology, 451 10 Ioannina Greece

BARU, MOSHE, molecular biologist, researcher; b. Pardes-Hana, Israel, Nov. 22, 1960; s. David and Amira (Rudin) B.; m. Einat Hamer, Sept. 12, 1989; children: Aviv, Or. BS, Hebrew U., Jerusalem, 1986; DSc, Technion, Haifa, Israel, 1992. Head R&D OMRI Labs., Rehovot, Israel, 1992—. Maj. Israel Def. Force, 1979-83. Home: Hadarim St, 37000 Pardes-Hana Israel Office: OMRI Labs PO Box 619, 76106 Rehovot Israel

BARUA, ALOK, engineering educator; b. Calcutta, India, June 6, 1953; s. Mrinal Kanti and Subinita Barua; m. Mausumi Barua, Dec. 8, 1983; 1 child, Arpita. BS, Calcutta U., 1972; B.Tech., Jadavpur U., India, 1977, M.Engring., 1980; PhD, Indian Inst. Tech., 1992. Lectr. Regional Engring. Coll., Rourkela, India, 1984-85; lectr. Indian Inst. Tech., Kharagpur, 1985-92, asst. prof., 1992-99, assoc. prof., 1999—. Author: Computer Aided Analysis, Synthesis and Expertise of Active Filters; contbr. articles to profl. jours. Mem. IEEE (sr.), System Soc. India (life). Buddhist. Avocations: reading, watching movies, visiting ruins of ancient civilizations. Office: Indian Inst Tech, Dept Elec Engring, Kharagpur 721302, India

BARUA, GAUTAM, environmental engineer educator; b. Jorhat, India, Dec. 4, 1965; s. Dina Nath and Bani (Sharma) B.; m. Monmee Bhattacherjee. B of Tech., Rajashan Agrl. U., Bikaner, India, 1989; M of Tech., Indian Inst. Tech., Kharagpur, 1991, PhD, 1995. Asst. prof. soil & water engring. Punjab Agrl. U., Ludhiana, India, 1996; lectr. soil & water engring. North Eastern Regional Inst. Sci. & Tech., Nirjuli, India, 1996—; rschr. in field. Contbr. articles to profl. jours. Avocation: reading. Home: KK Barooah Rd, Jorhat 785 001, India Office: North Eastern Regional Inst Sci & Tech, Dept Agrl Engring, Nirjuli 791 109, India

BARUCH, YEHUDA, educator; b. Haifa, Israel, Feb. 10, 1956; s. Moshe and Rachel (Gil) B.; m. Avital Schweitzer, Dec. 12, 1957; children: Ben, Aya, Neta, Avinoam. BSc in Electronic Engring., Ben Gurion U., 1981; MSc in Mgmt. Sci., The Technion, 1987, DSc in Mgmt. Scis., 1991. Rsch. fellow City U. Bus. Sch., 1991-92, London Bus. Sch., 1993-95; lectr. U. East Anglia, 1995—, sr. lectr., 1998—. Contbr. articles to profl. jours. Maj. Israeli Air Force, 1974-88. Grantee Ford Found., 1988, The Anglo Israeli Assn. British Coun., 1992. Office: U East Anglia, Earlham Rd, Norwich NR4 7TJ, England

BA-RUKAB, OMAR M., computer technology educator; b. Taif, Saudi Arabia, May 1, 1963; s. Mohammed Omar Ba-Rukab and Fatimah Mohammed Al-Amoudi; m. Nour Ahmed al-Amoudi, 1995; children: Mohammed, Osama. BSc in Elec. Engring. and Computer, King Abdullaziz U., Jeddah, Saudi Arabia, 1987; MSc in Computer Engring., Fla. Inst. Tech., 1993, PhD in Computer Engring., 1999. Tchg. asst. Jeddah Coll. Tech., 1987-91, lectr., 1993-95; head computer devision Jeddah Coll. of Electronic Tech., 1999—; mem. coll. bd. Jeddah Coll. Electronic Tech., 1999—; Contbr. articles to profl. jours. Cmty. svcs. tchr. computer programming, Jeddah Coll. of Electronics Tech., 2000. Muslim. Avocations: walking, reading, swimming. E-mail: obarukab@hotmail.com. Home: PO Box 109082, Jeddah 21351, Saudi Arabia

BARUSCH, LAWRENCE ROOS, lawyer; b. Oakland, Calif., Aug. 23, 1949; s. Maurice Radston and Phyllis (Rose) B.; m. Susan Amanda Smith, Aug. 7, 1983; children: Nathaniel M., Ariana G. BA summa cum laude, Harvard U., 1971, JD cum laude, 1975. Bar: Calif. 1975. Assoc. Cotton, Seligman & Ray, San Francisco, 1975-77; gen. counsel Jones & Guerrero Co., Inc., Agana, Guam, 1977-82; ptnr. Klemm, Blair & Barusch, P.C., Agana, Guam, 1982-85; assoc. Davis, Graham & Stubbs, Salt Lake City, 1986-87; counsel Parsons, Behl & Latimer, Salt Lake City, 1987-89, shareholder, 1989—; counsel Guam Tax Code Commn., 1990-94; adj. prof. U. Utah Coll. Law, 1998-99, 2000—, vis. assoc. prof., 1999-2000; mem. com. U.S. activities of foreigners and tax treaties, tax sect. ABA, 1994—. Contbr. articles to Guam Bar Jour., Utah Bar Jour. and Tax Notes. Chmn Dem. Party, Davis County, Utah, 1997-99. Sheldon fellow Harvard U., 1971. Mem. Guam Bar Assn. (pres. 1982-84), No. Marianas Bar Assn., Utah Bar Assn. (chmn. tax sect. 1994-95), Calif. Bar Assn., Phi Beta Kappa. Office: Parsons Behle & Latimer 201 S Main St Ste 1800 Salt Lake City UT 84111-2218

BARUZDIN, SERGEY ANATOLIEVICH, radioelectronics educator, researcher; b. St. Petersburg, Russia, Dec. 3, 1950; s. Anatoly Pavlovich and Ekaterina Nikolaevna (Liyazina) B.; m. Lubov Vladimirovna Ilinskaiya, Aug. 4, 1980 (div. Feb. 1990); children: Irina, Alexandr; m. Ludmila Ivanovna Nedumova, June 25, 1994. PhD of Tech. Sci., Inst. Elec. Engring., St. Petersburg, 1984. Engr. Main Geophys. Obs., Saint Petersburg, Russia, 1974-75; engr. Inst. of Elec. Engring., Saint Petersburg, 1975-77, jr. sci. worker, 1978-85, sr. sci. worker, 1985-89, docent, 1989—. Co-author: Functional Devices for Signal Processing, 1997; contbr. articles to profl. jours. Achievements include research in field of nuclear magnetic resonance and its applications for signal processing. Office: State Elec Engring U, LETI, 197376 Saint Petersburg Russia

BARWIG, REGIS NORBERT JAMES, priest; b. Chgo., Jan. 16, 1932; s. Ladislas-Joseph and Josepha Agnes (Neugebauer) B. AB, St. Procopius Coll., 1954; postgrad., Georgetown U., 1957, Pontifical Lateran U., Rome, 1959-61. Ordained priest Roman Cath. Ch., 1959. Sec. to abbot of Lisle, 1955-61; sec. gen. Christian Unity Apostolate, 1961-64; founding prior Claremont Priory, Cedarburg, Wis., 1964-67; prior Community of Our Lady, Oshkosh, Wis., 1968—; co-chmn. 1st Festival Faith, Milw., 1966; chmn. Ecumenical Conf. Spiritual and Liturgical Renewal Religious Life, 1969—; mem. Green Bay Diocese Ecumenical Commn., 1970-73; theol. cons. Consortium Perfectae Caritatis, 1974—; preacher, U.S. and Europe; U.S. liaison for beatification of Pope Pius IX, 1975—; assoc. Wanda Landowska Music Ctr., Lakeville, Conn., 1969; bd. dirs. Inter-Cath. Press Agy., N.Y., 1967-72. Author: Changing Habits, 1971, Waiting for Rain, 1975, Reflections on Spiritual Life for Order of Malta, 1982; translator: His Will Alone, 1971, Wanda Landowska Diaries, 1971, Pius XI-A Close-up, 1975, Pius IX-More than a Prophet, 1977, Writings of Blessed Maximilian Maria Kolbe, 1977, Evaluations of the Possibility of Constructing a Christian Ethic on the Assumptions of the Philosophy of Max Scheler, 1982; editor: Conferences of Mother Mary of Jesus, 1968; contbr. articles to religious publs. Decorated Bruderschaft, Collegio Teutonico, Vatican City, Knight Comdr., Order Isabel la Catolica, Spain, Grand Cross of Merit, Sovereign Mil. Order of Malta, Magistral Chaplain, Conventual Grand Cross Chaplain of Honor, Prelatial Councillor, Chief of Chaplains, Polish Assn., Sovereign Mil. Order of Malta, Knight Comdr. Ecclesiastical Grace, Gold Benemerenti medal Sacred Mil. Constantinian Order of St. George-Bourbon Two Sicilies, Chaplain Am. Del., Knight Equestrian Order Holy Sepulcher of Jerusalem, Grand Priory of Poland, Gold Cross Merit Primate of Poland, hon. Canon, Royal Coll. Chpt., Wilanow-Warsaw, Archbishop Weber H.S. Madonna award, Skowyrow Fdtn. award Pastoral Inst. Catholic Univ. Lublin, Spl. Fgn. award Warsaw Soc. Civitas Christiana, Person of Yr. award St. John Cantius Soc. Chgo. Mem. Selden Soc., Queen Mary Coll., Polish-Am. Assn. Wis. (chaplain 1979—), Polish Arts Club. Home and Office: 2804 Oakwood Ln Oshkosh WI 54904-8406

BARY, ETIENNE DE, artist, journalist; b. St. Avold, Moselle, France, Nov. 20, 1962; s. Jacques and Christiane (de Cazenove) de B.; m. Shayda Keliddarzadeh, Aug. 4, 1990; 1 child, Shad. Student, Atelier Met de Penninghen, Paris, 1981-82, Atelier Albers, Paris, 1982-83, Beaux Arts Paris, 1983-86. Illustrater, layout designer Femme Pratique, Paris, 1988; layout designer Creation mag., Issy-les Moulineaux, France, 1989, Glamour, Paris, 1990; Web master, creator Velodrama, a Parisian Cyberkusthalle, 1996—; tchr. HTML and CAO Paris Parson's Sch. Design, 1997, Ecole Multimedia, 1998. One-man shows include Ctr. Cultural Francais, Izmir, Turkey, 1996, Galerie Bosfroi, Paris, 1993, AAFA, 1997-99, Studio J. de Longerville, 1997, Galerie Art d Patruioine, 1998, Ctr. Culture Albert Chanot, 2000; exhibited in group shows Gilbert Brownstone Gallery, Paris, 1989, Ctr. Cultural Albert Ghanst, Clamart, 1994, 95; animation and realization of weekly contemporary art talk show Fréquence Protestante, FM 100.7, 1994-98. Avocations: playing Go, playing trumpet, roller riding, advertisement design. Home and Studio: 21 rue du Pt Wilson, 94250 Gentilly France

BAR-YAACOV, NISSIM, law educator; b. Sofia, Bulgaria, Apr. 21, 1926; arrived in Israel, 1949; s. Jacques and Rachel (Ezra) Nissimoff; m. Claire Aura Stonehill, May 25, 1961; children: Michael, Nomi, Dina. MA, The Hebrew U. Jerusalem, Israel, 1954; diploma in Internat. Law, U. Cambridge, Eng., 1955; PhD in Internat. Law, The Hebrew U. Jerusalem, 1961. Lectr. The Hebrew U. Jerusalem, Israel, 1961-67, sr. lectr., 1967-72, assoc. prof., 1972-80, prof., 1980-90; prof. emeritus The Hebrew U. Jerusalem, 1990—; vis. prof. U. Va., 1984-85; vis. scholar U. Cambridge, Eng., 1989-90; sec. Internat. Law Assn., Israel Branch, 1955-68; counsel for Israel Egypt-Israel Arbitration on Taba, 1986-88; head dept. Internat. Rels. The Hebrew U. Jerusalem, 1976-78. Author: Dual Nationality, 1961, The Israel-Syrian Armistice, 1967, The Handling of International Disputes by Means of Inquiry, 1974; contbr. articles to profl. jours. Recipient Arlosoroff prize Min. Fgn. Affairs, Israel, 1953, Bentwich prize Friends of Hebrew U., Eng., 1954. Mem. Am. Soc. Internat. Law, Internat. Law Assn., Israel Coun. for Fgn. Rels. Avocations: tennis, music. Home: 1 Rashba St, Jerusalem 92264, Israel Office: Dept Internat Rels, The Hebrew U Mount Scopus, Jerusalem 91905, Israel

BARYAH, GURKIRPAL SINGH, virologist, educator; b. Ahmedabad, India, Apr. 4, 1938; s. Pritam Singh and Beant Kaur Baryah; m. Darshan Kaur Ratti, Dec. 6, 1964 (dec. 1998); children: Gagandeep, Shelly. B of Vet. Sci., AM, Punjab Vet. Coll., Hisar, India, 1959; M of Vet. Sci., Bombay Vet. Coll., 1962; PhD, Indian Vet. Rsch. Inst., Izatnagar, India, 1968. Cert. Punjab State Vet. Coun., India. Asst. prof. G.B. Pant U. Agr. and Tech., Pantnagar, India, 1964-65; rsch. officer Virus Rsch. Ctr., Pune, India, 1967-70; sr. rsch. officer ICMR Virus Units, Madras, Agra, India, 1970-73; virologist Punjab Agrl. U., Ludhiana, India, 1973-85, sr. virologist, 1986-98, head dept. vet. microbiology, 1992-96; assoc. prof. U. Mastansiriyah, Coll. Medicine, Kufe, Iraq, 1980-82; prof. emeritus Christian Med. Coll., Ludhiana, India, 1998-99, head dept. vet. microbiology, 1992-96; prof., head dept. med. microbioloby DIR DS, Faridkot, India, 2000—; prin. investigator Govt. India Project, Ludhiana, India, 1991-94; cons., reviewer Dept. of Biotech., New Delhi, India, 1994-98; cons. Christian Med. Coll. and Hosp., Ludhiana, India. Contbr. articles to profl. jours. Fellow Danish Internat. Devel. Agy., Denmark, 1976-77; Fulbright fellow Indo-U.S. Subcommn. on Edn. and Culture, Wooster, Ohio, 1993; recipient Shakuntala Amir Chand award Indian Coun. Med. Rsch., 1972. Mem. Indian Virological Soc. (life), Indian Soc. Vet. Epidemiology and Preventive Medicine, Indian Assn. Advancement Vet. Rsch., Conf. Rsch. Workers Animal Diseases, N.Y. Acad. Scis. Avocations: physical fitness, reading, music, interior design, travel. Home: 456 B BRS Nagar, Ludhiana 141 004, India Office: Dasmesh Inst Rsch & Dent, Scis, Faridkot 151 203, India

BAR-YAM, YANEER, physicist; b. Boston, Aug. 29, 1959; s. Zvi Westreich and Miriam Bar-Y.; m. Naomi Bromberg, Aug. 14, 1983; children: Shlomiya, Yavni, Maayan, Taeer. SB, MIT, 1978, PhD, 1984. Rsch. asst. MIT, Cambridge, Mass., 1980-84, postdoctoral fellow, 1984-86; postdoctoral fellow IBM & MIT, Yorktown Heights, N.Y., 1986-87; sr. scientist Weizmann Inst. of Sci., Rehovot, Israel, 1988-91; assoc. prof. Boston U., 1991-97; pres. New Eng. Complex Sys. Inst., 1997—; mng. editor: InterJour., Cambridge, 1995—; vis. lectr. MIT, 1987-89, 90-91, 96, Cornell U., 1989, others. Author: Dynamics of Complex Systems, 1997; editor: Lattice Effects in High Tc Superconductors, 1992, Unifying Themes in Complex Systems, 1999; contbg. author: Some New Directions in Scienc on Computers, 1996; contbr. articles to profl. jours. Founding bd. dirs. Jewish Cmty. Day Sch., Newton, Mass., 1995-98; den leader Cub Scout Pack, Boy Scouts Am., Newton, 1996-98. NSF fellow, 1979-83, Bantrell Postdoctoral fellow MIT/Bantrell Found., 1984-86, Allon fellow Weizmann Inst. Sci., 1988-90, Revson fellow, 1988-90. Mem. Am. Phys. Soc., Phi Beta Kappa. Office: NECSI 24 Mt Augurn St Cambridge MA 02138

BARYLA, JEAN-MICHEL PIERRE, civil engineer; b. Domfront, France, July 29, 1947; s. Pierre Leopold and Juliette (Lemeur) B.; m. Christiane Ferret, July 6, 1973; 1 child, Aurore Melanie. BSCE, Inst. Nat. Sci. Appliquees, Lyon, France, 1968; MSCE, Ill. Inst. Tech., 1971. Soils engr. Ctr. Exptl. du Batiment et des Travaux Publics, Paris, 1972; civil engr. Inst. de Tech. des Travaux Publics et du Batiment, Kouba, Algeria, 1972-73; head lab. Gerland Rts., Lyon, 1973-75; hwy. engr. Louis Berger Internat., Inc., East Orange, N.J., 1975-80; sr. hwy. engr. Colas, Paris, 1980-83; project mgr. Louis Berger Sarl, Paris, 1983-91; tech. dir. Soc. de Constrn. d'Autoroutes de l'Ouest, Nanterre, France, 1991—; project mgr. Louis Berger Internat., Inc., 1994; sr. engr. PROFABRIL Internat., Lisbon, Portugal, 1996; hydraulic engr. Louis Berger SA, Paris, 1998. Contbr. articles to profl. publs.; author conf. procs. in field. With French Army, 1972-73. Mem. ASCE, Internat. Asphalt Pavements, Internat. Soc. for Soil Mechanics and Found. Engring. Roman Catholic. Achievements include French patent on slurry for filling trenches under pavements. Avocations: stamp collecting, travel, bridge, horseback riding. Home: 1 Place du Sud 1309 Eve, 92806 Puteaux France Office: SCAO, 106 Rue des Trois Fontanot, 92751 Nanterre France

BARYSHEVSKY, VLADIMIR GRIGORIEVICH, physicist, researcher; b. Minsk, Belarus, July 1, 1940; s. Grigorii Roobnich and Maria Baryshevskaya; m. Galina Dmitrievna Froltsova, June 18, 1970; children: Dmitryi, Innokentii, Elena, Vladimir. Diploma, Belarus State U., Minsk, 1962. Lectr., sci. rschr. dept. nuclear physics Belarus State U., Minsk, 1962-69, asst. prof. dept. nuclear physics, 1969-75, prof. nuclear physics, 1975-86; dir. Inst. Nuclear Problems, Minsk, 1986—; pres. Devel. and Security Rsch. Inst., Minsk, 1993-96; meritorious sci. worker of Belarus, 1996. Contbr. articles to profl. jours. Home: Voronianskaya 3-81, 220039 Minsk Belarus Office: Inst Nuclear Problems, Bobruiskaya Str 11, 220050 Minsk Belarus

BARYSHNIKOV, ANATOLY IVANOVICH, oil company executive, engineer; b. Pobeda, Kalininsky, Russia, Mar. 5, 1949; arrived in Italy, 1992; s. Ivan Ivanovich and Anna Mihailovna (Samarina) B.; m. Valentina Viktorovna Tokareva, July 27, 1978; children: Ekaterina, Anastasia. MS, Geol. Prospecting Inst., Moscow, 1971; PhD, Drilling Techniques Inst., Moscow, 1984; sr. rschr., All-Union Cert. Com. (VAK), Moscow, 1989. Drilling mgr. Prospecting Expedition, Chita, Russia, 1971-74; rschr. Geophys. Rsch. Corp., Tver, Russia, 1975-80; dept. mgr. Geophys. Rsch. Corp., Tver, 1984-89; mgr. Geotest Ltd., Tver, 1989-91; sr. engr. AGIP S.p.A., Milan, 1992—; educator Postgrad. Geol. Mgrs. Inst., Moscow, 1988-90; session chair Energy Week Conf., Houston, 1996. Contbr. articles to profl. jours.; patentee in field. Mem. Soc. Petroleum Engrs. Office: AGIP SPA, Via Emilia 1, 20097 San Donato Milanese Milan, Italy

BARYSHNIKOV, FEDOR FEDOROVICH, physicist, researcher; b. Tiraspol, Moldavia, Mar. 24, 1951; s. Fedor Vassilievich and Aleksandra Ivanovna (Krasilnik) B.; m. Galina Georgievna Tseplyaeva, Nov. 15, 1975; children: Dmitri, Aleksei. Master's, Moscow Phys. Tech. Inst., 1975, PhD, 1978. Minor rschr. Astrofizika, Moscow, 1979-82, sr. rschr., 1982-89; leading rschr. Granat, Moscow, 1992—. Contbr. articles to profl. jours. Home: Energeticheskaya 9/5, 111 116 Moscow Russia Office: SF SDB Granat, Volokolamskoye sh 95, 123 424 Moscow Russia

BARYSHNIKOV, MIKHAIL, ballet dancer; b. Riga, Latvia, Jan. 28, 1948; s. Nicholai and Alexandra (Kisselov) B.; 1 child, Aleksandra. Student, Ballet Sch. of Riga, Kirov Ballet Sch., Leningrad, Russia; DFA (hon.), Yale U., 1979; DHL (hon.), Columbia U., 1985. Mem. Kirov Ballet Co., 1969-74; prin. dancer Am. Ballet Theatre, 1974-78, N.Y.C. Ballet, 1978-79; dir. designee Am. Ballet Theatre, 1979-80, artistic dir., 1980-90; founder White Oak Dance Project, 1990—. Since 1974 guest artist with leading ballet cos. throughout world including Nat. Ballet of Can., Royal Ballet, Hamburg (Germany) Ballet, Ballet Victoria, Australia, Stuttgart (W.Ger.) Ballet, appeared at, Covent Garden, Spoleto (Italy) Festival; dances premier danseur roles in the traditional repertory; other repertory includes: Le jeune homme et la morte, Vestris, Medea, Push Comes to Shove, Hamlet Connotations, Other Dances, Pas de Duke, Santa Fe Saga, Pique Dame, Four Seasons, Opus 19, Rhapsody Apollo, Configurations, The Wild Boy, The Little Ballet, Follow the Feet, Sinatra Suite, Requiem; ballets staged for the Am. Ballet Theatre include The Nutcracker, 1976, Don Quixote (Kitri's Wedding), 1978, Cinderella, 1983; motion pictures include The Turning Point, 1976 (Acad. award nomination best supporting actor 1976), White Nights, 1985, That's Dancing, 1985, Dancers, 1987, The Cabinet of Dr. Ramirez, 1991, Company Business, 1992; actor on Broadway: Metamorphosis, 1989; numerous TV appearances including Dance in America series, Baryshnikov at the White House (Emmy award 1979), Baryshnikov on Broadway (Emmy award 1980), Baryshnikov in Hollywood, Baryshnikov by Tharp, A Salute to Fred Astaire, A Salute to Gene Kelly, Dance in America: Baryshnikov Dances Balanchine (Emmy award 1989); co-creator (with choreographer Mark Morris): White Oak Dance Project, 1990; author: Baryshnikov at Work: Mikhail Baryshnikov Discusses His Roles, 1976, Baryshnikov in Color, 1980; toured in Cutting Up (choreographed by Twyla Tharp), 1992-93. Gold medalist Varna Competition, Bulgaria 1966, First prize Internat. Ballet Competition, Moscow, USSR 1968; recipient Nijinsky prize at First Internat. Ballet Competition Paris Acad. Dance 1968, Dance mag. award 1978, Liberty award, N.Y.C., 1986. Address: care Vincent & Farrell Assocs 157 W 57th St Ste 502 New York NY 10019-2210*

BARZEL, ALEXANDER, retired philosopher; b. Budapest, Hungary, Sept. 17, 1921; arrived is Israel, 1945; m. Oscar and Irma (Eckstein) Vas; m. Shoshana Steiner; children: Gabriel, Yig'al, Orah, Rachel. PhD, U. Goethe, Frankfurt, Germany, 1971. Lectr. Oranim Coll., U. Haifa, Israel, 1967-72; sr. lectr. U. Haifa, 1971-80; prof. Technion-Israel Inst. Tech., 1980-90, dean humanities, 1980-84, 88-90. Author: Der Begriff "Arbeit" in der Philosophie der Gegenwart, 1971, The Great Conversation - Essays in Culture and Literature/Hebrew, 1971, Meaning and Form, 1976, Values, Humans, World, 1976, On Identity and World View - Being Jewish, 1978, 2d edit., 1979, Categories of Social Existence, 1984, The Structure of Judaism, 1994; contbr. over 80 articles to profl. jours. Mem., chmn. com. Israel Min. Edn., 1970-90; mem., chmn. coms. U. Haifa and Technion, 1967-90; sec. gen. Israeli Labor Youth Orgn., 1952-59; mem. com. The Kibbitz Movement. With Hungarian Mil., labor camp, 1942-44. Israeli Labor Party. Home: Kibbutz Hahoresh, 16960 Kfar Hahoresh Israel

BARZOV, YURI NIKOLAEVICH, executive recruiter; b. Nikolaev, Russia, Jan. 15, 1961; s. Nikolai Illarionovich and Evdokia Fillipovna (Selezneva) B.; m. Tatiana Victorovna Starostina, Oct. 12, 1984; children: Dmitri, Ekaterina, Elizaveta. MS, Moscow State Inst., 1978-83. Attache Russian consulate, Finland, 1983-88; third sec. Foreign Ministry of Russia, Moscow, 1988-89, adv., 1990-91, second sec., 1990-92; project dir. Inco Ltd., Moscow, 1992-93; exec. cons. H. Neumann Internat., Moscow, 1994-96; ptnr. Ward Howell Internat., Moscow, 1996—; cons. AIESEC, Moscow, 1998—. Lectr. Knowledge Soc., Moscow, 1988-90. Recipient recognition for profl. achievement, Pres. Russia, Moscow, 1989. Avocations: painting, travel.

BARZUN, JACQUES, author, literary consultant; b. Créteil, France, Nov. 30, 1907; came to U.S., 1920, naturalized, 1933; s. Henri Martin and Anna-Rose B.; m. Mariana Lowell, Aug. 1936 (dec. 1979); children: James Lowell, Roger Martin, Isabel; m. Marguerite Davenport, June 1980. Ed., Lycée Janson de Sailly, Paris; AB, Columbia U., 1927, MA, 1928, PhD, 1932. From lectr. history to assoc. prof. Columbia U., N.Y.C., 1927-45, prof., 1945, dean grad. faculties, 1955-58, dean faculties and provost, 1958-67, prof. emeritus, spl. adviser on arts, 1967-75; lit. adviser Scribner's, N.Y.C., 1975-93. Author: The French Race, 1932, Teacher in America, 1945, Berlioz and the Romantic Century, 1950, 3d edit., 1969, Pleasures of Music, 1951, 2d edit., 1977, God's Country and Mine, 1954, Music in American Life, 1956, Darwin, Marx, Wagner, 1941, The Energies of Art, 1956, Of Human Freedom, 2d edit, 1964, Race: A Study in Superstition, 1937, The Modern Researcher, 1957, 5th edit., 1993, The House of Intellect, 2d edit, 1975, Classic, Romantic and Modern, 1961, Science: The Glorious Entertainment, 1964, The American University, 1968, 2d edit., 1995, A Catalogue of Crime, 1971, 2d edit., 1986, On Writing, Editing and Publishing, 1971, The Use and Abuse of Art, 1974, Clio and the Doctors, 1974, Simple and Direct, 1975, 2d edit., 1993, Critical Questions, 1982, A Stroll With William James, 1983, A Word or Two Before You Go, 1986, The Culture We Deserve, 1989, Begin Here: On Teaching and Learning, 1990, An Essay on French Verse, 1991, From Dawn to Decadence: 1500 Years of Western Cultural Life, 2000; mem. editl. bd. The American Scholar, 1946-76, Ency. Brit, 1979—; editor: Selected Letters of Lord Byron, 1953, Nouvelles Lettres de Berlioz, 1954, The Selected Writings of John Jay Chapman, 1957, Follett's Modern American Usage, 1966. Trustee N.Y. Soc. Libr., 1968-97; mem. adv. coun. Univ. Coll. at Buckingham. Decorated Legion of Honor; Extraordinary fellow Churchill Coll., U. Cambridge (Eng.). Fellow Royal Soc. Arts, Royal Soc. Lit.; mem. Soc. Am. Historians, Mass. Hist. Soc. (corr.), AAAL (pres. 1972-75, 77-78), Am. Philos. Soc., Am. Acad. for Liberal Edn. (hon. pres.), Acad. Delphinale (Grenoble), Century Assn., Phi Beta Kappa.

BASAGOITI, ANTONIO GARCÍA-TUÑÓN, banker, lawyer; b. Madrid, Mar. 22, 1942; s. Antonio Amezaga and Angeles Garcia-Tuñon Basagoiti; m. Maria Josefa Pastor, Dec. 11, 1967 (div. 1988); children: Maria Jose, Antonio, Iciar, Carmen, Gonzalo, Marta, Maria, Leticia, Beatriz; m. Isabel Montes Moreno, June 24, 1991. LLD, Madrid U., 1966. Lawyer Banco Hispano Americano, Madrid, 1967-69, lawyer internat. divsn., 1970; asst. mgr. to regional mgr. Banco Hispano Americano, Bilbao, 1971-77; gen. mgr. Banco Hispano Americano, Madrid, 1977-91, Banco Ctrl. Hispano, Madrid, 1991—; chmn. Corporacion Borealis; vice chmn. Fabrica Española de Productos Quimicos y Farmaceuticos; bd. dirs. Proyectos y Desarrollos Urbanisticos y Financieros, Union Fenosa, Banco Santander, Central Hispano, Pescanova. 2d lt. Spanish Army, 1966-67. Mem. Real Academia de Jurisprudencia y Legislacion, Club La Moraleja, Club Neguri, Club Somosaguas, Club de Campo, Casino de Madrid. Roman Catholic. Avocations: golf, cycling, music, reading, sailing. Office: Banco Santander Ctrl Hispano, Plaza Canalejas 1, 28223 Madrid Spain

BASAK, AMULYA BIKASH, botany educator, mycologist, plant pathologist; b. Chittagong, Raozan, Bangladesh, Aug. 11, 1955; s. Benode Behari and Ananta Bala B.; m. Rupna Dutta, Dec. 6, 1987; children: Mowmita,

Paramita. BS in Botany with honors, U. Chittagong (Bangladesh), 1975, MS, 1976, PhD in Botany, 1994. Lectr. N.F. Degree Coll., Comilla, 1979-81; lectr. dept. botany U. Chittagong (Bangladesh), 1981-83, asst. prof. dept. botany, 1984-92, assoc. prof. dept. botany, 1992-95, prof. dept. botany, 1995—, house tutor Suharrowardhi Hall, 1994-95, provost, 1995-97; country rep. Internat. Mycol. Com. for Asia, Taiwan, 1998; gen. sec. Chittagong U. Tchrs. Rsch. Coun., 1982-83. Author: Crop Diseases and Their Control, 1989; editor: (jour.) Sandhan, 1983-85; mem. editl. bd. Udvid Bharta, 1997—; asst. editor Chattagram Vishwabidyalaya Bharta, 1982-83; contbr. numerous articles to profl. jours. Gen. sec. Basakpara Social Welfare Soc., 1982-87. Mem. Bangladesh Botanical Soc. (life), Bangladesh Soc. Microbiologists (life), Bangladesh Phytopathological Soc. (life), Bangladesh Assn. Advancement of Sci.(life), Bangladesh Soc. Seed Sci. and Tech. (life), Bangladesh Hort. Soc., Indian Soc. Seed Tech. (life), Asiatic Soc. Bangladesh. Hindu. Avocations: indoor games, singing, writing in newspaper. E-mail: vc-cu@spnetctg.com. Home: PO Unsattarpara Vill, Mahamuni Pahartali, Chittagong Bangladesh Office: U Chittagong, Dept Botany, Chittagong 4331, Banglaesh

BASAK, JAYANTA, computer engineer, researcher; b. Calcutta, India, Sept. 25, 1965; s. Gour and Santi (Lata) B.; m. Raktima Dey, Aug. 15, 1996. B in Engring., Jadavpur U., 1987; M in Engring., Indian Inst. Sci., Bangalore, 1989; PhD, Indian Statis. Inst., Calcutta, 1995. Computer engr. KBCS Project Indian Statis. Inst., 1989-91; vis. scientist Carnegie Mellon U., Pitts., 1991-92; programmer Indian Statis Inst., 1992-95, assoc. prof., 1996—; frontier rschr. Brain Sci. Group, Riken, Japan, 1997—; vis. fellow UN Devel. Program, 1991. Recipient Young Scientist award Indian Sci. Congress Assn., 1994, Young Scientist medal Indian Nat. Sci. Acad., 1996. Mem. IEEE (sr. mem.). Avocations: reading, listening to music. Office: Indian Statis Inst Machine Intelligence Unit, 203 BT Rd, Bengal Calcutta 700 035, India

BASAK, PRANAB, retired educator; b. Burdwan, W.Bengal, India, Dec. 1, 1931; s. Brindabon Behari and Usha Rani (Pramenik) B.; m. Sova Mukherjee, June 1, 1970; 1 child, Pratyay. BA, R.S.P. Coll., Jharia, India, 1960; MA, Calcutta U., 1963; PhD, Ranchi U., 1968. Headmaster Sr. Basic Sch., Purulia, India, 1955-60; lectr. Y.S.S.K. Vidyapith, Purulia, 1960-64, Ranchi Coll., 1964-65; lectr. Giridih (India) Coll., 1965-80, reader, 1980-85, univ. prof., 1985-93; ret.; rsch. guide Ranchi U., 1993-99. Author: Bharatpath O Dui Pathikrit, (poetry books): Kakataliya, 1992, Ek Jhinuk Mukto, 1993, Shamuk Shankha Habe, 1993 (Bengali Acad. award); editor: (anthology) Bandana Giti Shudha, 1991. Pres. Bihar Bengalee Assn. (cultural), 1987—. Recipient Bangla Bhasha Purashkar, Bihar Bangla Acad., 1996, fellow, 1997—. Hindu. Avocations: music composition, singing, gardening, yoga, religious discourses. Home: Barganda, 815301 Giridih Bihar, India Office: Giridih College, 815301 Giridih India

BASAVAIAH, DEEVI, chemistry educator, researcher; b. Tenali, India, Aug. 11, 1950; s. Deevi Nageswararao and Deevi Koteswaramma. BSc, Andhra Loyola Coll., Vijayawada, India, 1970; MSc, Banaras Hindu U., Varanasi, India, 1972, PhD, 1979. Postdoctoral fellow Purdue U., 1980-83; scientist Nat. Chem. Lab., Pune, India, 1984; lectr. U. Hyderabad, India, 1984-87, reader, 1987-96, prof., 1996—. Contbr. articles to profl. jours. Fellow Indian Acad. Scis. Avocations: bridge, chess. Office: U Hyderabad, Sch Chemistry, Hyderabad 500046, India

BASBAS, MONTE GEORGE, judge; b. Manchester, N.H., May 6, 1921; s. George and Rose (Economou) B.; m. Audrey Ann Vagiates, Jan. 10, 1948; children: John Thomas, Monte George, Audrey Ann. AB, Dartmouth Coll., 1944; JD, Boston U., 1949. Bar: Mass. 1949, N.H. 1949, U.S. Supreme Ct. 1969. Justice Dist. Ct. Newton, Mass., 1971—, presiding justice, 1976—; Bar: Mass. 1949, N.H. 1949, U.S. Dist. Ct. Mass. 1950, U.S. Dist. Ct. N.H. 1951, U.S. Supreme Ct. 1969. mem. Dist. Ct. Dept. Stds. Com., 1973—, chmn., 1984—, others. Mayor City of Newton, 1966-71; mem. Prs.'s Adv. Bd., Bentley Coll., 1983—; bd. dirs. Newton Community Svc. Ctrs., Inc. Capt. USAAF, 1942-45; PTO. Decorated Air medal with clusters, D.F.C.; named Newton C. of C. Man of the Year, 1966; numerous citations. Mem. ABA, Mass. Bar Assn., Boston Bar Assn., Waltham Bar Assn., Watertown Bar Assn., Weston Bar Assn., Newton Bar Assn., Mass. City Clks. Assn. (past pres.), Mass. Mayors Assn. (past pres.), Am. Legion, Masons, Boston U. Nat. Alumni Council, Boston U. Sch. Law Alumni Assn., NAACP, Alpha Omega, Phi Delta Phi, Chi Phi, Knights of St. Andrew. Avocations: photography, fishing, flying, computers. Home: 25 Jeffrey Rd Wayland MA 01778-2505

BASCETINCELIK, ALI, academic administrator, engineering educator; b. Ankara, Turkey, Dec. 25, 1946; s. Sevket and Seride Sarikaya B.; m. Ayse Dogru, July 22, 1974; children: Aylin, Aysun. Agrl. Engr., U. Ankara, 1970; PhD, U. Çukurova, Adana, Turkey, 1977; Prof., 1988; Assoc. Prof. (docent), U. Ege, Izmir, Turkey, 1982. Engr. TZDK, Ankara, 1971-72; researcher U. Çukurova, Adana, 1972—, head dept. agrl. machinery, 1994—; dir. Vocat. Sch. Antakya, Hatay, Turkey, 1988-92. Socialist. Muslim. Avocations: travel, music. Home: Çukurova Üniv, Lojmanlary no 45, Adana 01330, Turkey Office: Univ Çukurova Fac Agr, Balcaly, Adana 01330, Turkey

BASCH, RICHARD VENNARD, photographer, producer, writer, director; b. Inpls., Jan. 22, 1945; s. Richard and Helen Louise (Vennard) B.; m. Meredith Baker, Feb. 12, 1966; 1 child, Nicholas; m. Vicki Sylvester, Aug. 15, 1977. Cert., U. Fine Arts, Perugia, Italy, 1965, London Film Sch., 1966; BA, Antioch Coll., 1968; DFA, London Inst. for Applied Rsch., 1995. Dir. filmmaker tng. Am. Film Inst., Washington, 1968-69; instr. film history R.I. Sch. Design, Providence, 1970-73; cons. in theatre Antioch Coll., Yellow Springs, Ohio, 1976-77; prin., photographer Richard Basch Studio, Washington, 1979—; dir. film programs Brown U., 1972-73; cons. Smithsonian Instn., Washington, 1979—. Author: Faces of Fairmont Heights, 1970; producer (films) The Burning Issue, 1984, Faces from the Future, 1996. Mem. Am. Soc. Mag. Photographers. Episcopalian. Office: Richard Basch Studio 2627 Connecticut Ave NW Washington DC 20008-1545

BASCHAT, AHMET ALEXANDER, obstetrician, gynecologist; b. Hamburg, Germany, July 20, 1962; s. Mehmet and Nihal (Karahan) B.; m. Miriam Elisabeth Doyle, Mar. 5, 1993. B Medicine B Surgery, Royal Coll. Surgeons Ireland, Dublin, 1989. Med. intern Beaumont Hosp., Dublin, 1989; surg. intern Beaumont Hosp., 1990; resident in ob-gyn. Med. U. Lubeck, Germany, 1990-93, 94-97, 1994—; resident in internal medicine Newton-Wellesley Hosp., Boston, 1993-94; fellow in maternal-fetal medicine U. Md., Balt., 1997—. Contbr. articles to profl. publs., chpt. to book. Mem. Royal Coll. Surgeons Ireland (licentiate), Internat. Fetal Medicine and Surgery Soc., Internat. Soc. Ultrasound in Ob-Gyn., German Soc. Ob-Gyn. Avocations: golf, music. Office: U Md Sch Medicine Dept Ob-Gyn 405 W Redwood St Dept Ob Baltimore MD 21201-7005

BASCHNAGEL, JÖRG H., physicist, educator, researcher; b. Flörsheim, Germany, Apr. 2, 1965; s. Georg and Inge (Schmitt) B. Diploma in chemistry, Johannes-Gutenberg U., Mainz, Germany, 1990, PhD in chemistry, 1993; Habilitation in Physics, U. Mainz, 1999. Rsch. asst. dept. physics Johannes-Gutenberg U., 1990-93, scientific rsch. asst., lectr. dept. physics, 1993-95, 97-99; scientific rsch. asst. Inst. Charles Sadron, Strasbourg, France, 1995-97; guidance sci. rsch. Johannes-Gutenberg U., 1993-99; prof. physics U. Louis Pasteur, Strasbourg, France, 1999—. Author: (book) Stochastic Processes: From Physics to Finance, 1999; contbr. chpts. to books; contbr. articles to profl. jours. Recipient Johannes Gutenberg award U. Mainz, 1994. Mem. German Physical Soc., European Phys. Soc. Roman Catholic. Avocations: sports, table tennis. Office: Inst Charles Sadron, 6 rue Boussingault, 67083 Strasbourg Cedex, France

BASCHUNG, CHRISTINA MARIA, opera singer, voice educator; b. Kriegstetten, Solothurn, Switzerland, Nov. 8, 1940; arrived in Germany, 1969; d. Willi Adolf and Marie (Winistörfer) B. Superior cert., City Conservatory, Biel, Switzerland, 1965; final cert., Internat. Opera Studio, Zurich, 1966. Opera singer Städt. Buhnen, Biel-Solothurn, 1967-69, Regensburg, Germany, 1969-72, Flensburg, Germany, 1972-76; with Theater am Goetheplatz, Bremen, Germany, 1976-80; opera singer Staatstheater, Braunschweig, Germany, 1981-83; tchr. voice U Osnabrück, Germany, 1980—, U. Osnabrück, Germany, 1985—; with Kirchenmusikseminar, Osnabrück, 1986—. Concert performances and guest appearances in operas in Austria, The Netherlands, Switzerland, Denmark, Germany, United Arab Emirates, and Kenya, 1969—; appeared in operas include Cosi fan Tutte, Abduction of the Seraglio, Magic Flute, Marriage of Figaro (Mozart), Masked Ball (Verdi), Nightengale (Stravinsky), Barber of Seville (Rossini), Bohemee, Gianni Schicchi (Puccini), Carmen (Bizet), Tannhäuser, Parsival (Wagner), Tales of Hoffmann (Offenbach), Freischütz (Weber), Martha (Flotow), Ariadne auf Naxos (Richard Strauss), Raising of the Moon (1st performance in Germany), Schopfung (Hayden), Haendel (Messias) (Jephta), Mozart messe in c-moll, numerous others. Fax: 0049 541 261 53. E-mail: cbaschun@rz.uni-osnabrueck.de. Home: Süsterstrasse 43, D-49074 Osnabrück Germany

BASCIL TÜTÜNCÜ, NESLIHAN, endocrinologist; b. Adana, Turkey, Oct. 5, 1967; s. Nurhan and Solmaz Bascil; m. Tanju Tütüncü, July 28, 1996. MD, Hacettepe U., Ankara, Turkey, 1991, D of Internal Medicine, 1996; D of Endocrinology and Metabolism, Hacettepe U., 1999. Resident internal medicine Hacettepe U. Faculty Medicine, Ankara, 1992-96, fellow in endocrinology and metabolism, 1997-99; endocrinologist Baskent U. Hosp., Ankara, 1999—; cons. Baskent U. Hosp., Ankara. Author: (book chpts.) Adrenal Incidentaloma, 1998, Pancreas Diseases in AIDS, 1998; contbr. articles to profl. jours. Mem. Rotaract Club, Ankara/Cankaya, 1990-93. Mem. European Fedn. Endocrine Socs., Turkish Soc. Endocrinology and Metabolism, Assn. Hacettepe U. Faculty of Medicine Grads. Muslim. Fax: 90 312 2321360. E-mail: tt04-k@tr.net. Office: Baskent U Hosp, 1 Cadde Bahcelievler, Ankara Turkey

BASDEN, ANDREW, information technology educator; b. Edinburgh, Scotland, July 31, 1948; s. Eric Bernard and Joan Frances (Blacklocks) B.; m. Ruth Carol Angel, Sept. 22, 1973; children: Alastair Graham, Stuart Jeffrey. BSc, Southampton U., Eng., 1969, PhD, 1973. Programmer Warner Lambert, Ltd., Eastleigh, Eng., 1974, U. Southampton, 1974-80; sr. research scientist ICI plc., Runcorn, Eng., 1980-86; sr. research fellow U. Salford, Eng., 1986-87, lectr., sr. lectr., reader knowledge sys. and human factors, 1987—. Author: The Beauty of Original Sin, A Brief History of God, 1992-2000. Mem. Frodsham Parish Council, Cheshire, Eng., 1985-87, Frodsham Evang. Fellowship; Green Party candidate for Parliament, 1987. Avocations: photography, mountain walking, bird watching. Home: 24 Penrith Close, Frodsham, Cheshire WA6 7ND, England Office: Univ Salford, The Crescent, Salford England

BASDEO, SAHADEO, Trinidad and Tobago government official, educator, politician; b. Rousillac, Trinidad and Tobago, Sept. 10, 1945; s. Basdeo and Ramrajie (Mongru) Seusaran; m. Beverley Shirleen, Aug. 14, 1971; children: William Shastri Narin, Deven Marshall, Kristen Gene Santosh. BA in History and Polit. Sci., Brandon U., Manitoba, Can., 1970; MA in Caribbean Labor and Brit. Imperial History, U. Calgary, Alberta, Can., 1972; PhD in Caribbean Labor History, Dalhousie U., Halifax, N.S., 1975. Lectr. in history St. Benedict's Coll., La Romaine, Trinidad and Tobago, 1964-67; teaching asst. U. Calgary, Alberta, Can., 1970-72; analyst ednl. program Ministry of Edn., Manitoba, 1975-76; dir. rsch. in edn. Provincial Govt. Manitoba, 1976-78; cons. to sch. divs. Manitoba, 1976-78; lectr. in history and contemporary politics U. W.I., Trinidad and Tobago, 1978-88; senator Parliament of Trinidad and Tobago, 1981-86; senator Govt. of Trinidad and Tobago, 1986—, min. of external affairs and internat. trade, 1988-91; sr. lectr. inst. internat. rels. U. of The West Indies, 1992—; prof. history and internat. rels. Okanagan U. Coll., Kelowna, B.C., Can., 1994—; mem. pub. accountr com., pub. accounts enterprises com., Parliament of Trinidad and Tobago, 1981-86; mem. exec. com. Commonwealth Parliamentary Assn., Trinidad and Tobago, 1986—; chmn. standing ocm. Carribean Fgn. Mins., 1988-89; chmn. Carribean Community Coun. Trade Mins., 1989-90; leader nat. dels., internat. confs. on trade and polit. co-operation; participant spl. internat. peace assignments Orgn. of Am. States, Caribbean Community, Grenada, 1983, Panama, Haiti, 1989. Author: Labour Organization and Labour Reform in Trinidad, 1919-1939, 83; contbr. numerous articles to profl. jours. Chmn. Nat. Alliance for Reconstruction Party. Recipient Lions Club award Brandon U., 1968, Rotary Club award Brandon U., 1968, Meritorious and Yeoman Svc. to the Cause of the Sch., Community and Country award St. Benedict's Coll. Past Students' Assn., 1986; rsch. grantee U. Calgary, 1971; grad. teaching fellow U. Calgary, 1970-72; recipient numerous scholarships, Brandon U., Dalhousie U., 1967-75. Mem. Assn. Caribbean Historians, Trinidad Country Club, Trinidad Golf Club. Mem. Nat. Alliance for Reconstruction Party. Hindu. Avocations: golf, swimming, cricket. Home: 3172 Woodstock Dr, Westbank, BC Canada V4T 1S2 Office: Okanagan U Coll, 3333 Coll Way, Kelowna, BC Canada V1V 1V7

BASDEVANT, JEAN-LOUIS HENRI, physicist, educator; b. Bucharest, Romania, Sept. 18, 1939; s. Jean and Denise Basdevant; children: Nicolas, Olivier. Grad., Ecole Normale Supérieure, Paris, 1963; Agregation de Physique, U. Paris, 1963; PhD, U. Strasbourg, France, 1966. Rsch. assoc. Ctr. Nat. de la Rsch. Sci., U. Orsay, France, 1963-64, Lawrence Radiation Lab., Berkeley, Calif., 1964-65, U. Orsay and Commissariat a Atomic Energy, Saclay, France, 1966-70; prof. physics Ecole Poly., Palaiseau, France, 1969—; rsch. assoc. CERN, Geneva, 1970-72; dir. rsch. Ctr. Nat. Rsch. Sci. lab. theoretical physics U. Paris, 1972-92; bd. dirs. Ecole Poly., Palaiseau, 1978-2000, chmn. physics dept., 1992—; dir. lab. theoretical physics U. Paris, 1981-83; prof. physics Saint-Cyr Spl. Mil. Sch., Coetquidan, France, 1986-93. Author: Mécanique Quantique, 1986, Physique Quantique, 1997, The Quantum Mechanics Solver, 2000; editor 9 books; contbr. over 100 articles to profl. jours. on theoretical physics, particle physics, astro physics. Named to Order of Yugoslav Star, Yugoslav Presidency, Belgrade, 1984, Officier of Legion of Honor, French Pres., Paris, 2000; recipient La Cases prize French Acad. Sci., Paris, 1992. Mem. Alumni Ecole Normale Supérieure, Les Amis de Mozart. Avocations: pianist, history. Home: 134 rue D'Assas, 75006 Paris France Office: Ecole Polytechnique, Physics Dept, 91128 Palaiseau France

BASE, GRAEME ROWLAND, illustrator, author; b. Amersham, Eng., Apr. 6, 1958; s. Geoffrey Donald and Elizabeth Enid (Philips) B.; m. Robyn Anne Paterson, Aug. 1, 1981; children: James Geoffrey, Katherine Gabrielle, William Alexander. Art diploma, Swinburne Inst. Tech., 1978. Author, illustrator: My Grandma Lived in Gooligulch, 1983, Animalia, 1986 (Australian Children's Book award Children's Book Coun. Australia 1987, Kids Own Australia Literature award 1988), The Eleventh Hour: A Curious Mystery, 1988 (Australian Children's Book award Children's Book Coun. Australia 1989, Book Design award Australian Book Pub. Assn. 1988, Young Australian Best Book award 1989, Kids Own Australia Literature award 1989), The Sign of the Seahorse, 1992, The Discovery of Dragons, 1996, The Worst Band in the Universe, 1999; illustrator: Adventures With My Best Worst Friend, 1982, The Island Bike Business, 1982, Jabberwocky From "Through the Looking Glass," 1985, Jabberwocky: A Book of Brillig Dioramas, 1996. Office: Penguin Books Australia Ltd, 487 Maroondah Hwy PO Box 257, Ringwood VIC 3134, Australia

BASELT, RANDALL CLINT, toxicologist; b. Chgo., Feb. 12, 1944; s. Benjamin Oliver and Vivian Marie (Rende) B.; m. Lana Mak, June 11, 1966; 1 child, David. BS in Chemistry, U. Ill., 1965; PhD in Pharmacology, U. Hawaii, 1972. Cert. Am. Bd. Forensic Toxicology, Am. Bd. Clin. Chemistry, Am. Bd. Toxicology, forensic alcohol supr., clin. toxicologist technologist, clin. chemist, clin. lab. toxicologist. Forensic toxicologist Office of Coroner, County of Orange, Calif., 1965-69; rsch. fellow dept. pharmacology U. Hawaii Sch. Medicine, Honolulu, 1969-72; NIH postdoctoral rsch. fellow Medizinisch-Chemisches Inst., U. Bern (Switzerland) Sch. Medicine, 1972-73; rsch. toxicologist Office of Coroner, San Francisco, 1973-75; chief toxicologist Office of Med. Examiner, Farmington, Conn., 1975-78; dir. toxicology and drug analysis lab. U. Calif. Med. Ctr., Sacramento, 1978-84; dir. Chem. Toxicology Inst., Calif., 1984—; asst. prof. lab. medicine U. Conn. Health Ctr., Farmington, 1975-78; assoc. prof. pathology U. Calif. Sch. Medicine, Davis, 1978-84; cons. drug abuse USN, 1983—, USAF, 1984—; accredited lab. inspector Nat. Lab. Cert. Program, 1988—. Author: Disposition of Toxic Drugs and Chemicals in Man, 5th edit., 1999, Biological Monitoring Methods for Industrial Chemicals, 3d edit., 1997, Analytical Procedures for Therapeutic Drug Monitoring and Emergency Toxicology, 2d edit., 1987, (with M. Houts and R.H. Cravey) Courtroom Toxicology, 1980; editor 7 other books; founder, editor Jour. Analytical Toxicology, 1977—; mem. editl. bd. Jour. Forensic Scis., 1983—; contbr. articles to profl. jours. Mem. Am. Acad. Clin. Toxicology, Am. Assn. for Clin. Chemistry, Am. Indsl. Hygiene Assn., Calif. Assn. Toxicologists (past pres.), Internat. Assn. Forensic Toxicologists, Jour. Am. Med. Assn. (peer rev. com. 1985—), Soc. Forensic Toxicologists (bd. dirs. 1978-80, lab. survey com. 1982-83), Soc. Toxicology, Southwestern Assn. Toxicologists. Office: Chem Toxicology Inst 1167 Chess Dr Foster City CA 94404-1151

BASER, KEMAL HÜSNÜ CAN, pharmacist, educator; b. Cankiri, Turkey, July 15, 1949; s. Musa and Süheyla Baser; m. Hanife Düzgün, Apr. 26, 1971; children: Musa Emre, Bora. BSc in Pharmacy, U. Eskisehir, 1972; PhD of Pharmacognosy, U. London, 1978. Dir. Sch. Chem. Engring., Eskisehir, 1978-80; assoc. prof., prof., vice-dean faculty of pharmacy Anadolu U., Eskisehir, 1981-93, dean faculty of pharmacy, 1993—; lectr. Sch. Pharmacy, Eskisehir, 1978-81; dir. Medicinal and Aromatic Plant and Drug Rsch. Ctr. Anadolu U., Eskisehir, 1980—; cons. UNIDO, Tehran, Iran, 1996, Khartoum, Sudan, 1995, Freetown, Sierra Leone, 1993, Lagos, Nigeria, 1992, Accra, Ghana, 1991; sec.-gen. Internat. Coun. for Medicinal and Aromatic Plants, 1997—. Co-author: Herb Drugs and Herbalists in Turkey, 1986; editor, co-editor procs., 1993, 95. Lt. Turkish Land Forces, 1976. Recipient Disting. Svc. medal Internat. Fedn. Essential Oil and Aroma Trades, 1995. Fellow Linnean Soc.; mem. Am. Soc. Pharmacognosy, Phytochemistry Soc. Europe, Soc. Medicinal Plant Rsch., N.Y. Acad. Scis., Turkish Soc. Cosmetic Rschs. (pres. 1995—), Turkish Phytotherapy Soc. (sec.-gen. 1996—). Avocation: music. Office: Faculty of Pharmacy, Anadolu Univ, 26470 Eskisehir Turkey

BASHILOV, ALEXANDER SERGEYEVICH, mechanical engineer; b. Kimry, Russia, May 11, 1950; s. Sergey Vasilyevich and Alexandra Ivanovna (Volkova) B.; m. Olga Vladimirovna Filimonova, Mar. 25, 1989; 1 child, Sergey Alexsandrovich. Engr., Ural Polytech. Inst., 1972. From asst. foreman to sr. foreman Kalinin Engring. Work, Sverdlovsk, Russia, 1974-80; mgr. shop, chief engr. NPO Molniya JSC, Moscow, 1981—. Inventor in field. Lt. Soviet Army, 1972-74. Fellow AIAA. Avocation: chess. Office: NPO Molniya JSC, 6 Novoposelkovaya Str, 123459 Moscow Russia

BASHKIN, VLADIMIR NIKOLAYEVICH, science administrator; b. Dobrinka, Russia, Oct. 4, 1949; s. Nikolay V. and Anna A. (Grigirova) B.; m. Galina N. Aponitskaya, Oct. 2, 1970; children: Nataly, Darya. Diploma, Moscow State U., 1971, PhD, 1975, DSc, 1987. Cert. prof. diploma in biogeochemistry. Rschr. Inst. Soil Sci. & Photosynthesis, Acad. Scis. USSR, Pushchino, 1974-86, sr. rschr., 1986-88; head dept. gen. ecology and ecol. standardization Pushchino State U., 1992; head lab. of landscape biogeochemistry Inst. Soil Sci. & Photosynthesis, Russian Acad. Scis., Pushchino, 1988; advisor Cuban Acad. Scis., Havana, 1983-84; part-time head Russian Nat. Focal Ctr. for Effects, Ministry of Environ. Protection of Russian Fedn., Moscow, 1993; expert Vernadsky's Biospheric Ctr., Pushchino, 1992; prof. Seoul nat. U., 1998-99, JGSEE, Bangkok, 1999—. Author: (books) Agrogeochemistry, 1987, Biogeochemical Foundation of Ecological Standardization, 1993, Biogeochemistry of Snall Catchments, 1994, Acid Deposition and Ecosystems Sensitivity in East Asia, 1998, Practical Environmental Analysis, 1999; mem. editl. bd. Environ. Conservation Jour., 1992, Jour. Regional Ecol. Problems, Water Air, Soil Pollution Jour., 1998; contbr. papers to profl. jours. including Soviet Soil Sci. (USSR State prize for young scientists in ecology 1980). Vice-chmn. working group of effects Long-Range Transboundary Air Pollution Conv., UN/ECE, Geneva, Switzerland, 1996. Recipient Superoir Attectation Commn. of Russian Fedn., 1997. Mem. German Soil Sci. Soc., Soc. Environ. Toxicology and Chemistry, Nat. Geog. Soc., N.Y. Acad. Scis. Orthodox. Avocations: driving cars, sauna. Fax: 7-0967-79-0532. E-mail: bashkin@jgsee.kmutt.ac.th. Office: Inst Basic Biol Problems, Russian Acad Scis, Pushchino 142292, Russia

BASHKIROVA, ELENA IVANOVNA, public opinion administrator, consultant; b. Moscow, July 29, 1946; d. Ivan Jakovlevich Kozlov and Iraida Alexandrovna Shemelina; 1 child, Maria Jurievna. MS in Linguistics, Inst. Sociology, 1968, PhD, 1982. Interpreter Iran, 1968-69; rschr. Inst. Sociology, USSR, 1969, head dept., 1991; gen dir. ROMIR, Russia, 1992—. Mem. editl. bd. Pub. Opion Rsch.; expert Sovetnik, 1999; contbr. articles to profl. jours. Office: ROMIR Rsch Group, Novaya Basmannaya str, 6, 107078 Moscow Russia

BASHMAKOVA, LOUISA PETROVNA, literature educator, researcher; b. Perm, Urals, Russia, Aug. 8, 1942; d. Peter Andrianovich and Ledia Sergeevna (Sokolova) B. PhD, Moscow State U., 1973. Prof. Kuban State U., Krasnodar, Russia, 1973—, chairperson Russian studies, 1995-97, chairperson Russian/Comparative, 1997—; head dept. Russian/Am. studies Kuban State U., Krasnodar, 1993—, prof. Am. studies, 1993—, dir., founder Ctr. for History of Culture, 1992—; Lectr. Soc. Book Lovers, Krasnodar, 1985-90. Author: Problems of Contemporary American Novel, 1979, The Writers of Old South, 1997; translator, editor: American Humor (C. Rourke), 1994. Recipient fin. funding Soros Found., Moscow, 1991, grant NEH, Washington, 1995. Mem. Melville Soc., Am. Studies Assn., Soc. Studies in American Culture. Avocations: reading, writing, swimming. Home: Nevkipelogo St 21 Apt 35, 350065 Krasnodar Russia Office: Kuban State U, Stavropolskaya St 149, 350040 Krasnodar Russia

BASHORE, IRENE SARAS, research institute administrator; b. San Jose, Calif.; d. John and Eva (Lionudakis) Saras; m. Vincent Bashore (div.); 1 child, Juliet Ann. BA, Pepperdine U., 1950; MA in Theatre Arts, Calif. State U., Fullerton, 1977. Founder, exec. dir. Inst. for Dramatic Rsch., Fullerton, Calif., 1967—.

BASHOUR, FOUAD ANIS, cardiology educator; b. Tripoli, Lebanon, Jan. 3, 1924; s. Anis E. and Mariana (Yazigi) B.; m. Val Imm, Sept. 28, 1978. BA, Am. U. of Beirut, Lebanon, 1944, MD, 1949; PhD, U. Minn., 1957. Intern Am. U. of Beirut Hosp., Beirut, 1949-50; med. officer UNRWA, 1950-51; resident in internal medicine U. Minn. Hosps., 1951-54; rsch. fellow U. Minn. Med. Schs., 1954-55; instr. in medicine U. Minn., 1955-57; rsch. assoc. Am. U. Med. Sch., Beirut, 1957, asst. prof. medicine cardiopulmonary lab. sect., 1957-59; instr. internal medicine U. Tex. Southwestern Med. Ctr., Dallas, 1959-60, assoc. prof. internal medicine, 1963-71, dir. Cardiovascular Inst., 1967-78, prof. medicine, 1971-85, prof. medicine and physiology, 1985-95; mem. staff Parkland Meml. Hosp., Dallas; prof. emeritus of physiology and internal medicine, 1995-99; mem. staff Zale-Lipshy Univ. Hosp., Dallas, Ashbel Smith prof. medicine and physiology, 1999—; founder, pres. Cardiology Fund, Inc., 1972-93; program dir. consultation agreement lectrs. Univ. Kuwait, U. Tex., 1977-85; mem. chancellor adv. coun. U. Tex., 1982—; mem. bd trustees of coms. on promotions and med. sch. Am. U. Beirut, 1996—; cons. in field. Mem. editorial bd. Chest, 1963-69, Lebanese Med. Jour., 1957-59, cited in the Warren Commn. Pub., 1963; contbr. more than 200 articles to profl. publs. Elder Christ Luth. Ch., Dallas. Recipient Americanism award DAR, 1970; named Knight Order of Holy Cross Jerusalem; Fouad Bashour ann. lectr. disting. physiologist in his honor, 1974—, Fouad Bashour distinguished chair in physiology in his honor, 1990, eminent scholar, Tex., 1985, Wisdom Hall of Fame, eminent Wisdom fellow, 1998. Fellow Am. Coll. Chest Physicians (emeritus), Am. Physiol. Soc. (circulation group), Am. Heart Assn. (coun. on basic sci., coun. on circulation); mem. Am. Fedn. Clin. Rsch. (emeritus), Ctrl. Soc. Clin. Rsch. (emeritus), So. Soc. Clin. Investigation (emeritus), Tex. Med. Assn., Dallas County Med. Assn., Am. Soc. Internal Medicine, Tex. Med. Found., Order of Cedars of Lebanon (officer 1971), cons. Tex. Bd. of Med. Examiners. Fax: 214-648-9376. Office: U Tex Southwestern Med Ctr 5323 Harry Hines Blvd Dallas TX 75390-7208

BASILE, ADRIANA, plant biologist; b. Naples, Italy, Apr. 9, 1960; d. Mario and Giovanna (Campanaro) B.; m. Aniello de Ruberto, June 25, 1987; children: Alessandra, Francesca. MSc in Pharm. Tech. and Chemistry, U. Naples, 1983, MSc in Biol. Scis., 1988. Rschr. U. Naples, 1990—, botany educator, 1995—. Contbr. articles to profl. publs. Pharmacists' Assn. scholar, 1983. Mem. Italian Bot. Soc., Am. Bot. Soc. Roman Catholic. Avocation: Latin dancing. Home: via A D'Antona 36, 80 131 Naples Italy Office: Dept Biologia Vegetale, Via Foria 223, 80139 Naples Italy

BASILIO, MARGARIDA MARIA DE PAULA, linguistics and foreign language educator; b. Rio de Janeiro, May 17, 1944; d. Francisco de Paula and Lucia de Sá Freire B.; m. John Vincent Nicholson, Oct. 24, 1975. BA in

Classics, Cath. U., Rio de Janeiro, 1968; MA in Linguistics, Fed. U., Rio de Janeiro, 1974; PhD in Linguistics, U. Tex., 1977. Tchg. asst. Gama Filho U., Rio de Janeiro, 1965-68, tchr., 1968-73; asst. prof. Cath. U., Rio de Janeiro, 1972-77, assoc. prof., 1977-92, 95—; vis. prof. Fed. U., Rio de Janeiro, 1979-81, assoc. prof., 1981-95; cons. Coordination Devel. of Pers. in Higher Edn., Brasília, Brazil, 1982-98, Fed. Sponsor Studies and Projects, Brasília, 1985-98, Nat. Coun. Devel. Sci. & Tech., Brasília, 1987-98, Found. Rsch. Devel. Sao Paulo, 1995-98. Author: Estruturas Lexicais do Portugues, 1980, Teoria Lexical, 1987; editor Linguagens, 1981, A Delimitacao Das Unidades Lexicais, 1999; co-editor: Gramatica do Portugues Faiado, 1996. Ford Found. fellow Fed. U., 1974, Fulbright/Coordination Devel. Pers. in Higher Edn. fellow Fulbright Com., 1984; rsch. grantee Nat. Coun. Devel. Sci. & Tech. Com., Rio de Janeiro, 1987—. Mem. Soc. Brasileira Para Progresso da Ciencia, Assn. Linguistica e Filologia da Am. Latina, Assn. Brasileira de Linguistica. Avocations: photography, classical movies, samba, jazz, American pop art. Office: Cath Univ Rio de Janeiro, Rua Marques Sao Vicente 225, 22453900 Rio de Janeiro Brazil

BASILIOUS, NAGI MOUSSA, artist, painter; b. Cairo, Dec. 12, 1949. BA in Painting, Helwan U. Graphic designer Egyptian TV, 1973-75, graphic designer, scene painter, 1977-83, painter, designer, 1983—. Exhibited in one-man shows and in group shows. Recipient award Ministry of Culture, 1979, award Fine Arts Assn., 1976. Mem. Nat. Assn. Fine Arts, Cairo Atelier. Avocations: photography, electronics, reading. Office: 26 July St # 28, Flat # 24, Cairo Egypt

BASINGER, KIM, actress; b. Athens, Ga., Dec. 8, 1953; d. Don Basinger; m. Ron Britton, 1980 (div. Feb. 1990); m. Alec Baldwin, August 19, 1993. Student, Neighborhood Playhouse, N.Y.C. Model Eileen Ford Agy., N.Y.C., 1972-77; ind. actress, 1977—. Starring role (TV series) Dog and Cat, 1977; TV films include Katie-Portrait of a Centerfold, 1978, The Ghost of Flight 401, 1978, Killjoy, 1981, (TV miniseries) From Here to Eternity, 1979; (feature films) Hard Country, 1981, Mother Lode, 1982, Never Say Never Again, 1983, The Man Who Loved Women, 1983, The Natural, 1984, Fool for Love, 1985, 9 1/2 Weeks, 1986, No Mercy, 1986, Blind Date, 1987, Nadine, 1987, My Stepmother is an Alien, 1988, Batman, 1989, The Marrying Man, 1991, Final Analysis, 1992, Cool World, 1992, The Real McCoy, 1993, The Getaway, 1994, Ready to Wear (Prêt-à-Porter), 1994. Office: CAA 9830 Wilshire Blvd Beverly Hills CA 90212-1804 also: Hofflund Polone care Judy Hofflund 9465 Wilshire Blvd Ste 820 Beverly Hills CA 90212-2607

BASKAKOV, ALBERT PAVLOVICH, heat engineering educator; b. Village Mojjarino, Kalinin, Russia, Mar. 1, 1928; s. Pavel Nikitich and Anna Dmitrievna (Sazonova) B.; m. Nelli Grigorievna Martinova, Mar. 5, 1948; children: Anna, Sergei. Engr., Moskow Power Inst., 1950, Kandidate Scis., 1953; DSc, Ural State Tech. U., 1965. Engring. diplomate. Asst. Ural State Tech. U., Ekaterinburg, 1953-56, asst. prof., 1956-64, prof., head power engring. dept., 1964-98, prof. power engring., 1998—; head sci. lab. Ural br. Acad. Scis. Russia, Ekaterinburg, 1961-64. Mem. editl. bd. Jour. Powder Tech., Internat. Jour. Thermotechnica; author: Rapid Nonoxidizing Heating and Heat Transfer in Fluids Bed, 1968; (with others) Fluidized Bed Boilers and Combustors, 1996 (award Hon. Prof. Ural State Tech. U. 1997); author, editor: Heat Engineering, 2nd edit., 1991. Grantee Energy Ctr. European Union, Ekaterinburg, 1995. Mem. Sci. Metals Assn. (hon.), Internat. Power Acad. Avocation: skiing. Home: Visotskogo St 10 F46, 620072 Ekaterinburg Russia Office: Ural State Tech U, Mira St 19, 620002 Ekaterinburg Russia

BASKERVILLE, CHARLES ALEXANDER, geologist, educator; b. Jamaica, N.Y., Aug. 19, 1928; s. Charles H. and Annie M. (Allen) B.; m. Susan Platt, July 5, 1979; children: Mark Dana, Shawn Allison, Charles Morris, Thomas Marshall. BS, CCNY, 1953; MS, NYU, 1958, PhD, 1965. Cert. geologist, Maine, Ind.; cert. profl. geologist. Asst. civil engr. N.Y. State Dept. Transp., Babylon, 1953-66; prof. engring. geology CUNY, N.Y.C., 1966-79, dean sch. of gen. studies, 1970-79, prof. emeritus, 1979—; project rsch. geologist U.S. Geol. Survey, 1979-90; prof. geology Ctrl. Conn. State U., New Britain, 1990—, dept. chmn., 1992-94; Commonwealth vis. prof. George Mason U., Fairfax, Va., 1987-89; mem. U.S. Nat. Com. on Tunnelling Tech., NRC, chmn. subcom. on edn. and tng.; mem. Am. del Internat. Tunnelling Assn. to Internat. Colloquim of Tunnelling and Underground Works, Beijing, People's Republic of China, 1984; geol. cons. N.Y.C. Dept. Environ. Protection Water Tunnel #3; guest lectr. various colls., 1964—; geol. program evaluator for colls. seeking continued mid. states accreditation. Author numerous sci. papers. Mem. com. for minority participation in the geoscis. U.S. Dept. Interior, 1972-75; panelist Grad. Fellowship Program NRC; chmn. Minority Grad. Fellowship Program, 1979-80; mem. com. of visitors for edn. and human resources program divsn. earth scis. NSF, 1991; mem. N.Y. State Low Level Radioactive Waste Com. NAS, 1994-96. Recipient Founders Day award N.Y. U., 1966, 125th Anniversary medal The City Coll., 1973, award for excellence in engring. geology Nat. Consortium Black Profl. Devel., 1978, Recognition award Nat. Assn. Black Geologists and Geophysicists, 1998. Fellow Geol. Soc. Am. (sr., com. on minorities in geoscis., chmn. com. on coms. 1989), N.Y. Acad. Scis., Geol. Soc. Washington, Am. Inst. Profl. Geologists, Assn. Engring. Geologists (rep. to nat. bd. dirs. 1973-74, chmn. N.Y.-Phila. sect. 1973-74), Internat. Assn. Engring. Geology, Yellowstone-Bighorn Rsch. Assn., Sigma Xi. Office: Ctrl Conn State U Dept Physics and Earth Scis 1615 Stanley St New Britain CT 06053-2439

BASKIN, EDUARD MOISEEVICH, mathematician; b. Uljanovsk, Russia, Feb. 8, 1937; s. Moisey Izrajlevich Baskin and Rima Mendeleevna Rabkina; m. Lidija Nikitichna Utkina, May 23, 1963. B, Jr. Coll., Pezm, Russia, 1955; BS, St. Petersburg (Russia) Coll., 1960; MS, U. Moscow, 1966; PhD in Math. (hon.), Inst. Stds., Moscow, 1971. Engr. Design Office, Moscow, 1960-61; sr. engr. Planning Office, Moscow, 1961-62; sr. engr. Sci. Rsch. Inst., Moscow, 1972-78, sr. rsch. fellow, 1964—. Contbr. articles to profl. jours. Avocation: tennis. Home: Belomorskaja 18-4-281, 125195 Moscow Russia

BASKOUS, ATHAN A., retired environmental engineer; b. Schenectady, N.Y., June 12, 1921; s. Alexander and Beatrice B.; m. Dena Julia Xanthos, Feb. 7, 1945 (dec. Dec. 1968), children: Alexander, Patricia; m. Bertha Esther Caranikas, Aug. 26, 1973. B in Civil Engring., Cornell U., 1943; MPH, U. Mich., 1955. Profl. engr. N.Y., profl. land surveyor, N.Y. Engr. Havens & Emerson, Cleve., 1946-49; engr. N.Y. State Dept. Health, Albany, 1949-55, regional dir., 1955-71; regional engr. N.Y. State Dept. Environ. Conservation, Albany, 1971-83; cons. Schenectady, 1983-95. Merit badge counselor Boy Scouts Am., Schenectady, 1950-55. 1st Lt. U.S. Army, 1943-46. Mem. Classical Mandolin Soc. Am. Avocations: violin restoration, violinist, mandolinist, tennis, travel. Home: 825 Jamaica Rd Schenectady NY 12309-6411

BASKY, ZSUZSA, aphidologist, researcher; b. Orgovány, Hungary, July 20, 1946; d. Laszlo and Zsuzsanna (Gombar) B.; m. Jeno Müller (div. 1971); 1 child, Laszlo Gyula. Degree in hort. engring., Hort. U. Budapest, 1969; MSc, Hort. U., Budapest, 1978; degree in Plant Protection Engring., Agrl. U. Gödöllő, 1971; PhD, Hungarian Acad. Scis., Budapest, 1984. Entomologist Plant Protection Station, Tass, 1969-77; rsch. entomologist aphidologist Vegetable Crops Rsch. Inst., 1978-88, Plant Protection Svc. Szolnok, 1989-94, Plant Protection Inst., Hungarian Sci. Acad., Budapest, 1994—. Contbr. articles to profl. jours. including Protection Ecology, Crop Protection, among others. Recipient Excellence Work award Min. Agr., 1980. Fellow Royal Entomol. Soc. Eng.; mem. Hungarian Soc. Agr. (gov. body zoology sect. 1990—, gold badge 1990), Hungarian Acad. Scis. (plant protection com. 1996—), Ceral Aphid Working Group, Aphidological Soc. Home: Varosmajor u 51, 1122 Budapest Hungary Office: Plant Protection Inst, Hung Acad Scis/Herman O 15, 1022 Budapest Hungary

BASKYS, PAUL JOHN, airport manager; b. Sydney, NSW, Australia; s. Jonas Felix and Therese (Lichter) B.; m. Heather May Gill, July 2, 1988; 1 child, Mitchell. B in Bus. Mgmt., Charles Sturt U., Australia, 1996. Air traffic controller Dept. Aviation New South Wales, Sydney, Australia, 1983-87; regional search-rescue officer Dept. Aviation New South Wales, Sydney, 1987; ops. officer Fed. Airports Corp., Sydney, 1988-90, duty airport mgr., 1990-95; mgr. Ayers Rock Airport Ayers Rock Resort Co., Yulari, No. Terr., 1996; asst. mgr. ops.-air Cairns Internat. Airport, Australia, 1998—; sr. cons. Landside Inchon Internat. Airport, Rep. of Korea; mem. Civil Aviation Safety Authority Rev. Panel, Australia, 1996—. Vice chmn. Comty. Recreation and Lesiure Assn. Yulara, 1997; team mem. No. Territory Emergency Svc., 1997. Mem. Australian Inst. Mgmt. Avocation: pilot. Office: DLIA c/Parsons, FKI Bldg 16th Fl 28-1, Seoul 150-756, Korea

BASLÉ, JEAN-LUC LOUIS, apparel manufacturing executive; b. Angers, France, Sept. 14, 1942; s. Georges and Madeleine (Hunault) B.; m. Beryl Fenn Sturtevant, Mar. 15, 1975; children: Edward, Eleonore. BA, Ecole Superieure Scis. Commls., Angers, France, 1964; MBA, Columbia U., 1969; postgrad., Princeton U., 1982. Product mgr. Am. Can Co., Greenwich, Conn., 1969-71; asst. v.p. Citibank, Paris, 1972-76; v.p. Citibank, N.Y., 1976-78, 1984-92; sr. v.p. Indosuez Bank, Chgo., 1978-82; dep. mgr. Europe Indosuez Bank, Paris, 1983; gen. mgr. Citibank Pvt. Bank, Paris, 1992-94; cons. Maritime Investment Mgmt., Paris, 1995-96; chmn., CEO Yves Jacquier SA, Rohan, France, 1997—. Author: The International Monetary System-Challenges and Perspectives, 1982. Fellow Std. Athletic Club. Avocations: tennis, mythology. Office: Yves Jacquier SA, 6 Rue Notre Dame, 56580 Rohan France

BASOĞLU, METIN, psychiatrist, researcher; b. Kayseri, Turkey, Nov. 17, 1948; arrived in England, 1984; s. Ismail and Ziyaver B. MD, U. of Hacettepe Sch. of Med., Ankara, Turkey, 1973; Specialist in Psychiatry, U. Istanbul, Turkey, 1979; lectr. in Psychiatry, Inst. Psychiatry, U. London, U.K., 1987. M.D. Resident in psychiatry Dept. Psychiatry U. Istanbul, Istanbul, Turkey, 1974-79, specialist in Psychiatry, 1979-83; lectr. psychiatry Inst. Psychiatry U. London, London, U.K., 1987-94; hon. sr. lectr. Inst. Psychiatry U. London, 1994—, head sect trauma studies Dept. Psychiatry, 1999—. Contbr. articles to profl. jours.; editor: Torture and Its Consequences. Mem. AAAS, N.Y. Acad. Scis., World Fedn. Mental Health. Avocations: piano playing, sculpturing, skiing. Office: Sect Trauma Studies, 38 Carver Rd, SE24 9LT London England

BASOL, METE M., bank executive; b. Istanbul, Turkey, Feb. 7, 1957; s. Haluk and Fatos Basol; m. Serap H. Basol, Sept. 29, 1990. BSc in Econs., Ariz. State U., 1980. Assoc. Interbank A.S., Istanbul, 1984-85, area mgr., mgr., 1985-88; mgr. Turk Merchant Bank, Istanbul, 1988-91, dep. gen. mgr., 1991-96; chmn., CEO Bankers Trust AS, Istanbul, 1997-2000, Deutsche Bank AS (named change from Bankers Trust AS), Istanbul, 2000—. Mem. Assn. for Fgn. Capital Coordination, Jr. Businessmen and Mgrs. Assn., Rotary Club. Avocations: football, basketball. Office: Deutsche Bank AS, Cevdet Pasa CD 288 Bebek, 80810 Istanbul Turkey

BASOV, NIKOLAI GENNADIEVICH, physicist; b. Usman, nr. Voronezh, USSR, Dec. 14, 1922; s. Gennadiy Fedorovich and Zinaida Andreevna (Molchanova) B.; m. Ksenia Tikhonovna, Feb. 15, 1927; children: Gennadiy, Dmitriy. Grad., Moscow Mech. Inst., 1950, Can. Phys. Math. Sci., 1953, D. Phys. Math. Sci., 1956; LL.D. (hon.), Polish-Mil.-Tech. Acad., 1972, Jena U., 1974, Prague Poly. Inst., 1975, U. Pavia, Italy, 1977, Madrid Poly. U., 1985; Karl Marx Stadt Tech. U., 1988. With P. N. Lebedev Phys. Inst., USSR Acad. Sci., 1948—, vice dir. for sci. work, 1958-73, head lab. quantum radio physics, 1963—; prof. solid state physics Moscow Inst. Phys. Engrs., 1963—; dir. P. N. Lebedev Phys. Inst., 1973-89, dir. quantum radiophysics div., 1989-98; scientific leader Inst. Quantum Radiophysics, 1998—; mem. expert coun. of prime-minister of Russian Govt., 1991—. Author over 500 works. Research on principle of molecular generator, 1952, realized molecular generator on molecular beam of ammonia, 1955, 3-level system for receiving states with inversal population suggested, 1955, proposed use of semicondrs. for creation lasers, 1958, realized various types of semicondr. lasers with excitation through p-n junctions, electronic and optical pumping, 1960-65, research on obtaining short powerful pulses of coherent light; proposed thermal and chem. methods for laser pumping, 1962, gas dynamic lasers, 1966; research optical data processing, 1965—; proposed, 1961, realized thermonuclear reactions by using powerful lasers, 1968; developed main trends in optical frequency standards, 1967-68; inventor electron-beam pumped semicondr. laser projection TV, 1968; proposed, 1966, realized eximer lasers, 1970; realized stimulation of chem. reactions by infrared laser radiation, 1970; proposed and realized electro-ionization laser, 1971; proposed concept of low-entropy compression of high-aspect ratio multilayer thermonuclear targets, 1974, showed possibility of their stable compression, 1983; realized lasers with long-time stability of 2.10-14, 1982; chief editor Priroda, 1967-90, Kvantovaya Elektronika, 1971—. Chmn. bd. All-Union Soc., Znanie, 1978-90, hon. chmn., 1990—; dep. USSR Supreme Soviet, 1974-89; mem. presidium Supreme Soviet, 1982-89; v.p. exec. coun. World Fedn. Sci. Workers, 1976-83; v.p. WFSW, 1983-90, hon. mem., 1990—. Decorated Order Lenin (5), Order of Patriotic War hero twice Socialist Labour; recipient Lenin prize, 1959, Nobel prize for fundamental rsch. in quantum electronics resulting in creation of masers and lasers, 1964, Gold medal Czechoslovakian Acad. Scis., 1975, A. Volta's Gold medal, 1977, Order of Kirill and Mephodii (Bulgaria), 1981, E. Henkel Gold medal German Dem. Rep., 1986, Commodor's cross Order of Merit, Poland, 1986, Kalinga prize UNESCO, 1986, Gold medal Slovakian Acad. Scis., 1988, M.V. Lomonosov Gold medal USSR Acad. Scis., 1989, State prize of USSR, 1989, Edward Teller medal, 1991. Fellow Optical Soc. Am., Indian Nat. Sci. Acad., Amer. Phys. Soc., 1998; mem. European Acad. Scis. and Arts (Salzburg chpt.), Internat. Acad. Scis. (hon.), USSR Acad. Scis. (presidium 1967-90, advisor 1990—), Acad. Natural Scis. of Russian Fedn. (hon.) Acad. Scis. German Dem. Rep., Polish and Czechoslovakian Acad. Scis., German Acad. Natural Scis. Leopoldina, Bulgarian Acad. Scis., Royal Swedish Acad. Engring., European Acad. Arts, Scis. and Humanities (Paris chpt.), Acad. Scis. Ga., Acad. Scis. Belorussia, fell., Amer. Physical Soc., 1998. Office: PN Lebedev Phys Inst, 53 Leninsky Prospekt, Moscow Russia

BASQUIN, MARY SMYTH (KIT BASQUIN), museum administrator; b. N.Y.C., July 3, 1941; d. Joseph Percy and Virginia Sandford (Gibbs) Smyth; m. Maurice Hanson Basquin, Feb. 4, 1967 (div. Feb. 1984); children: Susan, Peter Lee, William. BA, Goucher Coll., Balt., 1963; MA, Ind. U., 1970. Asst. dir. pub. rels. Indpls. Mus. Art, 1971-72; dir. Washignton Gallery, Frankfort, Ind., 1972-79, Indpls., 1977-79; dir. Kit Basquin Gallery, Milw., 1981-83; curator edn. Haggerty Mus. Marquette U., Milw., 1988-95; dir. outreach Milw. Wis. Humanities Coun., 1995-98; curator Marvin Lowe Retrospective, Ind. U. Art Mus., 1998; mktg. William Doyle Galleries, N.Y.C., 1999, exhbn. mgr., 2000—; rsch. assoc. Bklyn. Mus. Art, 2000; asst. print study rm. Met. Mus. Art, N.Y.C., 2000—; instr. art history Concordia U., Mequon, Wis., 1991, instr. Marquette U., Gaza, 1996; pres. contemporary art soc. Milw. Art Mus., 1986-87, prints and drawings subcom., 1991-99, pres. Print Forum, 1996-97; mem. program com. Midwest Mus. conf., Milw., 1992. Wis. editor New Art Examiner, Chgo., 1980-81; contbr. articles to profl. jours. Trustee Ten Chimneys Found., Genesee Depot, Wis., 1997-99; mem. adv. bd. Ten Chimneys Found., 2000—. Mem. Univ. Club N.Y., Univ. Club Milw. Episcopalian. Avocations: fashion, theater, concerts, swimming, biking. Home & Office: 1675 York Ave Apt 19A New York NY 10128-6756

BASRA, DEVINDER SINGH, plastic surgeon; b. Thanabipur, India, Jan. 9, 1942; came to Eng., 1968; s. Bishan Singh and Harnam Kaur Basra; m. Sara Kaur, 1989; 1 child, Dev Santini; children by previous marriage: Devina, Sukhdev. M.B.B.S., Med. Sch., (India), 1966; F.R.C.S., Royal Coll. Surgeons, Edinburgh, Scotland, 1976; fellow Internat. Acad. Cosmetic Surgery, Switzerland, 1982. House surgeon Govt. Hosp., Amritsar, India, 1966-68; sr. house surgeon accident, orthopedics, plastics and surgery Nat. Health Hosps., Eng., 1968-74; registrar Health Authority, Dundee, Scotland, 1974-75; registrar surgery Noble Hosp., Douglas, Isle of Man, 1976-77; facial aesthetic surgeon, London, 1977—. Author: The Ageing Skin, 1986; also articles; editorial com. Internat. Jour. Aesthetic Surgery, 1981—. Recipient Best Artist prize Col. Brown Sch., India, 1958; Best Artist prize Med. Sch., India, 1964, 65. Fellow Royal Soc. Medicine; mem. Internat. Soc. Aesthetic Surgery (charter mem. 1981—) Japanese Assn. Aesthetic Surgeons, Fedn. Europeene des Societes Nat. de Chirurgie Esthetique (v.p. 1987—), Indian Assn. Cosmetic. Surgeons (pres. 1988—). Avocations: photography, interior designing, art, sculpture. Office: 111 Harley St, London W1N 1DG, England

BAS RAMALLO, FRANCISCO, psychotherapist, educator, researcher; b. Cartagena, Spain, Oct. 8, 1940; s. Jose Bas Solvez and Dolores Ramallo Esparza; m. Ascension Maestre Najera, Aug. 20, 1966 (div. 1983); children: Francisco Bas Maestre, Susana Bas Maestre; m Verania Andres Navia, Sept. 1, 1983. Diploma in elec. engring., Cartagena U., 1962; first degree in philosophy & ednl. sci., U. Madrid, 1979, D of Psychology with special distinction, 1991. Tech. sales dir. Cenit SA, Madrid, 1966-74; tech. dir. ITT-Control, Madrid, 1974-79; gen. dir. Ctr. Psychology Bertrand Russell, Madrid, 1979—; project mgr. Snamproy, Madrid, 1979-86; prof. U. Psychostatis UAM, Madrid, 1982-86; dir. psico-pedagogical office Col. Fuent, Madrid, 1986-93; invited prof. postgrad. studies, 1994— U. Autonoma Madrid, hon. prof., 1997. Author: Cognitive Behavioral Therapy of Depression, 1992, Children Eating Disorders, 1999, Trastornos de la Alimentacion en Nuestros Hijos, 2000; contbr. articles to profl. jours., book chpts. Mem. Spanish Social Cognitive-Behavioral Therapy Assn. (founder, hon. pres. 1997), Nat. Com. Creation of Profile Clin. Psychologist Health Care in Spain. Avocations: walking, writing, reading, travel, thinking. Home: C/ Oviedo 48, Pozuelo de Alarcon, 28223 Madrid Spain Office: Ctr Psicologia, c/Marques de Urquijo 10-1, 28008 Madrid Spain

BASRI, HASAN, religious organization leader. Chmn. Indonesian Ulama Coun., Jakarta; min. of state for land and agrarian affairs Govt. of Indonesia, Jakarta. Office: Min State Land/Agr Affairs, JL Sisingamangaraja No 2, Kebayoran Baru Jakarta 12110, Indonesia*

BASRI, MEER S., business executive; b. Baghdad, Sept. 19, 1911. Sec. Iraqi Ministry Fgn. Affairs, 1932; dir. Iraq Directory, 1935; sec., dir. Baghdad C. of C., 1935-45; contr. Comml. Exch., 1936-38; asst. Iraqi Commr. Internat. Exhbn., Paris, 1937; dir. Eastern Comml. Corp., 1945-49; asst. dir. gen. Date Assn., 1947-52; dir. various cos.; del. Internat. Bus. Conf., Rye, N.Y., 1944; mem. Gen. and Adminstrv. Councils, Baghdad. Editor C. of C. Jour., 1938-45, numerous books; author: Essays on Iraqi Economy, 1948, Glossary of Economic Terms and Theories, 1948, Leaders of Thought in Modern Iraq, 1971, (poetry) Echoes of the Lyre, Men and Shadows, 1955, Political Personalities in Modern Iraq, 1987, Thirsty Souls, 1998, Songs of Love and Eternity, 1991, Life's Journey, 1992, History of Iraqi Literature, 3 vols., 1994-99, Arab Nationalism, 1999, Baghdad Sketches, 1998, others. Address: 244 Dover House Rd, London SW15, England

BASS, DAVID STEVEN, lawyer, educational administrator; b. Bklyn., Dec. 10, 1946; s. Joseph and Thelma (Feingold) B.; m. Carol W. Palevsky, Aug. 17, 1969; children: Adam Brett, Wayne Jonathan. BA, Bklyn. Coll., 1967; JD, NYU, 1971, LLM, 1975. Bar: N.Y. 1972, U.S. Dist. Ct. (ea. dist.) N.Y. 1975. Atty. Office Labor Rels. and Collective Bargaining N.Y.C. Bd. Edn., 1973-80, dep. dir., 1980-84, dep. exec. dir., 1984—; adj. prof. edn. law and pers. adminstrn. City Coll. CUNY, 1992—. Mem. Am. Arbitration Assn., N.Y. State Bar Assn. Democrat. Jewish. Home: 31 Whitney Dr Marlboro NJ 07746-1249 Office: Office Labor Relations and Collective Bargaining NYC B d Edn 110 Livingston St Brooklyn NY 11201

BASS, FRIDRICH GERSHON, physicist, educator; b. Kharkov, Ukraine, Oct. 26, 1930; arrived in Israel, 1995; s. Gershon Israel Bass and Rebeka Mark Genkina; m. Larisa Boris Vatova; children: Olga, Gregory. PhD, U. Kharkov, 1958; DSc, Acoustical Inst. Moscow, 1963. Head rschr. Inst. Radio Physics, Kharkov, 1955-94; prof. Poly. Inst. Kharkov, 1971-94, Bar Ilan U., Ramat Gan, Israel, 1995—. Author: (with I.M. Fuks) Wave Scattering from Statistically Rough Surfaces, 1979; contbr. articles to profl. jours. 1st lt. Artillery Mil., 1948-53. Recipient Outstanding Achievements award Am. Inst. Radio Engring., 1969. Avocation: history. Home: Orlov 7/4, 49414 Petah Tiqwa Israel Office: Dept Physics, Bar Ilan Univ, 52900 Ramat Gan Israel

BASS, LUDVIK, mathematics educator, researcher; b. Prague, Czech Republic, Mar. 9, 1931; arrived in Australia, 1965; s. Antony and Agnes (Janda) B.; m. Nina Schmahl, Mar. 11, 1961; children: Karen Louise, Marianne. DPhil, U. Vienna, Austria, 1954; MA, Dublin U., Ireland, 1959; RNDr, Charles U., Prague, Czech Republic, 1992. Rsch. scholar Dublin Inst. for Advanced Studies, 1954-56; lectr. Trinity Coll., Dublin U., 1956-61; prin. mathematician and physicist BSA Group Rsch. Ctr., Birmingham, Eng., 1961-63; prin. lectr. Lanchester Inst. Tech., Coventry, Eng., 1963-65; prof. math. U. Queensland, Brisbane, Australia, 1965—; sr. fgn. fellow NSF, 1968-69; vis. fellow Danish Nat. Rsch. Found., 1972, 77, 86, 92, 96; mem. Ctr. for Theoretical Studies Charles U., Prague, 1992—; vis. positions in U.S., U.K., Germany, Czech Republic. Contbr. articles to Math. Physics, Math. Biology, Philosophy of Sci. Fellow Inst. of Physics; mem. Royal Danish Acad. of Scis. (fgn.). Avocations: music, squash, hiking. Office: U Queensland, Dept Math, QLD Brisbane 4072, Australia

BASS, LYNDA D., medical/surgical nurse, educator; b. Suffolk, Va.; d. H.M. and Katie Lea Bass. BSN, N.C. Agrl. and Tech. State U., Greensboro, 1968; MS in Nursing, Cath. U. Am., 1974; Gen. Surgery Clin. Specialist, George Washington U. Hosp., Washington. Cert. BCLS instr., CPR instr.-trainer. Clin. instr. Suburban Hosp., Bethesda, Md.; edn./tng. quality assurance coord. Howard U. Hosp., Washington; clin. educator Providence Hosp., Washington; edn. specialist VA Md. Healthcare Sys., Balt.; coord. clin. staff Devel. Mount Vernon Hosp., Alexandria, Va. Capt. U.S. Army, 1968-71, Vietnam. Mem. Nat. Nursing Staff Devel. Assn., Vietnam Vets. Am., Chi Eta Phi.

BASS, NEVILLE M., orthodontist; b. Manchester, Eng., June 8, 1938; s. Arthur and Ray B.; m. Mona Chong, Jan. 6, 1969; children: Alexander, Anton. LDS, Dental Sch., Manchester, Eng., 1960, B Dental Surgery, 1960; FDS, Royal Coll. Surgeons, Eng., 1964, Dip Orthodontics, 1963. Diplomate Brit. Orthodontic Bd., Royal Coll. of Surgeons in Orthodontics. Cons., orthodontist USAF, 1965-69; lectr. postgrad. orthdontic dept. Royal London Hosp., 1988—; orthodontist pvt. practice London, 1969—; bd. dirs. Orthomodules Ltd., London, 1985—. Patentee in field (10) in orthopedic appliances; contbr. numerous articles to profl. jours. Recipient Preston Gold medal Manchester U., 1960. Mem. European Orthdontic Soc., Brit. Orthodontic Soc. (pres. 2000—), Angle Soc. of Europe (sec. 1978-81, chmn. sci. com. 1994, pres. 2000—), Alpha Omega. Avocations: writing, sailing, skiing, travel, sculpture. Office: 4 Queen Anne St, London W1M9LE, England

BASSALO, JOSE MARIA FILARDO, physics educator, researcher; b. Belem, Para, Brazil, Sept. 10, 1935; s. Eladio and Rosa (Filardo) B.; m. Celia Coelho; children: Jose Maria, Adria Bassalo Aflalo. B in Physics, U. Brasilia, 1965; M in Physics, U. Sao Paulo, 1973, D in Physics, 1975. Civil engr. Roads Munich Dept. of Belém, 1958-85; full prof. DFUFPA, Belém, 1989—. Author: Crônicas da Fisica, 1987, 5th edit., 1998, Nascimentos da Física, 1997. Mem. Brazilian Physics Soc., Brazilian Soc. for Advancement of Sci., Brazilian Soc. History of Sci., N.Y. Acad. Scis. E-mail: bassalo@amazon.com. Home: Serzedelo Correa 347/1601, 66025240 Belém Pará, Brazil Office: UFPA, Campus U de Guama, 66075900 Belém Pará, Brazil

BASSANINI, PIERO, mathematician, educator; b. Milano, Italy, Sept. 23, 1941; s. Antonio and Sandra (Tremontani) B.; m. Lisa Longhi, Febr. 3, 1969; 3 children. MA in Physics, U. Milano, Italy, 1965; PhD in Math. Physics, U. Rome, Italy, 1969. Postdoctoral fellow U. Windsor, Ont., Can., 1968-69; asst. and assoc. prof. U. Perugia, Italy, 1969-75; full prof. U. Milano and Perugia, 1976-80, U. Rome, Italy, 1980—; chmn. dept. applied math. U. Perugia, 1977-80; sci. adv. Higher Math., Rome, 1990-94; sci. cons. Naval Basin, Rome, 1986—. Author: Partial Differential Equations, 1997; contbr. numerous articles to profl. jours. Lt. Italian Air Force, 1967-68. Mem. UMI, AIMETA, IABEM. Office: Dept Math U Rome I, P le A Moro 5, 00185 Rome Italy

BASSANO, CARLO, cardiac surgeon; b. Napoli, Italy, July 6, 1961; s. Giovanni Bassano and Elvira Cesareo; m. Maria Guilia Gagliardi, Oct. 7, 1995; 1 child, Federico. MD, U. Federico II, Napoli, 1986; D, Min. Univ. Sci. Rsch. & Tech., Rome, 1994. Resident in cardiac surgery Tor Vergata U., Rome, 1987-94, staff surgeon, 1995—, asst. prof., 1998—; prof. cardiac surgery Italian Red Cross Nursing Sch., Rome, 1995-98. Contbr. articles to profl. jours. Fax: 390665975117. Home: Via Calcutta 25, 00144 Rome Italy Office: European Hosp, Via Portuense 700, 00149 Rome Italy

BASSECHES, ROBERT TREINIS, lawyer; b. N.Y.C., Jan. 24, 1934; s. Jacob Thomas and Paula (Treinis) B.; m. Harriet Itkin, July 6, 1958; children: K.B., Joshua, Jessica. BA, Amherst Coll., 1955; LLB, Yale U., 1958. Bar: D.C. 1962, U.S. Ct. Appeals (D.C. cir.) 1962, U.S. Ct. Appeals (2d cir.) 1978, U.S. Ct. Appeals (4th cir.) 1998. Law clk. to judge David L. Bazelon U.S. Ct. Appeals (D.C. cir.), Washington, 1958-59; law clk. to justice Hugo L. Black U.S. Supreme Ct., Washington, 1959; assoc. Shea & Gardner, Washington, 1959-63, ptnr., 1963—, adminstrv. ptnr., 1980-86, chmn., exec. com., 1988-93. Trustee Green Acres Sch., Rockville, Md., 1971-76, pres., chmn. bd. trustees, 1973-75; pres. Chevy Chase (Md.) Village Citizens Assn., 1976. Mem. Maritime Adminstrv. Bar Assn. (pres. 1969-71, sec. 1967-69), Phi Beta Kappa. Office: Shea & Gardner Ste 800 1800 Massachusetts Ave NW Washington DC 20036-1872

BASSETT, DAVID CHARLES JEREMY, medical microbiologist, consultant; b. Southampton, Eng., Feb. 21, 1930; s. Reginald John and Pauline Margaret (Souter) B.; m. Marilyn Downton (div. July 1975); children: Stephen Charles, Judith Michal Bassett Carter, James Ralph (dec.); m. Seraphina Sandra Keekock, Feb. 6, 1984; children: Nicholas Francis, Naomi Kim. Assoc. in Bacteriology, Inst. Biomed. Sci., 1953; MB, BS, U. London, 1958, postgrad. acad. diploma in bacteriology, 1962. Ho. officer Whipps Cross Hosp., Hosp. SS John and Elizabeth, London, 1959-60; trainee bacteriologist Guy's Hosp., London, 1960-62; hon. sr. registrar in bacteriology Wrexham Hosp. Group, Wales, 1962-65; external mem. sci. staff Med. Rsch. Coun. U.K., Trinidad Regional Virus Lab., Port of Spain, Trinidad and Tobago, 1965-68; sr. bacteriologist Ctrl. Pub. Health Lab., Colindale, Eng., 1968-72, Cross-Infection Reference Lab., London, 1968-72; sr. lectr. bacteriology Inst. Child Health, U. London, 1972-76; med. officer, bacteriologist, head labs., acting dir. Caribbean Epidemiology Ctr., Port of Spain, 1977-89; sr. tchr. fellow Nat. U. Singapore, 1989-91; vis. sr. lectr. Chinese U. Hong Kong, 1991-95; hon. cons. microbiologist Great Ormond Street Hosp. Group, London, 1972-76, Hong Kong Hosp. Authority, 1994-95; assoc. cons. Nat. U. Hosp., Singapore, 1989-91. Contbg. author: AIDS: Profile of an Epidemic, 1989, Principles and Practice of Medical Laboratory Science, Vol. 2, 1997; contbr. articles to med. jours., including Brit. Jour. Dermatopathology, Procs. Royal Soc. Medicine. Fellow Royal Coll. Pathologists, Royal Soc. Tropical Medicine and Hygiene; mem. Path. Soc. Gt. Britain and Ireland (sr.), PanAm. Health Orgn. Avocations: music, history, natural history. Home: 5 Pear Tree Close, Cambridgeshire CB6 3UU, UK

BASSETT, TINA, communications executive; b. Detroit; m. Leland Kinsey Bassett; children: Joshua, Robert. Student, U. Mich., 1974, 76-78, 81, Wayne State U., 1979-80. Advt. dir. Greenfield's Restaurant, Mich. and Ohio, 1972-73; dir. advt. and pub. rels. Kresco, Inc., Detroit, 1973-74; pub's. rep. The Detroiter mag., 1974-75; pub. rels. dir. Detroit Bicentennial Commn., 1975-77; prin. Leland K. Bassett & Assocs., Detroit, 1976-86; intermediate job devel. specialist Detroit Coun. of the Arts, 1977; project dir. Detroit image campaign dept. pub. info. City of Detroit, 1975, spl. events dir., 1978, dep. dir. dept. pub. info., 1978-83, dir. dept. pub. info., 1983-86; pres., prin. Bassett & Bassett, Inc., Detroit, 1986—; bd. dirs. Diverse Steel Corp. Publicity chmn. Under the Stars IV, V, VI, VII, VIII, IX and X, Benefit Balls, Detroit Inst. of Arts Founders Soc., 1983-88, Detroit Inst. of Arts Founders Centennial Ball, 1985, publicity chmn. Mich. Opera Theater, Opera Ball, 1987; program lectr. Wayne County Close-Up Program, 1984; mem. ctrl. planning com. Am. Assn. Mus.; mem. Founders Soc., Detroit Inst. Arts, 1988—; mem., publicity chair Grand Prix Ball, 1989; co-chair, prodr. Mus. Hall Ctr. for Performing Arts; bd. dirs. arts coun. Detroit Inst. Arts, 1996, bd. dirs. cinema arts coun., 1996—; bd. dirs. Weizman Inst. Sci., 1996-97. Named Outstanding Woman in Agy. Top Mgmt., Detroit chpt. Am. Women in Radio and TV, 1989. Mem. AIA (hon., pub. dir. 1990-91, Richard Upjohn fellowship 1991), Detroit Hist. Soc., , Internat. Women's Forum, Music Hall Assn., Pub. Rels. Soc. Am. (Advt. Woman of Yr. 1989), Woman's Advt. Club Detroit, Cinematic Arts Coun., DIA Board of Dirs., 1996—. Home: 30751 Cedar Creek Dr Farmingtn Hls MI 48336-4989 Address: Bassett & Bassett 1502 Randolph St Ste 200 Detroit MI 48226-2295

BASSFORD, LYNN FOSTER, physicist, engineer; b. Webster, Mass., Jan. 23, 1969; d. George E. and Carolyn M. (Sherman) F. BS in Physics, U. Mass., Lowell, 1991. NASA cert. for Hubble Space Telescope's sci. instruments, data mgmt., instrumentation and comms., elec. power, shift supervisor, and thermal control subsystems. Satellite flight contr. Lockheed Martin Tech. Ops. Co., GSFC, NASA, Greenbelt, Md., 1991-95; Hubble Space Telescope satellite shift supervisor flight ops Lockheed Martin Tech. Ops., Goddard Space Flight Ctr., Greenbelt, Md., 1995-99, HST sci. instrument systems engr., 2000—. Mem. Nat. Soc. Physics Students.

BASSI, JEAN JACQUES, systems analyst; b. Metz, Lorraine, France, Dec. 18, 1950; s. Théodore and Germaine (Guérard) B.; m. Brigitte Lucie Langlade, June 15, 1975; children: Veronique Cecile Colette, Laurene-Marie Luce. DEA, U. Paris IV, 1974. Analyst Cebea, Metz, 1977-81; mem. task force Fabre, Metz, 1981-89; cons. Alone, Burgundy, 1990-96; analyst, cons. Bourgogne-Informatique, Vievy, France, 1996—. Author various software pkgs. Mem. City Coun., Vievy, 1989. Cmdr. lt. French Air Force, 1979. Republican. Roman Catholic. Avocation: aviation. Home: Dracy-Chalas, 21230 Vievy France

BASSILADZE, SERGEY GENNADIEVICH, laboratory administrator, nuclear engineer; b. Balkhash, Kazakhstan, Feb. 19, 1941; s. Gennadiy Silvestrovich and Evgenija Nikolaevna (Burakova) B.; m. Evgeniya Fedorovna Korabelnikova, Apr. 3, 1970; children: Timur Sergeevich, Irina Sergeevna. Grad., Moscow Engring. Phys. Inst., 1963, postgrad., 1969; DSc, Joint Inst. Nuc. Rsch., 1979; prof., Moscow State U., 1993. Rschr. Joint Inst. Nuc. Rsch., Dubna, Russia, 1963-66; head lab. Joint Inst. Nuc. Rsch., Dubna, 1970-80; head divsn. Nuc. Rsch. Computer Ctr. Moscow State U., 1981-88, vice-dir. Computer Ctr., 1988-89, head divsn. Internat. Ctr. Informatics and Electronics, 1990-92, head lab. Nuc. Physics Inst., 1992—. Author: Fast Nuclear Electronics, 1982, The Interfaces of Modular Multiprocessors Bus Systems, 1992; co-author: (with E.I. Rehin, P.S. Chernov) Coincidence Method, 1979. Mem. Internat. Informatization Acad. Office: Nuc Physics Inst, Moscow State Univ, 119899 Moscow Russia

BASSILI, SAFWAT SOBHY, ophthalmologist; b. Alexandria, Egypt, Feb. 13, 1954; arrived in Australia, 1985; s. Sobhy Bassili and Saphiia Hanna Meleika; m. Anna Claire Osinski, Nov. 12, 1989; children: Matthew Joel, Gabrielle Claire, Claire Elizabeth, Alexandra Sophie. M.B.Ch.B. with honors, Alexandria U., 1977; DO, Royal Coll. Surgeons of Eng., 1985. Lic. physician, Egypt, Eng., Australia, U.S.; lic. ophthalmologist, Australia. House officer Alexandria U., 1978-79; sr. house officer in gen. surgery S. Shields Gen. Hosp., Tyne and Wear, England, 1980-81; sr. house officer orthopaedic surgery Addenbrookes Hosp., Cambridge, England, 1981; sr. house officer in gen. surgery Huntingdon County and Hitchingbrooke Hosp., Cambridgeshire, England, 1981-82; sr. house officer in accident and emergency medicine Norfolk and Norwich Hosp., Norwich, England, 1982; sr. house officer in ophthalmology West Norwich Hosp., 1983-84, Southampton (England) Eye Hosp., 1984-85; registrar, sr. registrar in ophthalmology Royal Victorian Eye and Ear Hosp., Melbourne, Australia, 1985-88, fellow in vitreo-retinal surgery, 1989; cons. ophthalmologist Austin & Royal Victorian Eye and Ear Hosp., Melbourne, 1990-94, 95—; fellow in vitro retinal surgery La. State U. Eye Ctr., New Orleans, 1994-95; vitreo-retinal surgeon Austin & Repatriation Med. Ctr., Melbourne, 1995—; mem. Ednl. Commn. for Fgn. Med. Grads., U.S., 1993. Contbr. articles to profl. jours. Fellow Royal Australian Coll. Ophthalmologists, Royal Australian Coll. Surgeons, Royal Coll. Surgeons Eng.; mem. Am. Acad. Ophthalmology, Soc. of Apothecaries of London, Australian Med. Examining Coun., Gen. Med. Coun. Eng. Avocations: reading, music, golf, family. Office: No Specialist Eye Ctr, 47 Burgundy St, Heidelberg 3084 VIC, Australia

BASSILY, ELIJAH SARWAT, management executive; b. Aswan, Egypt, Nov. 19, 1967; s. Sarwat Sabet and Isis Fawzy (Shenouda) B.; m. Randa Guirguis Beshir; children: Virginia, Georgenia. Bachelor, Am. U. in Cairo, 1991. Dep. chmn. AMOUN Pharm. Co., Cairo, Egypt, 1991—. Mem. AAAS, IEEE, Am. Mgmt. Assn., N.Y. Acad. Scis. Democrat. Coptic Orthodox. Avocations: reading, soccer, table tennis, volleyball. Home: 146 El-Orouba St, Cairo Heliopolis, Egypt Office: AMOUN Pharm Co, 125 El-Hegaz St Heliopolis, Cairo Heliopolis, Egypt

BÄSSLER, HEINZ, chemistry educator; b. Angsburg, Germany, July 21, 1937; s. Richard and Wilhelmine Bässler. PhD, Tech. U., 1963. Prof. Philipps U., Marburg, Germany, 1970—. Contbr. articles to profl. jours. Home: Freiherr von Stein Str 12, D-35041 Marburg Germany Office: Philipps U, Inst Phys Chemistry, D-35032 Marburg Germany

BASSLER, MARKUS SYLVESTER, medical researcher; b. Freiburg, Germany, Jan. 16, 1954; s. Gerhard Wolfgang Bassler and Gerda (Wonhalla) Maidanidis; m. Annette Brünhild Lang, Apr. 8, 1980; children: Julia, Moritz, Dennis. Med. diploma, U. Heidelberg, Germany, 1980, Dr.med., 1981; habilitation, U. Mainz, Germany, 1995. Assoc. dr. U. Freiburg, 1980-84; asst. doctor, rschr. U. Mainz, 1984-94, Oberarzt, 1994—; presenter, organizer workshops in field. Contbr. articles to profl. jours. Recipient Richard-Merten prize Richard-Merten-Stiftung, 1995. Mem. Internat. Psychoanalytic Assn., Soc. for Psychotherapy Rsch. Avocation: chess. Fax: 0049-6131-176688. E-mail: bassles@psychosomatik.klinik.uni-mainz.de. Office: U Mainz Clinic Psychosomatic Medicine, U Mainz Clinic, Untere Zahlbacherstr 8, 55131 Mainz Germany

BASSNETT, PETER JAMES, retired librarian; b. Sutton Coldfield, Warwickshire, Eng., Nov. 16, 1933; emigrated to Can., 1966; s. Lionel and Phyllis (Mair) B.; m. Ann Gorham, Dec. 12, 1959; children: Madeline Jane, Sarah Catherine. A.Library Assn., N. Western Poly. Sch. Librarianship, London, 1963. Chartered librarian, U.K. Library asst. City of Westminster, London, 1958-61; tech. librarian Cement & Concrete Assn., London, 1963-64; librarian-in-charge London Borough of Haringey, 1964-66; adminstrv. asst. to dir. Calgary Pub. Library Bd., Alta., 1966-72; dir. systems and mgmt. North York Pub. Library Bd., Ont., 1972-75; CEO librs. Scarborough Pub. Library Bd., Ont., 1975-95; ret., 1995; exec. coordinator Ont. Pub. Libraries Programme Rev., Toronto, 1980-82. Contbr. articles to profl. jours. Chmn. adv. com. on library arts programme So. Alta. Inst. Tech., 1969-72. Fellow Libr. Assn. (U.K.); mem. Alta. Libr. Assn. (pres. 1969-70), Powys Soc. Home: 29 Highbridge Pl, Scarborough, ON Canada M1V 4R7

BASSO, CHRISTOPHE PAUL, electrical engineer; b. Paris, June 22, 1965; s. Paul and Michelle (Vidal) B.; m. Anne Guillon, June 2, 1990; children: Lucille, Paul. Baccalaureat, Clos-Banet, Perpignan, France, 1983; BSEE, U. Montpellier, France, 1985. Customer engr. Hewlett Packard, Paris, 1985-87; elec. engr. European Synchrotron, Grenoble, France, 1989-97; application engr. Motorola, Toulouse, France, 1997-99, ON Semiconductor, Toulouse, 1999—. Author: The IEEE 488 Bus, 1996; contbr. articles to profl. jours. Mem. IEEE. Avocations: basketball, windsurfing, mountain biking, snow shoeing. E-mail: cbasso@wanadoo.fr. Office: ON Semiconductor, BP 1056, 31023 Toulouse France

BASSOLI, MASSIMO, editor; b. Rome, June 27, 1954; s. Oddone Bassoli and Bianca Proietti; m. Francesca Romana Dolazza, Oct. 31, 1989; children: Brando Morris Richard, Greta Mies Domino, Vieri Francis Ford. D in Architecture, La Sapienza U., Rome, 1980. Editor Tutti Frutti, Rome, 1982—, Metal Shock, Rome, 1985—, Flash, Rome, 1985—, Calcio Calendario, Rome, 1985—, Il Giornale d'Italia, Rome, 2000—. Office: Tutti Frutti, via Ovidio 10, 00193 Rome Italy also: Il Giornale D'Italia, Via Boezio 17, 00193 Rome Italy

BASSOMPIERRE, PATRICE JOSEPH, physician, health facility administrator; b. Nancy, France, Aug. 11, 1945; arrived in South Africa, 1978; s. Roger and Andrèe (Weimerskirch) B.; m. Maryse Bastien, Nov. 9, 1968; 1 child, Luc. MD, U. Nancy, France, 1972. Med. practitioner Nice, France, 1972-77; CEO Servier Labs., South Africa, 1978-89, Italy, 1989-93; CEO, founder Tema Med., Cramerview, South Africa, 1994—. Pres. Rassemblement Pour La Republique, South Africa, 1995—. Office: PO Box 3467, Cramerview 2060, South Africa

BASSON, HENRY HAWKSWORTH, chemical company executive; b. Ladybrand, South Africa, Oct. 8, 1941; arrived in Belgium, 1982; s. Johannes J.M. and Miriel L.H. (Fawkes) B.; m. Sybil Margaret Schaffer, July 30, 1966; children: Penelope Jane, Louise Margaret, David Henry. BSc, Natal U., Pietermantzburg, South Africa, 1961, BSc with honors, 1962, MSc, 1964; PhD, Pa. State U., 1969. Rsch. officer African Explosives and Chem. Industries, Modderfontein, South Africa, 1965; sales mgr. Rohm & Haas, Pinetown, South Africa, 1970-74; mktg. mgr. Rohm & Haas, Paris, 1974-82; bus. mgr. Rohm & Haas, London, 1982-86; gen. mgr. Rohm & Haas, Antwerp, Belgium, 1986-92; pres. Rheox Europe, Brussels, 1992-97, Kronos Europe, Brussels, 1997—; bd. dirs. Kronos Internat. Inc., Leverkusen, Germany, Kronos Norge, Oslo. Mem. Am. Chem. Soc. Avocations: golf, skiing, jogging, opera, wine. Office: Kronos Europe SA/NV, 31 Rue De L'Hopital, 1000 Brussels Belgium

BASSOT, JACQUES, aesthetic surgeon; b. France, Sept. 5, 1924. Ex chirurgien Des Hopitaux de la Region, Sanitaire De Lille, France. Editor: La Revue de Chirurgie Esthetique de Langue Francaise; author: Le Bien Etre et la Beute, 1998. Mem. AAAS, De La Societe Francaise De Chirurgie Esthetique (hon. pres.), Internat. Acad. Cosmetic Surgery, Internat. Soc. Aesthetic Surgery (exec. bd.), La Fed. Europeene des Soc. Nat. de Chirugie Esthetique (pres., foundateur), N.Y. Acad. Scis. Home: 54 Ave LeFevre, 94420 Le Plessis Trevise France

BASSOUL, AZIZ MICHEL, financial executive; b. Beirut, Lebanon, Aug. 1, 1946; s. Michel Aziz and Helene Georges (Satel) B.; m. Claire Anwar Syriani, Aug. 11, 1977; 1 child, Michel. MS in Engring., Ecole Centrale, Paris, 1969; MS in Econs., U. Paris, 1970; MBA, Columbia U., 1972; PhD in Fin., U. Paris, 1976. Charge de mission Prefecture de Paris, 1969-70; staff officer Citibank, N.Y.C., 1972-73; cons. Contracting & Trading Group, Beirut, 1973-76; sec. gen. Contracting & Trading Group, Paris, 1976—, dep. fin. contr., 1981-86, gen. mgr. fin., 1986-96, CFO, 1996—; fin. contr., bd. dirs. C.A.T. Holding S.A., Luxembourg, 1994—; bd. dirs. Banque de l'Industrie et du Travail, Beirut, Dayacat Sdn. Bhd., Kuala Lumpur. Mem. Auto. Touring Club Du Liban, Rotary. Roman Catholic. Avocations: Asian art, Caucasian rugs, travel. Home: 38 Avenue Victor Hugo, 75116 Paris France Office: CAT Co, Al-Arz Str Saifi, Beirut Lebanon

BASSY, ALAIN MARIE, sales executive; b. Paris, Apr. 3, 1947; s. Auguste Henri and Marie-Thérése (Biais) B.; Brigitte Elisabeth Narjot, Sept. 10, 1974; 1 child, Aurore. Student, Ecole Normale Supérieure, Paris, 1966, L. és L., 1967, agrégation, 1969. Lectr. U. de Paris X, 1970-71; rschr. Ctr. Nat. Rsch. Sci., Paris, 1971-74; asst. sec. gen. Groupe Maison Familiale, Cambrai, France, 1974-76; sci. advisor Bibliotheque Publique d'Info., Paris, 1976-79; asst. sec. gen. Ctr. Nat. des Lettres, Paris, 1979-82; sales mgr. La Documentation Française, Paris, 1982—; cons. Caisse Nat. des Monuments Historiques et des Sites, Paris, 1982-86; sr. lectr. Ecole Normale Supérieure, Paris, 1972-74, Ecole Pratique des Htes Etudes, Paris, 1977-85, Ecole Nationale des Chartes, Paris, 1978-85. Author: Orbite Terrestre, 1972 (Laureate, Fondation Singer-Polignac award 1972), (book and dias) Le Texte et L'image, 1980, (illustrated book) Les Fables de La Fontaine, 1986; author, editor: Jean de La Fontaine, Contes et Nouvelles, 1982, Jean de La Fontaine, Fables, 1995; contbr. articles, reviews to profl. jours. Decorated chevalier Ordre Nat. Mérite, chevalier Legion of Honor, officer Palmes Académiques (France). Home: 127 rue Michel Ange, 75016 Paris France Office: La Documentation Francaise, 29 Quai Voltaire, 75007 Paris France

BAST, KENNETH GEORGE, healthcare executive; b. Milw., Oct. 31, 1949; s. George H. and Genevieve (Zimmel) B.; m. Patricia A. Hogan, Nov. 17, 1973. BSBA, Marquette U., 1971; MBA, U. Wis., 1977. Personnel asst. St. Joseph Hosp., Warren, Ohio, 1972-74; v.p. ops. Meml. Hosp., Burlington, Wis., 1974-80; pres. No. Ill. Med. Ctr., McHenry, Ill., 1980-82; v.p. TW3 Corp., Downer's Grove, Ill., 1982-84; v.p. health services John Knox Village, Lee's Summit, Mo., 1984-89; cons. Hamilton/KSA, Mpls., 1989-97; ind. cons. Burnsville, Minn., 1997-98; v.p. health care consulting Benedictine Health System, St. Paul, 1998-2000; ind. cons.; project dir. Mobile Intensive Care program Emergency Med. Services, McHenry, 1981-82; instr. Cen. Mo. State U., Kansas City, 1986-89; adj. faculty Master of Healthcare Adminstrn. program U. Minn., 1995-97; mem. review bd. of Swedish long term care health facilities, Jonkoping, Sweden, 1987; bd. dirs. Multi Hosp. Mut. Ins., Hamilton, Bermuda. Mem. McHenry Econ. Commn., 1982, Govs. Adv. Council on Aging, Mo., 1985-88. Mem. Am. Hosp. Assn., Nat. Council on Aging, Am. Coll. Health Care Execs. Roman Catholic. Avocation: photography.

BASTA, ANTONI, obstetrician/gynecologist, educator; b. Tabaszowa, Krakow, Poland, July 10, 1946; s. Stefan and Maria (Bajorek) B.; m. Maria Majchrowska, Nov. 19, 1973; children: Pawel, Marcin. Physician degree, U. Med. Acad. Krakow, Poland, 1972; 1st degree specialist ob-gyn., U. Med. Acad. Krakow, 1976, 2nd degree specialist ob-gyn., 1978, PhD, 1979. Asst. chmn. dept. ob-gyn. Med. Acad. Krakow, Poland, 1972-79; assoc. prof. ob-gyn. Med. Acad. Krakow, 1992-2000, prof., 2000—; head chmn. dept. ob-gyn. Jagellonian U., Krakow, 1997—; cons. ob/gyn. Krakow Region, 1997-98. Co-author: Selected problems of Intensive Obstetrics Cases 1998, 2000, Cervical Cancer, 1999, Colour Atlas of Cytology and Colposcopy, 1999, Vulvar Cancer, 2000; mem. internat. editl. bd. Gynecopathology; mem. editl. bd. European Jour. Gynecol. Oncology; contbr. 20 papers on gynecol. oncology, esp. carcinogenesis, diagnostic and therapeutic mgmt. of cervical and vulvar carcinoma. Mem. Polish Assn. Gynecologist Southern Poland (pres. 1997—), Polish Soc. Colposcopy Cervical Pathophysiology (pres. 1998—), Internat. Fedn. Cervical Pathology and Colposcopy (exec. com.), Polish Assn. Gynecology (exec. bd.), Polish Assn. Gynecol. Oncology (exec. bd.), European Assn. Gynecologists and Obstetricians, European Assn. Gynecol. Oncology. Roman Catholic. Avocations: skiing, swimming. E-mail: basta@gin.cm-uj.krakow.pl. Home: 30 C Praska St, 30-328 Krakow Poland Office: U Dept Ob/Gyn, Jagellonian U, 31-501 Krakow Poland

BASTAWROS, ASHRAF F., engineering educator; b. El Dakahlia, Egypt, May 29, 1966; s. Fawzy Bastawros and Suaad Michael; m. Hala F. Sorial, Jan. 10, 1993. BS, Cairo U., 1988; MS, Brown U., 1995, PhD, 1996. Instr. Cairo U., 1988-91; rsch. asst. Brown U., Providence, R.I., 1991-96; postdoctoral fellow Harvard U., Cambridge, Mass., 1996-99; asst. prof. Iowa State U., Ames, 1999—; rsch. asst./assoc. in exptl. micromechs. Recipient Best Paper award Jour. Electronic Packaging, 1999, award Sigma Xi; Ipert-Innovative Fund grantee Iowa State U., 1999. Mem. ASME, Soc. Exptl. Mechs., Materials Rsch. Soc. Avocations: laser and optics, cars, juggling. Fax: (515) 294-3262. E-mail: bastaw@iastate.edu. Home: 245 Sinclair Ave Apt 321 Ames IA 50014-7791 Office: Iowa State U 1200 Howe Hl Ames IA 50011-0001

BASTEN, ANTONY, health facility administrator; b. Singapore, Aug. 3, 1939; arrived in Australia, 1953; s. Sir Henry and Lady Mildred B.; m. Susan Basten, May 9, 1964. DPhil, St. Peters Coll.; B Medicine B Surgery, Adel U. RMO Royal Adelaide Hosp., 1964-65; clin. asst. Nuffield Dominions Trust U. Oxford, 1966-69; from sr. lectr. to prof. immunology U. Sydney, Australia, 1971-75, prof. immunology, 1975—; dir. Centenary Inst. Cancer Medicine and Cell Biology, Sydney, 1989—; dir. clin. immunology Royal Prince Alfred Hosp., 1971-99, Rsch. Ctr. Sydney, 1982-90; dir. clin. immunology and allergy Ctrl. Sydney Area Healthy Svc., 1996—; cons. Royal Prince Alfred Hosp., Sydney, The New Children's Hosp. Contbr. articles to profl. jours. Chmn. AIDS Task Force, 1987; chief Commonwealth Med. and Sci. Adv. on AIDS, 1988-89; active Nat. Health Med. Rsch., 1994-96; chair HIV vaccine working gorup ANCAHRO, 2000. Queen Elizabeth II Rsch. fellow Walter & Eliza Hall Inst. Melbourne, 1970-71; recipient Wellcome Australia medal, 1980, award for vocat. excellence Rotary Internat., 1996; apptd. officer in gen. divsn. Order of Australia, 1988. Fellow Australian Acad. Tech. Scis. and Engring., Royal Coll. Physicians, Royal Australasian Coll. Physicians, Royal Coll. Pathologists Australasia, Australian Acad. Sci.; mem. Australian Soc. Clin. Immunology and Allergy (pres. 1991-92), Australian Soc. Immunology (pres. 1979), Australian Soc. Med. Rsch. (pres. 1977), Union Club. Avocations: literature, music, golf. Home: Roseville, 34 Bromborough Rd, 2069 Sydney Australia Office: Centenary Inst Cancer Med, Locked Bag 6, 2042 Newtown Australia

BASTENHOF, DIRK, retired mechanical engineer, researcher; b. Rotterdam, The Netherlands, June 23, 1937; arrived in France, 1969; s. Johannes Bastenhof and Adriana Lauwaars; m. Cornelia Johanna Bunjes, Aug. 27, 1966; children: Anja Joelle, Lucia, Arnaud. MS, Tech. U. Delft, The Netherlands, 1962. Devel. engr., diesel engr. Stork-Werkspoor, The Netherlands, 1963-69; devel. engr., diesel engr., specialist for fuel injection-emissions SEMT-PIELSTICK, St. Denis, France, 1969-99. Contbr. sci. papers to confs.; patentee in field. Mem. ASME (Paper Presentation award 1986). Avocations: piano, yoga, swimming, cycling.

BASTIAANS, ROB J.M., mechanical engineering researcher; b. Mill, The Netherlands, May 19, 1965. BSc, Tech. Coll. Arnhem, The Netherlands, 1987; MSc, Eindhoven U. Tech., The Netherlands, 1991, PhD, 1997. Rschr. J.M. Burgers Ctr. Fluid Dynamics, Eindhoven, 1997-98, Eindhoven U. Tech., 1998—. Office: Eindhoven U Tech, PO Box 513, NL5600MB Eindhoven The Netherlands

BASTIAN, JEAN-PIERRE, historian; b. Ales, France, May 24, 1947; s. Paul and Olive (Michel) B.; m. Danielle Helene Vuille, July 3, 1976; two children. Diploma in Latin Am. studies, U. Sorbonne, 1976; DSc, El Colegio de Mexico, 1987. Prof. Inst. Internat., Mexico City, 1975-87, U. Autonoma Metropolitana, Mexico, 1988-93, U. Strasbourg II, France, 1993—. Mem. European Assn. Latin Am., Internat. Soc. Sociology Religion, Swiss Assn. Latin Am.

BASTIEN, JANE SMISOR, music educator; b. Hutchinson, Kans., Jan. 15, 1936; d. Herbert D. and Gladys I. (Haston) Smisor; m. James W. Bastien; children: Lisa Bastien Hanss, Lori Bastien Vickers. AA, Stephens Coll., 1955; BA, Barnard Coll., 1957; MA, Columbia U., 1958. Asst. prof. Tulane U., New Orleans, 1958-75; pvt. piano tchr., La Jolla, Calif., 1975—. Author/composer: Bastien Piano Books/Ednl. Piano Books for Children and Adults. Recipient Alumnae award Stephens Coll., 1960. Mem. Nat. Assn. Music Tchrs. (Lifetime Achievement award 1999), Music Tchrs. Assn. of Calif. (State Tchg. award 1996). Republican. Presbyterian. Avocations: gardening, collecting antiques. Home and Studio: 2431 Vallecitos Ct La Jolla CA 92037-3146

BASTIN, GUY SYLVAIN PAUL, retired clinical laboratory physician; b. Seraing, Belgium, Feb. 3, 1933; s. Eli Jean Julien and Yvonne Louise (Léga) B.; married; children: Nadine, Sandra, Anne, Pascale. Diploma doctor medicine, U. Liege, 1959, diploma médecin hygiénist, 1960, diploma génie sanitaire, 1962; diploma médecine tropicale, Inst. Médecine Tropicale, 1960. Clin. lab. physician Govt., Elisabethville, Katanga, 1961, WHO, Léopoldville, 1962-66, Assistance Publique, Liège, Belgium, 1967-85, Entr'aide et Prévoyance, Hermalle, Belgium, 1967-80, Lab. D'Analyses Médicales Cerba, Liège, 1982, Clinique Saint Vincent, Rocourt, Belgium, 1983-87, Clinique de L'Espérance, Montegnée, Belgium, 1985-97; ret. Mem. Mensa Belgium, 1971—. Avocations: painting, ancient greek coins, cryptozoology, parapsychology, extraterrestrials. Home: Rue Hansez 15, B4877 Olne Belgium

BASTINE, REINER H. E., psychotherapist, psychologist, mediator; b. Kassel, Hassia, Germany, Sept. 26, 1939; s. Erich F. O. and Johanna E. H. Bastine. Diploma, U. Marburg, Germany, 1964; PhD, U. Hamburg, Germany, 1969. Prof. U. Heidelberg, Germany, 1973—. Co-editor: Foundations of Psychotherapy, 1982; editor: Clinical Psychology, Vol. I, 1992; co-author: Family Mediation, 1993; author: Clinical Psychology, Vol. II, 3d edit., 1998. E-mail: reiner.bastine@urz.uni-heidelberg.de. Office: Psychol Inst, Haupstr. 47-51, D-69117 Heidelberg Germany

BASTO-GONÇALVES, JOSE, mathematics educator; b. Porto, Portugal, Jan. 28, 1952. BS, U. Porto, 1975; PhD, U. Warwick, Coventry, 1981. Asst. U. Porto, 1975-82, asst. prof. math., 1982-86, assoc. prof., 1986-91, prof., 1991—. Contbr. articles to profl. jours. Office: U Porto Dept Applied Math, Rua das Taipas 135, 4050 Porto Portugal

BASTOS, SUELENA VIEIRA DE MELO, psychologist; b. Rio de Janeiro, Dec. 1, 1946; d. Odyr Pontes and Cybele (Oliveira) Vieira; m. Celso Melo Bastos; 1 child, Athenea. Degree in psychology, Pontifica U. Catholica, Brazil, 1970. Lic. clin. psychologist. Cons. Am. Sch. of Rio de Janeiro, 1972-75, psychologist, 1975—, dir. student svcs., 1989—; pvt. practice Rio

de Janeiro, 1971—; regional rep. for Brazil Omni Referral Svcs., 1992—; supr. grad. students, Rio de Janeiro, 1982—; cons. various schs., 1970-80. Contbr. articles to profl. jours. Mem. APA, Conselho Regional de Psicologia. Avocations: writing children's plays, directing plays, travel, meeting new people, reading. E-mail: suelena@openlink.com.br. Home: Rua Maria Eugenia 196/501, 22261080 Rio de Janeiro Brazil Office: Am Sch of Rio de Janeiro, Estrada do Gavea 132, 22451260 Rio de Janeiro Brazil

BASU, JAYDEEP KUMAR, physicist; b. Calcutta, India, Feb. 2, 1970; s. Dilip Kumar and Anita Basu. BSc, St. Xavier's Coll., Calcutta, 1992; MS, U. Calcutta, 1994. Sr. rsch. fellow Saha Inst. Nuclear Physics, Calcutta, 1994—. Recipient Young Physicist award Indian Phys. Soc., 1999. Avocations: listening to music, watching games on TV. Fax: 0091 33 337 4637. E-mail: joy@cmp.saha.ernet.in. Office: Saha Inst Nuclear Physics, 1/AF Bidhannagar, Calcutta 700 060, India

BASU, SOMNATH, engineer; b. Calcutta, Apr. 30, 1951; arrived in U.S., 1984; s. Sibakali and Kalyani B.; m. Sumita Basu, June 11, 1981; children: Shiladitya, Saptarshi, Sruti. BE in Chem. Engring., Regional Engring. Coll., Durgapur, India, 1974; M Tech. Chem. Engring., Indian Inst. Tech., Kharagpur, India, 1976; MChemE, Miss. State U., 1986; MS in Environ. Engring., Northeastern U., Boston, 1989, PhD in Environ. Engring., 1996. Registered profl. chem. engr., Mass. Asst. project engr. Fertilizer Corp. of India, Durgapur, 1976-81; asst. plant mgr. Hindustan Fertilizer Corp., Haldia, India, 1981-83; tchg. and rsch. asst. Northeast U., Boston, Miss. State U., 1984-89; environ. engr. Camp Dresser & McKee, Cambridge, Mass., 1989-90; sr. environ. process engr. Badger Engrs., Inc., Cambridge, 1990-93; environ. process supr. Raytheon Engrs. and Constructors, Cambridge, 1993-94; program mgr. Deer Island, Mass. Water Resources Authority, Winthrop, 1994-99; project mgr. Parsons Engring. Sci., Canton, Mass., 1999—; adj. faculty mem. Sch. of Engring., Northeastern U., Boston. Contbr. articles to profl. jours. Vol. thcr. Boston Inner City Mid. and H.S. Children, 1998—. Recipient cert. appreciation Waste Mgmt. Edn. and Rsch. Consortium, Las Cruces, N.Mex., 1993. Mem. AIChE, Water Environ. Fedn. Avocations: stamp collecting, travel.

BASU, SUKUMAR, materials science educator, researcher; b. Calcutta, India, Aug. 6, 1942; s. Panchanan and Binapani Basu; m. Sumitra Sarkar, Dec. 9, 1974; children: Sukanya, Sudhanya. BSc, S.N. Coll., Calcutta, 1964; MSc, Sci. Coll., Calcutta, 1966; postgrad. diploma, Indian Inst. Tech., Kharagpur, 1968, PhD, 1973. Postdoctoral rsch. fellow U. Vienna, Austria, 1972-74; rsch. assoc. Max Planck Inst., Muelheim-Ruhr, Germany, 1975-78; sci. officer Coun. Sci. and Indsl. Rsch., Kharagpur, 1978-79; lectr. materials sci. Indian Inst. Tech., Kharagpur, 1979-81; asst. prof. Indian Inst. Tech., 1981-91, assoc. prof., 1991-94, prof., 1995—, head Materials Sci. Ctr., 1996-99; vis. assoc. Anna U. Madras, India, 1991-94; vis. fellow State U., Milan, 1995-96. Contbr. over 100 articles to internat. sci. jours., including Jour. Applied Physics, Jour. Semicondr. Sci. and Tech., Solid State Comm. Fellow Max Planck Soc., Germany, 1975. Fellow Sr. Sci. and Tech. Agy. (Japan); mem. Internat. Ctr. Theoretical Physics (life, Indian chpt.), Solar Energy Soc. of India (life), Semiconductor Soc. India (life). Avocations: music, travel, writing articles and poetry, watching football games. Office: Indian Inst Tech, Materials Sci Ctr, W Bengal Kharagpur 721 302, India

BASUMALLICK, AMITAVA, metallurgy educator; b. Chandannagore, India, Mar. 15, 1962; s. Amarendra Nath and Rita (Ghosh) B.; m. Jaya Sarkar, Feb. 20, 1994; 1 child, Sreetapa. BE in Metallurgy, Jadavpur U., Calcutta, 1986, ME in Metallurgy, 1988, M in Computer Application, 1991, PhD in Metallurgy, 1998. Cert. engr. Asst. engr. Bhartia Electric Steel, Calcutta, 1986-88; lectr. Bengal Engring. Coll., Howrah, India, 1990-98, asst. prof., 1998—; cons. India Foils Ltd., Calcutta, 1996. Contbr. articles to profl. jours. Recipient Gold medal Jadavpur U., Calcutta, 1988. Mem. Indian Inst. Metals (hon. sec. B.E. Coll. chpt. 1993-96), IACS (life). Avocations: listening to music, reading journals, playing cricket, football. Office: B E Coll Dept Metall Engr, PO Botanic Garden, Howrah 711103, India

BATA, RUDOLPH ANDREW, JR., lawyer; b. Akron, Ohio, Jan. 9, 1947; s. Rudolph Andrew and Margaret Eleanor (Ellis) B.; m. Genevieve Ruth Brannan, Aug. 25, 1968 (div. May 1985); 1 child, Seth Andrew; m. Linda Lee Waldo, May 7, 1985; 1 child, Sarah Ariel. BS, So. Coll., Collegedale, Tenn., 1969; JD, Emory U., 1972. Bar: D.C. 1973, N.C. 1978, U.S. Dist. Ct. N.C. 1991, U.S. Ct. Appeals (4th cir.) 1991; cert. mediator AOC. Assoc. ICC, Washington, 1972-73; in house counsel B.F. Saul Real Estate Investment Trust, Chevy Chase, Md., 1973-74; staff atty. Martha, Cafferky, Powers & Jordan, Washington, 1974-75; asst. corp. counsel Hardee's Food Systems, Inc., Rocky Mount, N.C., 1975-78; ptnr. Bata & Blomeley, Murphy, N.C., 1978-87, 88-90, Bata & Sumpter, Murphy, 1987-88; sole practice, 1990—. Bd. dirs. Cherokee County United Fund, Murphy, 1981-83. Mem. ABA, N.C. Bar Assn., D.C. Bar Assn., 30th Jud. Dist. Bar Assn., So. Soc. of Adventist Attys. (pres. 1984-85), Cherokee County C. of C. (bd. dirs. 1980-82). Avocations: golf, tennis, hiking. Office: 225 Valley River Ave Ste A Murphy NC 28906-3000

BATABYAL, BALARKA A., ancient Indian history educator, poet; b. June 26, 1966. BA, St. Xavier's Coll., Mumbai, India, 1988, HSC in Arts, 1985, MA, 1991; postgrad., U. Mumbai. Lectr. dept. history Kirti M. Doongursee Coll. Arts, Sci. and Commerce, Badar, Mumbai; lectr. Hitory in Govt. Law Coll., Churchgate, Mumbai; head dept. ancinet Indian culture Siddharth Coll. Arts, Sci. and Commerce, Mumbai; vis. prof. history of civilizations T.N. Med. Coll.; rsch. asst. health svcs. sector Tata Inst. Social Sci., Mumbai; freelance journalist. Contbr. articles to profl. jours., poetry to mags. Mem. Asiatic Soc. (life; pre-modern book selection com.). Home: 42 Buena Vista Apts, Jagannath Rao Bhosle Marg, Mumbai 400021, India

BATAMACK, PATRICE THEODORE DESIRE, chemistry educator, researcher; b. Douala, Littoral, Cameroon, Nov. 1, 1962; s. Joseph Etote Robert and Philomene Claire (Ngo Batadjam) B.; m. Ndjee Aurélie, Apr. 25, 1998. Grad. in chem. engring., Poly. Inst. Loraine, Nancy, France, 1988; cert. in computer sci., Indsl. Computer Sci. Inst., Brest, France, 1989; PhD in Chemistry, U. Pierre et Marie Curie, Paris, 1991; MBA, Arts et Metiers, Paris, 2000; diploma for directing postgrad. works, U. Pierre et Marie Curie, 1999. Postdoctoral fellow Loker Hydrocarbon Inst. U. So. Calif., L.A., 1992-94; lectr. chemistry U. Pierre et Marie Curie, 1994—. Contbr. articles to profl. jours. Mem. French Chem. Soc. (prize catalysis divsn. 1995), Am. Chem. Soc. Avocations: reading, meditation, sports. Office: U Pierre et Marie Curie, 4 Pl Jussieu, 75252 Paris France

BATCHELDER, ANNE STUART, former publisher, political party official; b. Lake Forest, Ill., Jan. 11, 1920; d. Robert Douglas and Harriet (McClure) Stuart; m. Clifton Brooks Batchelder, May 26, 1945; children: Edward, Anne Stuart, Mary Clifton, Lucia Brooks. Student Lake Forest Coll., 1941-43. Clubmobile driver ARC, Eng., Belgium, France, Holland and Germany, 1943-45; pub., editor Douglas County Gazette, 1970-75, 79-90; bd. dirs. Firstier Bank Omaha; dir., treas. U.S. Checkbook Com. Mem. Rep. Ctrl. Com. Nebr., 1955-62, 70-83, vice chmn. Ctrl. Com., 1959-64, chmn., 1975-79, mem. fin. com., 1957-64; chmn. women's sect. Douglas County Rep. Fin. Com., 1995, vice chmn. com., 1958-60; v.p. Omaha Woman's Rep. Club, 1957-58, pres., 1959-60; alt. del. Nat. Conv., 1956, 72, del., 1980, 84, 88; mem. Rep. Nat. Com. for Nebr., 1964-70; asst. chmn. Douglas County Rep. Ctrl. Com., 1971-74; 1st v.p. Nebr. Fedn. Rep. Women, 1971-72, pres., 1972-74; chmn. Nebr. Rep. Com., 1975-79; vice-chmn. Bldg. Fedn. Rep. Women, 1998—; mem. Nebr. State Bldg. Commn., 1979-83; Rep. candidate for lt. gov., 1974. Sr. v.p. Nebr. Founders Day, 1958; trustee Hastings Coll., 1977—; bd. dirs. YWCA, 1983-89, Omaha Libr. Found., 1991-2000, Libr. Found., 2000—; past trustee Brownell Hall, Vis. Nurse Assn.; past pres. Nebr. chpt. Freedoms Found. at Valley Forge; chmn. fin. George Bush for Pres., Nebr., 1987-88; apptd. Kennedy Ctr. Performing Arts, 1989, 94, Pres.' Adv. Com. on the Arts, 1990-92, Nat. Com. for the Performing Arts, 1992—; mem. Nebr. Rep. State Fin. Com., 1990, Nat. Fin. Com. Bush-Quayle, 1992; active Omaha Meth. Hosp. Found., Brownell-Talbot Sch. Found. Elected to Nebr. Rep. Hall of Fame, 1984; named Citizen of the Yr. Midlands Coun. Boy Scouts Am., 1997. Mayflower Soc., Colonial Dames, P.E.O., Nat. League Pen Women Omaha Country, Omaha. Presbyterian. Home: 6875 State St Omaha NE 68152-1633

BATCHELOR, JAMES KENT, lawyer; b. Long Beach, Calif., Oct. 4, 1934; s. Jack Morrell and Edith Marie (Ottinger) B.; m. Jeanette Lou Dyer, Mar. 27, 1959; children: John, Suzanne; m. Susan Mary Leonard, Dec. 4, 1976. AA, Sacramento City Coll., 1954; BA, Calif. State U., Long Beach, 1956; JD, Hastings Coll. Law, U. Calif., 1959. Bar: Calif. 1960, U.S. Dist. Ct. (cen. dist.) Calif. 1960, U.S. Supreme Ct. 1968; cert. family law specialist Calif. Bd. Legal Specialization, 1980. Dep. dist. atty., Orange County, Calif., 1960-62; assoc. Miller, Nisson, Kogler & Wenke, Santa Ana, Calif., 1962-64; ptnr. Batchelor, Cohen & Oster, Santa Ana, 1964-67, Kurilich, Ballard, Batchelor, Fullerton, Calif., 1967-72; pres. James K. Batchelor, Inc.; tchr. paralegal sect. Santa Ana City Coll.; judge pro-tem Superior Ct., 1974—; lectr. family law Calif. Continuing Edn. of Bar, 1973—. Contbr. articles to profl. jours. Fellow Am. Acad. Matrimonial Lawyers (pres. So. Calif. chpt. 1989-90); mem. ABA, Calif. State Bar (placque chmn. family law sect. 1975-76, advisor 1976-78), Orange County Barristers (founder, pres., placque 1963), Calif. State Barristers (placque 1965, v.p.), Orange County Bar Assn. (placque sec. 1977, pres. family law sect. 1968-71, Best Lawyers in Am. 1989-90, 91-92, 93-94, 95-96, 97-98, 99—). Republican. Methodist. Office: 765 The City Dr S Ste 270 Orange CA 92868-6908

BATCHELOR, JOSEPH BROOKLYN, JR., electronics engineer, consultant; b. Jersey, Ga., Apr. 11, 1922; s. Joseph Brooklyn and Mary Arlie (Reece) B.; m. Clara Owens, July 14, 1940; children: Joseph Brooklyn III, James Alfred, William Owens. Diploma, North Ga. Coll., 1940. Registered profl. engr., Ill., Ga. Owner, pres. JRS Electronics-Svc., Rsch. & Cons., Monroe, Ga., 1946-57; dir. rsch. and engring. Cen. Electronics, Inc., Chgo., 1957-61; rsch. engr. Hallicrafters Corp., Chgo., 1961-63; aircraft devel. engring. specialist Lockheed A/C Corp., Marietta, Ga., 1965-70; pres., chmn. BRECO Corp., Walnut Grove, Ga., 1972-75; cons. engr. Batchelor Labs., Libertyville, Ill., 1963-65; owner, mgr. Batchelor Labs., Walnut Grove, 1970-72, Jersey, 1975—; pres. PATRONIX-Patent Holding Corp., Chgo., 1958-61. Patentee in field; inventor radio-location device for lost student pilots WWII. Chmn. bd. Monroe Christian Ch., 1950-57. Sgt. USAF, 1945-46, World War II. Mem. AAAS, Citizens Adv. Coun. on Energy, Mensa. Avocations: amateur radio, classical music, reading. Home and Office: 106 Main St Jersey GA 30018

BATCHO, RONALD FRANK, automotive company executive; b. Hackensack, N.J., Mar. 31, 1947; s. Edward Stephen and Anna (Korley) B.; m. Michele Jean (Kosmider) McAndrew, Dec. 23, 1984; children: Ronald Frank, Rebecca Louise. AAS, Fashion Inst. Tech., 1967. Indsl. engr. Can. Garment Ltd., Winnipeg, Man., 1967-68; asst. product mgr. Ea. Isles, Inc., N.Y.C., 1968-73; product mgr. Windjammer Fashions, N.Y.C., 1973-77; pres. Crewco, Inc., Cornelius, N.C., 1977-83, United Sportswear, Inc., Locust, N.C., 1983-87; v.p. United Screen Printers, Locust, 1983-97; automotive after-market agt. Dealer Devel. Svcs., Charlotte, N.C., 1997—; mem. Cornelius bd. Piedmont Bank and Trust Co., Davidson, N.C., 1980-87. First lt. Maywood (N.J.) First Aid Squad, 1975-77; CPR instr. Am. Heart Assn., Englewood, N.J., 1975-77. Mem. Am. Mgmt. Assn., Ctrl. Piedmont Employers Assn. Democrat. Roman Catholic. Fax: 704-523-9311. Office: Dealer Devel Svcs 206 Woodlawn Rd Charlotte NC 28217

BATDORF, LYNN ROBERT, horticulturist; b. Lebanon, Pa., Aug. 4, 1954; s. Robert LeVoy Smith Jr. and Rudella Louise (Brandt) Batdorf; m. Holly A. Hamilton, Oct. 24, 1998; children: Jessica Zischka, Theodore Robert. AA in Horticulture, Inst. of Applied Agrl., 1974; BSBA, U. Coll., 1984; BS in Ornamental Horticulture, U. Md., 1994. Cert. profl. horticulturist. Agrl. rsch. technician U.S. Nat. Arboretum, Washington, 1977-80, horticulturist, 1980—; horticultural cons. TJ Horticultural Svcs., Washington, 1989—; instr. water garden mgmt. course Montgomery Coll., Germantown, Md., 1996—. Author: Boxwood Handbook: A Practical Guide to Knowing and Growing Boxwood, 1995, revised 1997; contbr. National Arboretum Book of Outstanding Garden Plants, 1989, Time-Life Gardener's Guide, Perennials, 1988, The Washington Star Garden Book, 1988. Recipient Cert. of Merit U.S. Dept. Agrl., 1980, 89, 91, (2) 93, 96. Mem. Am. Boxwood Soc. (hon. life, bd. dirs.) Internat. Registration Authority for Cultivated Boxwoods, Am. Hemerocallis Soc., Internat. Water Lily Soc., Internat. Soc. for Horticultural Sci., Am. Assn. of Botanic Gardens and Arboreta, Royal Horticulture Soc., European Boxwood and Topiary Soc. (hon. life),. Office: US Nat Arboretum 3501 New York Ave NE Washington DC 20002-1958

BATE, ANDREW JONATHAN, English literature educator; b. Sevenoaks, Kent, Eng., June 26, 1958; s. Ronald Montagu and Sylvia Helen (Tait) B.; m. Paula Jayne Byrne, Apr. 1, 1996; children: Thomas Montague, Elinor Clare. BA, Cambridge U., 1980, PhD, 1983. Harkness fellow Harvard U., Cambridge, Mass., 1980-81; research fellow St. Catharine's Coll., Cambridge, Eng., 1983-85; fellow Trinity Hall, Cambridge, 1985-90; King Alfred prof. English lit. U. Liverpool, Eng., 1991—. Author: Shakespeare and the English Romantic Imagination, 1986, Shakespearean Constitutions, 1989, Romantic Ecology, 1991, Shakespeare and Ovid, 1993, The Genius of Shakespeare, 1997, The Cure for Love, 1998, The Song of the Earth, 2000; contbr. articles to profl. jours. Avocations: opera, mountain walking, cricket. Office: U Liverpool, Dept English, Liverpool England

BATE, BRIAN R., psychologist; b. Cleve., July 4, 1940; s. Paul A. and Claire N. B.; children: Jennifer A., Julia L. BA in English, Western Res. U., 1963, MS in Psychology, 1965; PhD in Psychology, Case Western Res. U., 1972. Lic. psychologist, Ohio. Instr. Cuyahoga C.C. Western Campus, Parma, Ohio, 1969, from asst. prof. to prof. of psychology, 1970—; pvt. practice, Cleve., 1972-96. Contbr. articles to profl. jours. Nat. Merit Scholar Princeton U., 1958-61, Western Res. U., 1962-63; USPHS fellow, 1963-67. Mem. APA, Am. Fedn. Musicians, Edelweiss Ski Club, Cleve. Buddhist Temple. Achievements include development and teaching of the first underclass-level behavior modification course in United States, 1970-77. Home: 6511 Mill Rd Cleveland OH 44141-1560 Office: Cuyahoga Cmty Coll Western Campus Parma OH 44130-5199

BATE, JENNIFER LUCY, musician; b. London, Nov. 11, 1944; d. Horace Alfred and Dorothy Marjorie B. Student, Bristol U. Shaw libr. London Sch. Econs., London U., 1966-69; organizer numerous tchg. programs. Collaboration with Olivier Messiaen, 1975-92; designer portable organ with Mander Organs, 1984; designer prototype computer organ, 1987; compositions: Toccata on a Theme of Martin Shaw, Introduction and Variations on an Old French Carol, Four Reflections, Homage to 1685, Lament, An English Canon, Variations on a Gregorian Theme; recordings include concertos and solo works of all periods. Recipient F.J. Read prize Royal Coll. Organists, Grand Prix du Disque, Messiaen, Music Retailers' Assn. award for 18th century series From Stanley to Wesley; named Young Musician, 1972, Personnalité de l'Année, France, 1989, One of Women of Year, U.K., 1990-97. Avocations: cooking, theatre, philately, gardening. Fax: 020 8444 3695. E-mail: jenniferbate@classical-artists.com. Address: 35 Collingwood Ave, Muswell Hill, London N10 3EH, England

BATEL, RENATO, molecular toxicologist, researcher; b. Vodnjan, Croatia, Nov. 7, 1955; s. Vladimir Batel and Onorina Žužić; m. Nevenka Bihari, Sept. 15, 1979; children: Tea, Iris. BSc in Chemistry, Faculty Natural Scis., Zagreb, Croatia, 1979; MSc in Oceanology, U. Zagreb, 1982, PhD, 1987. Jr. asst. Rudjer Bošković Inst., Rovinj, Croatia, 1979-82; asst. Bošković Inst., Rovinj, Croatia, 1982-87, sr. asst., 1987-90, sci. assoc., 1990-94, sr. sci. assoc., 1994-97, sci. advisor, 1998—, head lab., 1993—; prof. biology U. Rijeka, Croatia, 1988-89; mem. Commn. Molecular Biology, Acad. of Scis. and Lit., Mainz,Germany, 1993—. Avocations: philately, numismatics. Home: Motovunska BB, 52210 Rovinj Republic of Croatia Office: Inst Rudjer Bošković, G Paliaga 5, 52210 Rovinj Republic of Croatia

BATEMAN, IAN JULIAN, economist, researcher; b. Birmingham, Eng., Sept. 14, 1961; s. Kenneth and Andrina B.; m. Fiona Bateman. B Social Sci., Birmingham U., 1985; MS, Manchester U., 1987; PhD, Nottingham U., 1996. Cert. environ. and agrl. economist. Lectr. U. Exeter, 1987-88; economist Boots PLC, 1988-89; lectr. U. East Anglia, 1989—; cons. to govt. and industry. Author: textbooks on environ. econs.; contbr. articles to profl. jours. Recipient grants from govternmental depts., agys., rsch. couns., cos. Avocations: outdoor recreation, time with family and children. Office: Sch of Environmental Science, U East Anglia, Norwich NR4 7TJ, England

BATEMAN, JEANNINE ANN, county official; b. Hillsboro, Kans., July 6, 1945; d. Forrest Edward and Alvina (Bernhardt) Skibbe; m. Rufus J. Bateman, Apr. 25, 1965; 1 child, Kristine Kay. AS in Bus., Butler County Cmty. Coll., El Dorado, Kans., 1996; student, Baker U., Baldwin City, Kans., 1963-64, Wichita State U., 1997—. Bookkeeper Marion County Coop., Marion, Kans., summer 1963; abstract asst. Hannaford Title Co., Marion, 1964-74, 79-84; clk., dep. Marion County Treas. Office, Marion, 1984-94, treas., 1994—. Treas. Marion Warrior Boosters, 1993, 1st Dist. Rep. Women, Kans., 1997—; bd. dirs. Leadership Marion County, 1994-95, sec., treas., 1995-96, v.p., 1996-97. Mem. North Ctrl. Kans. County Treasurers (sec., treas. 1996-97, v.p. 1997-98, pres. 1998-99), Kans. County Treasurer's Assn. (sec. 1999, v.p. 2000, pres. 2001), Marion County Rep. Women, Marion County Rep. Party, Order of the Purple, Kiwanis Club Marion, Phi Theta Kappa, Phi Kappa Phi. N.Am. Baptist. Avocations: walking, hiking, reading, basketball, football. Office: Marion County Treas PO Box 257 Marion KS 66861-0257

BATEMAN, PETER PATRICK, retired allergist; b. Cairo, Sept. 3, 1922; s. John Edwin and Susan Frances (Stevens) B.; m. Gweneth Merle Jones; children: Philip, Mary Anne, Michael (dec.), Matthew Peter. MB, BS, Adelaide (Australia) U., 1950. Resident med. officer Royal Adelaide Hosp., 1950-52, clin. asst. in allergy, 1952-70, vis. med. officer in allergy, 1971-86, staff specialist in allergy, 1987; ret., 1987. With Royal Australian Navy, 1942-45. Fellow Australian Coll. Allergists; mem. Australian Med. Assn., Australian Soc. Hypnosis, Australian Soc.Immunology and Allergy. Liberal. Anglican. Avocation: pottery. Home: 1A Young St, Burnside SA, Australia 5066

BATEMAN, WALTER SAMUEL GRONO, academic researcher; b. Cottesloe, Australia, May 4, 1938; s. Walter Martin and Frances Alice (Grono) B.; m. Lois Grace (Koch) Bateman, Feb. 23, 1962; children: Simon, Sarah, Emma. BS in Econ., U. Queensland, Australia, 1971; MS in Econ., U. Papua New Guinea, 1978; graduate diploma in Profl. Acct., U. Canberra, Australia, 1992. With Royal Australian Navy, 1954-94; rsch. fellow Ctr. for Maritime Pol. U. Wollongong, Australia, 1994—; co-chmn. Maritime Cooperation Working Gp. Council for Security Cooperation in Asia Pacific, 1994—. Editor: Maritime Change: Issues for Asia, 1993, Australia's Maritime Bridge into Asia, 1995, The Seas Unite: Maritime Cooperation in the Asia Pacific Region, 1996, Calming the Waters: Initiatives for Asia Pacific Maritime Cooperation, 1996. Recipient Order of Australia, 1993. Mem. Royal Queensland Yacht Squadron. Avocations: bridge, sailing, walking, writing. Home: 8 17 Falder Pl, Keiraville NSW 2500, Australia Office: U Wollongong, Northfields Av, Wollongong NSW 2500, Australia

BATES, ALAN (ARTHUR BATES), actor; b. Derbyshire, Eng., Feb. 17, 1934; s. Harold Arthur and Florence Mary (Wheatcroft) B.; m. Victoria Ward, May 1970 (dec. June 1992); 2 sons (twins, 1 dec.). Student, Royal Acad. Dramatic Art, London. Appeared in stage prodns. including Hamlet, London, Butley, London and N.Y.C. (Antoinette Perry award for Best Actor 1973, Drama League N.Y. award), Poor Richard, N.Y.C., Merry Wives of Windsor and Richard III, Stratford, Ont., Taming of the Shrew, Stratford-on-Avon, Eng., 1973, Life Class, 1974, Otherwise Engaged, 1975 (variety club awards), The Seagull, 1976, Stage Struck, 1979-80, A Patriot for Me, London and L.A., 1983, One for the Road, Victoria Station, 1984, The Dance of Death, 1985, Yonadab, Nat. Theatre, 1986, (with Patrick Garland) Down Cemetery Road, 1986, Melon, 1987, Ivanov, Much Ado About Nothing, 1989, Stages, Nat. Theatre, 1992-93, The Showman, London, 1993, Antony & Cleopatra, Stratford-on-Avon, 1999; films include The Fixer (Oscar award nomination), Women in Love, The Three Sisters, A Day in the Death of Joe Egg, The Go-Between, Second Best, Impossible Object, In Celebration, Royal Flash, An Unmarried Woman, The Shout, The Rose, Nijinsky, Quartet, The Return of the Soldier, 1982, The Wicked Lady, 1983, Duet for One, 1986, A Prayer for the Dying, 1987, We Think the World of You, 1988, Force Majeur, 1988, Mr. Frost, 1989, Dr. M., 1989, Hamlet, 1990, Shuttlecock, 1991, Losing Track, 1991, Silent Tongue, 1992, St. Patrick, 1999; TV shows include The Collection, 1977, The Mayor of Casterbridge, 1978, Very Like a Whale, The Trespasser, 1981, A Voyage Round My Father, 1982, An Englishman Abroad, 1985 (Brit. Acad. Film & TV Arts award, Ace award Nat. Cable TV Acad.), Separate Tables, 1983 (Ace award Nat. Cable TV Acad.), Dr. Fischer of Geneva, 1984, One for the Road, 1985, Pack of Lies, 1987, The Dog It Was That Died, 1988, 102 Boulevard Haussmann, 1990, Secret Friends, 1991, Unnatural Pursuits, 1992, Hard Times, 1994, Oliver's Travels, BBC-TV, 1994, (film) The Grotesque, 1995, (TV film) Nicholas' Gift, 1997, Arabian Nights, In the Beginning, The Prince & the Pauper, (U.S. TV film narration) The Arabian Nights, 1999, (British TV series narration) The Spying Game, 1999, (theater) The Master Builder (London), 1995, (Ont.), 1996, Simply Disconnected, 1996, Fortune's Fool, 1996, Life Support, 1997, (radio) Art, Murder in Paris, Man and Boy, 1998, (film) The Cherry Orchard, 1998, (TV) Nicholas' Gift, 1998, St. Patrick, 1999, (BBC TV) Love in a Cold Climate, 2000. Served with RAF. Recipient Clarence Derwent award, Evening Std. award, 1972. Office: Chatto & Linnit Ltd, 123A Kings Rd, London SW3 4PL, England

BATES, BARBARA J. NEUNER, retired municipal official; b. Mt. Vernon, N.Y., Apr. 8, 1927; d. John Joseph William and Elsie May (Flint) Neuner; m. Herman Martin Bates, Jr., Mar. 25, 1950; children: Roberta Jean Bates Jamin, Herman Martin III, Jon Neuner. BA, Barnard Coll., 1947. Confidential clk. to supr. Town of Ossining, N.Y., 1960-63, receiver of taxes, 1971-90; ret.; pres. BNB Assocs., Briarcliff Manor, N.Y., 1963-83, Upper Nyack Realty Co., Inc., Briarcliff Manor, 1966-71. V.p. Ossining (N.Y.) Young Rep. Club, 1958; pres. Young Womens Rep. Club Westchester County (N.Y.), 1959-61; regional committeewoman N.Y. State Assn. Young Rep. Clubs, 1960-62; mem. Westchester County Rep. Com., 1963-95; mem. Ossining Women's Rep. Club, 1960-92, pres., 1984-85; mem. Westchester County Women's Rep. Club, 1957-92. Mem. DAR, Jr. League Westchester-on-Hudson, Receivers Taxes Assn. Westchester County (legis. liaison, v.p., pres. 1984-85), Hackley Sch. Mothers Assn. (pres. 1968), R.I. Hist. Soc., Ossining Hist. Soc., Westchester County Hist. Soc., Briarcliff-Scarborough Hist. Soc., Ossining Woman's Club. Congregationalist. Home: 23 Bloomer Rd Brewster NY 10509-1060 also: 663 Reynolds Rd Chepachet RI 02814-1629

BATES, BENJAMIN JOHNSON, telecommunications educator, researcher; b. Chilcothee, Ohio, Jan. 25, 1954; s. Philip Knight and Myrna (Mademann) B. BA in Math. and Econ., Pomona Coll., Claremont, Calif., 1976; MS in Statistics, U. Wis., Madison, 1978; MA in Comms., U. Wis. Stevens Point, 1981; PhD in Comms., U. Mich., Ann Arbor, 1986. Instr. Rutgers U., 1985-86; lectr. U. Calif., Santa Barbara, 1986-88; vis. asst. prof. Mich. State U., 1988-89; vis. lectr. The Chinese U. of Hong Kong, 1992-93; asst. prof., dir. Inst. Comm. Rsch. Tex. Tech. U., 1989-94; assoc. prof. U. Tenn. Knoxville, 1994—. Contbr. articles to profl. jours. Mem. AEDMC, AAPOR, BEA, ICA, NCA. E-mail: bjbates@utk.edu. Office: Dept Broadcasting U Tenn 333 Communication Bldg Knoxville TN 37996-0001

BATES, CHARLES WALTER, human resources executive, lawyer; b. Detroit, June 28, 1953; s. E. Frederick and Virginia Marion (Nunneley) B. BA in Psychology and Econs. cum laude, Mich. State U., 1975, M in Labor and Indsl. Rels., 1977; postgrad., DePaul U., 1979-80; JD, William Mitchell Coll. Law, 1984. Bar: Wash. 1990, U.S. Dist. Ct. (we. dist.) Wash. 1992; cert. sr. profl. in human resources. Vista vol., paralegal Chanel Counties Legal Aid Assn., 1975-76; job analyst Gen. Mills, Inc., Mpls., 1977-78; plant pers. asst. II Gen. Mills, Inc., Chgo., 1978-80; plant asst. pers. mgr. Gen. Mills Inc., Chgo., 1980-81; pers. mgr. consumer foods mktg. divsn. Gen. Mills, Inc., Mpls., 1981-82, pers. mgr. consumer foods mktg. divsns. and Saluto Pizza, 1982-84; human resources mgr. Western divsn. Godfather's Pizza, Inc., Costa Mesa, Calif., 1984-85; human resources mgr. western U.S. and Can. Godfather's Pizza, Inc., Bellevue, Wash., 1985-91; dir. human resources Royal Seafoods, Inc., Seattle, 1991-92, dir. human resources and employee rels. counsel, 1992-94, dir. human resources and counsel, 1994-95; sr. internal auditor PACCAR, Inc., Bellevue, Wash., 1995-97; dir. field human resources, dir. human resources PACCAR Automotive, Inc., Renton, Wash., 1997; dir. human resources TransAlta Centralia Ops., Renton, Wash., 2000—, Wash., 2000—; instr. employee labor rels. Lake Washington Tech. Coll., 1992-94. Mem. editl. adv. bd. Recruitment Today mag., 1990-91. Candidate for lt. gov. of Minn., 1982; asst. scoutmaster Boy Scouts Am., 1971—, asst. advisor activities Order of Arrow chpt., 1989-92, 96-97; Sammamish Cmty.

Councilmem., Bellevue, 1990-93; mem. East Bellevue Transp. Study Adv. Group, 1989-92; mem. Bellevue Civil Svc. Commn., 1997-2000, vice chmn., 1999, chmn., 2000. Recipient Scouter's Tng. award Boy Scouts Am., 1979, Vantage Recruiting award Recruitment Today mag., 1989, Vigil Honor award Boy Scouts Am., 1990, Dist. Award of Merit, Boy Scouts Am., 1991. Mem. ABA (labor and employment law sect.), Wash. State Bar Assn. (labor and employment law sect.), Nat. Eagle Scout Assn., N.W. Human Resources Mgmt. Assn. (South Puget Sound chpt.), Soc. for Human Resources Mgmt. Home: 2237 113th Ave SW Olympia WA 98512-9178 Office: TransAlta-Centralia Ops 913 Big Hanaford Rd Centralia WA 98531-9101

BATES, CHRISTOPHER JOHN, nutrition researcher; b. London, Apr. 18, 1938; s. John Gordon and Irene Doris (Scantlin) B.; m. Catherine Elizabeth Crichton, Sept. 17, 1968; 1 child, Gemma. BA, Oxford (Eng.) U., 1961, MA, 1964, DPhil, 1964. Postdoctoral rschr. Yale U., New Haven, 1964-66; mem. sci. staff Dunn nutrition unit. Med. Rsch. Coun., Cambridge, Eng., 1966-98, human nutrition rschr., 1998—. Editor Nutrition Soc.; contbr. chpts. to books and articles to profl. jours. Office: MRC Human Nutrition Rsch, Downhams Ln Milton Rd, Cambridge CB4 1XJ, England

BATES, COLIN ARTHUR, physics educator; b. Norwich, Eng., May 7, 1935; s. Ralph Mehew and Annie Kathleen (Cooper) B.; m. Margaret Green, July 26, 1961; children: Karen Nicola, Julian Michael, Richard Daniel. BSc, Nottingham (Eng.) U., 1956, PhD, 1959. Demonstrator Nottingham U., 1958-59, rsch. asst., 1959-61, lectr. physics, 1962-70, sr. lectr., 1970-74, reader, 1974-84, prof., 1984-2000, head dept. physics, 1987-2000, emeritus prof., 2000—; rsch. assoc. Stanford (Calif.) U., 1961-62. Contbr. articles to profl. jours. Fellow Inst. of Physics. Avocations: aquarist, garden, sport. Home: 26 Lime Grove Av Chilwell, Nottingham NG9 4AR, England Office: Sch Physics & Astronomy, U Nottingham, Nottingham NG72RD, England

BATES, EDNA JEAN, biochemist, researcher; d. Kenneth Frederick and Sophie Woodward; m. David Jonathan Bates, Aug. 9, 1975; children: Janine, Simon. BSc with honors, Dundee (Scotland) U., 1975; PhD in Biochemistry, U. Coll., London, 1978. Assoc. rsch. asst. U. Coll., London, 1978-81; sr. tutor Monash U., Victoria, Australia, 1981-84; rsch. fellow U. Adelaide (Australia), 1985-94, 96—; rsch. officer Flinders (Australia) U., 1995. Contbr. articles to profl. jours. Office: Dept Animal Sci, U Adelaide Waite Campus, Glen Osmond 5064, Australia

BATES, GERALD EARL, bishop emeritus; b. Caldwell, Ohio, Sept. 12, 1933; s. Earl and Lillian Inez (Merritt) B.; m. Marlene Rachel Parsons, Aug. 21, 1954; children: David Earl, William Randall, Elizabeth Ann. AA, Spring Arbor Coll., 1953; AB, Greenville Coll., 1955; MDiv, Asbury Theol. Sem., 1958; ThM, Western Theol. Sem., 1964; PhD, Mich. State U., 1975; DD (hon.), Roberts Wesleyan Coll., 1986, Greenville Coll., 1998. Missionary with Gen. Missionary Bd. Free Meth. Ch. of N.Am., Winona Lake, Ind., 1957-85; area adminstrv. asst. for Cen. Africa Free Meth. Ch. of N.Am., 1973-85; bishop Free Meth. Ch. of N.Am., Indpls., 1985-99, bishop emeritus, 1999—; adj. prof. Union Inst., Cin. Author: Soul Afire, 1981, 2d edit., 1993; chmn. bd. editors: Book of Discipline, 1985. Trustee Asbury Theol. Sem., Wilmore, Ky., Spring Arbor Coll., Mich.; bd. dirs. King Trust N.A.; bd. dirs. India Missionary Tng. Bd., J. Wesley Bible Coll., Budapest, Hungary, Free Meth. Found.; pres. Free Meth. World Fellowship, 1989-95; pres. U.S. bd. Hope Africa U., Kenya. Recipient Alumnus of Yr. award Spring Arbor Coll., 1974, Goodwill Amb. award Noble County C. of C., 1988, Alumnus of Yr. award Asbury Theol. Sem., 1991. Mem. Phi Kappa Phi. Republican. Avocations: reading, travel, photography. Home: 6715 Oak Lake Dr Indianapolis IN 46214-2038

BATES, HAROLD MARTIN, lawyer; b. Wise County, Va., Mar. 11, 1928; s. William Jennings and Reba (Williams) B.; m. Audrey Rose Doll, Nov. 1, 1952 (div. Mar. 1978); children—Linda, Carl. m. Judith Lee Farmer, June 23, 1978. B.A. in Econs., Coll. William and Mary, 1952; LL.B., Washington and Lee U., 1961. Bar: Va. 1961, Ky. 1961. Spl. agt. FBI, Newark and N.Y.C., 1952-56; tech. sales rep. Hercules Powder Co., Wilmington, Del., 1956-58; investigator U.S. Def. Dept., Lexington, Va., Louisville, 1959-62; practice law, Louisville, 1961-62; sec.-treas., dir., house counsel Life Ins. Co. of Ky., Louisville, 1962-66; practice law, Roanoke, Va., 1966—; sec., dir. James River Limestone Co., Buchanan, Va., 1970-96; sec. Eastern Ins. Co., Roanoke, 1984-87. Pres., Skil, Inc., orgn. for rehab. Vietnam vets., Salem, Va., 1972-75; freshman football coach Washington and Lee U., 1958-60. Served to cpl. U.S. Army Airborne, 1946-47, PTO. Mem. Va. Bar Assn., Roanoke Bar Assn., William and Mary Alumni Assn. (bd. dirs. 1972-76), Soc. Former Spl. Agts. of FBI (chmn. Blue Ridge chpt. 1971-72). Republican. Home: 2165 Laurel Woods Dr Salem VA 24153-1807 Office: 406 Professional Arts Bldg Roanoke VA 24011

BATES, JAMES EARL, academic administrator; b. Ligonier, Pa., Aug. 10, 1923; s. Earl Barrington and Margaret (Kinsey) B.; m. Lauralou Courtney, Apr. 15, 1950; children: Susan Bates Jaren, Sara Bates Hudson, James Barrington, Willa Laurens. DSc, Temple U., 1946; DPM, Pa. Coll. Podiatric Medicine, 1970; EdD (hon.), Franklin Pierce Coll., 1972; DSc (hon.), Calif. Coll. Podiatric Med., 1995; LLD, Barry U., 1995; LHD (hon.), Pa. Coll. Podiatric Medicine, 1996. Practice podiatric medicine Phila., 1946-71; assoc. prof. roentgenology Temple U., Phila., 1948-60; prof., pres. Pa. Coll. Podiatric Medicine, Phila., 1962-95, chancellor, 1995-96, chancellor, CEO, 1997-98; cons. to dean Sch. Podiatric Medicine Temple U., 1998—; chancellor Temple Sch. Podiatric Medicine; cons. BHRD Region IX, HEW, San Francisco, 1973-74, Region V, Chgo., 1974-75; del. Nat. Commn. on Certifying Health Manpower; mem. health adv. com. HEW, 1972-73; adv. panel for podiatry Inst. Medicine, Nat. Acad. Scis., 1972-74; adv. council for comprehensive health planning Pa. Dept. Health, 1972-75, health manpower task force edn. com., 1976; mem. task force on health manpower distbn. Nat. Health Council, 1973, mem. com. on manpower, 1976-83; mem. Nat. Adv. Council on Health Professions Edn., 1983-87; cons. team So. Regional Ednl. Bd. Feasibility Study for So. Podiatry Sch., 1975-76; mem. Statewide Profl. Standards Rev. Council, 1976-82, Greater Phila. Com. for Med.-Pharm. Scis. Contbr. sci. articles to profl. jours. Trustee First United Meth. Ch. of Germantown, 1965-72, past chmn. fin. com.; v.p. bd. Germantown Businessmen's Assn., Disting. Service award, 1964; chmn. 277th and 278th Ann. Germantown Week, 1958-59; dep. service dir. Phila. CD Council, 1966-73; mem. Health Adv. Commn., Phila., 1976; past pres., bd. mgrs. Germantown YMCA; v.p. Phila. Boosters Assn.; trustee Univ. City Sci. Center, Phila. Served with M.C. AUS, World War II. Recipient citation Pa. Coll. Podiatric Medicine, 1970, citation Gov. Pa., 1973, lifetime achievement award Podiatric Mgmt. Mag., 1993. Fellow Internat. Acad. Preventive Medicine (dir. 1973-78), Brit. Soc. Podiatric Medicine (hon. 1991—), Royal Soc. Health (Eng.), Am. Coll. Foot Roentgenologists (pres. 1958-59), Coll. Physicians Phila.; mem. Am. Podiatry Assn. (Merit award 1962, gen. chmn. Region Three Ann. Conv. 1975—), Pa. Podiatry Assn. (pres. 1959-60, Man of Yr. award 1961, Spl. citation 1973), Greater Phila. Podiatry Soc. (pres. 1955-56), Fedn. Assns. Schs. of Health Professions (pres. 1975-76), Am. Assn. Colls. Podiatric Medicine (pres. 1969-72), Pyramid Club, Pi Epsilon Delta, Pi Delta. Republican. Clubs: Greate Bay Country, Union League, Pyramid Club. Office: Pa Coll Podiatric Medicine 810 N Race St Philadelphia PA 19107-2496

BATES, KATHY, actress; b. Memphis, June 28, 1948. BFA, So. Meth. U., 1969. Film appearances include Taking Off, 1971, Straight Time, Come Back to the Five and Dime, Jimmy Dean, Jimmy Dean, Summer Heat, Arthur 2: On the Rocks, Signs of Life, High Stakes, Men Don't Leave, Dick Tracy, White Palace, Misery, 1990 (Acad. award for Best Actress 1990, Golden Globe award), At Play in the Fields of the Lord, 1991, The Road to Mecca, Prelude to a Kiss, Fried Green Tomatoes, 1991 (Golden Globe nomination, BAFTA nomination), Used People, A Home of Our Own, North, Curse of the Starving Class, Dolores Claiborne, 1994, Angus, 1995, Diabolique, 1996, The War at Home, 1996, Primary Colors, 1998, Swept from the Sea, 1998, Titanic, 1998, Dash and Lilly, 1999, My Life as a Dog, 1999; stage appearances include Vanities, 1976, Semmelweiss, Crimes of the Heart, The Art of Dining, Goodbye Fidel, 1980, Chocolate Cake and Final Placement, 1981, 5th of July, 'night, Mother, 1983 (Tony nomination, Outer Critics Circle award), Two Masters: The Rain of Terror, 1985, Curse of the Starving Class, Frankie and Johnny in the Clair de Lune (OBIE award 1988), The Road to Mecca; TV appearances include (series) The Late Shift (Golden Globe award, Am. Comedy award, SAG award), The Love Boat, St. Elsewhere, Cagney & Lacey, L.A. Law, China Beach, Homicide, N.Y.P.D. Blue, (pilot) Fargo, (miniseries) Murder Ordained, The Stand, 1994, (movies of the week) Johnny Bull, No Place Like Home, Roe vs. Wade, Hostages, The West Side Waltz, 1995, The Late Shift, 1996; dir. Talking With, PBS Great Performances, (NBC). Office: Susan Smith & Assocs 121 N San Vicente Blvd Beverly Hills CA 90211-2303

BATES, LURA WHEELER, trade association executive; b. Inboden, Ark., Aug. 28, 1932; d. Carl Clifton and Hester Ray (Pace) Wheeler; m. Allen Carl Bates, Sept. 12, 1954; 1 child, Carla Allene. BSBA, U. Ark., 1954. Cert. constrn. assoc. Sec.-bookkeeper, then officer mgr. Assoc. Gen. Contractors Miss., Inc., Jackson, 1958-77, dir. adminstrv. svcs., 1977-98, asst. exec. dir., 1980-98; owner, Ditty Bag Supply Co., 1987-98; adminstr. Miss. Constrn. Found., 1977-98; sec. AIA-Assoc. Gen. Contractors Liaisonship Coms., 1977-98; sec. Carpenters Joint Apprenticeship Coms., Jackson and Vicksburg, 1977-98. Sec. Marshall Elem. Sch. PTA, Jackson, 1962-64, v.p., 1965; sec.-treas. Inter-Club Coun. Jackson, 1963-64; tchr. adult Sunday sch. dept. Hillcrest Bapt. Ch., Jackson, 1975-82; dir. Bapt. Women WMU, 1987—, sec., 1992—; tchr. adult Sunday sch. dept. 1st Bapt. Ch., Crystal Springs, Miss., 1989-98; mem. exec. com. Jackson Christian Bus. and Profl. Women's Coun., 1976-80, sec., 1978-79, pres., 1979-80. Named Outstanding Woman in Constrn. Miss., 1962-63, Outstanding Mem. Nat. Assn. Women in Constrn. Fellow Internat. Platform Assn.; mem. AAUW, NAFE, Nat. Assn. Women in Constrn. (life, chpt. pres. 1963-64, 76-77, 92-93, nat. v.p. 1965-66, 77-78, nat. dir. Region 5, 1967-68, nat. sec. 1970-71, 71-72, pres. 1980-81, coord. cert. constrn. assoc. program 1973-78, 83-84 guardian-contr. Edn. Found. 1981-82, chmn. nat. bylaws com. 1982-83, 85-88, nat. parliamentarian 1983-92), Nat. Assn. Parliamentarians, U. Ark. Alumni Assn. (life, pres. ctrl. Miss. chpt. 1992-93, 93-94, 94-95), Delta Delta Delta. Editor NAWIC Image, 1968-69, Procedures Manual, 1965-66, Public Relations Handbook, 1967-68, Profl. Edn. Guide, 1972-73, Guidelines & Procedures Handbook, 1987-88; author digests in field. Home: 1007 Lee Ave Crystal Springs MS 39059-2546 Office: 2093 Lakeland Dr Jackson MS 39216-5010

BATES, PETER GERALD, diplomat; b. London, Feb. 25, 1959; s. Ronald Gordon Nudell and Kirsti (Mottonen) B.; m. Margaret Irene Gibson; children: Frederick Thomas, Geoffrey David. BA (hons.), Univ. Toronto. Fgn. svcs. officer Dept. Fgn. Affairs and Internat. Trade, Ottawa, Can., 1989-91; 2d sec. Canadian Embassy, Moscow, Russia, 1991-94; desk officer for European and conventional arms control Dept. Fgn. Affairs & Internat. Trade, Ottawa, 1994-96; Can. rep. NATO High Level Task Force, Brussels, Belgium, 1994-96; deputy head Canadian Delegation to the 1996 CFE Treaty Rev. Conf., Vienna, Austria, 1996; 1st sec. Canadian Embassy, Washington, 1996-99. Recipient RadleyúWalters Sword Canadian Forces COmbat Training Ctr., 1981. Mem. Royal Canadian Military Inst. Avocations: home computing, scale modelling. E-mail: petergbates@cs.com. Office: Embassy of Can 501 Pennsylvania Ave NW Washington DC 20001-2114

BATESON, PATRICK, zoology educator; b. Oxfordshire, Eng., Mar. 31, 1938; s. Richard Gordon and Sölvi Helene (Berg) B.; m. Dusha Mathews; children: Melissa, Anna. BA, Cambridge (Eng.) U., 1960, PhD, 1963, DSc, 1977. Sr. asst. in rsch. Cambridge (Eng.) U., 1965-69, lectr., 1969-78, reader, 1978-84, prof., 1984—, head zoology dept., 1994-96, provost King's Coll., 1988—. Author: Measuring Behaviour, 1986, Design for a Life: How Behavior Develops, 1999; editor: Growing Point in Ethology, 1976, Mate Choise, 1983, Development and Integration of Behaviour. Fellow Zool. Soc. London (Sci. medal 1976), Royal Soc. London; mem. Assn. for the Study of Animal Behaviour (former pres.). Home and Office: Kings Coll, The Provosts Lodge, Cambridge CB2 1ST, England

BATEY, PETER WILLIAM JAMES, urban planning educator, urban and regional analysis consultant; b. West Hartlepool, Eng., Aug. 17, 1948; s. George Thomas and Ruth (Garstang) B.; m. Joyce Dover, Jan. 25, 1975; children: Rachel Alexandra, James Richard. BS, U. Sheffield, Eng., 1969; M of Civic Design, U. Liverpool, Eng., 1971, PhD, 1985. Planning officer Lancashire County Council, Preston, Eng., 1969-73; sr. planning officer Greater Manchester (Eng.) Council, 1973-75; lectr. civic design U. Liverpool, 1975-84, sr. lectr., 1984-87, reader, 1987-89, Lever prof. town and regional planning, 1989—, dean faculty social and environ. studies, 1997—; cons. Claritas, London, 1998—; vis. rsch. scholar geography U. Ill., Urbana, 1981-82; chmn. Conf. Heads of Planning Schs., 1990-96. Editor: Town Planning Rev., 1984-87, (book series) London Papers in Regional Science, 1984-90, European Research in Regional Science, 1990-97; contbr. articles to planning and regional sci. jours., chpts. to books. Mem. Mersey Basin Campaign Coun., 1999—. Recipient Silver Jubilee medal Hungarian Econ. Assn./Regional Sci. Assn., 1985; George A. Miller scholar, Fulbright scholar U. Ill., 1981-82. Fellow Royal Soc. Arts, Royal Statis. Soc., Royal Town Planning Inst.; mem. Regional Sci. Assn. Internat. (pres. 1997-98), Russian Acad. Arch. and Constrn. Scis. (fgn.), Acad. Learned Socs. in the Social Scis. (academician). Anglican. Home: 4 Agnes Rd Blundellsands, Liverpool L23 6ST, England Office: U Liverpool Dept Civic Design, Abercromby Sq PO Box 147, Liverpool L69 3BX, England

BATEY, ROBERT GORDON, hepatological specialist, educator; b. Sydney, Apr. 17, 1944; s. Charles Gordon and Thelma Irene (Cochrane) B.; m. Adrienne Edyth Brown, June 14, 1969; children: Stephen John, Virginia Michelle. BSc with honors, Sydney U., 1965, MB, BS with honors, 1969, MD, 1992. Intern Sydney Hosp., 1968, resident med. officer, 1969-70; registrar Royal Prince Alfred Hosp., Sydney, 1971, clin. supt. medicine, 1972-73, NH & MRC rsch. scholar, 1973-76, vis. med. officer, 1978-82; hon. lectr. in medicine Royal Free Hosp., London, 1976-78; dir. drug and alcohol unit Westmead, Sydney, 1982-91; dir. gastroenterology unit John Hunter Hosp., U. Newcastle, Newcastle, Australia, 1992—, assoc. prof. medicine, 1992-96, prof., 1996—, dep. dean, faculyt of medicine and health scis., 1998—; chmn. Western Sydney Drug and Alcohol Svc., 1989-91, Nat. Hepatitis C Com., 1999—. Contbr. numerous articles to profl. publs. Rsch. project grantee Rsch. into Drug, Alcohol and Liver Disease com., 1982-2001, Bushell Found., 1991-93, NH&MRC, 1979-89. Fellow Royal Australasian Coll. Physicians (chmn. bd. of continuing edn., 1994—, advisor drug and alcohol issues 1986—, coun. 1992—), Royal Coll. Physicians (U.K.), Am. Assn. for Study Liver Disease, Am. GE Assn., Biochem. Soc. U.K., GE Soc. Australia (hon. sec. 1989-90), Scientific Programme Com. (hon. sec.). Avocations: surfing, bonsai. Office: John Hunter Hosp, Lookout Rd, New Lambton Heights 2305, Australia

BATHERSBY, JOHN ALEXIUS, archbishop; b. Stanthorpe, Queensland, Australia, July 26, 1936; s. John Thomas and Grace Maud (Conquest) B. Lic. of Theology, Gregorian U., Rome, 1972, DTM, 1982. Ordained priest, 1961. Assoc. pastor Goondiwindi, 1962-69; spiritual dir. Pius XII Provincial Sem., Banyo, Queensland, 1973-86; bishop of Cairns Queensland, 1986-91, archbishop of Brisbane, 1992—. Avocations: walking, mountain climbing, sports, classical music. Home and Office: Archbishop's House, 790 Brunswick St, New Farm QLD 4005, Australia

BATHGATE, LIAM DONALD, communication executive; b. Sydney, Australia, Jan. 2, 1950; s. Donald Douglas and Joan Brenda (Hudson) B.; m. Jeanne Madeline Dunstan, July 14, 1979; children: John, Anna, Louisa. Polit. corr. Australian Associated Press, 1975-79; press sec. Deputy Prime Min. Australia, 1979-84; sr. pvt. sec. Leader Nat. Party Australia, 1984-87; pub. affairs mgr. Sydney Harbour Tunnel, Australia, 1987-92; gen. sec. NSW Nat. Party, Australia, 1992-97; mgr. group comm. Tenix Pty. Ltd., Australia, 1997—. Fellow Australian Inst. Profl. Communicators; mem. Royal Inst. Deaf and Blind Children (life). Anglican. Avocation: historic buildings. Office: Tenix Pty Ltd, 100 Arthur St, North Sydney 2074, Australia

BATHIAS, CLAUDE, materials science educator, consultant; b. Bénévent, France, Aug. 5, 1938; s. André and Gabrielle (Thienot) B.; m. Marie-Claude Leveque, Dec. 26, 1964; children: Anne Potter, Claire Besset. French PhD, U. Poitiers (France), 1964; postgrad., MIT, 1972. Engr., cons. Aerospatiale Co., Paris, 1973-85; material engring. dept. head French Ministry for Rsch. and Tech., Paris, 1978-82; prof. U. Technology, Compiègne, France, 1974-88, Conservatoire Nat. des Arts et Métiers, Paris, 1989—; vis. prof. Ga. Inst. Tech., Atlanta, 1988-98; dir. CNRS Lab. 914 U. Compiegne, 1980-85, Inst. for Tech. and Materials Sci., Paris, 1985—; chmn. numerous sci. confs., vis. prof. SWJ U., Chengdu, China, 1994—. Editor books from conf. proc.; contbr. numerous articles to sci. and profl. jours. Advisor Ministry for Rsch., Paris, 1978-82, Ministry for Def., Paris, 1983-86, Ministry for Fgn. Affairs, Paris, 1988-91; del. VAMAS-France, Paris, 1983-99. Decorated chevalier Ordre Nat. du Merite (France); recipient Oppenheim award Ingénieurs et Scientifiques de France, Paris, 1978, award Nat. Rsch. Inst. for Metals, Tokyo, 1988. Fellow Am. Soc. Materials; mem. ASTM, MIT Club of France. Avocations: tennis, music, international cooperation. Home: 80 Boulevard Bourdon, 92200 Neuilly Sur Seine France Office: Conservatoire Nat des Arts et Métiers, 292 rue Saint Martin, 75141 Paris France

BATHO, GORDON RICHARD, education educator; b. London, Feb. 27, 1929; s. Walter and Harriet Emily (Dymock) B.; m. Hilary Crowson, Sept. 5, 1959; children: Richard Clement John, Stephen Paul Gordon. BA, Univ. Coll. London, 1950, postgrad. cert. edn., 1951; MA, Royal Holloway Coll., London, 1953. Sr. history master Ilfracombe Grammar Sch., Devon, Eng., 1953-55; asst. lectr., lectr., sr. lectr. U. Sheffield, Eng., 1956-74; prof. edn. U. Durham, Eng., 1975-88, emeritus prof., 1988—; chmn. Durham Thomas Harriot Sem.; vis. lectr. various univs. Editor: Household Papers of Henry Percy (1564-1632), 1962, Talbot Papers in Coll ege of Arms, 1972, Advices to His Son, 2000, Durham Biographies, Vol. 1, 2000; author: Politics of Education, 1989; contbg. author: Thomas Harriot, Man of Science, 2000. Sec. Parochial Ch. Coun., St. Giles, Dham; mem. Gilligate Trust; editor Durham County Local History Soc.; lectr. Nat. Assn. Decorative and Fine Art Soc. Fellow Royal Hist. Soc.; mem. Hist. Assn. (v.p.). Avocations: gardening, hist. visiting. Home: 3 Archery Rise, Durham DH1 4LA, England Office: U of Durham Sch of Edn, Leazes Rd, Durham DH1 1TA, England

BATISLAM, ERTAN, urology educator; b. Kayseri, Turkey, Apr. 9, 1963; s. Muhsin and Eser Batislam; m. Yesim Akalin, July 19, 1986; 1 child, Baris Tan. MD, U. Ankara, Turkey, 1986. Cert. in medicine Ministry of Health, Turkey. Resident dept. urology U. Ankara, 1987-91; postgrad. fellow in urology U. Western Ont., London, Can., 1992; lectr. urology Urology clinic Ministry of Health Ankara Tchg. Hosp., 1993-97; transplant fellow divsn. organ transplantation U. Tex., Houston, 1997-98; chmn., assoc. prof. dept. urology U. Kirikkale, Turkey, 1998—; mem. univ. senate, assoc. dean Med. Sch. U. Kirikkale, 1999—; vice-head Univ. Hosp. Kirikkale, U. Kirikkale, 1998-99. Lt. urologist, Turkish mil., 1993. Fellow in transplantation U. Tex., 1997-98. Mem. Turkish Urol. Assn., Turkish Cancer Assn. Avocations: sports, scuba diving, traveling. Fax: 90-318-225 28 19. E-mail: ebatislam@superonline.com. Home: Kubilay sokak 35-9, Ankara 06570, Turkey Office: U Kirikkale Med Sch Dept Urology U Hosp, Millet cad, Kirikkale 71100, Turkey

BATISSE, MICHEL, physicist, international civil servant; b. Chateauroux, France, Apr. 3, 1923; s. Justin and Renee (Augereau) B.; m. Claude Bazin, Nov. 26, 1949; children: Laurence, Stephane-Isabelle. Diploma in engring., Ecole Ctrl. Paris, 1946; DSc in Physics, Sorbonne, Paris, 1951. Rsch. engr. Paris, 1950-51; sci. officer Middle East UNESCO, Cairo, 1951-56; arid zone program coord. UNESCO, Paris, 1957-61, natural resources divsn. dir., 1961-72, environ. dept. dir., 1973-83, asst. dir. gen. sci., 1983-84, sr. advisor environ., 1985—; pres. Blue Plan (for environ. and devel. in Mediterranean), Sophia-Antipolis, France, 1985—; sr. adviser UN Environ. Program, Nairobi, 1985-94; adv. on biodiversity Rio Conf., 1991-92, adv. Word Bank, Washington, 1991-92; sec. gen. Biosphere Conf., 1968; mem. Biosphere Reserves Adv. Com. Editor: Blue Plan publs.; contbr. articles to profl. jours. Bd. dirs. Conservation Internat., Washington, 1989—. With French Mil., 1944-45. Decorated officer Legion of Honor; recipient John Phillips medal World Conservation Union, 1988, UNESCO Gold medal, 1998, Global 500 Role of Honor. Mem. World Acad. Arts Scis. Avocations: ancient books, sea shells. Home: 9 Ave L Bucquet, 92380 Garches France Office: care UNESCO, 1 Rue Miollis, 75732 Paris France

BATISTUTA, GABRIEL OMAR, professional soccer player; b. Reconquista, Argentina, Feb. 1, 1969. With Newell's Old Boys, Argentina, 1988-89, River Plate, Argentina, Boca Jrs., Argentina; champion (with Boca Jrs.) Argentine League, 1990-91, top scorer, 1990-91; champion (with Argentina) America Cup, 1991; ctr. forward Fiorentina Football Club, Italy, 1991—; champion (with Fiorentina) Italian Cup, 1995-96. Named Argentina's all-time leading scorer. Office: Fiorentina Assn Calcio SpA, Piazza G Savonarola 6, 50132 Florence Italy*

BATLEY, EDWARD MALCOLM, language professional/educator, foreign languages; b. Holmfirth/Huddersfield, Yorkshire, U.K., Sept. 5, 1935; s. Ronald Emanuel and Anne (Hogley) B.; m. Margaret Tindle, July 29, 1961; children: Melanie Anne, David Marcus, Gareth Adam. BA with honours in German, U. Durham, U.K., 1957, Diploma of Edn., 1958, MLitt, 1965. Asst. tchr. English, Music, Sport Wilhelmsdorfer Gymnasium, Baden-Württemberg, Germany, 1958-59; master for modern langs. Honley Holme Valley Grammar Sch., Huddersfield, Yorkshire, U.K., 1959-62; head German dept. Highbury County Sch., London, 1962-64; lectr. in German Goldsmiths' Coll., U. London, 1964-70, sr. lectr., head German dept., 1970-87, head dept. European Langs., 1987-93; reader in German U. London, 1990-96, head German studies, 1994-96, reader emeritus, 1996; hon. dir. U. London Inst. Germanic Studies, 1993-98; pres. Fédn. Internat. des Profs. de Langues Vivantes, 1981-83, 84-86, 87-89, 90-92; chmn. internat. symposium on compact courses for modern langs. U. Marburg, Germany, 1981, numerous others. Author: (book) A Preface to the Magic Flute, 1969, Catalyst of the Enlightenment: Gotthold Ephraim Lessing, 1991; contbr. articles on music, theatre, freemasonry and German lit. to profl. and scholarly jours.; editor Modern Langs., 1970-79; co-author Lang. Policies for the World of the 21st Century, UNESCO, 1993. Chmn. Internat. Conf. on Langs. and Human Rights, Paris, 1989. Recipient Jacob and Wilhelm Grimm prize, Berlin, 1982, Jan Amos Comenius medal, Prague, 1992; Conseiller honoraire de la Fédn. Internat. des Profs. de Langues Vivantes, 1993. Mem. Assn. for Lang. Learning, Inst. Germanic Studies, English Goethe Soc., Lessing Akademie Wolfenbüttel, Schiller Gesellschaft Marbach, Goethe Gesellschaft Weimar, Internat. Vereinigung der Germanisten, Fédn. Internat. des Langues et Littératures Modernes, Fédn. Internat. des Professeurs de Langues Vivantes, Acad. Européene des Arts, des Scis. et des Lettres. Avocations: piano playing, composition, tennis. Home: Keruing, Mottingham Ln, London SE9 4RX, England Office: University of London, Goldsmith College, New Cross, London SE14 6NW, United Kingdom

BATLEY, GRAEME EDWARD, environmental analytical chemist, researcher; b. Young, Australia, Jan. 7, 1941; s. Jack and Ena Tait (Sutherland) B.; m. Ruth Margaret Beer, Mar. 13, 1966; children: Karen Sue, Steven Richard. BSc with 1st class honours, U. NSW, Australia, 1961, MSc, 1964, PhD, 1967, DSc, 1994. Postdoctoral fellow U. Ill., Urbana, 1967-69; rsch. scientist Australian Atomic Energy Commn., Lucas Heights, 1970-81; rsch. sci. Commonwealth Sci. and Indsl. Rsch. Orgn., Lucas Heights, 1981-94, mgr. Centre for Advanced Analytical Chemistry, 1989—, chief rsch. sci., 1994—; vis. scientist Can. Centre for Inland Waters, Burlington, Ont., 1980-81. Editor, author: Trace Element Speciation, 1989; author more than 150 papers in field. Fellow Royal Australian Chem. Inst. (v.p. NSW 1989-91, pres. 1991-93, Analytical Chemistry medal 1991, Govt. medal 1995), Australian Water and Wastewater Assn. (chmn. environ. div. 1995—), Soc. Environ. Toxicology and Chemistry (pres. Asia/Pacific 1996—), Internat. Assn. on Water Quality (dir. Australian nat. com. 1990-94), Internat. Union Pure and Applied Chemistry (nat. rep. to commn. on electroanalytical chemistry 1987-97). Avocations: tennis, photography. Office: Commonwealth Sci & Indsl Rsch Orgn, New Illawarra Rd, Lucas Heights 2234, Australia

BATLINER, GERARD, lawyer; b. Eschen, Liechtenstein, Dec. 9, 1928; married; two children. JD, U. Fribourg, Switzerland, 1957. V.p. Fortschrittliche Burgerpartei, 1958-62; dep. mayor Commune of Eschen, 1960-62; head of govt./Minister of Justice Principality of Liechtenstein, 1962-70; lawyer Liechtenstein, 1970—; pres. of the parliamentary del. of Liechtenstein Coun. of Europe, 1974-77, v.p. of parliamentary del. of Liechtenstein, 1978-81, v.p. parliamentary assembly, 1981-82; mem. European Human Rights Commn., 1983-90; chmn. sci. coun. Liechtenstein Inst., 1987-97, mem. sci. coun., 1998—; mem. European Commn. for Democracy Through Law, 1991—; arbitrator Ct. of the OSCE, 1995—. Author numerous publs. in field. Mem. Liechtensteinische Akademische Gesellschaft, Liechtensteinische Gesellschaft fur Umweltschutz, Historischer Verein, Genossenschaft Theater

am Kirchplatz, Liechtensteinische Kunstgesellschaft. Office: Am Schragen Weg 2, 9490 Vaduz Liechtenstein

BATMANABANE, MOUNISSAMY, anatomist, educator; b. Cuddalore, India, Apr. 22, 1948; s. Mounissamy and Pappathy; m. Gitanjali Sivaji Dorai, Feb. 11, 1981; 1 child, Vaishnavi. MBBS, Jawaharlal Inst. Postgrad. Med. Edn. and Rsch., Pondicherry, India, 1970, MS, 1975. Demonstrator Jawaharlal Inst. Posgrad. Med. Edn. Rsch., Pondicherry, 1972-78, from lectr. to prof., 1982-91, prof., 1991—; lectr. U. Calabar, Nigeria, 1978-82; med. undergrad. examiner, med. and non-med. postgrad. examiner, India, 1982; PhD examiner, U. Adelaide, Australia, 1997. Contbr. articles to profl. jours. Referee Indian Jour. Pharm., 1996. Under officer Nat. Cadet Corps., India, 1965-67. Nat. Merit scholar Govt. India, 1965-70; grantee U. Calabar, 1978-82. Mem. Jipmer Scientific Soc. (v.p. 1985-86), Indo-French Soc. Med. Allied Scis. (sec. 1976-78). Avocations: body building, volleyball, badminton, karate, philosophy. Office: JIPMER, Dept Anatomy, Pondicherry 605 006, India

BATNICK, MICHAEL ARNOLD, political economist, political consultant; b. N.Y.C., Dec. 3, 1916; s. Sanford and Esther (Jaffee) B.; m. Barbara Sarah Citron, May 15, 1936 (div. June 1954); children: Michael, Marguerite, Bonnie; m. Christl Wolf. PhD, U. Calif. Berkeley, 1979. From intern to dir. program and planning, dep. commr. U.S. Govt., 1932-53; chief economist, dir., cons. Haas Consult, Hanover, Germany, 1953—; pvt. practice econ. and polit. cons. Latin Am., Asian and African govts., pvt. industry; guest lectr. econs. and polit. sci. Calif. State Colls., U. Guadalajara, U. Autonoma, Mexico; commentator Spanish radio. Columnist pvt. newswellter; contbr. textbooks, articles to profl. jours. Home: Calle Alcoy 7-4F, 03590 Altea Alicante, Spain Office: Haas Consult, Apartado 27, 03590 Altea Alicante, Spain

BATOR, MARTHA ZACHRY MAYSON, artist; b. Atlanta, Feb. 12, 1930; d. James Lucian and Jane Crawford (Hancock) Mayson; m. Edmund Alexander Bator, June 11, 1952; children: Jane Crawford, Zachry Mayson. BA, Oglethorpe U., 1951; studies in painting, Helsinki (Finland) U.; studies in sculpture and pastel, various artists. Tchr. Dekalb County Schs., Atlanta, 1951-53, Prince Georges County Schs., Mt. Ranier, Md., 1954-56, D.C. Schs., 1967-70; pres. Design Studio, Kuwait, 1975-79; artist Atlanta, 1980—. One-woman shows at Mercer U., Oglethorpe U. Mus., Goodyear Ho.; two-person shows at DeKalb C.C., Quinlan Fine Arts Gallery; also various invitational and group exhbns.; represented in corp. collections including King and Spaulding, Atlanta, McRae and Holloway, Atlanta, Ganek, Wright and Dobkin, Atlanta, Ga. Coun. for Arts, Children's Hosp., Macon, Ga., Kuwait Embassy, Washington, Heathrow Country Club, Sarasota, Fla., John C. Campbell Folk Sch., Brasstown, N.C., Art Pl., Kuwait and Dubai, Oglethorpe U. Mus., Kaiser Permanente, Jean and Mack Henderson Women's Ctr. at Kennestone Hosp.; works included in publs. including So. Homes Mag., Peachtree Mag., Pastel Jour., 200 Great Painting Ideas for Artists (Carole Katchen), The Best of Pastel and A Gallery of Marine Art, others. Mem. Dekalb Coun. for Arts, 1982—. Recognized for Achievement by Ga. Woman in Visual Arts, Sec. of State, 1997; recipient 1st prize Ann. Heritage Fine Arts Competition, 3 Nat. Juried Best of Show awards, various nat. and internat. awards. Mem. Pastel Soc. Am. (signature), Southea. Pastel Soc. (v.p. 1987—), Knickerbocker Artists, U.S.A., Atlanta Artist's Ctr. (gallery chmn. 1986, 87, Mem. of Excellence), Art Sta., Plein Air Painters of Ga. Avocations: travel, photography. E-mail: eamzmbator@home.com. Home and Studio: 3432 Stratfield Dr NE Atlanta GA 30319-2567

BATOS, VEDRAN, computer consultant, information systems specialist, educator; b. Dubrovnik, Croatia, Nov. 18, 1960; s. Matko and Maria (Jakovic) B.; m. Maria Franulovic, Nov. 9, 1985; children: Dora, Matko. Degree in elec. engring., U. Zagreb, 1983, MS in Elec. Engring., 1986, PhD in Computing Sci., 1997. Electronics engr. Hosp. Ctr., Zagreb, 1983-84, Hitachi Ltd., Landsberg, 1986-87; sys. engr. Derc-Computing Ctr., Dubrovnik, 1987-88, mgr. info. tech., 1988-89; mgr. info. tech. devel. Dubrovnik Bank, 1990-94; dir. Nivel-Bus. Info. Technologies, Dubrovnik, 1994-99; dir. AS/400 sales and support divsn. Euronet Worldwide, Inc., Little Rock, 1999-20000, sr. Info. Technologies cons., 2000—; sr. lectr. Polytechnic, Dubrovnik, 1997; bus. ptnr. IBM, Austria and Croatia. Recipient Best IBM Bus. Ptnr. for Croatia, 1995. Mem. IEEE, IEEE Computer Soc., Assn. Computing Machinery, N.Y. Acad. Scis. E-mail: batos@attglobal.net. Home: Gorica SV, Vlaha 22, 20000 Dubrovnik Croatia

BÄTSCHMANN, OSKAR, art history educator; b. Lucerne, Switzerland, Sept. 15, 1943; s. Robert Oskar and Martha (Baldegger) B.; m. Marie Therese Bätschmann, Nov. 11, 1988. PhD, U. Zürich, Switzerland, 1975, habil., 1981. Lectr. U. Zürich, 1979-83; prof. art history U. Freiberg, Germany, 1984-87; chmn. dept. art history U. Giessen, Germany, 1988-90, U. Bern, Switzerland, 1991—; dir. d'études École des Hautes Études en Sciences Sociales, Paris, 1992; pres. Swiss Assn. Art Historians, 1980-86; pres. rsch. com. Swiss Acad., 1992-96; pres. rsch. com. Swiss Inst. Art Rsch., 1994—; sec. Comité Internat. d'Histoire l'Art, 1996. Author: Malerei der Neuzeit, 1988, Entfernung der Natur, 1989, Nicolas Poussin, 1990, Kunstgeschichtliche Hermeneutik, 1992, Hans Holbein 1493/4-1543, 1997, Ausstellungskünstler, 1997, The Artist in the Modern World, 1997, Bibliography of the History of Art, 1997, Ferdinand Hodler, Die Zeichenungen im Kunstmuseum Bern, 1999; mem. editl. bd. Zeitschrift für Kunstgeschichte, 1984-99. Getty scholar, Getty Ctr. for History of Art and Humanities, Santa Monica, Calif., 1990-91; P. Mellon sr. fellow CASVA, Nat. Gallery, Washington, 1995. Mem. Austrian Art Historian Assn. (hon.). Office: Inst für Kunstgeschichte, Hodlerstrasse 8, CH-3011 Bern Switzerland

BATSON, DAVID FREDERICK EDWARD, social studies educator; b. Seaton Carew, Durham, Eng., June 11, 1938; s. Sidney Edward and Ella Irene Lucy (Clarke Jackson) B. Assoc., Kings Coll., London, 1961; BD, U. London, 1969. Ordained priest Ch. of Eng., 1962. Non stipendiary min. Parish of Leigh with Bransford, Diocese Worcester, 1968-79; prin. Dept. Social Work Tng., Dumfries-Galloway, Scotland, 1984-94; lectr. and tutor Langside Cokego, Glasgow, Scotland, 1994-96; lectr. in social studies Dumfries and Galloway Coll., 1996—; hon. asst. chaplain Convent of the Holy Name, 1968-72. Bd. dirs. Crusaid Scotland, Edinburgh, 1993-97; vice chmn. South West Scotland Decorative and Fine Arts Soc., 1995-97. Fellow Soc. Antiquaries of Scotland; mem. N.Am. Patristics Soc. Conservative. Avocations: gardening, traveling. Home: Kindar House, New Abbey DG2 8DB, Scotland

BATSON, DAVID WARREN, lawyer; b. Wichita Falls, Tex., Jan. 4, 1956; s. Warren M. Batson and Jacqueline (Latham) Rhone. BBA, Midwestern State U., 1976; JD, U. Tex., 1979. Bar: Tex. 1980, U.S. Dist. Ct. (no. dist.) Tex. 1981, U.S. Tax Ct. 1981, U.S. Ct. Appeals (5th cir.) 1983, U.S. Ct. Appeals (D.C. cir.) 1983, U.S. Ct. Claims 1984, U.S. Supreme Ct. 1984. Atty. Arthur Andersen & Co., Ft. Worth, 1980-81; tax atty. The Western Co. of N.Am., Ft. Worth, 1981-85; sr. tax atty. Alcon Labs., Inc., Ft. Worth, 1985; gen. counsel Data Tailor, Inc., Ft. Worth, 1985-87; sr. tax atty. Arco, 1988-90; atty. pvt. practice, Wichita Falls, Tex., 1990—; lectr. U. of Tex., Arlington, 1984-85; of counsel Means & Means, Corsicana, Tex., 1985-86. Contbr. articles to profl. jours. Speaker A Wish With Wings, Arlington, Tex., 1984-85, Habitat for Humanity. Mem. Assn. Trial Lawyers Am., Tex. Bar Assn., Christian Legal Soc., Tex. Trial Lawyers Assn., State Bar at Tex. Coll., Phi Delta Phi. Avocations: negotiations, camping, self improvement. Address: PO Box 585 Stephenville TX 76401-0585

BATT, JÜRGEN OTTO HELMUT, mathematics educator; b. Gumbinnen, Germany, Aug. 18, 1933; s. Ulrich and Gerturd (Brummund) B.; m. Hannelore Edith Ulbricht, Dec. 20, 1966; children: Christiane, Astrid. Dr. rer. nat., Rein-Westfäl Tech. Hochsch. Aachen, 1962; Habilitation, Universität München, 1969, Ausserplanmässiger prof., 1974. Wiss. Mitarbeiter Kernforschungsanlage Jülich, 1962-64; wiss. asst. Universität Heidelberg, 1964-66; vis. prof. Kent State U., 1967-68, assoc. prof., 1970-71; Ordinarius Universität München, Fed. Republic Germany, 1976-99, mem. Acad. Senate, 1986-88, mem. Versammlung, 1988-98. Contbr. articles to profl. jours. Dekan Fakultät für Mathematik der Universitat München, 1977-79; co-editor Transport Theory and Statistical Physics. Mem. Am. Math. Soc., Deutsche Mathematiker Vereinigung. Office: Univ München Math Inst, Theresienstr 39, 80333 Munich Germany

BATT, RONALD ELMER, gynecologist, scientist; b. Buffalo, Sept. 24, 1933; s. Elmer Lawrence and Mary Catherine (Roll) B.; m. Carol Mary Schaab, Dec. 28, 1957; children: Paula, Douglas, Thomas, Neil, Jennifer, John; m. 2d, Kathleen Over Cansdale, May 19, 1982; stepchildren: William, James, Suzanne, Timothy, John, Mark. BS in Biology, Niagara U., 1954; MD, U. Buffalo, 1958. Intern Millard Fillmore Hosp., Buffalo, 1958-59; resident in ob-gyn SUNY, Buffalo, 1959-60, 62-66; rsch. fellow Harvard U. Med. Sch., 1963-64; asst. in surgery Peter Bent Brigham Hosp., Boston, 1963-64; fellow in gynecologic surgery Mayo Clinic, 1965; practice gynecology specializing in endometriosis and reproductive surgery Buffalo, 1966-98; researcher, 1966—; prof. clin. gynecology, clin. prof. social and preventive medicine SUNY Buffalo. Co-author: Another Era: A Pictorial History of the School of Medicine and Biomedical Sciences, State University of New York at Buffalo 1846-1996; contbr. chpts. to books, articles to profl. jours. With M.C., USN, 1960-62. Recipient Lifetime Career Achievement award Med. Alumni Assn. Sch. Medicine and Biomed. Scis. SUNY, 1998. Fellow Royal Coll. Surgeons Can., Am. Coll. Obstetricians and Gynecologists, ACS; mem. Am. Soc. Reproductive Medicine, Soc. Reproductive Surgeons, Am. Assn. History Medicine, Internat. Soc. History Medicine. Office: Buffalo Children's Hosp 219 Bryant St Buffalo NY 14222-2006

BATTENBERG, FRIEDRICH, archive director; b. Erbach, Deutschland, July 3, 1946; s. Friedrich Emanuel and Johanna (Reusch) B.; m. Hannelore Kuethe, May 14, 1971; children: Charlotte, Susanne, Eike. Dr. iuris utr., U. Frankfurt, Germany, 1973; prof., Tech. U. Darmstadt, Germany, 1990. Tech. U. Darmstadt, 1977-84; Archive dir. Staatsarchiv, Darmstadt, 1982—; prof. Tech. U. Darmstadt, 1990—. Author: (book) Das Europaeische Zeitalter der Juden, 2 vols., 1990, Herrschaft und Verfahren, 1995, Reichsacht und Anleite iml Spämittelalter, 1986; editor Aschkenas Zeitschrift für Geschichte und Kultur der Juden, 1991—. Mem. Arbeitsglmeinschaft geschichte und kultur der Juden, Vereinigung fuer Verfassungsgeschichte, Hessische Kirchengeschichtliche Vereinigung. Avocations: violin, viola, string quartet. Office: Haus der Geschichte, Haus der Gesichte, Karolinenplatz 3, Staatsarchiv, D-64289 Darmstadt Germany

BATTERMAN, STEVEN CHARLES, engineering mechanics and bioengineering educator, forensic engineering and biomechanics consultant; b. Bklyn., Aug. 15, 1937; s. Jacob and Anna (Abramowitz) B.; m. Judith Wilpon, Mar. 29, 1959; children: Scott David, Risa Karen, Daniel Adam. BCE, Cooper Union, 1959; ScM (NSF fellow), Brown U., 1961, PhD, 1964; MA (hon.), U. Pa., 1971. Mem. faculty U. Pa., 1964-97, prof. mech. engring. and applied mechanics, 1974-79; assoc. prof. orthopaedic surgery rsch. U. Pa. (Sch. Medicine), 1972-74, prof. orthopaedic surgery research, 1974-97; prof. biomechanics in vet. medicine U. Pa Sch. Vet Medicine, 1975-84, prof. bioengring., 1974-97; emeritus prof. Sch. Engring. and Applied Sci., Sch. Medicine U. Pa., 1997—; pres. Cons. Assocs., Inc., Cherry HIll, N.J.; forensic enring. and biomechanics cons. to govt., industry, ins. cos., attys. Contbr. numerous articles to profl. jours.; patentee apparatus for acoustically determining periodontal health. Recipient S.R. Warren Disting. Teaching award U. Pa., 1982. Mem. ASCE, ASME, Am. Acad. Mechanics, Am. Soc. Engring. Edn., Biomed. Engring. Soc., Soc. Exptl. Mech., Soc. Automotive Engrs., Am. Soc. Safety Engrs., Am. Acad. Forensic Scis. (Founder's award 1992, pres.-elect 1993-94, pres. 1994-95), Assn. for Advancement Automotive Medicine, Sigma Xi, Tau Beta Pi, Chi Epsilon. Jewish. Home: 109 Charlann Cir Cherry Hill NJ 08003-2906

BATTIAU-QUENEY, YVONNE, geography educator; b. Clermont-Ferrand, France, June 25, 1941; d. Paul and Paule (Thoumazou) Queney; m. Michel Battiau, June 30, 1969; 1 child, Nicole. LittD, U. Brest, France, 1978. Lectr. geography U. Lille, France, 1968-78, sr. lectr., 1978-91, head dept. geography, 1978-82, prof., 1992—. Author: Geomorphology of Wales. Pre-glacial inheritance in the present landscape, 1980, The landforms of France, 1993; mng. editor Hommes et Terres du Nord, 1979-93. Fellow Geol. Soc. London; mem. Soc. Geol. France, Assn. Geography France (mem. coun. 1993—), Assn. of French Geographers (vice pres.). Office: U Sci & Tech Lille, Cite Scientifique, 59655 Villeneuve d'Ascq Nord, France

BATTIGALLI, PIERPAOLO, ecomomics educator; b. Milan, Italy, June 18, 1961; s. Giancarlo and Letizia (Minio Paluello) B.; m. Alessandra Maria Cernuschi, Sept. 3, 1988. Laurea, U. Bocconi, Milan, Italy, 1987; MS, London Sch. Economics, 1989; Dottorato, Pooled Univs. Milan, 1992. Rsch. asst. U. Bocconi, Milan, Italy, 1991-92; asst. prof. Politecnico Di Milano, Milan, 1992-94, Princeton U., 1994-99; prof. European U. Inst., Fiesole, Italy, 1998—. Contbr. articles to profl. jours. Tenent, Italian Army, 1986. Mem. Am. Econ. Assn., Econ. Soc., Assn. Italian Economists in Foreign Countries, Game Theory Soc. Avocation: fencing. Office: European Univ Inst, 9 Via Dei Roccettini, 50016 Fiesole Italy

BATTIN, R(OSABELL) RAY (ROSABELL HARRIET RAY), audiologist, neuropsychologist; b. Rock Creek, Ohio; d. Harry Walter and Sophia (Boldt) Ray; m. Tom C. Battin, Aug. 27, 1949. AB, U. Denver, 1948; MS, U. Mich., 1950; PhD, U. Fla., 1959; postgrad., U. Miami (Fla.) Sch. Medicine, 1957, U. Iowa, 1958. Diplomate Am. Bd. Forensic Medicine, Am. Bd. Profl. Disability Cons., Am. Bd. Psychol. Spltys., Am. Bd. Forensic Examiners (cert. forensic examiner, cert. med. examiner); diploamte forensic neuropsychology, devel. psychology, psychol. assessment; lic. psychologist, Tex. Instr. in speech pathology U. Denver, 1949-50; audiologist Ann Arbor (Mich.) Sch., 1950-51, Houston Speech and Hearing Ctr., 1954-56; clin. fellow divsn. Clin. Svcs. U. Fla., Miama, 1952-54; dir. speech pathology/psychology Hedgecroft Hosp. and Rehab. Ctr., Houston, 1956-59; audiologist Drs. Guilford, Wright and Draper, Houston, 1959-63; pvt. practice psychology, audiology, and psycholinguistics Houston, 1959—; clin. instr. dept. otolaryngology U. Tex. Sch. Medicine, Galveston, 1964-80; dir. of audiology vestibulography and speech pathology lab. Houston Ear, Nose and Throat Hosp. Clinic, 1963-73; adj. clin. instr. U. Houston, 1981-86; lectr. The First Word program Sta. KUHT-TV, 1959; guest lectr. to various workshops and schs., 1959—; v.p. Behavioral Perceptual Ctr., 1986-90; neuropsychol. cons. edn. divsn. Environ. Health Screening Lab., 1989-99, mem. adv. bd., 1989-99. Author: (with C. Olaf Haug) Speech and Language Delay, 1964, Vestibulography, 1974, Private Practice: Guidelines for Speech Pathology and Audiology, 1971; editor (with Donna R. Fox) Private Practice in Audiology and Speech and Language Pathology, 1978; contbg. author: Seminars in Speech, Language, Hearing (Northern), Auditory Disorders in School Children (Roeser and Downs), Current Therapy of Communications Disorder (Perkins); editor Jour. Acad. Pvt. Practice in Speech Pathology and Audiology, 1981-84; contbr. articles in field to profl. jours.; author: (with Irvin A. Kraft) The Dysynchronous Child (film), 1971, Symposium Brain Plasticity As it Relates to the Remediation of Attention, Auditory Processing, Language and Reading Disorders, 1999; The Battin Clinic Language Learning Screening Test for Preschool Children, 1985, The Battin Scale of Parent's Attitude Toward Family Experience and Need for Child Cochlear Implant Candidates. Bd. dirs. Juvenile Ct. Vols., 1980-83, Children's Resource and Info. Ctr., 1981-85, Dyslexic Adult Support Svcs., 1986-90, Musicfest, 1991—, Houston repretory Theater, 1993—; mem. adv. bd. Caring Choices, 1993—, HSPVA Friends, 1998—. Recipient Gold award for Ednl. Exhibit, Am. Acad. Pediats., 1969, Lifetime Achievement award Houston Psychol. Assn., 1996. Fellow Am. Speech and Hearing Assn. (profl. svcs. bd. 1967-70, com. on pvt. practice 1971-74), World Acad. Inc.; mem. Internat. Assn. Applied Psychology, Am. Coll. Forensic Examiners, Acad. Pvt. Practice in Speech Pathology and Audiology (pres. 1968-70), Am. Psychol. Assn., Tex. Speech and Hearing Assn. (v.p. 1968), Tex. Psychol. Assn., Houston Psychol. Assn., Harris County Biofeedback Soc. (pres. 1984), Acad. of Aphasia, Internat. Assn. of Logopedics and Phoniatrics, Tex. Biofeedback Soc., Am. Acad. Audiology. Home: 3837 Meadow Lake Ln Houston TX 77027-4029 Office: Battin Clinic 4545 Post Oak Place Dr Ste 375 Houston TX 77027-3121

BATTISTELLA, LINAMARA, medical educator; b. São Paulo, Apr. 13, 1951; d. Gilberto and Maria de Lourdes Midoes Rizzo; m. Rubens Battistella, Dec. 20, 1973; children: Clarissa, Melissa, Fabio. Fellow U. São Paulo Sch. Medicine, 1974-77; clin. physician U. São Paulo Gen. Hosp., 1977-81, dir. rehab. svc., 1981-86, dir. rehab. dept., 1986; prof. postgrad. course U. São Paulo, 1990, São Paulo Cath. U. Med. Sch., 1995—; cons. mem. sci. bd. Haemophilia Jour., 1999; v.p. Internat. Fedn. Physical Rehab. Medicine. Editor: (book) Rehabilitation in Haemophilia, 1984, (jour.) Aeta Fisiatrica, 1994. Avocation: fitness. Office: HCUSP Div Medicine & Rehab, R Diderot 43, São Paulo Brazil

BATTISTI, ALFREDO, archbishop; b. Masi, Italy, Jan. 17, 1925. Ordained priest to Roman Cath. ch., 1947. Chancellor, vicar gen. Paduan (Italy) Diocese, 1947-73; archbishop City of Udine, Italy, 1994—; pres. Episcopal commn. for social problems and problems of the labour world Italian Episcopal Conf., 1979-82. Office: Arcivescovado, Via Treppo 7, 33100 Udine Italy*

BATTLE, JEAN ALLEN, writer, educator; b. Talladega, Ala., June 15, 1914; s. William Raines and Lemerle McLemore (Allen) B.; m. Lucy Troxell, Aug. 25, 1940; 1 dau., Helen Carol Battle Salmon. Student, Birmingham So. Coll., 1932-33; B.S., Middle Tenn. State U., 1937; M.A., U. Ala., 1941; Ed.D., U. Fla., 1952; postgrad., Oxford U., 1980. Dept. chmn., dean students Fla. So. Coll., 1940-55, dean coll., 1956-59; dean Coll. Edn. U. South Fla., Tampa, 1959-71; prof. higher edn. U. South Fla., 1971; guest lectr. Rewley House, Oxford U., 1981; editor, pub. Tenn. Valley News.; Mem. Fla. Tchrs. Edn. Adv. Council, Fla. Continuing Edn. Council; mem. courses study com. Fla. Bd. Edn.; mem. Tampa Bay Com. on Fgn. Affairs; adv. com. Hillsborough County Hosp.; bd. dirs. Fla. Univ. System Honduras Program, World Trade Council, Tampa, Poynter Found., St. Petersburg, Fla., Harold Benjamin Found., U. Md.; bd. dirs., v.p. Southeastern Edn. Lab., Atlanta. Author: Culture and Education for the Contemporary World, 1969, (with others) The New Idea in Education, 1974, Choices for an Intelligent and Humane School and Society, 1981, Education: The Fate of Humanity, 1982, rev., 1983; Contbr. papers to tech. lit. Served to capt. USAAF, 1942-46. Recipient Disting. Service awards Fla. So. Coll., 1952, Disting. Service awards Fla. Citizenship Clearing House, 1957; Outstanding Alumnus award Middle Tenn. State U. Mem. SAR, Fla. Hist. Soc., Nat. Edn. Assn., Fla. Edn. Assn. (co-chmn. tchr. recruitment com.), Tampa C. of C. (edn. com.), Acad. Polit. Sci., Oxford Soc. (sec. Fla. br. 1990—), Omicron Delta Kappa, Pi Gamma Mu, Kappa Delta Pi, Phi Delta Kappa, Sigma Alpha Epsilon. Methodist. Club: Carrollwood Village Golf and Tennis. Home: 11011 Carrollwood Dr Tampa FL 33618-3905

BATTLE, KATHLEEN DEANNA, soprano; b. Portsmouth, Ohio, Aug. 13, 1948; d. Grady and Ollie (Layne) B. MusB, U. Cin., 1970, MusM, 1971, D of Performing Arts (hon.), 1983; D of Performing Arts (hon.), Westminster Choir Coll., Ohio U.; D of Music (hon.), Xavier U., 1989; DHL, Amherst Coll., 1990. Appeared with Met. Opera, San Francisco Opera, Chgo. Opera, Salzburg Festival, N.Y. Philharm., Boston Symphony, Phila. Orch., Chgo. Symphony, Berlin Philharm., Vienna Staatsoper, Paris Opera, Royal Opera/Covent Garden, others; roles include Semele, Cleopatra in Julius Caesar, Pamina in Magic Flute, Susanna in Marriage of Figaro, Zerlina in Don Giovanni, Blonde in Abduction from the Seraglio, Rosina in Barber of Seville, Adina in Elixir of Love, Norina in Don Pasquale, Sophie in Der Rosenkavalier, Zerbinetta in Ariadne auf Naxos, Zdenka in Arabella; recordings include Salzburg Recital (Grammy, 1987), Kathleen Battle At Carnegie Hall (Grammy, 1992), Bel Canto, A Christmas Celebration, (with Jessye Norman) Spirituals in Concert, Pleasures of Their Company, Salzburg Recital, (with Placido Domingo) Live in Tokyo, (with Wynton Marsalis) Baroque Duet, (with Itzhak Perlman) The Bach Album. Recipient Grammy awards, 1987, 88. Mem. Delta Omicron. Methodist. Office: care Columbia Artists Mgmt Inc Epstein Divsn 165 W 57th St New York NY 10019-2201*

BATTLES, ROXY EDITH, novelist, consultant, educator; b. Spokane, Wash., Mar. 29, 1921; d. Rosco Jirah and Lucile Zilpha (Jacques) Baker; m. Willis Ralph Dawe Battles, May 2, 1941; children: Margaret Battles Holmes, Ralph, Lara. AA, Bakersfield (Calif.) Coll., 1940; BA, Calif. State U., Long Beach, 1959; MA, Pepperdine U., 1976. Cert. tchr. English, adult basic edn. and elem. edn., Calif. Free-lance writer 50 nat. and regional mags., 1940—; tchr. elem. Torrance (Calif.) Unified Schs., 1959-85; tchr. adult edn. Pepperdine U., Torrance, 1969-79, 88-89; free-lance children's author, 1966—; mystery novelist Pinnacle Publs., N.Y.C., 1980; with Tex. A&M U., 1988; instr. Mary Mount Coll., Harbor Coll., 1995; author-in-residence Young Authors Festival, Am. Sch. Madrid, 1991; lectr. in field. Author: Over the Rickety Fence, 1967, The Terrible Trick or Treat, 1970, 501 Balloons Sail East, 1971, The Terrible Terrier, 1972, One to Teeter-Totter, 1973, 2d edit., 1975, Eddie Couldn't Find the Elephants, 1974, reprints, 1982, 84, 88, What Does the Rooster Say, Yoshio?, 1978, The Secret of Castle Drai, 1980, The Witch in Room 6, 1987, 3d edit., 1989 (nominee Garden State, Nene, and Hoosier awards), The Chemistry of Whispering Caves, 1988, rev. edit., 1997, Computer Encryptions in Whispering Caves, 1997; playwright: Roxy, 1995, The Lavender Castle, 1996, mus. version, 1997, Sacred Submarine, 2000, Single Mothers, 2000. Active So. Calif. Coun. on Lit. for Children and Young People, 1973-80, 87—. Recipient Commendation UN, 1979; Hoosier award nominee, 1990; Garden State award nominee, 1990, Nene award nominee, 1992, 93. Mem. S.W. Manuscripters (founder), Surfwriters. Home: 560 S Helberta Ave Redondo Beach CA 90277-4353

BATTON, KENNETH DUFF, federal agency administrator, contractor, consultant; b. May 30, 1942; s. Roy L. and Heppie Duff (Mayson) B.; m. Deborah Dean Solsaa, Feb. 14, 1965; children: James Stanislaus, Michele Dean; m. June L. Baker Anderson, July 22, 1989. BS, Minn. State U., 1970. Naval aviator, 1959-63; EDP programmer operator Josten's, Inc., Owatonna, Minn., 1964-65; programmer, analyst, sr. analyst Minn. State U., 1965-70; EDP mgr. Associated Coll. Ctrl. Kans., 1971-72, U. Va., Charlottesville, 1973-74; sr. mgr. U. Va. Med. Ctr., Charlottesville, 1975-77; sys. cons. Glen Raven (N.C.) Mills, 1977; prin. PRC Data Svcs. Co., McLean, Va., 1977-78; dep. project dir. Computer Ctr. Exec. Office Pres., Washington, 1978; project dir. Alaska Fed. Data Processing Ctr., Anchorage for PRC Govt., Washington, 1978-83; mgmt. analyst NASA Hdqrs., 1983-84; data base adminstr. NASA Sci. and Tech. Info. Ctr., 1984-85; prin. cons. Govt. Info. Sys., Prince George's County, Md., 1985-86; configuration mgr. PRC/GIS NOAA GOES Project, Washington, 1986-88; freelance cons., pub., rschr., 1988—; instr. computer sci. Associated Colls. of Cen. Kans., McPherson, 1971-72. Mem. Data Processing Mgmt. Assn. (chpt. pres. 1977).

BATTY, PETER WRIGHT, television and film producer, director, writer; b. Sunderland, England, June 18, 1931; s. Ernest Faulkner and Gladys Victoria (Wright) B.; m. Anne Elizabeth Stringer, Mar. 21, 1959; children: David Alexander, Charlotte Elizabeth, Richard John. BA and MA, The Queen's Coll., Oxford U., 1954. Feature writer The Fin. Times, London, 1954-56; freelance journalist U.S.A., 1956-58; producer BBC, London, 1958-63; editor, Tonight Programme BBC TV, London, 1963-64; exec. producer, assoc. head factual programming ATV, London, 1964-68; chief exec. Peter Batty Prodns., London, 1968—. Author: The House of Krupp, 1966, La Guerre D'Algerie, 1989; co-author: The Divided Union, 1987; prodr., dir. and writer numerous TV programs, films and documentaries including The Quiet Revolution, 1961, The Big Freeze, 1963, The Fall and Rise of The House of Krupp, 1964 (Grand Prix, Venice Film Festival, Silver Dove, Leipzig Film Festival), The Road to Suez, 1965, Battle for the Desert, 1967, Battle for the Bulge, 1969, Birth of the Bomb, 1970, Superspy, 1974, The Rise and Rise and Laura Ashley, 1976, A Turn Up in a Million, 1981, The Algerian War, 1984, Fonteyn and Nureyev: The Perfect Partnership, 1985 (Internat. Emmy nomination), The Divided Union, 1987, A Time For Rememberance, 1989, Swastika Over British Soil, 1990, Tito, 1992, and many others, including 6 episodes of The World At War series. Mem. Dir.'s Guild, Garrick Club. Avocations: walking, reading, music. Home and Office: Claremont House, Renfrew Rd, Kingston Surrey KT2 7NT, England

BATULE, ROBERT JOHN, priest; b. Bklyn., May 23, 1958; s. Robert Philip and Ann Marie (Reilly) B. BA, Cathedral Coll., 1980; MDiv, Immaculate Conception, 1985; MA, Adelphi U., 1990, St. Johns U., 1996. Ordained priest Roman Cath. Ch., 1985. Parish priest St. Boniface Roman Cath. Ch., Elmont, N.Y., 1985-90, St. Martha Roman Cath. Ch., Uniondale, N.Y., 1990-93, Corpus Christi Roman Cath. Ch., Mineola, N.Y., 1993—; chmn., moderator Cath. Youth Orgn. Nassau and Suffolk, Hicksville, N.Y., 1997—. Contbr. articles to profl. jours. 2d lt. USAF, 1981-82. Mem. Fellowship of Cath. Scholars, Soc. Cath. Social Scientists, Nat. Assn. of Scholars. Roman Catholic. Avocations: athletics, reading. Office: Corpus Christi Roman Cath Ch 155 Garfield Ave Mineola NY 11501-2506

BATYGIN, GENNADY SEMYONOVITCH, sociologist, researcher; b. L'vov, Ukraine, USSR, Feb. 19, 1951; s. Semyon L'vovitch Gantman and Alexandra Ivanovna Batygina; m. Laryssa Alekseevna Kozlova; children: Edward, Gennady. Diploma, Moscow U., 1974; DSc, Inst. Sociology, Moscow, 1986, prof., 1991. Head, dept. sociology of knowledge Inst. Sociology, Russian Acad. Scis., Moscow. Author: The Lectures in Methodology of Sociological Research, The Foundations of Scietific Inference in Applied Sociology; editor-in-chief Jour. Sociology, 1994—. Grantee Russian Found. for Humanities, 1996-98, 00—, Russian Found. for Basic Rsch., 2000—, Nat. Tng. Found., 1999—, Soros Found., 1995. E-mail: gennady.batygin@msses.co.ru and batygin@isras.rssi.ru. Office: Inst Sociology RAS, 117259 Krzhizhanovskogo, 24/35 5 Moscow Russia

BATYGIN, YURI KONSTANTINOVICH, accelerator physicist; b. Moscow, Sept. 25, 1954; s. Konstantin Stepanovich and Valentina Fedorovna (Muhina) B.; m. Galina Zinov'evna Batunina, Oct. 6, 1979; children: Ekatherine, Konstantin. BS, Moscow Engring. Physics Inst., 1977, PhD, 1984; DSc in Physics and Math., Dubna Joint Inst. Nuc. Rsch., Russia, 1998. Researcher Moscow Engring. Physics Inst., 1977-86, sr. researcher, 1987-94; contract researcher Inst. Phys. and Chem. Rsch., Japan, 1994-99; sr. scientist high energy sys. divsn. Am. Sci. & Engring., Inc., Santa Clara, Calif., 2000—; vis. scientist Eindhoven U. Tech., The Netherlands, 1986-87. Editor: American Institute of Physics Proceedings Series, vol. 480, 1999; contbr. articles to profl. jours.; inventor in field. Mem. Am. Phys. Soc., N.Y. Acad. Scis. Home: 18045 Millwood Ln Morgan Hill CA 95037 Office: Am Sci & Engring Inc High Energy 3300 Keller St Bldg 101 Santa Clara CA 95054-2612

BAÚ, PLÍNIO CARLOS, surgeon, educator; b. Carazinho, Brazil, Jan. 1, 1953; s. Luiz João and Etelvina (Bozzetto) B.; m. Marilise Kostelnaki, Feb. 24, 1979; children: Patrícia, Plínio Carlos Baú Filho, Renata. MD, Porto Alegre U., Brazil, 1976, CM, 1978, DEd, 1991. Diplomate Brazilian Bd. Surgery. Asst. prof. dept. surgery Porto Alegre U., 1986—; judiciary dr. Ct. of Justice, Porto Alegre, 1988—. Mem. Surgeons' Brazilian Coll., Laparoscopic Surgery Brazilian Soc., Med. Assn. Rio Grande del Sul, Comenda Albert Sabin. Roman Catholic. Avocation: golf. Home: Rua Carajá 46, 91900-370 Porto Alegre RS, Brazil

BAUC, JAROSLAW, federal official; b. Lódz, Dec. 1, 1957; married, 2 children. M, Lódz U., 1982, PhD in Econs. and Sociology, 1991; MA in Econs., U. Windsor, Can., 1988. With Centre of Socio-Econ. Analyses, 1993-97, Bus. Rsch. and Promotion Ctr., 1993-97; adviser to fin. min. of Mongolia USAID; adviser to fin. min. of Romania, 1997; chmn. bd. suprs. Bank PKO BP, 1998-2000; sec. of state Ministry of Fin.; adj. Inst. of Econ. Growth Theories Lódz U., chair of econs.; chmn. bd. suprs. of Bank PKO BP; sec. of state Ministry of Fin., 1998. Contbr. articles to profl. jours. Avocations: classical music, sports. Office: Ministry of Fin, ul Swietokrzyska 12, 00-916 Warsaw Poland*

BAUCH, KARLHEINZ GEROLD, medical consultant; b. Chemnitz, Saxony, Germany, Feb. 19, 1936; s. Karl and Gerda (Martin) B.; m. Ursula-Ruth Naumann, May 30, 1974; children: Julia, Hendrik. MD, Med. Acad., Dresden, Germany, 1956; MD habil., U. Halle, Germany, 1982. Med. diplomate, subspecialist in diabetology and gastroenterology, subspecialist in endocrinology. Med. asst. dept. internal medicine Chemnitz, 1960; gen. practitioner Karl-Marx-Stadt, 1961, tng. in internal medicine, 1962-66; sr. registrar Clinic for Diabetes and Metabolic Diseases, 1967-81; head dept. gastroenterology and endocrinology, 1981; apptd. cosn. Med. Clinic, Chemnitz, 1990; pres. Soc. for Internal Medicine, Saxony Chemnitz, 1993-95. Editor: Interdisciplinary Issues of Iodine Deficiency, 1985, 89, 2000; contbr. chpts. to books and articles to profl. jours. Mem. Soc. for Advances in the Field of Internal Medicine, Acad. Scientists Leopoldina, Soc. for Metabolic Diseases and Endocrinology (pres. 1997-2000), German Soc. for Internal Medicine (mentor com. 1994-2000), N.Y. Acad. Scis. Lutheran. Avocations: literature, music. Home: Weydemeyerstrasse 13, 09117 Chemnitz Saxony, Germany Office: Med Clinic, Flemmingstrasse 2, 09116 Chemnitz Saxony, Germany

BAUCH, THOMAS JAY, lawyer, educator, financial/investment advisor; b. Indpls., May 24, 1943; s. Thomas and Violet (Smith) B.; m. Ellen L. Burstein, Oct. 31, 1982; children: Chelsea Sara, Elizabeth Tree. BS with honors, U. Wis., 1964, JD with highest honors, 1966. Bar: Ill. 1966, Calif. 1978. Assoc. Lord, Bissell & Brook, Chgo., 1966-72; lawyer, asst. sec. Marcor-Montgomery Ward, Chgo., 1973-75; spl. asst. to solicitor Dept. Labor, Washington, 1975-77; dep. gen. counsel Levi Strauss & Co., San Francisco, 1977-81, sr. v.p., gen. counsel, 1981-96, of counsel, 1996-2000; pvt. practice, Tiburon, Calif., 1996-2000; mng. dir. Laurel Mgmt. Co., L.L.C., San Francisco, 2000—; cons. prof. Stanford (Calif.) U. Law Sch., 1997—; ptnr. Ika Enterprises; mng. dir. Doughnet.com Inc.; dir., counsel Marine Desalinazation Svcs., LLC. Mem. U. Wis. Law Rev., 1964-66. Bd. dirs. Urban Sch., San Francisco, 1986-91, Gateway H.S., San Francisco, Charles Armstrong Sch., Belmont, Calif., San Francisco Opera Assn., Telluride Acad., Corinthian Acad.; bd. visitors U. Wis. Law Sch., 1991-95. Mem. Am. Assn. Corp. Counsel (bd. dirs. 1984-87), Bay Area Gen. Counsel Assn. (chmn. 1994), Univ. Club, Villa Taverna Club, Corinthian Yacht Club, Order of Coif, San Francisco Yacht Club. Office: Laurel Mgmt Co LLC Ste 1450 One Maritime Plaza San Francisco CA 94111

BAUCHET, PIERRE PAUL, retired social science educator; b. St Denis, France, Mar. 16, 1924; s. Ovide Bauchet and Elisabeth Marie Mazure; m. Jacqueline Griffon, June 23, 1953; children: Bernard, Emmanuelle, Pierre-Henri. Lic. in Law, U. Paris, 1945, LLD, 1949, agregation, 1958. Rschr. Nat. Ctr. Sci. Rsch., Paris, 1950-52, dir. human scis. and social scis., 1967-72, chmn. commn. econs., 1972-92; prof. U. Nancy, 1952-56; prof. dept. law U. Mohammed, Rabat, Morocco, 1956-58, U. Lille, France, 1958-62; dir. studies Ecole Nationale Adminstrn., Paris, 1962-66; prof. U. Paris, 1966—, chmn. dept. law, 1980-81, former pres., prof. emeritus, 1993—; mem. Inst. de France Academie des Scis. Morales et Politiques. Author: Les Tableaux Economiques: Analyse de la Région Lorraine, 1955, L'Experience Française de Planification, 1958, Propriété Publique et Planification, 1962, Bilan de Décentralisation Industrielle en France, 1964, Comptabilité Nationale et Analyse Economique, 1971, La Nouvelle Comptabilité Nationale, 1982, L'Economie du Transport International et Marchandises, Air et Mer, 1982, Le Plan dans l'Economie Française, 1986 (Prize Inst. France), Le Transport International dans l'Economie Mondiale, 1988, 2d edit., 1991, Le Transport Maritime, 1992, L'Imparfait Libéralisme, 1993, Les Transports de l'Europe, 1997, Les Transports Mondiaux, 1998, Comprendre l'Economie Française, 1999; contbr. articles to profl. jours. Scholar Columbia U., 1948-49; named Officer Legion Honor, Comdr. Order Merit, Officer Palmes Académiques. Mem. Académie Marine. Home: 12 Rue Pestalozzi, 75005 Paris France Office: CNRS, Rue Paul Bert, 94200 Ivry/Seine France

BAUCHOT, FREDERIC JACQUES, telecommunications engineer; b. Paris, May 8, 1959; s. Roland and Marie-Louise (Boutin) B.; m. Marie-Noëlle Basselier, Oct. 9, 1982; children: Jérôme, Lucie. PhD, CNRS, Paris, 1984. From design engr. to lead engr. IBM France, La Gaude, 1984-2000, chmn. CTS in CER, 1996—. Recipient Silver medal SEP, 1996; named French Engr. of Yr., 1996. Mem. IEEE (sr.). Home: 299 Chemin Du Vallon, 06640 Saint-Jeannet France Office: CER IBM France, Le Plan Du Bois, 06610 La Gaude France

BAUCHSPIESS, KARL RUDOLF, physicist; b. Cologne, Germany, Sept. 24, 1955; s. Rudolf and Gertrud (Dostert) B. Diplom, U. Koln, 1982; PhD, Simon Fraser U., Burnaby, B.C., Can., 1990. Vis. scientist IBM Almaden Rsch. Ctr., San Jose, 1989-90, Photon Factory, Nat. Lab. for High Energy Physics, Tsukuba, Ibaraki, Japan, 1990-92; rsch. fellow Murdoch U. (Western Australia), 1992-95, Curtin U. (Western Australia), 1995-96, Fla. A&M U., Tallahassee, 1996, U. Trento, Italy, 1997, U. Bonn, Germany, 1997-99; with Inst. Space Simulation German Aerospace Ctr., Koeln, Germany, 1999—; vis. prof. Simon Fraser U., Burnaby, B.C., Can., 1996. Contbr. articles to profl. jours. Mem. Am. Phys. Soc., German Phys. Soc. Roman Catholic. Office: German Aerospace Ctr (DLR), Inst Space Simulation, Linder Hoehe 51147 Koeln Germany

BAUDET, FRANCIS ANDRE, sociologist, educator; b. Les Autels-Villevillon, France, Oct. 11, 1946; s. Andre Louis and Marthe Eva (Durrat) B.; m. Danielle Nicole Maillot, Feb. 18, 1969 (separated); 1 child, Adrien-Karl. Gen. Cert. Edn., France, 1964, M in Philosophy, 1967, PhD Sociology, 1971. Tchr. ITA of Mostaganem, Algeria, 1971-73; asst. prof. U. Constantine, Algeria, 1973-83; qualified tchr. sociology U. Paris VIII, 1983—; pub.'s reader, OPU, Algiers, 1973-83. Contbr. articles to profl. jours. With Algerian mil., 1971-72. Home: 46 Ave Lemonnier, F-78160 Marly Le Roi France

BAUDET, JEAN CLAUDE, philosopher, editor; b. Brussels, May 31, 1944; s. Emile and Marguerite (De Souter) B.; m. Marianne Claire Allard, Sept. 18, 1965. Ing. Indsl., ISIB, Brussels, 1964; DSc, U. Paris, 1977. Rschr. Faculty of Agronomy, Gembloux, Belgium, 1968-77; editor-in-chief Technologia, Brussels, 1978-89; pres. APPS, Brussels, 1981-96; editor sci. and philosophy Revue G n rale, 1996—. Author: Les Cereales Mineures, 1981, Les Ingenieurs Belges, 1986; founder Technologia, 1978. Mem. Conseil Superieur de la Langue Française, Brussels, 1993—. Recipient chevalier Ordre de Leopold, officier Ordre de Leopold II (Belgium). Mem. Comite Belge D'Histoire des Sciences.

BAUDET, MONIQUE MARIE, chemistry educator; b. Souk-el-Khenis, Tunisia, July 22, 1941; d. Augustin Henri Marie and Marie Louise Adeline (Bollard) B.; m. Pierre Alfred Cyr Riviere, Sept. 7, 1967; children: Anne, Nicolas. Baccalaureat, Oratoire/Ste Marie, Auch, France, 1958; Lic. DSc, U. Toulouse, France, 1962, DS in Physics, 1972. Maitre asst. U. Toulouse, France, 1963-80, maitre de conferences, 1981-91, prof., 1992; postdoctoral fellow with P M.F. Lappert, Sussex, Eng., 1975. Co-author book in field; contbr. articles to profl. jours. Mem. Soc. Chem./France, Royal Soc. of Chemistry, Soroptimist. Roman Catholic. Avocations: lectr. in field, travel. Office: Heterochimie Fondamentale, Applique/U Paul Sabatier, 31062 Toulouse Cedex, France

BAUDHUIN, PIERRE, cell biologist, physician; b. Leuven, Belgium, July 17, 1934; s. Fernand Baudhuin and Madeleine Renoirte; m. Madeleine Van Aubel, Dec. 14, 1963; children: Alain, François, Vinciane, Frederic. MD, U. Cath. de Louvain, 1958. Charge de recherche Fonds Nat. de la Rsch. Sci., Louvain, 1963-64, 65-67, chercheur qualifie, 1967-71; rsch. assoc. Rockefeller U., N.Y.C., 1964-65; charge de cours U. Cath. de Louvain, 1971-72, prof., 1972-79; prof. ordinaire U. Cath. de Louvain, Brussels, 1979-99, prof. emeritus, 1999—; dir. Info. des Cliniques Univs. St. Luc, Brussels, 1989-91, Unite de Biologie Cellulaire-U. Cath. de Louvain, Brussels, 1989-99; cons. Cliniques Univ. St. Pierre, Louvain, 1971-72. Author: Cytologie et Biologie Cellulaire, 1994; contbr. over 200 articles to profl. jours. Recipient Laureat du Concours des Bourses de Voyage, Belgian Govt., 1958. Mem. AAAS, Am. Med. Info. Assn., N.Y. Acad. Scis., Internat. Soc. Cell Biology. Home: rue de la Cambre 151, B-1150 Brussels Belgium

BAUDIN, BRUNO, biochemist, educator; b. Charquemont, Doubs, France, Dec. 18, 1958; s. Jacques and Jeannine (Tanner) B.; m. Christine Oudot, May 4, 1996; children: Florian, Léna, Ludovic. D of Pharmacy, UFR Medicine/Pharmacy, Besançon, France, 1981; M in Biochemistry, Paris VI U., 1987; PhD of Pharm. Scis., Paris V U., 1989. Intern pharmacy Paris Hosp., 1981-88; biologist Saint Antoine Hosp., Paris, 1988-90; asst. educator UFR Pharmacy, Paris, 1989-2000, prof., 2000—; biologist Saint Antoine Hosp., Paris, 1990—. Contbr. articles to profl. jours. Commandant French Mil. Health Divsn., 1983. Grantee French Found. Med. Rsch., 1985. Mem. French Soc. Biochemistry and Molecular Biology. Office: Hosp St Antoine Biochimie A, 184 rue du Fanbourg St Antoine, 75571 Paris Cedex 12, France

BAUDIS, PAVEL, psychiatrist, researcher; b. Prague, Czech Republic, Oct. 2, 1930; s. Vaclav and Ludmila (Gabrielova) B.; m. Alena Kolouskova, Aug. 2, 1956; children: Pavel, Eva, Vaclava. MD, Charles U., Prague, 1955, PhD, 1966. Lic. in psychiatry Bd. Edn., Prague, 1960; cert. specialist in psychiatry and rsch. Resident in psychiatry Hosp. Karlovy Vary, Czech Republic, 1955-56; psychiatrist Psychiat. U. Hosp., Plzen, Czech Republic, 1958-62, vice dir., 1962-74; rsch. and clin. psychiatrist Psychiat. Rsch. Inst., Prague, 1974-86; dir. psychiat. dept. Psychiat. Ctr., Prague, 1986-93, rsch. psychiatrist, 1993—; cons. Ministry of Health Czech Republic, Prague, 1992-99; chmn. ethics com. Psychiat. Ctr., Prague, 1992—; mem. exec. bd. FOCUS, Prague, 1992—; mem. exec. bd. Ctr. for Devel. of Psychiatry, 1994—. Mem. editl. bd. Socijalna Psihijatrija, 1986—; contbr. articles to profl. jours. Recipient medal Mil. Acad. Lodz, Poland, 1978, medal Swedish Med. Soc., Stockholm, 1997. Mem. Czech Psychiat. Soc. (sec. 1997—), Vondracek's Found. (mem. sci. bd. 1993—), Czech Psychiat. Assn. (pres. 1990-94, sec., v.p. 1994—). Avocations: World War II history, travel, psychiatric jokes. Office: Psychiatricke centrum, Ustavni 91, 181 03 Prague 8, Czech Republic

BAUDLER, MARIANNE, chemistry educator, researcher; b. Stettin, Germany, Apr. 27, 1921; d. Fritz and Clara (Siermann) B. DiplChem, Tech. U., Dresden, Germany, 1943; DrRerNat, U. Göttingen, Germany, 1946. Asst. prof. chemistry U. Köln, Germany, 1949-62, assoc. prof., 1963-67, prof., 1968-86, dir. Inst. Inorganic Chemistry, 1968-86, prof. emeritus, 1986—. Contbr. more than 280 articles to various internat. jours. including Zeitschrift für Anorganische und Allgemeine Chemie, Angewandte Chemie, Chemische Berichte, Zeitschrift für Naturforschung, Chem. Rev. Mem. German Chem. Soc. (Alfred-Stock-Gedächtnispreis 1986), German Soc. for Sci. and Art, German Acad. Sci. Leopoldina, Acad. Sci. U. Göttlingen. Day time telephone: 0221/401445. Office: Inst Inorganic Chemistry, U Köln, Greinstr 6, D-50939 Köln Germany

BAUDOIN, TOMISLAV, otolaryngologist; b. Zagreb, Croatia, Mar. 25, 1964; s. Vladimir and Maja (Putanec) B.; m. Andrea Fiser, Sept. 3, 1994; children: Borna, Ivan, Marko. MD, Zagreb Sch. Medicine, 1989, Zagreb Sch. Medicine, 1996. Gen. practitioner Zagreb, Croatia, 1990-91; referee med. affairs Croatian Army, 1991-92; resident in otolaryngology Univ. Hosp. S.M., Zagreb, 1992-96, specialist ear, nose & throat physician, head/neck surgeon, 1996—; asst. Zagreb Sch. Medicine, 1997—; chief pediat. ENT dept. Univ. Hosp. S.M., 1996—. Editl. bd. Symposia Otorhinolaryngology, 1996. Mem. Croatian Assn. ENT/Head & Neck Surgery, European Rhinologic Soc. Office: Univ Hosp SM, Vinogradska 29, HR-10000 Zagreb Croatia

BAUDUSCH, RENATE, Germanist; b. Erfurt, Germany, June 4, 1929; d. Arthur and Margarete (Kahle) Walker; m. Heinz Baudusch, Nov. 26, 1957; 1 child, Sondra. PhD, Humboldt U., Berlin, 1956; DSc, Humboldt U., 1970. Germanist Akademie der Wissenschaften, Berlin, 1956-89. Author: Klopstock als Sprachwissenschaftler und Orthographiereformer, 1958, Die nominalen Kategorien in der danischen Grammatik, 1970, Punkt, Punkt, Komma, Strich, 1984. Mem. Goethe Gesellschaft, Internationale Vereinigung fur germanische Sprach- und Literaturwissenschaft, Gesellschaft fur deutsche Sprache, Deutscher Germanistenverband. Evangelisch. Home: Moldaustrasse 11, 10319 Berlin Germany

BAUER, ANTONIE GERTRUD, journalist; b. Munich, Germany, Dec. 12, 1961; d. Martin Simon and Gertrud (Wild) B. Diploma in Econs., Munich U., 1988, PhD in Econs., 1992. Journalist Sueddeutscher Rundfunk, Stuttgart, Germany, 1983-85, Bayerischer Rundfunk, Munich, 1985-86; editor-in-chief APF, Munich, 1986-91; asst. prof. Munich U., 1988-94; editor Forbes, Munich, 1994-95, Sueddeutsche Zeitung, Munich, 1995—. Author: Der Treibhauseffekt, 1993; co-author: Mikrooekonomie, 1994, Stichwort Spezial: Geld, 1996; contbr. articles to profl. jours. Home: Hans-Sachs-Str 12, 80469 Munich Germany Office: Sueddeutsche Zeitung, Sendlinger Str 8, 80331 Munich Germany

BAUER, A(UGUST) ROBERT, JR., surgeon, educator; b. Phila., Dec. 23, 1928; s. A(ugust) Robert and Jessie Martha-Maynard (Monie) B.; BS, U. Mich., 1949, MS, 1950, MD, 1954; M Med. Sci.-Surgery, Ohio State U., 1960; m. Charmaine Louise Studer, June 28, 1957; children: Robert, John, William, Anne, Charles, James. Intern Walter Reed Army Med. Ctr., 1954-55; resident in surgery Univ. Hosp., Ohio State U., Columbus, also instr., 1957-61; pvt. practice medicine, specializing in surgery, Mt. Pleasant, Mich., 1962-74; chief surgery Ctrl. Mich. Community Hosp., Mt. Pleasant, 1964-65, vice chief of staff, 1967, chief of staff, 1968; clin. faculty Mich. State Med. Sch., East Lansing, 1974; mem. staff St. Mark's Hosp., Salt Lake City, 1974-91; pvt. practice surgery, Salt Lake City, 1974-91; clin. instr. surgery U. Utah, 1975-91. Trustee Rowland Hall, St. Mark's Sch., Salt Lake City, 1978-84; mem. Utah Health Planning Coun., 1979-81. Served with M.C., U.S. Army, 1954-57. Diplomate Am. Bd. Surgery. Fellow ACS, Southwestern Surg. Congress; mem. AMA, Salt Lake County Med. Soc., Utah Med. Assn. (various coms.), Utah Soc. Certified Surgeons, Salt Lake Surg. Soc., Pan Am. Med. Assn. (affiliate), AAAS (affiliate), Sigma Phi Epsilon, Phi Rho Sigma. Episcopalian. Club: Zollinger. Contbr. articles to profl. publs., researcher surg. immunology. Office: PO Box 17533 Salt Lake City UT 84117-0533 Address: 1366 Murray Holladay Rd Salt Lake City UT 84117-5050

BAUER, BRENT A., physician; b. Madison, Wis., Apr. 5, 1962. BA, U. Minn., 1984; MD, Mayo Med. Sch., 1988. Diplomate Am. Bd. Internal Medicine. Physician Mayo Clinic, Scottsdale, Ariz., 1992-96, Rochester, Minn., 1996—. Recipient Young Rschrs. award Am. Heart Assn., Mpls., 1986. Mem. AMA (young physician rep.). Republican. E-mail: bauer.brent@mayo.edu.

BAUER, BRIGITTE LOUISE MARIA, linguistics researcher, educator; b. Oss, The Netherlands, May 25, 1960; d. Marius Gerardus Martinus and Maria Clara (Steinhauser) B.; m. Paul Leendert Clemens Winkes, Sept. 6, 2000. MA in French Linguistics and Lit., U. Nijmegen, The Netherlands, 1987, MA in Art History and Archaeology, 1988, PhD in Linguistics, 1992. Tchg. asst. U. Nijmegen, 1985-87, univ. asst., 1988-92; fellow Niels Stensen Found., Amsterdam, The Netherlands, 1992-93, Royal Netherlands Acad. Arts and Scis., Amsterdam, 1993-96; lectr. U. Nijmegen, 1996-98; asst. prof. French linguistics U. Tex., Austin, 1999—; vis. scholar U. Tex., Austin, 1992, 94, 96, 97; vis. scholar Wolfson Coll., Cambridge, Eng., 1992-93, 95, vis. fellow, 1996, 97. Author: The Emergence and Development of SVO Patterning in Latin and French. Diachronic and Psycholinguistic Perspectives, 1995, Archaic Syntax in Indo-European. The Spread of Transitivity in Latin and French, 2000; contbr. articles to internat. profl. jours. Mem. adv. bd. IE Doc. Ctr. U. Texas, 1998—, Sorority, Nijmegen, 1982-87, pres., 1985. Recipient Rsch. award Niels Stensen Found., Amsterdam, 1992. Mem. MLA, Linguistic Soc. Am., Indogermanische Gesellschaft, Soc. Linguistica Europaea, Philol. Soc. U.K., Internat. Soc. Hist. Linguistics. Avocations: sports, reading, gardening. Home: Staringstraat 34, 6521 AK Nijmegen The Netherlands Office: Dept French & Italian Univ Tex Austin TX 78712-1197

BAUER, ERNST GEORG, physicist, educator; b. Schoenberg, Germany, Feb. 27, 1928. MS, U. Munich, 1953, PhD in Physics, 1955. Rsch. asst. U. Munich, 1955-58; head crystal physics br. Michelson Lab., China Lake, Calif., 1958-69; prof. Tech. U. Clausthal, Germany, 1969-96; disting. rsch. prof. Ariz. State U., Tempe, 1993—. Author: Elektronenbeugung, 1958. Recipient Gaede prize German Vacuum Soc., 1988, Welch award Am. Vacuum Soc., 1992, Niedersachsenpreis, 1994. Fellow Am. Phys. Soc., Am. Vacuum Soc.; mem. Goettingen Acad. Sci., Materials Rsch. Soc., German Electron Microscopy Soc. Office: Ariz State Univ Dept Phys Astronomy Tempe AZ 85287-1504

BAUER, FRIEDRICH LUDWIG, mathematician, educator; b. Regensburg, Bavaria, Fed. Republic Germany, June 10, 1924; s. Ludwig and Elisabeth (Scheuermayer) B.; m. Irene Maria Theresia Laimer, June 15, 1949 (dec. Aug. 1973); m. Hildegard Vogg, Mar. 16, 1974; children: Gertrud Josefine, Martin Alston, Margret Elisabeth, Ulrich Alexander, Bernhard Klaus. PhD, U. Munich, 1952, DSc, 1954; DSc (hon.), Grenoble (France) U., 1974, Passau (Germany) U., 1989, Munich U. of the Armed Forces, 1998. Tchg. asst. Tech. U. Munich, 1952-54, lectr., 1954-58, prof. math., 1963-72, prof. math. and computer sci., 1972-89; prof. emeritus, 1989—; prof. applied math. Mainz (Fed. Republic of Germany) U., 1958-62; co-dir. Leibniz Computing Ctr., Munich, 1968—. Author: Kryptologie, Springer, Berlin, 1993, 2d edit., 1994, Decrypted Secrets, 1997, 2nd edit., 2000; contbr. articles to profl. jours. Served as 2d lt. German Army, 1943-45. Awarded Bavarian Order of Merit, 1971, Wilhelm Exner medal Republic of Austria, 1978, Fed. Cross of Merits, Fed. Republic of Germany, 1982, Goldener Ehrenring des Deutschen Mus., 1988, IEEE Computer Pioneer award 1988. Mem. Bavarian Acad. of Sci., Deutsche Akademie der Naturforscher Leopoldina, Bayerischer Maximiliansorden für Wissenschaft, Austrian Acad. Scis. Roman Catholic. Avocations: piano, organ. Home: Nördliche Villenstrasse 19, D-82288 Kottgeisering Germany

BAUER, GASTON EGON, cardiologist; b. Vienna, Austria, May 7, 1923; m. Phyllis Smith, Jan. 7, 1949; children: Christopher, Michael, Timothy. MB, BS, U. Sydney, Australia, 1946, MD, 1995. Hon. physician Sydney Hosp., 1956-76; hon. cons. physician Hornsby and Kuringai Hosp., Australia, 1964-81, Manly Dist. Hosp., Australia, 1964-88; hon. physician in cardiology Royal North Shore Hosp., St. Leonard's, Australia, 1976—; warden of clin. sch. Royal North Shore Hosp., Australia, 1979-85. Contbr. articles to profl. jours., chpts. to med. books. Fellow of senate U. Sydney, 1982-93. Recipient univ. medal and Arthur E. Mills grad. prize U. Sydney, 1946, Archie Telfer prize Sydney Hospitallers, 1963. Mem. Royal Coll. Physicians (London), Royal Australian Coll. Physicians (councillor 1975-81), Am. Coll. Cardiology, Cardiac Soc. Australia and N.Z. (councillor 1977-83), Australian Med. Assn., Royal Soc. Med. London (corr.), Order of Australia. Home: 115 Shirley Rd, Roseville New South Wales 2069, Australia

BAUER, GÜNTHER, science educator; b. Korneuburg, Austria, Mar. 26, 1936; s. Otto and Margit (Droppa) B.; m. Felicitas Molowa, July 22, 1965. Diploma Engring., Technische Hochschule, Vienna, 1962; Dr. techn., Tech. U., Vienna, 1965, U. Doz., 1975. Univ. asst. Tech. U., Vienna, 1964-78, univ. prof., 1978—; head Inst. Gen. Chemistry, U. Tech., Vienna. Author publs. in field. Avocations: ceramics, tennis, chess. Office: Inst Tech Electrochem/Solid St Chem, Gumpendorferstrasse 1a, Vienna A-1060, Austria

BAUER, HEINZ, mathematician; b. Nurnberg, Germany, Jan. 31, 1928; s. Hans and Elise (Buetler) B.; m. Irene Poellet, Oct. 4, 1957; children: Christian, Christine. Student, U. Nancy, France; DPhilNatural, U. Erlangen, Germany, 1953, Habilitation, 1956; DSc (hon.), Technische U. Dresden, Germany, Charles U., Prague, Czech Republic. Rsch. fellow Centre Nat. Recherche Scientifique, Paris, 1956; prof., dir. Inst. Versicherungmathematik/Mathematische Stat. U. Hamburg, 1962-65, dean Faculty of Sci., 1963-64; dozent U. Erlangen-Nurnberg, 1956-58, prof. math., co-dir. Math. Inst., 1965—; vis. assoc. prof. U. Wash., Seattle, 1961-62; vis. prof. U. Paris, 1964, 79, Calif. Inst. Tech., 1967, N.Mex. State U., 1968. Author: Wahrscheinlichkeitstheorie und Grundzuge der Masstheorie, 1964, 3d edit. 1973; Harmonische Raume und Ihre Potentialtheorie, 1966; Probability Theory and Elements of Measure Theory, 1972, 2d edit., 1981, Wahrscheinlichkeitstheorie, 4th edit., 1991, Probability Theory, 1996, Mass- und Integrationshteiroe, 2d edit., 1992, Measure and Integration Theory, 2000; co-editor: Mathematische Annalen; Expositiones Mathematicae, de Gruyter Studies in Mathematics; rsch., pubs. on contbns. to integration theory, functional analysis, probability theory and potential theory. Decorated Bavarian Order of Merit, Bavarian Maximilian-Order; recipient Chaubenet prize Math. Assn. Am., 1980. Mem. Bavarian Acad. Scis., Munich Acad., Acad. Leopoldina Halle, Austrian Acad. Sci., Royal Danish Acad. Sci., Finnish Acad. Sci., Deutsche Mathematiker-Vereinigung (pres. 1976-77), Am. Math. Soc., Soc. Mathematique de France. Home: 17 Eschenweg, D-91058 Erlangen Germany Office: 1 1-2 Bismarckstrasse, D-91054 Erlangen Germany

BAUER, JEROME LEO, JR., chemical engineer; b. Pitts., Oct. 12, 1938; s. Jerome L. and Anna Mae (Tucker) B.; children from previous marriage: children: Lori, Trish, Jeff. BSChemE, U. Dayton, 1960; MSChemE, Pa. State U., 1963; postgrad., Ohio State U., 1969. Registered profl. engr., Ohio. Asst. prof. chem. engring. U. Dayton, Ohio, 1963-67; mgr. advanced composites dept. Ferro Corp., Cleve., 1967-72; engring. material and process specifications mgr. Lockheed Missiles & Space Co., Inc., Sunnyvale, Calif., 1972-74; gen. dynamics design specialist Convair Div., San Diego, 1974-76, project devel. engr., 1976-77; dir. research Furane div. M&T Chems. Inc., Glendale, Calif., 1980-82; mem. tech. staff Jet Propulsion Lab., Calif. Inst. Tech., Pasadena, Calif., 1977-80, 82-90; mem. tech. staff mfg. engring. The Aerospace Corp., El Segundo, Calif., 1990—, engring. specialist, 1997—. Editor: Materials Sciences for Future, 1986, Moving Foreward With 50 Years of Leadership in Advanced Materials, 1994, Materials and Processes Challenges, 1996, Evolving & Revolutionary Technologies for the New Millennium, 1999; contbr. articles to profl. jours. Jr. warden St. Luke Episcopal Ch., La Crescenta, Calif., 1980, sr. warden 1981. Fellow Internat. Elec-

tronics Packaging Soc. (pres. L.A. chpt. 1982), Soc. Advancement of Material Process Engring. (membership chmn. no. Calif. sect. 1973-74, vice chmn. San Diego sect. 1974-75, chmn. 1975-76, chmn. 1976, chmn. L.A. sect. 1977, internat. nat. treas. 1978-82, gen. chmn. 31st internat. symposium exhbn., Las Vegas, Nev., 1986, Meritorious Achievement award 1983, internat. v.p. 1987-89, internat. pres. 1989-90); mem. Am. Inst. Chem. Engrs. (founder, chmn. Dayton sect. 1964-66, spl. projects chmn. Cleve. sect. 1968-69), Phi Lambda Upsilon, Delta Sigma Epsilon. Republican. Avocations: carpentry, photography, camping. Home: PO Box 3298 El Segundo CA 90245-8398 Office: The Aerospace Corp 2350 E El Segundo Blvd El Segundo CA 90245-4691

BAUER, JOHANN, biologist, researcher, consultant; b. Pestendorf, Germany, Apr. 9, 1952; s. Johann and Walburga (Schranner) B.; m. Sigrid Hildegard Bucher, Oct. 15, 1959; 1 child, Thomas. Diploma, U. Munich, 1978, PhD, 1981. Staff Max-Planck-Inst., Martinsried, Germany, 1978-81; rschr. Max-Planck-Inst., Martinsried, 1983-89, rschr., cons., 1991—; postdoctoral staff Duke U., Durham, N.C., 1982; rschr. U. Regensburg, Germany, 1989-91. Editor: Cell Electrophoresis, 1994. Mem. Fedn. Am. Socs. Exptl. Biology, Internat. Electrophoresis Soc., N.Y. Acad. Sci. Achievements include patent for table top elutriator for preparative cell purification. Office: Max Planck Inst Biochem, D-82152 Martinsried Germany

BAUER, MARIA CASANOVA, computer engineer; b. Cienfuegos, Las Villas, Cuba, Jan. 1, 1954; came to U.S., 1979; d. Manuel José and Loida Eugenia (Ojeda) Casanova; m. Lawrence D. Bauer, Feb. 14, 1997; 1 child, Ingrid. BSEE cum laude, U. Miami, 1985; MS, U. Cen. Fla., 2000. Software engr. Martin Marietta Corp., Orlando, Fla., 1986-89; computer engr., mgr. software acquisition, Tng. Sys. divsn. Naval Air Warfare Ctr., Orlando, 1989-97; project dir. U.S. Army Simulation, Tng. and Instrumentation Command, Orlando, 1997—; software arch. U.S. Army Simulation, Tng. and Instrumentation Command, Orlando, 1997. Mem. IEEE, Golden Key, Sigma Xi, Tau Beta Pi, Eta Kappa Nu, Phi Kappa Phi. Achievements include co-development of weapons system for Desert Storm. Home: 3212 Lake George Cove Dr Orlando FL 32812-6844

BAUER, PIERRE, electrical engineer; b. Paris, France, Sept. 3, 1941; s. Roger and Henriette (Hanauer) B.; m. Daniele Marguerite Pachoud; children: Sylvie, Isabelle, Jerome. BSEE, Poly. Inst. Grenoble, 1964; MS, U. Mich., 1965, PhD, 1968. From asst. dir. CRPE CNRS to dir. CESBIO, Toulouse, France, 1969-98; dir. rsch. LEGOS, Toulouse, 1999—. Mem. Internat. Union Radio Sci. (pres. 1993-96). Home: 17 Route des Bardis, 31320 Rebigue France Office: CNES BPI 2526, 18 Av Edouard Belin, 31401 Toulouse Cedex 4, France

BAUER, RAYMOND GALE, sales professional; b. Merchantville, N.J., June 19, 1934; s. Robert Iwrin and Florence Winifred (Guyer) B.; m. Jayne Whitehead, Feb. 15, 1955; 1 child, Linda Joan. AA, Monmouth Coll., 1955; BBA, U. Miami, 1958. Disvn. mgr. R.J. Reynolds Tobacco Co., Winston-Salem, N.C., 1959-68; mgr. Mid-Atlantic U.S. Envelope Co., Springfield, Mass., 1968-74; divsn. sales mgr. Eastern Tablet Corp., Albany, N.Y., 1974-75; owner Ray Bauer Assocs., mfrs. reps., Haddonfield, N.J. With USAFR, 1959-64; officer USAF Aux. Mem. Friends of Haddonfield Libr., Haddonfield Civic Assn., Smithsonian Assn., U. Miami Alumni Assn., Monmouth U. Alumni Assn., Nat. Philatelic Soc., Am. Security Coun., Air Force Assn., Am. Conservative Union, Am. Mgmt. Assn., Internat. Platform Assn., Sch. and Home Office Products Assn., Am. Legion, Rep. Club Haddonfield, U.S. Sentatorial Club, Arrowhead Racquet Club, Iron Rock Swim and Country Club, Lambda Sigma Tau, Lambda Chi Alpha. Home and Office: 132 Maple Ave Haddonfield NJ 08033-1432

BAUER, ROGER, literature educator; b. Seebach, France, Dec. 4, 1918; s. René and Francoise (Levy) B.; m. Edith Strasser, Apr. 24, 1948; 1 child, René Sebastian. Diploma, Ecole Normale Superieure, 1934; Agrege, U. Sorbonne, Paris, 1945; Dr. Letters, U. Sorbonne, 1965. Prof. U. Munster, W. Ger., 1948-49, U. Cologne, W. Ger., 1949-55, U. Bonn, W. Ger., 1955-62; dir. Institut Francais, Bonn, 1955-62; prof. comparative lit. U. Saarland, Saarbruecken, 1962-65; prof. Germanics Faculte des Lettres, U. Strasbourg, France, 1965-69; prof. comparative lit. U. Munich, 1969-88, prof. emeritus, 1987—; assesseur Bur. of Assn. Internat. Comparative Lit., 1976-82, v.p., 1982-88. Author: La Realite, Royaume de Dieu, 1965, Dir Schöne Dierdence, 2000; contbr. articles to profl. jours. Commandeur de l'Ordre des Palmes Academiques, Presidence du Conseil, Paris, 1988. Mem. Deutsche Akademie fur Sprache und Dichtung, Academia Scientiarum et Litterarum Moguntina. Home: Aiblingerstrasse 8, 80639 Munich Germany

BAUER, THOMAS GÜNTHER, travel and tourism educator, consultant; b. Erlangen, Bavaria, Germany, Apr. 11, 1954; arrived in Australia, 1986; s. Günther and Engelfriede (Dütsch) B.; m. Lina M. Wong, Jan. 20, 1984; children: Joseph, Sebastian. B of Bus., Fachhochshcule Landshut, Landshut, Germany, 1979, Fachhochschule, Munich, 1980; M of Bus. in Tourism Devel., Victoria U. Tech., Melbourne, Australia, 1991; PhD in Antarctic Tourism, Monash U., Melbourne, 1998. Apprentice Carlton Hotel, Nürnberg, Franconia, Germany, 1971-74; bus. mgr. KWG Devel., Marina, Calif., 1983-85; tutor Footscray Inst., Melbourne, 1988; lectr. in travel and tourism Victoria Union of Tech., Melbourne, 1989-94; sr. lectr., coord. undergrad. courses in tourism Victoria U., Melbourne, 1994-98, assoc. prof., 1999; asst. prof. Hong Kong Polytechnic U., 1999—; hon. prof. Shanghai Inst. Tourism, 1999—; German market specialist Victorian Tourism Commn., 1990-93; mng. dir. BAUAIR Pty. Ltd., Melton, 1992—. Prodr., photographer, editor: (video) Voyage to Antarctica, 1995; photographer, designer: (CD-ROM) Voyage to Antarctica, 1996. Fellow Footscray Inst. Tech. (hon.); mem. Pacific Asia Travel Assn. (edn. chmn. So. Australian chpt. 1996-98). E-mail: hmthomas@polyu.edu.hk. Home: 5 Madeleine Pl, 3337 Melton Victoria, Australia Office: Hong Kong Polytechnic U, Dept Hotel and Tourism Mgmt, Hung Hom Kowloon Hong Kong SAR, China

BAUER, VIKTOR, pharmacologist, researcher; b. Nové Zámky, Slovak Republic, May 31, 1942; s. Ferenc and Katalin (Kürthy) B.; m. Edit Fischer, Apr. 11, 1970; children: Kinga, Helga. MD, Comenius U., Bratislava, Slovakia, 1965; PhD, Czechoslovak Acad. Scis., Prague, 1969, ScD, 1985. Physician dept. internal medicine Dist. Hosp., Nové Zánky, 1965-66; rschr. Inst. Pharmacology Czechoslovak Acad. Scis., Prague, 1969-72; head dept. Inst. Exptl. Pharmacology, Slovak Acad. Sci., Bratislava, 1972-79, dep. dir., 1980-90, dir., 1990—; assoc. prof. CU. Bratislav, 1994, prof. pharmacology, 1995; chmn. Slovak Commn. Sci. Degrees, 1993-95; dep. secn. gen. Slovak Acad. Sci., 1986-88. Author: Pharmacology of Gastrointestinal Motility, 1988; contbr. over 300 articles to profl. jours.; patentee (8) in field. Mem. Slovak Parliament, Bratislava, 1990; pres. Cultural and Civic Soc. Hungarians in Slovakia, Bratislava, 1991-98; mem. presidium World Fedn. Hungarians, Budapest, 1992—. Mem. Slovak Physiol. soc., Slovak Pharmacology Soc. (sec.-gen. 1990—), Czechoslovak Acad. Sci., Slovak Acad. Sci., Hungarian Acad. Scis. Avocation: football. Fax: 421-7-54775928. E-mail: exfabauv@savba.sk. Home: Bratislavská 17, 931 01 Šamorín Slovakia Office: Inst Exptl Pharmacology, Dubravská cesta 9, 842 16 Bratislava Slovakia

BAUERLY, RONALD JOHN, marketing educator; b. Monroe, Wis., Oct. 31, 1953; s. Jack Leroy and Josephine (Wiegel) B.; m. Robin Rochelle Kramer, Aug. 8, 1981; children: Shannon Marie, Thomas Joseph. BBA, U. Iowa, 1975, MBA, 1977; DBA, Southern Ill. U., Carbondale, 1989. Asst. mgr. K-Mart Corp., Racine, Wis., 1977-78; instr. Metropolitan Tech. Community Coll., Omaha, 1978, Loras Coll., Dubuque, Iowa, 1979-81, Northwest Mo. State U., Maryville, 1981-82; asst. prof. Brescia Coll., Owensboro, Ky., 1983-86; asst. prof. mktg. Western Ill. U., Macomb, 1987-91, assoc. prof., 1991-96, prof., 1996—. Editor Jour. of Contemporary Business Issues; contbr. articles to jours. Mem. Am. Acad. Advt., Am. Mktg. Assn., Assn. for Consumer Rsch., Acad. Mktg. Sci., Mktg. Mgmt. Assn., Phi Kappa Phi, Beta Gamma Sigma. Office: Western Ill U 424 Stipes Macomb IL 61455

BAUERNFEIND, JAMES C., secondary education educator; b. N.Y.C., Aug. 23, 1948; s. James Charles and Genveive Anne (Fitzgerald) B.; m. Monica Lynne Hangey, Mar. 2, 1973; children: James III, Christina, Rebecca, Jessica. BE, S.W. Tex. State U., San Marcos, 1980. Cert. secondary tchr., Tenn. Tchr. Mt. Juliet H.S., Mt. Juliet, Tenn., 1994—. Maj. USAF, 1966-94. Mem. Kiwanis, Phi Delta Kappa. Republican. Roman Catholic. Avocations: reading, travel, computering. E-mail: bauernfeind@home.com. Home: 619 Noel Dr Mount Juliet TN 37122-2027 Office: Mt Juliet H S 3565 N Mount Juliet Rd Mount Juliet TN 37122-3047

BAUERSFELD, WALTER WOLFRAM, clinical chemist, laboratory professional; b. Heidenheim, Germany, May 10, 1951; s. Werner and Margarete (Gräfe) B.; m. Liane Kummer, Apr. 10, 1997; 1 child, Leonard. Dipl.chem., U. Stuttgart, Germany, 1981, Dr.rer.nat., 1984. Rschr. Rob-Borch-Krko, Stuttgart, 1981-84; asst. Kliuiken, Esslingen, Germany, 1984-95; lab. chief Kreiskrankenhaus, Loerrach, Germany, 1995—; scientific advisor clin. lab., 1997—. Mem. Berufsevereingigung der Naturwissenschaftler in der Labordiagnostik (pres. 1993-95, sec. 1995—), Deutsche Gesellschaft Klinishe Chemie, Deutsche Gesellschaft Transfusionsweduzin und Immunhaematologie. Avocation: piano. Office: Kreiskruuhenhaus, Spirtalstrasse 25, D-79539 Loerrach BW, Germany

BAUFRETON, CHRISTOPHE, cardiothoracic surgeon; b. Angers, France, Sept. 26, 1963; s. Robert and Nicole (Gaubusseau-Joubert) B.; m. Marie Sophie Marechal, July 8, 1988; children: Alexandre, Agathe. MD, U. Paris, 1994; PhD, U. Amsterdam, 1997. Resident Hosps. of Paris, 1988-94; chief resident Hosp. Henri Mondor, Créteil, France, 1994-96; surgeon U. Hosp., Angers, France, 1996-98, cons. surgeon, 1998—. Author: Heparin Coating Aprotinin and Blood Activation During Cardiopulmonary Bypass, 2d edit., 1998; contbr. articles to profl. jours. Capt. French Army Res., 1994-2000. Mem. European Assn. Cardio-Thoracic Surgery, French Soc. Thoracic and Cardiovascular Surgery, French Coll. Thoracic and Cardiovasc. Surgery. Home: 15 rue Merlet de la Boulaye, 49000 Angers France Office: U Hosp, 4 rue Larrey, 49000 Angers France

BAUGHAN, JULIAN JAMES, barrister, recorder; b. London, Feb. 8, 1944; s. Edward Christopher and Jacqueline Fors (Hodge) B. Student, Eton Coll., Berkshire, U.K., 1956-61; BA in History with Honors, Oxford (Eng.) U., 1965. Lawyer, 1967—; prosecuting counsel Dept. Trade and Industry, U.K., 1983-90; recorder Crown Ct., U.K., 1985—; Queen's counsel U.K., 1990—. Office: 13 Kings Bench Walk, Temple London EC4, England

BAUGHMAN, R(OBERT) PATRICK, lawyer; b. Zanesville, Ohio, Nov. 18, 1938; s. Robert G. and Kathryn E. B.; m. Joyce Hall, June 17, 1959; 1 dau., Patricia. B.S., Ohio State U., 1960, J.D., 1963. Bar: Ohio 1963. Assoc. firm Sindell & Sindell, Cleve., 1964-71, Jones, Day, Reavis & Pogue, Cleve., 1972-73; asst. atty. gen. State of Ohio, Columbus, 1971-72; pres., prin. firm Baughman & Assocs., Cleve., 1973—. Mem. ABA, Ohio Bar Assn., Cuyahoga County Bar Assn., Nat. Council Self-Insurers, Internat. Assn. Indsl. Accident Bds. and Commns., Internat. Platform Assn. Episcopalian. Club: Columbia Hills Country. Office: Baughman & Assocs 55 Public Sq Ste 2215 Cleveland OH 44113-1996

BAUKNIGHT, CLARENCE BROCK, consultant; b. Anderson, S.C., May 14, 1936; s. John Edward and Theodosia (Brock) B.; m. Harriet League, June 29, 1959; children: Harriet League, Clarence Brock. B.S., Ga. Inst. Tech., 1958. Dist. mgr. Wickes Corp., and predecessor, Atlanta, 1960-65; exec. v.p. Builder Marts Am., Inc., Greenville, S.C., 1965-87, pres., chief exec. officer, 1987-88, chmn. bd. dirs., 1987-88, now bd. dirs.; CEO, chmn. bd. dirs. Builderway, Inc., 1970-96; chmn. bd. dirs. Enterprise Computer Sys., Inc., Channelinx.com. Mem. policy adv. bd. Joint Ctr. Urban Studies Harvard U., 1982-87; trustee Bumcombe St. United Meth. Ch., 1985-90, chmn., 1989-90, Greenville Hosp. System, 1987-93, chmn., 1991-92; bd. dirs. Greenville Health Corp., 1994-97. Mem. Chief Exec. Orgn., Greenville Country Club, Poinsett (Greenville), Cullasaja and Highlands, Wild Dunes, Masons, Shriners, Phi Delta Theta. Methodist. Home and Office: PO Box 2183 Greenville SC 29602-2183

BAUM, CARL EDWARD, electromagnetic theorist; b. Binghamton, N.Y., Feb. 6, 1940; s. George Theodore and Evelyn Monica (Bliven) B. BS with honors, Calif. Inst. Tech., 1962, MS, 1963, PhD, 1969. Commd. 2d lt. USAF, 1962, advanced through grades to capt., 1967, resigned, 1971; project officer Air Force Rsch. Lab. (formerly Phillips Lab.), Kirtland AFB, N.Mex., 1963-71, sr. scientist for electromagnetics, 1971—; pres. SUMMA Found.; U.S. del. to gen. assembly Internat. Union Radio Sci., Lima, Peru, 1975, Helsinki, Finland, 1978, Washington, 1981, Florence, Italy, 1984, Tel Aviv, 1987, Prague, Czechoslovakia, 1990, Kyoto, Japan, 1993, Lille, France, 1996, Toronto, Can., 1999; mem. Commn. B U.S. Nat. Com., 1975—, Commn. E, 1982—, Commn. A, 1990—. Author: (with others) Transient Electromagnetic Fields, 1976, Electromagnetic Scattering, 1978, Acoustic, Electromagnetic and Elastic Wave Scattering, 1980, Fast Electrical and Optical Measurements, 1986, EMP Interaction: Principles, Techniques and Reference Data, 1986, Lightning Electromagnetics, 1990, Modern Radio Science, 1990, Recent Advances in Electromagnetic Theory, 1990, Direct and Inverse Methods in Radar Polarimetry, 1992, (with A.P. Stone) Transient Lens Synthesis: Differential Geometry in Electromagnetic Theory, 1991; editor: (with H.N. Kritikos) Electromagnetic Symmetry, 1995, (with L. Carin and A.P. Stone) Ultra-Wideband, Short-Pulse Electromagnetics 3, 1997, Detection and Identification of Visually Obscured Targets, 1998; contbr. articles to profl. jours. Recipient award Honeywell Corp., 1962, R&D award USAF, 1970, Harold Brown award Air Force Systems Command, 1990; Air Force Rsch. Lab. fellow, 1996; Electromagnetic pulse fellow. Fellow IEEE (Harry Diamond Meml. award, 1987, Richard R. Stoddart award, 1984); mem. Electromagnetics Soc. (pres. 1983-85), Electromagnetics Acad., Sigma Xi, Tau Beta Pi. Roman Catholic. Home: 5116 Eastern Ave SE Apt D Albuquerque NM 87108-5618 Office: AFRL/DEHE 3550 Aberdeen Ave SE Bldg 909 Kirtland AFB NM 87117-5748

BAUM, EDWARD JOSEPH, chemistry educator, consultant; b. N.Y.C., Sept. 1, 1938; s. Casper Edward and Julia Linslee (Culp) B.; children: Laura Anne O'Donnell, Jeanne Karen Raffety; m. Melissa Corrie Anne Brown, Aug. 12, 1991. BSc, UCLA, 1961; PhD, U. Calif., Riverside, 1965. Assoc. prof. chemistry Oreg. Grad. Ctr., Portland, 1967-78; chief tech. advisor UNESCO, São Paulo, Brazil, 1978-83; prof. chemistry Grand Valley State U., Grand Rapids, Mich., 1983—; affiliate, clin. prof. environ. medicine U. Oreg. Med. Sch., Portland, 1972-78; cons. Nat. Rsch. Coun. Fed. Hwy. Adminstrn. Author: Chemical Property Estimation: Theory and Application, 1998; contbr. 18 articles to profl. jours. Cpl. USAR, 1955-62. Mem. Am. Chem. Soc., Internat. Chemometrics Soc., QSAR & Modeling Soc. Achievements include patent for apparatus for removing pollutants from stack effluents. Avocations: scuba diving, skiing, sailing. Home: 1540 N Lasalle Blvd Chicago IL 60610-1349 Office: Grand Valley State U Chemistry Dept Allendale MI 49401

BAUM, RICHARD PAUL, nuclear medicine physician; b. Pirmasens, Germany, June 17, 1954; s. Richard Karl and Maria Luise (Ehrhardt) B.; m. Christiane Chini, July 1, 1977 (div. Oct. 1983); children: Christian, Daniel; m. Julitta Erna Rueck, Jan. 2, 1984. Abitur, Immanuel Kant U., Pirmasens, 1974; med. lic., Joh. Gutenberg U., Mainz, Germany, 1980, MD, PhD, 1985. Lic. specialty bd. Nuclear Medicine. Resident dept. nuclear medicine U. Med. Ctr., Frankfurt, Fed. Republic of Germany, 1984-88, vice-dir. dept. nuclear medicine, 1988-96; dir. Clin. PET Ctr., 1994-97; asst. prof. med. sch. U. Frankfurt, 1988-90, assoc. prof., 1990-95, prof., 1996—; v.p. Internat. Rsch. Group in Immunoscintigraphy, 1988-90; pres., 1990-92; chief sci. investigator Internat. Atomic Energy Agy., Vienna, 1991—; vis. prof. Med. Coll., China; chmn. clinic nuclear medicine/PET ctr. Zentralklinik Bad Berka, Germany. Author: Wandel Nuklearmed. Nieren Diagnostik, 1987; editor: Clinical Use of Antibodies, 1991; patentee in field. Recipient Mallinckrodt award German Soc. Nuclear Medicine, 1990, Sara Bhai Meml. Oration, Nuclear Medicine Soc. India, 1999. Mem. European Assn. Nuclear Medicine (adv. bd. 1991—, mem. task group 1988—), Soc. Nuclear Medicine, European Agy. for the Evaluation of Med. Products (EMEA), Internat. Soc. Radiolabelled Blood Elements (bd. dirs. 1992—), N.Y. Acad. Scis. Roman Catholic. Avocations: chess, computers, music, traveling, sports. Home: Bergweg 4, D-55595 Hargesheim Germany Office: Clinic Nuclear Medicine, Zentralklinik Bad Berka, 99437 Bad Berka Germany

BAUM, RICHARD THEODORE, engineering executive; b. N.Y.C., Oct. 3, 1919. BA, Columbia U., 1940, BS, 1941, MS, 1948. Registered profl. engr., N.Y., D.C., and 20 other states, Nat. Bur. Engring. Registration. Engr. Electric Boat Co., Groton, Conn., 1941-43; with Jaros, Baum & Bolles, N.Y.C., 1946—, ptnr., 1958-86, ptnr. emeritus, cons. to firm, 1986—; mem. adv. coun., faculty of engring. and applied sci. Columbia U., N.Y.C., 1972—. 1st lt. USAAF, 1943-46. Egleston medalist Columbia U., 1985. Fellow ASME, ASHRAE, AAAS, Am. Cons. Engrs. Coun.; mem. NAE (mech. engring. peer com. 1991-93), NSPE, N.Y. Acad. Scis., Nat. Soc. Energy Engrs., NRC (chmn. bldg. rsch. bd. 1987-91), Am. Arbitration Assn. (panel arbitrators 1973—), Coun. on Tall Bldgs. and Urban Habitat (vice chmn. N.Am. chpt.), Univ. Club N.Y.C. Office: Jaros Baum & Bolles 80 Pine St New York NY 10005-1702

BAUM, SANDRA BEATTIE, executive secretary; b. Buffalo, Oct. 9, 1948; d. Edwin Eugene and Margaret Virginia (Kinkead) Beattie; m. William Paul Baum, Nov. 30, 1968; 1 child, Robert B. Student, Lake Sumter C.C. Office mgr. C.L. Ossman Design, Buffalo, 1980-85; contracts specialist M/A Com, Inc., Burlington, Mass., 1985-89; exec. sec. Lake County Coop. Ext. Svc., Taveres, Fla., 1989—. Bd. dirs., sec., vice chmn. Keep Lake County Beautiful, Eustis, Fla., 1994—; sec. Agrl. Adv. Com., Tavares, 1989—. Mem. NAFE, Nat. Assn. Exec. Secs. Republican. Roman Catholic. Avocations: knitting, sewing.

BAUM, WILLIAM WAKEFIELD CARDINAL, archbishop; b. Dallas, Nov. 21, 1926; s. Harold E. and Mary Leona (Hayes) W. Student, Kenrick Sem., St. Louis, 1947-51, U. St. Thomas Aquinas, Rome, 1956-58; STD, U. St. Thomas Aquinas, Rome, 1958; STL, Muhlenberg Coll., Allentown, Pa., 1957, DD, 1967; LLD, Georgetown U., St. John's U., Bklyn. Ordained priest Roman Cath. Ch., 1951. Assoc. pastor St. Aloysius Parish, St. Therese's Parish and St. Peter's Parish, Kansas City, Mo., 1951-56, 61-64, 67-68; adminstr. St. Cyril's Parish, Sugar Creek, Mo., 1960-61; pastor St. James Parish, Kansas City, 1968-70; chancellor Diocese Kansas City-St. Joseph, 1967-70; bishop of Springfield-Cape Girardeau, Mo., 1970-73; archbishop of Washington, 1973-80; elevated to cardinal Roman Cath. Ch., 1976; prefect Sacred Congregation for Cath. Edn., Rome, 1980-90; grand penitentiary cardinal Apostolic Penitentiary, Rome, 1990—; instr., then prof. Avila Coll., Kansas City, Mo., 1954-56, 58-63; Hon. chaplain of the Pope, 1961; peritus 2d Vatican Council, 1962-65; hon. prelate of the Pope, 1968; 1st exec. dir. Bishops' Commn. Ecumenical and Inter-religious Affairs, 1964-67; mem. Joint Working Group; reps. Cath. Ch. and World Council Chs., 1965-69; mem. Mixed Commn.; reps. Cath. Ch. and Lutheran World Fedn., 1965-66; mem. Vatican's Congregations Cath. Edn., Doctrine of Faith and Secretariat for Non Christians, Bishop's Welfare Emergency Relief Com. Author: The Teaching of Cardinal Cajetan on the Sacrifice of the Mass, 1958, Considerations Toward the Theology on the Presbyterate, 1961. Trustee, chancellor Cath. U. Am.; chmn. bd. trustees Nat. Shrine Immaculate Conception. Mem. Nat. Conf. Cath. Bishops (adminstrv. com.). Address: Via Rusticucci 13, Rusticucci 13, 00193 Rome Italy

BAUMAN, JAN GEORGIUS JOSEF, cell biologist, histochemist; b. Vlaardingen, The Netherlands, Mar. 1, 1950; s. petrus W.M. and Maria (van Holstijn) B.; m. Marionne J.A. Th. van de Kruijs, June 14, 1976; children: Sanne Maartje, Eveline Sabine, Nadine Marieke. D of Biology, State U. Leiden, The Netherlands, 1975, PhD, 1980. Doctoral rschr. lab. histocytochemistry U. Leiden, 1975-80; rsch. sci. dept. radiobiology Erasmus U., Rotterdam, The Netherlands, 1980-85, Netherlands Cancer Found., Ryswyk, 1985-87; fellow Royal Netherlands Acad. Scis., Amsterdam; appt. at dept. radiobiology Erasmus U., Rotterdam, 1987-92; sect. head cytometry Inst. for Applied Radiobiology and Immunology, Ryswyk, 1990-92; postdoctoral rschr. E.C. Slater Inst. U. Amsterdam, 1992-96; instr. biology and info. tech. various colls., 1997-98; instr. info. tech. IT Higher Vocat. Coll., 1998—; vis. assoc. researcher dept. cell biology Univ. Mass. Medical Sch., Worcester, Mass., 1990. Mem. editl. bd. Histochemistry, 1993-95; contbr. articles to profl. jours. Recipient Robert Feulgen prize Gesellschaft fur Histochemie, 1983, Eleanor Roosevelt Inst. Cancer Rsch. fellowship Internat. Union Against Cancer, 1990. Mem. Soc. Histochemistry (bd. dirs. 1991-95), Internat. Soc. Analytical Cytology, Am. Soc. Cell Biology. Avocations: computer programming, tennis.

BAUMAN, ROBERT PATTEN, diversified company executive; b. Cleve., Mar. 27, 1931; s. John Nevin and Lucille (Patten) B.; m. Patricia H. Jones, June 15, 1961; children: John, Elizabeth. BA, Ohio Wesleyan U., 1953; MBA, Harvard U., 1955. Mktg. adminstrn. Maxwell House div. Gen. Foods, White Plains, N.Y., 1958-65, gen. mgr. Post div., 1967, corp. v.p., 1968, exec. v.p., 1968, pres., dir. internat. ops., 1973; dir. Avco Corp., Greenwich, Conn., 1980-85, chmn., CEO, 1981-85; vice chmn. Textron Inc., Providence, R.I., 1985-86; chmn. Beecham PLC, 1986-89; CEO SmithKline Beecham Plc., Brentford, Eng., 1989-94; chmn. Brit. Aerospace PLC, Farnborough, Eng., 1994-98, BTR plc, London, 1998-99; bd. dirs. Union Pacific Corp, CIGNA Corp., Morgan Stanley, Russell Reynolds, Hathaway Holdings Inc., Panorama, Invensys plc. Author: Plants as Pets, 1982; co-author: From Promise to Performance, 1997. Mem. Conf. Bd. Clubs: Webhannet Golf (Kennebunk, Maine); Blind Brook (Port Chester, N.Y.), Wisley Golf (Surrey, Eng.), Pine Valley Golf.

BAUMAN, WILLIAM ALLEN, pediatrician, educator, health systems consultant; b. N.Y.C., Nov. 23, 1923; s. Louis and Stella (Kraus) B.; m. Joan Carlsen, June 28, 1952; children: William Carlsen, Phillip Allen, Pamela Joan. Student, Harvard U., 1942-43, 46; MD, Columbia U., 1947; postgrad. in biostats., Sch. Pub. Health, 1960-63. Intern L.I. divsn. Kings County Hosp., Bklyn., 1947-48; resident The Babies Hosp., N.Y.C., 1948-50; chief pediatric clinic Vanderbilt Clinic, N.Y.C., 1954-65; practice medicine specializing in pediatrics N.Y.C., 1953-75; dir. med. data processing Presbyn. Hosp., N.Y.C., 1966-74, assoc. attending pediatrician, 1973-93, emeritus staff, 1994—; v.p. med. adminstrv. svcs. Group Health Inc., N.Y.C., 1974-77; chmn. bd. govs. Hillcrest Gen. Hosp.-Group Health Inc., 1975-79, attending pediatrician, 1975-79; sr. v.p. Health Svcs. Group Health Inc., 1977-79; v.p. med. affairs Danbury Hosp., Conn., 1979-90; mem. faculty dept. pediatrics Columbia U., 1952-73, assoc. clin. prof. pediatrics, 1973—; mem. med. bd. Maternity Ctr. Assn., 1969-95; chmn. faculty-student adv. bd. P&S Club, Coll. Physicians and Surgeons, Columbia U., 1970-90; chmn. com. on data processing N.Y. County Health Rev. Orgn., 1976-79. Contbr. articles to profl. jours. Mem. data protection rev. bd. N.Y. State Dept. Health, 1993—. With M.C. USAF, 1951-52. Fellow Am. Coll. Med. Informatics, N.Y. Acad. Medicine; mem. Am. Acad. Pediatrics, N.Y. County Med. Soc., AMA, Med. Soc. State N.Y. (chmn. com. info. tech. in medicine 1967-93), Assn. Ambulatory Pediatrics, Assn. Computing Machinery, Soc. Computer Medicine (bd. dirs.), Bioengring. Inst., Am. Soc. Info. Scis., N.Y. Acad. Scis., N.Y. State Assn. Professions, Am. Assn. Med. Systems and Infomatics (pres. 1983). Home and Office: 667 Heritage Hls Somers NY 10589-1927

BAUMAN, ZYGMUNT, sociologist; b. Poznan, Poland, Nov. 19, 1925; s. Maurice and Sophie (Cohn) B.; m. Janina Gustawa Lewinson, Aug. 18, 1926; children: Anna, Irena, Lydia. BA, U. Warsaw, Poland, 1950, MA, 1954, PhD, 1956, Habilitation, 1960; hon. degree, U. Oslo, U. Lapland, U. Uppsala. Lectr., sr. lectr. U. Warsaw, Poland, 1953-64, chmn. gen. sociology dept., 1964-68; prof. sociology U. Tel-Aviv, Israel, 1968-71, U. Leeds, Eng., 1971—; chief editor Studia Sociologizne quar., Warsaw, 1960-68, Studia Sociologicano-Polityczne, Warsaw, 1962-68. Author: Between Class and Elite, 1970, Culture as Praxis, 1972, Hermeneutics and Social Science, 1980, Memories of Class, 1982, Legislators and Interpreters, 1987, Freedom, 1988, Modernity and the Holocaust, 1989, In Search of Politics, 1999, Liquid Modernity, 2000; contbr. articles to profl. jours. Recipient European Amalfi prize, 1989, Theodore W. Adovno prize, 1998. Mem. Brit. Sociol. Assn. Avocation: photography. Office: Univ of Leeds, Leeds LS2 9JT, England

BAUMANIS, AIVARS, Latvian ambassador; b. Riga, Latvia, Dec. 23, 1937; s. Arturs and Elza (Finks) B.; m. Benita Schultz, July 7, 1962 (div. Oct. 1968); children: Laila, Gints, Ivo; m. Anita Rutka, Feb. 14, 1979; children: Filips. Law degree, Latvian State U., Riga, 1961. Investigator City Police Dept., Riga, 1961-65; corr. fgn. desk in radio, Riga, 1965-71; editor Liesma mag., Riga, 1971-74; editor, then editor-in-chief Jurmala (Latvia) Newspaper, 1980-88; head Latvian br. Novosti, news agy., Riga, 1988-90; dir. Latvian News Agy. LETA, Riga, 1990-91; amb. Permanent Mission of Latvia to UN, N.Y.C., 1991-97; Latvian amb. to Denmark Latvian Embassy, Copenhagen, 1997—. Mem. Latvian Journalists Assn. (chmn. 1988-91). Lutheran. Avocations: jazz, movies, art. Office: Embassy of Latavia, Rosboeksvej 17, 2100 Copenhagen Denmark*

BAUMANN, CHRISTOPHER ANTHONY, chemist, educator; b. Portland, Oreg., Dec. 22, 1955; s. Albert W. and Dorothy F. (Nudo) B.; m. Lisa Ahrens, July 13, 1985. BS, Oreg. State U., 1978; PhD, U. Fla., 1982. Postdoctoral fellow Ind. U., Bloomington, 1982-84; asst. prof. U. Scranton, Pa., 1984-89, assoc. prof., 1989-98; prof. U. Scranton, 1998—. Mem. Am. Phys. Soc., Am. Chem. Soc. (grantee 1985, 87), Sigma Xi, Acacia, Phi Lambda Upsilon (moderator 1987-90). Office: U Scranton Dept Chemistry Scranton PA 18510

BAUMANN, ERNST FREDERICK, college president; b. N.Y.C., Oct. 4, 1943; s. Ernst and Grace (Crowley) B.; m. Kathleen Ann Brennan, June 17, 1967; children: Ernst Frederick Jr., Lori Ann, Macushla, Katrinka, Victoria, Greta. BA, Harvard U., 1967; postgrad., Colo. U. Observer, rsch. asst. High Altitude Obs., Nat. Ctr. for Atmospheric Rsch., Boulder, Colo., 1967-69; uranium geologist, grade control engr. Kerr-McGee Corp., Casper, Wyo., 1969-71; mine geologist engr. Am. Smelting and Refining Co., Leadville, Colo., 1975; chief geologist, engr. Leadville (Colo.) Lead Corp., 1976-79; dir. adult basic edn. and gen. ednl. devel., counselor Upper Ark. Area Coun. Govts., Cañon City, Colo., 1987-96; corr. officer, supr. C.T.C.F./D.O.C., Cañon City, 1979-99; pres., chmn. Coll. of the Cañons, Cañon City, 1987-96; officer Colo. Territorial Correctional Facility, Dept. Corrections, Cañon City; recruiter Harvard U., Cañon City; pres., chmn. bd. Working in SETI Search for Extra-Terrestrial Intelligence. Co-author: Toward a New World: Powerful Proof of the Existence of God, 1995; editor: The Crucifixion; patentee mil. mountaineer's collapsible ski. Mayoral candidate City of Cañon City, 1983, 85. Maj. CAP, USAF Aux., 1980-99. Mem. K. of C. (scribe). Republican. Roman Catholic. Home: PO Box 118 Twin Lakes CO 81251-0118 Office: Coll of the Cañons Forge Rd/Indsl Park Canon City CO 81212

BAUMANN, GERD, physics educator, researcher; b. Heldenfingen, Germany, Jan. 3, 1956; s. Erwin and Anna (Wöhrle) B.; m. Carin Baumann, 1993. Diploma in physics, U. Ulm, Germany, 1985, Dr. rer. nat., 1988. Asst. U. Ulm, 1989-95, sr. asst. prof. physics, 1995—; cons. Wolfram Rsch., Champaign, Ill., 1994. Author: Mathematica in der Theoretischen Physik, 1993, Mathematica in Theoretical Physics, 1996, Symmetry Analysis of Differential Equations with Mathematica, 2000. Recipient award Verband der Metallindustrie, 1989, Merckle res. award, 1997. Office: U Ulm Dept Math Physics, Albert-Einstein-Allee 11, D-89069 Ulm Germany

BAUMANN, JURGEN, lawyer, educator; b. Essen, Germany, June 22, 1922; s. Wilhelm and Gertrud (Sieg) B.; m. Edith Muller, May 10, 1951 (div. 1979); children: Katharine, Christiane, Renate; m. Doris Haug, Aug. 31, 1979. Grad., U. Munster, Fed. Republic Germany, 1950, Habilitation, 1955. Asst. prof. U. Munster, 1951-55, lectr., 1955-59; pvt. practice law Detmold, Fed. Republic Germany, 1953—; prof. law U. Tubingen, Fed. Republic Germany, 1959-76, 1978-88; law senator City of Berlin, 1976-78; curator U. Hagen, West Germany; counselor Friedrich-Naumann Found., Gustav-Heinemann Inst. Vice chmn. Fed. Com. of Experts of Interior Right, Liberal Party. Avocation: modern art. Home: Eduard-Haber-Str 11, 72074 Tubingen Germany Office: U Fak of Law, Scholl Place, Tubingen Federal Republic of Germany

BAUMANN, MARTIN, religious studies educator; b. Swakopmund, Nambia, 1960; arrived in Germany, 1984; MA, U. Marburg, Germany, 1988; PhD, U. Hannover, Germany, 1993. D Habilitation U. Leipzig, 1999. Lectr. in study of religions U. Hannover, 1992—; editl. bds. various internat. jours. Author: Deutsche Buddhisten, 1993, Migration, Religion, Integration, 2000. Office: Sem for Religious Studies, U Hannover Str Moore 21, 30167 Hannover Germany

BAUMANN, MICHAEL ALFONS, dentist, scientist; b. Katzenelnbogen, Germany, July 7, 1962; s. Josef and Sigrid (Gros) B.; m. Uta Annette Giedziella, Dec. 27, 1997; children: Helena Uta Regina, Raffael Michael Alexander. DMD, U. Mainz, Germany, 1987, PhD, 1993. Asst. Dental Sch., U. Tübingen, Germany, 1989-90; asst. Dental Sch., U. Mainz, 1987-89, 90-91, sr. lectr., 1991-94; univ. prof. dentistry U. Köln, 1994—, dep. dir. Dental Sch., 1994—. Author: Grundlagen der Zahnerhaltungskunde, 1995, 97, Die Räumliche Darstellung des Endodonts, 1995; (with Beer) Praktische Endodontie, 1994, Endodontologie, 1997, Uendodontology, 2000. Mem. European Panel for Infection Control in Dentistry (chmn. rsch. 1993—), Internat. Assn. Dental Rsch., Am. Assn. Endodontists, Pierre Fauchard Acad. Avocations: music (piano, pipe organ), art. Fax: 49-221-478 6720. Office: Dental Sch Dept Restorative Dentistry, Kerpener Str 32, D-50931 Cologne Germany

BAUMANN, PIERRE KONRAD, biochemist, psychopharmacologist, educator; b. Lucerne, Switzerland, Mar. 16, 1944; s. Konrad O. and Kaethe (Schürhoff) B.; m. Marie-Héléne Verweyen-Thenagels, May 30, 1968; children: Kathrin, André. Dipl. in chemistry, U. Basle, Switzerland, 1968; dr rer nat., Max Planck Inst. Psychiatry, Munich, 1974; dipl. clin. pharmacology, Swiss Soc. Clin. Pharmacology, 1988. Postdoctoral fellow State Rsch. Hosp., Galesburg, Ill., 1972; head biochemistry and clin. psychopharmacology unit Univ. Adult Psychiatry Dept., Prilly-Lausanne, Switzerland, 1972—; from lectr. to prof. U. Lausanne, 1980—; sec. Swiss Soc. Biol. Psychiatry, 1981-87; v.p. Soc. Neuropsychopharm., Nurenberg, Germany, 1996-99. Editor: Biologische Psychiatrie der Gegenwart, 1992, Alpha Acid Glycoprotein: Genetics, Biochemistry, Physiological Functions and Pharmacology, 1989, Transport Mechanisms of Tryptophan in Blood Cells, Nerve Cells, and at the Blood-Brain Barrier, 1978; contbr. articles to profl. jours. Avocations: judo, hiking. Home: CH 1302 Vufflens-la-Ville Switzerland Office: Dept U Psychiatrie Adulte, Route de Cery, CH-1008 Pailly-Lausanne Switzerland

BAUMANN, THEODORE ROBERT, aerospace engineer, consultant, army officer; b. Bklyn., May 13, 1932; s. Emil Joseph and Sophie (Reiblein) B.; m. Patricia Louise Drake, Dec. 16, 1967; children: Veronica Ann, Robert Theodore, Joseph Edmund. B in Aerospace Engring., Poly. U., Bklyn., 1954; MS in Aerospace Engring., U. So. Calif., L.A., 1962; grad., US Army C&GS Coll., 1970, Indsl. Coll. of Armed Forces, 1970, US Army War Coll., 1979, Air War Coll., 1982. Structures engr. Glenn L. Martin Co., Balt., 1954-55; structural loads engr. N.Am. Rockwell, L.A., 1958-67; dynamics engr. TRW Systems Group, Redondo Beach, Calif., 1967-71, systems engr., 1971-75, project engr., 1975-84, sr. project engr., 1984-92; cons. SAAB-Scania Aerospace Div., Linkoping, Sweden, 1981-82; asst. dir. Dir. Weapons Systems, U.S. Army, Washington, 1981-85, staff officer Missile & Air Def. System div., 1975-81. Contbr. articles to Machine Design, tech. publs., tech. symposia. Asst. scoutmaster Boy Scouts Am., Downey, Calif., 1985-93; instr. Venice Judo Boys Club, 1966-86. Served from 2d lt. U.S. Army to col. USAR, 1954-88. Decorated Legion of Merit. Mem. AIAA; mem. Soc. Am. Mil. Engrs (life), Am. Legion, Res. Officers Assn. (life), U.S. Judo Fedn., Nat. Rifle Assn., Knights of Columbus. Republican. Roman Catholic. Achievements include developing a new method for the analysis and classification of random data; contbr. to air force ballistic missile program; devel. procedure for design of prestressed joints and fittings. Office: Theodore R Baumann & Assoc 7732 Brunache St Downey CA 90242-2206

BAUMANN, THOMAS, publishing company editor; b. Allmannsweier, Germany, Sept. 29, 1961; s. Helmut Oskar and Waltraud (Mundinger) B.; m. Claudia Heitz, Oct. 11, 1985; children: Lukas Michael, Judith Kornelia, Emily Rebecca. MA, U. Freiburg, Germany, 1988, Dr phil, 1990. Editor Verlag Johannis, Lahr, Germany, 1990-93, editl. dir., 1993—. Author: Zwischen Weltveränderung und Weltflucht, 1991; editor: Ambo. Forum für christliche Literatur, 1990-92. Baptist. Avocations: family, books. Office: Verlag Johannis, Heiligenstrasse 24, 77933 Lahr Germany

BAUMANN, WINFRIED, retired physics educator, researcher; b. Tarutino, Bessarabia, Romania, Feb. 13, 1929; came to U.S., 1959; s. Immanuel and Else (Schulz) B.; m. Gisela Buhl, June 18, 1959; children: Christine, Peter Helmut. Diploma in Physics, U. Goettingen, Germany, 1956, Dr. in Natural Scis., 1959. Jr. engr. U. Calif., Berkeley, 1959-60; sr. scientist Avco-Everett Rsch. Lab., Everett, Mass., 1960-65, Bell-Aerospace Co., Buffalo, N.Y., 1965-74; tchr. Gymnasium Bad Nenndorf, Germany, 1974-93. Contbr. articles to profl. jours. Mem. AIAA, Am. Physics Soc., Sigma Xi. Evangelical Lutheran. Home: Hinter den Hoefen 32, 315422 Bad Nenndorf Germany

BAUMANN, WOLFGANG HEINRICH, electrical engineer; b. Nossen, Germany, Mar. 4, 1946; s. Anton P. and Herta E. (Buhrig) B.; m. Monika Müller, Feb. 25, 1972. Degree in engring., Ing.-Schule, Aachen, Germany, 1969. Devel. engr. Siemens, München, Germany, 1969-71; svc. engr. Siemens, Düsseldorf, Germany, 1971-73; devel. engr. Litef, Freiburg, Germany, 1973-93; agt. engring. office Ingenieurbüro Wolfgang H. Baumann-Beratung & Vertrieb, Stegen, Germany, 1993—. Schatzmeister Sportverein Eschbach, Stegen, 1994-96; Beisitzer BDIC, Koblenz, Germany, 1988-97. Mem. Evangel. Ch. Avocation: travel. Home: Flaunserstr 15, 79252 Stegen Germany

BAUMANN-HOELZLE, RUTH ELLA, theologian, ethics consultant; b. Horgen, Switzerland, June 12, 1957; d. Richard Otto and Ella Alice (Oblak) Hoelzle; m. Robert Baumann, July 7, 1984; children: Simon, Ilona. Licentiate in theology, U. Zürich, Switzerland, 1983, Verbi Divini Ministra, 1983; D of Theology, U. Zürich, 1990. Min. Ch., Switzerland, 1983-84; scholar Harvard U., Cambridge, Mass., 1984-86, U. Zürich Inst. for Social Ethics, 1990—; pres. Interdisciplinary Inst. Ethics in Health Care, 1999. Author: Human-Gentechnologie, 1990 (Stehr-Boldt-Fonds award 1991); editor: Gentische Testmoglichkeiten (genetic testing in humans), 1990, Autonomie und Freiheit in de Meditin-Ethik, Immanuel kant und kae Barth, 1999. Pres. Ethics Forum, Zürich, 1990; pres. Pranatale Bagnorik Winksther, 1991; v.p. Swiss Soc. Biomedical Ethics, Switzerland, 1994—; mem. Ethic Commn. Swiss Acad. Med Scis., Bern, Switzerland, 1994—. Zwinglian. Avocations: jogging, hiking, swimming, skiing, gardening, music. Home: Säntisstrasse 1, CH-8633 Wolfhausen Switzerland Office: Dialogethics, Glonastrasse 18, CH-8028 Zürich Switzerland

BAUMBERGER, CHARLES HENRY, lawyer; b. Port Huron, Mich., Sept. 13, 1941; s. Peter Julius and Evelyn Margaret (Jackson) B.; m. Martha Carolyn Megathlin, Aug. 8, 1969; children: Peter Scott, Charles Henry Jr. BA, Vanderbilt U., 1963; JD, U. Fla., 1966. Bar: Fla. 1966, U.S. Dist. Ct. (so. dist.) Fla. 1967; cert. civil trial lawyer. Atty. Stephens, Demos & Magill, Miami, Fla., 1967-68; ptnr. Hastings, Goldman & Baumberger, Miami, 1969-74; founding ptnr. Rossman & Baumberger P.A., Miami, 1974—; lectr. various continuing legal edn. programs; guest on numerous radio, TV talk shows, 1987—. Contbr. articles to profl. jours. Mem. Gov's. Task Force on Emergency Room and Trauma Care, 1987; So. Fla. Health Action Coalition, Inc., 1984; task force on trauma and trauma systems Dept. Transp., 1987—. Served to 1st lt. U.S. Army Res., 1966-72. Mem. ABA, ATLA (past chair of Profl. Negligence Sect.), Fed. Bar Assn., Dade County Bar Assn. (bd. dirs. 1977-88, pres. 1989-90), Fla. Bar (exec. coun. trial lawyers sect. 1983-89, chmn. 1990-91), Acad. Fla. Trial Lawyers (bd. dirs. 1980-89), Dade County Trial Lawyers Assn. (founding mem. bd. dirs. 1981-84), Am. Bd. Trial Advocates (Miami chpt. past pres.), Fla. Lawyers Action Group, So. Trial Lawyers Assn., Trial Lawyers for Pub. Justice (founding mem. 1982—), Am. Coll. Trial Lawyers, Coral Reef Yacht Club, Univ. Club. Democrat. Methodist. Home: 5755 Suncrest Dr Miami FL 33156-5704 Office: Rossman Baumberger & Reboso 44 W Flagler St Fl 23 Miami FL 33130-1808

BAUME, MICHAEL EHRENFRIED, diplomat; b. Sydney, NSW, Australia, July 6, 1930; s. Alan Charles and Elizabeth Constance Baume; m. Ann Brigid Tancred, Feb. 20, 1963 (div. Oct. 1988); children: Andrew, Nicholas, Patrick; m. Toni Lyall Down, June 22, 1990. BA, U. Sydney, 1950. Assoc. Securities Inst. Australia. Fin. journalist various orgns., Sydney, 1949-69; t.v. panelist, author, radio commentator Australian Broadcasting Corp., Sydney, 1968-73; stockbroker Patrick Ptnrs., Sydney, 1970-75; dir. Tancred Bros. Industries, Brisbane, Queensland, Australia, 1970-83, Rothbury Wines, Pokolin, NSW, 1971-83; mem. parliament Parliament of Australian, Canberra, ACT, Australia, 1975-96; Austral.n consul-gen. Australian Govt., N.Y.C., 1996—; parliamentary sec. to treas. Australian Parliament, Canberra, 1982-83, shadow min., 1985-96; pres. Soc. Foreign Consuls in N.Y., 1999-2000. Author: Sydney Opera House Affair, 1967. Mem. for MacArthur, Ho. of Reps., Canberra, 1975-83; senator Australian Parliament, Canberra, 1984-96. Named Officer of Order of Australia, Queen of Australia, Canberra, 1999. Liberal. Avocations: tennis, skiing, cricket, theatre, music. E-mail: michael.baume@dfat.gov.au. Office: Australian Consultate Gen 150 E 42nd St Fl 34 New York NY 10017-5612

BAUME, PETER ERNE, medical educator; b. Sydney, Australia, Jan. 30, 1935; s. Sidney Erne and Jean (Brodziak) B.; m. Jennifer Broughton Tuson, Dec. 15, 1958; children: Sarah Jane, Ian Peter. M.B.B.S., U. Sydney, 1959, FRACP, 1971, MD, 1969. Med. practitioner. Resident and med. registrar Royal North Shore Hosp., Sydney, 1959-62, hon. asst. physician, 1966-74; fellow Vanderbilt U., Nashville, 1964-65; clin. supr. U. Sydney, 1966-69; fed. minister for aboriginal affairs Australia, 1980-82; fed. minister for health, 1982, fed. minister for edn., 1982-83; shadow minister for edn. and status of women Australia, 1982-83; shadow minister Community Svcs. and Youth Affairs, Australia, 1985-87; senator for NSW Parliament of Australia, Canberra, 1974-91; head of community medicine U. NSW, 1991-95, 97-00; chancellor Australian found. chmn. Australian Sports Drug Agy., 1991-99; chancellor Australian Nat. U., 1994—; emeritus prif., 1999; bd. mem. Sydney Water, 1998—. Contbr. articles to profl. jours. and publs. Chmn. senate standing com., Australian Senate, 1976-80; dep. chair Australian Nat. Coun. on AIDS, 1993-94; mem. Australian Group Amnesty Internat., NSW Coun. of Civil Liberties; commr. Australian Law Reform Commn.; hon. rsch. assoc. Social Policy Rsch. Ctr., U. N.S.W., 2000—; others. Officer Order of Australia, 1992. Mem. Liberal Party of Australia. Jewish. Avocations: writing, reading, music, lawn bowling. Home: 32/17 Raglan St, Mosman NSW 2088, Australia

BAUMEL, JOAN PATRICIA FRENCH, educator, writer, lecturer; b. Winona, Minn., Mar. 12, 1930; d. William Oswald and Gertrude Marie (Fitzgerald) French; m. Herbert Baumel, July 11, 1971. Student, l'Ecole du Louvre, France, 1950-51; student with high honors, Inst. Phonétique Sorbonne, Paris, 1950-51; BA magna cum laude, Douglass Coll., 1952; postgrad., U. Detroit, 1952-55, Case Western Reserve U., 1960, U. Akron, 1962, U. Notre Dame, 1963, Manhattanville Coll., 1971; MA in French, Rutgers U., 1965; PhD in Modern Langs., Fordham U., 1985. Tchr. French lang. and culture, elem. and coll. levels various schs. including Mother House of Religious of the Sacred Heart, Kenwood, Albany, N.Y., Ohio, Mich., 1955-66; tchr. French White Plains (N.Y.) Pub. High Sch., 1966-86; curricula creator Akron (Ohio) Pub. Schs., 1962-63; co-dir. Baumel Assocs., Yonkers, N.Y., 1984—, Concerts and Lectures with Herbert Baumel, 1991—, Words and Music Programs with Herbert Baumel, 1991—, Yonkers Pub. Libr., 1992, Waverly Heights, Gladwyne, Pa., 1993-95, Workmen's Circle Lodge, Sylvan Lake, N.Y., 1994, Thomas Paine/Huguenot Hist. Soc., New Rochelle, N.Y., 1995—; lectr. French lang. and culture Yonkers (N.Y.) Pub. Libr., 1992, Greenburgh (N.Y.) Pub. Libr., 1992, anti-semitism CUNY Grad. Ctr., B'nai B'rith Internat. Mus., Washington, 1st Unitarian Soc., Westchester, N.Y., Rockland (NY) Ctr. for Holocaust Studies, Unitarian Ch. of All Souls, N.Y.C., Temple Beth Israel, Port Washington, N.Y., Holocaust Resource Ctr. and Archives, Queensborough C.C., CUNY, 1991, Women's Am. ORT, Midchester Jewish Ctr., Yonkers, 1992, Ctrl. Queens YM & YWCA, N.Y.C., 1992. Author: Paul Claudel and the Jews: A Study in Ambivalence, 1985; lectr. topics include French Anti-Semitism; The Gallic Road to the Concentration Camp; Klaus Barbie and the Children of Izieu, numerous others. Mem. adv. bd. Mark Brent Dolinsky Meml. Found. Recipient Woodrow Wilson fellowship, 1958-59, Yearbook Dedication award White Plains (N.Y.) Pub. H.S., 1980. Mem. Am. Assn. Tchrs. French, White Plains Tchrs. Assn., N.Y. State Assn. Fgn. Lang. Tchrs., French Inst./Alliance Francaise, Alliance Francaise Westchester, Phi Beta Kappa. Avocations: tennis, gardening, music, reading. Home and Office: Baumel Assocs 86 Rosedale Rd Yonkers NY 10710-3033

BAUMER, MICHAEL V., lawyer; b. Austin, Tex., Mar. 25, 1958; s. Andrew Ronald and Sandra Kay Baumer; 1 child, Daniel Ryan. BA in History, Lamar U., 1981; JD, U. Houston, 1984. Bar: U.S. Ct. (so., we., no.) Tex. 1998, U.S. Ct. Appeals (5th cir.), U.S. Supreme Ct. Assoc. Harris, Cook, Browning, Jordan & hyden, Corpus Christi, Tex., 1984-87, Small, craig & Werkenthin, Austin, Tex., 1987-97; ptnr. Baumer & McHaney, Austin, Tex., 1997-99. Mem. Travis County Bar Assn. (former sec., pres., v.p. 1997-99, coun. mem. 1989-99 bankruptcy sect.). Avocations: hiking, climbing, driving, cooking. Office: Baumer & McHaney 1717 W 6th St Ste 290 Austin TX 78703-4789

BAUMGART, WINFRIED ECKHART, history educator; b. Streckenbach, Germany, Sept. 29, 1938; s. Emil and Anni (Hepke) B.; m. Gisela Thamm, Nov. 11, 1963; children: Anja, Matthias. PhD, U. Saarbrücken, Fed. Republic Germany, 1966. Rsch. asst. U. Saarbrücken, 1967-70, U. Bonn, Fed. Republic Germany, 1967-70; prof. history U. Bonn, 1970-73, U. Mainz, Fed. Republic Germany, 1973; Konrad Adenauer prof. history, Georgetown U., Washington, 1978-79; vis. prof., U. Paris, 1988-89, U. Glasgow, 1990-91. Author numerous books on 19th and 20th century European history. Mem. Vereinigung Erforschung Neueren Geschichte. Roman Catholic. Home: Südring 39, 55128 Mainz Germany Office: U Mainz History Seminar, Saarstrasse 21, D 55099 Mainz Federal Republic of Germany

BAUMGARTEN, STEPHEN ROBERT, physician, urologist; b. Bklyn., Jan. 18, 1945; s. Jack Milton and Diane (Perlman) B.; m. Anne Glanzman, Apr. 27, 1990; children: Kelly Elizabeth, Stephen Paul, Amy. BA, Queens Coll., 1966; MD, SUNY, Bklyn., 1970. Diplomate Am. Bd. Urology. Surg. intern Maimonides Med. Ctr., Bklyn., 1970-72, resident in urology, 1974-77; pvt. practice in urology Bklyn., 1977—; asst. teaching attending Maimonides Hosp. and Coney Island Hosp., Bklyn., 1977-87; clin. instr. urology N.Y. Hosp. Cornell Med. Sch., N.Y.C., 1988—; attending physician St. John's Hosp. South Shore, L.I. Coll. Hosp., Bklyn., Beth Israel Hosp., Bklyn. Lt. comdr. USN, 1972-74. Fellow ACS; mem. N.Y. State Med. Soc., Am. Fertility Soc., Bklyn. L.I. Urologic Assn. Office: 2301 Ocean Ave Brooklyn NY 11229-3149

BAUMGARTNER, HANS RUDOLF, retired pharmaceutical researcher, educator; b. Basel, Switzerland, June 10, 1934; s. Johann Jakob and Lina (Keller) B.; m. E. Regula Morf, Apr. 24, 1962; children: Meret, Matthias, Maja. Grad., U. Basel, 1961, MD, 1963; postgrad., U. Paris, 1958-59, U. Vienna, Austria, 1959-60, Roche, Basel, 1961-63. Resident dept. pathology U. Basel, 1963-64, resident dept. internal medicine, 1964-66; rsch. fellow Royal Coll. Surgeons, London, 1967; rsch. assoc. Montefiore Hosp. and Med. Ctr., N.Y.C., 1968-70; group leader thrombosis rsch. Roche, Basel, 1970-81, head thrombosis and atherosclerosis rsch., 1982-86, head cardiovascular rsch., 1987-97; prof. U. Bern, Switzerland, 1988-99. Contbr. articles to med. jours. Recipient Theodor Naegeli prize Naegeli Found., 1987. Mem. Internat. Soc. on Thrombosis and Hemostasis (coun. 1972-78, com. mem. 1973-79, sr. adv. coun. 1980—, Disting. Career award 1997), European Thrombosis Rsch. Orgn. (exec. com. 1980-88), European Atherosclerosis Soc. (exec. com. 1982-96), Am. Heart Assn. (corr. fellow arteriosclerosis coun. 1986, mem. thrombosis coun. 1986). Avocations: mountain climbing, mountain farming and gardening, arts, music.

BAUMGARTNER, JOHANN FRANZ, radiochemistry scientist, educator; b. Munich, May 3, 1929. Diploma in chemistry, Tech. U., Munich, 1954, D in Natural Sci., 1956. Prof. U. Heidelberg, Fed. Republic of Germany, 1964-76, U. Mainz, Fed. Republic of Germany, 1976-79, Tech. U., Munich, 1980-99; dir. Inst. Heisse Chemie Kernforschungszentrum, Karlsruhe, Fed. republic of Germany, 1964-79. Recipient Otto Hahn prize City of Frankfurt, Fed. Republic of Germany, 1989. Mem. Acad. Sci. Lit. (assoc.). Office: Tech U, Dept of Chemistry, 85748 Munich Germany

BAUROV, YURIY ALEXEEVICH, physicist, researcher; b. Slavyanka, Hasanskiy, Russia, Mar. 14, 1947; s. Alexeiy Mihaiylovich and Nina Iosifovna (Futera) B.; m. Larisa Viktorovna Murachenkova, Jan. 6, 1973; children: Alexeiy, Alexandr. Diploma, Moscow Aviation Inst., 1972; D in Tech. Sci., Ctrl. Sci. Rsch. Inst. Mach B, Kaliningrad, Russia, 1978. Engr. Ctrl. Sci. Rsch. Inst. Mach. B, Kaliningrad, 1973-80, chief of group, 1980-83, chief of sector, 1983-89, chief of lab., 1989—; pres. Coun. of Dirs. Closed Joint-Stock Co., Rsch. Inst. Cosmic Physics. Contbr. articles to profl. jours. Mem. N.Y. Acad. Scis., Phys. Soc. Russia. Avocation: travel. Office: Ctrl Sci Rsch Inst Mach B, Pionerskaya 4, 141070 Korolev Russia

BAUSCH, PINA, dancer, ballet director, choreographer; b. Solingen, Germany, July 27, 1940; 1 child: Rolf Salomon. Studied with K. Jooss, Folkwangschule, Essen, Germany, 1955-58; student, Juillard Sch. Music, New York, 1960-61. Dancer Paul Sanasardo and Donya Feuer Dance Co., 1960-61, New Am. Ballet, Spoleto, 1961, Met. Opera, N.Y.C., 1961; solo dancer Folkwang Ballet Co., 1962; artistic dir., choreographer, dancer Folkwang Dance Studio, 1969-73; dir., choreographer Wuppertaler Buhnen, 1973—; head dance dept. Folkwang Hochschule, Essen, 1983-89; guest tchr. Dance Co. Paul Sanasardo, N.Y.C., 1972. Choreographer Fragment, 1968, Im Wind der Zeit, 1969 (1st prize Cologne Choreography Competition), Nachnull, 1970, Aktionen für Tänzer, 1971, Wiegenlied, 1972, Tannhäuser-Bacchanals, 1972, Iphigenie auf Tauris, 1974, Zwei Krawateen, 1974, Fritz, 1974, Adagio - Funf Lieder Von Gustav Mahler, 1974, Ich Bring dich um die Ecke, 1974, Orpheus and Eurydike, 1975, Fruhlingsopfer, 1975, Die Sieben Todsünden, 1976, Blaubart, 1977, Komm tanz mit mir, 1977, Renate Wandert Aus, 1977, Kontakthof, 1978, Cafe Müller, 1978 (Critics award 1992), Er Nimmt Sie an Der Hand Und Führt Sie in Das Schloss, Die Anderen Folgen, 1978, Macbeth, 1978, Arien, 1979, Keuschheitslegende, 1979, Ein Stück Von Pina Bausch, 1980, Bandoneon, 1980, Walzer, 1982, Nelken, 1982, Auf Dem Gebirge Hat Man Ein Geschrei Gehört, 1984, Two Cigarettes in the Dark, 1985, Viktor, 1986, Ahnen, 1987, Palermo Palermo, 1987, Tanzabend II, 1991, Das StÜ4ck Mit Dem Schiff, 1993, Ein Trauerspiel, 1994, Danzón, 1995, Nur Du, 1996, Der Fensterputzer, 1997, Masurca Fogo, 1998, Herzog Bluebeard's Castle, 1998; dir. (film) Die Klage der Kaiserin, 1987-90; appeared in (film) E la nave va, 1982. Recipient Folkwang prize, North Rhine-Westphalian prize, 1973, Grand Cultrual prize, 1990, Fed. Republic Germany Ctr. prize, 1990, Piccasso medal UNESCO, 1993, German Dance prize Profl. Assn. Tchg. Dance, 1995, Joanna Maria Gorvin prize, 1995, many others; grantee German Acad. Exch. Svc., 1959, 60. Office: Tanztheater Wuppertal Pina Bausch, Spinnstr 4, D42283 Wuppertal Germany*

BAUSS, (KARL) FRIEDER, scientist; b. Kaiserslautern, Germany, July 27, 1955; s. Robert and Elfriede Amalie (Schmidt) B.; m. Sonja Ruth Mutschelknauss, Aug. 26, 1988. Diploma in biology, U. Kaiserslautern, Germany, 1982, Dr.rer.nat., 1985. Postdoctoral fellow German Cancer Rsch. Ctr., Heidelberg, 1985-86; head lab. Dr. K. Thomae GmbH, Biberach, Germany, 1987-88, Roche Diagnostics GmbH (formerly Boehringer Mannheim GmbH), 1988—; rsch. fellow Dept. Pathophysiology, Berne, Switzerland, 1988. Contbr. articles to profl. jours.; patentee in field. Recipient European prize Osteofluor, Merck-Clevenot, France, 1986; co-recipient European prize for clin. urology European Assn. Urology, 1999. Mem. Am. Soc. for Bone and Mineral Rsch., European Calcified Tissue Soc., German Soc. for Exptl. and Clin. Pharmacology and Toxicology, German Soc. Immunology. Home: Rottstrasse 11, D-67141 Neuhofen Germany Office: Roche Diagnostics GmbH, Sandhofer Strasse 116, D-68305 Mannheim Germany

BAUTIER, ROBERT-HENRI, archivist, curator; b. Paris, Apr. 19, 1922; s. Edgar Bautier and Suzanne Voyer; m. Anne-Marie Regnier, 1947; 1 child. Student, Ecole des Chartes, Sorbonne, Ecole des Hautes Etudes. Archivist Nat. Archives, 1943; head archivist Archives départementales de la Creuse, 1944; mem. Ecole Française de Rome, 1945; keeper Archives de France, 1948; prof. Ecole Nat. des Chartes, 1961-90; curator Musée Jacquemart-André, Chaalis Abbey, 1990-2000. Author numerous books; contbr. over 300 articles to profl. jours. Pres. Com. Internat. de Diplomatique, 1980, hon. pres.; pres. Com. Historic and Sci. Works, Min. Nat. Edn., 1989—, Soc. française d'Héraldique et Sigillographie. Recipient Chevalier Légion d'honneur, Officier Ordre nat. du Mérite, Comdr. des Palmes Acad. Arts and Letters, others. Fellow Brit. Acad. (assoc.), Medieval Acad. Am.; mem. Belgian Acad. (assoc.), Acad. Internat. d'Héraldique, Inst. de France, Acad. Inscriptions. Address: 13 rue de Sévigné, 75004 Paris France also: Les Rabuteloires, 45360 Chatillon-sur-Loire France

BAUTISTA, REYNALDO YASAY, civil and sanitary engineering educator; b. Espiritu, Ilocos N., The Philippines, May 24, 1961; s. Ricardo Discalzo and Aurelia (Yasay) B.; m. Genalyn Sanchez, Jan. 31, 1989; children: Joanna Marie, Reygene John, Joyce Reah, Mae Jen. BSCE, St. Louis U., Baguio City, The Philippines, 1978-83; grad. in math., U. Philippines, Baguio City, 1984; BS in San. Engring., U. Baguio, Baguio City, 1986, MA in Ednl. Mgmt. cum laude, 1996, EdD, 1998. Registered civil and san. engr., The Philippines. Project engr. Flores Constrn., Baguio City, 1983-84; prof. engring. U. Baguio, 1984-88, head dept. surveying, 1986-88; prof. civil and san.

engring. Philippine Mil. Acad., Baguio City, 1989—, course dir. reinforced concrete design, 1989—, structural cons., 1995—; rev. dir. for civil and san. engring. United Engrs. Rev. Ctr., Dagupan City, Laoag City, Baguio City, 1988; structural cons. Lagman Constrn., Isabela City, 1995—, Baguio City, 1997—;. Author: Workbook in Reinforced Concrete DEsign, 1990 (Outstanding Author award 1990). Chapel design cons. Congregatio Immaculati Cordis Mariae, Baguio City, 1988; mem. civil engring. works com. Pinehurst Parish, Pacdal-Baguio City, 1993; grad. sch. panelist U. Baguio, 1997—. Mem. Assn. Structural Engrs. Philippines (life), Philippine Inst. for San. Engrs. (life, Outstanding award 1989), Am. Concrete Inst., Pvt. Edn. Ret. Annuity Assn. (One of 10 Outstanding Mems. award 1996). Avocations: structural designing, playing basketball, estimating, interior decorating, layout artist. Office: Philippine Mil Acad, Fort del Pilar, Baguio City 2600 CAR, The Philippines

BAUTSCH, WILFRIED, medical microbiology educator; b. Berlin, July 22, 1957; s. Joachim and Wilfriede Ursula (Wendker) B.; m. Sabine Hofmann, June 1, 1987; children: Antonia Clarissa, Johannes Caspar, David Christian Walter. Diploma in biochemistry, U. Hannover, Germany, 1983, diploma in medicine, 1985, PhD in Biochemistry, 1989, MD, 1989. Rsch. asst. Inst. Biophys. Chemistry, U. Hannover Med. Sch., 1987-89, dir. Lab. Med. Microbiology, 1989-95, sr. registrar med. microbiology, 1995, asst. prof. med. microbiology, 1995—. Mem. German Chamber of Physicians, German Soc. of Hygiene and Microbiology, German Soc. Biochemistry and Molecular Biology, German Soc. Immunology. Roman Catholic.

BAVBEK, MURAD, neurosurgeon, educator; b. Ankara, Turkey, Apr. 23, 1959; s. Osman and Zülfiye Bavbek; m. Sevim Altin, July 8, 1982; two children. MD, Ankara U., 1982. Diplomate in medicine. Primary care physician Health Ministry, Kastamonu, Turkey, 1982-84; med. mil. physician Army, Çorlu, Turkey, 1984-86; resident in neurosurgery Hacettepe Med. Sch., Ankara, 1986-93; cons. in neurosurgery Social Assn.'s Hosp., Ankara, 1993-95; rsch. fellow in neurosurgery U. Va., Charlottesville, 1995-96; cons. in neurosurgery Baskent U., Ankara, 1997-98, asst. prof. in neurosurgery, 1998-99; assoc. prof. neurosurgery dept. Baskent U., 1999—. Contbr. articles to profl. jours. Mem. Turkish Neurosurg. Soc. Avocations: hiking, travel, biking, computer/Internet. E-mail: mbavbek@yahoo.com. Home: Angora Evler, Bulusmalar Cad C12A, 06530 Beysukent, Ankara Turkey Office: Baskent U Hosp #45, Fevzi Cakmak Bulvari 10 Sok, 06490 Bahçelievler Ankara, Turkey

BAVČAR, EVGEN-ANGEL, aesthetics researcher, writer, photographer; b. Lokavec, Slovenia, Oct. 2, 1946; became French citizen, 1982; s. Franc and Avgusta-Marija (Schlegel von Gottleben). M in history and philosophy, U. Ljubljana, Slovenia, 1972; PhD in Aesthetics, U. Sorbonne, Paris, 1976. Rschr. Nat. Ctr. Scientific Rsch. (CNRS), 1976-97; participant IX World Congress on Aesthetics, Dubrovnik, 1980; contbr. French-Culture radio programs, 1982; official photographer, Paris, 1988; organizer conf. Slovene lit., Ctr. Georges Pompidou, Paris, 1990; asst. prof., summer acad. in Berlin, 1992; lectr. on picture and the word, U. Complutense, Spain, 1993, lectr. Germany, Italy, 1993, mem. internat. jury for contemporary European video creations, Marseille, France, 1993; lectr. seminar on photography, Wiesbaden, Germany, 1994; participant confs. on image and thought, Rio de Janeiro and São Paulo, 1994. Author: Le Voyeur Absolu, 1992, Engel Unter dem Berg, 1996; collaborator (films) Narcis brez zrcala, 1987, Le regard ebloui, 1988, Jenseits der Schatten/Die Bilder von Anderswo, 1992, La chambre obscure, 1992, Das dunkle Licht, 1992, El rumor de la linea, 1994, (documentary film) Pictures of a Kingdom, 1992, (Grand Prix UNESCO, 1995), Le regard approché, 1995; collaborator, co-author (documentary film) Les Ailes de la Nuit, 1994; participant 5 radio programs for France Culture, 1989; contbr. articles to profl. jours.; subject numerous articles profl. jours. and mags.; one-man photographic exhbns. include Sunset Jazzclub, Paris, 1987, Galerie Finnegan's, Strasbourg, France, 1989, 92, Mus. fur Photographie, Braunschweig, Germany, 1990, 91, French Cultural Ctr. Ljubljana, 1990, FNAC Forum, Paris, 1990, Mcpl. Sch. Fine Arts, Boulogne-sur-mer, France, 1990, French Inst., Berlin, 1991, Städtische Galerie Wolfsburg, Germany, 1992, Cafe Aroma-Fotogalerie, Berlin, 1992, Galerie Niedlich, Stuttgart, Germany, 1992, Mus. Contemporary Art, São Paulo, 1993, Galeries Photo FNAC, French Inst., Naples, Italy, 1993, Galeries Photo FNAC, Berlin, 1994, Ezra and Cecile Zilkha Gallery, Calif., 1994, Mus. Chateau d'Annecy, France, 1994, Colombo Gallery, Milan, Italy, 1995, Galeries Photo FNAC, Caen, France, 1995, Galerie Christine Debras Yves Bical, Brussels, 1995, Pilonova galerija, Ajdovščina, Slovenia, 1996, Galerie Melweg, Amsterdam, The Netherlands, 1996, French Inst. Charles Nodier, Ljubljana, Slovenia, 1997, Centro de la Imagen, Mexico, 1999, many others. Mem. Slovene Writers' Assn. Home: 34 ave du General Leclerc, F-75014 Paris France

BAWDEN, NINA (MARY), author; b. Eng., 1925. Author: Who Calls the Tune (in U.S. as Eyes of Green), 1953, The Odd Flamingo, 1954, Change Here for Babylon, 1955, The Solitary Child, 1956, Devil by the Sea, 1957, Just Like a Lady (in U.S. as Glass Slippers Always Pinch), 1960, In Honour Bound, 1961, Tortoise by Candlelight, 1963, The Secret Passage (in U.S. as The House of Secrets), 1963, On the Run (in U.S. as Three on the Run), 1964, Under the Skin, 1964, A Little Love, A Little Learning, 1966, The White Horse Gang, 1966, The Witch's Daughter, 1966, A Handful of Thieves, 1967, A Woman of My Age, 1967, The Grain of Truth, 1968, The Runaway Summer, 1969, The Birds on the Trees, 1970, Squib, 1971, Anna Apparent, 1972, Carrie's War, George Beneath a Paper Moon, 1974, The Peppermint Pig, 1975, Afternoon of a Good Woman, 1976, Rebel on a Rock, 1978, Familiar Passions, 1979, Walking Naked, 1981, Kept in the Dark, 1982, The Ice House, 1983, The Finding, 1985, Circles of Deceit, 1987, Keeping Henry, 1988, The Outside Child, 1989, Family Money, 1991, Humbug, 1992, The Real Plato Jones, 1993, In My Own Time, 1994, A Nice Change, 1997, Off the Road, 1999. Author: Who Calls the Tune (in U.S. as Eyes of Green), 1953, The Odd Flamingo, 1954, Change Here for Babylon, 1955, The Solitary Child, 1956, Devil by the Sea, 1957, Just Life a Lady (in U.S. as Glass Slippers Always Pinch), 1960, In Honour Bound, 1961, Tortoise by Candelight, 1963, The Secret Passage (in U.S. as The House of Secrets), 1963, On the Run (in U.S. as Three on the Run), 1964, Under the Skin, 1964, A Little Love, A Little Learning, 1966, The White Horse Gang, 1966, The Witch's Daughter, 1966, A Handful of Thieves, 1967, A Woman of My Age, 1967, The Grain of Truth, 1968, The Runaway Summer, 1969, The Birds on the Trees, 1970, Squib, 1971, Anna Apparent, 1972, Carrie's War, George Beneath a Paper Moon, 1974, The Peppermint Pig, 1975, Afternoon of a Good Woman, 1976, Rebel on a Rock, 1978, Familiar Passions, 1979, Walking Naked, 1981, Kept in the Dark, 1982, The Ice House, 1983, The Finding, 1985, Circle of Deceit, 1987, Keeping Henry, 1988, The Outside Child, 1989, Family Money, 1991, Humbug, 1992, The Real Plato Jones, 1993, In My Own Time, 1994, Granny the Pag, 1995, A Nice Change, 1997. Address: care Curtis Brown Ltd 10 Astor Pl New York NY 10003-6935 also: 22 Noel Rd, London NI 8HA, England also: 19 Kapodistriou, Nauplion 21100, Greece

BAWDEN, RICHARD JOHN, agricultural studies educator; b. London, Aug. 13, 1939; arrived in Australia, 1962; s. Charles Richard and Lilian Ann (Hawkridge) B.; m. Diane Bryce, Nov. 7, 1964 (dec. July 1995); children: Marcus Kingsley, Fiona Rosemary, Lucinda Charlotte, Phoebe Diane. BSc in Agr. with honors, London U., 1961; PhD, U. Queensland, Brisbane, 1966. Unit rsch. mgr. Boots Co. Ltd. Pharms., Nottingham, Eng., 1966-67; lectr. U. New Eng., Armidale, Australia, 1968-70, dir. Drummond Coll., 1970-74, dean Faculty Rural Scis., 1977-78; dean Faculty Agr. and Rural Devel. Hawkesbury Agrl. Coll., 1978-93; prof. systemic devel. U. Western Sydney, 1988-2000, dir. Ctr. for Systemic Devel., 1993-2000, prof. emeritus, 2000—; cons. FAO, UN, Montevideo, Uruguay, 1975-76; dir. Hynwest Consulting, Richmond, Australia, 1979-96, Australia Bus. Network, Sydney, 1993—; Systemic Devel. Inst., 1999—; Systemic Devel. Assocs. 1999—; vis. disting. prof. Mich. State U., 2000—. Contbr. more than 200 articles to profl. jours. Convenor NSW Adv. Coun., Australian Broadcast Commn., Sydney, 1985-86; councillor NSW Pony Club Assn., Sydney, 1982-86. Fellow Royal Soc. for the Arts, mem. order of Australia. Avocations: music, reading philosophy, golfing, family. Office: Dept Resource Devel Mich State Univ East Lansing MI 48824

BAWN, KATHLEEN, political science educator; b. Lincoln, Nebr., Jan. 12, 1961; d. Robert and Janice Bawn; m. Roland Sturm; 1 child, Obin. BA, U. Chgo., 1982; PhD, Stanford U., 1992. Sys. analyst Commonwealth Edison, Chgo., 1982-87; asst. prof. polit. sci. UCLA, 1991-99, assoc. prof., 1999—. Contbr. articles to profl. jours., including Am. Polit. Sci. Rev., Am. Jour. Polit. Sci., Brit. Jour. Polit. Sci. Nat. fellow Hoover Instn., Stanford, 1995-96. Mem. Am. Polit. Sci. Assn., Midwest Polit. Sci. Assn. Avocation: running. E-mail: kbawn@polisci.ucla.edu. Office: UCLA Dept Polit Sci Los Angeles CA 90095-0001

BAXANDALL, PETER ROBERT, mathematician, educator; b. Liverpool, Eng., Apr. 28, 1938; s. Harry and Mary Hannah (Hillman) B.; m. Alison Jane Eady Surgey, July 3, 1963; children: John Surgey, James Peter. BSc, Manchester U., 1960; Diploma Advanced Studies in Sci., 1964; postgrad., Cambridge U., 1960-62. Lectr. U. Cape Town, South Africa, 1962-64, U. Keele, Eng., 1965-83; warden Horwood Hall, 1974-83; tchr. Bryanston Sch., Dorset, Eng., 1983-98; tutor, assoc. lectr. Open U., Eng., 1970—. Author: (with others) Proof in Mathematics, 1980, Differential Vector Calculus, 1981, Vector Calculus, 1986. Keele fellow, 1984-89. Fellow Royal Soc. Arts.; mem. Math. Assn. Avocation: canals. Home: Old Garden Cottage, Shorts Ln Blandford Forum, Dorset DT11 7BD, England

BAXTER, ALAN GEORGE, immunologist; b. Melbourne, Australia, Jan. 30, 1963; s. James and Brenda (Burstal) B.; m. Susan Margaret Munro, Mar. 3, 1991; 1 child, Robert Alexander. PhD, U. Melbourne, 1992, MB, BS, 1986. Resident Royal Melbourne Hosp., Australia, 1987-88; rsch. scholar Walter & Eliza Hall Inst., Australia, 1988-91; rsch. fellow Harvard U., Boston, 1991-92; rsch. officer Cambridge U., England, 1992-94; from rsch. officer to sr. rsch. officer Centenary Inst., Newtown, Australia, 1994—, head Autoimmunity Rsch. Group, 1998—; clin. tutor Royal Melbourne Hosp., 1988-89. Author: Germ Warfare: Breakthroughs in Immunology, 2000. Office: Centenary Inst, Locked Bag #6, 2042 Newtown NSW, Australia

BAXTER, BETTY CARPENTER, educational administrator; b. Sherman, Tex., Oct. 10, 1937; d. Granville e. and Elizabeth (Caston) Carpenter; m. Cash Baxter; children: Stephen Barrington, Catherine Elaine. AA in Music, Christian Coll., Columbia, Mo., 1957; MusB in Voice and Piano, So. Meth. U., Dallas, 1959; MA in Early Childhood Edn., Tchrs. Coll., Columbia, 1972, MEd, 1979, EdD, 1988. Tchr. Riverside Ch. Day Sch., N.Y.C., 1966-71; headmistress Episcopal Sch., N.Y.C., 1972-87, headmistress emeritus, 1987—; founding head Presbyn. Sch., Houston, 1988-94; dir. Chadwick Village Sch., Palos Verdes Peninsula, Calif. Author: The Relationship of Early Tested Intelligence on the WPPSI to Later Tested Aptitude on the SAT. Mem. ASCD, Nat. Assn. Episcopal Chs. (former gov. bd., editor Network publ.), Nat. Assn. Elem. Sch. Prins., Ind. Schs. Assn. Admissions Greater N.Y. (former exec. bd.), Nat. Assn. for Edn. of Young Children, L.A. Assn. Sch. Heads, Nat. Assn. Elem. Sch. Prins., Assn. Supervision and Curriculum Devel., Kappa Delta Pi, Delta Kappa Gamma. Republican. Presbyterian. Home and Office: 2737 Vista Mesa Dr Rncho Pls Vrd CA 90275-6323

BAXTER, GENE KENNETH, mechanical engineer, company executive; b. Emmett, Idaho, Sept. 4, 1939; s. Glen Wilton Sr. and Mable Velhelmina (Casper) B.; m. Laraine Marie Mitchell, Jan. 20, 1968; children: Gretchen Lynn, Aaron Gregory. AA in Mech. Engring. (scholar), Boise Jr. Coll., 1959; BS in Mech. Engring., U. Idaho, 1961; MS in Aero. Engring. (NDEA fellow), Syracuse U., 1966, PhD in Mech. Engring., 1971. Registered profl. engr., N.Y., Ariz. Engr. Pratt & Whitney Aircraft Co., East Hartford, Conn., 1961; tchg. and rsch. asst. Syracuse (N.Y.) U., 1962-67; engr. Galson & Galson Cons. Engrs., Syracuse, 1968; sr. mech. engr., staff engr. electronic sys. divsn. GE Co., Syracuse, 1968-77; advanced project mgr. mech. design engring. mgr., space div. GE Co., Daytona Beach, Fla., 1977-82; engring. dept. head Schlumberger Tech. Corp., Rosharon, Tex., 1982-83; mgr. engring., downhole svcs. divsn. Exploration Logging, Inc. divsn. Baker Internat. Corp., Sacramento, 1983-85; mgr. handling qualities sect. engring. and tng. simulation McDonnell Douglas Helicopter Co., Mesa, Ariz., 1985-87; mgr. projects mgmt. McDonnell Douglas Helicopter Co., Mesa, 1987-88, project mgr. Advanced Apache Simulation projects, 1988-91; pres. Exodyne Electric Motors, Inc., Tempe, Ariz., 1991-93, Baxter Engring., Mesa, 1993—; dir. mech. projects creating visual simulation and tng. sys., nuc. power controls, shipboard digital control sys.; dir. equipment for measurement, analysis and control of wellhead, formation and drilling parameters for oil well svcs. industry; dir. hardware sys. and software models of flight, avionics, displays, controls and aircraft subsys. for helicopter simulation and tng. sys.; dir. for design and manufacture of submersible electric motors and accessories for indsl. turbine pumping applications; dir. mech. engring. cons. for forensic applications; tchr. refresher course N.Y. State Profl. Engrs., Syracuse, 1975-76; spkr. numerous profl. confs. Contbr. articles to profl. jours. Chmn. fin. and stewardship com. United Ch. of Christ, Liverpool, N.Y., 1974-77, chmn. bd. trustees, 1977; ruling elder Ormond Beach (Fla.) Presbyn. Ch., 1979-82, chmn. stewardship com., 1979-80, pres. corp., 1980-82, chmn. fin. com., 1981-82; pres. bd. dirs. Hope Women's Ctr., 1995-2000. Recipient Design award Machinery Mag., 1961, Raymond J. Briggs award Idaho Bd. Engring. Examiners, 1961. Mem. IEEE (sr., treas. Daytona sect. 1978-79, chmn. 1979-80, treas. Phoenix Area Cons. Network 1995—), ASME, SAE, ASHRAE, NSPE, NAFE, Nat. Assn. Profl. Accident Reconstruction Specialists, Southwestern Assn. Tech. Accident Investigators, Ariz. Soc. Profl. Engrs., Phi Kappa Phi, Tau Beta Pi. Home: 1243 N Norwalk Mesa AZ 85205-4038

BAXTER, GLEN, artist; b. Leeds, Eng., Mar. 4, 1944; s. Charles and Florence B.; m. Carole Agis; 2 children. Student, Leeds Coll. Art. Exhbns. include N.Y.C., Modernism Gallery, San Francisco, Venice, Amsterdam, Tokyo, Paris; rep. U.K. at Sydney Biennale, 1986, Adelaide Festival, 1992, Hôtel Furkablick, Switzerland, 1993; retrospective at Musée de l'Abbaye Sainte-Croix, Les Sables d'Olonne, France, 1987, Maison Levanneur centre Nat. L'Esmmpe et L'Art Imprimé, Chatou, Paris, 1999, Chris Beetles Gallery, London, 1999, Modernism Gallery, 2000, Bastia, Corsica, 2000; illustrator Charlie Malarkey and the Bey Button Machine, 1986; author: The Impending Gleam, 1981, Atlas, 1982, Glen Baxter: His Life: The Years of Struggle, 1983, Jodhpurs in the Quantocks, 1986, Welcome to the Weird World of Glen Baxter, 1989, The Billiard Table Murders, A Gladys Babbington Morton Mystery, 1990, Glen Baxter Returns to Normal, 1992, The Collected Blurtings of Baxter, 1993, The Further Blurtings of Baxter, 1994, The Wonder Book of Sex, 1995, Glen Baxter's Gourmet Guide, 1997, (print catalogue) A Soul in Torment, 1999, Blizzards of Tweed, 1999, Podium, 2000. Avocations: croquet, dozing. Address: c/o Chris Beetles Gallery, 10 Ryder St St James's, London SW1Y 6QB, England

BAXTER, GLENN AUSTIN, engineer; b. Sacramento, Calif., Aug. 19, 1966; s. Gary Lyle and Joan Winafred (Reichard) B.; m. Leslie Ann Headington, June 18, 1994. Student, Multnomah Bible Coll., Portland, Oreg., 1992-94; Student, Deanza Coll., 1986-89, 94. Assembly tech. debugger Alpha Omega Computer Systems, Corvallis, Oreg., 1982-83; prototype devel. engr. Monolithic Memories, Inc., Santa Clara, Calif., 1983-87; R&D engr. Apple Computer, Inc., Cupertino, Calif., 1987-91; sr. engr. LaCie, Ltd., Beaverton, Oreg., 1991-93; cons., 1992-95; mgr. advanced devel. Xilinx, Inc., San Jose, Calif., 1994-97, staff rsch. engr., 1994—; cons. in field. Youth leader Scotts Valley Bible Ch., Calif., 1996-98. Mem. IEEE, Virtual Sockets Interface Alliance, U.S. Patent and Trademark Office. Republican. Avocations: astronomy, electronics, physics, hiking. Fax: 408-371-4264. Office: Xilinx Inc 2100 Logic Dr San Jose CA 95124-3450

BAXTER, JANET SCHWARTZ, motivational company executive, cinematographer; b. Chgo., Dec. 3, 1947; d. Joseph Robert and Marta Henrietta (Somlo) Schwartz; m. Richard Raymond Baxter, June 30, 1936. BA, U. Calif., Berkeley, 1969. Rsch. asst. Neuropsychiat. Inst. UCLA, 1967; tchr. Spaulding Youth Ctr., Tilton, N.H., 1969-73, Ind. Learning Sch., Corte Madera, Calif., 1974; mgr. office svc. Synanon, Marshall, Calif., 1974-77; tchr. Synanon Sch., Marshall, 1977-80; account exec. Synanon Fin. Mktg. Group, Badger, Calif., 1980-90; sr. mktg. cons. AdGap, Miramonte, Calif., 1990—; cons. in mktg., corp. motivation, drug rehab., operant psychology; participant numerous internat. films and TV workshops. Vol., VISTA, Harlem, N.Y.C., 1967. Mem. Advt. Splty. Inst., Nature Conservancy, World Wildlife Fund, Nat. Audubon Soc., Phi Sigma Sigma. Republican. Jewish. Avocations: hiking, tennis, flute, ecotravel, birdwatching. Home and Office: AdGap 9444 Waples St Ste 100 San Diego CA 92121-2940

BAXTER, JEFFREY Q., graphic artist, sculptor; b. Rockford, Ill., Sept. 25, 1959. Grad. high sch., Rockford. Painter, 1988—, sculptor, 1993—. Exhibns. include Gallery 10, Rockford, 1995, 96, 97, 98, 99, Art Guild of Rockford, 1995, 97, 98, 99, Arts Chatteau, Butte, Mont., 1996, 98, Joan Cawley Gallery, Scottsdale, Ariz., 1997, Charlene's Gallery 10 Ltd., Gills Rock, Wis., 1998, 99; commd. On The Water Front festival, Rockford, 1997, 98; represented in permanent collections Bachrodt Motors Inc., Ill., numerous pvt. collections; featured in International Encyclopedia Dictionary of Modern and Contemporary Art, 2000-2001. Recipient 1st and 2d place sculpture awards Minn. Aquarium Soc. Nat. Art Show, Mpls., 1993, award of Excellence, Manhattan Arts Internat. Art Competition, N.Y.C., 1996, 97, 99. Mem. Rockford Area Arts Coun., Internat. Sculpture Ctr. Home and Studio: 5299 Village Ct Rockford IL 61108-6617

BAXTER, MICHAEL ARLEN, statistician; b. Ilford, Essex, Eng., May 18, 1956; s. Herbert and Beatrice Jeanne (Fox) B.; m. Gillian Marcia Gelding, Aug. 30, 1990; children: David Charles, Samuel William. BSc in Math. with 1st class honors, U. Coll. London, 1976, MSc in Stats. with distinction, 1977, DSc in Stats., 1994. Chartered statistician, Royal Statis. Soc. Asst. statistician Office of Population Censuses and Surveys, London, 1977-83; sr. asst. statistician Dept. of Transport, London, 1983-89; head of methodology Ctrl. Statis. Office, London, 1989-94; head of rsch. Office for Nat. Stats., London, 1994—; external moderator MSc in Govt. and Bus. Stats., U. Westminster, London, 1991-93; referee various jours., 1980—; statisticians' rep., nat. exec. Assn. 1st Divsn. Civil Servants, 1991—. Author: Compulsory Seat Belt Wearing: Report by the Department of Transport, 1985, Reduction of Annual Data to Monthly or Quarterly Data, 1991, A Guide to Seasonal Adjustment of Monthly Data, 1991, 2d edit., 1994, A Guide to Seasonal Adjustment of Quarterly Data, 1991, 3d edit., 1994, A Brief Guide to Seasonal Adjustment with X-11 and QX11, 1991, Reduction of Annual Data to Monthly or Quarterly Data, 1994, A Guide to Interpreting X11ARIMA/88 Diagnostics, 1994, Interpolating Annual Data into Monthly or Quarterly Data, 1998; editor: The Retail Prices Index: A Technical Manual, 1998; contbr. articles to profl. jours. Nat. sec. B'nai B'rith Young Adults, U.K., 1982-83; young adult rep. on nat. exec. com. B'nai B'rith, U.K., 1982-84; sec. Jewish Cmty. Coun., Ilford and Dist., 1987-90; mem. nat. coun. United Synagogue, 1992-96. Recipient Jeffreys prize U. Coll. London, 1974, Stevenson prize, 1975. Fellow Royal Astron. Soc., Royal Statis. Soc.; mem. Lewis Carroll Soc. Jewish. Avocations: astronomy, Bible study, Lewis Carroll. Home: 74 Lynton Mead, London N20 8DJ, England Office: Office National Stats, 1 Drummond Gate, London SW1V 2QQ, England

BAXTER, MURDOCH SCOTT, nuclear geochemist, editor-in-chief, environmental consultant; b. Glasgow, Scotland, Mar. 12, 1944; s. John Sawyer Napier and Margaret Hastie (Murdoch) B.; m. Janice Henderson, Aug. 3, 1968; 1 child, John. BSc in Chemistry with honors, U. Glasgow, 1966, PhD in Nuclear Geochemistry, 1969. Chartered chemist, U.K. Rsch. fellow SUNY, 1969-70; lectr. in geochemistry and radiochemistry U. Glasgow, 1970-85; dir. Scottish Univs. Rsch. and Reactor Ctr., Glasgow, 1985-90, Internat. Atomic Energy Agy., Marine Environ. Lab., Monaco, 1990-97; sci. cons., editor Elsevier Sci. Ltd., 1982—; prof. U. Glasgow, 1985-95; cons. U.K. Rsch. Couns., Internat. Atomic Engergy Agy., local authorities and media; vis. fellow Internat. Atomic Energy Agy., Monaco, 1981-82. Founder and editor-in-chief Jour. Environ. Radioactivity; mem. edit. bd. Jour. Radioanalytical and Nuclear Chemistry; sr. editor Elsevier book series Radioactivity in the Environment; contbr. over 150 articles to profl. jours. Recipient rsch. grants U.K. Govt./Rsch. Couns., 1970-90; named Chevalier of Order of St. Charles for svcs. to Principality, Prince Rainier III of Monaco, 1997. Fellow Royal Soc. Edinburgh, Royal Soc. Chemistry, Internat. Union Eco-Ethics, Internat. Union Radioecology (hon., mem. adv. panel), Scotch Malt Whisky Soc., Scotish Assn. Marine Sci.; mem. Queens Pk. Football Club. Avocations: hill walking, sports, sailing, cars. Fax: 0044 1852 300 351. E-mail: baxter@j-e-r.demon.co.uk. Home and Office: Ampfield House, Clachan Seil, Argyll PA34 4TL, Scotland

BAXTER, ROGER GEORGE, boarding school consultant; b. Redditch, Eng., Apr. 21, 1940; s. Benjamin George and Gweneth Muriel Baxter; m. Dorothy Ann Cook, Mar. 29, 1967; children: Philip Leslie, Fiona Jane. BSc, Sheffield (Eng.) U., 1963, PhD, 1966. Jr. rsch. fellow U. Sheffield, 1965-66, lectr. dept. applied math., 1966-70; asst. math. master Winchester (Eng.) Coll., 1970-81, undermaster, 1976-81; headmaster Sedbergh Sch., Cumbria, Eng., 1982-95; boarding sch. cons. Select Edn., 1995—; gov. Bramcote Sch., Scarborough, 1982-95, Hurworth House Sch., Darlington, 1982-95, Cathedral Choir Sch., Ripon, 1984-95, Mowden Hall Sch., Northumberland, 1984-96, Cundall Manor Sch., York, 1988-98, Durham Sch., 1995—, Bow Sch., Durham, 1995—, Ch. Warden, Cartmel Priory, 1997—. Freeman, City of London; liverman Gunmaker co. Avocations: opera production, opera, music, cooking, wine. Home: The Rivelin, Lindale, Grange over Sands LA11 6LJ, England

BAXTER-SMITH, GREGORY JOHN, lawyer; b. Davenport, Iowa, Sept. 27, 1949; s. James Sanford Baxter and Doris Arlene (Olson) Smith; m. Carolyn Imes, June 10, 1975 (div. Oct. 1980); children: Bradley Imes, Brian McBride; m. Karen Ruth Thomas, Dec. 12, 1986. BA in English, Bucknell U., 1971; JD, U. Mo., 1974. Bar: Mo. 1974, U.S. Dist. Ct. (we. dist.) Mo. 1975, U.S. Tax Ct. 1975. Clk. Hon. Charles Shangler Mo. Ct. Appeals, Kansas City, 1974-75; assoc. Miller & Poole, Springfield, Mo., 1975-76; shareholder Poole & Smith, P.C., Springfield, 1976-78, Gregory J. Smith, P.C., Springfield, 1978-86, Poole, Smith & Wieland, P.C., Springfield, 1986-90, Smith & Fels, P.C., Springfield, 1990—. Mem. Springfield Met. Bar Assn., Greene County Estate Planning Coun., Mo. Bar Assn., Elks. Republican. Lutheran. Avocation: golf. Home: 5027 S Glenhaven Ave Springfield MO 65804-7800 Office: Smith & Fels PC 528 W Battlefield St Ste 103 Springfield MO 65807-4122

BAYANDOR, JAVID, aerospace engineer, researcher, educator; b. Tehran, Iran, 1969; s. Nozar and Fereshteh (Marashi) B.; m. Samra Sangari, 1995. Math. and Physics Diploma, Alborz Coll., Tehran, 1987; BSc in Aerospace Engring., Sharif U. of Tech., Tehran, 1992; PhD in Aerospace Engring., Royal Melbourne Inst. Tech., 2000. Aerospace engr., rschr. Sharif U. Tech., Tehran, 1992-94, engring. instr., 1992-94; engring. rschr. Swinburne U. Tech., Melbourne, Australia, 1995-96, vis. lectr., 1995; aerospace engr., rschr., educator Sir Lawrence Wackett Aerospace Ctr., Royal Melbourne Inst. Tech., 1995—; cons. Iran-Nat. Automobile Co., Tehran, 1992-94; propeller overhaul trainer Iran-Air Airline, Tehran, 1990. Contbr. articles to profl. jours. and internat. confs. Recipient various rsch. and scholarship awards. Mem. AIAA, ASME, Aus. Space Rsch. Inst., Space Assn. Aus., Iran Soc. Mech. Engrs. Achievements include development of a hydro-propulsive system (HYPS); aerodynamic design and optimization of a locally-manufactured automobile and an aircraft. E-mail: bayandorj@asme.org. Office: Royal Melbourne Inst Tech, 226 Lorimer St Port Melbourne, 3207 Melbourne Australia

BAYBAYAN, RONALD ALAN, lawyer; b. Paia, Hawaii, July 4, 1946; s. Celedonio Ladresa and Carlina (Domingo) B.; m. Dianne Lea, June 14, 1969 (div. June 1985); children: Alycia Kay, Amber Lea; m. Sharyn Dee Huckins, Dec. 31, 1985 (div. Oct. 1996). BA, Coe Coll., 1968; JD, Drake U., 1974. Bar: Iowa 1977, U.S. Dist. Ct. (so. dist.) Iowa 1977, U.S. Tax Ct. 1978, U.S. Dist. Ct. (no. dist.) Iowa 1980, U.S. Ct. Appeals (8th cir.) 1985, U.S. Supreme Ct. 1985, U.S. Dist. Ct. Hawaii 1986. Asst. law librarian Drake U., Des Moines, 1974-77; assoc. Law Office Mike Wilson, Des Moines, 1977-78; sole practice Des Moines, 1978—; bd. dirs. Berkley & Co. Amb.; presenter in field. Co-author: Paralegals in Family Law Practice in Iowa, 1995, How to Draft Wills and Trusts in Iowa, 1996, 99, A Practical Guide to Estate Administration in Iowa, 1997. Bd. dirs. Wakonda Christian Ch., 1989-90; dir. communique Victory Christian Ctr., 1991—; mem. bd. counselors Drake U. Law Sch., 1997—. Served with USAF, 1969-73. Mem. ABA, Iowa Bar Assn., Polk County Bar Assn., Am-Filipino Assn. Iowa (bd. dirs. 1986), Bass Anglers Sportsman Soc. (Iowa chpt. pres. 1979-82), Iowans for Better Fisheries (bd. dirs. 1991), Mid-Iowa Bassmasters (past pres., past v.p., past sec.). Republican. Home: 6217 Urbandale Ave Des Moines IA 50322-3541 Office: 4921 Douglas Ave Ste 3 Des Moines IA 50310-2749

BAYEFSKY, ABA, artist; b. Toronto, Ont., Can., Apr. 7, 1923; s. Samuel and Hetty (Simon) B.; m. Evelyn Swartz; children: Anne, Edra, Eban. Student, Ctrl. Tech. Sch., Toronto, Acad. Julian, Paris. Dir. art

classes Hart House, U. Toronto, 1957-69; staff mem. Ont. Coll. Art, Toronto, 1957-88; Mem. Internat. Jury for 2nd Internat. Exhbn. Prints, Tokyo, 1960. One-man shows include Albert White Gallery, Toronto, 1966, Can. Embassy, Washington, 1971, Art Gallery Hamilton, 1973, Can. Consulate, N.Y., 1973, Ont. Coll. Art, 1976, The Market Gallery, Toronto, 1982, Gustafsson Gallery, Toronto, 1983, Junstina M. Barnicke Gallery, Hart House, U. Toronto, 1986, Koffler Gallery, 1989; works exhibited at Can. Embassy, Washington, 1993, Can. House, London, 1994, Can. War Mus., Ottawa, 1998, Nat. Gallery Ottawa, Can., Nat. Gallery Victoria, Melbourne, Australia, Art Gallery Ont., Hamilton, London, Ont., Sarnia, Met. Mus., N.Y., Libr. Congress, Washington, Hebrew U., Jerusalem, Ecole des Beaux Arts, Que., Loyola Coll., Que., Concordia U., Montreal, Hart House, U. Toronto, Beaverbrook Gallery, Fredericton, N.B., The Holocaust Mus. at Yad Vashem, Jerusalem, colls. in Can., U.S. and India. Ofcl. Can. war artist RCAF, 1943—. With RCAF, 1942-46. Recipient Purchase prize Can. Soc. Painters in Watercolor, 1953, J.W.L. Forster award Ont. Soc. Artists, 1958, Order of Can., 1979, Commemorative medal 125th Anniversary, Can. Confedn., 1992; French Govt. scholar, 1947-48; Can. Coun. fellow, 1958. Mem. Can. Soc. Graphic Art (past pres.), Can. Soc. Painters in Watercolour, Can. Group Painters (past pres.), Fedn. Can. Artists (past pres. Ont. region). Home: 7 Paperbirch Dr, Don Mills, ON Canada M3C 2E6

BAYEKOVA, CHOLPON, judge. Chair. constitutional ct. Constitutional Ct. of Kyrgstan. Office: Constitutional Court, Orozbekova St 37, 720040 Bishkek Kyrgyzstan*

BAYER, EDWARD ALLEN, biochemist, researcher; b. Detroit, Jan. 4, 1947; arrived in Israel, 1971; s. Harmon Symond and Adele Ann (Allen) B.; m. Laurette Tami Amar, Aug. 9, 1968 (div. 1973); children: Tali, Havi; m. Anette-Hannah Tenenbaum, Oct. 29, 1974; children: Shiri, Karen, Roey. BS, U. Mich., 1969; MS, Wayne State U., 1971; PhD, Weizmann Inst., 1976. Postdoctoral tng. Tel Aviv U., 1977-82; with Weizmann Inst. Sci., Rehovot, Israel, 1982—; cons. Belovo Chems., Bastogne, Belgium, 1990—, Convatec, Bristol-Myers-Squibb, Clwyd, U.K., 1993—, STC Labs., Winnipeg, Can., 1994—, CBD Techs., Fort Lee, N.J., 1994—; chmn. Gordon Conf. on Cellulases and Cellulosomes, N.H., 1999. Editor: Avidin-Biotin Technology, Methods in Enzymology, 1990; assoc. editor Biotech. Advances, 1998—; contbr. articles to profl. jours.; co-inventor Avidin-Biotin systems; co-discoverer of cellulosomes. Recipient Sarstedt Rsch. award German Assn. for Clin. Chemistry, 1990; named Guest of Honor Doctoral Thesis awards Utrecht U., 1991. Mem. Internat. Soc. for Molecular Recognition (gen. coun. 1993-99). Jewish. Avocations: art, music, fossil collecting. Home: HaToot 5, Famot HaShavim 00000, Israel Office: Weizmann Inst Sci, Dept Biol Chemistry, Rehovot 76100, Israel

BAYER, ERNST, academic administrator, chemistry educator; b. Ludwigshafen, Germany, Mar. 24, 1927; s. Ernst and Maria (Schmeck) B.; m. Ingeborg Dedekind, Mar. 1953; children: Bettina, Carola, Andrea, Klaus, Tom. B in Chemistry, U. Heidelberg, Fed. Republic Germany, 1950, M in Chemistry, 1952; D in Natural Sci., U. Freiburg, Fed. Republic Germany, 1954. Head dept. biochemistry Govt. Rsch. Inst., Geiweilerhof, Fed. Republic Germany, 1954-57; lectr. U. Karlsruhe, Fed. Republic Germany, 1957-62; prof. U. Tübingen, Fed. Republic Germany, 1962—; Welch prof. U. Houston, 1967-71; v.p. U. Tübingen, 1976-79. Inventor sludge to oil process; contbr. numerous articles to profl. jours. Head Govt. Adv. Com. on Existing Chems., Munich, Tübingen and Bonn, Fed. Republic Germany, 1984. With German Navy, 1944-45. Decorated Merit Cross (Fed. Republic Germany); recipient A.J.P. Martin award Chromatography Soc., 1978, Tswett medal USSR Acad. Sci., 1978, BP Energy Rsch. award, London, 1982, Philip Morris prize, 1986, Internat. prize TUV, 1990, Fresenius prize, 1994, Maria Curie medal, 1997. Mem. German Chem. Soc. (bd. dirs. 1984—, v.p. 1992—, Richard Kuhn medal 1990), Rotary of Reutlingen and Tübingen, Austrian Soc. Analytical Chemistry (Pregl medal 1993). Lutheran. Home: Bei der Ochsenweide 17, D-72076 Tübingen Germany Office: U Tübingen Inst Organic Chem, Auf der Morgenstelle 18, D-72076 Tübingen Germany

BAYER, FERN PATRICIA, curator, writer; b. Montreal, Que., Can., Oct. 23, 1949; d. George James and Catherine Marie Gloria (Boucher) B. BA, McGill U., 1971; diploma in mus. sci., U. Internat. Art, Italy, 1972; MA, U. Toronto, 1975. tchg. asst. U. Toronto, 1975-76; freelance art cons., 1975-77; chief currator Govt. Ont. Art Collection, 1977-95; curator, mem. bd. dirs. Art Metropole, Toronto. Guest curator The Search for the Spirit: General Idea, 1968-75; ind. curator major internat. contemporary art exhbns., Can., U.S., Middle East, Japan and Europe; author: The Ontario Collection, 1984, (with E. Arthur) From Front Street to Queen's Park, 1979; contbr. articles to profl. jours. Roman Catholic. Office: Ste 1017, 131 Bloor St W, Toronto, ON Canada M5S 1S3

BAYER, JONATHAN LEVY, photographer; b. N.Y.C., Mar. 28, 1936; s. Julien Sampson Levy and Joella (Haweis) Bayer. AB, Harvard U., 1958; MA, U. Pa., 1963. Tchg. fellow U. Pa., Phila., 1963-65; staff writer Congl. Quar., Washington, 1965-67; chief publs. European Cmty. Info. Svc., Washington, 1967-71; freelance photographer London, 1971—; mem. visual arts panel, vice chmn., chmn. Greater London Arts Assn., 1978-81; trustee The Photographers' Gallery, London, 1985-95. Exhbns. include The Photographic Gallery, Southampton, U.K., 1975, Carlton Gallery, N.Y.C., 1975, The Photographer's Gallery, London, 1976, Parsons-Dreyfuss Gallery, N.Y.C., 1977, Ian Birksted Gallery, London, 1980, Hartnell Coll., Salinas, Calif., 1981, The White Gallery, Tel Aviv, 1981, Bank of Am., San Francisco, 1982, Camden Art Ctr., London, 1989; group shows include Studio Gallery, Washington, 1974, Midlands Group, Nottingham, U.K., 1976, 78, Gainsborough House, Sudbury House, U.K., 1979. Home: 29 Belsize Park, London NW3 4DX, England

BAYER, THOMAS ANDREAS, biologist; b. Esslingen, Germany, Nov. 20, 1961; s. Adolf and Hildegard (Berner) B.; m. Gudrun Schultz; 1 child, Maximilian. Diploma in Biology, U. Stuttgart (Germany), 1989; PhD in Biology, U. Cologne (Germany), 1993. Sr. scientist dept. psychiatry U. Bonn (Germany) Med. Ctr., 1993—. Contbr. articles to profl. jours. With Allied Mobile Force, Germany, 1983-84. Mem. Soc. for Neurosci., German Neurosci. Assn. Office: Dept Psychiatry, Sigmund-Freud Strasse 25, 53105 Bonn Germany

BAYERL, MAXIMILIAN, electrical engineer; b. Salzburg, Austria, Feb. 19, 1942; s. Maximilian and Berta (Muhr) B.; m. Karin Hertha Adolph, May 2, 1972 (div. 1993); children: Immanuel, Ilja. Grad., Coll. Higher Tech. Edn., Salzburg, 1961. Design engr. Tauernkraftwerke, Salzburg, 1965-70; from engr. to mgr., dir. Westinghouse Bell, Johannesburg, South Africa, 1971-84; mng. dir. Martech Holdings, Johannesburg, 1985-90; CEO IMS-Ionen-Mikofabrikations Sys., Vienna, Austria, 1990—. Avocations: art, traveling, skiing, tennis. Office: IMS Ionen Mikrofabrikations, Schreygasse 3, A-1020 Vienna Austria

BAYES, RONALD HOMER, English language educator, author; b. Freewater, Oreg., July 19, 1932; s. Floyd Edgar and Mildred Florence (Cochran) B. BS, East Oreg. State Coll., 1955, MS, 1956; postgrad., U. Pa., 1959-60; DDM, U. Delle Arti, Termi, Italy, 1982. Asst. prof. English Ea. Oreg. State Coll., LaGrande, 1955-56, assoc. prof. English, 1960-68; lectr. English U. Md., College Park, 1958-59, 66-67; prof. St. Andrews Presbyn. Coll., Laurinburg, N.C., 1968—; founder, exec. bd. St. Andrews Rev. & Press, Laurinburg, 1970-95; mem. N.C. State Arts Coun., Raleigh, 1987-89; master poet Atlantic Ctr. for Arts, New Smyrna Beach, Fla., 1988; cons. Nat. Coun. for Arts, Washington, 1969-71. Author: (poetry) Dust & Desire, 1961, Cages & Journeys, 1964, Child Outside My Window, 1965, History of the Turtle, 1970, The Casketmaker, 1972, Porpoise, 1974, Tokyo Annex, 1977, King of August, 1979, Fram, 1979, Beast in View, 1985, Guises, 1992; (fiction) Sister City, 1971. Chmn. Rep. Ctrl. Com., Union County, Oreg., 1967-68, Scotland County, N.C., 1980-81; bd. dirs. Scotland County Humane Soc., Laurinburg, 1993—. With U.S. Army, 1956-58. Woodrow Wilson Nat. fellow, 1959-60; named one of Outstanding Young Men of Am., 1960; recipient Outstanding Alumni award Ea. Oreg. State Coll., 1973; Roanoke-Chowan prize for poetry, 1973, N.C. Writers' Conf. award, 1987, master poet Atlana Ctr. for the Arts, 1988, N.C. arts grantee, 1988, N.C. award for Literature, 1989, cert. honor Poetry Coun. N.C., 1994; Disting. Prof. Creative Writing Chair named in his honor, 1999. Mem. Danforth Found. (assoc.), Internat. House Japan, Japan Soc., N.C. Poetry Soc. (life), Oregon Poetry Soc. (life), Mason. Episcopalian. Avocations: gardening, reading, jogging, travel. Home: PO Box 206 Laurinburg NC 28353-0206

BAYKAM, BEDRI, painter, writer, politician; b. Ankara, Apr. 26, 1957; m. Sibel Yagci, June 1997. Student, French Lycée, U. Paris, Calif. Coll. Arts and Crafts. Exhibitions include Ataturk Cultural Ctr., 1983, 85, 86, 88, 90, 92, 94, 97, 99, City Gallery, 1983, Martin/Molinary, Paris, 1984-85, Gallery Baraz, 1984, Gallery Wanda Reiff, Holland, 1985, Galerie Daniel Templon, Paris, 1985, Gallery Wirtz, San Francisco, 1986, E.M. Donahue, N.Y.C., 1988-92, Stedelijk Mus. Schiedam, Holland, 1993, Galerie Lavignes-Bastille, Paris, 1990-94, Mus. of Revolution, Havana, Cuba, 1999, Galerie Zafira, Paris, 1999; artist retrospective exhibit monography I'm Nothing but I'm Everything, 1999; author art books: The Brain of Paint, 1990, Monkey's Right to Paint, 1994, Fleeing Moments, Enduring Tastes, 1996, the Color of the era, 1997; author polit. books: May 27 Was Our First Love, 1994, Mustafa Kemal's on Duty Now, 1994, Secular Turkey Without Concession, 1995, His Eyes Rest on Us, 1997, The Years of 68, Vol. I, 1998, Vol. II, 1999, Che, the Last Condottiere of the Millenium, 2000; contbr. articles to profl. jours.; columnist Aksam (daily). Party assembly mem. Republican People's Party, 1995-98, Turkish Social Democrats. Named Painter of Yr. Nokta mag., 1987, 90, 95, 96, 97, 98, Best Artist Laureat winner, 1994 Art Junction, Art Festival Cannes, France. Avocations: tennis, football, pop-rock music. E-mail: bedbay@turk.net. Home: Palanga Cad 33/23, Ortakoy, Istanbul 80840, Turkey

BAYKUT, FATMA SACIDE, physical chemistry educator; b. Tarsus, Adana, Turkey, Aug. 28, 1923; d. Mehmet Mahir and Hatice Mergen; m. Muhiddin Fikret Baykut, June 23, 1949; children: Gökhan, Doğuhan. BS in Chem. Engring., U. Istanbul, Turkey, 1946, PhD in Phys. Chemistry, 1950. Asst. prof. U. Istanbul, Chemistry Faculty, 1950-55, assoc. prof., 1955-67, prof., 1967-90, prof. emeritus, 1990—, head phys. chemistry dept., 1967-80, 80-90, head chemistry dept., 1967-80, 80-90; mem. coun. mgrs. U. Istanbul, Engring. Faculty, 1967-89. Author: Physical Chemistry of Surfactants, 1967, (with others) Physical Chemistry, 1975, 2nd edit., 1980, Surfactants and Their Physico-Chemical Properties, 1986, Environmental Problems and Protection, 1987, Industrial Electrochemistry, 1989, Advanced Physical Chemistry I, 1991, Physical Chemistry I and II, 1994; contbr. 66 sci. publs. to profl. jours. Mem. Am. Chem. Soc., Turkish Chem. Soc., N.Y. Acad. Sci.

BAYLAC-DOMENGETROY, FRÉDÉRIC PIERRE DOMINIQUE, cardiologist; b. Boulogne, France, Apr. 27, 1960; s. Marcel and Marie-Josephe Louise A. (Emeriau) B.; m. Joelle Bernadette Riffaud, June 20, 1986; children: Emeline, Anne Sophie, Clotilde, Marie-Anais, Adelaide, Claire, Justine. Grad., Paris Med. Faculty, 1984. Med. intern Paris, 1984-85; med. intern in cardiology Poitiers, France, 1985-89, physiological D.E.A., 1987-88; hosp. practician Angouleme, France, 1989-90; liberal cardiologist Cognac, France, 1990—; cons. CNP, 1989—. Author: Flecainide/Acetate and Slow Inward Current, 1987, Relations Between Cardiac and Vascular Effects of Nitrendipine, 1989; contbr. articles to profl. jours. Mem. adminstrn. coun. APEL, Cognac, 1996, pres., 1998; mem. ADOT, Angouleme, 1993, Croix Rouge Française, 1990. Capt. Med., 1989. Recipient Young Investigator award, 1990, Young Student award Paris-West, 1982. Fellow French Cardiology Fedn. Paris; mem. Kiwanis (past sect., Cognac François 1991, Gold Kiwanis 1995). Avocations: jogging, archery. Home: 32 St Marguerite de Navarre, 16100 Cognac France Office: 4 North St, 16100 Cognac France

BAYLEN, JOSEPH O., retired history educator; b. Chgo., Feb. 12, 1920; s. Leo and Mary (Lakin) B.; m. Margaret Pringle, June 16, 1979; 1 son, James Leo; 1 stepdaughter, Julia. AA, Wright Jr. Coll., 1939; BE, No. Ill. U., 1941; MA, Emory U., 1947; PhD, U. N.Mex., 1949. Instr. history U. N.Mex., 1948-49; asst. prof. history N.Mex. Highlands U., Las Vegas, 1950-52; assoc. prof. N.Mex. Highlands U., 1952-54; prof. history, chmn. div. social sci. Delta State Tchrs. Coll., 1954-57; prof. history Miss. State U., 1957-61; prof. history U. Miss., 1961-66, chmn., 1963-66; chmn. dept. history Ga. State U., 1966-78, Regents' prof., 1969-83, emeritus Regents' prof. history, 1983—; lectr. in history Ctr. for Continuing Edn., U. Sussex, 1985-89; vis. asst. prof. U. Md. Overseas Program, Europe, 1952-53; vis. assoc. prof. Agnes Scott Coll., 1953; vis. prof. summers Emory U., 1952, U. Ala., 1960, Georgetown U., 1964, 65, Tulane U., 1966, 68, U. York, 1979; Fulbright-Hays lectr., U.K., 1961-62, 72-73; mem. Miss. Hist. Commn., 1954-57, 63-66; vice chmn. So. Humanities Conf., 1964-65, chmn., 1965-66; mem. Nat. Fulbright Adv. Screening Com., 1962-64, chmn., 1964-65; cons. NEH, 1969-83, BBC-TV, 1988—; mem. Fed. Govt. Regional Archives Com., 1971-74; chmn. adv. com. on history Univ. System of Ga., 1970-72, 76-78, British Libr., Consultative Group on Newspapers, 1990—; lectr. U. Sussex, City Univ., London. Author: monographs Mme. Juliette Adam, Gambetta, and the Idea of a Franco-Russian Alliance, 1960, Lord Kitchener and the Viceroyalty of India, 1910, 1965, Soldier-Surgeon; The Crimean War Letters of Dr. D.A. Reid, 1955-1856, 1968, W.T. Stead and the Russian Revolution of 1905, 1969; (with O.S. Pidhainy) East-European and Russian Studies in the American South, 1972; contbr.: (with others) Dictionary of Labour Biography, 1977, Biographical Dictionary of Internationalists, 1983, British Literary Magazines, 1984, Biographical Dictionary of Peace Leaders, 1985, Victorian Britain: An Encyclopedia, 1988, Papers for the Millions: The New Journalism in Britain..., 1988, Biographical Dictionary of American Journalism, 1989, Ency. of the British Press, 1992, Dictionary of Literary Biography (British Publishing Houses 1881-1965), 1992; co-editor: (with N.J. Gossman) The 1890's An Encyclopedia of British Literature, Art and Culture, 1993, Twentieth Century Britain: An Encyclopedia, 1995, Shaping the Collective Memory, Government and International Historians through Two World Wars, 1996, A Journalism Reader, 1997, American National Biography, 1999, New Dictionary of National Biography, 2000, Reader's Guide to British History, 2000; bd. editor: Encyclopedia of 1848 Revolutions; So. Humanities Rev.; mem. editl. adv. bd. Ency. of the World Press; contbr. over 150 articles to profl. jours., over 160 book revs. Capt. AUS, 1941-45. Guggenheim fellow, 1958-59, rsch. fellow Inst. Advanced Studies, Princeton U., 1966; summer fellowships and awards include So. Fellowship Found., 1955, Am. Philos. Soc., 1956, 65, Am. Coun. Learned Socs., 1961-62; English-Speaking Union, 1978; recipient Most Disting. Alumni award No. Ill. U., 1976, Disting. Prof. award Ga. State U., 1979, Disting. Prof. award Ga. State U. chpt. Omicron Delta Kappa, 1980, Hugh McCall award for disting. achievement in hist. studies, 1982. Fellow Royal Hist. Soc.; mem. Am. Hist. Assn. (exec. coun. 1972-75), So. Hist. Assn. (chmn. European history sect. 1972-73, exec. coun. 1983-86), N.Am. Conf. Brit. Studies (chmn. so. conf. 1977-79), European Movement, Travellers Club, London Press Club (bd. dirs. 1995—), Phi Kappa Phi, Omicron Delta Kappa, Phi Alpha Theta, Pi Gamma Mu, Kappa Delta Pi, Phi Kappa Tau. Home: 45 Saffrons Ct, Compton Place Rd, Eastbourne BN21 1DY, England

BAYLEY, STEPHEN, design consultant, author; b. Cardiff, Oct. 13, 1951; s. Donald and Anne B.; m. Flo Fothergill, 1981; 2 children. Student, Quarry Bank Sch., Liverpool, Manchester U., Liverpool Sch. Arch. Lectr. history of art The Open U., 1974-76, U. Kent, 1976-80; dir. Conran Found., The Boilerhouse Project, The Design Mus., 1980-90; prin. design cons. Eye-Q Ltd, 1991—; creative dir. New Millenium Experience Co., 1997-98; lectr. throughout U.K. and abroad. Author: In Good Shape, 1979, The Albert Memorial, Conran Directory of Design, Commerce and Culture, 1989, Labour Camp, 1998, General Knowledge, 2000, others; contbr. articles to newspapers and mags. Named Columnist of Yr., Periodical Pubs. Assn., 1995, Chevalier des Arts et des Lettres. Avocation: travel-related services. Fax: 02078209966. Address: 176 Kennington Park Rd, London SE11 4BT, England

BAYLISS, DAVID, transport studies educator, consultant; b. Cleveleys, Lancashire, Eng., July 9, 1938; s. Herbert and Anne Esther (Roper) B.; m. Dorothy Christine Crohill, Aug. 25, 1961; children: Mark Andrew, Jason Peter, Ruth Abigail. BS in Civil Engring., Manchester U., 1961, diploma in town planning, 1966; testamur, Inst. Mcpl. Engrs., 1963, diploma in traffic engring., 1964. Registered chartered engr. U.K. Chief transport planner Greater London Coun., 1972-84; dir. planning London Regional Transport, 1984-99; expert advisor OECD, World Bank, European Conf. of Ministers of Transport, WHO, European Commn.; vis. prof. Imperial Coll. London, 2000—. Author: Encyclopedia Brittanica Year Book (Transportation), 1978-87; contbr. numerous articles on urban and transport planning to profl. publs. Fellow Inst. Civil Engrs., Royal Town Planning INst., Chartered Inst. Transport, Inst. Hwys. and Transp., Inst. Transp. Engrs. (U.S.); mem. Sci. Rsch. Coun. (chmn. transport com. 1978-80), Regional Studies Assn. (chmn. 1980-82), Brit. Parking Assn. (pres. 1987), Inst. Logistics e Transport, Royal Soc. Arts, Royal Acad. Engring. Home: 37 Ledborough Ln, Beaconsfield Bucks HP9 2DB, England Office: Halerow Vineyard House, 44 Brook Green, London W6 7BY, England

BAYLISS, SIR RICHARD IAN SAMUEL, endocrinologist; b. Tettenhall, Eng., Jan. 2, 1917; s. Frederick William and Muryel Anne (Sanderson) B.; m. Joan Hardman Lawson, 1942 (dec.); children: Caroline, Christopher; m. Constance Frey, 1958 (div. 1979); children: Susan, Virginia; m. Marina Audrey de Borchgave D'Altena, 1979. BA, Cambridge U., 1938, MB, 1941, MD, 1946. Resident St. Thomas's Hosp., London, 1941-45; physician Royal Postgrad. Med. Sch., London, 1948-54, Westminster Hosp., London, 1954-81, Her Majesty the Queen's Household, London, 1964-70, Her Majesty the Queen, London, 1970-82; dean Westminster Med. Sch., London, 1960-65; cons. in medicine Royal Navy, 1977-82; gov. Merck Found., Rahway, N.J., 1973-89; dir. J.S. Pathology Svcs., London, 1981-90, Pvt. Patient's Plan, London, 1978-89; cons. endocrinologist; chmn. med. adv. panel Ind. TV Commn., London; cons. Biotech. Investments Ltd., London. Author: Practical Procedures, 3d edit., 1960, Thyroid Disease: The Facts, 3d edit., 1998; editor: Investigations in Endocrine Disease, 1974. Decorated knight comdr. Victorian Order; fellow Rockefeller Found., 1950-51. Fellow Royal Soc. Medicine (pres. endocrinology sect. 1966-68), Royal Coll. Physicians; mem. Assn. Physicians (pres. 1980-81), Thyroid Club (pres. 1972-78). Avocations: skiing, music. Home: 61 Onslow Sq Flat 7, London SW7 3LS, England

BAYNES, ROY DENNIS, hematologist, educator; b. Johannesburg, South Africa, Mar. 1, 1955; came to U.S., 1989; s. Roy Dennis and Theresa Mary (Chellew) B.; m. Jessica Alice Hellings, Oct. 5, 1979; children: Terry Louise, Richard Dennis. MB, BChir, U. Witwatersrand, Johannesburg, 1978, M of Medicine, 1986, PhD, 1987. Diplomate Am. Bd. Internal Medicine and Hematology, Am. Bd. Internal Medicine. Intern Johannesburg Hosp., 1979; medicine resident U. Witwatersrand Med. Sch., 1980-83, rsch. fellow Med. Rsch. Coun., 1984-85, lectr., cons. physician, 1986-89; rsch. prof. U. Kans. Med. Ctr., Kansas City, 1989-90, prof. medicine, 1990-97; prof. medicine & oncology, dir. bone marrow transplantation Wayne State U., Detroit, 1997—; cons. South African Inst. Med. Rsch., Johannesburg, 1986-89, Nat. Livestock Bd., Chgo., 1993-94; pres. Med. Grads. Assn., Johannesburg, 1988. Author: Iron Metabolism in Health and Disease, 1994; contbr. articles to profl. jours. Capt. S. African Def. Fource Med. Svcs., 1980, 85-86, Namibia. Recipient Suzman Gold Medal award Coll. Medicine, 1983, Blignault award Med. Assn., South Africa, 1990; Zoutendyk fellow Med. Rsch Coun., South Africa, 1985. Fellow ACP (diplomate); mem. Am. Soc. Hematology, Am. Soc. Clin. Oncology, Ctrl. Soc. Clin. Investigation, South African Soc. Med. Oncology (founding mem.), Sigma Xi (treas. 1992-95). Achievements include biochemical characterization of the serum form of transferrin receptor; definition of the mechanism of production of the serum form of transferrin receptor; discovery of a serum form of erythropoietin receptor; description of an enhancing effect of IL-II on iron absorption; defining the role of bone marrow transplantation in solid malignancies; evaluating the use of immunotheraphy in elimination of minimal residual malignancy after transplantation; establishment of major bone marrow transplant problem. Office: Karmanos Cancer Inst Bone Marrow Transplantation 4 Brush 3990 John R Detroit MI 48201

BAYOR, BERNARD KOFI, financial company executive; b. Daffiama, Ghana, June 10, 1955; s. Tobias and Angelina Bayor. BA in Sociology and Econs. with honors, U. Ghana, Legon, 1978. Cert. in budgeting and fin. mgmt. Ghana Inst. Mgmt. and Pub. Adminstrn. Project officer Ashanti Regional; tutor in English and econs. Toase Secondary Sch., 1985-88; budget analyst Bolgatanga (Ghana) Dist., 1988—; chief exec., dir. B&B Global Bus. & Commerce Ltd., Bolgatanga, 1992—; exec. dir., founder Devel. Network Ctr., Bolgatanga, 1994; tutor Navarongo Secondary Sch., 1978-79; exec. Devel. Corp., Kumasi, 1983-85; asst. export promotion officer Ghana Export Promotion Coun., Accra, 1979-80. Contbr. poems to periodicals. Chmn. Rural Aid/Upper East Rural Water Devel. Project, Bolgatanga, 1989-91. Mem. Sawan Kirpal Ruhani Mission Sci. of Spirituality (group leader Bolgatanga chpt.). Avocations: writing short stories and poems, travel, gardening, farming, reading. Office: B&B Global Bus, Commerce Ltd PO Box 102, Bolgatanga Upper East, Ghana

BAYOT, MARC, investment consultant, finance educator; b. Brussels, Belgium, Oct. 2, 1937; m. Maria Giuseppina Chiarelli, Dec. 2, 1961; children: Bernard, Ariane. Student humanities-Latin scis., Athenee Royal, Etterbeek, Belgium, 1949-55; Ingenieur Commercial, Free U., Brussels, 1959; grad. commerce and finance, Free U., 1960; grad. in econs., Johns Hopkins U., Bologna, Italy, 1960. Mgr. Generale Bank, Brussels, 1968-78, dep. mgr., 1978-90, gen. mgr., 1990-95, strategic adv. investment mgmt., 1995—, pres. investment funds; prof. Free U., Brussels, 1980. Mem. Belgian Investment Funds Assn. (internat. adv. 1991, chmn. pension com.), European Fedn. Investment Funds and Companies (hon. pres. 1994, chmn. pension com.). Home: Rue Hubert Coenen 5, 1160 Brussels Brabant, Belgium Office: Fortis Investment, 7A Nagement Blvd Albert 11, 1210 Brussels Brabant, Belgium

BAYOUMI, ABOUBAKR AHMED, mathematician, educator; b. Zakazik, Al-Sharkia, Egypt, Sept. 1, 1946; s. Ahamed Bayoumi and Amina Mohammad (Al-Bindary) H.; m. Thanaa Mohamed Ismail, Feb. 25, 1972; children: Eeman, Mohammad, Youmna. BSc, Cairo U., 1967; PhD in Math., Uppsala (Sweden) U., 1979; cert. assoc. prof., Basic Rsch. Inst., Fla., 1995, Basic Rsch. Inst., Molisa, Italy, 1995. Demonstrator math. Cairo U., 1967-73; asst. Uppsala U., 1973-75; rsch. fellow Mittag Leffler Inst., Stockholm, 1980-82; asst. prof. Cairo U., 1982-83, Bahrain U., 1983-85; asst. prof. King Saud U., Riyadh, Saudi Arabia, 1985-90, assoc. prof., 1990-98; prof. King Saud U., Riyadh, 1998—. Hon. mem. Al-Kaser Al-Anay Friendship Soc., Cairo U., 1993. Uppsala U. scholar, 1975-79. Mem. Am. Math. Soc., London Math. Soc., Inst. Basic Rsch. (hon., Fla. and Molisa). Muslim. Avocations: reading, playing football, painting. Home: 47 Abrag Al-Hana Flat 12, Zahraa Al-Halmia Cairo, Egypt Office: King Saud U Coll Sci, PO Box 2455, Dept Math, Riyadh 11451, Saudi Arabia

BAYRAMLAR, HUSEYIN, ophthalmologist; b. Izmir, Tepecik, Turkey, May 20, 1964; s. Bayram and Tenzile (Feratlar) B.; m. Hulya Çelik, Aug. 17, 1987; children: Osman Faruk, Murat Sinan, Mahnur. MD, Ege U., Izmir, 1987. Resident dept. ophthalmology Firat U. Med. Faculty, Elazig, Turkey, 1988-91; ophthalmologist Gumushane State Hosp., Turkey, 1992-94; asst. prof. ophthalmology Inonu U., Malatya, Turkey, 1994—; fellow pediat. ophthalmology and strabismus Albany (N.Y.) Med. Coll., 1995-96; head dept. ophathlmology Inonu U. Med. Faculty, Malatya, 1997-99. Contbr. articles to med. jours. Dr. Demir Basar grantee Jour. Cataract Retractive Surgery, 1997. Mem. Turkish Ophathlmol. Soc., European Soc. Cataracts and Refractive Surgeons. Avocations: reading, football, watching TV. Home: Cosnuk Mh Mehmet Buyruk Cd, Turay Apt 4, 44300 Malatya Turkey Office: Inonu U, Turgut Ozal Med Ctr, 44029 Malatya Turkey

BAYS, JUNE MARIE, counselor, social worker; b. LaSalle, Ill., Feb. 16, 1941; d. John Frederick and Esther Marie Nielsen; m. James Philip Bays, June 29, 1963; children: Timothy James, Daniel Mark. Diploma in Nursing, Evanston Hosp. Sch. Nursing, 1962; BS, Western Mich. U., 1983, MSW, 1986. Lic. clin. social worker, Ind. Med. surg. nurse Evanston Hosp., 1962-63; psychiat. staff nurse U. Hosp., Madison, Wis., 1963-65, Madison Gen. Hosp., 1965-66; therapist Madison Ctr., South Bend, Ind., 1986-90; social work clin. specialist U. N.C. Hosp., Chapel Hill, 1990-91; therapist Samaritan Counseling Ctr., South Bend, Ind., 1991-95, Bethel Coll. Counseling Ctr., Mishawaka, Ind., 1995—. Mem. NASW. Avocations: reading, sewing, travel, art. E-mail: Baysj@Bethel-in.edu. Office: Bethel Coll Counseling Ctr 1001 W Mckinley Ave Mishawaka IN 46545-5509

BAYSAL, CEM, energy executive; b. Istanbul, Turkey, Apr. 10, 1948; s. Hicri and Semiha (Bayulken) B.; m. Nurhan Nalbantoğlu, Apr. 1, 1991; 1 child, Kiraz. MSME, Mid. East Tech. U., Ankara, Turkey, 1972; MSc in Operational Rsch., U. London, 1975. Rsch. asst. U. London, 1974-75; prodn. mgr. Lassa Tyre Co., Izmit, Turkey, 1977-79; dept. mgr. Koç Holding R & D Ctr., Istanbul, 1979-83; mng. dir. Shrama, Istanbul, 1983-96, Rama Energy Svcs., Istanbul, 1989—; mem. Cogeneration Com., Istanbul, 1988-96, Energy Conservation Com., Ankara, 1981-86, EEC Energy Group,

Brussels, 1982-84. Author: Conservation at Personal Level, 1980, Industrial Energy Conservation, 1981, Conservation Faces Doomsday, 1990. Active World Wildlife Fund, 1976. Energy fellow U.S. Govt., 1983, Fgn. Student fellow British Coun., London, 1974; recipient Outstanding Effort in Energy Conservation award Ministry of Energy, 1989. Mem. Turkish Am. Businessmen Assn., U. London Alumni Assn. Avocations: cycling, travel, photography, gardening. Fax: 90-212-2939372. E-mail: shrama@superonline.com. Home: Garanti Koza Evleri, Çagla 1 Mah 2 Cad 21 Zekeriyaköy, Sariyer 80930 Istanbul Turkey

BAYSTON, ROGER, microbiologist, researcher, consultant; b. Sheffield, Yorkshire, Eng., Nov. 22, 1943; s. Stanley and Doris (Davies) B. M in Med. Sci., U. Sheffield, 1976, PhD, 1979; MSc in Clin. Microbiology, U. London, 1985. Rsch. asst. U. Sheffield, 1974-76, rsch. fellow, 1976-80; lectr. in microbiology U. London, 1980-85, sr. lectr. in microbiology, 1985-94; clin. microbiology U. Nottingham, Eng., 1994—; head biomaterials-related infections group U. Nottingham Med. Sch., 1996—. Author: Hydrocephalus Shunt Infections, 1989; contbr. chpts. to books; editor Jour. Antimicrobial Chemotherapy, 1994-97; patentee in field. Rsch. grantee NIH, Denver, 1986, Med. Rsch. Coun., London, 1985, Wade Charitable Trust, London, 1997. Fellow Royal Coll. Pathologists; mem. Soc. for Rsch. into Hydrocephalus (hon. treas., hon. sec. 1978-96), Nat. Working Party on Neurosurg. Infection, Nat. Working Party on Vascular Graft Infection (chmn.), Brit. Soc. Antimicrobial Chemotherapy (coun. mem.), Brit. Soc. for Infection, Assn. for Spina Bifida and Hydrocephalus (hon. cons. in hydrocephalus 1985—, med. com. 1993—), Biofilm Club (com. mem.). Avocations: archery, reading, music, Scandinavian history, gardening. E-mail: roger.bayston@nottingham.ac.uk. Office: U Nottingham Div Microbiol, Clin Scis Bldg City Hosp, Nottingham NG5 1PB, England

BAZAINE, JEAN, artist; b. Paris, Dec. 21, 1904; s. Léon Bazaine and Clémenece Temblaire. Prin. works include stained glass windows for ch. at Assy, 1946, Saint Séverin, Paris, 1966, Villeparisis, 1958, Ste Roseline Les Arcs, 1970, Berlens, Switzerland, 1979, La Madeleine, Brittany, 1981, cathedral of St Dié, Vosges, 1986, ceramic mural and windows at Audincourt, 1951-54, ceramic mural at UNESCO, 1960, Maison de la Radio, Paris, 1963, Sénat, Palais de Luxembourg, Paris, 1988, Cluny metro, 1988, ch. at Concarneau, Brittany, 1996, ceramic mural, Saint-Dié, 1999; exhbns. include Galerie Louis Carré & Cie, Maeght, Paris; retrospective exhbns. include Berne, 1958, Eindhoven, 1959, Hanover, 1963, Zürich, 1963, Oslo, 1963, Paris, 1965, Grand Palais, Paris, 1990, Halmstad, Sweden, 1992, Charlottenborg, Denmark, 1992; rep. at Biennali of Venice, São Paulo, Carnegie, Grand Palais, Paris; author: Notes sur la peinture d'aujourd'hui, 1948, Exercice de la peinture, 1973, Le Temps de la Peinture, 1990. Recipient Grand prix Nat. des Arts, 1964; named Comdr. Ordre des Arts et des Lettres, 1979. Home: 36 rue Pierre Brossolette, 92140 Clamart France Office: Galerie Louis Carré, et Cie 10 avenue de Messine, 75008 Paris France

BAŽANT, ZDENĚK JOSEF, civil engineering educator, scientist; b. Nové Město na Morave, Czech Republic, June 11, 1908; s. Zdeněk and Maria (Kadlecová) B.; m. Štěpánka Barbora Cuříková, Mar. 14, 1934 (dec. Sept. 1997); children: Zdeněk Pavel, Milada Obersteinová. Degree in civil engring., Czech Tech. U., Prague, 1930, DS, 1956. Designer Lanna a.s.s., Prague, 1932-41, chief designer, 1942-47; docent Czech Tech. U., 1939, prof. civil engring., 1947-75, chair dept. civil engring., 1955-57, 60-61; mem. Prague Subway Design Com., 1952-68, State Water Power Design Com., 1952-58. Author: Stability of Cohesionless Soil, 1953, Methods of Foundation Engineering, 1979; contbr. articles to profl. publs. Lt. Rwy. Engrs. regiment Czech armed forces, 1931-32.. Mem. Am. Soc. Civil Engrs., Czech Soc. Civil Engrs., Czech Soc. Mechanics. Roman Catholic. Achievements include first measurement of compaction and liquefaction of saturated sand during earthquake. Home: Ovci hajek 52, 15800 Prague Czech Republic

BAZARBASHI, MOHAMMAD SHOUKI, oncologist; b. Aleppo, Syria, Aug. 1, 1960; arrived in Saudi Arabia, 1967.; s. Ahmad Najdat Bazarbashi and Afaf Baki; m. Reem Adnan Bazarbashi; children: Najdat, Adnan, Malikah. MB, BChir, King Saud U., Riyadh, Saudi Arabia, 1982. Diplomate Am. Bd. Internal Medicine, Am. Bd. Internal Medicine for Med. Oncology, Am. Bd. Internal Medicine for Hematology. Intern, resident, fellow Wayne State U., Detroit; cons. oncologist King Faisal Specialist Hosp., Riyadh, 1991-98, head sect. med. oncology, 1998—; dep. chmn. Nat. Cancer Registry, Riyadh, 1996—. Editor Cancer Incidence Report, 1994. Recipient The Upjohn award for outstanding achievement in cancer rsch., 1990. Mem. Am. Soc. Clin. Oncology, European Soc. Med. Oncology. Avocations: squash, parasailing. Home: PO Box 53599, Riyadh 11211, Saudi Arabia Office: King Faisal Specialist Hosp, MBC 64 PO Box 3354, Riyadh 11211, Saudi Arabia

BAZES, MELVIN ISRAEL, electronics engineer; b. L.A., Apr. 9, 1947; s. Maury and Sylvia (Herman) B.; m. Yaffa Shuali, Sept. 24, 1981; children: Nahum Jacob, Revital Sarah. BS in Chemistry cum laude, UCLA, 1968; MS in Chemistry, U. Calif., Berkeley, 1969, MS in Engring. Sci., 1971. Design engr. Beta Engring. Ltd., Beer Sheba, Israel, 1971-72, Tel Aviv U., 1973-75; design engr. Intel Israel Ltd., Haifa, 1977-94, prin. engr., 1994—. Holder 26 patents in field; contbr. articles to profl. jours. and publs. Mem. IEEE. Jewish. Office: Intel Israel Ltd IDC-2E, PO Box 1659, 31015 Haifa Israel

BAZHANOV, VLADIMIR MARKOVICH, climatologist, researcher; b. Kharkov, USSR, Jan. 25, 1951; arrived in Sweden, 1993; s. Mark Igorevich and Inna Vladimirovna (Stolnik) B.; m. Tatyana Platonova, Sept. 3, 1977; children: Leonid, Darya. MSc, Coll. Radioelectronics, Kharkov, USSR, 1974; PhD, Inst. Applied Geophysics, Moscow, 1988. Cert. engr., physics and math. Chief engr., rschr. State Oceanographic Inst., Odessa, Ukraine, 1974-91; sr. rschr. Ctr. Marine Ecology, Odessa, 1992-93; rschr. Stockholm U., 1993—; lectr. Hydrometeorol. Coll., Odessa, 1989-93; cons. Municipality, Odessa, 1986-93; mem. Club of Sci., Odessa, 1990-93. Author: Modern Investigations of Atmospheric Ozone Over the Ocean, 1992. Recipient Charter of Honor, State Com. on Hydrometeorology and Environ. Control, 1986. Mem. N.Y. Acad. Scis., U.S. Nat. Geographic Soc. Avocations: sports, reading, music, travel.

BAZIK, EDNA FRANCES, mathematician, educator; b. Streator, Ill., Dec. 26, 1946; d. Andrew and Anna Frances (Vagasky) B.; BSEd, Ill. State U, 1969; postgrad. Hamilton Coll., summer 1971, Ill. State U., 1972, Augustana Coll., summer 1973; MEd, U. Ill., 1972; PhD, So. Ill. U., 1976, gen. adminstrv. cert., 1980. Tchr. math. Northlawn Jr. High Sch., Streator, 1969-74; instr. math. edn. So. Ill. U., 1974-76; asst. prof. math. Concordia U., 1976-78; asst. prof. math. Ill. State U., Normal, 1978-85; assoc. prof. math. Eastern Ill. U., 1985-88; math. specialist, coord. Oak Park (Ill.) Pub. Schs., 1988-89; math coord. Hinsdale Sch. Dist. 181, 1989—; coord. inservice presentations, workshops for tchrs.; cons. to sch. dists. NSF grantee, 1980—. Presdl. award NSF, 1990. Mem. AAUP, Ill. State Bd. Edn. (mem. assessment team math. 1998—), Assn. Tchr. Educators, Ill. Assn. Tchr. Educators, Nat. Coun. Tchrs. Math. (chair elections com. 1990-91, Ill. Coun. Tchrs. Math. (governing bd., dir. coll. and univ. level), Math. Assn. Am., Nat. Coun. Suprs. Math., NEA, Ill. Edn. Assn., Sch. Sci. and Math. Assn., U.S. Metric Assn., Am. Ednl. Rsch. Assn., Assn. Supervision and Curriculum Devel., Ill. Assn. Supervision and Curriculum Devel., Ill. Standards Achievement Test Math Validation Com., Ill. State Bd. Edn. Math. Assessment Com., Assn. Childhood Edn. Internat., Coun. Exceptional Children, Ill. Curriculum Coun., Rsch. Coun. Diagnostic and Prescriptive Math., Kappa Delta Pi, Phi Delta Kappa (pres. Ill. State U. chpt. 1982-83), Pi Mu Epsilon, Delta Kappa Gamma, Phi Kappa Phi. Republican. Lutheran. Co-author: Elementary Mathematical Methods, 1978, Mind Over Math, 1980, Teaching Mathematics to Children with Special Needs, 1983, Step-by-Step: Addition, 1984, Step-by-Step: Subtraction, 1984, Step-by-Step: Multiplication, 1984, Step-by-Step: Division, 1984, Problem-Solving Sourcebook, 1985, Step-by-Step: Fractions, 1987, Step-by-Step: Decimals, 1988. Home: 1501 Darien Lake Dr Darien IL 60561-5069 Office: Hinsdale Sch Dist 181 100 S Garfield Ave Hinsdale IL 60521-4252

BAZIN, PATRICK, library director; b. Besancon, France, Feb. 23, 1950; s. Joseph Bazin and Louisette (Le Goff) Lazar; m. Denyse Clavel, May 8, 1978; 1 child, Marianne. B in Philosophy, Lyon (France) 2 Univ., 1973, M in Philosophy, 1976; grad., Nat. Upper Libr. Sch., Lyon, 1976. Curator Ecole Nat. des Mines de Paris, Paris, 1976-78; curator Lyon Pub. Libr., Lyon, 1978-92, dir., gen. curator, 1992—; tchr. Nat. Upper Sch. Info. Sci. and Libs., Lyon, 1989—; vice-chmn. Rhone-Alpes Agy. for Book and Documentation, Rhone-Alpes Province, 1994—. Mem. Nat. Ctr. of Books. Office: Bibliotheque Municipale, 30 blvd VivierMerle, 69431 Lyon Cedex 03, France

BAZLER, FRANK ELLIS, retired lawyer; b. Columbus, Ohio, Jan. 17, 1930; s. Frank Hayes and Minnie Maybrum (Rucker) B.; m. Virginia Ann Hutchison, Oct. 17, 1954. BSBA, Ohio State U., 1951, JD, 1953. Bar: Ohio 1953, U.S. Dist. Ct. (we. dist.) Ohio 1956, U.S. Ct. Mil. Appeals 1957, U.S. Supreme Ct. 1957, U.S. Ct. Appeals (6th cir.) 1964. Assoc. Robert S. Miller, Atty., Troy, Ohio, 1955-57; ptnr. Miller, Bazler & Schlemmer, Troy, 1957-71; asst. corp. counsel Hobart Mfg. Co., Troy, 1971-74; corp. atty., asst. sec. Hobart Corp., Troy, 1974-95; ret., 1995; of counsel Dungan & LeFevre, Troy, 1995—; v.p. Bazler Transfer & Storage, Inc., Columbus, Ohio, 1950-58; sec., bd. dirs. Golden Triangle Farms, Inc., Troy, 1972—. Pres. Troy United Fund, Inc., 1960, Troy Mus. Corp., 1990; chmn. Miami County chpt. ARC, 1955-59, Miami County (Ohio) Rep. Fin. Com., 1981-84; mem. Miami County Gen. Bd. Health, 1992—, pres. pro-tem, 1998—; commn. on cert. of Attys. as Specialists of Supreme Ct. of Ohio, 1994-99, chmn., 1994-96. Capt. JAG, USAFR, 1953-61. Named one of Outstanding Young Men in Troy and Ohio, Troy Jaycees, 1957, Ohio Jaycees, 1961; recipient Disting. Citizen award Troy C. of C., 1985, Citizenship award Ohio State U., 1993. Fellow Am. Bar Found. (Ohio chair 1995—), Ohio State Bar Found. (pres. 1992); mem. ABA (ho. of dels. 1984-00, mem. gen. practice sect. 1968—, coun. 1976-80, mem. standing com. on specialization 1999—), Nat. Caucus State Bar Assns. (Ohio rep. 1993—, exec. com. 1997—, pres. 2000—), Ohio State Bar Assn. (pres. 1984-85, coun. of dels. 1979-88, Ohio Bar medal 1990), Miami County Bar Assn. (pres. 1966, Meritorious Svc. award 1985), Nat. Coun. Bar Pres. (exec. coun. 1988-91), Kiwanis (pres. 1964), Brukner Nature Ctr. (trustee 1998—, pres. 1999—), Indsl. Heritage Mus. of Miami County (trustee, sec. 1997—), Masons, Scottish Rite. Republican. Presbyterian. Avocations: photography, travel, golf. Home: 1156 Premwood Dr Troy OH 45373-3877 Office: Dungan & LeFevre 210 W Main St Troy OH 45373-3287

BAZOLI, GIOVANNI, banker; b. Brescia, Italy, Dec. 18, 1932; married; 3 children. Prof. pub. law instns. faculty econs. Cath. U. Milan; chmn. Mittel; dep. chmn. Banca San Paolo di Brescia and Editrice La Scuola; chmn. Nuovo Banco Ambrosiano (now Banco Intesa), Milan, 1982—; bd. dirs., exec. com. Italian Banking Assn. Office: Banca Intesa, Piazza Paolo Ferrari 10, 20121 Milan Italy*

BAZYLAK, GRZEGORZ BOHDAN, analytical chemist, educator; b. Wroclaw, Poland, Nov. 28, 1953; s. Henryk and Daniela (Antczak) B.; m. Teresa Babska, Oct. 7, 1978; 1 child, Dorota. MS in Food Chemistry cum laude, Tech. U. Lodz, Poland, 1979, PhD in Tech. Scis. cum laude, 1990. Rsch. scientist Tech. U. Lodz-Inst. Fundamental Food Chemistry, 1979-90, adj. prof., 1990-91; adj. prof. hygienics dept. Med. U. Lodz, 1991-97, dir. biochromatographic lab. hygienics dept., 1991-97, asst. prof. dept. gen. chemistry Inst. Physiology & Biochemistry, 1997—; mem. sci. bd. Rsch. and Developing Ctr., Oram-Osrodek Badawczo Rozwojowy Aparatury Manewrowej, Lodz, 1991—; primary mem., fellow establishers coun. Polish Supramolecular Chemistry Network Found., Warsaw, Poland, 1997—; vis. fellow dept. environ. medicine, Karolinska Inst., Stockholm, 1995; vis. scientist Ctr. for Analytical Chemistry, Imperial Coll. Sci., Tech. and Medicine, London, 1996; cert. pub. health nutritionist WHO Regional Office for Europe, Copenhagen, 1994; co-chmn. plenary session 9th Internat. Symposium on Chiral Discrimination, Nagoya, Japan, 1997; mem. rsch. bd. advisors Am. Biographical Inst., 1999—. Author: (poetry collections) Danzig Night, 1998, Dansing Polanica, 1999; co-author: (handbook) Trace Analysis of Toxic Components in Food Stuffs, 1992, Laboratory Manual for Bioorganic Chemistry, 1999; mem. editl. bd. AWERS, 1998—, Przeglad Artystyczno-Literacki, 1998—; contbr. numerous articles to profl. jours. and conf. publs. Mem. Nat. Young Writers Soc. Viaduct, Lodz, 1975-82, Lodz Literary Soc. Centauro, Lodz, 1984-90. Col. Polish Army, 1980-81. Scholar Internat. Assn. for the Exch. of Students for Tech. Experience, Solna, Sweden, 1978; Medulo Internal grantee Med. U. Lodz, Poland, 1992-96, 99, vis. grantee Swedish Inst., Stockholm, 1995, Exch. of Person grantee The Brit. Coun., London, 1996; travel grantee Stefan Batory Found., Warsaw, Poland, 1993, 95, 98, German Inst. for Human Nutrition, Potsdam, 1993, Dutch Fgn. Office, Haag, The Netherlands, 1994, 97, Crafoord Found., Lund, Sweden, 1995, Tswett Found., Edinburgh, Scotland, 1996, Nat. Swiss Found., Bern, Switzerland, 1998. Mem. Chromatographic Soc., Polish Chem. Soc., N.Y. Acad. Scis., Nat. Literati Assn. (co-chmn. Lodz br. 1998—), Poetry Soc. (London), Torun Artistic and Literary Soc. (co-chmn. 1999—). Achievements include quantitative characterization of topography of heterogeneity centers in magnesium oxide and magnesium carbonate adsorbents; invention of helically distorted chiral selectors for the enantioselective HPLC (High Performance Liquid Chromatography); contribution to chemometrically aided characterization of alkanolamines as lysosomotropic agents and enzyme inhibitors; design of micromachined chromatographic systems mimicking disrupted adrenergic receptor. Home: Mieszczanska 5 M32, PL-93322 Łódź Poland Office: Med U Lodz Inst Physiology & Biochemistry Dept Gen Chemistry, Lindleya 6, PL-90131 Łódź Poland

BAZZANELLA, CARLA, humanities researcher; b. Turin, Italy, Aug. 6, 1947; d. Giuseppe and Fernanda (Saggini) B.; m. Lovisolo Davide, Jan. 31, 1981; 1 child, Michele. Degree in Humanities, U. Turin, 1970. Tchr. Secondary Sch., Turin, 1970-76; postdoctoral fellow U. Pavia, Italy, 1976-81; rsch. fellow U. Turin, 1982. Mem. Internat. Assn. for Dialogue analysis (sci. bd.), Italian Soc. Linguistics (sci. bd. 1977-80), Soc. Philosophy of Lang., Cognitive Sci. Ctr. (sci. bd.). Office: U Turin Dept Philosophy, vS Ottavio 20, 10124 Turin Italy

BEACH, ARTHUR O'NEAL, lawyer; b. Albuquerque, Feb. 8, 1945; s. William Pearce and Vivian Lucille (Kronig) B.; BBA, U. N.Mex., 1967, JD, 1970; m. Alex Clark Doyle, Sept. 12, 1970; 1 son, Eric Kronig. Bar: N.Mex. 1970. Assoc. Smith & Ransom, Albuquerque, 1970-74; assoc. Keleher & McLeod, Albuquerque, 1974-75, ptnr., 1976-78, shareholder Keleher & McLeod, P.A., Albuquerque, 1978—; teaching asst. U. N. Mex., 1970. Bd. editors Natural Resources Jour., 1968-70. Mem. ABA, State Bar N.Mex. (unauthorized practice of law com., adv. opinions com., med.-legal panel, legal-dental-osteo.-podiatry com., jud. selection com., specialization bd.), Albuquerque Bar Assn. (dir. 1978-82). Democrat. Mem. Christian Sci. Ch. Home: 2015 Dietz Pl NW Albuquerque NM 87107-3240 Office: Keleher & McLeod PA PO Drawer AA Albuquerque NM 87103

BEACH, ROGER C., oil company executive; b. Lincoln, Nebr., Dec. 5, 1936; s. Melvin C. and L. Mayme (Hoham) B.; m. Elaine M. Wilson, Oct. 1954 (div. 1972); children: Kristi, Mark, Anne; m. Karen Lynn Ogden, July 27, 1974. BS, Colo. Sch. Mines, 1961. Profl. petroleum refining engr., Calif. With Unocal Corp., L.A., 1961—; mgr. spl. projects Unocal Corp., Los Angeles, 1976-77, dir. planning, 1977-80, v.p. crude supply, 1980-86, pres. refining and mktg., 1986-92, corp. sr. v.p., 1987-1992, pres., 1992-94, CEO, 1994—, now chmn. and COO, 1994-98, CEO, 1998—. Chmn. bd. trustees Nat. 4-H Coun. Mem. Pres.'s Interchange Exec. Alumni Assn. Office: Unocal Corp 2141 Rosecrans Ave Ste 4000 El Segundo CA 90245-4746

BEACH, SANDRA MARIE YUDICHAK, secondary education educator; b. Niagara Falls, N.Y., Jan. 21, 1946; d. Thomas Stephen and Helen (Kosko) Yudichak; m. Fred Ellsworth Beach, Aug. 28, 1965 (div., May, 1994); 1 child, Gary Nathan. BA, SUNY, Buffalo, 1969; MA in Tchg., Niagara U., 1973. Cert. secondary English tchr., N.Y. Tchr. Grand Island (N.Y.) Middle Sch., 1969-77, 83-99, Grand Island H.S., 1977-83, 99—; tutor, Lewiston, N.Y., 1969—; superintendent's advisory com., Lewiston-Porter H.S., N.Y., 1994-95, mem. decision making team; tchr. stakeholder Grand Island Middle Sch. Shared Decision Making, 1992-94. Named delegate to Spain, ASCD, 1995. Mem. ASCD (assoc.), Power of Positive Students, N.Y. State United Tchrs. Avocations: writing, needle crafts, travel. E-mail: sandebeach@gris.wnyric.org. Home: 5001 Forest Rd Lewiston NY 14092-1904 Office: Grand Island Sr High Sch 1100 Ransom Rd Grand Island NY 14072-1460

BEACHLEY, MICHAEL CHARLES, radiologist; b. Harrisburg, Pa., Nov. 14, 1940; s. Kenneth Gumbert and Carolyn Elizabeth (Jones) B.; m. Deborah Rowe Samson, July 27, 1963; children: Kenneth, Barbara, William. A.B., Dartmouth Coll., 1962, B.M.S., 1963; M.D., Harvard U., 1965. Diplomate: Am. Bd. Radiology. Intern in surgery Med. Coll. Va., Richmond, 1965-66, resident in radiology, 1966-69, instr. radiology, 1970, faculty, 1972—, acting chmn. dept. radiology, 1976, prof., 1977-87, chmn. dept. radiology, 1977-82, prof. radiation scis., 1981-87, prof. biophysics, 1980-82, prof. physiology and biophysics, 1982-87, clin. prof., 1987—; clin. prof. radiology U. Pitts., 1988—; chmn. Dept. Radiology St. Margaret Meml. Hosp., Pitts., 1987-97; pres. Three Rivers Imaging Cons., Ltd., 1993-94, Duquesne Imaging Ltd., 1994—; med. dir. Radiology Ptnrs.; chmn. dept. radiology U. Pitts. Med. Ctr., Saint Margaret, 1997-99; cons. McGuire VA Hosp., 1977—; fellow in radiol. pathology Armed Forces Inst. Pathology, Washington, 1969. Contbr. chpt. to book, revs. and med. articles to profl. jours. Vice-pres. College Hills Civic Assn., 1975-77. Served as maj. M.C. U.S. Army, 1970-72. Fellow Am. Coll. Radiology (pres. Va. chpt. 1982-83, chmn. com. on stds. and accreditation 1998—), Am. Coll. Angiology; mem. AMA, Am. Heart Assn., Radiol. Soc. N.Am. (chmn. bylaws com. 1994-96), Am. Roentgen Ray Soc., Pitts. Roentgen Soc. (chmn. com on fellowship nomination 1998-99), Pa. Radiol. Soc., Pa. Med. Soc. (alt. del., mem. med.-legal com.), Allegheny Med. Soc. (peer rev. bd. 1997-99), Pa. Radiol. MSO (chmn. by-laws com., exec. com.), Dartmouth Club Western Pa. (exec. com.), Harvard Club Western Pa. (treas.), Pitts. Field Club. Home: PO Box 331 Bakerstown PA 15007-0331

BEADEL, STEPHEN JAY, author; b. Sharpsburg, Iowa, Aug. 5, 1949; s. Walter Reldon and Katherine Margaret (Repplinger) B. BS, Iowa State U., 1971. Owner, mgr. Beadel Lumber, Lenox, Iowa, 1976-83; author, 1985—; guest on numerous talk shows, 1990. Author: The Prophetic Beast, The Predicted Fall of Berlin Wall, 1989, What the Church Won't Tell You About Christmas, 1989, The Four Horseman of the Apocalypse, 1989, What Do You Mean "Born Again"?, 1990, The Pagan Rituals of Easter, 1990, Where is the True Church, 1990, The Reward for Salvation, 1990. Avocations: photography, painting. Home: 1230 70th St Windsor Heights IA 50311

BEAHM, FRANKLIN D., lawyer; b. Independence, Kans., Jan. 18, 1953; s. Edgar Hiram and Dorothy S.; m. Tawny L. McIntyre, Jan. 7, 1994; children: F. David, Patrick Stuart, Kristin Sanders, Stephen McWilliams. BBA, So. Methodist U., 1975; JD, Tulane U., 1977. Bar: La. 1977, Colo. 1993, U.S. Dist. Ct. (ea. dist.) La. 1977, U.S. Dist. Ct. (mid. dist.) La. 1980, U.S. Dist. Ct. (we. dist.) La. 1985, U.S. Ct. Appeals (5th cir.), U.S. Tax Ct. 1989, U.S. Supreme Ct. 1993, Tex. 2000. Assoc. Manard & Scheonberger, New Orleans, 1977-80, Bourgeois, Bennett, Metairie, La., 1980; assoc. Hammett, Leake & Hammett, New Orleans, 1980-83, ptnr., 1983-85; ptnr. Thomas, Hayes & Beahm, New Orleans, 1985-95, Chehardy, Sherman, Ellis, Breslin, Murray, Metairie, 1995-97, Beahm & Green, New Orleans, 1997—. Mem. Am. Health Lawyers Assn., Am. Soc. Law and Medicine, La. Assn. Def. Counsel, La. Bar Assn. (Interprofl. com. 1997-98, professionalism com. 1999—), La. Med. Soc. (Interprofl. com. 1997-98), La. Soc. Hosp. Attys. of the La. Hosp. Assn., Denver Bar Assn., Def. Rsch. Inst. (med. malpractice com., product liability com.), Beta Alpha Psi. Office: 145 Robert E Lee Blvd Ste 408 New Orleans LA 70124-2581

BEAHRS, OLIVER HOWARD, surgeon, educator; b. Eufaula, Ala., Sept. 19, 1914; s. Elmer Charles and Elsa Katherine (Smith) B.; 1 child, Gean Beahrs Landy; m. Helen Edith Taylor, July 27, 1947; children: John Randolf, David Howard, Nancy Ann Beahrs Oster. BA, U. Calif., Berkeley, 1937; MD, Northwestern U., 1942; MS in Surgery, Mayo Grad. Sch. Medicine, 1949; D of Mil. Medicine honoris causa, Uniform Svcs. U. Health Sci., 1999. Diplomate Am. Bd. Surgery. Fellow surgery Mayo Grad. Sch. Medicine, Rochester, Minn., 1942, 46-49, prof. surgery, 1966-79, prof. emeritus, 1979—; asst. surgeon Mayo Clinic, 1949-50, head sect. gen. surgery, 1950-79, vice-chmn. bd. govs., 1964-75; Bd. dirs. Rochester Meth. Hosp.; trustee Mayo Found.; mem. cancer control and rehab. adv. com. Nat. Cancer Inst., 1975-84; mem. Am. Joint Com. on Cancer, 1975-78, exec. dir., 1980-92. Editor: Surgical Consultations; editorial bd.: Surgery, Surg. Techniques Illustrated; contbr. over 400 articles to profl. jours. Hon. life, bd. dirs. Am. Cancer Soc., 1975—; trustee Rochester Meth. Hosp.; adv. bd. Uniform Svcs. Univ. Health Scis.; med. cons. Pres. and Mrs. Reagan. Capt. USNR, 1942-64, ret. Recipient Leadership and Humanitarian awards Am. Cancer Soc. Fellow Royal Coll. Surgery in Ireland (hon.), Royal Australasian Coll. Surgery (hon.); mem. AMA, ACS (mem. exec. com., bd. govs., chmn. cen. jud. com., long-range planning com., chmn. bd. govs., chmn. bd. regents, pres. 1988-89), Am. Group Practice Assn. (sec.-treas. 1974-75), Minn. Surg. Soc. (pres. 1960-61), Am. Thyroid Assn., James IV Assn. Surgeons, Am. Surg. Assn. (pres. 1979-80, chmn. com. on issues 1980-83), So. Surg. Assn., Cen. Surg. Assn., Western Surg. Assn., Soc. Head and Neck Surgeons (pres. 1966-67), Am. Assn. Endocrine Surgeons (pres. 1986-87), Am. Assn. Clin. Anatomists (pres. 1986-87), Soc. Surgery Alimentary Tract, Soc. Pelvic Surgeons (pres. 1983-84), Soc. Surg. Oncology, Am. Assn. Clin. Anatomists (pres.), Philippine Coll. Surgeons (hon.), Hellenic Coll. Surgery (hon.), Assn. Française de Chirurgie Française, Northwestern U. Alumni Assn. (Merit award), Sigma Xi, Phi Kappa Epsilon, Phi Beta Pi, Theta Delta Chi. Republican. Methodist. Home: 2253 Baihly Ln SW Rochester MN 55902-1023 Office: 200 1st St SW Rochester MN 55905-0001

BEAL, JOHN EVERETT, composer, conductor; b. Santa Monica, Calif., Jan. 20, 1947; s. Ralph Raymond and Marjory May Beal; Karen Dale Laidlaw, Oct. 23, 1993 (dec. Mar. 1998); 1 child, Matthew David Laidlaw. Student, San Diego State Coll., UCLA. Composer, pub. Opus Pocus Music, N. Hollywood, Calif., 1978—; pres., sr. composer Reeltime Music, Inc., Beverly Hills, Calif., 1984—. Musician, 1966—; composer (film) Zero to Sixty, 1977, The Funhouse, 1981, Terror in the Aisles, 1984; composer, rec. artist: Coming Soon!, 1998 (Golden Score award 1998). Divsn. rep., coach Little League Am., Toluca Lake, Calif., 1985-89. Sgt. USMC, 1966-72, Vietnam. Decorated Air medal with bronze star, 8 Air medals, Naval Achievement with valor. Mem. NATAS, ASCAP, NARAS (gov. 1984-86), Soc. Composers and Lyricists. Avocations: film, travel, dining. Fax: 818-762-0045. Office: Reeltime Music Inc 9601 Wilshire Blvd Ste 340 Beverly Hills CA 90210-5206

BEAL, ROBERT LAWRENCE, real estate executive; b. Boston, Sept. 10, 1941; s. Alexander Simpson and Leona M. (Rothstein) B. BS cum laude, Harvard U., 1963, MBA, 1965. Vice pres., ptnr. Beacon Cos., Boston, 1965-76; ptnr. The Beal Cos., Boston; pres. Beal and Co., Inc., Boston, 1976—; corporator, dir., mem. exec. com., lending com. Provident Instn. Savs., 1975-86; chmn. bd. dirs. Mass. Devel. Fin. Agy., 1976—; instr. real estate Northeastern U., 1969-75; mem. East Cambridge rezoning adv. com., 1989—; dir. Artery Bus. Com., 1989—, chmn., 1995-99, treas., 1989-95. Bd. dirs. Boston Zool. Soc., 1972-86, pres., 1980, chmn., 1981-84, hon. chmn., 1985; mem. vis. com. Sch. Mus. Fine Arts, Boston, 1974-76, 88-89; overseer Boys Club Boston, 1975-93; mem. corp. Belmont Hill Sch.; trustee Beth Israel Deaconess Med. Ctr., 1981—, mem. bldg. and grounds com., 1976-82, 86-90; dir. Harvard Coll. Fund Coun., 1972-73, capital fund dir. Class '63, 1979-85, co-chmn. 25th reunion, co-chmn. 35th reunion, class gift; exec. bd. Boston chpt. Am. Jewish Com., 1987-96, mem. bd. govs., 1989-92; co-chair United Way of Massachusetts Bay; bd. dirs. Boston Mcpl. Rsch. Bur., 1978—, treas., 1988-89, 92, vice chmn., 1990-93, chmn., 1994-96; bd. dirs. Met. Boston Housing Partnership, Inc., 1983-95; trustee The Partnership, Inc., 1981-89, New Eng. Aquarium, 1987—, bd. govs., 1993-98; mem. adv. task force John F. Kennedy Libr., 1982; bd. overseers Mus. Fine Arts, Boston, 1988-97, 98—; mem. vis. com. Harvard Div. Sch., 1989—, adv. com. Taubman Ctr., John F. Kennedy Sch. Govt., Harvard U., 1989—; co-chair United Way Mass. Bay, 2000. Mem. Nat. Realty Com. (dir., past sec., mem. exec. com. 1974-99, v.p., vice chmn.), Mass. Assn. Realtors (dir. 1979-81), Greater Boston Real Estate Bd. (bd. dir. 1970-72, 76-90, pres. 1978-79), Am. Soc. Real Estate Counselors, Bldg. Owners-Mgrs. Assn. Boston (dir. 1970-72), Ripon Soc. (co-founder, nat. treas. 1968-73, nat. governing bd. 1979-85), Nat. Assn. Real Estate Appraiser (cert.), Mass. Taxpayers Found. (dir. 1980-86), Inst. Property Taxation (affliate), Internat. Assn. Assessing Officers (primary subscribing mem. 1982—), Beacon Hill Civic Assn. (bd. dir. 1975-79), Bostonian Soc. (life), Greater Boston C. of C. (bd. dirs.), The Vault (coord. com. 1978-97), Combined Jewish Philanthropies Greater Boston (exec. com. 1989—, vice chmn. 1992-93, chmn. com. on endowment fund 1999—), Greater Boston C. of C. (bd. dirs. 1992—), Alexis de Tocqueville Soc. (mem. cabinet 2000). Republican. Jewish. Home: 21 Brimmer St Boston MA 02108-1001 Office: Beal and Co Inc 177 Milk St Ste 2A Boston MA 02109-3410

BEALE, GEOFFREY HERBERT, geneticist; b. London, June 11, 1913; s. Herbert Walter and Elsie (Beaton) B.; m. Betty McCallum, Mar. 16, 1949 (dec. 1969); children: Andrew, Steven, Duncan. BSc, Imperial Coll., London, 1935; PhD, London U., 1938; DSc (hon.), Chulalongkorn U., Bangkok, 1996. Rsch. assoc. John Innes Hort. Inst., London, 1935-40, Carnegie Inst., Cold Spring Harbor, N.Y., 1947; Rockefeller fellow Ind. U., Bloomington, 1947-48; from lectr. to sr. lectr. U. Edinburgh, Scotland, 1948-63; Royal Soc. rsch. prof. U. Edinburgh, 1963-78. Author: Genetics of Paramecium Aurelia, 1954; co-author: (with J. Knowles) Extranuclear Genetics, 1978, (with S. Thaithong) Malaria Parasites, 1992; contbr. articles to profl. jours. Served with Brit. Army, 1941-46. Fellow Royal Soc. (London), Royal Soc. (Edinburgh). Avocations: music, languages. Home: 23 Royal Terr, Edinburgh EH7 5AH, Scotland Office: U Edinburgh, ICAPB W Mains Rd, Edinburgh EH9 3JT, Scotland

BEALE, JACK GORDON, engineering consultant, water research foundation administrator; b. Sydney, Australia, July 17, 1917; s. Rupert Noel and Esther Anderina (Green) B.; m. Stephania Toth-Dobrzanski, 1958; children: David John, Christopher William. Diploma in mech. engring. with honors, Sydney Tech. Coll., 1939; M of Engring., U. NSW, 1964, DS (hon.), 1997; LLD (hon.), Australian Nat. U., 1999. Chartered profl. engr., Australia. Prin. Hon. Jack G. Beale Cons. Chartered Profl. Engrs., Sydney, 1942—; bd. dirs. numerous pvt. and pub. cos., Australia; Min. for Conservation, Govt. NSW, Sydney, 1965-71, Min. for Environ. Control, 1971-73; mem. representing NSW, Australian Ministerial Water Resources Coun., Canberra, 1965-71, Australian Ministerial Forestry Coun., Canberra, 1965-71, Australian Ministerial Environ. Coun., Canberra, 1971-73; sr. adviser UN Environment Program, 1974-77, UN Devel. Program, 1975-77; chmn. Water Rsch. Found. Australia, Canberra, 1955—; mem. Nat. Water Rsch. Coun., 1982-83; chmn., bd. dirs. Zenith Investments, 1955—, FES (NSW) Pty. Ltd., 1987—, Energy Sys. Pty. Ltd., Sydney, 1987—, HydroCo Ltd., 1987-93, Hydro-Gen Ltd., Sydney, 1993—; mem. adv. coun. Ctr. for Resource and Environ. Studies Australia Nat. U., Canberra, 1990—; ptnr. HydroCo Partnership, 1993-98. Author: Environment Protection and Management, 1974, The Manager and The Environment, 1977. Active Legis. Assembly of NSW, Sydney, 1942-73. Jack Beale Chair of Water Resources named in his honor Australian Nat. U., 1989, Ann. Jack Beale Water Resources Lecture Series named in his honor, 1990, Jack Beale Global Environ. Lecture Series named in his honor U. N.S.W., 1997; apptd. Honorable for Life HM Queen, 1973; apptd. officer Order of Australia by HM Queen, 1999. Fellow Instn. of Engrs. Australia (hon., life); mem. ASME (life) ASCE (life) Am. Soc. Agrl. and Biol. Sys. Engrs. (life). Achievements include first nat. water plan for Australia; devel. of an integrated soil, water and vegetation program to rejuvenate the Australian landscape, "Green Australia", integrated program to mitigate the economical and social damage of national droughts, "Droughtproofing", integrated program to mitigate the economic and social damage of national droughts, integrated network of climatically distributed hydroelectric generating facilities to ensure economically viable electricity output (patent); advanced uniformity of precipitation from overlapping distribution patterns of irrigation sprinklers; devel. of whole river valley, governmental guidelines for environ. impact statements; initiator of comprehensive Australian state and nat. environ. policy, law and mgmt., comphrensive pioneer environ. policy, law and mgmt. initiatives in developing countries. Avocations: swimming, tennis, yachting, reading, education. Home and Office: 12/93 Elizabeth Bay Rd, Sydney NSW 2011, Australia

BEALE, JULIAN HOWARD, parliamentarian; b. Sydney, Australia, Oct. 10, 1934; s. Oliver Howard and Margery Ellen (Wood) B.; m. Felicity Irene Monderer, Dec. 17, 1962; children: Jennifer, Deborah. B in Engring., Sydney U., 1957; MBA, Harvard U., 1963. Engr. English Elec. Co. Australia, 1956-61; ops. engr. Esso Australia Ltd., 1963-65; gen. mgr. Imco Container Co., 1965-79; mgn. dir. The Moonie Oil Co., Ltd., Australia, 1979-84; federal mem. Ho. of Reps., Canberra, Australia, 1984-96; chmn. J T Campbell & Co. Plc Ltd., 1996-98. Lt. Royal Australian Navy, 1959-73. Home: 22 Hill St, 3142 Melbourne Australia

BEALE, SIR PETER JOHN, medical advisor; b. Romford, England, Mar. 18, 1934; s. Basil Hewett and Eileen Beryl (Heffer) B.; m. Julia Mary Winter, Apr. 13, 1935 (dec. Apr. 2000); children: Simon, Timothy, Andrew, Katie, Matthew. BA, Cambridge U., England, 1958. FRCP, FFOM, FFPHM, DTM&H, London. Dr. Armed Forces, 1960-94, surgeon gen., 1991-94; chief med. advisor Brit. Red Cross, London, 1994-00; govern Yeludi Sch., 1996—. Contbr. articles to profl. jours. Decorated Knight Brit. Empire. Fellow Royal Inst. Pub. Health & Hygiene; mem. Old Felstedian Soc. (pres. 1998—), Tidworth Garrison Golf Club (pres. 1989—). Mem. Ch. of England. Avocations: squash, golf, tennis, bridge, music. Home: The Old Bakery, Avebury SN8 1RF, England

BEALES, DEREK EDWARD DAWSON, historian, educator; b. Felixstowe, Eng., June 12, 1931; s. Edward and Dorothy Kathleen (Dawson) B.; m. Sara Jean Ledbury, Aug. 14, 1964; children: Christina Margaret, Richard Derek. BA, U. Cambridge, Eng., 1953, MA, PhD, 1957, LittD, 1988. Research fellow Cambridge U., 1955-58, fellow, 1958-62, asst. lectr., 1962-65, lectr., 1965-80, prof. modern history, 1980-97, prof. emeritus, 1997—; vis. prof. Harvard U., Cambridge, Mass., 1965, Ctrl. European U., Budapest, Hungary, 1995—. Author: England and Italy, 1859-60, 1961, From Castlereagh to Gladstone, 1969, The Risorgimento and the Unification of Italy, 1971, History and Biography, 1981, Joseph II, I: In the Shadow of Maria Theresa, 1987; editor: (with Geoffrey Best) History, Society and the Churches, 1985, Mozart and the Habsburgs, 1993, (with H.B. Nisbet) Sidney Sussex College Quatercentenary Essays, 1996; editor various hist. jours. Served as sgt. Royal Arty., Brit. army, 1949-50. Recipient Prince Consort prize U. Cambridge, 1960; Leverhulme 2000 rsch. fellow, 2001—. Fellow Royal Hist. Soc., Brit. Acad., European Sci. Found. (mem. standing com. for humanities 1994-99). Anglican. Avocations: music, bridge, walking. E-mail: deb1000@cam.ac.uk. Office: Cambridge Univ, Sidney Sussex Coll, Cambridge England

BEALES, PETER FREDERICK, tropical diseases physician, consultant, educator; b. London, June 16, 1935; s. Leslie John and Hilda Elizabeth (Jewell) B.; m. Sriutra Ketbhan, July 22, 1960; children: Philip Leslie, Serena Elizabeth. MB ChB, U. Liverpool, Eng., 1968; diploma in tropical medicine & hygiene, Liverpool Sch. Tropical Med., 1969; MD, U. Liverpool, 1987. Bd. cert. pub. health medicine Royal Colls. Medicine U.K. Dep. dir. Dept. Med. Svcs., Am. Samoa, 1970-72, dir., 1972-74; sr. WHO malariologist to Thailand, 1974-80; med. officer program and tng. Malaria Action Program, WHO, Geneva, Switzerland, 1980-83, chief programming and tng., 1983-90; chief tng. for control of tropical diseases WHO, Geneva, 1990-96; ret., 1996; tech. asst. entomology WHO, Geneva, 1956-60, Afghanistan, Ceylon, Burma, Cambodia, North Borneo, Thailand; short-term cons. WHO, Copenhagen, 1963-66; vis. prof. tropical hygiene faculty tropical medicine Mahidol U., Bangkok, 1996—; hon. fellow Liverpool Sch. Tropical Medicine, 1996—; asst. prof., clin. asst. prof. tropical medicine and pub. health U. Hawaii, 1970-74; vis. lectr. dept. parasitology Valencia U., Spain, 1993—; cons. in field. Co-editor: (books) Malaria and Planning for Its Control in Tropical Africa, 1989, Health, Information Society and Developing Countries, 1995, Severe and Complicated Malaria, 1990, 2000; contbr. numerous articles to profl. jours. and books. Chmn. Health Svcs. Regulatory Bd., Am. Samoa, 1972-74; chmn. med. rev. com. WHO, Geneva, 1984-96; mem. Regional Med. Program Hawaii and Pacific Basin Coun., 1972-74. NCO-cpl. Royal Army Med. Corps., 1954-56. Recipient Citation House Concurrent Resolution 98, 3d Regular Session 13th Legislature of Am. Samoa, 1974, Pin in recognition of svcs. to pub. health Ministry Pub. Health, Thailand, 1980. Fellow Royal Entomol. Soc. (pres.), Royal Soc. Medicine, Royal Soc. Tropical Medicine and Hygiene; mem. Am. Soc. Tropical Medicine and Hygiene, Brit. Med. Assn., Inst. Sci. Tech. Avocations: antiques, tennis, philately, woodworking, gardening. Home: Case Postale 102, 1218 Grand Saconnex Switzerland

BEALL, DONALD RAY, multi-industry high-technology company executive; b. Beaumont, Calif., Nov. 29, 1938; s. Ray C. and Margaret (Murray) B. BS, San Jose State Coll., 1960; MBA, U. Pitts., 1961; postgrad., UCLA; D of Engring. (hon.), GMI Engring. and Mgmt. Inst., 1994, Milw. Sch. Engring., 1994. With Ford Motor Co., 1961-68; fin. mgmt. positions Newport Beach, Calif., 1961-66; mgr. corp. fin. planning and contracts Phila., 1966-67; controller Palo Alto, Calif., 1967-68; exec. dir. corp. fin. planning N.Am. Rockwell, El Segundo, Calif., 1968-69, exec. v.p. electronics group, 1969-71; exec. v.p. Collins Radio Co., Dallas, 1971-74; pres. Collins Radio Group, Rockwell Internat. Corp., Dallas, 1974-76; corp. v.p., pres. Electronic Ops., Dallas, 1976-77; exec. v.p. Rockwell Internat. Corp., Dallas, 1977-79; pres., chief operating officer Rockwell Internat. Corp., Pitts., 1979-88; chmn. bd., chief exec. officer Rockwell Internat. Corp., Costa Mesa, Calif., 1988-98; chmn. Rockwell Internat. Corp., Seal Beach, 1997-98, chmn. of exec. com. of bd., 1998—; mem. bd. overseers and Grad. Sch. of Mgmt.; bd. visitors U. Calif., Irvine, 1988—; trustee Calif. Inst. Tech.; bd. dirs. Procter & Gamble Co., Amoco Corp., Times-Mirror Corp., L.A. World Affairs Coun.; mem. Bus. Higher Edn. Forum, Bus. Coun., Bus. Roundtable, SRI Adv. Coun., Coun. on Competitiveness. Recipient Exemplary Leadership in Mgmt. award John E. Anderson Sch. Mgmt., UCLA, 1991, Excellence in Tech. award Gartner Group, 1991, Spirit of Achievement award Jr. Achievement of So. Calif., 1993, Adm. Chester W. Nimitz award Navy League's Fleet, 1995, Inaugural Front and Ctr. award Calif. State U., Fullerton, 1996, Human Rels. award Am. Jewish Com., Orange County, 1996; named hon. chmn. Nat. Engrs. Week, 1994. Fellow AIAA, Soc. Mfg. Engrs.; mem. Navy League U.S., Young Pres.'s Orgn., Sigma Alpha Epsilon, Beta Gamma Sigma. Address: 777 E Wisconsin Ave Milwaukee WI 53202 Office: Rockwell Internat Corp Ste 1400 777 E Wisconsin Ave Milwaukee WI 53202*

BEALS, CLEM KIP, III, dentist; b. Springfield, Ohio, Mar. 7, 1949; s. Clem II and Betty Jane (Epley) B.; m. Mary Elizabeth Barry, June 10, 1974 (div. Feb. 1985); 1 child, Elizabeth Allison; m. Mary Margaret Ewing, June 8, 1985; 1 child, Andrew Jonathan. BS magna cum laude, Urbana (Ohio) Coll., 1971; DDS, Ohio State U., 1974. Resident in dentistry St. Elizabeth Hosp., Youngstown, Ohio, 1975-76; gen. practice dentistry Marion, Ohio, 1976—; exec. dir. Marion County Dental Clinic, Marion, 1979-94; chmn. dept. dentistry Marion Gen. Hosp., 1984-87. NSF grantee, 1970. Mem. ADA (ho. dels. 1997—), Ohio Dental Assn. (dist. coord. 1994-96), Coun. on Comms. and Pub. Svc., Acad. Gen. Dentistry, Ctrl. Ohio Dental Soc. (v.p. 1986-87, pres. 1988-89), Marion Acad. Dentistry (pres. 1977, sec./treas. 1979—), Jaycees (bd. dirs Marion chpt. 1978-79), Kiwanis, Psi Omega (Achievement award 1974). Republican. Methodist. Avocations: flying, skiing. Home: 1025 Brookpark Rd Marion OH 43302-6815 Office: 396 E Church St Marion OH 43302-4106

BEALS, L(OREN) ALAN, association executive; b. Glens Falls, N.Y., Jan. 10, 1933; s. Edgar Vernon and Ruth (Ackley) B.; m. Sandra Gale Campbell, Feb. 26, 1982; children by previous marriage: Vernon Alan, Catherine Ann, Kimberly Ruth; stepchildren: Vicki Lynn Adair, Steven Montgomery Campbell, Gary Britt Campbell, Toby Lane Poston. B.A., Colgate U., 1954; M.P.A., Syracuse U., 1955. Intern City of Richmond, Va., 1955-56; adminstrv. asst. City of Norfolk, Va., 1956; dir. publs., dir. town affiliations Nat. League of Cities, Washington, 1957-59; dir. congl. relations Nat. League of Cities, 1970, dir. fed. affairs, 1971, dep. dir., 1972-75, exec. dir., 1975-90; exec. sec. Md. Municipal League, College Park, 1959-65; dir. econ. ops. programs Met. Fund, Detroit, 1965-66; sec. Pub. Ofcls. Adv. Coun., Office Econ. Opportunity, Washington, 1966-67, Great Lakes regional dir., Chgo., 1967-70; lectr. govt. and politics U. Md., 1959-65; chmn. Fed. Regional Coun., Chgo., 1968-69; lectr. U. So. Calif., L.A., 1977-81; founding trustee Cmty. Found., Silver Spring, Md., 1971-75; bd. dirs. Nat. Tng. and Devel. Svc., Washington, 1975-82, chmn., 1976-77; bd. dirs. Nat. Assn. Regional Couns., Washington, 1975-79, Coun. for Internat. Urban Liaison, Washington, 1975-85, chmn., 1980-82; bd. dirs. Pub. Tech., Inc., Washington, 1975-90, chmn., 1978-80, 83-85, 86-90; bd. dirs. Acad. for State and Local Govt., Washington 1975-90, United Way of Coastal Empire, Inc., 1995-98; chmn. Acad. for Contemporary Problems, 1977-78; bd. dirs. Ctr. for Renewal Resources, 1980-83; exec. com. Internat. Union Local Authorities, The Hague, 1985-90; pres., CEO Savannah Area C. of C., 1990-99; mem. Ga. Partnership for Excellence in Edn., 1990-99; exec. com. Savannah Olympic Support Coun., 1991-96. Contbg. editor: Nation's Cities Weekly, 1970-75, Editor-in-chief, 1975-90; editor: Md. Municipal News, 1959-65. Pres. Savannah Area Conv. and Visitors Bur., 1990-99. Mem. Am. Soc. Pub. Adminstrn., Nat. Acad. Pub. Adminstrn. (trustee 1978-81), Internat. City Mgmt. Assn., Savannah First City Club, Savannah Golf Club, Savannah Chatham Club, Savannah Rotary Club. Home: 117 Mcintosh Dr Savannah GA 31406-5245

BEALS, MARK GRADEN, educator; b. Irvona, Pa., Aug. 11, 1936; s. George Bylle and Leila Elzeda (Eidell) B. B.A., Lycoming Coll., 1956; M.A., U. Hawaii, 1958; Ph.D., U. Ariz., 1968. Psychologist Yakima, Wash., 1961-64; instr. psychology Yakima Valley Coll., 1961-64; asst. prof., coordinator program in spl. edn. No. Ariz. U., Flagstaff, 1966-69; prof., dir. undergrad. curricula, coordinator student teaching and programs for gifted U. Nev., Las Vegas, 1969-85, assoc. dean Coll. Edn., 1985-91; dean Coll. Social Sci. Greenwich U., 1991—; cons. State of Ariz. Dists. 15, 16, 22, 1970-79, Navajo, Apache Nations, 1966-69; founder cons. New Horizons Ctr. for Learning, Las Vegas, 1971-95; cons. and lectr. in field; pioneer in field of learning disabilities. Author: Handbook for Teachers of the Culturally Deprived, 1966, Laughter of Children, 1968 (film); contbr. articles to profl. jours. Pres. So. Nev. Epilepsy Assn., Nev. Epilepsy Assn., 1972-75; mem. Com. on Rehab., 1969; mem. Gov.'s Com. on Gifted, 1975, Com. on Accreditation, 1981—, others. Served with U.S. Army, 1944-47. Recipient Gov.'s award State of Nev., 1968; Epilepsy Found. leadership award, 1975; award for leadership to children Ariz. Assn. Chronic Lung Disease, 1977, Outstanding Leadership in Edn., 1991; named Educator of Yr., 1991. Fellow Menninger Found.; mem. Am. Psychol. Assn., Western Psychol. Assn., Council for Exceptional Children, AAAS, Ednl. Research Assn., Assn. for Retarded Citizens, Orton Soc. Humanistic Psychology Assn., Mensa. Republican.

BEALS, PAUL ARCHER, religious studies educator; b. Russell, Iowa, Feb. 18, 1924; s. Archer Edwin and Myrtle Mae (Kelsey) B.; m. Vivian Brown, Sept. 29, 1945; children: Lois Ruth, Stephen Paul, Samuel Archer, Timothy Joel. AB, Wheaton (Ill.) Coll., 1945; diploma, Moody Bible Inst., Chgo., 1948; ThM with high honors, Dallas Theol. Seminary, 1952, ThD, 1964. Missionary in Cen. African Republic Bapt. Mid-Missions, Cleve., 1952-64; prof. of missiology Grand Rapids (Mich.) Bapt. Seminary, 1964-97, prof. emeritus missiology, 1998—, dir. continuing edn., 1977-90; theol. cons. Bapt. Mid-Missions, 1969—; conf. speaker. Author: A People for His Name, 1985, rev. edit., 1995; contbr. articles to profl. jours. Mem. Evang. Theol. Soc., Evang. Missiological Soc. (pres. 1990-93), Am. Soc. Missiology, Pi Gamma Mu. Home: 2111 Audley Dr NE Grand Rapids MI 49525-1517

BEAN, ALAN LAVERN, retired astronaut, artist; b. Wheeler, Tex., Mar. 15, 1932; s. Arnold H. B.; children: Clay, Amy. B.S. in Aero. Engring., U. Tex., 1955; grad., USN Test Pilot Sch.; Dr. Sci. (hon.), Tex. Wesleyan U., 1972, U. Akron; student, St. Mary's Coll., 1962; pvt. studies with various art tchrs. Commd. ensign U.S. Navy, 1955; advanced through grades to capt.; test pilot various aircraft U.S. Navy, Patuxent, Md., 1960-63; astronaut Manned Spacecraft Center, NASA, 1963—, lunar module pilot Apollo XII, 1969, ret., 1975; 4th man to walk on moon; comdr. 2d Skylab mission; set record 59 days in space; back up comdr. Apollo-Soyuz Test Project in 1975; held 10 world records in aeros. and astronautics; mem. Internat. Adv. Bd. Frederic Remington Art Mus., Ogdensburg, N.Y., 1986. Exhibited in group shows at Bryant Galleries, Houston, 1974, Nat. Air and Space Mus., Smithsonian Inst., Washington, 1978-80; 2 mall show with Alek Leonov; Astronaut/Cosmonaut art in LaGeode, Paris, 1985; Bus. in the Arts Awards, Hirshorn Mus. and Sculpture Garden, Washington, 1986; one man shows include Opera Assn., Ft. Worth, 1983, Meredith Long Gallery, Houston, 1984, 86; represented in numerous pubs. including Aviation Space mag., Time mag., Art Gallery International mag., S.W. Art mag., Omni mag.; host, narrator (video) The Safe and Succesful Use of Art Materials, 1986; subject of PBS spl. Alan Bean—Art Off This Earth, 1991. Decorated D.S.M. with cluster, Navy Astronaut Wings; Navy Disting. Service medal with cluster; recipient Man of Yr. award Tex. Press Assn., 1969, Rear Adm. William S. Parsons award, 1970, Disting. Engring. Grad. award U. Tex., 1970, Godfrey L. Cabot award, 1970, Spl. Trustees award Nat. Acad. TV Arts and Scis., 1970, Yuri Gagarin award AIAA, 1974, Merit award N.Y. Art Dirs. Club, 1985. Fellow Am. Astron. Soc.; mem. Delta Kappa Epsilon. Home and Studio: 9173 Briar Forest Dr Houston TX 77024-7222

BEAN, JOHN PERRIN, education educator; b. Cin., Apr. 25, 1946; s. William Bennett and Abigail Jane Shepard Bean; m. Barbara Ann Cottral, Dec. 20, 1969; children: David Shepard, Jeffrey Perrin. BA in Anthropology, Beloit (Wis.) Coll., 1968; MFA in Poetry, U. Iowa, 1970, MA in English, 1972, MAPA in Polit. Sci., 1976, PhD in Edn., 1978. Program asst. Internat. Writing Program U. Iowa, Iowa City, 1972-74; acad. program rev. and devel. specialist U. Nebr., Lincoln, 1978-81; asst. prof. edn. Ind. U., Bloomington, 1981-87, assoc. prof. edn., 1987—; program chair higher edn. and student affairs Ind. U., 1990-95. Co-author: The Strategic Management of College Enrollments, 1990; contbr. articles to profl. jours.; songwriter Last Go Round, 1999; mem. editl. bd. Jour. Coll. Student Retention, 1998—. Recipient Best in Show and Purchase award Swope Mus., Terre Haute, Ind., 1990, Best in Show award for oil painting Indpls. Art League, 1991. Mem. Assn. for Study of Higher Edn. (chair rsch. papers program 1997), Am. Ednl. Rsch. Assn. (chair rsch. papers program Divsn. J 1989). Avocations: playing old time music, oil painting, writing poetry and songs, building Cremonese-style violins. Office: Ind U Sch Edn 201 N Rose Ave Bloomington IN 47405-1005

BEAN, PHILIP THOMAS, educator; b. Southill, England, Sept. 24, 1936; s. Thomas William and Amy (Faulkner) B.; m. Anne Elizabeth Seller, Sept. 12, 1963 (div.); m. Valerie Winifred Davies nee Jones, Mar. 28, 1969 (dec. June 1999); children: Ian Thomas, Jonathan Lee. BS, U. London, 1966, MS in Econs., 1971; PhD, U. Nottingham, England, 1983. Probation officer London Probation Svc., 1963-70; rsch. officer Med. Rsch. Coun., Chichester, England, 1970-72; lectr., sr. lectr. U. Nottingham, England, 1972-90; prof. criminology U. Loughborough, England, 1990—; vis. prof. U. Western Australia, Perth, 1986, Luther Coll., Iowa, 1983, U. Manitoba, Can., 1979. Author: Rehabilitation and Deviance, 1974, Complusory Admissions to Mental Hospitals, 1980, Punishment, 1981, Mental Disorder and Legal Control, 1987, Mental Disorder and Community Safety, 2000. Vis. fellow U. Cambridge, England, 1968. Mem. British Soc. Criminology (pres. 1996-99, sec. 1993-96), Atheneum. Avocations: music, poetry. Home: 41 Trevor Rd, West Bridgford, Nottingham NG2 6FT, England Office: Midlands Ctr Criminology, U Loughborough, Loughborough LE11 3TU, England

BEANLAND, DAVID GEORGE, academic administrator; b. Yallourn, Victoria, Australia, Aug. 6, 1938; s. Charles H. and Florence L. (George) B.; m. Heather Lynette Toy, Aug. 5, 1961; children: Christine, Gregory, Matthew, Philip. BEng (hon.), U. Melbourne, Australia, 1951; MSc, U. Salford, 1975, PhD, 1977. Head dept. comm. engring. Royal Melbourne (Australia) Inst. Tech., 1968-79, dean faculty engring., 1979-84, assoc. dir., 1984-89, dir., 1989-92, vice chancellor, 1992-2000; rschr. Harwell Rsch. Lab., England, 1975-76; dir. IDP Edn. Australia, 1996—. Contbr. articles to profl. jours. Dir. Melbourne Conv. and Mktg. Bur. & Melbourne City Mktg., 1992-97, Com. for Melbourne, 1992-2000, Bus. Higher Edn. Roundtable, Melbourne, 1992-2000. Fellow Instn. Engrs. Australia, Instn. Radio and Electronic Engrs. Australia, Acad. Tech. Sci. and Engring. Avocations: building, hiking, sport, travel. Office: Royal Melbourne Inst Tech, 124 Latrobe St, 3000 Melbourne Victoria, Australia

BEAR, HENRY LOUIS, lawyer; b. Kansas City, Kans.; s. Max and Mary (Kagon) B.; m. Betty Jean Isenhart, Jan. 4, 1951; 1 child, Dinah. JD, U. Mo., 1939. Bar: Mo. 1939, Calif. 1949, U.S. Dist. Ct. (so. dist.) Calif. 1949, U.S. Supreme Ct. 1959. Assoc. O'Hern & O'Hern, Kansas City, Mo., 1939-42; ptnr. Bear, Kotob, Ruby & Gross, and predecessors, Downey, Calif., 1949—; sec., dir. Pyrotronics Corp.; dir. Bank of Irvine. Author: California Law of Corporations, Partnerships and Associations, 1970. Chmn. Midland dist. coun. Boy Scouts Am., 1954; active Cmty. Chest, Lynwood, Calif. Served to lt. USAF, 1942-46. Named Lynwood Man of Yr., 1952. Fellow Am. Coll. Probate Counsel; mem. ABA, Mo. Bar Assn., Calif. Bar Assn., Calif. Trial Lawyers Assn., L.A. County Bar Assn., Exec. Dinner Club (pres.), Rotary, Elks. Office: Bear Kotob Ruby & Gross 10841 Paramount Blvd PO Box 747 Downey CA 90241-0747

BEAR, JACOB, civil engineer, educator, consultant; b. Haifa, Israel, Feb. 2, 1929; s. Isac Bear and Ester Sternfeld; m. Siona Setton, June 14, 1951; children: Eitan, Alon, Iris. BSc, Technion-Israel Inst. Tech., Haifa, Israel, 1953, MSc, 1957; PhD, U. Calif., Berkeley, 1960; D in Technol. Scis. (hon.), U. Delft, The Netherlands, 1978, Eidgenössische Technische, Zurich, Switzerland, 1988. Registered profl. engr. Mem. faculty Technion-Israel Inst. Tech., Haifa, 1960-97, faculty emeritus, 1997—. Author: Dynamics of Fluids in Porous Media, 1972, Hydraulics of Ground Water, 1979; co-author: (with A. Verrujit) Modeling Groundwater Flow and Pollution, 1987, (with Y. Bachmat) Introduction to Modeling Transport Phenomena in Porous Media, 1990; founder, chief editor Internat. Jour. Transport in Porous Media; contbr. over 175 articles to profl. publs. Recipient M.K. Hubbert award Nat. Ground Water Assn., 1990, Rothschild prize in engring., 1998. Fellow Am. Geophys. Union. Achievements include research in water resources, groundwater, transport in porous media. Home: 28 Liberia St, 34980 Haifa Israel Office: Technion-Israel Inst Tech, Dept Civil Engring, 32000 Haifa Israel

BEAR, LARRY ALAN, lawyer, educator; b. Melrose, Mass., Feb. 28, 1928; s. Joseph E. and Pearl Florence B.; m. Rita Maldonado, Mar. 29, 1975; children: Peter, Jonathan, Steven. BA, Duke U., 1949; JD, Harvard U., 1953; LLM, (James Kent fellow), Columbia U., 1966. Bar: Mass. 1953, P.R. 1963, N.Y. 1967. Trial lawyer Bear & Bear, Boston, 1953-60; cons. legal medicine P.R. Dept. Justice, 1960-65; prof. law sch. U. P.R., 1960-65; legal counsel, then commr. addiction svcs. City of N.Y., 1967-70; dir. Nat. Action Com. Drug Edn. U. Rochester, N.Y., 1970-77; pvt. practice N.Y.C., 1970-82; pub. affairs radio broadcaster Sta. WABC, N.Y.C., 1970-82; U.S. legal counsel Master Enterprises of P.R., 1982-90; pres. Found. for a Drug Free Pa., 1991-92; adj. prof. markets, ethics and law Stern Sch. Bus., NYU, 1986-99, vis. prof. bus. ethics, 2000—; lectr. in legislation and ethics Wharton Sch. Exec. Program, 1996—; vis. prof. legal medicine Rutgers U. Law Sch., 1969; vis. prof. legal, social and ethical context of bus. Athens Lab. for Bus. Adminstrn., Greece, 1996; mem. alcohol and drug com. Nat. Safety Coun., 1972-82; cons. in field of substance abuse prevention, edn. programming, 1980—; mem. Atty. Gen.'s Med./Legal Adv. Bd. on Drug Abuse, Pa., 1992. Author: Law, Medicine, Science and Justice, 1964, The Glass House Revolution: Inner City War for Interdependence, 1990, Free Markets, Finance, Ethics, and Law, 1994; contbr. articles to profl. jours. Mem. adv. com. on pub. issues Advt. Coun., 1972-95; mem.-at-large Nat. coun. Boy Scouts Am., 1972-85; chmn. Bd. Ethics, Twp. of Mahwah (N.J.), 1990-91; mem. alumni admissions adv. com. Duke U., 1987—. Mem. ABA, N.Y. State Bar Assn., Forensic Sci. Soc. Great Britain, Acad. Colombiana de Ciencias Medico-Forenses, Harvard Club (N.Y.C.). Home: 95 Tam Oshanter Dr Mahwah NJ 07430-1526 Office: Dept Fin Mgmt Edn Ctr 44 W 4th St Ste 9-190 New York NY 10012-1106

BEARD, AMANDA, swimmer, Olympic athlete; b. Irvine, Calif., Oct. 29, 1981. Mem. Pan Pac Team, 1995; swimmer U.S. Olympic Team, Atlanta, 1996. Recipient 2 silver medals in 100 meter breaststroke and 200 meter breaststroke Olympic Games, Atlanta, 1996, gold medal in 4x100 medley relay Olympic Games, Atlanta, 1996; holder Am. record for 100 meter breastroke, 1996. Office: US Swimming Inc One Olympic Plz Colorado Springs CO 80909

BEARD, JONATHAN DAVID, vascular surgeon, consultant, educator; b. Chelmsford, Essex, Eng., Oct. 23, 1955; s. John Vincent and Joan Edith Beard; m. Mandy Sharon Sharpe, Feb. 13, 1987. BSc with honors, U. London, 1976; MB BS, Guys Hosp., London, 1979; ChM, U. Bristol, 1987. Vascular rsch. fellow Bristol (Eng.) U., 1984-86; surg. registrar Bristol Hosps., 1986-88; surgery lectr. Leicester (Eng.) U., 1988-90; vascular surgery cons. Sheffield (Eng.) Vascular Inst., 1990—. Assoc. editor European Jour. Vascular Surgery, 1990-99, sr. editor, 2000—; contbr. articles to profl. jours. including European Jour. Vascular and Endovascular Surgery, Brit. Med. Jour., and Brit. Jour. Surgery. Recipient Surg. award The Worshipful Co. of Cutlers, 1998. Fellow Royal Coll. Surgeons (Eng.); mem. Vascular Surg. Soc. Gt. Britain and Ireland (audit chmn. 1993-98), European Soc. for Vascular Surgery. Avocation: barbershop singing. Office: Sheffield Vascular Inst, Northern Gen Hosp, Sheffield S5 7AU, England

BEARDSLEY, THEODORE S(TERLING), JR., professional society administrator; b. East St. Louis, Ill., Aug. 26, 1930; s. Theodore Sterling and

Margaret (Kienzle) B.; m. Lenora J. Fierke, May 26, 1955; children: Theodore Sterling III, Mark A., Mary Elizabeth. BS, So. Ill. U., 1952; MA (Max Bryant fellow), Washington U., St. Louis, 1954; postgrad., U. Heidelberg, Germany, 1955-56; PhD, U. Pa., 1961; linguistic rsch., Inst. Caro y Cuervo, Bogota, Colombia, summer 1973. Asst. in English Lycee Wilson, Chaumont, France, 1952-53; mem. faculty Rider Coll., 1957-61, chmn. dept. modern lang., 1959-61; asst. prof. Spanish So. Ill. U., 1961-62, U. Wis., 1962-65; dir. Hispanic Soc. Am., N.Y.C., 1965-95, pres., 1995—; adj. prof. NYU, 1967-69, 80, Adelphi U., 1966, 68, Columbia U., 1969, Eckerd Coll., 1997—; Fulbright lectr., Ecuador, 1974; guest lectr. U. Complutense, Madrid, 1990, 94, U. Salamanca, 1994, 99, U. Rábida, Spain, 1996; diss. dir. U. Oviedo, Spain, 1992; vis. prof. U. Wis., 1995; chmn. Museums Coun. N.Y.C., 1972-73; spl. cons. Hispanic bibliography Libr. Congress, fall 1973, N.J. State Dept. Edn., spring 1975, NEH, 1978—. Narrator Spanish lang. recorded tours, Nat. Gallery Art, Met. Mus., Mus. Natural Sci., Boston Sci. Mus., Smithsonian Instn., Pouce de León, 2000; continuing series on Caribbean popular music in U.S, WBGO-FM, 1979; Xavier Cugat, 1980, USA Latino, 1981, Enrique Madriguera, Spanish Nat. Radio, 1985; author: Hispano-Classical Translations, 1482-1699, 1970, Tomas Navarro Tomas, A Tentative Bibliography, 1908-1970, 1971; librettist: Ponce de Leon, 1973; also articles; recordings include: Charla con Camilo José Cela, 1966, Visita a la Hispanic Society, 1969; editor: Enrique Madriguera, 1994; co-editor: Celestina: Early Text, 1997; narrator-author: 4 part series Hispanic Immigration to the United States (text pub. 1976), CBS-TV, 1972, Ponce de Leon, 2000; narrator: Charlotte Symphony, 2000; mem. adv. bd.: Hispanic Rev., Studia humanitatis, Boletín de ANLE, Hispanic Sem. of Medieval Studies, Revista Caribe. Served with AUS, 1954-56. Decorated Orden de Mérito Civil, Spain ; Fulbright grantee, 1952-53; Jusserand traveling fellow, 1962; research grantee Am. Council Learned Socs., 1964; travel grantee, 1974; recipient Premio Bibliofilia Barcelona, Spain, 1973, Merit award Noticias de Arte, 1999. Mem. ASCAP, Hispanic Soc. Am., Renaissance Soc. Am. (exec. coun., acting dir. 1981-82), Acad. Norteamericana Lengua Española, Internat. Inst. (Madrid), Internat. Linguistic Assn. (exec. coun.), Hispanic Sem. Medieval Studies (bd. dirs.), Ponce De Leon Conquistadors, Sigma Delta Pi, Sigma Tau Gamma; corr. mem. Royal Spanish Acad., Real Acad. Bellas Artes San Carlos (Valencia), Acad. Guatemalteca de Lengua, Assn. Bibliofilos Barcelona, Fundacion Odón Betanzos (Rociana), Fundacion Santa Maria de la Rabida, Fundacion Universitaria Espanola (Madrid), Inst. Valencia Don Juan (bd. dirs. Madrid). Office: Hispanic Soc Am 613 W 155th St New York NY 10032-7501

BEARE, GENE KERWIN, electric company executive; b. Chester, Ill., July 14, 1915; s. Nicholas Eugene and Minnie Cole (St. Vrain) B.; m. Doris Margaret Alt, Dec. 11, 1943 (dec.); children: Gail Kathryn, Joanne St. Vrain; m. Patricia Pfau Cade, Sept. 12, 1964 (dec.); m. Lee May Hollo, July 29, 1997. B.S. in Mech. Engring, Washington U., 1937; M.B.A., Harvard, 1939. Registered profl. engr., Ill. With Automatic Electric Co., Chgo., 1939-58, successively asst. to v.p. and gen. mgr., asst. to pres., mgr. internat. affiliated cos., gen. comml. mgr., 1939-54, v.p. prodn., 1954-58, dir., 1956-61; pres., dir. Automatic Electric Internat., Inc., Chgo., 1958-61; chmn., dir. Automatic Electric (Can.), Ltd., Chgo., Automatic Electric Sales (Can.), Ltd., 1958-61; pres., dir. Sylvania Internat., 1959-60; pres. Gen. Telephone & Electronics Internat., Inc., 1960-61, dir., 1960-72; also dir. numerous subs. in Gen. Telephone & Electronics Internat., Inc., Colombia, Mex., Venezuela, Argentina, Switzerland, Panama, Brazil, Bel; dir. Am. Research and Devel. Corp., 1967-74, Canadair Ltd., 1972-75; pres. Sylvania Electric Products, Inc., 1961-69, dir., 1961-72; exec. v.p. mfg., dir. Gen. Telephone & Electronics Corp., 1969-72; exec. v.p., dir. Gen. Dynamics Corp., St. Louis, 1972-77; pres. Gen. Dynamics Comml. Products Co., 1972-77; chmn. Asbestos Corp. Ltd., 1974-77; dir. Arkwright-Boston Mut. Ins. Co., Westvaco Corp., Emerson Electric Co., St. Joe Minerals Corp., Am. Maize-Products Corp., Datapoint Corp., Nooney Realty Trust, Inc. Served to lt. USNR, 1942-45. Mem. Pan Am. Soc., Nat. Elec. Mfrs. Assn. (bd. govs. 1963-72, v.p. 1964, pres. 1965-66), Armed Forces Communications and Electronics Assn., Nat. Security Indsl. Assn. (trustee 1969-72). Clubs: Wee Burn (Darien, Conn.) (gov. 1963-68); Union League (N.Y.C.), Econ. (N.Y.C.); St. Louis (dir. 1979—); Old Warson (Ladue, Mo.) (dir. 1979—), Univ. (St. Louis), The Ocean Club of Fla., Ocean Ridge. Home: 801 S Skinker Blvd Saint Louis MO 63105-3269 Office: Pierre Laclede Center 7701 Forsyth Blvd Ste 1070 Saint Louis MO 63105-1840

BEARE, WALTER ELLIOT, zoologist; b. Cork, Ireland, Nov. 16, 1971; s. William and Rose Alice (Hurley) B. BA in Zoology, Trinity Coll., Dublin, Ireland, 1994; MSc in Aquaculture, U. Coll., Cork, 1997. Rsch. asst. U. Coll., Cork, 1997-98. Mem. Irish Youth Choir, 1999—. Mem. Cork Backgammon Club (pres. 1998). Avocations: backgammon, cycling, reading, choral singing.

BEARN, DAVID RUSSELL, orthodontist; b. Sheffield, Yorkshire, Eng., Sept. 9, 1963; s. Andrew Russell and Margaret Edith (Morse) B.; m. Ruth Olga Hetherington, Apr. 14, 1984; children: Amelia, Russell, Elizabeth. B Dental Surgery, U. Sheffield, Eng., 1985; M Dentistry, U. Newcastle, Eng., 1993; PhD, U. Manchester, Eng., 2000. House surgeon U. Sheffield, 1986-87; sr. house physician Dumfries Infirmary, Scotland, 1987-88; registrar U. Glasgow (Scotland) Dental Sch., 1989-90; career registrar U. Newcastle Dental Sch., 1991-94; lectr. U. Manchester, Eng., 1994—; adj. assoc. prof. U. N.C., Chapel Hill, 1996; referee Brit. Jour. Orthodontics, 1996—; rsch. fellow U. Manchester/Royal Coll. Surgeons London, 1996-99. Contbr. articles to profl. jours. Fellow Royal Coll. Physicians and Surgeons Glasgow; mem. Brit. Orthodontic Soc., Manchester Med. Soc., Royal Coll. Surgeons London. Mem. Ch. of England. Avocations: family, fell walking, soccer. E-mail: david.bearn@man.ac.uk. Home: 41 Sheffield Rd, Glossop Derbyshire SK13 8QJ, England Office: U Manchester Dental Sch, Higher Cambridge St, Manchester M15 6FR, England

BÉART, EMMANUELLE, actress; b. St. Tropez, France, Aug. 14, 1965; d. Guy B.; 1 child. Student, drama sch. Appeared in films, including And Hope to Die, 1972, Demain les mômes, 1975, First Desires, 1983, Zacharius, 1984, Un amour interdit, 1984, Raison perdue, 1984, Love on the Quiet, 1985, Manon of the Spring, 1986, Date with an Angel, 1987, Door on the Left as You Leave the Elevator, 1988, Children of Chaos, 1989, Against Oblivion, 1991, Captain Fracassa's Journey, 1991, The Beautiful Troublemaker, 1991, I Don't Kiss, 1991, A Heart of Stone, 1992, Ruptures, 1993, Torment, 1994, A French Woman, 1995, Nelly and Mr. Arnaud, 1995, Le Dernier chaperon rouge, 1996, Mission Impossible, 1996, Don Juan, 1998, Stolen Life, 1998, Time Regained, 1999, Elephant Juice, 1999, La Bûche, 1999, Les Destinées Sentimentales, 2000. Office: care VMA, 20 Avenue Rapp, 75007 Paris France also: care William Morris Agy 151 S El Camino Dr Beverly Hills CA 90212-2704*

BEASLEY, JOHN JULIUS, child and family development educator; b. Raleigh, N.C., July 9, 1947; s. Julius Helland and Ruth Christine (Richardson) B.; m. Mary Sandra Wortham, June 21, 1969; 1 child, Elizabeth. BA, E. Carolina U., 1969; MS, Va. Tech., 1972, PhD, 1978. Extension agent 4-H Va. Tech., Blacksburg, 1971-74, instr. extension, 1974-78, asst. prof. extension, 1978-81; chair Appalachian State U., Boone, N.C., 1981-86; assoc. prof. Appalachian State U., Boone, 1981-88; prof. Ga. So. U., Statesboro, 1988—, chair, 1988-96; cons. Head Start, Vienna, Va., 1995—; spkr. in field. Editor rsch. sect. Jour. Extension, 1979-81; reviewer Jour. of Family and Consumer Scis., 1994—; contbr. articles to profl. jours. Pres., University Optimist, Statesboro, 1991-92, adv. bd., 1996—; pres. Child Abuse Coun., Statesboro, 1995-97. Grantee Children's Trust Fund, 1991, Ga. Child Care Coun., 1992. Mem. Future Homemakers of Am./HERO (hon.), Am. Assn. Family Consumer Sci. (cert. family consumer scientist), Ga. Family Consumer Scis., Statesboro C. of C., Optimist Internat. (life), Phi Delta Kappa, Phi Kappa Phi, Phi Upsilon Omicron. Episcopalian. Home: 108 Turkey Trl Statesboro GA 30458-8908 Office: Ga So U PO Box 8021 Statesboro GA 30460-1000

BEASOM, NANCY ANN, occupational therapist, consultant; b. Kansas City, Kans., Nov. 2, 1936; d. Albert Lawrence and Ruth Augusta (Badgley) Hibbs; m. Ronald Lightner Beasom, June 14, 1958; children: Kim Leslie Schwab, Jeffrey Craig Beasom, Bryn Ann Fay. BS, U. Pa., 1958. Registered and lic. occupational therapist, Pa., Fla. Artist/craftsman West Chester, Pa., 1965-75; occupational therapy cons. in pvt. practice West Chester, 1978-81; occupational therapist DPW/Embreeville Ctr., Coatesville, Pa., 1975-82, occupational therapy supr., 1982-85, mental retardationunit mgr., 1982-85, occupl. therapist, 1985-96; occupl. therapy cons. Chester County MH/MR Unit, West Chester, 1988-91; occupational therapy cons. Elwyn, Inc., Pa., 1989—; cons. in occupational therapy Brian's House, West Chester, 1978-81, Home Health Care Agy., West Reading, Pa., 1981-82. Mem. Am. Occupational Therapy Assn. Avocations: basketry, gardening, writing poetry, art work, growing orchids. Home: 2085 River Basin Ter Punta Gorda FL 33982-1106

BEATON, MEREDITH, enterostomal therapy clinical nurse specialist; b. Danvers, Mass., Oct. 5, 1941; d. Allan Cameron and Arlene Margaret (Jerue) Beaton; m. William Paul Hollingsworth, Nov. 19, 1983 (div.); 1 stepchild, Brendon R. Diploma, R.I. Hosp. Sch. Nursing, Providence, 1968; BS in Nursing, U. Ariz., 1976; MS in Human Resource Mgmt., Golden Gate U., 1984; postgrad., U. Tex., 1988; EdD, U. N.Mex., 1995; MS in Nursing, U. Phoenix, 1998. Cert. enterostomal therapy nurse, health edn. specialist. Commd. ensign USN, 1968, advanced through grades to lt. comdr., 1979; charge nurse USN, USA, PTO, 1968-88; command ostomy nurse, head ostomy clinic Naval Hosp. Portsmouth, Va., 1985-88; pres., chief exec. officer Enterostomac Therapy Nursing Edn. and Tng. Cons. (ETNetc), Rio Rancho, N.Mex., 1989-99; mgr. clin. svcs. we. area Support Systems Internat., Inc., Charleston, S.C., 1990-92; pres., CEO Paumer Assocs. Internat., Inc., Rio Rancho, N.Mex., 1992—; sr. cons. enterostomac therapy nursing, edn., & tng. cons.; dir./provost N.Mex. Sch. Enterostomac Nursing, Rio Rancho, 1996—; enterostomal therapy nurse, clin. nurse specialist, educator Presbyn. Health Care Svcs., Albuquerque, 1992-95; sr. cons. Enterstomal Therapy Nursing Edn. & Tng. Cons. A Divsn. of Paumer Assocs., Rio Rancho, N. Mex., 1995—; dir./provost N.Mex. Sch. ET Nursing, Rio Rancho, 1995—; lectr. in field. Mem. adminstrv. bd. Baylake United Meth. Ch., Virginia Beach, 1980-83; chmn. bd. deacons St. Paul's United Ch., Rio Rancho, also vice moderator; active Am. Cancer Soc.; mem. adv. bd. Keep Rio Rancho Beautiful, 1998—; mem. bd. dirs. Assn. Advancement of Wound Care. Mem. Wound, Ostomy and Continence Nurses Soc. (nat. govt. affairs com., govt. affairs com. Rocky Mountain region, newsletter editor, pub. rels. com., regional pres. 1989-93, nat. sec. 1994-95), United Ostomy Assn., World Coun. Enterstomac Therapists, N. Mex. Health Care Assn., N. Mex. Assn. for Home Care, N. Mex. Assn. for Continuity of Care, Assn. Advanced Wound Care (bd. dirs.). Republican. Avocations: hot air ballooning, gourmet cooking, flower arranging, interior design. Office: PO Box 44395 Rio Rancho NM 87174-4395

BEATON, REBECCA ANDREA, psychotherapist; b. West Covina, Calif., Dec. 3, 1964; d. Allen Ethan and Joan Delores (Graybill) Brogan; m. Robert Gifford Beaton II, Sept. 4, 1993. BA in Human Philosophy & Cultural Geog., U. Calif., Santa Barbara, 1986; MS in Cmty. Counseling, Ga. State U., 1995, specialist in edn., 1996, PhD in Counseling Psychology, 2000. Health counselor Bragg Health Sci., Santa Barbara, Calif., 1986-87; counselor intern Anxiety Disorders Inst./Atlanta Ctr. for Eating Disorders, 1994-95; counselor intern employee assistance program Lockheed Aero. Sys. Co., Marietta, Ga., 1994-95; psychotherapist Anxiety Disorders Inst. Atlanta, 1995-98; pvt. practice Ctr. for Psychotherapy and Healing Arts, 1998-2000; psychology resident Counseling and Testing Ctr. U. Ga., 1999-2000; pvt. practice Atlanta, 2000—; grad. rsch. asst. Ednl. Rsch. Bur., Ga. State U., Atlanta, 1993-94, dept. counseling and psychol. svcs., 1993-96; therapy group leader Trauma Abuse and Resource Program, Atlanta, 1995-98; psychotherapist Atlanta Ctr. for Eating Disorders, Atlanta, 1995-98; growth group leader Ga. State U., Atlanta, 1995-98, part-time faculty, 2000—; trainer Wellness Inst., 1997-2000; process group leader for med. interns Ga. Bapt. Med. Ctr., 1998-99; presenter in field. Contbr. articles to profl. jours. Vol. counselor Ga. Mental Health Inst., Atlanta, 1991-93; vol. rape crisis ctr. counselor, legal liaison Grady Meml. Hosp., Atlanta, 1992-98. Mem. APA (divsn. 17, divsn. 38, divsn. 30), ACA, Am. Ednl. Rsch. Assn., Assn. for Multi-cultural Counseling and Devel., Assn. for Transpersonal Psychology, Atlanta Assn. for Play Therapy, The Menninger Found. Avocations: wildlife photography, hiking, gardening, mountain bike riding, bird watching. Office: Ctr Psychotherapy/Healing Arts 1827 Powers Ferry Rd SE Bldg 7 Atlanta GA 30339-5621

BEATON, ROY HOWARD, retired nuclear industry executive; b. Boston, Sept. 1, 1916; s. John Howard and Mary Beaton (LaVoie) B.; m. Margaret Marchant, July 22, 1939 (dec. Oct. 4, 1978); m. Leora Lauer Schier, June 26, 1982; children: Constance Beaton Fegley, Roy Howard, Patricia Schier Briselden, Susan Schier Carter, Mary Schier Rieber. BS, Northeastern U., 1939, DSc (hon.), 1967; DEng, Yale U., 1942. Registered profl. engr., Wash., Wis., Fla., Calif. With E.I. DuPont, 1942-46, plant tech. supr. Manhattan (Nuclear Bomb) Project, 1943-44; chief chem. devel., chief engr., gen. mgr. constrn. engring. GE, Richland, Wash., 1946-56; gen. mgr. neutron devices dept. GE, Milw., 1957-63; gen. mgr. Apollo Systems, Daytona Beach, Fla., 1964-68; v.p., gen. mgr. def. electronics systems div. GE, Syracuse, N.Y., 1968-74; v.p., gen. mgr. energy systems and tech. div. GE, Fairfield, Conn., 1974-75; sr. v.p. and group exec. Nuclear Energy Group, San Jose, Calif., 1975-81. Chmn. industry div. United Way Campaign, Santa Clara County, Calif., 1978-79. Fellow Am. Inst. Chemists, AAAS; mem. NSPE, Nat. Acad. Engring., Am. Ordnance Assn., Am. Nuclear Soc., Am. Inst. Chem. Engrs., IEEE, AIAA, Navy League U.S., Air Force Assn., Soc. Mil. Engrs., Santa Clara County Mfg. Group, Sigma Xi, Tau Beta Pi. Home: 12 Fawn Ln Sequim WA 98382-3887

BEATRICE, PIER FRANCO, humanities educator; b. Padua, Italy, June 29, 1948; s. Alberto and Rachele (Zollo) B.; m. Paola Isaia, July 1, 1978; children: Charles, Philip. Degree in arts, U. Padua, 1970; PhD, Cath. U., Milan, 1978. Asst. prof. U. Padua, 1978-79, lectr., 1979-80, prof. early Christian lit., 1980—; vis. prof. U. Liège, Belgium, 1996, Boston Coll., 1998-99. Author: Tradux peccati, 1978, La lavanda dei piedi, 1983, L'eredità delle origini, 1992, Theosophia, 2000; contbr. articles to jours. in field; editor: L'intolleranza cristiana, 1993; mem. editl. bd. Cristianesimo nella Storia, Bologna, 1983-94, Studia Patavina, 1984-94; mem. adv. bd. Jour. Early Christian Studies, 1996—. Mem. Internat. Assn. Patristic Studies, Internat. Soc. for the Classical Tradition, N.Am. Patristics Soc., Studiorum Novi Testamenti Societas, Internat. Assn. for the History of Religions, Am. Acad. of Religion, Soc. of Biblical Lit. Roman Catholic. Avocations: sports, music, movies, theater, travels. Home: Via Metastasio 16, I-35125 Padua Italy

BEATRICE, RUTH HADFIELD, hypnotherapist, retired educator, financial administrator; b. Phila., Feb. 6, 1931; d. Claude and Alice Elizabeth (Smith) Hadfield; m. Michael Joseph Beatrice, May 29, 1954. BS, West Chester State U., 1953; MS, Marywood Coll., 1978; postgrad., Temple U., Pa. State U., 1978-80; cert. clinl. hypnotherapist, Phila. Hypnosis Union Inst., 1980. Cert. hypno-anaesthesia therapist Nat. Bd. Hypnotherapy and Hypnotic Anaesthesiology, 1991. Educator Bristol Twp. (Pa.) Sch. Dist., 1953-54, Phila. Sch. Dist., 1954-55; recreation dir. Phila. Dept. Recreation, 1953-57; educator Worcester (Pa.) Sch. Dist., 1958-59, Springford (Pa.) Joint Sch. Dist., 1960-61, Souderton (Pa.) Sch. Dist., 1961-63, Ctrl. Bucks Sch. Dist., Doylestown, Pa., 1970-1993; ret., 1993; clin. hypnotherapist in pvt. practice Perkasie, Pa., 1980—; clin. hypnotherapist, pvt. practice Avalon, N.J., 1980—, Port St. Lucie, Fla., Perkasie, Pa.; bus. adminstr. Beatrice Adminstrs. Co-author books on tutoring for Ptnrs. at Learning Series, 1978, 1979, 1983. Bd. mem. Pierce Free Libr., Hilltown, Pa., 1970-75; union del. Office and Profl. Employees Internat. Union Internat. Conv., Vancouver, B.C., Can., 1995; treas. Newcomers Civic Assn., Perkasie, 1964-85; me. Avalon (N.J.) Civic Assn., avalon Sr. Assn. Mem. NEA (life), Nat. Assn. Profl. Therapists, Am. Legion Aux., Pa. State Edn. Assn. (life), Hypnotism Soc. of Pa. (v.p. Phila. br. 1993-95), Phila. Hypnosis Union Local 476 (v.p. 1993-95), Nat. Guild of Hypnotists, Nat. Bd. for Hypnotherapy and Hypnotic Anaesthesiology. Democrat. Presbyterian. Avocations: tennis, walking, biking, fishing, boating, cooking, golf. Home and Office: 273 52nd St Avalon NJ 08202-1314 also: 3192 SE Carrick Green Ct Port Saint Lucie FL 34952-6042

BEATRIX, HER MAJESTY (BEATRIX WILHELMINA ARMGARD), Queen of The Netherlands; b. Soestdijk, The Netherlands, Jan. 31, 1938; d. Queen Juliana and Prince Bernhard; m. Prince Claus von Amsberg, Mar. 10, 1966; children: Prince Willem-Alexander (Prince of Orange), Prince Johan Friso, Prince Constantijn. D. Sociol., Juridical and Hist. Scis., U. Leiden, The Netherlands. Queen of The Netherlands, 1980—. Home: Paleis Noordeinde, PO Box 30412, 2500 GK The Hague The Netherlands*

BEATTIE, ANN, writer; b. Washington, Sept. 8, 1947; d. James and Charlotte (Crosby) B.; m. Lincoln Perry. B.A., Am. U., 1969; M.A., U. Conn., 1970; L.H.D. (hon.), Am. U., 1983. Vis. asst. prof. U. Va., Charlottesville, 1976-77, vis. writer, 1980; Briggs Copeland lectr. English Harvard U., Cambridge, Mass., 1977. Author: Chilly Scenes of Winter, 1976, Distortions, 1976, Secrets and Suprises, 1979, Falling In Place, 1980, Jacklighting, 1981, The Burning House, 1982, Love Always, 1985, Where You'll Find Me, 1986, Alex Katz, 1987, Picturing Will, 1990, What Was Mine, 1991, My Life Starring Dara Falcon, 1997, Park City: New & Selected Stories, 1998. Recipient Disting. Alumnae award Am. U., 1980, award in lit. Am. Acad. and Inst. Arts and Letters, 1980; Guggenheim fellow, 1977. Mem. Am. Acad. and Inst. of Arts and Letters, 1992, PEN, Authors Guild. Office: care Janklow and Nesbit 445 Park Ave New York NY 10022-2606

BEATTIE, SIR DAVID STUART, former New Zealand governor general; b. Sydney, Australia, Feb. 29, 1924; s. Joseph Nesbitt Beattie; m. Norma Macdonald; 7 children. LLB, U. Auckland, New Zealand, 1948. Called to bar, 1949; ptnr. firm Grierson, Moody, Jcakson and Beattie, 1953-58; individual practice law, 1958—; Queen's counsel, 1965; judge New Zealand Supreme Ct., 1969-80; gov.-gen. for New Zealand, 1980-85; chmn. Royal Commn. on Cts., 1977-78; chmn. Sir Winston Churchill Meml. Trust Bd., 1975-80; chmn. rules com. Supreme Ct., 1977-79; chmn. New Zealand Meat Industry Assn., 1987—; chmn. U.S. New Zealand 50th Commemoration Com., 1992; patron New Zealand Rugby Union, 1981-97. Mem. exec. bd. Crippled Children's Soc., Auckland, 1963-69; chmn. Dilworth Trust Bd., 1966-69, New Zealand Internat. Festival of the Arts, Ministerial Working Party on Sci. and Tech., several govt. commns.; treas. Auckland Cancer Soc., 1969; trustee Halberg Trust, Intellectually Handicapped Trust, 1971-80, McKenzie Found., 1970-80; chancellor Anglican Diocese of Auckland, 1967-69, 87-93; pres,. Harkness Found. in New Zealand, 1992—, New Zealand Olympic and Commonwealth Games Assn.; commr. of inquiry into Fijian cts., 1993-94. With New Zealand Army, 1941-43, Royal New Zealand Naval Vol. Res., 1943-46. Mem. Auckland Dist. Law Soc. (pres. 1964). Home: Heretaunga, 18 Golf Rd, Wellington New Zealand

BEATTIE, GREGORY NEIL, lawyer, archaeologist; b. Brisbane, Australia, July 9, 1960; s. Norman Thomas and Joyce Lillian (Low) B. LLB, U. Sydney, Australia, 1984, B in Econ., 1983; LLM, Cambridge (Eng.) U., U.K., 1987. Assoc. ptnr. Esplins Solicitors, Sydney, Australia, 1988-89; assoc. Price Brent Solicitors, Sydney, Australia, 1990-95; ptnr. Eakin McCaffery Cox Solicitors, Sydney, Australia, 1995-99; founding ptnr. Staunton Beattie Solicitors, Sydney, Australia, 1999—; mem. Law Soc., Sydney, Australia, 1984—. Recipient Walter Reid Meml. award U. Sydney, Australia, 1980-83. Mem. Law Soc. NSW, Near Eastern Archaeological Found. Avocations: reading, archaeology, ancient languages, history, arabic. Home: 111 Frazer St, Marrickville 2204, Australia

BEATTIE, JAMES ALEXANDER GORDON, physician; b. Aberdeen, Scotland, Apr. 23, 1943; s. Alexander Gordon and Margaret Taylor Beattie; m. Jennifer Barbara Nichols, July 1, 1968; children: Victoria, Alastair, Michael, Richard. MB BChir, Aberdeen U., 1967, DRCOG, 1970, DMRD, 1971. Ho. officer NHS, Aberdeen, 1967-69, registrar, 1969-71; gen. practitioner physician NHS, Edinburgh, Scotland, 1971-73, Invervrie, Scotland, 1973—. Fellow Royal Coll. GPS, Royal Coll. Physicians Edinburgh. Home: Birchfield Covenstone, Kintore, Aberdenshire AB51 049, Scotland Office: Invervrie Health Ctr, Constitution Stores, Invervrie AB51 4SV, Scotland

BEATTIE, JAMES KENNETH, chemist; b. Phila., June 8, 1939; arrived in Australia, 1972; s. Kenneth William and Madeline (Walzak) B.; m. Margaret Olive Hallo Beattie, Apr. 6, 1968; children: Andrew, Katharine. AB, Princeton U., 1961; MA, Cambridge (Eng.) U., 1963; PhD, Northwestern U., 1966. Asst. prof. U. Ill., Urbana, 1966-72; lectr. U. Sydney, Australia, 1972-73, sr. lectr., 1974-83, assoc. prof., 1984—, head divsn. inorganic chemistry, 1995-96; cons. Colloidal Dynamics Pty. Ltd., Australia, 1996—. Contbr.over 120 articles to profl. jours. Fellow Alfred F. Sloan Found., 1971-73. Fellow AAAS, Royal Australian Chem. Inst. (various offices 1983—), Royal Soc. Chemistry, Fedn. Univ. Staff Assns. (rsch. policy com. 1981-89). Office: Sch Chemistry, University of Sydney, Sydney NSW 2006, Australia

BEATTY, BARBARA RACHEL, education educator; b. Palo Alto, Calif., Mar. 7, 1946; d. Shelton Lee and Caroline (Burtis) B.; m. Michael Broeker Meyer, June 24, 1977; children: Douglas, Lucy. AB, Radcliffe Coll., 1968; EDM, Harvard U., 1973, EdD, 1981. Cert. tchr., Mass. Kindergarten tchr. Boston Pub. Schs., 1968-72; coord. Child Care Project Edn. Devel. Ctr., Newton, Mass., 1973; dir. Losley Ellis Sch., Cambridge, Mass., 1973-78; asst. prof. Lesley Coll., Cambridge, Mass., 1973-81; assoc. prof. Wellesley (Mass.) Coll., 1981—; coll. coord. Boston Higher Edn. Partnership, 1985—; coll. rep. Consortium for Excellence in Tchr. Edn., Wellesley, 1985—. Author: Preschool Education in America, 1995 (Choice Outstanding Acad. Book award 1996); assoc. editor History of Edn. Quar., 1999—. Bd. dirs. Roxbury Home for Aged Women, Boston, 1980-89, Mason-Rice Aftersch. Program, Newton, Mass., 1984-88, Ctr. for Rsch. in Women, Wellesley, Mass., 1998—; co-pres., bd. dirs. Boston Assn. for the Edn. Young Children, 1976-78. Fellow Radcliffe Rsch. Scholar Program, 1983-84, Spencer Found. (Chgo.), 1996-97; grantee Dept. Edn., 1986-87. Mem. Am. Ednl. Rsch. Assn. (sec. divsn. F 1996-99), ASCD, Mass. Assn. Colls. and Tchr. Edn., History Edn. Soc. (prize com. 1993-96), Phi Beta Kappa. Avocations: gardening, reading. Office: Wellesley Coll Dept Edn 106 Central St Wellesley MA 02481-8268

BEATTY, CRAIG DAVID, mechanical engineer; b. Grove City, Pa., Jan. 7, 1973; s. David Ralph and Linda Lou (Cribbs) B.; m. Tonya Marie Settlmire, Feb. 10, 1996. BSME, Grove City Coll., 1995. Engr. in tng., Ohio. Project engr. Republic Engineered Steels, Canton, Ohio, 1995—. Mem. Assn. Iron and Steel Engrs. Office: Republic Engineered Steels 2633 8th St NE Canton OH 44704-2311

BEATTY, FRANCES, civic worker; b. Chgo., Apr. 17, 1940; d. Pasquale and Rose (Brunetti) Calomeni; m. Robert Alfred Beatty, Aug. 24, 1963; children: Bradford, Roxanna Beatty Goebel. BA, Northwestern U., 1961; MA, U. Chgo., 1967. Tchr. math. Proviso West High Sch., Hillside, Ill., 1961-66. Active Oak Brook Dist. 53 Sch. Bd., 1979-85; mem. women's bd. Field Mus. Natural History, Chgo., 1985—, mem. founders coun., 1988—, treas. women's bd., 1991-93; mem. governing bd. Chgo. Symphony, 1985-92; trustee Chgo. Symphony Orch., 1992—; mem. women's bd. Ravinia Festival, Highland Park, Ill., 1987—, Northwestern U., Evanston, Ill., sec. women's bd., 1999—, mem. libr. bd., 1990-95; mem. women's bd. U. Chgo.; mem. coun. Wellness House, Hinsdale, Ill., 1994. Mem. The Antiquarian Soc. Art Inst. Chgo., Alumnae of Northwestern U. (pres. 1996-98), Woman's Athletic Club Chgo. (3d v.p. 1985-87, 1st v.p. 1992-94, pres. 1994-96), John Evans Club.

BEATTY, GRACE JOELY, author, consultant; b. Lynn, Mass., Feb. 11, 1947; d. Joseph B. and Shirley E. (Phillips) B.; m. David C. Gardner, Mar. 24, 1984. BA, Simmons Coll., 1968; MEd, Boston U., 1972, EdD, 1979; PhD, Columbia Pacific U., 1984. Diplomate Am. Bd. Med. Psychotherapists (fellow); lic. psychologist, Mass. Tchr. Braintree (Mass.) H.S., 1968-70; asst. prof. Quincy (Mass.) Jr. Coll., 1971-77; sr. rsch. assoc. Boston U., 1977-79; owner, mgr. Gardner Beatty Group, Rancho La Costa, Calif., 1979—; v.p. CyberHelp, Inc., Carlsbad, Calif., 1995—; pres. Self-Test Labs., Inc., 1999—. Author (with David C. Gardner) over 45 books, including Access for Windows 95, ACT 2.0 for Windows, Cruising American On-line (2.0 and 2.5), Cruising CompuServe, Cruising Microsoft Netowrk, Excel 5 for Mac: The Visual Learning Guide, Excel 5 for Windows: The Visual Learning Guide, Internet for Windows: The Visual Learning Guide (AOL 2.0 and 2.5 edits, Microsoft 95 edit.), Lotus 123 for Windows: The Visual Learning Guide (v4), Powerpoint for Windows 95: The Visual Learning Guide, Quicken 5 for Windows: The Visual Learning Guide, Windows 95: The Visual Learning Guide, WinFaxPro: The Visual Learning Guide (7.0), Wordd 7 for Windows 95: The Visual Learning Guide, WordPerfect 6 for DOS: The Visual Learning Guide, Works for Windows 95: The Visual Learning Guide, Dissertation Proposal Guidebook: How to write a research proposal and get it accepted, 1979, Career and Vocational Education, 1984, Stop Stress and Aging Now, 1986, Never Be Tired Again!, 1989 (Book-of-

Month Club selection), Discover Internet Explorer, 1997, Discover Netscape Communicator, 1997, Windows NT 4.0 Workstation: Visual Desk Reference, 1997. Office: Gardner Beatty Group 7618 Nueva Castilla Way Carlsbad CA 92009-8137

BEATTY, ROBERT ALFRED (R. ALFRED), surgeon; b. Colchester, Vt., May 7, 1936; s. George Lewis and Leila Margaret (Ebright) B.; m. Frances Calomeni, Aug. 24, 1963; children: Bradford, Roxanna. BA, U. Oreg., 1959, BS, 1960, MD, 1961. Diplomate Am. Bd. Neurol. Surgery. Intern U. Ill. Rsch. and Edn. Hosp., Chgo., 1961-62; resident neurosurgery U. Ill., Chgo., 1962-66; practice neurosurgery Hinsdale, Ill., 1967—; mem. staff Hinsdale Hosp., 1967—, Cmty. Meml. Hosp., LaGrange, Ill., 1967—, U. Ill. Hosp., Chgo., 1967—, Good Samaritan Hosp., Downers Grove, Ill., Elmhurst (Ill.) Hosp.; clin. assoc. prof. neurosurgery U. Ill., 1967—; founding adviser Marion Joy Rehab. Center, Wheaton, Ill., 1969-7; mem. State Ill. Spinal Cord Injury Adv. Coun., 1995, vice-chmn. 1997. Contbr. articles to profl. jours. Mem. founder's coun. Field Mus. Capt. USMC, AUS, 1968. Rsch. fellow St. George's Med. Sch., London, 1966-67. Mem. AMA, ACS, SAR, Ill. Med. Soc., Dupage County Med. Soc., Am. Assn. Neurol. Surgeons, N.Am. Spine Soc., Congress Neurol. Surgeons, Soc. Brit. Neurol. Surgeons, Internat. Microsurg. Soc., Nat. Assn. Spine Specialists, English Speaking Union, John Evans Club (N.W. U.), Theodore Thomas Soc., Chgo. Symphony Orch. (governing mem.), Hinsdale Golf Club, Phi Beta Kappa, Phi Beta Pi, Phi Kappa Psi. Republican. Achievements include research on intracranial aneurysms, lumbar discs; inventor medical instruments; profl. sculptor (under name R. Alfred). Office: 333 Chestnut St Hinsdale IL 60521-3247

BEATTY, (HENRY) WARREN, actor, producer, director; b. Richmond, Va., Mar. 30, 1937; s. Ira O. and Kathlyn (MacLean) Beaty; m. Annette Bening; 1 child, Kathlyn. Student, Northwestern U., 1956, Stella Adler Theatre Sch., N.Y.C., 1957. Actor films Splendor in the Grass, 1961, The Roman Spring of Mrs. Stone, 1962, All Fall Down, 1962, Lilith, 1963, Mickey One, 1965, Promise Her Anything, 1965, Kaleidoscope, 1966, The Only Game in Town, 1969, McCabe and Mrs. Miller, 1971, Dollars, 1971, The Parallax View, 1974, The Fortune, 1975, Town and Country, 1999; appeared in Broadway play A Loss of Roses, 1960; actor, producer films include Bonnie and Clyde, 1967 (Acad. award nomination for best actor), Ishtar, 1987; producer, co-screenwriter, actor Shampoo, 1975 (Acad. award nomination for best screenplay), Love Affair, 1994; producer, co-dir., co-screenwriter, actor Heaven Can Wait, 1978 (Acad. award nominations for best actor, best dir. and best screenplay); producer, dir., co-screenwriter, actor Reds, 1981 (Acad. award for best dir.), Bulworth, 1998; producer, dir., actor Dick Tracy, 1990; co-producer, actor: Bugsy, 1991; Love Affair (also producer and writer), 1996; Town and Country, 1998; Bulworth (also producer and writer); 1998; actor (TV) A Salute to Dustin Hoffman, 1999; TB guest appearances include Studio One, 1948, What's My Line, 1950, Vibe, 1997. Mem. Dirs. Guild Am. Democrat. Office: CAA care Risa Gertner 9830 Wilshire Blvd Beverly Hills CA 90212-1804

BEAUCHAMP, HARRY, internist, pulmonologist; b. Nuneaton, England, Feb. 8, 1960; s. Gerry and Barbara (Weyman-Jones) B.; m. Libby Maria O'Connor, Aug. 14,987; children: Kate, Conor, Patrick, Molly. MBBChB, Univ. Coll., Dublin, 1985. Diplomate Am. Bd. Internal Medicine, Am. Bd. Pulmonary Medicine; licensed Royal Coll. Physicians, Ireland, Royal Coll. Surgeons, Ireland. Asst. prof. medicine Tufts U., Boston, 1992-94; cons. physician Blackrock Clinic, Ireland, 1993—; med. officer Irish Youth Rugby Team, 1997—, Leinster Rugby Devel., Ireland, 1994-97. Med. dir. Christina Noble Children's Found., Mongolia, Vietnam, 2000. Fellow Am. Coll. Physicians, Am. Coll. Chest Physicians, Royal Acad. Medicine. Avocations: rugby, golf. Home: Brooke, Stillgoran Rd, Donnybrook Dublin 4, Ireland Office: Blackrock Clinic Ste 19, Rock Rd, County Dublin Ireland

BEAUCHAMP, VALDIVIA VÂNIA S., translator; b. Recife, Brazil, June 17, 1944; d. Francisco Targino and Angelica (Lucas) De Siqueira; m. Jimmie Willis Beauchamp (div. 1970); 1 child, Angélica R. Beauchamp-Ringeisen. BS in Journalism, CEUB, 1978; MA in Portuguese and Spanish Lit., NYU, 1992. Registered profl. journalist. Social comm. sec. Office of Brazilian Presidency, Brasilia, Brazil, 1984-90; portuguese translator Family Court, N.Y.C., 1993; v.p., translator, broker asst. Lucander & Co., N.Y.C., 1993-95; translator, broker asst. Josephthal Lion & Ross, N.Y.C., 1995, U.S. Securities and Futures, N.Y.C., 1995-96; in flight translator, internat. flight attendent TWA, N.Y.C., 1996—, Am. Airlines, 1999; reporter, corr. Revista Aerea, N.Y.C., 1984—; founder, tchr. Lang. Sch. Multi Lingua, Brazil, 1985-89; tchr. Portuguese and Spanish, Sigma Delta Pi, Purdue U., Ind., 1982-84, NYU, 1990-92. Founder literary hour NYU, 1990-92; mem. Leadership Com. Fifty Ave. Presbyn. Ch., 1994—; liberal artist Lafayette Art Mus., 1982-84. Mem. NYU Alumni, C. of C. of the Rockaways (exec. dir. 1998). Democrat. Presbyterian. Avocations: oil painting, piano, freelance writing, horseback riding, boating/fishing.

BEAUFORT, JEAN-LOUIS, lawyer, educator; b. Nancy, France, Jan. 8, 1946; s. Abel Raoul and Raymonde Marie (Jacquemin) B.; children: Eric, Nicolas. Degree in law, U. Nancy, 1969, M in Law, 1970, cert. adminstrn. of bus., 1971, D in Law, 1978. Tchr. Ste. Elisabeth Tech. H.S., Nancy, 1971-73; asst. Law Coll. U. Nancy, 1971-78, lectr., 1979—; pvt. practice law Nancy, 1972—. Mem. RPR. Mem. RPR. Avocations: stamp collecting, fishing, skiing, walking. Home: 5 Bis rue de la gare, 54950 Saint-Clement France Office: Cabinet D'Avocats, 11 Ave Victor Hugo, Nancy France

BEAUJEAN, JACQUES EUGENE, aviation products company executive; b. Liege, Belgium, Sept. 18, 1944; s. Pierre E. and L. (Kelleter) B.; m. Françoise H. Meunier; children: Olivier, Christophe. Home: 12 Ave Marie Louise, 1410 Waterloo Brabant Belgium Office: Champion Aviation, Chaussee de Louvain 490, B-1380 Lasne Belgium

BEAUMARIE, CARLOS FABIAN, food products executive; b. Buenos Aires, May 27, 1962; s. Juan Carlos and Elvira Maria (Moreira) B.; m. Florencia Maria Bellini, Dec. 6, 1991; children: Maria Milagros, Ines Maria, Maria Josefina, Sofia Maria. Indsl. engring. degree, U. Buenos Aires, 1986; MBA, Belgrano U., Buenos Aires, 1995. Purchaser Massuh, Buenos Aires, 1985-88, Massutt, 1988-91; indsl. engring. mgr. Project Stani.Cadbury, 1991-96; production mgr. Cadbury, Dublin, Ireland, 1996-97; supply mgr. Cadbury Stani SAIC, Buenos Aires, 1997—. Roman Catholic. Avocations: tennis, football, squash, reading, books. Office: Cadbury Stani SAIC, Uruguay 3911, 1644 Victoria Argentina

BEAUMESNIL, ARNAUD J., sales and marketing professional; b. Le Mans, Sarthe, France, Sept. 17, 1961; s. Michel M. and Elyane (Dolivet) B.; m. Betty M.A. Lefevre, July 10, 1982; children: Alexander, Prescylla, Leslie, Hamilton, Remington, Beverly-Betty. Automation and Industry Degree, LTE Washington, Le Mans, 1977, B in Automation, 1979; Superior Bachelor Degree in Automation, AFP, Le Mans, 1981. Sales exec. Canon, France, 1982-87; France sales mgr. Computer Assocs., 1987-91, Word Perfect, 1991-94; so. Europe sales mgr. Frame Tech., 1994-96, Interleaf, 1995-96; so. Europe regional mgr. On Tech., 1996-97; dir. ops. IBM Partitiel, 1998; sales and marketing mgr. Cisco Systems, 1998—; France channel sales cons. Globalink, 1994—, Citizen, 1995—. Team leader Youth Integration, Versailles, France, 1992. Mem. Internat. Fedn. of Automobiles, Internat. Confedn. de Karting, Automobile Club of the West, French Auto Racing Fedn. Roman Catholic. Avocation: car racing. Home: 2 Allée de la Roche les Campagnards, F-78690 Les Essarts le Roi France

BEAUMONT, BRYAN ALAN, Australian federal court; b. Brisbane, Australia, Dec. 29, 1938; s. Alan P. and Thora C. (Harrison) B.; m. Jeanette Alison (Wilkie) B.; m. Jan. 10, 1967; children: Justine, Madeleine, Nicholas, Eliane. LLB, Sydney (Australia) U., 1961. Solicitor, 1961-65, barrister,, 1965-78, Queen's counsel,, 1978-83; judge Supreme Ct. Australian Capital Ter., 1983—; presdl. mem. Adminstrv. Appeals Tribunal, 1983—; judge Supreme Ct., Norfolk Island, Australia, 1989-93, chief justice, 1993—; acting judge Supreme Ct., Vanuatu, Australia, 1993; judge Fed. Ct. Australia, Sydney, 1983—, Ct. of Appeal, Tonga, 1997—; vis. fellow Wolfson Coll., Cambridge (Eng.) U., 1990, 98, Harvard U., Boston, summer 1992. Mem. coun. Women's Coll., Sydney U., 1992-96; trustee Ensemble Theatre Found., 1996—. Fellow Australian Inst. Jud. Adminstrn. (hon., chmn. 1990-92); mem. Am. Law Inst. Avocations: tennis, music, theatre. Office: Fed Ct Australia, Queens Sq, Sydney NSW 2000, Australia

BEAUMONT, JOAN ERRINGTON, academic historian; b. Adelaide, Australia, Oct. 25, 1948; d. Clifford James and Edna Jean (Errington) Magor; children: Diana, Caroline, Julia. BA with honors, U. Adelaide, 1969; PhD, King's Coll., London, 1975. Lectr. Deakin U., Victoria, 1977-80, sr. lectr., 1980-84, 88-89, reader in history, 1989-95, prof. history, 1995-98, head Sch. Australian and Internat. Studies, 1993—, dean faculty arts, 1998—; lectr. Monash U., Victoria, Australia, 1985-87. Author: Comrades in Arms: British Aid to Russia, 1941-1945, 1980, Gull Force: Survival and Leadership in Captivity, 1941-45, 1988; editor: The New Europe: East and West, 1991, Australia's War, 1914-1918, 1995, Australia's War, 1939-1945, 1996; contbr. articles to profl. jours., chpts. to books. Australian Rsch. com. grantee, 1979-82, 93, 94-95, 97-99, Dept. Def. grantee, 1994—, Australian War Meml. grantee, 1992, others. Mem. Australian Historians Assn., Commn. of the History of Internat. Rels. Baptist. Office: Deakin U, Deakin U, Faculty Arts, 3217 Geelong, Victoria Australia

BEAUMONT, MONA, artist; b. Paris; d. Jacques Hippolyte and Elsie M. (Didisheim) Marx. m. William G. Beaumont; children: Garrett, Kevin. Postgrad., Harvard U., Fogg Mus., Cambridge, Mass. One-woman shows include Galeria Proteo, Mexico City, Gumps Gallery, San Francisco, Palace of Legion of Honor, San Francisco, L'Armitiere Gallery, Rouen, France, Hoover Gallery, San Francisco, San Francisco Mus. Modern Art, Galeria Van der Voort, San Francisco, William Sawyer Gallery, San Francisco, Palo Alto (Calif.) Cultural Ctr., Galerie Alexandre Monnet, Brussels, Honolulu Acad. Arts; group shows include San Francisco Mus. Modern Art, San Francisco Art Inst., DeYoung Meml. Mus., San Francisco, Grey Found. Tour of Asia, Bell Telephone Invitational, Chgo., Richmond Art Ctr., L.A. County Mus. Art, Galerie Zodiaque, Geneva, Galerie Le Manoir, La Chaux de Fonds, Switzerland, William Sawyer Meml. Exhibit, San Francisco, 1st Internat. Flash Art Mus. Exhbn., Trevi, Italy, 1999, Masks of Venice 2, Internat. Exhbn., 1999 (silver medalist), Masks of Venice 3 Internat. Exhbn., 2000; others; represented in permanent collections Oakland (Calif.) Mus. Art, City and County of San Francisco, Hoover Found., San Francisco, Grey Found., Washington, Bulart Found., San Francisco; also numerous pvt. collections. Mem. Soc. for Encouragement of Contemporary Art, Bay Area Graphic Art Coun., San Francisco Art Inst., San Francisco Mus. Modern Art, Capp Street Project, San Diego Mus. Contemporary Art, L.A. Mus. Contemporary Art. Recipient ann. painting award Jack London Square, 2 ann. awards San Francisco Women Artists, One-man Show award San Francisco Art Festival; purchase award Grey Found., San Francisco Women Artists (2), San Francisco Art Festival; included in Printworld Internat., Internat. Art Diary, Am. Artists, N.Y. Art Rev., Calif. Art Rev., Art in San Francisco Bay Area. Address: 11785 River Rim Rd San Diego CA 92126-1148

BEAUNE, PATRICK, publisher; b. Aix-Les-Bains, Savoie, France, July 8, 1952; s. François and Juliette (Tardy) B. Student, Ecole Supérieure Commerce, Paris1974. Pub. Editions Champ Vallon, Seyssel, France, 1979—. Home: Rue de Gérin, 01420 Seyssel France Office: Editions Champ Vallon, 01420 Seyssel France

BEAUPERE, RENE MAURICE, religious center administrator; b. Lyon, France, Mar. 2, 1925; s. Louis and Jeanne (Leclerc) B. Diploma, Instn. Des Chartreux, Lyon, 1941, U. Lyon, 1944, Dominican Collegium U., Chambery, 1952, Archaeol. and Biblical Sch., Jerusalem, 1953. Editor Lumiere et Vie, Lyon, 1957-70; prof. ISEO, Paris, 1965-75; co-dir. Cleo Travels, Lyon, 1961—, F.O.I. Courses, Lyon, 1965—; dir. Ctr. St. Irenee, Lyon, 1953—. Editor: (jours.) Lumiere et Vie, 1957-70, Foyers Mixtes, 1968—, Chretiens en Marche, 1966—; contbr. numerous articles to profl. jours. and books. Roman Catholic. Office: Ctr St Irenee, 2 Place Gailleton, 69002 Lyon France

BEAUVISAGE, PATRICK MICHEL, lawyer; b. Valenciennes, France, Mar. 26, 1944; s. Michel and Jacqueline (Herrent) B.; m. Marie-Odile Lardin, 1969 (div. 1974); children: Charlotte, Jean-Baptiste. Licencie en droit, U. Paris, 1967. Bar: Paris 1968. Lectr. U. Paris, 1969-73; mng. ptnr. Monahan Duhot, Paris, 1989-92, Stibbe Simont Monahan Duhot, Paris, 1993—; mem. ctrl. bd. Stibbe Simont Monahan Duhot, Paris/Amsterdam/Brusssels, 1993—. Roman Catholic. Avocations: hunting, shooting. Office: Stibbe Simont Monahan Duhot, 154 rue de l'Université, 75007 Paris France

BEAUZAMY, BERNARD M., mathematics association administrator; b. Paris, Jan. 8, 1949; s. Pierre E. and Ida (Moday) B.; m. Denise Pruvost; 1 child, Brigitte. PhD, U. Paris, 1976. Prof. U. Lyon, France, 1979-95; chmn., CEO Société du Calcul Mathématique SA, 1995—; researcher U. Paris, 1985—; bd. dirs. Inst. de Calcul Mathematique, Paris. Author: Espaces d'Interpolation, 1976, Introduction to Banach Spaces, 1982, 2d edit., 1985, Modèles Etalés, 1984, Operator Theory, 1988. Home: 27 Ave Parmentier, 75011 Paris France

BEAVAN, EVA VARIE, social worker, therapist; b. Frederick, Md., Sept. 14, 1966; d. Lawrence Eugene and Judy Varie Putman; m. Robert Allan Beavan, Jan. 31, 1987; children: Laurel Elizabeth, Patrick Allan, Calvert Elton. AA, Frederick (Md.) C.C., 1991; BA magna cum laude, Western Md. Coll., 1993; MSW, U. Md., Balt., 1994. Lic. cert. social worker, Md. Sr. crisis counselor Frederick County Mental Health Assn., 1990-94; outreach therapist Washington County Mental Health Ctr., Hagerstown, Md., 1994; family therapist Karma Ho., Inc., Frederick, 1995-96; therapist Citizens Assisting and Sheltering the Abused, Inc. (CASA), Hagerstown, 1996—. Vol. Brookhill Weekday Preschool, Frederick, 1999—. Predl. scholar Western Md. Coll., 1991-93. Mem. NASW (sec. western Md. region 1998—), Phi Beta Kappa, Pi Gamma Mu, Psi Chi. Republican. Methodist. Avocations: reading, writing, walking, doll collecting. Home: 100087 Quail Knob Ln Frederick MD 21702 Office: CASA Inc 116 W Baltimore St Hagerstown MD 21740-5439

BEAVER, ALLAN, travel and tourism educator, travel agency director; b. London, Feb. 12, 1934; s. Jack and Beatrice (Pearl) B.; m. Muriel Secker, Sept. 8, 1963. MSc, Birmingham (Eng.) U., 1986. Owner, operator Beaver Travel, Radlett, Eng., 1962—; chmn. Beaver Travel Pubs., Radlett, 1976—; vis. sr. lectr. Surrey U., Guildford, Eng., 1987—; vis. prof. Bournemouth (Eng.) U., 1996—; vis. lectr. Buckingham Coll., High Wycombe, Eng., 1996—; sr. Eng. expert in travel and tourism terminology Brit. Stds. Inst., 1996—; dir., treas. Travel, Tourism and Events Nat. Tng. Orgn., 1998—. Author: Mind Your Own Travel Business, 3 vols., 1975, 3d edit., 1993, Wages and Costs in the U.K. Travel Industry, 1987, Travel Agency Layout Equipment and Design, 1989, Charity Matters, 1989, Middlesex Matters—A History of Middlesex Freemasonry, 1995, Annual U.K. Travel and Industry Survey, 22d edit., 1999, A History of the Association of British Travel Agents, 2000. Fellow City and Guilds of London Inst., Chartered Inst. Transport, Tourism Soc., Inst. Travel and Tourism, Inst. Logistics, Chartered Inst. Mktg.; mem. Assn. Sci. Experts in Tourism, Assn. Brit. Travel Agts. (travel agts. coun. 1993—, chmn. edn. and tng. com. 1993—, chmn. coach and rail com. 1996—, chmn. Greater London Region, examiner cert. of travel agy. competence and travel agts. cert. 1976—), Galileo Users Coun. (vice chmn. 1980—), Travel, Tourism and Events Nat. Tng. Orgn. (treas., travel sector chmn.), Inst. Travel and Tourism (past chmn., past v.p.). Avocations: walking, chess, bridge. Office: Beaver Travel Pubs, 16 Loom Ln, Radlett WD7 8AD, England

BEAVER, DANIEL ROY, history educator; b. Hamilton, Ohio, Sept. 23, 1928. PhD, Northwestern U., 1962. Prof. history U. Cin., 1958—. Cpl. U.S. Army, 1946-47. Mem. Soc. Mil. History, Interuniv. Seminar for War and soc., Ohio Acad. History. Democrat. Office: U Cin Dept History Cincinnati OH 45221

BEAVERS, ROY LACKEY, retired utility executive, essayist, activist; b. Joplin, Mo., Apr. 24, 1930; s. Roy L. Sr. and Margarette Nellie (Loughlin) B.; m. Valerie Evelyn Gurney; children: Leslie Anne, Brendan G. BS in Bus., U. Mo., 1952; MA in Polit. Sci., U. Md., 1970. Commd. ens. USN, 1952, advanced through grades to comdr., 1966, retired, 1972; agt., broker ins. agy., Lebanon, Mo., 1972-77; field rep. Nat. Rural Electric Coop. Assn., Washington, 1977-84; mgr. pub. info. and legis. liaison wholesale power coop. KAMO Power, Vinita, Okla., 1984-93; moderator internet discussion list EMF-L concerning electromagnetic field health hazards, 1995-2000; advocate for regulation of electromagnetic radiation; assigned US Arms Control Disarmament Agy. (SALT I strategic arms negotiations), 1970-72. Contbr. polit. and mil. essays to newspapers and other publs. including An Absence of Accountability (U.S. policy failure in Vietnam), 1976. State hdqrs. dir. Va. Com. to Re-elect Nixon, Richmond, Va., 1972; mem. Bd. Mo. Cmty. Betterment Edn. Fund, 1990-93, Bd. Okla. Acad. for State Goals, 1990-93. Decorated Bronze, Silver, and Gold medals U.S. Naval Inst., Pres. Merit Svc. medal, Navy Commendation medal. Mem. U.S. Naval Inst., Internat. Platform Spkrs. Assn., Bioelectromagnetics Soc. Home: Lake Shore Estates 26555 Gene Dr Lebanon MO 65536-5776

BEAZLEY, KIM CHRISTIAN, Australian government official; b. Perth, Australia, Dec. 14, 1948; s. Kim Edwards and Betty Beazley; m. Mary Paltridge, 1974 (dissolved 1989); children: Jessica, Hannah, Rachel; m. Susanna Annus, 1991; 1 child, Rachel. Student, U. Western Australia, Oxford (Eng.) U. Lectr. social polit. theory Murdoch U., Perth; M.P., 1980—, min. for aviation, min. assisting the min. for def., 1983, spl. min. of state, 1983-84, min. for def., 1984-90, leader of the house, 1988—, v.p. exec. coun., 1988-91, min. of transp. and communications, 1990-91, minister for fin., 1991, 93—, min. for employment, edn. and tng., 1991-93, min. for fin., 1995-96; leader of the house ALP, 1996—. Co-author: The Politics of Intrusion, the Superpowers and the Indian Ocean. Rhodes scholar, Oxford U., 1973-76. Office: c/o ALP Centenary House, 19 Nat Circuit, Barton ACT 2600, Australia*

BEAZLEY, RONALD CHARLTON, lawyer; b. Sydney, Australia, Oct. 28, 1938; s. Samuel Charlton and Mavis Alma (Parkes) B.; m. Maureen Frances Dennis, Mar. 7, 1964; children: Matthew, Caroline, Alison. LLB, U. Melbourne, Australia, 1960. Barrister, soliciter, 1961. Solicitor Molomby & Molomby, Melbourne, 1961-63, Stewart & Constable, Wangaratta, Australia, 1964-65; prin. Just & Beazley, Wangaratta, Australia, 1965-76; ptnr. Deacons, Graham & James, Melbourne, 1976-91; solicitor Victorian Govt., Australia, 1991—, spl. counsel, 2000—; councillor Law Inst. Victoria, 1969-70; mem. Supreme Ct. Rules Com., 1985-89; chmn. Specialisation Bd. LIV, 1992-95; chmn. govt. practice com. IBA, 1994-98. Commr. Victorian Cricket Assn., 1991—. Fellow Australian Inst. Mgmt.; mem. Legal Practitioners Liability Com., Law Inst. Victoria (hon. life). Avocations: tennis, golf, skiing, horseracing. Home: 12 Bruce St, Toorak VIC 3142, Australia Office: Victorian Govt Solicitor, 55 St Andrews Pl, Melbourne VIC 3002, Australia

BEBCHICK, LEONARD NORMAN, lawyer; b. New Bedford, Mass., Dec. 11, 1932; s. Samuel and Frances (Hait) B.; m. Gabriela Meyerhoff, Aug. 31, 1968; children: Ilana, Brian. AB, Cornell U., 1955; LLB, Yale U., 1958. Bar: Mass. 1958, D.C. 1960, Md. 1989. Atty. CAB, Washington, 1959-60; assoc. Ginsburg & Leventhal, Washington, 1960-64; ptnr. Bebchick, Sher & Kushnick, Washington, 1964-74, Martin, Whitfield, Smith & Bebchick, Washington, 1974-82; pres. Leonard N. Bebchick P.C., Washington, 1982-88; ptnr. Leva, Hawes, Mason, Martin & Bebchick, Washington, 1988-89; pvt. practice as lawyer Washington, 1989—;, joint co. sec. Brit Caledonian Airways, Eng., 1963-88; bd. dirs. British Caledonian Group, Eng., 1978-88, London Transport Internat. Cons., U.S., 1990-92; spl. counsel D.C. Pub. Svc. Commn., Washington, 1965-66, V.I. Pub. Utilities Commn., 1967-70. Pres. Congregation Beth El of Montgomery County, 1993-95; bd. dirs. United Synagogue of Conservative Judaism, 1993—, Jewish Fedn. Greater, Washington, 1996—; bd. govs. coms. Jewish Agy. Israel, 1998—; v.p. Muss H.S., Israel, 1997—. Mem. ABA (chmn. adv. com. on aero. law 1982-83), FBA, Internat. Bar Assn., Inst. of Dirs. (London), U.S. Nat. Student Assn. (v.p. internat. affairs 1953-54). Democrat. Jewish. Home: 6321 Lenox Rd Bethesda MD 20817-6023 Office: 888 16th St NW Washington DC 20006-4103

BEBEAR, CLAUDE, insurance company executive; b. Issac, Dordogne, France, July 29, 1935; s. Pierre Andre Jean and Marie (Veyssiere) B.; m. Catherine Marie Louise Jeanne Dessagne, July 26, 1957; children: Guillaume, Héloise, Flavie. Grad., Ecole Poly., Paris, Actuaries Inst. of Paris. Various positions Ancienne Mutuelle, Roven, France, 1958-74; gen. mgr. Mutuelles Unies, Rouen, 1974-82; chmn., chief exec. officer AXA Group, Paris, 1982-89, AXA-Midi Assurances, Paris, 1989-90; chmn. AXA, Paris, 1990—; chmn., chief exec. officer AXA Assurances Iard Mutuelle, 1972, AXA Assurrances Vie Mutuelle, 1972, La Mutualite Generale Assurances Risques Divers, 1972; chmn. UNI Europe Assurances Mutuelle, 1980, AXA Can. Inc., 1985, Finaxa Belgium, 1986, Alpha Assurances Vie Muttuelle, 1990; rep. dir. Compagnie Fin. Delmas Vieljeux, 1989, Compagnie Fin. De Paris, 1989, AXA Ré, 1989, Axa Assurances Vie, 1991, Axiva, 1991, Uni Europe Assurance, 1991, AXA Assurances IARD, 1991, Direct Assurance IARD, 1990, Direct Assurance Vie, 1989, Cofilon, 1992; pres. d'honneur de l'Institut des actuaires Français, 1989—. Chmn. Inst. du Mécenat Humanitaire, Paris, 1986, AXA Atout Coeur, Paris. Lt. French Army, 1956-58. Decorated chevallier Legion of Honor, officer Ordre Nat. du Merite (France); named Mgr. of Yr., Nouvel Economisle, 1988. Mem. FFSA (v.p. Paris 1975-92), French Inst. Actuaries (hon. pres. Paris), Assn. de Geneve, Club des Prin. Assureurs Prives Europeens. Avocations: hung, golf. Office: AXA, 25 Avenue Mangnon, 75008 Paris France*

BEBIS, GEORGE, computer science educator; b. Athens, Greece, Jan. 13, 1966; came to U.S., 1991; s. Nikolaos and Chrysanti Bebis; m. Nektaria Kalykaki, Mar. 31, 1968. BS in Math., U. Crete, Heraklion, Greece, 1987, MS in Computer Sci., 1991; PhD in Engring., U. Ctrl. Fla., 1996. Vis. asst. prof. U. Mo., St. Louis, 1996-97; asst. prof. U. Nev., Reno, 1997—; colloquia organizer U. Nev., Reno., 1997—; presenter in field. Contbr. articles to profl. jours. Mem. IEEE (vice chair No. Nev. 1997—, program chair No. Nev. 1997—). Avocations: swimming, fishing, traveling. E-mail: bebis@cs.unr.edu. Office: Computer Sci Dept Univ Nev Reno NV 89557-0001

BECCAR VARELA, DAMIAN FERNANDO, lawyer; b. San Isidro, Buenos Aires, Argentina, Mar. 27, 1943; s. Damian and Solange (Soulas) B.V.; mem. Mercedes Ines Delfino; children: Mercedes Ines, Agustina, Mariana, Damian, Gonzalo. JD, Cath. U. Argentina, 1967. Ptnr. Estudio Beccar Varela, Buenos Aires, 1971—, chmn., 1986—. Hearings dir. Govt. of the Province of Buenos Aires, 1969. Avocation: woodworking. Office: Estudio Beccar Varela, Cerrito 740, 1309 Buenos Aires Argentina

BECERRA, SOFIA PATRICIA, biomedical research scientist; b. Lima, Peru, Mar. 3, 1953; d. Roger and Sofia (Gutierrez) B.; m. Vicente Notario, July 31, 1982; children: Patricia M., Rafael V. BSc, Cayetano Heredia U., 1976; PhD, U. Navarra, 1979. Vis. fellow Nat. Cancer Inst., Bethesda, Md., 1979-82, expert, 1987-91; vis. assoc. Nat. Inst. of Allergy and Infectious Disease, Bethesda, 1982-86; rsch. assoc. Georgetown Med. Sch., Washington, 1986-87; vis. scientist Nat. Eye Inst., Bethesda, 1991-94, investigator, 1994—. Contbr. articles to profl. jours. including Jour. of Biol. Chemistry, Biochemistry, Protein Expression and Purification, Proc. NAS, Jour. of Virology. Vis fellowship Fogarty Internat. Ctr., 1979-82. Mem. Am. Soc. Bichemistry and Molecular Biology, Assn. for Rsch. in Vision in Ophthalmology, NIH Structural Biology Interest Group, The Protein Soc. Roman Catholic. Achievements include rsch. in the field of identification of a non-AUG initiation codon that is used in mammalian translation systems and is present in a human adeno-associated viral genome, overexpression and purification of HIV-1 reverse transcriptase and structure-function studies on pigment epithelium-derived factor; inventor pigment epithelium-derived factor--characterization of its novel biological activity and sequences encoding and expressing the protein and methods of use, 1998. Office: NIH-NEI Rm 308 Bldg 6 Bethesda MD 20892-0001

BECHERER, HANS WALTER, retired agricultural equipment executive; b. Detroit, Apr. 19, 1935; s. Max and Mariele (Specht) B.; m. Michele Beigbeder, Nov. 28, 1959; children: Maxime (dec.), Vanessa. BA, Trinity Coll., Hartford, Conn., 1957; postgrad., Munich U., 1958; MBA, Harvard U., 1962. Exec. asst. office of chmn. Deere & Co., Moline, Ill., 1966-69; gen. mgr. John Deere Export, Mannheim, Germany, 1969-73; dir. export mktg. Deere & Co., Moline, 1973-77, v.p., 1977-83, sr. v.p., 1983-86, exec. v.p., 1986-87, pres., 1987-90, COO, 1987-89, CEO, 1989—, chmn., 1990—, also bd. dirs.; bd. dirs. Schering-Plough Corp., Honeywell Internat. Inc., Chase Manhattan Corp. and Chase Manhattan Bank; mem. industry sector adv. com. U.S. Dept. Commerce, 1975-81; mem. Bus. Roundtable, 1989—; mem. adv. com. Chase Manhattan Bank Internat., 1990-98; trustee Com. for Econ. Devel., 1990—. Trustee St. Katherine's/St. Mark's Sch., Bettendorf, Iowa,

1983—. 1st lt. USAF, 1958-60. Mem. Coun. on Fgn. Rels., Conf. Bd., Equipment Mfgs. Inst. (bd. dirs. 1987-90), Rock Island (Ill.) Arsenal Golf Club. Republican. Roman Catholic. Office: Deere & Co One John Deere Pl Moline IL 61265-8098

BECHERER, RICHARD JOSEPH, science consulting firm executive, physicist; b. Boston, Mar. 19, 1941; s. Edward Charles and Grace Elizabeth (Dalton) B.; m. Kathleen Quinn, June 26, 1965 (div. Aug. 1984) children: Joan Elizabeth, Christine Diane, Carolyn Jean; m. Susan Jaeger, Sept. 30, 1989 (div. Jan. 1999). BS in Physics, Boston Coll., 1962; MS in Physics, U. Ill., Champaign, 1964; NASA trainee, U. Rochester, 1969-71, PhD in Optics, 1972. Scientist Tech. Ops. Inc., Burlington, Mass., 1965-68, EIKONIX Corp., Bedford, Mass., 1968-71; sr. scientist, sect. mgr. Polaroid Research Labs, Cambridge, Mass., 1971-75; mem. tech. staff Lincoln Lab, MIT, Lexington, Mass., 1975-81; dir. optical sys. Sci. Applications Internat. Corp., Lexington, Mass., 1981-91; pres. Delta Sciences, Stow, Mass., 1991—; lectr. Northeastern U., Boston, 1966-83, U. Oulu, Finland, 1990, Nat. Tech. U., Ft. Collins, Colo., 1993—; cons. NAS Nat. Rsch. Coun., Washington, 1972-76; mem. Commn. Internat. l'Eclairage, Washington, 1973-76, USN Electro-Optics Working Group, 1977-80, NATO Rsch. Study Group, Munich, 1978-79; Strategic Def. Initiative Experimenters Working Group, 1986-91; instr. SPIE laser radar, sensor sys. courses Nat. Tech. U., 1983—; adj. prof. U. Conn., Storrs, 1992—; dep. dir. CONNECT-New Eng. Alliance Photonics Tech. Deployment, Storrs, 1994—; pres. coun. U. Ill., 1990—. Co-author: Optical Radiation Measurements, Vol. 1: Radiometry, 1979; editor: Adaptive Optics Systems and Technology, 1982, Laser Radar II, 1987, Laser Radar III, 1988, Laser Radar IV, 1989, Laser Radar V, 1990, Laser Radar VI, 1991, Laser Radar VII, 1992, Lidar for Remote Sensing, 1992, Lidar and Atmospheric Sensing, 1995; mem. editl. bd. Laser Focus, 1973-77; patentee optical filtering methods, optical heterodyne detection. Active Conservation Law Found., 1992—; com. mem. Rep. Nat. Com., Washington, 1994; campaign com. Mass. 5th Congl. Dist., Concord, 1994. Presidential scholar Boston Coll., 1962. Fellow Internat. Soc. Optical Engring.; mem. Optical Soc. Am. (chmn. edn. com.), Fides Soc., Pine Tree Soc., Sigma Xi, Sigma Pi Sigma. Roman Catholic. Avocations: history, politics, travel, tennis, skiing. Home: 13 Deer Path Apt 4 Maynard MA 01754-3412

BECHERT, DIETRICH WOLFGANG, aeronautics scientist, acoustician; b. Munich, Germany, Aug. 7, 1936; s. Karl Richard and Sibylle Mignon (Lepsius) B.; m. Armgard Schulze-Fielitz, Apr. 7, 1972; children: Stefan, Karoline. Diploma in Engring., Tech. U. Darmstadt, Germany, 1962; Dr. in Engring., Tech. U., Berlin, 1968, Habilitation, 1986. Scientist Tech. U. Darmstadt, 1962-64, Inst. Fluid Dyn. Tech. U., Berlin, 1964-65, DVL, Berlin, 1965-71, Max-Planck-Inst., Göttingen, Germany, 1971; scientist/group leader DFVLR, Berlin, 1971-80; visiting assoc. prof. U. Houston, 1980-81; scientist DLR, Berlin, 1981-89, chief scientist, 1989—; referee for U.S. and Swedish NSF, German DFG. Referee internat. jours.; contbr. articles to profl. jours. Recipient Ernst-Mach prize, 1986, Bionics prize, 1992, Philip Morris prize, 1998. Fellow Am. Phys. Soc.; mem. AIAA (sr.), Deutsche Gesellschaft für Luft-und-Raumfahrt. Achievements include patents for a household combustor, for a high-speed train pantograph, for drag reducing surfaces, for improved transonic wings and for improved turbomachines; discovery of jet noise amplification effect, of sound absorption by vortex shedding, of drag reduction mechanism of shark skin; research on acoustics of high speed trains. Office: DLR, Mueller-Breslaustr 8, 10623 Berlin Germany

BECHERT, HEINZ HELMUT, religious studies educator; b. Munich, June 26, 1932; s. Rudolf M. and Herta (Bade) B.; m. Marianne Wuerzburger, Aug. 20, 1963. PhD, U. Munich, 1956. Rsch. asst. U. Saarbruecken, 1956-61; rsch. asst. U. Mainz, 1961-64, lectr., 1964-65; prof., Indian and Buddhist studies U. Goettingen, 1965—; rsch. fellow Colombo, Ceylon, 1958-59, Japan Soc. for the Promotion of Sci., 1990; vis. prof. Yale U., New Haven, 1969-70, 74-75. Author: Buddhismus, Staat und Gesellschaft, 3 vols., 1966-73, Sinhalese Manuscripts, 2 vols., 1969-97, W. Geiger, 1976, 95; co-author, editor: The World of Buddhism, 1984, reprinted 1991, Pali Niti Texts of Burma, 1981, When Did the Buddha Live?, 1995, Buddhism in Ceylon, 1978, Einfuehrung in die Indologie, 1979, The Language of the Earliest Buddhist Tradition, 1980, Zur Schulzugehörigkeit von Werken der Hinayana-Literatur, 2 vols, 1985-87, The Dating of the Historical Buddha, 3 vols., 1991-97, Sanskrit Dictionary of the Buddhist Texts from the Turfan Finds, 1972-99, Burmese Manuscripts, 3 vols., 1979-96. Mem. Royal Swedish Acad. Lit. and History, Royal Belgium Acad., Acad. Europe (Cambridge), Acad. Wissenschaften Göttingen. Home: Hermann-Foege-Weg 1A, 37073 Göttingen Germany Office: Seminar Fuer Indologie, Hainbundstrasse 21, 37085 Göttingen Germany

BECHTEL, SHERRELL JEAN, psychotherapist; b. Birmingham, Ala., Sept. 23, 1961; d. Lewis Eugene and Sarah Rozelle (Sherrell) B. BS in Social Work, U. Ala., Birmingham, 1989; MSW, U. Ala., Tuscaloosa, 1990; DD, World Christianship Ministries, Fresno, Calif., 1997. Cert. addiction specialist; cert. group psychotherapist; lic. clin. social worker, Tenn., Ga.; ordained minister. Vol. counselor Planned Parenthood, Birmingham, 1986-88; intern Bradford Adult Chem. Dependency, Birmingham, 1989; rsch. staff asst. U. Ala., Tuscaloosa, 1989-90; intern counselor Bradford Adolescent Chem. Dependency, Birmingham, 1990; primary counselor The Crossroads, Chattanooga, 1990-92; owner S. J. Bechtel LCSW, CAS, Chattanooga, 1991—; rschr. Ala. Commn. Youth, Montgomery, 1989-90; trainer Legal and Jud. Aspects Child Welfare, Decatur, Ala., 1989; presenter Ala. Victim Compensation, Mobile, 1990; speaker Limestone Correctional Facility, Huntsville, 1990; lectr. Grad. Sch. Social Wk., Tuscaloosa, 1990, U. Tenn., Chattanooga. Subcom. mem. Atty. Gen. Alliance Against Drug Abuse, Birmingham, 1989; speaker Victims of Crime and Leniency, Tuscaloosa, 1990; planning com. Holistic Health Retreat, Birmingham, 1988; mem. Tenn. Coun. on Children and Youth-Legis./Policy; vol. ARC Disaster Mental Health/Direct Svcs. Mem. NASW (pres. student orgn. 1986-89), Tenn. Alcohol Drug Assn., Jewish Community Ctr., Phi Kappa Phi. Avocations: tennis, softball, bowling, water sports. Office: 109A Jordan Dr Chattanooga TN 37421-6732

BECHTELER, WILHELM, engineering educator; b. Immenstadt, Bavaria, Germany, July 1, 1939; s. Wilhelm and Anna (Nerlinger) B.; m. Edith Oechsl, Apr. 10, 1970 (dec. May 1970); m. Barbara Bueb, July 25, 1986; children: Georg W., Thomas A., Maximilian. Diploma, Tech. U., Munich, 1964; Dr in Engring., Tech. U., 1968, Habil, 1971. Engr. Dorsch Consult, Munich, 1971-73; prof. Armed Forces U., Munich, 1973—; dean of faculty Armed Forces U., 1973-74, dir. Inst. Hydrosci. Editor: Transport of Suspended Sediments, 1986; contbr. over 100 articles to profl. jours. Mem. City Coun., Eching, Germany, 1977-82. Mem. ASCE, Internat. Assn. Hydraulic Rsch., German Assn. for Water Resources (bd. dirs. 1985-90). Achievements include research on near nature river training, hydrodynamic-numerical models, physical modelling, sediment transport, river morphology. Office: Univ Fed Armed Forces, Munich, D-85577 Neubiberg Germany

BECHTER, KARL, psychiatrist; b. Ravensburg, Germany, 1950; m. Helga Kern, 1979; children: Clemens, Jonathan, Felix. MD, U. Ulm, Germany, 1977, Habilitation, PhD in Psychiatry, 1996. Rsch. fellow in neurology U. Ulm, 1977-79, rschr. in psychiatry, 1979-87, oberarzt in psychiatry, 1987-98, head dept. psychotherapy/psychosomatics, 1999—. Contbr. articles to profl. jours. Recipient Kurt-Schneider award Kuratorium, Bonn, 1996, Theodore and Vada Stanley Found. Rsch. Programs award, 1998. Mem. Assn. European Psychiatrists, Internat. Soc. for Neuroimaging in Psychiatry, German Soc. for Biol. Psychiatry. Avocation: performance of ancient music. E-mail: dr.bechter@bkh-guenzburg.de. Office: Univ of Ulm Dept Psychiatry, Ludwig-Heilmeyer-Str 2, 89312 Günzburg Bayern, Germany

BECHTEREVA, NATALIA PETROVNA, physiologist, research institute researcher; b. St. Petersburg, Russia, July 7, 1924; d. Piotr Vladimirovich and Zinaida Vasilievna (Pospelova) B.; m. Ivan Ilyich Kashtelian (dec. 1990); 1 child, Medvedev Sviatoslav. MD, 1st State Med. H.S., Leningrad, USSR, 1947; PhD in Biology, Pavlov Inst. Physiology, Leningrad, 1951; DSc in Medicine, Inst. Exptl. Medicine, Leningrad, 1959. Jr. rsch. fellow Inst. Exptl. Medicine, 1950-54, head human neurophysiology dept. dep. dir., then dir., 1962-90; sr. rsch. fellow, head physiology lab. Polenov State Neurosurg. Inst., Leningrad, 1954-62, dep. dir., 1960-62; sci. dir., head Lab. Neurophysiology of Thinking and Consciousness, St. Petersburg, 1990—; sci. dir. Human Brain Inst., Russian Acad. Scis., R, 1994—. Author: Neurophysiological Aspects of Human Mental Activity, 1974, 2d edit., transl. into English), 1978, Normal and Diseased Human Brain, 1980 (transl. into Spanish 1984), On the Human Brain, 1994, On the Human Brain: 20th Century and Its Last Decade in Human Brain Science (in Russian and English), 1997. Mem. USSR Supreme Soviet, Moscow, 1970-74, 89-91. Decorated 12 orders and medals of USSR, Russia and Germany; recipient McCulloch medal Cybernetics Soc., 1972, USSR State prize, 1985. Mem. Russian Acad. Scis. (Bechterev gold medal 1997), Russian Acad. Med. Scis., Internat. Acad. Geology, Human and Nature Protection Scis., Austrian Acad. Sci. (fgn.), Finnish Acad. Sci. (fgn.), Am. Acad. Medicine and Psychiatry (fgn.). Russian Orthodox. Avocations: collecting paintings, music. Home: Apt 33, Kronverkskaya St 29/37, 197101 Saint Petersburg Russia Office: Russian Acad Scis Human, Brain Inst, Pavlova St 9, 197376 Saint Petersburg Russia

BECI, BAHRI, linguist, editor, researcher; b. Shkodra, Albania, Mar. 6, 1936; s. Jonuz and Nadire (Hoxha) B.; m. Vlera Korbi, June 1, 1939; children: Benet, Entela. PhD, Paris U., 1977; sci. cand., Inst. Linguistics, Tirana-Albania, 1979, D in Scis., 1984, Habilitation, 1994. Sci. rschr. Inst. Linguistics, Tirana, Albania, 1958—; sci. sec. Inst. Linguistics, Tirana, 1974-76, chief dept. grammar, 1991-93, dir., 1993—; lectr. Tirana U., 1977-96; vis. lectr., Shkodra, Prishtina, 1977-81, Naples, St. Petersburg, Skopie, 1977-96; sec. editl. office Studio Albanica, 1993; mem. directing coun. Acad. Scis., Albania, 1993, chmn. Albanian com. for European Linguistic Atlas, 1993; vice-chmn. Albanian Com. of the Assn. Internat. for Studies of S.E. Europe, 1993; adj. dir. Centre d'Etudes Balkaniques of Paris, 2000. Author: Northwest Speeches of Albanian Language and the Phonetic System of the Speech of Shkodra, 1995, Problems of Language Policy and Language Planning in Albania, 2000; co-author: Albanian Language 2-8 class, 1996, 2d edit. 1999, Atlas Linguarum Europea, Grammar of Albanian Language, 1997, Atlas of Albanian Language. Decorated Order N. Frasheri 2d Class, People's Coun., 1986; recipient Naim Frasheri medal, People's Coun., 1973. Muslim. Avocation: nature sight seeing, music, pictures, sports. E-mail: bahri.beci@libertysurf.fr. Home: 25 Boulevard Maxime Gorki, 94800 Villejuif France

BECK, ANDREW JAMES, lawyer; b. Washington, Feb. 19, 1948; s. Leonard Norman and Frances (Greif) B.; m. Gretchen Ann Schroeder, Feb. 14, 1971; children: Carter, Lowell, Justin. BA, Carleton Coll., 1969; JD, Stanford U., 1972; MBA, Long Island U., 1975. Bar: Va. 1972, N.Y. 1973, Pa., 1992. Assoc. Casey, Lane & Mittendorf, N.Y.C., 1972-80; ptnr. Haythe & Curley, N.Y.C., 1982-99, Torys, N.Y.C., 1999—; exec. com. Torys, 2000—; bd. dirs. Capita Rsch. Group. Bd. dirs. Allied Devices Corp., 1994-98, Capita Rsch. Group, Inc., 2000—; trustee Bklyn. Heights Synagogue, 1980-81, Bklyn. Heights Montessori Sch., 1988-92, treas., 1990-92. Mem. ABA, Va. State Bar Assn., N.Y. Stat Bar Assn., Pa. Bar Assn., Assn. of Bar of City of N.Y., Nat. Stroke Assn. (gen. counsel 1992—, sec., bd. dirs. 2000—). Avocations: squash, bridge. Home: 71 Willow St Apt 1 Brooklyn NY 11201-1657 Office: Torys 237 Park Ave Fl 20 New York NY 10017-3140

BECK, ANGEL C., columnist, screenwriter, educator; b. Omaha, Aug. 18, 1951; d. James and Aleane (Fitz) Carter; m. Frank J. Beck, May 7, 1977 (div. May 12, 1988); children: Jaman, Angel Marie, Frank J. BGS, U. Nebr., 1975. Sports reporter Oakland (Calif.) Tribune, 1987-88; reporter Shoreline Times/Ft. Worth, 1988-89, Arlington (Tex.) Citizen Jour., 1989-90; talk show host WNET TV, N.Y.C., 1990-91; tchr. Stamford (Conn.) Pub. Schs., 1990—; syndicated columnist Tribune Media Svcs., Chgo., 1996-97, Zwita Prodns. Syndications, Stamford, Conn., 1997—; adv. I Have a Dream WCBS-TV, N.Y.C., 1995—. Author: History of Black Golfers, 1989, How To Play Bid Whist, 1995; film dir., screenplay writer: Center of Attention; contbr. articles to Black Enterprise jour. Mem. Nat. Assn. Black Journalists. Avocations: bid whist, jazz. Office: PO Box 112486 Stamford CT 06911-2486

BECK, BARBARA NELL, elementary school educator; b. Corpus Christi, Tex., Oct. 25, 1940; d. Marshall Joseph and Madie Ann (Spence) Robertson; m. Joel J. Beck, June 23, 1973. BA, Baylor U., 1964. Tchr. Killeen (Tex.) Ind. Sch. Dist., 1964—. Sunday sch. tchr., co-treas., ch. clk. First Bapt. Ch. of Nolanville. Mem. NEA, Tex. State Tchrs. Assn., Tex. Assn. for the Gifted and Talented, Killeen Edn. Assn. (treas., past pres., bd. dirs.), Clifton Park PTA (past treas.). Office: Clifton Park Elem Sch 2200 Trimmier Rd Killeen TX 76541-8599

BECK, CHRISTINE SAFFORD, photographer, publisher, volunteer; b. Phila., July 10, 1943; d. Elisha Jr. and Margaret (Tramdack) Safford; m. Leif Christian Beck, Nov. 21, 1964; children: C. Lars, Eric S., Anders. BA in German and French, Queens Coll., 1964; MA in German Lit., Bryn Mawr Coll., 1969; postgrad., N.Y. Inst. Photography. Co-founder, pres. Nat. Jr. Tennis League of Phila., 1969-79; pres., CEO Nat. Jr. Tennis League, N.Y.C., 1979-83; owner, photographer Christine S. Beck Photography, Villanova, Pa., 1990—; pub., owner Prism Light Press, Bryn Mawr, Pa., 1995—; stock photographer Garden Image Agy., Montreal, 1999—; pres. Phila. Tennis Patrons Assn., 1985-95, mem. adv. bd., 1995—; pres. Arthur Ashe Youth Tennis Ctr., Phila., 1985-95; chair adv. coun. Esperanza Health Ctr., Phila., 1994-97. Photographer (books): Beyond Me. Voices of the Natural World, 1993, Spirit of Summit County, Colorado, 1996; producer Broadway Comes to Queens benefit concert, Charlotte, N.C., 1999. Bd. dirs. Habitat for Humanity, Phila., 1988-90; coord. vols. Jimmy Carter Workcamp, North Phila., 1988; chair stewardship campaign Bryn Mawr Presbyn. Ch., 1992; trustee Queens Coll., Charlotte, N.C., 1995—; trustee Gesu Sch., Phila., 1996—, chair devel., 2000—; chair fundraising campaign Arthur Ashe Youth Tennis Ctr., 2000—; chair alumni phase fundraising campaign Queens Coll., N.C., 2000—. Recipient Kennedy award Robert F. Kennedy Pro Celebrity Tennis Tournament, 1975, Jimmy Carter Hammer award Habitat for Humanity, 1988, Merit award for women Internat. Tennis Hall of Fame, 1988, Svc. Bowl, U.S. Tennis Assn., 1991, Take the Lead award Girl Scouts of Greater Phila., 1992, First Phila. Youth Tennis Jerome Laroque award, 1999. Mem. U.S. Tennis Assn. Middle States (treas. 1986-89, Mangan award 1990, Coren award 1973), N.Am. Nature Photographers Assn. (charter mem.), Nikon Profl. Svcs. Avocations: golf, tennis, hiking. Office: Prism Light Press PO Box 766 Bryn Mawr PA 19010-0766

BECK, EARL RAY, historian, educator; b. Junction City, Ohio, Sept. 8, 1916; s. Ernest Ray and Mary Frances (Helser) B.; m. Marjorie Culbertson, Nov. 7, 1944 (dec. Feb. 1995); children: Ann, Mary Sue. A.B., Capital U., 1937; M.A., Ohio State U., 1939, Ph.D., 1942. Instr. Capital U., 1942-43, Ohio State U., 1946-49; asst. prof. Fla. State U., Tallahassee, 1949-52; assoc. prof. Fla. State U., 1952-60, prof. history, 1960-89, chmn. dept. history, 1967-72, chmn. grad. studies, 1982-87; prof. emeritus, 1989—; summer vis. prof. La. State U., 1955, Tulane U., 1959, Duke U., 1966. Author: Verdict on Schacht, 1956, The Death of the Prussian Republic, 1959, Contemporary Civilization I, 1959, On Teaching History in Colleges and Universities, 1966, Germany Rediscovers America, 1968, A Time of Triumph and of Sorrow: Spanish Politics During the Reign of Alfonso XII, 1874-1885, 1979, Under the Bombs: the German Home Front, 1942-1945, 1986, 99, European Homefronts, 1939-45, 1993, 98. Served with AUS, 1946-49. Mem. So. Hist. Assn. (chmn. European history sect. 1983-84), German Studies Assn. Presbyterian. Home: 2514 Killarney Way Tallahassee FL 32308-3163

BECK, EDWARD NELSON, minister; b. Washington, Aug. 19, 1949; s. Edward and Joyce Jacqueline (Wood) B.; m. Mona Faye Gandy, Jan 1, 1971; children: Rebecca Joyce, Jonathan Edward. BA, BTh, Gulf Coast Bible Coll., Houston, 1972; ThM, Fredericksburg Bible Inst., Va., 1985, ThD, 1986. carained to ministry Ch. of God, 1972. Pastor Hillcrest Ch. of God, Cody, Wyo., 1972-74; assoc. pastor Dunn Loring (Va.) Community Ch. of God, 1975-77; pastor Arwood Ch. of God, Fredericksburg, 1977-88, Taylortown Community Ch., Shelby, Ohio, 1988-95, 1st Ch. of God, Wert, Ohio, 1995—; dir. sr. high youth camp Ministerial Coun. the Ch. of God, Dunn Loring, Utica, Pa., 1975-95, Burnside, Pa., 1989—; second v.p. Lighthouse Bible Inst., Dunn Loring, 1977—; mem. exec. com. Billy Graham Evangelistic Assn. Ralph Bell Greater Fredericksburg Crusade, 1984; v.p. Ministerial Coun. Ch. of God, 1986; trustee The World Missionary Fellowship the Ch. of God, Can., 1986—; dir. community Christmas program Shelby Ministerial Assn., 1990—; evangelist, numerous so. and ea. states, 1975—. Author and editor booklet The Gift of Tongues and Other Tongues, 1984. Office: 1st Ch of God 314 S Harrison St Van Wert OH 45891-2020

BECK, ELAINE KUSHNER, elementary and secondary school educator; b. Phila., May 31, 1942; d. Joseph and Emma Kushner; m. Stuart Edwin Beck, June 20, 1964; children: Adam, Barry, Caroline. BS, Drexel U., 1963; Masters equivalent, Temple U., Pa. State U., West Chester U., 1984. Cert. tchr., Pa. Tchr. grades 4, 5, 6 Upper Darby (Pa.) Sch. Dist., 1963-64; tchr. high sch. Francis Hammond-Alexandria (Va.) Sch. Dist., 1964-65; tchr. adult edn. YMCA, Alexandria, 1966-67; tchr. mid. sch. Haverford Sch. Dist., Havertown, Pa., 1980—; bus. owner Lady Elaine Creations, Havertown, 1976-80. Contbg. editor: Passoverama, 1979-80; author (teaching program) The Equipment Scavenger Hunt, 1989. Mem. strategic plan com. Haverford Sch. Dist., Havertown, 1995-96; organizer sr. citizen dances, Havertown, 1992, 93, 94; pres., v.p., mem. adv. bds. sisterhood Temple Beth Hillel/Beth El, 1980-81. Recipient Dominick Recchiuti Humanitarian award, 1992; named one of Top 5 Home Econs. Tchrs. in U.S., Home Baking Assn., 1994; Ptnr. in Edn. grantee Sun Oil Co., 1989. Mem. NEA, Pa. Edn. Assn., Nat. Audubon Soc., Nature Conservancy, World Wildlife Fund, Sierra Club, Key and Triangle, Omicron Nu, Phi Sigma Sigma (honored Drexel U. chpt. 1998). Avocations: exotic bird training, wild bird watching, sailing, environmentalism, biking. Home: 624 Greythorne Rd Wynnewood PA 19096-2509 Office: Haverford Sch Dist 1701 Darby Rd Havertown PA 19083-3738

BECK, HANS, physicist; b. Zurich, Switzerland, Dec. 4, 1939; s. Hans and Marthy (Schnorf) B.; m. Ursula Urfer, Apr. 25, 1970. Diploma in Theoretical Physics, U. Zurich, 1967, PhD in Physics, 1970. Postdoctoral fellow U. Zurich, 1970-72; research assoc. Cornell U., Ithaca, N.Y., 1973; postdoctoral fellow IBM Research Lab., Ruschlikan, Switzerland, 1974; lectr. U. Basel, 1975-78; prof. physics U. Neuchatel, Switzerland, 1978—, vice rector, 1987-91, dean faculty sci., 1983-85; pres. planning com. Swiss U. Conf., 1993-2000. Contbr. articles to sci. jours. Mem. Swiss Phys. Soc. (sec. 1981-83), European Physical Soc. (treas. 1993-94). Home: Peupliers 6, 2014 Bole, Neuchâtel Switzerland Office: Inst de Physique, Rue Breguet 1, 2000 Neuchâtel Switzerland

BECK, HELMUT, retired librarian; b. Rudolstadt, Thuringia, Germany, Feb. 6, 1927; s. Alfred and Hedwig (Sturmfels) B.; m. Ursula Rosenhahn, Dec. 11, 1950; 1 child, Monika. Libr., Friedrich-Schiller U., Jena, Fed. Republic of Germany, 1950, diploma Germanist, 1960, PhD, 1961. Dir. Pub. Libr., Saalfeld, Fed. Republic of Germany, 1950-52; subject specialist, vice-dir. Pub. Libr. Ernst Abbe, Jena, 1952-61; dir. cataloguing dept. Friedrich-Schiller U. Libr., Jena, 1961-75; lectr. German lit. Libr. Sch. Erich Weinert Leipzig, 1961-66; lectr. libr. and info. sci. Friedrich-Schiller U., Jena, 1973-75, rsch. field libr. sci., 1975-92; ret., 1992. Author: Einfuhrung in die bibliothekarisch-bibliograph-Klassifikation, 1972, Sachkatalogisierung, 1973; contbr. articles to profl. jours. Mem. Thomas-Mann-Circle. Avocations: dog sport, walking, travel, swimming, music. Home: Netzstrasse,, Netzstrasse 67, D-07749 Jena Germany

BECK, IRENE CLARE, educational consultant, writer; b. N.Y.C., Dec. 18, 1944; d. James E. and Helen (Carroll) Clare; m. William J. Beck, Aug. 9, 1986; children: Daniel, James Chesire. BA, St. Mary's Coll., 1966; MA, Fairfield U., 1977; EdD, U. Rochester, 1982; Grad. Cert. Women's Studies, DePaul U., 1998. Cert. tchr., N.Y. Tchr. Elem. Sch., N.Y.C., 1966-68, Montessori Acad. N.Y., Bklyn., 1968-73; faculty Housatonic Community Coll., Bridgeport, Conn., 1975-77, Nazareth Coll., Rochester, N.Y., 1977-83; faculty dir. Sheppard Pratt Nat. Ctr. Human Devel., Balt., 1983-91; exec. dir. William & Irene Beck Found., 1987—; cons. Headstart Programs, Rochester, 1980-83, Family Day Care Tng., Rochester, 1980-83; mem. women's studies faculty program DePaul U., 1999—; presenter workshops and seminars. Author: Expect Respect, Let Me Tell You (manuals), (No Hang Ups (telephone audiotape), 1987, In Tune With Teens (booklet), 1990; weekly news col. Parents and Teens, 1987-90; freelance writer, 1986—; contbr. articles to profl. jours.; sr. editor What's Workikng for Girls in Illinois, 1996-99. Mem. AAUW, Assn. Childhood Edn. Internat. Avocations: hiking, swimming, biking. Home: 424 W Armitage Ave Apt F Chicago IL 60614-4682

BECK, IVAN GABRIEL, publishing company executive; b. Budapest, Jan. 27, 1945; s. Gyula and Livia (Graits) Guttman; m. Corinne Marie Rubies, Mar. 9, 1985 (div. Aug. 1990); 1 child, Joelle Julie Christine. Diploma, Brunel U., London, 1966; postgrad., John Cass Art Sch., London, 1966-68. From salesman to mgr. Sladden, Stuart & Powell, London, 1966-76; dir. Ibex Internat., London, 1976-86, World Aid, London, 1986-98, Ctrl. BB, London, 1998—. Mem. Inst. Internat. Rsch. Mem. Conservative Party. Jewish. Home: Sulgrave Rd, London W6 7PU, England Office: Ctrl BB, 111 Southwark St, London SE1 0JF, England

BECK, JOHN ROBERT, pathologist, information scientist; b. Cleve., Sept. 8, 1953; s. John Edward and Maralyn Janet (Smith) B.; m. Sharon Louise Dombkowski, Aug. 30, 1975; children: John Benjamin, Stefan Andrew, Meredith Louise. AB, Dartmouth Coll., 1974; MD, Johns Hopkins U., 1978. Diplomate Am. Bd. Pathology. Intern, then resident in pathology Dartmouth-Hitchcock Med. Ctr., Hanover, N.H., 1978-80, dir. bloodbank, 1984-89, dir. clin. pathology, 1987-89; fellow, clin. decision making New Eng. Med. Ctr., Boston, 1981; from asst. to assoc. prof. pathology Dartmouth Med. Sch., Hanover, 1982-89; prof., dir. biomed. info. communication ctr. Oreg. Health Scis. U., Portland, 1989-92; prof., v.p. info. tech. Baylor Coll. Medicine, Houston, 1992—; exec. dir. Houston Acad. Medicine-Tex. Med. Ctr. Libr., 1999—; cons. Nat. Libr. Medicine, Bethesda, Md., 1988-92. Editor-in-chief Med. Decision Making, 1989-94. Recipient Rsch. Career Devel. award Nat. Libr. Medicine, 1986. Fellow Am. Coll. Med. Informatics, Am. Soc. Clin. Pathologists (coun. chmn. 1991-93), Coll. Am. Pathologists (com. vice-chair 1997-2000); mem. Soc. for Med. Decision Making (sec.-treas. 1985-87, v.p. 1987-88, pres. 1995-96), Acad. Clin. Lab. Physicians and Scientists (exec. councilor 1989-91, Young Investigator award 1981), Am. Assn. Med. Colls., Group on Info. Resources (exec. com. 1997—). Republican. Avocations: golf, bridge, trumpet. Office: Baylor Coll Medicine Info Tech 1 Baylor Plz Houston TX 77030-3411

BECK, JOHN ROLAND, environmental consultant; b. Las Vegas, N.Mex., Feb. 26, 1929; s. Roland L. and Betty L. (Shrock) B.; m. Doris A. Olson, Feb. 9, 1951; children: Elizabeth J., Thomas R., Patricia L., John William. BS, Okla. A&M U., 1950; MS, Okla. State U., 1957; postgrad., U. Tex., 1954, George Washington U., 1965. Registered sanitarian, Ohio, Ariz.; cert. wildlife biologist. Wildlife researcher King Ranch, Kingsville, Tex., 1950-51; faculty Inst. Human Physiology U. Tenn., Martin, 1954-55; rsch. biologist FWS, USDI, Grangeville, Idaho, 1955-57; ctr. dir. Job Corps, OEO, Indiahoma, Okla., 1965-67; supr. animal control biology FWS, USDI, 1953-69; operating v.p. Bio-Svc. Corp., Troy, Mich., 1969-78; pres. BECS Ltd., Prescott, Ariz., 1981-85; spl. asst. USDA - APHIS, Washington, 1986-87; prin. cons. Biol. Environ. Cons. Svc. Inc., Phoenix, 1978-93; faculty assoc. Ariz. State U., Tempe, 1980-89; expert witness in bus. evaluations, 1979-98; expert witness in pesticide litigations, 1989-94; participant fin. seminars, 1980-85. Sr. author: Managing Service for Success, 1987, 2d edit., 1991; columnist mo. column on pest control in 2 mags., 1980-88; referee Internat. Health Related Jour., 1999—; contbr. articles to profl. jours. Life mem. Rep. Nat. Com., 1993—; mem. Rep. Senatorial Inner Cir., 1994-99, Rep. Presdl. Roundtable, 1995-97. Capt. USAR, 1950-62. Fellow Royal Soc. Health, N.Y. Explorers Soc.; mem. ASTM (chmn. pesticide com. 1979-81, chmn. vertebrate pesticides 1994-2000), Rotary (dist. treas. 1997-99), Wildlife Soc., Sigma Xi. Republican. Baptist. Avocations: botany studies, ornithology, mammalogy.

BECK, LUKE FERRELL WILSON, insurance specialist; b. Granbury, Tex., Feb. 2, 1948; s. Don Elder and Georgia Ferrell (Wilson) B.; m. Susan Villars, Nov. 14, 1970 (div. Feb. 1974). BA in Psychology, U. Tex., 1970. CPCU. Claims rep. Employers Ins. Tex., Beaumont, 1975-86; home office supr. Employers Ins. Tex., Dallas, 1986-89; litigation specialist CNA Ins. Co., Dallas, 1989-93, litigation supv., 1993—. 1st lt. U.S. Army, 1971-75. Mem. Soc. of CPCU. Presbyterian. Avocations: cooking, history. Home: 2108 Barton Dr Arlington TX 76010-4750 Office: CNA Ins PO Box 219046 Dallas TX 75221-9046

BECK, MARY VIRGINIA, lawyer, public official; b. Ford City, Pa., Feb. 29, 1908. BA, U. Pitts., 1929, LLB, 1932, JD, 1968. Bar: Mich. 1944. Elected to Common Coun., City of Detroit, 1950-70; mem. bd. suprs. County of Wayne, Mich., 1950-69; exec. dir. Ukrainian Info. Bur., Detroit, 1995, ret., 1995. Chmn. Policeman and Retirement Fund Commn., Detroit, 1958062; chmn. Wayne County Port Commn., 1962-68; mem. Gov.'s Commn. on Status of Women, 1962, Gov.'s Commn. on Econ. Devel., 1962. Recipient Cert. of Merit, Fashion Group of Detroit, 1955, Ruth Houston Whipple award Plymouth Bus. and Profl. Woman's Club, 1956, Sport Guild award Sports Guild Detroit, 1956, award Detroit Dental Soc., 1957, citation Detroit Cancer Fighters, 1959, Ukrainian Cmty. Svc. award Ukrainians of the Free World, 1960, Ukrainian of Yr. award Ukrainian Grad. Club of Detroit and Windsor, 1963, award Amvets of World War II, 1967, Woman of Yr. award Soroptimist Club, 1968; inducted into Detroit's Bowling Hall of Fame, 1974, Mich.'s Womens Hall of Fame, 1992, others; placement of 4 portraits in Ukrainian Mus. N.Y., 1999, Ukrainian Women's Ctr. in the Kiev Moayla Acad., 2000; Ukrainian Studies Scholarship established in her honor, 2000. Mem. Mich. State Bar, Detroit Bar Assn., Women Lawyers Assn. Mich., Nat. Assn. Women Lawyers, Detroit Bus. Women's Club, Nat. Fedn. Profl. and Bus. Women, Internat. Platform Assn., World Fedn. Ukrainian Women's Orgns. (hon.), Ukrainian Nat. Women's League Am. (hon.).

BECK, MICHAEL HAWLEY, dermatologist, consultant; b. Stoke-on-Trent, Stafford., Eng., Oct. 20, 1948; s. William Hawley and June Aldersey (Davenport) B.; m. Gerralynn Judith Harrop, Mar. 18, 1978; children—James John William, Robin Michael Davenport. M.B., Ch.B., Liverpool U. Med. Sch., 1972, M.R.C.P., 1977. House officer Clatterbridge Hosp., Merseyside, Eng., 1972-73, sr. house officer, 1973-74; sr. house officer in gen. medicine Salford Health Authority, Manchester, 1975-77; registrar of gen. medicine Trafford Health Authority, Manchester, 1977; registrar in dermatology Salford Health Authority, 1977-79, sr. registrar, 1979-81; cons. dermatologist Bolton and Salford Health Trusts, Manchester, U.K., 1981—; dir. dermatitis investigation unit, Manchester, U.K., 1981—; hon. assoc. lectr. U. Manchester, 1981-92; hon. clin. lectr., 1992—. Mem. editl. bd. Jour. of Dermatol. Treatment, 1998—; contbr. articles to med. jours. Fellow Royal Soc. Medicine (dermatol. sect. 1981—); mem. North of Eng. Dermatol. Soc., Dowling Club, Brit. Assn. Dermatologists, Ileostomy Assn. (dermatol. adv. 1982—), Brit. Contact Dermatitis Group (com. mem. 1981—, chmn. 1985-88). Ch. of Eng. Office: 57 Chorley New Rd, Bolton BL1 4QR, England

BECK, MORRIS, allergist; b. Miami, Fla., Oct. 12, 1927; s. Max and Anna (Luks) B.; m. Hollis Schwartz, Aug. 6, 1960; children: Gayle Beck Finan, Anne Lin. BA, UCLA, 1949; MD, U. Zurich, Switzerland, 1957. Diplomate Am. Bd. Allergy and Immunology, Am. Bd. Pediatrics. Intern Queens Hosp. Ctr., 1958, resident in pediatrics, 1959-60; preceptor in allergy U. Miami (Fla.) Med. Sch., 1961-77; pvt. practice pediatrician Miami, 1961-77, pvt. practice allergist, 1978—; chief dept. allergy Miami Children's Hosp., 1986—, Miami VA Hosp., 1994—; clin. prof. pediatrics Nova U. Southeastern Med. Sch., 1998—; clin. asst. prof. U. Miami Med. Sch. With U.S. Army, 1950-52. Fellow Am. Coll. Allergy & Immunology, Am. Acad. Pediatrics, Am. Assn. Cert. Allergists; mem. Am. Acad. Allergy & Immunology, Am. Coll. Chest Physicians. Republican. Jewish. Avocations: photography, fishing, travel. Office: 7800 SW 87th Ave # C-340 Miami FL 33173-3570

BECK, ROBERT RAYMOND, priest; b. Waterloo, Iowa, Aug. 28, 1940; s. Paul Clayton and Mildred Anne (Klein) B. BA, Loras Coll., Dubuque, Iowa, 1962; ThM, Aquinas Inst. Theology, Dubuque, 1965; cert. of study, Ecole Biblique, Jerusalem, 1978; DMin, Cath. U., 1983. Assoc. pastor St. Columbkille Parish, Dubuque, 1966-71; with campus ministry U. No. Iowa, Cedar Falls, 1971-73; instr. of Scripture Aquinas Inst. Theology, 1973-81; prof. religious studies Loras Coll., 1981—, chair dept. religious studies, 1992—, John Cardinal O'Connor endowed chair in Cath. thought, 1999-2000; co-founder, bd. dirs. Cath. Worker, Dubuque, 1976-94; co-founder, pastor Anawim Faith Community, Dubuque, 1981—; founder, dir. Ray Herman Peace Ctr., Dubuque, 1983-86. Author: Nonviolent Story: Narrative Conflict Resolution in the Gospel of Mark, 1996; composer: (rock opera) Mark, A Pop Opera 1975, 87, 99, Our Father, 1968; columnist: Sunday's Word, 1982-87; editor: Loras Faculty Review, 1989—; contbr. articles to profl. jours. Mem. Soc. Bibl. Lit., Am. Acad. Religion, Cath. Theol. Soc. Am. Democrat. Home: 1450 Alta Vista St Dubuque IA 52001-4327

BECK, ROLAND HERWIG FRIEDRICH, biotechnology engineer; b. Melk, Austria, Apr. 12, 1961; s. Herwig and Sieglinde (Botz) B.; m. Tarja Tuulikki Nissilä, Apr. 15, 1990; children: Markus, Tomas. Diploma, U. Bodenkultur, Vienna, Austria, 1985, PhD, 1987. Rsch. fellow U. Bodenkultur, 1985-87; rsch. coord. Cerestar, Vilvoorde, Belgium, 1987-90, sect. leader, 1990-95, application ctr. mgr., 1995-99; v.p. sales Cerestar USA, Hammond, Ind., 1999—; lectr. in field. Contbr. over 40 articles to profl. jours. Avocations: reviewer for research projects, PhD examiner, music. Home: Molenstraat 10, 3078 Everberg Belgium Office: Cerestar R&D, Havenstraat 84, 1800 Vilvoorde Belgium

BECK, TAMÁS, economic expert; b. Budapest, Hungary, Feb. 26, 1929; s. Géza and Ibolya (Lóránth) B.; m. Ilona Rákos, Apr. 18, 1963; 1 child, Ágnes Katalin Szilvás. MS in Econs., Tech. U., Budapest, 1951; postgrad., Princeton U., 1971-72, U. Econs., Budapest, 1974. Engr. Flax and Hemp Directory, Budapest, 1951-61; dir.-engr. Flax and Hemp Spinning Enterprise, Szeged, Hungary, 1961-70; mng. dir. Flax Spinning and Weaving Enterprise, Budapest, 1970-88; min. Minister of Trade, Budapest, 1988-90; mng. dir. Capegate Ltd., Budapest, 1990—; mem. Tech. Bd. Devel., 1970—, Indsl. Developing Cmty., 1984—; bd. dirs. Ing Bank. Author over 300 books and articles. Pres. Hungarian C. of C., 1982-88, Hungarian-Israeli C. of C. and Industry, 1996—, Hungarian-South African Assn., 1993—. Recipient Hungarian State award, 1985, Grosses Goldenen Ehrenzeichen mit dem Stern, Republic Osterreich, 1990. Mem. World Fedn. Hungarian Engrs., Architects Hungarian Assn. (v.p. 1992—), Sigma Xi. Avocation: sailing. Home: Méra u 5/7, 1121 Budapest Hungary Office: Kapgate Internat AG, Szechenyi u. 1/D, H-1054 Budapest Hungary

BECK, VAUGHAN RODNEY, fire safety systems and risk engineer; b. Melbourne, Victoria, Australia, Mar. 28, 1948; s. Maurice and Freda (Wall) B.; m. Ann Bolderston, Apr. 1971; children: Phillipa, Benjamin. Diploma of Mech. Engring., Footscray Tech. Coll., Melbourne, 1969; B Engring. in Mech. Engring., U. Melbourne, 1971, M Engring. Sci., 1978; PhD, U. N.S.W., Sydney, 1987. Plant engr. ICI Australia Pty. Ltd., Sydney, 1971-72; rsch. engr. BHP Steel, Melbourne, 1972-74, Dept. Housing and Constrn., Melbourne, 1974-78, Exptl. Bldg. Sta., Sydney, 1978-82; prin. lectr. Footscray Inst. Tech., Melbourne, 1982-91; prof. and dir. Ctr. Environ. Safety and Risk Engring. Victoria U. Tech., Melbourne, 1991-98, 99, pro vice-chancellor R&D, 1998, 99—; vis. scientist Nat. Rsch. Coun., Can., Ottawa, Ont., 1987; professorial fellow Warren Ctr. for Advanced Engring., U. Sydney, 1989. Prin. author: (monographs) Fire Safety and Engineering, 1989, Draft National Building Fire Safety Systems Code, 1991. Recipient Advance Australia Found. award, 1993, John J. Ahern award Soc. Fire Protection Engrs., Boston, 1994. Fellow Instn. of Engrs. Australia (dep. chair Soc. Fire Safety 1993-96, W.H. Warren medal 1976), Australian Inst. Bldg. (Fred Wilson Meml. prize 1988), Australian Acad. Technol. Scis. and Engring. Avocations: family, rural property, bushwalking, canoeing. Office: Victoria U Tech, PO Box 14428 MCMC, Melbourne VIC 8001, Australia

BECK, WOLFGANG MAXIMILIAN, inorganic chemistry educator; b. Munich, May 5, 1932; s. Emil and Johanna (Geistbeck) B.; m. Gerda Lesch, Aug. 8, 1958; children: Markus, Gunter, Kathrin. PhD in Chemistry, Tech. Hochschule Munich, 1960. Lectr. Tech. Hochschule Munich, 1963-68; prof. chemistry, head Inst. Inorganic Chemistry U. Munich, 1968-98, dean faculty chemistry and pharmacy, 1973-75; vis. prof. U. Wis., Madison, 1977. Contbr. over 550 articles to profl. publs. Recipient chemistry award Acad. Goettingen, 1967, Liebig Medal DCH, 1994. Mem. German Chem. Soc., Chem. Soc. London, Am. Chem. Soc. Office: U Munich Inst Inorganic Chemistry, Butenandtstr 5-13, 81377 Munich Germany

BECKENBAUER, FRANZ, former soccer player, professional soccer team executive; b. Sept. 11, 1945; s. Franz Sr. and Antonia Beckenbauer; m. Brigitte Wittmann; 3 children. Student, No. Coll. Ins. Studies. Player Bayern Munich Football Club, N.Y. Cosmos Soccer Team; mgr. West German Nat. Team, 1984-90; tech. dir. Marseilles team, 1990—; cons. Olympique Marseilles, U.S. Soccer Fedn., 1990—; former coach; founder Franz Beckenbauer Found., 19982; advisor Mitsubishi Mrawa Football Club, 1992—. Author: Einer wie ich (Someone Like Me). Winner (with Bayern Munich) West German Cup, 1966, 67, 69, 71, West German Championship, 1972, 74, European Cup, 1967, 1974-76, World Club Championship, 1976; (with West German Nat. Team) European Nations Cup, 1972, World Cup, 1974; (with N.Y. Cosmos) N. Am. Championship, 1977, 78-80; named Footballer of Yr., 1972, 76, West German Footballer of Yr., 1980, Profl. Football Man, 1977—; named to Order of Internat. Football Fedn., 1984. Office: DFB, Otto Fleck Schneise 6, 6000 Frankfurt Germany*

BECKER, BORIS, retired professional tennis player; b. Leimen, Germany, Nov. 22, 1967; s. Karl-Hinez and Elvira Becker; m. Barbara Feltus, Dec. 1993; 1 child. Mem. Fed. Republic Germany championship team Davis Cup Tournament, Goteborg, Sweden, 1988. Winner numerous tennis tournaments, including West German Jr. Championship, 1983, Young Masters Tournament, Birmingham, Eng., 1985, Grand Prix Tournament, Queen's, 1985, Men's Singles Championship, Wimbledon, Eng., 1985, 86, 89, U.S. Open Singles Tournament, N.Y., 1989, Australian Open, 1991, 96, ATP World Championship, 1995;(with Michael Stich) Men's Doubles Gold Medal, Olympics, 1992. Office: USTA 70 W Red Oak Ln White Plains NY 10604-3602*

BECKER, BRUCE CARL, II, physician, educator; b. Chgo., Sept. 8, 1948; s. Carl Max and Lillian (Podzamsky) B.; m. Irene Stepien-Thibault, 1991; 1 child, Joseph. BS in Aero. and Astron. Engring., U. Ill., 1970; MSME, Colo. State U., 1972; postgrad., Wright State U., 1973-74; MD, Chgo. Med. Sch., 1978; MS in Health Svcs. Adminstrn., Coll. of St. Francis, Joliet, Ill., 1984; Diploma in Spanish, U. Chgo., 1988; Diploma in Polish, Coll. of Du Page, 1989. Diplomate Am. Bd. Med. Mgmt.; cert. physician exec. Resident in surgery U. N.C., Chapel Hill, 1978-79; resident in family practice St. Mary of Nazareth Hosp. Ctr., Chgo., 1979-81, chmn., program dir. dept. family practice, 1985-90, asst. dir. med. edn., 1981-82, dir. family practice residency, 1983-90, chief Family Practice Ctr., 1983-85, chmn. dept. family practice, 1985-90, med. dir. home health svc., 1985—, med. dir. HMO-Ill., 1985—, mem. planning and devel. com. governing bd., 1987-91, v.p. med. affairs, 1989—; clin. instr. Chgo. Med. Sch., 1982, affiliate instr., 1982-83, asst. prof., 1983, vice chmn. dept. family medicine, 1983-91; mem. family practice residency act Adv. Com. Ill. Dept. Pub. Health, 1991—; mem. adv. com. family practice residency Ill. Dept. Health, 1991—. Mem. editl. rev. bd. Postgrad. Medicine, 1987-89; contbr. articles to med. jours. Mem. pub. health adv. network HHS, 1990-91; bd. dirs. Midwest region Inn Care Am., 1991—; mem. dinner com. Ill. chpt. Lupus Found. Am., 1991. Capt. USAF, 1970-75. Fellow Am. Acad. Family Physicians (rep. to accrediation rev. com. for physician assts. 1989-94, chmn., 1991-93), Am. Coll. Physician Execs., Am. Coll. Health Care Execs. (regents adv. coun. 1996-2000); mem. AMA, Ill. Acad. Family Physicians (commn. on internal affairs 1986, commn. pub. and govt. policy 1987-89, chmn. 1989-90, bd. dirs. 1988-92, chmn. pub. rels. and info. com. 1988-92, state rep. family practice res. act com. 1990-92, vice spkr. 1991-92), Soc. Tchrs. Family Medicine, Assn. Am. Med. Colls., Alliance Continuing Med. Edn., Am. Coll. Occupl. Medicine, Am. Acad. Med. Adminstrn., Chgo. Med. Soc. (councilor for Chgo. Med. Sch. 1986-91, alt. councilor 1991-95, mem. physicians stress ad hoc com. 1989-90, vice chmn. 1990-91, adv. com. on pub. health policy 1990—, presdl. adv. com. 1991—), Ill. Med. Soc. (coun. on edn. and manpower 1986-96, chmn. com. on CME activities 1991-96, chmn. subcom. physician placement and practice issues 1986-90, third party payment and processes com., Ill. Acad. Family Physicians rep. 1990-92), Phi Delta Epsilon. Roman Catholic.

BECKER, CARL BRADLEY, philosopher, educator; b. Chgo., Apr. 27, 1951; arrived in Japan, 1983; s. Paul Edward and Violet (Escarraz) B.; m. Akiko Ochiai. BA in Philosophy, Prin. Coll., St. Louis, 1971; MA in Philosophy, U. Hawaii, 1973, PhD in Philosophy, 1981; DLitt (hon.), Internat. U., Bombay, 1992. Rsch. asst. East-West Ctr., Honolulu, 1979-81; asst. prof. philosophy So. Ill. U., Carbondale, 1981-83; Fulbright lectr. Osaka (Japan) U., 1983-86; asst. prof. curriculum U. Hawaii, Honolulu, 1986-88; vis. prof. religions Tsukuba (Japan) U., 1988-92; prof. ethics Kyoto (Japan) U., 1992—; advisor Japan Assn. for Religious and Natural Healing Assn.; cons. in field. Author: Kanji Finder Index Japanese Dictionary, 1979, Japan: My Teacher, My Love, 1983, Christianity: History and Philosophy, 1985, Communication East and West, 1988, American and English Ideals, 1991, English Thinking, English Writing, 1992, Paranormal Experience, 1992, Breaking the Circle: Buddhist Views, 1993, At the Border of Death--Japanese Near-Death Experience, 1993, Buddhism and Environmental Ethics, 1995, American Businessman, 1996, Issues of Life and Death, 1998, Asian/Jungian Views of Ethics, 1999; translator: Practical Ethics for Our Time, 1998; contbr. articles to profl. jours. Recipient Robert Ashby award Soc. for Religious and Psychol. Rsch., 1982, Best Internat. Rsch. award Soc. for Internat. Edn., Tchg. and Rsch., 1986. Mem. N.Y. Acad. Sci., Soc. Values in Higher Edn., Holistic Medicine Assn. (dir. 1994—), Mind-Body Sci. Assn. (dir. 1994—), Biothanatology Assn. (dir. 1995—), Mensa, Japan Am. Forensics Assn. (founder), Internat. Assn. for Near-Death Studies, Mind-Body Rsch. Assn., Internat. Soc. Life Info. Sci. Achievements include invention of new dictionary system for Japanese hieroglyphs. Office: Kyoto U Human Sci, Yoshida Nihon Matsu-cho, Sakyo Kyoto 606-8501, Japan

BECKER, CONSTANCE DUSTIN, ecology educator, conservationist; b. Durham, N.C., Feb. 20, 1954; d. Roland Frederick and Florence Kingston (Courtis) B.; m. Mark David Hollingsworth, Aug. 18, 1984. BS in Sci. Edn., U. Va., 1977; MS in Forest Sci., Yale U., 1984; PhD in Zoology, U. Alta., Can., 1992. Faculty and program dir. Sch. for Field Studies Yale U., New Haven, Conn., 1984-92; grad. tchg. and rsch. asst. U. Alta., 1988-92; adj. prof. in biology Ind. U., Bloomington, 1992-93, rsch. assoc. in internat. forestry, 1993-98; asst. prof. Kans. State U., Manhattan, 1998—; vis. prof. Ind. U., 1993-96; co-dir. People Allied for Nature, N.Y.C., 1994-99. Contbr. articles to profl. jours. Tchr. U.S. Peace Corps, Kenya, 1977-80. Mem. Am. Ornithol. Union, Soc. Conservation Biology. Avocations: birdwatching, travel, organic gardening. E-mail: dbecker@oznet.ksu.edu. Home: 1931 Leavenworth St Manhattan KS 66502-3816 Office: Kans State Univ 2021 Throckmorton Manhattan KS 66502

BECKER, ELISABETH MARIA, artist, educator; b. Paris, Nov. 1, 1942; came to U.S., 1987; d. Henri Georges and Irene Maria (Tobler) B.; children: Mariette Schlegel, Natalie Schlegel Barker, Pascale Schlegel, Claudine Caviezel. Diploma, Internat. Acad. Arts, Basel-Bern, 1964. Tchr. arts and crafts Handecapt Sch., St. Gallen, Switzerland, 1974; artist Stage City Theater, St Gallen; substitute tchr. Internat. Orphin Coll., Pestalozzi Village, Trogen, Switzerland, 1973; lectr. U. St. Gallen, Switzerland, 1987-88; artist Elisabeth Maria Becker Fine Art Gallery, Taos, N.Mex, 1991—. One woman show and group shows in Teufen Switzerland, 1973, Gerona, Spain, 1974-76, Zurich, 1981, 82, Herisau, Switzerland, 1982, Lugano, Switzerland, 1982, Amsterdam, 1985, Bern, Switzerland, 1986, Basel, 1986, Zug, Switzerland, 1987, Nurnberg, Germany, 1987, Taos, 1990, Art Expo, N.Y., 1998, others; represented by Creighton Dacis Gallery, Washington. Mem. Soc. Swiss Painter Sculptors. Home: 212 Siler 5198 NDCBU Taos NM 87571-6108 Office: Elisabeth Maria Becker Fine Art Gallery 212 Siler Rd Taos NM 87571-6108

BECKER, GARY STANLEY, economist, educator; b. Pottsville, Pa., Dec. 2, 1930; s. Louis William and Anna (Siskind) B.; m. Doria Slote, Sept. 19, 1954 (dec.); children: Judith Sarah, Catherine Jean; m. Guity Nashat, Oct. 31, 1979; children: Michael Claffey, Cyrus Claffey. AB summa cum laude, Princeton U., 1951, PhD (hon.), 1991; AM, U. Chgo., 1953, PhD, 1955; PhD (hon.), Hebrew U., Jerusalem, 1985, Knox Coll., 1985, U. Ill., Chgo., 1988, SUNY, 1990, U. Palermo, Buenos Aires, 1993, Columbia U., 1993, Warsaw (Poland) Sch. Econs., 1995, U. Econs., Prague, Czech Republic, 1995, U. Miami, 1995, U. Rochester, 1995; PhD, Hofstra U., 1997, U. d'Aix-Marselles, 1999. Asst. prof. U. Chgo., 1954-57; from asst. to assoc. prof. Columbia U., N.Y.C., 1957-60, prof. econs., 1960-68, Arthur Lehman prof. econs., 1968-70; prof. econs. U. Chgo., 1970-83, Univ. prof. econs. and sociology, 1983—, chmn. dept. econs., 1984-85; Ford Found. vis. prof. econs. U. Chgo., 1969-70; assoc. Econs. Rsch. Ctr. Nat. Opinion Rsch. Ctr., Chgo., 1980—; mem. domestic adv. bd. Hoover Instn., Stanford, Calif., 1973-91, sr. fellow, 1990—; mem. acad. adv. bd. Am. Enterprise Inst., 1987-92; rsch. policy advisor Ctr. for Econ. Analysis Human Behavior Nat. Bur. Econ. Rsch., 1972-78, mem. and sr. research assoc., 1957-79; assoc. mem. Inst. Fiscal and Monetary Policy, Ministry of Fin., Japan, 1988—. Author: The Economics of Discrimination, 1957, 2d edit., 1971, Human Capital, 1964, 3d edit., 1993, Japanese transl., 1975, Spanish trans., 1984, Chinese trans., 1987, Romanian trans., 1997, Human Capital and the Personal Distribution of Income: An Analytical Approach, 1967, Economic Theory, 1971, Japanese transl., 1976, (with Gilbert Ghez) The Allocation of Time and Goods Over the Life Cycle, 1975, The Economic Approach to Human Behavior, 1976 (German transl., 1982, Polish transl., 1990, Chinese transl., 1993, Romanian transl., 1994, Italian transl. 1998), A Treatise on the Family, 1981, expanded edit., 1991, Spanish transl., 1987, Chinese transl., 1988, Accounting for Tastes, 1996 (Czech transl., 1998, Italian and Chinese transls. 1999, (with Guity Nashat Becker) The Economics of Life, 1996 (Chinese transl., 1997, German transl., 1998, Japanese transl., 1998), (in German) Family, Society, and State, 1996, (in Italian) L'approccio Economico al Comportamento Umano, 1998; editor: Essays in Labor Economics in Honor of H. Gregg Lewis, 1976; co-editor: (with William M. Landes) Essays in the Economics of Crime and Punishment, 1974; columnist, Bus. Week, 1985—; contbr. articles to profl. jours. Recipient W.S. Woytinsky award U. Mich., 1964, Profl. Achievement award U. Chgo. Alumni Assn., 1968, Frank E. Seidman Disting. award in Polit. Economy, 1985, merit award NIH, 1986, John R. Commons award Omicron Delta Epsilon, 1987, Nobel prize in Econ. Scis., 1992, Lord Found. award, 1995, Irene Taueber award, 1997. Fellow Am. Statis. Assn., Econometric Soc., Nat. Assn. Bus. Economists, Am. Acad. Arts and Scis., Am. Econ. Assn. (Disting., v.p. 1974, pres. 1987, John Bates Clark medal 1967); mem. NAS, NAE (founding mem., v.p. 1965-67), Nat. Assn. Bus. Economists, Am. Philos. Soc., Internat. Union for Sci. Study Population, Mont Pelerin Soc. (exec. bd. dirs. 1985-96, v.p. 1989-90, pres. 1990-92), Western Econ. Assn. (v.p. 1995-96, pres. 1996-97), Pontifical Acad. Scis., Econ. History Assn., Nat. Assn. of Bus. Economists, Phi Beta Kappa. Office: U Chgo Dept Econs 1126 E 59th St Chicago IL 60637-1580

BECKER, HORST-VINCENT DANIEL, financial executive; b. Hamburg, Germany, Mar. 23, 1941; s. Vincent and Margarete (von Elsner) B.; m. Uta Ingelore Hildegard Bartsch, Dec. 21, 1973; children: Olaf, Sina. Diplom-Kaufmann, U. Hamburg, Germany, 1969; student, Temple U., 1969-70. External auditor Price Waterhouse, Hamburg, 1971-74, team leader, sr. auditor, 1974-77; internal auditor UN Relief and Works Agy. for Palestine Refugees, Vienna, Austria, 1977-87; fin. officer UN Relief and Works Agy. for Palestine Refugees, Jerusalem, 1987-91; treas. UN Relief and Works Agy. for Palestine Refugees, Vienna, 1991-93; head budget and fin. Orgn. Prohibition Chem. Weapons, Den Haag, The Netherlands, 1993—. Mem. Inst. Internal Auditors. Avocations: reading, music, sports, travel. Home: Mesdagstr 59, 2596 XV Den Haag The Netherlands Office: Orgn Prohibition Chem Weap, Johan de Wittlaan 32, 2517 JR Den Haag The Netherlands

BECKER, ISIDORE A., business executive; b. N.Y.C., May 10, 1926; s. Max and Eva (Chester) B.; m. Adele Sandler, Dec. 20, 1947; children: Steven Richard, Carol Ann. B.A., Bklyn. Coll., 1949. Partner Herbert D. Silver & Co., N.Y.C., 1956-63; fin. v.p., chmn. financial com. Rapid-Am. Corp., N.Y.C., 1966-72; vice chmn. bd. Rapid-Am. Corp., 1967-72, 76-82, dir., 1964-82, pres., 1972-76; chief financial officer, treas. McCrory Corp., N.Y.C., 1964-70; dir. McCrory Corp., 1964-82; vice chmn. bd., dir. Glen Alden Corp., N.Y.C., 1967-72; chmn. bd., dir. Schenley Industries, Inc., 1968-82; pres. Riviera Hotel, Inc., 1973-83; chmn. bd. Shaw-Ross Internat. Importers, Inc., 1983—, Southern Wine & Spirits, 1983—. Vice chmn. bd. Boys Town Jerusalem; founder Albert Einstein Coll. Medicine; asso. chmn., bd. govs. Anti Defamation League B'nai B'rith. Served with USMCR, 1944-46. Home: 10155 Collins Ave Bal Harbour FL 33154-1655 Office: 15960 NW 15th Ave Miami FL 33169-5608

BECKER, JUERGEN CHRISTIAN, physician, researcher; b. Wihelmshaven, Germany, May 13, 1964; s. Ulrich Johann and Brigitte (Mueller) B. MD, U. Hannover, Germany, 1990; dozent, U. Würzburg, Germany, 1998. Intern dept. internal medicine U. Hannover, Germany, 1990; resident dept. dermatology U. Würzburg, 1990-93, cons., 1996—; rsch. assoc. Scripps Rsch. Inst., La Jolla, Calif., 1994-96. Contbr. articles to profl. jours. Mem. European Orgn. for Rsch. and Treatment Cancer, German Assn. Dermatologists (Oscar Gans award 1997), Am. Assn. Cancer Rsch. (Young Investigators award 1995). Office: U Würzburg, Josef Scheider Str 2, D-97080 Würzburg Bavaria, Germany Address: U Würzburg Dept Derm, Sch Med Josef Schneiderstr2, D-97080 Würzburg Germany

BECKER, KARLA LYNN, systems analyst; b. West Point, N.Y., Nov. 3, 1956; d. Fred. D. and Margaret Erika (Buckmann) Spinks; m. Eric Louis Becker; children: Erika Margaret Augusta Ashmore, Robert Loren Curtis II. BA, Ind. U.-Purdue U. at Indpls., 1982; MS, Ind. U., 1986. Cert. aerobics and fitness instr. Mgr. Eastside Chiropractic Clinic, Indpls., 1978-80; English tutor univ. div. Ind. U.-Purdue U. at Indpls., 1980-82, composition instr. English dept., 1982-83, tech. writer computing services, 1983-84; tech. writer Ind. U. Adminstrv. Computing, 1984-87; mgmt. info. svcs. cons., writer, support adminstr. Simon Property Group, Indpls., 1987-97; sys. cons. Source Svcs., Indpls., 1997-99; sr. sys. analyst Eli Lilly & Co., Indpls., 1999—. Author: Composing Technical Documents, 2000; contbr. articles, book revs., poems to various publs.; editor: Lit. Jour., Genesis, All-Am. Mag., Am. Collegiate Press Assn., 1983. Mem. Soc. Tech. Communication (Cert. of Achievement 1985), Sigma Delta Chi, Pi Lambda Theta. Democrat. Roman Catholic. Avocations: singing, teaching aerobics. Office: Eli Lilly & Co Lilly Corp Ctr Drop Code 6337 Ctr Indianapolis IN 46285-0001

BECKER, NANCY JANE, information science educator; b. Irvington, N.J., June 3, 1948; d. George Henry and Vida Jacqueline (Collins) B.; m. James Edward Weissinger, Sept. 4, 1971 (div. Aug. 1989); children: Jeffrey Michael, Erica Kathleen. BA, Seton Hall U., 1972; MLS with honors, Columbia U., 1992, EdD, 1999. Reference dept. intern Columbia U., N.Y.C., 1991-92, reference libr. Tchr. Coll., 1992-93, electronic info. resources libr., 1993-96; instr. info. sci. St. Johns U., Jamaica, N.Y., 1996-99; asst. prof. St. Johns U., Jamaica, 1999—. Mem. ALA, Assn. Coll. & Rsch. Librs. (com. chair 1995-96, 98-99, sect. chair 1997-98), Am. Ednl. Rsch. Assn., Assn. Libr. and Info. Sci. Edn., Beta Phi Mu. Dem. Roman Cath. Avocations: hiking, reading. Office: St Johns Univ 8000 Utopia Pkwy Jamaica NY 11432-1343

BECKER, ROBERT JEROME, allergist, health care consultant; b. Milw., May 29, 1922; s. Jacob and Sarah (Saxe) B.; m. June Granof, June 25, 1950; children: Scott M., Jill Becker Wilson, Jon G. BS, U. Wis., Milw., 1943; MD, Med. Coll. Wis., 1949. Intern Michael Reese Hosp., Chgo., 1949-50; resident in internal medicine VA Hosp., Wood, Wis., 1950-53; resident in allergy Roosevelt Hosp., N.Y.C., 1955-56; pvt. practice specializing in allergy Joliet, Ill., 1956-82; founder, chmn. bd. dirs. HealthCare COMPARE, 1982-90, chmn. bd. dirs. emeritus, 1990—; cons. health care utilization co., 1982-90; founder, pres. Becker Cons. Corp., 1990—; founder, chmn. bd. dirs. Healthcare Comm. Mgmt. Corp., 1990-93; med. dir. Quad river Found. Med. Care, 1976-84; pres. Am. Assn. Profl. Stds. Rev. Orgns., 1980-82; exec. v.p. Joint Coll. Allergy and Immunology, 1978-86; mem. adv. coun. Nat. Inst. Environ. Health Scis., 1984-88; bd. dirs. Impac Corp., Am. Psych Sys.; vice chmn, bd. dirs. Madison Info. Technologies, Inc.; chmn. Utilization Rev. Accreditation Commn., 1991-94, bd. dirs., 1994-96. Author articles in field. Pres. bd. edn. Joliet Twp. H.S. Dist. 204, 1969-70, 75-76; mem. bus. adv. com. U. Ill. Sch. Bus., Chgo., 1987—. Recipient Clemens von Pirquet award Georgetown U. Internat. Interdisciplinary Ctr. Immunology, 1978; named Entrepreneur of Yr. Arthur Young/Venture Mag., 1988. Fellow ACP, Am. Acad. Allergy, Am. Coll. Allergists (pres. 1987), Am. Coll. Chest Physicians; mem. Ill. Soc. Internal Medicine (pres. 1984-86), Asthma and Allergy Assn. Am. (bd. dirs. 1987—), Asthma and Allergy Found. Am. (bd. dirs. 1990-94), Am. Managed Care and Rev. Assn. (bd. dirs. 1989-95), Am. Assn. Preferred Providers Assn. (bd. dirs. 1989—), Utilization Rev. Accreditation Commn. (chair 1991-94, bd. dirs. 1991-96), Am. Assn. Preferred Provider Orgns. (bd. dirs. 1988-93), Am. Psychiat. Sys. (bd. dirs. 1994—), Alpha Omega Alpha, Alpha Sigma Nu. Office: 1S 045 Spring Rd Oakbrook Terrace IL 60181

BECKER, ROGER VERN, information science educator; b. Omaha, Apr. 12, 1947; s. LaVern Herman and Doris Bessie (Smith) B.; m. D'Lea Brauner; 1 child, Lindsey Vern. Student, U. Nebr., 1965-67, JD, 1970; LLM, U. Wash., 1971; Specialist in Libr./Info. Svcs., Ind. U., 1981. Dir. info. svcs. U.

Va. Sch. Law, Charlottesville, 1971-73; dir. legal rsch. U. N.D. Sch. Law, Grand Forks, 1973-80; dir. tech. U. Ark. Sch. Law, Fayetteville, 1981-83; planner, systems strategist, dir. tech. U. Puget Sound, Tacoma, Wash., 1983-94; dir. info. tech. Sch. Law Seattle U., 1994-97; chief info. officer, endowed prof., dean libr. info. svc. Centenary Coll. La., 1996—; bus. and mktg. advisor P.S. The Last Word in Personal Style, Mercer Island, Wash., 1984—. Prodr. various videos; program designer various computer programs; author articles in field. Mem. Govs. Commn. on Libraries, N.D., 1974-76. Mem. Order of Coif, Beta Phi Mu. Avocations: Christian radio, pastoral writing. Office: Centenary College PO Box 4118 2911 Centenary Blvd Shreveport LA 71104-3396

BECKER, SEYMOUR, hazardous materials and wastes specialist; b. Bronx, N.Y., Feb. 14, 1924; m. Ruth Schmitt, Aug. 30, 1958. MS, U. Wis., 1949; PhD, Pacific Western U., 1981. Nationally cert. hazardous materials mgr. and hazardous control mgr. Radiation control insp. Suffolk County Dept. Health Svcs., Hauppauge, N.Y., 1960-81; tech. cons., 1981-83; hazardous materials and wastes cons. Environ. Svcs., Portland, Maine, 1983-85, Mercy Hosp., Portland, 1985—; del. to China, People to People, Spokane, Wash., 1987, del. to Russia and Ukraine, 1992; advisor and cons. State of Maine Hosp. Assn., Augusta, 1988-90, Low Level Radioactive Wastes Authority, Augusta, 1989-93, Dept. Environ. Protection, Augusta, 1989-93. Contbr. articles to profl. jours. Cons. Emergency Mgmt. Agy., Windham, Maine, 1983—, Local Emergency Planning Com., Windham, 1989—, chair, Cumberland, Maine, 1996—; rep. State Emergency Response Commn., Maine, 1998—. Mem. APHA, Acad. Hazardous Materials Mgmt., Health Physics Soc., N.Y. Acad. Scis., Maine Pub. Health Assn. Achievements include development of N.Y. State radiation code; initiation of radiation control program in Suffolk County, N.Y. Home: 169 High St Apt 312 Portland ME 04101-2852 Office: Mercy Hosp 144 State St Portland ME 04101-3795

BECKER-HEIDMANN, PETER M., physicist, researcher; b. Mülheim, Germany, Dec. 30, 1953; s. Karl P. and Katharina B. (Zimmermann) Becker; m. Daniela I. Heidmann; children: Pascal, Frédéric. Diploma in physics, U. Hamburg, Germany, 1981, Dr.rer.nat. in soil sci., 1989. Rsch. scientist Inst. Soil Science U. Hamburg, 1981-84, head isotope dating lab., 1984—. Editor jour. Radiocarbon, 1996. Mem. Internat. Soil Sci. Soc. Office: Inst Soil Sci, Allende-Platz 2, 20146 Hamburg Germany

BECKERMAN, MILTON BERNARD, retired media broker; b. Bronx, N.Y., Sept. 3, 1917; s. Harris and Rachel (Barnett) B.; m. Bernice Smith, Aug. 29, 1937; children: Jay Harry, Dorothy Ann, Dana Charles (dec.), Susan Joyce. Student, NYU, 1935-37. Publicity, pub. rels. and advt. staff Lewis A. Jacobs, Buffalo, 1937-39; salesman Bennett Bros., Waycross, Ga., 1939-40; editor Lyons (Ga.) Progress, 1940-41; assoc. editor Swainsboro (Ga.) Forest-Blade, 1940-41, editor/pub., 1946-49; editor/pub. Claxton (Ga.) Enterprise, 1949-55, Natchitoches (La.) Enterprise, 1955-59; bus./fin. editor, columnist St. Petersburg (Fla.) Times, 1959-63; asst. to pres. Greenbaum & Assocs., St. Petersburg, 1963-68; v.p. EBS Tax Svc., St. Petersburg, 1968-70; co-owner Beckerman Assocs., Inc., Madeira Beach, Fla., 1970-96; assoc. Lindsey-Beckerman Media Cons., Inc., 1996—; pres. A Plus Wheelchair Transport, Inc., 1996—; ret. Corres./stringer 35 trade jours., 1959-69; contbr. articles to profl. jours.; contbg. author: The Last Linotype, 1985. Vice pres. bd. dirs. Fla. Philharmonic Soc., St. Petersburg, 1960-62; bd. dirs. Am. Cancer Soc., Claxton, 1953-55; chmn. Citizens Adv. Com. Elimination Slums/Blight, St. Petersburg, 1961-63; chmn. bd. trustees Gulf Beaches Pub. Libr., Madeira Beach, 1966-67; publicity chmn. Pinellas County Dem. Party, St. Petersburg, 1965; active boy Scouts Am. With U.S. Army, 1945-46. Named Hon. Lifetime mem. Free Cmty. Papers Fla., 1992, Disting. Journalism Alumnus, DeWitt Clinton H.S., 1997; recipient Ben Hammack Meml. Svc. award Ind. Free Pub.'s Assn., 1996. Mem. Soc. Profl. Journalists (chpt. pres. 1960-62), Fla. Advt. Pubs. Assn. (life), Southeastern Advt. Pubs. Assn. (Herb Campbell award 1992), Ind. Free Papers of Am., Assn. Free Cmty. Papers, Fla. Press Assn., Ga. Press Assn. (W. Trox Bankston Trophy 1947, Theron S. Shope Trophy 1947, Sam W. Wilkes Trophy 1952-53), Assn. of Free Newspapers (London), Syndicat National des Editeurs de Periodiques Gratuits (Paris). Avocation: writing. Home: 14001 Miramar Ave Madeira Beach FL 33708-2214

BECKERS, ALBERT MARIE, endocrinologist; b. Verviers, Liege, Belgium, Mar. 26, 1956; s. Albert A. and Claire (Chapelier) B.; m. Martine L. Rixhon, Oct. 5, 1985; children: Charlotte, Natacha, Pablo. MD, U. Louvain, Belgium, 1980; specialist internal medicine, U. Liege, 1985, PhD, 1986, specialist nuclear medicine, 1987. Asst., resident, clinic chief U. Liege, Belgium, 1980-93; asst. prof. U. Liege, 1993—, prof. agrégé, 1997—, assoc. head endocrinology svc., 1999. Contbr. articles to profl. jours. Mem. Belgian Pituitary Study Group (pres. 1987—), Endocrine Soc., Genem (v.p. 1993—), Belgian Endocrine Soc. (pres. 1999). Avocations: history, music, travel, nature. Office: Univ Liege, CHU-B35 Dept Endocrinology, 4000 Liege Belgium

BECKETT, HENRY DALE, consultant, psychiatrist; b. Bournemouth, Eng., Sept. 28, 1920; s. Lauderdale Carl Douglas and Ethel Mary (Stanger) B.; m. Lyn Hudd, June 30, 1943; children: Ann Carisso Josephine, John Lyndale, Jane, Elizabeth Julie. MRCS, LRCP, St. Mary's Hosp., London, 1946; diploma in psychiat. medicine, Margannwg Hosp., 1955, MRC Psych., 1971. House physician Brentwood Mental Hosp., Essex, 1947; registrar Morgannwg Hosp., Glamorganshire, 1948-55; sr. house med. officer Cane Hill Hosp., Surrey, 1955-63, cons. psychiatrist, 1963-81; hon. cons. psychiatrist London borough of Bromley, Eng., 1981-86; Mem. med. working group laying down guidelines for clin. practice treating narcotic addicts Dept. Health and Social Security, Gt. Britain, 1984; chmn. working party on rehab. of opiate abusers King's Fund Centre, London, 1969, working party on relationships between police and drug workers, 1972-73. Pub., editor People Line, 1984; contbr. articles to profl. jours. Mem. Assn. Prevention Addiction Gt. Britain (chmn. 1972-73, 85-89), Soc. Study Addiction, Brit. Soc. Med. and Dental Hypnosis, Soc. Study Normal Psychology, Sci. and Med. Network, Brit. Med. Assn. Avocation: walking. Address: 18 Ockendon Rd, Islington, London N1 3NP, England

BECKETT, MARTYN GERVASE, architect, artist; b. Yorkshire, England, Nov. 6, 1918; s. William Gervase and Marjorie Blanche (Greville) B.; m. Priscilla Leonie Brett, May 30, 1921; children: Lucy Caroline, Richard Gervase, Jeremy Rupert. BA, Cambridge U., 1939. Lic. Architect. Pvt. practice architecture, pvt. houses and scheduled bldgs. London, 1952—; architect Kings Coll. Cambridge U., 1961-91; cons. Gordonstoun (Scotland) Sch., 1957-61, Savoy Hotel Group, London 1980—, Temple Bar Trust, 1982—, Charterhouse Sch., 1983—, Eton (Eng.) Coll., 1986-91. One-man shows Royal Acad., Clarges Gallery, 1980, 83, Soan Gallery, 1986, 88, 89-97, Grape Lane Gallery, York, 1988; represented in permanent collections Sudbury Lake House, Derbyshire, 1966, Bruern Abbey, Oxfordshir, 1972, Hunton Ct., Kent., 1979, Mortham Tower, Durham, 1972. Chmn. bd. trustees Wallace Collection, London, 1972-93; trustee Brit. Mus., London, 1978-88; chmn. Nat. Trust, Yorkshire Region, 1980-85; mem. mgmt. council Chatsworth House Trust, Derbyshire, Eng., 1981—. Served to capt. Brit. Army, 1939-46, ETO. Decorated Mil. Cross. Fellow Royal Soc. Arts; mem. Royal Inst. Brit. Architects. Club: Brooks (London). Avocations: piano, painting. Home and Office: 3 St Albans Grove, London W8 5PN, England

BECKETT, ROY GEORGE, solicitor; b. Hull, Eng., Dec. 12, 1958; s. Harold and Ivy (Peck) B.; m. Suzanne Firth, May 26, 1984; children: James, Olivia. LLB with honors, Manchester (Eng.) U., 1980. Lic. solicitor. Trainee solicitor Graham & Rosen, Hull, Eng., 1981-83, asst. solicitor, 1983-84; asst. solicitor Bullivant & Co., Liverpool, Eng., 1984-85, Chaffe Street, Manchester, 1985-87; assoc. Dibb Lupton Alsop (formerly Alsop Wilkinson), Manchester, 1987-89, ptnr., 1989—, head comml. property, 1992-99, regional mng. ptnr., 1998—. Mem. Law Soc. Avocations: skiing, squash, gardening, reading, family. Office: Dibb Lupton Alsop, 101 Barbirolli Sq, Manchester M2 3DL, England

BECKETT, THEODORE CORNWALL, lawyer; b. Heidelberg, Fed. Republic Germany, Nov. 21, 1952; (parents Am. Citizens); s. Theodore Charles and Daysie Margaret (Cornwall) B.; m. Patricia Anne McKelvy, June 18, 1983; children: Anna Kathleen, Kerry Christine, Cooper Charles. BA, U. Mo., 1975, JD, 1978. Bar: Mo. 1978, U.S. Dist. Ct. (we. dist.) Mo. 1978. Ptnr. Beckett & Hensley L.C., Kansas City, Mo., 1994—. Bd. dirs. Kans. Spl. Olympics, 1979-84, legal advisor, 1984—, Kans. City Metro Spl. Olympics, 1993—. Mem. ABA, Mo. Bar Assn., Kansas City Bar Assn., Mo. Assn. Trial Attys., Assn. Trial Lawyers Am., Kansas City Club, Carriage Club, Beta Theta Pi. Democrat. Presbyterian. Office: Beckett & Hensley LC PO Box 13185 610 Commerce Tower Kansas City MO 64199

BECKETT, WILLIAM ALAN, plastics company executive, air safety campaigner; b. Sheffield, Eng., Jan. 5, 1946; s. William Alexander and Doris (Whitham) B.; m. Linda Sanders, Sept. 30, 1965; children: Marcus, Sarah (dec.), Richard, Clare. CEO William Beckett Plastics, Sheffield, 1972—, Leeds Display Ltd., Sheffield, 1992—; pres. William Beckett Plastics, Inc., Chgo., 1994—. Co-chmn. SCISAFE (Survivors Campaign to Improve Safety in Airline Flight Equipment), Eng., 1988—; chmn. Sheffield Cricket League, 1995, Yorkshire Amateur Cricket Alliance, 2000. Avocations: golf, theatre, dining, wine. Home: 274 Ecclesall Rd South, Sheffield S11 9PS, England Office: Wm Beckett Plastics Ltd, Tinsley Indsl Pk Shepcote W, Sheffield S9 1TH, England

BECKFORD, JAMES ARTHUR, sociologist, educator; b. Enfield, Middlesex, Eng., Dec. 1, 1942; s. John Henry and Elizabeth Alice (Gillman) B.; m. Julia Carolyn Hanson, Sept. 25, 1965; children: Louisa, Charlotte, Martin. BA in French, U. Reading, U.K., 1965, PhD, 1972, DLitt, 1985. Lectr. in sociology U. Reading, U.K., 1967-73, U. Durham, 1973-87; prof. sociology Loyola U. of Chgo., 1987-89, U. Warwick, Coventry, Eng., 1989—. Author: (books) The Trumpet of Prophecy, 1975, Cult Controversies, 1985, Religion and Advanced Industrial Society, 1989, (with S. Gilliat) Religion in Prison, 1999; editor: (book) New Religious Movements and Rapid Social Change, 1986. Gov. INFORM, London, 1992—. Rsch. grantee Social Sci. Rsch. Coun., 1978-80, Unesco, 1985-86, Leverhulme Trust, 1994-96. Mem. Assn. for Sociology of Religion (pres. 1988-89), Internat. Sociol. Assn. (v.p. 1994-98), Am. Sociol. Assn., Soc. for the Internat. Soc. Religion (pres. 1999—). Avocations: jogging, clarinet playing, steam locomotives. Home: 4 Dunvegan Close, Kenilworth CV8 2PH, England Office: U Warwick, Coventry CV4 7AL, England

BECK-FRIEDMAN, TOVA, artist; b. Tel-Aviv, Feb. 21, 1942; came to U.S., 1971; BA, Purdue U., 1974; MFA, Goddard Coll., 1976; postgrad., Tama U. Art, Tokyo, 1982-84. participant Boleslawiec (Poland) Internat. Symposium, 1996, Clay/Sculpt Gulgong Symposium, Australia, 1995, Environ. Sculpture Symposium, MuJu, Korea, 1994; artist in residence Grand Cayon U., Phoenix, 1992, Visual Arts Sch., Be'er Sheva, Israel, 1990, N.J. Mus. Archaeology, Drew U., 1988; vis. artist in sculpture, Skidmore Coll., Saratoga Springs, N.Y., 1990. Solo exhbns. include Herzliya Mus., Israel (catalogue), 1990, Visual Arts Sch. Gallery, Be'er Sheva, 1990, Newark Mus. (catalogue), 1991, Bill Bace Gallery, N.Y.C., 1991, 93, Quietude Gallery, East Brunswick, N.J., 1992, Schering-Plough Gallery, Madison, N.J., 1992, Lisa Parker Gallery, N.Y.C., 1996, N.J. State Mus. (catalogue), Trenton, 1996, Bergen Mus. Art, Paramus, N.J., 1997, Visual Arts Gallery, Coll. Morris, Randolph, N.J., 1998, Mitchell Mus., Mt. Vernon, Ill., 1998, Ben Shahn Gallery, William Paterson Coll., Wayne N.J., 1999, others; group exhbns. include Jersey City (N.J.) Mus., 1996, 97, Artemisia Gallery, Chgo., 1996, Quietude Gallery, 1996, Boleslawiec Culture Ctr., 1996, Manmouth (N.J.) Mus., 1996, Cesky Krumlov Culture Found., Czech Republic, 1997, Galeria Sztuki, Poland, 1997, Galeria de Arte Florida, Caracas, Venezuela, 1997, N.J. State Mus., 1999, Leigh Yawkey Woodson Art Mus., Wis., 2000, others; pub. sculpture installations and commns. include Zaklady Ceramiczne, Boleslawiec, William Paterson Coll., Riker Hill Art Park, Wayne, N.J., Newark Mus. Sculpture Garden, Schering-Plough Corp., Nat. Inst. Ossolinski's, Warsaw, Gan-Remez Park, Be'er Sheva, Be'er Sheva City Hall, Beit Ha'ribua Hakachol, Rosh Ha'ain, Israel, others; represented in pub. collections Ariz. State U. Mus., Tempe, Mus. Modern Art Libr., N.Y.C., Fukuoka Town Hall, Gifu-Ken, Japan, others; work featured in numerous newspaper and mag. articles and mus. catalogues; work included in 4 books. E-mail: tbfstudio@earthlink.net.

BECKHAM, DAVID, professional soccer player; b. Leytonstone, London, May 2, 1975. Profl. soccer mem. Manchester (Eng.) United. Recipient Winner medal Youth Cup team, 1992, Young Player of Yr. award PFA. Office: Manchester United Football, Sir Matt Busby Way, Manchester M16 0RA, England*

BECKHAM, WALTER HULL, JR., lawyer, educator; b. Albany, Ga., Apr. 18, 1920; m. Ethel Koger, Mar. 13, 1943; children: Barbara, Walter III, James K. AB, Emory U., 1941; LLB cum laude, Harvard U., 1948. Bar: Fla. 1949, U.S. Supreme Ct. 1956, D.C. 1978. Assoc. prof. law U. Miami, Fla., 1948-49; ptnr. Nichols, Gaither, Beckham et al, 1950-67; of counsel Podhurst, Orseck, Josefsberg, Eaton, Meadow, Olin & Perwin P.A., Miami, 1967—; prof. law U. Miami, 1967-82, prof. emeritus, 1982—. Editor Harvard Law Rev. Pres. Greater Miami YMCA, 1963-68, Crippled Children's Soc. Dade County, 1968-69; mem. Dade County Mental Health Bd., 1971-73; chmn. bd. trustees YMCA Blue Ridge Assembly, 1977-79; trustee Nat. Jud. Coll., 1990-96, trustee, chmn., 1995-96, chmn. emeritus, 1996—. With USNR, 1941-46; capt. USNR, ret. Recipient The Perry Nichols award, Acad. Fla. Trial Lawyers, 1984. Mem. ABA (spl. com. on tort liability system 1979-84, spl. commn. on assn. governance 1983-84, chmn. tort and ins. practice sect. 1974-75, Ho. of Dels. 1979-85, 87-95, sec.-elect 1986-87, sec. 1987-90), Am. Bar Found., Am. Coll. Trial Lawyers, Am. Law Inst., Assn. Trial Lawyers Am. (chmn. aviation sect. 1966-68), Fla. Bar Assn. (past mem. bd. of govs. jr. bar sect.), Dade County Bar Assn. (pres. jr. bar sect. 1952-53, exec. com. 1953-54), Internat. Acad. Trial Lawyers (pres. 1973), Internat. Acad. Law and Sci., Law Sci. Inst., Maritime Law Assn. U.S., Nat. Inst. Trial Adv. (trustee 1976-86, chmn. 1983-85), Inner Circle of Advs., Med. Inst. for Attys. (dir. 1968-83), Nat. Bd. Trial Adv. (founding mem.), Phi Beta Kappa, Omicron Delta Kappa, Phi Alpha Delta, Chi Phi, Kiwanis. Office: Podhurst Orseck Josefsberg Eaton Meadow Olin Perwin City Nat Bank Bldg 25 W Flagler St Ste 800 Miami FL 33130-1720

BECKHAUS, RUEDIGER W.H., chemist, educator; b. Boizenburg, Germany, Feb. 16, 1955; s. Friedrich Wilhelm and Melitta (Bretzmann) B.; m. Silvia Klein, Sept. 17, 1983; children: Katkarina, Julia. Diploma, Merseburg, Germany, 1980; PhD, 1984, Dr.sc.nat, 1989, dr.rer.nat. habilitation, 1991. Asst. Merseburg (Germany) U., 1980-84, sr. asst., 1984-91; rsch. fellow Munich Tech. U., 1991; prof. Aachen U., Germany, 1991-92, 1991-97, prof. chemistry, 1997-98; prof. and chair dept. inorganic chemistry Oldenburg (Germany) U., 1998—. Author: Metallocenes, 1998, Organometallics in Organic Synthesis, 1993; contbr. articles to profl. jours. Recipient Humboldt grant 1991, 92, Heisenberg grant, 1992, 97, Carl Duisberg award, 1998, Karl Ziegler award 1998. E-mail: ruediger.beckhaus@uni-oldenburg.de. Home: Luentjenweg 48, D 26131 Oldenburg Germany Office: Oldenburg U, D 26111 Oldenburg Germany

BECKMAN, BJORN INGEMAR, food products executive; b. Stromstad, Sweden, Apr. 19, 1942; s. Evert and Irene Ruth (Olsson) B.; m. Gunila Elisabeth Carlson, 1969; children: Minna, Jenny, Karl. Sec. Swedish West Coast Fishermen's Assn., 1959-76; editor Fishermen's Jour. Yrkesfiskaren, 1976-86; gen. sec., chief editor Swedish Fishermen's Fedn., 1986—; chmn. Swedish Fishermen's Unemployment Fund, 1994—; sec. Swedish West Coast Fishermen's Age Pension Fund, 1972—. Contbr. articles to profl. jours. and newspapers. Mem. Swedish Pubs. Club. Avocations: boating, fishing, horses. Home: Gorasvagen 15, S-443 91 Lerum Sweden Office: Sw Fish Fedn Yrkesfiskaren, Amerikaskjulet uppg G, S-414 63 Göteborg Sweden

BECKMAN, JAMES WALLACE BIM, economist, marketing executive, educator; b. Mpls., May 2, 1936; s. Wallace Gerald and Mary Louise (Frissell) B. BA, Princeton U., 1958; PhD, U. Calif., 1973. Ordained elder Presbyterian Ch. Pvt. practice Berkeley, Calif., 1962-67; cons. Calif. State Assembly, Sacramento, 1967-68; pvt. practice Laguna Beach, Calif., 1969-77; cons. Calif. State Gov.'s Office, Sacramento, 1977-80; pvt. practice real estate cons. L.A., 1980-83; v.p. mktg. Gold-Well Investments, Inc., L.A., 1982-83; pres. Beckman Analytics Internat., econ. cons. to bus. and govt., L.A. and Lake Arrowhead, Calif., 1983—, East European/Middle East Bus. and Govt., 1992—; adj. prof. Calif. State U. Sch. Bus., San Bernardino, 1989—, U. Redlands, 1992—, U. Calif., 1998—; cons. Eastern European environ. issues. Contbr. articles to profl. jours. Maj. USMC, 1958-67. NIMH fellow, 1971-72. Fellow Soc. Applied Anthropology; mem. Am. Econs. Assn., Am. Statis. Assn., Am. Mktg. Assn. (officer, Nat. Assn. Bus. Economists (officer). Democrat. Office: Beckman Analytics Internat PO Box 1753 Lake Arrowhead CA 92352-1753

BECKMAN, MICHAEL, lawyer; b. N.Y.C., Oct. 8, 1945; s. Albert Beckman and Cecille Bronson; m. Susan Liebowitz, June 26, 1970 (separated Dec. 1987); children: Andrew D., Jason D. Bar: N.Y. 1969, U.S. Dist. Ct. (so. dist.) N.Y. 1972. Atty. Gordon Brady Keller & Ballen, N.Y.C., 1969-71; ptnr. Wolkowitz & Beckman, N.Y.C., 1971-74; sr. ptnr. Bell Kalnick Beckman Klee & Green, N.Y.C., 1974-88; sole practice N.Y.C., 1988-92; sr. ptnr. Beckman & Millman PC, N.Y.C., 1992-96, Beckman Millman & Sanders LLP, N.Y.C., 1996—; adj. prof. law NYU, 1981-93. Dir. N.Y. Jr. Tennis League, N.Y.C., 1986-95, Sports & Arts in Schs. Found. Mem. West Side Tennis Club. Avocations: tennis, skiing. Home: 437 W 24th St New York NY 10011-1253 Office: Beckman Millman & Sanders LLP 116 John St Rm 1313 New York NY 10038-3303

BECKMANN, JOHN, architect, designer, writer; b. Mt. Kisco, N.Y., Sept. 3, 1960; s. Norman Peter and Margret Rose (Gorog) B.; m. divorced; 1 child, Kyra. BFA in Environ. Design, Parsons Sch. of Design, 1982. Established Axis Mundi, 1987; design cons. Met. Mus. of Art, N.Y.C., 1991-92; adj. prof. architecture N.J. Inst. Tech., 1999. Designer: included in group exhibitions, The Am. Crafts Mus., N.Y., 1988, The Nat. Arts Club, N.Y., 1988, Via Salon, Paris, 1989, Museo Alchimia, Milan, Italy, 1990, Gallery 91, N.Y., 1991, Mcpl. Art. Soc., N.Y., 1993; individual projects: Randolph Duke boutique, N.Y.C., 1987-88, Collaboration w/Uvegi Assoc., Final Image, N.Y., 1992, Aerotik Furniture Collection, 1990, Barbara Kramer Showroom, 1991, chinaware for Swid-Powell, 1992, Magnum, N.Y.C., 1998, Parlay, N.Y.C.; author: International Interiors: Showrooms, 1993; editor: the Virtual Dimension: Architecture, Representation and Crash Culture, 1998. Grantee Graham Found. for Advanced Visual Studies in the Fine Arts, 1996. E-mail: jbeckmann@axismundi.com. Office: Axis Mundi 72 Seaman Ave New York NY 10034-2822

BECKMANN, SUZANNE C., business executive, researcher, educator; b. Goettingen, Germany, June 1, 1959; d. Hans-Helmut and Ursula Waechter. Diploma, U. Bonn, Germany, 1983; DSc, U Hohenheim, Stuttgart, Germany, 1993. Cons. Commn. of the European Cmtys., Brussels, 1983-85; rsch. asst. U. Hohenheim, Stuttgart, 1985-87, rsch. assoc., 1987-90; rsch. fellow The Aarhus (Denmark) Sch. Bus., 1990-92; assoc. prof. Odense (Denmark) U., 1992-97; rsch. prof. Copenhagen (Denmark) Bus. Sch., 1997—; mem. exec. com. European Mktg. Acad., Brussels, 1996—; bd. dirs. Dansk Varefakta Naevn, Copenhagen, 1998—. Author: Essen und Emotionen, 1993; mem. editl. bd. Jour. Consumer Policy, 1991—, Jour. Econ. Psychology, 1997—, Internat. Jour. Rsch. in Mktg., 1997—. Recipient Rsch. award Funen Found. for Bus. Rsch., 1994, Best Paper award Europeand Mktg. Acad., 1996, Highest Quality Rating ANBAR Electronic Intelligence, 1998. Mem. European Mktg. Acad. (pres. 2000-2002). Office: Copenhagen Bus Sch, Solbjerg Plads 3, 2000 Frederiksberg Denmark

BECKWITH, GEORGE E., computer company executive; b. Shirley, Mass., May 8, 1955; s. Edward Furniss Beckwith and Lois Messenger Wright; m. Adria Mary Quinones, Nov. 22, 1997; 1 child, Tobias Joseph Beckwith-Quinones. BA, Bates Coll., 1978; MS, Columbia U., 1985. Supr. Columbia U. Librs., N.Y.C., 1983-86; libr. rschr. AT&T, Morristown, N.J., 1986-89; libr. sys. mgr. AT&T, Bernadsville, N.J., 1989-92; product mgr. AT&T, Parsippany, N.J., 1992-96; product mgmt. dir. About.com, N.Y.C., 1996—. Patron Met. Opera, 1994—. Mem. Bates Coll. Alumni Assn. (sec. 1993—). Democrat. Avocations: musician, flute player, hiker. E-mail: chipwith@aol.com. Home: 200 Cabrini Blvd Apt 44 New York NY 10033-1119

BECKWITH, LARRY EDWARD, mechanical engineer; b. Pierre, S.D., Oct. 21, 1943; s. Charles Edward and Junebelle Ann (Robley) B.; m. AnhTuyet Thi Pham, Mar. 3, 1970. BSME, S.D. Sch. Mines Tech., Rapid City, 1966. Mil. engring. officer USACE, 1967-69; from mech. engr. to ptnr. Dunham Assocs., Bloomington, Minn., 1966, 70—; bd. dirs. Beckwith Hardware, Inc., Presho, S.D., 1977-92. State chmn. S.D. Coll. Reps., 1965-66; life mem. Rep. Nat. Com., 1994—; bd. govs. Walden Assn., 1994-96, pres., 1996. Capt. U.S. Army, 1967-69, Vietnam. Recipient bronze star U.S. Army, 1968, w/oak leaf cluster, 1969. Mem. VFW (life), Am. Legion, Decathlon Club, Oxford Club. Avocations: chess, golf. Office: Dunham Assocs Inc 8200 Normandale Blvd Ste 500 Bloomington MN 55437-1075

BECOFSKY, ARTHUR LUKE, arts administrator, writer; b. N.Y.C., Sept. 17, 1950; s. Arthur and Frances (Oliva) B. BA in Polit. Sci., Duke U., 1972; MA in Polit. Sci., Columbia U., 1974. Adminstr. Cunningham Dance Found., N.Y.C., 1974-79, exec. dir., 1980-94; pres. Art Plus Mgmt. Svcs., 1994—; world booking agt. Merce Cunningham Dance Co., N.Y.C., 1976-94; cons. Found. for Ext. and Devel. of Am. Profl. Theatre, N.Y.C., 1985, Found. for Dance Promotion, 1995—, Ringside/Elizabeth Streb, 1995—, The Armitage Found., 1995, Cross Performance, Inc., 1995-98, Stephen Petronio Dance Co., 1995—, Gotham Dance, Inc., 1995, ODC/San Francisco, 1995—, Twyla Tharp, 1996, David Dorfman Dance, 1996—, Ballet Hispanico, 1996—, David Rousseve/Reality, 1996—, Susan Marshall Dance Co., 1996—, Rena Shagan Assocs., 1996—, Margaret Jenkins Dance Co., 1997—, Bill Young and Dancers, 1997—, Bridgehampton Chamber Music Assocs., 1997, Ananda Shankar Dance Co., Calcutta, 1997—, Nest/Tokyo, 1997—, Garth Fagan Dance, 1998—, Moving Education, 1998—, Richard Alston Dance Co., London, 1998-2000, Grupo Corpo/Brazil, 1998—, Rosy Co./Tokyo, 1998—, Siobhan Davies Dance Co., London, 1998-99, Lines Contemporary Ballet, 1998-2000, Joe Goode Performance Group, 1999—, Pentacle Help Desk, 1999—, Art Plus Care to Dance, 1999—, Expressions Dance Co., Brisbane, 1999—, Uno Man, Tokyo, 1999—, Kazco Takemoto, Tokyo, 1999—, Kenichi Tanno & Numbering Machine, Tokyo, 1999—, Jose Limon Dance Co., 1999—, Daniel Yeung, Hong Kong, 1999—; mem. dance panel NEA, 1983-94. Guitarist with Rhys Chatham & The Din, 1981; composer: Secretarial Suite, 1980, Track, 1983, Get Real, Cassandra, 1985, Space Into Action, 1986; author: The Road Show Abroad, 1985, On Commissioning New Art, 1989, MMerce, 1991, Lar Lubovitch: The Company We Keep, 1999. Bd. dirs. Dancing for Life, 1987, U.S. Performing Arts subcom. CULCON for U.S.-Japan cultural exch., 1989-93. Mem. Dance/U.S.A. (bd. dirs. 1983-88, 91-98, treas. 1983-86, vice chair 1993-96), World Dance Alliance (bd. dirs. 1993-97), Am. Arts Alliance (bd. dirs. 1983-87). Democrat. Avocation: photography. E-mail: ckdance@aol.com. Home: 324 E 9th St Apt 8 New York NY 10003-7962 Office: Stuyvesant Station PO Box 759 New York NY 10009-0759

BÉCOUARN, YVES HENRI, oncologist, researcher; b. Alger, Algeria, Mar. 1, 1954; s. Fernand and Andrée Jacqueline (Besse) B.; m. Marie Christine Lalague, July 12, 1986 (div. Feb. 1999); children: Romain, Antoine. Med. studies, U. Bordeaux (France), 1972-78; MD, 1984. Cert. Digestive Diseases Bd. Cert., Med. Oncology Bd. Cert., Gastrointestinal Tract Oncology Cert. Intern U. Hosp. Bordeaux, 1975-78, residency, 1978-84; chef de clinique des univs., hosp. asst. Bordeaux, 1984-88; med. asst. GI tract oncology dept. French Cancer Ctrs., Bordeaux, 1988-93; splst., chief GI tranct oncology dept. Inst. Bergonie Cancer Ctr., Bordeaux, 1993—; gen. sec. Digestive Group French Cancer Ctrs., 1997—, pres., 2000—; pres. Aquitaine Gastro Oncology Group, 1997; co-organizer Internat. Conf. GI Malignancies, 1994—. Contbr. more than 300 articles to med. jours. Mem. Am. Soc. Clin. Oncology, European Soc. Med. Oncology, European Organizaion Rsch. and Treatment of Cancer, others. Roman Catholic. Avocations: squash, motor racing, single seater cars, go-kart racing. Office: Inst Bergonie Cancer Ctr, 180 Rue de Saint-Genès, 33076 Boredeaux CEDEX, France

BECVAROVA, VĚRA, agricultural engineer, economist; b. Jaroměř, Czechoslovakia, June 11, 1944; d. Rubeš František and Rubešová Věra Grimová; m. Jaroslav Bečvář, Aug. 26, 1967; children: Věra, Markéta. Agrl. Engr., U. Agr., Prague, Czechoslovakia, 1968; PhD, Sch. Econs., Prague, Czechoslovakia, 1983; Ed Habilitation, U. Brno, 1995. Economist State Farm, Bezno, Czechoslovakia, 1967-71, Trade with Fruits and Vegetables, Prague, 1971-74; rschr. Rsch. Inst. Agrl. Econs., Prague, 1974-95, dir., 1989-92; bank expert Agrobank, Prague, 1995-98; prof. Mendel's Agr. U., Brno, 1995—; bank expert GE Capital Bank, 1998—; rschr. Rsch. Inst. Agrl. Econs., Prague, 1974-82, scientist, chief dept., 1982-89, dir. Inst., 1989-92; bd. cons. U. Agr., Prague, 1989-93; tchr. U. Agr., Prague, 1982-94, 95—,

Brno, 1984—. Author: Market and Its Control in Agriculture, 1991, Financial Market and Agriculture, 1993. Grantee Principles of Agr. Policy CSFR, Ministry Economy, 1991, Capital Profitability in Agr., Agri-food sector, 1993, Subsidy in Agr., 1995, MZLU Brno, 1996, 97, 98. Mem. Czech Acad. Agr. Avocations: music, history, arts. E-mail: vera.becvarova@ge-capital.com. FAX: 420 2 2444 6129. Home: Seifertova 27, 13000 Prague Czech Republic

BÉDA, GYULA, mechanical engineer, educator; b. Koncháza, Ung, Czechoslovakia, May 21, 1931; s. Gyula and Margit (Kelemen) B.; m. Rózsa Pálvögyi, July 11, 1957; 1 child, Péter. MSc, Tech. U., Miskolc, Hungary, 1953, Dr.techn., 1961; PhD, Hungarian Acad. Scis., Budapest, 1961, DSc, 1983. Asst. prof. Tech. U., Miskolc, 1956-61, assoc. prof., 1961-68; prof. Tech. U., Budapest, 1968—, head dept. tech. mechanics, 1970-95, dean mech. engring. faculty, 1972-81, head rsch. group for continuum mechanics, 1996-99, head sch. math. depts., 1986-95; vice dean mech. engring. faculty Tech. U. Miskolc, 1960-64, vice rector, 1964-67; mem. com. on sci. promotion of Faculty of Mech. Engring. of Tech. U. Budapest, 1994-00. Author: Continuum Mechanics, 1986, Elasticity, 1987 (Pubrs. award 1987), Kinematcs and Dynamics, 1989, 99, Continuum Mechanics, 1995 (pub.'s award 1999). Mem. Internat. Congress on Fracture (coun.), Hungarian Acad. Scis. (com. on theoretical and applied mechanics 1967—, com. on sci. promotion 1963-84). Home: Bognár St 4, H-1021 Budapest Hungary Office: Technical Univ of Budapest, Müegyetem rkp 5-7, H-1521 Budapest Hungary

BÉDARIDA, FRANÇOIS, historian; b. Lyons, Rhône, France, Mar. 14, 1926; s. Henri Bedarida and Germaine Vanderpol; m. Renée Mély, Aug. 25, 1949; children: Claire, Marc, Catherine. Grad., U. Paris, Ecole Normale Supérieure, Paris; MA (hon.), U. Oxford, England, 1967. Asst. prof. U. Paris, 1960-66; dir. Maison Française, Oxford, 1966-70; vis. fellow All Souls Coll., Oxford, 1971; prof. Institut d'Etudes Politiques, Paris, 1972-78; dir. Inst. d'Histoire du Temps Présent, Paris, 1978-90; dir. rsch. Ctr. Nat. Recherche Sci., 1979—; sec. gen. Com. Internat. Scis. Hist., 1990—. Author: L'Ère Victorienne, 1974, La Société Anglaise, 1976, Stratégie Secrète de la Drôle de Guerre, 1979, Vichy et les Français, 1992, L'Histoire et le Métier d'Historien en France, 1995, Churchill, 1999. Decorated chevalier de la Légion d'Honneur, officier de l'Ordre Nat. du Mérite, comdr. Brit. Empire. Home: 13 Rue Jacob, 75006 Paris France

BEDDOW, RICHARD HAROLD, judge; b. Springfield, Mass., Jan. 3, 1932; s. Richard Harold and Elizabeth Christine (Geehern) B.; m. Trudy C. Howells, Jan. 14, 1967; children: Catherine Elizabeth Almand, Elissa Christine. BS, U. Mass., 1953; LLB, Boston Coll, 1959. Bar: Mass. 1960. Atty. ICC, Washington, 1959-69, mem. rev. bd., 1969-73, adminstrv. law judge, 1973-81; adminstrv. law judge NLRB, Washington, 1981—. With USN, 1953-55. Roman Catholic. Avocation: landscape gardening. Home: 2406 Rockwood Rd Accokeek MD 20607-9584 Office: NLRB 1099 14th St NW Washington DC 20570-0001

BEDERSKI, KRZYSZTOF, physicist; b. Toruń, Poland, May 15, 1947; s. Arkadiusz and Janina (Firych) B.; m. Ewa Siekiera, Aug. 5, 1972 (div.); 1 child, Łukasz; m. Maria Teresa Zacharzewska, Aug. 18, 1995. M of Physics, Mariae Curie-Sklodowska U., Lublin, Poland, 1971, D of Physics, 1978. Asst. Inst. Physics, Mariae Curie-Sklodowska U., 1971-72, asst. lectr., 1972-78, scientist, 1978—. Contbr. over 25 articles to profl. publs., including Internat. Jour. Mass Spectrometry, Can. Jour. Chemistry, others. Mem. Polish Acad. Scis. (plasma physics sect.), N.Y. Acad. Scis., Polish Phys. Soc. Avocations: photography, computers, sports, reading. E-mail: bederski@tytan.umcs.lublin.pl. Home: Paryska 3 m 81, 20-854 Lublin Poland Office: MC-Sklodowska U Inst Physic, pl M Curie-Sklodowska 1, 20-031 Lublin Poland

BEDFORD, BARBARA J., Olympic athlete; b. Hanover, N.H., Nov. 9, 1972. Recipient Gold medal 4 x 100-meter medley (team) Sydney Olympics, 2000, 100-meter backstroke U.S. nats., Mpls., 1999; 3d pl. 100-meter backstroke Pan Pacific Championships, 1999. Office: USA Swimming 1 Olympic Plz Colorado Springs CO 80909-5746*

BEDFORD, COLIN THOMAS, bio-organic chemistry educator; b. Southsea, Hampshire, Eng., Aug. 14, 1937; s. Charles Albert and Anne (Allway) B.; m. Joan Alicia Mackintosh, Sept. 7, 1963; children: Kara Lesley, Vanessa, Lindsay Paul. BSc, U. Manchester, Eng., 1958, MSc, 1960; PhD, U. Glasgow, 1963. Chartered chemist. ICI rsch. fellow U. Oxford, Eng., 1963-65; Bristol rsch. fellow U. Sussex, Eng., 1965-67; teaching postdoctoral fellow U. B.C., Vancouver, Can., 1967-69; scientist, sr. scientist, prin. scientist Shell Biosci. Rsch., Sittingbourne, Eng., 1970-83; sr. lectr. U. Westminster, London, 1984—; cons. Ministry of Def., Eng., 1978-82; cons. Shell EXPRO, Aberdeen, Scotland, 1990-93. Contbr. over 50 articles to chem. and biochem. jours. Fellow Royal Soc. Chemistry; mem. Biochem. Soc., Marylebone Cricket Club. Avocations: cricket, golf, music, dining out. Office: U Westminster Div Molec Bio, 115 New Cavendish St, London W1W 6UW, England

BEDFORD, RONALD DAVID, English educator; b. London, Apr. 4, 1940; arrived in Australia, 1991; s. John William and Lilian Gladys (Hubbard) B.; m. Linda Ann Hilton, Aug. 13, 1966 (div. 2000); children: Jonathan Bentley, Oliver Newton. MA, Cambridge (Eng.) U., 1966, PhD, 1970. Lectr. Shrewsbury (Eng.) Tech. Coll., 1962-63; supr. in English St. Catharine's Coll., Cambridge, Eng., 1963-66; lectr. in English lit. Exeter (Eng.) U., 1966-90; prof. U. New Eng., Armidale, Australia, 1991—; vis. prof. Justus Liebig U., Giessen, Germany, 1980; chief examiner Oxford and Cambridge Schs. Exam. Bd., Cambridge, 1985-91; cons. NSW Bd. Studies, Sydney, Australia, 1992-93. Author: The Defence of Truth: Herbert of Cherbury and the Seventeenth Century, 1979, Dialogues with Convention: Reading Renaissance Poetry, 1989; contbr. articles to profl. jours. Rsch. grantee Brit. Acad., 1978; recipient Large grant Australia Rsch. Coun., 1999—. Mem. Australian Univs. Lang. and Lit. Assn., Australia and New Zealand Shakespeare Assn. Avocations: ornithology, bushwalking. Office: Dept English, U New England, Armidale NSW 2351, Australia

BEDFORD, STEUART JOHN RUDOLF, conductor; b. London, July 31, 1939; s. L.H. and Lesley (Duff) Bedford; m. Norma Burrowes, 1969 (div. 1980); m. Celia Harding, 1980; 2 children. BA, Lancing Coll., Sussex, Eng.; F.R.C.O., Oxford U.; F.R.A.M., Royal Acad. Music. Operatic tng. as repetiteur, asst. conductor Glyndebourne Festival, 1965-67, English Opera Group (later known as English Music Theatre), Aldeburgh and London, Eng., 1967-73; co-artistic dir. English Music Theatre, 1976-80; artistic dir. English Sinfonia, 1981-90; artistic dir. then exec. artistic dir. Aldeburgh Festival, 1974-99. Freelance conductor, numerous performances with English Opera Group, Welsh Nat. Opera, Met. Opera, N.Y. Opera, Royal Danish Opera, Royal Opera House, Convent Garden, Santa Fe Opera, Teatro Colón, Buenos Aires, Brussels, Lyon, others; conductor BBC, Netherlands Radio, Belgian Radio; recordings include works by Britten, Shostakovich, Saxton. Recipient medal Worshipful Co. Musicians. Avocations: golfing, skiing. Office: care Harrison-Parrott Ltd, 12 Penzance Pl, London W11 4PA, England

BEDFORD, SYBILLE, writer; b. Berlin, Mar. 16, 1911; d. Maximilian von Schoenebeck and Elizabeth Bernhard; m. Walter Bedford, 1935. Literary journalist, 1930s. Author: A Visit to Don Otavio, 1953, A Legacy, 1956, The Best We Can Do, 1958, The Faces of Justice, 1961, A Favourite of the Gods, 1968, A Compass Error, 1968, Aldous Huxley: A Biography, vol. 1, 1973, vol. II, 1974, Jigsaw, 1989, As It Was, 1990. Recipient Order of Brit. Empire, Companion of Lit. Royal Soc. Lit. Fellow Royal Soc. Lit. Avocations: wine, food, reading, traveling. Office: care Lutyens & Rubinstein, 231 Westbourne Park Rd, London W11 1EB, England

BEDI, MONA, research scientist; b. Delhi, India, Dec. 18, 1965; d. Ved Prakash and Lalita Rani Bedi; m. Rakesh Mayor, Feb. 5, 1988; 2 children. B Medicine B Surgery, Lady Hardinge Med. Coll., Delhi, 1987; MD, Maulana Azad Med. Coll., Delhi, 1995. Intern Lady Hardinge Med. Coll., 1987-89; pvt. practice gen. medicine Delhi, 1989-92; sr. resident in physiology Maulana Azad Med. Coll., 1995-98, sr. rsch. assoc. in physiology, 1989—, tchr., rschr., 1992-98; cons. in field, Delhi, 1989-92. Contbr. articles to profl. jours. Worker Pulse Polio Immunization, Delhi, 1996-98; field worker, organizer Matri Suraksha Abhiyan, Delhi, 1997-98. Grantee CSIR, Delhi, 1998—. Mem. Delhi Med. Assn., Maulana Med. Coll. Old Student Assn. Avocations: writing poetry, reading, research, watching BBC, discovery. Office: Maulana Azad Med Coll, Bahadur Shah Zafar Marg, Delhi 110 002, India

BEDI, RAJAN, electronics designer; b. Magherafelt, No. Ireland, June 30, 1968; s. Harminder Lal and Sita Devi (Punn) B. BEng with honors, DIS, U. Ulster, No. Ireland, 1991; PhD, U. Edinburgh, Scotland, 1994. Design engr. Nirad Ltd., No. Ireland, 1989-90; postdoctoral rsch. fellow IRCM, Montreal, Que., Can., 1995; sr. design engr. Arm Ltd., Cambridge, Eng., 1996—; prin. cons. V.B. Sys., U.K., 1991—. Contbr. papers to profl. jours. Sec. Indian Cmty. and Cultural Assn. of Cambridge, 1999—, trustee, 1999—; advisor Cambridgeshire Standing Adv. Coun. on Religious Edn., 2000—. J.S. Scott scholar Coll. Tech., 1985, 86, Cowan House scholar U. Edinburgh, 1993; J.M. Lessells fellow The Royal Soc., 1994. Mem. IEEE, IEE. Avocations: sports, music, Indian culture, history, astronomy. Home: 62 Silverwood Close, Cambridge CB1 3HA, England Office: Arm Ltd, 110 Fulbourn Rd, Cambridge CB1 9NJ, England

BEDJAOUI, M. MOHAMMED, judge International Court of Justice; b. Sidi Bel Abbes, Sept. 21, 1929; s. Benali and Fatima El-Oukili); m. Leila Francis, Oct. 21, 1962; children: Amal, Assia. Doctorate in Law, Grenoble U., France; diploma, Polit. Studies Inst. Lawyer Appeal Ct., Grenoble; attache researches internat. law sect. Nat. Ctr. Sci. Rsch., Paris; jur. counsellor provisional govt. of Algeria; dir. Cabinet Pres. Nat. Constituent Assembly, Algiers, Algeria, 1962; gen. sec. govt. Cabinet Pres. Nat. Constituent Assembly, 1962-64; pres. dir. Nat. Rys. Soc. Algeria, 1964; dean Faculty Law, Algiers, 1964-65; min. of justice Govt. of Algeria, 1964-70; amb. to France, Algerian Embassy, Paris, 1970-79; amb. to UN N.Y.C., 1979-82; judge Internat. Ct. Justice, The Hague, The Netherlands, 1982—, pres., 1994-97, mem., 1997—; mem. Internat. Law Commn., UN, 1965-82. Author: International Civil Service, 1956. Fonction Publique internationale et influences nationales, 1958; La Revolution Algerienne et le Droit, 1961; Problèmes récents de Succession d'Etats, 1970; Non-alignement et droit international, 1976; Pour un nouvel ordre economique international, 1978; contbr. articles to profl. jours. Recipient decorations UAR, France, Morocco, Algeria, Mali. Mem. Assn. Acad. Internat. Law. Office: Internat Ct Justice, Peace Palace, Carnegieplein 2, 2517 KJ The Hague The Netherlands*

BEDNAR, JAROMIR, biochemist; b. Drnovice, Moravia, Czechoslovakia, July 10, 1928; arrived in Germany, 1969; s. Antonin and Marie (Kumrova) B.; m. Helena Jaroslava Tresnakova, Sept. 4, 1970; children: Rene, Barbara. Diploma in engring., Tech. U., Prague, Czechoslovakia, 1951; D in Natural Scis., Tech. U., Munich, 1974, diploma in engring., 1967. Cert. rschr. and biochemist. Rschr. Rsch. Inst. Brew & Malt, Prague, 1953-67, commerce affairs asst., 1968-69; rschr., tchr. Tech. U., Munich, 1970-93, emeritus, 1993—. Author: Brew and Malt Analytical Tables, 1967; co-author: Brew-Malt Analytics, 1966; contbr. articles to profl. jours.; patentee in field. Mem. N.Y. Acad. Scis. Avocations: theater, concert, sports. Home: Na Rokytce 1113/12, 180 00 Prague Czech Republic

BEDNAREK, FRANCIS JOHN, pediatrician and neonatologist; b. Wilkes-Barre, Pa., July 29, 1944; s. Francis Joseph and Irene Margaret (Borawski) B.; m. Carole Ann Emerick, July 9, 1966 (div. May 1976); children: David, Brian, Erik; m. Sharon Marie Head, Nov. 3, 1979; children: Erin Marie, Meghan Marie, Christopher Ryan. BS, King's Coll., 1966; MD, Loyola U. Sch. Medicine, 1970. Intern, resident in pediatrics U. Mich., Ann Arbor, 1970-73; fellowship in neonatology U. Mich., 1973-75, inst. dept. pediat., 1973-75; asst. prof. pediat., Ob-Gyn U. Mass., Worcester, 1975-79; assoc. prof. U. Mass., 1979—; dir. perinatal fellowship U. Mass., 1985—; interim chief divsn. neurology, adv. com. NNPP Northeastern U., Boston, 1992—; ethics com. U. Mass. Meml., 1999—, Worcester, 1984-94; mem. adv. bd. HMBANA, Hartford, Conn., 1994—. Baptismal ministry St. George's Catholic Ch., Worcester, 1997—; bereavement team U. Mass. Meml., 1988—; GME com. U. Mass, 1999—. Fellow AAP-Neonatal-Perinatal Medicine; mem. AMA, AAAS, Mass. Med. Soc., Worcester Dist. Med. Soc., N.E. Perinatal Soc., Mass. Perinatal Assn., N.Y. Acad. Sci. Avocations: skiing, jogging, camping, racquetball, golf. E-mail: bednaref@ummhc.org. Office: U Mass Meml 119 Belmont St Worcester MA 01605-2982

BEDNARIK, ROBERT GERHARD, scientific publisher; b. Baden, Austria, Apr. 6, 1944; s. Robert Othmar and Olga Victoria (Halbhuber) B.; m. Elfriede Kaethe Schipfer, Feb. 8, 1971; children: Cathrin Olga, Robert Gerhard Franz. Prin. rschr. Pilbara Expedition, Western Australia, 1967-70, Parietal Markings Project, South Australia, 1975—; mng. dir. Archaeol. Publs. Inc., Melbourne, Australia, 1983—; gen. editor Australian Rock Art Rsch. Assn., Melbourne, 1984—; permanent chair Internat. Fedn. of Rock Art Orgns., Melbourne, 1988—; editor Archaeol. and Anthropol. Soc. Victoria, Melbourne, 1990—; nat. coord. ICOMOS-CAR (UNESCO), Melbourne, 1991—; adv. com. Rock Art Protection Program, Canberra, 1985-88, Australian Inst. Aboriginal Studies, Canberra, 1987-89; tech. adv. com. Australian Heritage Commn., Canberra, 1986-89; chief sci. advisor First Sailors Expdn.; vis. fellow, lectr. numerous univs. worldwide, 1983—. Contbr. over 400 scientific articles to profl. publs. Mem. Australian Rock Art Rsch. Assn. (sec. 1983—), Archaeol. and Anthropol. Soc. of Victoria (editor 1990—), Australian Archaeol. Assn., Com. Internat. d'Art Rupestre (nat. coord. 1991—), Am. Rock Art Rsch. Assn., Rock Art Soc. of India (hon. life mem.). Home: 3 Buxton St, Elsternwick 3185, Australia Office: Archaeol Publs, PO Box 216, Caulfield South 3162, Australia

BEDNARSKI, KRZYSZTOF, sculptor; b. Cracow, Poland, July 25, 1953; married; 2 children. Student, Acad. Fine Arts. With Lab. Theatre J. Grotowski, Wroclaw, Poland, 1976-82. Prin. works include monument of Fellini in Rimini, Krzysztof Kieslowski's grave, Warsaw; works in numerous collections. Fax: 06-6896068. Address: 28/55 Nowowiejska St, 02-010 Warsaw Poland also: Via Dei Banchi Vecchi 134, 00-186 Roma Italy

BEDNORZ, J. GEORG, crystallographer; b. May 16, 1950. Grad., U. Munster, Fed. Republic of Germany, 1976; PhD, Swiss Federal Inst. Tech., ETH Zurich, 1982. Rschr. IBM Zurich Rsch. Lab., Switzerland, 1982—; mgr. high temperature superconductivity rsch. group IBM Zurich Rsch. Lab., 1987—; lectr. Swiss Fed. Inst. Tech., U. Zurich. Co-recipient 13th Fritz London Meml. award, 1987, Nobel Prize in physics Royal Swedish Acad. Soc., 1987; recipient Dannie Heineman prize Minna James Heineman Stiftung, Acad. Scis. Gottingen, Fed. Republic of Germany, 1987, Robert Wichard Pohl prize German Phys. Soc., 1987, Hewlett-Packard Europhysics prize, 1988, Marcel-Benoist prize Marcel-Benoist Found., 1986, APS Internat. prize for new materials research, 1988, Viktor Moritz Goldschmidt prize German Mineral. Soc., 1987, Otto-Klung prize Otto-Klung Found., 1987. Office: IBM Zurich Rsch Lab, Saumerstrasse 4, Ruschlikon Zurich CH-8803, Switzerland*

BEDOIRE, FREDRIC KURT, architectural history educator and researcher; b. Stockholm, Sept. 1, 1945; s. Kurt Thorsten and Elsa Margareta (Brander) B.; 1 child, Johannes. BA, Stockholm U., 1969, PhD, 1974; Degree in Arch., Royal Acad. Fine Arts, 1972; docent, 1975. Curator Royal Armoury, Stockholm, 1969, Stockholm City Mus., 1970-73; antquarian Nat. Bd. Antiquities, Stockholm, 1974-78; assoc. prof. archtl. history Royal Inst. Tech., Stockholm, 1978-92; prof. archtl. history Royal U. Fine Arts, Stockholm, 1992—, pro-vice-chancellor, 1998—; engaged in internat. collaboration concerning Indsl. Archaeology, 1972-85. Author: Industriarkitektur i Stockholms Innerstad, 1972, Kiruna Kyrka, 1973, Stockholm: Architecture and Townscape, 1973, 77, 88, English edit., 1988, (together with Henrik O. Andersson) Arkitekten Gustaf Wickman, 1974, Bankbyggande i Sverige, 1981, Swedish Architecture Drawings 1640-1970, 1986, Stockholm University: A History, 1978, 87, I Skuggan av Blodskam, 1988, Jewish Patronage and Modern Architecture (Swedish edit.), 1998, Den stora Hälsingegården, 2000. Home: Peter Myndes Backe 20, SE-11846 Stockholm Sweden Office: Royal U Fine Arts, Konsthögskolan, Arkitekturskola, 111 49 Stockholm Sweden

BEDOUELLE, HUGUES, biologist, researcher; b. Bourg-La-Reine, Seine, France, Aug. 19, 1949; s. Jean and Monique (Fontaine) B.; m. Shamila Nair, Sept. 4, 1995. MS in Math., U. Paris VII, 1971, PhD in Microbiology, 1980, PhD in Natural Sci., 1983; Engr., Ecole Poly., Paris, 1974. Engr. Soc. Azote et Produits Chimiques, Rouen, France, 1975, Lab. Mutatest de l'Inst. Pasteur, Paris, 1976, Inst. Nat. Rsch. sur la Sécurité, 1977; mining engr. Min. of Industry, France, 1976-82; rschr. dept. biochemistry and molecular genetics Inst. Pasteur, 1978-83, 86—; rschr. lab. biochemistry Nat. Cancer Inst., Bethesda, Md., 1981; attaché of rsch. CNRS, Paris, 1982-83, head of rschs., 1983-89, dir. rsch., 1989—; rschr. lab. molecular biology Med. Rsch. Coun., Cambridge, Eng., 1984-86; cons. in biotech. Inst. Français du Petrole, 1983—; cons. in protein engring. Transfusion-Mérieux-Innovation, Lyon, France, 1990-91; dir. rsch. unit structural biology and infectious agts. CNRS, 2000—. Contbr. articles to profl. jours. Lt. French Mil., 1974. European Molecular Biology Orgn. fellow, 1984, Royal Soc. London fellow, 1985. Mem. Protein Soc., French Soc. Biophysics, French Soc. Biochemistry and Molecular Biology, French Soc. Microbiology. Avocations: music, swimming, horse riding. Home: 4 Rue Auguste Bartholdi, 75015 Paris France Office: Inst Pasteur, 28 Rue Docteur Roux, 75724 Paris Cedex 15, France

BEDRIJ, OREST, investment banker, scientist; b. Ukraine, May 24, 1933; arrived in U.S., 1949, naturalized, 1955; s. Eustachy and Olha (Banach) B.; m. Oksana Cymbalista, Nov. 10, 1956; children: Orest W., Roksasa Bedrij Arpa, Chrystyna Bedrij Stecyk. BSEE, Rochester Inst. Tech., 1956, MS in Humanities; PhD in Physics, Columbia Pacific U., 1986. Various mgmt. positions IBM Corp., Poughkeepsie, N.Y. and Los Angeles, 1956-68; IBM tech. dir. Space Flight Facility, Jet Propulsion Lab., Calif. Inst. Tech., 1962-63; founder, pres., dir. Securities Coun., Inc., 1965-83, Profit Tech., Inc., 1983-89, Griffin Capital Mgmt. Corp., N.Y.C., 1989-97; co-founder, dir. Advance Memory Sys. Inc. (merged with GE) as Intersil, Inc., Sunnyvale, Calif., 1968-72, Inst. for Math. Physics, 1972—, Internat. Jour. Nonlinear Math. Physics, Kiev, 1992; with Griffin Securities, Inc., N.Y.C., 1997—; mem. exec. com., treas., dir. Ukrainian Studies Fund, Harvard U., 1959-72. Author: Yes, It's Love: Your Life Can Be a Miracle, 1974, One, 1977, 2d rev. edit., 1978, You, 1988; contbr. articles to profl. jours.; patentee in field. Trustee, treas. John E. Fetzer Found., 1987-89. With USAR, 1954-60. Recipient Outstanding Contribution award IBM, 1967. Mem. Internat. Soc. for Study of Human Ideas on Ultimate Reality and Meaning, N.Y. Acad. Arts and Scis., Shevchenko Sci. Soc., Sci. and Med. Network, London, Am. Inst. Physics, The World Trade Ctr. Club. Achievements include research in physics of ultimate reality. Office: Griffin Securities Inc 140 Broadway Fl 29 New York NY 10005-1101

BEDROSIAN, GREGORY RONALD, venture capitalist; b. Phila., Sept. 14, 1966; s. Samuel D. and Agnes Bedrosian; m. Elena V. Mayorova, Sept. 3, 1999; 1 child, Nicholas G. BS in Econs., U. Pa., 1988; MBA, Harvard U., 1992. Investment banker Salomon Bros., Inc., N.Y.C., 1988-90; investment banker Credit Suisse First Boston Ltd., London, Moscow, 1992-95; co-founder, mng. dir. Sputnik Funds (Renaissance Capital), Moscow, 1995-99; co-founder, pres., CEO InVentures, London, 2000—. Mem. Coun. on Fgn. Rels., Harvard Club of N.Y., Met. Club. Republican. Home: 35 Bryan Ave Malvern PA 19355-3007

BEDROSSIAN, URSULA KAY KENNEDY, editor; b. Austin, Tex., Dec. 8, 1948; d. Richard Arch and Ursula Marie (Jones) Kennedy; m. Carlos Wanes Bedrossian, Aug. 8, 1970; children: Vanessa, Richard, Robert. BS, Jacksonville U., 1972; MEd, Vanderbilt U., 1984; PhD, St. Louis U., 1991. Registered med. technologist and cytotechnologist Am. Soc. Clin. Pathologists. Med. technologist Del Oro Med. Lab., Houston, 1977-78; edn. coord., lab. supr. dept. family practice U. Tex. Med. Sch., Houston, 1978-81; rsch. asst. VA Med. Ctr., Nashville, 1981-84; clin. instr. dept. pathology St. Louis U., 1985-89; dir. edn. and quality I DMC Univ. Labs., Detroit, 1991-97; mng. edtor Wiley-Liss, N.Y.C., 1989—. Mng. editor Diagnostic Cytopathology, 1984—; asst. editor The Prostate, 1992-95; contbr. articles to sci. jours. Dir. med. relief Armenian Gen. Benevolent Union, 1993-97. Recipient commendation U.S. Army 101st Workhorse Bn., Badhersfeld, Germany, 1985. Mem. Clin. Lab. Mgmt. Assn., Am. Soc. Cytotech. (liaison to Papunivolaou Soc. Cytopathology 1993—, scientist mem. Am. Soc. Cytopathology), Armenian Am. Bus. Coun. , Brazilian Cultural Club. Avocations: geology, natural sciences, travel, speaking Spanish and Portuguese. Office: Biomed Comm Oak Park IL 60302

BEDWORTH, DAVID ALBERT, health educator; b. Cortland, N.Y., Mar. 31, 1949; s. Albert Ernest and Agnes Sheldon (Franklin) B.; children: Jodi Michele, Michael David. BS, Butler U., 1971; MS, U. Ill., 1972, PhD, 1976. Instr. Russell Sage Coll., Troy, N.Y., 1973-75; asst. prof. SUNY, Brockport, 1976-78; program coord. Heart Health Edn. R.I., Pawtucket, 1978-79; prof. SUNY, Plattsburgh, 1979—; cmty. edn. cons. STOP Ctr. for Domestic Violence, Plattsburgh, 1982; drug edn. cons. Federal Correction Instn., Ray Brook, N.Y., 1982, Ticonderoga (N.Y.) Ctrl. Sch. Dist., 1985. Author: (with Albert E. Bedworth) Health Education: A Process for Human Effectivess, 1978, Health for Human Effectiveness, 1982, The Profession and Practice of Health Education, 1992; contbr. articles to profl. jours., chpts. to books. Task force on youthful alcohol abuse N.Y. State Dept. Mental Hygiene, 1977; profl. edn. com. Am. Lung Assn., 1980-84, exec. com., 1981-82. Mem. APHA, ASCD, N.Y. State Fedn. Profl. Health Educators (pres. 1977). Democrat. Avocations: antiques, travel. Office: SUNY Plattsburgh NY 12901

BEE, ANNA COWDEN, dance educator; b. Feb. 17, 1922; d. Porter Guthrie and Marion Irene (McCurry) Cowden; m. Alon Wilton Bee, Oct. 21, 1942; children: Anna Margaret Bee Foote, Alon Wilton. AB, Samford U., 1944; student, Chalif Sch. Dance, N.Y.C., 1950-54. Mem. faculty Byram H.S., JAckson, 1945-52, Hinds Jr. Coll., Raymond, Miss., 1952—; dir. Hi-Steppers, girls' precision dance group; chaperone Miss Mississippi to Miss Am. Pageant; condr. charm clinics for teenagers; judge beauty pageants. Prodr. half-time shows for Gator Bowl, 1958, 64, 81, Sugar Bowl, 1960, Hall of Fame Bowl, 1977-79, Mid-Am. Bowl, 1988, Sr. Bowl, 1988. Bd. dirs. Multiple Sclerosis Soc., Jackson, 1966-72; state chmn. Miss. Easter Seals Soc. campaign, 1966, 79; chmn. women's divsn. United Way, Jackson, 1973; commencement spkr. Hinds C.C., 1999. Recipient Hinds C.C. Svc. award, 1993, Miss Miss. Vol. of Yr. award, 1995, Miss Am. Vol. of Yr. award, 1995, Dance Tchrs. Unlimited Lifetime Achievement award, 1996, Dance Tchrs. United Achievement award in dance, 1996; named Woman of Achievement, Jackson Bus. and Profl. Women's Club, 1967-78, Outstanding Vol. Goodwill Industry Miss., 1997, Golden Isles Bowl Classic, 1997; Miss. Legislature commendation for contbn. to youth, 1981; Anna Cowden Bee Hall named in her honor Hinds c.C. Bd. Trustees, 1993. Mem. Nat. Faculty Dance Educators Am., Dance Masters Am., Miss. Edn. Assn., Miss. Assn. Health and Phys. Edn., Beta Sigma Omicron. Baptist. Home: 256 Azalea Ct Brandon MS 39047-7264 Office: Hinds Jr Coll Raymond MS 39154

BEEBE, SANDRA E., retired English language educator, artist, writer; b. March AFB, Calif., Nov. 10, 1934; d. Eugene H. and Margaret (Fox) B.; m. Donald C. Thompson. AB in English and Speech, UCLA, 1956; MA in Secondary Edn., Calif. State U., Long Beach, 1957. Tchr. English, Garden Grove (Calif.) High Sch., 1957-93, attendance supr., 1976-83, ret., 1993; tchr. watercolor courses, Asilomar, Calif., 1997; jury chmn. N.W.S., 1997. Contbr. articles to English Jour., chpts. to books; watercolor artist; exhbns. include AWS, NWS, Okla. Watercolor Soc., Watercolor West, Midwest Watercolor Soc., Butler Inst. Am. Art, Youngstown, Ohio, Kings Art Ctr., Audubon Artists N.Y.; cover artist Exploring Painting, 1990, title page Understanding Watercolor, American Artist, 1991. mem. faculty Asilomar, 1997; chmn. of jurors N.W.S. Open, 1997. Named one of the Top Ten Watercolorists The Artists Mag., 1994; recipient Best Watercolors award Rockport Press, 1995; chosen for Design Poster selection, 1995, 97. Mem. Am. Watercolor Soc. (dir. 1999—), Nat. Watercolor Soc., Midwest Watercolor Soc., Watercolor West, Allied Artists N.Y., Knickerbocker Artists N.Y., Audubon Artists N.Y., West Coast Watercolor Soc., Rocky Mountain Nat. Watermedia Honor Soc., Jr. League Long Beach, Kappa Kappa Gamma. Republican. Home: 7241 Marina Pacifica Dr S Long Beach CA 90803-3899 Studio: B-Q Gallery 3920 E 4th St Long Beach CA 90814-1656 also: 239 Mira Mar Ave Long Beach CA 90803-6153

BEEBY, THOMAS H., architect. Architect C.F. Murphy, Chgo., 1965-71; ptnr. Hammond, Beeby, Rubert, Ainge Inc., Chgo., 1971—; mem. faculty dept. architecture Ill. Inst. Tech., Chgo., 1973-80; dir. Sch. Architecture U. Ill.-Chgo., Chgo., 1980-85; dean, prof. archtl. design Yale U. Sch. Architecture, 1985-91; adj. prof. Archtl., Yale U., 1992—; mem. adv. bd. dept. arch.

Ill. Inst. Tech., 1993—, trustee, 1997—. Designs exhibited: Art Inst. Chgo., Mus. Contemporary Art, Chgo., Cooper-Hewitt Mus., N.Y.C., Walker Art Ctr., Mpls., Venice Biennale; contbr. articles to profl. jours. Recipient Progressive Architecture citation, 1976, 87, 89, Louis Sullivan award, 1989. Fellow AIA (mem. nat. com. on design, nat. honor award 1984, 87, 89, 91, 93); mem. Soc. Archtl. Historians (bd. dirs. 1996-2000), U.S. State, Office Fgn. Bldg., Archtl. adv. bd., 1989-93, Graham Found. (bd. dirs. 1992—). Office: Hammond Beeby Rupert Ainge Inc 440 N Wells St Ste 630 Chicago IL 60610-4546

BEECHEY, COLIN VICTOR, biologist, researcher; b. London, Mar. 11, 1949; s. Francis Victor and Florence (Milan) B.; m. Dianne Edith Jones, Sept. 16, 1972; children: Kim, Kathryn. Higher Nat. Cert., Oxford Poly., Eng., 1971. Chartered biologist Inst. Biology. Sr. scientific officer Med. Rsch. Coun., Didcot, Oxon, Eng., 1967—. Contbr. chpts. to books. Mem. Genet. Soc. Avocations: alpine mountaineering, rock climbing, hill walking, motorcycling. Office: Med Rsch Coun, Mammalian Genetics Unit, Harwell Didcot OX11 0RD, England

BEECHEY, GWILYM EDWARD, musician, educator; b. London, Jan. 12, 1938; s. William Rowland and Helen (Comley) B.; m. Joyce Mary Downing; children: Christopher, Jennifer, Margaret. MA, CANTAB, Cambridge, Eng., 1963, MusB, 1959, PhD, 1965; music scholar, rschr., Magdalene Coll., Cambridge, Eng. Asst. dir. music Dean Close Sch., Cheltenham, 1962-65; asst. lectr. music Glasgow U., Scotland, 1965-68; lectr. music Hull U., Eng., 1969-88; editor The Consort The Dolmetsch Found., 1986-91; composer, editor of 17th and 18th century music, organ recitalist. Contbr. New Grove Dictionary of Music and Musicians, 6th edit., 1980, New Grove Dictionary of Opera, 1992, Symphony Orchestras of the World, 1987; contbr. articles to profl. jours. Avocations: sports, reading literature and history. Home: 15 Hamlyn Ave, Hull HU4 6BT, England

BEECHEY, RONALD BRIAN, biochemist, researcher; b. Heckmondwike, Yorkshire, Eng., Apr. 24, 1931; s. Albert and Edna (Smith) B. BSc, U. Leeds, U.K., 1953, PhD, 1970. Chartered chemist, U.K. Rschr. Med. Rsch. Coun., London, 1956-58; lectr. U. Southampton, Eng., 1958-63; rsch. scientist Shell Rsch., Sittingbourne, Eng., 1963-83; head dept. biochemistry U. Wales, Aberystwyth, 1983-98; dir. Portland Press Ltd., London, 1992-98, Portland Press Inc., U.S., 1992-98; hon. rsch. fellow Hannah Rsch. Inst., Ayr, Scotland, 1993—, Inst. Environ. and Grassland Rsch., Aberystwyth, 1992; hon. rsch. prof. physiology lab. U. Liverpool, Eng., 1992—. Contbr. articles to profl. jours. Fellow Royal Inst. Chemistry; mem. Internat. Union Biochemistry and Molecular Biology (treas. 1998—), Biochem. Soc. (treas. 1992-96), Physiol. Soc., Am. Physiol. Soc., Am. Soc. Biol. Chemistry and Molecular Biology. Home: The Elm, Torpenhow, Montgomery Hill, Frankby Wirral L98 1NF, England Office: Dept Physiology, Univ Liverpool, Liverpool L69 3BX, United Kingdom

BEEKELAAR, GERHARD ALFONSUS MARTINUS, historian, educator; b. Hilversum, The Netherlands, Sept. 21, 1933; s. Jacobus A. Beekelaar and Maria Gesina Meemken; m. Rosa Maria Theresia De Beus, July 28, 1961; children: Pauline, Rutger. MA, U. Nijmegen, The Netherlands, 1960, PhD, 1964. Vice prin. St. Vitus Coll., Bussum, The Netherlands, 1964-73; history rschr. Rijksuniversiteit Utrecht, The Netherlands, 1971-73; assoc. prof. modern history U. Nijmegen, 1973-96; mng. dir. Ctr. Parliamentary History, Nijmegen, 1996-99; vice chmn. dept. Am. studies U. Nijmegen, 1996-99; vis. prof. history Johns Hopkins U., Balt., 1978-79. Author: Between the Revision of the Dutch Constitution (1848) and the Re-institution of the Episcopal Hierarchy (1853), 1964, The Liberal 'Arnhem Daily' (1811-1848), 1981, The Dutch Catholics between Isolation and Assimilation, 1989, The Province of Gelderland (1840-1850), 1997; editl. sec. Journal of History, 1996—, Analen van het Thijmgenootschap, 1967—. Bd. mem. Thomas More Acad., The Netherlands, 1989—; regional sec. Orde van den Prince, Nijmegen, 1998—. Recipient Faculty Enrichment award Govt. Can., 1987, Pro Ecclesia et Pontifice, 1992, bronze medal U. Nijmegen, 1998. Mem. Thijmgenootschap (sec. gen. 1975—). Roman Catholic. Avocations: jogging, biking, swimming. Home: Huygensweg 14, 6522 HL Nijmegen The Netherlands Office: U Nijmegen PB 9103, Erasmusplein 1, 6500 HD Nijmegen The Netherlands

BEEKMAN, FREEK J., research physicist; b. Markelo, The Netherlands, June 25, 1961; s. Jan Beekman and Ietje E. Ditzel. MS in Exptl. Physics, Nijmegen (The Netherlands) U., 1991; PhD in Med. Physics, Utrecht (The Netherlands) U., 1995. Engr. Philips Elcoma, Nijmegen, 1985-86; engr., dept. nuc. medicine Univ. Hosp., Nijmegen, 1986-88; sr. rsch. physicist, nuc. medicine staff Images Scis. Inst., Univ. Hosp., Utrecht, 1995—; chair 1999 Internat. Mtg. Fully 3D Reconstruction in Radiology and Nuc. Medicine, editor Procs.; chair Utrecht '98 Bi-lateral workshop on SPECT-imaging; mem. program com. Computer Graphics and Imaging 1999, Palm Springs, Calif. Contbr. chpts. to books, articles and revs. to profl. jours. and conf. procs.; patentee in field of med. imaging; editor issue IEEE Trans. Med. Imaging. Rsch. grantee ADAC Labs., 1997—; Advanced Clin. Rsch. award, ADAC Labs., Milpitas, Calif., 1995. Mem. IEEE Nuc. Soc. (program coms. Med. Imaging and Nuc. Sci. confs., 1998, 99, 2000, Young Investigator award 1999), IEEE Plasma Soc., Soc. Nuc. Medicine, Dutch Soc. Nuc. Medicine. Avocations: running, Flamenco guitar, diving. E-mail: fbeekman@azu.nl.

BEELEY, JOSIE ANN, biochemistry educator; b. Crewe, Cheshire, Eng., Jan. 30, 1939; d. Reginald and Olive Leslie (Barnes) Hollinshead; m. John Gervais Beeley, Sept. 15, 1965; 1 child, James Malcolm. BSc with honors, U. Manchester, 1961, MSc, 1962, PhD, 1964. Asst. lectr. U. Sheffield, 1964-65; rsch. assoc. U. Wash., 1965-67; asst. lectr. U. Glasgow, 1967-68, lectr., 1968-78, sr. lectr., 1978—. Contbr. more than 150 articles to profl. jours. Recipient Orca-Rolex prize, European Orgn. for Caries Rsch., 1975. Mem. Inst. Biology, Brit. Electrophoresis Soc. (sec., 1989-92, pres. 1994-97), Internat. Assn. for Dental Rsch. (councillor 1995-98), Assn. of Basic Sci. Tchrs. in Dentistry (sec.-treas. 1988—). Avocations: playing, referring, coaching, and umpiring tennis. Office: U Glasgow Dental Sch, 378 Sauchiehall St, Glasgow G2 3J2, Scotland

BEELMANN, ANDREAS, psychology educator, researcher; b. Haseluenne, Germany, May 23, 1962; s. Bernhard and Maria (van Berkum) B. MSc, U. Bielefeld, Germany, 1990, PhD, 1994. Rsch. assoc. U. Bielefeld, 1991-94; asst. prof. psychology U. Erlangen-Nuremberg, Germany, 1994—. Editor: Early Childhood Intervention, 1996; contbr. articles to sci. jours., including Jour. Clin. Child Psychology, Psychologische Rundschau, Jour. Abnormal Child Psychology, Research in Developmental Disabilities. Mem. German Psychol. Assn., European Assn. Psychology and Law, Assn. Behavior Modification. Office: U Erlangen-Nuremberg, Bismarckstr 1, Dept Psych, D-91054 Erlangen Germany

BEEM, JOHN KELLY, mathematician, educator; b. Detroit, Jan. 24, 1942; s. William Richard and June Ellen (Kelly) B.; m. Eloise Masako Yamamoto, Mar. 24, 1964; 1 child, Thomas Kelly. A.B. in Math., U. So. Calif., 1963, M.A. in Math., 1965, Ph.D. in Math., 1968. Asst. prof. math. U. Mo., Columbia, 1968-71, assoc. prof., 1971-79, prof., 1979—. Author: (with P. Y. Woo) Doubly Timelike Surfaces, 1969, (with P. E. Ehrlich) Global Lorentzian Geometry, 1981, (with P.E. Ehrlich and K.L. Easley), 2d edit., 96; condr. research in differential geometry and gen. relativity. Recipient Kemper Tchg. award, 1996; NSF fellow, 1965, 68. Mem. Math. Assn. Am., Am. Math. Soc., Phi Beta Kappa. Home: 5204 E Tayside Cir Columbia MO 65203-5191

BEEMAN, JOSIAH HORTON, diplomat; b. San Francisco, Oct. 8, 1935; s. Josiah Horton and Helen Virginia (Hooper) B.; m. Susan Louise Sturman, Oct. 28, 1995; 1 child, Olivia Louise. BA, Calif. State U., 1957. Adminstrv. asst. Congressman Phillip Burton, Washington, 1964-66; mem. San Francisco Bd. Suprs., 1967-68; sec. internat. affairs Presbyn. Ch., N.Y.C., 1969-70; dir. Washington Office Presbyn. Ch., Washington, 1970-75; staff dir. Democratic Caucus U.S. Ho. of Reps., Washington, 1975; chief dep. dir. fin. State Calif., Washington, 1975-80; polit. and legis. dir. Am. Fedn. State, County and Mcpl. Employees, Washington, 1980-83; dir. Dem. Nat. Conv., San Francisco, 1983-84; pres. Beeman and Assocs., Washington, Sacramento, 1983-94; U.S. amb. to New Zealand and Samoa, 1994-99; chief of staff U.S. Broadcasting Bd. Govs., 2000—. Chmn. gen. assembly coun. Presbyn. Ch. U.S.A., 1988-89. Democrat. Office: 3036 Beechwood Ln Falls Church VA 22042-3138

BEEMER, JOHN BARRY, lawyer; b. Scranton, Pa., Sept. 4, 1941; s. Ellis and Rose Mary (Costello) B.; m. Diane Montgomery Fletcher, July 18, 1964 (dec. July 1999); children: David, Bruce. BS, U. Scranton, 1963; LL.B., George Washington U., 1966. Bar: Pa. 1966, U.S. Supreme Ct. 1980; cert. civil trial adv. Nat. Bd. Trial Advocacy. Law clk. U.S. Ct. Claims, 1966-67; clk. to judge U.S. Dist. Ct. (mid. dist.) Pa., 1967-68; assoc. Warren, Hill, Henkelman & McMenamin, Scranton, 1968-72; ptnr. Beemer, Brier, Rinaldi & Fendrick, 1972-77; pres. Beemer, Rinaldi, Fendrick & Mellody, P.C., Scranton, 1977-83; ptnr. Beemer & Beemer, Scranton, 1984—; lectr. in law U. Scranton, 1969-70. Chmn. com. constn. and by-laws revision Lackawanna (county Pa.) United Fund., 1971; nat. chmn. U. Scranton Alumni Fund Drive, 1972. Mem. ABA, Pa. Bar Assn., Lackawanna Bar Assn. (bd. dirs. 1988—), Assn. Trial Lawyers Am., Pa. Trial Lawyers Assn., Phi Delta Phi. Office: 114-116 N Abington Rd Clarks Summit PA 18411

BEEMSTER, JOSEPH ROBERT, risk management consultant; b. Chgo., Nov. 11, 1941; s. Joseph Z. and Emily (Dehaus) B.; B.A., DePaul U., 1962; postgrad. Ill. Inst. Tech., 1976, 77, U. Minn., 1979, 80; m. Judith L. Scheffers, Sept. 7, 1963; children—David, Susan. Mfg. mgr. Johnson & Johnson, Chgo., 1967-71, mgr. safety and security, 1971-78; corporate dir. safety and health Pacific Dunlop GNB Inc., St. Paul, 1978-88; sr. v.p. Richard Oliver Risk Mgrs., 1988—. Author: Safe Work Practices for Workers Exposed to Lead; producer videotapes on health and safety tng. Chmn., Bolingbrook (Ill.) Human Relations Commn., 1971-77. Mem. Am. Soc. Safety Engrs., Am. Indsl. Hygiene Assn. Home: 1606 Hadley Ct Wheeling IL 60090-6916 Office: 10 South Lasalle St Ste 3000 Chicago IL 60603

BEEN, DEREK CRAIG, electrical engineer, consultant; b. Kingston, Jamaica, June 10, 1969; arrived in Bahamas, 1969; s. James Elmer and Dorothy Elizabeth (Smith) B. AA in Electronics, Coll. of the Bahamas, Nassau, 1988; BSEE, Fla. Inst. Tech., 1991, MSEE, 1993. Engrng. intern, Fla. Project mgr. Innovative Waves, Nassau, 1993-96; assoc. engr. Chris Symonette & Assocs., Nassau, 1996—; tchr., cons. The Tng. Ctr., Nassau, 1995-96. Asst. leader 1st Bahamas Sea Scouts, Nassau, 1986-88; mem. steering com. Chs. of Christ Young Adult Fellowship, Nassau, 1995-96. Mem. IEEE. Home: PO Box SS-6408, Nassau NP, Bahamas Office: Symonette & Assocs, PO Box CB-12394, Nassau NP, Bahamas

BEENACKERS, JOHN A.W.M., engineering consultant; b. Bavel, The Netherlands, Dec. 5, 1948; s. Frans and Anna (Van Vugt) B.; m. Tiny Oomen, June 23, 1953; children: Barend, Mariëlle. Ing., U. Profl. Edn., Breda, 1970; Jr., Tech. U., Eindhoven, 1976, Dr. Chem. Tech., 1980. Scientist Tech. U., Eindhoven, 1976-80; engr., project mgr. DSM, Galeen, The Netherlands, 1980-91; tech. dir. Dutch Fly Ash Corp., Hertogenbosch, 1991-94; owner, dir. Beenackers Milieu & Technologie, Schinnen, 1994—; external examiner Limburg U. Profl. Edn., Heerlen, 1990—; coord. Hogeschool Limburg Contracting, Heerlen, 1994—; lectr. in field. Author: The Kinetics of the Heterogeneous Alkaline Isomerization of Carbohydrates, 1980; contbr. articles to profl. jours. Mem. Club of Dutch Dirs., Internat. Soc. for Environ. and Tech. Implications of Constrn. with Alternative Materials (chmn. working group), Kiwanis. Avocation: long-distance running. Email: jhm@beenackers.nl. Office: Beenackers Milieu & Tech, Achter de Kerk 4a, 6365 CP Schinnen The Netherlands

BEENTJES, PANCRATIUS CORNELIS, religious studies educator; b. Heemskerk, The Netherlands, June 4, 1946; m. Lucienne Bauer; 2 children. Student in theology, U. Amsterdam, Katholieke Theol. U., Amsterdam. Tchr. of religion, 1970-73; editor Het Spectrum Pub. Ho., 1973-76; lectr. Katholieke Theologische U. Utrecht, 1976-91, prof. old testament, 1991—; v.p. com. New Interconfessional Dutch Bible Translation. Contbr. articles to profl. publs. Mem. bd. Bible Mus. at Amsterdam. Mem. Dutch Roman Cath. Bible Soc. (pres. bd. advisors). Office: Katholieke Theol U Utrecht, PO Box 80101, 3508 TC Utrecht The Netherlands

BEER, GILLIAN PATRICIA, writer and educator; b. Bookham, Surrey, Eng., Jan. 27, 1935; d. Owen Kempster Thomas and Ruth Winifred (Burley) Bell; m. John Bernard Beer, July 7, 1962; children: Daniel John, Rufus Bernard, Zachary William. BA, St. Anne's Coll., 1957; B. Litt., U. Oxford, 1960; Litt. D., U. Cambridge, 1989. Asst. lectr. Bedford Coll., U. London, 1959-62; lectr. U. Liverpool, 1962-64; fellow Girton Coll., Cambridge, 1965—; asst. lectr. U. Cambridge, 1966-87, reader in lit. and narrative, 1987-89, prof. English, 1989—, King Edward VII prof. English lit., 1994—; pres. Clare Hall Coll., 1994—.vis. prof. U. Calif., Berkeley, 1991. Author: Meredith: A Change of Masks, 1970, Darwin's Plots, 1983 (Crawshay prize 1984), George Eliot, 1986, Arguing with the Past, 1989, Open Fields: Science in Cultural Countries, 1996, Virginia Woolf: The Common Ground, 1996. Leverhulme fellow, 1986, Research reader Brit. Acad., 1987-89. Fellow Brit. Acad., Royal Soc. Arts. Avocations: music, travel. Home: 6 Belvoir Terr, Cambridge CB2 2AA, England Office: Girton Coll, Cambridge CB3 0JG, England

BEER, JOHN BERNARD, English language educator; b. Watford, Herts, Eng., Mar. 31, 1926; s. John Bateman and Eva (Chilton) B.; m. Gillian Patricia Kempster Thomas, July 7, 1962; children: Daniel John, Rufus Bernard, Zachary William. BA, Cambridge (Eng.) U., 1950, PhD, 1957, LittD, 1995. Rsch. fellow St. John's Coll., Cambridge, 1955-57; asst. lectr., lectr. Manchester U., 1958-64; lectr., reader, prof. Cambridge U., 1964-93, prof. emeritus, 1993—; fellow Peterhouse, Cambridge, 1964-93, emeritus fellow, 1993—, Leverhulme emeritus fellow, 1995-96. Author: Coleridge the Visionary, 1959, The Achievement of E.M. Forster, 1962, Milton, Lost and Regained, 1964, Blake's Humanism, 1968, Blake's Visionary Universe, 1969, Coleridge's Poetic Intelligence, 1977, Wordsworth and the Human Heart, 1978, Wordsworth in Time, 1978, Against Finality, 1993, Romantic Influences: Contemporary-Victorian-Modern, 1994, Providence and Love: Studies in Wordsworth, Channing, Myers, George Eliot and Ruskin, 1998; editor: Coleridge's Poems: 1963, 86, 93, Coleridge's Variety: Bicentenary Studies, 1974, A Passage to India: Essays in Interpretation, 1985, Aids to Reflection (The Collected Coleridge), 1993, Questioning Romanticism, 1995; co-editor: (with G.K. Das) E.M. Forster: A Human Exploration; Centenary Essays, 1979. Fellow Brit. Acad.; mem. Royal Over-Seas League. Avocations: walking, travel, music. Home: 6 Belvoir Terrace, Cambridge CB2 2AA, England

BEER, MICHAEL DOMINIC, psychiatrist, educator; b. Reading, Eng., Nov. 4, 1956; s. Michael and Susanna Elisabeth (Carson) B.; m. Naomi Rosemary Salter, June 29, 1985; children: Charles, Joshua, David, Esther. BA, Oxford (Eng.) U., 1978, MA, 1984; MB, BS, London U., 1985, MD, 1993. From house officer to sr. house officer Guy's Hosp., London, 1985-89, sr. registrar psychiatry, 1990-94; rsch. fellow Wellcome Inst. for History Medicine, London, 1989-90; sr. lectr. psychiatry Guy's King's and St. Thomas Hosp., London, 1994—; cons. Bexley Hosp., London, 1994—; chair U.K. Psychiat. Intensive Care Com. Editor: Christian Choices in Healthcare, 1995; mem. editl. bd. History Psychiat. Jour., 1993—; contbr. articles to profl. jours. Dep. chmn. Parish Ch., Bermondsey, London, 1991-95; gov. Leighton Park Sch., Reading, 1987-93. Mem. Royal Coll. Psychiatrists, European Assn. for the History Psychiatry, British Med. Assn., Marylebone Cricket Club, Old Leightonians Cricket Club (sec.-treas. 1987-96). Avocation: sports. Office: Bexley Hosp, Bracton Ctr Old Bexley Ln, Bexley Kent DA5 2BW, England

BEER, PETER HILL, federal judge; b. New Orleans, Apr. 12, 1928; s. Mose Haas and Henret (Lowenburg) B.; children: Kimberly Beer Bailes, Kenneth, Dana Beer Long-Innes; m. Marjorie Barry, July 14, 1985. BBA, Tulane U., 1949, LLB, 1952; LLM, U. Va., 1986. Bar: La. 1952. Successively assoc., ptnr., sr. ptnr. Montgomery, Barnett, Brown & Read, New Orleans, 1955-74; judge La. Ct. Appeal, 1974-79, U.S. Dist. Ct. (ea. dist.) La., New Orleans, 1979—; vice chmn. La. Appellate Judges Conf.; apptd. by chief justice of U.S. to state-fed. com. Jud. Conf. U.S., 1985-89; apptd. by chief justice of U.S. to Nat. Jud. Coun. State and Fed. Cts., 1993—. Mem. bd. mgrs. Touro Infirmary, New Orleans, 1969-74; mem. exec. com. Bur. Govtl. Rsch., 1965-69; chmn. profl. divsn. United Fund New Orleans, 1966-69; mem. New Orleans City Coun., 1969-74, v.p., 1972-74. Capt. USAF, 1952-55. Decorated Bronze Star. Mem. ABA (mem. ho. dels.), Am. Judicature Soc., Fed. Bar Assn., La. Bar Assn., Fed. Judges Assn. U.S. (bd. dirs. 1985, 5th cir. rep. bd. govs.), Nat. Lawyers Club, So. Yacht Club, St. John Golf Club. Jewish. Home: 133 Bellaire Dr New Orleans LA 70124-1008 also: 204 3rd Ave Pass Christian MS 39571-3214 Office: US Dist Ct US Courthouse 500 Camp St New Orleans LA 70130-3313

BEEREKAMP, JOHANNES BERNARDUS, film critic; b. Amsterdam, Nov. 5, 1952; s. Hendrik Wouter and Anna Elizabeth (Lindeman) B.; m. Marieke Korthof; children: Anna, Lucas, Eva. B.Psychology, U. Amsterdam, 1975. Editor-in-chief Spiegeloog, Amsterdam, 1974-77; rsch. asst. Rsch. Inst. voor Toegepaste Psychologie, Amsterdam, 1977-79; film editor NRC Handelsblad, Amsterdam, 1979—; guest tchr. in film criticism U. Groningen, 1999. Author: (essay book) De Kippen van Vader Abraham, 1992; editor: Filmdaarboek 1980-1999, De Filmkrant, 1981-99, Jaarboek Winkler Prins, 1985—. Chmn. Kring van Nederlandse Filmjournalisten, Amsterdam, 1998—. Chmn. Kring Van Ned. Filmdournalisten. Home: Roompotstraat 10-1, 1078 KU Amsterdam The Netherlands Office: NRC Handelsblad, Karthuizerdwarsstraat 18E, 1015 KP Amsterdam The Netherlands

BEERING, STEVEN CLAUS, academic administrator, medical educator; b. Berlin, Germany, Aug. 20, 1932; came to U.S., 1948, naturalized, 1953; s. Steven and Alice (Friedrichs) B.; m. Catherine Jane Pickering, Dec. 27, 1956; children: Peter, David, John. BS summa cum laude, U. Pitts., 1954, MD, 1958; DSc (hon.), Ind. Cen. U., 1983, U. Evansville (Ind.), 1984; ScD (hon.), U. Pitts., 1998; DSc (hon.), Ramapo Coll., 1986, Anderson Coll., 1987; ScD (hon.), Ind. U., 1988; LLD (hon.), Hanover Coll., 1986; DsC (hon.), Purdue U., 2000. Intern Walter Reed Gen. Hosp., Washington, 1958-59; resident Wilford Hall Med. Center, San Antonio, Tex., 1959-62, chief internal medicine, edn. coordinator, 1967-69; prof. medicine Ind. U. Sch. Medicine, Indpls., 1969—, asst. dean, 1969-70, assoc. dean, dir. postgrad. edn., 1970-74, dir. statewide med. edn. system, 1970-83, dean, 1974-83; chief exec. officer Ind. U. Med. Center, Indpls., 1974-83; pres. Purdue U. and Purdue U. Research Found., West Lafayette, Ind., 1983-2000, pres. emeritus, 2000—; prof. pharmacology and toxicology Purdue U.; bd. dirs. Arvin Industries, Eli Lilly Co., NISource, Inc., Am. United Life, Veridian Corp.; cons. Indpsl. VA Hosp., St. Vincent Hosp.; chmn. Ind. Commn. Med. Edn., 1973-83, Med. Edn. Bd. Ind., 1974-83, Liaison Com. on Med. Edn., 1976-81. Contbr. articles to sci. jours. Sec. Ind. Atty. Gen.'s Trust, 1974-83; regent Nat. Library Medicine, 1987-91; mem. Lafayette Community Council. Served to lt. col. M.C. USAF, 1957-69. Fellow ACP, Royal Soc. Medicine; mem. Am. Fedn. Clin. Rsch., Am. Diabetes Assn., Endocrine Soc., Assn. Am. Med. Colls. (chmn. 1982-83), Coun. Med. Deans (chmn. 1980-81), Assn. Am. Univs. (chair 1995-96), Nat. Acad. Sci. Inst. of Medicine, Ind. Acad., Indpls. Athletic Club, Columbia Club, Skyline Club, Woodstock Club, Meridian Hills Club, Phi Beta Kappa, Sigma Xi, Alpha Omega Alpha, Phi Rho Sigma (U.S. v.p. 1976-85). Presbyterian (elder). Fax: 765-496-7561. E-mail: scb@purdue.edu. Home: 3746 Westlake Ct West Lafayette IN 47906-8612 Office: Purdue U Office of Pres Emeritus Rm 218 Memorial Union West Lafayette IN 47906-3584

BEERMAN, JOSEPH, health educator; b. N.Y.C., Aug. 31, 1937; s. Herbert and Frances B.; m. Andrea Ellenhorn, Aug. 15, 1987; 1 child, Eric Hunter. BA, Hunter Coll., 1959; MA, NYU, 1963; diploma Tchr.'s Coll., Columbia U., 1970. Cert. in health and phys. edn., N.Y. Tchg. asst., track coach NYU, 1959-61; tchr. health edn. Herman Ridder Jr. H.S., N.Y.C., 1961-65; prof. health and phys. edn. Manhattan C.C.-CUNY, N.Y.C., 1965-96, assoc. dean faculty, 1978-79, prof. emeritus, 1996—, adj. prof., 1996—; cons. Nat. Coun. Jr. Colls., NEA, Washington, 1965—; rep. Coun. Health Educators, CUNY, 1965—. Author: Chemical Dependency and the Minorities, 1993, Basic Tennis: Skills and Strategies, 1995. Guest speaker YMCA and sr. citizen orgns., N.Y.C., 1965—; presenter tennis clins. Ea. Tennis Patrons, N.Y.C., 1965-75; presenter seminars N.Y.C. Bd. Edn., 1961-70. Sgt. U.S. Army, 1959-61. Nat. Humanities Faculty grantee, 1978; recipient McGovern award U.S. Tennis Assn., 1987; inducted into Hunter Coll. Athletic Hall of Fame, 1993. Fellow Internat. Inst. Cmty. Svc., Friends of Penn Relay's; mem. Am. Alliance Phys. Edn., Health, Recreation and Dance (mem. various coms. 1960—),. Democrat. Jewish. Avocations: philately, numismatics, antiques, tennis. Home: 16-70 Bell Blvd Apt 113 Bayside NY 11360 Office: CUNY 199 Chambers St New York NY 10007-1044

BEERSMANS, FRANS, language educator; b. Berchem, Belgium, Mar. 30, 1942. Degree, Cath. U., Louvain, Belgium, 1963. Asst. Cath. U., 1963-64; lectr. Philipps U., Marburg, Germany, 1966-74, Fontys Hogescholen, Tilburg, Holland, 1974—. Editor: (dictionary) Van Dale Groot Woordenboek Duits, 1990, Langenscheidts Taschenwörterbuch Niederländisch, 1996.

BEERY, ROGER LEWIS, II, risk management consultant; b. San Antonio, Apr. 9, 1957; s. Roger Lewis Sr. and Margaret (Dorrill) B.; m. Donna M. Hodgkinson. BBA, U. Tex., 1979, MBA, 1981. Founder, pres. Austin (Tex.) Cons. Group, Inc., Breckenridge, Colo., 1980—; lectr. U. Tex., Austin, 1979-87, Rice U., Houston, 1986-88; expert witness in ins. related lawsuits; speaker in field; guest cons. Rice U. Entrepeneur's Conf., 1986-88; speaker Nat. Automobile Dealers Assn. Conv., 1990; presenter in field. Author: Dealership Risk Mgmt. Newsletter; contbr. articles to profl. jours. including Automotive Exec., Automobile Dealer Mag. Founder Exec. Level Mgmt., Ltd., Bermuda, 1997—; bd. dirs. Summit Sch. Dist. RE-1, 1997—. Republican. Avocations: skiing, hiking, mountain biking. Office: Austin Cons Group Inc 130 Ski Hill Rd #140 Breckenridge CO 80424

BEEVOR, ANTONY ROMER, merchant banker; b. London, May 18, 1940; s. Miles and Sybil (Gilliat) B.; m. Cecilia Hopton, Oct. 2, 1970; children: Karen Louise, Mark Andrew. Degree in philosophy, politics and econs., Oxford (Eng.) U., 1962. Lic. solicitor. With Ashurst Morris Crisp, London, 1962-72, ptnr., 1968-72; dir. Hambros Bank, London, 1972-98; dir. gen. Takeover Panel, London, 1987-89; dir. The Rugby (Eng.) Group PLC, 1993-2000, Hambros PLC, London, 1990-98; mng. dir. S.G. Hambros Corp. Fin., 1998-2000, sr. advisor, 2000—; dir. Gerrard Group PLC, 1995-2000, Gerrar Xking Ltd., Croda Internat., Helical Bar PLC; dep. chmn. The Takora Panel, London, 1999—, chmn., Fairbridge, 2999—. Office: S G Hambros, 41 Tower Hill, London EC3N 4S9, England

BEG, ISMAT, mathematics educator, researcher; b. Gujrat, Punjab, Pakistan, Jan. 4, 1951; s. Mohammad Zaman and Kaniz Fatimah; m. Shahida Ismat Butt, Jan. 3, 1984; children: Usman Ismat, Abira Ismat, Nauman Ismat. BSc, Punjab U., Lahore, Pakistan, 1970, MSc, 1973; PhD, Bucharest U., Romania, 1982. Chartered mathematician. Lectr. Punjab Edn. Dept., 1973-78; lectr. Quaid-i-Azam U., Islamabad, Pakistan, 1982-83, asst. prof., 1984-91, assoc. prof., 1991—; prof. Kuwait U., Safat, 1998—; prin. investigator 9 rsch. projects. Author 80 rsch. papers. Named Best Mathematician Govt. Pakistan, 1986. Fellow Inst. Math. and Its Applications; mem. Am. Math. Soc., London Math. Soc., N.Y. Acad. Scis. Avocations: economics, chess, swimming. Home: Kuwait U, Apt 121 Shawaikh Campus, Safat Kuwait Office: Kuwait U, Dept Math PO Box 5969, Safat 13060, Kuwait

BEGELL, WILLIAM, publisher; b. Wilno, Poland, May 18, 1928; came to U.S., 1947, naturalized, 1953; s. Ferdinand and Liza (Kowarski) Beigel; m. Esther Kessler, May 27, 1948; children: Frederick Paul (dec.), Alissa Maya. BChemE, CCNY, 1953; MChemE, Poly. Inst. Bklyn., 1958; postgrad., Columbia U., 1958-59; DSc, Acad. Sci. BSSR, Minsk, 1984. Engrng. mgr. heat transfer research facility dept. chem. engring. Columbia U., 1953-59; co-founder, exec. v.p. Scripta Technica, Inc., Washington, 1959-74; founder, pres. Hemisphere Publishing Corp., Washington, 1974-91, Begell House, Inc., Pubs., N.Y.C., 1991—; pres., chief scientist Byelocorp Sci., Inc., 1991—; dir. Supco Internat. Engrng. Corp., Milan, 1994—; lectr. pub. George Washington U., Washington, also N.Y. U.; cons. Heat Transfer Research Lab., Columbia U.; cons. in field. Editor 7 books; contbr. numerous articles on heat transfer to profl. jours.; patentee in field. Mem. nat. adv. bd. ctr. for the Book, Libr. of Congress; chmn. exec. coun. Profl. and Scholarly Pubs.; bd. dirs. Am. Fedn. for the Blind. Recipient Benjamin Gomez award book pub. div. Anti-Defamation League, 1984. Mem. AAAS, Am. Inst. Chem. Engrs., Am. Soc. for Engring. Edn., ASME (communications bd. Fellow, 1996, Disting. Svc. award 1992), Assn. Am. Publishers (dir.), N.Y. Acad. Scis. (publs. bd.), Internat. Centre for Heat and Mass

Transfer, Washington Book Publishers (founder), Am. Assn. Engring. Socs. Jewish. Home: 46 E 91st St New York NY 10128-1350 Office: Begell House Inc Pubs 79 Madison Ave New York NY 10016-7802

BEGGS, HARRY MARK, lawyer; b. Los Angeles, Nov. 15, 1941; s. John Edgar and Agnes (Kentro) B.; m. Sandra Lynne Mikal, May 25, 1963; children: Brendan, Sean, Corey, Michael. Student, Ariz. State U., 1959-61, Phoenix Coll., 1961; LL.B., U. Ariz., 1964. Bar: Ariz. 1964, U.S. Dist. Ct. Ariz. 1964, U.S. Ct. Appeals (9th cir.) 1973, U.S. Ct. Appeals (fed. cir.) 1995, U.S. Supreme Ct. 1991. Assoc. Carson Messinger Elliott Laughlin & Ragan, Phoenix, 1964-69, ptnr., 1969-93; mem., mng. lawyer Carson Messinger Elliott Laughlin & Ragan, P.L.L.C., Phoenix, 1994—. Mem. editorial bd. Ariz. Law Rev. 1963-64; contbr. articles to profl. jours. Recipient award for highest grade on state bar exam. Atty. Gen. Ariz., 1964; Fegtly Moot Ct. award, 1963, 64; Abner S. Lipscomb scholar U. Ariz. Law Sch., 1963. Fellow Ariz. Bar Found. (founder); mem. State Bar Ariz., Ariz. Acad., Maricopa County Bar Assn. Office: PO Box 33907 Phoenix AZ 85067-3907

BEGHIN, FRANCOIS P., lawyer; b. Brussel, Brabant, Belgium, Feb. 11, 1968; s. Douchan Beghin and Marcelle Bikx. JD, U. Brussels, 1993. Atty. Beghin and Assocs., Brussels, 1993—. Avocation: soccer. Home: Square des Cicindeles 7, 1170 Brussels Belgium Office: Blvd de Liempereur 24, 1000 Brussels Belgium

BEGUIN, BERNARD AUGUSTE, columnist, retired broadcasting company executive; b. Sion, Valais, Switzerland, Feb. 14, 1923; s. Bernard and Clemence (Welten) B.; m. Antoinette Leonie Waelbroeck, Apr. 12, 1948; children—Pierre, Claude, Jean, Martine. Licence es lettres classiques, U. Geneva, 1945; postgrad. Grad. Inst. Internat. Studies, Geneva, 1945. Sec. World Student Relief, Geneva, 1945-46; editor Journal de Geneve, Geneva, 1947-59, editor-in-chief, 1959-70; UN corr. Fin. Times, Geneva, 1949-59; Radio and TV commentator Swiss Broadcasting, Geneva, 1955-70, dep. dir., 1970-86, sec. bd. dirs., 1980-86; vis. prof. profl. ethics U. Neuchatel, 1985-88. V.p. Press Ctr., Geneva, 1954-55. U.S. Dept. State Smith-Mundt fellow, Washington, 1952; pres. Ind. Complaints Authority on Broadcasting, 1991-92, Swallow Found. for unbiased info. in cases of emergency, Rwanda, 1995; cons. Unesco, 1994.np. Mem. Swiss Press Assn. (pres. 1959-60, hon. mem. 1970—), Swiss Press Council (pres. 1986-90), Cruising of Switzerland.

BEGUM, FORQUAN, government administrator; b. Jan. 22, 1951; d. Md. Tamijuddin Bhuiya and Al-Haj Rokeya Begum; adopted children: Saif Mohammad Ashraf Al Sade, Nadim Mohammad Towhid Al Rumi, Samia Afrin Nipa. BSc with honors, Dhaka (Bangladesh) U., 1972, MSc, 1974. Headmistress Kanchan Girl's High Sch., Narayanganj, Bangladesh, 1975; youth program officer Bangladesh Family Planning Assn., Dhaka, 1976-80; project devel. assoc. Family Planning Svcs. & Tng. Ctr., Dhaka, Bangladesh, 1980; rsch. assoc. Press Inst. Bangladesh, Dhaka, 1981; dy. dir. Dept. Youth Devel., Ministry Youth & Sports, Dhaka, Bangladesh, 1981-92; asst. sec. Ministry of Finance, Dhaka, 1993—; prof. physics Adarsa Coll., Dhaka, 1980, Islami Mohila Coll., Dhaka, 1981; self-employed, 1983-84; tutor Commonwealth Distance Tng. Course, 1991—; advisor Jatio Tarun Sangha, Dhaka, 1975-80, Family Planning Youth Assn., Dhaka, 1977-81, Swanirvar Youth Com., Dhaka, 1990-91. Author: The Contribution of Women in the Independence Movement and Liberation War of Bangladesh, Selected Poetry of Bangladesh, Women's Right and Honour in Islam, Women: The Ladder of the World and the Civilization; editor: The Society, 1990; contbr. to nat. dailies and periodicals. Active with Student League, 1968-74; freedom fighter in Liberation War of Bangladesh, 1971. Recipient Best Trainee award Bangladesh Jaycees, Dhaka, 1986. Mem. Bangladesh Red Crescent Soc. (life), Family Planning Assn. Bangladesh (life), Azimpur Community Ctr. (women's sec.), UNESCO Club (organizing sec.), OISCA, Purnimabasha Literary Orgn., Daudpur Union Women Orgn. (pres.), Swanirvar Bangladesh, Bangha Bhandhu Shancritic Chusty, Lions Club. Avocations: reading, children, working for the poor and peace, traveling, gardening. Home: 54(New)/E, Azimpur Estate, Dhaka Bangladesh Office: Ministry of Fin Budget Divsn, Bangladesh Secretariat, 1000 Dhaka Bangladesh

BEGUR, RAJESH NANJUNDIAH, lawyer; b. Mysore, Karnataka, India, Oct. 1, 1964; s. Hanumantarao and Sumitra Nanjundiah. B in Commerce, U. Bombay, 1984, LLB, 1987. Solicitor India, 1992, Supreme Ct. Eng. and Wales, 1994. Articled clk. Manilal Kher Ambalal & Co., Bombay, 1988-90; sr. assoc. Amarchand & Mangaldas & Hiralal Shroff & Co., Bombay, 1990-95, Nishith Madanlal Desai, Bombay, 1995-96; ptnr. A.R.A. LAW, Bombay, 1996—. Mem. Bar Coun. Maharashtra and Goa, Bombay Incorporated Law Soc., Law Soc. London. Avocations: reading, music, traveling. Office: ARA LAW Agra Bldg 1st Fl, 121 MG Rd Fort, Mumbai Maharashtra 400023, India

BEHAR, MAXIM, journalist, public relations and advertising executive; b. Shumen, Bulgaria, Dec. 10, 1955; s. Montcho Moshe and Rachel (Surozhon) B.; m. Mila Behar, 1985; children: Michael, Ralitsa. Advanced degree in econ. rels., Prague Econs. U., Czech Republic, 1983. Corr., reporter Mladez Daily, Mlady Svet Weekly, Prague, 1981-83; reporter internat. dept. Rabotnichesko delo Daily, 1983-85, spl. corr. Dist. of Shumen, 1985-89; corr. Duma Daily, Warsaw, Poland, 1989-91; internat. dept. chief Duma Daily, 1991-92; co-founder, mng. editor, 1st dep. editor-in-chief Standart Daily, Sofia, Bulgaria, 1992-95; owner, chief exec., bus. cons., media planning and mktg. M3 Comm. Group, Inc.; warr corr. during Soviet invasion in Lithuania, 1991. Interviews with Pres. Lech Walesa of Poland, Pres. Vaclav Havel of Czech Republic, Pres. Zhelju Zhelev of Bulgaria, King in exile Simeon II of Bulgaria, Dr. Zbigniew Brzezinski. Mem. Assn. Bulgarian Advt. Agys. and Profls. (founder, pres.), Journalists for European Union (founder, v.p.), Internat. Advt. Assn. (U.S.), Internat. Pub. Rels. Assn. Avocations: music, computers. Home and Office: 34 Vladajska St, 1606 Sofia Bulgaria

BEHARI, MADHURI, neurologist, educator; b. New Delhi, India, June 29, 1950; d. Krishna and Tara Krishna (Verma) B. MB, BS, Lady Hardinge Med. Coll., New Delhi, 1973, MD, 1977; D of Neurology, All India Inst. Med. Scis., New Delhi, 1980. Sr. resident All India Inst. Med. Scis., New Delhi, 1978-81, asst. prof., 1984-85, assoc. prof., 1986-89, additional prof., 1989-98, prof., 1998—; lectr. G.B. Pant Hosp., New Delhi, 1981-83, asst. prof., 1983-84; cons. G.B. Pant Hosp., New Delhi, 1981-84, All India Inst. Med. Scis., New Delhi, 1984—, researcher, 1984—, adminstr., 1988—. Author: (with others) MCQs in Medical Sciences, 1992, Progress in Neurology, 1994; assoc. editor: Neurology India jour., 1994—; contbr. articles to profl. jours. Mem. Nat. Acad. Med. Scis., N.Y. Acad. Med. Scis., Neurol. Soc. India, Indian Epilepsy Assn., Indian Acad. Neurology, Assn. British Scholars, Nat. Magnetic Resonance Soc., Youth Hostel Assn. India. Avocations: gardening, trekking, gliding. Office: All India Inst Med Scis, Ansari Nagar, New Delhi 110029, India

BEHBAHANI, ROYA, clinical pharmacist; b. Tehran, Iran, Mar. 1, 1963; came to U.S., 1984; d. Ziarddin B. and Farangis Kaveh; m. Craig Katz, Jan. 14, 1985 (div. 1994); 1 child: Kevin; m. Ramin Vassighi, Aug. 19, 1995; children: Shayan, Roxanna. Pre-pharmacy student, Camden County Coll., 1984-86; BS in Pharmacy, Phila. Coll. Pharmacy & Sci., 1989, D in Pharmacy, 1990. Licensed pharmacist N.J., Pa. Pharmacy intern Chapel Pharmacy, Cherry Hill, N.J., 1987, Amherst Pharmacy, Lumberton, N.J., 1988-89; clin. rsch. and pharmacokinetics fellow Phila. Coll. Pharmacy & Sci., Nat. Assn. Clin. Rsch., 1990-91; clin. pharmacist pharmacokinetics Cooper Hosp., Camden, N.J., 1991-96; drug info. product mgr. oncology group SmithKline Beecham Pharm., Phila., 1996—; part-time staff pharmacist Burlington Meml. Hosp., Mt. Holly, N.J., 1989-96; tchg. asst. clin. pharmacy Phila. Coll. Pharmacy and Sci., 1989-90, instr., 1990-91, clin. asst. prof., 1991-96; chair workflow com. SmithKline Beecham Pharm., 1998—; mem. safety com. Cooper Hosp., 1993-95, patient edn. com., 1991-96, pharmacy and Therapeutics com., 1991-96; mem. admissions com. Phila. Coll. Pharmacy & Scis., 1988-89; spkr. in field. Contbr. articles to pharm. jours. Mem. Am. Soc. Hosp. Pharmacists, Mid-Atlantic Coll. Clin. Pharmacy (chair program com. 1994-96), Am. Coll. Clin. Pharmacy, Rho Chi. Home: 20 Red Hill Ct Mount Laurel NJ 08054-3192 Office: Smithkline Beecham Pharm Product Info Dept 1 Franklin Plz Ste 1800 Philadelphia PA 19102-1225

BEHL, PREM, exhibitions organizer; b. New Delhi, Sept. 10, 1944; s. Puran Anand and Shakuntla (Nijhowne) B.; m. Anita Laroia; children: Nikhil, Dhruv. Student, La Martiniere Coll., Lucknow, India, 1960; BA in History, Delhi U., 1965. Area sales exec. India Foils Ltd., Calcutta, India, 1965-71; regional mgr. Singer Sewing Machine Co., Bombay, India, 1972-74; exec. dir. Usha Internat. Ltd., New Delhi, India, 1974-81; dir.-India Internat. Wool Secretariat, Bombay, India, 1981-84; mng. dir. Exhbns. India, New Delhi, 1987—; subcom. on exports Min. of Textiles, 1982-83. Governing coun. Wool Rsch. Assn., India, 1981-84. Mem. Fedn. Indian C. of C. and Industry, Indo Am. C. of C. and Industry, India Conv. Promotion Bur., Indo French C. of C., Indo German C. of C., Pacific Telecomm. Coun., Soc. Cable TV Engrs, Delhi Gymkhana Club Ltd., Associated C. of C. and Industry, All India Mgmt. Assn., Delhi Mgmt. Assn., Indo Canadian Bus. Coun., Joint Bus. Coun., Internet Soc., Royal Bombay Yacht Club. Avocations: philately, numismatics, music. Home: E-6 Defence Colony, New Delhi 110024, India Office: Exhibitions India, C-390 Defence Colony, New Delhi 100024, India

BEHNEY, CHARLES AUGUSTUS, JR., veterinarian; b. Bryn Mawr, Pa., Nov. 30, 1929; s. Charles Augustus and Victoria Parks (Wythe) B.; m. Judith Ann Boggs, May 26, 1979; children: Charles Augustus III, Keenan F. BS, U. Wyo.; DVM, Colo. State U., 1961. Owner Cochise Animal Hosp., Bisbee, Ariz., 1961—; veterinarian, dir. S.W. Trailsdust Zoo, Bisbee, 1966—; ownr Kazam Arabians, Bisbee, 1969—; assoc. prof. Cochise Coll.; chmn. Comprehensive Health Planning, Cochise County, Ariz., 1968. Mem. Ariz. Coun. for the Hearing Impaired, 1999. Mem. Am. Vet. Med. Assn., Soc. for Breeding Soundness, Internat. Platform Assn., Rotary, Elks. Republican. Episcopalian. Achievements include patents in ultrasound device and eye cover for treating infections, apparatus to alter equine leg conformation, external vein clamp, equine sanitation instrument; development of ear implant instrumentation system; patent for Farrier's rasp with measure. Home and Office: PO Box 4337 Bisbee AZ 85603-4337

BEHNKE, DOLEEN, computer and environmental specialist, consultant; b. Alameda, Calif., Sept. 23, 1950; d. Charles Joseph Ziegler and Dola Faye (Cushing) Peterson; m. Glen A.Pellett, June 26, 1971 (div. 1986); children: Mark Dolan, Michael Jay; m. Danny L. Carr, Dec. 29, 1986 (div. 1996); m. Jon T. Behnke, June 28, 1996. BA, U. Wis., Madison, 1973. Notary Pub., Mich. Budget analyst Ednl. Testing Svc., Princeton, N.J., 1979-80; tech. recruiter Uniforce Svcs., Inc., Rock Hill, S.C., 1983-84; mgr. tng. and documentation Electronic Data Systems Corp., Troy, Mich., 1985-87; tech. writer, trainer, analyst cons. CES, Inc., Troy, 1989-92; pres. D'Carr Co., Inc., Roseville, Mich., 1988-93; tech. writer, trainer, cons. Eaton Corp., Southfield, Mich., 1988-93; pres., CEO Carr-Ben Tech Ltd., Royal Oak, Mich., 1996-98; bd. dirs. Carr-Ben Tech Ltd., Royal Oak, 1999—; installer, instr. Gt. Plains Acctg., Fargo, N.D., 1990—; cons. Hazardous Materials Info. Exch., Washington, 1989—; cons., tech. writer Saturn Corp., 1991-92, Blue Cross Blue Shield, Southfield, Mich., 1992-93, 95-96; tech. writer FANUC Robotics, N.A., Inc., Auburn Hills, Mich., 1993-95. Co-author: CIW-Weld Monitor, 1990, 93. Mem. AAUP, NAFE, Greater Trenton Musicians Union, Profl. Bus. Women's Assn., Roseville Kiwanis (pres. 1995, lt. gov. elect 1996-97, clown 1994—), Royal Oak Kiwanis (Mich. dist. chairperson for K-Kids 1999-2000, 2000—, Mich. dist. chairperson for Young Children Priority One 2000—). Republican. Roman Catholic. Avocations: piano, swimming, computers, politics. Office: 222 Hi Hill Dr Lake Orion MI 48360-2429

BEHNKE, ROY HERBERT, physician, educator; b. Chgo., Feb. 24, 1921; s. Harry and Florence Alice (MacArthur) B.; m. Ruth Gretchen Zinszer, June 3, 1944; children: Roy, Michael, Donald, Elise. A.B., Hanover Coll., 1943; Ph.D. (hon.), 1972; M.D., Ind. U., 1946. Diplomate: Am. Bd. Internal Medicine. Intern Ind. U. Med. Center, 1946-47, resident, 1949-51, chief resident medicine, 1951-52; instr. medicine Ind. U. Sch. Medicine, Indpls., 1952-55, asst. prof. medicine, 1955-58, assoc. prof., 1958-61, prof., 1961-72; chief medicine VA Hosp., Indpls., 1957-72; prof. medicine U. South Fla. Coll. Medicine, Tampa, 1972—, chmn. dept. medicine, 1972-95, chmn. dept. head emeritus, 1995—; AMA rep. to residency rev. com. in internal medicine, 1970-75; mem. exec. and adv. com. Inter-Soc. Commn. Heart Disease Resources, 1968-72, chmn. pulmonary study sect., 1969-72; chmn. career devel. com. VA, 1980-83. Mem. Met. Sch. Bd. Washington Twp., 1968-72, pres., 1971; bd. dirs. Southside Community Health Center, 1968; trustee Tampa Gen. Hosp. Found., 1979-85; mem. research coordinating com. Am. Lung Assn., 1983-85, chmn., 1985-87, bd. dirs., 1983-87. Served with AUS, 1943-45, 47-49. Recipient Std. Oil Found. award Ind. U., 1971, Alumni Achievement award Hanover Coll., 1971; named Hon. Alumnus, USF Coll. Medicine, 1995; John and Mary Markle scholar, 1952, 57. Fellow and master ACP (gov. Fla. chpt. 1980-84, Laureate award 1991); fellow Am. Coll. chest Physicians; mem. AMA, Am. Fedn. Clin. Rsch., Ctrl. Soc. Clin. Rsch., So. Soc. Clin. Rsch., Alpha Omega Alpha. Home: 5111 Rolling Hill Ct Tampa FL 33617-1024 Office: Dept Internal Medicine 12901 N 30th St # 19 Tampa FL 33612-4742

BEHR, ARNO, chemist, educator; b. Aachen, Germany, Jan. 26, 1952. Cert. chemist, Tech. U. Aachen, 1977, Doctor, 1979, grad. in Edn., 1986. Head dept. Henkel Co., Düsseldorf, Germany, 1987-96; prof. U. Dortmund, Germany, 1996—. Author: Fundamentals of Industrial Chemistry, 1986, Carbon Dioxide Activation by Metal Complexes, 1988, Textbook of Technical Chemistry, 1996. Office: Univ Dortmund, Lehrstuhl Tech Chemistry A, D-44221 Dortmund Germany

BEHR, MARION RAY, artist, writer, business executive; b. Rochester, N.Y., Sept. 12, 1939; d. Justin Max and Sophie Gusta (Koffler) Rosenfeld. B.Art Edn., Syracuse U., 1961, M.F.A., 1962; m. Omri Marc Behr, June 24, 1962; children: Dawn Marcy Yael, Darrin Justin Mason, Dana Marisa Jana. Contbr. publs. for stories, crafts, mag. covers and toy designs to nat. mags. including McCall's, Good Housekeeping, Lady's Circle, 1962-77; one-woman shows include Douglas Coll., 1983, Pargot Gallery, 1989, Eldorado Gallery, 1992, Beamsderfer Gallery, 1992, Hunterdon Art Gallery, 1993; Hunterdon Mus. Art, 1998; Inst. Cultural Peruano Norteamericano, 1999; exhibited in group shows at Contemporary Am. Artists, Scarsdale, N.Y., 1964, Douglass Coll., 1977, John Szoke Gallery, 1989, Kanagawa Prefectual Gallery, Yokohama, Japan, 1989, 80 Washington Sq. East Gallery, N.Y.C., 1990, Juniper Gallery, Napa, Calif., 1991, Eldorado Gallery, Colorado Springs, Colo., 1992, B. Beamsderfer Gallery, Highland Park, N.J., 1992, Artsquad Gallery, Easton, 1993, Lever House, 1995, Audubon Artists, 1995, 97, 99, Cork Gallery, 1996, Cheltenham Ctr. for Arts, 1996, Krasdale Gallery, 1998, Nat. Acad. Mus., 1998, Stark & Stark, 1998, Zimmerli Art Mus., Rutgers U., New Brunswick; permanent print collection Smithsonian Instn. Nat. Mus. Art History, 1995, Jane Voorhees Zimmerli Art Mus., 1993, 96, Thai Royal Art Collection, Bangkok, 1995, Inst. Cultural Peruano Norteamericano, Peru, 1999; creator survey Women Working Home-the Invisible Workforce, 1978; pres. Women Working Home, Inc., Edison, N.J., 1980—; condr. workshops; author: (with others) Women Working Home: The Homebased Business Guide and Directory, 1981, 2nd edit., 1983; contbr. articles to popular mags., 1988-89, popular art jours., 1991-98, numerous articles to profl. jours.; illustrator Jewish Holiday Book, 1977; inventor (with Omri Behr) acid free, environmentally safe graphic etching process; installed Electrotech processor and taught first non toxic intaglio etching class at Stanford U., 1999; installed electroetch and established non-toxic etching in the Inuit Artists Holman Eskimo Co-op Art Center, Holman Island, NWT, Canada, 1999, U Al Moutamid IBN Abbad, Asilah, Morocco, 2000; extensive radio and TV appearances rep. Nat. Alliance Homebased Businesswomen. Mem. Kean for Gov. campaign, 1981; mem. White House Conf. on Free Enterprise Zones, 1982, Nat. Assn. of Women Artists, 1992, Soc. Am. Graphic Artists, So. Graphics Coun., 1992, Print Coun. N.J., 1993; trustee Women's Bus. Ownership Ednl. Conf., Inc., N.J., 1985; apptd. to N.J. Devel. Authority for Small, Minority and Women's Bus. Commn., 1986; Presdl. del. White House Conf. on Small Bus., 1986. Recipient N.J. Women in Bus. Advocate of the Yr. award SBA, 1984, Merit award Am. Artist Profl. League, Woman of Yr. in Bus. and Industry award, 1985, Audubon Artists Merit award, 1995; Syracuse U. alumni grantee, 1957; Arts and Humanities grantee Charles E. Lindbergh Fund, 1993-94. Mem. Nat. Alliance Homebased Businesswomen (pres. 1980-82, legis. chair 1982-85; originator, founder), Women's Caucus for Art, Audoban Artists. Jewish. Office: 325 Pierson Ave Edison NJ 08837-3123

BEHREND, WILLIAM LOUIS, electrical engineer; b. Wisconsin Rapids, Wis., Jan. 11, 1923; s. Albert and Eva Mae (Barney) B.; m. Manet Louise Whitrock, July 7, 1945; children: Jane Louise, Ann Behrend Luther. B.S. in Elec. Engring., U. Wis., 1946, M.S., 1947. Research engr. David Sarnoff Research Ctr., RCA, 1947-64; advanced devel. engr. comml. systems div. RCA, Meadows Lands, Pa., 1964-66, prelimanary design and systems analyst, 1966-84; ret., 1984, cons. engr., 1984-90. Contbr. articles on elec. engring. to profl. jours.; patentee in field. Served with USNR, 1944-46. Recipient RCA David Sarnoff Rsch Ctr. Outstanding Rsch. award, 1956, 59, 63, RCA Comml. Systems Div. Outstanding Contbns. to Product Tech. award, 1974. Fellow IEEE (Scott Helt award 1971); mem. N.Y. Acad. Scis., Sigma Xi. Address: 6436 Antietam Ln Madison WI 53705-2564

BEHRENDT, JOHN CHARLES, geophysicist, writer; b. Stevens Point, Wis., May 18, 1932; s. Allen Charles and Vivian Eulaine Behrendt; m. Dona Ebber, Oct. 6, 1961 (div. June 1989); children: Kurt Allen, Marc Russel. Student, Wis. State Coll., 1950-52; BS, U. Wis., 1954, MS, 1956, PhD, 1961. Cert. geophysicist, Calif. Asst. seismologist Arctic Inst. N.Am., Ellsworth Station, Antarctica, 1956-58; rsch. assoc. U. Wis., Madison, 1958-64; rsch. geophysicist U.S. Geol. Survey, Denver, 1964-68, 77-95, Monrovia, Liberia, 1968-70, Denver, 1970-72; rsch. geophysicist, br. chief U.S. Geol. Survey, Woods Hole, Mass., 1972-77; sr. rsch. assoc. Inst. Arctic U. Colo., Boulder, 1996—; mem. com. NAS, Washington, 1975-95; sci. advisor, mem. del. U.S. Del. to Antarctic Treaty, Washington, 1977-95. Author: Innocents on the Ice: A Memoir of Antarctic Exploration, 1957 (award 1999); contbr. more than 270 articles to profl. jours. Recipient Antarctic Svc. medal Dept. Def., 1965, Meritorious Svc. award Dept. Interior, 1992, F. Ippilito gold medal Italian Acad. Sci. and Antarctic Rsch. Program (Italy), 1999. Fellow Geol. Soc. Am.; mem. AAAS, Am. Geophys. Union, Soc. Exploration Geophysicists. Democrat. Unitarian Universalist. Avocations: photography, bicycling, mountaineering, outdoor activity, reading, music. Office: U Colo Instaar Boulder CO 80309-0001

BEHRENDT, THOMAS RUDOLF, lawyer; b. Halle, Fed. Republic Germany, July 14, 1951; s. Willy and Jutta (Kuska) B.; children: Halina, Carolyn. Diploma in econs., U. Munich, 1975, 1. jur. Staatsexamen, 1979; assessor jur, Bavarian Ministry Justice, Munich, 1981. Rsch. worker German Inst. for Econ. Rsch., Berlin, 1972-74, Ifo-Inst. for Econ. Rsch., Munich, 1974-75; acad. asst. U. Munich, 1976-82; pvt. practice lawyer Munich, 1982—; mem. several bd. dirs. Contbr. articles to profl. jours. Advisor elected govt. of German Dem. Republic, 1990; advisor to Treuhand, 1990. Mem. German Econ. Soc., Peutinger Collegium, Am. Coun. on Germany, Order of St. John (Ehrenritter), Export Club. Lutheran. Avocations: books, art, golf. E-mail: TBehrRA@aol.com.

BEHRENS, BERNHARD BALTHASAR, mathematics educator; b. Taufkirchen, Bayern, Germany, Jan. 21, 1944; arrived in Sweden, 1975; s. Albert and Lidwina (Meyer) B. Diploma in math., U. Tech., Berlin, 1969, D of Natural Scis., 1974. Asst. Tech. U., Berlin, 1969-74; asst. prof. Chalmers U. of Tech., Gothenburg, Sweden, 1975—. Home: Chalmersg 19, S-41135 Gothenburg Sweden Office: Chalmers U of Tech, Dept of Math, S-41296 Göteborg Sweden

BEHRENS, GEORG MARTIN NORBERT, immunologist, researcher; b. Friesoythe, Germany, July 29, 1968; s. Georg and Margarethe (Scheele) B.; m. Doris Anges Preut, Aug. 31, 1996; 1 child, Linus Philipp. Degree in medicine, Hannover (Germany) Med. Sch., 1995; Dr.med., U. Giessen, Germany, 1996. Rsch. fellow dept. clin. immunology Hannover Med. Sch., 1995—. Author: HIV-Infekt, 2000; contbr. articles to profl. jours. Mem. German Soc. Immunology. Office: Dept Clin Immunology, Carl-Neuberg-St 7, 30625 Hannover Germany

BEHRENS, HENRY WILLIAM, international business educator, investment executive; b. Scheessel, Germany, Aug. 4, 1935; came to U.S., 1955, naturalized, 1960; s. Claude William and Sophie Magdalena (Ellmers) B.; m. Eva Paeslack, June 12, 1960; children: Andrew M., Lawrence H. BS, Columbia U., 1961, MBA, 1962; PhD, New Sch. for Social Rsch., 1969. Economist Exxon Internat., N.Y.C., 1962-65; vis. lectr. econs. Columbia U., N.Y.C., 1965; asst. prof. econs. and fin. Fairleigh Dickinson U., Rutherford, N.J., 1965-68; assoc. prof. econs. and fin. Union Coll. and U., Schenectady, N.Y., 1968-72; pres. Algonquin Investors Corp., Niskayuna, N.Y., 1972-78; exec. dir. U.S.A.F.E.C., N.Y.C., 1979-81; prof. world bus. Am. Grad. Sch. Internat. Bus., Phoenix, 1982-84; prof. fin. and internat. bus. Nat. U., San Diego, 1984-96; prin., CEO The McCormack Group, San Diego, 1985—. Author: The Effects of Monetary Policy on Commercial Banks, Thrift Institutions and the Residential Mortgage Market, 1968; Export Guide, 1985; author various rsch. reports. Mem. U.S. Senate Club, Am. Mgmt. Assns., Am. Fin. Assn., Am. Econ. Assn., Columbia U. Club (N.Y.C.), Alpha Kappa Psi. Office: PO Box 27708 San Diego CA 92198-1708

BEHRENS, HILDEGARD, soprano; b. Oldenburg, Germany, 1937; m. Seth Scheidman. Student, Music Conservatory, Freiburg, Fed. Republic of Germany. Opera debut in Freiburg, 1971; resident mem. Deutsche Opera Am Rhein, Dusseldorf, Fed. Republic of Germany; debut Covent Garden, 1976, as Leonore in Fidelio, in Salzburg, 1977, as Salome; appeared in Tosca, N.Y. Met., 1985, as Brünnhilde in Siegfried, N.Y. Met., 1988, title role in Elektra, N.Y. Met., 1994; appeared in new Production of The Ring, Bayreuth, 1988; appeared with Frankfurt (Fed. Republic of Germany) Opera, Teatro Nacional de San Carlo, Lisbon, Portugal, Vienna Staatsoper, Met. Opera, N.Y.C., Orchestre Nat. de Paris, 1990; soloist Chgo. Symphony Orch., 1984. Office: Herbert H Breslin Inc 119 W 57th St New York NY 10019-2303

BEHRENS, JAMES WILLIAM, physicist, administrator, author; b. Litchfield, Ill., Apr. 29, 1947; s. George William and Norma Clara Marie (Boeker) B.; m. Pamela Jane Breese, July 7, 1973 (div. Jan. 1980); 1 child, Jaime Rhea; m. Linda Sue Lawrence, July 5, 1984. BS in Engring. Physics, U. Ill., 1970; MS in Engring and Applied Sci., U. Calif., Davis, 1976, postgrad., 1976-78. Physicist Lawrence Livermore (Calif.) Nat. Lab., 1969-78, U.S. Dept. Commerce, Nat. Bur. Stas., Gaithersburg, Md., 1978-89; sci. tech. advisor Joint Chiefs of Staff, U.S. Dept. Def. Joint Staff, Washington, 1989-91; asst. exec. program mgr. Office Asst. Sec. Def. U.S. Dept. Def., Washington, 1991-92; sr. spl. projects mgr. U.S. Dept. Def., USN, Indian Head, Md., 1992-93; asst. dir. U.S. Dept. Def., Interagy. Tng. Ctr., Ft. Washington, Md., 1993-95; dep. dir. Interagy. Tng. Ctr. U.S. Dept. Def., Ft. Washington, Md., 1995-97; dir. U.S. Dept. Def. Ft. Washington Facility, 1997-99; sr. rsch. scientist, engr. U.S. Dept. Def., Naval Rsch. Lab., Washington, 1999—; tech. cons., pres. I.Q. in Nuc. Electronics Sys. & Tech., Inc., Rockville, Md., 1983-89; guest scientist Commissariat à l'Energie Atomique (CEA), Bruyere-le-Chatel, France, 1984. Author: Symbols and Fragments, 1993, Record of the House of Braunschweig-Illinois-Hannover, 1995, The 1995 Behrens Chronicle: A Complete Work, 1996, The 1995 Boeker Chronicle: A Complete Work, 1996, The 1996 Behrens-Boeker Chronicles: A Combined Work, 1997; co-editor: Fifty Years with Nuclear Fission, 1989; contbr. tech. articles to profl. pubs. Mem. Nat. Geneal. Soc., Nat. Writers Assn., Internat. Platform Assn., Nat. Audubon Soc., Nat. Wildlife Fedn., Am. Nuc. Soc. (cert. Appreciation 1989). Independent. Lutheran. Achievements include investigation of fast neutron-induced fission cross section measurements of the actinide elements, improvement of accuracy of neutron-induced fission cross section values which are used in broad areas of applied nuclear physics. Home: 1 Spa Creek Lndg Unit A2 Annapolis MD 21403-2330 Office: Naval Rsch Lab 4555 Overlook Ave SW Washington DC 20375-0001

BEHRING, KENNETH E., professional sports team owner; b. Freeport, Ill., June 13, 1928; s. Elmer and Mae (Priewe) B.; m. Patricia Riffle, Oct. 16, 1949; children: Michael, Thomas, David, Jeffrey, Scott. Student, U. Wis., 1947. Owner Behring Motors, Monroe, Wis., 1953-56, Behring Corp., Ft. Lauderdale, Fla., 1956-72; owner Blackhawk Corp., Danville, Calif., 1972—, also chmn. bd. dirs.; owner Seattle Seahawks, NFL, 1988-97; Calif. land developer; mem. policy adv. bd. real estate and urban econs. U. Calif., Berkeley.; chmn. bd. dirs. Behring-Hofmann Ednl. Inst., Inc. U. Calif. Trustee U. Calif., Berkeley; regent St. Mary's Coll., Moraga, Calif., Holy Name Coll., Oakland, Calif.; hon. trustee Mt. Diablo Hosp. Found., Concord, Calif.; hon. chmn. Seattle Art Mus., Am. Cancer Soc., Muscular Dystrophy, Silverado Concours. Named Man of Yr. Boys Town Italy, En-

trepreneur of Yr. INC mag. Mem. Am. Acad. Achievement (honoree 1989), Assn. Wash. Bus., Seattle Master Builders Assn., Blackhawk Club, Vintage Club, Seattle Yacht Club, Wash. Athletic Club. Office: Blackhawk Corp PO Box 807 Danville CA 94526-0807

BEHRMAN, EDWARD JOSEPH, biochemistry educator; b. N.Y.C., Dec. 13, 1930; s. Morris Harry and Janet Cahn (Solomons) B.; m. Cynthia Fansler, Aug. 29, 1953; children—David Murray, Elizabeth Colden, Victoria Anne. B.S., Yale, 1952; Ph.D., U. Calif. at Berkeley, 1957. Research asso. biochemistry Cancer Research Inst., Boston, 1960-64; bd. tutors biochem. scis. Harvard, 1961-64; asst. prof. chemistry Brown U., Providence, 1964-65; mem. faculty Ohio State U., Columbus, 1965—; asso. prof. biochemistry Ohio State U., 1967-69, prof., 1969—; rschr. in peroxydisulfate and nucleotide chemistry. Contbr. articles profl. jours. USPHS fellow, 1955-56, 57-60; NSF grantee, 1966-73; NIH grantee, 1973-81. Mem. Am. Chem. Soc., Royal Soc. Chemistry, Phi Beta Kappa, Sigma Xi. Home: 6533 Hayden Run Rd Hilliard OH 43026-9642 Office: Ohio State U Dept Biochemistry Columbus OH 43210

BEICHELT, FRANK ERICH, mathematics educator; b. Hilbersdorf, Freiberg, Germany, Apr. 8, 1942; s. Erich Bruno and Gerda Johanna (Venus) B. Diploma in Math., F. Schiller U., Jena, Germany, 1966; D Natural Scis., Mining Acad., Freiberg, 1972; D Tech. Sci., Traffic U., Dresden, Germany, 1978. Asst. Tech. U., Dresden, 1966-68; head asst. Mining Acad., Freiberg, 1969-74; head engr. Lignite Mining Industry, Röblingen a See, Germany, 1974-79; asosc. prof. Traffic U., Dresden, 1979-81; prof. math. Ingenieurhochschule, Mittweida, Germany, 1981-93, head dept., 1981-93; sr. lectr. U. Witwatersrand, Johannesburg, South Africa, 1997-98, rsch. prof., 1998—; vis. prof. Maximilian U., Würzburg, Germany, 1990, U. Tech., Schweinfurt, Germany, 1991, U. Tribourg, 1995, 98, Ariz. State U., Tempe, 1995. Author: Reliability and Maintenance, 1970, Preventive Maintenance, 1976, Reliability of Complicated Systems, 1988, Reliability and Maintenance Theory, 1993, Stochastics for Engineers, 1995, Stochastic Processes for Engineers, 1997; co-author: Mathematic Models of Reliability and Maintenance, 1983, Stochastic Processes and Their Applications, 2000; contbr. more than 90 articles to profl. jours. Lt. German mil., 1968-69. Mem. IEEE Reliability Soc. Avocations: sports, mountaineering. Fax: (0027) 11 339 6640. E-mail: 010 Frank@cosmos.wits.ac.za. Office: U Witwatersrand, Pvt Bag 3, Wits 2050 Johannesburg South Africa

BEIER-HOLGERSEN, RANDI, physician, surgeon; b. Copenhagen, Denmark, Feb. 9, 1956; d. Frantz Frederik and Karen (Groentved) Verwohlt; m. Arne Beier-Holgersen, Apr. 22, 1978; children: Lars, Anders. MD, U. Copenhagen, 1983. Registrar Frederiksberg (Denmark) Hosp., 1983-88, K.A.S. Glostrup, Denmark, 1988-90, K.A.S. Herlev, Denmark, 1990-91; asst. surgeon K.A.S. Glostrup, Denmark, 1991-94, prin. investigator, 1994-95, asst. sr. surgeon, 1995-97; sr. surgeon H:S Bispebjerg Hosp., Copenhagen, 1998-99; asst. sr. surgeon K.A.S. Herlev, Denmark, 1999-2000; sr. surgeon H:S Bispebjerg Hosp., Copenhagen, 2000—. Cntbr. articles to profl. jours. Mem. Danish Soc. for Clin. Nutrition (sec. 1997—), Danish Soc. Gastroenterology, Danish Soc. Urology. Avocation: music. Home: Noeddehaven 30B, DK-2500 Valby Denmark Office: H:S Bispebjerg Hosp, Bispebjerg Bakke 23, DK-2400 Copenhagen Denmark

BEIERWALTES, WILLIAM HENRY, physician, educator; b. Saginaw, Mich., Nov. 23, 1916; s. John Andrew and Fanny (Aris) B.; m. Mary Martha Nichols, Jan. 1, 1942; children: Andrew George, William Howard, Martha Louise. AB, U. Mich., 1938, MD, 1941. Diplomate: Am. Bd. Internal Medicine and Nuclear Medicine. Intern, then asst. resident medicine Cleve. City Hosp., 1941-43; mem. faculty U. Mich. Med. Center, 1944-87, prof. medicine, 1959-87, prof. emeritus, 1987—; dir. nuclear medicine, also dir. Thyroid Research Lab., 1952-86, cons., 1987-95; cons. nuclear medicine depts. St. John Hosp., Detroit, Wm. Beaumont Hosp., Royal Oak and Troy, Mich., 1987-95, The UpJohn Co. Rsch. div., 1952-65, The Abbott Labs. Rsch. div., 1960-67; sr. med. cons. MD (Med. Fedn.), Bagdad, Iraq, 1963; mem. exec. com. Inst. Sci. and Tech., 1963; lectr. Nat. Naval Med. Ctr., 1964-88, Ctr. for Environ. Health Mich. State Dept. Health, 1988-89; Peter Heimann lectr. 34th meeting Internat. Congress Surgery, Stockholm, Sweden, 1991; adv. panel on radionuclide labeled compounds for tumor diagnosis Internat. AEC, 1974-75; mem. Mich. State Radiation Bd., 1980-84; co-chmn. Nat. Coop., Thyroid Cancer Therapy Group, 1978-81. Author: Clinical Use of Radioisotopes, 1957, Manual of Nuclear Medicine Procedures, 1971, Love of Life Autobiog. Sketches, 1996; contbr. numerous articles to profl. jours.; assoc. editor Jour. Lab. and Clin. Medicine, 1954-60; editl. bd. Jour. Nuclear Medicine, 1964-69, assoc. editor, 1975-81; editl. bd. Jour. Clin. Endocrinology and Metabolism, 1963; adv. bd. Annals of Saudi Medicine, 1986-90; patentee for monoclonal antibodies to HCG, and radionuclide in vivo biochem. imaging of endocrine glands, 1951; first to treat a patient for cancer with radio labeled antibodies, 1951; co-inventor radiopharms, 1971; originator of radioimmunodetection of human cancer; first description of cytogenetic evolution of thyroid cancer; first description of fall of serum antithyroid antibodies during pregnancy with rise after delivery, other med. techniques. Guggenheim fellow, 1966-67; Commonwealth Fund fellow, 1967; recipient Hevesy Nuc. Medicine Pioneer award, 1982, Disting. Faculty award U. Mich., 1982, Johann-Georg-Zimmerman Trust for Cancer Rsch. Sci. prize for greatest contbn. to treatment of thyroid cancer, 1983, WWJ 950 Detroit Citizen of Week award, 1994; named Internat. Man of Yr. Internat. Biog. Ctr., Cambridge, Eng., 1992-93. Mem. AMA (Outstanding Scientific Achievement award 1994), ACP, Am. Fedn. Clin. Rsch. (pres. 1954-55), Soc. Nuclear Medicine (pres. 1965-66, Disting. Educator's award 1989, The Best Doctors in Am. award 1993-95), Ctrl. Clin. Rsch. Club (pres. 1958-59), Am. Thyroid Assn. (v.p. 1964-65, 66-67, Disting. Svc. award 1972), Ctrl. Soc. Clin. Rsch. (councillor 1964-67, 67-71), Galens Med. Soc., Assn. Am. Physicians, Mich. Med. Soc., Am. Endocrine Soc., Am. Soc. Clin. Oncology. Home: 917 Whittier Rd Grosse Pointe MI 48230-1873

BEIGBEDER, YVES BAYARD, international organization educator, researcher; b. Morlaix, Finistere, France, July 16, 1924; s. Louis Jean Gustave and Madeleine Hélène (Engelhard) B.; m. Audrey Rosemary Robinson; children: Muriel, Thomas, Steven, Martin. Licencié en Droit, Sorbonne U., Paris, 1945; MSc in Edn., Indiana U., 1948; LLD, Grenoble U., France, 1973. Legal sec. to French judge Nuremberg Internat. Mil. Tribunal, 1946; pers. officer UN Food and Agr. Orgn., Rome, 1951-55; pers. officer WHO, Geneva, 1955-84, asst. chief of pers.; sr. fellow UN Inst. for Tng. and Rsch., Geneva, 1986—; adj. prof. Webster U., Geneva, 1979—; pres. conciliation bd. European Space Agy., Paris, 1986—; legal counsel to UN orgns., staff, 1994; vis. prof. France, Switzerland, U.S., Can., 1981—. Author: The Role and Status of International Humanitarian Volunteers and Organizations, 1991, Internal Monitoring of Referenda and National Elections, 1994, The International Management of United Nations Organizations, 1997, L'Organization Mondiale de la Santé, 1997, Judging War Criminals, 1999. Recipient Prix de l'Institut de France award, Paris, 1996. Mem. Acad. Coun. on UN Sys., Union Internat. Assocs., Soc. Française pour le droit Internat. Avocations: golf, chess. Home: 6 Rue de l'Hotel de Ville, 74200 Thonon Les Bains France

BEIGL, WILLIAM, physician, naturopath, hypnotist, acupuncturist, consultant; b. Chgo., July 9, 1950; s. William C. Beigl and Mary Tomlinson; m. Mavis Johnson, Aug. 5, 1977. BA in Elem. Edn., U. South Fla., 1971; D of Natural Medicine, Acad. Sci. of Man, Sussex, Eng., 1979. Founder "You Too Can Choose Happiness" System, 1975; pvt. practice hypnotherapy Chgo., 1977—, pvt. practice naturopathic medicine, acupuncture and oriental natural medicine, 1979—; mem. rsch. team Donsbach U., 1980; chief rschr. disease prevention B.P.H. Corp.; bd. dirs. Mid-West Hypnosis Conv.; cons. in field; 1st syndicated hypnosis columnist, 1982; CEO Bill Beigl Enterprises, Inc., 1992, World Hypnosis Orgn., Inc., 1992; guest presenter Paramedics 25th Anniversary Celebration, Phila., 1993, (with Lee Ramsey) Blair Cheese Fest, 1994; devised lowered casino game tables; expert witness on hypnosis Cook County Ct. Sys. Editor, pub. Portage Park News, 1980; originator Paramedic System, 1968 (honored by Pres. Johnson 1968, Pres. Nixon 1969, Pres. Reagan 1985); responsible for Ramped Curbs, Braille Markings on Elevators and Monuments, Handicapped Parking Space, Licence Plates and Pub. Accessibility for Wheelchairs, Lowered Casino Gaming Tables, licensing of naprapaths and naturopaths in Ill., 1994, licensing acupuncturists in Ill., 1997; author: Adventures in Hypnosis, 1990, 2d edit., 1991; contbg. author: Think & Grow Breasts, 1994; contbr. articles on natural healing and hypnosis to newspapers and mags.; patentee in field. Assoc. bd. mgrs. Robert R. McCormick chpt. Chgo. Boy's Club, 1975; mem. trauma unit Operation Desert Storm, 1991; vol. with Hurricane Andrew victims, 1992, Mississippi River flood victims, 1993, summer Centennial Olympics physician, Atlanta, 1996; bd. dirs. Kids Internat., 1996; mem. trauma unit Operation Desert Thunder, 1998; with Small Bus. Nonprofit Orgn. Credit Cards, 1998, Acceptance of Alternative Med. Fees by HMOs, 1999. Recipient award Congressman Sidney Yates, 1971, Disease Prevention award Better Positive Health Found., 1979, Pen and Quill award Nat. Bd. for Hypnotherapy and Hypnotic Anesthesiology, 1991, Excellence award Honeywell, 1994; named Chicagoan of Yr., Mayor Richard J. Daley, 1968, Chgo. Cath. of Yr., Cardinal John Cody, 1968, Illinoisan of Yr., Gov. Richard B. Ogilvie, 1968, One of 10 Outstanding Young Citizens, Chgo. Jaycees, 1980, Inspirational Mind of Four Profl. Championship Sports Teams, 1983-84, Citizen of Week, Sta. WBBM, 1984; appeared in Ripley's Believe It Or Not, 1984; honored by Gov. James R. Thompson, 1985, U.S. Senator Charles H. Percy, 1986; featured on CBS-TV Portrait Series, 1985, Cablevision's Good Neighbors, 1987; inducted into Internat. Hypnosis Hall of Fame, 1989. Mem. Internat. Naturopathic Assn. (cert., Naturopathic Physician Yr. 1985), Nat. Assn. Naturopathic Physicians (cert.), Nat. Guild Hypnotists (cert.), Assn. Advance Ethical Hypnosis (cert., past v.p., past sec. Ill. chpt., bd. dirs. 1986, participant the biggest hypnosis conv. 1988, co-chmn. world's largest and friendliest 1987-88, 89), World Hypnosis Orgn. (cert.), Am. Naturopathic Assn., Am. Soc. Clin. Hypnosis, Minn. Assn. Naturopathic Physicians (cert.), Hemlock Soc., Chgo. Meml. Assn., Boys Clubs Am. (life, Boy of Yr. 1968), Hospice, Midwest Pain Soc., Pain Clinic Physicians. Lodge: Moose. Office: 2521 W Montrose Ave Chicago IL 60618-1505

BEILIN, JOSEPH (YOSSI), member of parliament; b. Petach Tikva, Israel, June 12, 1948; s. Zvi and Zehava (Bregman) B.; m. Helena Einhorn, Aug. 12, 1969; children: Gil, Ori. BA in Hebrew Lit., Tel Aviv U., MA in Polit. Sci., 1976, PhD in Polit. Sci., 1981. Journalist Davar newspaper, Tel Aviv, 1969-77; lectr. polit. sci. Tel Aviv U., 1972-85; spokesman Israel Labour Party, Tel Aviv, 1977-84; sec. of govt. Office of Prime Minister, Jerusalem, 1984-86; dir. gen. fgn. affairs Israel Ministry Fgn. Affairs, Jerusalem, 1986-88; deputy min. of fin. Govt. Israel, 1988-90; dep. min. fgn. affairs Govt. Israel, Jerusalem, 1992-95; min. of econs. and planning Govt. of Israel, 1995, min. Office of the Prime Minister, 1996, min. of justice, 1999—; instr., researcher Tel Aviv U., 1972-85. Author: Sons in their Fathers' Shadow, 1984, The Price of Unity, 1985, The Roots of Industry in Israel, 1987, Israel: a Concise Political History, 1993, Touching Peace, 1997, The Manual for Leaving Lebanon, 1998, From Socialism to Social Liberalism, 1999, His Brother's Keeper, 2000. Recipient Gleitsman Found. Internat. Activist award, 1999. Mem. Assn. Polit. Sci. Office: Ministry of Justice, 29 Salah A-Din St PO Box 1087, 91010 Jerusalem Israel

BEILIS-MAJERFELD, RACHEL, painter, graphic artist; b. Paris, May 28, 1930; d. Baruch and Tauba (Mestelman) Majerfeld; married; children: Nava Beilis Fleisher, Michael Beilis. MA, Acad. Plastic Arts, Warsaw, Poland, 1957; diploma of edn., Bar Ilan U., Tel Aviv, 1976; studies in etching, Beaux Arts Acad., Paris, 1978-79. Apptd. tchr. art area high schs., also Levinsky Coll.; tchr. Amamit U., Tel Aviv and Amamit U. Bat Yam. One-woman shows include Ho. of Am. Zionists, Tel Aviv, 1968, Culture Ho., Rehovot, Israel, 1972, Beit Ha'am, Jerusalem, 1976, Tourel Gallery, Tel Aviv, 1976, Artists, Painters and Sculptors Assn. Gallery, Tel Aviv, 1992, Cultural Ctr., Netanya, Israel, 1995, Tzavta Cultural Ctr., Tel Aviv, 1995, D.S. Danon Gallery, Tel Aviv, 1996, Tzirum Gallery, Kibbutz Urim, Israel, 1996, Town Mcpl. Gallery, Jerusalem, 1997, Danon Gallery, Tel-Aviv, 1998, Kibutz Artists Studio, Tel Aviv, 2000; exhibited in various group shows, Israel, U.S., France, Spain, Chile, Sweden, Switzerland, Holland, Denmark, Germany, 1957—, Mus. Zahenta, Warsaw, 1951, Mus. of Holocaust, Jerusalem, 1973, Mus. of Art Holon, Israel, 1974, 75, 85, 89, Found. Napoleon, Paris, 1995, Eretz Israel Mus., Tel Aviv, 1996, Salon des Inds., Paris, 1995, 96, 97, 98, Mus. Haaretz, Tel Aviv, 1996, Mus. Hatanah, Tel Aviv, 1997, Gall. Herout Paris, 1997, Beit Amanim, Jerusalem, Israel, 1999, Mus. Holon, 1999, 2000. Recipient La Toile D'or, Nat. Fedn. French Culture, 1997, Gold medal, diploma first prize in internat. exbhn., Stockholm, 1996, Silver medal internat. d'Art Comtemporain, 1998, Gold medal France, 1998, La Croix d'argent du merite Arts-Scis.-Lettres, France, 1988, Createur d'Aujord 'hui, 1998, Federation Natl. of the Culture Francaise Gold Medal, Internatl. Art Contempo-rain, Grand Prix du Prestige European et Commandeur de l'Etoile d'Europe, 1998, Grand Prix du Prestige European with Grade de Commandeur in the Ordre de l'Etoile de l'Europe, Danemark, 1998, la'Toile dor, Federation Natl. de la Culture Francaise, 1997, 98, Consecration, 1999, Grand Concourse Internatl., 1999, France; other exhbn. awards. Mem. Assn. Painters and Sculptors, Assn. Tchrs. in Israel, Assn. Artists Miniaturists, Prof. mem., Acad. Internatl. Greci-Marino, Italy, 1999, mem., l'Assn. des Peintres Independants, Paris, Grand Palais of Arts. Avocations: music, books, folklore arts, black and white and French films, crafts. Home: Hatryah 26, 58403 Holon Israel

BEIMAN, YONG LING SUN, management consultant; b. Xiamen, China, Sept. 30, 1959; d. An Min and De Lan (Wang) Sun; m. Irv Harry Beiman, May 15, 1988. AA, Quanzhou (China) Tchrs. Coll., 1981; BA summa cum laude, Salem Coll., 1987; MBA, Duke U., 1989. Faculty dept. English Jimei Tchrs. Coll., Xiamen, 1981-84; systems analyst RJR Tobacco Internat., Inc., Winston-Salem, N.C., 1986-88; fin. analyst RJR Nabisco, Inc., Atlanta, 1989; asst. v.p. Wellington Mgmt. Co., Boston, 1989-93; gen. mgr. Hewitt Assocs. Consulting Co., Ltd., 1993-98; mgmt. cons. East Gate Cons., 1999—. Mem. Am. C. of C. in Shanghai, Expatriate Assn., Assn. Profl. Women. Avocations: reading, travel, swimming, taiji, music. Fax: (808) 249-8813. Office: 551 Polulani Dr Wailuku HI 96793-1561

BEISCHER, NORMAN ALBERT, retired medical educator, editor; b. Bendigo, Australia, Apr. 15, 1930; s. Albert Ludwig and Minna (Matchett) B.; m. Elizabeth Evizel Young, Apr. 8, 1961; children: David Albert, Andrew Donald, Anne Evizel. MB, BS, U. Melbourne, Australia, 1954; M in Ob-Gyn., U. Melbourne, 1963, MD, 1969. Resident med. officer Alfred Hosp., Melbourne, 1955, Royal Children's Hosp., Melbourne, 1956; registrar Royal Womens Hosp., Melbourne, 1957-59; registrar in ob-gyn. Royal Maternity Hosp., Belfast, No. Ireland, 1960-62; 1st asst. dept. ob-gyn. U. Melbourne, 1963-68, prof., chmn. dept. ob-gyn., 1968-95, emeritus prof., 1996—. Co-author: (with E.V. Mackay) Obstetrics and the Newborn, Colour Atlas of Gynaecology, Care of the Pregnant Woman and Her Baby, (with E.V. Mackay, C. Wood and R. Pepperell) Illustrated Textbook of Gynaecology; editor Australian and New Zealand Jour. Obstetrics and Gynecology, 1982-99; contbr. over 200 articles to profl. jours. Chmn. consultative coun. obstetric and pediatric mortality and morbidity, Victoria, Australia, 1984-2000; dir. rsch. found. Med. Rsch. Found. for Women and Babies, 1982—. Named to Order of Australia, 1994. Fellow Royal Coll. Surgeons (Edinburgh, Scotland), Royal Australasian Coll. Surgeons, Royal Australian Coll. Obstetricians and Gynaecologists, Royal Coll. Obstetricians and Gynaecologists (London); mem. Australian Med. Assn., Royal South Yarra Tennis Club, Melbourne Club. Anglican. Avocations: gardening, farming. Home: 26 Linda Crescent, Hawthorn 3122, Australia Office: 380 Victoria Parade, East Melbourne 3002, Australia

BEISEL, DIETER ERWIN, editor-in chief of periodical; b. Quedlinburg, Germany, Aug. 18, 1940; s. Hans Hermann Erwin and Elisabeth Maria (Feuerstein) B.; m. Dagmar Geralde Pfeiffer, Aug. 13, 1965 (div. 1974); children: Nicolai, Tatjana; m. Christina Sieglinde Mundt, July 14, 1983. Student in philosophy and German,, U. Heidelberg, U. Freiburg, Germany. Editor Rhein-Neckar-Zeitung, Mannheim, Germany, 1969-72; editor-in-chief Werk & Zeit, Berlin, 1973-76; staff prodn. and visualization Pardon, Frankfurt, Germany, 1977-78; sci. editor Westermann's Monatshefte, Braunschweig, Germany, 1978-80; staff prodn. Natur, München, Germany, 1981-89; editor-in-chief Kultur & Technik Mag., (München), Germany, 1990—. Author: Alternative Energien, 1988, Travelling into the Country of Rebel Tigray - an African Future, 1989; editor, co-author: Bauen und Wohnen, 1987, Das Ökohaus, 1988; contbr. articles to profl. pubs. Mem. German Journalists Assn., Utilization Assn. Word, Utilization Assn. Picture/Arts. Home: Occamstrasse 3, D 80802 Munich Bayern, Germany Office: Redaktion Kultur & Technik, Occamstrasse 3, D 80802 Munich Bayern, Germany

BEITER, THOMAS ALBERT, crystallographer, research scientist, consultant; b. Lancaster, Ohio, Jan. 21, 1947; s. Paul Clement and Marie Julia (Mullen) B. BS in Math., Ohio State U., 1970; MS in Physics, Miami U., Oxford, Ohio, 1984, PhD in Chemistry, 1992. Rsch. scientist, cons. in crystallography Mansfield, Ohio, 1992—. Mem. Am. Chem. Soc., Am. Crystallographic Assn., Am. Phys. Soc., Am. Math. Soc., Assn. for Symbolic Logic, Sigma Xi, Phi Beta Kappa. Achievements include development of new methods for solving mathematical problems in x-ray diffraction crystallography; structure determination from powder data; indexing of triclinic powder data; space group determination for atomic arrangements; analysis of disorder in crystalline samples; research in number theory (Fermat Conjecture). Avocation: flying. Office: PO Box 3532 Mansfield OH 44907-0532

BEITINGER, GUNTER, electronic engineer; b. Neumarut, Bavaria, Germany, Mar. 17, 1968; s. Guenther Friedrich and Silvia Annemaria Mai B.; m. Corina Saucedo. BA, U. Hagen, 1994; MA, U. Erlangen, 1994, D of Engring., diploma engring., 1999. Rsch. collaborator FAPS, Erlangen, 1994—; project leader prodn. planning Siemens Automotive, Regensburg, Germany, 1999-00; new project and svc. mgr. Siemens Automotive, El Paso, Tex., 2000—. Contbr. articles to profl. jours. Avocations: snowboarding, squash, painting. Office: FAPS Inst, Erlangdstr 7, 91058 Erlangen Germany

BEITLER, STEPHEN SETH, private equity and venture capital executive; b. N.Y.C., Oct. 1, 1956; s. Stanley Samuel and Arline (Mandell) B.; m. Deborah Joy Gottlieb, Jan. 16, 1982; children: Grace Jacqueline, Elinore Meredith. BA, cert. of Asian Study, Am. U. Sch. Internat. Studies, Washington, 1977; postgrad., U. Chgo., 1977-78; MS, Def. Intelligence Coll., 1986. Legis. aide U.S. Ho. of Reps., Washington, 1975-77; commd. 2d lt. U.S. Army, 1977, advanced through grades to maj., 1989; intelligence briefing officer to Sec. Def. and Chmn. Joint Chiefs of Staff, Washington, 1984-86; asst. to asst. sec. of def. Office Sec. Def., Washington, 1987-88, asst. to undersec. of def., 1988-89; resigned U.S. Army, 1989; mgr. ops. devel. Helene Curtis, Inc., Chgo., 1989-90, corp. mgr. strategy and devel., 1990-92, dir. strategy and devel., 1993; nat. mgr. operational planning and info. Sears Merchandise Group, Hoffman Estates, Ill., 1993-95; sr. dir. fin. processes and systems Sears, Roebuck and Co., Hoffman Estates, Ill., 1995-97, asst. corp. contr., 1997-98; ptnr. Trident Capital, Chgo., 1998—; comdr. 305th psychol. ops. bn. USAR, Arlington Heights, Ill., 1992-96; comdr. 16th psychol. ops. bn. USAR, Ft. Sheridan, Ill., 1996-98; cons. MGA, Inc., Chgo., 1985—; founding chmn. Conf. Bd. Coun. Competitive Analysis. Contbg. author: The Military Intelligence Community, 1986; contbr. articles to profl. publs. Bd. dirs. United Way of Highland Park-Highwood, 1999—; vol. Bus. Vols. for the Arts, Chgo., 1991-94. Lt. col. USAR, ret. 1998. Decorated Green Beret for valor and svc. Fellow Inter-univ. Seminar on Armed Forces and Soc., Soc. Competitive Intelligence Profls. (bd. dirs. 1991-94); mem. Spl. Forces Club, Army and Navy Club, Unions League Club of Chgo., The Execs. Club of Chgo., Fin. Execs. Inst. Home: 156 Lakewood Pl Highland Park IL 60035-5010 Office: Trident Capital 272 E Deerpath Rd Ste 304 Lake Forest IL 60045-1947

BEITNER, RIVKA, biochemistry researcher, educator; b. Warsaw, Poland, Mar. 10, 1939; arrived in Israel, 1950; d. Abram and Sarah (Eppelbaum) Rubinstein; m. Moshe Beitner, July 14, 1959; children: Esther, Joseph, Shai. BSc, Bar-Ilan U., Ramat-Gan, 1961, MSc, 1963; PhD, McGill U., Montreal, Can., 1970. Biochemistry instr. Bar-Ilan U., Ramat-Gan, 1961-67; rsch. fellow Lady Davis Inst. for Med. Rsch. Jewish Gen. Hosp., Montreal, 1967-70; life scis. lectr. Bar-Ilan U., Ramat-Gan, 1970-74, asst. prof. life scis., 1974-79, assoc. prof. life scis., 1979-83, prof. life scis., 1983—. Editor: Regulation of Carbohydrate Metabolism, Vols. I and II, 1985; mem. editl. bd. Molecular Genetic Metabolism, 1986—; contbr. articles to profl. jours. including Biochem. Sci.; inventor treatment of trauma to the skin. Grantee Med. Rsch. Coun., 1968-70, U.S.-Israel Binat. Sci. Found., 1974-76, Muscular Dystrophy Assn. Am., 1976-81, Ministry of Commerce and Industry, 1979-82, 88-90. Mem. N.Y. Acad. Sci., Israel Endocrine Soc., Israel Biochem. Soc., Israel Soc. Diabetes. Home: 39 Ahi Dakar St, 43259 Raanana Israel Office: Bar-Ilan U, Dept Life Scis, 52900 Ramat Gan Israel

BEIT-OR, BEN-ZION, company executive; b. Kfar-Saba, Israel, Nov. 16, 1942; s. Baruch and Phina Beit-Or; m. Amira Avisar; children: Tamar, Tal, Dan. BSc, Technion, Haifa, Israel, 1969. V.p. prodn. Electra Ltd., Israel, 1975-77; CEO, Shnitzky Ltd., Israel, 1977-78; chief R & D inf. and spl. operation forces br. Israeli Army, 1978-80, chief R & D, 1984-86; mil. attaché Israel Def. Forces, Washington, 1988-90; pres. Beit-Or Engring., Israel, 1990-93; v.p. Silver-Arrow, Israel, 1993-96; pres. Interchange Nets, Petach-Tikva, Israel, 1996—. Col. Spl. Forces, Armour, Israeli Army, 1978-90.

BEIYE, FENG, applied mathematics educator, researcher; b. Huaian, China, May 27, 1946; s. Feng Ding and Yuan Fang; m. Zhang Qingzhen, Dec. 24, 1971; children: Nannan, Dongdong. BSc, Peking U., 1980, MA, 1983. Rsch. asst. Inst. Applied Math., Beijing, 1983-86, asst. prof., 1986-90, rsch. assoc. prof., 1990-95, rsch. prof., 1995—; reviewer Math. Rev., 1990—. Author: Stability, Bifurcation and Chaos, 1995, Geometric Theory of Ordinary Differential Equations and Bifurcation Problems, 2000; contbr. articles to profl. jours. Mem. Am. Math. Soc. Home: Rm 106 Apt 6, Peking Univ, Beijing 100871, China Office: Inst Applied Math, Academia Sinica, Beijing 100080, China

BEIZER, LANCE KURT, lawyer; b. Hartford, Conn., Sept. 8, 1938; s. Lawrence Sidney and Victoria Merriam (Kaplan) B. BA in Sociology, Brandeis U., 1967; MA in English, San Jose State U., 1967; JD, U. San Diego, 1975. Bar: Calif. 1975. Selective svc. affairs coord. U. Calif., 1969-73, vet. affairs coord., 1973-75; vet. outreach coord. San Diego Community Coll. Dist., 1975-76; dep. dist. atty. Santa Clara County, Calif., 1976—. Bd. mgrs. Santa Clara Valley S.W. YMCA, Saratoga, Calif., 1988, chair, 1991-93; bd. dirs. The Lumen Found., San Francisco, 1985—. Bd. dirs. Fedn. Cmty. Ministries, Calif., 1992—, chair, 1996—. Lt. USNR, 1961-65. Mem. Calif. Dist. Attys. Assn., Santa Clara County Bar Assn., Am. Profl. Soc. on Abuse of Children, Nat. Assn. Counsel for Children, Am. Weil Soc., Mensa, Commonwealth Club. Republican. Episcopalian. Home: 1197 Capri Dr Campbell CA 95008-6002 Office: Santa Clara County Dist Atty 70 W Hedding St San Jose CA 95110-1768

BEJLEGAARD, NIELS MARTIN, retired metallurgy educator; b. Copenhagen, Feb. 23, 1939; arrived in Norway, 1982; s. Erik Bejlegaard and Gerda Solveig Mikaelsen Sund; m. Grete Lis HUjegaard, Mar. 30, 1972. Student, Acad. Kursus, Copenhagen, 1959, U. Copenhagen, 1961; M in Physics, D.T.U. Copenhagen, 1977; cert. engr., U. Copenhagen. Engr. Dansk Industri Syndikat Aktieselskab, Copenhagen, 1977-79, Elektriska Svetsning Aktie Bolag, Copenhagen, 1979-80, Charles Hude Patents, Copenhagen, 1980-82; lectr. metallurgy Stavanger (Norway) Tech. Sch., 1982-2000, censor, 1984-2000; ret., 2000; cons. Niels H. Abel Math. Competition, Stavanger, 1993—, Georg Mohr Math. Competition, Copenhagen, 1993—. Mem. London Math. Soc., Can. Math. Soc., Masons. Avocations: recreational mathematics, psychology, teaching. Home: Linde Alle 54, 2720 Vanløse Denmark

BEKASSY, ALBERT NANDOR, pediatrician; b. Pacser, Hungary, Nov. 25, 1942; s. Zoltan and Margit (Gaspar) B.; m. Zivile Dieninyte, Nov. 12, 1994; children: Bernard, Viktor; children from previous marriage, Margit Albert-Szabolcs. MD, Rijeka Med. Faculty, Croatia, 1967; MS, Belgrade U., 1975. Intern Sombor, Vojvodina, 1967-69; resident, Belgrade, Yugoslavia, 1971-75; sr. lectr. Univ. Hosp., Lund, Sweden, 1982—; rsch. fellow RFH Med. Sch., London, 1984; dir. World Hungarian Med. Acad., 1990; BMT coord. U. Hosp., 1986. Contbr. articles to profl. jours. Layman pres. elect Reformed Ch. Svc. for Hungarians in Western Europe, 1987. 1st class capt. former Yugoslav Army, 1967-68. Home: Jordabalksv 43, SE22657 Lund Sweden Office: Univ Hosp, Dept Pediatrics, S-22185 Lund Sweden

BEKER, HALUK, physicist, educator; b. Istanbul, Turkey, Sept. 19, 1944. BS, Robert Coll., Istanbul, 1967; PhD, U. Wyo., 1972. From asst. prof. to prof. Bogazici U., Istanbul, 1972—. Mem. Phi Kappa Phi. Office: Bogazici U Physics Dept, 80815 Bebek, Istanbul Turkey

BEKHOR, JAMIL SION, writer; b. Baghdad, Iraq, Mar. 15, 1918; came to U.S., 1948, naturalized, 1961; s. Sion I. and Missouda (Shouker) B.; m. Irene Wolpert, Mar. 24, 1956. BS in Civil Engrng., Baghdad Coll., 1938; corr. schs., Bennett Coll., Eng., 1939-40; Constrn. Engr., Pa. State U., 1959; postgrad., Churchman Bus. Coll., Easton, pa., 1960-61. Br. sec. David Sassoon & Co. Ltd. Eng., Baghdad, 1938-46; mgr. Victor Gareh & Co. Ltd., Baghdad, 1946-49; asst. to owner Rabico Import-Export, Inc., N.Y.C., 1949-52; purchasing mgr. Warren Pipe & Foundry divsn. Shahmoon Industries, Inc., Phillipsburg, N.J., 1952-71. Author, illustrator, editor, pub. Emanic Modulation, 1990, 91, 94; inventor tube dispenser device. Recipient award of merit 2d Internat. Inventors and New Products Exhbn., N.Y.C., 1966. Mem. Purchasing Agts. Assn. Lehigh Valley, Nat. Assn. Purchasing Agts. Avocations designing wood and metal work, violin, computer art.

BEKIESIŃSKA-FIGATOWSKA, MONIKA, radiologist; b. Warsaw, Poland, Apr. 22, 1966; d. Ryszard and Idalia Maria (Konarska) Bekiesiński; m. Dariusz Piotr Figatowski, June 4, 1993. MD, Med. Acad., Warsaw, 1990; PhD, Med. Acad., Lublin, Poland, 1995. Med. diplomate. Intern Ctrl. Rlwy. Hosp., Warsaw, Poland, 1990-91, resident, 1991-94, staff dept. diagnostic imaging, 1993—. Co-author: Contemporary Diagnostic Imaging of Central Nervous System Diseases, 1996, Magnetic Resonance and Computed Tomography in Clinical Practice, 1997, Neuroradiology, 2000; contbr. articles to profl. jours. Mem. Polish Med. Soc. Magnetic Resonance, Polish-German Radiol. Soc., European Soc. Neuroradiology. Avocations: photography, voyages, cinema. Office: Ctrl Rwy Hosp, Bursztynowa 2, 04-749 Warsaw Poland

BEKKER-NIELSEN, TONNES, history educator; b. Copenhagen, Denmark, Oct. 18, 1955; s. Hans and Else (Carbel) B.-N.; m. Marit Jensen, Nov. 15, 1981; children: Kirstine, Emilie. MA in History and Art History, Aarhus (Denmark) U., 1981, PhD in History, 1987. Editor Sfinx Mag., Aarhus, 1981-83; asst. curator Mus. of Antiquity, Aarhus, 1983-84; rsch. fellow Aarhus U., 1984-85; dir. Aarhus U. Press, 1985-2000; asst. prof. U. Bergen, Norway, 1994-2000; assoc. prof. U. So. Denmark, Ebsjerg, 2000—; dir. Historisk Revy, Aarhus, 1981-85. Author: Bydannelse i Det Romerske Gallien, 1984, Romerveje i Europa, 1985, The Geography of Power, 1989; co-author: Ancient Akamas, 1995, Gads Historieleksikon, 2001. Trustee Orbis Terrarum, Aarhus, 1983—; mem. bd. Jutland Hist. Soc., 1994—. Mem. Internat. Pubs. Assn. (Geneva, mem. exec. com. 1995-98), Internat. Assn. Scholarly Pubs. (Malibu, Calif., pres. 1991-98), Assn. European Historians, Soc. for Promotion of Roman Studies. Lutheran. Avocations: watercolors, hiking, piano. Home: Femhojevej 6, 6710 Esbjerg Denmark Office: U So Denmark, Niels Bohrs vej, 6700 Esbjerg N, Denmark

BEKOFF, OSCAR, psychotherapist; b. Bklyn., Aug. 27, 1917; s. Irving and Eva (Horowitz) B.; m. Beatrice Mendelow, June 9, 1940; children: Roberta, Marc, Marjorie. BA, City U. L.A., 1979, MS in Psychology, 1981, Litt.D (hon.), 1984, PhD in Psychology, 1986. Fellow and Diplomate Am. Bd. Med. Psychotherapists and Diagnosticians; fellow and diplomate Internat. Acad. Behavioral Medicine Counseling and Psychotherapy. Pvt. practice psychotherapy & behavioral medicine Tamarac, Fla., 1982—; exec. v.p. Clinton Oil Co., 1961-67; asst. to the chmn. of the bd. Real Petroleum Co., 1968-71; pres. Nantod Corp., Brookville, N.Y., 1963-77; bd. govs. Behavioral Sci. Ctr., Nova U., Ft. Lauderdale, 1985-88; instr. continuing edn. Broward Community Coll., Coconut Creek, Fla., 1985, L.I. U., Greenvale, N.Y., 1984-88; prof. psychology dept. L.I. U. Developed Intra-Persona Therapy. Author: It's Yours for the Asking, 1988. Dist. commr. Boy Scouts Am., 1938-42; commr. City of N.Y., 1948; adv. bd. Fla. State Crime Commn., 1985—; cons., advisor Fla. Pepper Commn. on Aging, Tallahassee, 1990—. Recipient Cert. of Merit Nat. Coun. ARC, 1985, 50-Yr. Svc. award, 1990, Letter of Honor for pro bono work with the elderly from Pres. Ronald Reagan, 1988. Fellow Internat. Acad. Behavioral Medicine Counseling and Psychotherapy; mem. APA (Am. Psychol. Soc.), Am. Assn. Counseling and Devel., Am. Assn. Family Counseling and Mediators (supr. 1986), Nat. Ski Patrol (life), Amateur Ski Instrs. Assn. (life, cert. ski instr. 1946—), Oddfellows, Masons (32 deg.). Jewish. Home: 7661 Granville Dr Tamarac FL 33321-8747

BEKUI, SEFIAMOR KWADZO MENSAH DOTSE, technical educator; b. Agotime-Kpetoe, Ghana, Feb. 28, 1955; s. Ason Alfred and Afua Theresia Bekui; m. Anna Zerkortia, Apr. 17, 1989 (div. Feb. 1993); 1 child, Afua Mawu Femor; m. Peace Dokosi, Apr. 10, 1993; 1 child, Yawa Mawuny-a. Cert. welder. Welder Kaiser Engring. Internat., Tema, 1975, Tema Steelworks Ltd., 1975, Mark Cofie Engring. Work Ltd., Accra, 1976-77; tutor, prin. supt. Ghana Edn. Svc., Ho, 1977—. Sec. Electricity Project Com., Wegbe Kpalime, Volta, Ghana, 1990-94. Mem. Wegbe Kpalime Youth Assn. (sec. 1986-94), Miwoe Nenyo Farmers Assn. (sec. 1989—). Presbyterian. Avocations: indoor games, horticulture, farming, reading. Home: Mount of Peace, PO Box 9, Wegbe Kpalime Kpamdo Volta, Ghana

BEKYAROVA, ELENA BORISSOVA, chemist, researcher; b. Gotze Delchev, Sofia, Bulgaria, June 27, 1966; d. Boris Stoyanov and Velika Pandova (Vodenova) B.; m. Christomir Yordanov, June 25, 1994. Magister, U. Chem. Tech., Sofia, 1989; PHD, Bulgarian Acad. Sci., Sofia, 1995. Cert. chemist. Rschr. Inst. Non-Ferrous Metals, Plovdiv, Bulgaria, 1989-91, Inst. Gen. & Inorganic Chemistry, Bulgarian Acad. Scis., Sofia, 1994—. Contbr. articles to profl. jours.; patentee in field. Grantee U. Trieste, Italy, 1995, U. Chiba, Japan, 1998-2000. Mem. Bulgarian Catalysis Club, Union Chemists in Bulgaria. Mem. Orthodox Ch. Avocations: literature, theatre. Office: Bulgarian Acad Scis, Acad G Bonchev Bl 11, 1113 Sofia Bulgaria

BELADI, ILONA, virologist; b. Szeged, Hungary, Aug. 6, 1925; d. Arpad and Ilona (Zimanyi) B.; m. Ferenc Olah, Dec. 22, 1949; children: Tamas, Tibor. MD, Med. U., Szeged, Hungary, 1950. Asst. prof. Inst. Microbiology Med. U., Szeged, Hungary, 1950-53, sr. asst. prof., 1953-57, assoc. prof., 1970-74, prof., 1974-94, prof. emeritus, 1994—. Author: Adenovirusok, 1967 (award 1971). Pres. Red Cross of Med. U., Szeged, 1974-95, Assn. Beautiful City, Szeged, 1984-95. Sr. rsch. fellow Inst. Microbiology Med. U., 1957-70. Avocations: gardening, bridge. Home: Dugonics u 3, 6721 Szeged Hungary Office: Dom ter 10, 6720 Szeged Hungary

BELAFONTE, HARRY, singer, concert artist, actor; b. N.Y.C., 1927; s. Harold George and Melvine (Love) B.; m. Julie Robinson, Mar. 8, 1957; children—Adrienne, Shari, David, Gina. Student pub. schs.; LHD (hon.), Park Coll., Mo., 1968; HHD (hon.), Park Coll.; Doctorate Liberal Arts (hon.), ArtsD (hon.), New Sch. Social Research; MusD (hon.), Morehouse Coll., 1987; DFA (hon.), SUNY, Purchase, 1987, Spelman Coll., 1990; DHL (hon.), CCNY, 1990, Columbia U., 1993; DSc (hon.), Tufts U., 1991, Brandeis U., 1991, Long Island U., 1991; DA (hon.), Bard Coll., 1993; DLitt, U. West Indies, Kingston, Jamaica, 1996; hon. degree, U. Mass., 1996; LLD(hon.), McMaster U., Hamilton, Ont., Can., 1996; D (hon.) in Civil Law, U. Newcastle, Britain, 1998; LHD (hon.), Bklyn. Coll., 1998. Pres. Belafonte Enterprises, Inc., N.Y.C. Singer, actor in Broadway shows John Murray Anderson's Almanac (Tony award 1953), Three for Tonight, 1955; motion pictures: Bright Road, 1952, Carmen Jones, 1954, Island in the Sun, 1957, The World, the Flesh and the Devil, 1958, Odds Against Tomoroow, 1959, The Angel Levine, 1969, Buck and the Preacher, 1971, Uptown Saturday Night, 1974, White Man's Burden, 1995, Kansas City, 1996; prodr. stage play To Be Young Gifted and Black, 1969; appeared in TV movies Grambling's White Tiger, 1981, Swing Vote, 1999; prodr. TV spls. A Time for Laughter, 1967, Harry and Lena, 1969; TV program Tonight with Belafonte, 1960 (Emmy award); appeared on German TV spl. I Sing What I See, 1980; concert performances in Cuba, Jamaica, Europe, 1980, Australia, N.Z., U.S., Europe, 1981, Can., 1982, U.S., Europe and with Can. symphony orchs., 1983, U.S., 1985, U.S., Can., Japan, Europe, 1986; prodr. Strolling Twenties-TV; co-prodr. Beat Street, 1984; appeared at Golden Nugget, Atlantic City and Las Vegas, 1985, 86; initiator, performer rec. We Are the World, 1985 (Grammy award 1985); performer concert tours, U.S., Can. and Europe including 60 city tour, 1988, concerts in U.S., Europe, Can., 1989, 90, 93, concerts in U.S., Japan and Can., 1991, concert tour U.S., 1992, concerts U.S., Can. and Europe, 1995, U.S., Can., Europe and Far East, 1996, 50-city European tour, 1998; 1st N.Y. appearance in 30 yrs. Avery Fisher Hall, Lincoln Ctr., 1993. Chmn. Martin Luther King, Jr. Holiday Commn., 1987; goodwill amb. UNICEF, 1987; bd. dirs. N.Y. State Martin Luther King, Jr. Inst. for Nonviolence, 1989—; N.Y. State Employees Brotherhood com. (Benjamin Potocker brotherhood award 1993). Recipient award of appreciation for initiation of and work for USA for Africa, Am. Music, 1986, Leader for Peace award Peace Corps, 1988, Danny Kaye award U.S. Com. for UNICEF, 1989, Africa's Future award, 1994, Whitney M. Young Jr. Svc. award Boy Scouts Am., 1989, Golden Acorn award Bronx Community Coll., 1989, Kennedy Ctr. honors, 1989, Mandela Courage award (inaugural presentation), 1990, Tribute to a Black Am. award Nat. Conf. Black Mayors, Inc., 1991, Bill of Rights award ACLU So. Calif., 1991, Internat. House Berkeley award, 1994, Food and Hunger Hotline award, 1994, Humanitarian award N.Y. Assn. New Americans, 1994, Brotherhood award 100 Black Men, 1994, Children's Champion award UNICEF Com. Greater Boston-joint award with Julie Belafonte, 1994, Nat. Medal of the Arts, 1994, Letelier-Moffitt Human Rights award, 1994, Best Supporting Actor (Kansas City), 1996, N.Y. Film Critics Cir., Jesse Owens Humanitarian award, 1996, Man of the Yr. award N.Y. chpt. Hadassah, 1996, Hadassah Internat. First Citizen of the World award, 1996, Medal of Distinction, Lenox Hill Hosp., N.Y.C., 1996, South African-Am. Orgn. Leadership award, 1996, Florinda Lasker Civil Liberties award, 1997, Living Landmark award N.Y. Landmarks Conservancy, 1997, Humanitarian of Yr. award WLIW/21, 1997, William Moses Kunstler Racial Justice award, 1997, N.Y. Arts & Bus. Coun. award, 1997, Chmn.'s award NAACP Image Awards, 1999, Ronald H. Brown award Nat. Child Labor Com., 1999; inducted into Miami Children's Hosp. Internat. Pediat. Hall of Fame, 1996.

BÉLAI, ISTVÁN, film director, writer; b. Budapest, Hungary, May 8, 1931; s. Béla and Maria (Kramer) Buchwald; m. Julianna Jako Belai, Apr. 25, 1970; 1 child, Krisztina. Degree in Sounding, Tech. U., Budapest, Hungary, 1957. Sound engr., film dir. Pannonia Filmstudio, Budapest, Hungary, 1956-85; head of studio Hungarian Acad. Sci., Budapest, 1985-89; exec. Artifolium Ltd., Budapest, Hungary, 1991—. Author: (films) Koncertissimo, 1968 (Silver Hugo 1968, nominated oscar 1970), Inauguration, 1970, Gloria Mundi, 1970, Event, 1970, Funeral, 1974, Parade, 1974, Carriage Driving-ship, 1984, What Can I Be? (Prix Nat. Cannes 1987), 1986, Cooexistentia, 1987 (1st prize Animation 1988), Tungsram (1st prize C. of C. 1996), 1988, The White Line (short story, 1st prize of short stories), 1996, Conzertissimo, 1997. Avocations: skiing, chess. E-mail: ibelai@hotmail.com. Home and Office: Frankel Leo 68b, 1023 Budapest Hungary

BELAISCH, JEAN GAGOU, gynecologist; b. Tunis, Tunisia, Mar. 28, 1927; s. Charles and Yvonne Belaisch; m. Andree Lucie Hottelet, Feb. 13, 1952; children: Joelle, France. MD, Faculty of Medicine of Paris, 1957. Resident Univ. Hosps. of Paris, 1953-57, chef de clinique en gynecologie, 1958, chef de clinique en endocrinologie, 1959; chef Centre de Sterilite de L'Hopital de l'Hotel Dieu, Paris, 1960-77; cons. Maternity of Hopital Saint Vincent de Paul, Paris, 1978—; charge d'enseignement Faculty of Medicine, 1962-77; with U. Rene Descartes, 1977-92. Author: L'Homme de Cinquante Ans, 1989, Questions D'Hommes, 1996; co-editor Jour. Contraception Fertilite Sexualite, 1969; co-editor: Endometriose, 1999, Endocrinologie Masculine, 1996; author 6 med. films (2 awards). Recipient Legion of Honor. Mem. French Spkg. Soc. of Andrology (gen. sec. 1982-86, hon. pres. 1993—), French Soc. of Gynecology (pres. 1995-97), French Soc. of Fertility (v.p. 1987). Avocations: archeology, astronomy, French literature. E-mail: jean.belaisch@wanadoo.fr. Office: 36 rue de Tocqueville, 75017 Paris France

BELAÏSCH-ALLART, JOËLLE, obstetrician-gynecologist; b. Paris, July 22, 1952; d. Jean and Andrée (Hottelet) B.; m. Jean-Paul Allart, June 18, 1982; children: Sarah, Alexandre. Intern hopitaux Paris, 1976-81, chef clinique asst., 1981-84; gynecologist Accouheme de hopitaux, 1984—; dir. Svc. Ob-Gyn Reproduction Humaine Hosp. Jean Rostand, Sèvres, France. Editor: Les enfants de l'impossible, 1988. Mem. French Soc. Gynecology (gen. sec. 1989—), Coll. Medicine Paris Hosps. Jewish. Home: 5 Ave Jean Monnet, 92130 Issy France Office: Hsop Jean Rostand, 141 Grande Rue, 92310 Sevres France

BELANI, KUMAR GIRDHARIDAS, anesthesiologist; b. Bangalore, India. MB BChir, St. John's Med. Coll., Bangalore, 1974; MS in Anesthesiology, U. Minn., 1983. Bd. cert. Am. Bd. Anesthesiology and Critical Care. Prof. anesthesiology and pediats. U. Minn., Mpls., 1997—; clin. prof. anesthesiology U. Calif., San Francisco, 1998—; dir. continuing med. edn. in anesthesiology dept. anesthesiology U. Minn., Mpls. Recipient Disting. Prof. award IKRDC, 1997; named as one of Best Drs. in Twin Cities and USA, Mpls. St. Paul Mag., 1999, 2000. Mem. Assn. Univ. Anesthesiologists, Am. Soc. Anesthesiologists, Minn. Soc. Anesthesiologists (pres. 1999-2000). Hindu. Avocations: travel, walking, biking, religion. Home: 4916 Ridge Rd Edina MN 55436-1012 Office: Dept Anesthesiology 420 Delaware St SE # 294 Minneapolis MN 55455-0374

BELASHOV, VASILY YURIEVICH, physics educator, researcher; b. Leningrad, Russia, July 8, 1956; s. Yury Grigorievich and Ludmila Vasilievna (Belousova) B.; 1 child, Andrei; m. Elena Semionovna Smychnikova, Apr. 24, 1978. Degree in engring. oceanology, Leningrad Adm. Makarov Engring. Marine Coll., Leningrad, 1978; PhD, Russian Acad. Scis., Moscow, 1989, DSc in Radiophysics, 1998. Engr., oceanologist Kolymskoe Hydrometeorol. and Nature Control Bd., Magadan, Russia, 1978-80; engr. N. Eastern Interdisciplinary Sci. Rsch. Inst. Far E. Br. Russian Acad. Scis., Magadan, 1980-84, rschr., 1984-92, sr. rschr., 1992-99, chief rschr., 1999—; assoc. prof. Internat. Pedagogical U., Magadan, 1992-97; prof. No. Internat. U., 1997—; mem. terrestrial and space noises group of Internat. Union Radio Sci. Commn., 1992—. Author: The KP Equation and its Generalization, Theory and Applications, 1997, Effective Algorithmns and Programmes of Numerical Mathematics, 1997; contbr. articles to profl. jours. Mem. N.Y. Acad. Scis. Avocations: poetry, music, painting, travel. Office: NEISRI FEB RAS, 16 Portovaya, 685000 Magadan Russia

BELCHER, MAX, social services administrator, college dean; b. East Lynn, W.Va., Mar. 16, 1942; s. George H. and Ella D. (Dickerson) B.; m. Linda L. Frey, Aug. 8, 1964; children: Kipling, Babbette, Andrew, Raleigh, Perry. BA, Berea (Ky.) Coll., 1969; ThM, Trinity Coll., 1972; ThD, Trinity Theol. Sem., 1973; MA, Liberty (Va.) U., 1994; DD, LLD (hon.), Internat. Free Prof. Episc. U., London, 1966; PhD, U. San Jose, 1996. From caseworker to dist. mgr. Mich. Dept. Social Svcs., Flint, 1964-97, dist. mgr., 1992-97; mem. faculty dept. psychology Baker Coll., Flint, 1987-98, 99—, dean for gen. edn., 1998-99. Bd. dirs. Consortium on Child Abuse and Neglect, Flint, 1993-97, 99. Recipient Cert. of Merit in Youth Employment, Genesee Intermediate Sch. Dist., 1979, Cert. of Appreciation, Health Care Access Project, 1990. Mem. Am. Counseling Assn., Ky. Counseling Assn., Am. Assn. Christian Counselors, Intercollegiate Studies Inst. (faculty advocate), Mich. County Social Svcs. Assn. (life). Home: 9421 McAfee Rd Montrose MI 48457-9123 Office: Baker Coll 1050 W Bristol Rd Flint MI 48507-5516

BELCHER, SAMUEL L., plastics engineer, manufacturing executive; b. Meyersdale, Pa., Dec. 15, 1933; s. Frank and Edna B.; m. Donna M. Belcher. BSME, U. Akron, 1958; MBA, U. Toledo, 1968; cert. mktg. mgmt., Stanford U., 1976. Licensec profl. engr., Ohio. Process engr. Rubbermaid, Wooster, Ohio; process engr., product devel. mgr. Owens Ill., Toledo; dir. rsch. Wheaton Industries, Millville, N.J.; devel. engr. mgr., product mgr. Cincinnati Milacron, Batavia, Ohio; pres., founder Sabel Plastech, Inc., Moscow, Ohio, 1988—. Editor: Practical Extrusion Blow Molding, 1999; contbr. chpts. to books and articles to profl. publs., including Modern Packaging, Modern Plastics, Plastics Tech., others.; patentee in field. Recipient Outstanding Alumni award U. Akron Coll. Engring., 1995. Fellow Soc. Plastics Engrs. (bd. dirs. blow molding divsn., Lifetime Achievement award in Blow Molding 1995); mem. Soc. Mfg. Engrs. (sr.). Fax: 513-553-4114. E-mail: sabelplastechs@fuse.net. Office: Sabel Plastechs Inc 2055 Weil Rd Moscow OH 45153-9641

BELCOURT, ALAIN BERNARD, research director; b. Aix-Les-Bains, France, Apr. 10, 1943; m. Nicole E. Grimm; children: Olivier, Cyrille, Philippe. DS, U. Louis Pasteur, Strasbourg, France, 1975. Dir. rsch. INSERM, Strasbourg, France, 1984—; vis. scientist UAB, Birmingham Ala., 1976, NIDR-NIH, Bethesda, Md., 1978-79, vis. expert, 1979-81; v.p. CEED, Strasbourg, 1996—. Contbr. over 100 rsch. articles to profl. jours. Home: 34 Rue Marc Aurele, 67200 Strasbourg France Office: Ctr European d'Etude Du Diabete, CHU 1 Pl de l'Hopital, 67000 Strasbourg France

BELDECOS, GEORGE JOHN, Hellenic air force officer, planning consultant; b. Athens, Greece, May 18, 1961; s. John George and Helen (Papanikolaou) B. MArch, Nat. Tech. U., Athens, 1985; MPhil in Town Planning, U. Coll., London, 1987; PhD in Town Planning, U. London, 1995. Registered arch., U.K.; chartered town planner, U.K. Town planner Ministry of Housing and Planning, Athens, 1986; town planning officer Western Macedonia Devel. Corp., Kozani, Greece, 1987-89; commd. 2nd lt. Greek Air Force, 1989, advanced through grades to maj., 1999, staff officer, 1989-91; aide-de-camp to chief Hellenic Nat. Def. Gen. Staff, Athens, 1991-93, def. planner, 1993-94; H.H. Humphrey fellow USIA, New Brunswick, N.J., 1994-95; rsch. fellow Rutgers U., 1994-95; head planning and constrn. quality assurance sect. Air Force Constrn. Wing, 1995-98, staff officer, 1998—. Author: History of Hellenic Air Force 1930-1941, 1990, Hellenic Orders, Decorations & Medals, 1991, Hellenic Armed Forces Commendation Medals, 1992, Hellenic Wings, 1999. Decorated Medal of Mil. Merit, officer Order of Phoenix, Officer Order of Merit, gold cross Ecumenical Patriarchal Throne, Order of Constantine the Gt. (Greece); H.H. Bartlett scholar U. London, 1987; A. Onassis Found. fellow, 1986-88. Fellow Royal Geog. Soc. (London); mem. Royal Town Planning Inst. (U.K.). Avocations: aviation, scuba diving, parachuting, military history. Home: 7 Trapezountos St, GR-11527 Athens Greece

BELDOTTI, DENNIS JASON, retired company executive; b. Needham, Mass., June 16, 1955; s. Charles J. and Tina N. (DeLeo) B. BS, Framingham State Coll., 1978; MLA, Boston U., 1998. Offshore capt.'s lic. USCG. Software engr. SofTech, Waltham, Mass., 1977-78; systems engr. IBM, Sudbury, Mass., 1978-79; sales support analyst Honeywell, Waltham, 1979-80; internat. mktg. analyst Prime Computer, Natick, Mass., 1980-86; pres., CEO Select Corp., Wellesley, Mass., 1986-89; ret.; chmn. bd. Image Charters, Hull, Mass., 1980-90, Studio Photography, Needham, Mass., 1978-89. Contbg. author: (anthology) At A Distance, 1996. Republican. Roman Catholic. Avocations: skiing, sport fishing, tennis, auto racing.

BELEA, ADONIS, retired geneticist, consultant; b. Kolozsvár, Romania, July 22, 1924; arrived in Hungary, 1930; s. György and Erzsébet (Hering) B.; m. Éva Nagy, July 30, 1949; children: Éva, Gyöngyi. BS in Agr., U. Agr., Hungary, 1948, MS in Agr., 1962; PhD in Biology, Hungarian Acad. Scis., Budapest, 1965, DS in Biology, 1977, hon. prof., 1988. Jr. clk. Min. Agr., Budapest, 1949-51; farm mgr. Mezőörs State Farm, Hungary, 1951-52, Exptl. Farm, Kecskemét, Hungary, 1952-53; rsch. worker Agrl. Rsch. Inst., Hungarian Acad. Scis., Martonvásár, 1953-70, sci. cons., 1982-98; sr. rsch. worker Biol. Ctr. Genetics Inst., Szeged, Hungary, 1970-82; sci. cons. Agrobotanical Inst., Tápiószele, Hungary, 1999—; mem. genetics com. Hungarian Acad. Scis., 1973—, mem. plant breeding com., 1970-73. ,uthor: Interspecific and Intergeneric Crossing in the Plant World, 1986, Tropical Crop Production, Gödöllő, Hungary, 1989, Interspecific and Intergeneric Crosses in Cultivated Plants, 1992; contbr. articles to profl. jours. Mem. Hungarian Acad. Sci. (mem. genetics com. 1973—, mem. plant breeding com. 1970-73). Avocations: literature, history, gardening. Home: 32 Erdő St, 2083 Solymàr Pest, Hungary

BELENKAYA, ELENA SEMENOVNA, physicist, researcher; b. Moscow, Dec. 10, 1946; d. Semen Zacharovich and Lubov Isaevna Belenky; m. Igor Borisovich Aingorn, Jan. 21, 1970; 1 child, Olga Igorevna Belenkaya. Diploma in astronomy, Moscow State U., 1971, PhD in Plasma Physics, 1985. Tchr. physics Sch. N863, Moscow, 1972-73; engr. Inst. Nuclear Physics, Moscow State U., 1973-81, jr. scientist, 1981-87, sci. rschr., 1987-90, sr. scientist, 1990—, sec. dept's coun., 1978—. contbr. articles to sci. jours., including Geomagnetism Aero., Jour. Geophys. Rsch., Jour. Atmospheric and Solar-Terrestrial Physics. Grantee Am. Astron. Soc., 1993, Soros grantee Internat. Sci. Found., 1993-94, Russian Basic Rsch. Found., 1995-97; recipient Silver medal NYYY, 1965. Mem. Am. Geophys. Union, European Astron. Soc., Russian Astron. Soc. Avocations: astronomy, psychology, psychoanalysis, poetry, biology. Office: Moscow State U, Inst Nuclear Physics, 119899 Moscow Russia

BELENKY, ALEXANDER SOLOMONOVICH, mathematician, consultant, researcher; b. Moscow, Mar. 16, 1946; came to the U.S., 1993; s. Solomon Yosefovich Belenkii and Sofia Meerovna Belenkaia. MS in Automation, Moscow Inst. of Chem. Engring., 1967; MA in Piano, Gnesyn's Coll. Music, Moscow, 1968; MS in Math. summa cum laude, Moscow State U., 1974; PhD in Math., Russian Acad. Scis., 1981, DSc in Applied Math., 1995, Prof. Math. Method Applications, 1997; Academician, Russian Acad. Transport, 1996. Lectr. All Union Soc. Znanie, Moscow, 1981-89; vis. rschr. MIT, Boston, 1991-92, 93-94; leading rschr. Inst. of Control Scis., Moscow, 1995-99; cons.; vis. lectr. U. Udina, Italy, Ecole Central, France, 1992-94. Author: Computer-Aided Systems for Container Transportation, 1981, Applied Mathematics in National Economy, 1985, Mathematical Models of Optimal Planning in Transportation Systems, 1988, Methods of Optimal Planning in Transport, 1988, Operations Research in Transportation Systems: Ideas and Schemes of Optimization Methods for Strategic Planning and Operations Management, 1998, others, (scenerios of documentories) Transport in the USSR, 1985, Engineer of a Nuclear Power Station, 1986, Oil-well Drilling Technology, 1987, Technology of Processing Waste Products, 1988, (senerio of advertising film) Water-Pipe Faucet, 1988; exec. editor Jour. Transport, Sci., Tech., Mgmt., 1990-94; contbr. articles on optimization methods and their applications in strategic mgmt. to profl. publs. Mem. Moscow House of Scientists. Home and Office: PO Box 1314 Brookline MA 02446-0010

BELESON, ROBERT BRIAN, marketing executive; b. N.Y.C., Sept. 28, 1950; s. Abraham Gilbert and Ruth (Zirman) B. BS, Cornell U., 1971; MBA, Harvard U., 1974. Personnel planning mgr. J.C. Penney Co., N.Y.C., 1971-72; product mgr. Gen. Foods Corp., White Plains, N.Y., 1974-79; v.p., mktg. Remy Martin Amerique, N.Y.C., 1979-81, pres., chmn., 1982-88; v.p., mgmt. supr. Ogilvy & Mather, N.Y.C., 1981-82; group v.p. Remy and Assocs., N.Y.C., 1988-89; pres., chief exec. officer RB Internat., N.Y.C., 1989-91; sr. v.p., chief mktg. officer Playboy Enterprises, Inc., Chgo., 1991-96; pres. M. Shanken Cornerstone, N.Y.C., 1996—. Jewish. Avocations: tennis, skiing, horseback riding, travel. Home: RB Internat 5 N Beech Tree Rd Brookfield CT 06804-3500

BELETZ, ELAINE ETHEL, nurse, educator; b. N.Y.C., Jan. 5, 1944; d. Harry and Rose (Friedman) B. RN, Mt. Sinai Hosp., N.Y.C., 1968; BSN, Fairleigh Dickinson U., 1970; MA, NYU, 1974; MEd, Columbia U., 1978, EdD, 1979. Staff nurse ICU Mt. Sinai Hosp., 1968-70, asst. head nurse, 1970, adminstrv. supervisory relief nurse, 1973-74, 77-78; clin. instr. Roosevelt Hosp. Sch. Nursing, N.Y.C., 1970-73; nurse gerontologist St. Luke's Hosp. Ctr., N.Y.C., 1974; asst. dir. nursing Bklyn. Hosp., N.Y.C., 1975-77; asst. prof. nursing Hunter Coll. CUNY, 1978-81; v.p. nursing Mt. Sinai Hosp. Med. Ctr., Chgo., 1982-83; assoc. prof. nursing Villanova (Pa.) U., 1983—; lectr.; cons. nursing adminstrn., labor rels. in health care; mem. task force on block grants Ill. Dept. Health. Contbr. articles to profl. jours.; internat. cons. and lectr. Bd. dirs. Hadassah Nurses Coun., Phila., 1993-94; pres.-elect, 1994-96, pres. 1996-98; Midatlantic Reg. v.p. nat. bd. Zionist Orgn. Am., 1998—, del. 91st nat. conv., 1998, nominating com., 1998; mem. religious affairs and fgn. rels. com. Am. Jewish Com., 1997—. Recipient Disting. Achievement award Columbia U. Nursing Edn. Alumni Assn., 1989; named to Hall of Fame, Columbia U. Nursing Edn. Alumni Assn., 1999. Fellow Am. Acad. Nursing; mem. Am. Nurses Assn. (bd. dirs. 1982-87, mem. polit. action com. 1982-86), N.Y. State Nurses Assn. (treas. 1977-78, pres.-elect 1978-79, pres. 1979-81, bd. trustees, cert. of appreciation 1981, hon. recognition award 1987), Pa. Nurses Assn. (nominating com. 1985-86, chair polit. action com. 1990-92), N.Y. Counties Registered Nurses Assn. (nominating com. 1973, dir. 1975-78, Amanda Silvers award 1981), Shershower Benevolent Assn., Nursing Edn. Alumni Assn. (Leadership award 1989), Sigma Theta Tau, Phi Kappa Phi, Phi Beta Delta (a founder 1998). Jewish. Office: Villanova U Grad Program Nursing Health Care Adminstrn Coll Nursing Villanova PA 19085

BELFIGLIO, VALENTINE JOHN, political science educator, pharmacist; b. May 28, 1934; s. Edmond Liberato and Mildred Elizabeth (Sherwood) B.; 1 child by previous marriage, Valentine Edmond. BS, Union U., 1956; MA, U. Okla., Norman, 1967; PhD, U. Okla., 1970. Registered pharmacist, Fla., Okla., Tex. Grad. asst., instr. U. Okla., 1967-70; prof. polit. sci. Tex. Woman's U., Denton, 1970—. Author: The United States and World Peace,

1971, American Foreign Policy, 1979, The Italian Experience in Texas, 1983, The Best of Italian Cooking, 1985, Alliances, 1986, Go for Orbit, 1987, Pride of the Southwest, 1991, Italian Experience in Texas: A Closer Look, 1994, Honor, Pride, Duty: A History of the State Guard, 1995, They Came from the Sea, 2000; contbr. numerous articles on internat. rels., Asian politics to profl. jours., as well as extensive rsch. and publs. about ancient Roman amphibious warfare; reviewer textbooks in internat. politics Holbrook Press, Boston, 1973-75. With USAF, 1959-67. Decorated knight Order of Merit, Republic of Italy; recipient Guido Dorso prize U. Naples, 1985, C.K. Chamberlain award East Tex. Hist. Assn., 1990; Tex. Woman's U. Instnl. Rsch. grantee, 1973-74, 76-77, NEH grantee, 1978; postdoctoral fellow Republic of South Africa, 1976;. Mem. AAUP, Internat. Studies Assn. (sec.-treas. region 1974-76), Am. Polit. Sci. Assn., Am. Italian Hist. Assn., Mensa, Kappa Psi. Republican. Roman Catholic. Avocations: chess, dancing, gourmet cookery. Home: 704 Camilla Ln Garland TX 75040-4622 Office: Tex Woman's U PO Box 425889 Denton TX 76204-5889

BELFOUR, ED, professional hockey player; b. Carman, Man., Can., Apr. 21, 1965. Student, U. N.D. Goalie Chgo. Blackhawks, 1988-97, Dallas Stars, 1997—; mem. NCAA All-Am. West second team, 1986-87, tournament team, 1986-87, WCHA All-Star first team 1986-87; player NHL All-Star game, 1992-93. Recipient Vezina trophy, 1990-91, 92-93, Calder Meml. trophy, 90-91, William M. Jennings trophy, 90-91, 92-93, Trico Goaltender award, 1990-91; co-recipient Garry F. Longman Meml. trophy, 1987-88; named Rookie of the Year, 1990-91, Sporting News All-Star 2nd team, 1992-93, NCAA All-Am. Second Team, 1986-87, NHL All-Rookie Team, 1990-91, NHL All-First Team, 1990-91, 92-93. Office: Dallas Stars 211 Cowboys Pkwy Irving TX 75063-5931

BELFRAGE, ANNA C., executive club president; b. Jönköping, Sweden, June 29, 1953; d. Mats R. and Tutta (Hansson) Carlberg; m. Erik J. Belfrage, Oct. 5, 1993. Diploma in Mktg., Chartered Inst. Mktg., U.K., 1987; MBA, Henley Mgmt. Coll., Eng., 1988. V.p.. Up With People, Oslo Norway, also Tucson, 1976-86; mktg. dir. Am. Express, Stockholm, 1988-89; cons. SEM, Glasgow, 1989-91; pres. Positive Sweden, Stockholm, 1991-94, Svenska Dagbladet Exec. Club, Stockholm, 1994—; sr. adv. The Kreab Group of Cos., Stockholm, 2000—; chmn. Megafon Annonsbyra AB, Stockholm, 1995—; dir. Up With People-AB, 1988—, Italian C. of C., Stockholm, 1994—, Hjo Grosshandel AB, 1995—, Destination Stockholm AB, 1995—, Internat. Coll. AB, Stockholm, 1997—. Mem. Assn. MBAs. Avocations: music, art, travel, skiing. Office: SVD Exec Club, Kreab Floragatan 13, SE 11475 Stockholm Sweden

BELGRANO, NÉSTOR JOSÉ, lawyer; b. Buenos Aires, May 1, 1955; s. Manuel and Hebe María (Lastra) B.; m. María Gloria Chozas, July 5, 1980 (div. 1991); 1 child, Nicolás; m. Josefina Bengolea, July 8, 1993; 1 child, Sofia. Degree in Law, Cath. U. Buenos Aires, 1981. Internat. officer Banco Galicia, Buenos Aires, 1979-83; assoc. M & M Bomchil, Buenos Aires, 1983-85, ptnr., 1985—. Contbr. articles to profl. jours. Mem. ABA, Colegio de Abogados de Buenos Aires, Circulo de Armas, Jockey Club, Golf Club Argentino. Avocations: golf, fishing. Office: M & M Bomchil, Suipacha 268 12th Fl, C1008AAF Buenos Aires Argentina

BELIAEVA, OLGA BORISOVNA, research scientist; b. Kirov, Russia, Apr. 1, 1940; d. Boris Yakovlevich and Vera Sergeevna (Shliravina) Kozminikh; m. Anatolii Ilyich Belyaev, Oct. 19, 1961 (div. 1974); 1 child, Julia. MSc, Lomonosov State U., Moscow, 1963, PhD, 1971, Superior Rsch. Scientist, 1983; DSc, Russian Acad. Scis., Moscow, 1994. Jr. rsch. scientist Inst. Photosynthesis, Moscow, 1964-66; rsch. scientist Lomonosov State U., Moscow, 1970-83, sr. rsch. scientist, 1983-92, leading rsch. scientist, 1992—. Author: Pigment Apparatus of Photosynthesis, 1988, Photobiosynthesis of Chlorophyll, 1989; contbr. articles to profl. jours. Grantee G. Soros Fund, 1993. Mem. Russian Soc. for Photobiology. Office: Biology Dept, Lomonosov State Univ, 119899 Moscow Russia

BÉLIARD, JEAN, diplomat; b. Colmar, Haut-Rhin, France, Mar. 22, 1919; m. Diana Jane Mowrer, Feb. 2, 1950 (div. July 1965); 1 child, Diana; m. Denise Marie Leboulleux, Oct. 13, 1967; children: Patrice Eric, Thiery. M of Law and Econs., U. Paris, 1939, degree in pub. adminstrn., 1949. French consul gen. Chgo., 1958-64; dir. gen. Radio-TV, Monte Carlo, Monaco, 1964-66; consul gen. N.Y., 1966-69; dir., spokesman French Info. Svc., 1969-73; amb. to Mex., 1973-77, amb. to Brazil, 1977-81, amb. to Can., 1981-84; sec. gen. Atlantic Treaty Orgn., Paris, 1985-97. Author: Vertige en eau profonde, 1964 (Best Crime Book of Yr. award 1964), Meurtre à Alpe d'Huez, 1968. Pres. France-Amérique, Paris, 1985-89, Inst. France Can., Paris, 1990—. Lt. Tank Corp, 1944-45, ETO. Decorated Croix de Guere, 1944-45, Comdr. French Légion of Honor, 1983, French Order Merit, 1964, Comdr. French Légion of Merit, 2 Bronze star, 1944-45; recipient Medaille de la Resistance, 1977. Home: 96 Ter rue de Longchamp, Neuilly 92200, France

BELIĆ WEISS, ZORAN, artist, educator; b. Beograd, Srbija, Yugoslavia, Apr. 24, 1955; came to the U.S., 1989; s. Milan and Ljubinka (Vidosavljević) Belić; m. Mila Djermanović, 1999. BFA in Painting, U. Arts, Beograd, Yugoslavia, 1981; BA in Philosophy, U. Beograd, 1985; MFA in Multimedia, Rutgers U., 1991. Pvt. practice Mission Viejo, Calif.; art dir. D'Arcy, Masius, Benton & Bowles, Inc., New York City, 1991-93; prof. Miss. State (Miss.) U., 1993-96, U. Denver, Colo., 1996-97, Art Inst. So. Calif., Laguna Beach, 1997—, U. Calif., Irvine, 1998—; dir. gen. Imperium DeSign, Cosmopolis, Calif., 1998—. Exhibited in 17 one-man shows; exhibited in 133 group shows; Author: Academy of Arts and Sciences Dictionary of Visual Arts, 1989; lectr. in field; contbr. articles to profl. jours. Tchr. Internat. Aikido Fedn., Mission Viejo, Calif., 1988—. Recipient II award Internat. Drawing Triennial, Wroclaw, Poland, 1981, IV award, Internat. Drawing Biennial, Rijeka, Yugoslavia, 1988; ULUS fellow Beograd, Yugoslavia, 1986-87, Rsch. grantee U.S. Dept. Interior, Washington, 1996. Mem. Internat. Assn. Aesthetics, Internat. Aikido Fedn., Coll. Art Assn., Udruzenje Likovnih Umetnika Srbije (v.p. 1989). Avocations: contemplation. E-mail: zbelic@home.com. Home: 21622 Marguerite Pkwy Apt 144 Mission Viejo CA 92692-4409

BELIKOVA, TATJANA PAVLOVNA, physicist, computer scientist, researcher; b. Moscow, Dec. 18, 1947; d. Pavel Semenovich and Valentina Karpovna (Belikova) Holavko; m. Alexei Grigorjevich Vitukhnovsky, Aug. 13, 1975; children: Lia, Mitia. MD, Moscow State U., 1972, Moscow Physics-Technics Inst., 1978; PhD, Inst. Info. Transm. Problem/, Russian Acad. of Sci., Moscow, 1981. Jr. scientist Inst. for Info. Transmission Problems/Russian Acad. Scis., Moscow, 1972-75; rsch. scientist IPPI RAN, Moscow, 1975-83, sr. rschr., 1983—, head group for med. image processing, 1989—; cons. Oncology Ctr., Moscow, 1997. Contbr. articles to profl. jours.; patentee in field. Recipient grant Russian Acad. Sci., 1993-95, grant Internat. Assn. for Promotion and Coord. with Scientists from the Ind. States of the Former Soviet Union (INTAS), 1994-95, 97—. Mem. Internat. Soc. Optical Engring., Internat. Optical Soc. Am., Soc. Computers Applications in Radiology, Moscow Scientific Soc. Roentgenology and Radiology. Avocations: music, art, literature, theatre. Home: 1 Radiatorskaya str 7-26, 125171 Moscow Russia Office: Inst Info Transmission, B Karetny 19, 101447 Moscow Russia

BELIN, DOMINIQUE MARIE, biologist, researcher; b. Geneva, May 24, 1952; parents Sacha and Jacqueline (Rougemont) B.; m. Martine Anne Collart, Mar. 22, 1986 (June 1997); children: Alexandre, Sarah. Grad., Coll. Geneva, 11969; diploma, U. Geneva, 1973, PhD, 1979. Asst. U. Geneva, 1973-78, maitre asst., 1982-88, rsch. master, 1988-98, asst. prof., 1999—; postdoctoral fellow Rockefeller U., N.Y., 1979-82; vis. asst. prof. Harvard Med. Sch., Boston, 1991-94. Mem. Univ. Coun., Geneva, 1976-78, 95—. Damon Runyon-Walter Winchell fellow, 1980-82; Swiss Nat. Found. of Sci. Rsch. grantee, 1992—. Mem. Union Schweizerische Gesellschaften Fur Experimentelle Biologie, N.Y. Acad. Scis., Internat. Soc. for Fibrinolysis and Thrombolysis. Home: 2 BD Pont-D'Arve, CH1205 Geneva Switzerland Office: CMU Dept Pathology, 1 rue Michel-Servet, CH-1211 Geneva Switzerland

BELIS, VLADIMIR, medical administrator, educator; b. Bucharest, Romania, May 1, 1930; s. Alexandru and Maria Belis; m. Margareta Tasiedanu, Sept. 17, 1965. MD, U. Medicine Carol Davila, Bucharest, 1954, PhD in Forensic Medicine, 1967. Asst. U. Medicine and Pharmacy, Bucharest, 1963-74, asst. prof., 1974-89, prof., 1989—; prof. Police Acad., Bucharest, 1974—. Author: Mechanical Trauma in Legal Medicine, 1985, Practical Guide of Legal Medicine, 1990, Forensic Medicine, 1992, Legal Medicine for Law Students, 1996. Capt. Med. Corps. Romanian armed forces, 1975-90. Recipient Victor Babes award for Microscopical Investigation in Legal Medicine, 1995. Mem. Romanian Soc. Legal Medicine (pres., chief editor), Control Commn. on Human Tissues and Organ Harvesting and Transplantation, Internat. Acad. Legal Medicine, N.Y. Acad. Scis., Am. Acad. Forensic Sci. Avocation: climbing. Office: Nat Inst Legal Medicine, Vitan Barzesti 9-11, 75669 Bucharest Romania

BELIZÁN, JOSÉ MIGUEL, obstetrician, researcher; b. Rosario, Santa Fe, Argentina, Dec. 1, 1945; s. Luciano Americo and Zulema Margarita (Chiesa) B.; m. Maria Hortensia Rouillon, Apr. 19, 1970; children: Maria, Florencia, José Miguel. MD, Sch. Medicine, Rosario, Argentina, 1970, PhD in Medicine, 1975; PhD in Reprodn., Del Salvador U., Buenos Aires, 1974. Bd. cert. in obstetrics Superior Rschr. of Argentinean Nat. Coun. Sci. and Tech. Fellow WHO, Montevideo, Uruguay, 1971-72; scientist L.Am. Ctr. Perinatology, Montevideo, 1972-74; asst. prof. Sch. Medicine, Rosario, 1974-77, 81-83; scientist Inst. Nutrition of Ctrl. Am., Guatemala City, Guatemala, 1977-81; dir. Centro Rosarino de Estudios Perinatales, Rosario, 1981-97, L.Am. Ctr. Perinatology and Human Devel., Montevideo, Uruguay, 1997—; cons. WHO, Geneva, 1990—, Swedish Agy. for Rsch. in Developing Countries, 1993—, NAS, 1984-86, UNICEF, Buenos Aires, 1992—. Contbr. articles to profl. jours.; mem. editl. bd. Am. Jour. Obstetrics and Gynecology, 1993—. Chmn. Nat. Bd. Obstetrics Records, Buenos Aires, 1974-76; mem. Nat. Bd. for Promotion of Breastfeeding, Guatemala, 1978-79; chmn. Com. for Promotion of Med. Rsch., City Govt. of Rosario, 1993-95; mem. Nat. Com. on Maternal Mortality, Buenos Aires, 1994—. Recipient Golden medal for collaboration in reproductive health Brasilian Ctr. for Population Dynamics, Rio de Janeiro, 1982; Rsch. grantee Internat. Devel. Rsch. Ctr., Ottawa, Ont., Can., 1986-93, WHO, Geneva, 1990-95; decorated Knight, Heraldry Order of Cristobal Colon, Pres. of Dominican Republic, 2000. Mem. AAAS, N.Y. Acad. Scis. Home: Apt 702, Juan Benito Blanco 811, 11300 Montevideo Uruguay also: Brassey 7611, Rosario 2000, Argentina Office: LAm Ctr Perinat-Human Devel, Casilla de Correo 627, Montevideo Uruguay

BELIZARIO, VICENTE YLANAN, JR., tropical medicine physician; b. Manila, Philippines, Nov. 13, 1959; s. Vicente and Waldetrudes (Ylanan) B.; m. Maria Bella Tumaliwan, Dec. 20, 1993; 3 children. BA cum laude, U. Philippines, 1981, MD, 1985; M in Tropical Medicine & Hygiene, Uniformed Svcs. U. Health Sci., 1991. Med. officer Malangas Coal Corp., Zamboanga Del Sur, Philippines, 1987; resident Philippine Gen. Hosp., Manila, 1988; assoc. prof. dept. parasitology Coll. Pub. Health U. Philippines, Manila, 1988—; cons., vis. lectr. in field. Mem. Philippine Med. Assn., Philippine Soc. Parasitology, Laguna Med. Soc. Roman Catholic. Avocations: piano playing, swimming, gardening. Office: Coll Pub Health U Philippin, 625 P Gil St, 1000 Manila Philippines

BELL, CHARLES D., lawyer; b. McKeesport, Pa., Jan. 23, 1923; s. Charles R. and Bertha Beatrice (Davis) B.; m. Mary Porter Wilkin, Mar. 17, 1945 (dec. 1971); children—Betty Bell Williams, Peggy Jean Hrach, Charles William, Julie Bell Caldwell; m. Marjorie Wicks, Mar. 26, 1977. BS in Chemistry, Bethany Coll., 1944; JD, U. Mich., 1949. Bar: W.Va., 1951. Assoc. Schroeder, Merriam, Hofgren & Brady, Chgo., 1950-51, Bell, McMullen, Wellsburg, W.Va., 1951—; asst. pros. atty. Brooke County, Wellsburg, 1960-68, 72-76, 81-90; bd. dirs., sec. Banner Fibreboard Co., Wellsburg. Past bd. dirs. W.Va. Rehab. Found., North Ctrl. region Boy Scouts Am.; mem. W.Va. Ind. Coll. Found., chmn., 1992-95; bd. trustees Bethany Coll., 1976-97, chmn., 1977-97. Served with AUS, 1944-46. Mem. ABA, Brooke County Bar Assn., W.Va. State Bar Assn., Wheeling Country Club, Masons, Elks. Republican. Home: 1140 Duval Hts Wellsburg WV 26070-1570 Office: Bell McMullen 67 Town Sq Wellsburg WV 26070

BELL, CHARLES EUGENE, JR., industrial engineer; b. N.Y.C., Dec. 13, 1932; s. Charles Edward and Constance Elizabeth (Verbelia) B.; B. Engring., Johns Hopkins U., 1954, M.S. in Engring., 1959; m. Doris R. Clifton, Jan. 14, 1967; 1 son, Scott Charles Bell. Indsl. engr. Signode Corp., Balt., 1957-61, asst. to plant mgr., 1961-63, plant engr., 1963-64, div. indsl. engr., Glenview, Ill., 1964-69, asst. to div. mgr., 1969-76, engring. mgr., 1976-93; cons., 1993—; host committeeman Internat. Indsl. Engring. Conf., Chgo., 1984, 92. Served with U.S. Army, 1955-57. Registered profl. engr., Calif. Mem. Am. Inst. Indsl. Engrs. (pres. 1981), Indsl. Mgmt. Club Central Md. (pres. 1964), Nat. Soc. Profl. Engrs., Ill. Soc. Profl. Engrs., Soc. Plastics Engrs. Republican. Roman Catholic. Home: 1021 W Old Mill Rd Lake Forest IL 60045-3749

BELL, CHRISTOPHER, physiology educator; b. Melbourne, Victoria, Australia, Sept. 30, 1941; s. Arthur Cruse and Betty (Coutts) B.; m. Christine Margaret Bell. BSc, U. Melbourne, 1962, MSc, 1964, PhD, 1967, DSc, 1980; MA, U. Dublin, Ireland, 1996. Lectr. U. Melbourne, 1973-76, sr. lectr., 1976-79, reader in physiology, 1979-95; prof. physiology U. Dublin, 1995—; dir. preclinical studies Trinity Coll., Dublin, 1996—; hon. treas. Australian Physiol. and Pharmacol. Soc., 1980-86, CEO, 1993-95. Author: Inside Ourselves, 1989; editor various books; mem. editl. bd. various biomed. jours., 1983—; contbr. chpts. to books and articles to profl. jours. Nat. Heart Found. rsch. fellow, Australia, 1967-73; fellow Trinity Coll., Dublin, 1997. Mem. Am. Physiol. Soc., Physiol. Soc., Brit. Pharmacol. Soc. (Sandoz prize 1972). Avocations: gardening,r eading, opera, military history, Georgian buildings. Office: Dept Physiology, Trinity Coll, Dublin 2, Ireland

BELL, DAVID ANDREW, philosophy educator; b. London, Apr. 24, 1947; s. Jack Martin and Kathleen Myra (Petty) B.; m. Diane Kelly, July 1, 1983; children: Edward, Madeleine. BA in Philosophy, Trinity Coll., Dublin, Ireland, 1970; MA in Philosophy, McMaster U., Hamilton, Can., 1973; postgrad., Göttingen (Germany) U., 1974; PhD in Philosophy, McMaster U., Hamilton, Can., 1975. Lectr. in philosophy Sheffield (Eng.) U., 1976-89, prof. philosophy, 1989—; vis. prof. Leuven (Belgium) U., 1987-88, Munich U., Munich, 1994; hon. prof. Keele (Eng.) U., 1994-97; fellow Wissenschaftskolleg, Berlin, 1995-96. Author: Frege's Theory of Judgement, 1979, Husserl, 1990; editor: The Analytic Tradition, 1990, Wissenschaft und Subjektivität, 1993. Radcliffe Trust rsch. fellow, Oxford, Eng., 1987, Alexander von Humboldt rsch. fellow, Berlin, 1988; rsch. readership British Acad., Sheffield, Eng., 1993-95, Alexander von Humboldt Forschungspreis, 1999. Mem. Mind Assn. (pres.-elect). Office: Sheffield U, Dept Philosophy, Sheffield S10 2TN South Yorkshire, England

BELL, DONALD WILLIAM, experimental psychologist; b. L.A., Apr. 28, 1936; s. Samuel Chamblis and Betty M. (Welz) B. BA, U. So. Calif., 1959, MA, 1963, PhD, 1966. Rsch. assoc. Subcom. on Noise Rschr. Ctr., L.A., 1962-66; postdoctoral fellow Stanford (Calif.) U., 1966-68; rsch. psychologist SRI Internat., Menlo Park, Calif., 1968-76, sr. rsch. psychologist, 1976-82, program mgr., 1982-83, dir. speech rsch. program, 1983-89, dir., sensory sci. and tech. ctr., 1989-93; pres. Digital Voice Corp., 1982—; prin., dir. Security Group Inc., 1996—; pres. Digital Voice Corp., 1982—; prin., dir. Security Group, Inc., 1996—. Contbr. articles to profl. jours. Mem. planning commn. Town of Portola Valley, Calif., 1980-92. Mem. IEEE, Acoustical Soc. Am., Psychonomic Soc., Am. Voice I/O Soc. (dir.). Home and Office: 1288 Spring Rd Montecito CA 93108-2831

BELL, DONNA LEDBETTER, guidance counselor; b. Biltmore, N.C., July 22, 1939; d. William Richard and Ruby Bache (Malday) Ledbetter; divorced; 2 children. BS in Home Econs., U. Tenn., 1960; MA in Guidance and Counseling, Western Carolina U., 1967; EdD in Counseling and Student Pers., Va. Poly. Inst. and State U., 1986. Tchr. Amherst County sch. sys., Amherst, Va., 1964-65, Buncombe County Sch. Sys., Asheville, N.C., 1965-66, Roanoke (Va.) City/County Sch. Sys., 1981-82; counselor reception unit Juvenile Evaluation Ctr., Swannanoa, N.C., 1966; instr. gen. psychology and child psychology Montreat (N.C.) Anderson Coll., 1967-68; group facilitator Title IV workshops St. Augustine Coll./N.C. State U. Human Rels. Ctr., Raleigh, 1969; instr. career-life planning U. Va. Regional Ctr., Roanoke, 1977-78; guidance counselor 9th-12th grade students Montgomery County Sch. Sys., Blacksburg, Va., 1984, Fairfax County Publ Schs., Springfield, Va., 1986—; grad. rsch. asst. Va. Poly. Inst. and State U., Blacksburg, 1984-85, rsch. assoc., 1985-86; instr. Asheville-Buncombe Tech. Inst., 1965-66. Lay eucharistic min. Cathedral of All Souls, 1998; bd. dirs. Guardian Ad Litem Program, 1999—. Mem. AACD, Nat. Assn. Women Deans, Adminstrs. and Counselors, No. Va. Counselors Assn., Va. Counselors Assn., Phi Delta Kappa, Phi Kappa Phi. Episcopalian. Avocations: reading, theater, travel, art, music. Home: 117 Lower Christ School Rd Fletcher NC 28732-9455

BELL, FRANCES LOUISE, medical technologist; b. Milton, Pa., Apr. 28, 1926; d. George Earl and Kathryn Robbins (Fairchild) Reichard; m. Edwin Lewis Bell II, Dec. 27, 1950; children: Ernest Michael, Stephen Thomas, Eric Leslie. BS in Biology cum laude, Bucknell U., 1948; MT, Geisinger Meml. Hosp., 1949. Registered med. technologist. Med. technologist Burlington County Hosp., Mt. Holly, N.J., 1949-50, Robert Packer Hosp., Sayre, Pa., 1950, Carle Hosp./Clinic, Urbana, Ill., 1951-52, St. Joseph Hosp., Reading, Pa., 1972-83. Vol. Crime Watch, City Hall, Reading, 1985-90, Am. Heart Assn., Reading, 1956—, March of Dimes, Reading, 1956-72, Am. Cancer Soc., Reading, 1956-71, Multiple Sclerosis, Reading, 1956-72, Reading Musical Found., 1985-90, Hist. Soc. Berks County; corr. sec. women's aux., 1986-90; fin. sec. aux. Albright Coll., 1988-95; hospitality co-chmn. women's com. Reading Symphony Orch., 1985-90, editor yearbook women's com., 1992-96; editor yearbook Reading Symphony Orch. League, 1996—; chmn. hospitality Reading-Berks Pub. Librs., 1988-91; mem. Friends Reading Mus., Berks County Conservancy. Mem. AAUW (assoc. editor bull. 1961-63, cultural interests rep. 1967-68), Woman's Club of Reading (treas. 1986-88, fin. sec. 1991—), United Meth. Women, World Affairs Coun. Berks County, Libr. Soc. Albright Coll., Phi Beta Kappa. Republican. Methodist. Avocations: music appreciation, photography, postcard art prints. Home: 1454 Oak Ln Reading PA 19604-1865

BELL, JOHN IRVING, medical researcher, educator; b. July 1, 1952. Student, Ridley Coll., Can., 1966-71; B Med. Sci. with honors, U. Alta., Can., 1975; BA in Physiol. Scis. with honors, Oxford (Eng.) U., 1976, BM BCh, 1979, DM, 1990. House officer John Radcliffe Hosp., Oxford, 1979-80; sr. house officer dept. clin. cardiology Hammersmith Hosp., London, 1980-81; sr. house officer renal unit Guy's Hosp., London, 1981; sr. house officer in neurology Nat. Hosp. Neurol. Diseases, London, 1982; rsch. fellow Nuffield dept. clin. medicine Oxford U., 1982, univ. lectr. Nuffield dept. clin. medicine, 1989, Nuffield prof. clin. medicine, 1992—; clin. fellow medicine, postdoctoral fellow med. microbiology Stanford (Calif.) U., 1982-87; Wellcome sr. clin. fellow, hon. cons. physician John Radcliffe Hosp., Oxford, 1987; Norbert Freinkel lectr. Am. Diabetes Assn., 1991; dep. chmn. Powderject Pharms., 1998—, Oxagen, 1998—. Editor: Genetics and Human Nutrition, 1990, T Cell Receptor Genes, 1998; mem. editl. bd. Trends in Genetics, Immumogenetics Monitor, 1991, Human Molecular Genetics, 1992, Quar. Jour. Medicine, 1992, Immunological Revs., 1998—; mem. various grant rev. coms.; contbr. numerous articles to profl. publs.; patentee in field. Founder Wellcome Trust Ctr. for Human Genetics. Rhodes scholar, 1975-78; John Radcliffe Rsch. fellow, 1982, Alta. Heritage Trust Fund for Med. Rsch. fellow, 1983-87, fellow Magdalen Coll., 1990, 92; grantee Wellcome Trust, Arthritis and Rheumatism Coun., EEC. Fellow Royal Coll. Physicians, Acad. Med. Sci. (founder); mem. Assn. Physicians Gt. Britain and Ireland, Human Genome Orgn., Brit. Soc. Rheumatology, Internat. T Cell REceptor Nomenclature Com., Oxford Exptl. Medicine Club. Office: John Radcliffe Hosp, Nuffield Dept Clin Medicine, Headington Oxford OX, England

BELL, JOHN NIGEL BERRIDGE, environmental pollution educator, researcher; b. Derby, Derbyshire, Eng., Apr. 26, 1943; s. John Edward Donald and Dorothy Elise (White) B.; m. Jennifer Margaret Pollard, Aug. 1970 (div. 1977); m. Carolyn Mary Davies, July 31, 1978 (div. July 1992); children: Glyn, Gareth, Owain. BSc, U. Manchester, Eng., 1964, PhD, 1969; MSc, U. Waterloo, Can., 1965, D Environ. Studies (hon.), 1998. Rsch. asst. Bedford Coll., London, 1968-70; rsch. asst. Imperial Coll., London, 1970-72, lectr., 1972-83, sr. lectr., 1983-87, reader in environ. pollution, 1987-89; prof. environ. pollution Imperial Coll. Sci., Tech. & Medicine, London, 1989—; specialist advisor House of Commons Select Com. on Environ., London, 1984, 88, 91, 98, House of Commons Select Com. on Agr., London, 1988, House of Lords Select Com. Sci. & Tech., 1996; mem. working group on air quality guidelines WHO, Neukirchen, Austria, 1985, Les Diablerets, Switzerland, 1994; mem. sci. and engring. com. Brit. Coun., Manchester, Eng., 1991-98; mem. safety, health and environ. coun. Brit. Nuclear Fuels Ltd., Risley, Eng., 1993-2000. Co-author: Air Pollution Injury to Vegetation, 1986; contbr. articles to profl. jours. Gov. Wilson Sch., Reading, Eng., 1988-92. Recipient contracts U.K. Nirex, 1988—, U.K. Dept. Environ., 1986-97, U.K. Overseas Devel. Adminstrn. Dept. for Internat. Devel., 1995—; grantee U.K. Natural Environ. Rsch. Coun., 1975-94, 97—, Engring. and Phys. Scis. Rsch. Coun., 1997—. Fellow Royal Soc. Arts; mem. Brit. Ecol. Soc., Internat. Union Radioecologists, Soc. Environ. Toxicology and Chemistry, European Environ. Mgmt. Assn. Avocations: travel, natural history, railways, classical music, literature. Home: 48 Western Elms Ave, Reading RG30 2AN, England Office: Imperial Coll Ctr Environ Tech, Royal Sch Mines, London SW7 2BP, England

BELL, JOHN PERRY, minister, religious organization administrator; b. Columbia, La., Feb. 8, 1948; s. John Dixon and Laverne (Beck) B.; m. Gwendolyn Jean McKay, Dec. 18, 1971; children: Felicia, Peter, Rachel. BA, N.E. La. U., 1970, MA, 1971; ThM, Southern Meth. U., 1973; DMin, Garrett Evang. Sem., 1989. Ordained to ministry United Meth. Ch., 1974. Min. youth United Meth. Ch., Athens, Tex., 1972; pastor United Meth. Ch., Argyle, Wis., 1973-76, Sheboygan Falls, Wis., 1976-84, Waupaca, Wis., 1984-91; assoc. conf. min. United Ch. of Christ, 1991-97; exec. dir. United Meth. Found., 1998—; bd. dirs. Bell Press, Waupaca, 1990—; sec. Coun. on Fin. Adminstrn., Sun Prairie, Wis., 1984-92; del. World Meth. Conf., Honolulu, 1981, Nairobi, 1986, New World Mission, Bangalore, India, 1989, UNCED, Rio de Janeiro, 1992, UN Conf. on Population, Cairo, Egypt, 1994. Pres. Am. Cancer Soc., Waupaca, 1988-90, Mental Health Assn., Waupaca, 1988-91. Recipient Superior award Am. Cancer Soc., 1989-90. Mem. World Future Soc., Kiwanis (local pres. 1983). Democrat. Home: 2212 Stockton Dr Springfield IL 62703-5268 Office: 1630 S State St Springfield IL 62704-3682

BELL, JOHN TEDFORD, civil engineer; b. Live Oak, Fla., May 18, 1960; s. Wilbur Seale and Mary Bond (Benson) B.; m. Kathryn Elizabeth Gill, July 21, 1993. BSCE, U. Fla., 1983; postgrad., U. S.C., Ga. Tech. Registered profl. engr., Fla., Ga., S.C., Tenn., Ala. Design engr. Campbell Wallace Cons. Engrs., Knoxville, Tenn., 1983-85, Jordan, Jones & Goulding, Inc., Charleston, S.C., 1985-89; pres., owner Gen. Inspection Svcs. Inc., Charleston, 1987; project mgr. Jordan, Jones & Goulding, Inc., Atlanta, 1989-90; regional mgr. Jordan, Jones & Goulding, Inc., Knoxville, 1991-95, Tallahassee, 1995-96; pres., owner The Coloney Co., Tallahassee, 1996—. Contbr. articles to profl. jours. Asst. scoutmaster Boy Scouts Am., Charleston, S.C., 1986-89; bd. dirs. So. Shakespeare Festival, Tallahassee, 1996—. Mem. ASCE, NSPE, Am. Water Works Assn., Governor's Club. Methodist. Achievements include successfull opening of engineering design office. Avocations: hunting, fishing, model railroading, skiing. Office: The Coloney Co 1014 N Adams St Tallahassee FL 32303-6133

BELL, JOSHUA, musician; b. Ind., Dec. 6, 1967. vis. prof. Royal Acad. Music. Youngest guest soloist Phila. Orch. Subscription concert, 1982; participant European tour St. Louis Symphony, 1985, German tour Indpls. Symphony, 1987; guest soloist with numerous orchs., U.S.A., Can., U.K., Germany, Czech Republic; recitalist U.S.A., Europe; recordings include Mendelssohn and Bruch concertos with Acad. St. Martin-in-the-Fields, Sir Neville Marriner, Tchaikovsky and Wieniawski concertos with Cleve. Orch. and Vladimir Ashkenazy, (recital album) Brahms, Paganini, Sarasate, Wieniawski with Samuel Sanders, Lalo Symphonie Espagnole and Saint-Saens Concerto with Montreal Symphony Orch. and Charles Dutoit, Franck, Fauré and Débussy, Chausson Concerto for violin, piano, string quartet with Thibaudet and Isserlis, Poème with Royal Philharmonic Orch. and Andrew Litton, Mozart Concertos 3 and 5 with English Chamber Orch. and Peter Maag, Prokofiev violin concertos with Montreal Symphony Orch. and Charles Dutoit, Barber and Walton concertos, Bloch Baal Shem, with Balt. Symphony and David Zinman; concerti with L.A. Philharm and Esa-Pekka Salonen; Gershwin Fantasy with London Symphony Orch., others. Avocations: chess, computers, golf, tennis, baseball. Address: care IMG Artists, Media House 3 Burlington Ln, Chiswick London W4 2TH, England

BELL, LINDA GWENN, periodical and magazine writer; b. Lakewood, Ohio, Dec. 26, 1942; d. J. David and Laura Elenor (Seefreid) Horsfall; m. Charles Lee Bell, Dec. 27, 1962; children: Amy Bell Mulaudzi, Peggy Gwenn Bell. BA in Journalism, Ohio State U. Editor Am. Assn. Fgn. Svc. Women Newsletter, Washington, 1978-80; house editor Royal Soc. New Zealand Acad. Sci., Wellington, 1981-85; English editor Adult Lit. Assn., Harare, Zimbabwe, 1986-88; mgr. Am. Mission Cmty. Assn., Lusaka, Zambia, 1988-90; corr. North Forty News, LaPorte, Colo., 1994—. Author: Hidden Immigrants, 1997, (chpt. in book) Strangers at Home, 1998. Mem. Internat. Friends of Colo. State U. Unitarian.

BELL, MARTIN, member of parliament; b. Redisham, Suffolk, Eng., Aug. 31, 1938; s. Adrian and Marjorie (Gibson) B.; m. Nelly Gourdon, 1971 (div.); 2 children; m. Rebecca Sobel, 1985 (div. 1993). Student, King's Coll., Cambridge, Eng.; DHC, Derby U., 1996, degree (hon); degree (hon), E. Anglia U., 1997, N. London U., 1998. Trainee news asst. BBC, Norwich, Eng., 1962; TV news journalist BBC, 1965-97, Washington corr., 1978-89, Berlin corr., 1989-93, Vienna corr., 1993-94, fgn. affairs corr., 1994-97; mem. parliament for Tatton at Chelsire Ho. of Commons, London, 1997—. Author: In Harm's Way, 1995, An Accidental MP, 2000. Named Officer of Brit. Empire, 1993, Reporter of Yr., Royal TV Soc., 1976, 92, Newscaster of Yr., TV and Radio Industries Club, 1995; recipient Pres.'s medal Inst. Pub. Rels., 1996. Avocations: swimming, walking, listening. Office: MP for Tatton Ho of Commons, Westminster, London England

BELL, MICHAEL GEOFFREY HARRISON, civil engineering educator; b. London, Oct. 27, 1953; s. Peter Robert and Elizabeth Mary (Harrison) B.; m. Reiko Ohnishi; children: Lawrence, Olivia, Martin. BA, Cambridge U., 1975; MSc, Leeds U., 1976, PhD, 1981. Rsch. asst. U. Coll., London, 1979-82; postdoctoral rsch. fellow U. Karlsruhe, Germany, 1982-84; lectr. Newcastle U., U.K., 1984-94, reader, 1994-96, prof., 1996—; dir. Transport Ops. Rsch. Group, 1996—, dep. dir., 1992-96. Author: Transportation Network Analysis, 1997; assoc. editor Transportation Research B, 1992—. Office: U Newcastle, Claremont Tower, Newcastle Upon Tyne NE1 7RU, United Kingdom

BELL, MICHELLE LANNETTE, floriculturist, researcher, educator; b. Willows, Calif., Mar. 4, 1967; m. Joseph Edward Flaherty, Aug. 16, 1997. BS in Agr., Calif. State U., Chico, 1989; MS in Hort. Sci., N.C. State U., 1992, PhD in Hort. Sci., PhD in Entomology, 1997. Asst. prof., extension floricultur specialist U. Fla., Bradenton, 1997—; ednl. advisor, sec., bd. dirs. S.e. Greenhouse Conf. and Trade Show, Greenville, S.C., 1997—; advisors floriculture divsn. Fla. Nurserymen and Growers Assn., Orlando, 1997—. Editor: Commerical Poinsettia Production in Florida, 1998; contbr. articles to web pages. John Carew Meml. scholar Bedding Plants Found., Inc., 1995. Mem. Am. Soc. Hort. Sci., Entomology Soc. Am., So. Region Am. Soc. Horticultural Sci., Fla. State Hort. Soc., Ohio Florists Assn., Sigma Xi, Gamma Sigma Delta, Pi Alpha Xi (chpt. treas. 1990-91), Phi Kappa Phi (chpt. v.p. 1988-89). Office: U Fla Gulf Coast Rsch and Edn 5007 60th St E Bradenton FL 34203-9511

BELL, NANCY LEE HOYT, real estate investor, middle school educator, volunteer; b. L.A., Oct. 25, 1929; d. James and Mabel Ruth (Lockard) Hoyt; m. Ralph Rogers Bell, July 3, 1953; children: Linda Lee, John Curtis, James Hoyt, Martha Chambers, Ralph Rogers II, Nancy Lee II. Student, Whittier Coll., 1948, San Jose State Coll., 1949; BA in Edn., U. Calif., Santa Barbara, 1950; postgrad., San Francisco State Coll., 1952, UCLA, 1953; MS in Edn., U. So. Calif., 1955. Tchr. John Adams Jr. H.S., Santa Monica, Calif., 1950-54; real estate investor. Pres. Santa Clarita Cmty. Concerts, Saugus, Calif., 1968-69; vol. worker USO, YWCA, 1944-45, Cancer Crusade, Calif. and Wash., 1960-90. Mem. AAUW (charter life; pres.), Big Bear Valley Hist. Soc. (life; sec.), DAR (charter life; treas.), Gen. Soc. Mayflower Descs. (life; bd. dirs.), Alpha Delta Pi. Republican. Methodist. Avocations: world travel, collecting antiques, genealogy researcher, activities with children and grandchildren, music. Home: 615 Main St Apt B Edmonds WA 98020-3804

BELL, NICHOLAS ANTHONY, translator, educator; b. London, Nov. 6, 1951; s. Anthony Newton and Penelope Mary (Sandberg) B.; m. Rebecca O'Driscoll (div. 1980); m. Inga Totzauer (div. 1985); m. Maggi Lussi, Apr. 10, 1992; stepchildren: Cathy, Patrick. Cert. in edn., Middlesex U., England, 1978; cert. ESL, RSA/Cambridge, England, 1989; MEd, Manchester U., England, 1997. Youth trainer Fulham Tng. Workshops, London, 1986; tchr. English Castle's English Inst., Baar, Switzerland, 1987-93, Volkshochschule, Zurich, Switzerland, 1992-94, Handelsschule Kaufmaennischen Verbandes, Zurich, 1994-97, U. Applied Scis., Winterthur, Switzerland, 1998—; ko-leiter Fachstelle fuer Fremdsprachenunterricht, Zurich, 1998—; translator Landis and Staefa, Switzerland, 1994-98; freelance translator. Bd. dirs. Lifespark; mem. death penalty coordination group Amnesty Internat., Switzerland, 1997—. Mem. Assn. Suisse de Traducteurs, et Interpretes. Avocations: writing, reading, jogging, music, cooking. Home: Spruemuelistrasse 1, 8816 Hirzel Switzerland

BELL, PATRICK MICHAEL, endocrinologist, researcher; b. Belfast, Northern Ireland, Mar. 9, 1953; s. Benjamin Jonathan and Jane (McIllveen) B.; m. Dorothy Patricia Walker, June 28, 1979; children: Jane, Kathleen Sarah, Jonathan Patrick. MB, BCh, BAO, Queens U. of Belfast, 1977, MD by thesis, 1984. Registered specialist in endocrinology and diabetes mellitus, Gen. Med. Coun., U.K. Rsch. fellow Royal Victoria Hosp., Belfast City Hosp., Belfast, 1981-82; sr. registrar Royal Victoria Hosp., Belfast, 1982-84; Mayo Found. fellow in endocrinology Mayo Clinic, Rochester, Minn., 1984-85; sr. registrar Belfast City Hosp., 1985-86; cons. physician Royal Victoria Hosp., 1986—; hon. clin. lectr. Queens U. Belfast, 1992—; hon. sec. Med. Staff, Royal Victoria Hosp., 1996-98; examiner Royal Coll. Physicians, Ireland and Edinburgh, 1994—. Author: Multiple Choice Questions in Medicine, 1981, 2 more edits.; contbr. articles on diabetes, glucose metabolism, and insulin resistance in med. jours. Exec. com. mem. Alliance Party of Northern Ireland, 1987-94, policy convenor, 1988-92. Fulbright Hays Traveling scholar 1984; named Graves Lectr. Royal Acad. Medicine in Ireland, 1992. Fellow Royal Coll. Physicians Glasgow, Royal Coll. Physicians Ireland, Royal Coll. Physicians London; mem. Am. Diabetes Assn., Brit. Diabetic Assn. (chmn. Northern Ireland com. 1992-98, mem. bd. trustees 1992-98), Assn. Physicians of Gt. Britain and Ireland (elected). Mem. Alliance Party Northern Ireland. Church of Ireland. Avocations: golf, Trollope novels, cricket. Office: Royal Victoria Hospital, Grosvenor Rd, Belfast BT12 6BA, Northern Ireland

BELL, PAUL BURTON, JR., academic administrator, zoology educator; b. Memphis, June 24, 1946; s. Paul Burton and Margaret Louise Bell; m. Terry Jane Carrel, Aug. 4, 1979; children: Peter Edward Schnaitman, Heather Margaret Louise. AB cum laude, Washington U., 1968; PhD, Yale U., 1975. Sci. tchr. Vashon High Sch., St. Louis, 1969-70; rsch. fellow Calif. Inst. Tech., Pasadena, 1974-76; adj. asst. prof. UCLA, 1976-79; asst. prof. zoology U. Okla., Norman, 1979-86, assoc. prof. zoology, 1986-93; univ. registrar U. Okla., 1990-97; assoc. provost U. Okla., Norman, 1991-97, prof. zoology, 1993—, dean arts and scis., 1997—, vice provost, 1997—; vis. researcher Linköping (Sweden) U., 1983-90. Contbr. articles to profl. jours. Home: 1025 Mcnamee St Norman OK 73069-5445 Office: U Okla 601 Elm Ave Rm 1100 Norman OK 73019-3111

BELL, PETER FRANK, surgeon, educator; b. Bangalore, India, June 12, 1938; arrived in England, 1948; s. Frank and Ruby Edna (Corks) B.; m. Anne Jennings, Aug. 25, 1961; children: Jane Marie, Louise Catherine, Mark Peter. MB ChB, U. Sheffield, 1961, MD, 1970. Registrar surgery Sheffield Health Bd., Eng., 1963-65; lectr. surgery U. Glasgow, Scotland, 1965-68, sr. lectr. surgery, 1969-74; found. prof. surgery U. Leicester, England, 1974—; treas., council mem. Brit. Jour. Surgery, London, 1982—; Mark Sharp and Dohme invited lectr. Australasian and Nephtol. Soc. Australia and New Zealand, 1977. Author: Operative Arterial Surgery, 1983, Surgical Aspects of Haemodialysis, 1985; editor European Jour. Vascular Surgery, 1985; contbr. articles to profl. jours. Sir Henry Wellcome travel fellow Wellcome Found., Denver, 1968-69. Fellow Royal Surgeons Coll. (coun.), Royal Coll. Physicians and Surgeons Glasgow; mem. Surg. Rsch. Soc. (past sec. and pres.), Vascular Soc. Gt. Brit. and Ireland (past pres.), Transplantation Soc. (sec.), European Soc. for Vascular Soc. (past pres.). Mem. Ch. of England. Avocations: horticulture, oil painting, tennis. Office: Leicester Royal Infirmary, Robert Kilpatrick Bldg, Leicester LE2 7LX, England

BELL, REBECCA, psychotherapist, journalist; b. N.Y.C., Dec. 20, 1942; d. Hiram Charles Bluming and Mildred Ann Good; m. Martin Bell, Feb. 7, 1986 (div. Apr. 1993); children: Michael Sobel, Jessica Sobel. BA, UCLA, 1993, MSW, 1995. Lic. clin. social worker. Reporter Hollywood Citizens News, L.A., 1969-70; news writer Sta. KTLA-TV, L.A., 1970-71; assignment editor Sta. KHJ-TV, L.A., 1971-72; anchor, reporter Sta. WXYZ-TV, Detroit, 1972-76; reporter Sta. WCAU-TV, Phila., 1976-78; anchor Sta. WNET-TV, N.Y.C., 1978; corr. NBC, N.Y.C., 1978-86; corr. war coverage, White House reporter NBC Network, London, N.Y., Washington, 1978-86; pvt. practice as psychotherapist Beverly Hills, Calif., 1995—. Author: (book) The Strange Disappearance of Jimmy Hoffa, 1974. Recipient Emmy award Am. Fedn. Radio and TV Artists, 1983, Deadline award, 1978, Golden Mike award, 1974. Mem. NASW. Avocations: painting, horseback riding.

BELL, ROBERT CHARLES, applied mathematician; b. Hobart, Australia, Feb. 13, 1949; s. Powell William and Margaret Gwenyth (Boyd) B.; m. Janet Hodge, June 22, 1974; children: Miranda Louise, Geraldine Sally, Jessica Ann. BS, Monash U., Melbourne, Australia, 1971; PhD, Monash U., 1977. Exptl. scientist CSIRO Divsn. of Atmospheric Rsch., Aspendale, Victoria, Australia, 1974-90; supercomputing support mgr. CSIRO Divsn. of Info. Tech., Carlton, Victoria, 1990-92; supercomputing facility mgr. CSIRO Divsn. of Info. Tech., 1992-97; dep. mgr. HPCCC, Melbourne, 1997—. Fellow Royal Meteorol. Soc.; mem. Australian Meterol. and Oceanographic Soc., Assn. for Computing Machinery. Baptist. Office: HPCCC 24th Fl, GPO Box 1289K, 3001 Melbourne Victoria, Australia

BELL, ROBERT CHARLES, retired plastic surgeon, author, civic worker; b. Sudbury, Ont., Can., Nov. 22, 1917; s. Robert Duncan and Violet Lydia (Clarke) B.; m. Phyllis Pearl Hunter Codling, June 28, 1941; children—Robert Graham, Geoffrey Duncan, Diana Mary. M.B. B.S., St. Bart's Hosp., London, 1941. House surgeon St. Barts Hosp., 1941-42; demonstrator anatomy U. Aberdeen, Scotland, 1942-43; registrar in surgery St. John's Hosp., London, 1944; sr. registrar in plastic surgery Royal Victoria Infirmary, Newcastle Upon Tyne, Eng., 1949-52; cons. plastic surgeon Newcastle Regional Bd., 1952-82, ret., 1982; hon. cons. Newcastle U., 1960-82. Author: Board and Table Games From Many Civilizations, 1960; Commercial Coins 1787-1804, 1963; Tyneside Pottery, 1971; The Board Game Book, 1979. Chmn. Northumberland and Durham br. English Speaking Union, Eng., 1983—. Served with Royal Can. Air Force, 1945-48. Fellow Royal Coll. Surgeons; mem. Royal Coll. Physicians, No. Surg. Soc. (hon.). Mem. Ch. of England. Avocations: numismatics; woodwork; gardening. Home: 20 Linden Rd, Tyne and Wear Gosforth NE3 4EY, England

BELL, ROBERT GRAHAM, microbiologist, researcher; b. Aberdeen, Scotland, Mar. 17, 1943; arrived in New Zealand, 1981; s. Robert Charles and Phyllis Pearl Hunter (Codling) B.; m. Janet Susan Miller, Sept. 19, 1968; children: Andrea Jane, Sylvia Gwendolyn, Penelope Caroline, Elizabeth Ann. BSc with honors, U. Durham, Newcastle-on-Tyne, Eng., 1965; PhD, U. Cambridge, Eng., 1968. Asst. prof. U. Guelph, Ont., 1968-72; sr. lectr. U. Otago, Dunedin, New Zealand, 1972-74; rsch. scientist Agr. Can., Lethbridge, 1974-77; sr. lectr. Nat. U. Singapore, 1977-81; microbiologist Meat Industry Rsch. Inst. of New Zealand, Hamilton, 1981-90, head microbiology and food safety, 1990-97, Mirinz fellow, 1997-99; microbiologist AgRsch., 1999—; New Zealand tech. cooperation coord. Saudi Arabian Stds. Orgn., Riyadh, 1986-92. Co-author: Product Life of Domestic and Imported Chilled Sheepmeats in Saudi Arabia, 1993; contbr. chpts. to books, articles to profl. jours.; patentee in field. Postgrad. award Agrl. Rsch. Coun., Eng., 1965-68. Mem. New Zealand Microbiology Soc., New Zealand Nat. Culture Collection Com., New Zealand Nat. Com. of Internat. Inst. of Refrigeration (commr. C2 1990—). Avocation: farming. Office: AgRsch, Pvt Bag 3123, Hamilton New Zealand

BELL, ROBERT MATTHEW, pharmaceutical company consultant; b. London, Dec. 3, 1932; came to U.S., 1972; s. George Frederick and Patricia (Brusso) B.; m. Jeanette Edna Head, Sept. 17, 1955; children: Adrian R., Colette M. MB,ChB, Birmingham U., Eng., 1968. Diplomate Am. Bd. Family Practice; cert. pharm. chemist Pharm. Soc. Great Britain. Relief mgr. Boots Chemists, Eng., 1955-57; owner Bell's Pharmacy, Rhodesia, 1958-61; joint owner Strachan's Pharmacy, Rhodesia, 1962-69; asst. lectr. Godfrey Huggins Sch. Medicine, Rhodesia, 1970-72; clin. project dir. Sterling Winthrop Rsch. Inst., Renesselaer, 1973-75; chief clin. pharmacology ICI Americas, Wilmington, Del., 1975-78; pres., owner RAMA Med. Clinic, Charlotte, N.C., 1980-86; from assoc. dir. to sr. dir. healthcare info. svcs. Searle, Inc., Skokie, Ill., 1986-96; prin. Bell and Assocs., Sedonia, Ariz., 1996—; mem. drug rev. com. Drugs Control Coun. of Rhodesia, Salisbury, 1971-72; mem. adv. bd. Upjohn Healthcare Servers, Charlotte, N.C., 1983-84; chmn. adv. bd. Med. Office Asst. Program Piedmont Comty. Coll., Charlotte, N.C., 1983-84; mem. exec. bd. Am. Acad. Pharm. Physicians, Raleigh, N.C., 1995-96. Co-author: (book) The Practical Management of Renal Failure, 1969; co-editor: (book) The Endorphins, Marcel Dekker, N.Y., 1982. Grantee Malvern Trust, Rhodesia, 1963; named Metrolina Vol. of Yr., Am. Lung Assn., N.C., 1985; recipient Outstanding Svc. award Drug Info. Assn., Ambler, Pa., 1997. Mem. AMA, DIA, Am. Acad. Pharm. Physicians (AMA SSS del.), Am.-Zimbabwe Med. Assn. (chmn. 1996-98). Avocations; postal history, reading, exercising. Office: Bell & Assocs PO Box 3668 Sedona AZ 86340-3668

BELL, ROBERT STANLEY, aerospace engineer; b. Kansas City, Mo., Apr. 30, 1951; s. Harold Stanley and Dorothy Mae Bell; m. Martha Jane Pujol, Apr. 14, 1971 (div. July 1977); m. Eva Elizabeth Horanyi, July 16, 1978; children: David, James. BS in Mech. Engring., U. Colo., 1982; cert. completion, Naval Nuc. Powerplant Sch., 1983; postgrad., USC, 1997-98. Cert. engr.-in-tng. mech. engring., Colo. Assoc. engr. Nat. Bur. Stds., Boulder, Colo., 1980-82; nuc. powerplant engr. Westinghouse Elec. Corp., Idaho Falls, Idaho, 1982-84; rsch. engr. Lockheed Corp., Palo Alto, Calif., 1984-88; sr. rsch. engr. Ball Aerospace, Boulder, 1988-92; sr. mgr. The Boeing Co., Huntington Beach, Calif., 1992—; cryogenic engring. instr. Cryoco, Inc., Boulder. Contbr. articles to profl. jours. Staff sgt. USAF, 1971-76. Named Outstanding Young Man of Am., 1982. Mem. AIAA, ASME, Soc. Automotive Engrs., Cyrogenic Soc. Am. Avocations: singing, skiing, bicycling, chess. E-mail: AdvRocket@aol.com and robert.s.bell@boeing.com. Fax: 714-896-6930.

BELL, ROBERT TREVOR, economics researcher, educator; b. Port Elizabeth, South Africa, Mar. 27, 1934; s. Robert and Violet (Thompson) B.; m. Brenda Margaret Edds, Apr. 25, 1970; children: Catherine Stroud, Margaret. B in Commerce, Rhodes U., South Africa, 1955, B in Commerce with honors, 1956, PhD, 1968; MA in Econs., Vanderbilt U., 1959. Prof. econs. U. Natal, South Africa, 1973-78, Grad. Sch. Internat. Studies, U. Denver, 1978-81; dep. dir. Inst. Social and Econ. Rsch. U. Durban-Westville, South Africa, 1982-84; prof. dept. econs. Rhodes U., 1984-94; prof. Inst. for Social and Econ. Rsch. U. Durban-Westville, 1995-2000, 2000—; vis. prof. U. Colo., Boulder, 1977-78. Author: Industrial Decentralization in South Africa, 1973; contbr. articles to profl. jours. Vis. fellow Carnegie, U. Chgo., 1964-65; grantee Anglo Am. & DeBeers Ednl. Trust, S.A., 1975, 87, 96, Liberty Life Ednl. Found., 1991. Mem. Am. Econ. Assn., Econ. Soc. South Africa. Home: 129 Juniper Rd Berea, Durban 4001, South Africa Office: U Durban-Westville, Private Bag 54001, Durban South Africa

BELL, ROGER ALISTAIR, astrophysicist; b. Walton-on-Thames, Eng.; came to U.S., 1963; s. William Ernest and Irene May (Elsley) B.; m. Sylvia Anne Gandine-Stanton, July 16, 1960; children: Alistair Michael, Andrew Christopher. BSc, U. Melbourne, Victoria, Australia, 1957; PhD, Australian Nat. U., Canberra, 1961; PhD (hon.), Uppsala (Sweden) U., 1982. Lectr. U. Adelaide, Australia, 1962-63; asst. prof. U. Md., College Park, 1963-69, assoc. prof., 1969-76, prof., 1976-98, dir. astronomy program, 1987-91, emeritus prof., 1998—; program dir. NSF, Washington, 1981-84. Contbr. sci. articles to profl. publs. Grantee NASA, NSF. Fellow Royal Astron. Soc.; mem. Am. Astron. Soc. (sec. 1989-95), Internat. Astron. Union, Am. Inst. Physics (governing bd. 1990-96). Office: U Md Astronomy Dept College Park MD 20742-0001

BELL, WILLIAM JACK, journalism educator; b. nr. Norcatur, Kans., Nov. 1, 1915; s. James S. and Ruth (Diefendorf) B.; m. Marjorie May Andrews, May 9, 1942 (dec. May 1991). B.A., B.S., Emporia (Kans.) State Tchrs. Coll., 1937, M.S., 1940; Ph.D., U. Mo., 1949. Tchr. high sch. Colby, Kans., 1937-42; reporter-editor Colby Free Press-Tribune, 1937-42; grad. asst., instr. U. Mo. Sch. Journalism, 1946-49; asst. prof. U. Okla. Sch. Journalism, 1949-51; photographer Daily Oklahoman, Oklahoma City, summer 1951; prof. journalism, head journalism and graphic arts dept. East Tex. State U., Commerce, 1951-83, prof. emeritus, 1985. City commr. Commerce, 1960-64, 74-84, mayor pro tem, 1964-67, 74-84, mayor, 1967-70, 84-86; bd. dirs. Sulphur River Mcpl. Water Dist., 1971-72, chmn. airport adv. bd., 1971-74; mem. exec. com. NetSeO Trails coun. Boy Scouts Am., 1953-57; pres. exec. bd. Commerce Pub. Libr., 1993—. Served with USNR, 1942-45. Recipient Faculty award East Tex. State U., 1976; Named Piper prof., 1982, Disting. Alumnus, Emporia State U., 1985; named to East Tex. State U. Athletic Hall of Fame, 1989. Mem. Sports Info. Dirs., Nat. Assn. Intercollegiate Athletics (pres. 1964-67, coord. 1968-82, named to Helms Found. Hall of Fame 1970), Commerce C. of C. (bd. dirs. 1955-57, 59-62, 69-71, bd. dirs. 1995—, v.p. 1985, pres. 1987-88, named Citizen of the Decade of 1980s, 1990), Lions (pres. Commerce 1959-60, dep. dist. gov. 1962-64, sec.-treas. 1987-95, club newsletter editor 1954—, Melvin Jones fellow), Phi Delta Kappa (historian 1957-69), Sigma Delta Chi. Home: 2500 Washington St Commerce TX 75428-3521

BELLA, DUSAN, diplomat; b. Martin, Slovak Republic, Mar. 2, 1958; s. Dusan and Maria (Sestakova) B.; m. Eugenia Kociscakova, Sept. 1, 1984; 1 child, Martin. MSc, Czech Tech. U., 1982. From researcher to mktg. mgr. ZTS Rsch. & Devel. Inst., Martin, 1982-92; dir., dir. gen. Min. Fgn. Affairs, Bratislava, 1993-96; head OECD sect. Embassy of the Slovak Republic, Paris, 1996-2000, head permanent del. OECD, 2000—. Avocations: music, arts, sports. Home: 28 Ave d'Eylau, 75016 Paris France Office: Min Fgn Affairs, Hlboka 2, 83336 Bratislava Slovakia

BELLA, JONATHAN NORIEGA, cardiologist; b. Cotabato City, The Philippines, Apr. 12, 1965; came to U.S., 1991; s. Primitivo Jr. and Patrocinio (Noriega) B. BA in Humanities, U. of Philippines, Manila, 1985; MD, U. of East, Manila, 1989. Cert. Am. Bd. Internal Medicine, Am. Bd. Cardiovasc. Disease. Intern Atlantic City Med. Ctr., N.J., 1991-92; resident Montefiore Med. Ctr., N.Y.C., 1992-94; fellow in cardiology N.Y. Hosp.-Cornell Med. Ctr., 1994-97; instr. medicine Weill Med. Coll. Cornell U.; fellow in echocardiography N.Y. Hosp.-Cornell Med. Ctr., 1997-98; instr. Weill Med. Coll. Cornell U.; dir. echocardiology Louis Stokes Cleve. VA Med. Ctr., 1998—; asst. prof. medicine Sch. Medicine Case Western Res. U., Cleve., 1998—. Fellow Am. Coll. Cardiology; mem. Am. Heart Assn., Am. Soc. Echocardiography. Roman Catholic. Office: Louis Stokes Cleve VA Med Ctr 10701 East Blvd Cleveland OH 44106-1702

BELLAICHE, GUY, gastroenterologist; b. Sarcelles, France, Oct. 10, 1964; s. Max and Dolly (Adda) B.; m. Corinne Taieb; children: Estelle, Xavier, Elise. MD, U. Paris VII, 1988. From specialist asst. to practicing gastroenterologist Hosp. Robert Ballanger; prof. Inst. Nursery. Co-editor rev. Gastroenterology, books Memento de Digestif, Cors Concrets de Digestif. Mem. French Nat. Soc. Gastroenterology, Assn. Gastroenterol. Gen. Hosps. Avocations: gardening, reading, chess. Home: 1 Allee Nungesser et Coli, 93420 Villepinte France Office: Hosp Robert Ballanger, Bd Robert Ballanger, 93602 Aulnay Sous Bois France

BELLAMINE, AOUATEF, biochemist; b. Lekef, Tunisia, July 2, 1963; came to U.S., 1996; d. Mustapha and Miriem Bellamine; m. Olivier Leroux, July 17, 1996. BS, U. Tunisia, Tunis, 1988; M in Toxicology, U. Paris V, 1991, PhD in Biochemistry, 1996. Rsch. fellow Vanderbilt U., Nashville, 1996—. Contbr. articles to profl. jours.; patentee in field. Mem. AAAS, Internat. Soc. Study of Xenobiotics. E-mail: aouatef@toxicology.mc.vanderbilt.edu. Home: 2215 Abbott Martin Rd Nashville TN 37215-2527

BELLAMY, CAROL, international organization executive; b. Plainfield, N.J., 1942. BA with honors, Gettysburg Coll., 1963; JD, NYU, 1968. Asst. commr. Dept. Mental Health and Mental Health Retardation Svc., N.Y.C.; with Peace Corps., Guatemala, Ctrl. Am.; assoc. Cravath, Swaine & Moore, N.Y.C.; mem. N.Y. State Senate; prin. Morgan Stanley & Co., N.Y.C.; mng. dir. Bear Stearns, N.Y.C.; dir. Peace Corps., Washington, 1993-95; exec. dir. UNICEF, 1995—. Office: UNICEF Office of Exec Director 3 United Nations Plz New York NY 10017-4486

BELLANGER, GILBERT, nuclear engineer; b. Le Mans, Maine, France, Jan. 12, 1944; s. Leon and Germaine (Verax) B.; m. Christiane Stahl, Oct. 5, 1965 (div. July 1975); 1 child, Christophe; m. Marie Claude Durand, Apr. 4, 1980; children: Arens, Franck. Diploma of Engr., Conservatoire Nat. Arts Metier, Paris, 1983; PhD with distinction, U. Dijon, France, 1989. Head nuclear materials analysis lab. Commissariat a l'Energie Atomique, Is sur Tille, France, 1965-85, dir. materials and corrosion lab., 1985—. Contbr. articles to profl. jours. Mem. Internat. Soc. Electrochemistry, Inst. Corrosion, Cefracor. Home: 10 Ave de la Paix, F21260 Selongey France Office: Commissariat a l'Energie, Ctr Etud Valduc, F21120 Is sur Tille France

BELLANGER, SERGE RENÉ, banker; b. Vimoutiers, France, Apr. 30, 1933; s. René Albert and Raymonde Maria (Renard) B. MBA, Paris Bus. Sch., 1957. With Citibank, 1966-73, mem. Paris br., 1966-69; world corp. rels. officer for Europe Citibank, N.Y.C., 1969-73, asst. v.p., 1969-71, v.p., 1972-73; sr. v.p., gen. mgr. Crédit Industriel et Commercial, N.Y.C., 1973-79, exec. v.p., gen. mgr., 1979—; U.S. gen. rep. CIC Group, N.Y.C., 1973—; prof. banking French Banking Inst., 1961-64; mem. adv. com. French House, Columbia U., 1976—, chmn., 1996—; mem. adv. com. Ctr. for Study of French Civilization and Culture, NYU, 1988—; mem. adv. bd. French Inst. Culture and Tech. U. Pa., 1992—, chmn. adv. bd., 1992-95; mem. adv. bd. Lycée Francais N.Y., 2000—; dir. Am. Ctr. in Paris, 1985-93; mem. U.S. Com. Fgn. Trade Advisors for France, 1979—, v.p. U.S. com., 1992-93, exec. v.p., 1985-93, mem. bd. dirs. nat. com., 1986—, mem. Paris exec. com., 1994-95; chmn. internat. banking course New Sch. Social Rsch., N.Y.C., 1981-83; adv. coun. French Abroad, 2000. With French Air Force, 1958-60. Decorated Algeria Commemorative medal, Officer Legion of Honor, Comdr. Nat. Order of Merit. Mem. French-Am. C. of C. (councillor 1973-74, exec. com. 1974-80, v.p. 1980-82, exec. v.p. 1982-83, nat. pres. 1983—, pres. N.Y. chpt. 1983—), European-Am. C. of C. (pres., CEO 1990-96, hon. chmn. 1996—), N.Y. C. of C. (mem. internat. bus. initiative 1994-95), N.Y.C. Partnership and C. of C. (ptnr. 1992—), Assn. French C. of C. and Industry Abroad (adminstr. 1984—, v.p. 1989-95, 1st v.p. 1995-99, pres. 1999—), French Overseas Assn., Inst. Fgn. Bankers (trustee 1975-77, v.p. 1977-79, chmn. legis. and regulatory com. 1977-79, chmn. 1979-80), Lyonnaise de Banque (bd. dirs. 1986-89), Assn. for Promotion of French Sci., Industry and Tech. (pres. 1986-91), Banque de l'Union Européenne, bd. dirs. 1989-90), Food and Wines from France (SOPEXA) (bd. dirs. 1983-93), N.Y. Futures Exchange (dir. 1980-87, chmn. fgn. exchange steering com. 1981-82), N.Y. Cotton Exchange (bd. dirs. fin. instrument exchange divsn. 1985-95), Bank Adminstrn. Inst. (mem. editl. bd. World of Banking Mag., 1981-87, columnist Banker's Mag. 1986-96), Univ. Club, River Club, Automobile Club de France. Home: 860 U N Plz Apt 2324C New York NY 10017-1810 Office: 520 Madison Ave New York NY 10022-4213

BELLAROSA, AARON JAMES, computer company executive; b. Newport Beach, Calif., Jan. 5, 1976; d. Alfred John and Patricia Ann (Feldner) Tharyk. BA in Govt., Dartmouth Coll., 1998. CEO, co-founder, advisor Granite of N.H. Investments, Hanover, 1996-98; econ. rsch. analyst The White House, Washington, 1997; bus. analyst A.T. Kearney, Inc., N.Y.C., 1998-99; sr. bus. analyst Am. Online, Inc., N.Y.C., 1999; mgr. E-Commerce Clickthebutton.com, Inc., N.Y.C., 2000—. Mem. N.Y. New Media Assn. Republican. Fax: 212-929-2642. Home E-mail: ajb@alum.dartmouth.org. Office E-mail: ajb.98@alum.dartmouth.org. Home: 353 W 51st St Apt 3 New York NY 10019-6484 Office: Clickthebutton.com Inc 38 W 21st St Fl 10 New York NY 10010-6906

BELLAS, STELIOS KIRIKOS, information engineer; b. Chios, Greece, Mar. 7, 1963; s. Kirikos and Aggeliki (Poulos) B.; married; two children. Degree in elec. engring., Tech. U. Kozani; postgrad., Nat. Tech. U., Athens, 1993—. Elec. engr. Kostalas Elec. Engring., Chios, 1982, Sigouros Elec. Engring., Athens, 1985; tech. elec. engring. Nat. Power of Electricity, Athens, 1986-87; programmer Am. Computers & Engrs., Athens, 1991; mktg. mgr., tech. support Bioghnostics, Athens, 1993-94; insp., info. engr. dept. mcht. ships' inspection svc. Ministry Mcht. Marine, 1994—, Internat.

Safety Mgmt. auditor, 1996—, pediat.-cardiovasc. disease stats. analysis, 1997-98; cons. mgr. Carriers Ships Agy., Athens, 1987; cons. tech. Technet Computer Installation, Athens, 1988; info. cons. Am. Computers & Engrs., 1991; tech. elec. engring. Legrand, Kozani, Greece, 1983, HAI Hellenic Aerospace Industry, Tanagra, Greece, 1985; tchr. computers-programming langs. pvt. sch., 1993-94; Y2K mgr. Tsakos Shipping and Trading S.A., 1998-2000. Author: Computer Peripherals, 1989. With Hellenic Navy, 1992-94. Scholar Tech. U. Kozani, 1984, 85, 86. Mem. IEEE, Tech. C. of C. Greece, Engr. Union Greece, Greek Inst. Naval Tech. Greek Orthodox. Avocations: painting, travel, repairing cars, mechanical construction, computer graphics. Home and Office: 12 Makrigianni, GR18537 Piraeus Greece

BELLASTELLA, ANTONIO, endocrinologist, educator; b. Caivano, Naples, Italy, Jan. 6, 1940; s. Luigi and Immacolata (Argiento) B.; m. Paola, July, 15, 1968; children: Luigi, Daniela, Giuseppe. Degree in medicine, U. Naples, Italy, 1964; diploma in endocrinology, Torino, Italy, 1966. Vol. asst. U. Naples, 1965-72, asst. prof to assoc. prof., 1972-90, prof., 1990—, chief endocrinology unit, 1988—; dir. internal medicine and nutrition diseases Inst. Endocrinology, U. Naples, 1997—. Author: Biological Rhythms in Endocrinology, 1981; editl. bd. Minerva Endocrinologica, 1995—; contbr. articles to profl. jours. Capt. Sanitary Army, Italy, 1965-66. Mem. Italian Soc. Endocrinology (coun. mem. 1992-97). Office: Inst Endocrinol 2d U Naples, Via Pansini 5, 80131 Naples Italy

BELLE, ALBERT JOJUAN, professional baseball player; b. Shreveport, La., Aug. 25, 1966. Student, La. State U. With Cleve. Indians, 1987-1996, Chgo. White Sox, 1997-99, Balt. Orioles, 1999—. Player Am. League All-Star Game, 1993-96; ranked 1st in Am. League for runs batted in, 1993; named to Am. League Silver Slugger Team, 1993-95, Sporting News Am. League All-Star Team, 1993-94; named Player of Yr. Sporting News, 1995. Achievements include leading the Maj. League in home runs, 1995; mem. Am. League champions, 1995. Office: Balt Orioles Oriole Park at Camden Yards 333 W Camden St Baltimore MD 21201-2435

BELLEGARDA, JEROME RENÉ, electrical engineer, scientist, consultant; b. Freiburg-in-Breisgau, Germany, Nov. 30, 1961; came to U.S., 1983; s. Denis Baptiste Bellegarda and Ginette Rolande Jeanne Grosjean; m. Eveline Jeannine Aymé, Sept. 3, 1988; children: Guillaume Denis Antoine, Mélodie Anne Pauline, Céline Claire Denise. Diploma in Engring., Ecole Nat. Sup. Elec. Mech., Nancy, France, 1984; PhD in Elec. Engring., U. Rochester, 1987; MBA in Internat. Bus., Santa Clara (Calif.) U., 1999. Rsch. assoc. U. Rochester, N.Y., 1984-87; rsch. staff mem. IBM T.J. Watson Rsch. Ctr., Yorktown Heights, N.Y., 1988-94; prin. scientist Apple Computer, Cupertino, Calif., 1994—. Assoc. editor IEEE Transactions on Speech and Audio Processing, 1999—; reviewer, referee numerous jours.; Author (with others): Advances in Handwriting and Drawing: an Interdisciplinary Approach, 1994, Automatic Speech and Speaker Recognition: Advanced Topics, 1996, Robustness in Speech and Language Technology, 2000; contbr. articles to more than 75 profl. jours. and confs. Fulbright scholar French Govt., Paris, 1983; Vogt fellow Ecole Nat. Superieure d'électricité et de Mécanique, 1983. Sr. mem. IEEE, Internat. Speech Comm. Assn. E-mail: jerome@apple.com. Office: Apple Computer Inc MS 302-2LF 2 Infinite Loop Cupertino CA 95014

BELLELLI, ANDREA, biochemist; b. Rome, Italy, Dec. 30, 1958; s. Luciano and Giovanna (De Paola) B.; m. Flavia Onofrii, Aug. 24, 1984; children: Elena, Valeria. MD, U. Rome, 1983. Health officer Italian Army, Rome, 1985-86; rschr. Nat. Coun. Rsch., Rome, 1988-97, 1st rschr., 1997—. Contbr. more than 40 articles to profl. jours. including Jour. Biol. Chem., Biochemistry USA, Biochem. Jour., among others. Mem. Italian Soc. Biochemistry. Home: P.za Trasimeno 2, 00198 Rome Italy Office: Centro di Biologia Mol CNR, P.za Aldo Moro, 00185 Rome Italy

BELLEMANS, MICHEL DOMINIQUE, financial services company executive; b. Ninove, Flanders, Belgium, June 25, 1968; s. Guido Victor and Nadine (De Strijcker) B. Degree in mktg. mgmt., U. Brussels, 1989, M in Fin. & Economical Scis. cum laude, 1993, degree in tax scis., 1994. Cert. internat. fin. specialist. Account mgr. Bank Brussels Lambert, Brussels, 1989-91, Fiduver, Brussels, 1992-94; mng. dir. Van Doorn Trust and Ptnrs., Brussels, 1994-97; dir. Van Doorn Trust and Ptnrs., Willemstad, Curacao, 1997—; dir. RAAD (Belgium), Luxemburg, 1996—, U.K., 1997—; mng. dir. Raad, Belgium, 1998—, Luxembourg, 1998—, U.K., 1998—, Curacao, 1998—, Bvi, 1998—; mng. dir. Raad Ventures & Consulting, 1998—. Mem. Nat. Assn. for Support to Handicapped Persons, Brussels, 1996—. Mem. Internat. Tax Planning Assn, Rotary (Vilvoorde chpt., youngest mem. award). Avocations: scuba diving, classical and contemporary arts, charity. Office: RAAD CSxM NV, Tervurenlaan 82, B-1040 Brussels Belgium

BELLENGER, GEORGE COLLIER, JR., physics educator; b. Gadsden, Ala., Oct. 15, 1926; s. George Collier Sr. and Corrie Anna (Sitz) B.; m. Anna Conwell Hubbard, July 4, 1959; children: Baily, George III, James Thomas. B in Indsl. Engring., Ga. Inst. of Tech., 1952. Constrn./indsl. engring. E.I. DuPont Co., Augusta, Ga., 1952-54, Richmond, Va., 1955-58; ops. rsch. E.I. DuPont Co., Wilmington, Del., 1958-63; group supr.-engring. E.I. DuPont Co., Chattanooga, 1963-65; sr. supr. systems E.I. DuPont Co., Wilmington, 1965-67; chief supr. E.I. DuPont Co., Deep Water, N.J., 1967-70; systems mgr. E.I. DuPont Co., Wilmington, 1970-78, mgr. project devel., 1978-87; math/physics educator Wilmington Coll., New Castle, Del., 1987-91; chair gen. studies divsn. Wilmington Coll., New Castle, 1991—, chair faculty senate, 1998—. PTA pres. Mt. Pleasant Sch. Dist., Wilmington, 1972-76; commr. North Brandywine Youth Baseball, Wilmington, 1974-77; head coach Mt. Pleasant Youth Football, Wilmington, 1977-79. Lt. U.S. Army, 1944-47. Mem. Rotary Internat. (pres. 1983-84, Paul Harris fellow 1987), Nat. Norwich/Norfolk Terrier Assn. (pres. 1993-96), Army and Navy Club, Phi Delta Theta. Achievements include rsch. on a micro/macro production and inventory system based on a stochastic deterministic, partial differential set of equations, a manufacturing capacity expansion plan based on combining a unique LP model and computer simulation methods. Home: PO Box 449 Unionville PA 19375-0449 Office: Wilmington Coll 320 Dupont New Castle DE 19720

BELLER, MARTIN LEONARD, retired orthopaedic surgeon; b. N.Y.C., Apr. 30, 1924; s. Abraham Jacob and Ida (Fishkin) B.; m. Wilma Gertrude Kjelgaard, June 29, 1947; children: Alan Lewis, Beatrice Ann Beller Foreman Heck, Peter James. AB with honors, Columbia U., 1944, MD, 1946. Diplomate Am. Bd. Orthopaedic Surgery. Intern Mt. Sinai Hosp., N.Y.C., 1946-47; resident in orthopaedic surgery Hosp. Joint Diseases, N.Y.C., 1949-52; pvt. practice Phila., 1952-87; asst. prof. orthopaedic surgery U. Pa. Sch. Medicine, Phila., 1967-72; assoc. prof. U. Pa. Sch. Medicine, 1972-80, clin. prof., 1980-87; attending orthopaedic surgeon Hosp. U. Pa., 1963-87; assoc. attending orthopaedic surgeon Albert Einstein Med. Center, Phila., 1960-70; chmn. dept. orthopaedic surgery Albert Einstein Med. Center (Daroff divsn.), 1970-79. Author: (with I. Stein and R. O. Stein) Living Bone in Health and Disease, 1955, (with I. Stein) Clinical Densitometry of Bone, 1970. Vestryman Episcopal Ch., 1966-87, 90-93, 96-99; trustee St. Paul's Episcopal Ch., Wellsboro, Pa., 1999—. Capt. M.C., AUS, 1947-49. Am. Orthopaedic Assn. exchange fellow Gt. Britain, 1963. Fellow ACS, Am. Acad. Orthopaedic Surgeons (bd. councilors 1978-81, Pa. rep. commn. on trauma 1984-87), Internat. Soc. Orthopaedic Surgery and Traumatology; mem. Am. Orthopaedic Assn., Pa. Orthopaedic Soc. (pres. 1975-77), Orthopaedic Rsch. Soc., Am. Coll. Rheumatology, N.Y. Acad. Sci., Phi Beta Kappa, Alpha Omega Alpha, Phi Delta Epsilon (nat. pres. 1975-76, chmn. bd. trustees 1984-85, assoc. sec. 1991-95, exec. com. 1995—). Republican. Home: RR 1 Box 256-B Gaines PA 16921-9768

BELLER, MATTHIAS HEINRICH, chemist, educator, researcher; b. Gudensberg, Hessen, Germany, Apr. 11, 1962; s. Horst and Anneliese (Keim) B.; m. Anja Fischer, Dec. 29, 1992. Chemistry Diplomate, U. Göttingen, Germany, 1987, PhD, 1989. Rsch. scientist Hoechst AG, Frankfurt, Germany, 1991-92, group leader, 1992-93, sect. leader homogeneous catalysis, 1993-95; prof. chemistry Tech. U. Munich, 1995-98, U. Rostock, Germany, 1998—; dir. Inst. for Organic Catalysis Rsch., Rostock, 1998—; cons. Hoechst AG, Frankfurt, 1995-99, Novartis, Basel, Switzerland, 1997—, Degussa-Huels AG, Frankfurt, 1998—. Editor: Transition Metals for Organic Synthesis, 1998; patentee (40) in field; contbr. articles to profl. jours. Mem. German Mil., 1981-82. Liebig grantee Found. of German Chem. Industry, 1990; recipient Otto Roelen award, 1997. Mem. German Chem. Soc., DECHEMA. Avocations: tennis, skiing, chess, modern literature. Home: Bernsteinweg 16, 18119 Rostock Germany Office: Inst Organ Catalysis Rsch, Buchbinderstr 5-6, 18055 Rostock Germany

BELLERS, ERWIN BEN, research scientist, researcher; b. Enschede, The Netherlands, Nov. 14, 1965; s. L.M. Bellers and A. Bellers-Ellenbroek; m. Dionyse Frederique Hartmann, May 10, 1996. MSc with honors, U. Twente, 1993; PhD, Delft U., 2000. Software engr. DHG, Deventer, 1993; rsch. scientist Philips Rsch., Eindhoven, 1993—. Author: De-Interlacing--A Key Technology of Scan Rate Conversion: Advances in Image Communication, Vol. 9, 2000; contbr. articles to profl. jours. With Netherlands Mil., 1988-89. Mem. IEEE, Internat. Soc. for Optical Engring. Avocations: tennis, dancing, mountain climbing, windsurfing, skiing. Office: Philips Rsch 345 Scarborough Rd Briarcliff Manor NY 10510-2099

BELLIER, OLIVIER, geologist; b. Auch, Gers, France, June 9, 1961; s. Guy and Monique (Ducas) B.; m. Catherine Dufau, May 14, 1994; children: Mathieu, Amelie. MS, U. Paris XI, 1985, PhD, 1989. Ative tectonics rschr. Ctr. Nat. Rsch. Sci., Orsay, France, 1985-89; rschr. French Spatial Inst., Paris, 1989-91, French Geog. Inst., Paris, 1991-92, French Rsch. Inst., Orsay, 1992-2000; prof. Univ. Aix-Marseille III, 2000—; oversea rschr. Orstom, Lima, Peru, 1986-87. Contbr. articles to profl. jours. Bd. dirs. remote sensing French-Indonesia Cooperation, 1992-97; pres. French com. Internat. Lithosphere Program, 1999-00. Mem. Am. Geophysical Union, European Union Geoscience, Geol. Soc. Office: Cerege UMR CNRS 6635, B280 Eur Medit de L'Arbois, 13545 Aix-En-Provence France

BELLIN, HOWARD, management consultant company executive; b. N.Y.C., Oct. 30, 1933; arrived in Australia, 1961; s. Paul and Anna (Sterner); m. Barbara Ann Box, May 12, 1962; children: Sara Lea, Paul. BSMetE, Carnegie Mellon U., 1955. Trainee Great Lakes Steel Corp., Detroit, 1955; dept. mgr. Kelsey Hayes Corp., Detroit, 1955-57; from indsl. engr. to dept. mgr. Gillette Co., Boston, 1957-64; factory mgr. Allied Corp., Richmond, Va., 1964-65, Sydney, Australia, 1966-67; mng. dir. Avin Plating, Melbourne, Australia, 1967-69; founder, chmn. I.F. Cons., Melbourne, Australia, 1969—; presenter in field. Mem. editl. bd. Jour. Mktg. Channels; contbr. articles to profl. jours. Active franchise divsn. Singapore Productivity Bd. With U.S. Army, 1957. Mem. Am. Club. Liberal Party. Jewish. Avocations: exercise, jogging, photography, reading, history. Home: 17 Moule Ave, 3186 Brighton Australia Office: I F Cons, 390 St Kilda Rd, 3004 Victoria Australia

BELLIN, HOWARD THEODORE, plastic surgeon; b. N.Y.C., Apr. 8, 1936; s. Maurice and Etta (Rosenbloom) B.; m. Christina Paolozzi, Oct. 27, 1964 (dec. Apr. 27, 1988); children: Marco, Andy. BA, Amherst Coll., 1957; MD, N.Y. Med. Coll., 1962. Diplomate Am. Bd. Plastic Surgery. Intern U. Calif. Hosp., San Francisco, 1962-63; resident Met. Hosp., N.Y.C., 1963-66; resident in plastic surgery Columbia Presbyn. Med. Ctr., N.Y.C., 1968-70; instr. in surgery Columbia Coll. Physicians and Surgeons, N.Y.C., 1968-70; asst. clin. prof. surgery N.Y. Med. Coll., N.Y.C., 1970-84, asst. clin. prof. demratology, 1975-83; chief plastic surbery Cabrini Med. Ctr., N.Y.C., 1973-80; pres. Cosmedica Plastic Surgery Ctr., N.Y.C., 1980—; pres. Cortec, Inc., N.Y.C., 1983—, Life Signs, Inc., N.Y.C., 1989—, Motor Vehicle Protection Systems, Inc., N.Y.C., 1993—, also chmn. bd.; bd. dirs. Novamed, Inc.; mem. sci. adv. com. Inst. Ecosystem Studies, 1998—; chmn. of bd. PerfectYourself.com. Author: Dr. Bellin's Beautiful You Book, 1981; patentee on cardiac monitoring system, 1991, portable EKG monitoring device, 1985, system for subliminal signals, 1992, systems for cancellation...artifacts, 1992, auto theft prevention system, 1995, patient monitor sheets, 1995, automobile security device, 1998. Capt. USAF, 1966-68. Fellow N.Y. Acad. Medicine; mem. AAAS, Am. Soc. Plastic and Reconstrv. Surgeons, Explorers Club (nominating com. 1985). Avocations: auto racing, helicopter flying, archaeology, computer programming. Office: Cosmedica 105 E 73rd St New York NY 10021-3502

BELLINGER, EDGAR THOMSON, lawyer; b. N.Y.C., Sept. 23, 1929; s. John and Margaret (Thomson) B.; children from previous marriage: Edgar Jr., Robert, Margaret; m. Ann Clark, Feb. 25, 1989. BA, Haverford Coll., 1951; JD with honors, George Washington U., 1955. Bar: D.C. 1955, Md. 1955. Law clk. to chief judge U.S. Dist. Ct. D.C., 1955-57; asst. U.S. aty for Washington, 1957-59; ptnr. Pope, Ballard & Loos, Washington, 1959-81, Zuckert, Scoutt and Rasenberger, Washington, 1981-94, Bellinger & Assocs., Washington and Md., 1995—; chmn. unauthorized practice com. D.C. Ct. Appeals, 1972-78; mem. D.C. jud. conf., 1972-90; bd. mgrs. Chevy Chase Village, 1983-86. Mem. ABA (mem. fidelity and surety com., mem. forum on constrn. industry, past chmn. bonds, liens and ins. divsn.), Am. Arbitration Assn. (panel of arbitrators), D.C. Bar Assn. (D.C. Ct. Appeals orgn. com. 1972), Md. Bar Assn., Talbot County Bar Assn., Nat. Assn. Securities Dealers (panel of arbitrators), Met. Club, Chevy Chase Club (bd. govs. 1972-77, pres. 1976-77), Barristers. Home: 27497 West Point Rd Easton MD 21601-8439 Office: 888 17th St NW Washington DC 20006-3939 also: PO Box 739 Easton MD 21601-8914

BELLINGER, JOHN B., JR., federal official; b. N.Y.C., May 21, 1926; s. John Bellinger and Margaret (Thomson) B.; m. Anne Taliafero Tynes, Dec. 19, 1953; 1 child, John Bellinger, III. BS, U.S. Mil. Acad., 1948; MA, Georgetown U., 1962, PhD, 1975; grad., U.S. Army War Coll., 1969. Commd. U.S. Army, 1948; advanced through grades to col., chief of strategy div. Joint Chiefs of Staff, 1978; sr. adviser Kien Giang Province Republic of Vietnam, 1966-67; comdr. 1st bn. 37th Armor, Ansbach, Fed. Republic Germany, 1967-68; chief, plans div. U.S. Army Vietnam Republic of Vietnam, 1971-72; dep. to army planner Washington, 1973-76, chief strategy div. joint chiefs of staff, 1976-77; ret., 1978; sr. staff mem., study dir. Pres.'s Def. Reorgn. Studies, Washington, 1978-79; dir. def. guidance and program planning Under Sec. Def. (policy), Washington, 1981-89; policy planner Under Sec. Def. (policy), 1989-94; ret., 1995. Author: Decision Making in Arms Control, 1975; contbr. articles to profl. jours.; lectr. in field. Chmn. budget and fin. com., vestryman St. Peter's Episc. Ch., 1981-84, chmn. ushers, 1986—. Decorated Def. Superior Svc. medal, Legion of Merit with oak leaf cluster, Air medal with oak leaf cluster, Bronze Star, Cross of Gallantry (Republic of Vietnam), Combat Infantry Badge. Mem. Assn. of the U.S. Army, Nat. Polit. Sci. Honor Soc., Cum Laude Soc., U.S. Squash Racquets Assn. (ranked 13th in Men's 65 plus singles 1993), U.S. Tennis Assn., Army Navy Country Club (tennis com. 1973-79, bd. govs. 1975-78), Pentagon Officers Athletic Club. Home: 4001 N Ridgeview Rd Arlington VA 22207-4615

BELLINZONI, RODOLFO CESAR, medical manufacturing company executive; b. Carlos Casares, Argentina, Jan. 6, 1957; s. Rodolfo and Catalina (Possamay) B.; m. Ana Gutierrez, Feb. 26, 1993; 1 child, Martin. DVM, UNCPBA, Tandil, Argentina, 1980; DSc, Nat. U. LaPlata, 1987. Fellow CEVAN, Buenos Aires, 1983-87; rsch. assoc. Baylor Coll., Houston, 1987-90; from rsch. & devel. to mfg. mgr. Biogenesis, Buenos Aires, 1990—. Office: Biogenesis, Auto Panamericana Rm 38.2, 1619 Garin Argentina

BELLIS, CARROLL JOSEPH, surgeon, educator; b. Shreveport, La.; s. Joseph and Rose (Bloome) B.; m. Mildred Darmody, Dec. 26, 1939; children: Joseph, David. BS summa cum laude, U. Minn., 1930, MS in Physiology, 1932, PhD in Physiology, 1934, MD, 1936, PhD in Surgery, 1941. Diplomate Am. Bd. Surgery. Fellow in physiology U. Minn., Mpls., 1930-34; resident in surgery U. Minn. Hosps., Mpls., 1937-41; pvt. practice surgery, Long Beach, Calif., 1945-87; mem. staff St. Mary Med. Ctr., Long Beach; prof., chmn. dept. surgery Calif. Coll. Medicine, 1962—; surg. cons. to surgeon gen. U.S. Army; adj. prof. surgery U. Calif. Author: Fundamentals of Human Physiology, A Critique of Reason, Lectures in Medical Physiology; contbr. numerous articles on surgery and physiology to profl. jours. Served to col. M.C. AUS, 1941-46. Recipient Charles Lyman Green prize in physiology, 1934, prize Mpls. Surg. Soc., 1938, ann. award Mississippi Valley Med. Soc., 1955; Alice Shevlin fellow U. Minn., 1932-34. Fellow ACS, Royal Soc. Medicine, Internat. Coll. Surgeons, Am. Coll. Gastroenterology, Am. Med. Writers Assn., Internat. Coll. Angiology (sci. council), Gerontol. Soc., Am. Soc. Abdominal Surgeons, Nat. Cancer Inst., Phlebology Soc. Am., Internat. Acad. Proctology, Peripheral Vascular Soc. Am. (founding); mem. AAAS, Am. Assn. Study Neoplastic Diseases, Mississippi Valley Med. Soc., N.Y. Acad. Scis., Hollywood Acad. Medicine, Am. Geriatrics Soc., Irish Med. Assn., Am. Assn. History Medicine, Pan Pacific Surgical Assn., Indsl. Med. Assn., L.A. Musicians Union (hon.), Pan Am. Med. Assn. (diplomate), Internat. Bd. Surgery (cert.), Internat. Bd. Proctology (cert.), Phi Beta Kappa, Sigma Xi, Alpha Omega Alpha. Home: PMB 808 904 Silver Spur Rd Rllng Hls Est CA 90274-3800

BELLIVEAU, GERARD JOSEPH, JR., librarian; b. Waltham, Mass., May 27, 1940; s. Gerard Joseph and Mary Teresa (Reilly) B. BA in English Lit., Boston Coll., 1963; MA in Philosophy, Boston U., 1972; MLS in Libr. Svc., Rutgers U., 1973. Lectr. U. Rouen (France), 1965-66; philosophy bibliographer Boston Pub. Libr., Boston, 1967-68; asst. libr. Racquet & Tennis Club: Libr. of Sport, N.Y.C., 1971-78, head libr., 1979—; libr. gen. rsch. div. N.Y. Pub. Libr., N.Y.C., 1973-79, libr. in charge gen. rsch. div., 1980-81, asst. chief pub. catalog sect. gen. rsch. div., 1981-88, asst. chief libr. gen. rsch. div., 1988-95; mem. coop. acquisitions program com. METRO Ref. and Rsch. Libr. Agy., N.Y.C., 1984-88, chair coop. acquisitions program com., 1985-86, mem. resources devel. com., 1986-89. Bd. dirs. Peabody-Mason Music Found., Boston, 1972-87. Mem. Williams Club. Democrat. Avocations: architecture, travel, French medieval history. Office: Racquet & Tennis Club Libr 370 Park Ave New York NY 10022-5968

BELLMER, HELMUT WILHELM KARL JOHANN, editor; b. Bremerhaven, Germany, Feb. 11, 1921; s. Wilhelm Carl Albert and Anna Frieda Emilie (Riekenberg) B.; m. Elfriede Luise Schroeder, Aug. 14, 1920; children: Hella, Anke. Diploma Verwaltungswirt, Oberpostdirektion, Hamburg, Germany, 1987. Radio operator Coastal Radio Sta., Germany, 1939-44, 47-52; officer in charge Coastal Radio Sta., Cuxhaven, Germany, 1967-82; chief Post & Telegraph Office, Heligoland, Germany, 1952-57; govt. inspector Hamburg and Kiel, Germany, 1657-67; chmn. commodore Trans-Ocean, Cuxhaven, Germany, 1989—; radio inspector German Life Boat Institution, 1949-89. Author: Trans-Ocean, 1970 (Silberne Ehrennadel award 1995), Unsere Alte Liebe, 1969-82 (Goldene Ehrennadel 1988). Active Nautischer Verein, Cuxhaven, 1970—, Verein der Funkamateure der Deutschen Bundespost, 1983—. Served with German Army, 1944-45. Recipient Bundesverdienstkreuz am. Bande, Bundespraesident, Bonn, 1983. Mem. Sail Tng. Assn. Germany (hon.), Press Club, Ocean Cruising Club (port officer 1974—). Avocations: sailing, amateur radio, stamp collecting, painting, swimming. Home: Strichweg 48A, D-27472 Cuxhaven Germany Office: Trans Ocean PB 728, zur Ford des Hochseesegelns, D-27457 Cuxhaven Germany

BELLO, JOSEPH YUSUF, academic administrator; b. Babanloma, Nigeria, June 20, 1940; s. Akanbi and Olawumi (Lagbile) B.; m. Funmilayo Alao; children: Folake, Sunday, Moji, Ayoola, Jide. B in Edn., U. Ibadan, 1969; M in Edn., Ahmadu Bello U., 1976, PhD, 1984. Tchr. U.M.S. Primary Schs., Zuru, Nigeria, 1962; tutor Mokwa Tchr.'s Coll., Nigeria, 1965-66, 69-70; prin. Govt. Comml. Coll., Kontagora, Nigeria, 1970-72; head edn. dept., dean, dep. provost Coll. Edn., Zaria, Nigeria, 1973-88; provost Kwara State Coll. Edn., Ilorin, Nigeria, 1988-96; gen. mgr. Kwara Printing & Pub. Corp., 1996—. Mem. Counselling Assn. Nigeria, Nat. Assn. Ednl. Planning & Adminstrn., Traditional Coun. Chiefs. Avocations: indoor games, art, game hunting. Home: 10 Okehi Close Box 5466, Adewole Housing Estate, Ilorin Nigeria

BELLOCH, JUAN ALBERTO, Spanish government official; b. Mora de Rubielos, Teruel, Spain, Feb. 3, 1950; married; 1 child. Judge La Gomera, Berga Vic y Alcoy, 1975—; magistrate, pres. Court of Justice of Biscay, 1981-90; mem. Gen. Coun. Judiciary, 1990-93; min. justice Govt. Spain, Madrid, 1993-96, min. interior, 1994-96; mem. legis. Govt. Spain, Zaragoza, 1996; pres. of Aragon Socialists Govt. Spain, 1997; with Socialist parliamentery group of Congreso de Disputados Ministries of Justice and of the Interior, Govt. of Spain, 1996; pres. of Socialist group Townhall of Zaragoza, 1999; Socialist candidate to Chamber of Senate for Zaragoza. Mem. Democratic Justice; founder Assn. Judges for Democracy, Assn. Magistrates Européens pour la démocratie et les libertés; founder, pres. Assn. for Human Rights of the Basque Country; congressman Partido Socialista Obrero Espanol, 1996—. Office: care PSOE, Ferraz 68 y 70, 28008 Madrid Spain also: Ayuntamiento de Zaragoza, Plaza del Pilar 18, 50071 Zaragoza Spain

BELLOMO, JO, social worker, school administrator, educator; b. N.Y.C., July 13, 1941; d. Patrick and Josephine Bellomo. BA, CUNY, 1974; MSW, Columbia U., 1976; postgrad., NYU. Tchr. Sch. of The Actor's Co., N.Y.C., 1964-70; social worker Children's Treatment Ctr., N.Y.C., 1976-82; clin. coord. The Reece Sch., N.Y.C., 1982—; assoc. prof. NYU Sch. Social Work, 1990—; acting tchr. Bellomo Studio, N.Y.C., 1970-76. Dir. Westbeth Feminist Theater, 1969-71, Town Hall, 1970 (outstanding work by female dir. award). Bd. dirs. The Colandra Inst., N.Y.C., 1978-84. Avocations: coaching actors, theater, gardening. Office: The Reece Sch 180 E 93d St New York NY 10128

BELLONI-COFLER, JACQUELINE DOLORÈS THÉRÈSE, physical chemist, radiation chemist, photographer; b. Arles, France, Oct. 27, 1935; d. Paul and Adrienne (Blayac) Cofler; m. Marcel Belloni, Apr. 8, 1958; children: Luc, Gilles, Irène, Paul. Lic es Scis Phys, U. Paris, 1956, Diplome Etudes Superieures, 1958, D es Scis Phys, 1961. Stagiaire de recherche CNRS/Inst. Radium, Paris, 1957-59, attachee de recherche, 1960, chargee de recherche, 1960-70; maitre de recherche CNRS-U. Paris XI, Orsay, France, 1971-74, 75-85, dir. rsch., 1985—; conseil dept. CNRS, Paris, 1992-95; v.p. rsch. U. Paris XI, Orsay, 1982-89; head of lab. CNRS-U. Paris Sud, Orsay, 1989-97; hon. prof. U.S.T.C., Academica Sinica, 1996. Contbr. articles to profl. jours. Recipient Silver medal Nat. Ctr. for Sci. Rsch., 1983, Grand prix Acad. of Scis., 1991, Bruylants medal U. Louvain la Neuve, 1992, Chevalier de l'Ordre Nat. du Mérite, 1995, Maria Sklodowska-Curie medal Polish Soc. Radioactive Rsch., 1998, Grand Prix Aimé Poirson Acad. Scis., Paris, 2000. Mem. French Phys. Chem. Soc. (coun. 1986-89). Roman Catholic. Avocations: antiques, museums, gardens. Office: Lab Chinie Physique, Bat 350 U Paris-Sud, 91405 Orsay France

BELLOT-ROSADO, FRANCISCO, mathematics educator; b. Madrid, Dec. 28, 1941; s. Francisco Bellot-Rodriguez and María Rosado Alvarez de Sotomayor; m. Maria Ascensión López Chamorro, July 27, 1968. Lic. in Math., U. Madrid, 1964. Prof. math. I.N.E.M. Marqués de la Ensenada, Logroño, Spain, 1966-70, I.N.B. Emilio Ferrari, Valladolid, Spain, 1970—; charged of course Faculty of Scis., Valladolid, 1972-75; assoc. prof. U. Va., 1991—; mem. jury Spanish Math. Olympiad, 1986-89, 95-97; dep. leader Spanish delegation Internat. Math. Olympiad, leader, 1990-97; reviewer Zentralblatt Didaktik D. Math., Karlsruhe, Fed. Republic Germany, 1987—; Europe rep. of World Fedn. Nat. Math. Competitions, 1996—; founder Mediterranean Maths. Competition, 1998—. Author: Olimpiada Matematica Española, 1992; co-author: Cien Problemas de matematicas, 1994; mem. jour. editorial staff Gaceta Matematica, 1987-89; editor Jour. Soc. Iberoamericana para la Promocion de la Matemática Iberoamericana, 1996; contbr. articles to profl. jours. Pres. Assn. de Catedráticos de Bachillerato, Valladolid, 1983—. Recipient Paul Erdös Internat. award World Fedn. Nat. Math Competitions, 2000. Mem. Real Soc. Math. Española, Math. Assn. (Eng.), Can. Math. Soc., Math. Assn. Am., Assn. Profs. Math. de l'Enseignement Pub., Math. Kangourou European (pres. 1997), Kangourou sans Frontières (bd. of govs. 1995—). E-mail: fbellot@hotmail.com. Office: INB Emilio Ferrari, La Sementera S/N, E-47009 Valladolid Spain

BELLOW, SAUL C., writer; b. Lachine, Que., Can., June 10, 1915; s. Abraham and Liza (Gordin) B.; m. Anita Goshkin, 1937 (div.); 1 child, Gregory; m. Alexandra Tschachasov, 1956 (div); 1 child, Adam; m. Susan Glassman, 1961 (div.); 1 child, Daniel; m. Alexandra Ionesco Tuleca, 1974 (div.); m. Janis Freedman, Sept., 1989; 1 child, Naomi Rose. Student, U. Chgo., 1933-35; BS, Northwestern U., 1937, LittD, 1962; LittD, Bard Coll., 1962, NYU, 1970, Harvard U., 1972, Yale U., 1972, McGill U., 1973, Brandeis U., 1974, Hebrew Union Coll.-Jewish Inst. Religion, 1976, Trinity Coll., Dublin, Ireland, 1976. Instr. Pestalozzi-Froebel Tchrs. Coll., Chgo., 1938-42; mem. editl. dept. "Great Books" project Ency. Brit., Inc., Chgo., 1943-46; mem. English dept. U. Minn., Mpls., 1946, asst. prof., 1948-49, assoc. prof. English, 1954-59; vis. lectr. NYU, 1950-52; creative writing fellow Princeton (N.J.) U., 1952-53; faculty mem. Bard Coll., Annandale-on-Hudson, N.Y., 1953-54; vis. prof. English U. P.R., Rio Piedras, 1961; celebrity in residence U. Chgo., 1962, Grunier Disting. Svcs. prof., 1962—, mem.

com. on social thought, 1962—, chmn. com. on social thought, 1970-76; Tanner lectr. Oxford U., Romanes lectr., 1990. Author: (novels) Dangling Man, 1944, The Victim, 1947, The Adventures of Augie March, 1953 (Nat. Book award 1954), Seize the Day, 1956, Henderson the Rain King, 1959, Herzog, 1964 (Prix Internat. de Litterature 1965, Nat. Book award 1964, Soc. Midland Authors Fiction award 1976), Mr. Sammler's Planet, 1970 (Nat. Book award 1970), Humboldt's Gift, 1975 (Pulitzer prize for fiction 1976), The Dean's December, 1982, More Die of Heartbreak, 1986, A Theft, 1989, The Bellarosa Connection, 1989, The Actual, 1997, (short stories) Mosby's Memoirs, and Other Stories, 1968, Him with His Foot in His Mouth, and Other Stories, 1984, Something to Remember Me By: Three Tales, 1991, Occasional Pieces, 1993; (plays) The Wrecker, 1954, The Last Analysis, 1964, Under the Weather, 1966, (nonfiction) To Jerusalem and Back: A Personal Account, 1976, It All Adds Up: From the Dim Past to the Uncertain Future, 1994, Ravelstein, 2000; contbr. fiction to Esquire and lit. quars.; criticisms appear in New Leader, others; short story to Atlantic's 125th Anniversary Edit., 1982. Decorated Croix de Chevalier, France, 1968, Comdr. Legion of Honour, France, 1983, Comdr. Order of Arts and Letters, France, 1985; Guggenheim fellow, 1948, Neil Gunn Internat. fellow, 1977; Nat. Inst. Arts and Letters grantee, 1952, Ford Found. grantee, 1959-61; recipient O. Henry prize for The Gonzaga Manuscripts, 1956, for A Silver Dish, 1980, Friends of Lit. Fiction award, 1960, James L. Dow award, 1964, Jewish Heritage award B'nai B'rith, 1968, Formentor prize, 1970, Nobel prize for lit., 1976, Gold medal Am. Acad. Arts and Letters, 1977, Brandeis U. Creative Arts award, 1978, Medal of Honor for lit. Nat. Arts Club, 1978, Malaparte Lit. award, 1984, Premio Scanno Lit. award Italy, 1988, Nat. Medal of Arts, 1988, Lifetime Achievement award Nat. Book Award, 1990, Lifetime Cultural Achievement award YIVO Inst. for Jewish Rsch., 1996. Mem. Am. Acad. Arts and Scis. (Emerson-Thoreau medal 1977).

BELLOWS, A. ROBERT, ophthalmologist, surgeon; b. Manchester, N.H., May 14, 1937; s. Arnold Leo and Eleanora Bellows; m. Jean Blunt Farley, May 30, 1964; children: Matthew, Kristen, Nathaniel. BA, Brown U., 1959; MD, Boston U., 1963. Diplomate Am. Bd. Ophthalmology. Intern Univ. Hosp., Boston, 1963-64; asst. resident in internal medicine VA Hosp., Boston, 1964-65; opthal. resident Yale New Haven (Conn.) Hosp., 1967-70, chief resident, 1970; W.M. Grant MD Glaucoma Fellowship Mass. Eye and Ear Infirmary, Boston, 1971-72; partner Ophthalmic Consultants of Boston, Inc., 1974—; surgeon Mass. Eye & Ear Infirmary, 1990—; instructor in ophthal. surgery, Yale U., 1969-70; asst. clin. prof. ophthal. Harvard U., 1972-92, assoc. prof., 1992-97, lectr., 1997—; asst. clin. prof. Tufts U., 1992—. Capt. USAF, 1965-67, Libya. Fellow Am. Acad. Ophthal. (Hon. award 1984, Sr. Hon. award 1996); mem. ACS, Mass. Med. Soc., Ophthal. Assn. in Rsch. to Prevent Blindness, Mass. Soc. Eye Physicians and Surgeons, Assn. for Rsch. in Vision and Ophthal., New England Ophthal. Soc., Am. Eye Study Club, Chandler Grant Glaucoma Soc. (pres. 1995-97). Home: 327 Commonwealth Ave Boston MA 02115-1900 Office: Ophthalmic Cons of Boston 50 Staniford St Ste 600 Boston MA 02114-2587 also: 88 Ansel Hallet Rd West Yarmouth MA 02673-2556

BELLOWS, THOMAS JOHN, political scientist, educator; b. Chgo., Aug. 15, 1935; s. Charles Everett and Dorothy (Morrison) B.; m. Marilyn Denise Corbell; children: Scott Anthony, Justin Thomas, Trevor Cullen, Ethan Forrest; children by previous marriage: Roderick Alan, Adrienne Marie, Jeannine Louise, Derek John, Marshall Everett. Student, Am. U., 1956, UCLA, 1956-57; BA, Augustana Coll., 1957; MA, U. Fla., 1958, Yale U., 1960; PhD, Yale U., 1968. Asst. prof. polit. sci. West Ga. Coll., Carrollton, 1962-64, 66; from asst. prof. to prof. polit. sci. U. Ark., Fayetteville, 1967-81; chmn. dept. U. Ark., 1971-78; dir. divsn. social policy scis. U. Tex., San Antonio, 1981-88, prof. polit. sci., 1981—; Vis. lectr. depts. history, polit. sci. Nanyang U., Singapore, 1965; vis. prof. Nat. Chengchi U., Taiwan, 1979. Author: The People's Action Party of Singapore: Emergence of a Dominant Party System, 1970, (with S. Erikson and H. Winter) Political Science: Introductory Essays and Readings, 1971, Taiwan's Foreign Policy in the 1970's, 1976, (with H. Winter) People and Politics: An Introduction to Political Science, 1985, Bridging Tradition and Modernization: The Singapore Bureaucracy, 1989, (with H. Winter) Conflict and Compromise, 1992; author, editor The Republic of China: The First Eighty Years, 1993, Taiwan and Mainland China, 2000; editor: Am. Jour. Chinese Studies, 1999—. Mem. Southwest Conf. Asian Studies (pres. 1995), Am. Assn. for Chinese Studies (pres. 1998—), Assn. Asian Studies, Phi Beta Kappa, Phi Alpha Theta, Phi Kappa Phi. Methodist. Office: U Tex Dept Polit Sci San Antonio TX 78249

BELLUCCI, GIANCARLO, planetary scientist, researcher; b. Rome, May 1, 1960; s. Giuseppe and Irma (Marinangeli) B. Grad., U. Rome, 1986. Rschr. Consiglio Nazionale delle Ricerche Inst Fisica dello Spazio, Rome, 1987—. Contbr. articles to profl. jours. Lance corp. Italian Army, 1986-87. Mem. European Geophys. Soc., Am. Astronomical Soc. (planetary scis. divsn.). Avocations: tennis, skiing. Office: Coun Nat Rsch Inst Physics, Via Del Fosso Del Cavaliere, 00133 Rome Italy

BELMARES, HECTOR, chemist; b. Monclova, Coahuila, Mex., Feb. 21, 1938; s. Armando and Guadalupe (Sarabia) B.; B.Sc., Instituto Tecnológico de Monterrey (Mex.), 1960; Ph.D. (Todd fellow 1961-63), Cornell U., 1963; postdoctoral student Calif. Inst. Tech., 1965; m. Eleanor Johanna Wold, Aug. 28, 1965; children: Michelle Anne, Michael Paul, Elizabeth Myrna, Mary Eleanor. Sr. research chemist Rohm and Haas Co., Phila., 1965-71; gen. mgr. tech. and quality control Fibras Químicas, S.A., Monterrey, Mex., 1972-75; sr. research chemist Centro de Investigación en Química Aplicada, Saltillo Coahuila, Mex., 1976-83, Sola Optical USA Inc., 1984—; mem. adv. panel Modern Plastics Mgmt., 1986-87; cons. on polymers for industry; cons. UN Indsl. Devel. Orgn. Community rep. Against Indsl. Air Pollution, Moorestown, N.J., 1968-70. Mem. Am. Chem. Soc., N.Y. Acad. Scis., AAAS, Sigma Xi. Mem. Christian Evangelical Ch. Patentee in field. Contbr. articles to profl. jours. Home: 1100 Shadyslope Dr Santa Rosa CA 95404-2743

BELMONDO, JEAN-PAUL, actor; b. Neuilly-sur-Seine, Apr. 9, 1933; s. Paul B.; divorced; 3 children. Student, Ecole Alsacienne, Paris, Cours Pascal and Conservatoire. pres. French Union Actors, 1963-66., Annabel Prodns., 1981—; dir. Théâtre des Variétés, 1991—. Appeared in plays, including L'hôtel du libre-échange, Oscar, Trésor-Party, Médée, La mégère apprivoisée, Kean, 1987, Cyrano de Bergerac, 1990, Tailleur pour Dames, 1993, La Puce à l'oreille, 1996; films include Sois belle et tais-toi, A pied, à cheval et en voiture, les Tricheurs, Charlotte et son Jules, Le Voleur, 1966, Casino Royale, 1967, The Brain, 1969, Borsalino, 1970, The Burglars, 1972, Le Magnifique, 1973, Stavisky, 1974, L'Incorrigible, 1975, Le Marginal, 1983, Les Morfalous, 1984, Hold-up, 1985, Le Solitaire, 1987, Les Cent et une Nuits, 1995, Les Misérables, 1995, Désiré, 1996, numerous others; author: (autobiography) 30 Ans et 25 Films, 1963. Recipient Prix Citron, 1972, Légion d'honneur; named Chevalier, Ordre Nat. du Mérite, Arts et des Lettres. Address: Annabel Prodns, 5 rue Clément Marot, 75008 Paris France also: Théâtre des Varietes, 7 blvd Montmartre, 75002 Paris France

BELMONT, JOSEPH, government official; b. Grand Anse, Mahe, Jan. 6, 1947; married. BSc in Agrl. Engring., U. Madagascar, Tanarive, 1966-70; MSc in Tropical Agrl. Devel., U. Reading, Eng., 1975. Rsch. officer Grand Anse Agrl. Rsch. Sta., 1970-71, agrl. ext. officer, 1971-74, sr. agrl. officer, 1976-79; chief agrl. officer Dept. of Agriculture, 1979-80; gen. mgr. Islands Devel. Co. Ltd., 1980-82; minister of labor and social security, 1982-85, minister of manpower and social svcs., 1985-86, minister of health and social svcs., 1986-88, minister of employment and social svcs., 1988-89, minister of adminstrn. and manpower, 1989—. Office: Ministry of Adminstrn and Manpower, Independence Ho PO Box 199, Victoria Mahe, Seychelles*

BELMONTÉ, KATHRYN (KIKI BELMONTÉ), writer, small business owner; b. Tallahassee. MEd, Fla. Atlantic U.; owner KiKi's Creative Assembly for Native Am. Arts & Crafts; developer, mgr. Helping Hands Classroom Sheltered Workshop for Mentally Handicapped Adults, 1988-97. Author: Black, Brown and Amber, 1979, Comes a Riderless Horse, 1983, reading home tutoring system Tutor Your Child, 1983; compiler, editor Where to Find Thrift Treasures, 1988, Where to Buy Antiques in Palm Beach County, 1989; author: American Heroes and Heroines, 1998. Dir. Kambi Youth Theatre, West Palm Beach, 1979-82, Creative Arts Workshop, Cities in Schs., 1985; organizer, dir. SRO Players Dramatics Club for Handicapped Adults; tech. dir. Performing Arts Summer Sch., Palm Beach Gardens, Fla., 1983-84, 85; workshop originator lecturer Seminole Indian History 1992, Mobile Art Craft Show 1993; active Palm Beach County Cultural Coun., Lake Worth Art League, Palm Beach County Art in Pub. Places Com., 1991-92, Nat. Mus. Am. Indian. Recipient 1st place award Cleveland Creative Arts, Tenn., 1981, Walter Bogle award Creative Arts Guild, 1983, Colored Pencil Painting Best in Show award Lake Worth Art League, 1993; grantee Palm Beach County Edn. Found., 1987, Community Found. Palm Beach and Martin Counties. Mem. NEA, Nat. Writers Club (hon. mention 1983), Fla. Freelance Writers Assn. (1st pl. awards 1984, 85, 3rd pl. 1990, honorable mention 1991), North Palm Beach C. of C., Norton Gallery Art, Armory Sch. Arts, Fla. Humanities Coun., St. Labre Indian Sch., Arrow Club. Avocations: drawing, painting, collecting Native Am. art, photography. Home: 7820 Canterbury Ln Plantation FL 33324-1934

BELMONTE-SERRANO, MIGUEL A., rheumatologist; b. Barcelona, Spain, Apr. 9, 1957. MD, U. Autonoma, Barcelona, 1980, PhD, 1991. Fellow in rheumatology Hosp. Bellitge, Barcelona, 1982-86; cons. in rheumatology Hosp. Gen. Castellon, Spain, 1987—, dir. bioinformatics unit; fellow Stanford (Calif.) U., 1991-92; prof. informatics U. Jaume I, Castellon, 1994-97. Editor: (CD-Rom book) Curso de Contracturas Musculares, 1999; editor booklet: Protocolos de Actuación en Reumatologia, 1999. Mem. Am. Coll. Rheumatology (internat. mem.), Spanish Soc. Rheumatology. Office: Hosp Gen, Reumatologia, 12004 Castellon Spain

BELO, CARLOS FELIPE XIMENES, apostolic administrator. Bishop, 1983. Nominated Nobel Peace prize, 1995, winner 1996. E-mail: ipjet@antenna.nl. Office: IPJET for East Timor, Gruttohoek 13, 2317WK Leiden The Netherlands*

BELOBORODOW, WLADIMIR WITALJEWITSCH, chemical engineer; b. Krasnodar, Russia, May 21, 1929; s. Witalij Petrowitsch and Tatjana Konstantinowna (Nowogilowa) B.; m. Eleonora Fedorowna Buchtarewa, Jan. 20, 1971. DS, H.certif.commn., Moscow, 1968. Scientific collaborator All Russian Rsch. Inst., St. Petersburg, Russia, 1952-62, chief dept., 1962-71; prof. Higher Polytech Sch., Krasnodar, Russia, 1971-74; chief dept. Cauch.h.sch. Ctr., Rostow, Russia, 1971-74; head chair H.comml.sch., St. Petersburg, 1974-83; chief dept. oils refining All Russian Rsch. Inst., 1983-95, chief scientific collaborator, 1995—; Author: MEthods of Calculation of Oil Extraction Proces, 1960, Main Processes of Vegetable Oils Production, 1966; co-author: Preparatory Processes of Oil Seeds Processing, 1974, Heat Equipment for Millsof the Popular Nutrition, 1983, Mass heat transfer in the solid porous bodies, 1999. Russian Acad. Scis. grantee, Moscow, 1994—. Avocations: history, swimming. Home: Marata 29-59, 191 002 Saint Petersburg Russia Office: All Russian Inst Fats, Tschernjachofsky 10, 191 119 Saint Petersburg Russia

BELOHLAVEK, JIRI, conductor, educator; b. Prague, Feb. 24, 1946; s. Jiri and Anna B.; m. Anna Fejerova, Feb. 6, 1971; children: Susanna, Marie. Grad., Conservatoire in Prague, 1966, Acad. Music Arts, Prague, 1972. Artistic dir., condr. Orch. Puellarum Pragensis, 1967-72; assoc. condr. Czech Philharm. Orch., 1970-72; condr. Brno (Czechoslovakia) Philharm. Orch., 1972-77; chief condr. Prague Symphony Orch., 1977-89; condr. Czech Philharm. Orch., 1981—, music dir., 1990-92; founder, music dir. Prague Chamber Philharm. Orch. (now Prague Philharm.), 1994—; prin. guest condr. BBC SO, London, 1995—, Nat. Opera Theatre in Prague, 1997—; prof. conducting class Acad. Music, Prague, 1995—. Winner first prize nat. competition young condrs. in Czechoslovakia, 1970; finalist H.V. Karajan Internat. Competition, 1971. Office: Prague Philharmonia, Krocínova 1, 11000 Prague 5, Czech Republic

BELOUSOV, VALERY VASILYEVICH, physicist; b. Chelyabinsk, Russia, Mar. 9, 1956; s. Vasily Ivanovich and Antonina Phedotovna Belousova; m. Elena Alexandrovna Spirodonova, Aug. 29, 1981; children: Alexander Valeryevich, July 14, 1983. MA, Chelyabinsk (Russia) State U., 1982; PhD, Ural State U., Ekaterinburgh, Russia, 1989; DSc, Moscow State Steel/Alloys Inst, 1997. Rsch. scientist Chelyabinsk State U., 1982-85, assoc. prof., 1989-91; sr. rsch. scientist MISA, Moscow, 1994-98; head materials dept. Rsch. Inst. of Steel, Moscow, 1998—; prin. rsch. scientist Russian U. of People's Friendship, Moscow, 1999, lectr., 1999—; cons. Bauman Tech. U., Moscow, 1996-98; cons. in field. Patentee in field. Office: Rsch Inst of Steel, Dubninskaya Str 81A, 127411 Moscow Russia

BELOUSOVA, ANNA PAVLOVNA, geology researcher; b. Lesogorsk, Sakhalin, Russia, Mar. 15, 1947; d. Pavel Gavrilovich and Nadezhda Andreevna (Salmashova) B. Degree in engring.-geology, Oil and Gas Indsl. Inst., 1971; DSc, All Russian Rsch. Inst., Moscow, 1981; degree in sci., Geol. Prospecting Inst., Moscow, 1988; degree in exptl. math., Phys. Engring. Inst., Moscow, 1988. Sr. geologist 2d Hydrogeol. Dept., Moscow, 1971-79; educator Geol. Prospecting Inst., Moscow, 1979-90; head rsch. group Water Problems Inst. Russian Acad. Scis., Moscow, 1990—; lectr. higher ecol. courses, Moscow, 1995—; head, cons. postgrads. Water Problems Inst., Russian Acad. Scis., 1995—, head sec. sci. coun. Ecol. Problems and Emergency. Author: Methods for Protecting Ground Water from Pollution and Depletion, 1985; contbr. articles to jours. in field; editor Internat. Ency., Abu Dhabi, 1994—. Grantee Internat. Sci. Found./Soros, 1994, Russian Basic Rsch. Found., 1995-97. Mem. Internat. Assn. Hydrological Scis., Internat. Assn. Hydrogeologists, N.Y. Acad. Scis. Eastern Orthodox. Avocations: travel, photography. Home: kop 1 apt 222, Warshavskoe Shosse bld 128, 113587 Moscow Russia Office: Water Problems Inst, 3 Gubkina St, 117735 Moscow Russia

BELOVEZHDOV, NICOLAY IVANOV, physician, researcher, consultant; b. Sofia, Bulgaria, July 24, 1928; s. Ivan Nicolov and Dimitrina Vasileva (Bratoeva) B.; m. Violete Ljubenova Milosheva; 1 child, Maria. MD, Med. U. Sofia, 1952; DrMedSci, Med. Acad. Sofia, 1984. Diplomate in medicine. Physician City Hosp., Ihtiman, Bulgaria, 1952-60, head dept. internal medicine, 1960-65; rsch. fellow Med. Acad., Sofia, 1965-78, assoc. prof., 1978-86, head dept. clin. pharmacology, 1983-86, prof., head clinic internal medicine and clin. pharmacology, 1986-93; cons. Transport Med. Inst., Sofia, 1993-99. Author: Drug Nephropathies, 1985, Clinical Pharmacology, 1993, Drug Therapy in Internal Medicine and Clinical Pharmacology, 1996, Drugs in Chronic Renal Failure, 1997, Practical Therapy of Internal Diseases, 1998, Therapy with Antimicrobial Drugs, 2000; author, editor: Therapy of Internal Diseases, 1994, Acutal Problems of Therapy, 1999, 2000. Mem. Bulgarian Soc. Internal Medicine (pres. 1985-95). Avocations: music, history.

BELŠAN, TOMÁŠ, radiologist; b. Prague, Czech Republic, Feb. 25, 1966; s. Ivo and Jarmila (Zásmucká) B.; m. Gabriela Tausová, July 25, 1998. MD, Charles U., Prague, 1990. Rsch. asst., intern Gen. Faculty Hosp.-Radiology, Prague, 1990-91, resident radiologist in tng., 1991-93, radiologist, 1993-97; radiologist, head magnetic resonance dept. Faculty Hosp. Motol-Radiology, Prague, 1997—; vis. physician St. Luke's Episcopal Hosp., Tex. Childrens Hosp., Houston, 1997; asst. prof. U. Hosp., Charles U., Prague, 1997—. Co-author: (with L. Vyhnánek) Radiology-Chapters From Clinical Practice, 1997. Mem. Czech Radiology Soc., Soc. Interventional Radiology, Soc. Magnetic Resonance. Home: Koštálkova 1361, 266 01 Beroun Czech Republic Office: Faculty Hosp Motol Radiol, V úvalu 84, 150 06 Prague Czech Republic

BELSEY, HUGH GRAHAM, museum curator; b. Hemel Hempstead, Eng., May 15, 1954; s. Graham Miles and Elizabeth Muriel (Pottage) B. BA with honors, Manchester U., 1976; MLitt, Birmingham U., 1982. Curator Bowood House, Calne, Wiltshire, Eng., 1978-80, Gainsborough's House, Sudbury, Suffolk, Eng., 1981—. Contbr. articles to profl. jours. Office: Gainsboroughs House, Sudbury Suffolk CO10 2EU, England

BELSKY, FRANTA, sculptor; b. Brno, Czechoslovakia, Apr. 6, 1921; arrived in Eng., 1939; s. Josef and Marta (Grunbaum) B.; m. Margaret Constance Owen, June 10, 1944 (dec. 1989). Diploma with honours, Royal Coll. Art, London, 1950. Tchr. art schs., 1950-55. Works collected in Nat. Portrait Gallery, collections throughout Europe and U.S.; works include fountains, statue of Sir Winston Churchill for Churchill Meml. and Libr. in U.S. at Westminster Coll., Fulton, Mo. and City of Prague, 1992, bust in Churchill Archives, Cambridge, 1971, Mountbatten Meml., Westminster, 1982, bust of Queen Elizabeth II, 1982, Airmen Meml., Prague, Czech Republic, 1995; contbr. to various books, and jours. Bd. govs. St. Martin's Sch. Art, 1967-88. Served in World War II. Churchill fellow Westminster Coll., Fulton, Mo. Fellow Royal Soc. Brit. Sculptors; mem. Soc. Portrait Sculptors (pres. 1964-68, 94—). Avocations: skiing, gardening, amateur archeology. Home: 4 The Green, Sutton Courtenay, Oxford OX14 4AE, England

BELSON, PATRICIA A., artist; b. San Francisco, Apr. 5, 1932; d. Joseph Patrick and Norma Stephanie (Bole) Gleeson; m. Dogan E. Belson, Sept. 2, 1961 (dec. July 1991); children: Linda, Susan. Office mgr. Psychiat. Group Offices, Seattle, 1958-63; pub. rels., brochure designer, English sec. Istanbul Hilton Hotel, Turkey, 1963-64; office mgr. Psychiat. Outpatient Facility, San Francisco, 1973-76; owner Wadyacallit, Sequim, Wash., 1980-85; corp. ptnr., mktg. dir. Fantasy Prodns., Inc., Seattle, 1985-90; self employed fine artist Seattle, Sequim, 1990—; vol. treas. Blue Whole Gallery, Sequim, 1997-98, artists' coop. mem., charter mem., 1997—. Solo exhbns. include Istanbul (Turkey) Intercontinental Hotel, 1978, Galerie du Soleil, Sequim, 1996, Gallery at the Fifth, Sequim, 2000; exhbns. include Bechtel Corp., 1976 (3d place award), A Contemporary Theater Gallery, Seattle, 1992, Juan de Fuca Festival of Arts, 1994, (hon. mention), Clallam Art League, Port Angeles, 1994 (2d place watercolor), 95, Northwest Watercolor Soc., 1994 (hon. mention), Juan de Fuca Festival Arts, 1995 (1st place watercolor), Clallam Art League Sr. Show, 1995 (Best of Show award), 98 (Best Still life winner), 1999 (Best Seascape), Sequim Arts Mem. Show, 1997 (1st place mems. choice, 2d place pub. choice), Blue Whole Gallery, Sequim, 1997-99, Olympic Nat. Resource Ctr. U. Washington, Forks, 1997—, Clallam Art League Gallery, 1999—, Frye Art Museum, Seattle, 2000; also pvt. galleries, Calif., Hawaii, Oreg. and Washington, others. Vol. tourist info. ctr. Sequim/Dungeness Valley C. of C., 1994-96; pub. rels. vol. Sequim Arts, 1996-97, vol. tutor Seattle Sch. Dist., 1991-92; vol. Sequim Arts Treas., 1997-99. Recipient Best of Show award Clallam Art League Sr. Show, 1995, 1st Pl. Sequim Arts Mem. Show, 1995, Best Seascape award Clallam Sr. Show, 1999. Avocations: sailing, canoeing, tennis, skiing, hiking. E-mail: pen4pat2@hotmail.com. Home: 101 Wilcox Ln Sequim WA 98382-8904

BELT, DAVID LEVIN, lawyer; b. Wheeling, W.Va., Jan. 13, 1944; s. David Homer and Mae Jean (Duffy) B.; m. Carolyn Emery Copeland Belt, July 22, 1967; children: David Clifford, Amy Elizabeth. BA, Yale U., 1965, LLB, 1970. Bar: Conn. 1970. Assoc. Jacobs, Grudberg, Belt & Dow, P.C., New Haven, Conn., 1970-74, mem., 1974—. Co-author: The Connecticut Unfair Trade Practices Act, 1994; contbr. articles to profl. jours. 1 lt. USAR, 1965-67, Vietnam. Fellow Conn. Bar Found. (life); mem. Conn. Bar Assn. (exec. com. antitrust and trade regulation sect. 1978—), Conn. Trial Lawyers Assn., Yale Club N.Y.C. Office: Jacobs Grudberg Belt & Dow PC 350 Orange St New Haven CT 06511-6415

BELTON, JOHN THOMAS, lawyer; b. Yonkers, N.Y., Feb. 24, 1947; s. Harry James and Anne Marie (Kupko) B.; m. Linda Susanne Cheugh, jan. 6, 1973; 1 child, Joseph Timothy. BA, Ohio State U., 1972, postgrad. in bus. adminstrn., 1972-73; JD, Ohio No. U., 1976. Bar: Ohio 1977, U.S. Ct. of Claims. Sole practice Columbus, Ohio, 1976-83; ptnr. Belton & Marlin, and predecessor firm Belton, Goldwin & Cheugh, Columbus, 1983—; arbitrator Franklin County Ct. Common Pleas, 1983—; dir. Weeks-Finneran Inc. Rep. precinct chmn., 1983; v.p. Far Northwest Coalition, 1984. Mem. ch. coun. St. Peter's Parish, 1984—, Pub. Bd. Zoning Appeals, 1991—; pres. Dublin Youth Athletics, 1985—. With USAF, 1968-71. Mem. ABA, ATLA, Columbus Bar Assn. (com. chmn. 1976—), U.S. Dist. Ct. Fed. Bar, U.S. Supreme Ct. Bar, Ohio Bar Assn. (bd. govs. 1993—), Dublin Jr. C. of C., The Pres., Ohio State Alumni, Republican Glee, Columbus Shamrock, K.C., Order of Barristers, Omicron Delta Kappa, Phi Alpha Delta (justice 1975). Roman Catholic. Avocations: reading, chess, golfing, racquetball, recreational activities. Home: 8649 Dunsinane Dr Dublin OH 43017-8757 Office: Belton Wherry & Marlin 2066 Henderson Rd Columbus OH 43220-2452

BELTON, PETER STANLEY, research institute administrator; b. London, June 19, 1947; s. Stanley Vulcan and Bertha Frances Belton; m. Teresa Laura Stutz, Sept. 4, 1976; children: Benjamin, Thomas, James. BSc, U. London, 1968, PhD, 1972. Postdoctoral rschr. U. East Anglia, Norwich, Eng., 1972-74; with Unilever Rsch., 1974-79; head group Inst. Food Rsch., Norwich, 1979-87, head dept., 1987-92, head lab., 1992—, dep. dir., 1992-99, head food materials Sci. Divsn., 1999—; hon. prof. U. East Anglia, 1992. Contbr. over 180 articles to sci. jours. Office: Inst Food Rsch, Norwich Rsch Park, Norwich NR4 7UA, England

BELTRAN, EUSEBIUS JOSEPH, archbishop; b. Ashley, Pa., Aug. 31, 1934; s. Joseph C. and Helen Rita (Kozlowski) B. Ed., St. Charles Sem., Overbrook, Pa. Ordained priest Roman Cath. Ch., 1960. Consecrated bishop, 1978; pastor chs. in Atlanta and Decatur, Ga., 1960; notary, then vice officialis Atlanta Diocesan Tribunal, 1960-62; vice chancellor Archdiocese Atlanta, 1962; officialis Archdiocesan Tribunal, 1963-74; pastor chs. in Atlanta and Rome, Ga., 1963-66; vicar gen. Archdiocese of Atlanta, 1971-78; pastor St. Anthony's Ch., Atlanta, 1972-78; bishop of Tulsa, 1978-92; archbishop of Oklahoma City Archdiocese of Oklahoma, 1992—; mem. com. liturgy Nat. Conf. Cath. Bishops; also com. for Am. Coll., Louvain, Belgium; bd. regents Conception Sem.; bd. dirs. St. Gregory's Coll., Shawnee, Okla. Mem. Equestrian Order Holy Sepulchre, NCCJ. Club: K.C. Office: Archdiocese of Oklahoma City PO Box 32180 Oklahoma City OK 73123-0380

BELTRAN, FELIX, graphic designer; b. Havana, Cuba, June 23, 1938; arrived in Mex., 1982; s. Joaquin and Carmen (Concepcion) B.; m. Lassie Sobera, Sept. 23, 1963; 1 child, Milena. BA, Sch. Visual Arts, 1960, Am. Art Sch., 1962; postgrad., New Sch. Social Rsch., 1961, Print Graphic Art Ctr., 1962; M (hon.), Europe Acad., Parma, Italy, 1982; D of Graphic Arts, Internat. U. Found., 1984. Assoc. art dir. Am. Pub. Co., N.Y.C., 1959-62, Cypress Books Co., N.Y.C., 1960-62; art dir. Exposicuba, Havana, Cuba, 1966-67; pres. fine arts sect. Union Cuban Artists, Havana, 1977-81; pres. nat. Cuban com. Internat. Assn. Art, Paris, 1979-82; dir. Felix Beltran & Assocs., DF, Mex., 1982—. Author: Desde of Diseno, 1970, Letragrafia, 1973, Acerca del Diseno, 1975, Diccionario de Diseno Grafico, 1996. Mem. Internat. Graphic Alliance, Internat. Trademark Ctr., Brno Biennale Assn. Avocations: reading, travel.

BELTRAN, LECY, plastic artist; b. São Paulo, Feb. 9, 1933; d. Cyro and Vanice (Angrimani) Laurenza; m. Antonio Beltran, June 13, 1953; children: Antonio Fernando, Maria Cristina. Student in sculpture, Master Dante di Giacomi, São Paulo; student in painting, Master Antonio Moraes, São Paulo; student in piano, Carlos Gomes Conservatory, São Paulo. Dir. Brazilian Mus. Sculpture, São Paulo. One-woman shows include U. Poitiers, France, 1996, (Personalitées honorific medal), Palais Palffy, Vienna, 1996, UNO, Vienna, 1996, Espaço Chiado, Lisbon, 1996, U. Complutense Madrid, 1996, Vatican, Palazzo del Vicariato, 1997, Miami Convention Ctr.- Art Americas 1997, Soho, Agora Gallery, N.Y.C., 1997, Brazilian Embassy, Tokyo, 1997, Cultural Ctr. of Brazilian Embassy, Moscow, 1998, many others; group shows include XV Sanjoanense Show Acad. Art Mcpl. Govt. São João da Boa Vista, 1991 (Gold medal 1991), Art Show U. São Judas Tadeu, Alberto Mesquita de Carvalho Inst., 1991 (Gold medal 1992), IV Art Show Pinheiros Dist. Region, São Paulo Trade Assn., 1991, V Art Show, 1992 (Silver medal 1992), VI Art Show, 1993 (Gold medal 1993), Campaign Sculpture Everyone's Reach III, Workteam Spl. Events, 1992, Petrópolis Abrarte Artistic Culture, 1992 (Gold medal 1992, Silver medal 1992), Brazilian Soc. Fine Arts, Rio de Janeiro, 1992, Sec. Edn. and Culture Franca, 1992, U. São Judas Tadeu, 1993 (Spl. mention 1993), José de Almeida Art Room, Petrópolis, 1994 (Gold medal 1994), Art Rm. Batista da Costa, Rio de Janeiro, 1994 (Gold medal 1994), La Pigna Gallery, Rome (Fra Angelico medal), Brazilian Consulate, Munich, 1994, Agora Gallery, N.Y.C., 1996; contbr. Internat. Art Guide, 1995; pub. monuments include Sao Paulo Internat. Airport, City Hall Sq., Sao Paulo, Palazzo de Vicariato, Vatican, represented in pvt. collections. Recipient gold medal Art Room U. São Judas Tadeu, Alberto Mesquita de Carvalho Inst., 1992, gold medal Petropolis Abrarte Artistic Culture, 1992, silver medal Petropolis Abrarte Artistic Culture, Summer Expo-Art, 1992, gold medal Batista da Costa Art Room, Rio de Janeiro, 1994, First prize Assn. Dos Artistas Plasticos de Santo Amaro, 1996, Distinction trophy, 1997, Excellent Work award China Art Expo, Peking, 1997, Silver Palette, Ethel Lowdes Art Show, 1997, Gold

medal Brazilian Soc. Fine Arts, 1997, 1st prize sculpture, public jury award, Coupe de la Ville de Beausoleil at Cannes-Azur, 1999, Croix de Vermeie, Mérite et dévoement Français, 2000. Mem. Nat. Mus. Women Arts, Museu Brasileiro de Escultura (dir.), Societe Amis du Salon D'Automne, Ordine Accademico Internat. Greci-Marino (acad. official knight of Verbano). Avocations: decoration. Home: Apt 131, R Joaquim Jose Esteves 60, 04740000 São Paulo Brazil Office: Atelier Lecy Beltran, Rua Darwin 814, 04741-011 São Paulo Brazil

BELTRAN, PATRIA ANTONIETA CASTRO, editor; b. Manila, Sept. 2, 1927; d. Melquiades Madrid and Victoria Felicidad (Bundalian) Castro; m. Pedro Nanquil Beltran, Oct. 27, 1951; children: Kathryn Beltran Abaño, Abel Luis, Brenda Ann Beltran Ortiz, Ruth Monserrat Beltran Tissino, Myra Victoria, Ida Genevieve Beltran Lucila, Joanna Claire. AB summa cum laude, Coll. Holy Spirit, Manila, 1948; postgrad., U. Philippines, Quezon City, 1948-49; MA with honors, Columbia U., 1950. Instr. English dept. U. Philippines, Quezon City, 1950-51; mng. editor In the Grade Sch., Manila, 1951—; editor The Modern Tchr., Manila, 1951—, SINAG Newsletter, Makati, Philippines, 1994—, Mother Butler Mission Guilds, Manila, 1957—; treas. Casbel Mktg. Corp., Quezon City, 1972-80; sec. Victoria Realty Co., Manila, 1953—. Coord. SINAG Hosp. Vols., East Ave. Med. Ctr. chpt., Quezon City, 1993—; chair unit IV Mother Butler Mission Guilds, Manila, 1960-62, 80-90, 1992—, nat. sec., 1965-76, sec. Manila coun., pres. Manila chpt., 1990-91; vol. Focolare Movement, 1967—. Roman Catholic. Avocations: sewing, needlework, reading, playing the piano. Home: West Triangle, 11 Bulletin St W Triangle, 1104 Quezon City Philippines Office: The Modern Teacher, Victoria Realty Co Box 1504, 1099 Manila Philippines

BELTRAO, ALEXANDRE FONTANA, coffee organization executive; b. Curitiba, Parana, Brazil, Apr. 28, 1924; s. Alexandre and Zilda (Fontana) B.; m. Anna Emilia, 1964; 2 children. Ed. Asst. engr. dept. soil mechanics Inst. de Pesquisas Tecnologicas, Sao Paulo, 1948; mem. staff Inst. Nat. d'Aerophotogrametrie, Ministere de la Reconstrn., Paris, 1950-51, Ministry of Works, London, 1950-51; founder, dir. Planning Svcs. Ltd., 1954-64; observer Govt. of State of Parana to UN Internat. Coffee Conf., 1962; spl. adviser to Pres. Brazilian Coffee Inst., 1964; chief Brazilian Coffee Inst. Bur., N.Y.C., 1965-66; pres. World Coffee Promotion Com. of Internat. Coffee Orgn., 1965-67; exec. dir. Internat. Coffee Orgn., 1968-94; sec. of sci. and tech. Internat. Coffee Orgn., Parana, Brazil, 1995-98, spl. sec. strategic issue, 1999—; coffee organization executive; b. Curitiba, Parana, Brazil, Apr. 28, 1924; s. Alexandre and Zilda (Fontana) B.; m. Anna Emilia, 1964; two children. Ed. Instituto Santa Maria, Curitiba, U. de Sao Paulo, Escola Nacional de Engenharia, Rio de Janeiro. Asst. engr. dept. soil mechanics Inst. de Pesquisas Tecnologicas, Sao Paulo, 1948; mem. staff Inst. Nat. d'Aerophotogrametrie, Ministere de la Reconstruction, Paris, 1950-51, Ministry of Works, London, 1950-51; founder, dir. Planning Services Ltd., 1954-64; observer Govt. of State of Parana to UN Internat. Coffee Conf., 1962; spl. adviser to Pres., Brazilian Coffee Inst., 1964; chief Brazilian Coffee Inst. Bur., N.Y.C., 1965-66; pres. World Coffee Promotion Com. of Internat. Coffee Orgn., 1965-67; exec. dir. Internat. Coffee Orgn., 1968-94; sec. of sci. and tech., Parana, Brazil, 1995-98, spl. sec. strategic issue, 1999—. Author: Parana and the Coffee Economy, 1963; (essay) Economy of States of Parana, Para and Ceara, 1958. Lt. Brazilian Army, 1945-46. Decorated comdr. Order of Rio Branco. Mem. Soc. Strategic Affairs. Author: Parana and the Coffee Economy, 1963, (essay) Economy of States of Parana, Para and Ceara, 1958. Lt. Brazilian Army, 1945-46. Decorated comdr. Order of Rio Branco. Mem. Soc. Strategic Affairs. Office: Assuntos Estrategicos, Edificio Castello Branco, Rua Marechal Hermes 999, 80530914 Curitiba Parana, Brazil Address: Praca Nossa Senhora da Salete s/n, Palacio Iguacu 3 andar, Cep 80-530-900 Curitiba Paraná, Brazil

BELTZNER, GAIL ANN, music educator; b. Palmerton, Pa., July 20, 1950; d. Conon Nelson and Lorraine Ann (Carey) Beltzner. BS in Music Edn. summa cum laude, West Chester State U., 1972; postgrad., Kean State Coll., 1972, Temple U., 1972, Westminster Choir Coll., 1972, Lehigh U., 1972. Tchr. music Drexel Hill Jr. High Sch., 1972-73; music specialist Allentown (Pa.) Sch. Dist., 1973—; tchr. Corps Sch. and Cmty. Devel. Lab., 1978-80, Corps Cmty. Resource Festival, 1979-81, Corps Cultural Fair, 1980, 81; Integrate music and scienceinto the curriculum to reiforce what has been learned from the scientists in the Growing With Science presentations with concepts such as the National Standards for Music dev. by MENC, Kodaly, Orff Schulwerk, Dalcroze Eurhythmics, Howard Garner's Multiple Intelligences, Heidi Hayes Jacobs Integrating the Curriculum, Dr. Sue snyder Intergrating Music into the Curriculum, Pam Robbins Brain Research. Mem. Mus. Fine Arts, Boston, aux. Allentown Art Mus., aux. Allentown Hosp.; mem. woman's com. Allentown Symphony, The Lyric Soc. of the Allentown Orch.; mem. Allentown 2d and 9th Civilian Police Acads.; bd. dirs. Allentown Area Ecumenical Food Bank; mem. Growing with Sci. partnership—Air Products and Chems., Inc. and Allentown Sch. Dist., Good Shepherd Home Aux. Decorated Dame Comdr., Ordre Souverain et Militaire de la Milice du St. Sepulcre; recipient Cert. of Appreciation, Lehigh Valley Sertoma Club; Excellence in the Classroom grantee Rider-Pool Found., 1988, 91-92. Mem. AAUW, NAFE, ASCD, Am. String Tchrs. Assn., Am. Viola Soc., Internat. Reading Assn., Internat. Platform Assn., Allentown Edn. Assn., Music Educators Nat. Conf., Pa. Music Educators Assn., Am. Orff-Schulwerk Assn., Phila. Area Orff-Schulwerk Assn., Soc. Gen. Music, Am. Assn. Music Therapy, Internat. Soc. Music Edn., Internat. Tech. Edn. Assn., Assn. for Tech. in Music Instrn., Choristers Guild, Lenni Lenape Hist. Soc., Lehigh Valley Arts Coun., Allentown Symphony Assn., Midi Users Group, Pa.-Del. String Tchrs. Assn., Nat. Sch. Orch. Assn., Lehigh County Hist. Soc., Confedn. Chivalry, Maison Internat. des Intellectuels Akademie, Order White Cross Internat. (apptd. dist. comdr. for Pa./U.S.A. dist., nobless of humanity), Airedale Terrier Club of Greater Phila., Kappa Delta Pi, Phi Delta Kappa, Alpha Lambda. Republican. Lutheran. Home: PO Box 4427 Allentown PA 18105-4427

BELVEDERE, MARIE, accountant, stock broker; b. N.Y.C., Dec. 31, 1935; d. Rocco and Lucia DiCapite; m. Anthony Belvedere, Oct. 25, 1958; children: Lyn Marie, Susan Pietri. BS, SUNY, Westbury, 1985. CFP. Stockbroker, 1975—; mem. exec. coun. Oppenheimer Fund, N.Y.C., 1996. Past pres. Nassau/Suffolk chpt. N.Y. State Soc. Enrolled Agts., Smithtown, N.Y. Recipient Founders award N.Y. State Soc. Enrolled Agts., 1989. Office: 53 Veterans Hwy Commack NY 11725-3481

BELYAEV, IGOR YAROSLAVOVICH, scientist; b. Poronaisk, Sakhalin, Russia, Oct. 25, 1958; s. Yaroslav Pavlovich and Lyubov Fedorvna B.; m. Svetlana Victorovna Belyaeva, July 28, 1984; children: Yaroslav, Olga. Engring. degree, Moscow Engring. Physics Inst., 1975-81; PhD in Radiobiology, Inst. Biophysics/Acad. of Sci., Moscow, 1986; ScD in Genetics, Sanct-Petersburg State U., Russia, 1994. Probationer Moscow Engring. Physics Inst., 1981-83, postgrad. student, 1983-86, jr. rsch. scientist, 1986-87, sr. rsch. scientist, 1987-88, head of lab., 1988—, head rsch. scientist, 1994—; guest scientist Stockholm U., Sweden, 1993—; lectr. in biophysics Moscow Engring. Physics Inst., 1990—. Mem. editl. bd.: Internat. Jour. Electro- and Magnetobiology. Recipient award Internat. Union for Pure and Applied Biophysics, Vancouver, Can., 1990, U.S. Radiation Rsch. Soc., Toronto, Can., 1991, Internat. Sci. Found., Moscow, 1993. Mem. European Soc. for Radiation Biology, European Bioelectromagnetics Assn., Swedish Soc. Radiobiology. Office: Dept Radiobiol/Stockholm U, Svante Arrhenius vage 16-18, 106 91 Stockholm Sweden

BELYAKOV, ANDREY NIKOLAEVICH, metallurgical engineer; b. Krasnoyarsk, USSR, Oct. 17, 1964; s. Nikolay and Galina Belyakov; m. Lidia Kudryavtseva, June 15, 1984; children: Maria, Daria. M, Ufa (USSR) Aviation Inst., 1987; D, Inst. Metals Superplasticity Problems, Ufa, 1995. Rschr. Ufa Aviation Inst., 1987-88; rschr. Inst. Metals Superplasticity Problems, Ufa, 1988-91, jr. rsch. assoc., 1991-95, rsch. assoc., 1995-96; rsch. assoc. U. Electro-Comm., Tokyo, 1996—. Postdoctoral fellow Japan Soc. Promotion Sci., 1996, Postdoctoral fellow Inoue Found. Sci., 1999; Sci. and Tech. Agy. fellow Nat. Rsch. Inst. for Metals, 2000. Mem. Japan Inst. Metals. Avocations: history, literature, photography. Office: U Electro-Comm, Chofugaoka 1-5-1, Chofu 182-8585, Japan

BELYAVSKIY, EVGENIY DANILOVICH, radio-physicist, researcher; b. Taganrog, USSR, Aug. 26, 1940; s. Daniil Grigorevich and Aleksandra Philippovna (Matsarenko) B.; m. Lyudmila Nikolaevna Volkova, Jan. 17, 1975; children: Viacheslav, Nikolay. Engring. degree, Kiev (USSR) Poly. Inst., 1964; PhD in Radiophysics, Saratov U., USSR, 1970, D of Phys.-Math. Sci., 1987. Worker Mech. Plant, Poltava, USSR, 1957-59; engr. Orion Rsch. Inst., Kiev, 1965-70, rschr., 1970-71, sr. rschr., 1971-89, head of lab., 1989-96; prof. physics Kiev Poly. Inst., 1996—; cons. Industry of Kiev, 1992—; expert State Com. Scis., Kiev, 1993-96. Contbr. articles to profl. jours.; patentee in field. Grantee Soros Found., 1993, Found. Fundamental Rsch., Ukraine, 1994-95. Avocations: traveling, history, arts, sports. Home: kv 212, Prospect Majokovskogo 79, 253232 Kiev Ukraine Office: Nat Tech U, Prospect Pobedy 37, 252056 Kiev Ukraine

BELZBERG, SAMUEL, investment professional; b. Calgary, Alta., Can., June 26, 1928; s. Abraham and Hinda (Fishman) B.; m. Frances Cooper; children: Cheryl Rae, Marc David, Wendy Jay, Lisa. B.Comm., U. Alta., Edmonton, 1948. Chmn. Balfour Holdings, Inc., 1992-97; pres. 1st City Fin. Corp. Ltd., Vancouver, B.C., Can., 1970-83, 86-91, chmn., 1983-91; pres. Gibralt Capital Corp., Vancouver, 1995—, Bel-Fran US Inc., 1997—; bd. dirs. e-Sim Ltd., Versaware Techs., Ltd., Westminster Capital, Inc., Metromedia Asia Corp., Bar Equipment of Am. Home: 3711 Alexandra St, Vancouver, BC Canada V6J 4C3 Office: 1177 W Hastings St Ste 2000, Vancouver, BC Canada V6E 2K3

BENABBES-TAARJI, JALIL ABBES, hotel executive; b. Fes, Morocco, Nov. 20, 1960; s. Ahmed and Zoubida (Belkahia) B.-T.; m. Sophia Benamour, June 15, 1990 (div. July, 1990); m. Siham Bennis, Feb. 29, 1992; children: Youssef, Hamza. Grad., HEC Paris, 1983; MS, U. Paris I, 1985. Asst. v.p. Credit Lyonnais, N.Y.C., 1987-88; sec. gen. Le Petit Soussin, Casablanca, 1988-90; gen. mgr. Hotel Tikida, Marrakech, Morocco, 1991-94, Tikida Hotels, Marrakech, Morocco, 1994—. Pres. CGEM-TENSIFT, Marrakech, 1995—; v.p. CGEM-Tourism, Casablanca, 1995-96. Mem. HEC Tourism Group, Assn. de l'Industrie Hoteliere (pres. 1997—). Avocations: golf, skiing. Office: Tikida Hotels, Circuit de la Palmeraie, 40007 Marrakech Morocco

BENACERRAF, BARUJ, pathologist, educator; b. Caracas, Venezuela, Oct. 29, 1920; came to U.S., 1939, naturalized, 1943; s. Abraham and Henriette (Lasry) B.; m. Annette Dreyfus, Mar. 24, 1943; 1 child, Beryl. B es L, Lycee Janson, 1940; BS, Columbia U., 1942; MD, Med. Sch. Va., 1945; MA, Harvard U., 1970; MD (hon.), U. Geneva, 1980; DSc (hon.), NYU, 1981, Va. Commonwealth U., 1981, Yeshiva U., 1982, U. Aix-Marseille, 1982, Columbia U., 1985, Adelphi U., 1988, Weizmann Inst., 1989, Harvard U., 1992, U. Bordeaux, 1993, U. Vienna, 1995. Intern Queens Gen. Hosp., N.Y.C., 1945-46; rsch. fellow dept. microbiology Med. Sch. Columbia U., 1948-50; charge de recherches Centre Nat. de Recherche Scientique Hosp. Broussais, Paris, 1950-56; asst. prof. pathology Sch. Medicine NYU, 1956-58, assoc. prof. Sch. Medicine, 1958-60, prof. Sch. Medicine, 1960-68; chief immunology Nat. Inst. Allergy and Infectious Diseases NIH, Bethesda, Md., 1968-70; Fabyan prof. comparative pathology, chmn. dept. Med. Sch. Harvard U., 1970-91; ret. Med. Sch., Harvard U., Cambridge, Mass., 1991; pres., CEO Dana-Farber Cancer Inst., 1980-91, Dana-Farber Inc., 1990-95; mem. immunology study sect. NIH; pres. Fedn. Am. Socs. Exptl. Biology, 1974-75; chmn. sci. adv. com. Centre d'Immunologie de Marseille. Bd. govs. Weizmann Inst. Medicine; mem. sci. adv. com. Children's Hosp. Boston; mem. award com. GM Cancer Rsch. Found., also chmn. selection com. Sloan prize, 1980. Capt. M.C. AUS, 1946-48. Recipient T. Duckett Jones Meml. award Helen Hay Whitney Found., 1976, Rabbi Shai Shacknai lectr. and prize Hebrew U. Jerusalem, 1974, Waterford award, 1980, Nobel prize, 1980, Corr. Emerite de l'Institut de la Sante et de la Recherche Scientifique, Nat. Medal of Sci. NSF, 1990. Fellow Am. Acad. Arts and Scis.; mem. NAS, Nat. Inst. Medicine, Am. Assn. Immunologists (pres. 1973-74), Brit. Assn. Immunology, French Soc. Biol. Chemistry, Internat. Union Immunology Socs. (pres. 1980-83). Home: 111 Perkins St Jamaica Plain MA 02130-4313 Office: Dana-Farber Cancer Inst 44 Binney St Boston MA 02115-6084

BENAGIANO, GIUSEPPE PINO, medical institute director, medical educator; b. Rome, Oct. 15, 1937; s. Andrea and Maria Luisa (Piergili) B.; m. Orietta Bianchini, Oct. 4, 1965 (div. 1984); children: Marisa, Andrea; m. Stephanie Canwell, June 29, 1985. MD, U. Rome, 1961, specialist in ob-gyn., 1965. Supranumerary asst. prof. U. Rome, 1962-63, from asst. to assoc. prof., 1968-73; Ford Fdn. fellow Karolinska Inst., Stockholm, 1964-67; rsch. specialist Population Coun., N.Y.C., 1967; med. officer WHO, Geneva, 1973-80, dir. spl. program rsch. in human reproduction, 1993-97; prof., dir. Inst. Ob-Gyn. U. La Sapienza, Rome, 1981-93; dir.-gen. Italian NIH, Rome, 1997—; cons. U.S. AID, Washington, 1982, 90. Editor: Progestogens in Therapy, 1982, Endocrine Mechanisms in Fertility Regulation, 1986, Immaginario Erotico e "Realta" Pornografica, 1989, Trattato di Fisiopatologia della Riproduzione Umana, 1993, The Evolution of the Meaning of Sexual Intercourse in the Human, 1996. Fellow ACOG (hon.), RCOG (hon.); mem. Soc. Italiana di Sessuologia Clinica (pres. 1986-89), Soc. Advancement of Contraception (pres. 1992-95), Italian Soc. Ob-gyn., Internat. Fedn. Gynecologists and Obstetricians (jour. assoc. editor. 1989—, sec.-gen. 1997—), Internat. Com. Rsch. in Reproduction (founding mem., bd. dirs. 1981-96). Roman Catholic. Avocation: gardening. Home: 28 Chemin des Massettes, 1218 Grand Saconnex Geneva, Switzerland Office: ISS, Viale Regina Elena 299, 00161 Rome Italy

BENAIM, FORTUNATO, surgeon, educator; b. Mercedes, BA, Argentina, Oct. 18, 1919; s. Simon and Alegrina (Bensadon) B.; m. Fernandez de Benaim Marta; children: Alejandra Gisela, Pablo Fortunato. MD, U. Buenos Aires, 1946. Cert. burn specialist. Staff surgeon Argerich Hosp., Buenos Aires, 1946-56; dir. Burn's Inst., Buenos Aires, 1956-84; pres., med. dir. Burn Found., Buenos Aires, 1981—; prof. surgery Buenos Aires U., 1956-84, hon. prof., 1984—; cons. prof. plastic surgery Salvador U., Buenos Aires, 1990—. Recipient Everet Idris Evans award Am. Burn Assn., 1980, Giusepe Whitaker Internat. Burn prize, Palermo, Sicilia, Italia, 1988, Tanner-Vandeput-Boswick Internat. Burn prize Internat. Burn Found., New Delhi, 1990. Mem. Argentine Acad. of Surgery (past pres. 1990), Nat. Acad. of Medicine Buenos Aires, Nat. Acad. Scis. Cordoba/Argentina (corrs.). Office: Found Del Quemado, Alberti, 1093 Buenos Aires Argentina

BENAK, JAMES DONALD, lawyer; b. Omaha, Jan. 22, 1954; s. James R. and Norma Lea (Roberts) B.; Patricia Ann Duffy, Mar. 1995; 1 child, James Duffy. BA, U. Nebr., 1977; JD, Creighton U., 1980. Bar: Nebr. 1980, U.S. Dist. Ct. Nebr. 1980, U.S. Ct. Appeals (7th cir.) 1988, U.S. Ct. Appeals (6th cir.) 1989, Ill. 1990, U.S. Dist. Ct. (no. and ctrl. dists.) Ill. 1991. Assoc. Kennedy, Holland, DeLacy & Svoboda, Omaha, 1980-84; asst. gen. atty. Union Pacific R.R. Co., Omaha, 1984-87, gen. atty., 1987-90; ptnr. Jenner & Block, Chgo., 1990—. Bd. dirs. Combined Health Agys. Drive/Nebr., 1985-90, Automated Monitoring and Control Internat., Inc., 1987-90, Coll. World Series, 1989-90. Mem. ABA (litigation sect.), Nebr. Bar Assn., Chgo. Bar Assn. (pub. utility and ins. law com.). Roman Catholic. Home: 335 N Garfield Ave Hinsdale IL 60521-3723 Office: Jenner & Block One IBM Plz Chicago IL 60611

BENAL, JOLANTA, editor, dog trainer; b. Hackensack, N.J., July 9, 1958; d. Władysław Franciszek Benal and Alicja Stefania Maliszewska; life ptnr. Sarah McDavitt Egan, July 19, 1989. AB, Cornell U., 1979; JD, N.Y. Law Sch., 1983. Editor Benal Editl. Svcs., Bklyn. Mem. Lesbian and Gay Cmty. Svcs. Ctr., 1989—; chair Friendship in the Interests of Dogs and Their Owners, Bklyn., 1998—. Mem. Assn. Pet Dog Trainers.

BEN ALI, ZINE EL-ABIDINE, president of Tunisia, international organization administrator; b. Sousse, Tunisia, Sept. 3, 1936; Married; 5 children. Degree in electronics, Saint-Cyr Military Acad., France, Chalons-sur-Marne Sch. Artillery, France, High Sch. of Intelligence and Security, U.S. Dir. mil. security Tunisia, 1964-74; mil. attaché Tunisian Embassy, Rabat, Morocco, 1974-77; gen. dir. nat. security, 1977-80, ambassador to Poland, 1980-84; sec. state nat. security Ministry of Interior, Tunisia, 1984, minister nat. security, 1985-86, minister of interior, 1986-87; min. state for the interior Ministry of Interior, 1987; prime minister, 1987; pres. Tunisia, 1987—; chmn. Orgn. of African Unity, Addis Ababa, 1994. Office: Palais de Carthage, Tunis 2016, Tunisia*

BENAM, JAVID FEIZOLLAH, engineering educator, researcher, consultant; b. Tabriz, Iran, Apr. 22, 1935; s. Esmail Feizollah and Sarieh Feizollah B.; m. Sharareh Mahootchian, Sept. 5, 1954; children: Mana, Morvarid. BSc in Mech. Engring., Tehran (Iran) Polytech, 1958, MSc in Mech. Engring., 1961; postgrad., Coll. Advanced Tech., Birmingham, Eng., 1961-62. Lab. instr.thermodynamics Tehran Polytech., Tehran, Iran, 1962-65; design engr. MECON Cons. Engrs. in Oil Industries, Tehran, Iran, 1965-67; fac. mem. Tehran Polytech., Tehran, Iran, 1967-76; tech. mgr. Arya Shipping Lines, Tehran, 1976-78; supr. instrumentation dept. Power Rsch. Ctr., Tehran, Iran, 1978-83; head mech. engring. dept. Amir Kabir U., Tehran, 1983-86; supr. instrumentation dept. OIEC Cons. Engrs., Tehran, 1986-89; rsch. dep. Mech. Engring. Dept. Amir Kabir U., Tehran, 1993-98; supr. Instrumentation Dept. Iranian Offshore Engring. Co., Tehran, 2000—; instr. B.C. Inst. Tech., Vancouver, Can. Contbr. articles to profl. jours., tutorials in instrumentation, control, hydraulics and pneumatics and automation techs. Mem. Soc. Control and Instrument Engrs. (bd. dirs. 1995-96), Internat. Fedn. Automatic Control (assoc. mem.), Soc. Mech. Engrs. Avocations; music, electronics. Home and Office: 105-460 West 15 St, North Vancouver, BC Canada V7M 1S6

BEN-AMI, ARNON, federal official; b. Tel-Aviv, Jan. 27, 1949. BA in Pre-Medicine, NYU, 1974; MBA, L.I. U., 1975; M in Polit. Sci., Haifa U., Israel, 1989. Commd. officer Israeli Def. Force, 1966, advanced through grades to brig. gen., 1990, battery bn. brigade comdr., 1966-87, comdr. field arty. sch., 1987-89, comdr. home front command, 1990-92, chief-of-staff home front command, 1992, sr. officer Mil. Mission to the Far East, 1992-94, ret., 1996; acting chmn. Supreme Emergency Econ. Bd., Tel Aviv, 1996—; cons. fin. and acad. projects Dominick & Dominick, N.Y., 1973-75; project mgr. Malam Sys. Ltd., Israel, 1995-96. Home: 32 Sheshet-Hayamim, 97804 Jerusalem Israel

BEN-AMOTZ, AMI, oceanographer, marine biologist, educator; b. Tel Aviv, Israel, July 30, 1943; s. Yehiam and Bracha (Frenkel) B.; m. Bat-Ami Goldenzail, May 30, 1968. BS, Hebrew U., 1967, MS, 1969; PhD, Weizmann Inst., 1973; postgrad., Brandies U., 1974. Asst. prof. Hebrew U., Jerusalem, Israel, 1975-76; sr. biologist Nat. Inst. Oceanography, Haifa, Israel, 1976-80, assoc. rsch. prof., 1980-86, head dept. marine biology, 1984-91, rsch. prof., 1986—; cons. prof. Weizmann Inst., Rehovot, Israel, 1976-90, coord. prof., 1992—; chief scientist NBT Ltd., Eilat, Israel, 1990—; adv. Nikken Sohonsha Co., Gifu, Japan, 1990—. Editor: Dunaliella: Physiology, Biochemistry and Biotechnology, 1992. Lady Davis Trust fellow, 1975-76. Mem. Nat. Acad. Sci. Home: 21 Hatomer, PO Box 3181, Savyon Israel Office: Israel Oceanographic & Limnological Rsch, PO Box 8030, 31080 Haifa Israel

BENANI, SAAD DYRAR, investment banking associate; b. Casablanca, Morocco, Sept. 22, 1972; came to U.S., 1993; parents: Latif and Amale B. BA, Columbia U., 1996. Fin. analyst Salomon Smith Barney, N.Y.C., 1996-98; assoc. Deutsche Banc Alex. Brown, N.Y.C., 1998—. Fax: 212-669-1555. E-mail: saad.d.benani@db.com. Office: Deutsche Banc Alex Brown 130 Liberty St New York NY 10006-1105

BENARDELLI DE LEITENBURG, MAINARDO ALVISE MARIA, diplomat; b. Gorizia, Italy, Dec. 18, 1964; d. Gualtiero and Luciana (PLastino) B. D in Polit. Scis., U. Padova, Italy, 1987. 2d sec. Ministry of Fng. Affairs, Rome, 1991-93; 1st sec. and dep. head of mission Italian Embassy, Uganda, Rwanda, Burundi, 1993-96; 1st sec. Italian Embassy, The Hague, The Netherlands, 1996-99, Sri Lanka, 1999—. Contbr. articles to profl. jours. Avocations: arts, reading, tennis. Office: Italian Embassy Sri Lanka, 55 Jawatta Rd, 5 Colombo Sri Lanka

BENATAR, LEO, packaging company executive; b. Atlanta, Feb. 21, 1930; s. Morris H. and Mary (Levy) B.; m. Louise Cure, Sept. 2, 1956; children: Morris L., Ann Marie, Ruth Eileen. B. Indsl. Engring., Ga. Inst. Tech., 1951; postgrad., Rochester Inst. Tech., 1956, Harvard Bus. Sch., 1970. Formerly pres. Mead Packaging Co., Atlanta; chmn. Engraph, Inc., Atlanta; bd. dirs. Sonoco Products Co., Johns Manville Corp., Interstate Bakeries Corp., Mohawk Industries, Inc., Aaron Rents, Inc.; past mem. internat. adv. coun. Trust Co. Ga., Trust Co. Bank; past mem. adv. bd. Arkwright-Boston Ins.; past chmn. Fed. Res. Bank Atlanta. Past bd. dirs. Rsch. Atlanta, Jr. Achievement, ARC, Nat. Minority Purchasing Coun., Keep Am. Beautiful, Peachtree Corners; past bd. visitors Emory U.; bd. dirs. Atlanta Partnership Bus. and Edn., Ga. Coun. on Econ. Edn.; steering com. Nat. Found. Ileitis and Colitis; past indsl. mgmt. adv. coun., nat. adv. bd. Ga. Inst. Tech.; mem. adv. coun. Coll. Bus. Adminstrn., Ga. State U.; mem. alumni adv. bd. Sch. Indsl. and Systems Engring. Ga. Tech.; bd. trustees Ga. Tech. Found.; past chmn. Pvt. Industry Coun.; past mem. DeKalb Reorgn. Com., Ga. Bd. Industry and Trade. With USN, 1951-53. Recipient Arcdiocesan medal of St. Paul Greek Orthodoc Archdiocese of North and South Am.; Lion of Judah award, Cmty. Achievement award ORT. Mem. Bus. Coun. Ga., Nat. Alliance Bus. (past chmn. Met. Atlanta, bd. dirs.), Japan-Am. Soc. Ga., Commerce Club, Standard Club, Buckhead Club. Home and Office: 121 Burdette Rd NW Atlanta GA 30327-4803

BENCHIMOL, MARCOS, emergency physician, internal medicine educator; b. Rio de Janeiro, Sept. 21, 1959; s. Hilbrio Simao and Cheva (Levy) B.; m. Maria Figueiredo, May 25, 1990; 1 child, Ilana. MD, U. Rio de Janeiro, 1986. Resident, then chief resident in internal medicine Hosp. des Servidores, Brazil, 1987-89, resident in cardiology, 1989-91; staff physician ICU Hosp. Miguel Couto, Brazil, 1991-93; mem. staff Hosp. Universitario, Rio de Janeiro, 1993—; prof. internal medicine, 1993—; chief emergency care unit Hosp. Universitario, 1994-95. Lt. Brazilian mil., 1990-91. Mem. ACP (Brazilian chpt.). Avocations: sailing, singing, travel. Home: R Prof Gastao Bahiana, 114/502, 22071030 Rio de Janeiro Brazil Office: Hosp Universitario CF Filho, R Brigadeiro Trompowski 5No, Rio de Janeiro Brazil

BENCHOFF, JAMES MARTIN, manufacturing company executive; b. Hagerstown, Md., May 18, 1927; s. J. Thompson and Marie (Hickey) B.; m. Brigitte R. Puhringer, July 1, 1978 (div.); children by previous marriage—Helen Marie, James Martin II. Student, U. Pa., 1944-45. With Grove Mfg. Co. div. Hanson Industries, Shady Grove, Pa., 1954—, v.p., 1962-66, 1st v.p., 1966, 1st v.p., asst. gen. mgr., 1966-68, exec. v.p., gen. mgr., 1968-69, pres., chief exec. officer, 1969-80, chmn., chief exec. officer, 1980-88, chmn. emeritus, 1988—; pres. Monta Vista Inc., Waynesboro, Pa., 1959—; pres., chmn. Ben Mar Holdings Ltd., Waynesboro, 1970—. Clubs: Waynesboro Country; Fountain Head Country (Hagerstown, Md); Met. (N.Y.C.). Office: PO Box 308 Waynesboro PA 17268-0308

BENCINI, SARA HALTIWANGER, concert pianist; b. Winston Salem, N.C., Sept. 2, 1926; d. Robert Sydney and Janie Love (Couch) Haltiwanger; m. Robert Emery Bencini, June 26, 1954; children: Robert Emery, III, Constance Bencini Waller, John McGregor. Mus. B., Salem Coll., 1947; postgrad. grad. Juilliard Sch. Music, 1948-50; M.A., Smith Coll., 1951; D In Mus. Arts, U. N.C., Greensboro, 1989. Head piano dept. Mary Burnham Sch. for Girls, Northampton, Mass., 1949-51; pianist, composer dance and drama dept. Smith Coll., 1951-52; head music dept. Walnut Hill Sch. for Girls, Natick, Mass., 1952-54; pvt. piano tchr., High Point, N.C., 1954-66; concert pianist appearing in Am. and Europe, 1948—; duo-piano performances with PBS-TV, Columbia, S.C., 1967, Winston Salem Symphony, N.C., 1964-68, Ea. Mus. Festival, Greensboro, N.C., 1969. Democrat. Presbyterian.

BENCKO, VLADIMIR, physician, researcher, educator; b. Rimavska Sobota, Slovakia, Czechoslovakia, Jan. 6, 1938; s. Viliam and Krista (Homolova) B.; m. Alena Trmalova, July 7, 1962; 1 child, Martin. MD, Charles U., Prague, Czechoslovakia, 1961, PhD, 1967, DSc, 1980. Med. diplomate; diplomate in hygiene (environ. medicine) and epidemiology. Jr. physician Dist. Hygiene Sta., Poprad, Czechoslovakia, 1961-63; postgrad. fellow Inst. of Hygiene Charles U., Prague, 1963-67; rsch. worker Inst. Hygiene and Epidemiology, Prague, 1967-73; asst. prof. Med. Faculty of Hygiene Charles U., Prague, 1974-86, head dept. hygiene Inst. Tropical Health, 1986-90; prof., head Inst. Hygiene and Epidemiology First Sch. of Medicine, Charles U., Prague, 1990—; temp. advisor WHO, 1972—; temp. cons. Com. Challenges to Modern Soc. NATO, 1994—. Mng. editor Jour. Hygiene, Epidemiology, Microbiology and Immunology, 1980-92; vice chair editorial bd. Ctrl. Europe Jour. Pub. Health, 1993—; assoc. editor Occupa-

tional Hygiene, Risk Mgmt. of Occupl. Hazards, 1992—; contbr. chpts. to books and ency., numerous articles to profl. jours. Advisor to min. Fed. Com. for Environment, Prague, 1990-92. Recipient awards for sci. publ. Czech Lit. Found., 1985, Czech Med. Assn., 1995, Outstanding Scholarly Achievment and Disting. Svc. award Internat. Inst. Advanced Studies Sys. Rsch. and Cybernetics, 1997. Mem. Internat. Soc. Environ. Epidemiology, Czech Med. Assn., N.Y. Acad. Scis., Hungarian Soc. Occupl. Health (life hon.), Internat. Soc. Indoor Air Quality and Climate (founding mem.), Slovak Med. Assn. (hon.). Roman Catholic. Achievements include biological monitoring of toxic metals in exposure assessment; environmental epidemiology of cancer. E-mail: vladimir.bencko@lf1.cuni.cz. Office: Charles U 1st Sch Med, Studnickova 7, CZ 12800 Prague 2, Czech Republic

BENCZE, LÁSZLÓ, chemist, educator; b. Dorog, Hungary, Sept. 26, 1962; s. László and Erzsébet (Fekete) B. MS, Eötvös U., Budapest, Hungary, 1985, PhD, 1989. Developing engr. Tungsram Rt., Budapest, 1988-90; rsch. assoc. dept. phys. chemistry Eötvös U., Budapest, 1990-94, adj. assoc. prof. dept. phys. chemistry, 1994-96, assoc. prof. dept. phys. chemistry, 1996—. Contbr. articles to profl. jours. Mem. Benedek Endre Speleol. Group, Dorog, 1995—, Brass Orch. of Dorog, 1976—. DAAD fellow, 1992-93; rsch. grantee Nat. Sci. Rsch. Fund, 1991-98, Hungarian-Slovenian Intergovtl. S&T Coop., 1997-98. Mem. Hungarian Chem. Soc., Sci. Assn. on Machinery, Mass Spectrometry Group. Roman Catholic. Avocations: playing saxophone, listening to music, excursions, researching and touring caves, playing badminton. Home: Féja Géza u 7, 2509 Esztergom-Kertvaros Hungary Office: Eötvös U, Pazmany P setany 2, 1117 Budapest Hungary

BENCZE, LORANT ANSELM, college president, linguist, educator; b. Sellye, Baranya, Hungary, Dec. 6, 1939; s. Sandor and Maria (Foldi) B.; m. Zsuzsanna Orsi, Nov. 16, 1975; children: Krisztina, Zsofia, David. Diploma, Lorand Eötvös U., Budapest, Hungary, 1969, PhD, 1972; CSc, Hungarian Acad. Scis., Budapest, Hungary, 1984. Form master Benedictine H.S. Benedictine Archabbey, Pannonhalma, 1969-75; sr. libr. Hungarian Acad. Scis., Budapest, 1975-81; asst. prof. modern Hungarian Eötvös U., Budapest, 1981-89, assoc. prof. head sect. hermeneutics, rhetoric and discourse, 1989-92; pres., head dept. lit. and linguistics Cath. Tchr. Tng. Coll., Zsambek, 1992—, univ. prof., 1997—; mem. Hungarian Accreditation Com., Spl. Com. Edn. of Humanities and Theology of Linguistics, Philology, and Oriental Studies, 1996—. Author: Style and Interpretation in Verbal Communication, Vols. 1-2, 1996; dep. editor-in-chief Annales Univ. Scientiarum Budapestinensis de Rolando Eötvös Nominatae, Sect. Linguistica, 1986-92; editor-in-chief Bibliotheca Septem Artium Liberalium Zsambek, Budapest, 1995—; contbr. articles to profl. jours. including New Testament Studies. Recipient Kuno Klebersberg award Inst. Edn., 1996. Mem. Assn. Ch. Colls. and Univs. in Hungary (pres. 1994-2000). Office: Vilmos Apor Cath Coll, Zichy Ter 3, H-2072 Zsambek Hungary

BENDECK-NIMER, ALBERTO COSTA, pediatrician; b. Teguciagalpa, Honduras, Feb. 7, 1936; s. Costantino Juan and Betty (Nimer) Bendeck; m. Isabel Widad, Jan. 8, 1961; children: Ingrid Mary, Costantino Juan, Rubèen Alberto, Marcía Irene, Adrian Alberto. BS, San Miguel Coll., 1952; MD, U. Chile, 1960. Resident Variety Children's Hosp., Miami, Fla., 1960-64; pediatrician San Felipe Hosp., 1964-67, chief emergency ward, 1967-69; chief infants Ward Hosp. Materno-Infantil, 1969-72, sub-chief pediat., 1972-76; chief pediat. dept. Social Security Hosp., Tegucigalpa, 1976-83, dir. materno-infantil, 1995-99; prof. pediat. U. Honduras Sch. Medicine. Editor: (with others) Pediatria, 1978; mem. editl. bd. Inter-Med., 1975; rsch. and publs. on pediat. Active Patronato for Welfare of Residents at Tegucigalpa. Mem. Honduran Med. Assn., Honduran Pediat. Assn., Am. Acad. Pediat., Colombia Pediat. Assn. (hon.), Dominican Republic Pediat. Assn. (hon.), Country Club, Club Hondureño Árabe, Club Campestre, Bosques de Zambrano. Home: 3202 Copan Lomas del Mayab, Tegucigalpa Honduras Office: Clínicas Médicas Colonia San Carlos, PO Box 724, Tegucigalpa Honduras

BENDELAC, ROGER E., investment executive, financial consultant; b. Oct. 5, 1956; s. David and Marie Bendelac; married; 2 children. Diplome, Institut D'Etudes Politiques, Paris, France, 1978; MBA, Columbia U., 1980. Lic. securities and commodities registered rep. Acct. exec. Oppenheimer & Co., Inc., N.Y.C., 1980-83, v.p. retail sales dept., 1983-84, sr. v.p. retail sales dept., 1984-85; sr. v.p. internat. br. Shearson Lehman Hutton, Inc., N.Y.C., 1985-87; pres., CEO REB Futures, Inc., N.Y.C., 1987-90; investment exec. Westminster Securities Corp., N.Y.C., 1988—; CEO Generis Capital Corp., N.Y.C., 1990-91; mng. dir. Genersis Assocs., Inc., N.Y.C., 1991—; mng. dir. internat. instnl. sales Laidlaw Global Securities, N.Y.C., 1997-98; pres., COO, dir. Laidlaw Global Corp., N.Y.C., 1998—, Global Electronic Exch., Inc., N.Y.C., 1998—. Editor bus. rev. Columbia U., 1979. Mem. N.Y. Acad. Scis. (elected mem.), Columbia Bus. Sch. Club. Avocations: running, team hand ball, readings in economics and history. Office: Laidlaw Global Securities 100 Park Ave New York NY 10017-5516

BENDELL, SIMON NEIL, radiographer; b. Bournemouth, Dorset, Eng., Dec. 13, 1958; m. Diane Button, Apr. 12, 1980; children: Sarah, Jayne. Diploma, Coll. Radiographers, 1978; diploma in med. ultrasound, Southampton Sch. Radiography, 1985. Radiographer High Wycombe (Eng.) Gen. Hosp., 1978-81, Poole (Eng.) Gen. Hosp., 1981-99, Lymington Hosp., 1999—; mem. bd. examiners for MSc in ultrasound Kings Coll., London, 1993-98; lectr., course coord. Southampton (Eng.) Sch. Radiography, 1990-93. Gov. Poulner Infant Sch., Ringwood, Dorset, Eng., 1991-93. Mem. Soc. Radiographers (dist. rep. 1983-85, health and safety rep. 1985-88), Brit. Med. Ultrasound Soc. Anglican. Office: Radiology Lymington Hosp, Southampton Rd, Lymington SO41 92H, England

BENDER, HAROLD, beverage company consultant; b. Boston, Oct. 2, 1910; s. Samuel and Clara Rebecca (Wernon) B.; m. Lilyan Alpert, Mar. 24, 1935; children: M. Barbara, Laurence Howard. BSBA, Boston U., 1931. Sales exec. Ideal Wine and Spirits Co., Inc., Boston, 1933-68; treas. John Gilbert Jr. Co., Boston, 1968-87, cons., 1987—. Grantee Lilyan Bender Endowment Fund, Boston, 1990. Mem. Assn. for Devel. Bordeaux Wines (Champagnon de Bordeaux 1955), Wine and Spirits Club (life, Boston U., Brandeis U., award of merit 1965), Masons (50 Yr. mel 1989). Republican. Avocation: researching major hist. events. Home: 250 Hammond Pond Pkwy Apt 16115 Chestnut Hill MA 02467-1533

BENDER, HOWARD JEFFREY, software engineering educator; b. Phila., Dec. 18, 1946; s. Irving Monroe and Ethel (Hellman) B.; m. Randi Laine Anderson, May 22, 1971; children: Rebecca Jennifer, Heidi Julia (dec.). BS, Pa. State U., 1969; MS, Polytech. Inst. N.Y., 1980; PhD, U. Md., 1992. Sr. programmmer, analyst ITEL Corp., White Plains, N.Y., 1977-80; computer scientist CSTA, Greenbelt, Md., 1980-82; systems engr. Lockheed Corp., Greenbelt, Md., 1982-85, CTA, Inc., Rockville, Md., 1985-93; instr. U. Md., College Park, 1981-85, adj. asst. prof., 1986-94, assoc. dir., 1994-98, cons., 1994—; pres. Edn. Process Improvement Ctr., Hyattsville, Md., 1995—. Author tech. articles; programmer (software) Personal Computing to Aid the Handicapped, 1981. Welcome wagon host University Park Civic Assn., 1989—. Mem. ASCD, Assn. for the Advancement of Computing in Edn., Computer Profls. Social Responsibility. Avocations: tennis, bridge, banjo. Home: 4200 Sheridan St Hyattsville MD 20782-2137

BENDER, JANET PINES, artist; b. Chgo., June 14, 1934; d. Nathan and Hana (Leff) Pines; m. Irwin Robert Bender, Feb. 25, 1966. BS, U. Wis., 1955; MA, Northwestern U., 1956; postgrad., U. Ill./Loyola U., Chgo., 1955-56, Tyler Sch. Fine Arts, Phila., 1957. One-woman shows include One Ill. Ctr., Chgo., 1979, 87, Olive Hyde Gallery, Fremont, Calif., 1980, 81, N.A.M.E. Gallery, Chgo., 1982, W.A.R.M. Gallery, Mpls., 1984, A.R.C. Gallery, Chgo., 1985, 87, 89, 94, 96, 98, 99, 2000, R.H. Love Galleries, Chgo., 1989, 92, Soho 20 Gallery, N.Y.C., 1990, Galerie Thea Fischer-Reinhardt, Berlin, Germany, 1990, 98, catalog, exhib. travels to Munich & Antwerp, R.H. Love Contemporary Gallery, Chgo., 1992, 97, Unitarian Ch. Evanston, Ill., 2000; exhibited in group shows at Creative Art Workshop, New Haven, CT, 2000, Sydney Coll. of Art, Australia, 1999-2000, Mus. Sci. and Industry, Cho., 1995, 96, 98, Atelierhof, Bremen, Atelier, Hamburg, Germany, 1999, Creative Art Workshop, New Haven, 2000, Artimesia Gallery, Chgo., 1996, Gallery 750, Sacramento, 1996, Women's Nat. Art Gallery, Washington, 1995, Rockford (Ill.) Art Mus., 1994, U. Wis. Art Gallery, Madison, Amos Enos Gallery, N.Y.C., 1993, Tonali Gallery, Mexico City, 1992, Renaissance Soc., Chgo., 1986, Ill. State Mus., 1983, 72nd Newport (R.I.) Nat. Exhbn., 1983, Chauttaqua Nat. Exhbn., 1981, Zolla Leiberman Gallery, Chgo., 1980, Holter Mus., Helena, Mont., 1997, Swan Gallery, Sydney (Australia) Coll. Art Gallery, 1998, Atelierhof Kunsthandwerkev, Bremen, Germany, 1999; represented in permanent collections at Mus. Sci. and Industry, Chgo., Young & Rubicam, Chgo., Brown-Forman Corp., Louisville, Nugent Wenckus Corp., Chgo., Louis Zahn Drug Co., Melrose Park, Ill, Fuller Comml. Brokerage Co., Chgo., Dynamark Inc., Chgo., Aabott Distbn., Miami, Art Beasley Inc., San Diego, Siegel, Denberg, Vanasco, Shivkovsky, Moses and Shoenstadt, Chgo., Altschuler, Melvoin & Glassner, Chgo., Shafer, Meltzer & Lewis Assocs., Wilmette, Ill., Schiff, Hardin & Waite, Chgo, art res. Byrdcliff Art Colony, 1998. Bd. dirs. Art Residents Chgo. Gallery, Chgo., 1984—; juror Ill. Assn. Fine Arts Awards, 1993. Recipient Ill. Arts Coun. Project Completion grants, 1979, 81-82, Visual Arts Fellowship grant Ill. Arts Coun., 1983; fellow Northwestern U., 1955-56. Mem. NAFE, Women's Caucus for Art, Nat. Woman's Mus., Mus. Contemporary Art, Art Inst. Chgo., Chgo. Artist Coalition, Ill. Arts Alliance, Met. Mus. Art (N.Y.), Coll. Art Assn., Peace Mus., Ill. State Gallery, Com. fr Artist Rights (organizing com. 1988), Siam House, Pi Lambda. Avocations: reading, tennis, swimming, travel, theater. Studio: 2001 N Elston Ave Chicago IL 60614-3901

BENDER, JOHN HENRY, JR. (JACK BENDER), editor, cartoonist; b. Waterloo, Iowa, Mar. 28, 1931; s. John Henry and Wilma (Lowe) B.; divorced; children: Thereza, John Henry IV, Anthony; m. Carole R. Humphrey, 1995. BA, U. Iowa, 1953; MA, U. Mo., 1962; postgrad., Art. Inst. Chgo., 1956, Washington U., St. Louis., 1957. Art dir., asst. editor Commerce Pub. Co., St. Louis, 1953-54, 56-58; editor Florissant Reporter, 1958-61; edit. cartoonist Waterloo Courier, 1962-84, assoc. editor, 1975-83; art. dir., editor Alpha VII Corp., Tulsa, 1984-87; head dept. prodn. art Platt Coll., Tulsa, 1987-92; cartoonist Don Martin Studio, Miami, Fla., 1989-92; cartoonist Alley Oop comic strip United Media Syndicate, N.Y.C., 1991—; sports cartoonist Basketball Weekly, Baseball Digest Mag., U. Iowa, others. Author: Pocket Guide to Judging Springboard Diving, (with Dick Smith) Inside Diving, (with Ed Gagnier) Inside Gymnastics. With USAF, 1954-56, col. USAFR, ret. Recipient Best Editl. award Mo. Press Assn., 1960, Grenville Clark Editl. Page award, 1968, Freedoms Found. award, 1969, 71, 75, Ignatz award Orlandocon, 1992, Air Force Commendation medal, 1981; named to Hall of Fame East H.S., Waterloo, Iowa, 1972, Names on Main, Cedar Falls, Iowa, 1997. Mem. Assn. Am. Editl. Cartoonists, Nat. Cartoonists Soc., Comic Art Profl. Soc., Sigma Chi. Home: RR 1 Box 540 Terlton OK 74081-9740 Office: 3289 S Cincinnati Ave Apt 499 Tulsa OK 74105-1960

BENDER, RALF, biostatistician; b. Siegen, Germany, July 6, 1962; s. Herbert and Edelgard (Koerth) B.; m. Katharina Nies, July 24, 1987. Diploma in stats., U. Dortmund, Germany, 1989; PhD, Hannover (Germany) Med. Sch., 1992. Rsch. assoc. Hannover Med. Sch., 1990-92, Heinrich-Heine-U. Düsseldorf, Germany, 1992-97, Ruhr-U. of Bochum, Germany, 1997-99, U. Bielefeld Sch. Pub. Health, Germany, 1999—. Contbr. articles to profl. jours. Mem. German Soc. for Med. Informatics, Biometry and Epidemiology (cert. biometry in medicine, cert. epidemiology), Internat. Biometric Soc., Internat. Soc. for Clin. Biostatis, European Callers and Tchrs. Assn. Avocations: square dancing, square dance calling. E-mail: Ralf.Bender@uni-bielefeld.de. Home: Jakobstr 72, D-57271 Hilchenbach Germany Office: Inst Epid and Med Stats, PO Box 100131, D-33501 Bielefeld Germany

BENDER, RANDI LAINE, occupational therapist; b. Omaha, July 17, 1947; children: Rebecca Jennifer, Heidi Julia (dec. Mar. 1991). BS, U. Ill., 1970; MS, Calif. Coll. for Health Scis., 1996. Registered occupational therapist. Occupl. therapist Westchester County Med. Ctr., Valhalla, N.Y., 1970-76, UCP Therapeutic Nursery, Washington, 1987-89, Edward Mazique Parent Child Ctr., Washington, 1989, Great Oak Ctr., Silver Spring, Md., 1989-93, Montgomery Primary Achievement Ctr., Silver Spring, 1993—, Pediat. Svcs. Am., Inc., Washington, 1996—. Active Easter Seals, 1999—. Mem. Coun. for Exceptional Children, Am. Occupational Therapy Assn., DAR, Riverdale Presbyn. Ch. Avocations: writing poetry, painting portraits, jigsaw puzzles. Home: 4200 Sheridan St Hyattsville MD 20782-2137

BENDER, TAMAS, rheumatologist; b. Budapest, Oct. 23, 1951; s. György Bender and Gertrud Baroti; m. Eva Rakovszky; 1 child, Krisztina. MD, Med. U., Budapest, 1976; PhD, Med. U., 1999. Rheumatologist, head physiotherapeutical dept. Inst. Rheumatology and Physiotherapy, 1992—; official expert Ministry of Health. Contbr. articles to med. jours. (Markusovszly prize 1992); co-author: The Theory and Practice of Physiotherapy, 1995 (Springer prize 1995). Mem. Internat. Soc. Med. Hydrology, Hungarian Balneological Soc. (gen. sec., pres. 1997—), Fedn. Internat. du Themal et Climatique, Hungarian Rheumatological Soc. Avocation: sports. Office: Inst Rheumatology Physiothe, 1025 Frankel L St 25-27, 1520 Budapest Hungary

BENDERITTER, THIERRY XAVIER, pathologist; b. Bamako, Mali, Mar. 23, 1955; s. Edmond and Marie Therese (Schneider) B.; m. Evelyne Giovo, Sept. 15, 1980; children: Philippe, Sophie. Grad. in immunology-tropical medicine, U. Marseilles, France, 1981, grad. in anatomic pathology and cytology, 1984, M Human Biology, 1986. Asst. pathologist U. Marseilles, 1984-88; chief dept. pathology Toulon (France) Hosp., 1988-92; pvt. practice, Toulon, 1992—. Mem. French Soc. Egyptology, Queen Elizabeth Found. for Egyptology. Avocations: egyptology, computers. Home: Campagne Lacoste-Boyere, 83 rue Pierre Delsol, 83130 La Garde France Office: Pathology Ctr, 9 rue Corneille, 83000 Toulon France

BENDHEIM, LEONORE CAROLINE, psychotherapist; b. Amsterdam, The Netherlands, Oct. 26, 1921; came to the U.S., 1943; d. Martin and Alice Sofia (Mayer) B. B in Art Edn. and Art Therapy, Kans. U., 1970; B in Social Work, Washburn U., 1972; MS in Clin. Counseling/Art Therapy, Emporia State U., 1974; MS in Clin. Gerontology, Kans. State U., 1983. Interior designer Mehagians, Phoenix, 1950-59; pvt. practice interior design Phoenix, 1959-63; rsch. vol. Menninger Rsch., Topeka, 1963-66; art therapy vol. Topeka State Hosp., 1966; vol. vocat. rehab. Ctr. for the Blind, Topeka, 1967; psychiat. evaluation team mem. Kans. Psychiat. Diagnostic Ctr., Topeka, 1970-73; counseling in psychotherapy Colmery-O'Neil VA Med. Ctr., Topeka, 1973-83, Phoenix South Mental Health, 1987-89; pvt. practice psychotherapist Scottsdale, Ariz., 1989-93. Edn. coord. Ashram Assn., Topeka, 1970-73; pres. Unitarian-Universalist Fellowship, Topeka, 1973-75, program chmn., 1975-78, chmn. bd. dirs., 1978-80.

BENDIKAT, ELFI, history educator; b. Berlin, Germany, Apr. 18, 1949; d. Kurt Röhling and Johanna (Braun) B.; m. Uwe Lehnert. PhD, Free U. Berlin, 1988. Asst. prof. Free U. Berlin, 1988-94; asst. prof. Humboldt U. Berlin, 1994-98, prof., 1998-99. Author: Öffentliche Nahverkehrspolitik, 1998, Wahlkämpfe in Europa, 1988. Mem. German and English Soc.; Com. Franco-Allemand de recherches sur l'histoire. Mem. Social Dem. Party. Home: Prinz-Friedrich, Leopoldstr 28, D-14129 Berlin Germany Office: Humboldt U, Unter den Linden 6, D-10099 Berlin Germany

BENDIX, KLAUS, brokerage house executive; b. Copenhagen, Denmark, Feb. 24, 1958; s. Axel and Jytle (Housen) B.; m. Lise Iverson, June 4, 1994. Banking degree, 1979; Master of Commerce, Copenhagen Bus. Sch., 1979. Asset mgr. Codan Insurance, Copenhagen, 1984-90; ptnr. P-H Bank, Copenhagen, 1990—. With Civil Defence, 1980-81. Mem. Danish Fin. Analyst Soc. (com. mem. 1988). Avocations: golf, tennis, dog training. Home: Nygade 4, 1164 Copenhagen Denmark Office: P-H Bank A/S, Nygade 4 4 Sal, 1164 København K, Denmark

BENDIX, LARS GOTFRED, software engineering educator, consultant; b. Herning, Denmark, Oct. 31, 1957; s. Knud Gybel and Birthe (Bendix) Pedersen. MSc, Aarhus (Denmark) U., 1986, PhD, 1996. Cons. BIT Cons., Denmark, 1986-91, 94—; lectr. European Bus. Sch., Italy, 1991-92; vis. prof. Siegen (Germany) U., 1993; rschr. Aalborg U., 1994-95, asst. prof. software engring., 1995—. Contbr. articles to sci. jours. and conf. procs., including Software Engring. Jour., Software Engring. and Knowledge Engring., Informatica, Software Configuration Mgmt. Avocations: music, film, swimming. Office: Aalborg U, Fredrik Bajers Vej 7E, 9220 Ålborg Øst, Denmark

BENDL, JIRI, scientist; b. Hradec Kralove, Czech Republic, Oct. 26, 1931; s. Leo and Marie (Smidova) B.; m. Yvonna Mrazkova; children: Jiri, Irena. PhD, Acad. Scis., Prague, Czech Republic, 1959, DSc, 1977; Dr.h.c., U. Pilsen, Czech Republic, 1997. Instr. Acad. Scis., Prague, Czech Republic, 1956-59, scientist, 1959-66, sr. scientist, 1966-77, head dept., 1977—; vis. prof. elec. machines U. Hannover, Germany, 1990; cons. in electric machines. Author: Electrodynamic Braking of Induction Machines, 1990; contbr. more than 110 papers to profl. pubs. Mem. Optimization of Elec. and Electronic Equipment Soc., Electromagnetic Phenomena in Nonlinear Circuits Soc., Advanced Methods in the Theory of Elec. Engring. Soc., Elec. Drives and Power Electronics Soc., and Power Electronics and Motion Control Soc. Roman Catholic. Avocations: sports, music, travel. Home: Famfulikova 1144, 18200 Prague Czech Republic Office: Inst Elec Engring Acad Scis, Dolejskova, 18202 Prague 8, Czech Republic

BENDORIUS, RIMGAUDAS ADOLFAS, physics educator, scientist; b. Vilnius, Lithuania, Feb. 26, 1942; s. Adolfas and Zofija (Matuseviciute) B.; m. Marija Bendoriene, Feb. 6, 1965; children: Renata, Laura. Grad., U. Vilnius, 1964, Doctor, 1974. Sci. worker Inst. Semiconductors Physic, Vilnius, 1963-76; lectr. physics Vilnius Gediminas Tech. U., Vilnius, 1976—; chmn. Fundamental Scis. Faculty Coun., 1993-97, 97—. Author: Fizikos minimumas (The Minimum of Physics), 1992, The Inclusion of Illusion Days, 1997, Collected Tasks of Physics, 2000. Mem. coun. Vilnius Gediminas Tech. U., 1997. Mem. Lithuanian Physics Soc. Avocations: poetry, gardening. E-mail: rabendor@uj.pfi.lt. Home: Architektu 25-70, 2043 Vilnius Lithuania Office: Vilnius Gediminas Tech U, Sauletekio 11, 2054 Vilnius Lithuania

BENDTSEN, PREBEN, medical educator; b. Copenhagen, Oct. 27, 1956; s. Bendt and Grethe Bendtsen; children: Maria, Marcus, Emma. MD, U. Copenhagen, 1984, PhD, 1994; assoc. prof., U. Linkoping, Sweden, 1999. Resident physician Växsjö Hosp., Sweden, 1983-84; med. officer Salvation Army, Zimbabwe, 1986-87; med. cons. SIDA, Uppsala, Sweden, 1989-90; resident physician Univ. Hosp., Linkoping, 1991-93, chief physician drug and dependency unit, 1994—; sr. lectr. U. Linkoping, 1997—, assoc. prof., 1999; advisor Merck AB, Stockholm, 1997—; med. cons. prison and probation authorities, Linkoping, 1997—. Author: Guide to Treatment of Alcohol Dependency, 1997; contbr. articles to profl. jours. Mem. Swedish Med. Assn. (bd. dirs. sect. for alcohol and drug abuse 1998). Avocations: golf, football. Fax: 46 13 221865. E-mail: preben.bendtsen@lio.se. Home: Igelknoppsvägen 8, S-590 62 Linghem Sweden Office: Univ Hosp, Social Medicine, S-581 85 Linkoping Sweden

BENEDECZKY, ISTVÁN, zoology educator; b. Tolna, Hungary, Nov. 4, 1931; s. József and Julianna (Kalmár) B.; m. Róza Pásztor, Mar. 25, 1955; children: Julia, Lilla. MS, U. Budapest, Hungary, 1955, PhD, 1959. Biol. diplomate. Asst. prof. med. faculty Med. Faculty Pécs, Hungary, 1957-65; assoc. prof. Med. Faculty Budapest, 1968-75; rsch. fellow Biol. Rsch. Inst., Tihany, Hungary, 1975-81; prof. zoology, dir. U Szeged, Hungary, 1982-92; pres. Tisza Rsch. Com., Szeged, 1982-92. Author: Apáthy the Scientist and Patriot, 1995, Lecture Notes, 1990, 92; contbr. articles to profl. jours., chpt. to book. Recipient Békésy awards Hungarian Oto-Laryngology Soc., 1976, Acad. awards Hungarian Acad. Scis., 1975. Roman Catholic. Avocation: tourism. Home: Othelló Str 7, 2000 Szentendre Hungary

BENEDETTI, SANDRO, architect; b. Marino, Rome, Sept. 2, 1933; s. Danilo Benedetti and Maria Pia Galbani; m. Maria Coronato, June 27, 1962; children: Simona, Emanuele, Irene. Degree in architecture, U. Rome, 1960; hon. degree, Acad. Virtuosi del Pantheon, Rome, 1985. Docent in archtl. history U. Rome Sapienza, asst. in archtl. history, 1969, prof. incaricato, 1972, prof., 1976. Editor mag. Palladio; prin. works include homes, schs., and churches in Italy, Ecclesiastic Sem., Potenza, Italy, restoration project Palazzo Senatorio, Rome, Cathedral in Paola, Calabria, Italy, restoration facades St. Peter in Vatican, New Entrance of Musei Vatican, Rome; author 9 books, including Giacomo Del Duca and the Sixteenth Century Architecture, Pietro da Cortona "stuccatore," Architecture Lectures, Current Sacred Architecture. Recipient Premio Nazionale InArch., Critica Storica, Premio Regional InArch. for ch. bldg. S. Gioacchino e Anna, Rome. Mem. Istituto Studi Romani, Centro Studi Storia Architettura (bd. dirs.). Roman Catholic. Home: Via Cilicia 8, 00179 Rome Italy Office: Studio Architettura, Via Vespucci 8, 00153 Rome Italy

BENEDICT, BARRY ARDEN, university administrator; b. Wauchula, Fla., Feb. 7, 1942; s. Clifford Allen and Caroline Mae (Watzke) B.; m. Sharon Gail Parker; children: Erin, Beau, Brooke, Mark. BCE, U. Fla., 1965, MS in Engring., 1967, PhD in Civil Engring., 1968. Rsch. assoc. U. Fla., Gainesville, 1968-69, prof., 1980-86; asst. prof. Vanderbilt U., Nashville, 1969-72, assoc. prof., program dir., 1972-75; assoc. prof. Tulane U., New Orleans, 1975-77, U. S.C., Columbia, 1978-80; prof., dept. head La. Tech. U., Ruston, 1986-88, dean., Jack Thigpen prof., 1988-98; v.p. acad. affairs Rose-Hulman Inst. Tech., Terre Haute, Ind., 1998—; project dir. La. NSF-EPSCoR, 1989-94; cons. to numerous industries; dir. Inst. Micromanufacturing, 1997-98. Contbr. articles to profl. jours. and chpts. to books. Mem. NSPE (gov.-at-large profl. engrs. in edn. divsn.), La. Dept. Econ. Devel., La. Transp. Rsch. Ctr. (vice chair 1993-98). Methodist. Avocation: jogging. Home: 212 Barton Ave Terre Haute IN 47803-1840 Office: Rose-Hulman Inst Tech 5500 Wabash Ave Terre Haute IN 47803-3999

BENEDICT, DOROTHY JONES, genealogist, researcher; b. Bronxville, N.Y., Mar. 23, 1916; d. Harry Edwin and Katherine Jones; m. Mark Charles Benedict; children: Ann Benedict Johnson, Sharon Benedict Bash, Gail Benedict Bain, Faye. BA, Goucher Coll., 1938. Statistician E.W. Axe Co., N.Y.C., 1938; with Nat. Labor Rels. Bd., N.Y.C., 1938-39. Leader Girl Scouts of Am., Glastonbury, Conn., 1957-64; creator convalescent homes Sunday mini-svc. Asbury Ch., Glastonbury, 1960-70. Mem. Nat. Soc. Magna Carta Dames, Arts Soc. Orlando Mus., DAR, Delta Delta Delta, Phi Beta Kappa. Methodist. Avocations: golf, walking, art. Home: 100 S Interlachen Ave Winter Park FL 32789-4438

BENEDICT, HELEN, journalism educator, writer; b. London, Nov. 5, 1952; came to U.S., 1978; BA, U. Sussex, Eng., 1975; MA, U. Calif., Berkeley, 1979. Reporter The Independent, Richmond, Calif., 1979-80; freelance reporter N.Y.C., 1981-86; prof. Columbia U., N.Y.C., 1986—. Author: A World Like This, 1990, Portraits in Print, 1991, Virgin or Vamp, 1992, Bad Angel, 1996, The Sailor's Wife, 2000. Mem. Poets, Essayists, Novelists. Home: 531 W 112th St Apt 4A New York NY 10025-1666 Office: Grad Sch Journalism Columbia U New York NY 10027

BENEDICT, JULIUS NIYI, education educator; b. Ogun State, Nigeria, Nov. 26, 1950; s. Matthew Osinuga and Celina Adewunmi (James) B.; m. Henrietta Titlola Osinubi, July 6, 1974; children: Mary, Samuel, Matthew, Daniel, Gabriel. BFA with honors, U. IFE, Nigeria, 1977; P.G.D.E., U. Lagos, Nigeria, 1981; M in Edn., U. Ibadan, Nigeria, 1983; PhD in Ednl. Tech., U. Ibadan, 1988. Lectr. Ogun State Coll. Edn., Nigeria, 1979-84; prof. Ogun State U., 1984-97, U. of the N. Qwa Qwa Campus, S. Africa, 1998—; supr. UNICEF, Ogun State, 1992; cons. instructional materials mass edn., Ogun State/UNDP, 1995—. Author: (books) Educational Technology Implication For Teachers, 1995, Elements of Curriculum Delelopment & Teaching Principles, 1995; editor-in-chief Uniqwa Rsch. jour., 2000; contbr. articles to profl. jours. Recipient scholarship Fed. Govt. Nigeria, 1974-77, Ogun State Govt., 1983-88. Mem. Nat. Assn. Profl. Educators (state chmn., nat. PRO), Nigeria Assn. Ednl. Media & Tech. (state chmn. 1993—). Avocations: reading, painting, singing, lawn tennis. Home: PO Box 1711, Lombard 20 Harrismith, 9880 Harrismith S. Africa Office: U of the North/Qwa Qwa, PM Bag X13, 9866 Phuthaditjhaba S. Africa

BENEDICT, LAWRENCE NEAL, foreign service officer; b. Independence, Mo., Dec. 17, 1942; s. Albert Michael and Audentia Elizabeth (Thomas) B.; m. Gloria Kay Bruning, July 2, 1966. BA, Calif. State U., Long Beach, 1974. V.p. A.M. Benedict & Assocs., Long Beach, Calif., 1966-72; vice consul Am. Embassy, Dahka, Bangladesh, 1974-77; comml. officer Am. Consulate Gen., Rio de Janeiro, 1977-79; desk officer for Bangladesh U.S. Dept. of State, Washington, 1979-80, desk officer for Turkey, 1980-82, dep. dir. devel. fin., 1986-89; fin./devel. officer Am. Embassy, Ankara, Turkey, 1982-86; counselor econ. affairs Am. Embassy, Islamabad, Pakistan, 1989-92; dep. chief of mission Am. Embassy, Khartoum, Sudan, 1992-95; amb. Am.

Embassy, Praia, Cape Verde, 1996—. Staff sgt. USANG, 1963-69. Mem. Am. Fgn. Svc. Assn. Avocations: tennis, reading, collecting books and wine. Home and Office: Pretoria Dept Of State Washington DC 20521-0001

BEN-ELISSAR, ELIAHU, Israeli government official; b. Radom, Poland, 1932. Diplomé l'Institut d'Etudes politiques, Diplomé l'Institut Hautes Etudes internationales, U. Paris; PhD in Polit. Sci., U. Geneva. With Govt. of Israel, 1965, elected to ctrl. com. Herut and Likud, 1970—, party spokesman, 1971-77, head info. dept. during Likud nat. election campaigns, 1973, 77, mem. Likud polit. bur., 1993-96, chmn. Likud polit. com., various positions Likud Party, del. World Zionist Congress, 1972, 87, 92, dir.-gen. office prime min., 1977-80; head Israel's 1st del. to Mena House talks Govt. of Israel, Cairo, 1977; Israel's 1st amb. to Egypt Govt. of Israel, 1980-81, mem. Knesset, 1981-96, chmn. com. fgn. affairs and def., 1982-84, 89-92, mem. com. fgn. affairs and def., 1981-82, 84-89, 92-96, mem. del. to Madrid Peace Conf., 1991, mem. del. to UN gen. assembly, 1992, amb. to U.S., 1996-98, amb. to France, 1998—; past corr. L'Aurore, Israel, Le Jour, Genéve, Israel. Author: La Guerre israélo-arabe, 1967, La Diplomatie du Troisiéme Reich et les Juifs (1969, 1981), Kesher Ha'hashmada, 1987, No More War, 1995. Named Grand Officer Ordre de l'Ethiopie, 1964, Grand Cruz Extraordinaria, Orden de la Democracia, Colombia, 1980.

BENELLO, DAVID, management consultancy director; b. Milan, Mar. 6, 1954; arrived in Eng., 1995; s. Franco Benello and Augusta Lange; 1 child, Sophie Angelica. BA, Oxford (Eng.) U., 1976; MBA, Harvard U., 1982. 2d lt. Italian Army, Milan, 1977-78; sr. assoc. Arthur Andersen, Milan, 1979-80; dir. McKinsey & Co., London, 1982—. Avocation: flying. Office: McKinsey & Co Inc, 1 Jermyn St, London SW1Y 4UH, England

BENES, BOHUSLAV, retired European ethnology educator; b. Brno, Czechoslovakia, Oct. 20, 1927; s. Bohuslav and Anna (Oslejsková) B.; m. Alena Kucerová; 1 child, Raduz. MPhil, Masaryk's U., Brno, 1950, PhD, 1952, CSc, 1966, DrSc, 1987. H.S. tchr. Ostrava, 1950-52; lectr. U. Brno, 1952-70, prof. asst., 1971-88, prof., 1989-93, ret. prof., 1993; cons. Waldviertel Akademie Waidhofen, Austria, 1990—, Arge Region Kultur, Horn, Austria, 1992—, Slovakian Acad. Sci., Bratislava, 1976—. Author: Temporal Street-Ballad, 1970, Listen to a Nice Song, 1983, Czech Folk-poetry, 1990, (with V. Hrníčko), Political Inscriptions in Streets, 1993, Introduction to Folklore Studies, 1980, 2d edit., 1989. Mem. Internat. Soc. for Folk Narrative Rsch. Home: Zemědělská 19, CR 61300 Brno Czech Republic

BENES, DANIEL MARKUS, computer company executive, consultant; b. Vienna, Austria, Apr. 18, 1969; came to U.S., 1999; s. Thomas and Hana (Kopecky) B. Magister, Vienna Sch. Bus. Adminstrn., 1998. Sales mgr. Nat. Lottery, Vienna, 1989-91; bus. developer Talk Consultancy, Vienna, 1992; rschr. A.C. Nielsen, Vienna, 1993-96; controlling investor rels. Auricon Group, Vienna, 1997-99; exec. officer Auricon Immobilien, Vienna, 1998-99; exec. officer bus. devel. Jenbacher Ltd., Farmington Hills, Mich., 1999—. Author: Quantitative Analysis of Consolidated Financial Statements, 1997; co-author: Company LAN in Austria, 1995. Avocations: arts, literature, music, golf. Office: Jenbacher Ltd West Tech Park 26602 Hagger Ty Rd Farmington Hills MI 48331

BENEŠ, IVAN, chemist; b. Prague, June 21, 1948; s. Karel and Vlasta (Černohorská) B.; m. Blanka Hlužová, July 19, 1973 (div. Apr. 1979); 1 child, Pavel; m. Jutta Maria Nickel, Aug. 10, 1979; children: Petra, Dagmar. MSc, Charles U., Prague, 1971; PhD, Czechoslovak Acad. Sci., Prague, 1983. Cert. lab. methods in hygiene. Scientist Inst. Organic Chemistry and Biochemistry, Prague, 1971-83; dept. head Inst. Hygiene, Teplice, Czech Republic, 1983—; head monitoring project Teplice Programme, 1992-99, head monitoring project in air pollution and health, 2000-2002. Adv. bd. mem. (jour.) Bioprospect, 1993—. Mem. Chem. Soc., Biotechnol. Soc. Home: Heleny Malířové 12, 415 01 Teplice Czech Republic Office: Inst Hygiene, Wolkerova 3, 416 65 Teplice Czech Republic

BENES, IVAN, economist; b. Prague, Czech Republic, Apr. 8, 1947; s. Eduard and Alena (Surova) B.; 1 child, Suzane. MSc, Czech Tech. U., Prague, 1970. Cert. engr. Engr. Energoprojekt, Prague, 1971-80, head dept., 1980-90, tech. dir., 1990-91; mng. dir. Cityplan, Prague, 1992—. Mem. Czech Assn. for Energy Econs. (pres. 1997—), Assn. Energy Mgrs., Cezchoslovak Fgn. Inst. (bd. dirs. 1997—). Office: Cityplan, Odboru 4, 12000 Prague 2, Czech Republic

BENES, SOLOMON, biomedical scientist, physician; b. Iasi, Romania, Mar. 28, 1925; came to U.S., 1978; s. Moritz and Cecilia (Abramovici) B.; m. Liudmila Topor, Mar. 27, 1954. MD, Sch. of Medicine, Bucharest, Romania, 1952. Intern microbiology lab. Mil. Hosp., Bucharest, 1949-50, fellow microbiology lab., 1950-51, dir. clin. lab. outpatient dept., 1951-52; dir. rsch. lab. Ctr. for Radiobiology Rsch., Bucharest, 1953-57, 59-66; chief physician microbiology lab. Mil. Hosp., Bucharest, 1967-73; chief physician clin. lab. Ctr. of Haematology, Bucharest, 1973-76; assoc. in medicine Havard Med. Sch., Boston, 1978-81; asst. rsch. scientist, asst. prof. SUNY Health Sci. Ctr., Bklyn., 1982-95; sr. rsch. scientist, asst. prof. SUNY Rsch. Found., Bklyn., 1995-98; ret., 1998. Author: (with others) Seminars in Infectious Diseases, 1983; contbr. articles to Sexually Transmitted Diseases, Antimicrobial Agts. and Chemotherapy, Jour. Clin. Microbiology, Proceedings of the 6th Internat. Symposium on Human Chlamydial Infections. Col., Romanian Army Med. Svc., 1946-73. Achievements include discovery that the Trachoma biovar of Chlamydia trachomatis is able to achieve intercellular propagation in cell culture and that, in a proper cell setting, this bacterium spreads from cell to cell in cell culture, contrary to what was generally believed. Home: 2421 Shellpot Dr Wilmington DE 19803-2547

BENET, LESLIE ZACHARY, pharmacokineticist; b. Cin., May 17, 1937; s. Jonas John and Esther Racie (Hirschfeld) B.; m. Carol Ann Levin, Sept. 8, 1960; children: Reed Michael, Gillian Vivia. AB in English, U. Mich., 1959, BS in Pharmacy, 1960, MS in Pharm. Chemistry, 1962; PhD in Pharm. Chemistry, U. Calif., San Francisco, 1965; PharmD (hon.), Uppsala U., Sweden, 1987; PhD (hon.), Leiden U., The Netherlands, 1995; DSc (hon.), U. Ill., Chgo., 1997, Phila. Coll. Pharm. & Sci., 1997, L.I. U., 1999. Asst. prof. pharmacy Wash. State U., Pullman, 1965-69; asst. prof. pharmacy and pharm. chemistry U. Calif., San Francisco, 1969-71, assoc. prof., 1971-76, prof., 1976—, vice chmn. dept. pharmacy, 1973-78, chmn. dept. pharmacy, 1978-96, dir. drug studies unit, 1977—, dir. drug kinetics and dynamics ctr., 1979-98, chmn. dept. biopharm. scis., 1996-98; mem. pharmacology study sect. NIH, Washington, 1977-81, chmn., 1979-81, mem. pharmacol. scis. rev. com., 1984-88, chmn., 1986-88; mem. generic drugs adv. com. FDA, Washington, 1990-94, mem. Sci. Bd., 1992-98; chair external rev. com. CBER, 1998, chair expert panel on individual equivalence, 1998—; mem. sci. adv. bd. SmithKline Beecham Pharms., 1989-92, Pharmetrix, 1989-92, Alteon, Inc., 1993—, TheraTech, Inc., 1993-96, Roche Biosci., 1998—, Pain Therapeutics, Inc., 1999—, UMD, Inc., 1999—, Silico Insights, Inc., 2000—; chmn. bd. AvMax, Inc., 1994—; bd. dirs. OxoN Medica, Inc., InforMedix, Inc., Josman Labs., Inc. Editor Jour. Pharmacokinetics and Biopharmaceutics, 1976-98; assoc. editor Pharmacology and Therapeutics, 1995—; mem. editl. bd. Pharmacology, 1979—, Pharmacy Internat., 1979-82, Pharm. Rsch., 1983-95, ISI Atlas of Sci.: Pharmacology, 1988-89, Pharm. News, 1994-98, AAPS PharmSci, 1999—, Chemistry and Pharm. Bull., 2000—, The Effect of Disease States on Drug Pharmacokinetics, 1976, Pharmacokinetic Basis for Drug Treatment, 1984, Pharmacokinetics: A Modern View, 1984, ISI Atlas of Sci.: Pharmacology, 1988-89, Integration of Pharmacokinetics, Pharmacodynamics and Toxicokinetics in Rational Drug Development, 1992, Clinical Applications of Mifepristone (RU486) and Other Antiprogestins, 1993; contbr. more than 400 articles to profl. jours. Appt. to Forum on Drug Devel. and Regulation, 1988. Fellow Acad. Pharm. Scis. (pres. 1985-86, chmn. basic pharmaceutics sect. 1976-77, mem.-at-large exec. com. 1979-83, Rsch. Achievement award 1982), AAAS (mem.-at-large exec. com. pharm. scis. sect. 1978-81, 91-95, chair 1996-97), Am. Assn. Pharm. Scientists (pres. 1986, treas. 1987, bd. dirs. 1988-93, Disting. Pharm. Scientist award 1989, Disting. Svc. award 1996, Wurster rsch. award in pharmaceutics 2000); mem. AAUP, Inst. Medicine NAS (forum on drug devel. and regulation 1988-94, chmn. com. on antiprogestins, 1993, membership com. 1994-97, chmn. other health professions sect. 1995-97, chmn. com. pharmacokinetics & drug interactions in elderly 1996-97, mem. Round Table R & D Drugs, Biologics & Med. Devices 1997-2000, bd. on health scis. policy 1999—), Am. Found. for Pharm. Edn. (bd. dirs. 1987—, Disting. Svc. "Profile" award 1993), Am. Coll. Clin. Pharmacology (Disting. Svc. award 1988), ISSX (councillor 1992-96, treas. 1998-99), Am. Pharm. Assn. (Higuchi Rsch. prize 2000), Am. Soc. Clin. Pharmacology and Therapeutics (Rawls-Palmer award and lectureship 1995), Am. Soc. for Pharmacology and Exptl. Therapeutics, Generic Pharm. Industry Assn. (mem. blue ribbon com. on generic medicines 1990), Internat. Pharm. Fedn. (bd. pharm. scis. 1988, chair 1996—), Drug Info. Assn., Am. Coll. Clin. Pharmacy (therapeutic frontiers lectr. 1995), Am. Assn. Colls. Pharmacy (Volwiler Rsch. Achievement award 1991, pres. 1993-94, bd. dirs. 1992-95), Sigma Xi, Rho Chi (Ann. Lecture award 1990), Phi Lambda Sigma. Home: 601 Van Ness Ave Apt 451 San Francisco CA 94102-3259 Office: U Calif San Francisco Dept Biopharm Scis San Francisco CA 94143-0001

BENETTON, GILBERTO, clothing manufacturing company executive; b. Treviso, Italy, June 19, 1941. Co-founder, chmn. Fratelli Benetton, Treviso, 1965—; vice chmn., mng. dir. Benetton Group; chmn. bd. dirs. Gruppo S.I.P.I. Cons. Svcs.; bd. dirs. Saes, Banca del Friuli; chmn. bd. dirs. Edizioni Holding, Sfera SpA. Office: Benetton Group, Via Villa Minelli 1, 31050 Ponzano Veneto Treviso, Italy*

BENETTON, LUCIANO, clothing manufacturing company executive; b. Treviso, Italy, May 13, 1935; four children. MBA (hon.), Inst. de Empresa, Madrid, 1992. Co-founder, chmn. Fratelli Benetton, 1965—; chmn. bd., pres. Benetton Group; bd. dirs. Eliolona. Co-founder Colors Publs. Elected sen. Italian Rep. Party, 1992. Office: Benetton Group, Via Villa Minelli 1, 31050 Ponzano Veneto Treviso, Italy*

BENEWITZ, MAURICE CHARLES, labor arbitrator, educator; b. Hartford, Conn., Nov. 16, 1923; d. Doris L. Benewitz; m. Lesley Frank Alan Benewitz. AB in Econs., Harvard U., 1947; PhD in Econs., U. Minn., 1954. From asst. prof. to prof., dept. chair Baruch Coll., N.Y.C., 1955-75; arbitrator Manhasset, N.Y., 1958—; dir. Nat. Ctr. for the Study of Collective Bargaining in Higher Edn., N.Y.C., 1970-73. Author: Higher Education Arbitration, 1988. Mem. Am. Arbitration Assn. (panel mem.), Fed. Mediation and Conciliation Svc. (panel mem.), N.Y. State Pub. Employee Rels. Bd. (panel mem.), N.Y.C. Office Collective Bargaining (panel mem.), N.J. State Med. Bd., Nat. Acad. Arbitrators, Phi Beta Kappa. Home and Office: 261 Thompson Shore Rd Manhasset NY 11030-2240

BÉNÉZECH, MICHEL HENRI, criminologist, researcher; b. Agen, France, Oct. 1, 1942; s. René and Marguerite (Charles) B.; m. Claude Christine Mandraut, Dec. 22, 1994. MD, U. Bordeaux, France, 1969, Forensic Physician, 1970, Psychiatrist, 1973, LLD, 1973. Diplomate in medicine and criminology. Lectr. Nat. Sch. Magistrature, Bordeaux, 1970-85; assoc. prof. forensic medicine U. Bordeaux, 1989-92; head dept. psychiatry Penitentiary System, Bordeaux, 1979—; lectr. law U. Bordeaux, 1980—; cons. in legal psychiatry, 1979—; expert in law cts., Bordeaux, 1974—; rsch. on mentally disordered offenders; assoc. prof. criminal law U. Bordeaux, 1997—. Author: L'information en médecine, 1993, Le Secret Médical, 1996; contbr. articles to profl. jours. Recipient Médaille Pénitentiaire, 1999, Palmes Académiques, 2000. Mem. World Forensic Psychiatry and Psychology Assn., Internat. Acad. Legal Medicine, N.Y. Acad. Scis. Office: Centre Hosp Charles Perrens, 121 Rue de la Béchade, 33076 Bordeaux France

BENFIELD, DAVID WILLIAM, philosophy educator; b. Des Moines, Jan. 12, 1941; s. Walter Edwin and Frances Louise (Brantley) B.; m. Kathleen Harris, June 22, 1980; 1 child, John David Bradshaw. BA cum laude, St. John's Coll., 1962; MA, Brown U., 1966, PhD, 1972. Instr. SUNY, Stony Brook, 1967-72, asst. prof., 1972-73; asst. prof. philosophy and religion Montclair State Coll., Upper Montclair, N.J., 1973-76, assoc. prof., 1976-91, chmn. conf. on methods in philosophy and the scis., 1983-84, chmn. acad. computing com., 1987-88; full prof., 1991—. Contbr. articles to profl. jours. Mem. Am. Philos. Assn., L.I. Philos. Soc. (pres. 1970-73), Soc. for Philosophy and Pub. Affairs (chmn. N.Y. group 1979-80), Leibniz Soc., Hume Soc., So. Soc. for Philosophy and Psychology, Phi Beta Kappa. Office: Montclair State U Dept Philosophy & Religion Upper Montclair NJ 07043

BENFIELD, ERNEST FREDERICK, ecology educator; b. Bangor, Maine, Feb. 1, 1942; s. Ernest Caldwell and Myrtle Baker Benfield; m. Elizabeth Marlene Reary, Dec. 22, 1963; children: Jonathan Frederick, Jennifer Leigh, Jason Patrick. BS in Biology, Appalachian State U., 1964, MA in Biology, 1965; PhD in Zoology, Va. Poly. Inst. and State U., 1970. Instr. Gordon Mil. Coll., Barnesville, Ga., 1965-67; asst. prof. ecology Va. Poly. Inst. and State U., Blacksburg, 1971-77, assoc. prof. ecology, 1977-85, prof. ecology, 1985—; presenter in field. Assoc. editor Am. Midland Naturalist, Notre Dame, Ind., 1982-85; contbr. articles to profl. jours. Rsch. grantee U.S. Forest Svc., 1976-81, NSF, 1979—, U.S. EPA, 1980-2000. Mem. N.Am. Benthological Soc. (assoc. editor jour. 1985-88, 93-96, interim mng. editor 1989-90, exec. chair 1988-89, pres.-elect 1993-94, pres. 1994-95), Soc. Internat. Limnologie (session chair 1989, 98), Ecol. Soc. Am. Avocations: traditional music, fishing, basketball, softball. E-mail: benfield@vt.edu. Office: Biology Dept Va Poly Inst & State Univ Blacksburg VA 24861

BENGE, PHILLIP JAMES, entrepreneur; b. London, Aug. 19, 1949; s. John Henry Rupert and Mary Catherine (Sage) B.; m. Catherine Duncan Smart, Apr. 9, 1977 (div.); children: Helena Jacqualine, Laura Marie; m. Penelope Ann Robinson, 1990. HNC Bus. Studies, North London Poly., 1969. Salesman Sealocrete, London, 1969-71; owner P.J. Benge Supplies, London, 1971-74, Resin Svcs., London, 1974-76; tech. dir. Basewise, Ltd., Norwich, Eng., 1976-78; sales mgr. Generale De Svc. Informatique, London, 1978-79; sales mktg. mgr. Applied Computing Svcs., London, 1979-81; div. mgr. Intelligence (UK) PLC, Wimbledon, Eng., 1981-83; founding dir. Dataflex, Ltd., London, 1983-86, Dataflex Design Group PLC, Wimbledon, 1986-96; mktg. dir. Reflex Magnetics Ltd., London, 1997-99; mng. dir. One Smart World Ltd, London, 1999—; dep. chmn. ISS Tech. AG, Germany, 1999—. Campaign mgr. Coombe Trust Fund, London, 1969-73; founder U.K. Modem Approvals Group, 1992—. Named Best Newcomer to Internat. Rallying, Isle of Man, 1974. Mem. Guild of Mktg., Inst. Dirs. Avocations: golf, chess, current affairs, property restoration.

BENGESSER, GERHARD, psychiatrist and neurologist; b. Wartberg, Austria, Dec. 14, 1939; s. Alois and Therese (Kaltenback) B.; m. Regina Schoeller, Aug. 26, 1989; children: Susanne, Valentina. MD, U. Innsbruck and Graz, Austria. Physician in charge of dept. Linz: Landesnervenklinik Wagner-Jauregg; speaker Med. Group, Amnesty Internat. Author: Wechselbeziehungen zwischen Psychiatrie, Psychologie und Philosophie, 2 vols.; main author: Pladoyer fuer eine mehrdimensional Psychiatrie; contbr. numerous articles to profl. jours. Fellow Internat. Acad. Eclectic Psychotherapists; mem. N.Y. Acad. Scis. Roman Catholic. Achievements include description of a superstructure in phobics. Home: Kremstalstr 15, A-4053 Haid/Ansfelden Austria Office: Wagner-Jauregg Hosp, Wagner-Jauregg Weg 15, A-4020 Linz Austria

BENGTSON, RICHARD LEE, agricultural engineer, educator; b. Clinton, Iowa, Dec. 23, 1942; s. Robert Eino and Helen Carolyn (Piper) B.; m. Neveena Jean Lee, June 27, 1970; children: Robert Lee, Rhonda Joy. BS in Agrl. Engring., U. Wyo., 1966; MS in Agrl. Engring., U. Ill., 1967; PhD in Agrl. Engring., Okla. State U., 1980. Registered profl. engr., La. Rsch. asst. dept. agrl. engring U. Ill., Urbana, Ill., 1966-67; commd. 2d. lt. U.S. Army, 1967, advanced through grades to capt., 1968; rsch. assoc. dept. agrl. engring. Okla. State U., Stillwater, Okla., 1977-80; from asst. prof. to prof. La. State U., Baton Rouge, La., 1980-92, prof. dept. biol. and agrl. engring, 1992—; adv. council Scotlandville High Sch. for Engring., Baton Rouge, 1991-94; cons. Baton Rouge (La.) Green, 1996. Contbr. articles to Transactions of the Am. Soc. Agrl. Engrs., Jour. Soil and Water Conservation, Jour. Irrigation and Drainage; assoc. editor Am. Soc. Agrl. Engrs. Recipient Tchg. award Nat. Assn. Coll. and Tchg. Agr., 1989, First Miss. Corp. award La. Agr. Experiment Station, Baton Rouge, 1995, Outstanding Advising award Nat. Acad. Advising Assn., 1995, Excellence in Environ. Rsch. award U.S. EPA, 1996, Sedberry award for Outstanding Undergrad. Tchg., 1999. Mem. Am. Soc. Agrl. Engrs. (div. chair 1995-96), Soil Water Conservation Soc., La. State U. Faculty Senate, Sigma Xi (chpt. pres. 1979-98), Gamma Sigma Delta (chpt. sec. 1965-98). Methodist. Achievements include development of subsurface drainage designs for Southern Louisiana, management practices for improved surface runoff water quality from sugarcane, GLEAMS-WT model to simulate water quality from different management practices. Assisted in the development of a new biological engineering curriculum. Office: Louisiana State U 177 Eb Doran Bldg Baton Rouge LA 70803-0001

BENGTSON, STEN OLOF, orthopedic surgeon; b. Stockholm; s. Olof and Eva (Westlund) B.; m. Hélène Lindberg, Apr. 5, 1977; children: Mårten, Jonas, Maria. BA, U. Stockholm, 1971; MD, U. Lund, Sweden, 1980, PhD, 1990. Registrar in orthops. Ctrl. Hosp. Kalmar, Sweden, 1980-85; sr. registrar, rsch. fellow U. Lund, Sweden, 1985-90; cons. orthop. surgeon Ctrl. Hosp., Växjö, Sweden, 1990—, head rheuma, shoulder and elbow surgery, 1996—. Author: The Infected Knee Arthoplasty, 1990. Recipient travelling award Swedish Soc. for Rheumatological Surgery, 1995. Avocations: bicycling, aerobics. Office: Ctrl Hosp, Dept Orthopedics, S-35185 Växjö Sweden

BEN-HAIM, SHLOMO AURAHAM, medical educator, physiologist; b. Haifa, Israel, Oct. 15, 1957; s. Avraham Bentlaum and Miriam (Tziag) Ben-H.; m. Simona Ernest; children: Yael, Yuval, Atalia, Revital. MD cum laude, Technion-Israel Inst. Tech., Haifa, 1982, DSc, 1987. Lectr. dept. physiology and biophysics Technion-Israel Inst. Tech., Haifa, 1987-90, sr. lectr. dept. physiology and biophysics, 1990-92, tenured sr. lectr. dept. physiology and biophysics, 1992-94, assoc. prof. dept. physiology and biophysics, 1994—; assoc. prof. medicine Harvard Med. Sch., Cambridge, Mass., 1993—. Reviewer Am. Heart Jour., Am. Jour. Cardiology, Am. Jour. Physiology, Circulation Rsch., Hypertension, Jour. Electrophysiology; contbr. chpts. to books and articles to profl. jours. Maj. Israeli Def. Force, 1981-89. Recipient Bernard Elkin prize for surgery, 1981, Rhoue Fellowship prize, 1987, Juludan prize for biomed. rsch., 1994, Andreas Grüntzig ETHICA award for best inventor, 1998; grantee Israel Ministry Health, 1987-89, Israel Acad. Scis. and Humanities, 1988-91, Med. Rsch. Coun., Israel-South Africa Rsch. Fund, 1988-91, Ben-Gurion Found. for Rsch., 1989, Israel Ministry Def., 1990, 91, Israel Ministry Health, 1990, German-Israel Binational Fund for Cardiovasc. Rsch., 1990-93, Am. Heart Assn.-Iowa Affiliate, 1992-93, Vital Heart Sys., 1994—. Mem. IEEE, N.Am. Soc. Pacing and Electrophysiology, Am. Fedn. Clin. Rsch., Am. Heart Assn., Fedn. Exptl. Biology, Biomed. Engring. Soc., Israel Med. Assn. Jewish. E-mail: liats@impulse.co.il. Avocations: ice skating, folk dancing, weight lifting, gourmet cooking, tree climbing. Office: 7 Etgar St, PO Box 2009, 39120 Tirat-Hacarmel Israel

BEN-HAIM, YAKOV, mechanical engineering educator, researcher; b. Chgo., Oct. 7, 1952; s. John Paul and Muriel Moulton; m. Miriam Rivka Ben-Haim, July 31, 1976; children: Zvi, Eitan, Rafael. BA, Beloit (Wis.) Coll., 1973; MA, U. Calif., Berkeley, 1978, PhD, 1978. Lectr. Technion/ Israel Inst. Tech., Haifa, 1978-85, sr. lectr., 1985-89, assoc. prof., 1989-98, prof. mech. engring., 1998—. Author: The Assay of Spatially Random Material, 1985, Robust Reliability in the Mechanical Sciences, 1996, (with Isaac Elishakoff) Convex Models of Uncertainty in Applied Mechanics, 1990; editor: (with H.G. Natke) Uncertainty: Models and Measures, 1997. Alexander von Humboldt fellow, 1992. Mem. Phi Beta Kappa. Office: Technion-Israel Inst Tech, Fac Mech Engring, Haifa Israel 32000

BENHOFF, EDWARD SPRENG, marketing professional; b. Cleve.; s. Homer E. and Helen (Spreng) B.; m. Barbara Anderson, June 28, 1958 (dec.); children: Mary Rebecca, Caroline Mae, Amy Helen; m. Jacqueline D. Chant, Aug. 21, 1993. BS, Colgate U., 1957. Claims adjuster Liberty Mutual Ins., Cleve., 1957-58, Erie, Pa., 1959—; export mgr. Hupp Corp., Cleve., 1959-70, Marus & Wimer, Cleve., 1969-70; pres. Tradecom Internat. Inc., Cleve., 1969--; bd. dirs., Cleve., Pappas & Assoc., Cleve. Contbr. articles to profl. jours. Gov. Gyro Internat. Dist. 1, 1987-88; mem. No. Ohio Dist. Export Council U.S. Dept. Commerce, Cleve., 1987--. Sgt. USNG, 1958-62. Export Devel. award Case western Res. U. sch. Mgmt. and dept. Commerce, 1970, Exporter of the Yr., U.S. Sml. Bus. Adminstrn., 1987, Disting. Svc. award, O.F.C.A. Mem. Ohio Fgn. Commerce Assn. (v.p., pres. 1974-76, 98-99), Cleve. World Trade Assn., Worldwide D-I-Y Coun. (chmn. 1997-98), Am. Soc. Internat. Execs., Nat. Assn. Export Coun., Internat. Gyro Club (dist. I gov. 1987-88). Presbyterian. Avocations: tennis, skiing, reading, walking. Home: 2967 Country Club Ln Twinsburg OH 44087-2951 Office: Tradecom Internat Inc 32750 Solon Rd Ste 9 Solon OH 44139-2846

BÉNIÈRE, FRANÇOIS JEAN-MARIE, physicist; b. Loudeac, France, May 28, 1944; s. Jean Maurice and Suzanne (Plesse) B.; m. Michelle Louise Bonnec; 1 child, Arnaud Marc-François. MS, U. Rennes, France, 1964; MS in Agrégation, U. Paris, 1966; DS, U. Orsay, France, 1970. Lectr. U. Orsay, France, 1965-68, reader, 1968-70; reader U. Paris, 1970-74; asst. prof. U. Lannion, France, 1974-79; prof. U. Rennes, France, 1979—. Author: Physics of Electrolytes, 1972; co-author: (series) Diffusion in Non-Metallic Solids, 1997; editor: Mass Transport in Solids, 1981. Comdr. French Navy Res., 1971—. Mem. Phys. French Soc., Anticorrosion Soc. Roman Catholic. Avocations: boating, fishing, shooting. Home: 28 Rue du Puits Mauger, 35000 Rennes France Office: U Rennes, 35042 Rennes France

BENIGNI, ROBERTO, actor, writer, director, producer; b. Misericordia, Arezzo, Italy, Oct. 27, 1952. Appeared in films, including Berlinguer ti voglio bene, 1977, I, Giorni cantati, 1979, Chiedo asilo, 1979, Womanlight, 1979, Luna, 1979, In the Pope's Eye, 1981, Il Minestrone, 1981, Tu mi turbi, 1983, F.F.S.S., 1983, Nothing Left To Do But Cry, 1984, Coffee and Cigarettes, 1986, Down by Law, 1986, The Little Devil, 1988, Voice of the Moon, 1989, Johnny Toothpick, 1991, Night on Earth, 1991, Son of the Pink Panther, 1993, The Monster, 1994, Life Is Beautiful, 1997 (Oscar Best Fgn. Film 1998, Oscar Best Actor 1998), Asterix and Obelix vs. Caesar, 1999; writer (films) Berlinguer ti voglio bene, 1977, Chiedo asilo, 1979; writer, dir. (films) Tu mi turbi, 1983, Nothing Left To Do But Cry, 1984, The Little Devil, 1988, Johnny Toothpick, 1991, Life Is Beautiful, 1997; writer, dir., prodr. (film) The Monster, 1994. Recipient Nastro d'Argento, David di Donatello, 1989; named hon. citizen of Cesena; Toronto Intl Film Festival, People's Choice Award, Life is Beautiful, 1998; Vancouver Intl Film Festival, Most Popular Film, Life is Beautiful, 1998; National Board of Review, NBR Award, Special Achievement in Filmmaking, Life is Beautiful, 1998; Montreal World Film Festival, People's Choice Award, Life is Beautiful, 1998; Los Angeles Intl Film Festival, Audience Award, Best Feature Film, Life is Beautiful 1998; European Film Awards, Best Actor, Life is Beautiful, 1998; Ft Lauderdale Intl Film Festival, Critic's Choice Award, Best Director, Best Actor, Life is Beautiful, 1998; Screen Actors Guild, SAG Award, Best Actor, Life is Beautiful, 1999; David di Donatello Awards, David (Italian Oscar), Best Actor, Best Director, Best Screenplay, Life is Beautiful, 1998; Cannes Film Festival, Grand Jury Prize, Life is Beautiful, 1998; Chicago Film Critics Assoc Awards, Best Foreign Language Film, Life is Beautiful, 1999; Cesar Awards, Best Foreign Film, Life is Beautiful, 1999; British Academy Awards, BAFTA Film Award, Best Actor, Life is Beautiful, 1999; American Comedy Awards, Best Comedic Actor, Life is Beautiful, 1999; American Academy Awards, Oscar for Best Actor, Life is Beautiful, 1999.

BENIGNO, MARY ANN, osteopath, surgeon; b. Paterson, N.J., Mar. 15, 1960; d. Joseph Benigno and Irene (Conte) Kundert. BA, Rutgers U., 1982; DO, Coll. Osteo. Medicine, Biddeford, Maine, 1986. Intern Doctors Hosp., Columbus, Ohio, 1986-87, resident surgery, 1987-92; fellow, resident breast oncologic surgery Meml. Sloan-Kettering Cancer Ctr., N.Y.C., 1992—; clin. instr. Ohio U. Coll. Osteo. Medicine, Athens, 1989-92. Contbr. articles to profl. jours. Named one of Outstanding Young Women of Am., 1987. Fellow Am. Coll. Osteo. Surgeons (cand.); mem. Am. Osteo. Assn. (Media Network spokesperson), AMA, Am. Cancer Soc. (spokesperson), N.J. Assn. Osteo. Physicians and Surgeons, Ohio Osteo. Assn., Internat. Skating Inst. Am., U.S. Figure Skating Assn., Bergen-Passaic Osteo. Med. Soc., N.Y. Met. Breast Cancer Group. Avocations: aerobics, weight lifting, figure skating. Office: 1265 Paterson Plank Rd Ste 3A Secaucus NJ 07094-3242

BENING, ANNETTE, actress; b. Topeka, May 29, 1958; m. Steven White (div.); m. Warren Beatty, 1992; children: Kathlyn Bening Beatty, Benjamin Beatty, Isabel Ashley Ira Beatty, Ella Corinne Beatty. Student, Mesa Coll.; theatre degree, San Francisco State U.; studied at, Am. Conservatory Theatre. Films include The Great Outdoors, 1988, Valmont, 1989, The Grifters, 1990 (Acad. award nomination best supporting actress 1990), Postcards from

the Edge, 1990, Guilty by Suspicion, 1991, Regarding Henry, 1991, Bugsy, 1991, Love Affair, 1994, Richard III, 1995, The American President, 1995, Mars Attacks!, 1996, The Siege, 1998, American Beauty, 1999 (Acad. award nom. best actress), In Dreams, 1999, What Planet Are You From, 2000; stage appearances Coastal Disturbances, 1986, (Tony award nomination 1986, Clarence Derwin award 1987, Theatre World award 1987), Spoils of War, 1988, Hedda Gabler, 1999; TV movies Manhunt for Claude Dallas, 1986. Avocations: scuba diving. Office: CAA c/o Kevin Huvane 9830 Wilshire Blvd Beverly Hills CA 90212-1804

BENIRSCHKE, KURT, pathologist, educator; b. Glueckstadt, Germany, May 26, 1924; came to U.S., 1949, naturalized, 1955; s. Fritz Franz and Marie (Luebcke) B.; m. Marion Elizabeth Waldhausen, May 17, 1952; children: Stephen Kurt, Rolf Joachim, Ingrid Marie. Student, U. Hamburg, Germany, 1942, 45-48, U. Berlin, Germany, 1943, U. Wuerzburg, Germany, 1943-44; M.D., U. Hamburg, 1948. Resident Teaneck, N.J., 1950-51, Peter Bent Brigham Hosp., Boston, 1951-52, Boston Lying-in-Hosp., 1952-53, Free Hosp. for Women, Boston, 1953, Children's Hosp., Boston, 1953; pathologist Boston Lying-in-Hosp., 1955-60; teaching fellow, assoc. Med. Sch. Harvard, 1954-60; prof. pathology, chmn. dept. pathology Med. Sch. Dartmouth, Hanover, N.H., 1960-70; prof. reproductive medicine and pathology U. Calif. at San Diego, 1970-94; chmn. dept. pathology U. Calif. at San Diego (Sch. Med.), La Jolla, 1976-79; ret. U. Calif. at San Diego, 1994; dir. research San Diego Zoo, 1975-86, trustee, 1986—, pres., 1998-2000; cons. NIH, 1957-70. Served with German Army, 1942-45. Mem. Am. Soc. Pathology, Internat. Acad. Pathology, Am. Coll. Pathology, Am. Acad. Arts and Scis., Teratol. Soc., Am. Soc. Zool. Vets. Home: 8457 Prestwick Dr La Jolla CA 92037-2023 Office: Univ Calif San Diego Pathology Dept 200 W Arbor Dr San Diego CA 92103-9000

BENISH, BARBARA LUCILLA, artist, educator; b. Orange, Calif., June 29, 1958; arrived in Czech Republic, 1993; d. Robert John Benish and Dola Mae (Holestein) Miller; life ptnr. Petr Kalny; children: Gabriela Benish-Kalná, Natalia Benish-Kalná. BA, U. Hawaii, Honolulu, 1982; MFA, Claremont U., Calif., 1988. tchr. Claremont (Calif.) U., 1987, 1991; with Acad. Applied Arts, Prague, Czech Republic, 1993, 95, 96; prof. Graphics Ateliér, Art Acad. Brno, Czech Republic. Artist: over 25 one-woman shows including: Saxon-Lee Gallery, L.A., 1989, Stadtgeschichtliche Museen Nurnberg, Germany, Galerie Behemot, Prague, Otis/Parsons Gallery, L.A., Artworks, L.A., Mánes Gallery, Prague; exhibited in over 60 group shows Santa Monica Mus. Art, L.A., Artists Mus., Lodz, 1993, P.S. 1 Mus., N.Y., 1993, Contemporary Art, London, 1995, Post Gallery, L.A., 1996, Mus. Modern Art, Prague, 1997, and many others internationally; represented in pvt. collections Stadtgeschichtliche Museen/DurerHaus, Nurnberg, Getty Mus., L.A., Libr. Congress, Washington, N.Y. Pub. Libr. Book Collection, So. Meth. U., Dallas, others. Recipient Fulbright award, Prague, 1993-94, Rsch. award Open Soc., Soros, Prague, 1995-97; grantee Cultural Affairs Dept., City of L.A., 1990, 92. Democrat. Avocation: gardening.

BENISTI, DIDIER LEON, physicist, researcher; b. Grenoble, France, Apr. 18, 1966; s. Roger and Mireille (Sadoun) B. BS, Ecole Normale Superieure, Lyon, France, 1989, MS, 1989; PhD in Physics, U. Provence, Marseille, France, 1995. Vol. nat. svc. French Ministry of Fgn. Affairs, Lisbon, Portugal, 1990-92; with French Ministry of Rsch., Marseille, 1993-96; rschr. Consorzio RFX, Padua, Italy, 1997-98; prof. physics Lycée Henri IV, Paris, 1998-2000; rschr. Commn. Atomic Energy Saclay, Gif-Sur-Yvette, France, 2000—; vis. scientist MIT, Cambridge, 1996-97. Contbr. articles to sci. jours. Lavoisier grant French Ministry Fgn. Affairs, 1996. Mem. Am. Phys. Soc., Soc. Francaise Phys., European Phys. Soc. Jewish. Avocations: piano, organ, tennis. E-mail: dbenisti@cea.fr. Office: CEA Saclay, Bât 133N, 91191 Gif-Sur-Yvette France

BENITEZ, BERTHA PRADA, bacteriologist; b. Barrancabermeja, Colombia, Oct. 21, 1964; d. Daniel and Bertha (Prada Duran) B. Degree as bacteriologist, U. Metropolitana, Barranquilla, 1989. Chief hosp. Pio XII Lab. Health Svc. Putumayo, Colon, 1991; bacteriologist Lab. Benitez Prada, Sincelejo, 1992-94, Rheuma-Immunology Lab., Sincelejo, 1994-95, Hosp. Bocagrande, Cartagena, 1991-93, Benitez Prada Lab. and Rheuma-Immunology Lab., 1994—. Bd. dirs. AIDS League, Sincelejo, 1992—; mem. Fundacion Colonia Santandereana, 1992; mem. Religious Instrn. Movement, 1993—. Roman Catholic. Avocations: aerobics, dancing, reading, television. Home: Calle 27 No 16A-46 Ap 402, Edificio Bulevar, Sincelejo Sucre, Colombia Office: Carrera 16, No 27A-28, Sincelejo Sucre, Colombia

BENITEZ, JORGE ANTONIO, microbiology educator; b. N.Y.C., July 9, 1949; s. Jose Antonio Benitez and Athala Mercedes Robles; m. Anisia Silva Cabrera, Oct. 23, 1951; children: Blanca Elena, Jorge Enrique. BS, U. Havana, Cuba, 1973, PhD, 1983. Asst. prof. Havana Higher Poly. Inst., 1973-79; rsch. scientist Nat. Ctr. Sci. Rsch., Havana, 1979-98; assoc. dir. U. Mo. Protein Core, 1998; asst. prof. Calif. State U., Fresno, 1999—; adj. assoc. prof. Havana Higher Poly. Inst., 1979-98, U. Havana, 1988-98. Rsch. grantee Internat. Found. for Sci., Sweden, 1979, 80; rsch. fellow Alexander von Humboldt Found., Germany, 1986. Mem. Am. Soc. for Microbiology. E-mail: jbenitez@csufresno.edu. Home: #212 5665 N Fresno St Apt 212 Fresno CA 93710-6057 Office: Calif State Univ Coll Sci M/S SB 73 2555 E San Ramon Ave Fresno CA 93740-8034

BENITEZ, JUAN CARLOS, technology researcher; b. La Plata, Argentina, Jan. 1, 1946; s. Juan Jose and Maria Olimpia (Gentile) B.; m. Graciela Monica Saldivar, Dec. 6, 1974; children: Juan Manuel, Maria Eugenia, Maria Juliana. Chem. Engr., Nat. U., La Plata, 1974, D in Engring., 2000. Registered chem. engr. Asst. profl. Consejo Nacional de Investigaciones Cientificas, La Plata, 1974-77, assoc. profl., 1977-80, prin. profl., 1980-82, asst. rschr., 1982-86; assoc. rschr. Commn. Investigaciones Cientificas Buenos Aires, La Plata, 1986-95, ind. rschr., 1995—; dir. Rsch. Group, La Plata, 1995-97; docent Tech. U., La Plata, 1995-97; cons. engr. Naval Rsch. Group, Puerto Belgrano, Argentina, 1980-90; cons. engr. pvt. orgn., Buenos Aires, 1980-97. Contbr. articles to profl. jours. Mem. Kindergarten Cooperation Assn., Gonnet, La Plata, 1986, First Aid Cmty. Assn., Gonnet, 1985-87, Sch. Family Cooperation Assn., Gonnet, 1988-90; sec. Commn. Club Estudiantes, La Plata, 1990-92. Recipient fellowship exch. DAAD, Bonn, Germany, 1974, CENIM/ISI, Madrid, 1992, fin. support for rsch. Rsch. Com. Buenos Aires, 1995-97. Mem. Buenos Aires Scientifics Assn., Argentine Corrosion Assn., Chem. Engr. Assn. Avocations: swimming, opera. Home: Calle 60 No411, 1900 La Plata Argentina Office: Cidepint, Av 52 e/ 121 y 122, 1900 La Plata Argentina

BENITO, GABRIEL R. GARCIA, management educator; b. Carcavelos, Portugal, Apr. 16, 1960; s. Luis and Eva (Robertstad) Garcia Benito; m. Marianne Vahl, Aug. 28, 1999. M Bus. and Econs., Norwegian Sch. Mgmt., Oslo, 1984; MPHil, Norwegian Sch. Econs., Bergen, 1992, PhD in Econs., 1995. Rsch. fellow Norwegian Inst. Rsch. in Mkgt., Oslo, 1990-91; asst. prof. Østfold Coll., Halden, 1992-94; asst. prof. Norwegian Sch. Mgmt., 1994-95, assoc. prof., 1997-99, prof., 1999—; rsch. assoc. prof. Copenhagen Bus. Sch., 1995-97; vis. rsch. scholar U. Melbourne, Australia, 1999; dir. MSc program Norwegian Sch. Mgmt., 1994-95, 97-99, head sect. internat. bus., 1997-98. Contbr. articles to profl. jours. Vis. scholar U. Melbourne, 1999; rsch. grantee Norwegian Rsch. Coun., 1999—, Norwegian Coun. Applied Social Rsch., 1990—. Mem. European Internat. Bus. Acad. (bd. dirs. 1996—), Acad. Internat. Bus., Internat. Soc. Mktg. and Devel., Acad. Mgmt. Office: Norwegian Sch Mgmt, Elias Smiths Vei 15, N-1302 Sandvika Norway

BENITO, MIGUEL, publishing executive; b. Tarancuena, Soria, Spain, May 4, 1943; arrived in Sweden, 1965; s. Gregorio Benito and Teresa Mozas; m. Vuokko Annikki Nikula, Oct. 13, 1968; children: Egil, Guisli, Gisela. Postgrad., Stockholm U., 1971. Libr. asst. Royal Libr., Stockholm, 1966-74; lectr. Sch. Librarianship, Boras, Sweden, 1974—; dir. Immigrant Inst., Boras, 1981—, Invandrarförlaget, Boras, 1978—; owner, editor Taranco Pub. House, Boras, 1985—; pres. Swedish Universal Decimal Classification Com., Stockholm, 1986-90. Author: Latinamerica in Swedish bibliography, 1971, Swedish Studies and Documents About Cuba, 1971, Manual to the Use of the UDC System, 1995, Bibliographic Control, 1995, Multilingual Dictionary in Librarianship, 1995, 97, 99, Classification Systems, 1999; editor: Swedish Universal Decimal Classification System Online. Mem. Asociacion Española de Archiveros, Bibliotecarios, Museólogos y Documentalistas, Spain, Swedish Libr. Assn., Swedish Migrant Writers Assn. (pres. 1996—), Fedn. Immigrant Assn. (pres. 1981—). Office: Immigrant Inst, Katrinedalsgatan 43, 50451 Borås Sweden

BENITO, ROBERTO PATRICIO, pulp and paper company executive; b. Buenos Aires, Argentina, Sept. 29, 1941; s. Roberto Pedro and Elena Agustina (Dominguez) B.; m. Maria Martha Devorik, Apr. 24, 1966; children: Maria Florencia, Fernando Roberto, Gonzalo Patricio. Bachelor, Nat. Coll., 1959; pub. acct., Nat. U. Buenos Aires, 1965. Sales analyst Esso S.A.P.A., Buenos Aires, 1965; fin. analyst mktg. dept. Esson S.A.P.A., Buenos Aires, 1966-67, fin. analyst treas. dept., 1968, chief of cash and banks, 1969, chief of exchange and internat. ops., 1970-71; fin. mgr. Propulsora Siderugica, Buenos Aires, 1971-75; gen. mgr. and ptnr. Cen. Nat. Argenina, Buenos Aires, 1975—. Mem. Golf Club Argentino. Roman Catholic. Avocation: golf. Home: Avenida Las Heras 1844, 1127 Buenos Aires Argentina Office: Cen Nat Argentina, Bartolone Mitre 734, 1426 Buenos Aires Argentina

BENITO-RUIZ, JESUS, plastic surgeon; b. Madrid, Spain, July 2, 1964; s. Jesus Benito and Isabel Ruiz. MD, U. Valencia, Spain, 1987, PhD, 1993, specialization in plastic surgery, 1993. Resident Hosp. Le Fe, Valencia, Queen Victoria Hosp., Eng., Emory U., Atlanta, 1987-92; asst. Hosp. Clin., Barcelona, Spain, 1993-94, adjoint in plastic surgery, 1994—. Contbr. articles to profl. jours. Recipient Gomez-Ferrer Navarro prize Acad. Medicine, Valencia, 1987, Med. Degree award U. Valencia, 1987. Mem. Spanish Soc. Plastic, Reconstructive and Aesthetic Surgery (exec. bd.), N.Y. Acad. Scis., Internat. Soc. Burn Injuries, Spanish Assn. for Microsurgery (exec. bd.). Office: Hosp Clin, C Villarroe 170 Plas Surg, 08036 Barcelona Spain

BENJAMIN, ADELAIDE WISDOM, community volunteer and activist; b. New Orleans, Aug. 23, 1932; d. William Bell and Mary (Freeman) Wisdom; m. Edward Bernard Benjamin Jr., May 11, 1957; children: Edward Wisdom, Mary Dabney, Ann Leith, Stuart Minor. Student, Hollins Coll., 1950-52; BA in English, Newcomb Coll., 1954; JD, Tulane U., 1956; student, Loyola U., New Orleans, 1980-81; grad. extension program Sewanee Theol. Sch., U. South, 1982. Assoc. Wisdom, Stone, Pigman and Benjamin, New Orleans, 1956-58; tchr. ext. courses Sewanee Theol. Sem., 1984-89; spkr., panelist on sch. issues various local and nat. groups. Mem. Tulane Law Rev., 1954-56; compiler, editor, pub. Trinity Ch. supplemental songbook, 1980. Pres. bd. New Orleans Symphony, 1984-89; mem. exec. bd. La. Philharm. Orch., 1992—; trustee, Mary Freeman Wisdom Charitable Found., sec., 1987-92, pres., 1990-94, treas., 1994—; pres. E&A Charitable Found., New Orleans, 1983—; bd. dirs. Nat. Symphony Orch., Washington, 1992-98, RosaMary Charitable Found., New Orleans, 1978—, Loyola U., New Orleans, 1989-99, mem. exec. com., 1996-99, bd. dirs. Nat. D-Day Museum, New Orleans, 1998—, La. Mus. Found. Bd., New Orleans, 1989—, mem. exec. com., 1991—, Children's Hosp., New Orleans, 1976-79, S.E. La. coun. Girl Scouts U.S., New Orleans, 1989-97, Louise S. McGehee Sch., New Orleans, 1990-97, v.p., 1991-97, hon. mem. bd. dirs., 1998—, Newcomb Children's Ctr., New Orleans, 1991-94, New Orleans Mus. Art Fellows Forum, 1991—; mem. adv. bd. dept. psychiatry La. State U. Med. Ctr., 1992—; active Trinity Episc. Ch., New Orleans, sec. parish coun., 1973-75, sec. vestry, 1975-79, leader Trinity Quartet, 1979-84; local YWCA, 1967-75, 76-79, sec. bd. dirs., 1967-68, 1st v.p., 1968-69; trustee Metairie Park Country Day Sch., 1971-79, sec., 1976-79, pres. PTA, 1975-76; mem. Loving Cup selection com. New Orleans Times Picayune, 1985; mem. adv. bd. Pub. Radio Sta. WWNO, 1980—; bd. dirs Parenting Ctr., 1981—; mem. adv. bd Tulane Summer Lyric Theatre, Tulane U., 1972—, pres. adv. bd., 1977-79; bd. dirs. Kingsley House, New Orleans, 1971-77. Recipient Weiss Brotherhood award Nat. Conf. Christians and Jews, 1986, Outstanding Philanthropist, Nat. Soc. Fundraising Execs., 1986, Volunteer Activist Award, St. Elizabeth Guild, 1986, Jr. League Sustainer award, 1987, Disting. Alumna award McGehee Sch., 1987, George Washington Honor Medal for Individual Achievement, Freedom Found. at Valley Forge, 1988, Living and Giving award Juvenile Diabetes Found. 1991, Outstanding Citizen New Orleans award La. Colonials, 1994, Jacques Yenni award Outstanding Community Svc. Sch. Bus. Adminstrn. Loyola Univ., 1994, Integritas Vitae award for outstanding cmty. svc. Loyola U., 1994, Classical Arts Patron award Tribut to the Classical Arts, 1998; named Goodwill Ambassador for Louisiana Gov.'s Commn. Internat. Trade, Industry and Tourism, 1987, Sweet Art, Contemporary Arts Ctr., 1988, Significant Role Model, Young Leadership Coun., 1988, Woman of Distinction S.E. La. Girl Scout Coun., 1992. Mem. ABA, LWV, La. Bar Assn., New Orleans Bar Assn., Jr. League New Orleans (exec. com. 1971-72, bd. dirs. 1967-72), Ind. Women's Orgn., Com. 21, Am. Symphony Orch. League, Quarante Club (2d v.p. 1978-79), Debutante Club, Le Debut des Jeunes Filles Club, New Orleans Town Gardners (pres. 1979-80), Thomas Wolfe Soc. (life mem.). Home: 1837 Palmer Ave New Orleans LA 70118-6215

BENJAMIN, ARLIN JAMES, physicist; b. Guthrie, Okla., Oct. 9, 1933; s. Harold Dinsmore and Lulu Martha (Black) B.; m. Patricia Ann Crabb, Oct. 10, 1964; children: Arlin James, Cynthia Denise, Deborah Dawn. BS, Sam Houston State Coll., 1955; MS, Okla. State U., 1957; postgrad., MIT, 1959, Wichita U., 1959-60. Rsch. engr. Boeing Co., Wichita, Kans., 1956-63; lead nuclear engr. LTV Corp., Dallas, 1963-64; ops. rsch. analyst Research Triangle Inst., Research Triangle Park, N.C., 1964-66; sr. ops. rsch. analyst Gen. Dynamics Corp., Ft. Worth, 1966-68; mgr. Control Data Corp., Honolulu, 1968-70; sr. scientist S.W. Rsch. Inst., San Antonio, 1970-78; prin. scientist Hittman Assocs. Inc., Sacramento, Calif., 1978-81; mgr., sr. staff mem. BDM Corp., Hawthorne, Calif., 1981-86; prin. engr. Northrop Grumman Corp., Midwest City, Okla., 1995—, Pico Rivera, Calif., 1986-95. Contbr. articles to profl. jours. Mem. Am. Geophys. Union, Am. Nuclear Soc., Am. Phys. Soc., Inst. Physics, Phys. Soc. London, European Phys. Soc., Inst. Mgmt. Sci., Alpha Chi, Pi Gamma Mu.

BENJAMIN, EDWARD BERNARD, JR., lawyer; b. New Orleans, Feb. 11, 1923; s. Edward Bernard and Blanche (Sternberger) B.; m. Adelaide Wisdom, May 11, 1957; children: Edward Wisdom, Mary Dabney, Ann Leith, Stuart Minor. BS, Yale U., 1944; JD, Tulane U., 1952. Bar: La. 1952. Practiced in New Orleans, since 1952; ptnr. Jones, Walker, Waechter, Poitevent, Carrere & Denegre, New Orleans, 1967—; pres. Am. Coll. Probate Counsel, 1986-87, Internat. Acad. Estate and Trust Law, 1976-78; vice chmn. bd. trustees Southwestern Legal Found., 1980-88, bd. dirs., 1988-90; chmn. bd. Starmount Co., Greensboro, N.C., 1968-88, chmn. emeritus, 1988—. Editor-in-chief Tulane U. Law Rev., 1951-52; mem. editorial bd. Community Property Jour., 1974-89. Trustee Hollins Coll., 1966-87; chancellor Episcopal Diocese of La., 1984—, Trinity Episcopal Ch., New Orleans, 1974-92; mem. adv. bd. CCH Estate & Fin. Planning Svc., 1982-88; chmn. Salavation Army City Commd. Adv. Bd., 1965-68; pres. New Orleans Jr. C. of C., 1953. 1st lt., F.A. pilot, U.S. Army, 1943-46. Mem. Am. Coll. Tax Counsel, Am. Law Inst., ABA (sec. taxation sect. 1967-68, coun. 1976-79, coun. real property, probate and trust law sect. 1978-81), La. Bar Assn. (chmn. taxation sect. 1959-60), La. Law Inst., La. Bar Found. (trustee 1998-99), New Orleans Country Club, Southern Yacht Club, New Orleans Lawn Tennis Clu. Home: 1837 Palmer Ave New Orleans LA 70118-6215 Office: Jones Walker Waechter Poitevent Carrere & Denegre 201 Saint Charles Ave Fl 51 New Orleans LA 70170-1000

BENJAMIN, GEORGE WILLIAM JOHN, composer, conductor, educator; b. London, Jan. 31, 1960; s. William and Susan (Bendon) B. Student, Westminster Sch., Paris Conservatoire, King's Coll., Cambridge, IRCAM, Paris. Prof. composition Royal Coll. of Music, 1986—; performed, lectr. Great Britain, Europe, U.S., and Far East; founding artistic dir. Wet Ink Festival, San Francisco Symphony Orch., 1992, Meltdown Festival, South Bank, 1993, Artistic Con., BBC Radio 3, Sounding the Century, 1996-99; composer in residence Tanglewood, 1999. Prin. guest artist Hallé Orch., 1993-96, Carte Blanche at Opéra Bastille, Paris, 1992; orchestra works Ringed by the Flat Horizon, 1980, A Mind of Winter, 1981, At First Light, 1982, Jubilation, 1985, Antara, 1987, Sudden Time, 1989-93, 3 Inventions for Chamber Orchestra, 1993-95, Sometime Voices, 1996, chamber music Sonata for Violin and Piano, 1977, Piano Sonata, 1978, Octet, 1978, Flight, 1979, Sortilèges, 1981, Three Studies for Piano, 1985, Upon Silence, 1990, Viola, Viola, 1997, Palimpsest, 2000; featured composer 75th Salzburg Festival, 1995; operatic conductor Pelléas et Mélisande, 1999. Recipient Lili Boulanger award, 1985, Koussevitzky Internat. Record award, 1987, Grand Prix du disque de l'Académie Charles Cros, 1987, Gramophone Contemporary award, 1990, Chevalier dans l'Ordre des Arts et Lettres, 1996, Edison award, 1998. Fellow Royal Coll. Music (London, hon.); mem. Bavarian Acad. Fine Arts. Office: Faber Music, 3 Queen Square, London WCIN 3AU, England

BENJAMIN, JAMES SCOTT, lawyer; b. Miami Beach, Fla., Aug. 28, 1954; s. Julian R. Benjamin and June Lois Garvin; m. Laura Cipolla, Mar. 5, 1989; children: Kaitlyn, Courtney. BS in Advt., U. Fla., 1976; JD, Samford U., 1979. Bar: Fla. 1980, U.S. Dist. Ct. (so. dist.) Fla. 1981, U.S. Dist. Ct. (mid. dist.) Fla. 1989, U.S. Ct. Appeals (11th cir.) 1989, U.S. Dist. Ct. (we. dist.) Tex. 1993, U.S. Supreme Ct. 1994. Assoc. Krause Reinhard & Pozen, Miami, Fla., 1980-81; asst. state atty. 17th Jud. Cir. Broward County, Ft. Lauderdale, Fla., 1981-84; shareholder Benjamin & Aaronston P.A., Ft. Lauderdale, 1984—; presenter/lectr. in field. Author, columnist Xcitement Mag., 19905, Screw Mag., 19985. Bd. dirs. Arthritis Found., Ft. Lauderdale, 1998, treas., 19995. Mem. Fla. Assn. Criminal Def. Attys. (bd. dirs. 19985), Broward County Assn. Criminal Def. Lawyers (v.p. 1997-98, pres. 1998-99), First Amendment Lawyers Assn., Free Speech Coalition, Inns of Ct. Avocation: fly fishing. Office: Benjamin & Aaronson PA Ste 1615 One Financial Plaza Fort Lauderdale FL 33394

BENJAMIN, RALPH, electronics researcher; b. Darmstadt, Hessen, Germany, Nov. 17, 1922; s. Charles and Claire (Stern) B.; m. Kathleen Ruth Bull, Sept. 8, 1951; children: John David (dec.), Michael Frank. BS with 1st class hons., London U., 1944, PhD, 1964, DS, 1970, D of Engring. (hon.), 2000. With Royal Naval Scientific Svc., U.K., 1944-60; head of rsch. Admiralty Surface Weapons Est., 1960-64; dir. Admiralty Underwater Weapons Est., 1964-71; supt. dir. Govt. Comms. HQ, 1971-82; head comms. techs. and networks Shape Tech. Ctr./NATO, 1982-87; vis. prof. electronics rsch. at various univs., 1988—; cons. to various dept. govt. Author: Modulation, Resolution and Signal Processing, 1966, (autobiography) Five Lives in One, 1996; patentee in field; contbr. articles to profl. jours. Companion Order of the Bath, HM The Queen, 1980. Fellow Royal Acad. of Engring., City and Guilds of London, Western Centre Inst. of Elec. Engrs. (ex-chmn.); mem. Ct. Brunell U. Avocations: hill walking, water sports, langs., work. Home: 13 Bellhouse Walk, Rockwell Park, Bristol BS11 OUE, England

BENJAMIN, RUTH, writer; b. Tacoma, Mar. 5, 1934; d. Samuel David Turteltaub and Rebecca Shallit; m. Arthur Isaac Rosenblatt, Aug. 5, 1956; children: Paul, Judy. BA, Sarah Lawrence Coll., 1956. Circulation dept. staff The Am. Inst. Physics, N.Y.C., 1953-54; prodn. asst. Esquire, Inc., N.Y.C., 1955-56; asst. editor Hillman Periodicals, N.Y.C., 1957-58; devel. dept. staff Poets & Writers, Inc., N.Y.C., 1983-84; adminstrv. asst. RKK&G Mus. & Cultural Facilities Cons., 1995—. Author: Naked at Forty, 1984, Movie Song Catalog, 1993. Mem. The Authors Guild, Inc., The Players. Avocations: reading, theater, cabaret. Home: 1158 5th Ave New York NY 10029-6917

BENKHOFF, JOHANNES, chemist, researcher; b. Rhede, Westfalen, Germany, Feb. 15, 1966; Karl and Liesel (Schröer) B. Diploma, U. Bochum, Germany, 1991; D Natural Sci., U. Essen, Germany, 1994. Sci. rschr. U. Bochum, 1991-92, U. Essen, 1992-95; postdoctoral fellow Harvard U., Cambridge, Mass., 1995-97; rsch. chemist Ciba SC, Basel, Switzerland, 1998—. Author: Synthesis and Properties of Sterically Rigid Macrocycles and Molecular Tweezers for the Study of Non Kovalent Interactions in Host-Guest-Komplexes, 1994. With German mil., 1985-86. Roman Catholic. Avocations: soccer, volleyball, jogging, playing the cello. E-mail: johannes.benkhoff@cibasc.com. Home: St Alban-Rheinweg 212, CH-4052 Basel Switzerland Office: R-1047.2.20, CIBA SC, CH-4002 Basel Switzerland

BENKIPUR, VIDYASHANKAR SADASIVARAO, mechanical engineer, consultant, researcher; b. Tumkurtown, Karnataka, India, Nov. 27, 1931; s. Sadasivarao Subbarao and Anasuyabai (Sadasivarao) B.; m. Champa Vidyashankar, Aug. 20, 1964; children: Meenakshi, Dayanand. BEng, Mysore (India) U., 1953. Jr. engr. Chambal Hydro-Electric Project, Kotah, India, 1955-57; asst. engr. Hindustan Steel Ltd., Bhilai, India, 1957-61; asst. exec. engr. Neyveli Lignite Corp., India, 1961-62; asst. plant engr. Fertilizer Corp. India, Bombay, 1962-67; chief project engr. Montreal Engring. Internat., Bombay, 1967-75; project mgr. Friedrich Uhde GmbH, Bombay, 1975-77; cons. Gohel Cons., Bangalore, India, 1978-80; head project engring. dept. Khoday Engring., Bangalore, 1980-83; cons. engr. self employed, Bangalore, 1983—; v.p. Riper Found., Bangalore, 1993—; co-author, dep. leader rsch. publ. Inernational Productivity Handbook, 1995. Mem. Indian Inst. World Culture, Bangalore, 1979—, Jayanagar Study Ctr., Bangalore, 1993—. Fellow Instn. Engrs. India; mem. ASME. Hindu. Avocations: photography, chess, spiritual quest, scientific studies. Home: 1337 32 E Cross 4th T Block, Jayanagar/Bangalore 560041, India Office: Riper Found, 19 Puttalingaiah Rd, Padmanabhanagar, Bangalore 560070, India

BENKO, LINDSAY, Olympic athlete; b. Elkhart, Ind., Nov. 29, 1976. Degree in comms., U. So. Calif., 1999. Recipient Gold medal 4 x 200-meter freestyle (team) Sydney Olympics, 2000, Silver medal 4 x 200-meter relay (team) World Championships, 1998, 200-meter backstroke, 400-meter freestyle summer nats., 1999, Silver medal 200-meter and 400-meter freestyle Pan Pacific Championships, 1999; winner NCAA title in 500-meter freestyle and 200-meter backstroke, 1996, 97, 500-meter freestyle. Office: USA Swimming 1 Olympic Plz Colorado Springs CO 80909-5746*

BENKOVITCH, BORIS ILICH, pharmacologist; b. Vladicacasus, Russia, Apr. 23, 1945; s. Ilia Lvovitch and Rose Iosiphovna (Bogatina) B. Diploma of physician, Med. Inst., Minsk, 1968; PhD in Biology, Latv U., Riga, 1973; D of Med. Scis., Russian Acad. Med. Sci., Moscow, 1990. Rschr. labor clinic psychopharm. Russian Acad. Med. Sci., Moscow, 1968-80, scholar labor clinic psychopharm., 1980-84; scholar dept. borderline psych. Serbsky Nat. Rsch. Ctr., Moscow, 1984-90, chief lab. psychophys. neureveget., 1990—; cons. in field. Author: Psychopharmacology Preparations and Nervous System, 1999; contbr. articles to profl. jours. Active Acad. People of the World, Montreal, 1996. Mem. Internat. Acad. Energyinformative, Moscow Acad. Nat. Sci., N.Y. Acad. Sci. Avocations: chess, swimming, travel, skiing.

BENMBAREK, JILANI, business executive; b. Tunisia, July 8, 1947; s. M'Barek M.B. and Meryem (Boundka) B.; children: Islem, Malek, Donia. M in Physics, U. Tunis, 1968; AEA, Thermodynamics U., Poitiers, France; postgrad., Ecole Nat. Superieur De Mechanique, France, 1971. Journalist for sports newspaper Tunisia, 1963-68; prin. engr. Tunis Air, Tunisia, 1971-73; resident rep. Tunis Air at Boeing Co., Seattle, 1973; chmn. bd. Oasis Tech. Corp., Tunisavia, mng. dir., 1974—; chmn. J.B. Holding, Sodesco Internat.; pres. GE Mech. Sys.; rep. in Tunisia of Reda Pumps Ltd.; pres. Utica Ariana, Tunis, PGD Gizak, P.D.6 Petromed, Groupement de Maintenance et de Gestion, Z.I., Ksau, Said; bd. dirs. Office de L'Aviation Civile et des Aeroports, Office de la Marine Marchande et Des Ports. Mem. Airlines Orgn. Planning Adminstrn. Assn. (exec. com.), Chamber Mixt Tuniso-Egyptian, C. of C. and Industrie Tunis (first v.p.). Home: 22 Rue 7131 El Manar 2, 2092 El Manar 2 Tunis Tunisia Office: ZI Ksar Saïd, 20 rue du Bois, 280 Ksar Said Tunis Tunisia

BEN-MENAHEM, ARI, geophysics educator, researcher; b. Berlin, Nov. 4, 1928; s. Ben-Menahem Moshe and Sarah Leah Schlanger Epelbaum; m. Batia Schneiderman; children: Shahar, Noga. MS, Hebrew U., 1954; PhD, Calif. Inst. Technology, Pasadena, 1960. Prof. Weizmann Inst. Sci., Israel, 1965—; vis. prof. MIT, 1983-84, 87-89, 90-93, 95, U. Paris, 1994, Stanford U., 1975-77; dir. Adolpho Bloch Geophys. Observatory, Israel, 1972-94; Samuel and Ayala Zacks chair Geophysics, Weizmann Inst. Sci., Israel, 1972—; chief seismologist, Prime Minister's Office, Israel, 1954-58. Contbr. articles to profl. jours.; author: (textbook) Seismic Waves and Sources, 1981. Office: Weizmann Inst Sci, 76100 Rehovot Israel

BENN, DOUGLAS FRANK, information technology and computer science executive; b. Detroit, May 8, 1936; s. Frank E. and Madeline (Pond) B.; m. Shirley M. Flanery, July 16, 1955; children—Christopher, Susan, Kathy. BS in Math., Mich. State U., 1960, MA, 1962; cert. data processing (NSF scholar), Milw. Inst. Tech., 1965; postgrad., U. Wis., 1965-66; Ed.Adminstrn., Washington U., 1972; MS in Computer Sci., So. Meth. U., 1982, D of Engring. in Computer Sci., 1990. Tchr. math. and sci. Lansing

(Mich.) Public Schs., 1960-64; chmn. computer sci. dept. Kenosha (Wis.) Area Tech. Inst., 1964-67, mgr. data processing, 1965-67; sr. project leader Abbott Labs., North Chicago, Ill., 1967-68, world-wide sr. IT cons. (67 countries), 1968-69; dir. data processing div. St. Louis Public Schs., 1969-74; dir. info. systems div. mental health State of Ill., Springfield, 1974-78; v.p., chief info. officer Med. Computer Systems, Inc., Dallas, 1978; dir. bus. adminstrn. Dallas County Mental Health Center, 1979-80; prof. computer sci. So. Meth. U., Dallas, 1979-82, 89-96; sr. dir. corp. research and devel. Blue Cross & Blue Shield of Tex., Dallas, 1980-83; v.p., chief info. services Western States Adminstrs., Fresno, Calif., 1984-88; chmn., pres. D.F. Benn & Assocs. Inc., 1989—; prof. Info. Tech. U. Tex., Dallas, 1990-92, 2000—; chief info. officer Tex. Natural Resource Conservation Commn., 1996-98; exec. dir. for tech. Corpus Christi Ind. Sch. Dist., 1998-99; lectr. and adv. coun. Great Cities Pub. Sch. Sys., 1969-74; chief info. officer Ill. Dept. Mental Health and Developmental Disabilities, 1974-78, Wis. Bd. Vocat. Tech. and Adult Edn., 1964-67; co-dir. mgmt. adv. group Ill. Dept. Mental Health, 1974-78; mem. adv. group Tex. Gov.'s Task on Mental Health, 1980; adj. prof. computer info. sys. Wash. U., 1972-74; expert witness/software appraisal svcs. U.S. Tax Ct., 1995, Info. Tech. State of Tex., 1997-99, Strategic Planning Coun., 1997, Geog. Info. Sys. Coun., 1997—, Nat. Gov.'s Assn./EPA Joint Task Force Electronic Commerce, 1997-99. Contbr. articles on info. techs., engring. mgmt., and software valuation to profl. jours. Arbitrator computer and bus. contract cases, 1976—. Mem. Data Processing Mgmt. Assn., Assn. for Sys. Mgmt. (Disting. Svc. award 1980, Merit award 1976, Achievement award 1978, chpt. pres. 1976-77, dist. dir. 1976-78), Am. Arbitration Assn., Data Processing Mgmt. Assn. (bd. dirs. 1987-89), Am. Soc. Engring. Mgmt. Presbyterian. E-mail: dougbenn@aol.com. Home and Office: 3417 Mount Vernon Way Plano TX 75025-3611

BENN, RAYMOND CHRISTOPHER, materials engineer; b. London, Oct. 20, 1946; came to U.S., 1977; s. Frank Abraham and Eileen Mabel (Ashford) B.; m. Pamela Scott Woodhouse, Apr. 8, 1979; children: Briana Crawford, Britanny Ashford. Chem. engring. candidate, London U., 1965-66; BSc with 1st class honors in Metallurgy, U. Surrey, Eng., 1970; MBA, U. New Haven, 1995. Chartered engr., U.K.; registered profl. engr., Conn. Devel. metallurgist Delta Materials Rsch., 1970-74; rsch. metallurgist Inco Alloys Ltd., Hereford, Eng., 1974-77; sect. mgr. Inco Alloy Products Co. Rsch. Ctr., Suffern, N.Y., 1977-82, prin. metallurgist, 1982-84; group leader, sr. metallurgist Inco Alloys Internat., Inc., Huntington, W.Va., 1984-89; staff engr. Allied Signal Engines (Textron-Lycoming), Stratford, Conn., 1989-95; chief technologist Wyman-Gordon Co., Groton, Conn., 1995-2000; prin. scientist United Techs. Rsch. Ctr., East Hartford, Conn., 2000—; tech. presenter in field. Contbr. more than 50 articles to profl. publs.; co-author 2 books in field. Recipient Innovative P/M award European Powder Metallurgy Assn., 1992. Fellow ASM (chmn. specialty materials divsn. 1988-92, chmn. W.Va. chpt. 1986-87, chmn. Hudson Valley chpt. 1983-84, chmn. heat resistant materials group 1983-88, Chpt. chmn. award 1984, 87, nominating com. 1985), Inst. Materials; mem. TMS-AIME, Sigma Xi. Congregational. Achievements include research in developing alloys (including mechanical alloying techniques) and materials technology for high temperature/performance applications in aerospace and industry; over 25 patents in field. Avocations: boating, archery, calligraphy, rowing. Office: United Techs Rsch Ctr 411 Silver Ln Hartford CT 06118-1127

BENNA, CARLO, astrophysicist, researcher; b. Turin, Italy, May 14, 1962; s. Giovanni and Olga Benna. PhD in Physics, U. Turin, 1991. External fellow European Space Agy., Paris, 1993, 94; vis. scientist Smithsonian Instn., Washington, 1993-94, 96-97; rschr. Inter-Univ. Consortium Spatial Physics, Turin, 1996-97; owner Benna Software, Turin, 1995-96; astrophysicist, rschr. Astron. Obs. of Turin, 1997—; software cons. Obs. of Turin, 1995-96, Arcetri Obs., Florence, Italy, 1995; assoc. Harvard U., Cambridge, Mass., 1993—; UVCS lead observer NASA Goddard Space Flight Ctr., Greenbelt, Md., 1997, 98, 99, 2000; assoc. scientist Ultraviolet Coronagraph Spectrometer/Solar and Heliospheric Obs. project European Space Agy./NASA, 1996—. Contbr. articles to profl. jours. Coord. environ. protection assn. Legambiente, Turin, 1988-90, Ischia (NA), 1999. Grantee NASA, 1995, European Space Agy., 1996. Avocations: tennis, skiing, canoeing, auto races, diving. Home: Strada Val San Martino 92, 10131 Turin Italy Office: Astron Observatory of Turin, Strada Osservatorio 20, 10025 Pino Torinese (To) Italy

BENNER, CHARLES HENRY, retired music educator; b. Fort Recovery, Ohio, Feb. 4, 1912; s. Henry Farraday and Ida Matilda (Denney) B.; m. Mary Arbutus Kautz; children: Charles Jonathan, Susan Elizabeth, Daniel Farraday. BS in Edn., Wittenberg U., 1935; MEd, U. Cinn., 1947; PhD, Ohio State U., 1963. Tchr. music, gen. subjects Pub. Schs., Butler County, Ohio, 1934-42; prin. Lemon-Monroe Sch., Ohio, 1946-48; tchr. music, math. Wyoming, Ohio, 1948-58; mem. faculty Sch. Music Ohio State U., Columbus, 1958-68; mem. faculty Coll. Conservatory Music U. Cinn., 1968-79, ret., 1979, prof. emeritus, 1979—; pres. N. Ctrl. Divsn. Music Educators Nat. Conf., 1965-67; U.S. del. internat. symposium October-Art-Children, Moscow, 1977; cons. to Australia Coun. and Australia Soc. Music Edn., Canberra, 1980; vis. prof. music edn. Cath. U., Washington, 1981-82; mem. faculty Brigham Young U., Provo, Utah, summer 1974. Author: From Research to the Classroom: Teaching Performing Groups, 1972; co-author: Music in General Education, 1965. Reader Radio Reading Svc., Cinn., 1990—. With USCG, Maryland, 1942-43, Deck Ofcr., Lt. jg., PTO, 1944-46. Recipient Disting. Svc. award Ohio Music Edn., 1971, Ohio Music Edn. Dist. Svc. Awd., 1971, Canticum Novum award Wittenberg U., Springfield, Ohio, 1973, U. Cincinnati Coll., Conservatory of Music, Dist. Svc. Awd., 1979. Mem. Ohio Music Assn. (pres. 1958-60, disting. svc. award 1971), Internat. Soc. Music Edn. (bd. dirs. 1974-76), Music Educators Nat. Conf. (life, pres. 1974-76). Home: 5610 Windridge Dr Cincinnati OH 45243-2987

BENNER, PETER CHARLES, solicitor; b. Cheshunt, Eng., June 1, 1937; s. Charles William and Joyce (Oldroyd) B.; m. Elizabeth Anne Kenyon, Jan. 16, 1965; children: Tracy Caroline Alice, Lucinda Diana Kate. Student, Ardingly Coll., Sussex, England, 1950-56; BA, Downing Coll., Cambridge, England, 1959, MA, 1963. Articled clk. Evan-Davies & Co., London, 1959-61; asst. solicitor Berry & Berry, Tunbridge Wells, Kent, Eng., 1963-65; asst. and ptnr. Charles Benner & Son, Crawley, Sussex, Eng., 1965-86; ptnr. Houseman Rohan & Benner, Crawley, Haywards Heath, Eng., 1986—; notary pub., 1979—; chmn. Mid Sussex Solicitors Group, Haywards Heath, 1983-84. Chmn. Sussex County Young Conservatives, 1965-66; treas. S.E. Area Young Conservatives, 1966-67. Mem. United Oxford & Cambridge Univ. Club, Law Soc. (London). Avocations: old cars, dog walking, Sussex local history. Home: Pear Trees Warninglid, Haywards Heath RH17 5TY, England Office: Houseman Rohan & Benner, Aberdeen House South Road, Haywards Heath RH16 4NG, England

BENNER, RICHARD BYRON, philosophy educator; b. Somers Point, N.J., Dec. 6, 1936; s. Theodore Roosevelt and Carolyn Mildred (Wilkinson) B.; m. Ethel Barbara Blair, June 7, 1958 (div. Oct. 1996); children: Richard Byron Jr., Kathryn Lynn, Cheryl Susan; m. Linda Jean Foster, Dec. 24, 1996; 1 stepchild, Genevieve Lynn Fox. BA, Villanova U., 1969; MS, Fla. State U., 1972; postgrad., U. Pa., 1972—. Clin. lab. chief Shore Meml. Hosp., Somers Point, N.J., 1961-62; med. rschr. Bryn Mawr (Pa.) Hosp., 1962-71; office mgr. O.C. Plumbers, Inc., Ocean City, N.J., 1972-79; plumbing contractor Doctor's Plumbing and Heating, Ocean City, 1979-85; hist. preservationist R.B. Benner and Son, Ocean City, 1985-93; animal care specialist Wildlife Aid, Inc., English Creek, N.J., 1993-95; instr. philosophy Atlantic Cape C.C. (formerly Atlantic C.C.), Mays Landing, N.J., 1995-99; asst. prof. philosophy and religion Atlantic Cape C.C. (formerly Atlantic C.C.), Mays Landing, 1999—; spkr. in field; adj. assoc. prof. philosophy Ocean County Coll., Toms River, N.J., 1998-99. Contbr. articles, photographs to profl. publs. Founder, pres. Ocean City Hist. Preservation Soc., 1986-90. With U.S. Army, 1958-61; vol. U.S. Dept. Interior, N.J. Divsn. Fish and Game. Recipient 1st place photo award Egg Harbor Twp., 1995, 96, cert. of recognition Exch. Club, 1991. Mem. Am. Philos. Assn., Philosophy Edn. Soc., Audubon Soc., Nature Conservancy, Nat. Wildlife Fedn., World Wildlife Fund, Sierra Club, Mensa. Avocations: outdoor and wildlife photography, conservation. E-mail: rbenner@atlantic.edu. Home: 6037 Main St Mays Landing NJ 08330-1896

BENNETT, BROOKE, Olympic athlete; b. May 6. Grad. high sch., Plant City, Fla., 1998. Swimmer; winner gold and silver medals Pan-Am Games, 1995; winner gold medal Pan Pacific Games, 1995, 97; gold medalist 800m freestyle Olympic Summer Games, 1996; sponsor Brandon Blue Wave; gold medalist 400m freestyle, Sydney, 2000, 800m freestyle, Sydney, 2000. Avocation: horse-back riding. Office: c/o USA Swimming 1 Olympic Plz Colorado Springs CO 80909-5746

BENNETT, CARL DOUGLAS, English language educator, writer; b. Waycross, Ga., July 22, 1917; s. George Alexander and Tivvie V. Spell Bennett; m. Margaret Weir, Apr. 10, 1942; children: Katharine B. Gregg, Susan B. Tucker, Patty B. Uffelman. AB with honors, Emory U., 1940, MA in English, 1944, PhD in English, 1962. Instr. in English West Ga. Coll., Carrollton, Ga., 1941-42; from asst. to assoc. prof. English Wesleyan Coll., Macon, Ga., 1944-59; prof. English St. Andrews Presbyn. Coll., Laurinburg, N.C., 1959-82, chmn. Afro-Asian cultures, 1963-67, chmn. humanities and fine arts divsn., 1973-78, disting. prof. English, 1982-88, disting. prof. English emeritus, 1988—; lectr. in lit. various instns., Africa and Asia, 1962, 79, 80; vis. prof. Seinan Gakuin, Fukuoka, Japan, 1980-81. Author: (book) Joseph Conrad, 1991; contbr. articles to ency. and profl. publs. Chmn. Macon Interracial Com., 1953-54; dir. interns in industry projects Am. Friends Svc. Com., Atlanta, 1953, 54; vol. Boy Scouts Am., Literacy Coun., Habitat for Humanity, others. Fulbright-Hays grantee Indian Civilization, New Delhi and Mysore, India, 1964, NEH grantee, 1978, Carnegie grantee. Mem. MLA, AAUP, South Atlantic chpt. MLA, Scotland County Inst. for Lifelong Learning. Democrat. E-mail: bennett@tartan.sapc.edu. Office: St Andrews Presbyn Coll Laurinburg NC 28352

BENNETT, DAVID HINKLEY, lawyer; b. Portage, Wis., Sept. 18, 1928; s. Ross and Helen (Hinkley) B.; m. LaVonne Wilson, Feb. 3, 1955; children: Mark H., Todd W., John D. BBA, U. Wis., 1952, LLB, 1956. Bar: Wis. 1956, U.S. Ct. Appeals (7th cir.) 1962, U.S. Supreme Ct. 1966. Ptnr. Bennett & Bennett, Portage, 1956—; dist. atty. Columbia County, Wis., 1959-67; regent Wis. State Univs., 1965-71. Served to 2d lt. AUS, 1953-56. Mem. ABA, Wis. Bar Assn. Republican. Presbyterian. Lodge: Masons. Home: 215 W Franklin St Portage WI 53901-1643 Office: Bennett and Bennett 135 W Cook St # 30 Portage WI 53901-2103

BENNETT, DOROTHY CATHERINE, cell biology educator, researcher; b. Leicester, Eng., Feb. 16, 1954; d. Herbert William and Eileen Mary (Talbot) B.; m. Robert Frederick Brooks, Apr. 4, 1981; children: Rachel, Helen. BA with honors, Cambridge (Eng.) U., 1975, MA, 1979; PhD, London U., 1979; rsch. student, Imperial Cancer Rsch. Fund, London, 1975-79. Postdoctoral fellow Salk Inst., Calif., 1979-80, Imperial Cancer Rsch. Fund, London, 1980-83; from asst. prof. to assoc. prof. St. George's Hosp. Med. Sch., London, 1987-93, chair in cell biology, 1999—; mem. adv. panel Vitiligo Soc., 1995—. Contbr. articles to sci., biomed., and cancer jours., also rev. chpts. to books. Mem. Amnesty Internat., Friends of the Earth, Save Brit. Sci. Soc. Cancer Rsch. Campaign grantee St. George's Hosp. Med. Sch., 1983-87; Runyon-Winchell Cancer Fund fellow, 1979, Imperial Cancer Rsch. Fund fellow, 1980-83; Fulbright-Hays sr. travel scholar, 1979-80. Mem. Coun. European Soc. for Pigment Cell Rsch., Brit. Assn. for Cancer Rsch., Brit. Soc. for Devel. Biology, Brit. Soc. for Cell Biology (Seiji Meml. award 1999). Avocations: music, literature, hiking. Office: St George's Hosp Med Sch, Cranmer Ter, London SW17 ORE, England

BENNETT, EDWARD VIRDELL, JR., surgeon; b. Nashville, July 17, 1947; s. Edward Virdell and Florence Elaine (Nelson) B. BA in Biology, Fisk U., 1969; MD cum laude, Ohio State U., 1973. Fellow in surgery Johns Hopkins U., Balt., 1973-75; intern, then resident Johns Hopkins Hosp., Balt., 1973-75; resident in surgery and cardiothoracic surgery Albany Med. Ctr. Hosp., N.Y., 1975-80; instr. in surgery Albany Med. Ctr. Hosp., 1976-80; asst. prof. surgery Health Ctr. U. Tex.-San Antonio, 1980-83; practice medicine specializing in cardiothoracic surgery Sayre, Pa., 1983-91; chief cardiac surgery Guthrie Clinic Ltd., Sayre, 1990-91; mem. Staff Robert Packer Hosp., Sayre, 1983-91; mem. Guthrie Clinic, Ltd., Sayre, 1983-91; cardiac surgeon Albany Cardiothoracic Surgeons, P.C., 1991—; mem. staff Albany Med. Ctr. Hosp., 1991—, St. Peters Hosp., Albany, 1991—; clin. asst. prof. Albany Med. Coll., 1991—; chief cardiac surgery St. Peter's Hosp., Albany, 1997—. Contbr. articles to med. jours. Producer med. motion picture. Mem. N.Y. State Cardiac Adv. Com., 1995—. Fellow Am. Coll. Chest Physicians, Am. Coll. Cardiology, ACS; mem. Soc. Thoracic Surgeons, Internat. Soc. for Heart Transplantation, Sigma Xi, Alpha Omega Alpha, Omega Psi Phi. Republican. Episcopalian. Avocations: sailing, scuba diving, skiing. Office: Albany Cardiothoracic Surgeons 319 S Manning Blvd Ste 301 Albany NY 12208-1790

BENNETT, SISTER ELSA MARY, secondary education educator; b. Muskegon, Mich., Dec. 13, 1930; d. Thomas B. and Elsa (Koelbel) B. BS, Our Lady of Lake Coll., San Antonio, 1955, MEd, 1971. Registered massage therapist, Tex.; Reiki master. Tchr. phys. edn. parochial schs., Abilene, Tex., Tulsa, San Antonio, Houston, Ennis, Tex., Alexandria, La., 1954-69; tchr., coach parochial schs., San Antonio, 1969-74, 86-87, pub. schs., Mich., 1974-78; tchr. St. Augustine Sch., Laredo, Tex., 1978-79; adminstr., coach Our Lady of Lake U., 1979-86; phys. therapy aide Warm Springs Rehab., San Antonio, 1989-90; tchr. San Antonio Ind. Sch. Dist., 1990—; with pub. rels. dept. San Antonio City Parks and Recreation Dept., 1987-89. Instr. ARC, San Antonio, 1952. Mem. AAHPER and Dance, Tex. Assn. Health, Phys. Edn., Recreation and Dance. Avocations: golf, swimming, sailing, bowling, travel. Home: 2318 Town Grove Dr San Antonio TX 78238-5023

BENNETT, GENEVIEVE, artist; b. Chgo., Feb. 11, 1927; d. Joseph and Mary Sieczka; m. William A. Bennett, Jan. 31, 1953; children: William George, J. Daniel, Gordon Dean. BA, Calif. State U., Fullerton, 1974; MA, Calif. State U., Long Beach, 1978. Artist Anaheim, Calif.; part-time tchr. art Ebell Club Anaheim, 1985-97, art tchr. Whittier and Anaheim, Calif.; lectr. on N.Am. temple mound builders. One-woman shows include Calif. Poly. U., Ponoma, 1995, Orange County Fair, Calif., 1995, Anaheim Mus., 1997. Recipient Grumbacher Gold medallion award, 1999, Celebrating Remarkable Women Among Us award Orange County chpt. Nat. Assn. Women Bus. Owners, 1999, Cert. Spl. Congl. Recognition, Loretta Sanchez, 1999. Mem. Nat. League Am. Pen Women (state v.p. 1997-98, Orange County br. pres. 1997-98, recipient State Women of Achievement award, 1998), Calif. State U. Art Alliance, So. Calif. Women's Caucus for Art, Orange County Fine Arts, Phi Delta Gamma (Phi chpt.). Avocations: archaeology, piano, music, travel, art meetings. Home: 2026 W Judith Ln Anaheim CA 92804-6511

BENNETT, HAROLD EARL, physicist, optics researcher; b. Missoula, Mont., Feb. 25, 1929; s. Edward Earl and Linda Queen (McCoy) B.; m. Jean Louise McPherson, Aug. 17, 1952 (div. Nov. 1984); m. Dorothy Jean Searles, Nov. 17, 1984; children: Jeanie Nybo, Dorothy Ann Picking. BA, U. Mont., 1951; MS, Pa. State U., 1953, PhD, 1955. Instrument-rated pilot. Grad. asst. Pa. State U., State College, 1951-55; physicist Wright Air Devel. Ctr., Dayton, Ohio, 1955-56; physicist Naval Air Warfare Ctr. (name Naval Weapons Ctr. 1964-93), China Lake, Calif., 1956-62, rsch. physicist, 1962-95, ret., 1995, assoc. head rsch. dept. physics div., 1972-91; cons. optical physics Quoin Inc., Ridgecrest, Calif., 1995-96; pres. Bennett Optical Rsch. Inc., Ridgecrest, 1995—; chair Space Applications Com., IWV 2000 Orgn., Ridgecrest, Calif., 1996—; co-chmn. Laser Induced Damage in Optical Materials Conf., Boulder, Colo., 1979-96. Adv. editor Optics Communications, 1969-86; contbr. over 100 articles on optics to profl. jours., chpts. to books; holder 12 patents on optical instruments and systems. Pres. Indian Wells Valley Community Concert Assn., Ridgecrest, Calif., 1974-75; sr. fellow Naval Weapons Ctr., 1990; former mem. Calif. Rep. State Ctrl. Com. Recipient LTE Thompson award Naval Weapons Ctr., 1974, Tech. Dir.'s award, 1983; Capt. Robert Dexter Conrad award Dept. Navy, 1979, Dep. Comdr.'s award for R & D, 1995, Tech. Leadership award Navy High Energy Laser Project, 1995, Navy Meritorius Civilian Svc. award, 1995. Fellow Optical Soc. Am. (assoc. editor Jour. 1968-79, bd. dirs. 1972-75), Internat. Soc. for Optical Engring. (bd. dirs. 1985-87, v.p. 1987, pres. 1988, Tech. Achievement award 1983, organizer and chair Laser Power Beaming II Conf. 1995, chair Free Electron Laser Challenges Conf. 1997, chair Free Electron Laser Challenges II 1999), Maturango Mus. (life). Republican. Achievements include research in interferometry, large optics, optical testing, thin film optics, laser power beaming to space. Home: 916 N Randall St Ridgecrest CA 93555-3007 Office: 201 N Sanders St Ridgecrest CA 93555-3867

BENNETT, HELEN DONELE, educator; b. Spartanburg, S.C., Feb. 24, 1948; d. Freddie and Julia Beatrice (Rogers) B. BA, U. S.C., 1969; MEd, Converse Coll., 1977, cert. in adminstr., edn. specialist, 1990. Cert. spl. edn. tchr., psychology, sociology, prin., supr. City planner Model Cities, Inc., Spartanburg, S.C., 1969-70, planning coordinator, 1970-71; tchr., learning disabilities, emotionally handicapped Teszler Learning Adjustment Spartan County Schs., Spartanburg, 1971-87, coord. transition program, 1987-92; asst. prin. Whitlock Jr. H.S., Spartanburg, 1992—. Active County Bd. Domestic Violence, Spartanburg, 1980-86; chmn. City of Spartanburg Civil Svc. Commn. Named Tchr. of Yr., Charles Lea Ctr., 1991, Spartanburg County Spl. Edn. Asssn., 1979. Mem. NEA, NAACP (sec. Spartanburg chpt.), Coun. on Exceptional Children (Spl. Educator of Yr. 1986), S.C. Edn. Assn., Assn. Suprs. and Curriculum Specialists, Sigma Gamma Rho (Tameochus-Xi Sigma chpt.), Civil Svc. Commn. (chairperson). Avocations: writing short stories and plays, architectural design, reading, tennis. Home: 113 Cornelius Rd Spartanburg SC 29301-2850 Office: Whitlock Jr HS 364 Successful Way Spartanburg SC 29303-2477

BENNETT, HERD LEON, lawyer; b. Portsmouth, Ohio, Oct. 17, 1934. BA, Duke U., 1956; JD, Cornell U., 1959. Bar: Ohio 1959. Ptnr. Bennett & Bennett, Eaton, Ohio, 1959—; asst. atty. gen. of Ohio, 1962-63; spl. counsel to atty. gen. of Ohio, 1963-70; trustee Ohio State Bar Found., 1984-92, chair planning and rsch. com., 1986-92, awards com., 1988-90, pres. 1991-92; trustee Preble County Law Libr. Assn., 1970-72; trustee Ohio Continuing Legal Edn. Inst., 1990-91, 93-99, treas., 1993-94, vice chmn., 1994-95, chmn., 1995-96; trustee Eaton Found., 1978—, v.p., 1980—; trustee Nat. Hummel Found. and Mus., 1982—; bd. dirs. Ohio Bar Title Ins. Co., 1991-98, Northedge Shopping Ctr., Inc., Miller's Super Markets, Inc. Trustee Eaton Cmty. Improvement Corp., 1981-94 (v.p. 1987-94), trustee Preble County Area Cmty. Improvement Corp., 1994— (pres. 1994—); mem. Eaton Area C. of C., 1959—; mem., moderator, Sunday Sch. tchr. Concord United Ch. of Christ, Eaton H.S. Alumni Assn. (pres. 1983-84, permanent advisor); exec. officer Duke U. Offie Devel., 1956-90, admissions interview chmn. for S.W. Ohio, 1994-97. Mem. ABA (real property, probate and trust law sect.), Nat. Assn. Criminal Def. Lawyers, Am. Judicature Soc., Ohio State Bar Assn. (mem. bd. govs. 1997—, mem. legal ethics and profl. conduct com. 1981—, coun. dels. 1981—), Preble County Bar Assn. (v.p. 1972-74, pres. 1974-76). Office: Bennett & Bennett 200 W Main St Eaton OH 45320-1748

BENNETT, JOHN CHARLES, farmer, former engineering-construction executive; b. Dover, N.J., Jan. 23, 1925; s. John and Therese Adele (Weiss) B.; m. Betty Evelyn Koenig, June 17, 1950; children: John Lance, Stephen Gary. BS in Engring., Swarthmore Coll., 1945. Registered profl. engr., 48 states, D.C., P;R., Venezuela, Greece; registered profl. planner, N.J.; registered land surveyor, La. Field engr., supt., dist. mgr., v.p., engring. ptnr., dir. The Austin Co., N.Y.C., Cleve., Can., 1946-75; v.p. spl. projects in Greece, Mid. East and North Africa, The Austin Co., 1975-79; pres., CEO, Structors, Inc., Chgo., 1979-82, Advanced Tech. Sys., Fairlawn, N.J., 1982-85; chmn. bd. Scandia, Inc., Atlanta, 1979-82; owner, operator Abacus Bennett Farm, Blairstown, N.J., 1985—; asst. sec. HUD, Washington, 1973. Pres., bd. dirs. N.J. Easter Seal Soc., Morris Plains, 1968-74, Morris County Rehab. Ctr., Morris Plains, 1971-74; bd. dirs. Morris Ctr. YMCA, Morristown, N.J., 1978—. Lt (j.g.) USN, 1943-46. Mem. Nat. Bd. Engring. Examiners, Newcomen Soc., Loyal Order Ky. Cols., Intrepids Club, Tau Beta Pi. Home and Office: 12 Moraine Rd Morris Plains NJ 07950-2711

BENNETT, JOHN K., lawyer; b. Newark, N.J., Apr. 4, 1955. BA magna cum laude, Lafayette Coll., 1977; JD cum laude, Seton Hall U., 1980; LLM in Labor Law with honors, NYU, 1988. Bar: N.J. 1980, U.S. Dist. Ct. N.J., U.S. Dist. Ct. N.Y. (ea., so. and no. dists.), U.S. Ct. Appeals (2d and 3d cirs.), U.S. Supreme Ct. Law sec. to Hon. Robert L. Clifford Supreme Ct. N.J., 1980-81; assoc. to sr. ptnr. Carpenter, Bennett & Morrissey, Newark, 1981-98; ptnr., chair labor and employment law practice Connell, Foley & Geiser LLP, 1998—. Articles editor Seton Hall Law Rev., 1979-80; contbr. articles to profl. jours. Mem. ABA (litigation and labor and employment law sects., state labor law devel. com.), N.J. State Bar Assn. (exec. com. labor and employment law sect.), Essex County Bar Assn. Fax: 973-535-9217. Office: Connell Foley & Geiser LLP 85 Livingston Ave Roseland NJ 07068-3702*

BENNETT, JOHN MAKEPEACE, information systems specialist, consultant; b. Warwick, July 31, 1921; s. Albert J. and Elsie W. (Bourne) B.; m. Rosalind Mary Elkington, Jan. 26, 1952; children: Christopher John, Ann Margaret, Susan Elizabeth, Jane Mary. BE in Civil Engring., 1942, BE in Mech. and Elec., 1947, BSc, 1947; PhD, Cambridge U., 1953. Computer specialist Ferranti Ltd. Manchester, London, 1950-55; sr. numerical analyst U. Sydney, NSW, Australia, 1956-61, prof. computer sci., 1961-86, prof. emeritus, 1987—; dir. Comfax Internat. Ltd., 1986-92, Knowledge Engring. Ltd., 1986-90; chmn. appointments bd. U. Sydney, 1969-74; mem. Australian Govt. Com. on Privacy, 1973-74, Computerization of Legal Data, 1973-74; mem. programs and organizing conf. various internat. computer cos.; expert adviser on customs adminstrn. and procedures, 1982-83. Contbr. over 100 articles to profl. publs. Patron U. Sydney Found. for Info. Tech., 1991—. With Royal Australian Air Force, 1942-46. Recipient Fulbright award, 1981. Fellow Australian Computer Soc. (life, founding pres., Chips award 1981), Brit. Computer Soc., Instn. Engrs. Australia, Inst. Math. and its Applications, Royal Statis. Soc.; mem. Internat. Coun. Computer Comm. (gov. 1989—, sec.-gen. 1989-93), Australian Nat. Com. Computation and Automatic Control (found chmn. 1959-63, medal 1984), Internat. Fedn. Info. Processing (v.p. 1975-77, Silver Core award 1977), Acad. Tech. Scis. and Engring. (chairperson NSW divsn. 1989-90), Sydney Univ. Club (hon. life), United Svc. Club (Brisbane chpt.). Avocations: recreational sailing, golf. Home: 26 Beatty St, PO Box 22, Balgowlah NSW 2093, Australia

BENNETT, JOHN RODERICK, consulting gastroenterologist; b. Wallasey, Eng., Sept. 15, 1934; s. William Henry and Janet Elizabeth (Earl) B.; m. Helen Dorothy Martin, June 22, 1963; children: Paul Martin, Mark Jonathan, Sarah Janet. MB, ChB, Liverpool (Eng.) U., 1957, MD, 1966; MD (hon.), 1997. House officer David Lewis No. Hosp., Liverpool, 1957-58; registrar Pub. Health Lab. Svc., Eng., 1959-61, Birmingham (Eng.) Gen. Hosp., 1961-62, hosp., Stoke-on-Trent, Eng., 1962-64; Sheldon rsch. fellow hosp., Worcester, Eng., 1965-66; fellow in gastroenterology Johns Hopkins Hosp., Balt., 1967-68; sr. registrar Broadgreen Hosp., Liverpool, 1968-69; cons. physician Hull (Eng.) Royal Infirmary, 1969-97; hon. prof. medicine U. Hull, 1994-97; treas. Royal Coll. Physicians, London, 1996—; v.p. World Orgn. of Gastroenterology, 1998—. Author, editor: Therapeutic Endoscopy and Radiology of the Gut, 1979, 2d edit., 1990, Reflux Oesophagitis, 1989; editor, author: Practical Problems in Gastroenterology, 1985; editor Gullet. Fellow Royal Coll. Physicians; mem. Brit. Soc. Gastroenterology (hon.), Italian Soc. Gastroenterology (corr.), Athenaeum Club, Am. Gastroenterology Assn. Anglican. Avocations: gardening, walking, sailing, music. Home: Kingpring House, Vicarage Ln, Long Compton CV36 5LH, England Office: Royal Coll Physicians, St Andrew's Place, London NW1 4LE, England

BENNETT, LESTER LAMAR, III, educator, writer; b. Alma, Ga., July 14, 1943; s. Lester Lamar and Lois Guinelle (Morris) B.; div. Feb., 1982; children: Lester Lamar IV, Morris Pafford, Catherine Guinelle, Elizabeth Allie Lee B. AB, U. Ga., 1973; studies in Travel and Tourism, Advanced Career Tng., Atlanta, 1978, Brit.-Am. Travel Inst., Coral Gables, Fla., 1988, Travel Agts. Internat., St. Petersburg, Fla., 1990; MA in Edn., Nat. Lewis U., 1992; PhD in English Composition, Union Inst., Cin., 1998. Real estate Cypress Bay Assocs., S.E. U.S., 1973-88; educator Hillsborough Pub. Schs., Tampa, Fla., 1989-90, Tampa Bay Acad., Fla., 1990-92, Hillsborough C.C., Plant City, Fla., 1993-94; instr. English Pazmany Peter Cath. U., Budapest, 1995-96, Spolecnost Pratel U.S.A., Prague, Czechoslovakia, 1996-97; creative writing specialist, 1985—. Author: (book) Reflections in the Still Water: The First Fairy Tale from the Realm of the Rim, 1998. Fellow in ESL, Found. for a Civil Soc. in Bratislana, Slovakia, 1996. Mem. TESOL, Nat. Conf. Tchrs. of English, Assembly Expanded Perspectives in Learning. Unitarian. Avocations: world travel, nature. Home: 3833 Peachtree Rd NE Apt 1101 Atlanta GA 30319-5226

BENNETT, MARK, software company executive; b. London, Apr. 21, 1971; s. David Michael and Carol Ann B. Degree in software engring., Bracknell (Eng.) U., 1991. Software engr. Racal, Hooks, Eng., 1987-91; sales engr.

GADC, Milton Keynes, Eng., 1991-92; acct. mgr. Telenex, Brackley, Eng., 1992-93, GEC Plessey Telecomm., Maidenhead, Eng., 1993-95; stategic acct. mgr. LTEQ Ltd., Frimley, Eng., 1995-98; sales dir. Europe, Newpoint Technologies Inc., Salem, N.H., 1998—. Mem. IEEE. Mem. Tory Party. Anglican. Avocations: golf, motor racing. Fax: 44 1908 669886. E-mail: mben3142@supanet.com. Office: Newpoint Technologies Inc 13 Red Roof Ln Salem NH 03079-2929

BENNETT, MARY See THOMPSON, DIDI CASTLE

BENNETT, MAX RICHARD, neuroscience; b. Melbourne, Australia, Feb. 19, 1939; s. Adler and Ivy Rosemary (Arthur) B.; m. Gillian Bennett; children: David, Nerida. B in Engring., Melbourne U., 1963; DSc, Sydney U., 1976. Lectr. Sydney U., 1969; sr. lectr., 1971, reader, 1974, prof., 1982; dir. Neurobiology Rsch. Ctr., 1982; founder Fedn. Australian Scientific and Technol. Soc., Sydney Inst. for Biomed. Rsch., Internat. Soc. for Autonomic Neurosci., Australian Neurol. Networks Soc.; Plenary lectr World Congress of Neurosci., 1995. Author: Autonomic Neuromuscular Transmission, 1972, Optimizing Research and Development, 1985, Idea of Consciousness, 1997, History of the Synapse, 2000. Recipient Goddard rsch. prize Nat. Heart Found., 1996, Ramaciotti Found. medal, 1996, Renesson rsch. prize Nat. Heart Found., 1997, Burnet Medal Lecture, 1998, Malcolm Rsch. prize Nat. Heart Found., 1999; Acad. Sci. Australia fellow, 1981. Mem. Internat. Soc. Autonomic Neurosci. (pres. 2000—), Internat. Brain Rsch. Orgn. (coun.).

BENNETT, PETER NORMAN, physician; b. Calcutta, India, Nov. 25, 1939; s. Norman and Elizabeth Jane (Ogston) B.; m. Jennifer Mary Brocklehurst, Aug. 31, 1963; children: Michael, Neil, Sally Anne. MB, Aberdeen U., 1963; MD, 1967. Lectr. in medicine Aberdeen U., U.K., 1967-71; rsch. fellow London U., 1971-73; lectr. Royal Postgrad. Med. Sch., London, 1973-76; sr. lectr. Bath U., U.K., 1976; cons. physician Royal United Hosp., Bath, U.K., 1976; reader Bath U., U.K., 1990; assoc. dean dept. med. scis., Bath U., U.K., 1989—. Editor: Drugs and Human Lactation, 1996; Ethical Responsibilities and Good Clinical Practice in European Drug Research, 1994; co-author: Clinical Pharmacology, 1997. Co-chair European Ethical Rev. Com., 1996. Office: Bath U Sch Postgrad Med, Bath U Dept Med Scis, Wolfson Ctr Ryl United Hosp, Bath BA1 3NG, England

BENNETT, ROBERT JOHN, geography educator; b. Southampton, Hampshire, Eng., Mar. 23, 1948; s. Thomas Edward and Kathleen Elizabeth (Robson) B.; m. Elizabeth Anne Allen, Sept. 11, 1971; children: Phillip, Richard. BA, U. Cambridge, Eng., 1970, MA, 1974, PHD, 1974. Lectr. U. London U. Coll., 1973-78, U. Cambridge, 1978-85; prof. geography U. London, London Sch. Econs., 1985-96; Leverhulme rsch. prof. U. Cambridge, 1996—; tutor Fitzwilliam Coll., Cambridge, 1982-85, dir. studies in geography, 1978-85. Author: (with R.J. Chorley) Environmental Systems, 1978, Geography of Public Finance, 1980, Central Grants to Local Governments, 1982, others. Recipient R.E. Murchison award Royal Geog. Soc., London, 1982, Founder's medal Royal Geog. Soc., 1998; named Profl. fellow St. Catharine's Coll., 1996—. Mem. Ch. of England. Office: Dept Geography U of Cambridge, Downing Place, Cambridge CB23 EN, England

BENNETT, VELMA JOYCE (JOYCE WILLIAMS), writer, poet; b. Chgo., Mar. 25, 1941; d. Floyd Theodore and Willie Belle (Williams) B. BA in Secondary Edn., Western Mich. U., 1964; MEd, Loyola U., 1975. Cert. secondary and elem. edn., coll. counseling. Tchr. English and social studies Wendell Phillips H.S., Chgo., 1964-65; editor Follett Pub. Co., Chgo., 1965-66; tchr. Bryant Elem., Chgo., 1966-72; H.S. tchr. Outward Bound, Grand Rapids, Mich., 1979-81; pvt. practice writer, poet Allegan, Mich., 1990—. Author: Everybody's Poetry, 1994. Past pres. NAACP, Allegan. Avocations: reading, listening to music, nature watching, people watching, spirits.

BENNETT-KASTOR, TINA L., linguist, educator; b. La Mesa, Calif., Feb. 8, 1954; d. Clayton Leon and Patricia Jean (Billups) Bennett; m. Frank Sullivan Kastor, Oct. 28, 1979; children: Kristina, Patrick, Liam, Mary Elisabeth, Caroline. BFA, Calif. Inst. Arts, 1973; AM, U. So. Calif., 1976, PhD, 1978. Rsch. assoc. John Tracy Clinic, L.A., 1977; asst. prof. Wichita State U., 1978-87, assoc. prof., 1987-97, prof., 1998—; vis. scholar Linguistics Inst. Ireland, Dublin, 1995; rsch. cons. Rehab. Ctr., UCLA, 1976; humanities cons. Children's Audio Svcs., Columbia, S.C., 1979-86; editl. cons. Lang. Speech and Hearing Svcs. in the Schs., Washington, 1999—. Author: Analyzing Children's Language, 1988; editor: Discourse Across Time and Space, 1977; contbr. articles to profl. jours. and mags. Pres. Little Red Wagon Child Care, Inc., Wichita, 1985; v.p. Celtic Cir./Irish-Am. Cultural Inst., Wichita, 1994-2000. Hall fellow Hallmark Found., U. Kans., 1987; rsch. grantee Wichita State U., 1979, 81, 88, 99. Mem. Am. Speech, Lang., and Hearing Assn., Linguistic Soc. Am., N.Y. Acad. Sci., Irish-Am. Cultural Inst., Irish-Am. Partnership. Democrat. Roman Catholic. Avocations: folk music, photography. Home: 115 N Fountain St Wichita KS 67208-3831 Office: Wichita State U 1845 Fairmount St # 14 Wichita KS 67260-0001

BENNICE, ANGELO PHILIP, county official, consultant; b. Brocton, N.Y., Aug. 13, 1931; s. Dominec and Anna (Greco) B.; m. Rosemary Terese Michalak, Jan. 17, 1953; children: Gretchen, Gregory, Benjamin. BS in Chemistry, SUNY, Fredonia, 1973; postgrad., Niagara U., Syracuse U., Pa. State U. Supt. Dunkirk (N.Y.) Water Pollution Control Facility, 1958-78; dir. South and Cen. Chautauqua Lake Sewer Dists., Celoron, N.Y., 1978—; chmn. adv. bd. Ohio River Valley Sanitation Commn., Cin., 1984; former mem. N.Y. State Commr.'s Task Force on Water Resources; former mem. N.Y. State Operators Award Com.; bd. dirs. Adams Art Gallery, Dunkirk. Editor newsletter County Mgrs. Assn., 1989. Chmn. Continuing Edn. Coun., 1977, Dunkirk CSC, 1988; councilman-at-large City of Dunkirk, 1990—; mem. Chautauqua County Emergency Planning Commn.; mem. coll. coun. SUNY, Fredonia, 1977-91; mem. parish coun. Holy Trinity Roman Cath. Ch.; mem. troop coun. Boy Scouts Am., Dunkirk; co-chmn. United Way, Dunkirk; mem., foreman Pioneer Hook and Ladder Co.; chmn. Dunkirk City Safety Co.; numerous others. With USN, 1952-56, Korea. Recipient Presdl. award of honor Dunkirk-Fredonia Jaycees, 1967, Jacyee of Yr. award, 1968; Honored Chemistry Alumnus award SUNY, 1980. Mem. Am. Chem. Soc., Water Pollution Control Fedn., Am. Pub. Works Assn., N.Y. Water Pollution Control Assn. (bd. dirs. Western sect. 1975, exec. bd.), Chautauqua Regional Profl. Wastewater Operators Assn., Dunkirk-Exempt Fireman's Assn. (life), Moose. Democrat. Avocations: boating, fishing, hunting, woodworking. Office: S & Ctrl Chautauqua Lake Sewer Dists PO Box 458 Celoron NY 14720-0458

BENNINGFIELD, CAROL ANN, lawyer; b. San Antonio, Dec. 8, 1952; d. Gordon Lane Benningfield and Ann Benningfield McCraw. BA in Polit. Sci., S.W. Tex. State U., 1975; JD, U. Tex., 1979. Bar: Tex. 1979, U.S. Dist. Ct. (so. dist.) Tex. 1995. Staff atty. Tex. Dept. Labor and Stds., Austin, 1979; staff counsel Tex. Chem. Coun., Austin, 1979-80; assoc. Wiley, Garwood, San Antonio, 1981-83; account exec. Dean-Witter Reynolds, San Antonio, 1983-89; pvt. practice Rockport, Tex., 1990—. Mem. gala com. San Antonio Stock Show and Rodeo, 1981-83; mem. Target 90 Goals for San Antonio, 1984-85; deacon First Presbyn. Ch., Rockport, 1992-95, mem. choir, 1990-96; mem. Rockport Art Assn., 1990—, Coll. State Bar of Tex.; trustee Aransas County Ind. Sch. Dist., Rockport, 1993-96, sec., 1993-96. Fellow Tex. Bar Found. Tex.; mem. San Antonio Young Lawyers (membership chmn. 1982), Rockport Fulton C. of C. (dir. 1992-94, awards com. chmn., v.p. 1993), Rotary. Office: 2602 Highway 35 N Rockport TX 78382-5707

BENOIDT, JEAN VICTOR GEORGES, financial consultant; b. Brussels, Apr. 15, 1931; s. Victor Georges and Leonie Pauline (de Moerloose) B.; m. Marguerite Georgette Verlinde, Aug. 18, 1971; 1 child, Catherine. Degree in Fin. and Econs., U. Brussels, 1955. Buyer Galeries Anspach, Brussels, 1957-59, Sarma, Brussels, 1959-62; pres. S.A. J. Benoidt, Brussels, 1962-79, Reals Estate Benoidt Ltd., Brussels, 1965-88, Euragex Ltd, Brussels, 1964-79; fin. cons. J. Benoidt Co., Montescot, France, 1979—; cons. Principality of Andorra. Mem. Lions Club, Dante Alighieri (sec. 1993—). Avocations: bridge, philatelist, golf. Home: La Cypriere Rt D'Elne, 66200 Montescot France Office: J Benoidt Cons, Rt D'Elne, 66200 Montescot France

BENOIT, HENRI, physicist, educator; b. Paris, Sept. 18, 1928; s. Jean Baptiste and Marguerite (Vincent) B.; m. Mar. U, 1964 (div. Oct. 1982); 1 child, Jean-Christophe; m. Marie Jose Asselin, Mar. 23, 1985. B, Ecole Alsacienne, Paris, 1947; postgrad., Lycee J. Decour, Paris, 1948-50; Agregation Scis. Physique, Ecole Normale Superieure, Paris, 1954; D d'Etat, U. Paris, 1959. Attache CNRS, Paris, 1955-63; maitre conf. Faculty of Scis., Paris, 1964-69; prof. U. Pierre et Marie Curie, Paris, 1969-95, ret., 1995; examinateur French Navy, 1994-98, French Air Force, 1999-2000. Author: Elements of Physics, 1967. Capt. Artillery, 1956-57, Algeria. postdoctoral fellow U. Calif. C.D. Jeffries Lab., Berkeley, 1960-61. Home: 5 rue Olivier Noyer, F75014 Paris France Office: U Pierre et Marie Curie, T12 E4 CC81 4 Place Jussieu, F-75252 Paris Cedex 05, France

BENOIT A LA GUILLAUME, CLAUDE JOSEPH, physicist; b. Septmoncel, Jura, France, Dec. 22, 1929; s. Luc and Madeleine (Benoit-Gonin) Benoit a la G.; m. Anne-Marie Escapil-Inchauspe, July 28, 1955; children: Jacques, Pierre-Yves, Michel, Luc. Degree in physics, Ecole Normale Superieure, Paris, 1954, DSc, 1958. Attache de recherche CNRS, Paris, 1954-57, charge de recherche, 1958-60, maitre de recherche, 1961-64, dir. de recherche, 1965-94, emeritus, 1995—; dir. Groupe de Physique des Solides, Paris, 1972-76. Contbr. more than 150 articles to profl. jours. in fundamental semiconductor physics. Recipient Prix de la Ville de Paris, 1985, Prix Robin, Soc. Francaise de Physique, 1991. Office: Groupe de Physique des solides, U Paris VII, 2 Place Jussieu, 75251 Paris France

BENON, JEAN FRANCOIS, economist, French local government official; b. Perpignan, Pyr Orient, France, Nov. 16, 1960; s. Guy and Marthe (Gouzy) B. M in Law, Paris. Assas U., 1982. Chief clk. office of chmn. Reunion Island County Coun., France, 1982-84; head econ. dept. Val D'Oise Prefectural Govt., France, 1984-90; mng. dir. Val D'Oise Econ. Devel. Agy., France, 1990—. Publs. dir. (econ. mag.) Decideurs in Val D'Oise. Mem. Cergy-Pontoise (France) Jr. Chamber Internat., 1984—, JCI senator, 1996, vice chmn. local welfare assn. Pontoise, France, 1986—; councillor Ile de France Regional, Econ. and Soc. Coun., Paris, 1989—. Avocations: golf, travel. Home: 1 Rue du Prieure, F-95000 Cergy ValDoise, France Office: Com Expansion Econ ValDoise, Com Expans Econ Val d'Oise, 2 Ave du Parc, F-95032 Val d'Oise France

BENOS, THEOFANIS EVANGELOS, economics educator; b. Athens, Jan. 20, 1938; s. Evangelos K. and Georgia K. (Palikari) B.; m. Maria C. Ikonomou, Jan. 4, 1979; children: Evangelos, Georgia. BA, Athens Econ. U., 1961; MA, U. Rochester, 1967, PhD in Econs., 1970. Rschr. Ctr. Planning, Athens, 1963-65; prof. econs. Fla. Atlantic U., Boca Raton, 1970-74, U. Macedonia, Greece, 1974-84, U. Pireaus, Athens, 1984—. 2d lt. Greek Army, 1961-63. Home: 3 Agelaou Str, 15343 Ag Paraskevi Greece Office: U Pireaus Dept Econs, Pireaus Greece

BENSAHEL, HENRI, pediatric orthopedics educator, researcher; b. Casablanca, Morocco, June 30, 1928; arrived in France, 1948; s. David and Angèle (Drai) B.; m. Alice Muller, Sept. 2, 1934; children: Jean-François, Pierre-Olivier. BS in Physics, Chemistry and Biology, Rabat, Morocco, 1948; med. faculty, U. Paris, 1962. Jr. resident country hosp. Creteil, France, 1955-56; resident in surgery Hosps. AP-HP, Paris, 1957-62; fellow in pediat. surgery Bretonneau Hosp., Paris, 1962-64, head pediat. orthopaedic unit, 1964-68, head dept. pediat. orthopaedics, 1968-96; prof. pediat. orthopaedics U. Paris VII, 1972—, Robert Debré Hosp., Paris, 1988-96; sr. cons. Robert Debré Hosp., Paris, 1996—, hon. prof. pediat. orthopaedics, Paris, 1996. Author numerous books including Current Concepts in Paediatric Orthopaedics, 5 edits., 1978, Techniques in Paediatric Orthopaedics, 1985, Children Trauma, 1986, Paediatrics and Paediatricians, 1990, Children & Sport, 1998, Sport in Childhood, 1998—; contbr. numerous papers to profl. jours.; editor-in-chief: Jour. Paediat. Orthopaedics, 1992. Advisor to Min. of Health, Paris, 1990-93; dep. mayor, Saint-Mande, 1995. Decorated Chevalier Legion d'Honneur, 1989, Officier Légion d'Honneur, 1999, Officier de l'Ordre National du Mérite, 1995; recipient Médaille de Ville de Paris, 1985. Mem. European Pediat. Orthopaedics Soc. (hon.; founder pres. 1981), Internat. Fedn. Pediat. Orthopaedics Soc. (pres. 1998), Sephardi Assn. in France (hon. pres.), AIDS, Cancer, Vaccine Devel. (pres. 1999). Avocations: golf, swimming. Home: 1 Ave Foch, 94160 Saint Mande France

BENSAL, MOSHE, electrical engineer; b. Istanbul, Turkey, Oct. 15, 1953; s. David and Beki (Boueno) B.; m. Ilana Senior, Feb. 27, 1985; children: Dudi, Adi, Eden. Technician, Orot Holon, Israel, 1971; BSEE, Tel-Aviv U., 1979. Project mgr. Intel, Haifa, 1980—; project mgr. 82596 Intel Israel, 1987-90. IDF, 1971-75, Israel. Mem. IEEE. Avocations: computers, radio amateur, hiking. Office: Intel Israel, MTM PO Box 1659, 31-015 Haifa Israel

BENSAOU, MUSTAPHA BEN, management science educator, researcher; b. Montbeliard, France, Dec. 27, 1958; s. Bachir and Fatma-Zohra (Soual) B.; m. Masako Kishida, June 7, 1986; children: Sophian, Alexis, Lennon. MS in Civil Engring., Ecole Nat. des TPE, Lyon, France, 1981; DEA in Mech. Engring., Inst. Nat. Polytech., Grenoble, France, 1981; MA in Mgmt. Sci., Hitotsubashi U., Tokyo, 1985; PhD in Mgmt., MIT, 1992. Assoc. prof. tech. mgmt. and Asian bus. INSEAD, Fontainebleau, France, 1992—, dir. Euro-Asia Ctr., 1999—; vis. assoc. prof. mgmt. Harvard Bus. Sch., Boston, 1998-99. Contbr. articles to profl. jours. Fellow Japanese Ministry of Edn., Tokyo, 1982-86; Rotary scholar, 1981-82. Mem. Acad. of Mgmt., INFORMS Acad., Internat. House of Japan. Avocations: marathon running, skiing, shorenji-kempo, reading, languages. E-mail: ben.bensaou@insead.fr. Office: INSEAD, Blvd de Constance, 77309 Fontainebleau France

BENSEN, ANNETTE WOLF, graphic art company consultant; b. Bklyn., Aug. 7, 1938; d. Isidor and Sylvia Wolf; m. Gene Bensen, Oct. 14, 1979. AAS, N.Y.C. C.C., 1958; postgrad., Pratt Inst., 1974-75, Sch. Visual Arts, N.Y.C. With Wagner-Ellsberg, Inc., N.Y.C., 1958-62; art dir. Island Pen Mfg. Inc., Stacie Pen, Curtis Rand Industries, Inc., N.Y.C., 1962-68; with G.S. Lithographers, Inc., N.Y.C., 1968-70; ptnr., pres. Rembrandt's Mother, Inc., N.Y.C., 1970-72; co-owner, pres. Film Comp., Inc., N.Y.C., 1972-75; mgr. Expertype, N.Y.C., 1975-90, Expertype & The Graphic Word Co., N.Y.C., 1990-92; sr. v.p. Expertype divsn. JCH Group Ltd., N.Y.C., 1992-93; v.p. prodn. Metro Creative Graphics, Inc., N.Y.C., 1993-97; v.p. ops. Digital Ops. Tech. Svcs., Inc., N.Y.C., 1997-98; owner, mgr. AnGen Svcs, N.Y.C., 1999—; adj. lectr. N.Y.C. C.C., 1971-75; adv. commn. dept. graphic arts and advtsg. tech. N.Y.C. Tech. Coll./CUNY, 1994—, adj. lectr.; mem.adv. commn. High Sch. Graphic Comm. Arts, 1999—. Mem. Found. for Graphic Arts, Inc., 1994—; mem. Graphic Arts Ednl. Commn., Bd. Edn., N.Y.C. Recipient Fellowship award N.Y. Club of Printing House Craftsmen, 1996. Mem. Assn. Publn. Prodn. Mgrs., Assn. Graphic Comm. (Outstanding Instr. recognition award 1999), Graphic Arts Profls., Women in Prodn., Printing Women N.Y. (pres.). Fax: 914-276-0666. Address: AnGen Svcs 585C Heritage Hills Dr Somers NY 10589-1908

BENSIGNOR, EMMANUEL JEAN, veterinarian, consultant; b. Versailles, France, Oct. 13, 1970; s. Pierre Bensignor and Lucile Clavel; 1 child, Clara. DVM, Alfort, France, 1993; diplomate, European Coll Vet. Dermatology, London, 1998; diploma in allergology and clin. immun., U. Limoges, 1998. Med. diplomate; cert. vet. dermatology. Resident European Coll. Vet. Dermatology, Bordeaux, France, 1996-98; asst. Alfort Vet. Sch., 1995-96; cons. Paris, Bordeaux, 1999—. Editor: Atlas of Canine Pyoderma, 2000; CD-ROM Canine Dermatology, 2000; contbr. articles to profl. jours. Treas. Group D'etudes en Dermatology des Animaux de Compagnie, Paris, 1997, Syndicat Francais des Vet. Membres des Coll. Europeens, Paris, 1998. Mem. Am. Acad. Vet. Dermatology, European Soc. Vet. Dermatology, Soc. Francaise Mycologie Med. Avocations: golfing, sailing, wine tasting. Home: 31 rue Victor Hugo, 94700 Maisons-Alfort France Office: Clinique Vétéinarian, 125 rue Vicille du Temple, 75003 Paris France

BENSON, DONALD ERICK, holding company executive; b. Mpls., June 1, 1930; s. Fritz and Annie (Nordstrom) B.; children: Linda K., Nancy A., Stephen D.; m. Roberta Mann, 1992. BBA in Acctg., U. Minn., 1955. CPA, Minn. From staff to partnership Arthur Andersen & Co., Mpls., 1955-68; pres. MEI Corp., Mpls., 1968-86, MEI Diversified Inc., Mpls., 1986-94; exec. v.p. Marquette Bancshares, Inc., Mpls., 1992—; also bd. dirs.; bd. dirs. Mesaba Holdings, Inc., Champion Air, Minn. Twins Baseball Club, Mass. Mut. Corp. Investors, Mass. Mut. Participation Investors, Capital Cargo Holdings, Inc., Delta Beverage Group, Inc., Nat. Merc. Bancorp.; past chmn. Health Systems Minn.; dir. Swedish Coun. Am. and its Royal Round Table. Chmn. Bethel Coll. Found., St. Paul, Park Nicollet Health Svcs.; past chmn. Health Sys. Minn., Mpls.; past pres. Boys and Girls Clubs Mpls. Served with U.S. Army, 1951-53. Mem. AICPA, Minn. CPA Soc., Mpls. Club, Interlachen Country Club. Office: Marquette Bancshares Inc 3900 Dain Rauscher Plz Minneapolis MN 55480-1000

BENSON, FRANK ATKINSON, electrical engineer; b. Grange-Over-Sands, Cumbria, Eng., Nov. 21, 1921; s. John and Selina (Atkinson) B.; m. Kathleen May Paskell, Sept. 23, 1950; children: Peter John, Trevor Mark. B Engring., U. Liverpool, Eng., 1942, M Engring., 1945; PhD, U. Sheffield, Eng., 1952, D Engring., 1957. Registered profl. engr. Rsch. officer Admiralty Signal Establishment, Witley, Eng., 1943-46; lectr. in elec. engring. U. Liverpool, England, 1946-49; lectr. to reader in electronics U. Sheffield, Eng., 1949-67, pro-vice-chancellor, 1972-76, dean engring., 1978-81, prof., head of dept. electronic/elec. engring., 1967-87, emeritus prof., 1987—. Co-author: Fields, Waves and Transmission Lines, 1991; author: Voltage Stabilized Supplies, 1957, Problems in Electronics with Solutions, 1958; editor/contbr. author: Millimetre and Submillimetre Waves, 1969; contbr. articles to profl. jours. Named dept. lt. of South Yorkshire, HM the Queen, 1979—, decorated Order Brit. Empire, 1988. Fellow IEEE, Instn. Elec. Engrs. Ch. of England. Avocations: hobbies, travel, gardening, music. Home: 64 Grove Rd, Sheffield S72GZ, England Office: Dept Elec/Electronic Engrin, Univ Sheffield/Mappin St, S1 3JD Sheffield England

BENSON, JOAN DOROTHY, secondary school educator; b. Paterson, N.J., Aug. 23, 1948; d. Arnold Albin and Dorothy Minnette Benson; m. Jacob A. Ritz, June 22, 1969 (div. Jan. 1995); children: Kristina, Julie. BA, Rowan Coll., 1975; cert. in math., William Paterson U., 1984; MS in Computer Sci., Iona Coll., 2000. Cert. tchr., N.J. Asst. to spl. edn. tchr. Pequannock Twp. Schs., Pompton Plains, N.J., 1981-84; computer instr. Pequannock Adult Sch., Pompton Plains, 1983-97; math. tchr. DePaul Cath. H.S., Wayne, N.J., 1984-98, media specialist, computer tchr., 1998—; guest tchr. Kathrinebergs Folkhögskola, Vessigebro, Sweden, summers, 1989—. Elder, deacon Pompton Reformed Ch. Mem. Nat. Coun. Tchrs. Math., Nat. Cath. Edn. Assn., Vasa Order Am., Kappa Delta Phi. Avocations: handbell choir, reading, computers, travel. E-mail: jbenson@depaulcatholic.org. Home: 93 Treetop Ct Bloomingdale NJ 07403-1024 Office: DaPaul Cath HS 1512 Alps Rd Wayne NJ 07470-3601

BENSON, JOHN RUSSELL, surgeon, researcher; b. Kingston-upon-Hull, Eng., Nov. 8, 1959; s. George Samuel and Elsie May (Bell) B. BA with honours, Oxford (Eng.) U., 1981, BM, BCh, 1984, MA (hon.), 1985, DM, 1997. Sr. house officer Hammersmith Hosp., London, 1988; dept. demonstrator, dept. anatomy U. Oxford, England, 1986; sr. house officer Radcliffe Infirmary, Oxford, 1987; registrar Newham Gen. Hosp., London, 1989-92; clin. rsch. fellow Inst. Cancer Rsch., London, 1992-94; sr. registrar Royal Marsden Hosp., London, 1994-96, Chelsea and Westminster Hosp., London, 1996-2000; cons. breast surgeon Addenbrookes, Hinching Brooke Hosps., Cambridge, Eng., 2000—; assoc. lectr. U. Cambridge, 2000—. Author: TGFB and Cancer (RG Landes Co.); contbr. articles to med. jours., including Lancet, Brit. Jour. Cancer. Grad. scholar St. Peter's Coll., Oxford U., 1983-84; grantee Brit. Oncological Assn., 1995, Ethicon Found. Fund, 1998; Travel fellow Royal Coll. Surgeons, Inc., N.Y., 1996. Fellow Royal Coll. Surgeons (Eng.), Royal Coll. Surgeons (Edinburgh), Royal Soc. Medicine; mem. Am. Assn. for Cancer Rsch. (corr., travel grantee 1994), Brit. Assn. Surg. Oncologists, Oxford Union Soc. (life), N.Y. Acad. Scis., N.Y. met. Breast Group. Avocations: piano, travel, collecting knick-knacks. Home: Upper Wolvercote, 26 Millway Close, Oxford OX2 8BL, England Office: Addenbrookes Hosp, Breast Unit, Hills Rd, Cambridge CB2 2QQ, England

BENSON, JUDI LAMAR, poet, magazine editor; b. Coronado, Calif., Dec. 20, 1947; arrived in Eng., 1978; d. Elliot Walter and Julia Searcy (Lamar) Parish; m. Peter Ross Benson, Aug. 15, 1966 (div. 1975); 1 child, Todd Parish; m. Kenneth John Smith, July 6, 1981; stepchildren: Nicole Smith, Danny Smith, Kate Smith. BA, U. North Fla., Jacksonville, 1975; MA, Antioch U., London, 1981. Sec. U. Fla., Gainesville, 1966-68, Johnson Control, Pensacola, Fla., 1968-69; dir. pub. rels. Jacksonville Symphony Orch., Jacksonville, 1975-78; asst. dir. Antioch U., London, 1980-87; freelance painter London, 1987-92; team sec. Nat. Soc. for Prevention of Cruelty to Children, London, 1992-97; tutor creative writing Arvon Found., Devon and Yorkshire, Eng., 1985, 87, 89. Author: (poetry) Somewhere Else, 1990, In the Pockets of Strangers, 1993, Call It Blue, 2000; co-editor: (anthology) Klaonica, 1993, What Poets Eat, 1994, The Long Pale Corridor, 1996, (periodical) Foolscap mag., 1987-96. Bereavement counsellor Royal London Hosp., 1992-94. Avocations: rug hooking, swimming, silk painting. Home: 78 Friars Rd, East Ham London E6 1LL, England

BENSON, LUCY WILSON, political and diplomatic consultant; b. N.Y.C., Aug. 25, 1927; d. Willard Oliver and Helen (Peters) Wilson; m. Bruce Buzzell Benson, Mar. 30, 1950 (dec. Mar. 1990). BA, Smith Coll., 1949, MA, 1955; LHD (hon.), Wheaton Coll., Norton, Mass., 1965; LLD (hon.), U. Mass., 1969; LHD (hon.), Bucknell U., 1972; LLD (hon.), U. Md., 1972; LHD (hon.), Carleton Coll., 1973; LLD (hon.), Amherst Coll., 1974, Clark U., 1975; HHD, Springfield Coll., 1981; L.H.D. (hon.), Bates Coll., 1982; L.L.D. (hon.), Lafayette Coll., 1999. Mem. jr. exec. tng. program Bloomingdale's, N.Y.C., 1949-50; asst. dir. pub. rels. Smith Coll., 1950-53; rsch. asst. dept. Am. studies Amherst Coll., 1956-57; pres. Amherst LWV, Mass., 1957-61; pres. Mass. LWV, 1961-65, nat. pres., 1968-74; mem. Gov.'s cabinet and sec. human svcs. Commonwealth of Mass., 1975; mem. spl. commn. on adminstrv. rev. U.S. Ho. of Reps., Washington, 1976-77; under sec. State Security Assistance, Sci. and Tech. U.S. Dept. State, Washington, 1977-80; cons. U.S. Dept. State and SRI Internat., Washington, 1980-81; pres. Benson and Assocs., Amherst, 1981—; vice-chair Citizen Network for Fgn. Affairs; trustee N.E. Utilities, 1971-74, 76-77; bd. dirs. Continental Group, Inc., Dreyfus Fund, Dreyfus Liquid Assets, Dreyfus Asset Allocation Fund, Dreyfus 401K Fund, Dreyfus Third Century Fund, Inc., Comms. Satellite Corp., Gen. Reins. Corp., Dreyfus Worldwide Dollar Money Market Fund, Inc., Logistics Mgmt. Inst. Steering com. Urban Coalition, 1968, exec. com., 1970-75, 80-84, co-chair, 1973-75; mem. Gov. Mass. Spl. Com. Rev. Sunday Closing Laws, 1961; mem. spl. commn. Mass. Legislature to Study Budgetary Powers of Trustees U. Mass., 1961-62; mem. Gov. Mass. Com. Rev. Salaries State Employees, 1963, Mass. Adv. Bd. Higher Ednl. Policy, 1962-65, Mass. Bd. Edn. Adv. Com. Racial Imbalance and Edn., 1964-65, Mass. adv. com. U.S. Commn. Civil Rights, 1964-73; vice-chair Mass. Adv. Coun. Edn., 1965-68; mem. Mass. Com. Children and Youth Com. to Study Report by U.S. Children's Bur., Mass. Youth Svc. Div., 1967; mem. pub. adv. com. U.S. Trade Policy, 1968; vis. com. John F. Kennedy Sch. Govt.; mem. Trilateral Commn., Coun. Fgn. Rels.; mem. town meeting, Amherst, 1957-74, 2000, mem. fin. com., 1960-66; trustee Edn. Devel. Center, Newton, Mass., 1967-72, Nat. Urban League, 1974-77, Smith Coll., 1975-80, Brookings Instn., 1974-77, Alfred P. Sloan Found., 1975-77, 81—, Bur. Social Sci. Rsch., Inc., 1985-87; bd. dirs. Catalyst, 1972-90, Internat. Exec. Svc. Corps, Atlantic Coun. of U.S., 1988—, vice-chair, 1993—; former bd. govs. Am. Nat. Red Cross, Common Cause, Women's Action Alliance; bd. govs. Internat. Ctr. on Election Law and Adminstrn., 1985-87; trustee Lafayette Coll., 1985—, vice-chair, 1990—. Recipient Achievement award Bur. Govt. Research, U. Mass., 1963; Distinguished Service award Boston Coll., 1965, Smith Coll. medal, 1969, Distinguished Civil Leadership award Tufts U., 1965, Distinguished Service award Northfield Mount Hermon Sch., 1976; Radcliffe fellow Radcliffe Inst., 1965-67. Mem. NAACP, ACLU, Nat. Acad. Pub. Adminstrn., UN Assn., Urban League, Assn. Am. Indian Affairs, East African Wildlife Soc., Jersey Wildlife Preservation Trust Channel Islands, Internat. Inst. Strategic Studies. Home and Office: 46 Sunset Ave Amherst MA 01002-2018

BENSON, STEVEN DONALD, sheet metal research and marketing executive, sheet metal mechanic, programmer, author; b. Longview, Wash., Oct. 11, 1953; s. Steven Hughes Benson and Donna Ruth (Johnson) McKinney; m. Patricia Joyce Krauss, Feb. 14, 1982; children: Steven William, Patricia Ann. AA in Drafting, South Salem Indsl. Arts Coll., 1973; AA in Robotics, AMADA Sch., Buena Park, Calif., 1997. Precision sheet metal mechanic Ariz. Precision Sheet Metal, Phoenix, 1980-86, Neilson Mfg. Inc., Salem,

Oreg., 1986—; owner, operator Time Honored Gifts, Salem, 1988—; pres. Advanced Sheet Metal Applications, Salem, 1986—; instr. Oreg. Advanced Tech. Consortium, Wilsonville, 1990—; sheet metal instr. Clackamas C.C., Oregon City, Oreg., 1997—; editor, pub. Precision Sheet Metal Chronicle, electronic mag., 1998—. Author: (textbooks) Introduction to Precision Press Brake, 1991, Intermediate Press Brake, 1992, Advanced Precision Press Brake, 1994, Press Brake Technology, 1997, (software) Advanced Sheet Metal Applications (ASMA 4.0), 1982, 90, 92, 95, 97. Sec., treas. Bike PAC of Oreg., Salem, 1988—, lobbyist, 1992; mem. A Brotherhood Against Totalitarian Enactments (ABATE), Oreg., Inc. Recipient edn. award Fabricators and Mfg. Assn. Internat., 1999. Master Masons; mem. Fabricators and Mfrs. Assn. (adv. com. precision sheet metal adv. 1997—, coun.), Soc. Mfg. Engrs., Internat. Sheet Metal Workers (local 16). Avocations: family activities, children, politics, Indian moto-cycles, British sports cars. Fax: 206-727-8729. E-mail: steve@asmachronicle.com. Home: 395 23d St NE Salem OR 97301-4440 Office: Advanced Sheet Metal Applications 398 Rose St NE Salem OR 97301-4468

BENSUSSAN, ARMAND, biologist, immunologist, researcher; b. Casablanca, Morocco, Sept. 10, 1954; s. Léon and Rosa (Abitan) B.; m. Elisabeth Eugenie Larbi, Nov. 21, 1981; 1 child, Florian Adrien. M Biochemistry, M Human Biology, U. Paris VII, 1979, D State in Human Biology, 1987. Rsch. assoc. Harvard U. Med. Sch., Boston, 1982-85; in charge rsch. Nat. Inst. Health and Med. Rsch. (INSERM), Paris, 1985-90, dir. rsch., 1991-95; dir. rsch. unit Nat. Inst. Health and Med. Rsch. (INSERM), Creteil, France, 1996—. Contbr. articles to sci. jours., including Jour. Exptl. Medicine, Nature, Procs. NAS, USA. Recipient European prize Balear Transplant Found., 1995, Bernard Halpern prize, Paris, 1995, French Acad. Scis. prize, Paris, 1986, Cancer Rsch. prize Val de Marne Region, Creteil, 1998; grantee Med. Rsch. Found., Paris, 1988. Mem. AAAS, Am. Assn. Immunologists, French Assn. Immunologists. E-mail: bensussan@im3.inserm.fr. Office: INSERM U 448 Fac Medicine, 8 Rue du General Sarrail, 94010 Créteil Cedex, France

BENSUSSAN, DENIS, radiologist; b. Marseille, Bouches du Rhone, France, Mar. 31, 1951; s. Roger Pierre B. and Jeanine Coulomb; m. Claudia Husson, July 7, 1983; children: Pierre-Brice, Marie-Albane, David-Edouard, Anne-Sophie. Baccalaureat Sci. Mention AB, Lycée Périer, Marseille, France, 1969; MD, Faculté Medecine Marseille, 1977. Nat. Diploma Radiology, Paris, 1982; Diplôme d'Univ. Réparation Juridique Dommage Corporel, Marseille, 1995. Asst. vascular radiology svc. CHU Timone, Marseille, France, 1978-82, attaché consultation hosps., 1982-92; vascular and interventional radiologist Ctr d'Angiographie Diagnostique et Thérapeutique; v.p. Assn. Pour la Promotion de la Radiologie Interventionnelle, Marseille, France, 1984; mem. adminstrn. coun. Assn. des Radiologues Angiographistes et Angioplastiens Libéraux, Paris, 1996. Contbr. article to med. jour. Medecin prin., comdr. French Navy, 1978-79. Mem. Assn. Eleveurs Chevaux de Sang du Sud-Est (pres. 1997—), Lions Club (pres. Marseille-Doyen 1997-98), RSNA, CIRSE, French Radiology Soc., Soc. Francaise d'Imagerie Cardiovasculaire, Coll. Francais de Radiologie Interventionnelle. Fax: 33 0491925834. Home: 408 Rue Paradis, 13008 Marseille France Office: Ctr Angiographie Therapeut, Rue Louis Astruc, 13005 Marseille France

BENTAHILA, ABDELALI, humanities educator; b. Fes, Morocco, Nov. 16, 1947; s. Tayeb and Habiba (Abdellaoui) B.; m. Eirlys Edwina Davies, 1983; 1 child, Sami Reda. MA, U. Wales, 1975, PhD, 1981. Tchr. Moroccan Ministry of Edn., Fez, 1970-74; ednl. adviser Ministry of Edn., Casablanca, 1975-76; lectr. Royal Mil. Acad., Meknes, Morocco, 1982-92; lectr. U. Sidi Mohamed Ben Abdellah, Fez, 1976-85, prof., 1985-97; prof. U. Abdelmalek Essaadi, Tetouan, 1997—; head dept. English U. Sidi Mohamed Ben Abdellah, 1982-88, dir. postgrad. studies, 1982-89. Author: Language Attitudes Among Arabic-French Bilinguals in Morocco, 1983; contbr. articles to profl. jours.; mem. editl. bd. Jour. Multilingual and Multicultural Development, 1996—, Bilingualism: Language & Cognition, 1997—. Mem. Internat. Sociol. Assn. Muslim. Avocations: gardening, running, travel. Home: BP 1220, Tangier Morocco Office: U Abdelmalek Essaadi, Faculté des Lettres, Tetouan Morocco

BEN-TAL, NIR, biochemist; b. Jerusalem, Israel, Sept. 15, 1961; s. Yona and Ruth (Cahana) B.; m. Sheshi Ben Ami; children: Gonnie, Nitzan. BS in Biology, Chemistry, Physics, The Hebrew U., Jerusalem, 1988; D Sci. in Chemistry, The Techion, Haifa, Israel, 1993; postgrad., Columbia U., N.Y., 1994-97. Sr. lectr. Tel Aviv U., Israel, 1997—. Recipient scholarship, Gutwirth Found., 1989-92; fellowship The Israeli Acad. Scis., 1997, Wolfson Found., 1998. Home: 6 Hakalir St, 64953 Tel Aviv Israel Office: Dept Biochemistry, Tel Aviv U, 69978 Tel Aviv Israel

BENTATA, DAVID JOSEPH, company executive; b. Gibraltar, Nov. 28, 1946; s. Joseph David and Esther (Benady) B.; m. Rachel Marsh, Sept. 7, 1975 (div. Jan. 1988); children: Asher, Kellie, Gideon; m. Camelia Magen; stepchildren: Eyal, Avi. Shop asst. The English Outfitters Ltd., Gibraltar, 1962-65, shop mgr., 1965-69, buyer, 1969-74; mng. dir. Tamarind Holdings Ltd., Gibraltar, 1974—; mng. dir. Rock Freeze Ltd., Gibraltar, 1973-75, Brit. Comml. Agy., Gibraltar, 1974-76, Baruta Holdings Ltd., Gibraltar, 1975—, The English Outfitters Ltd., Gibraltar, 1975—, Toyamo Ltd., Gibraltar, 1984—, TEO Dos S.L., Spain, 1992—. Mgr. Gibraltar Maccabi Football Team; pres. Main St. Assn., Gibraltar, 1996; Nuclear Specialist, Gibraltar Regiment, 1964. Avocations: writing, reading, clay pigeon shooting, photography, music. E-mail: teodos@arrakis.es. Office: Teo Dos Sl, Cent Com Gran Sur, 11300 La Linea Spain

BENTDAL, ØYSTEIN HAGEN, transplant surgeon; b. Oslo, Norway, June 29, 1948; s. Kåre Sigvart and Gudrun Hagen (Bentoal) H.; m. Ragnhild Emblem, Jan. 3, 1969; children: Yngvild, Ellisiv. MD, U. Oslo, 1973, Dr.med., 1996. Resident Sarpsborg Sykehus, 1976-80; resident Rikshospitaht, Oslo, Norway, 1980-83, rsch. fellow, 1983-86, cons., 1987—. Mem. Transplant Soc., ESOT, Scandia Transplant. Office: Surg Dept B Rikshospitaht, Pilestredit 32, Oslo 0027, Norway

BENTE, LYNN ALAN, chemist; b. Dover, Ohio, July 8, 1950; s. Francis E. and Madge A. B.; m. Francie K. Bente, Mar. 18, 1972; children: Joel F., Joshua L. B of Chemistry, Kent State U., B in Earth Scis.; MBA, Ashland Coll. Product mgr. Keystone Aniline, Dover, 1991-99; owner Buckeye Chem. & Color, Dover, 1991—. Patentee in field. With USAR, 1970-75. Mem. Am. Chem. Soc., Soc. Dyers & Chemists (editl. bd.), Soc. Plastics Engrs. E-mail: labente@bright.net. Office: Buckeye Chem & Color Co 4298 Boy Scout Rd NE Dover OH 44622-7529

BENTER, TERESA ANN, health facility administrator; b. Seymour, Ind., July 3, 1965; d. Alvin Willis and Wilma Ann (Tormoehlen) Benter. Student, Ivy Tech., Columbus, Ind., 1997—. Cert. med. mgr. Ins. clk. Weir, Bevers, Baxter, Seymour, Ind., 1984—; office mgr. Rosemary Weir, MD, Seymour, 1994—. Leader 4-H Club, Seymour, 1984—; Sunday sch. tchr. St. Paul Luth. Ch., Brownstown, 1986—. Mem. Assn. Health Care Mgrs., Phi Theta Kappa. Avocation: cross stitching. Office: PO Box 427 120 Saint Louis Ave Seymour IN 47274-2304

BENTHALL, JONATHAN CHARLES MACKENZIE, anthropologist, writer; b. Calcutta, Bengal, India, Sept. 12, 1941; s. Arthur Paul and Mary Lucy (Pringle) B.; m. Zamira Menuhin, Oct. 23, 1975; children: Dominic, William. BA, King's Coll. Cambridge U., Eng., 1962, MA, 1968. Sec. Inst. Contemporary Arts, London, 1971-73; dir. Royal Anthrop. Inst., London, 1974-2000; chair trustees Internat. NGO Tng. and Rsch. Ctr., Oxford, 1997—; trustee Alliance of Religions and Conservation, 1998—. Author: Science and Technology in Art Today, 1972, The Body Electric: Patterns of Western Industrial Culture, 1976, Disasters, Relief and the Media, 1993; editor Anthropology Today, 1985-2000; contbr. numerous articles to profl. jours. Mem. of many coms. Save the Children Fund, U.K. 1981-1996. Named Chevalier de L'Ordre des Arts et des Lettres, France, 1973, hon. rsch. fellow Univ. Coll., London, 1994; recipient Anthropology in Media award Am. Anthrop. Assn., 1993. Mem. Assn. Social Anthropologists of the Commonwealth. Avocations: music, swimming, mountain walking, books. Home: 212 Hammersmith Grove, London W6 7HG, England

BENTLEY, DOUGLAS PAUL, hematologist; b. Sheffield, Yorkshire, Eng., July 22, 1945; s. Edward Stainsby and Cynthia Jean (Crawley) B.; m. Nancy Dean Callow, Sept. 6, 1969; children: David Charles, Sarah Jane. M.B.Ch.B., U. Manchester, Eng., 1967; PhD, U. Wales, 1986. Lectr. Welsh Nat. Sch. Medicine, 1972-78, vis. sr. lectr., 1978-81; cons. hematologist Llandough Hosp., Penarth, Wales, 1981—; hon. clin. faculty U. Wales, 1981—. Sr. med. editor Jour. of Evaluation in Clin. Practice. Avocations: sailing, radio electronics. Office: Llandough Hosp, Penlan Rd, Cardiff CF64 4XX, Wales

BENTLEY, FRED DOUGLAS, SR., lawyer; b. Marietta, Ga., Oct. 15, 1926; s. Oscar Andrew and Ima Irene (Prather) B.; children from previous marriage: Fred Douglas, Robert Randall; m. Jane Morrill McNeel, Nov. 7, 1997. BA, Presbyn. Coll., 1949; JD, Emory U., 1948; HHD (hon.), Kennesaw State U., 1999, PhD (hon.), 2000, LHD (hon.), 2000. Bar: Ga. 1948. Sr. mem. Bentley & Dew, Marietta, 1948-51; ptnr. Bentley, Awtrey & Bartlett, Marietta, 1951-56, Edwards, Bentley, Awtrey & Parker, Marietta, 1956-75, Bentley & Schindelar, Marietta, 1975-80, Bentley, Bentley & Bentley, Marietta, 1975—; pres. Beneficial Investment Co., Newmarket, Inc., Happy Valley, Inc., Bentley & Sons, Inc.; founder, chmn. bd. Charter Bank and Trust Co.; founder, trustee emeritus Kennesaw Coll. Mem. Ga. Ho. Reps., 1951-57, Ga. Senate, 1958; past pres. Cobb County (Ga.) C. of C.; founder, hon. curator Bentley Rare Book Galleries-Brenau U., Kennesaw State U.; mem., past chmn. Ga. Coun. Arts, 1976-89; mem. Gov.'s Fine Arts Com., 1990-92, Cummer Mus. of Art (hon. life); attache Ghana Olympic Com.; founder Cobb Emergency Svcs., bd. advisors Emory U-Woodruff. Served with USN. Recipient Blue Key Cmty. Svc. award, Founder's award, 1992, Clarisse Baquell award for outstanding svc., Spl. Svc. award Kennesaw State U., Robert Cleveland award for lifetime achievement in law; named Citizen of Yr., C. of C., 1951, Leader of Tomorrow, Time mag., 1953, Vol. Citizen of Yr., Atlanta Jour./Constn., 1981, Kennesaw Hist. Soc. Man of Yr., 1996, Brenau U.. Man of Yr. award, 1996, President's award Kennesaw State U., 1999, Disting. Alumna Marietta H.S.; fellow J. Pierpont Morgan Libr.; Oct. 15 Fred Bentley Day City & Coun.; Bridge named in his honor, 2000. Mem. ABA, Ga. Bar Assn., Ga. Mus. Art (bd. advisors, hon. life mem.), Nat. PTA (hon. life), Cobb Landmarks Soc. (founder), Kennesaw Mountain Jaycees (founder), Rotary (hon. life), Georgian Club (bd. dirs.), The Grolier Club (hon.), Fellows of Marietta Cobb Mus. of Art (founder, chmn.). Republican. Methodist. Home: 1441 Beaumont Dr Kennesaw GA 30152-3201 Office: 241 Washington Ave NE Marietta GA 30060-1958

BENTLEY, GEORGE, orthopedics educator, researcher, consultant, surgeon; b. St. Albans, U.K., Jan. 19, 1936; s. George and Doris (Blagden) B.; m. Ann Gillian Hutchings, Apr. 6, 1960; children: Sarah, Paul, Stephen. MB, ChB, U. Sheffield, 1959, M in Surgery, 1972. Cert. orthopaedic surgeon. House surgeon, house physician Royal Infirmary, Sheffield, 1959-60, SHO in orthopaedics, 1960-61; lectr. in anatomy U. of Birmingham (U.K.), 1961-62; SHO in surgery Manchester Royal Infirmary, 1962-63; rotating surg. registrar Sheffield Royal Infirmary and Children's Hosp., 1963-67; registrar in orthopaedics Orthopaedic Hosp., Owenstry, U.K., 1965-67; sr. registrar in orthopaedics Nuffield Orthocentre Radcliff Infirmary, Oxford, Eng., 1967-69; instr. in orthopaedics U. Pitts., 1969-70; lectr., sr. lectr., clin. reader U. Oxford, 1970-76; prof. orthopaedics and accident surgery U. Liverpool, U.K., 1976-82; prof. orthopaedics Univ. Coll., London; hon. cons. orthopaedic surgeon Royal Nat. Orthopaedics Hosp., Middlesex Hosp., London, 1982—. Editor, author: Mercer's Orthopaedic Surgery, 1996, Robb & Smiths Operative Orthopaedics, 1991; contbr. papers on osteoarthritis, cartilage cell-engring. and biomaterials to profl. jours. Fellow Acad. Med. Scis., Royal Coll. Surgeons of Eng., Royal Coll. Surgeons Edinburgh; mem. British Orthop. Rsch. Soc. (pres. 1986-87), British Orthop. Assn. (pres. 1991-92), European Fedn. of Nat. Assns. of Orthopaedics and Traumatology (exec. com. 1995—), Soc. Francaise de Chirurgie Orthopédique et Traumatologique (hon.). Avocations: golf, tennis, music, horolgy. Office: Inst of Orthopaedics, Brockley Hill, Stanmore Middlesex HA7 4LP, England

BENTLEY, HELEN, nursing educator; b. Leicester, Eng., Dec. 26, 1945; d. Alexander and Mabel (Sturgess) Jordan; m. David Arthur Bentley, Apr. 1, 1967; children: Rachel Dawn Wright, Peter David. Diploma in nursing with distinction, De Montfort U., 1990; postgrad. cert. in edn. of adults, U. Surrey, 1991; MSc, U. Nottingham, 1993. Registered gen. nurse, midwife; nat. cert. in dist. nursing. Dist. nurse/midwife Leicestershire County Coun., 1968-70; gen. practice nursing G.P. Surgery, Leicester, 1971-72; staff nurse Leicester Gen. Hosp., 1973-77; dist. nursing sister Leicestershire Health Authority, 1977-90; nurse tchr. Charles Frears Coll. of Nursing and Midwifery, 1991-94; sr. lectr. DeMontfort U., Leicester, 1994—; founder nurse prescribing pilot project, 1997-98. Book reviewer, 1994—; contbr. articles to profl. jours. Councillor Fleckney Parish Coun., Leicestershire, 1980-95; sch. gov. Fleckney Primary Sch., Leicestershire, 1982-90; chmn., bldg. com. Fleckney Bapt. Ch., 1996—. Mem. Royal Coll. Nursing. Office: DeMontfort U, Scraptoft Campus, Leicester LE7 9SU, England

BENTLEY, JOHN, information, media and finance executive; b. Brighton, UK, Feb. 19, 1940; s. Jack and Peggy Bentley. Chmn. Barclay Securities Investment P/C, 1969-73, Mills and Allen, 1969-73, Brit. Lion Films, 1971-73, Intervision Video P/C, 1981-84, Faxcast Broadcast Corp. P/C, 1990-92, Viewcall Europe P/C, Viewcall Am. Inc., 1994-97; CEO Netmedia Corp. P.L.C.

BENTLEY, JON GILL, English and film educator, associate dean; b. Abilene, Tex., Oct. 9, 1945; s. Clarence Edward and Gloria Sue (Gill) B.; m. Cathy Lynne Bell, June 2, 1978 (div. Aug. 1980); m. Rebecca Ann Zerger, June 9, 1990; children: Laurel Anne Zerger Bentley, Emma June Zerger Bentley, Suzannah Claire Zerger Bentley. BA in English and Comparative Lit., U. N.Mex., 1979, MA in English, 1982, postgrad., 1996—. Editor, publ. English Plug, Austin, 1968-70; loans mgr. Abilene (Tex.) Savs. Assn., 1970-73; owner Tin Ear Music Collective, Nightship Press, Abilene, 1973-75; owner 23d Street Books, El Rito, N.Mex., 1975-77, Albuquerque, 1977-82; vis. lectr. U. N.Mex., Albuquerque, 1979-87; instr. English Albuquerque TVI C.C., 1986—, asst. dean, 1997-98, assoc. dean, 1998—. Author: Hearing Things, 1982, Severe Charm, 1985, New Poems, 1994; editor (lit. jour.) Weedy Teeth, 1985-87. Juror Assn. Am. Poets, 1990-92. Breadloaf fellow Middlwbury Coll., Vt., 1970. Mem. Nat. Coun. Tchrs. English, Nat. Coun. Instrnl. Adminstrs. Democrat. Episcopalian. Office: Albuquerque TVI CC 525 Buena Vista Dr SE Albuquerque NM 87106-4023

BENTLEY, RAYMOND, social studies of technology educator; b. Rochdale, Lancashire, Eng., Nov. 22, 1949; s. Clifford and Clara (Earnshaw) B.; m. Daniela Hoflehner, Dec. 29, 1998; 1 child, Christopher Philip. BS with honors, U. Wales, Bangor, 1971; MS, U. Sussex, Brighton, Eng., 1972, DPhil, 1982. Postgrad. rschr. Sci. Policy Rsch. Unit U. Sussex, 1975-77; guest rschr. dept. sci. studies U. Ulm, Germany, 1977-81; lectr. higher and adult edn. Ulm, 1982-86; sr. lectr. Liverpool (Eng.) Bus. Sch. Liverpool John Moores U., 1986-89; prof. Fachhochschule Ulm U. Applied Scis., 1989—, dep. head of faculty Fachbereich Grundlagen, 1993—; jour. referee Rsch. Policy, 1976—. Author: Technological Change in the German Democratic Republic, 1984, Research and Technology in the Former German Democratic Republic, 1992. Mem. Partnership with Third World, Ulm. Recipient Jean Monnet awards European Cmty., 1991, 92, 93, 96, 97, 98, 99; grantee Dept. Edn. Sci., 1971-72, postgrad. rsch. grantee Sci. Rsch. Coun., 1975-77; rsch. scholar German Acad. Exch. Svc., 1977-79. Mem. Verband Hochschule und Wissenschaft. Avocations: music, films, traveling. Office: U Applied Scis Fachhoch Ulm, Postfach 3860, 89028 Ulm Germany

BENTLEY, ROBIN ERIC, physicist; b. Sydney, Australia, Dec. 31, 1939; s. Eric Hindle and Victoria Eliza (Starr) B.; Glenys Robyn Prothero, Nov. 30, 1976 (div. Nov. 1990); 1 child, Celia Elziabeth. BSc, U. Sydney, Australia, 1960, MSc, 1974. Exptl. scientist CSIRO, Australia, 1960-73, sr. exptl. scientist, 1973-87, prin. exptl. scientist, 1987-91, sr. rsch. scientist, 1991-98, prin. rsch. scientist, 1998—; rschr. and cons. in field. Author: Theory and Practice of Thermoelectric Thermometry, 1998, Temperature and Humidity Measurement, 1998; editor: Resistance and Liquid-in-Glass Thermometry, 1998; contbr. articles to profl. jours.; inventor in field. Mem. Australian Inst. Physics. Avocations: ballroom dancing, Latin-Am. dancing. Office: CSIRO, Bradfield Rd, Sydney 2070, Australia

BENTON, EDWARD HENRY, lawyer; b. Norwalk, Conn., Dec. 1, 1950; s. Edward Failing and Margaret Theresa (Sabo) B. BA, Yale U., 1974; JD, Vanderbilt U., 1981. Bar: N.Y. 1982. Pres. POS Corp., New Haven, 1974-76; asst. account exec. Benton & Bowles Inc., N.Y.C., 1976-78; assoc. Simpson Thacher & Bartlett, N.Y.C., 1981-85, Skadden, Arps, Slate, Meagher & Flom, N.Y.C., 1985-86, Cadwalader, Wickersham & Taft, N.Y.C., 1987; chmn. bd. dirs., gen. counsel Video Cave, Inc., Catskill, NY; bd. dirs. Columbia County Indsl. Devel. Agy. Mem. Vanderbilt U. Law Rev., 1980-81. Patrick Wilson scholar, 1978-81. Mem. Yale Club (N.Y.C.), Royal Hong Kong Yacht Club. Episcopalian. E-mail: edwardbenton@mail.com. Home and Office: 88 Richmond Rd PO Box 88 Malden Bridge NY 12115-0088

BENTSEN, LLOYD, former government official, former senator; b. Mission, TX, Feb. 11, 1921; s. Lloyd M. and Edna Ruth (Colbath) B.; m. Beryl Ann Longino, Nov. 27, 1943; children: Lloyd M. III, Lan, Tina. J.D., U. Tex., 1942. Bar: Tex. 1942. Practice law McAllen, Tex., 1945-48; judge Hidalgo County, Tex., (hdqs. Edinburg), 1946-48; mem. 80th-83d congresses from 15th Tex. Dist.; pres. Lincoln Consol., Houston, 1955-70; U.S. Senator from Tex., 1971-93, chmn. senate fin. com.; mem. senate commerce, sci., transp. and joint com. on taxation and congl. joint econ. com.; sec. Dept. Treasury, Washington, 1993-94; ptnr. Verner, Lipfert, Bernhard, McPherson and Hand; Democratic nominee for Vice Pres. U.S., 1988. Served to maj. USAAF, 1942-45. Decorated D.F.C., Air Medal with 3 oak leaf clusters; recipient Presdl. medal of Freedom, 1999.

BENTZ, EDWARD JOSEPH, JR., energy, environment and transportation management consulting firm executive; b. N.Y.C., May 17, 1945; m. Carole. BS in Physics, Rensselaer Poly. Inst., 1966; vis. fellow Rockefeller Inst., 1966-67; MPhil., Yale U., 1969, PhD, 1971. Danmark-Amerika Fondet George C. Marshall fellow Neils Bohr Inst., Copenhagen, 1971-72; vis. fellow USSR Acad. Scis., 1972, mem. tech. staff David Sarnoff Research Center, RCA, Princeton, N.J., 1972-74; mem. policy staff EPA, Washington, 1974-77; Congl. fellow U.S. Senate com. Commerce, sci. and transp., Washington, 1976-77; dir. impact analysis Presidential-Congl. Nat. Transp. Policy Study Commn., Washington, 1977-79; exec. dir. Presidential-Congl. Nat. Alcohol Fuels Commn., Washington, 1979-80; pres. E.J. Bentz & Assocs., Inc., Springfield, Va., 1980—. appointed mem. Fairfax County Va. Wetlands Bd., 1986—, vice-chmn., 1988—. Author books; contbr. articles to profl. jours. Mem. NAS (transp. rsch. bd. rail tank care design com. 1992—), N.Y. Acad. Scis., Transp. Research Bd. , Va. Acad. Scis., Soc. Govt. Regulatory Economists, Sigma Xi, Sigma Pi Sigma. Office: EJ Bentz & Assocs Inc 7915 Richfield Rd Springfield VA 22153-2324

BENTZINGER, RUDOLF, history of German language educator; b. Erfurt, Thuringia, Germany, Aug. 22, 1936; s. Rudolf and Hermine (Kruse) B. State exam. for mid. sch. tchr., Tchrs. Tng. Coll., Erfurt, 1956; state exam. for secondary sch. tchr., Friedrich Schiller U., Jena, Germany, 1959, Dr phil, 1968, Habilitation, 1991. Tchr. mid. sch., Kirchscheidungen, Germany, 1956-61; sci. asst. Tchrs. Tng. Coll., Leipzig, Germany, 1961-67, lectr., 1968-76; sci. worker Acad. Scis. German Dem. Republic, Berlin, 1976-90, Berlin-Brandenburgische Acad. Scis., 1991—; headmaster team German Text Mid. Ages, Berlin, 1992—; hon. prof. U. Tech. Berlin; substitute prof. Johann Gutenberg U. Author: Mainz History of German Language & Medieval Literature des 15 Jahrhunderts, 1973, Die Wahrheit muss ans Licht, 1982, Untersuchungen zur Syntax der Reformationsdialoge 1520-1525, 1992, Studien zur Erfurter Literaturopractice, 1998-2000; editor Deutsche Texte des Mittelalters, 1982—; co-editor Internat. Jahrbuch für Germanistik, 1992—. Home: Hans Loch Strasse 64, D-99099 Erfurt Germany Office: Berlin-Brandenb Acad Scis, Jägerstrasse 22/23, D-10117 Berlin Germany

BENVENISTE, XAVIER, computer company executive; b. Paris, May 21, 1955; married; 2 children. PhD in Math., U. d'Orsay, 1984, M in Computer Scis., 1987. Tchr. ENS rue d'Ulm, Paris, 1974-78; researcher CNRS, Paris, 1978-86; engr. Dassault Système, Paris, 1986-87; engr. Computervision, Paris, 1987-94, R&D mgr., 1989-94; CAD/CAM Cascade Devel. Matra Datavision, 1994-98; CAD/CAM prin. engr. Parametric Tech., Waltham, Mass., 1998—. Avocations: swimming, painting, music. Home: 5 bis Rue Henri Thirard, BP-25, 94240 L'Hay les Roses Cedex, France Office: Parametric Tech France, Parc Buropale Bat 15, 91573 Brevres Cedex, France

BENVENUTI, ALBERTO GUGLIELMO, library director, archaeologist; b. Florence, Tuscany, Italy, Sept. 21, 1944; s. Giuseppe Feliciano Benvenuti and Aurora Bacchini. BSc, State U., Florence, 1972; MSc, Stanford U., 1974. Cert. dr. in archaeology. Editor-in-chief Olimpia Edits., Florence, 1968-74; asst. lectr. State U., Florence, 1975-76; sch. master State H.S., Athens, 1977-79; libr. Italian Sch. Archaeology at Athens, 1980-82, libr.'s dir., 1983—, archives dir., 1997—; sector dir. Italian Excavation Mission, Poliochni, Lemnos, Greece, 1987—, Italian Survey Mission, Kefalonia, Greece, 1996—; pub. adviser LM Edits., Athens, 1989—; mem. exam. bd. Ministry Culture, Athens, 1990—. Author: (book) Archaeology and Mythology, 1996; editor: (book) Il Museo di Lemno, 1995; mem. editl. staff Magna Graecia, 1999—; contbr. articles to profl. jours. Mem. Soc. for Study of Greek Ancient Tech., Greek Soc. Archaeology, German Inst. Archaeology, Italian Inst. for Exptl. Archaeology, Italian Inst. Prehistory and Protohistory, Soc. Roman Studies at Athens, Soc. for the Revival of the Nemea Games, Archaeol. Inst. Paros and Cyclads. Fax: 30 1 7240133. E-mail: algul@yahoo.com. Home: Patr Ioakeim 25, 10675 Athens Greece Office: Italian Sch Archaeol Athens, Pathenonos 14, 11742 Athens Greece

BEN-YAACOV, GIDEON, computer system designer; b. Bney Brack, Israel, July 26, 1941; came to U.S., 1979; s. Abraham and Henda (Natel) B-Y.; m. Miriam R. Schultz, May 11, 1967; children: David, Saul. BSEE, Technion Israel Inst. Tech., Haifa, 1966. R&D engr. Israeli Ministry of Def., Haifa, 1967-69; sci. asst. U. of the Witwatersrand, Johannesburg, Republic of South Africa, 1969-71; head office engr. ESCOM, Johannesburg, 1971-79; staff engr. Gibbs & Hill, Omaha, 1979-82; head process computer engring. HDR, Omaha, 1982-83; cons. engr. Power Utility Process Computer Engring., Omaha, 1983-92; sr. engr. advanced transp. techs. MFS Network Techs., Omaha, 1992-96, MFS Transp. Sys., Mt. Laurel, N.J., 1996—. Contbr. tech. articles to Process Computer Systems Engring.; author tech. papers. Mem. IEEE (sr.), Instrument Soc. Am. (sr., Philip P. Sprague Application award for devel. advanced operator interface, 1980). Achievements include research on human-factors in power and transportation industries; development of operator interface terminals for power plant computer systems, sound verification and validation procedures to enhance software QA process; technical and administrative leadership for the design of more than 30 advanced computer systems for the process industries; introduction of application of distributed controls for electrostatic precipitators. Home: 1870 Mayfair Dr Omaha NE 68144-1050

BEN YAHIA, HABIB, Tunisian government official; b. Tunis, Tunisia, July 30, 1938; married; 2 children. B.A., U. Tunis, 1962; postgrad. in internat. relations, Columbia U., 1964-65. With Tunisian Ministry Fgn. Affairs, 1963—, head econ. coop. with U.S., 1965-67; econ. counselor Tunisian embassy, Washington, 1967-70, Paris, 1970-73; div. chief Bilateral Fin. Coop. Ministry Tunisian embassy, 1973-75, asst. dir. internat. coop., 1975-76, chief staff ministry, 1976-77; 1st ambassador to Japan, 1977-81; ambassador to Belgium, 1981, to U.S., Washington, 1981-88; former min. fgn. affairs Tunis; min. Ministry of Nat. Def.; now min. fgn. affairs Ministry Fgn. Affairs, Tunis, Tunisia. Decorated comdr. de l'Ordre de la Republique, other fgn. medals. Office: Ministry Fgn Affairs, Pl du Gouvernement, Kasbah Tunis 1006, Tunisia*

BENYAMINI, DUBI, mechanical engineer; b. Haifa, Israel, July 26, 1941; s. Avraham Zupraner and Henya (Filozof) Benyamini; m. Ester Zilberfarb, Jan. 8, 1969 (div. Apr. 1983); children: Asaf, Talya; m. Lea Kremer, May 15, 1983; children: Avishai, Eran, Sigal. BSME, Hatechnion, 1963, MS in Aeronautical Engr., 1965. Maj. Israeli Airforce, 1963-92, ret., 1992. Author: A Field Guide to the Butterflies of Israel, 1990, 4th edit., 1997; editor News of the Israeli Lepidopterists Soc., 1983—. Chief ops. Aeroclub, Herzelia, 1974-84, pres., 1984-92. Active Israeli Def. Force, 1963-69, Reserves, 1969-92. Fellow Royal Entomol. Soc.; mem. Israeli Lepidopterists Soc. (pres. 1983—), Societas European Lepidopterologia, Am. Lepidopterists Soc., Linneana Belgica, Brit. Butterfly Conservation Soc., Assn. for Tropical Lepidoterra, Xerces Soc., Israeli Entomol. Soc., Chilean Entomol. Soc., Am. Soc. Mfg.

Engrs. (sr.). Avocations: gardening, lepidopterist, private pilot. E-mail: dubi ben@netvision.net.il. Home: 91 Levona St, 71947 Bet-Arye Israel Office: Dept 2629, 70100 Lahav Israel

BENYON, WILLIAM, landowner; b. London, Jan. 17, 1930; s. Richard and Eve (Cecil) B.; m. Elizabeth Hallifax, Aug. 24, 1957; children: Catherine, Richard, Edward, Mary, Susannah. Student, Royal Naval Coll., 1943-47. Lt. Royal Navy, 1947-57; exec. Couraulds Ltd., London, 1957-67; M.P. Ho. of Commons, 1970-92; chmn. Peabody Trust, London, 1992-97, Ernest Cook Trust, Gloucestershire, U.K., 1992—. Knight, Queen of Eng., 1994. Conservative. Mem. Ch. of England. Home: Englefield House, NR Reading, Berkshire RG7 5EN, England Office: Englefield Estate Office, Theale, Reading RG7 5DU, England

BENZ, CARL ARVELL, nuclear engineer, physics educator; b. Batavia, Iowa, Nov. 27, 1911; s. Charles William and Anna Mathilda (Erickson) B.; children: Beverly, Karen, William, Robert. BSc in Physics, Iowa Wesleyan U., 1932; MSc in Physics, U. Iowa, 1934; postgrad., U. Chgo., 1936. Cert. tchr. physics, Ind.; registered profl. engr., Calif. Devel. engr. Sinclair Refining Co., East Chicago, Ind., 1934-35, Anaconda Lead Products, East Chicago, 1935-36; physics instr. Hammond (Ind.) H.S., 1936-42, Lyons Twp. H.S., LaGrange, Ill., 1942-47; assoc. physicist Argonne (Ill.) Nat. Lab., 1947-52; nuclear engr. Blaw-Knox Co., Pitts., 1952-63; assoc. prof. State Coll. Iowa, Cedar Falls, 1963-65, Grove City (Pa.) Coll., 1965-67; nuclear engr. Stone & Webster, Boston, 1967-68, United Engring. and Constructors, Boston, 1968-69; engring. specialist Bechtel Power Corp., Gaithersburg, Md., 1969-76; ret. Contbr. articles to profl. jours. Mem. Am. Nuclear Soc. (chmn. D.C. sect. 1974-75), Kiwanis, Phi Delta Kappa. Methodist. Achievements include discovery of structure of liquid/isopentane disappeared at critical point; research on critical assembly leading to nautilus submarine determining cladding metals and control rod size. Home: 3314 Chiswick Ct Apt 1G Silver Spring MD 20906-1635

BENZ, JOCHEN WALTER, business administration educator, management consultant; b. Stuttgart, Germany, May 24, 1955; s. Walter and Inge (Zeininger) B. Diplom-Wirtschafts-Ingenieur, U. Karlsruhe, Germany, 1979, DrRerPol, 1981. Mem. rsch. staff U. Karlsruhe, 1980-81; mgr. Nagoldtal Reisen, Nagold, Germany, 1981-85; prof. F.H. fulda U., Fulda, Germany, 1985-92; prof. bus. mgmt. FH Konstanz U., Konstanz, Germany, 1992—; mktg. dir. EXTRATOURS, Nagold, 1982-85; mktg. cons. to several cos. in Europe, 1986-95; mgmt. cons. to several cos. in Europe, 1995—. Author: Optimale Werbebudget- und Werbeprogrammplanung, 1981; contbr. articles to profl. jours. Mem. German Assn. for Ops. Rsch., German Assn. for Computing, German Assn. for Classifications. Avocations: sailing, skiing. Office: Fachhochschule Konstanz, Brauneggerstr 55, D-78462 Konstanz Germany

BENZECRI, JEAN-PAUL, mathematics educator; b. Oran, France, Feb. 28, 1932; s. Emile and Odette (Benyamine) B.; m. Francoise Le Roy, Oct. 17, 1960; 1 child, Jean. Agrecation, Ecole Normale Superieure, Paris, 1953; PhD, U. Princeton, 1955; Doctorat D'Etat, Sorbonne, Paris, 1960. Asst. prof. ENS, Paris, 1955-58; oper. rsch. asst. French Navy, 1958-60; prof. U. Rennes, France, 1960-65, U. Sorbonne, Paris, 1965-92. Author/editor five vols. in economy, linguistics and medicine, with one translated into English: Correspondence Analysis Handbook; author: Treatise: L'Analyse Des Donnees Vols. 1-2, 1973; editor: Review: Cahiers de L'Analyse des Donnees, Vols. 1-22, 1975-97. Recipient awards in field.

BENZER, SEYMOUR, neuroscience educator; b. N.Y.C., Oct. 15, 1921; s. Mayer and Eva (Naidorf) B.; m. Dorothy Vlosky, Jan. 10, 1942 (dec. 1978); children: Barbara Ann Benzer Freidin, Martha Jane Benzer Goldberg; m. Carol A. Miller, May 11, 1980; 1 child, Alexander Robin. BA, Bklyn. Coll., 1942; MS, Purdue U., 1943, PhD, 1947, DSc (hon.), 1968; DSc, Columbia U., 1974, Yale U., 1977, Brandeis U., 1978, CUNY, 1978, U. Paris, 1983, Rockefeller U., N.Y.C., 1993, Cold Spring Harbor Watson Sch. of Biol. Scis., 1999. Mem. faculty Purdue U., 1945-67, prof. biophysics, 1958-61, Stuart disting. prof. biology, 1961-67; prof. biology Calif. Inst. Tech., 1967-75, Boswell prof. neurosci., 1975—; biophysicist Oak Ridge Nat. Lab., 1948-49; vis. assoc. Calif. Inst. Tech., Pasadena, 1965-67. Contbr. articles to profl. jours. Rsch. fellow Calif. Inst. Tech., 1949-51; Fulbright rsch. fellow Pasteur Inst., Paris, 1951-52; sr. NSF postdoctoral fellow Cambridge, Eng., 1957-58; recipient Award of Honor Bklyn. Coll., 1956, Sigma Xi rsch. award Purdue U., 1957, Ricketts award U. Chgo., 1961, Gold medal N.Y. City Coll. Chemistry Alumni Assn., 1962, Gairdner award of merit, 1964, McCoy award Purdue U., 1965, Lasker award, 1971, T. Duckett Jones award, 1975, Prix Leopold Mayer French Acad. Scis., 1975, Louisa Gross Horwitz award, 1976, Harvey award Israel, 1977, Warren Triennial prize Mass. Gen. Hosp., 1977, Dickson award, 1978, Rosenstiel award, 1986, T.H. Morgan medal Genetics Soc. Am., 1986, Karl Spencer Lashley award, 1988, Gerard award Soc. Neurosci., 1989, Helmerich award, 1990, Wolf Found. Prize (in medicine), Israel, 1991, Bristol-Myers Squibb Neurosci. award, 1992, Crafoord prize Royal Swedish Acad. Scis., 1993, Mendel award Brit. Genetical Soc., 1994, Alberto Feltrinelli prize Accademia dei Lincei, Italy, 1994, Internat. prize for biology, Japan, 2000. Fellow Indian Acad. Scis. (hon.); mem. Nat. Acad. Scis., Am. Acad. Arts and Scis., Am. Philos. Soc. (Lashley award 1988), Harvey Soc., N.Y. Acad. Scis., AAAS, Royal Soc. London (fgn. mem.), Royal Acad. of Scis. of Spain (fgn. mem.), Acad. des Scis. France (fgn. mem.). Home: 2075 Robin Rd San Marino CA 91108-2831

BENZIANE, KHALID, radiologist; b. Fes, Morocco, Feb. 26, 1959; arrived in France, 1978; s. Mohamed and Zineb (Ababou) B. MD, Med. U., Bordeaux, France, 1985; 3d degree (splty.), Med. U., Poitiers, France, 1989. Hosp. physician in radiology Châtellerault (France) Hosp., 1989—. Contbr. articles to med. jours. Mem. Assn. Formation Radiologic and Med. Imagery, Pontevin Radiology Study Group. Avocations: philately, numismatism, history of Arabic medicine, African arts. Office: Hosp Ctr Camille Guerin, 5 pl Ste-Catherine Rad Svc, F-86100 Cedex Chatellerault France

BEOM, HYEON GYU, engineering educator; b. Kwangju, Korea, Aug. 28, 1963; s. Hee Rok and Young Rye (Lee) B.; m. Seong Hee Oh, Nov. 16, 1991; children: Eugene, Euyoung. BS, Seoul Nat. U., 1985; MS, Korea Advanced Inst. Sci. and Tech., Taejon, 1988, PhD, 1993. Rsch. asst. Korea Advanced Inst. Sci. and Tech., Taejon, 1988-92, rschr., 1993, postdoctoral fellow, 1995; postdoctoral fellow Ga. Inst. Tech., Atlanta, 1993-95; sr. rschr. Hyundai Electronics Industries, Ichon, Korea, 1996; asst. prof. Chonnam Nat. U., Kwangju, Korea, 1997—. Contbr. articles to profl. jours. E-mail: hgbeom@chonnam.ac.kr. Fax: 82-62-530-1689. Office: Chonnam Nat U, 300 Yongbong-dong, Kwangju 500-757, Korea

BEPPU, KEIKO, American literature educator; b. Toyonaka, Osaka, Japan, June 3, 1936; s. Tsunekoto and Kimiko (Konishi) B.; m. Hiroshi Hirai, May 23, 1961 (div. May 1963). BA in English, Kobe Coll., Nishinomiya, Japan, 1959; MA in English Lang. and Lit., U. Mich., 1967, EdD in English Lang. and Lit., 1973. Asst., lectr. Kobe Coll., Nishinomiya, 1968-70, lectr., 1973-74, assoc. prof., 1974-82, prof., 1982-99, chair English dept., 1991-95, dir. Rsch. Inst., 1987-91, 95-99, dir. rsch., 1995-99; pres. Matsuyama Shinonome Coll., Japan, 1999—; vis. prof. Mich. State U., East Lansing, 1980-81; lectr. Kwansei Gakuin U., Nishinomiya, 1989-96; trustee Kobe Coll., Nishinomiya, 1993—. Author: The Educated Sensibility in Henry James and Walter Pater, 1979; author, editor: The Image of Woman in American Literature, 1985, The River and the American Imagination, 1992; co-author: As Others Read Us: International Perspectives on American Literature, 1991, Melville and Melville Studies in Japan, 1993; author, editor: New Essays on Edith Wharton, 1997; editl. staff Studies in English Literature, English Literary Soc. Japan, 1983-87. Internat. fellow AAUW, Washington, 1972-73. Mem. Am. Lit. Soc. Japan (pres. Kansai chpt. 1993-97, councillor 1988—, v.p. Japan 1998-2000, pres. 2000—), Emily Dickinson Soc. (trustee 1992—), Internat. Edith Wharton Soc., Rotary Club (Matsuyama). Avocations: skiing, oil painting, traveling. Office: Matsuyama Shinonome Coll Kuwabara, Matsuyama-shi Japan

BERA, RAJENDRA KUMAR, aerospace engineer, researcher; b. Kanpur, India, Nov. 27, 1945; s. Bankim Chandra and Saroj Kumari (Jana) B. BTech, Indian Inst. Tech., Kanpur, 1967, MTech, 1969, PhD, 1976. Scientist Nat. Aerospace Labs., Bangalore, India, 1971-95; cons. software specialist Tata-IBM Ltd., Bangalore, India, 1995-97, IBM Global Svcs., India, 1997—; vis. faculty Indian Inst. Tech., Kanpur, 1988; vis. asst. prof. U. Okla., Norman, 1979-80. Fellow Instn. of Engrs. India (mem. exec. com. 1986—); mem. N.Y. Acad. Scis. Avocations: journalism, music. Office: IBM Global Svcs, Golden Enclave, Airport Rd, 560 017 Bangalore India

BERAHO, ENOCH KAROBE, management educator; b. Mbarara, Uganda, Dec. 25, 1938; m. Leconcia Abahuje Gashongore, Aug. 12, 1993; children: Joseph B., Lorraine K., Nicole K., Nicholas B. BS with honors, U. London, 1965; MS in Genetics, Makerere U., Kampala, Uganda, 1972; MBA, Nat. U., San Diego, 1981; PhD in Mgmt., U.S. Internat. U., San Diego, 1978. Genetics rsch. fellow Ministry of Agr. Uganda, Kampala, 1966-72; asst. prof. mgmt. S.C. State U., Orangeburg, 1981-85, prof. mgmt., 1985-97, 1997—. Fin. advisor Euclare Health Ctr., Columbia, S.C., 1995—. Mem. Am. Stats. Assn., Western Acad. of Mgmt. Anglican. Avocations: swimming, reading, travel. Home: 8 Stamport Ct Irmo SC 29063-8455

BERAN, ROY GARY, neurologist; b. Sydney, Mar. 6, 1950; s. Frederick and Erica (Grosner) B.; m. Maureen Elizabeth Riley, Oct. 18, 1944; children: Ruth Elizabeth, Rachel, Esther, Joshua Robert. MBBS, U. New South Wales, Australia, 1972, MD, 1984; Diploma of Tertiary Edn., U. New Eng., Australia, 1982; B Legal Sci., Macquarie U., Sydney, 1992; diplome, Adeliade CAE, Australia. Training St. Vincents Hosp., Sydney, 1973-75; gen. practice Sydney, 1976-77; neurology trainee Public Hosp., Adelaide, Australia, 1978-80, Prince of Wales/Prince Henry Hosp., Sydney, 1980-82; neurologist Prince Henry Hosp., Sydney, 1982—; vis. neurologist Royal Rehab. Ctr., Sydney, 1982—; cons. neurologist Royal Australian Navy, 1982—; vis. neurologist South Western Health Area, Sydney, 1983—, Macquarie Hosp., 1984—; vis. fellow Cmty. Medicine U. NSW, 1993—. Contbr. numerous articles to profl. jours.; presenter in field; editor books. Rep. ACROD, 1990—; gov. bd. mem. World Assn. Medicine Law, 1996—; bd. dirs. Australian Inst. Health Law & Ethics, 1996—. Ltd. comdr. RANR. Recipient Public Health prize Univ. New South Wales, 1972; Francis Hardy Fauldings Meml. rsch. fellow, 1981, Winston Churchill Meml. Trust fellowship, 1982. Fellow Royal Australasian Coll. Physicians, Australian Coll. of Legal Medicine (exec. councilor 1995-97, v.p. 1998—, bd. editors jour. 1998—, censor in chief 1999—), Am. Acad. Neurology, Australian Faculty Pub. Health Medicine, Royal Australian Coll. Gen. Practitioners, Royal Coll. Physicians UK, Australian Coll. Biomed. Scientists , Royal Soc. Medicine; mem. Epilepsy Soc. Australia (bd. dirs. 1980-93, 99—), Epilepsy Assn. of NSW, Australian Assn. of Neurologists, Australian Mil. Assn. Jewish. Avocations: surfing, skiing, travelling, studying, writing. Office: 12 Thomas St Ste 5 6th fl, Chatswood 2067, Australia

BERAN, SAMUEL JONATHAN, plastic surgeon; b. Phila., June 5, 1966; s. Irving Nathan and Phyllis Elaine Beran; m. Nancy Reisman, Aug. 25, 1996; 1 child, Jacob Alexander. BS, Union Coll., 1988; MD, Albany Med. Coll., 1990. Diplomate Am. Bd. Plastic Surgery, Am. Bd. Surgery. Resident in gen. surgery Thomas Jefferson Hosp., Phila., 1990-95; resident in plastic surgery U. Tex. Southwestern, Dallas, 1995-97, asst. prof. plastic surgery, 1997-99; plastic surgeon White Plains, N.Y., 1999—; mem. staff No. Westchester Hosp. Ctr., Sound Shore Med. Ctr., United Hosp. Med. Ctr., White Plains Hosp. Ctr.; presenter in field. Author: Ultrasound-Assisted Liposuction, 1998; author chpts. to books; mem. editl. bd. Selected Readings in Plastic Surgery, 1997—; contbr. more than 25 articles to profl. jours. including Plastic and Reconstructive Surgery, Clin. Plastic Surgery. Mem. organizing staff Phila. chpt. Am. Cancer Soc., 1990-95. Grantee NIH, 1988. Mem. AMA, Am. Soc. for Laser Medicine and Surgery, Am. Soc. Plastic and Reconstructive Surgeons, Am. Soc. for Aesthetic Plastic Surgery, Med. Soc. State N.Y. (rep. Albany Med. Coll. 1987-90), Plastic Surgery Rsch. Coun., Westchester County Med. Soc., Alpha Omega Alpha. Avocations: scuba diving, traveling, roller blading. Office: 10 Chester Ave White Plains NY 10601-5112

BERANEK, LEO LEROY, acoustical consultant; b. Solon, Iowa, Sept. 15, 1914; s. Edward Fred and Beatrice (Stahle) B.; m. Phyllis Knight, Sept. 6, 1941 (dec. Nov. 1982); children: James Knight, Thomas Haynes; m. Gabriella Sohn, Aug. 10, 1985. A.B., Cornell Coll., 1936, D.Sc. (hon.), 1946; M.S., Harvard U., 1937, D.Sc., 1940; D.Eng. (hon.), Worcester Poly. Inst., 1971; D.Comml. Sci. (hon.), Suffolk U., 1979; LL.D. (hon.), Emerson College, 1982; Dr. Pub. Service (hon.), Northeastern U., 1984. Instr. physics Harvard U., 1940-41, asst. prof., 1941-43; dir. Electro-Acoustics and Systems Rsch. Labs., 1941-46; assoc. prof. communications engring. MIT, 1947-58; pres., dir., chief exec. officer Bolt Beranek & Newman, Cambridge, Mass., 1953-69, chief scientist, 1969-71, dir., 1953-84; pres., chief exec. officer, dir. Boston Broadcasters, Inc., 1963-79, chmn. bd., 1980-83; pres. Am. Acad. Arts and Scis., Cambridge, 1989-94, chair develop. com., 1995—; part-owner WCVB-TV, Boston, 1972-82; chmn. bd. Mueller-BBM GmbH, Munich, 1962-86; bd. dirs. Tech. Integration Inc., Bedford, Mass., 1987—. Author: Principles of Sound Control in Airplanes, 1944, Acoustic Measurements, 1949, 2d edit., 1986, Music, Acoustics and Architecture, 1962, Noise Reduction, 1960, Noise and Vibration Control, 1971, 2d edit., 1988, Noise and Vibration Control Engineering, 1992, Concert and Opera Halls: How They Sound, 1996; contbr. articles on acoustics, audio and TV comm. sys. to tech. publs. Charter mem. bd. overseers Boston Symphony Orch., 1968-80, chmn., 1977-80, trustee, 1977-87, chmn. bd. trustees, 1983-86, hon. chmn., 1987, life trustee 1994-2000; mem. bd. overseers Harvard U., 1984-90; mem. coun. for arts MIT, 1972—; mem. Mass. Commn. on Jud. Conduct, 1986-88, life trustee Cornell Coll., 1998—; others in past. Guggenheim fellow, 1946-47; recipient Presdl. certificate of merit, 1948; Cornell Coll. Alumni Citation, 1953; 1st Silver medal le Groupement des Acousticiens de Langue Francaise Paris, 1966; Abe Lincoln TV award So. Bapt. Conv., 1976; named Sta. WCRB Person of the Yr., 1987. Fellow NAE (bd. dir. marine bd., com. pub. engring. policy, aeros. and space engring. bd.), AAAS, IEEE (chmn. profl. group audio 1950-51), Am. Phys. Soc., Am. Acad. Arts and Scis., Audio Engring. Soc. (pres. 1967-68, Gold medal 1971, gov. 1966-71), Acoustical Soc. Am. (mem. coun. 1944-47, v.p. 1949-50, pres. 1954-55, Bienniel award 1944, Sabine award 1961, Gold medal 1975, Hon. mem. 1994); mem. Inst. Noise Control Engring. (charter pres. 1971-73, dir. 1973-75, 1st Disting. Noise Control Engr. 1997), Internat. Inst. Acoustics (hon. fellow), Mass. Broadcasters Assn. (bd. dirs. 1973-80, pres. 1978-79, Disting. Svc. award 1980), Cambridge Soc. Early Music (pres. 1963-71, dir. 1961-79), Acad. Disting. Bostonians, Greater Boston C. of C. (dir. 1973-79, v.p. 1976-79, Disting. Cmty. Svc. award 1980, 83), St. Botolph Club, Phi Beta Kappa, Sigma Xi, Eta Kappa Nu (eminent mem. 2000). Episcopalian. Home and Office: 975 Memorial Dr Ste 804 Cambridge MA 02138-5755

BERARDESCA, ENZO, educator, researcher; b. Borgosesia, Italy, Sept. 1, 1954; s. Alberto and Laura (Riganti) B.; m. Antonella Mezzadra, Dec. 12, 1981; children: Berardesca, Marta. MD, Univ. Pavia, Pavia, Italy, 1978, dermatology specialist, 1982. Asst. prof. Univ. Pavia, 1982-89; asst. research Univ. Calif., San Francisco, 1987; assoc. prof. Univ. Pavia, 1989, prof., 1990—; chmn. Int. Soc. Bioengineering Skin, 1990—; founder EEMCO Group, Bruselles, Belgium, 1994. Co-editor: Bioengineering of the Skin Series. Avocations: hiking, skiing. Office: U Pavia Dermatology, 27100 Pavia Italy

BERARDI, JORGE ENRIQUE, economist; b. Buenos Aires, June 8, 1937; s. Francisco and Ofelia Beatriz (Pinasco) B.; m. Maria Dolores de las Mercedes Lopez Narvaja; children: Fabiana Beatriz, Gabriela Leonor. Degree in pub. acctg., Buenos Aires U., 1960, lic. in econs., 1969, D in Econs., 1973. Min. economy Provincia de Santa Fé, Argentina, 1976-78; sec. of treas. Govt. of Argentina, Buenos Aires, 1981; econ. adviser Buenos Aires Stock Exch., 1982-85, sec., 1990-92, v.p., 1992-93, pres., 1993-94; adviser Inst. Argentino Mercado de Capitales, Buenos Aires, 1985-89; pres. Inver-Plus Diagonal Mut. Fund, Buenos Aires, 1993-95; pres. MBK Bursatil, 1994-99; owner Jorge Berardi Econ. Advisor, Buenos Aires, 1982—; trustee Acindar, S.A., Buenos Aires, 1983—; bd. dirs. Consultora Este Asiatico. Author: La Crisis del Mercado de Valores Argentino en la Capitalizacion Empresaria, 1974; contbr. more than 200 articles to profl. jours. Fellow Internat. Bank, 1963. Mem. Circulo de Armas, Consejo Argentino para las Relaciones Internacionales. Roman Catholic. Avocation: jogging. Office: Jorge Berardi Econ Adviser, Avda Corrientes 980 7oB, 1043 Buenos Aires Argentina

BERAUD, ALAIN, economics educator; b. Chabanais, France, Aug. 15, 1941; s. Albert and Marianne (Gounin) B.; m. Colette Samoyault, June 23, 1963; children: Ivan, Delphine. PHD, U. Poitiers, France, 1971. Asst. U. Rennes, France, 1964-68; maitre conf. U. Paris IX, 1969-90; prof. econs. U. Rouen, France, 1990-93, U. Cergy, France, 1993—; dir. dept. econs. U. Cergy, 1993-96, v.p. Author: Introduction to Macroeconomics Analysis, 1990; editor New History of Economic Thought, 1992-2000. Home: 7 Rue Petit, 75019 Paris France Office: U Cergy, 33 Blvd du Port, 95011 Cergy France

BERBARY, MAURICE SHEHADEH, physician, military officer, hospital administrator, educator; b. Beirut, Lebanon, Jan. 14, 1923; came to U.S., 1945, naturalized, 1952; s. Shehadeh M. and Marie K. Berbary; children: Geoffrey Maurice, Laura Marie. BA, Am. U., Beirut, 1943; MD, U. Tex., Dallas, 1948; MA in Hosp. Adminstrn., Baylor U., 1970; diploma, Army Command and Gen. Staff Coll., Leavenworth, Kan., 1963, Air Force Sch. Aerospace Medicine, San Antonio, 1964, Army War Coll., Carlisle, Pa., 1969. Diplomate Am. Bd. Ob-Gyn. Intern Parkland Meml. Hosp., Dallas, 1948-49, resident in ob-gyn., gen. surgery and urology, 1949-53; resident in ob-gyn. Walter Reed Army Hosp., Washington, 1955-57; fellow in obstetric and gynecologic pathology Armed Forces Inst. Pathology, Washington, 1959-60; practice clin. medicine in ob-gyn., 1953—; capt. MC U.S. Army, 1952, advanced through grades to col., 1968, sr. flight surgeon, 1970; chief dept. ob-gyn. U.S. Army Hosp., Ft. Polk, La., 1957-59, Womack Army Hosp., Ft. Bragg, N.C., 1960-62; div. surgeon 1st. inf. div., Ft. Riley, Kans., 1963-64, 3d. Armored div., Germany, 1964-65; corps surgeon V. Corps, Germany, 1965-67, 24th Army Corps, S. Vietnam Theater of Operation, 1970; comdr., hosp. adminstr. U.S. Army Hosp., Teheran, Iran, 1954-55; comdr. 43d Hosp. Group Complex, Vietnam, 1969-70; command surgeon U.S. Armed Forces Command and U.S. Army South, U.S. C.Z., Panama, 1970-73; comdr. 5th Gen. Hosp., Stuttgart, West Germany, 1973-77, Munson Army Hosp., Ft. Leavenworth, Kans., 1977-81; sr. staff officer dept. ob-gyn William Beaumont Army Med. Ctr., Ft. Bliss, Tex., 1981-83; ret., 1983, cons. health care adminstrn. and med.-legal affairs, 1984—; vis. lectr. ob-gyn. pathology Duke U. Med. Ctr., Durham, N.C., 1960-62; clin. instr. dept. ob-gyn. U. Kans. Coll. Medicine, Kansas City, 1963-80, advanced to clin. asst. prof., 1980—; instr. 5th Army NCO Acad., Fort Riley, Kans., 1963-64. Decorated Legion of Merit with three oak leaf clusters, Bronze Star medal, Meritorious Svc. medal, Army Commendation medal, Combat Air medal, Sr. Flight Surgeon's badge, Expert Field Med. badge. Fellow ACS, Am. Coll. Ob-Gyn., Am. Coll. Health Care Execs.; mem. AMA, Assn. Mil. Surgeons, Am. Occupational Med. Assn., Soc. U.S. Army Flight Surgeons, Am. Hosp. Assn., N.Y. Acad. Scis., Tex. State Med. Assn., Dallas County Med. Soc., Internat. Platform Assn., Masons (32 deg.). Home and Office: 7923 Abramshire Ave Dallas TX 75231-4712

BERCE, JARO, information and management consultant; b. Ljubljana, Slovenia, Oct. 23, 1954; s. Boris and Avgusta (Ropret) B.; divorced; children: Ziga, Jan; m. Aleksandra Zorc, June 8, 1991; children: Tim, Denis. BEE, U. Ljubljana, 1979; M of Computer Sci., U. Miss., 1986. Grad. asst. Inst. Josef Stefan, Ljubljana, Slovenia, 1979-82; system engr. Iskra Delta, Ljubljana, 1982-85; cons. Iskra Avtomatika, Ljubljana, Slovenia, 1985-88; dir. GRAD, Ljubljana, 1988-93; chief exec. officer S I P & A, Ljubljana, 1993-97; info. tech. expert Deloitte & Touche, Ljubljana, 1997-99; state under sec. Republic of Slovenia, Govt. Office for European Affaires, 1999—; bd. dirs. Phare Cons. for Mgmt. and Info. Tech.; tchr. Acad. for Entrepreneurs; cons. in field. Chair Slovene ISO/IEC, Ljubljana, 1992, Sect. at Beijing Conf., China, 1986; pres. ZSMS Ljubljana Bezigrad, 1974. Fellow Assn. Mgmt. Consulting Slovenia; mem. IEEE, Internat. Project Mgmt. Assn., Assn. Computing Machinery, Rotary. Avocations: tennis, skiing, paragliding, windsurfing. Home: Mlinska Pot 20, 1231 Ljubljana Slovenia

BERCEA, VLADIMIR, research scientist; b. Bucharest, Nov. 26, 1953; s. Gheorghe and Victoria Turcu B.; m. Lucia Ianc, Oct. 30, 1985; 1 child, Gheorghe Teodor. Head of Dept., Mech. Enterprise Prodn., Bucharest, 1984-85; Engr., Mktg. and Mgmt., Bucharest, 1990, 97-98. Head of dept. Mech. Enterprise Prodn., Resita, Romania, 1977-85; scientific rschr. Inst. of Projection and Devel. Rsch. in Mech. Equipments, Bucharest, 1985-89; supr. dept. CIES/Supervising Spl. Equipment, Bucharest, 1989-90; head of quality control dept. Radmil Mil. Engring., Bucharest, 1991-92; head of import-export dept. Radmil, Bucharest, 1992-94, councillor of gen. dir., 1994-96, dept. gen. dir., 1996-98; mktg. dir. Nat. Soc. Radmil Rsch., Bucharest, 1998—. Maj. Army Equipment Mgmt., 1988—. Avocations: fishing, hunting. Office: Comex 97 SA/Sector 3, SOS Garii Catelu nr 1974, Bucharest Romania

BERCELI, TIBOR, education educator; b. Budapest, Aug. 7, 1929; s. Bela and Ilona (Konyi) B.; m. Maria Balla, May 5, 1956; children: Zsuzsanna, Gyorgy. Diploma in Engring., Tech. U., Budapest, 1951; PhD, Acad. of Scis., Budapest, 1955, DS, 1965; Prof. Habilitation, Tech. U., Budapest, 1970. Rschr. Rsch. Inst. for Telecomms., Budapest, 1955-62, head of dept., 1962-87; asst. prof. Tech. U., Budapest, 1962-68, prof., 1970—; vis. prof. Drexel U., Phila., 1988-89; cons. Cen. Rsch. Inst. for Physics, Budapest, 1962-64, Rsch. Inst. for Telecomms., Budapest, 1987—; guest prof. Tech. U., Hamburg, Germany, 1991, Osaka U., Japan, 1992, Nat. Poly. Inst., Elec. Lab. Micromondes et Optoelectronique, Grenoble, France, 1994. Author: (books) Reflex Klystron Modulator, 1967, Nonlinear Microwave Active Circuits, 1987; inventor in field; contbr. articles to profl. publs. Local chmn. URSI Electromagnetic Wave Theory Symposium, Budapest, 1986; chmn. European Microwave Conf., Budapest, 1990; mem. Com. for Telecomm., Budapest, 1966—, URSI Nat. Com., Budapest, 1978—. Recipient State prize Pres. of Hungary, Budapest, 1980. Fellow IEEE. Avocations: hiking, tourism, gardening. Office: Tech U of Budapest, Goldmann Gyorgy ter 3, 1111 Budapest Hungary

BERCKMOES, FREDERIC-BENOIT, environmental and mechanical engineer; b. Lubumbashi, Zaire, Dec. 26, 1932; s. Auguste and Geredina-Marie (Bakker) B.; m. Surleau Claudette, June 19, 1954; children: Cecile, MarieChristine, Francoise. Engr., Arts-Metiers Sch., Brussels, 1956; Indsl. Engr., Belgium State U., Brussels, 1986. Engr. Union Miniere du Haut Katanga, Kolwezi, Republic of Congo, 1958-61, prin. engr., 1961-64, chief dept., 1964-66, mining sec., 1966-67; chief dept. Diamant Bd., Brussels, 1967-69; project engr. Nichols Engring. Co., Brussels, 1969-74, dept. mgr., 1974-80; chief engr. Krebs, Paris, 1980-86; dir. Servithen, Neauphle, France, 1986—; expert chartered to Ct. Appeal, Versailles, France. Patentee in field. Lt. Belgium Army, 1956-58. Decorated Knight of the Order Belgium Crown, 1972. Mem. Round Table Club West Africa (v.p. 1965-66), Lions. Roman Catholic. Avocations: minerals, humanitarian activities. Home: Parc des Bordes 25, 78760 Jouars-Pontchartrain France Office: Servithen, 8 Guillaume de Bois Nivard, 78640 Neauphle France

BERCKX, PAUL F. P. H., retired secretary general Flemish ministry; b. Mol, Fl Brabant, Belgium, Jan. 17, 1925; s. Louis and Louisa (Binje) B.; m. Raymonde Crokaert, Oct. 31, 1950; 1 child, Anna-Maria. BEd, Teachers Coll., Brussels, 1945; Lic. Adminstrn. Law, Higher Adminstrn. Sch., Brussels, 1950; Magister Adminstrn. (hon.), U. South Africa, Praetoria, 1958. Translator Ministry Edn., Brussels, 1945-50, dir., 1950-58, dir.-gen., 1959-80; adminstr. gen. Ministry Flemish Comty., Brussels, 1980-89, sec. gen., 1989-90; retired; founder, mgr. T.B.P., administr's perioiodical, Brussels, 1945-96; founder, pres. Civil Sch. for Civil Servants, Brussels; pres. bd. Cultural Ctr., Wemmel, Belgium, 1980—; v.p. Festival of Flanders, Mechelen, Belgium, 1995—. Chief of cabinet for various mins., Brussels, 1974-84; chief of cabinet for v.p. of Flemish Government, 1984-88. Served with Belgian Army, 1950-51. Mem. Liberal Party. Avocations: cultural and law studies and activities. Home: Markt 46/1, B-1780 Wemmel Brabant, Belgium

BERCOVIER, MICHEL, mathematician; b. Lyon, Rhone, France, Sept. 10, 1941; s. Henri and Nacha (Karmiol) B.; divorced; children: Ouri, Itai, Ido. Lic., U. Paris, 1964; D Sci, U. Rouen, France, 1976. Maitre asst. U. Rouen, 1969-73; dir. Computer Ctr., Jerusalem, 1973-77; lectr. Hebrew U., Jerusalem, 1977-79, sr. lectr., 1979-83, assoc. prof., 1983, prof., 1996; chmn. computer scis. Pole Universitaire Leonard de Vinci, Paris, 1996-98; head W3C Israel Office, 2000—; cons. Kleber Colombes, Paris, 1973-85, Hutchinson, 1992, L'Oreal, 1997; v.p. Bercom, Petah-Tikva, Israel, 1986-96; chmn. bd. dirs. Aleph-Yssum, Jerusalem, 1987-96. V.p. U.E.J.F., Paris, 1965. Recipient Chevalier des Palmes Academiques, French Ministry Edn., 1986, Conseiller du Commerce Exterieur, French Ministry Fgn. Affairs, 1993—.

Mem. S.I.A. (bd. dirs. 1994—), WUA-CFD (chmn. 1992—). Office: Hebrew U, Sch Compu Sci and Eng, Jerusalem 91904, Israel

BERCOVITCH, SACVAN, English language professional, educator; b. Montreal, Que., Can., Oct. 4, 1933; s. Alexander and Brytha (Avrutick) B.; children: Eytan, Alexander. B.A., Sir George William Coll., 1961; M.A., Claremont (Calif.) Grad. Sch., 1963, Ph.D., 1965; LittD (hon.), Concordia U., 1993. Asst. prof. English and Am. lit. Brandeis U., 1966-68; asso. prof. U. Calif., San Diego, 1968-70; prof. English and Am. Lit. Columbia U., 1970-83; Powell M. Cabot prof. Am. lit. Harvard U., 1983—; lectr., Kyoto, Tokyo, Shanghai, Beijing, Amsterdam, Frankfurt, Konstanz, Lisbon, Jerusalem, Tel Aviv, Salzburg, Coimbra, Montreal, Rome, Budapest, Paris, Venice, Bologna, Toronto, Oxford, Berlin, Yale U., Princeton U., U. Pa., U. Calif., Berkeley, L.A., San Diego, Irvine, Cornell U., Dartmouth Coll., Concordia Coll., Claremont Grad. Sch., many others; advisor, cons. in field. Author: Typology and Early American Literature, 1972, The American Puritan Imagination, 1974, The Puritan Origins of the American Self, 1975, The American Jeremiad, 1978, Reconstructing American Literary History, 1986, Ideology and Classic American Literature, 1986, The Office of the Scarlet Letter, 1991, The Rites of Assent: Transformations in the Symbolic Construction of America, 1992; gen. editor: Cambridge History of American Literature. Am. Philos. Soc. fellow, 1968-69, Guggenheim fellow, 1969-70, Am. Coun. Learned Socs. fellow, 1971-72, Nat. Humanities Inst. fellow, 1975-76, Ctr. for Advanced Study in Behavioral Scis. fellow, 1978-79, NEH fellow, 1978-79, 86-87, Woodrow Wilson Ctr. fellow, 1990-91, Time-Life fellow Huntington Libr., 1994—, Cabot fellow for achievement in humanities; recipient James Russell Lowell prize for scholarship, award for excellency in teaching. Fellow Am. Acad. Arts and Scis.; mem. MLA (mem. exec. com. Am. sect. 1976-78), English Inst., Am. Studies Assn. (pres. 1982-84).

BERCOVITZ, GEORGE EDWARD, international marketing consultant; b. N.Y.C., Apr. 6, 1933; s. Nathan and Alice (Wolf) B.; m. Yvette Mittler, Mar. 20, 1955; children: James Michael, Richard Allen. BA, NYU, 1954, MBA, 1961. Advt. and promotion and product mgmt. Joseph E. Seagram & Sons, N.Y.C., 1965-77; account supr. Smith-Greenland, N.Y.C., 1977; dir. advt. and promotions Am. Distilling Co., N.Y.C., 1978-79; sr. account exec. Shaller-Rubin Agy., N.Y.C., 1979-81; v.p. Contact Systems Corp., N.Y.C., 1982-90; pres. GEB Mktg., 1991—; adj. asst. prof. bus. York Coll., CUNY; contr. articles to profl. jours. Officer Hillcrest Jewish Ctr. Mem. Assn. U.S. Army, Am. Mktg. Assn., Global Bus. Assn., Res. Officers Assn., Squadron A Assn., NYU Alumni, AEP Alumni, Brit.-Am. C. of C. Jewish. Avocations: photography, music, reading. Home: 19540F Peck Ave Fresh Meadows NY 11365-2827

BERDOWSKA, EWA DANUTA, physicist, researcher, educator; b. Sosnowiec, Poland, Mar. 17, 1949; d. Władysław and Jozefa (Kecher) Koziol; m. Janusz Marek Berdowski, May 31, 1969; children: Agnieszka, Sylwia. MSc, Silesian U., Katowice, Poland, 1972; PhD in Physics, U. Mining and Metallurgy, Cracow, Poland, 1982. Asst. Silesian Tech. U., Gliwice, Poland, 1972-82, tutor, 1982-91; tutor Czestochowa (Poland) U., 1991—; head gas sensors rsch. and design group Ctrl. Mining Inst., Katowice, 1975-82; head sensors investigation group Exptl. Mine of Coal, Mikolow, Poland, 1982-90; vis. prof. W-R Tech. U., Aachen, Germany, 1994, U. Lvov, Ukraine, 1995, 97, 98. Author: Problems in Physics, 1990, Experiments in Physics, 1992; contbr. articles to profl. jours. Grantee Polish Com. for Sci. Rsch., 1994, 97, Govt. of Poland, 1985, 87. Mem. N.Y. Acad. Scis., European Acoustics Assn., Polish Phys. Soc. Avocations: history, literature. Office: Inst of Physics Czestochowa U, al Armii Krajowej 13, 42 200 Częstochowa Poland

BERDOWSKI, JANUSZ MAREK, physicist, educator, researcher; b. Częstochowa, Poland, Aug. 3, 1945; s. Ferdynand and Helena (Wajzer) B.; m. Ewa Danuta Kozioł, May 31, 1969; children: Agnieszka, Sylwia. MSc, Silesian U., Katowice, Poland, 1969; PhD in Physics, Gdańsk (Poland) U., 1977; DSc in Physics, Poznań (Poland) U., 1988. Asst. Silesian Tech. U., Gliwice, Poland, 1969-77; tutor Silesian Tech. U., Gliwice, 1977-89, asst. prof., 1989-91; assoc. prof. Częstochowa (Poland) U., 1991—; asst. prof. Polish Acad. Sci., Gliwice, Poland, 1994—; head of ultrasonic transd. rsch. and design group Milltronics, Peterborough, Can., 1989-90; mem. sci. couns. Inst. Coal Chemistry, Polish Acad. Scis., 1994—; head of ultrasonic investigation of coal materials dept. Polish Acad. Sci., Gliwice, 1996—; head solid state physics dept. Czestochowa U., 1997—, vis. prof. W-R Tech. Univ., Aachen, Germany, 1993, 97, 99, Lviv (Ukraine) State U., 1995, 97, 2000, Inst. Materials Sci. and Prodn. Enterprise "Carat", Lviv, Ukraine, 1997, 2000; prorector for sci. and rsch. Częstochowa U., 1996—. Author: (book) Influence of Isotope Effects and Phase Transitions on the Interactions of Light and Surface Acoustic Waves in Antiferroelectric Crystals, 1987 (award Minister Nat. Edn. 1989), Discoverer: Crystal Growth and Solid State Material Products and Rsch., 1977-79 (awards Minister of Sci., 1978, Pres. Polish Acad. Scis., 1979, Ultrasonics, 1991 (award Rector of Silesian Tech. U. 1991). Mem. Establishment Commn. of Solidarity, Silesian Tech. U., Gliwice, Poland, 1980-90, v.p. Częstochowa Univ., 1994-95. Grantee Govt. of Poland, Warsaw, 1986, 1988, Polish Com. for Sci. Rsch., Warsaw, 1994, 97. Mem. IEEE, Lasers Electro-Optics Soc. of IEEE, European Acoustics Assn. Paris, Polish Acoustical Soc. (sec. Silesian divsn.), Polish Phys. Soc. Avocations: tourism, music. Office: Częstochowa Univ Inst, Physics al Armii Krajowej 13, 42 200 Częstochowa Poland

BERECZKI, DANIEL, physician, consultant neurologist; b. Eger, Heves, Hungary, Feb. 7, 1960. MD, Debrecen (Hungary) Med. Sch., 1984; PhD, Hungarian Acad. Sci., Budapest, 1994. Bd. cert. in neurology and psychiatry. Vis. rschr. SUNY, Stony Brook, 1989-92; resident Debrecen Med. Sch., 1984-88, assoc. prof. neurology, 1992-96, 96—; vis. prof. Tohoku Gakuin U., Sendai, Japan, 1997-98. Mem. editl. bd. Clin. Neurosci./Ideggyogyaszati Szemle, 1999—; contbr. articles to profl. jours. Recipient Weszepremy award Coun. Univ. Med. Sch. Debrecen, 1984, ETT award Hungarian Ministry Edn., 1996, others. Mem. Hungarian Soc. Neurologists and Psychiatrists (mem. directorial bd. 1999—), Working Group on Evidence Based Medicine (v.p. 1997—). E-mail: bereczki@jaguar.dote.hu. Office: Univ Med Sch/Dept Neurology, Nagyerdei krt 98, H-4012 Debrecen Hungary

BERECZKY, ERZSÉBET, literary advisor; b. Budapest, Jan. 5, 1932; d. István Bereczky and Gizella Martinkó; m. György Gyorffy, Dec. 22, 1955; 1 child, Erzsébet. Dramaturg Déryné Theatre, Miskolc, Hungary, 1954-57, Hungarian Nat. Theatre, Budapest, 1957—. Editor: Imre Madách: The Tragedy of Man, 1983, Information on New Plays from 1983-91; editor (periodical) Review ofTheatre Periodicals from 1987-94; translator (book) Dürrenmatt: Play Strindberg E.M. Remarque: Die letzte Station, 1959, others. Recipient Mari Jászai award Hungarian Ministry of Culture. Mem. Internat. Theatre Inst. Avocations: travel, reading, swimming. Home: Ulloi-ut 130 v lép I em3, 1107 Budapest Hungary Office: Nat Theatre, Hevesi Sándor tér 4, 1077 Budapest Hungary

BEREDER, FRÉDÉRIC LAURENT, architect; b. Oran, Algerie, May 18, 1960; s. Antoine and Huguette (Dimech) B.; m. Jin Wu, 1991; children: Jean-Michel, Cristel. M in Architecture, U. Marseille, 1986. Architect diplomé par le Gouvernement, France; 1st class architect and bldg. engr., Japan, 1997. Dir. Duct Sarl, Marseille, 1986-89; rep. Dumez Japan, Tokyo, 1991-93; advisor SEC, Tokyo, 1993-96; pres., chmn. Nichi Futsu Sekkei, Tokyo, 1997—. Inventor artificial reef (First prize 1989). Mem. Am. C. of C. (Japan), French C. of C., Ordre des Architectes France, Coll. Internat. Des Experts Architectes Switzerland. Home: Hon-Moku Minami, 3-907 Bay City, Yokohama Naka-Ku, Japan Office: 2-4-2-1003 Oji-Cho, Naka-Ku Yokohama 231-0027, Japan

BEREGI, EDIT, retired gerontologist; b. Brassó, Romania, Mar. 3, 1926; d. Miklós Beregi and Ilona Róth; m. István Földes, Dec. 12, 1947; children: István, Éva. MD, Pázmány Péter Med. U., Budapest, Hungary, 1950; specialty degree in pathology, histopathology and cytology, Med. U., Budapest, 1956; cert. in med. sci., Hungarian Acad. Sci., Budapest, 1956, D in Med. Sci., 1969. Asst. dept. pathology Med. U., Budapest, 1950-53, asst. dept. pathol. medicine, 1956-60, dir. rsch. dept. gerontology, 1961-78, prof., dir. gerontology ctr., 1978-93, prof. gerontology Ctr. Semmelweis, 1993-96; acad. scholar Hungarian Acad. Sci., Budapest, 1953-56; ret., 1996. Author: Malignant Tumors of the Thyroid Gland, 1967, Renal Biopsy in Glomerular Diseases, 1978, Epidemiological Cross-Sectional and Longitudinal Studies on Health Conditions of the Elderly, 1989; editor: Centenarians in Hungary, 1990. Recipient Karger prize Karger Pubs., Basel, Switzerland, 1970, 3d Age award Internat. Assn. Gerontology, Mex., 1989, Anniversary medal for svc. to age rsch. and geriatric medicine Brit. Geriats. Soc., 1997. Mem. Internat. Assn. Gerontology (chmn. European clin. sect. 1981-85, pres.-elect 1989-93, pres. 1993-97, past pres. 1997—), Internat. Fedn. Aged Persons (sci. com. 1982—), Internat. Fedn. on Aging (bd. dirs. 1985—). Avocation: writing.

BEREND, ROLF, member European parliament; b. Gernrode/Eichsfeld, Germany, Oct. 1, 1943. Mem. European Parliament, Germany, 1999—; mem. Group of European People's Party (Christian Democrats) and European Democrats; mem. com. on regional policy, transport and tourism, com. on culture, youth, edn., the media and sport, delegation to EU-Slovak Republic Joint Parliamentary Com., mem. from the European Parliament to the Joint Assembly of the Agreement between the African, Caribbean and Pacific States and the European Union. Mem. Christian Democratic Union. Office: Lindeistrabe 17, D-37339 Gernrode/Eichsfeld Federal Republic of Germany*

BERENDI, ERLINDA BAYAUA, physician surgeon; b. Santiago, Isabela, The Philippines, Oct. 31, 1947; came to U.S., 1972; d. Jeremias Carreon and Amanda (Florentin) Bayaua; m. S. Alexander Berendi, Jan. 2, 1981. BS, U. Santo Tomas, Manila, 1966, MD, 1971. Med. dir. Great Pacific Life Ins. Co., Manila, 1971-72; intern, resident Michael Reese Hosp., Chgo., 1973-77; pres., physician, surgeon Consultative Exams., Inc., Chgo., 1980—; med. dir. Intracorp. Med. Rev. Svcs., Arlington Heights, Ill., 1987-89; pres. Finnegan's Choice, Inc., Chgo., 1985—; med. cons. Dept. Health and Human Svcs., Chgo., 1977-83, State of Ill., Dept. Rehab. Svcs., Chgo., 1981—; acting chmn. med. quality rev. com. Bur. of Program Integrity, Ill. Dept. Pub. Aid, Chgo., 1977—; physician cons. Comprehensive Health Svcs, Inc., Chgo., 1978-79; chief med. cons. U.S. R.R. Retirement Bd., 1981-95. Mem. AMA, Am. Acad. Family Physicians, Nat. Assn. Disability Examiners, N.Y. Acad. Scis. Avocations: running, weightlifting, piano. Home: 6666 N Tower Circle Dr Lincolnwood IL 60712-3221 Office: Consultative Exams Inc 55 E Washington St Ste 2101 Chicago IL 60602-2219

BERENT, STANLEY, psychologist, educator, researcher, consultant; b. Norfolk, Va., Mar. 10, 1941; s. David and Esther (Laibstain) B.; m. Joy McKeever; children: Melissa Virginia, Alison Reneé, Rachel Irene. BS, Old Dominion U., 1966; MS, Va. Commonwealth U., 1967; PhD, Rutgers U., 1972. Diplomate Am. Bd. Profl. Psychology. Prof. U. Va., Charlottesville, 1972-79, U. Mich., Ann Arbor, 1979—; chief of psychology, VA Med. Ctr., Ann Arbor, 1979-85; vis. prof. U. London, 1988-89, China Rehab. Rsch. Ctr., Beijing, 1998—; pres., CEO, bd. dirs. NeuroBehavioral Resources, Inc., 1998—. Author 4 books, 18 book chpts.; contbr. more than 200 articles to profl. jours. Bd. dirs. Arbor Hills Assn., 1986-88. Served with USMC, 1959-63. Fellow Am. Psychol. Assn.; mem. Assn. Advancement Sci., Neurosci. Soc., Am. Epilepsy Soc., Am. Acad. Neurology. E-mail: sberent@umich.edu. Office: U Mich Hosps Box 0840 Med Inn Bldg Suite 480 Ann Arbor MI 48109-0840

BERENZWEIG, JACK CHARLES, lawyer; b. Bklyn., Sept. 29, 1942; s. Sidney A. and Anne R. (Dubowe) B.; m. Susan J. Berenzweig, Aug. 8, 1968; children: Mindy, Andrew. B.E.E., Cornell U., 1964; J.D., Am. U., 1968. Bar: Va. 1968, Ill. 1969. Examiner U.S. Pat. Off., Washington, 1964-66; pat. adviser U.S. Naval Air Systems Command, Washington, 1966-68; ptnr. Brinks, Hofer, Gilson & Lione and predecessor firm, Chgo., 1968—. Editorial staff Am. U. Law Rev., 1966-68; contbr. articles to profl. jours. Mem. ABA, Chgo. Bar Assn., Ill. State Bar Assn., Bar Assn. 7th Fed. Cir., Va. State Bar, Internat. Trademark Assn. (bd. dirs. 1983-85), Brand Names Edn. Found. (bd. dirs. 1993-98), Meadow Club (Rolling Meadows, Ill.), Miramar Club (Naples, Fla., Delta Theta Phi. Home: 127 W Oak St Apt A Chicago IL 60610-5422 Office: Brinks Hofer Gilson & Lione Ltd Ste 3600 455 N Cityfront Plaza Dr Chicago IL 60611-5599

BERES, PERVENCHE, foreign diplomat; b. Paris, Mar. 10, 1957. Mem. European Parliament, 1999—, mem. com. on econ. and monetary affairs, substitute com. on constnl. affairs; vice-chmn. Group of the Party of European Socialists. Socialist Party. Office: 288 Blvd Saint-Germain, F-75007 Paris France*

BERESFORD, DOUGLAS LINCOLN, lawyer; b. Washington, June 1, 1956; s. Spencer Moxon and Ann (Lincoln) B.; m. Lori Anne Mainous, Sept. 22, 1990; children: Alexander Gould, Erik Mainous. AB cum laude, Harvard U., 1978; JD, Georgetown U., 1982. Bar: D.C. 1982, U.S. Ct. Appeals (D.C. cir.) 1984, U.S. Supreme Ct. 1986. Assoc. Morgan, Lewis & Bockius, Washington, 1982-83; assoc. Newman & Holtzinger, P.C., Washington, 1983-89, ptnr., 1989-94; ptnr. Long, Aldridge & Norman, Washington, 1994-2000, Hogan & Hartson LLP, Washington, 2000—. Office: Hogan & Hartson LLP 555 13th St NW Ste 800E Washington DC 20004-1161

BERESFORD-HILL, PAUL VINCENT, headmaster, international educator; b. Dublin, Ireland, May 15, 1949; came to U.S., 1974, naturalized, 1978; s. Francis John and Alexandra (de La Poer Beresford) H.; m. Kathryn Elizabeth Ernyei, Apr. 11, 1976; children: Christopher Tristram, Timothy Alexander. Cert. in Edn., BEd, Oxford (Eng.) U., 1971; MA, New U. for Social Rsch., 1979; MSc, Oxford (Eng.) U., 1991; MEd, Columbia U., 1996, EdD, 1997. Gov. Milton Keynes' Coll. Edn. (U.K.), 1969-71; curriculum coord. Buckinghamshire Edn. Authority, Milton Keynes, Eng., 1971-74; lectr. Bletchley (Eng.) Coll. of Further Edn., 1972-74; founder, headmaster Anglo-Am. Internat. Sch., N.Y.C., 1974-90; rsch. assoc. Ctr. for Comparative Studies Edn. Oxford U., 1991-98; project officer TEMPUS Programme for Ednl. Leadership in Eastern Europe, 1991-92; adj. lectr. ednl. adminstrn. Klingenstein Ctr. Sch. Leadership, Columbia U., 1996—; pres. Internat. Ctr. Mgmt. Edn., Inc., N.Y.C.; pres. bd. dirs. Am. Home Study Inst., 1981-88; dir. Wolsey Hall Oxford, N.Am. Ltd., 1981-88; mem. grad. faculty New U. Social Rsch., 1979; pres. GAP Activity Project, Inc., 1985—; chmn. Mountbatten Inst., 1985—; headmaster King and Low-Heywood Thomas Sch., Stamford, Conn., 1996-98; chief adminstr. The Global Learning Ctr., Dowing Coll., Oakdale, N.Y., 1998-2000; headmaster Bangkok Patana Sch., The Brit. Sch. in Thailand, 2000—; mem. local accreditation subcom., Ministry of Edn., Thailand; mem. com. on English lang. tchg. in Thai schs., Prime Min.'s Office, Thailand. Author: Teaching in Inner London-The American Experience, 1991; editor: American Culture and Institutions, 1994, Resource Sharing in Public Education: A Primer for Administrators, 1996, the Privatization Movement in Education-Eastern Europe and the Baltics, 1997, From Cooperation to Collaboration, 1998; contbr. articles to profl. jours. Mem. edn. com. Brit. Coun. Chs., 1970-74; bd. dirs. Internat. Baccalaureate N.Am. Inc., 1979-89, Riverside Shakespeare Co., N.Y.C., 1984-87, Malignant Hyperthermia Assn. U.S., 1984-95; vice chmn. bd. trustees Prew Sch., London, 1984-89; chmn. bd. dirs. Am. Friends of Shaftesbury Homes and Arethusa, 1987-90; founder English Speaking Union U.S. Nat. Shakespeare Recitation Competition; founder, chmn. N.Y.C. Coalition Concerned Students. Named Knight of Justice, Most Venerable Order St. John of Jerusalem, mem. Most Excellent Order of Brit. Empire. Fellow Royal Anthrop. Inst. (U.K.), Coll. of Tchrs., Inst. Dirs. London; mem. Am. Soc. Order Brit. Empire (pres. 1995—), Royal Soc. Lit., Guild Ind. Schs. (bd. dirs. 1985-89), European Coun. Internat. Schs., Oxford Union Sch., English-Speaking Union, St. George's Soc., Brit.-Am. C. of C., Brit. Schs. and Univs. Club N.Y. (dir.), Pvt. Schs. Comm. Ministry and Edn. (insp.), Spl. Parliamentary Com. nglish Tchg. in Thai Schs. Roman Catholic. Clubs: Metropolitan (N.Y.C.), Carlton (London), United Oxford and Cambridge (London), Racquet and Tennis (N.Y.C.), Royal Overseas League (London). Home: 21 White Pine Ln Setauket NY 11733-3953 also: Bangkok Patana Sch, Soi La Salle Sukhumvit 105, Bangkok 10260, Thailand

BERESWILL, STEFAN HORST, microbiologist, molecular biologist; b. Zweibrücken, Germany, Apr. 26, 1965; s. Horst and Ilse (Bradfisch) B.; m. Christina Müller, Mar. 10, 1990. Diploma, U. Kaiserslautern, Germany, 1991; PhD, U. Heidelberg, 1995. Biol. diplomate. Diplomand German Cancer Rsch. Ctr., Heidelberg, 1990-91; doctorand Max Planck Inst. Med. Rsch., Heidelberg, 1991-95; rsch. fellow Inst. Med. Microbiology and Hygiene U. Freiburg, 1995—, asst. prof. faculty medicine, 2000—, habilitation faculty medicine, 2000—. Contbr. articles to profl. jours.; patentee in field. Mem. Fedn. European Microbiol. Socs., Deutsche Gesellschaft Hygiene & Microbiology. Home: Sautierstr 63, D-79104 Freiburg Germany Office: Inst Med Microb/Hygiene, Hermann-Herderstr 11, D-79104 Freiburg Germany

BERETTA, GIOVANNI, urologist, andrologist, researcher; b. Cormano, Italy, Aug. 7, 1951; s. Salvatore and Rosa (Colombo) B.; m. Elisabetta M. Vittoria Chelo; children: Alberto, Giulio, Emiliano, Giacomo. MD, U. of Milan, 1977, degree in urology, 1980; degree in reproductive pathology and andrology, U. Parma, 1983, U. Turin, 1987. Dir. Ctr. Italiano Fertilitá, Unitá de Andrologiá, Milan, 1987—. Author: Rapporto imperfetto, 1988, Disfunzioni Sessuali Maschili Cerro, 1994, La Sessualité Maschile, 1997; co-author: Come curare la sterilitá Maschile e Feminile, 1986. Home: via Dela Fortezza 6, 50129 Florence Italy Office: Ctr Italiano Fertil/Sessual, viale Berengario 11, 20149 Milan Italy

BEREZANTSEVA, MARIA SERGEYEVNA, education educator; b. St. Petersburg, Russia, July 27, 1970; d. Elena Vsevolodovna and Sergey Borisovich (Dalmatov) B. MSc in Biology, St. Petersburg State U., 1992, PhD in Biology, 1999; diploma in Baltic Sea environ., The Baltic U., St. Petersburg, 1992; postgrad., Russian State Pedagogical U., 1992-96. From lectr. to sr. lectr. St. Petersburg State U., 1997—; supr. students rsch. St. Petersburg State U., 1995. Contbr. articles to profl. jours. Soros/Fgn. & Commonwealth Office scholar Linacre Coll., Oxford, Eng., 1993-94; Environ. Scis. grant Ctrl. European U. Found., Budapest, Hungary, 1992. Mem. Soc. Natural Scientists. Avocations: bird watching, piano music, hiking. Home: 34 Malyi Ave PS Apt 36, 197110 Saint Petersburg Russia Office: St Petersburg State Univ, 7/9 University Embankment, 199034 Saint Petersburg Russia

BEREZHNOY, YURI ANATOLIYOVICH, physicist; b. Kharkov, Ukraine, May 27, 1936; s. Anatoliy Semenovich and Valeriya Michaylovna (Zinkina) B.; m. Nataliya Nikolayevna Bichkova, Jan. 20, 1977; 1 child, Andrey. MS, Kharkov State U., 1958, PhD in Nuclear Physics, 1965, ScD, 1978. Rschr. Kharkov Inst. Physics and Tech., 1958-79; head of chair of theoretical nuclear physics Kharkov State U., 1979—. Author: (with A.I. Akhiezer) Nuclear Theory, 1995; book reviewer Nuclear Diffraction, 1997; contbr. articles to profl. jours. Am. Phys. Soc. grantee, 1993. Mem. Ukrainian Phys. Soc., Ukrainian Acad. Sci. (nuclear physics coun. 1992—). Office: Kharkov State U Dept Physic, Svobody Sq 4, 310077 Kharkov Ukraine

BEREZIN, ANDREY ALEXANDROVICH, physicist, researcher; b. Moscow, June 21, 1946; s. Alexander Alexeevich and Tatyana Nikitichna (Lazukina) B.; m. Svetlana Alexandrovna Mayakova, June 27, 1980 (div. Nov. 1985); 1 child, Kirill Andreevich; m. Natalia Valerievna Volkova, Jan. 11, 1986; children: Julia, Artiom. BS, Moscow Inst. Electronics/Math, 1969; PhD, Inst. Med. Biophysics, 1984. Rsch. scientist Oncol. Ctr. of Russian Acad. Med. Scis., Moscow, 1969-78; sr. rsch. scientist Inst. Chem. Physics, Moscow, 1978-84, Inst. Theoretical Problems, Moscow, 1984-91, 91-94; vis. fellow Princeton (N.J.) U., 1996-2000; sr. rsch. scientist Oil and Gas Rsch. Inst., Moscow, 1996—. Contbr. articles to profl. jours.; patentee in field. Avocation: comparaison of different editions of the Bible and New Testament texts (including translations). Home: Baryshiha St 36 23, 123368 Moscow Russia Office: Oil and Gas Rsch Inst, Gubkina St 8, 117125 Moscow Russia

BEREZYUK, ANATOLIY NIKOLAEVICH, civil engineer, educator, administrator; b. Loutsk, Ukraine, Feb. 18, 1940; s. Nikolai and Maria (Popelyshkina) B.; m. Yulia Berezyuk, 1963; children: Igor, Dmitriy. Diploma of Civil Engring., Inst. Civil Engring., Dniepropetrovsk, Ukraine, 1963, Cand.Sci.Techn., 1975, Prof., 1991. Head prodn. and tech., dep. work supr., sr. egnr. various Orgns. of Civil Engring., 1963-66; asst., sr. instr., asst. prof. Inst. Civil Engring., Dniepropetrovsk, 1966-75, dean of the archtl. dept., 1975-81, dean civil engring. dept., 1981-90; vice rector State Acad. Civil Engring., Dniepropetrovsk, 1990—. Author: Construction of Thermal Power Stations, 1983, The Assembly of Residential and Industrial Buildings from Prefabricated Reinforced Concrete, 1989, Technology of Construction--Assembly Works during the erection of buildings in winter conditions, 1992, Erection of the Agricultural Buildings from Local Building Materials, 1993, The Diagnostics and Estimation of Technical State of Building Structures and Foundations, 1996. Mem. coun. civil engring. and arch. Ministry of Edn. of Ukraine. Decorated Order of Honour, 1986; recipient medal Vet. of Labour, 1989; named Honorable Worker of Nat. Edn. of Ukraine. Mem. Club of Sport Vets. Avocations: volleyball, hunting. Home: 15 Chernyshevsky str 57, 49005 Dniepropetrovsk Ukraine Office: State Acad Civil Engring, 24-A Chernyshevsky Str, 49005 Dniepropetrovsk Ukraine

BERG, ANTHONY RICHARD, finance company executive; b. Sydney, NSW, Australia, Dec. 22, 1945; s. Charles Josef and Greta Erna B.; m. Carol Gordon, Nov. 2, 1972; children: Laurie, Karen. B of Econs. (hon.), U. Sydney, 1966; MBA, Harvard U., 1970. Analyst Schroder, Darling Ltd., Sydney, 1967; asst. to mng. ptnr. Loeb, Rhoades & Co., N.Y.C., 1970-72; mng. dir., CEO Hill Samuel/Australia Ltd., Sydney, 1972-85, Macquarie Bank Ltd., Sydney, 1985-93, Boral Ltd., Sydney, 1994-2000; dir. Gresham Ptnrs. Ltd., 2000—; chmn. Mercantile Mutual Holdings Ltd., 2000—. Mem. Australia Coun., Sydney, 1978-82, Australian Mfg. Coun., Melbourne, 1984-88; mem. coun. Nat. Gallery of Australia, Canberra, 1997—; chmn. Nat. Gallery of Australia Found., Canberra, 1999—; active Bus. Coun. of Austrlia, 1994-2000. Recipient BRW/Alcatel award for outstanding performance in the fin. industry, 1990; mem. Order of Australia, 1992; named Optus Banker of Yr., Australian Banking and Fin., 1993. Fellow Australian Soc. Cert. Practising Accts., Securities Inst. Australia, Australian Inst. Co. Dirs. Avocations: the arts, skiing, tennis, running.

BERG, GERTRUD ERIKA BIRGITTA, oncology educator; b. Vasteras, Sweden, Apr. 4, 1944; d. Arne Erik and Britt (Lundeberg) Björk; m. Björn Sölve Berg, Jan. 13, 1968; children: Asa Erika, Thorun Erika. PhD, U. Uppsala, Sweden, 1975; MD, U. Goteborg, Sweden, 1983. Tchr. Genetics U. Uppsala, Sweden, 1967; student U. Goteborg, Sweden, 1975-80; tchr. Anatomy, 1977-80; physician Sahlgenska Hosp., Goteborg, Sweden, 1981—; head on thyroid unit, 1994—; chmn. Swedish Assn. Isotope Treatment, 1994—. Contbr. research papers in field. Mem. Swedish Med. Rsch.:Thyroid Rsch. Group, Swedish Cancer Rsch. Neuroncology. Avocations: sailing, scuba diving, mountain touring. Office: Thyroid Unit, Sahlgenska Hosp Univ, S-41345 Goteborg Sweden

BERG, HÅKAN CARL ERIK, marine ecotoxicologist, researcher; b. Stockholm, Dec. 20, 1965; s. Lars and Inger Berg. MS, Stockholm U., 1990, PhD in Marine Ecotoxicology, 1996. Ecotoxicologist Swedish Environ. Rsch. Inst., Stockholm, 1990; rschr. dept. sys. ecology Stockholm U., 1991-97; ecotoxicologist Nat. Chems. Inspectorate, Solna, Sweden, 1997-98; assoc. prof. dept. chem. engring./indsl. ecology Royal Inst. Tech., Stockholm, 1998—. Contbr. articles to sci. jours. Home: Korsfararvägen 130, 181 40 Lidingö Sweden

BERG, HERMANN JOHANNES, laboratory administrator, researcher; b. Greifswald, Germany, July 16, 1924; s. Heinrich and Johanna (Meissner) B.; m. Liebgard Peuker, July 17, 1954; children: Angelika, Dorothea, Albrecht. Diploma, Tech. U., Dresden, Germany, 1952, Dr.rer.nat., 1953; Dr.habilitation, U. Jena, Germany, 1962. Mem. staff, head dept. biophysicochemistry Inst. Microbiology and Exptl. Therapy, Jena, 1954-89; head lab. bioelectrochem. IMB, Jena, 1989-96, pvt. lab., Jena, 1996-99, Inst. Virology, U. Jena, 1999—; lectr. phys. chemistry Friedrich-Schiller U., Jena, 1965. Editor: Bioelectrochemistry and Bioenergetics, 1987-99. Recipient S. Hiller medal Latvian Acad. Sci., 1994, J. Heyrovsky medal CSSR Acad. Sci., 1979, Wilhelm Ostwald medal, 1997. Mem. Biophysikalische Gesellschaft der DDR, Gesellschaft Deutscher Naturforscher u. Ärzte, Saxonian Acad. Scis., Bioelectrochem. Soc. (hon. v.p. 1979-92), Internat. Soc. Electrochemistry (officer divsn. V 1980-83), Acad. Oeconomica Tübingen. Avocations: gardening, history, old Egypt, China and Japan. Home: Greifberg 15, 07749 Jena Germany

BERG, PAUL, biochemist, educator; b. N.Y.C., June 30, 1926; s. Harry and Sarah (Brodsky) B.; m. Mildred Levy, Sept. 13, 1947; 1 son, John. BS, Pa. State U., 1948; PhD (NIH fellow 1950-52), Western Res. U., 1952; DSc (hon.), U. Rochester, 1978, Yale U., 1978, Washington U., St. Louis, 1986, Oreg. State U., 1989, Pa. State U., 1995. Postdoctoral fellow Copenhagen (Denmark) U., 1952-53; postdoctoral fellow Sch. Medicine, Washington U., 1953-54, Am. Cancer Soc. scholar cancer research dept. microbiology sch. medicine, 1954-57, from asst. to assoc. prof. microbiology, 1955-59; prof. biochemistry Sch. Medicine, Stanford (Calif.) U., from 1959, now prof. emeritus, Sam, Lulu and Jack Willson prof. biochemistry, 1970-94, Robert W. Cahill prof. cancer rsch., 1994—, chmn. dept. sch. medicine, 1969-74; dir. Stanford U. Beckman Ctr. for Molecular and Genetic Medicine, 1985—, Affymetrix, 1993—, Nat. Found. Biomed. Rsch., 1994—; non-resident fellow Salk Inst., 1973-83; adv. bd. NIH, NSF, MIT; vis. com. dept. biochemistry and molecular biology Harvard U.; bd. sci. advisors Jane Coffin Childs Found. Med. Rsch., 1970-80; chmn. sci. adv. com. Whitehead Inst., 1984-90; bd. sci. adv. DNAX Rsch. Inst., 1981—; internat. adv. bd. Basel Inst. Immunology; chmn. nat. adv. com. Human Genome Project, 1990-92. Contbr. profl. jours.; Editor: Biochem. and Biophys. Research Communications, 1959-68; editorial bd.: Molecular Biology, 1966-69. Trustee Rockefeller U., 1990-92. Served to lt. (j.g.) USNR, 1943-46. Recipient Eli Lilly prize biochemistry, 1959; V.D. Mattia award Roche Inst. Molecular Biology, 1972; Henry J. Kaiser award for excellence in teaching, 1969, 72; Disting. Alumnus award Pa. State U., 1972; Sarasota Med. awards for achievement and excellence, 1979; Gairdner Found. annual award, 1980; Lasker Found. award, 1980; Nobel award in chemistry, 1980; N.Y. Acad. Sci. award, 1980; Sci. Freedom and Responsibility award AAAS, 1982; Nat. Medal of Sci., 1983; named Calif. Scientist of Yr. Calif. Museum Sci. and Industry, 1963; numerous disting. lectureships including Harvey lectr., 1972, Lynen lectr., 1977, Priestly lectrs. Pa. State U., 1978, Dreyfus Disting. lectrs. Northwestern U., 1979, Lawrence Livermore Dir.'s Disting. lectr., 1983, Linus Pauling lectr., 1993. Fellow AAAS; mem. NAS, Inst. Medicine, Am. Acad. Arts and Scis., Am. Soc. Biol. Chemists (pres. 1974-75), Am. Soc. Cell Biology (chmn. pub. policy com. 1994—), Am. Soc. Microbiology, Am. Philos. Soc., Internat. Soc. Molecular Biology, Japan Biochem. Soc. (elected fgn. mem. 1978), French Acad. Sci. (elected fgn. mem. 1981), Royal Soc. (elected fgn. mem. 1992). Office: Stanford Sch Medicine Beckman Ctr B-062 Stanford CA 94305-5301*

BERG, STANTON ONEAL, firearms and ballistics consultant; b. Barron, Wis., June 14, 1928; s. Thomas C. and Ellen Florence (Nedland) Silbaugh; m. June K. Rolstad, Aug. 16, 1952; children: David M., Daniel L., Susan E., Julie L. Student, U. Wis., 1949-50; LLB, LaSalle Ext. U., 1951; postgrad., U. Minn., 1960-69. Claim rep. State Farm Ins. Co., Mpls., Hibbing and Duluth, Minn., 1952-57, claim supt., 1957-70; regional mgr. State Farm Fire and Casualty Co., St. Paul, Minn., 1970-84; firearms cons. Mpls., 1961—; bd. dirs. Am. Bd. Forensic Firearm and Tool Mark Examiners, 1980—; instr. home firearms safety, Mpls., 1975—; cons. to Sporting Arms and Ammunition Mfrs. Inst., 1974-84; internat. lectr. on forensic ballistics Adv. Bd. Milton Helpern Internat. Ctr. for Forensic Scis., 1975—; mem. bd. cons. Inst. Applied Sci., Chgo., 1974—; cons. for re-exam. of ballistics evidence in Robert Kennedy assassination/Sirhan case Superior Ct. L.A., 1975; ct. expert witness in most state cts., Mil. Gen. Ct. Martial Territorial Ct. at V.I. and U.S. Dist. Cts., Supreme Ct. of Ont., Can.; mem. Nat. Forensic Ctr., 1979—, internat. study group in forensic scis., 1985—; chmn. internat. symposiums on forensic ballistics, Edinburgh, Scotland, 1972, Zurich, 1975, Bergen, Norway, 1981, Dusseldorf, Germany, 1993. Contbg. editor Am. Rifleman mag., 1973-84; mem. editl. bd. Internat. Microform Jour. Legal Medicine and Forensic Scis., 1979—, Am. Jour. Forensic Medicine and Pathology, 1979-91; contbr. articles on firearms and forensic ballistics to profl. publs. With U.S. Army Counter Intelligence Corp., 1948-52. Fellow Am. Acad. Forensic Sci., Am. Coll. Forensic Examiners (life, bd. cert. forensic examiner and diplomate); mem. ASTM (criminalistics subcom. 1989—, non powder guns subcom. 1990—, paintball guns and sys. subcom. 1994—), NRA, Assn. Firearms and Tool Mark Examiners (exec. coun. 1970-71, charter mem., life mem., editl. com. AFTE jour., 1989-92, Disting. Mem. and Key Man award 1972, exam. and standards com. 1975-76, spl. honors award 1976, nat. peer group on cert. of firearms examiners 1978—), Forensic Sci. Soc., Internat. Assn. forensic Scis., Internat. Assn. for Identification (mem. firearms subcom. of sci. and practice com. 1961-74, 86-2000, chmn. firearm subcom. 1964-66, 69-70, 91-95, lab. rsch. and techniques subcom. 1980-81, life and disting. mem., life charter mem. Minn. divsn.), Internat. Wound Ballistics Assn. (full mem.), Western. Conf. Criminal and Civil Problems (sci. adv. com.), Am. Gunsmithing Assn. (life), Am. Legion (life), Army Counter-Intelligence Corp. Vets. Assn. (life), Browning Arms Collectors Assn. (life 1988—), Am. Ordnance Assn. (life), Minn. Weapons Collectors, Internat. Cartridge Collectors Assns. (life), Internat. Reference Orgn. Forensic Medicine and Scis., Internat. Assn. Bloodstain Pattern Analysts. Address: 6025 Gardena Ln NE Minneapolis MN 55432-5840

BERG, WERNER, agricultural engineer; b. Nauen, Germany, Feb. 28, 1962; s. Fritz and Charlotte (Richter) B.; m. Ines Kessner, May 24, 1985; children: Friederike, Richard. Diploma in engring., Dresden (Germany) U. Tech., 1985, PhD in Engring., 1990. Rschr. Max-Eyth-Inst. Agrl. and Environ. Engring., Potsdam, Germany, 1989-91, Inst. Agrl. Engring. Bornim, Potsdam, Germany, 1992—; lectr., presenter in field. Contbr. articles to profl. jours. Mem. German Engring. Soc., European Soc. Agrl. Engrs., Internat. Commn. Agrl. Engring. Avocations: nature, family, athletics, chess. Office: Inst Agrl Engring Bornim, Max-Eyth-Allee 100, D-14469 Potsdam Germany

BERGA, SARAH LEE, women's health physician, educator; b. San Benito, Tex., May 22, 1954; d. John Orrin and Nancy Estelle (Michael) B.; m. Frederick S. Sherman, Sept. 26, 1981 (div. 1994); children: Alexis Estelle, Nathaniel Abbott; m. Lockwood Hoehl, Oct. 28, 1995. BA, U. Va., 1976, MD, 1980. Diplomate Am. Bd. Ob-Gyn., Am. Bd. Reproductive Endocrinology. From asst. to assoc. prof. U. Pitts., 1988—; dir. reproductive endocrinology and infertility divsn. U. Pitts. Sch. of Medicine, 2000; med. dir. menopause ctr. Magee-Womens Hosp.; assoc. med. dir. Gen. Clin. Rsch. Ctr.; bd. dirs. U. Pitts. Physicians. Mem. Soc. Gynecologic Investigation (coun. mem. 1999—). Home: 5432 Northumberland St Pittsburgh PA 15217-1129 Office: U Pitts Reproductive Divsn 300 Halket St Pittsburgh PA 15213-3108

BERGAMINI, ETTORE, pathologist; b. Ferrara, Italy, Oct. 2, 1937; s. Aldo and Laura (Pasquali) B.; m. Zina Gori, June 8, 1975; 1 child, Laura. MD, U. Pisa, Italy, 1962; PhD, Scuola Normale Superiore, Pisa, 1965. Asst. prof. U. Messina, Italy, 1964-66, U. Siena, Italy, 1966-73; asst. prof. U. Pisa, Italy, 1974-80, prof., 1980—; dir. Ctr. Gerontological Rsch., Pisa, 1989-95; vice chmn. Gordon Rsch. Subcom. Europe, 1991-93, ad-hoc com., 1994. Editor: General Pathology and Pathophysiology of Aging, 1993; co-editor: Protein Metabolism in Aging, 1990. Mem. Rotary. Roman Catholic. Avocations: music, farming. Office: Inst Patologia Generale, via Roma 55, 56126 Pisa Italy

BERGAN, EDMUND PAUL, JR., lawyer; b. N.Y.C., May 6, 1950; s. Edmund Paul and Alice (Gordon) P. B.; m. Patricia Ann Gallagher, Jan. 31, 1987; children: Annabel (dec.), Caroline. BA, Holy Cross Coll., 1971; JD, Fordham U., 1975. Bar: N.Y. 1976. Staff atty. SEC, Washington, D.C., 1975-77; v.p., assoc. gen. counsel Securities Industry Assn., N.Y.C., 1977-81; v.p., asst. gen. counsel Alliance Capital Mgmt. LP, N.Y.C., 1981-88; v.p. gen. counsel Alliance Fund Distbrs., N.Y.C., 1988-94; v.p., gen. counsel Alliance Fund Svc. Subs., N.Y.C., 1988-94; sr. v.p., gen. counsel Alliance Fund Distbrs. and Alliance Fund Svcs., N.Y.C., 1994—. Mem. ABA (mem. fed. securities com. 1982—, investment advisers and cos. subcom. 1999—), Investment Co. Inst. (SEC rules com. 1986—, closed-end fund com. 1989—, chmn. 1992-97, various subcoms.), Bar Assn. City N.Y. (investment mgmt. com. 1999—). Republican. Roman Catholic. Avocations: historical studies, athletics. Office: Alliance Capital Mgmt LP 1345 Ave of Americas New York NY 10105-3198

BERGANT, BORIS MIRAN, journalist, broadcasting researcher; b. Maribor, Slovenia, Apr. 19, 1948; s. Eugen and Marija Bergant; m. Verena Bergant, 1969; 1 son, Damjan. Journalist, U. Ljubljana, Slovenia; student, Kenyon Coll. Editor for fgn. affairs Radio-TV Slovenia, Ljubljana, 1981-86, news editor, 1986-88, dep. dir. TV, 1988-92, dep. dir. gen., 1992—. Recipient award for Best Journalistic Achievement, 1976, for Best Documentary RV, 1978, TV award, 1981. Mem. European Inst. for Media, Slovenian Coun. of the European Movement (sec. gen.), Assn. of Journalists of Slovenia (pres. 1987-91), CIRCOM Regional (pres. 1990-92, sec.-gen. 1993—), European Broadcasting Union (adminstrv. coun., vice chmn. TV com. 1995-99, v.p. 1998—). Avocation: tennis. Home: Abramova 8, Ljubljana 1000, Slovenia Office: RTV Slovenia, Kolodvorska 2, Ljubljana 1550, Slovenia

BERGE, CLAUDE J., mathematician; b. Paris, June 5, 1926; s. André and Genevieve (Fourcade) B.; m. Jane Gentaz, Dec. 1952; 1 child, Delphine. PhD, U. Paris. Dir. rsch. Ctr. Nat. Rsch. Sci., France, 1954—; resident dir. Ctr. Nat. Rsch. Sci., Paris, 1960—; prof. Inst. Stat., Paris, 1967; dir. Internat. Computation Ctr., 1964-68. Author 12 books in field. Recipient Sci. prize Union Assurances de Paris, 1989, Gold medal European Fed. Operation Rsch. Soc., 1989. Mem. Oeuvres de Litterature Potentiale (founding). Home: Galvani # 10, 75017 Paris France

BERGE, HANS CORNELIS TEN, author, poet; b. Alkmaar, The Netherlands, Dec. 24, 1938. Tchr. Acad. Dramatic Art, Amsterdam, 1968-70, Art Acad., Arnhem, The Netherlands, 1970-90; vis. scholar Nat. Mus. of Man, Ottawa, Ont., Can., 1974-75; vis. prof. U. Tex., Austin, 1981, U. Coll. London, 1996. Writings include: (verse) Poolsneeuw, 1964, Zwartkrans, 1966, Personages, 1966, Gedichten 1964-67, 1969, De witte sjamaan, 1973, Va-banque, 1977, Nieuwe Gedichten, 1981, Tramontane: vijf triptieken en een liefdesverklaring, 1983, Texaanse elegieën, 1983, Acht liederen van angst en vertwijfeling, 1987, We dromen weg in blauw en grijs: een drieluik voor M.B., 1991, The White Shaman: Selected Poems, 1991, Overgangsriten, 1992, Een tuin in de winter, 1993, Materia Prima, gedichten, 1963-93; (fiction) Canaletto, en andere verhalen, 1969, Een geval van verbeelding, 1970, Het meisje met de korte vlechten, 1977, De beren van Churchill, 1978, Matglas, 1981, Zelfportret met witte muts, 1985, Het geheim van en opgewekt humeur, 1986, Een Italiaan in Zutphen, 1991, De honkuaste reiziger, dagbock bladen-veldnotities 1, 1995, Vrouwen, jaloezie en andere ongemakker, veldnotities 2, 1996, De jaren in Zeedorp: The Sea-town years, 1998; (other writings) Een schrijver als grenskozak: F.C. Terborgh over zichzelf en zijn werk, 1977, Levenstekens en doodssinjalen, 1980, De Mannenschrik: over het motief van de verslindende vrouw in literatuur en mythe, 1984, De verdediging van de poëzie, en andere essays, 1988, Zutphen, 1988; editor, transl.: 15 Cantos (Ezra Pound), 1970, Poëzie van de Azteken, 1972; editor: Mythen en fabels van noordelijke volken, 3 vols., 1974-79; transl.: De dood is de jager: Indiaanse mythen van Noordwestr-Amerika, 1974, Laat op aarde (Gunnar Ekelöf), 1975, In het geheime huis en andere gedichten (Christopher Middleton), 1983, De danseres van Izu (Kawabata Yasunari), 1983, Een lakse bries (Mark Strand), 1983, (with Margaret Törnqvist) De Byzantijnse trilogie (Gunnar Ekelöf), 1985, Canto XLIX (Ezra Pound), 1985, Kerkhof in de sneeuw (Xavier Villaurrutia y González), 1986, Mijn naam is Schurft, voorafgegaan door Het verhaal van Asdiwál, 1990; founder, editor Raster. Recipient Soc. Dutch Lit. prize, 1968, City of Amsterdam prize, 1971, Jan Campert Found. prize, 1972, Multatuli prize, 1987, Constantijn Huygens prize, 1996. Office: Meulenhoff Nederland, PO Box 100, 1000 AC Amsterdam The Netherlands

BERGEL, MENY, physician, researcher; b. Rosario, Santa Fe, Argentina, Mar. 26, 1925; s. Simon and Alegria Bergel. MD, U. Litoral, Rosario, 1947. Postdoctoral fellow, rsch. fellow U. Rochester, N.Y., 1952-53; dir. rsch. Sommer Leprosarium, Buenos Aires, 1958-63, Inst. Leprology, Rosario, 1963-85; prof. biology J.F.K. U., Buenos Aires, 1976—; prof. postgrad. studies Argentine Med. Assn., Buenos Aires, 1983—; med. dir. Leprosy Rsch. Inst., Buenos Aires, 1985—; guest investigator Rockefeller Inst., N.Y.C., 1959; cons. dermatologist Ferroviario Hosp. Rosario, 1956—, Pub. Health Svc.-Dermatology, Buenos Aires, 1960—; cons. researcher Centro Leprologico S. Araujo, Curitiba, Brazil, 1975—. Author: Elements of Leprosy, 1963, Leprosy as a Metabolic Disease, 1989, Leprosy: Etiology, Pathology, Treatment, 1990, Metabolic Theory of Leprosy, 1992. Recipient Rosendhal award of Weizman Inst., Mitsuda award Inst. of Leprology; Fulbright scholar, 1959; grantee Pub. Health Svc., U.S., 1961, WHO, Switzerland, 1972, Muscular Dystrophy Assn. Am., 1973; nominated for Gandhi Internat. award, 1993. Mem. Argentine Soc. Pharmacology (hon. pres. 1971), Nat. Acad. Scis. (Hansen award), Argentine Med. Assn. (Sommer award 1958), Soc. of Dermatology (hon., Peru), Soc. of Dermatology (hon., Greece), Soc. of Leprology (hon., Korea), Soc. of Leprology (hon., Philippines), Italian Soc. Pharmacology (hon.), Denmark Soc. of Biology (hon.), Order of Malta (comdr. 1973), Rotary (Order of Garay 1987), Lancisian Acad. (hon.). Jewish. Avocations: painting, sculpture. Office: Inst of Leprology, Paraguay 1365, 1057 Buenos Aires Argentina

BERGELT, PHILIP ROBERT, JR., printer, antiques dealer; b. Tampa, Fla., Dec. 3, 1962; s. Philip Robert and Honora Ann (Carey) B. Student, U. South Fla., 1980-82, Fla. Keys C.C., 1988-89. Mgr. Dunderbaks, Tampa, Fla., 1981-84; dir. purchasing Hyatt Hotels & Resorts, Tampa, 1984-92; pub. Oblivion Mag., Palm Desert, Calif., 1992-93; prodn. mgr. Kinko's, Palm Springs, Calif., 1993-95; printer Triangle Reprographics, Orlando, Fla., 1996—; antiques wholesaler self-employed, St. Cloud, Fla., 1995—. Recipient Eagle Scout award, Boy Scouts Am., St. Cloud, 1980. Mem. Sons Union Vetrans Civil War. Republican.

BERGEN, CHRISTOPHER BROOKE, opera company administrator, translator, editor; b. L.A., Jan. 11, 1949; s. Edward Grinnell Bergen and Alvina Ellen (Temple) Stevens; m. Mary Novella Tilman, Apr. 11, 1998. BA, UCLA, 1971; MA, Yale U., 1977. Conf. officer IAEA, Vienna, Austria, 1973-75, data analyst, 1979-81; import mgr. COBEC Trading Corp., N.Y.C., 1978-79; assoc. Geissler Engring. Co., Oakland, Calif., 1982-83; dir. Yale Cons. Assocs., San Francisco, 1983-84; editor INPUT, Mountain View, Calif., 1984; adminstr. surtitles San Francisco Opera, 1985-98. Editor profl. jours.; translator operatic texts for projection during performances at San Francisco Opera, Santa Fe Opera, Met. Opera, Lyric Opera of Chgo., Washington Opera, many other opera cos., symphonies and conservatories in U.S., abroad. Democrat. Avocations: literature, rowing. Home: 16 La Salle Rd Upper Montclair NJ 07043

BERGENHEIM, ANDERS TOMMY, neurosurgeon, educator; b. Gothenborg, Sweden, Dec. 30, 1951; s. Ingmar and Hillevi (Svensson) Eriksson; m. Åsa Bergenheim, Dec. 27, 1974; children: Mikael, Jon, Tove, Johannes, Sanna, Hampus. MD, Umeå U., 1985, PhD, 1994. Intern Karlstad (Sweden) Hosp., 1985-87; resident dept. neurosurgery Umeå U. Hosp., 1987-92; cons. dept. neurosurgery Umeå U., 1994, assoc. prof., 1995, sr. lectr., 1996; sec. Nat. Planning Group CNS Tumors, Sweden, 1992. Editl. bd. Jour. Neuro-Oncology. Mem. Scandinavian Neurosurg. Soc. (pres.), Scandinavian Neuro-Oncology Group (pres.). Home: Lingonvagen 16, S-903 39 Umeå Sweden Office: Umea U Hosp, Dept Neurosurgery, S-901 85 Umeå Sweden

BERGER, ANDRÉ LÉON, geophysics educator; b. Acoz, Belgium, July 30, 1942; s. Léon and Georgette (Pouleur) B.; m. Marie-Anne Lallemand, Sept. 28, 1968; children: Pascale, Valérie, Catherine. MS in Meteorology, MIT, 1971; DSc, U. Cath. Louvain, Belgium, 1973; Dr. Honoris Causa, U. Aix-Marseille, France, 1989, U. P. Sabatier Toulouse, 1999. Asst. U. Cath. Louvain, 1965-73, suppléant, 1973-76, chargé de cours, 1976-84, head Inst. of Astronomy and Geophysics, 1978—, prof., 1984-89, ordinary prof., 1989—; vis. prof. Free U., Brussels, 1982-92; maitre de conf. U. Liege, Belgium, 1985-93; chmn. panel spl. program on sci. of global environ. change NATO, 1992-93, chmn. spl. program panel in air-sea interactions, 1981; chmn. Internat. Commn. on Climate, 1987-93, Paleoclimate Commn., Internat. Quaternary Assn., 1987-95; mem. hearings bd. European Parliament and Belgium Ministry Rsch.; mem. sci. coun. Gaz de France, 1994-99, Petrofina, 1998—; mem. Environment Coun. Electricité de France, 1998—. Author: Le Climat de la Terre, un passé pour quel avenir?, 1992; editor: Climatic Variations and Variability: Facts and Theories, 1981; co-editor: Milankovich and Climate, Understanding the Response to Orbital Forcing, 1984, Understanding Climate Change, 1989; contbr. rsch. articles on climatic variations and climate modelling to profl. jours. Created knight, 1996; recipient Médaille d'Argent de Sa Sainteté, Pope Paul VI, Vatican, 1979, Prix de la première biennale Italian Soc. Physics, 1980, Prix Charles Lagrange, Classe des Sci. Acad. Royale Scis., des Lettres et des Beaux-Arts de Belgique, 1984, Norbert Gerbier-Mumm Internat. award World Meteorol. Orgn., 1994, Prix Docteur A. De Leeuw-Damry-Bourlart, 1991-95. Fellow Am. Geophys. Union; mem. European Geophys. Soc. (hon. mem., pres. 2000—, v.p. hydrospheres-atmospheres sect. 1984-88, Golden award 1989, Milutin Milankovitch medal 1994), Internat. Union of Geodesy and Geophysics (lectr. 1987), Academia Europaea (coun. mem. 1993-99), Koninklyke Nederlandse Akademie van Wetenschappen (fgn. mem.), Acad. Scis. Paris (fgn. assoc.), Am. Meteorol. Soc., Royal Meteorol. Soc. (fgn. mem.). Avocations: mountain hiking, collecting meteorological stamps. Office: Cath U Louvain, 2 Chemin de Cyclotron, B-1348 Louvain-la-Neuve Belgium

BERGER, BIRGIT, pharmacist; b. Landau, Germany, Sept. 23, 1966; d. Hans-Joachim and Barbara (Januscheck) Roehler; m. Markus Guenther Berger, June 17, 1995. Degree in pharmacy, aprobation, Albert Ludwigs U., Freiburg, Germany, 1992; PhD in Sci., U. Hamburg, Germany, 1995. Sci. coworker dept. toxicology U. Hamburg Med. Sch., 1992-95; pharmacist Pub. Pharmacy, Hamburg, 1992-95; scientific coworker Fraunhofer Inst. Toxicology Environ. Medicine, Hamburg, 1995-96; regulatory affairs mgr. Schwarz Pharma, Monheim, Germany, 1996-98; coord. postgrad. med. edn. EuMeCom dept. Glaxo Wellcome, Germany, 1998—. Contbr. articles to profl. jours. Mem. Rotaract, Hannover, Germany, 1983-86. Lutheran. Avocations: badminton, swimming, cooking, photography. Home: Hoherade 11, 20257 Hamburg Germany Office: EuMeCom, Alsterufer 1, 20354 Hamburg Germany

BERGER, CHARLES MARTIN, lawn and garden company executive; b. Wilkes-Barre, Pa., May 2, 1936; s. Edward and Sadie (Zwass) B.; m. Jane Elrod Purdy, June 5, 1960; children: Cary John Aaron, Elizabeth Anne, Valerie Ann. A.B., Princeton U., 1958; M.B.A., Harvard U., 1960. Mktg. mgmt. Procter and Gamble Co., Cin., 1960-64; with H.J. Heinz Co., 1964-96; gen. mgr. mktg. U.S.A. div. H.J. Heinz Co., Pitts., 1964-69, dir. corp. planning world hdqrs., 1969-70; mktg. dir. Heinz-London, 1970-72; mng. dir. Plasmon SpA, Milan, Italy, 1972-78; pres., CEO, chmn. Weight Watchers Internat. Inc., Jericho, N.Y., 1978-94; chmn., CEO Heinz India Pvt. Ltd., Bombay, India, 1994-96; chmn., pres. and CEO The Scotts Co., Columbus, OH, 1996-; bd. dirs. The Scotts Co., Inc., Com Scape Comms.; lectr. Carnegie-Mellon Grad. Sch. Indsl. Adminstrn., 1968-69. Chmn. bd. dirs. Am. Sch. Milan, 1975-78; bd. dirs. Buckley Country Day Sch., Manhasset, N.Y., 1983-89, Columbus Symphony Orch., 1997—. Mem. World Pres'. Orgn. (bd. dirs. 1994—), Am. Mgmt. Assn. (bd. dirs.), Princeton Club, Village Club of Sands Point (N.Y.), Columbus Club, Capital Club (bd. gov.'s), Port Royal Club. Republican. Jewish. Office: Scotts World Hdqrs 41 S High St Columbus OH 43215-6101

BERGER, DANIEL PHILIPPE, defense company executive; b. Lausanne, Switzerland, May 26, 1950; s. Emmanuel and Marie (Ecoffey) B.; m. Radhia Ayari, Oct. 8, 1992; children: Sarah, Cedric, Julien, Kevin. M.Physics, Fed. Poly. U., Lausanne, 1973, PhD in Physics, 1977; M.Math., U. Lausanne, Switzerland, 1973; MBA, Internat. Inst. Mgmt. Devel., Lausanne, 1996. Rsch. asst. Rsch. Ctr. of Plasma Physics, Lausanne, 1973-76; engr. Oak Ridge (Tenn.) Nat. Lab., 1977; sales engr. IBM, Lausanne, 1978-79; product mgr. Oerlikon-Contraves (OC), Zürich, Switzerland, 1980-85, v.p. sales, 1994—; gen. mgr. OC Dynatec, Zürich, 1986-93; mem. Air Def. Com., Berne, Switzerland, 1989—. Contbr. articles to profl. jours. Pres. AVIA-Def. Against Aircrafts, Lausanne, 1986-94, AVIA Air Force Officers Assn., 1997—. Col. Swiss Army, 1997—. Mem. Am. Mgmt. Assn., IMD Alumni Assn. Fax: 41 1 316 4122. E-mail: czbeda@ocag.ch. Avocations: jogging, cross-country skiing, lectures. Home: Mühlehaldenstrasse 3, CH 8956 Killwangen Aargau, Switzerland Office: Oerlikon-Contraves, Birchstrasse 155, CH 8050 Zürich Switzerland

BERGER, DAVID, lawyer; b. Archbald, Pa., Sept. 6, 1912; s. Jonas and Anna (Raker) B.; m. Barbara Simmons Wainscott, Nov. 5, 1997; children: Jonathan, Daniel. AB cum laude, U. Pa., 1932, LLB cum laude, 1936. Bar: Pa. 1938, D.C., N.Y. Asst. to prof. U. Pa. Law Sch., Phila., 1936-38, spl. asst. to dean; law clk. Pa. Supreme Ct., Phila., 1939-40; spl. asst. to dir. enemy alien identification program U.S. Dept. Justice, Washington, 1941-42; law clk. U.S. Ct. Appeals, 1946; pvt. practice Phila., Washington and N.Y.C.; city solicitor Phila., 1956-63; founder, chmn. Berger & Montague, P.C., Phila.; former counsel Sch. Dist. Phila.; former chmn. adv. com. Pa. Superior Ct.; mem. drafting com. fed. rules evidence U.S. Supreme Ct.; lectr. on legal subjects. Author numerous articles on law. Nat. commr. Anti-Defamation League; assoc. trustee U. Pa., mem. bd. overseers Law Sch.; Presdl. appointee U.S. Holocaust Meml. Coun.; dir. Internat. Tennis Hall of Fame; bd. dirs. ARC, Palm Beach, Fla.; founder, mem. Friends of Art and Preservation in Embassies. Decorated Silver Star and Presdl. Unit Citation; Fellow Duke of Edinburgh's Award World Fellowship; David Berger chair of law for the improvement of the adminstrn. of justice established at U. Pa. Law Sch.; enshrined in U. Pa. Tennis Hall of Fame, 1997. Fellow Am. Coll. Trial Lawyers, Internat. Acad. Trial Lawyers, Internat. Soc. Barristers; mem. ABA (vice-chair tort and ins. practice sect. com. on comml. torts 1988-89), Phila. Bar Assn. (pres., bd. govs., chancellor), Phila. Bar Found. (past pres.), The Athenaeum Phila., Penn Club (N.Y.C., founder), Order of Coif, The Queens Club (London), Royal Ascot Racing Club (Ascot, Eng.). Home: Elephant Walk 109 Jungle Rd Palm Beach FL 33480-4809 Office: Berger & Montague PC 1622 Locust St Philadelphia PA 19103-6305

BERGER, DEBORAH KORNBLUTH, educator, educational consultant; b. Chgo., Oct. 10, 1968; d. Ralph Ross and Anita Dubow Kornbluth; m. Burman Aaron Berger, Mar. 14, 1992; children: Benjamin Adam, Eli Matthew. BA, Emory U., 1990; MEd, Loyola U., Balt., 1993; Certificate, AMI Assn. Montessori Internat., Washington, 1993. Cert. tchr., Md. Youth advisor B'nai B'rith Youth Orgn., Rockville, Md., 1990-93; spl. asst. ABRH Cons., Washington, 1990-91; youth dir. Kadima Orgn., Rockville, 1991-93; tchr. Hebrew B'nai Shalom, Alexandria, Va., 1991-94, Kehilat Shalom, Gaithersburg, Md., 1992-94; ednl. cons., tchr. Jefferson Montessori, Gaithersburg, 1995-96; elem. directress, tchr. Manor Montessori Internat., Potomac, Md., 1993-98; ednl. tutor, cons., owner Tutoring & Test Preparation by Deborah K. Berger, North Potomac, Md., 1992—; ednl. cons. Flower Hill Sch., Gaithersburg, Butler Sch., 1999—; mem. adv. bd. B'nai Israel, Rockville, 1998—; tutor, ednl. cons. Butler Sch., 1999—. Mem. nursery bd. B'nai Israel,, 1998—; mem. leadership com. United Jewish Appeal, 1994-95. Recipient Internat. Gold Star award B'nai B'rith Orgn., 1986, Nat. Leadership Orgn. award of Honor, 1985. Mem. Hadassah, Potomac Chase Women's Assn., Bunco Club, Reading Club. Jewish. Avocations: reading, writing, skiing, dancing, volunteering at schools.

BERGER, FREDERICK JEROME, electrical engineer, educator; b. Szatmar, Hungary, Nov. 26, 1916; came to U.S. 1929; s. Joseph and Goldie (Weiss) B. BS, CCNY, 1959, BEE, 1961; MEE, NYU, 1964; LLD, Frank Ross Stuart U., 1981; DSc, Capitol Coll., Laurel, Md., 1986. Tool and die maker Brewster Aero. Co., 1935-39, chief tool, gauge and plant engr., 1939-45; process engr. Arma Co., 1946-51; entrepreneur Elec. Electronic Communication Systems and Machine Shop Equipments, 1952-61; prof., dep. chmn., chmn. and engring. sci. coord. CUNY, 1962-82; evaluator Accrediting Bd. Engring., 1962-81; cons. NSF, 1969-80. Editor Jour. of Tau Alpha Pi, 1975-95. With U.S. Army, WWII. Recipient Letter of Recognition for Outstanding Contbn. to Edn. Pres. Ronald Regan, 1987, Pres. William Clinton, 1993. Fellow Am. Soc. Engring. Edn. (Frederick J. Berger ann. scholarship award 1990—, James H. McGraw award in Engring. Tech. Edn. 1992, Centennial cert. and medallion 1993); mem. IEEE (life, Engring. Svc. award 1964-81), Am. Nuclear Engring. Soc., Instrument Soc. Am. (life), Masons, Tau Alpha Pi (founding exec. dir. 1973—), Tau Beta Pi.

BERGER, GERT ALEXANDER, neurologist; b. Gunzenhausen, Bavaria, Germany, Dec. 12, 1943; s. Raimund and Hanne (Thurn) B.; m. Martina Pfister (div. 1987); 1 child, Florian; m. Saskia Carissima Nöggerath, Dec. 9, 1988; children: Oliver, Carolin. BS, U. Innsbruck, 1969, U. Erlangen, 1969; MD, U. Erlangen, 1969. Cert. epileptologist, neurologist, psychiatrist. Resident Klinikum, Nürnberg, Germany, 1970-76; sr. house officer Neurol. Klinik, Nürnberg, 1976—. Contbr. articles to profl. jours. Fellow neurology and psychiatry Bayer. Landesärztekammer, Germany, 1974—. Mem. Internat. Liga gegen Epilepsie (Deutsche sect.), Internat. Fedn. Clin. Neurophysiology (German assn. supr. EEG edn. 1975—, supr. EMG edn. 1987—), German Assn. Ultrasound in Medicine (supr. UDS edn. 1988—). Avocations: riding, tennis. Office: Klinikum Nurnberg, Breslauer Str 201, D-90340 Nuremberg Bayern, Germany

BERGER, HAROLD, lawyer, engineer; b. Archbald, Pa., June 10, 1925; s. Jonas and Anna (Raker) B.; m. Renee Margareten, Aug. 26, 1951; children: Jill Ellen, Jonathan David. BS in Elec. Engring, U. Pa., 1948, JD, 1951. Bar: Pa. 1951. Practiced in Phila.; judge Ct. of Common Pleas, Phila. County, 1971-72; chmn., moderator Internat. Aerospace Meetings Princeton U., 1965-66; chmn. Western Hemisphere Internat. Law Conf., San Jose, Costa Rica, 1967; chmn. internat. Confs. on Aerospace and Internat. Law, Coll. William and Mary; permanent mem. Jud. Conf. 3d Circuit Ct. of Appeals; mem. County Bd. Law Examiners, Phila. County, 1961-71; chmn. World Conf. Internat. Law and Aerospace, Caracas, Venezuela, Internat. Conf. on Environ. and Internat. Law, U. Pa., 1974, Internat. Confs. on Global Interdependence, Princeton U., 1975, 79; mem. Pa. State Conf. Trial Judges, 1972-80, Nat. Conf. State Trial Judges, 1972—; chmn. Pa. Com. for Independent Judiciary, 1973—; adv. coun. Biddle Law Libr., U. Pa., 1991—; mem. bd. overseers Sch. Engring. & Applied Scis., U. Pa., 1998—. Mem. editorial advisory bd.: Jour. of Space Law, U. Miss. Sch. of Law, 1973—; contbr. articles to profl. jours. Mem. We the People 200 Com. for Constn. Bicentennial, 1991. Served with Signal Corps, AUS, 1944-46. Recipient Alumnus of Year award Thomas McKean Law Club, U. Pa. Law Sch., 1965, Gen. Electric Co. Space award, 1966, Nat. Disting. Achievement award Tau Epsilon Rho, 1972, Spl. Pa. Jud. Conf. award, 1981. Mem. Inter-Am. Bar Assn. (past chmn. aerospace law com.), Fed. Bar Assn. (past nat. chmn. com. on aerospace law, pres. Phila. chpt. 1983-84, mem. nat. exec. coun., past nat. chmn. fed. jud. com., Presdl. award 1970, Nat. Disting. Svc. award 1978, nat. com. 1987 bi-centennial of U.S. Constn., chmn. class action and complex litigation com. 3d cir. 1990—, nat. chmn., alternate dispute resolution com. 1992-95, pres. eastern dist. Pa. chpt. 1996—), ABA (Spl. Presdl. Program medal 1975, past chmn. aerospace law com., mem. state and fed. ct. com., nat. conf. of state trial judges), Phila. Bar Assn. (past chmn. jud. liaison com. 1975, chmn. internat. law com. 1977), Assn. U.S. Mems. Internat. Inst. Space Law Internat. Astronautical Fedn. (former bd. dirs.), Internat. Acad. Astronautics Paris. Office: 1622 Locust St Philadelphia PA 19103-6305

BERGER, JEROME MORRIS, communications executive; b. Cleve., Dec. 7, 1951; s. Jack and Beatrice Berger; m. Francine Ellis, Oct. 9, 1977. BA, Boston U., 1973; MS in Journalism, Columbia U., 1976. Editor, reporter Marlboro (Mass.) Enterprise, 1977-82; reporter UP Internat., Boston, 1982-87, statehouse bur. chief, 1987-90; asst. prof. Sch Journalism Northeastern U., Boston, 1990-96; comms. dir. com. on ways and means Mass. Senate, Boston, 1996-98; comms. dir. Mass. Cultural Coun., Boston, 1998—; developer, cons. Nat. Polit. Awareness Test, Project Vote Smart, Boston, 1993-96. Media columnist The Middlesex News, 1996; editor-in-chief: Insuring American Health for the Year 2000, 1992; contbr. articles to profl. publs. Mem. adv. network State Fiscal Analysis Initiative, Boston, 1993-94; media cons. Graduated Income Tax Campaign, Boston, 1994. Mem. Soc. Profl. Journalists. Avocations: reading, walking. E-mail: jfberger@world.std.com. Office: Mass Cultural Coun 120 Boylston St Boston MA 02116-4611

BERGER, JOHN PETER, author, art critic; b. London, Nov. 5, 1926; s. S.J.D. and Miriam (Branson) B. Attended, Central Sch. Art, Chelsea Sch. Art. Began career as painter, tchr. drawing; exhibited works at Wildenstein Gallery, Redfern Gallery and Leicester Gallery, London; art critic Tribune, New Statesman; scenario: (with Alain Tanner) La Salamandre, Le Milieu du Monde, Jonas (N.Y. Critics prize for best scenario of Yr. 1976), (with Timothy Neat) Play Me Something (BFI), 1989, (film scenario) Isabelle: A Story in Shots, 1998; author: Marcel Frishman, 1958, (novels) A Painter of Our Time, 1958, Permanent Red, 1960, The Foot of Clive, 1962, Corker's Freedom, 1964, The Success and Failure of Picasso, 1965, Lilac and Flag, 1990, Into Their Labours, 1991, To the Wedding, 1995, King. A Street Story, 1999, (with Patricia Macdonald) Once in Europa, 1999; (essays) Keeping a Rendezvous, 1991, (with J. Mohr) A Fortunate Man; the story of a country doctor, 1967; Art and Revolution, 1969, Moments of Cubism and Other Essays, 1969; (essays) The Sense of Sight, 1985 (pub. in Eng. as The White Bird), Photocopies, 1996, (poems) Pages of the Wound, 1996; essays and articles include: The Look of Things, 1972, G (novel), 1972 (Booker prize 1972, James Tait Black Meml. prize 1972), Ways of Seeing, 1972, (with J. Mohr) The Seventh Man, 1975 (Union of Journalists and Writers of Paris prize for best reportage 1977), Pig Earth (fiction), 1979; About Looking, 1980; (with J. Mohr) Another Way of Telling, 1982, (with Katya Berger) Titian: Nymph and Shepherd, 1996, (with John Christie) I Send You This Cadmium Red, 2000; work for theatre (with Nella Bielski) A Question of Geography, premiere Theatre National de Marseille, 1984, Goya's Last Portrait, 1989; (non-fiction) And Our Faces, My Heart, Brief as Photos, 1984, Steps Towards a Small Theory Of The Visible, 1996; Once in Europa (fiction) 1987 (award 1989); translator: (with A Bostock) Poems on the Theatre (B. Brecht), 1960, Return to My Native Land (Aime Cesaire), 1969; numerous TV appearances, including: Monitor, two series for Granada TV. Office: Quincy, Mieussy, 74440 Taninges France

BERGER, LINDA FAY, writer; b. Ft. Worth, Mar. 12, 1943; d. Walter Bob and Bertha Fay (Christensen) B. AA, Tarrant County Jr. Coll., Ft. Worth, 1976; BBA, U. Tex., Arlington, 1981; MBA, North Tex. U., 1987. Cert. profl. sec. Profl. Sec. Assn. Internat. With Tex. Refinery Corp., Ft. Worth, 1961-91, file clk., telex operator, departmental sec., exec. sec., asst. pers. dir., pers. dir. Co-author: A Joyful Journey, 1995. Mem. Profl. Secs. Internat. (sec. 1969-79), Tex. Assn. Bus. (sec. 1990), Order Ea. Star (Riverside chpt. 834). Republican. Mem. Unity Ch. Avocations: travelling, yoga, reading, cooking.

BERGER, MICHAEL GARY, lawyer; b. New Haven, Apr. 16, 1946; s. Jacob and Edith (Axelrod) B.; m. Miriam Janet Haines, July 24, 1977; children: Richard, Daniel. BS, Yale Coll., 1968; JD, Columbia U., 1973. Asst. dist. atty. New York County Office of Dist. Atty., N.Y.C., 1973-76; pvt. practice N.Y.C., 1981—; counsel Epstein, Becker & Green, P.C., N.Y.C., 1987—; arbitrator Am. Arbitration Assn., 1994—; mem. Criminal Justice Act Panel, N.Y.C., 1976-79; legal rep. clients in various fields icluding bus., medicine, profl. sports and entertainment; spkr. at cmty. client and bar groups. Mem. cons. bd.: Lawyers Cooperative Practice Guide—Handling a Criminal Case in New York, 1994; commentator on legal matters for Ct. TV, CNBC, Fox News, nat. and local TV programs; contbr. book revs. to law publs. Mem. ABA, Fed. Bar Coun., Nat. Assn. Criminal Def. Lawyers, N.Y. State Bar Assn., Assn. of Bar of City of N.Y. Avocation: tennis. Office: Law Offices 20th Fl 250 Park Ave Fl 20 New York NY 10177-0001

BERGER, NATHAN ALLEN, dean, university administrator; b. Phila., July 8, 1940; s. Meyer and Lillian (Salko) B.; m. Sosamma John, June 23, 1968; children: Joshua S., Ravi B., Sarina H. AB, Temple U., 1962; MD, Hahneman U., 1966. Intern Michael Reese Med. Ctr., Chgo., 1967-68; rsch. assoc. NIH, Balt., 1968-71; assoc. prof. Washington U. Sch. Medicine, St. Louis, 1971-82; prof. medicine, biochemistry, and oncology Case Western Res. U., Cleve., 1983-95, dir. cancer ctr., 1985—, interim dean, v.p. med. affairs, 1995-96, dean, v.p. med. affairs, 1996—; bd. trustees Edison Biotech. Am. Cancer Soc., U. Hosp. Cleve., Henry Ford Health System. Contbr. articles to profl. jours.; mem. editl. bd. Jour. Clin. Investigation, Jour. Biol. Chemistry, Cancer Rsch.; others. Lt. comdr. USPHS, 1968-71. Fellow Washington U. Sch. Medicine, 1971-82; Leukemia Soc. Am. scholar. Mem. Am. Soc. Hematology, Am. Soc. Biol. Chemists, Am. Soc. Clin. Oncology, Am. Soc. Cancer Rsch., Am. Soc. Clin. Investigation, Am. Assn. Physicians. Office: Case Western Res U 10900 Euclid Ave Cleveland OH 44106-1712

BERGER, PER ERIK, drilling service company manager; b. Oslo, Norway, May 16, 1962; s. Bjoern Willy and Berit (Haugan) B.; m. Elin Siglen, July 11, 1987; children: Ingvild, Eivind, Jon Even. BSL, Rogaland Regional Coll., Stavanger, Norway, 1984. Profl. petroleum engr. Field svc. engr. Baker Hughes Inteq, Stavanger, 1984-88, field tech. coord., 1988-92, ops. mgr., 1992-96, mgr. evaluation dept., 1996-97, technology devel. mgr., 1997-99, ops. mgr., 2000—. Inventor in field. Mem. Soc. Petroleum Engrs., Soc. Profl. Well Log Analysts, Norwegian Formation Evaluation Soc., Norwegian Petroleum Soc. Avocations: cross country skiing, running, jaguar classic cars. Office: Baker Hughes Inteq, Ekofiskveien 1, 4056 Tananger Norway

BERGER, RICHARD, obstetrician and gynecologist; b. Augsburg, Germany, Sept. 3, 1960; s. Richard and Maria (Brunner) B.; m. Carmen Prassler, July 15, 1988; children: Georg, Franziska. MD, U. Munich, 1987; PhD, U. Bochum, Germany, 1996. Rsch. fellow Inst. for Surg. Rsch., U. Munich, 1984-87; rsch., clin. fellow dept. gynecology Univ. Hosp. Giessen, Germany, 1987-94; rsch. fellow Max-Planck Inst. for Neurol. Rsch., Cologne, 1994-95; cons. dept. gynecology Univ. Hosp. Bochum, 1995—. Co-author: Fetus and Neonate, The Circulation, Vol. 1, 1993, Giessener Gynaekologische Fortbildung, 1993, Vom Accouchierhaus fur Frauenklinik, 1989, Geburtshilfe in Hessen, 1992, Emergency Surgery, 1986, Microcirculation - an update, Vol. 2, 1987; contbr. articles to profl. jours. Mem. Cartellverband (CV), Munich, 1981—. Recipient award European Congress of Anesthesiology, 1985, Sci. award Mittelrheinische Soc. Gynecology and Obstetrics, 1990, Sci. award German Soc. Perinatology, 1997; grantee Deutsche Forschungsgemeinschaft, 1993—, Max-Planck Soc., 1995—, U. Bochum, 1996—. Mem. German Soc. for Gynecology and Obstetrics (Sci. award 1992), German Soc. Physiology (sec. developmental physiology), Med. Faculty of U. Bochum. Roman Catholic. Avocations: modern art and history, hiking, skiing, guitar playing, cooking.

BERGER, STEVEN R., lawyer, state official; b. Miami, Aug. 23, 1945; s. Jerome J. and Jeanne B. B.; m. Francine Blake, Aug. 20, 1966; children: Amy, Charlie. BS, U. Ala., 1967; JD, 1969. Bar: Fla. 1969, Nev. 1991, U.S. Dist. Ct. (no. dist.) Fla. 1969, U.S. Dist. Ct. (so. dist.) Fla. 1971, U.S. Dist. Ct. (mid. dist.) Fla. 1989, U.S. Dist. Ct. Nev. 1991, U.S. Ct. Appeals (5th cir.) 1971, U.S. Ct. Appeals (11th cir.) 1981, U.S. Ct. Appeals (2nd and 9th cirs.) 1991, U.S. Supreme Ct. 1972, U.S. Ct. Claims 1977; cert. appellate specialist Fla. Bar Bd. Assoc. W. Dexter Douglass, Tallahassee, Fla., 1969-71, William R. Dawes, Miami, 1971; ptnr. Carey, Dwyer, Cole Selwood & Bernard, Miami, 1971-81; sole practice Steven R. Berger, P.A., 1981-89; ptnr. Wolpe, Leibowitz, Berger & Brotman, 1989-94, Berger & Chafetz, 1994-99; asst. atty. gen. State of Fla., 1999—; mem. faculty Nat. Appellate Advocacy Inst., Washington, 1980; vice chmn. bench and bar adv. com. Ct. Appeals. 4th Dist., 1986-92. Chmn. City Miramar Planning Bd., 1975-76. Mem. ABA (vice chmn. app. practice com. litigation sect. 1981-83, chmn. 5th cir. subcom. appellate practice com. 1978-81), Am. Judicature Soc., Am. Arbitration Assn., Tallahassee Bar Assn., Kendall-South Miami Dist. Bar Assn., Dade County Def. Bar Assn., Fla. Def. Lawyers Assn. (vice chmn. appellate rules com. 1989), Def. Rsch. Inst., Rep. Nat. Lawyers Assn., Internat. Assn. Def. Counsel, N.Y. State Bar Assn., State Bar Nev., N.Y. State Trial Lawyers Assn. Office: Office of Atty Gen 444 Brickell Ave Ste 950 Miami FL 33131-2407

BERGER, THOMAS LOUIS, author; b. Cin., July 20, 1924; s. Thomas Charles and Mildred (Bubbe) B.; m. Jeanne Redpath, June 12, 1950. BA with honors, U. Cin., 1948; postgrad., Columbia U., 1950-51; LittD (hon.), L.I.U., 1986. Librarian Rand Sch. Social Sci., N.Y.C., 1948-51; staff mem. N.Y. Times Index, 1951-52; assoc. editor Popular Sci. Monthly, 1952-53; disting. vis. prof. Southampton Coll., 1975-76; vis. lectr. Yale U., 1981, 82; Regent's lectr. U. Calif., Davis, 1982. Author: Crazy in Berlin, 1958, Reinhart in Love, 1962, Little Big Man, 1964, Killing Time, 1967, Vital Parts, 1970, Regiment of Women, 1973, Sneaky People, 1975, Who Is Teddy Villanova?, 1977, Arthur Rex, 1978, Neighbors, 1980, Reinhart's Women, 1981, The Feud, 1983 (Pulitzer Prize nomination 1984), Nowhere, 1985, Being Invisible, 1987, The Houseguest, 1988, Changing the Past, 1989, Orrie's Story, 1990, Meeting Evil, 1992, Robert Crews, 1994, Suspects, 1996, The Return of Little Big Man, 1999, (play) Other People, 1970. Served with AUS, 1943-46, ETO. Recipient Rosenthal award Nat. Inst. Arts and Letters, 1965; Western Heritage award, 1965; Ohioana Book award, 1982; Dial fellow, 1962. Office: Don Congdon Assocs 156 Fifth Ave New York NY 10010-7002

BERGERAC, JACQUES, real estate investment company executive; b. Biarritz, France, May 26, 1927; s. Charles and Alice (Romatet) B.; m. Ginger Rogers, Feb. 12, 1953 (div. 1957); m. Dorothy Malone, June 22, 1959 (div. 1963); children: Mimi, Diane; m. Edith Brennan, June 22, 1975. Law degree, U. Paris, 1952. Lawyer, Paris, 1952; motion picture actor MGM, Hollywood, Calif., 1952-61; motion picture producer, Hollywood, 1961-69; pres. Revlon-France, Paris, 1970-79, Balmain-Worldwide, Paris, 1979-87, Miguel Cruz, Paris, 1987-89, Belatxa, Paris, 1990-96, Tilia, S.A., Paris, 1996—. Mem. Racing Club France. Roman Catholic. Avocations: tennis, surfing, jai alai.

BERGER-KRAEMER, NANCY, speech and language pathologist, artist; b. N.Y.C., Aug. 15, 1941; d. George G. and Ruth (Kirsch) Berger; m. Aaron Kraemer, July 10, 1966; children: Lea, Steven. BA, Adelphi U., 1963; MS in Edn., Queens Coll., 1968; cert. clin. competency in speech pathology. Lic. and cert. speech and lang. pathologist, N.Y., N.J.; permanent cert. speech and hearing for handicapped, N.Y. Speech therapist Dist. # 24 Sch. Sys., Valley Stream, L.I., 1962-64; dir. speech and lang., hearing/speech pathologist Port Chester Sch. Dist., Rye, N.Y., 1965-66; speech and lang. pathologist Roselle Park (N.J.) Sch. Sys., 1966-67, Willis Sch. for Educationally Handicapped, Plainfield, N.J., 1967-68, St. Barnabas Med. Ctr., West Orange, N.J., 1971-97; pvt. practice Maplewood, N.J., 1968—, Andover Twp., 1998—; lectr., spkr. in field; cons. in field. Numerous one-woman shows, N.J., N.Y., N.Y.C., Chatham, N.J.; group shows include N.J. Ctr. Visual Arts, Summit, City Without Walls, Newark, Bergen Mus., Jersey City Mus., Trenton City Mus., N.J. State Mus., Montclair Art Mus., Noyes Mus., Phoenix Gallery, Veridian Gallery, Newark Mus., Pindar Gallery, Gallerie Ambiente, Germany, William Carlos Williams Ctr. Arts, N.J., San Diego Art Inst., Stedman Art Gallery, New Brunswick, N.J., Fordham U.-Lowenstein Libr., N.Y.C., Johnson & Johnson, N.J., Cali Assocs., Bellemead Devel. corp., AT&T, Nabisco Brands, Beneficial Ins. Co., Prudential Ins. Co., PleiadesGallery, N.Y.C., Art Ctr. No. N.J., Art Assn. Harrisburg, Pa., Stamford Art Assn., Ct., Princeton (N.J.) Art Assn., Bucknell U. Ctr. Gallery, Art Alliance 13th Ann. N.J. Statewide Exhibit, Skylands Ann. Art Exhibit, Sussex Arts, Heritage Coun., Sparta, N.J., Ceres Gallery, N.Y.C., others. Mem. Am. Speech Lang. Hearing Assn., Auditory Verbal Internat. (charter, lectr. 1975—), Alexander Graham Bell Assn., N.J. Speech and Hearing Assn., Sussex Co. Judicial Ctr., Newton, N.J.

BERGERON, EARLEEN FOURNET, actress; b. New Orleans, Aug. 7, 1938; d. Earl Joseph Fournet and Lucia (Cuccia) Wadsworth; m. James Ronald Bergeron Sr., June 17, 1961; children: Blanche Theresa, Michele Yvette, James Ronald Jr. B of Social Sci. in Theatre and Speech, Loyola U., 1960. bd. dirs. Port Players, Shreveport, La.; assoc. mem. The Co. Repertory Theatre, Inc., Project-Shakespeare in the Schs. Actor: (play) The Secret Affairs of Mildred Wilde, 1977, The Boyfriend, 1977, The Shadow Box, 1979, California Suite, 1980, Hay fever, 1985, Brighton Beach, 1986, Beyond Therapy, 1987, Steel Magnolias, 1988, 89, Nunsense, 1990, Broadway Bound, 1991, The Women, 1993, Nunsense II, 1995, Stomping Grounds, 1995, 96, Angels in America, Part I: Millenium Approaches, Part II: Perestroika, 1997, Spareribs, 1998, Come Back Little Sheba, 1999 (TV series) Rescue 911, 1991, (film) Man in the Moon, 1990, (comml.) Goodwill, 1988, Schumpert Medical Center, 1991, Cunningham and McDonald, Plastic Surgeons, 1991, JB Cable Ads, 1995, Pierre Bossier Mall, 1996. Mem. Shreveport Opera Guild, 1972-97; area leader fund drive Am. Cancer Soc., Shreveport, 1985-89; active Shreveport Med. Aux., 1968-97, exec. bd. 1976-78. Named one of Outstanding Team Capts., United Way Fund, 1969. Mem. Shreveport Little Theatre Guild (bd. dirs. 1985-86), Shreveport Little Theatre, Majorie Lyons Playhouse, Strand Theatre. Roman Catholic.

BERGERON, ELMO P., chemical engineer, consultant; b. Gray, La., Dec. 18, 1936; s. Elmo P. and Estelle F. Bergeron; m. Carolyn Gaudet, Nov. 30, 1963; 1 child, Ann Michele. BS in Chem. Engring., La. State U., Baton Rouge, 1960, MS, 1961, PhD, 1963. Registered profl. engr., La. Devel. engr. Allied Chem., Morristown, N.J., 1963-66; sys. engr., process specialist Dow Chem., Plaquemine, La., 1966-74; process cons. Dow Chem., Terneuzen, Netherlands, 1974-76; process cons., project mgr. Dow Chem., Plaquemine, 1977-93; cons., 1993—. Contbr. articles to profl. jours.; patentee in field. Named to Outstanding Young Men of Am., 1970. Mem. AIChE, La. Soc. Profl. Engrs. Republican. Roman Catholic. Avocations: reading, photography, woodworking.

BERGERON, LYNN HENRY, assistant principal, private school educator; b. New Orleans, Nov. 9, 1930; s. Hercules Joseph and Marcelle Claire (Couturie) B.; m. Jean Roberta Corvers; children: Roberta (Emmons) Stephen, Michael, Robert, Lynn Jr. Diploma, Gen. Staff Coll., 1978; BA in Social Sci., Cumberland U., 1988. Cert. tchr., La. Commd. 2d. lt. U.S. Army, 1952, advanced throuth grades to col., 1983; dir. personnel U.S. Army, New Orleans, 1969-88; tchr., asst. prin. Archdiocese New Orleans, 1988—; steamship line mgr. Tex. Transport & Terminal, New Orleans, 1960-69; pres. Apex Property Mgmt. LLC, Harahan, La., 1992-99. Author: The Bergeron and Couturie Families, 1999. Named Dist. Tchr. Northwestern U., Ruston, La., 1995. Republican. Roman Catholic. Avocations: genealogy, history, chess. E-mail: ljharahan@aol.com. Home: 101 Sedgefield Dr Harahan LA 70123-4720 Office: Apes Property Mgmt LLC 9605 Jefferson Hwy Ste I183 River Ridge LA 70123-2550

BERGERON, ROBERT FRANCIS, JR. (TERRY BERGERON), software engineer; b. Gloucester, Mass., Jan. 23, 1942; s. Robert Francis and Jean Ann (Francis) B.; children: Robert, Karin, Kristin; m. Marion Louise Pisarchuk, July 14, 1979; children: Steven, Tanya. ScB summa cum laude, Brown U., 1964; PhD math., MIT, 1968. Rsch. assoc. Bolt Beranek & Newman, Cambridge, Mass., 1968; instr. math MIT, Cambridge, 1969; mem. tech. staff Bell Lab., Whippany, N.J., 1969-72, supr., 1972-84; tech. mgr. AT&T Bell Lab., Warren, N.J., 1984-95; cons., sr. mgr. Cotelligent, Liberty Corner, N.J., 1996-2000. Patentee in field; contbr. articles to profl. jours. Home: 27 Kevin Dr Flanders NJ 07836-9762

BERGERSEN, FRASER JOHN, research scientist; b. Hamilton, New Zealand, May 26, 1929; s. Victor Emmanuel and Arabel Huntley (Young) B.; m. Gladys Irene Heather, July 5, 1952; children: Jennifer Anne, Philip John, Peter Richard. BS, U. Otago, Dunedin, New Zealand, 1951, MS, 1953; DSc, U. New Zealand, 1962. Assoc. U. Otago, Dunedin, 1952-54; rsch. scientist Commonwealth Sci. & Indsl. Rsch. Orgn. div. Plant Industry, Canberra, Australia, 1954-72; chief rsch. scientist CSIRO div. Plant Industry, Canberra, Australia, 1972-94; rsch. assoc. U. Wis., Madison, 1958-59; advisor Consejo Nacional de Pesquisas-Empressa Brasilera Agropecuarias, Brazil, 1970-77; cons. NSW Agrl., 1971-79, Rockefeller Found., N.Y., Food and Agrl. Orgn., Rome, UN Environ. Programme, Nairobi, UN Ednl., Sci. and Cultural Orgn., Paris, Internat. Inst. Tropical Agr., Ibadan; leader collaborative rsch. projects Australian Ctr. for Int. Agr. Rsch., 1984-91; vis. fellow Australian Nat. Univ., Canberra, 1994—. Author: Root Nodules of Legumes: Structure and Functions, 1982: editor: Methods for Evaluating Biological Nitrogen Fixation, 1980; editor (with J. Postgate) A Century of Nitrogen Fixation Research, 1987; contbr. 170 papers to profl. jours. Underwood fellow U. Sussex, Brighton, U.K., 1973; recipient David Rivett medal Commonwealth Sci. & Indsl. Rsch. Orgn. Officers Assn., Australia, 1968; mem. Order of Australia. Fellow Royal Soc. (London), Australian Acad. Sci. (coun. mem. 1987-93, fgn. sec. 1989-93). Baptist.

BERGFIELD, GENE RAYMOND, engineering educator; b. Granite City, Ill., July 11, 1951; s. Walter Irvin Bergfield and Venie Edith (Sanders) Bennett; m. Juanita Pauline Kapp, Sept. 19, 1970; children: Gene Raymond Jr., Timothy Shawn. BA in Applied Behavioral Scis., Nat. Coll. Edn., Chgo., 1988. Field engr. Westinghouse PGSD, St. Louis, 1979-81; instr. Westinghouse PGSD, Phila., 1982-84; asst. resource mgr. Westinghouse PGSD, Chgo., 1984-89; power plant instr. Westinghouse PGPD, Orlando, Fla., 1989-93; ops. and maintenance supr. Edison Mission O&M Inc., Auburndale, Fla., 1993-97; power plant cons. PenPower, Auburndale, Fla., 1997-99; ind. power plant cons., 1999—. With USN, 1971-79. Office: Penpower 1302 N 19th St # 4 Tampa FL 33605-5215

BERGGREN, BO ERIK GUNNAR, paper company executive; b. Falun, Sweden, Aug. 11, 1936; s. Tage B. and Elsa (Hoglund) B.; m. Gunbritt Haglund, 1962; children: Erik, Karin, Charlotta, Klas. MMetE, Royal Inst. Tech., Stockholm, 1962; PhD (hon.), Royal Inst. Tech., 1989, Dalhousie U., Halifax, Can., 1996. Metall. engr. R & D STORA Kopparbergs Domnarvet Steelwork, Sweden, 1962-68; mill mgr. STORA Söderfors Specialty Steelworks, Sweden, 1968-74; exec. v.p. STORA, Falun, 1975-78, pres., CEO, 19884-92, chmn. bd., CEO, 1992-94, chmn. bd., 1994-95; chmn. bd. STORA, Stockholm, 1995-98; pres. Incentive, Stockholm, 1978-84; bd. dirs., chmn. ASTRA, 1993-99, SAS Sverige AB/Fedn. Swedish Industries; bd. dirs. Danisco A/S Denmark; adv. coun. J.P Morgan Internat., 1989-99; adv. com. Robert Bosch Internat. Beteiligungen AG. Decorated King's medal of 12th Dimension with Ribbon of Order of Seraphim, comdr. 1st class Order of Lion of Finland. Mem. Royal Acad. Forestry and Agrl., Royal Swedish Acad. Engring. Scis., Royal Inst. Tech. (bd. dirs.). Avocations: music, arts, tennis, skiing. Office: Stora Kopparberget Found, PO Box 5501, S-114 85 Stockholm Sweden

BERGGREN, ERIC GRIFFITH, consulting company executive; b. Phila., Aug. 22, 1962; s. Ronald Bernard and Mary Beth B.; m. Deborah Logan, July 2, 1988; children: Allison Griffith, John Ericsson. BA, Kenyon Coll., 1984; M of Mgmt., Northwestern U., 1988. Analyst The MAC Group, Chgo., 1984-86, assoc., 1988-90; prin. Gemini Cons., Chgo., 1990-93; pres. Berggren & Co., Inc., Chgo., 1994—; asst. brand mgr. G.D. Searle & Co., Skokie, Ill., 1997; advisor ncognito.com, Chgo. Contbr. articles to profl. jours. Recipient Econs. Prize, Kenyon Coll., Gambier, Ohio, 1984. Avocations: tennis, sailing. E-mail: eric@berggrenco.com. Fax #: (312) 787-8801. Office: Berggren & Co Inc 1221 N Dearborn St Apt 402N Chicago IL 60610-8375

BERGHAHN, KLAUS LEO, German and Jewish studies educator; b. Duesseldorf, Germany, Aug. 5, 1937; arrived in U.S., 1967; s. Wilhelm and Anna (Bong) B.; m. Doris E. Beyer, Aug. 10, 1966; 1 child, Marcus J. Student, U. Cologne, Germany, 1957-59; Staatsexamen, U. Muenster, Germany, 1963, Dr phil, 1967. Tutor, asst. U. Muenster, 1963-67; asst. prof. German studies U. Wis., Madison, 1967-71, assoc. prof., 1971-73, prof., 19735, chmn. German dept., 1994-97, mem. senate, 1974-78, 85-87, dir. ctr. German European studies, 19985, Weinstein-Bascom prof. German and Jewish studies, 1999—; vis. prof. Free U. Berlin, 1978, U. Bielefeld, Germany, 1980-81, U. Giessen, Germany, 1983, 92, U. Mich., Ann Arbor, 1984, U. Calif., Davis, 1989, Hebrew U., Jerusalem, 1993; mem. adv. bd. German Am. Art Found., Chgo., 1995—; mem. German sect. Fulbright Commn., 1995-98; mem. adv. bd. German dept. Harvard U., 1994-95, 96-97; organizer spl. sessions, confs. and symposia, 1983—. Author: Formen der Dialogführung in Schillers klassischen Dramen, 1970, Friedrich Schiller: Vom Pathetischen und Erhabenen, 1970, Friedrich Schiller: Kallias oder über die Schönheit, 1971, Briefwechsel zwischen Schiller und Körner, 1973, Schillers Gedichte, 1980, G.E. Lessing: Hamburgische Dramaturgie, 1981, Schiller5Ansichten eines Idealisten, 1986, (with Beate Pinkerneil) Am Beispiel Wilhelm Meister, 2 vols., 1980, Grenzen der Toleranz, 2000; editor: (with Reinhold Grimm) Schiller5Zur Theorie und Praxis der Dramen, 1972, Wesen und Formen des Komischen im Drama, 1975, Utopian Vision5Technological Innovation5Poetic Imagination, 1990, (with Hans Ulrich Seeber) Literarische Utopien von Morus bis zur Gegenwart, 1983, 2d edit., 1985, (with Holub and Scherpe) Responsibility and Committment. Ethische Postulate der Kulturvermittlung. Festschift für Jost Hermand, 1996; editor: Schiller5Zur Geschichtlichkeit seines Werkes, 1976, The German-Jewish Dialogue-Reconsidered, 1996, Friedrich Schilles: Ueber die aesthetische Erzhichung des Menschen, 2000; mem. editl. bd. Monatshefte, 19705, Mich. Germanic Studies, 19855, Goethe Yearbook, 19885; contbr. articles and revs. to profl. jours., chpts. to books. Vol. for local and state polit. campaigns. Fellow VW-Found., Germany, 1965-67, Am. Philos. Soc., 1969, 73, Inst. for Rsch. in Humanities, U. Wis., 1972, 89-94, Ctr. for Interdisciplinary Rsch., Bielefeld, 1980-81, German Acad. Exch. Svc., 1990, 99, also others; 14 summer rsch. grants U. Wis. Grad. Sch. Mem. MLA (19th and early 20th century German lit. divsn. exec. com. 1974-78, chmn. 1977, mem. 18th and early 19th century German lit. divsn. 1983-88, chmn. 1987, mem. adv. bd. MLA Profession 1997-99), Am. Assn. Tchrs. German (program and selection com. 1990), Internat. Union Germanists (program com. 1995), Lessing Soc., Schiller Soc. (medal 1984), Goethe Soc. Avocations: reading, writing, music, theater, chess. Home: 2908 Oxford Rd Madison WI 53705-2220 Office: U Wis Dept German 860 Van Hise Hall 1220 Linden Dr Madison WI 53706-1525

BERGHMANS, JEAN-PIERRE, lime and dolomite company executive; b. Nameche, Namur, Belgium, Jan. 23, 1949; s. Jean and Elisabeth (Lhoist) B.; m. Katherine d'Aspremont Lynden, Apr. 22, 1972; children: Mélanie, Sibylle, Valentine. MA in Econs., U. Louvain (Belgium), 197l; MBA, European Inst. Bus. Adminstrn., Fontainebleau, France, 1974. Chmn. exec. bd. Group Lhoist, Limelette, Belgium, 1974—. Avocations: collecting paint-

ings and sculpture, music, skiing, shooting. Home: Château de Hoyoux, B-4560 Les Avins en Condroz Clavier, Belgium also: 69 Ave R Vandendriessche, 1150 Brussels Belgium Office: Saint Jean-des-Bois, 1342 Ottignies, Louvain Belgium

BERGHOLM, ERNST TAUNO HERMAN (BARON OF AMIDA), architect, company director, author; b. Helsinki, Mar. 21, 1935; s. Tauno Kaarlo Axel and Aune Elisabeth (von Freymann a.d.H. Nursie) B.; m. Kerstin Sandén, Mar. 25, 1955; children: Katri Birgitta, Maria Elizabeth; m. Ulla-Maija Kanerva, Mar. 14, 1975; children: Pia-Sofia Irja Johanna, Anna Aune Alexandra; m. Alli Anneli Hartikka, Jan. 22, 1982. Grad. architect, also advanced diploma, U.S.A., Can., 1957. Architect Sweden, 1953-54, 60-64, Can., 1956-59; owner, pres. Bergholm & Co., Helsinki, 1964—; chmn. or bd. dirs. several cos., Finland, Liechtenstein. Prin. works include hosps., schs., chs., residential bldgs. in several countries; author: Anor till Sofia Fleming Friherrinna af Liebelitz, 1971, Suomesta Saksittua, 1976, Prinkkalan Moniste eli Suomen Kansan Historia, 1976, Käsikirja Perhetalouden eri Aloilta, 1985, Mannerheim Kaskujen Kuvastimessa, 1997, Valtakunnan Valioita, 2000; contbr. articles to various publs.; writer TV and radio programs. Decorated Nat. Def. medal, Finland, knight comdr. Order Holy Sepulchre; recipient grand medal Order Cultural Merit, grand cross Order of Sports Merit, highest medal of honor VACRS, 1st class Social Svc. Order, grand cross Tunghai Order Friendship (Republic of China), knight of merit Order Cross of Constantin the Gt., Imperial House Order of Merit of Angelo-Comneno Dynasty, grand cross Order St. Lazarus, grand cross Order St. Eugene, grand cross Order Constantin the Great, plaque of merit Finnish Anti-Aircraft Sch., 1955, citation Tunghai U., Key to City, Taipei, 1983, Gold medal of merit Cen. Ch. Commerce, 1995, Blue Cross with sword and others. Mem. Humanist Soc. Finland (founding, bd. dirs. 1969-70), Finland-Liechtenstein Soc. (founder, pres. 1977-85, hon. pres., 1985—), Geneal. Soc. Finland (life), also bd. dirs. several Finnish assns. and socs. Liberal Royalist. Avocations: music, genealogy. Office: PO Box 159, SF-00141 Helsinki Finland

BERGHOLM, KARI AXEL, diplomat; b. Helsinki, Finland, Apr. 11, 1930; s. Tauno Axel and Aune Elisabeth (Von Freymann) B.; m. Aino Tuovi Pehu-Lehtonen, Dec. 21, 1951; children: Kaarlo, Jorma, Heikki, Tapio. MScEE, Helsinki Inst. Tech., 1952; cert. in indsl. adminstrn., Carnegie-Mellon U., 1971. With Helsinki City Adminstrn., 1953-71; mng. dir. Finnish Stds. Assn., Helsinki, 1971-77; spl. advisor Ministry for Fgn. Affairs, Helsinki, 1977-95, spl. counselor, 1984-95, ambassador, 1992-95, cons., 1995—. Senator Jr. Chamber Internat., 1967. Named Officer 1st Class Order of White Rose of Finland, 1989, Knight Comdr. Order of Lion of Finland, 1999. Mem. Internat. Folklore Orgn. (pres. 1997—), Finnish Folklore Assn. (pres. 1965-91, hon. pres. 1992). Avocation: folklore. Home: Runebergink 39A37, FIN00100 Helsinki Finland Office: Ministry for Fgn Affairs, PO Box 176, FIN00161 Helsinki Finland

BERGHS, HUBERT THEODOOR, rheumatologist; b. Bocholt, Limburg, Belgium, Feb. 20, 1945; s. Mathieu Willem Berghs and Maria Catharina Goyens; m. Irene Henriette Engelen, Oct. 10, 1969; children: Katrien, Ann. MD, Cath. U. Leuven, Belgium, 1968. Asst. internal medicine Dr. A.C.M. Lips, Eindhoven, The Netherlands, 1968-70; asst. rheumatology U. Hosp., Leiden, The Netherlands, 1970-72, Giso, Lariboisiere, Paris, 1972; pvt. practice Genk, Belgium, 1973—. Contbr. articles to profl. jours. Mem. Belgian Assn. Rheumatology (sec. 1982-84, pres. 1984-86, treas. 1988-96), Acknowledgment Com. Rheumatology. Home: Mosselerlaan 97, 3600 Genk Limburg, Belgium Office: Bretheistraat 149, 3600 Genk Limburg, Belgium

BERGIN, COLLEEN JOAN, medical educator; b. Foxton, New Zealand, May 13, 1953; came to U.S., 1981; d. Joseph Bernard and Mary Catherine (Butel) B.; m. Niall C.T. Wilton, May 22, 1992; children: Tessa, Sophie. MBChB, Auckland Med. Sch., 1979. Resident U. B.C., Vancouver, Can., 1981-87; faculty Stanford (Calif.) U., 1989-92; prof. U. Calif., San Diego, 1992—; cons. radiologist Auckland Hosp., 1998—. Contbr. articles to profl. jours. NIH Rsch. grantee, 1992—; Thoracic Radiology fellow Duke U., 1988. Mem. Am. Roentgen Ray Soc., Radiol. Soc. N.Am., Soc. Thoracic Radiology, Soc. Magnetic Resonance. Democrat. Roman Catholic. Avocations: golf, flying, photography, diving.

BERG-JOHNSEN, JON, neurosurgeon; b. Oslo, June 6, 1955; s. Per and Doris (Jensen) B.; m. Anne Moe Hagen, Sept. 27, 1986; children: Ida Kristine, Martin. MD, U. Oslo, 1983, PhD, 1991. Rsch. fellow Inst. Exptl. Med. Rsch., Oslo, 1982-84; resident in neurosurgery Ullevaal U. Hosp., Oslo, 1984-93, chief attending physician neurosurgery, 1993—. Contbr. articles to profl. jours. Capt. Norwegian Army, 1992. Mem. Norwegian Neurosurg. Soc. (leader 1997—). Home: Fuglelivn 20 A, 0667 Oslo Norway Office: Dept Neurosurgery, Nat Hosp, 0027 Oslo Norway

BERGKAMP, DENNIS, professional soccer player; b. Amsterdam, May 10, 1969. Forward Ajax Amsterdam Football Club, Holland, Inter Milan Football Club, Italy; with Holland's Nat. Team World Cup, 1990, 94, 98; forward Arsenal FC, Eng., 1995—. Named Dutch Footballer of Yr., 1992, 93, Eng. Footballer of Yr., 1997, 98. Office: Arsenal FC Arsenal Stadium, Avenell Rd, Highbury London N5 1BU, England

BERGKVIST, THOMAS A., lawyer; b. Des Moines, Aug. 20, 1960; s. Carl Ivar and Else (Bon Jespersen) B.; m. Laurie Varlotta, May 4, 1991; children: Kristen Nicole, Carolyn Paige. BA, Trinity Coll., 1982; JD magna cum laude, Boston U., 1985. Bar: Pa. 1985, N.J. 1987. Atty. Saul Ewing Remick & Saul, Phila., 1985-93, Law Office of Thomas A. Bergkvist, Phila., 1993—; of counsel Kahn Greenberg & Blau, Malvern, 1996—. Mem. ABA, Pa. Bar Assn., Phila. Bar Assn., Phila. Estate Planning Coun., Germantown Cricket Club, Pi Gamma Mu.

BERGLEITNER, GEORGE CHARLES, JR., investment banker; b. Bklyn., July 16, 1935; s. George Charles and Marie (Preitz) B.; m. Betty Van Buren, Oct. 29, 1966; children: George Charles III, Michael John, Stephen William. BBA, St. Francis Coll., Bklyn., 1959; MBA, CCNY, 1961; PhD in Bus. Adminstrn. (hon.), Colo. State Christian Coll. Dir. instl. sales A.T. Brod & Co., N.Y.C., 1965-66; dir. instl. sales Weis, Voisin & Cannon, Inc., N.Y.C., 1966-67, C.B. Richard, Ellis & Co., N.Y.C., 1967-68; pres. Stamford (N.Y.) Fin. Co., also bd. dirs.; pres. M.J. Manchester & Co., Fashion & Time, Inc., B.J.B. Graphics, Inc., First Coinvestors, Inc., Smart Fit Foundations, Inc., Jay Co., Computer Holdings Corp., Ltd., Delhi Mfg. Corp., Delhi Industries, Delhi Mfg., Inc., Delhi Internat., Inc., Luxemborg; bd. dirs. Alpha Capital Corp., Am. Energy Mgmt. Corp., Stamford Fin., Electronic Tax Ctrs., Inc., L.I.U.G., L.I. Venture Capital Group, L.I. Venture Group, High Tech Semiconductor Svcs., Del. County Indsl. Devel.; sponsor N.Y. Venture Group; bd. dirs. Indsl. Devel. Agy., Delaware County, N.Y. Chmn. Franciscan Fathers Devel. Program, 1967-71; mem. Pres's Coun., Franciscan Spirit award; 1959—; pres. South Kortright Ctrl. Sch.; chmn. No. Catskills Econ. Devel. Coun., Econ. Devel. Coun. Stamford, Econ. Devel. Coun. Delaware County; regent St. Francis Coll.; bd. dirs. Econ. Devel. Coun., Printing Trade Sch., Cmty. Hosp., Stamford, N.Y., Stamford Econ. Devel. Coun., Del. County Indsl. Devel. Agy., coun. sec.; chmn. Cath. Charities Am., v.p., 1999, pres., 1999—; bd. dirs., sec. Indsl. Devel. Authority Delaware County, 1999—; co-chair Project Strive, Albany, N.Y.; mem. fin. com. Sacred Heart Roman Cath. Ch.; pres. Otsego Del. Bd. Realtors, 2000; v.p. bd. dirs. Cath. Charities, 1999, pres., 1999-2001. With U.S. Army, 1952-55. Paul Harris fellow Rotary Internat.; Internat. Rotary Benefactor; recipient St. Francis Coll. Alumni Fund award, 1965, Del. County Youth award, 1991, John F. Kennedy Meml. award, 1972, Internat. award for Svc. to Investment Commn., 1982, Youth Bur. award, 1991, St. Francis Prep Sch. Alumni Achievement award, 1993; named Stamford Citizen of Yr., 1992, Realtor of Yr., 1992, Col. Harper Grange Citizen of Yr., 1993. Mem. N.Y. State Realtors Assn. (bd. dirs., chmn. polit. action, polit. action dir. 1999), Conn. Venture Capital Assn., Venture Assn. N.J. (bd. dirs.), Assn. Investment Bankers, Otsego-Delaware Bd. Realtors (P.A.F. chmn., bd. dirs., pres.-elect, pres. 1994, 99), Stamford C. of C. (pres. 1991-92), Am. Legion, Am. Inst. Mgmt., Cath. War Vets, Honor Legion N.Y.C. Police Dept., CCNY Alumni Assn., Elks, Loyal Order Moose, Univ. Club (Albany). Republican. Home: Red Rock Rd Stamford NY 12167 Office: Stamford Fin Bldg Off Bd Dirs Stamford NY 12167

BERGLEY, BRUCE ALLEN, certified public accountant; b. Mpls., Sept. 22, 1959; s. Kenneth Melvin and JoAnn Ruth (Fuller) B.; m. Peggy LouAnn Goodsell, May 1, 1980; children: Rebecca Ann, Rachel Marie. BS in Bus. Acctg., U. Minn., 1982. Cert. pub. acct. Audit jr. Defense Contract Audit Agy., Mpls., 1982-83; staff acct. Kaliher, Belanger, Passolt & Co., Hopkins, Minn., 1983-84, Lanigan & Kolb, CPA's, Coon Rapids, Minn., 1984-87, Apple & Apple, CPA's, St. Louis Park, Minn., 1987-89; shareholder Dutcher, Lee, Bergley & Assocs., Blaine, Minn., 1989-93; pres. Bruce Bergley, PA, CPA, Coon Rapids, Minn., 1993—; instr. CPA Review Course, Convisor Duffy CPA Review, 1988-93. CFO, budget and finance chair, PACT Charter Sch., Anoka, Minn., 1997-99; treas. Pond View Townhome Assn., Coon Rapids, Minn., 1988-91. 2d Lt. USAR, 1979-87. Mem. Am. Inst. CPA's, Minn. Soc. CPA's. E-mail: brucecpa@mn.state.net. Home: 1502 146th Ln NW Andover MN 55304-3401 Office: Bruce Bergley PA CPA 8990 Springbrook Dr NW Ste 150 Coon Rapids MN 55433-2734

BERGLUND, JAN ERIK, venture capitalist; b. Stockholm, June 1, 1938; arrived in Eng., 1983; s. David Elof and Mary Viola (Mannberg) B.; m. Agneta Marie-Louise Nylin, Aug. 26, 1967; children: David, Charlotte. MBA, Stockholm Sch. Econs., 1961; PhD in Engring., Royal Inst. Tech., Stockholm, 1963. Prof. Royal Inst. Tech., Stockholm, 1965-69; mng. dir. Tulwe, Sundsvall, Sweden, 1969-72; tech. dir. Beijerinvest, Stockholm, 1972-75; mng. dir. Sponsor, Stockholm, 1975-83, Habia Internat., Beaconsfield, Eng., 1983-86; CEO Indsl. Tech. Securities, London, 1986—; chmn. Applied Photophysics, Leatherhead, Eng., 1988—, Metrodata, Eggham, Eng., 1993—, Oregon Networks, Ashby, 1998—, Skankod, Stockholm, Sweden, 1975—, Arboga Industries Park, 1982—, Imagik, Letchworth, Eng., 1999—. Author: What is Operations Research?, 1965, Management Games - Play and Reality, 1968, The World of Production, 1969; contbr. articles to Swedish and Brit. tech. jours. Home: 3 Ben More Oak End Way, Gerrards Cross SL9 8DX, England Office: Indsl Tech Securities, Surrey Tech Ctr, Surrey Rsch Park, Guildford GU2 5YG, England

BERGLUND, JOEL, museum curator and director, researcher; b. Copenhagen, Sept. 9, 1938; s. Christian and Lilly Emogenia (Berglund) Petersen; m. Margrethe Knudsen, une 30, 1978 (dec. July 1989); m. Maria Hinnerson, Aug. 9, 1994. MA in Prehist. Archaeology, U. Copenhagen, 1976. Curator Provincial Mus., Middelfart, Denmark, 1978-80, Qaqortoq, Greenland, 1981-91; asst. curator Greenland Nat. Mus. and Archives, Nuuk, 1992—, vice dir., 1999—; dir. South Grenland Culture House Puilasoq, Qaqortoq, 1985-91; examiner Greenland U., Nuuk, 1993—; with Prince of Wales No. Heritage Ctr., Yellowsknife, Can., 1993-96; co-editor archaeol. field reports in Can. and Greenland. Contbr. articles to profl. jours. Mem. Kongelige Nordiske Oldskrifiselskab, Jysk Arkeologisk Selskab, Skandinavisk Museums Forbund. Avocations: travel, mountain hiking, art, modern history. Home: Tupaarnat 11, DK-3905 Nuussuaq Nuuk, Greenland Office: Greeland Nat Mus-Archieve, PO Box 145, DK-3900 Nuuk Greenland

BERGLUND, KÅRE NILS, rheumatologist; b. Stockholm, Apr. 2, 1917; s. Gustaf and Agnes (Johansson) B.; m. Joanna Michalik, Dec. 27, 1970; children: Jonas, Per, Pelle. MD, Stockholm U., 1946. Asst. prof. rheumatology Stockholm U., 1956-64; prof. rheumatology U. Lund, Sweden, 1964-82; prof. emeritus U. Lund, 1982—. Contbr. articles to profl. jours. Avocations: swimming, literature. Home: Kollegiev 73, 224 73 Lund Sweden Office: Dept Rheumatology, U Hosp Lund, 221 85 Lund Sweden

BERGLUND-NILSSON, BIRGITTA, French language educator; b. Göteborg, Sweden, Nov. 18, 1935; d. Harald and Margit Ingegerd (Holmgren) Berglund; m. Kurt Sjunne Nilsson, Feb. 26, 1966; children: Johan, Fredrik, Sofia. BA, U. Göteborg, 1961, tchrs. tng., 1967, D in French, 1987. Tchr. area h.s. Nassjo, Sweden, 1961-63, Göteborg, 1963-67; tchr. Adult Edn., Göteborg, 1967-74, asst. dir., 1974-84; lectr. U. Göteborg, 1984-88; sr. lectr. Karlstad (Sweden) U., 1988-97, asst. prof., 1997—; dir. dept. Karlstad U., 1991-94, mem. various bds., 1995—. Contbr. articles to various publs. Mem. Zonta. Office: Karlstad Univ, Dept Culture and Comm, 65188 Karlstad Sweden

BERGMAN, BO, quality management educator, researcher; b. Helsingborg, Sweden, May 27, 1943; s. Yngve and Signe Elisabeth (Lindbäck) B.; m. Elisabeth Vanäs; children: Anders, Göran. PhD in Math. Statistics, U. Lund, Sweden, 1978. Reliability engr. aerospace divsn. Saab, Linköping, Sweden, 1969-75; mgr. Saab-Scania AB, Linköping, 1975-84; prof. quality tech. and mgmt. Linköping U., 1983-99; SKF-prof. TQM Chalmers U. Tech., Gothenburg, 1999—; adj. prof. Royal Inst. Tech., Stockholm, 1981-83; chmn. numerous internat. confs. Author: Quality from Customer Needs to Customer Satisfaction, 1994; contbr. over 50 articles to profl. jours. Mem. Internat. Statis. Inst., Internat. Acad. for Quality. Office: Chalmers U Technology, SE-41296 Gothenburg Sweden

BERGMAN, CHARLES CABE, foundation executive; b. May 1, 1933; s. Sidney Meyer and Esther Rachel (Cabe) B. AB, Harvard U., 1954. Account asst. Ketchum, MacLeod & Grove, Inc., Pitts., 1955-57; assoc. dir. devel. and alumni affairs Browne & Nichols Sch., Cambridge, Mass., 1957-59; assoc. v.p. Lavin Co., Inc., Boston and N.Y.C., 1959-61; v.p. People to People Health Fedn., Washington, 1962-63, Inter-Am. Found. for the Arts, N.Y.C., 1963-65; exec. v.p., treas., trustee Acad. Religion and Mental Health, N.Y.C., 1965-72; exec. v.p., COO, dir. Insts. Religion and Health, 1972-78; sr. assoc. Jeffcoat Schoen & Morrell, 1981-82; exec. v.p., COO Pollock-Krasner Found., Inc., N.Y.C., 1985-99, chmn. bd., COO, 1999—; cons. UN Ctr. on Transnat. Corps., 1979-80; dir. George Nelson & Co., N.Y.C. Cons. Adminstrv. Psychiatry Program, Yale Med. Sch., New Haven, 1971, NIMH, Argentina, 1969, Ctr. for Studies Child and Family Mental Health, NIMH, Washington, 1971; spl. adviser Pres.'s Com. on Mental Retardation, Washington, 1971, White House Conf. on Children and Youth, Washington, 1970, Maurice Falk Med. Fund, 1971; vis. lectr. U. Colo.; Presdl. felow Aspen Inst. Humanistic Studies. Chmn. internat. coun. Am. Field Svc. Internat. Intercultural Programs; bd. dirs. The Alliance for Young Artists and Writers, Inc., N.Y., VSA Arts, Washington, Delfina Studios Trust, London, The Nat. Found. for Advancement in the Arts, Miami, Fla.; mem. bd. advisors Fund for Arts and Culture in Cen. and East Europe; bd. artistic advisors Creative Artists Network; former panelist N.Y. State Coun. on Arts Visual Arts Program; mem. N.Y. State Coun. on Arts, 1999—; sr. advisor Foursome Investments, Ltd., London; adv. bd. Lucy Daniels Found., Raleigh, N.C. Home: 24 E 82nd St # 4C New York NY 10028-0344 Office: 863 Park Ave New York NY 10021-0342

BERGMAN, FRITZ HILDING, forestry educator; b. Helsinki, Finland, Sept. 26, 1920; arrived in Sweden, 1952; s. Frans Crescens and Hilda Kristina (Grönholm) B.; m. Helga Matilda Hansson, Aug. 25, 1946; children: Gunilla, Solveig, Helena, Folke, Mårten. B of Agr. and Forestry, U. Helsinki, 1954, Licentiate of Agr. and Forestry, 1961; D of Forestry, Royal Coll. Forestry, Stockholm, 1976. Asst. Assn. Forest Tree Breeding, Sundmo, Sweden, 1952-56; dir. Assn. Forest Tree Breeding, Sundmo, 1957-62; chief silviculturist MoDo Co., Örnsköldsvik, Sweden, 1962-79; prof. forest regeneration Swedish U. Agrl. Scis., Umeå, Sweden, 1979-81, prof. silviculture, 1981-85; ret. Swedish U. Agrl. Scis., 1985. Author: Spruce in hard conditions, 1991; contbr. over 80 articles to profl. jours. Chmn. Finlands War Vets. in Västerbotten, Sweden, 1984—; vice-chmn. Fedn. Finlands War Vets. in Sweden, 1992—. 1st lt. Finnish Army, 1940-44. Recipient Mannerheims award Finlands Boy Scout Fedn., 1937, Cross of Freedom IV, Marshal of Finland Mannerheim, 1944, The Golden Twig award Swedish Forestry Assn., 1976, Finlands White Rose Order, Pres. of Finland, 1992, Cross of Merit Fedn. Finlands War Vets, 1997. Mem. Royal Swedish Acad. Agr. and Forestry, Royal Swedish Acad. Engring. Scis. Avocations: walking in the forest, photography, fishing. Home: Svedbergsgatan 20, S-913 31 Holmsund Sweden

BERGMAN, REUVEN, dermatologist; b. Tel-Aviv, May 15, 1953; s. Oscar and Shoshana (Stein) B.; m. Michal Gill, Apr. 16, 1953; children: Elad, Sivan. MD, Tel Aviv U., 1980, M Dermatology, 1990; Dermatopathology Fellow, NYU, 1986-87. Med. diplomate in dermatology. Dermatology resident Rambam Med. Ctr., Haifa, Israel, 1983-89, sr. dermatologist, 1989-95, vice-chmn. dept. dermatology, 1995-2000, chmn. dept. dermatopathology, 2000—; lectr. in dermatology Technion Faculty, Haifa, 1991-94, sr. lectr. in dermatology, 1994-99, assoc. prof. dermatology, 1999—; cons. dermatopathologist, Haemek Med. Ctr., Afula, Israel, 1991-94; chmn. Israel Nat. Exams. Com., 1995—. Mem. editl. bd. Am. Jour. Dermatopathology, 1996—, Dermatopathology - Practical and Conceptual, 1996—; editor more than 75 sci. papers in dermatol. lit. Mem. Israel Soc. Investigative Dermatology (pres. 1992-95), Internat. Soc. Dermatopathology (exec. bd. 1997—). Jewish. Office: Dept Dermatology, Rambam Med Ctr, Haifa Israel

BERGMANN, ARTHUR M., writer, investor, former county official, former newspaperman; b. N.Y., Nov. 24, 1927; s. Augustus H. Bergmann; m. Danielle Marie Dusseau. BS in Polit. Sci. and Pub. Adminstrn., Empire State Coll., SUNY, Old Westbury, 1974; M in Pub. and Gen. Adminstrn., L.I.U., 1979. Cert. arbitrator. With N.Y. Herald Tribune, 1945-63; asst. news editor Riverhead News, 1949-50; Suffolk County (N.Y.) corr. for N.Y.C. newspapers, 1949-63; news editor Moriches (N.Y.) Tribune, 1950-51; mem. staff Newsday, 1951-71, Suffolk County polit. editor, columnist, 1965-71; chief dep. Suffolk County Exec., Hauppauge, N.Y., 1972-79. Chmn. Suffolk Criminal Justice Coordinating Coun., 1975-79, Arson Action Com.-Suffolk Arson Task Force, 1975-77, MTA Permanent Citizens Adv. Com., 1978-79; adv. coun. N.Y. State Crime Victims Compensation Bd., 1978-79; trustee Suffolk Acad. Medicine, 1974. Served with USAAF, 1946-47. Recipient Disting. Svc. award United Jewish Appeal, 1976; Pub. Adminstrn. award C. W. Post Coll., 1977; Disting. Svc. plaque L.I. Assn. Commerce & Industry, 1977; Exemplary Svc. award Empire State Coll., SUNY, 1981; nominated for Pulitzer prize (2). Mem. Acad. Polit. Sci., Soc. Silurians, Am. Legion, Moriches Yacht Club (past commodore, Center Moriches, N.Y.), Pi Alpha Alpha. Address: 400 N Flagler Dr West Palm Beach FL 33401-4304

BERGMANN, CHRISTINE, German government official. Min. Govt. of Germany, 1991—; now min. family, women's and sr. citizens' affairs Govt. of Germany, Berlin. Office: Min Family Affairs, Postfach 11 0207, 10832 Berlin Germany*

BERGMANN, GUNTER FEDOR, Germanist; b. Riesa, Germany, Apr. 2, 1935; s. Hans and Johanna (Pietzsch) B.; m. Helga Hasselbach, Dec. 15, 1972; 1 child, Claudia. Diploma, U. Leipzig, 1957, PhD, 1961. Asst. scientist Saxon Acad. of Knowledge, Leipzig, 1957-61, scientific leader, 1961-91, chief sec., 1991—. Author: Wörterbuch der obersächsischen Mundarten, Sächsische Mundartenkunde, 1968, Kleines sächsisches Wörterbuch, 1986; co-author: The Dialects of Modern German, 1990. Recipient Theodor-Frings-Preis Saxon Acad. of Knowledge and U. Leipzig, 1996. Home: Preussenstr 15, 04289 Leipzig Germany Office: Saxon Acad of Knowledge, Karl-Tauchnitz-Str 1, 04004 Leipzig Germany

BERGMANN, HANS WILHELM, plant physiologist; b. Thamsbrueck, Germany, June 6, 1940; s. Karl Robert and Charlotte Therese (Meldau) B.; m. Eva Reich, Dec. 7, 1946; children: Martin, Katharina, Ulrike. MSc, U. Jena, Germany, 1966, PhD in Agrl. Chemistry, 1970, PhD in Plant Physiology, 1981, sr. lectr., 1991. Economist Coop. Farm, Langensalza, Germany, 1959-60; head rsch. group Acad. Sci., Berlin, 1972-89, state project leader, 1985-90; sr. lectr. U. Kassel, Jena, 1990-92, prof., 1992—, prof. food sci., 1999—; advisor rsch. coun. Ministry of Sci., Berlin, 1989-90. Author: Animal Nutrition, 1995, Amines in Nutrition, 1996; inventor activation of stress resistance; contbr. articles to profl. jours. Councillor Parish Coun. various towns, Germany, 1962-90, ch. elder, Mellingen, Germany, 1994; advisor internat. coun. Internat. Soc. Sustainable Agr. and Resource Mgmt., Delhi, India, 1998; mem. opposition Free Ch. Groups, 1985-90. State grantee, Berlin, 1964; recipient Roemer prize Acad. Sci. Berlin. Mem. AAAS, N.Y. Acad. Scis., German Soc. Botany, Soc. Applied Botany (v.p. 1996), Soc. Quality Rsch. (v.p. 1998). Avocations: music, singing, sports. E-mail: bergmann@mampf.ieu.uni-jena.de. Home: Schulgasse 131 a, D 99441 Mellingen Germany Office: U Jena, Dornburger Strasse 25/27, D 07743 Jena Germany

BERGMANN, RALF B., physicist; b. Haren, Germany, Oct. 6, 1962; s. Fritz and Thea (von Lintel) B.; m. Birgit C. Schmelzle, Sept. 14, 1985; children: Christian, Daniel, Anika. Diploma physics, U. Freiburg, 1988; PhD of Physics, U. Stuttgart, 1991. Rschr. Solar Energy Sys. Max Planck Inst., Stuttgart, Germany, 1988-91; rsch. assoc. U. NSW, Sydney, Australia, 1991-93; rschr. Max Plank Inst., Stuttgart, 1993-97; rschr., head Crystalline Silicon Tech. group U. Stuttgart, 1997—. Contbr. articles to profl. jours. Fax: 49-711-685-7143. E-mail: ralf.bergmann@ipe.uni-stuttgart.de. Office: Univ Stuttgart Inst Phys Electronics, Pfaffenwaldring 47, D-70569 Stuttgart Germany

BERGMARK, TORD, psychiatrist, psychotherapist; b. Skellefteå, Sweden, Dec. 9, 1941; s. Kjell and Gunnel (Flodmark) B.; m. Christina Anderson, Aug. 14, 1982; children: Agnes, Gustav, Anders, Emma. MD, Karolinska Inst., Stockholm, 1977. Asst. prof. dept. psychiatry Söder Hosp., Stockholm, 1991-92; gen. practitioner Stockholm, 1992-93; head Cognitive Psychiatry Stockholm, 1993—; mem. peer rev. groups for psychiatry, Stockholm, 1997—; bd. dirs. support group for schizophrenics, Stockholm, 1992-95; creator Care Burden Scale for Relatives, 1988, Self-Confidence Scale, 1995; bd. dirs. Stockholm Pvt. Psychatrist Team. Contbr. articles to profl. jours.; co-editor Empathy, 1992-94; creator introduction to TV program Living with Schizophrenia, 1992. Mem. Am. Psychiat. Assn. (internat.), Swedish Assn. Psychiatrists, Internat. Assn. Cognitive Therapy, Internat. Assn. for Study of Personality Disorders. Avocation: kayaking. Office: Cognitive Psychiatry Stockholm, Hogbergsgatan 33, 11620 Stockholm Sweden

BERGOGLIO, REMO MIGUEL, infectious disease physician; b. Cordoba, Argentina, July 9, 1917; s. Juan Bergoglio and Maria Alloatti; m. Yolanda Lucia Grasselli, Sept. 14, 1946; children: Maria Teresa, Maria Ines, Remo Miguel. Grad., Nat. U., Cordoba, 1964, Nat. U., Cordoba, 1972. Pres. Colegio Medico Cordoba, 1951-56; sec. gen. Federacion Medica de Cordoba, 1952-56; dir. Hosp. Rawson, Cordoba, 1958-63, 66-72; pres. Acad. Med. Scis., Cordoba, 1981-82, 95-96, prof. emeritus, 1983—. Author: Antibioticos, 1971, 5th edit., 1995, 3 de Diciembre Dia del Medico, 1988. Home: Av Colon 396 1 Piso, 5000 Cordoba Argentina

BERGOLD, ORM, medical educator; b. Nuremberg, Germany, Apr. 30, 1925; s. Friedrich and Wilhelmine (Schering) B.; m. Sylvia Patricia Sanchez, 1983; children: Heike, Timm. MD, Chgo. Med. Coll., 1974; DChemistry, Benjamin Franklin Inst., N.Y.C., 1976; MAcupuncture, Old Chinese Acupuncture Acad., Hong Kong, 1978; DSc (hon.), St. Andrew's Coll., London, 1965. REIKI Master, 1994. Pres. Orm Bergold Chemie, Langlau and Bochum, Germany, 1953-63; pres. Inst. Med. Biophysics and Biochemistry, Campione, Switzerland, 1963-81, San Jose, Costa Rica, 1982—; pres. Inst. Biocybernetic and Natural Therapy, San Jose, 1985—, Stress and Aging Control Inc., Panama, Costa Rica, 1986—, AIDS Control, Inc., Panama, 1989—; prof. cybernetic medicine Acad. Gen. Penticum pro Pace, Rome, 1977—, senator, 1979; prof. extraordinary U. Francisco Marroquin, Guatemala City, 1979—, senator, 1980—. Author: Kybernetische Medizin, 1977, Cancer prophylaxis: A problem of early recognition and treatment, 1980, Cancer Treatment with Human Fibroblast Interferon, 1982, Cancer Treatment by Natural Remedies, 1983, Stress, Cortisol and Stress Diseases, 1989, AIDS Treatment, 1989; contbr. articles to profl. jours. Named Hon. Pres. Acad. for Biocybernetic Holistic Medicine, Rheda, Germany, 1990—, Man of Yr. Am. biog. Inst., 1994; decorated grand cross Ordre Equestre de la San Croix de Jèrusalem, chevalier du Tastevin. Mem. N.Y. Acad. Sci. Home: PO Box 359-1250, Escazu Costa Rica

BERGQUIST, GENE ALFRED, farmer, rancher, county commissioner; b. Paynesville, Minn., Aug. 5, 1927; s. Albin and Viola (Heinrich) B.; m. Ann Dorothy Corwin, Aug. 2, 1958; children: Wayne A., Viola M. Grad. high sch., Rhame, N.D. Self-employed farmer-rancher Rhame, 1948—; Slope County commr. Amidon, N.D., 1982—; bd. dirs. Rhame, N.D. Cenex, 1970-82; bd. dirs. Harper Twp. Rhame; com. mem. Slope County Agrl. Stabilization and Conservation Svc.-USDA Commn., Amidon, 1968-84. Bd. dirs. Rhame Rural Fire Dept., 1976—, Bowman-Slope Social Svc. Bd., Bowman, N.D., 1991—, Deep Creek Twp., 1958-64, Richland Center Twp. Bd., 1952-57; elder Lyle Presbyn. Ch.; youth leader 4-H Slope County, 1950-57; mem. Bowman-Slope Revolving Loan Fund Com., 1998—; mem. job devel. bd. Slope and Bowman Counties, 1999—. Mem. N.D. Assn. Counties.

Presbyterian. Avocations: reading, painting, fishing, riding, gardening. Office: Courthouse Amidon ND 58620

BERGQUIST, NILS ROBERT, medical consultant; b. Uppsala, Sweden, Apr. 7, 1939; s. Nils Gunnar and Anna (Ekblom) B.; m. Margith Annita Elofsson, May 27, 1966 (div. Nov. 1992); children: Nils Rikard Samuel, Anna Vera Vilhelmina; m. Margaret-Anne Eddison, Apr. 10, 1999. MD, Karolinska Inst., Stockholm, 1967, PhD, 1974, cert. clin. immunology, 1979. Lab. physician Nat. Bacteriological Lab., Stockholm, 1967-71, 72-74; rsch. asst. prof. microbiology SUNY, Buffalo, 1971-72; acting prof. and chmn. dept. immunology Karolinska Inst., Stockholm, 1974-75; dir. Armauer Hansen Rsch. Inst., Addis Ababa, Ethiopia, 1975-76; sr. lab. physician Nat. Bacteriological Lab., Stockholm, 1976-85; sr. med. officer WHO, Geneva, 1985—; cons. WHO, Geneva, 1983-84, Ulleval Hosp., Oslo, 1984, Med. Bd. of the Armed Forces, Karlstad, Sweden, 1985. Contbr. articles to profl. jours. Served with Swedish Navy Reserve Corps, 1973—. Mem. Swedish Soc. Medicine, N.Y. Acad. Scis., Am. Soc. for Tropical Medicine and Hygiene. Lutheran. Avocation: orchid growing. Home: Versonnex au Bourg, F-01210 Versonnex France

BERGQUIST, OLOF BJARNE JÖRGEN, process engineer, researcher; b. Piteå, Norrbotten, Sweden, Jan. 4, 1965; m. Karin Maria Bergquist; children: Agnes, Oskar. MSc, Luleå (Sweden) Tech. U., 1991; Lic. in Tech., Linköping (Sweden) Tech. U., 1996, PhD, 1999. Technician Assidomän, Piteå, 1986-87, process engr., 1991-93; rschr. Linköping Tech. U., 1991-99; asst. prof. Luleå (Sweden) U. Tech., 1999—. Contbr. articles to profl. jours. Recipient Powder Metallurgy award of excellence, Copenhagen, 1996. Mem. European Powder Metallurgy Assn. Office: Luleå U Tech, Divsn Qual Tech & Stats, SE-97187 Luleå Sweden

BERGREEN, MORRIS HARVEY, lawyer, business executive, private investor; b. Passaic, N.J., Sept. 28, 1917; s. Harold and Jennie (Dolgen) B.; m. Adele G. Bergreen, Sept. 1, 1947; children: Laurence, John. Student, NYU, 1935-38; LLB, Fordham U., 1941; postgrad., NYU. Bar: N.Y. 1942. Sr. ptnr. Bergreen & Bergreen, N.Y.C., 1953-86, 95—; ret. of counsel Milbank, Tweed, Hadley & McCloy, N.Y.C., 1986-95; sr. ptnr. Bergreen & Bergreen, N.Y.C., 1995—; pres. Croydon Co., Inc.; gen. mgr. Grosvenor Investment Co., Skirball Investment Co.; chair pub. com. Commentary. Pres. The Skirball Found.; bd. dirs., founding mem. bd. trustees Skirball Cultural Ctr.; mem. adv. bd. Skirball Inst. on Am. Values; trustee, bd. dirs. Audrey Skirball Kenis Theatre, Inc.; life trustee NYU, mem. acad. affairs com., mem. devel. com., trustee NYU Sch. Med., trustee NYU Sch. Med. Found., mem. health initiatives com., trustee Bronfman Ctr. for Jewish Student Life; life trustee Mt. Sinai-NYU Med. Ctr.; bd. govs. Oxford Ctr. for Hebrew and Jewish Studies Oxford U.; trustee, mem. investment com. NCCJ, Inc.; bd. dirs., v.p. Grand St. Settlement; trustee Jewish Home and Hosp. for Aged; bd. dirs. Sarah R. Neuman Nursing Home; bd. govs. Hebrew Union Coll., The Am. Jewish Com., others. 1st lt. USAAF, 1942-46. Recipient Albert Gallatin medal for outstanding contbn. to society NYU, 1995. Mem. ABA, N.Y. State Bar Assn., Assn. Bar of City of N.Y., Fordham Law Rev. Assn., Harmonie Club (N.Y.C.), Sunningdale Country Club (Scarsdale, N.Y.), Club at Morningside (Rancho Mirage, Calif.), Tamarisk Country Club (Rancho Mirage, Calif.), Hillcrest Country Club (L.A.), N.Y. Athletic Club. Home: 24 Highland Farm Rd Greenwich CT 06831-2606 also: 980 Fifth Ave New York NY 10021-0126 Office: Bergreen & Bergreen 767 Fifth Ave Fl 50 New York NY 10153-0023

BERGRUN, NORMAN RILEY, aerospace executive; b. Green Camp, Ohio, Aug. 4, 1921; s. Theodore and Naomi Ruth (Stemm) B.; m. Claire Michaelson, May 23, 1943; children: Clark, Jay, Joan. BSME, Cornell U., 1943; LLB, LaSalle U. Ext., 1955; DSc, World U., 1983. Registered profl. mech. engr. Thermodynamicist Douglas Aircraft Co., El Segundo, Calif., 1943-44; rsch. scientist NACA Ames Rsch. Lab., Mt. View, Calif., 1944-56; mgr. analysis Lockheed Missile & Space Co., Sunnyvale, Calif., 1956-67, staff scientist, 1967-69; dir. mgmt. systems Nielsen Engring. and Rsch., Mt. View, 1969-71; CEO, scientist Bergrun Rsch. and Engring., Los Altos, Calif., 1971—; guest on radio and TV programs in the U.S., Can., Australia and Europe; spkr. L'Academie Europeene, 1987; Expo West lectr., 1996, Expos Bay Area lectr. 2000, CompuServe Conf. lectr.; instr. NASA Space Day, 1998; lectr. Independence H.S., San Jose, 1999, Bay Area Expn., 2000; founder Bergrun Rsch. (www co.), Concord, Calif., 1999. Author: Ringmakers of Saturn, 1986, Tomorrow's Technology Today, 1972, A Warming Trend for Icing Research, 1995, Air Travel Safety Forum Attracts Public Media Interest, 1997, The International Space Station: A Momentous Cultural, Scientific and Societal Undertaking, 1998, Earth's Moon...Why We Never Returned, 1999, Lunar Life Forms Do Exist, 2000; photographer including the Sir Francis Drake Collection, 1990; contbr. more than 90 articles and reports of profl. jours. Incorporator Aurora Singers Found., Palo Alto, Calif., 1989; co-founder NSPE Edn. Found., Sacramento, Calif., advisor to bd., 1985-92; mem. Steinman Coun., 1988—, steering com. mem. Congressional Visits Day, 1997, 98, 99, 2000; mem. Cornell U. Concert Musician Carnegie Hall, 1989. Named Man of Yr., Am. Biog. Assn.; recipient Archimedes award, 1988, Cert. of Appreciation, Eglin AFB, 1961. Fellow AIAA (assoc., sr. judge 7th and 8th grade essay contest 1992, 93, 94, 95, 97, 98, 99, 2000, chair nat. pub.-policy comm. subcom. 1992—, coord. nat. pub. policy com. task force, 1999, regional dep. dir.-at-large 1995—, pub. policy liaison rep. 2000, spl. svc. citation 1994, 98 (cert. of recognition 2000), advisor Airline Safety Initiative 1997, moderator Internat. Space Sta. Forum 1998); mem. NSPE (life), Profl. Engrs. Soc. (Calif. pres. 1988-89, Integrity award 1989, Outstanding Exec. Performance award 1986, Disting. Contbns. award 1985-86, 86-87, 98). Achievements include discoveries of existence of large, mobile cylindrical objects, identified at Saturn, Miranda, Iapetus, Mars, Neptune, Earth's moon, the Sun, and deep space; patents for Cyclic Electric Thermal Ice-Prevention System for Airplanes. Office: Bergrun Rsch and Engring 26865 Saint Francis Rd Los Altos CA 94022-1910

BERG-SCHLOSSER, DIRK, political science educator; b. Ruhlsdorf, Germany, Dec. 10, 1943; s. Gerhard and Ursula (Krefft) B.-S. Dipl.oec.publ., U. Munich, Germany, 1968, Dr.oec.publ., 1971; Dr.phil.habil., U. Augsburg, Germany, 1978; PhD, U. Calif., Berkeley, 1979. Asst. prof. U. Aachen, Germany, 1971-73; asst. prof. U. Augsburg, 1975-79, assoc. prof., 1985; vis. prof. U. Munich, 1980-82, U. Eichstaett, Germany, 1982-84; prof. polit. sci. U. Marburg, Germany, 1986—. Author: Politische Kultur, 1972, Tradition and Change in Kenya, 1984, Empirische Demokratieforschung, 1999; co-author: Einführung in die Politikwissenschaft, 6th edit., 1995. Mem. Wörthsee (Germany) City Coun., 1982-86. German Acad. Exch. Svc. scholar, 1968-69; German Sci. Found. fellow, 1973-75. Mem. Internat. Polit. Sci. Assn. (chair rsch. com. on democratization in comparative perspective 1994—). Fax: 49-6421-282 8991. E-mail: bergschl@mailer.uni-marburg.de. Home: Scheppe-Gewisse-Gasse 26, 35039 Marburg Germany Office: Philipps-U Marburg, Wilhelm-Röpke-Str 6, 35032 Marburg Germany

BERGSCHNEIDER, DAVID PHILIP, legal administrator; b. Springfield, Ill., Nov. 19, 1951; s. Fred J. and Ruby A. (Martin) B.; m. Dawn E. Combes, Sept. 23, 1989; children: Alec, Bryant, Cale. Student, Bradley U., 1969-71; BA, Ill. Coll., 1973; JD, Marquette U., 1976. Bar: Ill. 1976, Wis. 1976, U.S. Ct. Appeals (7th cir.) 1990, U.S. Supreme Ct. 1980. Mem. legis. staff Ill. Gen. Assembly, Springfield, 1976-77; asst. defender Office State Appellate Defender, Springfield, 1977-93, legal dir., 1993—. Co-author: Defending Illinois Criminal Cases, 1988, Illinois Criminal Practice, 1980, Brief Writing and Oral Argument Handbook, 1988, 94, 97; author: Illinois Handbook of Criminal Law Decisions, 1993, 2d edit., 1998; also articles. Recipient Award of Excellence Ill. Pub. Defender Assn., 1989. Mem. ABA, Ill. Bar Assn. (criminal justice sect. coun. 1987-91, 94-98, sec. 1995-96, chmn. 1996-97), Ill. Attys. for Criminal Justice, Aircraft Owners and Pilots Assn. Office: Office State Appellate Def PO Box 5780 Springfield IL 62705-5780

BERGSHOLM, PER, psychiatrist, neurologist; b. Tønsberg, Vestfold, Norway, Dec. 28, 1945; s. Svein Ollestad and Bodil Johanne (Paulsen) B.; m. Lillian Naustdal, Dec. 19, 1984; children: Line, Maria, Helene. Student Sch. Medicine, U. Oslo, 1971; MD, U. Bergen, Norway, 1995. Authorized specialist in neurology, authorized specialist in psychiatry, Norway. Intern in internal medicine Ctrl. Hosp. of Rogaland, Stavanger, 1971; intern surgery Diakonissehjemmet's Hosp., Bergen, 1972; intern gen. practice Rjukan, Telemark, 1972; staff neurologist Univ. Hosp. Haukeland, Bergen, 1974-79; staff psychiatrist Univ. Hosp. Haukeland and Univ. Hosp. Sanviken, Bergen, 1979-89; staff psychiatrist, clin. dir. Ctrl. Hosp. of Sogn og Fjordane, Førde, Norway, 1990—; asst. prof. psychiatry U. Bergen, Haukeland, 1981-82, 87; rsch. fellow Norwegian Rsch. Coun., Bergen, 1983-85. Contbr. rsch. and rev. articles to sci. jours.; contbr. chpt. on electroconvulsive therapy to book. Lt. M.C., Norwegian Army, 1973-74. Mem. Norwegian Med. Assn., Norwegian Psychiat. Assn., Norwegian Neurol. Assn. Office: Ctrl Hosp Sogn og Fjordane, Dept Psychiatry, N-6800 Førde Norway

BERGSMA, AD, journalist, psychologist; b. The Hague, The Netherlands, Jan. 26, 1965; s. Auke Bergsma and Tiny Bergsma-Duyvesteyn; m. Korina Van Petersen; 1 child, Thomas Kasper. D, Utrecht (The Netherlands) U., 1990. Freelance writer, 1990-97, journalist, editor, 1997—. Author: Emoties en kwaliteit van bestaan, 1995, Kinderen en psychotherapie, 1995, Het brein: ons innerlijke universum, 1996, Het gezicht: het visitekaartje van de ziel, 1996, Kyk op het Gozicht, 1999. Mem. APA, Netherlands Soc. Journalists. Office: Weekbladpers/Psychologie, Raamgracht 4, 1011 JV Amsterdam The Netherlands

BERGSMA, SYB, financial executive; b. Gravenhage, Holland, Oct. 6, 1936; m. Nettie Bieze-Bergsma; children: Joost Hessel Louis, Liesbeth Jeannette, Michiel Alexander. Dr.Econs., U. Amsterdam, 1965. With Kon. Zwanenbrg Organon, Oss, 1965; asst. sect. to bd. mgmt. Kon. Zwanenbrg Organon, 1966; head econ. research Kon. Zout Organon, Oss, 1967; head econ. affairs Akzo Chemie, Amersfoort, 1968-73; controller Akzo Chemie, 1973-77; treas. Akzo N.V., Arnhem, 1977-82; mem. mgmt. com., exec. v.p. fin. Akzo N.V., 1982-96; prof. fin. mgmt. U. Amsterdam, 1997—; chmn. bd. dirs. UPM Investments N.V.; mem. supervisory bd. ABN-Amro Mut. Funds; bd. dirs. Vander Moolen Holding, Koninklyke ANWB, Generali N.V., ASML Holding N.V., Van Melle N.V. Avocation: golf. Office: Apollaan 8, 6891 EC Rozendaal Holland

BERGSTEIN, JACK MARSHALL, surgeon; b. Duluth, Minn., Apr. 21, 1955; s. Sherman and Muriel (Gilder) B.; m. Mary Beth Bergstein, May 21, 1982; children: Lauren, Julian. BA in Journalism, U. Minn., 1978, MD, 1982. Diplomate Am. Bd. Surgery with added qualifications in surg. critical care; diplomate Am. Bd. Forensic Examiners, Am. Bd. Forensic Medicine. Resident surgery U. Minn., Charlotte Med. Ctr., 1982-85, 85-87; surg. critical care fellow Lincoln Med. and Mental Health Ctr., Bronx, N.Y., 1987-88; sr. attending surgeon Froedert Hosp., Milw., 1988-97; dir. trauma and surg. critical care St. Francis Med. Ctr., Peoria, 1997-99; assoc. prof. surgery U. Ill. Coll. Medicine, Peoria, 1997-99; dir. surg. critical care, assoc. dir. trauma Jon Michael Moore Trauma Ctr. W.Va. U. Hosp., Morgantown, 1999—; prof. surgery W.Va. Sch. Medicine, Morgantown, 1999—; active staff St. Francis Hosp., Peoria, 1997-99. Dir. at large Peace Studies Ctr., Milw., 1995-97; adv. bd. Peoria Safe Cmtys., 1997-99. Fellow ACS (chmn. Wis. com. on trauma 1995-97); mem. Am. Trauma Soc. (pres. Wis. 1992-97), Am. Assn. Surgery of Trauma, Ea. Assn. for the Surgery of Trauma (dir.-at-large 1999—, chmn. violence prevention task force, 1999—, vice chair violence prevention task force, 1994-99), Western Trauma Assn., Assn. Tchrs. Preventive Medicine, Assn. Acad.Surgery, Midwest Surg. Assn., Nat. Network Violence Prevention Practitioners. Avocations: bonsai, watercolor painting. Home: 264 Lakeside Dr Morgantown WV 26508-5604 Office: WVa Sch Medicine Jon Michael Moore Trauma Ct PO Box 8229 1 Stadium Dr Morgantown WV 26506-8229

BERGSTEN, C. FRED, economist; b. Bklyn., Apr. 23, 1941; s. Carl Alfred and Lois Halkaline (Kirk) B.; m. Virginia Lee Wood, June 16, 1962; 1 son, Mark. AB, Ctrl. Meth. Coll., Fayette, Mo., 1961, LHD, 1995; MA, Fletcher Sch. Law and Diplomacy, Medford, Mass., 1962, MA in Law and Diplomacy, 1963, PhD, 1969. Internat. economist Dept. State, 1963-67; vis. fellow Council Fgn. Relations, 1967-68; asst. for internat. econ. affairs NSC, 1969-71; sr. fellow Brookings Instn., 1972-76; asst. sec. treasury internat. affairs, 1977-81; sr. assoc. Carnegie Endowment Internat. Peace, 1981; dir. Inst. Internat. Econs., 1981—; bd. dirs. Consumers Union, 1976-77, Consumers for World Trade, 1982-90, Atlantic Ins., 1973-77, Ovrseas Devel. Coun., 1974-77, Ctrl. Meth. Coll., 1982-88, Ctr. Law and Social Policy, 1973-77, Worldwatch Inst., 1975-77, Fletcher Sch. Law and Diplomacy, 1992—; dir. Overseas Pvt. Investment Corp., 1977-81, U.S.-Israel Binat. Rsch. and Devel. Found., 1977-81; U.S. coord. U.S.-Saudi Arabia Joint Econ. Commn., 1977-81; mem. def. mgmt. bd. Task Force on Fgn. Ownership and Control, 1989-90, competitiveness policy coun., 1991-97, chmn., 1991-97; mem. panel on pub.-pvt. cooperation in civilian tech. NAS, 1990-91; mem. exec. com. Trilateral Commn., 1991—, Bretton Wood Com., 1989—, Carnegie Endowment, Nat. Commn. Am. and the New World Order, 1992, Commn. Govt. Renewal, 1992; chmn. APEC Eminent Persons Group, 1993-95; vice chmn. adv. com. on fgn. econ. policy Dept. State, 1996—. Author: The Future of the International Economic Order: An Agenda for Research, 1973, Toward a New World Trade Policy, 1975, World Politics and International Economics, 1975, Toward a New International Economic Order: Selected Papers of C. Fred Bergsten, 1972-74, 1975, The Dilemmas of the Dollar: The Economics and Politics of United State International Monetary Policy, 1976, American Multinationals and American Interests, 1978, Managing International Economic Interdependence:Selected Papers of C. Fred Bergsten, 1975-76, 1977, The International Economic Policy of the United States: Selected Papers of C. Fred Bergsten, 1977-79, 1980,The World Economy in the 1980s: Selected Papers of C. Fred Bergsten, 1981, The United State in the World Economy: Selected Papers of C. Fred Bergsten, 1981-82,1983, Bank Lending to Developing Countries: The Policy Alternatives, 1985, The United States-Japan Economic Problem, 1985, Global Economic Imbalances, 1985, Auction Quotas and United States Trade Policy, 1987, America in the World Economy: A Strategy for the 1990's, 1988, International Adjustment and Financing, 1991, Pacific Dynamism and the International Economic System, 1993, Reconcilable Differences? United States-Japan Economic Conflict, 1993, Global Econ. Leadship and the Group of Seven 1996, Whither APEC?, 1997; mem. editl. bd. Fgn. Affairs, 1972-77, Internat. Orgn., 1973-77, Jour. Internat. Econs., 1977-80, Foreign Policy, 1987—. Recipient Meritorious Honor award Dept. State, 1965, Disting. Alumnus award Central Meth. Coll., 1975, Exceptional Service award Treasury Dept., 1980, French Legion of Honor, 1987. Fellow Chinese Acad. Social Scis. (hon.); mem. Am. Econ. Assn., Coun. Fgn. Rels. Office: Inst Internat Econs Ste 620 11 Dupont Cir NW Washington DC 20036-1207

BERGSTROM, BETTY HOWARD, consulting executive, foundation administrator; b. Chgo., Mar. 15, 1931; d. Seward Haise and Agnes Eleanor (Uek) Guinter; m. Robert William Bergstrom, Apr. 21, 1979; children: Bryan Scott, Cheryl Lee, Jeffrey Alan, Mark Robert, Philip Alan. BS in Speech, Northwestern U., 1952, postgrad., 1983; postgrad., U. Nev., Reno, 1974. Dir. sales promotion and pub. rels. WLS-AM, Chgo., 1952-56; account exec. E.H. Brown Advt. Agy., Chgo., 1956-59; v.p. Richard Crabb Assocs., Chgo., 1959-61; pres., owner Howard Assocs., Calif. and Chgo., 1961-76; v.p. Chgo. Hort. Soc., 1976-90; pres. Bergstrom Assos., Chgo. and Carefree, Ariz., 1990—; exec. dir. Ariz. Found. for Women, 1996-98. Mem. editl. bd. Garden mag., 1977-84, Glenview Cmty. Ch., 1977-89, Fourth Presbyn. Ch., 1990—, trustee, 1994-97; editor Garden Talk, 1976-86; contbr. articles on fund devel., horticulture, edn. advt. and agr. to profl. jours.; editor Ill. AAUW Jour., 1966-67. Del. Ill. Constl. Conv., 1969-70, mem. com. legis. reform, 1973-74, cts. and justice com., 1971-74; apptd. mem. Ill. Hist. Libr. Bd., 1970, Ill. Bd. Edn., 1971-74. AAUW fellowship grant named in her honor; recipient Communicator of Yr. award Women in Comm., 1983; named Outstanding Fundraising Exec., 1997. Mem. AAUW, LWV (state v.p. Ariz. 1999), Nat. Soc. Fund Raising Execs. (cert. fund raising exec., bd. dirs. 1983-92, 96—, sec. 1986, v.p. 1990-92, pres.-elect, 1997, pres. 1999, nat. bd. dirs. 1990-92, nat. del. assembly 1997-99, Pres.'s award 1988, Outstanding Fund Raising Exec.-Ariz. 1997, internat. bd. dirs. 2000—), Fortnightly Club (bd. dirs. 1994-96), Nat. Women's History Mus. (nat. adv. coun., nat. bd. dirs. 2000—), Charter 100, Ariz. Women's Coun. (pres. 1999), Am. Assn. Museums, Am. Assn. Bot. Garden and Arboreta, Garden Writers. Am., Northwestern U. Alumni, U. So. Calif. Alumni Assn. Office: 111 E Chestnut St Apt 42H Chicago IL 60611-6020 also: PO Box 5253 Carefree AZ 85377-5253

BERGSTRÖM, MAGNUS LARS, scientist, chemist; b. Södertalje, Sweden, Apr. 14, 1966; s. Lennart Torsten and Runa Margareta (Svedberg) B. MSc. Royal Inst. Tech., Stockholm, 1990, PhD, 1995. Rsch. and tchg. asst. Royal Inst. Tech., Stockholm, 1990-95; postdoctoral scientist Risø Nat. Lab., Roskilde, Denmark, 1996-99; scientist Royal Inst. Tech., Stockholm, 1999—. Contbr. articles to profl. jours. including Langmuir, Jour. Colloid and Interface Sci. and Jour. Physical Chemistry. Home: Ekensbergsvägen 118 6, SE 11769 Stockholm Sweden Office: Royal Inst Tech, Dept Chemistry/ Surface Chem, SE 10044 Stockholm Sweden

BERGSTROM, ROBERT, chemist; b. Vasteras, Sweden, Dec. 26, 1968. MS, Uppsala U., 1992. Rschr. Swedish Meteor. Hydrol. Inst., Norrkoping, Sweden, 1997—. Editl. asst. Internat. Jour. Quantum Chemistry, 1994-97. 2d lt. Swedish Army, 1987-88. Office: SMHI-IF, 60176 Norrköping Sweden

BERGSTROM, ROLF OLOF BERNHARD, manufacturing company executive; b. Helsingborg, Skaane, Sweden, Jan. 20, 1934; s. Curt and Inga (Stalbrand) B.; m. Ingrid Haggstrom, June 23, 1959; children: Eva, Anders, Mats. MBA, Gothenburg (Sweden) U., 1957. V.p. adminstrn. AB Ifoverken, Bromolia, Sweden, 1965-68; asst. fin. mgr. Industri AB Euroc, Malmo, Sweden, 1968-70; exec. v.p. Ifo AB, Bromolla, 1970-71, pres., 1971-76; exec. v.p. Industri AB Euroc Malmo, Bromolla, 1976-77; pres. Dynapac AB, Solna, Sweden, 1977-86, HeatTech. AB, Danderyd, Sweden, 1986-97, Ursvik Industri AB, Danderyd, Sweden, 1996-99, Erima Invest AB, Danderyd, 1999—. Lutheran. Office: Erima Invest AB, Robertsviksvagen 2, 18235 Danderyd Sweden

BERGSTRÖM, SUNE K. D., retired biochemist; b. Stockholm, Jan. 10, 1916; s. Sverker B. and Wera (Wistrand) B.; m. Maj Gernandt, July 30, 1943. Docent physiol. chemistry, MD, Karolinska Inst., Stockholm, 1944, D. Med. Sci. in Biochemistry, 1944; D h.c., U. Basel, Switzerland, 1960, U. Chgo., 1960, Harvard U., 1976, Mt. Sinai Med. Sch., 1976, Med. Acad. Wroclaw, Poland, 1976, McMaster U., Hamilton, Can., 1988. Rsch. fellow U. London, 1938, Columbia U., N.Y.C., 1940-41, Squibb Inst. Med. Rsch., New Brunswick, N.J., 1941-42; asst. biochem. dept. Med. Nobel Inst., Karolinska Inst., Stockholm, 1944-47; rsch. fellow U. Basel, 1946-47; prof. physiol. chemistry U. Lund, Sweden, 1947-58; prof. chemistry Karolinska Inst., 1958-80, dean med. faculty, 1963-66, rector, 1969-77; chmn. bd. dirs. Nobel Found., Stockholm, 1975-87; pres. Royal Swedish Acad. Scis., 1983-85; chmn. WHO Adv. Com. Med. Research, Geneva, 1977-82; La Madonnina lectr., Milan, Italy, 1972; Dunham Lectr. Harvard U., 1972; Dohme lectr. Johns Hopkins U., 1972-73; Merrimon lectr. U. N.C., Chapel Hill, 1973; V.D. Mattia lectr. Roche Inst., 1974; Harvey lectr. Harvey Soc., N.Y.C., 1974; Gen. Amir Chand orator All India Inst., New Delhi, 1978; Cairlton lectr. U. Tex. Health Sci. Ctr., Dallas, 1979; mem. Swedish Med. Rsch. Coun., 1952-58, 64-70, Swedish Natural Sci. Rsch. Coun., 1955-62. Contbr. articles to sci. jours. Decorated Grand Officier de l'Ordre du Mérite, Paris, 1984; recipient Anders Jahre Med. prize, Oslo, 1972, Gairdner award U. Toronto, 1972, Louisa Gross Horwitz prize Columbia U., 1975, Francis Amory prize Am. Acad. Arts and Scis., 1975, Albert Lasker Basic Med. Rsch. award, N.Y.C., 1977, Robert A. Welch award, Houston, 1980, Nobel prize, 1982. Mem. Royal Swedish Acad. Scis., Swedish Acad. Engring. Scis., Am. Acad. Arts and Scis., Am. Philos Soc. (Benjamin Franklin medal 1988), Am. Soc. Biol. Chemists, Acad. Scis. USSR, Academia Leopoldina (German Democratic Republic), Royal Soc. Edinburgh, Med. Acad. USSR, Finska Vetenskaps-Societeten, Swedish Soc. Med. Scis., Inst. of Medicine (sr.), NAS, fgn. assoc. NAS, Pontifical Acad. Scis., Città del Vàticano. Office: Karolinska Inst, Nobel Forum Box 270, 17177 Stockholm Sweden

BERHANE, GEBRE-CHRISTOS, diplomat; b. Makalle, Ethiopia, Mar. 6, 1953; m. Ketema Redda; 3 children. Student, Haile Selassie Univ. From mem. polit. dept. to head adminstrn. mass movements Tigray People's Liberation Front, Ethiopia, 1976-83; head bur. fgn. rels. Ethiopian People's Revolutionary Dem. Front, 1988-91; amb. to U.S. Govt. Ethiopia, Washington, 1991—. Office: Embassy of Ethiopia 3506 International Dr NW Washington DC 20008-3035

BERIDZE GIORGI, THENGIZ, biochemist, educator; b. Tbilisi, Georgia, Oct. 26, 1939; s. Giorgi and Rusudan (Roinashvili) B.; m. Marina Ketsba, Jan. 22, 1986; 1 child, Giorgi. Diploma in chemistry with honors, State U. Tbilisi, 1962; PhD in Biochemistry, A.N. Bach Inst. Biochemistry, Moscow, 1967, 80. Predoctoral fellow A.N. Bach Inst. Biochemistry, Moscow, 1962-66; postdoctoral fellow Protein Rsch. Inst., Pouschino, Russia, 1967-68; sr. rschr. Inst. Plant Biochemistry, Tbilisi, 1968-69, head lab., 1969—; sr. lectr. State U. Tbilisi, 1969-89, prof., 1989—. Co-author: Satellite DNA, 1982, 2nd edit., 1986. Mem. Georgian Acad. Scis. (corr. 1988-93). Home: Al Kazbegi Ave 47A flat 10, 380077 Tbilisi Georgia Office: Inst Plant Biochemistry, D Agmashenebeli Ave 10th Km, 380059 Tbilisi Georgia

BERINGER, JOHN EVELYN, microbiologist, educator; b. Harrogate, United Kingdom, Feb. 14, 1944; s. William and Joan Beringer; m. Sheila Murray Gillies, July 11, 1970; children: David John, Richard Michael, Peter Alan. BSc, U. Edinburgh, 1970, diploma in agriculture, 1965; PhD, U. East Anglia, 1973. Rsch. scientist John Innes Inst., Norwich, United Kingdom, 1973-80; dept. head Rothamsted Exptl. Sta., Harpenden, United Kingdom, 1980-84; prof. molecular genetics U. Bristol, United Kingdom, 1984—. Contbr. articles to profl. jours. Chmn. Adv. Com. on Releases to Environ., UK, 1986-99. Fellow Inst. Biology; mem. Soc. for Gen. Microbiology (Fleming lectr. 1979), Soc. for Applied Bacteriology, Order British Empire (comdr. 1993, Knight Bachelor 1999). Avocations: travel, reading, gardening, classic cars. Home: 92 Church Ln, Backwell Bristol BS48 3JW, England Office: U Bristol, Woodland Rd, Bristol BS8 1UG, England

BERINSTEIN, WILLIAM PAUL, business executive; b. Elmira, N.Y., Dec. 25, 1935; s. Benjamin M. and Ann (Newhouse) B.; m. Phyllis Altman, Aug. 22, 1964; children: Benjamin M., Dorothy C. BA, U. Mich., 1957. Pres. Polk Properties, Inc., Syracuse, N.Y., 1960-89; ptnr. HLB Assocs. Investments, Syracuse, 1973—, ANB Assocs. Investments, Syracuse, 1964—; pres. Cortland Cinema Corp., Syracuse, 1967—, Cornell Theatres, Inc., Syracuse, 1973—; owner Euclid Enterprises, Syracuse, 1973—; pres. Bendor Mgmt. Ltd., 1992—; pres. 715 Realty Corp., 1990—. Trustee Temple Soc. of Concord, Syracuse, 1968-74, 90-92, treas, 1992-96, pres., 1997—. Named to Hall of Fame, Syracuse Men's Bowling Assn., 1990. Mem. Onondaga County Bowling Coun. (sec. 1985—), N.Y. State Bowling Proprs. Assn. (bd. dirs. 1958-65), Bowling Proprs. Assn. Am. (bd. dirs. 1958-64). Jewish. Avocations: genealogy, travel. Home: 5166 Pointe East Dr Jamesville NY 13078-8798 Office: 1067 W Genesee St Syracuse NY 13204-2244

BERK, HARLAN JOSEPH, numismatist, writer, antiquarian; b. Joliet, Ill., June 7, 1942; s. Sammy and Ruth (Press) B.; m. Ellen Landman, Sept. 20, 1966 (div. 1978); children: Aaron R., Shanna L.; m. Pamela Margaret Blade, June 22, 1982; 1 child, Sammy Blade. Student, U. Ill., 1960-64. Vice pres. New Star Jewelers, Joliet, 1964-85; pres. Harlan J. Berk Ltd., Joliet, 1964, Chgo.; bd. dirs. OLICON Imaging Systems, Inc., Louisville; lectr., treas. N.Y. Internat. Numis. Conv.; Am. rep. Numismatica Ars Classica, Zurich, 1990-94. Author: Roman Gold Coins, 1985, Eastern Roman Successors, 1987, Roman Gold Coins of the Medieval World 383-1453 A.D. (Robert Friedberg award 1987), Eastern Roman Successors of the Sestertius; columnist World Coin News, 1989—, What's Old (Best Fgn. Column Numismatic Literary Guild, 1989, 90, 91, 92). Mem. exec. com. World Heritage Mus., Champaign, Ill., 1988—. Mem. Internat. Assn. Profl. Numismatists (pub. rels. for Am., chmn. 2000 internat. congress Chgo.), Profl. Numismatist Guild (edn. chmn., bd. dirs., v.p., pres.-elect), Am. Numismatists Assn. (dealer liaison com., mem. editl. bd. Numismatist, advisor to authentication bd. 1975—). Democrat. Jewish. Avocations: art collecting, scuba diving, running, skiing, fishing. Office: 31 N Clark St Chicago IL 60602-2806

BERK, MEHMET CAGLAR, neurosurgeon; b. Ankara, Turkey, Jan. 19, 1966; m. Fatma Sen, Oct. 11, 1992. Med. diploma, Hacettepe U., Ankara, 1989. Med. diplomate Turkish State Bd. Neurosurgery, European Bd. Neurosurgery. Family practitioner Turkish Ministry of Health, Kayseri, 1990-91; resident in neurosurgery Ankara U., 1992-98; cons. in neurosurgery Marmara U., Istanbul, Turkey, 1998-99; pvt. practice Ankara, 1999—; acad. rschr. in neurosurgery dept. neurosurgery Ankara U., 1998—; dir. subdivsn. functional and stereotactic neurosurgery Marmara U., Istanbul, 1998-99; rsch. fellow PAWSLAB, St. Louis U., 1999-2000; clin. fellow subdivsn.

functional and stereotactic neurosurgery U. B.C., Vancouver, 2000—. Contbr. numerous rsch. and med. reports, as well as acad. papers to profl. jours. Mem. European Soc. for Functional and Stereotactic Neurosurgery, Turkish Neurosurg. Soc. Avocations: skiing, scuba diving, R/C model flight.

BERKARDA, BULENT, internist, hematologist, oncologist; b. Duzce, Turkey, May 18, 1932; s. Kemal and Nadire Berkarda; m. Nevin Tirnakci, Sept. 4, 1959; children: Hulya, Kemal. MD summa cum laude, U. Istanbul, Turkey, 1956; D hon. causa, U. Paris, 1997. Intern Haseki Therapeutics Clinic, Istanbul, Turkey, 1957-58; resident Haseki Therapeutics Clinic, 1958-61; succesively asst. prof. medicine, assoc. prof., head dept. hematology, prof. medicine, head dept. oncology, assoc. dean, dean Cerrahpasa Sch. Medicine, Istanbul, 1964-83, dir. dept. med. oncology, 1975—; pres. U. Istanbul, 1994-98; spl. Wilson fellow in oncology U. Rochester, N.Y., 1973-74. Author book on hematology in Turkish, 1977; developer global coagulation test, 1964; contbr. research writings in field to profl. publs. Served as med. officer Turkish Navy, 1962-64. Decorated Ordre du Merite Nat., Legion d'Honneur, France. Mem. Internat. Soc. Chemotherapy, Internat. Soc. Hematology, Am. Soc. Cancer Edn., European Soc. Med. Edn., various local socs. Moslem. Home: Spor Cd 96 Besiktas, Istanbul Turkey Office: Cerrahpasa Sch Medicine, Dept Oncology, Istanbul Turkey

BERKENBLIT, SCOTT IRA, orthopaedic surgeon; b. Bklyn., Jan. 3, 1964; s. Ronald Henry and Sarita (Daniels) B.; m. Gail Benson, Oct. 19, 1997. BS, MIT, 1986, MS, 1990, PhD, 1996; MD, Harvard U., 1996. Diplomate Nat. Bd. Med. Examiners; lic. in Md. Intern in gen. surgery Johns Hopkins Hosp., Balt., 1996-97, resident in orthopaedic surgery, 1997—. Author: (with others) Advances in Osteoarthritis, 1998; contbr. articles to profl. jours. Exec. bd. Roland Springs Cmty. Assn., Balt., 1999, chmn. residential issues com., 1999. NSF fellow 1987-90. Mem. AMA, Am. Acad. Orthopaedic Surgeons, Orthopaedic Rsch. Soc., Sigma Xi, Phi Beta Kappa, Tau Beta Pi. Jewish. Avocations: playing the trumpet, skiing, hiking, classical music, strategic games. E-mail: bblit@alum.mit.edu. Home: 4313 Roland Springs Dr Baltimore MD 21210-2756 Office: Johns Hopkins Outpatient Ctr 601 N Caroline St Rm 5165 Baltimore MD 21287-0006

BERKENSTADT, JAMES ALLAN, lawyer; b. Chgo., June 26, 1956; s. Edward Jules and Lois Marion (Solomon) B.; m. Holly Lynn Cremer, Aug. 3, 1985; children: Rebecca, Bradley. BA, Northwestern U., 1978; JD, So. Ill. U., 1981. Bar: Ill., Wis. Litigation atty. Pollina & Phelan, Chgo., 1982-85; atty. for security dept. Chgo. Cubs Nat. League Ball Club, Chgo., 1982-84; litigation atty. Axley & Brynelson, Madison, Wis., 1986-87; v.p., corporate counsel The Wisconsin Cheeseman, Inc., Madison, 1987—. Author: Black Market Beatles: The Story Behind The Lost Recordings, 1995, Nevermind: Nirvana, 1998; prodr. The Beatles Tapes CD, 1994—, The Best of the Big Bands CD, 1998, 2000; contbr. articles to Musician mag. Bd. dirs. Cremer Charitable Found., Madison, 1989—; historian/archivist for rock band Garbage. Mem. NARAS. Avocations: racquetball, golf, music archivist, writer. Office: The Wisconsin Cheeseman Inc 301 Broadway Dr Sun Prairie WI 53590-1799

BERKI, FERIZ, Hungarian Orthodox priest, journal editor; b. Kotor, Yugoslavia, Dec. 31, 1917; arrived in Hungary, 1930; s. Sándor Alexander and Sophie (Chuchak) B.; m. Mary Pournaras; children: Manuela, Adam. Diploma in theology, U. Athens, Greece, 1940; doctorate in theology, U. Preshov, Czechoslovakia, 1957; hon. doctorate, Theol. Acad. Moscow, 1973, Ref. Theol. Acad., Budapest, Hungary, 1988. Ordained priest, 1954. Referent Ministry of Edn. II Sect., Budapest, 1941-52; prof. theology Orthodox Theol. Acad., Budapest, 1942-44; referent Hungarian Orthodox Ch., Budapest, 1952-54, archpriest-dean, 1954—; mem. presidium Ecumenical Coun. Chs. in Hungary, Budapest, 1962—. Editor, translator orthodox liturgical and prier books in Hungarian, 1955—; author: The Organization of the Hungarian Orthodox Church, (in Hungarian and Greek) 1942, The Book of Canons, 1946, The Orthodox Christianity, 1975, 2d edit., 1984, Az el nem ásott talentum, 1985; contbr. numerous articles to internat. profl. jours.; editor (ch. jour.) Egyházi Krónika. Recipient Hungarian Flag, Hungarian Govt., 1957, 87, Cross Ord. Hungarian Rep. Officer, 1997.

BERKI, TIMEA, immunologist, researcher; b. Pecs, Hungary, Jan. 31, 1961; d. László and Anikó (Cséry) B.; m. Peter Németh, Mar. 21, 1987; children: David, Kinga. MD, U. Med. Sch. of Pecs, 1985; PhD, Hungarian Acad. Scis., 1993. Med. diplomate; lab. diagnostics specialist. Postdoctoral fellow Hungarian Acad. Scis., 1985-89, U. Tex.-Southwestern Med. Ctr., Dallas, 1989-91; asst. prof. Univ. Med. Sch. of Pecs, 1991—; mng. dir. Pannonia Rsch. Park Ltd., Pecs, 1993—. Co-inventor in the photo-immunotargeting method procedure for relieving cell mixtures and tissues of targeted populations, 1988; contbr. articles to profl. jours. Grantee Nat. Rsch. Fund, Hungary, 1993-95, Med. Sci. Coun., Hungary, 1994—. Mem. Hungarian Immunol. Soc., Hungarian Soc. Lab. Diagnostics, Hungarian Membrane Soc. Lutheran. Avocations: swimming, aerobics, sewing, hiking. Office: Univ Med Sch Pecs/Immunol, Szigeti ut 12, H-7643 Pécs Baranya, Hungary

BERKLEY, REGINALD MAURICE, surgeon, art historian; b. London, Feb. 20, 1931; arrived in Australia, 1951; s. Harris and Fedora (le Vine) B.; m. Valerie Anne Miles, Dec. 1, 1962; children: Dora Jane, Vanessa. B Medicine B Surgery, U. Melbourne, Australia, 1955, Diploma in Laryngology and Otology, 1966, BA, 1988, B.Litt. with honors, 1990. Resident med. officer Royal Melbourne Hosp., Australia, 1956-57, surg. registrar, 1959-62; lectr. anatomy U. Melbourne, Australia, 1958; surg. registrar Worcester Royal Infirmary, Eng., 1963, St. Mary Abbot's Hosp., London, 1964; sr. surgical registrar Postgrad. Med. Sch., London, 1965-66; consulting head and neck surgeon Melbourne, Australia, 1966—. Author: The Imagery of the Angry Penguins Movement, 1989; contbr. surgical and art historical articles to profl. jours. 2nd lt. Royal Norfolk Rgt., 1950. Fellow Internat. Coll. Surgeons, Royal Soc. Medicine (London), Royal Coll. Surgeons (Eng.), Royal Australasian Coll. Surgeons; mem. British Assn. Otorhinolaryngologists (life), European Rhinological Soc., European Acad. Facial Surgery (The Joseph Soc.), Pan-Pacific Surg. Assn., Art Assn. Australia, Assn. Art Historians. Avocations: fine arts, opera, Handel's oratorios, travel, English history. Home: 13 Jason Ct, North Balwyn VIC 3104, Australia

BERKLEY, WILLIAM ROBERT, insurance holding company executive; b. Oct. 31, 1945; m. Marjorie Adnepos, June 19, 1971; children: Lisa A., W. Robert Jr., Lauren E. BS, NYU, 1966; MBA, Harvard U., 1968. Founder, chmn., chief exec. officer W. R. Berkley Corp., 1967—; chmn. Pioneer Cos. Inc., The Greenwich Bank & Trust Co., Westport Nat. Bank; co-chmn. bd. dirs. Sabin Vaccine Inst.; chmn. Strategic Distbn., Inc.; bd. dirs. Middlesex Bank & Trust Co. Chmn. bd. overseers Stern Sch. Bus., NYU; trustee NYU, Georgetown U.; vice chmn. U. Conn. Office: W R Berkley Corp PO Box 2518 165 Mason St Greenwich CT 06830-6608 also: Pioneer Cos Inc 700 Louisiana St Houston TX 77002-2700

BERKLEY-CARTER, DEBORAH LYNNE HALL, counselor; b. Halifax, Va., June 14, 1952; d. Robert Lee and Madeline (Foster) Hall; m. Karl Edward Carter, Aug. 9, 1989; children: Jason Ryan Berkley, William Justin Berkley. BS, Longwood Coll., 1973; MS, Va. Poly. Inst. and State U., 1979; MEd, Lynchburg (Va.) Coll., 1988; EdS, Coll. William and Mary, 1994, EdD, 1999. Lic. profl. counselor. Tchr. Nottoway (Va.) County Pub. Schs., 1975-77; co-owner, dir. The Children's Dept., Lynchburg, 1980-86; co-owner Foods With a Flair, Lynchburg, 1979-86; tchr. Amherst (Va.) County, 1985-86; tchr., counselor Campbell County Pub. Schs., 1986-91; counselor Williamsburg-James City County Pub. Schs., Williamsburg, Va., 1991-93, New Vistas Sch., Lynchburg, 1993—; The Rivermont Sch., Lynchburg, Va., 1994; pvt. practice Deborah Berkley-Carter and Assocs., Lynchburg, 1993—; owner The Madeline Ctr., Lynchburg, Va., 1997—. Mem. ACA, Lynchburg Counseling Assn., Va. Counseling Assn., Mental Health Assn., Kappa Omicron Phi, Kappa Delta, Sigma Chi Iota. Avocations: colonial architecture, colonial handcrafts, writing, catering. Office: The Madeline Ctr 18697 Forest Rd Lynchburg VA 24502-4363

BERKOLAIKO, GREGORY, mathematician; b. Voronezh, Russia, Apr. 4, 1976; s. Mark Zinovyevich and Alexandra Eugenyevna (Rodkina) B. BSc, Voronezh State Univ., Russia, 1996; MPhil, Univ. Strathclyde, U.K., 1997; postgrad., Univ. Bristol, 1997—. Teaching asst. Voronezh State Univ., 1995-96, Univ. Bristol, 1997—. Contbr. articles to profl. jours. Recipient Soros Student award Internat. Soros Sci. Ednl. Program, 1995, 96, Young Scientist of Voronezh Region Voronezh Adminstrn., 1995. Office: U Bristol Sch Math, BS8 1TW Bristol United Kingdom

BERKOV, DMITRI VLADIMIROVITCH, physicist; b. Moscow, June 13, 1962; arrived in Germany, 1994; s. Vladimir Isaakovitch Goldin and Asja Veniaminovna Berkova; m. Natalia L'vovna Gorn, Aug. 31, 1993. MSc, Moscow Engring. Physics Inst., 1985; PhD in Physics, Moscow Inst. Radiotech./Elect., 1989; DSc, Moscow Lomonosow U., 1995. Rsch. assoc. Inst. Solid State Physics, Chernogolovka, Russia, 1988-89; sr. rsch. assoc. Inst. Chem. Physics, Chernogolovka, 1989-94; rsch. scientist Inst. Phys. High Tech., Jena, Germany, 1994-96, Innovent, Jena, 1997—. Co-author: Magnetism in Medicine; contbr. more than 30 articles to profl. jours. Cmty. Action Magnetic Storage Tech. fellow U. Regensburg, 1990-91, U. Keele, 1991, U. Erlangen, 1992-93, Lab. L. Neel, Grenoble, 1993; DAAD fellow U. Erlangen, 1992-93. Achievements include research in magnetism of disordered systems and micromagnetism. Avocations: photography. Home: An der Leite 3B, D 07749 Jena Germany Office: Innovent, Felsbachstr 5, D 07745 Jena Germany

BERKOVA, NADEJDA PETROVNA, biochemist, medical researcher; b. Sumy, Ukraine, Jan. 7, 1957; d. Petr Tichonovitch and Lidia Georgievna (Ponomareva) B.; m. Vladimir Petrovitch Zotov, Nov. 1983 (div. 1991); 1 child, Zotov Alexandre; m. Niklaus Anton Düzmüller, May 30, 1997; 1 child, Damien. BSc, Skrybin Acad., Moscow, 1979; PhD in Immunology, Inst. Bioorganic Chemistry, Moscow, 1990. Rschr. Inst. Bioorganic Chemistry, Moscow, 1981-90, sr. rschr., 1990-92; assoc. rschr. INSERM, Rennes, France, 1990-92; postdoctoral rschr. Laval U., Que., Can., 1992-94, St. Francis d'Assisi Hosp./Wyeth Ayerst Co., Que., 1994-96; assoc. prof. St. Francis d'Assisi Hosp./Laval U., 1996-97; assoc. rschr. CNRS, Rennes, France, 1997-2000; cons. BCM Biotech. Inc., Laval, 1990-92; prof. biochemistry Inst. Bioorganic Chemistry, Moscow, 1989-91. Contbr. articles to profl. jours. Grantee FRSQ, 1995-97; recipient other grants and scholarships. Mem. AAAS, Ob-Gyn. Soc. Can. Home: 25 Rue de la Grande Piocre, 35510 Cesson-Sévigué France Office: CNRS, 2 Ave du Prof Leon Bernard, 35043 Rennes France

BERKSON, JACOB BENJAMIN, lawyer, author, conservationist; b. Washington County, Md., Dec. 6, 1925; s. Meyer and Ida Evelyn (Berman) B.; m. Ann Goldstein, June 25, 1955 (div.); children: Daniel Jeremy, Susan Kay, James Meyer. BA, U. Va., 1947, LLB, 1949, JD, 1970; grad., Fed. Exec. Inst., Charlottesville, Va., 1972. Bar: Md. 1949, Va. 1949, U.S. Supreme Ct. 1965, Calif. 1975. Sole practice Hagerstown, Md., 1949-52, 54-64; ptnr. McCauley, Cooey, Berkson & Wright, Hagerstown, 1964-70; dep. gen. counsel U.S. GSA, Washington, 1970-76; pvt. practice law Hagerstown 1976—; instr. Law Hagerstown Bus. Coll., 1986; trial magistrate, Hagerstown and Washington County, Md., 1951-52; mem. Legis. Coun. Md., 1955-58; del. Md. Legislature, 1955-58; trial magistrate, Hagerstown, 1958-59. Recipient commendation for svc. to U.S. Naval Acad. and pub. interest Chief of Naval Personnel, 1956. Lt. USNR, 1944-46, 52-54. Author: Shingahi Saburo and Short Stories, 1978, Comin' Home, 1993, A Canary's Tale, 1996; case editor, co-founder Va. Law Weekly, 1948; contbr. articles to profl. jours., address to Congrl. Record. Scoutmaster local coun. Boy Scouts Am.; organizer, dir. County Youth Conservation Corps; active Big Bros.; bd. dirs. Doub's Woods County Park, Devil's Backbone County Park; assisted in establishment of C&O Canal Nat. Histo. Park, 1954-70; camp sponsor YMCA; adv. Model Youth Legis.; pres. PTA; chmn. Washington County Park Commn., 1961-66; bd. dirs. Rachel Carson Coun., Inc., Chevy Chase, Md., 1996—. Mem. ABA, Calif. Bar Assn., Va. Bar Assn., Md. Assn. County Civil Attys. (pres., award for svc. as pres. 1966), Washington County Bar Assn. (pres.), Am. Legion, Hagerstown Club, Lions (pres.), Speakers Soc., Elks, Torch Club (Hagerstown), Thomas Jefferson Soc. Alumni. Republican. Jewish. Home and Office: 1419 Potomac Ave Hagerstown MD 21742-3315

BERKY, ALBIN LOUIS, music educator, musician; b. Bratislava, Slovakia, Mar. 31, 1953; arrived in Australia, 1980; s. Albin Donath and Marta Vilma (Bitto) B.; m. Julia Anastazia Fekete, July 20, 1957; children: Richard, Jacqueline. Diploma in Music, State Conservatory Music, Bratislava, 1977. Mem. conservatorium choir, woodwind quintet, baroque quartet TV and Radio Bratislava Rec. Studios, 1975-77; prof. music Nat. Conservatorium Music, Bratislava, 1975; prof., conductor Sch. Music Bratislava, 1975-77; freelance musician Slovconcert Agy., 1977-80; oboist Australian Chamber Orch., Sydney, 1981; woodwind player, oboist, leader Riverina Trio Charles Sturt U., Wagga, 1981-86; lectr. woodwinds U. Sydney, St. George Campus, 1986; dir. Berky Music Acad., 1987; woodwind lectr. Australian Internat. Conservatorium Music, 1993-95; tchr. clarinet, saxophone, oboe, recorder, chamber music, 1978-96; accredited pvt. music tchr. Sydney U., Conservatorium of Music.; woodwind lectr., originator woodwind dept. Charles Sturt U., Riverina Conservatoium Ctr. Wagga and Albury, 1981; performed in approximately 250 recitals, ednl. concerts for NSW Edn. Dept., Trio Recitals, ABC broadcasts and local TV through NSW, Victoria, ACT, Sydney Opera House, St. Stephens Ch. Sydney, Sydney Conservatorium Music, Canberra Sch. Music, others; mem. mgmt. bd. Charles Sturt U. Conservatorium Ctr., Wagga.; ofcl. rep., project mgr. State Conservatorium of Music Bratislava, Slovakia, 1996. Mem. Internat. Double Reed and Clarinet, Saxophone Soc., NSW Music Tchrs. Assn., Slovak Art Assn. (pres.). Home: 23 Merinda Ave, Epping NSW 2121, Australia

BERLAMONT, JEAN E., engineering educator; b. Brugge, Belgium, Nov. 29, 1946; s. Aime and Henriette (Geerolf) B.; m. Lola Bosch, Apr. 7, 1972; children: Luc, Nicolas, Sophie. MS Civil Engring., Ghent State U., 1969, PhD Civil Engring., 1975. Rsch. engr. Ghent U., Belgium, 1969-74; lectr. hydraulics K.U. Leuven, Belgium, 1974-76, prof. hydraulics, 1976—, vice-dean, 1987-93, dean faculty of engring., 1993-99. Home: Bergstraat 103, Kessel-Lo 3010, Belgium Office: KU Leuven Hydraulics Lab, de Croylaan 2, Heverlee 3001, Belgium

BERLATO, SERGIO, foreign diplomat; b. Vicenza, Italy, July 27, 1959. Mem. European Parliament, 1999—, mem. com. on agr. and rural devel., substitute com. on budgets, substitute com. on fisheries; mem. Union for Europe of the Nations Group; mem. delegation to the EU-Slovak Republic Joint Parliamentary Com., delegation to the EU-Romania Joint Parliamentary Com. Home: Vicolo Noè Bordignon 3, I-36014 Santorso Italy*

BERLIANT, MARCUS CRAIG, economist; b. Chgo., July 16, 1956; s. Kenneth and Esther B.; m. Clara Frances Asnes, Sept. 16, 1984. BA, Cornell U., 1977; MA in Stats., U. Calif., Berkeley, 1981, PhD in Econ., 1982. From asst. to assoc. prof. econ. U. Rochester, N.Y., 1982-94; prof. econ. Washington U., St. Louis, 1994—. Assoc. editor Regional Sci. and Urban Econs., 1989—, Jour. Pub. Economy Theory, 1997—, Papers in Regional Sci., 1999—, Jour. Regional Sci., 2000—; contbr. numerous articles to profl. publs., including Jour. Econ. Theory, Jour. Math. Econ., others. Fulbright fellow Erasmus U., Rotterdam, The Netherlands, 1984, vis. fellow Australian Nat. U., Canberra, 1995, S.W. Brooks vis. fellow U. Queensland, Brisbane, Australia, 1995, fellow Ctr. Polit. Economy, Washington U., 1994—; vis. scholar U. Calif., Berkeley, 1988-89; grantee NSF, 1984, 86, 90, 93, 95, NATO, 1985. Mem. Am. Econ. Assn., Assn. Pub. Policy Analysis and Mgmt., Econometric Soc., Nat. Tax Assn., Regional Sci. Assn. Internat. E-mail: berliant@wueconc.wustl.edu. Office: Washington U Dept Econ CB 1208 1 Brookings Dr Saint Louis MO 63130-4899

BERLIN, ALEXANDER ALEXANDROVICH, polymer engineer, educator; b. Moscow, Sept. 27, 1940; s. Alexander Yakovlevich Berlin and Tat'yana Ivanovna Glivenko; m. Galina Mikhaylovna Trofimova, Jan. 9, 1965 (div. Feb. 25 1982); children: Aleksey, Dar'ya; m. Svetlana Zakharovna Rogovina, Nov. 19, 1982; children: Elena, Tat'yana. MSc, BSc, Moscow Inst. Physics Tech., 1963, PhD, 1967; DSc, Russian Acad. Scis., Moscow, 1974. Rsch. Inst. Chem. Physics Russian Acad. Scis., Moscow, 1963-78, head lab., 1978-89, head of divsn., 1989—, dep. dir., 1994—; dir., 1996—; prof. Moscow Inst. Physics and Tech., 1982—, Soros Found., N.Y.C., 1994. Author: Kinetic Method in Polymer Synthesis, 1973, Kinetics of Polymerization Processes, 1978, Principles of Polymer Composites, 1985, Fast Polymerization Processes, 1996. Mem. Russian Acad. Scis., N.Y. Acad. Scis. Home: 24 Donskaya Str 68, 117419 Moscow Russia Office: Inst Chem Physics, 4 Kosygin Str, 117977 Moscow Russia

BERLIN, YURI ALFREDOVICH, physicist, educator; b. Moscow, Dec. 12, 1944; s. Alfred Anisimovich and Zinaida Andreevna (Zinovjeva) B.; m. Natalja Shapiro, Dec. 12, 1975; children: Alexander, Mikhail. BSc, Moscow Phys. Engring. Inst., 1968; PhD, Moscow Inst. Physics and Tech., 1974. Engr., asst. Inst. Chem. Physics USSR Acad. Scis., Moscow, 1968-72, jr. sci. rschr., 1972-78, head rsch. group, 1978-83, head of lab., 1983-93; prof. physics and theoretical chemistry Inst. Molecular Sci., Okazaki, Japan, 1993-94; sr. rschr. N.N. Semenov Inst. Chem. Physics Russian Acad. Scis., Moscow, 1993—; prof. theoretical physics and biophysics Technische U., Munich, 1994-99; sr. rsch. assoc. Northwestern U., Evanston, Ill., 1999—; supr., cons. Moscow State U., 1992-93; lectr., supr. Moscos Inst. for Physics and Tech., 1977-91. Mem. editl. bd. Jour. Chem. Phys. Reports, 1995—; guest editor Chem. Physics, 1996; contbr. articles to profl. jours. including Phys. Rev., Jour. Chem. Physics, others. Grantee Interant. Sci. Found., 1993, 94, Deutsche Forschungsgemeinschaft, 1995, 96, 97, 98, 99. Mem. AAAS, Internat. Soc. for Study of Origin of Life, Royal Dutch Acad. Scis., N.Y. Acad. Scis. Avocations: arts, classical music. Home: 800 Hinman Ave Apt 611 Evanston IL 60202-2326 Office: Northwestern U Dept Chemistry 2145 Sheridan Rd Evanston IL 60208-0834

BERLUSCONI, SILVIO, Former prime minister, Italy; b. Milan, Italy, Sept. 29, 1936; m. Carla Dall'Oglio (div.); 2 children; m. Veronica Lario, 1990; 3 children. Law degree, U. Milan, 1971. Owner Finivest Group; worked on Milano 2 Housing Project, 1969; owner Canale 5 Network, 1980—, Italia 1 TV Network, 1983—, Rete 4 TV Network, 1984—, La Cinq Comml. TV Network, 1985—, Cinema 5 Chain, Estudios Roma, 1986—, Milan AC Football Club, 1986—, La Standa, 1988—; chmn. Arnoldo Mondadori Editore SpA, 1990, half-share, 1991—; Former prime min. Rome, 1994; mem. European Parliament, Brussels, Belgium. Office: Parlamento Europeo, Rue Wiertz, ASP 9E132 Brussels B-1047, Belgium*

BERMAN, ARTHUR LEONARD, retired state senator; b. Chgo., May 4, 1935; s. Morris and Jean (Glast) B.; m. Barbara Dombeck; children: Adam, Marcy Padorr. BS in Commerce & Law, U. Ill., 1956; JD, Northwestern U., 1958. Bar: Ill. 1958. Atty. pvt. practice, Chgo.; ptnr. White, White & Berman, Chgo., 1958-74, Chatz, Berman, Maragos, Haber & Fagel, Chgo., 1981-82, Berman, Fagel, Haber, Maragos & Abrams, Chgo., 1982-86, Karlin & FLeisher, Chgo., 1986-99; dir. labor mediations svcs. Chgo. Bd. Edn., 2000—; spl. atty. Bur. Liquidations, Ill. Dept. Ins., 1962-67; spl. asst. atty. gen. Ill., 1967-68; mem. Ill. Ho. of Reps., 1969-76, Ill. Senate, 1977-99. Pres. 50th Ward Young Dems., 1956-60; v.p. Cook County Young Dems., 1956-60, 50th Ward Regular Dem. Orgn., 1955-99; active 48th Ward Regular Dem. Orgn., 1967-99; exec. bd. Dem. Party, Evanston, Ill., 1973-99; bd. govs. State of Israel Bonds. Mem. ABA, Ill. Bar Assn., Chgo. Bar Assn. (bd. mgrs. 1988-89), Nat. Assn. Jewish Legislators (pres. 1987-89), Am. Trial Lawyers Assn., U. Ill. Alumni Assn., Phi Epsilon Pi, Tau Epsilon Rho. Office: 6007 N Sheridan Rd Chicago IL 60660-3039

BERMAN, BARRY, marketing educator; b. Bklyn., Dec. 2, 1944; s. Abraham Louis and Gussie Boyarsky B.; m. Linda Nancy Grossman,June 9, 1968; children: Glenna Laurie, Lisa Naomi. BBA, CCNY, 1966, MBA, 1968; PhD, CUNY, 1973; postgrad., Hofstra U., 1999—. Instr. mktg. Hofstra U., Hempstead, N.Y., 1967-71, asst. prof., 1971-74, assoc. prof., 1974-79, prof., 1979-80, 81—, Walter H. "Bud" Miller distin. prof. bus., 1989—, acad. dir. exec. MBA program, 1999—; assoc. prof. Rutgers U., Newark, N.J., 1980-81; cons. State Edn. Dept. N.Y., Albany, 1971—, N.Y. Telephone Corp., N.Y.C., 1978, Singer Co., Stamford, Conn., 1985, Fortunoff's, L.I., 1990, John Wiley and Sons, N.Y.C., 1992, NCR, 1998, Savvy Sys., 1998, Kohl's, 1999. Co-author: Principles of Marketing, 1995, Marketing, 1997; author: Marketing Channels, 1996. NDEA fellow; Bernard M. Baruch scholar. Mem. Am. Mktg. Assn., Am. Collegiate Retailing Assn., Acad. Mktg. Sci., So. Mktg. Assn., Beta Gamma Sigma. Avocations: photography, computers, baking. Home: 2037 Oliver Way Merrick NY 11566-5423 Office: Hofstra U Hofstra Univ 144 Weller Hl Hempstead NY 11549-0001

BERMAN, CAROL, commissioner; b. Bklyn., Sept. 21, 1923; d. Hyman and Sarah (Levy) B.; m. Seymour Jerome Berman, May 19, 1944; children: Elizabeth, Charles. BA, U. Mich., 1943. Trustee Bd. Edn., Lawrence, N.Y., 1973-77; senator State of N.Y., Albany, 1978-84; spl. rep. State Divsn. for Housing, Hempstead, N.Y., 1985-86; commr. N.Y. State Commn. on Lobbying, Albany, 1988-92, N.Y. State Commn. of Elections, Albany, 1992—. N.Y. co-chair Nat. Jewish Dem. Coun., 1988—, Met. Airport Noise Mitigation Rev. Commn., 1992—; del. Dem. Nat. Conv., N.Y., 1992; vice-chair Nassau Dem. County Com., Mineola, N.Y., 1970-72. Mem. Phi Beta Kappa, Phi Kappa Phi. Jewish. Avocations: grandchildren, golf. Home: 42 Lord Ave Lawrence NY 11559-1324 Office: NY State Bd Elections Empire State Plz Swan St Bldg Core 1 Albany NY 12223

BERMAN, DAVID, lawyer, poet; b. N.Y.C., Sept. 11, 1934; s. Joseph and Sophie (Hersh) B. BA with honors, U. Fla., 1955; postgrad. Johns Hopkins U., 1955-56; JD, Harvard U., 1963. Bar: Mass. 1963. Teaching fellow Harvard Coll., 1962-63, 66-67; law clk. to justice Mass. Supreme Ct., 1963-64; asst. atty. gen. Commonwealth of Mass., 1964-67; assoc. Zamparelli & Whyte, 1967, ptnr., 1968-74; pvt. practice, 1974-82, 1990—; ptnr. Berman & Moren, Medford, Mass., 1982-89. Author: Future Imperfect, 1982, Slippage, 1996, Early Mandamus in Massachusetts, Massachusetts Legal History, 1998. Trustee Cantata Singers, 1981—. Mem. ABA, Mass. Bar Assn., Mass. Bar Found., Middlesex Bar Assn. (Most Outstanding Trial Lawyer Appelate award, 1998), Harvard Club (Boston), Signet Soc., Confrerie de la Chaine des Rotisseurs, Ordre Mondial, Masons. Republican. Unitarian. Home: 33 Birch Hill Rd Belmont MA 02478-1729 Office: 100 George P Hassett Dr Medford MA 02155-3264

BERMAN, GEOFFREY LOUIS, management company executive; b. L.A., July 15, 1953; s. Geoffrey M. and Patricia A. (Meyer) B.; m. Autumn Joy Patton, Mar. 26, 1983; children: Arielle Louise, Michelle Elise. BA/BS in Bus. Adminstrn., U. of the Pacific, 1975; JD, Southwestern U., 1985. Loan officer Union Bank, L.A., 1975-80; adminstrv. asst. Credit Mgrs. Assn., L.A., 1980-82; asst. v.p. Mitsui Mfrs. Bank, L.A., 1982-86; asst. sec., mgr. adjustment bur. Credit Mgrs. Assn., Burbank, Calif., 1986-97; v.p. turnaround management Devel. Specialists, Inc., L.A., 1997—; dir. Comml. Fin. Conf. Calif., L.A., 1978-80; co-chair insolvency laws com. Am. Bankruptcy Inst., Alexandria, Va., 1994—; mem. panel of mediators Ctrl. Dist. Bankruptcy Ct., L.A., 1995—; chmn. Task Force on Gen. Assignments for Benefit of Creditors, 1995—. Co-author: (manual) ABI Creditor's Com. Manual, 1995; contbg. editor Am. Bankruptcy Inst. Jour., 1996—, Fed. CT Receiver, 1999—; contbr. articles to profl. jours. Task force mem. City of Buena Park (Calif.) Investment Policy Rev. Com., 1995. Recipient Recognition award Fed. Bar Assn., L.A., 1986. Mem. L.A. Bankruptcy Forum, Bay Area Bankruptcy Forum, Orange County Bankruptcy Forum. Office: Devel Specialists Inc 333 S Grand Ave Ste 2010 Los Angeles CA 90071-1524

BERMAN, JOSHUA MORDECAI, lawyer, manufacturing company executive; b. Rochester, N.Y., Aug. 4, 1938; s. Jeremiah Joseph and Rose (Rappaport) B.; m. Ruth Freed, Mar. 17, 1996; children: Marc Ethan, Eve. BBA summa cum laude, CCNY, 1958; JD cum laude, Harvard U., 1961. Bar: Mass. 1961, N.Y. 1984. With Goodwin, Procter & Hoar, Boston, 1961-80, ptnr., 1969-80; pres. Berman Engel P.C., 1980-85; counsel Kramer, Levin, Naftalis & Frankel, 1985—; adviser Fidelity Investments, 1971—, Rank Group Ltd., Auckland, New Zealand, 1996—; chmn. bd., CEO Tyco Internat. Ltd., 1970-73, bd. dirs., v.p. Founder, pres. Boston Children's Sch., 1965-66. Home: Alexandra La Frasse, 1837 Chateau d'Oex Switzerland

BERMAN, MONA S., actress, playwright, theatrical director and producer; b. Jersey City; d. Edward and Mary (Auster) Solomon; m. Carroll Z. Berman; children: Marcie S. Berman Ries, Laura Jane. BA, Beaver Coll., postgrad. Columbia U., MFA, Boston U. Tchr. English, drama Jersey City High Schs.; actress indsl., stage, TV, Valley Players, Holyoke, Mass., The Millbrook Playhouse, Mill Hall, Pa., 1991; owner, dir. The Theatre Sch. and Producing Co., Maplewood, N.J.; chmn. drama edn. YM-MWHA of Met.

N.J. Cons., Clark Ctr. for Performing Arts, N.Y.C., 1965-66; instr. South Orange, Maplewood Adult Sch., 1967; artistic dir. Children's Theatre Co. Inc., Maplewood, 1968-70; cons. The Whole Theater Co.; dir. pub. relations Co. 3 by 2. Playwright: Hello Joe, That Ring in the Center, The Big Show, Interim, Who Can Belong?, Sudden Changes, Without Malice, Interim 2; producer, dir. A Night of Stars; guest theatre reviewer El Paso Herald Post, 1980-82. Active Boston United Fund, 1955-59, chmn. Boston residential area, 1957; bd. dirs. Greater Boston Girl Scouts Am., 1956-58, Tufts Med. Faculty Wives, 1956-58; active S. Fla. Theatre League. Mem. Dramatist Guild, Actors Equity Assn., Profl. Actor's Assn. Fla., The Creative Alliance. Address: 8925 Collins Ave Surfside FL 33154-3530

BERMAN, RICHARD ANDREW, financial company executive; b. London, Apr. 3, 1956; s. Lawrence Sam and Kathleen Doreen (Lewis) B.; m. Susan Elizabeth Charles, Aug. 31, 1985; children: Charlotte Xara Louise, Theodore Frederic Charles. BA in Econs. with honors, U. Cambridge, Eng., 1978, MA, 1981. Mgr. Orion Bank Ltd., London, 1978-80; treas. Andrea Merzario Spa, London, 1980-83; group treas. Heron Corp. Plc, London, 1984; dir. IFM Investments Ltd., London, 1984-90; mng. dir. Pine St. Investments, London, 1986-90, Sabre Corp. Ltd., London, 1987—; bd. dirs. Delphis Fund Mgmt., Ltd., Buchanan Capital Mgmt. Ltd., Sainty Hird and Ptnrs. Ltd., SHP Assocs., Ltd., Tulloch Ptnrs., Ltd. Fellow Assn. of Corp. Treas., Securities Inst. Avocations: gardening, walking, family. Office: Sabre Corp Fin Ltd, Stratton House Stratton St, London W1X 5FE, England

BERMAN, RONALD CHARLES, lawyer, accountant; b. Chgo., July 7, 1949; s. Joseph and Helen Berman; m. Kristine K. Topp, May 1, 1993; children: Daniel J. Lohr, Joseph James. BBS with highest honors, U. Ill., 1971, JD with honors, 1974. Bar: Ill. 1974, Wis. 1976; CPA, Wis. Mem. tax staff Grant Thornton, Chgo., 1974-76; tax supr. Grant Thornton, Madison, Wis., 1976-78, tax mgr., 1978-81, ptnr. tax dept., 1991-94; assoc. Neider & Boucher, Madison, 1995, shareholder, 1996—; lectr. cont. legal edn. U. Wis., 1999—. Mem. editl. adv. bd. Physician's Tax Advisor Newsletter, 1986-89, Physician's Tax and Investment Advisor, 1989-93. Scoutmaster Boy Scouts Am., Middleton, Wis., 1978—, fin. chmn. Mohawk Dist. Four Lakes coun., Madison, 1981-85, chmn. endowment fund, 1984-92, v.p. fin., 1992-94, exec. bd., 1982—, treas., 1994-96, nat. rep., 1996—; bd. dirs. Scouts on Stamps Soc. Internat., 1986-96, v.p., 1996—; bd. dirs. Madison Pension Coun., 1986-98, pres., 1988-89. Recipient Silver Beaver award Boy Scouts Am., 1981, Middleton Good Neighbor award Middleton Good Neighbor Festival, 2000. Mem. ABA (employee benefits com. taxation sect.), AICPA, Wis. Soc. CPAs (chmn. fed. tax com. 1990-92), State Bar Wis., Ill. Bar Assn., Madison Estate Coun. (bd. dirs. 1991-97, pres. 1995-96), Wis. Planned Giving Coun., Nat. Com. Planned Giving, Web Network Benefits Profls., Optimists, Order of Coif, Alpha Pi Omega, Phi Kappa Phi, Phi Alpha Delta. Avocations: photogrphy, philately, camping. Home: 3906 Rolling Hill Dr Middleton WI 53562-1224

BERMAN, SANFORD SOLOMON, motion picture sound designer, composer, arranger, artist; b. Long Branch, N.J., Nov. 14, 1951; s. Jerome Sidney and Marion (Solomon) B. BFA, Phila. Coll. Art, 1974. Freelance sound designer, record prodr./arranger, musician/composer; vis. prof. UCLA. Sound designer, supr. (features) Double Jeopardy, Analyze This, Brokedown Palace, Neil Simon's Odd Couple 2, Hard Rain, Hush, Multiplicity, Jade, Virtuosity, Wings of Courage, Bad Girls, Tombstone, Striking Distance Aladdin (Golden Reel winner, FX Editl., Oscar nomination), Love Field, Unlawful Entry, J.F.K. (FX Editl., Brit. Acad. award, Golden Reel nominee), Hot Shots!, Back to the Future (The Ride), Revenge (Golden Reel nominee), Immediate Family, Oliver & Company (Golden Reel winner), The Princess Bride (Golden Reel nominee), The Seventh Sign (Golden Reel nominee), da, Big Bad John, Going Under Cover, Mac & Me, Weeds, Jaws III, Cloak & Dagger, The Stone Boy, Wolfen, Strange Invaders, That Championship Season, The Sword & The Sorcerer, History of the World Part I, Miss Lonelyhearts, Ten to Midnight, The House on Sorority Row, Evilspeak, Q, Summerspell, Suburbia, Roar, Sweet Sixteen, The Fatal Game, Radioactive Dreams, The Glory of Khan, (short subjects) A Hard Rain, Ballet Robotique (Oscar nomination), The Wizard of Change, The Quest, A Trip to Tomorrow, Bird & The Robot, The Water Engine, Lean Machine, Wind Tunnel, Environmental Effects, New Magic, The Collector, Niagara, Lets Go!, Tour of the Universe, Runaway Train, Zargon, Deep Water Rescue, Rollercoaster, Monte Carlo Race, Alpine Highway, Toyota, Chevrolet, Jet Helicopter, Call from Space; keyboardist for James Brown "Static", 1996; creator comic effects Eat It (Grammy nomination), Like a Surgeon (Grammy nomination), New Duck (Grammy nomination); prodr., arranger, keyboardist Secret Smiles; composer (feature film scores) Screamers, Cataclysm, (commls.) Toyota, 1986, Celica, 1986; appeared with Bruce Springsteen, Steel, Hall & Oates, Chuck Berry, Dwayne Eddy, Jr. Walker & The All-Stars, James Brown, others. Mem. ACLU, So. Calif., 1985—, People for the Am. Way, So. Calif., 1985—, Am. Jewish Congress, 1982—. Recipient Brit. Acad. award Brit. Acad. of Film and TV Arts, Gt. Britain, 1992. Mem. Motion Picture Sound Editors (pres. 1992—, Golden Reel award 1988, 92), Acad. of Motion Picture Arts and Scis., Nat. Acad. Recording Arts and Scis., Am. Soc. Music Arrangers and Composers, Motion Picture Editors Guild. Democrat. Avocations: drawing, antique and classic automobiles, books.

BERMAN, STEVEN RICHARD, computer company executive; b. N.Y.C., Dec. 30, 1947; s. Harold and Norma (Bystock) B.; m. Susan Segall, Aug. 3, 1969; 1 child, Russell T. BS in Meteorology, CCNY, 1968; postgrad., U. Chgo., 1968-69; MS in Tech. Mgmt., Pepperdine U., 1993. Programmer, analyst Logicon, Inc., San Pedro, Calif., 1970-73, 75-78, Hughes Aircraft Co., Culver City, Calif., 1973-75; sr. analyst Argosystems, Inc., Sunnyvale, Calif., 1978-80; mgr. software support Ultrasystems, Inc., Irvine, Calif., 1981-86; sr. rsch. engr. Northrop Grumman Inc., Hawthorne, Calif., 1986-98; software project mgr. TRW Inc., L.A., 1998—. Author (computer programs) Recording Input-Output, 1983, Batch Jobs from Fortran, 1988, Marking Files No Backup, 1988. NDEA Title IV fellow, Chgo., 1968. Mem. Am. Contract Bridge League, Mensa. Avocations: bridge, travel. Home: 17336 Flame Tree Cir Fountain Valley CA 92708-3522

BERMAN, SYLVIA, biochemist, researcher; b. Chernovtsy, Bukovina, Ukraine, Apr. 2, 1950; arrived in Israel, 1975; d. T'svi Hirsh and Gusta (Skayanski) Nagel; children: Ilana, Rinat. BA, State U., St. Petersburg, Russia, 1971; MSc in Biochemistry and Immunology, State U., Kishinev, Moldova, 1973. Lab. technician Assaf Harofeh Hosp., Zerifin, Israel, 1976-86, lab. supr., 1986-91; head Nephrology Lab. Assaf Harofeh Hosp., Zerifin, 1991—. Contbr. articles to med. jours., including Am. Jour. Nephrology, Renal Physiology and Biochemistry, Renal Failure, Jour. Cardiovasc. Pharmacology Therapeutics. Avocations: classical music, poetry, ballet, gardening, pets. Home: Haviva Reich St 8/4, Holon Kiriat Sharet Israel Office: Assaf Harofeh Med Ctr, Nephrology Dept, 70300 Zerifin Israel

BERMINGHAM, ANN CATHLEEN, art historian, educator; b. Wharton, N.J., May 22, 1948; d. John C. and Margaret H. B.; m. Mark A. Rose. BA, Manhattanville Coll., 1970; MA, U. Mass., 1972; PhD, Harvard U., 1982. Adj. lectr. U. Calif., Santa Cruz, 1981-82; vis. lectr. U. Calif., Riverside, 1982-83; from asst. prof. to assoc. prof. U. Calif., Irvine, 1983-93; prof. U. Calif., Santa Barbara, 1993—; chair dept. history of art & architecture U. Calif., Santa Barbara, 1998—; assoc. dean fine arts U. Calif., Irvine, 1989-91, 92-93. Author: Landscape and Ideology, 1986, Learning to Draw, 2000; co-author: The Photographic Vision, 1982; co-editor: The Consumption of Culture, 1995. Mem. Am. Soc. 18th Century Studies, Interdisciplinary 19th Century Studies, Coll. Art Assn., Phi Kappa Phi. ACLS fellow, 1997, J. Paul Getty fellow, 1991-92, 87-88. E-mail: aberming@humanities.ucsb.edu. Office: U Calif Santa Barbara Dept History Art/Arch Santa Barbara CA 93106

BERMUDEZ SOKOLICH, DIANA LOURDES, psychologist; b. Huanuco, Peru, Dec. 16, 1959; d. Alfonso B. and Anita Sokolich; m. Jesus Arturo Zagastizabal, Aug. 29, 1986; 1 child, Berenice. Degree in psychology, Cath. U. Peru, Lima, 1992. Psychologist Santa Cecilia Sch., Callao, Peru, 1984-87; cons. ONG Floratristan, Lima, Peru, 1987-92; prof. clin. psychology U. San Martin, Lima, Peru, 1993-99; prof. human resources Pontifica U., Lima, Peru, 1995-96; clin. psychologist Desarollo y Conducta, Lima, Peru, 1993-99; cons. in field. Mem. APA, Colegio Psicologis del Peru, Assn. Egrsadis Pintifica Univ. Roman Catholic. Avocations: reading, music, dancing, cycling, walking. Office: Desarrollo y Conducta, Laredo 110, Lima 33, Peru

BERN, MURRAY MORRIS, hematologist, oncologist; b. Montgomery, Ala., Feb. 26, 1944; s. Hymie and Ruth Edith (Schaeffer) B.; m. Nancy Frazee, Nov. 23, 1967; 1 child, Alan. BA, Vanderbilt U., 1966; MD, Tulane U., 1970. Diplomate Am. Bd. Internal Medicine, Am. Bd. Hematology, Am. Bd. Oncology. Intern, then resident New Eng. Deaconess Hosp., Boston, 1970-72; resident in medicine Boston City Hosp., 1972-73; fellow in hematology & oncology New Eng. Deaconess Hosp.; Am. Cancer Soc. fellow Ctr. for Blood Rsch., Boston, 1973-75; sect. chief hematology New Eng. Deaconess Hosp., Boston, 1975-86; co-founder Cancer Ctr. of Boston, 1986; lab. dir. bone marrow transplantation Cancer Ctr. Boston, Boston and Plymouth, Mass., 1986—; chmn. transfusion com., sect. chief hematology, oncology New Eng. Bapt. Hosp., 1999—; dir. Cancer Ctr. of Boston and its stem cell support care, 1990-97; sect. chief hematology New Eng. Bapt. Hosp., 1999—; asst. prof. medicine Harvard U., 1987-94, asst. clin. prof. medicine, 1978-87. Author, editor: Urinary Track Bleeding, 1985, Hematologic Disorders in Maternal and Fetal Medicine, 1990. Mem. bd. med. advisors Am. Cancer Soc., Mass., 1976-80, fellow, 1973-75; bd. dirs. N.E. region ARC, 1994—. Recipient Tullis award for rsch. Fellow ACP (jr. faculty fellow 1973-77); mem. Am. Soc. Hematology (clin. practice com. 1996—), Am. Soc. Clin. Oncology. Avocations: camping, fishing. Office: Cancer Ctr Boston 125 Parker Hill Ave Boston MA 02120-2847

BERNA, MARIE-ROSE, international organization executive. Dep. sec.-gen. Benelux Econ. Union, Brussels. Office: Benelux Econ Union, 39 rue de la Régence, B-1000 Brussels Belgium

BERNABÉ, FRANCO, telecommunications industry executive; b. Vipiteno, Italy, Sept. 18, 1948; s. Bruno and Clara (Frigerio) B.; m. Maria Grazia Curtetto; children: Marco, Lucia. Degree in Econs., U. Turin, 1973. Asst. econs. dept., polit. scis. faculty U. Turin, Italy, 1973-74, prof. econ. policy, 1975-76; sr. economist dept. econs. and stats. OECD, Paris, 1976-78; dir. econ. studies FIAT, Turin, 1978-83; asst. to pres. Ente Nazionale Idrocarburi, Rome, 1983-84, vice dir. planning and control, 1984-86, dir. planning and control, 1986-92; mng. dir., CEO Eni SpA, Rome, 1992-98; CEO Telecom Italia SpA, Rome, 1998—; chmn. Andala UMTS SpA; bd. dirs. French Inst. Pétrole; hon. chmn. OME. Bd. dirs. LUISS Univ. Mem. Italian Stock Co. Assn. (gen. coun., exec. com.), Gen. Confedn. Italian Industry (exec. com.), Italian Coun. Economy & Labour, Bocconi U. Inst. Energy Sourses Econs. (exec. com.), Conf. Bd. (internat. counsellor), W.E.F. Found. Office: ENI SpA Telecom Italia SpA, Via Flaminia 189, 00196 Rome Italy*

BERNABEI, LYNNE ANN, lawyer; b. Highland Park, Ill., Apr. 11, 1950; d. Guy and Anna (Tamarri) B. BA, Harvard U., 1972, JD, 1977. Bar: D.C. 1979, U.S. Supreme Ct. 1988, U.S. Dist. Ct. D.C. 1977, U.S. Ct. Appeals (D.C. cir.) 1979, U.S. Ct. Appeals (3d cir.) 1985, U.S. Ct. Appeals (fed. cir.) 1988, U.S. Ct. Appeals (4th cir.) 1992, U.S. Ct. Appeals (6th cir.) 1990. Clk. U.S. Dist. Ct. Judge William Bryant, Washington, 1977-78; assoc. Tigar & Buffone, Washington, 1978-80; clin. instr. Georgetown U., Washington, 1980-81; gen. counsel Govt. Accountability Project, Washington, 1981-85; ptnr. Newman, Sobol, Trister & OWens, Washington, 1985-87, Bernabei, Katz & Balaran, Washington, 1987—. Co-author: The High Citadel: On the Influence of Harvard Law School, 1978; author articles. Recipient Achievement award Lambda Legal Defense and Edn. Fund, Washington, 1990. Mem. ABA, ATLA, Nat. Lawyers Guild (bd. dirs. D.C. chpt. 1992-95). Office: Bernabei & Katz 1773 T St NW Ste 100 Washington DC 20009-7139

BERNABEU, PATRICK THIERRY, communications executive; b. The Tronche, France, May 20, 1960; s. Jean-Batiste Norbert and Stella Vitale Bernabeu. Tech. degree, France. Exploration miner of diamonds Can. Democrat. Roman Catholic. Avocations: computer internet, collecting stamps, money, antiques. Home: 387 TRC N41 Chomin, Hector Berliog II, F38190 Villard-Gonnod France Office: Info Bus Enterprises, 389 TRC 41 Chemin du, 38490 Berlioz France

BERNAL, RICHARD LEIGHTON, ambassador; b. Kingston, Jamaica, Nov. 30, 1949; m. Margaret Bernal; 2 children. BS in Econs., U. West Indies, 1971; M in Econs., New Sch. Social Rsch., 1979, PhD in Econs., 1988; M in Internat. Pub. Policy, Johns Hopkins U., 1996. With Bank of Jamaica, Nat. Planning Agy.; lectr. in internat. econs. U. West Indies, Kingston, Jamaica, 1979-86; gen. mgr. Workers Savs. and Loan Bank, 1987-91; amb. to U.S.A. Govt. of Jamaica, 1991—; ambassador, permanent rep. to Jamaica OAS, 1991—. Contbr. articles to profl. jours. Office: Embassy of Jamaica 1520 New Hampshire Ave NW Washington DC 20036-1210

BERNARD, ALBERT GERSHON, biologist, researcher; b. London, Jan. 22, 1929; s. Albert Francis and Ethel Grace (Ireland) B.; m. Ute Margarette Hartung, May 12, 1962; children: Juliet, Oliver. BSc in Math., Birkbeck Coll., London, 1974. Technician ARC, Babraham, Eng., 1954-59; rsch. asst. St. Thomas Hosp., London, 1959-62, Charing Cross Hosp./London U., 1962-67; sr. chief sci. officer Royal Free Hosp. Sch. Medicine/London U., 1967-82, head low temperature rsch. and human IVF lab., 1982-92; sr. rsch. fellow, head of rsch. U. Wales Coll. Medicine, Cardiff, 1992-95; sci. advisor London Female and Male Fertility Ctr., 1993-95; advisor/cons. Fakeeh Hosp., Jeddah, Saudi Arabia, 1984-92, Male and Female Fertility Ctr., 1993-95; advisor Cancer Rsch. Campaign, South Mimms, Eng., 1985-90. Author: Clinical Application of Cryobiology, 1992; contbr. articles to profl. jours. Vol. advisor Citizens Advice Bur., Potters Bar, Eng., 1996—; chmn. Royal Free Hosp. Rsch. Ctr., London, 1972—; mem. com. Deanery Synod, Hatfield, Eng., 1995—. Cpl. Parachute Regt., 1947-49, Palestine. Rsch. grantee in field. Fellow Inst. of Biology, Soc. Low Temperature Biology (hon.; treas.); mem. Royal Free Recreation Club (chmn. 1977—). Mem. Labour Party. Anglican. Avocations: grandchildren, theatre, golf, gardening, travel. Home: Pound Farm House, 37 Baker St, Potters Bar Herts EN6 2DZ, England

BERNARD, ANNE-JOSÉ See AUBRY, CECILE

BERNARD, BESS MARY, interior designer, consultant; b. Bklyn.; d. Hyman and Fannie Bernard. Formerly, with Melanie Kahane Assoc.; pres. Bernard Design Internat., Ltd., N.Y.C., 1960—; internat. cons. in field; lectr. in field. Prin. works include dining room for kindergarten children Marymount Sch., boutique for East Park Cultural Ctr., various projects for Waldorf Astoria hotel, apt. for pres. of Mitsubishi, numerous corp., hosp. and internat. projects. Chmn. Bklyn. Jewish Hosp.; lectr. interior design Sloan-Kettering Meml. Hosp. working with recuperating patients; mem. Sloan-Kettering Soc., PPSEAWA UN; com. mem. Cabrini Devel. Coun., Inner City Scholarship Fund, N.Y. Heart Assn., Waldemar Med. Rsch. Found., Inc. Recipient various vol. awards Bklyn. Jewish Hosp., United Hosp. Fund. Mem. Nat. Assn. Women Bus. Owners, Alliance Russian and Am. Women. Avocation: volunteer work. Office: Waldorf Astoria 301 Park Ave New York NY 10022-6897

BERNARD, CLAUDE CHARLES ANDRE, neuroimmunologist; b. Paris, Mar. 3, 1944; came to Australia, 1979; s. Pierre Charles and Leonie Albertine (Bollengier) B.; m. Ora Degani, Mar. 7, 1969; children: Tali, Eyal. PhD, U. Montreal, Can., 1973; DSc, Louis Pasteur, Strasbourg, France, 1978. Biologist Centre de'Immuno-Pathologie Hosp. St. Antoine, Paris, 1964-69; demonstrator Faculty Medicine U. Montreal, 1970-72; lectr. Faculty Biology U. Que.-Montreal, 1970-72; mem. Basel (Switzerland) Inst. Immunology, 1977-79; rsch. fellow La Trobe U., Bundoora, Australia, 1979-81, sr. rsch. fellow NH and MEC, 1981-86, prin. rsch. fellow, 1987-90, prof. neuroimmunology, 1990—; vis. rsch. fellow Walter and Eliza Hall Inst., Parkville, Australia, 1973-77; vis. scientist dept. chem. immunology Weizman Inst. Sci., Rehovot, Israel, 1985; cons. Little Co. Mary Hosp., Melbourne, Australia, 1988; bd. dirs. med. and sci. com. Anti-Cancer Coun. Victoria, Melbourne, 1990—. Editorial bd. Jour. Neuroimmunology, Eng., 1984—; founding editorial bd. Today's Life Sci., Sydney, Australia, 1989—, Immunol. Cell Biol., 1993, Devel. Neurosci., 1996; co-editor Asia-Pacific Multiple Sclerosis; contbr. articles to profl. jours., chpts. to books. Chair PTA Kew (Australia) Primary Sch., 1979-81, mem. sch. coun., 1983-85; mem. fund raising com. Balwyn (Australia) High Sch., 1987-90. Fulbright vis. scholar, U. Calif., San Francisco. Mem. Australian Assn. Weizmann Inst. (sec. 1982), Australian Acad. Sci. (Weizman fund com. 1984—), Internat. Soc. Neuroimmunology (bd. dirs. internat. exec. com. 1987), Multiple Sclerosis Soc. Australia (med. adv. bd. 1990—), Australian Soc. Immunology, Australian Behavioral Immunology Group. Achievements include research in the role of cellular and humoral immune responses in naturally occuring and experimentally induced deyelinating disorders, genetic regulation of myelin and other brain proteins in health and diseases. Office: La Trobe U, Bundoora Victoria 3083, Australia

BERNARD, DANIEL, retail executive. Ceo Carrefour, Paris. Office: Carrefour, 6 Ave Raymond Poincar, Paris 75116, France*

BERNARD, DERYCK MILTON, geographer, minister; b. Georgetown, Guyana, Apr. 12, 1950; s. James Augustus and Myrtle Evadne (Graham) B.; m. Myrna Cherly Morgan, Dec. 29, 1973; children: Denise Marcia, Ayanna Malene. BA with honors, U. Leicester, Eng., 1973; M Phil, U. Leicester, 1980. Asst. master Queen's Coll., Georgetown, 1972-74; lectr. U. Guyana, Georgetown, 1974-80, sr. lectr., dept. head, 1980-85, dean, 1981-83; permanent sec. Office of Prime Minister, Georgetown, 1985-86; minister Ministry of Edn., Georgetown, 1986-87, sr. minister, 1987-92; head dept. geography U. Guyana, 1993-96, dean faculty arts, 1999—; commr. Constn. Reform Commn., 1999; chmn. bd. dirs. Guyana Mgmt. Inst., Georgetown, 1985-87. Author: A New Geography of Guyana, 1999; editor: Guyana Pub. Service Jour., 1985-86; contbr. articles to profl. jours.; composer several nat. songs, 1974-76. Chmn. bd. govs. Kuru Kuru Coop. Coll., Guyana, 1986—; mem. gen. council People's Nat. Congress, Guyana, 1986-87. U. Guyana research grantee, 1979; Assn. Commonwealth Univs. fellow, 1983. Mem. Constn. Reform Commn. Methodist. Avocations: music, cricket, badminton. Office: Faculty Arts, Univ Guyana, Turkeyem Guyana

BERNARD, JAN HUS, mineralogist, researcher; b. Prague, Czech Republic, Sept. 7, 1928; s. Jindřich and Hana (Chlumecká) B.; m. Emilie Zelená, July 16, 1953; children: Iva, Olga. RNDr, MSc, Charles U., Prague, 1952, CSc in Geol. Sci., 1957. Rsch. scientist Czech Geol. Survey, Prague, 1954-90; lectr. Charles U., 1964; expert IAEA, Rabat, Morocco, 1964; vis. prof. UNESCO, Ankara, Turkey, 1967-71, Bukavu, Zaire, 1971-72, project dir. UN Devel. Program, Ibadan, Nigeria, 1979-81. Chief author: Mineralogy of Czechoslovakia, 1969, 2d edit., 1981 (Czech Lit. Fund award 1982), Ore Deposits and Metallogeny, 1986, Ency. of Minerals, 1992 (Czech Lit. Fund award 1993); author: Empirical Types of Ore Mineralization, 1991. Fellow Mineral. Soc. Am.; mem. Internat. Assn. on Genesis Ore Deposits (charter). Unitarian. Avocations: mineral collecting, gardening, swimming. Home: Lukešova 24, 142 00 Prague Czech Republic

BERNARD, MICHAEL MARK, lawyer, city planning consultant; b. N.Y.C., Sept. 5, 1926; s. H.L. and Henryetta (Siegel) B.; m. Laura Jane Pincus, Aug. 28, 1958; 1 dau., Daphne Michelle. AB, U. Chgo., 1949; JD, Northwestern U., 1953; MCity Planning, Harvard U., 1959. Bar: Ill. 1952, U.S. Dist. Ct. (no. dist.) Ill. 1953, N.Y. 1955, U.S. Ct. Appeals (1st cir.) 1956. Pvt. practice law Chgo. and N.Y.C., 1953-55; rsch. asst. Law Sch. Harvard U., 1955-56; city planning cons., atty.-adviser Puerto Rico, 1956-58; rsch. atty. Model Laws Project Am. Bar Found., 1959-60; city planner, legal adviser Chgo. Dept. City Planning, 1960-64; cons. planning and land regulation, 1964—; cons. Chgo. Area Transp. Study, 1964-65; mem. exec. faculty Boston Archtl. Ctr., 1967—; adv. to Gov.'s Exec. Office on reorgn. Commonwealth Mass., 1968-72; chmn. 1st Nat. Transp. Needs Study Mass.; cons. A.I.A. Rsch. Corp., 1974; cons. Mass. Atty. Gen., 1981—; mem. com. urban devel. and housing World Peace Through Law Ctr., 1965—; mem. com. transp. law transp. research bd. NRC-NAS, 1966—; cons. White House Policy Adv. Com. to D.C., 1966; del. World Congress Housing and Planning, Paris, France, 1962, Tokyo, Japan, 1966; fellow Ctr. Advanced Visual Studies, M.I.T.; prin. investigator Northwestern U. Transp. Ctr.; lectr. in field; vis. prof. urban and regional planning U. Iowa, 1969-70; vis. lectr. Harvard U., MIT, U. Mich.; mem. faculty Am. Law Inst., 1978—. Author: Constitutions, Taxation and Land Policy, 2 vols., 1979-80, Airspace in Urban Development, 1963; co-editor: Policy Studies Jour.; editor, pub.: Reflections on Space; revision project mgr.: Constitutional Uniformity & Equality in State Taxation, 2 vols., 1984, Transformation of Property Rights in the "Space Age", 1993, (U.S. Govt. manual) Transportation Planning for Small Cities, 1973; spl. editor: Urban Law Ann. Washington U. Sch. Law; columnist: Jour. Real Estate Devel.; bd. editors: Real Estate Fin.; contbr. articles to profl. jours. Patron Hull House Assn., Chgo., 1965; v.p., trustee Cambridge Community Art Ctr., 1971-73; mem. standing com. Unitarian Ch.; mem. founding site com. Mus. Contemporary Art, Chgo. With USN, 1944-46. Recipient cert. of commendation for teaching Boston Archtl. Ctr., 1984; grantee NRC-NAS, 1964-66. Fellow Lincoln Inst. Land Policy; mem. ABA (land use, planning and zoning com., chmn. T.D.R. subcom. 1984-89, air and space com.), Internat. Fedn. Housing and Planning, Am. Arbitration Assn. (cert., bldg. and constrn. arbitrator),Am. Soc. Pub. Adminstrn., Policy Studies Orgn., Am. Planning Assn. (chmn. legis. com. Met. Chgo. sect. 1963-65, Mass. state reporter planning and law div. 1990—), Boston Soc. Architects (affiliate), Nat. Space Soc. (bd. dirs., space law com. Boston chpt.), Am. Underground Space Assn., Internat. Ctr. for Land Policy Studies, Urban Affairs Assn. (jour. rev. editor), Am. Crafts Coun., Mass. Assn. Craftsmen (v.p. 1975-78). Boston Visual Artists Union (hon., sec.-gen. 1971-72), New England Poetry Club (life), U. Chgo. Club Boston (bd. dirs.), Boston Athenaeum (life, dir. Poetry program). Home: 25 Stanton Ave Auburndale MA 02466-3005

BERNARD, NORMAN PAUL, management consultant; b. Bath, Eng., June 29, 1945; s. Samuel and Elizabeth (Sherrif) B.; m. Elizabeth Joy Stockley (div. July 1990); children: Tamsin, Duncan; m. Claire Bernard-Gouzouli, Feb. 1991. MBA, Cranfield (Eng.) U., 1972. Assoc. McKinsey & Co. Inc., London, 1974-79; gen. mgr. Grindlays Bank, London, 1979-83; chmn. Citicorp Insce Brokers, London, 1982-84; v.p. Booz, Allen & Hamilton, London, 1985-90; chmn. First Cons. Ltd., London, 1990—. Mem. Chartered Inst. Bankers. Home: 13 Highfields Grove, Fitzroy Park, Highgate, London N6 6HN, England Office: First Cons Ltd, Vigilant Ho, 120 Wilton Rd, London SW1V 1JZ, England

BERNARD, PHILIPPE, molecular biologist; b. Malmedy, Belgium, Aug. 1, 1962; s. Pol and Maria (Widar) B.; partner Solange Heerinckx; children: Matthieu and Sophie. B of Zool. Scis., Brussels Free U., 1984, PhD, 1993. Rschr. U. National Autonoma de Mexico, 1985-87, U. Libre de Bruxelles, Belgium, 1987-95, Centre Nat. de la Recherche Scientifique, Montpellier, France, 1995-96; sci. educator U.C.L., Louvain-la-Neuve, 1996-97; molecular biologist BioRix, Rixensart, Belgium, 1997-99; rschr. U. de Liege, Belgium, 1999—. Contbr. articles to profl. jours.; patentee in field. Recipient Solvay prize in sci., 1993, Errera L. prize in biology, 1995. Avocation: music.

BERNARD, RICHARD MONTGOMERY, retired physician; b. Long Beach, Calif., Feb. 21, 1925; s. Francis M. and Irma V. (Phillips) B.; m. Virginia Marie Thompson, Sept. 19, 1946 (div. Mar. 1971); children: Richard Jr., David, Mary, Danielle; m. Nancy Johnston, Nov. 18, 1971; stepchildren: Vivienne Kouba, N. Catherine Thompson. BS in Chemistry, U. Calif. Berkeley, 1945; MD, U. Chgo., 1950. Charter Diplomate Am. Bd. Family Practice. Pvt. practice Westslope, Portland, Oreg., 1954-60, Beaverton, Oreg., 1960-86; assoc. with Dr. D. Graham, Beaverton, 1986-90; family practitioner St. Vincent Tanesbourne Med. Plz., Beaverton, 1990-91; locum tenens Oreg., 1991-92; family practitioner Providence Health Sys., Wilsonville, Oreg., 1992-98; clin. prof. medicine, family practice dept., Oreg. Health Sci. U., Portland, 1994—. Commr. transp. adv., 1994-96, Wilsonville Long Range Planning Commn., 1996-98; healthcare ombudsman Portland Metro Elders in Action, 2000—. Capt. USNR, WWII, 1942-46, Korea, 1950-53, ret., 1985. Recipient Meritorious Achievement award Oreg. Health Science U., 1988. Mem. Wilsonville Rotary. Republican. Avocations: fishing, golf, travel, photography, toy and model making. Home: 31530 SW Village Green Ct Wilsonville OR 97070-8426

BERNARD, WOLFGANG HEINRICH EDGAR, classical philologist, educator; b. Ingelheim on the Rhine, Germany, Apr. 23, 1960; s. Manfred and Brigitte (Salin) B.; m. Hildegund Stamm, Aug. 3, 1984; children: Katharina, Johanna. PhD, Mainz (Germany) U., 1984, PhD habil., 1992; privatdozent, Marburg (Germany) U., 1992. Lectr. Mannheim (Germany)

U., 1992; temporary prof. Greek U. Constance, Germany, 1992-93; prof. Greek Rostock (Germany) U., 1994—. Author: Rezeptivitaet und Spontaneitaet der Wahrnehmung bei Aristoteles, 1988, Spaetantike Dichtungstheorien, 1990. Grantee Deutscher Akademischer Austauschdienst, 1984, Deutsche Forschungsgemeinschaft, 1985, 88. Mem. Mommsen-Gesellschaft, Deutscher Hochschulverband, Deutscher Altphilologenverband. Avocations: sailing, volleyball, political journalism. E-mail: wolfgang.bernard@philfak.uni-rostock.de. Home: Gustav-Falke-Str 5, D-23562 Lübeck Germany Office: Rostock Univ, Universitaetsplatz 1, D-18051 Rostock Germany

BERNARDI, MAURO, educator, physician; b. Bologna, Italy, Oct. 18, 1947; s. Giancarlo and Elsa (Matteuzzi) B.; m. Carla Castegnaro, Oct. 6, 1973; children: Marcello, Francesca. MD, U. Bologna, 1972. Cert. medicine, Italy. Rsch. fellow U. Bologna, 1973, asst., 1978-83, assoc. prof. 1983-95, full prof. internal medicine, 1995—; asst. U. Chieti, Italy, 1974-78; rsch. fellow Liver Rsch. Unit, U. London, 1975; vis. prof. Technion, Haifa, 1984; dir. Specialization Sch. in Sports Medicine, U. Bologna, 1990-99, dir. Semeiotica Medica - Policlinico S. Orsola, 1997—. Contbr. articles to profl. jours. Grantee Consiglio Nazionale della Richerche, Rome, 1978, 95, 96, 97, Regione Emilia-Romagna, Bologna, 1991, U. Bologna, 1993-99, Ministry of U., Rome, 1995, 96, 98. Mem. European Assn. for the Study of the Liver (mem. sci. com. 1990-93), Italian Assn. for the Study of the Liver (mem. sci. com. 1978-81), Italian Soc. Gastroenterology, Italian Soc. Internal Medicine. Roman Catholic. Avocations: classical and operatic music, skiing, diving. E-mail: bernardi@med.unibo.it. Fax: 30 51 308966. Home: Viale Felsina 13, 40139 Bologna Italy Office: Policlinico S Orsola, Via Massarenti 9, 40138 Bologna Italy

BERNARDO, FERNANDO APELO, research institute administrator, educator; b. Cabagan, Isabela, Philippines, June 10, 1932; s. Francisco Ramos Sr. and Paz (Apelo) B.; m. Emiliana Novero, July 14, 1962; children: Dan, Rex, Ray, Amy. BSA, U. Philippines, Laguna, 1955; MS, U. Philippines, 1958; PhD, N.C. State U., 1962. Assoc. prof. U. Philippines, Laguna, 1969-72, prof., dean Coll. Agr., 1972-74; pres. Visayas State Coll. Agr., Leyte, Philippines, 1974-84; dir. S.E. Asian Regional Ctr. Grad. Tng. and Rsch. in Agr., Laguna, 1984-87; dep. dir. gen. internat. programs Internat. Rice Rsch. Inst., Laguna, 1987—; cons. Edn. Devel. Projects Implementing Task Force, Philippines, 1972-74, Bangladesh Agr. Rsch. Coun., 1981-82; chemn. bd. Leyte (Philippines) Sabah Basin Devel. Authority, 1978-84. Author: To Learn from the Japanese National System fo Education and Research in Agricultural Sciences, 1974, Visca: History and Analysis of Institution Building, 1985, Management of Research and Extension Programs in Agricultural Universities, 1986, Life, Nature and Science: Poetry. Dep. min. edn., culture and sports, Manila, Philippines, 1984-86; bd. dirs. Philippine Coconut R&D Found., Manila, 1977-85; chmn. bd. 8 colls., univs., Philippines, 1984-86. Recipient One of Ten Outstanding Young Men award for genetics Philippine Jaycees, 1966, Rizal Propatria award for ednl. adminstrn. Pres. F.E. Marcos, 1980, Pantas award for rsch. adminstrn. Phillipine Coun. for Agrl. and Resources R&D, 1982; named Most Outstanding Agrl. Educator of the Yr. Outstanding Hon. Soc. Philippines, 1978. Mem. Philippine Assn. Rsch. Mgrs., Assn. Colls. of Agr. Philippines (pres. 1973-74, 80-81), Philippine Assn. State Colls. and Univs. (pres. 1981-82), Asian Assn. Agrl. Colls. and Univs. (organizer, exec. sec. 1972-82, pres. 1982-84), Upsilon Sigma Phi (pres. 1991-94), Gamma Sigma Delta (pres. 1971-74). Avocations: tennis, gardening, poems, painting. Home: 8 Ilang-Ilang St, 4031 College Laguna, Philippines Office: Internat Rice Rsch Inst, 4031 Los Baños Laguna, Philippines

BERNASCONI, CHRISTIAN, chemical engineer; b. Paris, Oct. 29, 1946; s. Maurice and Germaine (Leboeuf) B.; m. Ginette Besse, Sept. 13, 1973; children: Christelle, Marilyne. Degree in chem. engring., Ecole Superieure Chimie, Lyon, France, 1971; PhD, U. Lyon, 1978. Assoc. prof. chemistry U. Lyon, 1971-82; chem. engr. Elf Antar France, Solaize, France, 1982—; speaker at internat. confs. and symposiums. Contbr. articles to Chemistry, Photochemistry, Photobiology, Petroleum Products Chemistry, Physico-Chemistry. Active Croix Rouge Francaise, Lyon, 1965; camp trainer, France, 1965-71. With French Army, 1973-74. Mem. Soc. Automotive Engrs., Internat. Assn. Stability and Handling of Liquid Fuels (steering com. 1990—). Roman Catholic. Achievements include several French and foreign patents for energetical products, petroleum products, processes and additives. Home: 168 Chemin du Bois Contal, 69390 Charly France Office: Elf Antar France Rsch Ctr, Elf Antar France Rsch Ctr, BP22 Rue du Canal, 69360 Saint Symphorien Ozo France

BERNAT, TIVADAR, retired geography educator; b. Zakany, Hungary, July 30, 1926; s. Jozsef and Rozalia (Jagozdics) B.; m. Iren Zuggo, July 5, 1955; 1 child, Borbala. Grad., U. Econs., Budapest, 1952, PhD, 1955; PhD in Acad. Sci., Hungarian Acad. Sci., 1975. Asst. econ. geography dept. U. Econs., 1952-56, first asst. to prof., 1956-67, lectr., 1967-70, dept. head, 1970-94. Co-author, editor: Economic Geography of Hungary, 1972, 81, Global Economic Geography, 1978, An Economic Geography of Hungary, 1985 (award Hungarian Acad. Sci. 1986). Recipient Gold Degree of Work award Hungarian State, 1986. Mem. Hungarian Geographic Soc. (v.p. 1980—). Avocation: gardening. Office: Budapest U Econs, Fovam Ter 8, 1093 Budapest Hungary

BERNATOWICZ, FRANK ALLEN, management consultant, expert witness; b. Chgo., Nov. 3, 1954; s. Chester and Pauline (Maciula) B.; m. Kathleen Ann Carlson, Apr. 29, 1978; children: Amy Elizabeth, Laura Ann. BSEE, U. Ill., 1976; MBA in Fin., Loyola U., Chgo., 1981, postgrad. in acctg., 1982-84. Registered profl. engr., Ill.; CPA, Ill. Engr. Commonwealth Edison Co., Chgo., 1976-79, gen. engr., 1979-82, prin. engr., 1982-84; sr. cons. Brenner Group, Chgo., 1984-85; supr. Ernst & Young (formerly Ernst & Whinney), Chgo., 1985, mgr., 1985-86; sr. mgr. Ernst & Young, Chgo., 1986-88, ptnr., 1989-96; prin. J. Alix & Assoc., Chgo., 1996-99; ptnr. PricewaterhouseCoopers, Chgo., 1999—; spkr. in field. Mem. bd. regents Mercy Boys Home, 1990—. Mem. AICPA, Ill. Soc. CPAs, Nat. Soc. Profl. Engrs., Turnaround Mgmt. Assn., Comml. Law League, Chgo. Soc. Clubs (Met.). Avocations: golf, racquetball, computers, investments. Home: 6543 Hillcrest Dr Burr Ridge IL 60521-5740 Office: PricewaterhouseCoopers 200 E Randolph St Chicago IL 60601-6436

BERNAY, BETTI, artist; d. David Michael and Anna Gaynia (Bernay) Woolin; children: Manette Deitsch, Karen Lynn. Grad. costume design, Pratt Inst.; student, Nat. Acad. Design, N.Y.C., Art Students League, N.Y.C. Exhibited one man shows at Galerie Raymond Duncan, Paris, France, Salas Municipales, San Sebastian, Spain, Circulo de Bellas Artes, Madrid, Spain, Bacardi Gallery, Miami, Fla., Columbia (S.C.) Mus., Columbus (Ga.) Mus., Galerie Andre Weil, Paris, Galerie Hermitage, Monte Carlo, Monaco, Casino de San Remo, Italy, Galerie de Arte de la Caja de Ahorros de Ronda, Malaga, Spain, Centro Artistico, Granada, Spain, Circulo de la Amistad, Cordoba, Spain, Studio H Gallery, N.Y.C., Walter Wallace Gallery, Palm Beach, Fla., Mus. Bellas Artes, Malaga, Harbor House Gallery, Crystal House Gallery, Internat. Gallery, Jordan Marsh, Fontainebleau Gallery, Miami Beach, Carriage House Gallery, Galerie 99, Pageant Gallery, Miami Beach, Rosenbaum Galleries, Palm Beach; exhibited group shows at Painters and Sculptors Soc., Jersey City Mus., Salon de Invierno, Mus. Malaga, Salon des Beaux Arts, Cannes, France, Guggenheim Gallery, Nat. Acad. Gallery, Salmagundi Club, Lever House, Lord & Taylor Art Gallery, Nat. Arts Gallery, Knickerbocker Artists, N.Y.C., Salon des Artistes Independants, Salon des Artistes Francais, Salon Populiste, Paris, Salon de Otono, Nat. Assn. Painters and Sculptors Spain, Madrid, Phipps Gallery, Palm Beach, Artists Equity, Hollywood (Fla.) Mus., Gault Gallery Cheltenham, Phila., Springfield (Mass.) Mus., Met. Mus. and Art Center, Miami, Fla., Planet Ocean Mus., Charter Club, Trade Fair Ams.; represented in permanent collections including Jockey Club Art Gallery, Miami, Mus. Malaga, Circulo de la Amistad, I.O.S. Found., Geneva, Switzerland, others. Bd. dirs. Men's Opera Guild, Project Newborn Neonatal unit Jackson Meml. Hosp.; mem. adv. bd. Jackson Meml. Hosp. Project Newborn; mem. women's com. Bascom Palmer Eye Inst., mem. adv. coun.; mem. working com. Greater Miami Heart Assn., Am. Heart Assn., Am. Cancer Soc., Alzheimer Grand Notable, 2nd Generation Miami Heart Inst., Sunrisers Mentally Retarded, Orchid Ball Com., Newborn Neonatal Intensive Care Unit, U. Miami, Jackson Meml. Hosp.; founder Mt. Sinai Hosp., Miami; benefactor Miami Heart Rsch. Inst.; grand benefactor Neonatal Project

Newborn, Jackson Meml. Hosp., Miami Opera, Am. Cancer Soc., Am. Heart Assn., Alzheimers Notable Care Unit, Greater Miami Opera Guild, March of Dimes, CancerLink, Sylvester Cancer Unit; adv. coun. Bascom Palmer Eye Inst.; founder Mt. Sinai Hosp. Recipient medal City N.Y., medal Sch. Art Leagues, N.Y.C., Prix de Paris Raymond Duncan, others. Mem. Nat. Assn. Painters and Sculptors Spain, Am. Women Artists, Société des Artistes Français, Société des Artistes Independants, Fedn. Francais des Sociétés d'Art Graphique et Plastique, Artists Equity, Am. Artists Profl. League, Am. Fedn. Art, Nat. Soc. Lit. and Arts, Met. Mus. and Arts Center Miami, Pres.'s Club U. Miami, Palm Bay Club, Jockey Club, Turnberry Club, Club of Clubs Internat. Address: 10155 Collins Ave Apt 1705 Bal Harbour FL 33154-1629

BERNAYS, RENÉ LUDWIG, neurosurgeon; b. Zurich, Switzerland, Jan. 29, 1959; s. Ludwig and Gabi (Steinmann) B.; m. Daniela Elisabeth Reutter, Sept. 16, 1989; children: Valerie, Florence, Catherine. MD, Med. Sch. U. Zurich, Switzerland, 1987; Neurosurgery bd. exam., U. Zurich, 1997. Resident Brain Rsch. Lab. U. Zurich, 1985-87, Neurol. Dept./Neurophysiol. Lab. Kantonsspital, St. Gallen, Switzerland, dept. Traumatology, U. Hosp., Zurich, 1992; resident/asst. med. dir. dept. neurosurgery U. Hosp., Zurich, 1993-99; vis. doctor Neurosurgical Dept. U. Calif. L.A., 1991. Contbr. articles to profl. jours. Chief lt. Swiss Army, 1990-98. Recipient fellowship in molecular neuroanatomy, Amsterdam, 1987, Health Sci. Ctr., U. Va., 1997, Mt. Sinai Hosp., N.Y., 1997. Mem. Swiss Neurosurgical Soc. Roman Catholic. Avocation: classical music. Office: Dept Neurosurgery U Hosp, Frauenklinikstrasse 10, 8091 Zurich Switzerland

BERNDTSSON, GUNILLA HELEN, acoustical engineer; b. Gothenburg, Sweden, June 3, 1958; d. Sven Valdemar and Emmy Elisabet (Olsson) Carlsson; m. Jan Olof Berndtsson, Mar. 15, 1992; children: Clara Elisabet, Siri Johanna. MS in Engring. Physics, Chalmers U. Tech., 1988; PhD, Royal Inst. Tech. Stockholm, 1995. Rsch. engr., rschr. Royal Inst. Tech., Stockholm, 1989-98; rschr. Ericsson Radio Sys., Stockholm, 1997—. Contbr. articles to profl. jours. Grantee Swedish Coun. for Work Life Rsch., 1997. Mem. Swedish Acoustic Soc., Acoustical Soc. Am. Avocation: singing. Home: Solstigen 20, 131 46 Nacka Sweden Office: Ericsson Radio Sys, Torshamnsgatan 23, 164 80 Stockholm Sweden

BERNE, MICHEL, educator; b. Saint-Etienne, France, June 2, 1954; m. Jacqueline; children: Emmanuel, Frederic, François. MS in Mining Engring., St.-Etienne Sch. Mines, 1976; MS in Petroleum Econs., Sch. Petroleum and Motors, 1977; PhD, U. Paris, 1979. Instr. King Fahad U. Petroleum and Minerals, Dhahran, Saudi Arabia, 1983-88; engr. French Petroleum Inst., Rueil, France, 1983-88; internat. councellor France Telecom U., Paris, 1988-92; head mgmt. dept. Nat. Telecomm. Inst., Evry, France, 1992-96; prof. Nat. Telecomm. Inst., Evry, 1996—; vis. prof. Mich. State U., 2000. Co-author: The Saudi Arabian Economy, 1986. Office: Inst Nat Des Telecomm, 9 Rue Charles Fourier, 91011 Evry France

BERNER, BOEL, sociology educator; b. Helsingborg, Sweden, Aug. 3, 1945; d. Carl and Karin (Sylwan) B.; m. Bengt Olle Bengtsson; 1 child, Sara. BA, U. Lund, Sweden, 1967, PhD, 1981, Docent, 1988. Editor Internat. Trade Press, London, 1967-68; asst. prof. Lund U., 1982-88, univ. lectr., 1988-91; univ. prof. Linköping (Sweden) U., 1991—. Author: The World of Technics, 1981, The Paths to Knowledge, 1989, The State of Things, 1996, Perpetuum Mobile?, 1999; editor: From Sewing Machine to Cyborg, 1996, Gendered Practices, 1997, Manoeuvring in an Environment of Uncertainty, 2000. Office: Dept Tech & Social Change, Linköping UK, S-58183 Linköping Sweden

BERNER, JOACHIM, editor-in-chief, publisher; b. Björketorp, Sweden, Nov. 26, 1962; m. Elisabet Hagardt; 1 child, Henrietta. MBA, Gothenburg (Sweden) Sch. Econ., 1993. Bus. editor Göteborg-Posten, 1990-92, mng. editor, dep. pub., 1993-96; sta. mgr., pub. Radio Rix, 1992-93; mng. editor, dep. pub. Dagens Nyheter, 1996-98; editor-in-chief, pub. Dagens Nyheter, Stockholm, 1998-2000, editor-in-chief, grn. mgr., pub., 2000—. Office: Dagens Nyheter, Gjörwellsgatan 30, 10515 Stockholm Sweden

BERNET, STEFFEN, engineering executive, electrical engineer; b. Ilmenau, Thuringia, Germany, Nov. 20, 1963; s. Dieter and Renate (Seeber) B.; m. Kerstin Barton, Feb. 20, 1987; children: Christiane, Daniel. Diploma, Tech. U. Dresden (Germany), 1990; PhD, Tech. U. Ilmenau (Germany), 1995. Scientific asst. Tech. U. Ilmenau, 1990-94; devel. engr. Siemens, Leipzig, Germany, 1994-95; hon. fellow U. Wis., Madison, 1995-96; scientist ABB Corp. Rsch., Heidelberg, Germany, 1996-98; head elec. drives groups ABB Corp. Rsch., Heidelberg, 1998—; sub-program mgr. power electronics sys. 1999—. Author: Semiconductors auZCS in Soft Switching Power Converters, 1995; contbr. 34 articles to profl. jours.; 5 patents in field of power electronics, 1999—. Lance cpl. German Army, 1983-84. Postdoc. grantee German Acad. Exch. Svc., 1995-96. Mem. IEEE (IAS, PES). Lutheran. Avocations: hiking, nature photography. Office: ABB Corp Rsch, Speyerer Str 4, 69115 Heidelberg Germany

BERNFELD, WENDY LYNN, media consultant company executive, lawyer; b. Montreal, Que., Can., May 16, 1957; arrived in The Netherlands, 1991; d. Edward Henry and Sybil Susan (Klions) B.; m. Eelke Peter Westra; children: Erik Stefan, Jesper Nils. Student, Vanier Coll., Montreal, 1974-76, McGill U., Montreal, 1977; LLB, Queens U., Kingston, Ont., 1980. Bar: Ont. Assoc. Silverstein & Selznick, Toronto, Ont., 1982-84; v.p. bus. affairs First Choice/The Movie Network, Toronto, 1984-91; mng. dir. Atlantis Films, Amsterdam, The Netherlands, 1991-93; v.p. bus. affairs and spl. projects ProNet/Nethold, Amsterdam, 1993-96; CEO Canal Plus Internat. Acquisitions, Amsterdam, 1996-98; mng. dir. Rights Stuff BV, Amsterdam, 1999—; law clk. to chief justice Supreme Ct., Ont., 1981-82. Bd. dirs. Theatre Works, Toronto, 1980-84. Mem. Law Soc. U.K. Jewish. Avocations: film, theater, hiking, cycling. Home and Office: Johannes Verhulstraat 197hs, 1075HA Amsterdam The Netherlands

BERNHARD, PRINCE (LEOPOLD FREDERIK EVERHARD JULIUS COERT KAREL GODFRIED PIETER), Prince of the Netherlands, Prince of Lippe-Biesterfeld; b. Jena, Germany, June 29, 1911; assumed Netherlands nationality, 1936; s. Prince Bernhard zur Lippe and Baroness Armgard von Sierstorpff-Cramm; m. Juliana Louise Emma Marie Wilhelmina, Princess of The Netherlands, Jan. 7, 1937; children: Beatrix Wilhelmina Armgard, Irene Emma Elizabeth, Margriet Francisca, Maria Christina. Referendar juris, U. Berlin; LLD, State U. Utrecht, 1946, U. Montreal, 1958, U. B.C., 1958, U. Mich., 1965; D.Econs, Free U. Amsterdam, 1965; D.Tech. Sci., U. Advanced Tech., Delft, 1951; D. Natural Sci., U. Basel, 1971. Appted. air cdre. (hon.) R.A.F.V.R., 1941; chief Netherlands liaison British Forces; col.; major gen., chief Netherlands Mission War Office; appted. supreme commdr. lt. gen. Netherlands Armed Forces, 1944; resigned, 1945; Royal commr. bd. Netherlands Trade and Industry Fair; hon. air marshal RAF, 1964—; inspector gen. Armed Forces; admiral gen. Royal Netherlands Air Force; gen. Army, 1954-76; hon. cdre. R.N.Z.A.F., 1973; ret. gen. Netherlands Army and Air Force; ret. adm. Netherlands Navy; founder, regent Prince Bernhard Fund, Praemium Erasmianum Found.; founder European Cultural Found.; founder, pres. World Wide Fund Internat.; councillor Netherlands Inst. Econs., Netherlands U. Econs., Rotterdam; hon. functions number over 200; mem. Coun. for Mil. Affairs of the Realm, Joint Def., Army, Admiralty and Air Force Couns. Mem. bd. Netherlands Trade and Industries Fair; pres., WWF, Netherlands, Rhino Rescue Trust; chair achievement bd. ICBP. Decorated knight grand cross Order of Bath, Royal Victorian Order, Order Brit. Empire; hon. commodore Royal N.Z. Air Force, 1973. Mem. Royal Aeros. Soc. (hon.), Royal Inst. Naval Architects, Aeromed. Soc., Royal Spanish Acad. Address: Soestdijk Palace, Baarn The Netherlands*

BERNHARD, ANDREAS PAUL, engineer; b. Johannesburg, South Africa, Jan. 6, 1971; came to US 1993; s. Andreas franz and Karin Maria B. BS in Aeronautical Engring., U. Witwatersrand, Johannesburg, South Africa, 1992; MS in Aerospace Engring., U. Md., 1995. Engr. Advanced Techs. and Engring., Midrand, South Africa, 1993. Gustave J. Hokeson fellow, 1996. Mem. Am. Helicopter Soc. (Lichten award 1996). Avocations: water polo, flying. Office: U Md Engring Classroom Bldg Rm 3181 College Park MD 20742-0001

BERNHARD, JEFFREY DAVID, dermatologist, editor, educator; b. Buffalo, Oct. 31, 1951. AB, Harvard Coll., 1973; MD, Harvard Med. Sch., 1978. Diplomate Am. Bd. Dermatology. Chief resident dermatology Harvard Med. Sch., Boston, 1982; fellow photomedicine Mass. Gen. Hosp., 1983; mem. faculty Med. Sch. U. Mass., Worcester, 1983—; dir. dermatology, assoc. prof. Sch. Medicine, 1986—; assoc. dean for admissions Med. Sch., 1989-95, prof. Med. Sch., 1992—. Author: Itch: Mechanisms and Management of Pruritus, 1994; asst. editor Jour. Am. Acad. Dermatology, 1993-98, editor, 1998—; mem. editl. bd. Jour. European Acad. Dermatology and Venereology, Yearbook of Cancer, 1981-88, Yearbook of Dermatology, 1988-97, Internat. Jour. Dermatology, Jour. Geriat. Dermatology, 1993-97. Knox fellow St. John's Coll., U. Cambridge, 1973-74. Mem. Am. Acad. Dermatology (Presdl. citation 2000), Soc. for Investigative Dermatology, European Acad. Dermatology and Venereology, Am. Dermatol. Assn., Royal Soc. Medicine, Sir James Saunders Soc., Aesculapian Club Boston, Assn. Profs. Dermatology, New Eng. Dermatol. Soc. (pres. 1990-91), Quinsigamond Dermatol. Soc., James C. White Club, Phi Beta Kappa, Sigma Xi. Office: U Mass Meml Med Ctr 55 Lake Ave N Worcester MA 01655-0002

BERNHARD, MANFRED EUGEN, publisher; b. Berlin, Apr. 19, 1917; came to U.S. 1932; s. Lucian and Margaret (van Rensselaer) B.; m. Joan Edgar, Aug. 21, 1947 (div. 1965); children: Manfred, Eugen, Lucienne, Damaris, Robert; m. Gwendolyn Harris, Aug. 25, 1975 (div.); 1 child, Royal. BA, Pratt Inst., Bklyn., 1935, U. Mo., 1942. Designer, builder N.Y. World's Fair, 1938-39; graphic designer Lucian Bernhard Studio, N.Y.C., 1940-42, dir. graphic sales, 1951-54; faculty dept. humanities Stephens Coll., Columbia, Mo., 1942-43; graphic designer MB Graphics, N.Y.C., 1944-50; pres. Webs Advt. Corp., 1954-96; founder, pres. Bernhard Ventures Corp., Palm Beach, Fla., 1996—; cons. Kids' Talk Comm., Old Lyme, 1987-93. Exec. prodr. motion picture Dr. Black/Mr. Hyde, 1975; prodr. numerous stage prodns., including Born Female, 1976, Love the Skin You're In, 1981, Chasing Rainbows, 1988. Recipient Kids Talk Day Proclamation City of L.A., 1988. Democrat. Lutheran. Avocations: counseling disadvantaged children, cooking, nature walks. Office: Bernhard Ventures Corp PO Box 549 Palm Beach FL 33480-0549

BERNHEIM, JAN L., medical scientific consultant, educator; b. Ukkel, Brussels, Belgium, Aug. 25, 1941; d. Gabriel M. Bernheim and Nelly S. Demey; m. Clara M. Castelyns, Aug. 14, 1968; children: Nathalie, Thomas, Nele, Sarah; 1 foster child, Guy van der Hofstadt. MD, U. Gent, Belgium, 1966; PhD, Vrije U., Brussels, 1978; M in Pub. Adminstrn., U. Libre, Brussels, 1989. Asst. pathology U. Gent, 1966-68; asst. internal medicine U. Amsterdam, The Netherlands, 1968-71; asst. J. Bordet Cancer Inst., Brussels, 1971-74; assoc. prof. U. Calif., San Diego, 1974-77; lectr. Vrije U., Brussels, 1978-87, prof., 1988—; med. sci. svc. cons. UCB-Pharma, Brussels, 1986-88; ind. cons. Brussels, 1998—; founding chmn. study group of quality of life European Orgn. Rsch. on Treatment of Cancer, Brussels, 1979-81; vis. prof. Nat. U. Rwanda Med. Sch., 1978-81. Contbr. numerous articles to profl. jours. Fellow ACP; mem. Royal Coll. Medicine (faculty pharm. physicians). Avocations: tennis, sailing. Office: Vrije U Brussels Med Sch, Laarbeeklaan 103, B 1090 Brussels Belgim

BERNHOLZ, PETER FERDINAND, economics educator; b. Bad Salzuflen, Germany, Feb. 18, 1929; arrived in Switzerland, 1971; s. Heinrich and Johanna (Jansen) B.; m. Elisabeth Homann, Aug. 25, 1960; children: Irina Siegrist, Juliane Bernholz Cavalli. MA, Marburg (Germany) U., 1953, D in Econs., 1955. Asst. Frankfurt and Munich (Germany) U., 1956-61; asst. prof. Frankfurt (Germany) U., 1962-66; prof. Tech. U., Berlin, 1966, U. Basel (Switzerland), 1970—; guest prof. MIT, 1969, Va. Poly. U., 1974, 78, Stanford (Calif.) U., 1981, UCLA, 1986-87, Australian Nat. U., 1993, U. Calif., Irvine, 1998; permanent rsch. assoc. Ctr. for Study of Pub. Choice, George Mason U., Fairfax, Va. Mem. Macro Econ. Policy Group, Brussels, 1988-90; mem., cons. Coun. of Advisors of the German Min. of Econs., 1974—. Mem. European Pub. Choice Soc. (pres. 1974-80), Mont Pelerin Soc. (bd. dirs. 1992-98), Bavarian Avad. Scis. E-mail: peter.bernholz@unibas.ch. Office: U Basel, Petersgraben 51, 4003 Basel Switzerland

BERNIÉ, JEAN-LOUIS, foreign diplomat; b. Querigut, France, Aug. 22, 1953. Mem. European Parliament, 1999—, mem. com. on employment and social affairs, substitute com. on environment, pub. health, consumer policy; mem. Group for a Europe of Democracies and Diversities; mem. delegation for relations with People's Republic of China. *

BERNIERI, FRANK JOHN, social psychology educator; b. Bklyn., May 2, 1961; s. Gene J. and Rose (Autunnale) B.; divorced; 1 child, Jennifer. BA, U. Rochester, 1983; PhD, Harvard U., 1988. Asst. prof. social psychology Oreg. State U., Corvallis, 1988-93, assoc. prof., 1993-94; assoc. prof. U. Toledo, Ohio, 1994—. Author: (with others) Coordinated Movement in Human Interaction, 1991; mem. editorial bd. Jour. Nonverbal Behavior, 1990—; contbr. articles to profl. jours. Fellow Harvard U., 1987; grantee NIH, 1988, Oreg. State U. Coll. Liberal Arts, 1990; NSF Young Investigator awardee, 1992. Mem. AAAS, APA, Am. Psychol. Soc., Soc. for Personality and Social Psychology, Soc. for Exptl. Social Psychology. Democrat. Office: U Toledo Dept Psychology Toledo OH 43606

BERNIK, FRANCE, science academy executive, literary historian; b. Ljubljana, Slovenia, May 13, 1927; s. Franc and Cecilija (Smole) B.; m. Marija Kanc, July 14, 1956; 1 child, Romana. Degree in Slavic Philology, U. Ljubljana, 1951, PhD in Lit. Scis., 1960. Teaching asst. Slovene lit. U. Ljubljana, 1951-57, prof., 1971—; editor, sec. Slovenska Matica, Ljubljana, 1961-72; with Slovenian Acad. Scis. and Arts. Rsch. Ctr., 1972—, sci. advisor Inst. Slovene Lit. and Lit. Scis., 1977—, ret.; pres. Slovenska Akademija Znanosti in Umetnosti, Ljubljana, 1992—; lectr., vis. prof. various univs. abroad. Author books and monographs: The Lyrics of Simon Jenko, 1962, Cankar's Early Prose, 1976, Simon Jenko, 1979, Problems of Slovene Literature, 1980, Typology of Cankar's Prose, 1983, Ivan Cankar: A Monograph, 1987, Slovene War Prose 1941-80, 1988, Studies on Slovene Poetry, 1993, Slowenische Literatur im europäischen Kontext, 1993, Ivan Cankar: Ein slowenischer Schriftsteller des europäischen Symbolismus, 1997, Horizons of the Slovenian Literature, 1999; editor-in-chief scholarly series Collected Works of Slovene Poets and Writers, 1981—; editl. bds. numerous scholarly jours. Named Amb. Republic of Slovenia in Science, 1994, Comdr. de l'Ordre de St. Fortunat, 1996; recipient Internat. Cultural Diploma of Honor, 1996, Eques commendator Ordinis sancti Gregorii Magni, the Vatican, 1996, Golden Hon. Decoration Freedom award Rep. Slovenia, 1997, Zois award Rep. Slovenia, 1999. Mem. Internat. Acad. Energy, L'Academia del Mediterraneo, Soc. Slovene Studies (hon.), Acad. Scientiarum et Artium Europaea (hon., sen.), Croatian Acad. Scis. and Arts. Office: Slovenian Acad Scis & Arts, Novi trg 3, 1000 Ljubljana Slovenia

BERNING, JESPER, lawyer; b. Copenhagen, Feb. 7, 1944; s. Sigurd Godvin and Ellen (Grum-Schwensen) B.; m. Karin Bak-Jensen, Aug. 5, 1967; children: Jakob, Christel, Emil. Grad., Gentoftestatsskole, Denmark, 1962; LLM, Copenhagen U., 1966, LLD, 1974. Bar: Denmark 1970, Supreme Ct. Denmark 1978. Law clk. B. Helmer Nielsen, Denmark, 1969-71; rsch. scholar U. Mich., Ann Arbor, 1971-72; assoc. prof. U. Copenhagen, 1972-75; ptnr. Berning Schlüter Hald, Copenhagen, 1975-98; chmn., bd. dirs. various internat. corps. Contbr. numerous articles to profl. publs.; author legal treaties. With Danish Air Force, 1966-67. Mem. IBA, Danish Bar Assn. Avocations: tennis, golf, skiing, sailing. Home: 6 Valleroedgade, DK-2960 Rungsted Kyst Denmark Office: Jesper Berning Ltd, 6B Valleroedgade, DK-2960 Rungsted Kyst Denmark Office: 10 bis rue de Chateau, F 83440 Fayence France

BERNING, ROBERT WILLIAM, librarian; b. Carroll, Iowa, Dec. 2, 1949; s. Norbert John and Marjorie Lavine (Miller) B. BSE, N.W. Mo. State U., 1972; MLS, Emporia State U., 1974. Cert. pub. libr., Iowa. Sch. libr. Mount Ayr (Iowa) Cmty. Schs., 1974-76, Wall Lake (Iowa) Cmty. Schs., 1977-79, West Point (Nebr.) Pub. Schs., 1979-81; dir. Dubuque County Libr., Farley, Iowa, 1981-82; sch. libr. HLV Cmty. Schs., Victor, Iowa, 1982-84; dir. Carlisle (Iowa) Pub. Libr., 1985—; mem. adv. bd. State Libr. Iowa, Des Moines, 1987, 89; mem. adv. com. Ctrl. Iowa Regional Libr., Clive, 1992-94, 98—. Libr. rep. Lanning Bequest com. City of Carlisle, 1995-97, Mng. Info. for Rural Am. (MIRA), 1998; mem. com., task force Iowans Can't Wait (Enrich Iowa), State Libr. Iowa, Des Moines, 1995-96. Mem.

ALA, KC, Iowa Libr. Assn. (govtl. affairs com. 1988-91), Iowa Small Libr. Assn. (sec. 1985-87), Carlisle Lion's Club, Carlisle C. of C. (libr. rep. 1990—), Mayor's Select Com. on Property Taxes, Des Moines, 1998-99. Roman Catholic. Avocations: collecting antiques, travel, gardening. Office: Carlisle Pub Libr 135 School St PO Box S Carlisle IA 50047

BERNING, VINCENT THEODOR, philosopher, educator; b. Berlin, July 25, 1933; s. August and Thea (Erhart) B.; m. Ursula Hendrina Baldeaux, Aug. 6, 1966; children: Katharina, Matthias. PhD, U. Munich, 1963. Sr. lectr., prof. Padagogische Hochschule Rheinland, 1971-80; prof. Rheinisch-Westfalische Technische Hochschule, 1980-87, prof. philosophy, 1987-98. Mem. Gen. Soc. Philosophy in Germany, Internat. Soc. Human Rights. Roman Catholic. Avocations: classical literature, theology, history of mind. Home: Waldstrasse 2, D-52159 Roetgen Germany Office: Rheinisch-Westfalische TH, Eilfschornsteinstrasse 16, D-52062 Aachen Germany

BERNOTH, MAREE ANNE, nursing educator; b. Newcastle, NSW, Australia, Apr. 18, 1954; d. Eris and Mary Catherine (McMahon) Blackford; m. Maxwell James Bernoth, May 17, 1975; children: Rebecca, Simone, Karl. BSN, Charles Sturt U., 1994; diploma adult edn. and tng., U. New Eng., 1997, postgrad. RN Psychiatry, RN Geriatrics; registered workplace assessor; accredited manual handling trainer. Nurse Morisset Psychiat. Hosp., Australia, 1980-85, Allandale Aged Care Facility, Cessnock, Australia, 1985-91, Mater Hosp., Waratah, Australia, 1991-92; educator Mercy Hospice, Newcastle, 1992-94, Allandale Aged Care Facility, Cessnock, 1994-97; lectr. U. Newcastle, 1997—; cons. Hunter Health, Newcastle, 1999. Contbr. articles to profl. jours. Named Nurse of Yr. North Ryde Psychiat. Ctr., Sydney, 1974. Mem. Australian Nurse Tchrs. Soc., Wound Found. Australia. Avocations: swimming, rugby, cycling, rowing, classical music. Office: Faculty of Nursing, Univ Newcastle, Newcastle 2308, Australia

BERNS, SANDRA SPELMAN, law educator; b. San Francisco, Dec. 9, 1940; d. James R. and Marilyn Spelman; m. Morton Leon Berns, June 29, 1962; 1 child, Dov. BA, U. Calif., Berkeley, 1962; LLB, U. Tasmania, 1986, PhD, 1992. Social worker Alameda County Welfare Dept., Oakland, Calif., 1963-67; tchr. Oakland Unified Sch. Dist., 1968-71, Mt. Scopus Coll., Burwood, Victoria, 1972-89, Sacred Heart Coll., Newtown, Tasmania, 1991; from law lectr. to assoc. prof. law U. Tasmania, Hobart, 1986-95; dean law Griffith U., Nathan, QLD, 1996—, prof. law, 1995—. Author: Concise Jurisprudence, 1993, Company Law and Governance: An Australian Perspective, 1998, To Speak as a Judge: Difference, Voice and Power, 1999. Mem. Queensland Women Lawyers. Office: Griffith U, Nathan Campus, Nathan QLD, Australia 4111

BERNSEN, NIELS OLE, information scientist, educator; b. Skanderborg, Denmark, July 14, 1947; s. Edmond Hviid and Gunder Kathrine Bernsen; m. Lone Adler, Jan. 31, 1969; children: Jonathan, Markus. MA, Odense (Denmark) U., 1972, PhD, 1976. Cert. philosophy. Jr. rsch. fellow Odense U., 1972-74, sr. rsch. fellow, 1974-77, rsch. fellow on the Danish state budget, 1977-80, lectr. philosophy, 1980-85, prof. natural interactive sys., 1997—, head dept., 1984-85; founder, dir. Natural Interactive Sys. Lab., 1998—; vis. rschr. in charge cognitive sci. European Commn. Divsn. Forecast & Assessment in Sci. & Tech., Brussels, 1986-87; co-founder Esprit long-term rsch., dep. head divsn. Esprit Programme in Info. Techs., Brussels, 1987-89; rsch. prof. cognitive sci. Roskilde (Denmark) U., 1989-97; vis. rschr. Oxford (Eng.) U., 1976, 80; founder, dir. Ctr. Cognitive Sci., Roskilde U., 1989-97; founding mem. coun. scientists Internat. Human Frontier Sci. Program, Strasbourg, France, 1989-96; chmn. bd. dirs. Ctr. for Lang. Tech., Copenhagen, 1991-95; dir. Ctr. for Cognitive Informatics, Roskilde U. and Risoe Nat. Lab., 1991-95; mem. 5-year evaluation panel European Commns. Programme for Internat. Cooperation in Sci. and Tech., Brussels, 1996; coord. European Network of Excellence in Intelligent Info. Interfaces, Esprit Long-Term Rsch., Brussels, 1996—. Author: Knowledge, A Treatise on Our Cognitive Situatiion, 1978, Heidegger's Theory of Intentionality, 1986, Designing Interactive Speech Systems: From First Ideas to User Testing, 1998; gen. editor: (five volumes) Research Directions in Cognitive Science: European Perspectives, 1989-93. Mem. working group Danish Health Authority and the Danish Ministry of Justice. With Danish Civil Def., 1974. Mem. OECD (working group bioinformatics Megasci. Forum 1996-98), European Network of Excellence in Lang. and Speech (founding mem. exec. bd., chmn. rsch. com. 1991—), Danish Acad. for the Tech. Scis., Danish Mountaineering Club (rock climbing instr.). Home: Skraeddervaenget 17, 5800 Nyborg Denmark Office: Odense Univ, Campusvej 55, 5230 Odense Denmark

BERNSTEIN, BASIL BERNARD, sociology educator; b. London, Nov. 1, 1924; s. Percival and Julia (Parks) B.; m. Marion Black, Nov. 24, 1954; children: Saul, Francis. BS in Econs., London Sch. Econs. and Polit. Sci., 1951; PhD, U. London, 1963; DLitt (hon.), U. Leicester, Eng., 1974, U. Rochester, 1989; FilHDr (hon.), U. Lund, Sweden, 1980; DUniv, Open U., London, 1983; PhD, U. Athens, 1996; LLD, U. East London. Tchr. City Day Coll., London, 1954-60; hon. rsch. asst. Univ. Coll. London, 1960-62; reader in sociology of edn. Inst. Edn., U. London, 1962-67, prof., 1967-79, Karl Mannheim prof., 1979—, sr. pro-dir., pro-dir. rsch., 1984-91, prof. emeritus sociology of edn., 1991—; active Social Sci. Rsch. Coun., U.K., 1968-72. Author: Class Codes and Control, Vol. I, 1971, rev. editl, 1974, Vol. II, 1973, Vol. III, 1975, rev. edit., 1977, Vol. IV, 1990, Pedagogy, Symbolic Control and Identity, 1996. Mem. Academia Europea. Mem. Labour Party. Jewish. Avocations: theatre, arts, good conversation. Home: 90 Farquhar Rd, London SE19 1LT, England Office: Inst Edn U London, Bedford Way, London WC1 HONS, England

BERNSTEIN, CARL, jewelry designer, artist; b. Botosani, Romania, Dec. 11, 1930; came to US, 1976; s. Shalom and Deborah B.; m. Lena Goldstein, Nov. 12, 1951 (div. June 1978); m. Sylvia Dorfman, Aug. 10, 1983; children: Shlomo, Selma, Rony. Student, Laurian, Romania, 1948, art sch., Bat Yam, Israel, 1965-70. Tchr. arts, art history art sch., Bat Yam, 1972-75; owner Gold Styles Inc., N.Y.C., 1982—; chmn. Jewelers Orgn. Tel-Aviv (Israel), 1970-75, Art Students Assn. Exhibited in shows at World Art Gallery, N.Y.C., 1998, N.Y. Tech. Inst. Show, 1999, Arts Forum, N.Y.C., 1999-2000, Flecher Gallery, Woodstock, N.Y., 2000, 4 West Gallery, Piermont, N.Y., 2000. Recipient Zahal award Israeli Army, 1953-58. Democrat. Jewish. Avocations: painting, travel, camping, archaeology. Home: 8200 Boulevard E Apt 24G North Bergen NJ 07047-6044 Office: Gold Styles Inc 64 W 48th St New York NY 10036-1708

BERNSTEIN, DONALD SCOTT, lawyer; b. Bklyn., July 11, 1953; s. Emanuel and Shirley (Smithline) B.; m. Jo Ellen Finkel, May 31, 1987; children: Daniel Emanuel, Julia Clare. BA, Princeton U., 1975; JD, U. Chgo., 1978. Bar: N.Y. 1979, U.S. Dist. Ct. (ea. and so. dists.) N.Y. 1979. Assoc. Davis Polk & Wardwell, N.Y.C., 1978-86, ptnr., 1986—; panelist Practicing Law Inst., N.Y.C., 1983—, Am. Law Inst., ABA, 1991—, Am. Bankruptcy Inst., 1991—; mem. vis. com. U. Chgo. Law Sch., 1995-98, chmn., 1997-98; mem. ofcl. U.S. del. Insolvency Working Group, UN Commn. on Internat. Trade Law. Contbg. author Collier on Bankruptcy, 1996—, bd. editors, 2000—. Bd. dirs. Altro Health and Rehab. Svcs., Bronx, N.Y., 1988-90, N.Y. chpt. Am. Diabetes Assn., 1992-96; mem. exec. com. bankruptcy lawyers div. United Jewish Appeal Fedn., 1985—. Mem. ABA (bus. bankruptcy com., com. on legal opinions), Am. Coll. Bankruptcy, New York County Lawyers Assn. (bd. dirs. 1992-94), Nat. Bankruptcy Conf. (exec. com. 1996-99), Am. Bankruptcy Inst., Assn. Bar City N.Y. (audit com., 2000—, com. on bankruptcy and corp. reorgn. 1979-83, 85-88, chmn. 1993-96, mem. tribar opinion com. 1988—, chmn. 1998—), Internat. Insolvency Inst. (bd. dirs.). Office: Davis Polk & Wardwell 450 Lexington Ave Fl 31 New York NY 10017-3982

BERNSTEIN, MARK R., retired lawyer; b. York, Pa., Apr. 7, 1930; s. Phillip G. Bernstein and Evelyn (Greenfield) Spielman; m. E. Louise Bernstein, May 10, 1955; children: Phillip, Cary, Adam, Andrew, Jonathan, Evan. BA, U. Pa., 1952; JD, Yale U., 1957. Bar: N.C., U.S. Dist. Ct. (we. dist.) N.C., U.S. Ct. Appeals, U.S. Custom Ct. Atty. Kennedy, Covington, Lobdell, & Hickman, Charlotte, N.C., 1957-60, Haynes, Graham, Bernstein & Baucom, Charlotte, N.C., 1960-67; atty. Parker, Poe, Adams & Bernstein, Charlotte, N.C., 1968-98, chmn., 1992-97; bd. dirs. Family Dollar Stores, Inc., Nat. Welders Supply Co., Inc. Bd. dirs., chmn. The Found. of the Carolinas, Inc., The Wildacres Found.; past pres. Charlotte Symphony Assn.; past chmn. mayor's com. for a Performing Arts Ctr., 1983-85, com. mem. Performing Arts Ctr. Task Force, 1987; chmn. N.C. Econ. Devel. Bd.; past pres. Temple Beth El, Charlotte Jewish Cmty. Ctr., Charlotte Civitan Club, Am. Symphony Orch. League, Golden Circle Theatre, Found. of Shalom Park; past mem. exec. com. Yale Law Sch.; past mem. bd. N.C. Blumenthal Performing Arts Ctr. Recipient Disting. Svc. award Jaycees, 1961, State of Israel Humanitarian award, 1981, Charlotte Fedn. of Jewish Charities A Man of the Ages award, 1985, Silver Medallion award NCCJ, 1995, Israel Humanitarian award, The Vanguard award for personal svcs. Arts and Sci. Coun., 1998. Mem. Mecklenburg County Bar Assn. (past pres.), Charlotte City Club, The Tower Club (bd. dirs.), Olde Providence Racquet Club (past pres.). Democrat. Home: 5300 Hardison Rd Charlotte NC 28226-6426

BERNSTEIN, ROBERT GEOFFREY, business consultant; b. Encino, Calif., May 24, 1967; s. Donald and Ann Bernstein. BA, U. Calif., San Diego, 1989; MBA, U. Rochester, 1993. Contr. Mike Glickman Realty, Woodland Hills, Calif., 1985-90; asst. to CFO Ctrl. Electric, L.A., 1990-91; mgr. Deloitte & Touche, L.A., 1993—. Mem. Beta Gamma Sigma. Fax: (113) 694-5113. E-mail: rbernstein@dttus.com. Home: 750 Penn St El Segundo CA 90245-3124 Office: Deloitte & Touche 1000 Wilshire Blvd Los Angeles CA 90017-2457

BERNSTEIN, ROBERT JAY, lawyer; b. Bklyn., July 1, 1948; s. Martin Emanuel and Vera (Muter) B.; m. Janet Rodolico, Oct. 28, 1978. BA cum laude, cert. in pub. and internat. affairs, Princeton U., 1970; JD cum laude, U. Mich., 1975. Bar: Colo. 1976, N.Y. 1977. Law clk. to judge Richard P. Matsch U.S. Dist. Ct., Denver, 1975-76; assoc. Fried, Frank, Harris, Shriver & Jacobson, N.Y.C., 1976-80; assoc. Cowan, Liebowitz & Latman, P.C., N.Y.C., 1980-82, ptnr., 1982—; mem. faculty, lectr. on copyright devels. Practicing Law Inst. Program, 1986, 88, 91, New Music Sem., 1987; guest lectr. on entertainment law U. Mich., 1987, 90; lectr. copyright law and litigation Copyright Soc. U.S.A., 1985, 87. Co-author column on copyright law N.Y. Law Jour., 1987—; contbr. articles on copyright law to Billboard mag., Entertainment and Sports Lawyer mag., others. Grantee Princeton U., 1969. Mem. ABA (sec. of patent, trademark and copyright lawyers, 1980—, forum com. on entertainment and sports law Music and Personal Appearances Div., 1980—, com. internat. copyright treaties and laws 1982-84, sub-com. on People's Republic of China., lectr. copyright law, forum com. on the entertainment and sports industries 1986), Am. Intellectual Property Law Assn. (sec., bd. dirs. 1990—, chmn. copyright law com. 1988-90, moderator panel on negotiation recording contracts, 1990, lectr. current devel. copyright law ann. meeting 1989, 93), Assn. Am. Pubs. (lawyers com. 1990—), Copyright Soc. of the USA (v.p. to pres.-elect, 1998-2000), Princeton Club, Fairview Country Club, Greenwich Reform Synagogue Men's Club. Avocations: tennis, jazz saxophone, piano, skiing, golf, Romance languages. Fax: (212) 575-0671. E-mail: RJB@CLL.com. Office: Cowan Liebowitz & Latman PC Fl 35 1133 Avenue Of The Americas New York NY 10036-6710

BERNSTEIN, SOL, cardiologist, educator; b. West New York, N.J., Feb. 3, 1927; s. Morris Irving and Rose (Leibowitz) B.; m. Suzi Maris Sommer, Sept. 15, 1963; 1 son, Paul. AB in Bacteriology, U. Southern Calif., 1952, MD, 1956. Diplomate Am. Bd. Internal Medicine. Intern Los Angeles County Hosp., 1956-57, resident, 1957-60; practice medicine specializing in cardiology L.A., 1960—; staff physician dept. medicine Los Angeles County Hosp. U. So. Calif. Med. Center, L.A., 1960—, chief cardiology clinics, 1964, asst. dir. dept. medicine, 1965-72; chief prof. services Gen. Hosp., 1972-74; med. dir. Los Angeles County-U So. Calif. Med. Center, L.A., 1974-94; med. dir. central region Los Angeles County, 1974-78; dir. Dept. Health Services, Los Angeles County, 1978; assoc. dean Sch. Medicine, U. So. Calif., L.A., 1986-94, assoc. prof., 1968—; med. dir. Health Rsch. Assn., L.A., 1995—; cons. Crippled Childrens Svc. Calif., 1965—. Contbr. articles on cardiac surgery, cardiology, diabetes and health care planning to med. jours. Served with AUS, 1946-47, 52-53. Fellow A.C.P., Am. Coll. Cardiology; mem. Am. Acad. Phys. Execs., Am. Fedn. Clin. Research, N.Y. Acad. Sci., Los Angeles, Am. heart assns., Los Angeles Soc. Internal Medicine, Los Angeles Acad. Medicine, Sigma Xi, Phi Beta Phi, Phi Eta Sigma, Alpha Omega Alpha. Home: 4966 Ambrose Ave Los Angeles CA 90027-1756 Office: 1640 Marengo St Los Angeles CA 90033-1036

BERNSTEIN, SUSAN See DVORA, SUSAN

BERNSTROM, RICHARD SVEN, investment banker, consultant; b. Paris, Sept. 27, 1941; came to the U.S., 1968; s. Sven Bror and Margareta Agaht (DeGeer) B.; div. Jan. 1986; 1 child, Erik. Grad., Lundsburgs Skola, 1961; M in Polit. Sci., Lund (Sweden) U., 1967; MBA, INSEAD, Fontainbleau, France, 1968. Investment officer Citiban, N.Y.C., 1968-71, Warburg-Paribas Becker, N.Y.C., 1971-78; exec. dir. Bank of Am. Internat., London, 1978-86; mng. dir. Prudential Bache Securities, London, 1986-92; cons. Price Waterhouse-Ctrl., Tashkent, Republic of Uzbekistan, 1993-94; pres., CEO Ctrl. Asian-Am. Enterprise Fund, Washington, 1994-98; independent cons., 1999—. Sgt. Swedish Infantry, 1961-62. Home: 35 Duchess of Bedford House, London W87QW, England

BERNTSON, KEVIN ANTON OLOF MARTIN, educational administrator, art historian, psychologist; b. St. Paul, May 18, 1951; s. Wilfred C. and Catherine (Sullivan) B. BA, St. Mary's Coll. Calif., 1973; MA, U. San Francisco, 1979; diploma in culinary arts, U. Johnson & Wales, 1982; MS, Mt. St. Mary's Coll., 1986; diploma in French cuisine, Le Cordon Bleu, London, 1996; PhD, U. Kent, Eng., 1998. Tchr. Sacred Heart H.S., San Francisco, 1973-76; dean of students Cretin H.S., St. Paul, 1976-77; guidance counselor Christian Bros. H.S., Sacramento, 1977-79; asst. prin. Providence H.S., Burbank, Calif., 1979-82; asst. dir. devel. Mt. St. Mary's Coll., L.A., 1982-83; dean discipline Mater Dei H.S., Santa Ana, Calif., 1982-85; prin. St. Anthony H.S., Long Beach, 1985-89; dir. internat. admissions U. Brussels, 1989-92; clin. psychotherapist NATO-European Union, 1991-94; art history instr. U. Kent, 1994—. Author: Cross-Cultural Counseling in the Classroom, 1988, History of Norton Hamlet, 1997, Communicating Persona Betwixt Medieval Monks, 1998. Mem. ASCD, Calif. Pers. and Guidance Assn., Master Chefs Gt. Britain, L.A. Pers. and Guidance Assn., Am.-Scandinavian Found., Nat. Coun. Tchrs. English, Calif. Assn. Marriage and Family Therapists, Faversham Soc., Sisters of Providence Assocs., Soc. Creative Anachronism. Home: La Maison des Lilas, rue des Druides, F 28170 Blevy France Office: U Kent, Internat Office, CT2 7NZ Canterbury CT2 TNZ Kent, England

BERNUS, PETER, researcher; b. Budapest, Hungary, Oct. 15, 1949; arrived in Australia, 1989; s. John Bernus and Maria-Valeria Nagy; m. Iren Pinter. MSc in Engring. in Electronic Tech., Budapest Tech. U., 1974; PhD in Engring. Scis., Hungarian Acad. Scis., 1986. Rsch. fellow Computer and Automation Inst. Hungarian Acad. Scis., 1976-79, sr. rsch. fellow Computer and Automation Inst., 1979-86; vis. rsch. fellow Stichting Matematisch Centrum, Amsterdam, The Netherlands, 1986-88; sr. rsch. fellow Queensland U., Brisbane, Australia, 1989-92; assoc. prof. Griffith U., Brisbane, 1992—; vis. fellow MIT AI Lab. and computer sci. dept. Brown U., Providence, 1979; rsch. asst. Computer and Automation Inst., Hungarian Acad. Scis., 1970-74. Series and volume editor: Springer Verlag Series of Handbooks in Information Systems; contbr. numerous articles to rsch. publs., jours. and internat. confs.; editl. bd.: Computers in Industry; guest editor Concurrent Engring. Rsch. and Applications Internat. Jour.; author, editor: Architectures for Enterprise Integration, International Handbook on Architectures of Information Systems. Recipient Yr.'s Best Thesis award Hungarian Telecomms. Assn., 1974. Mem. IFIP (foundation chair working group WG5.12 Enterprise Integration, chair IFIP-IFAC task force 1996—, chair Internat. Fedn. Automatic Control TC Architecture for Enterprise Integration). Office: Griffith U Nathan Campus, Sch Computing/Info Tech, 4111 Queensland Australia

BERO, JOSEPH MARTIN, manufacturing engineer; b. Chgo., Apr. 27, 1965; s. Stephen and Doris May (Bausch) B.; m. Dawn Maria Calvert; children: Maxwell Alexander, Nathanial Joseph, Quindlan Joseph. B-SChemE, U. Ill., 1987. Registered profl. engr., Calif., Md., Va. Design engr. Chevron, U.S.A., Richmond, Calif., 1987-88; staff mem. BDM Fed., Germantown, Md., 1992-93; project engr. Castol Heavy Duty Lubricants Inc., Balt., 1993-96, mgr. engring. and regulatory affairs, 1996-98, mfg. and engring. mgr., 1998—. Lt. USN, 1988-92. Mem. ASME, NSPE, Nat. Coun. Examiners for Engring. and Surveying. Avocations: woodworking, racquetball, basketball. Home: 4327 Federal Hill Rd Street MD 21154-1124 Office: Castrol Heavy Duty Lubricants Inc 9300 Pulaski Hwy Baltimore MD 21220-2418

BEROUAL, ABDERRAHMANE, electrical engineering educator, researcher; b. El-Khroub, Algeria, Oct. 30, 1951; came to France; s. Said and Chemama (Berkane) B.; m. Halina Juralojc, Oct. 21, 1978; children: Linda, Kamil Eddine. Grad. in Elec. Engring., Ecole Nat. Poly. Algiers, Algeria, 1976; PhD, Tech. U. Wroclaw, Poland, 1979; D of Phys. Scis., Inst. Nat. Poly. Grenoble, France, 1987. Cert. elec. engr., applied physicist. Rschr. Inst. Fundamental Electrotechnic and Electrotech. Tech. U. Wroclaw, 1977-80; asst. prof. Ecole Nat. Poly. Algiers, 1980-83; rschr. Lab. Electrostatique Matériaux Diélectriques Ctr. Nat. Sci. Rsch., Grenoble, 1983-87; assoc. prof. U. Joseph Fourier, Grenoble, 1985-87; prof. Ecole Nat. Poly. Algiers, 1987-92, Ecole Ctrl. Lyon, France, 1992—; cons. Algerian Ministry of H.S. and Sci. Rsch., 1980-83; dir. PhD theses in the area of high voltage tech. and elec. insulation Ecole Nat. Poly. Algiers, 1980—, Ecole Ctrl. Lyon, 1989—. Contbr. articles to profl. jours. Mem. IEEE, N.Y. Acad. Scis. Achievements include contributions to the understanding of prebreakdown and breakdown mechanisms in liquid dielectrics, the characterization of composite materials, models and simulators of discharges in long air gaps and on insulating interfaces; co-inventor of new capacitor structures: quadrupolars. Avocations: poet, polyglot. Office: Ecole Ctrl Lyon, Dept Electrotechnique, BP 163, 69131 Ecully France

BEROUARD, GILLES, advertising company executive; b. Talence, France, Mar. 25, 1962; s. Michel and Paula (Latrille) B.; m. Geraldine Favre, Aug. 25, 1990; children: Ludivine, Jade, Alicia. Grad., Trinity & All Saints Coll., 1983, SUP de C.C. Bordeaux, 1984. From dir. rsch. to regional CEO Euro Rscg New Europe, Czech Republic, 1985—. Office: Euro Rscg Prague, Vinohradska 60, Prague 3 Czech Republic

BERRA, LODOVICO EDOARDO, psychiatrist, psychotherapist; b. Turin, Italy, Sept. 11, 1960; s. Carlo Giuseppe Berra and Etta (Prestandrea) Dentis; m. Patrizia Pipino, Sept. 3, 1997. MD, U. degli Studi Turin, 1988; degree in sexology, Florence, Italy, 1993. Diplomate Italian Bd. Psychiatry and Psychotherapy. Resident in psychiatry U. Turin, 1988-92, intern in psychiatry, 1992-96; pvt. practice psychiatry and psychotherapy Turin, 1996—; cons. Clinica San Paolo, Turin, 1991-93, consultorio Ucipem, Venice, Italy, 1994-95, Centro di Psiicologia Cospes, Turin, 1995—. Author: L'Importenza Sessuale Maschile, 1996, Perversioni Sessuali, 1999; contbr. articles to profl. jours. Mem. Am. Psychiat. Assn., Am. Soc. Clin. Hypnosis, Soc. Existential Analysis. Avocations: golf, tennis. Office: Studio Medico Dott Berra, CSO Fiume 16, 10133 Turin Italy

BERREY, BEDFORD HUDSON, physician; b. Carrollton, Mo., Apr. 20, 1922; s. Robert Wilson and Elizabeth Mary (Hudson) B.; m. Marcia Lois Bagley, May 22, 1943; children: Elizabeth, Barbara, B. Hudson, Christopher, Michael. Student, Kansas City Jr. Coll., Mo., 1939-40; BS in Medicine, U. Mo., 1943; MD, U. Colo., 1945; MA in Internat. Rels., Am. U., 1969. Diplomate Am. Bd. Pediats. Intern Kansas City Gen. Hosp., Mo., 1945-46; resident in pediats. Denver Children's Hosp., 1946-47; practice medicine specializing in pediats. Kansas City, Mo., 1947-48, Harlingen, Tex., 1950-51; fellow in pediats. Ochsner Clinic, New Orleans, 1949; commd. capt. U.S. Army, 1951, advanced through grades to col., 1967; ret., 1976; dep. asst. chief med. dir. VA, Washington, 1976-77; asst. state health commr. Va. Health Dept., Richmond, 1977-84; med. dir. Nat. Alliance Sr. Citizen, 1986-91. Pres. South Tex. Amateur Athletic Union, 1962-63; pres. PTA, Berlin, 1954, Denver, 1952; bd. dirs. Rockbridge Area Hospice, Lexington, Va., 1999-02. Decorated Legion of Merit with 2 oak leaf clusters. Fellow ACP, Am. Acad. Pediats., Am. Coll. Physician Execs.; mem. Med. Soc. Va., Hudson Family Assn. (pres. 1989-90), Masons (32d degree), Shriners. Republican.

BERRI, MOHAMAD HUSSEIN, engineer, researcher; b. Tebnine, South, Lebanon, Mar. 5, 1959; came to U.S., 1987; s. Hussein Ali and Zahra Taleb (Fawaz) B.; m. Marine Adballah, July 27, 1973; children: Ali, Dena, Danny, Reem. BSEE, Gar-Younis U., Bengazi, Lebia, 1985; MSEE, Wayne State U., 1991, PhD, 1996. Rsch. asst. Wayne State U., Detroit, 1989-96, adj. prof., 1996—; rsch. engr. Ford Motor Co., Dearborn, Mich., 1994-97; sr. project engr. TRW Automotive Electronics, Farmington Hills, Mich., 1996-99; design specialist Ford Motor Co.-Visteon, Dearborn, Mich., 1999—. Recipient achievement award City of Dearborn, 1994, Nat. Collegiate Engring. award. Mem. IEEE, NAS, SAE, Control Sys. Soc., Am. Voice Input/Output Soc., Advanced Speech Application and Tech., Internat. Conf. on Acoustics Speech and Signal Processing, Soc. Automotive Engrs. (recognition award 1995), N.Y. Acad. of Sci. (Excellent Acad. Achievement award 1994), Wayne State Alumni Assn. Avocations: reading, swimming, social activity, traveling, music. Home: 4853 Argyle St Dearborn MI 48126-3141

BERRIDGE, MICHAEL JOHN, cell biologist, federal agency administrator; b. Oct. 22, 1938; s. George Kirton Berridge and Stella Elaine Hards; m. Susan Graham Winter, 1965; 2 children. BSc, U. Coll. Rhodesia and Nyasaland; PhD, U. Cambridge, Eng. Post-doctoral fellow U. Va., 1965-66, Case Western Reserve U., Cleve., 1966-69; prof. dept. zoology U. Cambridge, 1969—; dep. chief sci. officer The Babraham Inst., Cambridge, 1987—. Contbr. articles to profl. jours. Recipient Wolf Medicne prize Wolf Foundation, 1994, H.P. Heineken prize Royal Netherlands Academy of Arts and Sciences, 1994, Knight Batchelor, 1997. Avocations: golf, gardening. Office: Lab Molecular Signalling, The Babraham Inst, Cambridge CB2 4AT, England

BERRING, ROBERT CHARLES, JR., law educator, law librarian, former dean; b. Canton, Ohio, Nov. 20, 1949; s. Robert Charles and Rita Pauline (Franta) B.; m. Leslie Applegarth, May 20, 1998; children: Simon Robert, Daniel Fredrick. B.A. cum laude, Harvard U., 1971; J.D., U. Calif.-Berkeley, 1974, M.L.S., 1974. Asst. prof. and reference librarian U. Ill. Law Sch., Champaign, 1974-76; assoc. librarian U. Tex. Law Sch., Austin, 1976-78; dep. librarian Harvard Law Sch., Cambridge, Mass., 1978-81; prof. law, law librarian U. Wash. Law Sch., Seattle, 1981-82; prof. law, law librarian U. Calif., Boalt Hall Law Sch., Berkeley, Calif., 1982—, dean sch. library and info. scis., 1986-89, Walter Perry Johnson chair, 1998—; mem. Westlaw Adv. Bd., St. Paul, 1984-91; cons. various law firms; mem. on Legal Exch. with China, 1983—, chmn., 1991-93.; vis. prof. U. Cologne, 1993. Author: How to Find the Law, 8th edit., 1984, 9th edit., 1989, Great American Law Revs., 1985, Finding the Law, 1999; co-author: Authors Guide, 1981; editor Legal Reference Svc. Quar., 1981—; author videotape series Commando Legal Rsch., 1989. Chmn. Com. Legal Ednl. Exch. with China, 1991-93. Robinson Cox fellow U. Western Australia, 1988; named West Publishing Co. Acad. Libr. of Yr., 1994. Mem. Am. Assn. Law Libraries (pres. 1985-86), Calif. Bar Assn., ABA, ALA, Am. Law Inst. Office: U Calif Law Sch Boalt Hl Rm 345 Berkeley CA 94720-0001

BERRINGTON, HUGH BAYARD, political science educator; b. Surbiton, Surrey, Eng., Dec. 12, 1928; s. William Majilton and Grace Constance (Smith) B.; m. Catherine Margaret Smith, Aug. 9, 1965; children: Andrew William, Lucy Margaret, Sarah Constance, Mary Edith. BScEcon, London U., 1954; postgrad., Nuffield Coll., Oxford, Eng., 1954-56. Jr. clk. Barclays Bank, Merton Park, Eng., 1944-47; clk. Surrey County Coun., Epsom, Eng., 1949-52, Kingston, Eng., 1952-53; adminstrv. asst. Surrey County Coun., Wimbledon, Eng., 1953-54; asst. lectr. U. Keele, Staffordshire, Eng., 1956-59; lectr. U. Keele, Staffordshire, 1959-65; reader, head dept. politics U. Newcastle Upon Tyne, Eng., 1965-70, prof., head dept. politics, 1970-94, emeritus prof., 1994—. Author: Backbench Opinion in House of Commons, 1945-55, 1973; co-author: Backbench Opinion in House of Commons, 1955-59, 1961; editor: Britain in the Nineties: The Politics of Paradox, 1998. Ward assn. sec. Labour Party, Epsom Constituency, 1949-51. Cpl. Royal Air Force, 1947-49. Named Nat. Pub. Speaking Champion, Labour Party League of Youth, 1952; Personal Rsch. grantee Social Sci. Rsch. Coun., 1982-83. Mem. Polit. Studies Assn. U.K. (sec.-treas. 1958-61, treas. 1961-64, chmn. 1977-80, pres. 1981-83, v.p. 1983—), Internat. Soc. for Polit. Psychology. Anglican. Avocations: walking, theatre. Home: Townhead Cottage, Askham Cumbria CA10 2PG, England Office: Dept Politics, Univ Newcastle Upon Tyne, Newcastle Upon Tyne NE1 7RU, England

BERRINI, JEAN CHARLES, information scientist; b. Monthey, Valais, Switzerland, Apr. 11, 1954; s. Charles and Lydia (Brun) B. Engr., SFIT Lausanne, Switzerland, 1980; MBA, CRPM Lausanne, 1991. Asst. engr. SFIT, Lausanne, 1980-82; mgr., sales engr. Instrumatic SA/AG, Geneva and Zurich, Switzerland, 1983-86; mgr. sales, mktg. Landis & Gyr, Zug, Geneva, 1987-91; sales Elektrizitatsgeselschaft, Laufenburg, Switzerland, 1991-92; gen. mgr., dir. sales mktg. Semafor AG, Basel, Switzerland, 1996-98. Mem. IEEE, SIA, Mensa. Avocations: travel, languages. Home: Im Dorfli 10, 6343 Rotkreuz Switzerland

BERRUT, GILLES, internist; b. Neuilly, France, July 10, 1957; s. Jacques and Jacqueline (Rhifel) B.; m. Brigitte Ribes, July 11, 1981; 4 children. MD, France. Internist Praticien Hosp., Angers, France, 1992—. Office: Svc de Tedecine B, UF Gerontologie Clin, CHU 4 Rue Larrey, 49033 Angers France

BERRY, CLARE GEBERT, real estate broker; b. Carlisle, Pa., Oct. 4, 1955; d. George Robert and Helen (Davis) Gebert; m. James Isaac Vance Berry Jr., June 16, 1977; 1 child, James Isaac Vance Berry III. BA, Auburn U., 1977. Advt. assoc., circulation mgr. The News-Gazette, Lexington, Va., 1977-79; sales and editorial asst. Ponte Vedra (Fla.) Recorder Newspaper, 1979-81; co-founder, bus. mgr. The Sun-Times Newspaper, Jacksonville Beach, Fla., 1981-82; mgr. Arvida-Clearview Cable TV, Ponte Vedra Beach, 1982-85; broker/agt. Watson Realty Corp., Ponte Vedra Beach, 1985-90; broker agt. Marsh Landing Realty, Ponte Vedra Beach, 1990-93; founder, broker, owner Berry & Co. Real Estate, Ponte Vedra Beach, 1993—. Com. chmn. The Players Championship/TPC Charities, Ponte Vedra Beach, 1982 ; dir. Marsh Landing Homeowners Assn. Bd., Ponte Vedra Beach, 1989-90; dir. Ponte Vedra Pub. Edn. Found., 1994 . Recipient Realtor of Yr., Realtors' Assn., 1992, Residential Mem. of Yr., 1998. Mem. Fla. Assn. Realtors, Nat. Assn. Realtors, N.E. Fla. Builders Assn. Sales and Mktg. Coun., N.E. Fla. Assn. of Realtors (bd. dirs. 1998-00, chmn. edn. com. 200). Avocations: writing, promotions, beach activities, music, tennis. Home: 113 Linkside Cir Ponte Vedra Beach FL 32082-2032 Office: Berry & Co Real Estate 330 Hwy A1A Ste 200 Ponte Vedra Beach FL 32082-1824

BERRY, DAWN BRADLEY, writer, lawyer, jeweler; b. Peoria, Ill., Mar. 11, 1957; d. Raymond Coke and Clarette (Williams) Bradley; m. William Lars Berry, July 12, 1980. BS, Ill. State U., 1979, MS, 1982; JD, U. Ill., 1988. Bar: N.Mex. 1988, U.S. Dist. Ct. N.Mex. 1988, U.S. Ct. Appeals (10th cir.) 1993. Assoc. Modrall, Sperling, Roehl, Harris and Sisk, Albuquerque, 1988-90; pvt. practice Tijeras and Albuquerque, 1990—; assoc. Hinkle Law Offices, Albuquerque, 1995-96. Author: Equal Compensation for Women, 1994, The Domestic Violence Sourcebook, 1995, The Divorce Sourcebook, 1995, The Fifty Most Influential Women in American Law, 1996, The Divorce Recovery Source Book, 1998, The Estate Planning Sourcebook, 1999. Pres., bd. dirs. Talking Talons Youth Leadership, Tijeras, 1993-98, v.p., 1998-2000. Recipient Outstanding Young Alumni award Ill. State U., 1996; Rickert scholar for pub. svc. U. Ill., 1988. Mem. NAFE, Southwest Writers, Parrot Heads of N.Mex., F. Scott Fitzgerald Soc., Internat. Wench's Guild, Author's Guild. Avocations: travel, dance, falconry, gardening, Renaissance fairs. Home and Office: 222 Raven Rd Tijeras NM 87059-8016

BERRY, DIANE MARIE, science educator, medical technologist; b. Buffalo, Jan. 24, 1952; d. Edward Roy and Carol Ann (Rusin) B. AA summa cum laude, Villa Maria Coll., Buffalo, 1972; BS cum laude, Rosary Hill (Daemen) Coll., Buffalo, 1975; MS, Roswell Park Inst./SUNY, Buffalo, 1977. Cert. in infections control and barrier precautions; cert. ARC HIV-AIDS presentations. Med. technologist Our Lady of Victory Hosp., Lackawanna, N.Y., 1975—; instr. Villa Maria Coll., 1977-78, Hilbert Coll., Hamburg, N.Y., 1979; instr. Trocaire Coll., Buffalo, 1980-82, dir. med. tech. dept., 1982-86, prof. natural scis. divsn., 1986—; chair med. tech. adv. bd. Trocaire Coll., 1982-86, prof., 2000. Named to Outstanding Young Women of Am., 1983. Mem. Med. Egn. and Rsch. Found., Environ. Tech. Club, Phi Theta Kappa, Lambda Tau, Beta Beta Beta. Achievements include formulation and creation of State of New York Infectious Control Course Program; formation of a self-esteem course for women, formation of environmental chemistry course Trocaire College, 1999. Avocations: music, sports, stock car racing, classic cars. Office: Trocaire Coll 360 Choate Ave Buffalo NY 14220-2003

BERRY, GLENN, educator, artist; b. Feb. 27, 1929; s. B. Franklin and Heloise (Sloan) B. BA magna cum laude, Pomona Coll., 1951, BFA (Honnold fellow); MFA, Sch. Art Inst. Chgo., 1956. Faculty Humboldt State U., Arcata, Calif., 1956-69; prof. art Humboldt State U., Arcata, 1969-81, emeritus, 1981—. Exhibited one-man shows Ingomar Gallery, Eureka, Calif., 1968, Ankrum Gallery, L.A., 1970, Esther Bear Gallery, Santa Barbara, Calif., 1971, Coll. Redwoods, Eureka, 1989, Humboldt State U., Arcata, Calif., 1992, Morris Graves Mus. of Art, Eureka, Calif., 2000; exhibited in group shows Palace of Legion of Honor, San Francisco, Pasadena (Calif.) Art Mus., Rockford (Ill.) Coll., Richmond (Calif.) Art Mus., Henry Gallery U. Wash., Seattle, Morris Graves Mus. Art, Eureka, 2000; represented in permanent collections at Storm King Art Ctr., Mountainville, N.Y., Kaiser Aluminum & Chem. Corp., Oakland, Calif., Palm Springs (Calif.) Desert Mus., Hirshhorn Mus., Washington, others; mural Griffith Hall, Humboldt State U., 1978. Mem. Phi Beta Kappa. Home: PO Box 2241 Mckinleyville CA 95519-2241

BERRY, JAMES LEE, retired educator; b. Hollywood, Calif., May 19, 1939; s. Ralph (Red) Lee and Lillie Pauline (Pilkenton) B.; m. Sharon Joyce Hess, April 14, 1963; children: Jamie, Diana, Daniel. BS in Edn., Pitts. State U., 1961; MEd, Ga. Southern U., 1975; MBA, Webster U., 1983. Commd. ensign U.S. Army, 1962, advanced through grades to lt. col., 1982, ret., 1982; spl. agent Dept. Defense, San Antonio, Tex., 1983-84; sr. army instr. Northeast Military Magnet, Kansas City, Mo., 1986-2000; ret., 2000. Shooting coach U.S. Shooting, Colo. Springs, Colo. 1998; weightlifter U.S. Weightlifting, Colo. Springs, 1998-99. Decorated Bronze Star, Meritorious Svc. medal with 3 oak leaf clusters, Vietnam Cross of Gallentry. Avocations: shooting, weightlifting, painting. Home: PO Box 751 Lawrence KS 66044-0751

BERRY, L. CLYEL, lawyer; b. Twin Falls, Idaho, July 17, 1949; s. Clyel J. and Nellie B.; m. Jill Brunzell, July 17, 1970; children: Jacob Clyel, Matthew Robert. BABA, Wash. State U., 1973; JD, U. Idaho, 1975. Bar: Idaho 1976, U.S. Dist. Ct. (dis. Idaho) 1976, U.S. Ct. Appeals (ninth cir.) 1982. Assoc. Emil F. Pike, Twin Falls, 1976-78; ptnr. Pike and Berry, Twin Falls, 1978-83; prin. Twin Falls, 1983—; sec., dir. Theisen Motors, Inc., Twin Falls. Mem. Idaho State Bar Assn., Idaho Trial Lawyer Assn. (regional dir. 1981-82), Assn. Trial Lawyers of Am., Fifth Jud. Dist. Bar Assn. (sec.-treas. 1977-78). Avocations: whitewater rafting, kayaking, lic. Alaska guide, skiing, fishing, travel. Office: PO Box 302 Twin Falls ID 83303-0302

BERRY, PHILIPPA JANE, English literature educator; b. Barnet, Herts, England, Apr. 2, 1955; d. Thomas Edward and Celia Emily (Browne) B. BA with honors in English, King's Coll., Cambridge, England, 1977; MA with honors in English, U. Sussex, Brighton, England, 1978; D.Phil in English, U. Sussex, 1985. Lectr. English lit. U. Mohamad ben Abdallah, Fes, Morocco, 1980-84; lectr. English lit. U. E. Anglia, Norfolk, England, 1984-85, W. London Inst. Higher Edn., London, 1985-88, King's Coll., Cambridge, 1988—. Author: Of Chastity and Power: Elizabethan Literature and the Unmarried Queen, 1989, Shakespeare's Feminine Endings, 1999; co-editor: Shadow of Spirit: Postmodernism and Religion, 1993; contbr. articles to profl. jours. Fellow King's Coll. Cambridge. Avocations: swimming, yoga, walking, riding. Home and office: Kings Coll, Cambridge England CB21ST

BERRY, ROBERT, secondary school educator, art educator; b. Franklin, Ind., July 16, 1949; s. Robert Joseph and Esther Marie B.; m. Judith Ann Rabatin, June 14, 1975; children: Anne Estaire, Megan Rochelle, Katharine Mara. BS, Ball State U., 1974, postgrad. in gifted and talented edn., 1992-93; MA, DePauw U., 1982. Cert. life tchg., edn. Ind. Art instr. We. Boone High Sch., Thornton, Ind., 1974-76; instr. art, U.S. history Cloverdale (Ind.) High Sch., 1976-81; instr. art, gifted and talented Greencastle (Ind.) High Sch., Ind., 1981—; instr., mem. Earlham Coll., Richmond, Ind., 1987-88; state champion coach Acad. Super Bowl, Inc., Indpls., 1986, 87, 91; presenter in field. Precinct committeeman Dem. Party, Putnam Count, Ind., 1981—, city chmn. mcpl. election, 1991, 99. Fellow Ind. Acad. Sci., Maths. and Humanities (tchg. 1992-93); mem. Ind. Assn. Gifted, Putnam County Art League (pres. 1992-94), Elks (exalted ruler 1989-90, chair trustee com. 1996, Elk of Yr. 1990), Am. Legion (Mem. of Yr. 1992). Democrat. Avocations: tennis, sailing, yachting, painting. Home: 635 E Seminary St Greencastle IN 46135-1746

BERRY, ROBERT WORTH, lawyer, educator, retired army officer; b. Ryderwood, Wash., Mar. 2, 1926; s. John Franklin and Anita Louise (Worth) B. B.A. in Polit. Sci., Wash. State U., 1950; J.D., Harvard U., 1955; M.A., John Jay Coll. Criminal Justice, 1981. Bar: D.C. 1956, U.S. Dist. Ct. (D.C.) 1956, U.S. Ct. of Appeals (D.C. cir.) 1957, U.S. Ct. Mil. Appeals 1957, Pa. 1961, U.S. Dist. Ct. (ea. dist.) Pa. 1961, U.S. Dist. Ct. (ctrl. dist.) Calif. 1967, U.S. Supreme Ct. 1961, Calif. 1967, U.S. Ct. Claims 1975, Colo. 1997, U.S. Dist. Ct. Colo. 1997, U.S. Ct. Appeals (10th cir.) 1997. Research assoc. Harvard U., 1955-56; atty. Office Gen. Counsel U.S. Dept. Def., Washington, 1956-60; staff counsel Philco Ford Co., Phila., 1960-63; dir. Washington office Litton Industries, 1967-71; gen. counsel U.S. Dept. Army, Washington, 1971-74, civilian aide to sec. army, 1975-77; col. U.S. Army, 1978-87; prof., head dept. law U.S. Mil. Acad., West Point, N.Y., 1978-86; ret. as brig. gen. U.S. Army, 1987; mil. asst. to asst. sec. of army, Manpower and Res. Affairs Dept. of Army, 1986-87; asst. gen. counsel pub. affairs Litton Industries, Beverly Hills, Calif., 1963-67; chair Coun. of Def. Space Industries Assns., 1968; resident ptnr. Quarles and Brady, Washington, 1971-74; dir., corp. sec., treas., gen. counsel G.A. Wright, Inc., Denver, 1987-92, dir., 1987—; pvt. practice law Fort Bragg, Calif., 1993-96; spl. counsel Messner & Reeves LLC, Denver, 1997—; foreman Mendocino County Grand Jury, 1995-96. Served with U.S. Army, 1944-46, 51-53, Korea. Decorated Bronze Star, Legion of Merit, Disting. Service Medal; recipient Disting. Civilian Service medal U.S. Dept. Army, 1973, 74, Outstanding Civilian Service medal, 1977. Mem. FBA, Bar Assn. D.C., Calif. Bar Assn., Pa. Bar Assn., Colo. State Bar Assn., Denver Bar Assn., Army-Navy Club, Army-Navy Country Club, Phi Beta Kappa, Phi Kappa Phi, Sigma Delta Chi, Lambda Chi Alpha. Protestant.

BERRYHILL, HENRY LEE, JR., geologist; b. Charlotte, N.C., Nov. 6, 1921; s. Henry Lee and Viola Estelle (Johnston) B.; m. Louise Randall Russell, Sept. 13, 1947; children: Stuart Randall, Keith Courtney. B.S., U. N.C., 1947, M.S. in Geology, 1949. With U.S. Geol. Survey, 1948-86; chief publs. officer U.S. Geol. Survey, Denver, 1963-65; research marine geologist U.S. Geol. Survey, 1965-66; chief marine geology Gulf of Mexico-Caribbean region office U.S. Geol. Survey, Corpus Christi, Tex., 1967-70; chief Office Marine Geology, Washington, 1970-73; sr. research marine geologist Office Marine Geology, Corpus Christi, 1973-86; gen. cons., 1986-99, ret., 1999; Tech. adviser offshore prospecting com. ECAFE, 1972-73; Dept. Interior rep. Fed. Intragy. Com. on Marine Sci. and Engring., 1970-73; program mgr. integrated environ. assessment Outer Continental Shelf N.W. Gulf of Mexico, 1973-86; U.S. rep. marine geology panel U.S.-Japan Coop. Programs in Natural Resources, 1973-95; cons. Nat. Center for Geoscis., India, 1981-87. Author: Geology and Coal Resources of Belmont County, Ohio, 1963, Geology of the Ciales Area, Puerto Rico, 1965, Coal-Bearing Upper Pennsylvanian and Lower Permian Rocks, Washington Area, Pennsylvania, 1971, The Worldwide Search for Petroleum Offshore-A Status Report for the Quarter Century, 1947-72, 1974, Seismic Models of Late Qua ternary Facies and Structure, Northern Gulf of Mexico, 1986. Contbr. articles to sci. publs. Served with USAAF, 1942-45. Decorated DFC, Air medal with 3 oak leaf clusters; recipient Outstanding Performance award U.S. Geol. Survey, 1969, a seafloor feature of the Gulf of Mexico named Berryhill Basin in his honor, 1995. Fellow Geol. Soc. Am.; mem. Am. Assn. Petroleum Geologists (co-recipient Jules Braunstein meml. award 1987), Sierra Club (chmn. Coastal Bend group 1980-81, 86-89), Sigma Xi. Episcopalian. Home and Office: 231 Rosebud Ave Corpus Christi TX 78404-1734

BERSANI, PIERLUIGI, Italian government official; b. Bettola, Sept. 9, 1951; married; children: Elisa, Margherita. BA in Philosophy, Bologna (Italy) U. V.p. Aguinta Regionale Emilia Romagna; pres. Giunta Regionale dell'Emilia Romagna; regional sec. Dem. Party of Left; min. industry Govt. of Italy, Rome, from 1996, now min. transport; mem. standing conf. local and regional authorities Europe, mem. com. regional problems and devel. Coun. Europe, Strasbourg. Office: Ministry Industry, Via Molise 2, 00187 Rome Italy Address: Piazza della Croce Rossa 1, 00161 Rome Italy*

BERSELL, SEAN DEVLIN, trade association executive; b. Miami, Fla., 1959. AB, Dartmouth Coll., 1981; JD, U. N.Mex., 1985. Bar: Pa., 1985. Legis. counsel U.S. Senator Pete V. Domenici, Washington, 1985-91; asst. dir. Nat. Pk. Svc., Washington, 1991-93; sr. dir. pub. affairs AIChE, Washington, 1993-99; v.p. govt. affairs and mem. comm. Video Software Dealers Assn., Encino, Calif., 1999—; legis. counsel U.S. Senator Pete V. Domenici, Washington, 1985-91.

BERSET, DANIEL, analytical chemist; b. Berne, Switzerland, Sept. 6, 1951; s. Bernard B.; m. Giuliana Brignoli; children: Annic, Jeanne, Manon. U. Berne, Switzerland, PhD, 1984. Postdoctoral fellow U. B.C., Van Couver, Can., 1985-86; scientific co-worker IUL, Berne, 1990—. Office: Inst Environ Protection, Schwarzenburgstr 155, 3005 Berne Switzerland

BERSEUS, OLLE JAN OLOF, pathologist; b. Stockholm, Nov. 27, 1938; s. Stig and Birgitta (Berg) B.; m. Birgitta Holmberg, 1962; three children. Grad., coll., 1956; MD, Karolinska Inst., Stockholm, 1967, PhD in Med. Biochemistry, 1967. Clin. pathologist Orebro Med. Ctr. Hosp., Sweden, 1968-76; postgrad. tng. in blood banking, hemotherapy Dept. Transfusion Medicine Clin. Immunology Acad. Sjukhuset, Uppsala, Sweden, 1976-77; dir. dept. Transfusion Medicine & Immunohaemotherapy Orebro Med. Ctr. Hosp., 1977-97; head ctrl. lab. and blood bank Ostfold Hosp., Fredrikstad, 1997—. Mem. Swedish Soc. Transfusion Medicine, European Soc. Haemapheresis, Swedish Soc. Medicine. Office: Sentrallaboratoriet, Sykehuset Østfold, 1603 Fredrikstad Norway

BERSHITSKY, SERGEY YURIEVICH, physiologist; b. Yekaterinburg, Russia, Feb. 27, 1951; s. Yuri and Yekaterina (Ponomareva) B.; m. Olga Nikolaevna Poliakova, Jan. 22, 1976; children: Yelena, Anastasia. Grad., Med. Inst., Ekaterinburg, Russia, 1975; PhD in Biophysics, Moscow U., 1987. Rschr. Inst. Nat. Economy, Yekaterinburg, 1975-78; rsch. scientist Inst. Occupl. Disease, Yekaterinburg, 1978-79; rsch. fellow King's Coll., London, 1991-92, Nat. Inst. Med. Rsch., London, 1994-95; sr. rsch. scientist Russian Acad. Sci., Yekaterinburg, 1989—; internat. rsch. scholar Howard Hughes Med. Inst., 1995-2000. Mem. Physiol. Soc., Biophys. Soc. Office: Inst Physiology, 91 Pervomayskaya Str, Yekaterinburg Russia

BERSIA, JOHN CESAR, editorial writer, political science educator; b. Orlando, Fla., Nov. 23, 1956; s. Alfred and Rose-Marie (Idromasia) B. BA in Polit. Sci. and French, U. Ctrl. Fla., 1977, AA, 1977; MA in Govt., Georgetown U., 1979; MS in Pub. Info. Adminstrn., Am. U., 1980; MSc, London Sch. Econs., 1981. Distbr. Dexter Press Inc., Orlando, 1975-77; intern, analyst U.S. Dept. Labor, Washington, 1978-79; cons., staff assoc. Am. U., Washington, 1979-80; editor, cons. Global Perspectives, London, Washington, Orlando, 1981-83; pres. Global Perspectives Rsch. Group Inc., Casselberry, Fla., 1983-85; editorial bd. mem. The Orlando Sentinel, 1985—; dir. Transnat. Studies Assn., Orlando, 1982-85; adj. prof. polit. sci. U. Ctrl. Fla., 1990—, Rollins Coll., Winter Park, Fla., 1993—; chmn. Shadows Know Regional sch. to work partnership, Orlando, 1996—; coordinator U.S. A.I.D. Seminar, Winter Park, Fla., 1984-85; speaker in field; del. editorial page editors and writers seminar Am. Press Inst., 1987; chmn. Global Connections for Ctrl. Fla., Orlando, 1999—. Editor-in-chief: Global Perspectives: An Interdisciplinary Jour. Internat. Rels., 1982-85. Named to Outstanding Young Men Am., Jaycees, 1978, Outstanding Alumnus of Yr., U. Ctrl. Fla., 2000; fellow Knight Ctr. for Specialized Journalism, U. Md., 1991; recipient editl. award Florida Soc. Newspaper. Mem. London Sch. Econs. Soc., Am. Friends London Sch. Econs., Citrus Club, Georgetown Club Metro Orlando (bd. dirs. 1996—), Phi Kappa Phi, Omicron Delta Kappa. Roman Catholic. Avocations: hiking, travel, cooking. E-mail: jbersia@orlandosentinel.com. Office: Orlando Sentinel Comm 633 N Orange Ave Orlando FL 32801-1349

BERSIN, RICHARD LEWIS, physicist, plasma process technologist; b. N.Y.C., July 4, 1929; s. Maxwell Hilary and Virginia (Greenfield) B.; m. Lillian Freda Braudy, Mar. 21, 1954 (div.); children: Joshua Morris, Adam Samuel; m. Ruth Ann Hargrave, July 25, 1976; children: Jacob David Antonio, Rebekah Bersin Contreras. BS in Physics, MIT, 1950; MS in Maths. and Physics, Northeastern U., Boston, 1962. Physicist Tracerlab, Inc., Boston, 1950-58; divsn. mgr. Lab. for Electronics Corp., Waltham, Mass., 1968-69; pres., founder Internat. Plasma Corp., Berkeley, Calif., 1969-74; exec. v.p. Dionex Gas Plasma Sys., Hayward, Calif., 1974-79; dir. of dry processing Perkin Elmer Corp., Wilton, Conn., 1979-83, dir. tech. mktg., 1983-84; pres., cons. Emergent Techs. Corp., New Haven, Conn., 1985—; engring. specialist Ulvac Japan, Ltd., Chigasaki, Japan, 1989-92; sr. tech. staff mem. Ulvac Techs., Inc., Methuen, Mass., 1992—. Patentee in field. Mem. IEEE, Am. Vacuum Soc., Electrochem. Soc., Semi Internat., Am. Chem. Soc., Computer Soc., ASM Internat. Democrat. Episcopalian.

BERTA, PHILIPPE JEAN, biology and biochemistry educator; b. Besancon, Doubs, France, Apr. 11, 1960; s. Jean Charles and Henriette (Prince) B.; m. Brigitte Jeanne Ponsole, Aug. 31, 1990; children: Antoine, Julie. PhD, Montpellier U., France, 1986, Habilitation, 1992. Charge rsch. 2nd class Nat. Ctr. Sci. Rsch., France, 1988-90, charge rsch. 1st class, 1990-95; dir. rsch. Nat. Inst. Sci. & Med. Rsch., France, 1995—; prof. biology/biochemistry Inst. Human Genetics, CNRS-UPR, Montpellier, France, 1998—; mem. nat. com. Nat. Inst. Sci. & Med. Rsch., 1995-99; mem. French Panel for Med. Rsch., 1994; cons. 4 biotech. cos.; head DNA learning ctr., Nimes, Nimes-biotech-technopole. Co-discoverer of male sex determining gene in human/mammals; contbr. more than 85 articles to profl. jours. Mem. nat. com. Nouvelle UDF, 1996—; pres. Nimes, Neighbourg Planette, Nimes, France, 1995-97. Mem. French Soc. Genetics, French Soc. Biochemistry, French Soc. Endocrinology, N.Y. Acad. Scis. Home: 297 chemin Pied du Bon Dieu, 30000 Nimes France Office: Inst Human Genetics CNRSUPR 1142, 141 rue de la Cardonille, 34396 Montpellier France

BERTAGNA, JEAN-JACQUES HENRI PAUL, lawyer; b. London, Mar. 12, 1951; s. Paul Honore and Colette Adrienne (Guillot) B.; m. Chantal Jacqueline Simon, June 24, 1976; children: William, Edouard. Vienna internat. high sch. course, Vienna (Austria) U., 1971; degree in Bus. Law, Paris U., 1973, Diploma Higher Studies in Bus. Law, 1976; diploma in New Chinese Econ. Law, U. East Asia, Macao, 1987; diploma internat. rels. law, E.F.B., Paris, 1994. Bar: Paris, 1976. Adv. BD Law Firm, Paris, 1976-79; ptnr. BDBB Law Firm, Paris, 1979-91; sr. ptnr. Bertagna Gruia Dufaut Law Firm, Paris, 1991—; cons. Bertagna-Gruia Dufaut-Gruia, Bucharest, Rumania, 1994—; mng. dir. Berrymans Lace Mawer, EEIG, London. Overseas adv. editor The Company Lawyer; contbr. articles to profl. jours. Sch. pres. Parent's Assn. PEEP, Neuilly-Sur-Seine, France, 1995—. Mem. Tech. Lawyers Consortium, Brit. French Lawyers Assn., Paris Country Club. Home: 11 Rue Edouard Nortier, 92200 Neuilly-sur-Seine France Office: Bertagna Gruia Dufaut, 59 Ave Marceau, 75116 Paris France

BERTAIN, G(EORGE) JOSEPH, JR., lawyer; b. Scotia, Humboldt County, Calif., Mar. 9, 1929; s. George Joseph and Ellen Veronica (Canty) B.; m. Bernardine Joy Galli, May 11, 1957; 1 child, Joseph F. AB, St. Mary's Coll. Calif., 1951; JD, Cath. U. Am., 1955. Bar: Calif. 1957. Assoc. Hon. Joseph L. Alioto, San Francisco, 1955-57, 59-65; asst. U.S. Atty. No. Dist. Calif., 1957-59; pvt. practice of law San Francisco, 1966—; panel mem. Theodore Granik's Am. Forum of The Air, Washington, 1955. Editor-in-Chief, Law Rev. Cath. U. Am. (vol. 5), 1954-55. Mem. bd. regents St. Mary's Coll. Calif., 1980—; chmn. San Francisco Lawyers Com. for Ronald Reagan, 1966-78, San Francisco lawyers com. for elections of Gov./U.S. Pres. Ronald Reagan, 1966, 70, 80, 84; spl. confidential advisor to Gov. Reagan on jud. selection, San Francisco, 1967-74; chmn. San Francisco Lawyers for Better Govt., 1978—; confidential advisor to Senator Hayakawa on judicial selection, 1981-82, to Gov. Deukmejian, 1983-90, to Gov. Wilson, 1991-92; bd. dirs. St. Anne's Home, Little Sisters of the Poor, San Francisco. Recipient De La Salle medal St. Mary's Coll. Calif., 1951, Signum Fidei award, 1976. Mem. ABA, Calif. Bar Assn., Fed. Bar Assn. (del. to 9th cir. jud. conf. 1967-76), St. Thomas More Soc. San Francisco, U.S. Supreme Ct. Hist. Soc., Assn. Former U.S. Attys and Asst. U.S. Attys. No. Calif. (past pres.), Commonwealth Club, Wester Assn., Knights of Malta, KC. Republican. Roman Catholic. Address: 2314 9th Ave San Francisco CA 94116-1937

BERTELS, GUY LOUIS, electrical engineering company executive; b. Brussels, Dec. 28, 1953; m. Françoise Weber, June 13, 1981; children: Julie, Stephanie. Degree in Elec. Engring., U. Louvain, Belgium, 1977. Head studies dept. ENI, Antwerp, Belgium, 1977-82; chief installation dept. AEG, Brussels, 1982-83, mgr. systems div., 1983-90; mng. dir. Alstom Contracting, Brussels, 1990—. Mem. AIEB, Fabrimetal (bd. dirs.). Avocations: tennis, skiing, trekking, horse riding. Home: Rue Pierre Geruzet 11, 1160 Brussels Belgium Office: Alstom Contracting, 60 Blvd de la Woluwe, 1200 Brussels Belgium

BERTELSEN, AKSEL BROCKHUSEN, psychiatrist; b. Fredericia, Denmark, July 25, 1936; d. Bertel and Clara (Brockhusen) B.; m. Kamma Gerner Olsen, Aug. 22, 1959; children: Sören, Erik. MD, Århus U., 1963. Intern Dept. Surgery and Medicine Århus U. Hosp., Denmark, 1963-64; intern Dept. Neurology and Neurosurgery Århus U., Denmark, 1965-68; jr. registrar Psychiat. Hosp., Århus, Denmark, 1969-70, sr. registrar, 1976-82, supt., 1982—; rsch. fellow WHO Collaborative Ctr., Aarhus, 1970-92, dir., 1992—. Asst. Editor Acta Psychiatrica Scandinavia, 1976-82; contbr. articles to profl., acad. jours. Recipient James Shield Meml. award, 1985, Kurt Schneider award, 1992. Mem. Den Alm Danske Laegeforening, Fgn. Speciallaeger, Danish Psychiatric Selskab, Internat. Soc. for Twin Studies (founding). Lutheran. Avocation: geology. Fax: 011 45 77 89 2899. E-mail: de@psykiatri.aaa.dk. Home: Rosenvej 26, 8240 Risskov Denmark Office: Århus Psychiat Hosp, Skovagervej 2, 8240 Risskov Denmark

BERTENSHAW, WILLIAM HOWARD, III, radio and television producer; b. N.Y.C., Nov. 28, 1930; s. William Howard Jr. and Grace Annette (Miller) B.; m. Betty J. Underriner, July 7, 1956 (dec. Nov. 1975); children: Jane Ann, Judith Ann, Jo Ann; m. Bobbi C. Slachofsky, Dec. 16, 1984. BA in Communications, Ohio Wesleyan U., 1950. Asst. mktg. editor Bus. Week mag., N.Y.C., 1953-55; radio-TV dir. Hardy Burt Assocs., N.Y.C., 1955-57; radio-TV producer Empire Broadcasting Corp., N.Y.C., 1957-60, Nat. Episcopal Ch., N.Y.C., 1960-70; producer MBS, N.Y.C., 1970-75; dir. communications Council of Chs. City of N.Y., 1975-84; exec. producer, chief exec. officer Radio & TV Roundup Prodns., N.Y.C., 1984—; producer TKR Cable TV, N.Y.C., 1987—; guest lectr. So. Meth. U., Dallas, 1972, Seton Hall U., South Orange, N.J., 1974, Pace U., N.Y.C., 1980, Syracuse (N.Y.) U., 1982; vice chmn. dept. communications N.J. Coun. Chs., 1986—; host People Working for People, Sta. WOR-TV, N.Y.C., 1988; programmer Cable TV Network of N.J., 1985; producer The Jersey Cape TV series, 1990—. Host Inner-Dimension Community Concerns, Union Eyes and Perspective on the News Sta. WOR Radio, WOR Special Report, N.Y., 1970—. Pres. Rep. Club, West Cape May, N.J., 1986-87; vice chmn. communications N.J. Coun. Chs., 1986-89; committeman Cape May County N.J. Rep. Orgn., 1987-90, Essex Coun. N.J. Rep. Orgn., 1960-85. Sgt. U.S. Army, 1951-53. Recipient Gabriel award Washington Conf., 1966-67, Radio Programming award Ohio State U., 1969, Columbus Film Festival award Ohio Coun. Chs., 1970, Radio-TV award N.J. Coun. Chs., 1983, Olive award, 1984, Cape award Cable TV Network N.J., 1987, Angel award Excellence in Media, Hollywood, Calif., 1999, 2000. Mem. AFTRA, Nat. Lima Bean Assn. (founder), Alpha Sigma Rho, South Jersey Bird Club. Episcopalian. Club: Suburban Sports Car (N.J.) (v.p., co-founder 1956-61). Home: 653 Sun Haven Dr Clayton NJ 08312-1955

BERTEZ, BRUNO JACQUES, editor; b. Anzin, France, Sept. 20, 1944; s. Leon and Lallement B.; m. Françoise Lancelle, Aug. 31, 1964; children: Caroline, Conrad. Grad., Sch. Higher Study Commerce, 1967. Stock broker Rondeleux-Oudart, Paris, 1967-75; editor-in-chief La Vie Française, Paris, 1979-81, mng. editor, 1981-84; editor-in-chief Agefi, Paris, 1984—, La Tribune de l'Économie, Paris, 1984—. Mem. Soc. Editions Boursières, Agefi Suisse. Office: Soc Edits Boursières, 13 passage St Sébastien, 75011 Paris France

BERTHELOT, YVES M., international organization administrator; b. Paris, Sept. 15, 1937; m. Doris Yeatman, 1961; 3 sons, 1 dau. Grad., Ecole Polytechnique and Ecole Nationale de la Statistique et de l'Administration Economique. Dir. studies Ministry of Planning, Ivory Coast, 1965-68; from chief of the study of enterprises divsn. to chief of svc. of programmes Institut national de la Statistique et des Etudes Economiques, 1971-75; chief svc. des Etudes et Questions Int. French Ministry of Cooperation, 1976-78; dir. rsch. Devel. Ctr. OECD, Paris, 1978-81; dir. Prospective Studies and Int. Info. Ctr., 1981-85; dep. sec.-gen. UNCTAD, 1985-93; exec. sec. UN Comm. for Europe, 1993—. Contbr. articles to profl. jours. Avocations: sailing, skiing. Office: Econ Commn for Europe, Palais des Nations, CH-1211 Geneva Switzerland

BERTHELSDORF, SIEGFRIED, psychiatrist; b. Shannon County, Mo., June 16, 1911; s. Richard and Amalia (Morschenko) von Berthelsdorf; m. Mildred Friederich, May 13, 1945; children: Richard, Victor, Dianne. BA, U. Oreg., 1934, MA, MD, 1939. Lic. psychiatrist, psychoanalyst. Intern U.S. Marine Hosp., Staten Island, N.Y., 1939-40; psychiat. intern Bellevue Hosp., N.Y.C., 1940-41; psychiat. resident N.Y. State Psychiat. Hosp., N.Y.C., 1941-42; research assoc. Columbia U. Coll. Physicians and Surgeons, N.Y.C., 1942-43; asst. physician Presbyn. Hosp. and Vanderbilt Clinic, N.Y.C., 1942-51; supervising psychiatrist Manhattan (N.Y.) State Hosp., 1946-50; asst. adolescent psychiatrist Mt. Zion Hosp., N.Y.C., 1950-52; psychiat. cons. MacLaren Sch. for Boys, Woodburn, Oreg., 1952-84, Portland (Oreg.) Pub. Schs., 1952-67; clin. prof. U. Oreg. Health Scis. Ctr., 1956—; tng. and supervising analyst Seattle Psychoanalytic Inst., 1970—. Author: Treatment of Drug Addiction in Psychoanalytic Study of the Child, Vol. 31, 1976, Ambivalence Towards Women in Chinese Characters and Its Implication for Feminism, American Imago, 1988, (with others) Psychiatrists Look at Aging, 1992. Bd. dirs., v.p. Portland Opera Assn., 1960-64, Portland Musical Co., 1987-92; bd. dirs., pres. Portland Chamber Orch., 1964-70, 92-94, 96-97, exec., 1997—. Maj. USAF, 1943-46. Recipient Henry Waldo Coe award U. Oreg. Med. Sch., Portland, 1939, citation Parry Ctr. for Children, Portland, 1970, Child Advocacy award ORAPT, 1998. Fellow Am. Psychiat. Assn. (life), Am. Geriatrics Soc. (founding fellow); mem. Am. Psychoanalytic Assn. (life), Portland Psychiatrists in Pvt. Practice (charter, pres. 1958), Mental Health Assn. (bd. dirs., chmn. med. adv. com. 1952-60), Multnomah County Med. Soc. (pres.'s citation 1979), Oreg. Psychoanalytic Found. (founding mem.), Am. Rhododendron Soc. (bd. dirs., v.p. Portland chpt. 1956-58, Bronze medal and citation 1974), Am. Rhododendron Species Found. (bd. dirs. 1960-75), Phi Beta Kappa, Sigma Xi, Phi Sigma, Phi Mu Alpha. Avocations: farming, music. Home: 1125 SW St Clair Ave Portland OR 97205-1127

BERTHILLIER, MARC JEAN, aircraft engine company researcher; b. Paris, Oct. 17, 1962; s. Jacques Maurice and Denise Monique (Barbier) B.; m. Danielle Anne-Marie Ledermann, Feb. 14, 1987; children: Frederic, Claire, Christophe. MS, Ecole Centrale Nantes, 1986. Rsch. engr. Snecma, Paris, 1988-93, rsch. group leader, 1993-99, dep. mgr. design methodologies dept., 1999—. Office: Snecma, Centre de Villaroche, 77550 Moissy Cramayel France

BERTH-JONES, JOHN, consultant dermatologist, educator; b. London, Oct. 23, 1955; s. Harold Berth-Jones and Elizabeth Beesley. MB, BS, St. Bartholomews Hosp. Med. Sch., 1979. Sr. house officer in dermatology Univ. Hosp. Wales, Cardiff, 1986-87; registrar in dermatology Leicester Royal Infirmary, Coventry, Eng., 1987-89, rsch. fellow in dermatology, 1989-91; sr. registrar in dermatology Leicestershire Hosps., Coventry, 1991-94; cons. in dermatology Walsgrave Hosp., Coventry, 1994—. Contbr. articles on dermatology, atopic dermatitis and psoriasis to med. jours. Surg. lt. comdr. Royal Navy, 1979-86. Fellow Royal Coll. Physicians, Brit. Assn. Dermatologists, European Acad. Dermatology and Venereology, Am. Acad. Dermatology. Home: Cypresses, 15 South Ave Stoke Park, Coventry CV2 4DQ, England Office: Walsgrave Hosp, Dept Dermatology, Coventry CV2 2DX, England

BERTHOLD, FRANK, pediatrician and oncologist; b. Dresden, Germany, May 4, 1948; s. Harald and Ilse (Lembcke) B.; m. Rosemarie Schwarzer; children: Christiane, Susanne. MD, Med. Sch. Dresden, 1978; PhD, U. Giessen, Germany, 1985. Physician asst. Cmty. Children's Hosp., Dresden, 1972-78; rsch. assoc. Children's Hosp., U. Giessen, 1978-82, sr. physician, 1983-86; rsch. assoc. Children's Hosp., U. Phila., 1982-83; prof. Children's Hosp., U. Cologne, Germany, 1986è. Author: Clinical and Laboratory Investigations in Neuroblastoma. Bd. dirs. Psychosocial Network of Luth. Ch., Cologne, 1994è. Mem. German Soc. Pediatric Oncology and Hematology (treas. 1986è), German Soc. Pediatrics, Internat. Soc. Pediatric Oncology. Presbyterian. Avocations: hiking, table tennis, bicycling, modern theater. Office: U Cologne Children's Hosp, Joseph-Stelzmann-str 9, D-50924 Cologne Germany

BERTHON, GUY RENÉ, chemistry researcher, consultant; b. Azay-le-Ferron, France, June 15, 1942; s. Denis Marcel and Marcelline Marie (Bourin) B.; m. Nicole Jeanne Lecardonnel, July 11, 1964; children: Frédérique, François. Lic. in scis., U. Poitiers, France, 1964; D, U. Poitiers, 1966, DSc, 1970. Stagiaire rsch. Nat. Ctr. Sci. Rsch., Poitiers, 1966-68, attaché rsch., 1968-72, chargé rsch., 1972-82; maître rsch. Nat. Ctr. Sci. Rsch., Toulouse, France, 1982-84, dir. rsch., 1984—; postdoctoral fellow U. St. Andrews, Scotland, 1977; cons. Labs. Lucien, Colombes, France, 1989-91, Lancôme, Chevilly-Larue, France, 1992, Labs. Boiron, Ste. Foy les Lyon, France, 1996, Roche Consumer Health (Worldwide) S.A., Vernier-Geneva, 1997. Editor: Handbook of Metal-Ligand Interactions in Biological Fluids; Bioinorganic Chemistry, 2 vols., 1995, Handbook of Metal-Ligand Interactions in Biological Fluids; Bioinorganic Medicine, 2 vols., 1995; contbr. over 140 articles to profl. jours. Office: ICMPS-FR 1744, 38 rue des Trente-Six Ponts, 31400 Toulouse France

BERTHON, RENE MAX, corporate executive; b. Paris, May 4, 1914; s. Henri and Clemence (Lecomte) B.; m. Simone Sangaud, Apr. 23, 1946; children: Gerard, Patrick. Student, Ecole Polytechnique, 1935. Counsel chmn. Schneider S.A., Paris. Deocrated Officier de la Legion d'Honneur, Commandeur du Merite. Home: 2 av. Emile Bergerat, 75016 Paris 16, France

BERTHU, GEORGES, foreign diplomat; b. Angoulême (Charente), France, May 14, 1950. Mem. European Parliament, 1999—, mem. com. onc onstnl. affairs, substitute com. on econ. and monetary affairs; mem. Union for Europe of the Nations Group; vice chmn. delegation for relations with Can. Office: Parlement européen, Rue Wiertz ASP 6F155, B-1047 Brussels Belgium*

BERTI, GIOVANNI, diagnostics company executive; b. Marsciano, Perugia, Italy, Sept. 18, 1935; s. Ercole and Sofia (Bianconi) B.; m. Serenella di Marsciano, Dec. 11, 1965 (dec. 1991); children: Daniele, Lucia. D, U. Bologna, Italy, 1959. Cert. indsl. chemist. Mgr. Montedison Spa., Terni, Italy, 1960-70; exec. Bayer Diagnostici Spa., Cavenago Brianza, Italy, 1970-93, ret., 1994. Contbr. articles to profl. jours.; patentee in field. Mem. Am. Assn. Clin. Chemistry, Internat. Soc. Clin. Enzymology, Royal Soc. Chemistry, N.Y. Acad. Scis. Roman Catholic. Home: Via Provinciale 34, 23864 Malgrate Lecco, Italy

BERTINI, CATHERINE ANN, United Nations official; b. Syracuse, N.Y., Mar. 30, 1950; d. Fulvio and Ann (Vino) B.; m. Thomas Haskell, 1988. BA, SUNY; DSc (hon.), McGill U., Montreal, Can., 1997; DHL (hon.), SUNY, Cortland, 1999; DSc, Pine Manor Coll., 2000. Youth dir. N.Y. Rep. State Com., 1971-74; with Rep. Nat. Com., 1975-76; mgr. pub. policy Container Corp. Am., 1977-87; dir. Office Family Assistance, U.S. Dept. Health and Human Svcs., 1987-89; acting asst. sec. U.S. Dept. Health and Human Svcs., 1989; asst. sec. U.S. Dept. Agrl., 1989-92; exec. dir. UN World Food Programme, Rome, 1992—; UN panel mem. sec. gen.'s High Level Personalities on African Devel., UN, 1992-95. Commr. Ill. State Scholarship Comm., 1979-84; mem. Ill. Human Rights Comm., 1985-87; spl. envoy of Sec. Gen. to the Horn of Africa, 2000. Recipient Leadership in Human Svcs. award Am. Pub. Welfare Assn., 1990, Pub. Svc. award Am. Acad. Pediatrics, 1991, Leadership award Nat. Assn. WIC Dirs., 1992, Quality of Life award Auburn U., 1994, Disting. Alumni award Nelson A. Rockefeller Coll. Pub. Affairs and Policy, 1997. Fellow Harvard U., 1986. Office: UN World Food Program, Cesare Giulio Viola 68/70, 00148 Rome Italy

BERTINOTTI, FAUSTO, foreign diplomat; b. Milan, Italy, Mar. 22, 1940. Mem. European Parliament, 1999—, substitute com. on econ. and monetary affairs; mem. com. on legal affairs and internal mkt.; mem. Confed. Group of the European United Left/Nordic Green Left; mem. substitute delegation for relations with countries of South Asia and the South Asia Assn. for Regional Coop. Office: Dir Naz Rifondazione Comuni, Viale del Policlinico 131, I-00161 Rome Italy*

BERTMAN, SKIP, baseball coach; b. 1838; m. Sandy Bertman; children: Jan, Jodi, Lisa, Lori. BA in Health and Phys. Edn., U. Miami, 1961, M in Health and Phys. Edn., 1964. Asst. baseball coach U. Miami, 1976-83; head baseball coach La. State U., Baton Rouge, 1984—; led USA Baseball Team, 1995-96; asst. coach Olympic Baseball Team; asst. coach Interncontinental Baseball team, 1987, U.S. Olympic Baseball team, 1988; mgr. NCAA champion La. State U. Tigers, 1991, 93, 96, 97; head coach USA Baseball, 1995, 96. Author: Skip: The Man and The System, Coaching Youth Baseball. Named Nat. Coach of Yr., Baseball Am. and The Sporting News, 1986, Collegiate Baseball newspaper and Am. Baseball Coaches Assn., 1991, 93; named to U. Miami Sports Hall of Fame, 1994. Office: 7000 Exchequer Dr Baton Rouge LA 70809-4903

BERTOLAMI, ORFEU, physicist; b. Sao Paulo, Brazil, Jan. 3, 1959; s. Ader Bertolami and Ester Malka Fiks; m. Maria da Conceicao Apolonia Bento, Oct. 1992; 1 child, Marina Bento Bertolami. B in Physics, U. Sao Paulo, 1981; MS in Physics, Inst. Physics, Sao Paulo, 1983; Advanced Degree in Math., U. Cambridge, U.K., 1984; DPhil in Physics, U. Oxford, 1987. Postdoctoral fellow U. Heidelberg, Germany, 1987-89, Inst. Fisica e Math., Lisboa, Portugal, 1989-91; lectr. Inst. Superior Tecnico, Lisboa, 1991-97; sci. assoc. Theory divsn. CERN, Geneva, 1993-95; postdoctoral fellow Inst. Nat. Nuclear Physics, Turin, Italy, 1994-95; tenureship Inst. Supr. Tech., Lisboa, Portugal, 1997—. Contbr. over 75 pubs. in profl. jours.; co-editor tech. proceedings in field. Mem. Soc. Portuguese Fisica, Soc. Portuguese Astronomia. Office: Inst Superior Tech, Av Rovisco Pais, P-1096 Lisboa Codex, Portugal

BERTOLINI, ENIZO, engineering consultant; b. Verona, Italy, May 4, 1932; s. Guglielmo and Rosa (Leveghi) B.; m. Tullia Chiariomi, May, 1962 (div. 1977); m. Marisa Vincenzina Mion; children: Luca, Maddalena, Matteo. B, Liceo Massedaglia, Verma, 1951; D in Engring., U. Padova, Italy, 1958, PhD in Physics, 1959. Chartered engr. Rschr. IMFM/CERM, Geneva, 1959-62; sect. leader EMEA, Rome, 1965-69, group leader, 1969-70, head lab., 1970-73; prof. U. Calif., Davis, 1969-70; dep. mgr. Joint European, Abingdon, Eng., 1973-78, divsn. head, 1978-85, dep. dept. head, 1985-91, chief engr., 1991-97, tech. adviser to dir., 1997-99; tech. advisor UKAEA, Abingdon, 2000—. Contbr. articles to profl. jours. Recipient Valentino prize Puglia Govt., 1999. Fellow Inst. Elec. Engring.; mem. European Physics Soc. Roman Catholic. Avocations: skiing, swimming, hiking, music, theater. Home: 24 Jackman Close, Abingdon OX14 36A, England Office: UKAEA, Abingdon OX14 3EA, England

BERTOLINI, LUCA, urban planner, architect, artist; b. Rome, Apr. 7, 1963; s. Enzo and Tullia (Chiarioni) B.; m. Valentina Mazzucato, Nov. 1, 1992; children: Saskia, Mattia. MArch, Poly. Turin, Italy, 1989, PhD in Urban Planning, 1995. Lic. arch. and planner, Italy. Rschr. Poly. Turin, 1989-95, U. Utrecht, The Netherlands, 1995-99, U. Amsterdam, 1999—. Author: Cities on Rails, 1998; contbr. articles to profl. jours., including Internat. Planning Studies, European Planning Studies, Planning Practice and Research, Town Planning Review. Mem. Profl. Assn. Dutch Urban Designers and Planners. Avocation: travel. Fax: (31)(20) 5254051. E-mail: l.bertolini@frm.uva.nl. Office: AME, Nieuwe Prinsengrecht 130, 1018 VZ Amsterdam The Netherlands

BERTOLUCCI, BERNARDO, film director; b. Parma, Italy, Mar. 16, 1941; s. Attilio and Ninetta B.; m. Clare Peploe, 1978. Attended, Rome (Italy) U. Dir. films The Grim Reaper, 1962, Before the Revolution, 1964 (Young Critics award Cannes Film Festival), La Via del Petrolio, 1965, His Partner, 1968, The Conformist, 1970 (Nat. Film Critics Best Dir. award), The Spider's Strategem, 1970, Last Tango in Paris, 1972, 1900, 1976, Luna, 1979, Tragedy of a Ridiculous Man, 1981, The Last Emperor (Golden Globe award for Best Dramatic Picture, 1987, Best Dir., Best Screenplay, Best Original Score, Best Editor, Best Cinematography, Best Sound, Best Prodn. Design, Art Dir., Best Costume Design, Acad. award for Best Picture of Yr., Best Dir., Best Screenplay Adaptation, Best Film honor Brit. Acad. Film and TV Arts), The Sheltering Sky, 1990, Little Buddha, 1994, Stealing Beauty, 1996, Besieged, 1998 (Globo D'Oro award for Best Film 1999); author: poems In Search of Mystery, 1962 (Viareggio prize, Italy); Paradiso e inferno, 1999. Office: care Recorded Picture Co, 24 Hanway St, London W1P 9DD, England also: care Jeff Berg ICM 8942 Wilshire Blvd Beverly Hills CA 90211-1934

BERTON, GIUSEPPE STEFANO, physician, cardiologist; b. Zurich, Mar. 11, 1957; s. Giulio and Pia Sofia (Nardi) B. MD, U. Padua, Italy, 1983. Cert. specialist in cardiology, specialist in internal medicine. Fellow U. Padua, 1981-88; physician Conegliano City Hosp., Italy, 1988-89, cardiologist, 1993—; cardiologist Bassano City Hosp., 1990-93. Contbr. articles to med. jours. Fellow Nat. Soc. Italian Cardiologists, European Soc. Cardiology. Avocations: skiing, cycling. E-mail: giube@nline.it. Home: Via Colombo 74, 31015 Conegliano Veneto, Italy Office: Dept Cardiology, Conegliano Veneto, Treviso Italy

BERTON, TERESINHA MARISA, animal science researcher; b. Tenente Portela, Brazil, Oct. 3, 1961; d. Olderige Antonio and Maria (Gadenz) Bertol; m. Jonas Irineu Santos Filho. Degree in Animal Sci., Fed. U. Santa Maria, Brazil, 1983; MSc, Fed. U. Rio Grande do Sul, Porto Alegre, Brazil, 1988. Rschr. IAPAR, Pato Branco, Brazil, 1990-94, EMBRAPA, Concordia, Brazil, 1995—; cons. COOPERCENTRAL, Chapeco, Brazil, 1997—, Seara Alimentos, Brazil, 1998—. Avocations: reading, travel. E-mail: tbertol@cnpsa.embrapa.br. Office: CNPSA.Embrapa, BR 153 km 110 Vila Tamandua, Concordia SC, Brazil 89700

BERTONCELLO, IVAN, experimental hematologist, researcher; b. Melbourne, Victoria, Australia, Feb. 3, 1949; s. Settimo and Delfina (Rossetti) B.; m. Jane Margaret Slattery, Jan. 5, 1974; children: Paul Damien, Michael Joseph, Rebecca Jane, Anna Catherine. MSc, U. Melbourne, 1974, PhD, 1976. Postdoctoral fellow Royal Children's Hosp Rsch. Found., Melbourne, 1975-76; postdoctoral fellow dept. clin. physiology U. Ulm, Germany, 1977; rsch. fellow Peter MacCallum Cancer Inst., Melbourne, 1978-91, head stem cell biology, 1991—; assoc. pathology dept. U. Melbourne, 1997—. Contbr. articles to profl. jours., chpts. to books. Lady Latham fellow Royal Children's Hosp., Melbourne, 1975, 76, Alexander Von Humboldt fellow U. Ulm, 1977, Peter Crimmins fellow Peter MacCallum Cancer Inst., Melbourne, 1978-83. Mem. Internat. Soc. Exptl. Hematology (assoc. editor Exptl. Hematology 1994-98, chair nominating com. 2000), Am. Soc. Hematology, Australian and New Zealand Soc. Cell and Devel. Biology (pres. 1992-94), Australian Soc. Med. Rsch. Roman Catholic. Avocations: music, art, literature, tennis. Office: Peter MacCallum Cancer Inst, St Andrews Pl, East Melbourne VIC 3002, Australia

BERTONE, THOMAS LEE, management consultant; b. Pittsburg, Kans., Nov. 15, 1938; s. Anthony and Gaye Kittle Bertone; m. Ellen Reville Kniffin, Sept. 6, 1969; children: Elizabeth Reville, Katherine Logan. AB cum laude, Harvard U., 1960; MA, Stanford U., 1963; D Pub. Adminstrn., George Washington U., 1971. Budget examiner on def. U.S. Bur. Budget, Washington, 1964-67; cons., assoc. Booz Allen & Hamilton, Washington, 1967-69, 78-80; dir. budget rev. Office Fiscal Affairs, N.J. Legislature, Trenton, 1973-75, exec. dir. Office Fiscal Affairs, 1975-78; regional dir. state and local govt. cons. Coopers & Lybrand, Phila., 1980-82; dir. internat. cons. Grant Thornton, Chgo., 1986-90; pres. Thomas L. Bertone & Assocs., Pennington, N.J., 1982-86, 90—; World Bank decentralization advisor to permanent sec. Sri Lanka Ministry Local Govt., 1985-89; ADB advisor to budget dir. Budget Office, Federated States Micronesia, 1993-95; IMF budget advisor to min. fin. Palestine Authority, Gaza and West Bank, 1995; U.S. AID intergovtl. fiscal rels. advisor to prime min. and min. fin. Fedn. Bosnia Herzegovina, 1997. Sr. advisor on state fin. amd mgmt. to gov. candidate State of W.Va., Charleston, 1970-72; pro bono cons. N.J. Office Mgmt. and Budget, Trenton, 1999. 2d lt. U.S. Army, 1964, Korea. Mem. ASPA, Inst. Mgmt. Cons. (cert.), Assn. Govt. Accts. (cert. govt. fin. mgr.). Democrat. Avocations: scuba diving, skiing, horseback riding, shooting and gun collecting, dogs. E-mail: tom bertone ab60@post.harvard.edu. Home and Office: 153 E Delaware Ave Pennington NJ 08534-2304

BERTOSSI, ALAN ALBERT, computer scientist, educator; b. London, Jan. 7, 1956; s. Leslie Bertossi and Gemma Finzi; m. Fabiana Colombini, Dec. 7, 1985; 1 child, Sara. Degree, U. Pisa, Italy, 1979. System designer Italsiel, Rome, 1980-82; asst. prof. computer sci. U. Pisa, Italy, 1983-88, assoc. prof., 1989-94; prof. U. Trento, Italy, 1995—. Contbr. articles to profl. jours. Office: U Trento, Dept Mathematics, 38050 Trento Italy

BERTOTI, EDGAR FRIGYES, mechanical engineer, researcher; b. Miskolc, Hungary, Aug. 13, 1961; s. Edgar Aba and Julianna (Piti) B.; m. Réka Csilla Karczag, Aug. 17, 1984; children: Diana, Robert, Regina. MS, U. Miskolc, 1984, PhD in Engring., 1992. Engr. Tüki, Hungary, 1984-86; asst. rschr. U. Miskolc, 1986-89, sr. rschr., 1989—. Contbr. articles to sci. jours., including Internat. Jour. Numerical Methods in Engring., Internat. Jour. Solids and Structures. Sgt. Hungarian Land Forces, 1985-86. Rsch. fellow Tüv Rheinland, 1991; Humboldt fellow Humboldt Found., 1993, Fulbright fellow, St. Louis, 1995. Office: U Miskolc Dept Mechanics, Egyetemváros, H-3515 Miskolc Hungary

BERTRAM, CHRISTOPHER DAVID, engineering educator; b. Northampton, Eng., Jan. 22, 1950; arrived in Australia, 1980; BA, Oxford (Eng.) U., 1971, DPhil, 1975, MA, 1977. Chartered profl. engr. Tech. mgmt. apprentice Brit. Aircraft Corp., Bristol, Eng., 1968-72; postdoctoral fellow Johns Hopkins U., Balt., 1975-76, rsch. asst., 1976-77; rsch. assoc. Cambridge (Eng.) U., 1977-80; lectr., sr. lectr. U. NSW, Sydney, Australia, 1980-90, assoc. prof., 1991—; mem. adj. faculty Ga. Inst. Tech., Atlanta, 1992; invited prof. Swiss Fed. Inst. Tech., Lausanne, Switzerland, 1994. Contbr. chpt. to: Biological Fluid Dynamics, 1995; contbr. articles to profl. jours. Recipient grant-in-aid Australian Acad. Sci. to Math Inst., U. Warwick, 1991, Australian Dept. Industry, Sci. and Tourism to MIT and U. Ill.-Chgo., 1998, numerous rsch. grants Australian Rsch. Coun. Fellow I.E. Aust., World Coun. Biomechanics. Avocations: music, tennis. Office: U NSW, Grad Sch Biomed Engring, Sydney 2052, Australia

BERTRAM-DROGATZ, (PETER) ALEXANDER, microbiologist, pharmacologist; b. Hamburg, Germany, Feb. 10, 1966; m. Katrin Drogatz, Sept. 27, 1996. Student, U. Hamburg, 1986-89; MA in Microbiology, U. Kans., 1991; D Natural Scis., U. Marburg, Germany, 1994; cert. bus. adminstrn., Fern U Hagen, Germany, 2000; cert. in bus. adminstrn., Fern U., Hagen, Germany, 2000. Grad. tchg. asst. dept. microbiology U. Kans., Lawrence, 1990-91; lab. asst., grad. tchg. asst. U. Marburg, 1991-95, sci. employee Lab. for Microbiology,, 1992-95; asst. advanced lab. genetics course U. Bielefeld, Germany, 1996; asst. gen. pharmacology course Med. Hochschule Hannover, Germany, 1997, sr. sci., lab. head Inst. for Gen. Pharmacology,, 1996-97, lectr. pharmacology for dentistry students, 1997; rsch., scale up and prodn. mgmt. BioteCon GmbH, Berlin /Potsdam, Germany, 1997-99; investment mgr. Mediport VC Mgmt. GmbH, Berlin, Germany, 1999—; mng. dir. Ganomycin GmbH, Greifswald, Germany, 2000—; presenter sci. meetings, 1989—. Contbr. articles and abstracts to sci. jours., including Jour. Applied Bacteriology, European Jour. Biochemistry, Letters in Applied Microbiology, Archives Microbiology, Molecular and Gen. Genetics, BioEngring., Jour. Inorganic Biochemistry, Genes, Chromosomes, Genomes, Biol. Chemistry Hoppe-Seyler, European Jour. Clin. Microbiol. and Infectious Diseases; contbg. author: Encyclopedia for Food Microbiology. With German Army, 1985-86. Mem. Am. Soc. for Microbiology, German Soc. for Pharmacology and Toxicology, Union for Gen. and Applied Microbiology. Avocations: guitar, horseback riding. Fax: 49-30-76942109. Office: Mediport VC Mgmt GmbH, Wiesenweg 10, 12247 Berlin Germany

BERTRAND, JEAN-LOUIS, financial company executive, lecturer; b. Mulhouse, France, June 12, 1965; s. André G. and Michelle G. (Claudet) B.; m. Sylvie Tourenne, Dec. 29, 1990; children: Juliette, Tom. Engring. degree, Ecole Nat. Superieure, Paris, 1988; MBA, Mankato State U., 1989. Account mgr. Credit Comml. de France, Paris, 1989-90; dealer Credit Comml. de France, London, 1990-92; internat. treas. Carnaud Metal Box, Paris, 1992-95; mkt. ops. sr. corp. dealer Standard Charterd Bank, London, 1995-96; head treas. Levi Strauss & Co., Brussels, 1996—; lectr. in field. Recipient Amb. of Goodwill Rotary Found., 1989. Avocations: family, running, badminton, tennis. Office: Levi Strauss & Co, Ave Arnuad Fruieur 15-23, 1050 Brussels Belgium

BERTSCH, GARY KENNETH, political scientist, educator; b. Vallejo, Calif., June 8, 1944; s. Gideon and Freda (Hepper) B.; m. Joan Elizabeth Brubacher, Feb. 29, 1964; children: Dawn, Todd, Jason. BA, Idaho State U., 1966; MA, U. Oreg., 1968, PhD, 1970. Vis. prof. U. Zagreb, Yugoslavia, 1969-70; prof. polit. sci. U. Ga., Athens, 1970—; vis. prof. nat. security affairs Air U., Dept. Def., Maxwell AFB, Ala., 1981-82; Fulbright prof. politics U. Lancaster, Eng., 1984-85; dir. Ctr. Internat. Trade and Security, 1987—. Author numerous books, including East-West Strategic Trade and the Atlantic Alliance, 1983; Reform and Revolution in Communist Systems, 1991; editor: Engaging India, 1999, Dangerous Weapons, Desperate States, 1999, Crossroads and Conflict, 2000, also numerous articles. Recipient numerous awards for tchg. U. Ga., 1970—, profl. chair for disting. tchg., 1982—, numerous rsch. grants, 1970—. Mem. Am. Polit. Sci. Assn., Internat. Studies Assn. Home: 228 Henderson Ave Athens GA 30605-1037 Office: U Ga Dept Polit Sci Athens GA 30602

BESANÇON, ALAIN JUSTIN, political scientist, historian; b. Paris, Apr. 25, 1932; s. Justin Louis and Madeleine (De Lagrange) B.; m. Marie Goldstyn, Oct. 26, 1954; children: Sophie, Martin, Agnès, Serge. Diploma, Inst. Polit. Study, Paris, 1952; doctoral degree, U. Sorbonne, Paris, 1975. With Sch. of High Study, Paris, 1964—, dir. studies, 1975—; vis. assoc. prof. Columbia U., 1966, Rochester Inst. Tech., 1968; vis. fellow Kennady Inst., Washington, 1975, Hoover Instn., 1981-82, Princeton U., 1995, All Souls Coll., Oxford, Eng., 1987. Author 15 books, numerous articles; columnist l'Express, 1982-88. Recipient History prize Acad. Française, Paris, 1978, Essay prize, 1987. Mem. Acad. Moral and Polit. Scis. of Inst. of France (elected 1996), Le Siècle. Fax: 01 33 1 42 84 2569. Home: 97 Rue du Bac, 75007 Paris France

BESANCON, FRANCOIS JEAN, internist, gastroenterologist, educator; b. Paris, Sept. 16, 1927; s. Justin Louis and Madeleine Marie (Delagrange) B.; m. Béatrice Sabine Hoppenot, Apr. 4, 1951; children: Odile, Paul, Jean, Pascale, Hélène. MD, U. Paris, 1955, DSc, 1957, agrégé, 1963. Chief of staff Lariboisiere Hosp., Vaugirard Hosp., Paris, 1967-77, Hosp. Hôtel-Dieu, Paris, 1977—; prof. internal medicine U. Paris, 1973—; faculty Broussais Hôtel-Dieu, 1973—, ret., 1992. Author: L'anémie Pernicieuse, 1955, Votre Premiere Publication, 1973, Contre-Indic des Exam Complé, 1983, Conseils du Médecin á ses Malades, 1985, Communiquer avec une victime de l'alcool, 1996 (translated in Polish 1999, Spanish 2000), Conscious Motives of Moderate Drinkers, 1997, Conscious Motives of People Refusing Drugs and Suicide, 1999; contbr. more than 300 articles to profl. jours. Mem. Soc. Nat. Francaise Gastro-Entérologie, Sci. Soc. Belgium, Sci. Soc. Czechoslovakia, Sci. Soc. Poland, Sci. Soc. Bulgary, Soc. Francaise & Europe Alcoologies. Roman Catholic. Avocations: alpinism, jogging. Home: 14 Bd Emile Augier, 75116 Paris France

BESANCON, ROGER R., pharmacologist; b. Dole, France, May 28, 1967; s. Maxime Besancon and Jacqueline R. (Molle) Dubief. MS in Pharmacology, U. Paris VI, 1991; PhD in Neuroscis., Ecole Normale Superieure, Lyon, France, 1996. From monitor to tchr. Edn. Nationale, Lyon, 1993—. Sgt. French Infantry, 1991-92. Mem. Internat. Brain Rsch. Orgn., Soc. Neuroscis. Office: Lab Biol Psychopharm Faculty Pharmacy, 8 Ave Rockefeller, F-69373 Lyon France

BESANT, DEREK MICHAEL, artist, educator; b. Ft. MacLeod, Alta., Can., July 15, 1950; m. Alexandra Haeseker, Aug. 1, 1974. BFA, U. Calgary, 1973, postgrad., 1974. Exhbn. designer Glenbow-Alta. Inst. Art Gallery and Mus., 1973-77; instr. Alta. Coll. Art, 1977—; guest lectr. S.W. Tex. State U., San Marcos, 1982. Exhbns. include Can. Rep. Brit. Internat. Biennale, 1979, Bronx Mus., N.Y., Calgary Arch. and Urban Studies Alliance, Cabo Fio Internat. Biennial, Brazil, Premio Internat. Biella per L'Incisione, Italy, Salon des Nations, Paris, Biennale Internat. de Gravure, Yugoslavia, 4th Internat. Seoul (Korea) Biennale, Brit. Drawing Biennale, Middlesborough, Eng., Internat. Print Exhibit, China, 1983, Norske Internat. Biennale, Norway, 1984, Fredrikstad Biennale, Norway, 1984, 7th Tokyo Video Festival, 1985, Ethiopia Exhbn., Akron (Ohio) Art Mus., 1985, Ibiza (Spain) Internat., 1985, Kyoto (Japan) City Mus., 1985, Queensland Coll. Art Australian Tour, 1985, Artists' Response to Arch., Victoria, Tex., 1986, Para Mus. Art, Poland, 1986, Mira Godard Gallery, Toronto, 1986, U. New Delhi, 1986, Glenbow Mus., Banff, Alta., 1986, The Dong-A-Ilbo, Korea, 1986, Premio Biella Internat., Italy, 1987, Galantal Artpool Mus. Fine Arts, Budapest, Hungary, 1987, 12th Internat. Biennale, Krakow, Poland, 1988, Met. Mus., Miami, Fla., 1988, Internat. Buchkunst, Leipzig, 1989, S.W. Tex. Artforum, 1989, Mira Godard, Toronto, 1989, Wolujen/Udell/Vancouver, 1989, Gütersloh, Germany, 1989, Premio Biella, Italy, 1990, Art Gallery Hamilton, 1990, 3rd Biennale Intenrat., Cuba, 1990, 11th Brit. Internat. Biennale, 1991, Kharkov Art Mus., USSR, 1991, 1st Internat. Congress, Brussels, 1991, 6th Internat. Bapha Varna Biennale, Mus. Art, Bulgaria Internat. Triennale, 1991, Krakow Poland/Nünberg, Germany, 1991, Museu d'Arte de Sabadell, Barcelona, 1992, Ctr. de la Gravure, Et De L'Image Imprimee, Belgium, 1992, MECC, Maastricht, Holland, 1993, 8th Internat. Lodz Biennale, Poland, 1994, Flash Art Project, Berlin, 1994, Can. Festival Sao Paulo, Brazil, 1994, Wingfield Arts and Music Festival, Eng., 1994, Curs Internat. de Arquitectura, Spain, 1994, Mus. de'Arte Contemporaneo, Ags, Mex., 1995, Centrum voor Kunsten Openluchtmus., Gent, Belgium, 1995, Invitational Internat. Biella per l'Incisione, Italy, 1996, Deutsche Internat. Triennale Kunstverien Frechen Stadtsaal, Germany, 1996, Mus. Art, Yugoslavia, 1996, Art Contemporain et Multificiplinarité Found. Derouin, Val-David, Que., 1997, City Mus. Art, Poland, 1997, Centro de Arte Moderno, Buenos Aires, 2000, Mus. fuer Moderne Kunst Weddel, Germany, 2000, Florean Mus, Maramures, Romania, 2000, Kunstverein Bad Salzdetfurth, Germany, 2000; recent works include Flatiron Mural W. wall Gooderham Flatiron Bldg., Toronto, 1980, video documentation Christo-Surrounded Islands, Miami; commns.: Cineplex Odeon, N.Y.C., 1989, Scotia Plz., Toronto, 1989, Mount Royal Coll., Calgary, Can., 1989, Daydream Glass Skywalk, Calgary, 1995. Recipient 2nd prize Miami Internat. Biennale, 1977, World Culture prize for Letters, Arts and Sci., 1984, Centro Studi e Ricerche delle Nazioni, Italy; Can. Coun. grantee, 1985. Home: Box 48081 Midlake RPO, 40 Midlake Blvd SE, Calgary, AB Canada T2X 3C0 Office: 1407 14th Ave NW, Calgary, AB Canada T2N 4R3

BESCH, LORRAINE W., special education educator; b. Orange, N.J., June 27, 1948; d. Robert Woodruff and Minnie (Wrightson) B.; m. William Lee Gibson, July 10, 1982. AA in Liberal Arts, Mt. Vernon Coll., 1968; BA in Sociology, U. Colo., 1970; MA in Spl. Edn., U. Denver, 1973. Cert. handicapped thcr., N.J. Elem. resource rm. tchr. Beeville (Tex.) Ind. Sch. Dist., 1973-75; trainable mentally retarded tchr. Kings County Supt. Schs., Hanford, Calif., 1975-78; h.s. resource rm. tchr. Summit (N.J.) Bd. Edn., 1980-81; h.s. resource rm. tchr. Westfield (N.J.) Bd. Edn., 1981-99, head coach field hockey, 1981-83, mem. crisis mgmt. team, 1982-87, in class support tchr. English, 1993-99. Named to Women's Inner Circle Achievement, 1996; recipient Internat. Sash of Academia, ABI, 1997. Mem. AAUW, Smithsonian Nat. Mus. Am. Indian (charter), Sky Meadows Cir. Nat. Mus. Women in Arts, CEC (learning disabilities divsn.), Westfield Edn. Assn. (del. 1983-90, tech. com. 1993-94, conf. funds com. 1994-99), Hartford Family Found. (v.p., sec. 1991-97), Wrightson-Besch Found. (sec.-treas. 1994-99, pres. 1999—), Archaeology Conservancy (life), 1892 Founders Soc., Morristown Meml. Health Found., Col. Williamsburg Burgesses, Nat. Trust Historic Preservation, N.J. Hist. Society. Avocations: traveling, reading, gardening, tennis. Home: 8 Lone Oak Rd Basking Ridge NJ 07920-1613

BESEMERES, JOHN FRANK, public servant; b. Ballarat, Victoria, Australia, Apr. 29, 1941; s. John C. and Alice (Finlayson) B.; m. Anna Cecylia Wierzbicka, Mar. 26, 1972; children: Mary Christina, Clare Elizabeth. BA with honors, Melbourne (Australia) U., 1962; PhD, Australian Nat. U., Cnberra, 1976. Various pub. svc. appointments Canberra, 1977-81; head Polish studies Macquarie U., Sydney, 1982-85, head Slavonic studies, 1985; sr. Soviet analyst Office of Nat. Assessments, Canberra, 1986-88, spl. advisor Soviet affairs, 1989, head Europe, Americas, Middle East, Africa br., 1989—. Author: Socialist Population Politics, 1980; translator books and articles. Commonwealth Australia scholar, 1964-67; named commdr. Order of Merit, Poland, 1994. Avocations: reading, music, traveling, photography. Home: 13 Cockle St, ACT O'Connor 2602, Australia Office: Nat Assessments, PO Box E 346, Kingston ACT 2604, Australia

BESENHARD, JÜRGEN OTTO, chemistry educator; b. Regensburg, Germany, May 15, 1944; s. Josef Peter and Johanna (Becker) B.; m. Ursula Elvira Benz, Jan. 18, 1985; children: Maximilian, Sebastian, Florian, Hanna. Diploma in chemistry, Tech. U., Munich, 1970, PhD, 1973, Habilitation, 1979. Pvt. dozent Tech. U., Munich, 1980-85; prof. inorganic chemistry U. Münster, Germany, 1986-92, Tech. U. Graz, Austria, 1993—. Patentee electrochem. power sources; contbr. articles to profl. publs., 1971—; contbr. articles to profl. jours. Mem. Gesellschaft Deutscher Chemiker, Deutsche Keramische Gesellschaft, Internat. Soc. Sol. State Ionics, Internat. Soc. Electrochemistry (nat. sec. for Austria), Gessellschaft Osterreichischer Chemisker. Home: Zusertalgasse 62, A-8010 Graz Austria Office: Tech U Graz Inst Chem Tech, Stremayrgasse 16/III, A-8010 Graz Austria

BESENYI, CARLOS ARÓN, academic administrator; b. Kecskemét, Hungary, Mar. 10, 1935; s. Karoly and Katalin (Varga Kibedi) B.; m. Susana Gabriela Va'cz, June 20, 1964; children: Carlos Esteban, Susana Margarita C., Alejandro Nicolas, Sofia Gabriela. Traductor Público, U. Buenos Aires, 1961, Contador Público Nacional. Tchr. English and math Belgrano Day Sch., Goethe Schule, Buenos Aires, 1951-68; head math. and sci. St. Peter's Sch., Martinez, Argentina, 1968-72; head math. dept. St. Catherine's Sch., Buenos Aires, 1970-85; founder, dir. gen. St. Stephen's Coll., Bariloche, 1985—; adviser in math. St. Brendan's Coll., Buenos Aires, 1971-85; lectr. math. Internat. Baccalaureate Orgn., 1986—; local sec. U. Cambridge, Bariloche, Argentina, 1986—; asst. examiner Internat. Baccalaureate Orgn., 1985—; workshop presenter in field. Author: (book) Matemática Financiera y Actuarial, 1961, Elementary Mathematics for Primary Schools, Books 1 to 4, 1962, 63, 64, 65, Manual de Matemática del Maestro, Tomos 1, 2, 3, 1980, 81, 82. Active mem., lay preacher Meth. Ch. Knight of the Order of St. John, 1973. Avocations: travel, swimming, carpentry.

BESHEARS, CHARLES DANIEL, insurance executive; b. Vandalia, Mo., Sept. 6, 1917; s. Charles D. and Anabel (Baker) B.; m. Louise Davis Clarke, Sept. 1980; children: Jacqueline, Charles, Scott (dec.), Melanie; stepchildren: Crescente, Maria-Asuncion, Hernan Errazuriz. Grad. exec. program bus. mgmt., UCLA, 1968; advanced mgmt. program, Harvard U., 1971; diplomas in property and casualty ins. and mgmt., Ins. Inst. Am.; grad., Am. Coll. Life Underwriters, 1978. CLU. With Farmers Ins. Group, L.A., 1937-79, v.p. field ops., 1966-68, v.p. charge property and casualty ops., 1968-73; pres., dir. Farmers New World Life Ins. Co., Mercer Island, Wash., 1973-79; dir. Ohio State Life Ins. Co., 1973-79, Investors Guaranty Life Ins. Co., 1973-79; pres. Reaseguros Britania, Chile; ins. cons. Chile, 1980-92; bd. govs., honors. com. Internat. Ins. Soc. Inc. With USAAF, 1942-45. Mem. DAV, VFW, Am. Legion, Chile Club. Address: Casilla 331 Correo 12, La Reina Santiago Chile

BESHIR, MOHAMED YOUSSEF, industrial engineer, consultant; b. Cairo, Egypt, May 31, 1946; s. Ahmed Fouad and Entissar Mohamed El-Khateeb; m. Hala Hafez (div. Sept. 1990); chldren: Hisham, Mostafa. BSc, Ain Shams Univ., Cairo, 1968, MSc, 1972, PhD, 1978. Demonstrator Ain Shams Univ., Cairo, 1969-78, asst. prof., 1978-84, assoc. prof., 1984-85; dir., co-owner Montex, 10th of Ramadan City, Egypt, 1985-97, pres., 1997—; vis. asst. prof. Tex. Tech. U., Lubbock, 1979-83; cons. engr. Egyptian Engrs. Syndicate, 1985. Contbr. numerous articles to profl. jours. Mem. Inst. Industrial Engrs. (sr.), The Am. Industrial Hygiene Assn., Human Factors & Ergonomics Soc., The Ergonomics Soc., Egyptian Engrs. Syndicate. Avocations: soccer, football, basketball, hockey, fishing. Home: 12 Abdel Moniem Hafez, Almaza Cairo Egypt Office: Modern Co Textile Industries Montex, P O Box 177, 10th of Ramadan City Egypt

BESHTOEV, KHAMIDBI MUKHAMEDOVICH, physicist, researcher; b. Baksan, USSR, May 5, 1944; s. Mukhamed Mukhamatovich and Asli Pitirovna (Berdova) B.; m. Nina Victorovna Schogoleva, Mar. 5, 1970; children: Murat, Julia. PhD, Moscow U., 1974. Scientist State U., Nalchik, USSR, 1974-77; scientist Baksan Obs., Neutrino, USSR, 1977-83, sr. scientist, 1983-92; sr. scientist Joint Inst. Nuclear Rsch., Dubna, Russia, 1992—; sci. sec. Baksan Obs., Neutrino, 1983-87, vice-chmn. pub. control, 1989-91. Avocations: economic theories, walking. Office: Joint Inst Nuclear Rsch, Curie 6, 141980 Dubna Russia

BESIMO, CHRISTIAN EMANUEL, dentist, department head, educator; b. Zürich, Switzerland, May 23, 1957; s. Otto Emanuel and Denise Germaine (Claraz) B.; m. Ruth Henriette Meyer, Mar. 31, 1990; children: Luca Emanuel, Julia Henriette, Mario Christian. DMD, U. Zürich, 1983; privatdozent, U. Basel, Switzerland, 1993. Asst. prof. Sch. Dentistry U. Basel, 1987-92, assoc. prof., 1993—; head of dept. Aeskulap Clinic, Brunnen, Switzerland, 1999—. Author: Abnehmbarer Zahnersatz auf Implantaten, 1994, Removable Partial Dentures on Osseointegrated Implants, 1997. Mem. AAAS, Swiss Dental Soc. (pres. sci. com. 1999—), Swiss Prosthodontic Soc. (pres. 1993-97), Collegium Implantologieum (pres. 1994-98), Pierre Fauchard Acad., N.Y. Acad. Sci. Avocations: literature, sports, painting. Home: Riedstrasse 9, CH-6430 Schwyz Switzerland Office: Aeskulap Clinic, CH-6440 Brunnen Switzerland

BESING, RAY GILBERT, lawyer, writer; b. Roswell, N.Mex., Sept. 14, 1934; s. Ray David and Maxine Mable (Jordan) B.; m. Heather McEachern; children: Christopher, Gilbert, Andrew, Paul. Student, Rice U., 1952-54; B.A., Ripon Coll., 1957; postgrad., Georgetown U., 1957; J.D., So. Methodist U., 1960. Bar: Tex. 1960. Ptnr. Geary, Brice, Barron, & Stahl, Dallas, 1960-74; sr. ptnr. Besing, Baker & Glast, Dallas, 1974-77; prin. Law Offices of Ray G. Besing, P.C., Dallas, 1977—; lectr. trial procedures So. Meth. Sch. of Law, 1966-68; guest lectr. comm. law and policy, univs. and industry confs., 1984—; lectr. Bologna Ctr. of Johns Hopkins U., Nitze Sch. Advanced Internat. Studies, 1999. Author: Who Broke Up AT&T?: From Ma Bell to the Internet, 2000; mng. editor, So. Methodist U. Law Jour., 1959-60. Pres. Dallas Cerebral Palsy Found., 1970; bd. dirs. Dallas Symphony, 1972, Dallas Theatre Center, 1971; trustee Ripon Coll., 1969-76; mem. Tex. Gov.'s Transition Team on Telecom., 1982. Tex. Moot Ct. champion, 1958. Mem. Tex. Bar Assn., Dallas Bar Assn., Dallas Jr. C. of C. (v.p. 1964), Sigma Chi. Democrat. Episcopalian (mem. exec. council diocese Dallas, 1969-72). E-mail: rbesing@cybermesa.com. Home and Office: 400 Graham Ave Santa Fe NM 87501-1658

BESKOS, DIMITRI E., structural engineering educator; b. Athens, Greece, Jan. 26, 1946; s. Efthimios D. and Georgia (Bozou) B.; children: Niki, Denise, Mia. Diploma in civil engrng., Nat. Tech. U. Athens, 1969; MS, Cornell U., 1971, PhD, 1973. Instr. Cornell U., Ithaca, N.Y., 1973-74; asst. prof. U. Minn., Mpls., 1974-79, assoc. prof., 1979-82; prof. U. Patras, Greece, 1981—, dir. structural engrng., 1982-83, 86-88, 89-91, 93-99; vis. prof. U. Minn., Mpls., 1982-84, 89, Colo. State U., Ft. Collins, 1985-86. Author and/or editor 12 books; assoc. editor 4 internat. jours.; mem. editl. bd. 5 internat. tech. jours.; contbr. over 220 articles to profl. jours. Fellow ASCE, Internat. Assn. for Computational Mechanics (gen. coun.), Internat. Assn. for Boundary Element Methods, Internat. Soc. for Boundary Elements (steering com.), Greek Assn. Computational Mechanics (past pres.). Office: U Patras, Dept Civil Engrng, 26500 Patras Greece

BESKOVA, IRINA, research scientist; b. Tbilisy, USSR, July 21, 1954; d. Alexandr and Galina (Maminova) Padurov; m. Alexandr Beskov, July 3, 1976; 1 child, Daria. PhD, Moscow State U., 1980; D Habilitat, Russian Acad. Scis., 1993. Rsch. fellow Russian Acad. Scis., 1980-91, sr. rsch. fellow, 1991-95, leading rsch. assoc., 1995—; mem. expert coun. Inst. Philosophy Russian Acad. Scis., 1997—. Author: How Is the Creative Thinking Possible?, 1993; contbr. articles to profl. jours. Grantee in field, 1996-98, 2000-02. Mem. N.Y. Acad. Scis. Avocations: chi kung, tai chi chuan, painting, music, photography. Office: Russian Acad Scis Inst Phil, Volkhonka 14, 119842 Moscow Russia

BESLEY, MORRISH ALEXANDER (TIM BESLEY), civil engineer; b. New Plymouth, New Zealand, Mar. 14, 1927; arrived in Australia, 1950; s. Hugh Morrish and Isobel (Alexander) B.; m. Nancy Marguerite Cave, Feb. 15, 1952; children: Trevor J., Grant A., Rodney G. BE in Civil Engrng., U. New Zealand, 1950; B Legal Studies, Macuarie U., Sydney, Australia, 1984; Barrister at Law, Supreme Ct. NSW, 1985. Chartered profl. engr., Australia. Engr. Ministry of Works, New Zealand, 1950; with Snowy Mountains Hydro-Electric Authority, 1950-67; 1st asst. sec. Dept. External Territories, 1967-72; exec. mem. Fgn. Investment Review Bd., 1975-76; 1st asst. sec. Dept. of Treasury, 1973-76; sec. Commonwealth Dept. Bus. and Consumer Affairs, ACT, Australia, 1976-81; comptroller gen. Customs, 1976-81; mng. dir. Monier Ltd., Sydney, 1982-87, chmn., CEO, 1987; chmn. Monier Redland Ltd., 1988, Redland Australia, 1988-95; exec. chmn. Commonwealth Indsl. Gases Ltd., Sydney, 1988-90; chmn. The CIG Group, 1988-93, Commonwealth Banking Corp., 1988-91, Commonwealth Bank Australia, Sydney, 1991-99; pres. Metal Trades Industry Assn., Sydney, 1989-91; chmn. Leighton Holdings Ltd., Sydney, 1990—. Chmn. Royal Botanic Gardens, Sydney, 1989-92; dir. O'Connell St. Assocs. Pty. Ltd.; mem. Red Shield Appeal Com., Sydney, 1987—, Sydney Adv. Bd. The Salvation Army, 1994-99, Legacy Appeal Com., Sydney, 1988—; mem. mgmt. bd. Australian Grad. Sch. Mgmt., 1983-92, Chancellor Macquarie U., 1994—. Decorated mem. and officer Order of Australia. Fellow Australian Acad. Tech. Sci. and Engrng. (pres. 1998—); mem. Royal Sydney Yacht Squadron, Nat. Press Club, Union Club, Elanora Country Club, Australian Club Sydney. Home: Pvt Box 304, Cammeray NSW 2062, Australia Office: Leighton Holdings Ltd, PO Box 1002, Crows Nest NSW 2065, Australia

BESOLD, FLORIAN, lawyer; b. Munich, Apr. 15, 1949; s. Anton and Elisabeth (Heinrich) B. Grad., U. Norwich, Eng., 1969; law degree, U. Munich, U. Bonn, Germany. Pvt. practice Munich, 1975—. Editor jour. Bayernspiegel. Pres. Bayerische Einigung E.V., Munich, 1988—, Bayerische Volksstiftung, Munich, 1988—. Recipient Constitut medal Bavarian Parliament, 1993, Poetentaler award Unity of Bavarian Poets, 1996, Adalbert-Stifter medal Unity of Sudetendeutsche, 1997. Roman Catholic. Avocations: music, politics, history, painting, poetry, sports. Office: Bayernspiegel, Residenzstr 27, 80333 Munich Germany

BESOMI, DANIELE, historian of economic thought, author; b. Switzerland, June 27, 1960. Laurea in Econs., U. Pavia, Italy, 1983; MPhil, U. Cambridge, Eng., 1987; PhD in Econs., U. Loughborough, Eng., 1996. Ind. rschr. in econs., 1983—. Author: Equilibrio, Distribuzione e Crisi, 1995, The Making of Harrod's Dynamics, 1999 (Dorfman prize for best dissertation in history of econ. thought 1997, best European book in the subject European Soc. History Econ. Thought 2000); co-author: (with G. Rampa) Dal liberalismo al liberismo, 1998, 2d edit., 2000; contbr. articles to profl. jours. Grantee Swiss Nat. Fund for Sci. Rsch., 1986, 91, 94-97, Culture Com., Ticino Canton, Switzerland, 1997-99. Home: C P 7, 6950 Gola di Lago Switzerland

BESSAI, HORST JOACHIM, electrical engineering educator; b. Simmern, Germany, Apr. 22, 1956; s. Ludwig and Lieselotte (Wagner) B.; m. Ellen Jansohn, Feb. 28, 1986; 1 child, Jan. Diploma in Engring., Tech. U. of Darmstadt, Germany, 1980, DEng, 1985. Cert. in elec. engrng. Rsch. staff mem. Rsch. Inst. of Deutsche Bundespost, Darmstadt, Germany, 1980-85; project mgr., head of group Dornier-Deutsche Aerospace, Friedrichshafen, Germany, 1986-90; project cons. Acoustic Imaging, Phoenix, 1990-91; univ. prof. U. Siegen, Germany, 1991—; cons. to several German electronics cos., 1991—; spkr., session chair for various internat. coms.; dir. Europe, Africa, Mid. East com. IEEE Comm. Soc., 1998-99, v.p. 2000—; lectr., thesis advisor Ariz. State U., U. Siegen, 1991—. Patentee telecomm., signal and radar processing (16); contbr. over 20 tech. publs. to elec. engrng. jours. Mem. IEEE, N.Y. Acad. Scis. Avocations: piano, history, fgn. langs. Home: von-Galen-Strasse 3, 57250 Netphen Germany Office: U Siegen Inst Telecom, Holderlin Strasse 3, 57068 Siegen Germany

BESSELL, ERIC MICHAEL, medical practitioner, clinical oncology consultant; b. Stony Stratford, Eng., Dec. 17, 1946; s. William Henry and Doris Mabel (Willson) B.; m. Deborah Jane Lloyd, July 31, 1971; children: Laura Elizabeth, Andrew Thomas. BSc, U. Bristol, Eng., 1967; PhD, U. London, 1970; MB BS, St. Mary's Hosp. Med. Sch., London, 1978. Registrar in clin. oncology Royal Postgrad. Med. Sch./Hammersmith Hosp., London, 1980-83; sr. registrar Royal Marsden Hosp., London, 1983-85; cons. Nottingham (Eng.) Health Authority, 1985—; cons. Kings Mill Hosp., Sutton-in-Ashfield, Eng., 1985—, The Park Hosp., Nottingham; clin. dir. dept. clin. oncology Nottingham City Hosp., 1986-96. Contbr. articles to profl. jours. Fellow Royal Coll. Physicians, Royal Coll. Radiologists (examiner London and Hong Kong 1993-2000); mem. Brit. Oncol. Assn., European Soc. for Therapeutic Radiology and Oncology, Radiotherapy Club (pres. 1998-99). Anglican. Avocations: mountain walking, piano playing, opera. Home: 13 Dovedale Rd, Nottingham NG2 6JB, England Office: Nottingham City Hosp, Clin Oncol/Hucknall Rd, Nottingham NG5 1PB, England

BESSELL, JUSTIN RAYMOND, surgeon, researcher; b. Elizabeth, Australia, Jan. 10, 1964; s. Raymond Leonard and Raylee Joy (Hosking) B.; m. Sara May Falconer, Mar. 31, 1990; children: Olivia Sara, William, Imogen. MB, BS, U. Adelaide, Australia, 1987, MD, 1996. Surg. registrar South Australia Tchg. Hosps., 1987-97; rsch. fellow The Royal Adelaide Ctr. for Endoscopic Surgery, 1993-96; rsch. fellow dept. surgery The Queen Elizabeth Hosp., Adelaide, 1993-98; chief surg. resident N.W. Adelaide Health Svc., 1998; fellow in upper gastrointestinal surgery Princess Alexandra Hosp., Brisbane, 1999; fellow in hepato-biliary pancreatic surgery Leicester Gen. Hosp., U.K., 2000—; vis. rsch. fellow sect. minimal invasive surgery Eberhard-Karls-U., Tübingen, Germany, 1995; mem. Nat. Cancer Grant Applications Assessment Panel Anti-Cancer Coun., Victoria, Australia, 1995-99; vis. gen. surgeon Pt. Augusta Hosp., 1998; vis. gen. surgeon Mater Pvt. Hosp., 1999. Contbr. articles to profl. jours., chpts. to books. Officer Royal Australian Army Med. Corps., 1999—. Rsch. fellow Alexander Von Humboldt Found., 1995; Nat. Health and Med. Rsch. Coun. Med. Postgrad. scholar Australian Govt., 1994-95; project grantee Anti-Cancer Found. Univs. South Australia, 1995. Fellow Royal Australasian Coll. Surgeons (new tech. com. 1996); mem. European Assn. Endoscopic Surgeons, Surg. Rsch. Soc. Australia, Gastroent. Soc. Australia (exec. com. sect. alimen,ary tract surgery 1994-96), Australian Med. Assn., Internat. Soc. Minimally Invasive Therapy. Anglican. Avocations: tennis, information technology. Office: PO Box 1153, Glenelg South SA 5045, Australia

BESSERO, GILLES MARIE, government official; b. Montbeliard, France, July 27, 1952; s. Frederic Alfred and Muguette (Colin) B.; m. Annick Gaby Girousse, Dec. 29, 1973; children: Pierre, Sylvie. Degree in engring., Ecole Poly., Paris, 1974, ENSTA, Paris, 1976. Dep. dir. SHOM/MOA, Brest, France, 1985-87, dir., 1987-88; head sci. instruments sect. SHOM/EPSHOM, Brest, 1988-91; dir. SHOM/MOM, Toulon, France, 1991-94; head bur. gen. affairs SHOM, Paris, 1994-99; under dir. Dir. Coop. and Indsl. Affairs, Ministry of Def., Paris, 1999—; vice chmn. geodesy sect. CNFGG, Paris, 1997—. Author: Tides, 1980, Geodesy, 1985. Mil. engr. French armed forces, 1973—. Recipient Chevalier Ordre Nat. du Merite, 1990, Chevalier Legion D'Honneur, 1996, Chevalier Ordre du Merite Maritime, 1999. Office: DGA/DCI, 4 Bis rue de Porte d'Issy, 75509 Paris Cedex 15, France

BESSHO, KAZUHISA, oral surgeon; b. Kyoto, Japan, Oct. 25, 1957; s. Kiyoshi Koike and (Sumie) B.; m. Machiko Takahashi, May 12, 1996. DDS, Higashinihon Gakuen U., 1984; DMSc, Mie U., 1990. Doctor Kyoto U., 1984-85, Shizuoka Kenritsu Gen. Hosp., Shizoka, Japan, 1985-86; asst. prof. Mie (Japan) U., 1990-92, Kyoto U., 1992—. Author: Bone Morphogenetic Protein, 1996; contbr. articles to profl. jours. Leader Boy Scouts Kyoto, Japan, 1973—. Grantee Japanese Ministry of Edn., Sci. and Culture, 1997, The Implant Dentistry Rsch. and Edn. Found., 1997. Mem. Internat. Assn. for Dental Rsch., Asian Assn. of Oral and Maxillofacial Surgeons, Japanese Soc. for Biomaterials. Avocations: car racing, motorcycling, skiing, traveling, tennis. Home: 14-5 Miyanokami-cho, Hanazono Ukyo-ku, Kyoto 616-8047, Japan Office: Kyoto U Grad Sch Medicine, 54 Kawahara-cho Shogoin, Kyoto 606-8507, Japan

BESSIS, HUGH JOEL, finance educator, consultant; b. Cardiff, Wales, Sept. 22, 1946; s. Emile B. and Suzanne Kouby. Engr., Centrale-Paris, 1970; MBA, Columbia U., 1974; PhD, U. Paris, Dauphine, 1985. Engr. Louis Berger, Inc., N.J., 1971-73; engr. Louis Berger, Inc., NJ, 1972-74; asst. Insead, Fontainebleau, France, 1976; Doctorate prog. Groupe HEC, Paris Dauphine, 1977-79; prof. fin. Groupe HEC, Paris, 1980—; cons. risk mgmt. dept. Bank Paribas, Paris, 1993—. Author: Venture Capital, 1988, The Business Plan, 1993, Gestion Des Risques Des Banques, 1995, Risk Management in Banking, 1998. Armed Forces, Lt. res., France, 1970-71. Fellow Assets-Liabilities Mgmt. Assn.; mem. French Assn. Fin. Office: Groupe HEC, 1 Avenue de la Liberation, 78351 Jouy-en-Josas France

BESSMELTSEV, STANISLAV SEMIONOVITCH, physician, researcher; b. Voronegskaya, Russia, Jan. 18, 1952; s. Semion Ivanovitch and Alexandra Nicolaevna (Boldireva) B.; m. Olga Ivanovna Gangan, July 5, 1975; children: Elena, Maria, Ekatherine. MD in Internal Medicine, Krasnodar Med. Sch., 1975; PhD in Hematology, Rsch. Inst. of Hematology, 1988. Physician Hosp. in Grosnii, USSR, 1975-79, 81-82; resident Dagestan Med. Sch., Makhachkala, USSR, 1981; ambulance physician Hosp., Leningrad, USSR, 1982-87; physician Russian Rsch. Inst. Hematology and Transfusion, 1987-90, jr. rschr., 1990-91, sr. rschr., 1991-95, leading rschr., 1995—; prof. 1st Pavlov's Med. U., St. Petersburg, Russia, 1999—. Author: Aplastic Anemia, 1995, Sonography in Hematology, 1997, Chronik Myeloid Leukemia, 1998, Treatment of Chronik Myeloid Leukemia, 1999. Mem. N.Y. Acad. Sci., Acad. Natual Scis., Internat. Soc. for Fibrinolysis and Thrombolysis, Soc. for Supportive Care in Cancer, European Haematology Assn. Avocations: chess playing, historical literature. E-mail: bsshem@hotmail.com. Home: Vasilievsky Island, 9 Linie H 20 Ap 10, 199004 Saint Petersburg Russia Office: Russian Rsch Inst, 2nd Sovetskaya Str 16, 193024 Saint Petersburg Russia

BESSON, PHILIPPE GASTON, physician; b. Juan Les Pins, Alpes Mari, France, Aug. 8, 1948; s. Gaston Rene and Juliette Edmee (Percier) B.; m. Maria Luisa Louro De Matos Barrenho, May 8, 1991; children: Audrey, Helen, Sophia, Diana. MD, 1975; Ordem dos Medicos, Lisbon, Portugal, 1989; Diplome de Medecin, Geneva, 1996. Intern U. Dijon, France; resident Tonerre's Hosp., France; pvt. practice Geneva; hon. prof. Albert Schweitzer Internat. U., 2000—. Author: La Creme Budwig, 1994, Equilibre Acide/Base, Je Me Sens Mal..., 1997, J'ai Mal Partout, 1999, Je Suis Fatigue, 2000. Mem. N.Y. Acad. Scis. Office: Cabinet Medical, 14 Rue Etienne Dumont, 1204 Geneva Switzerland

BESSON, RAYMOND JEAN, electronics engineering educator; b. Villars St. Georges, Doubs, France, May 2, 1938; s. Raymond Adrien and Madeleine Henriette (Lenoir) B.; m. Colette Marie Reynaud, Dec. 23, 1969; children: Claire, Helene, François. Lic. in physics, U. Besançon, France, 1961, PhD, 1968, Dr. d'Etat, 1970. Tchr. physics, chemistry Dole, France, 1962-65; asst. prof. electricity U. Besançon, 1966-74; prof. École Nat. Supérieure Mecanique Microtechs., Besançon, 1974-80, 1st class prof. electronics, 1981-87, exceptional class prof. electronics, 1988—; rschr. U. Besançon, 1966-74, Ecole Nat. Supérieure Mecanique Microtechs., 1974-78, dir. lab., 1978—; co-creator, co-organizer European Frequency and Time Forum, 1987—; organizer Lab. de Chronométrie Électronique et Piézoélectricité; creator indsl. co. for industrialization of Lab. de Chronométrie Électronique et Piézoélectricité's main rsch. results BVA Industry S.A., 1991; regional dept. for rsch. and tech. Ministry of Rsch., 1982-99. Co-contbr. chpt. to: Physical Acoustics, 1975; contbr. over 80 articles on piezoelectric resonators, oscillators sensors to various publs. and procs.; inventor family of new resonators and oscillators; patentee piezoelectric resonators oscillators sensors, new specific quartz accelerometers. With French mil., 1965-66. Recipient Silver medal Nat. Ctr. Sci. Rsch., Paris, 1980, Grand prize in electronics Gen. Ferrié, Paris, 1980, Sci. and Def. prize French Dept. Def., Paris, 1984, W.G. Cady award IEEE and Ultrasonics, Ferroelectrics and Frequency Control Soc., 1992; named Officer Legion of Honor, Officer of Merit, Officer of Acad. Palms. Mem. IEEE (sr.), Elec. and Electronics Soc., French Soc. Microtechs. and Chronometry (pres.). Roman Catholic. Avocations: skiing, swimming, foreign languages. Home: 23 Rue Octave David,

25000 Besancon France Office: École Nat Supérieure Méconique Microtechs, 26 Chemin de l'Epitaphe, 25030 Besançon France

BESSONOV, EVGUENI GRIGORIEVICH, physicist; b. Moscow, Dec. 6, 1939; s. Grigorii Stepanovich and Lubov Georgievna (Evstigneeva) B.; m. Galina Grigorievna Afanasieva, May 5; children: Oksana Evguenievna. MSc, Phys. Engr. Inst., Moscow, 1963; PhD in physics, Lebedev Phys. Inst., Moscow, 1970, D in sci., 1988. Engr. Lebedev Physical Inst., Moscow, 1963-67, rsch. scientist, 1967-86, sr. scientist, 1986—. Contbr. articles to profl. jours. Home: Central St Home 16 flat 54, 142092 Troitsk Russia Office: Lebedev Physical Inst AS, Leninsky Prospect 53, 117924 Moscow Russia

BESSOS, HAGOP IBRAHIM, medical research scientist; b. Beirut, Dec. 22, 1949; arrived in the UK, 1976.; s. Ibrahim and Elizabeth (Mesrobian) B.; m. Kathleen Mary Duffy, June 9, 1979; children: Maureen-Eliz, Stephen-Bessilios. BSc, Am. U., Beirut, 1973, MSc, 1976; PhD, U. Edinburgh, 1980. Clin. scientist Scottish Nat. Blood Transfusion Svc., Edinburgh, 1980-83, sr. clin. scientist, 1983-90, prin. clin. scientist, 1990—. Contbr. articles to profl. jours.; patentee in field. Annie and Margaret McKenzie scholar U. Edinburgh, 1977-80. Mem. Am. Assn. Blood Banks, Internat. Soc. Thrombosis Haemostasis, British Blood Transfusion Soc. (co-chmn. blood components group 1991—), British Soc. for Haemostasis & Thrombosis, Assn. of Clinical Biochemists, British Soc. for Immunology. Mem. Armenian Evang. Ch. Avocations: squash, badminton, hiking, travelling, music. Home: 47 Marchmont Rd, Edinburgh EH9 1HU, Scotland Office: SE Blood Transfusion Svc, Lauriston Pl, Edinburgh EH3 9HB, Scotland

BESSOU, JEAN-PAUL, thoracic surgeon, medical educator; b. Neuilly sur Seine, Seine Ile, France, July 21, 1950; s. Raymond Pierre and Simone Claude (Lagadec) B.; m. Catherine Yvonne Bret, Oct. 4, 1975; children: Caroline-Sophie, Aurelien, Florence. MD, U. Paris, 1982; univ. prof. cert., U. Rouen, France. Intern Hopitaux de Paris; trainee in cardiovascular surgery Broussais Hosp., Paris; thoracic and cardiovascular surgeon Charles Nicolle Hosp., Rouen, prof. thoracic and cardiovascular surgery, 1986—. Office: Hosp Charles Nicolle, 1 Rue de Germont, 76000 Rouen France

BEST, FRANKLIN LUTHER, JR., lawyer; b. Lock Haven, Pa., Dec. 14, 1945; s. Franklin L. and Hazel M. (Yearick) B.; m. Kimberly R., May 1, 1982. BA, Yale U., 1967; JD, U. Pa., 1970; postgrad., Columbia U., 1994. Bar: Pa. 1970. Assoc. MacCoy, Evans & Lewis, Phila., 1970-74; asst. counsel Penn Mut. Life Ins. Co., Phila., 1974-77, asst. gen. counsel, 1978-84, assoc. gen. counsel, 1985-99, mng. corp. counsel, 1999—; counsel, asst. sec. Penn Ins. and Annuity Co., Phila., 1983-96, counsel, sec., 1996—; lectr. Pa. Bar Inst., 1976-84. Author: Pennsylvania Insurance Law, 1991, 2d edit., 1998; contbr. articles to profl. jours. Bd. dirs. Ctr. City South Neighborhood Assn., 1979-80, pres., 1978-79; mem. Com. of Seventy, 1978-84; sec. Washington Sq. Assn., 1977-87; mem. 30th Ward Rep. Exec. Com., 1972-84, West Pikeland Twp. Open Spaces Com., 1987-99, chairperson, 1995-99, planning commn., 1994—, chairperson, 1996—. Mem. ABA, Internat. Claim Assn. (sec. 1995—, exec. com. 1979-81, 85-88), Phila. Bar Assn., Yale Club of Phila. Baptist. Office: Penn Mut Life Ins Co 600 Dresher Rd Horsham PA 19044-2204

BEST, LAEL-ANSON ELIEZER, thoracic surgeon; b. Bombay, Aug. 11, 1951; s. Eliezer Moses and Ivy (Abraham) B.; m. Rebecca Abra, Dec. 25, 1977; children: Niv, Shere, Hila. MB, BChir, B.J. Med. Coll., Ahmedabad, India, 1975, MS, 1978. Lic. thoracic surgeon, Israel. Fellow Mayo Clinic, Rochester, Minn., 1987-88; dir. thoracic surgery Rambam Med. Ctr., Haifa, Israel, 1989—; cons., surgeon gen. Israel Def. Forces, 1993—. Contbr. articles to profl. jours. Lt. Israeli Def. Forces, 1985-87. Fellow ACS, Internat. Coll. Surgeons, Am. Coll. Chest Physicians; mem. Internat. Soc. Esophageal Diseases (nat. rep.), Gen. Thoracic Surg. Club. Office: Rambam Med Ctr, 8 Aliya St, 31096 Haifa Israel

BESTAOUI, YASMINA, electronic engineer, educator; b. Paris, June 7, 1960; d. Hammadi and Malika (Benhamed) B. BS, U. Tlemcen, Algeria, 1981, MS, 1984; PhD, ENSM, Nantes, France, 1989. Assoc. prof. U. Tlemcen, 1981-89, U. Nantes, 1989-99; vis. assoc. prof. Naval Postgrad. Sch., Monterey, Calif., 1997-98, U. Evry, France, 1999—. Contbr. articles to profl. jours. Mem. IEEE. Avocations: reading, music, sports, theater. Office: IUP U Evry, 40 rue Pelvoux, 91020 Evry courcouronnes France

BESTEHORN, UTE WILTRUD, retired librarian; b. Cologne, Germany, Nov. 6, 1930; came to U.S., 1930; d. Henry Hugo and Wiltrud Lucie (Vincentz) B. BA, U. Cin., 1954, BEd, 1955, MEd, 1958; MS in Library Sci., Western Res. U. (now Case-Western Res. U.), 1961. Tchr. Cutter Jr. High Sch., Cin., 1955-57; tchr., supr. libr. Felicity (Ohio) Franklin Sr. High Sch., 1959-60; with libr. sci. dept. Pub. Libr. Cin. and Hamilton County, 1961-78, with libr. info. desk, 1978-91; ret., 1991; textbook selection com., Felicity-Franklin Sr. High Sch., 1959-60; supr. Health Alcove Sci. Dept. and annual health lectures, Cin. Pub. Library, 1972-77. Book reviewer Library Jour., 1972-77; author and inventor Rainbow 40 marble game, 1971, Condominium game, 1976; patentee indexed packaging and stacking device, 1973, mobile packaging and stacking device, 1974. Mem. Clifton Town Meeting, 1988—; mem. Bookfest 90 com. Pub. Libr. Cin. and Hamilton County. Recipient Cert. of Merit and Appreciation Pub. Library of Cin., 1986. Mem. Cin. Chpt. Spl. Libraries Assn. (archivist 1963-64, 65-70, editor Queen City Gazette bull. 1964-69), Pub. Library Staff Assn. (exec. bd., activities com. 1965, welfare com. 1966, recipient Golden Book 25 yr. service pin, 1986), Friends of the Library, Greater Cin. Calligraphers Guild (reviewer New Letters pub. 1986-88), Delta Phi Alpha (nat. German hon. 1951). Republican. Mem. United Ch. of Christ. Avocations: calligraphy, painting and sketching, writing, photography, violin . Home: 3330 Morrison Ave Cincinnati OH 45220-1440

BESTWICK, WARREN WILLIAM, retired construction company executive; b. Missoula, Mont., June 27, 1922; s. William Andrew and Beatrice Anna (Eddy) B.; m. Glenette Haas, Sept. 11, 1949; children: Sharon Kaye, Carol Eddy, Jan Marie. Student, Glendale Coll., 1941, U. Mont., 1942; BA, U. Wash., 1949, postgrad., 1950. Sr. acct. Frederick & Nelson, Seattle, 1950; contr., bus. mgr. Va. Mason Hosp., Seattle, 1958-64; contr. Bumstead Woolford Co., Seattle, 1964-68; contr., treas. Wash. Asphalt Co., Seattle, 1968-72; exec. v.p., sec., treas. Wilder Constrn. Co., Inc., Bellingham, Wash., 1972-77, pres., COO, CFO, 1977-89, vice-chmn., 1989-92; ret., 1992. Past bd. dirs. Consumers Choice, Bellingham; bd. govs. Va. Mason Med. Ctr., Seattle; past chmn. Area IV adv. bd. Wash. Dept. Commerce and Econ. Devel.; past dir., vice chmn. Mt. Baker Bank, Bellingham; past bd. dirs. adv. bd. Mt. Baker Coun. Boy Scouts Am. Col., pilot USMCR. Decorated DFC (3), Air medal (7). Mem. Assn. Wash. Bus. (past dir.), Whatcom County Devel. Coun. (past dir. and pres.), Bellingham C. of C. (past dir.), Shukson Found. (past dir., pres., bd. dirs.), Marine Res. Officers Assn. (past dir. Seattle), Res. Officers Assn., Marine Corps League, The Beavers (Constrn. hon., emeritus), United for Wash., U. Wash. Alumni Assn., Ret. Officers Assn., Marine Aviation Assn., World Affairs Coun., Wash. Athletic Club (Seattle), Bellingham Golf and Country Club, Bellingham Yacht Club, Rotary (past pres.). Home: PO Box 2032 Rancho Santa Fe CA 92067-2032

BESUSCHIO, SANTIAGO CESAR, pathologist, epidemiologist; b. Buenos Aires, Oct. 12, 1931; s. Santiago and Carmen (Otero) B.; m. Isabel Casado, July 17, 1959; children: Susana, Adrian; m. Iliana Wlazlo, Sept. 9, 1995. MD, U. Buenos Aires, 1958, grad. hygienist, 1960; grad. pathologist, Pub. Health Dept. Sch., Buenos Aires, 1960. Intern, resident Pirovano Hosp., Buenos Aires, 1961-64; chief pathology dept. Inst. Microbiology/U. Buenos Aires, 1963-68, Inst. Cardiology/Nat. Acad. Medicine, Argentina, 1967-73, French Hosp., Buenos Aires, 1968—; dir. collaborating ctr. WHO Internat. Classification Tumors, Geneva, 1970-76; chief pathology dept. Inst. Hematological Rsch./Nat. Acad. Medicine, Buenos Aires, 1972-94; prof. pathology U. Buenos Aires, 1986—; assoc. prof. pathology U. Paris VI Pierre et Marie Curie, France, 1993-94; cons. pathologist Cancer Ctr. Buenos Aires Province, Gonnet, Argentina, 1985-93, Club Pathologie Hematologique, Paris, 1988—; hon. coord. nat. sci. and tech. dept. Nat. Program Health, Buenos Aires, 1989—; organizer Nat. Registry Cancer, Abidjan, Ivory Coast, 1969-70; assoc. rschr. epidemiology unit IARC/WHO, Lyon, France, 1969; coord. continuing edn. program Pub. Health Dept.; commn. study AIDS Nat. Acad. Medicine and Pub. Health Ministry, 1985, 90; vis. prof. Kiel U., Germany, 1970, 88. Author: Chronic Hydroarsenicism Regional Endemic, 1982, Argentine Hemorrnagic Fever, 1982 (Nat. Dept. Culture award 1990), General Pathology, 1992, Pathological Anatomy, 1993. Mem. Nat. Commn. Against Hemorrnagic Fever, 1971-74; OAS rep. UN Conf. on Tech. Coop. between devel. countries, Buenos Aires, 1978; v.p. Argentine br. Soc. Ingenieurs Scientifiques France, Paris, 1980—; pres. Hematol. Pathology Club, Buenos Aires, 1981. Recipient Sci. award Nat. Acad. Medicine, Buenos Aires, 1966, 72, 82, 91, Faculty Medicine-U. Buenos Aires, 1967-79, 70-71, 71-73, 73; Sci. Merit award Severo Vaccaro Found., Buenos Aires, 1990-91, Chevalier dans l'Ordre des Palmes Academiques French Prime Min., Paris, 1992. Fellow OAS, Leukemia and Lymphomas Epidemiology, Leukemia and Lymphomas; mem. Soc. Anatomique, European Acad. Scis., Arts and Humanities (corr. mem.), N.Y. Acad. Sci. Fax: 54-1-1-4824-0829. E-mail: funscb@fibertel.com.ar. Home: Las Heras 2931, 1425 Buenos Aires Argentina Office: Inst Pathology, Laprida 1708, 1425 Buenos Aires Argentina

BETANCOURT, HECTOR MAINHARD, psychology scientist, educator; b. Chile, Sept. 1, 1949; came to U.S. 1979; s. Hector and Eleonora (Mainhard) B.; m. Bernardita Sahli; children: Paul, Daniel. BA, Cath. U., Santiago, Chile, 1976; MA, UCLA, 1981, PhD in Psychology, 1983. From asst. prof. to assoc. prof. psychology Cath. U., Santiago, Chile, 1977-79, 83-85; from assoc. prof. to prof. psychology Loma Linda U., Riverside, Calif., 1985-93, chmn., 1990-93; prof. psychology, founding chmn. Grad. Sch. Loma Linda U., Calif., 1993—; internat. cons. in higher edn./tng. in psychology, 1997—. Editor Interam. Psychologist, 1982-86; mem. edit. bd. Jour. Cmty. Psychology, 1986-89, Spanish Jour. Social Psychology, 1986—, Conflict and Peace, 1993-99, Jour. Personality and Social Psychology, 1997-98; contbr. articles to profl. jours. Recipient Rotary Found. award for Internat. Understanding, Rotary Internat., 1976-77; Fulbright fellow, UCLA, 1979-80. Mem. APA (exec. com. and chmn. task force on ethnicity, divsn. 48 peace psychology 1994-95, pres. 1997-98), Internat. Soc. Polit. Psychology, Internat. Soc. Cross-Cultural Psychology (exec. com. 1984-86), Interam. Soc. Psychology (sec.-gen. 1983-87, v.p. U.S. and Can. 1999—), Soc. for Psychol. Study Social Issues, Soc. Personality and Social Psychology, Psychologists for Soc. Responsibility (nat. steering com., 1999—). Avocations: internat. politics, literature, philosophy. Office: Loma Linda U Dept Psychology Grad S Loma Linda CA 92350-0001

BETANCOURT LOPEZ, ANTONIO L., association executive; b. Belen de Umbria, Colombia, Jan. 9, 1944; came to U.S., 1967; s. Angel Maria and Pastora (Lopez) B.; m. Kyoko Funayama-Kagawa, July 1, 1982; children: Kiantar, Annika, Kyboter, Isaac. Sec. gen. CAUSA Internat., N.Y.C., 1979-89; asst. to pres. New World Comms., N.Y.C., 1980-83; exec. v.p. Internat. Security Coun., Washington, 1984-90; exec. dir. Assn. for the Unity of Latin Am., Washington, 1983—, Summit Coun. for World Peace, Washington, 1981—; dep. sec. gen. Fedn. for World Peace, Washington, 1991—; pres. Young Gruppe, Inc., Washington, 1992—, News & Communication, Inc., 1993—; pres. Group Internat. Arte, Washington, 1996—, World Inst. for Devel. and Peace, 1996—. Exec. editor jour. Global Affairs, 1984-90; exec. dir. conf. procs. Mem. Family Fedn. for World Peace and Unification, N.Y.C., 1996—. Recipient commendation Cath. U., La Plata, Argentina, 1984, Acad. award Mexican Acad. Internat. Law, 1985, Grand Medal of Peace, Dem. People's Republic of Korea, 1996; named hon. citizen Santo Domingo City, 1987. Mem. Am. Fgn. Svc. Assn. (internat. assoc.), Corcoran Gallery, N.Y. Acad. Sci., Oxford Club, Asia Soc., Korea Soc., Wilson Ctr. for Scholars. Avocations: gardening, antique collecting and restoration, hiking, fishing. Home: 6305 Queens Chapel Rd University Park MD 20782-2131 Office: Summit Coun for World Peace 3600 New York Ave NE Washington DC 20002-1947

BETBEZE, JEAN-PAUL, economist; b. Bagnéres, France, Sept. 6, 1949; s. Georges and Juliette (Lapierre) B.; m. Joselyne Desroches; children: Georges-Henri, Paul-Hadrien. Hautes Etudes Comml., France, 1972; D in Econ. Sci., 1979; agregation, Faculty Econ. Sci., 1984. Prof. U. Besançon, France, 1984-87, U. Paris II, 1987-90; chief economist Credit Lyonnais Group, Paris, 1990—, head of strategy, 1996—. Author: La Conjoncture Economique, rev. edit., 1989, L'Investissement, 1990; contbr. articles to profl. jours. Mem. French Assn. Bus. Economists (pres. 1994-97), Cercle des Economistes. Office: Credit Lyonnais, 81 Rue de Richelieu, 75002 Paris France

BETHE, HANS ALBRECHT, physicist, educator; b. Strassburg, Alsace-Lorraine, Germany, July 2, 1906; came to U.S., 1935; s. Albrecht Theodore and Anna (Kuhn) B.; m. Rose Ewald, 1939; children: Henry, Monica. Ed. Goethe Gymnasium, Frankfurt on Main, U. Frankfort; Ph.D., U. Munich, 1928; D.Sc., Bklyn. Poly. Inst., 1950, U. Denver, 1952, U. Chgo., 1953, U. Birmingham, 1956, Harvard U., 1958. Instr. in theoretical physics univs. of Frankfort, Stuttgart, Munich and Tubingen, 1928-33; lectr. univs. of Manchester and Bristol, Eng., 1933-35; asst. prof. Cornell U., 1935, prof., 1937-75, prof. emeritus, 1975—; dir. theoretical physics div. Los Alamos Sci. Lab., 1943-46; Mem. Presdl. Study Disarmament, 1958; mem. Pres.'s Sci. Adv. Com., 1956-60. Author: Mesons and Fields, 1953, Elementary Nuclear Theory, 1957, Quantum Mechanics of One-and Two-Electron Atoms, 1957, Intermediate Quantum Mechanics, 1964; contbr. Handbuch der Physik, 1933, Revs. Modern Physics, 1936-37, Phys. Rev., Astrophys. Jour. Recipient A. Cressy Morrison prize N.Y. Acad. Sci., 1938-40; Presdl. Medal of Merit, 1946; Max Planck medal, 1953; Enrico Fermi award AEC, 1961; Nobel Prize in physics, 1967; Nat. Medal of Sci., 1976; Vannevar Bush award NSF, 1985; Einstein Peace prize Albert Einstein Peace Prize Found., 1993, Oersted prize Am. Assn. Physics Tchrs. Fgn. mem. Royal Soc. London; mem. Am. Philos. Soc., NAS (Henry Draper medal 1968), Am. Phys. Soc. (pres. 1954), Am. Astron. Soc. Office: Cornell U Newman Lab Ithaca NY 14853

BETHEL, DAVID PERCIVAL, education professional; b. Bath, Somerset, U.K., Dec. 7, 1923; s. William George and Elsie Evelyn (Cossins) B.; m. Margaret Elizabeth Wrigglesworth, May 8, 1943; children: Paul David, Ruth Rebecca. NDD, West of Eng. Coll. of Art, Bristol, 1950; ATD, Univ. Bristol, 1951; LLD (hon.), Univ. Leicester, 1982; DLitt, U. Loughborough, 1987; EdD, UWE, 1998. Design certs.: FSAE, FSTC, FCSD, FRSA, RWA. Lectr. Coll. of Art, Stafford, U.K., 1951-56; vice-prin. Coll. of Art, Coventry, 1956-65, prin., 1965-69; dep. dir. Leicester Polytechnic, Leicester, 1969-73, dir., 1973-87; chmn. Coun. for Nat. Acad. Awards, Art/Design Rsch. Degrees Com., London, 1975-81, Com. of Dirs. of Polytechnics, London, 1978-80, Hong Kong Coun. for Acad. Accreditation, 1987-92; mem. Hong Kong Univ. Grants Com., 1982-92; coun. mem. Royal West of Eng. Acad., v.p., 1996—. Author: A CAse of Sorts, 1985, An Inudstrious People, 1992, 120 Woodcuts and the Bard, 1994; works have appeared in numerous shows including Gloucester City Art Gallery, 1960, Elizabeth Gallery, Coventry, 1960, Coun. for th Encouragement of Music and the Arts Gallery, Belfast, 1962, Herbert Art Gallery, Coventry, 1963; represented in permanent collections Royal West of Eng. Acad., Gloucester City Librs., Stafford City Librs., U. Leicester, Leicestershire Art Gallery, others. Commdr. of the Most Excellent Order of the Brit. Empire, HM The Queen, 1983; ct. mem. Worshipful Co. of Framework Knitters, London, 1994. Conservative. Ch. of England. Avocations: design history, travel, genealogy. Home: 48 Holmfield Rd, Leicester LE2 1SA, England

BETHEL, MARILYN JOYCE, librarian; b. Detroit, Jan. 14, 1935; d. Thomas Agmey and Mary Helen (Lisek) Hepfner; m. Herschel Earl Bethel, June 20, 1960 (div. Mar. 1969); 1 child, Mary Joyce. BA in Edn., Fla. Atlantic U., 1974; MLS, La. State U., 1975, MEd, 1976; postgrad., Fla. Atlantic U., 1977-78. Cert. reading specialist, Fla. Cons. Fla. Diagnostic and Learning Resources, Ft. Lauderdale, 1979-80; librarian Cocnut Creek (Fla.) Elem. Sch., 1980-82; cons. Fla. Coll. Bus., Pompano, 1982-84; librarian Broward County Librs., Hallandale, Fla., 1983; cataloger Broward County Librs., Ft. Lauderdale, 1983-90; br. head Broward County Librs., Deerfield, 1990-92; librarian Broward County Librs., Pompano, 1992-95, Ft. Lauderdale, 1995-2000; cons. Fla. Diagnostic and Learning Resources, 1979-80; mem. behavioral objectives writing team Broward County Spl. Edn., 1981. Advisor to periodical Biography Today, 1992—; writer newsletter Exceptional Student, 1979-80. Vol. crisis counselor Sexual Assault Treatment Ctr., Broward County, Fla., 1977-78; lectr., instr. New Covenant Ch., Pompano, 1984-87. With USAF, 1954-55. Recipient Cert. of Appreciation, Bd. County Commrs., Ft. Lauderdale, 1978. Mem. ALA (com. for cataloging for children 1989-95, liaison Freedom to Read 1979-80), Fla. Libr. Assn., Broward County Libr. Assn., Nat. Alzheimers Assn. Republican. Presbyterian. Avocations: floral arranging, snorkeling, swimming, reading. Home: 272 NE 39th Ct Pompano Beach FL 33064-3545 Office: Broward County Librs 100 S Andrews Ave Fort Lauderdale FL 33301-1830

BETHELL, HUGH JAMES NEWTON, general practitioner; b. Berwick St. James, Eng.; s. Richard Bryan Wyndham and Jacquamina Alice (Barton) B.; m. Astrid Jill Short (dec. 1979); children: Katharine Emma, Christina Louise; m. Lesley Harris. MB, BChir with distinction in physic, Cambridge (Eng.) U.-Guys Hosp., 1966; MD, Cambridge U., 1995. House physician Addenbrookes Hosp., Cambridge, 1967; sr. house officer in medicine Bolingbroke Hosp., London, 1969; registrar in cardiology Charing Cross Hosp., London, 1969-72; registrar in dermatology Guys Hosp., London, 1972-74; pvt. practice, Alton, Eng., 1974—; dir. Basingstoke and Alton Cardiac Rehab. Unit, 1976—' chmn. secondary prevention and rehab. com. Coronary Prevention Group, London, 1987—; mem. rehab. com. Brit. Heart Found., London, 1992—. Author: Exercise-Based Cardiac Rehabilitation, 1996; contbr. numerous articles and revs. to med. jours. and chpts. to books. Decorated mem. Order Brit. Empire. Fellow Royal Coll. Physicians, Royal Coll. Gen. Practitioners; mem. Brit. Assn. for Cardiac Rehab. (founder pres. 1993-95), Brit. Cardiac Soc. (working party on cardiac rehab. 1989-91), Hawks Club. Home: Timbers, Boyneswood Rd, Madstead Alton GU34 5DY, England Office: Health Ctr, Alton Hants GU34 2QX, England

BETHELL, JOHN, company executive; b. Nuneaton, Warwicksh., Eng., Apr. 30, 1939; arrived in France, 1997; s. William Arthur and Elizabeth Marshall (Green) B.; m. Gillian Stewart Robertson McCartney, Aug. 22, 1964; children: Kim, John Hugh, Julie Jean, Rebecca Anne. BSc in Geology with honours, Glasgow (Scotland) U., 1962. Geologist Govt. of Sierra Leone, 1962-64; mktg. asst. Texco, 1964-68; dist. mgr. Texaco Africa Ltd., Sierra Leone, 1968-72; mng. dir. Argus of Ayr Ltd., Scotland, 1972-82; chief exec. Scottish Seed Potato Devel. Coun., 1982-97; chmn. Delco Rus Ltd., Céret, France, 1995—; chmn. Argoventure Ltd., Scotland, 1973-85; sec. S.E. Growers Ltd., Scotland, 1989-94, Clantweed, Ukraine, 1994—. Bd. dirs. Internat. Sch., Freetown, Sierra Leone, 1968-72; chmn. computer forum Scottish Conservative and Unionist Assn., 1986-90; founder chmn. River Tyne Trust, Scotland, 1990-94. Recipient Paul Harris award Rotary Internat., 1995; hon. fellow Edinburgh U., 1988-97. Mem. Rotary (hon. Kiev, Ukraine, sec. Perpignan-Agly 1990-00). Avocations: mountain climbing, classical music. Home: La Châtaigneraie, 66400 Céret P-O, France

BETHELL, LESLIE MICHAEL, historian, educator; b. Leeds, Yorkshire, Eng., Feb. 12, 1937; s. Stanley and Bessie (Stoddart) B.; divorced; children: Ben, Daniel. BA, U. London, 1958, PhD, 1963. Lectr. in history U. Bristol, Eng., 1961-66; lectr. in history U. Coll. U. London, 1966-74, reader in history, 1974-86; prof. Latin Am. history U. London, 1986-92, dir. Inst. Latin Am. Studies, 1987-92; sr. rsch. fellow St. Antony's Coll., 1993-96; dir. ctr. Brazilian Studies U. Oxford, 1997—. Author: The Abolition of the Brazilian Slave Trade, 1970; co-author: Latin America between the Second World War and the Cold War, 1992, A Guerra do Paraguai, 1995; editor: The Cambridge History of Latin America, Vols. I and II-Colonial Latin America, 1984, Vol. III-From Independence to circa 1870, 1985, Vols. IV and V-Circa 1870 to 1930, 1986, Vol. VI Parts land 2- Latin America 1930: Economy Society and Politics, 1994, Vol VII Mexico, Central America, Caribbean Since 1930, 1990, Vol. VII Spanish South America Since, 1930, 1991, Vol. X-Latin America Since 1930: Ideas, Culture and Society, 1995, Vol. XI- Bibliographical Essays, 1995. Home: The East Stair, Wytham Abbey Oxford OX2 8QE, England

BETHMONT, MICHEL, manufacturing executive, materials engineer, consultant; b. Domont, France, Apr. 15, 1951; s. Victor Bethmont and Micheline Cornec; m. Sylvie Gallerand, Dec. 10, 1978; children: Sandrine, Pierre-Laurent, Anne-Claire, Thomas. Grad. in engring., Inst. Supéerieur Matériaux Constrn. Mécanique, Saint-Ouen, France, 1974; grad., Université Tech. Compiègne, France, 1977. Rsch. engr. FRAMATOME, Paris, 1977-82; mgr. study group EDF Rsch. and Devel. Divsn., Ecuelles, France, 1982-96; project mgr. in maintenance EDF Conventional Thermal Dept., Saint-Denis, France, 1996. Mem. Am. Soc. for Testing and Materials, Soc. Parents (pres. 1984, 90), Soc. Française Métallurgie. Roman Catholic. Avocations: bicycle, boat, cross country, philosophy reading. Fax: 33 1 43 69 34 87. Home e-mail: michel.bethmont@compuserve.com; office e-mail: michel.bethmont@edfgdf.fr. Home: 15 rue Labrouste, Paris 75015, France Office: EDF Mission Thermique, 1 Pleyel Pl, Saint Denis 93282, France

BETHOUX, FRANÇOIS ANDRE, physiatrist, researcher; b. Paris, May 31, 1964; s. Pierre Andre and Janine Gabrielle (Monin) B.; m. Sandrine Christine Delclaud, Apr. 9, 1988; children: Nicolas, Ambre. MD, A. Carrel Med. Sch., Lyon, France, 1990; Bd. Phys. Med. and Rehab., J. Monnet U., St. Etienne, France, 1994; DEA Handicap and Rehab., Bourgogne U., Dijon, France, 1994. Med. diplomate specializing in phys. medicine and rehab. Resident U. Hosps., St. Etienne, France, 1991-94; academic physiatrist U. Hosps., St. Etienne, 1995-97; rsch. fellow Case We. Res. U., Cleve., 1994-95; fellow in neuroimmunology Mellen Ctr. Multiple Sclerosis, Cleve., 1997—; rschr. Jean Monnet U., St. Etienne, France, 1992-97, tchr., 1995-97; tchr. Sch. Phys. Therapy, St. Etienne, 1992-97, Inst. Social Scis., St. Etienne, 1996-97. Contbr. chpt. to book, articles to profl. jours. Grantee French Assn. Paralyzed People, 1994. Mem. French Soc. Phys. Medicine and Rehab., Internat. Soc. Quality of Life. Avocations: music, reading, cycling. Fax: 216-445-6259. E-mail: BETHOUF@cesmtp.ccf.org. Home: 2179 Cottage Grove Dr Cleveland Hts OH 44118-2873 Office: Cleve Clin Found 9500 Euclid Ave Cleveland OH 44195-0001

BETINIS, EMANUEL JAMES, physics and mathematics educator; b. Oak Park, Ill., Oct. 31, 1927; s. James Emanuel and Ioanna Helen (Kallas) B.; children: Demetrios, Joanna, Markos. BS in Chemistry and Math., Northwestern U., 1950; MS in Applied Math., U. Ill., 1952; MS in Physics, U. Chgo., 1979. Aerodynamicist Northrop Aviation, Hawthorne, Calif., 1953-54; theoretical reactor physicist Atomics Internat., Canoga Park, Calif., 1954-57; applied sci. rep. IBM, Chgo., 1957-61; math. cons. Math. Cons. Svc., Chgo., 1961-81; adj. prof. math. and physics IIT, Roosevelt U., Chgo., 1981-88; mathematician Batelle Meml. Labs., Willowbrook, Ill., 1988-89; asst. prof. physics Elmhurst (Ill.) Coll., 1990—. Contbr. articles to Jour. Geophys. Rsch., Jour. Brit. Interplanetary Soc., Hadronic Jour., Matrix, Lensor Soc. Great Britain. Mem. PTO. With U.S. Army, 1946-47. Fellow Brit. Interplanetary Soc.; mem. Am. Nuclear Soc., Sigma Pi Sigma, Pi Mu Epsilon. Republican. Orthodox. Achievements include patent in golf ball trajectory with lift and drag; research in analytic solution of boundary-value problems in arbitrary geometry, special relativity, quantum mechanical proof of speed of light limitation, analytic solution of 3 dimensional heat conduction equation in arbitrary geometry, nuclear potential and prediction of 470MeV elementary particles, analytic solution of non-linear hydrodynamics equations; development and manufacture of devices for entropy and Biot-Savart physics experiments, calculation of velocity of nucleons in the deuteron, EM theory relativistic time dilation and removal of velocity of light speed limit, Em theory relativistic Schroedinger equations, scattering cross-section for superluminal particles, faster than light quantum mechanics. Office: Elmhurst Coll Dept Physics Box 47 190 Prospect Ave Elmhurst IL 60126-3271

BETLEJEWSKI, STANISLAW, physician; b. Torun, Poland, Dec. 16, 1933; s. Jan and Agnieszka (Bledzka) B.; m. Maria Glinska, Sept. 19, 1959; 1 child, Andrew. Physician, Med. U., Gdansk, Poland, 1957, MD, 1966, PhD, 1972; Prof., Med. U., Bydgoszcz, Poland, 1984. Asst. Med. U., Gdansk, 1957-59, asst. prof., 1972-81; asst. prof., chmn. Med. U., Bydgoszcz, 1981-84, prof., chmn., 1984—; physician Navy, Poland, 1959-61; adj. prof. Med. U., Gdansk, 1961-72.; pro-rector Med. U., Bydgoszcz, Poland, 1984-90. Contbr. articles to profl. jours. Capt. Polish Navy, 1959-61. Mem. Polish Soc. Otorhinolaryngology (pres. 1989-92), Polish Soc. Rhinology (pres. 1996—), Internat. Fedn. Otorhinolaryngological Socs. (mem. exec. com. 1989—), Polish Soc. Laryngectomised (hon. pres. 1986—), Am. Acad. Otolaryngology, Head and Neck Surgery, European Acad. of Otology and Neuro-Otology, European Rhinologic Soc. Avocations: painting, sculpture, skiing. Home: Powstancow Wielkopols 44/36, Bydgoszcz Poland Office: Dept Otolaryngology/Med U, Sklodowska Curie Str 9, 85-094 Bydgoszcz Poland

BETTA, PIER-GIACOMO, pathologist; b. Alessandria, Piedmont, Italy, Dec. 24, 1949; s. Mario and Caterina (Balbi) B.; m. Patrizia Longo, Sept. 7, 1990; 1 child, Beatrice. Degree in medicine, U. Turin, Italy, 1975; degree in anatomic pathology, U. Parma, 1979; degree in oncology, U. Turin, 1982; degree in exptl. pathology, U. Genoa, Italy, 1986. Asst. dept. pathology City Hosp., Alessandria, Italy, 1976-82, dep. chief dept. pathology, 1982-89; chief svc. of pathol. anatomy and cytopathology Santo Spirito Hosp., Casale Monferrato, Italy, 1989-97; chief pathology unit dept. oncology City Hosp., Alessandria, Italy, 1997—; mem. asbestos group Nat. Oncology Commn., Ministry of Health. Mem. Am. Soc. Clin. Oncology, Internat. Mesothelioma Interest Group, N.Y. Acad. Scis., European Soc. Mastology, Italian Soc. of Anatomic Pathology and Cytopathology, Italian League Against Cancer (pres. Alessandria sect.). Office: City Hosp, Via Venezia 16, 15100 Alessandria Italy

BETTENCOURT, LILIANE, cosmetics company executive; d. Eugéne Schueller. Vice chmn. bd. Gesperal; also bd. dirs. L'Oreal, Paris, 1995—. Office: L'Oreal, 41 Rue Martre, 92117 Clichy France*

BETTI, ROBERTO, physician; b. Milan, Italy, Mar. 8, 1949; s. Marco and Anna Maria (Turati) B.; m. Marilena Invernizzi, Dec. 19, 1974. MD, U. Milan, 1974. Resident U. Milan, 1972-74, 74-77; asst. Hosp., Milan, 1977-89, attending physician, 1989—; cons. in field. Author: Accessory Mammary Tissue in Clinical Practice, 1996; contbr. over 200 articles to profl. jours. With Italian Army, 1975-76. Mem. Internat. Soc. Dermatology, Italian Soc. Dermatology, Italian Hosp. Soc. Dermatology. Roman Catholic. Avocation: cycling. Office: Derm Clinic/S Paolo Hosp, Via di Rudini 8, Milan Italy

BETTOCCHI, CARLO, urologist; b. Rome, Oct. 7, 1964; s. Silvio Bettocchi and Angela Gamberini. Degree in medicine, U. Bari, Italy, 1989, degree in urology, 1994; hon. degree in andrology, U. London, 1995. Cert. in medicine. Rsch. registrar U. Maastricht, The Netherlands, 1991; clin. asst. U. London, 1992-95; sr. registrar U. Bari, 1995—; locum cons. U. London, 1998-99; kidney transplantation dept. U. Bari, 1992—. Field editor male congenital surgery: Italian Jour. Andrology, 1998—; contbr. more than 15 chpts. to sci. books; numerous articles to sci. jours. Mem. Italian Nat. Obs. on Gender Disphoria (treas. 1998-00), Italian Soc. Andrology (councillor 1999-01). Democrat. Roman Catholic. Avocations: golf, tennis, music, arts. Fax: 39 080 5478880. E-mail: bettocchi@urologia.uniba.it. Home: Corso A De Gasperi 292, 70125 Bari Italy Office: Policlinico Dept Urology, Piazza G Cesare 11, 70124 Bari Italy

BETTS, BARBARA STOKE, artist, educator; b. Arlington, Mass., Apr. 19, 1924; d. Stuart and Barbara Lillian (Johnstone) Stoke; m. James William Betts, July 28, 1951; 1 child, Barbara Susan (dec.). BA, Mt. Holyoke Coll., 1946; MA, Columbia U., 1948. Cert. tchr., N.Y., Calif., Hawaii. Art tchr. Walton (N.Y.) Union Schs., 1947-48, Presidio Hill Sch., San Francisco, 1949-51; freelance artist San Francisco, 1951; art tchr. Honolulu Acad. Arts, summer 1952, 59, 63, 85, spring 61, 64; libr. aide art rm. Libr. of Hawaii, Honolulu, 1959; art tchr. Hanahauoli Sch., Honolulu, 1961-62, Hawaii State Dept. Edn., Honolulu, 1958-59, 64-84; owner Ho'olaule'a Designs, Honolulu, 1973—. Illustrator: Cathedral Cooks, 1964, In Due Season, 1986; exhibited in Hawaii Pavilion Expo '90, Osaka, Japan, State Found. of Culture and Arts, group shows since 1964, one person shows 1991, 96, 99; represented in Arts of Paradise Gallery, Waikiki, 1990—; traveling exhbns. include Pacific Prints, 1991, Printmaking East/West, 1993-95, Hawaii/Wis. Watercolor Show, 1993-94. Mem. Hawaii Watercolor Soc. (newsletter editor 1986-90), Nat. League Am. Pen Women (art chmn. 1990-92, sec. 1992-94, 2000—, nat. miniature art shows 1991, 92, 93, 95), Honolulu Printmakers (dir. 1986, 87), Assn. Hawaii Artists, scholarship aid programs, Mount Holyoke Coll., Mary Lyon Soc., Rutgers Univ., Col. Henry Rutgers Soc. Republican. Episcopalian. Avocations: art, travel, writing, photography. Home: 1434 Punahou St Apt 1028 Honolulu HI 96822-4740

BETTS, BERT A., former state treasurer, accountant; b. San Diego, Aug. 16, 1923; s. Bert A. and Alma (Jorgenson) B.; m. Barbara Lang; children: Terry Lou, Linda Sue, Sara Ellen, Bert Alan, Randy Wayne, LeAnn, John Chauncey, Frederick P., Roby F., Bruce H. BBA, Calif. Western U., 1950. CPA, Calif. Accountant John R. Gillette, 1946-48; ptnr. Gillette & Betts, 1949-50; pvt. accounting practice, 1951-54; ptnr. Betts & Munden, Lemon Grove, Calif., 1954-57; sr. ptnr. Bert A. Betts & Co., 1958-59; treas. State of Calif., 1959-67; prin. Bert A. Betts & Assos., 1967-77; chief exec. officer Internat. Prodn. Assos., 1970-87; dir. Lifetime Communities Inc.; gen. partner Sacramento Met. Airport Properties 4, Ltd., 1970—. Author (with Barbara Lang Betts): A Citizen Answers. Mem. Lemon Grove Sch. Bd., 1954-57; Calif. chmn. Max Baer Heart Fund; state employees chmn. Am. Cancer Soc., 1962-64, bd. dirs. county br., 1963-69, Sacramento County campaign chmn., mem. exec. com., 1965, pres. Sacramento chpt., 1967-68; sponsor All Am. B-24 Liberator Collings Found. Served as 1st lt. USAAF, 1942-45. Decorated D.F.C., Air medal with four clusters; recipient Louisville award Municipal Finance Officers Assn. U.S. and Can., 1963; honored by Calif. Municipal Treas.'s Assn., 1964; inductee Hoover H.S. Hall of Fame, San Diego, 1998. Mem. Nat. Assn. State Auditors, Comptrs. and Treas's Mcpl. Forum N.Y., Calif. Soc. CPAs, San Diego Squadron Air Force Assn. (past vice comdr.), Am. Legion, 2d Air Div. Assn., 8th Air Force Hist. Soc., VFW, Confederate Air Force (col.), Native Sons. Golden West, Internat. B-24 Liberator Club, Foresters, Lemon Grove Masonic Lodge, Calif. Scholarship Fedn. (life), Disting. Flying Cross Soc., Sigma Phi Epsilon, Beta Alpha Psi (hon.), Alpha Kappa Psi (hon.). Presbyn. Clubs: Eagles; Men's (Lemon Grove) (pres.), Lions (Lemon Grove) (treas.); Commonwealth. Home: 441 Sandburg Dr Sacramento CA 95819-2559 Also: 1830 Avenida Del Mundo Coronado CA 92118-3018

BETTS, JAMES WILLIAM, JR., financial analyst, consultant; b. Oct. 11, 1923; s. James William and Cora Anna (Banta) B.; m. Barbara Stoke, July 28, 1951; 1 child, Barbara Susan (dec.). BA, Rutgers U., 1946; postgrad., New Sch. for Social Rsch., 1948-49; MA, U. Hawaii, 1957. With Dun & Bradstreet, Inc., 1946-86, svc. cons., 1963-64, reporting and svc. mgr., 1964-65; sr. fin. analyst Dun & Bradstreet, Inc., Honolulu, 1965-86; owner Portfolio Cons. of Hawaii, 1979—; cons. Saybrook Point Investments, Old Saybrook, Conn., 1979—; owner James W. Betts and Co., 1996—. Contbr. articles to mag. With AUS, 1943. Mem. Am. Econ. Assn., Nat. Assn. Bus. Economists, Western Econ. Assn., Atlantic Econ. Soc., Col. Henry Rutgers Soc., Internat. Inst. Forecasters, Transp. Rsch. Forum. Republican. Episcopalian.

BETZ, JOCHEN NICOLAY, physicist, researcher; b. Ludwigshafen, Germany, Sept. 12, 1968; s. Walter Karl and Helga (Lenk) B. European diploma Initation in Rsch., U. Joseph Fourier, Grenoble, France, 1993, PhD with first class honors, 1997; diploma in Physics, U. Fridericiana, Karlsruhe, Germany, 1994. Physicist R&D Lab. Louis Néel, Nat. Ctr. Sci. Rsch., Grenoble, 1993-97; physicist rsch. & devel. Forschungszentrum, Karlsruhe, Germany, 1997-98; physicist R&D OMRON Electronics, Nufringen, Germany, 1998—; coord. devels. within a European Project, European Union, Grenoble, 1994-97. Patentee in field. Authorized rep. German census Ministry Dept. of Interior, Ludwigshafen, Germany, 1987. Recipient Am. Materials Rsch. Soc. Spl Student award, 1996, German-French Coll. award U. Karlsruhe, 1997. Avocations: skiing, photography, music. Office: OMRON Electronics, Carl-Benz-Str 4, D-71154 Nufringen Germany

BETZ, ULRICH ACHIM KARL, molecular biologist; b. Mutlangen, Germany, Jan. 26, 1967; s. Helmut and Christa (Eschinger) B.; m. Heike Rahel Deinzer, July 30, 1992; children: Melinda, Julian. Diploma, U. Tubingen, Germany, 1994; PhD, U Cologne, 1998. Rschr. Max-Planck Inst. Biology, Tubingen, Germany, U. Koln, Germany, Bayer Ag, Wuppertal, Germany. Contbr. articles to profl. jours.; patentee in field. Stipend scholar U. Tubingen. Roman Catholic. Avocation: research. Office: Bayer Ag, PH-R Ai II, D-42096 Wuppertal Germany

BETZER, ROY JAMES, retired national park service ranger; b. Rapid City, S.D., June 9, 1936; s. Bruce and Virginia Rose (Coppo) B.; m. Jeanette Menegas, Dec. 23, 1962 (div.). BS, Black Hills State Coll., 1959, BS in Edn., 1961; MA, U. S.D., 1966. Nat. pk. svc. ranger, 1992-98, tchr., coll. instr.; Mus. Tech. Living History interpreter U.S. Dept. Army; acting coach San Antonio Performing Arts, Barbizon; actor, cabaret singer, photographer; promotion specialist City of San Antonio; facilitator photographic workshop; cons. living history. With USN. Avocation: living history consulting, presenting 35 mm SLR workshops. Home: PO Box 840 Stonewall TX 78671-0420

BETZJITOMIR, SUSAN MARIE, financial consultant, lawyer, adult education educator; b. Bangor, Maine, Apr. 7, 1961; d. Roger Dennis and Trudy Louise (Box) Runyan; m. Howard Steven Jitomir; children: Roxanne, Jennifer, Jean, Susan. AS with distinction, Corming C.C., 1994; BS, Cornell U., 1997, LLD, 2000. Model Vogue Agy., N.Y.C., 1980-81; elder deacon Campbell (N.Y.) Presbyn. Ch., 1982-86; farmer Thurston, N.Y., 1985-93, Beaver Dams, N.Y., 1995—; supplemental instrn. leader Corming (N.Y.) C.C., 1991-94; fin. svcs. rep. 1st Investors, Elmira, N.Y., 1997. Contbr. articles to newspaper and periodical. Lectr. Merchantville Grange, Thurston, 1986-91; councilman Tsp. of Thurston, 1987-93, coord. CD, 1989-93; bd. dirs. Neighborhood Justice Project, Elmira, 1996. Mem. AAAS, Nat. Assn. Securities Dealers. Avocations: farming, photography, writing, politics, research. Home: Fish Hill Rd Beaver Dams NY 14812

BEUCHOT, MAURICIO, philosopher, priest; b. Torreon, Mexico, Mar. 4, 1950; s. Hardie and Martha (Puente) B. BA in Philosophy, Inst. Superior Autonomo Occidente, Guadalajara, Mex., 1977; MA in Philosophy, U. Iberoamericana, 1978, PhD in Philosophy, 1980. Asst. lectr. St. Thomas Aquinas Sem., Mexico City, 1975-76; lectr. U. Iberoamericana, Mexico City, 1976-79; asst. prof. Inst. Investigation Philosophy Univ. Nat. Autónoma Mex., Mexico City, 1979-84; prof. Inst. Investigation Philology, Mexico City, 1984-90; dept. head Ctr. Study of Classics, Mexico City, 1990—; Mem. Brit. Soc. History of Philosophy, Internat. Soc. Thomas Aquinas, Soc. Medieval Spanish Study, Mex. Acad. History. Roman Catholic. Home: Calzada de las Brujas 51 Col Nueva Oriental, Tlalpan, 14300 Mexico City Mexico Office: UNAM, Circuito Mario de la Cueva, 04510 Mexico City Mexico

BEUERLEIN, DAVID LEWIS, executive recruiter; b. Topeka, Kans., June 8, 1963; s. John Baptist and Arlene Struble Beuerlein; m. Sheila Davis, Nov. 5, 1988; 1 child, Craig David. BS, U. Kans., Lawrence, 1985; MS, U. Tex., Arlington, 1991; MBA, U. Tex., Austin, 1993. Program mgr. Gen. Dynamics, Ft. Worth, 1985-91; sr. engagement mgr. McKinsey & Co., Dallas, 1993-98; dir. high tech. Spencer Stuart, Dallas, 1998—. E-mail: dbeuerlein@spencerstuart.com. Office: Spencer Stuart 1717 Main St Ste 5600 Dallas TX 75201-7369

BEUKEMA, JAN JAKOBUS, marine biologist; b. Groningen, The Netherlands, Apr. 23, 1935. PhD, State U. Groningen, 1968. Fishery biologist Orgn. for Improvement of Inland Fisheries, The Netherlands, 1963-67; marine biologist Netherlands Inst. for Sea Rsch., Den Burg Texel, 1967—. Editor Jour. Sea Rsch., 1984—; contbr. over 100 articles to profl. jours. Home: Linieweg 19, 1783BA Den Helder The Netherlands Office: Netherlands Inst for Sea Rsch, PO Box 59, 1790 AB Den Burg Texel The Netherlands

BEUKEN, WILLEM ANDRÉ, retired theology educator, priest; b. Helmond, N Brabant, The Netherlands, May 13, 1931; arrived in Belgium, 1989; s. Willem Hendrik and Philomena Johanna (Spoorenberg) B. BA in Classical Langs., U. Amsterdam, The Netherlands, 1958; STL in Theology, Canisianum, Maastricht, The Netherlands, 1962; cand. laureate Biblical Exegesis, Pontifical Biblical Inst., Rome, 1965; DD in Theology, Rijks U. Utrecht, The Netherlands, 1967. Joined Order of Soc. of Jesus, 1949, ordained, 1961, professed, 1967. Sr. and ordinary prof. Catholic Theol. U., Amsterdam, The Netherlands, 1967-85; ordinary prof. Catholic U., Nijmegen, The Netherlands, 1985-89, Leuven, Belgium, 1989-96; rector Theol. Sem. of the Dutch Jesuit Province, Amsterdam, 1976-84; sec. Oudtestamentische Werkgezelschap Netherlands, 1978-81, pres. 1989-92; mem. Pontifical Biblical Commn., Vatican City, 1996—. Author: literary-hist. study of books Zechariah Haggai and Haggai- Sacharja 1-8, 1967, (commentary book of Isaiah, chpts. 40-66, 4 vols.) Jesaja deel IIA, 1979, Jesaja deel IIB, 1983, Jesaja deel IIIA, 1989, Jesaja deel IIIB, 1989, The Book of Job, 1994, Isaiah II/2 Chapters 28-39, 2000. Mem. Soc. Biblical Lit., Europese Vereniging van Katholieke Theologen. Afdeling Vlaanderen. Home: Waversebaan 220, 3001 Leuven-Heverlee Belgium Office: Kath U Faculty Godgeleerdh, St Michielsstraat 6, 3000 Leuven Belgium

BEUMLER, HENRY WEBER, lawyer; b. Douglas, Ariz., May 27, 1913; s. Henry Conrad Andrew and Susan Alberta (Weber) B.; m. Mary Estelle Collins, June 11, 1939 (dec.); children: Henry Collins, Timothy Collins, Edward Collins, Candyce Collins. BA, U. Ariz., 1934, JD, 1936; postgrad., U. Mex., 1937, Ariz. State U., 1960. Bar: Ariz. 1936, U.S. Dist. Ct. (Ariz.) 1936. Ptnr. Beumler & Beumler, Douglas, 1936-58; pvt. practice, Douglas, 1958-78, Portal, Ariz., 1978—; tchr. Douglas High Sch., 1958-78; mayor City of Douglas, 1950-60; city atty. Douglas, 1939-42; dep. atty. Cochise County, Ariz., 1940-42; commr. U.S. Dist. Ct., Tucson, 1948-68. Mem. Ariz. Devel. Bd., 1954-58, Ariz. Civil Rights Commn., 1956-58, San Simon Unified Dist. Sch. Bd., pres., 1985-88. Served to lt. col. AUS, 1942-46. Paul Harris fellow Rotary Internat. Mem. ABA, Ariz. Bar Assn., Cochise County Bar Assn., Ret. Tchrs. Assn., Masons, Phi Delta Kappa. Address: PO Box 16166 Portal AZ 85632-1166

BEUNEN, GASTON PRUDENCE, physical education educator; b. Berchem, Antwerpen, Belgium, June 26, 1945; s. René and Gerda (De Wachter) B.; m. Christiane Schueremans, July 19, 1969; children: Joeri, Mick, Ine. M Phys. Edn., Katholieke U., Leuven, Belgium, 1967, tchrs. diploma, 1967, PhD, 1973. Rsch. asst. K.U. Leuven, 1967-74, sr. researcher, 1974-75, asst. prof., 1975-82, prof. phys. edn., 1982—. Contbr. articles to profl. jours. Recipient award Van Clé Found., Belgium, 1971, Lynn Vendien award Am. Acad. Kinesiology and Phys. Edn.; fellow European Coll. Sport Scis., 1992-96; Fulbright-Hays rsch. scholar Commn. Ednl. Exch. between U.S.-Belgium, 1983-84. Fellow Am. Coll. Sports Medicine; mem. Internat. Soc. for Advancement of Kinanthropometry (pres. 1988-92, past pres. 1992-96). Roman Catholic. Office: KU Leuven Faculty Phys Edn & Physiotherapy, Tervuursevest 101, B-3001 Leuven Belgium

BEURMAN, ALBERT LEROY, retired corrections officer; b. Pueblo, Colo., Sept. 18, 1935; s. William Franklin and Mildred Leona (Smith) B.; children: Leann, Bert, Frank, Chris, Connie, Richard. Student, Midwest Bus. Coll., 1968-69. Usher Mesa Drive Theater, Pueblo, Colo., 1951-53; meat cutter Pueblo Meat and Provisions, 1953-54; rolling mill laborer Colo. Fuel and Iron, Pueblo, 1955-68; clk. Farmers Union Coop., Belt, Mont., 1970-72; corrections officer Ariz. Dept. Corrections, Florence, 1972-76; security officer Transp. Test Ctr., Pueblo, 1977-82; corrections officer Colo. Dept. Corrections, Canon City, 1982-88, ret. Author: (book) The Ride of a Lifetime, 1995. Recipient Cert. of Recognition, U.S., 1995. Avocations: motorcycle touring, fishing, writing, video camera photography, pilot. Home: 1104 Beulah Ave Pueblo CO 81004-2728

BEUSAN, MARIO, architect, educator; b. Zagreb, Croatia, June 25, 1944; s. Petar and Angela (Gorischek) B.; m. Ivna Svoboda, Aug. 28, 1976; children: Filip, Damjan. Diploma B.C.E., U. Zagreb, 1974, MCE, 1983, MSc, 1989. Arch., designer Industroprojekt, Zagreb, 1975-77; arch., designer Inst. Arch., Faculty Arch., Zagreb, 1977-93, rsch. fellow, 1993-99, asst. prof., mentor, 1999—. Mem. counseling bd. Com. for Revitalization of the Old City Klanjec, 1990, Gallery A. Augustincić, Klanjec, 1990, Local Cmty. Coun. M.Z. A. Cesarec, Zagreb, 1990-95. Mem. Croatian Archs. Assn., Croatian Assn. Artist Applied Arts, Matrix Croatica. Roman Catholic. Home: Pod Zidom 3/III, 10 000 Zagreb Croatia Office: Faculty Arch, Kacićeva 26, 10 000 Zagreb Croatia

BEUSSE, JACQUELINE, writer, marketing company executive; b. Albany, N.Y.; d. H. A. and Christina M. (Collins) B. Student mgmt. program for women, Pa. State U.; BA magna cum laude, Caldwell Coll.; MA magna cum laude, N.Y. Inst. Tech.; bus. degree, The Wood Sch., N.Y.C. Sr. ct. stenographer Middlesex County Prosecutors Office, New Brunswick, N.J.; adminstrv. asst. to Sen. John A. Lynch New Brunswick, adminstrv. asst. to Judge John J. Rafferty; product mgr. Johnson & Johnson, New Brunswick; dir. devel. and pub. rels. Caldwell (N.J.) Coll.; pres., writer Mktg. by Objectives, Inc., Caldwell; cons. Gucci, Inc., Fraunces Tavern, Constn. Hall, JFK Ctr., Washington, 6 Frank Sinatra concerts; cons., pub. N.Y. Cornell Med. Ctr. Concert Series; cons., prodr., pub. Urban League, Lincoln Ctr. Concerts. Contbr. articles to mags. and newspapers. Chmn. Theater on the Hill; bd. dirs. John F. Kennedy Trust; N.J. state commr. Motion Picture and TV; chmn. Grover Cleveland Bicentennial Celebration-Presdl. Tribute; media cochair N.J. State Dem. Com.; publicity chair Garden State Arts Ctr.-Irish Festival and Found.; cons. Meml. Sloan Kettering Cancer Ctr., Expo 2000; prodr. 4 Bob Hope shows for charity; prodr., cons. Am. Cancer Soc. Recipient ASTRA 1st prize award for TV documentary We Are the Music Makers. Mem. USO (bd. dirs.), AAUW (bd. dirs.), N.J. Soc. to Prevent Blindness (bd. dirs.), West Essex C. of C. (v.p.). Democrat. Roman Catholic. Avocations: art, music, literature, historical research, ice-skating. E-mail: gissane@webtv.net. Office: Mktg by Objectives Inc PO Box 136 Caldwell NJ 07006-0136

BEUTIN, PAUL WOLFGANG, humanities educator; b. Bremen, Germany, Apr. 2, 1934; s. Paul Gustav and Charlotte Louise (Teitge) B.; m. Elsbeth Eleonore Gebhard, Dec. 31, 1963 (div. Feb. 1977); 1 child, Friedrich Olaf; m. Heidi Elise Seifert, Mar. 10, 1978; 1 child, Lorenz Gösta. Diploma in civil svc., U. Hamburg, Germany, 1961; D, U. Hamburg, 1963; privatdozent, U. Bremen, Germany, 1996. Asst. U. Hamburg, 1963-68, lectr., 1971-99; prof. U. Göttingen, Germany, 1973; lectr. U. Oldenburg, Germany, 1981-82, U. Lüneburg, Germany, 1990—. Author: Sexuality and Obscenity, 1990, Barlach or the Access to the Unconscious, 1994, The Democrat Fritz Reuter, 1995, History of the Peace Idea Since Immanuel Kant, 1996, ANIMA Inquiries into Women's Mysticism of the Middle Ages, 3 vols., 1997-99. Recipient prize Kurt Tucholsky Soc., 1956, 57. Mem. Union of Authors (Germany)(functionary 1991—), Union Edn. and Sci., Oswald von Wolkenstein Soc., Forum Vormärz Rsch. Avocation: Alpine trekking. Home: Hohenfelder Str 13, D-22929 Köthel/Stormarn Germany

BEUTLER, ARTHUR JULIUS, manufacturing company executive; b. LaCrosse, Wis., Sept. 2, 1924; s. Arthur Julius and Augusta Henrietta (Dobe) B.; m. Carolee Yvonne Crawford, Dec. 28, 1952; 1 child, Karen Elizabeth. BSEE, U. Wis., 1948, Grad. in EE, 1968. Registered profl. engr., Wis. Trainee inventor program Gen. Electric Co., Schenectady, N.Y., 1948-51; devel. engr. Gen. Electric Co., Milw., 1951-59, project engr., 1959-61, sr. engr., 1961-64; chief engr. Dings Magnetic Separator Co., Milw., 1964-67; pres., owner Creative Engring. Assocs., Inc., Greendale, Wis., 1967-72, 88—; v.p. mfg. Gettys Mfg. Co., Racine, Wis., 1972-79, v.p. internat., 1979-81; v.p. tech. planning div. motion control div. Gould, Inc. (formerly Gettys Mfg. Co.), Racine, 1981-88; cons. engr. mfg. control systems, robotics. Patentee elec. controls. Served with U.S. Army, 1943-46, PTO. Mem. IEEE (sr., chpt. chmn. 1969-72), NSPE, Soc. Mfg. Engrs. (cert.), Tau Beta Pi, Eta Kappa Nu.

BEVAN, RICHARD JUSTIN WILLIAM, retired canon, church executive; b. St. Harmon, Radnor, Wales, Apr. 21, 1922; s. Richard Henry and Margaret Mabel (Pugh) B.; m. Sheila Rosemary Barrow, Sept. 4, 1949; children: Roderick, Nicholas, Timothy, Christopher (dec.), Rosemary. Attended, St. Augustine's Coll., 1939; BA, LTh, U. Durham, 1945; PhD (hon.), Columbia Pacific U., 1980; ThD (hon.), Geneva Theol. Coll., 1972, U. Greenwich, 1990. Ordained to ministry as deacon 1945, priest 1946. Asst. curate Stoke Parish Ch., Stoke-on-Trent, Eng., 1945-49; chaplain Aberlour Orphanage, Banff, Scotland, 1949-51; asst. master Towneley Tech. H.S., Burnley, Lancashire, Eng., 1951-60; hon. asst. curate Ch. Kirk, Diocese of Blackburn, Lancashire, 1951-56, Whalley, Diocese of Blackburn, 1956-60; rector St. Mary-Le-Bow, Durham City, County Durham, Eng., 1960-64; vicar United Benefice St. Oswald with St. Mary-Le-Bow, 1964-74; rector Grasmere, Lake Dist., Eng., 1974-82; canon residentiary, treas., libr. Carlisle Cathedral, Cumbria, Eng., 1982-89, vice dean, acting dean, 1986-89, canon emeritus, 1989—; chaplain to Her Majesty the Queen Royal Coll. Chaplains, 1986-92; chaplain U. Durham, 1961-74, convenor, 1966-76, Durham Girls H.S., 1966-74, St. Mary's Coll. U. Durham, 1961-72, St. Cuthbert's Soc. U. Durham, 1966-74, St. Aidan's Soc. U. Durham, 1960-64, Trevelyan Coll., Durham, 1966-72; examining chaplain to Bishop of Carlisle, 1970—; gov. St. Chad's Coll., Durham, 1969-89; theol. cons. Churchman Pub. Ltd., 1986. Author: (poetry) Unfurl the Flame, A Twig of Evidence: Does Belief in God Make Sense?, 1986; editor: Steps to Christian Understanding, 1959, The Churches and Christian Unity, 1964, Durham Sermons, 1964. First pres., founder Grasmere Village Soc., 1976; mem. com. Dove Cottage Wordsworth Trust, Grasmere, 1966-74. Mem. Victory Svcs. Club (London). Avocations: poetry reading and composing, travel. Home: Beck Cottage, Burgh-by-Sands Carlisle Cumbria CA5 6BT, England

BEVAN, ROBERT LEWIS, lawyer; b. Springfield, Mo., Mar. 23, 1928; s. Gene Walter and Blanche Omega (Woods) B.; m. Ronice Diane Gartin, Jan 25, 1977; children: Matthew Gene, Lisa Ann. AB, U. Mo., 1950; LLB, U. Kansas City, 1957. Bar: Mo. 1957, D.C. 1969. Adminstrv. asst. U.S. Senator T. Hennings Jr., Washington, 1957-60; legis. asst. U.S. Senator E.V. Long, Washington, 1960-69; sr. govt. relations counsel Am. Bankers Assn., Washington, 1970-84; ptnr. Hopkins & Sutter, Washington, 1984-95; of counsel Stinson, Mag and Fizzell, Kansas City, Mo., 1995—. Ghost author: The Intruders, 1967; contbg. editor U.S. Banker, 1985-88. Fieldman Dem. Nat. Com., 1968. Served with U.S. Army, 1946-47, 1951-53. Mem. ABA (bus. law sect., chmn. banking law com. 1988-92, commn. on IOLTA 1997-2000, co-chmn. joint banking com. 1999-2000), Echequer Club. Avocations: art and antiques. Office: 1201 Walnut St Fl 28 Kansas City MO 64106-2117

BEVC, CAROL-LYNN ANNE, advertising executive; b. Jam, N.Y., Oct. 6, 1952; d. Joseph F. and Dorothea Mae (Kirshe) Bova; m. Frank P. Bevc, May 11, 1974; children: Christine, Elizabeth. Bookkeeper J. Rolfe Davis Ins., Orlando, Fla., 1987-89; CFO Wordwise, Inc., Winter Park, Fla., 1989-2000; acct. exec. Inner/g, Winter Park, 2000—. Leader Citrus coun. Girl Scouts U.S.A., 1986-96. Mem. AAUW (pres. Seminole County br. 1985-87, 95-97, bd. dirs., dir. comm. Fla. state 1998—), DAR. Avocations: camping, biking. Home: 1511 Black Bear Ct Winter Springs FL 32708-3860 Office: Inner/g Ste 208 1177 Lousiana Ave Winter Park FL 32789

BEVC, FRANK PETER, electrical engineer; b. Johnstown, Pa., Mar. 5, 1952; s. Frank Henry and Mildred (Gallo) B.; m. Carol-Lynn Bova, May 11, 1974; children: Christine, Elizabeth. BSEE, U. Pitts., 1973, MBA, 1976. Design engr., program mgr. Westinghouse, Pitts., 1973-83; mgr. tech. projects Westinghouse, Orlando, Fla., 1983-90, mgr. steam sys. engring., 1990-92, mgr. emerging tech., 1992-97; mgr. emerging tech. Siemens Westinghouse, Orlando, 1998—; treas. Gasification Tech. Coun., 1998-2000; treas. Energy Frontiers Internat., Arlington, Va., 1996-98; bd. dirs. Gasification Techs. Coun. Contbr. articles to profl. jours. Mem. IEEE (sr.), World Energy Congress (mem. tech. bd. 1995-98), Gas Turbine Assn. (v.p. 1992—), Am. Nat. Stds. Inst. (mem. stds. bd. 1974-80), U.S. Advanced Ceramics Assn. (bd. dirs.), Nat. Biomass Industries Assn. Home: 1511 Black Bear Ct Winter Springs FL 32708-3860 Office: Siemens Westinghouse 4400 N Alafaya Trl Orlando FL 32826-2398

BEVER, TIMOTHY MICHAEL, systems software engineer; b. Eaton Rapids, Mich., Nov. 10, 1953; s. Harry S. and Jean A. (Cramer) B.; m. Dorothy J. Farrell, Apr. 22, 1977; 1 child, Sharon E. BBA with honors, Saginaw Valley State Coll., 1981. Computer programmer Saginaw (Mich.) Steering Gear, 1981-83, systems analyst, 1983-84; systems engr. Electronic Data Systems, Saginaw, 1984-86, systems software engr., 1986-95; advanced software engr. Saginaw (Mich.) Steering Gear, 1995—. With USN, 1971-76. Mem. VFW, Disabled Am. Vets., Vietnam Vets. Am., Am. Legion, Nat. Space Inst., U.S. Naval Inst. Home: 4440 Lynndale Dr Saginaw MI 48603-2090 Office: Electronic Data Systems 5225 Exchange Dr Flint MI 48507-2935

BEVERIDGE, JO-ANNE FAY, laboratory director; b. Toronto, Ont., Can., Aug. 19, 1955; d. Denis F. and Olga L. Hagon; m. Jan. E. Beveridge, Aug. 21, 1976 (div. May 1992); children: Rachel E., Peter I. BS in Med. Tech., Mich. Technol. U., 1977. Med. technologist All Saints Episcopal Hosp., Ft. Worth, Tex., 1980-83, Mansfield (Tex.) Cmty. Hosp., 1984-87; lab. mgr. Arlington (Tex.) Diagnostic and Imaging Ctr., 1987-89; asst. lab. mgr. Allied Clin. Lab., Hurst, Tex., 1989-94; med. technologist North Hills Hosp., North Richland Hills, Tex., 1992-97; quality assurance coord. Ft. Worth Health Dept., 1995-97; lab. dir. Plaza Med. Ctr. Ft. Worth, 1997—; advisor diabetes adv. bd. Plz. Med. Ctr. Ft. Worth; adj. instr. Tarleton State U., Stephenville, Tex. Standing chairperson handbook Birdville PTSA, North

Richland Hills, 1999; leader troop 1205 Girl Scouts Am., North Richland Hills, 1990-97. Mem. Am. Soc. Clin. Pathologists (assoc., cert.), Clin. Lab. Mgmt. Assn., South Cen. Assn. Blood Banks, Am. Assn. for Clin. Chemistry. Episcopalian. Avocations: scuba, sewing, gardening. Fax: (817) 347-5764. E-mail: joanne.beveridge@lonestarhealth.com. Home: 6504 Parkway Ave N Richlnd Hls TX 76180-4309 Office: Plaza Med Ctr Ft Worth 900 8th Ave Fort Worth TX 76104-3901

BEVERIDGE, WILLIAM IAN, former veterinary medicine educator; b. Junee, NSW, Australia, Apr. 23, 1908; s. James William and Ada (Beardmore) B.; m. Patricia Dorothy Thomson; 1 child, John Caldwell. B Vet. Sci., U. Sydney, 1931, D Vet. Sci., 1949; ScD, U. Cambridge, Eng., 1975; DVM (hon.), U. Hanover, Germany, 1963. Rsch. officer CSIRO, Australia, 1931-38; Harkness fellow, 1938-89; rsch. officer W. & E. Hall Inst., Melbourne, Australia, 1942-45; vis. worker Pasteur Inst., Paris, 1936-37, 46; prof. U. Cambridge, 1947-75; cons WHO, 1964-74; vis. prof. Ohio State U., 1953. Author: The Art of Scientific Investigation, 1950, Frontiers of Comparative Medicine, 1972, Influenza, The Last Great Plague, 1977, Seeds of Discovery, 1980, Fighting Diseases: My Varied Scientific Career, 1997. Recipient Gold headed cane Am. Vet. Assn. Fellow Australian Vet. Assn. (life); mem. World Vet. Assn. (pres. 1957-75, Gamge gold medal). Home: 5 Bellevue Rd, Wentworth Falls Australia

BEVERLEY, PETER CHARLES LEONARD, head science facility; b. Farnham, Surrey, U.K., Mar. 7, 1943; s. Samuel and Elinor (Verity) B.; m. Elisabeth Ann Copleston, Nov. 10, 1967; children: William, Christopher, Emma. BS, U. Coll., London, 1964, MBBS, 1967, DS, 1986. Jr. rsch. fellow MRC, London, 1969-72; rsch. fellow Sloan Kettering Inst., N.Y.C., 1972-73; rsch. fellow ICRF, London, 1973-78, staff scientist, 1978-92, head tumour immunology unit, 1992-95; scientific head Edward Jenner Inst. for Vaccine Rsch., Compton, U.K., 1992—; cons. Transgene, Strasburg, France, 1993—, Stanford Rook, London, 1996—. Contbr. articles to profl. jours., books chpts. and reviews. Mem. Brit. Soc. Immunology, Brit. Assn. Cancer Rsch., Brit. Transplantation Soc. Office: Edward Jenner Inst, Vaccine Rsch, Compton Berkshire RG20 7NN, United Kingdom

BEVERLY, LAURA ELIZABETH, special education educator; b. Glen Jean, W.Va., Nov. 26; d. Sidney and Alma Logan. BA in Elem. Edn., W.Va. State Coll., 1960; MS in Spl. Edn., Bklyn. Coll., 1969; postgrad., Oxford (Eng.) U., 1974, N.Y.U., 1982. Cert. elem./spl. edn. tchr., N.Y. Tchr. Bd. Coop. Ednl. Svcs., Westbury, N.Y., 1966—; mem. adv. bd. Am. Biographical Inst. Inc., Raliegh, N.C., 1985—. Mem. ASCD, Am. Inst. of Parliamentarians, Royal Soc. Health, Phi Delta Kappa. Avocations: reading, traveling. Home: PO Box 346 Glen Jean WV 25846-0346

BEVERS, THERESE BARTHOLOMEW, physician, medical educator; b. Amarillo, Tex., Apr. 5, 1960; d. James Oliver Bartholomew and Ruth Ann Berg. BS, Tex. Woman's U., 1981; MD, U. Tex. Health Scis. Ctr., San Antonio, 1987. Intern, then resident U. Tex. Health Sci. Ctr., San Antonio/Bexar County Hosp., 1987-90; physician pvt. practice, Wichita Falls, Tex., 1990-91, Dallas, 1991-94; chief med.dir. Medi Clinic, Houston, 1994-96; asst. prof. clin. cancer prevention, med. dir. cancer prevention ctr. U. Tex., M.D. Anderson Cancer Ctr., Houston, 1996—; mem. expert panel Nat. Comprehensive Cancer Network Breast Screening and Diagnosis Com., Nat. Comprehensive Cancer Network Breast Cancer Prevention Com. Mem. editl. bd. Oncolog, Breast Diseases: A Year Book Quarterly. Mem. AMA (task force on prevention), Am. Cancer Soc. Tex. div. (mem. breast cancer detection com., colorectal cancer detection com.), Am. Acad. Family Physicians, Tex. Acad. Family Physicians (mem. com. health care svcs. 1992-96, mem. com. clin. preventive medicine 1996-98, commr. pub. health and clin. affairs 1998—). Avocations: skiing, hiking, antiques, decorating, reading. Office: U Tex M D Anderson Cancer Ctr 1515 Holcombe Blvd # 336 Houston TX 77030-4009

BEVERSDORF, ANNE ELIZABETH, astrologer, author, educator; b. Houston, Tex., Aug. 14, 1949; d. S. Thomas and Norma (Beeson) B. BA, U. Tex., 1972; MLS, Ind. U., 1974. Founding librarian Social Studies Devel. Ctr. Ind. U., Bloomington, 1975-79, info. specialist, 1980-82; co-founder Ind. Clearinghouse for Computer Edn., Indpls., 1983-86; Calif. mktg. rep. Minn. Ednl. Computing Corp., San Marcos, Calif., 1986-88; pres., chief exec. officer Beversdorf Assocs., Ltd., Vista, Calif., 1988-93; writer, lectr., astrologer Vista, Calif., 1993—; cons. Procter & Gamble Ednl. Services, Cin., 1981-85, Brazil Office of Tech. Edn., Rio de Janeiro, Porto Alegre, 1986; mem. faculty Ind. U., Indpls., 1986, San Diego State U., 1988-91. Contbr. over 30 articles to U.S. and internat. profl. jours. Mem. Am. Coun. Vedic Astrology, Am. Fedn. Astrologers, San Diego Astrol. Soc. Avocations: reading, weaving, needlework, piano music. Home and Office: 1119 Anza Ave Vista CA 92084-4517

BEVERSDORF, DAVID QUENTIN, neurologist, researcher; b. Bloomington, Ind., May 28, 1965; s. Samuel Thomas and Norma (Beeson) B.; m. Sheri Anderson, Dec. 26, 1990. BS, Ind. U., 1987; MD, Ind. U., Indpls., 1992. Med. resident Meth. Hosp. Ind., Indpls., 1992-93; neurology resident Dartmouth-Hitchcock Med. Ctr., Lebanon, N.H., 1993-96; behavioral neurology fellow U. Fla. Coll. Medicine, Gainesville, 1996-98; asst. prof. neurology Ohio State U. Med. Ctr., Columbus, 1998—. Contbr. articles to med. jours., including Procs. Nat. Acad. Scis., Lancet, Neurology, Psychiatry Rsch.-Neuroimaging, Jour. Neurology, Neurosurgery and Psychiatry, and Physiology and Behavior. Recipient rsch. grant for autism rsch. Stallone Fund, L.A., 1994. Mem. AMA, Am. Acad. Neurology, Cognitive Sci. Soc., Soc. for Neurosci., Cognitive Neurosci. Soc., Phi Beta Kappa. Office: Ohio State U Med Ctr Dept Neurology 1654 Upham Dr Columbus OH 43210-1250

BEVILACQUA, ANTHONY JOSEPH CARDINAL, archbishop; b. Bklyn., June 17, 1923; s. Louis and Maria (Codella) B. Student, Cathedral Coll., Bklyn., 1941-43, Sem. of Immaculate Conception, Huntington, N.Y., 1943-49; JCD, Gregorian U., Rome, Italy, 1956; MA in Polit. Sci, Columbia U., 1962; JD, St. John's U. Sch. Law, 1975. Ordained priest Roman Cath. Ch., 1949; ordained bishop, 1980. Bar: N.Y. 1976, U.S. Dist. Ct. (we. dist.) Pa. 1984, Pa. 1988, U.S. Dist. Ct. (ea. dist.) Pa. 1988, U.S. Supreme Ct., 1989. Asst. pastor Sacred Heart, St. Stephen's Ch., St. Mary's Ch., 1949-50; prof. history Cathedral Prep. Sem., Bklyn., 1950-53; prof. canon law Sem. of Immaculate Conception, Huntington, N.Y., 1968-80; adj. prof. law St. John's U. Sch. Law, Queens, N.Y., 1976-80; successively asst. chancellor, vice-chancellor, chancellor Diocese of Bklyn., 1965-83, dir. Cath. migration and refugee office, 1971-83, ordained aux. bishop, 1980; bishop Diocese of Pitts., 1983-88; archbishop Archdiocese of Phila., 1988—; elevated to cardinal Coll. of Cardinals, 1991; mem. com. pro-life activities, 1989—; mem. Pontifical Congregation for Causes of Saints, 1991—; mem. Pontifical Coun. "Cor Unum", 1991—. Contbr. articles to profl. jours. Bd. dirs. Mercy Home for Children. Mem. Canon Law Soc. Am., Pa. Bar Assn., Fellowship of Am. Cath. Scholars. Office: Archdiocese Phila 222 N 17th St Philadelphia PA 19103-1295

BEVINGTON, DAVID MARTIN, English literature educator; b. N.Y.C., May 13, 1931; s. Merle Mowbray and Helen (Smith) B.; m. Margaret Bronson Brown, June 4, 1953; children: Stephen, Philip, Katharine, Sarah. B.A., Harvard U., 1952, M.A., 1957, Ph.D., 1959. Instr. English Harvard U., 1959-61; asst. prof. U. Va., 1961-65, asso. prof., 1965-66, prof., 1966-67; vis. prof. U. Chgo., 1967-68, prof., 1968—, Phyllis Fay Horton distng. svc. prof. in the humanities, 1985—; vis. prof. N.Y. U. Summer Sch., 1963, Harvard U. Summer Sch., 1967, U. Hawaii Summer Sch., 1970, Northwestern U., 1974. Author: From Mankind to Marlowe, 1962, Tudor Drama and Politics, 1968, Action is Eloquence, Shakespeare's Language of Gesture, 1984; editor: Medieval Drama, 1975, The Complete Works of Shakespeare, 4th edit., 1997, The Bantam Shakespeare, 1988. Served with USN, 1952-55. Guggenheim fellow, 1964-65, 81-82; sr. fellow Southeastern Inst. Medieval and Renaissance Studies, summer 1975; sr. cons. and seminar leader Folger Inst. Renaissance and Eighteenth-Century Studies, 1976-77. Mem. MLA, AAUP, Renaissance Soc. Am., Shakespeare Assn. Am. (pres. 1976-77, 95-96), Am. Acad. Arts and Scis., Am. Philos. Soc. Home: 5747 S Blackstone Ave Chicago IL 60637-1823 Office: Univ Chgo English Dept 5801 S Ellis Ave Chicago IL 60637-5418

BEVIR, WILLIAM MARK, political science educator; b. London, Feb. 18, 1963; s. William Lawrence and Phebe (Belton Cobb) B.; m. Laura Grant, Apr. 7, 1990; children: Lawrence Antony, Harry John. BA, Exeter U., U.K., 1985; DPhil, Oxford U., U.K., 1989. Rsch. fellow Madras U., India, 1990-92; Sir James Knott fellow Newcastle U., U.K., 1992-98, reader in polit. theory, 1998—; asst. prof. U. Calif., Berkeley, 2000—. Author: The Logic of the History of Ideas, 1999; contbr. articles to profl. jours. Mem. Next Generation Leaders Forum, South Korea, 1995. Mellon fellow Ransom Ctr., 1999, Spl. Rsch. fellow Leverhulme Trust, 1996-98. Office: Dept of Polit Sci U Of Calif Berkeley CA 94720-0001

BEWES, PETER CECIL, surgeon; b. Nairobi, Kenya, Sept. 21, 1932; arrived in Eng., 1946; s. Thomas Francis Cecil and Nellie Sylvia Cohu (Berry) B.; m. Hilary Stansfeld Bryant, Dec. 10, 1966; children: Carol Mary, Anna Elisabeth, Helen Catherine. MB BCh, Cambridge U., 1956, M of Surgery, 1966. Sr. surg. registrar Min. Health, Uganda, 1969-70; sr. lectr. surgery Makerere U., Uganda, 1971-72; cons. surgeon Kilimanjano Christian Med. Ctr., Moshi, Tanzania, 1973-79; cons. trauma surgeon Birmingham (Eng.) Accident Hosp., 1973-93; dir. continuing med. edn. Min. of Health, Uganda, 1994-98; retired. Author: Surgery, 1984; asst. editor: Primary Surgery, vol. 1, 1990, Vol. II, 1987, Primary Anesthesia, 1986. Capt. Royal Army M.C., 1957-59. Recipient Albert Hopkinson Anatomy prize Emmanuel Coll., 1953. Fellow Assn. Surgeans East Africa, Royal Coll. Surgeons Eng. Anglican Christian Ch. Avocation: photography. Home: Park House, 32 Tuns Rd, Necton Norfolk PE37 8EL, England

BEWES, RICHARD THOMAS, minister, writer; b. Nairobi, Kenya, Dec. 1, 1934; s. Thomas Francis Cecil and Nellie Sylvia Cohu (Berry) B.; m. Elisabeth Ingrid Jaques, Nov. 9, 1942; children: Timothy, Wendy, Stephen. MA, Cambridge (Eng.) U., 1957. Ordained to ministry Ch. of Eng., 1959. Vicar St. Peter's Ch., Harold Wood, Essex, Eng., 1965-74, Emmanuel Ch., Northwood, Middlesex, Eng., 1974-83; rector All Souls Ch., Langham Place, London, 1983—; chmn. African Enterprise, U.K., 1978—, Ch. of Eng. Evang. Coun., 1992—; bd. dirs. Billy Graham Evangelistic Assn., U.K. Author: Talking About Prayer, 1979, The Pocket Handbook of Christian Truth, 1981, The Church Overcomes, 1983; compiler: John Wesley's England, 1981, Does God Reign?, 1995, Speaking in Public-Effectively, 1998, Great Quotations of the 20th Century, 1999, The Lamb Wins, 2000, Open Home Open Bible, 2000. Prebendary St. Paul's Cathedral, London, 1988. Recipient Freedom of City award Charlotte, N.C., 1984. Mem. Guild of Brit. Songwriters. Avocations: broadcasting, photography, writing, tennis. Home: 2 All Souls Pl, London W1N 3DB, England Office: All Souls Ch, Langham Pl, London W1N 3DB, England

BEWLEY, ANTHONY PAUL, dermatologist; b. Liverpool, Eng., June 21, 1963; s. Gerard and Viola Margaret (Murphy) B. MBChB, Bristol (Eng.) U., 1987. Trainee in dermatology Westminster Hosp., London, 1992, Univ. Coll. Hosps., London, 1992-94; sr. registrar in dermatology Royal Southampton (Eng.) Hosp., 1994-96; cons. dermatologist Whipp's Cross Hosp., London, 1996—. Contbr. articles to profl. jours. Mem. Royal Coll. Physicians. Office: Whipp's Cross Hosp Dermatol, Leystonstone, London E11 1NR, England

BEX, BRIAN WILLIAM LOUIS, educational administrator; b. Chgo., Feb. 5, 1943; s. John and Jeanne Rowena Bex; children: Jay, Charles, Kristophor. Student, Ind. U.; LLB, U. Chgo., 1965, JD, 1967. Pres., founder Am. Comms. Network-Brian Bex Report, Inc., Hagerstown, Ind., 1966—; pres., treas., founder The Remnant Trust, Hagerstown; spkr. and lectr. Author: The Individualist Declaration, 1968, Decline and Fall of the American Republic, 1974, The Road, Never the Inn, 1976, The Vanishing Dinosaur, 1985, Out of Bounds, 1992, The Teeter Totter Equation, 1998, others. Address: 100 N Woodpecker Rd Hagerstown IN 47346-1431

BEX, JEAN-PIERRE, cardiovascular surgeon, consultant; b. Marseille, France, Dec. 1, 1942; s. Albert and Andree (Magna) B.; m. Francoise Algoud; children: Nathalie, Anton, Elvire, Nora, Boris. MD, U. Paris, 1973. Chief of clinic Faculty Medicine, Paris, 1973-80; asst. prof. cardiovasc. surgery Hosp. Laënnec, Paris, 1973-80; head Mediterannean Inst. Cardiology, Marseille, 1979—; dir. Cardiostar Comm. and Info. Network. Editor-in-chief European Rev. for Med. Biotech., 1978-90, Cardiotecho News, 1990-98. Fax: 33 0 1 42 22 32 77. Office: Cliniche Garazzeni, 21 Via Garazzeni, Bergamo Italy

BEXELL, ANNA KERSTIN ELIN, physician; b. Solna, Sweden, Apr. 22, 1942; d. Erik and Gun (Helander) B.; m. Jan Andersson; children: Kajsa, Erik. Lic. Physiotherapist, Lund Sch. Physiotherapy, 1965; MD, U. Lund, 1975. Med. adviser Swedish Internat. Devel. Authority, Ministry of Health, Lusaka, Zambia, 1989-92; sr. cons. Malmö (Sweden) Red Cross, 1992-95, Malmö City Coun., Malmö U. Hosp., 1983-97, U. Lund, 1997—; cons. Swedish Internat. Devel. Authority, 1989—. Contbr. articles on women and health, immigrant health, health and devel. to profl. jours.

BEXTERMILLER, THERESA MARIE LOUISE, architect, computer graphics; b. St. Charles, Mo., Feb. 9, 1960; d. Charles Frederick and Loretta Joan (Unterreiner) B. BArch, Kans. State U., 1983; MFA Computer Graphics/Interactive Media, Pratt Inst., 1990. Lic. architect, N.Y., 1989, Mo., 1990; cert. Nat. Coun. Archtl. Regis., 1996; real estate salesperson, Mo., 1995-98, broker, 2000—. Grad. architect Mackey/Mitchell, St. Louis, 1983-84, Fleming Corp., St. Louis, 1984-85; project architect, prototype mgr. Casco Corp., St. Louis, 1985-87; grad. architect HBE Corp., St. Louis, 1987-88; freelance architect N.Y., 1988-90, St. Louis, 1991-92, 99; with telecomm. Western Union, 1992-93, AT&T Network Systems, 1993-94; contract architect M.K.-Ferguson Group, 1994-95, Fru-Con Engring. Inc., St. Louis, 1995-96; prin. TMB Architecture/Computor Graphics, 1997—, Theresa Marie Bextermiller, RA, MFA, NCARB, Broker, 2000—, Le Pique and Orne Architects-Inc., 1998—, Hellmuth, Obata & KassaBaum, Inc., St. Louis, 1998—, Tom Whitaker with Infante Assocs., Inc., 1999—; cons. Alias/Wavefront, Washington U., 1991-97; active SIG Computer Human Interaction. Mem. Nat. Trust Historic Preservation, League of Our Lady of Sacred Heart, Assn. Holy Souls, Legion of 1000-W, St. Louis, AIA. Roman Catholic. Avocation: volunteer artwork. Home: 1120 Blendon Pl Saint Louis MO 63117-1911

BEY, PIERRE, oncologist; b. Marnay, France, Dec. 30, 1944; s. Henri Bey and Marie Madeleine F. Desjours; m. Annick Cardot, Dec. 30, 1966; children: Frederique, Julien, Celine, Benoit. MD, Nancy U., 1974. Cert. radiation oncologist, 1976. Radiation oncologist Anti Cancer Ctr., Nancy, France, 1976—; prof. U. Nancy, 1980—; dir. Anti-Cancer Ctr., Nancy, 1991; gen. sec. French Fedn. Anti Cancer Ctrs., Paris, 1996—. Contbr. articles to profl. jours. Home: Rue Henri Poincare 42, 54000 Nancy France Office: Ctr Alexis Vautrin, Ave de Bourgogne, 54500 Vandoeuvre Nancy, France

BEYA, ZOUBIER, soccer player; b. 1972. Formerly with Etoile de Sahel, Tunisia; midfielder Soccer Club Freiburg, Germany, Tunisia. Named Tunisia's Footballer of the yr. Address: 16 rue de la Ligue Arabe, El Menzah VI, D-60492 Tunis 1004, Tunisia*

BEYEN, ROLAND ENGELBERTUS, humanities educator; b. Nieuwpoort, Belgium, Jan. 13, 1935; s. August Eugeen and Marie-Louise (Coulier) B.; m. Jozefa Alberta Van Bragt, July 25, 1960 (div. Mar. 1990); children: Gil, Sophie, Clotilde, Marnix. Licentiate in Romance Philology, Katholieke U. Leuven, Belgium, 1959, PhD in Romance Philology, 1968. French tchr. Secondary Sch. St. Jozeph, Brussels, 1960-61, Secondary Tchr. Tng. Sch. St. Thomas, Brussels, 1961-63, Royal Cadet Sch., Brussels, 1963-64; rsch. asst. Katholieke Univ. Leuven, Belgium, 1965-68, prof., 1968-74, ordinary prof., 1974-2000, dir. Ctr. for the Study of the French Lit. in Belgium, 1969-2000. Author: Michel de Ghelderode ou La Hantise du Masque, 1971, Ghelderode, 1974, (bibliography) de Michel de Ghelderode, 1987, (corr.) de Michel de Ghelderode, 6 vols., 1991, 92, 94, 96, 98, 2000. Mem. Acad. Royale de Langue et de Lit. Françaises de Belgique. Home: Sleestraat 25, B-2820 Bonheiden Belgium Office: Katholieke Univ Leuven, Blijde Inkomststraat 21, B-3000 Leuven Belgium

BEYENE, TILAHUN, educator, writer, researcher; b. Adwa, Ethiopia, Nov. 27, 1949; came to U.S., 1973; PhD with distinction, U. Md., 1982. Assoc. dean U. Md., College Park, 1989—; bd. dirs. Internat. Peace & Devel., Princeton, N.J.; pres. Tchrs. Assn. ASMARA/Ethiopia, 1971-73; chair rsch. com. Acad. Achievement Programs, College Park, 1996—; mem. faculty Coll. Edn., College Park, 1990—. Author: 99 Kilometers, 1971, Fitwote Siga, 1972, Lisan, 1973. Vice chmn. Tigray Devel. Assn., Washington, 1989-91; bd. dirs. Save War Victims, Washington, 1998—. Mem. Nat. Coun. Ednl. Opportunity Assn., Black Faculty & Staff Assn., Phi Delta Kappa. Home: 9201 New Hampshire Ave Apt 402 Silver Spring MD 20903-3607 Office: U Md 112 Chemistry Building College Park MD 20742-2000

BEYER, CLAES GUNNAR LOUIS, lawyer; b. Göteborg, Sweden, Nov. 24, 1936; s. Gunnar Robert and Kerstin (Bauer) B.; m. Anita Grönkvist, 1961 (div. 1992); 1 child, Hans; Marianne G. Lindqvist, Aug. 6, 1994. LLB, U. Lund, Sweden, 1961; LLM, U. Ill., 1962; diplomé, Inst. de Droit Comparé, Paris, 1962. Bar: Sweden. Law clk. Ct. of First Instance, Stenungsund, 1962-63; assoc. Mannheimer & Zetterlöf, Göteborg, 1963-70; ptnr. Mannheimer Swartling Advokatbyrå (merger Mannheimer & Zetterlöf and Carl Swartling), Göteborg, 1970—; mem. Securities Coun., Sweden, 1988—, Swedish Industry and Commerce Stock Exch. Com., 1991—; expert Swedish Govt. Com. on Due Process in Taxation, 1993-95, Com. on the Securities, 1987-89, Com. on Reorganisation Swedish Ct. Sys., 1996-98; designated by Swedish Govt. to panel of conciliators Internat. Ctr. for Settement of Investment Disputes, 1999—. Acting bd. mem. Volvo Environment Prize Found., 1990—, Volvo Rsch. and Ednl. Founds., 1986—. Mem. Swedish Bar Assn., Inst. for Co. and Securities Law (bd. dirs. 1984—), Assn. of the Bar of N.Y., Internat. Bar Assn., Union Internat. des Avocats. Mem. Liberal Party. Avocations: literature, sailing, tennis. Office: Mannheimer Swartling, Box 2235, S-40314 Göteborg Sweden

BEYER, DONALD STERNOFF, JR., state official; b. Trieste, Free Territory of Trieste, June 20, 1950; came to U.S., 1952; s. Donald Sternoff Sr. and Nancy Prew (McDonald) B.; m. Carolyn Anne McInerney, July 15, 1972 (div.); children: Donald III, Stephanie; m. Megan Carroll, Sept. 19, 1987; children: Clara, Grace. BA in Econs. magna cum laude, Williams Coll., 1972. Former pres., v.p. and other positions Don Beyer Volvo, Falls Church, Va., 1974—; lt. gov. Commonwealth of Va., Richmond, 1990-98; urban at large mem. Commonwealth Transp. Bd., Va., 1987-90; chmn. Va. Econ. Bridge Initiative, Va., 1990—. Chmn. Baliles for Gov., No. Va., 1985, Paul Simon for Pres., Va., 1988, Bill Clinton for Pres., Va., 1992; mem. 11th Dist. Dem. Com., Vienna, Va., 1992; Dem. nominee Gov. of Va., 1998. Named Time Mag. Quality Dealer of Yr. for Va., 1991. Mem. Land Rover Alexandria (pres. 1997—). Democrat. Epsicopalian. Avocations: golf, skiing, climbing. Office: Don Beyer Volvo 1231 W Broad St Falls Church VA 22046-2167

BEYER, HANS-GEORG, computer scientist, educator; b. Ludwigslust, Germany, May 31, 1959; s. Georg and Marie (Ritter) B.; m. Rea Katharina Süssmann, Oct. 9, 1987; 1 child, Josephine. MSc in Elec. Engring., Tech. U. Ilmenau, Germany, 1982; PhD in Physics, Bauhaus U. Weimar, Germany, 1989; habilitation in computer sci., U. Dortmund, Germany, 1997. Cert. lectr. in computer sci. R & D engr. in semiconductor electronics Gleichrichterwerk Stahnsdorf, Germany, 1982-84; rsch. scientist, physics dept. Bauhaus U. Weimar, 1984-89; rsch. scientist Tech. U. Darmstadt, Germany, 1990-92; rsch. scientist, dept. computer sci. U. Dortmund, 1993—; lectr. computer sci., U. Dortmund, 1997—. Contbr. articles to profl. jours.; patentee in field of elec. engring.; assoc. editor IEEE Trans. on Evolutionary Computation, 1997—. Heisenberg fellow, German Rsch. Found., 1997. Office: U Dortmund, Informatik XI, D-44221 Dortmund Germany

BEYER, MARY EDEL, primary education educator; b. Winona, Minn., July 16, 1932; d. Edmund Aloysious and Gertrude Cecilia (Knopick) Edel; m. Argene Lester Beyer, June 7, 1958 (dec. Aug. 1985); children: Jason Edel Beyer, Trudy Edel Beyer, Gerard Edel Beyer, Jeremy Edel Beyer. AS in Edn., Winona State U., 1952, BS, 1967, MS, 1978. Cert. elem. tchr., Minn. Tchr. 1st grade Dodge Ctr. (Minn.) Sch., 1952-55; tchr. 1st grade, kindergarten Dist. 857, Lewiston, Minn., 1955-63; tchr. kindergarten Dist. 861, Winona, 1968-95, Stockton (Minn.) Sch., 1966-70; tchr. Rollingstone Elem. Sch., 1970-95; owner MEME's Doll Mus.; sch. del. Minn. Edn. Effective Program, 1987-95; pres. Winona Dist. 861 Reading Com. Contbr. to Poland Today Pol-Am. Jour., 1993; celebrity reader Children's Books Reading on the mall, 1990; photographer, writer School News Winona Post, 1985-95; freelance writer. Spencer, cadet mem. USO Group, Winona, 1950-52; leader Girl Scouts-Boy Scouts, 1952-70; mem. Sweet Adelines, 1978—; sings lead Hiawatha Valley Sweet Adelines, sec. 1994-97; apptd. commr. City of Winona Hist. Preservation Commn., 1996—; soprano St. Stanislaus Kostka choir, 1996—; sec. activity coun. Sr. Citizen Friendship Ctr., 1999—; tour guide riverboats on Miss. River, Winona Port. Recipient Pres.'s award Lakeside St. Machines, Winona, 1992, Disting. Svc. award, 1993, Diamond award 4-H Club, Winona, 1995; named Master Knitter Extension Office, Winona, 1985, Ky. Belle of the Blue Grass Gov. of Ky., 1951. Mem. PTA (pres.), Minn. Reading Assn. (del. 1985-95), Polish Heritage Soc. (sec. 1967—), Am. Legion Aux., Knights Columbus (4th degree lady). County Hist. Soc. (mus. vol.), Winona Athletic Club, C. of C. (bus. edn. intern 1995). Avocations: photography, fashion modeling, music, art, doll collecting. Home: 260 W Broadway St Winona MN 55987-5224

BEYER, MORTEN STERNOFF, airlines executive; b. N.Y.C., Nov. 13, 1921; s. Otto Sternoff and Clara (Mortenson) B.; m. Jane I. Hartman, Sept. 29, 1945 (div. 1989); children: Barbara, Nancy (Mrs. James Henry Evans), James, William; m. Catherine Frick Randall, Nov. 30, 1990. B.A. with honors, Swarthmore Coll., 1943. Various positions Pan Am. World Airways, 1943-48; asst. to v.p. operations and maintenance Capital Airlines Inc., Washington, 1948-60; sr. v.p. operations, maintenance and sales Riddle Airlines Inc., Miami, Fla., 1960-63; dep. dir. gen., gen. mgr. Saudi Arabian Airlines, Jeddah, Saudi Arabia, 1964-67; exec. v.p. Modern Air Transport, Inc., Miami, 1967-70; pres. Modern Air Transport, Inc., 1970-71, Capital Internat. Airways, Inc., Nashville, 1971-72, Phoenix Airlines Inc., Detroit, 1972-73; pres., chief exec. officer Johnson Internat. Airlines, Inc., Missoula, Mont., 1974-75; chmn. AVMARK Inc., Arlington, Va., 1975-92, AVMARK Internat. Ltd., London, 1985-92, Morten Beyer & Agnew, 1992—; also editor AVMARK Newsletter, Comml. Aircraft Fleets, Transport Aircraft Values, other publs.; cons. USAF, 1954-55, Miami, Fla., 1963-64. Democratic candidate U.S. Reps., 1956; pres. Fairfax County Young Democrats, 1956-57. Club: Toastmasters Internat. (pres. 1952-56). Home: 50270 Dove Cove Rd PO Box 179 Dameron MD 20628-0179 Office: MBA Inc 2107 Wilson Blvd Ste 750 Arlington VA 22201-3042

BEYER, SUZANNE, advertising agency executive; b. N.Y.C.; d. Harry and Jennie Hillman; m. Isadore Beyer; children: Pamela Claire, Hillary Jay. Grad., Conservatory of Mus. Art, N.Y.C., 1947; student, Nassau C. C., N.Y.C., 1963-65. Singer, tchr. piano N.Y.C., 1947-66; asst. to v.p. media dir. Robert E. Wilson, Advt., N.Y.C., 1967-72; media planner, media buyer frank J. Corbett div. BBDO Internat., N.Y.C., 1972-77, Lavey/Wolff/Swift divsn. BBDO Advt., N.Y.C., 1977-80; sr. media planner Lavey/Wolff/Swift (divn. BBDO Advt.), N.Y.C., 1980-83, media supr., 1983-94; media supr. Lyons, Lavey, Nichel, Swift, N.Y.C., 1995-96; pharm. advt. med. media cons., 1996—. Soprano Opera Assn., Nassau, 1976-99, United Choral Soc., Woodmere, L.I., 1970-99, Armand Sodero Chorale, Baldwin, L.I., 1980-86, Rockville Centre Choral Soc., 1986—. Mem. Pharm. Advt. Coun., L.I. Advt. Club, Healthcare Bus. Women's Assn. Home: 66 Fonda Rd Rockville Centre NY 11570-2751

BEYER, WAYNE CARTWRIGHT, lawyer; b. Bklyn., Feb. 21, 1946; s. Gerhard Robert and Barbara Janeway (Fein) B. AB, Dartmouth Coll., 1967; MAT, Harvard U., 1970; Jd, Georgetown U., 1977. Bar: N.H. 1978, U.S. Dist. Ct. N.H. 1978, U.S. Tax Ct. 1986, U.S. CT. Appeals (1st cir.) 1979, U.S. Supreme Ct. 1986, D.C. 1996. Mem. staff U.S. Ho. of Reps., Washington, 1973-75; atty. McLane, Graf, Raulerson, P.A., Manchester, N.H., 1978-83; chief of staff GSA, Washington, 1983-84, dep. gen. counsel, 1984-86; atty. Cleveland, Waters & Bass, P.A., Concord, N.H., 1986-94, Wayne C. Beyer & Assoc., Manchester, N.H., 1994-96; asst. corp. counsel Dist. of Columbia, 1996—; lectr. civil rights. Contbr. articles to profl. jours. Mem. ABA, N.H. Bar Assn., Assn. Trial Lawyers Am., Def. Rsch. Inst., Internat. Assn. Chiefs of Police, Harvard Club, Bar Assn. of D.C. Home: 2501 Porter St NW Apt 527 Washington DC 20008-1254 Office: Office Corp Counsel 441 4th St NW Fl 6 South Washington DC 20001-2714

BEYER-ENKE, SIEGFRIED, magazine editor, publisher; b. Berlin, Nov. 2, 1917; s. Robert Beyer and Gertrud (Philipson) Enke; m. Marta junker, 1944 (div. 1966); 1 child, Stefan; m. Sigrid Quabbe, Oct. 1, 1967; 1 child, Caroline. Diploma, U. Frankfurt, Germany, 1944, degree in pharmacy, 1947. Founder, owner, editor Der Deutsche Apotheker, Oberursel, Hessen, 1948—. Home and Office: Verlag Der Deutsche Apothek, Postfach 1650, 61406 Oberursel Hessen, Germany

BEYER-MEARS, ANNETTE, physiologist; b. Madison, Wis., May 26, 1941; d. Karl and Annette (Weiss) Beyer. B.A., Vassar Coll., 1963; M.S., Fairleigh Dickinson U., 1973; Ph.D., Coll. Medicine and Dentistry N.J., 1977. NIH fellow Cornell U. Med. Sch., 1963-65; instr. physiology Springside Sch., Phila., 1967-71; teaching asst. dept. physiology Coll. Medicine & Dentistry N.J., N.J. Med. Sch., 1974-77, NIH fellow dept. ophthalmology, 1978-80; asst. prof. dept. ophthalmology U. Medicine and Dentistry N.J., N.J. Med. Sch., Newark, 1979-85, asst. prof. dept. physiology, 1980-85, assoc. prof. dept. physiology, 1986—, assoc. prof. dept. ophthalmology, 1986—; vis. assoc. prof. dept. ophthalmology and vision sci. U. Wis., Madison, 1995—; cons. Alcon Labs. Contbr. articles in field of diabetic lens and kidney therapy to profl. jours. Chmn. admissions No. N.J., Vassar Coll., 1974-79; mem. minister search com. St. Bartholomew Episcopal Ch., N.J., 1978, fund-raising chmn., 1978, 79; del. Episc. Diocesian Conv., 1977, 78; long range planning com. Christ Ch., Ridgewood, N.J., 1985-87, vestry, 1994-95. Recipient NIH Nat. Rsch. Svc. award, 1978-80, Found. CMDNJ Rsch. award, 1980; grantee Juvenile Diabetes Found., 1985-87, NIH, NEI grantee, 1980-95, Pfizer, Inc. grantee, 1985-89, 93—. Mem. Am. Physiol. Soc., N.Y. Acad. Scis., Soc. for Neurosci., Am. Soc. Pharmacology and Exptl. Therapeutics, Assn. for Rsch. Vision & Ophthalmology, Internat. Soc. for Eye Research, AAAS, The Royal Soc. Medicine, Internat. Diabetes Found., Am. Diabetes Assn., European Assn. Study of Diabetes, Aircraft Owners and Pilots Assn., Sigma Xi. Home: 120 Ely Pl Madison WI 53705-4015

BEYGELZIMER, YAKIV EFIMOVICH, materials science researcher, educator; b. Odessa, Ukraine, Aug. 21, 1952; s. Efim Izrailevich and Doroteya Emmanuilovna (Rozengarten) B.; m. Galyna Iosifovna Nosovytska, Jan. 8, 1977; 1 child, Alina. Diploma with highest honors, Donetsk (Ukraine) U., 1974; candidate technical scis., Physics & Tech. Inst. Byelorussian Nat. Acad. Scis., Minsk, 1982; D in Technical Scis., Physics & Tech. Inst. Ukrainian Nat. Acad. Scis., Donetsk, 1994. Rsch. mem. High Pressure Dept., Physics & Tech. Inst., Ukrainian Nat. Acad. Scis., Donetsk, 1975-84, sr. rsch. mem., 1984-96, leading rsch. mem., 1996—; prof. Donetsk Technical U., 1995—; chmn. acad. bd. Donetsk Sci. Tech. Co. Ukrainian Nat. Acad. Scis., 1992—; mem. drs. acad. bd. Physics and Tech. Inst. Ukrainian Nat. Acad. Scis., 1994—; sr. rsch. cons. Sintra Ltd., Donetsk, 1994—, Joint Stock Co. NORD, Donetsk, 1994—; chmn. Physics Dept., Youth Rsch. Ctr., Donetsk, 1995—; mem. drs. dissertation def. com. Donetsk Technical U., 1996—, Donbass State Mech. Engring. Acad., Donetsk, 1996—; com. mem. Internat. Conf. "High Pressure-2000: Material Sci. and Tech.", Kiev, Ukraine, 2000. Mem. editl. bd. Mechanics, Moscow, 1988-92; mem. founding editl. bd. Physics & Tech. High Press Engring., Ukraine, 1992—, Heuristics and Didactics of Scis., Donetsk, 1996—; contbr. over 150 articles to profl. jours. Grantee Ukrainian State Sci. & Tech. Com., 1992-94, Ukrainian Nat. Acad. Scis., 1994—. Mem. Russian Acad. Scis. Avocations: books, jogging, swimming, cooking. E-mail: tean@an.dn.ua. Office: Ukrainian Nat Acad Scis Physics & Tech Inst, 72 R Luxembourg St, Donetsk 83114, Ukraine

BEYREUTHER, ROLAND, mechanical engineer, scientist; b. Dresden, Saxony, Germany, Jan. 15, 1938; s. Rudi and Hanna Fischer (Rickers) B.; m. Ute Vogel, Oct. 12, 1963; children: Jens, Elke. Diploma in engring., U. Mech. Engring., Karl-Marx-Stadt, Germany, 1962; degree in engring., Tech. U., Dresden, 1968, Habilitation, 1971; Prof., Acad. Sci. German Dem. Rep., 1983. Sci. asst. Inst. Fiber Tech., Dresden, 1962-68, sci. collaborator, 1968-79, dept. head fiber formation, 1981—; dept. head fiber formation Inst. Polymer Tech., Dresden, 1984-92, Inst. Polymer Rsch., Dresden, 1992—. Author: Dynamik von Fadenbildungs-und Fadenverarbeitungs-Prozessen, 1986; contbr. more than 80 articles to profl. jours. Recipient Sci. and Technique Nat. prize, 3rd grade (in team) Govt. German Dem. Rep., 1989. Mem. Polymer Processing Soc. E-mail: probey@ipfdd.de. Fax: 49-0351-4658219. Office: Inst Polymer Rsch, Hohe Strasse 6, D-01069 Dresden Germany

BEYSENS, DANIEL ANDRÉ-MARIE, physicist; b. Paris, Aug. 11, 1945; s. René Mathieu and Germaine (Gerard) B.; m. Chantal Nicole Faniel, Nov. 3, 1967; 1 child, Cyril. Degree in Engring., Institut d'Optique, Paris-Orsay, 1969; D in Physics, U. Paris, 1973. Physicist, chmn. condensed matter div. Commissariat à l'Energie Atomique, Saclay, France, 1973-95; commissariat l'Energie Atomique, Grenoble, France, 1995—; scholar UCLA, 1986; investigator ESA, NASA, CNES, 1984—; pres. OPUR Assn. Editor: Fundamental Properties of Interfaces in Single and Complex Liquids, 1991, Dynamical Phenomena at Interfaces, Surfaces and Membranes, 1992, Fragmentation Phenomena, 1993, Interplay of Genetic and Physical Processes in the Development of Biological Form, 1994, Dynamical Networks in Physics and Biology, 1998; contbr. sci. articles to profl. jours. Decorated Chevalier des Palmes Académiques. Mem. Soc. Française de Physique (ANCEL prize 1985), Am. Phys. Soc., European Colloid and Interface Soc., European Low Gravity Rsch. Assn. Avocations: sailing, biking, skiing.

BEZANSON, THOMAS EDWARD, lawyer; b. Hartford, Conn., Aug. 1, 1945; s. Philip Thomas and Lillian (Carlson) B.; m. Janie R. Bezanson, Aug. 10, 1969; children: Philip, Jeffrey. BA, Grinnell, 1967; MA, Rutgers U., 1971, JD, 1974. Bar: N.Y. 1975, U.S. Dist. Ct. (ea. dist.) 1975, U.S. Dist. Ct. (so. dist.) N.Y. 1975, U.S. Ct. Appeals (2d cir.) 1975, U.S. Ct. Appeals (6th cir.) 1980, U.S. Supreme Ct. 1991. Assoc. Chadbourne & Parke, N.Y.C., 1974-81, ptnr., 1981—. Author: 42 Poems, 1993. Bd. dirs. Westchester Philharm., 1992-98, N.Y. Lawyers for the Pub. Interest, Inc., 1997—, The Legal Aid Soc., 1999—. Served in U.S. Army, 1967-69, Thailand. Mem. ABA, N.Y. State Bar Assn., Assn. of Bar of City of N.Y. Office: Chadbourne & Parke 30 Rockefeller Plz Fl 31 New York NY 10112-0129

BEZARES, EDUARDO, brewery company executive, educator; b. Bilbao, Vizcaya, Spain, May 2, 1963; s. Fernando Bezares and Marisa Carretero; m. Maria Del Mar F. Claverie, Oct. 31, 1996; 1 child, Maria. Indsl. engr., U. Basque Country, Bilbao, 1988; diploma in indsl. orgn., London Sch. Econs., 1994; MBA, U. La Laguna, Tenerife, Spain, 1996. Cert. in indsl. engring. Tng. engr. Royal Dutch Shell, The Netherlands, 1988; logistics dir. Compaqia Cervecera de Canarias, Tenerife, 1989—; logistics tchr. Tenerife C. of C., 1994—, U. La Laguna, 1998—, Las Palmas (Spain) C. of C., 1998; transport and R&D tchr. Am. U. Preston, Tenerife, 1995—; bd. dirs. Tenerife Pt. Authority, 1994—. Advisor AIESEC, Tenerife, 1987-91; mem. IAESTE, Bilbao, 1986-88; chmn. Canary Islands Shipping Coun., Tenerife, 1994—; vice chmn. Spanish Shippers Coun., Madrid, 1994—. Sgt. Engr. Army, 1987. Mem. Am. Prodn. and Inventory Control Soc., Inst. Logistics U.K., Brewery Transport Adv. Com. Eng., Canary Island Indsl. Assn. (bd. dirs. 1994—). Roman Catholic. Avocations: nautical sports, golf, books, music. Fax: 34 922 305084. E-mail: ebezarezc.cervecera@nexo.es. Home: Campoamor, 38006 Tenerife Spain Office: Compaqia Cervecera Canarias, Avda Angel Romero 18, 38008 Tenerife Spain

BEZBORODNYI, SERGEI DMITRIEVITCH, physician, researcher, journalist; b. Donetsk, Ukraine, July 8, 1973; s. Dmitryi Vladlenovitch Bezborodnyi and Maia Borisovna (Golish) Bezborodnyay. MD with honors, Moscow Med. Acad., 1996; PhD in Clin. Pharmacology, Sci. Ctr. Med. Ctr., Moscow, 1998. Postgrad. fellow, physician, researcher Moscow State Med. U., 1996-97, sr. rschr., 1997-98, assoc. prof. clin. pharmacology, 1998—. Author: Therapeutic Monitoring in Clinical Pharmacology of Cardiovascular and Gastrointestinal Drugs on REMEDi HS Drug Profiling System, 1999; contbr. articles to profl. jours.; contbr. to Moscow mcpl. nespapers, 1993—. Recipient State prize Moscow State Govt., 1999. Mem. Internat. Fedn. Journalists, N.Y. Acad. Scis., Moscow Acad. Natural Scis. Home: UL 1905 D 4 Kw 56, 123022 Moscow Russia

BEZERRA, MARCIO L. S., military officer; b. Rio de Janeiro, Oct. 21, 1975; s. Nauricio Severo and Nelma Soares Bezerra. Student, Coll. Nossa Senhora Rosario, Rio de Janeiro, 1985, Coll. Belisario dos Santos, Rio de Janeiro, 1989, Coll. Podium, Rio de Janeiro, 1992, Acad. Mil. Agulhas Negras, Resende, Brazil, 1997. Army officer Brazilian Army, Rio de Janeiro, 1993—; cadet Acad. Mil. Agulhas Negras, Resende, 1994-97. Lt. Brazilian Arty., 1998-99. Avocations: sports, reading. Office: Brazilian Army, Av Sco Sebastico S/Nr, Rio de Janeiro 21650210, Brazil

BEZIC, IRENA, psychologist; b. Zadar, Yugoslavia, Aug. 26, 1960; d. Jerko and Eva (Rudolf) B.; m. Darko Marin, Sept. 10, 1988; children: Hana, Jan. M of Psychology, U. Zagreb, Croatia, 1991. Rsch. asst. Clin. Rsch. Ctr. Sandoz, Basel, Switzerland, 1985; clin. psychologist Rehab. Clinic, Zagreb, Croatia, 1986-90; clin. psychologist, supr. Merkur Hosp., Zagreb, Croatia, 1986—; sci. and tech. asst. U. Zagreb, 1990-92; psychol. program officer UNICEF, Zagreb, 1993-94; psychologist pvt. practice, Zagreb, 1994—; cons. in field. Contbr. articles to profl. jours. Recipient Rector's award U. Zagreb, 1986. Mem. European Assoc. Psychotherapy, Croatian Assoc. Psychology, European Union for Coaching, Organizational Consulting, Organizational Devel. and Supr. Avocations: painting, guitar, mountaineering, sailing. Home: B Adžije 28, 10000 Zagreb Croatia Office: Idemo Dalje, B Adzije 28, 10000 Zagreb Croatia

BEZIRTZOGLOU, CHRISTOS, intergovernmental organization administrator; b. Athens, Greece, Nov. 12, 1966; s. Venizelos-Eleutherios C. and Elissabet (Rafailidou) B.; m. Anna I. Katrami, Jan. 3, 1997. BSc in Physics, U. Patras, Greece, 1991; postgrad., Open U., U.K., 1996—, Inst. Info. Strategy Devel., Greece, 1993; PGC in Applied Software Engring., Hellenic Mgmt. Assn., Greece, 1994; diploma analysis & design info. sys., Athens Econ. U., Greece, 1993; diploma design/mgt. computer networks, Nat. Tech. U. Athens, 1993. Freelance analyst, programmer Greece, 1989-92; trainer Hellenic Mgmt. Assn., Athens, 1993-94; cons. Alexander Young Horwath, Piraeus, Greece, 1994-95; 2d line support mgr. European Union, Brussels, 1995-98, asst. to dir. DG IV.C, 1999—; organizing com. microbial ecology and disease Internat. Congress, 1990, organizing com. anaerobic bacteria and anaerobic infections Internat. Congress, 1996; com. mem. Standarison Body, 1989—. Editor New Tech., 1994-95. Served with Greek mil., 1992-93. Mem. IEEE (stds. com. 1988—), Assn. Computing Machinery, Greek Computer Soc., Hellenic Physics Assn., Greek-French Sci. Soc., The Brain Club, Mensa. Christian Orthodox. Avocations: travel, photography, music, genetic art, linguistics. Home: Warandelaan 24, B-3090 Overijse Belgium

BEZLEPKIN, ANATOLIY ANDREEVICH, physicist, researcher; b. Zaporozhye, Ukraine, Aug. 30, 1948; s. Andrej Ivanovich and Olga Efimovna (Kaplya) B.; m. Valentina Michailovna Galkina, Jan. 26, 1973; children: Alexej, Nataliya, Igor. Degree in phys. sci. and math., Kharkov (Ukraine) State U., 1991. Jr. rschr. Kharkov State U., 1975-77, sr. rschr., 1977—. Contbr. articles to profl. jours. Sgt. Soviet Army, 1967-69. Avocations: amateur radio operator, fishing, volleyball, collecting mushrooms. Office: AM Gorkii State U, sq Svobodi 4, 310077 Kharkov Ukraine

BEZRUKOV, VLADISLAV VIKTOROVICH, gerontologist, researcher; b. Kujbyshev, USSR, Feb. 25, 1940; s. Viktor Vasiljevich and Tatjana Petrovna (Vostrova) B.; m. Ludmila Ivanovna Polotnenko, June 29, 1963 (dec. Mar. 1996); 1 child, Irina (dec.). MD, Med. Inst., Kiev, Ukraine, 1963; PhD, Inst. Gerontology, Kiev, 1970, D Med. Sci., 1983. Physician Regional Hosp., Cherkassi, Ukraine, USSR, 1963-65; jr. and sr. rschr. Postgrad. Inst. Gerontology, Kiev, 1968-73; social affairs officer UN/CSDHA, Vienna, 1983-88; dir. Inst. of Gerontology, Kiev, 1988—; corr. mem. Acad. Med. Sci. Ukraine, 1997, prof., 1998. Co-author: Aging of the Central Nervous System, 1979, Hemodynamics and Aging, 1984, Aging and Age-Related Experimental Pathology of Cardiovascular System, 1994, The Aging Cardiovascular System: Physiology and Pathology, 1996. Pres. USSR Gerontological and Geriatric Soc., 1988-91, Health and Charity Found., Kiev, 1989—. Named Honored Scientist of Ukraine, 1998. Mem. Ukrainian Gerontol. and Geriatric Soc. (pres. 1995—). Home: 4 Kondratjuk St Apt 15, 254201 Kiev Ukraine Office: Inst of Gerontology AMS, 67 Vyshgorodskaya Str, 254115 Kiev Ukraine

BEZRUKOVA, ALEXANDRA GENNADIEVNA, ecological optician, biophysicist; b. Leningrad, Russia, June 20, 1944; d. Gennadii Alexandrovich Drozdov and Larissa Pavlovna (Voevodina) Drozdova; m. Sergei Feodorovich Bezrukov, Apr. 26, 1968; 1 child, Pavel Sergeevich Bezrukov. Diploma of Physics, Leningrad State U., 1969; Candidate of Biol. Scis., Coun. Ctrl. Rsch. Inst. of Roentgenology and Radiology, Leningrad, 1976; D of Physico-Math. Scis., Supreme Cert. Com. of Russian, Fedn., Moscow, 1997. Jr. rsch. scientist CRIRR, Ministry of Pub. Health of USSR, Leningrad, 1969-80, Leningrad Polytech. Inst., Leningrad, 1980-84; sr. rsch. scientist St. Petersburg (Russia) State Tech. U., 1984-97, prof., 1997—. Contbr. articles to profl. jours. Recipient grant Internat. Sci. Found., 1993, European Sci. Found., 1994, Nordic Coun. Ministers, 1999, German Rsch. Found., 2000; named Internat. Woman of Yr., Internat. Biog. Ctr., Cambridge, Eng., 1997-98. Office: St Petersburg State Tech U, Dept Bioengring Fac Med Phy, 195251 Saint Petersburg Russia

BEZUGLOV, VLADIMIR VILENOVICH, chemist, researcher; b. Magadan, Russia, Nov. 9, 1949; s. Vil Vasiljevich and Valentina Ivanovna (Maslennikova) B.; m. Natalja Vladimirovna Komarova, Nov. 20, 1975. MS, Moscow Inst. Fine Chem. Tech., 1972, PhD in Chemistry, 1982, DSc in Chemistry, 1997. Rschr. Inst. Bioorganic Chemistry, Moscow, 1972-80, jr. scientist, 1980-84, sr. scientist, 1984-97, head lab., 1997—; mem. sci. coun. Inst. Bioorganic Chemistry, 1989—; vis. prof. U. Montpellier, France, 1999-2000. Co-author: Prostaglandins and Cardiovascular System, 1986; contbr. articles to profl. jours.; patentee in field. Mem. mgmt. bd. People's Party "Free Russia", Moscow, 1991-93. Recipient Sr. Rsch. Worker award Russia Acad. Scis., 1987. Mem. Russian Biochem. Soc., Mendeleev Chem. Soc., Internat. Rsch. Cannabinoid Soc. Avocations: computer programming, music disk collection. E-mail: vvbez@oxylipin.siobc.ras.ru. Office: Inst Bioorganic Chemistry, ul Miklukho-Maklaya 16/10, 117871 GSP7 Moscow Russia

BEZUIDENHOUT, PIETER JACOBUS, construction company executive; b. Randfontein, Gautena, S. Africa, Jan. 29, 1960; s. Johannes Andries and Martha Magdalena (van der Merwe) B.; m. Anna-Luisa Rossetti, Nov. 28, 1992; 1 child, Liezl. Constable S. African Police Force, 1977-80; sales rep. Nampak, S. Africa, 1980-82; co. dir. Multi-Distributors, S. Africa, 1982-84; bldg. contractor Skoubou, S. Africa, 1984-92; labour contractor PJB Enterprises, S. Africa, 1995-99. Avocations: golf, cycling, jogging. Office: PO Box 6583, Greenhills 1767, South Africa

BEZUIDENHOUT, PIETER JACOBUS SCHALK, investment consultant, researcher; b. Bloemfontein, South Africa, Jan. 4, 1947; s. Pieter Jacobus and Martha Susanna (Bekker) B.; m. Christine Mary Williams, Dec. 30, 1975; children: Maryke, Louise. BJuris, U. Port Elizabeth, South Africa, 1974; BA with honors, U. South Africa, 1982. Lawyer Marquard & Keet, Cape Town, South Africa, 1971-74; pvt. sec. South African Embassy, London, 1975-79; 2d sec. South African Embassy, Rome, 1981; counsellor South African Permanent Mission, Geneva, Switzerland, 1982-86; dep. head of mission South African Embassy, Vienna, 1989-93; dep. resident rep. IAEA, Vienna, 1989-93; pvt. cons., 1998—; lectr. U. Pretoria, South Africa, 1999—; lawyer, 1970-74, 98—. Contbr. articles to profl. jours. Maj. South African Citizen Force, 1968-74. Christian. Avocations: archaeology, history, music. Home: 887 Arcadia St, Arcadia 0083 Pretoria, South Africa Office: Genesis Internat, PO Box 13118, Hatfield 0028 Pretoria, South Africa

BEZZAOUCHA, ABDELDJELLIL, epidemiologist; b. Kasr El Bokhari, Algeria, Nov. 28, 1951; s. Mohamed and Rihana (Bouziane) B.; m. Nadjet Tabet-Derraz, Nov. 27, 1981; children: Ilham, Ahmed-Chawki, Mohamed, Abdelaziz. MD, Faculty of Medicine, Algiers, Algeria, 1976, cert in epidemiology, 1981, PhD, 1987. Chief of projects Nat. Inst. Pub. Health, Algiers, Algeria, 1985-92; head dept. epidemiologie Ctr. Hosp. Univ., Algiers, 1993—, Blida, 1997—. Author: Epidemiologie et Biostatistique, 1995; contbr. articles to profl. jours. Mem. N.Y. Acad. Scis. Avocations: reading, history. Home: Houchi Moulound No 8, 16000 Algiers Algeria Office: CHU Blida, Hôpital Frantz-Fanon, Zabana Blida Algeria

BHADORIA, PRATAPBHANU SINGH, agriculture and food engineering educator; b. Manhad, M.P., India, July 7, 1952; s. Maharaj Singh and Raja (Chauhan) B.; m. Madhuri Kushwah, May 5, 1980; children: Prachi, Prebal. BSc, U.W. Gwalion, India, 1971, MSc, 1973; D, Indian Inst. Tech. Kharagpur, 1974, PhD, 1981. Lectr. Indian Inst. Tech. Kharagpur, 1981-90, asst. prof., 1990-96, assoc. prof., 1996—. Recipient Alexander von Humbold award, Germany, 1988, ICRA fellowship, Holland, 1985. Avocation: research. Office: Indian Inst Tech, Agr & Food Engring Dept, Kharagpur 721302, India

BHAGIA, VASDEV, physician, consultant; b. Karachi, Pakistan, July 28, 1943; s. Shewakram Pahlajrai Bhagia and Parpati Thawani; m. Veena Hingorani Gopi, June 7, 1972; children: Vijay, Vinita. MBBS, All India Inst. Med. Scis., New Delhi, 1965. Diplomate Am. Bd. Pediats. Intern All India Inst. Med. Scis., New Delhi, 1965, house surgeon, 1966; sr. house officer pediats. Eng., 1967; sr. resident in pediats. Meadowbrook Hosp., Long Island, N.Y., 1968; chief resident N.Y. Med. Coll., N.Y.C., 1969; fellow in pediats. Harvard Med. Sch. Children's Hosp., Mass., 1970; joint chief med. officer Indian Airlines, New Delhi, 1970—. Fellow Inst. Aero-Space Medicine, Am. Acad. Pediats.; mem. Indian Acad. Pediats., Med. Club (sec. gen. 1984-86). Avocation: travel. Home: B4/167 Safdarjung Enclave, New Delhi 110029, India Office: Indian Airlines, Gurdwara Rakabgangj Rd, 110001 New Delhi India

BHAI, RAJA MOHAMMAD, oil company executive; b. Dhaka, Bangladesh, Aug. 24, 1953; s. Mohammad and Khatija Mohammad Bhai; m. Safinaz Husain, Feb. 23, 1980; children: Ahad Mohammad, Omar Mohammad, Leia. MBA, U. Ont., Can., 1977. Mng. dir. Panther Steel Ltd. and Panther Internat. Ltd., Dhaka, 1979—, Panther Textile Ltd., Dhaka, 1984-92, Panther Flour and Food Ind. Ltd., Dhaka, 1989—, Q.E. Ltd. and RMB Fisheries Ltd., Dhaka, 1996—; bd. dirs. Olympic Industries Ltd. (formerly Bengal Carbide Ltd.), Dhaka, Tripti Industries Ltd. (formerly Bengal Food Ltd), Dhaka. Office: Tripti Industries Ltd, 62-63 Motijheel C A, 1000 Dhaka Bangladesh

BHAKDI, SUCHARIT PUNYARATABANDU, microbiology educator; b. Washington, Nov. 1, 1946; arrived in Germany, 1963; citizen of Thailand.; s. Luang Dithakar and Tanpuying Saiyude (Gengradomying) B.; m. Birgit Elfriede Lehnen, Mar. 9, 1973 (div. 1999); children: Sebastian Chakrit, Johannes Suriya, Benjamin Suchinda, Jeremias Ramet; m. Verena Gerl, May 25, 2000. MD, Bonn U., 1970. Diplomate in Med. Microbiology. Postdoctoral Max-Planck Inst., Freiburg, Germany, 1972-76, Copenhagen (Denmark) Univ., 1976-77; postdoctoral Giessen (Germany) Univ., 1977-82, asst. prof., 1982-87, assoc. prof., 1987-90; prof., head dept. Mainz (Germany) Univ., 1990—; advisor Ctr. for Molecular Medicine, Siriraj Hosp., Bangkok Univ., 1991—. Editor Med. Microbiology and Immunology, 1990—; contbr. numerous articles to profl. jours. Recipient Justus-Liebig award U. Giessen, 1979, Constance award U. Constance, 1980, German Soc. for Microbiology award German Soc. for Microbiology, 1987, Dr. Sasse award U. Berlin, 1988, Robert-Koch award Clausthal-Zellerfeld, 1989, Schunk award, 1989, Alexander-von Humboldt award Alexander von Humboldt-Stiftung, 1991, Schettler award 1999, German Soc. Angiology award, 1999. Avocations: sports, music, history medicine and science. Office: U Mainz Inst Med Microbiology, Augustusplatz, 55101 Mainz Germany

BHALERAO, SUDHAKAR KASHINATH, education educator; b. Chalisgaon, Maharashtr, India, Mar. 27, 1932; s. Kashinath Gopal and Ganga Kashinath B.; m. Usha Gopal Kharwandikar, Feb. 23, 1958; children: Vivek, Medhavini. BA, Christian Coll., Indore, India, 1953; BT, Grad.'s Basic Tng. Ctr., Dhulia, India, 1956. FRAS, Royal Astron. Soc. London. Vice-prin. Pethe H.S., Nasik, India, 1960-90; lectr. in field. Author 65 books, including: Our Solar System, 1972 (Book State award 1972), Artificial Satellites and Space Science, 1972 (Book State award 1979), Scientific Temper Promotion Trust Soc. Work, 1996; producer numerous slide shows; contbr. more than 2000 articles to profl. jours. and publs.; arranger 3000 telescopic observations for masses and children. Recipient Nat. award for tchrs. Govt. of India, 1978, 92; numerous book awards including Balkumar Sahitya Sammelan awards 1990, 93, Nanasaheb Bhare award, 1992, others. Mem. Sky and Telescope Assn. Nasik (pres. 1992—). Avocations: signing, hiking, writing, oratory, sky observing. Home: Sudhanshu, New Bombay-Agra Rd, Nashik 422011, India

BHALLA, CHAMAN LAL, insurance broker; b. Aur, Punjab, India, Dec. 19, 1936; arrived in Eng., 1963; s. Tara Chand and Maya Wanti (Dhir) B.; m. Promil Abbey, Apr. 27, 1960; children: Susan Vedhera, Sanjay, Salil. BA, Punjab U., 1958. Reg. ins. broker British Ins. Broker Registration Coun. Clerk Sch. Internat. Studies, New Delhi, 1959-60; auditor Atlas Cycle Industries, Sonepat, India, 1960-63; storekeeper, buyer Taylor and Ptnrs., Maidenhead, Eng., 1963-64; asst. cost acct. Ronald Trist Control, Slough, Eng., 1964-68; mng. dir. Lawley Ins. Brokers Ltd., Slough, Reading, others, 1968—; cons. Asian Bus. Assn., Slough, 1990—. Gen. sec. Young Indians Assn., 1964-75; trustee Hindu Temple, Slough, 1988-92; non exec. dir. Berkshire Health Auth., 1994-96; mem. complaints and discipline com. Health Commn., 1996—. Fellow Inst. Sales Mktg. Mgmt., Corp. Ins. Fin. Advisors; mem. British Ins. Brokers Assn. (hon. regional treas.). Avocations: golf, gardening, music, opera. E-mail: info@lawleyinsurancebrokers.com. Office: 325 High St, Slough Berkshire SL1 1TX, England

BHARADWAJ, BALAJI, automotive engineer; b. Kirkee, Maharashtra, India, May 1968; s. Madura Rangaswamy Iyengar and V. Lakshmi; m. J. Lakshmi. BSME, Bangalore U., India, 1990; MS in Mfg. Engring., Syracuse U., 1995, PhDME, 1998. Registered profl. engr. Engring. intern SVL Industries Ltd., India, 1987; rsch. engr. Bangalore U., 1990-91; rsch. asst., fellow mech. and aerospace engring. dept. Syracuse (N.Y.) U., 1991-97; rsch. intern Xerox Palo Alto (Calif.) Rsch. Ctr., 1996-97; project engr. Visteon Automotive Systems-Ford Motor Co., Allen Park, Mich., 1997—; Author: (with others) Industrial Knowledge Management Model Framework for Sharing of Engineering Practices Through Ubiquitous 2000; contr. articles to profl. publs.; patentee in field. Senator, mem. student life com. Grad. Student Orgn. Syracuse U., 1996-97. U. fellowship Syracuse U., 1996-97; recipient Best Outstanding Project prize, 2 certs. of merit Karnataka State Coun. for Sci. and Tech., 1991. Avocations: photography, gardening (rose crafting), Indian classical music, philatelly. Fax: 313-323-8149. E-mail: bbharadw@hotmail.com. Home: 515 Tobin Dr Apt 310 Inkster MI 48141-3503 Office: Visteon Automotive Systems 16630 Southfield Rd Allen Park MI 48101-2555

BHARADWAJ, PREM DATTA, physics educator; b. Gorakhpur, India, May 20, 1931; came to U.S., 1960; s. Ganga Dhar and Bhagwati Devi (Sharma) B.; m. Vidya Wati Sharma, Feb. 14, 1949; children: Rakesh Kumar, Rajnesh Kumar, Vidhu Rani Eranki, Sudha Kar. BS 1st class with merit, NREC Coll. Khurja, India, 1950; MS 1st class 1st, Agra (India) Coll., 1952; PhD, SUNY, Buffalo, 1964. Asst. prof. physics B.R. Coll. Agra, 1952-54; lectr. physics GPIC Tehri, Tehri Garhwal, India, 1954-56, Govt. Coll. Meerut, India, 1956-59; asst. prof. physics B.R. Coll. Agra, 1959-60; grad. asst. physics SUNY, Buffalo, 1960-62; from asst. prof. physics to assoc. prof. physics Niagara U., Niagara Falls, N.Y., 1962-66, prof. physics, 1966—, chmn. dept. physics, 1976-86; cons. NSF, 1966-71; reviewer N.Y. State Regents Exams. in Medicine and Dentistry, 1976; summer rsch. participant NSF, La. State U., Baton Rouge, 1965; vis. prof. dept. crystallography Rosewell Park Cancer Inst., Buffalo, N.Y., 1970-71. Co-author: Intermediate Agriculture Physics and Climatology, 1954; contbr. articles to profl. jours. Pres. Sathya Sai Ctr. Buffalo, Amherst, N.Y., 1990-93, Hindi Samaj of Greater Buffalo, Amherst, 1996-97; mem. trust com. Hindu Cultural Soc. Western N.Y., 1999—. Recipient Rajiv Gandhi Nat. Unity award for excellence Govt. India, 1995, Hind Rattan (Jewel of India) award Govt. of India, 1995; named Internat. Man of Yr. Internat. Biog. Ctr., Cambridge, England, 1999. Mem. India Assn. of Buffalo (co-founder 1961, award for outstanding work in edn. and cmty.), Hindi Samaj of Greater Buffalo (co-founder 1986), Am. Phys. Soc. Democrat. Hindu. Home: 100 N Parrish Dr Amherst NY 14228-1477 Office: Niagara U Physics Dept Lewiston Rd Niagara Falls NY 14109

BHARADWAJ, RENU SATISH, educator, medical researcher; b. Ambala, Haryana, India, Aug. 14, 1954; d. Ved and Suraksha (Khunghar) Prakash; m. Satish Narayan Bharadwaj, Oct. 17, 1978; children: Deepti, Nilkhil. MBBS, Armed Forces Med. Coll., Pune, India, 1976; MD in

Microbiology, B.J. Med. Coll., Pune, 1980. Registered med. practitioner; specialist in med. microbiology. Lectr. B.J. Med. Coll., 1977-81, assoc. prof., 1981-99, prof., chair, 1999—. Assoc. editor Med. Jour. West India, 1996-97; staff editor Byjeemic, 1985; contbr. articles to Lancet, Indian Jour. Med. Rsch., others. Mem. Indian Assn. Med. Microbiologists (exec. coun. 1995-97, sec. Maharashtra chpt. 1997-98), Am. Soc. Microbiology, Hosp. Infection Soc. India (life). Mem. Soka Gakkai Internat. Avocations: swimming, reading, writing. Home: 182 Narayani, Ganesh Nager, Pune 411038, India Office: BJ Med Coll, 411001 Pune, Maharashtra India

BHARATI, SUNIL YOVESHCHANDRA, geologist, geochemist, educator; b. Moradabad, India, June 2, 1960; arrived in Norway, 1986; s. Yovesh Chandra and Shanta (Agarwal) Sharma; m. Sangeeta Bhargava, Dec. 29, 1991; children: Shipra, Shruti. BSc, U. Bombay, 1980; MSc, Indian Inst. Tech., Bombay, 1982; CSc, U. Oslo, 1989; PhD, Norwegian U. Sci. Tech., Trondheim, 1997. Geologist Oil Natural Gas Corp Ltd., Bombay, 1983-86; sr. geochemist Geolab Nor, Trondheim, 1990-98, lab. mgr., ops. mgr., 1998—; cons., tchr. India, 1994-95, Nigeria, 1995-96, Tanzania, 1995-96; organizer, chair Nat. ACS Meeting, 1994. Contbr. several articles to profl. jours. Mem. cultural com., vol., 1997 Nordic World Ski Championships, Trondheim, 1997. Mem. Am. Assn. Petroleum Geologists, European Assn. Geoscientists Engrs. (founding), European Assn. Organic Geochemists. Avocations: mountaineering, photography, traveling. Office: Horneberg vn 5, PB 5740 Fossegrenda, N 7437 Trondheim Norway

BHARDWAJ, ANIL, astrophysicist; b. Aligarh, India, June 1, 1967; s. Shyam Sunder Sharma and Asha Sharma; m. Preeti Sharma, Apr. 21, 1995; children: Misha, Anusha. BSc, Lucknow U., 1985, MSc, 1987; PhD, Banaras Hindu U., 1992. From rsch. fellow to sr. rsch. fellow Banaras Hindu U., Varanasi, India, 1987-92; scientist Vikram Sarabhai Space Ctr., Trivandrum, India, 1993—. Grantee UN Office of Outer Space Affairs, 1996. Mem. Am. Geophys. Union, Indian Space Scientist Assn. Avocations: travel, driving, listening to music, gardening. Home: Vrindavan TC 5/808 (2), GC Nagar 121 2d St Manamoola Rd, Peroorkada 695005, India Office: Vikram Sarabhai Space Ctr, Space Physics Lab, 695022 Trivandrum Kerala, India

BHARGAVA, RAJ RANI, mathematician, educator; b. Kota, Rajasthan, India, June 15, 1949; d. Rajeshwar Dayal and Sneh Lata Bhargava. BS, Kanpur U., 1967, MS, 1969; PhD, Indian Inst. Tech., Bombay, 1974. Lectr., reader U. Roorkee, India, 1975-95; prof. U. Roorkee, 1996—; head computer ctr. Kota Open U., 1989-90; vis. prof. Kagoshima (Japan) U. Dept. Mech. Engring., 1997-98. Author: Introduction to Numerical Techniques, 1982. Alexander von Humboldt fellow, 1980, 84. Avocations: reading, swimming, music, dancing. Home: 132/3 Vikas Nagar, Roorkee 247 667, India Office: Dept Math, Univ Roorkee, Roorkee 247 667, India

BHARGAVA, SUNITA WADEKAR, journalist; b. Mumbai, India, Sept. 14, 1964; d. Bhagwan T. and Pushpa B. (Dhodapkar) Wadekar; m. Neeraj Bhargava, July 17, 1989; children: Saahil Wadekar Bhargava, Kunaal Wadekar Bhargava. BA in English with honors, Lady Shri Ram Coll., 1986; BA, MA in Journalism, NYU, 1991. Reporter, editor Dataquest/Telematics, New Delhi, India, 1985-88; spl. corr. Econ. Times, New Delhi, 1985-88, India Today, N.Y.C., 1992-94; asst. editor Bus. Week, N.Y.C., 1991-96; columnist Rediff-On-the-Net, Mumbai, India, 1998—. Recipient Maurice Feldman award N.Y. Fin. Writers Assn., 1990. Fellow South Asian Journalists Assn.; mem. Soc. Profl. Journalists (pres. NYU chpt. 1990-91), Assn. for Rehab. of Battered Women, Phi Beta Kappa, Kappa Tau Alpha. Avocations: collecting antique teapots, sketching, photography, reading, movies. Home: 93 Chitrakoot Altamount Rd, Mumbai 400026, India

BHARUCHA, NADIR EDDIE, neurophysician; b. Bombay, India, Feb. 5, 1948; s. Eddie Phiroz and Piloo (Kohiyar) B.; m. Roberta Harrison Raven, May 1, 1980; children: Perin, Kate, Amy. B Medicine B Surgery, U. Bombay, 1973, MD, 1976. Diplomate Am. Bd. Neurology and Psychiatry. Resident KEM Hosp., Bombay, 1973-76; registrar, sr. house officer St. Thomas Hosp./Nat. Hosp. for Nervous Diseases, London, 1976-80; registrar, lectr. Nat. Hosp. for Nervous Diseases, London, 1976-80; tchr. fellow U. Hosp., Boston, 1981; vis. scientist Nat. Inst. Neurol. and Communicative Disorders and Stroke, Bethesda, Md., 1981-83; asst. prof. neurology KEM Hosp., 1983-93; assoc. prof. neurology Bombay Hosp. Inst. Med. Scis., 1993—, cons. neurologist, 1983—; head dept. neuroepidemiology Med. Rsch. Ctr., Bombay Hosp., Mumbai, 1983—; hon. cons. neurologist Children's Hosp., Mumbai, 1983—, Parsee Gen. Hosp., Mumbai, 1983—. Author: Epilepsy: A Comprehensive Textbook, 1997; assoc. editor: Neurology in Clinical Practice, 2d edit., 1996; contbr. over 100 articles to profl. jours., chpts. to books. Fellow Royal Acad. Physicians Can., Am. Acad. Neurology, Assn. Brit. Neurologists, Australian Assn. Neurologists, Royal Coll. Physicians. Avocation: reading. Office: Bombay Hosp, 12 Marine Lines, Mumbai 400020, Mumbai

BHARUCHA, NILUFER ERUCH, postcolonial literature educator, researcher; b. Bombay, Jan. 24, 1952; d. Eruch Phirozshah and Daisy Eruch (Tata) B. BA with honors, U. Bombay, 1972, MA, 1974; MEd, U. Manchester, Eng., 1982; PhD, U. Bombay, 1990. Lectr. Maniben Nanavati Women's Coll., Bombay, 1975-86, Regional Inst. English, Bangalore, India, 1986-88; sr. lectr. dept. English U. Bombay, 1988-90, reader dept. English, 1990-95, prof. dept. English, 1995—; vis. prof. Otto-Von-Guericke U., Magdeburg, Germany, 1996—, U. Siegen, Germany, 2000, U. Avignon, France, 2000; hon. dir. tchr. devel. project Indian Edn. Soc., Bombay, 1990-92; cons. lang. devel. project Bombay Mcpl. Corp., 1992-93, text book project Shivaji U., Kolhapur, India, 1991-92; lectr. in field. Co-editor: Indian English Fiction 1980-90: An Assessment, 1994, Postcolonial Perspectives on the Raj and its Literature, 1994; contbr. articles to profl. jours. Hon. program officer Nat. Social Svc., Bombay, 1976-86; hon. editor AVEHI, Ednl. Resources Ctr., Bombay, 1994—; hon. coord. Nat. Adult Edn. Program, Bombay, 1984-86. Recipient TCTP scholarship Brit. Coun., 1981-82, Acad. Staff fellowship Assn. Commonwealth Univs., Eng., 1994-95. Mem. Indian Assn. Commonwealth Lit. and Lang. Studies (exec. com. 1996—), Assn. Brit. Coun. Scholars (sec. 1993—), Bombay English Assn. (joint sec. 1976-78). Parsi Zoroastrian. Avocations: hiking, travel, theatre, classical Indian music. Home: Block D-9 Captain Colony, Tardeo Rd, Mumbai 400 034, India Office: Univ Bombay Dept English, Vidyanagari Kalina, Mumbai 400 098, India

BHASKARWAR, ASHOK NIWRITTI, chemical engineer, educator; b. Pusad, India, Dec. 23, 1959; s. Niwritti and Malati Bhaskarwar; m. Madhumati Omprakash Sharma, May 19, 1992. B Tech., Laxminarayan Inst. of Tech., Nagpur, India, 1981; ME, Indian Inst. of Sci., Bangalore, 1983, PhD, 1987. Rsch. assoc. Indian Inst. Sci., Bangalore, 1987-88, 89-90; asst. prof. Indian Inst. Tech., New Delhi, 1990-95, 96-97, assoc. prof., 1997—; mem. sci. staff Lab. voor Petrochemische Tech., Ghent, Belgium, 1988-89; vis. asst. prof. U. Minn., Mpls., 1995-96; cons. Deluxe Corp., Shoreview, Minn., 1995-96. Mem. editl. bd. ACH-Models in Chemistry. Recipient young scientist award Ind. Nat. Sci. Acad., 1991; Boyscast scholar Dept. Sci. and Tech., New Delhi, 1994. Mem. Indian Inst. Chem. Engrs. (assoc.). Hindu. Avocations: reading, music, painting, sketching. Office: Indian Inst Tech, Dept Chem Engring/Hauz Khas, New Delhi 110 016, India

BHAT, G. M., sedimentologist, educator; b. Srinagar, Kashmir, India, July 2, 1959; s. Haji Rashee and Azeezi Bhat; m. Raja Bano, Sept. 19, 1973; children: Manzoor, Gulshan, Muzaffar, Shahnawas; m. Hajra Bano, Feb. 24, 1993; 1 child, Mufaiz. BSc, Kashmir U., Srinagar, India, 1979; MSc, Jammu U., 1981, MPhil, 1983, PhD, 1987. Lectr. higher edn. Srinagar, 1986-87; lectr. Jammu U., 1987-92, sr. lectr., 1992-98, reader in sedimentology, biostratigraphy, 1997-99; reader dept. geology and geophysics U. Kashmir, Srinagar, 1999—; chmn. Siwalik Rsch. Group; convener Convention of Indian Assn. Sedimentologists, 1999; convener Internat. Rsch. Working Group on Mitigation of Natural Hazards, Jammu and Kashmir, 1999; lectr. in field. Contbr. articles to profl. jours.; editor The IAS Newsletter, 1996—. Joint sec. J—K Gandhi Samarak Nidi, Jammu, 1980-89; founder, gen. sec. Nat. Ednl. and Rsch. Soc., J&K State, India, Srinagar, Kashmir, 1994—. Fellow Geol. Soc. India (life), Indian Assn. Sedimentologists (life, mem. governing coun. 1997—); mem. Inst. Engrs. (bd. govs. 1987-92), Indian Acad. Scis. Avocations: trekking, gardening, music, reading, creative writing. Home: Pampore, Srinagar Kashmir 192121, India Office: PG Dept Geology & Geophysic, Univ Kashmir, Srinagar 190006, India

BHAT, KESHAVA, botanist, consultant; b. Pallathadka, Kerala, India, Jan. 3, 1940; arrived in Venezuela, 1969; s. Subraya and Lakshmi Bhat; m. Devaki Bhat, May 24, 1969; children: Pavan Kumari, Suma, Kumar Prasad, Anasuya Devi. BSc, Madras (India) Christian Coll., 1959, MSc, 1961; PhD in Botany, Presidency Coll., Madras, 1966. Rsch. asst. Presidency Coll., Madras, 1966-68; prof. on contract U. de Oriente, Cumana, Venezuela, 1969-73; prof. aggregate U. de Oriente, Cumana, 1973-75, assoc. prof., 1975-80, prof., 1980-87; founder dir. Jardin Etnobotánico Chara Chakra, Cumana, 1979—; mem. com. of experts on medicinal plants in developing countries, Arusha, Tanzania, 1990. Author: Ayuda Para El Estudio De Las Plantas Con Flores, 1982, Herbolario Tropical, 1985, 6th edit., 1994, French edit., 1990, Holistic Life: A Simple Way of Better Living, 1991, 2d edit., 1994, Las Bases Del Naturismo, 1991, Basics of Natural Health, 1991, 2d edit., 1994, El Sentido de la Vida, del Embarazo hasta la Muerte, 1994 La Vuelta al Conuco: Producción Naturista para un Mundo en Crisis, 2d edit., 1998, Goodbye to the Ruling Scientific Model: Proposal for a New Science, 1998; chief editor Ediciones Vivir Mejor, Caracas, 1987—. Founder, promoter A Simple Way of Better Living, Caracas, 1969—; founder, hon. pres. Fundavime, Caracas, 1989—. Sr. rsch. fellow CSIR, India, 1968; named Best Ethnobotanist, Christian Cazabone Found., Caracas, 1997. Mem. Internat. Soc. Plant Morphologists (life), Internat. Assn. for Plant Taxonomists (life). Avocations: ethnobotany, astronomy, teaching. Home: Opp Indsl Estate, Alevoor Rd, Manipal 576119, India Office: Fundavime, Av Trujillo 12/39 Urb Mariperez, Caracas Venezuela

BHAT, NIRANJAN CHIDANAND, inspections executive; b. Sangli, India, Feb. 12, 1972; p. Chidanand Gururaj and Laxmi Chidanand Bhat. Diploma in welding tech., Dnyaneshwar Vidyapeeth, Pune, India, 1989; degree in mech. engring., U. Pune, 1993; diploma in Bus. Mgmt., Brit. Insts., Bombay, 1994; diploma in Quality Control Mgmt., Nat. Inst. Indsl. Rsch. Devel., Madras, India, 1995; advanced diploma in Total Quality Mgmt., Nat. Open Sch. Mgmt. Studies, Madras, India, 1997; PhD in Welding Tech., Internat. U. Calif., 1998; diploma in Environ. Mgmt., Nat. Inst. Labor Edn. & Mgmt., Chennai, India, 1998; diploma in Indsl. Safety, Indian Coun. Labor Mgmt., Chennai, 1999; diploma Quality Assurance & Quality Sys., All India Coun. Mgmt. Studies, Chennai, 2000. Cert. quality engr., cert. boiler and pressure vessel inspector, internal quality auditor, Non-Destructive Evaluation level-II; cert. welding inspector. Quality assurance in charge D.D. Enterprises, Pune, 1993-94; inspection engr. Sys. Engrs. & Adv. Svcs., Pune, 1995; exec. inspections engr. Société Générale de Surveillance India Ltd., Pune, 1996—; chief cons. Weldcon, Pune, 1995—; cons. in field on boiler, pressure vessel, piping and spl. projects. Editl. asst. Jour. Process Equipment & Piping Tech., 1996—. Fellow Indian Soc. Mech. Engrs., Indian Soc. Engrs. and Technicians, Indian Soc. Bus. Mgmt., Electrochem. Soc. India, Indian Inst. Plant Engrs., United Writers' Assn., Inst. Chartered Mgrs. (India), Mgmt. Studies Promotion Inst.; mem. ASME (affiliate), Am. Soc. Non-destructive Testing (cert. radiography testing, magnetic-particle testing, ultrasonic testing, penetrant testing, visual testing, leak testing, eddy-current testing Level II), Am. Welding Soc., Deutscher Verband fur Schweiben, Internat. Assn. Quality Practitioners, The Welding Inst.-Welding & Joining Soc., Indian Inst. Indsl. Engring., Indian Inst. Welding, Indian Soc. Non-destructive Testing (cert. welding insp.), Quality Circle Forum India, Gramya Rsch. Analysis Inst., Indian Vacuum Soc. Avocations: music, technical books, movies, driving, socializing. E-mail: niranjan bhat@usa.net. Home: 4 Akash Apts, Karve Rd, Pune 411029 Maharashtra India

BHAT, RAJIV, biophysical chemist, educator; b. Kathua, Jammu, India, Aug. 16, 1960; s. Mohan Lal and Krishna (Kachru) B.; m. Anjli Nehru, Oct. 31, 1991; 1 child, Ayush. BS, U. Jammu, 1978, MS, 1980; PhD, Indian Inst. Tech., Delhi, 1986. Lectr. Thapar Inst. Engring. and Tech., Patiala, India, 1985-86; postdoctoral assoc. Brandeis U., Waltham, Mass., 1986-89; lectr. U. Delhi, India, 1989-90; asst. prof. Jawaharlal Nehru U., Delhi, 1990—. Contbr. articles to profl. jours. and books. Grantee Dept. Sci. and Tech. India, 1993, Dept. Biotech., India, 1999; recipient Disting. Leadership award Am. Biog. Inst., 1989, Young Investigator Travel award Protein Soc., 1988. Mem. Soc. Biol. Chemists (life), Indian Biophys. Soc. (life). Home: T-011 Jawaharlal Nehru U, New Delhi 110067, India Office: Centre Biotechnology, Jawaharlal Nehru Univ, New Delhi 110067, India

BHATIA, ARATI, pathologist; b. Poona, India, July 23, 1948; d. Shiv and Savitri (Khosla) B.; m. Arun Mathai Chacko; 1 child, Adil. MBBS, Amritsar Med. Coll., 1971; MD, All India Inst. Med. Scis., Delhi, 1976. Resident in pathology All India Inst. Med. Scis., New Delhi, 1974-76; demonstrator Univ. Coll. Med. Scis., Delhi, 1976-79, lectr, reader, 1979-91, prof. pathology, 1991—. Home: G36 Sainik Farms, 110062 New Delhi India Office: Univ Coll Med Sci, Divsn Cytology, 110095 Delhi India

BHATIA, SUKHWANT KAUR, geneticist, researcher; b. Dehragopipur, India, Feb. 11, 1950; s. Rawel Singh and Balwant (Kaur) B. BSc, Panjab U., Chandigarh, India, 1969; MSc, Punjabi U., Patiala, India, 1971; PhD, Kurukshetra U., Haryana, India, 1983. Demonstrator Nat. Dairy Rsch. Inst., Karnal, India, 1971-75; scientist Nat. Dairy Rsch. Inst. & Nat. Bur. Animal Genetic Resources, Karnal, 1975-85; sr. scientist Nat. Bur. Animal Genetic Resources, Karnal, 1985—; presenter 75 papers to internat. and nat. confs. Author: (with V. Shanker) Compendium, 1995, Sex Chromatin Test: Some Practical Applications in Farm Animals; contbr. over 78 articles to profl. jours. Recipient Jawahar Lal Nehru award Indian Coun. Agrl. Rsch., New Delhi, 1984, Best Paper awards Indian Dairy Assn., New Delhi, 1991, 92. Mem. Agrl. Rsch. Svcs. Scientists Forum (life), Soc. Cons. Dom. Animal Biodiversity (life, exec. mem.). Office: Nat Bur Animal Genetic Res, Makram Pur, PB No 129, Karnal 132 001, India

BHATIA, SURESH KUMAR, chemical engineering educator; b. Delhi, India, Sept. 8, 1952; arrived in Australia, 1996; s. Narsingh Dev and Nirmala (Devi) B.; m. Meena Jhuraney, Mar. 12, 1986; children: Nimisha, Nirav. B of Tech., Indian Inst. of Tech., 1974; MSE, U. Pa., 1976, PhD, 1981. Sr. engr. Booz Allen Applied Rsch., Bethesda, Md., 1976-78; sr. staff engr. Mobil R&D Co., Paulsboro, N.J., 1981-82; vis. asst. prof. U. Fla., Gainesville, 1982-84; asst. prof. Indian Inst. of Tech., Bombay, India, 1984-90, prof., 1990-96; reader U. Queensland, Brisbane, 1996-2000, prof., 2000—; cons. Glaxo Labs., Bombay, 1992-94, Tata Chems., Bombay, 1987-89, Lubrizol India, Bomba India, 1988-89, Bundaberg Distilling Co., 1997-98. Contbr. articles to profl. jours. Recipient Herdillia award Indian Inst. of Chem. Engrs, S.S. Bhatnagar award Govt. of India, 1993. Fellow Indian Acad. of Scis.; mem. Internat. Adsorption Soc. Avocations: tennis, swimming. Office: Dept Chem Engring, U Queensland, Brisbane QLD 4072, Australia

BHATIA, VANRAJ ANANDJI, composer; b. Bombay, May 31, 1927. MA in Eng. (hon.), Elphinstone Coll., Bombay, 1949; study with Howard Ferguson, Royal Acad. Music, London, 1950-54; study with Nadia Boulanger, Paris Conservatoire, 1954-59. Reader in musicology Western Music Dept. Faculty of Music U. Delhi, 1960-65; freelance composer Bombay, 1965—; participant Indian Del. to East-West Music Encounter, Japan, 1960. Western classical works include Cyclic Variation-Cello and Harpsichord, 1954, Violin Sonata, 1956, Woodwind Quintet, 1957, Piano Concerto, 1958, Scena for Voice, Violin and Piano, 1959, Music for Six Instruments (composed for Edinburgh Festival), 1963, Kaleidoscope-String Quartet and Prepared Piano, 1965, Rudranam and Vasansi for three unaccompanied choirs, 1974-75, Jaisalmer, 1976; music for feature films: Ankur, Nishant, Manthan, Bhumika, Junoon, Kalyug, Sazaye Maut, 36 Chowringhee Lane, Ed Dad Mithi; music for about 6000 advertisements: films, radio and TV. On panel for Commonwealth Scholarships, 1964, Programme Awards, All India Radio, 1973-75, Time and Talent Prize, 1972. Recipient Lilly Boulanger Meml. prize, 1958, Bengal Film Journalists award for music in film Bhumika, 1976, Bengal Film Journalists award for music in film Manthan, 1977, Sur Singar Sansad award, 1986, 87, Pres. Gold medal for Tamas, 1988, Sangeet Natak Acad. award, 1989, Maharashtra Rajya Puraskar, 1990. Home and Office: Rungtra House-Grnd Floor, 68 Nepean Sea Rd, 6 Bombay India

BHATIA, VIPAN, urologist, educator; b. New Delhi, July 14, 1957; s. Lakshmi Chand and Shukla Bhatia; m. Rupila Ahuja, Nov. 25, 1984; 1 child, Simran. MBBS, Med. Coll., Amritsar, India, 1978, MS in Surgery, 1982; MCh in Urology, All India Inst. Med. Scis., New Delhi, 1986. Registrar surgery Med. Coll., Amritsar, 1979-82; sr. registrar urology All India Inst. Med. Scis., New Delhi, 1984-86; head urology dept. RG Stone Clinic Urol. Rsch. Inst., New Delhi, 1986-92; clin. tutor urology faculty medicine Kuwait U., 1993-95; asst. clin. prof. urology faculty medicine Tawam Hosp., United Arab Emirates U., Al Ain, 1996—; internat. invited faculty 12th World Congress on Endourology and ESWL, Washington, 1994, 13th World Congress on Endourology and ESWL, Israel, 1995; dep. nat. del. Kuwait chpt. Soc. Internat. Urology, 1994-95; vis. internat. fellow Katharinen Hosp., Stuttgart, Germany, 1987, Oberhause Hosp., Fulda, Germany, 1986; lectr. undergrad. and postgrad. continuing urol. edn. programs; guest lectr. sci. presentations at various meetings. Internat. referee Brit. Jour. Urology, 1998—; internat. reviewer Urology News, Scotland, 1998—; mem. editl. bds. Brit. Jour. Urology, Urology News, Medicine Digest, Brit. Med. Jour. Surgery; contbr. articles to profl. jours., chpts. to books. Recipient merit rsch. scholarship Punjab Govt. India, Amritsar, 1980-82, disting. rsch. award Kuwait Found. for Advancement Scis., 1995. Fellow ACS, Internat. Med. Scis. Acad., Internat. Coll. Surgeons; mem. Surgeons of India, Assn. Surgeons India, Urol. Soc. India, Urolithiasis Soc. India, Soc. Internat. D'Urologie (internat. scholarship 1996). Hindu. Avocations: western classical music. Office: Tawam Hosp Urology Dept, PO Box 15258, Al-Ain United Arab Emirates

BHATKAL, MARUTI NARAYAN, lawyer; b. Bhatkal, India, Apr. 5, 1933; s. Narayan Manjunath and Laxmi Narayan B.; m. Madhumati Maruti Bhatkal, Apr. 30, 1961; 1 child, Supriya. BA, Wilson Coll., 1955; LLB, Govt. Law Coll., Mumbai, India, 1958. Bar: Maharashtra, 1958. Legal advisor All India Trade Union Congress unions, Mumbai, 1956-58; asst. labour officer Sankey Elec. Stampings Pvt., Ltd., Mumbai, 1958-62; asst. commr. of labour and concilliation Govt. of Maharashtra, Mumbai, 1962-63; advocate Mumbai, 1963—; dir. RCI (India) Pvt., Ltd., Bangalore, 1995-97, Airsonic Travels Pvt., Ltd., Mumbai, 1994—. Fellow Indian Soc. Arbitrators (trustee 1993—); mem. Indian Coun. Arbitration. Avocations: music, reading, sports. E-mail: bhatkal@bom7.vsnl.net.in. Home: #42 Veena Towers, Near Colaba Post Office, Mumbai/Maharashtra 400005, India Office: Bhatkal Assocs, #42 Veena Twrs/Colaba PO, 400005 Mumbai/Maharashtra India

BHATNAGAR, DEEPAK, biochemist, researcher; b. Ratlam, India, Oct. 19, 1951; s. Mahavir Prasad and Pushpa Bhatnagar; m. Sadhna Bhatnagar, Apr. 4, 1982. BSc, U. Jodhpur, India, 1971; MSc, Maharaja Siyajirao U. Baroda, India, 1973; PhD, Banaras Hindu U., Varanasi, India, 1981. Lectr. Govt. Med. Coll., Faridkot, India, 1974-77; rsch. fellow Banaras Hindu U., Varanasi, 1978-81; lectr. Govt. Med. Coll., Patiala, India, 1982-88; sr. lectr. Devi Ahilya U. Indore, India, 1989-91, reader, 1991—. Contbr. articles to profl. jours. Recipient award U. Grants Commn. Rsch. Project, New Delhi, 1991-94, Madhya Pradesh Coun. Sci. and Tech., Bhopal Rsch. Project, 1991-96. Avocations: reading, writing, sports, social activities. Office: Devi Ahilya Univ Dept Biochemistry, Khandwa Rd, Indore 452017, India

BHATNAGAR, MAHENDRA PRASAD, patent agent, consultant; b. Saharanpur, India, July 1, 1936; s. Ayodhia Prasad and Shanti Devi Bhatnagar; m. Usha Bnatnagar, Jan. 20, 1963; children: N. Carrae, Anupama, Preetima, Vijay. BSc, Agra U., India, 1954; B in Engring., U. Roorkee, India, 1960; MBA, U. Delhi, India, 1977. Registered engr., India. Examiner of patents and designs Patent Office of India, 1960-69; chief engr. Nat. Rsch. Devel. Corp., India, 1969-95; patent agt. Lall, Lahiri & Salhotra Attys., New Delhi, 1995—; cons. Ctr. Devel. Telematics, India, 1995—. Contbr. articles to profl. jours. Fellow Inst. Electronics and Telecomm. Engrs.; mem. Internat. Assn. Advancement Teaching and Rsch. Intellectual Property. Avocations: chess, billiards. Home: 161 Vigyan Vihar, Delhi 110092, India Office: Lall Lahiri & Salhotra, N-128 Panchsheel Park, New Delhi 110017, India

BHATNAGAR, OM PRAKASH, English language educator, retired; b. Agra, India, May 30, 1932; s. Ganga Swarup and Lakshmi B.; m. Parvati Hingorani, Oct. 21, 1959; children: Deepak, Jyoti. MA in Econs., Hitkarini U., Saugar, India, 1954; MA in English, U. Saugar, 1956; postgrad. diploma in tchg. English as fgn. lang., Ctrl. Inst. English, Hyderabad, India, 1969; PhD in English, U. Nagpur, India, 1992; DLitt (hon.), World U., N.Y.C., 1979. Lectr. in English Vidarbha Mahavidyalaya, Amravati, India, 1956-70; prof. English Vidarbha Mahavidyalaya, Amravati, 1974-92, dir. continuing edn., 1974-90; prof. English State Inst. English, Bombay, 1970-71, State Inst. Arts Social Scis., Nagpur, 1972-73. Author: (poetry) Thought Poems, 1976, Feeling Fossils, 1977, Angles of Retreat, 1979, Oneiric Visions, 1980, Shadows in Floodlights, 1984, The Audible Landscape, 1986; (criticism) Perspectives on Indian Poetry in English, 1986, Studies in Indian Drama in English, 1987, Indian Literature in English, 1990; editor (poetry) Intercontinental Poetry, 1978, New Dimensions in Indo-English Poetry, 1980, Rising Columns, Some Indian Poets in English, 1980. Recipient G.R. award Ctr. Devel. Edn., 1986. Avocations: languages, poetry. Home: Rituraj A 478 Sarita Vihar, New Delhi 110044, India

BHATNAGAR, SURENDRA PRASAD, company executive; b. Saharanpur, India, Feb. 13, 1941; s. Ayodhya Prasad and Shanti (Devi) B.; m. Kulsrestha Sudha, May 8, 1966; children: Anjali, Aparna. BSc, Agra U., Muzzefernagar, India, 1957; MSc, Aligarh (India) U., 1962, PhD, 1967. Sr. rsch. assoc. Indian Inst. Sci., Bangalore, 1971-72; doctoral rsch. fellow U. Southampton, Eng., 1972-74; rsch. assoc. Cornell U., 1974-75; vis. scientist Nat. Inst. Health, 1975-77; doctoral rsch. assoc. Ctrl. Rsch. Lab., Antibiotics Plant, IDPL, Rishikesh, India, 1967-71; gen. mgr. Ministry Fin., Govt. India, Madhya Pradesh, India, 1977-79, Reckitt & Colman India Ltd., Bangalore, 1979-87; pres. Chems. & Plastics India Ltd., Bangalore, 1987-92; mng. dir. Tech-Dry Pvt. Ltd., Bangalore, 1992—; bd. dirs. Drachem, India. Contbr. articles to internat. jours.; patentee in field. Fellow Royal Soc. Chemistry, Nat. Acad. Scis.; mem. London Chem. Soc., Am. Chem. Soc. Avocations: reading, badminton. Home: Brentwood Apts 1st Fl, 2d Main, 35 Defence Colony, Indiranagar/Bangalor 560 038, India Office: Tech Dry India Pvt Ltd, 769 I Cross, Indiranagar, Bangalore 560 038, India

BHATNAGAR, VED PRAKASH, physicist, researcher; b. Meerut, India, June 30, 1944; arrived in U.K., 1985; s. Hariom Prakash and Shanti Devi Bhatnagar; m. Sunita Raizada, Nov. 6, 1973; 1 child, Seema. BSc, Agra (India) U., 1961, MSc in Physics, 1963; MSc (Tech.) in Electronics, Birla Inst. Tech. & Sci., Pilani, India, 1965; MS in Applied Math, U. Mich., 1970, PhD in Elec. Engring., 1971. Sr. rsch. fellow Ctrl. Electronic Engring. Rsch. Inst., Pilani, 1965-67; rsch. asst. U. Mich., Ann Arbor, 1967-71; rsch. assoc. Ecole Royale Militaire, Brussels, 1971-76, chef de travaux, 1976-81, maitre de rsch., 1981-88; sr. radio frequency physicist Joint European Torus Joint Undertaking, Abingdon, U.K., 1988-93; asst. head heating and operations dept. Joint European Torus Joint Undertaking, Abingdon, 1993-98; prin. sci. officer nuclear fission and radiation protection European Atomic Energy Cmty., European Commn., Brussels, 1998—; mem. Tokamak adv. group European Atomic Energy Cmty., Brussels, 1978-84; project leader Joint European Torus/European Atomic Energy Cmty./Etat Belge Ecole Royale Militaire, Brussels, 1981-84, Next European Torus/European Atomic Energy Cmty./Etat Belge Ecole Royal Militaire, Brussels, 1985-86; ion cyclotron resonance heating dep. task area leader Internat. Tokamak Exptl. Reactor-European Union Home Team, European Atomic Energy Cmty., Brussels, 1995-98. Contbr. articles to profl. jours.; patentee in field. Fellow Am. Phys. Soc.; mem. Eta Kappa Nu, Sigma Xi. Hindu. Avocations: cricket, badminton. Office: European Commn Mo 75 5/51, RTD/DII3 rue de la loi 200, Brussels 1049, Belgium

BHATT, BALSWAROOP, mathematics educator; b. Hindaun, India, Sept. 24, 1949; s. BAlchendra and Dhanni Bhatt; m. Snehlata Nagar, May 23, 1975; children: Anju, Anita, Ashish. BSc, U. Rajasthan, 1969, MSc, 1971, PhD, 1976. Lectr. U. West Indies, St. Augustine, Trinidad, 1978-83, sr. lectr., 1983-93, lectr., 1996-98, sr. lectr., 1998—; assoc. prof. Sultan Qaboos U., Oman, 1991-95; prof. U. Antioquia, Medellin, Colombia, 1995-96. Author: Non-Newtonian Fluid Flows, 1982. Mem. Allahabad Math. Soc., Indian Soc. Theoretical and Applied Mechanics, Am. Math. Soc., Caribbean Congress Fluid Dynamics, Caribbean Acad. Scis., N.Y. Acad. Scis. Office: U WI, Dept Math & Computer Sci, Saint Augustine Trinidad

BHATT, DEVENDRA KUMAR, geologist; b. Lucknow, Uttar Pradesh, India, June 6, 1944; s. Urba Datt and Madhavi (Pande) B.; m. Jaya Pant, Feb. 2, 1972; 1 child, Vivek. BS, Lucknow U., India, 1960, BS in Geology, 1961, MS, 1963, PhD, 1982. Sr. tech. asst. Oil and Natural Gas Corp., Ltd., India, 1963-67; scientific officer Oil and Natural Gas Corp., Dehradun, India, 1967; jr. geologist Geol. Survey India, 1968-77, sr. geologist, 1978-91, dir. geology, 1991-92, dir. geol. selection grade, 1993—. Contbr. articles to profl. jours. Fellow Geol. Soc. India (life), Pal Soc. India (life). Avocations: reading biographies and autobiographies, mountain trekking, classical music. Office: Geol Survey of India, Jhalana Instnl Area, 302004 Jaipur/Rajasthan India

BHATT, DEVENDRA PRAKASH, chemist, researcher; b. Pithoragarh, India, Jan. 12, 1958; s. Kedar Datt and Kunti (Devi) Bhatt; m. Neema Joshi, May 9, 1983; children: Yogesh, Deepti. BSc, Govt. Postgrad. Coll., Pithoragarh, 1976, MSc, 1978; PhD in Chemistry, Kumuan U., Nainital, India, 1985; cert. in German, Goethe Inst., Berlin, 1989. Lectr. chemistry Kumaun U., Almora, India, 1979-80, rsch. fellow, 1981-83; sci. asst. Ctrl. Electrochemical Rsch. Inst., Madras, India, 1983-84; sci. asst. Ctrl. Electrochemical Rsch. Inst., Karaikudi, India, 1984-87, scientist, 1987-94; scientist Nat. Physical Lab., New Delhi, 1994—; convenor Swadeshi Sci. Movement India, Delhi, 1995—. Editor: Electroplating and Metal Finishing, 1997; contbr. articles to sci. jours., including Jour. Electrochem. Soc., Electrochim. Acta; patentee in field. German Acad. Exch. Svc. fellow Free U., Berlin, 1989-90; recipient World 2000 Millennium award Internat. Assn. Educators World Peace Am. Fellow Soc. Advancement Electrochem. Sci. & Tech. (life); mem. Carbon Soc. India (life). Hindu. Avocations: popularizing ancient Indian sciences, playing cards, music. Fax: 91-11-5852678. Home: DRH-20, Nat Phys Lab Colony, New Delhi 110060, India Office: Nat Phys Lab IPR Mgmt Group, KS Krishnan Rd, New Delhi 110012, India

BHATT, HARISH CHANDRA, astrophysicist, educator; b. Pithoragarh, India, Dec. 24, 1954; s. Amba Dutt and Prabha (Joshi) B.; m. Prabha Pant, May 25, 1989; children: Namita, Anamika. BS, U. Rajasthan, 1974; MS, Indian Inst. Tech., 1977; PhD, Phys. Rsch. Lab., Ahmedabad, India, 1984. Postdoctoral fellow Phys. Rsch. Lab., Ahmedabad, India, 1983-85; fellow Indian Inst. Astrophysics, Bangalore, 1986-90, reader, 1990-96, assoc. prof., 1996—; vis. scholar Queen Mary Coll., London, 1980, 82; vis. scientist Indian Inst. Astrophysics, 1985-86; lectr. Indian Inst. Sci., Bangalore, 1986-96. Assoc. editor. Bull. Astronomical Soc. India, 1996—; contbr. articles to profl. jours. Mem. Internat. Astronomical Union, Astronomical Soc. India. Avocations: writing, trekking in Himalayas. Home: Koramangala, 518 1 Fl 1st A Main 8 Block, Bangalore 560-095, India Office: Indian Inst Astrophysics, Koramangala, Bangalore 560-034, India

BHATT, NAVINCHANDRA BALDEVRAM, electrical engineer; b. Saniad, Gujarat, India, June 1, 1950; came to U.S., 1973; s. Baldevram B. and Jamnaben N. B.; m. Tarangini I. Patel, July 23, 1977; children: Rachna, Rishee. BEE, M.S. U. Baroda, Vadodara, India, 1972; MSEE, W.Va. U., 1975, PhD, 1978. Registered profl. engr., Ohio, N.Y. Engr. Am. Electric Power, N.Y.C., 1977-80; sr. engr. Am. Electric Power, Columbus, Ohio, 1980-91; prin. engr. Am. Electric Power, 1991-93, sect. mgr., 1993—. Named Tech. Champion Electric Power Rsch. Inst., Palo Alto, Calif., 1996. Mem. IEEE (sr.). Office: Am Electric Power 700 Morrison Rd Gahanna OH 43230-6642

BHATTA, GAMBHIR, political science and management educator; b. Baitadi, Nepal, Jan. 10, 1960; s. Megh Dev and Krishna (Bista) B.; m. Bhawana Dhungana, Feb. 22, 1992; 1 child, Ashwin. BA, Tribhuwan U., Kathmandu, Nepal, 1982; MA in Econs., Bowling Green State U., 1985, MA in Polit. Sci., 1985; PhD, U. Pitts., 1990. Sr. cons. Dept. City Planning, Pitts., 1990-91; rsch. scholar U. Ctr. for Social and Urban Rsch., Pitts., 1991-93; program officer UN Devel. Program, UN Vols., Uganda, 1993-96; vis. fellow Nat. U. of Singapore, 1996-98, lectr., asst. prof., 1998—; cons. Internat. Mgmt. Devel. Inst., Pitts., 1989-92, UNDP, Uzbekistan, 1994, UN Devel. Program, Nepal, 1996-98, Singapore Inst. Mgmt., 1997-99, Sch. of Mgmt., Open Poly. U. of New Zealand, 2000. Author: Reforms at the United Nations, 2000; contbr. articles to profl. publs. Leader Election Monitoring Mission, UN, ctrl. region, Uganda, 1994. Office: Nat U Singapore Polit Sci, 10 Kent Ridge Crescent, Singapore 119260, Republic of Singapore

BHATTACHARJEE, AJIT KUMAR, mechanical engineer, engineering company executive; b. Faridpur, Bengal, India, Jan. 2, 1933; s. Surech Chandra and Santana Devi (Saraswati) B.; children from previous marriage: Maya, Ranjit; m. Padmaja Patil, Dec., 1989. BSc in Engring., Calcutta (India) U., 1956. Chartered engr., U.K. Works metallurgist Internat. Combustion Ltd., Eng., 1956-64; works mgr. Structural Engring. Works Ltd., India, 1964-68, Larsen & Toubro, Ltd., India, 1968-75; gen. mgr. Voltas Ltd., India, 1975-78; CEO G.R. Engring. Works, Ltd., India, 1978-88; mng. dir. Plastcon Engring. Pvt. Ltd., India, 1988—; mem. Breach Candy Bath Trust, 1967—. Fellow Inst. of Material (U.K.); mem. ASME, The Bombay Presidency Golf Club. Achievements include pioneering fabrication capacity of Indian industry to fabricate nuclear reactor components for electricity generation.

BHATTACHARJEE, GURU PRASANNA, mathematics educator, researcher; b. Syllet, Bangladesh, Apr. 1, 1939; s. Upendra Nath and Surabala Bhattacharjee; m. Niyati Bhattacharjee, Aug. 1, 1968; children: Gaurab, Nirveek. BSc with honors, Gauhati U., 1958, MSc, 1960; PhD, Indian Inst. Tech., Kharagpur, 1965. Assoc. lectr. Indian Inst. Tech., Kharagpur, 1962-65, lectr., 1965-72, asst. prof., 1972-80, prof., 1980—, head dept. math., 1995-98; chmn. JEE-2000, IIT, Kharagpur; Author: Applied Statistics Algorithms, 1970, 73; mem. editorial rev. bd. Internat. Jour. Computer Math., 1986—; contbr. articles to jours. including Technometrics, Biometrika, Ann. Math. Stats., Applied Stats., Microprocessor and Microprogramming, Computer Jour., Computing, BIT, Parallel Algorithms and Applications, others. contbr. articles to profl. jours. Mem. Am. Math. Soc. Hindu. Avocations: magazines, books, television. Home: Flat B6/5, 66/A Govindapur Rd, Calcutta 700045, India Office: IIT Kharagpur, Dept Math, 721 302 Kharagpur India

BHATTACHARYA, DEBESH, economics educator; b. Calcutta, India, Mar. 15, 1940; arrived in Australia, 1970; s. Jogesh Chandra and Bina Bhattacharya; m. Ellen Mary McEwen, Nov. 15, 1980; children: Rita, Bina. BA in Econs. and Polit. Sci. with honors, Calcutta U., 1958, MA in Econs., 1960; postgrad., Manchester U., 1965, PhD in Econs., 1968. Lectr. in econs. Goenka Coll., Calcutta, 1961-63, Vidyasagar Evening Coll., Calcutta, 1961-64, U. Otago, Dunedin, New Zealand, 1968-70; fellow U. Western Ont., London, Can., 1965; lectr., sr. lectr., prof. U. Sydney, Australia, 1970—, now dir. South Asian studies; lectr. in econs. Simon Fraser U., Barnaby, Can., 1974; cons. Australian Broadcasting Corp. Radio/TV, Sydney, 1970—, UN Inst. Devel. Econ. Planning, Madagascar, Malagasy Republic, 1975, UN Devel. Program, Algiers, Algeria, 1976, UN Conf. Trade and Devel., Geneva, 1977; fellow Rsch. Inst. Asia and Pacific Studies, Sydney. Author: A Comparative Study of Economic Development in India and China, 1975, Economic Development and Underdevelopment, 1989, The Political Economy of Development, 1993, The Role of Technological Progress in Indian Economic Development, 1972. Acting gen. sec, Calcutta U. Students Union, 1958-60; gen. sec. Mancher U. Indian Students Union, 1965-66; convenor Anti-Apartheid Movement, Sydney U., 1970-71; pres. Sydney U. Palestine Human Rights, 1980-83. Lt. Nat. Civic Corps., 1963-64. Recipient stipend Govt. West Bengal, 1954-58, free studentship Manchester U., 1965-67, rsch. assistance, 1968. Mem. Internat. Inst. for Devel. Studies (life), Econ. Soc. of Australia and New Zealand, Ctr. for Indian Studies Sydney (treas. 1989-94). Avocations: swimming, cricket, football, music, chess. Home: 17 Cheltenhan Rd, Croydon 2132 NSW, Australia Office: U Sydney, Dept Econs, Sydney NSW 2006, Australia

BHATTACHARYA, PURUSOTTAM, political science educator; b. Howrah, India, Dec. 30, 1950; s. Kanai Lal and Bani (Biswas) B.; m. Anindita Sanyal, Feb. 10, 1982; children: Priyadarshi, Chandreyee. BA in History with honors, Calcutta U., India, 1970; BS in Econs., London Sch. Econs., 1974; MPhil, Nehru U., New Delhi, 1980, PhD, 1989. Lectr. history Calcutta U., Nabagram Coll., India, 1981-82; lectr. internat. rels. Jadavpur U., Calcutta, India, 1982-88; reader internat. studies Pondicherry U., India, 1988-90; reader internat. rels. Jadavpur U., 1990—; joint dir. Internat. Rels. and Strategic Studies Jadavpur U., 1993—; participant internat. visitor program USIA, Washington, 1993; fellow session 322 Slzburg Sem., 1995; participant numerous nat. and internat. seminars and confs., vis. fellow Sch. Internat. Studies & Law, Coventry (Eng.) Univ., Jan.-March, 2000. Author: Britain in the European Community, 1994; contbr. articles to profl. jours. Rsch. grantee Univ. Grant Commn. New Delhi, 1986-87; internat. visitor USIA, Washington, 1993; fellow Salzburg seminar, session 322, 1995. Mem. Calcutta Hist. Soc., West Bengal Polit. Sci. Assn., London Sch. Econs. Soc. Avocations: reading, current affairs, music, travel, photography. Home: B-3/1 Parijat, 24 Mandeville Gardens, Calcutta 700 019, India Office: Jadavpur U, Internat Rels, Calcutta 700 032, India

BHATTACHARYA, SUKUMAR, accountant; b. Calcutta, India, Apr. 1, 1923; s. Durgamohan and Bhavani Bhattacharya; m. Renuka Battacharya, Mar. 4, 1945 (dec.); children: Ajay, Sanjay, Ranjan. BA, Scottish Ch. Coll., Calcutta, India, 1941; MA, Presidency Coll., Calcutta, 1943; LLB, Calcutta U., 1957. Chartered acct. Inst. Chartered Accts. India. Prof. math. Rajendra Coll., Faridpur, India, 1943-44, Scottish Ch. Coll., 1944-46; statistician Govt. Bengal, Calcutta, 1944-46; income tax officer Govt. of India, 1946-52; sr. tax advisor Lovelock Lewes, Calcutta, 1952-64; sec., CRO McLeod & Co. Ltd., Calcutta, 1964-70; bd. dirs. Jardine Henderson Ltd., Calcutta; chmn. East India Pharms. Works, Calcutta, 1984—. Editor: Finance and Commerce; author: Indian Income Tax: Law and Practice, Indian Wealth Tax and Gift Tax, Wealth Tax in India; contbr. over 100 articles on taxation to profl. jours. Scholar Calcutta U., 1941, 43. Mem. India Internat. Ctr., Calcutta Club. Avocations: chess, writing. Home: 64/1/25A Belgachia Rd, Calcutta 700037, India Office: Sukumar Bhattacharya & Co, 21 Old Court House St, Calcutta 700001, India

BHATTACHARYA, TANMAY, researcher, educator; b. Hardwar, India, May 1, 1970; s. Nirmal Kumar and Mamta Bhattacharya; m. Anuradha Bhattacharya, June 28, 1999. BA, Gurukul Kangri U., India, 1991; MA, Gurukul Kangri U., 1993, PhD, 1997. Lectr. Gurukul Kangri U., 1993-96, Alemaya U., Ethiopia, 1996-98; postdoctoral fellow Indian Inst. Tech., Kharagpur, India, 1998—. Author: (chpt. book) Life Events and Schizophrenia, 1999; contbr. papers to profl. jours. and confs. Mem. APA (grantee 1998), Indian Sci. Congress Assn. Avocations: playing cricket, soccer, music, making friends. Home: N-286 Shivalik Nagar, 249403 Hardwar India Office: Indian Inst Tech, Dept Humanities Social Sci, 721302 Kharagpur India

BHATTACHARYYA, SOUVIK, engineering educator; b. Calcutta, India, Oct. 26, 1959; s. Sailendranath and Pratima Bhattacharya; m. Tamali Sarkar, Nov. 21, 1992; 1 child, Shambhobi. BME, Jadavpur U., Calcutta, 1981; MS, U. Cin., 1985; PhD, Tex. A&M U., 1991. Lectr. Indian Inst. Tech., Kharagpur, India, 1991-93, asst. prof., 1993-97, assoc. prof., 1998—; sr. lectr. U. Canterbury, Christchurch, New Zealand, 1998-99; cons., Tisco, India, 1997, NZAA, Christchurch, New Zealand, 1999; lectr. U. Canterbury, Christchurch, 1998—. Contbr. articles to profl. jours. Project grantee Coun. of Scientific and Indsl. Rsch., India, 1998; Univ. Rsch. grantee U. Canterbury, Christchurch, 1999. Mem. ASME, Am. Soc. Heating, Regrigeration and Air-Conditioning, New Zealand Automobile Assn. E-mail: souvik@mech.canterbury.ac.nz. Home: 1/9 Bowen St, Christchurch New Zealand Office: U Canterbury, Mech Engring, PB 4800, Christchurch New Zealand

BHATTACHARYYA, UTPAL, electric power industry executive; b. Calcutta, West Bengal, India, May 27, 1956; s. Amal Kanti and Srilekha Bhattacharyya; m. Meena Saha, Jan. 23, 1984; 1 child, Ritabrata. BEE, Jadavpur U., Calcutta, 1978; diploma in mgmt., Indira Gandhi Nat. Open U., Delhi. Lic. engr. Grad. engr., trainee Larsen & Toubro, Calcutta, India, 1978-80; trainee engr. CESC Ltd., Calcutta, 1980-82, sr. engr. planning, 1982-90, dep. mgr. planning, 1990-94, mgr. comml. engring., 1994-97, exec. asst. to mng. dir., 1997-98, dep. gen. mgr. corp. svcs., 1998-2000, gen. mgr. corp. svcs., 2000; dir. Fedn. Electricity Undertaking, Mumbai, 1999; vis. lectr. in field. Contbr. articles to profl. jours. V.p. Assn. Creative Theatre, Calcutta, 1999. Recipient Nat. scholarship Govt. of India. Mem. Energy Subcom. Confedn. India Industry, Energy Subcom. Bengal C. of C. & Industry, 1996—, Internat. Assn. Electricity Generation Transmission, Instn. Engrs., Indian Soc. Lighting Engrs. Avocations: theatre, music, reading. Fax: (91)(33) 236-8263. Office e-mail: ub@rpgnet.com. Home: AE-525 Sector 1 Salt Lake, 700064 Calcutta West Bengal, India Office: CESC Ltd, CESC House Chowringhee Sq, 700001 Calcutta West Bengal, India

BHATTAD, SITARAM MANIKALAL, food industry technical executive; b. Ambada, India, June 23, 1941; s. Manikalal J. and Kashi B. BS, Nat. Dairy Rsch. Inst., India, 1967; MS in Food Sci., U. Sask., CAn., 1970; postgrad., Ohio State U., 1970-72. Rsch. assoc. Ohio State U., 1970-72; quality control supr. Shasta Beverages divsn. Consol. Foods Corp., Columbus, Ohio, 1972-73; food technologist, project coord. Kitchens of Sara Lee divsn., Deerfield, Ill., 1973-74; microbiologist, mgr. lab. svcs. canned meat divsn. Libby McNeill & Libby divsn. Nestle Enterprises, Inc., Chgo., 1974-78; gen. mgr. tech. svcs. Foodways Nat. divsn. N.J. Heinz Co., Wethersfield, Conn., 1978-80; v.p. rsch. and tech. svcs. Iroquios Brands Ltd., Carteret, N.J., 1980-82; founder C&S Importers & Exporters, Northbrook, Ill., 1976—, Jay Innovative Ingredients, Carteret; mng. dir. Prime Solvents Extractions, Ltd., India, 1984-91, dir. food and agrl. U.S. Tech. Inc., Livonia, Mich., 1975—; founder, editor Dairy Sci. Mag., 1967—; chief exec. Internat. Tech. Transfer, Carteret, 1985; chmn., pres. Balaji Banana Products, Ltd., 1991; cons. Info. and Software Tech., 1999. Named Outstanding Citizen of Yr., Chgo., 1977. Mem. Inst. Food Technologists, Am. Soc. Quality Control, Am. Soc. Microbiology, Am. Assn. Cereal Chemists, Toastmasters Internat. (pres. 1977, Outstanding Toastmaster of Yr. award 1976, 77, area gov. 1978). Address: Jay Innovative Enterprises, 151/1 Yashwant Nagar, Talegao Dabhade Pune 410507, India

BHATTARAI, RISHI R., civil engineer, researcher; b. Ramechhap, Nepal, Oct. 10, 1966; s. Narayan P. and Pratibha Bhattarai; m. Rashmi Ghimire, June 19, 1998. BS in Civil Engring., Kakatiya U., Warangal, India, 1991; MS in Civil Engring., La. Tech. U., 1997. Engring. intern cert., La. Design engr. S.K.R.N. & Assocs., Kathmandu, Nepal, 1992-94; rsch. engr. La. Tech. U., Ruston, 1997—. Contbr. articles to profl. jours. Mem. ASCE (assoc.), Water Environment Fedn., La. Water Environ. Assn. Avocations: trekking, reading, soccer, chess. E-mail: rajbhattarai@hotmail.com and rishi@coes.latech.edu. Office: La Tech Univ College St Ruston LA 71272-0001

BHATTI, BAQAR HUSSAIN, public sector executive, educator; b. Lahore, Pakistan, July 17, 1962; s. Faqir Hussain and Riaz-Ul Jannah; m. Hafsa Baqar Iftikhar, Oct. 9, 1992; 1 child, Daniyal. BCommerce, Hailey Coll. Commerce, Lahore, 1985; LLB, Univ. Law Coll., Lahore, 1988; student, Chartered Inst. Mgmt. Accts., Londo, 1998. Chartered mgmt. acct. Asst. cost mgr. Punjab Livestock Devel. Bd., Lahore, 1984-85; tax cons. Bhatti Law Assocs., Lahore, 1988-90; probationer officer Civil Svcs. Acad., Lahore, 1990-92; asst. contr. mil. accounts Pakistan Mil. Accounts Dept., Lahore, 1992-96; dep. dir. audit Pakistan Audit Dept., Lahore, 1996-98; dep. dir. accounts Nat. Hwy. Authority, Lahore, 1998—; founder, coordinator Zenith Sch. Accountancy, Lahore, 1997—, Zenith Assn. Comrades, Lahore, 1999—. Author: Economic Environment, 1999, Cost Accounting, 1999. Recipient Silver medal Fed. Bd. Intermediate and Secondary Edn., 1981; Merit scholar, 1981-83. Mem. Chartered Inst. Mgmt. Accts., Nat. Geographic Soc. Muslim. Avocations: reading, photography, trekking, playing keyboard. E-mail: bagarbhatti@hotmail.com. Office: Zenith Sch Accountancy #18, 24-Civic Ctr/Garden Town, Lahore Pakistan

BHATTI, JAWED IQBAL, utility company executive; b. Gujranwala, Punjab, Pakistan, Nov. 1, 1957; s. Irshad Ulhaque and Nazir Begum Bhatti; m. Irum Jawed. BEEE, N.E.D. U. Engring., Karachi, Pakistan, 1980; MSEE, U. Engring., Lahore, Pakistan, 1998. Design engr. Philips Elec. Co. of Pakistan, Karachi, 1980-82; telecom. engr. Saudian Air Def. Forces, Dahran, Saudi Arabia, 1985-87; exec. engr. Water and Power Devel. Authority, Lahore, Pakistan, 1987—. Author: Designing of Flood Forecasting Telemetry Network Using Meteorburst Communication, 1997; also articles. Capt. Pakistan Army, 1982-84. Mem. IEEE, IEEE Pakistan, Pakistan Amateur Radio Soc. Avocations: reading, designing electronics, fishing. Office: Pakistan Water/Power Devel, 144-G Model Town, Lahore 54700, Pakistan

BHATTI, ZAHEER, broadcast company executive; b. Raja Sansi, Pakistan, Oct. 6, 1940; s. Mohammed Ismail Bhatti and Sardar Begum; m. Zia Sultana Mirza, Apr. 14, 1965; children: Mujahida yasmin, Rabia Bhatti, Ahmed Zulfiqar. Student, Govt. Coll. Lahore, 1960; postgrad., Punjab U., 1962. Program prodr. Radio Pakistan, Lahore, 1962-66, Pakistan TV, Lahore, 1966-72; program mgr. PTV, 1972, gen. mgr., 1972-74; head of documentaries PTV HQ, Rawalpindi, 1974-75; contr. program internat. rels. PTV HQ, 1975-87, dir. tng. internat. rels., 1987—; bd. dirs. pakistan Orgn. for Comm. Devel.; cons. ILO-IPEC, Islamabad, Pakistan, 2000—; bd. dirs. pakistan TV, Islamabad, Shalimar Recording and Broadcasting Co.; mem. censor bd. for commls. PIV/SRBC. Dir., prodr. documentaries Life Beat, 1968, Silhouettes for Fortune, 1979, Double Happiness 1983 (Best Documentary PTV 1983). Mem. Family Planning Assn. of Pakistan, Islamabad club. Avocations: writing, swimming, music, hiking. Office: Pakistan TV Tng Acad, 47 H9, 44000 Islamabad pakistan

BHAUMIK, SABYASACHI, psychiatrist; b. Calcutta, India, Dec. 20, 1952; s. Gopal and Uma (Bose Mazumdar) B.; m. Susmita Hoare, Dec. 5, 1981; 1 child, Sugato. MBBS, U. Calcutta, India, 1980; diploma in psychiatry, U. London, 1988. Resident R.G. Kar Med. Coll., Calcutta, India, 1978-79, 79-80; sr. house officer Gwynedd Hos., Bangor, England, 1985; sr. house officer, registrar Dartford & Gravesham Health Authority, England, 1985-88; sr. registrar Leicestershire Health Authority, England, 1989-92; cons. psychiatrist Fosse Health Trust, Leicester, 1992—, clin. tutor, lead clinician, 1998—; hon. sr. lectr. U. Leicester, 1998—. Contbr. articles to profl. jours. Mem. Royal Coll. Psychiatry U.K., Overseas Dr.'s Assn., Penrose Club. Hindu. Avocations: poetry, travel, reading, cricket. Office: Leicester Firth Hosp, Groby Rd, Leicester LE3 9QF, England

BHIGJEE, AHMED IQBAL, neurology educator; b. Durban, South Africa, July 11, 1951; m. Rokaya Chohan; 3 children. MB ChB, U. Natal, 1975; FRCP, Royal Coll., 1978; MD, U. Natal, South Africa, 1993. Intern King Edward Hosp., Durban, 1976, registrar in anat. pathology, 1977; registrar U. Durban, 1978-79, physician, lectr., 1982; clin. asst. Royal No. Hosp., London, 1978; registrar in neurology U. Cape Town, South Africa, 1983-85; specialist in neurology Wentworth Hosp., Durban, 1986-91, prin. specialist, 1992; assoc. prof. neurology Univ. Natal, Durban, 1993-96, prof. neurology, 1997—. Editor Jour. of Islamic Med. Assn. South Africa, (newsletter) Neuropen. Co-founder Radio Azaania, Durban, 1995. Islam. Avocations: swimming, jogging, reading. Office: Wentworth Hosp Dept Neurology, Pvt Bag, Jacobs 4026, South Africa

BHISE, SATISH, pharmacy educator; b. Masur, India, Aug. 3, 1952; s. Balkrishna Shankar and Laxmibai Balkrishna Bhise; m. Manjiri Satish Bhise; children: Sourabh, Suhas. BPharm, Govt. Coll. Pharmacy, Karad, Maharashtra, 1974; MPharm, Haffkine Inst. Tng. Rsch./Test, Mumbai, 1977; PhD, Birla Inst. Tech. & Scis., Pilani, 1983; diploma in info. tech., C-DAC, Pune, Maharashtra, India, 1998. Cert. in pharmacy. Clin. rsch. assoc. Searle (India) Ltd., Mumbai, 1976-78; lectr. Birla Inst. Tech. Scis., Pilani, 1979-84; asst. prof. K.M.K. Coll. Pharmacy, Mumbai, 1984-87; prin. Govt. Coll. Pharmacy, Karad, 1987—; chmn. bd. studies pharmacy faculty Shivaji U., Kolhapur, 1987-93; dean faculty pharm. scis. Maharashtra U. Health Scis., Nashik, 1999—; chief coord. ISTE-short-term courses Govt. Coll. Pharmacy, Karad, 1993, 95, 97, 98, chief coord. AICTE-short-term course, 1996, 97, 98, 99, APTI pres. Maharashtra br., 1998—. Author: (books) Human Anatomy and Physiology, 1996, Health Education and Community Pharmacy, 1996; contbr. articles to profl. jours. Recipient Best Essay award Pudhari-Pune U., 1998. Mem. Internat. Therapeutic Drug Monitoring and Clin. Toxicology, Indian Pharm. Assn., Am. Chem. Soc., Assn. Pharm. Tchrs. of India (mem. exec. coun. 1998—). Avocations: reading, carrom, classical Indian instrumental music. Fax: 9102164-71196. E-mail: gcopk@scpl.net.in. Home: 15 Parijat Vidyanagar, Karad 415124, India Office: Govt Coll Pharmacy, Vidyanagar, Karad 415 124, India

BHOBE, ATUL D., structural engineer; b. Mumbai, India, Sept. 5, 1964; s. Damodar Narayan and Meenakshi Damodar (Rajadhyaksha) B.; m. Nimishaa Sharmila, May 25, 1989; children: Vinayita, Anaya, Ameya. B of Engring., U. Mumbai, India, 1985; M of Structural Engring., U. Mich., 1986. Ptnr. S N Bhobe & Assocs., Mumbai, India, 1986—. Mem. Indian Inst. Bridge Engrs., Indian Rds. Congress. Achievements include designed and engineered the construction of more than 100 major bridges all over India. Office: S N Bhobe & Assocs, 62 Mahavir Ctr Sector 17, Navi Mumbai 400705, India

BHOGAL, CHARANJIV SINGH, automotive company executive; b. New Delhi, Oct. 28, 1960; s. Avtar Singh and Surjit Kaur (Jetla) B.; m. Anu Nagi, Dec. 15, 1985; 1 child, Jasmehr Singh. Grad., Inst. Cost & Working Accts., 1981. Ptnr. Pritam Singh Hari Singh, New Delhi, 1978-95, prin., owner, 1995—. Recipient Bharat Shree award Coun. for Nat. Devel., 1996,Bharat Gaurav award, 1996, Nat. Trade Excellence award, India Solidarity Coun., 1996. Avocations: stamp collecting, reading, hiking. Office: Pritam Singh Hari Singh, 31/1A St 2 New Rohtak rd, New Delhi 110005, India

BHOJWANI, ROMY LAXMIKANT, hotel executive; b. Ahmednagar, India, Mar. 1, 1975; s. Laxmikant Rewachand and Mona Laxmikant B. BS, Pune U., India, 1995; Hotel Adminstrn. and Food Tech. Grad., Sophia Poly., Pune, 1995; postgrad., Pune U., 1995—. Indsl. trainee The Golden Gate, Bombay, 1993, 94; indsl. trainee Hotel President, Bombay, 1994; mgmt. trainee The Oberoi, Bombay, 1995; dir. Bhojwani Hotels Pvt. Ltd., Pune, 1996—, Hotel Krishna Internat. Pvt. Ltd., Bangalore, India, 1996—; dir. ops. Hotel Amir Pvt. Ltd., Pune, 1996—; bd. dirs. Bhojwani Group, Pune. Founding mem. Emerging President's Group, Pune, 1996. Mem. Cornell Hotel Soc. (founding mem. emerging pres. group 1996), Royal Connaught Boat Club, Poona Club Ltd., Colada Sailing Club. Avocations: public speaking, swimming, sailing, tennis. Office: Bhojwani Group, 7 M G Rd, Pune 411 001, India

BHONGIR, MADAN MOHAN, public health engineer; b. Hyderabad, India, Aug. 11, 1941; s. Ramakrishna Rao and Yesboda Bai (Nampally) B.; m. Suguma Samudrala, Apr. 30, 1967; children: Y.V. Aparna, B. Vandana, B. Anuparna, B. Lakshmi Priya. B in Civil Engring., Osmania U., Hyderabad, 1964. Cert. in engring. Jr. engr. C.E (P.H), Govt. Andhra Pradesh, Hyderabad, 1965-75, dep. exec. engr., 1975-84, exec. engr., 1984-95; supt. engr. E.N.C.(P.H), Govt. Andhra Pradesh, Hyderabad, 1995-98, chief engr., 1998—; Under officer Nat. Credit Corps, 1965. Sec. Andhra Pradesh Soma Kystriya Sangham, Hyderabad, 1960-67; exec. mem. Chikkad Pally Youth Club, Hyderabad, 1965-67, Andhra Pradesh Youth Congress, Hyderabad, 1960-65; convenor All India Youth Assn. Nat. Conf., Hyderabad, 1960-65, Nimibaba Heri Temple Trust, Hyderabad, 1999-00. Recipient Peace award Forum for Hindu and Muslim Unity, 1980, Meritorious Svc. award Hyderabad Met. Water Supply and Sewage Bd., 1987, disting. Svc. award HMWSESB and ODA, 1995. Mem. Inst. Engrs. India, All India Water Supply Orgn., Andhra Pradesh Pollution Control Bd., Hare Krishna Internat. Country Club (patron life mem.). Indian Nat. Congress. Hindu. Avocations: sight-seeing, touring. Home: Chikkadpally #1-8-105, Hyderabad 500020, India

BHORE, JAY NARAYAN, psychiatrist; b. Kavalapur, Bombay, India, Sept. 12, 1915; came to U.S. 1958; s. Narayan Suleman and Chandra (Nandrekar) B.; m. Mary Elizabeth Singleton, June 17, 1960. BS, Govt. Coll., India, 1939; M.B.B.S., BJJ Med. Coll., India, 1943; MD, Northwestern U., Chgo., 1967. Med. officer Student Health Ctr., Bishop Coll., Calcutta, India, 1947-51; resident physician Jubar Sanatorium, Simla Hills, India, 1951-53; resident diseases of chest Mcpl. T.B. Sanatorium, Chgo., 1958-60; fellow neurology/psychiatry Northwestern U. Med. Sch., Chgo., 1960-61; rotating intern Augustana Hosp., Chgo., 1962; resident in psychiatry St. Joseph Hosp., London, Ont., Can., 1964-65, Northwestern U., Chgo., 1965-67; staff psychiatrist Downey (Ill.) VA Hosp., 1968-71, West Side VA Hosp., Chgo., 1970-73, VA Hosp., Woods, Wis., 1973; pvt. practice psychiatry Milw., 1974—; founder, pres. Rev. N.S. Bhore Meml., Kavalapur, India, 1975; pres. Rev. N.S. Bhore Mem. Evang. Assocs., Milw., 1976. Founder Free Pub. Libr., Kavalapur, 1980, Med. Clinic Day Care Ctr., Kavalapur, 1981, Chandra Hosp., Kavalapur, 1990. Mem. APA, AMA, Wis. Psychiat. Assn.,

Christian Med. Dental Soc., Am. Assn. Physicians from India. Presbyterian. Avocations: fishing, travel, writing. Home and Office: 1543 N Prospect Ave Milwaukee WI 53202-2367

BHOSALE, CHANDRAKANT HARI, physics educator, researcher; b. Maswad, Satara, India, June 1, 1952; s. Hari Dhondiram and Chhababai Hari Bhosale; m. Sunanda Chandrakant; children: Rupali, Sonali, Amit. BS, Shivaji U., India, 1974, MS, 1976, MPhil, 1983, PhD, 1988. Lectr. Rayat Shikshan Sanstha, India, 1979-92; reader in physics India, 1992—; vis. fellow Indian Nat. Sci. Acad., New Delhi, 1998-99. Editor procs. Solid State Energy Conversion, 1986. Mem. Semiconductor Soc. India (life), Soc. Advancement Electrochem. Sci. & Tech. (life), Marathi Vidnyan Parishad (life). Avocations: popularization of science, reading, scientific research. Office: SUK, Vidyanagar, 416 004 Kolhapur Maharashtra India

BHOSLE, USHADEVI NARENDRA, math educator, researcher; b. Dhule, India, Mar. 30, 1949; d. Vamanrao Chindhuji and Susheela (Sonawane) Patil; m. Narendra Balramji Bhosle, May 25, 1976; children: Chandrashekhar, Trupti. BSc, Poona U., 1969; MSc, Shivaji U., 1971; PhD, Tata Inst., 1980. Rsch. asst. T.I.F.R., Bombay, 1971-74, rsch. assoc. II, 1974-77, rsch. fellow, 1977-82, fellow, 1982-90, reader, 1990-95, assoc. prof., 1995-98; prof., 1998—; vis. scholar Math. Inst., Erlangen, Germany, 1989, Liverpool U., 1989, vis. prof., 1991, 97, U. Mex., 1995; prof. U. Paris, 1994. Contbr. articles to profl. jours. Rsch. grant Scis. and Engring. Rsch. Coun., 1989, Royal Soc., London, 1991, Indo-French Ctr. of Advanced Rsch., 1994, European Internat. Sci. Rsch. Coop., 1997. Fellow Indian Acad. Scis.; mem. Am. Math. Soc. Avocations: drawing, painting, reading, music. Office: Tata Inst Fundamental Rsch, Homi Bhabha Rd, Mumbai 400005, India

BHUGRA, DINESH KUMAR MAKHAN LAL, psychiatrist, educator; b. Yamunanagar, Haryana, India, July 8, 1952; arrived in U.K., 1980; s. Makhan Lal and Shanta (Chugh) B. MA, MSc, MLN Coll., Yamunanagar, 1969; MBBS, Armed Forces Med. Coll., Poona, 1976; MPhil, U. Leicester, 1989; PhD, U. London, 1999. Sr. house officer H. F. Hosp., New Delhi, 1977-79, Cork Regional Hosp., Eire, 1979-80, Harborough Regional Hosp., Eng., 1980-81; sr. house officer, registrar Leicestershirew Hosp., Eng., 1981-86; sr. lectr. Maudsley Hosp, Eng., 1986-92, Inst. Psychiatry, London, 1992—. Author: SAOs in Psychiatry, 1992; co-author: Case Management in Psychiatry, 1993; co-editor: Principles of Social Psychiatry, 1993, Troublesome Disguises, 1997, Ethnicity: An Agenda for Mental Health, 1999, Annotated Bibliography Ethnic Mental Health, 1999; editor: Religion and Psychiatry, 1996, Internat. Rev. Psychiatry, Internat. Jour. Social Psychiatry. Mem. mgmt. com. BCP, London, 1993-95, CRA, London, 1994—. Fellow Royal Soc. Medicine, Royal Coll. Psychiatrists (chair coll. trainees com. 1987-88, hon. sec. gen. psychiatry sect. 1993-97, chair faculty gen. and cmty. psychiatry of RC psych.). Office: Inst Psychiatry, De Drepigny Park, London SE5 8AF, England

BHUIYAN, ABDUS SALAM, zoology educator; b. Jagatpur, Bangladesh, Dec. 31, 1947; s. Talebur Rahman and Pirzadi Umme (Qulsum) B.; m. Begum Mahmuda, Dec. 8, 1974; children: Tahmina Sultana, Nur-Al-Safa, Nur-Al-Mehdi. BS with honors, Dhaka U., Bangladesh, 1969, MS, 1970; PhD, Rajshahi U., Bangladesh, 1985; postgrad., Newcastle Upon Tyne, England, 1992. Lectr. zoology Feni Coll., Bangladesh, 1972-74; lectr. zoology Rajshahi U., Bangladesh, 1974-77, asst. prof., 1977-86, assoc. prof., 1986-91, prof. zoology, 1991—, chmn. dept. zoology, 1989-92; dir. Summer Sci. Inst. Zoology, 1991. Contbr. articles to profl. jours. Nat. Environ. Sci. Acad. fellow, New Delhi, 1996. Fellow Zoolol. Soc. Bangladesh. Muslim. Avocations: travel, wildlife, history. Office: Rajshahi U, Dept Zoology, Rajshahi 6205, Bangladesh

BHUIYAN, MD. SHOAIB, electronics engineer, computer engineer, educator; b. Chandpur, Commilla, Bangladesh, Apr. 13, 1964; s. Md. Giasuddin and Fatima Zohra B.; m. Runa Lisa Munni, Mar. 13, 1996; 1 child, Sadida Bhuiyan Deea. BS with honors, U. Dhaka, Bangladesh, 1987, MS, 1989; diploma in Japanese, Nagoya U., 1992; DEng, Nagoya (Japan) Inst. Tech., 1996. Sci. officer Bangladesh Atomic Energy Commn., Dhaka, 1990; lectr. Univ. Grants Commn., Dhaka, 1990-92; postgrad. rschr. Nagoya Inst. Tech., 1992-96, rsch. assoc., 1996-2000, postgrad. supr., 1997—; asst. prof. computer sci. Suzuka U. of Med. Sci. and Technology, 2000—; adj. faculty Nagoya Coll., Toyoake, 1996—. Contbr. articles to sci. jours. and conf. procs. on neurocomputing and computer vision. Rsch. grantee Prin. Investigator award: The Hori Info. Sci. Promotion Found., 1998; Merit scholar U. Dhaka, 1985, postgrad. rsch. scholar Govt. Japan, 1992-96. Mem. IEEE, Computer Soc. of IEEE (mem. tech. com. on pattern analysis and machine intelligence), Internat. Neural Network Soc., Inst. Electronics, Information and Comm. Engrs. Japan. Muslim. Avocations: reading, gourmet food, music. Home: Kyuuban Danchi 7-1004, 2-11-1 Shichiban, Minato Nagoya 455-0001, Japan Office: Suzuka U Med Sci/Tech, Info Processing Ctr 1001, Kishioka Suzuka MIE 510-0293, Japan

BHULLAR, SUKHDEV SINGH, biotechnology educator and researcher; b. Madrassa, Punjab, India, Dec. 10, 1956; s. Tehal Singh and Pritam Kaur Bhullar; m. Surinder Kaur Pandher, Feb. 23, 1985; children: Karamdeep Kaur, Gursimrat Kaur. BSc, D.A.V. Coll., Jalandhar, India, 1977; MSc in Biochemistry, Punjab Agrl. U., Ludhiana, India, 1980; PhD in Plant Scis., U. Adelaide, Australia, 1985. Profl. officer Waite Agrl. Rsch. Inst., Australia, 1984; pool officer Punjab Agrl. U., 1985-86, asst. prof. dept. biochemistry, 1986-91; head dept. biotech. Guru Nanak Dev U., Amritsar, India, 1991-94, 98—, in-charge Distributed Informatics Sub-Ctr., 1994—, prof., 1999—. Office: Guru Nanak Dev U, Dept Biotech, Amritsar, Punjab India

BHUNCHET, EKAPOT, pathologist; b. Photalei, Thailand, July 23, 1963. MD, Tokyo Med. and Dental U., 1988, PhD, 1992. Resident Tokyo Med. and Dental U., 1992-96; staff dept. pathology Tsuchiura Kyodo Hosp., Ibaraki, Japan, 1996—. Contbr. articles to profl. jours. Buddhist. Avocations: tennis, music. Home: 2-32-22 Kasuga, Tsukuba Ibaraki 305-0821, Japan Office: Tsuchiura Kyodo Hosp, 11-7 Manabeshinmachi, Tsuchiura Ibaraki 300, Japan

BHUSHAN, SHASHI, physics educator; b. Deoria, India, Sept. 30, 1946; s. Bindhyeshwari Lal and Deoyani (Devi) S.; m. Indira Shrivastava, Apr. 30, 1953; children: Shailaja, Bhawana. BSc, U. Allahabad, India, 1965; MSc, U. Gorakhpur, India, 1967, PhD, 1972. Lectr. Davd Coll., Gorakhpur, 1971-72; lectr. Ravishankar Shukla U., Raipur, India, 1972-79, 81-84, reader, 1984—; prof. Inelec, Boumerdes, Algeria, 1979-81; vis. scientist Moscow State U., 1987; lectr. Coll. Tchrs. India, 1992-97, Navodaya Sch. Tchrs. India, 1994-96, others. Editor Jour. of Ravishankar U., 1990—; contbr. articles to profl. jours. Fellow Indian Cryogenics Soc.; mem. Semicondr. Soc. (life), Luminescence Soc. (life), Cryogenics Soc. (life), Disordered Systems Soc. (life), Luminescence Soc. India (coop. v.p. 1996-97). Avocations: talking about Indian philosophy, singing, reading literature, science, religion. Home: L-2,Pt Ravishankar Shukla U, Raipur 492010, India Office: Pt Ravishankar Shukla U, GE Rd, Raipur 492010, India

BHUTANI, KAMLESH KUMAR, chemist, researcher, educator; b. Ambala City, Haryana, India, Dec. 25, 1951; s. Sardari Lal and Krishna Wati (Ahuja) B.; m. Ruby Madan, June 27, 1980; children: Priyanka, Ritika. BS, Panjab U., Chandigarh, India, 1971; MS, Panjab U., 1973, PhD, 1978. Sr. tech. officer Panjab U., Chandigarh, 1977-78; mgr. rsch. and devel. Pharm. Ltd. Co. SAS, Nagar, India, 1978-80; sr. scientist Regional Rsch. Lab., Jammu, India, 1980-88; asst. dir. Reg. Rsch. Lab., Jammu, 1988-94; assoc. prof. Nat Inst Pharm. Edn. Rsch., Sas Nagar, 1994-99; prof., head dept. natural products, 1999—; chmn. Nat Inst Pharm. Edn. Rsch., Sas Nagar, 1996—; exec. com. CSIR Lab., Jammu, 1983-87; policy group med. chem. AAPS, 1991-92; vis. scientist Howard U., Washington, 1991-92. Contbr. over 86 articles to profl. jours. Patentee in field. Fellow Sigma Xi (expert natural products based drugs and pharms.). Home: NIPER Campus Sector 67, Sas Nagar 160062, India Office: Nat Inst Pharm Edn Rsch, SAS Nagar 160062, India

BHUTTA, AMJAD PERVAIZ, chemistry educator; b. Multan, Punjab, Pakistan, Jan. 5, 1959; s. Muhammed Bakhsh Bhutta; m. Farkhanda Amjad Bhutta; children: Awaisamjad, Usmanamjad, Hafsa, Aqsa. Grad., Govt. Coll., Multan, 1979; M in Chemistry, B.Z. U., Multan, 1982. Prodn. mgr. Pakistan Fruit Juice Co., 1982-85; asst. prof. Pakistan Air Force Coll., Mianwali; lectr. chemistry Govt. Coll. Civil Lines, Multan. Avocation: reading. Home: Willayat Abad Colony I, Multan Punjab, Pakistan Office: Govt Coll Civil Lines, Postgrad Coll, Multan Punjad, Pakistan

BHUTTO, IMRAN AHMED, ophthalmologist, researcher; b. Larkana, Pakistan, Feb. 10, 1963; s. Khuda Dad Khan and Farida (Mughal) B.; m. Lubna Mughal, Feb. 18, 1993; 3 children. MB, BS, Med. Coll. of Larkana, 1988; PhD in Ophthalmology, Nagasaki U., 1996. Resident med. ophthalmologist LRBT Trust, Karachi, 1990-91; rsch. assoc. Nagasaki U., 1996—. Mem. ARVO, Japanese Electron Microscope Soc. (adv. bd. 1999—). Avocations: travel, sports. Office: Nagasaki U Sch Medicine, 1-7-1 Sakamoto, 852-8501 Nagasaki Japan

BHUYAN, MUHAMMAD AYUBUR RAHMAN, economics educator; b. Dhaka, Bangladesh, July 12, 1938; s. Abedullah and Raushan Akhter (Khan) B.; m. Tahmina Miah, Oct. 18, 1964; children: Taslima, Rezaur, Sajedur. MA in Econs., Dhaka U., 1960; PhD in Econs., Lancaster U., Eng., 1975. Banker Ea. Mercantile Bank Ltd., Dhaka, 1961-68; lectr. econs. Chuadanga (Bangladesh) Coll., 1968-70; lectr. econs. Dhaka U., 1970-76, assoc. prof., 1976-84, prof. econs., 1984—, chair dept., 1983-87, dir. Bur. Econ. Rsch., 1987-90; cons. UNCTAD, Geneva, 1981-82; chair Bur. Econ. Rsch., 1995-99. Contbr. articles to profl. jours.; author 6 books. Mem. Bangladesh Econ. Assn., Internat. Studies Assn. Bangladesh, Bangladesh Soc. Economists, Dhaka U. Tchrs. Assn., Dhaka U. Club. Muslim. Avocations: bridge, swimming, yoga, gardening. Home: 34-C Shahid Minar Rd, Dhaka 1000, Bangladesh Office: Dept Econs Dhaka U, Nilkhet, Dhaka 1000, Bangladesh

BI, GUANGGUO, education educator; b. Dinghai, Zhejiang, China, Feb. 5, 1939; s. Maoxiang and Xiuzhen (Wang) B.; m. Yin Chen, Dec. 17, 1967; children: Hao, Xin. BE, Nanjing Inst. Tech., 1960. Asst. prof. Nanjing Inst. Tech., Jiangsu, 1961-77, lectr., 1978-84, assoc. prof., 1985-86; prof. Southeast U., Nanjing, Jiangsu, 1987—; cons. HP-SciTech. Joint Software Devel. Ctr. Co., Ltd., Beijing, 1997. Author: (book) Digital Communications, 1987; holder Chinese patent, 1990; contbr. articles to profl. jours. Recipient 2d class award on progress in sci. and tech. State Edn. Commn., Beijing, 1990, 1st class award on progress in sci. and technology, 1994, 2d class award on progress in sci. and tech. State Coun. of Peoples Republic of China, Beijing, 1995. Fellow China Inst. Comms. (bd. dirs.); mem. IEEE (sr.). Avocations: reading, travel, photography. Office: Southeast Univ, Nanjing 210096, China

BI, JIA JU, engineering educator, researcher; b. Shanghai, China, Sept. 29, 1933; s. Fung Chang and Bao Xian (Wang) Bie; m. Yong Hua Wei, Aug. 2, 1958; children: Hong Qiu, Hai Feng. BA in Engring., Tongji U., Shanghai, 1956; MA in Engring., Tsinghua U., Beijing, 1961. Dept. head Tongji U., Shanghai, 1982-84, dir. undergrad. edn., 1984-86, vice-provost, 1987-89; vice-dean Tongji U. Grad. Sch., Shanghai, 1989-93; dir. Tongji U. Rsch. Inst., Shanghai, 1993-96; sr. rschr. Tongji U., Shanghai, 1993—, prof., 1989—; vis. scholar N.C. State U., Raleigh, 1981-82; vis. prof. U. NSW, Sydney, Australia, 1986, 89; subject specialist Hong Kong Coun. for Acad. Accreditation, 1993—; sr. advisor Shanghai Instn. Higher Edn. Evaluation, 1996—; higher edn. evaluation expert Ministry Edn., China, 1998—. Author: Introduction to Offshore Mechanics, 1989; co-author: Higher Education Evaluation in Different Countries, 1997; contbr. articles to profl. jours. Recipient First prize for sci. and tech. achievement State Edn. Commn. China, 1986, award for Disting. Contbn. to Higher Edn., State Coun. China, 1992; grantee Internat. Visitor Program, U.S. Info. Agy., 1995. Mem. Chinese Soc. Mechanics, Chinese Soc. Ocean Engring., Chinese Soc. Higher Edn. Evaluation (individual coun.), Internat. Network Quality Assurance Agencies in Higher Edn. (bd. dirs. 1998-99). Avocations: photography, classical music, traveling. E-mail: jjbic@online.sh.cn. Home: Ste 201 Apt 89, Lane 258 Luo Jin Rd, Shanghai 201100, China Office: Tongji Univ Grad Sch, Siping Rd, Shanghai 200092, China

BI, RU-CHANG, crystallographer, educator; b. Shinze, Hebei, China, Aug. 4, 1940; s. Yu-Tian Bi and Jian Wang; m. Bi-Cheng Chen, June 26, 1969; children: Qun, Lei. MS, Leningrad U., USSR, 1965. Rsch. asst., assoc. Inst. Biophysics Acad. Sinica, Beijing, 1966-80, assoc. prof. Inst. Biophysics, 1983-93, prof. Inst. Biophysics, 1994—, dir. dept. protein crystallography Inst. Biophysics, 1986-92; rsch. fellow dept. chemistry York (Eng.) U., 1980-82; mem. expert group protein engring. Nat. High-Tech Devel. Program, China, 1990-93. Contbr. articles to profl. jours. Fax: 86-10-64871293. E-mail: rcbi@iname.com. Office: Acad Sinica Inst Biophysics, 15 Datun Rd Chaoyang Dist, Beijing 100101, China

BIALASIEWICZ, ALEXANDER ARTHUR, ophthalmologist, educator; b. Palembang, Sumatra, Indonesia, May 4, 1956; s. Arthur and Helga Bialasiewicz; m. Ingrid Katharina Deberitz, Dec. 22, 1989; 1 child, Alexandra Simone. MD, Hannover (Germany) U., 1978, PhD, 1981. Fellow Wilmer Ophthal. Inst. Johns Hopkins U., Balt., 1979-80; mem. head, transfusion and immunohematology dept. Armed Forces Med. Ctr., Hamburg, Germany, 1980-81; resident in ophthalmology U. Eye Hosp., Erlangen, 1982-85, asst. prof. ophthalmology, 1986-89; asst. prof. ophthalmology U. Eye Hosp., Münster, 1990-92; prof. U. Eye Hosp., Hamburg, 1993—; organizer internat. congress meetings on infectious diseases, Münster, 1989, Mannheim, 1992, 93, U. Hamburg, 1993, 97; mem. Nat. and European adv. bds. Ophthalmic Antiinfectives, 1990-92; mem. com. Bundesgesundheitsamt Berlin, 1988-94. Author: Chlamydial Infections, 1989, Infectious Diseases of the Eye, 1994, 95, Manual of Laboratory Diagnosis in Ophthalmology, 1994, Hygiene Issues in Ophthalmology, 1999; editor-in-chief Ocular Infection and Hygiene; editor: Ophthalmic Research. Mem. Am. Acad. Ophthalmology, Ocular Microbiology and Immunology Group, Assn. for Rsch. in Vision and Ophthalmology, N.Y. Acad. Sci., Wilmer Residents Assn., Internat. Soc. for Eye Rsch., Am. Soc. for Microbiology, German Ophthalmol. Soc., Assn. for Eye Rsch., Internat. Orgn. Against Trachoma, Internat. Soc. for Preventive Oncology, German Soc. Endocrinology, Am. Uveitis Soc. Avocations: tennis, skiing, scuba diving. Office: U Eye Hosp Hamburg, Martinistr 52, 20246 Hamburg Germany

BIALCZYK, JAN, plant physiologist, researcher; b. Targanice, Poland, May 27, 1948; s. Franciszek and Magdalena (Swietek) B.; m. Ewa Maria Liniowska, Oct. 30, 1976; 1 child, Agnieszka. MS, Jagiellonian U., Cracow, Poland, 1973, PhD, 1976. Asst. rsch. worker Jagiellonian U., 1973-76, asst. prof., 1976-82, assoc. prof., 1996—, head dept. plant physiology and devel., 2000—; postdoctoral position Max-Planck Inst. fur Biochemie, Martinsried, Germany, 1982-84; sci. sec. Inst. Molecular Biology, Cracow, 1976-80; organizer 5th European Physarm Meeting, Cracow, 1981. Reviewer various internat. jours.; contbr. articles to profl. jours. Mem. Mcpl. Coun. of Cracow, 1998—. Grantee Polish Acad. Scis., 1988-90, Ministry Nat. Edn., 1991, Ministry Sci. Rsch., 1992—. Mem. Am. Soc. Plant Physiolgists, Japanese Soc. Plant Physiologists, N.Y. Acad. Scis. Avocations: sailing, tourism. E-mail: bialczyk@mol.uj.edu.pl. Office: Jagiellonian U Inst Mol Biology, Al Mickiewicza 3, 31 120 Cracow Poland

BIALIK, VIKTOR, pediatric orthopediatric surgeon; b. Levoca, Slovak Republic, Mar. 1, 1942; arrived in Israel, 1968; s. Herman and Anna (Eckmann) B.; m. Sara Lerer, Oct. 6, 1969; 1 child, Moshe Gad. MD, Komensky U., Slovak Republic, 1965. Asst. prof. Inst. Forensic Medicine, Bratislava, 1965-68; orthopedic surgeon Rambam Med. Ctr., Haifa, Israel, 1968-74, sr. orthopedic surgeon, 1974-90, head pediat. orthopedic unit, 1990—, clin. assoc. prof., 1995—; lectr. Technion Faculty of Medicine, Haifa, among others; reviewer Israel Jour. Med. Scis., Jour. Pediat. Orthopedics. Mem. editl. bd. Jour. Pediat. Orthopedics, 1992—, Italian Jour. Pediat. Orthopedics, 1995—, guest editor-in-chief, 1993; contbr. more than 70 articles to profl. jours. Mem. Israel Orthopedic Assn., Israel Pdait. Orthopedic Soc., European Pediat. Orthopedic Soc. (historian 1994-95, gen. sec. 1995-98), Am. Inst. Ultrasound in Medicine, Internat. Soc. for the Devel. of Ultrasonography (pres. 1994-97), Slovak Orthopedic Soc. (hon.), Czech Orthopedic Soc. (hon.), Hungarian Orthopedic Soc. (hon.). Avocations: classical music, travel. Home: 43 Margalit St, 34464 Haifa Israel Office: Rambam Med Ctr, PO Box 9602, 31096 Haifa Israel

BIALLOZOR, SVETLANA, chemistry educator, researcher; b. Wilno, Poland, June 28, 1932; d. George and Maria (Kaszubska) B. MSc, Tech. U. Gdańsk, Poland, 1956, PhD, 1963, DSc, 1975. Asst. Tech. U. Gdańsk, 1956-75, prof., 1996—. Author: (student handbook) Kinetics and Catalysis, 1971; editor: (student handbook) Podstawy chemii—Elementary Aspects of Chemistry, 1994; contbr. numerous articles and reports to profl. publs. Recipient 2 honors Pres. of Poland. Fellow Polish Chem. Soc. Orthodox. Achievements include research in electrochemistry and kinetics of electrodic reactions. Avocations: travel, cats. Home: Podmłyńska 1-5 A/m6, 80-885 Gdańsk Poland Office: Tech U Gdańsk, ul G Narutowicza 11/12, 80-953 Gdańsk Poland

BIANCHI, ETTORE FULGENZIO, textile engineer; b. Como, Italy, Nov. 24, 1920; s. Giuseppe and Giuseppina (Sordelli) B.; m. Daniela Molteni, Oct. 22, 1951; children: Giuseppe, Anna. D in Textile Engring., Politecnico, Milan, 1946. Textile engr. Seteria Bianchi, Capiago Intimiano, Como, 1946-57, chmn. mng. dir., 1957—. Author: International Vocabulary of Fabrics, 1997; co-author: History of Capiago Intimiano, Vols. I-VII, 1981-97; inventor silk jacquard paintings named "Microarazzi", Cooper-Hewitt Mus., Smithsonian Instn., N.Y. Town engr. Capiago Intimiano, Como, 1947-52, town councillor, 1964-69. Office: Seteria Bianchi, Via Majetto 2-4, 22070 Capiago Intimiano Italy

BIANCHI, GIOVANNI ANTONIO, mechanical engineering educator; b. Como, Italy, Mar. 11, 1924; s. Francesco and Teresa (Di Martino) B.; m. Barbara Jane Epstein, Dec. 6, 1954; children: Paola, Sara, Elisabetta, Michele, Giacomo, Davide. D Engring., Tech. U., Milan, 1950; M Mech. Scis., Cornell U., 1953. Registered profl. engr. Rschr. Tech. U., Milan, 1954-58, asst., 1958-81, assoc. prof., 1961-71, prof., 1971-97, emeritus prof., 1997—; sec. gen. Internat. Ctr. Mech. Scis., Udine, Italy, 1977—; co-founder Internat. Fedn. Theory Machines and Mechanics, 1969. Editor Meccanica, 1968-82; contbr. articles to profl. jours. Paul Harris fellow Rotary Club, Udine, 1989. Mem. Internat. Fedn. Theory Machines and Mechanisms (pres. 1983-89), Italian Assn. Mech. Theory and Application (pres. 1982-85), Internat. Union Theoretical and Applied Mechanics (Italian rep. 1980—), Inst. Lombardo Scienze e Lettere, Polish Acad. Scis. Home: Viale Gran Sasso 48, 20131 Milan Italy Office: Internat Ctr Mech Scis, Piazza Garibaldi 17, 33100 Udine Italy

BIANCHI, MARCO E., research scientist, educator; b. Milan, Nov. 18, 1957; s. Aldo Bianchi and Maria Toscano; m. Monica Beltrame; 1 child, Laura. Laurea in biol. scis., U. Milan, 1980. Postdoctoral assoc. Yale U. Sch. Medicine, New Haven, Conn., 1981-83; postdoctoral fellow CNR, Milan, 1983-86; staff scientist EMBL, Heidelberg, Germany, 1986-89; assoc. prof. U. Pavia, Italy, 1989-92, U. Milan, 1992-99, U. San Raffaele, Milan, 1999—; group leader DIBIT San Raffaele Sci. Inst., Milan, 1992—. Mem. Soc. Italiana di Biofisica & Biologia Molecolare (sec. 1994—). Office: DIBIT, via Olgeltina 58, 20132 Milan Italy

BIANCHI, MARIA, critical care specialist, adult nurse practitioner, acute care nurse practitioner. Grad., Catherine Laboure Sch. Nursing, 1979, Fitchburg (Mass.) State Coll., 1985; postgrad., Russell Sage Coll., Troy, N.Y.; adult nurse practitioner, Mass. Gen. Hosp., Boston. Cert. post-anesthesia care nurse; critical care clin. specialist. Recovery as mgmt. educator, mktg. and recruitment cons., cons. in critical care nursing; adminstr. dept. spl. svcs., mgr. critical care Baystate Med. Ctr., Springfield, Mass., 1980-89; recruitment and sr. faculty St. Francis Med. Ctr. Sch. of Nursing, Hartford, Conn., 1989-92; grad. faculty U. Mass. Med. Ctr., Worcester, 1995-97; per diem nurse practitoner dept. surgery U. Mass. Sch. of Nursing, Worcester, 1995-97, 99—; faculty U. Mass. Sch. of Nursing, Amherst; clin. faculty Am. Internat. Coll., Springfield; asst. prof. Grad. Sch. U. Mass., Amherst, 1998-99; rsch. in pain, burn trauma, stress reduction, holistic methods for high risk individuals in maximum security penitentiary and critical care patients; nat. cons. for critical care/post anesthesia issues, pres. TransInternat. Healthcare; nat. lectr. AHI, Balt.; expert witness, Mass. and Conn.; medicolegal cons.; lectr. on critical care and post anesthesia issues, empowerment, acute pain, holistic techniques, medicological documentation, trauma. Mem. AACN, Am. Soc. Post-Anesthesia Nursing (Boston chpt. editl. cons.), Soc. Critical Medicine, Mass. Gen. Hosp. Alumni Assn., Catherine Laboure Alumni Assn., Sigma Theta Tau. Office: PO Box 614 Suffield CT 06078-0614

BIARY, NABIL M., neurologist; b. Damascus, Syria, Jan. 16, 1949; s. Mohamad and Kamar B.; m. Maha Soudan, Oct. 1, 1982; children: Rana, Nora, Tamara, Rasha. Degree in Physics, Chemistry, Biology, Damascus U., 1967, MD, 1972. MD; bd. cert. neurology, EEG, evoked potentials, clin. neurophysiology; spl. competence in paediatric EEG; Am. Bd. Psychiatry and Neurology with added qualifications in clin. neurophysiology, Am. Bd. Electrodiagnostic Medicine. Intern Christ Comm. Hosp., Oak Lawn, Ill., 1973-74; neurology resident Howard U., Washington, 1974-77; fellow in electroencephalography U. Ill. Hosp., 1977-78, attending physician, 1978-89; attending physician West Side VA Hosp., Ill., 1977-88; cons. neurologist Riyadh Armed Forces Hosp., Saudi Arabia, 1988—; instr. in neurology U. Ill., Chgo., 1977-78, asst. prof., 1978-89. Contbr. articles to profl. jours. Named to Outstanding Young Men of Am., 1983; named one of best 10 students in country, Syria, 1966; Acad. scholar Damascus U., 1967-72. Fellow Am. Acad. Neurology, Am. Electroencephal. Soc., Am. Assn. Electrodiagnostic Medicine; mem. Movement Disorders Soc., AMA. Avocations: swimming, reading, chess, sight-seeing, cycling. Office: Armed Forces Hosp, PO Box 7897, Riyadh 11159, Saudi Arabia

BIASCI, ANDREA, chemist; b. Livorno, Italy, Apr. 18, 1959. BSc in Chemistry, U. Pisa, Italy, 1986. From R & D asst. to export mgr. Laviosa Chimica Mineraria Spa, Livorno, Italy, 1987-94; gen. mgr. Bentec Spa, Livorno, 1995—, also bd. dirs.; sales mgr. Laviosa Chimica Mineraria Spa, 2000—; bd. dirs. Laviosa Chimica Mineraria Spa. E-mail: abiasci@laviosa.it. Home: Piazza della Vittoria 50, 57125 Livorno Italy Office: Bentec Spa, Via L Da Vinci 21, 57123 Livorno Italy

BIASE, FRANCISCO DI, neurosurgeon, researcher; b. Barra do Pirai, Rio, Brazil, July 25, 1949; s. Walter Di and Maria (Diogo) B.; m. Tereza Maldonado Roland, May 15, 1976; children: Fabiano Di, Rodrigo Di, Francisco R. Di, Daniel R. Di. MD, U. Brazil, Rio de Janeiro, 1973; postgrad., Cath. Pontificia U., Rio de Janeiro, 1986-87. Resident in neurosurgery Dr. Paulo Niemeyer's Svc., Rio de Janeiro, 1974-76; specialization in EEG, Drs. Helio Bello-Niemeyer, Rio de Janeiro, 1977; prof. anatomy and physiology Faculty Philosophy and Scis., Barra do Pirai, 1974-76, Volta Redonda, Brazil, 1975-76; mem. attending staff Nat. Inst. Social Security, Barra do Pirai, 1977—; chief postgrad. dept., editor-in chief Aleph mag. Ednl. Found. R. Pimentel, Rio de Janeiro, 1977—; chief neurosurgery and neurology dept. and computed tomography svc. Santa Casa Hosp., Barra do Pirai, 1978—; med. dir. Di Biase Clinic, Barra do Pirai, 1984—. Author: O Homem Holistico, 1995, Caminhos da Cura, 1998; co-author: Science and the Primacy of Consciousness, 1999; contbr. articles to profl. jours. Mem. AAAS, Brazilian Med. Assn., Brazilian Soc. Neurosurgery, Brazilian EEG Soc., Brazilian Soc. for Progress of Sci., N.Y. Acad. Scis., Internat. Holistic U., Coll. Internat. des Therapeutes. Avocations: tennis, jogging, tai chi chuan, meditation. E-Mail: biase@attglobal.net. Office: Di Biase Clinic, Paulo de Frontin 280, 27123120 Barra do Pirai Brazil

BIASI, MARIAPAOLA, personnel recruitment company executive; b. Conegliano, Italy, Sept. 5, 1969; d. Enzo and Luisa (Pizzinat) B. Degree in polit. econ., Bocconi U., Milan, 1995. Human resources mgr. Seris SPA, Milan, 1995-97; CEO, Selecting SPA, Milan, 1997—. Mem. Sales and Mktg. Mgrs. Assn. Roman Catholic. Avocations: reading, theatre, cooking, creative works, fitness. Office: Selecting SPA, Viale Stelvio 5, 20159 Milan Italy

BIASUTTI, MICHELE, composer, psychologist; b. Udine, Italy, Feb. 14, 1963; s. Bruno and Clotilde (Miniscalco) B.; m. Cristina Donofrio, Nov. 16, 1996. Degree in psychology, U. Padua, Italy, 1987, PhD, 1997. Tchr. Conservatory of Music, Novara, Italy, 1989-90, High Sch., Udine, Italy, 1990-91, 91-93, Conservatory of Music, Venice, Italy, 1991-92; rsch. Padua U., Italy, 1993—; artistic dir. Computer & Arts Festival, Padova, 1993—. Composer Ritmi Biologici, 1987, Tavola IV, 1993. Avocations: basketball, soccer, travel. E-mail: biasutti@ux1.unipd.it. Home: Via Viotti 19 BIS, 35132 Padua Italy Office: U Padua, Piazza Capitaniato 3, 35132 Padua Italy

BIBB, DANIEL ROLAND, antique painting restorer and conservator; b. Gadsden, Ala., June 10, 1951; s. Cassius Roland and Louise Selma B. Student, Jefferson State, 1969-70, DeKalb Coll., 1971-72. Sales cons. Macy's Antique Gallery, Atlanta, 1973; dir. Collector's Gallery, Atlanta, 1974-76, Connoisseur's Gallery, New Orleans, 1977-79; painting conservator Daniel R. Bibb Fine Painting Conservation & Restoration, Atlanta, 1980—; chief fund raiser Atlanta Rabbit Rescue; researcher for pvt. collectors and museums, Atlanta, 1977-89; listed conservator, New Orleans Museum List of Restorers, New Orleans, 1988. Discovered a lost major painting of Philip IV of Spain, from workshop of Valasquez; exhibited lost painting Atlanta High Mus. Art, 1980; publication of discovered paintin, High Mus. Monthly, 1980; conservator Anglo-Am. Art Mus., Baton Rouge, New Orleans Mus. Art.; owner Fabergè collection on loan to New Orleans Mus. Art, 1996; icon collection touring mus'., Louisiana, Miss. and Alabama, 1998—; writer on various subjects to nat. mags. Fund raiser Am. Heart Assn., Atlanta, 1987, 88, March of Dimes, 1987, 88, Atlanta Rabbit Rescue, 1984—; mem. High Mus. of Art, Atlanta; vol. ARC Disaster Relief Team, Atlanta, 1992, Art Care Art Auction for fight against AIDS, 1992, 93, chmn. Live Auction, 1993. Recipient Design award, Most Authentic Design, Patio Planters of the Vieux Carre, New Orleans, 1977. Mem. Nat. Trust for Historic Preservation. Republican. Baptist. Achievements include raising funds and pub. awareness of animal cruelty. Avocations: antique collecting, collecting Royal portraits, pre-revolutionary Russian icons, porcelain, paintings. Home and Office: Bibb Painting Restoration 807 Summit North Dr NE Atlanta GA 30324-5641

BIBBY, THOMAS FREDERICK ALLEN, physicist; b. Caracas, Venezuela, Feb. 17, 1955; came to U.S., 1955; s. T.F. Allen Bibby and Joan Francis Keefer; m. Yu Wang, Oct. 20, 1990; 1 child, Keefer. BS in Physics, Marlboro Coll., 1978; MSEE, U. Vt., 1982; PhD in Physics, Drexel U., 1992. Assoc. mem. tech. staff RCA Corp., Palm Beach Gardens, Fla., 1984; asst. mem. tech. staff David Sarnoff Rsch. Ctr., Princeton, N.J., 1985-90; postdoctoral fellow USN Naval Air Warfare Ctr., Warminster, Pa., 1993-95; sr. process engr. IPEC Westech, Phoenix, 1995; mgr. process R&D Integrated Prcoess Equipment Corp. Planar, Phoenix, 1996-97; mgr. strategic tech. Integrated Prcoess Equipment Corp., Phoenix, 1997-99; sr. tech. mgr. SpeedFam-Integrated Process Equipment Corp., Chandler, Ariz., 1999; sr. intellectual property engring. mgr. Venture Info. Capital, Williston, Vt., 1999—. Contbr. articles to profl. publs. Mem. IEEE, Am. Phys. Soc., Optical Soc. Am. Achievements include patents in field. Avocations: hiking, running, photography. Fax: (602) 288-9468. E-mail: tbibby@venture-infocapital.com. Office: Venture Info Capital 400 Cornerstone Dr Ste 325 Williston VT 05495-4046

BIBEAULT, DONALD BERTRAND, business executive, investor; b. Woonsocket, R.I., Nov. 14, 1941; s. George Bertrand and Renee (Herbert) B.; m. Gigi Loving, June 18, 1994; 1 child, Zachary James. BSEE, U. R.I., 1963; MBA, Columbia U., 1965; PhD, Golden Gate U., 1979, JD (hon.), 2000. COO Pacific States Steel, Union City, Calif., 1975-78, PLM Internat., San Francisco, 1979-81; turnaround advisor Varity Corp., 1981-82; pres., CEO Best Pipe and Steel Co., San Francisco, 1983-86; workout advisor Bank of Am., 1987-89; chmn. Am. Nat. Petrol, Houston, 1990-91; chmn., CEO Tyler Dawson Supply Co., Tulsa, 1990-91, Iron Oak Supply Co., Sacramento, 1990-93; pres. Bibeault and Assocs., Inc., San Rafael, Calif., 1976—; bd. trustees Golden Gate U., San Francisco, 1986-97; bd. advisors U. R.I. Bus., Kinston, 1993—; bd. overseers Columbia Grad. Sch. Bus., N.Y.C., 1994—; bd. visitors Golden Gate U. Law Sch., San Francisco, 2000—. Author: Corporate Turnaround, 1982 (Fortune award 1982); contbr. articles to profl. jours. Mem. adv. bd. on trade Dept. of Commerce, Washington, 1988-92. Lt. U.S. Army, 1963-65. Mem. Turnaround Mgmt. Assn. (founding dir. 1987-91), Bankers Club San Francisco. Home and Office: Bibeault Assocs 60 Peacock Dr San Rafael CA 94901-1505

BIBIKOV, NIKOLAY GRIGORIEVITCH, neurophysiologist, educator; b. Moscow, Feb. 13, 1940; s. Grigory Nikolaevitch and Irina Michailovna (Nasarevskaya) B.; m. Margarita Vasilievna Rybasenko, Sept. 5, 1940; children: Tatiana, Maria, Grigory. B, Moscow U., 1963; M, Acoustics Inst., Moscow, 1969, Candidate in Physics, 1971; D in Biology, St. Petersbourgh (Russia) U., 1992. Minor sci. rschr. Acoustics Inst., Moscow, 1963-67, sci. rschr., 1967-76, sr. sci. rschr., 1976-90, leading sci. rschr., 1990—; lectr. Moscow Pedagogical U., 1993—. Author: Auditory Processing in Vertebrates, 1987. Mem. Russian Assembly of Nobility, Moscow, 1991; v.p. Kutusoff's Union, Moscow, 1995. Grantee Internat. Sci. Found., 1994-95. Mem. Internat. Brain Rsch. Orgn., Acoustical Soc. Am., Russian Acoustical Soc. (head bioacoustical dept. 1996), Russian Acad. Natural Scis. (corr.). Orthodox Christian. Home: ap 28, Krasnoarmeiskaiya St 26-1, 125167 Moscow Russia Office: Acoustics Inst, Schvernik St 4, 117036 Moscow Russia

BIBLE, GEOFFREY CYRIL, tobacco company executive; b. Canberra, Australia, Aug. 12, 1937; s. Cyril Edward Bible and Dorothea Elizabeth (O'Brien) McGrath; m. Sara Curtis Anderson-Emery, Sept. 10, 1965; children—Mary, Tom, Kim. Chartered acct., Australia; cost and mgmt. acct., U.K. Fin. dir. UN, Lebanon and Jordan, 1959-64; budget mgr. ILO, Switzerland, 1965-66; fin. mgr. Esso Med., Switzerland, 1966-68; mgr. corp. planning Philip Morris Europe, Switzerland, 1968-70; mgr. R.W. King & Yuill, Stockbrokers, Switzerland, 1970-76; dir. corp. planning Philip Morris Europe, Switzerland, 1976-78; v.p. Philip Morris Internat., N.Y.C., 1976-81, exec. v.p., 1984-87; , pres., chief exec. officer, 1987-90, 94-95, chmn., 1995—; mgr., dir. Philip Morris Austria, Benson Hedges Can., 1981-84; pres., chief auditor officer Kraft Gen. Foods, Glenview, Ill., 1990—. Chmn. Geneva English Sch., 1971-77. Roman Catholic. Office: Philip Morris Co Inc 120 Park Ave New York NY 10017-5592

BIČÁK, JIŘÍ, theoretical physicist, educator; b. Prague, Czech Republic, Jan. 7, 1942; s. Josef and Marie (Linhová) B.; m. Jana Kudrnová, June 23, 1964; children: Jitka, Alena. MS, Charles U., Prague, 1964, PhD, 1968, DSc, 1982. From asst. to assoc. prof. dept. mathematical physics Charles U., Prague, 1965-91, prof. dept. mathematical physics, 1991—, head dept. theoretical physics, 1986—; vis. prof., rschr. U. Cambridge, A. Einstein Inst., Caltech, U. Utah, others; Sackler vis. astronomer U. Cambridge, 2000. Author: Einstein and Prague, 1979, Gravitational Waves in General Relativity, 1987; mem. editl. bd. Czechoslovak Jour. Physics, 1968-96, Gen. Relativity and Gravitation, 1980-89, European Jour. Physics, 1985-88; contbr. articles to profl. jours. Lt. Czech Mil., 1964-65. Recipient Copernicus medal Czech Astron. Soc., Prague, 1973, Honorable mention Gravity Rsch. Found., Mass., 1977, medal Union of Czech Mathematicians and Physicists, 1987. Fellow Inst. Physics U.K.; mem. Internat. Com. for Gen. Relativity and Gravitation, Internat. Union for Pure and Applied Physics (mem. astrophysics commn. 1990-96), Am. Phys. Soc., Czech Learned Soc. (founder). Roman Catholic. Achievements include discovery and interpretation of solutions of general relativity equations; description of properties of gravitational waves, black holes and cosmological models. Home: Francouzská 6, 12000 Prague 2, Czech Republic Office: Charles U Inst Theoret Phys, V Holešovičkách 2, 18000 Prague 8, Czech Republic

BICAKCIC, EDHEM, government official. Prime min. Fedn. Govt. of Bosnia and Herzegovina, 1996—. Office: Office of Prime Minister, Alipasina 41, 71000 Sarajevo Bosnia-Herzegovina*

BICHEVIN, VICTOR VASILY, research scientist; b. Krasnojarsk, Russia, Mar. 25, 1935; s. Vasily Ivan and Hilda Henrik (Pelt) B.; m. Aleksandra Andrei Popov, July 18, 1960 (div. May 1976); children: Natalja, Pjotr. BS, Tartu U., Estonia, 1959, PhD, 1972. Jr. rsch. assoc. Inst. Physics, Tartu, 1960-63, 66-73, sr. rsch. assoc., 1973—. Contbr. over 50 articles to profl. jours. Mem. European Phys. Soc. Home: Aardla 144/49, EE2400 Tartu Estonia Office: Inst Physics, Riia 142, EE2400 Tartu Estonia

BICK, KATHERINE LIVINGSTONE, neurobiologist, international liaison, consultant; b. Charlottetown, Can., May 3, 1932; came to U.S., 1954; d. Spurgeon Arthur and Flora Hazel (Murray) Livingstone; m. James Harry Bick, Aug. 20, 1955 (div.); children: James A., Charles L. (dec.); m. Ernst Freese, 1986 (dec. 1990). BS with honors, Acadia U., Can., 1951, MS, 1952; PhD, Brown U., 1957; DSc (hon.), Acadia U., 1990. Rsch. pathologist UCLA Med. Sch., 1959-61; asst. prof. Calif. State U., Northridge, 1961-66; lab. instr. Georgetown U., Washington, 1970-72, asst. prof., 1972-76; dep. dir. neurol. disorder program Nat. Inst. Neurol. and Communicative Disorders and Stroke, NIH, Bethesda, Md., 1976-81, acting dep. dir., 1981-83, dep. dir., 1983-87; dep. dir. extramural rsch. Office of Dir. NIH, 1987-90; sci. liaison Centro Studio Multicentrico Internazionale Sulla Demenza, Washington, 1990-95; cons. Nat. Rsch. Coun., Italy, 1991-97, The Charles A. Dana Found., N.Y.C., 1993-98, Edn. Commn. of the States, 1996-99. Editor: Alzheimer's Disease: Senile Dementia and Related Disorders, 1978, Neurosecretion and Brain Peptides, Implications for Brain Functions and Neurol. Disease, 1981, The Early Story of Alzheimer's Disease, 1987, Alzheimer Disease, 1994, 2d edit., 1999, Alzheimer Disease: The Changing View, 2000; contbr. articles to profl. jours. Pres. Woman's Club, McLean, Va., 1968-69; bd. dirs. Fairfax County (Va.) YWCA, 1969-70; pres. Avenel Homeowner's Assn., 1998; pres. Emerson Unitarian Ch., 1964-66; mem. Bethesda Pl. Cmty. Coun., 1992-95, pres., 1993-94; mem. Dana Alliance for Brain Initiatives, 1993—; bd. dirs. Wilmington N.C. Child Advocacy Commn., 1998—. Recipient Can. NRC award Acadia U., 1951-52, NIH Dir.'s award, 1978, Spl. Achievement award NIH, 1981, 83, Superior Svc. award USPHS, 1986, Presdl. Rank award meritorious sr. exec., 1989; Universal Match Found. fellow Brown U., 1956-57, Fed. Exec. Inst. Leadership fellow, 1980. Fellow AAAS; mem. Am. Neurol. Assn., Am. Acad. Neurology, Assn. for Rsch. in Nervous and Mental Disease, Internat. Brain Rsch. Orgn., World Fedn. Neurology Rsch. Group on Dementias (exec. sec. Am. region 1984-86, chmn. 1986-93), Alzheimer's Disease Internat. (mem. scientific and med. adv. bd.), Soc. for Neurosci., Acad. of Medicine (Washington), Dana Alliance for Brain Initiatives.

BICK, RODGER LEE, hematologist, oncologist, researcher, educator; b. San Francisco, May 21, 1942; s. Jack Arthur and Pauline (Jensen) B.; m. Marcella Bick, Mar. 3, 1980 (dec. Feb. 1995); 1 child, Shauna Nicole. MD, U. Calif., Irvine, 1970; PhD, Acad. Medicine, Bialystok, Poland, 1995. Diplomate Am. Bd. Quality Assessment, Am. Bd. Forensic Medicine in Oncology, Hematology, Thrombosis, Hemostasis and Product Liability, Internat. Bd. Thrombosis, Hemostasis & Vascular Medicine, Am. Bd. Pain Mgmt. Med. intern Kern County Gen. Hosp., UCLA, Bakersfield, Calif., 1970-71, internal medicine resident, 1971-72; fellow in hematology-med. oncology Bay Area Hematology Oncology Med. Group, West Los Angeles, Calif., 1974-76; med. staff various hosps., Calif., 1974-77; med. staff, extensive adminstrv. and com. work various hosps., Bakersfield, Calif., 1977-92; med. dir. oncology hematology Presbyn. Comprehensive Cancer Ctr., Presbyn. Hosp., Dallas, 1992-95; staff hematologist/oncologist Bay Area Hematology Oncology Med. Group, Santa Monica, Calif., 1976-77, med. dir. Calif. Coagulation Labs., Inc., Bakersfield, 1977-92, San Joaquin Hematology Oncology Med. Group, 1977-92, Regional Cancer and Blood Disease Ctr. Kern, Bakersfield, 1986-92; asst. clin. prof. to clin. prof. medicine UCLA Ctr. Health Scis., 1976-94, assoc. prof. to prof. allied health profns. Calif. State U., Bakersfield, 1980-92, clin. prof. nursing and health scis., 1982-92; adj. assoc. prof. medicine/physiology, Wayne State U., Detroit; adj. clin. faculty Wesley Med. Ctr. and U. Kans. Med. Sch., Wichita, 1984-86; clin. prof. medicine U. Tex. Southwestern Med. Ctr., 1993—, clin. prof. pathology, 1993—; prof. haematology U. Tasmania Sch. Medicine, 1996; hematology cons. NASA; med. dir. UCLA/Kern Cancer Program, 1991-92, Ctrl. Calif. Heart Inst., 1990-92; invited spkr. and presenter in field, numerous internat. symposia and confs.; dir. numerous workshops in field. Author: Disseminated Intravascular Coagulation and Related Syndromes, 1983, Disorders of Hemostasis and Thrombosis: Principles of Clinical Practice, 1985, 2d. edit., 1992, 3d edit., 1997; guest editor, contbr.: Thrombohemorrhagic Disorders Perplexing to the Hematologist Oncologist, 1992; guest editor: Laboratory Diagnosis of Hemostasis Problems, I, 1994, II, 1995, (monograph) Seminars in Thrombosis and Hemostasis, 1994, Common Bleeding and Clotting Problems for the Internist, 1994; editor-in-chief: Hematology: Princples of Clinical and Laboratory Practice, 2 vols., 1993, Paraneoplastic Syndromes, Hematology Oncology Clinics of North America, 1996; editor: Current Concepts of Thrombosis, 1998; contbr. numerous chpts. to books; author monographs and lab. manuals; contbr. over 250 articles and papers and numerous revs. to profl. jours. and conf. procs.; patentee in field; editor-in-chief Jour. Clin. and Applied Thrombosis/Hemostasis & Vascular Medicine; mem. editl. bd. Am. Jour. Clin. Pathology, Internat. Jour. Haematology. Bd. dirs., exec. com. Bakersfield Symphony Orch., 1988-92. Fellow ACP, Am. Soc. Clin. Pathologists, Assn. Clin. Scientists, Am. Soc. Coagulationists, Internat. Soc. Hematology, Am. Coll. Angiology, Internat. Coll. Angiology, Nat. Acad. Clin. Biochemistry, Am. Heart Assn. (coun. on thrombosis, circulation and atherosclerosis; rsch. and grnat peer rev. com. 1980-86), Am. Geriat. Soc. (founding fellow); mem. AMA, AAAS, Am. Assn. Blood Banks, Am. Soc. Internal Medicine, Am. Soc. Hematology, Internat. Soc. Thrombosis and Haemostasis, Am. Assn. Study of Neoplastic Disease, Am. Assn. Clin. Rsch., Am. Cancer Soc., Internat. Assn. Study of Lung Cancer (founding mem.), Fedn. Am. Scientists, N.Y. Acad. Scis., Calif. Soc. Internal Medicine, Calif. Med. Assn., Calif. Thoracic Soc., Haematology Soc. Australia, Internat. Consensus Com. on Autithrombotic Therapy, numerous others. Lutheran. Avocations: ocean sailing, classical piano, brass musical instruments, photography, target archery, astronomy and astrophotography. Office: 10455 N Central Expy Ste 109 Dallas TX 75231-2215

BICKEL, DAVID ROBERT, statistician, physicist; b. Dallas, Oct. 15, 1970; s. Samuel Herman and Sharon Elizabeth B. BS in Physics with honors, Baylor U., 1993; MA in Computational Physics with honors, U. North Tex., 1994, PhD in Biostatistical Physics with honors, 1997. Physics tchg. asst. U. North Tex., Denton, 1993-95, physics rsch. asst., 1995-97; biostatistician U. Tex.-Houston Health Sci. Ctr., 1997—, asst. prof., 2000—. Rev. statistics book proposal Wiley-Interscis., 1999; contbr. articles to profl. jours. Mem. Am. Statistical Assn., Am. Phys. Soc., Nat. Assn. Advancement Sci., Soc. Molecular Biology and Edn., Sigma Xi (bd. dirs. 1999-00). Presbyterian. Avocation: teaching the Bible at church. Office: U Tex-Houston Health Sci Ctr 1100 Holcombe Blvd # 4430 Houston TX 77030-3906

BICKEL, FLOYD GILBERT, III, investment counselor; b. St. Louis, Jan. 10, 1944; s. Floyd Gilbert and Mary Mildred (Welch) B.; m. Martha Wohler, June 11, 1966; children: Christine Carleton, Susan Marie, Katherine Anne, Jennifer Anne, Laura Elizabeth, Andrew Barrett (dec.). BS in Bus. Adminstrn., Washington U., St. Louis, 1966; MS in Commerce, St. Louis U., 1968. Rschr. Yates, Woods & Co., St. Louis, 1966-67; asst. br. mgr. E.F. Hutton & Co., Inc., St. Louis, 1967-70, v.p. dir. consulting svcs., 1980-88; asst. v.p., resident mgr. Bache & Co., Inc., St. Louis, 1970-72; pres. Donelan-Phelps Investment Advisors, Inc., St. Louis, 1972-80; v.p. Merrill Lynch & Co., St. Louis, 1988—; bd. dirs. Data Rsch. Assocs., Inc, Summit Mktg. Group, Huntleigh Assocs., Eagle RiveR LLC. Mem. City of Des Peres (Mo.), Planning and Zoning Commn., 1975-76; chm. St. Louis County Bd. Equalization, 1976-79; pub. safety commr. City of Des Peres, 1977-80, mem. audit and fin. com., 1980-86; mem. State of Mo. Gov.'s Crime Commn., 1981-92; bd. dirs. Villa Duchesne Sch., 1986-92; aldeman City of Huntleigh, 1998—. Mem. Internat. Soc. Cert. Employee Benefit Specialists, Investment Mgmt. Cons. Assn., St. Louis Soc. Fin. Analysts, Bellerive Country Club, Beaver Creek Club, Cordillera Golf Club, Eagle Springs Golf Club, John M. Olin Bus. Sch. Washington U. Alumni Assn. (pres. 1995-96), John's Island Club. Republican. Roman Catholic. Home: 30 Huntleigh Woods Saint Louis MO 63131-4813 Office: Merrill Lynch & Co 1630 S Lindbergh Blvd Saint Louis MO 63131-3501

BICKEL, MINNETTE DUFFY, artist; b. New Bern, N.C., June 24, 1921; d. Richard Nixon and Minnette (Chapman) Duffy; m. William Croft, Jan. 3, 1947; children: Minnette B. Boesel, Susan B. Scioli. Exhibited in one-person shows N.C., statewide portrait exhbns. (two 1st place awards), regional juried shows, (winner three internat. awards); portraits include Gen. Claude Larkin, Tyrone Power, Thomas Graham, James Beckwith, Arthur Rolander, Frederick E. Fox, Senator Jesse Helms, Rachel Carson, R. Bud Dwyer, William Genge, Allison Williams, Dennis O'Connor. Mem. Am. Soc. Portrait Artists (affiliated), Stroke of Genius Gallery, Washington Soc. of Portrait Artists and Portrait Inst. Republican. Home: 816 Saint James St Pittsburgh PA 15232-2113

BICKELHAUPT, FRIEDRICH MATTHIAS, chemistry educator; b. Amstelveen, The Netherlands, Nov. 24, 1965; s. Friedrich and Annemarie Martel (Schwarzt) B.; m. Célia Fonseca Guerra, Sept. 8, 1999. M in Chemistry, Free U., Amsterdam, 1988; PhD in Chemistry, U. Amsterdam, 1993. Postdoctoral assoc. U. Erlangen, Nürnberg, Germany, 1993-95, Cornell U., N.Y.C., 1995-96; rsch. assoc. Vrije U., Amsterdam, The Netherlands, 1996-97; asst. prof. Vrije U., Amsterdam, 1999—, Philipps U., Marburg, Germany, 1997-99. Asst. editor Jour. Computational Chemistry, 1998; contbr. articles to profl. jours. Rsch. fellow Deutsche Forschungsgemeinschaft, 1993, Habilitation fellow Deutsche Forschungsgemeinschaft, 1997. Mem. Am. Chem. Soc., Gesellschaft Deutscher Chemiker, Koninklijke Nederlandse Chemische Vereniging. Avocations: literature, films, traveling, skiing, tennis. Office: Scheikundig Lab Vrye Univ, De Boelelaan 1083, NL1081HV Amsterdam The Netherlands

BICKERS, PATRICIA EVELYN, editor, lecturer; b. Portsmouth, Eng., Dec. 26, 1950; d. Norman Sefton Reece and Evelyn (Hill) B. BA in History & Theory of Art with honors, U. Sussex, Eng., 1973; postgrad., Birkbeck Coll., London, 1992. Lectr. Harrow Sch. Art, London, 1974-89; sr. lectr. Poly. Ctrl. London, 1989-92, U. Westminster, 1993—; assoc. editor Art Monthly, 1989-91, editor, 1991—; trustee Matt's Gallery, London, 1991—, Serpentine Gallery, London, 1995—; external examiner Glasgow Sch. Art, 1998-2000, St. Martin's Sch. Art, London Inst., 2000—. Author The Brit Pack: Contemporary British Art, the View from Abroad, 1995, revised and extended, 1997; exhbn. catalogues; contbr. criticism articles and interviews to Art Monthly, Artpress, Beaux Arts and other jours. and books; broadcaster BBC Radio and TV; co-selector New Contemporaries, 1994. Mem. Assn. Art Historians, Assn. Internat. Critiques d'Art, Lansdowne Club. Office: Art Monthly, 26 Charing Cross Rd Ste 17, London WC2 H0DG, England

BICKERTON, DAVID MARSHALL, languages educator; b. Castleford, Yorkshire, Eng., Jan. 22, 1944; s. Leonard Marshall and Mary Elisabeth (Crabtree) B.; m. Helene Monfort, Aug. 3, 1968; children: Claire, Paul, Christopher, Emilie. BA, French U. Leeds, Eng., 1967, PhD, 1978. Lectr. U. Glasgow, Scotland, 1969-83, dir. Lang. Ctr., 1983-93; dir. modern langs. U. Plymouth, Eng., 1993-98; rsch. prof. U. Plymouth, 1999—; mem. sci. coun. Inst. Nat. Rsch. Pedagogy, France, 2000—. Author: (book) Marc-Auguste and Charles Pictet and the Bibliotheque Brittanique (1796-1815), 1986; co-editor: (conf. procs.) The Transmission of Culture 1750-1850, 1999, Correspondence-Sciences et Techniques-Marc-Auguste Piclet, vol. 3, 2000; dir.: (TV documentary) La Batalha de la Lenga, 1990 (1st prize Festival of Aixe sur Vienne 1990). Sec. gen. Cercles, Plymouth, 1995-00; exec. mem. U. Coun. for Modern Langs., U.K., 1998—. Recipient Rapido Project award European Union, 1997. Mem. Assn. Univ. Lang. Ctrs. Avocations: traveling, building, wine. Home: 13 Thorn Park, PL3 4TG Plymouth England Office: U of Plymouth, Plymouth Bus Sch, PL4 8AA Plymouth England

BICKLEY, JOHN S., insurance association executive, educator, writer; b. Bethlehem, Pa., Dec. 30, 1917; m. Mary Louise Loftis; 1 child, Mary Carter. Student, Columbia U., Harvard U., U. Chgo.; BA, MBA, PhD, U. Wis. Life underwriter Coll. divsn. Mass. Mut. Life Ins. Co., 1939, Lincoln Nat. Life Ins. Co., 1940; dir. edn. State Auto Ins. Co., 1957-85; Frank Parker Samford chair ins. emeritus U. Ala., 1975—; emeritus dir. Columbus Life Ins. Co., 1963—; prof. ins. U. Ala., 1940-42, 47-48, 68-86, emeritus prof., 1986—, chmn. com. on internat. corp. rels., 1986—; prof. ins. U. Wash., 1948-50, Ohio State U., 1950-59, U. Tex., Austin, 1959-68; vis. prof. ins. Stanford U., 1953, U. Colo., 1957, U. Hawaii, 1962; chmn. dept. fin. U. Tex., Austin, 1965-68; spkr. in field in 30 nations. Author 3 books and monographs, numerous articles in profl. jours; founding editor Jour. of Risk and Ins., 1956-60. Trustee, founding bd. dirs. Griffith Found. for Ins. Edn., 1950—; founder, elector Ins. Hall of Fame, 1957—; bd. dirs. U. Ala. Cmty. Music Sch., 1999—; mem. internat. adv. bd. U. Ala., 1993—; bd. dirs. Tuscaloosa Symphony Orch., 1990—, chmn. pers. com., 1993—; bd. dirs. Tuscaloosa String Quartette Soc.; mem. bd. pensions Evang. Luth. Ch. in Am., 1966-78; founding mem. chancellor's coun. U. Tex. System, founding chmn. com. on property-liability ins. terminology, 1959-69. 1st lt. USAAC, 1942-46. Decorated Order of Sacred Treasure with gold rays and neck ribbon (Japan); recipient decorations Min. of Fin., Republic of China, 1979, Min. of Fin., Republic of South Korea, 1986; Gold medal award named in his honor Ins. Hall of Fame (laureate 1988), Gold medal De La Salle U., The Philippines, Lifetime Achievement award Nat. Profl. Fraternity; recipient numerous awards and honors; rsch. fellow FTC, 1968-69, Fed. Home Loan Mortgage Corp., 1972. 7em. Am. Econ. Assn., Am. Fin. Assn. (exec. com.), Ins. Co. Edn. Dirs. Soc., Am. Meteorol. Soc., Am. Risk and Ins. Assn. (pres. 1958-59), Ala. Ins. Planning Commn. (resident), Ala. Acad. Sci., Ohio State U. Inst. Soc. (founder, faculty sponsor), U. Tex. Austin inst. Soc. (founder, faculty sponsors), U. Ala. Ins. Soc. (founder, faculty sponsor), Newcomen Soc. (Ala. com.), Assn. Internat. Droit des Assurances, Corp. Ins. Agts. London (hon.), Internat. Assn. Accident and Health Underwriters (hon.), Am. Soc. for Ins. Mgmt. (hon.), Internat. Ins. Soc. (founder, chmn. emeritus, dir. for life), North River Yacht Club (Tuscaloosa, Ala., dir.), Univ. Club (Tuscaloosa), Jasons, Mortar Board, Sigma Phi, Alpha Kappa Psi, Gamma Iota Sigma, Phi Mu Alpha, Beta Gamma Sigma, Omicron Delta Kappa. Address: 1310 Indian Hills Tuscaloosa AL 35406

BICKNELL, BARBARA ANN, mechanical engineer, executive, consultant; b. Elyria, Ohio, Mar. 18, 1958; d. Joseph Robert and Doris Genevieve (Urig) Lach; m. Kris D. Bicknell, July 2, 1983. BS in Mech. Engring., U. Notre Dame, 1981; MS in Engring., U. Colo., 1993. Engring. mgr. Lockheed Martin, Denver, 1981-92; pres. Bicknell Consulting, Inc., Golden, Colo., 1992—; adj. instr. U. Denver, 1992—. Contbg. author: Basic Statistics, 1993; co-author: The Road Map to Repeatable Success, 1995. Mentor Asian Am. Corp. Experience Devel., Denver, 1992-95. Recipient Tech. award NASA, 1989. Mem. AIAA, Internat. Coun. Sys. Engrs. Achievements include experiments in low-gravity. Avocations: hiking, volleyball. Office: Bicknell Consulting Inc 433 Park Point Dr Ste 200 Golden CO 80401-5752

BICUDO, JOSÉ EDUARDO PEREIRAWILKEN, science educator; b. São Paulo, Brazil, Mar. 10, 1955; s. Hélio Pereira and Déa Pereira (Wilken) B.; m. Maria Heloisa Ribeiro, Aug. 10, 1981 (div. 1997). BSc, U. São Paulo, 1978, PhD, 1984; MA, Duke U., 1981. From instr. to asst. prof. to assoc. prof. U. São Paulo, 1979-96, prof., 1996—; postdoctoral fellow Harvard U., Cambridge, Mass., 1985-86, U. Berne, Switzerland, 1986-87; vis. prof. U. Calif., Davis, 1991-92; hon. vis. prof. U. NSW, Sydney, Australia, 1997. Editor: (book) The Vertebrate Gas Transport Cascade, 1993, (book chpt.) Phenotypic and Evolutionary Adaptation to Temperature, 1996 (Travel award Soc. for Exptl. Biology 1995); contbr. rsch. articles to profl. jours. Fellow Danish Internat. Devel. Agy., Denmark, 1977. Mem. Am. Physiol. Soc., Brazilian Soc. Advancement of Sci. (treas. São Paulo sect. 1992-94), Brazilian Physiol. Soc. (coun. mem. 1998-01), Faculty Assn. (v.p. 1989-91). Roman Catholic. Avocations: reading, hiking, photography, wine tasting. Office: U São Paulo, Rua Do Matão Trav 14 321, 05608900 São Paulo Brazil

BIDAN, GÉRARD MARIE, laboratory director; b. Paris, Jan. 15, 1951; s. Michel Henry and Christiane Marie-Thérèse (Alexandre) B.; m. Brigitte Simone Layous, June 26, 1976; children: Yann, Maelle. Diploma ESPCI engring., U. Paris VII, 1975, DEA, 1980; PhD, U. J. Fourier, 1980. Rschr. France Atomic Energy Coun., Grenoble, 1980-85, dir. lab., 1985—, dep. head of the unit, 1996—; expert sr. Commissariat a l'Energie Atomique, Grenoble, 1998—; rep. dept. Grenoble U. Coun., 1996—; mem. CNRS Scientific Coun., Paris, 1989-96. Author: (with others) Developments of Applications of Electronic Conducting Polymers, 1993, Polymer Films in Sensor Applications, 1995; guest editor Synthetic Metals, 1998, 99; patentee in field. Mem. French Soc. of Chemistry, Internat. Soc. of Electrochemistry. Avocations: entomology, swimming, body building, cross country skiing. Home: 3 rue des Trois Epis, 38100 Grenoble France Office: CEA-Grenoble DRFMC/SI3M, 17 rue des Martyrs, 38054 Grenoble Cedex 09, France

BIDDISS, MICHAEL DENIS, history educator; b. Farnborough, Kent, U.K., Apr. 15, 1942; s. Daniel and Eileen Louisa (Jones) B.; m. Ruth Margaret Cartwright, Apr. 8, 1967; children: Clare, Katherine, Sarah, Beth. BA, Queens' Coll., Cambridge, U.K., 1964, MA, PhD, 1968; student, U. Strasbourg, 1965-66. Fellow, dir. studies in history and social/polit. sci. Downing Coll., Cambridge, 1966-73; lectr., reader in history U. Leicester, U.K., 1973-79; prof. history U. Reading, U.K., 1979—; vis. prof. U. Victoria, B.C., Can., 1973, Capetown, S. Africa, 1976, 78, Monash, Australia, 1989, Nanjing, China, 1997. Author: Father of Racist Ideology, 1970, The Age of the Masses, 1977, The Nuremberg Trial and the Third Reich, 1992; co-author: Disease and History, 1972, 2d edit., 2000; editor: Gobineau: Selected Political Writings, 1970, Images of Race, 1979; co-editor: Thatcherism, 1987, Uses and Abuses of Antiquity, 1999, The Humanities in the

New Millennium, 2000. Fellow Royal Hist. Soc. (joint v.p. 1995-99); mem. Faculty of the History and Philosophy of Medicine/Soc. Apothecaries of London (hon. fellow, 1986—, pres. 1994-98, Osler medal 1989, Locke medal 1996), Coun. of Hist. Assns. (pres. 1991-94.). Avocations: mountain walking, music and opera, cricket. Office: Dept History, Univ Reading/ Whiteknights, Reading RG6 6AA, England

BIDDLE, ANTHONY JOSEPH DREXEL, III, investment banker; b. Washington, Nov. 30, 1948; s. Anthony Joseph Drexel Biddle Jr. and Margaret (Atkinson) Biddle Robbins; m. Karen M. Erskine, Dec. 23, 1970; children: Anthony Joseph Drexel IV, Cordelia Erskine Drexel. BS in Econs., Cornell U., 1970; MBA in Fin., U. Pa., 1975. 2d v.p. Chase Manhattan Bank, N.Y.C., 1975-77; mgr. Chase Manhattan Ltd., London, 1977-79; v.p. Flint Hills Drilling Co., Winfield, Kans., 1979-81; ptnr. Hale and Assocs., Washington and Winfield, 1979-81; pres. Drexel Biddle and Co. Inc., Phila., 1982-89; mgr. Global Environtl. Tech. Strategy Chase Manhattan Bank, N.A., N.Y.C., 1989-98; mng. dir. The Hanseatic Group Inc., Phila., 1988-89; dir. Constn. Cruise Lines Inc., Phila., 1988-89; founding dir. Resicontrol S.A., Sao Paulo, 1994-98, Recycomb S.A., Buenos Aires, 1995-98p; pres. ELM Capital LLC, Phila., 1999—; bd. dirs. Angelika Films; dir. Poly-Tek Rubber & Recycling Inc., Phoenix, 1999—; dir. U.S. Environtl. Export Coun., Washington, 1995-97; mem. environtl. tech. trade adv. com. U.S. Dept. Commerce, Washington, 1997—; advisor UN Conf. on Climate Change, N.Y., 1998; mem. U.S.-China Environtl. Energy and Bus. Roundtable, Washington, 1999. Contbg. author: Legal Aspects of the Management Process, 1976. Bd. advisors Andalusia Found.; bd. dirs. Boys Harbor Inc., N.Y.C., 1972—, Charity Ball Inc., Phila. 1981—, Phila. Ship Preservation Guild, 1982-91, Independence Hall Assn., 1984-91, Drexel U. Friends, Phila., 1987—, Hero Scholarship Fund, Phila.; founding co-chmn. Arthur Ross Gallery, U. Pa., 1982—; assoc. trustee U. Pa., 1983-87, Nat. Inst. for Music Theater, Kennedy Ctr., Washington, 1985-87. Lt. USN, 1970-73. Mem. Wharton Olympus Inc. (chmn. Europe-Mid East and Asia 1978-79), Soc. of Cin., Phila. Club, Athenaeum, Army-Navy Club, U. Club, Royal Automobile Club, Travellers Club. Avocations: sailing, skiing. Home: 638 Panama St Philadelphia PA 19106-4107

BIDDLE, DAN A., human resources executive; b. Saugus, Calif., Jan. 27, 1969; s. Richard Earl Biddle and Joyce Louise McInturff; m. Jennifer Ellen Biddle, Nov. 10, 1990; children: Makaela Vivian, Alyssa Marie. BS in Organizational Behavior, U. San Francisco, 1994; MA in Organizational Psychology, Calif. Sch. Profl. Psychology, 1999, postgrad., 1999—. Dir. Biddle & Assocs., Inc., Sacramento, 1990—; pres. Firefighter Seletion, Inc., Sacramento, 1998—. Mem. Soc. Indsl.-Organizational Psychology, Personnel Testing Coun. E-mail: dabiddle@biddle.com. Office: Firefighter Selection Inc 1333 Howe Ave Ste 212 Sacramento CA 95825-3362

BIDDLE, LIVINGSTON LUDLOW, JR., former government official, writer, consultant; b. Bryn Mawr, Pa., May 26, 1918; s. Livingston Ludlow and Eugenia (Law) B.; m. Cordelia Frances Fenton, Mar. 15, 1945 (dec. May 1972); children: Cordelia Frances, Livingston Ludlow IV; m. Catharina Van Beek Baart, Nov. 3, 1973. AB, Princeton U., 1940; LHD (hon.), Mt. St. Mary's Coll., N.Y., 1978; LLD (hon.), Catholic U., 1979; DFA (hon.), U. L.I., 1979, U. Cin., 1979, Providence Coll., 1980, U. Notre Dame, 1980; DL (hon.), Drexel U., 1980. Reporter Phila. Evening Bull., 1940-42; with Am. Field Service, Middle East, North Africa, Italy, France, Germany, 1942-45; spl. asst. to U.S. Senator Claiborne Pell, 1963-65; dep. chmn. Nat. Endowment for Arts, Washington, 1965-67; chmn. div. arts Liberal Arts Coll., Fordham U., Lincoln Center, N.Y.C., 1967-70; spl. asst. to Senator Claiborne Pell, 1973-74; liaison dir. Nat. Endowment for Arts, Washington, 1974-75; chmn. Nat. Endowment for Arts, 1977-81; staff dir. subcom. on edn. arts and humanities U.S. Senate, 1975-77. Author: Main Line, 1950, Debut, 1952, The Village Beyond, 1956, Sam Bentley's Island, 1960, Our Government and the Arts: A Perspective From Inside, 1988. Pres. Children's Service, Inc., Phila., 1960-62; chmn. bd. Pa. Ballet, 1971-72. Decorated Order of Leopold II Belgium, Jubilee medal, Bulgaria; recipient Phila. Athenaeum Best Novel award, 1956. Mem. Chevy Chase Club, Washington Club, Cosmos Club, Century Assn. Club (N.Y.C.). Democrat. Episcopalian. Home: 3050 P St NW Washington DC 20007-3052

BIDDLE, MARTIN, archaeologist; b. North Harrow, Middlesex, Eng., June 4, 1937; s. Reginald S. Biddle and Gwladys F. Baker; m. Birthe Kjølbye, 1966; 4 children, 2 from previous marriage. Student, Merchant Taylors' Sch., Pembroke Coll., Cambridge (Eng.) U. Asst. insp. ancient monuments Ministry of Pub. Bldgs. and Works, Eng., 1961-63; lectr. medieval archaeology U. Exeter, Eng., 1963-67; vis. fellow All Souls Coll. Oxford (Eng.) U., 1967-68; dir. Winchester Rsch. Unit, 1968—; dir. Univ. Mus., prof. anthropology and history of art U. Pa., 1977-81; lectr. of The House Christ Ch., Oxford, 1983-86; Astor sr. rsch. fellow in medieval archaeology, tutor Hertford Coll., Oxford, 1989—; dir. investigations Holy Sepulchre, Jerusalem, 1989—; prof. medieval archaeology U. Oxford, 1997—; dir. excavations and investigations Nonsuch Palace, 1959-60, Winchester, 1961-71, Repton, 1974-88, 93, St. Alban's Abbey, 1978, 82, 84, 91, 94-95; archaeol. cons. Canterbury Cathedral, St. Alban's Abbey, Eurotunnel, others; Trevelyan lectr. U. Cambridge, 1991. Author: Nonsuch Palace: Domestic Material, 1998, King Arthur's Round Table, 1996, Approaches to Urban Archaeology, 1996, Object and Economy in Medieval Winchester, 1990; co-author: (with C. Heighway) The Future of London's Past, 1973, (with others) Winchester in the Early Middle Ages, 1976, The History of the King's Works, Vol IV, Part 2, 1982; contbr. articles to profl. jours. Commr. Royal Commn. on Hist. Monuments for Eng., 1984-95. Recipient Frend medal Soc. of Antiquaries, 1986; decorated Order of Brit. Empire. Fellow Brit. Acad., Soc. Antiquaries, Royal Hist. Soc. Avocations: travel, architecture, Renaissance art. Office: Oxford U/Hertford Coll, Catte St, Oxford OX1 3BW, England*

BIDDLE, TIMOTHY MAURICE, lawyer; b. San Jose, Calif., Dec. 1, 1940; s. Maurice Francis and Hazel Eda (Bold) B.; m. Florence Elizabeth Hickey, June 15, 1963; children: Elizabeth, Timothy Mark, Matthew, Rebecca. BA in History, Georgetown U., 1962; JD, Cath. U., 1971. Assoc. Jones, Day, Reavis & Pogue, Washington, 1971-77, ptnr., 1977-79; ptnr. Crowell & Moring LLP, Washington, 1979—. Contbr. articles to profl. jours. Capt. USAF, 1962-67. Recipient Disting. Lawyer for 1991 Nat. Coal Assn., 1991. Mem. ABA, Energy and Mineral Law Found. (trustee), Helicopter Assn. Internat. (bd. dirs., spl. advisor 1990—). Office: Crowell & Moring LLP 1001 Pennsylvania Ave NW Washington DC 20004-2505

BIEBUYCK, BRIAN STUART, lawyer; b. Cape Town, South Africa, Oct. 3, 1957; s. Allan Leslie and Zoe Elaine (Adams) B.; m. Dec. 14, 1985 (div. Feb. 1996); children: Megan Penelope, Anton Allan; m. Reneé Dente, Mar. 21, 1996; children: Lauren, Caryn. BA, Stellenbosch U., 1978, LLB, 1980. Articled clk. Sonnenberg Hoffmann & Galombik, Cape Town, 1983-84, profl. asst., 1985-87, co. dir., 1987—. Lt. South African Air Force, 1981-82. Mem. Western Province Cricket Club (chmn. 1991-99), Kelvin Grove, Milnerton Aquatic Club, Plettenberg Bay Angling and Boat Club. Avocations: cricket, rugby, water skiing, working out at the gym. Home: 10 Whimbrel Ave, Flamingo Vlei, Cape Town 7441, South Africa Office: Sonnenberg Hoffmann & Galombik, Norwich on St Georges, Cape Town 8001, South Africa

BIECHL, HELMUTH, electrical engineer, educator; b. Starnberg, Germany, May 4, 1959; s. Peter and Erika (Plötz) B.; m. Anne Kohls, July 7, 1994. MS, Tech. U., Munich, 1985, PhD in Engring., 1989. Asst. prof. Tech. U., Munich, 1986-90; devel. engr. Siemens AG, Erlangen, Germany, 1990-91; project leader Bayernwerk AG, Munich, 1991-94; prof. U. Applied Scis., Kempten, 1994—; cons. ENCAL, Kempten, 1995—. Mem. German Assn. Elec. Engrs. Avocations: theatre, classical music, history. E-mail: helmuth.biechl@fh-kempten.de. Home: Am Denzlerpark 19, 87437 Kempten Germany Office: Fachhochschule Kempten, Bahnhofstr 61-63, 87435 Kempten Germany

BIEDERMAN, DONALD ELLIS, lawyer; b. N.Y.C., Aug. 23, 1934; s. William and Sophye (Groll) B.; m. Marna M. Leerburger, Dec. 22, 1962; children: Charles Jefferson, Melissa Anne. AB, Cornell U., 1955; JD, Harvard U., 1958; LLM in Taxation, NYU, 1970. Bar: N.Y. 1959, U.S. Dist. Ct. (so. dist.) N.Y. 1967, Calif. 1977. Assoc. Hale, Russell & Stentzel, N.Y.C., 1962-66; asst. corp. counsel City of N.Y., 1966-68; assoc. Delson & Gordon, N.Y.C., 1968-69; ptnr. Roe, Carman, Clerke, Berkman & Berkman, Jamaica, N.Y., 1969-72; gen. atty. CBS Records; N.Y.C., 1972-76; sr. v.p. legal affairs and adminstrn. ABC Records, L.A., 1977-79; ptnr. Mitchell, Silberberg & Knupp, L.A., 1979-83; exec. v.p., gen. counsel Warner/Chappell Music Inc., L.A., 1983-99, cons., 1999—; gen. counsel Warner/Chappell Music Inc., 2000—; adj. prof. Sch. Law Southwestern U., L.A., 1982-2000, prof. law, dir. entertainment and media law inst., 2000—, Pepperdine U., Malibu, Calif., 1985-87, Loyola Marymount U., L.A., 1992; lectr. Anderson Sch. Mgmt. UCLA, 1993, U. So. Calif. Law Ctr., 1995-97. Editor: Legal and Business Problems of the Music Industry, 1980; co-author: Law and Business of the Entertainment Industries, 1987, 2nd edit., 1991, 3d edit., 1995. Bd. dirs. Calif. Chamber Symphony Soc., L.A., 1981-92; dir. Entertainment Law Inst. U. So. Calif., 1993-2000. 1st lt. U.S. Army, 1959. Recipient Hon. Gold Record, Recording Industry Assn. Am., 1974, Trendsetter award Billboard mag., 1976, Gold Triangle award Am. Acad. Dermatology, 1999; named. Mem. N.Y. Bar Assn., Calif. Bar Assn., Riviera Country Club, Cornell Club. Democrat. Jewish. Avocations: golf, skiing, travel, reading. Home: 2406 Pesquera Dr Los Angeles CA 90049-1225 Office: Warner/Chappell Music Inc 10585 Santa Monica Blvd Los Angeles CA 90025-4921

BIEDERMAN, EDWIN WILLIAMS, JR., petroleum geologist; b. Stamford, Conn., June 30, 1930; s. Edwin Williams and Thelma Frances (Morrow) B.; m. Margaret-Jane Bell White, Aug. 23, 1958; children: Robert, Mary, Jane, James. BA, Cornell U., 1952; PhD, Pa. State U., 1958. Cert. petroleum geologist. Project leader Cities Svc. Co., Tulsa, 1958-68; pres. staff Cities Svc. Co., Cranbury, N.J., 1968-72; asst. dir. Pa. Tech. Assistance program, University Park, Pa., 1972-77, sr. tech. specialist, 1980—; field ctr. dir. NSF Chautauqua Courses, University Park, 1977-80; field ctr. dir. NSF Chautauqua Courses, University Park, 1977-80. Author: Atlas of Oil and Gas Reservoir Rocks From North America, 1986; contbr. articles to profl. jours.; holder 5 patents for geochem. exploration, in situ acidulation of phosphate rock, grate for vertical oil shale kiln, fire retardant foam, lightweight cement for oil wells. With USAF, 1952-54. Pa. State U. scholar 1956-58; am. Assn. Petroleum Geologists grantee 1957; recipient First Place award Project of Yr. Nat. Assn. Mgmt. and Tech. Assistance Ctrs., 1985. Mem. AAAS, Am. Assn. Petroleum Geologists, Soc. Econ. Paleontologists and Mineralogists, Geochem. Soc., Assn. Profl. Geol. Scientists. Office: Pa State U 232 Hosler Bldg University Park PA 16802-5001

BIEDERMAN, ROBERT WALLACE WILLIAMS, cardiologist; b. Kansas City, Mo., June 25, 1962; s. Edwin W. Jr. and Margaret Jane (White) B.; m. Kimberly Pauline Stuskey, Aug. 2, 1986; children: Brittani, Addison, Caroline. BS, Charleston So. U., 1985; MD, U. S.C., 1993. Diplomate Am. Bd. Internal Medicine. Sr. resident Dr. Gerald M. Pohost, Hershey, Pa., 1993-96; assoc. cardiology U. Ala., Birmingham, Ala., 1996-98, chief cardiology, fellow, 1998—; cardiologist Ctr. Cardiovas Nuc. Magnet Rsch. and Devel., Birmingham, 1998—. Contbr. articles to profl. jours. Recipient Frank E. Tressler Humanitarium award Carson Long Mil., 1980. Mem. Ala. Coll. Cardiology (Young Investigator Yr. 1998, 99), Am. Heart Assn. (Ala. chpt., Young Investigator Yr. 1998), Citadel (Jr. Sword Drill award 1984). Avocations: track, outdoor exploration, reading. E-mail: RWBKPS@AOL.COM. Home: 10319 Ridgecrest Pt Wexford PA 15090-9600 Office: U Ala Cardiovas Nuc Maget Rsch BOB 101 1808 7th Ave S Birmingham AL 35294-0001

BIEGANOWSKA, MARIA LUCYNA, chemistry educator; b. Pawłów, Lublin, Poland, Sept. 12, 1926; d. Jan and Zuzanna (Przychodzka) B. Diploma in Pharmacy, Med. Acad., Lublin, Poland, 1951, PhD, 1963. Asst. Med. Acad., Lublin, 1951-64, sr. sci. worker, 1964-77, asst. prof., 1977-91, assoc. prof., 1991-96, prof., 1996—. Contbr. articles to profl. jours. Recipient Golden Cross of Merit, 1976, Badge of Honor of Med. Acad., Lublin, 1978, Chevalier's Cross of the Order Polonia Restituta, awards Polish Ministry Health, 1987, 92, 96. Mem. N.Y. Acad. Scis., Polish Pharm. Soc. Roman Catholic. Avocation: tourist. Office: Med Acad Dept Inorganic, Analytical Chemistry, Staszica 6, 20-081 Lublin Poland

BIEGMAN, NICOLAAS H., ambassador; b. Apeldoorn, The Netherlands, Sept. 23, 1936; s. Nicolaas and Aukje (de Boer) B.; m. Mirjana Cibilic, Feb. 18, 1961; children: Nicolaas, Ivo. BA in Arabic, Leiden U., The Netherlands, 1958, MA in Turkish, 1961, PhD in Balkan History, 1967. With ministry fgn. affairs Govt. of The Netherlands, 1963—, amb. to Egypt, 1984-88; amb. to UN Govt. of The Netherlands, N.Y.C., 1992-97; amb. to NATO Govt. of Netherlands, 1998—; dir. Gen. Internat. Coop., 1988-92. Author: The Turco-Ragusan Relationship, 1967, Egypt: Moulids, Saints and Sufis, 1990, (photobooks) Egypt's Sideshows, 1992, An Island of Bliss, 1993, Mainly Manhattan, 1997. Recipient various awards, The Netherlands and Egypt. Office: NATO Hdqrs, Blvd Leopold III, 1110 Brussels Belgium

BIELE, HUGH IRVING, lawyer; b. Bridgeport, Conn., July 28, 1942; s. Ray James and Blanche (McClellan) B.; m. Pamela Althea Johnson, Aug. 21, 1965 (div.); children: Jonathan Christopher, Melissa Lynne. BA, St. Lawrence U., Canton, N.Y., 1965; JD, U. Utah, 1968. Bar: Utah 1968, U.S. Dist. Ct. Utah 1968, Calif. 1972, U.S. Dist. Ct. Calif. 1972, U.S. Ct. Appeals (9th and 10th cirs.). Instr. San Francisco Law Sch., 1971-73; atty. United Calif. Bank, San Francisco, 1971-74; v.p., sr. counsel First Interstate Bank, L.A., 1974-81; ptnr. Biele & Stuehrmann, L.A., 1981-83; sr. ptnr. Biele, Stuehrmann & Lapinski, L.A., 1983-84; founding ptnr. Biele & Lapinski, L.A., 1985-89; ptnr. Barton, Klugman & Detting, L.A., 1989-91; ptnr., dir. comml. law and litigation Grace, Skocypec, Cosgrove & Schirm, L.A., 1992-95; bd. govs. Fin. Lawyer Conf., L.A., 1976—, pres. 1984-85, original developer, ptnr. Engine Co. No. 28 rehabilitation, 1982—, ptnr. Engine Co. No. 28 Restaurant, 1988—, owner Biele Enterprises, bd. dirs. Vege-Kurl, Inc., 1990—. Author screenplay: Corporate Cancer, 1989, Hedge of Thorns, 1990. Bd. dirs. Community Counseling Svc., L.A., 1989—, pres., 1993-95, chmn. bd. dirs., 1995—; bd. dirs. Casa de Rosa and the Sunshine Mission, 1997—; bd. dirs., v.p., sec. Project New Hope, Inc., L.A., 1990-92; commr. Episc. Diocese AIDS Ministry, L.A., 1988-93; chmn. Vols. in Parole, L.A., 1979-80, 89-90, Lawyers for Human Rights, 1988—, co-pres. elect, 1999. Maj. U.S. Army, 1968-70. Decorated Bronze Star with oak leaf cluster, Army Commendation medal. Mem. ABA, Fed. Bar Assn., Internat. Bar Assn., L.A. County Bar Assn. (internat. sect. exec. com. 1978-97, chmn. 1981-82, exec. com. comml. law and bankruptcy sect. 1986—, chair 1992-93), Calif. State Bar (fin. inst. com.), Internat. Bankers Assn. Calif., St. Lawrence U. Alumni Assn. (pres. 1979-91). Republican. Episcopalian. Avocations: skiing, jogging, aerobics, travel. Home and Office: PO Box 2068 Hollywood CA 90078-2068

BIELIŃSKA-WAŻ, DOROTA JOANNA, physicist; b. Bydgoszcz, Poland, June 9, 1968; d. Franciszek Wiesław and Eugenia (Jagodzińska) B.; m. Piotr Henryk Waż, Sept. 14, 1991. M of Physics, U. Toruń, 1992, specialist on European law, 1995, D of Physics, 1998. Asst. U. Torun, 1997-98; rsch. assoc. Med. U., Bydgoszcz, Poland, 1998—. Contbr. articles to profl. jours. Pres. govt. body Grad. Students, 1995-97. Rsch. grantee Polish Rsch. Coun., 1998, European Sci. Found., 1997; Tempus fellowship European Cmty., 1993, 95, Humboldt Fellowshp., 1999—. Avocations: ballet, judo, science fiction literature, politics. Home: Krasińskiego 21/23/51, 87-100 Toruń Poland Office: Instytut Fizyki UMK, Grudziadzka 5-7, 87-100 Toruń Poland

BIELLIK, ROBIN JULIAN, epidemiologist; b. London, Feb. 11, 1949; d. Cyril and Rose (Barnard) B.; m. Peggy L. Henderson, May 9, 1985. BSc, U. London, 1971; DrPH, U. Tex., Houston, 1983. Devel. officer, nutritionist various non-govtl. orgns., Guatemala, 1972-78; health project officer UNICEF, Kampala, Uganda, 1983-85; epidemiologist Ctrs. Disease Control and Prevention, USPHS, Atlanta, 1985-87; epidemiologist Pan Am. Health Orgn. WHO, Brasilia, Brazil, 1987-90; epidemiologist WHO, Kathmandu, Nepal, 1991-93, Harare, Zimbabwe, 1994—; nutrition cons. UN High Comm. Refugees, Mogadishu, Somalia, 1980; pub. health cons. CARE, Bogota, Colombia, 1982; pub. health cons. United Chs., Santa Cruz, Bolivia, 1976. Contbr. articles to profl. jours. Mem. leadership coun. So. Poverty Law Ctr., Ala., 1980's—. Mem. Greenpeace, Survival Internat., Nat. Adv. Group of Immunization, South Africa Nat. Pub. Health Assn. Zimbabwe. Avocations: photography, travel. Office: WHO, 95 Park Ln, PO Box 5160, Harare Zimbabwe

BIELY, DEBRA MARIE, retired military officer; b. Columbus, Ohio, June 8, 1957; d. Joseph Richard and Mary Narcissus (Quin) Szulewski; m. Robert Lee Biely, July 31, 1977; children: Kevin Lee, Kelsey Lynn, Kerry Logan. BS, Ohio State U., 1979; MBA, Averett Coll., 1993. Commd. 2d lt. USMC, 1979, advanced through grades to lt. col.; bn. adjutant 3d recruit tng. bn. USMC, Parris Island, S.C., 1980-82; asst. div. personnel officer 2d Marine div. USMC, Camp Lejeune, N.C., 1982-84, regimental adjutant 10th Marines, 1984-85; group adjutant 3d Force Serv SPT group USMC, Okinawa, Japan, 1986-88; squadron exec. officer hdqrs. squadron MCAS USMC, Futenma, Japan, 1988-89; div. adminstrv. officer human resources div. USMC, Washington, 1989-90, sect. mgr./adminstrv. officer requirements and programs div. HQMC, 1990-92, analyst Office Program Appraisal Sec. Navy, 1992-93; congressional fellow Office of Senator Howell Heflin, Washington, 1993-94; joint requirements oversight coun. programs/resources dept. USMC, 1994-99, ret., 1999; prin. cons. CapGemini Ernst & Young, N.Y.C., 1999—. Instr. Presdl. Classroom, Washington, 1991. Mem. Women Officers Profl. Assn. (ex officio, bd. dirs.), Woodlake Country Club, Army & Navy Club (Washington). Avocation: golf. Office: Cap Gemini Ernst & Young 29th Flr 1114 Ave of the Americas New York NY 10036

BIEN, AMOS, ecologist; b. N.Y.C., Feb. 12, 1951; s. Saul M. and Mina (Schneider) B.; m. Damaris Reyes; children: Natasha, Samantha, Pablo. BA in Biology, U. Chgo., 1973; MA in Ecology and Evolution, SUNY, Stony Brook, 1982. Systems programmer Met. Life Ins. Co., N.Y.C., 1973-74; software developer GTE Info. Systems (PMI), N.Y.C., 1975-77; rsch. asst. Dr.Barbara Bentley, Sarapiquí, Costa Rica, 1979-80; sta. mgr. La Selva Biol. Sta., Sarapiquí, 1980; prof. Sch. for Field Studies, Oriente, Ecuador, 1984-85; pres. Rara Avis S.A., Horquetas, Costa Rica, 1983—; cons. ecotourism US-AID, Inst. Guat. Turismo, others, San José, Costa Rica, 1985—; lectr. rain forest conservation, 1983—. Author: Fallos y Aciertos en el Ecoturismo: Casos Concretos, 1999; contbr. articles to profl. jours. Pres. Costa Rican Youth Hostel Assn., San José, 1990-92; co-founder Hyde Park-Kenwood Recycling Ctr., Chgo., 1971-73; founder, pres. Costa Rican Pvt. Nature Res. Orgn., 1995-2000; founding mem. CONAGEBIO Nat. Commn. REgulation of Access to Biodiversity, 1999—; active Environment Liaison Ctr. Internat., 1999-2000; treas. Fedn. Costa Rican Environ. Orgns., 1998—. Mem. Internat. Soc. Tropical Foresters, Camara Nacional de Turismo, Assn. Tropical Biologists. Office: Rara Avis SA, Apartado 8105-1000, San Jose Costa Rica

BIENAYMÉ, ALAIN M., economics educator; b. Toulon, Var, France, May 22, 1934; s. André M. and Marie-Cécile (Knall-Demars) B.; m. Marie-Hélene Sifflet, Dec. 13, 1958; children: Sophie, Françoise, Jean. PhD in Econs., U. Paris, 1957; C.P.E. in English, Brit. Inst. Paris/Cambridge, 1955; Agrégation in Econs., France, 1964. Asst. prof. U. Paris, 1959-60; jr. prof. U. Rennes, France, 1960-64; prof. U. Dijon, France, 1964-68, U. Paris-Dauphine, 1969—; advisor to pres. E. Faure, various instns. Ministerial Office, 1966-78; mem. Conseil Économique et Social, France, 1974-84; trustee Internat. Coun. Ednl. Devel., N.Y., 1975-95. Author: La Croissance Des Entreprises, 2 vols., 1971-73 (Silver medal C.N.R.S. 1977), Entreprises, Marché, Etat, 1982 (Prix Gaston Le Duc Acad. Scis. Morales et Politiques 1988), Le Capitalisme Adulte, 1992 (Prix Emile Girardeau 1992), L'Economie Des Innovations Technologiques, 1994, Principes de Concurrence, 1998, eight other books. E-mail: alain.bienayme@dauphina.fr. Home: 5 Rue D'Estrées, 75007 Paris France Office: U Paris-Dauphine, Place Marechal Lattre Tassigny, 75116 Paris France

BIENER, ERNST, civil engineering educator, consultant; b. Haseluenne, Germany, June 26, 1954; s. Ernst and Maria (Koester) B.; m. Renate Peiler, May 11, 1984; 1 child, Jil. Diploma in engring., U. Aachen, 1981, PhD in Engring., 1983. Cert. waste disposal tech., examination and rehab. contaminated sites. Acad. asst. U. Aachen, Germany, 1981-83; project mgr. Hochtief Essen, Germany, 1983-89, Thiess, Brisbane, Australia, 1989; prof. civil engring. Tech. U., Aachen, 1989—; cons. engr., ptnr. UMTEC, Aachen, Bremen, Berlin, 1998—. Author: Wendehorst, 1994, Bautechnische Zahlentafeln, 1998. Mem. German Soc. Waste Mgmt., German Soc. Geotechnics, German Soc. Waste Water Engring., German Soc. Engrs. Roman Catholic. Avocations: travel, tennis, books. Office: UMTEC, Purweider Winkel 63, D-52070 Aachen Germany

BIENZ, MARIANN, scientist; b. Winterthur, Switzerland, Dec. 21, 1953; arrived in England, 1991; d. Jurg and Lilly (Gubler) B.; children: Maya Joanne, Benjamin Peter. Diploma in zoology, U. Zurich, 1976, PhD, 1981. Asst. prof. U. Zurich (Switzerland), 1986-90, assoc. prof., 1990-91; sr. staff scientist Med. Rsch. Coun., Lab. Molecular Biology, Cambridge, England, 1991-94; spl. appointment Med Res. Coun., Lab. Molecular Biology, Cambridge, England, 1994—. Contbr. articles to profl. jours. Postdoctoral fellow Med. Rsch. Coun., Lab. Molecular Biology, 1981-86; recipient friedrich Miescher prize Swiss Biochem. Soc., 1990. Mem. European Molecular Biology Orgn. (mem. coun. 1994—). Avocations: family, mountain walking. Office: MRC LMB, Hills Rd, Cambridge CB2 2QH, England

BIER, LOUIS HENRY GUSTAV, minister; b. Chgo., Jan. 12, 1933; s. Louis Wilfred and Ethel Lea (Laue) B.; m. Helene Mueller, July 29 ,1962; children: Richard Allen, Karen Elizabeth, Lisa Anne. B. of Edn., Chgo. Tchrs. Coll., 1954; B. and M. of Theology, Concordia Sem., 1959; MEd, Boston State Coll., 1962; DRE, Smith Bapt. U., 1987, DD, 1986. Ordained to ministry Luth. Ch. 1959; lic. soc. worker. Vicar Redeemer Luth. Ch., Phila., 1957, 1st Lutheran Ch., Holyoke, Mass., 1957-58; pastor St. Paul's Luth. Ch., West Frankfort, Ill., 1959-61; pastor Trinity Luth. Ch., Boston, 1961-98, emeritus, 1999—; chaplain VA New Eng. Health Care Sys., Boston, 1965—; instr. psychology Boston State Coll., 1967-81; mem. adj. faculty Holy Cross Greek Orthodox Sem., Brookline, Mass., 1998; chaplain West Roxbury VA Hosp. 1978-86, The Arbour, Boston, 1969; chaplain German Home for Elderly, Boston, 1962, also trustee, 1971—; bd. dirs. Interfaith Bible Readings, Inc.; circuit counselor Luth. Ch. Mo. Snyod; trustee Chapel of the Four Chaplains, Valley Forge, Pa., 2000. Incorporator, Faulkner Hosp., 1981; br. pres. A.A.L., 1980; mem. Arboretum dist. Boston coun. Boy Scouts Am., 1976-79, USO Coun. New Eng.; bd. mgrs. Sophia Snow House; served to lt. col. CAP, 1975—; chaplain, col. Mass. State Def. Fort; mem. animal studies com. Beth Israel-Deaconess Hosp., Harvard Med. Sch., 2000. Recipient Honored Citizen award Kennedy VFW, 1973, Lamb award Luth. Council, 1975, Community Service award Greater Boston Assn. of Retarded Citizens, 1974, George Meany Youth Service award AFL-CIO, 1983, Disting. Eagle Scout award, 1993; Emerson fellow Mil. Chaplains Assn. U.S.A., 1999, West fellow Boy Scouts Am., 1999. Mem. German Soc. Boston (trustee), Luth. Edn. Assn. (life), Mil. Chaplains Assn. (life, treas., v.p., pres.), Assn. Profl. Chaplains (cert., 25th Anniversary citation 2000), Mass. Chaplains Assn., Concordia Sem. (Servus Ecclesia Christi award), Profl. Chaplains Assn. Avocations: swimming, golf, reading. Home: 169 Nahatan St Westwood MA 02090-3607

BIERCE, JAMES MALCOLM, retired judge; b. Columbus, Ohio, July 5, 1931; s. Bruce Wallace and Glyde Vivian (Brown) B.; m. Frances Marilyn Ruth, June 19, 1953 (div. Sept. 1963); children—James M., Teresa Anne; m. 2d, Fern C., July 22, 1967. LL.B., U. Akron, 1963. Bar: Ohio 1965, Mich. 1971, U.S. Dist. Ct. (no. dist.) Ohio 1969, U.S. Ct. Appeals (6th cir.) 1966, U.S. Supreme Ct. 1972. Employment officer Trans World Airlines, Kansas City, Mo., 1955-58; asst. dir. law City of Cuyahoga Falls (Ohio), 1966-68; sr. mng. ptnr. Bierce, Holland, Manning, Metz & Wilson, Akron, 1968-77; judge Cuyahoga Falls Mcpl. Ct., 1977-95; instr. Ohio Jud. Coll., 1979-95; faculty adviser Nat. Jud. Coll., 1983—; chmn. mentor com. Ohio Jud. Conf., 1992—, vice chmn. ret. judges com., 1996-97. Bd. dirs. Am. Diabetes Assn., 1982-83; pres. Cuyahoga Valley Community Mental Health Center, 1983-85, Cuyahoga Falls Fraternal Order of Police Assn., 1977; trustee Cuyahoga Falls Sch. Found., 1985-86; pres. Akron Crime Clinic, 1993. With USNR, 1953-57. Mem. ABA, Ohio Bar Assn., Akron Bar Assn., Am. Judges Assn., Am. Judicature Assn., Akron Area Mcpl. Judges Assn. (pres. 1982-84), Am. Diabetes Assn., Lions, Phi Alpha Delta (officer 1969-78, named Outstanding Alumni 1985). Republican. Avocations: power boating, travel, computers.

BIERHOFF, OLIVER, professional soccer player; b. Karlsruhe, Germany, Jan. 5, 1968. Forward AC Milan, Italy; ctr. forward AC Milan; profl. soccer player Nationalelf, Germany. Office: AC Milan, Via Turati 3, 20100 Milan Italy*

BIERLY, SHIRLEY ADELAIDE, communications executive; b. Waterbury, Conn., Jan. 19, 1924; d. Samuel and Frances Ada (Bogorad) Brown; m. Leroy Elwood Bierly, Jan. 19, 1946 (div. 1951); children: Lee Jr., Dennis Ray, David Lincoln. Student, Orange Coast Coll., 1963-66, L.A. City Coll., 1967-69. Mgr. Pacific Telephone, San Francisco, Calif., 1953-82; exec. dir. Sr. Power Office, San Francisco, 1982—. Pres. Calif. Legis. Coun. for Older Am., San Francisco, 1984—, treas. Calif. Assn. of Older Am., 1984—, sec., bd. mem. Sr. Action Network, San Francisco, 1991—, Congress of Calif. Sr., Sacramento, 1994—; bd. trustees Agape Found., policy bd. Nat. Coun. Sr. Citizens, 1995—; commr. San Francisco Residential Arbitration and Stabilization Bd., 1997-2000, Calif. Commn. on Aging, 2000—. Mem. Am. Civil Liberties Union, Older Women's League, Gray Panthers. Avocations: photography, theatre, reading, philately. Fax: 415-541-9630. Office: Calif Assn for Older Ams (aka Sr Power) 325 Clementina St San Francisco CA 94103-4104

BIERMACHER, KENNETH WAYNE, lawyer; b. Hartford, Conn., Oct. 15, 1953; s. Donald David and Ethel Pearl (Biermacher) Lawton; m. Joan; children: Carl Joseph II (dec.), Matthew Robert, Michelle Renee; 1 step child Brent Cohen. BS summa cum laude, U. New Haven, 1976; JD with honors, Drake U., 1979. Bar: Iowa 1980, Tex. 1985, U.S. Dist. Ct. (so. dist.) Iowa 1980, U.S. Dist. Ct. (no. dist.) Iowa, 1981, U.S. Ct. Appeals (8th cir.) 1981, U.S. Supreme Ct. 1983, U.S. Dist. Ct. (no. dist.) Tex. 1984, U.S. Dist. Ct. (so. and we. dists.) Tex. 1985, U.S. Dist. Ct. (ea. dist.) Tex. 1993, U.S. Ct. Appeals (5th cir.) 1985. Assoc. Whitfield, Musgrave, Selvy, Kelly, Eddy, Des Moines, 1980-84; shareholder Geary, Stahl & Spencer, P.C., Dallas, 1984-89, Leonard Marsh Hurt Terry & Blinn, Dallas, 1989-90; ptnr.-in-charge Dallas office Small, Craig & Werkenthin, P.C., Dallas, 1990-93; v.p., ptnr., dir. Kane, Russell, Coleman & Logan, P.C., Dallas, 1993—; pres., dir. Frontrunner Capital Corp., Dallas, 1999—; sec., dir. MT Auctions.com, Inc., Dallas, 1999—; lectr. Iowa Defense Counsel Assn. Annual Meeting, 1982, Des Moines Area Community Coll. Legal Asst. Program, 1981-82, Human Resources Forum, Am. Electronics Assn., Dallas, 1986; legal research asst. Iowa State Bar Assn. Com. on Study Fed. Rules Evidence, 1982; chmn. spl. com. on Friends of Moot Ct. Drake Law Sch. Bd. Counsellors, 1983-84. Contbg. author: Understanding Iowa Law, 1984; editor: Energy and Nat. Resources Guide for Iowa, 1979; contbr. articles to law jours. Adv. U. New Haven Law Enforcement Explorers Post Boy Scouts Am., 1975; coach Johnston Sr. High Sch. Mock Trial Teams, Iowa, 1984; del. Polk County Rep. Conv., Des Moines, 1980, Iowa Rep. State Conv., 1980; deacon Canyon Creek Bapt. Ch., 1986-87; chmn. scholarship and fin. aid com. Canyon Creek Christian Acad., 1985-87; v.p., dir. Boys and Girls Clubs of Greater Dallas, Inc., 1997—, chmn. circus com., 1998—, chmn. resource devel. com., 1999—; bd. dirs. Henry C. Lee Inst. Forensic Sci., 1996—; adv. bd. Dallas Tower Club. Recipient Acad. Scholarship U. New Haven, 1973-76; semi-finalist Midwest Regional Moot Ct. Competition, 1979. Mem. ABA (sub-com. on fraudulent and deceptive trade practices, sect. tort and ins. practice 1985-86, vol. atty. post-conviction death penalty representation project 1988-89), ATLA, FBA, Iowa State Bar Assn. (mem. Young Lawyer Sect. ethics com. 1981, law schs. panel com. 1982, law-related edn. com. 1983-84), Def. Rsch. Inst., Iowa Assn. Trial Lawyers (founding dir., chmn. Drake U. Law Sch. student bd. dirs. 1978-79, ex-officio mem. bd. dirs. 1978-79), Dallas Bar Assn. (mock trial com., law in changing soc. com. 1985, speech com. 1985-86, bus. litigation sect. ethic and courtesy com. 1988, qualified mediator 1989—, mem. cts. com. 1995, mem. fee dispute com. 1995), State Bar Tex. (legal assts. com. 1988-91), Dallas Assn. Young Lawyers (liaison with other profls., fed. opinions com. 1986), Order of Barristers, Atty.-Mediator Assn., Drake U. Law Sch. bd. counselors (regional v.p. for Tex. and Okla. 1986-89), Alpha Chi (vice chmn. Conn. chpt. 1975-76). E-mail: biermak@krcl.com. Home: 4324 Hollow Oak Dr Dallas TX 75287-6847 Office: Kane Russell Coleman & Logan PC 1601 Elm St Ste 3700 Dallas TX 75201-7207

BIERMAN, JAMES NORMAN, lawyer; b. St. Louis, Nov. 23, 1945; s. Norman and Margaret (Loeb) B.; m. Catherine Best, Apr. 10, 1983; 1 child, James Norman. AB magna cum laude, Washington U., 1967; JD, Harvard Law Sch., 1970. Assoc. Hogan & Hartson, Washington, 1970-72; asst. dean Harvard Law Sch., Cambridge, Mass., 1973-75; assoc. Foley & Lardner, Washington, 1975-79, ptnr., 1979-85, ptnr. in charge, 1985—, mem. mgmt. com., 1989-98; mem. nat. coun. Washington U. Coll. Arts and Scis., 1999—. Mng. editor Harvard Jour. Legis., 1969-70. Mem. Civil Rights Reviewing Authority HEW, Washington, 1979-80. Mem. ABA, Fed. Bar Assn., D.C. Bar Assn., Supreme Ct. Bar, Washington Lawyers Com. for Civil Rights and Urban Affairs (bd. dirs.), Phi Beta Kappa, Omicron Delta Kappa, Pi Sigma Alpha, Phi Eta Sigma, City Club (Washington). Home: 906 Peacock Station Rd Mc Lean VA 22102-1021 Office: Foley & Lardner 3000 K St NW Fl 5 Washington DC 20007-5109

BIERMANN, THOMAS, science educator; b. Bonn, Germany, Jan. 22, 1954; s. Berthold and Anne Luise (Ipsen) B.; m. Edda Bongers; 1 child, Nora. Diploma volkswirt, U. Bonn, 1981; Dr.rer.pol., U. Koeln, Germany, 1986. Planning expert Lufthansa, Koeln, 1981-86, head mgmt. cons., 1987-90; regional dir. Lufthansa, Stuttgart, Germany, 1990-93; prof. Tech. Fachhochschule, Wildag, 1994—; mng. dir. Svc. Mgmt. Inst., Berlin, 1993. Co-editor: Kursweschsel Richtung Kunde, 1996; editor: Innovation mit System, 1997; co-author: Marketing Management, 1998; author: Dienst Leisturg Management, 1999. Mem. Schmalenbach Gesellschaft. Avocations: modern art, boating. Office: Svc Mgmt Inst, Bundesplatz 4, 10715 Berlin Germany

BIERON, JACEK, physicist; b. Krakow, Poland, Oct. 1, 1957; married; four children. MSc, Jagiellonian U., 1982, PhD, 1988. Rsch. asst., grad. asst, tchg. asst. dept. atomic physics Jagiellonian U., Krakow, 1982-91; guest scientist Ruhr U., Bochum, Germany, 1990-91; postdoctoral fellow U. Windsor, Ont., Canada, 1992-93; vis. asst. prof. computer sci. Vanderbilt U., Nashville, 1993-94; guest scientist atomic physics Nat. Inst. Standards & Technology, Gaithersburg, Md., 1994-95; vis. fellow Math. Inst. Oxford U., England, 1996-97; adj. prof. atomic physics Jagiellonian U., Krakow, 1995—. Office: Jagiellonian U Dept Physics, Reymonta 4, 30-059 Krakow Poland

BIERRING, OLE, ambassador; b. Copenhagen, Nov. 9, 1926; s. Knud and Ester Marie (Lorck) B.; m. Bodil Elisabeth Kisbye, Mar. 2, 1960; children—Christina, Jens, Marie Louise, Arendse. LL.M., U. Copenhagen, 1951; postgrad. Princeton U., 1956. With Danish Ministry of Fgn. Affairs, Copenhagen, 1951, attache Danish Embassy, Washington, 1956-58, 1st sec., Vienna, 1960-63, head dept. Ministry Fgn. Affairs, Copenhagen, 1967-68, min. councellor, alt. permanent rep. Denmark to North Atlantic Coun., Brussels, 1968-72; head dept. Ministry Fgn. Affairs, Copenhagen, 1972-74; dep. under-sec. state for polit. affairs, 1974-75, undersec., 1976-80, dep. permanent undersec., 1980; Danish amb. to France, 1980-84; permanent rep. of Denmark to UN, 1984-88, rep. of Denmark in security council, 1985-86; permanent rep. of Denmark to North Atlantic Coun., Brussels, 1988-95; permanent observer to WEU; amb. at large, adviser on Baltic Security, 1995-96; spl. rep. chmn.-in-office OSCE, 1997; cons. Ministry for Defense. Decorated grand cross Order St. Olav (Norway), comdr. First Class Order of Dannebrog, Legion d'Honneur (France), Merite National (France), others.

BIERS, MARTIN HENRY, physician; b. Bklyn., Oct. 10, 1931; s. Louis and Sarah (Naidich) Bierfass; m. Elizabeth Jaros Biers, Feb. 11, 1962; children: Eric, Carl, John. BA, NYU, 1951; MD, SUNY, Bklyn., 1955. Cert. in internal medicine and hematology, Am. Coll. Physicians. Intern Kings County Hosp., Bklyn., 1955-56; med. resident Bklyn. Vets. Hosp., 1956-57, Montefiore Hosp., Bronx, N.Y., 1957-58; hematology resident Mt. Sinai Hosp., N.Y.C., 1958-59; pvt. practice White Plains, N.Y., 1961—; attending medicine and chief emeritus hematology dept. White Plains Hosp. Capt. USAF, 1959-61. Mem. Am. Soc. Internal Medicine, N.Y. Med. Soc., Westchester Med. Soc. Office: 15 Chester Ave White Plains NY 10601-5115

BIERSACK, GERTRUD MARIA, obstetrician, gynecologist, hospital administrator; b. Hanover, Germany, Jan. 27, 1934; d. Johann Ferdinand and Serotina (Lutter) B. MD, med. states exam., U. Munich, 1959, Approbation, 1961, specialist in ob-gyn., 1970. Intern hosp., Germany, 1959-61, med. officer, 1961-62; mission physician Cath. Mission, Ghana, 1962-66; sr. med. officer hosp., Stuttgart, Germany, 1966-68; sr. med. officer Mission Med. Clinic, Würzburg, Germany, 1968-70, mem. staff, 1970—; staff ob/gyn. Sacred Heart Hosp., Abeokuta, Nigeria, 1970—; cons. SHH, 1985—, med. dir., 1985—. Recipient honor Govt. of Germany, 1983, 1st degree honors, 1994, award Chieftancy Alake of Egbal, Abeokuta, 1983. Mem. Royal Soc. Medicine (London). Home and Office: Sacred Heart Hosp, PO Box 816, Abeokuta Ogun St, Nigeria

BIERSCHENK, BERNHARD FRIEDRICH, psychologist, researcher; b. Kassel, Hesse, Germany, May 5, 1941; arrived in Sweden, 1967; s. Friedrich Johannes and Gertrude Alma (Eckhart) B.; m. Inger Kristina Ericson, June 21, 1973. Tchr. tng., Sch. Edn., Goettingen, 1967; Candidate in Psychology, U. Lund, Sweden, 1969, lic. in Psychology, 1972, PhD, 1972, docent in social sci., 1972. Rsch. asst., assoc. project leader Sch. of Edn., Malmö, Sweden, 1967-72; dep. assoc. prof. Lund (Sweden) U., 1973-74, dep. prof., 1974-81; sr. rschr. Lund U., 1981—; prof. Erlangen U., Nüremberg, Germany, 1976; sessional lectr. U. Alberta, Edmonton, Can., 1979-80; resident Theoretical Psychology, Edmonton, Can., 1979-80; v.p. Computing Ctr., Lund, Sweden, 1981; vis. fellow Nat. Sci. Engrings. Rsch. Coun., Ottawa, Can., 1981-82, Psychol. Lab., Copenhagen, Denmark, 1994-95; founding mem. Copenhagen Competence Rsch. Ctr., 1994. Author 100 pubs.; editor Cognitive Sci. Rsch, 1984—. Sgt. Police Corps (Lower Saxony, Germany), 1962-66. Recipient rsch. award Swedish Coun for Soc. Sci. Rsch., Stockholm, 1973, Nat. Bur. Edn., Stockholm, 1976, Danish Rsch. Couns., Copenhagen, 1996. Mem. German Soc. Psychology, Am. Psychol. Assn., N.Y. Acad. Scis. Avocations: skiing, swimming, hiking. Home: Ljungsaetersvaegen 10, 23641 Höllviken Sweden Office: Lund U Dept Psychology, Paradisgatan 5P, 22350 Lund Sweden

BIERWAGEN, RAINER MICHAEL, lawyer, associate; b. Weinheim, Germany, Apr. 23, 1957; s. Rudolf Walter and Trudel Emmie (Schaerlinger) B. First State Exam, U. Freiburg, Germany, 1981; Second State Exam, Land Baden-Wuerttemberg, Germany, 1987; PhD, U. Konstanz, Germany, 1989. Rsch. asst. U. Konstanz, Germany, 1987-89; assoc. Van Bael & Bellis, Brussels, 1989-95, Kemmler Rapp Boehlke & Crosby, Brussels, 1995—. Contbr. numerous articles to profl. law jours. Home: Ave Albert Jonnart 37, B-1200 Brussels Belgium Office: Kemmler Rapp Boehlke & Crosby, 9 Rond Point Schuman, B-1040 Brussels Belgium

BIERWISCH, MANFRED, linguist, educator; b. Halle, Germany, July 28, 1930; s. Wilhelm and Hedwig (Wand) B.; m. Monika Fischinger, Dec. 12, 1975. PhD, U. Leipzig, Germany, 1960; DSc, Acad. Scis., Berlin, 1982; Dr. honoris causa, Friedrich-Schiller-U., Jena, Germany, 1992. Rsch. asst. Acad. Scis., Berlin, 1957-61, rsch. fellow, 1961-79, head of rsch. group cognitive linguistics, 1980-91; head rsch. unit structural grammar Max-Planck Soc., Berlin, 1991-96; prof. Humboldt U., Berlin, 1993—; external mem. Max-Planck Inst. for Psycholinguistics, Nijmegen, The Netherlands, 1985—. Author: Grammatik des deutschen Verbs, 1963, Modern Linguistics, 1966; author, editor: Dimensional Adjectives, 1989, Economy Principles in Linguistic Theory, 1996. Mem. Linguistic Soc. Am. (hon.), Hungarian Acad. Scis. (hon.), Saxonian Acad. Scis. (hon.), Goethe Inst. (mem. presidium 1992), Berlin-Brandenburg Acad. Scis. (v.p. 1993-98). Avocation: hiking. Home: Rüdesheimer Strasse 6, D-14197 Berlin Germany Office: Humboldt U, Jägerstrasse 10-11, D-10117 Berlin Germany

BIES, DAVID ALAN, mechanical engineering educator; b. L.A., Aug. 15, 1925; s. Milton Irving and Frances E. (Mitchell) B.; m. Helen Margret Ormerod, Nov. 24, 1954 (div. 1985); 1 child, Carolyn Ann. BA, UCLA, 1948, MA, 1951, PhD, 1953. Staff physicist Bodine Soundrive, L.A., 1954-59; cons. Bolt Beranek & Newman, L.A., 1959-72; reader dept. mech. engring. U. Adelaide, Australia, 1972-90, vis. rsch. fellow dept. mech. engring., 1991—. Co-author: Engineering Noise Control, 1988, 2d edit., 1996; contbr. articles to profl. jours. Fellow Acoustical Soc. Am., Australian Acoustical Soc., Internat. Inst. Sound and Vibration; mem. AAAS, Inst. Noise Control Engring., Sigma Xi. Office: U Adelaide, Dept Mech Engring, Adelaide SA 5005, Australia

BIESBROUCK, MAURITS ALBERT GEORGES, pathologist; b. Roeselare, Belgium, Feb. 15, 1946; s. Albert Biesbrouck and Paula Monteyne; m. Maria Verstraete; children: Evelyne, Bernard. Kandidaat Natuur-en Medische Wetenschappen, U. Louvain, Belgium, 1968, MD, 1972. Cert. in clin. pathology Belgian Dept. Health. Dir. Lab. Clin. Pathology, Roeselare, 1985—, Blood Bank, Roeselare, 1989-97; assoc. dir. Blood Banks, Flanders, Belgium, 1995—; chmn. Med. Coun. Blood Banks, Belgium, 1996-97; chmn. Societas Scientifica Transfusionis Flandriae, 1997—. Avocations: history of medicine, translation work of Vesalius' Fabrica. Home: Koning Leopold III Laan 52, B-8800 Roeselare Belgium

BIESELE, JOHN JULIUS, biologist, educator; b. Waco, Tex., Mar. 24, 1918; s. Rudolph Leopold and Anna Emma (Jahn) B.; m. Marguerite Calfee McAfee, July 29, 1943 (dec. 1991); children: Marguerite Anne, Diana Terry, Elizabeth Jane; m. Esther Aline Eakin, Mar. 9, 1992. B.A. with highest honors, U. Tex., 1939, Ph.D., 1942. Fellow Internat. Cancer Research Found., U. Tex., 1942-43, Barnard Skin and Cancer Hosp., St. Louis, also; Fellow U. Pa., 1943-44, instr. zoology, 1943-44; temporary research assoc. dept. genetics Carnegie Instn. of Washington, Cold Spring Harbor, 1944-46; research assoc. biology dept. Mass. Inst. Tech., 1946-47; asst. Sloan-Kettering Inst. Cancer Research, 1946-47, research fellow, 1947, assoc., 1947-55, head cell growth sect., div. exptl. chemotherapy, 1947-58, mem., 1955-58, assoc. scientist div., 1959-78; asst. prof. anatomy Cornell U. Med. Sch., 1950-52; assoc. prof. biology Sloan-Kettering div. Cornell U. Grad. Sch. Med. Scis., 1952-55, prof. biology, 1955-58; prof. zoology, mem. grad. faculty U. Tex., Austin, 1958-78; also mem. faculty U. Tex. (Coll. Pharmacy), 1969-71, prof. edn., 1973-78; prof. emeritus zoology U. Tex., Austin, 1978-99; prof. emeritus sect. molecular cell and developmental biol. U. Tex. Sch. Biol. Scis., Austin, 1999—; cons. cell biology M.D. Anderson Hosp. and Tumor Inst., U. Tex. at Houston, 1958-72; dir. Genetics Found., 1959-78; mem. cell biology study sect. NIH, 1958-63; Sigma Xi lectr. NYU Grad. Sch. Arts and Scis., 1957; Mendel lectr. St. Peter's Coll., Jersey City, 1958; featured spkr. on first Earth Day, Old Westbury Campus of N.Y. Inst. Tech., 1970; Mendel Club lectr. Canisius Coll., Buffalo, 1971; mem. adv. com. rsch. etiology of cancer Am. Cancer Soc., 1961-64, pres. Travis County unit, 1966, mem. adv. com. on personnel for rsch., 1969-73; counsellor Cancer Internat. Rsch. Coop., Inc., 1962-90; mem. cancer rsch. tng. com. Nat. Cancer Inst., 1969-72; gen. chmn. Conf. Advancement Sci. and Math. Teaching, 1966. Author: Mitotic Poisons and the Cancer Problem, 1958; mem. editorial bd. Year Book Cancer, 1959-72; mem. editorial adv. bd. Cancer Rsch., 1960-64, assoc. editor, 1969-72; cons. editor: Am. Jour. Mental Deficiency, 1963-68; mem. editorial bd. The Jour. of Applied Nutrition, 1987-91; contbr. articles to profl. jours. Research Career award NIH, 1962, 67, 72, 77. Fellow N.Y., Tex. acads. scis., AAAS; mem. Am. Assn. Cancer Research (dir. 1960-63), Am. Soc. Cell Biology, Am. Inst. Biol. Scis., Phi Beta Kappa, Sigma Xi (pres. Tex. chpt. 1963-64), Phi Eta Sigma, Phi Kappa Phi. Achievements include provision of early evidence for abnormal chromosome numbers in cancer cells, for occasional excessively multiple-stranded state of cancer chromosomes; demonstration of a direct relation of chromosomal size in mammalian tissues and organs to the local metabolic activity, as evidenced by the local content of B vitamins, of differential toxicity in certain antimetabolites to cancer cells in culture. Home: 2500 Great Oaks Pky Austin TX 78756-2908

BIETENHOLZ, WOLFGANG PETER, physicist; b. Basel, Switzerland, Sept. 23, 1962; s. Alfred Georg and Johanna (Greiner) B.; m. Helvia Marlene Velasquez Bietenholz, Dec. 7, 1989; children: Diego Guido, Alan Philippe. Diploma in Physics, ETH Zuerich, Switzerland, 1988; PhD in Theoretical Physics, U. Bern, Switzerland, 1992. Summer student CERN, Geneva, Switzerland, 1985, scientific collaborator, 1989; grad. student U. Bern, Switzerland, 1989-92; vis. scientist ITEP, Moscow, USSR, 1993; rsch. assoc. MIT, Cambridge, Mass., 1994-96; vis. scientist HLRZ/DESY, Juelich, Germany, 1996-98; rsch. assoc. NORDITA, Copenhagen, 1998—; asst. U. Bern, Switzerland, 1989-93; lectr. CBPF, Rio de Janeiro, Brazil, 1993-94. Contbr. articles to profl. jours. Mem. exec. bd. Verein der Mathematiker und Physiker, Zuerich, Switzerland, 1984-87. Recipient H.S. award Merian Found., Basel, Switzerland, 1979-81. Avocations: philosophy, history, bicycling, chess. E-mail address: biefenho@nordita.dk. Fax: 0045/35389157. Home: Kastelsvej 5, DK-2100 Copenhagen 0 Denmark Office: NORDITA, Blegdamsvej 17, DK-2100 Copenhagen Denmark

BIFFA, RICHARD CHARLES, waste management company executive; b. London, Dec. 23, 1939; s. Richard Frank and Alice Ethel Amiens (Berryman) B.; m. Sandra Lesley Taylor, Mar. 6, 1968 (div. 1978); children: Richard Matthew, Anthony Charles; m. Gillian Louise Poole-Warren, Feb. 19, 1983; 1 child, Harriet Grace. Student, Berkhamsted Sch. Mem. staff Biffa Ltd., Loudwater, Eng., 1958-60, plant ops. and maintenance staff, 1960-63, mgr. waste divsn., 1963-71, dir., mgr., 1971-74, gen. mgr., 1974-75; mng. dir. Biffa Waste Svcs., Loudwater, 1975-85; chmn. Rechem Inst., Bourne End, 1985-91; dep. chmn. Shanks & McEwan, Bourne End, 1991—; mem. exec. com. White Ensign Co.; non-exec. dir. Try Group. Mem. Inst. Waste Mgmt., Royal Southampton Yacht Club, Phyllis Ct. Club. Office: Shanks & McEwan Group PLC, Shanks Group PLC, Astor House Station Rd, Bourne End Bucks SL8 5YP, England

BIFFI, GIACOMO CARDINAL, archbishop; b. Milan, June 13, 1928. Ordained priest Roman Cath. Ch., 1950. Consecrated bishop of Fidene and aux. of Milan, 1975, consecrated, 1976; archbishop of Bologna, Italy, 1984; created cardinal, 1985. Office: Archivescovdo, Via Altabella 6, I-40126 Bologna Italy*

BIFULCO, ANTONIA TERESA, psychiatrist, researcher; b. Derby, Eng., Mar. 18, 1955; d. Jerzy Tadeusz Czechowski and Christine Elizabeth (O'Neill) Czechowska; m. Vincent Bifulco, Sept. 9, 1976; 1 child, Lucia. BA, Exeter (Eng.) U., 1976; PhD, U. London, 1985. Groupworker Psychiat. Rehab., London, 1976-77; research asst. Bedford Coll., U. London, 1980-85; research officer Royal Holloway and Bedford New Coll., U. London, 1985—. Contbr. articles to profl. jours. and chpts. to books. Office: U London Royal Holloway, and Bedford New Coll, London WC1 B3RA, England

BIGALKE, HANS GÜNTHER, mathematician, educator; b. Celle, Germany, Feb. 23, 1933; m. Gisela Mahnke, 1958; children: Matthias, Sebastian. Staatsex, Tech. Hochschule Hannover, Germany, 1957, D Natural Scis., 1967; staatsex, Studiensem. Hannover, 1958. Studienref. OstRat Gymnasium, Hannover, Germany, 1957-68; cons. Stiftung Volkswagenwerk, Hannover, 1968-71; StDir. Gymnasium, Hannover, 1971-72; prof. Paed. Hochschule, Hannover, 1972-78; prof. U. Hannover, 1978-98, prof. emeritus, 1998—. Author: Kugelgeometrie, 1984, Heinrich Heesch-Kristallgeometrie Parkettierungen, Vierfarbenforschung, 1988; co-author: Didaktik der Mathematik, vol. 1, 1977, vol. 2, 1978, Regulaere Parkettierungen, 1994, Fachwerkhäuser, 2000. Mem. Deutsche Mathematiker-VereivigUng Gesellschaft fur Didaktik der Mathematik (chmn. 1975-80). Home: Leuschnerstr 24, D-29223 Celle Germany Office: Univ Hannover, Bismarckstr 2, D-30173 Hannover Germany

BIGANZOLI, ELIA MARIO, biostatistician; b. Tradate, Varese, Italy, Apr. 18, 1966; s. Antonio and Maria Luisa (Bisiach) B.; m. Caterina Santoro, Dec. 6, 1992; children: Davide, Giacomo. PhD, U. Milan, 1994. Biostatistician Istituto Nazionale Tumori, Milan, 1995—; cons. rschr. Marion Merrel Dow, Milan, 1989-95; bd. dirs. Italian com. for the evaluation of quality in the oncological lab., 1997. Contbr. articles to profl. jours. Mem. civil svc. Cascina Verde, Milan, 1991. Rsch. grant G. Lorenzini Found., Milan, 1989-94. Mem. Internat. Biometric Soc., Internat. Soc. of Clin. Biostatistics. Avocations: skiing, Alpinism, gardening. Home: Via Mazzini 4, 21036 Gemonio Varese, Italy Office: Istituto Nazionale Tumori, Via Venezian 1, 20133 Milan Italy

BIGAZZI, MARIO AMELIO, endocrinologist; b. Reggello, Italy, Feb. 5, 1938; s. Enrico and Iolanda (Giannini) B.; m. Maria Stella Reali, July 4, 1970; children: Benedetta, Prospero, Martino, Bernardo. Degree in medicine, U. Florence, 1962, cert. specialist in cardiology, 1965, cert. specialist in endocrinology, 1967. Mem. med. staff Army Sch. Medicine, Florence, Italy, 1963-64; asst. U. Florence, 1964-69; med. rsch. assoc. U. Chgo., 1969-71; assoc. prof. Poggiosecco Hosp. INRCA, Florence, 1971-86; gen. mgr. Prosperius Inst., Florence, 1975—; lectr., U. Milan, 1964-89, U. Florence, 1971-89. Patentee in field; editor: Relaxin in Humans, 1983; contbr. 150 articles to med. jours. Pres., Salviatino Park Com., Florence, 1985-89; mem. coun., USLN 10/A, Florence, 1986-88. Lt. Italian armed forces, 1983-84. NATO fellow, Rome, 1969. Mem. Endocrine Soc., N.Y. Acad. Scis., Italian Soc. Endocrinology, Soc. Andrologia, Rotary, Yacht Club Punta Ala. Roman Catholic. Avocations: gardening, skiing, sailing, painting. Office: Prosperius Inst, Viale Fratelli Rosselli 62, 50123 Florence Italy

BIGELOW, DANIEL JAMES, aerospace executive; b. Harrisville, Pa., Mar. 26, 1935; s. Raymond James and Hilda Irene (Graham) B.; m. Elizabeth Jane Allison, Sept. 10, 1955; 1 child, Allison Jane. BFA in Art Advt., Kent (Ohio) State U., 1957; MA in Edn., La. Tech. U., 1974; MS in Polit. Sci., Auburn U., 1986; MS, Air U., 1987; postgrad., Ohio State U., 1989—. Commd. 2d lt. USAF, 1957, advanced through grades to col., 1979, ret., 1987; command pilot 167 combat missions Vietnam; air attaché to Soviet Union, 1983-85; dir. Soviet program Air War Coll. Air U., Ala., 1985-87; gen. mgr. aerospace divsn. Modern Techs. Corp., Dayton, Ohio, 1988-98; dir. programs corp. hdqrs. Modern Techs. Corp., Dayton, 1998—. Contbr. articles to profl. jours.; author, editor: Soviet Studies, 1986-88. Decorated Legion of Merit with one oak leaf cluster, DFC, 14 Air medals, Def. Superior medal; recipient U.S. Am. Nat. award CIA Dir., William J. Casey, 1985. Mem. Acad. Polit. Sci., Air Rescue Assn. (mem. nat. bd. dirs., historian), Air Force Assn., Am. Def. Preparedness Assn., Discussion Club Dayton (v.p.), Internat. Platform Assn., F-86 Sabre Pilots' Assn., B-52 Stratofortress Assn., The Ret. Officers' Assn., Order Daedalians, Shriners, Airlift/Tanker Assn., Dayton Area Def. Contractors Assn. (pres.), Armed Forces Comms. and Electronics Assn., Def. Planning and Analysis Soc., Miami Valley Mil. Affairs Assn., Inst. of Navigation, Pararescue Assn., Royal Air Force Club, Electronic Engring. and Mfg. Group, Air Force Museum Found., Nat. Def. Indsl. Assn., Dayton Art Inst., Assn. Old Crows, Air Force Assn. of Cmty. Ptnrs., Dayton Area C. of C. Presbyterian. Avocations: art, photography, jogging. Home: 2537 Indian Wells Trl Xenia OH 45385-9373

BIGELOW, JOHN CHRISTOPHER, philosophy educator; b. Montreal, Que., Can., Feb. 4, 1948; arrived in Australia, 1978; s. Robert Sidney and Moyra Frances (Hale) B.; m. Elizabeth Ruth Cardno, Dec. 7, 1968; children: Stephen John, Benjamin David. BA, U. Canterbury, Christchurch, New Zealand, 1968; MA, Simon Fraser U., Vancouver, Can., 1970; PhD, U. Cambridge, Eng., 1973. Lectr. Victoria U., Wellington, New Zealand, 1973-78; lectr. La Trobe U., Melbourne, Australia, 1978-79, sr. lectr., 1980-88, reader, 1989-91; vis. lectr. Simon Fraser U., Vancouver, 1989; prof. Monash U., Melbourne, 1991—. Author: The Reality of Numbers, 1989; (with R.J. Pargetter) Science and Necessity, 1990; assoc. editor Australasian Jour. Philosophy, 1990—. Rsch. grantee Australian Rsch. Coun., Canberra, 1992; Daniel Taylor fellow U. Otago, Dunedin, New Zealand, 1991. Fellow Australian Acad. Humanities, Australasian Assn. Philosophy (pres. 1994). Office: Monash U Sch Philos Linguis, Wellington Rd, Clayton VIC 3800, Australia

BIGELOW, ROBERT WILSON, trial lawyer; b. L.A., Oct. 22, 1964; s. William Phillips and Dona (Heath) B.; m. Madeline Garcia, Sept. 24, 1995; children: William, Emma. Student, UCLA, 1982-84; BA with distinction, U. N.Mex., 1990; JD, Georgetown U., 1993. Bar: N.Y. Intern FTC, Washington, 1992; mem. Georgetown Criminal Justice Clinic, Washington, 1992-93; sr. staff aty. Criminal Def. divsn. Legal Aid Soc., Bronx, N.Y., 1993-2000, supervising atty., 2000—; mentor John Jay Legal Svcs., Inc., White Plains, N.Y., 1997—. Mem. ABA (criminal justice sect. 1996—, def. function/svcs. com. 1996—), Assn. Legal Aid Attys. (rep. 1997-99, alt. v.p. 1999—). Democrat. Episcopalian. Avocation: baseball research. Home: 154 Ferry St Newark NJ 07105-2111 Office: Legal Aid Soc Criminal Def Divsn 1020 Grand Concourse Bronx NY 10451-2605

BIGERELLE, MAXENCE, material science educator; b. Douai, France, Nov. 16, 1964; s. Willy-Max and Antoinette (Lachambre) B.; m. Isabelle Prouveur, July 4, 1993; children: Maximilien, Lorelei. Diploma 1st cycle technique, Nat. Conserv. Arts & Materials, Lille, France, 1992, diploma d'etudes superieures techniques, 1994, degree in engring., 1995, D with honors, 1999. Chemist Beghin, Corbehem, 1988-89; statistician Sollac, Biache, France, 1989-95; prof. Ecole Nat. Supérieure d'arts et Métriers, Lille, 1995—; cons. Fedn. Biomaterials, France, 1997—; mgr. surface and interface

ENSAM, Lille, 1996-99. Contbr. articles to profl. jours. Served with French mil., 1987-88. Avocation: aquariology. Home: 102 rue Marcel Prouveur, 59111 Lieu St Amand France Office: ENSAM, 8 Blvd Louis XIV, 59046 Lille France

BIGGER, STEPHEN WILLIAM, chemistry educator; b. Melbourne, Australia, Sept. 1, 1955; s. William Samuel and Kathleen (Armstrong) B.; m. Elizabeth Margaretha Maria Veenker, July 22, 1989; children: Andrew, David, Myra and Leah (twins). B of Applied Sci. with honors, U. Melbourne, 1978, PhD, 1983. From sr. demonstrator to lectr. phys. chemistry U. Melbourne, 1983-91; lectr. chemistry Victoria U. Tech., Melbourne, 1991-92, sr. lectr. chemistry, 1993-97, assoc. prof., 1998—; lectr. and presenter in field. Co-author: (with others) Photophysics of Polymers, 1987, Progress in Pacific Polymer Science, 1991; (with K.P. Ghiggino and A.D. Scully) The Effects of Radiation on High-Technology Polymers, 1989; (with J. Scheirs and O. Delatycki) Integration of Fundamental Polymer Science and Technology, 1991, Die Makromolekulare Chemie, Macromolecular Symposium, 1993; book rev. Am. Chem. Soc., Trends in Polymer Sci., Australian Jour. Chemistry, Chemistry in Australia; contbr. articles to profl. jours. Recipient numerous rsch. grants, 1988-96; recipient Commonwealth Postgrad. award Australian Govt., 1978. Mem. Royal Australian Chem. Inst., Soc. Chem. Industry Victoria, Am. Chem. Soc., Chemistry Edn. Assn., Inc. (life). Avocations: running, music, family. Office: Victoria Univ Tech, PO Box 14428 MCMC, 8001 Melbourne Australia

BIGGS, BRENDAN JOHN HOWARD, language and literature educator; b. Bristol, Eng., Oct. 22, 1963; s. Kenneth John and Barbara (Emms) B. BA in English Lang. and Lit., U. Oxford, 1985, MA, 1989, DPhil, 1992. Lectr. in English Keble Coll. U. Oxford, 1988-89; lectr. in English Corpus Christi Coll. U. Oxford, 1989-96, asst. dean, 1994-96; lectr. in English Christ Ch. U. Oxford, 1996-97, 99-2000, Trinity Coll. U. Oxford, 1996—. Editor: The Imitation of Christ: The First English Translation of the Imitatio Christi, 1997. Sec. parochial ch. coun. St. Andrew's Ch., Oxford, 1995-2000, church warden, 2000—. Mem. Oxford Medieval Soc. (sec. 1988-92). Office: Trinity College, Oxford OX1 3BH, England

BIGGS, JOHN HERRON, insurance company executive; b. St. Louis, July 19, 1936; s. Peter Willis and Lillian (Herron) B.; m. Penelope Frances Parkman, June 13, 1959; 1 child, Henry. AB magna cum laude, Harvard U., 1958; PhD in Econ., Wash. U., 1983. V.p., contr. Gen. Am. Ins. Co., 1970-77; vice chancellor for adminstrn. and fin. Washington U., St. Louis, 1977-85; chmn., pres., chief exec. officer Centerre Trust Co., 1985-89; pres., COO Tchrs. Ins. and Annuity Assn./Coll. Retirement Equities Fund, 1989-93, chmn., pres., CEO, 1993—; bd. dirs. Boeing Co., Ralston Purina Co.; trustee Tchrs. Ins. and Annuity Assn./Coll. Retirement Equities Fund, 1982—; emeritus trustee, former pres. Mo. Bot. Garden; mem. Fin. Acctg. Found., N.Y.C. Partnership. Trustee Washington U., Getty Trust & Fgn. Policy Assn.; chmn. Nat. Bur. Econ. Affairs, Danforth Found., Ch. Pension Fund; bd. dirs., chmn. United Way of N.Y.C. Fellow Soc. Actuaries; mem. Am. Acad. Arts and Scis., Am. Acad. Actuaries (bd. dirs. 1970-73), Bus. Higher Edn. Forum, Westchester Country Club, Sky Club, Harvard Club N.Y., Log Cabin Club, St. Louis Club. Home: 240 E 47th St Apt 23D New York NY 10017-2137 Office: TIAA/CREF 730 3rd Ave New York NY 10017-3206

BIGGS, PETER MARTIN, veterinary scientist, virologist; b. Petersfield, Hampshire, Eng., Aug. 13, 1926; s. Ronald and Cecile Agnes (Player) B.; m. Alison Janet Molteno, Sept. 9, 1950; children: Alison Sarah Stanley, Andrew Martin, John Philip. BSc, London U., 1953, DSc, 1975; PhD, Bristol (Eng.) U., 1958; DVM (hon.), Ludwig-Maxmillian U., Munich, Germany, 1976; D (hon.), U. Liege, 1991. Rsch. asst. Bristol U., 1953-55, lectr., 1955-59; head leukosis unit Houghton Poultry Rsch. Sta., Eng., 1959-73, dep. dir., 1971-73, dir., 1974-86; dir. Agrl. and Food Rsch. Coun. Inst. Animal Health, Eng., 1986-88; vis. prof. Royal Vet. Coll., U. London, 1982—; Andrew D. White prof. at large Cornell U., Ithaca, N.Y., 1988-94. Cpl. RAF, 1944-48. Recipient Joszef Marek medal Vet. U. Budapest, Hungary, 1979, Wolf Internat. prize for agr. Wolf Found., Israel, 1989; named Comdr. of Order of Brit. Empire, 1987. Fellow Acad. Med. Scis., Royal Coll. Vet. Surgeons, Royal Coll. Pathologists, Inst. Biology and Chartered Biologist (pres. 1990-92), Royal Soc.; mem. Internat. Assn. Comparative Rsch. on Leukemia and Related Diseases (pres. 1981-83), World Vet. Poultry Assn. (pres. 1981-85), Farmers Club, Athenaeum. Avocations: music, choral singing, boating, gardening, natural history. Home and Office: Willows, London Rd, St Ives PE27 5ES, England

BIGLIARDO, ROBERTO FELICE, foreign diplomat; b. Pomigliano d'Arco, Italy, Jan. 28, 1952. Mem. European Parliament, 1999—, mem. com. on employment and social affairs, com. fgn. affairs/human rights/common security/def. policy; mem. Tech. Group of Ind. Mems.; mem. del. for relations with Australia and N.Z. *

BIGNON, YVES-JEAN, oncologist, geneticist; b. Paris, Aug. 5, 1955; s. Michel and Marcelle (Guillaumin) B.; m. Edith Amiot, Mar. 21, 1999; children: Anne, Jean-Luc, Alice. MD, U. Clermont-Ferrand, 1984, PhD, 1991. From intern in medicine to asst. U. Auvergne, France, 1980-89; INSERM fellow U. Calif., San Diego, 1989-90; conf. master U. Auvergne, 1991-92; prof. U. Blaise Pascal, France, 1992—; prof. oncology, biology U. Auvergne, Clermont-Ferrand, France, 1997—; pres. Genetics and Cancer Group, France, 1993—; scientific bd. Nat. League Against Cancer, 1994—, Nat. Fedn. Cancer Ctrs., 1994—; founding mem. INSERM genetics com., 1995—. Recipient gold medal Internat. Jour. Medicine, 1994. Mem. European Soc. Human Genetics, Am. Assn. Cancer Rsch., French Soc. Genetic Counseling, Am. Soc. Human Genetics. Roman Catholic. Avocations: theology, long distance running, wine, music. Office: Ctr J Perrin BP392 Oncol, 58 rue Montalembert, 63011 Clermont-Ferrand France

BIGSBY, CHRISTOPHER WILLIAM, humanities educator, writer, broadcaster; b. Dundee, Scotland, June 27, 1941; s. Edgar Edward Leo and Ivy May (Hopkins) B.; m. Pamela Joan Lovelady, Oct. 9, 1965; children: Gareth Christopher, Kirsten Rebecca, Bella Juliet Natasha, Ewan James. BA, Sheffield (Eng.) U., 1962, MA, 1964; PhD, Nottingham U., 1966. Lectr. U. Wales, Aberystwyth, Wales, 1966-69; from lectr. to prof. U. East Anglia, Norwich, Eng., 1969—. Critical works include Confrontation and Commitment: A Study of Contemporary American Drama, 1967, The Black American Writer Vols. I and II, 1971, Superculture, 1975, Edward Albee, 1975, Approaches to Popular Culture, 1976, The Second Black Renaissance 1980, Contemporary English Drama, 1981, A Critical Introduction to 20th Century American Drama, 3 Vols., 1982, 84, 85, David Mamet, 1982, Modern American Drama 1945-1990, 1992, (novels) Hester, 1994, Pearl, 1995, Still Lives, 1996; editor: The Portable Arthur Miller, 1995, The Cambridge Companion to Arthur Miller, 1997, (with Don Wilmeth) The Cambridge History of American Theatre, 3 vols., 1998-2000, Contemporary American Playwrights, 1999; also TV and radio plays, short stories, cassettes, documentaries and contributed to reference works. Fulbright scholar, 1963. Fellow Royal Soc. Literature. Home: 3 Church Farm Colney, Norwich, Norfolk NR4 7TX, England Office: Univ East Anglia, Sch English & Am Studies, Norwich NR4 7TJ, England

BIH, HERNG-DAR, environmental psychologist; b. I-Lan, Taiwan, Sept. 15, 1959; s. Tien-Sen Bih and Hsiu-Chin Chang. BS, Nat. Taiwan U., 1980, MS, 1982; PhD, CUNY, 1992. Tchg. asst. Nat. Taiwan U., Taipei, 1984-86; dir. Rsch. Ctr. of Gender and Space, 1995—. Author: Women Who Search for Spaces, 1996, The Story of Things, 1996. Mem. com. Ministry of Edn., Taiwan, 1997, Taipei City Govt., 1996. Mem. Am. Psychol. Assn. (Dissertation award 1990), Environ. Design Rsch. Assn. Avocations: badminton, jogging. Office: Grad Inst Bldg/Nat Taiwan U, 1 Sec 4 Roosevelt Rd, Taipei 106, Taiwan

BIHARI, IMRE, physician; b. Szombathely, Hungary, Mar. 4, 1950; s. Erno and Anna Veronika (Kreismann) B.; m. Zsofia Adam, Oct. 12, 1974; children: Peter, Anna, Andras. MD magna cum laude, Semmelweis Med. U., Budapest, Hungary, 1974; PhD, SOTE, Budapest, Hungary, 1989. Cert. in gen. surgery and vascular surgery. Resident HIETE Postgrad. Med. Sch., Budapest, 1974-78, surgeon, 1978-95, asst. prof., 1995-98, assoc. prof., 1998—; mem. sci. coms. World Congress of Phlebology, London, 1995, Sydney, 1998, European Congress of Phlebology, Brema, 1999. Founder, editor-in-chief Vascular Diseases, 1994—; contbr. more than 150 articles to profl. jours. Mem. Hungarian Soc. for Surgery, Hungarian Soc. for Angiology and Vascular Surgery (bd. dris.), Internat. Coll. Angiology (mem. sci. coun.), Internt. Soc. for Study of Vascular Anomalies, European Lymphology Group. Home: Czako 11, 1016 Budapest Hungary Office: HIETE Postgrad Med U, Szabolcs St, 1389 Budapest Hungary

BIJNENS, JOHAN L., theoretical physics researcher; b. Tongeren, Belgium, Sept. 3, 1960; arrived in Sweden, 1997; s. Jos and Nicole (Bollars) B.; m. Anna K. Tollsten, Oct. 6, 1990; children: Sara, Peter. Lic. Physics, U. Leuven, Belgium, 1978; PhD, Calif. Inst. Tech., 1985; Dr.rer.nat.habil., U. Munich, Germany, 1993. Asst. prof. theoretical physics Nordisk Inst Teoretisk Fysik, Copenhagen, 1992-2000; now assoc. prof. theoretical physics Lund (Sweden) U., 2000—. Contbr. articles to profl. jours. Office: Nordita, Lund U, Theoretical Physics, Solvegatan 14A, S22362 Lund Sweden

BIJUR, PETER I., petroleum company executive; b. N.Y.C.; children: Kristin Anne, Matthew Montgomery, David Barrett. BA in Polit. Sci., U. Pitts., 1964; MBA, Columbia U., 1966. Various dist. and regional sales positions Texaco, Inc., 1966-71, mgr. Buffalo sales dist., 1971-73, asst. to sr. v.p. for pub. affairs, 1973-75, staff coord. dept. strategic planning, 1975-77, asst. to exec. v.p. Buffalo sales dist., 1977-80; mgr. Rocky Mountain Refining & Mktg., 1980-81, asst. to chmn. bd., 1981-84; pres. Texaco Oil Trading and Supply Co., 1984, v.p. spl. projects, 1984-86; pres., chief exec. officer Texaco Can. Inc., Don Mills, Ont., 1987-89; chmn. Texaco Ltd., London, 1989-91; pres. Texaco Europe, 1990-92; sr. v.p. Texaco, Inc., White Plains, N.Y., 1992-96, vice chmn. bd., 1996, chmn. bd. dirs., CEO, 1996—; dir. Am. Petroleum Inst., Internat. Paper Co.; chmn. bus. coun. N.Y. State. Trustee The Conf. Bd., Middlebury Coll., Mt. Sinai-NYU Med. Ctr.; mng. dir. Met. Opera; bd. mgrs. N.Y. Botanical Garden. Fellow Inst. Petroleum, Royal Soc. Arts (London); mem. Bus. Coun., Bus. Roundtable, Nat. Petroleum Coun., Coun. Fgn. Rels., Country Club of New Canaan. Office: Texaco Inc 2000 Westchester Ave Purchase NY 10577-2530

BIK, AART JOHANNES CASIMIR, software engineer; b. Gouda, The Netherlands, May 31, 1969; came to U.S., 1996; s. J.J.H. Bik and A.E.A. Huls. MS cum laude in Computer Sci., Utrecht (The Netherlands) U., 1992; PhD in Computer Sci., Leiden (The Netherlands) U., 1996. Postdoctoral rschr. Ind. U., Bloomington, 1996-97; sr. software engr. Intel Corp., Santa Clara, 1997—. Lutheran. Avocation: chess. Office: Intel Corp SC12-301 2200 Mission College Blvd Santa Clara CA 95054-1549

BIKALES, NORBERT M., chemist, science administrator; b. Berlin, Jan. 7, 1929; came to U.S., 1946; s. Salomon and Bertha (Bander) B.; m. Gerda V. Bierzonski, Apr. 28, 1951; children: Marguerite Sarlin, Edward A. BS in Chemistry, CCNY, 1951; MS in Chemistry, Polytech. U., 1956; PhD in Chemistry, Poly. U., 1961. Rsch. chemist Am. Cyanamid Co., Stamford, Conn., 1951-62; tech. dir. Gaylord Assocs., Newark, 1962-65; pres. N.M. Bikales & Co., Cons., Livingston, N.J., 1965-76; prof. chemistry, dir. continuing edn. in scis. Rutgers U., New Brunswick and Newark, N.J., 1973-79; dir. polymers program NSF, Washington, 1976-95; head Europe office NSF, Paris, 1995-98; trustee Gordon Rsch. Conf., 1990-97, Fedn. Materials Soc., 1998—. Editor Encyclopedia of Polymer Science and Technology, 1962-77; mem. editorial bd. Encyclopedia of Polymer Science and Engineering, 1982-90; contbr. articles to profl. jours., chpts. to books. Pres., Friends of Livingston (N.J.) Libr., 1968-72, Livingston Symphony Orch., 1970-76; judge Internat. Tech. Film '89 Festival, Pardubice, Czechoslovakia, 1989. Recipient award Twp. of Livingston, 1976, Great Medal City of Paris, 1985, Disting. Alumnus award Poly. U., Bklyn., 1986, Disting. Lectr. award Soc. Polymer Sci., Tokyo, 1986, Chevalier des Palmes Académiques award French Govt., 1993, Medal Polish Acad. Scis., 1997, Disting. Svc. award, NSF, 1999. Fellow AAAS, Internat. Union Pure and Applied Chemistry (titular mem., sec. 1979-87, 93-97, chmn. commn. on recycling of polymers 1993-98, fellow 1998—), Am. Phys. Soc., N.Y. Acad. Sci.; mem. Am. Chem. Soc. (councilor 1987-89, chmn. polymer divsn. 1983, emeritus 2000—), Soc. Plastics Engrs. (sr., bd. dirs. 1979-82), Polish Chem. Soc. (hon.), Groupe Français des Polymères (sci. counselor 1994-99). Achievements include 26 patents in materials, chemicals and chemical processes.

BILACEROĞLU, SEMRA, pulmonary specialist; b. Demirci, Manisa, Turkey, Apr. 12, 1960; d. Hüseyin and Ülker (Aysan) B. Grad., Am. Coll. Inst., Izmir, Turkey, 1978; MD, Aegean U., 1984. Head doctor Bogazliyan Tb Dispensary, Yozgat, Turkey, 1984-87; practitioner Karsiyaka Tb Dispensary, Izmir, 1987, Ali Halim Bayer Tb Dispensary, Izmir, 1987; physician-in-trainee Izmir Chest Diseases and Surgery Tng. and Rsch. Hosp., 1987, pulmonary specialist, 1992, head trainees, 1992—. Asst. editor Izmir Chest Hosp. Jour., Izmir, Turkey, 1989. Recipient awards Turkish Soc. Respiratory Rsch., Istanbul, 1998, Am. Thoracic Soc., San Diego, 1999. Mem. Turkish Thoracic Soc., European Respiratory Soc. (mem. diagnostic methods sci. group 1992—, congress sponsorship 1994). Avocations: walking, reading, travel, exercising, medical and social exchange through internet. Home: Inonu Cad No 656/15, 35290 Izmir Turkey Office: Izmir Gogus Hast Hastanesi, 35110 Izmir Turkey

BILAL, NASER ELDIN, microbiologist, consultant; b. Abu-Hugar, Sudan, July 1, 1952; s. Bilal Mohamed Ehaimir and Halima El-Bushari El-Nagi; m. Fatma Emam Othman, Dec. 29, 1979; children: Mohamed, Hana, Abdul, Rahman, Yousef, Ibrahim. BSc, Khardoum (Sudan) U., 1975; MPH, Alexandria (Egypt) U., 1983; DPH, Mansoura (Egypt) U., 1990. Med. lab. technologist Nat. Health Lab., Khartoum, 1975-76; demonstrator Inst. Med. Lab. Tech., Khartoum, 1975-76; sr. lab. technologist Nat. Coun. Rsch., Khartoum, 1976-78; demonstrator Riyadh (Saudi Arabia) U., 1979-81; lectr. King Saud U., Riyadh, 1984-99; asst. prof. microbiology, cons. King Khalid U., Abha, Saudi Arabia, 1999—; cons. and chmn. microbiology lab., Abha Maternity and Tchg. Hosp., 1995—, infection control officer, chmn. infection control and surveillance team, 1995—; cons. microbiologist Asir Ctrl. & Tchg. Hosp., Abha, 1990—. Contbr. over 27 articles to internat. profl. jours. Active Umma Party, Sudan, including mem. augmented coun., 1998; chmn. Sudanese cmty. sect., southwestern region Saudi Arabia, 1990—. Mem. Am. Soc. Microbiology, N.Y. Acad. Scis. Moslem. Avocation: soccer. Office: Abha Med Coll King Khalid U, PO Box 641, Abha Saudi Arabia

BILBAO, JESÚS MARIO, mathematics educator; b. Bilbao, Basque, Spain, Apr. 17, 1954; s. Jesús and Maria Luisa (Arrese) B.; m. Encarnación Rodriguez, Mar. 3, 1968. Grad., Faculty of Math., Seville, Spain, 1978; PhD in Applied Math., U. Seville, 1981. Asst. rschr. U. Seville, 1978-81, assoc. prof., 1982-84, prof., 1984—; assoc. prof. U. Alicante, Spain, 1981-82; vice rector U. Seville, 1987-88, dir. rsch. group on game theory, 1995—. Author: Cooperative Games on Combinatorial Structures, 2000; editor: Advances in Game Theory, 1999 (rsch. prize U. Seville 1998). Grantee U. Seville, 1997, Andalusian Govt., 1999. Mem. Game Theory Soc., Math. Programming Soc., Spanish Soc. of Operational Rsch., Amnesty Internat. E-mail: mbilbao@cica.es. Office: Escuela Super Ingenieros, Camino de los Descubrimient, 41092 Seville Spain

BILFINGER, THOMAS VICTOR, surgeon, educator; b. Ridgewood, N.J., May 4, 1952; s. Victor Wilhelm and Heidi Erika (Muser) B.; m. Celia Betty Dameron; children: Elizabeth, Christine, Michael. MD, U. Zurich, Switzerland, 1978, ScD, 1979. Intern U. Chgo., 1980-81, rsch. fellow, 1981-82; resident in surgery U. Tex. Med. Br., Galveston, 1982-86, resident in cardiovascular surgery, 1986-88, instr. in surgery, 1988-89; asst. prof. surgery SUNY, Stony Brook, 1989-92, assoc. prof. surgery, 1992-99, prof. surgery, chief thoracic surgery, 1999—; bd. dirs. cardiovascular intensive care unit SUNY, Stony Brook; rsch. assoc. Neurosci. Inst., SUNY, Old Westbury; sr. rsch. scientist Mind/Body Med. Inst., Harvard med. Sch., Mass.; mem. spl. populations rsch. dept. faculty NIDA, 1994—. Co-author: Evaluation of the Cardiac Surgical Candidate, 1992; mem. editl. bd. Advances in Neuroimmunology; guest editor: Inst. Jour. Cardiology, 1996, 98. Recipient Rsch. grant U. Chgo., 1981, Rsch. grant Eli Lilly, 1989, Rsch. grant NIH, 1991, Career Opportunity Rsch. Tng. award NIMH. Fellow ACS, Am. Coll. Cardiology, Am. Coll. Chest Physicians; mem. Am. Assn. Thoracic Surgeyr, Assn. for Acad. Surgery, Soc. Critical Care Medicine, Swiss Soc. Thoracic and Cardiovasc. Surgery, Soc. Thoracic Surgery. Office: SUNY Stony Brook Health Sc Ctr T19 Rm 080 Stony Brook NY 11794-0001

BILGER, DORINNE POTTER, musician, educator; b. Penn Yan, N.Y., Apr. 9, 1945; d. Lyndon Wainwright and Anna Emma Sarah (Salecker) Potter; m. David Victor Bilger, Dec. 30, 1966; 1 child, Daniel Victor. MusB, Ithaca Coll., 1967; postgrad., U. Hartford, 1970. Music specialist Haverling Schs., Bath, N.Y., 1967-68; mucis specialist Gov. Mifflin Schs., Shillington, Pa., 1968-70; piano instr. Bilger Music Studio, Shillington, 1968—; ptnr., pres. Bilger Products, Shillington, 1980—; piano performer, 1970-96. Recorded several chamber music repertoires, 1977-94. Mem. Am. Coll. Musicians, Piano Tchrs. Guild, Reading Music Tchrs. Assn., Music Tchrs. Nat. Assn., Sigma Alpha Iota. Home: 1200 Bedford Ave Shillington PA 19607-2353

BILGIC, ATTILA MICHAEL, physics researcher; b. Marl, Germany, Mar. 17, 1968; s. Agah and Margarete B.; m. Filiz Yildirim, June 10, 1994; children: Nora, MEral. Diploma in physics, U. Dortmund, Germany, 1996. Rsch. asst. U. Dortmund, Germany, 1996—. Contbr. articles to profl. jours.; patentee in field. Office: U Dortmund, Otto-Hahn Str 6, 44221 Dortmund Germany

BILGIN, NUH, mining engineer, educator; b. Lapseki, Ganakkale, Turkey, June 26, 1949; s. Mustafa and Nezihe (Bellibas) B.; m. Ayfer Uslu; 1 child, Damlanur. BSc in Mining Engring., Istanbul (Turkey) Tech. U., 1973; PhD in Mining Engring., U. Newcastle Upon Tyne, Eng., 1977. Lectr. mining engring. dept. Istanbul Tech. U., 1978-88, 89-93, 1994—, head Faculty Mines and Mining Engring. Dept., 1998—; vis. prof. U. Witwatersrand, Johannesburg, South Africa, 1988-89, Colo. Sch. Mines, Golden, 1993-94. Avocation: numismatics. Home: Erde Cad 18/31, Istanbul Turkey Office: Istanbul Tech Univ, 80626 Maslak-Istanbul Turkey

BILGIN, YASAR, physician; b. Mersin, Icel, Turkey, June 15, 1950; s. Ömer and Hatice Bilgin; m. Esra Akay, Apr. 17, 1986 (div. Jan. 1991); m. Cigdem Hayat Guuenc; children: Hatice, Nazli. MD, Justus Liebig U., 1978, PhD, 1981. Physician Justus Liebig U., Giessen, Germany, 1978-80, specialist of internal medicine, 1983—; physician Max Planck Assn., Bad Nauheim, Germany, 1980-83; guest prof. Humana Heart Inst., Ky., 1984; cons. Turkish Radion TV, Ankara, 1990-95, Turkish U., 1988—. Editor (newspaper) Saglik, 1990-95, Tercuman, 1988-92. Pres. Turkish-German Health Found., 1988—, The Coun. of Turkish Citizen Germany, 1993; mem. integration adv. coun. Social Min. of Hessen. Mem. AIDS-HILFE, German Lipid Liga, Am. Heart Assn. Office: Turkish German Found Health, Friedrich Str 13, 35392 Giessen Germany

BILGINOGLU, FARUK, marketing professional, human resources specialist; b. Istanbul, Turkey, Mar. 24, 1972; s. Mehmet and Ayse Ifakat (Basaran) B.; m. Emine Sarikaya, Sept. 3, 1996, 1 son, Mehmet. BBA, Marmara U., Istanbul, 1995, M in Human Resources, 1997. Mktg. mgr. Rotasoto, Istanbul, 1990—, Güzeloto, Istanbul, 1994—, Otoplast, Istanbul, 1992—. Author: Modern and Primary Warehouses, 1994, Marketing Economy, 1995, International Marketing, 1996, Performance Appraisal and Rewards Compensation, 1997, Human Resources Management and Development, 1997, Channels of Distributions, 1997, Leadership, 1998, Assertiveness, 1998. Home: Öztopuz cd Nigbolu sk, Cam Apt # 4 D10 Etiler Ulus, Istanbul Turkey Office: Rotas Ototic AS Davutpasacd, Sercekalesk No13 Cevizlibag, 34020 Istanbul Turkey

BILINSKY, YAROSLAV, political scientist; b. Lutsk, Ukraine, Feb. 26, 1932; s. Peter Bilinsky and Natalia (Balabaj) Bilinska; m. Wira Rusaniwskyj, Feb. 18, 1962; children: Peter Yaroslav, Sophia Vera Yaroslava, Nadia Yaroslava, Mark Paul Yaroslav. A.B. magna cum laude, Harvard U., 1954, postgrad. in Soviet affairs, 1956-57; Ph.D., Princeton U., 1958. Asso. Harvard U. Russian Research Center, 1956-58; instr. polit. sci. Douglass Coll., Rutgers U., New Brunswick, N.J., 1958-61; asst. prof. U. Del., Newark, 1961-65; asso. prof. U. Del., 1965-69, prof., 1969—; vis. instr. U. Pa., 1961; vis. prof. Columbia U., 1976. Author: The Second Soviet Republic: The Ukraine after World War II, 1964, Endgame in NATO's Enlargement: The Baltic States and Ukraine, 1999. Corr. sec. Peter and Paul Ukrainian Orthodox Ch., Wilmington, Del., 1965-66, trustee, 1967-71. Mem. Am. Polit. Sci. Assn., Am. Assn. Advancement Slavic Studies (pres. Mid-Atlantic Slavic Conf. 1992-93), Ukrainian Acad. Arts and Scis. in U.S. (pres. 1987-90). Home: 2 Mimosa Dr Newark DE 19711-7523 Office: U Del Polit Sci and Internat Rels Newark DE 19716-2574

BILIRAKIS, MICHAEL, congressman, lawyer, business executive; b. Tarpon Springs, Fla., July 16, 1930; s. Emmanuel and Irene (Pikramenos) B.; m. Evelyn Miaoulis, Dec. 27, 1959; children: Emmanuel, Gus. BS in Engring., U. Pitts., 1959; student, George Washington U., 1959-60; JD, U. Fla., 1963; JD (hon.), Stetson U.; hon. degree, U. Tampa. Bar: Fla. 1964; cert. coll. tchr., Fla. Atty., small businessman Pinellas and Pasco Counties, Fla., 1968—; mem. 98th-104th Congresses from 9th Dist. Fla., 1983—; mem. commerce com., vets. affairs com., chair health and environment subcom. Mem. Rep. Task Force on Social Security; co-chmn. Task Force on Infant Mortality; founder, charter pres. Tarpon Springs Vol. Ambulance Service; dir. Greek Studies program U. Fla.; dir. emeritus Juvenile Diabetes and Hospice; mem. Pres.' Coun. U. Fla. Sgt. USAF, 1951-55. Named Citizen of Yr. Greater Tarpon Springs, 1972-73, Man of Yr. United Way, 1989-90. Mem. Am. Legion (comdr. 1977-79), VFW, Amvets, USAF Sgts., NCOA, Air Force Assn., Greater Tarpon Springs C. of C. (past pres., dir.), Pinellas C. of C. (gov.), West Pasco Bar Assn., Am. Judicature Soc., Fla. Bar Assn., Gator Boosters, Fla. Blue Key (hon.), Mason (33 degree), Shriner, Jester, Moose, Elks, Rotary, Eastern Star, Phi Alpha Delta, Sigma Pi. Greek Orthodox. Lodges: Masons; Shriners; Moose; Tarpon Springs Rotary; Elks; Eastern Star; White Shrine of Jerusalem. Office: US Ho of Reps 2369 Rayburn House Ofc Bldg Washington DC 20515-0001

BILLARD, AUDE GEMMA, physicist, researcher; b. Lausanne, Switzerland, Aug. 6, 1971; d. Guiseppe Buttice and Odette Billard. BSc in Physics, EPFL, Switzerland, 1994, MSc in Physics, 1995; MSc in Knowledge Based Sys., U. Edinburgh, Scotland, 1996, PhD in Artificial Intelligence, 1998. Rschr. U. Lausanne, 1994-95, U. Edinburgh, 1997; lectr. Open U., U.K., 1997-98; rsch. assoc. IDSIA-EPFL, Switzerland, 1998-99, U. So. Calif., L.A., 1999—. Author: (book chpt.) Imitation in Animals and Artifacts, 2000; designer, creator: (robot toy) The Robota Toys, 1998; contbr. articles to profl. jours. and internat. confs. Sunburst scholar EPFL and Sunburst Found., 1995; young rschr. fellow Swiss Nat. Found., 1996-97, fellow Medicus Found., 1999. Mem. Soc. for Study of Artificial Intelligence (program com. symposium on imitation), Internat. Conf. on Machine Learning (program com.), European Conf. on Artificial Life (program com.). Office: U So Calif Computer Sci Dept SAL 230 941 W 7th Pl Dept Sal230 Los Angeles CA 90089-0001

BILLAZ, ANDRÉ, education educator; b. Lyon, France, Sept. 14, 1931; s. Adrien and Jeanne (Sibuet) B.; m. Christiane Cabarat Billaz, Apr. 22, 1965; children: Catherine, Anne. PhD, Paris-Sorbonne, 1973. Prof. French Inst. U., Vienna, Austria, 1960-65; dir. French Inst., Stuttgart, Germany, 1965-71; prof. Lille U., France, 1971-96; tchr. U. Lille, France, 1971-95; dir. Atelier Nat. Reproduction des Theses, Lille, 1981-96. Author: Voltaire et le romantisme en France, 1973. Lt. Armee de Terre, 1955-58, North Africa. Roman Catholic. E-mail: abillaz@nozdnet.fr. Home: 9 rue Lalo, F59170 Croix France Office: Univ Charles de Gaulle, 9 rue Angellier, 59046 Lille France

BILLÉ, JEAN-GEORGES, neurologist; b. Marseilles, France, Nov. 12, 1931; s. Francois and Victoria (Guilerme) B.; m. Mathilde Gavalda, June 6, 1959; children: Jacques, Francoise, Dominique. Grad., Faculté de Medecine, Marseilles. Interne Hopitaux de Marseilles, 1958-63; chef de clinique Faculté de Medecine, Marseilles, 1963—, dr. en medecine, 1963—, laureat, prof. assoc. univ.; médecine-chef du service de neurologie L'Hosp. St. Joseph, Marseilles; organizer neurogeriatric and gerontopsychiatric congress. Editor: Le Cerveau du 3ème Age, 1976, Le Cerveau du 3e Age, 1979, Neurogeriatrie, 1992. Mem. Soc. Française de Neurologie, Internat. Psychogeriatric Assn. Roman Catholic. Avocations: tennis, golf. Home: 11 Parc Mermoz, 13008 Marseilles France Office: 255 Ave du Prado, 13008 Marseilles France

BILLET, REINHARD, chemical engineer, consultant; b. Karlsruhe, Germany, Feb. 23, 1929; s. August and Wilhelmine (Küffner) B. Diploma in

engring., U. Karlsruhe, 1953, D in Engring., 1957. Rsch. engr. BASF Aktiengesellschaft, Ludwigshafen, Germany, 1960-67, prodn. engr., 1967-69, plant design, 1969-73, environ. engr., 1973-75; prof. Ruhr U., Bochum, Germany, 1975—, dean mech. engr. faculty, 1983-84; cons., 1995—. Author: Distillation Engineering, 1973, Evaporation Technology, 1981, Energy Saving in Seperation Processes, 1983, Packed Towers in Processing and Environmental Technology, 1995; contbr. articles to profl. jours. Recipient Merits medal Tech. U. Wroclaw, Poland, 1984. Mem. German Instn. Engrs. (Ring of Honor award 1964), Dechema, European Fedn. Chem. Engring., N.Y. Acad. Scis. Avocations: foreign languages, natural medicine. Home: Laerholz str 53, 44801 Bochum NRW, Germany Office: Ruhr Univ Bochum, 44780 Bochum NRW, Germany

BILLETER, ERNEST PETER, statistics and informatics educator, consultant; b. Basle, Switzerland, Apr. 7, 1919; s. Ernest and Maria (Massa) B.; m. Annelis Frey, Jan. 25, 1951 (dec. 1993); children: Peter, Martin, Gabrielle, Felix. D in Econs., U. Basle, 1948. Asst., Statis. Office City of Zurich, Switzerland, 1949-56; prof. stats. Fribourg (Switzerland) U., 1956—; founder Inst. Informatics, Fribourg, 1958; cooperator several internat. congresses (Italy, The Netherlands, Germany); vis. prof. Pa. State U., 1970. Author several books on stats. and informatics; contbr. numerous articles to internat. profl. jours.; mem. editl. bd. Metron (Italy), Kybernetes (Eng.). Scientific advisor mil. planning activities. Recipient award Cowles Commn., Chgo, 1950. Mem. AAAS, Internat. Statis. Inst. (The Hague). Avocations: astronomy, astrophysics, aircraft engineering. Home: Rte Belle Croix 13, CH-1752 Villars-sur-Glâne Switzerland

BILLETER, ROBERT JAMES, newspaper publisher; b. Clarksburg, W.Va., Aug. 16, 1926; s. Arch and Mabel Edith (Westfall) B.; m. Eileen Billie Horvath, Apr. 14, 1972; 1 child, William Fletcher. BS, W.Va. U., 1951. Editor Pendleton Times, Franklin, W.Va., 1951-53; copy editor Herald-Dispatch, Huntington, W.Va., 1953-54; reporter The Post, Morgantown, W.Va., 1954-56; copy editor Sun-Telegraph, Pitts., 1956-60; copy editor Post-Gazette, Pitts., 1960-81, night city editor, 1981-85, makeup editor, 1985-91; pub. The Weston (W.Va.) Democrat, 1992—. With U.S. Army, 1945-47. Episcopalian. Avocations: wine tasting, sailing, hiking, skiing. Home: One E 4th St Weston WV 26452 Office: The Weston Democrat 306 Main Ave Weston WV 26452-2046

BILLICK, L. LARKIN, marketing executive; b. Des Moines, Sept. 15, 1948; s. Lyle Larkin and Florence Carlson B.; m. Kathryn Rose Gildner, Aug. 14, 1971; children: Kelly Lynne, Brett Larkin. BS, U. Kans., Lawrence, 1970; grad. Inst. Bank Mktg., U. So. Calif., Lake State U., 1978. Group ins. trainee Bankers Life Co., Des Moines, 1970-71; nat. advt. rep. Stoner Broadcasting Co., Des Moines, 1971-74; advt. account supr. Mid-Am. Broadcasting, Des Moines, 1974-75; dir. pub. rels. and mktg. Iowa Bankers Assn., Des Moines, 1975-77; asst. v.p., advt. mgr. corp. staff Marine Banks, Milw., 1977-79, v.p. advt., 1979-81; pres. Billick Fin. Mktg. Group, 1981-82; sr. v.p. mktg. Univ. Savs. Assn., Houston, 1982-84; mgmt. supr. W.B. Doner Advt./S.W., Houston, 1984-86; pres. The Strategists, Inc., Houston, 1986-89, Rotan Mosle Div. Paine Webber, Inc., Houston, 1990-91, Oppenheimer & Co., Houston, 1991-94, LeMail Direct Marketing of Houston, 1994-95, Collectech Sys., Inc., 1995-96, Prime Co. Personal Comm., 1996-98; bus. sales mgr. GTE Wireless, 1998—. Bd. dirs. Grad. Inst. Bank Mktg., La. State U., 1978-79; chmn. comm. Milwaukee County Performing Arts Center, 1978-79; advt., promotion cons. to polit. candidates; chmn. comm. coun. United Performing Arts Fund Milw., 1978-79; dist. coord. State Del. for Jimmy Carter, 1972-80; chmn. comm. com. Milwaukee County coun. Boy Scouts Am., 1979-80; bd. dirs. Katy (Tex.) Nat. Little League, 1984-91, Katy Youth Football, 1984-86, Katy Taylor High Sch. Athletic Booster Club, 1989-94, pres., 1989-94, Pacesetters Drill Team Boosters Club, 1989-92, Nottingham Country Club Swim Team, 1984-92, Katy Bus. Assn., 1994—. Mem. Bank Mktg. Assn. (chmn. advt. council 1980-81, mem. nat. conv. com. 1980-82), Am. Bankers Assn. (mem. nat. mktg. conf. com. 1980), Am. Advt. Fedn. (public service com. 1980-81), Am. Mktg. Assn., U. Kans. Alumni Assn. (life), Milw. Advt. Club (v.p., bd. dirs. 1978-81). Republican. Roman Catholic. Home: 21415 Park Post Ln Katy TX 77450-5319 Office: 100 Glenborough Dr Ste 700 Houston TX 77067-3600

BILLIG, FRANKLIN ANTHONY, chemist; b. L.A., Feb. 11, 1923; s. Frank Henry and Hazel (Rockwell) B.; m. Tetsuko Morinaga, Apr. 23, 1957; 1 child, Patricia Ann Kikuko Billig-Harvey. BS, U. So. Calif., L.A., 1954. CPC, CSS. Sr. rsch. chemist Am. Potash & Chem. Corp., Whittier, Calif., 1954-64; rsch. chemist/lab. mgr./safety officer, Dept. Chemistry U. So. Calif., L.A., 1964—; cons. Flintridge Cons., Inc., Calif., 1980—, Hanson Lab. Furniture, Newberry Park, Calif., 1989; cons./staff assoc. Enterprise Environ. Svcs., L.A., 1981—. Author: Advances in Chemistry, 1959, 61, Organic Synthesis, 1959, Infra Red Spectra of Organic Sulfur Compounds, 1964, Infra Red Spectra of Sulfur Compounds, 1966; patentee in field. Master sgt. USAF, 1942-53, PTO, Korea. Fellow AAAS, L. Pasteur Inst. Advanced Med. Studies, Am. Inst. Chemists; mem. Sigma Xi. Republican. Roman Catholic. Avocations: quantum mechanics, Egyptology, archaeology, geology, paleontology. Home: 12722 Spindlewood Dr La Mirada CA 90638-2735 Office: U So Calif Dept Chemistry University Park Los Angeles CA 90089-0001

BILLIG, MICHAEL, social psychologist, educator; b. London, Sept. 8, 1947; s. David and Rossi (Hill) B.; m. Sheila Lisbeth Crawford, Jan. 1, 1971; children: Daniel, Rebecca, Rachel, Benjamin. BA, Bristol (Eng.) U., 1968, PhD, 1971. Rsch. fellow Bristol U., 1972-73; lectr. Birmingham (Eng.) U., 1973-84; prof. social scis. Loughborough (Eng.) U., 1985—; vis. prof. Temple U., Phila., 1991, U. Calif.-Santa Barbara, 1992, U. Rome, 1996; head dept. social scis. Loughborough U., 1986-90, co-dir. Comms. Rsch. Ctr., 1993—; mem. Conseil Sci. Ctr. Rsch. d'Info. and Documentation Antiraciste, Paris, Searchlight Info. Svcs., London, 1995. Author: Arguing and Thinking, 1987, Ideology and Opinions, 1991, Talking of the Royal Family, 1992, Banal Nationalism, 1995, Freudian Repression, 1999, Rock 'n' Roll Jews, 2000; contbr. articles to profl. jours. Recipient Erik Erikson award Internat. Soc. for Polit. Psychology, Gustavus Myers Ctr. award for study of human rights in N.Am., 1996. Mem. Assn. Study of Ethnicity and Nationalism, Brit. Psychol. Soc. Office: U Loughborough, Dept Social Scis, LE11 3TU Loughborough England

BILLIMORIA, RUSI PESTON, specifications engineer; b. Aden, British Colony, Apr. 5, 1931; s. Peston Shapur and Dosan B.; m. Gul Kharset Byramji, June 20, 1968; children: Kaerveen, Aadil. Marine Radio Officer, St. Xavier's Tech. Inst., Bombay, India, 1951; grad., Inst. Electronics/Radio Engrs., U.K., 1970; PhD, Coventry U., U.K., 1973; Chartered Engr., Inst. Engrs., Calcutta, India, 1977. Cert. telecomms. advanced tech. engr., advanced PG in microelectronics. Tech. author Racal Brit. Commn., Wembley, London, U.K., 1981-82; vis. lectr. Brixton Coll., London, U.K., 1982-83; inspector Plessey Naval Systems, Erith Kent, U.K., 1983; tech. author London, U.K., 1983-85, Cossor Electronics, Harlow Essex, U.K., 1986-87; sr. tng. asst. Inner City Tng., London SW 9, U.K., 1988-89; employment officer Dept. of Employment, London SW1, U.K., 1990-91; job search officer Tng. Factory, London SW4, U.K., 1992-93; radio contr. Queensway Cars, Prince's Trust, London, 1993—; engr. 2, Civil Aviations Authority, West Drayton, U.K., 1979-80; sr. tech. author Plessey Avionics, Ilford Essex, U.K., 1978-79; sr. acad. instr. Ngee Ann Tech. Coll. Singapore, 1971-73; tech. officer Govt. India, Bombay, 1958-63, Tech. 2A Cable and Wireless, Dubai, 1968-71. Editor Radio Svcs. Mag., 1958-68. Mem. Brit. Conservative Party, London, 1982—. Named Ednl. panelist Southwark Coun., London, 1992—; named radio officer Mercantile Marine U.K., India, 1951; Advanced Sci. Engring. Rsch. Coun. scholar, 1985-86/. Fellow Soc. Engrs., Inst. Electronics and Telecoms Engrs., Brit. Inst. Mgmt. Parsee Jarthosti. Home: 22 Saint Matthews Rd, London SW2 1NJ, England Office: Queensway Cars, Porchester Gardens, London W2, England

BILLING, RONALD JAMES, immunologist, researcher; b. U.K., July 23, 1943; came to U.S., 1970; s. James Jackson and Margaret Isobel (O'Connor) B.; m. Angela Mary Gillett, July 9, 1965; children: Peter, Michael, Janet. BS, U. Liverpool, 1965; PhD, U. Glasgow, 1969. Postdoctoral fellow Cal Inst. Tech., Pasadena, 1970-72; asst. prof., assoc. prof. UCLA, 1972-85; rsch. dir. C V Cancer Ctr., San Marcos, Calif., 1985—; rschr. in field. Patentee in field; contbr. numerous articles to profl. jours. Gosney fellow, 1970-72; grantee NIH, 1974-77, 77-88. Avocations: tennis, chess, backpacking, fishing, golf.

BILLINGS, HAROLD WAYNE, librarian, editor; b. Cain City, Tex., Nov. 12, 1931; s. Harold Ross and Katie Mae (Price) B.; m. Bernice Schneider, Sept. 10, 1954; children: Brenda, Geoffrey, Carol. BA, Pan Am. Coll., 1953; MLS, U. Tex., 1957. Tchr. Pharr-San Juan-Alamo (Tex.) High Sch., 1953-54; catalog librarian U. Tex., Austin, 1954-57; asst. chief catalog librarian U. Tex., 1957-65, chief acquisitions librarian, 1965-67, asst. univ. librarian, 1967-72, asso. dir. gen. libraries, 1972-77, acting dir. gen. libraries, 1977-78, dir. gen. libraries, 1978—; sec. Tex. Bd. Libr. Examiners; mem. adv. com. Tex. Higher Edn. Coordinating Bd. Libr. Formula, 1987-92, acad. support formula adv. com., 1993-94; mem. steering com. Tex-Share Project, 1993-94; trustee Amigos Bibliographic Coun., 1980-83; chmn. Coun. Acad. Rsch. Libr., 1979-81; chmn. rsch. libr. adv. com. Online Computer Libr. Ctr. (OCLC), 1980-82, 87-88, mem. OCLC Users Coun.; bd. dirs. Ctr. Rsch. Libr., Chgo., 1989-96, Assn. Rsch. Libr., 1989-92; mem. Tex. Coun. State Univ. Libr., Assn. Rsch. Libr. Preservation Com., Collection Devel. Com., Coun. on Libr. Resources Preservation and Access Com., Coun. on Libr. Resources/Assn. Am. Pubs. Joint Working Group on Electronic Info., 1993-94; mem. adv. bd. Project Muse-Johns Hopkins U. Press, Balt., 1995-98; mem. N.Am. adv. bd. Lit. Online, 1997—; assoc. Tex. Telecomms. Policy Inst., 1996—; mem. coun. on libr. and info. studies area studies materials task force ACLS, 1998—; mem. adv. coun. for Stanford U. Libr., 1998-2000; mem. steering com. Digital Libr. Fedn., 1999—, mem. adv. com., 1999—; project dir. numerous fed. grants. Author: Education of Librarians in Texas, 1956, Edward Dahlberg: American Ishmael of Letters, 1968, A Bibliography of Edward Dahlberg, 1972, The Shape of Shiel, 1865-1896, 1983, The Leafless American, 2d edit., 1986, Magic and Hypersystems, 1990, The Bionic Library, 1991, Supping with the Devil, 1993, The Information Ark, 1994, The Tomorrow Librarian, 1995, Libraries, Language and Change, 1998; editor books in field; contbr. to jours.; mem. editorial bd. Libr. Chronicle, 1970-97. Sec., trustee Littlefield Fund for So. History. Mem. ALA, Tex. Libr. Assn., Assn. Coll. Rsch. Libr. Democrat. Office: U Tex Libr PO Box P Austin TX 78713-8916

BILLINGS, STEPHEN ALEC, engineering educator; b. Staffordshire, U.K., Aug. 14, 1951; s. George and Annie Betty (Campbell) B.; m. Catherine Grant Jagger, Sept. 7, 1972; children: Simon Grant, Clare Grant Billings. BEng, Liverpool U., 1972, DEng, 1990; PhD, Sheffield U., 1976. Lectr. U. Sheffield, 1975-83, sr. lectr., 1983-85, reader, 1985-90, prof., 1990—. Contbr. articles to profl. publs. Fellow Inst. Elec. Engrs., Inst. Math. and its Applications; chartered Engr., chartered Mathematician. Office: Dept Engring, Univ Sheffield, Sheffield S1 3JD, United Kingdom

BILLINGSLEY, JOHN, electronics engineer, educator; b. Cheltenham, Eng., Aug. 14, 1939; arrived in Australia, 1992; s. Wilfred Richard and Agnes Aldington (Green) B; m. Rosalind Elizabeth Wilson, May 18, 1964; children: Berry Anne, Richard John, William Henry. BA with honors, Cambridge (Eng.) U., 1960, MA, 1964, PhD, 1968. Grad. apprentice Smiths Aviation Divsn., Cheltenham, Eng., 1960-62, engr. II autopilot sys. and circuit specification and design, 1962-64; demonstrator dept. engring. Cambridge U., 1967-71, asst. dir. rsch. dept. engring., 1971-76; reader elec. and electronic engring. Portsmouth (Eng.) Poly., 1976-86, personal chair robotics dept., 1986-92; prof. engring. U. So. Queensland, Toowoomba, Australia, 1992—; rsch. dir. Nat. Ctr. Engring. in Agr., Toowoomba, 1992—. Author: DIY Robotics and Sensors with the BBC Computer, 1983, Controlling With Computers, 1989; editor: Robots and Automated Manufacture, 1985, Mechatronics and Machine Vision, 2000; contbr. chpts. to books, numerous articles to profl. jours. Fellow Instn. Engrs. Australia, Inst. Elec. Engrs.; mem. IEEE (sr.). Home: 10 Glencoe Ct, Toowoomba QLD 4350, Australia Office: U So Queensland, Toowoomba QLD 4350, Australia

BILLINGSLEY, MARY LEE, health facility administrator, counselor; b. Oak Park, Ill., Sept. 30, 1952; d. Harvey Bernard Wilson and Louise May Allessi; m. Thad Hoffman Billingsley, Dec. 29, 1977; children: Amy, Andrew, Anne, Mary Lynn. BA cum laude, Loretto Heights Coll., 1975; MA, U. Mo., Kansas City, 1978. Bd. cert. counselor, lic. profl. counselor; bd. cert. cognitive-behavioral therapist. Psychometrician Psychiat. Assocs., Kansas City, Kans., 1975-78, counselor, 1978-83; exec. dir. Advanced Human Assessment, Mission, Kans., 1980-82; co-founder, clin. dir., counselor The Benessere Ctr., Leawood, Kans., 1983-93; pvt. practice counseling, Overland Park, Kans., 1993—. Co-author: The Bethany Ctr. Workbook, 1983, Depression: The Way Out, 1987, Eating Disorders: The Way Out, 1988. Bd. dirs. Vine St. Shelter Homeless Project, Kansas City, 1989, Ursuline Motherhouse, Paola, Kans., Ursuline Assoc. Mem. Am. Assn. Counseling and Devel., Kans. Assn. Counseling and Devel., Am. Assn. Specialist in Group Work, Kans. Assn. Specialist in Group Work (pres. 1987-88, 97-99), Johnson County Med. Aux., Wyandotte County Med. Aux., Undersea Med. Soc. (assoc.). Avocations: scuba diving, Americana book collecting, writing, quilting. Office: 11409 Ash St Ste B Shawnee Mission KS 66211-1753

BILLINGTON, BARRY E., lawyer; b. Bruceton, Tenn., June 24, 1940; s. Charles Raymond and Edith Virginia (Bowles) B.; m. Bonnie Leslie Johnson; Oct. 16, 1971 (div. Mar. 23, 1990); children: Erin Alexis, Barry E., Jr. AB in Econs., Davidson Coll., 1964; JD, Emory U., 1968. Bar: Calif. 1969, Ga. 1971, U.S. Dist. Ct. (ctrl. dist.) Calif. 1969, U.S. Dist. Ct. (no. dist.) Ga. 1971; diplomate Nat. Assn. Coll. Advocacy Trial Lawyers. Assoc. Surr & Hellyer, San Bernardino, Calif., 1968-70; with Mfrs. Life Ins. Co., Atlanta, 1970-71; assoc. Carter, Ansley, Smith & McClendon, Atlanta, 1971-72; of counsel Raiford & Hills, Decatur, Ga., 1972-75; ptnr. Raiford, Hills, Billington & McKeithen, Atlanta, 1975-77; mem. Rich, Bass, Kidd, Witcher & Billington, Decatur, 1977-82; ptnr. Billington & Beasley, Decatur, 1982-83, Billington & Turner, Atlanta, 1983-85; owner Barry E. Billington & Assocs., Atlanta, 1985—. Editor: Ga. Rep. Party Newsletter, 1968. Rep. publicity dir. San Bernardino County Rep. Party, 1969-70, San Bernardino County for Ronald Reagan Com., 1970; alt. del. Rep. Ctrl. Com. of Calif., 1969-70; chmn. 4th dist. Conservative Caucus, 1977-79; candidate for Ga. Ho. Reps., 52nd dist., 1978, U.S. Congress, 4th dist., Ga., 1980. With U.S. Army Mil. Police Corps, 1958-60. Mem. Atlanta Bar Assn. (spkr.'s com., litigation, family law, criminal law sects. 1974-77), Decatur-DeKalb Bar Assn. (chmn. spkr.'s com. 1977-78), ABA (litigation sect. 1969-89), Ga. Trial Lawyers Assn., Assn. Trial Lawyers Am., Ga. Assn. Criminal Def. Lawyers, Nat. Assn. Criminal Def. Lawyers, Diplomat of Nat. Coll. of Advocacy Trial Advocacy Course. Home: 878 Sherwood Cir Forest Park GA 30297-3035 Office: 3 Dunwoody Park Ste 103 Atlanta GA 30338-6709

BILLINGTON, DAVID, computer science educator; b. Melbourne, Victoria, Australia, July 23, 1950; s. Christopher and Bridget A. (Hellier) B. BS with honors, Monash U., Melbourne, Australia, 1972, MS, 1975; PhD, U. Melbourne, 1981; diploma in Computer Sci., U. Queensland, Brisbane, Australia, 1983. Lectr. U. Queensland, 1981, rsch. asst., 1981-84; lectr. Griffith U., Brisbane, 1985-91; sr. lectr. Griffith U., 1992—. Contbr. articles to profl. jours. Recipient grant Australian Rsch. Coun., 1992-93, 96-98, 98—. Mem. Australian Computer Sci. Assn. Avocation: bird watching. Office: Griffith U, Sch Computing Info Tech, Brisbane 4111, Australia

BILLINGTON, JAMES HADLEY, historian, librarian; b. Bryn Mawr, Pa., June 1, 1929; s. Nelson and Jane (Coolbaugh) B.; m. Marjorie Anne Brennan, June 22, 1957; children: Susan Billington Harper, Anne Billington Fischer, James Hadley, Jr., Thomas Keator. BA, Princeton U., 1950; D Phil., Oxford (Eng.) U., 1953; LittD (hon.), Lafayette Coll., 1981, U. Pitts., 1988, Williams Coll., 1991, Duke U., 1995; LHD (hon.), LeMoyne Coll., 1982, Rhode Island Coll., 1982, Cath. U. Am., 1983, NYU, 1987, Va. Theol. Sem., 1990, Hood Coll., 1992, U. Scranton, 1992, SUNY, Albany, 1993, Georgetown U., 1993, Bates Coll., 1993, The Am. U., 1995, Mt. Holyoke Coll., 1995; HHD (hon.), Furman U., 1986, Ball State U., 1988; D Pub. Svc. (hon.), George Washington U., 1990; LLD (hon.), Dartmouth Coll., 1990, U. Notre Dame, 1995. Instr. history Harvard U., Cambridge, Mass., 1957-58, fellow Russian Research Ctr., 1958-59, asst. prof. history, 1958-61; assoc. prof. history Princeton (N.J.) U., 1962-64, prof., 1964-73; dir. Woodrow Wilson Internat. Ctr. for Scholars, Washington, 1973-87; Librarian of Congress Libr. of Congress, Washington, 1987—; chmn. Bd. Fgn. Scholarships (Fulbright program), 1971-73, mem. 1973-76; vice-chmn. Atlantic Council's Working Group on the Successor Generation, 1982-86; trustee St. Alban's Sch., 1979-82; dir. Am. Assn. for the Advancement of Slavic Studies, 1968-71; spl. cons. to Chase Manhattan Bank on East-West Matters, 1971-73; vis. rsch. prof. to Inst. History of Acad. Scis. of USSR in Moscow, 1966-67, U. Helsinki, 1960-61, École des Hautes Études en Sciences Sociales, Paris, 1985, 88; vis. lectr. to various univs. in Europe and Asia. Author: Mikhailovsky and Russian Populism, 1958, The Icon and the Axe: An Interpretive History of Russian Culture, 1966, (Serbian transl., 1988), The Arts of Russia, 1970, Fire in the Minds of Men: Origins of the Revolutionary Faith, 1980, (Italian transl., 1986), Russia Transformed: Breakthrough to Hope, Moscow, August 1991, 1992, The Face of Russia, 1998; writer, host: (3-part TV series) The Face of Russia, 1998; mem. adv. bd. Fgn. Affairs, 1974-92, Theology Today, 1974-84; script writer and host of Humanities Film Forum, 1973; contbr. chpts. to books, numerous articles to profl. jours. Trustee John F. Kennedy Ctr. for Performing Arts, Ctr. Theol. Inquiry, Nat. Bldg. Mus., Woodrow Wilson Internat. Ctr. for Scholars, Am. Folklife Ctr.; bd. regents Nat. Libr. Medicine. 1st lt. U.S. Army, 1953-56. McCosh faculty fellow Princeton U., Guggenheim fellow, 1960-61; Rhodes scholar, 1950-53; Fulbright rsch. professor U. Helsinki, 1960-61; decorated Chevalier 1985 and Comdr. 1991 Order of Arts and Letters of France; recipient Gwanghwa medal Republic of Korea, 1991, Woodrow Wilson award Princeton U., 1992, Knight Comdr.'s Cross of Order of Merit, Fed. Republic of Germany, 1996. Mem. Am. Philos. Soc., Am. Acad. Arts and Scis., Cosmos Club, Phi Beta Kappa. Office: The Library of Congress 101 Independence Ave SE Washington DC 20540-0002

BILLIS, EURIPIDES CHRISTOS, communications executive; b. Nicosia, Cyprus, Aug. 26, 1936; s. Christos Michael and Athina Anna (Neofitou) B.; m. Maria Evmorfia, Sept. 19, 1965; children: Melina, Christos. Diploma, Tech Univ., Athens, 1961. Chief Athens Exch. Inst. Hellenic Telecom. Orgn., Athens, 1962-76, chief telecom. area, 1977-78, chief Greece Exch. Inst., 1978-80, chief Greece Exch. Maintenance, 1981-85, chief of factory, 1985-87, chief Telecom. Adminstrn. Bldg., 1987-90, dir. maintenance, 1991-92, dir. exch. dept., 1992—, dir. maintenance, 1993-97; advisor, 1998—; sr. lectr. Tech. U. Athens, 1965-66, sci. cooperator, 1966—; prof. telecom. Greek Army, Athens, 1968-75; pres. planning Athens New Digital Network, 1991. Author: Digital Exchanges, 1984, Programming of Stored Program Control Exchanges, 1985, Automatic Telephony, 1994, Telecommunication Systems, 1994, Supplement of Telephony, 1994, Introduction to Telecommunications Networks, 1995, The Open Systems Interconnection Data Link Layer, 1995, The Performance and Faults of Plesichronous Digital Hierarchy PCM Systems, 1995, The Need of Asynchronous Transfer Mode and Its Processes, 1995, The AXE-LO Switching System, 1996, The Electronic Whal System Digital-Local Switching System, 1997, Analysis of Signalling System Common Channel Signalling, 1997, The Access Network and the Modulation Asymetric Digital Subscriber Line, 1998, Synchronous Telecommunication Subjects, 1999. Mem. Tech. Chamber of Greece, Panellinium Union Diplom. Telecomm. Engrs. of OTE, Fed. Telecomm. Engrs. of European Cmty. Home: Michalacopoulou 118, Athens 11527, Greece Office: Hellenic Telecom Orgn, Kifisias 99-Marousi, Athens 15124, Greece

BILLOT, ERIC GUY, bank executive; b. Douarnenez, Brittany, France, Aug. 28, 1952; s. Etienne Henry and Nicole (Odouard) B.; m. Roselyne Louise Gerard, July 1, 1978; children: Charlotte, Henri, Hortense, Ellen. Student, ESCP, Paris, 1975, Inst. d'Etudes Politiques, Paris, 1977; Diplome d'etudes, U. Paris, 1979; student, INSEAD, Fontainebleau, France, 1989. Trainee Union de Banques à Paris, 1977-78, asst. mgr., 1978-79, mgr., 1979-82; mgr. Banque Martin Maurel, Marseille, France, 1982-86; asst. gen. mgr. Christiania Bank, Luxembourg, 1986-88, dep. gen. mgr., 1988-90; sr. v.p. Credit Suisse, Paris, 1990-94; gen. ptnr. Banque Arjil, France, 1995-99; ptnr. Price Waterhouse Coopers Corp. Fin., Paris, 1999—; tchr. Inst. d'Etudes Politiques, Paris, 1983-87, Ecole Nationale des Ponts et Chaussees, 1993—. Fellow Les Amis de la Republique Francaise Nat.; mem. Etrier de Paris, Cercle des Habits Rouges, Soc. de Venerie, Maison de la Chasse de la Nature. Roman Catholic. Avocations: sports, show-jumping, stag hunting, sailing. Home: 21 Avenue Emile Deschanel, 75007 Paris France Office: Price Waterhouse Coopers, 15 Rue Beaujon, F 75008 Paris France

BILLSON, FRANK ALFRED, ophthalmologist, educator; b. Melbourne, Victoria, Australia; s. Edward Fielder and Penelope Irene (Gaunson) B.; m. Gail Patricia Morell-Nodrum, Sept. 2, 1966; children: Francis Mark, Susanna Penelope. MD, U. Melbourne, 1959. Prof., chmn. dept. ophthalmology U. Sydney, 1977—, dir. Save Sight Inst., 1985—; prof. ophthalmology Tianjin Med. Coll., China, 1984—; pres. Foresight Australian Internat. Overseas Aid Prevention Blind, 1989—. Contbr. articles to profl. jours., chpts. to books; rsch. development and aging of human eye and associated diseases. Named Officer Order of Australia, Australian Govt., 1987, Life Gov. Royal Victorian Inst. for Blind, 1983; recipient Dunlop Asia medal Asia Link Australia, 1994. Fellow Am. Acad. Ophthalmology, Royal Australian Coll. Ophthalmologists, Royal Australian Coll. Surgeons; mem. Internat. Coun. Ophthalmology (councilor 1983-92), Internat. Acad. Ophthalmology, Royal Blind Soc. (councilor), Internat. Agy. for Prevention of Blindness (chmn. West Pacific region 1990-99). Avocations: music, photography, tennis. Office: Ophthalmology & Eye Health, PO Box 4337, Sydney NSW 2001, Australia

BILSKY, EDWARD GERALD, clinical social worker; b. Framingham, Mass., Jan. 31, 1961; s. Morton Edgar and Lois Ruth (Dunn) B. BA in Psychology, BA Sociology cum laude, Boston Coll., 1982; MSW, Simmons Coll. Sch. Social Work, 1991. Lic. ind. clin. social worker. Psychol. student intern Met. State Hosp., Waltham, Mass., 1981-84; family co-therapist Office of Michael A. Sperber, Newton, Mass., 1982; psychol. cons. Mentor, Inc., Cambridge, Mass., 1983-84; mental health worker II St. Elizabeth's Hosp., Brighton, Mass., 1984-85; sr. mental health worker, emergency rm. cons. Metrowest Med. Ctr., 1985-91; clin. social worker Heritage Hosp., 1991-92, dir. admissions, 1992-93, dir. intern tng., 1991-93; clin. social worker Wayland Clin. Assocs., 1991-97; asst. dir. psychiatric emergency svcs. Advocates, Inc., 1993-95; dir. clin. ops. Psychiat. Emergency Svc. Advocates, Inc., 1995-97; dir. mktg. and bus. devel. Behavioral Health Svcs. Divsn., Advocates, Inc., 1997; v.p. ops. Behavioral Health Mgmt. Solutions, Inc., 1993-97; profl. rels. mgr. New England Regional Care Ctr., CIGNA Behavioral Health, Holyoke, Mass., 1997—. Author: (with others) Managing the Balance: Looking at Work and Home Responsibilities, 1991. Mem. NASW. Home: 5 Blueberry Cir Framingham MA 01701-3711 Office: 300 Whitney Ave Ste 400 Holyoke MA 01040-2718

BILSTON, LYNNE ECKERT, biomedical engineer, reseacher; b. Cooma, NSW, Australia, Oct. 9, 1967; d. Kenneth and Flora (Margot) B.; m. Michael Patrick Eckert, 1993. B Engring., U. Sydney, Australia, 1989; MS in Engring., U. Pa., 1992, PhD, 1994. Rsch. asst. U. Sydney, 1990, lectr. mech. engring., 1994-98; rsch. fellow U. Pa., Phila., 1990-94; sr. lectr. U. Sydney, 1998—. Contbr. articles to profl. jours. Fulbright scholar, 1990-94. Mem. ASME, Neurotrauma Soc., Am. Soc. Biomechs. Office: U Sydney Dept Mech Engring, Bldg J07, Sydney NSW 2006, Australia

BILSTON, PAUL, engineering executive, consultant; b. Looma, NSW, Australia, June 16, 1966; s. Kenneth John Maynard and Flora Margot (Lyndon) B.; m. Susan Marguerite Manger, Sept. 3, 1994; children: Simon David, Timothy Jack. BME, Melbourne U., 1989; PhD, Monash U., Melbourne, 1993. Mng. dir. Advanced Pipeline Tech., Melbourne, 1993-94; gen. mgr. Allform Products, Melbourne, 1994-96; mgr. pipelines Worley Ltd., Brisbanne, Australia, 1996-98; gen. mgr. Integrated Pipeline Svcs., Brisbane, 1999—; dir. Cairngorm Securities, Melbourne, 1993-97. Mem. APIA. Avocations: skiing, renovating, walking.

BILU, YURI F., mathematician, consultant; b. Minsk, Belarus, Aug. 29, 1964; arrived in Israel, 1990; s. Felix N. and Klara Yu (Fruman) Belotserkovski; m. Elina Wojciechowska, Sept. 30, 1990; children: Margaret, Marie Rachel. BS, MS, Belorussian State U., Minsk, 1986; PhD, Ben Gurion U., Beer Sheva, Israel, 1994; habilitation, U. Basel, 2000. Asst. Ben Gurion U., 1990-93; rschr. U. Bordeaux II, France, 1993-94, Göttingen (Germany) U., 1994-95, Max Planck Inst., Bonn, Germany, 1995-96, ETH Zürich, 1996-97; asst. U. Basel, Switzerland, 1998-2000; prof. U. Bordeaux I, France, 2000—; vis. prof. U. Graz, Austria, 1996; vis. rschr. Macquarie U., Sydney, Australia, 1995, IMPA, Rio de Janeiro, 1996, Tech. U. Graz, 1997-99. Scholar Wolf Found., Israel, 1993; Bourse Chateaubriand scholar French Govt., 1993; Lise Meitner fellow Austrian Sci. Found., 1997. Mem. Am.

Math. Soc., Israel Math. Union. Avocations: cats, tourism, Russian literature. Home: Steinenvorstadt 12, 4051 Basel Switzerland Office: Math Inst Basel U, Rheinsprung 21, 4051 Basel Switzerland

BILYALOV, RENAT, physicist; b. Tashkent, Uzbekistan, May 22, 1963; Parents Remzi and Idiliya (Kazakova) B.; m. Gulnara Velilyaeva, Apr. 19, 1991; children, Rustem and Arsen. MS, Tashkent St. U., Uzbekistan, 1985; PhD, Physics-Tech. Inst., Tashkent, 1994. Cert. in physics. Rschr. Inst. Electronics, Tashkent, 1985-87, engr., 1987-88, tech. engr., 1991-93, rsch. scientist, 1993-95; post- doctoral fellow Fraunhofer Inst. Solar Energy Sys., Freiburg, Germany, 1995-97, vis. scientist, 1997-98; rsch. scientist Inter Univ. Micro-Electronics Ctr., Leuven, Belgium, 1998—; sr. sci. cons. Usbek St. Space Rsch. Agy., Tashkent, 1994-95. Patentee in field. Recipient best invention award Uzbek Acad. Sci., 1992; postdoctoral grantee German Sci. Exch. Office, 1995, Alexander von Humboldt Found., 1996, Sci. Travel grant MacArthur Found., 1996. Mem. Internat. Solar Energy Soc. Avocations: skiing, literature, music. Fax #: 32 (0) 16-281-501. E-mail: bilyalov@imec.be. Home: Koetsweg 95/2, 3010 Leuven Belgium Office: IMEC, Kapeldreef 75, 3001 Leuven Belgium

BIMBERG, GUIDO, musicologist, music educator, music executive; b. Halle, Germany, Mar. 3, 1954; s. Siegfried and Ortrud B.; m. Christiane Binder. PhD, Martin Luther U., Halle, Germany, 1979, habilitation, 1981. Assoc. prof. U. Halle, 1979-95; chair, prof. musicology Music Acad., Dortmund, 1995—; pres. German Acad. Humanities, Bonn, Germany, 1998—; vis. prof. U. Havana, 1983-86, U. Moscow, 1992—; sr. program cons. M.R.I., Inc., 1991—; v.p. Media Svcs., Inc., 2000—; bd. dirs. Digital Misoc Corp. Author over 20 books; contbr. over 200 articles to profl. jours. Recipient gold crown medal Hong Kong Music Assn., 1995, German Nat. prize for music and musciology, 2000, Innovation prize for music and media tech., 2000. Mem. German Soc. Musicology (v.p.), German Music Rsch. Found. (pres.). Fax: 0049-2330-974153. Office: German Acad for Humanities, Postfach 550133, D-44209 Dortmund Germany

BIMBOT, RENE, physicist, researcher; b. Poincy, France, June 19, 1939; s. Georges and Ernesta (Brambilla) B.; m. Nicole Fontaine, July 28, 1962; children: Frederic, Stephane. Lic. Physics, U. Paris, 1960, Agregation de Physique, 1962; PhD, U. Orsay, France, 1966; M Psychology, U. Paris V, 1976. Eleve maitre Ecole Normale, Paris, 1954-58; eleve prof. Ecole Normale Superieure, St. Cloud, 1958-62; stagiaire/attache de recherche CNRS, Orsay/Paris, 1962-66, charge de recherche, 1966-73, maitre de recherche, 1973-90, dir. rsch., 1990—; charge de cours U. Orsay, 1971-74; dir. Alice Accelerator, Orsay, 1980-85; dep. dir. rsch. dept. IPN, Orsay, 1988-92; dir. sci. comm. IN2P3, Paris, 1992-95; main organizer Nat. (French) Commemorative Radioactivity Discovery Centennial, 1996-98. Author 10 sci. films including Alice and the Heavy Ion Boom, 1989; author: Cent Ans Apres La Radioactivite, 1999; contbr. over 105 articles to profl. jours. Recipient Marie Curie medal UNESCO, Paris, 1998; Marie-Sklodowska-Curie medal Polish Marie Curie Orgn., Warsaw, 1998. Mem. Haut Comite Nat. pour le Centenaire de la Decouverte de la Radioactivite (sec. gen. 1995-99), Comite executif pour le Centenaire de la Découverte de la Radioactivite (pres. 1995-99). Home: 27 Av du Plessis, F92290 Chatenay-Malabry France Office: Inst Nuclear Physics, IPN-Orsay, 91406 Orsay France

BIMKOVÁ, ANNA, librarian; b. Plzeň, Czechoslovakia, Jan. 5, 1941; d. Ladislav and Anna (Vrátniková) Mašek; m. Josef Bimka, Feb. 25, 1967; children: Jana, Hana. Student, Charles U., Prague, 1966. Librarian The City Libr., Prague, Czechoslovakia, 1965-68, dir. dist. libr., 1968-78, dir., 1978—; cons. The Charles U., 1982—. Mem. Assn. Libr. and Info. Profls. Czechoslovakia. Avocations: literature, theatre. Home: Lucemburská 1, 130 00 Praha Czech Republic Office: Městská knihovna v Praze, Mariánské nám 1, 115 72 Prague 1, Czech Republic

BINDÉ, JÉRÔME, international official, educator, futurist; b. Friedrichshafen, Germany, Jan. 11, 1951; s. Maurice and Jeanne (Bourdet) B.; m. Lou Møllgaard, July 21, 1989; 1 child, Joséphine. Student, Ecole Normale Superieure, Paris, 1970-75; MPhil in Philosophy and Aesthetics, U. Paris, 1972; higher degree in Humanities, Agrégé Univ., France, 1974. Sr. lectr., dir. of seminar history of ideas Ecole Polytech., Paris, 1977-89; journalist The Quotidien de Paris, 1977-78; fellow French Acad. in Rome (Villa Medici), 1978-80; program planning officer, sr. program planning officer UNESCO, Paris, 1984-92, exec. sec., dir. World Commn. on Culture and Devel., 1992-94, dir. analysis and forecasting unit, 1994-98, dir. analysis and forecasting office, 1998—, sec. gen. Coun. on the Future, 1999—; contbr. cultural dept. Nouvel Observateur, Paris, 1979-96; cons. for planning and studies UNESCO, Paris, 1983-84. Editl. bd. UNESCO Courier, 1997—, Foresight, 1999—; editor: Les Clés du XXIe Siècle (Keys to the 21st Century), 2000; prin. co-author (with Federico Mayor): The World Ahead: Our Future in the Making, 2000; contbr. articles to profl. jours. and newspapers. Mem. Latin Acad. (founding). Avocations: reading, arts, swimming. Home: 75 Ave Denfert Rochereau, F-75014 Paris France 07SP Office: UNESCO, 7 Place de Fontenoy, F-75352 Paris France

BINDENAGEL, JAMES DALE, diplomat; b. Huron, S.D, June 30, 1949; s. Gordon Dean and Patricia Jean (Williams) B.; m. Jean Kathleen Lundfelt, Dec. 26, 1971; children: Annamarie, Carl Jakob. BA, U. Ill, 1971, MPA, 1977. With U.S. Consulate, Bremen, Germany, 1977-79; econ. officer Office Ctrl. European Affairs U.S. Dept. State, Washington, 1980-83; acting dir. Can. affairs U.S. Dept. State, 1988-89; dir. Office Ctrl. European Affairs U.S. Dept. State, Washington, 1992-94; polit. officer Am. Embassy, Bonn, Germany, 1983-86, dep. chief mission, 1994-96; acting dir. Can. affairs U.S. Dept. State, 1988-89; dep. chief mission Am. Embassy, Berlin, 1989-90; chargé d'affaires, acting amb. Am. Embassy, Bonn, 1996-97; divsn. chief developing countries and trade orgns. U.S. Dept. State Econ. and Bus. Affairs Bur., 1991; dir. Rockwell Internat., 1991-92; chargé d'affaires, acting amb. Am. Embassy, Bonn, 1996-97; sr. coord. New Transatlantic Agenda German Marshall Fund, 1997-98; dir. Washington Conf. on Holocaust-era Assets, 1998, amb., 1999—. Capt. USAR, 1971-74. Congl. fellow Am. Polit. Sci. Assn., 1987-88. Mem. Am. Polit. Sci. Assn. (congl. fellow 1987-88, Nat. Performance award 1998), Am. Coun. on Germany, Coun. on Fgn. Rels., Woodstock Bus. Conf., Pi Sigma Alpha. Roman Catholic. Avocation: tennis, hiking. Office: 202 Northmoor Dr Silver Spring MD 20901-2645

BINDER, HENRY J., internist, educator; b. N.Y.C., Dec. 5, 1936; s. Samuel Binder and Rose Divak; m. Joan W. Binder, May 26, 1961; children: Stephen E., Sarah A. AB, Dartmouth Coll., 1957; MD, NYU, 1961; MA, Yale U., 1978. Lic. MD, Conn. Asst. prof. medicine U. Chgo., 1968-69; asst. prof. medicine Yale U., New Haven, 1969-72, assoc. prof. medicine, 1972-78, prof., 1978—; vis. prof. U. Zurich, Switzerland, 1984-85, U. Lausanne, Switzerland, 1991-92, Pasteur Inst., Paris, 1999. Capt. USAF, 1966-68. Office: Yale U PO Box 208019 New Haven CT 06520-8019

BINDER, KURT, educator in theoretical physics; b. Korneuburg, Austria, Feb. 10, 1944; arrived in Germany, 1969; s. Eduard Victor and Anna (Eppel) B.; m. Marlies Ecker, July 15, 1977; children: Martin, Stefan. Diploma in Engring., Tech. Inst., Vienna, Austria, 1967, D in Tech., 1969; habilitation, Tech. U. Munich, Germany, 1973. Rsch. assoc. Tech. Hochschule, Vienna, Austria, 1969, Tech. U., Munich, 1969-74; IBM Zurich postdoctoral fellow Reuschlikon, Switzerland, 1972-73; prof. U. des Saarlandes, Saarbruecken, Germany, 1974-77; dir. inst. Theorie II IFF/KFA, Juelich, Germany, 1977-83; prof. Univ. Mainz, Germany, 1983—; speaker Sonderforschungsbereich 262, Mainz, Germany, 1987—; external mem. Max Planck Inst. for Polymer Rsch., 1989—; mem. tech. adv. bd. State Rheinland Pfalz, Mainz, 1988-93. Author: (book) Monte Carlo Simulation in Statistical Physics: An Introduction, 1988, 2d rev. edit. 1992; editor, co-author: Monte Carlo Methods in Statistical Physics, 1979, 2d rev. edit. 1986, Applications of the Monte Carlo Method, 1984, 2d rev. edit. 1987, Monte Carlo and Molecular Dynamics Simulation in Statistical Physics, 1995; also contbr. more than 500 articles to profl. jours. Mem. European Phys. Soc., German Phys Soc. (Max Planck medal 1993), Austrian Acad. Scis. (corr. mem.). Office: Inst Phys Univ Mainz, Staudinger Weg 7, D-55099 Mainz Germany

BINDER, LEO OTTO, chemistry educator; b. Linz, Austria, July 13, 1946; s. Leopold Florian and Anna (Hamberger) B.; m. Helga Zeipelt, Feb. 12, 1983; Claudia, Veronika. PhD, Tech. U., Graz, 1971-86. Cert. chem. engring. Univ. asst. Tech. U., Graz, 1971-86, asst. prof., 1986-88, assoc. prof., 1988-97, prof., 1997—. Contbr. articles to profl. jours. Mem. Internat. Soc. Electrochemistry (individual). Roman Catholic. Avocation: scuba diving. Office: Tech U, Stremayrgasse 16, A-8010 Graz Austria

BINDER, MILDRED KATHERINE, retired public welfare agency executive; b. York, Pa., Jan. 5, 1918; d. Jemie Irving and Emma Jane (Billet) B. BA in Sociology magna cum laude, Hood Coll., 1940. Sec., mgr. Stock's Appliances, York, 1940-42; from caseworker, supr. to exec. dir. York County Bd. Assistance/Pa. Dept. Public Welfare, 1942-83; ret., 1983; Past exec. com. York County Employment and Tng. Com.; past mem. dept. task forces state Social Service Delivery to Client Info. System, also mem. state ops. rev. bd.; co-chair Cmty. Dialogue Com., 1968-69; human svcs. planning coalition United Way, 1978-83, chair coun. agy. execs., 1967-71, 76-78; past mem. consumer adv. couns. Gen. Telephone, Met. Edison. Bd. dirs. Literacy Coun. York County, 1985-86; active York County Human Svcs. Adv. Com., 1983-87, York county Area Agy. on Aging Adv. Com., 1989-95. Recipient Commendation award Pa. gov., Pa. Ho. of Reps. Mem. AAUW (bd. dirs. York br. 1984-96), Am. Public Welfare Assn., York County Hist. Soc. (bd. dirs 1989-97), York Transp. Club (bd. dirs. 1987-91), Coll. Club York (bd. dirs. 1994—), Hood Coll. Club (pres. 1993-97). Home: 1611 W Market St York PA 17404-5416

BINDER, PATRICE, governmental executive; b. Nerac, France, Sept. 10, 1949; d. Fernando and Magali (Comolet) B.; m. Anne DuPoux, Sept. 16, 1972; children: Carole, Frederic, Alexia. PhD, Lyon U., France, 1975. Physician Nigerian Army, Agadez, 1976-78, French Army, Strasbourg, 1978-80; rschr. French Army, Lyon, 1980-85; rsch. mgr. French Army, Vert-Le-Petit, 1985-93; rsch. coord. Ministry Defense, Paris, 1993—. Contbr. articles to profl. jours. Mem. ISM, Soc. French Microbiology. Avocations: horseback riding, gardening. Office: DRET/STROT, DCSSA/AST/REC, PO Box 125, 00459 Armees France

BINDMAN, LYNN JANICE, neurophysiologist; b. London, July 14, 1938; d. Alan Arly (Weiner) and Nettie (Prevezer) Winton; m. Geoffrey Lionel Bindman; children: Jonathan Paul, Daniel Mark, Miriam Ruth. BSc, U. Col. London, 1960, PhD, 1964. Asst. lectr. U. Coll. London, 1965-69, rsch. asst., 1969-72, lectr., 1972-82, sr. lectr., 1982-93, reader, 1993—; mem. congress exec. com. Internat. Union Physiol. Scis., 1991-93. Author: (with O. Lippold) Neurophysiology of the Cerebral Cortex, 1981, (with others) Multiple Choice Questions in Physiology, 1997 (3d. edition), Women Physiologists, 1993; contbr. articles to profl. jours. including Jour. Neurophysiology, Jour. Physiology, Synapse, Hippocampus. Sch. governor, London, 1980-87; subject program reviewer Quality Assurance Agy., Gloucester, 1998—. Recipient project grant The Wellcome Trust, 1992-97. Mem. The Physiology Soc., Brain Rsch. Assn., Soc. Neuroscience. Avocations: walking, travel, art. Office: U Coll London, Gower St, London WCIE6BT, England

BINFIELD, JOHN CLYDE, historian, educator; b. Fulmer Chase, Buckingham, Eng., Dec. 5, 1940; s. Edward John and Margaret Florence (Goodfellow) B.; m. Noreen Helen Maycock, June 18, 1969; children: Emma Victoria, Anna Alexandra. BA, Emmanuel Coll., Cambridge, Eng., 1961, MA, PhD, 1965. Asst. lectr. U. Sheffield, Eng., 1964-67, lectr., 1967-74, sr. lectr., 1974-84, reader, 1984-88, dept. head, 1988-91; assoc. prof. U. Sheffield, 1999—. Author: George Williams and YMCA, 1973, So Down to Prayers, 1977, Pastors and People, 1984; editor Jour. United Reformed Ch. History Soc., 1976—; contbr. numerous articles to profl. jours. Vice chmn. Nat. Council YMCA's, London, 1982—, chmn. 1992-97, hon. v.p. 1999—; mem. Exec. World Alliance YMCA's, Geneva, 1985—; chmn. bd. govs. Silcoates Sch., Wakefield, Eng., 1983-93, chmn. Voluntary Action, 1990-93. Fellow Royal Hist. Soc., Soc. Antiquaries; mem. Royal Overseas League Club (London). Liberal Democrat. Avocations: chapels, houses, opera. Office: U Sheffield, Dept History, Western Bank, Sheffield S10 2TN, England

BINGEMAN, JOHN MERVYN, retired military officer, nautical archaeologist; b. London, Dec. 27, 1933; s. Alfred Mervyn and Grace Marjorie (Lanchester) B.; m. Jean Heather Sturgess (div. Mar. 1982); children: Michael John, Robin Mervyn; m. Jane Elizabeth Lucas Evans, June 1, 1982. Grad., Royal Naval Coll., Dartmouth, Eng., 1951, Royal Naval Engring. Coll., Plymouth, Eng., 1957. Chartered engr., Eng. Commd. ensign British Royal Navy, 1951; sr. engr. H.M.S. Daring, 1960-61; tech. officer Ghana Navy Base, Takoradi, 1966-67; tradesmaster Royal Naval Dockyard, Chatham, Eng., 1968-69; gen. mgr. Nigerian Naval Dockyard, Lagos, 1970-71; chief engr. H.M.S. Exmouth, 1972-73, H.M.S. Fearless-Intrepid, 1975-77; project mgr. Royal Naval Dockyard, Portsmouth, Eng., 78-80; staff officer Ministry of Def. Navy, London, 1981-84; ret. British Royal Navy, 1986; diving dir. historic British shipwreck sites, 1986—; lectr. on nautical archaeology. Contbr. articles to profl. jours. Mem. Inst. Mech. Engrs., Council Nautical Archaeology (hon. sec. 1982-83), Nautical Archaeology Soc. (hon. sec. 1983-86), Soc. Nautical Rsch. (vice-chmn. 1989-95, pres. 1996—). Pioneer in excavation of historic shipwreck sites including the Assurance (from the year 1753) and the Pomone, 1811. Currently licensee for the excavation of the wreckage of the Invincible, 1758. Home and Office: 5 Rumbolds Close, Chichester PO19 2JJ, England

BINGHAM, CHARLOTTE (MARY THERESE), writer; b. Haywards Heath, Sussex, Eng., June 29, 1942; d. John Michael Ward and Madeleine (Ebel) B.; m. Terence Joseph Brady, Jan. 15, 1964; children: Candida, Matthew. Student, U. Paris, Sorbonne, 1959-60. Author: Coronet Among the Weeds, 1963, Lucinda, 1966, Coronet Among the Grass, 1972, No, Honestly!, 1974, Belgravia, 1983, To Hear a Nightingale, 1988, The Business, 1989, In Sunshine or In Shadow, 1990, Stardust, 1991, By Invitation, 1991, Country Life, 1991, Nanny, 1991, At Home, 1992, Change of Heart, 1994, Debutantes, 1995, The Nightingale Sings, 1996, Grand Affair, 1997, Love Song, 1998, The Kissing Garden, 1999, The Loveknot, 2000, The Blue Note, 2000; (with Terence Brady) Rose's Story, 1972, Victoria, 1972, Victoria and Company, 1974, No, Honestly, 1976, Yes, Honestly, 1977; (scripts for TV series with Brady) One Two Sky's Blue, 1967, Take Three Girls, 1968-71, Upstairs, Downstairs, 1971-73, Such a Small Word, 1973, No, Honestly, 1974-75, One of the Family, 1975, Yes, Honestly, 1975-76, Making the Play, 1977, Pig in the Middle, 1980, Nanny, 1981-83, Father Matthew's Daughter, 1986, Forever Green, 1989, Lorna Doone, 1997; (films with Brady) Love With A Perfect Stranger, 1985, Magic Moments, 1986; (stage plays with Brady) The Sloane Ranger's Revue, 1986, The Shell Seekers, I Wish I Wish, 1990, Coming of Age; creator: (TV series) Oh, Madeline, (USA), 1983. Mem. Soc. of Authors. Office: United Authors Garden Studios care Peters Fraser & Dunlop, Studios 11-15 Betterton St, London WC2H9BP, England

BINGHAM, GEORGE WALTER CHANDLER, sales executive; b. Cambridge, Mass., Jan. 1, 1925; s. George Hutchins Jr. Bingham and Audrey Wellington (Wack) Bingham Suter; m. Carolyn Susan Webb, Nov. 25, 1967; 1 child, Susan Cordelia. Student, Dartmouth Coll., 1943-44, 46-48; BA, Gettysburg Coll., 1950; postgrad., Columbia U., 1950-51. With CBS TV, N.Y.C., 1951-55; account exec. Gill-Perna Sta. Reps., N.Y.C., 1955-56, Walker Representation Co., N.Y.C., 1956-57; v.p., mgr. New Eng. sales Walker-Rawalt, Inc., Boston, 1957-61; pres. New Eng. Spot Sales, Inc., Belmont, Mass., 1961—; mgr. New. Eng. sales Stone Reps., 1960-70; mgr. New Eng. sales Jack Masla & Co., Boston, 1970-80, Weiss & Powell, Boston, 1983-86; mgr. New Eng. sales Katz & Powell, Boston, 1987-95, ret.; treas., co-owner So. Maine Broadcasting Corp., Sanford/York County, 1975-83, Essex Broadcasting Corp., Newburyport, Mass., 1977-83. Mem. exec. com. Dartmouth Coll. Class of 1947; officer, dir. Camp Allen, Bedford, N.H., 1983—. With USNR, 1943-46. Mem. NATAS (founding mem. Boston, New Eng. chpt.), Broadcast Pioneers Internat., Radio and TV Soc., New Eng. Broadcasting Assn., New Eng. Assn. Radio and TV Sta. Reps. (pres. 1963-64), Maine Assn. Broadcasters, N.H. Assn. Broadcasters, Mass. Soc. SAR, Mass. Soc. Mayflower Descs. (officer, dep. gov. 1976-87), Am. Legion (comdr. post 281 1974-76, 85-92), Boston's Advt. Post, Harvard Faculty Club, Kiwanis, Phi Alpha Theta, Kappa Kappa Kappa (hon.). Democrat. Episcopalian. Avocations: history, theatre, fishing, sailing. Home and Office: New Eng Spot Sales Inc 208 Lewis Rd Belmont MA 02478-3833

BINGHAM, J. PETER, electronics research executive; married; 2 children. BS in Physics cum laude, Polytechnic Inst., N.Y.; MS in Exptl. Physics, U. Md., PhD in Elec. Engring. With RCA Consumer Electronics, David Sarnoff Rsch. Ctr.; exec. v.p., tech. Thomson Consumer Electronics; v.p. engring. Philips Consumer Electronics Co., 1982-91; with Philips Rsch. Philips Electronics N.Am. Corp., 1991; pres. Philips Rsch., 1991—; bd. dirs. Indsl. Rsch. Inst. Recipient David Sarnoff award, RCA Lab. Achievements award; Named in his honor Bingham Peak in Antarctica, Arctic Inst. of North Am. Office: 23 Brookwood Dr Briarcliff Manor NY 10510-2040

BINGHAM, JAMES STEWART, genitourinary physician; b. Belfast, No. Ireland, July 31, 1945; s. William and Nora Mary (Beckett) B.; m. Elizabeth Eleanor Stewart, Sept. 21, 1974; 1 child, Stewart. MB BCh, Queen's U., Belfast, 1969. Resident in ob-gyn. Vancouver (B.C., Can.) Gen. Hosp., 1975; cons. in genitourinary medicine Middlesex Hosp., London, 1977, St. Thomas' Hosp., London, 1992—. Recipient Terr. Decoration of Brit. Army, 1982. Fellow Royal Coll. Ob-Gyn., Royal Coll. Physicians London, Royal Coll. Physicians Edinburgh, Brit. HIV Assn. (chmn. 1996-2000), Med. Soc. Study of Venereal Diseases (pres. 1993-95), Soc. Apothecaries of London (convenor of examiners 1992-95), Internat. Union Against Sexually Transmitted Infections (chmn. 1995-99, pres. elect 1999—). Office: Lloyd Clinic Guy's Hosp, St Thomas' St, London SE1 9RT, England

BINGHAM, JUNE, author, playwright; b. White Plains, N.Y., June 20, 1919; d. Max J.H. and Mabel (Limburg) Rossbach; m. Jonathan B. Bingham, Sept. 20, 1939 (dec. July 1986); children: Sherry B. Downes, Micki B. Esselstyn (dec. 1999), Timothy, Claudia B. Meyers; m. Robert B. Birge, Mar. 28, 1987; 1 stepchild, Robert R. Student, Vassar Coll., 1936-38; BA, Barnard Coll., 1940. Writer, editor U.S. Treasury, Washington, 1943-45; editorial asst. Washington Post, 1945-46; writer Tarrytown (N.Y.) Daily News, 1946. Author: Do Cows Have Neuroses?, Do Babies Have Worries?, Do Teenagers Have Wisdom?, Courage to Change: An Introduction to Life and Thought of Reinhold Niebuhr, 1961, paperback, 1992, U Thant: The Search for Peace, 1970, (play) Triangles, 1986, You and the I.C.U., 1990, (play) Eleanor and Alice, 1996, (with others) The Inside Story: Psychiatry and Everyday Life, 1953, The Pursuit of Health, 1985, (musical) Squanto and Love, 1992, Young Roosevelts, 1993, The Other Lincoln, 1995; contbr. articles to nat. mags., newspapers and profl. jours. Bd. dirs. Barnard Coll., 1970-76, African-Am. Inst., N.Y.C., 1973-90, Riverdale Mental Health Assn., 1983—, Woodrow Wilson Found., Princeton, N.J., 1959-64, 83-89, Lehman Coll. Found., 1983-90, Ittleson Ctr. for Childhood Rsch., 1958-90, Franklin and Eleanor Roosevelt Inst., 1992—; founder T.L.C.; trained liaison comforter Vol. Program of Presbyn. Hosp., N.Y.C. Named Alumna of the Yr., Rosemary Hall, 1976. Mem. Authors Guild (nominating com. 1987-90), Dramatists Guild, PEN, Cosmopolitan Club. Democrat. Avocations: tennis, golf, theatre, movies, reading. Home: 5000 Independence Ave Bronx NY 10471-2804

BINGHAM, PARIS EDWARD, JR., electrical engineer, computer consultant; b. Aurora, Colo., Sept. 26, 1957; s. Paris Edward and Shirley Ann (Blehm) B.; m. Laurie Sue Piersol, May 9, 1981 (div. Sept. 1987); m. Helen Naef, Aug. 7, 1993. BS in Elec. Engring. and Computer Sci., U. Colo., 1979. Mem. tech. staff Western Electric Co., Aurora, 1979-81, system engr., 1981; mem. electronic tech. staff Hughes Aircraft Co., Aurora, 1981-83, staff engr., 1983-85, sr. staff engr., 1986-93, scientist, engr., 1993-94; area systems support engr. Sun Microsystems, Inc., Englewood, Colo., 1994—; cons. RJM Assocs., Huntington, N.Y., 1987-91; cons. Aurora, 1988—. Mem. IEEE, Assn. for Computing Machinery. Republican. Presbyterian. Achievements include research on artificial intelligence applications, distributed networking and computing, next generational software technologies. Office: Sun Microsystems Inc 9800 Mt Pyramid Ct Ste 300 Englewood CO 80112-2668

BINGHAM, RICHARD GEORGE, physicist, optical designer, consultant; b. Norwich, England, July 15, 1940; s. Thomas Frederick and Emma Maud (Lusher) B.; m. Elizabeth Anne Epps, Sept. 24, 1977; children: Amanda, Rachel. BA, Cambridge U., Eng., 1962, MA, 1966, PhD, 1966. Chartered engr. Optical engr. Royal Greenwich Obs., Cambridge, 1966-97; co. dir. Optical Generics Ltd., 1994-97, tech. dir., 1997-2000; co-dir. Optical Investments Ltd., 1997-2000. Editor: Metal Mirrors, 1993. Hon. rsch. fellow U. Coll. London, 1986—. Fellow Royal Astron. Soc. (past councillor); mem. Inst. Physics. Office: Dept Phys and Astr Univ Coll London, Gower St, London WC1E 6BT, England

BINGHAM, THOMAS HENRY (LORD BINGHAM OF CORNHILL), judge; b. Oct. 13, 1933; s. T.H. and C. Bingham; m. Elizabeth Loxley, 1963; 3 children. Student, Sedbergh Sch., Balliol Coll., Oxford. Bar: Gray's Inn, 1959, Bencher 1979. Standing jr. counsel Dept. Employment, 1968-72; with Queen's Counsel, 1972; recorder Crown Ct., 1975-80; judge High Ct. of Justice Queen's Bench Divsn., 1980-86; lord justice of appeal, 1986-92, master of the rolls, 1992-96; Lord Chief Justice of Eng. and Wales House of Lords, London, 1996-2000, sr. law lord, 2000—; mem. Lord Chancellor's Law Reform Com.; chair inquiry into supervision of BCCI, 1991-92. Asst. editor: Chitty on Contracts, 22d edit., 1961. Spl. trustee St. Mary's Hosp., 1985-92, chair, 1988-92. Office: House of Lords, Office Law Lords, London SW1, England

BINGYUAN, CAO, mathematician, educator; b. Chang De, China, Oct. 30, 1951; s. Cao Changming and Li Changyin; m. Wang Peihua, Jan. 25, 1980; 1 child, Cao Chang. Grad., Hunan Normal U., 1977, postgrad., 1977-79. Asst. math. dept. Hunan Normal U., 1978-86; lectr. dept. math. Changsha U. Water Resources and Electric Power, 1987-92, assoc. prof., 1992-96, prof., 1996—; chmn. math. dept. Shantou U., 1999—. mem. evaluation com. for higher profl. title Electric Industry Ministry, 1992-98. Compiler, author: Lectures in Economic Mathematics, 1994, others; contbr. numerous articles to profl. jours. Recipient 1st prize Econ. Math. Assn. Hunan, 1991, Fuzzy Math. and Sys. chpt. South China, 1994, 3d prize Zeng Xianzi Nat. Edn. Found. Normal U., 1997, Advanced Progress Sci. and Tech. Hunan Province Ednl. Com., 1997. Mem. Chinese Assn. Math., Chinese Assn. Ops. Rsch. (dir.), Chinese Assn. Indsl. and Applied Math., Rsch. Assn. Hunan Econ. Maths., Gesellschaft fur Angewandte Math und Mechanik, Elements Analysis China (standing com. dir.), Fuzzy Math. and Sys. Chpt. South China (pres.). Communist. Avocations: swimming, watching TV, fishing, holding academic congress.

BIN MAHFOUZ, MAHFOUZ MAREI, company executive; b. Mecca, Saudi Arabia, Dec. 15, 1969; s. Marei Mubarak and Khadija Omar Bin Mahfouz; m. Faiza Abdul Aziz Gabbaa, July 15, 1993; children: Balgis, Mohammed, Soliman. BA in Law, King Abdul Azia U., Jeddah, Saudi Arabia, 1993; LLM, Am. U., London, 1997; diploma in mgmt., Alexander Hamilton Inst., 1998; MBA in Fin., Washington Internat. U., 1998; postgrad., Glasgow (Scotland) U., 1999—. Exec. gen. mgr. Bin Mahfouz & Al Amoudi Group, Jeddah, 1993-97; exec. gen. mgr., CEO M. Bin Mahfouz Group & Co. Ltd., Mecca, Saudi Arabia, 1997—; legal cons. Bin Mahfouz Law Firm, Jeddah, 1993—, gen. mgr., 1993—; gen. mgr. Kindah Pub. & Info. Co., Jeddah, 1997—; bd. mem., exec. mgr. World Trade Ctr., Mecca, 1999—; dep. gen. mgr. Jeddah Internat. Exhbn. Co., 1999—; pres. Sudanese Trade Ctr., Jeddah, 1999—. Author: Arbitration in International and Islamic Law, 1998. Recipient Best Rsch. award King Abdul Aziz U., Jeddah, 1993. Mem. Internat. Bar assn., Internat. Assn. Young Lawyers, London Ct. Internat. Arbitration Ctr., Saudi Environ. Soc. (hon.), Saudi Umran Soc., Mecca Judiciary and Legal Juristic, Mecca C. of C. Avocations: reading, traveling, car racing, playing football, classical music. Fax: 0096625420633-5564776. Home: Al Aziziah Rd PO Box 734, Mecca Saudi Arabia Office: M Bin Mahfouz Group & Co, PO Box 734, Mecca Saudi Arabia

BINNEMANS, KOEN, chemist, researcher; b. Geel, Belgium, Jan. 27, 1970; s. Marcel Binnemans and Margaretha Wuyts. Lic. in chemistry cum laude, Cath. U. of Leuven, Belgium, 1992, PhD in Chemisty cum laude, 1996. Rsch. asst. Nat. Sci. Found. of Belgium, Leuven, 1992-96; postdoctoral fellow Fund for Scientific Rsch.-Flanders, Leuven, 1996—; vis. scientist U. Exeter, Eng., 1997, U. Rennes, France, 1996. Contbr. over 50 articles to profl. jours., chpts. to books. Recipient DSM award for chemistry and tech. 2nd prize, 1996. Mem. Internat. Liquid Crystal Soc., European Rare-Earth and Actinide Soc., Royal Flemish Chem. Soc. (youth prize 1992), Brit. Liquid Crystal Soc., Royal Soc. Chemistry (grad.), Am. Chem. Soc. Avocations: collecting minerals, determination of gemstones, travel, writing. Home: In't Eegdeken 53, B-2440 Geel Belgium Office: Cath U Leuven Dept Chem, Celestijnenlaan 200F, B-3001 Heverlee Belgium

BINNEMANS, PHILIPPE-HENRI, lawyer; b. Wilrijk, Antwerpen, Belgium, Feb. 23, 1961; s. Henri-Auguste and Marie-Anne (Crismer) B.; m. Nathalie Brunet, Aug. 14, 1987; children: Chloe, Maxime. Dir. Fiduciaire H.B., Antwerp, Belgium, 1981-82, Philax, Knokke, Belgium, 1982-86; lawyer Brussels Bar, 1986; sr. ptnr. Binnemans Law Firm, Brussels, 1989—. Recipient Hugo Van Eecke prize Pro-Stafhouder H. Van Eeke, 1988; winner Plead contest Brussels Bar, 1987, Laureate Plead contest S. Netherlands, Breda Bar, 1989. Mem. Brussels Bar, Vlaams Pleitgenootschap, Royal Leopold Club, Country Riding Club. Home and Office: Ave Louise 131/1, 1050 Brussels Belgium

BINNIE, COLIN DAVID, neurophysiology educator, consultant; b. London, Jan. 23, 1938; s. Horace David and Doris Amy (Read) B.; m. Florence Margaret Shields, Oct. 29, 1964; children: Caroline Joy, Jonathan Nicholas. MA, Cambridge (Eng.) U., 1962, BChir, 1963, MD, 1966. Registered med. practitioner; specialist registration in clin. neurophysiology. Sr. registrar in clin. neurophysiology St. Bartholomews Hosp., London, 1966-69; cons. in clin. neurophysiology Runwell (Eng.) Hosp., 1969-76; physician in charge dept. clin. neurophysiology St. Bartholomews Hosp., London, 1970-76; head clin. neurophysiology Inst. voor Epilepsiebestrijding, Heemstede, The Netherlands, 1976-86; cons. clin. neurophysiologist Bethlem Royal and Maudsley Hosp., London, 1986-95; prof. clin. neurophysiology King's Coll. Sch. Medicine, London, 1995—; chmn. Surgery Commn., Internat. League Against Epilepsy, 1993—; chmn. Electroencephalography and Clin. Neurophysiology Ednl. Bd., U.K., 1994—; vis. prof. physiology Univ. Coll., London, 1996—. Contbr. over 500 articles on clin. neurophysiology and epilepsy to med. jours., including Brain, Epilepsia, Jour. Neurology, Neurosurgery and Psychiatry, EEG and Clin. Neurophysiology, also numrous chpts. to books. Trustee Fund for Epilepsy, London, 1992—, Epilepsy Rsch. Found., London, 1993—. Recipient Ralph Nobel prize Cambridge U., 1969, Michael Stiftung prize, 1982, gold award Dutch Epilepsy Assn., 1986, Grey Walter medal, 1997. Fellow Royal Coll. Physicians and Surgeons (Glasgow), Royal Coll. Physicians (London), Royal Coll. Surgeons (London); mem. Royal Soc. Medicine (coun. sect. neurology 1994—), Brit. Soc. for Clin. Neurophysiology (coun. 1989-92, pres. 1992-96), Electrophysiol. Technologists Assn. (coun. 1964—). Avocations: languages, opera, walking. Office: King's Coll Hosp, Denmark Hill, London SE5 9RS, England

BINNIG, GERD KARL, physicist; b. July 20, 1947; m. Lore Binnig, 1969; 2 children. Diploma in Physics, Goethe U., Frankfurt, Fed. Republic Germany, PhD, 1978. Rsch. staff mem. IBM Zurich Rsch. Lab., 1978—, group leader, 1984—; with Stanford U., 1985-86; hon. prof. physics U. Munich, 1987—; vis. prof. Stanford U., 1986-88; mem. tech. coun. IBM Acad., adv. bd. Bild der Wissenschaft, 1990—. Author: Aus dem Nichts, 1989; mem. editorial bd. Rev. Sci. Instruments, 1990-92. Co-recipient Nobel prize in physics, 1986; recipient physics prize German Phys. Soc., 1982, Otto Klung prize, 1983, Joint King Faisal Internat. prize for sci., Hewlett-Packard Europhysics prize, 1984, Elliot Cresson medal Franklin Inst., 1987, Grosses Verdienstkreuz mit Stern und Schulterband des Verdienstordens, 1987, Minnie Rosen award Ross U., 1988; named to Nat. Inventors Hall of Fame, 1994. Fellow Royal Microscopical Soc. (hon. 1988); Acad. Scis. (fgn. assoc. 1987). Avocations: music, tennis, soccer, golf. Office: IBM Schweiz, Baendiweg 21 Post fach, Ruschlikon Zurich CH-8010, Switzerland*

BINNING, BETTE FINESE (MRS. GENE HEDGCOCK BINNING), athletic association official; b. Brandon, Man., Can., Sept. 20, 1927 (father Am. citizen); d. Henry Josiah and Beatrice Victoria (Harrop) Ames; grad. Brandon Collegiate, 1944; student Brandon, U., 1944-46; m. Gene Hedgcock Binning, May 3, 1952; children: Gene Barton, Barbara Jo, Bradford Jay. Exec. sec. to mgr. Gardner-Denver Co., Denver, 1950-52; mem. age group swimming com. Amateur Athletic Union U.S., 1966-68, 70-72, women's swimming com., 1968-69, 72—, age group swimming objectives subcom., 1970-71, del. conv., 1971, 72, 73, 74, 75, 76, 77, 79, 80; Okla. state chmn. age group swimming Amateur Athletic Union, 1966-68, 70-72, chmn. women's swimming com., 1968-69, 72-79, mem. Okla. exec. bd. for all amateur sports, also registration com., 1971-79; mem. U.S. Olympic com., 1972-80; nat. dir. swimming records, 1972-81; U.S. rep. to records com. Amateur Swimming Assn. Ams., 1975-83, dir. records com., 1975-83; dir., sec. records com. Union Amateur de Natacion de las Americas, 1979-83; tech. ofcl. Pan Am. Games, Mexico City, 1975, San Juan, P.R., 1979; ofcl. XXI Olympiad, Montreal, Que., Can., 1976; mem. interim organizing com. U.S. Olympic Festival, 1986; athletic adv. dir. U.S. Olympic Festival '89, 1987-88. Team capt. YMCA fund drives, 1966-78; mem. adv. com. Internat. Gymnastics Hall of Fame, 1996—. Mem. Kerr-Mcgee Swim Club (dir. 1968-75), Quail Creek Golf and Country Club, Oklahoma City Ski Club (Oklahoma City), Vail Athletic Club (Colo.). Presbyterian. Home: 3101 Rolling Stone Rd Oklahoma City OK 73120-1841 also: Vail Internat 205 300 E Lionshead Cir Vail CO 81657-5204

BINNING, GENE BARTON, computer company executive; b. Denver, Feb. 7, 1953; s. Gene Hedgecock and Bette Finice (Ames) B. BA in Econs. and Bus. Adminstrn., Vanderbilt U., 1975; MBA, U. Okla., 1977; EdD, Okla. State U., 1996. Br. controller Trane Air Conditioning Dist. Office, Okla. City, 1977-86; cons. pvt. practice, Okla. City, 1986-99; instr. U. Cen. Okla., Edmond, Okla., 1988-99; tech. dir. Vectrix Corp., Oklahoma City, 1999—. Tech. editor On the Horizons, 1996-99. Vol. coord. Sooner State Games, Okla. City, 1985-87; state regents faculty adv. com., 1992-93. Mem. AAUP, Assn. Info. Tech. Profl., Assn. Info. Sys., Okla. Higher Edn. Faculty Assn. of U. Ctrl. Okla. (pres. 1992-93), Faculty Assn. U. Ctrl. Okla. (pres. 1991-92), Quail Creek Golf and Country Club. Republican. Home: 2933 Rolling Stone Rd Oklahoma City OK 73120-1921 Office: Vectrix Corp 6440 Avondale Dr Ste 200 Oklahoma City OK 73116-6416

BINNION, JOHN EDWARD, education educator; b. Paris, Tex., July 14, 1918; s. Roy Cecil and Johnnie Mary (Garner) B.; m. Doris Lee Campbell, Mar. 30, 1945; children: Margaret Ann, John Edward II, Mary Virginia, Dianna Lee. AA, Chaffey Coll., Ontario, Calif., 1936; BBA, U. Tex., 1945; MA, N.Mex. Highlands U., 1951; EdD, Okla. State U., 1953; MBA, U. Denver, 1972. CPA, Okla., Tex.; cert. adminstrv. mgr. Acct. D&B Emsco Mfg. Co., Dallas, 1945-46; acct., office mgr. Lumber Dealer's Supply Co., Long Beach, Calif., 1946-47; tchr. Sawyer (Kans.) H.S., 1947-50; asst. prof. bus. edn. and bus. adminstrn., supr. USAF clk.-typist program N.Mex. Highlands U., 1950-52; assoc. prof. bus. edn. and acctg. Southwestern State U., Weatherford, Okla., 1953-55; prof. bus. edn., chmn. dept. U. Denver, 1955-65; prof. bus. edn. charge grad. program bus. edn. Tex. Tech. U., Lubbock, 1965-68; nat. dir. edn., edn. divsn Lear Siegler, Inc., 1968-72; prof., chmn. dept. bus. edn. Cleve. State U., 1972-79, prof. acctg., 1979-81; assoc. dean James J. Nance Coll. Bus. Adminstrn., 1980-81, prof. emeritus, 1981—; pres. Tex. Ednl. and Adminstrv. Mgmt. Systems, Crowell, Tex., 1981—; textbook cons. U.S. Armed Forces Inst., 1955-68; test coordinator, profl. standards program Nat. Assn. Ednl. Secs., 1965-69; mem. Policies Commn. Bus. and Econ. Edn., 1962-66; commr. Accrediting Commn. Assn. Ind. Colls. and Schs., 1963-69; mem. Colo. Adv. Com. Bus. Edn., 1955-65, U.S. Office Edn. Adv. Council Insured Loans to Vocat. Students, 1966-69; cons. Acad. Ednl. Devel., 1965-67, Ednl. Testing Service; chmn. mgmt. com. Inst. Certifying Secs., 1970-73. Author: Equipment Standards for Business Classrooms, 1954, Selected Authorities in Business Education, 1965; co-author: College Accounting for Secretaries, 1971; editor Western Bus. Rev, 1958-62, Colo. Study Guides for Bus. Edn, 1957-65, Purple Heart Mag., 1980-85; contbr. articles to profl. jours. Chmn. Foard County Dem. Com., 1982-88, 96—. Capt. AUS, 1940-44; lt. col. Colo. State Guard. Recipient Purple Heart and decorations for valor, Vets. Small Bus. Advocate of Yr. award U.S. Small Bus. Adminstrn., 1993; named to Ohio Vets. Hall of Fame, 1996. Mem. AICPA, Tex. Soc. CPAs, Okla. Soc. CPAs, Adminstrv. Mgmt. Soc. (Diamond Merit award 1976), Mountain Plains Bus. Edn. Assn. (pres. 1964-65), Nat. Bus. Edn. Assn., Nat. Assn. Bus. Tchr. Edn. (nat. sec. 1957-59), Assn. Ind. Colls. and Schs. (recipient award of merit Accrediting Commn. 1978), Svc. Corps Retired Execs. (SCORE), Mil. Order Purple Heart (nat. comdr. 1973-74, pres. svc. found. 1988-92, chmn. bd. 1992-95), Rotary, Delta Pi Epsilon (nat. treas. 1958-61, nat. exec. sec. 1962-66), Beta Gamma Sigma, Pi Omega Pi, Phi Beta Lambda, Alpha Kappa Psi, Beta Alpha Psi, Kappa Kappa Psi, Delta Tau Delta, Phi Delta Kappa. Democrat. Methodist. Fax: 940-684-1785.

BINNS, WALTER GORDON, JR., investment management executive; b. Richmond, Va., June 8, 1929; s. Walter Gordon and Virginia Belle (Matheny) B.; m. Alberta Louise Fry, Apr. 1, 1972; 1 child, Amanda; 1 stepdau., Clarissa. AB, Coll. William and Mary, 1949; AM, Harvard U., 1951; MBA, NYU, 1959. Trainee Chase Nat. Bank, N.Y.C., 1953-54; with GM, N.Y.C., 1954-94, asst. treas., 1974-82, chief investment funds officer, 1982-94, v.p., 1986-94; pres., CEO GM Investment Mgmt. Corp., 1990-94; bd. dirs. Options Clearing Corp., Inc., Equity Fund Latin Am., Commonwealth Equity Fund; investment adv. com. N.Y. State Common Retirement Fund, 1987-94; mem. pension mgrs. adv. com. N.Y. Stock Exch., 1988-94; mem. Gov. Cuomo's Task Force on Pension Fund Investment, 1988-89; mem. adv. com. Pension Benefit Guaranty Corp., 1991-95; mem. adv. com., bd. Chgo. Mercantile Exch., 1988-97, Chgo. Bd. Trade, 1992-93, Commodity Futures Trading Commn., 1992-94; mem. investment adv. com. Va. Retirement Systems, 1994—, Barings/ING Pvt. Equity Ptnrs., 1996—, SUN Asset Mgmt. Ltd., 1997—; mem. fiduciary panel Prudential Ins. Co., 1994-95. Trustee ARC Retirement System, 1987-90, Citizens Budget Commn., N.Y.C., 1982-94, Endowment Assn., Coll. William and Mary, Med. Coll. Va. Found., Maymont Found., Nat. Coun. Econ. Edn., 1982-94, Futures Ind. Assn., 1988-90; bd. dirs. Alcoholism Coun. Greater N.Y., 1982-92; bd. dirs. Cmty. Fund. of Bronxville, Eastchester Tuckahoe, Inc., 1986-92, Friends of Libr. Coll. William and Mary Coll., 1991-97, Fin. Execs. Rsch. Found., 1988-91, Christian Children's Fund, Nat. Coun. on Alcoholism and Drug Dependence, Vellore Christian Med. Coll. & Hosp. Bd.; founder, interim chmn. Friends of Higher Edn. Va., 1997—. Mem. Fin. Execs. Inst. (chmn. com. on employee benefits 1977-80, com. on investment of employee benefit assets 1985-88, treas. 1991-93), Bronxville Field Club, Harvard Club (N.Y.C.), Grolier Club, Commonwealth Club, Westwood Racquet Club, N.Y. Athletic Club, Phi Beta Kappa, Beta Gamma Sigma. Home: 115 Oxford Cir W Richmond VA 23221-3224 also: 120 Central Park S New York NY 10019-1560 Office: PO Box 17308 Richmond VA 23226-7308

BIN SULAIMAN, HAJI ZAKARIA, Brunei government official. Past permanent sec. Ministry Fgn. Affairs, dep. min. fgn. affairs Govt. of Brunei, min. comm., 1988—. Office: Min Comm Telecom Bldg 2d Fl, Old Airport, Jalan Berakas, Bandar Seri Begawan 1150, Brunei*

BINSWANGER, HANS CHRISTOPH, economist, educator; b. Zurich, Switzerland, June 19, 1929; s. Robert and Margarethe (Goetz) B.; m. Elisabeth Adis, Oct. 6, 1960; three children. BS, U. Zurich, 1956; MSc, U. St. Gallen, 1967. Prof. U. St. Gallen, 1968-94, dir. Inst. Economy and the Environment, 1992-94. Home: Guisanstrasse 15, CH-9010 Saint Gallen Switzerland

BINTLEY, DAVID, ballet company artistic director, choreographer; b. Huddersfield, Eng., 1957. Student, Royal Ballet Sch., Eng., 1974-76. Mem. Sadler's Wells Royal Ballet (now Birmingham Royal Ballet), 1976-82, resident choreographer, 1982-86; resident choreographer Covent Garden, Eng., 1986-93; freelance choreographer, 1993-95; artistic dir. Birmingham Royal Ballet, 1995—. Performed in La Fille Mal Gardée, The Dream, Cinderella, Checkmate, Rake's Progress, Sadler's Wells Royal Ballet; choreographer, The Outsider, 1976, Sadler's Wells Royal Ballet, Swan of Tuonela, 1982, The Snow Queen, 1986, Hobson's Choice, 1989, Consort Lessons, 1983, Flowers of the Forest, 1985, Sadler's Wells Royal Ballet; choreographer Galanteries, Covent Garden, 1986, Allegri diversi, 1987, Still Life at the Penguin Café, 1988, Cyrano, 1991, Tombeaux, 1993, Carmina Burana, Birmingham, 1995, Far from the Madding Crowd, 1996, Edward II, Stuttgart Ballet, 1995, The Nutcracker Sweeties, 1996, The Protecting Veil, 1998, The Shakespeare Suite, 1999, Arthur part 1, 2000. Office: Birmingham Royal Ballet, Birmingham Hippodrome Thorp St, Birmingham B5 4AU, England

BINYAMINI, NISSAN, retired botanist, educator; b. Jerusalem, Israel, Oct. 10, 1930; s. Vehuda dn Devora B.; m. Atalia Kolberg, Mar. 21, 1959; children: Ehud, Yoav. MS, Hebrew U., Jerusalem, 1958, PhD, 1968. With Min. Agrl., 1958-59; asst. Tel Aviv U., Dept. Botany, 1959-62, instr., 1962-70, lectr., 1970-73, sr. lectr., 1973-79, assoc. prof., 1979—; head dept. botany Tel Aviv U., 1986-88. Author: The Flehsy Fungi of Israel, 1975, Poison Plants of Israel, 1977, Larger Fungi of Israel, 1984, Mycology, 1987, Myxomycetes Fungi of Israel, 1991, The Larger Fungi of Israel. Mem. Israel Bot. Soc., Israel Phytpathological Soc., Brit. Mycological Soc., The Mycological Soc. Am., Mycological Soc. Japan. Office: Tel Aviv U Dept Botany, George S Wise Fac Life Sci, 69978 Tel Aviv Israel

BIOLCHINI, ROBERT FREDRICK, lawyer; b. Detroit, Sept. 22, 1939; s. Alfred and Erma (Barbetti) B.; m. Frances Lauinger, June 5, 1965; children: Robert F., Douglas C., Frances E., Tobin m., Thomas A., Christine M. BA, U. Notre Dame, 1962; LLB, George Washington U., 1965. Bar: Okla., Mich., 1965. Assoc. Doerner, Stuart, Saunders, Daniel, Anderson & Biolchini, Tulsa, 1968-71, ptnr., 1971-94; ptnr. Stuart, Biolchini, Turner & Givray, Tulsa, 1994—; pres., CEO Pennwell Corp.; chmn. bd. dirs. PennNet, Inc., Valley Nat. Bank, Ameritrust Holding Co., Old Faithful Underwriting Ltd.; mem. Lloyds of London, 1979—; bd. dirs. Lumen Energy Corp., Bank of The Lakes, Bank of Jackson Hole. Bd. dirs. Thomas Gilcrease Mus., past pres., chmn. bd., 1977-80, dir. emeritus, 1980—; bd. dirs., sec., legal clk. Tulsa Ballet Theatre, Inc., 1976-84; trustee Monte Cassino Endowment, 1978—; pres. Monte Cassino Sch. Bd., 1970-77; chmn. Christ the King Parish Coun., 1974-75; mem. adv. coun. U. Notre Dame Law Sch., 1982—; chmn. Cath. Diocese Tulsa Fund for Future, 1998—; bd. dirs. legal counsel Tulsa Area United Way, 1986—; mem. pres.'s coun. Regis Coll., 1986—. Capt. U.S. Army, 1965-67. Mem. Okla. Bar Assn., Mich. Bar Assn., Met. Tulsa C. of C. (bd. dirs. 1992—), Summit Club, Southern Hills Country Club, Club Ltd., Knights of Malta, Knights of the Holy Sepulchre. Roman Catholic. Home: 1744 E 29th St Tulsa OK 74114-5402 Office: First Place Tower 15 E 5th St Ste 3300 Tulsa OK 74103-4340

BION, JULIAN FLEETWOOD, intensive care and anaesthetist educator; b. Croydon, U.K., July 30, 1952; s. Wilfred R. and Francesca C. (Purnell) B.; m. Nitya Tangchurat, June 15, 1985; children: Alexander, Victoria. MBBS, Charing Cross Hosp., London, 1976; MD, London U., 1990. Cardiology registrar Northampton Gen. Hosp., U.K., 1979-80; sho anaesthetist Northwick Park Hosp., London, 1981; registrar anaesthetist Radcliffe Infirmary, Oxford, 1982; anaesthetist Red Cross, Geneva, 1981, 83; rsch. fellow Clin. Shock Study Group, Glasgow, Scotland, 1984-85; sr. registrar anaesthetist Bristol Royal Infirmary, 1985-87; sr. lectr. intensive care medicine Birmingham U., 1987—; mem. intercollegiate bd. for tng. in intensive care medicine. Editor: Current Topics in Intensive Care, 1993—; mem. editl adv. bd. Intensive Care Medicine, 1992—, Intensive and Critical Care Nursing, 1995-99; mem. editl bd. Clin. Intensive Care, 1990—, Brit. Jour. Hosp. Medicine, 1990—; contbr. articles to profl. jours. Advisor Commonwealth Scholarships Commn., London, 1992-99. Named Dr. of Yr. Bupa Med. Found., 1985. Fellow Royal Coll. Anesthetists, Royal Coll. Physicians; mem. Intensive Care Soc. (coun.), Brit. Med. Assn., European Soc. Intensive Care Medicine (coun., U.K. rep., sec., mem. exec. com.). Home: Stratford House, 13 Arthur Rd Edgbaston, Birmingham B15 2UN, England Office: U Dept Anaesthesia & Intensive Care, N5 Queen Elizabeth Hosp, Birmingham B15 2TH, England

BIRABUZA, ANDRÉ, pediatrician; b. Jenda, Bujumbura, Burundi, July 25, 1952; s. Joseph Birabuza and Nundana Ntimarishavu; m. Angèle Mugozi, Sept. 17, 1983; children: Cesar, Fabrice, Hannibal. MD, Kinshasa U., Congo, 1981; pediat. specialization, U. Dakar, Senegal, 1988. Med. dr. Ministry of Health, Bujumbura, 1981-83, pediatrician, 1988-91; dir. of prevention of contagious diseases project Burundi, 1991-93; councilor Ministry Pub. Health, Burundi, 1994-95; pvt. practice Bujumbura, 1996—; dir. Nat. Reproductive Health Programme, 1998—; cons. World Bank, Bujumbura, 1991-92. Author: (books) Africa Ill of Racism, 1991, Betrayal of African Intellectuals, 1994, The Burundian Illness, 1999, Poetry Collection, 1999; editor: (mags.) Intore, 1993-95, The Renaissance, 1996-97. Mem. Polit. Bur. of Uprona Party, Burundi, 1992-93, Nat. Econ. and Social Coun., Burundi, 1990-91, Constn. Commn., Burundi, 1991-92; gen. sec. Burundian Writers' Assn., 1994—. Mem. Nat. Physician's Order Coun. (gen. sec. 1989-94), Media Assn. Roman Catholic. Avocations: reading, jogging, swimming. Home: 19 Matana Ave, BP 2524 Bujumbura Burundi Office: Editions Intore, 14 Av P Lumumba, BP 525 Bujumbura Burundi

BIRADES, MICHEL CLAUDE, oil company professional, researcher; b. Tarbes, France, Mar. 1, 1959; s. Urbain Osment and Gabrielle Marie (Labourdenne) B.; m. Cécilia Paule Bertrand, Apr. 27, 1991; children: Sophie Marine, Manon Emilie. Sci. degree, Paris VI U., 1982, postgrad. diploma, 1983; engr., Ecole Nat. Ponts Chaussees, Paris, 1983; PhD, Ecole Centrale de Paris, 1985. Cert. engring. Drilling rsch. engr. ELF, Pau, France, 1985-89, structural rsch. engr., 1989-92, structural reliability expert, 1992-94; tech. site mgr. ELF, Dubai, United Arab Emirates, 1994-95; offshore structures expert ELF, Pau, 1995—; lectr. Inst. Francais du Pétrole, Paris, 1987-96; prof. Pau U., 1989-94. Author: Le Grand Livre De L'Oric, 1984, (software) Orphee: Directional Behavior of Bottom Hole Assemblies, 1989; contbr. articles to profl. jours. Fellow Soc. Petroleum Engrs., Assn. Française Techniciens du Pétrole, Clarom. Roman Catholic. Avocations: archery, chess, dance, squash, windsurfing. Home: 14 Rue de Tursan, 64000 Pau France Office: Elf Aquitaine, Ave Larribau, 64018 Pau France

BIRCA-GALATEANU, SERBAN, electronics educator; b. Urziceni, Romania, May 21, 1944; s. Dumitru and Lucia Birca-G. Grad., U. Poly. Bucharest, 1967, PhD, 1976; PhD, U. Nantes, 1993. From asst. to assoc. prof. U. Poly. Bucharest, 1967-90; assoc. prof. U. Nantes, France, 1990-93, IUFM, Nantes, 1993—; Author: Industrial Electronics, 1976, 2d edit., 1983, Optoelectronics, 1983, 2d edit., 1986; contbr. articles to profl. jours. Mem. IEEE (sr.). Avocations: music, traveling, bicycle. Home: 9 Pl V Mangin, Nantes France 44200

BIRCH, DIANA ELIZABETH, publisher; b. Doncaster, England, Nov. 24, 1944; d. Cecil Burt and Elizabeth Wright (Cowling) Robinson; children: Joshua Daniel Christian, Samuel Tobias Gabriel. BA in South East Asian History, U. London, 1968, MA in South East Asian History, 1969. Editor Medal News, London, 1979—; dir. Whiting & Birch Ltd., London, 1987—; cons. Medal Yearbook, London, 1995—; dir. Laay Svcs. Ltd., London, 1994—, Latchmere Press Ltd., London, 1996; ptnr. Mango Pub., 1997—; owner Savannah Publs., 1998—. Mem. Orders & Medals Rsch. Soc., Caribbean Ctr. Internat. Network, Orders & Medals Soc. Am. Avocations: all things Caribbean, collecting second-hand books about the Caribbean.

BIRCH, GORDON GERARD, food technologist, educator; b. Kingston, Jamaica, W.I., June 19, 1934; arrived in U.K.; s. Gerard Lawrence and Catherine Frances (Mahan) B.; m. Margaret Kathleen Martin, Dec. 29, 1959; children: John David, Ian Philip. BSc in Chemistry, U. London, 1956, PhD in Chemistry, 1966, DSc in Chemistry and Food Sci., 1977. Chemist U.K. Atomic Energy Authority, Sellafield, 1956-60; biochem. asst. Lister Inst. Preventive Medicine, London, 1960-61; lectr. U. reading, U.K., 1961-74; reader U. Reading, U.K., 1974-93, prof. food chemistry, 1993-99, prof. emeritus, 1999—. Mng. editor Food Chemistry Jour.; contbr. over 220 articles to profl. jours. European Union grantee, 1995—. Fellow Royal Soc. Chemistry (chartered chemist, Sr. medal in food chemistry 1992), Inst. Food Sci. and Tech., ELRO (hon.); mem. European Chemoreception Rsch. Orgn. (pres. 1990-94), Camberley Chess Club (chmn.), Desborough Sailing Club (capt.). Home: Monkton Wyld, 27 Crosby Hill Dr, Camberley GU15 3TZ, England Office: Univ Reading Dept Food Sci, PO Box 226 White Knights, Reading RG6 6AP, England

BIRCH, NICHOLAS JOHN, pharmacology consultant; b. Birmingham, Eng., Feb. 4, 1944; s. George Alfred and Constance (Hill) B.; m. Jennifer Grylls, Aug. 3, 1968 (div. 1983); children: Susanna Clare, Catherine Emma; m. Vance Joy Lomax, Dec. 14, 1988. BSc with honors, U. London, 1967; PhD, U. Sheffield, England, 1971. Rsch. fellow psychiatry U. Sheffield, England, 1971; rsch. fellow biochemistry U. Leeds, England, 1971-80, sr. rsch. fellow biochemistry, 1980-81; reader biomed. scis. Wolverhampton (England) Poly., 1981-88; prof. biomed. scis. U. Wolverhampton, 1988-97, emeritus prof. biomed. sci., 1997; cons. pharmacologist Acad. Consultancy Svcs. Ltd., Wolverhampton, Eng., 1997—; vis. prof. faculty pharmacy U. Montpellier, France. Author: 6 books, over 250 publs. in sci. and med. jours. Recipient Bronze medal Acad Medicine, Paris, 1980; named Ky. Col, Commonwealth of Ky., 1992, hon. prof. U. Ky., Lexington. Fellow Inst. Biology (mem. coun. 1992-95); mem. Biochem Soc., Brit Pharmacol. Soc., The Physiol. Soc., Expert Witness Inst., London. Office: Acad Consultancy Svcs Ltd, Codsall, Wolverhampton WV8 2ER, England

BIRCH, RICHARD ARTHUR, research scientist; b. Hythe, Kent, Eng., Aug. 26, 1951; s. Richard John and Marion Sarah (Burchett) B.; m. Sylvia Betty Lancaster, Jan. 28, 1978; children: Daniel Richard, Benjamin Charles, Matthew James. BSc in Applied Chemistry with honors, Brighton (Eng.) Poly., 1973; MSc in Analytical Chemistry, U. London, Eng., 1976. Chartered chemist. Lab. asst. Abbott Labs., Queenborough, Eng., 1973-75; rsch. scientist Quest Internat., Ashford, Eng., 1975—. Patentee in field. Church warden St. Leonard's Ch., Hythe, 1989-94. Mem. Royal Soc. Chemistry, Controlled Release Soc. Anglican. Avocations: campanology, photography. Office: Quest Internat, Kennington Rd, Ashford TN24 OLT, England

BIRCHBY, KENNETH LEE, banker; b. Columbus, Ind., Feb. 1, 1915; s. Ernest Lee and Constance Douglas (Pinsent) B.; m. Julia C. Barsch, Apr. 12, 1941; children—Kenneth Lee, John D. LL.B., St. Johns U., 1949; postgrad., Grad. Sch. Banking, Rutgers, 1956; LL.D. (hon.), St. Johns U., 1988. With Brevoort Savs. Bank, Bklyn., 1936-42; comptroller Brevoort Savs. Bank, 1945-48; spl. agt. FBI, 1942-45; auditor, v.p. Jamaica (N.Y.) Savs. Bank, 1948-66; exec. v.p. Hudson City Savs. Bank, Jersey City, 1966-68, pres., 1968-89, chmn., chief exec. officer, 1981-89, chmn., 1989-96, chmn. emeritus, 1996—, dir.; also dir., past instr. Grad. Sch. Savs. Banks, Brown U.; past adv. counsel Conf. State Bank Suprs. V.p., bd. dirs. Hudson County chpt. ARC., Bergen council Boy Scouts Am., Bergen/Rampo chpt. ARC, 1991—; past bd. dirs. N.J. Coll. Fund Assn.; past regent St. Peter's Coll. Mem. Savs. Banks Assn. N.J. (pres. 1970-72), Jersey City C. of C. (past pres., dir.), Assn. Former FBI Agts., Savs. Banks Auditors and Comptrs. Assn. N.Y. (past pres.), Nat. Assn. Mut. Savs. Banks (com. chmn., pres. 1974-75), C. of C. and Industry No. N.J. (dir.), Northampton Colony Yacht Club (Southampton, L.I.) (dir.), Ridgewood Country Club. Home (summer): RR 1 Box 648 Sag Harbor NY 11963-9100 Home: 12 Pine Tree Dr Saddle River NJ 07458-2907 Office: Hudson City Savs Bank Adminstrv Dept 80 W Century Rd Ste 2 Paramus NJ 07652-1473*

BIRCHER, ANDREA URSULA, psychiatric-mental health nurse, educator, clinical nurse specialist; b. Bern, Switzerland, Mar. 6, 1928; came to U.S., 1947; d. Franklin E. Bircher and Hedy E. Bircher-Rey. Diploma, Knapp Coll. Nursing, Santa Barbara, Calif., 1957; BS, U. Calif., San Francisco, 1961, MS, 1962; PhD, U. Calif., Berkeley, 1966. RN, Calif., Ill. Staff nurse, head nurse Cottage Hosp., Santa Barbara, 1957-58; psychiatric nurse, jr., sr. Langley-Porter Neuropsychiatric Inst., San Francisco, 1958-66; asst. prof. U. Ill. Coll. Nursing, Chgo., 1966-72; prof. U. Okla. Coll. Nursing, Oklahoma City, 1972-93, prof. emeritus, 1993—. Contbr. articles and papers to profl. jours. Recipient award for Outstanding Contributions to Faculty Governance U. Okla. Faculty Senate 1985, 93, others. Mem. AAUP, ANA, AAUW, NAFE, Am. Psychotherapy Assn. (cert. diplomate), Internat. Soc. Psychiat.-Mental Health Nursing, Nat. League for Nursing, N.Am. Nursing Diagnosis Assn., Calif. Assn. of Psychiat. Nurses in Advanced Practice, Ventura County Writers Club, Sigma Theta Tau, Phi Kappa Phi. Republican. Avocations: indoor gardening, cooking, reading, yoga, writing. Home: 1161 Cypress Point Ln Apt 201 Ventura CA 93003-6074

BIRCHER, MARTIN M(AXIMILIAN), foundation director, German language educator; b. Zurich, Switzerland, June 3, 1938; s. Willy and Lucie (Schwarzenbach) B. PhD, U. Zurich, 1965, Habilitation in German Lit., 1971. Assoc. prof. McGill U., Montreal, Que., Can., 1968-75; prof. German lit. U. Zurich, 1971—; dir. Martin Bodmer Found., Cologny-Geneva, Switzerland, 1996—; dir. rsch. Herzog August Bibliothek, Wolfenbüttel, Germany, 1975-96; vis. prof. U. Calif., Berkeley, 1970. Co-editor Daphnis, 1986—; editor Librarium, 1994—; contbr. numerous books, articles and revs. on 17th-20th centuries German and Swiss lit. Office: Martin Bodmer Found, 19-21 route du Guignard, CH-1223 Cologny Geneva Switzerland

BIRD, DONALD C., college administrator; b. Glendale, Ariz., Sept. 19, 1937; s. Eldred Holloway and Edith Maire Bird; m. Bonnie J. Bird, Aug. 2, 1962; children: Tawnya, Ninette, Jace Farrah, Danielle. AAS, Ricks Coll., 1962; BS, Utah State U., 1965; MS, Brigham Young U., 1968; EdD, Tex.

A&M U., 1973. Faculty mem. Ricks Coll., Rexburg, Idaho, 1965-74, chmn. dept., 1966-71; dir. edn. and tng. EG&G of Idaho, Idaho Falls, 1974-79; dean divsn. engring. and tech. EG&G of Idaho, 1979-88, faculty, 1988-95, acad. v.p., 1995—. Mem. city coun. Sugar City, Idaho, 1975-79; mem. sch. bd. Sugar-Salem Sch. Dist., Sugar City, 1987-93; mem. Higher Edn. Adv. Com., Idaho Falls, 1995—. Mem. Kiwanis. Republican. Mem. LDS Ch. Avocations: travel, R-ball, spectator sports of all kinds. E-mail: birdd@ricks.edu. Office: Ricks Coll Kimball 200 Rexburg ID 83460-0001

BIRD, ERIC CHARLES FREDERICK, environmental adviser; b. Tunbridge Wells, Kent, Eng., Sept. 2, 1930; arrived in Australia, 1957; s. Charles Thomas and Iris Olive (Biggs) B.; m. Juliet Frances Wain, June 30, 1962; children: Catherine, Philippa, Jennifer. BS, King's Coll., London, 1953, MS, 1955; PhD, Australian Nat. U., Canberra, Australia, 1960; MS (hon.), U. Melbourne, Australia, 1970. Asst. lectr. King's Coll., 1960; lectr. U. Coll., London, 1960-63; sr. lectr. Australian Nat. U., 1963-66; assoc. prof. U. Melbourne, 1966-92; dir. Geostudies Proprietary, Ltd., Victoria, Australia, 1977—; vis. prof. UNU, Tokyo, 1977-82; project coord. UN Environment Program, Nairobi, Kenya, 1982-95; prin. fellow U. Melbourne, 1993—. Author: Coasts, 1968, 2d edit., 1976, 3d edit., 1984, Coastline Changes, 1985, Submerging Coasts, 1993, Writers on the Coast, 1993, The Coast of Victoria, 1993, Writers on the Southwest Coast, 1994, Geology and Scenery of Dorset, 1995, Phillip Island, 1996, Beach Management, 1996, Isle of Wight, 1997, Coasts of Cornwall, 1998, Coastal Geomorphology: An Introduction, 2000; co-editor ency. The World's Coastline, 1985. Mem. Port Phillip Authority, Melbourne, 1970-81; adviser Sandringham Environment Panel, Melbourne, 1975-89. Officer Royal Air Force, 1955-57. Mem. Coastal Edn. and Rsch. Found. (editorial panel 1975—), Ocean and Coastal Rsch. Group (editorial panel 1989—). Avocations: walking, cricket, photography. Home and Office: 343 Beach Rd, Victoria Black Rock 3193, Australia

BIRD, L. RAYMOND, investor; b. Plainfield, N.J., Jan. 22, 1914; s. Lewis Raymond and Bessie (MacCallum) B.; student N.Y. U., 1946-47; m. May Ethel Siercks, June 5, 1949. With shipping dept. Horn & Hardart Co., 1936-46, control auditor, 1946-49, gen. supt. in commissary, 1949-51; asst. to treas. fin. and legal Lockheed Electronics Co. (formerly Stavid Engring., Inc.), 1951-55, treas., 1955-60; pres., dir. State Bank of Plainfield (N.J.), 1960-62; investor, 1962—; treas. Route Twenty Two Corp. Plainfield area committeeman Young Life Campaign, Inc.; pres. Plainfield Camp of Gideons; mem. exec. com., treas. Christian Bus. Men's Com. of Cen. Jersey; bd. dirs. Child Evangelism Fellowship N.J., Sudan Interior Mission; chmn. bd. trustees, chmn. exec. com., chmn. fin. and investments com. Barrington Coll.; trustee Evangelistic Com. Newark and Vicinity; bd. dirs., treas. Friends in Christ. Served as gen. staff officer from pvt. to 1st lt. 6th Armored Div., AUS, 1941-45. Mem. Am. Mgmt. Assn., Internat. Christian Leadership, Plainfield Area C. of C. Baptist (deacon). Home and Office: 625 Robert Fulton Hwy Quarryville PA 17566-1400

BIRD, LARRY JOE, professional basketball coach, former professional basketball player; b. West Baden, Ind., Dec. 7, 1956; s. Joe and Georgia B; m. Dinah Mattingly Oct. 1, 1989. Student, Ind. U., 1974, Northwood Inst., West Baden, Ind., 1974; BS, Ind. State U., 1979. Player Boston Celtics, 1979-92, spl. asst. to exec. v.p., 1992-97; head coach Ind. Pacers, 1997—; mem. U.S. Olympic Basketball Team, 1992. Author: (with Bob Ryan) Drive, 1989; actor (film) Blue Chips, 1994. Mem. U.S. Gold Medal team World Univ. Games, Sophia, Bulgaria, 1977, Nat. Basketball Assn. championship team, 1981, 84, 86, Nat. Basketball Assn. All-Star Team, 1980-92; named Collegiate Player of Yr. AP, UPI and Nat. Assn. Coaches, 1978-79; Rookie of Yr. Nat. Basketball Assn., 1980; Most Valuable Player Nat. Basketball Assn. All-Star Game, 1982, Nat. Basketball Assn., 1984-86, Nat. Basketball Assn. Playoffs, 1984, 86. Office: Ind Pacers 300 E Market St Indianapolis IN 46204-2603

BIRD, LESTER, prime minister of Antigua and Barbuda; b. Feb. 21, 1938; married; 7 children. BA, U. Mich., 1962; barrister at law, Gray's Inn, London, 1969. Pvt. practice law, Antigua and Barbuda, 1969-76; chmn. Antigua Labour Party, 1971-93, leader, 1993; nominated senator, opposition leader Upper House Parliament, 1971-76; M.P., 1976—; dep. premier, min. econ. devel., tourism and energy Antigua and Barbuda, 1976-81; dep. prime minister, 1981-94, min. fgn. affairs, econ. devel., tourism and energy,, 1981—, prime minister, 1994—; 1st chmn. Orgn. Ea. Caribbean States, 1982; chmn. Spl. Conf. in Devel. Needs of LDC's of Caribbean, 1981; chmn. Commonwealth Caribbean Countries Standing Com. of Mins. Fgn. Affairs, 1983, Commonwealth Caribbean Countries Coun. Mins. Industry, 1984; leader Conf. of Caribben Heads of Govt., 1994—; del. We. Hemisphere Heads of Govt., 1996, Commonwealth Heads of Govt. Conf., 1997. Methodist. Office: Office of Prime Min, Queen Elizabeth Hwy, Saint John's Antigua and Barbuda

BIRD, STEPHEN CHRISTOPHER, microcomputer company executive, consultant; b. Jan. 8, 1959; s. Charles James and Violet Amey (Green) B. Trainee technician Post Office Telephones, Oxford, Eng., 1975-78, technician 2A, 1978-79; designer engr. Posum Controls, Aylesbury, Eng., 1979-80; proprietor Magnus Microcomputers, Oxford, Eng., 1980—; microcomputer cons. Govt. Jamaica, Kingston, 1982-86, Club Caribbean, Jamaica, 1986-88, South Milan Bus. Co., Italy, 1988-90, Gov. of Zimbabwe, Ministry of Transport, Harare, 1990-92, Gov. North Sinai, Sinia Desert, Egypt, 1993, Argos Catalogue Syores, Milton Keynes, Eng., 1994-96, Flat Glass Industry, Worcester, Eng., 1996-97; microcomputer specialist Citibank, London, 1997-98, Dell Computers, Germany, 1998-99. Mem. Inst. Mgmt. Info. Sys., Inst. Analyst and Programmers. Democrat. Roman Catholic. Avocation: model railways. Home and Office: Magnus Microcomputers, 139 The Moors, Kidlington Oxford 0X5 2AF, England

BIRD, TREVOR STANLEY, electrical engineer; b. Donald, Victoria, Australia, Aug. 27, 1949; s. Roy Murray and Norma May (Beckham) B.; m. Valerie Irene Grant, May 17, 1975; children: Katherine May, Nicholas Trevor, Alison Rose. B in Applied Sci., U. Melbourne, Australia, 1971; M in Applied Sci., U. Melbourne, 1973, PhD, 1977. Reg. profl. engr. Postdoc. rsch. fellow U. London, 1976-78; lectr. James Cook U. N. Queensland, Townsville, Australia, 1978-83; sr. rsch. scientist CSIRO Divsn. Radiophysics, Sydney, 1984-88, prin. rsch. scientist, 1988-91, sr. prin. rsch. scientist, 1991-95, chief rsch. scientist, 1995—; cons. Plessey Radar Plc, Eng., 1982-83; rsch. mgr. electromagnetics of antennas CSIRO Divsn. Radiophysics, Sydney, 1989-97, gen. mgr. antennas and microwave sys., 1997—. Contbr. over 100 articles to profl. jours.; patentee in field; guest editor. Recipient CSIRO medal, 1990, 98; named hon. professorial fellow Macquarie U., 1996-99. Fellow Inst. Engrs. (Madsen medal 1988, 92, 95, 96), Inst. Elec. Engrs., IEEE (chpt. chmn. 1995-98, Disting. lectr. AP-S Soc. 1997-99, vice chmn. NSW sect. 1999—), Australian Acad. Tech. Engring. Scis. Avocations: reading, tennis, German language, book collecting. Office: CSIRO Telecomm Indsl Physic, PO Box 76, Epping NSW 1710, Australia

BIRD, WENDELL RALEIGH, lawyer; b. Atlanta, July 16, 1954; s. Raleigh Milton and R. Jean (Edwards) B. BA summa cum laude, Vanderbilt U., 1975; JD, Yale U., 1978. Bar: Ga. 1978, Ala. 1980, Calif. 1981, Fla. 1982, U.S. Ct. Appeals (2d, 3d, 4th. 5th, 6th, 7th, 8th, 9th, 10th and 11th cirs.) 1979-83, U.S. Supreme Ct. 1983. Law clk. to judge U.S. Ct. Appeals (4th cir.), Durham, N.C., 1978-79, U.S. Ct. Appeals (5th cir.), Birmingham, Ala., 1979-80; pvt. practice San Diego, 1980-82; atty. Parker, Johnson, Cook & Dunlevie, Atlanta, 1982-86; sr. ptnr. Bird & Assocs., P.C., Atlanta, 1986—; adj. prof. Emory U. Law Sch., Atlanta, 1985—; lectr. Washington Non-Profit Tax Conf., 1982—. Author: The Origin of Species Revisited, 2 vols., 1987; contbg. author: Federal and State Taxation of Exempt Organizations, 1994, CCH Federal Tax Service, 1988—; mem. bd. editors Yale U. Law Jour., 1977-78, others; contbr. articles to profl. jours. Bd. govs. Coun. for Nat. Policy, Washington, 1983—. Recipient Egger prize Yale U., 1978, Vanderbilt U. award, 1972. Mem. ABA (litigation sect., taxation sect., com. on exempt orgns., past chmn. subcom. on religious orgns., past chmn. subcom. on state and local taxes, chmn. subcom. on charitable contbns., sect. on real property probate and trust, com. charitable gifts), Am. Law Inst., Ga. Bar Assn., Fla. Bar Assn., Calif. Bar Assn., Ala. Bar Assn., Assn. Trial Lawyers Am., Phi Beta Kappa. Republican. Avocations: science, skiing, photography, genealogy, piano, architecture. Home: 92 Blackland Rd NW Atlanta GA 30342-4420 Office: Bird & Assocs PC 1150 Monarch Plz 3414 Peachtree Rd NE Atlanta GA 30326-1153

BIREN, ISIK, project development and construction executive; b. Istanbul, Oct. 1, 1933; s. Adnan Huseyin and Nezahat Fatma Biren; m. Ulker Atiye Uzsoy, Jan. 15, 1962; 2 children. BS, Naval Acad., 1952; MS, U.S. Naval Postgrad. Sch., 1960. Comdr. NATO Squadron, 1972-73; commandant naval war coll. Turkish Gen. Staff, Istanbul, 1975-77; chief plans and policy Turkish Gen. Staff, Ankara, 1986-88; undersec. of defense Ministry of Defense, Ankara, Turkey, 1979-82; comdr. combat fleet Turkish Navy, Golcuk, 1982-83; comdr. so. sea area Turkish Navy, Izmir, 1983-86; CEO Atakoy Tourism Galleria, Istanbul, 1988-90; head del. Turkish Govt., Athens, 1987-88; chief naval planning NATO, Brussels, 1968-70, allied staff officer, 1962-64, sr. strategic adv. U. Inst. Internat. Strategic Studies Ctr., 1997; bd. dirs. Intes Inc., Net Holding, Basketn Inc.; pres. IBTD, Mirage Inc. Contbr. articles to profl. jours. V.p. Liberal Dems., Ankara, 1995—; bd. dirs. Am. Turkish Coun. Washington, 1996—; bd. dir. Tatko Inc., 1996; founder Tutav, Ankara, 1982; chmn. Tourism Incentive Legislation Commn., 1982. Vice admiral Turkish Navy, 1983-88. Decorated Silver medal of heroism and disting. svc. Fellow Turkish Armed Forces Found.; mem. Rotary, Open Sea Yacht Club (hon.). Avocations: tennis, sailing, bridge, computers, travel. Home: Bagdat Caddesi # 237/9, Istanbul Turkey Office: Intes AS, Kore Sehitleri Cad Yzb Kaya, Aldogan Istanbul Turkey

BIRENDRA BIR BIKRAM SHAH DEV, HIS MAJESTY, King of Nepal; b. Kathmandu, Nepal, Dec. 28, 1945; s. King Mahendra Bir Bikram Shah and Crown Princess Indra Rajya Laxmi Devi Shah; m. Her Majesty Queen Aishwarya Rajya Laxmi Devi Shah, Feb. 27, 1970; children: Crown Prince Dipendra Bir Bikram Shah Dev, Princess Sruti Rajya Laxmi Devi Rana, Prince Nirajan Bir Bikram Shah. Ed., St. Joseph's Sch., Darjeeling, India, Eton (Eng.) Coll., U. Tokyo, Harvard U.; LLD (hon.), U. Delhi. Supreme comdr.-in-chief Royal Nepalese Army, 1972—; became king, Jan. 31, 1972, crowned, 1975. Chancellor, Tribhuvan U., Mahendra Sanskrit U.; patron Royal Nepal Acad. Sci. and Tech., King Mahendra Trust for Nature Conservation, Pashupati Area Devel. Trust, Lumbini Devel. Trust. Decorated hon. Field Marshall, Brit. Govt., 1980. Avocations: nature conservation, painting, riding. Address: His Majesty the King, Narayanhity Royal Palace, Durbar Marg Kathmandu Nepal*

BIRK, LEE (CARL BIRK), psychiatrist, educator; b. New Albany, Ind., Feb. 8, 1935; s. Glover McMurtrey and Marie Clyde (Carpenter) B.; m. Emily Perkins Gantt, June 21, 1958 (div. Jan. 1970); children: Elizabeth Waring, Alexandria Lee; m. Ann Harrison Wegner, June 15, 1973 (div. June 1990); children: Lara Blakiston, Jeffrey Lee. Student, Speed Scientific Sch., 1952-53, U. Louisville, 1953-54; BA in Zoology & Chemistry, Valparaiso U., 1956; MD, Johns Hopkins U., 1960. Intern U. Va. Hosp., Charlottesville, 1960-61; resident Harvard Med. Sch., Mass. Mental Health Ctr., Boston, 1961-62, 63-66; instr. psychiatry Harvard Med. Sch., Cambridge, Mass., 1968-69, asst. prof. psychiatry, 1969-73, asst. clin. prof. psychiatry, 1973-76, assoc. clin. prof. psychiatry, 1976—; dir. Learning Therapies, Inc., Newton, Mass., 1971-89, Concord, Mass., 1989-98, Burlington, Mass., 1998—; vis. prof. Inst. Living, Hartford, Conn., 1975; Rhoads lectr. Duke U. Sch. Medicine, 1994. Author/editor: Behavior Therapy in Psychiatry, 1972, Psychoanalysis and Behavior Therapy, 1973, Biofeedback: Behavioral Medicine, 1973; mem. editorial bd. Psychotherapy & Psychosomatics, 1974—, Family Process, 1975-78, 82-83, Jour. of Marital & Family Therapy, 1983-90, Jour. of Psychotherapy Integration, 1989—. Capt. USAF, 1962-63. Mem. Am. Family Therapy Assn., Am. Coll. Psychiatrists, Am. Soc. Clin. Psychopharmacology, Soc. Exploration of Psychotherapy Integration (cofounder). Independent. Avocations: helicopter skiing, whitewater rafting/kayaking. Home and Office: Learning Therapies Inc 8 Hart St Burlington MA 01803-1525

BIRKAVS, VALDIS, Latvian government official, law educator; b. Riga, Latvia, July 28, 1942; s. Voldemars and Veronika (Zihelmane) B.; m. Aina Zileva, Aug. 24, 1967; 1 child, Gatis. JD, U. Latvia, 1969, cand. iur., 1978, PhD, 1993. Dept. head, lab. head Lab. for Forensics and Criminology, Riga, 1969-86; lectr., assoc. prof. U. Latvia, Riga, 1969-86, dep. dean dept. law, 1986-89; dep. chmn. Supreme Coun. Republic of Latvia, 1992-93; prime minister Republic of Latvia, Riga, 1993-94, min. of fgn. affairs, 1994-99, dep. prime min., 1994-95, chmn. Coun. of Baltic Sea States, 1996-97, min. of justice, 1999—. Author: Criminology, Power and Society, Criminality: Causes and Consequences; contbr. articles to profl. jours. Chmn. Union Latvia's Way Party, 1993-97; v.p. Liberal Internat., 1997—. Mem. Lawyers Soc. Latvia (pres. 1988-95). Lutheran. Avocations: tennis, yachting, reading, mountain skiing. Office: Ministry of Justice, Brivibas Bulvaris 36, Riga LV-1536, Latvia

BIRKBECK, JOHN ADDISON, nutritionist, consultant; b. Broughty Ferry, Scotland, Jan. 24, 1933; arrived in New Zealand, 1975; m. Adele Margaret Birkbeck; children: Andrew, Fiona, Neil, Adrian. MB BChir, Edinburgh (Scotland) U., 1957. Adj. prof. Massey U., Auckland, New Zealand, 1999—. Fellow Royal Coll. Physicians (Can.); mem. Rotary Club Kumeu (sec./v.p.). Fax: 6494129163. E-mail: john@foodinfo.org. Home: PO Box 17 Waimauku, Auckland 1250, New Zealand Office: InforMed Sys Ltd, 8 Shamrock Dr, Kumeu 1250, New Zealand

BIRKELBACH, KLAUS W., sociologist; b. Wuppertal, Germany, Sept. 8, 1958; s. Dieter Birkelbach and Waltraud (Weber) Kraus; m. Margit Juliane Ruhland, Oct. 4, 1985; 1 child, Robert. Abitur, Abendgymnasium, Dusseldorf, Germany, 1983; Magister Artium, U. Dusseldorf, 1991, PhD, 1996. Social scientist U. Dusseldorf, 1991-96, U. Cologne, Germany, 1996—. Author: Occupational Success and Family Foundation, 1998; contbr. articles to profl. jours. Mem. Sektion methoder der Empirischen Sozialforschung der deutschen Gesellschadt fur Soziologie. Home: Moltkestr 401, 40477 Dusseldorf Germany Office: U Cologne Inst Angew Social, Greinstr 2, 50939 Cologne Germany

BIRKEN, JOSEPH GHM, marketing executive; b. Boxtel, Noord-Brabant, Netherlands, June 26, 1958; s. Hendrikus H. and Martina Maj (Pluk) B.; m. Karin Stekelenburg, May 22, 1987; children: Linda, Patrick. Degree in Law, U. Groningen, Netherlands, 1985. Various mktg. positions Unilever, Rotterdam, Netherlands, 1986-92; sr. cons. Experian Mktg. sys., Utrecht, Netherlands, 1992-93; CEO Experian Mktg. Svcs., The Hague, Netherlands, 1993-94; CEO, co-founder Claritas Netherlands, Zoeterwoude, 1995-97; CEO, founder Mktg. Sci., Rotterdam, 1997—. Lt. Royal Dutch Army, 1984-85. E-mail: JBIrken@MarketingScience.com. Office: Mktg Sci, Weena 290, Rotterdam Netherlands 3012 NJ

BIRKENHEAD, THOMAS BRUCE, theatrical producer and manager, educator; b. N.Y.C., Dec. 19, 1931; s. Thomas A. and Florence (Morison) B.; m. Susan Leslie Arkin, Dec. 3, 1954 (div. 1983); m. Maria Martins, May 26, 1999; children: Peter Lawrence, David Andrew, Richard James, Alison Jane, Leila Alessandra. BA, Bklyn. Coll. CUNY, 1954, MA, 1958; PhD, New Sch. Social Rsch., 1963. From lectr. to prof. econs. Bklyn. Coll. CUNY, 1957-72, prof., 1972-75; dean Sch. Social Scis., 1972-75; prof. emeritus Bklyn. Coll. CUNY, 1975—; bus. mgr. Theatre II of Glen Cove, N.Y., 1970-74; gen. mgr., cons. Keystone Ctr. of Music and the Arts, 1999. Co-mgr.: Do Black Patent Leather Shoes Really Reflect Up?, Present Laughter, Master Harold and the Boys, Children of a Lesser God, Ain't Misbehavin, Brighton Beach Memoirs, Biloxi Blues, Broadway Bound, Barbara Cook in Concert, Run For Your Wife, Rumors, Lost in Yonkers, Jake's Women, Goodbye Girl: gen. mgr.: Cape Cod Melody Tent, Hyannis, Mass., 1969-71, Twyla Tharp on Broadway, 1980, 81, Joe Egg, 1985, Social Security, 1986, Long Days Journey Into Night, London and Tel Aviv, 1986, Ain't Misbehavin, N.Y.C., 1988-89, Japan, 1990, Fresh Air Taxi, 1993, Honky Tonk Highway, 1994-96, Dream a Little Dream, 1994-95; co-prodr. 1995 Tony award broadcast, N.H.K. Japan; producer High Mountain Ghost, 1996-98; sec.-treas. Highly Ent., 1995—; mgmt. cons. Keystone Ctr. Performing Arts, 1999-2000. Founding mem., sponsor U.S. Shooting Team, U.S. Holocaust Meml. Mus., Am. Air Mus., Eng., U.S. Naval Meml. Found., WWII Meml., U.S. Olympic Com. T. Bruce Birkenhead scholarship in performing arts established by Performing Arts Mgmt. Program Bklyn. Coll. Mem. NRA, U.S. Naval Inst., Jimmy Carter Inst., Amnesty Internat., Women in Mil. Svc. for Am., Rover P4 Drivers Gild, W.P. Chrysler Club, Chrysler Products Restorers Club, Vintage Triumph Register, Groucho Club (Eng.), World Jewish Congress. Home: 353 W 44th St Apt 1A New York NY 10036-5416 Office: 145 W 45th St Rm 500 New York NY 10036-4008

BIRKETVEDT, GRETHE STØA, medical scientist, writer, musician; b. Sarpsborg, Norway, Sept. 17, 1942; d. Arne and Aase (Oscarsdatter) Støa; 1 child, Camilla Støa. MEd, Tchrs. Tng. Coll., Stord, Norway, 1964; MMus, Oslo U./Antioch Coll., 1969; M of Phys. Edn., U. of Sport, Oslo, 1972; MD, Oslo U. Medicine, 1983; MD, PhD, U. Tromsø, Norway, 1995. Cert. tchr. phys. edn.; music diplomate; med. diplomate. Tchr. Norwegian Tchg. Assn., Sarpsborg, 1964-67; Fulbright scholar U.S., 1968-69; musician, composer Norwegian Composers Assn., Oslo, 1969-83; gen. practitioner Med. Assn. Oslo, 1983-92; med. scientist Gen. Practice Orgn., Oslo, 1992-93; asst. prof. Tromsø Hosp., 1993-95; vis. scientist U. Pa., Phila., 1995—; rschr. U. Tronse, Norway; assoc. rsch. prof. Mount Sinai Med. Ctr., N.Y.C., 2000—; hon. prof. Albert Schweitzer Internat. U., Geneva, 2000—. Author: (books of poetry) On a Distance, 1976, 2d edit., 1977, There Are Days, 1978, Hildelin, A Symphonic Poem, 1980, (art and poetry) In the Light of the Planet, 1994; composer (music play) Musikklek, 1980, Laughing Street No. 2, 1986, Circus in Town, 1994, Vriompeisen, 1997, Pott og Sokk, 2000, Treatment of Overweight and Obesity in General Practice, 1999, Textbook for medical student and general practitioners, Pott ag Sokk, 2000; contbr. articles to profl. jours. and med. books. Recipient Writer's awrd U. Altertumskunde, Munich, Germany, 1980, Golden Acad. award, Lifelong Achievement Am. Biog. Inst., 1999; Norwegian Coun. Med. Rsch. grantee, 1996. Mem. AAAS, Fulbright Alumni Assn., Norwegian Writers Assn. Ctr., Soc. Study Ingestive Behavior, TONO Assn. Protection of Musical Original Work, Norwegian Assn. Gastroenterology, Norwegian Assn. Gen. Practitioners, Norwegian Assn. Music Composition, N.Y. Acad. Scis., Am. Assn. for Advancemtn Sci, Am. Diabetes Assoc. Avocations: music, writing, riding, painting, reading. E-mail: gsb42nor@aol.com. Home: Ole Messelts Vei 134, 0676 Oslo Norway also: 1630 Thomas Rd Ivy Hollow Farm Wayne PA 19087 Office: Mt Sinai Med Ctr Hypertension Dept # 23 1 Gustave Lerry Pl Box 1030 New York NY 10029

BIRKS, DOREEN ANN, retired ophthalmic surgeon; b. Beckenham, England, Mar. 3, 1925; d. Cyril Douglas and Ivy May (Bartholomew) B. MB BS, Royal Free Hosp., London, 1949; DO, Royal Eye Hosp., 1953. Resident, registrar, then sr. registrar Royal Eye Hosp., London, 1952-62; cons. ophthalmic surgeon Boling Broke Hosp., London, 1961-65, Royal Eye Hosp., London, 1962-73, Dist. Eye Unit, Sutton and Merion, Surrey, Eng., 1965-85, St. Thomas' Hosp., London, 1973-85; ret., 1985; hon. cons. ophthalmic surgeon, Royal Sch. of Blind, Leatherhead, Surrey, 1967-85, St. Thomas' Hosp., 1985—. Chmn., Cuckmere Valley Soc., Sussex, 1988-89. Freeman, City of London, 1989. Fellow Royal Soc. Medicine London; mem. So. Ophthalmol. Soc., Irish Ophthalmol. Soc., Intraocular Soc. U.K., Worshipful Soc. Apothecaries London (Liveryman), Sloane Club. Roman Catholic. Avocations: travel, photography, music, woodwork. Home: FRensham Cottage, Berwick Polegate BN26 6SP, England

BIRLESON, PETER, psychiatrist, educator; b. Darlington, Durham, Eng., Apr. 15, 1947; arrived in Australia, 1981; s. Eric Philip and Marjory (Nelson) B.; m. Geraldine Tait Bagguley, Aug. 18, 1973; children: John, Joanna, Michael. MB, BChir, Edinburgh, Scotland, 1971, MPhil, 1978; M Bus., Melbourne, 1996. Registrar Royal Edinburgh Hosp., 1973-76; sr. registrar dept. psychol. medicine Royal Hosp. for Sick Children, Edinburgh, 1976-81; cons. psychiatrist dept. child psychiatry Royal Children's Hosp., Melbourne, Australia, 1981-86; dep. dir. dept. child psychiatry Royal Children's Hosp., Melbourne, 1986-91; dir. clin. svcs. Royal Children's Hosp. Mental Health Svc., Melbourne, 1991-95; dir. Maroondah Hosp. Child & Adolescent Mental Health Svc., Melbourne, 1995—; sr. program advisor mental health br. Dept. Human Svcs., Victoria, Australia, 1995-98; adj. prof. Faculty Health Scis. Deakin U., Melbourne, 1997—. Contbr. articles to profl. jours. Designer child and adolescent mental health sys., Victoria, 1995-96. Fellow Royal Australian and New Zealand Coll. Psychiatrists, Australian Coll. Health Svc. Execs. (assoc.); mem. Royal Coll. Psychiatrists. Office: Maroondah Hosp CAMHS, 21 Ware Crescent, Ringwood East VIC 3135, Australia

BIRMAN, ALEXANDER, physicist, researcher; b. Moscow, May 23, 1946; came to U.S., 1994; s. Yakov and Rozaliya (Krimerman) B.; m. Emily Freydman, Dec. 25, 1980; children: Igor, Eugene. MSc, Moscow Physico-Tech. Inst., 1970; PhD, Inst. Applied Physics, Moscow, 1975. Sr. rsch. scientist Inst. Applied Physics, Moscow, 1970-85; leading rsch. scientist Astrophysics Corp., Moscow, 1985-93; sr. optical scientist Dicon Fiberoptics, Inc., Berkeley, Calif., 1995—; lectr. Moscow Physico-Tech. Inst., 1987-92. Contbr. articles to profl. jours. Mem. IEEE, Optical Soc. Am., Internat. Soc. for Optical Engring. Achievements include work on theory of waves diffraction in ring lasers; contribution to design of laser and fiber-optic gyroscopes; development of passive fiberoptic components for advanced communication systems. Home: 535 Pierce St Apt 2105 Albany CA 94706-1055 Office: Dicon Fiberoptics 1331 8th St Berkeley CA 94710-1453

BIRMINGHAM, BRUCE R., bank executive; b. Montreal, Que., Can., Dec. 22, 1941. BComm, Sir George Williams U., 1970; MBA, U. B.C., 1971. Various positions Bank of Nova Scotia, 1971-79, sr. v.p. corp. banking, gen. mgr. N.Am. internat. regional office, 1980-83, exec. v.p. corp. banking, 1983-91, sr. exec. v.p., 1991-92, vice chair bd. dirs., 1992—, now pres., bd. dirs.; bd. dirs. Scotia Leasing, Scotia Securities Inc., Bank of N.S. Jamaica Ltd., Scotiabank Jamaica Trust & Mcht. Bank Ltd., West India Co. of Mcht. Bankers Ltd., Bank of N.S. Trinidad & Tobago Ltd., Bank of N.S. Trust Co. of Trinidad & Tobago Ltd., Scotia Investment Mgmt. Ltd.; trustee, mem. exec. com. bd. trustees Scotiabank Pension Plan. Office: Bank of Nova Scotia, 44 King St W, Toronto, ON Canada M5H 1H1*

BIRMINGHAM, PATRICK MICHAEL, lawyer; b. St. Paul, Apr. 2, 1947; s. George Thomas and Nona Birmingham; m. Karen Ann Moir, Oct. 17, 1992. BS, Portland State U., 1970; JD, Western State U., 1975. Bar: Calif. 1975, U.S. Dist. Ct. (ctrl. dist.) Calif. 1975, U.S. Supreme Ct. 1978, Oreg. 1978, U.S. Dist. Ct. Oreg. 1978. With Riverside County (Calif.) Office of Pub. Defender, 1975-78; pvt. practice Portland, Oreg., 1978—. With U.S. Army N.G., 1970-75. Named in Best Lawyers in Am. and Nar. Directory Criminal Def. Lawyers. Mem. Oreg. Criminal Def. Lawyers (life), Calif. Attys. for Criminal Justice, Nat. Assn. Criminal Def. Lawyers, Multnomah Defenders Inc. (bd. dirs. 1990-92), Multnomah County Bar Assn. (mentor program 1994-99). Office: 1001 SW 5th Ave Ste 1625 Portland OR 97204-1132

BIRNBAUM, IRWIN MORTON, lawyer; b. Bklyn., July 15, 1935; s. Sol N. and Rose (Cohen) B.; m. Arlene R. Burrows, June 8, 1957; children: Bruce J., Leslie R. Birnbaum Ventura, Amy G. Birnbaum Heath. BS in Acctg., Bklyn. Coll., 1956; JD, NYU, 1961. Bar: N.Y. 1962. Budget officer Montefiore Med. Ctr., Bronx, N.Y., 1962-70, v.p., chief fin. officer, 1970-86; counsel Proskauer & Rose LLP, N.Y.C., 1986-89, ptnr., 1989-97; COO Yale Univ. Sch. Medicine, New Haven, Conn., 1997—; bd. dirs. N.Y. Regional Transplant Program, N.Y.C., treas., exec. com.; bd. dirs. FFH/N.E. Ins. Com., MCIC Vt., Inc.; adj. prof. Robert Wagner Sch. Pub. Svc., NYU; lectr. pub. health, health policy, adminstrn. Sch. Medicine Yale U. Editor: Health Care Law Treatise, 1990. Bd. trustees, treas., exec. com. Malmonides Med. Ctr., Bklyn., 1988—; sec./treas., exec. com. Hosp. Trustees N.Y. State, 1990-97. Fellow N.Y. Acad. Medicine; mem. Assn. of Bar of City of N.Y. (sec. com. on medicine and law 1989-90, sec. health law com. 1995-96), Am. Acad. Hosp. Attys. (spl. com. in health care systems). Avocations: sailing, tennis, reading, travel. Office: Yale Univ Sch Medicine 333 Cedar St I-209 SHM PO Box 208049 New Haven CT 06520-8049

BIRNBAUM, PHILIP, development economist; b. Union City, N.J., Oct. 3, 1928; s. henry J. and Lena B.; m. Joan Elaine, Feb. 7, 1959; children: Frederic, Nicholas. BBS, Rutgers U., 1950; MA, Columbia U., 1952; PhD, Harvard U., 1960. From program economist to asst. adminstr. U.S. AID Mission, Tunisia, Algeria, 1960-72; asst. adminstr. U.S. AID Mission, Washington, 1972-77; sr. v.p. Internat. Fund for Agrl. Devel., Rome, 1978-83; minister U.S. Sr. Foreign Svc., Rome, 1984—; adv. World Bank, Washington, 1985-94; cons. Inter-Am. Devel. Bank, Washington, 1995—. With U.S. Army, 1955-57. Fulbright scholar 1951. Avocations: tennis, gardening, travel. E-mail: pbjb@aol.com. Home: 5409 Audubon Rd Bethesda MD 20814-1203

BIRÓ, GÉZA, food scientist; b. Tatabánya, Komárom, Hungary, Dec. 20, 1933; s. Géza and Gézáné (Szlávik Erzsébet) B.; m. Klára Herczeg, July 23, 1970; 1 child, Krisztina. Vet., Vet. U. Budapest, 1957. Rschr. Meat Rsch. Inst., Budapest, Hungary, 1957-60, Vet. U., Budapest, 1960-70; dept. head Ministry Agr., Budapest, 1970-80; prof., dept. head Vet. U., Budapest, 1980—. Author: Food Hygiene, 1994, Food Safety and Public Health Nutrition, 2000; editl. bd. mem. Microbiologie Aliments Nutrition, 1985. Mem. Budapest Acad. Sci. (vet. sect., food sci. sect.), Codex Alimentarius Budapest. Home: Fodor u 12, 1126 Budapest Hungary Office: Veterinary Univ, Istvan u 2, 1078 Budapest Hungary

BIRÓ, GYÖRGY, food scientist, educator; b. Szolnok, Hungary, July 23, 1928; s. Sándor and Sándorné (Pásztor) B.; m. Györgyné Diviaczky, Aug. 6, 1952; 1 child, Tamás (dec.). MD, U. Med. Sch., Budapest, Hungary, 1952; PhD, Sci. Qualification Com., Budapest, 1958; DSc, Hungarian Acad. Scis., Budapest, 1979. Lic. in pub. health and epidemiology, also in occupational health. Epidemiologist Ministry of Def., Budapest, 1953-74; prof., head U. Med. Sch., Pécs, Hungary, 1975-81; dir. gen. Nat. Inst. Food Hygiene and Nutrition, Budapest, 1982-98; prof., head U. Health Scis., Budapest, 1982-98; indep. expert on nutrition, 1999—; pres. nutritional com. Hungarian Acad. Scis., Budapest, 1985-99. Mem. editl. bd. Acta Cardiologica, Belgium, 1994—, Ernahrungsforschung, 1986—; editor: Hungarian Food Composition Tables, 1988, 95, 98, 99. Col. M.C. Hungarian mil., 1953-74. Recipient Fodor József award Hungarian Soc. Hygiene, Budapest, 1977, Széchenyi award Ministry of Environ. Protection, Budapest, 1980, Sigmond Elek award Hungarian Sci. Soc. for Food Industry, Budapest, 1988. Fellow Internat. Union Nutritional Scis.; mem. Hungarian Soc. Nutrition (pres. 1983-97, hon. pres. 1997—, Sós József award 1987, Tangl Ferenc award 1992, Tarjan Robert award 1997, Pro Sanitate award 1999). Roman Catholic. Avocations: photography, carpentry, tourism. Home: Lehel utca 24/c, H-1135 Budapest Hungary Office: Semmelweis U, Horánszky U 24, H-1085 Budapest Hungary

BIROL, YUCEL, scientist; b. Elazig, Turkey, Aug. 19, 1959; cons. Assan Aluminum, Istanbul, 1995—; s. Rifki and Fatma (Tureyen) B.; m. Esin Dincer, 1985 (div. 1989); m. Feriha Sertcelik, Jan. 10, 1996; 1 child, Baris. BS, Istanbul (Turkey) Tech. U., 1982; MS, Case Western Res. U., 1984, PhD, 1987. Mgr. R&D Nasas Aluminum, Istanbul, 1988-92; sr. scientist Marmara Rsch. Ctr., Kocaeli, Turkey, 1992—. Contbr. articles to profl. publs. Achievements include patent in field. Avocations: music, movies, traveling. Office: Tubitak, Marmara Rsch Ctr, 41470 Gebze Kocaeli, Turkey

BIRÓNÉ-NAGY, EDIT, education educator; b. Budapest, Sept. 2, 1929; d. János Aladár Nagy and Maria Németh; m. Peter Biró, Apr. 25, 1953; children: Zoltán, Krisztina. Diploma in phys. edn., Hungarian Coll. Phys. Edn., 1951; MSc in Pedagogy, Eotvös U., Budapest, 1961, DPhil, 1965, PhD in Pedagogic Sci., 1975. Tchr. phys. edn. primary and secondary schs., Budapest, 1951-53; asst. Hungarian Coll. for Phys. Edn., Budapest, 1953-57, 1st asst., 1957-65, assoc. prof., 1965-80; prof. pedagogy Hungarian U. for Phys. Edn., Budapest, 1998-2000; prof. emeritus Semmelweis U., Budapest, 2000—; coach in athletics and dance; chmn. section pedagogy Hungarian Accreditation Commn., Budapest, 1997-2000; pro-rector of sci. Hungarian U. of Phys. Edn., 1994-98, head dept. pedagogy, 1991-94; chmn. subcommn. for phys. edn. Hungarian Acad. Sci., Budapest, 1990-94. author: Sportpedagogia, 1977, 3d edit., 1995; contbr. articles to profl. jours.; mem. editl. bd. New Pedagogic Rev., 1990-2000. Named Honoured Educator in Higher Edn., Ministry of Edn., Budapest, 1968; sci. prize Hungarian U. Phys. Edn., 1995, award, 1999. Mem. Hungarian Pedagogic Soc. (presidium mem. 1980-90, chmn. sect. phys. edn. 1980-90). Roman Catholic. Avocations: hiking, classical music, gardening. Office: Semmelweis U Fac Phys Edn, Sport Sci Alkotas utca 44, 1123 Budapest Hungary

BIRRELL, MARK ALEXANDER, government minister; b. Melbourne, Australia, Feb. 7, 1958. B in Econs., Monash U., Australia, 1979, B in Law, 1981. Barrister. M.P. Australia, 1983—, min. major projects, 1992-96, min. conservation, 1992-96, min. industry, sci. and tech., 1996—; solicitor, Australia, 1981-83. Editor: The Australian States, 1987. Australian pres. Young Liberal Movement, 1981-82; dir. Playbox Theatre, 1991-92; dir. Australian Inst. Polit. Sci., 1982-88. Mem. Liberal Party of Australia. Avocation: photography. Office: 173 Canterbury Rd, Canterbury 3124, Australia

BIRSHTEIN, TATIANA MAXIMOVNA, physicist, educator, researcher; b. Leningrad, USSR, Dec. 20, 1928; d. Max M. Birshtein and Maria I. Babin; m. David N. Mirlin, May 2, 1952; children: Helene Mirlina, Alexander Mirlin. Grad., Leningrad (USSR) U., 1951; postgrad., Pedagogical Inst., Leningrad, 1954-58; PhD, Inst. Macromol. Comp., Leningrad, 1960, Dr.Sci. (hon.), 1974. Indsl. engr. Leningrad, 1951-54; jr. rschr. Inst. Macromolecular Compounds, Russian Acad. Scis., Leningrad, 1958-66, sr. rschr., 1966-86, prin. rschr., 1986—; prof. St. Petersburg (Russia) U., 1965—; mem. adv. bd. sci. jours. Acta Polymer, Polymer Sci., Macromol. Theory Simul.; chmn. Internat. Sci. Symposium, St. Petersburg, 1996. Author: Conformation of Macromolecules, 1964; contbr. over 200 articles to sci. jours. Russian grantee for Prominent Sci. and Prominent Sch., 1995-98, 96—; named Soros prof., 1995-98. Office: Inst Macromol Comp RAS, Bolshoi pr 31, 199004 Saint Petersburg Russia

BIRT, BARON JOHN, broadcasting executive; b. Liverpool, Surrey, Eng., Dec. 10, 1944; s. Leo Vincent and Ida Birt; m. Jane Frances Lake, Sept. 14, 1965; children: Jonathan, Eliza. Student, St. Mary's Coll., Liverpool, Eng.; MA, Oxford U., 1966; D (hon.), Liverpool John Moores U., 1992, City U. London, 1998. Prodr. Nice Time, 1968-69; joint editor World in Action, 1969-70; prodr. The Frost Programme, 1971-72; exec. prodr. Weekend World, 1972-74; head current affairs LWT, 1974-77, contbr. current affairs, 1977-81, dir. programmes, 1982-87; dep. dir. gen. BBC, London, 1987-92, dir. gen., 1992-2000; mem. Ho. of Lords, London, England, 2000—; mem. Wilton Park Acad. Coun., 1980-83, Media Law Group, 1983—, Working Party on New Technols Broadcasting Rsch Unit, 1981-83, mem. exec. com., 1983-87; mem. Bus. in the Community's Women Econ. Target Team; vis. fellow Nuffield Coll. Oxford; hon. fellow St. Catherine's Coll. Oxford, 1992. Created knight, 1998, baron, 2000. Fellow Royal TV Soc. (v.p.). *

BIRT, MICHAEL CAMERON ST. JOHN, government official of Jersey; b. Godalming, Surrey, Eng., Aug. 25, 1948; s. St. John Michael Clive and Mairi Araminta (Cameron) B.; m. Joan Frances Miller Birt, Aug. 9, 1973; children: Benjamin, Alexa Robin. Student, Marlborough Coll.; MA in Law, Magdalene Coll., 1969, Cambridge. Bar: Middle Temple 1970, Jersey 1977, Q.C. 1995. Pvt. practice London, 1971-75; Jersey advocate Ogier & Le Cornu, St. Helier, 1976-93; crown advocate Jersey, 1987-93, atty. gen., 1994—, dep. bailiff. Mem. Royal Channel Islands Yacht, Royal Jersey Golf. Avocations: skiing, yachting, golf, tennis, sailing. Home: Maofant Manor, Saint Saviour Isle of Jersey Office: Bailiffs Chambers, Royal Ct House Royal Sq, St Helier Jersey JE1 1BA, Channel Islands*

BIRTH, PAULA ILENE, telecommunications executive; b. Kingston, Pa., Oct. 5, 1960; d. Paul Harvey and Ann B. (Beuka) Farver; m. Brent Lee Birth, June 14, 1980; 1 child, Joshua. Student, Pa. State U., Wilkes Barre. Cert. profl. in quality assurance. Account exec. Commonwealth Long Distance, Dallas, Pa., 1991-93; sales mgr. Commonwealth Long Distance, Allentown, Pa., 1994-95; mgr. mktg. and sale support Commonwealth Comm., Wilkes Barre, Pa., 1995-96; sales adminstr. PenTeleData, Palmerton, Pa., 1996-97, sales mgr., 1997-98, dir. bus. devel., 1998-99, chief adminstrv. officer, 1998-99, asst. gen. mgr., 1999—; network sales engr. Charter Bus. Network, Uniontown, Pa., 2000; cons. EdNet, Lancaster, Pa., 1998—; presenter in field. Den leader Boy Scouts Am., Lehman, Pa., 1987-90; soccer coach Lehighton (Pa.) Soccer Club, 1994-98. Mem. NAFE Soc. Cable Telecomms. Engrs. Inc. Republican. Evangelical. Avocations: golf, swimming, walking. E-mail: pbirth@chartercom.com. Office: PenTeleData 320 Bailey Ave Uniontown PA 15401-2461

BIRTWISTLE, DAVID THOMAS, computer company executive, consultant; b. Colwyn Bay, Wales, July 21, 1943; s. Thomas and Hanna (Rogers) B.; m. Cecilia Barbara Hakewill, Oct. 14, 1972; children: Thomas John, Katharine Jane. BSc in Physics, U. Manchester, Eng., 1965, PhD in Theoretical Physics, 1969; MSc in Stats., U. London, 1978. Chartered info. systems engr. Dir. DTB Computer Ltd., 1989—, Satnet Computing Ltd., 1997—; cons. software engr. to various cos. Contbr. numerous articles to profl. jours. Mem. Assn. for Computing Machinery. Avocations: reading, writing, langs. Address: 42 Wellesley Close, Ash Vale Avondale GU12 5SW, England

BIRTWISTLE, SIR HARRISON, composer; b. Accrington, Lancaster, Eng., July 15, 1934; m. Sheila Birtwistle, 1958; 3 children. Student, Royal Manchester Coll. Music, Royal Acad. Music, London. Dir. music Cranborne Chase Sch., 1962-65; vis. fellow Princeton U., 1966; Cornell vis. prof. music Swarthmore Coll., Pa., 1973-74; Slee vis. prof. N.Y. State U., Buffalo, 1975; assoc. dir. Nat. Theatre, 1975-88; Purcell prof. composition Kings Coll., London; composer-in-residence London Philharm. Orch., 1993-98; dir. contemporary music Royal Acad. Music, London. Compositions include (cantata) The Mark of the Goat, 1965-66, (1-act opera) Punch and Judy, 1966-67, (orch. works) Chorales for Orchestra, 1962-63, Three Movements with Fanfares, 1964, Nomos, 1968, Triumph of Time, 1972, Earth Dances, 1986, (instrumental ensemble) Refrains and Choruses 1957, Ring a Dumb Carillon, 1965, (choral works) Carmen Paschale, 1965, (opera) The Mask of Orpheus, 1974-81, Gawain, 1990, The Second Mrs. Kong, 1995, Cry of Anubis, 1995, Antiphonics, 1996, Exody, 1998, Pulse Shadows, The Woman and the Hare, 1999, numerous others; works performed at maj. festivals in Europe including Venice Biennale, Internat. Soc. Contemporary Music Festivals in Vienna and Copenhagen. Recipient Grawemeyer award U. Lousville, 1987, Siemens prize, 1995; hon. fellow Royal No. Coll. Music, 1990, Harkness Internat. fellow, 1966. Office: 42 Montpelier Sq, London SW7 1JZ, England address: care Boosey & Hawkes MP Ltd, 295 Regent St, London W1R 8JH, England

BISANZO, MARK THOMAS, sales executive; b. Port Chester, N.Y., Sept. 28, 1941; s. Dominic Daniel and Pauline Ann (Zak) B.; m. Mary Jane Ann Baldino, July 2, 1966; 1 child, Mark Christopher. AAS, Westchester C.C., 1963; BSME, N.Y. Inst. Tech., 1966; MBA, Fordham U., 1972. Instrument engr. Bechtel, N.Y.C., 1966-68, M.W. Kellogg, N.Y.C., 1968-70; sr. controls engr. Power Gas Corp., N.Y.C., 1970-71, Am. Electric Power, N.Y.C., 1971; sr. v.p. Control Assocs., Allendale, N.J., 1971—, 2000—; mem. adv. bd. Fisher Controls Co., Marshalltown, Iowa, 1997—; bd. dirs. Control Assocs. Pres. Bergen Cath. H.S. Fathers' Club, Oradell, N.J., 1991-94; coach Park Ridge (N.J.) Athletic Assn., 1980-90; mem. Our Lady of Mercy Roman Cath. Ch. Noctornal Adoration Soc., Park Ridge, Middlebury Collegiate Alumni Coll. Parents Alumni Assn. Mem. Soc. Gas Operators, Instrument Soc. Am. (v.p. N.Y. chpt. 1984-85). Avocations: skiing, photography, travel. Home: 67 Degroff Pl Park Ridge NJ 07656-1406 Office: Control Assocs 20 Commerce Dr Allendale NJ 07401-1600

BISCHOFF, MARILYN BRETT, clinical social worker; b. Mt. Vernon, N.Y., Apr. 16, 1930; d. Arthur Cushman and Mary Kathryn (Clark) Brett; m. Walter A. Bischoff, Mar. 25, 1961; children: Holly, Robert. BA magna cum laude, CCNY, 1959; MSSW, Columbia U., 1961; PhD in Social Work, Boston Coll., 1985; cert. in gerontology, U. Mass., Dartmouth, 2000. Diplomate in clin. social work Am. Bd. Examiners in Social Work. Clin. social worker Providence Child Guidance Clinic, 1961-65, 69-73; pvt. practice clin. social worker Attleboro, Mass., 1994—, Providence, 1965-94; instr. Providence Coll., 1988-89; speaker in field. Active Attleboro (Mass.) Area Mental Health Assn., 1975-94. Columbia Univ. fellow, N.Y.C., 1959-60; Nat. Inst. Mental Health fellow, 1960-61. Mem. NASW (sec.-treas. S.E. Mass. chpt. 1967-68, mem. speaker's bur. R.I. chpt. 1987, diplomate clin. social work), Acad. Cert. Social Workers, R.I. Group Psychotherapy Soc. (chair membership com. 1985-96), Columbia U. Alumni Assn., Attleboro Ski Club, Phi Beta Kappa. Avocations: camping, traveling, photography, sewing, bridge. Home and Office: 10 Norfolk Row Attleboro MA 02703-1629

BISCHOFF, WINFRIED FRANZ WILHELM, merchant banker; b. Aachen, Germany, Oct. 5, 1941; s. Paul Hellmut and Hildegard (Kuhne) B.; m. Rosemary Elizabeth Leathers, 1972; two children. B Comm., U. Witwatersrand, Johannesburg, South Africa, 1961. Mng. dir. Schroders Asia Ltd., Hong Kong, 1971-83; group chief exec. Schroders plc, London, 1984-95, chmn., 1995—; chmn. J. Henry Schroder & Co. Ltd., 1983-94; bd. dirs. Schroder & Co., Inc.; dep. chmn. Cable and Wireless plc, 1995—, non-exec. dir., 1991—. Roman Catholic. Avocations: opera, music, golf. Office: Schroders plc, 31 Gresham St, London EC2V 7QA, England*

BISCOE, TIMOTHY JOHN, academic administrator, physiologist; b. Harlow, Essex, England, Apr. 28, 1932; s. William Henry and Mary (Middleton) B.; m. Daphne Miriam Gurton, Sept. 17, 1955; children: Sarah, Mandy, Max. BS, London U., 1953, MBBS, DSc. Sr. scientific officer ARC Inst. Animal Physiology, Cambridge, Eng., 1962-65; rsch. fellow John Curtin Sch. Med. Rsch., Canberra, Australia, 1965-66; assoc. rsch. physiologist Cardiovascular Rsch. Inst. UCSF, 1966-68; rsch. assoc. dept. physiology U. Bristol (Eng.), 1968-70, prof. dept. physiology, 1970-79, head dept. physiology, 1975-70; Jodrell prof. physiology, head of dept. U. Coll., London, 1979-90, vice-provost, 1990-92, pro-provost, 1995—; dep. vice-chancellor U. Hong Kong, 1992-95; McLaughlin vis. prof. Mc Master U., 1986, Hooker vis. prof., 1990. Contbr. numerous articles to profl. jours. Capt. RAMC, 1958-62. Fellow Royal Coll. Physicians; Academia Europea, Physiol. Soc. (hon., hon. sec. 1977-82), Garrick Club. Avocations: reading, writing, looking, talking. Office: c/o Provost Office U Coll, Gower St, WC1E 6BT London England

BISHAI, AUGENIE MIKHAIL, physicist; b. Assuit, Egypt, Dec. 7, 1927; d. Farag Mikhail and Girgis Zakia (Bastawroos) B.; m. Gamal Ibrahim Habeeb, Aug. 3, 1961; children: Amgad, Eiman. BS, Ain Shams U., Cairo, 1958; MSc, Cairo U., 1965, PhD, 1971. Rsch. asst. Nat. Rsch. Ctr., Cairo, 1959-71, rschr., 1971-78, assoc. rsch. prof., 1978-87, rsch. prof., 1987—; lectr. physics Baghdad U., Iraq, 1978-83. Contbr. numerous articles to profl. jours. Mem. Egyptian Phys. Soc., Egyptian Math. Soc., Sci. Professions Syndicate. Avocations: family, reading, sewing clothes, visiting ancient places. Home: 17 El Tahrir St, 12311 Cairo Dokki, Egypt Office: Nat Rsch Ctr, El Tahrir St, 12311 Cairo Dokki, Egypt

BISHAI, HELMY MIKHAIL, fishery biologist, researcher, consultant; b. Manfalout, Assiout, Egypt, Feb. 20, 1926; s. Mikhail Bishai Farag and Zakieh Basta Guirgus; m. Soheir Sami Makar, Dec. 20, 1959; children: Amani, Hani. BSc in Zoology, Chemistry with honors, Cairo U., Arab Republic of Egypt, 1946, MSc in Zoology, 1950; PhD in Applied Sci. (hon.), Durham U., New Castle on Tyne, Eng., 1954. Demonstrator dept. zoology Cairo U. Faculty Sci., 1946-49, lectr. zoology, 1955-65, asst. prof., 1966-72, prof. fish biology, aquaculture, 1973-83, prof. emeritus, 1984—; mem. mission Durham U., Newcastle on Tyne, 1951-54; cons. Ministry Agr. and Fisheries, Khartoum, Sudan, 1958-61; cons. constrn. marine biol. sta. U. Tripoli, Libya, 1971-74; cons. biol. weed control Ministry Irrigation, Cairo, 1976-78; chmn. com. marine and fisheries resources Authority Rsch. So. East Egypt; chmn. com. marine & environ. scis. Egyptian Acad. Sci. Rsch. and Tech. Co-author: Principles of Animal Biology, 1970, Glossary of Zoological Terms, 1958, 3d rev. edit., 1979, Practical Systematic Zoology; translator 5 books, several sci. jour. articles. Mem. coun. environ. R&D Egyptian Acad. Sci. and Tech., rsch. coun. animal resources and fisheries. Recipient cert. of appreciation King Abdulaziz U., Saudi Arabia, 1982. Mem. Ecol. Soc. Am., Zool. Soc. Egypt, African Aquaculture and Fisheries Soc. (hon.), Pan African Fish and Fisheries Assn., Syndicate Sci. Professions Egypt (cert. of appreciation for pioneers in biol. sci. 1989), Acad. Sci. Rsch. and Tech. (v.p. com. for natural fishery resources 1984—), Supreme Coun. Univs. (pres. com. for promotion to professorship in zoology and biol. oceanography 1989—). Coptic Orthodox. Achievements include first to do studies on the River Nile at Sudan and inland Egyptian lakes, to evaluate results of projects in the field of fishery and aquaculture in Egypt. Home: 24 Imam Ali St, Heliopolis 11341, Arab Republic of Egypt Office: Cairo U Faculty Sci, Elgiza Cairo 12613, Arab Republic of Egypt

BISHNOI, UDAI RAM, agronomy and seed technology educator; b. Sukh Chain, Punjab, India, Aug. 15, 1942; came to U.S., naturalized, 1967; s. Ram Lal and Anchai Devi (Delu) B.; m. Sukh Devi Isarwal, May 11, 1966; children: Rita Rani, Raj Deep. BS, Rajasthan U., Jaipur, 1961; MS, Punjab Agrl. U., Ludhiana, 1963; PhD, Miss. State U., Starkville, 1971. Cert. profl. agronomist. Asst. prof. agronomy Rajasthan Agrl. U., Jobner, 1963-67; grad. rsch. asst. Seed Tech. Lab. Miss. State U., 1968-71; seed physiologist Hulsey Seed Labs., Inc., Decatur, Ga., 1971-72; assoc. prof. agronomy/seed tech. Ala. A&M U., Normal, 1972-80, prof., 1980—; seed technologist FAO/UN, Sudan and India, 1980, 88, 93; seed technologist, agronomist USAID/USDA-OICD, Keyna, Poland, 1980-83, 86; seed technologist, agronomist USAID, The Gambia, 1986, Denmark, 1995; U.S. del. to internat. crop sci. Congress, 1996; Titular prof. Nat. U. of South Argentina, 1997; mem., advisor promotion/tenure com. Ala. A&M U., Normal, 1991-93; vis. prof., Argentina, 1997. Author: Handbook of Seed Technology, 1982; assoc. editor Agronomy Jour., 1994—, Egerton Coll. Rsch. Bull., 1981-83; contbr. over 70 rsch. papers to profl. jours.; author: (documentary video) Farming System Research-An Approach to Conserve Soil and Increase Income on Limited Resource Farms, 1988. Bd. chmn., trustees Huntsville (Ala.) India Assn., 1990-92; sec.-treas. Agrl. Scientists Indian Origin, 1988-91. Recipient Scholarships Govt. India, Miss. State and Egypt, 1961, 68, 71, Rsch. Grants USDA, USAID, USDoEd, CIMMYT, State Ala., 1972-95, Outstanding Farming Sys. Rsch. award Rural Devel. Ctr., Tuskegee (Ala.) U., 1987, Outstanding Rsch. Scientist award 1991. Fellow Am. Soc. Agronomy, Crop Sci. Soc. Am.; mem. AAAS (bd. dirs. 1994-98), Assn. Ofcl. Seed Analysts, Am. Soc. Agronomy. Hindu. Achievements include prin. agronomist in release and devel. of two triticale (hybrid of wheat and rye) cultivars; development of several prodn. practices for soybeans, sorghum, triticale crops which helps to increase yields. Avocations: horseback riding, driving. Home: 6315 Havenwood Dr SE Huntsville AL 35802-1967 Office: Ala A&M U Dept Plant & Soil Sci Meridian St Normal AL 35762

BISHOP, BRONWYN, administrator; b. Sydney, Australia, Oct. 19, 1942; divorced; 2 children. Elected Senate of New South Wales, Australia, 1987-94, Ho. of Reps., Australia, 1994; shadow min. Dept. Pub. Adminstrn., Fed. Affairs & Local Govt., Australia, 1989-90, Dept. Urban and Regional Strategy, Australia, 1994, Dept. Health, Australia, 1994-95, Dept. Privatization and Commonwealth/State Rels., Australia, 1995-96; min. Dept. Defense Industry, Sci. & Personnel, Australia, 1998, Ministry Aged Care, Australia, 1998—. Office: Ministry Aged Care, Parliament House Ste MG48, Canberra ACT 2600, Australia*

BISHOP, BRUCE TAYLOR, lawyer; b. Hartford, Conn., Sept. 13, 1951; s. Robert Wright Sr. and Barbara (Taylor) B.; m. Sarah M. Bishop, Aug. 31, 1974; children: Elizabeth, Margaret. BA in Polit. Sci., Old Dominion U., 1973; JD, U. Va., Charlottesville, 1976. Bar: Va. 1977, U.S. Supreme Ct., Va. 1976, U.S. Dist. Ct. (ea. dist.) Va., U.S. Dist. Ct. (we. dist.) Va., U.S. Ct. Appeals (4th cir.); diplomate Am. Bd. Trial Advocates. Law clk. to chief judge U.S. Dist. Ct. (ea. dist.) Va., 1976-77; assoc. Willcox & Savage, P.C., Norfolk, Va., 1977-82; ptnr. Willcox & Savage, P.C., Norfolk, 1983—; bd. dirs. Nautical Adventures, Inc., Norfolk FestEvents, Ltd., 1981—, pres., 1982-85; pres. Va. OpSail 2000 Found.; mem. bd. visitors Old Dominion U., 1972-83, sec., 1979-81, chmn., mem. various coms.; speaker in field. Treas. Norfolk Reps., 1978-82, also mem. numerous coms.; bd. dirs., chmn. regional Key Club campaign United Way South Hampton Roads; chmn., cochmn. United Negro Coll. Fund, 1981, Four Cities United Way Campaign; trustee Va. Stage Co., 1982; pres. Community Promotion Corp.; commr. Norfolk Redevel. and Housing Authority; active numerous other community orgns. Named Outstanding Young Man, Norfolk Jaycees; recipient Disting. Alumni award Old Dominion U., Dominion Vol. of Yr. award, 1993. Mem. ABA (mem. various sects.), Fed. Bar Assn. (pres. Tidewater chpt. 1980-81), Am. Bd. Trial Advocates, Va. Assn. Def. Lawyers, Va. Bar Assn., Va. Trial Lawyers Assn., Norfolk-Portsmouth Bar Assn., Def. Rsch. Inst., Internat. Assn. Def. Counsel, Assn. Def. Attys., Def. Rsch. Inst., Old Dominion U. Alumni Assn. (bd. dirs. 1978-83), Old Dominion U. Ednl. Found. (bd. dirs. 1987—), Norfolk C. of C. (chmn. downtown devel. com. 1980-81), James Keat Am. Inn of Ct. (master). Avocations: basketball, tennis, gardening. Office: Willcox & Savage PC One Commercial Place Norfolk VA 23510

BISHOP, BRYAN EDWARDS, lawyer; b. Providence, Nov. 29, 1945; s. Charles Frederick Jr. and Emma Kirtley (Edwards) B.; m. Martha Jo Maben, June 12, 1970; children: Jennifer, Adam. BSME, U. Tex., Arlington, 1968; JD, Harvard U., 1972. Bar: Tex. 1972, U.S. Ct. Appeals (5th cir.) 1972. Ptnr. Rain, Harrell, Emery, Young & Doke, Dallas, 1972-87, Locke Purnell Rain Harrell, Dallas, 1987-98, Locke Liddell & Sapp LLP, Dallas, 1999—. Mem. ABA, State Bar Tex. (corp. law com., corp. banking and bus. law sect.), Tex. Bus. Law Found. (bd. dirs.). Club: Dallas Petroleum. Home: 7031 Roundrock Rd Dallas TX 75248-5144 Office: Locke Liddell & Sapp LLP 2200 Ross Ave Ste 2200 Dallas TX 75201-6776*

BISHOP, CHRISTOPHER C. R., surgeon, consultant; b. Paris, Nov. 17, 1952; s. Michael Rigby and Beatrice (Villemer) B.; m. Anthea Jane Tilzey, Sept. 17, 1977; children: Charles, Hugo, Lucie, Gabrielle. BA, Cambridge (Eng.) U., 1974, MB, BChir, 1977, MA, 1978, MChir, 1987. Cons. surgeon UCL Hosps., London, 1991—; hunterian prof. Royal Coll. Surgeons, London, 1991. Fellow Royal Coll. Surgeons. Office: 149 Harley St, London W1N 2DE, England

BISHOP, CLAIRE DEARMENT, small business owner, former librarian; b. Youngstown, Ohio, Oct. 12, 1937; d. Eugene Howard and Ruth (Bright) DeArment; m. Carl R. Meinstereifel, 1956 (div. 1964); children: Paul, Dawn; m. Olin Jerry Dewberry, Jr., 1974 (div. 1979); m. J. Bruce Bishop, May 6, 1992. BS, Clarion State U., 1967; MLS, Ga. State U., 1977. Cert. libr. media specialist, Ga. Libr. Henry County, Stockbridge, Ga., 1967-69; head libr. Russell H.S., East Point, Ga., 1969-84; engring. libr. Rockwell Internat., Duluth, Ga., 1984-88; rep. Govt. Industry Data Exch. Program, Corona, Calif., 1984-88; libr. Raytheon Co., 1990, Missile Sys. Divsn., Bristol, Tenn., 1988-90; owner, mgr. Claire's Collectibles, rubber stamp store, St. Augustine, Fla. Author newsletter Grin and Stamp It. Sec. San Marco Avenue Mchts. Assn. Mem. St. Augustine IBM Users Group (sec.), Six-Ninety-Six Investment Club (fin. officer), Mensa. Democrat. Avocations: computers, writing, information broker. Office: Claire's Collectibles 78B San Marco Ave Saint Augustine FL 32084-3258

BISHOP, ELIZABETH ANONA, history educator, consultant; b. Midland, Mich., Aug. 2, 1964; d. Jack Lawson and Donna Norine (Leavens) B.; m. Wael Hafez Mohammed Hafez Abu Sheikh; children: Yeh'a, Youssef. MA, Northwestern U., 1988; BA, Earlham Coll., 1986; PhD, U. Chgo., 1997. Manuscripts asst. dept. spl. collections U. Chgo. Joseph Regenstein Libr., 1989-92; asst. prof. Auburn (Ala.) U., 1996-97, Am. U. Cairo, 1998—; lectr. U. Md., 1995, 99; lectr. U. Chgo., 1996; cons. SRI Internat., Menlo Park, Calif., 1997—. Editor, author: Soraya Duval de Damperre Gulf and Gender: Migration and Women's New Roles in Rural Egypt, 1996; editor: Europe-Middle East Business: The New Alliance, 1995, (with Beckwith) Readings in Technology and Civilization, 1997. Recipient McNeill Fund award U. Chgo., 1990; fellow Am. Rsch. Ctr., Egypt, 1993; Wilkinson scholar in social scis. Earlham Coll., 1982-86. Mem. Assn. for the Advancement Slavic Studies, Middle East Studies Assn., Am. Hist. Assn.

BISHOP, GEORGE DAVID, psychology educator; b. South Haven, Mich., May 30, 1949; s. Rex R. and Lillian Carlene (Bidwell) B.; m. Jane Andrew, June 9, 1973; one son, one dau. BA, Hope Coll., 1971; MS, Yale U., 1973, PhD, 1976. Rsch. psychologist Walter Reed Army Inst. Rsch., Washington, 1975-79; asst. prof. psychology Am. U., Cairo, 1979-81; asst. prof. psychology U. Tex., San Antonio, 1981-87, assoc. prof., 1987-91; assoc. prof. Nat. U., Singapore, 1991—. Contbr. articles to profl. jours., chpts. to books. Capt. U. S. Army, 1975-79. Mem. APA, Singapore Psychol. Assn., European health Psychology Soc., Soc. for Behavioral Medicine, Am. Psychol. Soc., Soc. Psychol. Study Social Issues, Soc. Personality and Social Psychology. Episcopalian. Office: Nat U Singapore, 10 Kent Ridge Crescent, 119260 Singapore Republic of Singapore

BISHOP, JOHN MICHAEL, biomedical research scientist, educator; b. York, Pa., Feb. 22, 1936; married 1959; 2 children. AB, Gettysburg Coll., 1957; MD, Harvard U., 1962; DSc (hon.), Gettysburg Coll., 1983. Intern in internal medicine Mass. Gen. Hosp., Boston, 1962-63, resident, 1963-64; rsch. assoc. virology NIH, Washington, 1964-66, sr. investigator, 1966-68; from asst. prof. to assoc. prof. U. Calif. Med. Ctr., San Francisco, 1968-72, prof. microbiology and immunology, 1972—, prof. biochemistry and biophysics, 1982—; dir. G.W. Hooper Rsch. Found. G.W. Hooper Rsch. Found., 1981—; Univ. prof. U. Calif. Med. Ctr., San Francisco, 1994-2000; chair. Nat. Cancer Adv. Bd., San Francisco; chancellor U. Calif. Med. Ctr., San Francisco, 1998—. Recipient Nobel prize in physiology or medicine,

1989, Biomed. Rsch. award Am. Assn. Med. Colls., 1981, Albert Lasker Basic Med. Rsch. award, 1981, Armand Hammer Cancer award, 1984, GM Found. Cancer Rsch. award, 1984, Gairdner Found. Internat. award, Can., 1984, Medal of Honor, Am. Cancer Soc., 1984; NIH grantee, 1968—. Fellow Salk Inst. (trustee 1991—); mem. NAS, Inst. Medicine, Nat. Cancer Adv. Bd. Achievements include research in biochemistry of animal viruses, replication of nucleic acids, oncogenesis, control of cell growth, and molecular genetics. Office: U Calif Hooper Rsch Found Dept Microbiology PO Box 552 San Francisco CA 94143-0001

BISHOP, KIM IRENE, pharmaceutical executive, psychopharmacologist; b. Williamsport, Pa., Nov. 12, 1960; arrived in Switzerland, 1996; d. Harold Dane and Irene (Pelletier) B. BA, Franklin and Marshall Coll., 1982; MS, Villanova (Pa.) U., 1986; PhD, U. London, 1995. Coord. clin. rsch. Scheie Eye Inst. U. Pa., Phila., 1984-88; sr. clin. rsch. assoc. Allergan Pharms., Irvine, Calif., 1988-90; cons. Clin. Trials Rsch. Ltd., Maidenhead, Eng., 1994; sr. drug safety scientist Novartis, Basel, Switzerland, 1996-97, global project liaison mgr. for dermatology, transplantation, immunology, infectious diseases, 1997—. Contbr. articles to profl. jours. Alumni regional amb. Villanova U. Overseas rsch. scholar Brit. com. for Vice Chancellors and Prins., London, 1991-94; European Behavioral Pharmacology Soc. scholar, 1994; scholar Brit. Assn. Psychopharmacology Bursary, Eng., 1993, 94. Mem. Drug Info. Assn., Collegium Internationale Psychopharmacologium, Internat. Club of Basel, Profl. Women's Assn. Avocations: skiing, scuba diving, dancing, horseback riding, cycling.

BISHOP, MALCOLM GRAHAM HAMILTON, medical essayist; b. Montgomery, U.K., Aug. 10, 1944; s. Stanley Graham and Irene (Doughty) B.; m. Polly Ann Badman Bishop, Nov. 27, 1971; children: Auriol Caroline Ann, Olivia Frances Mary. BDS, U. London, 1968; LDS, Royal Coll. Surgeons, 1968; MSc, U. London, 1983; DGDP, Royal Coll. Surgeons, 1993. Dental surgeon in gen. practice Hertford, Eng.; lectr. in dental radiology Kings Coll. Hosp., London, 1968-99; pres. British Soc. Dental and Maxillo-Facial Radiology, 1993-94; lectr. ethics applied dentist Kings Coll. Hosp., London, 1998-99. Contbr. articles on ethics, philosophy and lit. to profl. jours. Mem. Royal Soc. Medicine London, N.Y. Acad. Scis., Athenaeum Club London. Office: Queen Anne House, 2A St Andrew St, Hertfordshire England

BISHOP, MARK ALAN, airline pilot, flight instructor; b. Cin., Apr. 2, 1960; s. Edward Dean and Helen Jean Bishop; m. Brenda Bishop, Aug. 24, 1985 (div. Aug. 1999; 1 child, Megan Christine. Flight instr. Cin. Flight Tng., 1986-88; charter pilot Exec. Jet Mgmt., Cin., 1988-89; airline pilot Enterprise Airlines, Cin., 1989-91, DHL Airways, Cin., 1991, Am. Airlines, DFW Airport, Tex., 1991—; flight instr. SimuFlite Internat., Dallas, 1994-96. Active in local poliitcs; precinct committeeman Rep. Party of Ind., Indpls.; mem. Greater Indpls. Rep. Fin. Com., 1999—. Mem. NRA, Aircraft Owners and Pilots Assn. Christian. Avocations: reading, travel, jogging, cycling. E-mail: Lindbergh7@aol.com. Home: 1319 Kings Cove Ct Indianapolis IN 46260-1671

BISHOP, NIGEL TEMPEST, mathematician, educator; b. London, Sept. 11, 1951; arrived in South Africa, 1976; s. Michael and Françoise Marie (Garat) B.; m. Judith Mary Mullins, Dec. 17, 1977; children: William, Michael. BA with hons., U. Cambridge, Eng., 1973; MA, U. Cambridge, 1977; PhD, U. Southampton, Eng., 1977. Lectr. U. Witwatersrand, Johannesburg, South Africa, 1976-79; sr. lectr. U. Witwatersrand, Johannesburg, 1980-85, assoc. prof., 1986-91; prof. U. South Africa, Pretoria, 1992—, vice dean, 1994-2000; adj. prof. U. Pitts., 1997-2000. Co-author: Pascal Precisely for Engineers and Scientists, 1990, Java Gently for Engineers and Scientists, 2000; contbr. articles to profl. jours. Grantee Nat. Rsch. Found., 1989—. Fellow Royal Astron. Soc.; mem. South Africa Math. Soc. Roman Catholic. Avocations: windsurfing, wine tasting. Office: UNISA, PO Box 392, Pretoria 0003, South Africa

BISHOP, PETER ORLEBAR, neurophysiologist; b. Tamworth, NSW, Australia, June 14, 1917; s. Ernest John Hunter and Mildred Alice Havelock (Vidal) B.; m. Hilare Louise Holmes; children: Phillippa Leslie, Elisabeth Clare, Roderick Owen. MB, BS, U. Sydney, Australia, 1940, DSc, 1967, MD (hon.), 1983. Jr. resident, med. officer Royal Prince Alfred Hosp., Sydney, 1941, neurol. registrar, 1941-42, clin. asst. in neurosurgery, 1946; fellow postgrad. com. in medicine U. Sydney, 1946-50; fellow Nat. Hosp., Queen Sq., Univ. Coll., London, 1946-50; fellow nat. health and med. rsch. coun. dept. surgery U. Sydney, 1950-51, sr. lectr. dept. physiology, 1951-54, reader in physiology, 1954-55, prof. physiology, head dept. physiology, 1955-67; prof., head dept. physiology Australian Nat. U., Canberra, 1967-82, prof. emeritus, 1983—; rsch. fellow Dept. Anatomy U. Coll., London, 1947-50; vis. prof. Dept. Neurophysiology Osaka U. Med. Sch., 1974, Keio U. Sch. Medicine, Tokyo, 1982, Katholieke U. Leuven, Belgium, 1984-85, U. Zurich, Switzerland, 1985, Dept. Physiology, Cambridge, Eng., 1986; vis. fellow Dept. Behavioural Biology, Rsch. Sch. Biol. Scis., Australian Nat. U., 1983-87; rsch. assoc. Dept. Anatomy, U. Sydney, 1987—; cen. coun. Internat. Brain Rsch. Orgn., 1986-92. Editoral bd. Physiology and Behavior, 1966-89, Exptl. Brain Rsch., 1966-89, Jour. of Neurophysiology, 1970-75, Exptl. Neurology, 1971-75, Vision Rsch., 1978-87, Hist. Records of Australian Sci., 1983-98, chmn. 1983-98. Surg. lt. Navy, 1942-46. Fellow Nat. Vision Rsch. Inst. Australia, 1983; named officer Order of Australia, 1986; recipient Australia prize Fed. Parliament of Commonwealth of Australia, 1993. Fellow Australian Acad. Sci., Royal Soc. of London; mem. Australian Neurosci. Soc., Australian Physiol. and Pharm. Soc. (treas. 1960-64), The Physiol. Soc. Home: 139 Cape Three Points Rd, Avoca Beach NSW, Australia 2251 Office: U Sydney, Dept Anatomy & Histology, Sydney NSW, Australia 2006

BISHOP, ROSALINDA MATUBIS, information manager, choreographer; b. Naga, The Philippines, Oct. 18, 1950; d. Rodrigo B. Matubis and Gregoria N. (Nacario) Bulalacao; m. Roy Bishop, Aug. 15, 1981 (div. Sept. 1989); 1 child, Raynor. BS in Edn., U. Nueva Caceres, The Philippines, 1969, MA in Edn., 1974; MBA, Ortanez U., Philippines, 1979; Assoc. Diploma Arts, Sydney Tech. and Further Edn., 1990; M in Info. Mgmt., Charles Sturt U., Wagga, Australia, 1997. Tchr. Dept. Edn., Pili, The Philippines, 1969-74; rsch./analyst Armed Forces of The Philippines, Manila, 1974-75; fgn. exchange officer Ctrl. Bank The Philippines, Manila, 1975-80; libr. officer Parliament House, Canberra, Australia, 1981-82; adminstrv. svc. officer Australian Bur. Stats., Canberra, 1982-86; libr. officer Australian Cath. U., Sydney, 1987-94, U. Western Sydney, 1986-87; supr. State Libr. NSW, Sydney, 1994—; Folk lore dir. Philippine Australian Assn., Canberra, 1981-84; dir., choreographer Philippine Dance Ensemble, Sydney, 1986—; pub. rels. officer Filipino Womens Assn., Sydney, 1986-90; protocol mgr. Mrs. Philippines Australia Beauty Pageant, Sydney, 1994—; treas. Philippine Australian Entertainment Network, 1997—. Choreographer/dir. Interpretative Dance (Lit. Musical Competition), 1973 (Nat. Winner 1973); contbg. editor Pilipino Mag. and Newspaper; occasional contbr. to Filipino media. Recipient Outstanding Filipino Migrant award ECC, Canberra, 1984, Best Cultural Performance award Philippine Australian Sports Coun., 1991, Mrs. Philippines Australia award Filipino Herald, Sydney, 1993. Mem. ALA, Australian Libr. and Info. Assn. (pres. acquistions NSW), Assn. Libr. Collection and Tech. Svcs., Filipino Womens Assn. (pub. rels. officer), Philippine Australian Country Club (sec.), Sydney Morning Herald/Dymocks Lit. Luncheon Club. Avocations: reading, ballroom dancing, travel, cooking, community work. Home: 7A Eulo Pde, 2112 Ryde NSW, Australia Office: State Libr NSW, Macquarie St, 2000 Sydney NSW, Australia

BISHOP, SUSAN KATHARINE, executive search company executive; b. Palm Beach, Fla., Apr. 3, 1946; d. Warner Bader Bishop and Katharine Sue (White) McLennan; m. Robert Uchitel, Dec. 27, 1973 (div. 1979); 1 child, Rachel. B.A., Briarcliff Coll., 1968; M.B.A., Fordham U., 1985. Actress N.Y.C., 1968-72; producer, hostess Sta. KIMO-TV, Anchorage, 1972-74; dir. programming Visions Pay TV, 1974-79; recruiter Joe Sullivan & Assocs., N.Y.C., 1980-82; prin. Johnson, Smith & Knisely, 1982-88; ptnr. Schmitt Bishop Tolette, N.Y.C., 1989-91; pres. Bishop Ptnrs., Ltd., N.Y.C., 1991—. Mem. Cable TV Adminstrn. and Mktg. Soc., Women in Cable, Assn. Exec. Search Cons. (bd. dirs.). Office: Bishop Ptnrs 708 3rd Ave New York NY 10017-4201

BISHOP, WILLIAM ARCHIE, solicitor; b. Bridgwater, Somerset, Eng., July 21, 1937; s. Evelyn Archie and Gertrude (Pocock) B.; m. Joan Beatrice Skerman, Aug. 2, 1961 (div. Nov. 1996); children: Paula Denise, Mark Russel; m. Anne Carolyn Edwards, June 26, 1998. Solicitor, Coll. Law, Guilford, Eng., 1970. Deck officer P&O Line, 1954-60; mgr. Holman Fenwick Willan, London, 1960-70, ptnr., 1970—, sr. ptnr., 1989—; legal adv. Internat. Salvage Union, London, 1979—; freeman City of London, 1988; examiner in admiralty High Ct. of Justice, London, 1996—. Mem. Law Soc., Royal Automobile Club. Avocations: horseback riding, golf, painting. Office: Holman Fenwick and Willan, Marlow House Lloyds Ave, London EC3N 3AL, England

BISHOP-GRAHAM, BARBARA, secondary school educator, journalist; b. Angwin, Calif., Apr. 22, 1941; d. Will Francis and Esther Clara (Blisserd) Bishop; children: Gregory Mark, Steven Bishop. BA in Journalism, U. Hawaii, 1975, BA in English, 1975, BA in Art History, 1975, BFA in Painting and Drawing, 1975; nat. cert. in journalism, Kans. State U., 1994; MA in Tech. Curriculum & Instrn., Calif. State U., Sacramento, 1999. Cert. tchr., Hawaii. Photography instr., art tchr. Hawaii Sch. for Girls, Honolulu, 1974-76; substitute tchr. English State Dept. Edn., Oahu, 1977-78; English and grammar instr. Hawaii Sch. for Bus., Honolulu, 1979-80; media dir., exec. asst., historian Oriental Treasures and Points West, Honolulu, 1981-82; legal asst. Goodsill, Anderson, Quinn, Honolulu, 1983-84; lang. arts and photography tchr. Lodi (Calif.) H.S., 1984-88, writing and lang. arts tchr., 1988-93, creative writing tchr., 1989—, journalism adviser, 1993-95, lang. arts tchr., 1993—, Brit. lit. tchr., 1996—; mem. curriculum coun. Lodi Unified Sch. Dist., 1989-92, 97-2000; liaison to PTSA Lodi H.S., 1991-92, mentor tchr., 1991-94; student literary mag. advisor Lodi H.S., 1989-2000. Sportswriter Oakland Tribune, 1957-60, Author Three Poems, 1998; contbr. articles to profl. publs. Fundraiser chmn. Big Bros. of Am., San Francisco, 1967; media dir. Clements (Calif.) Cmty. Cares, 1985-89. Recipient Edn. Contbn. award Masons 1988-92, 20th Century Achievement award Am. Biographical Inst., 1999; grantee Nat. Endowment of Arts, rsch. Japanese Lit. 1989; social rschr. grantee Brazil, U. So. Calif. grantee, 1992; grantee S. Joaquin County Office Edn., 1996-97; champion Hawaii State barrel racing, 1980. Mem. NEA, Calif. Tchrs. Assn. (Calif. state tchrs. coun. rep. 1996-97), Lodi Edn. Assn. (conf. fund chair 1989-97). Republican. Seventh-Day Adventist. Avocations: writing, dressage riding and showing, growing roses. Office: Lodi HS 3 S Pacific Ave Lodi CA 95242-3020

BISHT, PREM B., physics educator; b. Champawat, India, Jan. 15, 1965; s. Amba Datt and Saraswati (Joshi) B.; m. Mamta Pandey, Mar. 8, 1994. BSc, Dev Singh Bisht Coll., Nainital, India, 1983; MSc, Dev Singh Bishl Coll., Nainital, India, 1985, PhD, 1991. Rsch. assoc. Dept. Sci. and Tech., New Delhi, 1993-95; asst. prof. Indian Inst. Tech., Madras, 1997—; vis. scientist Tata Inst. for Fundamental Rsch., Bombay, 1993. Contbr. some 45 articles to profl. jours. Monbusho fellow Inst. Molecular Sci.a, Okazaki, Japan, 1991-93, Japan Soc. for Promotion of Sci. fellow Kyoto (Japan) Inst. Tech., 1995-97. Mem. Indian Assn. Physics Tchrs. Avocations: music, hiking, cricket, soccer, baseball. Office: Physics Dept, Indian Inst Tech, Madras 600036, India

BISIACHI, IRENE MARIA GIULIA, press office consultant; b. Rovereto, Trento, Italy, May 15, 1943; d. Ermanno and Albertina (della Rocca) B.; m. Luigi Valperga Count di Masino e di Caluso, Dec. 28, 1988. Cambridge proficiency in English, Brit. Sch., Milan, 1967; diploma laws and econs., Centro Studi e Documentazione delle Comunitá Europee, Milan, 1971; Doctor honoris causa in Reporting Sci., Pro-Deo U., N.Y.C., 1995. Free lance journalist La Notte, Milan, 1969-72; editor, pub. rels. Tempo Economico, Milan, 1972-74; corr. United Feature Syndicate, N.Y.C., 1976-80, La Revue de la Mercerie, Paris, 1979-81; mktg. rschr. Intermarket, Frankfurt-Am-Main, Germany, 1977-81; press office pub. rels. agt. Intersew, Monte Carlo, Monaco, 1978-79, Dactex, Birmingham, Eng., 1978-79, Simolia, Paris, 1979-81; owner editor responsible Notiziario Tessile Abbigliamento, Milan, 1979-92; press office cons. GUS Gruppo Giornalisti Uffici Stampa, Milan, 1977—; sec. Unione Italiana Stampa Tessile dell' Abbigliamento, Milan, 1974-78; observer in Milan, Italian fashion for Italy Am. C. of C., N.Y.C., 1979-80; advt. agt. Milan Spanish monthly Confeccion Española, Barcelona, 1978-83; dep. gov. in Italy for Am. Biog. Inst., Raleigh, N.C., 1995—; dep. dir. gen. in Italy for Internat. Biog. Ctr., Cambridge, Eng., 1996—. Recipient Bronze medal U.S. Trade Ctr., Milan, 1974, A.B.I. Key of Success award for Press Consultancy, 1996, Prize Dante Alighieri, 1999; named Honors. Grad. to Be Istituto Promozioni Internat., Rome, 1991, honors grad. in reporting sci. Univs. Internat. Studiorum Superiorum Pro-Deo, N.Y.C., 1995. Fellow Ordine dei Giornalisti della Lombardia, Gruppo Giornalisti Uffici Stampa, Assn. Lombarda Giornalisti; mem. German C. of C. in Milan, American C. of C in Italy, 1979-92, 1997—. Roman Catholic. Avocations: attending musical events, siamese cats, collecting outstanding porcelain, fashion shopping, photography. Home: Clotilde 6, Piazzale Principessa, 20121 Milan Italy Office: Via Monte di Pieta' 21, I-20121 Milan Italy

BISKUP, JOACHIM, psychoanalyst, psychologist; b. Salzgitter, Germany, Jan. 19, 1949; s. Ernst and Christine (Wieja) B.; m. Christiane Hering, Apr. 4, 1975; children: Joscha, Nina. Diploma in psychology, U. Göttingen, Germany, 1977, D in social sci., 1982. Pvt. practice psychology, Hardegsen, Germany, 1978-82; tng. in client-centered therapy Gesellschaft fuer Wissenschaftliche Gesprachstherapie, Braunschweig, 1978-84; postdoctoral fellow U. Göttingen, 1982-99; tng. in psychoanalysis Lou Andreas Salome Inst., Göttingen, 1985-91; pvt. practice psychoanalysis, Hardegsen, 1987—. Author: Die psychosoziale Situation von Koronarpatienten, 1982; contbr. articles to profl. jours. Mem. exec. bd. various clubs. 1st lt. German Air Force, 1967-71. Scholar Student Found. German People, 1974-80. Mem. German Psychoanalytic Assn. (exec. bd. 1997—), Lou Andreas Salome Inst. (exec. bd. 1994—, tng. analyst 1997—). Avocations: basketball, volleyball, tennis. Home: Drei-Eichen-Weg 16a, 37181 Hardegsen Germany Office: Göttingen, Nikolausberger Way 17, 37073 Göttingen Germany

BISMARCK, BEATRICE VON, art historian; b. Wiesbaden, Germany, Mar. 15, 1959; d. Gunther von and Swantie von (Becker) B.; m. Sebastian Victor Louis, Aug. 31, 1996. MA, Courtauld Inst. of Art, London, 1983; PhD, Freie U., Berlin, 1989. Rsch. asst. Solomon R. Guggenheim Mus., N.Y.C., 1983; asst. lectr. Freie U., Berlin, 1985; curator Staedelsches Kunstinsti, Frankfurt, Germany, 1989-93; asst. prof. U. Lueneburg, Germany, 1993-99; lectr. Acad. Visual Arts, Leipzig, Germany, 1999-2000; freelance art critic Flash Art, Milan, Italy, 1984-88, Noema, Wien-Salzburg, Austria, 1987-90. Editor/author: Games Fights Collaborations, 1996, Clegg & Guttmann: The Open Public Library, 1994; author: Bruce Nauman: The True Artist, 1998, others. Rsch. grantee German Acad. Exch., Bonn, 1980-81, Hilla Rebay Found., N.Y.C., 1983, Berlin Grant, 1985-87.

BISMUTH, FAVRE CHANTAL, medical educator; b. Cornimont, France, July 27, 1932; d. Jean and Noelle (Cuny) F.; m. Henri Bismuth (div. 1984); 1 child, Anne. With Hosp. Fernand Widal, Paris, 1980—, Hosp. Lariboisiere, Paris, 1996—; defense councillor Ministry of Health, Paris, 1989-95. Author: Paraquat Poisoning, 1995, Toxicologie Clinique, 5 edits. Fellow Am. Acad. Toxicology, Internat. Union Toxicology (v.p. 1992-95), French Soc. Toxicology (pres. 1987-89). Home: 10 Rue De La Cure, 75016 Paris France Office: Hosp Fernand Widal, U Paris 7, 200 Faubourg Saint-Denis, 75010 Paris France

BISNAUTH, DALE, Guyana government official; b. Better Success, Dec. 30, 1938; m.; 4 children. BA in History, U. West Indies, PhD in History; MDiv, U. London. Dean United Theol. Coll. West Indies; sr. lectr. U. West Indies, U. Guyana; sr. min., 1992; min. of edn. Govt. of Guyana, Georgetown, 1992—. Assoc. gen. sec. Caribbean Coun. Chs.; chmn. Guyana Coun. Chs. Office: Ministry of Edn, PO Box 1014 26 Brickdam, Stabroek Georgetown Guyana

BISNOVATYI-KOGAN, GENNADI SEMYONOVICH, astrophysicist, researcher; b. Mikhailovka, Saratov, Russia, Dec. 6, 1941; s. Semyon Bisnovatyi and Sofia Kogan; m. Linna Aikadjevna Fridman, 1969 (div. 1990); 1 child. Diploma, Moscow Phys.-Tech. Inst., 1964; PhD Phys. Math., Inst. Applied Math., Moscow, 1968; Doctor Scis., Space Rsch. Inst., Moscow, 1977. Jr. sci. rschr. Inst. Applied Math., Moscow, 1967-74; sr. sci. rschr. Space Rsch. Inst., Moscow, 1974-86, leading sci. rschr., 1986-95, main sci. rschr., 1995—; prof. Moscow State U., 1990-96. Editl. bd. Astrophysics, 1988—, Astronomy and Astrophys. Transactions, 1992—, Gravitation and Cosmology, 1997—; author: Physical Problems of Theory of Stellar Evolution, 1989; contbr. articles to profl. jours. Named Perren Prof., Queen Mary Westfield Coll., London, 1995; Kapitza fellow Royal Soc., Cambridge U., 1994; INTAS, CRDF, DFG grantee, 1994-97. Mem. Internat. Astron. Union, European Astron. Soc., Euro-Asian Astron. Soc. Fax: 7 095 3107093. E-mail: gkogan@mx.iki.rssi.ru. Office: Space research Inst, Profsoyuznaya 84/32, 117810 Moscow Russia

BISPO, ANTONIO ALEXANDRE, musicologist, architect; b. São Paulo, Brazil, Mar. 17, 1949; arrived in Fed. Republic Germany, 1974.; s. Antonio and Ermelinda (Rego) B. Lic. in Mus. Edn., Inst. Mus. de São Paulo, 1972, Lic. Condr., 1973; Diploma Architect, U. São Paulo, 1972; D Musicology, U. Cologne, Fed. Republic Germany, 1979. Dir. Conservatorio Jardim Am., São Paulo, 1971-73; lectr. Faculdade de Musica, São Paulo, 1973-74; researcher Institut für Hymnologische und Musikethnologische Studien Maria Laach, Cologne, 1979—; bd. dir. Musikschule der Stadt, Leichlingen, Fed. Republic Germany, 1981-84; mem. council Consociatio Internationalis Musicae Sacrae, Rome, 1980-85; lectr. U. Köln, 1998—. Author: Die Katholische Kirchenmusik in der Provinz São Paulo, 1979, Collectanea Musicae Sacrae Brasiliensis, 1981, Grundlagen christlicher Musikkultur in der aussereurop. Welt der Neuzeit, 1987-88, Martin Braunwieser, 1991, Beitraege uber Volkstraditionen u. Synkretismus, 1996, Die Musikkulturen der Indianer, I, 1997, II, 1999, Christliche Musikantropologie, 1999, Brasil-Europa e Musicologia, 1999, Brasil-Europa 500 Jahre: Musik und Visionen, 2000; editor: Correspondencia Musicológica, 1989—; contbr. articles to profl. jours. Mem. Soc. Brasileira de Musicologia (bd. dirs. 1981-93), Acad. Paulistana de Historia, Ordem Nacional dos Bandeirantes (honor), Associacao Brasileira de Folclore (honor), Institut fur Studien der Musikkultur des portugiesischen Sprachraumes (bd. dirs.), Inst. Brasileiro de Estudos Musicologicos (bd. dirs.), Akademie Brasil-Europa für Kultur-und Wissenschaftsforschung (bd. dirs.). Home: Theodor Heuss Ring 14, D50668 Cologne Germany

BISQUERRA, RAFAEL, education educator; b. Arta, Spain, Feb. 11, 1949; s. Andres and Isabel (Alzina) B.; m. Catalina Prohens, May 11, 1980; children: Aina, Marta. Degree in pedagogy, U. Barcelona, 1976; degree in psychology, U Autonoma de Barcelona, 1979; D in Ednl. Sci., U. Barcelona, 1980. Prof. U. Barcelona, Spain, 1976—; founder Grup de Recerca en Orientació Psicopedagogica (GROP), 1997—. Author: Metodos de investigacion educativa, 1989, Analisis Multivariable, 1989, Orientacion psicopedagogica para la prevencion y el desarrollo, 1990, Origenes y desarrollo de la orientacion psicopedagogica, 1996, Orientacion y tutoria, 1996, Modelos de orientacion e intervencion psicopedagogica, 1998, Educación Emocional y Bienestar, 2000. Avocations: reading, music, cinema, travel, swimming. Home: Cardenal Reig 42-46 8 3, 08028 Barcelona Spain Office: U Barcelona Dept Edn, Vall d'Hebron 171, 08035 Barcelona Spain

BISSA, RAMAN, accountant, editor; b. Jodhpur, Rajasthan, India, Apr. 1, 1958; s. Shri Krishna and Keshar (Purohit) B.; m. Suman Vyas, Dec. 8, 1984; children: Pratibha, Saurabh. BCom with honors, Jodhpur (India) U., 1977, LLB, 1982. Chartered acct. Inst. Chartered Accts., 1984. Asst. editor Current Tax Reporter, Jodhpur, India, 1981-86, editor, 1987-88, editor-in-charge, 1988—; asst. adminstrv. officer Oriental Ins. Co., Delhi, India, 1986. Author: CTR Ency. of Direct Taxes on CD-ROM; co-author: Law of Income Tax and Its Procedural Aspects, 1985, CTR Taxation Manual, 1994—; editor: All India Tax Tribunals Judgments, 1981—, CTR Year Book, 1982—; editor, scrutinizer: Tax Compendium, Vols. 1 through 73, 1992—, Analysis of Tax Cases, Vols. 1 through 5, 1992-96; coord. Indian Taxation, Vols. 1 through 7, 1988-92, 2d edit., 1999-2000. Treas. Saur Urjha Vikas & Maru Paryavaran Sansthan, Jodhpur, 1996-2000. Nat. scholar Govt. of India, 1973-77. Mem. Inst. Chartered Accts. India (exec. mem. Jodhpur br. 1984, treas. Jodhpur br. 1985, v.p. Jodhpur br. 1986), Indian Coun. Arbitration. Hindu. Avocations: reading, games, music. Home: Flat #6 Aakas Deep Bldg, 3rd D Rd Sardarpura, 342003 Jodhpur India Office: Current Tax Reporter, Archana 34 Heavy Indsl Area, 342003 Jodhpur India

BISSADA, NABIL KADDIS, urologist, educator, researcher, author; b. Cairo, Sept. 2, 1938; s. Kaddis B. and Negma Bissada; m. Samia; children: Sally, Nancy, Mary, Amy, Andrew. M.D., Cairo U., 1963. Diplomate Am. Bd. Urology. Intern Cairo Univ. Hosp., 1964-65; resident in surgery Babelsharia Gen. Hosp., 1965-69; resident in urology U. N.C. Hosp., 1970-72, chief resident, 1972-73; asst. prof. urology U. Ark., 1973-77, assoc. prof., 1977-79; cons. urologist King Faisal Specialist Hosp. and Rsch. Ctr., Riyadh, Saudi Arabia, 1979-87; prof., chief urologic oncology Med. U. S.C., 1987—, vice-chmn. dept. urology, 1999—; chief urologic surgery Ralph H. Johnson Med. Ctr., 1987—; co-chmn. Div. U., U.S. Sect. Internat. Coll. Surgeons, 1989-91, chmn., 1991-93, pres. Carolina Urol. Assn., 1997-99; pres. Egyptian-Am. Urol. Assn., 1990-92, Arab-Am. Urol. Assn., 1993—; frequent spkr. to regional, nat. and internat. med. groups. Author: Lower Urinary Tract Function and Dysfunction: Diagnosis and Management, 1978; Pharmacology of the Urinary Tract and the Male Reproductive System, 1982; cons., guest editor several med. jours. and periodicals; contbr. to hundreds of articles and book chpts.; pioneered several significant surgical and med. urologic treatment methods, developed the Charleston Pouch Technique for continent urinary diversion; conducted numerous local, nat., and internat. tchg. courses on urologic reconstructive techniques. Fellow ACS, Internat. Coll. Surgeons; mem. Am. Urol. Assn., , Egyptian-Am. Urol. Assn. (pres. 1990-92), Arab-Am. Urol. Assn. (pres. 1993—), Carolina Urol. Assn. (pres. 1997-99), Soc. Internat. D'Urologie, Soc. Urologic Oncology, Urodynamic Soc., Soc. Urology and Engring., Sigma Xi. Fax: 843-792-8523. Office: Med U of SC Med Ctr PO Box 250620 96 Jonathan Lucas St Charleston SC 29425-8900

BISSELL, BRENT JOHN, advertising and direct marketing executive; b. Dearborn, Mich., July 10, 1950; s. Ernest Ross and Virginia Jane (Pete) B.; m. Libby Schulak, Dec. 4, 1971; children: John, Sarah, Elizabeth, Daniel. BA, U. Toledo, 1971. Pres. Bissell Advt., Inc., Toledo, 1975-78; creative dir. Stark Bros. Nurseries & Orchards Co., Louisiana, Mo., 1979-80; divisional gen. mgr. Consumer Pub. Co., Canton, Ohio, 1980-82; mng. dir. D'Arcy, MacManus, Massius Direct Mktg., Bloomfield Hills, Mich., 1982-85; v.p., mng. dir. Bozell Direct, Chgo., 1985-87; sr. v.p., gen. mgr. McCann-Erickson Direct, Troy, Mich., 1988-93; pres. Direct Target One, Minnetonka, Minn., 1993-99; sr. v.p., gen. mgr. McCann Relationship Mktg., 1999—; lectr. in field; instr., bd. advisors Direct Mktg. Assn. Contbg. author: Direct Marketing Handbook, 2d edit., 1991, Next Step in Database Marketing: Consumer Guided Marketing, 1996. Mem. communications bd. Nat. Assn. Congl. Chs., 1990-93. Fellow ISSM (sr.); mem. SAR, Mayflower Descendants, Toledo Club, Masons. Office: McCann Erickson Direct 755 W Big Beaver Rd Ste 2500 Troy MI 48084-0230

BISSET, GORDON WOOD, pharmacology educator, researcher, retired; b. London, July 20, 1922; s. James Thomas Milne and Hilda Kathleen (Baillie) B.; m. Jean Morris, July 8, 1958; children: Yvonne Margaret, Jennifer Anne. MB, BS, Charing Cross Hosp. Med. Sch., London, 1952; PhD, U. Oxford, Eng., 1955. Sr. lectr. Charing Cross Hosp. Med. Sch., 1955-61; rsch. worker, mem. sci. staff Med. Rsch. Coun. Nat. Inst. Med. Rsch., London, 1961-70; prof. pharmacology U. London, 1971-85; vis. scientist Med. Rsch. Coun. Nat. Inst. Med. Rsch., 1985-95; dep. chmn., chmn. bd. studies in pharmacology U. London, 1974-84. Contbr. articles to profl. jours. Lt. Royal Navy Vol. Res., 1941-46. Recipient Rsch. scholarship Med. Rsch. Coun., 1952. Mem. Royal Coll. Surgeons Eng., Royal Coll. Physicians London (lic.). Avocations: golf, gardening, bridge, fishing, walking. Home: 16 Nascot Wood Rd, WD1 3SA Watford England

BISSLER, RICHARD THOMAS, mortician; b. Ravenna, Ohio, Nov. 23, 1953; s. Richard Samuel and Ruth Marion (Cowan) B.; m. Jane H. Vair, Aug. 23, 1975; children: Stephanie Ann, Carlie Jane. BS in Mortuary Sci., U. Minn., 1976; grad., Nat. Found. Funeral Svc. Mgmt., 1983. Lic. funeral dir. and embalmer Ohio; cert. crematory operator Cremation Assn. N.Am. Funeral svc. asst. Bissler & Sons Funeral Home, Kent, Ohio, 1970-74, mortician, 1976—, corp. sec., 1983-86, corp. sec.-treas., 1986-88, pres., 1988—; bd. dirs. Home Savs. Bank, Kent; bd. dirs., treas. NSM Ins. Co. Ltd. Trustee Kent Free Libr., 1986—, St. Patrick's Sch. Endowment Fund, 1994—, Nat. Selected Morticians Ins. Trust, 1995—; past bd. dirs., pres. Portage County A.C.S., Kent; past treas. NEO-SIDS Found., Akron, Ohio; mem. adult edn. adv. com. Kent City Schs.; steering com. Portage County

Hospice; devel. com. United Christian Ministries, 1996-98; mem. Vision 2000 com. City of Kent; mem. Kent Bus. and Edn. adv. com. Recipient Disting. Svc. award Kent Jaycees, 1986. Mem. Nat. Funeral Dirs. Assn., Ohio Embalmers Assn., Ohio Funeral Dirs. Assn., Nat. Selected Morticians (meeting chair 1989), Funeral Ethics Assn., Kent Area C. of C. (dir. 1985-89, Outstanding Bus. Person award 1992), Order of the Golden Rule, Kent Rotary (dir. 1991-93, pres. 1995-96), K.C. Republican. Roman Catholic. Avocations: golf, photography, travel. Office: Bissler & Sons Funeral Home 628 W Main St Kent OH 44240-2212

BISWAS, DHRUBES, electrical engineer; b. Durgapur, India, Sept. 11, 1964; s. Samaresh and Mamata (Chakraborty) B.; m. Subhra Biswas. B Tech. in Elec. Engring., Indian Inst. Tech., 1987; MSEE, U. Ill., 1991, PhD, 1992. Mgr. processing & devel. Northeast Semicondr. (EG&G), East Fishkill, N.Y., 1992-93; rsch. assoc. Cornell U., Ithaca, N.Y., 1993-94; prin. engr. AMP Inc., Clarksburg, Md., 1994-97; mgr. gallium arsenide molecular beam epitaxy materials Alpha Industries, Woburn, Mass., 1997-99; mgr. advanced materials Anadigics, Warren, N.J., 1999—. Mem. IEEE, Materials Rsch. Soc., Lasers and Electooptics Soc., Electron Devices Soc., Tau Beta Pi, Phi Kappa Phi. Avocations: volleyball, hiking, writing poetry, car racing. Home: 70 Bedford St Burlington MA 01803-3657 Office: Anadigics 35 Technology Dr Warren NJ 07059-5197

BISWAS, DILIP KUMAR, engineering company executive; b. Sylhet, Assam, India; s. Birendra Chandra and Subarnalata (Kar) B.; m. Laxmi Dilip Chatterjee-Sikdar, Dec. 14, 1966; 1 child, Monisha Dilip. B of Engring., Calcutta U., 1956; M of Engring., Sheffield U., 1960; degree in mgmt., Inst. of Mgmt., 1962. Gen. mgr. chems. divsn. ICI India Ltd., Calcutta, 1984-85; chief exec. tech. divsn. ICI India Ltd., Delhi, 1986-87; exec. v.p. mfg. divsn. Sandoz India Ltd., Bombay, 1987-95; chief cons. DB Assocs., Bombay, 1995-96, mng. dir., 1996-98; sr. v.p. Saurashtra Chems. Ltd., Porbandar, India, 1999—; mem. guest faculty Indian Inst. Tech., Madras, 1980-83, Bombay, 1987-95, Anna U. Madras, 1984—, Nat. Productivity Coun., Madras, 1980-83, Adminstrv. Staff Coll., Hydrabad, 1980-95. Patentee in field. Recipient Sir Ashutoah Mookherjee prize, Trevor Testimonial medal Calcutta U. Fellow Inst. of Chartered Engrs., Inst. Mech. Engrs. of Eng., Inst. of Mgmt., Am. Welding Soc., Inst. Quality Assurance (lead assessor, Eng.). Avocations: internet, reading, horticulture, yoga, travel. Achievements include work on environ. protection, energy conservation and mgmt. of appropriate technologies in field. E-mail: duleep@bom3.vsnl.net.in. Home: B-1 503 Valley Towers, Gladys Alvares Rd Thane W, Thane West 400607, India Office: Saurashtra Chems Ltd, Birla Sagar, Porbandar 360576, India

BISWAS, MUKUL, retired chemistry educator, researcher; b. Calcutta, W. Bengal, India, Nov. 1, 1935; s. Mohini Mohan and Gouri Biswas; m. Manjulika Sinha, June 1, 1960; children: Chaitali, Pubali. BSc with honors, Calcutta U., 1955, MSc, 1957, PhD, DSc, 1974. Cert. chem. sci. Postdoctoral rsch. assoc. Duke U., N.C., 1961-1963; lectr. in chemistry U. Kalyani Nadia, W. Bengal, 1963-64; from lectr. to prof. I.I.T. Kharagpur, India, 1964-1996; fellow Japan Soc. Promotion Sci. U. Tokyo, 1982-1983; emeritus scientist CSIR Presidency Coll., Calcutta, 1996—; vis. scientist U. Akron Inst. Polymer Sci., Ohio, 1983-1984. Contbr. articles to profl. jours. CSIR rsch. grantee IIT Kharagpur. Indian Assn. Cultivation Sci. (life). Hindu. Avocation: music. Home: Flat C-2/3 594/1 Dakshindari Rd, 700048 Calcutta West Bengal, India Office: Presidency Coll Dept Chemistry, 86/1 Coll St, 700073 Calcutta West Bengal, India

BITENSKY, VALERIY S., psychiatrist, educator; b. Ufa, Russia, Feb. 14, 1943; s. Semeon I. and Helena T. (Loshakova) B.; m. Irina G. Olchovskaya, Aug. 14, 1963 (div. Feb. 1979); 1 child, Anna; m. Victoria A. Shevchenko, Nov. 1987; 1 child, Konstantin V. MD, Med. Inst., Kharkov, Ukraine, 1966; Candidate Med. Sci., Rsch. Inst., St. Petersburg, Russia, 1978; PhD in Med. Sci., Union Ctr. Narcology, Moscow, 1991. Clin. psychiatrist Regional Mental Hosp., Sumy, Ukraine, 1966-70, Odessa, Ukraine, 1970-76; head doctor Regional Mental Hosp., Odessa, 1976-87; asst. prof. State Med. U., Odessa, 1987-90, prof., head chair psychiatry, 1990—; clin. dir. Mental Hosp., Odessa, 1997—. Author: Effecting Mechanisms of Anxiolytic, Anticonvulsive and Soporofi Drugs, 1988. Chmn. Ukrainian Physicians for the Prevention Nuc. War. Mem. Ukrainian Soc. Psychiatrists and Narcologists (bd. dirs.), Odessa Regional Sci. Soc. Psychiatrists (chmn.), Odessa Assn. Psychiatrists (chmn.), Rsch. Soc. on Alcoholism, European Assn. Psychiatrists. Avocations: music, sports. Office: Odessa Regional Mental Hosp, 1 Academica Vorobjeva St 9, 270006 Odessa Ukraine

BITNER, JOHN WILLIAM, banker; b. Jersey Shore, Pa., July 6, 1948; s. John W. and Gertrude Elizabeth (Brownlee) B.; m. Joy A. Lin, Apr. 4, 2000. BS in Econs., Lebanon Valley Coll., Annville, Pa., 1970; MBA, Boston Coll., Chestnut Hill, Mass., 1983. V.p. Commonwealth Bank, Williamsport, Pa., 1970-78, Neworld Bank, Boston, 1978-81; fixed income mgr. Digital Equipment Co., Maynard, Mass., 1981-84; sr. v.p. Ea. Bank, Malden, Mass., 1984—. Author: Successful Bank Asset/Liability Management, 1992; fin. columnist The Salem Evening News; contbr. articles to profl. jours. Past pres. Boys and Girls Club Greater Salem; bd. dirs. Salem YMCA. Kellogg fellow, 1973-75. Mem. Fin. Analysts Fedn., Boston Security Analysts Soc., North Shore C. of C. (econ. devel. com.), Salem Rotary.

BITO, JANOS FERENC, corporate executive, educator; b. Szeged, Hungary, July 21, 1936; s. Janos Jozsef and Iren (Katona) B.; m. Katalin Kaposi, May 11, 1974; children: Katinka, Janos Laszlo. MSc in Physics, Jozsef Attila Univ., Szeged, 1958, Dr Rer. Nat. summa cum laude, 1960; DSc in Tech. Sci., Hungarian Acad. Sci., Budapest, 1971. Sci. co-worker, sci. worker, head dept. plasma and electron physics, head of divsn., mem. sci. coun. Rsch. Inst. of Electronics, Budapest, 1958-71; with Roland Eötvös U., Budapest, 1965—, prof. physics, 1986—; head tech. divsn., dir. R&D Tungsram Co. Ltd., Budapest, 1971-86, exec. dir. sci. and prodn. ctr. of robotics and automation, 1986-93; dep. gen. dir. Tungsram T.H. Co. Ltd., Budapest, 1990-93, dep. dir., 1993-94; exec. dir. Ctr. of Robotics and Automation, Hungary, 1993—; chief advisor on Info. Tech. Minister of Telecomm., Transport and Water Mgmt., 1996-99; mem. Nat. Com. for Accreditation of Hungarian Univs. and High Schs. in field of Elec. Engring. and Info. Tech.; mem. Com. Habilitation at Faculties of Elec. Engring. and Info. Tech. of Tech. Univ. Budapest; chmn. Elec. and Electronical Jury of Nat. Sci. Rsch. Fund, 1999—; mem. PhD program coun. Hungarian Univ. Phys. Edn.; registered expert by UNIDO/UNDP, EC in info. tech., automation (robotics) and electronics. Author 5 academic guides; contbr. over 200 articles and books about physics and robotics. Recipient Imre Brody prize Roland Eotvos Phys. Soc., 1967, Pro Mundi Beneficia medal and diploma Acad. Brasileira de Ciencias Humanas, 1975, Gold medal Science Propagation Soc. Hungary, 1984, Roland Eotvoes prize Hungarian Coun. Ministers, 1991, Dennis Gabor prize, 1997; named one of 2000 Men of Achievement, 1973. Fellow IEEE (vice-chmn. Hungary Session); mem. N.Y. Acad. Scis., Hungarian Robotics Assn. (chmn.), Sci. Soc. Measurement and Automation (sci. coun.). Roman Catholic. Avocations: autos, space rsch. Office: Centre of Robotics and Automation, Nepszinhaz UTCA 8, H-1081 Budapest Hungary

BITON-POUSSIN, CATHERINE JEANNE, health facility administrator; b. Royan, France, Feb. 23, 1959; d. Jean and Yvonne (Bouchet) Poussin; m. Daniel G. Biton; children: Aurélie, Damien. MS in Tech., U. Poitiers, France, 1980; diploma d'etudes de scis. and tech. approfondies, U. Poitiers, 1982; MS in Biology, U. Oreg., 1982; D in Zoology, U. Munich, Germany, 1984. Tchg. asst. in biology U. Oreg., 1980-82; rsch. asst. U. Munich, 1982-84; exec. Servier, Suresnes, 1984-96, CEO, 1990—; quality mgr. Hosp. Univ. Genevois, Geneva, Switzerland, 1996—. Contbr. articles to profl. jours.; patentee in field. Mem. Internat. Brain Rsch. Orgn. Avocations: model airplanes, sailing, swimming. Home: 175 rue de Gex la ville, 01170 Gex France Office: Hosp Univ Genevois Divsn Pathology Clinic, Rue Michel Servet 1, CH1211 Geneva 4, Switzerland

BITOV, ANDREI GEORGEVICH, writer; b. Leningrad, Russia, May 27, 1937; m. Inga Petkevich; 1 child. Student, Leningrad Mining Inst. Stevedore, lathe operator, 1958-62; rschr. Leningrad Mining Inst., 1962; pres. Russian PEN Ctr., 1992—; writer, 1962—. Author: (novels) The Big Balloon, 1963, Such a Long Childhood, 1965, A Summer Place, 1967, Apothecary Island, 1968, Way of Life, 1972, Seven Journeys, 1976, Days of Man, 1976, Pushkin House, 1978, A Man in the Landscape, 1987, The Flying Monakhov, 1990, We Woke Up in a Strange Country, 1991, Awaiting Monkeys, 1993; (short stories) Sunday, 1980. Recipient Andrey Bely prize, Russia, Best Fgn. Book prize, Paris, Pushkin prize, Germany. Home: Apt 14, Krasnoprudnaya Str 30/34, 107140 Moscow Russia Office: Russian PEN Ctr, Neglinnaya St 18/1, Bldg 2, 103031 Moscow Russia*

BITRAN, JACOB DAVID, internist; b. Thessaloniki, Greece, Sept. 23, 1947; came to U.S., 1952; s. David Jacob and Martha (Faratzi) B.; m. Linda Sue Androw, Dec. 26, 1970; children: Lauren, Dina. BS, U. Ill., Chgo., 1968, MD, 1971. Diplomate Am. Bd. Internal Medicine with subspecialties in med. oncology, hematology. Intern in medicine Michael Reese Med. Ctr., Chgo., 1971-72, resident in internal medicine, 1973-75, clin. asst. prof. medicine, 1977-81, clin. assoc. prof. medicine, 1981-84; resident in pathology Rush Presbyn. St. Luke's Med. Ctr., Chgo., 1972-73; fellow in hematology/oncology U. Chgo., 1975-77, assoc. prof. medicine, 1984-88, prof. medicine, 1988-91; dir. divsn. hematology/oncology Luth. Gen. Hosp., Park Ridge, Ill., 1991—; prof. medicine U. Ill., Chgo., 1996-98; mem. sci. adv. bd. Lederle Labs., Wayne, N.J., 1986-89. Editor: Lung Cancer, 1988. Fellow ACP, Am. Coll. Chest Physicians; mem. Am. Assn. for Cancer Rsch. (program chmn. 1988-89), Am. Soc. Clin. Oncology (program chmn. 1990-91). Democrat. Achievements include development of usable chemotherapy regimen for non small cell lung cancer that has been in clinical use since 1976; exploration of dose intensive chemotherapy in breast cancer. Avocations: tennis, rowing. Office: Lutheran General Hospital 1700 Luther Ln Park Ridge IL 60068-1270

BITRAN, LEONARDO ALEJANDRO, rabbi; b. La Serena, Chile, Jan. 14, 1960; s. Raul Bitran and Cora Damiana Carreño. M in Econs., U. Chile, 1984; M in Hebrew Letters, Jewish Theol. Sem., 1992. Ordained rabbi, 1992. Rabbi Congregation Shaarey Zedek, W. Bloomfield, Mich., 1992—. Pres. region 1 Rabbinical Assembly, Mich. Mem. Knollwood Country Club, Franklin Hill Country Club. Avocations: skiing, photography. Home: 5784 Plum Crest Dr West Bloomfield MI 48322-1727 Office: Congregation Shaarey Zedek 4200 Walnut Lake Rd West Bloomfield MI 48323-2772

BITSAKIS, EFTICHIOS IOANNIS, philosophy educator, theoretical physics educator; b. Kakodiki, Chania, Greece, July 5, 1926; s. Joannis Markos and Despina Christos (Zouridakis) B.; m. Maria Efstratios Kokkinou, Dec. 26, 1962; 1 child, Ioannis. Grad. Chemistry, U. Athens, Greece, 1958; diplome de Physique Théorique, U. Paris, 1967; PhD, U. Paris VIII, 1973; D d'Etat en Philosophie, U. France, 1976. Cert. physicist, philosopher. With Abbott Labs., Athens, 1958-65, Lab. Nuc. Physics Coll. France, 1968-70; chargé de cours math. U. Paris XI, 1970-76; chargé de cours philosophie scis. U. Paris VIII, 1970-76; theoretical physicist Nat. Rsch. Found., Greece, 1976-78; asst. prof. theoretical physics U. Athens, 1979; prof. philosophy U. Ioannina, Greece, 1981-93, dean faculty philosophy, 1982-87. Author: Being and Becoming, 1965, Physique Contemporaine et Matérialisme Dialectique, 1973, The Conceptual Foundations of Quantum Mechanics, 1979, Theory and Praxis, 1980, Les Potentialités du Minime, 1980, Physique et Materialisme, 1983, Philosophical Anthropology, 1991, The Evergreen Tree of Knowledge, 1995, Le Nouveau Réalisme Scientifique, 1997, The Hidden Demon of Einstein, 2000. Grantee French Govt., 1965; rsch. fellow Boston U., 1992. Avocation: agriculture. Home: 6 C Palaiologou Str, 16232 Byronas Greece

BITSKEY, ISTVAN, literary history educator; b. Eger, Hungary, Mar. 26, 1941; s. Aladar and Eva (Grober) B.; m. Katalin Domboroczki, Aug. 18, 1973; children: Istvan, Peter. D, Kossuth U., Debrecen, Hungary, 1970; PhD, Acad. Sci., Budapest, Hungary, 1976, DS, 1991. Asst. prof. Kossuth U., Debrecen, Hungary, 1975-80, assoc. prof., 1980-92, prof., 1992—; invited prof. U. Vienna, 1984-86; dean faculty arts Kossuth U., 1993-98, head dept. old Hungarian lit., 1980—. Author: Hitvitak Tüzeben, 1978, Humanista Erudicio, 1979, Pázmany Peter, 1986, Eszmek, 1996, Il Collegio Germanico-Ungarico, 1996, Püspökök irók, 1997, Virtus és Religio, 1999, Konfessionen und liter gattangen, 1999. Recipeint Apaczai prize for edn., 1999. Mem. Soc. Hungarian Philology. Avocation: swimming. Office: Kossuth U, Egyetem Ter 1, 4010 Debrecen Hungary

BITTENCOURT, JOSE AUGUSTO, space science researcher, physics educator; b. Araguari, Brazil, June 8, 1947; s. Marinho and Alva Oliveira (Santos) B.; m. Izabel Alessi, July 22, 1972 (div. Oct. 1985); children: Marcus Alessi, Alexandre Alessi; m. Rosangela Maria Gomes, Dec. 1, 1995. BSc, Fed. U. Minas Gerais, Belo Horizonte, Brazil, 1970; MSc, Nat. Inst. Space Rsch., Sao Jose dos Campos, Brazil, 1972; PhD in Space Sci., U. Tex., Dallas, 1975. Rsch. asst. U. Tex., 1972-75, vis. scientist, 1976; rsch. asst. Nat. Inst. Space Rsch., 1971-72; rsch. scientist, prof. space and plasma physics Nat. Inst. Space Sci., 1975—, head space sci. Acad. Grad. Sch., 1982-87, head aeronomy dept./substitute dir. atmospheric & space sci., 1989-92, mem. adv. coun. for atmospheric and space scis., 1989—. Author: Fundamentals of Plasma Physics, 1986, 2d edit., 1995; editor Advances in Space Rsch., Vol. 12, 1992; assoc. editor Brazilian Jour. Geophysics, 1994—. NASA Internat. U. fellow in space sci., 1972-75. Mem. Internat. Union Radio Sci. (nat. rep. 1983—). Avocations: playing piano and guitar, music through computers. Home: Rua Taquaritinga 22, 12243180 São José dos Campos SP, Brazil Office: Nat Inst Space Rsch, CP 515, 12201970 São José dos Campos SP, Brazil

BITTENCOURT, PAULO L., gastroenterologist, hepatologist; b. Salvador, Bahia, Brazil, Aug. 20, 1966; s. Paulo M. and Achirea L. (Lisboa) B. MD, Fed. U. Bahia, Salvador, 1990; PhD, U. Sao Paulo, Brazil, 1999. Fellow in gastrointestinal endoscopy Free U. Brussels, 1996-97; fellow in gastroenterology and hepatology U. Sao Paulo Sch. Medicine, 1991-95, transplantation physician, 1997—. Contbr. articles to med. jours., including Am. Jour. Gastroenterology, Amyloid. Avocations: literature, arts, movies, swimming, travel. Home: Ouro Branco 129 Apt 105, 01425080 Sao Paulo Brazil

BITTNER, MICHAEL, physicist; b. Wilhelmshaven, Germany, June 21, 1960; s. Alfred and Elisabeth (Wietzorke) B.; m. Ulrike Elke Karrenberg, Jan. 26, 1988; children: Ramona, Lara. Diploma in physics, U. Wuppertal, Germany, 1987, PhD, 1993. Asst. U. Wuppertal, 1993-94, project scientist, 1994-96; project scientist German Aerospace Ctr., Oberpfaffenhofen, Germany, 1996-97; project mgr. German Aerospace Ctr., Oberpfaffenhofen, 1997—; vis. scientist NASA-Goddard Space Flight Ctr., Wallops, Va., 1989, Andoya (Norway) Rocket Range, 1990, Nat. Ctr. Atmospheric Rsch., Boulder, Colo., 1999; project mgr. NASA-Kennedy Space Ctr., Cape Canaveral, Fla., 1994. Editor: CRISTA/MAHRST Campaign Handbook, 1994. Assoc. Com. on Space Rsch., 1990—; nat. del. program adv. com. European Space Agy., 1995—, Com. on Earth Observing Satellites, 1997—. Scholar Albert-Magnus Soc., Archdiocese, Cologne, 1985-88. Mem. German Phys. Soc., N.Y. Acad. Scis. Avocations: swimming, biking, philosophy. E-mail: Michael.Bittner@dlr.de. Home: Ringstrasse 27, D-86929 Untermühlhausen Germany Office: German Aerospace Ctr DLRDFD, Oberpfaffenhofen, D-82234 Wessling Germany

BIUK-RUDAN, NEVENKA, veterinarian, researcher; b. Knin, Dalmatia, Croatia, Apr. 16, 1963; d. Vlado and Pera (Klepo) Biuk; m. Damir Rudan, Sept. 3, 1988; children: Dominik, Petar, Marina. BS in Vet. Sci., U. Zagreb, 1987, MS in Vet. Sci., 1990, DSc in Vet. Sci., 1997. Asst. instr. vet. sci. U. Zagreb, 1987-97, sr. asst. vet. sci., 1997—. Contbr. articles to profl. jours. Mem. Croatian Microbiol. Soc., Fedn. European Microbiology Socs., European Soc. Vet. Virology. Roman Catholic. Avocations: art, travel. Home: Ravenec 11a, 10 000 Zagreb Croatia Office: U Zagreb Vet Fac, Heinzelova 55, 10 000 Zagreb Croatia

BIVAS, ROBERT, chemical company executive; b. Paris, May 29, 1940; s. Albert and Laure (Dinar) B.; m. Michele Eripret, Sept. 7, 1963; children: Pierre, Philippe. BS in Engring., Ecole Poly., Paris, 1960; DSc, Faculté de Scis., Paris, 1968. Researcher Centre Nat. d'Etudes Spatiales, Paris, 1963-68; cons. Sligos, Puteaux, France, 1969-81; group info. systems mgr. Rhône Poulenc, Courbevoie, France, 1983-91; cons. in field, 1981-82, 92—; bd. dirs. Club Informatique des Grandes Entreprises Francaises. Contbr. articles to profl. jours. Named MIS Mgr. of Year, 1988. Mem. Com. for Space Research, Internat. Union Geodesy and Geophysics. Home: Clos St Michel Damply, Montalet Le Bois, F78440 Gargenville France

BIYA, PAUL, president of Cameroon; b. Mvomeko, Cameroon, Feb. 13, 1933; m. Jeanne Atyam; 1 child. Licence en Droit Public, U. Paris, 1960; diplome, Institut d'Etudes Politiques Paris, 1961, Institut des Hautes Etudes d'Outre-Mer, 1962, Etudes Superieures en Droit Public, 1963. Head Dept. Fgn. Devel. Aid, 1962-63; dir. cabinet in Ministry Nat. Edn., 1964-65, mem. goodwill mission to Ghana and Nigeria, 1965; sec.-gen. Ministry Edn., Youth and Culture, 1965-67; dir. Civil Cabinet of Head of State, 1967-68, sec.-gen. to pres., 1968, minister of state, sec.-gen. to pres., 1968-75, prime min., 1975-82; president Republic of Cameroon, 1982—. Decorated chevalier Order de la Valeur Ccmerounaise; comdr. Nat. Order Fed. Republic Germany, Nat. Order Tunisia; Grand-Croix Nat. Order of Merit Senegal; grand officer Legion of Honor (France). Mem. Union Nat. Camerouaise. Office: Office of Pres, care Ctrl Post Office, Yaoundé Cameroon*

BIYARI, KHALED HUSAIN, electronics company executive; b. Riyadh, Saudi Arabia, May 5, 1962; s. Husain Saleh and Fatima Abdulrahman (Shamekh) B.; m. Sameera Mustfa Adham, Jan. 18, 1986; children: Majid, Mazin, Rawan. BSEE, King Fahd U., Dhahran, Saudi Arabia, 1983, MSEE, 1985; PhD, U. So. Calif., 1989. Grad. asst. King Faud U., Dhahran, 1983-85, lectr., 1985-89, asst. prof., 1990-94, assoc. prof., 1994-95; v.p. R&D Advanced Electronic Co., Riyadh, 1995—; cons. Saudi Stds. Orgn., Riyadh, 1993—, KA City for Sci. and Tech., Riyadh, 1990-93, Royal Saudi Air Force, Riyadh, 1994-95; mem. engring. com., Riyadh, 1995—. Mem. IEEE (sr., chmn. Saudi sect. 1991-95), IEEE Communication Soc. (sr.), Saudi Engring. Soc. Avocations: chess, computers, volleyball. Office: Advanced Electronics Co, PO Box 90916, Riyadh 11623, Saudi Arabia

BIZIAGOS, EVANGELOS, virologist, researcher; b. Hara, Larissa, Greece, July 20, 1958; s. Athanasios-Menelaos and Vassiliki (Galazos) B.; m. Helena Anastassiadou, Feb. 18, 1993. BSc in Cell Biology, Claude-Bernard U., Lyon, 1983, MSc in Microbiology, 1984, DEA in Microbiology, 1985, PhD in Microbiology and Virology, 1989. Charge de cours Claude-Bernard U., Lyon, 1985-89; rschr. C.R.S.S.A., Grenoble, 1985-89, Clonatec S.A., Paris, 1988-89; asst. prof. Sch. Medicine U. Crete, Heraklion, 1991-94; in charge virology lab. U. Gen. Hosp., Heraklion, 1991-94; head virology-immunology Lab. Diagnostic Med. Ctr., Rethymnon, 1995-98, Asklepeion Crete Gen. Clinic and Diagnostic Med. Ctr., Heraklion, 1999—. Co-author: Virologie des Milieux Hydriques, 1991; contbr. articles to profl. jours. including Antiviral Rsch., Jour. Med. Virology, Jour. Viral Hepatitis, European Jour. Epidemiology, Antimicrobial Agents Chemotherapy, Arch. Virology, Applied Environ. Microbiology, Water Rsch., Water Sci. Tech., others. With Greek Med. Corps, 1990-91. Fellow Clonatec SA, Paris, 1986-88. Mem. Hellenic Soc. virology (responsible for Crete Island dept. 1994—), Hellenic Assn. for Study and Control of AIDS, Comité Français de la Recherche sur la Pollution de l'eau, Internat. Assn. on Water Quality. Christian Orthodox. Achievements include research in methodologies of detection of hepatitis A virus and other enteroviruses from environ and food samples, antiviral substances, monoclonal antibodies, cell cultures, modern methods in clin. lab. diagnosis of viruses (including PCR), epidemiology of hepatitis viruses in Greece, and viral pollution of the Mediterrean Sea. Home: 44 Atlandidos St, 71305 Heraklion Greece Office: U Crete Virology Lab, PO Box 1393, 71110 Heraklion Greece

BIZIUK, MAREK KAROL, educator; b. Sokotka, Poland, June 25, 1947; s. Czestaw and Jadwiga (Wisniewska) B. MS, Tech. U. Gdansk, Poland, 1969, PhD, 1977, DS, 1994. Asst. Tech. U. Gdansk, Poland, 1969-71, asst. lectr., 1971-77, tutor, 1977-94, reader, 1994-97, prof., 1997—; sec. Comm. Trace Organic Analysis, Poland, 1980-97. Co-author: (chpts.) River Quality: Dynamics and Restoration, 1997, Internat. River Water Quality, 1997, Encyclopedia of Analytical Chemistry, 2000. Recipient Ministry Nat. Edn. award, 1980. Mem. Romanian Assn. Analytical Chemistry. Avocations: literature, cinema, horseback riding, skiing, music. Home: Blizbora 29/5, 81-170 Gdańsk Poland Office: Tech U Gdansk Chem Faculty, Narutowicza 11/12, 80-952 Gdańsk Poland

BIZIULEVICHIUS, GEDIMINAS ARVYDAS, enzymologist, researcher; b. Vilnius, Lithuania, Mar. 31, 1949; s. Stasys and Alexandra (Liubauskaite) B.; m. Nijole Aldonyte, May 15, 1986; 1 child, Raminta. Avocations: scientific literature, nature, sports, cards. Home: 1-4 L Asanavičiūtes, Vilnius Lithuania Office: Inst Immunology, 12 Moksliniku St, LT-2600 Vilnius Lithuania

BJARNASON, BJÖRN, government official; b. Reykjavík, Iceland, Nov. 14, 1944; s Bjarni Benediktsson and Sigridur Bjornsdottir; m. Rut Ingolfsdottir, Sept. 21, 1969; children: Sigridur, Bjarni Benedikt. JD, U. Iceland, 1971. Editor Almenna Bokafelagid, Reykjavík, 1971-73; fgn. editor Visir, Reykjavík, 1973-74; dep. sec. gen. Office of Prime Minister, Reykjavík, 1974-79; journalist, dep. editor Morgunbladid, Reykjavík, 1979-90; v.p. Althingi, Reykjavik, Iceland, 1991—; min. culture, sci. and edn. Govt. of Iceland, Reykjavik, 1995—; chmn. Almenna Bokafelagid, Atlantic Treaty Assn. Contbg. author: Five Roads to Nordic Security, 1973, Strategic Factors in the North Atlantic, 1979, Deterence and Defense in the North, 1985. Mem. Rotary. Mem. Independence Party. Lutheran. Avocations: swimming, hiking, reading, films. Home: Hauhlid 14, 105 Reykjavik Iceland Office: Althingi, 150 Reykjavik Iceland

BJARNASON, GUDMUNDUR, government official; b. Hùsavik, Northern, Iceland, Oct. 9, 1944; s. Bjarni Stefänsson and Jakobina Jönssdöttir; m. Vigdis Gunnarsdöttir, Dec. 25, 1965; children: Jokobina, Arna, Silja Rùn. Grad., Co-operative Coll., Bifröst, Iceland, 1963. With Coop. Soc., Husavik, 1963-67, Coop. Bank of Iceland, Husavik, 1967-77; dir. br. Keflavik, Iceland, 1977-80; member Althingi-Progressive Party, NE Constituency, 1979-99; minister of health and social security Govt. of Iceland, 1987-91, M.P., 1979-99; mem. Icelandic Del. to Coun. of Europe, 1991-95; min. for environ & agr., 1995-99, dir. State Housing Fin. Fund, Iceland, 1999—. Office: Ibúdalánasjódur, Borgartun 21, 105R Reykjavik Iceland

BJARUP, JES, lawyer educator; b. Aarhus, Denmark, Feb. 17, 1940; arrived in Sweden, 1995; s. Alfred and Marie Elisabeth (Madsen) B.; m. Kirsten Nielsen, Apr. 10, 1963 (div. Nov. 1983); children: Tine, Pernille; m. Bodil Høegh, May 31, 1984. Comml. exam., Aarhus Handelstandsforgening, 1961; diploma in commerce, Aarhus Købmandskole, 1963; gen. cert. A-level, 1964; PhD, U. Edinburgh, Scotland, 1982. Shipping-man Poul Nørholt, Aarhus, 1958-61; lectr. in law Aarhus U., 1970-74, sr. lectr. in jurisprudence, 1974-96; prof. in jurisprudence faculty of law Stockholm U., 1996—; tutor in jurisprudence U. Edinburgh, 1976-78; Jean Monnet fellow European Univ. Inst., Florence, Italy, 1989-90; lectr. Acad. Legal Theory, Brussels, 1991-94; vis. prof. faculty law Stockholm U., 1994-96; bd. dirs. Curren Legal Theory, Tilburg, The Netherlands, 1991; auditor Iur. Internat. Assn. for Philosophy and Social Philosophy, Bologna, Italy, 1991-99. Author: Skandinavischer Realismus, 1978, Reason Emotion and the Law, 1982, Skandinavisch Realisme, 1984, Retsbegreb, Retsvidenskab, 1994; contbr. articles to profl. jours. Mem., chmn. Venstre Danmaks Liberale Parti, Skanderborg, 1985-89. Mem. Acad. Legal Theory. Avocations: music, art, golf. Home: Eskadervögen 46 7, S 18358 Täby Sweden Office: Stockholm U Dept Jurisprudence, Faculty of Law, S 10691 Stockholm Sweden

BJENNING, CHRISTINA ANNA, neuroscientist; b. Södertälje, Svealand, Sweden, May 31, 1962; came to U.S., Jan. 28, 1993; d. Arne Astley Elias and Anna Elisabeth (Jönsson) B. BS, U. Linköping, Sweden, 1987; PhD, U. Göteborg, Sweden, 1992. Lectr. U. Göborg, Sweden, 1990-93; postdoctoral assoc. Cornell U. Div. Neurobiology, N.Y.C., 1992-94, Cornell U. Div. Pharmacology, N.Y.C., 1992-94; postdoctoral fellow The Aaron Diamond Found. Rockefeller U., N.Y.C., 1994-97. Contbr. articles to profl. jours. Recipient postdoctoral award Swedish Rsch. Coun., 1993-95. Mem. AAAS, N.Y. Acad. Scis., N.Am. Assn. Shidiesan Obesity. Avocations: contemporary art, nature conservation. Office: Novo Nordisk A/S, G85 21, DK-2760 Malou Denmark

BJERCKE, ALF RICHARD, business executive, publisher; b. Oslo, May 30, 1921; s. Richard and Birgit (Brambani) B.; m. Berit Blikstad, Mar. 15, 1946; children: Leif Richard, Haakon Richard, Ingerid, Berit. Student, MIT, 1939-41. With Alf Bjercke A/S, Oslo, 1945—, ptnr., 1950—, vice chmn., 1966-69, chmn., 1969—; dir. A/S. Jotungruppen, 1972-83, chmn. corp. coun., 1983-88; chmn. bd. Nydalens Compagnie, 1982-88, Addis Ababa Nat.

Chem. Ind. Ltd., 1966-75, Norwater (Norske Vannkilder A/S), ABC Produkter A/S, Scanpump A/S, 1972-78, Vallenova, Inc., Oslo, 1984-88; chmn., dir. Oplandske Dampskibsselskab, 1981-91; dir. Norwegian Shipping & Trade Jour., 1962-81; chmn. Jotungruppen A/S, Kolding, Denmark, 1966-88, A/S Habil, vice chmn., Akershus Broiler Co.; chmn. Chilinvest A/S., Pan Art Gallery, Vinland Film A/S & Co.; dir. Atheneum Pub. Co., Mosvold Overseas Trading Co., Atheneum Comm., Inc., Alamo Co.; hon. consul gen. Tunisia in Norway, 1963-93; chmn. bd. A/S Norsemeter, 1992-96; bd. dirs. Alvern-Norway A/S, 1993-95, JMB A/S Parfumes, Spydeberg, Chimpundu Mine, Ltd.; chmn. bd. dirs. Norgem Mining Ltd., Kitwe, Zambia, Nor-art A/S, Sandefjord, 1993-97, Hamper A/S, Fredrikstad, 1995-98, Ide-Ko A/S, Fredrikstad, 1995, Ice Maker A/S Kristians, 1996-97; bd. dirs. Moelster Internat. A/S, Florö, Mineral Resources A/S, Aalesund, Fröyna Industries; chmn. UniClip A/S, 1995-97; vice chmn. Norwegian Spring Water Assn. Author: From the Diplomatic World, 1983, Dragonene, 1988, Norway, 1991, Norge, Norwegen, Norvege, Norvegia, 1992, la Noruega and Russian Norvegija, 1993, Japanese, Chinese edits., 1995, Portuguese edit., 1998, (CD-ROM) Nordic Establishing and Development Partners, Inc. (chmn.); contbr. articles to profl. jours.; columnist jour. Farmand. Chmn. coun. Kofoed Sch., 1962-80; mem. Olympic Com. of Norway, 1971-74; exec. com. Norwegian UNIDO Coun., del. conf.; Norway del. Econ. Commn. for Africa; mem. Norwegian Arbitration Bd. for Competitive Questions; chmn. Soc. for Protection of Ancient Towns, Soc. for Reconstrn. of Old Christiania, 1968-96; mem. coun. Norsk Sjofartsmuseum; chmn. bd. Norway Bus. Mus., 1980-88; Normwegian mem. adv. com. Sail Tng. Assn., London; past chmn. Nordic Adv. Coun. for Industry; mem. Commn. 3 CIOR, Norwegian chmn. Rotary Internat. Campaign Polio Plus (eradicating polio); mem. campaign com. Norwegian Conservative Party, 1974; bd. dirs. Artists Gallery of Oslo, 1957-69; vice chmn. East Norway Sailing Sch. Ship Assn., 1961-78; chmn. Norwegian-Ethiopian Soc., 1954-70, Sammen for Salinas Fund, 1995; chmn. coun. Norway-Am. Assn.; chmn. fin. com. Norwegian World Wildlife Fund Bd. Reps.; Norwegian rep. Operation Sail 76; bd. dirs. A Smoke-free Generation, 1980; chmn. Norwegian Ch. Coun., 1984; bd. dirs. Care (Norway), 1984, Norwegian Orgn. Asylum Seekers, 1984-87. Wity Royal Norwegian Air Force, 1941-45; maj. Res. Mem. Norwegian Assn. Industries (past dir.), Norwegian Inventors Assn. (hon., chmn. arbitration), Color Coun. Norway (chmn. 1958-69, 72-81), Norwegian Paint Mfrs. Assn. (past chmn.), Norway Athletic Assn. (chmn. 1968-72), Internat. Wine and Food Soc. (pres.), Peace Park Soc. (charter), World Wildlife Fund 1001 Club, MIT Club Norway, Phi Gamma Delta, Oslo Bus. Men's Club (dir. 1968-70), Oslo Mil. Soc. (mgr. 1997), Rotary (dist. gov. 1980-81, vice chmn. world cmty. svc., European Area coord. Family and Cmty. Concerns Task Force 1995-96), Norwegian Inventors Soc. (hon.), Norway-Tunisan Soc. (chmn. 2000). Email: bjercke@online.no. Home: 14 President Harbitzgate 0259, Oslo Norway Office: Sollivelen 55, 1366 Lysaker Norway

BJERKAAS, CARLTON LEE, technology services company executive; b. Fergus Falls, Minn., Apr. 17, 1948; s. Jay Oscar and Anna Marie (Bangert) B.; children: Kristopher Scott, Eric Stefan, Todd Philip. BS, U. N.D., 1970; MS, MIT, 1977; MPA, Auburn U., Montgomery, Ala., 1983. Commd. 2d lt. USAF, 1970, advanced through grades to col., 1992; weather forecaster Weather Detachment, Homestead AFB, Fla., 1971-73; flight examiner Weather Reconnaissance Squadron, Andersen AFB, Guam, 1973-75; radar rsch. meteorologist A.F. Geophysics Lab., Hanscom AFB, Mass., 1976-82; chief support br. operational requirements & testing Hdqrs. Mil. Airlift Command, Scott AFB, Ill., 1983-85; chief aerospace environ. requirements Hdqrs. A.F. Systems Command, Andrews AFB, Md., 1985-87; comdr. Weather Detachment, Lajes Field, Azores, Portugal, 1987-89; asst. chief of staff Hdqrs. Air Weather Svc., Scott AFB, 1989-91, dir. resource mgmt., 1991-92, dir. program mgmt., integration, 1992-94; dir. sys. and comm., 1994-95, dir. tech., plans and programs, 1995—; sr. scientist Hdqrs. Air Weather Svc., Scott AFB, Ill., 1995-96; divsn. mgr. Sci. Applications Internat. Corp., O'Fallon, Ill., 1996—. Contbr. articles to profl. jours. Com. chmn. Boy Scouts Am., O'Fallon, Ill., 1991-92; coach, referee youth sports, O'Fallon, 1989—; chmn. Sch. Bd., Lajes Field Azores, 1988-89; mem. Sch. Dist. Com., Lajes Field Azores, 1987. Fellow Am. Meteorol. Soc.; mem. AAAS, ASPA, N.Y. Acad. Scis., Acad. Polit. Sci., Air Weather Assn., Air Lift and Tanker Assn., Phi Beta Kappa, Sigma Xi, Phi Eta Sigma, Pi Alpha Alpha, Rotary. Methodist. Avocations: computers, soccer coaching, Boy Scouts. Office: Science Applications Intl Corp 731 Lakepointe Centre Dr O'Fallon IL 62269-3073

BJERKE, H. SCOTT, surgeon; b. Mpls., Dec. 26, 1956; s. Robert Edward and Darline McMartin B.; m. Janet Anne Sikora, Sept. 25, 1995; 1 child, Duncan. BS with honors, U. Mich., 1979; MD, U. Hawaii, 1983. Resident New Eng. Med. Ctr., Boston, 1983-88; chief divsn. surg. critical care U. Nev., Las Vegas, 1991-99; med. dir. trauma svcs. Clarian Health, Indpls., 1999—; bd. trustees Univ. Surgery Profls., Las Vegas, 1992-99. Co-author: (chpt.) Trauma, 4th edit., 1999. Med. dir. tactical medics Indpls. Police SWAT Team, 1999—; med. dir. Clark County Fire Dept., Las Vegas, 1992-99; IST physician FEMA Urban Search & Rescue, Oklahoma City, 1995; med. dir. Nye County Vol. Ambulance, Amargosa Spring, Nev., 1995-99. Recipient Congrl. Recognition Svc., Sen Bryan, 1995; Rsch. fellow UCLA Med. Ctr., L.A., 1988-90, Trauma fellow Cedars Sinai Med. Ctr., L.A., 1990-91. Fellow Am. Coll. Surgeons, Assn. Surgery Trauma, Ea. Assn. Surgery Trauma; mem. Internat. Assn. Police Surgeons (life). Avocations: sports cars, scuba diving. Office: Meth Hosp B-233 1701 N Senate Blvd Indianapolis IN 46206

BJERNE, MATTS GÖSTA, business executive; b. Malmoc, Sweden, Mar. 16, 1944; s. Gosta Wilhelm and Anna Margot (Hedman) B.; m. Anne Christina Elizabeth Sundblad, June 15, 1974; children: Caroline, Louise, Sophie. MBA, U. Lund, Sweden, 1967. Trainee Kodak, 1967; client dir. Foote, Cone & Belding, Sweden, 1968-73; mng. dir. Schjaerven AB, Sweden, 1974-80, J. Walter Thompson, Sweden, 1981-85; sales dir. Levi Strauss, 1986-90; mng. dir. Scholl Norden, 1991-96, Swatch Sweden AB, 1997-98; chmn. Pocketgrossisten AB, Sweden, 1999—. Mem. Reform Club. Avocations: golf, sailing. Home: Ymervagen 52, 18267 Djursholm Sweden

BJERNEROTH, GUNNEL BIRGITTA, anesthesiologist; b. Strängnäs, Sweden, May 2, 1961; d. Gunnar and Anna Maria (Sjöberg) B. MD, Uppsala U., 1988, PhD, 1992, Assoc. Prof., 1997. European Diploma in Anesthesiology and Intensive Care. Intern U. Hosp., Uppsala, 1991-93, resident, 1993-95, attending physician, 1995-96; assoc. prof. dept. anesthesiology U. Uppsala, 1997—; attending physician Axess Elisabeth Hosp., Uppsala, 1998—. Office: Axess Elisabeth Hosp, Geijersgatan 20, 75226 Uppsala Sweden Office: Dept Anesthesiology, Univ Hosp, 75185 Uppsala Sweden

BJERRE, MIKKEL BERG, marketing executive; b. Glostrup, Copenhagen, Denmark, July 21, 1967; s. Mogens and Connie (Berg) B.; m. Pernille Rask, June 12, 1999; 1 child, Oskar Rase Bjerre. BS, Copenhagen Bus. Sch., 1991, MBA, 1994. Mktg. coord. Klanrud A/S, Vedbaek, Denmark, 1994-95; planner Option Comm. A/S, Copenhagen, 1995-98; mktg. mgr. Scandinavia Egmont Entertainment, Copenhagen, 1998—; mktg. dir. Egmont Entertainment, Copenhagen, 2000—; cons. Brøste A/S, Lyngby, Denmark, 1994-96; bd. dirs. Varpelev Tomater A/S., Varpelev, Denmark. Patentee in field. Avocations: soccer, golf, skiing, scuba diving, backgammon. Home: Vagtelvej 12, 2000 Frederiksberg, Copenhagen Denmark Office: Egmont Entertainment, Halmtorvet 29, 1700V Copenhagen Denmark

BJERREGAARD, ENA, defense and aerospace industries association executive; b. Copenhagen, Dec. 27, 1949; m. Henrik Schou Christensen, Dec. 17, 1970; 1 child, Anders. Asst. def. procurement adviser Dansk Industri, Denmark, 1980-86, def. procurement adviser, 1986-90, head def. procurement svcs., 1990-96; dir. Def. & Aerospace Industries Assn. Denmark, Copenhagen, 1996—; sec. gen. Assn. Danish Aerospace Industries, Denmark, 1989, Danish C-31 Industry Group, 1989; head Danish EDIG Delegation, 1999, Danish NIAG Delegation, 1994. Contbr. articles to profl. jours. Mem. Danish Def. Material Com., Danish NATO CIS Com. Avocations: jogging, U.S. and U.K. Literature, opera, rock music. Office: Confedn Danish Industries, DI HC Andersens Blvd 18, DK-1787 Copenhagen V, Denmark

BJERREGAARD, PETER, medical researcher, educator; b. Copenhagen, May 28, 1947; s. Knud-Eyvind and Estrid Bente (Jensen) B.; m. Beth Zachariae, June 8, 1967; children: Bine, Tobias, Silas. MD, U. Copenhagen, 1972, 91. Cert. gen. physician and specialist in pub. health. Registrar Municipality Hosps., Copenhagen, 1972-78; chief med. officer Upernavik, Greenland, 1978-80; asst. med. officer Ministry of Health, Copenhagen, 1980-85; sr. advisor Danida, Nairobi, Kenya, 1985-89; sr. epidemiologist Danish Inst. for Clin. Epidemiology, Copenhagen, 1989-95, prof., 1996—; chmn. Greenland Med. Rsch. Coun., Nuuk, 1996—. Author: Living Conditions, Life Style, and Health in Greenland, 1995, The Circumpolar Inuit: Health of a Population in Transition, 1998; editor Internat. Jour. Circumpolar Health, 1997—; contbr. articles to profl. jours. Mem. Internat. Union for Circumpolar Health (sec. 1996-2000, pres. 2000—), Danish/Greenlandic Soc. for Circumpolar Health (pres. 1991—), Danish Med. Assn. Office: Nat Inst Pub Health, Svanemøllevej 25, DK-2100 Copenhagen Denmark

BJERREGAARD, RITT, Danish government official; b. Copenhagen, May 19, 1941. Mem. Danish Parliament, Copenhagen, 1971—; Minister of Edn. Danish Govt., Copenhagen, 1973, 75-78; Minister of Social Affairs Danish Govt., 1979-81, Minister of Food, Agr. and Fisheries, 2000—; Commr. Environment and Nuc. Security European Cmtys., Brussels, 1995-99; chair Parliamentary Group Social Dem. Party, 1987-92. Author several books on politics and role of women in politics. Mem. Parliamentary Assembly Coun. of Europe, 1990-95; pres. Danish European Movement, 1992-94; former v.p. Parliamentary Assn. CSCE; mem. Trilateral Commn., Ctr. for European Policy Studies. Office: Commn of European Cmtys, 200 rue de la Loi, 1049 Brussels Belgium

BJÖRCK, ANDERS PER-ARNE, Swedish government official; b. Nässjö, Sweden, Sept. 19, 1944; s. Arne and Ann-Marie (Svensson) B.; m. Py-Lotte von Zweigbergk, July 19, 1975; 1 child, Anne. Mem. parliament, 1968—; v.p. standing com. on constn., 1982-91; mem. bd. moderate party, 1981—, vice chmn. moderate party parliamentary group, 1985-91, 94—; min. of def. Govt. of Sweden, Stockholm, 1991-94; 1st dep. spkr. Swedish Parliament, Stockholm, 1994—; pres. Parliamentary Assembly of the Coun. Europe, 1989-91; chmn. European Dem. Group of the Assembly, 1985-89; bd. mem. Swedish Broadcasting Corp., 1978-91, Swedish Nat. TV Co., 1979-91, Swedish Press Subsidies, 1976-91, mem. regional bd. Nordbanken, 1995—; pres. internat. bd. Internat. Found. Airline Passengers' Assn., 1985-89. Pres. Swedish Young Moderates, 1966-71, Nordic Union Young Moderates, 1968-70; v.p. European Union Young Moderates, 1970-72; mem. Swedish Arms Export Control Bd., 1995-98. Recipient Diplomatic Svc. Order (Korea), Isabel La Catolica (Spain), Order of Merit (Austria), Grand Cross of Merit (Germany). Conservative. Office: Swedish Parliament, S-100 12 Stockholm Sweden

BJORCK, MARTIN GUSTAF, vascular surgeon; b. Stockholm, Sept. 2, 1952; s. Carl-Henrik and Elise (Akerberg) B.; m. Pia Margareta Olsson, Nov. 13, 1982; children: Lisa, Carl-Henrik, Anja. MD, U. Lund, 1978; Specialist in Surgery, U. Umea, 1990; PhD in Vascular Surgery, U. Uppsala, 1998. Medical diplomate. Cons. in gen. and vascular surgery Skelleftea Gen. Hosp., 1992. Recipient Swedish Vascular award, 1997. Mem. Swedish Soc. for Vascular Surgery, Swedish Surg. Soc. (bd. dirs. 1999—, editor jour. Swedish Surgery 1999). Office: Dept Surgery, Gen Hosp, S-93186 Skelleftea Sweden

BJØRGEENGEN, KJELL, artist, educator; b. Sandvika, Baerum, Norway, June 4, 1951; s. Per and Birgit Jitte Ebba (de Linde); m. Sissel Bakken; 1 child, Jari Bakken. Prof. Nat. Acad. Fine Arts, Oslo, Norway; artist in residence, Exptl. TV Sta., Owego, N.Y. 1982-95. Artist: solo exhbns. include: Henie-Onstad Artcenter Høvikodden, 1972, 82, Art Aid Galleri, Oslo, 1982, Photgallery, Oslo, 1983, Galleri Trekanten København, 1987, Mala Galeria, Warsaw, Poland, 1987, Video installation, Randers kunstmus., Porin Taidemus., Pori, 1990, Vido installation Rogalan Kunstnersenter, 1991, Stavanger Centrum Sztuki, Warsaw, 1991 Videosculptures Galleri K, Oslo, 1991, 95, Trondhjem Kustforening, Video installation, 1994, State Libr., Mariehamn, Aland, 1995, Eisfabrik, Hannover, 1996, E. House, Ghent, Belgium, Phase I True Blaning, Kunstnernes Hus, Oslo, 1997; group exhbns. and video festivals, Tokyo Video Art Festival 1984, 85, 86, 87, 88, Videofest 89, Internat. Filmfespiele, Berlin, 1989, 90, 92, Electric Cinema, Berlin, 1990, European Media Art Festival, Osnabruck, 1992, Ctr. of Contemporary Art, Warsaw, Poland, 1994, 97, The Nat. Mus. of Contemporary Art, Oslo, 1995, Haags Gemeentemus., World Wide Video Festival, 1996, Lab 6, Ctr. Contemporary Art Walsawa, Extended Points, Hara Mus. of Contemporary Art, Tokyo, 1997, Rogaland Kunst Mus., 2000; included in pub. and pvt. collections: Nat. Mus. Contemporary Art, Oslo, Norwegian Cultural Assn., Oslo, Nat. Gallery of Canada, Baerum kommunale kunstsamlinger, Sandvika, Louisiana, Humlebaek. Fax: 47-67-124002. Home: Kyrres Vei 37-B, N-1369 Stabekk Norway Office: Nat Acad Fine Arts, N-0166 St Olavs GT 23, Norway

BJORK, JENS NIKLAS KRISTOFER, systems engineer; b. Finspang, Sweden, Dec. 24, 1971; s. Jens Ola Greger and Riitta-Liisa Bjork. MS in Engring. Physics, Uppsala U., 1999. Tchr. tech. computer sci. U. Uppsala, 1996; software engr. Ericsson Telecom AB, Stockholm, 1997, software sys. engr., 1997-98, sys. mgr., 1998—. Contbr. articles to profl. jours.; inventor video transcoder. Acct. Local Tenant-Ownership Assn., Uppsala, 1996; treas. Local Music Club, Sandviken, 1990. 2d lt. Swedish Mountain Rangers, 1990-91. Grantee Goranssonka Fonden, 1992-97. Mem. IEEE Signal Processing Soc. Avocations: floor-ball, squash, trumpet. E-mail: niklas.bjork@etx.ericsson.se. Office: Ericsson Telecom AB, Gotalandsvagen 230, 12625 Alvsjo Sweden

BJÖRK, LARS MIKAEL, anesthesiologist, consultant; b. Malmö, Sweden, Jan. 16, 1958; s. Percival and Siv Anna (Beckers) B.; m. Britt Agneta Flenhagen, Aug. 10, 1985; 1 child, Emelie. MD, U. Lund, Sweden, 1983. Resident in anesthesiology and intensive care Malmö Gen. Hosp., 1983-84, sr. resident, 1989-93; intern Ängeholm (Sweden) Hosp., 1984-86; cons. Trelleborg (Sweden) Hosp., 1993-98, Malmö Gen. Hosp., 1998—. Author: Low Flow Anesthetics, 1991. Mem. Swedish Soc. Anaesthesia and Intensive Care. Avocations: art, music, computers, outdoor life.

BJÖRK, RAGNAR KARL VILHELM, historian, researcher; b. Västeras, Sweden, May 20, 1948; s. Bengt KA and Ruth (Girell) B. PhD, Uppsala (Sweden) U., 1983, docent, 1987. Rschr. Uppsala U., 1984-87, rschr., assoc. prof., 1987—. Author: Historical Argumentation, 1983, co-author, editor: Contemplating Evolution and Doing Politics, 1993; co-author, co-editor: Conceptions of National History, 1994, Societies Made Up of History, 1996; mem. editl. bd. Swedish Hist. Rev., 1983-99. Recipient rsch. grants, 1984-88, 1989-92, 1992-98. Mem. Swedish Hungarian Hist. Com. (sec. 1988—). Home: Granitvagen 24 D, S 75243 Uppsala Sweden Office: Uppsala Univ Dept History, St Larsgatan 2, S 75310 Uppsala Sweden

BJORK, ROBERT DAVID, JR., lawyer; b. Evanston, Ill., Sept. 29, 1946; s. Robert David and Lenore Evelyn (Loderhose) B.; m. Linda Louise Reese, Mar. 27, 1971; children: Heidi Lynne, Gretchen Anne. BBA, U. Wis., 1968; JD, Tulane U., 1974. Bar: La. 1974, U.S. Dist. Ct. (ea. dist.) La. 1974, U.S. Ct. Appeals (5th cir.) 1974, U.S. Dist. Ct. (mid. dist.) 1975, U.S. Supreme Ct. 1977, U.S. Dist. Ct. (we. dist.) 1978, U.S. Ct. Appeals (11th cir.) 1981, Calif. 1983, U.S. Dist. Ct. (no. dist.) Calif. 1983, U.S. Dist. Ct. (ea. dist.) Calif. 1984. Ptnr. Adams & Reese, New Orleans, 1974-83; assoc. Crosby, Heafey, Roach & May, Oakland, Calif., 1983-85; ptnr. Bjork Lawrence, Oakland, 1985—; instr. paralegal studies Tulane U., New Orleans, 1979-82. Mem. Tulane U. Law Rev., 1973-74; editor Med. Malpractice newsletter, 1983—. Bd. dirs. Piedmont (Calif.) Coun. Camp Fire, 1984-92, pres., 1987-89; treas. Couhig Congl. Com., New Orleans, 1980-82; bd. dirs. Camp Augusta Trust, 1990—. Lt. USNR, 1968-71. Mem. ABA, Internat. Assn. Def. Counsel, Calif. Bar Assn., La. Bar Assn. (chmn. young lawyers sect. 1982-83), Am. Soc. Law and Medicine. Home: 1909 Oakland Ave Piedmont CA 94611-3706 Office: Bjork Lawrence 1901 Harrison St Ste 1630 Oakland CA 94612-3501

BJÖRKELUND, CECILIA, family practice physician; b. Lund, Sweden, Feb. 16, 1948; d. Einar Nenne and Britt (Åkesson) B.; m. Christian Roger Ylander, Oct. 29, 1973; children: John, Christina. MD, U. Göteborg, 1990. Ward physician Stockholm County Coun., 1973-79; gen. practitioner Primary Health Care, Stromstad, Sweden, 1979-87, Students' Health Ctr., Uppsala, Sweden, 1987-91; clin. lectr. U. Göteborg, 1991-99, prof., 1999—. Avocation: golf. Office: Dept Primary Health Care, Vasa Sjukhus, S-41133 Göteborg Sweden

BJÖRKMAN, ANDERS B., naval architect; b. Stockholm, Apr. 28, 1946; s. Staffan E. and India I. (Sjögren) B.; m. Ilona M. Klars, Apr. 4, 1971 (div. 1993); children: Anna, Caroline, Hermine. MSc, Chalmers U. Tech., Gothenberg, Sweden, 1969. Ship surveyor Lloyd's Register, Eng. and Japan, 1971-79; naval architect V. Ships, Monte Carlo, Monaco, 1980—; advisor The El Salam Group, Cairo, 1989—. Author: Lies and Truths of the M/V Estonia Accident, 1998, Nya Fakta om Estonia, 1999; patentee Coulombi egg tanker. Bd. dirs. Swedish Ch. of the Cote d'Azur, 1981—; advisor IMO/ICS, London, 1991-93, IMO/Liberia, London, 1994, IMO/Sweden, London, 1995-96; candidate for Swedish Parliament, Moderate Party, 1970. Ens. Royal Swedish Navy, 1970. Mem. Propeller Club U.S.A., Monte Carlo Country Club. Avocations: tennis, bridge, skiing, literature. Home: 6 rue Victor Hugo, F06240 Beausoleil France Office: V Ships, BP 639, MC 98013 Monte Carlo Monaco

BJÖRKMAN, ANDERS ERIK GUSTAF, retired engineering educator; b. Stockholm, May 4, 1920; arrived in Denmark, 1961; s. Carl-Gustaf A. and Ebba M.T. (Petterson) B.; m. Kerstin C. Odqvist, May 4, 1948; children: Cecilia, Agneta, Gunilla, Birgitte. MS in Chem. Engring., Royal Inst. Tech., Stockholm, 1942, PhD, 1948; DSc, Chalmers Inst. Tech., Gothenburg, Sweden, 1957. Rsch. asst. AB Kabi, Stockholm, 1942-43; asst. prof. Royal Inst. Tech., Stockholm, 1944-48; R & D assoc. Billeruds AB, Säffle, Sweden, 1948-60; prof. chem. reaction engring., combustion, wood sci. & tech. Tech. U. Denmark, Lyngby, 1961-90, prof. emeritus, 1990—; pres. Internat. Acad. Wood Sci., Lyngby, 1993-96; chmn. bd. Danish Paint and Varnish Inst., Copenhagen, 1961-67; active Tech. Sci. Found., Copenhagen, 1967-70; treas. Internat. Union Pure and Applied Chemistry, Oxford, Eng., 1984-91. Author: Hydrogenation of Sulfite Waste Liquor, 1950; contbr. articles to profl. jours. Active Swedish Ch., Copenhagen, 1961—. Recipient Albert Wallin prize Sci. and Lit. Soc., Gothenburg, 1959, Gold medal Danish Industry, Copenhagen, 1991. Fellow Danish Acad. Tech. Scis., Royal Swedish Acad. Engring. Sci., Internat. Acad. Wood Sci. (Spl. Recognition award 1997). Lutheran. Achievements include extraction of lignin from milled wood; research on theories of pyrolysis/gasification of coal and pulping liquors, deactivation of catalysts, wood ultrastructure. Home: Langebakken 8, DK-2960 Rungsted Kyst Denmark

BJÖRKMAN, JAN OLOF, sociology educator, researcher, administrator; b. Västerås, Sweden, Oct. 15, 1939; s. Evert Axel and Viola Karin (Bergstrand) B.; m. Agneta Birgitta Linné, Sept. 11, 1966; children: Lotta, Sofia. BA, Uppsala (Sweden) U., 1963, Lic. Philosophy, 1969, PhD, 1974. Tchg. asst. Uppsala Univ., 1963-64, 67-68, adminstrv. asst., 1968-69, lectr., 1969—; head dept. sociology Uppsala U., 1971-72, 74-79; dir. studies Uppsala U., 1990-93, 1995-98. Editor (rsch. reports) Dept. Sociology, Univ. Uppsala, 1985-90; contbr. articles to profl. jours. and other publs. Avocations: classical music, antique books, arts and crafts. Office: Univ Uppsala, Dept Sociology Box 821, S-75108 Uppsala Sweden

BJORKMAN, JONAS, tennis player; b. Vaxjo, Sweden, Mar. 23, 1972. Profl. tennis player, 1991—. Recipient 4 Singles titles, 20 Doubles titles. Avocations: golf, hockey, soccer. Office: c/o ATP Tour 201 Atp Tour Blvd Ponte Vedra Beach FL 32082-3211*

BJÖRKMAN, LARS, dental educator; b. Lund, Sweden, Feb. 15, 1958; s. Ulf and Marianne (Tengwall) B.; m. Marit Bakke, Aug. 20, 1994. DDS, Karolinska Inst., 1983, PhD, 1995. With Public Dental Care, 1983-86; pvt. practice in dentistry Stockholm, 1986-89; rsch. asst. Karolinska Inst., Stockholm, 1989-95, asst. prof., 1995-99, assoc. prof., 2000—; head Norwegian Nat. Dental Biomaterials Adverse Reaction Unit, 1999—; mem. reference group Swedish registry of side effects from dental materials Swedish Nat. Bd. of Health and Welfare, Sweden, 1996. Contbr. articles to profl. jours. Mem. Internat. Assn. of Dental Rsch., Swedish Soc. of Toxicology. Fax: 47-555-898-62. E-mail: Lars.Bjorkman@odont.uib.no. Office: U Bergen Biomaterials, Årstadveien 17, N-5009 Bergen Norway

BJÖRKMAN, PER ABRAHAM, lawyer; b. Stockholm, Jan. 8, 1951; s. Staffan A. and India (Sjögren) B.; children: Cecilia, Martina; m. AnnaBell Dahlberg, 1996. LLB, U. Lund, Sweden, 1974. Assoc. Advokatfirman Landahl, Stockholm, 1976-81; ptnr. G. Sandströms Advokatbyrå, Stockholm, 1982-90, Per Björkman Advokataktiebolag, Stockholm, 1991, Gunnar Lindhs Advokatbyrå, Stockholm, 1992-98, Advokatfirman Björkman AB, 1998—; chmn. various fgn.-owned subs. in Sweden, 1978—. Mem. Swedish Bar Assn., Stockholm Bar Assn. (sec., bd. dirs. 1985-91), Internat. Bar Assn.

BJÖRKSTÉN, BENGT H., medical educator, consultant; b. Linköping, Sweden, Feb. 7, 1940; s. Bengt J. and Ulla A-M. (Ekholm) B.; m. Marianne Gerner, Oct. 5, 1964 (div. 1986); children: Johan, Ulrika, Mikael, Tove; m. Karin M. Sparring, Jan. 29, 1990. MD, Lund (Sweden) U., 1967; PhD, Umeå (Sweden) U., 1974, Tartu (Estonia) U., 1996; MD (hon.), Tartu (Estonia) U. Resident, fellow Umeå U., 1968-74, assoc. prof., 1976-78; vis. asst. prof. U. Minn., Mpls., 1975-76; dir. rsch. Pharmacia, Uppsala, Sweden, 1979-84; prof. Linköping U., 1984-99; exec. dir. Ctr. for Allergy Rsch. Karolinska Inst., Stockholm, 1999—; chmn. dept. pediat. Linköping U., 1984-96. Contbr. over 300 articles to profl. jours., over 100 chpts. to books. Chmn. regional chpt. sect. for immigrants Liberal Party, 1993-98. Served with Swedish mil., 1967-80. Fellow Am. Acad. Allergy and Immunology (corr.), German Allergology Soc. (corr.); mem. Scandinavian Pediat. Fedn. (pres. 1992—), European Acad. Allergy and Clin. Immunology, Finnish Allergology Soc. (hon.), Estonian Pediat. Assn. (hon.), South African Pediat. Assn. (hon.). Jewish. Avocations: theater, cinema, history, kayaking. Home: Vastmannagatan 12, 11124 Stockholm Sweden Office: Karolinska Inst, Ctr for Allergy Rsch, 17177 Stockholm Sweden

BJØRKUM, PER ARNE, geologist, educator, scientist; b. Vardø, Norway, Apr. 30, 1952; s. Alf and Bjørg Bjørkum; m. Aud-Mari Fladaas, July 26, 1975 (div. Aug. 1992); children: Per-Torkel, Geir-Vegar; m. Aud Sørskog, Apr. 8, 1994. BSc, U. Bergen, Norway, 1977, MSc, 1984; DSc, U. Oslo, Norway, 1992. Tchr. Gjøvik (Norway) H.S., 1979-82; sr. geologist Esso Norge, Norway, 1984-85; dept. mgr. Rogaland Rsch., Stavanger, Norway, 1985-87, rsch. supr., 1987-90; dept. mgr. Statoil a.s., Stavanger, 1990-94, tech. advisor, 1994—, rsch. geoscientist, 2000—; prof. geology Rogaland Coll., Stavanger, 1993—. Contbr. articles to profl. jours. Mem. Soc. Sedimentary Geology. Office: Statoil as, 4035 Stavanger Norway

BJORLING, EWA HELENA, dental researcher; b. Stockholm, May 3, 1961; d. Lars Henrik and Birgitte Ing-Britt (Blomquist) Klippmark; m. Nicke Lars Richard Bjorling, May 5, 1990; children: Gustav, Kristina. Dental Degree, Karolinska Inst., Stockholm, 1986, Dentist License, 1987, PhD in Virology, 1993. assoc. prof., bd. dirs. rsch. com., dental faculty Karolinska Inst., 1995; lectr. in virology, 1999. Contbg. author: Immunochemistry of AIDS, 1993, Immunology of HIV Infection, 1996. Grantee Swedish Soc. for Med. Rsch., 1995, Tobias Found., 1997. Mem. Moderate Party. Avocations: sailing, downhill skiing, formula cars, classical music. Office: Microbiology/Tumorbiol Ctr, Karolinska Inst, S-171 77 Stockholm Sweden

BJØRN, DINNA, choreographer, artistic director. Joined The Royal Danish Ballet, 1964; tchr. of Bournonville technique, 1975—; co-founder The Soloists of The Royal Danish Ballet, 1976, artistic dir., 1985-90; tchr. The Royal Theatre Ballet Sch., Denmark, 1985—; artistic dir. Norwegian Nat. Ballet, Oslo, 1990—; guest tchr. Boston Ballet, Berlin Opera Ballet, Munich Opera Ballet, The Israel Ballet, CID Danza Mex., Paris Opera Ballet Sch., English Nat. Ballet Sch.; tchr. master classes various univs. & ballet schs. in U.S., Europe and Asia. Soloist debut in Afternoon of a Faun, Royal Danish Ballet, 1966; choreographer numerous works. Recipient Bronze medal and Spl. prize Varna Internat. Ballet Competitions, Bulgaria, 1968. Office: Black Box Theater Alex Brygge, Stranden 3, 2050 Oslo Norway also: Norwegian National Ballet, PO Box 8800 Yougstorget, N-0028 Oslo 1, Norway*

BJÖRNHAG, GÖRAN OSKAR INGEMAR, animal physiology educator; b. Bredaryd, Sweden, Mar. 31, 1939; s. Oskar Birger and Effie Antonia

Henrietta (Ahlström) B.; m. Gunnel Margareta Gustafsson, Aug. 15, 1964; children: Ulrica, Oscar. Student, Hvilan, Åkarp, Sweden, 1963; degree in agronomy, Agrl. Coll. Sweden, Uppsala, 1967, lic., 1969, PhD in Agr., 1972. Assoc. prof. Swedish U. Agrl. Scis., Uppsala, 1974-2000, prof. animal physiology, 2000—, head dept. animal physiology, 1994—. Author, editor textbooks in field of animal physiology (in Swedish); contbr. articles to profl. jours., chpts. to books. Mem. Comparative Nutrition Soc. (U.S.), European Soc. for Comparative Physiology and Biochemistry (Belgium). Avocations: art, music, history. Office: Swedish U Agrl Scis, Box 7045, S-75007 Uppsala Sweden

BJORNSDOTTIR, INGIBJORG ELSA, environmental scientist; b. Edinburgh, Scotland, May 22, 1966; d. Bjorn Bjornsson and Svanhildur Sigurdardottir. BA, U. Iceland, 1991, BSc, 1995; MSc, Chalmers U. Technology, 1996. Environ. cons. Linuhonnun, Reykjavik, Iceland, 1997—. Mem. Icelandic Geol. Assn., Icelandic Glaciol. Soc., N.Y. Acad. Scis., Planetary Soc. Lutheran. Avocations: music, world water awareness.

BJORNSON, EDITH CAMERON, foundation executive, communications consultant; b. Orlando, Fla., Sept. 12, 1937; d. Hilliard Francis and Edith Muriel (McBride) Cameron; m. Carroll N. Bjornson, Jan. 11, 1963; children: Lisa Carol, Karl Cameron (dec.). BA, U. Fla., Gainesville, 1953, MA, 1956; profl. cert., Ecole de Cuisine LaVerenne, Paris, 1983. Copywriter Sta. WGGG, Gainesville, Fla., 1953-54; exec. asst. Actors' Studio, N.Y.C., 1956-58; prodn. asst. Omnibus, N.Y.C., 1958-59; assoc. prodr. Robert Saudek Assocs., N.Y.C., 1958-60, ABC News Adlai Stevenson Reports, N.Y.C., 1960; asst. gen. mgr. Sta. WNDT-TV, N.Y.C., 1960-63; co-prodr. The Open Mind, N.Y.C., 1963-69; dir. local programming Telepromter, Inc., N.Y.C., 1979-80; corporate v.p. programming Westinghouse Broadcasting and Cable, N.Y.C., 1980-83; cons. Sta. WNYC-TV, N.Y.C., 1984-86; v.p., sr. program officer The Markle Found., N.Y.C., 1986-98; mem. working group Carter Commn. on Radio and TV, Atlanta, 1992-96; mem. strategic planning bd. Conn. Pub. TV; bd. dirs. N.Y. New Media Assn., N.Y.C., 1998—; bd. dirs. Conn. Pub. TV and Radio, 1999—; cons. in new media profit and non-profit orgns.; exec. dir. Fulfilling the Promise project on digital comm., Century Found. and Carnegie Corp., 2000—; sr. advisor Morningside Ventures, Columbia U., 1999—; exec. dir. Fulfilling the Promise The Century Found. Carnegie Corp. Project advisor: (computer software) Voyager Co., 1993, SimHealth, 1994, (Internet software, multi-player online games) ReInventing America, 1995, President '96, (Columbia U. internet project) Morningside Ventures; contbr. articles to profl. jours. Vice chmn. bd. dirs. HealthCare Chaplaincy, N.Y.C., 1989-96; bd. dirs. Pro-Natura USA, N.Y.C., 1995-99; life trustee Health Care Chaplaincy, N.Y.C., 1997; exec. dir. Digital Promise, 2000—. Recipient Emmy award Acad. TV. Arts and Scis., 1960. Mem. Internat. Assn. Culinary Profls., Night Kitchen (computer software developers bd. dirs. 1996-98), Ocean Reef Club, Mortar Board, Delta Gamma. Republican. Avocation: cooking. Home: 34 E Lyon Farm Dr Greenwich CT 06831-4349

BJÖRNSSON, OLAFUR GRIMUR, biochemistry researcher; b. Reykjavik, Iceland, Jan. 6, 1944. Cand. Real., Coll. of Reykjavik, 1964; Cand. Phil., U. Iceland, 1965, BA, 1966, MD, 1973; PhD, U. London, 1982. Diplomate in clin. biochemistry and clin. physiology, Iceland. Intern various hosps./affils. of U. Iceland, 1973-75; med. resident, dept. clin. biochemistry U. Hosp. Iceland, Reykjavik, 1975-77; rsch. fellow Hammersmith Hosp./U. London/Royal Postgrad. Med. Sch., U.K., 1977-82; sr. rsch. fellow MRC Lipid Metabolism Unit/Hammersmith Hosp., London, 1982-84; rsch. assoc. dept. biochemistry and biophysics U. Pa., Phila., 1984-89; rsch. assoc. U. Oxford, Metabolic Rsch. Lab., Oxford, 1989-94; sr. investigator dept. physiology U. Iceland, Reykjavik, 1994—. Editor: Festschrift in honor of Prof. emeritus David Davidsson, Reykjavik, 1996; contbr. numerous articles to profl. jours. Project grantee Icelandic Govt., The Icelandic Sci. Found. and U. Hosp. of Iceland. Mem. Am. Soc. Biochemistry and Molecular Biology, Biophys. Soc., European Soc. for Clin. Investigation, The Icelandic Soc. London. Avocations: history of sci. Office: U Iceland/Dept Physiology, Vatnsmyrarvegur 16, Reykjavik Iceland

BJÖRNSSON, PER ANDERS, journalist; b. Stockholm, Sept. 27, 1951; s. Per Ludvig and Birgit Ingeborg (Bergstrom) B.; m. Eva Ingeborg Ulveson, July 1, 1978 (div. 1984); children: Karin, Adam; m. Gunhild Margareta Hölne; Feb. 1, 1996. MA, U. Stockholm, 1976. Lectr. econ. history U. Stockholm, 1977-78; free-lance journalist Tempus, Malmö, 1980-81; prodr. sci. and arts programs Swedish Nat. Radio, 1982-93; dept. head Svenska Dagbladet, 1994—; chmn. bd. dirs. Ordfront Pub. House, 1987-88. Author: Was the Twentieth Century in Vain?, 1993, The Short March, 1996, Managing the Future, 1997; editor: (anthology) Turning Points Europe After 1989, The Eternal Human Values, 1996, Sweden—a Media Society, 1997, Abdicating Elites, 1998; editor-in-chief Clio Mag., 1988-90. Recipient Lars Salvius award, 1994. Mem. Swedish Coun. Rsch. Humanities Social Scis., Swedish Inst. Contemporary History (bd. dirs.), Swedish Hist. Conv. (cofounder, bd. dirs.), Swedish Literary Soc. Finland (corr.), New Club (chmn. 1994-97), Nat. Classical Assn. (chmn. 1997—). Avocations: piano, travel, book collecting. Home: Lötsjövägen 85, 17443 Sundbyberg Sweden Office: Svenska Dagbladet, 10517 Stockholm Sweden

BJÖRNSSON, SVEINN, diplomat; b. Reykjavík, Iceland, Aug. 18, 1942; m. Magnea Sigurdardóttir. Grad., Comml. Coll. Iceland, 1963; diploma in Spanish and Spanish Lit., U. Barcelona, 1964; grad. in Econs. and Bus. Adminstrn., U. Iceland, Reykjavík, 1970. Asst. divsn. chief Ministry of Commerce, 1970, divsn. chief, 1973, dep. sec. gen., 1982; comml. counselor Embassy of Iceland, Paris, 1978, min. counsellor, dep. chief of mission, 1992; dep. chief mission Embassy of Iceland, Washington, 1997; min. counsellor Ministry for Fgn. Affairs, 1987; dep. permanent rep. Coun. Europe, Strasbourg, 1992, OECD, UNESCO, 1992; chmn. Price Coun. and Competition Authority, 1982-88, chmn. Bilateral Trade Commns. for Iceland and Soviet Union, Russian Fedn., Czechoslovakia, Poland, 1982-87; State Dept. Scholar Fellow GATT, 1986. Home: Vesturberg 155, Reykjavik Iceland

BLAABJERG, FREDE, engineering educator, researcher; b. Erslev, Denmark, May 6, 1963; s. Egon and Gertrud (Østergård) B.; m. Ina Vibeke Mathiasen, Nov. 10, 1990; children: Anja, Jakob. MSEE, Aalborg (Denmark) U., 1987, PhD, 1995. Project engr. Ascan Scandia, Randers, Denmark, 1987-88; asst. prof. Inst. Energy Tech. Aalborg U., Denmark, 1992-96; assoc. prof. Aalborg U., 1996-98, prof. power electronics and drives, 1998—; mem. Danish Tech. Rsch. Coun., Copenhagen, 1997—; annual tchr. award Energy Sector Aalborg U., 1995; chmn. Danfoss Prof. Programme, 1997—; bd. dirs. Danish Space Rsch. Inst., Copenhagen, 1998—; cons., lectr., tutorials in field; vis. prof., Padova, Italy, 2000; chmn. various internat. confs. Contbr. numerous articles to profl. jours., books; patent single current sensor in inverters; associated editor IEEE transactions on industry applications, Elteknik. Chmn. Nordie 2000, Aalborg. Recipient A.R. Angelo award, 1995. Mem. IEEE (sr., Paper award 1997, Outstanding Young Power Electronics Engrng. award 1998, reviewer, 2 Industry Application Soc. Paper awards 1998, Power Electronics Soc.), European Power Electronics Assn., Indsl. Electronics Soc. E-mail: fbl@iet.auc.dk. Home: Nissumvej 13, DK-9220 Aalborg East Denmark Office: Aalborg U Inst Energy Tech, Pontoppidan Straede 101, East Ålborg DK-9220, Denmark

BLACHERE, GÉRARD PIERRE HENRI, civil engineer; b. Chalette, France, Oct. 10, 1914; s. Henri G. and Madeleine (Le Roy) B.; m. Elisabeth Bumb, Apr. 20, 1950; children: Oliver (dec.), Hughes, Yvain. Student, Ecole Poly., France, 1933-35; grad., Ecole Nat. des Ponts Chaussees, France, 1938. Del. French Rebldg. Ministry, Berlin, 1945-46, Ministry for Rebldg. the Haut Rhin Dept., Colmar, France, 1946-49; commr. reconstrn. Govt. Tunisien, Tunis, 1949-54, Chef de la construction et de l'Urbanisme, Alger, Algérie, 1954-55; dir. constrn. French Ministry, Paris, 1955-57; dir. Ctr. Sci. du Bâtiment, Paris, 1957-74; pres., dir. studies Inst. de la Constrn. Industrielsee, Paris, 1970—; sect. pres. Coun. Gen. des Ponts et Chaussées, Paris, 1982-83; pres. de l'Auxirbat, Paris, 1976—; prof. Ecole Nat. des Ponts et Chaussées, Paris, 1960-70, Conservatoire Nat. Arts et Métiers, Paris, 1967-70. Author: Savoir Bâtir, 1965, Vers un Urbanisme Raisonné, 1968, Technologies of Industrialized Construction, 1975, Building Principles, 1987. V.p. Union Nationale des Camps de Montague, Paris, 1945-46. Capt. French mil., 1939-44. Decorated Croix de Guerre, comdr. Legion of Honor. Mem. Groupe de Haute Montagne. Home: Residence Dauphine, 78430 Louvecie France Office: Auxirbat, 8 rue des Saussaies, 75008 Paris France

BLACK, BARBARA ANN, publisher; b. Eureka, Calif., Dec. 11, 1928; d. William Marion and Letitia (Brunia) Black; m. Vinson Brown, June 18, 1950 (dec Dec. 1991); children: Tamara Pinn, Roxana Hodges, Keven Brown. BA, Western State Coll., Gunnison, Colo., 1950. Cert. tchr., Colo. Editor/proofreader Naturegraph Pubs., Los Altos, Calif., 1950-53; co-owner, mgr. Naturegraph Pubs., San Martin, Calif., 1953-60, Healdsburg, Calif., 1960-76; owner/mgr. Naturegraph Pubs., Happy Camp, Calif., 1976—. Author: Barns of Yesteryear, 1993; co-author: Sierra Nevada Wildlife, 1996, The Californian Wildlife Region, 1999; pub. over 100 titles on wildlife and Native Ams. Mem. Am. Booksellers Assn. Baha'i Faith. Avocations: gardening, backpacking, animal training.

BLACK, CAROL MARY, rheumatologist, educator; b. Leicester, Eng.; d. Edgar and Annie (Freer) Herbert; m. James Black, 1973 (div. 1983). BA, U. Bristol, 1962, MBChB, 1970, MD, 1974. Cons. West Middlesex U. Hosp. Nat. Health Svc., U.K., 1981-89; cons. Royal Free Hosp. Nat. Health Svc., London, 1989-94, prof. rheumatology Royal Free Hosp., 1994—; mem. Prince of Wales Adv. Group on Disability, London, 1998—; mem. clin. interest group Wellcome Inst., London, 1996—; mem. regional health authority adv. bd. Nat. Health Svc., London, 1997—, Nat. Specialist Commissioning Adv. Group, 1999—. Recipient Heberden Roundman's medal Brit. Soc. Rheumatology, 1999. Fellow Acad. Med. Scis., Royal Coll. Physicians (v.p.); mem. Royal Soc. Medicine (pres. immunology sect. 1997-99). Avocations: classical music, opera, walking, running, travel. Home: 2 Ferncroft Ave Flat 3, London NW3 7PG, England Office: Royal Free Hosp, Pond St, London NW3 2QG, England

BLACK, CHARLIE J., technical writer, author, educator, business consultant; b. Beatrice, Ala., Apr. 19, 1934; s. Napoleon and Mattie Ethel (Stallworth) B.; m. Lola P., June 12, 1960; children: Lisa Yvonne, LaSonya Ann. BS, Ala. State U., 1956; MBPA, Southea. U., Washington, 1978; postgrad., Tuskegee U., 1959-60, Atlanta U., 1962-63, 66, George Washington U., 1968-69, U. D.C., 1978-79, Cath. U., Washington, 1979-80. Band dir. Talladega (Ala.) Pub. Schs., 1956-58; math. tchr. West Point (Ga.) Pub. Schs., 1958-62, Atlanta Pub. Schs., 1962-63; cartographer USAF, St. Louis, 1963-65; edn. adv. U.S. Army, Ft. Leonard Wood, Mo., 1965-66; math. tchr. St. Louis Pub. Schs., 1966; edn. specialist U.S. Navy, Washington, 1966-67; tech. writer Tracor Inc., Rockville, Md., 1967-68; program dir. Ogden Tech. Lab., Washington, 1968-71; math. tchr. Washington Pub. Schs., 1971-72, 76-79, Montgomery County Schs., Rockville, 1981-84; ins. agent Equitable Life, Washington, 1972-73; securities agent Investors Fin., Washington, 1973; dist. mgr. So. Aid Life, Washington, 1973-75; bus. cons. C.J. Black Enterprises, Washington, 1979-81; syndicated columnist Washington Provider, 1984—; bd. dirs. Napoleon and Mattie Black Family Farm, Inc.; chmn. Ga. Ave. Devel. Corp., Washington, 1978-82; cons. to U.S. atty. for D.C., 1996—, Fedn. So. Coops., 1975-76, Green-Hale Sewing Ctr., 1976-80, with U.S. Senate Jud. Com., 1980, with D.C. Fin. Control Bd., 1996—, with U.S. atty. gen., 1996, with FBI dir. 1997, with U.S. Pres. Bill Clinton, 1997, others; spon., produced Hosteds Radio Program, WUST-AM, 1989; advisor supt. Monroe County Pub. Schs., 1998, editor Hornet Tribune, 1998, Mrs. Hillary Rodham Clinton, 1998, Washington D.C. City Coun., 1998, Washington D.C. Inspector Gen., 1998, Washington D.C. Police Chief, 1998, Senator Joseph Biden, 1998, Rep. J.C. Watts, 1998; advisor to Pres. Clinton, 2000—, FBI, 2000—, Robert Pitofsky Chmn. U.S. Fed. Trade Commn., 2000—, Comdr. Abraham Parks, D.C. Met. Police, 2000—, Linda Moody, Pres., D.C. Congress of Parents and Tchrs., 2000—. Author: Mathematical Needs, 1971, After the Fact, 1987; columnist New Observer, 1971—, Washington Provider Syndicate, 1991—. Pres. West Elem. PTA, Washington, 1971-73, Brightwood Cmty., Washington, 1974-80; mem. Assn. MBA Execs., 1978-84, Am. Airlines Admiral Club, 1979-83, D.C. C. of C., 1972-81, DCCC Investment Club, 1974-80, Concord Coalition, 1994—; chmn. Civil Protection Com., Washington, 1977; mem. Met. Washington C&P Consumer Coun., 1980-81; active D.C. Civic Assn.; mem. Dem. Senatorial campaign com. Brightwood Cmty. Assn.; advisor D.C. Fin. Control Bd., 1996—; advisor to Pres. Clinton, Senate Majority Leader, Congressman Stokes, Senator Moynihan, 1997—; exec. dir. D.C. Fin. Control Bd., 1998—; advisor D.C. Bd. of Edn., 1998—, D.C. Inspector Gen., 1998—, FTC, 1998—, Mrs. Hillary Rodman Clinton, 1998—, D.C. Coun., 1998—, SEC, 1999—, FCC, 1999, Fed. Res. Bd. Govs., 1999—, Eugene Kinlow, D.C. Fin. Mgmt. Responsibility and Assistance Authority, 1999, Ben Johnson, Dir.'s Pres.'s Initiative for One Am., 1999—, E.R. Shipp, Ombudsman, The Washington Post, 1999, James N. Rosanau, George Washington U., 1999, Ole R. Holsti, Duke U., 1999, Yale H. Ferguson, Rutgers U., 1999, Delia C. Bourne, Libr. for Allen County Pub. Libr., Ft. Wayne, Ind., 1999; advisor to editor The Hornet Tribune, 1998—, pub. The Mobile Beacon, 1999—; advisor to Pres. Clinton, 2000, Sen. Richard Shelby, chmn. selected intelligence com., 2000, Gen. Willie Alexander, comdr. Ala. NG, 2000, Abraham Parks comdr. 4th Dist. Met. Dept. Police, 2000, eds. AP, 2000; Robert Pitofsky chmn. Fed. Trade Commn., 2000—; Abraham Parks commdr. 4th police dist. D.C. Met. Police, 2000—; U.S. rep. Eleanor Holmes-Norton, 2000—. NSF fellow, 1959-60; named Top PTA Pres., Washington PTA, 1973; recipient plaques ASU Alumni, 1970, 73, Equitable Life, 1972, Lewis Black Family, 1987, Stallworth Family, 1987, D.C. Fedn. Civic Assns., 1997, Brightwood Cmty. Assn., 2000; reient cert. USAF, 1963, U.S. Army, 1966, Urban League, 1967, R.R. Moton High Reunion, 1990, DCFCA, 1993, Newspaper Inst. Am., 1970. Mem. Internat. Platform Assn. Democrat. Avocations: reading, writing, sports, speaking. Home: 6435 13th St NW Washington DC 20012-2959

BLACK, CLINTON LEANDER, education educator, author; b. May 30. BS in Biology, Fla. A&M U., 1993. Tchr. h.s. biology, science Ft. Lauderdale. Author: We As A Black People "Our Time Has Come". E-mail: clintii@excite.com.

BLACK, CONRAD MOFFAT, publishing corporate executive; b. Montreal, Aug. 25, 1944; s. George Montegu and Jean Elizabeth (Riley) B.; m. Barbara J.E. Amiel. BA, Carleton U., 1965; LLL, Laval U., 1970; MA in History, McGill U., 1973; LLD (hon.), St. Francis Xavier U., 1979, McMaster U., 1979; LittD (hon.), U. Windsor, 1979; LLD (hon.), Carleton U., 1989. Chmn., co-owner Ea. Twps. Pub. Co., Ltd., Knowlton, Que., 1966—; chmn. Sterling Newspapers Ltd., Vancouver, 1971—; pres., chmn. exec. com. Argus Corp. Ltd., 1978-79; chmn. bd., chmn. exec. com. Argus Corp. Ltd., Toronto, 1979—, CEO, 1985; chmn. The Ravelston Corp. Ltd., 1978; chmn. Hollinger, Inc., 1985, CEO, 1987; chmn., CEO Telegraph Group Ltd., 1987; chmn. Saturday Night Mag. Ltd., 1987; dep. chmn. Am. Pub. Co., 1987; chmn. and CEO Hollinger Internat. Inc.; chmn., CEO Southam Inc., 1994—, dir.; bd. dirs. Brascan Ltd., Can. Imperial Bank of Commerce, Ltd., The Spectator (1828) Ltd., Inc., UniMedia, Inc., Jerusalem Post Publs. Ltd., Sotheby's Holdings Inc.; chmn. bd. Nat. Interest, Washington, Coun. Fgn. Rels. Author: Duplessis, 1977, reprinted as Render Unto Caesar, 1998, A Life in Progress, 1993. Patron Malcolm Muggeridge Foun. Decorated officer Order of Can., apptd. to Privy Coun. of Can., 1992. Mem. Trilateral Commn., Americas Soc. (chmn.'s coun.), Internat. Inst. for Strategic Studies, Bilderberg Meetings (steering com.), Toronto Club, York Club, Toronto Golf Club, Granite Club, Univ. Club (Montreal), Mt. Royal Club (Montreal), Everglades Club, Beach Club (Palm Beach), Athenaeum, Beefsteak, Whites (London), Garrick (London). Office: Hollinger Inc, 10 Toronto St, Toronto, ON Canada M5C 2B7 also: Telegraph Group Ltd, Canary Wharf, 1 Canada Sq, London E14 5DT, England also: Hollinger Internat 712 5th Ave New York NY 10019-4108

BLACK, CORA JEAN, evangelist, wedding consultant; b. Mt. Pleasant, Pa., July 30, 1941; d. Alfred John and Ruby Isabel (Waugaman) B.; m. Arthur Byron Everett, Mar. 27, 1974. Student, Greensburg Bus. Coll., 1962, Moody Bible Inst., 1966; DD, Internat. Bible Inst., 1972; postgrad., Seton Hill Coll., 1986. Cert. bereavement facilitator, Am. Acad. Bereavement, 1999; ordained evangelist; notary public. Advt. display silk-screen artist West Penn Power Co., Greensburg, Pa., 1962-63; missionary to W.I. Gospel Light Ministry, New Stanton, Pa., 1964; pers. dir., Pa. state chair Assn. Internat. Gospel Assemblies of DeSota, Mo., 1970-80; founder, pres. America for Christ Ministry, New Stanton, 1974—; owner, founder Sea-Jay's All Faith Wedding Chapel, New Stanton, 1979—; chaplain Westmoreland County Prison, 1999—; coord. Holy Land tours, 1971-83; chaplain Westmoreland County Prison; mem. Kathryn Kuhlman Concert Choir, Pitts., 1955-62; owner Sea-Jay All Pet Hotel, New Stanton. Author of Christian literature; composer of published and recorded Gospel music including Christ is Coming! Are You Ready?, America for Christ, and The Joy of Life; weekly radio broadcasts. Chaplain for women inmates Westmoreland County Prison, Greensburg, Pa., 1998—. Mem. BMI, Am. Acad. Cert. Forensic Counselors, Am. Assn. Gospel Assemblies (internat. pub. rels. dir., Pa. chmn. for Women in Christ), Am. Psychotherapy Assn. (cert.), Am. Acad. Bereavement Assoc. (cert. bereavement facilitator), Ctrl. Westmoreland C. of C., Westmoreland Hist. Soc., New Stanton Hist. Soc. (sec.-treas. 1995—), Am. Assn. Christian Counselors (charter, counselor), Pa. Assn. Notaries, Internat. Platform Assn., DAR, Daus. Union Vets. of Civil War 1861-1865, Aux. Sons Union Vets. Civil War, Laides Grand Army Rep., Assn. Internat. Gospel Assemblies (pub. rels. dir. for U.S. and 40 some countries), Tri-State Gospel Music Assn. (treas. 1998—). Republican. Avocations: travel, photography, decorating and designing, painting, animals. Home: 440 N Center Ave PO Box 192 New Stanton PA 15672-0192 Office: Sea-Jays 440 N Center Ave New Stanton PA 15672-9416

BLACK, DAVID LUTHER, writer, consultant; b. Plainview, Tex., Apr. 3, 1934; s. Mac Truman and Wilman (Bailey) B.; m. Gloria Loyola, Mar. 31, 1984; 1 son by previous marriage, David Roger. AB, Baylor U., 1954; postgrad., U. Tex.-Austin, 1959-80. With S.W. Rsch. Inst., San Antonio; asst. to pres., dir. spl. programs, chief of party U.S. Agy. for Devel. Projects in Low Cost Housing Irrigation, Tanzania, Botswana, Colombia, 1980-84; dep. dir. regional program for sci. and tech. devel. OAS, Washington, 1984-87, advisor to sec. gen. for external affairs, 1987-96; sr. rsch. fellow Coun. on Hemispheric Affairs, Washington, 1996—; chief of mission, U.S. rep. Interam. Inst. Cooperation on Agr.; resident rep. in U.S.A. Interam. Inst., 1971-77; cons. to UNIDO, UNESCO, UNEP; advisor to Univ. in Chile Obtaining Projects with USAID Nat. Rsch. Coun., 1992—. Contbr. articles to profl. jours. on sci., Latin Am. affairs and culture. Extensive devel. experience in Latin Am., Africa, Caribbean; pres. OAS Fed. Staff Credit Union, 1989-92, v.p. 1992-96; pres. San Antonio Chamber Music Soc., 1973-76; active Cmty. Guidance Ctr. Recipient Centennial award for sci. and tech. ASME, 1980. Mem. Am. Soc. Metals (chmn. Latin Am. divsn. 1974-84), U.S. Assn. UN (bd. dirs.), Soc. Internat. Devel., U.S. Club of Rome, Nat. Press Club. Home: 3595 Poinciana Ave Coconut Grove FL 33133-6526

BLACK, DON, lyricist; b. London, June 21, 1938; s. Morris and Betsy (Kersh) Blackstone; m. Shirley K. Berg, July 12, 1958; children: Grant Howard, Clive Darren. chmn. Vivian Ellis Prize; mem. devel. com. Soho Theatre Co.; dir. Kings Head Theatre, Islington, Eng. Lyricist over 100 songs for films including James Bond Thunderball, Diamonds are Forever, The Man with the Golden Gun, also Ben (film Willard), To Sir with Love; worked with many composers including Jule Styne, Henry Mancini, Quincy Jones, elmer Bernstein, Michel Legrand, Marvin Hamlisch; artists who have recorded songs include Barbara Streisand, Frank Sinatra, Ray Charles, Smokey Robinson, Tony Bennett, Ray Charles, Michael Bolton, Meat Loaf etc. Recipient 2 Tony awards, 1995, Oscar (song Born Free), 5 Acad. award nominations, 3 Tony nominations, Golden Globe award, 5 Ivor Novello awards; named to Order of Brit. Empire, 1999. Mem. Brit. Acad. Songwriters Composers and Authors (v.p.), Royal Automobile Club. Avocation: snooker. Home: 18 Melbury Rd, London W 148LT, England

BLACK, FREDERICK EVAN, lawyer; b. N.Y.C., Oct. 1, 1944; s. Harry Newhouse and Gertrude (Marston) B.; m. Christine Barron MacKinnon, Aug. 26, 1967; children: Alexis MacKinnon, Caroline Frances Dorothy. BA in History, U. N.C., 1967; JD, Syracuse U., 1973. Bar: Pa. 1973, U.S. Dist. Ct. (ea. dist.) Pa. 1973, U.S. Supreme Ct. 1978, N.J., 1986, U.S. Dist. Ct. (mid. dist.) Pa. 1989. Atty. Nationwide Ins. Co., Phila., 1973-75, Margolis, Edelstein & Scherlis, Phila., 1975-77; ptnr. Post & Schell, Phila., 1977—. Bd. dirs. Friends of Holy Cross Monastery, Inc., 1986-91. Served to lt. USNR, 1967-82. Mem. Pa. Bar Assn., Pa. Def. Inst., Def. Rsch. Inst. Office: 240 Grandview Ave Camp Hill PA 17011-1706

BLACK, GENEVA ARLENE, social services agency administrator; b. Dazell, S.C., Apr. 30, 1932; d. Isaac and Carrie Lee (Hollimon) Sanders; children: Ronald D., Robert J., Clarissa D. Black Wells, Michael A., Steven G. Diploma Soc. Svc. Adminstrn., Temple U., 1970-73; Diploma Bus. Adminstrn., U. Detroit, 1981-82. Housing coord. Haddington Leadership Orgn., Phila., 1970-73, exec. dir., 1973; co-founder, exec. dir. Haddington Multi Svcs. for Older Adults, Inc., Phila., 1975—. host monthly radio program Sr.'s Hour, Sta. WDAS, 1996—. Pres., block capt. 5500 Block Poplar St.; chmn. Emergency Fund Coalition; mem. human svc. com. Empowerment Zone West Phila.; 192d legis. dist. chmn. Com. on Aging, trustee, treas. inspiration choir Vine Meml. Bapt. Ch., co-chmn. ch. anniversary com., sec. Fed. Credit Union; sec. West Phila. Planning Com.; sec. bd. dirs. Spectrum Health Svcs.; bd. dirs., v.p. Housing Assn. Authority Delaware Valley; bd. dirs. Mayor's Commn. on Svcs. to Elderly, 1996—; coord. sr. programs. Recipient numerous awards, including Leon S. Rosenthal award for humanitarian and cmty. svc. West Phila. C. of C., 1983, citation for outstanding cmty. svc. Pa. Ho. of Reps., 1985, 87, 90, 95, Cmty. Svc. award Phila. chpt. Nat. Assn. Negro Bus. and Profl. Women's Club, 1989, citation for outstanding cmty. svcs. gov. State of Pa., 1990, Pa. Senate, 1990, Cmty. Svc. award Emergency Fund for Older Philadelphians, 1991, Phila. Bapt. Ch., 1993, Allan Yaffe svc. award Phila. Corp. for Aging, 1994, cert. of appreciation U. Pa., 1995; named to Afro-Am. Hall of Fame, Drexel U., 1996; named Top Ladies of Distinction, Inc. Phila. Chpt., 1998; recipient Trail Blazer award 2000 Black Women, 1998. Mem. AARP (1st sec. Overbrook chpt. 1993-96), Phila. Corp. Aging (cert. mental health, 1987). Office: Haddington Multi Svcs for Older Adults Inc 5502 Haverford Ave Philadelphia PA 19139-1431

BLACK, JAMES ISAAC, III, lawyer; b. Lakeland, Fla., Oct. 26, 1951; s. James Isaac Jr. and Juanita (Feemster) B.; m. Vikki Harrison, June 15, 1973; children: Jennifer Leigh, Katharine Ann, Stephanie Marie. BA, U. Fla., 1973; JD, Harvard U., 1976. Bar: Fla. 1976, N.Y. 1977, U.S. Tax Ct. 1984. Assoc. Sullivan & Cromwell, N.Y.C., 1976-84, ptnr., 1984—. Mem. ABA, N.Y. State Bar Assn. (persons under disability com. trusts and estates law sect. 1984-87), Assn. of Bar of City of N.Y. (sec. 1980-81, trusts and estates and surrogates ct. com. 1980-83), Scarsdale Golf Club. Home: 23 Chesterfield Rd Scarsdale NY 10583-2205 Office: Sullivan & Cromwell 125 Broad St Fl 28 New York NY 10004-2489

BLACK, JAMES ROBERT, industrial engineer; b. Davenort, Iowa, Feb. 17, 1948; s. Robert James and Anne Louise (Johnson) B.; m. Mary Ann O'Malley, June 5, 1971; 1 child, Robert Joseph. BS in Indsl. Engring., Iowa State U., 1970, MS, 1971; MBA, U. Chgo., 1976. Indsl. engr. Inland Steel Co., East Chicago, Ind., 1971-76, sr. indsl. engr., 1976-77; indsl. engring. supr. Clark Equipment Co., Jackson, Mich., 1977-78; indsl. engring. mgr. Harrison plant Graphic Sys. divsn. Rockwell Internat., Rockford, Ill., 1978-83; corp.supr. adminstrv. work mgmt. Kohler Co., Wis., 1983-87; mgr. mfg. svcs. Frigidaire Co.-Wet Products, Jefferson, Iowa, 1987-91, assembly ops. mgr., 1991-93; Kaizen facilitator Frigidaire Co.-Wet Products, Webster City, Iowa, 1993, paint process mgr., 1993, plant engring. mgr., 1993-95; sr. project mgr. Ctr. for Indsl. Rsch. and Svc., Iowa State U., 1995—; pres. James R. Black & Assocs., 1997—; co-leader, guest lectr. Am. Mgmt. Assn., 1979-80; mem. adv. coun. Iowa State U. Ctr. Indsl. Rsch. and Svc., 1992-94; mem. planing com. Iowa conf. Mfg., 1991-93, chmn., 1993. Contbr. articles to profl. jours. Cons. Project Bus. divsn. Jr. Achievement, 1980; chmn. pack com. Cub Scouts, Boy Scouts Am., 1980-83, Webelos leader, 1982-83, asst. scoutmaster, 1983-84, scoutmaster, 1984-88, dist. vice chmn., 1984-86, dist. scouting chmn., 1986-88; asst. soccer coach, 1981-83, coach, 1984-85. Fisher Governor scholar, 1968-69, Maytag scholar, 1969-70. Mem. Inst. Indsl. Engrs. (sr.; treas. 1979-80, pres. 1980-81, bd. dirs. 1989-91, v.p. 1991-92), Am. Soc. for Quality, Assn. for Mfg. Excellence, Mainstream Living and Story County Devel. Ctr. (phonathon co-chmn. 1993-95, bd. dirs. 1994—, treas. 1995-97, v.p. 1997-99, pres. 1999—), Kohler Engring. and Tech. Orgn. (program chmn. 1986, chmn. 1987) K.C., Phi Kappa Phi, Tau Beta Pi, Gamma Epsilon Sigma, Psi Chi, Beta Gamma Sigma. Home: 3416 Valley View Rd Ames IA 50014-4613 Office: CIRAS/Iowa State U Coll Engring 2272 Howe Hl Ste 2620 Ames IA 50011-0001

BLACK, SIR JAMES (WHYTE), pharmacologist; b. June 14, 1924. MB, ChB, U. St. Andrews; MD (hon.), U. Edinburgh, 1989; DSc (hon.), U. Glasgow, 1989. Asst. lectr. physiology U. St. Andrews, 1946; lectr. physiology U. Malaya, 1947-50; sr. lectr. U. Glasgow Vet. Sch., 1950-58; with ICI Pharms. Ltd., 1958-64; head biol. rsch., dep. rsch. dir. Smith, Kline & French, Welwyn Garden City, 1964-73; prof., chmn. dept. pharmacology

Univ. Coll., London, 1973-77; dir. therapeutic rsch. Wellcome Rsch. Labs., 1978-84; prof. analytical pharmacology King's Coll. Hosp. Med. Sch., U. London, 1984—; chancellor Dundee (Scotland) U., 1992—. Decorated Knight, 1981; recipient Nobel prize for medicine, 1988. Fellow Royal Coll. Physicians, Royal Soc. (Mullard award 1978); mem. Royal Coll. Vet. Surgeons (hon. assoc.). Office: U Dundee, Chancellor's Office, Dundee DD1 4HN, Scotland

BLACK, JOHN HARRY, astronomer; b. Indpls., May 7, 1949; arrived in Sweden, 1996; s. John Wesley Jr. and Margaret Anne (Ross) B.; m. Cathy Horellou, July 21, 1995; 1 child, Steven John. BA, Harvard U., 1971, AM, 1973, PhD, 1975. Asst. prof. U. Minn., Mpls., 1975-78; rsch. assoc. Harvard Coll. Obs., Cambridge, Mass., 1978-83; assoc. prof. U. Ariz., Tucson, 1983-89, prof., 1989-95; prof. Chalmers U. Tech., Gothenburg, Sweden, 1996—. Contbr. over 100 articles to profl. jours. Recipient R.J. Trumpler award Astron. Soc. of the Pacific, 1977. Mem. Am. Astron. Soc., Royal Astron. Soc. (Eng.), Internat. Astron. Union, Royal Swedish Acad. Scis. (fgn.), Am. Geophys. Union. Office: Onsala Space Obs, 43992 Onsala Sweden

BLACK, KRIS SUSAN LYNN, marketing company executive, speaker, author, poet; b. Ladysmith, Wis., Sept. 19, 1950; d. Bruce Roger and Christine Mae (Sweet) B. AA with honors, Bakersfield Coll.; student, Phoenix Coll. Asst. mgr. jewelry dept. K Mart, Rapid City, S.D., 1965-68; beauty titilist, actress, model, tchr. Patricia Stevens, Phoenix, 1968-72; Country Musics' 1st lady internat. promotional dir. for TV series Hee Haw (Buck Owens), Bakersfield, Calif., 1972-76; dir. K.B. Properties, Dallas, 1976-78; v.p. Wynn Investments, Dallas, 1978—; pres. Sunflower Mktg., Dallas, 1982—; cons. CBI Labs., Aloe Labs. of Tex., 1979—, Richard Simmons, 1983, March of Dimes, 1976; dir. mktg. Colibri Skin Care Coming Home, healing retreat ctr.; internat. spkr. on mktg. and bus., relationships, mental health and illness, bi-polar rsch., healing from rape to internat. prosecution; Reiki master. Featured in Acting Naturally (Eileen Sisk). Mem. DAR, M.K. Gandhi Inst. for Non-Violence. Avocations: horseback riding, water sports, singing, human and animal rights, environment protection.

BLACK, LAVONNE PATRICIA, special education educator; b. West Palm Beach, Fla., Sept. 28, 1924; d. Harvey Francis Paul and Elsie Marguerite (Theegarten) B. Diploma, Palm Beach Jr. Coll., 1945; BA in Edn., Fla. State Coll. for Women, 1947; MA in Edn., George Peabody Coll. Tchrs., 1964. Cert. tchr. elem. edn. reading, hearing disabilities, motor disabilities, Fla.; cert. tchr. social studies, elem. edn., Kans.; cert. elem. edn. spl. hard of hearing-orthopedic, Ky. Tchr. physically handicapped Bd. Pub. Instr., West Palm Beach, 1947-58; tchr. deaf and hard of hearing Royal Palm Sch., West Palm Beach, 1952-58; tchr. physically handicapped/learning disorders Bd. Pub. Instrn. Exceptional Child Ctr., Ft. Lauderdale, Fla., 1958-69; dir., tchr. Scenicland Sch., Chattanooga, 1969-70; occupational edn. tchr. John Currie Jr. High Sch., Jacksonville, Fla., 1970-71; substitute tchr. Iliff Pre-Sch., Denver, 1972, University Park Coop., Denver, 1973, Austin Presch., 1973; house mother Sigma Alpha Epsilon Fraternity, U. Denver, 1971—; organizer, mgr. Sigma Alpha Epsilon Summer Rental Program, 1976—. Inventor portable sound chart for Lang., reading, speech, 1964. Active Jr. Welfare League, Inc., Palm Beach and Ft. Lauderdale.; secret spl. messenger Morrison Field, West Palm Beach, World War II, summer 1942. Recipient Thomas G. Goodale award for disting. svc. U. Denver, 1991. Mem. Coun. Exceptional Children, PEO, Palm Beach Jr. Coll. Alumni Assn., Kappa Alpha Theta. Democrat. Methodist. Avocations: swimming, dancing, backgammon, walking, travel. Home and Office: Sigma Alpha Epsilon 2050 S Gaylord St Denver CO 80210-4306

BLACK, LISA, artist; b. Lansing, Mich., June 19, 1934; d. W. Eugene and Eugenia (Anikeeff) Hunter; m. Thomas Howard Black, June 6, 1959; children: Kelly Windsor, Leslie Cheney. Diploma, d'etudes de civilisation, Paris, 1955; BA, U. Mich., 1956. One-woman shows include Wildwood Studios, Lake Orion, Mich., Conn. Bank & Trust Co., New Canaan, Noroton Gallery, Darien, Conn., Gates Gallery, New Canaan, Easter Seal Rehab. Ctr., Stamford, Conn., Landmark Lobby Gallery, Stamford, Barnes & Noble Gallery, Darien, Town Hall Gallery, Fairbanks Shop Gallery; group shows include Terrain Gallery, N.Y.C., 1970, Stamford Mus., 1972, Williams Gallery, Darien, 1974, Greenwich Art Barn, Conn., 1976, New Haven Paint and Clay Ann. Juried Exhbn., Conn., 1983, Darien Sport Shop, Gallery Group, White Plains, N.Y., Landmark Tower, Stamford, Conn., Hospice of Branford, 1987, Eagle Tower, Stamford, 1987, Invited Artists of Westport Ctr., Bridgeport (Conn.) Hilton, 1988, Silvermine Guild, Art of N.E. 50th Juried Exhbn., 1999; represented in permanent collection Conn. Bank & Trust Co. Vol. tchr. art, performance art, drawing Arts in Action program in local schs. Recipient over 100 art show and art society awards including 1st prize Rowayton Arts Ctr., 1989, 91, 93, Fred Kraus award for painting Stamford Mus., 1992, 1st prize Rowayton Arts Ctr., 1996, Best in Show Rowayton Arts Ctr., 1997, 1st prize watercolors Greenwich Art Soc., 1999, Old Greenwich Art Soc., 1999, 2000, many others. Mem. Greenwich Art Soc., Old Greenwich Art Soc., Vicious Cir., Conn. Graphic Arts Ctr., Rowayton Arts Ctr., New Canaan soc. for Arts, Darien Art Ctr., New Haven Paint and Clay Club. Republican. Avocations: handicrafts, family, antique shows. Home: 17 Brushy Hill Rd Darien CT 06820-6008

BLACK, MARK D., neuroscientist; b. Withernsea, Yorkshire, U.K., Jan. 4, 1968; came to U.S., 1996; s. David Joseph and Hilary Black. BSc, Liverpool (Eng.) U., 1989; PhD, Manchester (Eng.) U., 1992. Postdoctoral fellow Cambridge (Eng.) U., 1992-95, Marion Merril Dow, Strasbourg, France, 1995-96; assoc. scientist Hoechst Marion Roussel, Bridgewater, N.J., 1999—. Mem. Brit. Pharmacology Soc., Soc. Neurosci. E-mail: mark.black@h-mrag.com. Office: Hoechst Marion Roussel Rt 202 206 Invivo Cns Bridgewater NJ 08807

BLACK, MICHAEL DARRYL, pediatric cardiac surgeon, educator; b. Hamilton, Ont., Can., June 25, 1960; s. Emil and Elenor Black; m. Lisa Heather Goodman, Oct. 25, 1989; children: Daniel Corey, Jacqueline Page, Madelene Eve. BSc, U. Western Ont., 1982; MD, U. Toronto, 1986. Fellow U. Toronto-Hosp. for Sick Children, 1993-94; instr. surgery U. Calif., San Francisco, 1994-95; asst. prof. surgery, mem. staff divsn. cardiovasc. surgery U. Toronto, 1995-98; chief pediat. cardiovasc. surgery Stanford U., Stanford, Calif., 1999—, assoc. prof. surgery, 1999—; clin. assoc. prof. surgery U. Calif., San Francisco, 1999—; pres. Black Med. Innovations Inc. Contbr. articles on congenital heart disease in newborn to med. jours., chpts. to books. Recipient humanitarian award Hosp. for Sick Children; McClaughlin fellow U. Toronto; various grants, Can. Fellow Royal Coll. Surgeons Can. Achievements include pioneering minimally invasive surgical techniques for children, utilization of robotic assistance, research in prevention of cerebral deficits (neurological morbidity) following open heart surgery. Avocations: cycling, running. E-mail: michael.black@stanford.edu. Office: Stanford U Falk Cardivasc Rsch Ctr Stanford CA 94305-5407

BLACK, PAGE MORTON, civic worker; b. Chgo.; d. Alexander and Rose Morton; m. William Black, Mar. 27, 1962. Student, Chgo. Mus. Coll. Singer, pianist, Pierre Hotel, N.Y.C., Warwick Hotel, One Fifth Ave. Sherry Netherland Hotel; singer radio show and comml. Chock Full o' Nuts Corp.; rec. artist Atlantic Records, Den Records; co-founder Page and William Black Post-Grad. Sch. Medicine, Mt. Sinai Med. Sch., 1965—; chmn., mem. exec. bd. Parkinsons' Disease Found., Columbia U. Med. Ctr. (mem. adv. coun.); mem. nat. vis. coun. Columbia U. Health Scis. Faculties; hon. chmn. Chock Full O' Nuts Corp., 1983-90; active Columbia Presbyterian Health Scis. Adv. Coun.; founding mem. ASPCA. Recipient Am. award Parkinsons' Disease Found., 1987, Police Athletic League, 1992, Mahattan Mag. award, 1992, Lifetime Achievement award Parkinson's Disease Found., 1997, Dean's award for Disting. Svc., Columbia U. Coll. Physicians & Surgeons, 1998. Home: Premium Pt New Rochelle NY 10801

BLACK, PAUL JOSEPH, retired science educator; b. La Cumbre, Pavas, Colombia, Sept. 10, 1930; arrived in Eng., 1933; s. Walter and Susie (Burns) B.; m. Mary Elaine Weston, Aug. 3, 1957; children: Simon, John, Jeremy, Michael, Mary-Jane. BSc, U. Manchester, Eng., 1950; PhD, U. Cambridge, Eng., 1954; Doctorate (hon.), U. Surrey, Eng., 1991. Royal Soc. studentship U. Cambridge, 1953-56; lectr. in physics U. Birmingham, Eng., 1956-70; reader in physics U. Birmingham, 1970-74, prof. physics, 1974-76; prof. sci. edn. Chelsea Coll., London, 1976-85; prof. sci. edn. King's Coll., London, 1985-95, prof. emeritus, 1995—; Chair U.K. Govt. Task Group on Assessment and Testing, 1987-88; cons. Orgn. Econ. Coop. and Devel., Paris Ednl. R&D, 1988-96; vis. prof. edn. Stanford U., Palo Alto, Calif., 1998—. Joint project dir.: (with J. Ogborn) Nuffield Advanced Physics Course, 1973, (with W. Harlen) Nuffield Primary Science, 1993; author, co-editor: (with A. Lucas) Children's Informal Ideas in Science, 1993, (with J.M. Atkin) Changing the Subject, 1996, Testing: Friend or Foe, 1998, (with D. Wiliam) Inside the Black Box, 1998. Named Knight of St. Gregory, Roman Cath. Ch., 1974, Officer of the Order of Brit. Empire, 1983, Fellow of King's Coll., London, 1989; recipient Bragg medal U.K. Inst. Physics, 1973, medal of Internat. Commn. on Physics Edn., 2000. Fellow Inst. Physics U.K.; mem. Internat. Commn. on Physics Edn. (chair 1994-99), Internat. Union Pure and Applied Physics (v.p. 1997-99), Grubb Inst. Behavioral Studies (coun. mem. 1982, hon. v.p. 1997), U.S. Nat. Acad. Scis. (bd. testing and assessment 1996-99), Assn. for Sci. Edn. (hon. life, hon. pres. 1986), 1+1 Marriage Rsch. (chair of trustees 1997—). Roman Catholic. Office: Kings Coll London Sch Edn, 150 Stamford St, London SE1 8WA, England

BLACK, PHILIPPA, science academy executive. Pres. Royal Soc. New Zealand, Wellington. Office: Royal Society Chief Exec, PO Box 598, Wellington New Zealand*

BLACK, RAYMOND ALEXANDER, financial director; b. Wirral, Cheshire, Eng., Jan. 30, 1956; s. Albert Alexander and Edith Elizabeth (Turner) B.; m. Anne Theresa Duffy, July 6, 1985; children: Joseph, William. BSc with honors, U. Hertfordshire, Eng., 1984; MBA, Durham, Eng., 1993. Factory mgr. Evisons Veneers Ltd., Winnal, Eng., 1976-80; fin. dir. Chase Pers. Plc, London, 1984-93, Clark Scott-Harden, Yorkshire, Eng., 1994—. Mem. Assn. MBAs, Durham U. Alumni. Avocations: mountaineering, travel, natural history, classic and contemporary literature. Office: Clark Scott-Harden, 11 Osborne Terr Tesmond, Newcastle Upon Tyne NE1 2NE, England

BLACK, RILLA ALMA, violinist, library assistant, poet; b. Quincy, Ill., June 23, 1920; d. Frank and Georgia Eleanor (Stewart) Darnell; m. Albert Black, Nov. 9, 1944 (dec. Aug. 1998); children: Diana, Linda, Robert. BA, Culver-Stockton Coll., Canton, Mo.; MA in English, Chapman Coll., Orange, Calif., 1991; student, Eastman Sch. Music, Rochester, N.Y., 1943-44. Cert. tchr., Ill. Tchr. Bowen (Ill.) H.S., 1942-43; libr. asst. Orange County Pub. Libr., Santa Ana, Calif., 1977-91. Contbr. poetry to anthologies. Mem. Chapman Symphony, Orange, Calif., concertmaster, 1958. Mem. Internat. Soc. Poets, Am. Collegiate Poets Anthology. Achievements include being listed in Nat. Libr. Poetry Selection: Outstanding Poets of 1998.

BLACK, WILLIAM REA, lawyer; b. N.Y.C., Nov. 4, 1952; s. Thomas Howard and Dorothy Chambers (Dailey) B.; m. Kathleen Jane Owen, June 24, 1978; children: William Ryan, Jonathan Wesley. BSBA, U. Denver, 1978, MBA, 1981; JD, Western State U., Fullerton, Calif., 1987. Bar: Calif., U.S. Ct. Appeals (fed. cir.), U.S. Dist. Ct.; lic. real estate broker. Bus. mgr. Deere & Co., Moline, Ill., 1979-85; dir. Mgmt. Resource Svcs. Co., Chgo., 1985-86; sr. v.p. Geneva Corp., Irvine, Calif., 1986-91; pvt. practice Newport Beach, Calif., 1991-92; gen. counsel Sunclipse, Inc., 1992-98; spl. counsel Amcor, Ltd., 1992-98; dir. gen. Amcor de Mex., S.A. de C.V., 1993-98; secretario KHL de Mex. S.A. de C.V., 1995-98; CEO Kuroi Kiku Corp., Kuroi Ryu Corp., First Reconnaissance Co., 1997—; v.p., gen. cousnel Thomson-CSF Sextant, 1999—; bd. dirs. Am. Employers Def., Inc., United Studios Self Def., Inc. Mng. editor Western State U. Law Rev., Fullerton, 1984-87. Instr. Pai Lum Kung Fu Karate, Hartford, Conn., 1970-75, U.S. Judo Assn., Denver, 1975-80, United Studios Kenpo, L.A., 1995—. Recipient Am. Jurisprudence award Bancroft-Whitney Co., 1984, 85, 86; Pres.'s scholar full acad. merit scholarship, 1983. Mem. ABA, Am. Soc. Appraisers, Inst. Bus. Appraisers, Assn. Productivity Specialists, Am. Employment Law Coun., Profls. in Human Resources Assn., Am. Mgmt. Assn., Orange County Bar Assn., L.A. County Bar Assn., Mu Kappa Tau. Avocations: karate (2d degree black belt), skiing, scuba, golf. Office: 17481 Red Hill Ave Irvine CA 92614-5630

BLACKBOURN, DAVID GORDON, history educator; b. Spilsby, Eng., Nov. 1, 1949; s. Harry and Pamela Jean (Youngman) B.; m. Deborah Frances Langton; 2 children; BA with honors, Cambridge U., Eng., 1970, PhD, 1976. Rsch. fellow Jesus Coll., Cambridge, 1973-76, Inst. European History, Mainz, Fed. Republic Germany, 1974-75; lectr. Queen Mary Coll., U. London, 1976-79, Birkbeck Coll., U. London, 1979-85; reader in history Birkbeck Coll., 1985-89, prof. history, 1989-92; prof. history Harvard U., Cambridge, Mass., 1992-97, Coolidge prof., 1997—; vis. Kratter prof. history Stanford (Calif.) U., 1989-90; guest lectr. U.S., Eng., Italy, Yugoslavia, Fed. Republic Germany, 1976—, ann. lect. German Hist. Inst., London, 1998; mem. acad. adv. bd. Inst. for European History, Mainz, 1995—; hist. cons. Channel 4 TV (U.K.), History Channel (U.S.). Author: Class, Religion and Local Politics in Wilhelmine Germany, 1980, (with G. Eley) The Peculiarities of German History, 1984, Populists and Patricians: Essays in Modern German History, 1987, (edited with R.J. Evans) The German Bourgeoisie, 1991, Marpingen: Apparitions of the Virgin Mary in Bismarckian Germany, 1993 (Am. Hist. Assn. prize for best book), The Long Nineteenth Century: A History of Germany, 1780-1918, 1998. Numerous appearances on Brit. Broadcasting System, 1977—. Contbr. articles to profl. jours. Gov. Goodrich Sch., London, 1983-86. Alexander von Humboldt Found. fellow, 1984-85; German Acad. Exchange grantee, 1977, John Simon Guggenheim Meml. Found. fellow, 1994-95. Fellow Royal Hist. Soc.; mem. German History Soc. (com. 1981-85, sec. 1979-81), German Hist. Inst. (London) (com. 1983-92), Inst. for European History (Mainz, Germany). Avocations: writing, reading, jazz, politics, classical music.

BLACKBURN, JOHN GILMER, lawyer; b. Opelika, Ala., Oct. 21, 1927; s. John A. and Vera (Isley) B.; m. Phyllis Blackburn, May 12, 1951; children: Gay Blackburn Maloney, Allison Blackburn Akins, Lisa Blackburn Ayerst. BS in Acctg., Auburn U., 1950; JD, U. Ala., 1954; LLM in Taxation, NYU, 1956. Bar: Ala. 1954. Sole practice Decatur, Ala., 1955-79; ptnr. Blackburn, Maloney & Schuppert, P.C., Decatur, 1979—; lectr. various tax seminars. Mayor, City of Decatur, 1962-68; mem. exec. com. Ala. Dems.; chmn. Auburn U. Found.; chmn. Ala. Rev. Com. on Higher Edn. With U.S. Army, 1946-47, to 1st lt., 1951-52, ETO. Mem. ABA (com. on life ins., cos. sect. taxation), Ala. Bar Assn. (chmn. tax sect.). Methodist. Lodge: Kiwanis. Office: PO Box 1469 Decatur AL 35602-1469

BLACKBURN, JOHN LESLIE, small business owner; b. Malta Bend, Mo., Dec. 21, 1924; s. Clarence Oliver and Vivian (Mitchener) B.; m. Gloria Bullington, June 10, 1950; 1 child, Holly. BS, Mo. Valley Coll., 1950; MEd, U. Colo., 1952; PhD, Fla. State U., 1969. Counselor to men Fla. State U., Tallahassee, 1952-56; from asst. dean of men to dean student devel. U. Ala., Tuscaloosa, 1956-69, v.p. devel., 1978-90; vice chancellor student affairs U. Denver, 1969-74, vice chancellor univ. resources, 1974-78; pres. Blackburn Ednl. Techs., Tuscaloosa, 1990—; gen. sec. Am. Assn. of U. Administrators, Tuscaloosa, Ala., 1993-97; interim dir. Challenge 21, Tuscaloosa, 1998-99; mem. Model City Mayor's Adv., Denver, 1970-73, Nat. Adv. Coun. on Extension and Continuing Edn., Washington, 1976-78; cons. to sec. HEW, Washington, 1976; mem. Ala. Commn. on Aging; mem. Gov.'s Task Force on Devel. of Economically Distress Counties. Contbr.: Pieces of Eight, 1978. Sgt. AUS, 1943-46, CBI. The Blackburn Inst. was created in his honor by U. Ala., 1995, John L. Blackburn Exemplary award in his honor by AAUA, 1991. Mem. AAUA (pres. 1977-79), Am. Coun. on Edn. (acad. affairs commn. 1970-73), Nat. Assn. Student Pers. Adminstrn. (pres. 1973-74), Nat. Inst. Rsch. and Devel. (founder 1974). Home: 1601 St Andrews Dr Tuscaloosa AL 35406-2058 Office: Blackburn Ednl Techs PO Box 2615 Tuscaloosa AL 35403-2615

BLACKHAM, ANN ROSEMARY (MRS. J. W. BLACKHAM), realtor; b. N.Y.C., June 16, 1927; d. Frederick Alfred and Letitia L. (Stolfe) DeCain; m. James W. Blackham Jr., Aug. 18, 1951; children: Ann C., James W. III. AB, St. Mary of the Springs Coll.(now Ohio Dominican Coll.), 1949; postgrad., Ohio State U., 1950. Mgr. br. store Filene & Sons, Winchester, 1950-52; broker Porter Co. Real Estate, Winchester, 1961-66; sales mgr. James T. Trefrey, Inc., Winchester, 1966-68; pres., founder Ann Blackham & Co. Inc. Realtors, Winchester, 1968—; mem. bd. econ. advisors to Gov., 1969-74; participant White House Conf. on Internat. Cooperation, 1965; mem. Presdl. Task Force on Women's Rights and Responsibilities, 1969; mem. exec. coun. Mass. Civil Def., 1965-69; chmn. Gov.'s Commn. on Status of Women, 1971-75; regional dir. Interstate Assn. Commn. on Status of Women, 1971-74; mem. Gov. Task Force on Mass. Economy, 1972; mem. Gov.'s Jud. Selection Com., 1972, Mass. Emergency Fin. Bd., 1974-75; mem. bd. registration Real Estate Brokers and Salesman Commonwealth of Mass., 1991-94, chmn. 1994—. Bd. visitors Ohio Dominican Coll., 1995—, nat. fund raising chair, 1998-99; corporator, trustee Charlestown Savs. Bank, 1974-84; corporator Winchester Hosp., 1983—; dir., chair fund raising emergency room, Winchester Hosp. Found., 1998—; mem. Winchester 350th Anniversary Commn.; mem. design rev. commn. Town of Winchester; bd. dirs. Phoenix Found., Bay State Health Care, Mass. Taxpayers Found., Speech and Hearing Found., Baystate Health Mgmt., Realty Guild Inc., v.p. 1995-96, pres. 1997, 98, bd. dirs. 1996, 97, 98, 99; mem. regional selection panel White House Fellows, 1973-74; mem. com. on women in svc. U.S. Dept. Def., 1977-80; 2d v.p. Doric Dames, 1971-74, bd. dirs. 1974—; dep. chmn. Mass. Rep. State Com., 1965-66, 96—; sec. Mass. Rep. State Conv., 1970, del., 1960, 62, 64, 66, 70, 72, 74, 78, 90, 98; state vice chmn. Mass. Rep. Fin. Com., 1970; alt. del.-at-large Rep. Nat. Conv., 1968, 72, del., 1984; Rep. State Committeewoman, 1996—; pres. Mass. Fedn. Rep. Women, 1964-69; v.p. Nat. Fedn. Rep. Women, 1965-79; pres. Scholarship Found., 1976-78, Mass. Fedn. Women's Clubs; dir.; alumnae liaison The Beaumont Sch. for Girls. Recipient Pub. Svc. award Commonwealth of Mass., 1978, Merit award Rep. Party, 1969, Pub. Affairs award Mass. Fedn. Women's Clubs, 1975; named Civic Leader of Yr. Mass. Broadcasters, 1962, Banker and Tradesman Leader Making a Difference, 1999; recipient Bus. Owner of Yr. award New England Women Bus. Owners, 1995, Disting. Alumnae award Ohio Dominican Coll., 1999. Mem. Greater Boston Real Estate Bd. (hon., bd. dirs.), Eastern Middlesex Bd. Realtors (life mem. multi-million dollar club), Mass. Assn. Realtors (bd. dirs.), Nat. Assn. Realtors (women's coun.), Brokers Inst. (cert.), Coun. Realtors (cert., pres. 1983-84), Winchester C. of C. (bd. dirs.), Greater Boston C. of C., Nat. Assn. Women Bus. Owners, ENKA Soc., Rotary Internat., Tequesta Fla. Country Club, Capitol Hill Club, Ponte Vedra Club, Winchester Boat Club, Winchester Country Club, Wychmere Harbor Club, Womens City Club, Boston Coll. Club, Winton Club (sec., bd. dirs.), Hyannis Yacht Club, Boston Coll. Club. Home: 60 Swan Rd Winchester MA 01890-3747 Office: Ann Blackham & Co Inc 9 Thompson St Winchester MA 01890-2903

BLACKIE, PETER ANTONY, international administrator; b. London, Apr. 7, 1943; s. Lawrence and Simone (Beauchemin) B.; m. Jennifer McNaughton, Jan. 25, 1944 (div. 1980); children: Robert Alexander; m. Martine Rogival. Diploma, Sorbonne, Paris, 1962. Chartered acct. (FCA), 1967. Audit clk. Deloitte & Co., London, 1962-68; adminstr. Commn. European Communities, Brussels, 1976-83; prin. adminstr. Commn. European Communities, Brussels, 1983-92; advisor Commn. European Communities, Brussels, 1992—; alternate dir. European Bank for Reconstrn. and Devel., London, 1991—. Lt. Royal Arty, 1969-75. Avocations: running, opera. Office: European Commn, 200 Wetstraat, 1049 Brussels Belgium

BLACKIE, SPENCER DAVID, physical therapist, administrator; b. Endicott, N.Y., Sept. 27, 1946; s. Norman and June (Spencer) B.; m. Bonnie Jean Randall Moulton, June 11, 1967 (div. Apr. 1985); children: Rhonda, Randy, Brenda; m. Sharon Joan Clingman, May 10, 1986; children: Kristen, Sean, Alex. BS, Loma Linda U., 1968; MA, U. So. Calif., 1973; MS, Boston U., 1980. Cert. in manual therapy, clin. specialist in orthop. phys. therapy. Clin. dir. Loma Linda (Calif.) U. Med. Ctr., 1972-74; dir. rehab. svcs. New Eng. Meml. Hosp., Stoneham, Mass., 1974-84, Mt. Carmel Hosp., Colville, Wash., 1984-92, Regina Med. Ctr., Hastings, Minn., 1992—. Mem. Pool Com., Hastings, 1994; chmn. Parks and Recreation Bd., Colville, 1991-92. Capt. U.S. Army, 1969-71. Cmty. Fitness grantee Perrier Mineral Waters, Stoneham, 1978; decorated U.S. Army commendation medal. Mem. Am. Phys. Therapy Assn., Am. Occupl. Therapy Assn., Am. Acad. Orthop. Manual Phys. Therapy, Am. Soc. Hand Therapists, Minn. and Wis. Occupl. Therapy Assn., Rotary. Seventh-Day Adventist. Avocations: bicycling, classical guitar, karate, hiking/backpacking. Office: Regina Med Ctr 1175 Nininger Rd Hastings MN 55033-1056

BLACK-KEEFER, SHARON KAY, telecommunications executive; b. Denver, Jan. 23, 1949; d. Benoni Franklin and Loretta Marie (Meals) Black; m. Stephen Malone Keefer, Aug. 3, 1974; children: Sean M., Craig L., Elisabeth A. Student, U. Costa Rica, 1969; BA in Internat. Affairs magna cum laude, U. Colo., 1971, MS in Telecommunications, 1972. Rsch. positions U. Colo., Boulder, 1968-71; policy analyst telecommunications Office Telecommunications U.S. Dept. Commerce, Boulder, Colo., 1971-76; sr. systems analyst Norwest Info. Services Inc., Mpls., 1976-84, cons. data ops., 1984-85; mgr. voice communications Northwestern Nat. Life Ins. Co., Mpls., 1985-88; v.p. telecommunications svcs. COREMAR/Northwestern Nat. Life Ins., Mpls., 1989; sr. cons. Hatfield Assocs., Boulder, Colo., 1989-91; pres. Telecom Mgmt. Internat., Richfield, Minn., 1991—; adj. faculty mem. U. Denver Grad. Sch., Pace U., U. Minn. Sch. Mgmt., St. Mary's Coll. Grad. Ctr., and telecommunications adv. bd., mem. adv. bd. U. Colo. Telecommunications Program. Chairperson Community Action Com., Stillwater, Minn., 1984-86; mem. communications adv. com. Met. Coun. Twin Cities, St. Paul, 1977-78; pack chairperson Cub Scouts Am., Stillwater, 1987-89; elder 1st Presbyn. Ch., Stillwater, 1984-86. Mem. Internat. Communications Assn. (academic devel. com.), Nat. Rolm Users Group (chair Maintenance com. 1985-88), Minn. Telecommunications Assn. Avocations: skiing, sailing, hiking, genealogy, art history. Office: Telecom Mgmt Internat 2439 Norwood Ave Boulder CO 80304-1335

BLACKMAN, SIR COURTNEY NEWLANDS, diplomat; b. 1933; m. Gloria Mckoy, 1958; 3 children. BA, U. West Indies, Barbados; MBA, Inter-American U, P.R.; PhD, Columbia U. Jr. administr. ALCAN, Jamaica, 1956-58; secondary sch. tchr. Ghana, Barbados, Jamaica, 1958-63; economist Irving Trust Co., N.Y.C., 1968-71; assoc. prof. mgmt. Hofstra U., Long Island, N.Y., 1971-72; gov. Ctrl. Bank Barbados, 1972-87; amb. of Barbados to U.S.A. Govt. of Barbados, Washington, 1995—; internat. bus. con. 1987-94. Author: The Practice of Persuasion, 1982, Central Banking in Theory and Practice: A Small State Perspective, 1998. Office: Embassy of Barbados 2144 Wyoming Ave NW Washington DC 20008-3928

BLACKMAN, DAVID LEE, research scientist; b. Chgo., Jan. 4, 1948; s. Sol and Carol Edith (Rothman) B. BS in Maths., U. Ariz., 1973; student, Laney Coll., Oakland, Calif., 1977-79; MS in Chemistry, San Francisco State U., 1983. Lic. technician. Rsch. cons. Detox Assn., San Bernadino, Calif., 1973-74; peer counselor Laney Coll., 1977-79; lectr. San Francisco State U., 1979-83; staff rsch. assoc. U. Calif., Berkeley, 1984—; speaker PEW Found., N.Y., 1989; hon. prof. Albert Schweitzer Internat. U.; presenter papers in field. Author: Flourescent Spectroscopy..., 1983; contbr. articles to profl. jours. Mem. adv. bd. P.P. Land Conservancy, Berkeley, 1984-86; bd. dirs. Cmty. Svcs. United, Berkeley, 1985-86; vol. No. Alameda ARES/RACES, Berkeley, 1992-95. NSF grantee, 1989, 91. Mem. AAAS, Am. Assn. Physics Tchrs., Am. Radio Relay League, Co-op. Am., N.Y. Acad. Sci., Golden Gate Nat. Park Assn., Sierra Club, Mensa. Democrat. Jewish. Avocations: photography, computers, water coloring, swimming, non-linear dynamics. Home: 307 2nd St Phoenix OR 97535-7733

BLACKMAN, DEANE ROBERT, engineering educator, consultant; b. Melbourne, Australia, Nov. 3, 1935; s. Cecil Robert and Clara Louise (Deane) B.; m. Janice Veronica Callander, Nov. 12, 1959; children: Leon Deane, Guy Arthur, Lisa Veronica. B of Mech. Engring. with honors, U. Melbourne, 1957, M of Engring. Sci., 1959; PhD, Southampton U., Eng., 1964. Asst. lectr. U. Melbourne, 1959-60; rsch. asst. U. Southampton, 1960-64; sr. lectr. Monash U., 1964-90; vis. scientist USMS Eltanin, Antarctica, 1968, Royal Australian Navy Rsch., Sydney, Australia, 1972; resident Brit. Sch., Rome, 1976; vis. scientist Australian Numerical Meterology Rsch. Ctr., 1982; reader Monash U., Australia, 1990-94, dept. chmn., 1994-99; founder Demesne Computing, Australia, 1987—. Author: SI Units in Engineering, 1969, A Concordance to Tacitus, 1986. Recipient U.S. Antarctic medal NSF, 1976. Avocations: music, Olympic equestrian. Home: Sonoma 1210 Wellington Rd E, Narre Warren East 3804, Australia Office: Monash Univ, Dept Mech Engring, Clayton 3168, Australia

BLACKMON, RONALD H., biologist, science educator; b. Elizabeth City, N.C., Sept. 26, 1953; s. Henry L. and Lillian Rayford Blackmon. BS, Del.

State U., 1980; MS, Howard U., 1985, PhD, 1988. Postdoctoral rsch. assoc. USDA-Insect Attractants, Behavior/Basic Biology Rsch. Lab., Gainesville, Fla., 1988-89; asst. prof. Elizabeth City State U., 1989-94, assoc. prof., 1994-96, prof., 1996—, chmn., 1995—; mem. acad. ops. com. Program for Minority Advancement in Biomolecular Scis., Chapel Hill, N.C., 1991—; mem. Historically Minority Univs. program adv. bd. N.C. Biotech. Ctr., Research Triangle Park, N.C., 1997—. Mem. adv. bd. State Employees' Credit Union, Elizabeth City, 1999. Recipient Biotech. Leadership award N.C. Inst. for Minority Econ. Devel., Durham, N.C., 1993. Mem. AAAS, Soc. for In Vitro Biology, N.C. Acad. Sci., Sigma Xi. Avocations: reading science fiction, piano. E-mail: blackmrh@hotmail.com. Fax: 252-335-3697. Office: Elizabeth City State Univ ECSU Campus Box 970 Elizabeth City NC 27909

BLACKMORE, JAMES HERRALL, clergyman, educator, author; b. Warsaw, N.C., Feb. 15, 1916; s. Willie Richard and Martha Janie (Sansbury) B.; m. Ruth May Lillick, Jan. 26, 1945; children: Julia, John. BA cum laude, Wake Forest Coll., 1937; BD, Colgate Rochester Div. Sch., 1940; postgrad., Duke U., 1940-41, U. Iowa, 1949; PhD, U. Edinburgh, 1951; postgrad., Princeton U. Inst. Theology, 1975. Ordained to ministry Bapt. Ch., 1940. Dir. religious edn. Parsells Ave. Bapt. ch., Rochester, N.Y., 1938-40; pastor King (N.C.) Bapt. Ch., 1941-43, Masonboro Bapt. ch., Wilmington, N.C., 1947-49, First Bapt. Ch., Spring Hope, N.C., 1951-61; dir. pub. rels. Southeastern Bapt. Theol. Sem., Wake Forest, N.C., 1963-69, dir. publs., spl. instr., 1969-83, prof. assoc. div. studies, 1983-84; editor Outlook, 1963-84; vis. prof. Southeastern Bapt. Theol. Sem., 1985-96; interim minister Trinity Bapt. Ch., Bitburg-Metterich, West Germany, 1984; study tour with Dr. B. Elmo Scoggin, Israel, 1976; active archaeological excavations, Tel-Areor, Tel-Dan, Israel, 1981. Author: The Cullom Lantern, A Biography of W.R. Cullom, 1963, A Preacher's Temptations, 1966, A reticule, A Collection of Short Stories and Essays, 1969, Sermons at Warsaw, 1975, Conversations About Jesus, 1977, The Wayfarer, 1977, A Flight of Sparrows, 1978, Sermons at Masonboro, 1978, Biblical Orientation, 1981, Sermons at Spring Hope, 1983, Second Acts, 1984, The A.C. Reid Legacy, 1988, Reflections on the Temptations of Christ, 1992, others; contbr. articles to religious and learned jours., also to encys. Sec. bd. dirs. Bibl. Recorder, 1959-62; chmn. hist. com. Bapt. State Con., N.C. 1970-72. Served to maj. chaplain AUS, 1943-46. Scholarship in his honor est. Southeastern Bapt. Theol. Sem., 1984; named hon. citizen King, N.C., 1993. Mem. Bapt. Pub. Rels. Assn., Lions, Kappa Delta Alpha, Chi Eta Tau. Home: 209 S Wingate St Wake Forest NC 27587-2531

BLACKMORE, STEPHEN, garden director, botanist; b. Store-On-Trent, Eng., July 30, 1952; s. Edwin Arthur and Josephine (Henwood) B.; m. Patricia Jane Melrose Hawley, July 7, 1973; children: Elizabeth Jane, Roger Arthur. Regius keeper Royal Botanic Garden, Edinburgh; vis. prof. botany U. Reading, Eng.; vis. prof. plant scis. U. Glasgow. Fellow Linnean Soc. (Trail-Crisp medal 1989, Bicentennary medal 1992); mem. The Systematics Assn. (pres. 1994-97), U.K. Systematics Forum (chmn. 1992-99). Avocations: blues guitar, photography, hill walking. Office: Royal Botanic Garden, 20 A Inverleith Row, Edinburgh EK3 5LR, Scotland

BLACKNEY, ARTHUR BRUCE, Middle East defense and aviation consultant; b. London, Nov. 29, 1934; s. Roy Belsham and Winifred Emma (Treble) B.; m. Valerie Florence Laws, Aug. 20, 1960; children: Karen Jane, Sarah Louise. Postgrad. Cert. Advanced Study Engrng., Cambridge (U.K.) U., 1968; MBA with distinction, Westminster U., London, 1985, MA, 1988. European engr.; chartered engr. Commd. Royal Air Force, 1961-85, advanced through ranks to group capt., 1980; chief engr. RAF Brize Norton, Oxford, Eng., 1977-79; head maint. analysis and computing establishment Royal Air Force Swanton Morley, Norfolk, Eng., 1979-82; asst. dir. Ministry of Def., London, 1982-85; dir. adminstrn. and pers. Forsyte Kerman, London, 1985-87; gen. mgr. Airwork Ltd., Muscat, Oman, 1988-92; bus. strategy advisor Airwork Ltd., Bournemouth, Eng., 1992-93; internat. bus. mgr. Short Bros. Plc, Bournemouth, Eng., 1993-94; Middle East defense and aviation cons. Blackney Consultancy Svcs. Ltd., Oxford, 1994—. Chmn. Brit. Scholarships for Oman, Muscat, 1991-92. Fellow Instn. of Mech. Engrs., Inst. of Mgmt., Royal Geog. Soc., Royal Soc. of Arts. Ch. of Eng. Avocations: local history, genealogy, mountaineering, family activities. Home: The Cottage, Swan Ln, Burford Oxfordshire OX18 4SH, England Office: Blackney Consultancy Svcs, The Tannery, Burford Oxfordshire OX18 4DQ, England

BLACKSTOCK, LEROY, lawyer; b. El Reno, Okla., Apr. 19, 1914; s. Herbert Austin and Ethel Mae (Gwin) B.; m. Virginia Lee Lowman, Dec. 29, 1939; children: Craig, Priscilla, Burch, Lore, Trena. Grad., Draughon's Bus. Inst., Tulsa, 1933; LL.B., U. Tulsa, 1938. Bar: Okla. 1938. With Phillips Petroleum Co., Tulsa, 1933-41; asst. credit mgr. Phillips Petroleum Co., 1939-41; practiced in Tulsa, 1941-74; counsel Blackstock & Montgomery; dir., gen. counsel Tulsa Homebuilders Assn., 1959-68; dir. Fourth Nat. Bank, Tulsa, 1969-76, Owasso 1st State Bank, Okla., 1967-70; pres. Skelly Stadium Corp., 1964-70; pres., trustee Gt. Western Investment Trust; mem. nat. adv. com. Practising Law Inst., 1969-70; pres. Jud. Reform Inc., 1966-70; lectr. law office mgmt., econs. U. Tulsa Coll. Law, 1970-75; chmn. Okla. Coun. on Jud. Complaints, 1974-84; pres. Tulsa Sci. Center, 1968-73; chmn. Tulsa U. Law Schs. Com., 1960-74, Citizens Adv. Com. County Commrs., 1963-66; pres., bd. dirs. Tulsa County Bar Found., 1962-66; patron Okla. Bar Found., trustee, 1966; mem. Gov.'s Acad. for State Govt., 1966-68; chmn. Okla. Supreme Ct. Bar Com., 1966. Author: Managing Partner Approach, Paper Dolls and Lawyers' Fees. Pres. Tulsa council Camp Fire Girls, 1971-72; pres. Tulsa Baptist Laymen's Corp., 1962-66; Bd. dirs. Tulsa County Mental Health Assn., 1963-70, Tulsa Psychiat. Found., 1964-67; pres. Tulsa County Legal Aid Soc., 1961-62, bd. dirs., 1958-66. Served with USNR, 1943-46. Recipient Disting. Citizens award Okla. Psychol. Assn., 1963; Disting. Alumni award U. Tulsa, 1969, 78; Disting. Alumni award Tulsa U. Coll. Law, 1978; Boss of Year award Tulsa County Assn. Legal Secs., 1978. Fellow Am. Coll. Probate Counsel; mem. ABA (ho. dels. 1965-67, mem. spl. com. on nat. coordination of disciplinary enforcement 1969-72, standing com. profl. discipline 1973-77), Okla. Bar Assn. (bd. govs. 1965-67, pres. 1966), Tulsa County Bar Assn. (pres. 1962, Outstanding Atty. award 1961), World Assn. Lawyers (charter mem.), Tulsa County Hist. Soc. (founding mem.), Photog. Soc. Am., Soc. Amateur Cinematographers, Phi Alpha Delta. Republican. Baptist (chmn. deacons 1962, chmn. bldg. com. 1951-53). Club: Petroleum (dir. 1974-77). Home: 7213 S Atlanta Tulsa OK 74136 Office: 320 S Boston Ave Ste 2000 Tulsa OK 74103-4709

BLACKWELL, BRUCE BEUFORD, lawyer; b. Gainesville, Fla., July 23, 1946; s. Benjamin B. and Doris Juanita (Heagy) B.; m. Julie McMillan, July 12, 1969; children: Blair Allison, Brooke McMillan. BA, Fla. State U., 1968, JD with honors, 1974. Bar: Fla. 1975, Ga. 1977, U.S. Supreme Ct. 1979, N.Y. 1980. Atty. So. Bell Tel. & Telegraph Co., Charlotte, N.C., 1975-76, Atlanta, 1976-78; antitrust atty. AT&T, Orlando and N.Y.C., 1978-80; atty. Sun Banks, Inc., Orlando, Fla., 1980; assoc. Peed & King, P.A., Orlando, 1981-84; shareholder King & Blackwell, P.A., Orlando, 1984-97, King, Blackwell & Downs, P.A., 1997—; counselor to First Ctrl. Fla. Inns of Ct., 1999—. Bd. dirs. Legal Aid Soc., Orlando, 1986-88; chmn. Winter Park (Fla.) Civil Svc. Bd., 1992-94; trustee Fla. State U. Found., 1985-86. Capt. USAF, 1968-72. Recipient award of excellence Legal Aid Soc., 1993, Judge J.C. Stone Pro Bono Disting. Svc. award, 1996, Annual Friend of FAWL award Fla. Assn. Women Lawyers, 1998. Mem. Fla. Bar (chmn. 9th cir. grievance com. 1985-87, chmn. mid-yr. meeting 1986, chmn. 9th cir. fee arbitration com. 1992-94, bd. govs. 1994-98, vice chair statewide disciplinary rev. com. 1995-96, co-chair 1997-98, vice-chmn. access to cts. com. 1995-97, chmn. annual meeting com. 1997, mem. supreme ct. spl. com. on pro bono svcs. 1996-97, mem. com. to determine need for a new DCA 1998, Fla. Bar Presidents' Pro Bono Svc. award 1997, chair spl. com. on solo/small firm practice 1997-98, mem. rules com. 1997-98, mem. edn. work force 1996-97), Fla. Bar Found. (bd. dirs. 1998-2001), Orange County Bar Assn. (exec. coun. 1983-86, pres. 1987-88, co-chair fair campaign practices com.), Fla. State U. Alumni Assn. (nat. pres. 1985-86), Orlando Touchdown Club (pres. 1996-97), Gold Key, Order of Omega, Omicron Delta Kappa. Democrat. Presbyterian. Avocation: study of China. Home: 1624 Roundelay Ln Winter Park FL 32789-4042 Office: PO Box 1631 Orlando FL 32802-1631

BLACKWELL, DALE BASCOM, physicist; b. Toledo, Ohio, Nov. 1, 1930; s. Clyde Bascom and Minnie Velma (Myers) B.; m. Elizabeth Nell Dawson (div.); children: Marka Blackwell Barbour, Victoria Blackwell Bush; m. Nina Marie Gover, Sept. 10, 1967. BS, Ind. U., 1956. Acoustic engr. Electro-Voice, Inc., Buchanan, Mich., 1956-58; R&D engr. Kawneer, Co., Niles, Mich., 1958-61; acoustic engr. Empire Scientific, Garden City, N.Y., 1961-63; sr. engr. Fairchild Camera and Instrument Corp., Hauppage, N.Y., 1963-73; chief engr. Comml. Radio Sound Corp., N.Y.C., 1973-78, Dumont Instrumentation, Inc., Hauppage, N.Y., 1978-84; R&D engr. Northrop-Grumman Corp. assignment, Star Wars Sys. Los Alamos Nat. Lab., 1984-91; owner Design Group Ltd., Brazil, Ind., 1991—; cons. Fairchild Graphics Corp., Plainview, N.Y., 1964-66, 3M Corp., Woodbury, Minn., 1995, Japan Electronics Mfg. Agy., Wilmette, Ill., 1996—, Protech Comms., Fort Pierce, Fla., 1993—. Contbr. articles to profl. jours. including Electrical Design News, Radio Electronics mag., Electronics Now mag. Bd. dirs. Brazil Pub. Libr. With USAF, 1951-52. Mem. Wabash Valley Amateur Radio Assn., Terre Haute, 1994—. Achievements include inventor Cockpit Voice Recorder (Black Box) used in all commercial airline planes, high speed, rotational magnetic detent with accuracy of 2 seconds of arc, transistorized version of the Color Film Analyzer that allows printing movie film with proper color balance, movie film projection system with an electronically driven mirror tracking film rather than a CAM-driven claw movement of film. Avocations: computer programming, photography, classical music. Office: Design Group Ltd 1123 E Northwood Dr Brazil IN 47834-1232

BLACKWELL, DONALD EUSTACE, retired astrophysicist, educator; b. London, May 27, 1921; s. John and Ethel (Bowe) B.; m. Nora Louise Carlton, Mar. 26, 1951; children: Gillian, Elizabeth, Christopher, Martin. BA, MA, U. Cambridge, 1943, PhD, 1949. Jr. sci. officer Royal Aircraft Establishment, Farnborough Hants, U.K., 1943-46; asst. dir. Solar Physics Observatory, U. Cambridge, Eng., 1949-60; Savilian prof. astronomy U. Oxford, Eng., 1960-88, fellow New Coll., 1960-88, emeritus fellow, 1988—, prof. emeritus, 1988—. Contbr. articles to profl. jours. Fellow Royal Astron. Soc. (pres. 1973-75). Office: Dept Physics, Keble Rd, Oxford OX1 3RH, England

BLACKWELL, JULIE ABBOTT, financial analyst; b. Birmingham, Ala., Sept. 29, 1973; d. Paul Leslie Abbott and Martha Jane Jernigan; m. James Boyd Blackwell, Jr., May 31, 1997; 1 child, James Boyd III. BS, Clemson U., 1994; M in Accountancy, U. S.C., 1996. CPA, S.C. Asst. acct. AgFirst Farm Credit Bank, Columbia, S.C., 1994-96; staff auditor Price Waterhouse, LLP, Columbia, 1996-97; internal auditor Policy Mgmt. Sys. Corp., Blythewood, S.C., 1997-2000; sr. financial analyst Mynd Corp., Blythewood, S.C., 2000—. Mem. AICPA, Inst. Internal Auditors, S.C. Assn. CPA. Republican. Baptist. Avocations: snow skiing, water skiing, reading, music. E-mail: julieblackwell@pmsc.com.

BLACKWELL, THOMAS GEORGE, military police officer; b. Buffalo, N.Y., Aug. 7, 1960; s. Roger Inman Blackwell and Geneva Evelyn (Averett) Short; married. BA in Political Sci., English, Canisius Coll., 1982; MA in Russian & East European Studies, Univ. Kansas, 1992; postgrad., Defense Lang. Inst., Garmisch, Germany, 1990, U.S. Army Russian Inst., Garmisch, Germany, 1992-93; postgrad. Armed Forces Staff Coll., Nat. Def. U., Norfolk, Va., 1999. Commd. 2d lt. U.S. Army, 1982, advanced through grades to maj., 1994; exec. officer 523d Military Police Co., Aberdeen Proving Ground, Md., 1982-83, platoon leader, 1983-85; company commander U.S. MP Co., Johnston Island, 1986-87; adj. 759th Military Police Battalion, Ft. Carson, Colo., 1987-88, deputy ops. officer, 1988-89; mission comdr. U.S. On-Site Inspection Agy., Washington, 1993-95; chief force protection section HQ U.S. Army Europe, Provost Marshal's Office, Mannheim, Germany, 1996-97; chief staff actions divsn. HQ U.S. Army Europe, Office of the Chief of Staff, Heidelberg, Germany, 1997-99; sr. Balkans analyst Jt. Analysis Ctr., U.S. European Command, RAF, Molesworth, Eng., 1999—. Decorated Defense Meritorious Svc. medal U.S. Dept. Defense, 1995, Armed Forces Svc. medal, 1996, Army Commendation medal Dept. Army, 1985, 87, 89, 90, NATO medal, 1996, Meritorious Svc. medal Dept. Army, 1999, Armed Forces Expeditionary medal Dept. Def., 1999, Joint Svc. Commendation medal U.S. Dept. Def., 2000; Army ROTC scholarship U.S. Army, 1979. Mem. Am. Legion, Profl. Ski Instrs. Am. Avocations: snow skiing, racketball, running, golf.

BLACKWOOD, JAMES HIRAM, retired pastor; b. Hartstown, Pa., Nov. 12, 1908; s. James Milligan and Margaret Alverde Williams B.; m. Jean McLean English; children: James English, Jeanne Williams Blackwood Rowe. AB, Westminster Coll., New Wilmington, Pa., 1930, DD (hon.), 1948; ThB, Pitts.-Xenia Theol., 1933, ThM, 1949. Pastor Rennerdale (Pa.) United Presbyn. Ch., 1933-35, Germantown United Presbyn. Ch., Phila., 1935-41; chaplain U.S. Army/Air Force, 1941-45; pastor Sunset Hills United Presbyn. Ch., Pitts., 1945-50, Graystone United Presbyn. Ch., Indiana, Pa., 1950-52; chaplain USAF, 1952-55; pastor Third United Presbyn. Ch., Pitts., 1955-58; assoc. pastor Shadyside Presbyn. Ch., Pitts., 1958-64, 1972-87; pastor Whitehall United Presbyn. Ch., Pitts., 1964-72; rep. to Alliance of Reformed Chs., United Presbyn. Ch., mem. numerous coms.; moderator Pitts. Presbytery; exec. com. Westminster Coll.; ordained by Monoghela Presbytery of the United Presbyn. Ch. N.Am., Rennerdale, Pa. Author: Eucharistic Terminology of Presbyterian Churches, Christian Marriage, Book of Daily Devotions and Occasional Prayers. Lt. col. U.S. Army Air Forces 1941-45, USAF, 1952-55. Mem. Masons. Republican.

BLADEN, EDWIN MARK, lawyer, judge; b. Detroit, Feb. 2, 1939; s. Philip and Ruth Sara (Millstein) B.; m. Paula Dee Maskin, Sept. 2, 1962; children: Philip, Sara, Jeffrey. BA, Wayne State U., 1962, JD, 1965. Asst. atty. gen. State of Mich., Lansing, 1965-86; mng. atty. Moran & Bladen, Lansing, 1987-93; pvt. practice, East Lansing, Mich., 1994-97; adminstrv. law judge USCG, 1999—. Author: Consumer Law of Michigan, 1978. Mem. Dem. Polit. Reform Comm., Mich., 1968. With US Army Security, 1957-60, Korea. Recipient Alexander Freeman scholarship Wayne State U., Detroit, 1962-65. Mem. State Bar Mich. (chmn. anti-trust sect., treas./sec. 1990-94), Nat. Assn. Fraud Units (pres. 1985-86). Office: 3448 Jackson Fed Bldg 915 2nd Ave Seattle WA 98174-1009

BLÁHA, MILAN, hematologist; b. Brno, Moravia, Czech Republic, June 24, 1938; s. Jindřich and Julie (Prudilova) B.; m. Jitka Kocourková, Feb. 10, 1962; children: Vladimir and Alena (twins). MD, Charles U., Prague, Czech Republic, 1962. Resident Mil. Hosp., Jaroměr, Czech Republic, 1962-64; asst. Cen. Mil. Hosp., Prague, 1965-76; chief dept. intensive hematolog. care Mil. Med. Acad., Hradec Kralove, Czech Republic, 1977-92; chief ctr. for hemapheresis Charles U., Hradec Kralove, Czech Republic, 1993-96; chief dept. std. care, hematol. dept. Faculty Hosp., Hradec Kralove, Czech Republic, 1997-99, chief ctr. for hemapheresis, 1999—; state examination com. internal medicine Charles U., 1998—; state examination com. South-Czech U., 1999—. Author: Treatment of Bone Marrow Aplasia, 1986 (Czech Literary Coun. award 1988); patentee in field. Col. Czech Army. Mem. Czech Hematol. Soc. (hon.), Czech Assn. for Blood Transfusion, European Group for Blood and Marrow Transplants. Avocations: literature, nature, sciences, history. Home: K sokolovne 438, 50341 Hradec Kralove Czech Republic Office: Faculty Hosp Haematol Dept, Sokolskastreet 408, 500 05 Hradec Kralove Czech Republic

BLAHA, VERLE DENNIS, golf course executive, electrical engineer; b. Detroit, Nov. 21, 1929; s. Maurice Lee and Clarice Annette Blaha; m. LuVeral Alma Blaha, Aug. 11, 1956; children: Bryan Jay, Lynn Renee Blaha Melchior. BS in Bus., U. Minn., 1966, MBA, 1969. Field supr. Aero. Radio Inc., Washington, 1952-56; mgr. quality assurance Gen. Mills Electronics, Mpls., 1956-63; sr. v.p. Litton Microwave Cooking, Mpls., 1963-82; v.p., gen. mgr. Holaday Industries Inc., Eden Prairie, Minn., 1982-86; pres. Celsion Corp., Columbia, Md., 1986-91, New Opportunities Ltd., North Oaks, Minn., 1991—, Thumper Pond Golf Course, Ottertail, Minn., 1998—; cons. New Opportunities Ltd., 1970—; lectr. on investments. With USN, 1947-50, PTO. Fellow Internat. Microwave Power (chmn. bd. dirs. 1976-82). Republican. Lutheran. Avocations: hunting, fishing, building wildlife habitat. E-mail: verle77@aol.com. Office: New Opportunities Ltd 14 Sunset Ln North Oaks MN 55127-6454

BLÁHA, VLADIMÍR, internist, researcher; b. Jaroměř, Náchod, Czech Republic, July 15, 1964; s. Milan and Jitka (Kocourková) B.; m. Jana Kristková, Sept. 27, 1997; 1 child, Richard. MD, Charles U., Hradec Králové, Czech Republic, 1988; PhD, Charles U., Prague, 1991. Asst. Charles U., Hradec Králové, 1988-90, asst. prof., 1990-92, asst. specialist, 1992—; assoc. prof. internal medicine Charles U., Prague, 1999; cons. nutrition team Faculty Hosp., Hradec Králové, 1993—; rsch. scholar SUNY, Syracuse, 1996. Contbr. articles to profl. jours. Recipient Dean's award Charles U., 1988, Cert. of Recognition, Czech Lit. Found., 1990. Mem. Czech Med. Soc., N.Y. Acad. Sci., European Atherosclerosis Soc., Internat. Atherosclerosis Soc. Avocations: sports, nature, music. Home: M Horákové 1738, 500 06 Hradec Králové Czech Republic Office: Fac Hosp Dept Metab Care, Sokolská 408, 500 05 Hradec Králové Czech Republic

BLAIH, SALAH MOUSTAFA, chemist, pharmacist, educator; b. Shabrakheet, Egypt, Oct. 24, 1950; came to U.S., 1994; s. Moustafa F. Blaih and Esmat A. El-Zemrany; m. Joan D. Paglialunga, Dec. 20, 1980; children: Yasmin, Hani. BS in Pharm. Scis., Alexandria (Egypt) U., 1971, MS in Pharm. Scis., 1976; PhD, Ohio State U., 1988. Vis. asst. prof. Denison U., Granville, Ohio, 1988; assoc. prof. Alexandria U., 1989—; asst. prof. Kent State U.—Trumbull, Warren, Ohio, 1997—; cons. Resource Internat., Columbus, 1986, Amriya Rhone-Poulenc Pharm. Ind., Alexandria, 1989-95, WHO Egypt, Alexandria, 1991; adj. asst. prof. Ohio State U., Columbus, 1988, 89; adj. assoc. prof. Waynesburg (Pa.) Coll., 1995, U. Wis., Eau Claire, 1997; reviewer Alexandria Jour. Pharm. Sci., 1989-95. Contbr. articles to profl. jours. Soccer coach Morgantown (W.Va.) Youth Soccer Assn., 1994-95, basketball coach, Menomonie, Wis., 1997; vol. Boy Scouts Am., Warren, Ohio, 1997—. Recipient medal of Rsch. Excellence, Alexandria U., 1995. Mem. AAAS, ACS (Penn-Ohio Border Section chair 2001), Pharm. Soc. Egypt, Ohio Acad. Sci., Rho Chi. Avocations: raquetball, soccer, tennis. Office: Kent State U Trumbull 4314 Mahoning Ave NW Warren OH 44483-1931

BLAIKIE, PIERS MACLEOD, social studies educator; b. Helensburgh, Scotland, Jan. 29, 1942; s. Francis William Lang and June Fleming (Watson) B.; m. Sally Laura Bigland, Dec. 7, 1968; children: Freya Mary, Calum Macleod. BA, U. Cambridge, Eng., 1963, MA, 1964, PhD, 1971. Lectr. Dept. Geography, Reading, U.K., 1967-72; lectr. Sch. Devel. Studies, U. EAst Anglia, Norwich, U.K., 1972-80, sr. lectr., 1980-85, reader, 1985-93, prof., 1993—. Author: Family Planning in India, 1975, Political Economy of Soil Erosion, 1985; co-author: Land Degradation and Society, 1987, Nepal in Crisis, 1980; mem. editl. bd. Econ. Geography, 1992—, Land Degradation and Rehab., 1989—, Devel. and Change. Recipient Edward Heath award Royal Geog. Soc., London, 1994. Mem. Inst. Brit. Geographers. Labour Party. Avocations: writing, sailing. Office: Univ of East Anglia, Sch Devel Studies, Norwich NR4 7TJ, England

BLAIN, ALEXANDER DAVID, merchant banker; b. Featherston, Wellington, New Zealand, Aug. 10, 1925; arrived in Australia, 1960; s. James Blain and Ethel Jane (Burt) B.; m. Marjorie Ena McLeay, Nov. 25, 1950; children: David McLeay, Martin McLeay. B Commerce, Victoria (New Zealand) U., 1948. CPA, Australia; Fellow Chartered Acct., New Zealand. Banking rep. Burroughs Corp. (now Unysis), Wellington, 1952-60; mgr. product promotion Burroughs Corp. (now Unysis), Sydney, Australia, 1960-64; mktg. dir., then mng. dir. Jantzen Australia Ltd., Sydney, 1964-72; fin. dir. EZ Industries Ltd., Melbourne, Australia, 1972-84; gen. mgr. mktg. and smelting North Broken Hill Ltd., Melbourne, 1984-87; mng. dir., dep. chmn. Credit Suisse Bullion Pacific Ltd., Melbourne, 1987-94; chmn., mng. dir. First Internat. Securities Ltd., Melbourne, 1980—, First Internat. Capital Group Mcht. Bankers, Melbourne, 1994—. Flying officer Royal New Zealand Air Force, 1943-45, PTO. Fellow Australian Inst. Co. Dirs. (found.), Chartered Accts. New Zealand; mem. Australian Soc. CPAs., Australian Club, Met. Golf Club, Royal Geelong Yacht Club. Avocations: yachting, golf. Home: 685 Orrong Rd, Toorak Vic 3142, Australia

BLAIN, PETER CHARLES, lawyer; b. Milw., Nov. 15, 1949; s. Emile Octave and Mary Catherine (Usalis) B.; m. Katherine Stauber, June 12, 1971; children: Thomas Peter, Timothy Charles, Katherine Elizabeth, Peter James. BS, Wis. State U., Stevens Point, 1971; JD, Georgetown U., 1978. Bar: Wis. 1978. Budget analyst VA, Washington, D.C., 1974-78; atty. Reinhart, Boerner, Van Deuren, Norris & Rieselbach S.C., Milw., 1978—; chmn. Wis. State Bar Insolvency Sect., 1995-97; lectr. U. Wis., Milw., 1984—. Contbr. articles to profl. jours. 2d Lt. U.S. Army, 1972-74. Listed Best Lawyers in Am., Woodward/White, 1987—. Mem. Milw. Bar Bankruptcy Sect. (prog. chmn. 1984-85, sect. chmn. 1986-87, co-chair bankruptcy sect. bench/bar com. 1998—). Democrat. Roman Catholic. Avocation: reading. Office: Reinhart Boerner Van Deuren Norris & Rieselbach SC 1000 N Water St Ste 1800 Milwaukee WI 53202-6650

BLAINEY, GEOFFREY NORMAN, historian, educator; b. Melbourne, Australia, Mar. 11, 1930; s. Samuel and Hilda (Lanyon) B.; m. Ann Heriot, Feb. 15, 1957; 1 child, Anna. Free-lance author Australia, 1951-61; reader econ. history U. Melbourne, 1962-68, prof. econ. history, 1968-76, Ernest Scott prof., 1977-88, prof. emeritus, 1988—; prof. Harvard U., 1982-83; chmn. Australia Coun., 1977-81, Govts. Australia-China Coun., 1979-84; chmn. Australian selection com. Harkness Fellowships, 1983-89; gov. Ian Potter Found., 1991—, coun. Australian War Meml., 1997—; pres. coun. Queen's Coll., U . Melbourne, 1971-89. Author The Tyranny of Distance, 1966, The Causes of War, 1973, A Land Half Won, 1979, A Short History of the World, 2000. Decorated officer Order of Australia; recipient Gold medal Australian Lit. Soc., 1965, Britannica award, N.Y., 1988. Fellow Australian Acad. Humanities, Australian Acad. Social Scis., Royal Hist. Inst. Office: 43 Hotham St, E Melbourne, Victoria 3002, Australia

BLAIR, ANTHONY CHARLES LYNTON (TONY BLAIR), prime minister of United Kingdom; b. Edinburgh, Scotland, May 6, 1953; s. Leo Charles and Hazel Blair; m. Cherie Booth, Sept. 23, 1954; children: Euan, Nicholas, Kathryn. BA, St. John's Coll., Oxford, 1975. Cert. barrister-at-law. Pvt. practice barrister London, 1976-83; M.P. Brit. Parliament, London, 1983—; prime min., first lord of treas. London, 1997—; front bench spokesman Labour Party, 1984-88, shadow cabinet mem., 1988-97. Mem. Ch. of England. Office: Prime Mins Office, 10 Downing St, London England SW1A 2AA*

BLAIR, BETSY, actress; b. Cliffside, N.J., Dec. 11, 1923; d. Willett Kidd and Frederica (Ammon) Boger; m. Gene Kelly, Sept. 20, 1941 (div. 1957); 1 child, Kerry Kelly Novick; m. Karel Reisz, Sept. 5, 1963; stepchildren: Matthew, Toby, Barney. BA in Speech Therapy, London U., 1979. Chorus dancer in Panama Hattie, 1940; N.Y.C. theatre appearances include The Beautiful People, 1941, The Glass Menagerie, 1944, My Fiddle Has Three Strings, 1945, Richard III, 1956, Face of a Hero, 1958; London appearances include The Trial of Mary Dugan, 1959, Spoon River Anthology, 1963, Danger Memory!, 1989; also Tchin-Tchin, Paris & Spoleto, 1962; appeared in films A Double Life, 1949, Snakepit, 1950, Mystery Street, 1951, Another Part of the Forest Kind Lady, 1951, Marty, 1955 (Acad. award nomination 1955), Il Grido, Calle Mejor, All Night Long, Senilita, Best Actress-British Film Insts., Best Actress Cannes Film Festival; TV appearances in U.S. and U.K. include Philco, Kraft, Am. Theatre, Thirtysomething, Death of a Salesman, Portrait of a Lady, Abe Lincoln, Blue Movie, others. Mem. Actors Equity (Am. & British), Screen Actors Guild, Am. Film Acad., Coll. Speech Therapy. Avocations: books, bridge, swimming.

BLAIR, KATHIE LYNN, social services worker; b. Oakland, Calif., Sept. 29, 1951; d. Robert Leon Webb and Patricia Jean (Taylor) Peterson; m. Terry Wayne Blair, Dec. 29, 1970 (div. 1972); 1 child, Anthony Wayne. Eligibility worker Dept. Social Services, San Jose, Calif., 1974-76; adult and family svcs. worker State of Oreg., Portland, 1977-90; guest speaker welfare advocacy groups, Portland, 1987. Translator: Diary of Fannie Burkhart, 1991; contbr. articles to profl. jours.; developer word game for children. Mem. ACLU, Nat. Geog. Soc., A Brotherhood Against Totalitarian Enactments, Oreg. State Pub. Interest Rsch. Group, Nat. Headache Found., Clan Chattan Assn., Portland Highland Games Assn., Nature Conservancy, Nat. Wildlife Fedn., Harley Owners Group, Ladies of Harley, Sierra Club. Democrat. Avocations: history, women's studies, writing, photography, motorcycles.

BLAIR, MICHAEL REED, science educator, consultant; b. Des Moines, Oct. 3, 1953; s. Stanley James and Alice Ruth Blair; m. Susan Monaghan, May 21, 1977; children: Sean, Shannon. BS, U. Iowa, 1975; MS, Iowa State U., 1978. Sci. instr. Manilla (Iowa) Cmty. Schs., 1977-78; math and sci. instr. Levaula Coll., Faleula, Western Samoa, 1979-81; physical and earth sci.

instr. East Dubuque (Ill.) Pub. Schs., 1981-82; earth sci. educator Ralston (Nebr.) Pub. Schs., 1982-87; adv. sci. instr. Escuela Mazapan, La Ceiba, Honduras, 1987-91; sci. educator Des Moines Indep. Sch. Dist., 1991-95, staff devel. instr., 1993—, adv. physics instr., 1995—; coord. talented and gifted program Des Moines Pub. Schs., 1999—, advisor sci. bound program, 1995—; sponsor Earth Club, Roosevelt H.S., Des Moines, 1995—; presentor in field. Author: The Geology of Des Moines, 1991; contbr. articles to profl. jours. Recipient Tchr. Recognition award Iowa Math. and Sci. Coalition, 1995, Tchg. award Iowa Gov.'s Office, 1995, Environ. Educator Yr. award Iowa Conservation Bd., 1998, Radio Shack/Tandy Tchr. of Yr. award, 2000; Educator grante Earthwatch Orgn., 1999. Mem. Nat. Sci. Tchrs. Assn., Ctrl. Iowa Mineral Soc. (treas.), Blair Soc. Geneal. Rsch., Polk Environ. and Ednl. Consortium (advisor). Avocations: archeology, genealogy, kayaking. E-mail: michael.blair@dmps.k-12.ia.us. Home: 11248 NW 150th Ave Madrid IA 50156-7508 Office: Roosevelt HS Des Moines Indep Sch Dist 4419 Center St Des Moines IA 50312-2234

BLAIR, PHYLLIS E., artist, sculptor, illustrator; b. N.Y.C., Oct. 5, 1922; d. Franz Joseph and Marian Jane (Burke) Emmerich; m. Thomas Slingluff Blair, Sept., 17, 1946; children: Joan Dix, George Dike, Hadden Slingluff. Student, Skidmore Coll., 1940-42, Art Students League, 1945, Westminster Coll., 1970-72, Bennington Coll., 1989. Asst. art dept. Skidmore Coll., Saratoga Springs, N.Y., 1940-42; art illustrator & engring. draftsman GE, Schenectady, N.Y., 1942-44, Bell Labs., N.Y.C., 1944-46; elem tchr. Clinton, Tenn., 1946-47. One-woman shows include Hoyt Inst. Fine Arts, New Castle, Pa., 1971, 93, Butler Inst. Am. Art, Youngstown, Ohio, 1982, Westminster Coll., New Wilmington, Pa., 1983, Butler Inst. Am. Art, Salem, Ohio, 1994. Art curator Human Svcs. Ctr., New Castle, 1968-89, Jameson Meml. Hosp., 1978-99, Jameson Care Ctr., Jameson Retirement Pl., 1978-99, Jameson Rehab Ctr., 1978-99, Jameson Care Ctr., 1978-99, Jameson Retirement Place, 1978-99, Almira Home, New Castle, 1990-99, Lawrence County Children and Youth Svcs., 2000, The Soup Kitchen, Boynton Beach, Fla., 2000; founding mem. Nat. Mus. of Women in the Arts, Washington. Recipient Benjamin Rush award Pa. Med. Soc., 1991. Mem. Hoyt Inst. Fine Arts (chair art com. & permanent collection 1967-99, trustee, 1967-99, Blair Sculpture Walkway named in her honor 1996), Am. Heart Assn. (Disting. Svc. award Lawrence County chpt. 1978). Avocations: golf, painting, sculpting. Home: 1611 Cold Spring Rd Williamstown MA 01267-2771

BLAIR, ROBIN LEITCH, otolaryngologist, educator; b. Gourock, Scotland, Nov. 28, 1945; s. John and Catherine Blair; m. Elizabeth Anne Manson; children: Jennifer, Elinor. MB BChir, U. Edinburgh, Scotland, 1968. Diplomate Am. Bd. Otolaryngology. Resident U. Toronto, Ont., 1971-74, fellow, 1974-75, asst. prof., 1977-84; staff otolaryngologist Tchg. Hosps., Toronto, 1975-84; head dept. otolaryngology U. Dundee, Scotland, 1984—; cons. Tayside Health Bd., 1984—; mem. Scottish nat. panel, chmn. Specialist Adv. Com. in Otolaryngology. Author: Surgery-2, 1997; contbr. articles to profl. jours. Hon. sec. Edinburgh Angus Club, 1996-99. Recipient Honor award Can. Soc. Otolaryngology-Head and Neck Surgery, 1985. Fellow Royal Coll. Surgeons Edinburgh (chmn. bd. 1996—, examiners), Royal Coll. Surgeons Can.; mem. Scottish Otolaryn. Soc. (mem. coun. 1989-93), Royal Soc. Medicine (pres. sect. laryngology and rhinology 2000-2001). Home: Torwood Clarendon Dr, DD2 1JU Dundee Scotland Office: Ninewells Hosp & Med Ctr, Dept Otolaryngology, DD1 9SY Dundee Scotland

BLAIR, WARREN, artist, educator; b. Phila., Oct. 13, 1922; s. Mortimer Warren and Olive (Wilkinson) W.; m. Jane, Dec. 13, 1947; children: Heidi Beth Vassar. Cert., Phila. Mus. Sch. Indsl. Art, 1942, 47. Art mgr. to art dir. Smith, Kline & French Labs, Phila, 1950; design dir. SmithKline Corp., Phila., 1950-81; ret.. , 1981; design dir. World Corp., Phila., 1975-81. Design dir. The Fine Old House, 1980; Exhbns. include Am. Watercolor Soc., 1986, 88, 89, 90, 95, 99, Phila. Watercolor Club, 1984-96 (Hahn Gallery award 1992), John H. Geisel Watercolor Exhibit, 1987, 89, 90, 91, 92, Woodmere Art Mus., 1984-92 (Harrison Morris prize 1991), Reading Mus., 1992, 93, 98 (Merit award 1992), Mann Gallery, Reading, Pa., 1990, Phillip's Mill Annual, 1990, 91 (Cmty. Assn. award), Am. Coll. Life Underwriters, Bryn Mawr, Pa., 1991, 97, 98, Yellow Springs Annual, 1991, 92, 93, Reading Area C.C., 1994, 96. Sgt. U.S. Army, 1942-45, PTO. Decorated D.S.M. with two bronze stars; recipient Alumni award Univ. of the Arts, 1959, various other awards for advt. design. Mem. Art Dirs. Club Phila. (pres. 1959, 60, 61, Svc. award 1971, Man of Yr. award 1984, lifetime hon. mem.), Am. Watercolor Soc. (hon. mem.), Phila. Watercolor Soc. (life mem., Dana award 1981, Grumbacher award 1994, Winsor E.Newton Painting award 1995). Republican. Methodist. Avocations: golf, bridge, bowling.

BLAIS, BERNARD RAYMOND, ophthalmologist, occupational health physician, educator; b. Colchester, Vt., Sept. 19, 1931; s. Frederick Emille and Marguerite (Duffany) B.; m. Claire Aileen, Sept. 5, 1955; children: Stephanie A. McMahon, Kristine F. Miller. BS in Chemistry cum laude, St. Michael's Coll., 1953; MD, U. Vt., 1958. Diplomate Am. Bd. Ophthalmology, Nat. Bd. Med. Examiners, Am. Bd. Preventive Medicine; bd. qualified occupl. medicine. Med. intern Naval Hosp., Portsmouth, Va., 1958-59; resident in ophthalmology Naval Hosp., Phila., 1961-64; fellow in ophthalmic pathology Armed Forces Inst. Pathology, Washington, 1967-68; resident in occupl. medicine U. Cin. Sch. Medicine, 1980-83; assoc. ophthalmic pathologist Wills Eye Hosp., Phila., 1967-77; med. dir. Allied Health Sch., Naval Hosp., San Diego, 1968-72; chair ophthalmology dept. Naval Hosp., Phila., 1972-77; Nat. Naval Med. Ctr., Bethesda, Md., 1977-78; prof. surgery and ophthalmology USUHS, Bethesda, Md., 1977-87; dir. surface and sealift medicine Bur. Medicine and Surgery, 1978-82; force med. officer Mil. Sealift Command, Washington, 1978-87; regional med. dir. Lockheed-Martin Corp., Niskayuna, N.Y., 1988-96; clin. prof. ophthalmology Albany (N.Y.) Med. Coll., 1989—; cons., pres. Blais Consulting, Ltd., Clifton Park, N.Y., 1996—. Co-author: Basic Principles of Industrial Ophthalmology, 1999; contbr. articles to profl. jours. Decorated Air Force Bronze Medal; recipient Gen. Chmn. award Nat. Safety Coun., 1986. Fellow Am. Acad. Ophthalmology (liaison 1996—), ACS, Am. Coll. Occupl. and Environ. Medicine (chmn. eye and vision com. 1989—), Soc. Mil. Ophthalmologists (pres. 1975, sec.-treas. 1981-87). Republican. Roman Catholic. Avocations: skiing, photography, lecturing, volunteerism. Office: Blais Consulting Ltd 4 Innisbrook Dr Clifton Park NY 12065-2909

BLAIS, ROGER NATHANIEL, physics educator; b. Duluth, Minn., Oct. 3, 1944; s. Eusebe Joseph and Edith Seldina (Anderson) B.; m. Mary Louise Leclerc, Aug. 2, 1971; children: Christopher Edward, Laura Louise. BA in Physics and French Lit., U. Minn., 1966; PhD in Physics, U. Okla., 1971; cert. in computer programming, Tulsa Jr. Coll., 1981; cert. in bus., UCLA, 1986. Registered profl. engr., Okla. Instr. physics Westark C.C., Ft. Smith, Ark., 1971-72; asst. prof. physics and geophys. scis Old Dominion U., Norfolk, Va., 1972-77; asst. prof. engring. physics U. Tulsa, 1977-81, assoc. prof., 1981-98, prof., 1998—; assoc. dir. Tulsa U. Artificial Lift Projects, 1983—, chmn. physics, 1986-88, vice-provost, 1989-92, provost, v.p. acad. affairs, 1998—. Contbr. articles to profl. jours. Fellow Instrument Soc. Am. (dir. test measurement divsn. 1995-97, v.p. elect automation and tech. dept. 2000—); mem. AAAS, AAUP, NSPE, Am. Phys. Soc., Am. Geophys. Union, Soc. Petroleum Engrs., Am. Assn. Physics Tchrs., Am. Soc. Engring. Edn., N.Y. Acad. Scis., Iron Wedge Soc., Phi Beta Kappa, Sigma Xi, Sigma Pi Sigma, Tau Beta Pi, Phi Kappa Phi. Home: 5348 E 30th Pl Tulsa OK 74114-6314 Office: U Tulsa Office of Provost 600 S College Ave Tulsa OK 74104-3126

BLAIVE, BRUNO JEAN, chemistry researcher, numerical analysis educator; b. Chateauroux, Berry, France, May 23, 1950; s. Alphonse Jean and Hélène Marie (Lorrette) B. Grad. in engring., Poly. Sch., Paris, 1973; DSc in Chem. Physics., U. Aix-Marseilles, France, 1980. Rsch. attaché Nat. Ctr. Sci. Rsch., Marseilles, 1975-82, in charge rsch., 1982-91, dir. rsch., 1991—. Contbr. articles to sci. jours., including Phys. Rev., Jour. Math. Physics; author sci. computer programs. Mem. Am. Phys. Soc. Avocations: kites, collecting pickaxes, studying antiquity. Home: 4 rue Fontaine-Sainte-Anne, F-13012 Marseille France Office: Ecole Nat Sup Chimie, Faculty St Jerome, F-13397 Marseille Cedex 20, France

BLAKE, BARRY JOHN, educator; b. Melbourne, Victoria, Australia, Sept. 5, 1937; s. John Douglas and Kathleen Clare (Dolan) B.; m. Marie Therese Quilty, Nov. 18, 1963; children: Laurence, Hilary, Alice, Celia. BA with honors, U. Melbourne, 1958; MA, Monash U., Australia, 1967, PhD, 1975. Research fellow Monash U., Australia, 1966-67; lectr. U. Sydney, NSW, Australia, 1968-69; lectr. Monash U., Clayton, Victoria, Australia, 1970-72, sr. lectr., 1973-81, assoc. prof., 1982-87; prof. La Trobe U., Victoria, Australia, 1988—. Author: Case in Australian Languages, 1977, Australian Aboriginal Languages, 1981, Australian Aboriginal Grammar, 1987, Relational Grammar, 1990, Case, 1994; co-author: Language Typology, 1981; co-editor: Handbook of Australian Languages, 1979-81, 83, 91, 2000. Fellow Australian Acad. of Humanities. Avocation: gardening.

BLAKE, DAVID LEONARD, composer; b. London, Sept. 2, 1936; s. Leonard Arthur and Dorothy Violet (Bristow) B.; m. Rita Mary Muir, Sept. 24, 1960; children: Andrew, Claire, Daniel. BA, Gonville and Caius Coll., Cambridge, 1960, MA, 1963. Meisterschüler German Dem. Republic Akademie der Künste, 1960-61; tchr. London Sch. Dist., 1961-63; fellow U. York, Eng., 1963-64, lectr. music, 1964-72, sr. lectr., 1972-76, prof., 1976—. Editor: Hanns Eisler-A Miscellany, 1995; contbr. numerous articles to profl. jours.; composer four operas, concertos for violin and cello, several cantatas, orchestral works, works for choir and chamber music. Home: Mill Gill, Askrigg N Yorks DL8 3HR, England Office: U York Dept Music, U York Dept Music, Heslington, York Y010 5DD, England

BLAKE, GERALD HENRY, geography educator; b. Southampton, Eng., Feb. 1, 1936; s. Geoffrey Thomas and Grace (Dibben) B.; m. Brenda Jane Peach, Apr. 17, 1965; children: Robert Thomas, Carolyn Rachel, Julia Louise. MA, Oxford U., 1960; PhD, Southampton U., 1964. Tchr. St. John's Coll., Johannesburg, South Africa, 1960-61; lectr., sr. lectr., reader in geography, prof. U. Durham, Eng., 1964-94; prin. Collingwood Coll., Eng., 1987—; dir. Internat. Boundaries Rsch. Unit, Durham, Eng., 1989—. Co-author: The Middle East, 1976, Cambridge Atlas of the Middle East, 1987, Political Geography of the Middle East and North Africa, 1985; editor: Maritime Boundaries and Ocean Resources, 1987, Imperial Frontier, 1995, Maritime Boundaries, 1994; co-editor: Boundaries and Energy, 1998, Peaceful Management of Transboundary Resources, 1995, International Boundaries and Environmental Security, 1997. Justice of the Peace, County of Durham, 1973-93. Fellow Royal Geog. Soc., Brit. Soc. for Middle Eastern Studies; mem. Inst. Brit. Geographers, Internat. Geog. Union Commn. on World Polit. Map, Consortium on Internat. Dispute Resolution (dir.), Leander Club. Anglican. Avocations: rowing, walking, maritime museums, family history. Home: Collingwood Coll, South Rd, Durham DH1 3LT, England Office: U Durham Internat Boundaries Rsch Unit, Mountjoy Centre, Durham DH1 3UR, England

BLAKE, JOHN MICHAEL, publisher, writer; b. London, Nov. 6, 1948; s. Edwin F. and Evelyn J. (Meadows) B.; m. Diane S. Campbell, June 29, 1968; children: Emma, Charlotte, Adam. Student, N.W. London U., 1968. Reporter Hackney Gazette, London, 1966-69, Evening Post, Luton, Eng., 1969-70, Fleet Street News Agy., London, 1970-71; columnist London Evening News, 1971-80, London Evening Std., 1980-82; columnist, asst. editor The Sun, London, 1982-85, Daily Mirror, London, 1985-89; editor The People, London, 1989-90; pres. Mirror Group Newspapers USA, 1990-91; mng. dir. Blake Pub., London, 1991—. Author: Up and Down with The Rolling Stones, 1978, All You Needed Was Love, 1981. Avocations: boats, diving, skiing. Office: Blake Pub Ltd, 3 Bramber Ct 2 Bramber Rd, London W14 9PB, United Kingdom

BLAKE-INADA, LOUIS MICHAEL, cardiologist, researcher; b. Osaka, Japan, June 4, 1956; came to U.S., 1959; s. Edward Kneeland, Sr. and Setsuko (Inada) Blake. BA in Biochemistry and Molecular Biology, U. Calif., Santa Barbara, 1979; MD, Case Western Res. U., 1983. Diplomate Am. Bd. Internal Medicine, Am. Bd. Nuc. Medicine. Intern in gen. surgery Letterman Army Med. Ctr., San Francisco, 1983-84; resident in internal medicine Sch. Medicine Stanford U., Calif., 1988-90, resident in nuc. medicine, 1990-92, chief resident in nuc. medicine, 1991-92; fellow in cardiology Calif. Pacific Med. Ctr., San Francisco, 1992-93; fellow in cardiology, cardiac imaging U. Calif., San Francisco, 1993-95; fellow in invasive cardiology U. N.Mex. Health Sci. Ctr., 1997-98; asst. prof. medicine (cardiology), asst. prof. radiology U. Nev. Sch. of Medicine, Reno, 1998-2000; dir. echocardiography lab. Sierra Nevada VA Med. Ctr., Reno, 1999-2000; dir. nuclear cardiology Sierra Nevada Med. Ctr., Reno, 1999-2000; staff cardiologist Swedish Heart Inst., Seattle, 2000—. Contbr. articles to med. jours. including Am. Jour. Radiology, Jour. Nuc. Medicine, others; contbr. editor Jour. Am. Coll. Cardiology, 1993-95. Capt. U.S. Army, 1979-88. Evelyn Neizer rsch. fellow Stanford U., 1992, Prof. of the Year, UMV of Nevada sch. of med., 1999. Fellow ACP, Am. Coll. Angiology, Am. Coll. Cardiology (assoc.); mem. Am. Coll. Nuc. Physicians, Am. Heart Assn. (coun. on cardiovascular radiology), Am. Heart Assn. (coun. on vascular biology, coun. on cardiovascular and critical care medicine 1999—. coun. on vascular and molecular biology 1999—), Soc. Nuc. Medicine, Assn. Military Surgeons of the U.S., Stanford U. Alumni (life). Republican. Roman Catholic. Avocations: stocks and bonds, skiing, running, piano, languages. Home: 1855 Joy Lake Rd Reno NV 89511-8718 Office: U Nev Sch Of Med Reno NV 89557-0001

BLAKELEY, DAVID, chemical engineer; b. Oxford, Eng., Feb. 1, 1944; s. Kenneth and Kathleen Rose (Williamson) B.; children: Caroline, Matthew Paul; m. Ann Keightley, Nov. 22, 1986; children: Joanne, George. BS with honors, Birmingham (Eng.) U., 1965, PhD, 1968. Tech. svcs. engr. Monsanto Chems., Newport, Eng., 1968-70; sr. chem. engr. Burmah Engring., Manchester, Eng., 1971-72; internat. coord. Flexibox Internat., Manchester, 1973-75, systems mgr., 1976-77; mktg. mgr. Mass. Transfer Internat., Kirky Stephen, Eng., 1978-84; mktg. dir. Glitsch U.K., Ltd., Kirky Stephen, 1985-88; mng. dir. APV Pasilac, Ltd., Carlisle, Eng., 1989-94, Royston Lead, 1995-96, Begg Cousland & Co. Ltd., Glasgow, Scotland, 1998—. Mem. No. Engring. Employees Assn. Anglican. Avocations: squash, jogging, photography, ornithology. Home: Fernholme, Station Rd Brampton, C481EX Cambria CA8 1EX, England Office: Begg Cousland & Co Ltd, 636 Springfield Rd, Glasgow G40 3HS, Scotland

BLAKELEY-PEREZ, JOSE ALFREDO, software engineer; b. Cd. Madero, Mexico, Dec. 17, 1956; s. Jose A. Blakeley-Arrieta and Josefina Pérez-Orozco; m. Lucinda Eva Ruiz-Gonzalez, Aug. 13, 1981; 1 child, Jose Alfredo Blakeley-Ruiz. Computer sys. engr., Tech. de Monterrey, Mexico, 1978; M in Math. (computer sci.), U. Waterloo, Canada, 1983; PhD in Computer Sci., U. Waterloo, 1987. Asst. prof. Ind. U., Bloomington, 1987-89; tech. staff Tex. Insts., Dallas, 1989-94; software design engr. Microsoft Corp., Redmond, Wash., 1994—; assoc. editor Asssn. Computing Machinery, N.Y., 1993—. Contbg. author: (book) Modem Database Systems; contbr. articles to profl. jours.; 4 patents in field. Avocations: soccer, running. Fax: 425-936-7329. E-mail: joseb@microsoft.com. Office: Microsoft Corp One Microsoft Way Redmond WA 98052-6399

BLAKEMORE, COLIN (BRIAN), neuroscientist, writer, broadcaster; b. Stratford-upon-Avon, England, June 1, 1944; s. Cedric Norman (dec.) and Beryl Ann B.; m. Andrée Elizabeth Washbourne, 1965; three daus. Student Cambridge U.; PhD (Harkness fellow), U. Calif.-Berkeley; MA, Cantab, 1969, Oxon, 1979; ScD, Cantab, 1988, DSc, Oxon, 1989; DSc (hon.) Aston U., 1992, Salford U., 1994. Univ. demonstrator Physiol. Lab., Cambridge U., 1968-72, lectr. in physiology, 1972-79; fellow, dir. med. studies Downing Coll., 1972-79; vis. prof. NYU, 1970, MIT, 1971; Locke research fellow Royal Soc., Cambridge, 1976-79; Waynflete prof. physiology Oxford (Eng.) U., 1979—, professorial fellow Magdalen Coll., 1979—; dir. McDonnell-Pew Centre for Cognitive Neuroscience, Oxford, 1990—; dir. MRC Interdisciplinary Rsch. Ctr for Cognitive Neuroscience, Oxford, 1996—; hon. prof. China Acad. Mgmt. Sci.; Sir. Douglas Robb lectr. U. Auckland, 1991; BBC Reith lectr., 1976; Lethaby prof. R.C.A., London, 1978; Storer lectr. U. Calif.-Davis, 1980; Macallum lectr. U. Toronto, 1984; Osler lectr. Royal Coll. Physicians, 1993, Ellison-Cliffe lectr. Royal Soc. Medicine, 1993, James Law lectr. Cornell U., 1994, lectr. U. Manchester Inst. Sci. Tech., 1997, lectr. South Place Ethical Soc., 1997, Regents' prof. U. Calif., Davis, 1995-96; founder, bd. govs. Internat. Brain Injury Found. Inc., Washington, 1993; Spinoza prof. U. Amsterdam, 1996, Fellow Acad. Med. Scis., 1998—; founding mem. Com. Harkness Fellowships Assn., 1997. Author: Handbook of Psychobiology, 1975; Mechanics of the Mind, 1977; Mindwaves, 1987, The Mind Machine, 1988, rev. edit., 1994, Images and Understanding, 1990, Vision: Coding & Efficiency, 1990, Sex and Society, 1999; contbr.: Constraints on Learning, 1973, Illusion in Art and Nature, 1973, The Neurosciences Third Study Program, 1974; contbr. articles to profl. jours.; editorial bd. Perception, 1971—; Behavioral and Brain Scis., 1977—, Jour. Developmental Physiology, 1978-86, Exptl. Brain Research, 1979-89, Lang. and Communication, 1979-90, News in Physiol. Scis., 1986-88, Advances in Neurosci., 1989, Clin. Vision Scis., 1986-92, Internat. Rev. Neurobiology, 1996—; editor-in-chief IBRO News, 1986—; editorial adv. bd. Trends in Neuroscis., 1977-83, Chinese Jour. of Physiol. Scis., 1988—, Network, 1989-94, Vision Rsch., 1994—; assoc. editor NeuroReport, 1990—; series editor: Perspectives in Vision Research, 1981—; lectr. Common Sense, Christmas Lectures for Young People, Royal Inst., 1982; presenter BBC TV series The Mind Machine, 1988. Mem. nat. com. Brain Rsch. Assn., 1973-77, profl. adv. com. Schizophrenia: A Nat. Emergency, 1989; exec. com. and governing coun. Internat. Brain Rsch. Orgn., 1973—; mem. com. BBC Sci. Cons. Group, 1975-79; mem. sci. adv. bd. Cognitive Neurosis. Inst. N.Y., 1981—; hon. assoc. Rationalist Press Assn., 1986—); U.K. pub. adv. panel IRL Press, 1987-91; mem. exec. com. Dana Alliance for Brain Initiatives, 1996—, Worshipful Co. Spectacle Makers, 1997—, Livery, 1998—; chief exec. European Dana Alliance for Brain, 1997; patron sci., advisor Bristol 2000, 1996—; Freeman City of London, 1997—; patron Assn. Art Sci., Engring., Tech., 1997; patron mem. Profl. Advisory Panel Headway (Nat. Head Injuries Assn.), 1997. Leverhulme fellow, 1974-75; recipient Robert Bing prize Swiss Acad. Med. Scis., 1975; Dr. Robert Netter prize Académie Nationale de Médicine, Paris, 1984; Cairns medal, 1986, John Locke medal, 1983, Norman McAlister Gregg medal Royal Australian Coll. of Ophthalmologists, 1988, Michael Faraday award Royal Soc., 1989, Robert Doyne medal, 1989, John P. McGovern Sci. & Soc. medal, 1990, Montgomery medal, 1991, Osler medal Royal Coll. Physicians, 1993, Ellison-Cliffe medal Royal Soc. Medicine, 1993, Charles F. Prentice award Am. Acad. Optometry, 1994, Alcon prize for Rsch. Relevant to field of ophthalmology Alcon Rsch. Inst., 1996, Meml. medal Charles U., Prague, Czech Republic, 1998—, hon. mem. Physiological Soc., 1998; Hon. fellow Corpus Christi Coll., Cambridge U., 1994, Cardiff U., 1998, Downing Coll., 1999—, patron, Clifton Sci. Trust, Bristol. Fellow Royal Soc., World Econ. Forum, Acad. Med. Scis.; mem. Brit. Assn. Advancement Sci. (v.p. 1990-97, pres. 1997-98), Royal Netherlands Acad. Arts and Scis. (foreign mem.), European Brain and Behaviour Soc. (com. 1974-76), Cambridge Philos. Soc. (council 1975-79), Physiol. Soc. (hon., G.L. Brown prize, 1990, annual review prize, 1995), Exptl. Psychology Soc., Soc. Neurosci., European Neurosci. Assn., Assn. for Sci. Edn. (Royal Soc. Lectr., 1995), Acad. Europea.ad. Europea. Office: U Lab Physiology, Parks Rd, Oxford OX1 3PT, England

BLAKEMORE, JOHN STEWART, international management consultant; b. Newcastle, NSW, Australia, Nov. 30, 1939; s. Harold and Jessie (Stewart) B.; m. Deirdre June Flynn, Apr. 10, 1965; children: Scott Stewart, Nigel Campbell. BSc, U. NSW, Sydney, 1964; MSc, U. Newcastle, NSW, 1966, PhD, 1969; postgrad., Australian Sch. Nuclear Tech., 1970, Nomura Sch., Tokyo, 1985. Cert. mgmt. cons.; cert. engr. Rsch. scientist AAEC, Lucas Heights, N.S.W., 1969-70; chief metallurgist John Lysaght, Newcastle, 1970-77, Tubemakers, Newcastle, 1977-79; engring. mgr. Wormald Machinery Group, 1979-82; gen. mgr. Pyrotek, Sydney, 1982-84; mktg. dir. John Morris Sci., Sydney, 1983-84; div. gen. mgr. GEC, Sydney, 1984-85; mng. dir. Blakemore Cons., Sydney, 1985—; dir. MASC P/L, NSW, Blakemore Fin. Svcs., Leading Edge Initiatives, Australian Inst. Mgmt., Australian Inst. Mgmt. Tng., Ltd., NSW; lectr. U. Sydney, 1992, 93, 94, U. NSW; assoc. Australian Grad. Sch. Engring. Innovation; cons. Supply Chain Partnerships Program Dept. Industry Sci. Resources; condr. workshops in field; program mgr. DISR Value Chain Mgmt. Program. Author: The Quality Solution, 1989, The Quality Solution for the Plastics Industry, 8 vols., 1991, The Service Champion, 1993, Quality Habits of Best Business Practice, 1995, Strategic Planning for Business, 1998; author 85 tng. manuals in mgmt. and supply chain mgmt., quality and leadership, and statis. process control; patentee in field. Pres. Liberal Party, Newcastle, 1970-73, fed. conf. pres., 1973-75, pres., 1978-79; pres. Citizens Group, 1980-81. Commonwealth scholar, 1957, postgrad. scholar, 1965-66, U. Newcastle scholar, 1965; Internat. Nickel fellow, 1966-69. Fellow Australian Inst. Mgmt. (bd. dirs., chmn. adv. edn. and tng. com.), Australian Inst. Mgmt. Cons., Quality Soc. of Australia, Australian Orgn. for Quality, Australian Inst. Co. Dirs.; mem. Instn. of Engrs., Inst. Materials. Avocations: tennis, sailing, politics, piano, sea kayaking. E-mail: masc@blakemore.com.au. Home: 31A Macmasters Parade, Macmasters Beach NSW 2251, Australia Office: Blakemore Cons, L67 MLC Ctr, Martin Pl, Sydney NSW 2000, Australia Mailing Address: PO Box 473, Surry Hills NSW 2010, Australia

BLAKEMORE, MICHAEL HOWELL, theatre and film director; b. Sydney, June 18, 1928; s. Conrad and Una Mary (Litchfield) B.; m. Shirley Bush, 1960; 1 child; m. Tanya McCallin, 1986, 2 children. Student, Kings Sch., Sydney U., Royal Acad. of Dramatic Art. Actor Birmingham Repertory Theatre, Shakespeare Meml. Theatre, 1952-66; co-dir. Glasgow Citizen's Theatre, 1966-68; assoc. artistic dir. Nat. Theatre, London, 1971-76; dir. Players, N.Y.C., 1978; resident dir. Lyric Theatre Hammersmith, London, 1980. Dir.: A Day in the Death of Joe Egg, 1967, Arturo Ui, 1969, The National Health, 1969, Long Day's Journey into Night, 1971, The Front Page, Macbeth, 1972, The Cherry Orchard, 1973, Design for Living, 1973, Separate Tables, 1976, Privates on Parade, 1977 (also film, 1982), Candida, 1977, Make and Break, 1980, Travelling North, 1980, The Wild Duck, 1980, All My Sons, 1981, Noises Off, 1982 (Drama Desk award 1983-84), Benefactors, 1984, Lettic and Lovage, 1987, Uncle Vanya, 1988, Tosca (Welsh Nat. Opera), 1992, The Sisters Rosenweig, 1994, City of Angels, 1989, Lettice and Lovage, 1990, After the Fall, 1990, The Ride Down Mount Morgan, 1991, Life, 1997, Copenhagen, 1998 (Tony Award), Alarms and Excursions, 1998, Kiss Me Kate (Broadway, 1999, Copenhagen, 2000) (Tony Award, Drama Desk award); writer, dir.: (film) A Personal History of the Australian Surf, 1981 (Std. Film award), Country Life; author: Next Season, 1969. Named Best Dir. London Critics, 1972. Avocation: surfing. Home: 18 Upper Park Rd, London NW3 2UP, England

BLAKERS, KENNETH ROGER, farmer, former military officer; b. Sydney, NSW, Australia, Dec. 24, 1942; s. Ernest Alfred and Doris (Newbold) B.; m. Cathryn Claire Brasnett, Dec. 17, 1966. BSc, Melbourne (Australia) U., 1963. Farmer Wenonah Headland, NSW, Australia. Named Officer of the Order of Australia, Gov. Gen., Canberra, 1992. Office: Wenonah Headland, NSW 2455, Australia

BLAKEWAY, JOHN MURRAY, cosmetic company executive; b. Southampton, Eng., Oct. 1, 1927; s. Walter Richard and Violet Mary (Pearson) B.; m. Monique Frederique Delafon; children: Gael Carol, Gwendoline, Fiona, Alaric. BSc, Victoria U., Manchester, Eng., 1948. Rsch. chemist Lankro Chem. Co., Manchester, 1948-53; rsch. mgr. Colgate Palmolive Co., Manchester, 1953-63; rsch. dir. Chesebrough Ponds, London, 1963-75; dir. applied rsch. Roure S.A., Paris, 1975—. Editor Internat. Jour. Cosmetic Sci.; contbr. articles to profl. publs.; patentee in field. Fellow Soc. Cosmetic Scientists (silver medal 1989); mem. Royal Soc. Chemistry, Soc. Francaise Cosmetology (Pierre Velon medal 1979), Japan Cosmetic Sci. Soc. (hon.). Mem. Anglican Ch. Avocations: bridge, golf, restoration of ancient monuments. Home: Chateau de Nucourt, 95420 Nucourt France Office: Roure SA, 55 Voie du Bans, 95102 Argenteuil France

BLAKEY, MICHAEL LOUIS, anthropologist, educator; b. Washington, Feb. 23, 1953; s. Katus Reginald and Thelma Mildred (Mosley) B.; m. Cecelie Edith Counts, May 8, 1988; 1 child, Tariq Kevin Counts Blakey. BA, Howard U., 1978; MA, U. Mass., 1980, PhD, 1985; DSc, CUNY, 1995. Asst. prof. Howard U., Washington, 1985-89, assoc. prof., 1989-97, curator W.M. Cobb Collection, 1989—, dir. African burial ground project, 1992—, prof. anthropology, 1997—; rsch. assoc. Smithsonian Instn., Washington, 1985-94; vis. prof. Spelman Coll., Atlanta, 1989, La Sapienza U., Rome, 1990; disting. vis. scholar Columbia U., N.Y.C., 1997. Author: Socio-Politics of Archaeology, 1983; contbr. articles to profl. jours. Permanent rep. to Washington African Bur. Ednl. Scis., 1997—. NSF grad. fellow, 1979-82; recipient Robert L. Stigler Lectureship U. Ark., 1998. Mem. World Archaeol. Congress (U.S. coun. rep. 1999), Soc. Med. Anthropology (mem. exec. coun. 1989-92), Assn. Black Anthropologists (pres. 1987-89). Achievements include founding of W.M. Cobb Biol. Anthropology Lab. at Howard U.; invented method for determining duration of dental enamel hypoplasia; established African Burial Ground Project. Avocation: sailing.

Office: The Cobb Lab Howard U 2441 6th St NW Washington DC 20059-0001

BLAKLEY, JOHN CLYDE, telecommunications consultant; b. Bogota, Colombia, Sept. 14, 1955; came to U.S., 1964; s. Arthur C. and Dorothy M. (Balcome) B.; m. Jean M. Padden, May 21, 1983. BS, U. Miami, 1977, MEd, 1979. Notary at large, Fla. Mgr., adminstrv. asst. U. Miami Student Union, Coral Gables, Fla., 1977-79; mgr. Aladdins Castle, Inc., South Miami, Fla., 1979-80; adminstrv. mgr., cons. Lexow Brackins, CPA's, Hollywood, Fla., 1981-84; firm adminstr., cons. Lexow, Brackins, Koffler, CPA's, Hollywood, 1985-89; firm adminstr., computer mgr. Dohan/Simon, CPA's, Miami, 1989-92; product mgr. Expert Software, Inc., 1992-93, IS mgr., 1993-96; sr. cons. Trien & Assocs., 1996—; pres. Miami Apple Users Group, 1983; cons. YMCA, 1983. Chmn. Multiple Sclerosis Project Dance Marathon, Coral Gables, 1977-79; coord. United Way Miami, 1975-79. Recipient Whitten award Assn. Coll. Unions, 1977, Outstanding Leadership award C. of C., 1973, Outstanding Vol., United Way, 1975, Outstanding Alumni award U. Miami, 1986, 92. Mem. Assn. Acctg. Adminstrs., Fla. Inst. CPA's, Assn. Coll. Unions Internat. (chmn. region 6, 1975-77), U. Miami Young Alumni Club (bd. dirs., pres.), U. Miami Alumni Assn. (bd. dirs.), Hurricane Club, Gold Coast Macintosh Computer Club (bd. dirs.). Home: 11501 SW 92nd Ct Miami FL 33176-4247 Office: Trien & Assocs PO Box 402488 Miami Beach FL 33140-0488

BLANC, DARLITA JUDITH, counselor; b. Enid, Okla., Oct. 25, 1942; d. Curtis Darwin Blanc and Barbara Lee Rasmussen; m. Leon Wayne Taylor, Aug. 12, 1960 (div. June 1967); 1 child, Roger Wayne Taylor. BS, Okla. State U., 1967; MEd, Ctrl. State U., Edmond, Okla., 1975. Tchr. Ponca City (Okla.) Sch. Sys., 1966-70; supr. guidance counselor Bur. Indian Affairs, Navajo Indian Reservation, 1972-90; mental health specialist Window Rock Unified Sch. Dist. 8, Ft. Defiance, Ariz., 1991—; adj. prof. Navajo C.C., Navajo Indian Reservation, 1980—; cons., Ca., Ariz., Okla., N.Mex., 1991-00; presenter. Mem. Gov.'s Task Force Women and Behavioral Health, Phoenix, 1982-84; pub. rels. chair NOW, Phoenix, 1982-84, mem. com. combat racism, Washington, 1982-86. Mem. ACA, Assn. Transpersonal Psychology, Inst. Noetic Scis., Ariz. Sch. Counselor's Assn. Avocations: reading, painting, traveling, camping, hot air balloon crewing. Home: PO Box 246 Fort Defiance AZ 86504-0246 Office: Window Rock Unified Sch Dist 8 Spl Edn Dept PO Box 559 Fort Defiance AZ 86504-0559

BLANC, LAURENT, professional soccer player; b. Alès, France, Nov. 19, 1965. Defender Montpellier Football Club, France, Napoli Football Club, Italy, St. Etienne Football Club, France, Auxerre Football Club, France, Barcelona Football Club, Italy, Olympique Marseille Football Club, France, France Nat. Team, Inter Milan, Italy, 1999—; winner 1998 World Cup. Office: Olympique de Marseille, Via Durini 24, 20122 Milano Italy*

BLANCHAERT, REMY HENRY, JR., oral and maxillofacial surgeon; b. Kansas City, Mo., July 3, 1965; s. Remy Henry and Alice Noretta Blanchaert. BA in Chemistry, William Jewell Coll., 1987; DDS, U. Mo., Kansas City, 1991; MD, U. Conn., 1994. Diplomate Am. Bd. Oral and Maxillofacial Surgery. Asst. prof. oral and maxillofacial surgery U. Md., Balt., 1996—. Editor: Oral Cancer, 1999; contbr. chpt. to book. Vol. Health Vols. Overseas, India, 1997. Fellow Am. Assn. Oral and Maxillofacial Surgery, Am. Coll. Oral and Maxillofacial Surgery; mem. AMA, Psi Omega, Omnicron Kappa Upsilon. Republican. Roman Catholic. E-mail: rhb001@dental.umaryland.edu. Home: 401 W Redwood St Apt 206 Baltimore MD 21201-1726 Office: U Md Oral & Maxillofacial Surgery Assocs 419 W Redwood St Ste 410 Baltimore MD 21201-7002

BLANCHARD, BENOIT MARIE-REGIS, cardiologist; b. Sainte Adresse, Normandy, France, Nov. 9, 1959; s. Michel Blanchard and Jacqueline Huet. MD, St. Antoine Hosp., Paris, 1986. Intern Hopitaux de Paris, 1986-90; asst. head heart transplantation clinic Hosp. Pitie, Paris, 1990-92; cardiologist Cabinet Med. St. Roch, Le Havre, France, 1993—. Mem. N.Y. Acad. Scis. Office: Cabinet Med St Roch, 2 Rue Raoul Dufy, 76600 Le Havre France Also: Clinique du Petit Colmoulins, Rue Robert Ancel, 76700 Harfleur France

BLANCHARD, BRUCE, environmental engineer, government official; b. Ft. Stotsenburg, Philippines, Dec. 26, 1932; s. Wendell and Marcella (Palmer) B.; m. Mary Josie Cain, July 31, 1992; children: Wendell, Laura, Renee. SB in Civil Engring., MIT, 1957, SM in Civil Engring., 1964; honor. grad., Commd. and Gen. Staff Course, Ft. Leavenworth, Kans., 1980. Tchg. and rsch. asst. MIT, 1957-59, asst. lacrosse coach, 1958-59, 64; hydraulic engr. Bur. Reclamation, Dept. Interior, Denver, 1959-60, 60-61; water resources planning engr. Phoenix, 1961-66; sr. staff specialist Water Resources Coun., Washington, 1966-69; environ. specialist Office of Sec. Dept. Interior, Washington, 1970-71; dir. Office Environ. Project Rev., Washington, 1971-89; dep. dir. U.S. Fish and Wildlife Svc., Dept. of Interior, Washington, 1989-97; spl. asst. for tribal self-governance Office of Sec. of Interior, 1997—. Editor: The Nation's Water Resources, 1968. With U.S. Army, 1951-53, 60; col. Md. N.G., 1967-85; lt. Ariz. N.G., 1961-66. Decorated Army Commendation medal, Army Meritorious Svc. medal, Army Achievement medal; recipient Commendation medal State of Md., 1976, 78, 79, Meritorious Svc. medal State of Md., 1983, Meritorious Svc. medal Dept. Interior, 1985, Disting. Svc. medal, 1999. Fellow AAAS; mem. ASCE, Am. Geophys. Union, Am. Water Resources Assn., N.G. Assn. U.S., Soc. Am. Mil. Engrs., U.S. Armor Assn., Am. Soc. Pub. Adminstrn., Sr. Execs. Assn. Explorers Club, Phi Gamma Delta. Home: 80 Observatory Cir NW Washington DC 20008-3611 Office: Interior Bldg Ms2548 Washington DC 20240-0001

BLANCHARD, MELINDA, entrepreneur; b. N.Y.C., Oct. 1, 1952; d. Murray Leon and Myra Joy (Taylor) M.; m. Robert Morrison Blanchard, Nov. 18, 1973; 1 child, Jesse. BS in Behavioral Sci., Lyndon State Coll., Lyndonville, Vt., 1974. Owner/mgr. Board & Basket, West Lebanon, N.H., 1976-78, Kid's Connection, West Lebanon, N.H., 1979-82; v.p., majority shareholder Blanchard & Blanchard, Ltd., Norwich, Vt., 1983-88; owner/mgr. Artech, Quechee, Vt., 1989; owner, chef Mango's Restaurant, Anguilla, B.W.I., 1990-93, Blanchard's, Anguilla, B.W.I., 1994—. Chmn. Norwich (Vt.) Day Care Ctr., 1977-78; bd. dirs. Norwich Youth Coun., 1980-83; co-chmn. Ford Sayre Ski Team, Hanover, N.H., 1984-88. Recipient award for best retail store design Playthings Mag., 1981, award for retail package design Nat. Assn. for Specialty Foods, 1984, Trade Show Booth Design award, 1985, Award of Excellence Wine Spectator Mag. Democrat. Jewish. Avocations: travel, cooking, writing, reading, landscaping. Home: PO Box 158 Norwich VT 05055-0158 Office: Blanchard's, PO Box 898, Meads Bay Anguilla

BLANCHARD, RICHARD EMILE, SR., retired management services executive, consultant; b. Thompson, Conn., July 13, 1928; s. Lionel A. and Bernadette L. (Jolicoeur) B.; m. Lorraine Patricia Lachapelle, July 3, 1954; children: Michele Welling, Richard E., Danielle Wornstaff, Marie Blanchard Oser, Robert Allen, Janine. BS in Biology, Providence Coll., 1952; postgrad., U. Conn. Sch. Law, West Hartford, 1952-53. Cert. mgmt. cons. Chemist Charles Pfizer Co., Inc., N.Y.C., 1953-56, med. salesman, 1956-60, coll. rels. mgr., 1960-63, pers. mgr., 1963-67; dir. manpower and orgn. devel. Sky Chef divsn. Am. Airlines, N.Y.C., 1967-70; dir. manpower ARA Svcs., Inc., Phila., 1970-72, v.p., 1972-76; v.p. pers. Jerrico, Inc., Lexington, Ky., 1976-78; chmn., CEO Career Mgmt., Inc., C.M. Temporary Svcs., C.M. Mgmt. Svcs., Lexington, 1978-99; ret., 1999; cons. pers. svcs. Bd. dirs. Ky. Higher Edn. Coun., Bluegrass United Way, 1978—, Jr. Achievement, 1979—, Better Bus. Bur., 1985—, United Way of the Bluegrass, 1998—, U. Ky. Small Bus. Devel. Ctr., Ky. Econ. Devel. Coun.; v.p. Bluegrass Ednl. Work Coun., 1980—, Bluegrass Better Bus. Bur., 1990—, bd. dirs., past pres.; chmn. adv. bd. U. Ky. C.C., 1987—; divsn. chmn. United Way, 1990, 92—; Bd. dirs., vice-chmn. Human Rights Commn., 1991-94; co-chmn. bd. dirs. Bluegrass MS Soc., 1996; mem. adv. bd. C.C. divsn. U. Ky., Muscular Dystrophy Bluegrass Coun. With USN, 1946-48. Mem. Inst. Mgmt. Cons., Am. Mgmt. Assn., Am. Soc. Pers. Assocs. (past pres. N.Y. chpt.), Nat. Assn. Temporary Svcs., Ind. Temporary Svcs. Assn., Ky. Assocs. Temporary Svcs. (past pres.), Ky. State C. of C. (bd. dirs.), Lexington C. of C. (bd. dirs. 1996—), Lexington Country Club, Exec. Fitness and Sports Ctr., Lexington Tennis Club, Rotary (bd. dirs. 1996—). Republican. Roman Catholic. Home: 16279 Edgemont Dr Fort Myers FL 33908-3658 Office: 698 Tally Rd Lexington KY 40502-2727

BLANCHARD, RONALD JOSEPH, food service executive; b. Camden, N.Y., June 27, 1946; s. Earl Roland and Margaret Virginia (Platt) B. AS in Hotel and Restaurant Tech., SUNY, Canton, 1968; BA in Human Svcs., U. Mass., Boston, 1990. Gen. mgr. restaurant Howard Johnson Co., Miami, Fla., 1968-83, gen. mgr. hotel, 1983; mgr. tng. and devel. Marriott Family Restaurants, Quincy, Mass., 1984-87; sr. mgr. tng. and devel. Ground Round, Inc., Braintree, Mass., 1987-96; corp. dir. tng. B.E. Restaurant Group, N.Y.C., 1996—. Bd. dirs. Worcester Sq. Area Neighborhood Assn., Boston, 1988—, pres. 1992—; block leader East Brookline St. Neighborhood, Boston, 1988—; mem. Boston Redevel. Authority Working Group for Master Plan, Boston, 1991—. Mem. ASTD, Zeta Alpha Phi. Democrat. Roman Catholic. Avocations: electronics, music, computers, gardening, biking. Home: 66 Pearl St Apt 407 New York NY 10004-2444 Office: Windows on the World Fl 107 1 Worldtrade Ctr New York NY 10048-0202

BLANCHER, ANTOINE PASCAL, immunologist, educator; b. Rodez, Aveyron, France, May 4, 1954; s. Jean Joseph and Janine Alice (Chaix) B.; m. Marie Madeleine Sardou, Dec. 21, 1976; children: Guillaume, Nicolas. MD, U. Paul Sabatier, Toulouse, France, 1984, PhD, 1991. Resident Teaching Hosp. Purpan, Toulouse, France, 1978-84; asst. prof. Med. Sch. UPS, Toulouse, France, 1984-92; prof. immunology Med. Sch., UPS, Toulouse, 1992—; rsch. asst. prof. NYU Med. Ctr., N.Y.C., 1991—; cons. blood Transfusion Ctr., Toulouse, 1994—; dir. Rsch. Lab. of Human Immunogenetics, Toulouse, 1992—, Dept. Immunology, Teaching Hosp. Purpan, 1992—; cons. Eurobio Labs., Les Ulis, France, 1994—. Editor: Molecular Biology on Evolution of Blood Group and MHC Antigens in Primates, 1997; contbr. articles to profl. jours. Capt. French Army, 1980-81. Mem. French Soc. Immunology, N.Y. Acad. Scis. Achievements include research on production of macaque monoclonal antibodies. Avocations: painting, sculpture, music. Home: 16 Bld de Strasbourg, 31000 Toulouse France Office: Service D'Immunol Chu Purpan, Place du Dr Baylac, 31059 Toulouse France

BLANCHET, BERTRAND, archbishop; b. Montmagny, Que., Can., Sept. 19, 1932; s. Louis and Alberta (Nicole) B. B.A., Coll. Ste-Anne-de-la-Pocatiere, 1952; L.Th., Laval U., 1956, D.Sc., 1975. Ordained priest Roman Catholic Ch., 1956, consecrated bishop, 1973; tchr. biology Coll. and Coll. d'Enseignement Gen. et Profl., La Pocatiere, 1963-73; bishop of Gaspe Que., 1973-92; archbishop of Rimouski, 1992—. Mem. Chevaliers de Colomb, Rimouski. Address: CP 730, 34 Eveche Ouest, Rimouski, PQ Canada G5L 7C7

BLANCHET, JEAN-DIDIER FRANÇOIS, civil engineer; b. Angouleme, France, Dec. 2, 1939; s. François and Simone Marie (de Berghe) B.; m. Adeline Marie Rosier-Chopin, Jan. 15, 1962; children: Jérôme, Alexis, Aliénor. Student, Ecole Polytechnique, Paris, 1959-61, Ecole Nat. Ponts et Chaussees, Paris, 1962-64. Cert. civil engr. Head of harbors and airports DDE of Calvados, Caen, France, 1964-68; head of gen. studies Directorate of Air Transport, Paris, 1969-72; head corp. planning RATP, Paris, 1972-73; tech. counsellor Pvt. Office of Sec. of State for Transport, Paris, 1975, dir., 1975-77; dep. sec. gen. Air France, Paris, 1977-78, transport dir., 1978-81, exec. v.p. mktg., 1982-88; chmn., CEO Air Charter, Paris, 1982-88; CEO Air France, Paris, 1988-93; chmn., CEO Societé Hotels Meridien, Paris, 1993-94; dir. Societé Hotels Meridien, Forte, France, 1995-97; mem. coun. gen. Ponts et Chaussees at Min. for Transport, 1997-2000; sr. advisor airport devel. Egis, Guyancourt, France, 2000—. Lt. French Air Force, 1961-62. Decorated Chevalier, Legion d'Honneur, Chevalier, Mérite Maritime, Officier, Ordre Nat. du Mérite. Mem. Pine Valley Golf Club (overseas mem.), Golf de Saint Cloud. Avocations: skiing, sailing, golf, cycling. Home: 16 rue de Civry, 75016 Paris France Office: Egis, 11 Ave du Centre, 78286 Guyancourt Cedex France

BLANCHETT, CATE, actress; b. Melbourne, Australia. Grad., Nat. Inst. Dramatic Art, Australia, 1992. With Sydney Theatre Co., Belvoir St. Theatre Co. Appeared in theatre prodns., including Top Girls, Kafka Dances (New Comer award Sydney Theatre Critics Circle 1993), Oleanna (Rosemont Best Actress award), Hamlet, 1995, Sweet Phoebe, The Tempest, The Blind Giant is Dancing; actress (TV appearances) Heartland, Bordertown; actress (films) Parklands, 1996, Paradise Road, 1997, Thank God He Met Lizzie, 1997 (Best Performance by an Actress in Supporting Role award Australian Film Inst. 1997), Oscar and Lucinda, Elizabeth, 1998 (Nominated Oscar 1999, winner Best Performance by an Actress in a Leading Role award Brit. Acad. Awards 1999, Best Actress award Broadcast Film Critics Assn. Awards 1999, Best Actress award Chgo. Film Critics Assn. Awards 1999, Best Actress award London Film Critics Assn., Best Performance by an Actress in a Motion Picture award Golden Globe 1999, Best Actress in Motion Picture award Golden Satellite Awards 1999, Actress of Yr. 1999, Nominated Screen Actors Guild award 1999), Talented Mr. Ripley, 1999, Ideal Husband, 1999, Pushing Tin, 1999, The Man Who Cried, 2000, The Gift, 2000. Office: care Robyn Gardiner, PO Box 128, Surry Hills NSW2010, Australia

BLANCK, J. GUILLERMO, psychiatrist, philosopher; b. Bahia Blanca, Argentina, Apr. 8, 1950; s. Julio and Marta De Pietro B.; m. Adriana Silvestri, 1980 (div. 1990). Founder, mem. Assn. Argentina Terapia Comportamiento, 1980, Assn. Argentina Neuropsicologia, 1984, Argentinian Athenaeum for Study of Culture & Cognition, 1983; del. Latin Am. World Congress Behavior Therapy, Scotland, 1988; prof. U. Bs. As., 1989-95; chmn. Assn. Argentina Terapia Cognitiva Conductual, 2000—; mem. presdl. bd. ALAMOC, Latin Am. Assn., 1984-89. Author: Vygotsky, 1984, 89, 98, 2000; co-author: Bakhtin & Vygotsky, 1993; contbr. articles to profl. jours. socialist polit. activist, Argentina, 1968—. E-mail: ghalvarez@ciudad.com.ar. Office: Sucursal 13 B, PO Box 90, 1413 Buenos Aires Argentina

BLANCKAERT, JOHNNY FRANÇOIS, manufacturing executive; b. Aalst, Belgium, May 25, 1952; s. Paul Blanckaert and Lydia Romaschka; m. Lutgarde de Dobbeleer, Aug. 8, 1975; 1 child, Nele. Degree in Tech. Designing, VTI, Aalst, 1974. Chief prodn. control Honda, Aalst, 1985-90, asst. mgr. logistics, 1990-92, logistics mgr., 1992-94, prodn. mgr., 1994-95, prodn. and logistics mgr., 1995-97, mfg. mgr., 1997—. Avocations: tennis, hunting, waterskiing, swimming. Home: Kastanjelaan 25, 9290 Berlare Belgium Office: Honda Belgium NV, Wijngaardveld 1, 9300 Aalst Belgium

BLANCO, CARLOS, allergist, researcher; b. Teror, Spain, Oct. 28, 1963; s. Juan Blanco and Milagros Guerra; m. Pilar Mota, Apr. 27, 1995; children: Carlos, Ana. MBBS, U. La Laguna, Tenerife, Spain, 1987. Resident in allergy and clin. immunology Hosp. La Paz, Madrid, Spain, 1987-91; allergist Hosp. Dr. Negrin, Las Palmas, Spain, 1992—. Contbr. articles to med. jours. Grantee Spanish Health Svc., Madrid, 1996, 2000. Mem. Spanish Soc. Allergy (grantee 1994, 2000), European Acad. Allergy and Clin. Immunology, Am. Acad. Allergy, Asthma, and Immunology. Avocations: swimming, martial arts, chess, music. E-mail: cblancog@meditex.es. Office: Hosp Dr Negrin, C/Bco de la Ballena s/n, 35020 Las Palmas Canary Islands, Spain

BLANCO, JOSE, medical educator; b. Havana, Cuba, Nov. 26, 1949; s. Jose Antonio Blanco and Georgina Herrera; m. Barbara Frejomil, Apr. 19, 1969 (div. 1981); m. Ileana Zorrilla, Sept. 24, 1981; children: Michele, Edigema, Karenia, José Hector. Degree, U. Havana, 1974, M in Sports Medicine, 1977, PhD, 1987. Physician Inst. de Medicine Deportiva, Havana, 1975-80, 86-93, dir., 1980-86; prof. U. do Amazonas, Manaus, Brazil, 1994-96, U. Catolica de Brasilia, Brazil, 1996—, U. do Brasilia, 1997-99; advisor Aquatic Sports, Cuba, 1980-93, Federação Amazonense de Natação, Manaus, 1993-96, Federação Brasilense de Natação, Brasilia, 1996-97. Author: Sports Medicine Program, 1986; mem. editl. staff Revista Cubana de Med. Deportiva, 1986-93; inventor in field. Recipient Silver Pin award Internat. Swimming Fedn., Atlanta, 1996. Mem. Internat. Swimming Fedn. (med. com. 1986-96, Silver Pin 1996), N.Y. Acad. Scis. Roman Catholic. Avocations: swimming, chess, travel. Office: FIT 21, Comercio Local QI 21 BLB, 71655-120 Brasilia Brazil

BLANCO, JOSEFA JOAN-JUANA (JOSSIE BLANCO), social services administrator; b. Havana, Cuba, Jan. 31, 1954; came to U.S., 1962; d. Oscar Manuel and Josefa (Rodriguez) B.; m. John Franklin Hurt III, Nov. 18, 1979 (div. June 1985); children: John Franklin IV, Jeaninne Bernadette; 1 child, Richard Manuel Tejeda. BA in Psychology and Religion, Fla. Internat. U., 1975, MA in Sch. Psychology, 1976, postgrad. in pub. adminstrn., from 1983; MS in Human Resource Adminstrn., Villanova U., 1979; PhD in Adminstrn., West Coast U. Lic. tchr., Fla.; tng. lic. clin. and child care svcs. Psychometrician Mailman Ctr. for Child Devel., U. Miami, 1975-76; supr. adoptions Health and Rehabilitative Svcs. Fla., Miami, 1972-75, 76-80; instr. psychology Draughons Jr. Coll., Memphis, 1980-81; spl. project dir. Children's Psychiat. Ctr., Miami, 1981-84; exec. dir. Community Habilitation Ctr., Miami, 1984-86; shelter dir. Miami Bridge, Inc., Miami, 1986-89; regional dir. Luth. Ministries Fla., Ft. Lauderdale, 1989-90; exec. dir. Residential Pla. at Blue Lagoon Inc., Miami, 1990; grant writer, researcher, speaker at confs., 1990—; instr. Dade County Pub. Sch. System, 1991—; health ctr. adminstr. Dade County Pub. Health Dept. State of Fla. Dept. Health and Rehab. Svcs., 1992-94; instr. Dade County Pub. System, 1994—; instr. psychology Fla. Nat. Coll., 1998—, acad. adv., 1999—; facilitator nat. confs. Nat. Justice Dept. Bd. dirs. S.E. Region Com. To Study AIDS and AIDS Prevention; mem. Adult Congregate Living Facility. Recipient award for svc. to runaways Fla. Network, 1989, plaque for work with troubled youth Friends Fla. Network, 1989; Miami Herald scholar, 1969. Mem. Residential Child Car Assn. (bd. dirs., chmn. advocacy com.), Fla. Network Youth and Family Svcs. (quality assurance com., tng. com.), NAFE. Republican. Roman Catholic. Avocations: water sports, tennis. Address: 10521 SW 48th St Miami FL 33165-5649

BLANCO, LILIAN DELOS REYES, biologist; b. Manila, Nov. 21, 1953; arrived in Australia, 1988; d. Delmar Vitancor and Gloria (delos Reyes) B. BS cum laude, U. of the East, Manila, 1975; M in Biology, U. of the Philippines, Quezon City, 1979; PhD, Macquarie U., Sydney, Australia, 1995. Cert. sci. specialist in biology Presdl. Decree Philippines. Sci. rsch. specialist I Philippine Atomic Energy Commn., Quezon City, 1978-81, sci. rsch. specialist II, 1982-84, sci. rsch. specialist III, 1985-87, sr. sci. rsch. specialist, 1988; profl. officer Macquarie U., Sydney, 1989, Australian postgrad. rsch. staff, 1990-93; interpreter various orgns., Australia, 1995; rschr. Macquarie U., 1995; rschr. Biol. and Chem. Rsch. Inst. NSW Dept. Agriculture, Rydalmere, 1995; rsch. officer Inst. Respiratory Medicine U. Sydney, 1996; rsch. officer U. Tech., Sydney, 1997-2000, external cons., Insearch Ltd. Pty., 1997—; co-propr. Interwoven Expressions, 1998; health care interpreter Westmead Hosp. and Cmty. Health Svcs., 1993—; translator pvt. agys., 1999—. Author: String of Words and Solitude, Love Across the Sky. Founder CARE fellowship, Granville, New South Wales, Australia, 1991. Grad. scholar Nat. Sci. Devel. Bd., U. of the Philippines, 1975-77, Fgn. Lang. scholar Fgn. Svc. Inst. Ministry of Fgn. Affairs, Philippines, 1985-86, scholar Japan Internat. Coop. Agy., Tsukuba Science City, Japan, 1987, Postgrad. scholar Australian Govt., Sydney, 1990-93; fellow Internat. Atomic Energy Agy., U. Fla., Gainesville, 1984. Mem. Order of Internat. Fellowship. Adventist. Avocations: singing Gospel music, listening to classical music, foreign language studies. Home: 1 Torres Cres, Whalen 2770, Australia

BLANCO LOPEZ, DESIDERIO, secondary school educator, investigator; b. Sta. Ma. de al Vega, Zamora, Spain, Feb. 11, 1929; s. Secundino Blanco and Adelina López; m. Evelyne Dejardin, June 25, 1966; children: Desiderio, Marianne, Dominique. Doctor degree, U. Nac. Mayor de San Marcos, Lima, 1973. Dir. Decano U. de Lima, Peru, 1972-84, vice rector, 1984-89, rector, 1989-94; supt. Decano Escuela de Postgrado, 1994—. Author: (essays) Imagen por imagen, 1987, Claves semióticas, 1989; co-author: (manual) Metodologia del análisis semiótico, 1980, 83, 89. Mem. Sociedad Peruana de SemiÓtica. Home: Berlín 675, Lima Peru Office: Universidad de Lima, Avda Javier Prado Este s/n, Lima 33, Peru

BLANCO MENDOZA, HERMINIO, Mexican government official; b. Chihuahua, Mex., July 25, 1950; married; 2 children. BA in Econs., Monterrey Inst. Tech., Mex., 1971; student, U. Colo., 1971-72; MA, PhD, U. Chgo., 1978. Analyst U. Chgo., 1975-78; asst. sec. treas. Govt. Mex., 1978-80; prof. economy Rice U., Houston, Tex., 1980-85; advisor to presidency Govt. Mex., 1985-88, undersec. for fgn. trade Secretariat of Trade and Industry, 1988-90, head negotiator Free Trade Treaty, 1990-93, undersec. for trade negotiations, 1993-94, sec. of commerce and indsl. devel., 1995—; rschr. MIT, 1981. Office: Sec Commerce, Piso 10 Col Hip Condesa, 06179 Mexico City Mexico*

BLANC-TALON, JACQUES, scientific manager; b. L'Hay-Les-Roses, France, May 3, 1962; s. Roger Bernard and Suzanne (Jeannin) B.-T.; m. Nathalie Paulette Degouy, Dec. 31, 1965. Degree in engring., French Sch. Radio Electricity & Info., Paris, 1984; MS, Paris XI U., 1985, PhD, 1991. Scientist Suptelecom/CNRS, Paris, 1985; engr. SFIM, Massy, France, 1986-87; postdoctoral fellow CSIRO/DIT, Canberra, Australia, 1991-92; cons. DGA/DCE/CTA/GIP, Arcueil, France, 1993-97, sci. mgr., chief of robotics group, 1997—; prof. Parix XI U., Orsay, France, 1995-99; founding mem. Electronlab, Paris, 1985; chmn. conf. Advanced Concepts for Intelligent Vision Sys., 1999, 2000. Recipient Outstanding Paper award Soc. for Computer Simulation, San Francisco, 1993, Excellence Millennium award Internat. Inst. Advanced Studies, 2000. Mem. IEEE (mem. signal processing bd.). Avocations: piano, chess, karate, cooking, writing. Office: DCE/CTA/GIP, 16 bis Ave Prieur Cote d'Or, 94114 Arcueil France

BLAND, SIR CHRISTOPHER (FRANCIS BUCHAN BLAND), freight company executive; b. May 29, 1938; s. James Franklin MacMahon and Jess Buchan (Brodie) B.; m. Jennifer Mary May, 1981; 1 child; 4 stepchildren. Ed., Oxford (Eng.) U. Gov. Prendergast Girls Grammar Sch. and Woolwich Poly., 1968-70; chmn. Bow Group PLC, 1969-70; dir. Northern Ireland Fin. Corp., 1972-76; dep. chmn. Ind. Broadcast Authority, 1972-80; chmn. Sir Joseph Causton & Sons, 1977-85, London Weekend TV Holdings, 1984-94, Century Hutchinson Group, 1984-89, Life Scis. Internat. PLC (formerly Philcom PLC), 1987—, Nat. Freight Consortium PLC, London, 1994—, BBC, London; mem. bd. govs. BBC, 1996—. Editor Crossbow, 1971-72. Mem. Greater London Coun., Lewisham, 1967-70, Burnham Com., 1970, Prime Min.'s Adv. Panel on Citizen's Charter, 1991-94; mem. Chancellor's Pvt. Fin. Panel, 1994—, chmn., 1995—; chmn. rev.group on nat. tng. coun. and nat. staff coms. Nat. Health Svc., 1982; chmn. Hammersmith and Queen Charlotte's Hosps., 1982-94, Hammersmith Hosps. Nat. Health Svc. Trust, 1994—; mem. coun. Royal Postgrad. Med. Sch., 1982—, St. Mary's Med. Sch., 1984-88; mem. Irish Olympic Fencing Team, 1960; capt. modern pentathlon team Oxford U., 1959-60, capt. fencing team, 1961. 2nd lt. 5th Royal Inniskilling Dragoon Guards, 1956-58; lt. North Irish Horse Territorial Arty., 1958-69. Mem. Beefsteak Club. Office: BBC Broadcasting House, Portlands Pl, London W1A 1AA, United Kingdom*

BLAND, JOHN HANNAM, editor; b. Silsden, Yorkshire, Eng., Dec. 1, 1930; s. Herbert Hannam and Lucy Margaret (Anderson) B.; m. Olive Mary Hirst, Mar. 17, 1954; children: Paul Alastair, Andrew James, Helen Fiona. BA with honours, U. Manchester, Eng., 1953. Reporter, feature writer The Yorkshire Post, Leeds, Eng., 1955-59; foreign correspondent Reuters News Agy., London, Cuba, Caribbean, Mexico, 1959-72; features editor The Daily Telegraph Mag., London, 1973-74; editor in chief World Health Mag., Geneva, 1974-90; journalist pvt. practice, Geneva, 1991—. Mem. European Assn. Sci. Editors, Cercle des Attachés Info. Internat. Episcopalian. Avocations: skiing, walking, Arthurian Legends, classical music. Home: Côte de Mourex, 01220 Mourex France Office: World Health Orgn, Avenue Appia, 1211 Geneva 27, Switzerland

BLAND, TERESA P., financial analyst, consultant; b. N.Y.C., Oct. 19, 1957; d. Richard James and Janet (Myers) B. BA in Art History and Comparative Lit., Fordham U., 1989. Adminstrv. asst. Juilliard Sch., N.Y.C., 1988-90; bursar Grad. Sch. Figurative Art, N.Y.C., 1990-91; registrar Cunningham Dance Found., N.Y.C., 1993-94, fin. officer, 1994-95; contr. Stephen Gaynor Sch., N.Y.C., 1995-96; internal controls analyst Office of the Comptr., City of N.Y., 1998—; archivist Found. for Dance Promotion, N.Y.C., 1996. Vol. Kids and the Power of Work. Charlotte W. Newcombe Found. scholar, 1988, 89. Mem. Film Soc. Lincoln Ctr., Mus. Modern Art, Fordham U. Alumni Fedn. Democrat. Avocations: opera, ballet, cinema, travel, museums. Home: 3900 Greystone Ave Bronx NY 10463-1937 Office: Comptr's Office Mcpl Bldg One Centre St New York NY 10007

BLANDINO, BAYARDO MARTIN, artist; b. Carazo, Nicaragua, Aug. 22, 1969; arrived in Honduras, 1985; s. Bayardo Blandino and Leslie Madri-

gal. B in graphic arts, Escuela Nacional de Bellas Artes, Honduras, 1990. One-man shows include Alianza Francesa, Tegucigalpa Honduras, 1991, Gallery Portales, Tegucigalpa, 1992, 95, Gallery Los Toldos, Monterrey, Mex., 1993, Museo de Arte Contemporaneo, Panama, 1999, Fragmentaciones Proyecto de Exhibicion/Inst. Italo, Taipei Fine Arts Mus., 2000; exhibited in group shows, Oxfam, Eng., 1992, Seville, Spaing, 1992, San Jose, Costa Rica, 1992, Galeria Arte Moderno, Santo Domingo, Dominican Republic, 1992, 94, Gallery Portales, 1993, Nicaragua, 1991, 92, 94, Honduran Inst. Interam. Culture, 1992, 94 (award 1992, hon. mention 1994), Jakarta, Indonesia, 1995, Taipei, 1996, Centro Cultural la Beneficencia Valencia, Spain, 1998, Istituto Italo-Latinoamericano Italia, Rome, 1999, Taipei Fine Arts Mus., 1999. Recipient Rodrigo Peñalba award, 1991, 92, 94. Mem. Unión Nicaragüense de Artistas Plasticos Leonel Vanegas.

BLANDY, JOHN PETER, retired urological surgeon; b. Calcutta, Brit. India, Sept. 11, 1927; (parents English citizens); s. Edmond Nicolas and Dorothy Kathleen (Marshall) B.; m. Anne Mathias, Aug. 6, 1953; children: Susan Elizabeth, Caroline Anne, Nicola Jane, Kitty Helen. BA, Oxford U., 1948, BM, BCh, 1951, MA, 1953, DM, MCh, 1963. Exchange fellow Presbyn. St. Luke's Hosp., Chgo., 1960-64; consultant surgeon St. Peter's Hosp., London, 1968; consultant surgeon London Hosp., 1964-68, house surgeon, 1952, registrar, 1955-60; prof. urology London Hosp. U. London, 1969-92. Contbr. articles to profl. publs. and profl. books. Capt. M.C., Royal Army, 1953-55. Decorated comdr. Brit. Empire; recipient Freyer medal Galway U., 1976, Francisco Diaz medal Spanish Urol. Assn., 1988. Mem. European Assn. Urology (pres. 1986-88), Royal Coll. Surgeons Eng. (coun. 1982, Hunterian prof. 1963, v.p. 1992-94), Brit. Assn. Urol. Surgeons (pres. 1984-86, St. Peter's medal 1982); hon. mem. Am. Urol. Assn., Australasian Urol. Assn., Danish Urol. Soc., Mexican Acad. Urology, Can. Urol. Assn. Avocations: painting, sculpture.

BLANDY, RICHARD JOHN, economics educator; b. Vila, Vanuatu, Dec. 8, 1938; arrived in Australia, 1946; s. Richard Denis and Agnes Maxwell (Douglas) Blandy; m. Roslyn Anne Shepherd, June 24, 1941; children: Karen Jane, Alison Ingrid, Joanna Susan. B.Econ. with honors, Adelaide U., Adelaide, Australia, 1961; MA, Columbia U., N.Y.C., 1966; PhD, Columbia U., 1969. Tutor in Econ. U. Adelaide, 1962-63; profl. economist Internat. Labour Orgn., Geneva, 1963-66; sr. lectr. Flinders U. S. Australia, Adelaide, 1969-74; dir. Nat. Inst. Labour Studies, Adelaide, 1972-75, 80-92; reader in econs. Flinders U. South Australia, Adelaide, 1974; prof. econs. Flinders U. South Australia, 1975-97; emeritus prof. econs. Flinders U. South Australia, Adelaide, 1998—; Henderson prof. applied econ. and social rsch. U. Melbourne, 1992-94; CEO South Australian Devel. Coun., Adelaide, 1995-97; exec. dir. AustralAsia Econs. Pty. Ltd., Bedford Park, 1998—; assoc. commr. Industries Assistance Commn., Canberra, Australia, 1987—; adj. prof. econs. Curtin U., Perth, 1994—, No. Territory U., Darwin, 1998—, U. South Australia, 1999—. Editor, co-author: Australia At The Crossroads, 1980, How Labour Markets Work, 1982, Structured Chaos,1 985, Budgetary Stress, 1989, Fiji: Opportunity From Adversity, 1988, Labour Productivity and Living Standards, 1990, The Population Growth Prospects of the Darwin Region, 1998. Mem. State Devel. Coun., Adelaide, 1980-86, Australian Coun. for Population and Ethnic Affairs, 1981-84; gov. Seymour Coll., Adelaide, 1981-88; chmn. So. Devel. Bd., Adelaide, 1988-90. Named Giblin Lectr., Econ. Soc. Australia, 1985. Fellow Acad. of Social Scis. Australia; mem. Nat. Inst. Labour Studies (life). Anglican. Avocations: tennis, golf, bridge, gardening. Home: 88B Queen St, Norwood Australia 5067 Office: Flinders U, Bedford Park Australia 5042

BLANK, ARTHUR M., home and lumber retail chain executive; b. 1942. Acct. Arthur Young & Co., N.Y.C., 1963-67; with Daylin Inc., Los Angeles, 1967-74; v.p., treas. Handy Dan Home Improvement Ctrs. Inc., Los Angeles, 1974-78; with Home Depot Inc., Atlanta, 1978—, now pres., CEO, also bd. dirs. Office: Home Depot Inc 2455 Paces Ferry Rd Atlanta GA 30339-4024*

BLANKE, MICHAEL MARTIN, plant physiologist, researcher; b. Berlin, June 17, 1955; s. Martin Wolfgang Blanke and Edith Petrusch. MSc in Agr., Bonn U., 1980, PhD in Agr., 1984, postdoctoral, 1994—. Vis. prof., reader in fruit physiology U. Osnabrück, 1993-94; sr. scientist, reader U. Bonn, Germany, 1994—; organizer internat. workshops, 1990—; cons. PPSystems, U.S., 1995—; vis. fellow in plant physiology, U. Bristol, Eng., 1991—; rsch. assoc. U. Calif., Riverside, 1995; rsch. fellow Dept. Agr., Govt. of South Africa, 1989. Editor: Nitrat in Pflanze und Boden, 1990, Pome Fruit Quality Acta Horticulture, 1998, Fruit Production in the Tropics Acta Horticultura 531, 2000; contbr. articles to profl. jours.; editor procs. Mem. European Fruit Rsch. Inst. Network (sec.-gen. 1994-97), Gesellschaft für Angewandte Botanik, French Soc. European Plant Physiologists, East Malling Rsch. Assn., Soc. Exptl. Botany, Internat. Soc. Hort. Sci. Avocations: sailing, skiing. Fax: 49 228 73 5764. Email: MMBLANKE@uni-bonn.de. Office: Inst Obstbau Gemüsebau, Auf dem Hügel 6, D-53121 Bonn Germany

BLANKENBURG, ERHARD R., sociology of law educator; b. Duisburg, Germany, Oct. 20, 1938; arrived in The Netherlands, 1980; s. Kurt and Anna (Schlang) B. MA, U. Oreg., 1964; PhD, U. Basel, Switzerland, 1965; Dr.phil.habil., U. Freiburg, Germany, 1974. Ptnr. Quickborner Team, Hamburg, Germany, 1969-71; sr. rschr. Prognos AG, Basel, 1971-73; fellow Max Planck Inst., Freiburg, 1973-75, Wissenschaftszen Frum, Berlin, 1975-80; prof. Vrije U., Amsterdam, The Netherlands, 1980—. Author books on cts., criminology, comparative law, legal behavior; editor: Zeitschrift Rechtssoziologe. Mem. Law and Soc. Assn., Internat. Socoil. Assn. Soc. of Law, other European profl. orgns. Home: Keizersgracht 732, 1017 EW Amsterdam The Netherlands Office: Vrije U, 1081 HV Amsterdam The Netherlands

BLANKENSHIP, RICHARD EUGENE, communications company executive; b. Steubenville, Ohio, July 20, 1948; s. Alonzo Willard and Virginia Cornelia (Sczcepkowski) B.; m. Linda Lee Friesen, may 25, 1991. BS in Aerospace Engring., W.Va. U., 1971; student, U. Mo., 1972-73; MBA, San Diego State U., 1978; student, U. Kans., 1980. Civil engr. Starvaggi Industries, Inc., Weirton, W.Va., 1971-72; commd. U.S. Army, 1975-81, advanced through grades to capt., 1976; analysis officer Combined Arms Ctr., U.S. Army, Ft. Leavenworth, Kans., 1981-83, program mgr., 1981-83; resigned U.S. Army, 1983; prin. mktg. rep. Honeywell Inc., Mpls., 1983-87; sr. mktg. rep. Honeywell Inc., McLean, Va., 1987-90; market devel. mgr. Alliant Techsystems Inc., Arlington, Va., 1990-93; dir. govt. programs Microelectronics and Computer Tech. Corp., 1993-94; govt. acct. mgr. Met. Fiber Sys., 1994-98; telecom sales mgr. MCI Worldcom, Vienna, Va., 1998—; cons. Mead Resources Inc., Mpls. Author: Heavy Divisions, 1982. Vol. Spl. Olympics, Minnetonka, Minn., 1984, 1985. Decorated Meritorious Service medal Oak Leaf Cluster. mem. Am. Def. preparedness Assn., Assn. U.S. Army, Navy League (v.p. nat. capital coun.), nat. Security Indsl. Assn., W.Va. U. Alumni Assn. (bd. dirs., sec. 1990, nat. chpt. treas. 1991), Electronics Indsl. Assn. Republican. Roman Catholic. Clubs: Sporting, Tysons Corner, Athletic. Avocations: photography, music, basketball, golf. Home: 2769 Oakton Plantation Ln Vienna VA 22181-5924 Office: Worldcom 8100 Boone Blvd Vienna VA 22182-2642

BLANKFORT, LOWELL ARNOLD, newspaper publisher; b. N.Y.C., Apr. 29, 1926; s. Herbert and Gertrude (Butler) B.; m. April Pemberton; 1 child, Jonathan. BA in History and Polit. Sci., Rutgers U., 1946. Reporter, copy editor L.I. (N.Y.) Star-Jour., 1947-49; columnist London Daily Mail, Paris, 1949-50; copy editor The Stars & Stripes, Darmstadt, Germany, 1950-51, Wall St. Jour., N.Y.C., 1951; bus., labor editor Cowles Mags., N.Y.C., 1951-53; pub. Pacifica (Calif.) Tribune, 1954-59; free-lance writer Europe, Asia, 1959-61; co-pub., editor Chula Vista (Calif.) Star-News, 1961-78; co-owner Paradise (Calif.) Post, 1977—; co-owner Monte Vista (Colo.) Jour., Ctr. (Colo.) Post-Dispatch, Del Norte (Colo.) Prospector, 1978-93, Plainview (Minn.) News, St. Charles (Minn.) Press, Lewiston (Minn.) Jour., 1980-98, Summit (Colo.) Sentinel, New Richmond (Wis.) News, 1981-87, Yuba City Valley Herald, Calif., 1982-85, TV Views, Monterey, Calif., 1982-87, Summit County Jour., Colo., 1982-87, Alpine (Calif.) Sun, 1987-93, Bassics Mag., 1998—, Fingerstyle Guitar Mag., 1999—. Columnist, contbr. articles on fgn. affairs to newspapers. Active Calif. Dem. Ctrl. Com., 1963. Recipient awards Best Editls. in Calif., non-dailies, 1st or 2nd place seven consecutive years (Calif. Newspaper Pub. Assn.), Best Editl. in U.S. (Nat. Newspaper Assn.), Best Editl. U.S. Suburban Newspapers (Suburban Pubs. Newspapers Am.), Headliner of Yr. (San Diego Press Club), John Swett award (Calif. Edn. Assn.) and Citizen of the Yr. (Sweetwater Edn. Assn.), Spl. Media award (Nat. Conf. Christians and Jews), for articles on South America; named Outstanding Layman of Yr., Sweetwater Edn. Assn., 1966, Citizen of Yr., City of Chula Vista, 1976, Headliner of Yr., San Diego Press Club, 1980. Mem. ACLU (pres. San Diego chpt. 1970-71), Calif. Newspaper Pubs. Assn., World Affairs Coun. San Diego (pres. 1996-99), Ctr. Internat. Policy (bd. dirs. 1991—), Internat. Ctr. Devel. Policy (nat. bd. 1985-90), UN Assn. (pres. San Diego chpt. 1991-93, nat. coun. 1992-97, nat. bd. 1997—), World Federalist Assn. (nat. bd. 1992-2000, pres. San Diego chpt. 1984-86), Soc. Profl. Journalists, East Meets West Found. (nat. v.p. 1992-98), Inst. of the Ams. (assoc. 1989—, mem. internat. coun. 1994—). Achievements include widely travelled writer: more than 100 nations on all continents; nterviewed many heads of state including Fidel Castro in Cuba, Li Peng and Li Ziannin in China, Benezir Bhutto in Pakistan, Kim Dae Jung in Korea. Home: 4008 Old Orchard Ln Bonita CA 91902-2337 Office: 315 4th Ave Ste S Chula Vista CA 91910-3816

BLANKSON, VICTOR EMMANUEL ROBERTS, music educator, researcher church and choral music; b. Winneba, Central, Ghana, Feb. 24, 1946; s. Oman Ghan and Jane (Arthur) B.; m. Sarah Baawah Idan, Dec. 23, 1972; 5 children. Music Edn. diploma, Specialist Tng. Coll., Winneba, Ghana, 1972; BA with hons., U. Ghana, Legon, 1980. Edn. officer (music) Ministry of Edn., Jinja, Uganda, 1973-75; music tchr. Winneba Secondary Sch., Ghana, 1975-77, Univ. Ghana Primary Sch., Legon, 1980-82; vol. music specialist UN Devel. Program (Nat. Tchr. Tng. Coll.), Maseru, Lesotho, 1982-84; head of music dept. Maluti Coll., Matatiele, R.S.A., 1984-88, Cicira Coll, Umtata, South Africa, 1989—; radio performer Ghana, 1968-80, Lesotho 1974; adjudicator, Winneba, 1969-82, Uganda, 1973-75; pianist Transkei Tchrs. Assn., Umtata, 1985—. Guest organist Cath. Ch., Winneba, Organ Dedication, 1972; composer, performer (LP record) Robertsville Hymns, 1977; Author: (book) The Syncretic Church Music, 1980; co-editor Ghana Praise: Tunes from Ghana Abroad, 1979. Ch. organinst Meth./Lesotho Evang. Ch., Maseru, Lesotho, 1982-84, Meth. Ch., Umtata, South Africa, 1989—; sec. Fantse Korye Kuw Assn., Umtata, 1989-94. Recipient Symphony Submission Ghana Arts Coun., 1973. Mem. So. African Music Educators Conf., Internat. Soc. Music Edn. Methodist. Avocations: reading, music, (listening, improvising), tennis, organ playing, organizing functions. Home: 939 John Beer Dr, Umtata 5100, South Africa

BLANSJAAR, BEN A., psychiatrist, researcher; b. Leiden, The Netherlands, Apr. 3, 1956; s. Robert P. and Maria L. (De Boer) B. MD, U. Leiden, 1981, PhD, 1992. Psychiatrist Gemeentelyke Geneeskundige en Gezondheidsdienst, The Hague, The Netherlands, 1986-90; psychiatrist St. Joris Gasthuis, Delft, The Netherlands, 1990—, dir. tng. and rsch., 1991—. Mem. Assn. European Psychiatrists, Nederlandse Vereniging Voor Psychiatrie. Office: St Joris Gasthuis, St Jorisweg 2, 2612 GA Delft The Netherlands

BLANTON, JOHN ARTHUR, architect; b. Houston, Jan. 1, 1928; s. Arthur Alva and Caroline (Jeter) B.; m. Marietta Louise Newton, Apr. 10, 1954 (dec. 1976); children: Jill Blanton Milne, Lynette Blanton Rowe, Elena Diane. BA, Rice U., 1948, BS in Architecture, 1949. With Richard J. Neutra, L.A., 1950-64; pvt. practice architecture Manhattan Beach, 1964—; lectr. UCLA Extension, 1967-76, 85, Harbor Coll., Los Angeles, 1970-72. Archtl. columnist Easy Reader newspaper, 1994-96; designed nine bldgs. included in L.A.: An Architectural Guide; works featured in L'architettura mag., 1988; design philosophy included in American Architects (Les Krantz), 1989. Mem. Capital Improvements Com., Manhattan Beach, 1966, city commr. Bd. Bldg. Code Appeals; chmn. Zoning Adjustment Bd., 1990, Planning Commn. 1993-99. With Signal Corps, U.S. Army 1951-53. Recipient Best House of Yr. award C. of C., 1969, 70, 71, 83, Preservation of Natural Site award, 1974, design award, 1975, 84. Mem. AIA (contbr. book revs. to jour. 1972-76, Red Cedar Shingle/AIA nat. merit award 1979). Office: John Blanton AIA Architect 1456 12th St Apt 4 Manhattan Beach CA 90266-6187

BLANTON, PATRICIA LOUISE, periodontal surgeon; b. Clarksville, Tex., July 9, 1941; d. Ben E. and Mildred L. (Russell) B. MS, Baylor U., 1964, PhD, 1967, DDS, 1974, cert., 1975. Diplomate Am. Coll. Bd. Oral Medicine. Teaching asst. Baylor Coll. of Dentistry, Dallas, 1963-67, asst. prof., 1967-70, spl. instr., 1970-73, assoc. prof., 1974-76; resident periodontics VA Hosp., Dallas, 1975; prof. Baylor Coll. of Dentistry, Dallas, 1976-85, Baylor U. Grad. Sch., Dallas, 1976—; prof., chmn. Baylor Coll. of Dentistry, Dallas, 1983-85; prof. emeritus; cons. VA Hosp., Dallas, 1979-82; adj. prof. Baylor Coll. of Dentistry, Dallas, 1985—; cons. Commn. on Dental Accreditation and Coun. of Dental Edn., 1981—; v.p. State Anatomical Bd., Tex., 1983-85; mem. ADA-AADS Liaison Com., 1983—; chmn. Nat. Insts. Health, Oral Biology and Medicine Study Sect. II, 1985-86. Author: Periodontics for the G.P., 1977, Current Therapy in Dentistry, 1980, An Atlas of the Human Skull, 1980 (1st place honors 1981). Invited participant Am. Coun. on Edn., Austin, 1984; mem. liaison com. Dallas County Dental Soc.-Am. Cancer Soc., Dallas, 1976-78; bd. dirs. Dallas Dental Health Programs, 1992-93, S.W. Med. Found., 1992-93; bd. devel. Hardin-Simmons U., 1995—. Named one of Outstanding Young Women in Am., 1976. Fellow Am. Coll. Dentists, Internat. Coll. Dentists; mem. ADA (alt. del.), Tex. Dental Assn. (bd. dirs. 1995-97, v.p.), Am. Assn. Anatomists, Am. Acad. Periodontology, Am. Acad. Oral Medicine, Am. Acad. Osseointegration, Tex. Soc. Periodontists (pres. 1998-99), S.W. Soc. Periodontology (pres. 1999-00), Dallas County Dental Soc. (pres. 1992-93), Xi Psi Phi, Omicron Kappa Upsilon (pres. 1992-93). Avocations: reading, traveling. Office: 4514 Cole Ave Ste 902 Dallas TX 75205-4172

BLANUŠA, MAJA, medical researcher, educator; b. Zagreb, Croatia, May 1, 1940; d. Danilo and Sofija (Mileusnić) B.; m. Zvonimir Vrtodušić, Nov. 16, 1968 (dec. Oct. 1993); children: Tomislav, Mirjana. BS in Chem. Engring., U. Zagreb, 1963, MS in Natural Sci., 1967, PhD in Natural Sci., 1974. Rsch. asst. Inst. Med. Rsch. Occupational Health, Zagreb, 1963-74, rsch. assoc., 1974-83, sci. advisor, 1983—; dep. head Dept. Mineral Metab, Zagreb, 1975-89, head dept., 1989—. Contbr. articles to profl. jours. Cons. WHO, Copenhagen, 1989, EPA, Research Triangle Park, N.C., 1992. Recipient Ruder Bošković Republic Rsch. Coun., Zagreb, 1980. Mem. Croatian Chem. Soc., Internat. Soc. Exposure Analysis. Roman Catholic. Achievements include research on atomic absorption spectrometry and toxicology. Home: 40 Kneza Trpimira, 10432 Bregana Croatia Office: Inst Med Rsch Occupl, Health 2, Ksaverska St, 10000 Zagreb Croatia

BLASCO, AGUSTIN, agricultural engineering educator; b. Valencia, Spain, Aug. 14, 1955; s. Agustin and Maria Luisa (Mateu) B. Degree in Agrl. Engring., Valencia Agr. Sch., 1979, PhD, 1982. Lectr. U. Valencia, 1984-93, prof., 1993—; vis. scientist FAO, Rome, 1997-98. Author: Mejora Genetica del Conejo, 1988; contbr. articles to profl. jours. Spanish Govt. grantee, Edinburgh, 1985-86, Paris, 1994-95. Mem. Brit. Soc. Animal Sci., Am. Soc. Animal Sci. Avocations: music (classical guitar), writing poetry and short stories, ballroom dancing, learning languages. E-mail: ablasco@dca.upv.es. Office: U Politecnica de Valencia, Animal Sci PO Box 22012, Valencia 46071, Spain

BLASER, ARTHUR WESTON, political science educator, writer; b. Seattle, July 1, 1953; s. Henry Weston and Jeanne (LeCrenier) B.; m. Barbara Ann James, Apr. 22, 1995; 1 chid, Christan Amalya. BA, U. Wash., 1974; MA, Ohio Satte U., 1977, PhD, 1979; JD, Southwestern U., L.A., 1990. Bar: Calif. Asst. prof. Augustana Coll., Sioux Falls, S.D., 1977-79; vis. assoc. prof. U. Notre Dame, Ind., 1987-89; from asst. prof. to assoc. prof. dept. polit. sci. Chapman U., Orange, Calif., 1981—; cons. Augustana Rsch. Inst., Sioux Falls, 1981. Writer reference articles Salem Press, Pasadena, Calif., 1990-92, M.E. Sharp, Boston, 1995-97; contbr. articles to L.A. Times, Ragged Edge, The Futurist, Human Rights Quar. Chair edn. task force So. Calif. Coalition Against the Death Penalty; area coord. Unitarian Universalist Svc. Com. So. Calif. Served with USCG, 1973-75. Recipient Human Rels. award Orange County Human Rels. Commn., 1999, Scudder Disting. Faculty award Chapman U., 1991. Mem. Soc. for Disability Studies, Internat. Studies Assn., Amnesty Internat., Calif. Bar Assn., Phi Beta Kappa. Mem. Disciples of Christ Ch. Avocations: cycling, disability-related civic activities, parenting. E-mail: blaser@chapman.edu. Home: 532 N Maplewood St Orange CA 92867-6917 Office: Chapman U Dept Polit Sci 1 University Dr Orange CA 92866-1005

BLASER, MARCO, broadcasting executive; b. Lugano, Switzerland, May 6, 1935; s. Rudy and Anne Blaser; m. Renata Blaser-Pelossi; 1 child, Anthony. Reporter Swiss Broadcasting Corp., Lugano-Besso, dir.-prodr., head pub. affairs, head programming, mem. direction bd.; prodr./dir. Bavaria Film GmbH, Germany, 1961-62. Author/journalist various newspapers, 1962-89. Col. Swiss Spl. Svc. Intelligence, 1962-89. Recipient Documentary prize Porto Roz Koper, 1976, Golden Rose, Space Apollo Mission. Roman Catholic. Office: Direzione Radiotv Svizzera Ital, Office of the Director, 6903 Lugano Besso, Switzerland

BLASHFORD-SNELL, JOHN NICHOLAS, career officer, explorer, author, broadcaster; b. Hereford, England, Oct. 22, 1936; s. Leland and Gwendoline (Sadler) Blashford-S.; m. Judith Sherman, Aug. 27, 1960; children: Emma, Victoria. Student, Victoria Coll., Jersey Channel Islands, Royal Mil. Acad., Sandhurst, Eng.; DSc (hon.), Durham U., 1986; D Eng. (hon.), Bournemouth U., 1998. Commd. 2d lt. British Army, 1955-91, advanced through grades to col.; leader Blue Nile Expedition, 1968, Dahlak Quest Expedition, 1970; officer The British Transamericas Expedition, 1971-72, The Zaire River Expedition, 1974-75, Operation Drake, 1976-81; dir. gen. Operation Raleigh, 1984-91, Jade Venture to Mt. Xixabangma, Tibet, 1990, Kalahari Quest Expdn., 1990, Karnali Quest Expdn. to Nepal, 1991, Karnali Gorges Expdn. to Nepal, 1992, Raja Gaj Expdn. to Nepal, 1993, El Dorado Expdn. to Guyana, 1993, Giant Elephant Quest, India and Nepal, 1994-99, Kota Mama Expedition, 1998-2001. Author tech. publs. in field. Recipient Darien medal Com. Action Pro-Darien, Bogota, 1972, Segrave Trophy, London, 1975, Gold medal Instn. Royal Engrs., 1994; named Freeman of City of Hereford, 1984, La Paz medal, Bolivia, 2000. Mem. Order Brit. Empire, Sci. Exploration Soc. (chmn.), Explorers Club (Sweeney medal 1992), Royal Scottish Geog. Soc. (Livingston medal 1975), Royal Geog. Soc. (Patron medal 1993), Bucks Club, Rotary (Paul Harris fellow). Avocations: shooting, exploration, photography. Fax: 01747-851351. E-mail: expeditions@ses-explore.org. Office: Expedition Base, Motcombe, Nr Shaftesbury, SP7 9PB Dorset England

BLASI, ALBERTO A., statistical mechanics educator, physics educator; b. Terni, Umbria, Italy, Apr. 25, 1943; s. Bernardino Blasi and Elda Ramozzi; m. Livia Ornella Musso, July 1, 1975; 1 child, Elisabetta. Grad. in physics, U. Genoa, Italy, 1965. Vis. prof. CERN, Geneva, 1988; staff mem. U. Trento, Italy, 1991-92; vis. prof. LAPP, Annecy, France, 1993; asst. prof. physics U. Genoa, 1970-74, prof. math., 1975-77, prof. physics, 1978-87, 89-90, full prof. statis. mechanics, 1994—, head physics dept., 1994-97, chmn. physics rsch. area, 1998—; mem. organizing com. Congress on Wind Energy and Landscape, 1997. Editor: Constrained Dynamics and Quantum Gravity, 1996. Avocations: reading, scuba diving, sailing. Office: U Genoa Dept Physics, Via Dodecaneso 33, 16146 Genoa Italy

BLASINGIM, CHARLOTTE OREN DESHAZOR, counselor, consultant; b. Port Lavaca, Tex., Nov. 13, 1943; d. Tom and Lois DeShazor; m. Roy Blasingim, June 19, 1976; children: Vernon Neal III, Ken Stierley, Tim Blasingim, Tenya Blasingim, Trina Preuss. BS in Psychology and Sociology, Houston Bapt. U., 1993; MA in Counseling, Prairie View A & M U., 1997. Advt. salesperson Port Lavaca Wave Newspaper, 1975-76; advisor, censor media prodns. and ops. dept. Arabian Am. Oil Co., Dhahran, Saudi Arabia, 1981-85, sec. transp. dept., 1985-88; counselor clin. group therapy LifeGuide Cmty. Health Ctr., Houston, 1998; couselor Connections/STAR Program, Rockport, Tex., 2000—; lay Christian counselor on call Interdenominational Ch., Dhahran; vol. grief assistance program Houston Hospicee; intern counselor St. Judes Personal Care Home, Silver Ridge Partial Hosp.; group counselor Life Guide, Cmty. Mental Health Ctr. supr. vols. Reaser campaign for Tex. State Rep., Victoria, 1998. Mem. ACA, Assn. Multicultural Counseling and Devel., Assn. Spiritual, Ethical and Religious Values in Counseling, Assn. Specialists in Group Work, Internat. Assn. Marriage and Family Counselors, Am. Assn. Christian Counselors, Tex. Counseling Assn., Tex. Assn. Multicultural Couseling and Devel., Tex. Assn. Marriage and Family Counselors, Chi Sigma Iota. Democrat. Presbyterian. Avocation; writing. Home: 6909 King Arthur Corpus Christi TX 78413-5313 Office: Star Program Connections 1913 Rockport Plaza Hwy 35N Rockport TX 78382

BLÄSIUS, NIKOLAUS HERIBERT ARNOLD (KLAUS BLÄSIUS), orthopedic surgeon, medical educator, researcher; b. Daun, Eifel, Germany, Dec. 6, 1952; s. Walter Matthias and Johanna (Meyers) B.; m. Gerlinde Böhm, Oct. 1, 1987; children: Saskia, Felix, Pascal. MD, U. Aachen (Germany), 1978; Privatdozent Dr. med. habil., U. Heidelberg (Germany), 1989. Asst. surgeon U. Bonn (Germany), 1979-80; asst. orthopedics surgeon U. Freiburg (Germany), 1980-84; cons. orthopedic surgeon U. Heidelberg (Germany), 1985-92; vice-dir. Sch. Nurses, 1986-92; asst. prof. U. Heidelberg (Germany), 1989-94; dir. orthopedic dept. Bethlehem-Krankenhaus, Stolberg, Germany, 1992—; prof. U. Aachen (Germany), 1994—; med. dir. Sch. Physiotherapists, Horrem, Germany, 1994—; cons. Rehaklinik Heidelberg (Germany) for Blood Diseases, 1989-92; founder Stolberger Orthopaedics award; spkr. in field. Author: Endoprothenatlas Hüfte, 1989, Endoprothesenatlas Knie, 1995, Intertrochantere Osteomien zur Behandlung der Coxathrose, 1990, Oberonadie und Sport, 1999; editor Orthopadie und Sport, 1999; patentee in field; inventor cementless Neck preserving system hip. Bd. dirs. Overseas Student Coord., Germany, 1976. Recipient award Internat. Soc. Biomechanics, 1990, N.Y. Acad. Scis., 1995, European Soc. Foot and Ankle Surgeons, 1995. Mem. Internat. Stolberger Orthopädietag (founder, pres.), CLS-Hip-Multicenterstudy Germany (in charge), German Orthopedics Soc., Internat. Cartilage Repair Soc., German Soc. Innovative Orthopedics (v.p.). Roman Catholic. Avocations: history, modern-art, horseriding, skiing. Office: Bethlehem-Krankenhaus, Steinfeldstr 5, 52222 Stolberg Germany

BLASS, ELIZABETH VICTORIA, writer, editor; b. Little Rock, Aug. 30, 1949; d. Noland, Jr. and Elizabeth (Weitzenhoffer). Student, Fla. Presbyn. Coll., 1969. Columnist, editor Ark. Gazette, Little Rock, 1968-77; copywriter, account exec. Robert Landau Assocs., N.Y.C., 1981-83; sr. copywriter Hanley Ptnrship., N.Y.C., 1983-84; v.p., creative dir. Lintas, N.Y., 1988-90. Trustee Village of Pomona, 1997; bd. dirs. Little Rock Drug Abuse Coordinating Com., 1975, Community Photo-Film Workshop, Newburgh, N.Y., 1979-80. Mem. Nat. Assn. Female Execs., Soc. Profl. Journalists, Jr. League Litte Rock. Home and Office: 78 Pomona Rd Suffern NY 10901-1917

BLATT, CECÍLIA TERUMI, biologist, researcher; b. Braganca Paulista, São Paulo, Brazil, Apr. 10, 1960; d. Masato and Fumiko (Tanikawa) Teradaira; m. Celso Ronaldo Blatt, May 17, 1985. BSc in Biol. Scis., Unicamp, Campinas, Brazil, 1981; MSc in Phytochemistry, U. São Paulo, Brazil, 1986, PhD in Phytochemistry, 1991. Prof. botany Oswaldo Cruz Coll. Pharmacy, São Paulo, 1986-92; assoc. prof. U. Fed. Lavras, Brazil, 1997-98; sci. rschr. Bot. Inst., São Paulo, 1993—; vis. asst. prof. Coll. Pharmacy, Chgo., 1999-2000. Recipient grant Fundacao Amparo Pesquisa Estado São Paulo, 1993-98, postdoctoral fellowship, Chgo., 1999-2000. Mem. São Paulo Bot. Soc. (treas. 1997-98). Avocations: eco-tourism, physical exercises. Home: R Carlos Lisdegno Carlucci, 420-PA82, 05536000 São Paulo Brazil Office: Inst Botany, Av Miguel Estéfano 3687, 04301902 São Paulo Brazil

BLATT, MORTON BERNARD, medical illustrator; b. Chgo., Jan. 9, 1923; s. Arthur E. and Hazel B. Student Central YMCA Coll., 1940-42, U. Ill., 1943-46. Tchr., Ray-Vogue Art Schs., Chgo., 1946-51; med. illustrator VA Center, Wood, Wis., 1951-57, Swedish Covenant Hosp., Chgo., 1957-76; med. illustrator Laidlaw Bros., River Forest, Ill., 1956-59; cons., artist health textbooks, 1956-59; illustrator Standard Edn. Soc., Chgo., 1960; art editor Covenant Home Altar, 1972-83, Covenant Companion, 1958-82. Served with USAAF, 1943-44. Mem. Art Inst. Chgo. Club: Chgo. Press. Illustrator: Atlas and Demonstration Technique of the Central Nervous System, also numerous med. jours.; illustrator, designer Covenant Hymnal, books, record jackets. Address: 373 Eliseo Dr Greenbrae CA 94904-1326

BLATTER, JOSEPH S., sports association administrator; b. Visp, Switzerland, Mar. 10, 1936. BBA in Econs., U. Lausanne. Soccer player, 1948-71; dir. tech. devel. programs Fedn. Internat. Football Assn., 1975-81, gen. sec.,

CEO, 1981-98, pres., 1998—; head of pub. rels. Valaisan Tourist Bd., Switzerland; gen. sec. Swiss Ice Hockey Fedn., 1964; mem. Internat. Olympic Com. Named to Order of Good Hope, Olympic Order. Mem. Swiss Assn. of Sportswriters, Panathlon Club. Office: FIFA House, PO Box 85, 8030 Zurich Switzerland

BLAU, JOSEPH NORMAN, neurologist; b. Oct. 5, 1928; s. Moses Abraham and Reisla (Vogel) B.; m. Jill Elise Seligman, Dec. 19, 1968; children: Justin, Adrian, Rosie. MB, BS, St. Bartholomews Hosp. Med. Sch., London, 1952; MD, U. London, 1968. Registrar in neurology London Hosp., 1957-58; sr. registrar London Hosp. and Maidavale Hosp., London, 1959-61; Nufield med. rsch. fellow Mass. Gen. Hosp., Boston, 1962; cons. neurologist Nat. Hosp. and Maidavale Hosp., London, 1962-93; cons. neurology Royal Nat. Throat Nose and Ear Hosp., London, 1965-93; cons. Northwick Park Hosp., Harrow, Middlesex, Eng., 1972-93; hon. cons. neurologist and hon. dir. City of London Migraine Clinic. Author: Headache and Migraine Handbook, 1986, Migraine—Clinical Therapeutic Conceptual and Research Aspects, 1987, Understanding Headaches and Migraines, 1991; contbr. numerous articles to profl. publs. Capt. med. corps Royal Army, 1953-55. Rsch. grantee Med. Rsch. Coun., London, 1963-69. Fellow Royal Soc. Medicine (mem. neurology coun. 1994-97), Assn. Brit. Neurologists, London Jewish Med. Soc. (pres. 1985); mem. Migraine Action Assn. (hon. advisor 1980—), Brit. Assn. Study of Headache (chmn. 1997-2000). Avocations: cello, history of ideas. Home: 5 Marlborough Hill, London NW8 0NN, England Office: St John & St Elizabeth Hosp, 60 Grove End Rd, London NW8 9NH, England

BLAU, RICHARD MILES (DICK BLAU), performing arts educator, photographer, filmmaker; b. N.Y.C., Sept. 4, 1943; s. Albert and Beatrice Mandell (Manley) Freedberg, Herbert Blau (stepfather). BA, Harvard Coll., 1965; PhD, Yale U., 1973. From instr. to assoc. prof. Am. Studies SUNY, Buffalo, 1968-75; from assoc. to prof. dept. film U. Wis., Milw., 1975—, dept. chmn., 1979-99; steering com. photography coun. Milw. Art Mus., 1998—; co-creator program in Am. studies SUNY, Buffalo; co-founder dept. film U. Wis., Milw. Co-author: Polka Happiness, 1992; dir., editor (film) Jidyll, 1990; creative cons. (film) American Movie, 1998 (Grand Jury prize for documentary Sundance Film Festival 1999, Best of Festival prize Edinburgh Film Festival 1999); one-person shows include de Saisset Mus., Santa Clara, Calif., 1975, CEPA, Buffalo, 1975, Perihelion Gallery, Milw., 1983, Scala Galerie, Brno, Czechoslovakia, 1992, Paratiritis Gallery, Thessalonika, Greece, 1994, Midwest Express Ctr., Milw., 1998; exhibited in group shows Basquin Gallery, Milw., 1983, Nexus Gallery, Atlanta, 1985, W.A. Graham Gallery, Houston, 1986, Houston Internat. Foto Fest, 1988, Art Inst./Field Mus., Chgo., 1990, Milw. Art Mus., 1994, New Mus., 1999; represented in collections Art Inst. Chgo., Bklyn. Mus., Finnish Folk Music Inst., Kosciuszko Found. Archive of Polish-Am. Life, Macedonian Mus. Contemporary Art. Co-founder Ctr. for Exploratory and Perceptual Arts, Buffalo, 1973, Perihelion Art Gallery, Milw., 1978, Art Futures, Milw., 1987; founder Cmty. Media Project, Milw., 1986. Fulbright scholar, 1965; Wis. Arts Bd. fellow for photography, 1978, 80, Woodrow Wilson fellow, 1966-67. Mem. Phi Beta Kappa. E-mail: dickblau@uwm.edu. Home: 2723 N Farwell Ave Milwaukee WI 53211-3759 Office: Univ Wis Dept Film PO Box 413 Milwaukee WI 53201-0413

BLAUENSTEINER, ALBERT, computer scientist; b. Vienna, Austria, Sept. 9, 1949; s. Peter and Charlotte Emilie (Lauer) B.; m. Felicitas Nossek, May 27, 1977; children: Bibiane, Björn Christian. Diploma, Tech. U., Vienna, 1972. Programmer Tech. U., 1972-74, systems analyst, 1974-80, chief analyst, 1980-90, sr. mgr., 1990—; cons. in field, Austria, Germany, U.S., and France, 1976—. Contbr. articles to profl. publs. Avocations: astronomy, chess, philosophy. Home: Felix-Dahnstrasse 41, A-1190 Vienna Austria Office: Tech U, Karlsplatz 13, 1040 Vienna Austria

BLAUSEY, JEANNE MARTHA, accountant, financial systems analyst, fraud examiner; b. Toledo, Ohio, Aug. 21, 1958; d. Richard Herman and Dorothy Lucille (Flury) B. A in Bus. Tech. summa cum laude, Tiffin U., 1978; BA summa cum laude, Siena Heights Coll., 1983; MA, George Washington U., 1990. Cert. fraud examiner. Acct. The Prestolite Co., Toledo, 1978-83, SCA Svcs., Inc., Boston, 1983-84; enlisted USN, 1984, advanced through grades to lt., 1991; data processor USN, Norfolk, Va., 1984-89; systems analyst Electronic Data Systems, Detroit, 1990; plant acct. Prestolite Electric, Inc., Dearborn Heights, Mich., 1990; fin. systems analyst USN, Bethesda, Md., 1991-94; cons. acctg. software Solomon Software, Findlay, Ohio, 1994-95; sys. bus. analyst/cons. Omnicare Health Plan, Detroit, 1995-97; project mgr. U. Chgo. Hosps., 1998-99; fin. sys. analyst Amerigroup, Virginia Beach, Va., 1999-2000, mgr. operational audit, 2000—; adj. prof. acctg. Univ. Md., College Park, 1991-92. Lt. comdr. USNR, 1999—. Mem. Inst. Mgmt. Accts., Am. Legion, Assn. Cert. Fraud Examiners. Republican. Roman Catholic.

BLAUW, GERARD JAN, physician; b. Delft, The Netherlands, Nov. 9, 1959; s. Gerrit and Tini (Krul) B.; m. Sandra Wijnands; children: Lisanne, Alexander. MD, Leiden U., The Netherlands, 1986; PhD, U. Amsterdam, 1989. Internist tng. Leiden U. Med. Ctr., The Netherlands, 1990-94, internist, 1995—; project leader Cardiovascular Disease in Elderly, 1996—; prin. investigator Internat. Mulli Ctr. Study, 1998—. Recipient Young Investigator award Intenat. Soc. Hypertension, 1992. Office: Leiden U Med Ctr, PO Box 9600, 2300 RC Leiden The Netherlands

BLAUW, PIETER WILHELMUS, sociologist; b. Voorburg, The Netherlands, July 18, 1942; s. Jakob and Gerritje (Hortensius) B.; m. Gezina Cornelia Bruil; children: Anouk, Simone. Student, Christian Tchrs. Coll., The Hague, 1963; DSc cum laude, Erasmus U., Rotterdam, 1971, PhD, 1986. Tchr. comml. scis. Rutgers Mulo, Rotterdam, 1964-66; asst. prof. sociology Erasmus U., 1971-77, assoc. prof. sociology, 1977—; vis. prof. Swinburne U., Melbourne, Australia, 1993; pres. GS-Group, 1989-94, NWO Rsch. Group, Bldg. and Housing, 1992-94; v.p. ISA Rsch. Group Housing and the Built Environment, 1994—; bd. dirs., pres. Housing Corp. of Schoonhoven. Author: Suburbanisation and Social Contacts, 1986; co-author: Air Pollution and the Social Responsibility of Industrial Leaders, 1970, Emigration, 1983, The Opening of Two Polders. A History on Traffic and Transport, 1989; editor: Space for Public Life, 1989, Spatial Segregation as a Social Problem, 1980, Temporar Mutantur. On Social Change and Developments of Social Thoughts, 1992; co-editor: Urban Housing Segregation of Minorities in Western Europe and the United States, 1991, others; contbr. articles to profl. jours. Cornet Arnhem Artillery, 1963-64. Office: Erasmus Univ, PO Box 1738, 3000 DR Rotterdam The Netherlands

BLAZ, LUDWIK MARIAN, metallurgist, educator; b. Sanok, Poland, Aug. 24, 1946; s. Tadeusz and Boguslawa (Gorgon) B.; m. Teresa Brzysko, July 12, 1970; children: Ewa, Piotr, Joanna. MSc, Acad. Mining & Metallurgy, Cracow, 1971, PhD, 1979, DSc, 1990. Asst. prof. Acad. Mining & Metallurgy, Cracow, 1971-79, adj., 1979-95, prof. phys. metallurgy, 1995—. Author: Dynamic Recrystallization, 1988, Dynamic Structural Processes, 1998; contbr. articles to profl. jours. Office: Acad Mining and Metallurgy, Al Mickiewicza 30, PL30-059 Cracow Poland

BLAZEVIC, MIROSLAV, professional soccer coach; b. Feb. 9, 1934. Coach Grasshoppers Zurich Football Club, Switzerland, Dynamo Zagreb Football Club, Yugoslavia; winner Championship, 1982, Croatian Title, 1994; coach Nantes, France, 1989-91, Croatia Nat. Team, 1994—, World Cup, France, 1998. Office: Croatian Football Fedn, Ilica 31/11, Cro10000 Zagreb Croatia*

BLAZEVICH, LESLIE MATTHEW, financial consultant; b. Lewistown, Mont., May 4, 1943; s. Matthew R. and Beulah (Hoover) B.; m. Marilyn N. Pheiffer, June 15, 1963; children: Rene, Lisa. BS in Acctg., U. Mont., 1968. Cert. fin. planner. Asst. v.p. First Nat. Bank, Missoula, Mont., 1965-1985; sr. fin. advisor Am. Express F.A., Missoula, 1985—. Avocations: fly fishing. E-mail: caddis@bigsky.net. Office: Am Express Fin Advisors 2529 N Reserve St Missoula MT 59808-1313

BŁAZEWICZ-PASZKOW, MAGDALENA, biologist; b. Łodz, Poland, July 10, 1970; d. Jan and Elzbieta Krystyna (Guźdź) Błazewicz; married. MSc, U. Łodz, 1994. Asst. U. Łodz, 1996—; vis. rschr. Smithsonian Inst., Washington, 1995, 99, Inst. Royal des Scis. Naturelles de Belgique, Brussels, 1996, 97, 98; biologist Polish Arctic Expedition, Spitsbergen, 1998. Co-editor Cumacean Newsletter, 1996, 99. Grantee Polish Acad. Sci., 1996, 97. Home: Wypoczynkowa 22, 91-614 Łodz Poland Office: U Lodz Lab Polar Biology, and Oceanbiology, 90-237 Łodz Poland

BLAZHEVICH, SERGEY VLADIMIROVICH, physicist, educator, researcher; b. Makarov City, Russia, Apr. 7, 1948; s. Vladimir Antonovich and Zinaida Yakovlevna (Zhameitki) B.; m. Tatyana Nikolayevna Garelaya, Sept. 12, 1971; children: Alina, Yulia. PhD, Kharkov (Ukraine) State U., 1993. Young rschr. Inst. Physics and Tech., Kharkov, 1972-75, rschr., 1976-95; asst. prof. Belgorod (Russia) State U., 1995-98, assoc. prof., 1998—. Contbr. articles to profl. jours. Recipient grant Russian Found. for Basic Rschs., 1996-98. Mem. United Phys. Soc. of Russian fedn. Avocations: swimming, tourism, gardening. E-mail: blazh@bgpu.belgorod.su. Home: 87 Nekrasov str 17B, 308007 Belgorod Russia Office: Belgorod State Univ, Studencheskaya str 1, 308007 Belgorod Russia

BLAZIN, MICHAEL JOSEPH, banking executive; b. Lancashire, England, Nov. 22, 1955; came to U.S., 1957; s. Atlee Raymond and Felice Mary (Pado) B. BS, U.S. Naval Acad., 1977; MBA, Harvard U., 1985; MS, Johns Hopkins U., 1995. Cert. cash mgr., naval nuclear engr. Distbn. mgr. Procter & Gamble Mfg. Co., Balt., 1985-86; lockbox mgr. Equitable Bank, N.A., Balt., 1986-88, MNC Fin., Balt., 1988-93; project mgr. NationsBank, Balt., 1993-94; project mgr. receivables svcs. Bank of Am., Dallas, 1994—. Lt. USN, 1977-83. Mem. Assn. for Fin. Profls., Naval Inst., Harvard Club (Dallas), Harvard Bus. Sch. Club (Dallas), VFW, Am. Legion. Republican. Roman Catholic. Home: 2604 Hartman St Apt 5208 Dallas TX 75204-2673 Office: Bank of Am MS TX1-492-15-10 901 Main St Fl 15 Dallas TX 75202-3714

BLÁZOVICS, ANNA, biochemist, researcher; b. Budapest, Hungary, Jan. 21, 1951; d. László and Anna von (Kállay) B.; m. Tibor Horváth, Oct. 24, 1981 (div. 1985); 1 child, Balázs Zsigmond Horváth. Diploma, Karl Marx U. Econs., Budapest, 1974; MS, Eötvös Lóránd U., Budapest, 1983; PhD, Hungarian Acad. Sci., Budapest, 1989. Head of Lab. Chinoin, Budapest, 1975-79; asst., Biochem. Inst. Semmelweis Med. U., Budapest, 1979-83, rschr., Arteriosclerosis Rsch. Group, 1983-92, sr. lectr., Dept. of Medicine, 1992—; mem. editl. bd. Med. Jour. of Hungary, 1998—, Folia Hepatologica, 1998—; mem. PhD program Semmelweis U., 1993—, Flavonoid Rsh. Group Hungarian Acad. Sci., 1996—. Recipient Falk prize, Liver Rsch. Found, 1998, Falk II prize, Falk Found., 1996. Mem. Hungarian Sect. Soc. for Free Radical Rsch. (sec. 1993—), Hungarian Gastroent. Soc., Hungarian Arteriosclerosis Soc. Office: Semmelweis Univ, Szenthirályi 46, H-1088 Budapest Hungary

BLAZY, PIERRE FRANÇOIS, science educator; b. Foix, France, May 18, 1931; s. Martial and Suzanne (Rouan) B.; m. Andrée Baptiste, July 25, 1955. Ingenieur geologue degree, Ecole Nationale Superieure Geologie, Nancy, France, 1954; PhD, U. Nancy, 1958. Prof. U. Nancy, 1964-71, Inst. Nat. Poly., Nancy, 1971—; cons. Panamerican Union, Washington, 1967-68; adminstr. Société Nouvelle Acieries Pompey (Steel), Paris, 1984, Ascometal (Steel), Paris, 1984 geology operation systems, Paris, 1986, Guyanor Gold and Diamond Resources, Cayenne, 1998, Golden Star Resources, Denver, 1998; expert European Commns., Brussels, 1985—; bd. dirs., pres. Ecole Nationale Si—eroeire Geologie, Nancy, 1971; bd. dirs. Ctr. Valorisation des Matières Premières, Nancy, 1974—. Author: Valorisation des Minerais, 1970, El Beneficio de los Minerales, 1976, La Métallurgie Extractive des Métaux Non Ferreux, 1979, Energétique Industrielle II, 1981; contbr. 175 articles to profl. jours. With French Mil., 1958-60. Mem. Russian Acad. Scis. Achievements include 17 patents in the fields of flotation reagents, ionic flottation, phosphate roasting and removal of metals contained in phosphoric acid, environ. engring. Office: Ecol Nationale euperieure, de Geologie BP 40, 54501 Vandoeuvre France

BLECHA, KARL, social science administrator, former minister of interior; b. Vienna, Austria, Apr. 16, 1933; s. Karl-Matthias and Rosa Blecha; m. Rosa Nimmerrichter. DPh (hon.), U. Vienna. Mng. dir. Inst. Empirical Social Sci. Rsch., Vienna, 1963-75; M.P. Austrian Socialist Party for Lower Austrian Constituency, 1970-83, 89; chmn. drafing com. Austrian Socialist Party program, 1978, gen. sec. hdqrs., 1975-81, chmn. exec. com., 1977—, dep. chmn. parliamentary group, 1979-83, dep. chmn. of party, 1981-89; minister of interior Austria, 1983-89; mng. dir. Mitropa Inst. Social Sci. Rsch., 1989—. Author: Der durchleuchtete Wahler, Opinion Leaders in Austria, Recht und Menschlichkeit, Die Nationalratswahl. Mem. Austrian coun. Srs. (pres. 1999—), Pensionidenverband Österriche (pres. 1999—). Office: Mitropa Inst, Rainergasse 38, A-1050 Vienna Austria

BLECHMAN, ISAAK HAIM, civil engineer; b. Moscow, Feb. 15, 1934; s. Haim and Clara (Zechtzer) B.; m. Elen Gurevich, Dec. 11, 1974; children: Gaya, Eli. Degree in engring., Poly. Inst. Civil Engring., 1955; PhD, Bldg. Rsch. Inst. Moscow, 1968. Engr. math.-econ. optimization model for steel molds, Russia, 1955-59; rschr. Bldg. Rsch. Inst., Moscow, 1959-73, Haifa, Israel, 1974—; rschr. Bldg. Rsch. Inst. and Transp. Rsch. Inst., 1983—. Co-author: Technology of Precast Concrete Elements, 1963; author articles on modeling construction processes, on the theory of transp., and on the theory of behavior and strength of brittle solids.

BLECK, JORGE MARIA, lawyer; b. Lisbon, Portugal, Dec. 27, 1954; s. João Mayer and Helena (Pinto-da-Cruz) B.; m. Helena Quintela-de-Saldanha, July 25, 1981. Grad., U. Lisbon, 1980. Bar: Portugal 1982. Assoc. J.M. Galvão Teles, Bleck, Pinto Leite & Assocs., Lisbon, 1983-90, ptnr., 1990-93; ptnr. Morais Leitão, J. Galvão Teles & Assocs., Lisbon, 1993—. Mem. bd. Social Dem. Party, Lisbon, 1996-99. Avocation: golf. Office: Morais Leitão Teles Asso, Rua Castilho 75-1st, 1250-068 Lisbon Portugal

BLECK, WOLFGANG PETER, metallurgy educator; b. Duisburg, Germany, May 8, 1951; s. Fritz Rudolf and Pauline Wilhelmine (Baumgarten) B.; m. Elisabeth Agnes Thesing, Jan. 7, 1977; children: Katharina, Monika. Diploma in Engring., Tech. U., Clausthal, Germany, 1975, D Engring., 1979. Group leader rsch. Thyssen, Duisburg, Germany, 1980-93; univ. prof., head dept. ferrous metallurgy RWTH Aachen U. Tech., 1994—; hon. prof. Northeastern U., Shenyang, China, 1995. Chmn. editl. bd. Steel Rsch., 1998—; editor: (conf. book) Modern LC and ULC Sheet Steels, 1998, (book) Werkstoffpruefung in Studium und Praxis, 1999; contbr. articles to more than 100 prof. jours. Recipient Charles Hatchett award Inst. Metals, London, 1990. Mem. VDEM, DGM, DVM. Office: Inst Eisen HuettenKunde, Intzestrasse 1, 52072 Aachen Germany

BLEDZKI, LESZEK ANDRZEJ, limnologist, researcher; b. Gdansk, Poland, Sept. 12, 1953; came to U.S., 1992; s. Jozef Roman and Helena (Chadzynska) B.; m. Maria Stanislawa Bedryj, Apr. 17, 1982; 1 child, Alicja. MS, N. Copernicus U., Torun, Poland, 1978, PhD, 1989. Scientist Exptl. Fish Culture Sta. Polish Acad. Sci., Golysz, Poland, 1978-79; asst. dept. marine ecology Rsch. Inst. on Environ. Devel., Gdansk, 1979-81; sr. asst. N. Copernicus U., Torun, 1981-89, asst. prof., 1989-93; rsch. asst. Mt. Holyoke Coll., South Hadley, Mass., 1995-96, rsch. assoc., 1997—; mem. intergov. com. for marine environ. monitoring of Baltic Sea, Helsinki Conv., Gdansk, 1980-81; mem. Environ. Protection Com. for Local Govt., Torun, 1991-92. Recipient Congress award Soc. Internat. Limnologiae, 1989. Mem. Soc. Internat. Limnologiae-Internat. Assn. Theoretical and Applied Limnology (award 1989), Polish Hydrobiol. Soc. (sec. Torun chpt. 1982-93), Am. Soc. Limnology and Oceanography, Ecol. Soc. Am., Sigma Xi. Achievements include research in amount of phosphorous and nitrogen released by bdelloids rotifers. Avocations: heraldry, family history, photography, traveling, taxonomy. Home: 270 Granby Rd Chicopee MA 01013-3528 Office: Mount Holyoke Coll 50 College St South Hadley MA 01075-1423

BLEEHEN, NORMAN MONTAGUE, oncologist, educator; b. Manchester, Eng., Feb. 2, 1930; s. Soloman and Lena (Shlosberg) B.; m. Tirza Loeb, Sept. 2, 1969. BA, MA, BSci., Exeter Coll., 1947-1952; BM, BChir, Middlesex Hosp., 1955; doctorate (hon.), U. Bologna, Italy, 1989. Intern in medicine and surgery Middlesex Hosp., 1955-57, rsch. fellow, 1957-59, cons., 1967-69, prof. of radiotherapy Med. Sch., 1969-75; intern in medicine Hammersmith Hosp., London, 1956-57; surgery and radiology trainee Middlesex Hosp. Med. Sch., London, 1959-65; Lilly fellow dept. radiology Stanford (Calif.) U., 1966-67; prof. clin. oncology Cambridge U., 1975-95; cons. WHO, Geneva, Internat. Atomic Energy Authority, Vienna. Editor: Radiation Therapy Planning, 1983, Tumours of the Brain, 1986, Investigational Techniques in Oncology, 1987, Radiobiology in Radiotherapy, 1988; contbr. articles to profl. jours. Acting Maj. M.C., Royal Army, 1956-59. Recipient Gotch Meml. medal and prize Oxford U., 1953, Rontgen prize Brit. Inst. Radiology, 1986; named Commdr. of the British Empire, 1994. Fellow Royal Coll. Radiologists, Royal Coll. Physicians, Am. Coll. Radiology (hon.); mem. Internat. Soc. Radiation Oncology (pres. 1985-89), Internat. Assn. Study of Lung Cancer (v.p. 1988-92), Med. Rsch. Coun. Cancer Therapy Com. (chmn. 1972-78), Brit. Assn. Cancer Rsch. (chmn. 1977-80), Royal Soc. Medicine. Jewish. Avocations: gardening, skiing, reading. Office: Addenbrooke's Hosp, St John's Coll, Cambridge CB2 1TP, England

BLEIBERG, LEON WILLIAM, surgical podiatrist; b. Bklyn., June 9, 1932; s. Paul Pincus and Helen (Epstein) B.; m. Beth Daigle, June 7, 1970; children: Kristina Noel, Kelley Lynn, Kimberly Ann, Paul Joseph. Student, L.A. City Coll., 1950-51, U. So. Calif., 1951, Case Western Res. U., 1951-53; DSc with honors, Temple U., 1955; D in Podiatric Medicine, Pa. Sch. Podiatric Medicine, 1965; PhD, U. Beverly Hills, 1970. Served rotating internship various hosps., Phila., 1954-55; resident various hosps., Montebello, L.A., 1956-58; surg. podiatrist So. Calif. Podiatry Group, Westchester (Calif.), L.A., 1956-75; health care economist, researcher Drs. Home Health Care Svcs., 1976—; chmn. bd. Unltd. Healthcare, Metro Manila, Philippines; v.p. pub. rels. Bilboa Wellness Found., Upland, Calif.; CEO Med. Trianon, Newbury Park, Calif.; dir. biomechanics dept. Anit-Aging and Rejuvenation Clinic, Torrance, Calif.; podiatric cons. U. So. Calif. Athletic Dept., Morningside and Inglewood (Calif.) High Schs., Internet Corp., Royal Navy Assn., Long Beach, Calif. Naval Sta.; exec. cons. Thomas Med. Group, Pomona, Calif., 1995, Cardiotel, Van Nuys, Calif., 1995; lectr. in field; healthcare affiliate Internat. divsn. CARE/ASIA, 1987; pres. Medica, Totalcare, Cine-Medics Corp., Strategic World-Wide Health Care Svcs.; exec. dir. Internat. Health Trust, developer Health Banking Program; adminstr. Orthotic Concepts, 1993; prof. health care econs. and med. rehab. Global U., Ontario, Calif., chmn. dept. health care econs., chmn. dept. biomechanics and phys. rehab.; CEO Integrated Wellness Ctrs.; exec. dir. wellness divsn. Crown Golden Eagles; mem. nat. leadership Temple U., Phila.; exec. dir. The Med. Trianon. Producer (films) The Gun Hawk, 1963, Terrified, Day of the Nightmare; contbr. articles to profl. jours. Hon. Sheriff Westchester 1962-64; commd. mem. Rep. Senatorial Inner Circle, 1984-86; co-chmn. health reform com. United We Stand Am., Thousand Oaks, Calif.; mem. exec. coun. State of Calif., United We Stand Am.; active 1st Security and Safety, Westlake Village, Calif., 1993—; lt. comdr. med. svcs. corps Brit.-Am. Sea Cadet Corps, 1984—; track coach Westlake High Sch., Westlake Village; exec. sec. Nat. Coalition Parents for Anti-Drug/Violence Corp., Inc. L.A. World Affairs Coun.; county inspector U.S. Election Com., Calif.; exec. sec. Nat. Coalition of Parents Against Drug Abuse and Violence, Exec. award, 1999. With USN, 1955-56. Recipient Medal of Merit, U.S. Presdl. Task Force, Grand award Top Personalities mag., 1999. Mem. Philippine Hosp. Assn. (Cert. of Appreciation 1964, trophy for Outstanding Svc. 1979), Calif. Podiatry Assn. (hon.), Am. Podiatric Med. Assn. (hon.), Acad. TV Arts and Scis., Royal Soc. Health (Eng.), Western Foot Surgery Assn., Am. Coll. Foot Surgeons, Am. Coll. Podiatric Sports Medicine, Internat. Coll. Preventive Medicine, Hollywood Comedy Club, Sts. and Sinners Club, Westchester C. of C., Hals Und Beinbruch Ski Club, Beach Cities Ski Club, Orange County Stamp Club, Las Virgenes Track Club, Masons, Shriners, Scottish Rite. Fax: 805-499-8877. Home: 55 N Wendy Dr Newbury Park CA 91320-4351

BLEICHER, SHELDON JOSEPH, endocrinologist, medical educator; b. N.Y.C., Apr. 9, 1931; s. Max and Fannie (Klieger) B.; m. Diane D. Cole, Aug., 1990; children from previous marriages: Erick Max, Phillip Thaddeus Samuel, Deborah Ann Cote, Sandra Lynn Gable, Jodie Lisa Cole. A.B., NYU, 1951; M.S., Western Ill. U., 1952; M.D., SUNY Downstate Med. Center, Bklyn., 1956. Intern L.I. Jewish Hosp. Ctr., New Hyde Park, N.Y., 1956-57; resident Boston City Hosp., 1959-60; chief rsch. fellow in medicine Harvard-Thorndike Meml. Lab., Boston, 1962-63; chief metabolic research unit Jewish Hosp. Med. Center, Bklyn., 1963-67, chief div. endocrinology and metabolism, 1967-77; pvt. practice specializing in endocrinology and diabetes Woodbury, N.Y., 1990—; prof. medicine SUNY Downstate Med. Center, 1975—; chmn. dept. internal medicine Bklyn.-Cumberland Med. Center, 1978-83, Bklyn.-Caledonian Med. Ctr., 1983-90; cons. IAEA, Vienna, Austria, 1966—; mem. attending staff North Shore Univ. Hosp. at Syosset, North Shore Univ. Hosp. at Plainview, North Shore Univ. Hosp. at Manhasset. Mem. editorial bd. Diabetes in News, Practical Diabetes; contbr. articles to profl. jours. Vice pres. Locust Valley Central Sch. Bd., 1981-82, pres., 1982-85. Served to capt. M.C., USNR, 1957-92, ret. NIH fellow, 1960-63; NIH research career devel. award, 1970-75; recipient Torch of Liberty award Anti-Defamation League of B'nai Brith, 1982 . Fellow ACP, Am. Coll. Endocrinology; mem. AMA, N.Y. State Soc. Medicine, Nassau County Med. Soc., Am. Soc. Internal Medicine, Am. Diabetes Assn. (bd. dirs. 1979-85, Achievement award 1986, 90), N.Y. Diabetes Assn. (bd. dirs. 1965-93), pres. 1976-78), L.I. Diabetes Assn. (pres. 1978-81), N.Y. State Soc. Internal Medicine (state bd. dirs., treas. Bklyn. chpt., chmn. continuing edn. com.), Bklyn. Soc. Internal Medicine (treas. 1983-85, sec. 1985-87, pres. 1987-89), Endocrine Soc., Am. Assn. Clin. Endocrinologists, Am. Coll. Endocrinologists, Internat. Diabetes Fedn., Juvenile Diabetes Found. Internat., Sagamore Yacht Club (L.I., fleet surgeon 1983-86). Jewish. Office: 165 Froehlich Farm Blvd Woodbury NY 11797-2906

BLEILER, CHARLES ARTHUR, lawyer; b. Boston, Mar. 16, 1945; s. Charles Edward and Grace Rita Bleiler; m. Joyce Ann Kohlmyer, Oct. 6, 1972; children: Charles Edward. BS, Tufts U., 1967; JD, U. San Diego, 1973. BAr: Calif. 1973, U.S. Dist. Ct. (so. dist.) Calif. 1973. Commd. ensign U.S. Navy, 1967, advanced through grades to lt. comdr., resigned, 1978; ptnr. Williams, Clodig & Bleiler, San Diego, 1974-85, Bleiler & Reiter, San Diego, 1985-91, Malowney, Chialtas & Bleiler, San Diego, 1991-93; pres. Charles A. Bleiler A.P.C., San Diego, 1987—; lectr. San Diego Trial Lawyers Assn., 1982. Bd. dirs. Rancho Santa Fe (Calif.) Cmty. Ctr., 1990-94, pres., 1993-94; mem. San Dieguito Soccer Bd., Encinitas, Calif., 1991-92; bd. dirs. Torrey Pines H.S. Found., Del Mar, Calif., 1996-98, pres., 1997-98; founding mem., lector Nativity Ch., Rancho Santa Fe; fundraiser for charitable orgns.; bd. dirs. Rancho Santa Fe Little League, 1989-92. Mem. ATLA, Calif. State Bar, San Diego County Bar Assn., Optimist Club (charter pres. Kearny Mesa club 1987-89). Republican. Roman Catholic. Avocations: sailing, horseback riding, skiing, coaching youth baseball and soccer. Home: PO Box 1653 Rancho Santa Fe CA 92067-1653 Office: 12770 High Bluff Dr Ste 380 San Diego CA 92130-2060

BLENCOWE, PAUL SHERWOOD, lawyer, private investor; b. Amityville, N.Y., Feb. 10, 1953; s. Frederick Arthur and Dorothy Jeanne (Ballenger) B.; m. Mary Frances Faulk, Apr. 11, 1992; 1 child, Kristin Amanda. BA with honors, U. Wis., 1975; MBA, U. Pa., 1976; JD, Stanford U., 1979. Bar: Tex. 1979, Calif. 1989. Assoc. Fulbright & Jaworski, Houston, 1979-86; assoc. Fulbright & Jaworski, London, 1986-87, ptnr., 1988-89; ptnr. Fulbright & Jaworski L.L.P., L.A., 1989-2000, of counsel, 2000—. Editor: China's Quest for Independence: Policy Evolution in the 1970s, 1980; editor-in-chief Stanford Jour. of Internat. Law, 1978-79; contbr. articles on U.S. securities and corp. law to profl. jours. Mem. ABA, The Calif. Club, Phi Beta Kappa, Phi Kappa Phi, Beta Theta Pi. Office: Fulbright & Jaworski LLP 865 S Figueroa St Fl 29 Los Angeles CA 90017-2543

BLENDIS, LAURENCE MORTON, internist, educator, consultant; b. London, Oct. 7, 1936; s. Benjamin and Doris Blendis; m. Maxine Cicely Jose Swan, June 15, 1965; children: Dani, Emma Ronit. MB, BS with honours, U. London, 1961, MD, 1970. Cons. physician Ctrl. Middlesex Hosp., London, 1973-76; sr. physician Toronto (Ont., Can.) Gen. Hosp., 1976—; assoc. prof. medicine U. Toronto, 1976-83, prof., 1983—; vis. prof. Technion U. Med. Sch., Haifa, Israel, 1983-84, Hebrew U., Jerusalem, 1993-94, Ichilov Hosp., U. Tel Aviv, 1996—; ann. lectr. Can. Assn. for Study Liver Ascites and Pathophysiology. Co-editor: Cardiovascular Complications of Cirrhosis, 1990; guest co-editor: HepatoRenal Disorders in Seminars in Liver Disease, 1994; assoc. editor Hepatology, 1997—. Recipient gold medal Can. Assn. for Study Liver Ascites and Pathophysiology, 1996. Fellow Royal Coll. Physicians (London and Can.); mem. Am. Assn. for Study Liver Disease

(publ. com. 1990-93). Jewish. Office: Ichilov Hosp Inst Ge, 6 Weizman St, 64239 Tel Aviv Israel

BLENDON, ROBERT JAY, health policy educator; b. Dec. 19, 1942; s. Edward and Theresa B.; m. Marie C. McCormick, Dec. 31, 1977. BA, Marietta (Ohio) Coll., 1964; MBA, U. Chgo., 1966; MPH, Johns Hopkins U., 1967, DSc, 1969. Fellow Ind. U. Med. Ctr., Indpls., 1965-66; instr. dept. med. care and hosps. Johns Hopkins U. Sch. Hygiene and Pub. Health, Balt., 1969-70, also asst. to asso. dean for health care programs Sch. Medicine, 1969-70, asst. prof. dept. med. care and hosps., 1970-71; asst. dir. planning and devel. Office of Health Care Programs, Johns Hopkins Med. Instns., Balt., 1970-71; spl. asst. for health affairs to dep. undersec. for policy coordination HEW, Washington, 1971-72; and spl. asst. for policy devel. to asst. sec. to health and sci. affairs, 1971-72; sr. v.p. Robert Wood Johnson Found., Princeton, N.J., to 1987; prof. health policy and polit. analysis Harvard U. Sch. Pub. Health and Kennedy Sch. of Govt., Boston, 1987—; dep. dir. health policy Harvard U.; vis. lectr. Princeton U., 1972-87; sr. policy analyst com. on health svcs. industry Cost of Living Coun., Washington, 1971. Mem. editorial bd. Jour. of Am. Med. Assn., 1992—. Mem. Council Fgn. Relations, Inst. Medicine, Nat. Acad. Scis. Home: 478 Quinobequin Rd Newton MA 02468-2127 Office: Harvard U Sch Pub Health 677 Huntington Ave Boston MA 02115-6028

BLENKO, WALTER JOHN, JR., lawyer; b. Pitts., June 15, 1926; s. Walter J. and Ardis Leah (Jones) B.; m. Joy Kinneman, Apr. 9, 1949; children: John W., Andrew W. BS, Carnegie-Mellon U., 1950; JD, U. Pitts., 1953. Bar: Pa. 1954. Pvt. practice law Pitts., 1954—; ptnr. Eckert, Seamans, Cherin & Mellott, Pitts., 1984-93, of counsel, 1993—; mem. adv. bd. dept. mech. engrng. Carnegie-Mellon U., 1992—. Active Churchill Vol. Fire Co., 1970-82; charter and hon. mem. Wilkinsburg Emergency Med. Svc.; sec. Hampton Twp. Zoning Hearing Bd., 1991-92, vice-chmn., 1993; mem. Hampton Twp. Sch. Bd., 1993-97, pres. 1996; mem. adv. bd. Allegheny County Parks, 2000—. With U.S. Army, 1944-46, ETO. Decorated Bronze Star; recipient Disting. Svc. award Carnegie-Mellon U. Alumni Assn., 1993. Fellow Am. Coll. Trial Lawyers; mem. ASME, Pa. Bar Assn., Allegheny County Bar Assn., Assn. Bar of City of N.Y., Pitts. Intellectual Property Law Assn. (pres. 1977-78), Engrs. Soc. Western Pa., Internat. Patent and Trademark Assn., Carnegie-Mellon U. Alumni Assn. (exec. bd. 1996—, exec. com. 1997—), Duquesne Club, Univ. Club, Princeton Club (N.Y.), Rolls-Royce Owners Club (bd. dirs. 1982-84, v.p. publs. 1984-87, treas. 1987-89). Avocation: old cars. Home: 4073 Middle Rd Allison Park PA 15101-1207 Office: Eckert Seamans Cherin & Mellott 600 Grant St Pittsburgh PA 15219-2702

BLENNOW, ANDREAS, researcher; b. Burlöv, Skåne, Sweden, June 1, 1961; s. Hans and Barbro (Åkerlund) B.; m. Kristina Carlsson, Mar. 23, 1991; 1 child, Georg. BSc in Biology/Chemistry, Lund (Sweden) U., 1988, MSc in Biotech., 1988, PhD in Biochemistry, 1992. Asst. prof. Kalmar (Sweden) U., 1993; rsch. engr. Lund U., 1994, asst. prof., 1995; vis. fellow Oreg. State U., Corvallis, 1994; postdoctoral fellow RSBS, ANU, Canberra, Australia, 1995-96; asst. rsch. prof. Royal Vet. and Agrl. U., Copenhagen, Denmark, 1996-98, assoc. rsch. prof., 1998—; project coord. Cereal Starch Network Øresund, Copenhagen, 1999—. Author: Methods of Enzymology, 1994; contbr. articles to profl. jours. Postdoctoral grant Swedish Coun. for Agrl. and Forest Rsch., 1995. Mem. Amnesty Internat. Avocations: music, jazz orchestras. Office: Inst of Plant Biol, 40 Thorvaldsensvej, DK-1871 Copenhagen Denmark

BLESSING, MAXINE LINDSEY, secondary education educator; b. Skirum, Ala., Mar. 27, 1920; d. John Amos and Lizzy Maude (Croft) Lindsey; m. Alvin Reed Blessing, June 24, 1939; 1 child, Deanna Dawn Blessing Gilbert. BS in Secondary English Edn., Jacksonville (Ala.) U., 1956; postgrad., Auburn U., 1974-75. Tchr. DeKalb County (Ala.) Schs., 1943-97; ret., 1997; Beta Club sponsor Crossville (Ala.) H.S., 1960—, drama dir. jr. and sr. plays, 1960—, interim counselor. Sunday sch. tchr., pianist, organist Skirum Bapt. Ch., Crossville. Mem. AAUW, NEA, Nat. Coun. Tchrs. English, Ala. Coun. Tchrs. English, Ala. Edn. Assn., DeKalb County Edn. Assn. (mem. English textbook com. 1988-89), Ea. Star (worthy matron 1944-45), Skirum Cmty. Club (various coms.). Democrat. Baptist. Avocations: music, church and community activities, bridge, reading, attending plays. Home: 2314 County Road 46 Dawson AL 35963-3400 Office: Crossville HS PO Box 38 Crossville AL 35962-0038

BLEUMINK, ERIC, academic administrator, educator; b. Dieren, The Netherlands, May 19, 1935; m. Berendina Tyssen, May 30, 1963; children: Johan Arthur, Marianne Erica. MS in Biochemistry, U. Utrecht, The Netherlands, 1963, PhD, 1967. Rsch. asst. U. Utrecht, 1959-63; jr. scientist Orgn. for Applied Rsch., Zeist, The Netherlands, 1963-67; sr. scientist Acad. Hosp., Utrecht, 1967-71; head of lab. U. Groningen, The Netherlands, 1971-77; asst. prof. U. Groningen, 1977-80, prof., 1980—, vice chancellor, 1984-88, pres., 1988—; bd. dirs. Dutch Inst. Firenze, Italy, Dutch Inst. Cairo, Dutch Inst. Athens, Greece, Dutch Inst.-Tokyo, Japan; v.p. Orgn. Dutch Univs., 1995. Author: Food Allergy, 1967, Side Effects of Drugs Annuals, 1975-81; contbr. articles to profl. publs. Bd. dirs. Christian Dem. Party, The Netherlands, 1965-81; pres. Aid and Health Care Orgn., Drente, The Netherlands, 1991—, Pantheon Health Care Group, 1996—. Sgt.-maj. Dutch Army, 1954-56. Mem. Internat. Orgn. for Dermatol. Rsch., European Acad. Immunology and Clin. Allergy, N.Y. Acad. Sci. Avocations: gardening, hiking. Office: Univ of Groningen, Broerstraat 5 PO Box 72, 9700 AB Groningen The Netherlands*

BLEYN, JACQUES ARMAND, vascular surgeon; b. Paris, Mar. 17, 1946; arrived in Belgium, 1946; s. Aimé and André (Van Dorpe) B.; m. Nicole De Cock, July 3, 1971. MB, Rijksuniversiteit Gent, Ghent, Belgium, 1971, postgrad., 1977. Intern, resident Risksuniversiteit (Belgium) Gent, 1971-77; fellow in cardiovascular surgery Meth. Hosp., Houston, 1976; staff vascular surgeon U. Antwerp, Belgium, 1978-86; chief vascular surgeon O.L.V. Middelares, Deurne, Belgium, 1986—; dir. ABC Antwerp Bloodvessel Ctr., 1998—. Contbr. articles to profl. publs. ties Internat. Soc. Endovascular Special, European Soc. Vascular Surgery (founder), Internat. Soc. CardioVascular Surgery. Avocations: bicycling, hiking. Home: Cogels-Osylei 41, B-2600 Antwerp Belgium Office: OLV-Middelares Ziekenhuis, Florent Pauwelslei 1, B-2100 Deurne Belgium also: Euwfeestkliniek, Harmoniestraat 68, B-2018 Antwerpen Belgium

BLICHERT-TOFT, MOGENS, professor of surgery; b. Spöttrup Castle, Salling, Denmark, Sept. 9, 1936; s. Peter Arild and Jenny (Petersen) Blichert-T.; m. Birthe Janne; one child. Anatomy dissection diploma, Bristol (Eng.) U., 1959; MD, Copenhagen U., 1964. Cert. qualified surgeon, 1975, diploma in surg. gastroenterology, 1979, diploma in endocrine surgery, 1979. Intern Nästved Hosp., Denmark, 1964-68; surg. trainee Copenhagen U. Hosp., 1968-72, sr. surgeon, 1974-79; sr. surgeon Rigshospitalet, Copenhagen, 1972-74, surgeon-in-chief, 1991—; surgeon-in-chief Odense (Denmark) U. Hosp., 1979-91; prof. surgery Odense U. Hosp., 1983-91; pres. Danish Breast Cancer Group (DBCG), Rigshospitalet, 1989—, dir. endocrine and breast unit, 1991—; lectr. surgery Copenhagen U., 1991—. Contbr. articles to profl. jours. Lt. Royal Horse Guard, 1966. Recipient August Krogh prize, 1990, Danish oncology prize, 1997. Hon. fellow Royal Coll. Surgeons Edinburgh; mem. Internat. Surg. Group, Danish Surg. Soc. (pres. 1990-92, Hon. medal 1992), Endocrine Soc. (pres. Scandinavian sect. 1981-85). Fax: 45-35453642. E-mail: mbt@rh.dk. Office: Rigshospitalet 3104, Blegdamsvej 9, 2100 Copenhagen Denmark

BLINKEN, DONALD, ambassador, investment banker; b. N.Y.C., Nov. 11, 1925; s. Maurice Henry and Ethel (Horowitz) B.; m. Vera Evans, Oct. 15, 1975; 1 child, Antony John. B.A. magna cum laude, Harvard U., 1947. Cons. Marks & Spencer, Ltd., London, 1950-51; pres. Exchange Trading Corp., N.Y.C., 1952-53; v.p. Stein's Stores, Inc., N.Y.C., 1953-58, E.M. Warburg & Co., Inc., 1961-72; sr. v.p., chmn. exec. com. E.M. Warburg, Pincus & Co., Inc., N.Y.C., 1970-81, mng. dir., 1981-86, dir., 1987-94; U.S. amb. Budapest, Hungary, 1994-97; dir. Ion Tracking Instruments, Inc., 2000—; mem. adv. com. on internat. econ. policy Dept. of State, 1998—. Author: Wool Tariffs and American Policy, 1948; chmn. publ. com. Commentary, 1984-87. Co-chmn. Concerned Citizens for Arts N.Y. State, 1972-82; pres. Bklyn. Acad. Music, 1971-76, Mark Rothko Found., 1976-88; mem. trustees' coun. Nat. Gallery Art, 1984-94; trustee SUNY, 1976-90, chmn. bd., 1978-90; bd. dirs. N.Y. Philharmonic Soc., 1986-94, vice chmn. 1989-94; mem. U.S. 2d Circuit Nominating Panel, 1979; trustee Manville Personal Injury Settlement Trust, 1986-91; trustee N.Y. Pub. Libr., 1990-94; dir. Inst. Internat. Edn., 1990-94, hon. trustee, 1999—; trustee Isamu Noguchi Found., 1987-94; bd. overseers Nelson Rockefeller Inst. of Govt., 1985-94; chancellor Internat. Coun. of Cen. European U., 1998—; mem. adv. bd. Sch. Internat. and Pub. Affairs, Columbia U., 1998—; mem. exec. com. Citizens Democracy Corps, 1999—; hon. bd. dirs. N.Y. Philharm. Soc., 1999—; hon. trustee Inst. Internat. Edn., 1999—. With USAAF, 1944-45. Mem. Century Assn. Club, River Club (N.Y.C.), Coun. Fgn. Rels., Coun. Am. Ambs. Home: 435 E 52nd St New York NY 10022-6445 Office: 466 Lexington Ave New York NY 10017-3140

BLINKEN, ROBERT JAMES, manufacturing and communications company executive; b. N.Y.C., Apr. 18, 1929; s. Maurice Henry and Ethel (Horowitz) B.; m. Jeanne Pagnucco, Mar. 5, 1955 (div. Jan. 1967); children: Robert James, Rachel; m. Allison Matsner, Dec. 14, 1967; children: Anna, Ingrid. Grad., Horace Mann Sch., N.Y.C., 1946; B.A. cum laude, Harvard U., 1950. Pres. Teleprinter Corp., Paramus, N.J., 1953-61; v.p. Mite Corp., New Haven, 1961-63, pres., 1963-75; chmn. Mite Corp., 1975-85, Comm. Network Enhancement, Mountainside, N.J., 1986—; trustee Albright Inst. Archeol. Rsch., N.Y. Blood Ctr. Served to 1st lt. USAF, 1950-53. Office: 230 Park Ave Fl 26 New York NY 10169-2699

BLINKOVA, OLGA I(GOR), financial educator; b. Moscow, July 12, 1954; d. Igor and Nadezhda Blinkov. Grad., Moscow Acad. Fin., 1976, PhD of Econs., 1986. Dep. head of dept. Gosbank (Cen. Bank), 1976-90; pres., exec. first deputy-chmn. ELBIM-Bank, Moscow, 1990—. Author numerous publs. and monographs on fin., econs., and banking. Mem. Internat. Union Econs., Russian Acad. Econs., Fin. and Law., British Inst. of Dirs. (MInstD). Office: ELBIM-Bank, 3/1 Troilinsky per Arbat, Moscow 121002, Russia

BLINOV, MICHAEL NIKOLAEVICH, biochemist, researcher; b. Leningrad, Russia, Oct. 20, 1939; s. Nikolay Ilich and Lidia Michailovna (Tokareva) B.; m. Tamara Semenovna Kib, Dec. 3, 1961 (dec. Nov. 1991); 1 child, Veronika; m. Ludmila Nikolaevna Pakhomova, Feb. 17, 1993. Physician, magister, 1st Pavlov Med. Inst., Leningrad, 1962; Candidate of Med. Scis., Inst. Haematology Transfusiol., Leningrad, 1965, D in Med. Scis., 1977. Cert. lab. rschr. of higher category. Post-grad. staff Inst. Haematology & Transfusiology, Leningrad, 1962-65, jr. sci. worker, 1965-72; head lab. biochemistry Russian Rsch. Inst. Haematology and Tranfusiology, St. Petersburg, 1972—. Contbr. articles to profl. jours. Avocations: grandchildren, Internet, working in the country. E-mail: spb1077@spb.sitek.net. Home: Apt 40, Basseinaya 81, 196211 St Petersburg Russia Office: Russian Rsch Inst Haematology & Transfusiology, 2nd Sovietskaya 16, 193024 St Petersburg Russia

BLIN-STOYLE, ROGER JOHN, physicist; b. Leicester, Eng., Dec. 24, 1924; s. Cuthbert Basil and Ada Mary (Nash) Bl-St.; m. Audrey Elizabeth Balmford, Aug. 30, 1949; children: Anthony Roger, Helena Anne. BA, Oxford (Eng.) U., 1949, MA, DPhil, 1951; DSc (hon.), U. Sussex, Eng., 1990. Rsch. fellow U. Oxford, 1951-53, sr. rsch. officer, 1954-62, fellow, lectr. physics Wadham Coll., 1956-62; lectr. in mathematical physics U. Birmingham, Eng., 1953-54; prof. theoretical physics U. Sussex, Brighton, Eng., 1962-88, founding sci. dean, 1962-68, dep. vice-chancellor, 1970-72, pro-vice-chancellor of sci., 1977-79, hon. prof. physics, 1988-90, emeritus prof. physics, 1990—; chmn. Standing Conf of Profs. Physics, London, 1974-76, Sch. curriculum Devel. Com., London, 1983-88; pres. Inst. of Physics, 1990-92, Assoc. of Sci. Edn., 1993-94. Author: Theories of Nuclear Moments, 1957, Fundamental Interactions and the Nucleus, 1973, Nuclear and Particle Physics, 1991, Eureka! Physics of Particles, Matter and the Universe, 1997; contbr. articles to nuclear physics edn. to various publs. Lt. Royal Corps Signal, 1943-46, ETO. Hon. fellow Wadham Coll., 1987. Fellow Royal Soc., Inst. Physics (Rutherford medal and prize 1976). Avocation: music. Home: 14 Hill Rd, 14 Hill Rd, BN7 1DB Lewes East Sussex BN7 1DB, England Office: Univ Sussex, Univ Sussex, BN1 9QH Brighton East Sussex BN1 9QH, England

BLIRUP-JENSEN, SOREN, veterinarian, researcher; b. Copenhagen, Sept. 9, 1947; m. Birgit Christiansen, July 22, 1972; children: Niels, Dorthe. Diploma in Vet. Medicine, Vet. U., Copenhagen, 1972, PhD, 1976. Lectr. protein lab. Copenhagen U., 1976-83; rsch. mgr. DAKO A/S, Copenhagen, 1983-96, rsch. dir. clin. immunochemistry and microbiology, 1996—; participant Internat. Standardisation Group for Proteins in Human Serum which resulted in the BCR Ref. Material Cert. Reference Material 470-Coll. Am. Pathologists/Internat. Fedn. Clin. Chemistry; purified the world stds. for human transferrin, Orosomucoid and prealbumin together with Dr. P. Just Svendsen. Recipient Hoppe Seyler prize German Assn. for Lab. Medicine, 1994. Office: DAKO A/S, Produktionsvej 42, 2600 Glostrup Denmark

BLITT, RITA LEA, artist; b. Kansas City, Mo., Sept. 7, 1931; d. Herman Stanley and Dorothy Edith (Sofnas) Copaken; m. Irwin Joseph Blitt, Apr. 18, 1951; 1 child, Chela ne Connie. Student, U. Ill., 1948-50; BA, Kans. City U., 1952; postgrad., Kans. City Art Inst., 1951-55. Freelance painter, sculptor Aspen, Co., Emeryville, Colo., Leawood, Kans., 1958—. Author: Nessie the Sculpture, 1978, 1993, Rita Blitt: The Passionate Gesture, 2000; (video) Creating Drawings and Sculptures with Rita Blitt (formerly called Dancing Hands: Visual Arts of Rita Blitt), 1984; collaborations with dancers and musicians such as St. Joseph Ballet, Santa Ana, Calif., 1995, dancer/choreographer David Parsons, 1996, and cellist Yehuda Hanani, 1986; creator of words and paintings for internat. distributed posters "Kindness is Contagious, Catch It!", led to the founding of the Kindness Program sponsored by The Stop Violence Coalition; One-woman exhbns. include Unitarian Gallery, Kansas City, Mo., 1965, Hall's, Kansas City, Mo., 1967, Spectrum Gallery, N.Y.C., 1969, Johnson County C.C., Overland Park, KS, 1974, 79, Angerer Gallery, Kansas City, Mo., 1974, Battle Creek (Mich.) Civic Art Ctr., 1975, Harkness Gallery, N.Y.C., 1977, Martin Schweig Gallery, St. Louis, 1977, Gargoyle Gallery, Aspen, Colo., 1978, Tumbling Waters Mus., Montgomery, Ala., 1978, St. Louis U., 1980, Rockhurst Coll., Kansas City, Mo., 1984, Jewish Cmty. Ctr., Omaha, Nebr., 1984, Ctrl. Exchange, Kansas City, Mo., 1985, 91, 95, Leedy-Voulkos Gallery, Kansas City, Mo., 1987, Joy Horwich Gallery, Chgo., 1987, Goldman Gallery, Haifa, Israel, 1989, Bet Shmuel, Jerusalem, 1989, Mark Twain Bank, Kansas City, Mo., 1989, 90, Goldman Kraft Gallery, Chgo., 1990, Singapore Nat. Mus., 1991, Albrecht-Kemper Mus., St. Joseph, Mo., 1991, Aspen (Colo.) Inst., 1992, Foothills Art Ctr., Golden, Colo., 1992, Mackey Gallery, Denver, 1992, Jewish Cmty. Campus, Overland Park, KS, 1992, Aspen Inst., Aspen Colo., 1992, U. Ill., Urbana, 1994, Kennedy Mus. U. Ohio, Athens, 1994, Krasl Art Ctr., St. Joseph, Mich., 1994, La Quinta Sculpture Park, La Quinta, Calif., 1994, Baker U., Baldwin, Kans., 1995, Ctrl. Exch., Kansas City, Mo., 1995, Atchison (Kans.) Muchnik Gallery, 1996, Marines Meml. Theater, San Francisco, 1997, Resourceful Women, San Francisco, 1997, City Ctr., N.Y., 1998, Brandeis U., Waltham, Mass., 2000; group exhbns. include Kansas City (Mo.) Mus., 1959, Ringling Mus., Sarasota, Fla., 1967, Springfield (Mo.) Mus., 1967, Joslyn Mus., Omaha, 1972, Doug Drake Gallery, Kansas City, 1975, Conry Gallery, Kansas City, Mo., 1976, Cyvia Gallery, New Haven, 1977, Gargoyle Gallery, Aspen, Colo., 1979, Putney Gallery, Aspen, 1979, Carrefour Gallery, N.Y.C., 1979, Elaine Benson Gallery, Bridgehampton, N.Y., 1980, Tall Grass Fine Arts Gallery, Kansas City, Mo., 1980, 81, Art and Design Gallery, N.Y.C., 1982, Winter Manhattan (Kans.), Streker, Gallery, 1983, Joanne Lyons Gallery, Aspen, 1984, Banaker Gallery, 1987, 88, Andrea Ross Gallery, Santa Monica, Calif., 1990, LA 90, L.A., 1990, Eva Cohon, Chgo., 1995, Obere Galerie, Berlin, 1995, Din Deutsches Inst., Berlin, 1995, Nat. Mus. Women in Arts, Beijing, China, 1995, Dance Aspen, Colo., 1997, The Art Source, Indianapolis, Ind., 1998, Paula Vincenti Gallery, Marbella, Spain, 1999; permanent collections include Albrecht-Kemper Mus., St. Joseph, Mo., Am. Embassy, Barbados, Ga. Inst. Tech., JFK Libr., Cambridge, Mass., Kennedy Mus. Ohio U., Athens, Nat. Mus. Singapore, Skirball Mus., L.A., Spencer Mus. Art U. Kans., Lawrence, Spertus Mus., Chgo., Kansas City (Mo.) Children's Mus., Kennedy Mus., Ohio U., Ga. Tech. Ctr. for the Arts, I-Lan Taiwan City Hall and other numerous pvt. and pub. collections; sculptures in numerous pub. places including, Calif., Ill., Kans., Mo., Md., N.J., N.Y., Japan, Singapore, Israel; print sent to every country in the UN and Palestine Liberation Orgn. in honor of Norway helping Israel and the Palestinians Liberation Organization's first steps toward peace. Mem. Soc. Fellow The Nelson Gallery Found., The Aspen Inst.; bd. dirs. Trio Found.; mem. The Stop Violence Coalition; rsch. assoc. The Internat. Rsch. on Jewish Women. Co-honoree Parsons Dance Co., 2000. Mem. Internat. Sculpture Ctr., Kansas City Artists Coalition. Avocations: music, dance, travel, walking.

BLITZER, WOLF, anchor, news correspondent. BA in History, SUNY, Buffalo; MA in Internat. Rels., Johns Hopkins U.; doctorate (hon.), King's Coll., Gannon Univ., Quinnipiac Coll., SUNY, Buffalo. With Reuters New Agy., 1972; Washington corr. Jerusalem Post; mil. affairs corr. at the Pentagon CNN, Washington, 1990-92, sr. White House corr., 1992-99, host Late Editition, 1998—, sr. anchor, The World Today, 1999—. Author: Between Washington and Jerusalem: A Reporter's Notebook, 1985, Territory of Lies, 1989 (most notable book 1989); contbr. articles to profl. publs. Recipient Emmy for Coverage of Oklahoma City bombing, 1996, Best in the Bus. award Am. Journalism Rev., 1994, Disting. Alumnus award Johns Hopkins U. Alumni Assn., 1999. Office: Cable Network News 820 1st St NE Washington DC 20002-4243

BLIX, ARNOLDUS SCHYTTE, Arctic biologist; b. Borre, Vestfold, Norway, Oct. 4, 1946; s. Erik Schytte and Marie Schytte (Helle) B. Cand. Real U. Oslo, 1973; DrPhilos., U. Tromsø, Norway, 1975; grad., Royal Norwegian Def. Coll., Oslo, 1987. Rsch. physiologist Tromsø, Gothenburg, Fairbanks, 1974-76; assoc. prof. U. Alaska, Fairbanks, 1977-78; dir. dept. arctic biology U. Tromsø, 1979—, prof. physiology, 1980—; active in establishing Polar Mus., Tromsø, 1986; leader or participant over 30 polar expdns. to Alaska, Can., Greenland, Svalbard, and Antarctica, also to sealing and whaling expdns. in North Atlantic; chmn. Norwegian Nat. Com. for Polar Rsch.; del. to Sci. Com. for Antarctic Rsch., European Polar Bd.; former mem. Internat. Arctic Sci. Com.; mem. sci. com. Internat. Whaling Commn., Norwegian Royal Commns. on Sealing and Legislation for Environ. Protection in Svalbard, also numerous others. Contbr. over 150 articles to internat. jours., mainly on physiol. adaptations in arctic mammals and birds. Served with Norwegian Mil., 1971-73. Recipient U.S. Antarctic Svc. Medal, 1995. Mem. Norwegian Nat. Acad. Scis. and Letters (Fram com. Nansen award 1985, Nansen prize 1994, Nansen medal 1996), Royal Norwegian Soc. Scis. and Letters. Fax: 47 77 64 57 70. Office: U Tromsø, Dept Arctic Biology, N-9037 Tromsø Norway

BLIX, HANS MARTIN, retired international atomic energy official; b. Uppsala, Sweden, June 28, 1928; s. Gunnar and Hertha (Wiberg) B.; m. Eva Kettis, Mar. 17, 1962; children—Marten, Goran. LL.B., U. Uppsala, 1951; Ph.D., Cambridge U., 1959; LL.D., Stockholm U., 1960. Assoc. prof. U. Stockholm, 1960; legal adviser Ministry Fgn. Affairs, Stockholm, 1963-76, under sec. of state in charge of internat. devel. coop., 1976-78, 79-81; minister fgn. affairs Sweden, 1978-79; dir. gen. Internat. Atomic Energy Agy., Vienna, Austria, 1981-97; exec. chmn. UN Monitoring, Verification and Inspection Commn., 2000—; mem. Swedish Del. UN Gen. Assembly, N.Y., 1961-81, Swedish Del. Conf. Disarmament, Geneva, 1962-78; chair Assembly States Mems. Chernobyl Shelter Fund, 1998—. Author: Treaty Making Power, 1959; Statsmyndigheternas Internationella Forbindelser, 1964; Sovereignty, Aggression and Neutrality, 1970; The Treaty Maker's Handbook, 1974. Mem. Inst. de Droit Internat. Office: Internat Atomic Energy Agy, Wagramerstrasse 5 PO Box 200, A-1400 Vienna Austria

BLIZARD, SUSAN KENNEDY, biology educator; b. Omaha, Apr. 21, 1949; d. George L. and Bernice E.A. Kennedy; m. John S. Blizard, Mar. 8, 1980. BS in Zoology, U. Nebr., Lincoln, 1972, MS in Zoology, 1974; MBA in Mgmt., Golden Gate U., 1985; ArtsD in Biology, Idaho State U., 1994. Rsch. technician Eppley Cancer Inst., U. Nebr. Med. Ctr., Omaha, 1975-80; rsch. technician U. Calif., Davis, 1980-82; adj. prof. biology C.C. So. Nev., North Las Vegas, 1983-88, prof., 1990—, chmn. sci. dept., 1996-99. ArtsD fellow Idaho State U., 1988-90, fellow C.C. So. Nev. chpt. Phi Theta Kappa, 1992. Avocation: reading mystery novels. E-mail: sue blizard@ccsn.nevada.edu. Office: CC So Nev Biol Scis Dept S2B 3200 E Cheyenne Ave North Las Vegas NV 89030-4228

BLOBEL, GÜNTER, cell biologist, educator; b. Waltersdorf, Silesia, Germany, May 21, 1936. MD, U. Tübingen, Germany, 1960; PhD in Oncology, U. Wis., 1967. Intern Germany, 1960-62; fellow lab. cellular biology Rockefeller U., 1967-69; asst. prof. cell biology Rockefeller U., N.Y.C., 1969-73, assoc. prof., 1973-76, prof., 1976—; investigator Howard Hughes Med. Inst., 1986—; founder, pres. Friends of Dresden, Inc. Contbr. articles to profl. jours. and chpts. to books. Recipient Gairdner Found. award, 1982, Warburg medal German Biochem. Soc., 1983, Wilson medal Am. Soc. Cell Biology, 1986, U.D. Mattia award Roche Inst. Molecular Biology, 1986, Louisa Gross Horwitz prize Columbia U., 1987, Waterford Biomedical Sci. award, 1989, Albert Lasker Basic Med. Rsch. award, 1993, King Faisal internat. prize for sci., 1996, Mayor's award for Excellence in Sci. and Tech., 1997, Massry Prize, 1999, Nobel Prize for Medicine, 1999, Ellis Island Medal of Honor, 2000. Mem. Nat. Acad. Scis. (U.S. Steel award in molecular biology 1978, Richard Lounsbery award 1983), Am. Acad. Arts and Scis., Japan Biochem. Soc. (hon.), Am. Soc. Cell Biology (pres. 1990), German Soc. Cell Biology (hon.), Am. Philos. Soc., European Molecular Biol. ORgn. (assoc.). Office: Rockefeller U Cell Biology Lab 66th and York Ave New York NY 10021-6339

BLOCH, ANDREW CHARLES DANBY, publisher; b. Bognor Regis, Sussex, Eng., Dec. 19, 1945; s. Moishe Rudolf and Mary Hall Bloch; m. Sandra Wilkinson; children: Adam, Hester. MA in Philosophy, Politics & Econs., Oxford (Eng.) U., 1968. Rschr. Oxford (Eng.) Ctr. for Mgmt. Studies, 1969-70; asst. to chmn. Film Prodn. Assn. Great Britain, London, 1970-71; dir. Grosvenor Adv. Svcs. Ltd., London, 1971-74, Raymond Godfrey Ptnrs. Ltd., London, 1974—, Taxbriefs Ltd., London, 1976—; chmn. Helm Godfrey Ptnrs. Ltd.; mem. steering com. for investment advice cert. Securities Inst., London, 1994—; freelance journalist. Author: Providing Financial Advice, 1996; co-author: Planning for School and College Fees, 1988; editor: Taxation and Trusts, 1995—, Personal Investment Planning, 1995—, Pensions, 1995—, Business Financial Planning, 1995—, Financial Advice, 1996—, Investment Portfolio Management, 1997—. Bd. govs. Oxford (Eng.) Brookes U., 1989—, chmn., 1998—; mem. coun. Mus. Modern Art, Oxford, 1989—; trustee Oxford Inst. Legal Studies, 1994-99. Mem. Soc. Fin. Advisers. Avocations: helping to start small businesses, attending the opera, art and antiques, theatre. Fax: 020-7251-8867. E-mail: danby@block.com. Home: 17 Norham Rd, Oxford OX2 6SF, England Office: Taxbriefs Ltd, 2-5 Benjamin St, London ECIM 5QL, England

BLOCH, ANTOINE, cardiologist; b. Lausanne, Switzerland, Aug. 9, 1938; s. Paul and Herta (Sonnenfeld) B.; MD, U. Lausanne, 1963; m. Josee Sánchez, Aug. 25, 1973. Intern, U. Lausanne Hosp., 1964-66; med. resident St. Antonius Hosp., Utrecht, Netherlands, 1966-67, univ. hosps., Lausanne and Geneva, 1967-70; chief resident Univ. Cardiac Center of Geneva, 1970-73, physician, 1975-80; cardiac fellow Mass. Gen. Hosp., Boston, 1973-75; privat-docent Geneva Med. Sch., 1975-80, charge de cours, 1980—; chief cardiac unit Hopital de la Tour, Geneva, 1981—, chief cardiovasc. medico-surg. dept., 1997—. Swiss Nat. Fund grantee, 1977-79. Fellow Am. Coll. Cardiology, European Soc. Cardiology; mem. Am. Heart Assn., Am. Soc. Echocardiography, Swiss Med. Assn., Swiss Soc. Cardiology, French Soc. Cardiology, Swiss Soc. Intensive Care, Swiss Soc. Ultrasound, Internat. Soc. Cardiovascular Ultrasound. Contbr. numerous articles to profl. pubs. Home: 33 Crêt-de-Choully, CH-1242 Choully Switzerland Office: Hosp de la Tour, Cardiac Unit, Geneva CH-1217, Switzerland

BLOCH, ERICH, retired electrical engineer, former science foundation administrator; b. Sulzburg, Germany, Jan. 9, 1925; came to U.S., 1948, naturalized, 1952; s. Joseph and Tony B.; m. Renee Stern, Mar. 4, 1948; 1 child, Rebecca Bloch Rosen. Student, Fed. Poly. Inst., Zurich, Switzerland, 1945-48; BSEE, U. Buffalo, 1952; hon. degrees, U. Mass., George Washington U., Colo. Sch. Mines, SUNY Buffalo, U. Rochester, Oberlin Coll., U. Notre Dame, Ohio State U., Rensselaer Poly. Inst., 1989, Washington Coll., 1989, CUNY, N.Y.C., 1991; hon. degree, Poly. U., Bklyn., N.Y., 1993. With IBM, 1952-84; v.p. gen. mgr. IBM, East Fishkill, N.Y., 1975-80; v.p. tech. personnel devel. IBM, Armonk, N.Y., 1980-84; mem. com. computers in automated mfg. NRC, 1980-84; dir. NSF, Washington, 1984-90; fellow Coun. on Competitiveness, 1990—; prin. Washington Adv. Group, 1998—;

past vis. disting. prof. George Mason U.; bd. dirs. Motorola Inc., Convex Computers, Quality Edn. for Minorities Network, Telogy Network. Patentee in field. Recipient U.S. medal of tech., 1985, Computer World/Smithsonian award for innovation, 1991, Swedish Royal Order of the Polar Star, NAE Buche award statesmanship tech., Robert Noyce award Semiconductor Industry Assn., 1999. Fellow IEEE (Founder's award 1990, Computer Pioneer awards 1993, 94), AAAS; mem.NAE (Arthur M. Bueche award 1997), Am. Soc. Mfg. Engrs. (hon., Eugene Merchant Mfg. medal ASME and Soc. Mfg. Engrs.), Am. Soc. Engring. Edn., Royal Swedish Acad. Engring. Scis., Japan Acad. Engring. E-mail: ebloch@theadvisorygroup.com.

BLOCH, FRANCOIS M(ARC), lawyer; b. Rueil Malmaison, France, Aug. 4, 1964; s. Michel and Nicole (Geneix) B.; m. Laurence Brecher, July 9, 1994; children: Salomé, Adam, Noé. Bar: France 1990. Jr. atty. Bull H.N., Boston; atty. Baker & McKenzie, Paris, 1992-93; ptnr. heading comm./tech. practice Clifford Chance, Paris, 1993-2000; pres. Willkie Farr & Gallagher, Paris, 2000—; spkr. at confs. Contbr. articles to profl. jours. With French Army, 1990-91. Mem. IBA. Office: Willkie Farr & Gallagher, 21-23 rue Ville l'Evegne, 75008 Paris France

BLOCH, HERBERT, classicist, medievalist, historian, educator; b. Berlin, Germany, Aug. 18, 1911; came to the U.S., 1939, naturalized, 1946; s. Ludwig and Alice (Gutmann) B.; m. Clarissa Coolidge Holland, Nov. 23, 1943 (dec. Aug. 1958); children: Anne Coolidge, Nini; m. Ellen Cohen, Aug. 25, 1960 (dec. May 1987). Dottore in Lettere, U. Rome, 1935, diploma di Perfezionamento, 1937; LLD, U. Cassino, Italy, 1989. Instr. Greek and Latin Harvard U., Cambridge, Mass., 1941; asst. prof. Greek and Latin Harvard U., Cambridge, 1942-47, assoc. prof. Greek and Latin, 1947-53, prof. Greek and Latin, 1953-73, Pope prof. Latin lang. and lit., 1973-82, Pope prof. Latin lang. and lit. emeritus, 1982—; with excavation Ostia, Italy, 1938-39; mem. Inst. for Advanced Study, Princeton, N.J., 1953-54; prof.-in-charge Sch. Classical Studies, Am. Acad. Rome, 1957-59; mem. bd. Syndics Harvard U. Press, Cambridge, 1961-65; trustee Loeb Classical Libr. Harvard U., Cambridge, 1964-73, sr. fellow Soc. of Fellows, 1964-79. Author: I bolli laterizi e la storia edilizia romana, 1948, 2d edit., 1968, Supplement to Volume XV1 of the Corpus Inscriptionum Latinarum Including Complete Indices to the Roman Brick-Stamps, 1948, 2d edit., 1967, Monte Cassino in the Middle Ages, 3 vols., 1986 (Haskins medal The Medieval Acad. Am. 1988, Praemium Urbis, Rome, 1987), The Atina Dossier of Peter the Deacon of Monte Cassino. A Hagiographical Romance of the Twelfth Century, 1998. Recipient Fulbright award, Italy, 1950-51; Guggenheim fellow, 1950-51; fellow for ind. study and rsch. NEH, 1976-77. Fellow Am. Acad. Arts and Scis., Med. Acad. Am. (pres. of fellows 1990-93); mem. Am. Philological Assn. (dir. 1959-64, 66-70, v.p. 1966-68, pres. 1968-69), Am. Philos. Soc., Deutsches Archaeologisches Inst., Pontificia Accademia Romana di Archeologia (hon.), Zentraldirektion der Monumenta Germaniae Historica (corr.), Finnish Acad. Sci. and Letters, Premio Cultori di Roma, Rome, 1999. Home: 524 Pleasant St Belmont MA 02478-3201

BLOCH, JULIA CHANG, educator, former ambassador, former bank executive; b. Mar. 2, 1942; came to U.S., 1951, naturalized, 1962; d. Fu-yun and Eva (Yeh) Chang; m. Stuart Marshall Block, Dec. 21, 1968. BA, U. Calif., Berkley, 1964; MA, Harvard U., 1967; postgrad. in mgmt., 1987; DHL (hon.), Northeastern U., Boston, 1986. Vol. Peace Corps, Sabah, Malaysia, 1964-66; tng. officer East Asia and Pacific region, Washington, 1967-68; evaluation officer East Asia and Pacific region, 1968-70; mem. minority staff U.S. Senate Select Com. on Nutrition and Human Needs, Washington, 1971-76, chief minority counsel, 1976-77; dep. dir. Office of African Affairs U.S. Internat. Comm. Agy., Washington, 1977-80; fellow Inst. Politics Harvard U., Cambridge, Mass., 1980-81; asst. adminstr. Bur. for Food For Peace and Voluntary Assistance AID, Washington, 1981-87; asst. administr. Bur. for Asia and Near East, 1987-88; assoc. U.S.-Japan Rels. Program, Ctr. for Internat. Affairs Harvard U., Cambridge, Mass., 1988-89; amb. Kingdom of Nepal, 1989-93; group exec., v.p. Bank Am., San Francisco, 1993-96; pres. The U.S.-Japan Found., 1996-98; dir. Am. West Airlines, 1994-98, Penn Mutual Life Ins., 1997; prof. amer. studies Beida Univ., Beijing, China; trustee Eisenhower Exchange Fellowship, 1995-97, U.S. Chila Rels. Com., 1998—; U.S. Senate rep. World Conf. on Internat. Women's Yr., Mex., 1975; advisor U.S. Del. to Food and Agr. orgn. Conf., Rome, 1975; rep. Am. Council Young Polit. Leaders, Peoples Republic China, 1977; charter mem. Sr. Exec. Svc., 1979; head U.S. del. Biennial Session World Food Programme, Rome, 1981-86, Devel. Assistance Com. Meeting on Non-Govtl. Orgns., Paris, 1985, Intergovtl. Group on Indonesia, The Hargue, The Netherlands, 1987, World Bank Consultative Group Meeting, Paris, 1987, mem. exec. women in govt., 1988-93, mem. coun. fgn. rels., 1991—; vis. prof. internat. rels. Peking U., 1998. Author: A U.S.-Japan Aid Alliance, 1991; co-author: Chinese Home Cooking, 1986. Exec. bd. mem. Internat. Ctr. for Rsch. on Women, 1974-81; mem. adv. bd. Women's Campaign Fund, 1976-78; mem. nat. adv. coun. Experiemtn in Internat. Living, 1981-83; mem. U.S. Nat. Com. for Pacific Econ. Cooperation, 1984—, Nat. Presdl. Debate Forum, 1987-92; mem. presdl. adv. couns. Peace Corps, 1988-89; mem. com. to visit art mus. Harvard U., 1989; founder Women Fgn. Policy Group; mem. Am. Refugee Com. Bd., 1993; mem. Am. Himalayna Found. Bd., 1994; commr. Asian Art Mus., San Francisco, 1994; trustee, bus. leadership circle, 1994—. Hon Fulbright fellow, 1996; recipient Hubert Humphrey award for internat. svc., 1979, Humanitarian Svc. award AID, 1987, Leader for Peace award Peace Corps, 1987, Asian Am. LEadership award, 1989, Brotherhood/Sisterhood award Nat. Conf. on Christians and Jews, 1996; named Outstanding Woman of Color, Nat. Inst. for Women of Color, 1982, Woman of Distinction, Nat. Conf. for Coll. Women Student Leaders and Women of Achievement, 1987, Disting. Pub. Svc. award Nat. Assn. Profl. Asian Pacific Am. Women, 1989; Ford Found. Study fellow for internat. devel. Harvard U., 1966, Paul Harris award Rotary, 1992, Award of Honor Narcotic Enforcement Assn., 1992. Mem. Orgn. Cinese Am. Women (founder, chair 1977—, bd. dirs., Woman of Yr. 1987), Asia Soc. (pres. coun. 1989, trustee, 1994), Am. Studies Ctr. (vice-chair), Prytannean Honor Soc., Coun. Fgn. Rels., Mortar Bd., Cosmos Club. Republican. Avocations: ceramics, gourmet cooking, collecting art.

BLOCH, KONRAD EMIL, biochemist; b. Neisse, Germany, Jan. 12, 1912; came to U.S., 1936, naturalized, 1944; s. Frederick D. and Hedwig (Streimer) B.; m. Lore Teutsch, Feb. 15, 1941; children—Peter, Susan. Chem. Engr., Technische Hochschule, Munich, 1934; Ph.D., Columbia U., 1938. Asst. prof. biochemistry U. Chgo., 1946-50, prof., 1950-54; Higgins prof. chemistry Harvard U., Cambridge, Mass., 1954-82, prof. emeritus, 1982—. Recipient Nobel prize in physiology and medicine, 1964, Ernest Guenther award in chemistry of essential oils and related products, 1965, Nat. Medal of Sci., 1988. Fellow AAAS; mem. Am. Chemistry Soc. (Fritsche award 1964), Am. Soc. Biol. Chemists (pres. 1967), Nat. Acad. Scis., Am. Philos. Soc., Royal Sci. (fgn.). Office: Harvard U Dept Chemistry/Chem Biology 12 Oxford St Cambridge MA 02138-2902

BLOCH, KONSTANTIN OLEG, biologist, researcher; b. Samara, USSR, Apr. 25, 1953; s. Oleg Beer Bloch and Ella Moshe Shoor. MSc, Kharkov (USSR) State U., 1975; PhD, Inst. Med. Radiology, Obninsk, USSR, 1982. Rschr. Inst. Med. Radiology, 1975-84; head lab. Inst. Endocrynology, Kharkov, 1984-92; head rsch. group Technion, Haifa, Israel, 1992-93, Tel Aviv U., 1993—. Author: Lessons from Animal Diabetes, 1996; contbr. articles to profl. jours. Mem. European Assn. for the Study of Diabetes, N.Y. Acad. Scis. Avocations: travel, sports. Office: Tel Aviv U Beilinson Campus, Felsenstein Med Rsch Ctr, 49100 Petach-Tikva Israel

BLOCH, OLIVIER, philosopher; b. Paris, May 1, 1930; s. René and Odette (Cahen) B.; m. Marie-Louise Paillard, Sept. 6, 1960; children: Isabelle, Jérôme. DSc, U. Sorbonne, 1970. Prof. emeritus U. Paris I, Panthéon-Sorbonne. Author: La Philosophie de Gassendi, 1971, Le Matérialisme, 1981, 2d edit., 1995, Parité de la Vie et de la Mort—La Réponse du Médecin Gaultier, 1993, Matière à Histoires, 1997, Molière/Philosophie, 2000. Home: 23 rue du Chemin Vert, 75011 Paris France

BLOCH, PETER CONRAD, economist, educator; b. N.Y.C., June 8, 1944; s. Konrad Emil and Lore (Teutsch) B.; m. Marianne Nieman; children: Benjamin, Emilie. AB, Harvard U., 1967; MA, Johns Hopkins U., 1969; PhD, U. Calif., Berkeley, 1974. Maitre asst. assoc. U. Dakar, Senegal, 1974-76; vis. assoc. prof. Fletcher Sch. of Law and Diplomacy, Tufts U., Medford, Mass., 1977-80; asst. prof. Grinnell (Iowa) Coll., 1980-83; sr. scientist Land Tenure Ctr., U. Wis., Madison, 1984—, vis. asst. prof. dept. econ., 1983-85, faculty assoc. dept. forest ecology, 1999—; pres. Terra Inst., Ltd., Mt. Horeb, Wis., 1994-97; cons. Swedish Govt., Stockholm, 1989-98, U.S. Agy. Internat. Devel., Washington, 1975—, World Bank, Washington, 1985—. Contbr. articles to profl. publs. and chpts. to books. Grantee British Know How Fund, Lincoln Inst. Land Policy, U.S. Agy. Internat. Devel., World Bank. Mem. Assn. Recherches et Etudes sur le Foncier en Atrique. Avocations: gardening, travel. E-mail: pcbloch@facstaff.wisc.edu. Home: 21 Foxboro Cir Madison WI 53717-1201 Office: U Wis Land Tenure Ctr 1357 University Ave Madison WI 53715-1054

BLOCH, RENE M., naval officer, high technology and political economy consultant; b. FrancFort, Germany, Feb. 18, 1923; s. David and Irma (Benjamin) B.; m. Lucienne Marino, Feb. 18, 1973. Advanced Engring. degree, Ecole Polytechnique, Paris, 1946; Advanced Sci. degree, Sorbonne, Paris, 1946; MA in Engring. Sci., Harvard U., 1947; postgrad., Ecole Nat. Superieure Genie Maritime, Paris, 1949, Ecole Nat. Superieure Aeronautique, Paris, 1950; advanced mgmt. program, Harvard U., 1968. Enlisted Free French Forces, 1942; advanced in grades to vice-admiral French Navy, 1973; overhaul and repair officer Naval Air Sta., Toulon, France, 1950-52; tech. dir. French Naval Aviation, 1952-61; asst. dir. aeronautics for internat. affairs French Dept. Defense, 1961-64; asst. sec. defense for internat. affairs Govt. of France, 1965-66; personal adviser to sec. defense Dept. Defense, Govt. of France, 1967-68; comdr. Centre d'Essais des Landes, Biscarrosse, France, 1969-81; personal adviser to Dep. Sec. Def. Govt. of France, 1981-84; cons. Paris, 1984—; lectr. in field. Decorated comdr. Legion of Honor, Medal of Vol. Fighting in the Underground, Medal of Free France, Medal of Monte Cassino, Medal of Aeronautics, officer Order of Agrl. Merit, Grand Cross of the Order of Merit Fed. Republic Germany, Grand Cross of Mil. Order Aviz Portugal, comdr. Royal Order Orange-Nassau of The Netherlands, comdr. Royal Order Leopold I of Belgium, comdr. Order Italian Solidarity. Fellow AIAA, Royal Aeronautical Soc. London; mem. IEEE, French Naval Inst. (chmn.), Assn. Aéronautique et Astronautique France, Racing Club, St. James' Club. Jewish. Home: 6 Rue Benouville, 75116 Paris France Office: 59 blvd Lannes, 75116 Paris France

BLOCH, THOMAS ANTHONY, librarian; b. U.S.A., Dec. 15, 1939; s. Karl and Herta (Smejbidl) B.; children: Michael, Daniel, Camilo, Marilyn. MA in Libr. Sci., U. Chgo., 1963. Asst. libr. Pahlavi U., Shiraz, Iran, 1965-67; assoc. libr. Haile Selassie I U., Addis Ababa, Ethiopia, 1967-69; dir. libr. Internat. Ctr. Tropical Agr., Cali, Colombia, 1969-71; dir. librs. Cen. Am. Inst. Bus. Adminstrn., Alajuela, Costa Rica, Managua, Nicaragua, 1971—; internat. cons. Contbr. articles to profl. publs. Office: INCAE Libr, Apartado 960-4050, Alajuela Costa Rica

BLOCK, ALVIN GILBERT, journal executive editor; b. Moline, Ill., Sept. 15, 1946; s. Sylvan Emory Block and Pauline (Kutten) Salzman; m. Sarah Cannon Michael, June 17, 1977 (div. 1984); m. Ellen Marie Chapman, Jan. 19, 1992; children: Will Chapman, Thomas Chapman. BA, Bradley U., 1968. Editl. asst. Playboy mag., Chgo., 1970; exec. Salzman & Co., Davenport, Iowa, 1971-74; editor Ketchum (Idaho) Tomorrow, 1975-77; reporter Idaho Statesman, Ketchum, 1978-80; freelance writer, Sacramento, 1980-82; mng. editor Calif. Jour., Sacramento, 1983-94, editor, columnist, 1995-2000, editor-in-chief news and publs., 2000—; co-editor Calif. Polit. Almanac; editor Calif. Govt. and Politics Annual; v.p., editor-in-chief State Net, 1996—; commentator Sta. KXPR-FM, Sacramento, 1985-88. Councilman City of Ketchum, 1979. With U.S. Army, 1969-74. Recipient award for column Idaho Newspaper Assn., 1975, Soc. Profl. Journalists, 1995. Avocations: baseball, military history, railroading, writing. Home: 1133 Marian Way Sacramento CA 95818-3718 Office: Calif Jour 2101 K St Sacramento CA 95816-4920

BLOCK, DAVID JEFFREY, lawyer, investment manager; b. Bklyn., Aug. 22, 1951; s. Herbert and Ruth Block. BA in Polit. Sci., SUNY, Buffalo, 1973; JD, Emory U., 1976. Bar: N.Y. 1977, D.C. 1978, Calif. 1979. Atty. advisor U.S. Comptroller of the Currency, Washington, 1977-79; assoc. Rosenblum, Parish and Bacigalupi, San Francisco, 1979-81; ptnr. Rosen Wachtell & Gilbert, San Francisco, 1983-86; pvt. practice law San Francisco, 1981-83, 86-90; of counsel Adams, Sadler & Hovis, San Francisco, 1990-94, Leland Parachini Steinberg Matzger & Melnick, San Francisco, 1994—; investment mgr. Graver, Bokhof, Goodwin & Sullivan, investment counsel, San Francisco, 2000—; lectr. in field. Contbr. articles to profl. jours. Mem. Olympic Club. Avocations: golf, cooking, wine collecting. Office: 333 Market St San Francisco CA 94105-2102 also: 345 California St San Francisco CA 94104-2606

BLOCK, FRANCINE ELLEN, educational association administrator, consultant; b. Barre, Vt., Apr. 10, 1947; d. Joseph and Anna (Moisoff) Rome; m. Alan Joseph Block, July 27, 1969; children: Justin Andrew, Darren Stuart. BS, U. Vt., 1969, MAT, 1972. Tchr. Burlington High (Vt.) Sch., 1969-72; dir. career and coll. resource ctr. Westborough (Mass.) High Sch., 1979-84; ednl. cons., chief exec. officer Am. Coll. Admissions Cons., Richboro, Pa., 1984—; alumni admissions rep. U. Vt., Burlington, 1978—; co-founder No-Name Conf., FRanklin and Marshall Coll., 1992—; faculty mem. Bucknell Summer Inst., 1999—. Mem. Alliance to Build Coms., 1992—; co-chairwoman Bucks County Women's History award, 1991—; regional officer Assn. Jr. League Internat., N.Y.C., 1987-88; bd. dirs., officer Jr. League, Worcester, Mass., 1980-86, Princeton, N.J., 1989-90; chmn. allocations United Way Bucks County, 1990—, bd. dirs., 1997—. Mem. AAUW (bd. dirs. 1989-97), Am. Coll. Counseling Assn., Am. Sch. Counselors Assn., Am. Bus. Women's Assn., Nat. Assn. Coll. Admission Counseling (assembly del. 1998—), Nat. Assn. Fgn. Student Affairs, New Eng. Assn. Coll. Admissions Counselors, Pa. Assn. Secondary Schs. and Coll. Admissions Counselors (admissions practices com., profl. devel. com., exec. bd. 1997—), N.Y. Assn. Coll. Admissions Counselors, N.J. Assn. Coll. Admissions Counselors, Bucks County C. of C. (chmn. per. com. 1993-96, bd. dirs. 1996—), Hadassah Internat. (bd. dirs. Newton chpt. 1990-93, v.p. Hosp. Guild chpt. 1990-94, pres. 1994-96, v.p. Hosp. Guild exec. bd., pres. 1998-2000, supt. sch. adv. panel 1991-96). Office: Am Coll Admissions Cons PO Box 701 Richboro PA 18954-0701

BLOCK, MICHAEL KENT, economics and law educator, public policy association executive, former government official, consultant; b. N.Y.C., Apr. 2, 1942; s. Philip and Roslyn (Klein) B.; m. Carole Arline Polansky, Aug. 30, 1964 (div.); children: Robert Justin, Tamara Nicole; m. Olga Vyborna, Dec. 1, 1996. A.B., Stanford U., 1964, A.M., 1969, Ph.D., 1972. Research analyst Bank of Am., San Francisco, 1965-66; research assoc. Planning Assocs., San Francisco, 1966-67; asst. prof. econs. U. Santa Clara, 1969-72; asst. prof. econs. dept. ops. research and adminstrv. sci. Naval Postgrad. Sch., Monterey, Calif., 1972-74, assoc. prof., 1974-76; research fellow Hoover Instn., Stanford U., 1975-76, sr. research fellow, 1976-87; dir. Center for Econometric Studies of Justice System, 1977-81; ptnr. Block & Nold, Cons., Palo Alto, Calif., 1980-81; assoc. prof. mgmt., econs. and law U. Ariz., Tucson, 1982-85, prof. econs. and law, 1989—; mem. U.S. Sentencing Commn., Washington, 1985-89; exec. v.p. Cybernomics, Tucson, 1991—; pres. Goldwater Inst. for Pub. Policy, Phoenix, Ariz., 1992—; sr. policy adviser State of Ariz. Gov. Symington, 1996-97; chair Basis Sch. Bd., 1998—; mem. Ariz. Residential Utility Consumer Bd., 1995-96, chmn. Ariz. Constl. Def. Coun., 1994-97, Ariz. Juvenile Justice Adv. Coun., 1996-97; seminar dir. Econ. Devel. Inst./World Bank, 1992-95; cons. in field. Author: (with H.G. Demmert) Workbook and Programmed Guide to Economics, 1974, 77, 80, (with James M. Clabault) A Legal and Economic Analysis of Criminal Antitrust Indictments, 1955-80; contbr. articles to profl. publs. Fellow NSF, 1965, Stanford U. Fellow Progress and Freedom Found.; mem. Am. Econ. Assn., Phi Beta Kappa. Office: U Ariz Econ Dept Mcclelland Hl Rm 401 Tucson AZ 85721-0001

BLOCK, ROBERT MICHAEL, endodontist, educator, researcher; b. Ann Arbor, Mich., Oct. 15, 1947; s. Walter David and Thelma Violet (Levine) B.; m. Anne Powell Marshall, Sept. 4, 1977. BA, DePauw U., 1969; DDS, U. Mich.-Ann Arbor, 1974; cert. in endodontics, Va. Commonwealth U., 1977; MS in Pathology, Va. Commonwealth U., 1978. Diplomate Am. Bd. Endodontics. Clin. instr. Va. Commonwealth U., 1975-77, instr. pathology, 1977-78; rsch. assoc. endodontics U. Conn.-Farmington, 1975—; vis. sr. scientist Nat. Med. Rsch. Inst., Bethesda, Md., 1976-78; rsch. assoc. McGuire Vets. Hosp., Richmond, Va., 1975-78; vis. rsch. scientist U. Conn.-Farmington, 1978—; lectr. endodontics Flint Community Schs.; bd. dirs. Republic Bancorp, S.E., Republic Bank-S.E. div. Republic Bancorp. Contbr. articles profl. jours., chpt. in book. Exec. mem. campaign com. candidate for U. Mich. Bd. Regents, 1980; candidate for Mich. State Bd. Edn., 1982. HEW and NIH summer research fellow, 1970-71; research grantee McGuire Vets. Hosp., 1976-78. Fellow Am. Coll. of Endodontics; mem. Internat. Assn. Dental Rsch. (Edward P. Hatton award 1977), Am. Assn. Dental Rsch., Am. Assn. Endodontists (Meml. Research award 1977), Va. Dental Assn. (VAPAC com., state com. on infection control), Lapeer Dental Study Club (treas. 1978-82), ADA (Preventive Dentistry award 1973), Loudoun County Dental Soc. (v.p.). Office: Loudoun Tech Ctr 21525 Ridgetop Cir Sterling VA 20166-6510

BLOCK, SANDRA LINDA, special education educator; b. Inglewood, Calif., Aug. 29, 1947; d. Milton and Anne (Leiderman) Berenbaum; divorced; 1 child, Rina Ann Hunter. BS, U. So. Calif., 1969. Cert. tchr., Calif. Tchr. L.A. Unified Sch. Dist., 1969-87; mentor tchr. Calif.; comty. tchr. Irvine, Calif., 1987—. Mem. AAUW. Democrat. Jewish. Avocations: reading, traveling. Home: 4 Del Rey Irvine CA 92612-2961

BLOCK, WILLIAM KENNETH, lawyer; b. N.Y.C., Oct. 23, 1950; s. Louis and Catherine Veronica (Kerr) B. BA, Colgate U., 1973; JD, Union U., Albany, N.Y., 1976. Bar: N.Y. 1977. Gen. counsel N.Y.C. Tax Commn., 1978-81; asst. commn. fin. N.Y.C. Dept. Fin., 1981-84, dep. commr. fin., 1984-89; assoc. Schwartz, Weiss, Steckler & Hoffman, P.C., N.Y.C., 1989-91; pvt. practice, William K. Block, P.C., N.Y.C., 1992—; adj. lectr. real estate NYU, 1992—. Contbr. articles on real property tax law and procedure to profl. jours. Mem. ABA, Internat. Assn. Assessing Officers (chmn. met. jurisdiction coun. 1987-88, presdl. citation 1986, McCareen award 1988), N.Y. State Assessors Assn., N.Y. State Bar Assn., New York County Bar Assn. (com. on City of N.Y., real property com., govt. counsel com.), Real Estate Rev. Bar Assn., dir. 1995—), Assn. Bar City of N.Y. (com. on tax certiorari), Real Estate Bd. N.Y. (com. on taxation). Democrat. Roman Catholic. Home: 115 E 34th St Apt 20K New York NY 10016-4631 Office: 295 Madison Ave Fl 38 New York NY 10017-6304

BLOCKLEY, DAVID IAN, civil engineer; b. Ashbourne, Derbyshire, Eng., Sept. 18, 1941; s. Harold Gwynne and Olive Lydia (Kirkland) B.; m. Karen Elisabeth Bailey; children: Andrew David, Alison Mary. B Engring., U. Sheffield, Eng., 1964, PhD, 1967; DSc, U. Bristol, Eng., 1987. Devel. engr. BCSA Ltd., London, 1967-69; lectr. U. Bristol, 1969-82, reader, 1982-89, prof., 1989—, dean engring., 1994-98; cons. Craddy & Ptnrs., Bristol, non exec. dir. Bristol Water Holdings plc., 1998. Author: Structural Design and Safety, 1980; (with P.S. Godfrey) Doing it Differently, 2000; author: editor: Engineering Safety, 1990; contbr. articles to profl. jours. Fellow Royal Acad. Engring., Instn. Civil Engrs. (Telford gold medal 1978, George Stephenson medal 1981), Instn. Structural Engrs. (v.p., 1997—, Oscar Faber diploma 1986), Royal Soc. Arts.

BLODGETT, JULIAN ROBERT, small business owner; b. Honolulu, Nov. 21, 1919; s. Harry Hoagland and Esther Julia (Lyons) B.; m. Eleanor Anne Fischer, Nov. 4, 1941 (dec. 1983); children: Eric, Julie, Byron, Paul. BA, UCLA, 1940. Stock clk. Northrop Aircraft Co., Hawthorne, Calif., 1941-42; spl. agt. FBI, Washington, 1942-44, 46-57, Standard Oil Calif., San Francisco, 1945-46; gen. mgr. Western Indsl. Security Co., L.A., 1961-63; chief bur. investigation L.A. Dist. Atty., 1957-61; owner, operator Julian R. Blodgett Investigations, L.A., 1961—, Grey Fox Ltd., 1995—. Chmn., commr. L.A. City Housing Authority, 1963-65. Mem. Former Agts. FBI. Office: PO Box 49658 Los Angeles CA 90049-0658

BLOEMBERGEN, NICOLAAS, physicist, educator; b. Dordrecht, The Netherlands, Mar. 11, 1920; came to U.S., 1952, naturalized, 1958; s. Auke and Sophia M. (Quint) B.; m. Huberta D. Brink, June 26, 1950; children: Antonia, Brink, Juliana. BA, Utrecht U., 1941, MA, 1943; PhD, Leiden U., 1948; MA (hon.), Harvard U., 1951; D of Sci. (hon.), Laval U., 1987, U. Conn., 1988, U. Hartford, 1991, Moscow State U., 1997, Harvard U., 2000; LHD (hon.), U. Mass., Lowell, 1994, U. Ctrl. Fla., 1996, N.C. State U., 1998. Teaching asst. Utrecht U., 1942-45; research fellow Leiden U., 1948; mem. Soc. Fellows Harvard U., 1949-51, assoc. prof., 1951-57, Gordon McKay prof. applied physics, 1957—, Rumford prof. physics, 1974, Gerhard Gade univ. prof., 1980, prof. emeritus, 1990; vis. prof. U. Paris, 1957, U. Calif., 1965, Collège de France, Paris, 1980; Lorentz guest prof. U. Leiden, 1973; Raman vis. prof. Bangalore, India, 1979; Fairchild Disting. scholar Calif. Inst. Tech., 1984; von Humboldt Sr. Scientist, Munich, Fed. Republic Germany; hon. prof. Fudan U., Shanghai, People's Republic of China; Disting. Vis. Prof. CREOL, U. Ctrl. Fla., 1995. Author: Nuclear Magnetic Relaxation, 1948, Nonlinear Optics, 1965, Encounters in Magnetic Resonance, 1996, Encounters in Nonlinear Optics, 1996; also articles in profl. jours. Recipient Buckley prize for solid state physics Am. Phys. Soc., 1958, Dirac medal U. New South Wales (Australia), 1983, Stuart Ballantine medal Franklin Inst., 1961, Half Moon trophy Netherlands Club N.Y., 1972, Nat. medal of Sci., 1975, Lorentz medal Royal Dutch Acad., 1978, Frederic Ives medal Optical Soc. Am., 1979; von Humboldt sr. scientist award Munich, 1980, von Humboldt medal, 1989, Nobel prize in Physics, 1981; Guggenheim fellow, 1957. Fellow Am. Phys. Soc., Am. Acad. Arts and Scis., IEEE (Morris Liebmann award 1959, Medal of Honor 1983), Indian Acad. Scis. (hon.); mem. Optical Soc. Am. (hon.), Nat. Royal Dutch Acads. Scis., Nat. Acad. Engring., Am. Philos. Soc., Deutsche Akademie der Naturforscher Leopoldina, Koninklyke Nederlandse Akademie von Wetenschappen (corr.), Paris Acad. Scis. (fgn. assoc.), Royal Norwegian Soc. Scis. and Letters (fgn.). Office: Harvard U Div Applied Scis Pierce Hall Cambridge MA 02138

BLOEMER, ROSEMARY CELESTE, bookkeeper; b. St. Louis, Jan. 26, 1930; d. Edward J. and Leslie F. (McCreary) Walsh; m. Edward H. Bloemer, Sept. 4, 1948; children: Stephen, Diane, Janet. Cert. in court reporting, Bayside Coll., San Francisco, 1948; student, U. Mo., St. Louis, 1949-51, 83. Profl. singer Harvey Kincer Band, St. Louis, 1945-49; teller Roosevelt Savs. & Loan, 1967; income tax sec. Boatmen's Nat. Bank, St. Louis, 1968-73; sec. psychology dept. Washington U., St. Louis, 1978; beverages contr. Chase-Park Plaza Hotel, St. Louis, 1977-81; owner Bloemer Tax Svc., St. Louis, 1975—; legal sec. Lickhalter Law Office, St. Louis, 1970-88, Law Office of James K. Steitz, St. Louis, 1981-83; bookkeeper, tax advisor Mo. Hwy. Patrol Assn., Inc., St. Louis, 1981-83; bookkeeper, tax acct. Mo. State Hwy. Patrol Civilian Employees Assn., St. Louis, 1983-92; acct. Clarion Hotel, St. Louis, 1986, Bel-Air Hilton Inn, St. Louis, 1984-85; consignment standard stock machine screws, contr. accounts receivable Consol. Aluminum Co., 1973-75; sec. to 5 fin. specialists Cmty. Devel. Agy., St. Louis, 1980-81; tax preparer H&R Block, 1991-95; mem. team of reporters Price Waterhouse, 1990-96. Arbitrator, shopper, speaker Better Bus. Bur. St. Louis, 1980—; sec. to pres. Bd. Higher Edn., Christian Ch., 1975-77; vol. in choir Shrine of St. Joseph, St. Louis. Mem. Nat. Soc. Tax Profls., Nat. Assn. Tax Practitioners, Am. Soc. Notaries; Internat. Platform Assn. Roman Catholic. Avocations: gardening, sewing. Home and Office: 1435 Trampe Ave Saint Louis MO 63138-2541

BLOEMSMA, MARCO PAUL, investor; b. Heemstede, The Netherlands, July 20, 1924; s. Philippus and Wilhelmina Geertruida (Bonebakker) B.; LLM, Leyden U., 1948; m. Mieke Harten, Sept. 23, 1955; children: Marco Reinier, Barbara Patricia, Michiel Alexander. Lawyer firm van der Feltz, Voûte & Riechelmann, 1948-49; assoc., then ptnr. Blackstone, Rueb & van Boeschoten, 1951-72; pres. C. Harten Holding B.V., The Hague, 1972-85; bd. dirs. Mauritshuis Found.; positions formerly held include chmn. KTI-Group, Ten Doesschate-group, Euroma Holding; dir., pres., chmn. Patino-group; chmn. Lips United-group, ICL Nederland B.V., Auto-Palace-group, Bloemsma Holding B.V., Nebim Handelmaatschappy B.V.; bd. dirs. Mobil Chemie B.V., Ambac B.V., Volvo Bedryfswagens B.V., Ned. Mij. Mijnbouwkundige Werken N.V., Polak & Schwarz N.V., Lockheed Europe N.V., Vulcaansoord N.V., Merck Sharp en Dohme Nederland N.V., Rockwool Lapinus B.V., Svenska Metallverken/Granges Nederland B.V., Winthrop Europe N.V., Packard Instruments Europe N.V., Foster Grant Europe N.V., Anchor Found. (Verolme). Author nat. reports on fiscal and corp. subjects. Served with Dutch Naval Reserve, 1949-51. Hon. Ky. col. since 1962. Clubs: Cercle Interalliée (Paris), Cercle Litteraire (Lausanne). Home: 5 Ave de Crousaz, 1010 Lausanne Switzerland

BLOESCH, JÜRG, limnologist, consultant; b. Olten, Switzerland, Oct. 31, 1943; parents Max Gottfried and Aline (Hottiger) B. MSc, Swiss Fed. Inst. Tech., Zürich, 1968, PhD, 1974. From teaching asst. to sr. rsch. scientist Swiss Fed. Inst. Environ. Sci. & Tech. (EAWAG), Dübendorf, 1968—; cons. NOK, Baden, Switzerland, 1970-75, AKV, Lucerne, Switzerland, 1986-94, World Bank, Fed. Office Fgn. Econ. Affairs, Swiss Agy. Devel. and Coop., Macedonia, 1995—. Bd. dirs. Rheinaubund, Schaffhausen, Switzerland, 1993—, co-pres., 1995—; v.p. ASA, Solothurn, Switzerland, 1984—; active World Wildlife Fund, Greenpeace. 1st lt. Swiss infantry, 1970-95. Mem. Internat. Assn. Theoretical and Applied Limnology (nat. rep. 1992—), Internat. Assn. for Sediment-water Sci. (bd. dirs. 1993—), Internationale Arbeitsgemeinschaft Donauforschung (nat. rep. 1995-98, pres. 1998—), Am. Soc. Limnology and Oceanography. Avocations: traveling, skiing, cycling, music, reading. Home: Stauffacherstrasse 159, CH-8004 Zürich Switzerland Office: Swiss Fed Inst Env Sci/Tech, Uberlandstrasse 133, CH-8600 Dübendorf Switzerland

BLOK, HARMEN, mechanical engineer, consultant; b. Amsterdam, Sept. 9, 1900; s. Pieter Engel Johannes Blok and Wikje Harmina Poort; m. Aleida Schut, Jan. 30, 1935; children: Pieter J.J., Hendrika A., Hendrik P., Johannes, Jacobus A. Degree in mech. engring., U. Tech. Delft, The Netherlands, 1932. Chartered engr., Inst. Mech. Engrs., London. Rsch. and devel. engr. Royal Dutch Shell Group, Delft, 1933-51; prof. mech. engring. U. Tech. Delft, 1951-81; cons. machinery and tribology Ryswyk, The Netherlands, 1981—. Contbr. over 60 articles to sci. and profl. jours. Officer spl. svcs., Netherlands Army, 1947. Fellow Am. Soc. Mech. Engrs., inst. Mech. Engrs.; mem. Soc. Tribologists and Lubrication Engrs. (hon.). Avocations: cosmology, world history, geography, seismology, comparative linguistics. Home and Office: 4 Dr H Colynize Flat 19, 2283XM Ryswyk The Netherlands

BLOKH, ALEXANDRE (JEAN BLOT), writer; b. Moscow, USSR, Mar. 31, 1923; s. Arnold and Anne (Berlinrote) B.; m. Nadine Chamourine-Zagoska Blokh, Dec. 17, 1956. Student, Bromsgrove Pub. Sch., Worcester, U.K., 1939; PhD, Faculté de Droit de Lyon, France, 1945, Faculté des Lettres de Paris, France, 1946. Dir. interpretation svcs. U.N., N.Y.C., 1946-56, Geneva, 1958-61; head artistic creation dept. UNESCO, Paris, 1962-81; internat. sec. Internat. P.E.N., London, 1982-98; v.p. Internat. P.E.N., 1998—; pres. French P.E.N. Club, 1999; Officier des Arts et Lettres. Author: (fiction novel) Le Soleil de Cavouri, 1956, Les Enfants de New york, 1959, Obscur Ennemi, 1961, Les Illusions nocturnes, 1964, La Jeune Géante, 1968, La Difficulté d'Aimer, 1971 (Prix des Critiques), Les Cosmopolites, 1976 (Prix Valley Larbaud, Sporades, 1979, Gris du Ciel, 1981 (Prix Cazes)), Moi Graf Bouby, chat de gouttière, Tout l'ète, 1985, Sainte-Imposture, 1988, (non-fiction) Marguerite Yourcenar, 1971, 80, Le Grand Siècle russe et ses prolongements, 1971, Ossip Mandelstam, 1972, Là ou tu iras, 1973, Sporade, 1979, Ivan Gontcharov ou le rèalisme impossible, 1986 (Grand Prix de la Critique), Albert Cohen, 1986, Bloomsbury, 1992, Vladimir Nabokov, 1994 (poetry collection Vue du train, 1989, le Juif Margolin, 1998, Moise, 1999. Home: 34 Square Montsoures, 74014 Paris France

BLOKHIN, ALEXANDER MIKHAJLOVICH, mathematician, researcher; b. Krasnojarsk, Former USSR, Nov. 11, 1945; s. Mikhail Andreevich and Vera Sergeevna (Korshunova) B.; m. Rufina Makarovna Selina, Apr. 22, 1967. MS in Gas Dynamics, State U. of Novosibirsk, Former USSR, 1970; Phd in Mechs. of Liquid and Gas, Inst. Theoret. & Applied Mechs, 1975; DSc in Differential Equations, Inst. Math., 1984. Jr. rschr. Inst. Theoretical and Applied Mechs., Novosibirsk, Former USSR, 1970-73, rsch. worker, 1973-78, sr. rschr. computer ctr., 1978-80, sr. rsch. inst. math., 1980-87, head lab. computational problems in math., physics, 1987—; asst. State U. Novosibirsk, 1977-83, assoc. prof. differential equations, 1983-87, prof. differential equations, 1987-90, chmn. dept. differential equations, 1990—. Author: Energy Integrals and their Applications to Gas Dynamics Problems, 1986, Strong Discontinuities in Magnetohydrodynamics, 1993; editor: Mathematical Modelling and Differential Equations, 1996, Differential Equations, 1996. Home: Zolotodolinskaja Str 33-10, 630090 Novosibirsk Russia Office: Inst Math, pr Koptyuga 4, 630090 Novosibirsk Russia

BLOM, AART, non-profit organization administrator; b. Amsterdam, The Netherlands, Dec. 18, 1938; s. Christian and Aaltje (Veenenga) B.; m. Gonnie Starrenburg Blom, Jan. 30, 1967. PHd In Econ. Scis., U. Netherlands, Amsterdam, 1965. Deputy mgr. Nederlandse Bibliotheek Dienst, 1970-78, gen. mgr., 1978—. 2nd lt. Military Fin., 1965-67. Office: Nederlandse Bibliotheek Dienst, PO Box 437, 2260AK Leidschendam The Netherlands

BLOM, BIRGITTA, judge; b. Stockholm, June 22, 1929; d. Wilhelm and Inga (Wadell) Bergstrand; m. Lennart Blom, Jan. 1, 1955; 1 child, Kerstin. LLB, Stockholm U., 1954, JD, 1992. Legal advisor Ministry of Justice, Sweden, 1966-69, head divsn. internat. affairs, 1969-76; head divsn. Ct. Appeal, Stockholm, 1976-83, chief justice, 1983-96; chmn. com. of whole Internat. Maritime Conf., IMO, U.K., 1976; pres. Arbitration Inst. C. of C., Stockholm, 1988-99, Swedish Inst. Arbitration, Stockholm, 1985-90. Author: Maritime Code: The Liability of Shipowners, 1985; contbr. articles to profl. jours. Pres. Swedish Heart and Lung Found., Stockholm, 1987-99. Decorated His Majesty's Gold Medal King of Sweden. Mem. Rotary (pres. Stockholm club 1994-95). Home: Asbacken 29, 167 66 Bromma Sweden

BLOM, DANIEL CHARLES, lawyer, investor; b. Portland, Oreg., Dec. 13, 1919; s. Charles D. and Anna (Rener) B.; m. Ellen Lavon Stewart, June 28, 1952; children: Daniel Stewart (dec.), Nicole Jan Heath. BA magna cum laude, U. Wash., 1941, postgrad., 1941-42; JD, Harvard U., 1948; postgrad., U. Paris, 1954-55. Bar: Wash. 1949, U.S. Supreme Ct. 1970. Tchg. fellow speech U. Wash., 1941-42; law clk. to justice Supreme Ct. Wash., 1948-49; since practiced in Seattle; assoc. Graves, Kizer & Graves, 1949-51; gen. counsel Northwestern Life Ins. Co., 1952-54; ptnr. Case & Blom, 1952-54; assoc., ptnr., of counsel Ryan, Swanson & Cleveland, 1956—; exec. v.p., gen. counsel Family Life Ins. Co., 1977-85, spl. counsel, 1985-91; vice chmn. Wash. Bd. Bar Examiners, 1970-72, chmn., 1972-75; mem. industry adv. com. Nat. Assn. Ins. Commrs., 1966-68; pres. Wash. Ins. Coun., 1971-73, gen. counsel, 1975-78; mediator Arbitration Forums, Inc. Editor Wash. State Bar Jour., 1951-52; assoc. editor The Brief, 1975-76; author: Life Insurance Law of the State of Washington, 1980, Banking and Insurance, Deregulatory Cross-Currents, 1985, Hostile Insurance Company Takeovers: New Frontier of the Law, 1990, Administrative Finality Under the Washington Insurance Code, 1991, Business and Professionalism, 1994, The Civility Problem, 1995, Technics and the Civilization of Law Practice, 1997, Varieties of Regulatory Experience, 1998. Chmn. jury selection Wash. Gov.'s Writer's Day Awards, 1976; bd. dirs. Crisis Clinic; trustee Bush Sch., 1971-79, v.p., 1976-77; trustee, v.p. Frye Mus., Seattle, 1976-82, World Affairs Coun. Seattle, 1972-94, Friends of Seattle Pub. Libr., 1982-87; bd. visitors U. Wash. Libr., 88-92, Friends of U. Wash. Librs., bd. dirs., 1991-95, pres., 1991-92. 2d lt. AUS, 1942-45, PTO. Decorated Bronze Star; Rhodes scholarship finalist, 1949. Fellow Am. Bar Found.; mem. ABA (vice chmn. com. on life ins. law, sect. tort and ins. practice 1971-76, chmn. 1976-78, sect. program chmn. 1978-79, mem. coun. 1979-83, chmn. pub. rels. com. 1981-83, chmn. com. on profl. independence of the lawyer 1984-85, chmn. com. on scope and correlation 1985-86, chmn. com. on handbook and by-laws 1987-88, chmn. hist. com. 1991-94, del. ABA to Union Internat. Des Avocats 1986-91, policy coord. tort and ins. practice sect. 1986-90), Wash. Bar Assn. (award of merit 1975, chmn. legal edn. liason com. 1977-78), Seattle Bar Assn., Union Internat. Des Avocats (v.p. 1987-92), N.Am. Found. for Internat. Legal Practice (dir. 1987-95, pres. 1987-89, chmn. 1990-95), Am. Judicature Soc., Assn. Life Ins. Counsel, Harvard Law Sch. Assn., Am. Coun. Life Ins. (legis. com. 1982-85), Am. Arbitration Assn., Found. UIA (coun. 1990-97), Fedn. Regulatory Counsel, (dir. 1995-97), Harvard Assn. Seattle and Western Wash. (trustee 1976-77), Rainer Club, Phi Beta Kappa, Tau Kappa Alpha. Home: 100 Ward St # 602-3 Seattle WA 98109-5613 Office: Ryan Swanson & Cleveland 1201 3rd Ave Ste 3400 Seattle WA 98101-3034

BLOMBERG, DAGMAR CATHARINA MARIA, Japanologist; b. Orebro, Sweden, Dec. 4, 1946; d. Carl Harald Oriel and Dagmar Marta Maria (Tygnaeus) B. BA, Upsala (Sweden) U., 1970, PhD, 1977; BA, Cambridge U., England, 1972, MA, 1977. Lectr. Upsala U., Sweden, 1974-81, Umea U., Sweden, 1979-82; assoc. prof. Gothenburg U., Sweden, 1983; assoc. prof., lectr. Stockholm U., 1994—. Author: The Heart of the Warrior, 1994; editor: The West's Encounter With Japanese Civilization 1800-1940, 14 vols., 2000. Adolf Lindgrens Stiftelse rsch. grantee, Orebro, 1984, Nordic Inst. Asian Studies travelling grantee, Copenhagen, 1993, Found. Famiglia Rausing travelling grantee, Rome, 1996; vis. scholar Harvard U., 1984; Matsumae fellow Tokai U., Japan, 1978-79, Hambro fellow Clare Hall, Cambridge, 1986-87, Japan Found. fellow, Keio U., Tokyo, 1980-81, 91-92. Mem. Swedish Pan-European Assn. (founding mem. 1991—), Royal Soc. Asian Affairs, Asiatic Soc. Japan, Katharine Briggs Dining Club (corr. 1986—). Lutheran. Avocations: literature, classical music, art. Office: Stockholm U Inst Oriental Langs, Dept Japanese Kraftriket 4, S-106 91 Stockholm Sweden

BLOMBERG, DOUGLAS GORDON, education educator; b. Sydney, Australia, June 30, 1951; m. Heather Anne Goldsworthy, Aug. 18, 1984; children: Rebecca, Marijke, Jessica. BA with honors, U. Sydney, 1974, PhD, 1980; grad. diploma in edn., Gippsland Coll. Edn., Churchill, Australia, 1980; MEd, Monash U., Melbourne, Australia, 1995. Cert. tchr., Victoria. Coord. sr. sch. Mt. Evelyn Christian Sch., Melbourne, 1978-82, curriculum cons., 1983, vice-prin. curriculum, 1987-91; prin. Inst. Christian Edn., Melbourne, 1978-91; prin. Nat. Inst. Christian Edn., Melbourne and Sydney, 1992-98, acad. dean, 1999—; sr. mem. in philosophy of edn. Inst. for Christian Studies,, Toronto, 1998—; trustee Assn. Christian Scholarship, 1985—; hon. dir. Christian Parent Controlled Schs., Ltd., Sydney, 1989-91; vis. fellow Calvin Coll., Grand Rapids, Mich., 1991-92. Co-author, editor: A Vision with a Task, 1993, Humans Being, 1996, Reminding, 1998; editor Radix jour., 1974-78; contbr. to profl. publs. Fellow Australian Coll. Edn.; mem. Assn. for Reformational Philosophy, ASCD, Philosophy Edn. Soc. Australasia, Australian Curriculum Studies Assn., Australian Assn. Rsch. in Edn., Internat. Assn. Promotion Christian Higher Edn., Nat. Soc. Study of Edn., Am. Ednl. Rsch. Assn. Avocations: music, theater, rugby. Home: 21 Gibbs Rd, Montrose 3765, Australia Office: Nat Inst Christian Edn, 58 Douglas Rd, Blacktown 2148, Australia

BLOMHOFF, HEIDI KIIL, immunology educator; b. Porsgrunn, Norway, Jan. 1, 1958; d. Bjarne and Dagmar Christine (Amundsen) Kiil; m. Rune Blomhoff; children: Maia, Henrik. MS, U. Oslo, 1981, PhD, 1984; PhD, U. Oslo, 1987. Rsch. fellow The Norwegian Radium Hosp., Oslo, 1983-86, rschr., 1986-95, sr. rsch. scientist, 1995-96; prof. U. Oslo, Norway, 1996—; cons. World Health Orgn., Geneve, 1986-91, Norwegian Cancer Soc., 1987—; bd. dirs. The Norwegian Radium Hosp. Rsch. Found., Oslo, 1987—; editor: Norwegian Biochem. Newsletter, Oslo, 1990-92. Contbr. about 80 articles to profl. jours. Mem. Norwegian Biochem. Soc., Norwegian Immunology Soc., Am. Cancer Soc. Home: Havnabakhen 35, 0874 Oslo Norway Office: U Oslo Inst Med Biochemistry, PO 1112 Blindern, 0317 Oslo Norway

BLOMHOFF, RUNE, biochemist educator, researcher; b. Drammen, Norway, Jan. 22, 1955; s. Thor and Randi (Olsen) B.; m. Heidi Kiil, Aug. 16, 1978; children: Maia Kiil, Henrik Kiil. BS in Biochemistry, U. Oslo, 1981, PhD in Biochemistry, 1985. Rsch. fellow Norwegian Cancer Soc., Oslo, 1981-85, sr. rsch. scientist, 1986-91; prof. Inst. Nutrition Rsch. U. Oslo, 1992—; mem. Med. Rsch. Coun. unit Norwegian Rsch. Coun. for Sci. and Humanities, 1990-96. Editor: Vitamin A in Health and Disease, 1994; contbr. numerous articles to profl. jours. Recipient Anders Jahres prize for med. scis., 1991, King Olav V's prize for cancer rsch., 1996. Mem. Am. Inst. Nutrition (Mead Johnson award 1988), Norwegian Biochem. Soc., Biochem. Soc. U.K. Home: Frognerseterveien 5B, Havnabakken 35, 0874 Oslo 3, Norway Office: U Oslo Inst Nutrition Rsch, PO Box 1046, 0316 Oslo 3, Norway

BLOMJOUS, DRÉ J.G.M., army officer; b. Breda, Noordbraba, The Netherlands, Dec. 15, 1943; s. Dré J.M. and Maria J.H. (Sassen) B.; m. Rosita M.P. Fick, May 2, 1970; children: Willem-Jan, Sabine. Student, Royal Mil. Acad., 1968, Hogere Krygsschool, Den Haag, 1978. 2d lt. Royal Netherlands Army, 1968-70, dep. squadron comdr. 101 Tankbattalion, 1970-71; platoon comdr. Cavalry Tng. Ctr. Royal Netherlands Army, Amersfoort, 1971-73; capt. Bravo-squadron Royal Netherlands Army, Bergen, Germany, 1973-76; gen. staff officer, project officer Directorate of Material Royal Netherlands Army, 1976-80; logistics instr. Army Staff Coll. Royal Netherlands Army, The Hague, 1980-83; dep. head tng. matters divsn. Royal Netherlands Army, Amersfoort, 1983-85; lt. col., comdr. 101 Tankbattalion Royal Netherlands Army, 1985-87; dep. head intelligence and security divsn. Royal Netherlands Army, The Hague, 1987-88, dep. head. plans divsn., 1988-89; head major equipment divsn., col. Royal Netherlands Army, 1989-91, brigadier gen., dep. dir. major equipment, 1991-94; asst. chief of staff Intelligence divsn., maj. gen. Royal Netherlands Army, Mons, Belgium, 1994-96; dep. comdr.-in-chief RNLA, inspector res. pers. Royal Netherlands Army, 1996-98, lt. gen., 19986; head Netherlands' Permanent Mil. Representation at NATO's Mil. Com., 1998—; mil. del. Western European Union, 1998—. Decorated Officer in the Order of Orange-Nassau with Swords, Her Majesty the Queen, 1993. Mem. Rotary. Liberal Party. Avocations: sailing, golf, history. Office: NATO-HQ, Blvd Leopold III, 1110 Brussels Belgium

BLÖNDAL, THORSTEINN, internist; b. Reykjavik, Iceland, Aug. 5, 1946; s. Sölvi and Elsa Maria (Hedberg) B.; m. Sif Sigurôardottir, Oct. 13, 1968; children: Sjöfn, Arni, Edda. MD, U. Iceland, 1973; D Med. Edn., U. Uppsala, Sweden, 1982. Cert. lung medicine. Med. physician U. Hosp., Uppsala, 1975-82; lung specialist U. Hosp., Reykjavik, 1982—; physician in charge for TB in Iceland, Reykjavik Centre Cmty. Health, 1982—. Author: Quit Smoking, 1987. Mem. com. for smoking cessation Icelandic Govt., Reykjavik, 1984-88; internat. cooperation with Nordic Tb Baltic Project, 1997—. Office: Dept Internal Medicine, Landspitalinn, Reykjavik Iceland

BLONDEL, JEAN FERNAND, political science educator; b. Toulon, Var, France, Oct. 26, 1929; s. Fernand Albert and Marie Clemence (Santelli) B.; m. Michele Hadet, Oct. 4, 1954; m. Teresa Ashton, May 27, 1982. Diploma, Inst. Etudes Politiques, Paris, 1953; lic., Faculty of Law, Paris, 1954; B.Litt., St. Antony's Coll., Oxford, Eng., 1955. Lectr. in politics U. Keele, Eng., 1958-63, Am. Coun. Learned Socs.; fellow Yale U., New Haven, Conn., 1963-64; prof. govt. U. Essex, Colchester, Eng., 1964-84; vis. scholar Russell Sage Found., N.Y.C., 1984-85; prof. polit. sci. European U. Inst., Florence, Italy, 1985-94; prof., 1994—; exec. dir. European Consortium for Polit. Research, Colchester, 1970-79; mem. council, chmn. govt. and law com. Econ. and Social Research Council, London, 1986-90. Author: Voters Parties and Leaders, 1963, Introduction to Comparative Government, 1969, Comparative Legislatures, 1973, Political Parites, 1978, World Leaders, 1980, The Discipline of Politics, 1983, The Organisation of Governments, 1982, Government Ministers in the Contemporary World, 1985, Political Leadership, 1987, Comparative Government, 2nd edit., 1995, People and Parliament in the European Union, 1998; co-editor: Democracy and Economic Governance, 1999. Avocations: travel. Home: 15 Marloes Rd, London W86LQ, England Office: European Univ Inst Badia Fiesolana, Via dei Rocdettini 9, I-50016San Dominico di Fiesole Florence Italy

BLONDIAUX, JOKL, forensic anthropologist, educator; b. Caudry, France, Apr. 20, 1949; s. Pierre and Christianne (Servin) B.; m. Togor Mondol, Apr. 24, 1976; children: Elionore, Pierre-Elie, Marie. MD, Dijon U., 1979; PhD, Charles de Gaulle U., 1989. Med. advisor Brothers to All Men, Shariakandi, Bangladesh, 1975-77; anthropologist Walincourt, France, 1979—; assoc. prof. forensic anthropology Lille II U., France, 1998—. Pres. Assn. Housing for the Elderly, 1990—; v.p. Friends of Mus. Cambrai, 1993-94. Avocation: jogging. Office: Forensic Inst, Pl Theo Varlet, Lille Nord, France 59127

BLONDIN, JOAN, nephrologist educator; b. Beaumont, Tex., Nov. 28, 1936; d. Joseph Albert and Ona Mae (Williamson) B. BS, La. Tech U., 1959; MNS, Cornell U., 1961; MD, La. State U., 1969. Diplomate Am. Bd. Internal Medicine. Instr. U. Ala., Tuscaloosa, 1961-62; rsch. assoc. Cornell U., Ithaca, N.Y., 1962-63; asst. specialist La. State U., Baton Rouge, 1963-65; intern Barnes Hosp., St. Louis, 1969-70, resident, 1970-72; fellow Washington U., St. Louis, 1972-74, asst. prof., 1974-78; ptnr. Nephrology Cons., Monroe, La., 1978—; assoc. prof. La. State U. Sch. Medicine, Shreveport, 1978-98; adj. prof. human ecology La. Tech. U., 1988; adj. prof. medicine La. State U. Health Scis. Ctr., 2000—; active staff St. Francis Med. Ctr., 1978—, North Monroe Cmty. Hosp., 1984—; adj. prof. Coll. Pharmacy, Northeast La. U., 1996. Contbr. articles to profl. jours. Bd. dirs. Central Bank; mem. adv. bd. Bank One; bd. trustees Nat. Kidney Found. of La., 1988-97; mem. La. Bd. Regents, 1989-94, chmn., 1992; med. dir. North La. Dialysis Ctr., 1992-97, Ruston Kidney Ctr. Fellow La. Cancer Society, 1966, NIH, 1968; recipient Disting. Svc. award La. Dietetic Assn., 1998. Mem. AAAS, ACP, End Stage Renal Disease (chmn. quality consensus com. 1994-96), Internat. Soc. Nephrology, Am. Soc. Internal Medicine, Am. Soc. Nephrology, Am. Soc. Tropical Medicine and Hygiene, Am. Soc. Parenteral and Enteral Nutrition, Am. Heart Assn. (coun. on hypertension), Renal Physicians Assn. (bd. dirs., fin. com. 1991-94, chmn. quality care com.), N.Y. Acad. Scis., La. Med. Soc. (del. 1988—), Ouachita Med. Soc. (pres.-elect 1998-99, pres. 1999-2000, immediate past pres., exec. com. 2000—), Sigma Xi, Alpha Omega Alpha, Phi Kappa Phi, Omicron Nu. Republican. Episcopalian. Avocations: music, needlepoint, reading. Home: 5516 Bent Tree Dr Shreveport LA 71115-9564 Office: Nephrology Cons 711 Wood St Monroe LA 71201-7549

BLOODWORTH, A(LBERT) W(ILLIAM) FRANKLIN, lawyer; b. Atlanta, Sept. 23, 1935; s. James Morgan Bartow and Elizabeth Westfield (Dimmock) B.; m. Elizabeth Howell, Nov. 24, 1967; 1 child, Elizabeth Howell. AB in History and French, Davidson Coll., 1957; JD magna cum laude with 1st honors, U. Ga., 1963. Bar: Ga. 1962, U.S. Supreme Ct. 1971. Asst. dir. alumni and pub. relations Davidson Coll., N.C., 1959-60; assoc. Hansell & Post, Atlanta, 1963-68, ptnr., 1969-84; ptnr. Bloodworth & Nix, Atlanta, 1984-95, Bloodworth & McSwain, Atlanta, 1996—; counsel organized crime com. Met. Atlanta Commn. on Crime, 1965-67; asst. sec., counsel Met. Found. Atlanta, 1968-76. Bd. dirs. Atlanta Presbytery, 1974-78; trustee Synod of S.E., Presbyn. Ch. in U.S.A., Augusta, Ga., 1982-87; trustee Big Canoe Chapel, Ga., 1983-86, 88-91, chmn. bd. trustees, 1985-86, 90-91; mem. pres.'s adv. coun. Presbyn. Homes, 1989—; mem. president's adv. coun. Thornwell Home and Sch. for Children, 1998—. elder North Ave Presbyn. Ch., Atlanta. 1st lt. Intelligence Corps, USAR, 1957-59. Recipient Jessie Dan MacDougal Scholarship award U. Ga. Found., 1963, Outstanding Student Leadership award Student Bar Assn., U. Ga., 1963. Fellow Am. Coll. Trust and Estate Counsel; mem. ABA, State Bar Ga., Atlanta Bar Assn., Atlanta Estate Planning Coun., North Atlanta Estate Planning Coun., Capital City Club, Lawyers Club, Sphinx Club, Gridiron Club, Phi Beta Kappa, Phi Kappa Phi, Omicron Delta Kappa, Alpha Tau Omega (pres. chpt. 1957), Phi Delta Phi (grad. of yr. 1963, pres. chpt. 1963). Republican. Presbyterian. Home: 3784 Club Dr NE Atlanta GA 30319-1108 Office: 706 Monarch Plz 3414 Peachtree Rd NE Atlanta GA 30326-1153

BLOODWORTH, GLADYS LEON, educator; b. Natchitoches, La., July 9, 1946; d. Rudolph and Mary (LeRoy) Leon; m. John Edward Bloodworth, Aug. 14, 1971; children: John, Jeremy. BA, Southern U., Baton Rouge, 1968; MA, Calif. State U., Dominguez Hills, 1989. Lang. arts tchr. grades 6-10 Natchitoches Parish Schs.; categorical program adviser L.A. Unified Schs., mentor tchr., 1999—, coord. gifted coord., 1988. Named Outstanding Math Tchr., 1987-88. Mem. NEA, United Tchrs. L.A., Calif. Tchrs. Assn., Women in Ednl. Leadership, Kappa Kappa Iota. Methodist.

BLOODWORTH, J(AMES) M(ORGAN) BARTOW, JR., physician, educator; b. Atlanta, Feb. 21, 1925; s. J.M. Bartow and Elizabeth (Dimmock) B.; m. G. Jean Stone, Nov. 26, 1947; children: Lowell Ann, Joyce Lynn, Elizabeth Carol; m. Joan G. Wiltgen, July 8, 1972; children: Allison Joan, Ellen Lucy. Student, Emory U., 1942-43, 44-48, MD, 1948; student, Stanford U., 1943-44. Intern, then asst. resident pathology Columbia-Presbyn. Med. Ctr., N.Y.C., 1948-50; instr. pathology Columbia U., 1949-50; asst. resident medicine U. Iowa Hosp., 1950-51; mem. faculty Ohio State U. Coll. Medicine, 1951-62, prof. pathology, 1960-62; chief divsn. pathologic anatomy Ohio State U. Hosp., 1954-61; pathologist Columbus State Hosp., 1954-57; prof. pathology and lab. medicine U. Wis., Madison, 1962-95, prof. emeritus, 1995—; chief lab. svc. Madison VA Hosp., 1962-89, pathologist, 1989-95. Editor: Endocrine Pathology, 1968, 2d edit., 1982, 3rd edit., 1996; contbr. numerous articles to publs. in field. Served with AUS, 1941-45. Recipient Fight for Sight citation Am. Assn. Rsch. in Ophthalmology, 1964. Mem. AMA, Wis. Med. Assn., Am. Assn. Clin. Endocrinologists (charter), Dane County Med. Soc., Wis. Soc. Pathologists (pres. 1977-79), Am. Soc. Investigative Pathologists, Histochem. Soc., Am. Diabetes Assn. (Lilly award 1963, Profl. Svc. award Wis. affiliate 1982), So. Wis. Diabetes Assn., Am. Heart Assn., Wis. Heart Assn., Soc. Exptl. Biology and Medicine, Internat. Acad. Pathology, Am. Soc. Clin. Pathology, Am. Assn. Neuropathologists, Nat. Soc. Med. Rsch., Am. Soc. Cell Biology, Gyro Internat. Club (pres. Columbus chpt. 1962, pres. Madison chpt. 1980, 95). Home: 4514 Crescent Rd Madison WI 53711-4721

BLOOM, GORDON ALLAN, psychologist, educator; b. Toronto, Ont., Can., Sept. 12, 1966; s. Samuel Saul and Carolyn H. B.; m. Bonnie Ann Bloom, Aug. 8, 1993; children: Jacob Austin, Alexis Peninah. BA, U. We. Ont., London, 1988; MA, York U., N. York, Ont., 1993; PhD, U. Ottawa, Ont., 1997. Asst. prof. Calif. State U., Fresno, 1996—, sport psychologist, 1997—. Author: Great Job Coach!, 1996, Psychological Foundations of Sport, 2d edit., 2000; contbr. articles to profl. jours. Recipient Dr. G. Arthur Broten Young Scholar award We. Coll. Phys. Edn. Soc., 1998; team bldg. in sport grantee Social Scis. and Humanities Rsch. Coun., 1999; Rsch. scholar U. Ottawa, 1993-95. Mem. Internat. Soc. Mental Tng. and Excellence, Assn. Advancement Applied Sport Psychology, Can. Soc. Psychomotor Learning and Sport Psychology, Calif. Assn. Health, Phys. Edn., Recreation and Dance, Soc. Internat. Hockey Rsch., Can. Mental Tng. Registry. Avocations: ice hockey, reading, traveling, baseball. E-mail: gordonb@csufresno.edu. Office: Calif State U Fresno Dept Kinesiology Fresno CA 93740-0001

BLOOM, JACK SANDLER, investment banker; b. Boston, Mar. 20, 1957; s. Joseph and Inez (Sandler) B.; m. Jennifer Kingson, May 14, 1964; 1 child, Valerie. BA, Harvard U., 1979; MBA, MIT Sloan Sch., 1983. V.p. Allied Ventures, N.Y.C., 1983-85, Kaufman & Co., Boston, 1985-88; pres. Alpha Capital Corp., N.Y.C., 1988—; mng. dir. corp. fin. Commonwealth Assocs., 1994-95; pres. Auto Am., 1996—. Office: Alpha Capital Corp 950 3rd Ave Ste 2600 New York NY 10022-2705

BLOOM, JULIAN, artist, editor; b. Cleve., May 6, 1933; s. John Bernard and Lillian Judith (Finkel) B.; m. Shirley Ann Harper, Nov. 29, 1954; children: Sandra Layne Walker, Andrea Sue Wells. AA, Cypress Coll., 1972; student, U. LaVerne (Calif.), 1983-86. Lab tech. Harvey Aluminum, Torrance, Calif., 1956-64, foreman, 1964-66; sr. draftsman Northrop Corp., Anaheim, Calif., 1966-67; designer Northrop Aircraft, Anaheim, Calif., 1967-69, facilities engr., 1969-81, design to corp. cost designer, 1982-84; mfg. engring. mgr. Northrop Aircraft, Anaheim, 1984-85, mfg. mgr., 1985-92; artist, owner Realistic Watercolors, Cypress, 1992—; instr. watercolor Huntington Beach Art Ctr., 1997—, City of Cypress, 1998—. Featured in The Best of Watercolor, 1995; columnist Event Newspapers, 1998—. Co-chmn. Cypress (Calif.) Cultural Arts Planning Com., 1993-95; pres. Cypress Art League, 1993-96; commr. Cypress Cultural Arts, 1999—. Served with U.S. Army, 1954-56. Fellow Am. Artists Profl. League (Signature award 1993); mem. Nat. Watercolor Soc. (assoc. mem. 1989—, editor newsletter 1994-97), Watercolor West (bd. dirs. 1999—), Am. Soc. Marine Artists (artist mem., Signature award 2000). Republican. Jewish. Avocations: travel, computers, photography. Home and Office: 4522 Cathy Ave Cypress CA 90630-4212

BLOOM, STEPHEN ROBERT, medical educator, biomedical researcher; b. Maidstone, Kent, Eng., Oct. 24, 1942; s. Arnold and Edith Nancy (Fox) B.; m. Margaret Janet Sturrock, July 10, 1965; children: Sarah, Nicholas, Chloe, James. MB, Cambridge (Eng.) U., 1967, D in Surgery, 1967, MA, 1968, MD, 1979; DSc (hon.), London U., 1982. Gastro house physician Middlesex Hosp., 1967-68, cardiology house physician, 1968, casualty med. officer, 1969; Leverhulme rsch. scholar Inst. Clin. Rsch., 1970; house surgeon Mount Vernon Hosp., 1968-69; endocrine house physician Hamm Hosp., 1969-70; med. unit registrar Middlesex Hosp., London, 1970-72, MRC clin. rsch. fellow, 1972-74; sr. lectr. Royal Postgrad. Med. Sch., Hammersmith Hosp., London, 1974-78, reader in medicine, 1978-82, prof. endocrinology, 1982—, chmn. Divsn. Investigative Sci., 1997—; chmn. sci. com. Nat. Inst. Biol. Stds. and Control, London, 1993—; mem. subcom. biologicals Medicines Control Agy., London, 1992—; mem. grants subcom. Med. Rsch. Coun., London, 1990—. Editor: Gut Hormones, 1978, Endocrine Tumours,

1985, Surgical Endocrinology, 1993, Toohey's Medicine, 15th edition, 1994; editor-in-chief jour. Regulatory Peptides, 1979-84; lectr. in field. Fellow Royal Coll. Physicians (acad. v.p., sr. censor 1999), Royal Coll. Pathologists; mem. Bayliss & Starling Soc. (chmn. 1980-92), Assn. Physicians, Soc. Endocrinology (gen. sec. 1999). Avocations: walking, jogging, travelling, opera. Office: Royal Postgrad Med Sch, Hammersmith Hosp Campus, Du Cane Rd, London W12 0NN, England

BLOOM, VICTOR ROY, physician; b. Mar. 13, 1932; s. Froim and Jesse Selina (Parker) B.; m. Chloe Ann Rich, 1964 (div. 1976); children: Marston, Emma; m. Vanessa Lee Gale, Apr. 16, 1994. MA, U. Oxford, BM BChir, 1957. Med. tng. Bristol (Eng.) Royal Infirmary, 1958-59, Hosp. for Sick Children Gt. Ormond St., 1959-60, Nat. Heart Hosp., 1960, Hammersmith Hosp., 1960-62, Ctrl. Middlesex Hosp., 1962-64; physician Harley House, London, 1964-97; v.p. Hornsby Ednl. Trust. Mem. adv. panel Pro-Dogs, Dartmoor Preservation Soc. Freeman, City of London; liveryman Worshipman Soc. Apothecaries. Mem. Royal Coll. Physicians, Med. Soc. London, Torquay Pottery Collectors Soc. Avocations: opera, theatre, ceramics, cricket, football. Office: Little Brook, Buckland in the Moor, Ashburton Devon TQ13 7HN, England

BLOOM, WALTER RUSSELL, mathematics educator; b. Auckland, New Zealand, Dec. 2, 1948; came to Australia, 1960; s. Harry and Norma (Morris) B.; m. Lynette Myra Butler, Nov. 3, 1971; children:Alyson Claire, Monica Dita. BSc with honors, U. Tasmania, 1971, DSc, 1994; PhD, Australian Nat. U., 1974. Tchr. of math. Hobart Matriculation Coll., Tasmania, Australia, 1967; lectr. in math. U. Tasmania, 1974; lectr. in math. Murdoch U., Perth, Western Australia, 1975-81, sr. lectr., 1982-87, assoc. prof. math., 1988-95, dean Sch. Math. and Phys. Scis., 1991-96; prof. math. Murdoch U., Perth, 1995—; vis. Fulbright scholar U.Wash., 1976-77; vis. prof. U. Tübingen, Germany, 1980, 87, 91, 98. Contbr. articles to profl. jours. Alexander von Humboldt research fellow, 1987, 91, 98, 99; hon. assoc. in numismatics Western Australia Mus., 1998—. Fellow Australian Math. Soc. (sec. 1980-90), Royal Numismatic Soc.; mem. Am. Math. Soc., Perth Numismatic Soc. (editor). Office: Murdoch U, Perth Western Australia 6150, Australia

BLOOM, WILLIAM HERMAN, neurosurgeon, author; b. Granville, N.Y., Jan. 18, 1926; s. Samuel William and Lillian Anna (Pinsker) B.; m. Barbara Renee Miller, Nov. 28, 1960; children: Deborah Jane, Jeffrey Martin, Sharon Ann, Jonathan Richard. BS, Union Coll., 1944; MD, U. Buffalo, 1948. Diplomate Am. Bd. Neurol. Surgery. Intern Buffalo Gen. Hosp., 1948-49; residetn Mt. Sinai Hosp., 1949-50, Bellevue-NYU Med. Ctr., 1955-59; pvt. practice neurosurgeon Bay Shore, N.Y., 1961—; hon. clin. asst. faculty St. George Hosp., U. London, 1959-60; pres. Suffolk County med. Soc., Hauppauge, N.Y., 1976-77, Suffolk Acad. Medicine, Hauppauge, 1977-78, Nassau-Suffolk 2nd Dist. Br., M.S.S.N.Y., 1986-88; founder, pres. L.I. Neuroscis. Soc., Nassau-Suffolk, 1985-88. Collaborator: Atlas of Positive Contrast Myclography, 1961; author: The Great American Malpractice Dilemma 1988, The Life and Times of Samuel W. Bloom, 1996, Songs of the Sea and the Shore, 1999. Lt. USNR, 1950-52. Fellow Am. Coll. Surgeons; mem. Am. Assn. Neurol. Surgeons, Med. Soc. State of N.Y., Internat. Soc. of Poets, Congress Neurol. Surgeons, Sigma Xi. Republican. Jewish. Avocations: writing, music. Office: 270 E Main St Bay Shore NY 11706-8403

BLOOMBERG, MICHAEL RUBENS, finance and information services company executive; b. Boston, Feb. 14, 1942; divorced; 2 children. Graduate, Johns Hopkins U., 1964, Harvard U., 1966. Processing clerk Salomon Brothers, 1966; gen. ptnr. sys. devel. Salomon Brothers, N.Y.C.; pres. founder Bloomberg L.P., N.Y.C., 1981—, pres., CEO; pub. Bloomberg Business News, N.Y.C.; gen. mgr. Bloomberg Television, Bloomberg Radio, Sta. WBBR-AM 1130, N.Y.C.; pub. Bloomberg Mag./Bloomberg Personal Mag., Princeton, N.J., Bloomberg Personal, Skillman, N.J. Chmn. bd. trustees Johns Hopkins U.; trustee Big Apple Circus, Ctrl. Park Conservancy, Met. Mus. Art, H.S. Econs. And Fin., Inst. Advanced Study, Lincoln Ctr. Performing Arts, Jewish Mus., N.Y. Police and Fire Widows' and Children's Fund, Spence Sch., Prep for Prep, S.L.E. Found., U.S. Ski Team Ednl. Found., Serpentine Gallery, London. Mem. U.S. C. of C. (trustee). Office: Bloomberg LP 499 Park Ave 15th Fl New York NY 10022-1240*

BLOOMER, JONATHAN, insurance company executive. With Arthur Andersen; sr. ptnr. fin. markets divsn. Arthur Andersen, London; group fin. dir. Prudential plc, 1995-2000, group chief exec., 2000—; mem. City panel on takeovers and mergers, urgent issues task force, 1997—; dir. Railtrack plc, 1999—. Office: Prudential Plc, Laurence Pountney Hill, London EC4R OHH, England*

BLOOMFIELD, SIR KENNETH PERCY, educational administrator; b. Belfast, No. Ireland, Apr. 15, 1931; s. Harry Percy and Doris (Frankel) B.; m. Mary Elizabeth Ramsey, July 9, 1960; children: Caroline Elizabeth, Timothy Kenneth. MA, Oxford U., 1956; LLD (hon.), Queen's U., Belfast, 1991; Hon. fellow, St. Peter's Coll., Oxford, Eng., 1991. Asst. and dep. prin. Ministry of Fin., No. Ireland, 1952-56, pvt. sec. to minister of fin., 1956-59; dep. dir. Brit. Indsl. Devel. Office, N.Y.C., 1960-63; asst. to dep. sec. to cabinet Cabinet Office, 1963-72; undersec. No. Ireland Office, 1972-73; permanent sec. No. Ireland Civil Svc., 1976-86, head, 1984-91; nat. gov. for No. Ireland BBC, U.K., 1991-99; chmn. No. Ireland Higher Edn. Coun., Bangor, 1999—; chmn. N. Ireland Higher Edn. Coun., 1993—, Chief Execs. Forum, 1991-97; bd. dirs. Green Park Healthcare Trust; adv. bd. Bank of Ireland. Contbr. articles to profl. jours. Chmn. Children in Need Trust, London, 1992-98; bd. dirs. Opera N. Ireland, Belfast, 1991-97; pres. Ulster People's Coll., 1996—; N.I. Victims commr., 1997-98; pres. N.I. Coun., The Stationery Office, 1998—; chmn. Rev. of Criminal Injuries Compensation, 1998-99; mem. Joint Commn. for Recovery of Victims Remains, 1999—; mem. rev. panel on Jersey Machinery of Govt., 1999—; cons. Ch. of Eng. Rev. of Crown Appts. Commn., 1999—. Named Companion of the Bath, Queen of Eng., 1982; decorated Knight Commdr. of the Bath, Queen of Eng., 1987; recipient award for personal excellence, N. Ireland C. of C. and Industry, 1990. Mem. Oxford and Cambridge U. Club. Episcopalian. Avocations: reading history and biography, opera, theatre, swimming. Office: BBC No Ireland Higher Edn Coun, Rathgael House/Balloo Rd, Bangor, County Down BT19 17P, Northern Ireland

BLOOMFIELD, LINCOLN PALMER, political scientist; b. Boston, July 7, 1920; m. Irirangi Pamela Coates, 1948; children: Pamela, Lincoln, Diana. SB, Harvard U., 1941, MPA, 1952, PhD, 1956. With Dept. State, Washington, 1946-57, spl. asst. to asst. sec., 1952-57; sr. staff ctr. for internat. studies MIT, Cambridge, 1957—; prof. polit. sci. MIT, 1963-91, prof. emeritus, 1991—; dir. global issues Nat. Security Council, Washington, 1979-80; mem. Presdl. Commn. on 25th Anniversary of UN, 1970-71; vis. prof. Grad. Inst. Advanced Internat. Studies, Geneva, 1965, 72, 77, 79, Salzburg Seminar faculty, 1982, 86, 92, 95, moderator State Dept. seminar on fgn. policy and global issues, 1992-99; disting. vis. lectr. State Dept. Fgn. Svc. Inst., 1995. Host Christian Sci. Monitor TV program Fifty Years Ago Today, 1989-92; moderator EcoForum TV series, 1997-99; author: Evolution or Revolution?, 1957, The UN and U.S. Foreign Policy, rev. edit., 1967, In Search of Am. Foreign Policy, 1974, The Foreign Policy Process: A Modern Primer, 1982; co-author, editor: International Military Force, 1964, Kruschchev and the Arms Race, 1966, Outer Space: Prospects for Man and Society, rev. edit., 1968, Controlling Small Wars, 1969, The Management of Global Disorder, 1987, Prospects for Peacemaking, 1987, Managing Internat. Conflict, 1997. Bd. dirs. Unitarian-Universalist Assn., 1958-64, World Affairs Council of Boston, World Peace Found., Nat. Def. U., 1984-89, Can. Inst. Internat. Peace and Security, 1989-92. Lt. USNR, 1942-46. Recipient Chase prize Harvard U., 1956, EDUCOM prize Disting. Software, 1988, New Eng. Emmy award, 1992; Littauer fellow, 1952; Rockefeller fellow, 1954, 75. Fellow World Acad. Art and Sci. (elected); mem. Coun. on Fgn. Rels. Achievements include research on foreign policy, international organizations, political gaming, conflict-minimizing and policy planning strategies and systems. Home: 37 Beach St Cohasset MA 02025-1421 Office: 30 Wadsworth St Cambridge MA 02142-1320

BLOOMQUIST, DENNIS HOWARD, lawyer; b. Mpls. Sept. 18, 1942; s. Howard Richard and Ingrid Marit (Brostrom) B.; m. Shirley Anne Ruemele, Aug. 22, 1964; children—Michael Dennis, Eric William. B.A., Albion Coll., Mich., 1964; M.B.A., Mich. State U., 1965; J.D. cum laude, Wayne State U., 1968; LL.M., NYU, 1975. Bar: Mich. 1968, U.S. Dist. Ct. (ea. dist.) Mich. 1968, N.Y. 1971, Va. 1995. Assoc. Parsons, Tennent, Hammond, Hardig & Ziegelman, Detroit, 1968-70, Alexander and Green, N.Y.C., 1970-73; tax counsel Mobil Oil and Mobil Corp., N.Y.C., 1973-81, gen. counsel Mobil Land Devel. Corp., N.Y.C., 1981-88, real estate and land devel., Mobil Corp., 1984-88, asst. gen. tax counsel, Fairfax, Va., 1988—; lectr. continuing legal edn. Mem. ABA, Bar Assn. Mich., N.Y. State Bar Assn. Congregationalist. Home: 11136 Rich Meadow Dr Great Falls VA 22066-1417 Office: 3225 Gallows Rd Fairfax VA 22037-0001

BLOOR, DAVID, physics educator, researcher; b. Dover, Kent, Eng., July 25, 1937; s. Alfred Edwin and Gladys Ellen (Collins) B.; m. Margaret Anne Avery, July 2, 1960; children: Richard Edwin, Philip Douglas, James William, Thomas John. BS with honors, U. London, 1958, PhD, 1961. Chartered physicist. Lectr. U. Canterbury, Christchurch, New Zealand, 1961-64; lectr. Queen Mary Coll., London, 1964-80, reader, 1980-84, prof., 1984-89; prof. applied physics U. Durham, Eng., 1987-93; coord. molecular electronics initiative Sci. and Engring. Rsch. Coun., Swindon, Eng., 1987-93; cons. Gec-Marconi, Chelmsford, Eng., 1984-92; external examiner Trinity Coll., Dublin, Ireland, 1990-94; mem. expert coun. Ommel, Moscow, 1994—; external examiner U. Salford, 1996—. Editor: Polydiacetylenes, 1985, Organic Materials for Non-Linear Optics, 1991, Introduction to Molecular Electronics, 1994, (ency.) The Encyclopedia of Advanced Materials, 1994. Humboldt fellow U. Stuttgart, 1975, U. Bayreuth, 1997, Erskine fellow U. Canterbury, 1983, indsl. fellow Royal Soc., Gec Marconi Rsch. Ctr., 1984, Sir Derman Christopherson Found. fellow U. Durham, 1996. Fellow Inst. Physics; mem. Dielectrics Soc. (com. mem. 1992-98). Avocations: hill walking, gardening. Office: U Durham, Dept Physics South Rd, DH1 3LE Durham England

BLOSSER, HENRY GABRIEL, physicist; b. Harrisonburg, Va., Mar. 16, 1928; s. Emanuel and Leona (Branum) B.; m. Priscilla May Beard, June 30, 1951 (div. Oct. 1972); children: William Henry, Stephan Emanuel, Gabe Fawley, Mary Margaret; m. Mary Margaret Gray, Mar. 16, 1973 (dec. Jan. 1995); m. Amy June Conley, May 11, 1995 (div. Feb. 1997); m. Lois Pearlena Lynch, Oct. 17, 1998. BS, U. Va., 1951, MS, 1952, PhD, 1954. Physicist Oak Ridge (Tenn.) Nat. Lab., 1954-56, group leader, 1956-68; assoc. prof. physics Mich. State U., East Lansing, 1958-61, prof., 1961-90, Univ. Disting. prof., 1990—, dir. Cyclotron Lab., 1961-89; cons. Harper Hosp., Detroit, 1983—, Ion Beam Applications, Belgium, 1996—, others; adj. prof. radiation oncology Wayne State U., Detroit, 1996—. Bd. dirs. Midwest Univs. Rsch. Assocs., 1960-63. With USNR, 1946-48. predoctoral fellow NSF, 1953-54, sr. postdoctoral fellow, 1966-67; Guggenheim fellow, 1973-74. Fellow Am. Phys. Soc. (Bonner prize 1992); mem. Sigma Xi, Phi Beta Kappa, Kappa Alpha. Home: 2350 Emerald Forest Cir East Lansing MI 48823-7200 Office: Mich State U Nat Cyclotron East Lansing MI 48824-1321

BLOSSEY, MAUREEN B., mental health administrator; b. Lewistown, Pa., Dec. 30, 1944; d. Richard John and June (Brannan) Bojalad; m. P. Blossey, June 3, 1967 (div. Aug. 1977); children: Damian, Danielle, Jeremy; m. John J. Palovick, May 13, 1984; children: Pamela, Nicole, Jaclyn. BS, Clarion (Pa.) State Coll., 1967; MS, Bloomsburg U., 1989; postgrad., Mansfield U., 1978-80; PsyD in Profl. Studies, So. Cal. Univ., 2000. Spl. edn. tchr. youth ctr. Springfield State Hosp., Sykesville, Md., 1967-68; tchr. Union/Snyder Assn. Retarded Citizens, Danville, 1976; adminstr. Snyder County Assn. for Retarded Citizens, Danville, Pa., 1977-78; dir. community residential rehab. program Columbia Montour Snyder Union Mental Health/Retardation, Danville, 1978-82, mental health/retardation svcs. coord., 1982-91; mental health/retardation program adminstr. Schuylkill County Mental Health/Retardation Program, Pottsville, Pa., 1991—; adj. prof. Bloomsburg U., 1988-89, Kutztown (Pa.) U., 1993; tchr. Snyder County Assn. Retarded Citizens, 1977; established Community Housing and Support Program, 1978, dir. expansion, 1982; dir. establishment of TAPline, crisis intervention program; co-chair Columbia County Children's Task Force; mem. State Mental Health Coords., State Mental Retardation Coords., spl. edn. task force Susquehanna Valley; mem. positive approaches com. Pa. Office Mental Retardation, Pa. office Mental Health. Contbr. profl. jours. Chair Snyder County Child Abuse & Neglect Com., 1974-76; mem. parish coun. Divine Redeemer Parish, Mt. Carmel, Pa., Substance Abuse Task Force on Children's Issues, 2000; cub scout leader Boy Scouts Am., Middleburg, Pa., 1976-80, Pa. offi MR Waiting List Initiative Task Force, 1999. Mem. APA, Nat. Case Mgmt. Assn., Nat. Rural Mental Health Assn., Pa. Assn. Rehab. Facilitators, Pa. Crisis Intervention Assn., Mental Health/Mental Retardation Adminstrs. Assn. (mental retardation sub-com.), Pa. Mental Health/Mental Retardation Assn. (bd. dirs. 1994—) Nat. Counc. for Commty. Behavioral Healthcare Schuylkill Co. Child Death Review Team; Am. Psychological Assn, OMR Steering Com. on Self Determination, Nat. Behavioral Health Adminstrn. Assoc. Home: 327 W 2nd St Mount Carmel PA 17851-1211 Office: Schuylkill County MH-MR Prog Rm 2 420 N Centre St Pottsville PA 17901-1729

BLOT, JEAN See BLOKH, ALEXANDRE

BLOUNT, GREGORY JAMES, publishing executive, consultant; b. Washington, July 5, 1969; s. James C. Blount and Janet Delores Heath. Grad., U. S.C., 1991. Pub. Peter Glenn Pubs., Westport, Conn., 1993-2000; hon. com. mem. Dept. Media Arts, Columbia, S.C. Pub. pgdirect.com, Model and Talent Directory, Film and TV Directory, Fashion and Print Directory, Screen and Stage Directory, Modeling Handbook, Model-The Complete Guide. Avocations: guitar, golf, basketball. Office: Peter Glenn Pubs 49 Riverside Ave Westport CT 06880-4227

BLOUSTEIN, PETER EDWARD, entertainment management consultant, producer; b. N.Y.C., June 19, 1937; s. Francis Jerome and Jean (Pinsky) B.; m. Ariadne Natalie Jeon, June 17, 1962; children: Arlyn Sofia, Rachel Jean. AA, Boston U., 1957. Stage mgr. Radio City Music Hall, N.Y.C., 1959-63; advance dir. Time-Life Inc., N.Y.C., 1963; stage mgr. N.Y. Worlds Fair, N.Y.C., 1964; script analyst and dir. various studios L.A., 1964-69; mgr. Walt Disney, L.A. and Orlando, 1969-78; dir. entertainment Walt Disney World, Orlando, 1978-84; producer PremierCruise Lines/NCL, Miami/Cape Canaveral, Fla., 1984-88; producer various dinner theatres Orlando, 1984—; producer Entertainment Lotte World, Seoul, Korea, 1989—; cons. in entertainment PEB Assocs., Inc., Windermere, Fla., 1988—; producer AmeriFlora '92, 1990—; entertainment cons. to Opryland, 1990—; owner World Famous Rocket Belt; dir. reopening Navy Pier, Chgo., 1995; producer Fable Fantasy Parade Samsung Corp., Korea, 1996, 97, 98; cons. Walt Disney Entertainment; pres. Am. Gladiators Orlando Live!, 1996; pres. Gladco Corp., 1996; prodr. Parade Lotte World, Korea, 2000—, Parade Discovery World, Taiwan, 2000—. Producer opening celebration Jr. Olympics, Tampa, 1990; dir. opening Alamo Dome, 1993, Olympic Festival, 1993; producer, dir. Parade at World Expo, Taejon, Korea, 1993; hosp. visitor Congregation of Liberal Judaism, Winter, Park, Fla., 1988, bd. dirs., 1974-76; pres. Theme Park Mgmt. Inst., 1991—. With U.S. Army, 1960-66. Jewish. Avocations: reading, travel, sports.

BLOWER, PETER ROBIN, pharmacologist, educator; b. Romford, Essex, England, June 1, 1948; s. Ernest and Hilda Florence (Dowsett) B.; m. Margaret Alison Holden, Aug. 5, 1972; children: James Rupert, Michael Edward. MS in Biology, Inst. Biology, London, 1972; PhD, Aston U., Birmingham, Eng., 1977; DSc (hon.), U. East London, 1997. Chartered biologist Inst. Biology, 1986. Rsch. biologist Beecham Rsch. Labs, Harlow, Eng., 1969-73; sr. rsch. scientist Beecham Pharmaceuticals, Harlow, Eng., 1973-79, rsch. mgr., 1979-87; scientific advisor Smithkline Beecham, Harlow, Eng., 1987-92, dir. scientific support programs, 1992-96, dir. neurosci. product devel., 1996-2000; ind. pharm. cons., 2000—; owner Biophar Consulting; mng. dir. Blower & Cook Ltd., London, 1978-93; external examiner U. London, 1981-87, U. Marseille, France, 1994. Contbr. more than 50 articles to sci. jours., chpts. to books; patentee in field. Chmn. govs. U. East London, 1994-97, dep. chmn. govs. 1993-94, gov., 1988-93; sci. advisor Hertford Regional Coll., Turnford, Eng., 1983-93. Inst. Biology fellow, London, 1994, Royal Soc. Medicine fellow, London, 1993. Mem. Brit. Pharmacological Soc., Brit. Soc. Gastroenterology, East India Club London (social). Methodist. Avocations: English mediaeval history, cartography, hill walking, gardening. Home: Poole House Great Yeldham, Halstead CO9 4HP, England

BLUCHER, PAUL ARTHUR, lawyer; b. Youngstown, Ohio, Aug. 1, 1958; s. Arthur E. and Lillian L. (McQuillan) B.; m. Brenda Lee Kilgore, Aug. 25, 1990. AS with honors, Youngstown State U., 1984, BS magna cum laude, 1986; JD, U. Pitts., 1990. Bar: Fla. 1990, U.S. Dist. Ct. (mid. dist.) Fla. 1997, U.S. Ct. Appeals (11th cir.) 1998. Police officer Mahoning County Sheriff, Youngstown, 1979-85, police detective, 1985-87; assoc. Brigham, Moore, et al., Sarasota, Fla., 1990-96; ptnr. Brigham, Moore, et al., Sarasota, 1996-97; pvt. practice Law Office of Paul A. Blucher, P.A., Sarasota. Mem. allocations & admissions com. United Way, Sarasota, 1996— (Pathfinder Club Recognition award 1996); mem. Amyotrophic Lateral Sclerosis Assn. 1995—. Mem. ABA (state and local gov. com. 1990-99, real property sect. condemnation com. 1999—), Fla. Bar Assn. (stress mgmt. com. 1997—, young lawyers 1990-95, eminent domain com. 1990—), Fla. Restaurant Assn., Assn. Eminent Domain Profls., Sarasota County Bar Assn. (chair 1990—, spkrs. bur. 2000—). Democrat. Roman Catholic. Avocations: scuba diving, boating, flying. E-mail: pblucher@fifthamendment.com. Office: Law Offices of Paul A Blucher PA 2d Fl 434 S Washington Blvd Fl 2D Sarasota FL 34236-7100

BLUE, ADRIANNE, writer; b. Washington, July 17, 1942; d. Harry and Ruth (Thaler) B. BA, Am. U., 1963; MA, Stanford U., 1969. Literary editor Time Out Mag., London, 1978-79; sports editor City Limits Mag., London, 1979-80; freelance cultural journalist, 1980—; lectr. internat. journalism City U., London, 1998—; sports corr. Sunday Times, London, 1980-90; cons. in field. Author: (children's book) Field Events, 1988, Grace Under Pressure, 1987, Faster, Higher, Further: Women's Triumphs and Disasters at the Olympics, 1988, Queen of the Track, 1992, Martina Unauthorized, 1994, On Kissing: From the Metaphysical to the Erotic, 1996, pub. in 16 langs.; co-author: Fatima: The Autobiography of Fatima Whitbread with Adrianne Blue, 1989; editor: A Women's History of Sex, 1987. Mem. Soc. Authors, Authors Guild. Democrat. Avocations: hiking, roof gardening. Home and Office: 68 Northdown St, London N1-9BS, England

BLUE, DELAWRENCE CHARLES, investment banker, accountant, automobile dealer; b. Abaco, The Bahamas, Nov. 27, 1966; came to U.S., 1971; s. Frank and Ann Marie (Dassas) B. AA, Miami-Dade U., 1988; BS, Barry U., 1992, MPA, 1993. Pres. D.C. Blue & Co., Miami, 1982—, DCB Computers, Miami, 1992—; notary pub. State Fla., Tallahassee, 1995—. Contbr. articles to profl. jours. Sec. North Miami Health Facilities Auth., 1996—, Westside Property Owners, Miami, 1996—; panelist Miami-Dade Cultural Affairs Coun., 1996—; vice chmn. Haitian Polit. Action Com. Mem. Rep. Nat. Com. (charter, Eisenhower Commn. 1997), Los Amigos Club, Chess Club. Home: 155 NW 125th St Miami FL 33168-4616 Office: DC Blue Group 801 Brickell Ave Miami FL 33131-2951

BLUE, JAMES MONROE, lawyer; b. St. Petersburg, Fla., Oct. 5, 1941; s. James Monroe and Mildred (Hobbs) B.; m. Barbara Ann Alderson, Jan. 3, 1981; children: Tammy Marlene, Kelli Christine, Shannon Kathlene. BA, Fla. State U., 1963; JD with honors, Stetson Coll., 1967. Bar: Fla. 1967, U.S. Dist. Ct. (mid. dist.) Fla. 1968, U.S. Ct. Appeals (11th cir.) 1968, U.S. Supreme Ct. 1978. Assoc. Carlton, Fields, Ward, Emmanuel, Smith & Cuttler, Tampa, Fla., 1967-69; ptnr. Alley, Alley & Blue, Miami, Fla., 1969-75, Smith, Young & Blue, Tallahassee, 1975-79, Allen, Norton & Blue, Tampa, 1979—. Mem. ABA, Fla. Bar Assn., Fla. Bar (chmn. labor law sect. 1978-79, Fla. C. of C. (human resources com. 1989—), Tampa C. of C. (com. of 100, 1987—). Republican. Presbyterian. Avocations: golf, boating, reading. Office: 324 S Hyde Park Ave Ste 350 Tampa FL 33606-4110

BLUE, ROBERT LEE, secondary education educator; b. Columbiaville, Mich., Apr. 23, 1920; s. Arthur Floyd and Elma (Ellis) B.; BA, Mich. State U., 1941; MA, U. Mich., 1952; m. Dorothy L. Seward, July 15, 1961. Tchr., Chesaning (Mich.) H.S., 1941-42, 45-57; prin. Ricker Jr. H.S., Saginaw, Mich., 1957-59, Buena Vista H.S., Saginaw, 1960-69; asst. prof. secondary edn. Central Mich. U., Mt. Pleasant, 1969—. Bd. dirs. Hartley Edn. Nature Camp. 1957-69; pres. Saginaw County Assn. Ret. Sch. Pers., Mich. Assn. Ret. Sch. Pers. (chmn. awards com., Disting. Svc. award 1995). With U.S. Army, 1942-45. Decorated Bronze Star. Mem. NEA (life), Mich. Edn. Assn., Assn. Tchr. Educators, Mich. Assn. Tchr. Educators, Nat. Assn. Secondary Sch. Prins., Mich. Assn. Secondary Sch. Prins., Mich. PTA (hon. life), Am. Legion, Mich. Hist. Soc., Saginaw County Hist. Soc., Lapeer County Hist. Soc., Optomist, Pit and Balcony, Masons, Phi Delta Kappa. Republican. Methodist. Author: Footsteps Into The Past, A History of Columbiaville, 1979, also articles. Home: 1437 Lathrup Ave Saginaw MI 48603-4787 Office: 3037 Davenport Ave Saginaw MI 48602-3652

BLUEFARB, SAMUEL MITCHELL, physician; b. St. Louis, Oct. 15, 1912; s. Sol and Pauline (Brown) B.; m. Grace Parsons, Jan. 1, 1944; 1 son, Richard Alan; m. Leah Rose Vendig Pollock, Jan. 24, 1968; children—Fred, Nancy Pollock. B.S., U. Ill., 1936; M.D., 1937. Diplomate Am. Bd. Dermatology and Syphilology. Intern Cook County Hosp., Chgo., 1937-38; resident Bellevue Hosp., N.Y.C., 1939-41; practice medicine specializing in dermatology, 1941-78; sr. attending dermatologist, chmn. dept. Cook County Hosp., 1952-58; attending dermatologist VA Lakeside Hosp., 1954-78; sr. attending staff Chgo. Wesley Meml. Hosp., Passavant Hosp.; prof., chmn. dept. dermatology Northwestern U. Med. Sch., 1962-78; prof. dermatology U. South Fla., 1985-88; chmn. dept. dermatology Bay Pines VA Hosp., Fla., 1984-87. Author books and articles. Fellow Am. Acad. Dermatology and Syphilology (dir. 1969), ACP; mem. AMA, Ill. Med. Soc. (past pres. dermatol. sect.), Chgo. Med. Soc., Soc. Investigative Dermatology, Chgo. Dermatol. soc. (past pres.), Am. Dermatol. Assn., Noah Worcester Dermatology Soc. Home: Kenwood of Lakeview 3101 Sheridan Rd Chicago IL 60657

BLUEM, VOLKER, zoologist, educator; b. Eschwege, Germany, May 20, 1937; s. Hans and Anna (Meyer) B.; m. Mary Lang, July 23, 1965; two children. PhD, U. Frankfurt, 1965. Rsch. scholar J.W. Goethe U., Frankfurt, Germany, 1965-67; from rsch. asst. to prof. Ruhr U., Bochum, Germany, 1967—; head endocrinology rsch. sect. CEBAS Ctr. of Excellence, Bochum. Author: Vertebrate Reproduction, 1986; contbr. more than 200 articles to profl. jours. Mem. European Soc. Comparative Endocrinology, German Soc. Endocrinology, Internat. Acd. Astronautics (life).

BLUESTONE, ANDREW LAVOOTT, lawyer; b. N.Y.C., Feb. 16, 1951; s. Henry Robert and Joan (Lavoott) B.; m. Janet Francesca Whelehan, May 1987; 1 child, Gabrielle. BA, Alfred U., 1973; MA, SUNY, Oswego, 1975; JD, Syracuse U., 1978. Bar: N.Y. 1979, U.S. Dist. Ct. (so. and ea. dists.) N.Y. 1979. Sr. trial asst. dist. atty. Kings County Dist. Atty., Bklyn., 1978-84; sr. assoc. Davis & Hoffman, N.Y.C., 1984-86, Donald Ayers, N.Y.C., 1986, Alexander, Ash, Schwartz & Cohen, N.Y.C., 1986-88, Trolman & Glaser, N.Y.C., 1988-89; pvt. practice, N.Y.C., 1989—; arbitrator Small Claims Civil Ct. City of N.Y. Bd. dirs. Scandia Symphony, N.Y.C., St. Luke's AME Ch., N.Y.C. Mem. ABA, N.Y.C.T.L.A., Def. Assn. N.Y., Assn. Trial Lawyers Am. (lectr.), N.Y. State Trial Lawyers Assn., Bklyn. Bar Assn. Office: 233 Broadway Fl 51 New York NY 10279-5199

BLUESTONE, BARRY ALAN, economics educator; b. Bklyn., Dec. 27, 1944; s. Irving Julius and Zelda B.; m. Mary Ellen Colten, Jun 14, 1987; 1 child, Joshua. BA in Econs., U. Mich., 1966, MA in Econs., 1968, PhD in Econs., 1974. Prof. econs. Boston Coll., Chestnut Hill, Mass., 1971-86; dir. pub. policy PhD program U. Mass., Boston, 1987-98; Russel B. and Andrée B. Stearns trustee/prof. polit. economy Northeastern U., Boston, 1999—; dir. Nommus Cons. Group, Salem, Mass., 1990—. Author: (books) The Deindustrialization of America, 1982, The Great U-Turn, 1988, Negotiating the Future, 1992, Growing Prosperity, 2000. Sr. advisor House Dem. leader Washington, 1995; founding dir. Econ. Policy Inst., Washington, 1985—. Recipient Outstanding Merit award U. Mass., Boston, 1995. Mem. Gorbachev Found. (sr. fellow), Internat. Ctr. for Social Studies (scientific com. 1997—), Urban Outreach Coun./Northeastern U. (com. chair 1999—). Democrat. Avocations: bicycle racing, tennis. E-mail: bluestone@neu.edu.

BLUHER, GREGORY, computer scientist, mathematician; b. Odessa, Ukraine, May 9, 1960; came to U.S., 1979; s. Froim and Alla (Shvetz) Blyukher; m. Antonia Rose Wilson, May 25, 1986; children: Andrew Emmanuel, Julia Elizabeth, Sarah Elena. MA in Math. with honors, Johns Hopkins U., 1983; PhD in Math., Princeton U., 1988; MS in Computer Sci., UCLA, 1992. Asst. prof. The Coll. of N.J., Trenton, 1987-88, Whittier

(Calif.) Coll., 1988-89; programmer The Software Toolworks, L.A., 1989-90; rschr. computer sci. dept. UCLA, 1990-92; staff programmer IBM, San Jose, 1992-93; project leader ORACLE, Redwood City, Calif., 1993-95; sr. computer scientist Dept. of Def., Washington, 1995—. Translator: Introduction to the Classical Theory of Abelian Functions, 1990. Interviewer alumni coun. Johns Hopkins U., Balt., 1985-89. IBM scholar, 1983. Mem. IEEE-Computer Soc., Assn. Computing Machinery, Phi Beta Kappa. Home: PO Box 252 Simpsonville MD 21150-0252

BLUITT, KAREN, software engineering director; b. N.Y.C., Oct. 25, 1957; d. James Bertrand and Beatrice (Kaufman) B.; m. Kenneth Mark Curry, Nov. 24, 1979 (div. Dec. 1991). BS, Fordham U., 1979; MBA, Calif. State Poly. U., 1982; postgrad., George Mason U., 1994-98; PhD, Kennedy Western U., 2000. Software engr. Hughes Aircraft Co., Fullerton, Calif., 1979-81; microprocessor engr. Beckman Instruments Co., Fullerton, 1981-82, Singer Co., Glendale, Calif., 1982-83; sr. software engr. Sanders Assoc., Nashua, N.H., 1983-85; software project mgr. GTE Corp., Billerica, Mass., 1985-86; sr. software engr. Wang Labs., Lowell, Mass., 1986-87; project task leader Vanguard Rsch., Lexington, Mass., 1987-88; program mgr. Applied Rsch. & Engring., Bedford, Mass., 1989-91, Sparta, McLean, Va., 1992-93; prin. software engr. Sci. Applications Internat., Arlington, Va., 1993-94; tech. mgr. CACI, Arlington, 1994, Booz-Allen & Hamilton, Vienna, Va., 1995, MRJ Tech. Solutions, Inc., Fairfax, Va., 1996-97, Softek Systems, Inc., Fairfax, 1998—. 1st lt. USAF, 1979-88. Scholar Gov. N.Y. Scholarship Com., 1975-79, Beta Gamma Sigma, 1978—. Mem. IEEE, AAUW, Am. Women in Sci., Am. Brokers Network, Assn. Computing Machinery, Soc. Women Engrs., Wash. Soc. of Engrs. Office: Softek Sys Inc 4114 Legato Rd Fairfax VA 22033-4002

BLUM, BARBARA DAVIS, investor; b. Hutchinson, Kans.; d. Roy C. and Jo (McKinnon) Davis; children: Devin, Hunter, Ragan, Davis. BA, Fla. State U., 1960, MSW, 1961. Faculty Pediat. Psychiatry Clinic, U. Kans. Med. Ctr., Lawrence, 1961-63; acting adminstr. Suffolk County (N.Y.) Mental Health Clinic, Huntington, L.I., 1963-65; founder, ptnr. Mid-Suffolk Ctr. for Psychotherapy, Hauppage, L.I., N.Y., 1965-67; v.p. Restaurant Assocs. Ga., Inc., Atlanta, 1967-75; dep. adminstr. U.S. EPA, Washington, 1977-81; mem. Pres.'s Interagy. Coordinating Coun.; chair, pres., CEO Abigail Adams Nat. Bancorp and Adams Nat. Bank, Washington, 1983-98; CEO BDB Investment Partnership, 1998—; chair U.S./Japan Environ. Agreement, 1977; head 1st U.S. Environ. Del. to China, 1978; chmn. Environ. Policy Inst., 1981-84; sr. advisor UN Environ. Program, 1981-84; chair emeritus Ctr. for Policy Alternatives; trustee Fed. City Coun., 1988-99; nat. adv. bd. U.S. SBA. Chair D.C. Econ. Devel. Fin. Corp., 1986; founder Leadership Washington; del. UN Mid Decade Conf. on Women, 1980; bd. dirs. Kaiser Permanente Mid Atlantic, 1985—; dir. D.C. Retirement Bd.; dir. City 1st Bank; dep. dir. Carter-Mondale U.S. presdl. campaign, 1976, Carter/Mondale Transition Team, Washington, 1976-77; panelist Clinton-Gore Econ. Conf., Little Rock and Atlanta; presdl. appointee bd. dirs., treas. Inst. for Am. Indian Art; trustee, treas. Southeastern U.; trustee Dist. Columbia Pension Fund. Decorated comdr.'s cross Order of Merit W. Ger.; recipient Disting. Service award Federally Employed Women, Spl. Conservation award Nat. Wildlife Fedn., Orgn. of Yr. award Ga. Wildlife Fedn., 1974, Disting. Service award Americans for Indian Opportunity; named Bus. Woman of Yr. Nat. Assn. Bus. Women, Leukemia Soc., Assn. Women Contractors. Mem. Washington Women's Forum, Internat. Women's Forum, Cosmos Club, Econs. Club. Democrat.

BLUM, GEORGES, bank executive; b. Feb. 11, 1935; 2 children. V.p. Swiss Bank Corp., 1971-76, 1st v.p., 1976-80, sr. v.p., 1980-82, ctrl. mgr., mem. exec. bd., 1982-84, gen. mgr., mem. exec. bd., 1984-93, group CEO, 1993-96, later chmn. bd. dirs.; pres. bd. of dirs. Energie de l'Ouest-Suisse S.A., Lausanne, Switzerland, 1998S; bd. dirs. Sulzer AG, Winterthur, Swissair, Zurich, Tetra Alfa, Pully/Lund, Grande Dixence SA, Sion, Soc. Agence Econ. Fin. SA, Lausanne; chmn. S.A. Energie Ouest-Suisse EOS, Lausanne, Alp Trasit Gotthard SA, Bern, Internat. BM Biomedicine Holdings SA, Geneva. Avocations: skiing, reading, music. Office: Energie de l'Ouest-Sussie SA, Place de la Gare 12, Lausanne Switzerland*

BLUM, JEAN-YVES MARIE, dentist, researcher; b. Mostaganem, Algerie, France, Aug. 26, 1958; s. André and Yvette (Salivas) B.; m. Françoise Bianchi, Sept. 17, 1984; children: Guillaume, Stephanie. DDS, Montpellier (France) U., Montpellier, France, 1985; PhD, U. Paris, Paris, 1998. Cert. specialized studies in bacteriology, restorative dentistry, prosthodontics, biomecanics. Pvt. practice dentist St. Gilles, France, 1986—; instr. Montpellier U. Dental Sch., Montpellier, 1991-94. Contbr. articles to profl. jours.; inventor in field. Mem. Adminstrn. Coun., Montpellier, 1998—. Aspirant Armée de Terre, 1985. Mem. French Endodontic Soc. (regional pres. 1997—), European Soc. Endodontic. Home: 12 Rue de L Aubier, 34130 Saint Aunes France Office: Rue Eyminy, 30800 Saint-Gilles France

BLUM, MORDECHAI (MOTKE), painter, sculptor; b. Racaciuni, Romania, May 4, 1925; arrived in Israel, 1944; s. Arye Leib and Lea Lora (Josef) B.; m. Shoshana Antmann, Jan. 13, 1954; children: Anat Blum Galili, Ofer Hanoch. Grad., Bezalel Acad. Arts, Jerusalem, 1956; postgrad., Gerristen and Van Kempen Royal Silverworks, Zeist, The Netherlands, 1956-58. Youth counselor City of Jerusalem, 1951-54; restorer ancient mosaics Dept. Antiquities, Israel Mus., UNESCO, East Jerusalem Devel. Co. One-man shows include Rina Gallery, Jerusalem, 1959, Artists' House, Jerusalem, 1961, 69, 74, 86, 90, Atelier 97, Tel Aviv, 1961, Netanya Art Gallery, Israel, 1963, Hageffen Gallery, Haifa, Israel, 1964, Woodstock Gallery, London, 1964, Benei-Brith Gallery, Antwerpen, Belgium, 1964, Merenciano Gallery, Marseille, France, 1964, Nora Gallery, Jerusalem, 1964, 65, Union Am. Hebrew Congregations, N.Y.C., 1965, Sutton Club, Phila., 1965, Henry St. Gallery, N.Y.C., 1966, Emerging Artists Gallery, N.Y.C., 1967, Art Mus., Eilat, Israel, 1973, Rehovot (Israel) Gallery, 1975, Morgan Gallery, Edmonton, Alta., Can., 1981, Judaic Treasures Gallery, Millburn, N.J., 1989, Judaic Internat. Gallery, N.Y.C., 1989, Gallery B, Jerusalem, 1989, Webb Gallery, North Haven, Conn., 1991, Paulskirche, Frankfurt, Germany, 1991, Ceska Sporitelny Gallery, Prague, Czech Republic, 1992, Jerusalem Mcpl. Gallery, 1994, Schamretta Gallery, Frankfurt, Germany, 1996, FAH Gallerie, Maastricht, The Netherlands, 1996, Murakami Gallery, N.Y.C., 1997, Avero Toren, Leeuwarden, The Netherlands, 1998, Jerusalem Theater, 1999, Diocesan Museum, Vienna, Austria, 1999, FAH Gallery, Maastricht, The Netherlands, 1999, many others; group shows include Mus. Modern Art, Sao Paulo, Brazil, 1960, Mus. Modern Art, Rio de Janeiro, 1960, Tel Aviv Mus., 1963, 64, Galleria I.B.E.U., Rio de Janeiro, 1965, Galleria Asteria, Sao Paulo, 1965, Galleria Longchamps, Marseilles, 1965, Israel Art Gallery, Phila., 1965, Rose Sheskin Gallery, N.Y.C., Smithsonian Instn., Washington, 1965, UNESCO Brandeis Internat., Washington, 1966, NAD, N.Y.C., 1966, Israel Mus., Jerusalem, 1967, 93, David's Tower, Jerusalem, 1967, Paul-Louis Weiller Sculpture Exhibit-Acad. Fine Arts, Paris, 1972, Biennale Graphic Arts, Florence, Italy, 1972, Phila. Art Alliance, 1973, Helmhaus, Zurich, Switzerland, 1973, Ribenfeld Gallery, Tel Aviv, 1976, Arti et Amicitiae, Amsterdam, The Netherlands, 1978, Campbell & Franks Gallery, London, 1978, Artists' House, Jerusalem, 1986, 94, Del Bello Gallery, Toronto, 1987, Marble Arch Gallery, Toronto, 1990, many others; author: Jerusalem Reflections of Eternity, 1990. Sgt. Inf., 1948-49. Sonneborn grantee Bezalel Acad. Arts, 1954; recipient Mezuza Design 1st prize Accadia Hotel, 1955, Sonnenborn prize Bezalel Acad. Arts, 1956. Mem. Jerusalem Artists Assn., Internat. Artists Assn. Avocations: walking, visits to archaeol. sites, Jerusalem mysticism. Home: 4 Narkis St, 92461 Jerusalem Israel Office: Khutzot Ha-Yotzer Artist Colony, # 20, Hativat Yerushalayim St, Jerusalem Israel

BLUMBERG, BARBARA SALMANSON (MRS. ARNOLD G. BLUMBERG), retired state housing official, housing consultant; b. Bklyn., Oct. 2, 1927; d. Sam and Mollie (Greenberg) Salmanson; m. Arnold G. Blumberg, June 19, 1949 (dec. June 1989); children: Florence Ellen Schwartz, Martin Jay, Emily Anne. BA, De Pauw U., 1948; postgrad., New Sch. for Social Rsch., N.Y.C. Mem. pub. rels. dept. Nate Fein & Co., N.Y.C., 1948-51; freelance pub. rels. cons., 1960—; councilwoman North Hempstead, N.Y., 1975-82; adviser to energy com. N.Y. State Assembly, N.Y.C., 1982-84; dir. spl. needs housing Divsn. Housing and Cmty. Renewal, State of N.Y., 1984-89, ret., 1989; mem. bd. visitors Pilgrim State Hosp. Pres. UN Assn. Great Neck, N.Y., 1967-69, chmn. China Study Workshop, 1966-67; pres. Shalom chpt. Hadassah, 1955-57; exec. v.p. Lakeville PTA, Great Neck, 1963-65, Great Neck South Jr. H.S., 1965-66; co-chair UNICEF, Great Neck, 1968-70, spkrs. bur., 1971—; v.p. Herricks Cmty. Life Ctr., 1976-77, B'nai B'rith, Lake Success, N.Y.; coord. 6th Congl. Dist., N.Y. McGovern for Pres.; bd. dirs. New Dem. Coalition Nassau, Am. Jewish Congress, Day Care Coun. Nassau County, Citizens Sch. Com., Great Neck; active Reform Dem. Assn. Great Neck; platform com. Nassau Dem. Com.; del. Dem. Nat. Conv., 1992; adv. com. to spkr. N.Y. State Assembly; resource coun., housing devel. com. Cmty. Advocates; chair North Hempstead Housing Authority; trustee L.I. Power Authority, 1994-96. Recipient award Anti-Defamation League, New Hyde Park, N.Y., 1975, Alumni award DePauw U., 1977, Hadassah New Life award, 1980, Women's Pole of Honor, North Hempstead, 1994. Mem. North Shore Archeol. Assn. (chmn. study group), Women in Comm., Internat. Platform Assn., L.I. Womens Network (co-convenor), Interfaith Nutrition Network (v.p.), Cmty. Advocates (bd. dirs.), Mental Health Assn. Nassau County (bd. dirs.), North Shore NAACP, N.Y. Alumni Club DePauw U. (trustee), Alpha Lambda Delta. Home: 12 Birch Hill Rd Great Neck NY 11020-1309

BLUMBERG, BARUCH SAMUEL, academic research scientist; b. N.Y.C., July 28, 1925; s. Meyer and Ida (Simonoff) B.; m. Jean Liebesman, Apr. 4, 1954; children: Anne, George, Jane, Noah. BS, Union Coll., Schenectady, 1946; MD, Columbia U., 1951; PhD, Oxford (Eng.) U., 1957; 20 hon. doctoral degrees. Intern, then resident Columbia div. Bellevue Hosp., N.Y.C., 1951-53; fellow in medicine Columbia-Presbyn. Med. Ctr., N.Y.C., 1953-55; chief geog. medicine and genetics sect. NIH, Bethesda, Md., 1957-64; assoc. dir. clin. rsch. Fox Chase Cancer Ctr., Phila., 1964-86, v.p. population oncology, 1986-89, Fox Chase disting. scientist, 1989—; sr. advisor to pres. Fox Chase Cancer Ctr., 1989—; univ. prof. medicine and anthropology U. Pa., 1977—; dir. NASA Astrobiology Inst., Moffett Field, Calif., 1999—; George Eastman vis. prof. Oxford U., 1983-84; Raman vis. prof. Indian Inst. Scis., Bangalore, 1986; Ashland vis. prof. U. Ky., Lexington, 1986, 87; master Balliol Coll., Oxford, Eng., 1989-94; disting. vis. Nat. U. Singapore, 1992; vis. prof. U. Otago, Dunedin, New Zealand, 1994; James W. McLaughlin vis. prof. U. Tex.; vis. prof. dept. medicine Stanford U. Med. Ctr.; sr. advisor to pres. Fox Chase Cancer Ctr., 1989—; fellow Ctr. Advanced Study Behavioral Scis., Stanford U., Calif.; Larry Lokey disting. vis. prof. human biology Stanford U. Contbr. articles to profl. jours. Lt. USNR, 1943-46. Recipient Albion O. Berstein, M.D. award Med. Soc. State of N.Y., 1969, Grand Sci. award Phi Lambda Kappa, 1972, Ann. award Eastern Pa. br. Am. Soc. Microbiology, 1972, Passano award Williams & Wilkens Co., 1974, Modern Medicine Disting. Achievement award, 1975, Internat. award Gairdner Found., 1975, Karl Landsteiner Meml. award Am. Assn. Blood Banks, 1975, Nobel prize in physiology or medicine, 1976, Scopus award Am. Friends of Hebrew U., 1977, Strittmatter award Philadelphia County Med. Soc., 1980, Disting. Service award Pa. Med. Soc., 1982, Zubrow award Pa. Hosp., 1986, Achievement award Sammy Davis Jr. Nat. Liver Inst., 1987, John P. McGovern award Am. Med. Writers Assn., 1988, Gov.'s Award in the Scis. Commonwealth of Pa., 1989, John Blundell award Brit. Blood Transfusion Soc., 1989, Gold Medal award Can. Liver Found. and Can. Assn. Study of Liver, 1990, Showa Emperor Meml. award Japan, 1994; elected to Nat. Inventor Hall of Fame, 1993. Fellow ACP, Royal Coll. Physicians; mem. NAS, AAAS, Inst. Medicine of NAS, Am. Acad. Arts and Scis. (inst. medicine), Assn. Am. Physicians, Am. Soc. Clin. Investigation, Am. Soc. Human Genetics, Explorers Club N.Y., Athenaeum (London). Office: Fox Chase Cancer Ctr 7701 Burholme Ave Ste 2 Philadelphia PA 19111-2497

BLUMBERG, EDWARD ROBERT, lawyer; b. Phila., Feb. 15, 1951. BA in Psychology, U. Ga., 1972; JD, Coll. William and Mary, 1975. Bar: Fla., 1975, U.S. Dist. Ct. Fla. 1975, U.S. Ct. Appeals, 1975, U.S. Supreme Ct. 1979. Assoc. Knight, Peters, Hoeveler & Pickle, Miami, Fla., 1976-77; ptnr. Deutsch & Blumberg, P.A., Miami, 1978—; adj. prof. U. Miami Sch. Paralegal Studies. Author: Proof of Negligence, Mathew Bender Florida Torts, 1988. Mem. ABA (ho. of Dels. 1997—), ATLA, Dade County Bar Assn., Fla. State Bar (bd. govs., pres. elect 1996-97, pres. 1997-98), Acad. Fla. Trial Lawyers, Nat. Bd. Trial Advocacy (cert. civil trial adv.), Fla. Bar Found. (bd. dirs. 1996—, bd. govs. 1996-99). Office: Deutsch & Blumberg PA 100 Biscayne Blvd Fl 28 Miami FL 33132-2304

BLUMBERG, GRACE GANZ, law educator, lawyer; b. N.Y.C., Feb. 16, 1940; d. Samuel and Beatrice (Finkelstein) Ganz; m. Donald R. Blumberg, Sept. 9, 1959; 1 dau., Rachel. B.A. cum laude, U. Colo., 1960; J.D. summa cum laude, SUNY, 1971; LL.M., Harvard U., 1974. Bar: N.Y. 1971, Calif. 1989. Confidential law clk. Appellate Div., Supreme Ct., 4th Dept., Rochester, N.Y., 1971-72; teaching fellow Harvard Law Sch., Cambridge, Mass., 1972-74; prof. law SUNY, Buffalo, 1974-81, UCLA, 1981—; reporter Am. Law Inst., Prins. of the Law of Family Dissolution. Author: Community Property in California, 1987, rev. edit., 1999, Blumberg's California Family Code Annotated (ann.); contbr. articles to profl. jours. Office: UCLA Sch Law Box 951476 Los Angeles CA 90095-1476

BLUMBERG, HERBERT HASKELL, psychology educator; b. Phila., Dec. 8, 1941; s. Daniel and Sara Freda (Peiper) B.; m. Alison Jean Britton, Oct. 9, 1980; 1 child, Joanna Britton. BA, Haverford Coll., 1963; PhD, Johns Hopkins U., 1967. Lectr., asst. prof. Wilson Coll., Chambersburg, Pa., 1967-69; rsch. psychologist, addiction rsch. unit Inst. of Psychiatry, U. London, 1969-77; lectr., sr. lectr. Goldsmiths Coll., U. London, 1977—; vis. scholar Harvard U., 1988, 89; rsch. assoc. Ctr. for Nonviolent Conflict Resolution, Haverford (Pa.) Coll., 1970-71, vis. prof., 1992-93; mem. exec. com. Initiative for Peace Studies in the U. London, 1989-92; mem. editorial cons. bd. Cahiers Internationaux de Psychologie Sociale, Liege, Belgium, 1989—. Coauthor: Small Group Research: A Handbook, 1994, Small Groups: An Introduction, 1996; co-editor: Nonviolent Direct Action, 1969, Liberation without Violence, 1977, Small Groups and Social Interaction, 2 vols., 1983, Peace: Abstracts of the ... Behavioral Literature, 1992. Niwano Peace Found. grantee, 1993. Fellow Brit. Psychol. Soc. (assoc.); mem. APA (bibliographer, rev. editor Peace and Conflict Jour. of peace psychology divsn. 1995—), Am. Psychol. Soc., Brit. Sociol. Assn., Scientists for Global Responsibility, Soc. for the Psychol. Study of Social Issues, Psychologists for Social Responsibility. Achievements include preparation of a viable taxonomy of peace-psychology research. Home: 71 Harvist Rd, London England NW6 6EX Office: U London Goldsmiths Coll, Psychology Dept, London SE14 6NW, England

BLUMBERG, JUNE BETH, artist; b. Abington, Pa., May 14, 1959; d. Frederick Blumberg and Elin (Brunswick) Binder. A of Gen. Studies, Montgomery Community Coll., 1985; BFA, Moore Coll. of Art, Phila., 1991; AAS, C.C. of Phila., 2000. Stats. clk. Crime Prevention Assn., Phila., 1980-81; workshop tchr. Jefferson Hosp. Evening Program, Phila., 1986-87; art asst. Mildred Greenberg, Phila., 1988-89; vis. artist Moore Coll. of Art & Design, Phila., 1990; admission rep. Franklin Inst., Phila., 1990-92; rsch. scientist, artist Phila., 1979—; sec. fellowship Pa. Acad. Fine Art, 1995, 96. Shows include Nexus Art Gallery, Phila., 1979, Moore Coll. Art & Design, Phila, 1985-90, upper Saddle Cultural Ctr., N.J., 1986, Art Ctr. N.J., Milford, 1986, Ky. Highlands Mus., Ashland, 1988, Studio Arts Ctr. Internat., Florence, Italy, 1989, Palette and Chisel Acad. Fine Arts, Chgo., 1990, West Bend Gallery, Wis., 1990, Rittenhouse Fine Arts Ann., Phila., 1985-87, 90, Pen and Brush Club, N.Y.C., 1987, 89, 90, Clinton St. Gallery, Schenectady, N.Y., 1990, Pa. Acad. Fine Arts, Phila., 1991, 93, Phila. Print Club, 1991-97, Reno Gazette Jour. Bldg., Nev., 1991, Woodmere Art Mus., Phila., 1991, 92, 98, 99, Axis Gallery, Phila., 1992, Artcetera, Auburn, Calif., 1992, Dellora Norris Cultural Ctr., St. Charles, Ill., 1992, Gallery Cedar Hollow, Malvern, Pa., 1993, 479 Gallery, Phila., 1993, City Hall, Phila., 1993, Art Initiatives, N.Y.C., 1993, 94, Border Book Store, Phila., 1994, 95, 98, 99, Mills Pond House, St. James, N.Y., 1994, Nat. Arts Club, N.Y.C., 1994, Highwire Gallery, Phila., 1993, 94, The Police Bldg. Gallery, N.Y.C., 1995, Internat. Platform Assn., Washington, 1995, Riverbank Arts, Stockton, N.J., 1997, The Bear and Koala Tea Co., Bordentown, N.J., 1998, Main Line Art Ctr., Haverford, Pa., 1998, Phila. Sketch Club, 1998, N.Y. Law Sch., N.Y.C., 1998, 99, Cmty. Arts Ctr., Wallingford, Pa., 1999, Cumberland County Coll., Vineland, N.J., 1999, Wilmington Pub. Libr., 1999, Gallery One, Auburn, Calif., 1999, La. State U. Sch. Vet. Med., Baton Rouge, 1999, Gallery 402, N.Y.C., 1999, Salon des Amis, Malvern, Pa., 1999, Walter Greer Gallery, Hilton Head, S.C., 1999, Gallery One, Auburn, Calif., 1999, Mayer, Brown Platt, N.Y.C., 2000, others. Tutor Homeless Shelter, 1986. Recipient scholarship, 1983-85, Spl. Merit award Pen and Brush Club, 1990, cert. of merit Manhatt Art Internat. Mag., 1999, cert. of excellence Manhatt Art Internat. mag., 1999. Mem. NAFE, APHA, World Affairs Coun., Pastel Soc. West Coast, The Internat. Platform Assn. (Best of Show 1995), Toastmasters, Phi Theta Kappa. Democrat. Avocations: politics, reading, swimming, philosophy. Address: PO Box 148 Bala Cynwyd PA 19004-0148

BLUME, ARTHUR WALTER, IV, addictive behaviors researcher, therapist; b. Port Hueneme, Calif., May 23, 1959; s. Arthur Walter Blume III and Mary Kathleen Edwards; m. Karen B. Schmaling, May 14, 1994; children: Amanda Kathleen, Rachel Frances. MDiv, McCormick Sem., Chgo., 1985; MS in Psychology, U. Wash., 1999. Substance abuse therapist St. John's Med. Ctr., Springfield, Mo., 1986-91; pvt. practice Springfield, 1991-94; psychometrist, dual diagnosis therapist U. Wash., Seattle, 1994-97, addictive behaviors rschr., 1997—, rsch. therapist, 1999—; therapist Tulalip Tribes, Marysville, Wash., 1999—; substance abuse cons. St. John's Med. Ctr., Springfield, 1991-94. Co-author: Harm Reduction, 1998; contbr. articles to profl. jours. Summer youth mission worker Presbyn. Ch., 1973-82; civil rights activist People's Ch., Chgo., 1982-85; instr. ESL Doremus Cmty. Ctr., Chgo., 1983-84; bd. dirs. Met. Coun. Chs., Springfield, 1991-93; vol. homeless shelter Jewish League, Seattle, 1995-97. Rsch. grantee Alcohol and Drug Abuse Inst., Seattle, 1997; pre-doctoral rsch. fellow NIH, Rockville, Md., 1998-99. Mem. APA, Assn. for Advancement of Behavior Therapy, Assn. Profl. Psychometrists (bd. dirs. 1995-97). Avocations: poetry, backpacking, softball, snorkeling, travel. Office: Addictive Behaviors Rsch Ctr U Wash PO Box 351525 Seattle WA 98195-1525

BLUMENREICH, MARTIN SIGVART, oncologist; b. Oslo, Norway, Dec. 1, 1949; came to U.S., 1975; s. Sane and Bluma (Nomberg) B.; m. Patricia Estela Dulman, Dec. 23, 1978; children: Hannah Vardit, Arnina Mirit, Aryeh Moshe. MD, U. Uruguay, Montevideo, 1975. Diplomate Am. Bd. Internal Medicine, Am. Bd. Med. Oncology, Am. Bd. Med. Hematology. Intern Jewish Hosp. and Med. Ctr. Bklyn., 1975-76, resident, 1976-78; fellow med. oncology Meml. Sloan-Kettering Cancer Ctr., N.Y.C., 1978-81; asst. prof. medicine U. Louisville, 1981-85, N.J. Med. Sch., Newark, 1985-88; assoc. prof., prof. U. Louisville, 1988-95; med. oncologist Mankato (Minn.) Clinic, 1995-99; oncologist Minn. Oncology Hematology, P.A., Waconia, 1999—. Fellow ACP; mem. Am. Assn. Cancer Rsch., Am. Soc. Clin. Oncology. Office: MOHPA 490 S Maple St Ste 111 Waconia MN 55387-1762

BLUMHARDT, JON HOWARD, college official; b. Ft. Benning, Ga., Oct. 3, 1951; s. Howard Jerome and Joan (Tisdal) B.; m. Lisette Susan Vinet, Jan. 26, 1973; children: Matthew, Malia, Mark. BA in History, U. Hawaii, 1973, MA in Sociology, 1978, MEd, 1979, postgrad.; EdS, U Va., 1984; EdD in Edn., LaSalle U., 1998. Media specialist U.S. Army JAG Sch., Charlottesville, Va., 1980-85; adminstr. officer OPM Fed. Exec. Inst., Charlottesville, 1985-86; chief resources mgmt. IRS Honolulu Dist., 1986-87; dir. ednl. media svcs. Honolulu C.C., 1987—; owner Media Works, 1996—. Unit commr., Koolau dist., Aloha coun. Boy Scouts Am., 1996. Named one of Outstanding Young Men in Am., 1989, Eagle Scout, 1965; recipient Mahalo award Mayor of Honolulu, 1978, Cert. of Merit Aloha Coun. Boy Scouts Am., 1978, Wood Badge, 1978 Scoutmaster award of Merit Nat. Eagle Scout Assn., 1990, Boy Scout Leader's Tng. award, 1998, 20 yr. vet. award Boy Scouts Am., 1999; Arrowhead honor Boy Scouts Am., 2000. Mem. DAV (life), German Benevolent Soc. (Honolulu), Am. Legion, U. Va. Alumni Assn. (life), Disabled Am. Veterans (life mem.), Am. Legion (post 0009). Republican. Roman Catholic. Avocations: gardening, camping, sailing, fishing, woodworking. E-mail: jon@hcc.hawaii.edu. Home: 1150 Kamahele St Apt A Kailua HI 96734-3334 Office: Honolulu CC 874 Dillingham Blvd Honolulu HI 96817-4505

BLUMROSEN, ALFRED WILLIAM, law educator; b. Detroit, Dec. 14, 1928; s. Sol and Frances (Netzorg) B.; m. Ruth L. Gerber, July 3, 1952; children: Steven Marshall, Alexander Bernet. BA, U. Mich., 1950, JD, 1953. Bar: Mich. 1953, N.J. 1961, N.Y. 1981. Solo practice Detroit, 1953-55; mem. faculty Rutgers Law Sch., Newark, 1955—, prof., 1961—, acting dean, 1974-75, Herbert J. Hannoch scholar, 1984, Thomas A. Cowan prof., 1986—; dir. fed.-state rels., chief conciliations U.S. EOOC, 1965-67, cons. to chmn., 1977-79; advisor U.S. Dept. Justice, HUD, 1968-72, U.S. Dept. Labor, 1995-96; of counsel Kaye, Scholer, Fierman, Hays & Handler, N.Y.C., 1979-82; dir. Ford Found. intentional discrimination project Rutgers U., Law Sch., 1998—. Author: Black Employment and the Law, 1971, Modern Law: The Law Transmission System and Equal Employment Opportunity, 1993, Downsizing and Employee Rights, Vol. 50, 1998; ; contbr. articles to profl. jours., including Rutgers Law Rev. Fulbright scholar, South Africa, 1993, Rockefeller Inst. Resident scholar Bellagio Conf. Ctr., 1995. Mem. ABA (Ross essay prize 1983), Internat. Soc. for Labor Law and Social Security, Indsl. Relations Rsch. Assn., Order of Coif. Office: Rutgers U Sch Law 123 Washington St Newark NJ 07102-3026

BLUMSTEIN, ALFRED, urban and public affairs educator; b. N.Y.C., June 3, 1930; m. Dolores Reguera, Jan. 26, 1958; children: Lisa, Ellen, Diane. BS in Engring. Physics, Cornell U., 1951, PhD in Ops. Rsch., 1960; MS in Stats., U. Buffalo, 1954; JD (hon.), John Jay Coll., 1996. Prin. ops. analyst Cornell Aeronautical Lab., Buffalo, 1951-61; rsch. staff Inst. Def. Analyses, Arlington, Va., 1961-69; dir. sci. and tech. task force Pres.'s Commn. Law Enforcement and Adminstrn. Justice, Washington, 1966-67; J. Erik Jonsson Univ. prof. urban sys. and ops. rsch. H. John Heinz III Sch. Pub. Policy and Mgmt. Carnegie-Mellon U., Pitts., 1969—, dean, 1986-93, dir. Nat. Consortium on Violence Rsch., 1996—; overseas fellow Churchill Coll. Cambridge U., 1983—; chmn. various panels NRC Com. Rsch. Law Enforcement and Adminstrn. Justice, 1982-86, chmn. com., 1980-83; mem. NRC Commn. Behavioral and Social Scis. and Edn., 1994—. Mem. editl. bd. Ops. Rsch. Letters, Jour. Rsch. in Crime and Delinquency, Evaluation Rev., Jour. Criminal Justice, Sci. Commn. of Internat. Soc. of Criminology, 1985-91, others; co-editor Cambridge Criminology Series; contbr. articles to profl. jours. Chmn. Pa. Commn. Crime and Delinquency, Harrisburg, 1979-90; mem. Pa. Commn. on Sentencing, 1986-96; bd. dirs. Police Found., 1990-96; nat. adv. com. Inst. Rsch. on Poverty at U. Wis., 1989-94. Fellow AAAS, Am. Soc. Criminology (pres. 1991-92, Sutherland award 1987); mem. NNAE, Ops. Rsch. Soc. Am. (pres. 1977-78, Kimball medal 1985, Pres.'s award 1993), Am. Statis. Assn., Inst. Ops. Rsch. and Mgmt. Scis. (pres. 1996), Law and Society Assn., The inst. Mgmt. Scis. (pres. 1987-88), Internat. Fedn. Operational Rsch. Socs. (v.p. N.Am. 1992-94), Consortium of Social Sci. Assns. (pres. 1999—), Cosmos Club, Omega Rho (hon.). Home: 1455 Wightman St Pittsburgh PA 15217-1260 Office: Carnegie-Mellon U H John Heinz III Sch Pub Policy Mgmt Pittsburgh PA 15213*

BLUNDELL, DEREK JOHN, environmental geology educator; b. London, June 30, 1933; s. Frank Herbert and Irene Mary (Davie) B.; m. Mary Patricia Leonard, 1960. BS in Physics 1st class, U. Birmingham, Eng., 1954; PhD, U. London, 1957. Chartered geologist. Rsch. fellow in geology U. Birmingham, 1957-59, lectr. in geology, 1959-70; sr. lectr. U. Lancaster, 1970-72, reader in geophysics, 1972-75; head of geology dept. Chelsea Coll., U. London, 1975-85, prof. environ. geology, 1975-85; prof. environ. geology Royal Holloway U. London, 1985-98, head of dept., 1992-97; Royal Soc. vis. prof. U. Ghana, 1974, Leverhulme Emeritus fellow, 1998-2000, emeritus prof. geophysics, 1998—. Author, editor: A Continent Revealed: The European Geotraverse, 1992; editor: Tectonic Evolution of the North Sea Rifts, 1990; co-editor: Tecton Evolution of Southeast Asia, 1996, Lyell: the past is the key to the present, 1998; contbr. sci. papers to profl. jours. Mem. Geol. Soc. London (pres. 1988-90, Coke medal 1993), Athenaeum. Avocations: golf, traveling. Office: U London Royal Holloway, Dept Geology, Egham Surrey TW20 OEX, England

BLUNDELL, JAMES EDWARD, radiologist; b. Sydney, Australia, May 19, 1934; s. James and Winifred Anne (Lee) B.; m. Rosemary Aboud, May 25, 1985; children: Linda, Simon, Matthew. MBBS, Sydney U., Australia, 1956. Resident med. officer St. Vincent Hosp., Sydney, 1957-58; med. officer Australian Dept. Immigration, Greece & Italy, 1959-61; med. registrar Hackney Hosp., London, 1961-63; radiology registrar Sydney Hosp., 1963-66; dir. Gen. Publishers Ltd., Sydney, 1996—. Fellow Royal Australasian Coll. Radiologists; mem. Royal Sydney Golf Club, Australian Golf Club, Cruising Yacht Club of Australia. Fax: 02-9387-5758. Email: jimxray@ozemail.com.au. Home: Bellevue Hill, 32A Drumalbyn Rd, 2023

Sydney Australia Office: Bondi Junction Radiology, Plz Tower-Bondi Junction, 2022 Sydney Australia

BLUNDELL, RICHARD WILLIAM, economics educator; b. Shoreham, Sussex, Eng., Jan. 5, 1952; s. Lionel and Marjorie (Davies) B.; m. Anne Aberdeen; children: Katie, Jack. BSc in Econs., U. Bristol, Eng., 1973; MSc in Econometrics, London Sch. Econs., 1975. Lectr. U. Manchester, Eng., 1975-84; prof. econs. Univ. Coll. London, 1984—, dir. rsch. Inst. for Fiscal Studies, 1986—, dir. ESRC Ctr. for Micro-Econ. Analysis of Fiscal Policy, 1991—, head dept., 1988-92, Leverhulme Personal Rsch. prof., 1999; vis. assoc. prof. U. B.C., Vancouver, 1980-81, MIT, Cambridge, 1993, U. Calif., Berkeley, 1994-99. Author: The Measurement of Household Welfare, 1994; editor Jour. Econometrics, 1993-97, Econometrica, 1997—; contbr. articles to profl. jours. Recipient Jahnsson prize Jahnsson Found., 1995, Yrjo Johnsson prize, 1995. Fellow Econometrics Soc., British Acad., Coun. of Econometric Soc.; mem. European Econ. Assn. (coun. 1997—). Avocations: music, theatre, cycling, travel. Office: Univ Coll London Dept Econs, Gower St, London WC1E 6BT, England

BLUNDELL, WILLIAM RICHARD CHARLES, retired electric company executive; b. Montreal, Apr. 13, 1927; s. Richard C. and Did Aileen (Payne) B.; m. Monique Audet, Mar. 20, 1959; children: Richard, Emily, Michelle, Louise. BA in Sci., U. Toronto, 1949. Registered profl. engr., Ont. Sales engr. Can. Gen. Electric Co., Toronto, 1949-51, travelling auditor, 1951, various fin. positions, 1951-66, treas., 1966-68, v.p.-fin., 1968-70, v.p., exec. consumer div., 1970-72; v.p., exec. apparatus div. Can. Gen. Electric Co., Lachine, Que., 1972-79; pres., CEO, Camco Inc., Weston, Ont., 1979-83; pres., COO, Can. Gen. Electric Co. Ltd., Toronto, 1983-84; chmn., CEO Gen. Electric Can. Inc., Toronto, 1985-90; ret., 1991; chmn. Mfrs. Life Ins. Co., 1994-98, chmn. pub. sector pension investment bd., 2000—; bd. dirs. Seaside Cable TV, Purolator Courier Ltd., Sceptre Investment Counselling Ltd., Kasten Chase Applied Rsch. Ltd., Cedara Software, Inc., Triple Crown Electronics Inc. Decorated officer Order of Can.; recipient Engring. Alumni medal U. Toronto, 1990. Home: 29 Rothmere Dr, North York, ON Canada MAN-IV3

BLUNK, JOYCE ELAINE, artist, educator; b. Moorland, Iowa, May 13, 1939; d. George Daniel and Burnice Margaret (Taylor) Blunk. BA, U. Iowa, 1963, MA, 1970, MFA, 1971. Cert. tchr., Iowa. Grad. tchg. asst. U. Iowa, Iowa City, 1970-71; instr. Western Carolina U., Cullowhee, N.C., 1978-82; adj. instr. U. N.C., Asheville, 1992; artist, tchr. Vt. Coll. of Norwich U., Montpelier, 1997-98 99-2000; artist Joyce Blunk Studio, Asheville, N.C., 1975—; mem. exhbn. com. Asheville Area Arts Coun., 1999—. Exhibited in solo shows at Mint Mus. Art, Charlotte, N.C., 1991, U. Alaska, Anchorage, 1999; group shoes include Künstlerhaus, Schwandorf, Germany, 1990, Chateau de la Napoule, France, 1994. Poll. clk. local and nat. elections Buncombe County, N.C., 1999—; campaign worker Mayoral Election, Asheville, 1997. Va. Ctr. for Creative Arts fellow, Salzburg, Austria, 1999; Visual Artist fellow N.C. Arts Coun., 1996-97; Pollock-Krasner Found. grantee, 1991-92; material on file Archives on Women Artists, The Libr. and Rsch. Ctr. of the Nat. Mus. of Women in the Arts. Mem. Asheville Art Mus., Internat. Sculpture Ctr. Democrat. Avocations: reading, attehding classical music concerts, hiking, travel. Home: 31 Samayoa Pl Asheville NC 28806-2913

BLUTEL, XAVIER HERVÉ, cement group executive; b. Abidjan, Côte d'Ivoire, July 19, 1954; French citizen; s. Yves Albert Blutel and Christiane Marie De Courbeville; m. Karin Françoise Maleika, Oct. 8, 1981 (div. 1987); 1 child, Jean-Maxime; m. Isabelle Verschueren; 1 child: Zoé. BA in Law, U. Paris II-Assas, 1973; diploma in Chinese, Inst. Ea. Langs., Paris, 1974; M in Fin., U. Paris IX-Dauphine, 1976, engring diploma-applied math., 1977. Mgmt. cons. Alexander Proufoot, Paris and Brussels, 1979-81; contr. Exxon Chems. (France), Paris, 1981-86; dep. v.p. N.Am. divsn. Ciments Français, Bath, Pa., 1987-88; v.p. U.K. and Eire Ciments Français, London, 1988-91; v.p. Czech Republic Ciments Français, Prague, 1992-93; v.p. Greece, Cyprus and Balkans Italcementi, Athens, Greece, 1995-98; v.p. Thailand, Bangkok Italcementi, 1999; mem. adv. bd. for rsch. Ecole des Hautes Etudes Commerciales Bus. Sch., 1993-95; bd. dirs. Gacem Ltd., Banjul, The Gambia; exec. chmn. Halyps Bldg. Materials plc, Athens, 1995-98; exec. vice chmn. Vassiliko Cement Works plc, Nicosia, Cyprus, 1997-99. Lt. French Intelligence Svc., 1978-79. Mem. Fedn. Creek Cement Industries (bd. mem. 1995-98), French-Hellenic C. of C. (vice gen. sec. 1997-98). Avocations: classical guitar, mountain hiking, genealogy and regional history. Home: 35 Rue Vaneau, 75007 Paris France Office: Jalaprathan Cement PC Ltd, 2974 New Petchburi Rd Huai Khwang, Bangkok 10320, Thailand

BLY, CAROL MCLEAN, writer, educator; b. Duluth, Minn., Apr. 16, 1930; d. Charles Russell and Mildred Barr (Washburn) McLean; m. June 24, 1955 (div. 1979); children: Mary, Bridget, Noah, Micah. BA in English, Wellesley Coll., 1951; DHL, Northland Coll., 1985. Instr. writing U. Minn., Mpls., 1981—; vis. disting. Benedict prof. Carleton Coll., U. Minn., 1990, Edelstein-Keller disting. author, 1998-99; dir. The Loft, Mpls.; co-founder Collaborative of Tchrs. & Sch. Social Workers, St. Paul, 1993. Author: Letters from the Country, 1981, 1999, My Lord Bag of Rice, 2000, others. Bd. dirs. Episc. Cmty. Svcs., Mpls., 1980. Democrat. Avocation: tree planting. Home: 1668 Juno Ave Saint Paul MN 55116-1415

BLY, JAMES CHARLES, JR., financial services executive; b. Kane, Pa., Jan. 24, 1952; s. James Charles Bly Sr. and Dorothy Rose Hau Smith; m. Laurie Ann Ramadon, June 6, 1987; children: Alana W., Bridget R., James C. III, Chase N. BA, St. Bonaventure U., 1973. CLU, ChFC. Mgmt. trainee Conn. Gen. Life, Washington, 1974-76; rep. CIGNA Fin. Svcs., McLean, Va., 1976-79; mng. exec. Integrated Resources Equity Corp., N.Y.C., 1980-82; pres. Source Capital, Ltd., Pitts., 1982—; chmn., CEO Source Cos., LLC, 1998—; mem. adv. bd. John J. Kirlin, Inc., Rockville, Md., 1980—, Royal Bank of Can., Global Fin. Svcs., Network, 1991-97, Internat. Advisors Network, Ltd., 1998—; bd. dirs. Holgate Toy Co., Liberty-Pitts. Sys., Inc. Active Rep. Nat. Com. Mem. Soc. Fin Svcs. Profls., Family Firm Inst., Assn. Corp. Growth, Nat. Assn. Securities Dealers, Estate Planning Coun. (Pitts.), Fin. Planning Assn., Y Group, Duquesne Club, The Stonedale Guns, Edgeworth Club, St. James Club, Sewickley Heights Golf Club. Republican. Avocations: music, automobiles, history, travel. Home: Spanish Tract Rd Sewickley PA 15143 Office: Source Capital Ltd 1 Gateway Ctr # 1850 Pittsburgh PA 15222-1435

BLYAKHMAN, YEFIM MOISEI, chemist, researcher; b. Leningrad, Russia, Dec. 11, 1937; came to U.S., 1986; s. Moisei Isaak Blyakhman and Anna S. (Itzkov) Lohs; m. Irina A. Teverovskaya, Mar. 25, 1958; 1 child, Alexander. M in Chem. Engring., Leningrad Inst. Tech., 1960, PhD in Polymer Chemistry, 1965. Chem. engr. R&D Prodn., Leningrad, 1960-64; group leader Assn. Plast-Polymer, Leningrad, 1965-71, lab. dir., 1972-84; staff scientist Ciba-Geigy, Ardsley, N.Y., 1987-92; sr. staff scientist Ciba Specialty Chemicals, Brewster, N.Y., 1993—; adv. bd. Org. Sci. Tech. Advancement, Leningrad, 1965-81; scientific technological counsel Plast-polymer R&D and Prodn., Leningrad, 1972-78. Contbr. 154 articles to books and profl. jours.; contbr. article to Polymer Encyclopedia, 1977. Recipient 3 Gold medals Govt. Russia, Moscow, 1968, 72, 73. Mem. Am. Chem. Soc., Soc. Advancement Materials Process Engrs. Achievements include 197 patents in the area of thermoset polymers chemistry and tech. New routes to materials having high thermal stability, mechanical strength, and corrosion resistance for structural composites, adhesives coatings, electrical and electronic. Designer of numerous inventions from 1961-98 with 3 gold medals awarded in 1965, 67, 71. Home: Apt 2L 4705 Henry Hudson Pkwy Bronx NY 10471-3231 Office: Ciba Specialty Chemicals 281 Fields Ln Brewster NY 10509-2624

BLYTH, NICOLA, trading company executive; b. Sheffield, Yorkshire, England, Oct. 6, 1956; d. Peter Eden and Rosemary (Goodswen) B. BS in Agrl. Econs. with honors, U. Newcastle-on-Tyne, England, 1979; PhD in Agrl. Econs., U. Canterbury, Christchurch, New Zealand, 1982. Cert. meat quality assurance accreditation. English instr. English House, Madrid, 1975; adminstrv. asst. Combe House, Exeter, England, 1976; grad. fellow Agrl. Econs. Rsch. Unit, Christchurch, 1979-81, cons., 1981-83; chief mgr. Australian Meat & Livestock Corp., Sydney, Australia, 1983-86; dir. Blyth & Co. Ltd. Internat., Phila., 1987—; cons. Australian Meat & Livestock Corp., San Francisco, 1987; corp. planner A.M.L.C., Australia, 1985-86. Contbr. articles to profl. jours.; editor All AMLC Publs. (Reports), 1984-86. Mem. com. of rev. NSW Higher Edn. Bd., Sydney, 1985; pres. Postgrad. Students Soc. Lincoln, Christchurch, 1980-82; counsellor Samaritans, U.K., 1976-79. Fellow Sir Jorin Ormond Trust, New Zealand, 1979, Agrl. Econs. Rsch. Unit Post Grad. fellow; recipient Cert. of Merit, Outward Bound., U.K., 1974, Hill Award (Langs.), Maltby Grammar Sch., U.K., 1975. Mem. Agrl. Econs. Soc. (Australia, U.K.), Fedn. of Univ. Women (chmn. Sydney 1983-86, v.p. NSW), Post Grad. Soc. Lincoln (past pres.), Lincoln Coll. Old Students Assn., Australian Shippers Coun. (exec. mem. 1985-86), Industry Negotiating Com., Meat Industry Shipping Com. Avocations: sports, cultural activities. Home: Stone Mill Maltby, South Yorkshire S668NU, England

BLYTHE, MAX (GRAEME), clinical sciences educator; b. Rotherham, Yorkshire, Eng., Feb. 9, 1939; s. Frank Gibson and Gwen (Murdoch) B.; m. Gillian Margaret Moore, Dec. 18, 1973; 1 child, J.N. St.J. BSc with honours, U. Sheffield, Eng., 1968; MLitt, Oxford (Eng.) U., 1987; DLitt, Fairfax U., Baton Rouge, 1991, DUniv (hon.), 1997. Chartered biologist, U.K. Head biology dept. Queen Elizabeth's Grammar Sch., Gainsborough, Eng., 1962-65; lectr. biology Totley Coll. Edn., Sheffield, 1968-69; head biology Charterhouse, Godalming, Surrey, Eng., 1969-76; sr. edn. adviser Oxfordshire Edn. Authority, Oxford, 1976-82; prin. lectr. Oxford Brookes U., 1983-95, univ. reader clin. scis., 1995—; adviser, chief examiner Oxford and Cambridge Schs. Exams. Bd., 1976-82; mem. Faculty Clin. Medicine, Oxford U., 1979—, mem. Green Coll., 1980—; Holtermann fellow Sydney (Australia) Ch. of Eng. Grammar Sch., 1987, 92, 96; Royal Instn. lectr., London, 1982. Author: Web of Life, 1977, One Man's Medicine, 1989. Sr. rsch. fellow Wellcome Trust, London, 1995-97. Fellow Inst. Biology; mem. N.Y. Acad. Scis., Royal Over-Seas League, Marylebone Cricket Club (London). Avocations: listening to opera, travel, good food. Office: Oxford Brookes U, Sch Biol Scis, Oxford OX3 0BP, England

BLYUMAN, BORIS ALEXANDROVICH, geologist, researcher; b. Leningrad, Russia, Jan. 25, 1935; s. Alexandr Matveevich and Mariya Pavlovna (Antonjeva) B.; m. Inga Fedorovna Sukhorukova, Oct. 3, 1956; children: Natalia, Andrei. Grad., Leningrad Mining Inst., 1957; MS, Geol.-Mineral. Sci. Inst., Leningrad, 1969; DSc, Geol.-Mineral. Sci. Inst., St. Petersburg, 1992. Geologist West-Siberian Geol. Expedition, Stalinsk-Novokusnetsk, Russia, 1957-62; maj. rschr. All Union Geol. Sci. Rsch. Inst., St. Petersburg, 1962—. Author: Endogenic Regimes and Types of the Methamorphism of the Folded Belts, 1985, Earth Crust of the Continents and Oceans, 1998; coauthor: Polymetamorphic Complexes Pre-cambrian Fundamental Paleozoic and Mezozoic Fold Belts Middle Asia, 1974, Magmatic Formations of the USSR, 2 vols., 1979, Regional Metamorphic-Methasomatic Formations, 1983, Geological-Mineragenetic Map of the World scale 1:15000000 with explanatory note, 2000, Geology and Mineral Resources of Russia, vol. 2, 2000. Home: Nalichnaya 37/1 Apt 4, 199406 Saint Petersburg Russia Office: All Union Sci Rsc Geol Inst, Sredny prospect 74, 199106 Saint Petersburg Russia

BO, MARIO EDOARDO, geriatrician, cardiologist; b. Turin, Italy, Jan. 15, 1959; s. Giuseppe and Anna (Vergnano) B.; m. Simona Capello, June 22, 1991; children: Gianmaria, Maddalena. MD, U. Turin (Italy), 1984; D in Geriatric Therapy, U. Turin, 1991. Specialist in geriat. and gerontology. Asst., U. Turin Inst. Gerontology and Geriat. San Giovanni Battista Hosp., 1984-88; physician, specialty in geriat. and gerontology U. Turin, 1988—, physician, specialty in coronology, 2000—. Contbr. 100 articles to scientific pubs. Lt., Med. Official, 1986-87. Fellow Internat. Coll. Angiology; mem. European Atherosclerosis Soc. Home: Via Palmieri 14, 10143 Turin Italy Office: Inst Gerontology, C Bramante 88, 10126 Turin Italy

BOADELLA, DAVID JOHN, psychotherapist; b. London, July 6, 1931; arrived in Switzerland, 1988; s. Harold Frederick and Jessie Irene (Marsh) B.; m. Elsa Beatrice Corbluth, Sept. 29, 1952 (div. Feb. 1988); children: Adam, Eilidh; m. Silvia Eleni Specht, May 16, 1988; 1 child, Till. BA, U. London, 1953; MEd, U. Nottingham, 1960; DSc, Open U., Colombo, Sri Lanka, 1995. Registered psychotherapist, U.K. Head tchr. Abbotsbury Sch., Weymouth, Dorset, 1963-81; lectr. Coll. Higher Edn., Weymouth, 1970-73, U. Antioch, London, 1977-83, U. Tokyo, 1982-86; tutor U. Bath, Eng., 1981-86; co-dir. Internat. Inst. für Biosynthese, Heiden, Switzerland, 1988—; dir. Inst. for Devel. Human Potential, London, 1976-81; cons. Inst. for Biodynamic Psychology, London, 1968-85, Chiron Ctr. for Holistic Psychotherapy, London, 1995—; co-pres. Inst. for Psycho-Corporal Therapy, Naples, Italy, 1993. Founder, editor Energy and Character Jour., 1970; editl. staff European Jour. Psychotherapy Counselling and Health, 1997, Internat. Jour. Psychotherapy, 1997; author: Lifestreams: An Introduction to Biosynthesis, 1986, Wilhelm Reich: Re-evaluation of His Work, 1981, The Spiral Flame, 1956, Biosynthese Therapie, 1988. Founding mem. Internat. Green Cross, Geneva, 1993. Mem. Assn. for Humanistic Psychology London, Swiss Psychotherapy Assn., World Coun. Psychotherapy (bd. dirs. 1996—), European Assn. for Psychotherapy (bd. dirs. 1996—), European Assn. for Body Psychotherapy (pres. 1989-93), Internat. Assn. Somatotherapy (pres. of hon. 1993). Avocations: mountain climbing, poetry, chess. Office: Internat Inst für Biosynthese, Benzenrüti 6, CH 9410 Heiden Switzerland

BOAKYE, FRANCIS, physicist, educator, researcher; b. Kumasi, Ashanti, Ghana, June 3, 1943; s. Emmanuel Kofi and Margaret (Akon) B.; m. Ruth Asafo-Agyei, Aug. 15, 1971; children: Emmanuel Kwasi, Ama Kyerewah, Kwasi Minta. BSc, Univ. of Sci. and Tech., Kumasi, Ghana, 1968, MSc, 1973, PhD, 1987. Teaching asst. Univ. Sci. and Tech., 1969-71, asst. lectr., 1971-74, lectr., 1974-82, sr. lectr., 1982-88, 90—; assoc. prof. U. Liberia, Monrovia, 1988-90; assoc. prof. physics U. Sci. and Tech., Kumasi, Ghana, 1996—; moderator in physics West African Exams. Coun., Accra, Ghana, 1990-94, chief examiner in physics, 1990-94; external examiner in physics U. of Devel. Studies, Tamale, Ghana, 1995; mem. Ghana Optics Commn., 1996—; assoc. coord. Laser and Fibre Optics Ctr., U. Cape Coast, Ghana, 1996 —; coord. optometry program U. Sci. & Tech., Kumasi, Ghana, 1993—; mem. coun. West African Examinations Coun., Ghana, 1997—. Contbr. articles to profl. jours. Avocations: gardening, collecting foreign currencies. Home: Plot 14 Block II, Kumasi, Ashanti Ghana Office: Univ Sci and Tech, Dept Physics, Kumasi, Ashanti Ghana

BOAL, BERNARD HARVEY, cardiologist, educator, author; b. May 14, 1937., 1995-2000; Assoc. prof. medicine N.Y. Med. Coll., 2000—. Office: Cath Med Ctr Bklyn and Queens Jamaica NY 11432

BOARDMAN, SIR JOHN, classical archaeology educator, historian, art educator; b. Ilford, Eng., Aug. 20, 1927; s. Frederick Archibald and Clara (Wells) B.; m. Sheila Joan Lyndon Stanford, Oct. 26, 1952; children: Julia, Mark. BA, Magdalene Coll., Cambridge (Eng.) U., 1948, MA, 1951; PhD (hon.), U. Athens, Greece, 1991, U. Paris, 1994. Asst. dir. Brit. Sch. at Athens, Greece, 1952-55; asst. keeper at Ashmolean Mus. Oxford (Eng.) U., 1955-59, reader, 1959-78, fellow Merton Coll., 1963-78; hon. fellow Merton Coll., 1978; Lincoln prof. emeritus of Classical Archaeology and Art, fellow Lincoln Coll. Oxford (Eng.) U., 1978-94; hon. fellow Lincoln Coll., 1995; pres. Fédération Internationale pour Études Classiques, 1994-97; Geddes-Harrower prof. U. Aberdeen, Scotland, 1974; conductor excavations Chios, 1953-55, Tocra, Libya, 1964-65; del. OUP, 1979-89; vis. prof. Australian Inst. Archaeology, 1987; prof. ancient history Royal Acad., 1989—; Andrew W. Mellon lectr. Washington, 1993; hon. fellow Magdalene Coll., Cambridge U. Writings include: The Cretan Collection in Oxford: The Dictaean Cave and Iron Age Crete, 1961, Island Gems: A Study of Greek Seals in the Geometric and Early Archaic Periods, 1963, (with Leonard Robert Palmer) On the Knossos Tablets, 1963, Greek Art, 1964, The Greek Overseas: The Archaeology of Their Early Colonies and Trade, 1964, (with Josse Doerig, Werner Fuchs and Max Hirmer) Die griechische Kunst, 1966, (with John Hayes) Excavations at Tocra, 1963-1965, Vol. I: The Archaic Deposits, 1966, Vol. II: Archaic Deposits II and Later Deposits, 1973, Excavations in Chios 1952-1955: Greek Emporio, 1967, Pre-Classical: From Crete to Archaic Greece, 1967, Archaic Greek Gems: Schools and Artists in the Sixth and Early Fifth Centuries B.C., 1968, Engraved Gems: The Ionides Collection, 1968, Greek Painted Vases: Catalogue of an Early Exhibition in the Mappin Art Gallery, 1968, Greek Gems and Finger Rings: Early Bronze Age to Late Classical, 1970, (with Donna C. Kurtz) Greek Burial Customs, 1971, Athenian Black Figure Vases, 1974, Intaglios and Rings: Greek, Etruscan and Eastern, From a Private Collection, 1975, Athenian Red Figure Vases: The Archaic Period, 1975, (with Diana Scarisbrick) The Ralph Harari Collection of Finger Rings, 1977, (with Marie-Louise Vollenweider) Catalogue of the Engraved Gems and Finger Rings, 1978, (with Eugenio La Rocca) Eros in Greece, 1978, Greek Sculpture: The Archaic Period, 1978, (with Martin Robertson) Corpus vasorum antiquorum: Great Britain, Castle Ashby, Northampton, 1979, Escarabeos de Piedra de Ibiza, 1984, La Ceramica Antica, 1984, Greek Sculpture: The Classical Period, 1985, (with D. Finn) The Parthenon and Its Sculptures, 1985, Athenian Red Figure Vases: The Classical Period, 1989, Classical Art in Eastern Translation, 1994, The Diffusion of Classical Art in Antiquity, 1994, Greek Sculpture: Late Classical Period, 1995, Greek Art, 1996, The Great God Pan, 1997, Early Greek Vase Painting, 1998, Persia and the West, 2000; editor: T.J. Dunbabin, The Greeks and Their Eastern Neighbors: Studies in the Relations between Greece and the Countries of the Near East in the Eighth and Seventh Centuries B.C., 1957, The European Community in later Prehistory: Studies in Honor of C.F.C. Hawkes, 1971, The Oxford History of the Classical World, 1986, Chios: A Conference at the Homereion in Chios, 1984, 87, The Oxford History of Classical Art, 1993; editor Jour. Hellenic Studies, 1958-65; translator: Crete and Mycenae (Spyridon N. Marinatos), 1960; contbr. articles to profl. jours. 2nd lt. Brit. Army, Intelligence Corps, 1950-52. Decorated Knight Bachelor, 1989. Fellow Soc. Antiquaries, Brit. Acad. (Cromer Greek prize 1959, Kenyon medal 1995), Bavarian Acad. Scis. (corr.); mem. Hellenic Soc., Libya Exploration Soc., Soc. South Asian Studies, Royal Danish Acad. (fgn.), Acad. des Inscriptions et Belles Lettres, Inst. de France (assoc.), Royal Irish Acad., Athens Archeol. Soc. (v.p. 1998—), Accademia dei Lincei, Rome, Am. Philosophical Soc. Office: Ashmolean Mus, Oxford OX1 2PH, England

BOARTS, LAIRD SPEER, retired insurance company executive; b. Whiteburg, Pa., Apr. 29, 1908; s. Howard M. and Elsie Grace Boarts; widowed. Grad. h.s. Agy. mgr. State Farm Ins. Co., Bloomington, Ill., 1939-73; bd. dirs. Apollo (Pa.) Trust Co., 1949-95; bd. dirs. Pitts. Life Ins. Underwriters Assn.; tchr. life ins. program. Pres. Apollo Area Hist. Soc., 1970-77; sec. Apollo C. of C. With USN, 1945. Mem. Apollo C. of C. (organizer), Masons, Lions. Republican. Presbyterian. Avocations: golf, softball, horse shoes, church and civic work. Home: 1747 Pebble Beach Dr Fort Myers FL 33907-5774

BOAS, FRANK, lawyer; b. Amsterdam, North Holland, The Netherlands, July 22, 1930; came to U.S., 1940; s. Maurits Coenraad and Sophie (Brandel) B.; m. Edith Louise Bruce, June 30, 1981 (dec. July 1992); m. Jean Scripps, Aug. 6, 1993. AB cum laude, Harvard U., 1951, JD, 1954. Bar: U.S. Dist. Ct. D.C. 1955, U.S. Ct. Appeals (D.C. cir.) 1955; U.S. Supreme Ct. 1958. Atty. Office of the Legal Adviser U.S. State Dept., Washington, 1957-59; pvt. practice, Brussels and London, 1959-79; of counsel Patton, Boggs & Blow, Washington, 1975-80; pres. Frank Boas Found., Inc., Cambridge, Mass., 1980—. Mem. U.S. delegation to UN confs. on law of sea, Geneva, 1958, 60; vice chmn. Commn. for Ednl. Exch., Brussels, 1980-87; mem. vis. com. Harvard Law Sch., 1987-91, Ctr. for Internat. Affairs, 1988—; dir. Found. European Orgn. for Research and Treatment of Cancer, Brussels, 1978-87, Paul-Henri Spaak Found., Brussels, 1981—, East-West Ctr. Found., Honolulu, 1990—, Law of the Sea Inst., Honolulu, 1992-97, Pacific Forum CSIS, Honolulu, 1996—, Honolulu Acad. Arts, 1997—, U. Hawaii Found., 2000—; hon. sec. Am. C. of C. in Belgium, 1966-78. With U.S. Army, 1955-57. Decorated Officer of the Order of Leopold II, comdr. Order of the Crown (Belgium), comdr. Order of Merit (Luxembourg); recipient Tribute of Appreciation award U.S. State Dept., 1981, Harvard Alumni Assn. award, 1996. Mem. ABA, Fed. D.C. Bar Assn., Pacific and Asian Affairs Coun. (pres.), Honolulu Com. Fgn. Relations, Pacific, Outrigger Canoe (Honolulu), Travellers (London), Am. and Common Market (Brussels pres. 1981-85), Honolulu Social Sci. Assn. Home: 4463 Aukai Ave Honolulu HI 96816-4858

BOAS, JOHN ROBERT, banker; b. London, Feb. 28, 1937; s. Edgar Henry and Mary Katherine (Beattie) B.; m. Karen Elisabeth Gersted, Sept. 25, 1965; children: Helena, Christopher, Nicholas. Student, U. Cambridge, 1960. Exec. Price Waterhouse, London, 1960-65, ICI, London, 1965-66; exec. S.G. Warburg & Co. Ltd., London, 1966-71, dir., 1971-90, vice chmn., 1990-95; mng. dir. SBC Warburg, 1995-97; advisor UBS Warburg, 1997—; bd. dirs. Heritage Lottery Fund, Invesco Continental Smaller Co. Office: UBS Warburg, 2 Finsbury Ave, London EC2M 2PA, England

BOATENG, KWAME OSEI, information system engineer; b. Kumasi, Ghana, Dec. 28, 1962; parents Kwabena Osei Tutu and Adwoa Afoa; m. Mavis Osei Boateng, Feb. 4, 1994; 1 child, Akua. BSEE, U. Sci. & Technology Kumasi, 1991; M in Engring., Ehime U., 1997, D Engring., 2000. Tchg. asst. U. Sci. & Technology Kumasi, 1991-94; cons. engr. Computer Processing Co. Ltd., Kumasi, 1991-94; rsch. asst. Ehime U., Matsuyama, Japan, 1997-2000; rschr. Fujitsu Labs., Ltd., Kawasaki, Japan, 2000—. Avocations: music, badminton, TV, movies. Home: Fujitsu Sobudai House # 216, 3-4770-20 Sobudai Zama, 228-0011 Kanagawa Japan

BOATMAN, ROBERT WAYNE, lawyer; b. Ventura, Calif., Nov. 24, 1959; s. Wayne Lee and Dorothy Joan (Mann) B.; m. Priscilla, June 6, 1986; children: Matthew, Katie, Becky, Ellie, Sam, Jack. AB, Stanford U., 1981; JD, Ariz. State U., 1984. Lawyer Gullagher & Kennedy PA, Phoenix, 1984-85, 89—. Office: Gallagher & Kennedy PC 260 N Central Ave Phoenix AZ 85004-2201

BOBAL, PAL, lawyer; b. Salgstarjan, Hungary, Apr. 26, 1950; parents Gyula and Gyulani B.; m. Palni Veress, Oct. 1, 1977; children: David, Katalin. JD, Univ. Juristic Budapest, 1974; degree in econs., U. Economy, 1990. Journalist Assn. Journalists, Budapest, 1974-75; employee Min. Fgn. Affairs, Budapest, 1976-80; atty. County Coun., Budapest, 1980—; dept. head govt. office Budapest, 1990—; cons. Johns Hopkins U., Balt., 1992—, CUCHAN Co., Paris, 1995—. Author: Development for Local Governments, 1994; editor: Training of Trainers, 1992. Mem. N.Y. Acad. Scis., Nat. Geographic Soc. Office: Govt Office Pest County, Varoshaz 7, Budapest Hungary 1052

BOBAN, ZVONIMIR, soccer player; b. Imotski, Croatia, Oct. 8, 1969. Capt. Dinamo Zagreb, Bari, Italy, 1990-91; midfielder, forward AC Milan, Italy, 1991—. Address: Fed Italiana Giuoco Calcio, Via Gregorio Allegri 14, CP 2450 Rome I-00918, Italy Address: Giusappe Meazza San Siro, via Piccolomini 5, 20151 Milan Italy*

BOBBITT, JUANITA MARILYN CRAWFORD, international organization executive; b. N.Y.C., Sept. 4, 1938; d. Philip Theodore and Lillian Beatrice (Nelson) Crawford; 1 child, Edmund Michael. BA in Romance Lang., CUNY, Bklyn., 1959; MA in Econ., NYU, 1982; MPA, Harvard U., 1984. Pub. adminstrn. officer UN, N.Y.C., 1974-84, econ. affairs officer, 1984-92, sr. pub. adminstrn. officer, 1992-97, head gender adv. svcs. unit, 1998, internat. devel. cons., 1999—. Contbr. articles to profl. jours. Exec. com. St. George's Cmty. Devel. Corp., Bklyn., 1994-99; rep. provincial coun. Episcopal Ch., 1993-96. Mem. ASPA (exec. com., sect. internat. comparative adminstrn.), Harvard Club (N.Y.C. chpt., program com. 1991-99), Tri-State J.F. Kennedy Alumni Assn., (exec. com. 1987—), Delta Sigma Theta (pres. Bklyn. chpt. 1966-68, chair internat. com. 1993-99, nat. projects com. 1973-74). Episcopalian. Avocations: reading, walking, dancing, arts. Office: UN One United Nations Plz New York NY 10017

BOBCO, WILLIAM DAVID, JR., consulting engineering company executive; b. Chgo., Aug. 11, 1946; s. William David and Eleanor Josephine (Dvojack) B.; m. Donna Domenica DiFrancesca, Sept. 13, 1969; 1 child, Christina Marie. BS in Engring., U. Ill., Chgo., 1969; MBA in Prodn. Mgmt., U. Chgo., 1983. Prodn. mgr. Am. Can Co., Maywood, Ill., 1972-73; with Footlik & Assocs., Evanston, Ill., 1973—; exec. v.p. Footlik & Assocs., Evanston, 1986—; mem. indsl. adv. bd. U. Ill. Coll. Engring., Chgo., 1992—, chmn. alumni devel. com., 1991-95, mem. dean selection com., 1994. Vol. Art Inst. of Chgo., 1983-84; mem. facilities and grounds com. St. Giles Parish, 1995—, co-chair, 1997—, treas. golf com., 1997—. Mem. ASME (bd. dirs. Chgo. sect. 1984—, newsletter editor 1987-98, vice chmn. 1991, chmn. Chgo. sect. 1992-94, region VI rep. to A World in Motion K-12 tng. program, SAE (co-sponsor 1993), Engring. Alumni Assn. U. Ill. Chgo. (pres. 1984-88, bd. dirs. 1975-99), U. Ill. Alumni Assn. (bd. dirs. 1985-91,

nominating com. 1991, Loyalty award 1988, Constituent Leadership award 1991, Disting. Svc. award 1994); vol. Animal Care League, Oak Park, Ill., 2000. Roman Catholic. Avocations: travel, art, music. Office: Footlik & Assocs 2521 Gross Point Rd Evanston IL 60201-4993

BOB-DURU, ROBERT C., geography and environmental sciences educator; b. Awomama, Nigeria, Feb. 24, 1941; s. Gabriel Aweze and Angelina Nawanyimma (Obioma) Duru; m. Claret Ubani-Ukoma. BA with honors, U. London, 1964; MA, U. Ibadan, 1971, U. Pa., 1972; PhD, Temple U., 1978. Diplomate in microprocessors and informatics; grad. in surveying. Assoc. prof. Voorhees Coll., Denmark, S.C., 1975-78; prof. geography and environ. scis. U. Nigeria, Nsukka, 1986—, dean of faculty, 1985-93, head dept., 1993-95; chmn. accreditation panel Nat. Univ. Commn., 1999. Author: Maps and Map Making, 1980, Map Work and Laboratory Geography, 1984, The Nigerian Green Revolution. Mem. Nat. Com. on Space Applications, Fed. Govt. Nigeria, Lagos, 1993,. UN fellow, Tokyo and Dublin, 1986-87; Population Coun. fellow, 1971-72. Mem. Third World Assn. for Remote Sensing, African Remote Sensing Assn. (coord. Eastern Nigeria 1990), Nigerian Cartographic Assn. (Eastern zone chmn. 1987—). Christian. Avocations: photography, boating/fishing, badminton, soccer, music. Home: 11 Eni Njoku St, Nsukka, Enugu State Nigeria Office: U Nigeria, PO Box 3170, Nsukka Nigeria

BOBEK, STANISLAW EMANUEL, science educator, researcher; b. Tarnowskie Góry, Silesia, Poland, Dec. 25, 1930; s. Emil and Aniela (Lison) B.; m. Helena Węgrzyniak, Mar. 14, 1963; children: Janusz, Marcin. MS, U. Agr., Cracow, Poland, 1956; PhD, U. Agrl., 1962. Asst., Dept. Animal Physiology U. Agr., 1956-62, lectr., Dept. Animal Physiology, 1962-70, asst. prof., 1971-78, assoc. prof., 1978-86, prof., 1986—; chief Isotopic Lab., U. Agr., 1960-94; head Dept. Animal Physiology, U. Agr., 1983-94. Contbr. articles to profl. jours. Mem. ESNA, Polish Endocrine Soc., Polish Physiol. Soc. Roman Catholic. Avocations: mountain tourism, yachting. Home: Krowoderskich Zuchów, 31-271 Cracow Poland Office: U Agr, Al Mickiewicza 24-28, 30-059 Cracow Poland

BOBIC, MILOS, architect; b. Belgrade, Yugoslavia, June 30, 1946; s. Dobrivoje and Cveta (Mircevic) B.; m. Neda Nikolic, Nov. 20, 1972 (div. May 1988); children: Uros, Relja; m. Mirjana Milanovic, Dec. 20, 1992; 1 child, Igor. BArch, U. Belgrade, 1972, PhD, 1988. Ptnr. G&B Studio, Belgrade, 1970-78; rschr., mgr. CEP, Belgrade, 1978-88; docent U. Belgrade, 1989—; rschr. Urhahn Planners, Amsterdam, The Netherlands, 1992-96; adviser Kuiper Compagnons, Rotterdam, The Netherlands, 1996-99, DRO Amsterdam, 1999—; cons. DRO Town Planning, Amsterdam, 1988-89; docent Acad. van Bouwkunst, Amsterdam, 1993—. Author: Roof Above the Head, 1985, The Role of Time in City Spatial Structures, 1992, A Pattern Image, 1994, Strategy for Urbanity, 1996; editor: Communication, Profl. mag., 1982-87. Mem. Belgrade's Circle, Yugoslavia, 1991—; cons. Open Soc. Inst., N.Y.C., 1992—. Recipient Belgrade City award City Counsel, Belgrade, 1979, Award Belgrade's Arch. Saloon, 1984-87. Mem. Internat. Corp. Graphic Designers. Democrat. Avocations: tennis, basketball, sailing, woodcarving. E-mail: milanov@xs4all.nl. Home: Prinsengracht 689, 1017JV Amsterdam The Netherlands

BOBICH, ZELJKO, psychologist, psychotherapist; b. Karlovac, Croatia, July 7, 1954; arrived in Eng., 1992; s. Vladimir and Katarina (Mavrovich) B.; 1 child, Gordan. Prof. Psychology, Zagreb (Croatia) U., 1979, Diploma in Social Psychiatry, 1980, MSc in Med. Sci., 1981, MSc in Spl. Clin. Psychology, 1985, PhD in Med. Sci., 1989. Chartered clin. psychologist. Psychologist Jugoturbina, Karlovac, 1980; clin. psychologist Med. Ctr., Karlovac, 1980-84, cons. in psychodiagnostics, 1984-91; clin. psychologist Univ. Clinic, Belgrade, Yugoslavia, 1991, Oxfordshire Health Authority, Oxford, Eng., 1992-93; head psychology svc. for elderly Heathlands MH NHS Trust, Camberley, Surrey, Eng., 1993-98; clin. dir. brain injury rehab. unit Huntercombe Manor Hosp., Maidenhead, Berkshire, Eng., 1998; cons. clin. psychologist ICU Huntercombe Manor Hosp., Maidenhead, Berkshire, 1998—; pvt. practice, 1998-2000. Author: (books) Multiphasic Personality Inventory Karlovac, 1990, Anxiety - Patient's Manual, 1996, Recognize Your Enemy, 2000; author several psychometric tests and questionnaires; contbr. numerous articles to profl. jours. Mem. Brit. Psychol. Soc. Home: 6 Strathmore Ct, Upper Gordon Rd, Camberley Surrey GU15 2HN, England

BOBIER, CLAUDE-ABEL, scientist, educator; b. St. Etienne, France, Mar. 18, 1934; s. Pierre-Abel and Paulette Pierrette (Esquis) B.; m. Arlette Georgette Manissier, Sept. 4, 1959; children: Sylvie, Christine, Valerie. Agregation ScNat, Ecole Normale Superieure, St. Cloud, Paris, 1956-60; Dr es Sci., U. Paris VI, 1971, MS, 1958. Cert. marine geologist. Asst. U. Paris VI, 1960-63, maitre asst., 1963-75; prof. U. Tunis, Tunisia, 1975-86; maitre de conf. U. Bordeaux I, France, 1986-99; ret., 1999; sous dir. Sta. Geodynamique Sous-marine, Villefranche, France, 1963-75; chief mission academique formation des enseignants Rectorat Academie de Bordeaux, 1990-92; chief Insts. U. Tchrs. Formations Project, 1991-92. Sec.-gen. Assn. Parents d'Eleves, Villefranche, 1974-75; active other civic orgns. Served with French mil. Mem. Am. Geophys. Union, Am. Assn. Petroleum Geologists, N.Y. Acad. Scis., Geol. Soc. France, Internat. Ambs. Order. Home: 6 Square du Gue, F-33170 Gradignan France

BOBILLO MARTINEZ, ALFREDO, international business educator; b. Zamora, Spain, Mar. 3, 1953; s. Onesimo Martinez and Joaquina Bobillo; m. Celestina Rodriguez. Bachelor Degree, U. Valladolid, Spain, 1975, PhD in Econs. and Bus., 1990; Doctoral Degree, U. Deusto-Bilbao, Spain, 1982. Prof. U. Valladolid, 1982—. Author: Multinational Enterprises Financial Structure. Avocations: sports, gardening, collecting, music. Home: Urb Pago La Barca Parc 25, 47151 Boecillo Spain Office: Univ Valladolid, Campus Miguel Delibes, 47011 Valladolid Spain

BOBIN, NIKITA E., mining engineer; b. Leningrad, July 31, 1937; s. S. Bobin Yevgeny and Nataly K. Fanderflit; m. Nataly D. Pravosudovitch, May 12, 1962; children: Ann N. Semenova, Daria N. Mamaeva. Grad., Leningrad Mining Inst., 1959; DSc, St. Petersburg Mining Inst., Russia, 1996, Prof., 1997. Engr., scientist Inst. of Tech. Rschrs., Leningrad, 1961-69; scientist SPb Mining Inst., St. Petersburg, 1969-96, prof., 1996—. Author: (book) Tormojenie jiznedeyatelnos-ti kletok, Zinatne, Riga, 1987; contbr. articles to profl. jours. Office: St Petersburg Mining Inst, 21-Linia 2, 199026 Saint Petersburg Russia

BOBO, LEN DAVIS, musician; b. Vicksburg, Miss., Feb. 1, 1949; s. Samuel Redus and Eugenia (Causey) B.; m. Pamela Jeannine Moore, Apr. 13, 1974; children: Celeste Nichole, Brittany Noelle. AA, Hinds Jr. Coll., 1969; MusB, Miss. Coll., 1971; MusM, U. Tenn., 1975. Consecrated diaconal minister Meth. Ch. Dir. music Lakewood United Meth. Ch., No. Little Rock, Ark., 1976-79; music instr. U. Ark., Little Rock, 1975-90; ch. organist Pulaski Heights United Meth. Ch., Little Rock, 1979-93; music instr., coll. organist Hendrix Coll., 1983-98; minister of music First United Meth. Ch., Maumelle, Ark., 1993-94; instr. computer sci. The Anthony Sch., Little Rock, Ark., 1994-96; assoc. dir. music, organist, dir. Music and Arts Inst. First Presbyn. Ch., Pine Bluff, Ark., 1996—; vis. instr. music U. Ctrl. Ark., Conway, 1998-99; dir. music Covenant Presbyn. Ch., Jackson, Miss., 1999—. Composer (organ solo) Psalm 23, 1973, Praise to the Lord, 1977, Enchamatics, 1987, Fantasie pourle Trompette en chamade, 1990, (choral piece) The Lord's Prayer, 1979, (vocal solo) The Magnificat and Nunc Dimitis, 1979. Organist Ark. Celebration of 150 Yrs. Statehood, 1986. Sgt. Ark. Air N.G., 1974-76. Recipient Disting. Alumnus, Dept. Music, Miss. Coll., 1997. Mem. Am. Guild Organists, Fellowship Meth. Musicians (pres. 1978-79), Presbyn. Assn. Musicians, Nat. Fedn. Music Clubs (pres. Hot Springs chpt. 1981-82, Ark. Ch. Musician of Yr. award 1986), USCG Aux., Lions. Avocations: boating, fishing, photography, biking. Home: 335 Stonecastle Dr Brandon MS 39047-8073 Office: Covenant Presbyn Ch 4000 Ridgewood Rd Jackson MS 39211-6425

BOBOC, LOREDANA, Olympic athlete. Winner Gold medal gymnastics - pommel horse Sydney, 2000. Office: Federatia Romana Gimnastica, Str Vasile Conta 16 Sector 11, 70139 Bucarest Romania*

BOBROVNIK, SERGEY AFANASIEVICH, immunologist, researcher; b. Ukraine, Mar. 13, 1948; arrived in Portugal, 1999; s. Afanasiy Trofimovich Bobrovnik and Taiana Minovna Mosia; m. Tikhonova Tatiana Nikolaevna, May 15, 1970 (div. July 1990); children: Natalia, Elena; m. Elena Nikoaevna Artiomenko, May 8, 1998. Diploma in biophysics, Kiev State U., USSR, 1970, phD, 1974; DSc, Gamaleya Inst. Epidem. Micro., Moscow, 1989. Jr. rschr. Inst. Microbiology and Virology, Kiev, 1970-76; sr. rschr. dept. microbiology immunology Kiev State U., 1976-90; leading rschr. dept. molecular immunology Inst. Biochemistry, Kiev, 1990-99; rschr. scientist Gulbenkian Inst. Sci., Oeiras, Portugal, 1999—. Avocations: chess, ping-pong, reading. Fax: 351-21-440-79-70. Home: Rua Jose Henriques, Coelho 7-5D, Paco d'Arcos Portugal Office: Gulbenkian Inst Sci, Rua da Quinta Grande, 6, 351-21 Oeiras Portugal

BOCCARDI, LOUIS DONALD, news agency executive; b. Bronx, N.Y., Aug. 26, 1937; s. Louis and Delphine Boccardi; m. Joan M. Quinlan, Jan. 18, 1964; children—Susan, Lynn, Paul, Mark, Lauren. BA, Fordham Coll., 1958; MS, Columbia U. Grad. Sch. Journalism, 1959. Reporter/desk editor N.Y. World Telegram & Sun, 1959-64; asst. mng. editor N.Y. World Jour. Tribune, 1966-67; asst. gen. news editor AP, N.Y.C., 1967-69, mng. editor, 1969-73, v.p., exec. editor, 1973-85, pres., 1985—, now pres., CEO; mem. Pulitzer Prize bd.; bd. visitors Columbia U. Sch. Journalism, Northwestern U. Medill Sch. Mem. nat. adv. bd. Media Studies Ctr. Recipient Alumni Achievement award Fordham Coll., 1967, Outstanding Alumnus award Fordham U., 1968. Mem. Am. Soc. Newspaper Editors (Disting. Svc. mem.). Office: Associated Press 50 Rockefeller Plz Fl 7 New York NY 10020-1605

BOCCARDO, JAMES FREDERICK, lawyer; b. San Francisco, July 1, 1911; s. John Humbert and Erminia Gemma (Ferrando) B.; m. Lorraine Dimmett, Nov. 21, 1936; children: Leanne Boccardo Rees, John Humbert II. AB, San Jose State U., 1931; JD, Stanford U., 1934. Bar: Calif. 1934, D.C. Sole practice San Jose, Calif., 1934—. Mem. ABA, Calif. Bar Assn., D.C. Bar Assn., Internat. Acad. Trial Lawyers, Assn. Trial Lawyers Am., Calif. Trial Lawyers Assn., Santa Clara County Trial Lawyers Assn., Inner Circle Advs. (past pres.). Republican. Avocations: golf, aviation. Fax: 408-354-1021. Office: 985 University Ave Ste 12 Los Gatos CA 95032-7639

BOCCHI, EDIMAR ALCIDES, physician, researcher; b. Quintana, Brazil, Jan. 10, 1956; s. Alcides and Ercilia (Bizzarri) B.; m. Marlene Campanhola, Nov. 15, 1979; children: Brenda, Bruno, André. MD, Sao Paulo U., 1979. Med. diplomate. Resident in cardiology Sao Paulo U. Med. Sch., 1980-83; clin. head transplantation unit Heart Inst., Sao Paulo, 1988-98, head heart failure unit, 1998—. Contbr. articles to Jour. Heart Lung Transplantation, Circulation, others. Mem. Am. Heart Assn., Brazilian Soc. Cardiology. Avocations: sports (tennis, soccer), cinema. Home: Apto 161, Rua Oscar Freire 2077, 05409 01 São Paulo Brazil Office: Heart Inst, Av Dr Eneas Carvalho Aguiar, 05403-00 São Paulo Brazil

BOCCHICCHIO, JENNIFER DAWN, software engineer, physicist; b. Flushing, N.Y., July 15, 1974. BA in French, Hiram Coll., 1996, BA in Physics, 1996; MS, Fla. Inst. Technology, 1998. Software engr. Software Technology, Inc., Alexandria, Va., 1998—. Mem. AIAA, Am. Phys. Soc., Am. Geophys. Union, Zonta Internat. Avocations: hiking, singing opera, playing piano, creative writing.

BOCCIA, JUDY ELAINE, home health agency executive, consultant; b. San Diego, Aug. 29, 1955; d. Robert Garrett and Jerry Athalee (Carruth) Stacy; 1 child, Jennifer Lynn. BSN, Calif. State U., San Diego, 1978. RN, Calif.; lic. pub. health nurse, Calif. Staff nurse Univ. Hosp., U. Calif., San Diego, 1978-80, 81-82, Moffitt Hosp., San Francisco, 1980-81, Humana Huntington, Huntington Beach, Calif., 1982-84; intravenous and hospice vis. nurse Town & Country Nursing, Garden Grove, Calif., 1984-85; vis. nurse Vis. Nurse Assn., Orange, Calif., 1985-86; v.p. Doctors and Nurse Med. Mgmt., Newport Beach, Calif., 1986-89; dir. nursing HMSS, So. Calif., 1989-90; pres. Premier Care, Irvine, 1990-91, Homelife Nursing & Staffbuilders, Lake Forest, Calif., 1991—; cons., Calif., 1987—; pres., adminstr. Homelife Nursing-Staff Builders, O.C., 1991-97; AIDS educator; presenter in field; guest radio spkr. Parrish nurse. Mem. Oncology Nursing Soc., Intravenous Nurse Soc., Calif. Nurses Assn. Avocations: singing, walking with daughter, gardening. Home: 19 Stone Pine Aliso Viejo CA 92656-2131 Office: 19 Stone Pne Aliso Viejo CA 92656-2131

BOCCON-GIBOD, DOMINIQUE CHRISTIAN, communications executive, consultant; b. Paris, Apr. 11, 1937; s. François and Simone (Taillefer) B.-G.; m. Claude Terisse; children: Matthieu, Grégoire, Malvina. BS, U. Paris, 1962, MS, 1969. Staff engr. Philips, France, 1964-69, 1969-73, case leader, 1973-76, group leader, 1976-79, divsn. leader, 1979-83, unit mgr., 1983-88; dep. mgr. Alcatel, Marcoussis, France, 1988-97, divsn. mgr., 1997-99. Contbr. articles to profl. jours. Sub-lt. French Navy, 1962-64. Mem. IEEE, SPIE, OSI. Home: 132 Bd Malesherbes, F-75017 Paris France Office: Alcatel, Route de Nozay, F-91461 Marcoussis France

BOCCUZZI, JOSEPH, electrical engineer, educator; b. Bklyn., Dec. 23, 1965; s. Giacomo and Maria B.; m. Nina Marie Boccuzzi, Nov. 30, 1996; 1 child, Giovanni. BSEE, Polytechnic U. of N.Y., 1989; MSEE, Fla. Atlantic U., 1991. Design engr. Motorola, Boynton Beach, Fla., 1989-92; mem. tech. staff AT&T Bell Labs, Holmdel, N.J., 1992-96; sr. design svcs. mgr. Cadence Design Sys., Inc., San Jose, Calif., 1996—; adj. prof. Polytechnic U. of N.Y., Bklyn., 1998—; treas. IEEE vehicular technology N.J. sect., Holmdel, 1995-96. Avocations: reading, martial arts, all sports. Office: Cadence Design Systems Inc 230 Half Mile Rd Red Bank NJ 07701-5683

BOCHE, BERNHARD, process engineer; b. Munich, Bavaria, Germany, Feb. 19, 1966; s. Gernot and Anne-Marie (Geiger) B.; m. Silke Scholz, Oct. 21, 1994; children: Anika, Morits, Lena. Diploma in elec. engring., Tech. U. Munich, 1991, PhD in Elec. Engring., 1997. Staff R & D Tech. U. Munich, 1991-96; GaAs process tech. Infineon Technol. AG, Munich, 1996—. Avocations: music, photography. Office: Infineon Technol, Otto-Hahn-Ring 6, 81739 Munich Germany

BOCHETTO, GEORGE ALEXANDER, lawyer; b. Bklyn., Oct. 7, 1952; m. Paula Agins, Aug. 6, 1987; children: David, Evan. BA, SUNY, Albany, 1975; JD cum laude, Temple U., 1978. Bar: Pa. 1978, N.Y. 1995, U.S. Dist. Ct. (ea. dist.) Pa. 1979, U.S. Supreme Ct. 1992, U.S. Tax Ct. 1986. Pvt. practice, 1979-90; assoc. Pelino & Lentz, P.C., Phila., 1978-79, Monteverde & Hemphill, P.C., Phila., 1990-93, Bochetto & Lentz, P.C., Phila., 1993—. Contbr. articles to profl. jours. Bd. dirs. Pa. Spl. Olympics, 1986—; mem. Rep. State Com., Pa., 1992—; appt. Pa. State Athletic Commr. Gov. Ridge, 1995—. Mem. ABA, Pa. Bar Assn., Phila. Bar Assn. (subcom. chairperson profl. responsibility com. 1978—). Avocations: amateur boxing, boating, sports. Office: Bochetto & Lentz PC 1524 Locust St Philadelphia PA 19102-4401

BOCHNOVICH, JOHN ANDREW, entrepreneur; b. Carbondale, Pa., Oct. 21, 1941; s. John and Pauline (Kelachava) B. Student, MIT, 1959-62, Columbia U., 1963-64; BA, Binghamton U., 1968. Lic. mgmt. cons., Fla., 1980. Entrepreneur Johnson City, 1989—. Author: Thoughts From a Friend, 1991, Best Octal Digits in the Whole Universe, 1995, A Revolutionary View of Mental Illness, 1996. Mem. AIAA. Avocations: crossword puzzles, walking, astronautics. Home and Office: 425 Robinson St Binghamton NY 13901-4101

BOCKER, HANS JURGEN, editor, analyst, consultant, management educator; b. Thuringia, Germany, July 13, 1939; s. Hans Alfred and Liselotte (Böttcher) B.; m. Megan Elizabeth Sutton, Jan. 4, 1960; children: Adrian Alexander, Chloe April. MS in Engring., Tech. Univ., Darmstadt, 1964; MBA, Tech. Univ., Munich, 1968; Dr. Commerce, Univ. S. Africa, Pretoria, 1978. Cert. mech. engr., mgmt. prof., editor. Lectr. Univ. S. Africa, Pretoria, 1968-72, sr. lectr., 1972-78; pvt. practice indsl. and economic cons. various internat. companies and govts., 4 continents, 1969-86; assoc. prof. Wilfrid Laurier U., Waterloo, Ont., Can., 1978-84, Western Ill. U., 1984-86; editor-in-chief Finanz und Wirtschaft (Finance and Economy), London, 1986-91, Zollikerberg, B.C., Switzerland, 1992—; prof. EBS, London, 1986-91, Internat. Sch. Mgmt., 1993—; front-page columnist for Finanz und Wirtschaft; permanent vis. prof. bus. schs.; work with Treuhand Anstalt, Berlin; presenter in field; pres. Internat. Sch. Mgmt., Dortmund, 1993—; cons. to Internet Initial Pub. Offerings; chmn. bd. numerous cos. Author: books, study guides, case studies, interviews with famous personalities. Sometime TV and radio performer. Grantee Volkswagen Found. W. Germany 1964-66, many rsch. grants. Mem. Inst. Mgmt. Sci, Am. Inst. Decision Scis., Acad. Mgmt., Canadian Purchasing Assn., Swiss Fedn. Journalists, Inst. Corp. Orgn. and Comm. Switzerland (pres.), British Assn. Fgn. Journalists, Surrey Country and Tennis Club, Rotary Internat. Avocation: classical pianist. Office: Postfach 188, CH-8125 Zollikerberg Switzerland

BOCKERIA, LEO ANTONOVICH, cardiac surgeon; b. Ochamchira, Abkhasia, USSR, Dec. 22, 1939; s. Anton Ivanovich and Olga Ivanovna Bockeria; m. Olga Alexandrovna Soldatova Oct. 10, 1964; children: Olga Leonidovna, Ekaterina Leonidovna. Student, Acad. Moscow Med., 1959-65, postgrad., 1965-68, Candidate of Med. Scis., 1968, DMS, 1973. Sr. sci. worker Russian Acad. Med. Scis. Bakoulev Inst. Cardiovas. Surgery, Moscow, 1968-74, chief lab. for hyperbaric oxygenation, 1973-77, dep. dir., 1977-93, prof. surgery, 1978; head, chmn. inst. cardiac surgery Bakoulev Ctr. Cardiovas. Surgery, Moscow, 1993—; head, chmn. Bakoulev Inst. Cardiovas. Surgery, Moscow, 1994—; chief cardiac surgeon Ministry of Pub. Health, 1996—; head, chmn. dept. cardiovasc. surgery Sechenov Moscow Med. Acad., 1996—; dir. Ctr. Surgical and Interventional Arrhythmology Ministry of Pub. Health, 1998—. Author: Tachyarrhythmias, 1989, (with V. I. Bourakovsky) Hyperbaric Oxygenation, 1974, Textbook of Cardiovascular Surgery, 1989, 96, History of Cardiovascular Surgery, 1998, Cardiomyoplasty, 1997, Surgery of the Heart and Vessels in Children, 1999, Surgery in Patients with Simultaneous Pathology of Coronary and Carotid Arteries, 1999, Lectures on Cardiovascular Surgery, 1999; co-editor: Y. Jhorac a Cardiovascular Surgery, 1994—; editor: Annals of Surgery, 1996—. Recipient Lenin's prize, 1976, State prize, 1986; named Honored Sci. Worker, 1994. Mem. ACS (hon.), Russian Soc. Cardiovasc. Surgeons (pres. 1995—), Am. Assn. Thoracic Surgery, All-Russian Found. Assisting Sick Children with Congenital Heart Diseases (pres 1994—), Russian Acad. Med. Scis. (academician). Fax: 7-095-2377856. Home: Leninsky pr 11 app 64, 117049 Moscow Russia Office: Bakoulev Ctr Cardiovasc Sur, Leninsky pr 8, 117931 Moscow Russia

BOĆKOWSKI, MICHAŁ STANISŁAW, research scientist; b. Milanówek, Warsaw, Poland, May 3, 1964; s. Włodzimierz Jerzy and Maria Anna (Krawiec) B.; m. Beata Maria Pawłowska, Feb. 20, 1993; children: Maria Anna, Wojciech Wyodzimierz. MSc in Applied Sci., Warsaw U. Tech., 1989; PhD in Chemistry of Solids, U. Montpellier II, France, 1995. Rschr. High Pressure Rsch. Ctr. Unipress, Poland, 1989-92, 95—. Contbr. articles to profl. jours. Recipient award European High Pressure Rsch. Group, 1998. Avocations: ballroom dancing, Latin American dancing, sports. Office: High Pressure Rsch Ctr, Sokołowska 29/37, 01-142 Warsaw Poland

BOCKSERMAN, ROBERT JULIAN, chemist; b. St. Louis, Dec. 20, 1929; s. Max Louis and Bertha Anna (Kremen) B.; m. Clarice K. Kreisman, June 9, 1957; children: Michael Jay, Joyce Ellen, Carol Beth. BSc, U. Mo., 1952; postgrad., Far East Intelligence Sch, Tokyo, 1954; MSc, U. Mo., 1955. Chemist Sealtest Corp., Peoria, Ill., 1955-56; prodn. mgr. Allan Drug Co., St. Louis, 1957-59; rsch. chemist Monsanto Co., St. Louis, 1960-65; purchasing agt. Monsanto Co., Sauget, Ill., 1966-67; founder, pres. Pharma-Tech Industries, Inc., Union, Mo., 1967-84; tech. dir. Overlock-Howe Consulting Group, St. Louis, 1984-85; founder, pres. Conatech Consulting Group, Chesterfield, Mo., 1985—; sec., mem. industry packaging adv. com. Sch. of Engring., U. Mo., Rolla, 1979—; adj. prof. dept. food sci./nutrition U. Mo., Columbia; adj. prof. engring. mgmt. U. Mo., Rolla; vis. lectr. U. Mo., Clayton, Northwestern U., Evanston, Ill.; vol. Tutor-Ladue Sch. Dist., St. Louis; mem. spkrs. bur. Inst. Food Technologists, Inst. Packaging Profls. Tech. reviewer Jour. Inst. of Packaging Profls., Jour. Packaging Tech., Mo. Waste Control Scholarship Grants and Research, Medical Device and Diagnostic Industry Jour., Medical Plastics and Biomaterials Publication.; mem. editl. adv. bd. The Forensic Examiner; panelist (Help Desk column) Medical Device and Diagnostic Industry mag., The Forensic Examiner; contbg. author: Packaging Forensics - Package Failure in the Courts. Mem. Mo. Waste Control Coalition; mem. stormwater engring. com. City of Creve Coeur, Mo.; nat. mem. Libr. Congress, Mo. Hist. Soc. With U.S. Army, 1952-54, Korea. Small Bus. Innovation rsch. grantee. Mem. ASTM, Am. Coll. Forensic Examiners, Cons. Packaging Engring. Coun., Inst. Packaging Profls. (cert. packaging profl.), Am. Technion Soc., Inst. Food Technologists Arrangements (St. Louis), Nat. Forensic Ctr., Teltech Resource Network, Am. Chem. Soc., Am. Plastics Coun., Mo. Acad. Scis., N.Y. Acad. Sci., Acad. Sci. St. Louis, Assn. Cons. Chemists and Chem. Engrs., Am. Nutraceutical Assn., Nat. Dir. Expert Witnessess, Sigma Xi. Achievements include research on toxicological effects of additives from packaging materials upon foodstuffs, on biological and photo degradation of polymers, on technology of form/fill/seal packaging engineering, new sterilization technologies for medical devices and pharmaceuticals, barrier properties of polymer films, toxicology of chemical dusts and fumes, and food irradiation effects on humans. Home: 54 Morwood Ln Creve Coeur MO 63141-7621 Office: Conatech Cons Group 287 N Lindbergh Blvd Creve Coeur MO 63141-7849

BOCKSTAELE, PAUL PIETER, retired mathematics educator; b. Melle, Belgium, Feb. 7, 1920; s. Leon and Maria Alice (Leenesonne) B. Grad. in theology, Roman Cath. Sem., Ghent, Belgium, 1944; PhD in Math., U. Louvain, 1951. Instr. math. St. Vincentius Coll., Eeklo, Belgium, 1947-53, Tchrs. Coll., Sint Niklaas, Belgium, 1953-62; assoc. prof. math. and history of math. Cath. U. Leuven, Belgium, 1963-67; prof. Cath. U. Leuven (Belgium), 1967-85, prof. emeritus, 1985—. Contbr. articles on history of math. to profl. jours. Decorated officer amd great officer Order of Leopold, comdr. Order of Crown (Belgium); named canon Diocese of Ghent, 1967. Mem. Internat. Acad. History of Sci., Koninklijke Academie voor Wetenschappen, Letteren en Schone Kunsten van Belgie (award 1948), Deutsche Gesellschaft für Geschichte Medizin, Naturwissenschaft und Technik (corr.). Roman Catholic. Home: Graetboslaan 9, B-3050 Oud-Heverlee Belgium

BÖCKSTIEGEL, KARL-HEINZ, law educator, arbitrator; b. Engers, Germany, Aug. 2, 1936; s. Heinrich and Helene (Bedbur) B.; m. Ali Kort, July 29, 1971. JD, U. Cologne, Germany, 1962. Qualification as lawyer and judge, Germany. Law clk. cts. and law firms Germany, 1962-65; ptnr. law firm Düsseldorf, Germany, 1965-71; prof. internat. law U. Cologne, 1971-75, chair internat. bus. law, 1975—, dir. Inst. Air and Space Law, 1975—; pres. Iran-U.S. Claims Tribunal, The Hague, The Netherlands, 1984-88, London Ct. Internat. Arbitration, 1993-97, German Instn. Arbitration, 1996—. Editor: (publ. series) Internat. Bus. Law, Series of the German Instn. of Arbitration, Studies in Air and Space Law, German Jour. of Air and Space Law, 1975—; author 12 books on various fields of internat. law, air and space law, internat. bus. law, and arbitration; editor 31 books on various fields of internat. law, air and space law, internat. bus. law, and arbitration; contbr. articles to profl. jours. Hon. pres. Bürgergemeinschaft Alt-Frankenforst, Bergisch Gladbach, Germany, 1997—. Mem. German Assn. Internat. Law (pres. 1994—), London Ct. of Internat. Arbiration (hon. v.p. 1998), Assn. Arbitrators (hon. v.p. 1997), Internat. Law Assn. (exec. coun. 1985—), Internat. Coun. for Comml. Arbitration, The Athenaeum Club (London). Avocations: literature (James Joyce, Arno Schmidt), golf. Home: Parkstr 38, D-51427 Bergisch Gladbach Germany Office: U Cologne, Albertus-Magnus-Platz, D-50923 Cologne Germany

BOCZKAJ, BOHDAN KAROL, structural engineer; b. Kowel, Poland, Nov. 14, 1930; came to U.S., 1973, naturalized, 1979; s. Walenty and Anna (Sarnecka) B.; m. Teresa Marcela Bioniosek, Aug. 23, 1955; 1 child, Boleslaw. MS in Civil Engring., Tech. U. of Silesia, Gliwice, Poland, 1962; PhD, Tech. U. Lodz (Poland), 1969. Registered profl. engr., Pa. Asst. prof. Tech. U. of Silesia, 1969-73, Tech. U., Rzeszow, Poland, 1970-71; sr. engr. Dravo Engrs., Pitts., 1973-83; vis. prof. Birzeit U., West Bank, Israel, 1984-86; prin. engr. Schneider Engrs., Bridgeville, Pa., 1986-88; design engr. Rust Internat., Pitts., 1988-90; prin. engr. S.E.I. Engrs. and Cons., Pitts., 1990-91; cons., 1992-94; specialist Hoogovens Tech. Svcs., 1995-97; civil engring. mgr. CV Engring., Pitts., 1997; structural engring. cons., 1998—. Contbr. articles on prestressed concrete and theory of plates, concrete fatigue, structure on mine subsiding area to profl. jours.; co-author: Defense of Poland-Today and Tomorrow, 1993, Vision of Poland, 1995. Teaching grantee Fulbright Found. Coun. for Internat. Exch. of Scholars, Birzeit U., 1985-86. Mem.

ASCE, Polish Inst. Arts and Scis. in Am. Roman Catholic. Achievements include patent on Coke Oven Machinery. Home: 728 Riehl Dr Pittsburgh PA 15234-2511

BOCZKAJ, BOLESLAW FRANCISZEK, electrical engineer, consultant; b. Zabrze, Poland, May 16, 1957; came to U.S., 1973, naturalized, 1979; s. Bohdan Karol and Teresa Marcela (Bieniosek) B. BSEE, U. Rochester, 1979; MS, Ga. Inst. Tech., 1988. Registered profl. engr., Pa. Mgmt. assoc. U.S. Steel Corp., Rankin and Duquesne, Pa., 1979-83; elec. engr. Internat. Paper Co., Lewisburg, Pa., 1984; elec. and instrumentation engr. Belcan Corp., Bridgeville, Pa., 1984-86; elect. design engr. Centerline Engring. Corp., Wexford, Pa., 1988-89; elec. engr. Voest-Alpine Industries, Pitts., 1989-91; PLC programmer AEG Automation Systems Corp., Oakdale, Pa., 1991-92; elec. engr. John Carollo Engrs., Santa Ana, Calif., 1992; software engr. Varco Drilling Systems, Orange, Calif., 1993-96; PLC programmer Verteq, Santa Ana, Calif., 1996; controls engr. Process Analysts, Van Nuys, Calif., 1997-98. Co-author: Obrona Polski Dzis i Jutro, 1993, Wizja Polski, Pierwsze Przyblizenie, 1995, 2d edit., 1997; contbr. articles to profl. jours. and conf. publs. Mem. IEEE, Instrument Soc. Am. (stds. com. 1994—), SME. Achievements include development of software for programmable controller used as part of control system for state-of-the-art pipe transfer system machine on off-shore oil rigs. Home: 21 Greco Aisle Irvine CA 92614-0272 Office: PO Box 17027 Irvine CA 92623-7027

BODA, DOMOKOS ISTVÁN, retired pediatrics educator; b. Alistal, Czechoslovakia, Apr. 19, 1921; arrived in Hungary, 1938; s. Domokos and Lenke (Kosár) B.; m. Lenke Bányai, Oct. 4, 1947; children: Christina, Marta, Theodora. MD, U. P. Pázmány, Budapest, Hungary, 1944; specialist in Pediatrics, U. Pécs, Hungary, 1950; specialist in Infectious Diseases, Postgrad. Faculty, Budapest, Hungary, 1958; D in Med. Scis., Hungarian Acad. Scis., Budapest, 1965. Asst. physician Children's Hosp., Budapest, 1946-49, chief asst. physician, 1949-52; head physician pediatric dept. Ctrl. Hosp. for Infectious Diseases, Budapest, 1952-63; prof., head of univ. pediatric dept. A. Szent-Györgyi Med. U., Szged, Hungary, 1963-91; vis. prof. UCLA Ctr. Med. Sci., 1971; pres. European Soc. Pediatric Rsch., 1975, Hungarian Pediatric Soc., 1982-86, European Soc. Pediatric Nephrology, 1987; standing com. mem. Internat. Pedatric Assn., Paris, 1980-86. Author: (books) Fluid and Electrolyte Therapy, 1958, Respiration Therapy, 1963, Textbook of Pediatrics 1981, 2d rev. edit. 1985; contbr. numerous articles to profl. jours. Recipient Jancsó Miklós award U. Med. Sch. Szeged, 1982, Széchenyi prize Rep. of Hungary, Budapest, 1992; named Hon. Citizen, Senate City of Szeged, 1995. Avocations: tennis, guitar, chamber music. Home: Roosevelt ter 10, H-6720 Szeged Hungary Office: Univ Pediatric Dept, Korányi Fasor 14, H-6701 Szeged Hungary

BODA, ZOLTAN, internist; b. Miskolc, Hungary, Oct. 5, 1947; s. Jenó and Ilona (Schön) B.; m. Emese Ujvarosi, July 5, 1975; 1 child, Judit. MD, U. Med. Sch., Debrecen, 1972, PhD, 1987; DSc, Hungarian Acad. Scis., 1996. Staff physician U. Med. Sch., Debrecen, 1972-77, resident 2d dept. medicine, 1972-75, asst. prof., 1977-83, sr. asst. prof., 1983-92, docent, 1993-98, prof., 2000—, dept. head, 1999—; intern Rikshospitalet, Oslo, 1978; cons. Reanal Fine Chemist Factory, Budapest, Hungary, 1989—; chmn. hemostasis com. Hungarian Acad. of Sci., Debrecen, 1992-96. Author, editor: Clinical Hemostaseology, 1999 (Springer award 2000); author: (with others) Diagnosis of Arterial and Venous Thrombosis, 1987; patent Ristomycin as Platelet Aggregating Agent (award 1985); contbr. articles to profl. jours. Sub-lt. Hungarian Army. Mem. Internat. Soc. of Thrombosis and Hemostasis, Mediterrenian League Against Thrombosis and Hemostasis, Danubian League Against Thrombosis and Hemostasis, Hungarian Soc. of Thrombosis and Hemostasis (gen. sec. 1994-97), Hemostasis Club of Debrecen (chmn. 1985-96). Avocations: tennis, fishing, collecting Old Hungarian paintings. Home: Sestakert 1, 4032 Debrecen Hungary Office: U Med Sch 2 Dept Med, Nagyerdei krt 98, 4012 Debrecen Hungary

BODANSZKY, HEDVIG EROS, pediatrician, educator; b. Budapest, Hungary, Nov. 11, 1933; d. Marton and Rozalia (Surman) B.; m. Gyula F. Erös, Oct. 29, 1960 (dec. Nov. 1987); 1 child, Janos. Cert. Semmelweis U. Med. Sch. Asst. prof. Semmelweis U., Budapest, 1958-73, adj. prof., 1973-90, assoc. prof., 1990-98, prof., 1998—. Author: The Samll Intestine's Diseases in Childhood, 1985 (Nivo award 1986). Mem. European Soc. Pediat. Gastroenterology and Nutrition, Hungarian Pediat. Gastroenterology of Children. Avocations: music, travelling. Office: Univ Semmelweis 1 st Dept Pediat, Bókay j u 53, 1083 Budapest Hungary

BODDIE, ARTHUR WALKER, JR., surgeon, cancer researcher; b. Detroit, Dec. 21, 1941; s. Arthur Walker Sr. and Ellena Louise B.; m. Joy Marie Marchbanks, Aug. 20, 1966; children: Elise Catherine, Ellena Lois. BA, Yale U., 1963, MD, 1967. Diplomate Am. Bd. Surgery. Commd. capt. USAF, 1968, advanced through grades to lt. col., 1976, ret., 1980; assoc. prof. surgery M.D. Anderson Hosp., Houston, 1980-90; assoc. prof. surgery U. Ill., Chgo., 1990-93, prof. surgery, 1993—, vice-chair dept. surg. oncology, 1997—. Patentee in field; contbr. articles to profl. jours. Recipient Med. Instrumentation award Am. Assn. for Advancement Med. Instrumentation, 1984. Fellow Internat. Coll. Surgery (mem. Japanese sect., hon.); mem. Am. Mensa Soc., Chgo. Surg. Soc. (pres. 1997-98), Sixteen Prof. Socs., VA (mem. oncology subcom. merit rev. bd. 1996—), Sigma Pi Phi. Avocations: golfing, sailing. Office: Dept Surg Oncology U Ill (m/c 820) 840 S Wood St Chicago IL 60612

BODDIE, DON O'MAR, recording company executive, producer, recording artist; b. St. Louis, Nov. 22, 1944; s. George Palmer and Lucille (Owens) Johnson-Boddie; m. Martha Lee Brown, Oct. 11, 1970 (div. Dec. 1979); children: Don O'Mar, Anthony, Shawn, Shellie. BS in Bus. Mgmt. Tarkio Coll., 1988; BS in Mgmt., 1988, St. Louis Music Inst., 1968. Rec. artist Bamboo Records, St. Louis, 1966-70; producer, writer Puzzletown Prodns., St. Louis, 1970-77, James Earl World Prodns., East St. Louis, Ill. and Memphis, 1975-79, Hi Records, Memphis, 1975-79, Motown Records, Los Angeles, 1976-78; owner, producer, writer, artist Chrome Records, St. Louis, 1978—; cons. Archway Studios, St. Louis, 1970-85, Music Assocs. in Mo. Corp, Jefferson City, Mo., 1978—, JD Mgmt., St. Louis, 1978—; v.p. Scorpio Prodns., Pine Lawn, Mo., 1980-82, music producer, 1980-84. Producer: Lets Be Lovers, 1985 (Heritage award), The Legend, 1986 (Heritage award); rec. artist Can't Stop the Fire, 1987 (Heritage award), New Thing Between Us (chartered Top 5 on Midwest Survey 1990, 91), True Love (charted Top 5 on Midwest Survey 1990, 91); host, presenter Gateway Music Awards Ceremony, 1991; headliner for Cigarettes/Salem Spirit Festival, 1985; featured performer Shock Wave Music TV Show, Friends of The Black Music Society Gateway Awards Lacledes Landing, 1991. Recipient Named New R&B Rec. Artist of Yr. Gateway Music Award, 1990, 91. Mem. entertainment com. to elect Irene Smith, St. Louis, 1982., Music Assocs. Mo. (pres. 1986—),St Louis Bd. od Edn. State Mo., 1991, Chpt. 1 reading tchr. (basic skills), 1995, secondary edn. gen. edn. devel. (ABE), sr. master tchr, Adult Basic Edn., 1997, 98, music dir., Clay Cmty. Edn.Ctr. Democrat. Roman Catholic. Avocations: basketball, martial arts. Office: Chrome Records 6112 Hancock Ave Saint Louis MO 63134-2116

BODDUPALLI, SADASIVUDU, biochemistry consultant; b. Vijayanagaram, Asia, Feb. 11, 1928; s. Rao Veerabhadra and Sarvanamma (Gabbita) B.; m. Rukmabai Prasanna Varanasi, May 4, 1945; children: Ramabhadra, Kamala, Sarala, Karuna, Krishna Bharath. BS in Chemistry, Andhra Christian Coll., Guntur, India, 1948; MBBS, Andhra Med. Coll., 1954; Md in Biochemistry, All India Inst. of Med. Scis., New Delhi, 1961. Lectr. in biochemistry Andhra Med. Coll., Visakhapatnam, India, 1956-59; rsch. fellow All India Inst. med. Scis., New Delhi, 1959-61; prof., head dept. biochemistry Med. Colls. of Andhra Pradesh Med. Svcs., Hyderabad, India, 1963-83; rsch. scientist N.Y. State Rsch. inst. for Neurochemistry/Drug Addiction, N.Y.C., 1967-68; prof. lab. medicine Arab Med. U., Benghazi, Libya, 1985-86; prof. of biochemistry MR Med. Coll., Gulburga, India, 1991-94; chief cons. biochemistry Vijaya Diagnostic Ctr., Secunderabad, India, 1996-98; prof. biochemistry and dir. Advance Ctr. for Neuro Biochemistry, Osmania Med. Coll., Hyderabad, 1982-83; cons. ITL Biotech, Hyderabad, 1987-91. Contbr. articles to profl. jours. Rsch. grantee Indian Coun. of Med. Rsch., New Delhi, 1972-83; recipient award Guntur Med. Coll. Old Students Assn., 1978, Dr. B.C. Roy Nat. award as Eminent Med. Tchr., Med. Counsil of India, New Delhi, 1982. Mem. N.Y. Acad. Scis., 1997, Assn. of Clin. Biochemists of India, Assn. of Med. Biochemists of India (pres. 1993-94). Avocations: music concerts, spiritual discourses, watching internat. cricket and tennis. Office: Vijaya Diagnostics Ctr, Market St, Secunderabad 5000003, India

BODDY, KEITH, medical physicist, educator; b. Stockton-on-Tees, Eng., Nov. 1, 1937; s. Ernest and Edith Mary (Ball) B.; m. Sylvia Mary Goodier, Aug. 20, 1960; children: Christopher Stephen, Graham Stuart. BSc, U. Liverpool, 1959; MSc, U. London, 1961; PhD, U. Glasgow, 1969; DSc, U. Strathclyde, 1976; DSc (hon.), De Montfort U., 1998. Head of health physics Associated Electrical Industries, Aldermaston Court, Eng., 1959-63; univ. lectr. to sr. lectr. Scottish Univs. Rsch. and Reactor Ctr., East Kilbride, Scotland, 1963-67; head regional med. physics dept. Newcastle upon Tyne, Eng., 1978-97; prof. med. physics U. Newcastle-Upon Tyne, Eng., 1978-97; cons. expert panels IAEA, Vienna. Contbr. articles to profl. jours. Mem. Radioactive Waste Mgmt. Adv. Com., 1989—; mem. com. on med. aspects Radiation in the Environ., 1989—; mem. Ionizing Radiations Adv. Com., 1988—. Decorated officer Order Brit. Empire, comdr. Order Brit. Empire. Fellow Royal Soc. of Edinburgh Inst. Phys. Scis. in Medicine (pres. 1986-88), Inst. Physics and Engring. in Medicine (hon.), Inst. of Physics (Glazebrook medal, prize 1991), Soc. for Radiol. Protection (hon.; mem. coun. 1981-84), Brit. Nuclear Medicine Soc. (hon.), Royal Coll. Radiologists (hon.; Skinner medal 1999), Brit. Inst. Radiology (hon.), Internat. Orgn. for Med. Physics (pres. 1994-97), Internat. Union for Physics and Engring. in Medicine (pres. 1997-2000, IUPESM award of merit). Avocations: walking, music, gardening, crossword and logic puzzles, family.

BODE, DIETRICH KARL ERNST, publishing company executive; b. Giessen, Hessen, Germany, June 27, 1934; s. Ernst and Karoline (Veek) B.; m. Margaret Ella Louise Hassel, Sept. 16, 1960; children: Eva Beate, Theodor Felix. Dr. Phil., U. Marburg, Germany, 1960. Asst. U. Heidelberg, Germany, 1960-62; lectr. Philipp Reclam jun., Stuttgart, Germany, 1962-80, dir., 1981-84, pub., 1985-99. Author: Georg Britting: Geschichte seines Werkes, 1962; editor: Ferdinand Freiligrath. Gedichte, 1964, Gedichte des Expressionismus, 1966, 150 Jahre Reclam, 1978, Deutsche Gedichte, 1984, 125 Jahre Reclams Universal-Bibliothek, 1992, Rainer Maria Rilke: Gedichte, 1997. Mem. Evang. Ch. Office: Philipp Reclam jun Verlag, Postfach 1349, D-71252 Ditzingen Germany

BODE, JOHANN CHRISTIAN, internist, gastroenterologist; b. Bonn, Germany, Sept. 5, 1935; s. Hans Robert and Lotte Edith Clara (Schulze-Berge) B.; m. Christiane Bücher, Aug. 14, 1965; children: Johannes Georg, Konrad Alexander, Barbara Dorothee. MD, U. Marburg, 1964. Resident Free U., Berlin, 1963-64; resident to sr. resident U. Marburg Med. Sch., 1965-70, asst. prof. internatl medicine, 1971-80, assoc. prof. of internal medicine, 1981-82; chief dept. internal medicine sect. gastroenterol./hepatol. Robert-Bosch-Krankenhaus, Stuttgart, Germany, 1982—; prof. medicine U. Marburg, 1971-82, U. Tübingen, 1983—; chmn. 5th Congress European Soc. for Biomed. Rsch. on Alcoholism, 1995; pres. nutritional adv. bd. German Fish Industry. Editor: Metabolic Changes Induced by Alcohol, 1970, Gut and the Liver, 1998; contbr. articles to profl. jours. and textbooks. Recipient Heinrich-Wieland award Coun. for the Heinrich Willand award, 1970, Homburg award Coun. on Med. Edn., 1972, Curt Adam award Soc. for Med. Congress, 1976. Mem. European Assn. for the Study of the Liver (bd. dirs. 1970-74), Deutsche Gesellschaft für Verdaungs und Stoffwechselkrankheiten (bd. dirs. 1972-78), S.W. German Soc. for Gastroenterology (pres. 1994), European Assn. for Study of Liver, European Soc. for Biomed. Rsch. on Alcoholism (bd. dirs.), Internat. Soc. for Biomed. Rsch. on Alcoholism. Avocation: hiking, painting. Office: Robert Bosch Hosp, Auerbachstrasse 110, D-70376 Stuttgart Germany

BODE, JUERGEN, biochemistry educator, researcher; b. Uelzen, Germany, Mar. 27, 1944; s. Otto Wilhelm and Magdalena (Liebrecht) B.; m. Verena Claassen, July 22, 1977. Abitur, Neue Oberschule, Braunschweig, Germany, 1963; diploma, Tech. U. Braunschweig, 1968, PhD in Organic Chemistry, 1971, habilitation in biochemistry, 1981. Postdoctoral Calif. Inst. Tech., Pasadena, 1971-74, U. Oreg., Eugene, 1974; scientist Gesellschaft für Biotechnologische Forschung, Braunschweig, 1974—; prof. Tech. U., Braunschweig, 1987; group leader Epigenetic Regulation, 1999—; guest lectr. Hebrew U., Jerusalem, 1993; participant German Human Genome Project; mem. Genomatix Adv. Bd., Munich, 1998—. Contbr. chpts to books and more than 80 articles to profl. jours.; editor Nuclear Magnet Resonance, 1974-85, Molecular Biology Reports, 1995—, Gene Therapy Molecular Biology, 1997—. Mem. German Chem. Soc., Soc. Biol. Chemistry, Internat. Soc. for Gene Therapy and Molecular Biology. Avocations: collecting antique cameras. Email: jbo@gbf.de. Office: GBF Ges f Biotech Forschung, Mascheroder Weg, D-38124 Braunschweig Germany

BODEMANN, H(EINZ) HARM, physician; b. Hamburg, Feb. 5, 1943; s. Heinz and Gerda O. (Koepke) B.; m. Eva Regina Birkenmaier, May 21, 1971; children: Gerit, Basil, Gwendolin, Clara. MD, U. Hamburg, Germany, 1969; privatdozent, U. Freiburg, Germany, 1977. Sci. asst. U. Saarland, 1969-70, Max Planck Inst. Biophysics, Frankfurt, Germany, 1970-71; postdoctoral fellow Yale U. Dept. Physiology, New Haven, Conn., 1971-73, Yale U. Dept. Hematology, New Haven, Conn., 1972-73; sci. resident Dept. Internal Medicine U. Freiburg, Germany, 1973-81, oberarzt, 1982-86; head, chief dept. internal medicine Stadtishces Krankenhaus Acad. Hosp. U. Tübingen, Sindelfingen, Germany, 1986—; med. dir. Staedt Krankenhaus, Sindelfingen, 1999—. Contbr. articles to profl. jours. Mem. Deutsche Gesellschaft fuer Innere Medizin, Deutsche Gesellschaft fuer Haematologie und Internistische Onkologie, Deutsche Krebsgesellschaft, European Soc. Med. Oncology, Rotary Internat. Deutschland. Avocations: cello, golf. Office: Staedtisches Krankenhaus, Arthur Gruber St 70, D-71065 Sindelfingen Germany Address: Stadtishces Krankenhaus, Postfach 445, D-71046 Sindelfingen Germany

BODEN, FERNARD, government official; b. Echternach, Luxembourg, Sept. 13, 1943; married; 2 children. PhD in Math. and Physics, U. Liege, Belgium. Tchr. Lycee Classique, Echternach, 1966-78; 1st dep. burgomaster Echternach, 1970-76; mem. Mcpl. Coun., Echternach, 1976-78, Chamber of Deps., 1978—; min. nat. edn., tourism and youth Govt. of Luxembourg, 1979-89, min. family and social affairs, 1989—, min. tourism, 1989—, min. mid. class affairs, 1989—, min. solidarity, min. status of somen and sr. citizens, 1994—, min. civil svc., 1994-95, min. agr., viticulture and rural devel., 1995—, min. housing, 1995—, min. environ. Office: Min Agr, Viticulture, 1 rue de la Congregation, L-2913 Luxembourg Luxembourg*

BODENCHAK, FRANK LESLIE, investment company executive; b. Short Hills, N.J.; s. Frank Joseph and Irene Diane (Ivanow) B. BA in Econs. cum laude, Williams Coll., 1991; M in Acctg., NYU, 1992, MBA, 1993. CPA, N.Y. Acct. Ernst, Young, N.Y.C., 1991-93; investment analyst Furman Selz, N.Y.C., 1993-96, Morgan Stanley, N.Y.C., 1996—. Recipient Number 1 Instnl. Investor rankings in broadcasting Greenwich Rsch. and Reuters, 1997, 98, 99. Office: Morgan Stanley 1585 Broadway Fl 15 New York NY 10036-8200

BODENHAM, MARTIN FRANCIS, sales executive; b. Lincoln, Eng., Nov. 8, 1947; s. John Kenneth and Gertrude Mary (Fieldhouse) B.; m. Joan Marsh; children: Michael, David, Richard. Capital projects engr. GKN, 1971-74, tech. supt., 1974-85; tech. mgr. GKN Bolts, 1985-90; tech. mgr. Armstrong Atlas, West Midlands, Eng., 1990-96, tech. dir., 1994-96; tech. dir. Armstrong Fastenings, West Midlands, 1996—. Fax: 0121 224 2071.

BODENHOEFER, HANS JOACHIM, economics educator; b. Stuttgart, Fed. Republic Germany, July 30, 1941; arrived in Austria, 1975; s. Doris V. Von Srebrnicki, Apr. 4, 1970; children: Constanze C., Ariane B. Diploma Volkswirt, U. Tubingen, Fed. Republic Germany, 1965; D in Econs., Tech. U. Berlin, 1968. Rsch. asst. Inst. F. Bildungsfo, Berlin, 1965-68; postdoctoral fellow U. Chgo., 1968-69; asst. prof. Tech. U. Berlin, 1970-75; prof. econs. U. Klagenfurt, Austria, 1975—; rector U. Klagenfurt, Austria, 1983-87. Office: U Klagenfurt, Universitaetsstr 65-67, 9022 Klagenfurt Austria

BODENMANN, REINHARD, church history scholar; b. Koza, Cameroun, Aug. 31, 1955; s. Albert and Katharina (Fleischer) B.; m. Joëlle Simon, Aug. 1, 1978 (div. an., 1994); children: Siegfried, Franck-Johann, Laurence, Chantal; m. Marianne Ray, Oct. 1, 1994. G.C.M. in Math., U. Nantes, France, 1974; degree in Theology, France, 1978; MA in Theology, Eng., 1979; PhD in Theology, Prot. Faculty U. Strasbourg, France, 1984. Rsch. asst. U. Geneva, Switzerland, 1982-85; instr. in theology and catechism Luth. Ch., Consistory of Brumath, Alsace, France, 1985-87; ind. scholar Strasbourg, France, 1987-91; co-editor Theodore Beza's Correspondence U. Geneva, Switzerland, 1991-98; ind. scholar Geneva, 1998—. Author: (books) The Birth of an Exegesis. The Book of Daniel in the Christian Church of the First Three Centuries, 1987, Critical Bibliography of François Lambert's publications, 1987; Correspondence of Theodore de Beze, 5 vols. 1993, 94, 95, 96, 98, A Biography of Wolfgang Musculus 1497-1563, 2000; contbr. articles to publications in field. Home: 11 rue Victor-Hugo, 74100 Ambilly France Office: Inst d'Histoire Reformation, Uni-Bastion, 1211 Geneva Switzerland

BODENSTEDT, ANDREAS, retired sociologist, educator; b. Hannover, Germany, Feb. 5, 1934; s. Heinrich and Agnes (Middelberg) B.; married, Apr. 28, 1959 (dec. May 1978); children: Andrea, Véronique, Rafaela, Natalie; m. Ute Wasmund, Sept. 26, 1980. Diploma in German philosophy, U. Hamburg, Germany, 1959; PhD, U. Muenster, Germany, 1967. Rsch. officer Rsch. Inst. Agrl. Devel., Heidelberg, 1967-71, dir., 1971-78; prof. rural sociology U. Giessen, Germany, 1971-99; ret., 1999. Mem. German Assn. Sci.

BODEREAU, XAVIER JACQUES, ophthamologist, surgeon; b. Le Mans, Sarthe, France, July 29, 1951; s. Pierre and Jeanne (Perrotel) B.; m. Frederique Mainette, June 21, 1986; children: Antoine, Maximilien, Eva. Baccacaureat, 1963, MD, 1982. Med. Diplomate Ophthamologic surgeon. Intern Ancille (France) Hosp., 1978-82, chief of clinic, 1983-86; asst. surgeon Ancille Hosp., 1983-86. Contbr. articles to profl. jours., 1982-83. Recipient Prix Chibret Soc. of Ophthamology. Avocations: golf, chasse, aviation. Home: 11 Rue du Chanoine, Lelievre Sarthe, Sarthe, 72000 Le Mans France

BODEWITZ, HENDRIK WILHELM, Sanskrit educator, university dean; b. Gramsbergen, The Netherlands, Oct. 13, 1939; s. Johan Adriaan and Jennigjen (Lenters) B.; m. Janneke van Uchelen, Oct. 24, 1964; children: Johan Adriaan, Wanda Alida. MA, U. Utrecht (The Netherlands), 1966, LittD, 1973. Sr. lectr. U. Leiden (The Netherlands), 1969-76; prof. Sanskrit, 1992—; lectr. U. Utrecht, 1966-68, prof. Sanskrit, 1976-92, dean faculty, 1980-82, 84-86. Author: Jaiminiya Brahmana I, 1-65, 1973, Daily evening and morning offering, 1976, The Jyotistoma Ritual, 1990, Light, Soul and Visions in the Veda, 1991; editor Indo-Iranian Jour., Gonda Indological Studies. Mem. Royal Netherlands Acad., Academia Europaea (founder). Home: Stolberglaan 29, 3583 XL Utrecht The Netherlands Office: Kern Inst Dept Indology, PO Box 9515, 2300 RA Leiden The Netherlands

BODHARAMIK, ADISAI, communications executive; b. Bangkok, Apr. 23, 1940; married. PhD in Elec. Engring., U. Md. With Ministry of Transport and Comms.; chief network plant design ctr. Telephone Orgn. of Thailand; chmn. Jasmine Internat. PLC, Bangkok, 1978—; advisor to several pub. utilities. Bd. govs. Engring. Inst. Thailand; mem. coun. Internat. U. Thailand; trustee Nat. Tech. U., Thailand; appt. senator by King Bhumibol Adulyadej; dep. party leader Chartpattana Polit. Party, 1999—; min. to Prime Min.'s Office in charge of Tourism Authority of Thailand, 2000. Named Outstanding Internat. Alumnus U. Md.; recipient Hall of Fame award U. Md. Alumni Assn., 2000. Fax: 662-502-3152. Office: Jasmine Intl Tower 29-30 Fl, 200 Moo 4 Chaengwatana Rd, Pakkred Nonthaburi 11120, Thailand

BÓDI, ALEXANDER CHARLES, physics educator; b. Szatmárnémeti, Szatmár, Romania, Dec. 25, 1925; arrived in Hungary, 1986; s. András Bódi and Etelka Irma Moldvai; m. Mária Tóth, Apr. 20, 1952; children: Enikö, Tibor. BSc, Hungarian H.S., Szatmárnémeti, 1948; MSc, Bolyai U., Kolozsvár, Romania, 1952; PhD in Physics, Babes-Bolyai U., Kolozsvár, 1964. Asst. prof. Bolyai U., 1951-56, adj. prof., 1956; adj. prof. Babes-Bolyai U., 1960-68, assoc. prof., 1968-70, prof., head electronics dept., 1971-75; prof. physics Kossuth U., Debrecen, Hungary, 1986-96, with Inst. Expt. Physics, 1996—; vis. prof. Nat. U. Kinshasa, Zaire, 1974-78. Editor: Elektronikai Alafogalmak, 1983, (with others) Fizikai Kislexikon, 1976, Electronica, 1983. Mem. Eotvös Loránt Fizikai Társulat. Avocations: watercolor painting, gardening, tennis. E-mail: acbodi@moon.atomki.hu. Home: Békessy Béla 10 IX/75, 4032 Debrecen Hungary Office: Kossuth U Inst Exptl Physics, Bem tér 18/A, PO Box 105, 4001 Debrecen Hungary

BODI, LESLIE, language educator; b. Budapest, Hungary, Sept. 1, 1922; arrived in Australia, 1957; s. Bruchsteiner Istvan and Klara (Pongracz) Wertheimer; m. Marianne Marton, June10, 1950; 1 child, Anna. Dr. phil., U. Budapest, 1948, Diploma in Edn., 1949; Hon.D.Litt., Monash U., 1990; Dr. honoris cause, ELTE, Budapest. Tutor, lectr. dept. German U. Budapest, 1946-57; tchr. grammar sch. Melbourne, Australia, 1957-58; lectr. in German Newcastle (New South Wales, Australia) U. Coll., 1958-60; sr. lectr. in German Monash U., Clayton, Victoria, Australia, 1961-63, prof., chmn. dept., 1963-87, prof. emeritus and rsch. asst., 1988—; vis. prof. Vienna, Graz, ELTE and CEU Budapest; vis. fellow IFK Vienna, 1994; Humboldt fellow Berlin, 1999. Author: Heinrich Heine, 1951, Tauwetter in Wien, 1977, enlarged edit., 1995; co-author: Image of a Continent, 1990; editor: P. Weidmann: Der Eroberer, 1997; co-editor: Das Problem Osterreich, 1982, The German Connection, 1985; contbr. numerous articles to scholarly jours. Recipient Officer's Cross, Order of Merit, Fed. Republic Germany, 1973, Order for Art and Lit., Republic of Austria, 1976, Goethe medal Goethe Inst., 1991, Humboldt Rsch. award, 1997; Festschrift published in his honor Antipodean Enlightenments, 1987, Friedrich-Gundolf-Prize for German studies abroad Acad. of German Lang. and Lit., 1989. Fellow Hungarian Acad. Scis.; mem. Internat. Assn. Germanists, Australian Langs. and Lit. Assn., Heinrich Heine Soc., 18th Century Austrian History Soc., PEN, Inst. Erforschg. österr.u.internat.Lit.prozese, Öst.Ges. für Germanistik. Home: 25 Beddoe Ave, Clayton, Victoria 3168, Australia Office: Monash U Dept German, Clayton, Victoria 3168, Australia

BODIFORD, VINCENT W., newspaper publisher, automotive journalist; b. Dallas, Sept. 4, 1962; s. Jack Warren and Barbara Jane (Mavilia) B.; m. Jeanette Marie Sanders Bodiford, July 31, 1993; children: Monique Elizabeth, Alexander Justin. BBA, Columbus U., Metairie, La., 1988, MBA, 1999. Editor, pub. Bodiford Newspaper Co., LaFeria, Tex., 1993-96; pres., pub. Golden (Colo.) Media, Inc., 1996-98, Jeffco Pub. Co., Golden, Colo., 1998, Sidney (Nebr.) Daily Sun, 1998—; conv. spkr. Colo. Press Assn., Denver, 1998. Author: At the Wheel, 1993-98, The Weekend Drive, 1998—(Weekly syndicated auto. columns), Air Force One, 1999. Mem. Safari Club Internat., Ducks Unltd., Denver. Recipient John A Heselden Fellowship, Am. Press Inst. Reston, Va., 1998. Mem. AP, Nat. Newspaper Assn., Nebr. Press Assn., Automotive Press Assn., Denver Press Club, Needles Masonic Lodge # 326 F&AM, Motor Press Guild, Colo. Press Assn. (chmn. Diversity Com), 1997-98, Rocky Mountain Auto. Press (pres. 1997-99). Republican. Methodist-Episcopalian. Avocations: motorsports, aviation, travel, big game hunting and safari. E-mail: publisher@sidneysun.com. Home: PO Box 426 Sidney NE 69162-0426 Office: Sidney Daily Sun 817 12th Ave Sidney NE 69162-1625

BODIN, LARS-GUNNAR, composer; b. Stockholm, Sweden, July 15, 1935; s. Gunnar Fredrik and Anna Margareta (Sandberg) B.; m. Margareta Hervor Bäckström, Apr. 6, 1957; children: Charlotta, Axel. Grad., Katarina Real, Stockholm, 1952. Chmn. Fylkingen, Stockholm, 1969-72; prof. State Coll. Music, Stockholm, 1972-76; dir. EMS, Stockholm, 1977-89; jury mem. GMEB, Bourges, France, 1978-95, ARS Electronica, Linz, Austria, 1993-95. Compositions include Compositional Output, 1960 (The Rosenberg prize 1984), Clouds, 1976 (Stockholm Artist award 1986), Best Wishes Fro the Lilac Grove, 1994 (Magisterium prize 1996). Recipient State Income Guarantee for Artists award Swedish Govt., 1988. Mem. Royal Acad. Music, Internat. Confederation Electro-Acoustic Music (founder). Avocations: old house renovation, traveling, mushroom picking, strolling in the woods. Home: Helgalunden 17, S-11858 Stockholm Sweden Office: Semicolon: HB, Svalörtsvägen 21, S-64691 Gnesta Sweden

BODIN, MANFRED, banker; b. Münster, Germany, Nov. 14, 1939; married. Dr honoris causa. With Stadtsparkasse, Münster, Germany, 1960-64,

Witten, Germany, 1964-70; mem. mgmt. bd. Kreissparkasse, Recklinghausen, Germany, 1970-75; chmn. mgmt. bd. Kreissparkasse, Recklinghausen, 1976-83, Sparkasse Essen, 1984-91, Norddeutsche Landesbank, Girozentrale, Germany, 1991—. Office: Norddeutsche Landesbank, Georgsplatz 1, 30159 Hannover Germany

BODINSON, HOLT, conservationist; b. East Orange, N.J., Nov. 14, 1941; s. Earl Herdien and Hermoine (Holt) B. BA, Harvard, 1963; m. Ilse Marie Maier, Feb. 29, 1970. Sr. asso. Am. Conservation Assn., Inc., N.Y.C., 1966-70; dir. Office of Policy Analysis, N.Y. State Dept. Environ. Conservation, Albany, 1970-71, dir. div. ednl. services, 1971-77; dir. Ariz.-Sonora Desert Mus., 1977-78; exec. dir. Safari Club Internat./Safari Club Internat. Conservation Fund, Tucson, 1980-89; conservation dir. Safari Club Internat., Tucson, 1991-94, dir. wildlife and govtl. affairs, 1994-96; committeeman, Montgomery Twp. Conservation Commn., 1967-70; sec. N.Am. del. Conseil Internat. de la Chasse et de la Conservation du Gibier, 1988—; gen. sec. World Hunting and Conservation Congress, 1988; dir. Internat. Wildlife Mus., 1991-96; nat. sec. United Conservation Alliance, 1994-96. Served with arty. AUS, 1964-66. Mem. Stony Brook-Millstone Watershed Assn. (dir.), Safari Club Internat. (dir. Ariz. chpt.), N.Y. Outdoor Edn. Assn. (dir.), Outdoor Writers Assn. of Am., N.Y. State Rifle and Pistol Assn. (dir.). Episcopalian. Club: Harvard of So. Ariz. (pres.). Author: (with Clepper and others) Leaders in American Conservation, 1971. Contbg. editor Jour. Environmental Edn., 1968-94; dir. Conservationist mag. 1971-77, N.Y. State Environment newspaper, 1971-74. Home: 4525 N Hacienda Del Sol Tucson AZ 85718-6619 Office: 5683 N Swan Rd Tucson AZ 85718-4565

BODIS, JOZSEF FERENC, obstetrician/gynecologist; b. Csurgo, Hungary, July 12, 1953; s. Jozsef and Rozsa (Varga) B.; m. Katalin Zambo, May 7, 1977; children: Viktoria, Richard. MD, U. Med. Sch., Pécs, Hungary, 1977; D of OB-Gyn., U. Med. Sch., Budapest, Hungary, 1981; PhD, Hungarian Acad. Scis., Budapest, Hungary, 1989, DSc, 1999. Resident U. MEd. Sch., Budapest, Hungary, 1977-81, deputy, 1981-87, cons., 1987-91; dozent U. Womens Hosp., Tubingen, Germany, 1991-92; assoc. prof. U. Med. Sch., 1994-95; head dept. ob-gyn. County Teaching Hosp., Pécs, 1995—; cons. in field. Contbr. articles to profl. jours. Mem. Civic Club, Hunary, 1992—. Capt. Hungarian Army, 1978-79. Mem. Hungarian Assn. Gynecologic Endoscopy (gen. sec.), European Soc. Human Reproduction Embryology, European Assn. Ob-Gyn. Roman Catholic. Avocations: table tennis, tennis, swimming, art collecting, ballroon dancing. Home: Kurt, H-7624 Pécs Hungary Office: Dept Ob-gyn, Dischka Gy U 7, H-7621 Pécs Hungary

BODIS, STEPHAN B., radiation oncologist, educator, researcher; b. Basel, Switzerland, Feb. 16, 1958; s. Istvan and Ruth (Kipfer) B.; m. Mirjam Christeler, Sept. 30, 1989; 4 children . BS, U. Baden, Switzerland, 1978; MD, U. Basel, 1985. Lic. cert. profl. physician, Switzerland; diplomate Am. Bd. Radiation Oncology, Swiss Bd. Radiation Oncology. Resident physician Dist. Hosp., Baden, 1985-87, Univ. Hosp., Zurich, 1987-89; clin. fellow, rsch. fellow Inst. Gustave Roussy, Villejuif/Paris, 1989-91; resident, rsch. fellow Harvard Med. Sch. Joint Ctr. Radiation Therapy, Boston, 1991-95; attending physician Joint Ctr. for Radiation Therapy, Boston, 1995; head rsch. lab., dept. radiation oncology U. Zurich, 1995-99, assoc. physician, 2000—, asst. prof., 1999—. Contbr. articles to med. jours., including Jour. Clin. Oncology, Blood, Cancer. Grantee Swiss NIH, 1997, Swiss Cancer League, 1995, 99. Mem. Swiss Soc. Sci. Radiation Oncology (sec. 1997), Am. Soc. Therapeutic Radiation Oncology (bd. dirs.), European Soc. Therapeutic Radiation Oncology (mem. radiobiology com. 1999—, mem. internet com. 1999—), European Soc. Med. Oncology. Avocations: family, classical music, Elton John, Disney, travel. Office: Radiation Oncology, Ramistrasse 100, 8091 Zurich Switzerland

BODIZS, ARPAD KALMAN, chemical engineer; b. Brasov, Romania, Mar. 29, 1970; s. Kalman Bodizs and Rita Rohay. Grad., Indsl. H.S. Marghita, Romania, 1988; MSc, U. Babes-Bolyai, Cluj-Napoca, Romania, 1994; PhD, U. Veszprem, Hungary, 1997. Cert. in chem. engring., specialization in organic chem. techs. Chem. engr. dept. chem. engring. cybernetics U. Veszprem, 1997-98; software engr. SoftControl Ltd., Budapest, 1998-99; patent atty. asst. S.B.G.&K. Patent and Law Offices, Budapest, 1999—; cons. MSc theses dept. chem. engring. cybernetics U. Veszprem, 1994-95. Contbr. sci. articles to jours. chem. process control. Master-sgt. Mil. Unit Slobozia, 1988-89. Calvinist. Avocations: tennis, swimming, film aesthetics. Fax: 36 1 3428194. E-mail: mailbox@sbgk.hu. Office: SBG&K Patent and Law Office, Andrassy St # 113, 1062 Budapest Hungary

BODKIN, LAWRENCE EDWARD, research development company executive, gemologist, inventor; b. Sapulpa, Okla., May 17, 1927; s. Clarence Elsworth and Lillie (Moore) B.; m. Ruby Emma Pate, Jan. 15, 1949; children: Karen Bodkin Snead, Cinda, Lawrence Jr. Student, Fla. State U., 1947-50; grad., Gemological Inst., 1969. Chief announcer, program dir., mgr. various radio stations, Winter Haven, Fla., Tallahassee and Jacksonville, Fla., 1947-60; ind. jewelry salesman and appraiser Underwood Jewelers, 1961-87; pres. Bodkin Jewelers and Appraisers, Jacksonville, 1984—, Telanon, Jacksonville, 1981—, Bodkin Co., Jacksonville, 1974—; chmn., chief exec. officer Bodkin Corp., Jacksonville, 1975—; dir. elec. safety R&D in U.S. and Orient Innovative Designer Products Div. Brooke Shields Beauty Care, Kendall Park, N.J., 1989-92; cons. gem and mineral groups, Jacksonville, 1960—, numerous corps. and industries (on inventions); lectr. in field. Author: Dual Imagery of Ultra Speed Bodies, 1971, Miniatures, 1976, Bodkin's Revised Law of Buoyancy, 2000; contbr. articles to sci. publs.; inventor Universal-Fault Circuit-Interrupter (Bodkin Circuit), TIP (tested immersion protection), Auto Test and Reset GFCI (ground fault cir. interrupter), Bodkin Jewelry Clasp, Height Measure, others. Mem. Jacksonville Mus. Sci. and Hist., 1981—, Jacksonville Symphony Assn., 1985—, Cummer Gallery Art, Jacksonville, 1985—, Ye Mystic Revellers, 1997—. Served with U.S. Army, 1945-47, ETO. Mem. Fla. State U. Alumni Assn., Mensa Internat., San Jose Country Club. Avocations: fossil collecting, beach combing, philosophy, writing, theoretical physics. Home: 1149 Molokai Rd Jacksonville FL 32216-3273 Office: CJR Co 8381 Dix Ellis Trl Ste 103 Jacksonville FL 32256-8295 also: PO Box 16482 Jacksonville FL 32245-6482

BODKIN, RUBY PATE, corporate executive, real estate broker, educator; b. Frostproof, Fla., Mar. 11, 1926; d. James Henry and Lucy Beatrice (Latham) P.; m. Lawrence Edward Bodkin Sr., Jan. 15, 1949; children: Karen Bodkin Snead, Cinda, Lawrence Jr. BA, Fla. State U., 1948; MA, U. Fla., 1972. Lic. real estate broker. Banker Barnett Bank, Avon Park, Fla., 1943-44, Lewis State Bank, Tallahassee, 1944-49; ins. underwriter Hunt Ins. Agy., Tallahassee, 1949-51; tchr. Duval County Sch. Bd., Jacksonville, Fla., 1952-77; pvt. practice realty Jacksonville, 1976—; tchr. Nassau County Sch. Bd., Jacksonville, 1978-83; sec., treas., v.p. Bodkin Corp., R&D/Inventions, Jacksonville, 1983—; assoc. Brooke Shields Innovative Designer Products, Inc., Kendall Park, N.J., 1988-92. Author: 100 Teacher Chosen Recipes, 1976, Bodkin Bridge Course for Beginners, 1996, Class Conscious, 1999, (autobiography) Grandma Bodkin, 2000; published poet. Mem. Jacksonville Symphony Guild, 1985—; mem. Southside Bapt. Ch. Recipient 25 Yr. Svc. award Duval County Sch. Bd., 1976, Tchr. of Yr. award Bryceville Sch., 1981, Edn., Volunteerism, Employment award finalist, 1974. Mem. Am. Contract Bridge League, Nat. Realtors Assn., Southside Jr. Woman's Club, Garden Club Sweetbriar (bd. dirs.), Riverside Woman's Club Jacksonville (bd. dirs. 1991-92), UDC (Martha Reid chpt. #19), Fla. Edn. Assn. (pers. problems com. 1958), Duval County Classrooms Tchrs. (v.p. membership 1957), Woman's Club Jacksonville Bridge Group, Fla. Ret. Tchrs. Assn., Fla. Realtors Assn., N.E. Fla. Realtors Assn., Jacksonville Geneal. Soc. (practicing genealogist, family historian 1986—), Friday Musicale of Jacksonville, San Jose Golf Country Club, Jacksonville Sch. Bridge. Baptist. Avocations: reading, writing, genealogy, photography, club bridge, walking, travel. Home: 1149 Molokai Rd Jacksonville FL 32216-3273 Office: Bodkin Jewelers & Appraisers PO Box 16482 Jacksonville FL 32245-6482

BODLEY, HARLEY RYAN, JR., editor, writer, broadcaster; b. Dover, Del., Nov. 24, 1936; s. Harley Ryan and Mildred Olivia (Carver) B.; m. Patricia Jean Hall, Dec. 4, 1981. B.A., U. Del., 1959; postgrad., Am. U., 1960. Sports editor Del. State News, Dover, 1959-60; sports dir. Radio WDOV, Dover, 1958-62; sports writer News-Jour. Papers, Wilmington, Del., 1960-63; night sports editor News-Jour. Papers, 1963-67, asst. sports editor, 1967-71, sports editor, 1971-82; baseball editor USA Today, Washington, 1982—; discussion leader Am. Press Inst., Reston, Va., 1967-76; TV host Sta. WHYY-TV, Wilmington, 1967-74; columnist The Sporting News, St. Louis, 1978-83; commentator NBC-TV, Baseball: An Inside Look, 1987, USA Today: The TV Show, 1988-89; USA Today Radio Report, 1987-89; baseball analyst CNN, 1989—; commentator and host Baseball Sunday, United Syndications Radio Network, 1988-90; commentator CBS Radio Network baseball pre-game, 1990—, Comcast Sports Net, 2000—. Author: I Learned To Fly, So Can You, 1967; The Team That Wouldn't Die, 1981, Countdown to Cobb, 1985; writer Best Sports Stories, 1967-71, 1977-79, 1982, 1985. Flight safety counselor FAA, Phila., 1968-72. Served as sgt. U.S. Army N.G. 1956-64. Named Sportswriter of Yr., Nat. Sportscasters and Sportswriters Assn., 1961, 63, 65, 67-70, 73-75, 78-79; recipient Best of Gannett award Gannett Co., Inc., 1981, Mark Twain award AP, 1980, 25th Year award Baseball Commr., 1983, USA Today All-Star award, 2000. Mem. AP Sports Editors (pres. 1981-82, Best Sports Story award 1981, 1st place award 1982), Baseball Writers Assn. Am. (Phila. chpt. chmn. 1977-78), Wilmington Sportswriters and Broadcasters (pres. 1963 sec-treas. 1965-83), Sigma Delta Chi (Top Sports award 1982). Episcopalian. Clubs: Wilmington Country; Northeast Yacht. Avocations: golf; pilot; boating. Office: USA Today 1000 Wilson Blvd Ste 600 Arlington VA 22209-3905 also: care Athletes & Artists 421 7th Ave New York NY 10001-2002

BODMANN, HANS WALTER, education educator; b. Siedenburg, Niedersach, Germany, July 1, 1928; s. Alois and Alwine (Harms) B. Diploma in Physics, U. Kiel, Germany, 1955, Dr.rer.nat., 1955. Scientific asst. U. Cologne, Germany, 1955; scientific staff mem. Philips, Hamburg, 1956-61, head of light rsch. lab., 1961-63; head of light rsch. lab. Philips, Aachen, Germany, 1964-67; prof. U. Karlsruhe, Germany, 1967-93, dir. Lighting Inst., 1967-93; pres. Internat. Commn. on Illumination CIE, 1987-91, DIN-FNF, 1968-74. Editor: Aspekte der Informationsverarbeitung, 1985; contbr. articles to profl. jours. Dr. Honoris Causa U. Tucuman, Argentina, 1992, U. for Constrn., Bucharest, 1994. Mem. German Lighting Engr. Soc. (hon. mem., pres. 1973-74). Office: Lichttechnisches Inst, Kaiserstr 12, D-76131 Karlsruhe Germany

BODMER, WALTER FRED, cancer research administrator; b. Frankfurt-am-Main, Germany, Jan. 10, 1936; s. Ernest Julius and Sylvia Emily B.; m. Julia Gwynaeth Pilkington, Aug. 11, 1956; children: Mark William, Helen Clare, Charles Walter. BA, U. Cambridge, Eng., 1956, PHD, 1959; laurea honoris causa, U. Bologna, Italy, 1987; DSc (hon.), U. Oxford, 1988, U. Bath, Eng., 1988, U. Edinburgh, 1990, U. Surrey, 1990; Hon DSc, U. Hull, 1990; DSc (hon.), U. Bristol, 1991; Dr. honoris causa, U. Leuven, 1992; LLD (hon.), U. Dundee, 1993; DSc (hon.), U. Loughborough, 1993, U. Lancaster, 1994, U. Aberdeen, 1994; Dr. honoris causa, Masaryk U., Brno., 1994; DSc (hon.), U. London, 1996; Dr. honoris causa, U. Salford, 1996, U. UMIST, 1997, U. Haifa, 1998; DSc (hon.), U. Witwatersrand, Johannesburg, 1998. Rsch. fellow Clare Coll., U. Cambridge, Eng., 1958-60; fellow Clare Coll., U. Cambridge, 1961; demonstrator Dept. of Genetics, U. Cambridge, 1960-61; vis. asst. prof. to prof. Dept. of Genetics Stanford U. Sch. of Medicine, Palo Alto, Calif., 1961-70; prof. Dept. Genetics U. Oxford, Eng., 1970-79; dir. rsch. Imperial Cancer Rsch. Fund, London, 1979-91, dir. gen., 1991-96; prin. Hertford Coll., Oxford, 1996—; head ICRF cancer, immunogenetics IMM, Oxford, 1996—; hon. fellow Keble Coll., Oxford, 1981, Clare Coll., Cambridge, 1989; pres. Orgn. European Cancer Insts., 1990-93, v.p. the Parliamentary and Sci. Com., 1990-93; hon. v.p. Rsch. Defence Soc., 1990—; 1st pres. Internat. Fedn. of Assns. for Advancement of Sci. and Tech., 1992-94; pres. European Assn. for Cancer Rsch., 1994-96; chancellor Univ. Salford, 1995—; vis. prof. UMDS, 1996—; chmn. Nat. Radiol. Protection Bd., 1998—; chmn. bd. dirs. Laban Ctr., London, 1999. Co-author (with others) The Genetics of Human Populations, 1971, Our Future Inheritance - Choice or Chance?, 1974, Genetics Evolution and Man, 1976, The Book of Man, 1994; contbr. numerous articles to profl. jours. Recipient the William Allen Meml. award, Am. Soc. Human Genetics, 1980, The Conway Evans prize Royal Coll. of Physicians, 1982, Rabbi Shai Shacknai Meml. lectureship in immunology and cancer rsch., 1983; John Alexander Meml. prize and lectureship, U. Pa. Med. Sch., 1984, Rose Payne Disting. Scientist lectureship, Am. Soc. for Histocompatability and Immunogenetics, 1985, Ellison Cliffe lecture and medal, Royal Soc. Medicine, 1987, The Michael Faraday award, 1994; named Knight Batchelor, 1986, hon. fellow Green Coll., Oxford U., 1993,. Fellow Royal Soc., Royal Coll. of Pathologists, Royal Coll. of Surgeons (hon.), Royal Coll. Physicians (hon.), Royal Soc. Medicine (hon.), Internat. Inst. Biotech.; mem. Acad. Europea, Assn. for Sci. Edn. (pres. 1989-90), Brit. Assn. for the Advancement of Sci. (pres. 1987-88, v.p. 1989—, chmn. coun. 1996—), Brit Soc. for Histocompatibility and Immunogenetics (pres. 1990-91), Am. Acad. Arts and Scis. (fgn. hon. mem.), U.S. Nat. Acad. Sci. (assoc.), Am. Assn. Immunologists, Am. Philos. Soc. (fgn. mem.), Human Genome Orgn. (pres. 1990-92), Brit. Assn. Cancer Rsch. (pres. 1998—). Home and Office: Hertford Coll, Catte St, Oxford OX1 3BW, England

BODNAR, PETER O., lawyer; b. Queens, N.Y., Mar. 19, 1945; s. John and Edith (Schultz) B. BA in Govt., NYU, 1966; JD, Fordham U., 1970. Bar: N.Y. 1971, U.S. Dist. Ct. (so. dist.) N.Y. 1973. Confidential law sec. to Hon. Evans V. Brewster Family Ct. and County Ct. Westchester County, N.Y., 1970-73; pvt. practice White Plains, N.Y., 1973-77; ptnr. Bodnar & Greene, P.C., White Plains, N.Y., 1977-80, Bender & Bodnar, White Plains, N.Y., 1980-98; prin. Law Offices of Peter O. Bodnar, White Plains, N.Y., 1998—, Bodnar, Bradley & Milone LLP, White Plains, N.Y., 1999—; pres., CEO P.A.J. Am. Ltd./The Olo Corp., 1990-97, CEO Organica, USA, Inc., 1998—. Trustee Village of Ossining, N.Y., 1975-77. Fellow Am. Acad. Matrimonial Lawyers; mem. ABA (family law sect.), N.Y. State Bar Assn. (family law sect., exec. com. 2000—), Westchester County Bar Assn. (family law sect., exec. com. 1992—, chair 2000—). Office: 140 Grand St White Plains NY 10601-4831

BODNER, BRUCE IRA, ophthalmologist; b. Norfolk, Va., Nov. 5, 1945; s. Herman Bodner and Freda Glazier; m. Joanne Berson, Mar. 5, 1983; 1 child, Holly Michelle. BA in Biology, Va. Mil. Inst., 1967; MD, U. Va., 1971. Diplomate Am. Bd. Ophthalmology. Intern U. Mich. Hosp., Ann Arbor, 1971-72; resident in ophthalmology Emory U. Sch. of Medicine, Grady Meml. Hosp., others, Atlanta, 1975-78; chief resident in ophthalmology Emory U. Sch. of Medicine, Grady Meml. Hosp., Atlanta, 1977-78; various ednl. and staff positions to dir. Cornea and Contact Lens Clinic Sentara Hosps., 1980—; asst. to assoc. prof. dept. ophthalmology Ea. Va. Med. Sch., 1980—; founder, med. dir. Lions Med. Eye Bank and Rsch. Ctr. of Ea. Va., 1979—; commr. Joint Commn. of Allied Health Pers. in Ophthalmology, 1990-97; adv. bd. Contact Lens Coun., Washington, 1992-98; bd. councillors Am. Acad. Ophthalmology, 1993-95; founder, med. dir. Lions Med. Eye Bank & Rsch. Ctr. Ea. Va., Inc., 1979—; med. dir. Laser Optic Ctr. Norfolk, Va., 1996—; presenter in field. Contbr. articles to profl. jours. Named in Best Doctors in Am., S.E. region, 1996-97, nat. listing, 1998-99; Norfolk Found. scholar U. Va., 1967-71; Cornea & External Disease fellow Emory U. Sch. Medicine, Atlanta, 1978-79, Melvin Jones fellow, Lions, 1989. Fellow Am. Acad. Ophthalmology; mem. Am. Assn. Ophthalmology, Contact Lens Assn of Ophthalmologists (dir. 1992-97), Eye Bank Assn. of Am. Castroviejo Soc., Internat. Soc. Keratorefractive Surgery, Ocular Immunology and Microbiology Study Group, Am. Soc. Cataract and Refractive Surgery, Tidewater Ophthalmology and Otolaryngology Soc., Va. Soc. Medicine, Norfolk Acad. of Medicine, Va. Ophthalmology and Otolaryngology Soc., AMA (Physicians Recongition awards 1978, 91, 90, 93), Alpha Omega Alpha. Republican. Avocations: computers, investment tech. analysis, gardening.

BODNER, GEORGE MICHAEL, chemistry and education educator; b. Rochester, N.Y., Mar. 8, 1946; s. Max W. and Bess L. Bodner; m. Connie Cox, June 10, 1973 (div. July 1989). BS, SUNY, Buffalo, 1969; PhD, Ind. U., 1972. Vis. prof. U. Ill., Champaign-Urbana, 1972-75; mem. faculty Stephens Coll., Columbia, Mo., 1975-77, Purdue U., West Lafeyette, Ind., 1977—. Author: (textbook with Pardue) Chemistry, 2d edit., 1995, (with Spencer and Rickand) Chemistry: Structure and Dynamics, 1998. Recipient Catalyst award Chem. Mfrs. Assn., 1989. Avocation: motorcycling. E-mail: gmbodner@purdue.edu. Home: 220 Hartman Ct West Lafayette IN 47906-1626 Office: Purdue U 1393 Brown Bldg West Lafayette IN 47907

BODOKY, TAMÁS JÁNOS, geophysicist, researcher; b. Budapest, Hungary, July 2, 1941; s. Richard Felix and Agnes (Zombory) B.; m. Annamaria Krause, Mar. 30, 1970; children: Tamás Richard, Gergely Mark. MSc in Physics, Eötvös Lorand U., Budapest, 1964; candidate for tech. scis., Hungarian Scientific Acad., Budapest, 1974; doctor rerum naturalium, Eötvös Lorand U., 1974. Party chief in field exploration Eötvös Lorand Geophys. Inst., 1964-70; sr. rschr., head geophys. interpretation Eötvös Lorand Geophys. Inst., Budapest, 1971-80, sr. rschr., head rsch. in-mine seismic techniques, 1981-89, mgr., head divsn. seismics and computer tech., 1990-93, dir., 1994—. Co-author: (textbook) New Methods in Applied Geophysics, 1982; contbr. over 50 articles to profl. jours., including Magyar Geofizika, Annales Universitas Scientiarium Budapestiensis, Geophys. Prospecting, others. Chmn. presbyterium Presbyn. Ch., Leányfalu, Hungary, 1988—. Recipient Outstanding Svc. award Ctrl. Bur. Geology, Budapest, 1969, Hungarian State Dept. Industry, 1980, Pro Facultate Rerum Metallicarum award Univ. Miskolc, 1999, Borbá award Hungarian State Dept. of Economy, 2000. Mem. Assn. Hungarian Geophysicists (pres. 1990-91, editor-in-chief 1992—, Renner Janos award 1989, Best Paper award 1986), European Assn. Exploration Geophysicists (coun. mem. 1991-92, v.p. 1993, pres. 1994), European Assn. Geoscientists and Engrs. (chmn. geophys. divsn. 1995), Soc. Exploration Geophysicists, Hungarian Geol. Soc., Romanian Soc. Geophysics (Diploma Jubilara 1995). Presbyterian. Avocations: painting, music, water sports, excursions. Home: Moricz Zsigmond ut 90, H-2016 Leanyfalu Hungary Office: Eotvos Lorand Geophys Inst, Kolumbusz utca 17-23, H-1145 Budapest Hungary

BODOR, GÉZA, chemistry educator, researcher; b. Rakosliget, Hungary, July 21, 1930; s. Ferenc and Irén (Hummel) B.; m. Maria Müller, Mar. 9, 1968. Diploma in chem. engring., Tech. U. Budapest, Hungary, 1952, Candidate Chem. Sci., 1958, D Chem. Sci., 1969. Asst. sci. co-worker Polymer Rsch. Inst., Budapest, 1952-57, sci. co-worker, 1957-59, sr. sci. co-worker, 1959-61, head sci. dept., 1961-81, head sci. sect., 1981-92; prof. part-time Tech. U. Budapest, 1973-92, rsch. prof., 1993—. Author: Structural Investigations of Polymers, 1993 (award for high level); head editl. bd. Plastics and Rubber, 1989—. Fellow Ford Found., 1964-65. Home: Sárköz u 3/c, H-1142 Budapest Hungary Office: Tech U Budapest Polymer Tec, Müegyetem rkp 9, H-1111 Budapest Hungary

BODRATO, GUIDO, Italian government official; b. Montaldo Roero, Cuneo, Italy, Mar. 27, 1933. Degree in law. Econs. researcher IRES, Turin; mem. town coun. Turin; M.P. Chamber of Deps., 1968—, mem. budget and programming com. for state shares, 1980-82; min. Ministry of State Edn., Rome, 1982-83, Ministry of State Shares, Rome, 1983, Ministry of Industry, Rome, 1988—; mem. European Parliament, Brussels, Belgium. Office: Via Roaschia 133, I-10023 Chieri (TO) Italy*

BODYCOMB, JOHN FRANCIS, minister, consultant, theologian, sociologist; b. Melbourne, Victoria, Australia, Aug. 12, 1931; s. John Rhys and Annie Mayne (Francis) B.; m. Mavis Marjorie Forward, Dec. 15, 1956; children David Rhys, Janet Lynne, Robyn Jean, Helen Ruth. Lic. in Theology, Melbourne Coll. Divinity, Australia, 1956, Diploma in Religious Edn., 1957, ThD, 1983; MST, Boston U., 1969. Ordained to ministry, 1957. Pastor City Congl. Ch., Geelong, Australia, 1957-61; dir. christian edn. Congl. Union of South Australia, 1961-67; pastor First Congl. Ch., Kensington, N.H., 1967-69, Elizabeth United Parish, Australia, 1970-76; dean Uniting Ch. Theol. Sem., Melbourne, Australia, 1977-86; freelance preacher, tchr. Australia, New Zealand, 1987-88; chaplain U. Melbourne, Australia, 1989-97. Author: A Matter of Death and Life, 1986, The Prayer That Could Change the World, 1989, The Teaching That Could Change the World, 1991, The One With Many Names, 1993. Exec. mem. World Conf. on Religion and Peace, Australia, Victorian Coun. of Chs.; found. mem. Action Group for Religious Liberty; mem. Coun. of Christians and Jews. Recipient Order of Australia medal Fed. Govt. Australia, Canberra, 1997; fellow Australian Coll. Edn., Canberra, 1996. Mem. Assn. Religion and Intellectual Life, Assn. for the Sociology Religion, Australian Assn. for Study Religions, Australia-New Zealand Soc. for Theol. Studies, Australian Coll. Edn., Australian Sociol. Assn., Soc. for Sci. Study Religion, N.Y. Acad. Scis., Religious Rsch. Assn., Order Australia Assn., Royal Victorian Hist. Soc., U. Melbourne Staff Club. Mem. Uniting Ch. Australia. Avocations: opera, sports, outdoors, camping. E-mail: bodycomb@netspace.net.au.

BOE, MYRON TIMOTHY, lawyer; b. New Orleans, Oct. 30, 1948; s. Myron Roger and Elaine (Tracy) B. BA, U. Ark., 1970, JD, 1973; LLM in Labor, So. Methodist U., 1976. Bar: Ark. 1974, Tenn. 1977, U.S. Ct. Appeals (4th, 5th, 6th, 7th, 8th, 9th, 10th, 11th cirs.) 1978, U.S. Supreme Ct. 1978. City atty. City of Pine Bluff, Ark., 1974-75; sec.-treas. Ark. City Atty. Assn., 1975; sr. ptnr. Rose Law Firm, Little Rock, 1980—. Author: Handling the Title VII Case Practical Tips for the Employer, 1980. Served to 2d lt. USAR, 1972-73. Recipient Florentino-Ramirez Internat. Law award, 1975. Fellow Coll. Labor and Employment Lawyers, Inc., Ark. Bar Found., Ark. Bd. Legal Specialization (sec. 1982-85, chmn. 1985-89, labor, employment discrimination, civil rights).; mem. ABA (labor sect. 1974—, employment law com. 1974—), Ark. Bar Assn. (sec., chmn. labor sect. 1978-81, ho. of dels. 1979-82, Golden Gavel award 1983), Def. Rsch. Inst. (employment law com. 1982—), Am. Employment Law Coun. (charter), Ark. Assn. Def. Counsel. Office: Rose Law Firm 120 E 4th St Little Rock AR 72201-2893*

BOECK, HARALD CHRISTIAN ANANDO VON HAMM, cement company executive, consultant; b. Ringkoebing, Jutlandia, Denmark, 1925; s. Philip Lewin von Beck Boeck and Eva Sophie Constantia von Hamm; m. Ellen Marie Lassen, Apr. 2, 1953 (div. Aug. 1984); children: Eva Margot von Hamm, Henrik von Hamm; m. Remedios Dueno Sanico, Mar. 1, 1985; 1 child, Philip Christian von Hamm Sanico. Mech. Engr., Copenhagen Higher Tech. Inst. Engring., 1955. Engr. supervision and commissioning F.L. Smidth & Co. Ltd., Denmark, 1955-70; chief engr. Hasle Klinker & Chamottestensfabrik Ltd., Denmark, 1970-71; cement cons. U.N. Indsl. Devel. Orgn., Vienna, Austria, World Bank, Washington, Internat. Fin. Corp., Washington, Inter-Am. Devel. Bank, Washington, Asian Devel. Bank, Metro Manilla, Philippines, Arab Funds Econ. and Social Devel., Kuwait, 1971-83; mng. dir., chief exec. Benue Cement Co., Nigeria, 1983-86. 1st lt. Arty, 1953-58. Fellow Internat. Biog. Assn. (life). Conservative. Avocations: do-it-yourself activities, gardening, travel. E-mail: hcboeck@info.com.ph. Home and Office: 2215 F Zobel St, San Miguel Village, Makati City 1208, The Philippines

BOEDEKER, DANIEL ARTHUR, retired contractor; b. Sheboygan, Wis., Mar. 2, 1924; s. Arthur C. and Norma E. B.; m, Carolyn E., Aug. 20, 1950 (dec. 1950); children: Michael D., Cathryn ., Laurel L.; m. Jeanette E., Dec. 26, 1982. Student, Lakeland Coll. Prin., owner Boedeker Ditching and Trenching, Sheboygan, Manitowac, 1951-93, retired, 1993. Assessor, mpl. clk. Twp. of Herman, Wis., 1956, Sheboygan County, 1980. Republican. Avocation: wood crafts. Home: 716 Roosevelt Ave Howards Grove WI 53083-1015

BOEDEKER, DEBORAH D., classicist, educator; b. St. Louis, Dec. 31, 1944; d. John Thomas and Sarah (Chase) Dickmann; m. Kurt A. Raaflaub, July 14, 1978; children: Edgar Boedeker, Nancy Boedeker. BA, Wellesley Coll., 1966; MA, St. Louis U., 1967, PhD, 1973. Asst. prof. Georgetown U., Washington, 1974-76, Bklyn. Coll., CUNY, 1977-79, Wellesley (Mass.) Coll., 1979-81; asst. prof. to full prof. Coll. of the Holy Cross, Worcester, Mass., 1981-92; prof. classics Brown U., Providence, 1992—; joint dir. Ctr. for Hellenic Studies, Harvard U., Washington, 1992-2000. Author: Aphrodite's Entry into Greek Epic, 1974, Descent from Heaven, 1984; editor, co-author Herodotus and the Invention of History, 1987; co-editor, co-author: The New Simonides, 1996; editor: The World of Troy, 1997, The Iliad, the Odyssey and the Real World, 1999; co-editor, co-author: Democracy, Empire and the Arts in Fifth Century Athens, 1998; editl. bd. The Classical World, 1993-97; contbr. numerous articles to profl. jours. Ctr. for Hellenic Studies Jr. fellow, 1976-77; NEH Rsch. Conf. grantee, 1985-86. Mem. Am. Philol. Assn., Am. Inst. of Archaeology, Soc. for Preservation of the Greek Heritage (bd. dirs. 1993-2000), Classical Assn. of New Eng. E-mail: deborah boedeker@brown.edu. Home: 3100 Whitehaven St NW Washington DC 20008-3614 Office: Brown Univ Dept of Classics PO Box 1856 Providence RI 02912-1856

BOEDT, PHILIPPE, management consultant; b. Bruges, Belgium, July 30, 1945; s. Henry and Monique (Verstraete) B.; m. Françoise Drion, Sept. 19, 1970; children: Henri-François, Olivier, Stephane. MME, U. Cath. Louvain,

Belgium, 1970, M in Indsl. Mgmt., 1971. Indsl. engr. Procter & Gamble Benelux, Mechelen, Belgium, 1971-73, prodn. mgr., 1973-75, ops. mgr., 1975-82, plant indsl. engr., 1982-85, materials mgr., 1985-90; practice mgr. Bekaert Stanwick Cons., Kortryk, Belgium, 1990-92; European dir. purchasing and logistics Mactac Europe, Soignies, Belgium, 1992-99; mgmt. cons., exec. temp. mgmt. Lens, Belgium, 1999—; prof. indsl. mgmt. Univ. Fucam Mons, Belgium, 2000—. Founder Boy Scouts, Warneton, 1968, Comines, Belgium, 1962; tchr. youth catechism Cath. Ch. Mem. Univ. Engrs. Assn. Avocations: tennis, windsurfing, skiing, photography, reading. Home and Office: Rue de Cambron 3, B7870 Lens Belgium

BOEHM, PETER MICHAEL, ambassador, diplomat; b. Kitchener, Can., Apr. 26, 1954; s. Michael and Anna (Markus) B.; m. Julia Wayand, Dec. 19, 1981; children: Andreas, Alexander, Nikolas. Ba (hons.) in History, Eng. Lit., Wilfrid Laurier U., Can., 1977; Ma in Internat. Affairs, Carleton U., Can., 1978; PhD in History, U. Edinburgh, Scotland, 1983. From desk officer to dir. Dept. Foreign Affairs, Ottawa, Can., 1981-1995, dir.; 2d sec., vice consul Canadian Embassy, Havana, Cuba, 1983-86; counsellor and consul Canadian Embassy, San Jose, Costa Rica, 1988-92; ambassador, permanent rep. Permanent Mission of Can. to Org. Am. States, Washington, 1997—. Contbr. articles to profl. jours. Mem. Profl. Assn. Foreign Svc. Officers, Canadian Inst. Internat. Affairs, Inter-Am. Dialogue, Transylvania Club. Avocations: travel, reading, outdoor sports, alternative music. E-mail: peter.boehm@dfait-maeci.gc.ca. Office: Permanent Mission of Canada to the OAS 501 Pennsylvania Ave NW Washington DC 20001-2114

BOEHNE, EDWARD GEORGE, banker; b. Evansville, Ind., May 15, 1940; s. Edward John and Lucy Naomi (Strieter) B.; m. Patricia Graffis, Jan. 24, 1960; children: Lisa Elena, Edward Mark. BS, Ind. U., 1962, MBA, 1963, MA, 1967, PhD in Econs, 1968; LLD (hon.), Widener U., 1989. Economist Fed. Res. Bank, Phila., 1968-70, rsch. officer, economist, 1970-71, v.p., dir. rsch., 1971-73, sr. v.p., 1973-81, pres., 1981-2000; tchr. Bradley U., 1963-65, Ind. U., 1965-67, Temple U., 1969-70; bd. dirs. Ritlenhouse Trust, Toll Bros., AAA Mid-Atlantic. Chmn. Pa. Hosp., 1993-97; chmn. University City Sci. Ctr., 1998-99; bd. dirs. AAA Midlantic, Rittenhouse Trust, Toll Bros. Recipient Lieber award Ind. U., 1967, Gov.'s citation for outstanding svc. to Pa., 1978, Whitney Young Leadership award 1986, Stephen Girard award, 1987. Mem. Am. Econ. Assn., Nat. Assn. Bus. Economists. Office: 313 Devon State Rd Devon PA 19333-1411

BOEHNEN, DANIEL A., lawyer; b. Mitchell, S.D., Aug. 5, 1950; s. Lloyd and Mary Elizabeth (Buche) B.; m. Joan Bensing, May 22, 1976; children: Christopher, Lindsey. BS in Chem. Engring. cum laude, Notre Dame U., 1973; JD, Cornell U., 1976. Bar: Ill, U.S. Dist. Ct. (no. dist.) Ill., U.S. Ct. Appeals (7th and fed. cirs.), U.S. Supreme Ct. Atty. Allegretti, Newitt, Witcoff & McAndrews Ltd., Chgo., 1976—, assoc., 1982—; ptnr., exec. officer Allegretti & Witcoff, Ltd., Chgo., 1986—, bd. dirs., 1993-96; founder, mng. ptnr. McDonnell Boehnen Hulbert & Berghoff, Chgo., 1996—. Bd. dirs. Mitchell (S.D.) Prehist. Indian Village Soc., 1983—; commr. Northbrook Planning Commn., 1993—. Mem. ABA, AIPLA, Cornell Law Assn. Chg. (chmn.), Fed. Cir. Bar Assn. (bd. dirs.), Assn. Patent Law Firms (bd. dirs.). Avocations: skiing, photography, scuba diving. Office: McDonnell Boehnen Hulbert & Berghoff 300 S Wacker Dr Ste 3200 Chicago IL 60606-6709

BOEHNER, JOHN A., congressman; b. Reading, Ohio, Nov. 17, 1949; m. Deborah Gunlack, 1973; children: Lindsay M., Tricia A. BS, Xavier U., 1977. Pres. Nucite Sales, Inc.; mem. Ohio Ho. of Reps., 1984-90, 102nd-106th Congresses from 8th Ohio dist., Washington, D.C., 1991—; chmn. subcom. on employer-employee rels. 102nd-105th Congresses from 8th Ohio dist., Washington, D.C., 1998—; exec. com. mem. Nat. Rep. Congl. Com.; chmn. Ho. Rep. Conf. Com.; mem. Ag. Com., Ho. Oversight Com. Active Ohio Farm Bur. Mem. KC, Cin., Dayton, Middletown C. of C. Roman Catholic. Republican. Office: US Ho of Reps 1011 Longworth Bldg Washington DC 20515-3508

BOEHNSTEDT, SUSAN, transportation executive; b. Douglas, Az., Sept. 27, 1967; d. Daryl and JoAnne Dahlmeier; m. Curtis Michael Boehnstedt, Nov. 1, 1997. BS in Sociology, Az. State U., Tempe, 1991. Supr. Am. West Airlines, Tempe, Az., 1996-97; mgr. Am. West Airlines, Tempe, 1997; gen. mgr. Am. West Airlines, 1997-99, dir., 1999—; edn. bd. Am. West Airlines, Tempe, 1997—. Mem. E. Valley Bible Ch., 1997—. Independent. Avocations: running, travel, cooking. E-mail: susan.boehnstedt@americawest.com.

BOEKER, HERBERT RALPH, JR., urban planner; b. Cotulla, Tex., Dec. 4, 1951; s. Herbert Ralph and Doris (Franklin) B. BS in Sociology, Tex. A&M U., 1973, M in Urban and Regional Planning, 1975; MA in Energy and Mineral Resources, U. Tex., 1983. Project mgr. Tex. Dept. Water Resources, 1984-85, Tex. Water Commn., 1985-87; environ. coord. Gov.'s Office, Budget and Planning, Austin, Tex., 1987-89, asst. dep. dir. environ. planning, 1989; water resources planner Tex. Water Devel. Bd., Austin, 1990, unit head, policy, 1991-92, sect. chief, water rsch., 1992, sect. chief, water rsch. and policy, 1992-94, sect. chief, water policy, 1994-98, project mgr. water resources planning, 1998—; mem. Nueces River Basin Clean Rivers steering com., Uvalde, Tex., 1992-98; mem. Sulphur River Basin Authority steering com., Texarkana, 1992—; mem. Gov.'s Border Working Group, 1993-98; mentor Mickey Leland Environ. Internship Program, 1992; mem. "Region C" water planning group (non-voting), Grand Prairie, Tex., 1998—, North East Tex. regional water planning group (non-voting), Mt. Pleasant, 1998—. Contbr. chpt. to book. Chmn. Arkansas-White-Red Basins Inter-Agency com., 1998. Recipient Disting. Svc. award State of Tex., 1989; recipient 1st Place student paper award, Mining and Metall. Soc. of N.Am., N.Y.C., 1982. Mem. La Salle County Fair Assn., Assn. Former Students of Tex. A&M U., Tex. Friends of the U. Librs., Chihuahuan Desert Rsch. Inst. Baptist. Avocations: books, Western collectibles. Home: 2800 Bartons Bluff Ln Apt 904 Austin TX 78746-7932

BOELAERT, MARLEEN, tropical medicine researcher; b. Ukkel, Belgium, Oct. 21, 1960. D Medicine, Surgery and Obstetrics, Cath. U. Louvain, Belgium, 1985; diploma in tropical medicine, Prince Leopold Inst. Tropical Medicine, Antwerp, Belgium, 1986; DEA in statis. methods of epidemiology, Free U. Brussels, Brussels, 1991; D Pub. Health, U. Nancy, France, 1992; PhD, U. Ghent, Belgium, 1999. Physician Drs. without Borders, Brussels, 1986-94, pres., 1995-98; rsch. assoc. Prince Leopold Inst. Tropical Medicine, 1994—; lectr. U. Antwerp, 1999—. Pres. Physicians without Borders, Belgium, 1995-98; lectr. U. Antwerp, Belgium, 1999—.

BOER, ROGER WILLIAM, lawyer; b. Holland, Mich., July 2, 1934; s. William H. and Frances (Hulst) B.; m. Judith L. Jaqua, June 21, 1957; children; William, James, Charles, Martha, Karen. BA, Calvin Coll., 1956; JD, Wayne State U., 1960. Bar: Mich. 1961, U.S. Dist. Ct. Mich. 1961, U.S. Tax Ct. 1966. Atty. Mitts, Smith, Haughey & Packard, Grand Rapids, Mich., 1960-61; founding ptnr. McKee & Boer, Grand Rapids, Mich., 1961-63; asst. prosecuting atty., dep. prosecuting atty. Kent County Office, Grand Rapids, Mich., 1961-62, 63-64; founding ptnr. Rhoades, Garlington, McKee & Boer, Grand Rapids, Mich., 1963-65, Rhoades, McKee & Boer, Grand Rapids, Mich., 1965-87; founding shareholder Rhoades, McKee, Boer, Goodrich & Titta, Grand Rapids, Mich., 1987—, pres., 1994-99; spl. counsel Mich. Joint House Senate Investigating Com. on Worker's Compensation, 1964-65; spl. prosecutor one-man grand jury, 1977-78; sec. Grand Rapids Pub. Edn. Fund, 1989; bd. dirs., sr. shareholder Rhoades, McKee, Boer, Goodrich & Titta. Bd. dirs. Wedgewood Acres Home for Boys, 1969-71; bd. trustees Pine Rest Christian Hosp., 1971-83. bd. pres., 1981-83; study com. on abortion Christian Reformed Ch., 1973-74; bd. dirs. BBG Corp. Mem. State of Mich. Bar Assn., Grand Rapids Bar Assn. (trustee 1980-82, adv. com. in family law for Grand Rapids social agencies), Am. Trial Lawyers Assn., Green Ridge Country Club (bd. dirs. 1977-79), Egypt Valley Country Club, Peninsular Club. Home: 961 Gladstone Dr SE Grand Rapids MI 49506-3392 Office: Rhoades Mckee Boer Goodrich & Titta 161 Ottawa Ave NW Grand Rapids MI 49503-2701

BOERS, RENE, editor; b. Apeldoorn, The Netherlands, June 10, 1957; s. Jan Boers and Truus Meezen; children: Milan, Nena. Atheneum, K.S.A., Apeldoorn, 1976; D Dutch Lang., U. Utrecht, The Netherlands, 1985. Editor AV Press, Nymegen, The Netherlands, 1985-89, Media Nederland, Amsterdam, 1989-91; editor-in-chief/Meridian Internat. Audax Pub., Amsterdam, 1992-99; editor Plus Mag., SPN, Bussum, The Netherlands, 1999—. Home: A Thaerlaan 48, 3571EG Utrecht The Netherlands Office: Sr Publs Nederland, Olmenlaan 8, 1404 DG Bussum The Netherlands

BOERSMA, JUNE ELAINE (JALMA BARRETT), writer, photographer; b. N.Y.C., Apr. 27, 1926; d. Arthur Oscar and Gertrude Ann (Connolly) Schiefer; m. Kenneth Thomas McKim, June 8. 1946 (div. 1957); children: Kenneth Thomas Jr., Mark Rennie; m. Lawrence Allan Boersma, Nov. 22, 1962; children: Juliana Jaye, Dirk John. Student, Edgewood Park Jr. Coll., 1944-46. Writer non-fiction; co-owner, photographer Allan/The Animal Photographers, San Diego, 1980—. Author: (series) Wildcats of North America-Bobcat, Cougar, Feral Cat, Lynx, 1998, The Dove Family Tale, A True Story, 1998, Wild Canines-Coyote, Foxes, Wolf, 2000; contbr. articles to Ladies' Home Jour., Horse Illus., Cat Fancy, Dog Fancy, Popular Photography, Studio Photography, Petersen's Photographic, Dog World, others. Home: 3503 Argonne St San Diego CA 92117-1009

BOERSMA, LAWRENCE ALLAN (LARRY ALLAN), animal welfare administrator, photographer; b. London, Ont., Can., Apr. 24, 1932; s. Harry Albert and Valerie Kathryn (DeCordova) B.; m. Nancy Noble Jones, Aug. 16, 1952 (div. 1962) children: Juliana Jaye, Dirk John; m. June Elaine Schiefer McKim, Nov. 22, 1962; children: Kenneth Thomas McKim, Mark Rennie McKim. BA, U. Nebr., Omaha, 1953, MS, 1955; PhD, Sussex U., 1972; postgrad., U. Oxford, Eng., 1996. Journalism tchr. Tech. High Sch., Omaha, Nebr., 1953-55; dir. pub. rels., chair journalism dept. Adams State Coll., Alamosa, Colo., 1955-59; advt. sales analyst, advt. salesman Better Homes and Gardens, Des Moines, N.Y.C., 1959-63; advt. account exec. This Week Mag., N.Y.C., 1963-66; eastern sales dir., mktg. dir. Ladies' Home Jour., N.Y.C., 1966-75; v.p. assoc. pub., v.p. pub. Saturday Evening Post and The Country Gentleman, N.Y.C., 1975; v.p., dir. mktg. and advt. sales Photo World Mag., N.Y.C., 1975-77; advt. mgr. LaJolla (Calif.) Light, 1977-80; owner, photographer Allan/The Animal Photographers, San Diego, 1980—; pres., CEO The Photographic Inst. Internat., 1982-86; dir. comty. rels. San Diego Humane Soc./Soc. for Prevention Cruelty to Animals, 1985-94; assoc. exec. dir. The Ctr. for Humane Edn. for So. Calif., 1994-98; owner Animal Art, Shandaken, N.Y., 1999—; adj. asst. prof. Grad. Sch. Bus., Pace U., N.Y.C., 1964-65; adj. instr. N.Y. Inst. of Advt., 1974-77, others; adj. prof. Sch. Bus. Mesa Coll., San Diego, 1981-84, City Coll., San Diego, 1982-86, Winona Internat. Sch. Profl. Photography, Des Plaines, Ill., 1984-87, U. Calif. at San Diego, 1985; adj. prof. Coll. Bus. Adminstrn. U. LaVerne, San Diego, 1985; tchr. photography Winona Internat. Sch. of Profl. Photography, The Photographic Inst. Internat., U. Calif. San Diego, Adams State Coll. of Colo.; pres., CEO United Animal Welfare Found., San Diego, 1992-94; bd. dirs. Escondido Humane Soc. Found., 1994-99; chmn., CEO Internat. Dolphin Project, 1995; spkr. in field. Author: Strange Events at the House on Park Avenue: A Jack and Jimmy Mystery, 1996; photographer: (as Larry Allan) Wildcats of North America book series, 1998, Wild Canines book series, 2000; contbr. photography and articles to mags.; photographer calendars, books, and greeting cards; photographer: (motion picture) The Truth About Cats and Dogs; exhbns.: Art Photo Expo, L.A., 1999, others. Spokesperson Coalition for Pet Population Control, San Diego, 1990, 93, Com. Against Proposition C-Pound Animals for Med. Rsch., San Diego, 1990; spokesperson Spay-Neuter Action Project, 1991, mem. steering com., 1991, bd. dirs., 1992-93; mem. evaluation subcom. County of San Diego Dept. Animal Control Adv. Com.; founder, chair Feral Cat Coalition of San Diego County, 1992-93; Calif. State Humane Officer; vol. in pub. info. San Diego/Imperial Counties chpt. ARC, 1993—, mem. chpt. centennial com., 1996-97; mem. pub. info. officers San Diego County Emergency Svcs. Orgn., 1993-95; vol. photographer Calif. Wolf Ctr., 1999—; numerous others. Recipient 1st place Mobius Advt. award The U.S. Festivals Assn., 1991, Gold Mercury award Internat. Acad. of Comm. Arts & Scis., 1991, commendation for Disting. Humanitarian Pub. Svc. San Diego County Bd. Suprs., 1994, spl. commendation for Love and Concern for All Animals, San Diego City Coun., 1994, others. Fellow Royal Photog. Soc. Gt. Britain, Profl. Photographers Am. (Master of Photography award 1985, Photog. Craftsman award 1986), Profl. Photographers of Calif.; mem. PRSA (chmn. So. Tier N.Y. chpt. 1971-72), Soc. Animal Welfare Adminstrs., Nat. Soc. Fund Raising Execs. (cert., bd. dirs. 1988-89, treas. San Diego chpt. 1990-91, mem. nat. faculty 1992-93), Shriners (pres. Al Bahr chpt., Businessmen's Club), Masons. Republican. Presbyterian. Home: 3503 Argonne St San Diego CA 92117-1009

BOESCH, DIANE HARRIET, elementary education educator; b. Erie, Pa., July 3, 1942; d. William Jacob and Dorothy Gertrude (Call) B. BS, Edinboro (Pa.) State U., 1964; MA, Kent (Ohio) State U., 1968; postgrad., So. Ill. U., Carbondale, 1969, CUNY, 1972, Norwalk State Tech. Coll., 1979, Northeastern U., Boston, 1982, Fla. State U., 1988. Tchr. math. Iroquois Area Sch. Dist., Erie, 1964-67; grad. asst. Kent State U., 1967-68; tchr., writer Comprehensive Sch. Math. Project, Carbondale, Ill., 1968-70; tchr. math. Weston (Conn.) Pub. Schs., 1970—, dept. chmn. math., 1989—; dir. Weston Tchr. Ctr., 1983-84; condr. workshops on math. and writing, Conn., 1970—. Contbr. articles to profl. publs. Vol. nat. elections, Erie, 1960, West Haven, Conn., 1972. Recipient Celebration of Excellence award Conn. State Dept. Edn., 1988, Presdl. award NSF, 1990. Fellow Conn. Acad. for Edn. in Math. and Sci.; mem. NEA, Nat. Coun. Tchrs. Math., Conn. Educator Talent Pool, Conn. Edn. Assn., Weston Tchr. Assn., Coun. Presdl. Awardees in Math., Pi Mu Epsilon, Kappa Delta Pi. Republican. Lutheran. Avocations: genealogy, writing, music, reading, Atlanta Braves baseball. Office: Hurlbutt Elem Sch 9 School Rd Weston CT 06883-1696

BOËTHIUS, ULF CARL JAKOB, comparative literature educator; b. South Kedum, Skaraborg, Sweden, Dec. 2, 1933; s. Erik Gustaf Albert and Astrid Helena (Norberg) B.; m. Anna Fanny Hedenius, 1956 (div. 1978); children: Elin, Frida, Fanny; m. Carola Birgitta Hansson, 1979; children: Emma, Simon. BA, U. Uppsala, Sweden, 1955; MA, U. Uppsala, 1957, lic. of philosophy, 1962; PhD, Stockholm U., 1969. Lectr. Rudbeckian Sr. H.S., Västerås, Sweden, 1964-69; lectr. Stockholm U., 1970-90, prof., 1990-98; dir. studies dept. lit. Stockholm U., 1988-90. Author: Strindberg and the Woman Question Up to Giftas I, 1969, When Nick Carter Was Put to Flight. The Campaign Against Gutter Literature in Sweden, 1908-1909, 1989; contbr. articles to profl. jours.; editor: Modernity, Modernism and Children's Literature, 1998; co-editor: (with Johan Fornäs and Sabina Swejman) Method Questions in Youth Culture Research, 1990, (with Johan Fornäs) Youth and Cultural Modernization, 1990, (with Johan Fornäs and Sabina Cwejman) Gender and Identity in Change, 1991, (with Johan Fornäs, Hillevi Ganetz and Bo Reimer) Young Styles and Modes of Expression, 1992, (with Johan Fornäs and Bo Reimer) Youth in Different Areas, 1993, (with Johan Fornäs, Michael Forsman, Hillevi Ganetz and Bo Reimer) Youth Culture in Sweden, 1994. Past bd. dirs. Ctr. Mass Culture Studies, Ctr. Study of Childhood, U. Stockholm; past bd. dirs. Swedish Inst. for Children's Books, Stockholm, Strindberg Soc., Stockholm, Swedish Coun. for Rsch. in Adult Edn., Linköping, Sweden, Youth Studies Group of Swedish Coun. for Rsch. in Humanities and Social Scis. Mem. Children's Lit. Assn., Internat. Rsch. Soc. for Children's Lit., Strindbergssällskapet, Swedish Network for Youth Culture Studies. Address: Noreens väg 80, 75362 Uppsala Sweden

BOEV, ZLATOZAR NIKOLAEV, zoologist, researcher; b. Sofia, Bulgaria, Oct. 20, 1955; s. Nikolay Kroumov and Nadezhda Kostova (Karabadzhakova) P. Degree, Sofia U., 1980, DSc, 1999. Curator birds Nat. Mus. Natural History-Bulgarian Acad. Scis., Sofia, 1986—, assoc. prof., 1992—, sci. sec., 1999—; chmn. biology sect. Union of Scientists of Bulgaria, Sofia, 1998—; cons. Regional Environ. Ctr. for East and Ctrl. Europe, Ctrl. Office, Budapest, 1997. Author: What Do We Know About Birds, 1990, In the World of Fishes, 1994, In the World of Amphibians, 1994, In the World of Butterflies, 1995, others; contbr. over 370 articles to sci. publs. Found. mem. Friends of the U.S.A. in Bulgaria Soc., 1990—. Mem. Bulgarian Soc. Protection of Birds (sec. 1988-90), Bulgarian Zool. Soc. (sec. 1990—), Bulgarian Ornithological Soc. (sec. 1995), Soc. Avian Paleontology and Evolution (grantee 1988, 92), Bird Working Group of Internat. Coun. Archaeozoology (grantee 1992, 95), others. Avocations: photographing nature, archaeology, books, travel. Office: Nat Mus Natural History BAS, 1 Blv Tsar Osvoboditel, 1000 Sofia Bulgaria

BOFFERT, JOYCE D., chiropractor; b. Bklyn., May 5, 1949; d. Morris and Beatrice Boffert. D Chiropractic, N.Y. Chiropractic Coll., 1988. Cert. naturopath, acupunctурist, herbologist. Pvt. practice Colony Chiropractic, Syosset, N.Y., 1988—; adj. instr. Queensborough C.C., Bayside, N.Y., 1999—. Vol. Dem. Club, Nassau County, N.Y., 1999. Address: 72 Colony Ln Syosset NY 11791-4721

BOGADI-SARE, ANA, occupational medicine specialist, researcher; b. Bjelovar, Croatia, Oct. 17, 1953; d. Milan and Stefania (Kadoic) Bogadi; m. Miroslav Sare, Dec. 20, 1986; 1 child, Mislav. MD, U. Zagreb, Croatia, 1978; M in Occupl. Medicine, U. Zagreb, 1985; PhD in Occupl. Medicine, U. Rijeka, Croatia, 1997. Physician Indsl. Clinic for Prevention & Treatment Working Population, Zagreb, 1978-81; occupl. medicine specialist Inst. Med. Rsch. Occupl. Health, Zagreb, 1982-98; head divsn. for occupl. diseases and indsl. toxicology Croatian Inst. Occupl. Health, Zagreb, 1998—; prof. Coll. of Safety at Work, Zagreb, Croatia, 1999; cons. occupl. medicine Retirement Ins. Fund, Zagreb, 1993—; occupl. medicine legal expert, Zagreb, 1995—; mem. pub. adv. bd. Work and Safety, Zagreb, 1997—. Co-author: Sporadic Lung Diseases, 1991; contbr. articles to profl. jours. Mem. Croatian Soc. for Occupl. Health (managerial bd. 1996—), Croatian Soc. for Promotion Human Protection in Labour and Living Surrounding (v.p. 1997—), Archieves Indsl. Hygiene and Toxicology (exec. editl. bd. 1995—). Roman Catholic. Avocations: chorus singing, classical music, mountaineering. Fax: 385 1 65 58 704. E-mail: ana.bogadi-sare@zg.hinet.hr. Office: Croatian Inst Occupl Health, Av V Holjevca 22, 10020 Zagreb Croatia

BOGAERTS, COUNT ARTHUR FLORENT, diplomat, scientist; b. Gent, Belgium, Dec. 20, 1937; s. Count Francois zur Muide, Swyngerde de Lgon and Countess Ludovica (Verselder de Bruyne de Wondelghem) B.; DDiv and Theology S.U. Baptist Sem., 1959, B.Sc.M.E., Belgian Mil. Acad., 1960; Ph.D. Acoustics & Vibrations U. London, 1962; M.S., Case Western Res. U., 1963; Ph.D., MIT, 1964; M.D., Harvard U., 1964; Ph.D. (hon.), So. U., 1978, Am. U., 1978; Lic. physician, Germany, India, Nepal, Guatamala, Panama, Burundi, Liberia; cert. profl. engr., U.S., U.K., Germany, Belgium. Chmn. Fla. Interstate, Jacksonville, 1972-85; v.p. Heather Banking Corp., N.Y.C., 1979-83; chmn. Heraldic Rsch. Acad., 1980—; CEO Albert Schweitzer Soc., U.S. and Internat., 1968—; founder, CEO Black Diamond Peace Found., 1989—; pres. Signum Fidei Med. Air Corps, 1970—; co-dir., founder Sunderpore Leprosy Village, Bihar, India, 1980-85; v.p. Internat. Low Level Satellites Comp., Seattle, 1994-96; consul of Panama, Birmingham, Ala., 1985-88; consul Gral Panama, Guatemala, 1990-95; dir. internat. relief Internat. Assn. Edn. World Peace; v.p. United Towns Agy. North South Cooperation; permanent rep. UN (ECOSOC-NGO) 1975-2000; amb. Republic of Liberia, 1999—, State of Ariz., 1979-82; advisor to v.p. El Salvador, 1987-89, Brussels Embassy & pres. Liberia, 1974-80; pres. and min. def. Guatemala, 1982-88; expert advisor to Gov. of Chad, Kenya, Burundi, Liberia, others; apptd. peace mediator in Burundi Conflict, 1996-98, UN Peace Observer, 1980-98; hon. pres. Burundi Olympic Com.; v.p. Internat. Relief Red Cross, Burundi, 1997-99; spl. envoy Evangelical Chs. Burundi; internat. rep. Luth. Ch. Burundi, 1978—; amb. City Bjumbura, Burundi, 1997; min. Household of the Princes of Lippe, 1989—; vis. prof., lectr., cons. to profl. and edn. instns. Author many books on acoustics, solar energy, leprosy, missionary work, forensic sciences; contbr. articles to profl. jours. Co-founder, 1st dean applied sci. European U., Antwerp (affiliated U. Dallas); co-founder Albert Schweitzer Internat. U. (Ctrl. Am.) 1983, Inst. Forensic Medicine & Scis Guatemala, 1986, Sch. Medicine U. Santa Ana El Salvador, Nuevo U. San Salvador, 1986-89; co-founder 3 med. schs. in Ctrl. Am. Served to col. Belgium Army, 1956-61, reserve 1961—. Decorated Grand Collar Order of Signum Fidei, of St. Lazarus of Jerusalem; knight Grand Cross Order of Merit of St. Lazarus, Grand Cross Order of Merit of Lippe; knight Grand Cross of Justice Order of St. John, Grand Cross of Orthodox Order of St. Sepulchre; knight of Justice Order of Constantine St.Georges, Naples; Govt Knighthood's in ranks of grand Cross of Comdr. include Lion of Zaire, Red Cross of Japan, Red Cross of Portugal, Burundi, of the Liberator (Liberia), St. Stanislas, Poland, Order of Merit of Italy, UN (Burundi) Peace medal, 1978, others; named hon. citizen cities of L.A., San Francisco, Rome, Jasper, Ala., Cordova, Ala., states of Tenn., Miss., La., Tex., Ga., Ark., Kans., Okla., Fla.; named clan chief Bethel, Bushrod Island, Monrovia, Liberia. Recipient Royal Sci. Rsch. award Belgium, 1976, Cultural award, 1978, King Baudewijn Royal medal, 1986, UN Peace award, 1978; recipient numerous internat. sci. and cultural awards. Fellow AIAA, IEEE (sr., editl. bd. Inst. Forensic Scis. and Medicine 1978-84, 85-88), World Acad. Arts and Scis., Acad. Scis. Guatemala, El Salvador, Moscow, Flanders, Rome, Pro Pace (Vatican) N.Y., San Francisco, Inst. Physics, Inst. Acoustics (U.S., Germany, U.K.), VDI-Germany, Eng. Inst. VDT, Inst. KVIV, Royal Belgian Engrs. Inst.; mem. Internat. Ct. The Hague, Internat. Press Assn., numerous others. Clubs: Royal Yacht (Belgium), Royal Cano, Gent, Royal Golf (Belgium and Hannover, Germany), Mt. Kenya Safari (bd. dirs.), St. Johns (London), Mt. Crest County (S.C.), Royal Air Force (UK), Army and Navy (U.S., UK, France). E-mail: Blaisen@getnet.com. Home: 265 Kimberly Dr Dayton OH 45458-4134 Office: PO Box 752073 Dayton OH 45475-2073 also: Am Maximinenkreuz 25, Erftstadt 50374, Germany

BOGATAJ, LUDVIK, mathematics and economics educator, researcher; b. Murska Sobota, Prekmurje, Slovenia, Apr. 15, 1949; s. Franc and Irma (Čisar) B.; m. Marija Alma Zupančič, Dec. 4, 1950; children: David, Eneja. MSc in Ops. Rsch., U. Ljubljana, Slovenia, 1975, PhD in Ops. Rsch., 1980, PhD in Math., 1989; MSc in Math., U. Zagreb, Croatia, 1985. Asst. U. Maribor, Slovenia, 1973-74; asst. U. Ljubljana, 1974-81, asst. prof. math. and ops. rsch., 1981-91, assoc. prof., 1991-96, prof., 1996—, head dept., 1992—. Editor: Inventory Modelling, Vols. 1-2, 1995; contbr. articles to profl. jours., including Internat. Jour. Prodn. Econs., Glasnik Matematički, Engring. Costs and Prodn. Econs. Scholar U. Ljubljana. Mem. Soc. for Indsl. and Applied Math., Am. Math. Soc., Internat. Soc. for Inventory Rsch. (internat. referee 1982—), Slovenian Soc. for Informatics (v.p. sect. for ops. rsch. 1992-98), Soc. Univ. Tchrs. (pres. fin. fund, mem. exec. com. 1993—). Avocations: playing violin, music, hiking, jogging. Fax: 386 61 1892 698. Home: Kidriceva 1, 8210 Trebnje Slovenia Office: U Ljubljana Faculty Econs, Kardeljeva Ploscad 17, 1000 Ljubljana Slovenia

BOGATOV, ALEXANDER PETROVICH, physicist, educator; b. Suchan, Russia, Sept. 15, 1947; m. Anna Haimovna Lapidus, June 19, 1971; children: Matthew, Sophia, Alexei. Grad., Moscow Inst. Physics and Tech., 1971; CandPhysMathSci, Lebedev Phys. Inst., Moscow, 1977, DPhysMathSci, 1996. Cert. in elec. engring. Jr. rschr., sr. rschr., leading rschr., chief rschr. Lebedev Phys. Inst., 1971—; adj. assoc. prof. U. N.Mex., Albuquerque, 1996-97; prof. Moscow Inst. Physics and Tech., 1997—. Contbr. more than 100 articles to profl. jours.; patentee in field. Recipient award Acad. Sci. USSR and Acad. Sci. German Dem. Republic, 1979, State prize in physics USSR, 1984. Home: 14 Ordzhonikidze 6, 117071 Moscow Russia Office: PN Lebedev Phys Inst, 53 Leninsky prospect, 117924 Moscow Russia

BOGATUROV, ALEXEY NICOLAEVICH, physicist, researcher; b. Nizgnii Novgorod, Russia, Aug. 10, 1956; s. Nicolai Erastovich and Raisa Petrovna (Golneva) B.; m. Liliya Anatolyevna Simonova, Nov. 9, 1984. BS in Physics, Moscow State U., 1979. Rschr. Inst. Atmospheric Physics Russian Acad. Scis., Moscow, 1984—. Contbr. numerous articles to profl. jours. Home: Novo-Shichovo 3-33, 143092 Moscow Russia Office: Inst. Atmospheric Scis., Pyzhevskii 3, 109017 Moscow Russia

BOGATYREV, VLADIMIR LVOVICH, inorganic chemist; b. Perm, Russia, Feb. 20, 1935; s. Lev Ivanovich and Anna Ivanovna (Sevastyanova) B.; m. Valentina Andreevna Ivanchenko, Dec. 7, 1959; 1 child, Svetlana. Diploma in higher edn., Moscow State U., 1959; PhD in Chemistry, Inst. Inorganic Chemistry, Novosibirsk, Russia, 1964. Jr. scientist Inst. Inorganic Chemistry, Novosibirsk, 1959-61, sr. scientist, 1962-68, head rsch. lab., 1968—; mem. sci. coun. Inst. Inorganic Chemistry, Novosibirsk, 1965—, State U., Kemerovo, Russia, 1986—; prof. Novosibirsk State U., 1972-82, Siberian U. Consumers Coop. Socs., Novosibirsk, 1997—. Author: Ion-Exchangers in Mixed Bed, 1968, Principals of Reseiving of Ultra-Pure Substances, 1981; co-author: Extraction of Inorganic Substances, 1970, X-Ray Analysis of the Ion-Exchangers, 1982, Physical and Colloidal Chemistry, 1999. Soros Found. grantee, 1993. Avocations: fishing, gardening. Home: Morskoi Prospekt 64-21, 630090 Novosibirsk Russia Office: Inst Inorg Chem Acad Scis, 3 Acad Lavrentyev pr, 630090 Novosibirsk Russia

BOGDANOV, ROMAN VASILIEVITH, radiochemist, researcher; b. Leningrad, Russia, Nov. 19, 1936; s. Vasiliy Nikolaevith and Luebov Filippovna

(Neuman) B.; m. Natalia Alexeevna Schipkova, Dec. 30, 1969 (div. Dec. 1994); 1 child, Rodionova Ekaterina Romanovna. MS, St. Petersburg State U., Russia, 1959, PhD in Chemistry, 1966. Lab. asst. chemistry dept. St. Petersburg State U., 1959-60, rsch. asst. Inst. Chemistry, 1964-66, rschr., 1967-76, sr. rschr., 1977-94, head scientist, 1995—, assoc. prof. chemistry dept., 1997—; vice-chmn. pub. Soviet of chemistry dept. St. Petersburg State U., 1989-91. Author, co-author: (in Russian) From Molecule to Crystal, 1972, Vom Molekuel zum Kristall, 1976, Energie und Chemischer Prozes, 1975, Energia a Chemicke Procesy, 1976, 77 (Deed of Thanks of Russian Soc. Accomplishment, 1979), (in Russian) Prospectus About the Chemistry Department, 1984; author, editor: At the Crossing of Chemistry, 1980 (Hon. Deed of High Edn. Ministry 1982); co-author: Vom Atom zum Molekul, 1978, 80, 82 (Deed of Thanks of Russian Soc. Accomplishment, 1984); author, editor: Chemistry-Traditional and Paradoxical, 1985 (Hon. Deed of High Edn. Ministry 1988); assoc. editor Jour. Ecol. Chemistry, 1992—. Recipient Hon. Deeds, Rector of St. Petersburg State U., 1999, Edn. Ministry, Moscow, 1999. Avocations: boating, nature, fishing. Home: Zvezdnaya 14 Apt 108, 196233 Saint Petersburg Russia Office: St Petersburg State U, University Embank 7/9, 199034 Saint Petersburg Russia

BOGDANSKY, BETSY BOUGESS, professional society administrator; b. Everett, Mass., Nov. 18, 1948; d. Ernest Sydney and Gwendolyn (Rubenstein) Bougess; m. Alan Martin Bogdansky, Feb. 13, 1971; children: Mark, Erica, Judd. BA, Fairleigh Dickinson U., 1970; MA cum laude, Columbia U., 1975. Tchr. Malden (Mass.) Pub. Schs., 1970-72; asst. adminstr. Columbia U., N.Y.C., 1972-75; adminstr. Mass. Gen. Hosp., Boston, 1980-83; dir. membership N.Am. Soc. Pacing & Electophysiology, Natick, Mass., 1983—. With Beth-El AteReth Israel Sisterhood, Newton, Mass., 1980-90; bd. dirs. Maimonides Sch. PTA, Brookline, Mass., 1985—, v.p., 1992. Mem. Am. Soc. Assn. Execs. Jewish. Office: NAm Soc Pacing & Electophysiology 6 Strathmore Rd Natick MA 01760-2419

BÖGE, REIMER, member of European parliament; b. Hasenmoor, Fed. Republic Germany, Dec. 18, 1951. Mem. European Parliament, Kiel, Germany, 1999—; mem. Group of the European People's Party (Christian Democrats) and European Democrats; vice-chmn. com. on budgets; substitute mem. com. on agr. and rural devel.; mem. delegation for rels. with Japan; substitute mem. delegation to the EU-Estonia Joint Parliamentary Com. *

BOGEN, BJARNE, immunologist, educator; b. Oslo, Jan. 18, 1951; s. Victor and Birgit (Nesheim) B.; m. Gunn Irene Andersen, May 30, 1980 (div. May 1990); 1 child, Runar; m. Ida Elisabeth Dypvik, May 3, 1991; children: Ellen, Erik. MD, U Oslo, 1977; D Medicine, U. Tromsø, Norway, 1984. Cert. specialist in immunology and blood transfusion. Rsch. fellow U. Tromsø, 1979-84; sci. investigator Basel (Switzerland) Inst. for Immunology, 1985-86; assoc. prof. immunology U. Oslo, 1986-92, prof., 1993—; assoc. prof. Norwegian Coll. Vet. Medicine, Oslo, 1989—; chief attending physician Nat. Hosp., Oslo, 1995—; vis. prof. Stanford (Calif.) U., 1996-97; cons. Norwegian Cancer Soc., Oslo, 1996-98. Contbr. articles on recognition of antibodies by T lymphocytes to mem. jours., including Procs. NAS (U.S.), Cell, EMBO Jour.; editl. bd. Scandinavian Jour. Immunol., 1999—. Recipient Sr. Rsch. award Multiple Myeloma Rsch. Found., 1999. Mem. Norwegian Soc. for Immunology (pres. 1993-94), Scandinavian Soc. for Immunology (coun. 1995—), N.Y. Acad. Scis. Avocations: tennis, sailing, skiing. Home: Pelvikveien 28, 1335 Snarøya Norway Office: Inst for Immunology, Rikshospitalet, 0027 Oslo Norway

BOGER, DAN CALVIN, statistical and economic consultant, educator; b. Salisbury, N.C., July 9, 1946; s. Brady Cashwell and Gertrude Virginia (Hamilton) B.; m. Gail Lorraine Zivna, June 23, 1973; children: Gretchen Zivna, Gregory Zivna. BS in Mgmt. Sci., U. Rochester, 1968; MS in Mgmt. Sci., Naval Postgrad. Sch., Monterey, Calif., 1969; MA in Stats., U. Calif., Berkeley, 1977, PhD in Econs., 1979. Cert. cost analyst, profl. estimator. Rsch. asst. U. Calif., Berkeley, 1975-79; asst. prof. econs. Naval Postgrad. Sch., Monterey, 1979-85, assoc. prof., 1985-92, prof., 1992—, chmn. dept. command, control and comm., 1995—, chmn. dept. computer sci., 1997—, chmn. dept. info. warfare, 1997—, dean divsn. computer and info. scis. and ops., 1997—; bd. dirs. Evan-Moor Corp.; cons. econs. and statis. legal matters CSX Corp, others, 1977—. Assoc. editor The Logistics and Transp. Rev., 1981-85, Jour. Cost Analysis, 1989-92; mem. editl. rev. bd. Jour. Transp. Rsch. Forum, 1987-91; contbr. articles to profl. jours. Lt. USN, 1968-75. Flood fellow Dept. Econs. U. Calif., Berkeley, 1975-76; dissertation rsch. grantee A.P. Sloan Found., 1978-79. Mem. IEEE, Internat. Coun. on Sys. Engring., Am. Econ. Assn., Am. Statis. Assn., Econometric Soc., Inst. for Mgmt. Sci. and Ops. Rsch. (sec., treas. mil. applications soc. 1987-91), Sigma Xi. Home: 27 Cramden Dr Monterey CA 93940-4145 Office: Naval Postgrad Sch Code CC Monterey CA 93943

BOGER, DAVID VERNON, chemical engineering educator; b. Kutztown, Pa., Nov. 13, 1939; s. Charles D. and Edna G. Boger; m. Elizabeth A. Mannix, Oct. 7, 1967; children: Stephen, Samantha, Brooke. BSChemE, Bucknell U., 1961; MSChemE, U. Ill., 1964, PhDChemE, 1965. Lectr. dept. chem. engring. Monash U., Clayton, Australia, 1965-71, sr. lectr. dept. chem. engring., 1971-80, reader dept. chem. engring., 1980-82; dep. dean faculty of engring. U. Melbourne, Parkville, Australia, 1988-90, assoc. dean rsch. faculty of engring., 1990-92, prof. dept. chem. engring., 1982-99, laureate prof. chem. engring., 2000—; dep. dir. Advanced Mineral Products Ctr., Melbourne, Australia, 1991-99; dir. Particulate Fluids Processing Ctr., 2000. Author books, book chpts., jour. articles and motion picture films. Basketball coach Berwick Jr. Basketball Assn., Melbourne, 1991; sch. coun. mem. St. Margarets Sch., Melbourne, 1990. Recipient rsch. medal Royal Soc. Victoria, 1985; fellow Australian Acad. of Technol. Scis., 1989, USA Environtl. Excellence award Alcoa, 1995, External medal CSIRO, 1998, Flinders medal Australian Acad. Sci., 2000, Chemeca medal, 2000; named for Excellence in Chem. Engring., Instn. Chem. Engrs. and Esso Australia, 1991, POL Eurkea prize for Environ. Engring., 1993, Walter Ahlstrom Environ. prize, 1995. Fellow Instn. Chem. Engrs. UK, Australian Acad. Sci.; mem. Australian Soc. Rheology (pres. 1976-78, com. mem. 1978-88, medallion 1994), Brit. Soc. Rheology (Ann. award 1983), Am. Soc. Rheology, Internat. com. Rheology (Australian del.). Avocations: trout fishing, tennis, farming. Office: U Melbourne, Dept Chem Engring, Parkville VIC 3010, Australia

BOGERT, TRACY JOSEPH, adult probation officer; b. Olathe, Kans., Dec. 12, 1963; s. Gerald Neal and Barbara Rae B.; m. Rachel Alderate, June 14, 1997; children: Melody Audrina, Serenity Autumn. BS, U. Tex., 1997. Inventory control Pioneer Flour, San Antonio, 1982-91; probation officer Bexar County, San Antonio, 1997—. Media dir. Dem. Party, Bexar County, 1993-97; pres. South Metro Dems., 1997-99; v.p. Women's Polit. Caucus, Bexar County, 1996-98. Roman Catholic. Avocations: politics, hunting, fishing, target shooting, basketball. e-mail: cc7bogert@yahoo.com. Office: Bexar County Cmty Supervision & Correction Dept 601 Dolorosa San Antonio TX 78207-4536

BOGGAN, JEFFREY SCOTT, college administrator; b. Asheville, N.C., May 30, 1960; s. Robert Edmond Jr. and Patricia Ann (Kirkpatrick) B. BA in Govt., Wofford Coll., Spartanburg, S.C., 1982; MA in Higher Edn. Adminstrn., Appalachian State U., Boone, N.C., 2000. Account rep. Quaker Oats Co., Greensboro, N.C., 1985-86; adminstrv. officer City of Charlotte, N.C., 1986-88; dir. alumni and parents programs Wofford Coll., 1988-95; dir. devel. and alumni programs Montgomery Acad., 1995-96; dir. advancement, COO Phi Kappa Phi Found., 1996-97; agt. coll. fund divsn. Universal Insurance Co. Inc., Charlotte, 1997-98; sr. dir. devel. Lees-McRae Coll., Banner Elk, N.C., 1998—. Author quar. alumni article Wofford Today, 1988-91. Dir. Spartanburg Youth Theater, 1990; bus. cons. Jr. Achievement, Spartanburg, 1991; campaign exec. United Way of the Piedmont, Spartanburg, 1991, loaned exec., 1993; class mem. Leadership Spartanburg, 1991-92, grad., 1992, mem. bd. regents; active Spartanburg 2000 Task Force Literacy and Lifetime Learning; v.p. Spartanburg AWARE, Inc., 1993-94, pres., 1994-95. 1st lt. U.S. Army, 1982-85. Decorated Army Commendation medal (2). Mem. Nat. Soc. Fundraising Execs., Soc. Fund Raising Execs., N.C. Planned Giving Coun., Coun. for Advancement and Support of Edn., S.C. Assn. Alumni Dirs. (sec. treas. 1993-94, pres. 1994-95), Rotary of Spartanburg (com. chmn. 1991-92, chmn. Community Literacy Project, Gov.'s award 1991), Pi Kappa Phi (Alumnus of Yr. 1989, 90, 97, chpt. advisor 1989-91). Republican. Methodist. Avocations: music, sports, reading, community service. Home: PO Box 1805 Banner Elk NC 28604-1805 Office: PO Box 128 Banner Elk NC 28604-0128

BOGGS, BETH CLEMENS, lawyer; b. Dubuque, Iowa, July 28, 1967; d. Theodore Alan and Mary Ann (Fleckenstein) Clemens; m. T. Darin Boggs, Mar. 9, 1991. BA, Govs. State U., 1987; JD, So. Ill. U., 1991. Bar: Ill. 1991, Mo. 1992, U.S. Dist. Ct. (so. dist.) Ill. 1991, U.S. Dist. Ct. (ea. dist.) Mo. 1992, U.S. Dist. Ct. (cen. dist.) Ill. 1997. Clk. R. Courtney Hughes & Assocs., Carbondale, Ill., 1990-91; lawyer Sandberg Phoenix & von Gontard, St. Louis, 1991-93; assoc. LaTourette, Schlueter & Byrne, St. Louis, 1993-95; mng. ptnr. Landau, Omahana & Kopka, P.C., St. Louis, 1995-99; mng. and founding ptnr. Boggs, Backer & Bates, LLC, St. Louis, 1999—; adj. faculty Webster U., 1995—. Editor student articles So. Ill. U. Law Jour., 1991; contbr. articles to profl. jours. Mem. Young Lawyers divsn. of ABA (vice chair corp. counsel com. 1991-92, editor Corp. Counsel Newsletter 1991-92), Bus. Women St. Louis, Women Lawyers Assn., Lawyers Assn. St. Louis, Def. Rsch. inst., Mo. Orgn. Def. Lawyers. Avocations: tennis, softball, golf. Office: BBB 7912 Bonhomme Ave Ste 400 Saint Louis MO 63105-3512

BOGGS, DAVID JEROME, business educator, consultant; b. Ironton, Ohio, July 28, 1967; s. Boxley Burl and Joyce Elaine B.; m. Elisabeth Ann Strommer, June 26, 1999. BS, John Brown U., 1989; MBA, U. Tex., Richardson, 1991, PhD, 1998. Tchr. Quisqueya Christian Sch., Port-au-Prince, Haiti, 1991, Am. Coop. Sch., Paramaribo, Surinam, 1992; rsch. asst. U. Tex., Richardson, 1992-95, lectr., 1995-98, asst. prof. internat. bus., 1998—; cons. Boeing Corp., Seattle, 1999—. Contbr. articles to profl. jours. Avocations: sports, music, travel. Home: 5373 Reber Pl Saint Louis MO 63139-1418 Office: Boeing Inst Internat Bus 3674 Lindell Blvd Saint Louis MO 63108-3302

BOGGS, JOSEPH DODRIDGE, pediatric pathologist, educator; b. Bellefontaine, Ohio, Dec. 31, 1921; s. Walter C. and Birdella Z. (Coons) B.; m. Donna Lee Shoemaker, June 12, 1964; 1 son, Joseph Dodridge. A.B., Ohio U., 1941, Litt.D., 1966; M.D., Jefferson Med. Coll., 1945. Intern Jefferson Med. Coll. Hosp., Phila., 1945-46; resident Peter Bent Brigham Hosp., Boston, 1946-48; asso. pathologist Peter Bent Brigham Hosp., 1947-51; instr. pathology Harvard Med. Sch., Boston, 1948-51; with Children's Meml. Hosp., Chgo., 1951—; dir. labs. Children's Meml. Hosp., 1951—; prof. pathology Northwestern U., Chgo., 1952-92, prof. emeritus, 1992—; dir. BSP Ins. Co., Phoenix. Contbr. articles to profl. jours. Mem. med. adv. bd. Ill. Dept. Corrections, Springfield, 1971-77; bd. dirs. Blood Systems Inc., Phoenix, 1972-94, Community Hosp., Evanston, Ill., 1958-61, Lorretto Hosp., Chgo., 1971-72; chmn. Chgo. Regional Blood Program, 1978-80; bd. dirs. Ben Venue Labs., 1985—. Capt. M.C., U.S. Army, 1948-51. Mem. Am. Soc. Study of Liver Disease, N.Y. Acad. Scis., Midwest Soc. Pediatric Research, Inst. Medicine, Ill. Soc. Pathologists (pres. 1965), Ill. Assn. Blood Banks (pres. 1969-70). Office: 1448 N Lake Shore Dr Chicago IL 60610-6655

BOGGS, STEVEN EUGENE, lawyer; b. Santa Monica, Calif., Apr. 28, 1947; s. Eugene W. and Annie (Happe) B. BA in Econ., U. Calif., Santa Barbara, 1969; D of Chiropractic summa cum laude, Cleveland Chiropractic, L.A., 1974; PhD in Fin. Planning, Columbia Pacific U., 1986; JD in Law, U. So. Calif., 1990. Bar: Calif. 1990, U.S. Dist. Ct. (cen. dist.) Calif. 1990, Hawaii 1991, U.S. Ct. Appeals (9th cir.), Colo. 1999; CFP; lic. chiropractor Hawaii, Calif.; lic. radiography X-ray supr. and operator. Faculty mem. Cleveland Chiropractic Coll., 1972-74; pres. clinic dir. Hawaii Chiropratic Clinic, Inc., Aiea, 1974-87; pvt. practice Honolulu, 1991—; mem. faculty Hawaii Pacific U., 1997-99; cons. in field; seminar presenter 1990—. Contbr. articles to profl. jours. Recipient Cert. Appreciation State of Hawaii, 1981-84. Fellow Internat. Coll. of Chiropractic; mem. ABA, Am. Trial Lawyers Assn., Consumer Lawyers of Hawaii, Am. Chriopractic Assn., Hawaii State Chiropractic Assn. (pres. 1978, 85, 86, v.p. 1977, sec. 1979-84, treas. 1976, other coms., Valuable Svc. award 1984, Cert. Appreciation 1986, Cert. Achievement 1986, Chiropractor of Yr. 1986, Outstanding Achievement award 1991), Consumer Lawyers of Hawaii (bd. dirs.). Democrat. Avocation: bicycling. Office: 19050 Archers Dr Monument CO 80132-2807

BOGHOSIAN, SOGHOMON B., chemical engineer, educator; b. Athens, Greece, May 11, 1961; s. Boghos K. and Vartoui S. (Takesian) B.; m. Marina N. Koussathana, May 16, 1992; 1 child, Artemis. MS in Chem. Engring., U. Patras, Greece, 1984, PhD in Chem. Engring., 1988. Postdoctoral assoc. Norwegian Inst. Tech., U. Trondheim, Norway, 1988-89; assoc. rschr. Found. Rsch. & Tech.-Inst. Chem. Engring., Greece, 1991-95; adj. lectr. chem. engring. U. Patras, 1991-95; mem. faculty Forth/ICE-HT, 1995—; lectr. chem. engring. U. Patras, 1995-99, asst. prof. chem. engring., 1999—. Hon. fellow Greek State Fellow Found., 1981-84, Calouste Gulbenkian fellow, 1982-88; recipient Panhellenic prize Greek Math. Soc., 1978. Office: U Patras, Dept Chemical Engring, GR-26500 Patras Greece

BOGLAR, LUIZ, anthropology educator; b. Sao Paulo, Brazil, Dec. 27, 1929; s. Lajos Boglar and Anna Ratz; m. Eva Horváth, July 7, 1966; children: Andrea, Gábor. MA in Ethnology, U. Budapest, 1969; PhD in Ethnology, Acad. of Scis., 1969, PhD in Sociology, 1999. Museologist/curator. Head curator Budapest Mus., 1953-79; head rschr. Acad. of Scis., Hungary, 1979-90; chmn. U. Budapest, 1990-96; pres. Symbiosis Found., Budapest, 1994—; v.p. Bezeredj Found., Budapest, 1996—. Author: (books) Myth and Culture, 1996, Nekrei, 1997, Religion and Culture, 1995; reviewer publs. Recipient Samuel Teleki medal Soc. for Geography, Budapest, 1996, Republican Order, Ministry of Culture, Budapest, 1994, Life-Work Condecoration, Ministry of Culture, 1972. Mem. Soc. for Anthropology (pres. 1996), Brasilian-Hungarian Soc. (pres. 1993). Avocation: filmmaking. Office: Dept Cultural Anthropology, 1052 Budapest Hungary

BOGLE, JOHN CLIFTON, investment company executive; b. Montclair, N.J., May 8, 1929; s. William Yates, Jr. and Josephine (Hipkins) B.; m. Eve Sherrerd, Sept. 22, 1956; children: Barbara, Jean, John Clifton, Nancy, Sandra, Andrew. AB magna cum laude, Princeton U., 1951; LHD (hon.), Widener U., 1997; HHD (hon.), Albright Coll.; LLD (hon.), U. Del., U. Rochester, 2000. With Wellington Mgmt. Co., Phila., 1951-74, asst. to pres., 1954-62, sec., adminstrv. v.p., 1962-66, exec. v.p., 1966-67, pres., CEO, 1967-74; CEO, chmn. Vanguard Group Investment Cos., Valley Forge, Pa., 1974-96; sr. chmn., founder Vanguard Group, Valley Forge, 1996-99; pres. Bogle Fin. Makerts Rsch. Ctr., Valley Forge, 2000—; Kaufman vis. prof. NYU, 1999-00; former bd. dirs., mem. exec. com. CGU; bd. dirs., chmn. corp. objectives com. Mead Corp.; bd. dirs. Chris Craft Industries. Author: Bogle on Mutual Funds: New Perspectives for the Intelligent Investor, 1993, Common Sense on Mutual Funds: New Imperatives for the Intelligent Investor, 1999, John Bogle on Investing: The First 50 Years, 2000; subject of biography: John Bogle and the Vanguard Experiment: One Man's Quest to Transform the Mutual Fund Industry, by Robert Slater, 1996; numerous articles to profl. jours., chpts. to books. Chmn. bd. trustees Blair Acad.; chmn. bd. dirs. Nat. Constn. Ctr., Am. Indian Coll. Fund.; former mem. adv. coun. econs. dept. Princeton U.; dir. Independence Standards Bd. Recipient Woodrow Wilson medal Princeton U., 1999; named One of Four Investment Giants of the 20th Century Fortune mag., 1999. Mem. Nat. Assn. Securities Dealers (investment cos. com. 1967-74, long-range planning com. 1973-74), Investment Co. Inst. (gov. 1969-81, chmn. 1969-70), Securities and Exch. Commn. (market oversight and fin. svcs. adv. com.), Merion Cricket Club (Haverford), Merion Golf (Ardmore). Office: Vanguard Group PO Box 2600 Valley Forge PA 19482-2600

BOGLE, MICHAEL MACLAINE, curator; b. Winston-Salem, N.C., Sept. 13, 1944; arrived in Australia 1981; s. Jack MacLaine and Bessie (Fulton) B.; m. Susan Beland, Aug. 25, 1979 (div. Oct. 1986); m. Peta Landman, Jan. 6, 1987; 1 child, Ariel Bogle. BS in Textiles, Calif. State U., Northridge, 1971; MS in Textiles, Kans. State U., 1972; MA in History, Boston U., 1981. Asst. prof. Syracuse (N.Y.) U.; textile conservator Mus. Am. Textile History, Australian War Meml., Canberra; editor Craft Australia mag.; curator Hist. Houses Trust, NSW. Author: Textile Dyes, Finishes and Auxilliaries, 1981, Modern Australian Furniture, 1989; contbg. author, Cultivating The Country, 1988, Design in Australia 1880-1970, 1998, Convicts, 1999; contbr. articles to profl. jours. Bd. dirs. Strawbery Banke Hist. Village, Portsmouth, N.H., 1979-81. With U.S. Army, 1965-67, Vietnam. Recipient grad. fellowship, Kans. State U., 1972. Mem. Mus. Assn. of Australia, Art Assn. Australia. Moravian. Home: 31 Taylor St, 429 Riley St Surry Hills, Sydney 2010 NSW, Australia Office: Hist Houses Trust NSW, 61 Darghan St Glebe, Glebe 2061 NSW, Australia

BOGOD, YURI ABRAHAM, physicist; b. Ukraina, Aug. 4, 1939; s. Abraham Joseph and Fira Isaac (Zobin) B.; m. Maria Lev Amstislavsky; 1 child, Liburkin Irena Yuri. MS, State U. Kharkov, 1957; PhD, Inst. Low Temperature Physics, Kharkov, 1969; DS in Physics and Math., Inst. Low Temperature Physics, 1984. Jr. rschr., leading rschr. Inst. of Low Temperature Physics, Kharkov, 1962-90; rschr. Weizman Inst. of Sci., Rehovot, Israel, 1991-96; supr. PhD students Inst. of Low Temperature Physics, Kharkov, 1974-87. Contbr. articles to profl. jours.

BOGOEV, KSENTE MELE, scientific research organization executive; b. Leunovo, Gostivar, Macedonia, Oct. 20, 1919; s. Mele Lazarov and Fimia Noveva (Jakovleva) B.; m. Mileva Miceva, Dec. 22, 1947; children: Milćo, Žarko. Grad. in econs., U. Belgrade, Yugoslavia, 1951, PhD in Econs., 1962; hon. dr., Martin Luther U., Halle, Germany, 1976. Dir. Inst. Econs., Skopje, Macedonia, 1945-47; vice min. Macedonian Ministry Fin., Skopje, 1945-52; prof. econs. U. Skopje, 1952-85, vice dean faculty econs., 1953-54, dean, 1960-63, rector univ., 1965-68; pres. Govt. of Macedonia, Skopje, 1968-74; academician Macedonian Acad. Scis. and Arts, Skopje, 1974—, pres., 1992—; advisor permanent Yugoslav del. to OECD, Paris, 1955-57; mem. Presidium of Macedonia, 1974-77; bd. govs. Nat. Bank Yugoslavia, Belgrade, 1977-81. Author: Local Finances in Yugoslavia, 1964, Fiscal Policy, 1964, Finances and Budget, 1975, Coordination of Public Finances, 1976, Theory a Praxis of Regional Development in Yugoslavia, 1977, System of Public Finances in Yugoslavia, 1984, International Monetary and Financial System Reforms: Urgent and Fundamental Needs, 1985, Balance of Payments Adjustment in Yugoslavia, 1986, Foreign Debts in Developing Countries, 1986, Fiscal Harmonization and Fiscal Federalism, 1987, Study on Fiscal Policy, 1988, Taxation System of the Republic of Macedonia, 1994, Perspectives of the Republic of Macedonia, 1996 Economic Transition: Concepts, Achievements, Problems, 1994, Ecology and Fiscal Measures, 1994, The Neoliberal Theory on Tax System Functions, 1995, Perspectives of the Republic of Macedonis-Actual Possibilities and Perspectives for the Economic Development of the Republic of Macedonia in the Period 1996-2010, 1996, Essential Issues and Challenges of Fiscal Policy, 1996, The Achieved and the Forthcoming in Transition, 1996, National Development Strategy for Macedonia: Development and Modernization, 1997, Thirty Years of the Macedonian Acad. Scis. and Arts, 1997, Consolidation of the Fiscal System of the Republic of Macedonia, 1998, Priorities and Dilemmas in Post-privatization years, 1998; mem. editl. bds. Economist, Stopanski pregled, Finansije, Ekonomska analiza, Finansiska prakša, until 1991. Decorated Order of Labour with red flag, Order of Merit with golden star, Order of Republics with golden wreath (Yugoslavia), cavaliere di gran croce nell Ordine al Merito della Repubblica Italiana, grand officer Ordre de Leopold (Belgium); recipient nat. sci. award 11 Oct., Parliament of Macdeonia, 1965; grantee Ford Found., U.S., 1963-64. Mem. Internat. Inst. Pub. Fin., Inst. Fin. (collaborator), Internat. Bankers Assn., Assn. Yugoslav Economists (pres. 1964-67), Acad. Scientiarum et Artium Europeae, Union Yugoslav Univs. (pres. 1966-68). Christian Orthodox. Home: Aco Karamanov 24, 91000 Skopje Macedonia Office: Madedonian Acad Scis-Art, Bd Krste Misirkov 2 POB 428, 91000 Skopje Macedonia*

BOGOLUBOV, NIKOLAI NIKOLAEVICH, JR., mathematics physicist; b. Kiev, Ukraine, Mar. 7, 1940; s. Nikolai Niholaevich and Eugenia Aleksandrovna (Pirachhova) B.; m. Titiana Vasilievna Stirova, 1981; children: Eugenia Nikolaevna, Nickolas Bogolubov. M in Theoretical Physics, Moscow State U., 1962, D in Theoretical Physics, 1966, postdoctoral in theoretical physics, 1970. Rschr. Mathemation Inst., Stecklov, 1963-75; lab. head Statistral Mechanics for Matium Inst., 1976-86; head dept. of statis. mechanics VA Steclov Math. Inst., 1987—; cons. mem. Joint Inst. for Nuclear Rsch., Lab. of Theoretical Physics, Dubna, 1970-96, 96—. Contbr. over 160 articles to profl. publs. Engr. It. Radiadcation, 1983-90. Recipient State Prize of USSR Govt. of USSR, 1983, Acad. Krylov prize Ukrainian Acad. Sci., 1986. Mem. Russian Acad. of Sci., Acad. Creative Endeavour (pres. 1990), Schevehenko Soc. (Ukraine), Internat. Acad. Scis. Fax: 095 135-05-55. Office: Dept Statis Mechanics, VA Steklov Math Inst, 117966 Moscow Russia

BOGOMOLOV, EDWARD ALEXANDROVICH, physicist, researcher; b. Leningrad, USSR, Sept. 19, 1940; s. Alexander Vasilyevich and Eugenia Semenovna (Tiigonen) B.; m. Galina Dmitrievna Stratilova, Feb. 20, 1963; 1 child, Maryanna. Grad. in physics, Leningrad State U., 1963; PhD in Astrophysics, Ioffe Physico-Tech. Inst., Leningrad, 1984. Practical rschr. Ioffe Physico-Tech. Inst., 1963-65, scientist, 1965-86; sr. scientist Ioffe Physico-Tech. Inst., St. Petersburg, Russia, 1986—, head cosmic spectrometry lab., 1999—; mem. Baloon Investigations Commn., Moscow, 1980—; mem. sect. cosmic ray physics, space coun. Russian Acad. Scis., Moscow, 1997—, mem. sci. coun. on complex problem cosmic rays, 1997—. Author Procs. 16th Cosmic Ray Conf., Kyoto, Japan, 1979, 20th, Moscow, 1987, 21st, Adelaide, Australia, 1990, 24th, Rome, 1995, others. Grantee Soros Found., 1992, Russian Found. for Basic Rsch., 1997, 2000, INTAS, 1997. Mem. N.Y. Acad. Scis. Avocations: art, slides, books, mushroom picking. Fax: (812)247-19-63. E-mail: edward.bogomolov@pop.ioffe.rssi.ru. Home: 2d Line, House 41, Apt 22, 199053 Saint Petersburg Russia Office: Ioffe Physico-Tech Inst, Politekhnicheskaya 26, 194021 Saint Petersburg Russia

BÖGRE, LASZLO, biologist, educator; b. Gödöllö, Hungary, Feb. 11, 1960; s. János and Jánosné Deák (Ildikó) B.; m. Irute Sikorskyte; 1 child, Meskys Domantas. MD, U. Agr., Gödöllö, 1984; PhD, Biol. Rsch. Ctr., Szeged, Hungary, 1989. Rsch. assoc. Biol. Rsch. Ctr., Szeged, 1989-91; postdoctoral staff Alberta U., Edmonton, Can., 1991-92; postdoctoral staff Vienna (Austria) U., 1992-97, asst. prof., 1997-99; sr. lectr. Royal Holloway U. London, 2000—. Contbr. articles to profl. jours. Achievements include patentee in field. Avocations: photography, hiking, music. Home: 95 a Chertsey Ln, Staines Middlesex England Office: Royal Holloway U London, Sch Biol Scis Egham Hill, Egham TW20 0EX, United Kingdom

BOGSCH, ERIK, pharmaceutical company executive; b. Budapest, Hungary, Oct. 31, 1947; s. Aristides and Eva (Szentmártony) B.; m. Annamária Pohl, June 27, 1971; children: Erik, Judit, Nóra. Degree in chem. engring., Tech. U., Budapest, 1970, degree in econ. engring., 1974. Devel. mgr. Richter, Budapest, 1970-77, devel. dir., 1983-87, mng. dir., 1992—; dir. Medimpex, Mex., 1977-83; mng. dir. Medimpex U.K. Ltd., London, 1988-92. Recipient Small Cross, Order of Merit of Hungarian Republic, 1997. Mem. Hungarian Pharm. Mfrs. Assn. (vice chmn. bd. dirs. 1993, chmn. mfr.'s sect. 1993). Office: Gedeon Richter Ltd, Gyömrói út 19-21, 1103 Budapest Hungary

BOGUNOVIC, NIKOLA, computer engineering educator; b. Varazdin, Croatia, Aug. 31, 1944; s. Branko and Hedviga (Ozeg) B.; m. Mira Kastelan, Nov. 9, 1971; children: Maja, Hrvoje. BS, U. Zagreb, 1967, MS, 1971, PhD, 1984. Rsch. asst. Ruder Bošković Inst., Zagreb, 1968-71; rsch. assoc. Ruder Bošković Inst., 1972-84, lab. head, 1987—; prof. U. Zagreb, 1987—; vis. rschr. Culham Lab., Abingdon, Eng., 1971-72; vis. prof. Vanderbilt U., Nashville, Tenn., 1985-87. Editor: Artificial Intelligence in Measurement and Control, 1992; contbr. over 5o papers to profl. jours. Patentee in field. Mem. IEEE, Assn. for Computing Machinery, Digital Equipment Computer Users Soc. Roman Catholic. Avocations: scuba diving, skiing. Home: Srebrnjak 166, 10000 Zagreb Croatia Office: Ruder Boškovic Inst, Bijenicka 54, 10000 Zagreb Croatia

BOGUSLAVSKII, ILYA ZELIKOVICH, machine manufacturing executive, educator; b. Saint Petersburg, Russia, Jan. 25, 1933; s. Zelik and Sarra (Leszczinskaja) B. Elec. Engr., Tech. U. St. Petersburg, Russia, 1957; cand. Tech. Scis., Inst. Elec. Machinery, St. Petersburg, Russia, 1968, D in Tech. Scis., 1988; prof., Tech. U. St. Petesburg, Russia, 1989. Elec. engr. Electrosila Works, St. Petersburg, Russia, 1957-60, sr. elec. engr., 1961-64; chief electromagnetic and heat calculations divsn. Electrosila Works, St. Petersburg, 1965-2000; chief electrician Work Novaja Sila, St. Petersburg, 2000—; prof. elec. machines Tech. U. St. Petersburg, 1989—. Author: (book) Integral Method of Calculation of Electrical Machines tooth zone, 1968 (Russian); contbr. 140 articles to Russian Jour. Fuel, Power and Heat Systems, Electricity and others., 1960—; Patentee: Improvements in consruction

of A.C. machinery--patents in Russia, Germany, Switzerland, Austria, England, France. ; contbr. 20 articles to Power Engring. and other Mfg. Publs., 1980-97. Honored Sci. and Tech. Man of Russian Fedn. Mem. IEEE, St. Petersburg Electrotech. Soc. (pres. elec. machines divsn.). Avocations: jazz, symphony, opera, bicycling. Office: Electrosila Works AC Divsn, Moskovsky Prospekt 139, Saint Petersburg Russia

BOGUSLAVSKII, JOSIF ARKADJEVICH, mathematician, researcher; b. Poltava, Ukraine, Sept. 24, 1921; s. Azkadii Semenovich and Vera (Grigorievna) B.; m. Galina Gordeevna Lavrova, Nov. 29, 1957; children: Nadezgda, Azkadii, Stanislav. Kandidat, Jukowsky Air Force Acad., Moscow, 1951, PhD, 1961. Chief of sect. State Rsch. Inst. Aviation Sys., Moscow, 1946-55, chief lab., 1955—; prof. Phys.-Tech. Inst., Moscow, 1980—. Author: Methods of Navigatoin and Control, 1970, Applied Problems of Filtering and Control, 1983, Filtering and Control, 1988; contbr. articles to profl. jours. Recipient State Prize of USSR, 1983; CRDF grantee, 1997. Home: Victorenkostr h 2/1 apt 18, 125167 Moscow Russia Office: State Inst Aviation Sys, Victorenko str 7, 125319 Moscow Russia

BOGUSLAVSKY, GEORGE WILLIAM, psychologist, educator; b. Razdolnoye, Maritime, Russia, Oct. 17, 1911; came to U.S., 1930.; s. Vasilii P. and Anna (Lysenko) B.; m. Geneva K. Bowers, Jan. 8, 1943. BA, U. Wash., 1939, MS, 1941; PhD, Cornell U., 1953. Lic. psychologist, N.Y. Instr. U. Conn., Storrs, 1947-51; asst. prof. Cornell U., Ithaca, N.Y., 1953-57; prof., chmn. dept. psychology Rensselaer Poly. Inst., Troy, N.Y., 1957-77; cons. Am. Inst. Rsch., Pitts., 1952-77, Pergamon Inst., London, 1959-62; adv. N.Y. State Edn. Dept., Albany, 1957-59, Rensselaer Family Court, Troy, 1958-60. Contbg. author: Group Processes, 1957, Physiological Bases Psychiatry, 1958; also articles. Capt. Adjutant Gen.'s Dept., 1942-46, PTO. Rsch. grantee HEW, 1962-65. Mem. AAAS, APA, Assn. N.Y. Acad. Scis., Pavlovian Soc., Archives of History of Am. Psychology, Sigma Xi.

BOGUSŁAWSKI, PIOTR, physicist; b. Warsaw, Poland, Aug. 5, 1949; s. Jan and Aniela (Załeska) B.; m. Grażyna Sławińska, May 27, 1978; children: Magda, Wojtek, Julia. BSc in Physics, Warsaw U., 1972; PhD in Physics, Polish Acad. Scis., 1976. Asst. Inst. Physics Polish Acad. Scis., 1976-80, adj., 1981—, mem. sci. coun., 1990—; adj. prof. N.C. State U., Raleigh., 1994—. Recipient Sec.'s award Polish Acad. Scis., 1977, award of sect. math. and physics Polish Acad. Scis., 1986. Mem. Polish Phys. Soc. Home: Frascati 1, 00-492 Warsaw Poland Office: Polish Acad Scis Inst Phys, Al Lotników 32/46, 02-668 Warsaw Poland

BOGUTZ, JEROME EDWIN, lawyer; b. Bridgeton, N.J., June 7, 1935; s. Charles and Gertrude (Lahn) B.; m. Helene Carole Ross, Nov. 20, 1960; children: Marc Lahn, Tami Lynne. BS in Fin., Pa. State U., 1957; JD, Villanova U., 1962. Bar: Pa., U.S. Dist. Ct. (ea. dist.) Pa., U.S. Ct. Appeals (3d cir.), U.S. Supreme Ct. Assoc. Dash & Levy, Phila., 1962-63, Abrahams & Loewenstein, Phila., 1963-64; dep. dir., chief of litigation Community Legal Svcs., Phila., 1964-68, dir., 1968-78; emeritus, 1978—; pvt. practice law Phila., 1968-71; ptnr. Bogutz & Mazer, Phila., 1971-81, Fox Rothschild O'Brien & Frankel, Phila., 1981-98; judge Pro Tem Phila. Ct. Common Pleas, 1992—; ptnr. Christie, Pabarue, Mortensen & Young, P.C., Phila., 1998—; adj. clin. prof. law Villanova (Pa.) U., 1969-72, lectr., 1987—, bd. consultors Law Sch., 1983—; pres. Internat. Mobile Machines, Phila., 1980-81, Interdigital Comm., 1980-81, also bd. dirs. ABA-JAD Lawyers Conf., 1987-92, mem. exec. coun., 1986-92, vice chmn., 1987-88, chmn., 1989-90, chmn. nominating com., 1989-90, mem. long range planning com., 1989-90; mem. adv. bd. Pa. Med. Profl. Liability Catastrophe Loss Fund, 2000—; bd. dirs. Jefferson Park Hosp., Phila. Bd. dirs. Am. Friends of Hebrew U., 1988-93, chmn. exec. com., 1991-93, pres., 1993-95, chmn. bd. 1995-98, chair steering com., pres. Pa. Futures Commn. on Justice in the 21st Century, 1993—, chmn. of bd., 1993-97. With USAR, 1956-60. Fellow Am. Bar Found. (life), Pa. Bar Found. (life, pres. 1986-88, bd. dirs. 1983—, lifetime dir. 1991—), Am. Judicature Soc. (life, bd. dirs. 1990—); mem. ABA (ho. of dels. 1980-84, 86-96, credentials and admissions com. 1987-88, nominating com. 1992, 93, chair ABA/JAD bench bar com., vice chmn. lawyer's conf. 1987-89, chair 1988-90, co-chair mid-yr. meeting com. 1987-88, planning com., conf. sect. officers, 1988-90, bd. mem. consortium on legal svcs. and pub. 1987-91, mem. disaster relief task force, bd. dirs., commr., chmn. ABA Commn. on Advt. 1988-91), Pa. Bar Assn. (pres. 1985-86, bd. dirs. 1983-90, chair Governance Com., 1996-98), Phila. Bar Found. (pres. 1981), Phila. Bar Assn. (v.p. 1978, pres.-elect 1979, chancellor 1980, sec. 1975-78, trustee 1979—), Pa. Bar Trust (chair 1993—), Pa. House of Dels. (life; chair governance com. 1996-98), Nat. Met. Bar Leaders (founder, pres. 1979-82, pres. emeritus 1983—), Nat. Conf. Bar Pres. (exec. coun. 1981-84), Phila. C. of C. (bd. dirs. 1980-83). Republican. Jewish. Avocations: golf, sailing. Home: 110 S Somerset Ave Ventnor City NJ 08406-2848 Office: Christie Pabarue Mortensen & Young 1880 JFK Blvd Fl 10 Philadelphia PA 19103-7424

BOGZA, NADEZHDA FEDOROVNA, librarian, bibliographer; b. Lymany, Mykolayiv, USSR, Dec. 25, 1949; d. Fedor Terentievich and Yelena Sergeevna (Zarechanskaya) Shvets; m. Alexandre Michailovich Leonov, Nov. 8, 1973 (div. Mar. 1989); 1 child, Alina Alexandrovna Bezzubenko-Leonova; m. Yevgeny Michailovich Bogza, Dec. 12, 1994. Higher edn. diploma, The Inst. Culture, Kharkov, Ukraine, USSR, 1974. Libr.-bibliographer diplomate. Head libr. Sovkhoz, Zhovtnevoye, USSR, 1968-71; libr. shipyard, Mykolayiv, USSR, 1971-72, sch., Mykolayiv, 1972; libr. Gmyryov Nikolaev State Regional Scientific Libr., Mykolayiv, 1972-73, dir., 1987—; dir. Dist. Libr., Zhovtnevoye, USSR, 1973-87; presenter in field. Contbr. numerous articles to profl. jours. Named Honorable Worker of Culture Ukraine Pres. Decree , 1998. Mem. All-Ukrainian Libr. Assn. (bd. dirs. 1998), Trade Union Workers of Culture (mem. presidium regional com. 1987-99). Avocations: rose cultivation. Home: Glinka 6a Apt 58, Oktyabr'skoye Ukraine Office: Gmyryov Regional Libr, Moskovskaya 9, Mykolayiv Ukraine

BOHACEK, JAROSLAV, metrologist, educator, researcher; b. Roudnice, Czech Republic, Dec. 5, 1942; s. Jaroslav and Marie (Snejdarova) B.; m. Marcela Dolezalova, Apr. 15, 1976; children: Roman, Marcela. MS, Czech Tech. U., Prague, 1964, PhD, 1977, DSc, 1991. Asst. prof. Czech Tech. U., Prague, 1964-80, assoc. prof., 1980-93, prof. metrology, 1993—; guest scientist Physikalisch-Technische Bundesanstalt, Braunschweig, Germany, 1992, Nat. Phys. Lab., Teddington, Eng., 1993, 94, Bur. Internat. des Poids et Mesures, Sevres, France, 1995, Electrotech. Lab., Tsukuba, Japan, 1997, Nat. Rsch. Coun., Ottawa, Can., 1998; cons. Czech Metrological Inst., Brno, 1993—; advisor Czech Office for Standards, Metrology and Testing, Prague, 1993—. Author: Metrology of Electrical Quantities, 1994; contbr. articles to profl. jours. Recipient award Czech Office for Standards, Metrology and Testing, 1995; Grant Agy. of the Czech Republic grantee, 1996-97, 98—. Avocations: theatre, tennis. Home: Mazurska 520/9, Prague 8, Czech Republic CZ18100 Office: Czech Tech U Fac Elec Engrg, Technicka 2, Prague 6, Czech Republic CZ16627

BOHAN, THOMAS LYNCH, physicist, lawyer; b. Terre Haute, Ind., Feb. 12, 1938; s. Richard Timothy and Anna Elizabeth (Lynch) B.; m. Linda Ann Sian, Nov. 26, 1960 (div. Dec. 1981); children: Richard Michael, Cecilia Anne, John Charles; m. Rhonda Beth Berg, July 4, 1987. BS in Physics, U. Chgo., 1960; MS in Physics, U. Ill., 1964, PhD in Physics, 1968; JD, Franklin Pierce Law Ctr., 1980. Bar: Maine 1980, Mass. 1980, U.S. Dist. Ct. Maine 1980, U.S. Patent Office 1980, U.S. Ct. Appeals (1st cir.) 1992, U.S. Ct. Appeals (2nd cir.) 1994, U.S. Supreme Ct., 1996. Research assoc. U. Ill., Urbana, 1968-69; asst. prof. physics Bowdoin Coll., Brunswick, Maine, 1969-76; assoc. Sunenblick, Fontaine and Reben, Portland, Maine, 1980-82; ptnr. Med. and Tech. Cons., Portland, 1982-86, sole propr., 1986—; propr. Thomas L. Bohan & Assoc., Portland, 1985—. Editor (with A. Damask) Forensic Accident Investigation: Motor Vehicles-1, 1995; editor Forensic Accident Investigation: Motor Vehicles-2, 1997; contbr. articles to profl. jours. Chmn. Community Devel. Com., Brunswick, 1976-78; organizer, treas., pres. Peaks Island Land Preserve, Inc., 1994-97. Research grantee Am. Heart Assn., 1970-76, The Research Corp., 1972-74, NSF/NATO, 1967; fellow Tex. Instruments, 1965; Fulbright scholar, Peru, 1972-73. Fellow Am. Acad. Forensic Sci. (chair engring. sci. sect. 1997-98, bd. dirs. 1999—); mem. AAAS, Am. Chem. Soc., Am. Phys. Soc., Cumberland County Bar Assn., Maine Trial Lawyers Assn. Sigma Xi. Home: 54 Pleasant Ave Peaks Island ME 04108-1188 Office: Med & Tech Cons and Thomas L Bohan & Assocs 371 Fore St Portland ME 04101-5010

BOHANNON, CHARLES TAD, lawyer; b. Dallas, June 25, 1964; s. Charles Spencer and Donna Pauline (Smith) B.; m. Gayle Renee Alston, July 26, 1986. BA, Hendrix Coll., 1986; JD, U. Ark., Little Rock, 1992; LLM, Washington U., St. Louis, 1993. Bar: Ark. 1992, Tex. 1993, U.S. Dist. Ct. (ea. and we. dists.) Ark. 1992, U.S. Dist. Ct. (no. dist.) Tex. 1994, U.S. Ct. Appeals (5th and 8th cirs.) 1994, U.S. Tax Ct. 1994. Staff atty. U.S. Ct. Appeals (8th cir.), St. Louis, 1992-94; assoc. Gill Law Firm, Little Rock, 1994-98, Wright, Lindsey & Jennings, LLP, Little Rock, 1998—. Contbr. articles to profl. jours. Mem. ABA, Ark. Bar Assn., Pulaski County Bar Assn., Nat. Transp. Safety Bd., Bar Assn. Fifth Cir., Bar Assn. State Bar of Tex., Am. Judicature Soc., Nat. Assn. Bond Lawyers, Ark. State Soccer Assn., Ctrl. Ark. Referees Assn., Aircraft Owners and Pilots Assn. Avocations: soccer (player, referee, coach), flying, fly fishing, home renovation. Office: Wright Lindsey & Jennings 200 W Capitol Ave Ste 2200 Little Rock AR 72201-3699

BOHANNON, JOHN NEIL, III, psychology educator, researcher; b. White Plains, N.Y., Nov. 7, 1948; s. John Neil Jr. and Elizabeth Sadler (Morgan) B.; m. Rosemary Ridder, July 1, 1972 (div. Mar. 1986); children: John Neil IV, Catherine Ridder. AB, Fairfield U., 1970; MA, U. Hartford, 1972; PhD, SUNY, Stony Brook, 1975. Asst. prof. Emory U., Atlanta, 1975-78, Ga. Inst. Tech., Atlanta, 1978-84; assoc. prof. Va. Poly. Inst. and State U., Blacksburg, 1984-88; prof. psychology Butler U., Indpls., 1988—, head dept., 1988-96, A. Dunn prof., 1994—; mem. rev. panel NIMH, Washington, 1984-95. Author: The Development of Language, 1984, 5th edit., 1999; editor: Psychology Research, 1985; contbr. articles to profl. jours. With USN, 1966-67. Recipient Friend of Forensics tchg. award Barkely Forum, Emory U., 1977, M.A. Furst rsch. award Ga. Inst. Tech. chpt. Sigma Xi, 1984. Mem. Am. Psychol. Soc., Soc. for Rsch. in Child Devel., Southeastern Psychol. Assn., Southeastern Workers in Memory (pres. 2000). Avocation: swimming. E-mail: bohannon@butler.edu. Office: Butler U 4600 Sunset Ave Indianapolis IN 46208-3487

BOHANNON-KAPLAN, MARGARET ANNE, publisher, lawyer; b. Oakland, Calif., July 6, 1937; d. Thomas Morris and Ruth Frances (Davenport) Bohannon; m. Melvin Jordan Kaplan, Feb. 2, 1961; children: Mark Geoffrey, Craig Andrew, Stephen Joseph, David Benjamin, Jonathan Michael. Student, Smith Coll., 1955-56, U. Cin., 1956; B.A. in Philosophy, U. Calif.-Berkeley, 1960; LL.B., LaSalle Extension U., 1982, Coll. Fin. Planning, 1985. Bar: Calif. 1982. Engaged in property mgmt., real estate investment Kaplan Real Estate, Berkely and San Francisco, 1961-77; investment exec. Wellington Fin. Group, San Francisco, 1977—; cons. fin. planning and law San Francisco and Carmel, Calif., 1982—; pres. Wellington Publs., Carmel, 1983—, Exec. Advt., Carmel, 1983—; talk show host stations KNRY, KIEZ, 1999. Carmel, 1983—. Author: Another Way, 1997, (pseudonym Helen P. Rogers), Everyone's Guide to Financial Planning, 1984, Social Security: An Idea Whose Time Has Passed, 1985, The American Deficit: Fulfillment of a Prophecy?, 1988, The Election Process, 1988, The Deficit: 12 Steps to Ease the Crisis, 1988, (series) Taking A Stand On, 1991, Alternatives, 1992; editor: What Role if Any, Should Government's Role be Regarding Child Care in the United States?, 1991, What if Any, Should Governments Role Be Regarding Health Care in the United States, 1992, What Role Does, And What Role Should Media Play in Choosing Our Candidates for National Office?, 1993, Doesn't Anyone Care About the Children?, 1994, Responsibility: Who Has It and Who Doesn't and What That Means to The Nation, 1994, 97, White Hats: People Who Try To Make A Difference, 1994, Governments Struggling with Limited Resources, 1995, Should Government Intervene to Help Children and Teens In Trouble, If so How?, 1996, Excerpts From the Harry Singer Foundation High School Essay Contests, 1996-2000, Students Consider Whether It's Time For a Rite of Passage For American Teens and How We Might All Improve Our Local Communities, 2000. Co-founder The Harry Singer Found., Carmel, Calif., 1988; ind. candidate for U.S. Senate, 1992. Dir. Singer Online internat. programs, 1993—, web master, 1997—. Mem. ABA, Calif. Bar Assn., Calif. Real Estate Assn., Internat. Assn. Fin. Planners, Inst. Cert. Fin. Planners, Ind. Sector, Philanthropy Round Table, Nat. Coun. Soc. Studies Internat. Assn. Public Participation. Club: Commonwealth (San Francisco). Office: PO Box 223159 Carmel CA 93922-3159

BOHL, ERICH GUSTAV, mathematics educator; b. Hamburg, Germany, July 22, 1936; s. Oscar Adolf and Maria Anna (Plaas) B.; m. Uta Irene Unkelbach, Oct. 11, 1963; children: Barbara, Benjamin. Abitur, Bismarck-Schule, Hamburg, 1957; diploma in math., U. Hamburg, 1962, Dr.rer.nat., 1963, habilitation, 1965. Asst. U. Hamburg, 1963-70; assoc. prof. math. U. Calgary, Can., 1970-71; prof. math. U. Münster, Germany, 1971-79, U. Konstanz, Germany, 1979—; vis. asst. prof. math. UCLA, 1966-67. Author: Lösbarkeit und Numerik bei Operatorgleichungen, 1974, Finite Modelle gewöhnlicher Randwertaufgaben, 1981, Mathematische Grundlagen für die Modellierung biologischer Vorgänge, 1987; editor: Numerik und Anwendungen von Eigenwertaufgaben und Verzweigungsproblemen, 1977. Recipient medal of the Charles U., Faculty Math. and Physics Charles U., Prague, 1996, Meml. Medal, 1999. Mem. Gesellschaft Angewandte Mathematik und Mechanik, Deutsche Mathematiker-Vereinigung, Heidegger-Gesellschaft. Avocations: philosophy, classical music, theater. Home: Ringstr 83, 78465 Konstanz Germany Office: Univ Konstanz, Univ 10 Postfach 5560, 78434 Konstanz Germany

BOHL, FRIEDRICH, former German government official, lawyer; b. Rosdorf, Germany, Mar. 5, 1945; married; four children. Grad. law, 1969, 1972. Sci. asst. Marburg Inst. Comml. and Bus. Law, 1969; mem. Hesse State Assembly, 1970-80; lawyer, 1972—; mem. Fed. German Parliament, 1980—; min. without portfolio, chief Fed. Chancellery Govt. of Germany, from 1991; mem. Heinrich-Böll Found. Pub. notary. Recipient Promotion prize for state fine art trade German Dem. Republic, Karl Hofer prize West Berlin Fine Arts Acad., 1989, Democracy prize Blätter für deutsche und internationale Politik, 1990, Dr. Bruno Kreisky prize for svcs. to human rights, 1991, Peace prize World Coun. Meth. Ch., 1991. Home: Finkenstrasse 11, 35043 Marburg Cappel, Germany Office: Bundesminister a D, Platz der Republik, 11011 Berlin Germany*

BÖHLE, ANDREAS, urologist, educator, research scientist; b. Frankfurt/Main, Hessen, Germany, June 8, 1955; s. Eberhard and Lore (Niemann) B.; m. Anne Hohn, Aug. 9, 1990; children: Jan Lukas, Max Christian. MD magna cum laude, U. Hamburg, Germany, 1984; specialist in urology, U. Lübeck, Germany, 1989; venia legendi, U. Lübeck, 1994. Physician U. Berlin, 1983-85, U. Bochum, Germany, 1985-86; physician U. Lübeck, 1986—, sr. physician, univ. lectr., 1991-2000, dep. dir., full prof. urology, 2000—. Editor: (with D. Jocham) Optimal Therapy for Patients with High-Risk Superficial Bladder Cancer Controversy and Consensus, 1997; author: (with D. Jocham) Die Intravesikale Immuntherapie mit Bacillus Calmette Guérin, 1998. Active German Mil., 1975-76. Recipient C.E. Alken prize, 1997, Prof. Dr. Heinz Spitzbart prize European Gynecology-Urology Assn. for Infections, München, 1999, Erwin Fertig prize Justus-Liebig U., Giessen, 1999. Mem. European Assn. Urology, German Assn. for Urology, Am. Urologic Assn. Avocation: sailing. Office: Univ Lübeck, Ratzeburger Allee 160, 23538 Lübeck Germany

BOHLEY, PETER, biochemistry educator; b. Sulzbach-Rosenberg, Germany, Oct. 31, 1935; s. Karl and Margarete (Ehrlicher) B.; m. Dorothea Heinecke, July 22, 1961; children: Elisabeth, Johanna, Konrad. MD, Univ. Halle, Germany, 1959, D of Sci. Med., 1974. Asst. Univ. Halle, 1960-83; prof. biochemistry Univ. Tübingen, Germany, 1986—. Author: Tissue Proteinases, 1971, Erlebte DDR-Geschichte, 1994; editor: Intracellular Protein Catabolism, 1974. Mem. Biochem. Soc., N.Y. Acad. Scis. Achievements include co-discovery of Cathepsin L and Cathepsin H; isolation and characterization of these lysosomal proteases, surface hydrophobicity as signal for proteolysis. Avocations: history of science, writing, painting, etching. Home: Mohl-Str 58, D-72074 Tübingen Germany Office: U Tübingen Physiol Chem, Hoppe-Seyler Str 4, D-72076 Tübingen Germany

BOHLINGER, LEWIS HALL, state government official; b. Little Rock, July 8, 1942; s. Lewis Hall Bohlinger and Helen Elisa (Reid) Bragg; m. Kathleen Ann Klein, Jan. 30, 1967; children: Lewis Hall, Reid Watson. BS, Southeastern La. U., 1965; MS, Tulane U., 1970, ScD, 1975. Rsch. asst. Delta Primate Rsch. Ctr., Covington, La., 1965-69; health physicist La. Bd. Nuclear Energy, Baton Rouge, 1971-80; asst. adminstr. La. Nuclear Energy Divsn., Baton Rouge, 1980-87; dep. asst. sec. La. Office of Environ. Affairs, Baton Rouge, 1983-89; asst. sec. La. Office of Air Quality, Baton Rouge, 1984-86; dep. sec. La. DEQ, Baton Rouge, 1987-88; adminstr. La. Radiation Protection Divsn., Baton Rouge, 1989-94, La. Hazardous Waste Divsn., Baton Rouge, 1994-96; dep. sec. La. Dept. Environ. Quality, Baton Rouge, 1996—; adj. asst. prof. Tulane U., New Orleans, 1988—; chair Cen. Interstate Low Level Radioactive Waste Compact Commn., 1983-89, 91, chmn./mem. various state and fed. tech. coms. Grantee USPHS, 1969-71. Mem. Am. Nuclear Soc., La. Environ. Health Assn., Health Physics Soc., La. Air and Waste Mgmt. Assn., Delta Omega Soc. Home: 11930 Parkbrook Ave Baton Rouge LA 70816-4672 Office: LA Dept Environ Quality PO Box 82263 Baton Rouge LA 70884-2263

BÖHM, WINFRIED FRANZ, education educator; b. Schluckenau, Bohemia, Mar. 22, 1937; s. Oskar and Elisabeth (Liebsch) B.; m. Ingrid Katharina Goel-, Jan. 29, 1961 (dec. Mar. 1979); children: Birgitta, Guido; m. Regina Klepper, Oct. 2, 1982; 1 child, Katharina Elisabeth. BEd, U. Bamberg, Germany, 1964; PhD, U. Würzburg, Germany, 1969, prof. in Edn., 1973; Dr Honoris Causa (hon.), U. Catolica, Córdoba, Argentina, 1984. Prof. U. Würzburg, 1974—; prof. various internat. univs., 1974—; dir. Inst. für Pädagogik, Würzburg, 1974—; pres. Deutsche Montessori Gesellschaft, 1987—, Inst. for European Edn., Gardone Riviera, Italy, 1985—. Author: 32 books on Edn. and Philosophy in German, English, Spanish, Italian and Korean; over 350 articles in profl. jours; scriptwriter TV films; dir. stage and TV. Mem. Messina (Italy) Acad. Sci., Córdoba (Argentina) Acad. Sci., Prague (Czechoslovakia) Acad. Sci., Rotary Internat. Avocation: music. Home: Matth-Ehrenfried Str 46, D-97074 Würzburg Germany Office: Inst fü Pädagogik, Am Hubland, D-97074 Würzburg Germany

BOHMAN, MICHAEL CARL, child psychiatrist, researcher; b. Stockholm, Sweden, June 28, 1917; s. Gunnar Carl and Signe Helene (Eriksson) B.; m. Ingalill Levin Bohman, Feb. 13, 1964; children: Helene, David, Jenny, Hannes. MD, Karolinska Inst., Stockholm, Sweden, 1945. Asst. prof. Karolinska Hosp., Stockholm, Sweden, 1971-72; prof., chmn. Univ. Hosp., 1972-83, 84-89; cons. U. Stockholm, 1996—; scientific adv., cons. Swedish Socio-med. bd., 1978-83. Contbr. articles to profl. jours. Recipient Internat. Soc. for Biomedical Rsch. on Alcoholism award, Bristol, 1990. Mem. Swedish Soc. Child Psychiatry (chmn. 1976-78). Avocation: painting. Home: Hogbergsgatan 40A, S-11826 Stockholm Sweden

BÖHMDORFER, DIETER, Austrian minister of justice; b. Trutnov, Czech Republic, May 11, 1943; arrived in Austria, 1945; Law degree, U. Vienna, Austria, 1967. Bar: Austria, 1973. Pupil barrister law firm of Harald Eggstain, Harald Ofner, Karl Leutgeb, 1967-73; mem. supervisory bd. Austrian Airlines Lufterverkehrs, 1987-89, Vienna Airport, 1991-98; with ERP Loan Commn., 1991—; mem. gen. mng. bd. Carinthian Landesholding, 1999—; fed. min. justice Austria, 2000—. With Austrian armed forces. Office: Fed Ministry Justice, Museumstrasse 7, 1070 Vienna Austria*

BÖHME, GERNOT, philosophy educator; b. Dessau, Germany, Jan. 3, 1937; s. Friedrich Wilhelm and Gudrun (Freiin von Bothmer) B.; m. Karen Schmerschneider, 1965 (div. 1977); children: Anja, Kora, Rhea; m. Farideh Akashe, Jan. 31, 1951; 1 child, Rebecca. Abitur, Gymnasium für Jungen, Goslar, Germany, 1957; Dr phil, U. Hamburg, Germany, 1965; Habilitation, U. Munich, 1972. Asst. prof. U. Hamburg, Germany, 1965-66, U. Heidelberg, Germany, 1966-69; rschr. Max Planck Inst., Starnberg, Germany, 1969-77; prof. philosophy Tech. U. Darmstadt, Germany, 1977—. Author: Anthropology in Pragmatic Perspective, 4th edit., 1994, Letters to My Daughters, 1995, Kant's Critique of Judgement in a New Perspective, 1995, Idea and Cosmos. Plato's Doctrine of Time, 1996, Atmospheres Essays in New Aesthetics, 3d edit., 2000, Ethics in Context. On the handling of serious questions., 2d edit., 1998, The Type of Socrates, 2d edit., 1998, Introduction to Philosophy, 3rd edit., 1998, Pictoral Theory, 1999; co-author: The Other of Reason. The development of rationality in Kantian philosphy., 2d edit., 1992, Fire, Water, Earth, Air. A Cultural History of the Four Elements., 1996; editor: (with N. Stehr) The Knowledge Society, 1986, Plato's Theoretical Philosophy, 2000. Mem. Gen. Soc. Philosopny in Germany, Kant Soc., Soc. for New Phemonology, German Soc. for Aesthetics. Office: Tech U Darmstadt, Inst Philosophy, Schloss, D-64283 Darmstadt Germany

BÖHME-DÜRR, KARIN, communications educator; b. Erfurt, Germany, Feb. 16, 1949; d. Werner Böhme and Anna Weiss; m. Alfred Dürr, Sept. 29, 1983; children: Celina, Lillian. MA in Linguistics, U. Ariz., 1973; diploma in psychology, U. Heidelberg, Germany, 1975; PhD in Social Sci., U. Nijmegen, The Netherlands, 1983; PhD in Comm. Sci., U. Leipzig, Germany, 1998. Asst. prof. U. Munich, Germany, 1980-89; comm. rschr. Internat. Zentralinstitut, Germany, 1990-91; prof. U. Bamberg, Germany, 1994-96; prof. comm. and media rsch. U. Dusseldorf (Germany), 1999—; cons. VBZ, Germany, 1986-90, Zweites Deutsches Fernsehen, Germany, 1986-94, Stiftung Lesen, Germany, 1988-90, Bayerischer Rundfunk, Germany, 1976—; vis. prof. U. Minn., 1984; media cons. Author: Children's Understanding and Awareness of German Possessive Pronouns, 1983, Knowledge Changes by Media, 1990, In Search of the Audience, 1995, Looking for Perspectives: How the Image of Germany Has Changed in American Newspapers After the End of the Cold War, 2000. Rsch. fellow U. Calif., San Diego, 1990-91, Harvard U., 1991-92; grantee German Sci. Found. Mem. DGPuK, German Soc. Semiotics (first prize award 1984), Internat. Comm. Assn. (Top Paper award 1988). Avocation: media. Home: Kornwegerstr 47, 81375 Munich Germany

BÖHMER, THOMAS, internist; b. Narvik, Norway, Sept. 10, 1936; s. Einar and Ellen Marie (Arthur) B.; m. Liv Eyde, June 23, 1961 (div. 1976); children: Agnethe, Catherine, Benedict; m. Ingeborg Wikborg, May 31, 1991. MD, U. Oslo, 1960, PhD, 1969. Specialist in internal medicine, cardiology and endocrinology. Rsch. fellow Norwegian Heart Assn., Oslo, 1965-69; postdoctoral fellow U. Calif. Med. Ctr., San Francisco, 1969-70; resident/sr. resident Riks Hosp., Oslo, 1970-74, 76-79, assoc. prof. Rsch. Inst. Medicine, 1974-76; prof. dept. medicine Kroghstotten Hosp., Oslo, 1979-80; sr. resident Ullevål Hosp., 1980-83; sr. cons. dept. medicine Aker Hosp., Oslo, 1983—; sr. cons. physician Norske Liv, Oslo, 1983—; rsch. dir. WHO, Oslo, 1976-79. Fellow Am. Coll. Nutrition; mem. Norwegian Endocrine Soc. (pres. 1987-89). Avocations: skiing, tennis, music. Home: Holmend Terasse 32, 0773 Oslo Norway Office: Aker Univ Hosp, Dept Medicine, 0514 Oslo Norway

BOHN, DIETER EUGEN, engineering educator, researcher; b. Hagen, Germany, July 5, 1942; s. Friedrich and Gertrud (Nattermann) B.; m. Marianne Langohr, Dec. 9, 1971; children: Birgit, Anja. Diploma engr., Aachen U. (Germany) Tech., 1971, PhD in Engring., 1977. Rsch. engr. Aachen U. Tech., 1971-77; head compressor group Siemens KWU, Mülheim, Germany, 1978-87, head gas turbine rsch. dept., 1987-90; prof. Aachen U. Tech., 1990—, dir. Inst. Steam and Gas Turbines, 1990—, senator, 1992—; mem. adv. coun. VGB, Essen, Germany, 1995—; pres. B&B-AGEMA GmbH, Aachen, 1995—; cons. Gas Turbine Study Group for Economical and Ecol. Energy Conversion, 1991—; sr. reviewer German Rsch. Found., 1996—; chmn. rev. group materials for Gas Turbines and Jet Engines, Helmholtz-Gemeinschaft, 1997—. Contbr. articles to profl. jours. Chair City Coun. Energy Affairs, Aachen, 1992—; bd. dirs. Parish Coun. Moers, 1994—. Mem. AIAA, ASME (Best Paper award Heat Transfer 1994), Verein Deutscher Ingenieure, German Soc. Aeronautics and Astronautics. Office: Aachen Tech U Inst Steam-Gas Turbs, Templergraben 55, 52056 Aachen Germany

BOHNER, GERD WALTER, psychologist, educator; b. Karlsruhe, Baden, Germany, Oct. 11, 1959; s. Herbert Gustav and Beate Ingeburg Braun Bohner; m. Johanna Maria Dinger, Dec. 27, 1996. Dipl.psych., U. Heidelberg, Germany, 1986; Dr.Phil., U. Heidelberg, 1990; Dr.Phil.habil., U. Mannheim, Germany, 1997. Lectr. U. Mannheim, 1988-91, 92-98; vis. scholar NYU, 1991-92; prof. U. Würzburg, Germany, 1998; sr. lectr. U. Kent, Canterbury, U.K., 1998—; dir. grad. studies U. Kent, Canterbury, 1999—. Auhtor: Rape Myths, 1998, (with M. Wänke) Attitudes and Attitude Change, 2000; cons. editor European Jour. of Social Psychology, 1995—, British Jour. of Social Psychology, 1997—. Feodor Lynen fellowship Alexander von Humboldt Found., 1991-92. Mem. European Assn. for Exptl. Social Psychology, Am. Psychol. Soc., Soc. for Exptl. Social

Psychology. Avocations: travel, cooking, photography, darts. Office: U Kent, Dept Psychology, Canterbury CT2 7NP, United Kingdon

BOHORQUEZ, JOAQUIN, banker; b. Colombia, June 14, 1942; came to U.S., 1989; s. Joaquin and Marta Bohorquez; 3 children. Law degree, econs. degree, Pontifica Javeriann U., Bogota, Colombia, 1964; econs. degree, Am. U., 1966. Advisor to min. Ministry of Fin., Bogota, 1967-71, internal revenue commr., 1970-72, vice min. and acting min. fin., 1974-77; mgr. Citibank, Bogota and Mex., 1972-74; mng. dir. Bohorquez Assocs., Bogota, 1977-82; mng. dir. Caribbean area Proexpo, San Juan, P.R., 1983-89; mng. dir. Bohorquez Assocs., Washington, 1989-95, Westsphere Capital, N.Y.C., 1996—; chmn. bd. dirs. Banco Bopular, Bogota. Author: (book) Wages, 1964. Bd. trustees Nat. U., Bogota. Mem. Nat. Def. Coun. Avocations: tennis, golf, polo, diving. E-mail: jbohorquez@westsphere.com. Office: Westsphere Capital 13th Fl 55 E 59th St Fl 13 New York NY 10022-1112

BOHOSKEY, BERNICE FLEMING, mineral-land owner, writer; b. Seattle, Feb. 9, 1918; d. W. R. and Katherine E. (Emmeluth) Blair; stepdau. E. Charles Fleming; m. Woodward Bohoskey, Aug. 6, 1942 (dec. 1979); children: Charles W., Katherine A., Michael J., Constance E. Student, Mills Coll., Oakland, Calif., 1935-36, Cornish Sch. Arts, Seattle, 1936-38. Model various newspapers. mags., 1936-38; splty. dancer Earl Carroll's Vanities; actress various radio shows, stage plays and movies, Hollywood, Calif.; ptnr. Yakima Sheep Co. Composer: (hymn) Blessed Trinity, 1948, (song) God's on His Throne, 1948, (song) Just Give Me the Merry-Go-Round, 1949; contbr. articles to profl. jours. Founder, pres. Young First Voters Groups, 1940; spkr., organizer, Yakima County, Wash.; pres. Young Reps. Club, Wash., 1940. Mem. Jr. League (sustaining). Republican.

BOHR, AAGE NIELS, physicist, educator; b. June 19, 1922; s. Niels and Margrethe (Nörlund) B.; m. Marietta Bettina Soffer (dec. 1978); 3 children: m. Bente Meyer Scharff, 1981. Ph.D., U. Copenhagen, Denmark, 1954; D honoris causa, Manchester U., 1961; hon. degrees, Oslo U., 1969, Heidelberg U., 1971, Trondheim U., 1972, Uppsala U., 1975. Jr. sci. officer Dept. Sci. and Indsl. Research, London, 1943-45; research assoc. Inst. Theoretical Physics U. Copenhagen, 1946—, prof. physics, 1956—; dir. Niels Bohr Inst., 1962-70; mem. bd. Nordita, 1958-74, dir., 1975-81. Author: Rotational States of Atomic Nuclei, 1954; (with Ben R. Mottelson) Nuclear Structure, Vol. 1, 1969, Vol. 2, 1975. Recipient Dannie Heineman prize, 1960; Pope Pius XI medal 1963; Atoms for Peace award, 1969; H.C. Ørsted medal, 1970; Rutherford medal, 1972; John Price Wetherill medal, 1974; Nobel prize in physics, 1975; Ole Römer medal, 1976. Mem. Danish, Norwegian, Yugoslavian, Polish, Swedish acads. scis., Royal Physiograph. Soc. Lund, Sweden, Am. Acad. Arts and Scis., Nat. Acad. Scis. (U.S.), Deutsche Akademie der Naturforscher Leopoldina, Am. Philos. Soc., Finska Vetenskaps-Societeten, Pontifical Acad. Principal research areas include nuclear physics and quantal physics in general. Office: Niels Bohr Inst, Blegdamsvej 15-17, DK-2100 Copenhagen Denmark

BOHRER, RICHARD WILLIAM, religious writer, editor, educator; b. N.Y.C., June 17, 1926; s. Jacob William and Elsie Marie (Wahlstad) B.; m. Elizabeth Anne Spencer, July 8, 1955; children: Joel Stephen, Janice Joy Bohrer Pruitt. BA, Westmont Coll., 1947; MSc, U. So. Calif., L.A., 1956; MA, Calif. State U., Long Beach, 1962. Tchr. grades 3, 4, 5 Haile Selassie I Elem. Sch., Gondar, Ethiopia, 1947-50; tchr. grades 9, 10, 11 Alhambra (Calif.) High Sch., 1954-55; tchr. grade 6 Maple Ave. Sch., Fullerton, Calif., 1955-56; tchr. grades 9, 10, 11 Orange (Calif.) High Sch., 1956-63; news editor Anaheim (Calif.) Gazette, 1961-62; prof., dir. journalism Multnomah Sch. of the Bible, Portland, Oreg., 1963-79; broker Dick Bohrer Realty Inc., Portland, 1968-81; sr. editor, mng. editor Moody Monthly mag., Chgo., 1979-83; pub. Glory Press, 1981—; prof. Liberty U., Lynchburg, Va., 1983-89, 91-94; asst. prof., head mag. sequence Ball State U., Muncie, Ind., 1989-90; dir. Maranatha Writers Conf., Muskegon, Mich., 1980-89; prof. Inst. Bibl. Studies, Lake Grove, Oreg., 1996-97. Author: Easy English, 1977, Edit, Yourself and Sell, 1980, They Called Him Shifta, 1981, 21 Ways to Write Stories for Christian Kids, 3rd edit., 1997, 4th edit., 2000, John Newton, 1983, Bill Borden, 1984, How to Write What You Think, 1985, How to Write Features Like a Pro, 1986, Be an Editor Yourself, 1987, J. Edgar Beanpole: Football Detective, 1991, J. Edgar Beanpole: Volleyball Spy, 1991, J. Edgar Beanpole: Soccer Sleuth, 1991, J. Edgar Beanpole: Night Watcher, 1991, No Frills Editing Skills, 1993, John G. Mitchell: Lion of God, 1994, J. Edgar Beanpole and Friends: Basketball Hawkeye, 2000, J. Edgar Beanpole and Friends: Stage Snoop, 2000, Hey Kids! Let's Write Some Stories, 2000, Hey Kids! Let's Write Some True Stories, 2000, Four and Twenty Ways to Write Stories for Christian Kids, 2000, Sink It! Sink It! Becky P., 2000; editor: The Battle for Your Faith (Willard M. Aldrich), The Schemer and the Dreamer (Luis Palau), Down to Earth (John Lawrence), Parables by the Sea (Pamela Reeve), An Everlasting Love (John G. Mitchell), Plague in Our Midst (Gregg Albers, MD), Right With God (John G. Mitchell), What Do You Say When.... (Nellie Pickard), Counseling the Terminally Ill (Gregg Albers, MD), The Self-Study of Liberty University, Maranatha, Our Lord, Come! (Renald Showers), Let's Revel in John's Gospel (John G. Mitchell), Let's Revel in Romans (John G. Mitchell), Priceless Pearls (John and Esther Nader Smit), Luke (Beverly Williams West); acting editor Moral Majority Report, 1983-85, copy editor, 1985-88. Choir dir. Ctrl. Bible Ch., 1963-66. Recipient Pres.'s Svc. award Liberty U., 1985, Tchr. of Yr. award, 1987, 89. Mem. Northwest Assn. of Book Publ. Republican. Mem. Plymouth Brethren Ch. Avocations: oil painting, cooking, swimming. Home: PO Box 624 West Linn OR 97068-0624

BÖHRINGER, KARL FRIEDRICH, computer scientist, electrical engineer, educator. Diploma, U. Karlsruhe, Germany, 1990; MS, Cornell U., 1993, PhD, 1997. Cons. Apollo Computers, Lowell, Mass., 1988; tchg. asst. computer sci. dept. Cornell U., 1989-92, rsch. asst. robotics lab., 1994-96; postdoctoral rschr. U. Calif., Berkeley, 1996-97, lectr., 1997, asst. rsch. engr., 1997-98; asst. prof. dept. elec. engring. U. Wash., 1998—; vis. scholar Stanford U., 1994-95. Contbr. articles and book chpts. to profl. jours. and books. Recipient NSF Career award 1999. E-mail: karl@ee.washington.edu. Office: Dept Elec Engring Univ Washington PO Box 352500 Seattle WA 98195-2500

BOHUŠ, ONDREJ, anesthesiologist, consultant; b. Hnusta, Slovakia, Sept. 28, 1933; s. Ondrej Bohuš and Elza (Hlošková) Bohušová; m. Elena Kinková, July 4, 1957; children: Elena, Blanka. MD, Komensky U., Bratislava, Slovakia, 1957. Cert. in Surgery, Cert. Anesthiology and Resuscitation. Resident Dist. Hosp., Zvolen, Slovakia, 1957-61, cons. anesthesiologist, 1961-67, head dept. anesthesiology and intensive care, 1967-93, dir., 1971, 92; sr. cons. City Hosp., Banská Štiavnica, Slovakia, 1993—; vis. lectr. Postgrad. Med. Sch., Bratislava, Slovakia, 1967-90. Author: Anestéziologické komplikácie, 1990 (prize Slovak Med. Assn. 1991), Anestesiologie a resuscitace v České a Slovenské republice na cestě k oborové samostatnosti, 1996, Cinnost' revízneho lekara u spinálneho pacienta, Maly; author, editor: Anestéziológia, intenzívna starostlivost a resuscitológia, 1987, 2d edit., 1992 (prize OSVETA pub. 1987, prize Slovak Med. Assn. 1988). Mem. Slovak Med. Assn. (Hon. Acknowledgement 1985, Silver medal 1988, 89, Gold medal 1993), Slovak Soc. Anesthesiology and Resuscitation (pres. 1977-90), Czechoslovak Soc. Anesthesiology and Resuscitation (pres. 1979-83, 85-87), Slovak Soc. Anesthesiology and Intensive Medicine (hon.), Slovak Med. Assn. (hon. mem.). Home: Šafárikova 6, 96001 Zvolen Slovak Republic

BOICE, CRAIG KENDALL, management consultant; b. Portland, Oreg., June 25, 1952; s. Charles A. and Audrey (Larson) B.; m. Jacinta E. Remedios, Nov. 21, 1979. BA summa cum laude, Beloit Coll., 1973; MA, Yale U., 1974, M.Phil., 1976, M in Pub. and Pvt. Mgmt., 1979. Instr. fellow philosophy Yale U., New Haven, 1978-79; economist Overseas Pvt. Investment Corp., Washington, 1978; sr. cons. Coopers and Lybrand, Washington and London, 1979-81; v.p. ops. Internat. Licensing Network, N.Y.C., 1981-82; pres., chmn., chief exec. officer Boice Dunham Group, N.Y.C., 1983—; adj. asst. prof. NYU, 1984-99. Cons. Lake Placid Olympic Organizing Com., (N.Y.), 1979, New Haven Homesteading Program, 1979. Mem. Am. Mktg. Assn., Assn. Energy Engrs., Automated Meter Reading Assn., Computer and Automated Sys. Assn., Soc. Mfg. Engrs., Strategic Leadership Forum, World Future Soc., Geospatial Info. & Tech. Assn. Democrat. Office: Boice Dunham Group 30 W 13th St Apt 3C New York NY 10011-7988

BOICHENKO, ALEXANDER MIKHAILOVICH, physicist, researcher; b. Scherbinka, Russia, Oct. 17, 1963; s. Mikhail Nikolaevich and Mariya Nikolaevna (Alifanova) b.; m. Marina Emmanuilovna Yankovskaya, July 16, 1992; children: Tatyana, Ivan. Grad. with honors, Moscow Engring. Physics Inst., 1986; PhD, Inst. Gen. Physics, Moscow, 1992. Researcher Inst. Gen. Physics, Moscow, 1991-94, sr. researcher kinetic dept., 1994-99, head Lab. Atomic Spectrocopy, 1999—. Contbr. articles to profl. jours. Home: Bolshoi Predtechenskii per, 27/29 39, 123022 Moscow Russia Office: Inst Gen Physics, Vavilova St 38, 117942 Moscow Russia

BOIKO, VITALY PETROVICH, chemist, researcher; b. Krolevets, Ukraine, June 2, 1941; s. Petro Prokopovich and Nadiya (Semenivna) B.; m. Tetyana Volodymyrivna Luss, July 4, 1949; 1 child, Maxim. Engr., Poly. Inst., Kiev, Ukraine, 1962; CandChem, Inst. Macromolecular Chemistry, Kiev, 1975. Foreman, head of shift Chem. Plant, Kiev, 1962-65; sr. engr. Ukrainian Coun. of Nat. Economy, Kiev, 1965-66; head of group Inst. of Chlorine Industry, Kiev, 1966-67; sr. engr., jr. rschr., sr. rschr. Inst. Macromolecular Chemistry, Kiev, 1967—; sr. rschr. Presidium # of Acad. of Sci. of USSR, 1988. Author, co-author some 70 works in Soviet, Russian, Ukrainian and fgn. jours. including High Polymers, Jour. Applied Polymer Sci., Jour. Chem. Edn. Lectr. The Znanie Soc., Kiev, 1980-88. Recipient medal In Memory of 1500th Anniversary of Kiev, Presidium of Moscow Supreme Soviet of USSR, 1982, Inventor of USSR award Com. in Invention of USSR, 1983. Mem. Ukrainian Chem. Soc., Kiev Scientists House. Orthodox Christian. Avocations: travel, exercise, popularization of knowledge, composing comic stories. Home: Geroev Dnipra Str, 044214 Kiev Ukraine Office: Inst Macromolecular Chem, Kharkovskoe sh 48, 023160 Kiev Ukraine

BOIKOV, ILYA VLADIMIROVICH, mathematician, educator; b. Krementchug, USSR, Mar. 19, 1941; s. Vladimir Ilich Liberman and Nadezda Andreevna Boikova; m. Svetlana Zelmanovna Brusilovskay, Mar. 29, 1968; 1 child, Alla. Degree in computer engring., Poly. Inst., Penza, USSR, 1963; degree in math., U. Kazan, USSR, 1968, Cand. Sci., 1973; DSc, Siberian br. Acad. Sci., Novosibirsk, 1991. Engr. Computer Plant, Penza, 1963-65, Rsch. Inst., Penza, 1965-68; asst. Poly. Inst., Penza, 1971-72, assoc. prof., 1971-74; head higher math., chmn. Poly. Inst. (now named State U.), Penza, 1974—; prof. State U., Penza, 1991—; prof. Tchr.'s Coll., Penza, 1991—, head of state exam. com., 1974-77, 83-86, 92-99, 2000; chmn. coun. def. of doctor thesis in sci. Penza State U., 1998—. Author: Optimal Exactness Algorithms of Singular Integral Calculations, 1983, Optimal Calculation Methods in Automatic Control Tasks, 1983 (diploma of republic exhbn. 1985), Analytical Methods of Dynamical Systems Identification, 1992, Passive and Adaptive Algorithms of Calculation Singular Integrals, 1995; (with L.N. Domnin and N.F. Dobrunina) Approximate Methods of Calculation of Hadamard Integrals and Decision of Integral Equations with Hadamard Integrals, 1996; editor: (collection) Optimal Methods of Calculations and Its Applications to Processing of Information, 1982, 83, 84, 85, 87, 90, 91, 92, 96; patentees: equipment to restore output signals, 1989, device for computation of unit impulse response, 1996. Grantee Internat. Sci. Found., 1993, Novosibirsk U., 1994, 98, Russian Found. Fundamental Investigation, 1994, 97, State Sci., 1997, 2000, Soros Prof., 1999, Internat. Soros Sci. Edn. Program, 1999. Mem. Am. Math. Soc., N.Y. Acad. Scis., European Math. Soc. Avocation: historical and classical literature. Home: Kirov str 71-58, 440600 Penza Russia Office: Chr High Math, Krasnaya str 40, 440017 Penza Russia

BOILEAU, JACQUES, engineer, scientific expert; b. Sarrebruck, Germany, Feb. 20, 1924; French citizen; s. Louis and Marcelle (Ordinaire) B.; m. Agnès Perret, Oct. 27, 1950; children: Véronique, Blandine, Cécile, Isabelle, Xavier. Engr., Ecole Polytechnique, Paris, 1946; D of Phys. Scis., U. Paris, 1953; grad., Institut Sciences Politiques, Paris, 1952; LLM, U Aix-Marseille, France, 1962. Engr. R&D Service des Poudres, Dept. Def., Sorgues and Paris, France, 1953-67; tech. mgr. Service des Poudres, Dept. Def., Paris, 1967-71; sci. dir. Société Nationale des Poudres et Explosifs, Paris, 1971-83, sci. adviser to pres., 1983-89; sci. advisor French Dept. Def., other state orgns., 1989—; teaching lectr. Ecole Polytechnique, Paris, 1964-81; mem. mng. team Centre des Hautes Etudes de l'Armement, Paris, 1964-68; mem. mission for materials Ministry of Industry, Paris, 1982-84. Contbr. numerous articles to profl. jours.; patentee in field. Lt. gen. French Army, 1971-86. Decorated comdr. of Merit, officer Legion of Honor, officer Acad. Palms (France); recipient Grand Prix Lamb, French Acad. Scis., 1982. Mem. Société Francaise de Chimie, Groupe Francais des Polymères (v.p. 1981-85), N.Y. Acad. Scis., Am. Phys. Soc., Am. Materials Rsch. Soc. Roman Catholic. Avocation: singing in choir, hiking. Home and Office: 15 rue des Lions St Paul, 75004 Paris France

BOILLAT, GUY MAURICE GEORGES, mathematical physicist; b. Pontarlier, France, May 18, 1937; s. Georges Paul Charles and Lucie Marguerite Charlotte (Jubin) B. Licence scis., U. Besançon, France, 1959; postgrad., Inst. Henri-Poincaré, Paris, 1959-60, Inst. Theoretical Physics, Copenhagen, 1960-62, Norwegian Tech. U., Trondheim; DSc, Sorbonne U., Paris, 1964. Assoc. prof. dept. math. U. Clermont, Aubière, France, 1966-69, prof., 1969—; lectr., Italy, 1970—; researcher U. Messina, U. Catania, U. Bologna, Italy, 1970—. Co-author: Recent Mathematical Methods in Nonlinear Wave Propagation, 1996; contbr. 98 rsch. articles on nonlinear waves and fields to profl. jours. Dep. mem. Internat. Parliament for Safety and Peace. Recipient Commemorative Millennium Meml. award Albert Einstein Internat. Acad. Found. Mem. Maison Internat. Intellectuels (senator), Acad. M.I.D.I., Acad. Peloritana dei Pericolanti (Messina, corr.), French Horological Assn. (bd. dirs. 1983—, sec. gen. 1998—), Unione Matematica Italiana, Am. Math. Soc., Internat. Assn. Mathematical Physics, Internat. Soc. for the Interaction of Mechanics and Math., Knight Templar Order. Roman Catholic. Home: 16 rue Ronchaux, 25000 Besançon France

BOISARD, MARCEL A., United Nations official. Exec. dir. UN Inst. for Tng. and Rsch., Geneva, 1994—. Office: UNITAR Hdqs, Palais des Nations, CH-1211 Geneva Switzerland also: UNITAR Liaison Office One United Nations Plaza New York NY 10017*

BOISJOLY, RICHARD THOMAS, plastics engineer, educator; b. Lowell, Mass., Dec. 10, 1952; s. Joseph Antonio and Isabelle Evelyn B.; m. Karen Joyce Dureault, Aug. 17, 1974; children: Jennifer Rebecca, Elissa Sue. BS in Plastics Engring., Lowell Tech. Inst., 1974. Polymer chemist Anchor Hocking Corp., Lancaster, Ohio, 1974-77; project engr. King-Seeley Thermos Co., Norwich, Conn., 1977-79, Nashua (N.H.) Corp., 1979-83; quality engring. mgr. Nypro, Inc., Clinton, Mass., 1983-85; pres. Vt. Iron, Waterbury, 1985-86; sr. quality engr. Simmonds Precision Products, INc., Vergennes, Vt., 1986-88; sr. molding engr. Teradyne Connections Sys., Nashua, 1988-93; sr. project engr. Nypro, Inc., Clinton, Mass., 1993—; dir. Automated Assemblies, Clinton. Inventor in field. Vol. Girl Scouts Am., Waterbury, Vt., 1987; advisor Youth Softball League, Waterbury, 1986. Avocations: golf, gardening, model making. E-mail: elissaboisjoly@worldnet.att.net, rick.boisjoly@nypro.com. Fax: 978-365-7078. Home: 62 Musket Dr Nashua NH 03062-1441 Office: Nypro Inc 101 Union St Clinton MA 01510-2935

BOISJOLY, RUSSELL PAUL, dean, educational consultant; b. Lowell, Mass., Sept. 3, 1950; s. Antonio Joseph and Isabelle Boisjoly; m. Diana Blanchard, Aug. 1973 (div. Sept. 1980); m. Carol Somers, Aug. 15, 1987. BS in Indsl. Mgmt. with honors, U. Mass., Lowell, 1972; MBA in Fin. with high honors, Boston U., 1973; DBA in Fin., Ind. U., 1978. Asst. prof. fin. U. Md., College Park, 1976-77, 78-82; assoc. prof., chair dept. mgmt. Simmons Coll., Boston, 1982-85; assoc. prof., chair fin. dept. U. Mass., Lowell, 1985-89; prof. fin. Fairfield (Conn.) U., 1989-99, assoc. dean Sch. Bus., 1989-93, dean Sch. Bus., 1993-97; dean Sch. Bus., prof. fin. Adelphi U., Garden City, N.Y., 1999-2000; vis. asst. prof. Ind. U., Bloomington, 1977-78; sr. staff analyst OAO Corp., Beltsville, Md., 1980-81; mem. bus. edn. com. Charter Oak Coll., 1992-97, mem. accreditation com. New Eng. Assn. of Schs. and Colls. accreditation com., 1995, mem. accreditation visitation team Am. Assemlby of Collegiate Schs. of Bus.; with Barry U., 1998-2000, St. Joseph's U., 1998-99, Fairleigh Dickinson U., 1999, Winthrop U., 1999-2000; internat. cons. in field; presenter in field. Exec. editor Jour. Bus. and Econ. Studies, 1990-96; manuscript reviewer Jour. Econs. and Bus., Jour. Fin. Rsch., Jour. Acctg. and Pub. Policy, Fin. Rev., N.E. Jour. Econs. and Bus., Rev. Quantitative Fin. and Acctg.; contbr. articles to profl. jours. Trustee 1580 House Trust, 1984-85, 86-94, pres., 1985, co-treas., 1986-94; fin. svcs. planning com. Mass. Photovoltaic Ctr., 1987-88; bd. dirs. N.E. Bus. and Econs. Assn., 1990-96; ops. evaluation planning com. Town of Stratford, Conn., 1991-92; planning bd. Town of Sturbridge, Mass., 1994-97, chair Rte. 15 study com., 1996-97; edn. com. Conn. Tech. Coun., 1995-97; steering com. for consortium MBA in China, Assn. Jesuit Bus. Sch. Deans, 1995-97, bd. dirs., at-large rep., 1996-97; mem. design com. Magnet H.S. for Bus. Computer Sci. and Enterpreneurship, Cambria Heights, N.Y. Jacob Ziskind Meml. scholar U. Mass., Lowell, 1971, MBA scholar Boston U., 1972, Boston U. scholar, 1972; Ind. U. fellow, 1975-76, Bur. Bus. and Econ. rsch. fellow U. Md., 1979, Wilson Elkins rsch. fellow U. Md., 1981; instrnl. aid grantee U. Md., 1978; grantee Bay State Skills Corp., 1985, Mass. Photovoltaic Ctr., 1987, 1988, Am. Pub. Power Assn., 1987, Seed Grant for Rsch., 1988, United Auto Workers/Chrysler Ergonomics Risk Factors and Job Design, 1989, U.S. Dept. Edn., 1992-94, GE Found., 1994-98, PepsiCo Found., 1994-99. Mem. Am. Fin. Assn., Acad. Internat. Bus., Fin. Execs. Inst., Fin. Mgmt. Assn., Western Fin. Assn., Garden City C. of C. (bd. dirs. 2000—), Beta Gamma Sigma, Tau Epsilon Sigma. Roman Catholic. Avocations: golf, bird watching. Address: 1580 Massachusetts Ave Apt 4E Cambridge MA 02138-2925

BOISMENU, RICHARD, immunologist, researcher; b. Montreal, Sept. 7, 1962; came to U.S., 1992; s. Roger and Marcelle (Daoust) B.; m. Sherri Zeichick, Sept. 27, 1997. PhD, McGill U., 1992. Asst. prof. dept. immunology The Scripps Rsch. Inst., La Jolla, Calif., 1996—; rsch. dir. Strohm IBD Ctr., La Jolla, Calif., 1998—. Mem. AAAS, Am. Assn. Immunologists, Am. Gastroenterol. Assn. Achievements include contributions to the understanding of the function and specificity of intraepithelial lymphocytes. Office: The Scripps Rsch Inst 10555 N Torrey Pines Rd La Jolla CA 92037

BOISSERIE, JEAN-MARIE, researcher; b. Paris, July 8, 1932; s. Andre and Nicole (Bonnamy) B.; m. Violaine Jardin, June 9, 1965; children: Etienne, Anne-Laure. Diploma in engring., Ecole Nat. Ponts et Chaussees, 1956. Rschr. Elec. France Inst. Rsch., Paris., 1956-92; cons. Inst. Nat. Rsch. Info., Le Chesnay, France, 1971-97; asst. Ecole Nat. Ponts et Chaussées, Paris, 1971-77; referee Internat. Jour. Numerical Methods, 1971-88. Author: The Finite Element Method in Thin Shell Theory, 1982; contbr. articles to profl. jours. With French Mil. Val., 1961-63. Mem. N.Y. Acad. Scis. Roman Catholic. Avocations: tennis, skiing. Home: 2B Rue Debussy, 78100 Saint-Germain-en-Laye France

BOISSET, NICOLAS, biochemist, researcher; b. Chateaudun, France, June 2, 1963; s. Michel and Arlette (Hasle) B. Cert. in structural biochemistry, U. Tours, France, 1983; diploma d'etudes approfondies, Pierre and Marie Curie U., Paris, 1986; thesis in pharmacy, U. Tours, 1987; D of Univ., Pierre and Marie Curie U., 1990. Postdoctoral fellow N.Y. State Dept. Health, Albany, 1991-92; rsch. assoc. Centre Nat. Recherche Scientifique, Tours, 1992—, Paris. Contbr. rsch. articles to profl. jours. Lt. Health Dept., French Army, 1990. Mem. French Crystallography Assn., N.Y. Acad. Sci. Home: 4 Rue Thouin, 75005 Paris France Office: CNRS UMR 7590 Univs, Paris 6, 75252 Paris Cedex, France

BOISSON, JACQUES LOUIS, diplomat, ambassador. Permanent rep. to UN Govt. Monaco, N.Y.C., 1993—. Office: Monaco's Perm Mission UN 866 United Nations Plz Rm 520 New York NY 10017-1822

BOIVIN, GEORGES YVES PAUL, research scientist; b. Choisy-le-Roi, France, Nov. 3, 1948; s. Claude and Elise (Caillié) B.; m. Françoise Valverde, Apr. 19, 1975; children: Céline, Valérie. BS, U. Paris, 1966, MS, 1970, postgrad., 1974, PhD, 1982. Rsch. asst. U. Geneva, 1972-74, master asst., 1974-76, chargé rsch., 1976-82; chargé rsch. INSERM, Lyon, France, 1982-90, dir. rsch., 1990—. Co-author: Industrial Fluorosis, 1975-77 (F. Tissot prize 1978). Councillor 4th dist. City of Lyon, 1989—, 2d vice mayor, 1995—. Decorated Acad. Palms French Ministry of Edn., 1998. Mem. Am. Soc. for Bone and Mineral Rsch., Internat. Assn. for Dental Rsch., European Calcified Tissue Soc. Roman Catholic. Office: INSERM Unité 403, Faculté R Laennec, 69372 Lyon Cedex 08, France

BOJARIU, ROXANA, climatologist; b. Bucharest, Romania, Jan. 8, 1962; d. Alexandru and Rojy Clary (Demeter) V.; m. Gelu Bojariu, June 4, 1988; children: Irina, Gelu. Diploma in physics, U. Bucharest, 1984, Phd in geophysics, 1999. Tchr. Fundulea Sch., Romania, 1984-87; physicist Nat. Inst. of Meteorology and Hydrology, Bucharest, 1987-90, rschr., 1990-95, sr. scientist 3d degree, 1995-99, sr. scientist 2d degree, 1999—; vis. scientist Observatoir Midi-Pyrenee, Toulouse, France, 1997-98. Exec. editor Romanian Jour. of Meteorology, 1997—; contbr. articles to profl. jours. Grantee Ministry of Sci. and Tech., 1997. Mem. Romanian Meteorol. Soc., Romanian Phys. Soc., European Phys. Soc. Avocations: painting, music, science-fiction literature, mineralogy. Fax: 40 1 230 31 43. E-mail: bojariu@meteo.inmh.ro. Home: Jean Steriadi no 8, Bucharest Romania Office: Nat Inst Meterology and Hydro, Sos Bucuresti-Ploiesti 97, 71552 Bucharest Romania

BOJER, JORGEN, diplomat. Perm. rep. of Denmark to UN N.Y.C., 1997—. Office: Perm Mission of Denmark to UN 1 Dag Hammarskjold Plz 885 2nd Ave Fl 18 New York NY 10017-2201

BOJIN, JACQUES, management executive, consultant; b. July 25, 1939; s. Simon and Geneviève (Chabaud) B.; m. Danièle Perrin, Dec. 20, 1971; children: Marie-Hélène, Séverine. ME, Ecole Nat. Supérieure d'Arts & Métiers, 1961; MA, Inst. d'Etudes Politiques, Paris, 1963; MBA, MIT Sloan, 1964. Analyst 1st Nat. Bank Boston, 1964-65; asst. rep. 1st Nat. Bank Boston, Paris, 1967-68; internat. officer 1st Nat. Bank Boston, Boston, 1968-69, asst. v.p. Boston Overseas Fin. Corp., 1969-70; mgmt. cons. McKinsey & Co., Paris, 1970-74, J.B. & Associés, Paris, 1975—; pres. Terrin Group, Marseilles, France, 1977-78; founder, chmn., CEO A.B.C. Group, Paris, 1979—; chmn., CEO Def. Internat., Paris, 1985—. 1st lt. French Navy, 1966-68. Mem. Interallié Club, MIT Club of France (bd. dirs.). Avocations: travel, skiing, photography. Home: 5 Avenue Erlanger, 75016 Paris France Office: ABC Group, 9 Rue Beaujon, 75008 Paris France

BOJTÁR, ENDRE, literary studies educator; b. Budapest, Hungary, May 26, 1940; s. Bela Bernstein and Margit (Konya) Dely; m. Anna Farkas, Dec. 15, 1962; children: Endre, Peter. Student, Eotvos Lorand U., 1963. Researcher Inst. Literary Studies Hungarian Acad. Scis., Budapest, 1963-86, dept. head, 1986—; prof. comparative lit. Jozsef Attila U., Szeged, Hungary, 1977-80. UCLA rsch. fellow, 1985-86. Mem. Internat. Comparative Lit. Assn. Avocation: gardening. Home: 17 Lōnyay, 1093 Budapest Hungary Office: Inst Literary Studies, 11-13 Menesi, 1118 Budapest Hungary

BOK, IVAN, special effects and computer animation specialist; b. Liberec, Czech Republic, Oct. 5, 1966; s. Ivan Kamenár and Marie Hana Boková. MA, Acad. Performing Arts, Prague, Czech Republic, 1993; leaving examination, Aero Vodochody H.S., Vodochody, Czech Republic, 1995. Aeromechanic Aero Vodochody, 1985-86; asst. to exec. prodr. Art Centrum-5D Studio, Prague, 1988-90; CEO, exec. prodr. Factory Art, Prague, 1990—. Sponsor Christian Children's Fund, Switzerland, 1994—, Caritas, Czech Republica, 1995—. Fellow Rotary Internat. (Praga Caput Regni); mem. Union Czech Audio-Visual Prodrs., Czech Mgrs. Assn. Avocations: squash, literature, cinema, music. Office: Factory Art, Vinohradská 37, 120 00 Prague 2, Czech Republic

BOK, SONG HAE, biotechnologist, researcher; b. Chongyang, Chungnam, Korea, Apr. 25, 1943; s. Chichan and Soon (Yoo) B.; m. Yon Hee Kim, Sept. 2, 1972; children: Jayne, Eugene H., Jonathan. BS in Biology, Seoul (Korea) Nat. U., 1966; MS in Biochem. Engring., MIT, 1972; PhD in Microbiology, Pa. State U., 1976. Sr. microbiologist A.E. Staley Mfg. Co., Decatur, Ill., 1976-79; rsch. fellow Hoffman La Roche, Inc., Nutley, N.J., 1980-85; sr. rsch. specialist Monsanto Co., St. Louis, 1986-87; dir. biotech. Korea Rsch. Inst. Chemical Technology, Taejeon, 1987-92; dir. biotech. products Biotech. Biosci. Rsch. Inst., KIST, Taejon, 1992-99; pres. Korea Rsch. Inst. Biosci. and Biotech., Taejon, 1999—; adj. prof. biology Montreal U., Que., Can., 1998—. Recipient Ministry Sci. and Tech. award, Korea, 1988, King Se-Jong award Ministry Korean Patent Office, 1997, Prime Ministers award, Korea, 1997, Prime Ministers cert., 1998, Gold medal

Internat. Exhibition Ideas, Inventions, and New Products, Nuremberg, Germany, 1998, UTC Bioventure Idea award, 1999; named Most Outstanding Rsch. of Yr., Korea Rsch. Inst. Biosci. and Biotechnology, 1997. Fellow Am. Acad. Microbiology; mem. Am. Chem. Soc., Am. Soc. for Microbiology, Soc. for Indsl. Microbiology. Achievements include patents for non-toxic bioencapsulated biopesticides mfg. technology, non-toxic cholesterol lowering, antiatherogenic, blood pressure lowering compound JBB; discovery of acyl CoA-cholesterol acyltransferase inhibitor GERI BP001, inhibitor of farnesyltransferase, arteminolide. Office: Korean Rsch Inst Biosci and Biotech, PO Box 115 Yusong, Taejeon 305-600, Republic of Korea

BOKEMEYER, CARSTEN, physician, researcher, medical educator; b. Braunschweig, Germany, Sept. 15, 1962; s. Peter Klaus and Gisela (Ratsch) B.; m. Baerbel Ziesmann, Aug. 4, 1993; children: Frederike Alina, Neele Konstanze. MD, Hannover U., 1991, Habil, 1996. Med. asst. U. Hannover, 1989-95; attending physician U. Tuebingen, 1995—, prof. medicine, 2000—; bd. dirs. Wilsede Sch. for Oncology and Hematology, Oldenburg, Germany, 1991—; cons. Tumor Ctr. Tuebingen, 1995—. Author: Medicine Oncology, 1996; co-author: Testicular Cancer, 1996; editor: Supportive Care in Cancer, 1998, Paraneoplastic Syndromes, 1998; mem. editl. bd. Oncologie, 1995—, Oncology Reports, 1995—; contbr. articles to profl. jours. including Jour. Clin. Oncology, Jour. Nat. Cancer Inst. Recipient German Studien Stiftung, Rep. of Germany, 1982-89, award for molecular biol. rsch. in urol. cancer German Cancer Soc., 2000, Cancer award, 2000. Mem. German Cancer Soc. (grantee 1991), Am. Soc. Clin. Oncology, European Soc. Med. Oncology (ednl. and exam. com.). Avocations: tennis, skiing, philosophy. Office: U Tübingen, Otfried Mueller Strasse 10, 72076 Tübingen Germany

BOKHARI, SHAHID HUSSAIN, electrical engineer, educator; b. Lahore, Pakistan, Jan. 17, 1953; s. Riyaz and Khawar (Rashid) B.; m. Ambreen Fatima Qadir, Jan. 2, 1981; children: Saniyah, Saba. BSc, U. Engring. Lahore, 1974; MS, U. Mass., 1976, PhD, 1978. Rsch. asst. U. Mass., Amherst, 1975-78; vis. scientist NASA, Hampton, Va., 1978—; prof. U. Engring., Lahore, Pakistan, 1980—; vis. prof. U. Colo., 1999—; cons. in field. Author: Assignment Problems in Parallel and Distributed Computing, 1987; contbr. articles to profl. jours. Fellow IEEE, Assn. Computing Machinery. Muslim. Office: U Engring, Dept Elec Engring, Lahore 54890, Pakistan

BOKLUND, JOHN UNO, chemist, educator, researcher; b. Lund, Sweden, July 31, 1932; s. Uno Johan and Gunhild Elisabeth (Björklund) B. BS, U. Stockholm, 1962, MS, 1964, PhD, 1969. Scientist The Wenner-Gren Inst. for Exptl. Biology, Stockholm, 1964-69; microbiologist Nat. Bacteriol. Lab., Stockholm, 1971-73; chem. educator Inst. Edn., Stockholm, 1977-95, scholar in history of 18th century chemistry, 1995—; scientific leader marine biol. expdn. Mus. Natural History, Stockholm, 1967. Recipient Medal for zealous and devoted svc. State of Sweden, 1997. Avocations: etching, nature and culture, experimental photography. Home: Jungfrudansen 28, S-17156 Solna Sweden

BOKLUND-LAGOPOULOU, KARIN MARGARETA, English language educator, researcher; b. Uppsala, Sweden, Dec. 14, 1948; d. Karl Gunnar and Gjordis Vanja (Sandin) B.; m. George Coffer, 1970 (div. 1975); m. Alexandros Phaidon Lagopoulos, July 23, 1979; 1 child, Katerina Margarita. BA in French, U. Colo., 1969, MA in Comparative Lit., 1971, PhD in Comparative Lit., 1975; diploma in English, U. Thessaloniki, Greece, 1980. Teaching asst. U. Colo., Boulder, 1970, teaching assoc., 1971-75; lectr. U. Thessaloniki, 1981-84, asst. prof., 1984-85, assoc. prof., 1985-91, prof., 1991—. Co-author: Meaning and Geography, 1992; editor: Semiotics & Society, 1980, (with others) The Dynamics of Signs, 1982; contbr. articles to profl. jours. U.S. Ednl. Found. rsch. grantee, 1987. Mem. Modern Lang. Assn., Internat. Soc. for Semiotic Studies, Hellenic Semiotic Soc. (sec. 1986—). Office: U Thessaloniki, Sch of English, 540 06 Thessaloniki Greece

BOKOR, MAGDOLNA, neurologist; b. Szeged, Csongrad, Hungary, May 8, 1957; d. István and Mária A. (Szabó) B.; m. Tamás Garam, Mar. 24, 1990; children: Garam, Nóra. MD, Szent-Györgyi Albert Med. U, Szeged, 1981; Degree in Neurology, Postgrad. Med. U., Budapest, Hungary, 1985, Degree of Addictology, 1994; PhD, Hungarian Acad. Scis., Budapest, 1992. Med. diplomate. Clinician Mcpl. Hosp., Szentes, Hungary, 1981-83; chief physician Nyírő Gyula Mcpl. Hosp., Budapest, 1983—. Recipient István Apáthy Meml. award Szent-Györgyi Albert Med. U., Szeged, Hungary, 1979. Mem. N.Y. Acad. Scis., Hungarian Soc. Neurologists and Psychiatrists, Hungarian Soc. Addictologists, European Fedn. Neurol. Socs. (mem. sci. panel neuroepidemiology 1996—), Hungarian Soc. Headache, Hungarian Soc. Parkinson's Disease, Hungarian Soc. Stroke. Avocations: sailing, theater, classical music. Home: Varosmajor u 16, H-1122 Budapest Hungary Office: Hosp Nyírő Gyula, Lehel út 59, H-1135 Budapest Hungary

BOKOR, PAL, journalist; b. Budapest, Hungary, May 2, 1942; s. Mihaly and Rozsa (Steiner) B.; m. Alla Shikyaeva; children: Klara, Julia, Marton, Katalin. Student, Budapest Sch. Journalisn, 1961-62, U. Marxizm, Budapest, 1963-65, U. Lomonosov, Moscow, 1964-66. Journalist Hungarian News Agy., Budapest, 1960-64, Moscow, 1971-77; correspondent Hungarian News Agy., Washington, 1980-84; mng. fgn. editor Magyar Hirlap, Budapest, 1986-93; editor-in-chief Atlantic Press, 1993—. Author: Vladivostok, Kamchatka, Szahalin, 1978, A Chinese Summer, 1980, Washington, 1984, The Panda (novel), 1985, The Silver Malibu, 1988. Recipient Excellence award Hungarian TV, 1982. Mem. Hungarian Assn. of Journalists. Avocations: arts, photography. Home: Bereqsasz u 68, 1116 Budapest Hungary Office: Atlantic Ltd, 1126 Budapest Hungary

BOLAND, RAYMOND JAMES, bishop; b. Tipperary, Ireland, Feb. 8, 1932; came to U.S., 1957; Ed., Nat. U. Ireland and All Hallows Sem., Dublin. Ordained priest Roman Cath. Ch., Dublin, 1957. Vicar gen., chancellor of Washington archdiocese; ordained bishop Birmingham, Ala., 1988-93; transferred as bishop Kansas City, St. Joseph, Mo., 1993—. Address: PO Box 419037 Kansas City MO 64141-6037

BOLAND, ROY C., language educator; b. Opelika, Ala., July 28, 1950; s. Roy Boland and Rina E. Osegueda Funes. MA, Flinders U., Australia, 1976, PhD, 1986. Tutor Monash Univ., Victoria, Australia, 1977-79; lectr. Auckland (New Zealand) U., 1980-90; prof. La Trobe U., Bundoora, Victoria, Australia, 1991—; dir. Prince of Asturias Study Abroad program, Spain, Ctr. Galician Studies Australia and New Zealand, 1999. Author: Mario Vargas Llosa: Oedipus and the Papa State, 1988; editor: Mario Vargas Llosa, 1988, Antipodas Jour. Hispanic Studies; co-editor: War and Revolution in Hispanic Literature, 1990. Recipient Buho de Vox Escuela Universitaria Vox, Madrid, 1991; fellow Universidad Complutense, Madrid, 1987; grantee Xunta de Galicia, 1993. Avocations: reading, tennis, gastronomy, wine tasting, travel. Office: La Trobe U, Dept Spanish, Melbourne 3083, Australia

BOLANOS, MICHAEL TEMPLETON, new media executive; b. Denville, N.J., Jan. 29, 1965; s. Henry and Jean Mary (Chardi) B. Mng. dir. Bell and Barter Theater/Arts Ctr., Rockaway, N.J., 1981-83; pres. The Musicom Corp., N.Y.C., 1981—, U.S./Soviet Exch. Initiative, 1985-86; ptnr. Hart-Bolanos and Assocs., N.Y.C., 1987-88; pres. Global Programming Inc., N.Y.C., Tokyo, 1990-93; pres., CEO Entertainment Drive LLC, N.Y.C., 1995—; artistic coord. U.S./Soviet Exchange Initiative; mem. bd. Friends of Am. Theatre Wing, 1991-92; cons. NHK-TV, Tokyo, Fujisankei Group, Osaka, Japan, 1989-91, CompuServe, Columbus, Ohio, 1993-94. Creator/reporter Kidcast, KAMR-TV, Amarillo, Tex., 1975-76; co-creator, patentee eDrive Movie Viewer, 1994; creator Entertainment Drive (eDrive) on CompuServe, 1994 (Visionary Citation award Smithsonian/Computerworld 1995), eDrive Japan on NiftyServe, 1997; creator Offcl. Cindy Crawford website, 1998, StarClubs.com.; creator, exec. prodr. www.cindy.com., the Ofcl. Cindy Crawford Web site, www.britneyspears.com, the Ofcl. Britney Spears Web site. Artist coord. Rally for Soviet Jewry, Coalition to Free Soviet Jews, 1987; exec. prodr. on-line coverage of telethon Muscular Dystrophy Assn., 1994-95, exec. prodr. on-line chat Artists' Rights Found., 1995. Recipient Cyber 60 award N.Y. Mag., 1995, CyberStar award Virtual City Mag., 1996. Mem. The Japan Soc. (concert prodr. 1987), Am. Acad. Children's Entertainment (bd. outside advisors), Actor's Fund Am. (Inner Cir.), Internet Content Coalition, Young Entrepreneurs Assn., N.Y. New Media Assn., Sales and Mktg. Execs. N.Y., Assn. for Interactive Media. Avocations: acting, singing, travel, Japanese language and art. Office: Entertainment Drive 61 E 8th St # 388 New York NY 10003-6450

BOLDUC, J. EMILIEN, bank executive; b. Roberval, Que., Can., Mar. 10, 1939; s. François N. and Georgette N. (Neron) B.; m. Gisèle d. Benoit Pigeon, Dec. 11, 1976; children: Chantal, Eric. BS, Laval U., Can., MS, 1967. Joined Roberval (Can.) br. Royal Bank, 1957; various positions Royal Bank, Ste. Foy, Gagnon, others, Can.; credit officer Montreal main br. Royal Bank, 1967-68, asst. mgr. St. James (Can.) br., 1968-69, credit officer Canadian loans head office, 1969-73, mgr. mgmt. devel., personnel, 1973-76, sr. asst. mgr. Montreal main br., 1976-78, dep. mgr., 1978-79; v.p. ea. U.S.A. Royal Bank, N.Y.C., 1979-82; mng. dir. Banque Belge pour l'Industrie (formerly Royal Bank), Belgium, 1982-85; sr. v.p. World Corp. Banking, Eng., 1985-86, sr. v.p., chief inspector, 1986-88, exec. v.p. fin., 1988-90, v.p., CFO, 1990-94; vice chmn., CFO Royal Bank Can., Montreal, 1994-97, vice chmn., 1997-99. Roman Catholic. Avocations: fishing, tennis. Home: 350 Chemin Pinacle Est, Sutton, PQ Canada J0E2K03

BOLDYREFF, CORNELIA, computer science educator, consultant; b. Ludington, Mich., Mar. 16, 1948; arrived in U.K., 1965; d. Ephraim Basil and Margaret Ellen (Granger) B. BA in Philosophy with honours, Leeds (Eng.) U., 1971; MPhil in Computing, U. Durham (Eng.), 1986, PhD in Computer Sci., 1994. Sr. computer officer, head microsystems software unit. S.W. Univs. Regional Computer Centre, 1979-83; software product mgr. Sphinx Ltd., 1983-84; sr. cons. Imperial Software Tech., 1984-85; sr. lectr. in computing Slough Coll. Higher Edn., 1985-86; Gould fellow in software engring. Surrey U., Eng., 1986-88; rsch. fellow Brunel U. and Liverpool U., Eng., 1988-91; lectr. computer sci. div. Sch. Engring. and Computer Sci. U. Durham, Eng., 1992-94, lectr. dept. computer sci., 1994-98, sr. lectr., 1998-2000, reader, 2000—. Author book chpts., conf. procs. and numerous sci. articles. Mem. Brit. Computer Soc., Assn. for Computing Machinery, IEEE Computer Soc. Home: 16 High Wood View, Durham DH1 3DT, England Office: U Durham Dept Computer Science, Science Site, Durham DH1 3LE, England

BOLDYREV, ALEXANDER ALEXANDROVITCH, biological educator; b. Arkhangelsk, Russia, Sept. 5, 1940; s. Alexander Philipovich and Claudia Akimovna (Kopyrina) B.; m. Valeria Victorovna Maltseva, Sept. 28, 1963; children: Maria, Irina. MS, U. Moscow, 1963, PhD, 1967, DSci, 1977. Rsch. scientist U. Moscow, 1964-77, sr. rsch. scientist, 1977-87, prof. biochemistry, 1987—; head lab. Inst. Neurology, Moscow, 1992—; head internat. sci. project in frame Japanese-Russian Govt., 1995—. Author: Biological Significance of Histidine-Containing Dipeptides, 1995, Carnosine and Tissue Protection against Oxidative Stress, 1999; author manual and monograph; mem. editl. bd. Proc. Exptl. Biology and Medicine (Russia) 1998—, Neurochemistry (Russia). Soros professorship, 1994-2000; Fogarty grantee NIH/USPHS, 1993-95; Fulbright Found. fellow, 1996-97. Mem. N.Y. Acad. Sci., European Soc. Neurochemistry. Avocations: history, music, travel. Home: Krylatsky Hills, Bldg 36 Ap 271, 121614 Moscow Russia Office: Inst of Neurology, Volokolamskoje shosse 80, 123367 Moscow Russia

BOLENE, (MARGARET) ROSALIE STEELE, bacteriologist, civic worker; b. Kingfisher, Okla., July 11, 1923; d. Clarence R. and Harriet (White) Steele; m. Robert V. Bolene, Feb. 6, 1948; children: Judith Kay, John Eric, Sally Sue, Janice Lynn, Daniel William. BS, U. Okla., 1946. Technican bacteriology dept. Okla. Dept. Health, Oklahoma City, 1946-48; asst. bacteriologist Henry Ford Hosp., Detroit, 1948-49; bacteriol. cons., also asst. bus. mgr. Ponca Gynecology and Obstetrics, Inc., 1956-92, ret. Organizing dir. Bi-Racial Coun., 1963; lay adviser Home Nursing Svc., 1967-68; mem. exec. bd. PTA, 1956-71; active various cmty. drives; sponsor Am. Field Svc.; patron Ponca Playhouse; bloodmobile vol. ARC; vol. Helpline; Rep. precint organizer, 1960. Mem. AAUW (treas. 1964-66), DAR (life, sec.-treas. 1961-67, 1st vice regent 1972-73, chpt. treas. 1974-84, chpt. chaplain 1991-2000, state schs. chmn. 1990-94), Kay-Noble County Med. Aux. (treas. 1957-58, 66-67), Ponca City Art Assn., Pioneer Hist. Soc., Okla. Heritage Assn., Okla. Hist. Soc., Friends Cultural Ctr., Mus. Found., Inc. (publicity chmn. 2000), Friends Md. Mansion, Daus. Founders and Patriots (life, state pres. 1980-84, registrar 1993—), Nat. Huguenot Soc. (corr. sec.), Hereditary Order First Families Mass. Daus. Am. Colonists (chpt. regent 1982-84, state flag chmn. 1990-92), Magna Charta Dames (treas. Okla. chpt. 1984, life), Plantagenet Soc., Order Colonial Physicians and Chirurgiens (life), Ancient and Honorable Arty. Co. Women Descs. Okla. Ct. (life, treas. 1983-84, registrar 1986—), Dames of Ct. of Honor, Colonial Dames of 17th Century, Daus. of Colonial Wrs (registrar 1998—), Colonial Daus. 17th Century, U. Okla. Assn. (life), Ponca City Music Club, Red Rose Garden Club (pres. 1983-84, treas. 1993-95), Twentieth Century Club (rec. sec. 1992-94, treas. 1999), Wall St. Ladies Investment Club, Lambda Tau, Phi Sigma, Alpha Lambda Delta. Presbyterian (elder 1983-86, trustee 1998—). Home: 2116 Juanito Ave Ponca City OK 74604-3813

BOLES, ERIC PAUL, staffing company executive; b. Albany, Ky., July 10, 1965; s. Don Howard and Doris L. (Claborn) B.; m. Tabitha Hope Appleby, Oct. 22, 1992 (div. Aug. 1995). AA in Computer Sci., U. Ky., 1990; Real Estate Cert., Cumberland Real Estate Acad., N.C., 1986; cert. paralegal, So. Career Inst., 1989; BS in Computer Sci., Am. Inst. Computer Sci., 1997. Cert. network engr. Network suport splst. Long John Silvers, Lexington, Ky., 1990-92; network engr. Pomeroy Computer Resources, Lexington, 1992-95; MIS mgr. Studio Plus Hotels, Lexington, 1995-97; v.p. Alliance Staffing, Lexington, 1997-98; owner, pres. Techsource Inc., Lexington, 1998—; co-owner Consig4u, 1999—. With U.S. Army, 1983-85. mem. Soc. Human Resources, Lexington (Ky.) C. of C., Masons, Disabled Am. Vets. Home and Office: 1023 Creekford Dr Weston FL 33326-2834

BOLES-CARENINI, BRUNO, ophthalmologist, educator; b. Bergamo, Italy, Dec. 13, 1925. MD, U. Pavia (Italy), 1950; specialist diploma Clin. Ophthalmology, U. Parma (Italy), 1953. Asst. eye clinic Parma U., 1950-56, 59-60; sr. asst. eye clinic Cagliari (Italy) U., 1956-59; sr. asst. Genoa (Italy) Eye Clinic, 1960-65; dir. eye clinic U. Sassari (Italy), 1965-67; chair clin. ophthalmology U. Cagliari (Italy), 1967-74; prof. clin. ophthalmology and chair, dir. Inst. Opthalmology U., Turin, Italy, 1974-98; dir. ophthal. specialization Turin U., 1998—. Contbr. over 400 articles to profl. jours. Fulbright scholar dept. ophthalmology U. Cin., 1953-54; recipient Golden medal Health Ministry, 1983; named Knight Comdr. Rep. Italy, 1985. Mem. Italian Social Ophthalmology Studies Com., Genoa Med. Acad., Sassari Med. Scis. Soc., Cagliari Followers of Med. Scis. Soc., Italian Soc. Study of Arteriosclerosis, Turin Med. Acad., Italian Ophthalmol. Soc. (founder), Internat. Soc. Cryosurgery, Soc. of Eye Surgeons, Internat. Assn. Ophthalmic Surgery, Italian N.W. Ophthalmol. Soc. , Italian Assn. Study of Glaucoma (pres.), European Glaucoma Soc. (Italian rep.), EUPO (European Univ. of Prof. of Opthalmology, Italian Ref.). Office: Inst Ophthalmology, U Turin Via Juvarra 19, Turin Italy

BOLESLAW, NAGAY, physician and surgeon; b. Lwow, Ukraine, Jan. 27, 1927; s. Stalislaw and Balbina (Hess) N.; m. Kamilla Pawlak, May 16, 1946; children: Zbigniew, Leszek, Tomasz. Doctor, Med. Acad., Gdansk, Poland, 1951, MD, 1964; postgrad., Med. Acad., Szczecin, Poland, 1973, 86. Diplomate in medicine, 1951, in gen. surgery, 1959. Asst. 1st Surg. Clinic, Gdansk, 1950-51; dep. chief surgeon Provincial Hosp., Koszalin, 1957-64; lectr. II Surg. Clinic/Pomeranian Med. Acad., Szczecin, 1964-73, asst. prof., 1973-83; head, clin. prof. I Surg. and Hand Surg. Clinic/Pomeranian Med. Acad., Szczecin, 1983—; sr. asst. Mil. Hosp., Koszalin, Poland, 1952-57; provincial cons. surgeon Health Authority, Gorzow Wkp., 1976-87; Polish del. IFSSH, 1983—, pioneer in hand surgery, 1998. Author: Modified Guide for Kuentscher Nails, 1962, New Extractor for Kuentscher Nail Surgery, 1965, Hand Surgery, 1996, General Surgery Compendium, 1998. Head Pomeranian Med. Acad. Com. Maj. Mil. Health Svc., Koszalin, 1952-57. Decorated Polonia Restituta medal; recipient Ednl. Commn. medal Ministry of Edn., 1984. Mem. Soc. Surgery of the Hand, Polish Surg. Assn. Mem. Unia Wolnosci. Roman Catholic. Avocations: travel, angling. Home: Jacka Malczewskiego 9-7, 71-616 Szczecin Poland Office: Gen Hand Surgery Clinic, Unii Lubelskiej 1, 71-344 Szczecin Poland

BOLGER, GRAEME BARRETT, medical educator; b. Montreal, Que., Can., Aug. 26, 1955; came to U.S., 1981; s. Kenneth B. Bolger and June Barrett Harrison. BSc, McGill U., Montreal, 1977, MD, 1981. Diplomate Am. Bd. Internal Medicine. Resident Johns Hopkins Hosp., Balt., 1981-84; fellow Fred Hutchinson Cancer Ctr., Seattle, 1984-85, Cold Spring Harbor (N.Y.) Lab., 1985-93, Meml. Sloan Kettering Cancer Ctr., N.Y.C., 1990-92; asst. prof. U. Utah, Salt Lake City, 1994—. Contbr. over 25 articles to profl. jours. E-mail: graeme.bolger@m.cc.utah.edu. Office: Huntsman Cancer Inst U Utah 2000 Circle Of Hope Dr Salt Lake City UT 84112-5550

BOLGER, JAMES BRENDAN, New Zealand government official; b. New Zealand, 1935; m. Joan Bolger; nine children. Sheep and cattle farmer Te Kuiti, 1965-72; elected M.P. King Country, 1972-98; parliamentary undersec. to min. agr. and fisheries, min. Maori affairs, min. in charge of Rural Banking and Finance Corp. Govt. of New Zealand, Wellington, 1975-77, min. fisheries, assoc. min. agr., 1977-78, min. labour, 1978-84, min. immigration, 1978-81, prime min., 1990-97; leader Nat. Party, New Zealand, 1986-98; leader of opposition New Zealand, 1986-90; ambassador to U.S.A., 1998—; chmn. coms. of appointments and honors, edn., training and employment, enterprise industry and environment strategy Security Intelligence Svc., 1990-97. Pres. Internat. Labour Orgn., 1983. Decorated Order of New Zealand. Mem. Internat. Labor Orgn. (pres. 1983). Avocations: fishing, reading, rugby, cricket. Office: New Zealand Embassy 37 Observatory Cir NW Washington DC 20008-3627

BOLIN, RICHARD LUDDINGTON, industrial development consultant; b. Burlington, Vt., May 13, 1923; s. Axel Birger and Eva Madora (Luddington) B.; m. Jeanne Marie Brown, Dec. 18, 1948; children: Richard Luddington, Jr., Douglas, Judith, Barbara, Elizabeth. BSChemE, Tex. A&M U., 1947; MSChemE, MIT, 1950; postgrad. advanced mgmt. program, Harvard Bus. Sch., 1969. Jr. rsch. engr. Humble Oil & Refining Co., Baytown, Tex., 1947-49; staff mem. Arthur D. Little, Inc., Cambridge, Mass., 1950-56; Caribbean office mgr. Arthur D. Little, Inc., San Juan, 1957-61; gen. mgr. Arthur D. Little de Mex., Mexico City, 1961-72; pres. Internat. Parks, Inc., Flagstaff, Ariz., 1973-94, chmn., 1995—; bd. dirs. Parque Indsl. de Nogales, Nogales, Sonora, Mex.; dir. The Flagstaff Inst., 1976—, Secretariat World Econ. Processing Zones Assn., 1985—; mem. adv. bd. Lowell Obs., Flagstaff, 1993-94, Astrogeology Mus., Flagstaff, 1998—. With U.S. Army, 1942-46. Mem. Univ. Club of Mex. Office: PO Box 986 Flagstaff AZ 86002-0986

BOLIN, VLADIMIR DUSTIN, chemist; b. Inglewood, Calif., Feb. 25, 1965; s. Vernon Spencer and Barbara Sue (Chase) B.; m. Elizabeth Lynne Boswood, May 18, 1985; children: Ragnar Spencer, Roark Morgan. BS, U. Ariz., 1987. Chemist, microbiologist Bolin Labs., Inc., Phoenix, 1987-93; bd. dirs., pres. Aerotech Labs., Inc., Phoenix, 1993—, pres., 1993—; pres. Kalmar Labs., Inc., Phoenix, 1993—, also bd. dirs.; v.p. lab ops. Aqualab Inc., Phoenix, 1996—; bd. dirs., pres. Kalmar Labs., Inc., Phoenix; bd. dirs. Aqualab Inc., v.p., 1996—; bd. dirs. Ariz. Indoor Quality Coun., v.p. 1995—. Mem. ASTM, AAAS, Am. Water Works Assn. (pres.), Assn. Official Analytical Chemists, Am. Soc. Microbiolgoy, Am. Chem. Soc., N.Y. Acad. Scis. Home: 2020 W Lone Cactus Dr Phoenix AZ 85027-2624 Office: Aerotech/Kalmar Labs Inc 2020 W Lone Cactus Dr Phoenix AZ 85027-2624

BOLING, ELDON AVERY, physician; b. Elma, Wash., Aug. 29, 1925; s. Dawson and Nellie (Beam) B.; m. Lenore Altschule, Feb. 13, 1948; children: Peter, Alice, Lucy, Sarah, Deborah, Eli. BA, Whitman Coll., Walla Walla, Wash., 1946; MD, U. Calif., San Francisco, 1950. Intern San Francisco Gen. Hosp., 1950-51; rsch. fellow Peter Bent Brigham Hosp., Boston, 1952-54; resident in medicine Boston VA Hosp., 1954-57; staff physician Boston VA Med. Ctr., 1959-95, cons. physician, 1995—. Patentee in field. Lt. comdr. USNr, 1957-59. Avocation: music. Office: Boston VA Med Ctr 150 S Huntington Ave Boston MA 02130-4817

BOLKHOVITINOV, NIKOLAI NIKOLAEVICH, historian; b. Moscow, Oct. 26, 1930; s. Nikolai and Lidia (Komarova) B.; m. Liudmila Povel'nenko, Apr. 3, 1965. Candidate hist. scis., Moscow City Pedagogical Inst., 1959; DSc, Inst. History USSR Acad. Sci., 1966. Editl. staff Archive Fgn. Policy Russian Empire, Moscow, 1957-58; jr., then sr. staff mem. Inst. History Russian Acad. Scis., 1958-88; chmn. dept. history USA & Canada Inst. World History Russian Acad. Scis., 1988-92, dir. Ctr. N.Am. Studies, 1992—; academician Russian Acad. Scis. Author: The Beginnings of Russian-American Relations, 1775-1815, 1975, Russia and the American Revolution, 1976, Russia and the United States: Analytical Survey of Archival Documents and Historical Studies, 1986, Russian-American Relations and the Sale of Alaska, 1834-1867, 1996, Russian-American Relations, 1815-1832, 1975, The Monroe Doctrine, 1959, The USA: Problems of History and Contemporary Histopiography, 1980, History of Russian America, 1732-1867, Vols. 1-3, 1997-99, more than 300 other works. Recipient State prize Russia, 1997. Office: Inst World History, Leninski prospect 32a, 117334 Moscow Russia

BOLKIAH, PRINCE MOHAMED, Bruneian government official; b. Bandar Seri Begawan, Brunei, Aug. 27, 1947; s. Sultan Haji Omar Ali Saifuddin III and Raja Isteri Pengiran Anak Damit; m. Pengiran Anak Hajjah Zariah. Attachment Irish Guards/Ministry Def., London, 1971, Ministry Fgn. Affairs, Singapore, 1980; min. fgn. affairs Bandar Seri Begawan, 1984—; chmn. Ministerial Econ. Coun., 1998, Constl. Rev. Com., 1992. Chmn. Brunei Darussalam's Coun. Succession, 1985; mem. Brunei Darussalam's Coun. Mins., 1970, Brunei Darussalam's Privy Coun., 1968. Avocations: badminton, martial arts. Office: Ministry Fgn Affairs, Jalan Subok, Bandar Seri Begawan 1210, Brunei*

BOLLA, MICHEL MAURICE, physician, consultant; b. Seyssinet-Pariset, Isére, France, June 13, 1944; s. Michel François and Paulette Therése (Richiero) B.; m. Chantal Lucie Simiand, Sept. 6, 1969; children: Anne-Laure, Pier-Laurence. Baccalaureat Math., Coll. de la Salle, Grenoble, France, 1963. Asst. radiation oncology Grenoble Hosp., France, 1976-80; chief of clinic Faculty of Medicine, Grenoble, France, 1977-80, asst. prof. oncology, 1980-86; sr. radiation oncologist Grenoble Hosp., France, 1980-97; prof. oncology Joseph Fourier U., Grenoble, France, 1986—; head radiotherapy dept. Grenoble Hosp., France, 1997—. Author: De dépistage au Diagnostic Précore le Cancer du sein Aujourd Hui, 1998; co-author: Cancers de l'endometre, 1983; co-editor (with John Libbey): Growth Factors and Oncogenes, 1989; co-editor: Local Prostatic Carcinoma, 1994; contbr. articles to profl. jours. Military doctor, Cooperation, Morocco, 1971-72. Grantee, Ministery of Health, Paris, 1993, 95, 99. Chmn. European Orgn. for Rsch. and Treatment of Cancer Radiotherapy Group; assoc. ed. European Jour. Cancer; mem. European Soc. Therapeutic Radiation Oncology, European Orgn. for Rsch. and Treatment of Cancer. Avocation: opera. Office: Ctr Hosp U, Svc Radiotherapie BP 217X, 38043 Grenoble France

BOLLEN, L(AMBERTUS) J(ACOBUS), semiconductor laser industry executive; b. Maastricht, The Netherlands, July 25, 1946; s. J. L. and E. (Van Deijck) B.; m. M. M. Rikers, Dec. 22, 1969; 1 child. Degree in engring., Tech. U., Eindhoven, The Netherlands, 1970. Scientist Philips Rsch., Eindhoven, 1971-79; devel.engr. Philips/Elcoma, Eindhoven, 1979-83; head devel. Philips/Elcoma SSL, Eindhoven, 1983-86; head devel./products Philips/Pglod, Eindhoven, 1986-90; head ops. Philips POC, Eindhoven, 1990-98; dir. waferfab Uniphase, Eindhoven, 1998-99; dir. spl. waferfab project JDS Uniphase, Eindhoven, 2000—. Avocations: tennis, skiing, golfing. Office: Philips Rsch POC, JDS Uniphase, Prof Holstlaan 4, 5656AA Eindhoven The Netherlands

BOLLENBECK, GEORG, literary educator; b. Bruehl, Germany, Dec. 10, 1947; s. Hans and Regina (Schmidt) B.; m. Ida Kleinert, Dec. 5, 1973; 1 child, Felix. MS in Edn., U. Bonn, 1973; PhD, U. Siegen, Fed. Republic Germany, 1976, postgrad., 1982. Asst. prof. U. Siegen, 1976-84, prof. modern German lit., 1984—, prof. cultural studies, 1987—; co-mgr. spl. rsch. project U. Siegen, 1985—. Author: Zur Theorie und Geschichte der Arbeiterlebenserinnerungen, 1976, Armer Lump und Kunde Kraftmeier. Der Vagabund in der Literatur der zwanziger Jahre, 1978, Oskar Maria Graf. Eine Bildmonographie, 1985, Till Eulenspiegel. Der dauerhafte Schwankheld. Zum Verh(ä)ltnis von Produktions-und Rezeptionsgeschichte, 1985, Theodor Storm. Eine Biographie, 1988, Bildung und Kultur. Glanz und Elend eines deutschen Deutungsmusters, 1994, Tradition-Avantgarde-Reaktion. Deutsche Kontroversen um die Kulturelle Moderne 1880-1945, 1999; contbr. articles to profl. jours. Mem. Theodor Storm Soc., Soc.

Internat. German Studies, Eulenspiegel Soc. Office: U Gesamthochschule Siegen, Adolf Reichwein Str, D-57076 Siegen Germany

BOLLEY, ANDREA, artist; b. Guelph, Ont., Can., Aug. 15, 1949; d. Hildo and Laura Pia (Maurino) B. BFA, U. Windsor, 1975. tchr. Activity Ctr. Art Gallery Ont., 1979, 80, Arts Sake, Toronto, 1982. One-woman shows include IDA Gallery York U., 1976, Art Gallery Brant, 1977, Pollock Gallery, Toronto, 1977, 78, 80, Agnes Etherington Art Ctr., Kingston, 1981, Gallery One, Toronto, 1984, 85, 86, Klonaridis Gallery, Toronto, 1989, 90, 91, Upper Can. Brewing Co., 1993, Studio Show, 1994, 95, 96, 97, 98, 99; group exhbns. include Grapestake Gallery, San Francisco, 1980, Alta. Coll. Art, Calgary, 1980, Art Gallery Ont., 1981, Art Gallery Hamilton, 1981, Gallery One, 1984, 85, 86, Triangle N.Y., 1985, 91, Klonaridis Gallery, 1988, John Schweitzer Gallery, Montreal, 1989, Mississauga Civic Ctr. Art Gallery, 1990, Magnum Books, Ottawa, 1991, Bennington Coll., Vt., 1991, Upper Can. Brewing Co., 1992, Robert Kidd Gallery, Birmingham, Mich., 1999, others; represented in permanent collections Can. Coun. Art Bank, Art Gallery Windsor, Labatt's Can. Ltd., Citicorp Ltd., Can., Can. Imperial Bank Commerce, Max Factor Ltd., Chatelaine Mag., J.E. Seagram Ltd., McGill Club, Imperial Oil, Citibank Can., Toronto-Dominion Bank, Casey House, Am. Express, Guaranty Trust, Abitibi Paper, Triangle, Toronto Sund, Arthur Gelgoot and Assoc., Premiere Mag., Bells & Whistles, and various pvt. collections. Grantee Ont. Arts Coun., 1975, 76, 78, 79, 84, 85, Can. Coun., 1976, 80; recipient Ont. Soc. Artists Purchase award J.E. Seagram and Son Ltd., 1980. Office: 3 Riverdale Ave, Toronto, ON Canada M4K 1C2

BOLLICH, ELRIDGE NICHOLAS, investment executive; b. Eunice, La., Sept. 10, 1941; s. Nicholas Joseph and Caroline (Manuel) B.; m. Shirley Anne Yackel, July 14, 1973; children: Jennifer, Brian, Sandra. BBA in Fin., Tex. A&M U., 1963. Registered rep. N.Y. Stock Exchange. Asst. v.p. Rotan Mosle, Houston, 1969-74, v.p., 1975-86; 1st v.p. Rotan Mosle Paine Webber, Houston, 1986-88, Smith Barney, Houston, 1988-97; sr. v.p. Paine Webber, Houston, 1997—; dir. devel. bd. Nat. Commerce Bank, Houston, 1987-88. Cubmaster Boy Scouts Am., Houston, 1987-91; mem. troop com. troop 642 Boy Scouts Am., 1992—. 1st lt. U.S. Army, 1963-65, Vietnam, capt. USAR, 1967-69. Mem. VFW, Houston Security Dealers, Stock and Bond Club, Houston Racquet Club, KC. Roman Catholic. Avocations: hunting, tennis, plays, coaching boys and girls basketball, Boy Scouts. Office: Paine Webber Inc 5 Post Oak Park Ste 900 Houston TX 77027-3409

BOLLIGER, EUGENE FREDERICK, retired surgeon; b. Detroit, Sept. 19, 1923; s. Eugene Hans and Julia Frederick (Larson) B.; m. Lois Ann Doan, Dec. 16, 1946; children: Mark, Glen, Cynthia. MD, U. Mich., 1946. Diplomate Am. Bd. Surgery. Intern, then surg. resident Grace Hosp., Detroit, 1947-52; ward surgeon Madigan Army Hosp., Ft. Lewis, Wash., 1952-54; asst. chief surgery 2d Gen. Hosp., Munchweiler, Germany, 1954-55; chief surgery U.S. Army Hosp., Pirmasson, then Wurzburg, Germany, 1955-57; attending surgeon Northwestern Hosp., Mpls., 1957-58; chief of surgery Dickey County Meml. Hosp., Ellendale, N.D., 1958-82; surgeon SHARE HMO, Mpls., 1982-87; chief of surgery Mid-Dakota Hosp., Chamberlain, S.D., 1988-91, Gregory (S.D.) Community Hosp., 1991-94; retired, 1994; surg. cons. West Holt Hosp., Atkinson, Nebr., 1992-94, St. Anthony's Hosp., O.Neill, Nebr., 1992-94; real estate cons. Westin-Reid, Mpls., 1987-88. Major U.S. Army, M.C., 1949-57. Fellow ACS; mem. AMA. Republican. Lutheran. Avocations: piano, singing, woodworking, former pilot.

BOLLINGER, ALFRED, internist, researcher; b. Herisau, Appenzell, Switzerland, Jan. 23, 1932; s. Alfred and Nelly (Müller) B.; m. Verena Elisabeth Roth; children: Franziska Elisabeth, Bettina Veronika. MD, U. Zürich, Switzerland, 1959, docent, 1969, prof. medicine, 1977. Med. diplomate. Resident Nat. Heart Inst., Mexico City, Mex., 1963; chief resident U. Hosp., Zürich, 1969-76; docent U. Zürich, 1969-76, prof. medicine, 1977-95, prof. emeritus, 1995—; vis. prof. U. Calif., San Diego, 1989. Author: Funktionelle Angiologie, 1979, Clinical Capillaroscopy, 1990; editor: Praxis der Dopplersonographie, 1990, Laser Doppler, 1994. Recipient Sci. award Dutch Found. for Circulation, 1988, Max Ratschow Gold medal Curatorium Angiologiae Internat., 1995. Mem. Internat. Soc. Lymphology (hon. mem.), European Soc. Microcirculation (hon. mem., pres. 1990-92, Malpighi award 1992), German Soc. Angiology (hon. mem.). E-mail: boll@goldnet.ch.

BOLLINGER, KENNETH JOHN, aerospace engineer, computer and space scientist; b. Warren AFB, Wyo., Nov. 6, 1954; s. John Henry and Charleen Edna (Wallick) B.; m. Christine Faye Ferguson, May 11, 1973; children: Kelly Raun, Orion Grant, Sara Selene. BS, Calif. Poly. U., 1987. Aerospace engr. Voyager Project, ops. engr. Magellan Project Jet Propulsion Lab., Pasadena, Calif., 1986-93; asst. mgr., PDS Rings Node NASA Ames, Moffett Field, Calif., 1993-98; web svcs. mgr. NASA Ames, Moffett Field, 1998—, project mgr., lunar prospector, dept mgr. IT svcs., 2000—; pres. Web Frontiers, Space Frontiers San Jose, Calif., 1993—. Mem. Amateur Radio Civil Emergency Svc., 1988. Mem. Amateur Radio Club, NASA Ames.

BOLMARO, RAUL EDUARDO, physicist; b. San Martin, Argentina, Jan. 25, 1953; s. Felipe and Olga Velia (Ferreyra) B.; m. Liliana Raquel Divincenzo, Jan. 24, 1975; children: Barbara Rebeca, Celeste. PhD in Physics, Nat. de la Plata, Argentina, 1986. Tchg. asst. U. Rosario, Argentina, 1979-88; prof. Inst. Profesorado, Rosario, 1979-95, U. Rosario, 1988—; sci. collaborator Los Alamos (N.Mex.) Nat. Lab., 1988-90; sec. sci. and tech. Faculty of Sci. and Engring., 1994-98. Contbr. articles to profl. jours. Grantee U. Rosario, 1994, Nat. Coun. Rsch., 1994, Argentine-German Agreement, 1996, 2000; rsch. fellow Nat. Coun. Rsch., 1982-87, external fellow, 1988-90, Fulbright fellow, 1998. Mem. Physicist Assn. Argentina, The Materials Soc. Achievements include research in physics metallurgy and material science in field of plastic deformation. Office: Inst Fisica Rosario, Bv 27 de Febrero 210 BIS, 2000 Rosario Argentina

BOLOGA, OCTAVIAN CONSTANTIN, engineering educator; b. Sibiu, Romania, Dec. 15, 1948; s. Lucian and Elena (Florea) B. Engr., Tech. U., Cluj-Napoca, Romania, 1971; ScD, Poly. U., Timisoara, Romania, 1986. Cert. engr. Engr. I.R.A. Grivita, Bucuresti, Romania, 1971-76; tchg. asst. Lucian Blaga U., Sibiu, 1976-79, lectr., 1979-90, asst. prof., 1990-93, prof., 1993—, head dept. engring., 1994—, sci. sec., 1990-92; sci. sec. Sch. Engring., Sibiu, 1981-84; dir. Ctr. Metal Forming, Sibiu, 1991—. Co-author: Typified Processing Technologies, 1995; editor Jour. Plastic Deformation, 1994—; patentee in field. Pres. Astra Cultural Assn., Sibiu, 1990—. Recipient awards Tempus, Stuttgart, Hannover, Germany, 1992-93, London, 1992, Madrid, 1997-98, Nottingham, England, 1998. Mem. Romanian Gen. Assn. Engrs. (pres. Sibiu br. 1996—), Romanian Scientist Assn. Avocation: history. Home: Dobrun 10, 2400 Sibiu Romania Office: Lucian Blaga U, Blvd Victoriei 10, 2400 Sibiu Romania

BOLOGNESI, PIETRO, theologian, editor; b. Bologna, Italy, Apr. 22, 1946; s. Loris Bolognesi and Gina Nanni; m. Lydia De Wolf, Aug. 18, 1973; children: Micael, Davide. Diploma in engring., Aldini-Valeriani, Bologna, 1969; BTh, Faculté Libre Thélogie, Paris, 1975, ThM, 1978. Prof. systematic theology Istituto Biblico Evangelico, Rome, 1975-88; pres. Istituto di Formazione Evangelica e Documentazione, Padua, Italy, 1988—. Editor Studi di Teologia, 1978, La Libertà della Disciplina, 1994, Le Ali Pesanti, 1995, Repertorio Bibiografico su Bibbia e Teologia, 1994, Liberi di credere, 1997, Dichiarazioni Evangeliche. Il Movimento Evangelicale 1966-1996, 1997; contbr. articles to prof l. jours. Pastor Evang. Ch., Padua, 1980—. Mem. Fellowship of European Evang. theology. Home: Via J Quercia 81, 35134 Padua Italy Office: IFED, CP 756, 35100 Padua Italy

BOLORINOS, JOSE, airline executive, researcher; b. Aspe, Alicante, Spain, Apr. 27, 1956; s. Jose and Nieves (Cremades) B.; m. Gayle Jean Allard, Aug. 25, 1984; children: Elisabeth, José, John, Christian, Victoria. MS in Aero. Engring., U. Politecnica, Madrid, 1978; MS in Mgmt., MIT, 1988. Power plant engr. Iberia, Madrid, 1980-85, mgr. repair grup, 1985-86, adviser v.p. customer svc., 1986-90, adviser v.p. strategy, 1990-93, mgr. network optimization, 1994-97, v.p. network mgmt., 1997—; writer The Economist Group, London, 1991-96; cons. Market Access, Brussels, 1993-94; rschr. Insead, Fontainbleau, France, 1993. Author: Spain to 2000: A Question of Convergence, 1992, Spain to 2005: Making Room for the Private Sector, 1996. Roman Catholic. Avocations: skiing, skating, horseback riding. Home: Read Pleate Viveroi 27, 28860 Madrid Spain Office: Iberia, Velazquez 130, 28006 Madrid Spain

BOLOS, ADORACION MENDOZA, librarian; b. Manila, Jan. 6, 1936; d. Doroteo and Dionisia Leyva (Bayani) Mendoza; m. Eladio Teodoro Bolos, Nov. 13, 1929; children: Rubuena Bolos-Angeles, Ma. Ariel Bolos-Owen, Divina Bolos-Chingcuanco, Annabel Bolos-Sy, Charity Bolos-Andres. Elem. Tchr. Cert., Philippine Normal Coll., 1955; BSEd, Far Eastern U., Philippines, 1968; postgrad., U. of the Philippines, 1971; Career Exec. Svc. Officer, Devel. Acad. of Philippines. Jr. libr. The Nat. Libr., Philippines, 1956-57, 1957-60, reference libr., 1960-62, sr. reference libr., 1962-67, sr. libr., 1967-69, supervising libr. I, 1969-73, chief libr., 1973-76, acting asst. dir., 1976-86, asst. dir., 1986-89, dir. III, 1989-92, acting dir. IV, 1992-95, dir., 1995—. Mem. Philamlife Homeowners Assn., Inc., Las Pinas, Philippines; bd. mem. Nat. Hist. Inst., Nat. Commn. for Culture and the Arts, Philippine Bd. on Books for Young People; commr. Nat. Commn. for Culture and the Arts. Fellow UNESCO, 1974, Colombo Plan scholarship, 1976. Mem. Philippine Librs. Assn., Pub. Librs. Assn. of Philippines, Assn. of Spl. Librs. of the Philippines, Philippine Assn. of Acad. and Rsch. Librs., Philippine Bd. on Books for Young People, Alumni Assn. (mem. career exec. svc. devel. program). Avocations: reading, cooking, sewing, listening to music. Office: Nat Libr of the Philippines, POB 2926 T M Kalaw 1000 Ermita, Manila The Philippines

BOLÓS, JORDI, chemist, pharmacist; b. Barcelona, Spain, June 27, 1959; s. Joaquin and Ana (Gener) B.; m. Esther Argerich, Sept. 6, 1998. BSc in Pharmacy, U. Barcelona, 1981, MSc, 1982, BSc in Chemistry, 1984, DSc, 1987. Asst. prof. organic chemistry U. Barcelona, 1982-84; rschr. Lab. Uriach S.A., 1984-85, Lab. Vita S.A., 1985-87, Indsl. Comml. Quimica, 1987-89; rschr. Ferrer Internat. S.A., 1989—, dir. dept. medicinal chemistry. Avocation: drawing. Home: Josep Tarradellas 35 4-1, 08029 Barcelona Spain Office: Ferrer Internat, Juan de Sada 32, 08028 Barcelona Spain

BOLOTIN, ADOLF BORISOVICH, physics educator; b. Kharkow, May 20, 1925; s. Boris Lvovich and Sofya Isaakovna (Starzoselskaya) B.; m. Nelly Viktorovna Shengay, May 24, 1945; children: Viktor, Inna. PhD, Vilnius U., Lithuania, 1954; habil. dr. in physics and math., Acad. Sci., Byelorussia, Minsk, 1966. Asst. Vilnius U., 1949-50, sr. tchr., 1950-54, docent, 1954-67, prof., 1967—; head Lab. Atomic and Molecular Spectroscopy, Vilnius, 1979-93; mem. Sci. Coun. Chem. Kinetics and Structure, Moscow, 1974-93, Quantum Net Pub. Assn., Ukraine, 1995—. Author 7 books; contbr. over 343 articles to profl. jours.; mem. editl. bd. Fizika Mozekul, Kiev, 1976-84. Lt. Soviet Army, 1943-44. Internat. Sci. Found. grant, 1991, 13 medals Soviet Partiotic War Orders of 1st and 2d degrees. Mem. Lithuanian Phys. Soc., N.Y. Acad. Scis. World Assn. Theoretical Organic Chemistry. Avocations: locksmithery, music. Office: Vilnius U, Sauletekio 9, 2056 Vilnius Lithuania

BOLOTIN, HERBERT HOWARD, physics educator, consultant; b. N.Y.C., Jan. 11, 1930; arrived in Australia, 1971; s. Harry Bolotin and Gussie Botwinick; m. Charlotte Marilyn Pearlman, Feb. 11, 1951; children: Andrew Matthew, Allison Jane Weinmann. BS, CCNY, 1950; MS, Ind. U., 1952, PhD, 1955; DSc, Melbourne U., Australia, 1980. Physicist U.S. Naval Defense Lab., San Francisco, 1955-58, Brookhaven Nat. Lab., Upton, N.Y., 1958-61, Argonne (Ill) Nat. Lab., 1962-71; assoc. prof. Mich. State U., 1961-62; prof. physics U. Melbourne, 1971-95, prof. emeritus, 1996—; adj. prof. med. radiation scis. RMIT U., 2000—. Contbr. over 100 articles in field of nuc. structure physics to profl. publs.; inventor in field. Fellow Australian Inst. Physics (chmn. 1977-78); mem. Royal Soc. Victoria (rsch. medal 1989, pres. 1997—, found. fellow 1995). Office: U Melbourne, Sch Physics, Parkville VIC 3052, Australia

BOLOTIN, VLADIMIR VASILYEVICH, mechanical engineer, educator; b. Tambov, Russia, Mar. 29, 1926; s. Vasiliy Petrovich and Lyubov Yakovlevna (Poleyeva) B.; m. Kira Sergeyevna Guseva, June 19, 1953; children: Sergey and Yuri. Civil engr., Moscow Inst. Railway Engrs., 1948, PhD in Engring., 1950, DSc, 1952; D (hon.), Tech. U. Budapest, 1975. Registered profl. engr., Russia. Asst. prof. Moscow Inst. Railway Engrs., 1950-53; prof. Moscow Power Engring. Inst./Tech. U., 1953—; bd. mem. USSR Soc. Civil Engrs., Moscow, 1960-86, Russian Nat. Com. on Mechanics. Author: Dynamic Stability of Elastic Systems, 1956, Nonconservative Problems in the Theory of Elastic Stability, 1961, Statistical Methods in Structural Mechanics, 1961, 2d edit., 1965, Prediction of Service Life for Machines and Structures, 1984, 2d edit., 1991, Stability Problems in Fracture Mechanics, 1996, Mechanics of Fatigue, 1999. Recipient Order of Lenin USSR Govt, 1970, State Prize in Sci. and Tech., 1984, Order of Friendship, Russian Govt., 1999, Alfred Freudenthal medal ASCE, 1999; Gold Medal Czechoslovakia Acad. Scis. Prague, 1977. Mem. Russian Acad. Scis. (head lab. reliability Inst. Mech. Engring. 1980—, chmn. Coun. Structural Mechanics 1976—, vice-chmn. Joint Coun. Mechanics 1986—), Russian Acad. Engring., Russian Acad. Architecture and Structural Scis., U.S. Nat. Acad. Engring. (fgn. assoc.). Avocations: classical music, languages, travel. Office: Russian Acad Scis Inst Mech Engring Rsch, M Kharitonyevsky per 4, 101830 Moscow Russia

BOLOTOV, VLADIMIR NIKOLAI, physicist, educator, researcher; b. Moscow, Dec. 9, 1933; s. Nikolai Stepan Bolotov and Alexandr Evstaphi Bolotova; m. Svetlana Vladimir Volgina, Apr. 17, 1970; children: Yuri, Jaroslav. Diploma physics, Moscow Engr. Phys. Inst., 1958; postgrad., Inst. High Energy Physics, Moscow, 1968; D, Inst. Nuc. Rsch., Moscow, 1980. Engr. Phys. Inst. Acad. Sci. USSR, Moscow, 1958-64; head cosmic rays sta. Erevan (USSR) Phys. Inst., 1964-66; head lab. Inst. High Energy Physics, Moscow, 1966-74; chief lab. Inst. Nuc. Rsch., Moscow, 1975—. Contbr. articles to profl. jours. Fax: 135-22-68. Home: Shipilovskaya, 115569 Moscow Russia Office: Inst Nuc Rsch, 60th October Anniversary, 117312 Moscow Russia

BOLOTOWSKY, ANDREW ILYITCH, flutist, composer; b. N.Y.C., Aug. 20, 1949; s. Ilya Yulevitch and Meta (Cohen) B. Studied with William Kincaid, Phila., 1963-67; studied with Elaine Schaffer, N.Y.C., 1967; studied with Jean-Pierre Rampal, France, 1967; BA, New Sch. Social Rsch., 1971. 1st flute Pan Am. Orch., 1982—; flutist Am. Festival of Microtonal Music, N.Y.C., 1983-99, Downtown Music Ensemble, N.Y.C., 1983-84, 92-94, Downtown Music Prodns., 1983-96, 2000—; 1st flute Philharm. Symphony Westchester, 1987-90; with Am. Landmark Festivals, 1973—; baroque flutist Muse, 1987—, Am. Landmark Festival Concerts, 1973—, New Amsterdam Baroque, 1998—, Wood Hill Players, 1999—; performer over 2500 concerts, U.S.a., 1967—; vis. artist Beloit (Wis.) Coll., 1970-73; mime and flute in concert, 1974-84; Delbarton Baroque Ensemble, 1978-81; Criterion Concerts Guggenheim Mus., N.Y.C., 1979; artist N.Y. Com. for Young Audiences, N.Y.C., 1980-87; artist in residence summer mus. theater workshop NYU, 1981; pres. SoHo Baroque Opera Co., N.Y.C., 1983—, Laurel Arts Festival, Jim Thorpe, Pa., 1991, 92, 93, 94. Rec. artist (Orion master recording) 6 Serenades by Fernando Carulli, 1978, (Orion master recording) 20th Century Music for Flute and Guitar, 1978, Music for Flute and Mime, 1982, Behavioral Drift by Franz Kamin, 1980, What The Wind Told, 1979, Scribble Music Sampler by Franz Kamin, 1983, Poetry Music Quilts by Beth Anderson, 1982, Mark Steven Brooks: Compositions 1973-87, 1987; recs. include Pitch, Vol. I No. 3, 1988-89, Indian Summer by Tui St. George Tucker, Opus 1 records No. 107, Timepieces by Rita Falbel, 1991, Between the Keys, Newport Classic CD, 1992, Open Secrets (by Jackson Maclow), 1993 XICD, The Music of Frank Wigglesworth, CRI CD 733, Raj Kapoor's CD Kathmandu Embrace, 1997, Crayon (Jackson Maclow issue), 1997, Melody Sumner Carnahan The Time IS Now, Frog Peak Music CD, 1998, Johnny Reinhard's Raven, Stereo Soc. CD, 1999, Judith St. Croix's Vision of Light and Mystery, Sonic Muse CD, 1999, (4tayCD) Elodie Lauten's The Deus Ex Machina Cycle, 1999, also others; editor Flute Charts for "Pitch", vol. I number 4, 1990; live performances on radio and tv including Stas. WBAI, WQXR, WNYC New Sounds, WKCR, WFUV, NBC, CBS, NYC-TV; extra (films) Eyewitness, 1980, Godfather III, 1990. Grantee Carnegie Recital Hall, Tully Hall Criterion Found., 1976, 77, 78, 79, Meet the Composer, 1978, 80. Avocations: study of earlier flute systems, walking tours, Russian literature. Office: PO Box 492 New York NY 10003

BOLSHAKOV, VLADIMIR IVANOVICH, metallurgist, educator; b. Dnepropetrovsk, Ukraine, May 13, 1946; s. Ivan Fedorovich Bolshakov and Tatyana Fedorovna Starodubova; m. Irina Vasil'evna Rossikhina, Mar. 9, 1968. Diploma in engring. and metallurgy, Dnepropetrovsk, 1969; postgrad., Moscow Inst. Civil Engring., 1969-72; candidate of scis., Inst. Ferrous Metallurgy, Dnepropetrovsk, 1973; DSc, Dnepropetrovsk Metall. Inst., 1985. From jr. to sr. rschr. Dnepropetrovsk Civil Engring. Inst., 1973-74, asst. prof. metal and wooden structures, 1975-86, head of metal tech., 1986, prof. metal tech., 1987, rector, 1987—; Dr./visitor UMIST, Manchester, Eng., 1980-81; cons. INSA, Lyon, France, 1989-98, Lakehead U., Thunder Bay, Ont., Can., 1994-98. Author: Structure and Properties of Construction Steels, 1983, Thermal Treatment of Strengthened Construction Steel, 1987, Strengthening Construction Steels, 1993, Thermal and Thermomechanical Treatment of Construction Steels, 1994, Substructural Strengthening of Structure Steels, 1998. Dep. head coordination coun. Renaissance Found.; mem. dist. com. Trade Union of Workers of Ednl., Higher Sch. and Sci. Instns.; dep. head Knowledge Soc. Adminstrv. Bd. Named hon. worker of sci. and tech. of Ukraine, Pres. of Ukraine, 1992; named officer of French Order of the Palm Branch, Prime Minister of France, 1994; recipient Starodubov's award Internat. Engring. Acad., Moscow, 1996. Mem. Iron and Steel Soc., Can. Inst. Mining, Metallurgy and Petroleum, Inst. of Materials (London), European Soc. Math. and Mechanics. Avocation: philately. Home: 5/11 Acad Lazarian St, 320010 Dnepropetrovsk Ukraine Office: Pridneprovsk State Acad, Civil Engring and Arch, 320600 Dnepropetrovsk Ukraine

BOLSTER, JACQUELINE NEBEN (MRS. JOHN A. BOLSTER), communications consultant; b. Woodhaven, N.Y.; d. Ernest William Benedict and Emily Claire (Guck) Neben; student Pratt Inst., Columbia U.; m. John A. Bolster, May 8, 1954. Promotion mgr. Photoplay mag., 1949-53; merchandising mgr. McCall's, N.Y.C., 1953-64; dir. promotion and merchandising Harper's Bazaar, N.Y.C., 1964-71; dir. advt. and promotion Elizabeth Arden Salons, N.Y.C., 1971-76; dir. creative services Elizabeth Arden, Inc., 1976-78, dir. communications Elizabeth Arden Salons, 1978-87, communication cons., 1987—. Recipient Art Director's award 1961, 66. Mem. Fashion Group, Fashion Execs. Roundtable, Inner Circle, Advt. Women N.Y. (life), Women's Nat. Rep. Club (life). Episcopalian. Home and Office: 8531 88th St Woodhaven NY 11421-1308 also: Halsey Neck Ln Southampton NY 11968

BOLT, CHRISTINE ANNE, history educator; b. Nelson, England, Aug. 10, 1940; d. William Eastwood and Vera (Stuttard) Jackson; m. Ian Geoffrey Bolt, Aug. 18, 1962. BA in History with honors, Westfield Coll., London, 1961; PhD in Am. History, U. Coll. London, 1966. Asst. lectr. history U. Kent-Canterbury, England, 1966-67, lectr., 1967-73, sr. lectr., 1973-78, reader, 1978-84, prof. Am. history, 1984—, pro vice chancellor, 1988-91; vis. asst. prof. Wayne State U., Detroit; vis. assoc. prof. Northern Ill. U., 1970-71. Author: The Anti-Slavery Movement and Reconstruction, 1969, Victorian Attitudes to Race, 1971, A History of the U.S.A., 1974, American Indian Policy and American Reform, 1987, The Women's Movements in the United States and Britain, 1993, Feminist Ferment, 1995 ; co-author: Power and Protest in American Life, 1980; co-editor: Anti-Slavery, Religion and Reform, 1980. Office: Rutherford Coll, U Kent Canterbuty, Kent 7NX 7NS, England

BOLT, DAWN MARIA, financial coach; b. Bklyn., June 12, 1949; d. Gulick Arthur B. and Georgette Helen (Werner) Bolt-Wiggs; widowed; children: Robert B. Williams, Wesley A. Williams. BA, Bklyn. Coll., 1971. Cert. fin. planner; chartered fin. analyst. Fin. analyst Blyth Eastman Dillon, N.Y.C., 1971-77; rating agy. analyst Fitch Investors Svc., N.Y.C., 1977-78; bank analyst Merrill Lynch, N.Y.C., 1978-80; fin. analyst Moodys Investors Svc., N.Y.C., 1980-86; real estate sales agt. J.R. Silvers Realty, N.Y.C., 1987-95, Coldwell Banker Hunt Kennedy, N.Y.C., 1995-98; pvt. practice fin. planning and coaching, 1998—. Avocations: bowling, tennis, skiing, reading, coaching.

BOLT, HERMANN MAXIMILIAN, toxicologist, educator; b. Kirchen, Germany, Jan. 13, 1943; s. Wilhelm and Anna-Maria (Pohlmann) B.; m. Mechtild Ruppel, Feb. 1, 1968. MD, U. Cologne, Germany, 1968; PhD in Biochemistry, U. Tuebingen, Germany, 1973. Asst., lectr. U. Tuebingen, 1972-79; prof. toxicology U. Mainz, Germany, 1979-82; dir. Inst. Occupational Health, Dortmund, Germany, 1982—; prof. toxicology and occupational medicine U. Dortmund, 1982—; pres. FEST/EUROTOX, 1988—. Contbr. over 500 articles to profl. jours. Mem. Sci. Com. on Occupational Exposure Limits. Decorated Fed. Order of Merit, Germany, 2000; recipient Felix-Haffner prize U. Tuebingen, 1974, Marius-Tausk award German Soc. Endocrinology, 1976. Roman Catholic. Office: U Dortmund IFADo, Ardeystr 67, D-44139 Dortmund Germany

BOLT, MICHAEL GERALD, metallurgist; b. Sharon, Pa., Mar. 3, 1953; s. Thomas Bennett and Mary Jane (Lyons) B.; m. Roberta Ann Taylor, Oct. 14, 1972; 1 child, Jennifer Lynn Bolt. BA, Mansfield U., 1975; MS in Student Pers., Slippery Rock U., 1991. Sci. tchr. Cranford (N.J.) Sch. Dist., 1975-76; metall. lab. technician Wheatland (Pa.) Tube Co., 1976—. Treas. Mercer Crawford County Rails to Trails; mem. Canal Mus. Recipient Citizenship award Mercer (Pa.) County Govt., 1974. Mem. ACA, Nature Conservancy, Western Pa. Conservancy, Shenago Conservancy (bd. dirs.), Rails to Trails. Democrat. Roman Catholic. Avocations: bicycling, running, cross country skiing, reading. Home: RD2 Box 252 Patricia Dr W Transfer PA 16154-9305 Office: Wheatland Tube Co Council Ave Wheatland PA 16161

BOLTCHI, FARHAD ESLAM, periodontist, researcher; b. Tehran, Iran, Dec. 12, 1965; s. Mehdi and Mehri (Ochovat) Eslamboltchi; m. Fasaneh Payervand, June 18, 1994. DMD, Med. U. Hannover, Germany, 1990; MS in Oral Biology, Tex. A&M U./Baylor U., 1997. Asst. prof. Med. U. Hannover, 1991-94, Tex. A&M U./Baylor Coll. Dentistry, Dallas, 1997—; pvt. practice clin. periodontist Dallas, 1998—. Contbr. abstracts and sci. articles to med. jours. Rsch. grantee Baylor Coll. Dentistry, 1994, Guidor Co., Sweden, 1995, ITI Found., 2000. Mem. Am. Dental Assn., Am. Acad. Periodontology, Acad. Osseointegration. Office: 8335 Walnut Hill Ln Ste 210 Dallas TX 75231-4204

BOLTHO, ANDREA, economics educator; b. Berlin, Oct. 13, 1939; arrived in Italy, 1940; s. Alexander Boltho von Hohenbach and Ellis (von Hedenstroem) Boltho; m. Maya Nandi, July 15, 1967; children: Fabrice, Alexei. BSc, London Sch. Econ., 1962; MA, U. Paris, 1963; BLitt, U. Oxford, Eng., 1968; Diplome d'Etudes Universitaries Gen., BA, Inst. Oriental Lang./Civ., Paris, 1977. Divsn. head Orgn. for Econ. Coop. and Devel., Paris, 1966-77; fellow, tutor, reader in econs. Magdalen Coll., Oxford, 1977—; vis. rschr. EPA, Tokyo, 1973-74; vis. prof. Johns Hopkins U., Bologna, Italy, 1992, U. Paris, 1991, U. Venice, Italy, 1984, Internat. U. Japan, 1985, INSEAD, France, 1998-99; cons. World Bank, Washington, 1987. Author: Foreign Trade Criteria in Socialist Economies, 1971, Japan-An Economic Survey, 1975; editor: The European Economy: Growth and Crisis, 1982; contbr. articles to profl. jours. Japan Found. fellow, 1973, Ctr. Nat. Rsch., Venice, 1985. Mem. IFO Inst. (acad. coun. 1997-99). Office: Magdalen Coll, High St, OX1 4AU Oxford England

BOLTON, BRUCE DOUGLAS, museum director; b. Montreal, Que., Can., Oct. 21, 1950; s. Charles Wilfred and Mary Bolton; m. Roberta Margaret Cascadden, May 25, 1985; children: Sarah Catherine, Laura Margaret. BSc, McGill U., 1972. Dir. The David M. Stewart Mus., 1982—; pres. bd. dirs. Montreal Mus. Dir.; founding mem., former v.p. Que. Mus. Soc.; life. gov. Chateau Ramezay Mus.; adv. bd. Fort Ticonderoga Assn.; adjutant 78th Fraser Highlands. Dir. Trafalgar Sch. for Girls. Comdg. officer, lt.-Col. Black Watch, Royal Highland Regiment Can. Recipient Queen's Jubilee medal, Can. 125 medal. Mem. Order Mil. Merit, Mt. Stephan Club. Office: PO Box 1200 Stn A, Montreal, PQ Canada H3C 2Y9

BOLTON, THOMAS BRUCE, pharmacologist, educator; b. Sunderland, Eng., Nov. 14, 1941; s. Thomas and Winifred Bolton; m. Patricia Bolton; 3 children. BSc, U. London, 1964, PhD, 1967, BVM, 1969; MA (hon.), U. Oxford, 1971. Asst. lectr. Royal Vet. Coll. Univ. London, 1965-66; rsch. fellow Dept. Pharmacology Oxford U., 1969-76; sr. lectr., prof. Univ. London, 1976—; head pharmacology and clin. pharmacology dept. St. George's Hosp. Med. Sch., 1985—; external examiner U. Aston, U. Poitiers, U. Melbourne, U. Glasgow, U. Manchester, Oxford U., U. Ireland, U. Strathc-

lyde, Univ. Coll. London, Sch. Pharmacy London, Edinburgh U., U. Bordeaux, Cambridge U., Kings Coll. London; mem. physiol. and pharmacol. panel The Wellcome Trust, 1985-90, mem. Internat. Interest Group, 1991-94; mem. Univs. Funding Coun. Med. Com., 1991-92; mem. Higher Edn. Funding Coun. for Eng. Joint Med. Adv. Com., 1993-95; chmn. basic med. and dental scis. panel Higher Edn. Funding Coun.. Rsch. Assessment Exercise, 1992, 96. Editor Brit. Jour. Pharmacology, 1975-81, Jour. Physiology, 1985-92; contbr. articles to profl. jours. Mem. chairs and rsch. group com. Brit. Heart Assn., 1994—. Fellow Brasenose Coll., 1971-76, Royal Soc. Locke Rsch., 1972-76. Fellow Acad. Med. Scis.; mem. Brit. Pharmacol. Soc., Physiol. Soc., Biophys. Soc., Save Brit. Sci., Biochem. Soc., Univ. Fedn. Animal Welfare, Royal Coll. Vet. Surgeons, Acad. Europea. Avocations: building, sports. Office: Univ London St Georges Hosp, U London St Georges Hosp, Dept Pharm/Cranmer Terr, London SW17 0RE, England

BOLTON-HOLIFIELD, ALICE RUTH, basketball player; b. Lucedale, Miss., May 25, 1967; d. Linwood and Leola Bolton; m. Mark Holifield. B of Exercise Physiology, Auburn U., 1989. Basketball player C.A. Faenza, Italy, 1993, Erreti Faenza, Italy, 1994-95, Sacramento Monarchs, 1997—; mem. U.S.A. Women's Nat. Basketball Team. Lead singer Antidum Tarantula, Italy. 1st lt. USAR. Recipient gold medal 1994 Goodwill Games, 1994, World Championship Qualifying Team FIBA World Championship, 1993, World Univ. Games, 1991, U.S. Olympic Fesitval, 1986; bronze medal World Championship, 1994; named USA Basketball's Female Athelete of Yr., 1991, 1st Am. woman to play profl. basketball in Hungary and Sweden, 1990-91; named to NCAA 1989 Mideast Region All-Tournament Team, 1988, 89, NCAA Final Four All Tournament Team, 1988, SEC All-Academic Team, 1988, 89, All-SEC second team, 1989; earned SEC All-Tournament Team honors, 1988, All-WNBA 1st team, 1997, named first ever WNBA player of week, 1997, mem. gold medal winning Olympic team Atlanta, 1996, mem. U.S. Basketball Women's Nat. Team, 1995-96. Office: Sacramento Monarchs Arco Arena Sacramento CA 95834

BOLY, JEFFREY ELWYN, lawyer; b. Portland, Oreg., Mar. 16, 1942; s. Elwyn and Frances Rolland (Hulse) B.; m. Mary Ione Van Beckum, Sept. 4, 1965; children: Jeffrey Elwyn, Justin; m. Linda Diehl, Sept. 4, 1993; 1 child, Brian. AB, Georgetown U., 1964; JD, U. Calif.-San Francisco, 1967. Bar: U.S. Dist. Ct. (no. dist.) Calif. 1967, Calif. 1967, U.S. Ct. Appeals (9th cir.) 1967, U.S. Tax Ct. 1968, Oreg. 1971, U.S. Dist. Ct. Oreg. 1971, U.S. Supreme Ct. 1971. Trial atty. Office of Chief Counsel to Commr. IRS, San Francisco, 1967-71; ptnr. Wood Tatum Mosser Brooke & Landis, Portland, Oreg., 1971-87; ptnr. Hanna, Urbigkeit, Jensen, Goyak & O'Connell, Portland, 1987-88, Hanna, Murphy, Jensen & Holloway, 1988-89, Garvey, Schubert & Barer, Portland, 1989—. Bd. dirs. Oreg. Advocates for Arts, 1980-87, pres. bd. dirs., 1981-82; bd. dirs. Ballet Oreg., 1983-88, chmn., 1984-85; mem. parents' bd. Jesuit H.S., 1985-88, pres. parents' bd., 1988, mem. alumni bd., 1986—, chmn. planned giving com., 1993—; mem. estate planning coun. City of Portland, chmn. seminar com., 1988; mem. adv. coun. Oreg. Shakespeare Festival, 1991-94; mem. planned giving com. Am. Lung Assn. of Oreg., 1991—; bd. dirs. Portland Center Stage, 1994—, sec., 1995—. Mem. ABA (mem. tax sect.), Calif. Bar Assn., Western Region Bar Assn. (Oreg. rep., IRS liaison 1987—, chair 1991-92), Multnomah County Bar Assn., Oreg. State Bar Assn. (mem. estate planning sect., mem. exec. com. 1983-87, chair 1985-86, newsletter editor 1985-86; mem. taxation sect., mem. exec. com. 1981-83, 87-94, mem. IRS and Oreg. Dept. Revenue liaison subcom. 1987—, sec. 1989-90, chair-elect 1990-91, chair 1991-92), Georgetown U. Alumni Assn. (pres. Portland chpt. 1977). Democrat. Roman Catholic. Home: 2879 SW Champlain Dr Portland OR 97201-1833 Office: Garvey Schubert & Barer 121 SW Morrison St Fl 11 Portland OR 97204-3117*

BOLY, YÉRO, government official; b. Kompi-Ipala, Bazèga, Burkina Faso, 1954; married; 3 children. Degree, Ouagadougou Nat. Sch. Adminstr, 1975. Gen. sec. Namentenga Province, Burkina Faso, 1984-86; amb. to Ivory Coast Govt. Burkina Faso, 1986-88, amb. to Libya, 1988, minister of territorial adminstrn., 1995—. Named Officer of Nat. Order of Ivory Coast. Office: Ministry Territorial Admin, 03 BP 7034, Ouagadougou Burkina Faso*

BOLZ, GEORGE MICHAEL, engineering executive, consultant; b. Vienna, Austria, Mar. 22, 1948; arrived in Australia, 1952; s. George Adolf and Elizabeth (Mayer) B.; m. Glenda Jean Johnstone, Aug. 30.1998. B of Elec. Engring., U. Melbourne, Australia, 1970, B of Commerce, 1977. Chartered profl. engr. Engr. Dept. Civil Aviation, Melbourne, 1971-87; prin. engr. Civil Aviation Authority, Melbourne, 1987-89, Avtel Pty Ltd., Brunei Darussalam, Melbourne, 1989-92; pvt. practice cons. engr. Melbourne, 1992-96; exec. dir. Mayer Bolz Pty Ltd., Melbourne, 1996—; comms. engring. cons. Internat. Civil Aviation Orgn., Karachi, Pakistan, 1991; sys. engring. cons. Sydney (Australia) Airport Devel. Project, 1993-94, Australian Advanced Air Traffic Sys. project, France and Australia, 1995-98. Life mem. Nat. Gallery Victoria. Mem. IEEE, Australian French Assn. Profl. and Tech. Specialists (br. treas. 1978-80, br. sec. 1981-83, br. pres. 1984-86), Instn. Engrs. Australia (sr.), Air Traffic Control Assn., Australian Inst. Mgmt., Nat. Trust Australia (life). Roman Catholic. Avocations: opera, balet, fine arts. Office: Mayer Bolz Pty Ltd, PO Box 578, 3101 Kew Victoria, Australia

BOLZANI, LUCIANO GUISEPPE, psychiatrist; b. Pavia, Italy, Jan. 11, 1924; s. Giovanni Bolzani and Assunta Maria Passadori; m. Serena Maria Annovazzi, April 7, 1953; children: Giovanni, Lorenza. Student, Univ., Basel, Switzerland, 1943-45, Univ., Pavia, Italy, 1943-49; asst. qualified, Univ., Pavia, Italy, 1949-53. Med. diplomate. Asst. Univ., Pavia, 1944-53, tchr., 1958-77; asst. Viarnetto Psychiatric Clinic, Lugano Pregassona, Switzerland, 1954-60; dir. Viarnetto Clinic, Lugano Pregassona, 1960-93. Author: A Clinic History, 1997. Hon. mem. Swiss Red Cross, 1970-85. Roman Catholic. Home: Ceresio 34b, 6963 Pregassona/Lugano Switzerland

BOM, HEE-SEUNG, nuclear physician, educator; b. Kwangju, South Korea, Nov. 22, 1957; s. Dae-Soon Bom and Ok-Young Kim; m. Jong-Hee Shin; children: Sun-Yoon, Kyung-Yoon, Joon-Suk. MD, Chonnam U., Kwangju, Korea, 1982, PhD, 1988. Cert. Korean Bd. Internal Medicine, Korean Bd. Nuclear Medicine. Chmn. dept. nuclear medicine Chonnam U. Hosp., Kwangju, 1993—, dir. divsn. med. informatics, 1996—, assoc. prof., 1997—; fellow dept. radiology Emory U. Hosp., Atlanta, 1994-95. Author: Case Studies of Nuclear Medicine, 1997, Nuclear Imaging of the Chest, 1997; editor, author: A Guide to Medical Fellowship in USA, 1997; contbr. articles to profl. jours. Condr. Chonnam U. Med. Sch. Orch.; pres. Dongmyung Mid. Sch. PTA, Kwangju, Korea, 1998. Capt. Korean Army, 1988-90. Recipient Acad. award Congress of Korea, 1982. Mem. Korean Soc. Nuclear Medicine (bd. info. 1998—, Acad. award 1994), Korean Soc. Med. Informatics. Home: 85-62 Gyerim 2 Dong, Kwangju 501-082, South Korea Office: Chonnam U Hosp Nuclear Med, 8 Hakdong, Kwangju 501-757, South Korea

BOMAN, HANS G., biochemist, educator; b. Sweden, Aug. 16, 1924; married; 2 children. BS, U. Uppsala, 1950, PhD, 1953, DSc, 1958. Various tchg. and rsch. asst. positions Inst. Biochemistry U. Uppsala, 1952-58; rsch. assoc. Rockefeller U., 1958-60; asst. prof. biochemistry Uppsala U., 1960-63; rschr. molecular biology Swedish Natural Sci. Rsch. Coun., Uppsala, 1963-66; prof. microbioology Med. Faculty U. Umea, 1966-76, chmn. dept. microbiology, 1966-71; prof., chmn. microbiology U. Stockholm, 1976-90, prof. emeritus, 1990—; vis. prof. biology MIT, Cambridge, 1971-72. Contbr. more than 100 articles to profl. jours. Mem. sci. adv. coun. Swedish Prime Min., 1969-79; mem. study group for grants Swedish Cancer Soc., 1969-78; Swedish rep. Scandinavian Govt., 1973-76. Recipient Insect Biochemistry prize U. Umea, 1985, Bjorken prize U. Uppsala, 1988, Nils Rosen Linne prize in zoology Kungl. Fysiog. Sallskapet, Lund, 1992. Mem. Royal Swedish Acad. Engring. Scis., Royal Swedish Acad. Scis., Academia Europa. Achievements include research in protein chromatography and studies of different phosphoesterases, protein synthesis and RNA methylation, penicillin resistance and bacterial cell envelopes, insect immunity, and bacillus thuringiensis. Office: Karolinska Inst Ctr Microb, Box 280, 17177 Stockholm Sweden

BOMAN, (JOHN) ROBERT, educator; b. Hernosand, Sweden, Feb. 15, 1926; s. John Ragvald and Anna Sofie (Nordenberg) B. JD, Uppsala U., Sweden, 1964. Docent faculty law Uppsala U., Sweden, 1964-66, assoc. prof., 1966-72, prof. jud. procedure, 1972-91; prof. emeritus, 1991. Author: Om åberopande och åberopsbörda i dispositiva tvistemål, 1964, Deldom, 1975; contbr. articles to profl. jours. Avocation: history ships and shipping. Home: Vaderkvarnsgatan 38A, S 753 29 Uppsala Sweden

BOMBELLES, JOSEPH THOMAS, economics educator, consultant; b. Zagreb, Croatia, June 2, 1930; came to U.S., 1956; s. Joseph Hugo and Ljuba (Grzin) B.; m. G. Nina Bombelles, July 7, 1955; children: Thomas George, Mark Brian. LLB, U. Zagreb, 1952; MA, Case Western Res. U., 1960, PhD in Econs., 1965. Instr. Case Inst. Tech., Cleve., 1960-63; asst. prof. John Carroll U., Cleve., 1963-66, prof. econs., 1971-98, chmn. dept. econs., 1985-89, dir. chair in econs. energy and environment, 1974-86; assoc. prof. U. Ill., Normal, 1968-71; cons. LW Internat. Fin. Rsch. Inc., N.Y.C., 1968-92. Author: Economic Development of Communist Yugoslavia, 1968; contbr. articles to profl. jours. Fulbright fellow USIA, 1991-92, 95-96, tchg. fellow, 1998-99. Mem. Am. Econ. Assn., Am. Assn. for Advancement Slavic Studies, Croatian Acad. Arts and Scis. (corr.), Am.-Croatian Acad. Soc. (pres. 1963-65, 72-82), Assn. for Croatian Studies (pres. 1976-86, 91-99). Avocations: reading, travel. Home: 3295 Daleford Rd Shaker Heights OH 44120

BOMBERGER, RUSSELL BRANSON, lawyer, writer; b. Lebanon, Pa., May 1, 1934; s. John Mark and Viola (Aurentz) B.; divorced; children—Ann Elizabeth, Jane Carmel. BS, Temple U., 1955; MA, U. Iowa, 1956, M.A., 1961, PhD, 1962; MS, U. So. Calif., 1960; LLB, JD, LaSalle U.; grad., U.S. Marine Corps Command and Staff Coll., 1987, U.S. Naval War Coll., 1991. Bar: Calif. 1970, U.S. Supreme Ct. 1975. Mem. editorial staff Phila. Inquirer, 1952-54; lectr. U. Iowa, 1955-57, U. So. Calif., 1957-58; asst. prof. U.S. Naval Postgrad. Sch., Monterey, Calif., 1958-62; assoc. prof. U.S. Naval Postgrad. Sch., 1963-75, prof., 1975-89, prof. emeritus, 1989—; practice law, 1970—; free lance writer, 1952—, communications cons., 1963—; safety cons. internat. program U. So. Calif. Inst. Safety and Systems Mgmt., 1983—; cons. Internat. Ctr. for Aviation Safety, Lisbon, 1984—. Author: (novel) The Alternate Candidate, (broadcast series) The World of Ideas, (motion picture) Strokes and Stamps, (stage play) Closely Held; abstracter-editor: Internat. Transactional Analysis Assn. Capt. USNR, 1966-94. Decorated Meritorious Civilian Svc. medal, 1989; Am. Psychol. Found. fellow Columbia U., 1954-55, CBS fellow U. So. Calif., 1957-58. Office: PO Box 8741 Monterey CA 93943-8741

BOMBET, JEAN-PIERRE, executive; b. Boulogne Billancourt, France, June 30, 1947; s. Louis and Leone Bombet; m. Hermine Molière; children: Isaure and Louis-Hugues (twins). JD, U. Paris, Paris, 1969; MBA, Northwestern U., Evanston, Ill., 1972. Asst. to mktg. gen. mgr. P.L.M., Paris, 1972-74; mktg. mgr. Kronenbourg (BSN Group), Strasbourg, 1974-79, Roussel Uclaf, Washington, 1979-81; gen. mgr. Delsey, Paris, 1981-94; mng. dir. for Europe, Mid. East and Africa A.T. Cross, Lincoln, R.I., 1994—. Avocations: gastronomy, wines. Office: A T Cross European Hdqs, 12 bis rue Keppler, 75116 Paris France

BOMBICZ, PETRA ALEXANDRA, crystallographer, researcher; b. Budapest, Hungary, May 30, 1966; d. Sándor and Edit (Kaponya) B. BS, Tech. U. Budapest, Hungary, 1987; MS, Tech. U. Budapest, 1989, PhD, 1993, 97. chem. engr. Scholar scientific com. Hungarian Acad. Scis., Budapest, 1989-91; rschr., scientist Ctrl. Rsch. Inst. Hungarian Acad. Scis., 1993—; scholar Tech. U. Budapest, 1991-93, tchr., 1989-95; rschr. Free U., Berlin, 1998-99. Contbr. articles to profl. jours. Recipient Hungarian Acad. Scis. award, 1996. Mem. Hungarian Chem. Soc. (Standard award 1989), Internat. Union Crystallography (sec. nat. com. 1996). Avocations: travel, history of architecture, classical music, literature, gymnastics. Home: Üllöi ut 16/b, H-1085 Budapest Hungary Office: Chemistry Inst Chem Rsch Ct, Pusztaszeri ut 59-67, POB 17 Budapest H-1525, Hungary

BOMCHIL, MÁXIMO LUIS, lawyer; b. Buenos Aires, May 13, 1950; s. Máximo Bomchil and Sara Lydia (Garcia) Martin; m. Ana Lucrecia de Las Carreras, Nov. 24, 1982; children: Máximo José, Miguel, Martin. LLB, Univ. Catolica, Argentina, 1973; JD, U. Munich, Germany, 1976; M of Laws, London U., 1977. Mng. ptnr. M. & M. Bomchil, Buenos Aires, 1973—. Contbr. articles to profl. jours. Decorated Nat. Order of Merit, French Govt., 1993; named Outstanding Young Man, Camara Jr. de Buenos Aires, 1980. Mem. Internat. Bar Assn., Circulo de Armas, Golf Club of Argentina, Jockey Club. Office: M&M Bomchil, M & M Bomchil, Suipacha 268 Piso 12, 1355 Buenos Aires Argentina

BOMHOF, MARTIN A. M., neurologist, consultant; b. Rotterdam, The Netherlands, June 1, 1948; s. Reinder and Wilhelmina (Engelhard) B.; m. Ursula Fabrie, Aug. 25, 1973; children: Jeroen, Maarten, Eline. MD, U. Utrecht, The Netherlands, 1971, diploma in neurology, 1978; diploma in psychiatry, U. Groningen, The Netherlands, 1975; diploma in cultural scis., Open U., The Netherlands, 1991. Med. officer Dutch Army, The Netherlands, 1971-72, commd. maj., 1972-94; psychiatrist Ignatius Hosp., Breda, The Netherlands, 1978-84, neurologist, 1984—; cons. Psychogeriatrics Lucia, Breda, 1985—; active in clin. drug trails, 1985—. Author books on headache; reviewer 300 books, 1975—, various medical articles, 1980—. Mem. Neurol. Soc. The Netherlands, Leage Epilepsy Holland, Migraine Stichting The Netherlands (pres.), Anglo-Dutch Migraine Assn., Dutch-Belgian Study Club Extrapyramidal Disorders, Internat. Headache Soc., Dutch Headache Soc. (founding mem.), Dutch Neuro-Ophthal. Study Club, Dutch Child Neurology Club, Rotary (pres. Breda 1991). Roman Catholic. Avocation: art history study. Fax: 0031-765201354. E-mail: mambomhof@wxs.nl. Home: Schubertlaan 11, 4837 CP Breda The Netherlands Office: Ignatius Hosp, Ignatius Hosp, Molengracht 21, 4818 CK Breda The Netherlands

BOMMARCO, ANTONIO VITALE, former archbishop of Roman Catholic Church; b. Cres, Yugoslavia, Sept. 21, 1923. Ordained priest Roman Cath. Ch. 1949; consecrated bishop 1983. Office: Via Arcivescovado 2, 34170 Gorizia Italy*

BOMPART, FRANCOIS RENE, pharmaceutical company executive; b. Oran, Algeria, Nov. 14, 1959; s. Germain Bompart and Colette Cathala. MD, U. Angers, France, 1984. Clin. rsch. fellow Univ. Coll. London, 1985-87; clin. pharmacologist Hosp. Cochin, Paris, 1988-89; dir. clin. studies Smith Kline and French, Paris, 1989-90; dir. clin. devel. anti-infectives Rhone Poulenc Rorer, Paris, 1991, 97; dir. anti-infectives clin. rsch. Rhone Poulenc Rorer, Collegeville, Pa., 1992-96; med. dir. internat. Aventis Pasteur, Lyon, France, 1998—. E-mail: francois.bompart@aventis.com. Office: Aventis Pasteur, 2 Ave Pont Pasteur, 69007 Lyon France

BOMPAS, ANTHONY GEORGE, barrister; b. Penang, Malaysia, Nov. 6, 1951; s. Donald George and Freda Vice (Smithyman) B.; m. Donna Linda James, Jan. 16, 1981; children: Samuel Henry, Abra Mae, Caleb George. MA in Jurisprudence, Oxford (Eng.) U., 1974. Barrister, 1975—, jr. counsel to DTI Chancery, 1989-94; Queen's counsel London, 1994—. Mem. Worshipful Co. of Merchant Taylors (liveryman). Office: Lincoln's Inn, 4 Stone Bldgs, London WE2A 3XT, England

BOMPAS, DONALD GEORGE, charitable organization executive, consultant; b. Southgate, Eng., Nov. 20, 1920; s. Edward Anstie and Sissie Mary (Fraser) B.; m. Freda Vice Smithyman, Aug. 31, 1946; children: Catherine, Anthony George. MA, Oxford (Eng.) U., 1947. With Overseas Audit Svc., Nyasaland, 1942-47; with Overseas Audit Svc., Singapore, Malaya, Malaysia, 1947-66, dep. auditor-gen., 1956-60, auditor-gen., 1960-66; dep. sec., then sec. Guy's Hosp. Med. Sch., London, 1966-82; dep. sec. United Med. and Dental Schs. Guy's and St. Thomas Hosps., London, 1982-84, sec., 1984-86, hon. fellow, 1996; mng. exec. Philip and Pauline Harris Charitable Trust, 1986—. Decorated companion Order St. Michael and St. George; hon. Johan Mangku Negara (Malaysia); hon. fellow King's Coll., London, 1998. Home: 8 Birchwood Rd, Petts Wood BR5 1NY, England

BON, ALEXANDR IVANOVICH, chemical engineer; b. Saratov, Russia, June 16, 1941; s. Ivan Ivanovich and Julia Alekseevna (Kabankova) B.; m. Ludmila Nikolaevna Brovtcina (div. 1966); 1 child, Stanislav; m. Valentina Alekseevna Manankova, Nov. 26, 1971 (div. 1995); children: Ivan, Elena; m. Galina Leonidovna Fedorova. Diploma, Polytech. Coll., Tchelyabinsk, Russia, 1961; degree, Chem. Tech. Inst., Ivanovo, Russia, 1967, Cand. Sc., Russia, 1984. Technician, chief technician Chemical Plant, Kirov, Russia, 1961-66, engr., chief process engr., 1966-77; chief scientific assoc. NPO Polymersintez, Vladimir, Russia, 1977-86; head of lab. Polymersintez, Vladimir, Russia, 1986-97, mgr. of NPO Membranes, 1997-98; dir. Aquapore Scientific Mfg. Enterprise, Vladimir, 1992—; dep. gen. dir. Scientific Tech. Ctr., Vladipor, 1998. Contbr. articles to profl. jours. Recipient 14 Decorations for Achievement in Labor Gov. Russia, 1972-84, Medal for Distinction in Labor, 1970, Reward in sci. and engring. for membrane prodn. Russian govt., 1995. Fellow Membrane Club; mem. Russian Acad. Sci. and Art, N.Y. Acad Sci. Roman Catholic. Avocations: photography, video, cultivation of flowers & fish in aquariums. Fax: 216913. Office: ZAO STC Vladipor, 77 B.Nizhegorodskaya St, 600016 Vladimir Russia

BON, MICHEL MARIE, telecommunications executive; b. Grenoble, France, July 5, 1943; s. Emmanuel and Mathilde (Aussedat) B.; m. Catherine de Sairigné, June 18, 1971; children: Charles Emmanuel, Eleonore, Domitille, Adelaide. Grad., Ecole Superieure des Sciences Economiques et Commerciales, 1966, Ecole Nationale d'Administration, 1971, Stanford U., 1986. Inspecteur Inspection des Finances, Paris, 1971-75; chief of staff Credit Nat., Paris, 1975-78; v.p. credit Credit Agricole, Paris, 1978-81, dep. CEO, 1981-85; dep. CEO Carrefour, Paris, 1985-87, CEO, 1987-90, chmn., CEO, 1990-92; CEO Agence Nationale Pour L'Emploi, Paris, 1993-95; chmn., CEO France Telecom, Paris, 1995—; bd. dirs. LaFarge, France, Air Liquide, France, Le Monde, France, Bull, France. Chmn. Essec Bus. Sch., France; treas. Inst. Pierre Mendes France; vice chmn. Inst. Pasteur. Home: 4 Ave de Camoens, 75116 Paris France Office: France Telecom, 6 Place D'Alle Ray, 75505 Paris 15, France

BONABELLO, PIETRO, political scientist; b. Alessandria, Piedmont, Italy, June 20, 1937; s. Domenico and Rosa (Donna) B.; m. Piera Machetta, Sept. 22, 1962; children: Fabrizio, Emanuele, Marco. Grad. in Polit. Scis., U. Turin, Italy, 1968; postgrad., War Coll., Civitavecchia, Italy, 1973, Royal Coll. Def. Studies, London, 1985. Cadet Mil. Acad., Modena, Italy, 1955-57; officer cadet Svc. Br. Sch., Turin, 1957-59; commd. lt. Italian Army, 1959, advanced through grades to maj. gen., 1995; platoon-co. comdr. Italian Army, Italy, 1959-70; attendant to gen. staff course Italian Army, Civitavecchia, 1970-73; bn., regiment comdr. staff officer Italian Army, Italy, 1973-84; attendant Royal Coll. Def. Studies, London, 1985; sr. mil. adviser Italian Mission to CSCE and CFE Negotiations, Vienna, Austria, 1986-90; dep., then head Italian Verification Ctr., Viterbo, Italy, 1990-93; sr. mil. adviser Italian Mission to OSCE, Vienna, 1993-95; reduction coord. OSCE Art IV Dayton Agr. Implementation, Vienna, 1996-97; expert on OSCE bus. and activities Ministries of Def. and Fgn. Affairs, Rome, 1997-99—. Contbr. articles to profl. jours. Recipient Mauriziana medal Min. Def., Rome, 1988, Commendatore Italian Rep., Rome, 1994. Avocations: alpinism, travel, skiing, cycling. Home: Via Carlo Emilio Gadda 97, 00143 Rome Italy

BONATTI, CARLO ALBERTO, air conditioning company manager; b. Massa, Italy, Sept. 15, 1962; s. Augusto and Giovanna (Montagna) B.; m. Cristina Cazzetta, Dec. 16, 1989; children: Elisa, Valentina, Tommaso. MSEE, Poly. U. Milan, 1988. Software devel. team leader Aermacchi, Varese, Italy, 1987-92; from elec. engr. to product delivery sys. site mgr. Carrier, Villasanta, Italy, 1992—. Mem. IEEE. Home: Via Solari 50, 20144 Milano Italy

BONATTI, LUCA LORENZO, psychology educator, researcher; b. Milan, Aug. 10, 1960; arrived in France, 1994; s. Gabriele and Luciana (Nolli) B.; 2 children: Matteo and Livio. PhD, U. Degli Studi, Milan, 1986, Rutgers U., 1994. Assoc. rschr. Milan Hosp. San Raffaele, 1993-94, Nat. Ctr. Sci. Rsch., Paris, 1994-96; prof. U. Paris 8, 1996—; vis. prof. NYU, N.Y.C., 1996—; bd. dirs. Cognition; assoc. Behavioral Brain Sci., 1996—. Editor, cons. Ganzanti Editre, 1985-88; editor, translator Mondadori Editore, 1983-84; contbr. articles to profl. jours. Human Capital and Mobility individual fellow EEC, 1994-96, Ministero Ricerca Sci. fellow. Mem. Soc. for Philosophy and Psychology. Office: U Paris 8 UFR Psychology, 2 rue de la Liberté, 93525 Paris France

BONAVENTURA, ANTONINO, oncologist; b. Linguaglossa, Italy, Jan. 20, 1954; arrived in Australia, 1965; s. Salvatore and Caterina (Vecchio) B.; m. Majella Anne Kriukelis, Oct. 6, 1985; children: Kathleen Margaret, Louisa Shirley, Carmel Teresa, Sam Anthony, John-Paul, Rebecca Mary. MB, BChir, U. Queensland, 1979. Resident Royal Brisbane (Australia) Hosp., 1979-81; registrar Greenslopes Repatriation Hosp., Brisbane, 1982-86; fellow in medicine Wesley Hosp. Brisbane, 1987; registrar oncology Woden Valley Hosp., Canberra, Australia, 1988, Mater Misericordiae Hosp., Newcastle, Australia, 1989-90; staff specialist oncology Mater Misericordiae Hosp., Newcastle, 1991-98, sr. staff specialist oncology, 1999—. Author: Selected Schedules of Therapy for Malignant Tumors, 1993; contbr. articles to profl. jours. Fellow Royal Australian Coll. Physicians; mem. Am. Soc. Clin. Oncology, Clin. Oncology Soc. Australia, European Soc. Clin. Oncology, Internat. Assn. for Study of Lung Cancer. Roman Catholic. Avocations: family, golf, tennis, reading, computers. Office: Mater Misericordiae Hosp, Dept Med Oncology, Newcastle 2298, Australia

BONCI, ANDREW S., chiropractor; b. Yonkers, N.Y., Apr. 27, 1963. BA, U. Denver, 1986; D Chiropractic, Cleveland Chiropractic Coll., Kansas City, Mo., 1989. Diplomate Am. Acad. Pain Mgmt., Am. Acad. Experts in Traumatic Stress. Pvt. practice, N.Y.C., 1990-95; assoc. prof. Cleveland Chiropractic Coll., Kansas City, Mo., 1995—, also chmn. dept. diagnosis. Office: Cleveland Chiropractic Coll 6401 Rockhill Rd Kansas City MO 64131-1122

BONCIOCAT, NICOLAE ULPIU, chemist, educator; b. Arad, Romania, June 26, 1931; s. Nicolae and Aurelia (Foias) B.; m. Ileana Cornelia Nicoara, Dec. 29, 1960; children: Alina Aurelia Iovescu, Nicolae Ciprian, Amalia Maria. MS in chem. engring., Poly. U., Timisoara, Romania, 1954, PhD in Electrochemistry, 1971; BA in math, physics, West Univ., Timisoara, Romania, 1958. Asst. prof. Poly. Univ., Timisoara, 1954-58; chem. engr. Solventul, Timisoara, 1958-60; prof. Gh. Doja, Timisoara, 1960-62; rschr. Pharm. Rsch. Inst., Bucharest, Romania, 1962-70; chief corrosion dept. Ctr. Physical Chemistry, Bucharest, 1970-80; chief electrochemistry dept. Inst. Chem. Biochem. Energetics, Bucharest, 1980-96; dir. rsch. nat. Inst. Electrochemistry, Bucharest, 1996—; supr. for PhD in phys. chemistry U. Bucharest, 1990; mem. scientific coun. Inst. Chem. Rsch., Bucharest, 1990—, Inst. Microtech., Bucharest, 1992—, Nat. Inst. Electrochemistry, Bucharest, 1996—; assoc. prof. Mil. Tech. Acad., 1992—; cons. prof. Poly. Univ., Bucharest, 1992—. Co-author: An Introduction to Electrochemical Science, 1974; author: Electrochemistry and Applications, 1996; contbr. articles to profl. jours.; holder 90 patents in field. Mem. Civic Alliance, Bucharest, 1990. Fulbright scholar Univ. Pa., 1971-72; recipient Gheorghe Spacu prize Roumanian Acad., 1977, Honor medal West U., 1997. Mem. Internat. Soc. Electrochemistry, N.Y. Acad. Sci., Roumanian Soc. Electrochemistry, Sci. and Microsystems Commn. of Romanian Acad. Christian Orthodox. Avocations: classical music. Home: Block 71 Apt 37, Str Apusului 60-70, 77561 Bucharest Romania Office: Poly Univ CAEL, POB 17-112, Bucharest Romania

BONCOEUR-MARTEL, MARIE PAULE, neuroradiologist; b. La Souterraine, Limousin, France, Jan. 26, 1961; d. Pierre Louis and Paule (Migliori) Martel; m. Pascal Pierre Boncoeur. Radiologist, Toulouse III, 1989; 1st degree of PhD, U. Paris V, 1993. Resident Hosp. Toulouse, 1984-89; attending Hosp. Limoges, 1989—. Contbr. articles to med. jours. Mem. Radiol. Soc. N.Am. (corr. mem.), Am. Soc. Neuroradiology, European Soc. Neuroradiology. Avocation: horseback riding. Home: 5 Bis BD Victor Hugo, 87000 Limoges France Office: Radiologie B Chu Dupuytren, 2 Ave Martin Luther King, 87000 Limoges France

BONCU, SIMION, military officer; b. Breaza, Prahova, Romania, Aug. 1, 1950; s. Ion and Natalia B.; m. Rodica Munteanu, Aug. 19, 1976; 1 child, Cosmin. Grad., Air Force and Air Def. Acad., 1972; diploma mil. sci., Acad. Advanced Mil. Studies, 1976; diploma law, U. Bucharest, 1983; grad., Nat. Def. Coll., 1994; PhD, Mil. Acad., 1996. Commd. Air Force, 1972, advanced through grades to brig. gen.; various command positions Air Force and Air Def., 1972-76; rschr. and sr. rschr. dept. Mil. Doctrine Ctr. Studies

and Rschrs. on Mil. History and Theory, 1978-90; chief dept. Mil. Doctrine and Security Studies Inst. of Mil. History and Theory, 1990-91; chief Info. and Pub. Rels. Sect. MoD, 1991-93, chief of Mil. Info. and Pub. Rels. Directorate, 1993-98, chief Internat. Mil. Rels. Directorate, 1998-2000; lectr., assoc. prof. Acad. of Advanced Mil. Studies, Bucharest, 1980-89; lectr. Nat. Sch. of Polit. and Adminstrv. Studies, Bucharest, 1994, Dimitrie Cantemir, 1999-2000; minister counsellor Romania's Mission UN, N.Y.C., 2000. Author: Media-Watchdog of Democracy, 1998, Media Contribution in the Democratic Control Over the Armed Forces in Societies in Transition, 1997, A Changing European Security, Challenges and Solutions, 1995; co-author: Psychological Warfare in Contemporary Military Confrontations, 1988, The Technical Scientific Factor and Its Impact on Strengthening the National Defence Capability, 1983, Studies of Military Strategy, 1986, The Political-Diplomatic Factor and Its Role in Strengthening the National Defence Capability, 1985, Romanian Doctrinal Ideas and Concepts. A Historical Approach, 1990. Scholarship NATO, 1996-97. Mem. Assn. of Law and Internat. Rels. (scientific sec. 1980-89), Manfred Worner Euro-Atlantic Assn., Romanian Assn. of Pub. Rels. Profls. (founding mem., exec. bd. 1996-98, Prize and Plaque 1997). Avocations: climbing, fine arts.

BOND, ALAN MAXWELL, chemist, educator; b. Cobden, Australia, Aug. 17, 1946; s. Ian Thomas and Joyce Myrtle Bond; m. Tunde-Maria Szegedy; children: Stephen, Andrew. BSc, U. Melbourne, 1966, PhD, 1971, DSc, 1977. Sr. demonstrator dept. inorganic chemistry U. Melbourne, 1970-73, rsch. fellow, 1973-78; Found. prof. chemistry, div. chem. and phys. scis. Deakin U., Geelong, Australia, 1978-90; prof. chemistry La Trobe U., Bundoora, Australia, 1990-95, Monash U., Clayton, Australia, 1995—; vis. assoc. prof. dept. chemistry Northwestern U., Evanston, Ill., 1972, vis. prof., 1976; vis. prof. inorganic chemistry lab. Oxford (Eng.) U.; Royal Soc. Chemistry lectr., Australia, 1990; mem. com. Australian Rsch. Coun., Canberra, 1993—. Author: Modern Polarographic, 1980; contbr. more than 350 articles to profl. jours.; patentee in field; mem. editorial bds. various jours. Recipient Rennie medal, 1975, David Syme prize, 1978, Stokes medal, 1992, Liversidge award, 1992, numerous others; recipient numerous grants and fellowships, including Erskine fellowship Canterbury U., 1993, Japan Soc. for the Promotion of Sci. fellowship, 1990. Fellow Australian Acad. Sci. (coun. 1993—), Royal Australian Chem. Inst., Royal Soc. Chemistry (London); mem. Am. Chem. Soc., Electrochem. Soc. Office: Monash U, Dept Chemistry, Clayton Victoria, 3168, Australia

BOND, ALMA HALBERT, psychoanalyst, author; b. Phila., Feb. 6, 1923. BA in Psychology (with honors), Temple U., 1944; MA in Psychology, NYU, 1951; PhD in Devel. Psychology, Columbia U., 1961. Diplomate Am. Bd. Psychotherapy. Pvt. practice psychoanalysis pvt. practice, N.Y.C., 1953-91; tng. analyst Inst. Psychoanalytic Tng. and Rsch., N.Y.C., 1963—. Author: Who Killed Virginia Woolf, A Psychobiography, 1989, 2000, (with Lucy Freeman) America's First Woman Warrior: The Courage of Deborah Sampson, 1992, Dream Portrait, 1992, Is There Life After Analysis?, 1993, On Becoming a Grandparent, 1994, Profiles of Key West, 1996, the Autobiography of Maria Callas, a Novel, 1998, 2000; sr. writer CAYO mag.; contbr. Key West Citizen, Solaris Hill, Tropic Keys, Time Out, Remember. Lt. USN, 1944-46. Recipient Honors in Psychology Temple U., 1944, Winner Am. Literary Press Contest, 1993, Runner up First Novel Contest, 1995, Hemingway award, Fla. State awards for fine writing. Mem. Internat. Psychoanalytic Assn. Fax: 305-292-6457. Home and Office: 606 Truman Ave # 1 Key West FL 33040-3284

BOND, ANDREW H., research chemist; b. Lake Forest, Ill., Feb. 24, 1968; s. Rowland J. and Helen E. Bond. BS in Chemistry, No. Ill. U., 1990, PhD in Chemistry, 1995. Postdoctoral rschr. dept. chemistry Fla. State U., Tallahassee, 1995-96, Eichrom Industries, Inc., Darien, Ill., 1996-97; postdoctoral rsch. scientist chemistry divsn. Argonne (Ill.) Nat. Lab., 1997—; co-organizer Symposium Proc. Indsl. and Engring. Chemistry Rsch., 1999. Co-editor: Metal Ion Separation and Preconcentration, 1999; patentee in field. Poster Award winner Materials Rsch. Soc., Boston, 1999. Mem. Am. Chem. Soc. (gen. poster session organizer indsl. and engring. chemistry divsn., program com. mem., organizer various symposia), Am. Nuclear Soc., Sigma Xi. Avocations: reading, writing, outdoorsman. Office: Argonne National Lab Chemistry Divsn Argonne IL 60439

BOND, BRIAN JAMES, military historian, educator; b. Marlow, Eng., Apr. 17, 1936; s. Edward Herbert Bond and Olive Sartin; m. Madelene Joyce Carr, Sept. 15, 1962. BA in History, Oxford U., 1959; MA in History, London U., 1962. Lectr. King's Coll., London, 1966-77, reader, 1977-86, prof., 1986—; vis. prof. U. Western Ont., Can., 1972-73; vis. fellow All Souls Coll., Oxford, 2000; military historian for books including War & Society in Europe 1870-1970, 1984, The Pursuit of Victory, 1996, others. Fellow Royal Historical Soc., British Commn. for Mil. History (pres.). Avocations: gardening, country houses. Office: King's Coll Dept War Studie, Strand, London WC2RSLS, England

BOND, FRANCES CURTIS, retired editor; b. Chgo., Feb. 9, 1909; d. Vine Harlan Sr. and Frances Lay (Watson) Curtis; m. Bradford Austin Bond, Mar. 8, 1940 (dec. Nov. 1991); 1 child, David Bradford. B Journalism, U. Mo., 1932. Editor Nutrilite News Mytinger & Casselberry, Inc., Long Beach, Calif., 1948-58; dir. pub. info. and cmty. rels. Long Beach Commn. on Econ. Opportunities, 1967-77; cmty. editor Long Beach Rev. mag., 1978-90; ret., 1990. Bd. dirs., historian Ch. Women United, Long Beach, 1996; mission coord. United Meth. Women, Long Beach, 1996; mem. adminstrv. bd. Grace United Meth. Ch., Long Beach, 1996; former bd. dirs., exec. com. Pacific Coast Press Club; former adv. coun. com. on aging United Way; former mem. Calif. Atty. Gen.'s Adv. Com. on Consumer Info. and Crime Prevention for Sr. Citizens; former bd. dirs., sec. Calif. Dirs. Aging Programs; former mem. adv. bd. Sr. Opportunities and Svcs. Elderly Nutrition Program; former mem. adv. bd. Long Beach Children's Mus.; former bd. dirs. Internat. Cmty. Coun. of Calif. State U., Long Beach, Long Beach Ballet; former bd. dirs., exec. com. South Bay Indian Svcs., NAACP, Long Beach, Pacific Coast Press Club; docent, vol. Long Beach Aquarium of the Pacific, 1998—. Recipient 4 1st Pl. and 3 2d Pl. awards Internat. Indsl. Publs. Contest, 1951, Blue Pencil award for Outstanding Govt. Publs., Fed. Editors Assn., 1974, 75, 1st and 2d Pl. award Calif. Cmty. Action Exec. Dirs. Assn., 1976, Merit award Pacific Coast Press Club, 1988, Mission Recognition award United Meth. Ch., 1990; named Safe Driver of Yr. Long Beach, Nat. Safety Coun., 1963, Vol. of Mo., Long Beach Sr. Ctr., 1991, Lay Person of Yr., Grace United Meth. Ch., 1996. Mem. DAR (life, bd. dirs. Susan B. Anthony chpt. 1989-90), NAACP (life), Fulton County Hist. Soc. (life), Ind. Hist. Soc., Soroptomist Internat. (life, Soroptomist of Long Beach Hall of Fame 1997), Soc. Mayflower Descendants. Democrat. Avocation: photography. Home: 1625 E Appleton St Apt 3C Long Beach CA 90802-4069

BOND, GEOFFREY COLIN, chemistry educator; b. Ottery, U.K., Apr. 21, 1927; s. William Henry and Kate (Digby) B.; m. Angela Mary Ingram, Aug. 29, 1953; children: Richard D., Martin D., Andrew L., Rosemary A. BSc in Chem. (hon.), Birmingham U., U.K., 1948, PhD in Chem., 1951, DSc in Chem., 1966. Chartered chemist. Rsch. fellow Princeton (N.J.) U., 1951-53, Leeds (U.K.) U., 1953-55; lectr. Hull (U.K.) U., 1955-62; head catalysis rsch. Johnson Matthey and Co., Wembley, U.K., 1962-70; prof. in Chemistry Brunel U., Uxbridge, U.K., 1970-92, emeritus prof., 1992—. Author: Catalysis by Metals, 1962; Heterogeneous Catalysis-Principles and Applications, 1987, Catalysis by Metals and Alloys, 1995. Chmn. S.W. Herts (U.K.) Liberal Assn., 1973-75. Fellow Royal Soc. Chemistry (Catalysis by Noble Metals 1979); mem. Soc. Chem. Industry. Mem. Ch. Eng. Avocations: philately, chemistry, gardening. Home: 59 Nightingale Rd, Rickmansworth, Herts WD3 2BU, United Kingdom Office: Inst for Phys & Envirn Sci, Brunel University, Uxbridge UB8 3PH, United Kingdom

BOND, GORMAN MORTON, ornithologist, researcher; b. Elkridge, Md., Apr. 6, 1921; s. Morton Bradley Bond and Mary Agnes (Soper) Olfky; m. Leona Steinberg, Apr. 9, 1957; 1 child, Alissa. BA, George Washington U., 1963. Ornithologist U.S. Fish and Wildlife Svc., Washington, 1948-55; exhibits planner, birds Smithsonian Inst., Washington, 1956-63, rsch. asst. to sec., 1964-81; ret., 1981; instr. Dist. of Columbia Literacy Program, 1977-78. Staff sgt. USAAF, 1943-45. Decorated Air medal; recipient Smithsonian documentary film award, 1963, Merit Badge counselor Boy Scouts Am., 1974-75. Mem. Am. Ornithologists Union (chmn. archives com. Washington 1969-79), Nat. Audobon Soc. (editor bird census 1953-59), Biol. Soc. Washington (corr. sec. 1950-55). Avocations: birdwatching, photography. Home: 7361 Swan Point Way Columbia MD 21045-5010

BOND, JOHN (REGINALD HARTNELL), bank company executive. Student, Tonbridge Sch., Kent, Cate Sch., Calif.; hon. degree, Am. Internat. U., London. With Hong Kong and Shanghai Banking Corp., 1961; chief exec. Wardley Group Hong Kong and Shanghai Banking Corp., various locations, 1984-98; exec. dir. Hong Kong and Shanghai Banking Corp., 1988-89; with Hong Kong and Shanghai Banking Group, 1990-91; pres., chief exec. Marine Midland Bank Inc. (now HSBC Bank USA), Buffalo, 1991-92; group chief exec. Hong Kong and Shanghai Banking Holdings Plc, 1993; with Hang Seng Bank Ltd., 1990-96, Hong Kong Bank Malaysia Bhd, 1996; group chmn. HSBC Holdings PLC, London, 1998—. Decorated knights bachelor in honor of Her Majesty the Queen's birthday, 1999. Office: HSBC Holdings, 10 Lower Thames St, EC3R 6AE London England

BOND, JULIAN, civil rights leader; b. Nashville, Jan. 14, 1940; s. Horace Mann and Julia Agnes (Washington) B.; m. Pamela S. Horowitz, Mar. 17, 1990; children by previous marriage: Phyllis Jane, Horace Mann, Michael, Jeffrey, Julia. BA, Morehouse Coll., 1971; LLD (hon.), Dalhousie U., 1969, U. Bridgeport, 1969, Wesleyan U., Conn., 1969, U. Oreg., 1969, Syracuse U., 1970, Eastern Mich. U., 1971, Tuskegee Inst., 1971, Howard U., 1971, Morgan State U., 1971, Wilberforce U., 1971, Patterson State Coll., 1972, N.H. Coll., 1973, Detroit Inst. Tech., 1973; DCL (hon.), Lincoln (Pa.) U., 1970, Bates Coll., 1998, Northeastern U., 1999, Edward Weters Coll., 1995, Gonzege Sch. Law, 1997, Calif. State U., Monterey Bay, 1998, Washington U., 2000. A founder Com. Appeal for Human Rights, 1960, exec. sec., 1961; a founder Student Nonviolent Coordinating Com., 1960, communications dir., 1961-66; reporter, feature writer Atlanta Inquirer, 1960-61, mng. editor, 1963; mem. Ga. Ho. of Reps., from Fulton County, 1965-75, Ga. State Senate, 1975-87; vis. prof. history and politics Drexel U., 1988-89; Pappas fellow U. Pa., 1989; vis. prof. Harvard U., fall 1989, 91; prof. U. Va., fall 1990, 1993—, Am. U., 1991—, Williams Coll., fall 1992. So. corr. Reporting Racial Equality Wars; narrator Parts 1 and 2, Eyes on the Prize. Bd. dirs. So. Conf. Edn. Fund, Robert F. Kennedy Meml. Fund, Crisis Mag., Coun. for Liveable World; pres. emeritus So. Poverty Law Ctr.; chmn. bd. dirs. NAACP, 1998—. Office: 5435 41st Pl NW Washington DC 20015-2911

BOND, MALCOLM JAMES, medical educator; b. Clare, Australia, Jan. 11, 1959; s. Leslie Edgar and Ruth Elaine (Maynard) B.; m. Carolyn Ann Warren, Apr. 30, 1994; children: Cameron James, Verity Elise. BA, Flinders U., Adelaide, Australia, 1981, BA with honors, 1982, PhD, 1990. Sr. tutor Flinders U., Adelaide, 1987-90, lectr., 1991-97, sr. lectr., 1998—; cons. Paradigm Cons., Adelaide, 1987-99. Contbr. numerous articles to med. and psychology jours. Mem. Australian Psychol. Soc., Australian Coll. Edn., N.Y. Acad. Scis. Avocations: gardening, music, sports. Office: Sch Medicine, Flinders U GPO Box 2100, Adelaide 5001, Australia

BOND, MYRON HUMPHREY, investment executive; b. Chickasha, Okla., Jan. 12, 1938; s. Reford and Jane Embick (Humphrey) B.; m. Janice Wootten, July 1, 1961; children: Richard Allen, Lori Elizabeth. BS in Petroleum Engring. summa cum laude, U. Okla., 1961, MS in Petroleum Engring., 1965. Registered profl. engr., Okla. Staff engr. Exxon, Houston, 1960-68; sr. v.p. Paine Webber, Inc., Dallas, 1968—; pres., chmn. Four Bees Ranch Inc., 1989—; dir. Am. Pub. Communications, Inc., 1991-92. Bd. dirs. Dallas Epilepsy Assn., 1980-82, Dallas Campfire Girls, 1980-82. Lt. (s.g.) USN, 1961-64. Mem. Nat. Assn. Securities Dealers (prin., mem. Dist. 6 com. 1994-96), Dallas C. of C., Dallas Country Club, Brook Hollow Golf Club, Phi Eta Sigma, Pi Eta Tau, Tau Beta Pi, Sigma Tau, Omicron Delta Kappa, Kappa Alpha Order. Avocations: sports, ranching. Home: 4536 Belfort Pl Dallas TX 75205-3619 Office: Paine Webber 5950 Sherry Ln Ste 600 Dallas TX 75225-6551

BOND, NIGEL WILLIAM, psychologist; b. Peterborough, Eng., Aug. 30, 1949; arrived in Australia, 1973; s. William Frederick and Norma Ellen (Dean) B.; m. Judith Myhill, Sept. 19, 1970. BSc with honors, Nottingham (U.K.) U., 1970, PhD, 1974. From sr. tutor to assoc. prof. Macquarie U., Australia, 1973-92; prof. Flinders U., Adelaide, Australia, 1992-96, U. Western Sydney, Australia, 1996—. Editor: Animal Models of Psychopathology, 1984, Psychobiology: Issues and Applications, 1989, Readings in Australian Psychology, 1991; author: (CD-ROM) A Multimedia Course in Associative Learning, 1995. Fellow Acad. Social Scis. Australia; mem. Australian Psychol. Soc., Nat. Com. for Psychology, Australian Rsch. Coun. (panel mem.). Avocations: walking, reading, music, rugby. Home: 14 Edward St, Oatley NSW 2223, Australia Office: U Western Sydney, PO Box 555, Campbelltown NSW 2560, Australia

BOND, NILES WOODBRIDGE, cultural institute executive, former foreign service officer; b. Newton, Mass., Feb. 25, 1916; s. George Wood and Clara Mehitabel (Bonney) B.; m. Julia Rice Folsom, June 25, 1940 (dec. Sept. 1986); children: Ellen Dudley, Nancy Kenneth; m. Pamela Guest Bird, Sept. 17, 1988. A.B., U. N.C., 1937; A.M., Fletcher Sch. Law and Diplomacy, Medford, Mass., 1938. U.S. fgn. service officer, 1939-68; vice consul Havana, Cuba, 1939-40, Yokohama, Japan, 1940-41; 3d sec., vice consul Madrid, Spain, 1942-45; 2d sec., 1945-46; adviser to U.S. delegation to 4th session Econ. and Social Council, 1947; 2d sec., vice consul Bern, Switzerland, 1947; 1st sec. and consul, 1947; asst. chief div. N.E. Asian affairs Dept. State, 1947-49, officer in charge Korean affairs, 1949-50; adviser to U.S. delegation to 4th session UN Gen. Assembly, 1949; 1st sec. Office of U.S. Polit. Adviser to Supreme Comdr. Allied Powers, Tokyo, Japan, 1950; acting chmn. Allied Council for Japan, 1952; counselor embassy Tokyo, 1952, Seoul, Korea, 1953-54, Rome, Italy, 1956-58; dir. Office UN Polit. and Security Affairs, Dept. State, 1954-56; counselor of embassy, vis. lectr. Bologna Center, Johns Hopkins U., 1957-58; research fellow Ctr. for Internat. Affairs, Harvard, 1958-59; minister-counselor embassy Rio de Janeiro, Brazil, 1959-63; coordinator interdeptl. seminar Dept. State, 1963; minister, consul gen. São Paulo, Brazil, 1964-68; sec. bd. trustees Corcoran Gallery Art, Washington, 1973-86; pres., bd. dirs. Brazilian-Am. Cultural Inst., 1976-86; mem. ct. sys. study com. D.C. Bar, 1979-81, exec. dir. fee arbitration bd., 1981-87; exec. dir. Project Orbis, 1972; adviser São Paulo Bienal, 1969; dir. internat. exhbns. com. Am. Fedn. Art, 1976-77. Author: poetry Arcanum, 1965, Elegos, 1967, Dreams From a Wintry Night, 1993. Decorated commendatore Al Merito della Repubblica Italiana, grand officer Order So. Cross (Brazil). Mem. Univ. Club, Army and Navy Club (Washington), Harvard Club (N.Y.C.). Interned in Japan upon outbreak of war, repatriated on S.S. Gripsholm, Aug. 1942. Home: 35 Sill Ln Old Lyme CT 06371-1132

BOND, PETER DESMOND ROLLAND, civil engineer; b. Colombo, Sri Lanka, Sept. 14, 1939; s. Cyril Wilfrid and Kathleen Lucy (Loudoun-Shand) B.; m. Hilary Mary Heseltine, Feb. 27, 1971; children: Katherine, Edward. BSc with honors, St. Andrews U., Scotland, 1963; MSc, Imperial Coll., London, 1970. Engr. Sir. M. MacDonald & Ptnrs., London, 1963-69, Ove Arup & Ptnrs., London, 1970-74; from tech. adviser to group leader European Investment Bank, Luxembourg, 1974-94, dir. projects directorate, 1994—. Fellow Royal Soc. of Arts; mem. Instn. Civil Engrs., Instn. Structural Engrs., Chartered Instn. of Water and Environtl. Mgmt. Avocations: sailing, golf, archeology, music.

BOND, WILLIAM LAURIE, insurance executive; b. Pretoria, South Africa, Apr. 18, 1941; arrived in Zimbawe, 1962; s. William Robert and Penelope Elfreda (Bright) B.; m. Jane Irene Clements, Nov. 30, 1968 (div. Mar. 1979); children: Andrew Punell, Belinda Jane; m. Maureen Yvonne Keefer, Nov. 30, 1997; children: Ashleigh Keefer, Kate Keefer, David Keefer. Chartered ins. practitioner. Clk. Price Forbes, South Africa, 1959-62; broker Alfred Blackmode & Co., Zimbabwe, 1962-65; broker Minet Ins. Brokers, Zimbabwe, 1965-76, dir., 1976-89; dir. Cen. African Ins. Brokers, Zimbabwe, 1989-92; mng. dir. Progroup Ins. Brokers, Bulawayo, Zimbabwe, 1992—, also bd. dirs.; mng. dir. Gordon & Gordon Lloyds Agts., Zimbabwe, 1996—. Chmn. Matabele Area of Automobile Assn., Zimbabwe, 1982-87. Lt. Rhodesian Army, 1963-80. Recipient Top Paper prize Brit. Ins. Brokers Assn., 1985. Fellow Chartered Ins. Inst. U.K., Ins. Inst. of South Africa; mem. Ins. Inst. Bulawayo (pres. 1988), Rotary Club of Bulawayo (past pres. 1995-96, Paul Harris fellow 1997), Bulawayo Club (chmn. 2000—). Anglican. Avocations: bagpipe playing, motor sports, art.

BONDARENKA, VLADIMIRAS, physicist; b. Vilnius, Lithuania, June 5, 1950; s. Michail and Vera (Kutchinskaja) B.; m. Nadejda Krasnikova, Sept. 13, 1969; children: Julija, Vladimiras. Tchr. physics, Vilnius State Pedag. Inst., 1972, cand. phys.-math. scis., 1980; D of phys.-math. scis., Russian Acad. Scis., 1992; D of nature scis., Lithuanian Sci. Coun., 1993, D habilitatus of nature scis., 1994. Tchr. physics Vilnius Secondary Sch., 1972-75; sr. rschr. Semiconductor Physics Inst., Vilnius, 1975—. Inventor in field; contbr. articles to profl. jours. Home: Antakalnio 83/1-10, LT-2040 Vilnius Lithuania Office: Semiconductor Physics Inst, A Gostauto 11, LT-2600 Vilnius Lithuania

BONDAREV, VICTOR N., physicist, educator; b. Fürstenwalde, Germany, May 14, 1946; s. Nikolay E. and Nadezhda F. Bondarev. Degree in phys. theory, Odessa (Ukraine) U., 1968, PhD, 1974, DSc in Phys. Math., 1993. Lectr. Odessa U., 1968-82, sci. rschr., 1971-74, head lab. Phys. Inst., 1975—; prof. physics Odessa Tech. U., 1999—. Contbr. articles to profl. jours. Mem. Russian Soc. Solid State Ionics. Office: Phys Inst Odessa U, Pasteur St 27, 65026 Odessa Ukraine

BONDAREVSKII, SVJATOSLAW IGOREVICH, physics educator; b. Rostov-on-Don, Russia, June 22, 1938; s. Igor Zakharovich and Antonina Stepanovna (Abramova) B.; m. Nina Alexandrovna Tupikina, June 14, 1969; 1 child, Olga. MS, Leningrad (USSR) State U., 1961, PhD, 1969, DSc, 1983. Engr. A.N. Krylov Rsch. Inst., Leningrad, 1962-65, rsch. asst., 1967-69, rsch. scientist, 1970-97; prof. radiochemistry State Tech. U., St. Petersburg, Russia, 1997—. Contbr. articles to sci. publs., including Radiochemistry, Physics of the Solid State. Mem. Nuc. Medicine Soc., Mendelev Chem. Soc. (bd. dirs. 1995-98). Home: Bldg 23, Prospect Stacheck Apt 2, 198095 Saint Petersburg Russia Office: State Tech U, Bld 29 Polytechnicheskaya, 194251 Saint Petersburg Russia

BOND-BROWN, BARBARA ANN, musician, educator; b. Kansas City, Mo., July 1, 1955; d. John Bartley, Jr. and Tressie Laverne (Nichols) Bond; m. Lance Elliott Brown, Mar. 11, 1979. Student, Ctrl. Mo. State U., 1973-74, 75-77, U. Mo., 1974, William Jewell Coll., 1975; studies with Karen Halverhout, Prarie Village, Kans., 1995—. Dist. accompanist Kansas City Pub. Schs., 1979-82; ind. music tchr. Independence, Mo., 1982-84; ind. music tchr., accompanist San Francisco, 1984-92; ind. music tchr. Barbara Bond-Brown Music Studio, Lee's Summit, Mo., 1992—; developer method for young music beginners; spkr. at workshops and confs.; active adjudicator for competitions and auditions. Mem. Kans. City Music Tchrs. Assn. (v.p. achievement auditions 1994—, v.p. fall festival 1994—, chmn. pre-coll. honors auditions 1995—), Mo. Music Tchrs. Assn. (chmn. honors auditions 1993—, officer 1995—), Music Tchrs. Nat. Assn., Federated Music Tchrs. Avocations: reading, writing, cooking, traveling. Home and Studio: 906 SE 5th Ter Lees Summit MO 64063-4343

BONDE, COUNT PEDER CARLSSON, investment company executive; b. Stockholm, Sept. 2, 1923; came to U.S., 1992; s. Carl Gustaf and Ebba (Wallenberg) B.; m. Ylva M. Jenssen, June 18, 1948 (div. Jan. 1956); children: Johan, Ulrika, Hans; m. J. Madeleine Rouchier, Sept. 27, 1957 (div. May 1988); m. Clarissa Leggett, July 2, 1989; children: Helena, Amelie, Sophia. Student exam, Sigtunaskolan, Sigtuna, Sweden, 1942; res. officer, Royal Horse Guard, Cavalry, Stockholm, 1946; Lic.Jur., Uppsala U., 1948. Asst. judge Dist. Ct. Askim, Göteborg, Sweden, 1948-51; banking trainee U.S., France, Germany, 1952-56; from asst. v.p. to exec. v.p. Stockholms Enskilda Bank, 1957-71; dep. chief exec. Skandinaviska Enskilda Banken, Stockholm, 1972-73, Salén Shipping Group, Stockholm, 1973-76; spl. rep. Skandinaviska Enskilda Banken, Zürich, Switzerland, 1977; pres., CEO Banque Scandinave en Suisse, Geneva, 1978-82; exec. vice-chmn. Investor AB, Providentia AB, Stockholm, 1983-91; vice-chmn. Investor AB, Stockholm, 1992-93; chmn., CEO Investor Internat. AB, Washington, 1993-98; bd. dirs., vice-chmn., chmn. Alfa-Laval AB, Stockholm, 1961-91; vice-chmn. Stora AB, Falun, Sweden, 1985-91, Skandia Ins. Group AB, Stockholm, 1985-92, Astra AB, Sodertalje, Sweden, 1987-92; chmn. Forestal Valdivia, Santiago, Chile, 1991-94; chmn. European-Am. Bus. Coun., Washington, 1994-99. Governing bd. Nat. Cathedral Sch. for Girls, Washington, 1999—; adv. bd. Korn/Ferry Internat., L.A. Capt. Cavalry, Sweden, 1952-76. Decorated Knight Royal Order of Vasa, 1972, The King's Gold Medal, 1994, grand officer Portuguese Order of Henry the Seafarer by Pres. of Portugal, 1991, grand cross Order of St. Gregorius the Great by His Holiness the Pope, 1991, grand cross Order of Leopold II by H.M. the King of the Belgians, 1994; named Lord in Waiting, Ct. of His Majesty the King of Sweden. Mem. Royal Bachelors Club (Göteborg), Royal Swedish Yacht Club, Met. Club, Nat. Press Club, Chevy Chase Club. Home: Oak View 3201 36th St NW Washington DC 20016-3143

BONDEBJERG, IB, film and media studies educator; b. Brønderslev, Jutland, Denmark, Aug. 16, 1947; s. Kaj and Kirsten Bondebjerg (Hansen) Sørensen; m. Ulla Marie Christensen, Apr. 25, 1969; children: Katja, Jon. BA, U. Copenhagen, 1969, MA, 1973, PhD, 1978. Rsch. fellow U. Copenhagen, 1974-76, asst. prof., 1976-78, assoc. prof., 1978-88, docent, 1988-96, rsch. prof., 1996-99, prof., 2000—; Fulbright lectr. UCLA, 1986; chmn. Danish Rsch. Coun. for the Humanities, 1994-96, Com. of Heads of Danish Rsch. Couns., 1995-96; Norfa prof. U. Bergen, Norway, 1997-98; chmn. bd. dirs. Danish Film Inst., 1997-00. Author: (with U. Bondebjerg) Medier og Samfund, 1990, Elektroniske Fiktioner, 1993; co-author: Dansk Litteraturhistorie, vol. 7, 1984; editor, author: (with F. Bono) Television in Scandinavia, 1996, Moving Images, Culture and the Mind, 2000; co-editor (with K.B. Jensen); co-author: Dansk Mediehistorie, vol. 3, 1997; co-editor Kultur & Klasse, 1978-82, Mediekultur, 1989-95; co-editor, author Dansk Film 1972-1997, 1997, Intertextuality and Visual Media, 1999. Mem. Media and Popular Culture Group (convenor), European Sci. Found. (mem. standing com. for the humanities 1994-96), Internat. Assn. Media Rchrs., Internat. Comm. Assn., Soc. Cinema Studies. Office: Dept Film & Media Studies, Njalsgade 80, 2300 Copenhagen S, Denmark

BONDEMARK, LARS JOHAN, dental surgeon, orthodontist, consultant; b. Kristianstad, Skåne, Sweden, June 8, 1955; s. Yngve Karl and Siv Barbro (Larsson) B.; m. Inger Ann-Margret Palm, May 28, 1982; 1 child, Johan. Gen. cert. edn. advanced level, Coll. Kristianstad, Sweden, 1974; DDS, Ctr. for Oral Health Sci., Malmö, Sweden, 1979; specialist in orthodontics, Inst. Postgrad. Dental Edn., Jönköping, Sweden, 1990; D of Odontology, U. Lund, Sweden, 1994. Head Gen. Practice Clinic, Bjärnum, Sweden, 1979-88; asst. dept. orthodontics Inst. for Postgrad. Dental Edn., Jönköping, 1988-90; sr. cons., specialist in orthodontics Orthodontic Clinic, Hässleholm, Sweden, 1991-96, head, 1997-99; assoc. prof. and tchr. dept. orthodontics Faculty of Odontology, Malmö U., Malmö, 1998—; referee, cons. Am. Jour. Orthodontics and Dentofacial Orthopedics, 1995—; assoc. cons. Dept. Oral Radiology, Kristianstad, 1988-91. Author: Orthodontic Magnets, 1994; contbr. articles to profl. jours. Sec. Dental Soc. Kristianstad County, 1991-96. Mem. European Orthodontic Soc., Swedish Assn. Orthodontists, Swedish Dental Soc. Avocations: golf, knowledge of wine, music. Home: Västerbogatan 5B, 281 47 Hässleholm Sweden Office: Malmö U Fac Orthodontics, Carl Gustavs väg 34, SE-21421 Malmö Sweden

BONDESON, JAN, physician; b. Malmoe, Sweden, Dec. 17, 1962; s. Sven and Greta (Akesson) B. MD, Lund U., 1988, PhD, 1996. Resident Malmoe U. Hosp., Sweden, 1988-90, registrar, 1990-95, sr. registrar, 1995-96; rsch. fellow Kennedy Inst. Rheumatology, London, 1996-2000; sr. lectr., cons. rheumatologist U. Wales Coll. Medicine, Cardiff, 2000—. Author: The Prolific Countess, 1996, Cabinet of Medical Curiosities, 1997, The Feejee Mermaid, 1999, The Two-Headed Boy 2000, The London Monster, 2000. Hennerlof scholarship Swedish Soc. of Medicine, 1987, Rheumatology scholarship Astra-Boots, 1993. Fellow Royal Soc. Medicine; mem. TVR Car Club UK, Morgan Sports Car Club. Avocations: sports cars, wine, book collecting. Office: Dept Rheumatology U Wales, Coll Medicine Heath Park, Cardiff CF14 4XN, United Kingdom

BONDI, SIR HERMANN, mathematician; b. Vienna, Nov. 1, 1919; s. Samuel and Helene (Hirsch) B.; m. Christine Mary Stockmann, Nov. 1, 1947; children: Alison, Jonathan, Elizabeth, David, Deborah. BA, Trinity Coll., Cambridge U., Eng., 1940, MA, 1944; DSc (hon.), U. Bath, 1974, U. Sussex, 1974, U. Surrey, 1974, U. York, 1980, Southampton U., 1981, U. Salford, 1982, U. St. Andrews, 1985, U. Vienna, 1993. Lectr. math. U. Cambridge, 1948-54; prof. applied math. King's Coll., U. London, 1954-85;

vis. prof. Cornell U., Ithaca, N.Y., 1960; dir. gen. European Space Rsch. Orgn., 1967-71; chief sci. adviser Ministry of Def., 1971-77; chief scientist Dept. of Energy, 1977-80; chmn. Offshore Energy Bd., 1977-80; chmn., chief exec. Nat. Environ Rsch. Coun., 1980-84; master Churchill Coll., Cambridge, 1983-90, fellow, 1990—; Raman prof. Indian Acad. Scis., 1996; chmn. astronomy policy and grants com. Sci. Rsch. Coun., 1965-67; chmn. Nat. Com. for Astronomy, 1964-67; pres. Internat. Com. on Gen. Relativity and Gravitation, 1965-68; chmn. adv. coun. Sci. Policy Found.; pres. Inst. Math. and Its Applications, 1974-75 (Gold medal 1988, hon. fellowship 1993); mem. Adv. Coun. Rsch., Dept. for Fuel and Power, 1977-80; chmn. Severn Barrage Com., 1978-81. Author: Cosmology, 1960, The Universe at Large, 1961, Relativity and Common Sense, 1964, Assumption and Myth in Physical Theory, 1968, Science, Churchill & Me, 1990; also numerous articles. Decorated knight (KCB), 1973; recipient Birla Humanism prize, India, 1990, Planetary award Assn. Space Explorers, 1993, President's award for Sci. and Art, Govt. of Austria, 1997. Fellow Royal Soc., Royal Astronomy Soc., Cambridge Philos. Soc., Indian Acad. Scis. (hon.); mem. British Humanist Assn. (pres. 1982-99), Internat. Fedn. Insts. of Advanced Studies (chmn. 1984-96). Primary areas of research in constitution of stars, structure and evolution of universe, general relativity, especially propagation of gravitational disturbances; known for steady state theory of expanding universe. Office: Churchill Coll, Cambridge England also: care Royal Soc, 6 Carlton House Ter, London SW1Y 5AG, England

BONDING, PER, otolaryngologist, researcher; b. Copenhagen, Oct. 5, 1938; s. Ole E. and Tove E. (Kjaer) B.; m. Inger Holm, June 14, 1961; children: Nina, Jakob, Joachim. MD, U. Copenhagen, 1964, PhD, 1981. Specialist in otorhinolaryngology, Denmark. Postdoctoral fellow surgery/medicine hosps. Copenhagen, 1964-70, postdoctoral fellow otorhinolaryngology/audiology hosps., 1970-78; cons. ear, nose and throat dept. Glostrup Hosp., Copenhagen, 1979—, chmn. ear, nose and throat dept., 1986—. Author: On Auditory Frequency Selectivity, 1981; contbr. numerous papers to med. jours. Lt. Danish Air Force, 1967-68. Mem. European Acad. Otology and Neuro-otology, Danish Soc. Otolaryngology (chmn. continued med. edn. com. 1982-87), Danish Soc. Otolaryngology, Head and Neck Surgery (pres. 1994-97), Danish Soc. Ear Surgeons (pres. 1987-94), Politzer Soc. Avocations: skiing, fishing, opera, jazz. Fax: 45 4323 3949. Home: Skovvangen 13, DK 2920 Charlottenlund Denmark Office: Glostrup Hosp, Ear Nose Throat Dept, DK 2600 Copenhagen Denmark

BONDOC, ROMMEL, lawyer; b. Pomona, Calif., June 23, 1938; s. Nicholas Rommel and Gladys Sue (Buckner) B.; m. Ariel Guiberson, Aug. 20, 1960 (div. 1963); m. Alberta Linnea Young, Dec. 13, 1967; children—Daphne, Patience, Margaret, Nicholas. A.B., Stanford U., 1959, J.D., 1963. Bar: Calif. 1964, U.S. Ct. Appeals (9th cir.) 1965, U.S. Supreme Ct. 1969. Assoc. Melvin Belli, San Francisco, 1964-66, Vincent Hallinan, San Francisco, 1966-69; sole practice, San Francisco, 1969—. Mem. San Francisco Bar Assn. (judiciary com. 1982-85), No. Calif. Criminal Trial Lawyers Assn. (bd. dirs. 1972—, pres. 1978-79), Calif. Attys. for Criminal Justice (bd. dirs. 1975-80). Democrat. Methodist. Home: 509 Canyon Rd Novato CA 94947-4330 Office: 819 Eddy St San Francisco CA 94109-7701

BONDS, BARRY LAMAR, professional baseball player; b. Riverside, Calif., July 24, 1964; s. Bobby B. Student, Ariz. State U. With Pitts. Pirates, 1985-92, San Francisco Giants, 1992—. Named MVP Baseball Writers' Assn. Am., 1990, 1992, 1993, Maj. League Player Yr. Sporting News, 1990, Nat. League Player Yr. Sporting News, 1990, 91, mem. Sporting News Coll. All-Am. team, 1985, mem. All-Star team, 1990, 1992-96; recipient Gold Glove award, 1990-94, 96, Silver Slugger award, 1990-96. Achievements include leading the Nat. League in intentional walks, 1992-94. Office: San Francisco Giants Candlestick Point 24 Willie Mays Plz San Francisco CA 94107-2199

BONDYBEY, VLADIMIR EDMUND, chemistry educator; b. Prague, Czech Republic, Jan. 4, 1940; s. Edmund T. and Marie (Kovarikova) B.; m. Dinny Burian, June 29, 1966; children: Renée Marie, Andrea Lynn, Frances Caroline. Student, Charles U., Prague, 1963-65; MSc, Charles U., 1968; BSc, U. Rostock, Germany, 1966; PhD, U. Calif., Berkeley, 1972. Asst. prof. Charles U., 1966-69; postdoctoral fellow Oreg. State U., 1972-73; mem. tech. staff AT&T Bell Labs, Murray Hill, N.J., 1973-86; prof. chemistry Ohio State U., Columbus, 1986-92, Tech. U. Munich, 1988—; chmn. Gordon Confs. on matrix isolation; prof. invité U. Paris, 1993; Miller prof. U. Calif., Berkeley, 1997-98; adj. prof. U. Calif., Irvine, 1995—. Co-editor book on molecular ions; contbr. over 300 articles to profl. jours.; mem. editl. bd. Chem. Physics Letters, Jour. Chem. Physics, Phys. Chemistry, Chem. Physics, PCCP, Low Temperature Physics and Molecular Physics; patentee in field. Fellow Am. Phys. Soc.; Mem. Am. Chem. Soc., Optical Soc. Am. (chmn. spectroscopy group), Deutsche Bunsengesellschaft für Phys. Chemie. E-mail: bondybey@uci.edu. Office: Tech U Munich Dept Phys Chem, Lichtenbergstr 4, D-85748 Garching Germany

BONE, LAWSON MITCHELL, songwriter, poet; b. Fayetteville, Tenn., Feb. 13, 1954; s. John Davis and Ester Eugene Bone. BA in Bus. Lit., Ala. A&M U., 1976. 1st asst., mgr. Big K Dept. Stores, Nashville, 1976-90; underwriter Prudential Ins. Co., Huntsville, Ala., 1990-91; songwriter Columbine Records, Hollywood, Calif., 1995—, HillTop Records, Hollywood, 1995—. Songwriter: Hey Writer—Keep It Up, Song Business, Flesh Tight, Got To Be The One; author: (screenplays) Make Bones About It, 1994, Disaster Relief, 1994; contbr. poetry to anthologies. Sponsor Children Internat. Honduras, Kansas City, Mo., 1995—, Childreach, Cali, Colombia, Warwick, R.I., 1995—. Named Famous Poet for 1996, 98, 99, 2000, Famous Poets Soc., 1996, Poet of the Yr., 1999, 2000. Home: 306 Hamilton St Fayetteville TN 37334-3316

BONEE, JOHN LEON, III, lawyer; b. Hartford, Conn., Dec. 16, 1947; s. John Leon, Jr. and M. Elaine (Sheridan) B. BA, Trinity Coll., Hartford, 1970; JD, Suffolk U., Boston, 1974; postgrad., Hague Acad. Internat. Law, The Netherlands, 1975. Bar: Conn. 1974, U.S. Dist. Ct. Conn. 1974; U.S. Ct. Appeals (2d cir.) 1975, U.S. Supreme Ct. 1979. Assoc. McCook, Kenyon and Bonee, Hartford, 1974-78; ptnr. The Bonee Law Offices, Hartford, Conn., 1979—. Contbr. articles to profl. jours. Mem. bd. edn. Town West Hartford, 1981-83, corp. counsel, 1983, mem. community planning adv. com., 1984, mem. town coun., 1985-89; bd. dirs. World Affairs Coun., Hartford, 1980-91. Mem. ABA (gen. practice and internat. law sects., mem. ho. dels. 1996—), Conn. Bar Assn. (editor-at-large jour. 1978-84, probate and family law sects., mem. ho. of dels. 1995—), Hartford County Bar Assn. (bd. dirs. 1991-97, treas. 1992-93, sec. 1993-94, pres. elect 1994-95, pres. 1995-96, past pres. 1996-97, co-chair bench/bar leadership conf. com. 1992-93). Office: 1 State St Hartford CT 06103-3100

BONER, DONALD LESLIE, information systems executive; b. Lawton, Okla., June 3, 1944; s. Jessie Edward and Violet (Cravens) B.; m. Carol Ann Stevens, Oct. 25, 1966 (div. June, 1973); children: Freda L., Zirque M.; m. Suellen Jackson, Dec. 1, 1973. Student, Area Vocat. Tech. Sch., Nashville, Tenn., 1967, Tenn. Inst. Broadcasting, Nashville, 1969; AS, Ind. Vocat. Tech. Coll., Indpls., 1983. Acting dir. Near East Side Community Orgn., Indpls., 1971-74; sgt. Marion County Sheriff's Dept., Indpls., 1975-76; acquisition mgr. Colonial Discount, Indpls., 1977-80; community organizer Christamore House, Indpls., 1978-79; pres., co-founder Smoner Investment Co., Indpls., 1979-80; sgt. Pinkerton, Inc., Indpls., 1980-82; computer programmer Group VI Marketing, Indpls., 1982-83; dir. product devel., operation mgr. Adman, F.A.S., Indpls., 1983—; freelance programmer Programmers Guild, Indpls., 1980-82. Author: 5 computer games, 1980-82. Mem. adv. com. Purdue U. Dept. of Computer Tech. Industry; dcampaign coord. Small Claims Ct. judge, Indpls., 1974; mem. Dem. precinct com., Indpls., 1974-78. Recipient Caspar award Community Svc. Coun., Indpls., 1972, first prize for winemaking, Ind. State Fair, 1975. Mem. Nat. Assn. for Computing Machinery (bd. dirs. cen. Ind. chpt. 1986-87, vice chmn. 1987-88, chmn. 1988-89), Indpls. Computer Soc., IEEE Computer Soc., Cellar Master Club (treas. Indpls. 1975-91). Avocations: wine making, video, music, theatre. Home: 516 E 15th St Indianapolis IN 46202-2634 Office: Adman F A S VNU Bus Info Sys Inc 151 N Delaware St Ste 1750 Indianapolis IN 46204-2512

BONEV, HRISTO, professional soccer coach, former player; b. Feb. 3, 1947. Player, capt. Bulgaria Nat. Team; player then coach Lokomotiv Plovdiv Football Club; coach Panathinaikos Football Club, Greece; winner League Championship double, Cup double; coach Bulgaria Nat. Team, 1996—. Named Bulgarian Footballer of Yr.; Bulgarian Record Holder for scoring 206 goals in 410 appearances for Lokomotiv Plovdiv. Office: Bulgarian Football Union, Karnigradska 19, BG-1000 Sofia Bulgaria*

BONFIELD, ARTHUR EARL, lawyer, educator; b. N.Y.C., May 12, 1936; s. Louis and Rose (Lesser) B.; m. Doris Harfenist, June 10, 1958 (dec. 1995); 1 child, Lauren; m. Eva Tsalikian, Apr. 8, 2000. BA, Bklyn. Coll., 1956; JD, Yale U., 1960, LLM, 1961, postgrad. (sr. fellow), 1961-62; DHL (hon.), Cornell Coll., 1999. Bar: Conn. 1961, Iowa 1966. Asst. prof. U. Iowa Law Sch., 1962-65, assoc. prof., 1965-66, prof., 1966-69, Law Sch. Found. prof., 1969-72, John Murray prof., 1972—, assoc. dean for research, 1985—; summer vis. prof. law U. Mich., 1970, U. Tenn., 1972, U. N.C., 1974, Hofstra U., 1977, Lewis and Clark U., 1984; gen. counsel spl. joint com. state adminstrv. procedure act Iowa Gen. Assembly, 1974-75; spl. counsel adminstrv. procedure exec. br. State of Iowa, 1975; chmn. com. constl. law Nat. Conf. Bar Examiners Multi-State Bar Exam, 1977—; reporter 1981 Model State Adminstrv. Procedure Act, Nat. Conf. Commrs. Uniform State Laws, 1979-81; cons. Ark. State Constl. Conv., 1980; chmn. Iowa Gov.'s Com. State Pub. Records Law, 1983; Iowa commr. Nat. Conf. Commrs. on Uniform State Laws, 1984-2000; chmn. Iowa Gov.'s Task Force on Uniform Adminstrv. Rules, 1985-92; chmn. Iowa Gov.'s Task Force Team on Regulatory Process, Rule Making, and Rules Rev., 1999-2000. Prin. draftsman Iowa Civil Rights Act, 1965, Iowa Fair Housing Act, 1967, Iowa Adminstrv. Procedure Act, 1974, Iowa Open Meetings Act, 1978, Iowa Civil Rights Act, 1978, Amendments to Iowa Public Records Law, 1984, Amendments to Iowa Administrative Procedure Act, 1998; author: State Administrative Rule Making, 1986, State and Federal Administrative Law, 1989; contbr. numerous articles to law jours. Recipient Outstanding Service to Civil Liberties award Iowa Civil Liberties Union, 1974, Hancher Finkbine Outstanding Faculty Mem. award U. Iowa, 1980, Faculty Excellence award Iowa Bd. Regents, 1995, Outstanding Law Sch. Tchg. award U. Iowa, 1996; Frederick Klocksiem fellow Aspen Inst. Humanistic Studies, summer 1978. Mem. ABA (chmn. divsn. state adminstrv. law 1976-80, coun. 1980-84, chmn. sect. 1987-88, sect. adminstrv. law and regulatory practice), Am. Law Inst. (life), Iowa State Bar Assn. (chmn. com. adminstrv. law 1971-85, coun. sect. adminstr. law 1990-93, 94-97, 98-99, 2000—, reporter and mem., task force on state adminstrv. law reform 1994-96, Pres. award Outstanding Svc. to Bar and Public 1996), Am. Coun. Learned Soc. (del. from Assn. Am. Law Schs. 1984-94). Home: 206 Mahaska Dr Iowa City IA 52246-1606 Office: U Iowa Sch Law Iowa City IA 52242

BONFIELD, SIR PETER LEAHY, telecommunications industry executive; b. June 3, 1944; married. Degree in engring. with honors, Loughborough U. Tech., 1966; D (hon.), U. Loughborough, U. Surrey, 1994, U. Mid Glamorgan, 1995, U. Nottingham & Trent, 1996, Brunel, 1997, Open U., 1997. With Texas Instruments, Inc., divsnl. dir., 1974-81; mem. bd. Internat. Computers Ltd., Plc, 1981-84, mng. dir., 1984-85, chmn., CEO, 1985-96; mem. bd. Std. Telephones and Cables, Plc, 1985-87, chmn., 1986-87, dep. chief exec., 1987-90; dir. Brit. Insulated Calendar Calles, Plc, 1992-96; non-exec. dir. ZENECA Group, Plc., 1995—; CEO British Telecom., Plc, London, 1996—; non-exec. dep. chmn. Internat. Computers Ltd., Plc, 1997—; participant High Level Working Group, European Commn., 1994. Past mem. Civil Svc. Coll. Adv. Bd.; liveryman Worshipful Co. Info Technologists; freeman, London. Decorated comdr. Order of the Lion of Finland; recipient Mountbatten medal Nat. Electronics Coun., 1995, Outstanding Exec. award Tex. Tech U.; named Comdr. of Order of Brit. Empire, 1989. Fellow Royal Acad. Engring., Inst. Electrical Engrs., British COmputer Soc., Chartered Inst. Mktg., Royal Society Arts; companion Inst. Mgmt.; mem. Confederation of British Industry (pres.'s com.), British Coun., Co. Info. Technologists, Tilateral Commn., European Round Table. Avocations: music, history, sailing. Office: British Telecom plc, BT 81 Newgate St, EC1A 7AJ London England

BONG, MIMI, psychologist; b. Washington, Sept. 8, 1966; d. Du-Wan and Ok-Sun (Kim) Pong; m. Jong-Bum Kim; children: Kim, Suzie. BA, Ewha Womans U., Seoul, Korea, 1989; MA, Columbia U., N.Y., 1991; PhD, U. So. Calif., 1995. Assoc. prof. U. S.C., 2000—; ad hoc reviewer Contemporary Ednl. Psychology, Ednl. Psychologist, 1999. Contbr. articles to profl. jours.; mem. editl. bd. Jour. Ednl. Psychology, 1999—. Recipient Educare Scholar award, U. So. Calif., 1994. Mem. APA, Am. Ednl. Rsch. Assn., Assn. Ednl. Comms. Tech. Roman Catholic. Office: Dept Ednl Psychology Univ SC Columbia SC 29208

BONGO, EL HADJ OMAR, president of Gabon; b. Lewai, Franceville, Gabon, Dec. 30, 1935; married; 3 children. Ed., Tech. Coll., Brazzaville. Civil servant; entered Ministry Fgn. Affairs, 1960; dir. Office of Pres. Leon M'Ba, 1962, in charge of Info., 1963-64, in charge of Nat. Def., 1964-65; minister-del. Presidency in charge Nat. Def. and Coordination, Info. and Tourism, 1965-66; v.p. in charge of coord., nat. def. planning, info. and tourism, 1966-67, v.p. of Republic of Gabon, 1967, pres. of Gabon, 1967—, min. nat. def., 1967-81, min. of info., 1967-80, min. of planning, 1967-77, prime min., 1967-75, min. of the interior, 1967-70, min. of devel., 1970-77, min. of women's affairs, 1976-77; founder, sec.-gen. Parti Democratique Gabonais, 1968. With Gabon Air Force, 1958-60. Decorated High Chancellor Ordre Nat. de l'Etoile Equatoriale, Grand Cross Ordre Nat. de Cote d'Ivoire, Ordre Nat. du Niger, high officer Ordre Nat. Centrafricain, comdr. Ordre Nat. Francais du Merite, officier du Merite Combattant, Grand Cross Nat. Order of Chad, Grand Cross Nat. Order of Cameroon, Grand Cross Nat. Order of Togo, Grand Ribbon Nat. Order Leopard (Congo). Mem. UDEAC (pres. 1981). Office: Office of the President, BP 546, Libreville Gabon*

BONHAM-CARTER, HELENA, actress; b. Eng., May 26, 1966. Ed., Westminster. TV appearances include A Pattern of Roses, Miami Vice, A Hazard of Hearts, The Vision, Arms and the Man, Beatrix Potter, Dancing Queen, Fatal Deception, A Dark Adapted Eye; films include Lady Jane, A Room with a View, Maurice, Francesco, The Mask, Getting It Right, Hamlet, Where Angels Fear to Tread, Howard's End, Mary Shelley's Frankenstein, A Little Loving, Mighty Aphrodite, Margaret's Museum, 1994, Portraits Chinois, 1995, Twelfth Night, 1995, Wings of a Dove, 1996, Revengers Comedies, 1996, Keep the Aspidistra Flying, 1997, The Theory of Flight, 1997, Fight Club, 1998, Women Talking Dirty, 1999, Novacaine, 2000, Til Human Voices Wake Us. Office: Adam Isaccs United Talent 9560 Wilshire Blvd Beverly Hills CA 90212-2427 also: Conway Van Gelder, 18-21 Jermyn St, London SW1Y 6HP, England

BONHAM-CARTER, NORMAN ALBERT, retired solicitor; b. Farnborough, Eng., May 28, 1928; s. David William Frederick and Joyce Angela (Palmer) B.-C.; m. Dorothy Lorna Harcombe, Apr. 14, 1956 (div. Mar. 1974); children: Miranda Jane, David Edgar, Henry John; m. Eirian Whittington Jenkins, Mar. 6, 1974. Grad., Charterhouse, Godalaming, Eng. Clk. Nat. Provincial Bank Mayfair, London, 1947-50; articled clk. Thorold Brodie Bonham-Carter & Mason, London, 1950-55; asst. solicitor Trower Still & Keeling, London, 1956-59; ptnr. Thorold Brodie Bonham-Carter & Mason, 1959-73; merged with Radcliffes & Co., London, 1973-90, cons., 1990-93; owner vigneron, nr. Bordeaux, France. Mem. Law Soc. (coun. 1980-89), Royal Anglo Belgian Soc. (coun. 1967-90, former chmn., v.p. 1990—), Westminster Law Soc. (hon. mem., former sec. and pres.), Solicitors Wine Soc. (pres. 1991-96), Ordre de Coteau de Champagne (officer 1980—). Avocations: wine, travel, entertaining, sports. Home: 54 Priory Rd, London W4 5JA, England also: Marianne, 47250 Cocamont France

BONHEIM, HELMUT, English literature educator; b. Free City Danzig, Jan. 6, 1930; s. Walter C. and Kate (Selbiger) B.; m. Jean Ornstein, Nov. 23, 1951; 1 child, Jill. BA, Cornell U., 1951; MA, Columbia U., 1952; PhD, U. Wash., 1959; postgrad., U. Vienna, 1956-58. Asst. prof. English, U. Calif., Santa Barbara, 1958-63; guest prof. U. Munich, West Germany, 1963-65; prof. English U. Cologne, Germany, 1965—. Author: The King Lear Perplex, 1960, Joyce's Benefictions, 1964, Two Dozen Beasts, 1965, The Narrative Modes, 1982,92, Literary Systematics, 1990; editor: The European English Messenger, 1991-94; adv. editor James Joyce Quar., 1963-98. Mem. Wolfson Coll., Cambridge. Recipient Presdl. medal for svcs. to East-West Rels., 1995. Mem. European Soc. for Study of English (pres. 1994-2000). Home: Klosterstrasse 75, 50931 Cologne Germany Office: U Cologne Dept English, Albertus Magnus Platz 1, 50923 Cologne Germany

BONHOEFFER, SEBASTIAN, physicist, researcher; b. Tübingen, Germany, Oct. 16, 1965; s. Friedrich and Dorothee (Spatz) B. Konzertdiplom, Musikakademie, Basel, Switzerland, 1988; diploma in physics, U. Vienna, Austria, 1992; D.Phil., U. Oxford, Eng., 1995. Rsch. asst. in zoology U. Oxford, 1995—. Florey Rsch. fellow Lady Margaret Hall, Oxford, 1995. Avocation: classical music.

BONILLA VARGAS, JOSÉ ALBERTO, microbiology researcher; b. San José, Costa Rica, May 10, 1955; s. Alvaro Bonilla and Mercedes Vargas; m. Lissette Hernández, Apr. 7, 1978; children: Sergio, Irene, Daniel. Lic. microbiology, U. Costa Rica, San José, 1980, MSc in Immunology, 1985; PhD in Immunology, Goethe U., Frankfurt, Fed. Republic Germany, 1990. Rsch. asst. U. Costa Rica, San José, 1976-79, instr., 1979-81, adj. prof., 1982-89, assoc. prof., 1990-96, prof., 1996—, dir. Rsch. Ctr. Cellular & Molecular Biology, 1998—. Scholar U. Costa Rica, 1974-77, 85-90, Japan Internat. Coop. Agy., Osaka, 1978-79, German Acad. Svc., Frankfurt, Fed. Republic Germany, 1985-90. Mem. Virology Assn. Social Democrat. Roman Catholic. Avocations: tennis, basketball, science fiction, music. Home: 21 Urb Vista Allegre, B Hori Zonte Escazu, San José 85-1200, Costa Rica Office: U Costa Rica, CIBCM, San Pedro 2060, Costa Rica

BÖNING, KLAUS WALTER, dentist, educator; b. Aachen, N Westfahl, Germany, June 11, 1959; s. Walter and Wilhelmine Anna (Hausmann) B.; m. Elke Elisabeth Zimmermann, Feb. 22, 1990. Lic. dentist, Free U., Berlin, 1984, MD in Dentistry, 1987; Habil., Tech. U., Dresden, Germany, 1997. Asst. tchr. Free U., Berlin, 1984-88, asst. prof., 1988-94; assoc. prof. Tech. Univ., Dresden, Germany, 1994—; vis. assoc. prof. Northwestern U., Chgo., 1989. Contbr. articles to Jour. Oral Rehab., Dental Materials, Jour. of Dentistry, Jour. of Prosthetic Dentistry. Mem. Assn. for Rebuilding Dresden Ch. of Our Lady, 1991—. Roman Catholic. Mem. European Prosthodontic Assn., Internat. Assn. Dental Rsch. Avocations: piano, music of the baroque, electronics. Home: Löscherstr 1a, D-01309 Dresden Saxony, Germany Office: U Dresden Dpt Prosthodontic, Fetscherstr 74, D-01307 Dresden Saxony, Germany

BONINO, EMMA, foreign diplomat; b. Bra, Switzerland, Mar. 9, 1948. Mem. European Parliament, com. fgn. affairs/human rights/common security/def. policy; mem. Tech. Group of Ind. Mems.; mem. Joint Asembly of Agreement between African, Caribbean and Pacific States and the European Union. Office: Partito Radicale, Via di Torre Argentina 76, I-00186 Rome Italy*

BONINO, SERGE THOMAS, priest; b. Marseille, France, Mar. 11, 1961; s. Jacques and Jacqueline (Gouaty) B. D in Theology, U. Fribourg, 1992; PhD, U. Poitiers, 1993. Prof. philosophy U. Toulouse, France, 1990—; dir. Dominican House of Studies, Toulouse, 1993—, Inst. St. Thomas Aquinas, Toulouse, 1995. Mem. Pontifical Acad. St. Thomas Aquinas. Roman Catholic. Home: 1 impasse Lacordaire, 31400 Toulouse France

BONITZ, MICHAEL MANFRED, physicist; b. Leningrad, Russia, July 9, 1960; s. Manfred and Natalya Moiseevna (Aptekar) B.; m. Christine Jäkel, Aug. 1, 1981; children: Sebastian, Martin. Degree in physics, Moscow State U., 1987; PhD in Physics, Rostock (Germany) U., 1991, Habil in Physics, 1998. Rsch. asst. U. Rostock, 1987-2000, sr. rschr., privatdozent, 2000—; postdoctoral rschr. Optical Scis. Ctr. U. Ariz., Tucson, 1992-93, 95-96. Author monographs; contbr. articles to profl. jours. Mem. Am. Phys. Soc., German Phys. Soc., Orgn. Internat. Confs. Avocations: music, writing, alpinism. Office: Univ Rostock FB Physik, Universitätsplatz 3, 18051 Rostock Germany

BONMATÍ-PONT, MANUEL, chemistry educator; b. Figueres, Spain, Apr. 18. 1946; s. Miquel Bonmatí-Romaguera and Neus Pont-Lorenzo; m. Dolors Noguer-Costal, Aug. 3, 1996. PhD, U. Barcelona, Spain, 1988. Lic. pharmacist. Rschr. Inst. Biologia Fonamental, Barcelona, 1969-71; mem. rsch. dept. Laboratorios Grifols, S.A., Barcelona, 1973-75; rschr. Autonomous U. Barcelona, 1975-77; prof. chemistry and biochemistry H.S. Agr./Poly. U. Barcelona, 1979—; sr. fellow Istituto per la Chimica del Terreno, Pisa, Italy, 1984-86; invited prof. U. Burgos, Spain, 1999. Contbr. articles to profl. publs. Avocation: theater. Home: Sant Eudald 10, 08023 Barcelona Spain Office: Ceib-Escola D'Agricultura, Urgell 187, 08036 Barcelona Spain

BONNAUD, OLIVIER ANDRE, education educator; b. Marseille, France, May 4, 1950; s. Roger Adolphe and Danielle Marie (Lamotte d' Incamps) B.; m. Maryvonne Denise Lesne Bonnaud, July 26, 1995; children: Delphine, Alexandrina. MS, U. Orsay, Paris, 1973; degree, Ecole Normale Superieure, Cachan, France, 1971-75; PhD, U. Lyon, Ecole Centrale, France, 1978, U. Lyon, Ecole Centrale, France, 1984. Prof. Ecole Normale Superieure, Paris, 1971-75; asst. Ecole Centrale de Lyon, Lyon, France, 1976-83, asst. prof., 1983-89; prof. U. Rennes (France) 1 Supelec, 1984—. Author: Solid State Electronics, 1981, 92, 95, 96; co-editor: Polycrystalline Semiconductor III, 1994; inventor: 1999. V.p. Rennes (France) U. Air Club, 1992-97. Mem. Club EEA (pres. 1999—), EAEEIE Assn., IEEE. Avocations: pilot, sailing, skiing, diving. Home phone: 33 (0) 299831295. Office phone: 33 (0) 299286071. Home: 15 rue de la Tremblaie, 35510 Cesson-Sevigne France Office: Groupe de Micro & Visual, Upresa 6076 U Rennes 1, 35042 Rennes France

BONNECHERE, FRANCOIS JOSEPH, civil engineer, educator; b. Ombret, Liege, Belgium, Mar. 8, 1937; s. Albert-Jean and Jeanne (Dukers) B.; m. Luigina-Maria Santin, Apr. 21, 1969; children: Francoise and Olivier. Degree in civil engring., U. Liege, 1960; MS, U. Minn., 1967; D in Applied Scis., U. Liege, 1971. Teaching assoc. U. Minn., Mpls., 1965-67; asst. U. Liege, 1960-68, chief asst., 1968-74, asst. prof., 1974-80, prof., 1980-97; dir. Lab Géomécanique, U. Liege; prof. polytechnical faculty U. Mons, 1993-97. Alderman City of Amay, Belgium. Mem. Royal Commn. for Monuments, Sites. Home: Bas-Thiers 14, B-4540 Ombret-Amay Belgium Office: City Hall, 74 Chaussee Freddy Terwagne, B-4540 Amay Belgium

BONNELLY, CLAUDE, library director; b. Quebec, Can., Feb. 4, 1946; s. Emmanuel and Gabrielle (Lepine) B.; m. Lise Lebeuf, Dec. 29, 1969; children: Mathieu, Simon. PhB, U Laval, Quebec, 1966, Lic. Philosophy, 1968; MLS, U. Montreal, Que., Can., 1973. Ref. libr. Libr. U. Laval, Sainte-Foy, Que., 1968-75, head ref. dept., 1975-78, assoc. libr., 1978-88, dir., 1988—; dir. Abcdef Internat., Paris, 1997—, Can. Inst. Hist. Microprodns., Ottawa. Contbr. articles to profl. jours. Mem. Assn. Rsch. Librs., Can. Assn. Rsch. Librs. (dir. 1990-91), Assn. Pour L'Advancement des Scis. et des Techniquer de la Documentation, Corp. des Bibliothecaires Profls. du Que., Can. Libr. Soc., Internet Soc. Home: 929 Brown, Quebec, PQ Canada G1S 2Z6 Office: U Laval Libr, Pavillon Bonenfant, Sainte Foy, PQ Canada G1K 7P4

BONNER, CHARLES WILLIAM, III, community services executive, newspaper writer; b. N.Y.C., Feb. 24, 1928; s. Charles William and Priscilla (Kerley) B.; m. Margaret Lawrence, Aug. 21, 1954 (div. 1957); 1 child, Keith Lawrence; m. Theresa Frances Cipriani, July 25, 1959 (div. May 1970); children: Caroline Cipriani, Charles IV, Ian F. van der Laan; m. Jane Baldwin Gillespie, June 6, 1970 (div. 1974). Student, Columbia U., 1952-54. Fin. news staff N.Y. World-Telegram, 1952-55; public relations dir. N.Y. Multiple Sclerosis Soc., 1955-56; sect. dir. Greater N.Y. Fund, 1956-57; v.p. public relations Campbell, Inc., N.Y.C., 1957-71; v.p. public relations, dir. spl. projects Broadcasting div. Campbell, Inc., 1971; exec. v.p. Popular Publs., Inc., 1972-73; pres. Communications Control Corp., N.Y.C., 1973-75; free-lance writer, artist, 1975-77; exec. dir. Voluntary Action Center, 1978-80, Neighbor-to-Neighbor, 1980-89. Bd. dirs. Assn. Help Retarded Children, N.Y.C.; chmn. N.Y. exec. com. Hands Across the Sea. Served with U.S. Army, 1948-52, Far East Command. Recipient Vol. of Yr. award United Way, 1982, 85, 87, Vol. of Yr. award Meridian House Found., 1982, 85, 86. Mem. Public Relations Soc. Am., Nat. Soc. Fund Raising Dirs., Environ. Writers Assn., Greenwich Power Squadron, Fairfield County Public Relations Assn., St. Nicholas Soc., Conn. Press Club. Episcopalian. Home: PO Box 3054 New York NY 10163-3054

BONNER, GERALD, theologian, educator; b. London, June 18, 1926; s. Frederick John and Constance Emily (Hatch) B.; m. Priscilla Jane Hodgson; children: Jeremy, Damaris Rosamund Margaret. BA, U. Oxford, Eng., 1952, MA, 1956. Asst. keeper of manuscripts Brit. Mus., London, 1953-64; lectr. in theology U. Durham, Eng., 1964-69, reader in ch. history, 1969-90; Disting. Prof. of early Christian studies The Cath. U. of Am., Washington, 1991-94; vis. prof. Autustinian studies Villanova (Pa.) U., 1999. Author: (books) The Warfare of Christ, 1962, St. Augustine of Hippo: Life and Controversies, 1963, God's Decree and Man's Destiny, 1987, Church and Faith in the Patristic Tradition, 1996; editor: (book) Famulus Christi: Essays in Commemoration of the Thirteenth Centenary of the Venerable Bede, 1976; co-editor: St. Cuthbert: His Cult and His Community to A.D. 1200, 1989; contbr. articles to profl. jours. Lt. The King's Dragoon Guards, Brit. Army, 1944-48. Recipient The Johannes Quasten medal for Excellence and Leadership in Theology, Sch. of Religious Studies, The Cath. U. of Am., 1994. Fellow Soc. of Antiquaries of London; mem. Eccles. History Soc. Anglican. Avocations: reading, archaeology, wine, military history. Home: 7 Victoria Terr, DH1 4RW Durham England

BONNER, JACK WILBUR, III, psychiatrist, educator, administrator; b. Corpus Christi, Tex., July 30, 1940; s. Jack Wilbur and Irldene (Turner) B.; m. Myra Lynn Taylor; children: Jack Wilbur, IV, Katherine Lynn, Shelley Bliss. AA, Del Mar Coll., Corpus Christi, 1960; BA with honors, U. Tex., Austin, 1961; MD, S.W. Med. Sch., U. Tex., Dallas, 1965. Diplomate Am. Bd. Psychiatry and Neurology. Intern U. Ark. Med. Center, 1965-66; resident Duke U. Med. Center, 1966-69; assoc. in psychiatry Highland Hosp. divsn. Duke U. Med. Center, Asheville, N.C., 1971, asst. prof. psychiatry, 1972-80, dir. outpatient services, 1972-75, med. dir., 1975-81; chmn. bd. dirs., CEO, med. dir. Highland Hosp., Asheville, N.C., 1981-92; med. dir. The Oaks Psychiat. Health Sys., Austin, Tex., 1992-93, exec. med. dir., 1993-94; med. dir. Behavioral Health Svcs. Greenville (S.C.) Hosp. Sys., 1994—, adminstr. Behavioral Health Svcs., 1996—, acad. chair, 1999—; asst. clin. prof. Duke U. Med. Ctr., Durham, N.C., 1982-87, asst. cons. prof. psychiatry, 1987—; clin. assoc. prof. U. N.C. Sch. Medicine, Chapel Hill, 1986-92, Quillen-Dishner Coll. Medicine, Johnson City, Tenn., 1989-92, U. Tex. Health Sci. Ctr., San Antonio, 1993-94, U. S.C. Sch. Medicine, Columbia, 1995—. Author: (with others) The Psychology of Discipline, 1983, Unmasking the Psychopath: Antisocial Personality and Related Syndromes, 1986; contbr. articles to profl. jours. Chmn. bd. dirs. The Highland Found., 1980-93; bd. dirs. Western N.C. Med. Peer Rev. Found., 1975-78; trustee La Amistad Found., Maitland, Fla., 1985-95, N.C. Symphony, 1987-92. Fellow Am. Psychiat. Assn. (trustee 1999—), So. Psychiat. Assn. (v.p. 1984-85, chmn. bd. regents 1988-89, pres.-elect 1991-92, pres. 1992-93), Am. Coll. Psychiatrists (treas. 1992-95, 2d v.p. 1999-2000, 1st v.p. 2000—, E.B. Bowis award 2000); mem. AMA, Nat. Assn. Psychiat. Health Sys. (trustee 1989-94, 1st v.p. 1990-91, pres.-elect 1991-92, pres. 1991-93), Am. Group Psychotherapy Assn., Nat. Acads. Practice, Buncombe County (N.C.) Med. Soc. (pres.-elect 1982, pres. 1983), N.C. Psychiat. Assn. (pres.-elect 1981-82, pres. 1982-83), Nat. Anorexic Aid Soc. (nat. anorexia adv. coun. 1979-86), So. Med. Assn. (sec. sect. on neurology, neurosurgery and psychiatry 1977-80, chmn.-elect 1980-81, chmn. 1981-82), Ctrl. Neuropsychiat. Hosp. Assn. (councillor 1981-85, pres.-elect 1982-83, pres. 1983-84), Group Advancement Psychiatry (treas. 1991-99, pres.-elect 1999—), U. Tex. Southwestern Med. Sch. Alumni Assn. (bd. dirs. 1988-95, pres. 1989-91), Benjamin Rush Soc., Phi Theta Kappa. Home: Four Brookside Way Greenville SC 29605-1212 Office: Greenville Hosp Sys Behavioral Health Svcs 701 Grove Rd Greenville SC 29605-5601

BONNET, ALEXIS FRANTZ, mathematician, research administrator; b. Marseille, France, July 2, 1966; came to Eng., 1996; s. André and Jocelyne (Calliat) B.; m. Sandrine Baslé, 1987; children: Amélie, Pauline, Julien. Engr., Ecole Poly., France, 1988, Corps. Nat. des Mines, France, 1990; PhD in Math., U. Paris VI, 1992; accreditation to supervise rsch., U. Paris VI, Paris, 1994. Engr., rschr. Corps. Nat. des Mines CERMICS and Ecole Normale Supérieure, Paris, 1991-94; prof. math. U. Cergy-Pontoise, 1994-96; exec. dir., head of arbitrage rsch. Goldman Sachs Internat., London, 1996—; sci. advisor CISI, France, 1994; vis. scholar Courant Inst. Math. Scis., N.Y.C., 1989-90. Contbr. articles to profl. jours. Recipient 2d prize Internat. Math. Olympiads, 1983, 84, Rivot prize Acad. Sci., 1988, Laplace medal Acad. Sci., 1988, Louis Armand prize Acad. Sci., 1994, Henri Poincaré prize, 1988, Jeune Chercheur prize DRET, 1993, European Math. Soc. prize, 1996. Avocations: plane and helicopter pilot, skiing, waterskiing, tennis. Office: Goldman Sachs, 133 Fleet St, London EC4A 2BB, England

BONNETERRE, JACQUES M., health facility administrator, oncologist; b. Aubenton, Aisne, France, July 21, 1950; s. Maurice and Simonne (Claude) B.; m. Marie Edith A. Couteaux, Sept. 30, 1995; children: Vincent, Loic, Capucine. MD, Lille (France) U., 1976, PhD, 1986; M in Med. Mgmt., Ecole Superieure Commerce, Paris, 1992. Diplomate French Bd. Oncology. Resident U. Hosp., Lille, 1973-78; cons. med. oncology Ctr. Oscar Lambret, Lille, 1978-84, head med. dept., 1985—; prof. med. oncology Lille U., 1993; expert French Drug Agy., 1990—, European Drug Agy., 1995—, Nat. Fedn. Cancer Ctrs., Inserm, others; dir. Ctr. Oscar Lambret, Lille, 1996—. Author: Human Plasmocytoma, 1981, Professional Cancer, 1982. Mem. French Cancer Soc. (pres. 1998-99), Am. Soc. Clin. Oncology, Am. Assn. Cancer Rsch., European Soc. Med. Oncology, European Assn. Cancer Rsch. Office: Ctr Oscar Lambret, 3 rue Frederic Combemale, F-59020 Lille France

BONNETT, RAYMOND, organic chemist; b. London, July 13, 1931; s. Harry and Maud (Rolph) B.; m. Shirley Rowe, Aug. 25, 1956; children: Helen, Paul, Alastair. BSc, Imperial Coll., London, 1954; PhD, Cambridge (Eng.) U., 1957; DSc, London U., 1972. Rsch. fellow Harvard U., Cambridge, Mass., 1958-59; asst. prof. U. B.C., Vancouver, Can., 1959-61; lectr. Queen Mary Coll., London, 1961-66, reader, 1966-74, prof., 1974-76, 1976—; cons. Scotia Pharms. Ltd., U.K., 1988—. Inventor porphyrin photosensitiers. With RAF, 1949-51. Fellow Royal Soc. of Chemistry. Home: 19 Station Rd epping, Essex CM16 4HG, England Office: Queen Mary & Westfield Coll, Queen Mary & Westfield Coll, Mile End Rd, London E1 4NS, England

BONNEY, BRIAN HENRY, biology and mathematics educator; b. Great Yarmouth, Norfolk, Eng., Sept. 20, 1944; s. James Henry and Kate Elizabeth (Collins) B.; m. Helen Louise Cooke, Aug. 6, 1993; m. Lesley Roma Murrell, Dec. 14, 1968 (div. Jan. 1992); children: Catherine Sarah, David James Leslie. BSc in Zoology with honors, King's Coll., U. London, 1965; BA in Math. with honors, The Open U., Eng., 1978; MSc in Math., Brunel U., Uxbridge, Eng., 1986. Asst. lectr. in scis. and gen. studies West Suffolk Coll. Further Edn., Bury St. Edmunds, Eng., 1966-68; lectr. sci. and math. Sutton Coldfield Coll. Further Edn., Birmingham, Eng., 1971-75; lectr. in sci. Redhill (Eng.) Tech. Coll., 1976-83; sr. lectr. Cambridge (Eng.) Coll. Further Edn., 1983-84, head dept. engring. and sci., 1984-94; adminstr. City and Guilds of London Inst., 1995—; dir. tng. for Europe R&D projects Cambridgeshire County Coun., 1989-91; nat. mgr. Pickup Europe project South Bank U., London, 1991-93; mem. adv. group U.K. Ctr. for European Edn., London, 1991-95. Author: Cell Biology, 1982; author rsch. projects. Recipient Maj. award Gt. Yarmouth County Borough Coun., 1962-65, 65-66, Profl. Devel. grantee Surrey County Coun., 1979-81. Anglican. Avocations: mountaineering, photography, guitar and banjo playing, radio-controlled model flying, reading. Home: 3 Clover Ct, Linton Cambridgeshire CB1 6YW, England Office: City and Guilds, 1 Giltspur St, London EC1A 9DD, England

BONNEY, HAL JAMES, JR., federal judge; b. Norfolk, Va., Aug. 27, 1929; s. Hal J. and Mary (Shackelford) B.; m. Marie McBee, July 4, 1963 (div. 1979); children: David James, John Wesley. BA, U. Richmond, 1951, MA, 1953; JD, Coll. William and Mary, 1969. Bar: Va. 1969. Instr. Norfolk public schs., 1951-61; supt. Douglas MacArthur Acad., 1961-67; practiced law, 1969-71; law clk. U.S. Dist. Ct., 1969; prof. U. Va., 1964-71, Coll. William and Mary, 1969-71; U.S. bankruptcy judge Norfolk, 1971-95; ret., 1995; adj. prof. law Regent U. Sch. Law, 1987—; prodr. Hal Booney Presents. Tchr. Wesleymen Bible class Sta. WTAR-AM, 1962-98, tchr. emeritus, 1998; tchr. Good News TV Network, 1989—; treas. Wesleymen Found., Inc., Billy Graham Crusades, 1974-76; pres. adv. coun. CBN U., 1986-95; vice-chmn. Va. Meth. Bd. Edn., Inc., 1991-99; bd. visitors Duke Div. Sch., 1991—; bd. dirs. Norfolk Union Mission, 1994—; mng. dir. The Tidewater Winds; mem. City of Norfolk Task Force on Pub. Housing, 1995-96; advisor Film Sch., Regent U., 1996-2000, assoc. prodr. 2000—; mem. rules com. Va. United Meth. conf., 1996—; bd. ordained ministry United Meth. Ch., Va. Recipient S.A.R. Good Citizenship medal, Woodmen of the World History medal, U. Richmond Gold medal, George Washington honor medal Freedoms Found., Alli award Cultural Alliance Greater Hampton Rds., 1998; Judge Hal Bonney Day named in honor by City of Norfolk, Jan. 27, 1998. Mem. Nat. Conf. Bankruptcy Judges (pres. 1983, chmn. editl. bd. The Am. Bankruptcy Law Jour.), Va. State Bar, Norfolk and Portsmouth Bar Assn., Nat. Film Soc., Am. Film Inst., Brit. Film Inst., Am. Cinematheque (mem. moving picture ball benefit com.), James Kent Inn of Ct. (pres. 1994-96, hon. mem.), Phi Alpha Theta, Pi Sigma Alpha, Phi Alpha Delta, Mason, Shriners, Elks. Methodist. Home: 1357 Windsor Point Rd Norfolk VA 23509-1311 Office: The Wesleymen 408 Boush St Norfolk VA 23510-1215

BONNICI, ALBERT VICTOR, orthopedic surgeon; b. Malta, Jan. 18, 1956; arrived in Eng., 1977; s. Francis and Melita (Farrugia) B.; m. Jill Northgraves, Sept. 7, 1988; children: Andrew, Daniel, Rachel. Diploma, Sheffield (Eng.) U., 1979, Edinburgh (Scotland) U., 1985. Sr. registrar in orthopedic surgery Eng., 1991-94; clin. fellow in upper limb surgery Toronto, Can., 1993; cons. orthopedic surgeon Dist. Gen. Hosp., Eastbourne, Eng., 1995—. Contbr. articles to profl. jours. Fellow Royal Coll. Surgeons, British Orthopedic Assn. Home: Mylor Cottage Upper Dicker, East Sussex BN27 3QJ, England Office: Dist Gen Hosp, King's Dr Eastbourne, East Sussex BN21 2UD, England

BONNIEL, CHARLES ERIC, accountant, educator; b. Marseille, France, July 15, 1957; s. Yves and Claude Jeanne (Bellescize) B.; m. Marie-Aude Duparc, June 7, 1995. Grad., Paris U., 1980. Asst. sec. Parliament, Paris, 1982-85; info. ctr. asst. Le Figaro, Paris, 1985-90; head of projects Epargne de France, Paris, 1990-93; jr. prof. Arts & Metiers, Paris, 1994—; cons. Régnauld Communication, Paris, 1989—. Translator: Le Figaro, 1985—, Dielavoye Lioudi, 1984. With French Air Force, 1980-81. Home and Office: 25 Rue Saint-Didier, 75115 Paris France

BONNIERE, CHRISTOPHE JULIEN JEAN ANTOINE, artist; b. Ottawa, Ont., Can., Dec. 11, 1956; s. Rene and Claude (Caubet) B. Student, U. Toronto. Exhibited in permanent collections Bibliothèque Nat. de France. Curator See Gallery, Toronto; prodr. more than 50 photographic exhbns. Avocations: wilderness adventurer, social anthropologist, travel, philosophy. Office: 441 Bathurst St, Toronto, ON Canada M5T 2S9

BONOMETTI, ROBERT JOHN, technology management and strategy executive; b. N.Y.C., Sept. 29, 1953; s. Joseph Patrick and Fortunata Mary (Barba) B.; m. Virginia Anne Scyphers, Oct. 26, 1997; stepchildren: Jessica, Michael. BS summa cum laude, U.S. Mil. Acad., 1975; MS in Physics, MIT, 1981, PhD in Physics, 1985; MBA, L.I. U., 1987. Registered profl. engr., Va. Assoc. prof. physics U.S. Mil. Acad., West Point, N.Y., 1985-88; program mgr. Def. Advanced Rsch. Projects Agy., Arlington, Va., 1988-93; sr. policy analyst White House Sci. and Tech. Office, Washington, 1993-95; exec. dir. technology strategy Bell Atlantic Corp., Arlington, 1995-98; pres. MGB Enterprises, LLC, Winchester, Va., 1998—; prof. info. sys. and computer tech. Shenandoah U., Byrd Sch. Bus., 1999—; mem. industry adv. bd. Ctr. for Satellite and Hybrid Comm. Networks, U. Md., 1994—; chmn. rev. com. commercialization of space NASA, Washington, 1996; exec. dir. info. and comm. R&D com. Nat. Sci. and Tech. Coun., Washington, 1993-95; adj. prof. various univs., 1981—; chmn. Tek-Xam content exec com. VFIC, 2000—. Contbr. articles to profl. jours. Active various animal rights and environ. orgns. Lt. col. U.S. Army, 1975-95. Recipient Laurel award Aviation Week and Space Tech., 1990; Sci. and Tech. fellow Dept. Commerce, 1993-94; Hertz Found. fellow, 1981-85. Mem. IEEE (sr.), AIAA (sr.), Am. Phys. Soc., Am. Astron. Soc. Avocations: music, weightlifting, tennis, running. Home and Office: Majestik Global Bus Enterprises LLC 260 Golds Hill Rd Winchester VA 22603-3129

BONOMI, FERNE GATER, public relations executive; b. Council Bluffs, Iowa, July 27, 1923; d. Roy Winfield and Leona Hazel (Bays) Gater; m. Robert Foch Bonomi, Sept. 3, 1949 (div. 1974); children: Robert Duff, David Scott; m. Wayne P. Davis, Apr. 20, 1991. BA magna cum laude, U. Iowa, 1948. Editor Silver City (Iowa) Times, 1940-41; reporter, photographer, Sunday editor Cedar Rapids (Iowa) Gazette, 1943-47; dir. pub. info. Iowa Devel. Commission, Des Moines, 1950-51; pub. info. officer Gov. William S. Beardsley, Des Moines, 1951-53; v.p. Bonomi Assocs. Inc., Des Moines, 1954-72; adminstr. Mid-Iowa Drug Abuse Council, Des Moines, 1972-74; cons. Plain Talk Pub. Co., Des Moines, 1974-75; communications dir. Iowa Assn. Sch. Bds., Des Moines, 1975-86; owner, operator Bonomi & Co., Des Moines, 1986—; chmn. pubs. evaluation Am. C. of C. Execs., Washington, 1977-81; workshop presenter various nat. and state confs., 1976—. Author: Show Me A Man, 1969, National Curriculum for Accreditation, 1998; editor Iowa Sch. Bd. Dialogue, 1975-86; assoc. editor Leader's Mag., 1964-72. Chmn. comms. Des Moines Area Religious Coun., 1980-82; mem. Gov.'s Com. on Employment Handicapped, 1968-74; mem. adv. bd. Luth. Social Svcs. Ames Area, 1999—. Named Iowa Sch. Communicator of Yr., Iowa Sch. Pub. Rels. Assn., 1997. Fellow Pub. Rels. Soc. Am. (developer mentoring program 1994—, chmn. 1995, pres. Iowa chpt. 1980-82, chmn. accreditation 1982—, writer nat. curriculum for accreditation 1998, Outstanding Contbr. award 1983, commendation for meaningful rsch. Bronze Anvil competition 1997); mem. Nat. Sch. Pub. Rels. Assn. (cert., gold medallion award 1987), Phi Beta Kappa, Alpha Delta Pi (nat. editor 1959-62, Outstanding Alumna award 1977). Mem. United Ch. Christ. Avocations: canoeing, horseback riding, church choir, dancing, theater. E-mail: ferne@bonomi.com. Office: Bonomi & Co 1003 Kennedy St Ames IA 50010-4247

BONORA, ENZO, medical educator, researcher, consultant; b. Mantua, Lombardy, Italy, Mar. 18, 1953; s. Gianfranco and Elisabetta (Iannoni) B.; m. Cristina Pancera, June 11, 1981; children: Giovanni, Benedetta, Federica, Alessandra. MD, U. Pavia, Italy, 1979; PhD, U. Florence, Italy, 1987. Cert. bd. internal medicine, bd. metabolic diseases, bd. endocrinology. Postdoctoral fellow U. Parma, Italy, 1979-83; rsch. fellow U. Verona, Italy, 1983-86; asst. prof. U. Verona, 1986-92, assoc. prof., 1992—; vis. asst. prof. U. Tex., San Antonio, 1989-90; cons. Hosp. of Verona, 1983-89, sr. cons., 1989—. Recipient Sci. Achievement award Italian Diabetes Soc., 1992. Mem. European Assn. for Study of Diabetes, European Assn. for Study of Obesity, Am. Diabetes Assn. (Michaela Modan Meml. award 1997). Home: Galleria E Ferri 6, 46100 Mantova Italy Office: Endocrinologia e Malattie del Metabolismo, Ospedale Maggiore, 37126 Verona Italy

BONOTTO, DANIEL MARCOS, geochemistry educator; b. Dois Córregos, Brasil, Apr. 12, 1957; s. Odair and Apparecida (Mazziero) B.; m. Dalva Maria Bianchini, Sept. 3, 1983; children: André, Adriano, Sandra. BSc, UNESP, Rio Claro, Brasil, 1978; MS, U. São Paulo, Brasil, 1982, PhD, 1986; postdoctoral, Bath (U.K.) U., 1987. Cert. physicist. Educator, rschr. UNESP, Rio Claro, Brasil, 1980—; cons. nuclear geophysics UNESP, Rio Claro, 1986—, hydrochemistry, 1986—; head of lab. UNESP, Rio Claro, 1991-97; adviser in Isotope hydrology Internat. Atomic Energy Agy., Vienna, Austria, 1996-98; vis. fellow U. Bath, Eng., 1987. Contbr. articles to profl. jours. and chpt. to book Trends in Hydrology, 1994. Grantee CNPq, Brasilia, Brasil, 1995, FAPESP, São Paulo, 1997, IAEA, Vienna, Austria, 1997. Mem. Brazilian Geophys. Soc., Brazilian Geochem. Soc., Brazilian Geol. Soc. Home: Rua 15 No 421, 13501320 Rio Claro Brazil Office: UNESP, Av 24-A No 1515, 13506900 Rio Claro Brazil

BONOVSKA-MATEEVA, KRASSIMIRA VASSILEVA, agriculturist; b. Vidin, Bulgaria, Apr. 14, 1950; d. Vassil Lozanov and Galutka Natcova (Antova) B.; m. Velko Nikolov Ninov, Nov. 12, 1968 (div. 1980); children: Nikola, Irina; m. Plamen Danailov Mateev, June 18, 1980. MS, Tech. U. Sofia, 1974, Minsk U., 1977. Scientist Ministry of Labor, Sofia, Bulgaria, 1974-82; engr. Enterprise for Svc. and Maintenance of Computer Equipment, Sofia, 1982-83; dept. head Nat. Coord. Ctr., Sofia, 1985-87, Technoinvest, Sofia, 1987-95, MAFI, Sofia, 1997; sr. expert info. and pub. rels. dept. Fgn. Investment Agy., Sofia, 1997-98; dir. info. tech. and svcs. Ministry of Edn. and Sci., Sofia, 1998—; cons. PHARE-EU Project, Sofia, 1997—, UNDP Office, Sofia, 1992-93; tech. advisor UNDP Project, Sofia, 1994-95, 1984-88. Author: DOS Use Debugging Facilities, 1986, DIGSP System Manual, 1987, DIGSP User Guide, 1988, EXACT Essential, 1992. Mem. DECUS, STU, Eurographics, WG for Inf. Technologies to Coun. Ministries. Avocation: swimming. Home: 7 D-r Stoimen Grigorov str, 1113 Sofia Capital, Bulgaria Office: Min Edn & Sci Rep Bulgaria, Knjas Dondukov Str, 1000 Sofia Bulgaria

BONSALL, JOHN LYTTON, medical officer; b. Halifax, Yorkshire, Eng., Sept. 30, 1950; s. George Lytton and Phyllis Marion (Hoyle) B.; m. Arline Mary Towns, Sept. 23, 1973; children: Benedict Noel Lytton, Tristan Louis Jean-Yves. MB, BS, London U., 1975. Divsn. med. officer Turner & Newall PLC, Manchester, Eng., 1977-80, Schering Ltd., Cambridge, Eng., 1980-86; mgr. safety, health and environ. ICI Agrochems., Haslemere, Eng., 1986-91; chief med. officer IBM (U.K.) Ltd., Portsmouth, 1991-95; occupl. health cons. Royal Surrey County Hosp.; lectr. various univs., U.K., 1985—. Editor: Occupational Hazards of Pesticide Exposure, 1985, also papers in field. Mem. mgmt. bd. distance learning course in occupl. health Manchester (Eng.) U. Fellow Royal Coll. Physicians (faculty occupational medicine, mem. exam. bd. in occupational medicine 1990); mem. Royal Coll. Med. and Surgery (diploma indsl. health 1981), Soc. Occupational Medicine. Avocations: pilot, arts, metabolising. Office: IBM (UK) Ltd, PO Box 40 North Harbour, Portsmouth PO6 3AU, England

BONSIGNORE, MICHAEL ROBERT, electronics and computer company executive; b. Plattsburg, N.Y., Apr. 3, 1941. BA, US Naval Acad., 1963; postgrad., Tex. A&M U. Various mktg. and bus. devel. positions aerospace group Honeywell Inc., 1969-72, various mktg. and ops. mgmt. positions marine sys. divsn., 1972-81, gen. mgr. marine sys. divsn., 1981-82, pres. Honeywell Europe, 1982-87, exec. v.p. internat. divsn., 1987-90, exec. v.p., COO internat. and bldg. ctrl., 1990-93, chmn., CEO, 1993-2000; chmn., CEO Honeywell Inc. (merged with Allied Signal), 2000—; bd. dirs. Honeywell Medtronic Inc., New Perspective Fund Inc., U.S.-Russia Bus. Coun., Investment and Svc. policy Advt. Com., U.S.-China Bus. Coun., Alliance to Save Energy. Office: Honeywell Inc Internat 101 Columbia Rd Morristown NJ 07960-4658

BONSKY, JACK ALAN, lawyer; b. Canton, Ohio, Mar. 12, 1938; s. Jack H. and Pearl E. Bonsky; m. Carol Ann Portmann, Sept. 2, 1960; children: Jack Raymond, Cynthia Lynn. AB, Ohio U., 1960; JD, Ohio State U., 1964. Bar: Ohio 1964, U.S. Dist. Ct. (so. dist.) Ohio 1969. With Metcalf, Thomas & Bonsky, Marietta, Ohio, 1964-69, Addison, Fisher & Bonsky, Marietta, 1969-70; asst. counsel GenCorp., Inc. (formerly Gen. Tire & Rubber Co.), Akron, Ohio, 1970-75, assoc. gen. counsel, 1975-86, asst. sec., 1977-86, v.p., sec., 1986; v.p., sec., gen. counsel DiversiTech Gen., Inc., 1986-87; v.p., gen. counsel GenCorp Polymer Products, 1988-94; asst. gen. counsel, dir. environ. affairs GenCorp, Inc., 1994-96; pvt. practice, 1996—; solicitor City of Marietta, 1966-67; legal advisor City of Marietta Bd. of Edn., 1966-67; police prosecutor, Belpre, Ohio, 1969-70; comml. law instr. Am. Inst. Banking, 1969; dir. Frontier Holdings, Inc., Denver, Frontier Airlines, Denver, 1985 (merged with People Express Airlines, 1985). Mem. Marietta Income Tax Bd. of Rev., 1966-67; mem. Traffic Commn., 1966-69, chmn., 1967; mem. Civil Svc. Commn., 1969; trustee Urban League, 1978-81, pres., 1980-81; trustee Akron Comty. Svc. Ctr., 1978-81, United Way of Summit County, 1982-89; mem. Bath Twp. Merger Commn., 1995-96; v.p. Bath Twp. Home-owners' Assn., 1999; pres. Bath Twp. Homeowners Assn., 2000; bd. dirs. Washington County Soc. for Crippled Children, 1964-70, S.E. Ohio unit Arthritis Found., 1967-70, chmn., 1968-70; mem. Washington County Health Planning Com., 1968-70; ho. of dels. Ohio Easter Seal Soc., 1968-70; mem. econ. devel. revenue com. Bath Twp., 1999-2000. Recipient Akron Comty. Svc. Ctr. and Urban League Leadership award, 1981. Mem. Ohio Bar Assn. Home and Office: 4234 Idlebrook Dr Akron OH 44333-1726

BONTHA, JAGANNADHA RAD, scientist, development engineer; b. Srikakulam, India, Nov. 21, 1966; came to U.S., 1988; s. Murali Mohana Rao and Suryakumari Bontha; m. Madhuri Tripurana, Dec. 19, 1997; 1 child, Naveena Aishwarya. B of Tech., Andhra U., Visakhapatnam, India, 1988; M of Engring., Tulane U., 1990, PhD in Chem. Engring., 1997. Rsch. asst. Tulane U., New Orleans, 1988-93; devel. engr. Battelle, Pacific N.W. Nat. Lab., Richland, Wash., 1994-96, sr. devel. engr., 1997—. Contbr. articles to profl. jours.; patentee in field. Recipient scholarship Tulane U., 1988-93. Mem. AIChE, Am. Chem. Soc., Am. Soc. Engring. Edn., Electrochem. Soc., Sigma Xi. E-mail: j.r.bontha@pnl.gov. Office: Battelle PNNL Sixth and West Sts Richland WA 99352

BONTOZOGLOU, VASILIS, chemical engineering educator; b. Thessaloniki, Greece, Apr. 1, 1958; s. Andreas and Elektra (Mavromati) B.; m. Paraskevi Hatjigiannaki, June 30, 1984; children: Andreas, Christos. Diploma in chem. engring., U. Thessaloniki, 1982; MSChE, U. Ill., 1986, PhD, 1988. Rschr. CPERI-FORTH, Thessaloniki, 1988-93; asst. prof. U. Thessaly, Volos, Greece, 1993-97, assoc. prof., 1997—. Contbr. articles to profl. jours. Mem. AIChE, Euromech, Tech. Chamber Greece. Avocations: jogging, literature, mountain hiking. Office: U Thessaly Mech Engring, Pedion Areos, GR38334 Volos Greece

BONUGLI, BEULAH EVELYN, finance company executive; b. Cape Town, South Africa, July 7, 1947; d. Cyril Stanley and Helena May (Rudden) Thomas; divorced; children: Allen, Amanda. PA to CEO Edgars Group, Johannesburg, South Africa, 1980-84; dir. Techrent-Fin., Johannesburg, 1984-87; mng. dir. Union Fin., Johannesburg, 1987—. Named Marketer of Yr., Inst. Mktg. Mgmt., 1999. Mem. Exec. Bus. Women. Roman Catholic. Avocations: private pilot, sky diving, bungee jumping, scuba diving, dancing. Office: Union Fin Holdings, 322 Rivonia Blvd, Rivonia South Africa

BONUTTI, ALEXANDER CARL, architect, urban designer; b. Cleve., June 25, 1951; s. Karl Borromeo and Hermina (Rijavec) B. BArch, Ill. Inst. Tech., 1974; MSArch in Urban Design, Columbia U., 1978. Registered architect, Ohio, W.Va., Calif. With William B. Morris, AIA, Shaker Heights, Ohio, 1973; designer Stouffer's Hotels, Cleve., 1974, Ellerbe, Dalton, Dalton and Newport, Bethesda, Md., 1975-76; designer, asst. project mgr. Dalton, Dalton and Newport, Shaker Heights, 1976-79; prin. ACB Design, Cleve., 1980, Kaplan, McLaughlin and Diaz, San Francisco, 1981-91; sr. v.p., mng. prin. Hellmuth Obata Kassabaum, San Francisco, 1991—. Contbr. articles to profl. jours. Bd. dirs. Archtl. Found. San Francisco, 1997—, ARCPAC, 1996-99. Recipient Honor award Architects Soc. Ohio, Bay Village, 1979. Mem. AIA (steering com. 1989 Monterey Design Conf., Hon. awards U.S. Univ. Health Sci., Naval Facilities Command, Honor award for Pacific Presbyn. Profl. Bldg. 1987, Citation for Excellence, Urban Design Embarcadero Corridor Study, bd. dirs. Calif. coun. 1986-97, chmn. urban design com. San Francisco chpt. 1986-88, v.p., pres.-elect 1989, pres. 1990, chmn. Five Bay Area chpt. leaders forum 1991, Calif. Coun. Bldg. and Constrn. Legis. Commn. 1991), Urban Land Inst. (assoc.), Nat. Trust Hist. Preservation, Inst. Urban Design, Calif. Archtl. Polit. Action Com. (trustee 1997—), Archtl. Found. San Francisco (sec. 1998—), Phi Kappa Sigma (sec. 1970-71). Democrat. Avocations: jogging, cycling.

BONVOISIN, JACQUES JEAN, chemist, researcher; b. Malakoff, France, Mar. 21, 1961; s. Jacques Edmond and Henriette Marie-Louise (Di Meo) B.; m. Catherine Bocherens, July 21, 1990 (div.); children: Margot, Arthur. M Physics and Chemistry, U. Orsay, France, 1984, diploma d'etude approfondie, PhD, 1989. In chrge rsch. Nat. Ctr. Sci. Rsch., Toulouse, France, 1989—. Contbr. articles to profl. jours. E-mail: jbonvoisin@cemes.fr. Fax: 05 6225 7999. Office: CEMES/CNRS, 29 rue Jeanne Marvig, 31055 Toulouse Cedex France

BONYNGE, RICHARD, opera conductor; b. Sydney, Australia, Sept. 29, 1930; s. Carl Bonynge; m. Joan Sutherland, 1954; 1 child, Adam. Trained as pianist; specialist in bel canto and 19th century repertoire. Debut as condr. Santa Cecilia Orch., Rome, 1962, as opera condr. Faust, Vancouver, Can., 1963; condr. world opera houses Met. Opera, San Francisco Opera, Chgo. Opera, Teatro Liceo, Royal Opera House Covent Garden, Teatro Colon, Edinburgh Festival, Vienna Festival, Florence Festival; performed Tokyo, Seoul, Hong Kong, Warsaw, Lisbon, Paris, Rome, Stockholm, Copenhagen, Madrid, Hamburg, Munich, Dublin; prin. condr., artistic and music dir. various cos. including: Sutherland-Williamson Internat. Grand Opera Co., 1965, Vancouver Opera, 1974-78, Australian Opera, 1975-85; opera recs. include: Beatrice di Tenda, Norma, I Puritani, La Sonnambula, Lakmé, L'Elisir D'Amore, La Fille du Régiment, Lucia di Lammermoor, Lucrezia Borgia, Maria Stuarda, Faust, Alcina, Giulio Cesare, The Merry Widow,

L'Oracolo, Esclarmonde, Le Roi de Lahore, Thérèse, Les Huguenots, Don Giovanni, Les Contes d'Hoffmann, Suor Angelica, Semiramide, Die Fledermaus, Hamlet, I Masnadieri, Rigoletto, La Traviata, Il Trovatore, Anna Bolena, Ernani, Adriana Lecouvreur, others; ballet recs. include: Le Diable a Quatre, Giselle, Marco Spada, La Péri, Coppelia, Sylvia, Le Carillon, La Cigale, Le Papillon, La Boutique Fantasque, Aschenbrödel, The Nutcracker, Sleeping Beauty, Swan Lake, La Source, Le Corsaire, La Flute Enchantée, Le Reveil de Flore, Manon, others; recital discs with Sutherland, Tebaldi, Tourangeau, Pavarotti. Decorated comdr. Order Brit. Empire, officer Order of Australia; comdr. Arts and Letters (France). Office: care Colbert Artists Mgmt Inc 111 W 57th St New York NY 10019-2211

BOO, SUNG MIN, biology educator; b. Cheju, Republic of Korea, July 25, 1951; s. Du Young Boo and Geun Bae Koh; m. Apr. 5, 1982; children: Hyo Jin, Ga Hun. BSc in Biology, Kongju Tchrs. Coll., Republic of Korea, 1974; MSc in Botany, Seoul Nat. U., Republic of Korea, 1981, PhD in Botany, 1985. Asst. prof. Kengreung (Republic of Korea) Nat. U., 1983-87; prof. Chungnam Nat. U., Daejon, Rebublic of Korea, 1988—; vis. scientist Oslo U., 1986-87, Nat. Natural History Mus., Paris, 1992, Bamfield Marine Sta., Vancouver Island, Can., 1995-96; chairperson dept. biology Chungnam Nat. U., Daejon, 1992-94, 99—; rsch. prof. LG Yonam Cultural Found., Seoul, 1995; spkr. Internat. Weed Soc., 1998, Internat. Bot. Soc., 1999. Assoc. editor Phycological Rsch., 1997—; editor-in-chief Korean Jour. Environ. Biology, 1998—. Sgt. Republic of Korea Army, 1975-77. Mem. Internat. Phycological Soc. (mem. exec. com. 1999—), Korean Soc. Phycology (chairperson acad. com. 1997—), Phycological Soc. Am. Avocation: reading. Home: Dongsan Apt 1-201, Seogu, Daejon 305-764, Republic of Korea Office: Chungnam Nat U, Kungdong, Youseongu, Daejon 305-764, Republic of Korea

BOOBEKOV, KACHKYNBAI D., judge. Chmn. Supreme Ct. of Kyrgyzstan, Bishkek. Office: Supreme Ct of Kyrgyzstan, Orozbekova St 37, 720040 Bishkek Kyrgyzstan*

BOOCOCK, STEPHEN WILLIAM, lawyer; b. Wilkinsburg, Pa., Sept. 25, 1948; s. William Samuel and Zelda Elizabeth (Heginbotham) B.; m. Carol Ann Bennett, July 11, 1970; children: Eric Alan, Allison Anne, Megan Leigh. BS in Acctg., Pa. State U., 1970; JD, U. Pitts., 1973. Bar: Pa. 1974, U.S. Dist. Ct. (we. dist.) Pa. 1973. Supervising tax specialist Coopers & Lybrand, Pitts., 1973-76; tax counsel Incom Internat., Inc., Pitts., 1977-81; asst. treas., dir. tax Allegheny Ludlum Corp., Pitts., 1981-93, asst. v.p. taxes, 1994-96; asst. v.p. taxes, chief tax officer Allegheny Technologies, Inc., Pitts., 1996—. Treas. Meadow Wood Homeowner's Assn., 1990—. Served to capt. U.S. Army, 1970-79; with USAR. Mem. ABA, AICPA, Pa. Bar Assn., Allegheny County Bar Assn., Pa. Inst. CPAs, Pa. Chamber Bus. and Industry (tax subcom.), Pitts. C. of C. (tax subcom.), Com. on State Taxation, Tax Execs. Inst. (treas. Pitts. chpt. 1985-86, sec. 1986-87, sr. v.p. 1987-88, pres. 1988-89, nat. inst. dir. 1989-91, 99-2001, mem. nat. exec. com. 99-2001, v.p. region VI 1992-93, mem. IRS adminstrv. affairs com. 1993—, vice chmn. 1995-97, chmn. 1997-99, membership com. 1993-97, mem. alternative tax sys. com. 1995-97, tax info. sys. com. 1995-97, nominating com. 1994-95, 97-98, 50th ann. task force 1993-95). Republican. Avocations: golf, hunting, fishing. Home: 2625 Woodmont Ln Wexford PA 15090-7978 Office: Allegheny Technologies Inc 1000 Six PPG Pl Pittsburgh PA 15222-5479

BOODHRAM, PARDHOMUN, police officer; b. Savanne, Surinam, Mauritius, Sept. 15, 1950; s. Bhim and Rookmeen (Goburdhun) B.; m. Satiavtee Nathoo, Nov. 25, 1974; children Meera, Preeya, Sandya, Jamuna. B in modern mgmt., U. Cambridge, 1978. Police constable Mauritius Police Force, 1971, police sergeant, 1986; chief clerk Spl. Mobile Force, Vacoas, 1988-94; police officer Police Hdqs., 1994; officer in charge, registry PF 100 Ctrl. CID Hdqs., Port Louis, 1995—. activist, mem. SMF Hearts and Minds Campaign, 1988-94. Fellow Inst. Adminstrv. Mgmt. Avocations: football, volleyball, carrom, billiard, snooker. Home: N40 SMF Married Quarters, Vacoas Mauritius Office: Ctrl CID Hdqs, Registry PF 100, Port Louis Mauritius

BOOGAARD, PIETER JOHANNES, toxicologist, researcher; b. Zwyndrecht, The Netherlands, Mar. 8, 1960; s. Lein Adriaan Boogaard and Wilhemina Dipkelina A.C. Van Den Hout; m. Aaltje Dubbledam, Oct. 13, 1989; children: Lein Adriaan, Johanna Paulina, Arend Jaap. MS in Pharmacy, Leiden (The Netherlands) U., 1984, MS in Analyt. Chem., 1984, PharmD, 1985, PhD in Toxicology, 1990. Lic. pharmacist; registered toxicologist. Biomed. adv. Shell Internat. Petroleum Co., The Hague, The Netherlands, 1990-93; head biomed. lab. Shell Internat. Petroleum Co., The Hague, 1993-94; sr. scientist Shell Rsch., Amsterdam, 1995-96, Shell Internat. Chems., Amsterdam, 1996-2000; sr. toxicologist Shell Internat. Chems., 2000—; assoc. prof. occupl. toxicology and environ. health U. Amsterdam, 2000—; vis. scientist Chem. Industry Inst. Toxicology, Rsch. Triangle Park, N.C., 1994-95. Author: Development of Proximal Tubular Cell Systems to Study Nephrotoxicity, 1990. Recipient KNMP award Royal Dutch Society of Pharmacy, 1985. Mem. Netherlands Soc. Toxicology (sec. 1999—), Royal Netherlands Soc. Chemistry, Soc. Toxicology U.S.A., Internat. Soc. Study Xenobiotics, Health Coun. Netherlands. Mem. Dutch Reformed Ch. Avocations: mountaineering, singing. Office: Shell Interna, Carel van Bylandtlaan 30, 2596 HR The Hague The Netherlands

BOOHER, ALICE ANN, lawyer; b. Indpls., Oct. 6, 1941; d. Norman Rogers and Olga (Bonke) B. BA in Polit. Sci., Butler U., 1963; LLB, Ind. U., 1966, JD, 1967. Bar: Ind. 1966, U.S. Dist. Ct. (so. dist.) Ind. 1966, U.S. Tax Ct. 1970, U.S. Ct. Customs and Patent Appeals 1969, U.S. Ct. Mil. Appeals 1969, U.S. Ct. Appeals (D.C. cir.) 1969, U.S. Supreme Ct. 1969; cert. tchr., Ind. Rsch. asst., law clk. Supreme and Appellate Cts. Ind., Indpls., 1966; legal intern, atty., staff legal advisor Dept. State, Washington, 1966-69; staff legal adviser Bd. Vets. Appeals, Washington, 1969-78, sr. atty., 1978—, counsel, 1991—; former counselor D.C. Penal Facilities and Shelters. Author: The Nuclear Test Ban Treaty and the Third Party Non-Nuclear States, also children's books; contbr. articles to various publs., chpts. to Whiteman Digest of International Law; exhibited crafts, needlepoint in juried artisan fairs; originator U.S. postage stamps Women in Mil. Svc., 1980-97, POWs/MIAs, 1986-96. Bd. dirs. numerous community groups, including D.C. Women's Commn. for Crime Prevention, 1980-81; pres., legal adviser VA employees Assn. Recipient various awards; named Ky. Col., 1988. Mem. DAV (life), VFW Aux. (life), LWV, Women's Bar Assn. D.C., D.C. Sexual Assault Coalition (chmn. legal com.), Judge Advocates Assn., Butler U. Alumni Assn., Nat. Mus. Women in Arts, Kennedy Ctr. Stars, Sackler Gallery (patron), Women in Mil. Svcs. to Am. Found. (charter), Bus. and Profl. Women (pres. D.C. 1980-81, nat. UN fellow 1974, nat. bd. dirs. 1980-82, 87—, Woman of Yr. award D.C. 1975, Marguerite Rawalt award D.C. 1986), USO, Women Officers Profl. Assns., Navy League U.S.A., Am. Legion Aux. (life), Nat. Task Force on Women of the Mil. and Women Mil. POWS (chair Esther Peterson Tribute 1995, panel, paper moderator conf. 1997, book reviewer, contbr. to Stars & Stripes, Ex POWs Bull., others), U.S. Naval Inst., Army Women Officers Profl. Assn., Am. News Womens Club, Alliance Nat. Defense.

BOOHER, ROBERT BONKE, dentist; b. Indpls., Sept. 8, 1949; s. Norman R. and Olga M. (Bonke) B.; m. Shirley D. Hillman, July 1, 1989; 1 child, Megan Ann. BS, Purdue U., 1971; DDS, Ind. U., 1975. Assoc. dentist Dental Health Assocs., Indpls., 1977-79, co-owner, 1979-80; owner Assocs. in Family Dentistry, Indpls., 1980—. Bd. dirs. Julia Jameson Health Camp for Children, Indpls., 1978—. Maj. U.S. Army, 1977—. Mem. ADA, Ind. Dental Assn., Indpls. Dist. Dental Soc., Masons. Presbyterian. Avocations: singing, golf, tennis. Home: 10442 Fox Trce Zionsville IN 46077-9792 Office: 7800 E Us Highway 36 Avon IN 46123-7174

BOOKER, BRUCE ROBERT, theology educator, author, educational consultant; b. St. Paul, Dec. 14, 1951; s. Robert Max Booker and Elaine Mae Hinzie; m. Barbara Jean Toelaer Burns, Oct. 28, 1971 (div. Aug. 1982); children: Justin Eric, Rebecca Lynn; m. Patricia Gardner, Nov. 26, 1983; 1 child, David Ray. BS in Theology, Carolina Christian U., 1981; MA in Bus. Edn., Columbia Pacific U., 1985, PhD, 1988; postgrad., Union Messianic Jewish Yeshiva, 1990-93. Tech. instr. Mitel Corp., Irvine, Calif., 1980-85; chief engring. Johnston Telcomms., Walnut, Calif., 1985-87; Messianic rabbi Beth Shalom Messianic Congregation, Colton, Calif., 1989-91; mktg. analyst Norstar Telcomms., Wilkes-Barre, Pa., 1991-94; pres. Sar Shalom Ministries, Inc., Scranton, Pa., 1991-94; adj. prof. Carolina Christian U., Linwood, N.C., 1992—; dir. of tng. and tech. support Genesis Comms., Memphis, Tenn., 1994-97; pres. Booker Ednl. Svcs. Corp., Memphis, 1997-98; dir. trng. Hartford Comms., 1998—; exec. dir. N.E. Pa. Christian Task Force Against Anti-Semitism, Scranton, 1993-94. Author: Mitel Generic 1000 Automatic Route Selection, 1989, Mitel Automatic Route Selection Made Easy, 1989, To the Jew First, 1989, Towards a Jewish Evangelism, 1991, The Lie - The Satanic Origins of Anti-Semitism, 1993, A Call To Holiness, 1994, A Merciful Severity - A History of the Christian Persecution Against the Jew, 1995. Messianic rabbi Etz Chaim Messianic Fellowship, 1991-94. Staff sgt. USMC, 1972-80. Mem. SAR, ASTD, Disabled Am. Vets. (life). Republican. Messianic Judaism. Avocations: computer studies, biblical studies. Home and Office: PO Box 1946 Priest River ID 83856-1946

BOOM, HANS, information, communications specialist; b. Alkmaar, The Netherlands, July 26, 1954; s. Loek and Ed (Karels) B.; m. Wil B. Janssens; children: Edy, Loes, Ted-Jan. CEO Treecomm B.V., Bilthoven, The Netherlands, 1979—. Mem. nat. bd. Scouting Nederland. Mem. Dutch Pub. Rels. Assn., Internat. Pub. Rels. Assn. E-mail: hb@treecomm.com. Home: Kapellestraat 7, 3421 CT Oudewater The Netherlands Office: Treecomm BV, PO Box 30, 3420 DA Oudewater The Netherlands

BOOM, WILLEM HENRY, physician, biomedical researcher; b. L.A., Nov. 5, 1952; s. Willem B.K. and Florence Ann (Hopper) B.; m. Anne Louise Batzell, July 7, 1984; children: Alexander, Katherine. Cert. d'Etudes Politiques, Inst. D'Etudes Politiques, Paris, 1972; BA, Amherst Coll., 1975; MD, U. Rochester, 1979. Bd. cert. in internal medicine and infectious diseases Am. Bd. Internal Medicine. Intern and resident in internal medicine George Washington U. Sch. Medicine, Washington, 1979-82, chief resident in medicine, 1982-83; clin. and rsch. fellow in infectious diseases Harvard U., Boston, 1983-88; asst. prof. Case Western Res. U., Cleve., 1988-95, assoc. prof., 1995-2000, vice chmn. rsch. dept. medicine, 1999—, dir. Tuberculosis Rsch. Unit, 1999—, prof., 2000—. Editor Jour. Immunology, 1995-99; contbr. articles to profl. jours. Recipient grants NIH, 1985—. Mem. AAAS, Am. Assn. Immunologists, Infectious Diseases Soc. Am. Avocations: playing squash, gardening, travel, cinema. Office: Case Western Res U 10900 Euclid Ave Cleveland OH 44106-1712

BOON, JEAN PIERRE, physicist, researcher; b. Brussels, Nov. 20, 1935; s. Julien Emile and Colette (De Cuyper) B.; m. Francoise C. Wolter, July 30, 1960; children: Alexandra, Nathalie, Yannic. PhD, U. Brussels, 1964, DSc, 1975. Cert. physicist. Rsch. asst. U. Brussels, 1960-64; rsch. assoc. U. Chgo., 1964-67; rsch. assoc. Brussels U., 1967-75, rsch. fellow FNRS, 1975—, prof., 1975—; cons. Bell Telephone Labs., Summit, N.J., 1967-70; vis. prof. MIT, Cambridge, 1970-78, Kern Forschung Anslagg, Julich, Germany, 1978-79, U. Nice, France, 1979—. Author: Molecular Hydrodynamics, 1980, 91, Lattice Gas Hydrodynamics, 2000; editor: Redecouvrir le temps, 1988; contbr. more than 100 articles to profl. jours. Served with Belgium Navy, 1962-63. Recipient Jean Stas prize, Belgium, 1965. Mem. N.Y. Acad. Scis. Avocation: music. Office: Brussels U, Campus Plaine CP 231, Brussels 1050, Belgium

BOON, YVES MARIE, lawyer; b. Antwerp, Belgium, Feb. 16, 1947; s. Leon and Gabrielle (Garitte) B. B of Philosophy, U. Louvain, Belgium, 1966, LLD, 1969; MLitt, U. Aberdeen, 1971. Lectr. comml. law U. Constantine, Algeria, 1971-73; legal counsel Phillips Petroleum Co. Europe-Africa, Brussels, 1974-77; legal counsel Phillips Petroleum Co. Europe-Africa, London, 1977-84, v.p. gen. counsel, 1988-94; legal dir. Phillips Petroleum Co. Far East, Singapore, 1984-86; mgr. internat. negotiations Phillips Petroleum Co., Bartlesville, Okla., 1986-88; internat. legal cons., 1995—. Author: Energy Law Ivory Coast, 1982. Mem. Belgian Assn. of Corp. Lawyers, Internat. Bar Assn., Law Asia.

BOONCHAI, WARANYA, dermatologist; b. Bangkok, Thailand, Aug. 31, 1965; parents Kawee and Kanchana (Leelasiri) B.; m. Chunhakasem Chotinaiwattarakul, Jan. 9, 1998. MD, Siriraj Mahidol, Bangkok, 1989; MMedSci in Pathology, U. Queensland, Australia. Diplomate Thai Bd. Dermatology. From cons. dermatologist to asst. prof. Siriraj Med. Sch., 1995—. Author: Update in Dermatology, 1999. Office: Dept Dermatology, 2 Prannok, Bangkok-Noi Thailand 10700

BOONE, JAMES VIRGIL, retired engineering executive, researcher; b. Little Rock, Sept. 1, 1933; s. Virgil Bennett and Dorothy Bliss (Dorough) B.; m. Gloria Marjorie Gieseler, June 5, 1955; children: Clifford B., Sandra J. Smyser, Steven B. BSEE, Tulane U., 1955; MSEE, Air Force Inst. Tech., Ohio, 1959. Assoc. elec. engr. Martin Co., Balt., 1955; R&D engr. USAF, 1955-62; electronics engr. Nat. Security Agy., Fr. Meade, Md., 1962-77, dep. dir. for rsch. and engring., 1978-81; spl. asst. to gen. mgr. mil. electronics divsn. TRW, Inc., San Diego, 1981-83, asst. gen. mgr., 1983-85; dir. program mgmt. and group devel. TRW Electronic Sys. Group, 1985-86, v.p., dir. program mgmt. and group devel., 1986-87, v.p., gen. mgr. def. comm. divsn., 1987-91; v.p. requirements and group devel. Sys. Integration Group, 1993-95, v.p. tech. and engring., 1995-96; v.p., gen. mgr. TRW Sys. Svcs. Co., 1994-96; assoc. dir. Armed Forces Comm. and Electronics Assn., 1991-94, dir., 1994-96; bd. dirs. Advanced Hi Tech Corp., El Segundo, Calif.; mem. adv. bd. Tulane U. Coll. Engring., 1991—, pres., 2000—; adj. prof. sch. information tech. and engring. George Mason U., 1995-96; prin. rsch. scientist C3I Ctr., 1996-99, chair acquisition com. Nat. Cryptologic Mus. Found., Inc., 1997—. Served to capt. USAF, 1955-62. Recipient Exceptional Civilian Svc. award Nat. Security Agy., 1975, Disting. Alumnus award Tulane U. Sch. Engring., 1994. Mem. IEEE (sr.), AIAA (sr.). Republican. Presbyterian (elder). Home: 4905 Oakcrest Dr Fairfax VA 22030-4548

BOONE, WALTER LEE, JR., music educator. BA, Albany (Ga.) State U., 1982; MusM, Columbus (Ga.) State U., 1997. Minister of music Sts. Peter and Paul Parish, Decator, Ga., 1988-92; chorus tchr. Southside Middle Sch., Albany, Ga., 1992-98, Monroe High Sch., Albany, Ga., 1992-98; music specialist, chorus tchr. Turner Middle Sch., Atlanta, 1998—. Home: 1254 Defoor Village Ct NW # 221 Atlanta GA 30318-2992

BOONSTRA, CORNELIUS, electronics company executive; b. 1938; married. With Unilever NV, 1955-62; with Zwivel Handelmij NV, 1962-74, v.p., 1965-66, pres. SRV ops., 1966-74; pres. Intradal NV, 1974-83; vice chmn. bd. Date Douwe Egberts NV, 1983-84, chmn., 1984-86; sr. v.p. Sara Lee Corp., Chgo., 1986-88, exec. v.p., 1988-93, pres., COO,, 1993-95; pres. Royal Philips Electronics N.V., Amsterdam, The Netherlands, 1996—. Office: The Rembrandt Tower, Amstelplein 1, 1096 HA Amsterdam The Netherlands*

BOOPATHY, RAMARAJ, environmental scientist; b. Sobanapuram, India, May 14, 1960; came to U.S., 1988; s. Ramaraj Reddiyar and Saraswathy Ramaraj; m. Rosemary Rieger, Nov. 15,. 1990. BSc, U. Madras, India, 1979, PhD, 1986; MSc, Tamil Nadu Agrl. U., Coimbatore, India, 1981. Levenhulme Commonwealth fellow U. Strathclyde, Glasgow, Scotland, 1986-87; vis. scientist Italian Commn. for Nuclear Energy, Bologna, Italy, 1987-88; postdoctoral fellow U. Mo., Columbia, 1988-89; rsch. assoc. U. Iowa, Iowa City, 1989-90, U. Notre Dame, South Bend, Ind., 1991-92; scientist Argonne (Ill.) Nat. Lab., 1993-98; prof. dept. biol. scis. Nicholls State U., Thibodaux, La., 70301. Contbr. articles to profl. jours. including Applied and Environ. Microbiology, Archives of Microbiology, Water Environment Rsch., Water Rsch. Mem. AAAS, Am. Soc. Microbiology, Water Environment Fedn., Soc. Indsl. Microbiology, Am. Chem. Soc. Achievements include development of method for cleaning up explosives contaminated soil using natural soil bacteria. Home: 1025 Bayou Blue Bypass Rd Thibodaux LA 70301-6101 Office: Nicholls State U Dept Biol Scis Thibodaux LA 70310-0001

BOOR, MYRON VERNON, psychologist, educator; b. Wadena, Minn., Dec. 21, 1942; s. Vernon LeRoy and Rosella Katharine (Eckhoff) B. BS, U. Iowa, 1965; MA, So. Ill. U., 1967, PhD, 1970; MS, U. Pitts., 1981. Lic. psychologist, Kans., Mo. Research psychologist Milw. County Mental Health Ctr., 1970-72; asst. prof. clin. psychologist Ft. Hays State U., Hays, Kans., 1972-76; assoc. prof. Ft. Hays State U., Hays, 1976-79; NIMH postdoctoral fellow in psychiat. epidemiology U. Pitts., Western Psychiat. Inst. and Clinic, 1979-81; research psychologist R.I. Hosp. and Butler Hosp., Providence, 1981-84; clin. psychologist Newman Meml. County Hosp., Emporia, Kans., 1985-93, Heartland Health Sys., St. Joseph, Mo., 1994—; clin. psychologist Ft. Hays State U., 1972-79; asst. prof. psychiatry and human behavior Brown U., Providence, 1981-84; adj. faculty Emporia State U., 1985-94. Contbr. articles to profl. jours. U.S. Pub. Health Service fellow, 1965-67, NIMH fellow 1979-81. Mem. Am. Psychol. Assn., Soc. for Psychol. Study of Social Issues, Internat. Soc. for Study of Multiple Personalities (charter). Office: Heartland Health Sys 801 Faraon St Saint Joseph MO 64501-1868

BOORMAN, JOHN, film director, producer, screenwriter; b. Shepperton, Middlesex, Eng., Jan. 18, 1933; s. George and Ivy (Chapman) B.; m. Christel Kruse, 1957; 4 children. Broadcaster, critic BBC Radio; film editor ITN London, 1955-58; dir., producer So. TV, 1958-60. Contbr. articles to Manchester Guardian and mags.; 1950-54; head documentaries, Bristol, BBC-TV; dir. (documentary) The Citizens series The Newcomers, 1998; Lee Marvin: A Personal Portrait by John Boorman 1960-64, 1997; dir. films Catch Us If You Can, 1965, Point Blank, 1967, Hell in the Pacific, 1968, Leo the Last, 1969, Deliverance, 1970, Zardoz, 1973, Exorcist II: The Heretic, 1976, Excalibur, 1981, Emerald Forest, 1985, Hope and Glory, 1987 (Golden Globe award 1988 and Nat. Soc. Film Critics award), Where The Heart Is, 1989, I Dreamt I Woke Up, 1991, Beyond Rangoon, 1995, Two Nudes Bathing, 1995, Lumiere et Compagnie, 1995, The General, 1997, The General, 1998, The Tailor of Panama, 2000; founder: TV mag. Day by Day; author: fiction The Legend of Zardoz, 1973, Money into the Light, 1985, Hope and Glory, 1987, Projections 1, 1992, Projections 2, 1993, Projections 3, 1994, Projections 4, 1995, Projections 4 1/2, 1995, Projections 5, 1996, Projections 6, 1997, Projections 7, 1997, Projections 8, 1998, Projections 9, 1999. Decorated Comdr. of Brit. Empire, 1994; recipient Best Dir. prize Cannes Festival, 1970, 98. Office: care Edgar Gross Internat Bus Mgmt 9696 Ruhver Blvd # 203 Culver City CA 90232 also: Merlin Films, 16 Upper Pembroke St, Dublin Ireland*

BOORSMA, PETER BAUKE, public finance educator, Netherlands senator; b. Bergen, The Netherlands, July 15, 1944; s. Arnold and Niesje (van der Molen) B.; m. Simonette Gerarda Landweer, Sept. 4, 1969; children: Arnoud Jan, Michiel Christiaan, Vincent Rogier. DRS in Econs., Free U. Amsterdam, The Netherlands, 1969, DR in Econs., 1973. Jr. lectr. Free U. Amsterdam, 1969-74; with Ministry Fin., The Hague, The Netherlands, 1974-78; prof. pub. fin. Twente U., Enschede, The Netherlands, 1978—; senator Dutch First Chamber, The Hague, 1987—; mem. non-exec. bd. dirs. van Leeuwen Pipes & Tubes Group, Zwyndrecht, The Netherlands; advisor Moret Ernst & Young, Rotterdam, 1985-96, ABN-Amro Bank, Amsterdam, 1993-98; chmn. ABC Cons. Found., 1989-2000. Contbr. numerous articles to profl. jours., chpts. to books. Chmn. Cristina Deutekom Contest (for young opera singers). Mem. Internat. Inst. Fin. (bd. dirs.). Mem. Christian Democratic Appeal Party. Mem. Dutch Reformed Ch. Avocations: reading, music. Home: Kievitstraat 22, 7491 CN Delden The Netherlands Office: Twente U, PO Box 217, 7500 AE Enschede The Netherlands

BOORSTEIN, LAURENCE, economist; b. Neuilly, France, Jan. 22, 1951; s. Edward and Regula (Simons) B. BA, Columbia U., 1972, MS, 1974; CE, 1978, MBA, 1988. Sys. analyst Frederic R. Harris, Inc. engring. divsn. Planning Rsch. Corp., N.Y.C., 1974-77, prin. sys. engr. Frederic R. Harris, Inc. divsn., 1977-79; sr. systems planner Frederic R. Harris Engring. Div., N.Y.C., 1979-83; sr. economist Frederic R. Harris, Inc. divsn. Planning Rsch. Corp., N.Y.C., 1983-86; sr. economist Soros Assocs., N.Y.C., 1988-94; prin. economist Frederic R. Harris, Inc. divsn. AECOM Tech. Corp, N.Y.C., 1994—. Mem. Soc. Civil Engrs., Am. Mgmt. Assn. Home: 1 Ipswich Ave Apt 112 Great Neck NY 11021-3260 Office: Frederic R Harris Inc 605 3rd Ave New York NY 10158-0180

BOORSTIN, DANIEL JOSEPH, historian, lecturer, educator, author, editor; b. Atlanta, Oct. 1, 1914; s. Samuel and Dora (Olsan) B.; m. Ruth Carolyn Frankel, Apr. 9, 1941; children: Paul Terry, Jonathan, David West. AB summa cum laude, Harvard U., 1934; BA with honors, Balliol Coll., Oxford U., 1936, BCL with honors, 1937; postgrad., Inner Temple, London, 1934-37; JSD, Yale U., 1940; LittD (hon.), Cambridge U., 1967; LLD (hon.), Harvard U., 1993; other hon. degrees. Bar: Mass. 1942; barrister-at-law, Inner Temple, 1937. Instr., tutor history and lit. Harvard and Radcliffe Coll., 1938-42; lectr. legal history Harvard Law Sch., 1939-42; asst. prof. history Swarthmore Coll., 1942-44; from asst. prof. to prof. Am. history U. Chgo., 1944-64, Preston and Sterling Morton Disting. Service prof., 1964-69; Walgreen lectr. Am. instns., 1952; dir. Nat. Mus. History and Tech., Smithsonian Instn., Washington, 1969-73, sr. historian, 1973-75; libr. of Congress Libr. of Congress, 1975-87, libr. of Congress emeritus, 1987—; Fulbright vis. lectr. Am. history U. Rome, Italy, 1950-51, Kyoto U., Japan, 1957; cons. Social Sci. Research Center, U. P.R., 1955; lectr. for U.S. Dept. State in Turkey, Iran, Nepal, India, Ceylon, 1959-60, Indonesia, Australia, New Zealand, Fiji, 1968, India, Pakistan, Iceland, 1974, Philippines, Thailand, Malaysia, India, Egypt, 1975; 1st incumbent of chair Am. history U. Paris, 1961-62; Pitt prof. Am. history and instns. U. Cambridge, 1964-65; Shelby and Kathryn Cullom Davis lectr. Grad. Inst. Internat. Studies, Geneva, 1973-74; sr. fellow Huntington Library, 1969; mem. Commn. on Critical Choices for Ams., 1973-77, Dept. State Indo-Am. Joint Subcommn. Edn. and Culture, 1974-81, Japan-U.S. Friendship Commn., 1978-84; mem. Am. Revolution Bicentennial Commn.; sr. attorney Office Lend Lease Adminstr., Dept. Justice, Washington.; Fellow Trinity Coll., 1964-65; mem. task force on exploration NASA, 1989. Author: The Mysterious Science of the Law, 1941, new edit. 1996, Delaware Cases, 1792-1830, 3 vols., 1943, The Lost World of Thomas Jefferson, 1948, The Genius of American Politics, 1953, The Americans: The Colonial Experience, 1958 (Bancroft award 1959), America and the Image of Europe, 1960, The Image or What Happened to the American Dream, 1962, The Americans: The National Experience, 1965 (Francis Parkman prize 1966), The Landmark History of the American People, 2 vols., 1968, 70, 87, The Decline of Radicalism, 1969, The Sociology of the Absurd, 1970, The Americans: The Democratic Experience, 1973 (Pulitzer prize 1974, Dexter prize 1974), Democracy and Its Discontents, 1974, The Exploring Spirit, 1976, The Republic of Technology, 1978; (with Brooks M. Kelley) A History of the United States, 1981, 88, 91, The Discoverers, 1983 (Watson-Davis prize History of Sci. Soc. 1986), illus. edit., 1991, Hidden History, 1987, The Creators, 1992, Cleopatra's Nose, 1994, The Daniel J. Boorstin Reader, 1995, The Seekers, 1998; editor: An American Primer, 1966, American Civilization, 1972; editor Am. History; editor Ency. Britannica, 1951-55, mem. bd. editors, 1981—; contbr. articles and book revs. to various publs. Trustee Colonial Williamsburg, Kennedy Ctr., Cafritz Found., Woodrow Wilson Ctr., Thomas Gilcrease Mus.; mem. bd. visitors USAF Acad., 1968-70. Decorated Japanese Order of Sacred Treasure, 1st class; Grand Officer (Portugal); Legion of Honor (France); Order of Cultural Merit (Belgium); Rhodes scholar Balliol Coll., Oxford U., 1936; Sterling fellow Yale U., 1940; recipient Bowdoin prize Harvard Coll., 1934, Jenkins prize Balliol Coll., 1935, Younger prize, 1936, Charles Frankel prize NEH, 1989, Nat. Book award Nat. Book Award Com., 1989, numerous others. Fellow Am. Geog. Soc. (hon.), Royal Hist. Soc. (corr.); mem. Am. Acad. Arts and Scis., Am. Philos. Soc. (Thomas Jefferson medal 1999), Am. Antiquarian Soc., Am. Studies Assn. (pres. 1969-71), Orgn. Am. Historians, Colonial Soc. Mass., Internat. House Japan, Nat. Press Club, Cosmos Club, Elizabethan Club (Yale U. chpt.), Phi Beta Kappa (Disting. Svc. to Humanities award 1988). Jewish. Home: 3541 Ordway St NW Washington DC 20016-3173 Office: Libr Congress Libr Emeritus Washington DC 20540-0001

BOOS, HERMAN, theoretical physicist; b. Almaty, Kazakhstan, Jan. 28, 1965; s. Ernst and Elena (Knauer) B.; m. Uliana Soboleva, July 20, 1990 (div. 1994); 1 child, Christine; m. Elena Lezina, Feb. 20, 1998. Bachelors degree, Moscow State U., 1988; candidate of sci., Inst. for High Energy Physics, Protvino, Russia, 1996. Sci. rschr. Inst. for High Energy Physics, 1991—; Humboldt fellow U. Bonn, Germany, 1998—. Contbr. articles to sci. jours. Grantee, Internat. Sci. Found., 1995, Russian Found. Fundamental Rsch., 1996, Alexander von Humboldt Found., 1998. Avocations: skiing, badminton, basketball, learning foreign languages. Home: Festivalny Proezd 23/59, Protvino 142284, Russia Office: Inst High Energy Physics, Dept Theoretical Physics, Protvino 142284, Russia

BOOTH, ALAN RUNDLETT, history educator; b. Manchester, N.H., Mar. 20, 1934; s. Robert Plues and Lois (Rundlett) B.; m. Beatrice Edgcomb, Jun 23, 1956 (div. June 1978); children: Thomas E., Samuel R., Holly; m. Mai

garet Zoller, Aug. 6, 1988; 1 child, Grace Marie. AB, Dartmouth Coll., 1956; MA, Boston U., 1962, PhD, 1964. Asst. prof. history Ohio U., Athens, 1964-68, assoc. prof. history, 1968-73, prof. history, 1973—, prof. emeritus history, 1999, Hamilton/Baker & Hostetler prof. humanities, 1994-99, Hamilton/Baker & Hostetler prof. humanities emeritus, 1999—; manuscript cons. Jour. of Devel. Areas, Kalamazoo, 1965-97, Internat. Jour. African Historical Studies, 1970-97, African Econ. History, Mpls., 1980-95; Fulbright lectr. Swaziland, 1980-81, 89-90. Author: The United States Experience in South Africa, 1976, Swaziland: Tradition and Change in a Southern African Kingdom, 1983, Historical Dictionary of Swaziland, 2000; contbr. articles to profl. jours. Lt. USNR, 1956-60. Fulbright lectr., Basutoland, 1965-66, Swaziland, 1980-81, 89-90. Mem. Ohio Acad. History (exec. com. 1994-95), African Studies Assn. Democrat. Roman Catholic. Home: 1213 Bourgogne Ave Bowling Green OH 43402-1508 Office: Ohio U Dept History Bentley Hall 118 Athens OH 45701

BOOTH, ANNA BELLE, accountant; b. Homesville, Ohio, Jan. 15, 1912; d. John Wilson and M. Pearl (Toomey) B.; m. Guy DiAmbrosio, Apr. 29, 1930; 1 child, Guy Booth. BA, Taylor Coll., 1930. Office mgr. in charge of mfg. Jacobs Tailored Clothes, Inc., Phila., 1931-41; acct., corp. cashier Lehigh Coal and Navigation Co., Phila., 1941-55; acct. Bishop & Hedberg, Phila., 1955-57; acct., office mgr. The Camax Co., Phila., 1957-60; office mgr., cashier New Eng. Mutual Life Ins. Co., Phila., 1960-67; acct. Wall & Ochs, Inc., Phila., 1967-71; comptr. Bisler Packaging Div./Pet, Inc., Phila., 1971-82; ret. Mem. Am. Soc. Women Accts. (Phila. pres. 1956-58, dir. 1952-54, 62-64, 73-75), LWV (Phila.). Home: 2122 Sansom St Philadelphia PA 19103-4429

BOOTH, BENJAMIN KEITH WILLOUGHBY, information systems specialist; b. Banbury, England; s. Keith Willoughby and Heather (Stannard) B.; m. Octavia Jennings, 1995; 1 child, Elcanor Rachael. BA, U. Cambridge; PhD, U. Coll., London. Head info. systems The Sci. Mus., London, 1989-96; head ops. ICIS-LOR Group Reed-Elsevier, 1996—; chair IT Working Party. Fellow Mus. Assn., Royal Soc. Arts; mem. Brit. Computer Soc., Inst. Info. Scientists, Inst. Field Archaeologists, Leander Club, Hawks Club. Avocations: rowing, cookery past and present.

BOOTH, DAVID ALLENBY, psychology educator; b. Newark, England, Aug. 1, 1938; s. Philip Arthur and Miriam Gladys Ann Earl (Simpson) B.; m. Francis Ruth Brooking, Dec. 10, 1966; children: Philip Alphaeus, William Michael Lincoln. BA, Oxford (Eng.) U., 1958, BA with honors, 1959, BSc in Chemistry, 1960; BA in Psychology and Philosophy with first class honors, London (Eng.) U., 1962, MA, 1963, PhD in Biochemistry, 1964; DSc in Psychology, Birmingham (Eng.) U., 1977. Chartered health psychologist; registered pub. health nutritionist. Rsch. worker Inst. Psychiatry and Neurology, London, 1959-64; rsch. faculty Yale U., New Haven, 1964-66; asst. prof. Rockefeller U., N.Y.C., 1966; rsch. fellow U. Sussex, Brighton, Eng., 1966-72; sr. lectr. U. Birmingham, Eng., 1972-75; reader U. Birmingham, 1975-89, prof. psychology, 1989—; dir. Nutritional Psychology Rsch. Group, 1991—; series coord. Food Choice Confs., 1992—. Editor: Hunger Models, 1978, Neurophysiology of Ingestion, 1993, (spl. issue) Tactile Pattern Recognition, 1993; co-editor: Thirst: Physiology and Psychology, 1992, Appetite, 1994; author: Psychology of Nutrition, 1994; contbr. chpts. to books and articles to sci. jours. Rsch. grantee Med. Rsch. Coun., Mental Health Rsch. Trust, Sci. and Engring. Rsch. Coun., Agrl. and Food Rsch. Coun., Biotech. and Biol. Scis. Rsch. Coun., Brit. Nutrition Found., and Ministry of Agr., Fisheries and Food, U.K., 1966—. Fellow British Psychol. Soc. (health psychology divsn., divsn. of tchrs. and rschrs. com., grad. qualifications accreditation com.); mem. Exptl. Psychology Soc., European Chemoreception Rsch. Orgn., Soc. for Neuroscience, Soc. Chem. Industry Consumer and Sensory Rsch. Group, Nutrition Soc. (nutrition and behavior group), Soc. for Study Ingestive Behavior (long range planning com.), Assn. Univ. Tchrs. Office: U Birmingham Sch Psychology, Edgbaston, Birmingham B15 2TT, England

BOOTH, JOHN GRAHAM, physicist, educator; b. Stoke-on-Trent, Eng., Jan. 21, 1934; m. Mary Caroline Godfrey, Dec. 27, 1962; children: Rebecca, Patrick, Christian. BSc, Sheffield (Eng.) U., 1956, PhD, 1959, DSc, 1989. Lectr. Nottingham (Eng.) U., 1959-62; sr. scientist Battelle Inst., Columbus, Ohio, 1962-66; prof. physics Salford (Eng.) U., 1966—; vis. prof. Colo. State U., Ft. Collins, 1986; editor Elsevier Publ., The Netherlands, 1990—. Author: Ferromagnetic Materials, vol. 4, 1986; editor: Jour. Megnetism and Magnetic Materials, 1990—. Fellow Inst. Physics. Avocations: music, golf. Office: U Salford, The Crescent, Salford M5 4WT, England

BOOTH, MARK, broadcasting executive. Pres. UIH programming, mng. dir., CEO Maxwell Entertainment; inaugural CEO MTV Europe, 1986—; past mem. mgmt. team MTV Networks, U.S.; CEO Foxtel, Australia, 1994; COO JSkyB, Japan; CEO Brit. Sky Broadcasting, London, 1997-99, epartners, London, 1999—. Office: epartners, 14 Flood Walk, London SW3 5RG, England*

BOOTH, PENELOPE PARTRIDGE, educator, school principal, author; b. Niskayuna, N.Y., Dec. 7, 1943; d. Leonard Charlton and Elizabeth Jane (Russ) Partridge; m. John Robert Booth, Sept. 10, 1966 (div. 1975); children: Elizabeth Ashley, Patricia Anne. BS in Math., Mary Washington Coll., 1965; MEd, Towson State U., 1981. Comml. supr. Chesapeake & Potomac Telephone Co., Washington, 1965-66, Richmond, Va., 1967-68; math. tchr. Havelock (N.C.) High Sch., 1966-67, Jack Jouett Jr. High Sch., Charlottesville, Va., 1968-70; math. tchr. Baltimore County Pub. Schs., Towson, Md., 1974-81, supr. math., 1987-93; prin. Catonsville (Md.) Middle Sch., 1993-96; tchr. gifted and talented resource Office Of Math., Towson, 1981-84; chmn. math. dept. Hereford Mid. Sch., Monkton, Md., 1984-87; coord. office of maths. Baltimore County Pub. Schs., 1996—; instr. Baltimore county Pub. Schs., 1976-88, Md. Acad. Scis., Balt., 1984-86, Inst. for the Gifted Talented, Towson, 1983-85; cons. Md. State Dept. Edn., Balt., 1981—; adj. prof. Johns Hopkins U., 1996—, Coll. Notre Dame Md., 1997—; co-owner Conversation Pieces, 1997—. Author: Essentials of Mathematics, 1988, Consumer Mathematics, 1988, Foundations of Algebra and Geometry, 1998, (booklet) First Book of Testing. Adult leader troop 336, Girl Scouts U.S.A., Towson, 1972-88; mem. Lutherville (Md.) Recreation Coun., 1979-89; cons. Md. Math. League, 1982-87; chmn., co-founder Christa McAuliffe Scholarship Found., 1986—; mem. alumni adv. coun. Towson State U.; mem. adv. bd. MAT Program Johns Hopkins U., 1992—. Recipient Presdl. award NSF, 1985, Disting. Alumni award Towson State U., 1989. Mem. ASCD, Nat. Coun. Suprs. Math. (sec.-treas. Md. coun. 2000—), Nat. Coun. Tchrs. Math., Coun. Presdl. Awardees (scholarship chmn.), Optimists, Phi Delta Kappa, Delta Kappa Gamma (v.p.). Republican. Presbyterian. Avocations: traveling, needlepoint. Home: 135 Greenridge Rd Lutherville Timonium MD 21093-6124

BOOTHROYD, THE RIGHT HON. BETTY, secretary to speaker House of Commons; b. Dewsbury, Yorkshire, Eng., Oct. 8, 1929; d. Archibald and Mary (Butterfield) B. Student, Dewsbury Coll. Commerce and Art, 1940-45; LLD (hon.), Cambridge (Eng.) U., 1994; DCL (hon.), Oxford (Eng.) U., 1995. Sec. Labour Party Hdqs., Eng., 1948; sec., personal asst. to Baroness (Barbara) Castle, Lord Walston, Sir Geoffrey de Freitas; elected to Ho. of Commons, 1973; mem. Ho. of Commons Comm., 1983-87; dep. spkr. Ho. of Commons, 1987-92, spkr. of house, 1992-2000, spkr.'s sec., 2000—; del. to North Atlantic Assembly, 1974; accompanied Labour Party dels. to European Confs., 1955-60, Soviet Union, China and Vietnam, 1957; del. to North Atlantic Assembly, 1974; mem. European Parliament, 1975-77. Active Kennedy-for-Pres. campaign, U.S., 1960-61; asst. to Congressman, Washington, 1960-61; Labour Party councillor Hammersmith (London) Borough Coun., 1965-68; chancellor The Open Univ., London, 1994—. Anglican. Home and Office: care Speakers Office, London SW1A OAA, England

BOPANNA, K. N., pharmacist, marketing specialist; b. Apr. 28, 1972; m. Latha Bopanna. B Pharmacy with distinction, U Mysore, India, 1994; Pharm M with distinction, M.S. U. Baroda, India, 1996; diploma data prep. and computer softwwae, Nat. Inst. Indsl. Edn., Mysore, 1990; postgrad. diploma in tng. and devel., Inst. Health Care Adminstrn., Madras, India, 1998; advanced diploma in mktg. mgmt., Nat. Sch. Mgmt. Studies, Madras, 1998; postgrad., Mgmt. Studies Promotion Inst., Delhi, India, 1999; diploma in total quality mgmt., Nat. Inst. Labor Edn.-Mgmt., Madras. Product exec. ASTRA-IDL Ltd., Bangalore, 1997, sr. exec. med. svcs. dept., 1997-98, asst. mgr., 1998—; referee Indian Jour. Pharmacology; mem. vis. faculty Alliance Bus. Acad., Bangalore, Annamalai U., Chidambaram, Inda., also other acad. instns. Recipient outstanding achievement award Mgmt. Studies Promotion Inst., 1999. Fellow United Writers Assn.; mem. Indian Pharm. Soc., Indian Pharm. Assn., Soc. Biochemists India, Indian Soc. Tng. and Devel., Decan Phrm. Soc., Kodava Samaj, Mgmt. Studies Promotion Inst. (patron), N.Y. Acad. Scis. (hon.), Garden City Spkrs. Forum-Toastmasters (v.p. membership, award 2000). Avocations: cricket, music. Fax: 91-080-2252894. E-mail: knb@astraidl.sprintsmx.ems.vsnl.net.in. Home: 325 2d Fl II State 8th A Mn, Rd, Malleswaram (West), Bangalore 560 055, India Office: ASTRA-IDL Ltd 32/ 1-2, Crescent Towers Crescent Rd, Balgalore 560 001, India

BOQUET-JIMENEZ, ERNEST, clinical microbiologist, educator; b. Ripollet, Barcelona, Spain, Jan. 12, 1946; s. Alfonso Boquet Bussoms and Maria Reyes Jimenez Bigas; m. Maria Dolors Figueras Gonzalez, June 20, 1970; children: Meritxell, Ernest. Grad. in pharmacy, U. Barcelona, 1971, diploma in pub. health, 1972, D in Pharmacy, 1974. Adj. prof. U. Barcelona, 1974-75, aggregate prof., 1975-77, prof. microbiology, 1978-82, specialist in clin. biology, microbiology and parasitology, 1986; dir. microbiology lab. Hospitalary Ctr., Manresa, 1974-83, Gen. Hosp. of Catalonia, Sant Cugat, 1985-89; prof. U. Nursery Sch., Manresa, 1990-95; dir. Echevarne Lab., Manresa, 1991-96; adviser San Juan de Dios Hosp., Manresa, 1978-89, San Andres Hosp., Manresa, 1980-89, Clinica Sagrada Familia, Barcelona, 1990-96, Clinica Platon, Barcelona, 1990-96, Clinica Teknon, Barcelona, 1992-96, Ministry of Health, Spain, Paho. Author: Manual de Tecnicas en Microbiologia, 1990; author, co-editor: Garantia de Calidad, 1993, Curso de Microbiologia Clinica, 1993 and 11 more books; contbr. more than 125 articles to sci. jours. Mem. Am. Soc. Microbiology, Asociacion Espanola Farmaceuticos Analistas (v.p. 1987-91), Microbiology Quality Assurance of Spain (dir. 1978-97), N.Y. Acad. Sci. (life), European Conf. External Quality Assessment Organizers (v.p. 1992-95), European Ligand-Assay Soc. (bd. dirs. 1992-96), Fedn. Specialists of Colombia (hon.), Royal Acad. Pharmacy of Catalonia (hon.), Biochem. Fedn. of Argentina (hon.), Cuban Soc. Clin. Pathology (hon.), others. Home: Avda Pla de Bages 15, 08272 Sant Fruitos de Bages Spain Office: F Boquet, La Lluna 6, 08291 Ripollet Spain

BOR, SHEAU-SHONG, electrical engineer, educator, researcher; b. Kweiyang City, China, Sept. 20, 1948; s. Yu-Shong and Pao-Ning (Feng) B.; m. Yeh-Hwa Yih, Jan. 1, 1977. BS, Chung-Cheng Inst. Tech., Taiwan, 1970; MS, Tsing Hua U., Taiwan, 1976; PhD, Ohio State U., 1985. Tchg. asst. Chung-Cheng Inst. Tech., 1970-74, instr., 1976-81, assoc. prof., 1985-92; assoc. prof. Feng Chia U., Taiwan, 1992-96, prof., 1996—; chmn. dept. elec. engring. Chung-Cheng Inst. Tech., 1988-91, dean engring., 1991-92; chmn. dept. elec. engring. Feng Chia U., 1995—. Contbr. articles to profl. jours. Mem. Chinese Inst. Elec. Engring., Phi Tau Phi Scholastic Honor Soc. Avocations: reading, music, bridge. Office: Feng Chia Univ, Dept Elec Engring, 470 Taichung Taiwan

BORAH, KRIPANATH, pharmacist; b. Calcutta, India, Mar. 1, 1931; s. Ambicanath and Gunabati (Barooah) B.; married; children: Shambhunath, Arun. BS, Calcutta U., 1952, MS, 1956; PhD, U. Munich, 1961. Mgr. R&D Ciba-Geigy, Bombay, 1962-76; rsch. assoc. Boston Coll., 1976-77; group leader W.H. Rorer & Co., Ft. Washington, Pa., 1977-80; dir. pharm. devel. Organon Inc., West Orange, N.J., 1980-91; assoc. dir. Enzon Inc., South Plainfield, N.J., 1991-92; sci. dir. G & W Labs., South Plainfield, 1992-96; dir. R & D, Tomer Labs., Somerset, N.J., 1997—; adj. prof. Temple U. Sch. Pharm., Phila., 1991—. Fellow Alexander von Humboldt Found., 1959-61. Mem. Am. Chem. Soc., Am. Assn. Pharm. Sci., Am. Assn. Indian Pharm. Scientists. Home: 34 Overlook Trl Morris Plains NJ 07950-1924 Office: Tomer Labs 350 Campus Dr Somerset NJ 08873-1126

BORALLI ROCHA, EDUARDO, psychologist; b. Sao Paulo, Brazil, Feb. 19, 1956; s. Henrique Osualdo and Josephina (Boralli) R.; m. Adriana Magalhaes (Gouvea), May 31, 1996. BA in Clin. Psychology, U. Paulista, Sao Paulo, Brazil, 1981; MA in Clin. Psychology, Pontificia U. Cath., Sao Paulo, Brazil, 1990. Clin. psychologist pvt. practice, Sao Paulo, Brazil, 1982—; prof. U. Paulista, Sao Paulo, Brazil, 1987—. Co-author: (book) Contra-transferencia, 1994; contbr. articles to profl. jours. Mem. N.Y. Acad. Scis. Office: Al Min Rocha Azevedo 1077 cj52, 01410003 Sao Paulo Brazil

BORAN, ROBERT PAUL, JR., orthopedic surgeon; b. Pottsville, Pa., May 21, 1952; s. Robert Paul Sr. and Ellen Elizabeth (Reisig) B.; m. Catherine Virginia Kling, Oct. 18, 1980; children: Catherine, Ellen, Mary. BS, St. Joseph U., 1974; MD, Jefferson Med. Coll., 1978. Diplomate Am. Bd. Orthop. Surgery. Lab. technician Pottsville Hosp., 1972-74; disc jockey WPPA-AM and WAVT-FM, Pottsville, 1972-75; intern Pa. Hosp., Phila., 1978-79; resident in orthop. surgery Thomas Jefferson U. Hosp., Phila., 1979-83; chief resident Alfred I. DuPont Inst. of Nemours Found. Crippled Children, Wilmington, Del., 1981, U.S. VA Hosp., Wilmington; pvt. practice Pottsville, 1983—; mem. clin. adj. faculty dept. allied health sci. Kings Coll., Wilkes Barre, Pa. Bd. dirs. Schuylkill Rehab. Ctr., 1987—, chmn. bd. dirs., 1988—. Fellow ACS, Internat. Coll. Surgeons, Am. Acad. Orthopaedic Surgeons; mem. AMA, Pa. Med. Soc., Internat. Soc. for Technology in Arthroplasty,Schuylkill County Med. Soc., Am. Assn. Hip and Knee Surgeons, Assn. Arthritic Hip and Knee Surgeons, Ea. Orthopaedic Assn., Pa. Orthopaedic Soc., N.Am. Faculty of Swiss Assn. for Study of Internal Fixation of Fractures, AO Alumni N.Am., Jefferson Orthopaedic Soc., Alfred I. DuPont Inst. Alumni Assn., Thomas Bond Soc. of Pa. Hosp., Union League of Phila., Schuylkill Country Club, Vesper Club, Pottsville Club, Skytop Club, Ancient Order of Hibernians, Elks, Alpha Sigma Nu. Republican. Roman Catholic. Avocations: golf, cards. Home: 146 Glenworth Rd Pottsville PA 17901-8888 Office: Bldg 100 101 Schuylkill Medical Plz Pottsville PA 17901-3661

BORBOLA, GEORGE, radiologist; b. Szeged, Csongrad, Hungary, Feb. 21, 1950; s. Joseph and Eva (Székely) B.; m. Arató Katalin, Mar. 8, 1975; children: Kinga, Bence. MD, Szentgyörgyi Albert Med. U., Szeged, Hungary, 1974. Cert. radiologist Hungarian Bd. Radiology. Resident Szentgyörgyi Albert Med. U., Szeged, 1974-75; resident Gen. Hosp., Békéscsaba, 1975-79, staff radiologist, 1979-82, registrar of radiology, 1985-88; chief of radiology Polyclinic No. 5, Tripoli, Libya, 1982-85; chief of radiology Réthy Pál Gen. Hosp., Békéscsaba, 1989—, asst. dir., 1991-92; ultrasounder Thomas Jefferson U., Ultrasound Inst., Phila. Named Diagnostic Ultrasounder, U.S. Agy. Internat. Devel. and Thomas Jefferson U. Ultrasound Inst., Phila., 1994. Mem. Hungarian Soc. Radiology, Hungarian Soc. Ultrasound. Avocations: skiing, playing football, fishing. Home: Felsökörös sor 46, 5600 Békéscsaba Békes, Hungary Office: Réthy Pál Hosp, Gyulai ut 18, 5600 Békéscsaba Békes, Hungary

BORCH, CHRISTIAN, television correspondent, writer, educator; b. Bergen, Norway, June 2, 1944; s. Thor Christian and Karen Margrethe (Troye) B.; m. Ragnhild Louise Lie, July 4, 1969 (dec. Apr. 1988); children: Karen Janken, Ina Louise; m. Lella Hvinden Nilssen, June 20, 1992. Degree in nat. law, U. Oslo, 1965, degree in journalism, 1968; degree in polit. sci., London Sch. Econs., 1970; grad., Nat. Def. Coll., Oslo, 1983. Reporter Morgenbladet, Oslo, 1964-68, London corr., 1968-70, news editor, 1974-78; editor Confedn. of Norwegian Industries, Oslo, 1970-74; fgn. editor Norwegian Broadcasting Corp., Oslo, 1978-90, diplomatic corr. TV, 1990—; corr. AP, 1969-77; lectr. Nat. Def. Coll., 1983—, Atlantic Com., Oslo, 1983—. Author: Crown Prince Harald: A Political Biography, 1987, The Peace Makers: On International Disarmament, 1988, The European Community, Yesterday, Today and Tomorrow, 1991, 2d edit., 1993; co-author: They Rule the World: 50 Political Biographies, 1994. Mem. chief defs. Submarine Commn., 1984, Com. on Govts. Info. Policies, 1985; bd. govs. Norwegian Inst. Fgn. Studies, 1989—; mem. steering com. German-Norwegian Soc., 1989—, Norwegian Governments Permanent Advisory Commission on Disarmamentet. Recipient prize Norwegian Textiles Industries Fedn., 1978, Ann. Pres. Hon. award European Movement, 1986, Outstanding Reporting Hon. prize Assn. Norwegian Listeners, 1988. Mem. Rotary (pres.). Avocations: sports fishing, wildlife activities, painting, creative writing. Office: Norwegian Broadcasting Corp, N-0340 Oslo Norway

BORCH, OLE, lawyer; b. Odense, Denmark, May 8, 1956; s. Thorbjorn and Jette (Jorgensen) B.; m. Charlotte Elverdam, June 18, 1983; children: Nicoline, Ulrik. Cand.juris, U. Copenhagen, 1981. Advocate J. Hoffmeyer Law Firm, Copenhagen, 1984-89, Petersen & Jantzen Law Firm, Copenhagen, 1990-92; ptnr. Dragsted Schlüter Aros, Copenhagen, 1992—; pres. Brøndby F.C., 1996—. Pres. The Danish Com. Concerning Profl. Football, 1993-96, Com. for Sponsor Contracts under Danish Football Assn., 1996; arbitrator Arbitration Ct. under Danish Olympic Com. Mem. Internat. Bar Assn. (chmn. insolvency com. 1996—), Chmn. Danish Assn. Insolvency Law. Avocations: music, sports. E-Mail: Ob@dragsted.com. Home: Ellinorsvej 38, 2920 Charlottenlund Denmark Office: Dragsted Schlüter Aros, Bredgade 6, 1260 Copenhagen Denmark

BORCHARDT, DUKE, federal labor relations professional; b. Pinneberg, Germany, Mar. 29, 1941; came to the U.S., 1954; s. Karl Heinrich and Martha (Kreuzfeld) B.; m. Nancy Ann Saskas, Dec. 26, 1964; children: Lisa Marie Borchardt Baker, Marc. JD, La Salle U., 1968. Adminstrv. specialist N.Y. NG, Rocky Point, 1964-74, Fla. NG, Orlando, 1974-78; recruiting and retention specialist Fla. NG, St. Augustine, 1978-83, pers. mgmt. specialist, 1983, labor rels. mgr., 1983—; discipline and adverse action appeal hearing examiner Nat. Guard Bur., 1989—, chmn. labor rels. adv. coun., 1995—; mediator 7th jud. cir. small claims ct. St. Augustine, 1997—. Arbitrator 1st time juvenile offenders 7th Jud. Cir. State's Atty., St. Augustine, 1984—, guardian ad litem, 1989—, vice chair, 1992—; bd. dirs. St. Johns County Blood Bank, St. Augustine, 1994—; vice chair St. Johns County Juvenile Justice Com., St. Augustine, 1994—; mem. mental health/substance abuse adv. com. St. Johns County, 1988—, mem. health & human svcs. adv. coun., 1995—. Republican. Roman Catholic. Avocations: antique collecting, walking, working with and representing abused and neglected children. Home: 7 Grandview Rd Saint Augustine FL 32080-5339 Office: Fla NG Saint Francis Barracks PO Box 1008 Saint Augustine FL 32085-1008

BORCHARDT, MARLIES MARGARETE GERTRUD, mathematician, educator; b. Wohlmirstedt, Sachsen-Anhalt, Germany, June 9, 1950; d. Helmut and Gertraud Pallaske; divorced; children: Torsten, Björn. Dipl-Math, Martin-Luther U., Halle-Wittenberg, Germany, 1973; Dr. rer. nat., Tech. U. Ilmenau, Germany, 1980, facultas docendi, 1984, Dr. sc. nat., 1988, acknowledged as habilitation, 1991. Mathematician Faculty Math. and Natural Sci., Tech. U. Ilmenau, Germany, 1973-97. Vice-chmn. Gewerkschaft Erziehung und Wissenschaft, Thüringen, 1990-91. Mem. Am. Mat. Soc., European Math. Soc., Deutsche Math. Vereinigung, Gesellschaft Ops. Rsch., N.Y. Acad. Scis., Deutsche Herzstiftung, Weisser Ring. Home: Am Stollen 10, Thüringen Ilmenau D-98693, Germany

BORCHGREVINK, HANS MELCHIOR, hospital administrator, research scientist; b. Oslo, Aug. 27, 1949; s. Henrik and Bjoerg (Roenneberg) B.; m. Hanne Kristensen, Aug. 30, 1974; children: Hild, Henrik, Julie. BA, MD, U. Oslo, 1975, MHA, 1999. Research scientist Nat. Hosp. Inst. Audiology, Oslo, 1975-80; cons. audiology, asst. prof. Joint Med. Svc. Hdqs. Def. Command, Oslo, 1980-82; head dept. R&D Ministry of Environment, Oslo, 1982-83; cons. audiology, assoc. prof. Joint Med. Svc. Hdqs. Def. Command, Oslo, 1983-93; project mgr. to the dir. Nat. Hosp., Oslo, 1993—; cons. neuropsychology dept. neurosurgery Nat. Hosp., Oslo, 1978—; from asst. to assoc. prof. Norway State Acad. Music, Oslo, 1979—; internat. conf. organizer in field of hearing and neuropsychology, Oslo, Italy, Sweden, Australia; guest lectr. various univs., Europe, U.S., Asia, Australia, 1978—; founder Hearing Prophylaxis Program of Norwegian Armed Forces, 1980—; mem./invited expert rsch. study groups and coms. NATO, Internat. Orgn. Standardization, European Com. Standardization, Am. Conf. Govtl. Indsl. Hygienists's Threshold Limit Values for Phys. Agts. Com., Internat. Commn. Biol. Effects Noise, 1980—; project mgr. for the establishment of interventional ctr. Nat. Hosp., Oslo, 1994-96, clin. coord. yr. 2000 initiatives, 1999. Author: Voice and Song, 1982, (book chpts.) Music, Mind and Brain, 1982, Noise Induced Hearing Loss-Basic and Applied Aspects, 1986, Attention Deficit Disorder, 1989, Music, Language, Speech and Brain, 1991, Man and Environmental Noise-International Advanced Research Workshop, 1995, The Workplace-Fundamentals of Health, Safety and Welfare, 1997; editor, author: Hearing and Hearing Prophylaxis, 1982, Effects of Noise and Blasts, 1991, Scientific Basis of Noise-Induced Hearing Loss, 1996, Regional Health Programme for Health Region 2, 1996, Strategic Programs for the National Hospital, General Strategy, 1998, Activity Profile, 1999, Research Strategy, 1999. Co-founder Nature and Youth, Oslo, 1967; choir condr. Consortium Vocale Oslo Cathedral, 1995—, Expo 2000 Hanover; Lt. Joint Med. Svc. Hdqs. Def. Command, 1978. Recipient Gutzmann medal Humboldt U., 1980, Norwegian Grammy award "Spellemannsprisen", 1975; student/rsch. grantee Norwegian Rsch. Coun., 1971-79. Mem. Internat. Brain Rsch. Orgn., European Neurosci. Assn., European Brain and Behaviour Soc., N.Y. Acad. Scis. Avocations: music, history of art, skiing, mountain tracking, sailing. Fax: 47 22 868011. Home: Sofies Gt 74, N-0454 Oslo Norway Office: Nat Hosp Rikshospitalet, Pilestredet 32, N-0027 Oslo Norway

BORDELEAU, LISA MARIE, human services professional, consultant; b. Providence, Mar. 28, 1960; d. Roland John and Nancy Vivien (McIntosh) B.; m. John Theodore Endler, Sept. 8, 1991; children: Ian Endler Bordeleau, Meaghan Endler Bordeleau. BA cum laude, R.I. Coll., 1987; M in Liberal Arts, Harvard U., 1995. Devel. activities instr. Northern R.I. Assn. Retarded Citizens, Woonsocket, R.I., 1980-82; residential counselor Live In a Freer Environ., Mansfield, Mass., 1981-82; staff advocate, asst. program coord. Beta Hostel Corp., Attleboro, Mass., 1983-85; program mgr., residential dir. Alternatives Unlimited, Inc., Whitinsville, Mass., 1985-86; mental health worker Butler Hosp., Providence, 1986-87; program mgr. Work Inc., North Quincy, Mass., 1987-89; dir. residential svcs. Beta Cmty. Svcs., Attleboro, Mass., 1989-94, dir. devel., 1995-98; facilitator cmty. membership project Eunice Kennedy Shriver Ctr., Waltham, Mass., 1993-95, cons., 1995-96; policy evaluator Eunice Kennedy Shriver Ctr., Waltham, 1997-98, tng. initiate coord. cmty. membership project, 1998-99; cons. Cooperative for Human Svcs., Malden, Mass., 1989-91, Optima Cons., Inc., Cranston, R.I., 1991-96; cons. in field. Mem. North Attleborough Teen Ctr. Com., Mass., 1995. Mem. AAUW, NOW, The Feminist Majority. Avocations: weightlifting, body building, whale watching. Home: 11 Anthony E Greco Cir North Attleboro MA 02760-4745

BORDELON, CAROLYN THEW, elementary school educator; b. Shelby, Ohio, Dec. 28, 1942; d. Burton Carl and Opal Mae (Harris) VanAsdale; m. Clifford Charles Spohn, Aug. 28, 1965 (div. Feb. 1982); m. Al Ramon Bordelon, Oct. 26, 1985. BA in History and Polit. Sci., Otterbein Coll., 1966; MA in Edn., Bowling Green State U., 1972; postgrad., Ohio State U., 1986—. Cert. tchr. grades 1-8, Ohio. Elem. tchr. Allen East Schs., Harrod, Ohio, 1966-68; elem. tchr. Marion (Ohio) City Schs., 1968-78, chpt. I reading tchr., 1978-86, reading recovery tchr., 1986-88; reading recovery tchr. Dublin (Ohio) City Schs., 1988—; adj. instr. reading dept.grad. studies Ashland (Ohio) U., 1996. Author: The Parent Workshop, 1992, Octopus Goes to School, 1995. Vol. Am. Heart Assn., Worthington, Ohio, 1991; mem. Rep. Nat. Com., Washington, 1994-95; mem. Royal Scots Highlanders, Mansfield, Ohio, 1976—. Recipient Excellence in Edn. award Dublin City C. of C., 1991-93, 96, 97; Dublin City Schs./Ohio Dept. Edn. Tchr. Award grantee, 1993; Martha Holden Jennings Found. scholar, 1978. Mem. Archaeol. Inst. Am., Ohio Edn. Assn., Reading Recovery Coun. N.Am., Opera/Columbus, Mus. of Art, Columbus, Phi Delta Kappa, Phi Alpha Theta. Presbyterian. Avocations: bagpiping and Scottish activities, archaeology, interior design, harpsichord. Home: 3958 Fairlington Dr Columbus OH 43220-4531 Office: Griffith Thomas Elem Sch 4671 Tuttle Crossing Blvd Dublin OH 43017-3575

BORDEN, AMANDA, gymnast, Olympic athlete; b. Cin., May 10, 1977. Student, U. Ga., 1998, Ariz. State Univ., 1998—. Mem. Nat. Team, 1990, 92-93, 93-94, 94-95, 95-96, 96—, Pan Am. Games Team, U.S. Olympic Gymnastics Team, Atlanta, 1996. Recipient Silver medal Team World Championships, 1994, Gold medal team competition Olympic Games, Atlanta, 1996; placed 1st in the floor exercise and 2d in the balance beam jr. divsn. Am. Classic, Salt Lake City, 1991, 1st in the floor exercise U.S. Classic, Knoxville, 1992, 2d for team Pacific Alliance Championships, Seoul, Korea, 1992, 3rd in all around and balance beam, 3rd for team in vault Am. Classic-World Championships Trials, Salt Lake City, 1993, 1st for team Hilton Challenge, L.A., 1993, 94, 3rd in uneven bars Tokyo Cup, 1993, 2d in all around Am. Classic-World Championships Trials, Orlando, 1994, 2d for team Team World Championships, Dortmund, Germany, 1994, 1st in the all

around U.S. Classic, Palm Springs, Calif., 1994,, 3rd in all around, uneven bars and floor exercise Coca-Cola Nat. Championships, Nashville, 1994, 3rd in all around NationsBank World Team Trials, Richmond, Va., 1994, 2d for team in all around, 3rd for team in uneven bars, 2d in balance beam and floor exercise Am. Classic-Pan Am. Games Trials, Oakland, Calif., 1995, 1st in floor exercise, 2d in uneven bars Reese's Internat. Gymnastics Cup, Portland, 1995, 3rd in all around, 1st in balance beam and floor exercise McDonald's Am. Cup, 1995, 2d in all around Pan Am. Games, Mar del Plata, Argentina, 1995, 2d in all around and balance beam, 3rd for team in vault, 1st for team in uneven bars U.S. Classic, Colorado Springs, Colo., 1996, 1st for team and balance beam, 1st for team Budget Rent-a-Car Gymnastics Invitational USA vs. France, Miami, 1996. Avocations: bicycling, reading, shopping, playing on computer. Office: care USA Gymnastics Pan Am Plz 201 S Capitol Ave Ste 300 Indianapolis IN 46225-1058 also: Cin Gymnastics Acad 3536 Woodridge Blvd Fairfield OH 45014-6613

BORDES, ARMONIA, foreign diplomat; b. Toulouse, France, May 3, 1945. Mem. European Parliament, 1999—, mem. com. on econ. and monetary affairs, mem. com. on women's rights and equal opportunities, substitute com. on environment, pub. health, consumer policy; mem. Confederal Group of the European United Left/Nordic Green Left; mem. delegations to the parliamentary coop. coms. and delegations for relations with Kazakhstan, Kyrgyzstan, Uzbekistan, Tajikistan, Turkmenistan and Mongolia. Office: c/o Lutte Ouvrière, BP233, F-75865 Paris Cedex 18, France*

BORDES-BOURET, ELISABETH FRANÇOISE, engineering and chemistry educator; b. Ancy-le-Franc, Yonne, France, Oct. 28, 1944; d. Jean Etienne and Madeleine Antoinette (Bachelier) Bouret; m. François Bordes, Sept. 18, 1965 (div. Oct. 10, 1989); 1 child, Isabelle. M in Phys. Scis., U. Paris, 1970, diploma d'etudes approfondies, 1971, Docteur 3d cycle, 1973; Docteur d'Etat, U. Compiegne, France, 1979. Tchr., rschr. U. Paris (France) 6, 1971-73; asst. prof. U. Tech. Compiegne, France, 1973-84, prof. 2d class, 1984-93, full prof. 1st class, 1993—; cons. Elf-Atochem, Mazingarbe, France, 1982-88, DuPont de Nemours, Wilmington, Del., 1989—, Rhône-Poulenc, Aubervilliers, France, 1990—; tchr. Ecole Nat. Sup. de Chimie de Lille, 1999—; European Cmty. expert, 1988—. Mem. Am. Chem. Soc., Materials Rsch. Soc., Soc. Francaise de Chimie (exec. com. divsn. catalyse 1994), soc. Francaise Gènie de sProcédés. Avocation: yachting. E-mail: Bordes@univ-lille1.fr. Office: Lab de Catalyse, USTL, 59655 Villeneuve d Ascq France

BORDIN, NINEL, physicist, researcher; b. Moscow, Dec. 27, 1930; arrived in Israel, 1992; d. Miney Bordin and Sofia Plotkina; m. Grigoriy Ratner, Nov. 10, 1932 (dec. 1991); 1 child, Evgeniy. MS, Moscow Pedagogic Inst., 1952; PhD, All Union Sci. Rsch. Inst., 1966. Tchr. Sch., Moscow, 1952-58; engr., scientist All Union Sci. Rsch. Inst. of Current Sources, Moscow, 1958-92; rschr. Jerusalem Coll. Tech., 1993—. Author: Modeling of Solar Cells and Solar Arrays I-V Characteristics, 1986; translator: Direct Conversion of Heat in Electric Energy and Fuel Cells, 1965-80, Solar Cells, 1980-90; inventor in field of photovoltaics; contbr. more than 80 articles to profl. jours. Recipient Bronze medal Exhbn. Nat. Econ. Achievement, 1980, Astronaut Yh.A. Gagarin medal USSR Astronaut Fedn., 1986. Jewish. Office: Jerusalem Coll Tech, 21 Havaad Haleumi St #16031, 91160 Jerusalem Israel

BORDO, VLADIMIR GEORGIEVICH, physicist, researcher; b. Sevastopol, USSR, Sept. 10, 1958; s. Georgii and Zoya Vladimirovna (Litovkina) B.; m. Elena Vladimirovna Gretzkaya, Oct. 5, 1985; 1 child, Kirill. Grad., Leningrad State U., Russia, 1981, postgrad. studies, 1981-84, cand. scis., 1984. Rsch. assoc. Vavilov State Optical Inst., St. Petersburg, USSR, 1985-87, Inst. Gen. Physics, Moscow, USSR, 1987-89; sr. rsch. assoc. Inst. Gen. Physics, Moscow, Russia, 1989—; lectr. Moscow State U., Russia, 1991-94; mem. organizing com. Internat. Confs. on Advanced Laser Techs, Prague, Czech. Republic, 1993, Kontanz, Germany, 1994. Contbr. articles to profl., internat. jours including: Phys. Rev. A, Opt. Lett., Chem. Phys. lett., Optics and Spectroscopy, Jour. Exptl. and Theoretical Physics, Optics Comm., Laser Techs. for Surface Sci. Grantee: Internat. Scis. Found., 1993, 94, Internat. Sci. Found. and Russian Govt., 1995, Deutsche Forschungsgemeinschaft, Germany, 1996, 97, 99. Mem. N.Y. Acad. Scis. Avocations: classical music, travel. Office: Inst Gen Physics, Vavilov Str 38, 117942 Moscow Russia

BORDUSA, FRANK, scientist, biochemist; b. Markrandstadt, Germany, Mar. 16, 1969; s. Lothar and Kerstin (Behringer) B. BSc, U. Leipzig, Germany, 1992, MSc, 1995, PhD, 1997. Postdoctoral fellow U. Leipzig, 1997-99; sci. employee Max-Planck Soc., Halle, Germany, 1999—; Contbr. chpt. to book, articles to Biochemistry, FEBS Letters, others. Liebig scholar, 1999-2000. Mem. European Peptide Soc., Gesellschaft Deutscher Chemiker. Avocations: science, sailing, skiing. Home: Selliner Str 2, 04207 Leipzig, Saxony Germany Office: Max-Planck Soc Rsch Unit, Weinbergweg 22, 06120 Halle Germany

BORDY, MICHAEL JEFFREY, lawyer; b. Kansas City, Mo., July 24, 1952; s. Marvin Dean and Alice Mae (Rostov) B.; m. Marjorie Enid Kanof, Dec. 27, 1973 (div. Dec. 1983); m. Melissa Anne Held, May 24, 1987; children: Shayna Robyn, Jenna Alexis, Samantha Falyn. Bar: Calif., 1986, U.S. Dist. Ct. (cen. dist.) Calif., 1986, (so. dist.) Calif., 1987, U.S. Ct. Appeals (9th cir.), 1986. Tchg. asst. biology U. Kans., Lawrence, 1975-76, rsch. asst. biology, 1976-80; post-doctoral fellow Johns Hopkins U., Balt., 1980-83; tchg. asst. U. So. Calif., L.A., 1984-86; assoc. Thelen, Marrin, Johnson & Bridges, L.A., 1986-87, Wood, Lucksinger & Epstein, L.A., 1987-89, Cooper, Epstein & Hurewitz, Beverly Hills, Calif., 1989-93; ptnr. Jacobson, Runes & Bordy, Beverly Hills, 1994-96, Jacobson, Sanders & Bordy, LLP, Beverly Hills, 1996-97, Jacobson White Diamond & Bordy, LLP, Beverly Hills, 1997—. Bd. govs. Beverly Hills (Calif.) Bar Barristers, 1988-90, chair real estate law sect. 1998—, exec. com. 2000—; bd. govs. Cedars-Sinai Med. Ctr., L.A., 1994—; bd. dirs. Sinai Temple, 1998—; cabinet United Jewish Fund/Real Estate, L.A., 1995—; mem. planning com. Am. Cancer Soc., 1996—; mem. Guardians of the Jewish Home for the Aging, 1995—, Fraternity of Friends, 1997-99; active Lawyers Against Hunger, 1995—. Pre-Doctoral fellow NIH, Lawrence, 1977-80; post-doctoral fellow Mellon Found., Balt., 1980-83. Mem. ABA, State Bar Calif., L.A. County Bar Assn., Beverly Hills Bar Assn. (gov., barrister 1988-92, chair real estate sect. 1998—), Profl. Network Group. Democrat. Jewish. Avocations: running, reading. Office: Jacobson White Diamond & Bordy LLP 9777 Wilshire Blvd Ste 918 Beverly Hills CA 90212-1902

BORE, CLIFFORD LESTER, aircraft designer; b. London, Nov. 11, 1928; s. Lester and Violet Lillian (Fleece) B.; m. Betty Patricia Hall, July 7, 1951; children: Caroline Sylvia Janet, Chris Frank, Susan Jean, Marian Jane. BSc in Engring., U. London, 1951, MSc in Engring., 1959. Chartered engr. Rsch. engr. Hawker Aircraft (later Hawker Siddeley Avi., Brit. Aerospc.), Kingston, U.K., 1951-55; sr. project engr. design of P.1121 supersonic fighter, 1955-58; sr. project engr. design of P.1127 Kestrel V.T.O.L. N.B. Orgn., Kingston, U.K., 1958-62, sr. project engr. design of P.1154 supersonic V/Stol, 1962-65, sr. project engr. design of wings/intakes of Harrier V/Stol, 1965-67, engr. in charge design of Hawk, 1968, head of rsch., 1969-88; U.K. Soc. of British Aerospace Constructors rep. on fluid dynamics panel of NATO's adv. group on aerospace R&D, 1969-84; mem. econ. com. to reconcile Brit. pound with euro for industry, 2000; lectr. in field. Contbr. articles to profl. publs. Chmn. constituency and ward, candidate for local town coun., 1961-86. Recipient Pilcher Meml. prize Royal Aeronautical Soc., 1960. Fellow Royal Aeronautical Soc., Instn. of Mech. Engrs. Avocations: economics, nutrition, walking, photography, water sports. Home: 41 Kelvedon Close, Kingston upon Thames KT2 5LF, England

BORECZEK, KRZYSZTOF ANDRZEJ, history educator, editor; b. Kurow, Poland, Feb. 4, 1955; s. Mieczyslaw and Alicja Helena (Drazkiewicz) B.; m. Anna Maria Guzowska, June 28, 1987; 1 child, Jedrzej. PhD, U. Marie Sklodowska-Curie, Lublin, Poland, 1995. Tchr. Primary Sch., Kurow, Poland, 1979-80, H.S., Lublin, Poland, 1980—; sec. Wojewódzka Rada Towarzystw Regionalnych, Lublin, 1990-93; editor-in-chief Zeszyty Kurowskie, Kurów, Poland, 1990—. Contbr. articles to profl. jours.; author (monograph) Kurów from the Beginning of the 18th Century to 1956, 1996, District of Kurów—The Rise, Organisation and Functioning, 2000. Lt. Polish Army, 1978-79. Recipient medal Ministry Nat. Edn. Poland, Lublin, 1995, Silver Cross of Merit, 1999. Avocations: musics, model-making. Home: Dziewanny 5/27, 20-539 Lublin Poland Office: Kurowskie Towarzystwo Reg, Kilińskiego 2, 24-170 Kurów Poland

BOREEN, HENRY ISAAC, computer company executive; b. Warsaw, Poland, Mar. 7, 1927; came to U.S., 1949; s. Isaac and Grina (Goldstein) B.; m. Lois Adele Golwyn, June 22, 1958; children: Stuart Michael Boreen, Susan Tobey Hailman. BSEE, Drexel U., 1956, MSEE, 1958. Asst. prof. Drexel Univ., Phila., 1958; v.p. engr. Vector Mfg. Co., Inc., Trevose, Pa., 1958-64; chmn., CEO Solid State Sci., Inc., Montgomeryville, Pa., 1964-86; chmn. US-Tech, Inc., Valley Forge, Pa., 1987—; chmn., CEO AM Comm., Inc., Quakertown, Pa., 1990-99; chmn. Integrated Circuit Systems Inc., Valley Forge, Pa., 1993-99; bd. trustees A. Roth Found., Meadowbrook, Pa., 1980—; chmn. Combex, Inc., San Jose; bd. dirs. Integrated Cir. Sys., Inc. Co-author: Aerospace Telemetry, 1961. Recipient Centennial medal Drexel Univ., 1991. Avocations: gardening, photography, car racing, hiking, bird watching. Office: Integrated Circuit Systems 2435 Blvd of the Generals Valley Forge PA 19482-0968

BOREI, KARIN ELISABET, librarian; b. Stockholm, Mar. 7, 1939; came to U.S., 1953; d. Hans Georg and Maj Ellen (Osterlin) Borei; children: Susan Elizabeth Hodges, Erich Michael Hodges. BA, Brown U., 1961; MLS, Drexel U., 1972; postgrad., Boston U., 1982--. Asst. libr. Univ. Mus. Libr., Phila., 1966-68; Anglo-Germanic cataloger U. Pa., Phila., 1968-72, catalog editor, 1973-76; circulation libr. U. Va., Charlottesville, 1977-79; copy cataloging coord. Boston U., 1980, systems libr., 1980-83, assoc. dir. librs., 1983-87, mem. instnl. rev. bd., 1984-91; asst. univ. libr. Boston Coll., Chestnut Hill, Mass., 1987-91, assoc. univ. libr., 1991-92; cons. Boston Libr. Consortium, 1992, Mass. State Libr., 1993; libr. dir. Trinity Coll. Vt., Burlington, 1993-98; univ. libr. Millikin U., 1999—; organizer libr. confs.; presenter at confs., 1982—. Contbr. articles to libr. jours. Mem. ALA, Assn. Coll. and Rsch. Librs. (bd. dirs. 1990-94, White House Conf. com. 1990-92, pres. New Eng. chpt. 1988-89), Libr. Adminstrn. and Mgmt. Assn. (chmn. women adminstrs. group 1984-85), New Eng. Libr. Assn. (chmn. acad. librs. sect. 1984-85), Libr. and Info. Tech. Assn., Beta Phi Mu, Pi Lambda Theta. Office: Staley Libr Millikin U 1184 W Main St Decatur IL 62522-2039

BOREI, SVEN HANS EMIL, translator; b. Stockholm, Dec. 21, 1941; s. Hans Georg and Maj Ellen (Österlin) B.; m. Gisela Wilms Möller; children: Bethany, Rolf, Emil. AA, Valley Forge Mil. Acad., 1961; BA in English, U. Pa., 1964; postgrad., Syracuse U. English and writing tchr. Meadowbrook Sch. for Boys, Phila., 1964-65; basic skills instr. adult edn. Syracuse (N.Y.) Pub. Schs., 1965-67; assoc. dir. Ednl. and Cultural Ctr. Onondaga and Oswego Counties, Syracuse, 1966-67; English instr. Maria Regina Jr. Coll., Syracuse, 1967-68; pres., founder, trustee, CEO Ctr. for Literacy, Inc., Phila., 1968-78; literacy project coord. Appalachia Ednl. Lab., Charleston, W.Va., 1980-81; founder, pres., CEO Literacy Inst., Inc., Syracuse, 1981-88; co-prop. H.E.S. Konsult AB, Transförlag, Lerum, Sweden, 1986—; English lang. coord. Språkverket AB, Göteborg, 1987-89; cons., presenter workshops, seminars in field. Author: Appalachian Adult Literacy Programs Survey, 2 vols., 1981, LLA Finance Handbook, 1982, A Measure of Freedom, 1995; editor: Quality Thinking, 1998; translator: Art at Astra, 1997, Jan Johansson, a Visionary Swedish Musician, 1998, Travel Guide for Westwauland, 2000; contbr. articles to profl. jours. Supervisory tutor trainer Laubach Literacy Action, Syracuse, 1975, master tutor trainer, 1977, regional trainer Literacy Action, Syracuse, 1975; co-founder, chair Tutors for Literacy in Pa., cons., 1985, bd. dirs. 1972-80; co-founder, chair Tutors for Literacy in Pa., 1975-76, W.Va. Literacy Coalition, 1980-82, Tenn. Literacy Coalition, 1982-85; mem. Lerum Mcpl. Coun., 1991-98, mcpl. exec. com., 1995-98, mcpl. bldg. bd. 1999-02; bd. govs. Am.-Swedish Hist. Found., 1973-80, v.p., 1975-77, treas., 1977-78. Mem. Swedish Assn. Profl. Translators (bd. dirs. 1997—, vice chmn. 1998-99, chmn. 1999—), Nat. Adv. Coun. Interpreting and Translating. Avocations: music, local history, poetry, renovating furniture. Home: PL 3181, S-443 38 Lerum Sweden

BOREL, GEORGES ANTOINE, gastroenterologist, consultant; b. Neuchatel, Switzerland, Oct. 13, 1936; s. Jean and Alice Marie (Perrenoud) B.; m. Beatrice de Przysiecki, Apr. 7, 1964 (div. 1980); children: Pascal, Sibylle, Fabienne. MD, U. Zürich, 1963; Privat Docent (hon.), U. Lausanne, Switzerland, 1977. Rsch. fellow Univ. Hosp., Ann Arbor, Mich., 1968-69; cons. physician Univ. Hosp., Geneva, 1975—; pvt. practice gastroenterologist Lausanne, 1976—. Author: Comprendre son appareil digestif, 1994; contbr. articles to profl. jours. Mem. Swiss Soc. Gastroenterology. Avocation: furniture making. Office: Blvd Grancy 7, 1006 Lausanne Vaud, Switzerland

BOREL, JACQUES, writer; b. Paris, Dec. 17, 1925; s. Pierre and Lucie (Dubee) B.; m. Christiane Idrac, Sept. 25, 1948; children: Denis, Anne, Helene, Claude, Claire. Licence des Lettres, Sorbonne, U. Paris, 1948, Maitrise Lettres, 1949. Cert. tchr., France. Tchr., Lycee Blaise Pascal, Clermont-Ferrand, France, 1952-54; tchr. Lycee Paul Lapie, Courbevoie, France, 1954-56, Lycee Rodin, Paris, 1956-67; lit. adviser Editions Gallimard, Paris, 1969-75, Editions Balland, Paris, 1979-82; cultural attaché French Embassy, Belgium, 1984-86; vis. prof. Middlebury Coll. (Vt.), summer 1966, U. Hawaii, Honolulu, 1968-69, Portland State U. (Oreg.), summer 1967, U. Calif.-Irvine, fall 1969, U. Calif.-Riverside, fall 1980, NYU, N.Y.C., 1983. Author: (novels) L'Adoration (The Bond), 1965, Le Retour, 1970, Histoire de mes Vieux Habits, 1979, Petite Histoire de mes Reves, 1981, L'Attente, La Clôture, 1989, Le Déferlement, 1993, L'Aveu Différé, 1997, (diary) La Depossession, 1973, Journal de la Mémoire, 1994, (essays) Marcel Proust, 1972, Commentaires, 1974, Poesie et Nostalgie, 1979, Un Voyage Ordinaire, 1975, Paroles Écrites, Commemorations, 1990, Propos sur l'Autobiographie, 1994, L'Effacement, 1998, Sur Les Poètes, 1998, (poems) Sur Les Murs Du Temps, 1990, playwright Tata ou de L'education, 1967, translator James Joyce's Collected Poems, 1967; editor Verlaine's Complete Works, 1958, 1962, 1972. Decorated officier Ordre Nat. Des Arts et Lettres; recipient prix Goncourt, Academie Goncourt, Paris, 1965, Grand pri Soc. des Gens de Lettres pour l'Ensemble de l'Oeuvre, 1994. Mem. PEN Club.

BOREL, JOSEPH PAUL ANDRE, retired business executive; b. St. Etienne en Devoluy, enDevoluy, France, Feb. 8, 1938; s. Paulin Joseph and Marie Colombe (Girard) B.; m. Rosette Munoz, Apr. 24, 1965; children: Philippe, Sandrine. Engr., Ecole Nat. Superieure Elect., 1961; DSc in Physics, 1967. Rschr. Cealeti, Grenoble, 1961-67, rsch. team mgr., 1967-77, rsch. lab mgr., 1977-79; mgr. R & D Etude et Fabrication de Circuits Integres Silicium, Grenoble, 1979-81; tech. dir. Thomson-SC, Grenoble, 1981-87; exec. v.p. ctrl. R&D ST Microelectronics, Grenoble, 1987-99; expert R&D French Govt., Paris, 1977-79; mem. GCIS, 1977-79; chmn. steering com. Essderc/Esscirc, Europe, 1980-81; chmn. European com. ISSCC, 1983-84; spkr. in field. Contbr. articles to profl. jours.; patentee in microelectronics. Mem. conseil mcpl. St. Etienne en Devoluy, 1970. Recipient Grand Prix L'Electronique Gen. Ferie, Paris, 1979, Prix Chaptal Soc. Pour la Promotion de Lindustrie, 1997, Bronze medal INPG, Ministry of Edn., 1997. Mem. IEEE (sr., 3d Millennium medal 2000), Comite des Applications de L'academie des Scis. Home: 12 Rue du Drac, 38120 Saint Egreve France Office: SGS Thomson, 850 Rue Jean Monnet BP16, 38926 Crolles France

BOREL, RICHARD WILSON, communications executive, consultant; b. Columbus, Ohio, June 10, 1943; s. Richard Alfred and Margaret (Wilson) B.; m. Kathy Teaford, July 17, 1965; 1 child, Meredith Lynn. BS in Mktg., Ohio State U., 1964; MBA in Fin., U. Pa., 1966. Mgr. sales and svcs. budgets TWA, N.Y.C., 1966-69; mgr. planning and devel. John Blair & Co., N.Y.C., 1969-76; v.p., sta. mgr. Sta. WHOH Corp., Boston, 1976-84; sr. v.p., chief oper. officer Ea. Exclusives, Inc., Boston, 1984-85; pres., chief oper. officer Borel & Co., Dover, Mass., 1985-86, Metro Net, Inc., Boston and Vt., 1986-89; exec. v.p., chief operating officer Target Prodns., Inc., Boston, 1989-92; pres., CEO Borel & Co., Dover, Mass., 1992—. Author: (with others) Broadcast and Cable Management, 1986. Mem. New Eng. Broadcasting Assn. (pres. 1977-78), Wharton Club (bd. dirs. 1988—), Beta Gamma Sigma. Republican. Episcopalian. Avocation: sailing. Home: 6 Circle Dr Dover MA 02030-2106

BORELLA, FRANCOIS CHARLES, law educator; b. Nancy, France, Feb. 16, 1932; s. Denis and Jeanne (Gounot) B.; m. Marie Claire de Thomassin de Montbel, Aug. 27, 1955; children: Marie-Christine, Vincent, Cecile, Laurent, Sabine. DLaw, U. Nancy, 1957. Asst. Faculty of Law, Nancy, 1955-58, asst. prof., 1958-62, prof., 1967—; pres. U. Nancy, 1973-78; prof. Faculty of Law, Algiers, Algeria, 1962-66, vice dean, 1962-66. Author 11 books; contbr. more than 70 articles to profl. jours. Mem. Town Coun., Nancy, 1983—; mem. Regional Coun., Lorraine, France, 1986-92; mem. nat. coun. Socialist Party, France, 1974-79, chmn. com. on settlement of disputes, 19[illegible]-94. Decorated officier Nat. Order of Merit, comdr. Order Acad. Palms (France). Mem. French Assn. Polit. Sci., French Soc. Internat. Law. Roman Catholic. Office: Faculty of Law, Case Officielle No 26, 54035 Nancy France

BORELLI, GIORGIO, economic history educator; b. Verona, Italy, Sept. 19, 1940; s. Luigi and Gabriella (Facchinelli) B.; m. Ernesta Ballottin; children: Andrea, Filippo. Degree in law, U. Bologna, 1963. Vol. lectr. econ. history U. Padua, Verona, 1966, lectr. modern history, 1966, asst. prof. econ. history, 1968, prof., 1978-81; prof. Faculty of Law U. Sassari, 1976-78; dir. Inst. Econ. and Social History, U. Verona, 1982-91, dean Faculty of Econ., 1982-94, prof., 1982—; mem. sci. com. F. Datini Internat. Inst. Econ. History, Prato. Author: Un Patriziato della Terraferma Veneta Tra XVII e XVIII Secolo, 1974, Stato, Economia e Società nella Repubblica Veneta tra '400 e '700, 1976, Città e Campagna in Età Preindustriale (XVI-XVIII Secolo), 1986, Temi e Problemi di Soria Economica Europea, 1993, La forma e l'organizzazione, 1997; mem. editl. bd. Il Pensiero Economico Moderno. Commdr. of the Order of Merit, Italian Rep. Mem. Acad. Agrl. Scis. and Letters Verona, Inst. History Studies of Verona (pres.), Deputazione Veneta di Storia Patria, Italian Historians Soc., Econ. History Soc., Rotary. Home: via Calatafimi 2, 37126 Verona Verona, Italy Office: Inst Economic History, Lungadige Porta Vittoria 41, I 37129 Verona Verona, Italy

BOREN, DAVID LYLE, academic administrator; b. Washington, DC, Apr. 21, 1941; s. Lyle H. and Christine (McKown) B.; m. Molly Shi, Dec. 1977; children: David Daniel, Carrie Christine. B.A. summa cum laude, Yale, 1963; M.A. (Rhodes scholar), Oxford (Eng.) U., 1965; J.D. (Bledsoe Meml. prize as outstanding law grad.), U. Okla., 1968. Bar: Okla. 1968. Practiced law in Seminole, 1968-74; prof. polit. sci., chair divsn. social scis. Okla. Bapt. U., Shawnee, 1969-74; mem. Okla. Ho. of Reps., 1967-75; gov. Okla., 1975-79; mem. U.S. Senate from Okla., 1979-94; pres. U. Okla., Norman, 1994—; mem. Senate Fin. Com., Senate Agrl. Com.; chmn. Senate Select Com. on Intelligence, govt. dept. Okla. Bapt. U., 1969-74. Trustee Yale U., 1988-97. Named One of 10 Outstanding Young Men in U.S., U.S. Jaycees, 1967. Mem. Assn. U.S. Rhodes Scholars, Phi Beta Kappa. Methodist. Office: U Okla 660 Parrington Oval Rm 110 Norman OK 73019-3003

BOREN, KENNETH RAY, endocrinologist; b. Evansville, Ind., Dec. 31, 1945; s. Doyle Clifford and Jeannette (Koerner) B.; m. Rebecca Lane Wallace, Aug. 25, 1967; children: Jennifer, James, Michael, Peter, Nicklas, Benjamin. BS, Ariz. State U., 1967; MD, Ind. U., Indpls., 1972; MA, Ind. U., Bloomington, 1974. Diplomate Am. Bd. Endocrinology, Am. Bd. Nephrology, Am. Bd. Internal Medicine. Intern in pathology Ind. U. Sch. Medicine, Indpls., 1972; intern in medicine Ind. U. Sch. Medicine, 1972-73, resident in medicine, 1975-77, fellow in endocrinology, 1977-79, fellow nephrology, 1979-80, instr., 1980; physician East Valley Nephrology, Mesa, Ariz., 1980—; chief medicine Mesa Luth Hosp., 1987-89, chief staff, 1990-91; med. dir. RenalWest, 1996—. regional med. dir. RenalWest, 1996—. Bd. dirs. Ariz. Kidney Found., Phoenix, 1984—, pres. 1993-94. Lt. USN, 1973-75. Fellow ACP, Am. Coll. Clin. Endocrinology; mem. AMA, Maricopa County Med. Assn., Ariz. Med. Assn., Am. Soc. Nephrology, Internat. Soc. Nephrology, Am. Diabetes Assn. Republican. Latter Day Saints. Home: 4222 E Mclellan Rd Ste 10 Mesa AZ 85205-3119 Office: East Valley Nephrology 560 W Brown Rd Ste 3006 Mesa AZ 85201-3225

BORENSTEIN, MILTON CONRAD, lawyer, manufacturing company executive; b. Boston, Oct. 21, 1914; s. Isadore Sidney and Eva Beatrice B.; m. Anne Shapiro, June 20, 1937; children: Roberta, Jeffrey. AB cum laude, Boston Coll., 1935; JD, Harvard U., 1938. Bar: Mass. 1938, U.S. Dist. Ct. 1939, U.S. Ct. Appeals 1944, U.S. Supreme Ct. 1944. Pvt. practice law Boston, 1938—; officer, dir. Sweetheart Paper Products Co., Inc., Chelsea, Mass., 1944-61; pres. Sweetheart Paper Products Co., Inc., Chelsea, 1961-83, chmn. bd., 1984; with Sweetheart Plastics, Inc., Wilmington, Mass., 1958—; v.p. Sweetheart Plastics, Inc., Wilmington, 1958-84, also dir.; v.p. Md. Cup Corp., Owings Mills, 1960-77, exec. v.p., treas., 1977-84, also dir.; ptnr. Concorde Assocs., Boston. Bd. dirs. Am. Assocs. Hebrew U., 1968—; trustee Combined Jewish Philanthropies, Boston, 1969—, N.E. Sinai Hosp., Stoughton, Mass., 1974—, Ben-Gurion U., 1975-85, 87—, Boston Coll., 1979-87, chmn. estate planning coun., 1981-83, mem. coun. exec. com. 1984—, assoc. trustee, 1987-96; mem. pres.'s coun. Sarah Lawrence Coll., 1970-79; bd. overseers Jewish Theol. Sem. Am., 1971—; mem. pres. Congregation Kehillath Israel, Brookline, Mass., 1977-79, hon. pres., 1979—; mem. pres's coun. Brandeis U., 1979-81, fellow, 1981—; v.p. Assoc. Synagogues of Mass., 1980-81; exec. com. New Eng. region Anti-Defamation League, 1980—; bd. dirs., nat. governing coun. Am. Jewish Congress, 1984—; assoc. chmn. scholarship com. Harvard Law Sch., 1964-66, mem. spl. gifts com., 1990, mem. Langdell com., 1991, 92, 93, 94, 95, 96, 97, 98, 99, Boston regional campaign com., 1992, chmn. class reunion gift, 1993, 98. Recipient Community Svc. award Jewish Theol. Sem. Am., 1970, Am. Jewish Congress, 1993, Bald Eagle Outstanding Alumnus award Boston Coll., 1991; named Rofeh Internat. Man of Yr., 1996. Fellow Mass. Bar Found.; mem. ABA, Mass. Bar Assn., Boston Bar Assn. (mem. bicentennial com. 1986-87), Harvard Club (Boston and N.Y.C.), Harvard Faculty Club. Office: Concorde Assocs 1 Devonshire Pl Ste 2912 Boston MA 02109-3533

BORG, ALAN CHARLES NELSON, museum director; b. Jan. 21, 1942; s. Charles Nelson and Frances Mary Olive (Hughes) B.; m. Ann Blackmore, 1964 (div.); 2 children; m. Caroline Hill, 1976; 2 children. Ed., Westminster Sch.; MA, Brasenose Coll., Oxford U.; PhD, Courtauld Inst. Art. Lectr. English U. d'Aix-Marseille, 1964-65; lectr. history of art Ind. U., 1967-69; asst. prof. history of art Princeton U., 1969-70; asst. kkper of the Armouries H.M. Tower of London, 1970-78; keeper Sainsbury Centre for Visual Arts, U. East Anglia, 1978-82; dir. IMperial War Mus., 1982-95, Victoria and Albert Mus., London, 1995—. Author: Architectural Sculpture in Romanesque Provence, 1972, European Swords and Daggers in the Tower of London, 1974, Torture and Punishment, 1975, Heads and Horses, 1976, Arms and Armour in Britain, 1979; editor: (with A.R. Martindale) The Vanishing Past: studies presented to Christopher Hohler, War Memls.; contbr. articles to profl. jours. Avocations: music, travel. Office: Victoria and Albert Mus, South Kensington, London SW7 2RL, England

BORG, BJORN, professional tennis player; b. Sodertlage, Sweden, June 6, 1956; s. Rune and Margaretha Borg; 1 child, Robin; m. Loredana Berte, Sept. 4, 1989 (div. 1992). Mem. Sweden's Davis Cup Team; joined World Championship Tennis circuit, 1974; retired from professional tennis, 1983, returned to profl. tennis, 1991—. Named World Champion of Men's Tennis Internat. Tennis Fedn., 1978. Won Italian Open, 1974, Swedish Open, 1974, 78, French Open, 1974, 75, 78, 79, 80, 81, U.S. Profl. Tennis championship, 1974, 75, 76, Wimbledon championship, 1976, 77, 78, 79, 80, U.S. Nat. Indoor Tennis championship, 1977, World Championship Tennis, 1976, Can. Open, 1979, Colgate Grand Prix Masters, 1980, ATP Sr. Tour, 1992, Champions Tour, 1992-99. Office: care IMG 126 Riverside Dr Rumson NJ 07701*

BORG, GUNNAR ANDERS VALDEMAR, psychophysics educator; b. Stockholm, Nov. 28, 1927; s. Wiktor and Elna Maria (Johansson) B.; m. Vivi-Anne Johansson, Jan. 1, 1961 (div. 1984); children: Elisabet Maria, Per Gunnar Wiktor; m. Yvonne Margareta Wahllöf, Oct. 11, 1991. PhD in Psychology, U. Lund, Sweden, 1962. Psychologist, lectr. Umeå Tchrs. Coll., Sweden, 1951-62; assoc. prof., dean. Grad. Sch. Social Work/Pub. Adminstrn. Umeå Med. Sch., 1962-68; dir., univ. prof. Stockholm U., 1968-87, prof. perception and psychophysics, 1987-94, prof. emeritus, 1994—; vis. prof., rsch. assoc. U. Pitts., 1967, 73, Pa. State U., State College, 1968, U. Pa., Phila., 1968; vis. prof. U. Wis., Madison, 1973; Disting. vis. prof. N.Mex. State U., Las Cruces, 1984, 91. Author: Physical Performance and Perceived Exertion, 1962, The RPE Manual, 1985, Borg's Perceived Exertion and Pain Scales, 1998; editor: Physical Work and Effort, 1977, 86; contbr. more than 200 articles to profl. jours. Chmn. of symposia Wenner-Gren Ctr., Stockholm, 1975, 85. Served to capt. Engring. Corps., Sweden, 1951-70. Mem. Royal Swedish Acad. Engring. Scis., Internat. Assn. Applied Psychology (organizer, chmn. symposia, award 1998), Internat. Soc. for Psychophysics, Swedish Med. Assn., Rotary Internat., Internat. Assn. for the Study of Pain. Avocations: golf, tennis. Home: Furuholmen 1027, Rimbo

762 91, Sweden Office: Stockholm U Dept Psychology, Frescati Hagvag 14, Stockholm 106 91, Sweden

BORG, KIM, basso; b. Helsinki, Finland, Aug. 7, 1919; s. Kaarlo and Hilkka (Stenius) B.; student Inst. Tech., Helsinki, 1937-45; MSc, Sibelius-Acad., Helsinki, 1948-49; Dr.h.c., Helsinki; m. Ebon Ringblom, Feb. 10, 1950; children: Mette, Matti. Engaged as scientist, 1945-48, as photographer, 1948-49, as singer, 1949—; debut, Helsinki, 1947; with Finnish Nat. Opera, Royal Theatre, Copenhagen, 1952-70; tours in Europe, N.Am., South Am., Asia, Australia, Africa; operatic appearances Met. Opera Co., State Opera Hamburg (Germany), Royal Opera, Stockholm, Sweden; guest appearances Bolshoi Theatre, Moscow, USSR, State Opera Vienna (Austria); composer orchestral and chamber music; prof. Royal Conservatory, Copenhagen, 1972-89. Bd. dirs. Danish-Finnish Soc. Served to 1st lt. with Finnish Army, 1940-44. Decorated Cross of Liberty, Pro Finlandia medal, knight White Rose (Finland); hon. cross for scis. and arts (Austria); knight Dannebrog (Denmark); comdr. North Star (Sweden), Finland's Lion. Composer: String Quartet, 1968, Trios, 1974, 75, 76, Concerto for Trombone, 1977, String Sextet, 1977, Concerto for Double Bass, 1983, Trombone Quartet, 1983, String Quartet II, 1984, Quintet for Wood Winds, 1985, Suite for Flute and Harp, 1987, Symphony, 1991, Symphony No. 2, 1992, Symphony No. 3, 1995. Recipient Sibelius medal (Finland); decorated Mil medal (Finland). Author: Suomalainen Laulajanaapinen, 1972, Muistelmia, 1992.*

BORG, MARK GERARD, psychology educator, consultant; b. St. Venera, Malta, Nov. 22, 1956; s. Constantino and Josephine (Balzan) B. BA in Edn. with honors, U. Malta, 1981; MEd, U. Birmingham, Eng., 1984; PhD, U. Birmingham, 1992. Cert. psychologist, tchr. Tchr. Dept. Edn., Malta, 1981-84; part-time lectr. U. Malta, 1981-82, 83-84, full-time lectr., 1984-90, sr. lectr., 1990—, head Psychology Dept., 1996—, dep. dean faculty of edn., 1997-99, dean faculty of edn., 1999—; Senate mem. U. Malta, 1994-97; mem. adoption and fostering panel Nat. Commn. for the Disabled Ministry for Social Devel., 1996-97; cons. editor European Psychologist, 1996—; mem. editl. bd. Mediterranean Jour. Ednl. Studies, 1995—. Contbr. articles to profl. jours. V.p. sec. Malta Union of Profl. Psychologists, 1993-96, v.p., 1996—. Recipient George Cadbury prize Faculty of Edn. and Continuing Studies, U. Birmingham, 1993, Commonwealth Acad. Staff scholarship Assn. Commonwealth Univs., 1982, 89. Fellow Brit. Psychol. Soc. (assoc.); mem. APA (internat. affiliate), Internat. Coun. Psychologists, Am. Ednl. Rsch. Assn., Brit. Ednl. Rsch. Assn., Internat. Assn. Aplied Psychologists. Avocations: baroque music, reading, scuba diving. Office: Dept Psychology U Malta, Tal QROQQ, MSD 06 Msida Malta

BORG, OLAVI ALLAN, political scientist; b. Janakkala, Finland, Mar. 30, 1935; s. Villehard and Hilja Lydia (Ahola) B.; m. Anja Mirjami Paljakka, Oct. 6, 1959; children: Arto Olavi, Ale Ilari, Sami Antero. MA, Helsinki (Finland) U., 1958, PhD in Polit. Sci., 1964. Rschr., lectr. Helsinki U., 1958-66; assoc. prof. Jyväskylä and Tampere (Finland) U., 1966-69; prof. methodology of social sci. Tampere U., 1969-73, prof. polit. sci., 1973-99; dean social sci. faculty Tampere U., 1976-77, 91-93, vice-rector, 1978-80, 93-96; TV and radio commentator, 1961—; mgmt. cons. in field; mem. social scis. and humanities coun. Finnish Acad., 1995-97; chmn. Finnish Future Acad., 1998-99. Author: Finnish Parties and Party Programmes, 1965, Which Party I Should Vote For?, 1970, The Idea of Progress and Republic, 1995; co-editor: Green Politics, 1988; co-author: The Risks of Entrepreneurship, 1989. Mem. Parliament, Finland, 1972-75, Tampere City Coun. and Govt., 1969-2000, UNESCO Commn., 1979-85; v.p. Liberal Party Finland, 1970-80. Decorated Finnish Order SL K. Mem. Rsch. Soc. Vol. Assns. and Orgns. (chmn. 1987-95), Future Rsch. Soc. Finland (governing bd. mem. 1985-95), Tampere House (governing coun. mem. 1993-2000), Ins. Co. Kaleva (governing coun. mem. 1992—). Lutheran. Avocations: baseball, golf, history. Office: Tampere Univ, PL 607, 33710 Tampere Finland

BORG, ROBERT FREDERIC, civil engineer; b. N.Y.C., Jan. 10, 1923; s. Herman Leo and Pauline (Leibman) F.; children: Christina Borg-Gordon, Lisa Borg-Broe, Eric (dec.), Kiri Borg-Henry, Neil, Dean. B in Civil Engring., NYU, 1944, JD, 1949. Bar: N.Y. 1950; lic. profl. engr., N.Y., 1950, Ohio, 1950. Field engr. Turner Construction Co., Rome, N.Y., 1942, Spencer White & Prentis, N.Y.C., 1946-48; office engr. various gen. contractors, N.Y.C., 1948-55; co-founder, ptnr., chmn. Kreisler Borg Florman Gen. Construction Co. & affiliates, Scarsdale, N.Y., 1955--; co-founder Kensico Construction Co., Scarsdale, 1957--, pres., 1966--; structural engr. Chance Vought Aircraft, 1944; mem. bldg. rsch. adv. bd. Nat. Acad. Engring., Washington, 1963; adj. prof. NYU, 1971-79, Pratt Inst., Bklyn., 1983-86, Columbia U., N.Y.C., 1987-90; mem. US/USSR joint com. on coop. in housing and other forms construction U.S. Dept. Housing and Urban Devel., Washington, 1976-87; mem. Sino-US Trade Delegation to China, 1993. Contbg. author: (handbook) Building Design and Construction, 1999, Construction Project Management, (handbook) Temporary Structures in Construction, 1996, Technical and Business Practices; founder Photo Bulletin DeWitt Clinton H.S., N.Y.C.; photo editor Clinton News, 1940; editor-in-chief Quadrangle, NYU Coll. of Engring., 1943; one-man photography shows in various locations 1980-85, including Gallery Show in Soho, N.Y.C., 1985. Chmn., founder Garth Woods Conservancy, Scarsdale, N.Y., 1991—; co-developer, ptnr. Bethune Tower Apts., N.Y.C., 1970, Heywood Tower Apts., 1972, Univ. Riverview Apts., 1973, Cooper Gramercy Apts., 1975, Marcus Garvey Park Village, 1976, Cove Club Apts., 1992; staff mem., docent Internat. Ctr. Photography, N.Y.C., 1994—. Served with USN, 1944-46. Recipient Outstanding Builder Developer award Associated Builders and Owners Greater N.Y., 1989-90, 91, Builder of Yr. award, 1996, Emma Lazarus award, 1997; finalist Entrepreneur of the Yr. award So. New Eng., 1996, 97, 98, Entrepreneur of the Yr. Inst. Fellow ASCE (mem. com. on contract administrn. 1952, 63-67, founder, 1st chmn. constrn. group met. sect. 1962, chmn. tech. activities met. sect. 1963, met. sect. bd. dirs. 1962-67, mem. exec. com. nat. constrn. div. 1971, chmn. exec. com. nat. constrn. div. 1973-74, founding chmn. com. on social and environ. concerns in constrn. 1971), Am. Arbitration Assn. (mem. nat. panel arbitrators 1957—, mem. nat. constrn. industry arbitration com. 1972—, chmn. 1974-76, nat. bd. dirs. 1974-84, mem. de Jur Mediation Ctr. 1974—). Fax: 914-725-0346. E-mail: kbfgeneral@aol.com. Office: Kreisler Borg Florman Gen Constrn Co 97 Montgomery St Scarsdale NY 10583-5104

BORG, RUTH I., home nursing care provider; b. Chgo., Mar. 29, 1934; d. Axel Gunner and Charlotte (Benston) B. Diploma, West Suburban Sch. Nursing, 1956; tchr.'s degree, Chgo. Conservatory, 1958; BSN, Alverno Coll., 1981. Staff nurse Boath Meml. Hosp., Chgo.; head nurse psychiatry, head nurse long-term medicine VA North Chgo. Med. Ctr.; staff nurse, night supr. intermediate care VA Clement Zabiocki Med. Ctr., Milw.; pool nurse, in-home nursing care provider Milw. County Mental Health Complex; home nurse care provider Dr. Ghonsham Sooknandan, Kenosha, Wis., 1994—; in-home nursing care provider. Contbr. 2 articles to profl. jours. Recipient Mary D. Bradford Disting. Alumni award, 1998. Avocation: teaching and performing music.

BORGAONKAR, HEMANT PRABHAKAR, meteorologist; b. Pune, India, Apr. 26, 1956; s. Prabhakar Rangnath and Nirmala Prabhakar (Kulkarni) B.; m. Varsha Hemant Deshmukh, June 14, 1985; children: Madhavi, Malvika. Cert. meterol. tng., Pune (India) U., BSc, 1977, MSc, 1979, PhD, 1997. From sci. asst. to jr. sci. officer Indian Inst. Tropical Meteorology, Pune, 1981-96, sr. sci. officer, 1996—; rschr. in palaeoclimatology and dendroclimatology. Contbr. articles to profl. jours. Mem. Indian Meteorol. Soc. Avocations: reading, mountaineering, games, TV, climate variability. Office: Indian Inst Tropical Meter, Dr Homi Bhabha Rd, 411008 Pune India

BORGATTA, ISABEL CASE, sculptor; b. Madison, Wis., Nov. 21, 1921; d. Harold Clayton and Naomi Olive (Newburn) C.; m. Robert Edward Borgatta, Apr. 24, 1948 (div. Mar. 1976); children: Francesce, Paola, Mia. Student, Smith Coll., 1939-40; BFA, Yale U., 1944; postgrad., NYU, N.Y.C., 1944-48, Art Students League, N.Y.C., 1944-48. tchr. Halsted Sch., Yonkers, N.Y., 1948-50; lectr. CCNY, 1959-65, adj. prof., 1965-70; adj. prof. Coll. New Rochelle, 1973-77, prof., dept. chairperson, 1977-80. One-women shows include Village Art Ctr., N.Y.C., 1951, Galerie St. Etienne, N.Y.C., 1954, 57, Tyrringham (Mass.) Gallery, 1955, Gallery 10, N.Y.C., 1960, Mus. Hastings-on-Hudson, N.Y.C., 1961, Hudson River Mus., Briarcliff, N.Y., 1961, Frank Rehn Gallery, N.Y.C., 1968, 71, 75, 77, Briarcliff Coll. Mus., 1970, Laurel Gallery, N.Y.C., 1970, Roko Gallery, N.Y., 1972, Seton Coll., Yonkers, 1974, Elaine Benson Gallery, Bridgehampton, N.Y., 1974, 79, 83, Bridge Gallery, White Plains, N.Y., 1975, Mus. in the Mall, Bridgeport, Conn., 1975, Cathedral Mus., St. John the Divine, 1978, City U. Grad. Ctr., N.Y.C., 1977, Galerie Coach, Paris, 1978, Sid Deutsch Gallery, N.Y.C., 1986, 87, Camp Gallery Sweet Briar Coll., Va., 1986, Va. Ctr. for the Arts, 1987, Closson Gallery, Cin., 1987, Westbeth Gallery, N.Y.C., 1988; group exhbns. include Whitney Mus., Bklyn. Mus., Nat. Acad., Met. Mus., Hartford Atheneum, Women Choose Women, N.Y. Cultural Ctr., Pa. Acad. Fine Arts, Union Coll., San Francisco Mus. Modern Art, Walker Art Ctr., Mpls., others; represented in permanent collections Hartford Atheneum, Norfolk Mus., Yeshiva U., Kranert Mus., U. Ill., Benton Mus., U. Conn., Coll. New Rochelle, City U. Grad. Ctr., Okla. Art Ctr., Smith Coll. Mus., Book of the Month Club, Galina Co. Milan, Italy, Miller Assocs., N.Y., Collins & Aikman, N.Y.C., NYNEX Hdqrs., Grand Hyatt Hotel, N.Y.C., Zolfital Spa, Rome, H.I. Feldman Corp., N.Y.C., Transnational Devel. Corp. Sculpture grantee Govt. of Greece, Delphi, 1990, 93, Govt. of Greece, Crete, 1995, 96, 2000; Edward MacDowell fellow The Macdowell Colony, Peterborough, N.H., 1968, 73, 74, Yaddo fellow, Saratago Springs, N.Y., 1971, 73, Va. Ctr. for the Creative Arts fellow, 1985, 86, 89, 90, 91, 92. Mem. Nat. Sculpture Soc. (Alex J. Ettl grant for lifetime achievement in Am. sculpture 1995, Victor Meml. prize 1997), Sculptors Guild (exec. bd.), Women's Caucus for Art. Democrat. Home: 463 West St Apt 1105 New York NY 10014

BORGER, JOHN PHILIP, lawyer; b. Wilmington, Del., Apr. 19, 1951; s. Philip E. and Jane (Smyth) B.; m. Judith Marie Yates, May 24, 1974; children: Jennifer, Christopher, Nicholas. BA in Journalism with high honors, Mich. State U., 1973; JD, Yale U., 1976. Bar: Minn. 1976, U.S. Dist. Ct. Minn. 1976, U.S. Ct. Appeals (8th cir.) 1979, U.S. Supreme Ct. 1982, N.D. 1988, U.S. Dist. Ct. N.D. 1988, Wis. 1993. Editor-in-chief Mich. State News, East Lansing, 1972-73; assoc. Faegre & Benson, LLP, Mpls., 1976-83, ptnr., 1984—; bd. dirs. Milkweed Edits.; adj. prof. U. Minn. Sch. Journalism and Mass Comm., 1999. Mem. ABA (chmn. media law and defamation torts com. torts and ins. practice sect. 1996-97), Minn. Bar Assn., State Bar Assn. N.D., Wis. Bar Assn., Hennepin County Bar Assn. Office: Faegre & Benson LLP 2200 Norwest Ctr 90 S 7th St Ste 2200 Minneapolis MN 55402-3901

BORGER, MICHAEL HINTON IVERS, osteopathic physician, educator; b. Kirksville, Mo., Nov. 10, 1951; s. Donald L. Borger and Dorothy M. Hinton. BA in Sociology, U. Akron, 1974; DO, Coll. Osteo. Medicine and Surgery, Des Moines, 1977. Diplomate Nat. Bd. Examiners in Osteo. Medicine and Surgery, Am. Coll. Osteopathic Family Physicians; ordained elder Presbyn. Ch., 1969. Rotating extern Youngstown (Ohio) Osteo. Hosp., 1976; extern in family medicine Dietz Diagnostic Clinic, Des Moines, 1977; rotating intern South Bend (Ind.) Osteo. Hosp. (now St. Mary's Cmty. Hosp), 1977-78; active staff South Bend (Ind.) Osteo. Hosp. (now St. Mary's Cmty. Hosp.), 1978-79, assoc. staff, 1979-82; pvt. practice Nappanee, Ind., 1978--; mem. staff Elkhart (Ind.) Gen. Hosp., 1978—, Goshen Gen. Hosp., 1981—; clin. asst. prof. gen. practice Kirksville (Mo.) Coll. Osteo. Medicine, 1990-93; apptd. clin. preceptor Kansas City U. of Health Scis. Coll. of Osteo. Medicine, 1993—; asst. clin. prof. family practice Kansas City U. of Health Scis. Coll. of Osteo. Medicine, Kansas City, 1995—; pres. Northwood Physicians, Inc., 1992—; assoc. manuscript reviewer Jour. Respiratory Diseases, 1986-88, Jour. Musculoskeletal Medicine, 1989—; pres. Northwood Profl. Assocs., Inc., 1995—; mem. quality improvement com. Ptnrs. Health Plan, 1996-99; founder Circle of Care Healthcare Sys., 1996. Bd. dirs. Nappanee chpt. Families in Action, 1980-82; bd. dirs., chmn. Mission and Svcs. Commn., 1st Mennonite Ch., Nappanee, 1984-90, chmn. pastoral search com., 1989-90; mem. screening com. for elem. prin. Wa-Nee Sch. Dist., 1988; med. advisor United Presbyn. Ch. Nursery Sch., Nappanee, 1995—. Recipient Physician of Yr. award Ind. Assn. Emergency Med. Technicians, 1981, Good Citizens award Tower Savs., 1982, 1st degree black belt Tae Kwon Do, 1988, Tae Kwon Do Student of Yr. award, Hong's USA Tae Kwon Do, 1988; Burroughs-Wellcome Osteo rsch. fellow, 1980-81. Mem. Am. Osteo. Assn., Ind. Assn. Osteo. Physicians and Surgeons, Am. Acad. Applied Osteopathy, Nat. Honor Soc., Masons (3d degree), York Rite. Home: 353 N Hartman St Nappanee IN 46550-1417

BORGES, PAULO ALEXANDRE, biologist; b. Maputo, Mozambique, Jan. 25, 1965; s. Manuel and Lucia (Fatima) B.; m. Rosalina Maria Gabriel, Mar. 22, 1991; 1 child, Ana. BS, U. Lisbon, 1988; MS, A. Agores, 1991; PhD, London U., 1991. From asst. to prof. U. Agores, Angra do Heroismo, Azores, 1988—. Office: U Agores Terra-cha, Angra do Heroismo, Terceira Azores 9700-851, Portugal

BORGHI, BATTISTA, anesthesiologist; b. Faenza, Italy, May 8, 1952; s. Domenico Borghi and Lina Fagnocchi; m. Maria Pia Rainaldi; 1 child, Raffaele. MD, U. Bologna, Italy, 1977, diploma in anesthesiology/intensive care, 1980, specialist's diploma in cardiology, 1985. Vis. doctor med. clinic St. Orsola's Polyclinic, Bologna, 1977-78; attending physician Maggiore Hosp., Bologna, 1978, Maccabelli di Russi Hosp., Ravenna, Italy, 1978-79; physician in tng. Rizzoli Inst., 1978-79; jr. asst. intensive care and anesthesia Rizzoli Hosp., 1979-88, Bellaria Hosp., 1979; sr. asst. intensive care and anesthesia Rizzoli Hosp., 1988-91; head dept. anesthesia and intensive care Istituti Ortopedia Rizzoli, Bologna; instr. local health depts., 1980-85; cons. in field. Fellow Inst. Bloodless Surgery. Office: Istituti Ortopedia Rizzoli, v Pupilli 1, 40136 Bologna Italy

BORGSTAHL, KAYLENE DENISE, health facility administrator; b. Hampton, Iowa, May 21, 1951; d. Harry Dell and Berniece Irene (Muhlenbruck) Crabb; children: Elliot Michael, Brett Andrew. BS in Nursing, U. Iowa, 1973; MPA, Iowa State U., 1986. Asst. adminstr. Linn County Vis. Nurse Assn., Cedar Rapids, Iowa, 1975-85; v.p. program svcs. Voluntary Hosps. Iowa Home Health Care, Cedar Rapids, 1985-86; adminstr. Norell Home Health Svcs., Edina, Minn., 1986-87; case mgr. In Home Health Svcs., Mpls., 1987-88; adminstr. Sundance Med. Clinic Ltd., Shakopee, Minn., 1988-94, Apple Valley (Minn.) Med. Ctr., 1995-97, Resource Mgmt., Shakopee, Minn., 1997—. Mem. Sigma Theta Tau. Republican.

BORGSTEIN, PAUL JUSTUS, surgeon, oncologist; b. Deventer, The Netherlands, Apr. 7, 1959; s. Jan Adriaan Anthonie Borgstein and Anna Catherina Van Wyk. MD, State U., Groningen, The Netherlands, 1986. Surg. registrar Elizabeth's Gasthuis, Haarlem, The Netherlands, 1988-90; sr. surg. registrar Acad. Hosp. Free U., Amsterdam, The Netherlands, 1990-94, surgeon, 1994-96, surg. oncologist, 1996—; cons. Integral Cancer Orgn., Amsterdam, 1996—. Contbr. articles to profl. jours., chpts. to books. Mem. Dutch Soc. Surgery, European Soc. Surg. Oncology. Home: Overdiemerweg 12, 1111 PN Diemen The Netherlands Office: Onze Lieve Vrouwe Gasthuis, 1o Oosterparkstraat 279, 1091 HA Amsterdam The Netherlands

BORIE, BERNARD SIMON, JR., physicist, educator; b. New Orleans, June 21, 1924; s. Bernard simon and Ruth (Lastrapes) B.; m. Martine Edith Descamps, May 2, 1957 (div. May 1964); children: Kathleen, Fabienne, Marianne. BS, U. S.W. La., 1944; MS, Tulane U., 1949; PhD, MIT, 1956; Fulbright fellow, U. Paris, 1956-57. Rsch. physicist metall. divsn. Oak Ridge Nat. Lab., 1949-53, group leader x-ray diffraction Metals and Ceramics Divsn., 1957-60, head fundamental rsch. sect., 1960-69, sr. scientist, 1969-85; prof. U. Tenn., 1963—; vis. prof. Cornell U., 1971-72, U. Calif., Berkeley, 1980. Lt. USNR, 1944-45. Fellow AAAS; mem. AIME, Am. Soc. Metals, Am. Crystallographic Assn., Sci. Rsch. Soc. Am. Achievements include research in diffraction effects of thermal motion, x-ray diffraction studies of imperfect solids; order-disorder effects in solid solutions. Home: 13 Brookside Dr Oak Ridge TN 37830-7616 Office: U Tenn Materials Sci & Engring Dept Dougherty Hl Knoxville TN 37996-0001

BORIN, JEFFREY NATHAN, real estate developer; b. Detroit, Jan. 10, 1949; s. Ralph and Phyllis (Robinson) B.; m. Barbara Shapiro, Sept. 4, 1988; 1 child, Samuel. BS, U. Pa., 1971. Ptnr. Borin Investment Co., Livonia, Mich., 1971—; owner Jeffrey N. Borin Constrn. Co., Livonia, 1973—, Jeffrey N. Borin & Co. Real Estate Brokerage, Livonia, 1980—; pres. Borin Constrn. Mgmt., Inc., Livonia, 1987—, Turov Imports, Inc., Livonia, 1990—. Author: Turover Residences and Other Landmarks of Interest in Detroit, 1991, The Turover Aid Society of Detroit and the Turover Shul: Congregation B'nai Jacob, A Pictorial and Documentary History, 1993. Pres. jr. divsn. Jewish Welfare Fedn., Detroit, 1977-78; pres. Jewish Hist. Soc. of Mich., 1979-81. Mem. Western Wayne Oakland Assn. Realtors, Kiwanis, Skyline Club, Alpha Kappa Psi. Avocation: antiquing. Office: Borin Investment Co 11900 Globe St Ste 100 Livonia MI 48150-1152

BORIN, RALPH, real estate developer; b. Detroit, July 2, 1923; s. Samuel and Anna (Shifman) B.; m. Phyllis Robinson, Feb. 19, 1948; children: Jeffrey, Anne, Deborah. Grad., U.S. Maritime Svc. Tng. Sch., Gallups Island. Sec.-treas. Borin Builders Supply, Inc., Detroit, 1946-71; ptnr. Borin Investment Co., Livonia, Mich., 1971—; radio officer U.S. Merchant Marine, WWII; chmn. Borin Constrn. Mgmt., Inc., Livonia, 1987—. Office: Borin Investment Co 11900 Globe St Ste 100 Livonia MI 48150-1152

BORISON, SCOTT CRAIG, lawyer; b. N.Y.C., Feb. 8, 1961; s. E.B. and Joan B. Borison; m. Janet S. Legg, May 22, 1988; children: Ian, Madison. BA in Russian Studies, Fairleigh Dickinson U., 1982; JD, U. Okla., 1987. Bar: Okla. 1987, D.C. 1994, Md. 1995, U.S. Dist. Ct. Md., U.S. Dist. Ct. D.C., U.S. Ct. Appeals (4th and 10th cirs.), U.S. Tax Ct., U.S. Ct. Vets. Appeals. Law clk. Okla. Ct. Appeals, Oklahoma City, 1987-89; counsel Centurion Oil, Inc., Oklahoma City, 1989-93; atty., mem. Legg Law Firm, LLC, Frederick, Md., 1994—; bd. dirs. Religious Coalition for Emergency Human Needs. Mem. Nat. Assn. Consumer Bankruptcy Attys., Frederick County Bar Assn., Bankruptcy Bar Dist. Md. Office: Legg Law Firm LLC 5500 Buckeystown Pike Frederick MD 21703-8331

BORISOV, ALEXANDER ILYICH, priest; b. Moscow, Oct. 13, 1939; s. Ilyia Afanasievitch Blokhin and Daria Sergeevna Zaytceva; m. Nonna Ivanovna Borisova, Dec. 17, 1960; twins: Vera and Maria. Diploma, State Pedagogical Inst., 1964; Candidate Biol. Scis., 1969; grad., Theol. Sem., Moscow, 1973; Candidate Theology, Theol. Acad., Moscow, 1978. Scientist, rschr. Acad. Scis. of the USSR, Moscow, 1965-72; deacon The Sign of our Lady Ch., Moscow, 1973-89, priest, 1989-91; head priest Ch. of St. Cosmas and Damian, Moscow, 1991—. Author: The Ripen Fields, 1994; translator: Gene Activity in Early Development, 1972, Evolution by Gene Duplication, 1973, Life After Life, 1991. Dep. Moscow City Coun., 1990-93. Mem. Bible Soc. Russia (pres. 1991—), Commn. for Mercy (pres. 1992—). Home: Vishniakovsky per d 27 kv44, 109017 Moscow Russia Office: Bible Soc Russia Box 403, 51/14 Pyatnitskaya ul, 109017 Moscow Russia

BORISOV, VASILII PETROVICH, science historian; b. Oryol, Russia, Mar. 6, 1937; s. Petr Alexandrovich and Vera Vladimirovna (Govorova) B.; m. Svetlana Arkadievna Alimova, Jan. 28, 1961 (div. June 1992); 1 child, Maxim Vasilievich. Engr., State Tech. U., Moscow, 1961; PhD, Inst. History of Sci. & Tech., Moscow, 1966; sr. rschr., Rsch. Inst. Vacuum Tech., Moscow, 1980. Engr. Krasnaya Zwezda, Moscow, 1961-63; postgrad. rschr. Inst. History of Sci. & Tech., Moscow, 1963-67; chief of lab., chief of dept. Rsch. Inst. Vacuum Tech., Moscow, 1967-90; chief of dept. Inst. of History of Sci. & Tech., Moscow, 1990—; fellow of coun. Coun. on Cultural Heritage, Russian Acad. Scis., 1994—, fellow sci. coun. on history of tech., 1990—. Author: (book) Serguei A. Vekshinksy, 1988; author, editor: (Books) Russian Scientists and Engineers in the Emigration, 1993 (diploma Russian Acad. Scis. 1993), Modern Radio and Electronics (1950s-80s), 1993 (diploma Russian Acad. Scis. 1993); editor: (book) Russia Abroad: A Golden Book of the Russian Emigration, 1997; fellow editl. bd. Priroda, 1999—. Pres. Russian Squash Fedn. Recipient medal Exhbn. of Nat. Econ. Achievements, 1982. Mem. Russian Soc. Historians of Sci. and Tech. (fellow of presidium 1992—), Russian Soc. for Radio, Electronics and Comm. (fellow of coun. 1991—). Home: 2d Spasonalivkovski 16 kv61, 117049 Moscow Russia Office: Inst History of Sci, 1/5 Staropanski per, 103012 Moscow Russia

BORISOV, VICTOR VASIL'EVICH, physicist, researcher; b. St. Petersburg, Russia, Oct. 31, 1937; s. Vasiliy Nikolayevich Borisov and Anastasiya Yakovlevna Demenkova; 1 child, Marina Victorovna. Diploma in physics, St. Petersburg State U., 1961, PhD in Physics, 1971, DSc, 1987. Sr. rschr. St. Petersburg U., 1984-92, leading rschr., 1992—. Author: Nonsteady-State Electromagnetic Waves, 1987, Nonsteady-State Fields in Waveguides, 1991, Electromagnetic Fields of Transient Currents, 1996. Mem. N.Y. Acad. Scis., Russian Geog. Soc. Home: Vvedenskaya str 7, apt. 34, 197198 St Petersburg Russia Office: Inst Physics State U, Ulyanovskaya 1, 198904 St Petersburg Russia

BORISYUK, ANDRIY OLEXANDROVYCH, mechanical engineer, researcher; b. Kiev, Ukraine, Jan. 6, 1965; s. Olexandr Ivanovych and Rajisa Apolinarivna Borisyuk. Diploma in mechs. with honors, Kiev (Ukraine) State U., 1989; PhD, Inst. Hydromechs., Kiev, 1993. Engr. Inst. Hydromechs., Kiev, 1989, jr. rsch. fellow, 1992-93, rsch. fellow, asst. prof., 1993-97, assoc. prof., 1997—. Rsch. grantee Nat. Acad. Scis. Ukraine, 1995, 96, Alexander von Humboldt Found., 1997, 98, Consorzio per lo Sviluppo Interat. dell'Univ. Degli Studi di Trieste, Italy, 2000. Mem. European Mechs. Soc. E-mail: oibor@nas.gov.ua. Fax: 380-44-455-6432. Home: Semashko St 21 88, 03142 Kiev Ukraine Office: Inst Hydromechs, Zhelyabova St 8/4, 03680 Kiev 180 MSP Ukraine

BORJAS, GEORGE J(ESUS), economics educator; b. Havana, Cuba, Oct. 15, 1950; came to U.S., 1962; s. Juan V. Borjas and Edita F. Diaz; m. Jane Maureen Walsh, Nov. 11, 1989; children: Sarah Jane Irene, Timothy Jorge, Rebecca Kathryn. BS, St. Peter's Coll., Jersey City, 1971; MA, M in Philosophy, PhD, Columbia U., 1975. Asst. prof. Queens Coll., Flushing, N.Y., 1975-77; research assoc. Nat. Bur. Econ. Research, Cambridge, Mass., 1983—; prof. econs. U. Calif., Santa Barbara, 1978-90, San Diego, 1990-95; prof. pub. policy Kennedy Sch. Govt., Harvard U., Cambridge, Mass., 1995-97; Pferzheimer prof. pub. policy Kennedy Sch. Govt., Harvard U., Cambridge, 1998—; cons. Unicon Rsch. Corp., Santa Monica, Calif., 1982-94; econs. adv. panel NSF, 1988-90; mem. Gov.'s Coun. of Econ. Advisers, 1993-98. Author: Wage Policy in the Federal Bureaucracy, 1980, International Differences in the Labor Market Performance of Immigrants, 1988, Friends or Strangers: The Impact of Immigrants on the U.S. Economy, 1990, Labor Economics, 1995, Heaven's Door: Immigration Policy and the American Economy, 1999; editor: Hispanics in the United States, 1985, Immigration and the Work Force: Economic Consequences for the United States and Source Areas, 1992, Issues in the Economics of Immigration, 2000, Rev. of Econs. and Statistics, 1998—; mem. editl. bd. Quar. Jour. Econs., 1992-98, Internat. Migration Rev., 1992—, Review of Economics and Statistics, 1997-98; contbr. articles to profl. jours. Fellow Columbia U. Alumni Fund, 1973, NIMH, U. Chgo., 1977; grantee Rockefeller Found., 1983-85, Sloan Found., 1986-93, NSF, 1986—, Russell Sage Found., 1991-93; vis. scholar Harvard U., 1988-89. Fellow Econometric Soc.; mem. NAS (panel 1984-85, 95-97, Estrada fellow in immigration studies 2000), Am. Econ. Assn., Soc. Labor Econs., Assn. for Pub. Policy Analysis and Mgmt. (exec. coun. 2000-2005). Roman Catholic. Office: Kennedy Sch Govt Harvard U 79 Jfk St Cambridge MA 02138-5801

BORKERT, CLOVIS MANUEL, soil scientist, research agronomist; b. Porto Alegre, Brazil, June 17, 1942; s. Arlindo and Eli Eronia (Hagewiesche) B.; m. Jussara Teresinha Jacques, July 24, 1971; 1 child, Shandra de Cassia Jacques Borkert. BS in Agronomy, U. Fed. do Rio Grande do Sul, Porto Alegre, 1968, MS in Soils, 1973; PhD in Agronomy, Purdue U., 1983. Rsch. agronomist Ministry of Agr., Passo Fundo, Brazil, 1970-75; asst. prof. U. Passo Fundo, 1970-75; rsch. agronomist EMBRAPA Soja, Londrina, Brazil, 1975—; prof. soil sci. U. Estadual de Londrina, Brazil, 1995—. Editor: Enxofre e Micronutrientes na Agricultura Brasileira, 1988; contbr. chpt. to book, articles to profl. jours. 1st lt. Brazilian Army, 1964-65. Mem. Brazilian Soc. Soil Sci., Am. Soc. Agronomy, Soil Sci. Soc. Am., Internat. Soil Sci. Soc., Gamma Sigma Delta. Baptist. Avocations: reading, listening to music, jogging, beach resort vacations. Home: Rua Santos 1000 Apt 1202, 86020-021 Londrina Parana, Brazil Office: EMBRAPA-Soja, Caixa Postal 231, 86001-970 Londrina Parana, Brazil

BORKOVIĆ, IVO, law educator; b. Sinj, Croatia, Jan. 30, 1933; s. Filip and Roza (Matanović) B.; m. Ivanka Marunčić, Apr. 25, 1970; 1 child, Filip. Dipl., Sch. Econs. Makarska, 1954; LLB, Faculty Law Belgrade, 1959; LLD, Faculty Law Zagreb, 1965. Sec. Municipality Makarska, Croatia, 1959-62; lectr., asst. prof., assoc. prof. Faculty Law Split, Croatia, 1962-77; prof. Faculty Law Split, 1977—; mem. presidency Croatian Law Ctr.; counselor Constnl. Ct., Republic of Croatia. Author: Maritime Demesne, 1979, Administrative Law, 1st edit., 1982, 6th edit., 1997, (State

award for Sci., 1984), Procedure and Techniques of Drafting Legal Rules, 1982, Nomotehnics, 1995. Expert for pub. adminstrn. OUN, N.Y., 1970—; mem. presidency Inst. for Human Rights, Novi Vinodolski, 1996—. Hon. citizen City of Indpls., 1983. Mem. Adminstrv. Law Assn. Avocations: hunting, fishing. Home: Starčevićeva 17, 21000 Split Croatia Office: Faculty of Law, Domovinskog rata 8, 21000 Split Croatia

BORLAND, RAYMOND M., researcher; b. Chester, Pa., Nov. 23, 1948; s. Raymond Milton Jr. and Eleanor D. Borland; m. Joanne Yonkondy, 1977 (div. 1980). BS in Biology, St. Joseph's Coll., Phila., 1969; PhD in Developmental Biology, U. Del., 1974; MD, Harvard U., 1980. Postdoctoral fellow Harvard Med. Sch., Boston, 1974-77; asst. dir. clin. rsch. ICI Ams., Wilmington, Del., 1983-84; assoc. dir. clin. rsch. DuPont Pharm. Co., Du-Pont/Merck Pharm. Co., Wilmington, 1984-93; self-employed rschr., 1993—. Contbr. articles to profl. jours. Mem. SAR (v.p., surgeon gen. Kirkwood chpt. 1998-2000). Home and Office: 695 Colora Rd Colora MD 21917-1121

BORLAUG, NORMAN ERNEST, agricultural scientist; b. Cresco, Iowa, Mar. 25, 1914; s. Henry O. and Clara (Vaala) B.; m. Margaret G. Gibson, Sept. 24, 1937; children: Norma Jean (Mrs. Richard H. Rhoda), William Gibson. BS in Forestry, U. Minnesota, Minneapolis, 1937, MS in Plant Pathology, 1940, PhD in Plant Pathology, 1941; ScD (honoris causa), Punjab (India) Agrl. U., 1969, Kanpur U., India, Royal Norwegian Agrl. Coll., Luther Coll., 1970, Michigan State U., U. de la Plata, Argentina, Uttar Pradesh Agrl. U., India, 1971; Sc.D. (honoris causa), U. Arizona, Phoenix, 1972, U. Florida, 1973, U. Católica de Chile, 1974, U. Hohenheim, Germany, 1976, U. Agr., Lyallpur, Faisalabad, Pakistan, 1978, Columbia U., N.Y.C., 1980, Ohio State U., Columbus, 1981, U. Minnesota, Minneapolis, 1982, U. Notre Dame, 1987, Oreg. State U., 1988, U. Tulsa, 1991; L.H.D., Gustavus Adolphus Coll., 1971, Iowa State U., 1992; LL.D. (hon.), New Mexico State U., 1973; D. of Agriculture (hon.), Tufts U., 1982; D. of Agricultural Sciences (hon.), U. Agricultural Sciences, Hungary, 1980, Tokyo U. Agriculture, 1981; D. Agricultural Sciences (hon.), U. Nacional Pedro Henriques Turena, Dominican Republic, U. Cen. del Estes, Dominican Republic, 1983; D. Honoris Causa, U. Mayor de San Simón, Bolivia, U. de Buenos Aires, 1983, U. de Cordoba, Spain, U. Politécnica de Catalunya, Barcelon, Spain, 1986, Colegio Postgraduadas, Mexico, 1990; Rector U. Dubuque, 1992-93; honoris causa, U. Studi de Bologna, Italy, 1991, Warsaw Agrl. U., Poland, 1993. With U.S. Forest Service, 1935-38; instr. U. Minn., 1941; microbiologist E.I. DuPont de Nemours, 1942-44; research scientist in charge wheat improvement Coop. Mexican Agrl. Program, Mexican Ministry Agr. Rockefeller Found., Mexico, 1944-60; assoc. dir. assigned to Inter-Am. Food Crop Program Rockefeller Found., 1960-63; dir. wheat research and prodn. program Internat. Maize and Wheat Improvement Ctr., Mexico City, 1964-79; cons. Internat. Maize and Wheat Improvement Ctr., 1980—; disting. prof. internat. agronomy Texas A&M Univ, College Station, Tex.; cons., collaborator Inst. Nacional de Investigationes Agricolas, Mexican Ministry Agr., 1960-64; cons. FAO, North Africa and Asia, 1960; ex-officio cons. wheat research and prodn. problems to govts. in Latin Am., Africa, Asia, 1960—; mem. Citizen's Commn. on Sci., Law and Food Supply, 1973, Commn. Critical Choices for Am., 1973, Council Agr. Sci. and Tech., 1973—, Presdl. Commn. on World Hunger U.S.A., 1978-79, Presdl. Coun. Advisers Sci and Tech., 1990-93; dir. Population Crisis Com., 1971-92; asesor especial Fundacion para Estudios de la Poblacion A.C., Mexico, 1971-80; mem. adv. council Renewable Natural Resources Found., 1973; A.D. White Disting. prof.-at-large Cornell U., 1983-85; Disting. prof. Internat. Agr., Dept. Soil & Crop Scis., Tex. A&M U., Jan.-May, 1984—; adj. prof. dept. biology Emory U., Atlanta, 1991-92; advisor The Population Inst., U.S.A., 1978; bd. trustees Winrock Internat. U.S.A.; life fellow Rockefeller Found., 1983—. Recipient Disting. Service awards Wheat Producers Assns., and state govts. Mexican States of Guanajuato, Queretaro, Sonora, Tlaxcala and Zacatecas, 1954-60; Recognition award Agrl. Inst. Can., 1966; Recognition award Instituto Nacional de Tecnologia Agropecuaria de Marcos Juarez, Argentina, 1968; Sci. Service award El Colegio de Ingenieros Agronomos de Mexico, 1970; Outstanding Achievement award U. Minn., 1959; E.C. Stakman award, 1961; named Uncle of Paul Bunyan, 1969; recipient Disting. Citizen award Cresco Centennial Com., 1966; Nat. Disting. Service award Am. Agrl. Editors Assn., 1967; Genetics and Plant Breeding award Nat. Council Comml. Plant Breeders, 1968; Star of Distinction Govt. of Pakistan, 1968; citation and street named in honor Citizens of Sonora and Rotary Club, 1968; Internat. Agronomy award Am. Soc. Agronomy, 1968; Distinguished Service award Wheat Farmers of Punjab, Haryana and Himachal Pradesh, 1969; Nobel Peace prize, 1970; Diploma de Merito El Instituto Tecnologico y de Estudios Superiores de Monterrey, Mexico, 1971; medalla y Diploma de Merito Antonio Narro Escuela Superior de Agricultura de la U. de Coahuila, Mexico, 1971; Diploma de Merito Escuela Superior de Agricultura Hermanos Escobar, Mexico, 1973; award for service to agr. Am. Farm Bur. Fedn., 1971; Outstanding Agrl. Achievement award World Farm Found., 1971; Medal of Merit Italian Wheat Scientists, 1971; Service award for outstanding contbn. to alleviation of world hunger 8th Latin Am. Food Prodn. Conf., 1972; Nat. award for Agrl. Excellence in Sci. Nat. Agri-Mktg. Assn., 1982, Disting. Achievement award Council for Agrl. Scis. and Tech., 1982; inaugural lectr., medal recipient Dr. S.B. Hendrick's Meml. Lectureship., 1981, other honored lecturships; named to Halls of Fame Oreg. State U. Agrl., 1981, Agrl. Nat. Ctr., Bonner Springs, Kans., 1984, Scandinavian-Am., U.S.A., 1986, Nat. Wrestling, 1992; dedicated in his name Norman E. Borlaug Centro de Capitación y Formación de Agrs., Santa Cruz, Bolivia, 1983, Borlaug Hall U. Minn., 1985, Borlaug Bldg. Internat. Maize and Wheat Improvement Ctr., 1986; numerous other honors and awards from govts., ednl. instns., citizens groups. Hon. fellow Indian Soc. Genetics and Plant Breeding; mem. Nat. Acad. Sci., Am. Soc. Agronomy (1st Internat. Service award 1960, 1st hon. life mem.), Am. Assn. Cereal Chemists (hon. life mem., Meritorious Service award 1969), Crop Sci. Soc. Am. (hon. life mem.), Soil Sci. Soc. Am. (hon. life mem.), Sociedad de Agronomia do Rio Grande do Sul Brazil (hon.), India Nat. Sci. Acad. (fgn.), Royal Agrl. Soc. Eng. (hon.), Royal Soc. Edinburgh (hon.), Hungarian Acad. Sci. (hon.), Royal Swedish Acad. Agr. and Forestry (fgn.), Academia Nacional de Agronomia y Veterinaria (Argentina), Sasakaws African Assn. (pres. 1986—); hon. academician N.I. Vavilov Acad. Agrl. Scis. Lenin Order (USSR.), Am. Council on Sci. and Health (trustee 1978—), Internat. Food Policy Research Inst. (trustee 1976-82), Royal Soc. Eng., Chinese Acad. Agrl. Scis., 1994. Home: 15611 Ranchita Dr Dallas TX 75248-4982 Office: Tex A&M U 2474 Tamu Dept Soil & Crop Science College Station TX 77843-2474

BORLETTI, MAURIZIO, metals company executive; b. Milan, Italy, June 6, 1967; s. Ferdinando and Rosalinda (Bettoja) B. Student, Sir James Henderson Sch., Milan; D Econs., Luigi Bocconi U., Milan; degree (hon.), Internat. Sch., London. CEO Migri SRL, Milan, 1985—; COO Fin Promotion SRL, Milan, 1986—; pres., CEO Christofle and subs. cos., Paris, 1993—; chmn. Christofle Silver Inc., N.Y., 1993-99, Luxury Brand Devel. SA, Gland, Switzerland, 1999—. mem. indsl. rels. commn. Assolombarda, Milan, 1989—; mem. indsl. rels. com. Confindustria, Milan, 1989-91. V.p. indsl. rels. Young Mgrs. Assn., Milan, 1989-91. Office: Orfevrerie Christofle, Luxury Brand Development, Route des Avouillons 30, 1196 Gland Switzerland

BORMAN, EDWIN MILES, anesthetist consultant; b. Port Elizabeth, Republic of South Africa, Sept. 9, 1961; arrived in Eng., 1986; s. David Bevil and Sophia (Miller) B. MB, BChir with honors, U. Cape Town, South Africa, 1984. House officer Groote Schuur Hosp., Cape Town, 1985; sr. house officer in surgery Plymouth (Eng.) Health Authority, 1986-89, sr. house officer in anesthetics, 1989-91; registrar in anesthetics Queen Elizabeth Hosp., Birmingham, Eng., 1991-95; sr. registrar in anesthetics Walsgrave Hosps., Coventry, Eng., 1995-97; cons. anesthetist Walsgrave Hosps., Coventry, 1997—; U.K. rep. to European Union Med. Specialists, 1998—; mem. Ministerial Working Group on Working Hours; chief med. officer's working group on splst. tng., overseas drs., 1992-94. Contbr. papers to jours. in field. Fellow Royal Coll. Anesthesiologists, Royal Coll. Surgeons in Ireland; mem. Brit. Med. Assn. (jr. drs. com. 1989—, chmn. 1991-94, coun. 1991—, chmn. internat. com. 1999—), Gen. Med. Coun. U.K. (coun. mem. 1994—), European Bd. Anesthesiology (Brit. rep.). Avocations: Oriental art, classical music, Renaissance painting. E-mail: edwin@borman.demon.co.uk. Home: 30 Clover Dr, Birmingham B32 3DJ, England Office: Walsgrave Hosps NHS Trust, Clifford Bridge Rd, Coventry CV2 2DX, England

BORMAN, FRANK, former astronaut, laser patent company executive; b. Gary, Ind., Mar. 14, 1928; s. Edwin Borman; m. Susan Bugbee; children: Fredrick, Edwin. B.S., U.S. Mil. Acad., 1950; M. Aero. Engring., Calif. Inst. Tech., 1957; grad., USAF Aerospace Research Pilots Sch., 1960, Advanced Mgmt. Program, Harvard Bus. Sch., 1970. Commd. 2d lt. USAF, advanced through grades to col., 1965, ret., 1970; assigned various fighter squadrons U.S. and Philippines, 1951-56; instr. thermodynamics and fluid mechanics U.S. Mil. Acad., 1957-60; dir. Continental Airlines Holdings Inc. (formerly Tex. Air Corp.), Houston, 1992—; instr. USAF Aerospace Research Pilots Sch., 1960-62; astronaut Manned Spacecraft Ctr., NASA, until 1970; command pilot on 14 day orbital Gemini 7 flight, Dec. 1965, including rendezvous with Gemini 6; command pilot Apollo 8, 1st lunar orbital mission, Dec. 1968; sr. v.p. for ops. Eastern Air Lines, Inc., Miami, Fla., 1970-74, exec. v.p., gen. operations mgr., 1974-75, pres., chief exec. officer, 1975-85, chief exec. officer, 1975-86, chmn. bd., 1976-86; vice chmn., dir. Tex. Air Corp., Houston, 1986-92; chmn., CEO, dir. Patlex Corp., Las Cruces, N.Mex., 1992—; chmn. bd. Autofinance Group, Inc., Westmont, Ill.; Chm of Bd of Dir DBT OnLine Inc., Fort Lauderdale, FL, 1996-present; bd. dirs. Continental Airlines, Home Depot, Outboard Marine Corp. Recipient Disting. Svc. award NASA, 1965, Collier trophy Nat. Aeros. Assn., 1968, Congl. Space Medal of Honor, Harmon Internat. Aviation trophy. Office: Patlex Corp 745 Leonard Bryran Alley Las Cruces NM 88005 also: Autofinance Group Inc Ste 350 Oakmont Cir 1 601 Oakmont Ln Westmont IL 60559-5549

BORMONTOV, EVGENY NIKOLAEVICH, physicist, consultant; b. Olhovatka, Voronezh, Russia, June 24, 1951; s. Nikolay Alexandrovich and Anna Andreyevna (Krasnorutskaya) B.; m. Galina Alexeyevna Bondarenko, Sept. 15, 1973; children: Irina, Alexander. Diploma, Voronezh State U., 1973, candidate phys. and math. sci., 1983. Engr. Voronezh State U., 1973-82, asst., 1983-89, docent, 1989—; cons. Electronika, Yoronezh, 1989—. Contbr. articles to profl. jours. Grantee Russian Minisry Edn., Moscow, 1992, 94, 96. Avocation: chess. Home: Mayskaya St IIa, 394083 Voronezh Russia Office: Voronezh State U, Universitetskaya Sq I, 394693 Voronezh Russia

BORN, BROOKSLEY ELIZABETH, lawyer; b. San Francisco, Aug. 27, 1940; d. Ronald Henry and Mary Ellen (Bortner) B.; m. Alexander Elliot Bennett, Oct. 9, 1982; children: Nicholas Jacob Landau, Ariel Elizabeth Landau, Andrew E. Bennett, Laura F. Bennett, Peter J. Bennett. AB, Stanford U., 1961, JD, 1964. Bar: D.C. 1966. Law clk. U.S. Ct. Appeals, Washington, 1964-65; legal rschr. Harvard Law Sch., 1967-68; assoc. Arnold and Porter, Washington, 1965-67, 68-73, ptnr., 1974-96, 99—; chair U.S. Commodity Futures Trading Commn., Washington, 1996-99; lectr. law Columbus Sch. Law, Cath. U. Am., 1972-74; adj. prof. Georgetown U. Law Center, Washington, 1972-73. Pres. Stanford Law Rev, 1963-64. Chair bd. visitors Stanford Law Sch., 1987; bd. dirs. Nat. Legal Aid and Defenders Assn., 1972-79, Washington Legal Clinic for Homeless, 1993-96, Lawyers Com. for Civil Rights Under Law, 1993-96, Am. Bar Found., 1989-99, Washington Lawyers Com. for Civil Rights and Urban Affairs, 1992-96, Nat. Women's Law Ctr., 1981—; trustee Ctr. for Law and Social Policy, Washington, 1977-96, Women's Bar Found., 1981-86. Mem. ABA (chair sect. ind. rights and responsibilities 1977-78, chair fed. judiciary com. 1980-83, chair consortium on legal svcs. and the pub. 1987-90, bd. govs. 1990-93, chair resource devel. coun. 1993-95, chair coun. Fund for Justice and Edn. 1995-96, state del. from D.C. 1994—), D.C. Bar (sec. 1975-76, mem. bd. govs. 1976-79), Am. Law Inst., Southwestern Legal Found. (trustee 1993-96), Order of Coif. Office: Arnold & Porter 555 12th St NW Washington DC 20004-1206

BORN, GUNTHARD KARL, aerospace executive; b. Marienwerder, Germany, Mar. 31, 1935; s. Karl A. and Elise (Kuczewski) B.; m. Gertraud A. Forstner, Dec. 17, 1963. Diploma in physics, Tech. U. Munich, 1961; DEng, Tech. U. Stuttgart, Fed. Republic of Germany, 1967. Researcher Beckman Instruments, Munich, 1961-63, U.S. Army Electronics Command, Ft. Monmouth, N.J., 1963-69; div. head Messerschmitt-Bolkow-Blohm, Munich, 1969-93, tech. dir. high-energy laser rsch. program, 1980-93; presenter European, Asian, African, U.S. tours on lasers and musicology Goethe Inst. Fed. Republic of Germany, Munich, 1972—. Author: Mozarts Musiksprache, 1985; inventor in field of linguistics, numerous in fields of lasers and electrooptics; contbr. numerous articles to sci. and tech. publs. Avocation: travel. Home: Donarweg 22, D-81739 Munich Germany

BORN, GUSTAV VICTOR RUDOLF, medical researcher; b. Göttingen, Germany, July 29, 1921; arrived in U.K., 1933; s. Max and Hedwig (Ehrenberg) B.; m. Ann Plowden-Wardlaw, 1950 (div. 1960); children: Max, Sebastian, Georgina; m. Faith Elizabeth Maurice-Williams, Dec. 8, 1962; children: Carey, Mattew. BM BCh, Edinburgh Med. Sch., 1943; MA, Oxford (Eng.) U., 1951; MD (hon.), U. Münster, 1980, U. Leuven, 1981, U. Edinburgh, 1982, U. München, 1989, Brown U., 1987; DSc, U. Bordeaux, 1999, U. Paris, Loyola U., Chgo., 1995, U. Paris, 1987. Vandervell Prof. Pharmacology Royal Coll. Surgeons, 1960-73; Sheild Prof. Pharmacology Cambridge (Eng.) U., 1973-78; prof. pharmacology King's Coll. London U., 1978-86, prof. emeritus, 1986—; rsch. dir. William Harvey Rsch. Inst., London, 1986—; former prof. Fondation de France; hon. fellow St. Peter's Coll., Oxford; fellow King's Coll., London. Decorated chevalier de l'Ordre Nat. du Mérite; recipient medals U. Göttingen, 1979, U. Graz, 1984, Royal medal, Paul Moravitz prize, 1980, Robert-Pfleger prize, 1990, Alexander von Humboldt prize, 1994, Sr. Internat. Aspirin award, 1995, Fahraeus medal, 2000. Fellow Royal Soc., Royal Coll. Physicians; mem. N.Y. Acad. Scis. (hon.), Ehrenmitglied der Gesellschaft für Forschritte in der Inneren Medizin, Leopoldina, Rheinisch-Westfälische Acad., Club of Rome (hon.). Office: William Harvey Rsch Inst, Charterhouse Sq, London EC1M 6BQ, England

BORN, ROBERT HEYWOOD, consulting civil engineer; b. L.A., Nov. 7, 1925; s. Robert Bogle and Mignon Mary (Heywood) B.; m. Marilyn Alice Simpson, Aug. 15, 1947; 1 child, Stefanie Born. Student, Stanford U., 1943; BE, U. So. Calif., 1949, MSCE, 1956. Registered civil engineer Calif., Ariz., Nev., Utah, Tenn., Guam; registered agriculture engr. Calif. Assoc. hydraulic engr. Calif. Dept. of Water Resources, L.A., 1949-58; chief engr., county hydraulic engr. County Flood Control/Water Conservation Dist., San Luis Obispo, Calif., 1958-70; dir., exec. v.p., regional mgr. Camp, Dresser & McKee, Inc., Pasadena, Calif., 1970-78; v.p., regional mgr. Born, Barrett & Assoc./Barrett Cons. Group, Newport Beach, Calif., 1978-86, Memphis, 1978-86; prin. Robert H. Born Cons. Engrs., Memphis, 1986—, Irvine, Laguna Niguel, Calif., 1986—, Asheville, N.C., 1997—. Chmn. World Affairs Coun., San Luis Obispo, 1965. 1st lt. U.S. Army, 1943-47. Decorated Bronze star medal, 1944. Fellow ASCE (life, Engr. of Merit 1994); mem. Am. Water Works Assn. (com. chmn.), U.S. Com. on Large Dams, Am. Pub. Works Assn. (cert. outstanding pub. works achievement 1969, Floodplain Mgmt. Assn. Calif. Democrat. Presbyterian. Avocations: historical research, travel. Office: Robert H Born Cons Engrs 15 Little Cedar Ct Asheville NC 28805-2487

BORNE, PIERRE EMILE, mathematics and computer science educator; b. Corbeil, France, June 3, 1944; s. Paul Claude and Gisele Emelie (Besancenot) B.; m. Marguerite Jacqueline Plane, July 2, 1966; children: Olivier, Francois, Helene, Claire. MS, U. Lille, France, 1968, PhD, 1970, DS, 1976; PhD (hon.), nat. Inst. Math. and Elec., Moscow, 1999. Assoc. prof. U. Lille, 1969-79; assoc. prof. Inst. Industriel du Nord, Lille, 1979-81, prof., 1981-91; prof. automatic control Ecole Centrale de Lille, 1991—; invited prof. Ain Chock U., Casablanca, Morocco, 1986-92, Ecole Nationale d'Ingenieurs de Tunis, Tunisia, 1979-89, Tianjin (China) U., 1996—, Ecole Polytechnique de Tunisie, Tunis, 1997—. Editor: (series) Methodes et Pratiques de L'Ingenieur, 1990—; contbr. over 260 articles to profl. jours. and author of 14 books. Recipient Kulman prize, 1994, Russian Acad. Non-Linear Scis. fellow, 1996. Fellow IEEE (Contbn. award 1996, Svc. award 1998, Norbert Wiener prize 1998, Third Millenium medal 2000, sys. man and cybernetics pres, 2000—); mem. Internat. Assn. Math. and Computer Simulation, French Soc. Electriciens et Electroniciens (v.p.). Avocations: sports, dancing. Fax: 33 3 20 33 54 99. E-mail: p.borne@ec-lille.fr. Office: EC Lille, Bd Paul Langevin BP 48, F 59651 Villeneuve d'Ascq France

BORNEAS, MARIUS, physics educator; b. Sannicolaul, Romania, Feb. 16, 1921; s. Iulian Livius and Viorica (Oprean) B.; m. Otilia Voiticeanu, Dec. 22, 1956. Engr., Poly. U., Timisoara, Romania, 1946, Doctor, 1968. Asst. Poly. U., 1946-48, lectr. physics, 1948-51, dep. prof., 1951-69, prof., 1969—, head dept. physics, 1967-76, dean Faculty Physics and Chemistry, 1967-68; head dept. physics Pedagogic Inst., Timisoara, 1963-68. Author and co-author 12 books, also over 100 papers to sci. jours. Mem. Soc. Advancement of Physics, Romania Soc. Physics. Home: Str Zborului N 1 Sc C Ap 4, 1900 Timisoara Timis, Romania

BORNHARDT, CRISTIAN, chemical engineer, environmental engineering educator; b. Mulchén, Chile, Jan. 4, 1955; s. Klaus and Agnes (Brachmann) B.; m. Ruth Schürch, Jan. 7, 1978; children: Stephanie, Tanja. Degree in Chem. Engring., U. Concepción, Chile, 1979, MSc in Chem. Engring., 1981; D in Engring., Tech U., Berlin, 1996. Assoc. prof. U. de La Serena, Chile, 1984-88, U. de La Frontera, Temuco, Chile, 1988—; planning dir. U. de La Frontera, Temuco, 1997-99; initiator first formal program in environ. engring. in Chile, 1992; rsch. asst. Tech. U., Berlin, 1993-95. Author: Untersuchungen zur Entfernung von HOV durch Pulverkohlen, 1997. Recipient scholarship German Acad. Exch. Svc., 1981-83. Mem. Assn. Interamericana de Ingenieria Sanitaria y Ambiental, Internat. Water Assn. Office: U de La Frontera, Av Francisco Salazar, 01145 Temuco Chile

BORNMANN, WILLIAM GERARD, organic chemist; b. Bklyn., Nov. 16, 1951; s. William Gustof and Martha (Windolf) B.; m. Daria Rae Luth, June 19, 1976. BS, U. Wis., 1975; MS, Mont. State U., 1978; PhD, U. Vt., 1988. Postdoctoral fellow U. Vt., Burlington, 1988-91; lab. mgr. Lab. Bio-Organic Chemistry Meml. Sloan-Kettering Cancer Ctr., N.Y., 1991-93, head preparative synthesis core facility, 1993—. Contbr. 25 papers, articles to profl. jours. Mem. AAAS, Am. Chem. Soc., Internat. Soc. Heterocyclic Chemistry, Am. Assn. Pharm. Scientists, Am. Inst. Chemists, Am. Assn. Cancer Rsch., Soc. Medicinal Plant Rsch., Am. Soc. Pharmacognosy, N.Y. Acad. Scis., Royal Soc. Chemistry, Sigma Xi. Achievements include rsch. in the total synthesis of oxo-tabersonine, cephalotaxine, camptothecin, vindoline, catharanthine, tabersonine, vincadifformine and taxol as well as in enantioselective syntheses of vinblastine, leurosidine, vincovaline, organic chemistry. Office: Meml Sloan Kettering Cancer Ctr Preparative Synthesis Core Facility 1275 York Ave # 93 New York NY 10021-6094

BORNS, ROBERT AARON, real estate developer; b. Gary, Ind., Oct. 24, 1935; s. Irving Jonah and Sylvia (Mackoff) B.; m. Sandra Solotkin, Mar. 30, 1958; children: Stephanie, Elizabeth, Emily. BS, Ind. U., 1957; hon. degree, U. indpls., 1987. Account exec. Reynolds & Co., Chgo., 1957-59, Francis I duPont co., Indpls., 1960; owner, operator Borns & Co., Indpls., 1960-63; chmn. Borns Mgmt. Corp., Indpls., 1963—, Correctional Mgmt. Co., L.L.C., 1996—; bd. dirs. Artistic Media Ptnrs. L.L.C., Indpls. Power and Light Co., Mid Am. Capital Resources Corp., Standard Mgmt. Corp., IPALCO Enterprises. Bd. dirs. Indpls. Mus. of Art, Indpls. Symphony Orch., Ind. U. Found.; mem. bd. visitors Borns Jewish Studies Program, Ind. U.; past bd. dirs. Indpls. Children's Mus., I.W.C. Resources Corp., Indpls. Water Co.; past trustee St. Vincent's Hosp., mem. adv. bd.; past trustee St. Vincent's Hosp. Found. Recipient Enterprise award Indpls. Bus. Jour., 1982, Peace award State of Israel, 1979. Mem. Confrerie des Chevaliers du Tastevin, Econ. Club (bd. dirs.), Thunderbird Country Club (Rancho Mirage, Calif.). Office: Borns Mgmt Corp 21 Beachway Dr Indianapolis IN 46224-8566

BORNSTEIN, LAURA LEE, artist; b. Cleve., Nov. 9, 1948; d. Andrew Clark Lee and Beatrice Laura (Barna) Robinson; m. Miguel Andres Bornstein, Apr. 16, 1983; children: Michael Andrew, Nicolas Lee, Isabel. BFA, Miami U., Oxford, Ohio, 1970. Designer Avon Cosmetics, Liancour, France, 1970-72; ptnr., designer Harbinger Studio, Aspen, Colo., 1972-74; freelance graphic designer Los Angeles, 1974-80; art dir. ABC Leisure mags., N.Y.C., 1980-84; freelance artist, painter, book designer Buenos Aires, 1984—. Co-author: Amanantando a Su/Bebe & Alimentando a Su Hison, 1995. Home: Terrero 2238, San Isidro Argentina

BORNSTEIN, RITA, academic administrator; b. N.Y.C., Jan. 2, 1936; d. Carl and Florence (Gates) Kropf; children: Rachel, Mark, Per; m. Harland G. Bloland. BA in English, Fla. Atlantic U., 1970, MA in English, 1971; PhD in Ednl. Leadership and Instrn., U. Miami, 1975. Tchr., adminstr. Dade County Pub. Schs., Fla., 1971-75; adminstr. dept. edn. U. Miami, Coral Gables, 1975-81, adminstr. divsn. of devel., 1981-85, v.p., 1985-90; pres. Rollins Coll., Winter Park, Fla., 1990—; bd. dirs. Barnett Banks Ctrl. Fla., 1990-98, Barnett Banks, Inc., 1991-98, dir. emeritus, 1998—, Tupperware Corp., 1997—, NationsBank Corp., 1998. Author: Freedom or Order: Must We Choose?, 1976; Title IX Compliance and Sex Equity: Definitions, Distinctions, Costs and Benefits, 1981; contbr. articles to profl. jours. Mem. Am. Coun. on Edn. (com. leadership devel. 1991-93, bd. dirs. 1995-98), Nat. Assn. Ind. Colls. and Univs. (bd. dirs. 1992-95, chair govt. rels. com. 1994-95), Fla. Coun. of 100, Associated Colls. of the South (bd. dirs. 1992—, treas. 1993-95, sec. 1995-97, vice chair 1997-99, chair 1999—), Ind. Colls. and Univs. Fla. (coun. pres. 1990—, chair 1997-98), So. Assn. Colls. and Schs. (commn. colls. 1998—, exec. coun. 1999—), Annapolis Group (exec. com. 1999—). Office: Rollins Coll Office of Pres 1000 Holt Ave # 2711 Winter Park FL 32789-4499

BORNTRAGER, JOHN SHERWOOD, principal; b. Oak Harbor, Wash., July 3, 1953; s. George H. and Norma E. Borntrager; m. Linda Diane, Aug. 30, 1975; children: Melissa, Shanna. BA, San Diego State U., 1975; MA, U. Ctrl. Ark., 1984. Cert. elem. educator, Ariz., Mo., Ark.; cert. prin., Mo., Ark. Tchr. Alhambra Pub. Schs., Phoenix, 1976-79; tchr., prin. Norfork (Ark.) Pub. Schs., 1979-87; prin. Cedarville (Ark) Pub. Schs., 1987—. Mem. ASCD, Ark. Edn. Assn., Ark. Christian Educators Assn., Ark. Assn. Elem. Sch. Prins., Phi Delta Kappa.

BOROCHOFF, IDA SLOAN, artist; b. July 29, 1922; d. Louis and Eva (Bistrick) Sloan; m. Charles Zachary Borochoff, Jan 11, 1942 (dec. July, 1990); children: Lynn Borochoff Gould, Jean Sue Borochoff Shapiro, Toby Ann Borochoff Bernstein, Lance Mark. Student, U. Ga., 1939-40, Ga. State U., 1940, Chgo. Sch. Interior Decorating, 1966, Allegro Sch. Ballet, Chgo., Atlanta Ballet, 1948-54, Emory U., 1971-72. Investor, owner real estate, 1941—; v.p. Designs Unltd., Inc., Atlanta, 1964—; pres. Sloan Borochoff Gallery, Atlanta, 1970—; art lectr. Met. Ednl. Svc.; art tchr. Ga. Inst. Tech., 1991; prodr. live talk health show on cable TV, Atlanta, 1983-87. One woman shows include Lovett Sch., 1972, 75, Ga. Inst. Tech., 1972, 75, Atlanta Mdse. Mart, Saginaw Art Mus., 1998-99; group shows include Gwinnett Art Mus., Duluth, Ga., 1999, Ind. U., 1999, Purdue U., Indpls., 1999; art rev. columnist Northside Neighbor Newspapers; columnist Around Ga. with Ida. Bd. dirs. Atlanta Ballet, 1950-57; bd. dirs. Atlanta Music Club, co-editor newsletter; hostess Atlanta Arts Festival; capt. Heart Fund, 1968-76, area chmn. dr.; elected to bd. dirs. Am. Cancer Rsch. Ctr. Atlanta chpt.; active various multi-media groups; artistic dir. Atlanta Playhouse Theatre, chmn., trustee; artistic dir. Little Miss Ga. Pageant, Little Mr. Dogwood Festival Pageant; judge 17th Internat. Dogwood Festival Art Show, 1989; mem. U.S. cong. adv. bd. Am. Security Coun., 1983—; archivist nat. oral history nat. Coun. Jewish Women, 1990—; Ga. dir., chairperson Levi Hosp. Art Auction, Hot Springs, Ark., 1993-94; with Archives Exhibit Atlanta Jewish Fedn., 1994; donor Borochoff Libr. of A.A. Synagogue; com. mem., patron AJCC Book Festival, 1995-96. Recipient several art awards including Caber award, 1984; named hon. alumnus Atlanta Art Inst., 1968, One of Ten Leading Ladies of Atlanta, J.C. Singles, 19876, honored by Barbara Bush, White House, Washington, 1989, 90; City grantee, 1985. Mem. Atlanta Press Club, Atlanta Writers Club (membership com.), Atlanta Artists Club, Atlanta Women's C. of C. (chmn. fine arts 1977-78), LVW, High Mus. Art, Ga. Writers Assn., Arts High Mus. (patron), Corcoran Gallery (patron), Nat. Mus. Women in Arts (charter mem.), Internat. Platform Assn., B'nai B'rith Women (pres. chpt. 1975, mem. S.E. regional bd.), Ga. Hist. Soc., AAUW, Women in the Arts, Jockey Club, Progressive Club, Capitol Hill Club (Washington). Home: 3450 Old Plantation Rd NW Atlanta GA 30327-2426 Office: 733 Glendale Rd Scottdale GA 30079-1409

BORODIN, LEV SERGEEVICH, geologist; b. Ekaterinburg, Ural, Russia, Feb. 6, 1927; s. Sergei Pavlovich and Maria Zacharovna Borodin; m. Irene Ivanovna Nazarenko, Jan. 27, 1957; children: Tatyana, Catherine. Engr., Geol. Prospecting Inst., Moscow, 1950; cand. sci., Russian Acad. Sci., 1955, DS, 1966. Rschr. Geol. Inst. Mineral. Geochem. Rare Elements, Moscow, 1950-60; lab. chief Inst. Mineralogy Geochem. Rare Elements, Moscow, 1960-67, dep. dir. Inst. Mineralogy, 1967-71, lab. chief Inst. Mineralogy,

1971-87, lab. chief Inst. Lithosphere, 1988-94; chief rschr. Inst. Lithosphere Russian Acad. Sci., Moscow, 1994—; cons. UN, India, 1968-69; expert Russian Found. Basic Rsch., 1995—. Author: (mem. editl. bd.) Geochemistry Mineralogy and Gen. Deposits Rare Elements, vol. 1-3, 1966, Geochemistry of Major Ser. Igneous Rocks, 1981, Petrochemistry of Magm. Series, 1987, Geochemical Evolution of Granitoids, 1993; mem. editl. bd. Jour. Geol. Ore Deposits, 1993—. Recipient Order of Red Banner of Labour, 1986, Medal for Achievements in Geol. Prospecting Ministry of Geology, 1977, Medal for Merits in Prospecting of Mineral Resources, 1982. Avocations: classical music, gardening. Home: Leninsky prospect 87-378, 117313 Moscow Russia Office: Russian Acad Sci Lithosp In, Staromonetnyi per 22, 109180 Moscow Russia

BORODIN, YURIY IVANOVISH, gynecologist, obstetrician; b. Urussu, Russia, Aug. 28, 1953; s. Ivan Stepanovish and Antonina Nikolaevna (Romanova) B.; children: Olga, Yuliya; m. Irina Lelevna Borodina, May 5, 1995. MD, Kazan (Russia) Med. U., 1976, specialization in ob-gyn., 1978. Head immunology lab. Rep. Clin. Hosp., Kazan, 1978-80; resident Kazan Med. U., 1976-78, asst. prof., 1982-95, head dept. ob-gyn., 1995—. Contbr. articles to med. jours. Mem. Am. Assn. Immunology and Reproduction, Internat. Assn. Immunology and Reproduction, N.Y. Acad. Scis. Avocations: music, swimming, skiing. Home: Ad Kutuja 6 64, 420073 Kazan Tatarstan Russia Office: Kazan Med U, 49 Butlerov str, 420012 Kazan Tatarstan Russia

BORODINA, ELENA L'VOVNA, physician, acoustical researcher; b. Gorky, Russia, Mar. 26, 1963; d. Lev Vasil'evich and Roza Vasil'evna Borodina; m. Mikhail Gershevich Raikin, Oct. 15, 1988. Student, Gorky State U., 1980-85, Pub. U. Design, Gorky, 1988-90. Cert. radiophysician, designer. Engr. Sci. Rsch. Inst. Radio Comm., Gorky, 1985-91; engr., programmer Inst. Applied Physics, Russian Acad. Sci., Nizhny Novgorod, Russia, 1991-94; jr. rschr. Inst. Applied Physics, Russian Acad. Sci., Nizhny Novgorod, 1994-96, rschr., 1996—; translator Office Sci. and Tech. Translation, Nizhny Novgorod, 1989-95. Author: The Formation of Acoustical Fields in Oceanic Waveguides, 1991, 97; author, editor: The Formation of Acoustical Fields in Oceanic Waveguides, 1994, 95; contbr. articles to profl. jours. Grantee George Soros Found., 1994, Russian Found. for Basic Rsch., Moscow, 1996, 97, 98, 99. Mem. Acoustical Soc. Russia. E-mail: bel@hydro.appl.sci-nnov.ru. Fax: 8312-365976. Office: Inst Applied Physics RAS, 46 Uljanov St, 603600 Nizhny Novgorod Russia

BORODY, THOMAS JULIUS, gastroenterologist, consultant; b. Cracow, Poland, Jan. 12, 1950; arrived in Australia, 1960; s. John and Danuta Alina (Wawrzonek) B.; m. Susan Brandl, Dec. 3, 1973 (div. Feb. 1993); 1 child, Julie-Ann; m. Karen Marie Borg, May 23, 1993; 1 child, Danielle Monique. BSc in Medicine, U. NSW, Sydney, Australia, 1971, MB BS, 1975, MD, 1981. Med. diplomate. Resident St. Vincent's Hosp., Sydney, 1974-77, sr. med. registrar, 1981-82; rsch. fellow Garvan Inst. Med. Rsch., Sydney, 1979-81; postgrad. fellow Mayo Clinic, Rochester, Minn., 1982-84; dir. Ctr. for Digestive Diseases, Sydney, 1984—; bd. dirs. Exomed Internat., Sydney. Patentee treatment for human ulcer disease, endoscopic oxygenating device. Med. missionary ATOIFI Hosp., Solomon Islands, 1978. Fellow Royal Australian Coll. Physicians, Am. Coll. Gastroenterology; mem. Gastroent. Soc. Australia (Young Investigator award 1981). Mem. Seventh-Day Adventist Ch. Avocations: tennis, skiing. Office: Ctr for Digestive Diseases, 144 Great North Rd, Five Dock NSW 2046, Australia

BORONICO, JESS STEPHEN, management science educator, academic dean; b. Bronx, N.Y., Oct. 23, 1956; s. Stelio and Helen (Michaels) B. BS in Math., Fairleigh Dickinson U., 1978, MS in Math., 1980; PhD in Ops. Rsch., U. Pa., 1992. Prof. mgmt. scis. Rutgers U., Camden, N.J., 1987-88, Phila. Coll. Textiles and Scis., 1988-92; prof. mgmt. scis. Monmouth U., West Long Branch, N.J., 1993—, assoc. dean Sch. Bus., 1998—; cons. United Postal Svc., 1990-92, Reality Techs., 1991, N.J. Hwy. Authority, 1991-92, Kennedy Western U., Calif., 1994-97; mem. adv. bd. to various jours., 1993—. Author: Computer Simulation in Operations Management, 1996; contbg. author: The Service Productivity and Quality Challenge, 1995; editor: Studies in the Strategy and Tactics of Competitive Advantage, 2000; contbr. articles to profl. jours. Fellow U. Pa. Wharton Sch., 1983-87; recipient three Anbar citations of excellence for refereed publs., 1996-98. Mem. Inst. for Ops. Rsch. and Mgmt. Scis., Decision Scis. Inst., Am. Statis. Assn., Mensa. Avocations: softball, computer simulations. Home: 525 East St Long Branch NJ 07740-6815 Office: Monmouth U Sch Bus Adminstrn Bey Hall 213 West Long Branch NJ 07764

BORONOW, RICHARD CARLTON, gynecologist, educator; b. Appleton, Wis., Dec. 18, 1933; children: Robert, Thomas, Amy. BS in Medicine, Northwestern U., 1956, MD, 1959. Diplomate Am. Bd. Ob/Gyn. with cert. in gynecologic/oncology. Intern Cook County Hosp., Chgo., 1959-60; resident in ob/gyn Evanston Hosp., 1960-63; resident in surgery Meml. Hosp. Cancer, N.Y.C., 1963-64; fellow in gynecology Anderson Tumor Inst., Houston, 1964-65; mem. staff Miss. Baptist Med. Ctr., Jackson; clin. prof. gynecology U. Miss. Med. Ctr.; mem. med. alumni adv. bd. Northwestern U. Med. Sch. Author book; contbr. articles to profl. jours., chpts. to books. Fellow ACS, Am. Coll. Ob/Gyn; mem. Am. Radium Soc. (exec. com.), Soc. Gynecologic Oncologists (past pres.), Soc. Surg. Oncologists, Soc. Pelvic Surgeons (past pres.). Address: 1190 N State St Ste 402 Jackson MS 39202-2413

BOROSS, ZOLTÁN, accountant, educator; b. Pécs, Hungary, Apr. 10, 1929; s. István and Istvánné Antonia (Lovrics) B.; m.Cecilia Rozgonyi, Aug. 22, 1953 (div. 1972); children: András, István; m. Anna Salamon, July 28, 1973; 1 child, Attila. D iur. and rer. pol., U. Pécs, 1951; D in Econs., U. Econs., Budapest, 1967; DSc, Acad. Scis., Budapest, 1978. CPA. Asst. Tech. U., Budapest, 1951-56; head dept. Indsl. Cos., Budapest, 1956-61; vice-dir. Ctrl. Rsch. Inst. for Physics, 1962-75; gen. dir. Office of Hungarian Acad. Scis., 1972-77, State Office for Tech. Devel., 1978-82; prof. Tech. Univ. Budapest, 1982—; exec. pres. Hungarian Nat. Com. for Mgmt. Edn., 1986—. Co-author: Challenges for Sciene and Technology, 1985; contbr. articles to profl. jours. Mem. European Acctg. Assn., European Engring. and Mgmt. Assn. (treas. 1987—), Sigma Xi. Avocations: swimming, sailing. Home: Margit krt 40, H-1027 Budapest Hungary Office: Tech U Budapest, Muegyetem rkp 9, H-1111 Budapest Hungary

BOROVICK, ROMAN VLADIMIROVICH, biotechnologist; b. Pytalovo, Russia, July 3, 1942; s. Vladimir and Galina (Sorokina) B.; m. Lidija Michailovna, June 4, 1970; 1 child. DVM, Latvian Agrl. Acad., 1963; PhD, Kazan Vet. Inst., Russia, 1969; D in Vet. Sci., Rsch. Inst. Applied Microbio., Obolensk, Russia, 1980. Scientist Kazan Vet. inst., 1965-76; sr. scientist, dep. dir. sci. affairs Rsch. Inst. Applied Microbiology, Obolensk, 1976-93; dir. Toxicol. Ctr., Serpukhov, Russia, 1993—. Home: Lunacharsky Str Bld 37 Ap 9, 142200 Serpukhov Russia

BOROVIČKA, JIŘÍ, astronomer; b. Prague, Czechoslovakia, Jan. 16, 1964; s. Vítězslav and Hana (Toužimská) B. MSc, Charles U., 1987, PhD, 1993. Scientist Astronomical Inst., Ondřejov, Czech Republic, 1993—. Contbr. articles to profl. jours. Recipient Learned Soc. Czech Republic award, 1997. Mem. Internat. Astron. Union, Czech Astron. Soc. (pres. 1998—). Office: Astron Inst Acad Scis, of the Czech Republic, Ondřejov Czech Republic

BOROVIKOV, VALERIY VASILJEVICH, military officer, aerospace engineer, researcher; b. Bogdanovka, Ukraine, Nov. 16, 1958; s. Vasiliy Yakovlevich and Zinaida Ivanovna (Shevelieva) B.; m. Ljudmila Maratovna Kozlovskaya, 2000. Student, Kharkov Aviation Inst., 1979-83; engr.-mechanic, A.F. Mozhayskiy Mil. Eng. Inst., Leningrad, Russia, 1983; candidate of tech. sci., A.F. Mozhayskiy Mil. Eng. Inst., St. Petersburg, Russia, 1991, D of Tech. Scis., 1997. Mil. cadet A.F. Mozhayskiy Mil. Engring. Aerospace Inst., 1983-84; aero. engr. Cosmodrome Baykonur, Leninsk, Kazakhstan, 1984-87; comdr. Guard Co. Cosmodrome, Leninsk, Russia, 1987-88; tchr., doctorant A.F. Mozhayskiy Mil. Engring. Aerospace Acad., 1988-97, docent of sub-faculty, 1997-99, holder chair of cosmodromes, 1999—; col. A.F. Mozhayskiy Mil. Engring. Aerospace Inst., 2000; comdr. Guard Co. of Cosmodrome, Leninsk, 1987-88; mem. scientific coun. on conferment of bachelor and DSc degrees, A.F. Mozhayskiy Mil. Engring. Aerospace Acad., 1997—. Contbr. monographs and numerous articles to profl. jours. and conf. procs.; patentee in field of tech. transporting of dry materials; sci. discovery. Decorated medals for irreproachable svc. Supreme Soviet of USSR, 1986, 88, medal for distinction in mil. svc., Ministry of Def., 1991. Fellow N.Y. Acad. Scis. Russian Orthodox. Avocations: gymnastics, classical music. Home: Bogatyrskiy prospekt, 53-3, kv. 115, 197372 St Petersburg Russia Office: AF Mozhayskiy Mil Eng Acad, Zhdanovskaya St 13, 197082 St Petersburg Russia

BOROVTSOV, PYETR VASILJEVICH, physicist, educator; b. Chelyabinsk, Russia, Dec. 25, 1944; s. Vasily Trofimovich and Ekaterina Yakovlevna (Davydova) B.; m. Antonina Vasiljevna Andreeva, June 7, 1975; children: Vasily Petrovich, Ilja Petrovich. Candidate in Tech., NPO FONON, Moscow, 1981, DSc in Tech., 1994. Engr. Perm (Russia) Tech. U., 1968-70, asst., 1970-81, lectr., 1981-94, prof., 1994-96; chief dept. physics Perm Mil. Inst., 1996—; head sci. programs in holography and interferometry Acad. Scis., Moscow, 1981-91. Achievements include patentee in field. Avocation: reading. Home: Kovolyov Str 12 F 33, 614013 Perm Russia

BORREGO, CARLOS SOARES, environmental engineering educator; b. Malanje, Angola, June 25, 1948; arrived in Portugal, 1966; s. Alberto Soares and Maria Idalina (Diogo) B.; m. Maria Noémia Campos Soares, Sept. 16, 1972; 1 child, Filipa. Cert. mech. engring., Tech. U. Lisbon, 1972; MSc, Free U. Brussels, 1978, PhD, 1981; cert. in habilitation, U. Aveiro, 1991. Head Rsch. Inst., U. Aveiro, Portugal, 1981, assoc. prof., 1987-91, head of dept., 1989, prof., 1991—; pres. Coastal Zones and Sea Rsch. Ctr., 1994-2000; dir. IDAD Inst. Environ. and Devel., 1993; vice-rector U. Aveiro, 1998—; chmn. NATO/CONS ITM Series Air Pollution Modelling and Its Applications, 2000—. Author: Atmospheric Pollution in the Lisbon Airshed, 1994; editor: la CNQA, 1987, IV ENSB, 1989, 5a CNQA, 1996, Integrated coastal zone strategy: Need for a more quantitative approach, Coastal Environment 96, 1996, Urban Transport and Environment for the 21st Century, 1998, Analysis of the GHG Emission Trends and Climate Change Impacts on Air Quality, 2000. Min. of environ., Lisbon, 1991-93. Mem. Am. Chem. Soc., Am. Meteorol. Soc., European Assn. for Sci. of Air Pollution, European Coastal Zone Assn. for Sci. and Tech. Office: U Aveiro, Dept Environment & Planning, 3810-193 Aveiro Portugal

BORREGO, JESUS GARCIA, engineer; b. El Paso, Tex., Nov. 12, 1953; s. Jesus F. and Maria Luisa (Garcia) B.; children from previous marriage: Maria M., Cristina, Jesus Jr.; m. JoAnne Borrego, Feb. 20, 1999. BSEE, Calif. State U., Fullerton, 1984; BS in Computer Sci., Calif. State U., Dominguez Hills, 1987; MS in Computer Sci., Loyola Marymount, L.A., 1992. Cert. tchr., Calif. Enlisted USMC, 1972-83; mem. tech. staff Logicon, Inc., San Pedro, Calif., 1983-87; tech. lead Advanced Tech., Inc., El Segundo, Calif., 1987-88; staff engr. Hughes Aircraft, El Segundo, Calif., 1988-89; sr. prin. engr. Arinc Rsch. Corp., Fountain Valley, Calif., 1989-94; prof. Webster U., Colorado Springs, Colo., 1995-99; sr. mgr. Arinc Inc., Colorado Springs, 1994-97; with DataVision, Inc., 1997-98; prof. Regis U., Colorado Springs, Colo., 1995—; with DMW Worldwide, 1998—; adj. faculty El Camino Coll., Torrance, Calif., 1988-94; cons. JMB Cons., Gardena, Calif., 1988-94. Contbr. articles to profl. jours. With USMC Res., 1983-92. Mem. IEEE, IEEE Computer Soc., Assn. for Computer Machinery. Republican. Roman Catholic. Avocations: teaching, reading, racquetball, camping, travel. Office: Noochee Solutions Inc 7250 Campus Dr Colorado Springs CO 80920-6517

BORRELL, ANDREW KENNETH, agricultural scientist; b. Melbourne, Australia, Jan. 28, 1959; s. Murray Howard and Delma Joan (Ranson) B.; m. Carolyn Joy Leslie, Nov. 28, 1981; children: Stephen, Christopher, Leigh. B of Agrl. Sci., U. Melbourne, 1982, M of Agrl. Sci., 1986; PhD, U. Queensland, Australia, 1994. Cert. practicing agriculturist. Grad. rsch. asst. U. Melbourne, 1982; rsch. agronomist Queensland Dept. Primary Industries, Ayr, Australia, 1985-92; prin. rsch. scientist Queensland Dept. Primary Industries, Warwick, Australia, 1993—; lectr. James Cook U., Townsville, Australia, 1990-92; mem. internat. com. Australian Inst. Agrl. Sci., Warwick, 1995, 96; mem. steering com. Farming Systems Inst., Brisbane, Australia, 1996. Editor: Lessons and Opportunities from the Drought, 1994; contbr. articles to profl. jours. Mem. allocations com. TEAR Australia, Brisbane, 1993—; cons. Svc. Fellowship Internat., Indonesia, 1993-98; deacon Bapt. Ch., Warwick, 1994-95; lt. Boys Brigade, Warwick, 1998—. Churchill fellow, 1988; recipient Group Exchange award Rotary Internat., 1997. Mem. Australian Inst. Agrl. Sci. and Tech. (v.p. North Queensland br. 1989-91), Australian Sorghum Conf. Organising Com., Australian Agronomy Soc. Avocations: mountaineering, surfing, writing, music, photography. Home: 21 Weewondilla Rd, Warwick 4370, Australia Office: Queensland Dept Primary Ind, Hermitage Rsch Sta, Warwick 4370, Australia

BORRELLI, JOHN FRANCIS, architect; b. Buffalo, Nov. 6, 1955; s. Peter and Maria (Raimondo) B. BSCE, Columbia U., 1977; postgrad., Pratt Inst., 1977-81. Registered arch., N.Y., N.J., Conn., Vt., Ill., Va., Pa., Fla., Md., Mich. Project coord. C. Raimondo and Sons, Ft. Lee, N.J., 1971-78; project mgr. DAT Cons., N.Y.C., 1978-81, Litchfield Grosfeld Assocs., N.Y.C., 1981-83; project arch. Design Mgmt., Inc., N.Y.C., 1983-87; ptnr. Sys. Collaborative, Inc., N.Y.C., 1987-88, Davis Borrelli Assocs., N.Y.C., 1987-91; exec. v.p. Karco-Davis, Inc., N.Y.C., 1987-91; v.p. Rampart Constrn. Assocs., N.Y.C., 1987-91; prin. Meli Borrelli Assocs., N.Y.C., 1991-94; pres. John Francis Borrelli Arch., P.C., N.Y.C., 1991—; prin. MBA Mcpl., Inc., 1993, MBA Internat., Inc., 1991, SPGA MBA, Inc., 1993, Walter M. Ballard, Ltd., 1993, MBA&A, Inc., 1995, Vici Group, Ltd., N.Y.C., 1995. Prin. works include ING/Barings Securities, Inc. Hdqs., N.Y.C., Credit Suisse Hdqs., N.Y.C., Schonfeld Securities Inc. (various offices including N.Y.C., Chgo., N.J., Boca Raton, L.I. Hdqrs.), Netscape Comms. Corp. (various offices including N.Y., Chgo., Detroit, and Bethesda, Md.), H.S. for Environ. Scis., N.Y.C., Burlington Industries Hdqs., N.Y.C., Walt Disney Book and Product Licensing Offices, N.Y.C., Jefferson Ins. Corp. Hdqs., N.J., Western Union Corp. Hdqrs., N.J., Parade Publs. Corp. Hdqrs., N.Y.C., Covington Fabrics Corp. Hdqrs., N.Y.C., Otterbourg, Steindler, Houston and Rosen, P.C., N.Y.C., Lalique (N.Y.C. flagship boutiques and offices), Macromedia, Inc., N.J. Recipient 1st prize Gabriel Industries, 1976; Columbia U. scholar, 1973-77. Mem. AIA, ASCE, Nat. Trust for Hist. Preservation, World Wildlife Fund, Greenpeace. Avocations: woodworking, antique collecting, book collecting, gardening, tennis. Office: John Francis Borrelli Architect PC 13 E 37th St New York NY 10016-2821

BORRELLI, MARIO ALFREDO, sociologist; b. Naples, Italy, Sept. 19, 1922; s. Gennaro and Lucia (Morvillo) B.; Licentiate in theology Theol. U. Naples, 1965; postgrad. Tufts U., 1967-68; M. Social Adminstrn. and Social Work Studies, London Sch. Econs., 1970; m. Jilyan West, Sept. 19, 1971; 1 dau., Luciana. Dir., Casa dello Scugnizzo, 1950-70, Centro Communitario Materdei, 1970-92; pres. Italian Peace Research Inst., Naples, 1977-88; prof. sociology U. Md., 1973-76. Pres. Casa dello Scugnizzo Found., 1993-96; Hon. mem. Kiderschutzbund; recipient Lane Bryant Internat. Vol. citation, 1963, Stella della Bonta, 1963, Penna d'argento, 1981. Mem. Pontaniana Acad. Naples, Associazione Italiana della Stampa. Author 40 works in field. Home: Pozzuoli, 100A Via Vecchia San Gennaro, Naples Italy*

BÖRRESEN, TORGER ANDREAS, biochemist, researcher, science administrator; b. Bömlo, Norway, July 31, 1947; arrived in Denmark, 1983; s. Bjarne and Inga (Amundsen) B.; m. Sölvi Karin Larsson, July 3, 1971; 1 child, Maria. MSc, Norwegian Inst. Tech., 1970, PhD, 1976. Cert. chem. engr. Rsch. asst. Norwegian Inst. Tech., Trondheim, 1971-76; postdoctoral fellow U. Calif., Davis, 1977-78; sr. rschr. Inst. Fish Technol. Rsch., Tromsö, Norway, 1978-83; sr. rschr. Ministry of Fisheries Technol. Lab., Copenhagen, 1983-88, dir., 1988-95; rsch. dir. dept. for seafood rsch. Danish Inst. Fisheries Rsch., Copenhagen, 1995—; assoc. prof. Tech. U. Denmark, Copenhagen, 1985-96, prof., 1999—; ctr. leader Ctr. Marine Biotech., Copenhagen, 1987-88. Contbr. articles to profl. jours., chpts. to books. Mem. Am. Chem. Soc., Inst. Food Technologists, Danish Acad. Tech. Scis., Sigma Xi. Office: Danish Inst Fisheries Rsch, Bldg 221 Tech U, DK-2800 Lyngby Copenhagen, Denmark

BORRILLO, DANIEL ANGEL, law educator, researcher; b. Buenos Aires, Jan. 12, 1961; arrived in France, 1987; s. Angel Bruno Borrillo and Elida Angélica Rodrigues. Law degree, U. Buenos Aires, 1985, M of Sociology of Law, 1987; PhD in Law cum laude, U. Strasbourg, France, 1991; postgrad., Consejo Superior Invest. Sci., Spain, 1995. Lawyer, mem. Bar of Buenos Aires, 1985-93; asst. prof. Buenos Aires, 1985-87; mem. Nat. Acctg. Office, Argentina, 1980-87; tchg. asst. Strasbourg, France, 1988-90; vis. prof. Strasbourg, 1990-92; prof. law Paris U., 1992—; cons. European Union, 1993; vis. prof. Boston Coll., Daito Bunka U., Tokyo. Author: L'Homme Proprietaire de Lui-Même, 1992; editor: Sida et Droits de L'Homme, 1989, Sciences et Democratie, 1993, Genes En El Estrado, 1996, Droit et Homosexualités, 1999, Au-delà du PACS: l'expertise familiale à a l'epreuve de l'homosexualité, 1999, L'Homophobie, 2000. Vol. Atty. AIDS Assn., 1996. With Argentine Navy, 1979. Recipient prize Found. Rio de la Plata, 1986, Found. France, 1989, Human Capital and Mobility, 1992. Avocation: dancing the tango. Home: 11 rue Charles V, 75004 Paris France Office: U Paris X, 200 Ave Republique, 92001 Nanterre France

BORRINI, FRANCESCO, military officer, writer; b. Novara, Italy, May 15, 1945; s. Geo Alberto and Giuseppina (Rossi) B.; m. Mariarita Chelli; children: Alessandro, Andrea, Chiara. Degree in aeronautical engring., Poly., Milan, 1972; degree in aerospace engring., U. Rome, 1978. Tchr. Air Force War Sch., Florence, Italy, 1973-75; rschr. Air Force Study and Rsch. Ctr., Rome, 1975-84, Air Force Study, Rsch. and Experimentation Divsn., Pratica di Mare, Italy, 1984-92; mgr. Air Force Study, Rsch. and Experimentation Divsn., Pratica di Mare, 1992-99; with Air Force Flight Experiment Ctr, Pratica di Mare, 1999—. Author: Elements of Aerotechnique, 1975; contbr. articles to profl. jours. Served with Italian Air Force, 1988—. Home: Via Sassari 29, 00040 Ardea Italy Office: CSV, Pratica di Mare Airport, 00040 Pomezia Italy

BORRMAN, HÉLÈNE INGER MARIA, forensic odontologist, educator; b. Göteborg, Sweden, Apr. 24, 1951; d. Stig Erik and Solveig Lilian (Kjellberg) B. DSc, Göteborg U., 1975, D Odontology, 1987. Asst. prof. oral and maxillo-facial radiology U. Göteborg, 1977-84, assoc. prof., 1987-91, dir. rsch. hist. odonotology; dir. rsch. hist. odontology Swedish Dental Assn. Mus. Nat. Antiquities, Stockholm; guest scientist Mineral Metabolism Lab. VA Hosp.; vis. asst. prof. faculty dentistry, dir. sect. radiology Loma Linda (Calif.) U., 1984-86; invited lectr. in field. Reviewer numerous jours. in field; contbr. articles to profl. publs. Bd. dirs. U. Info. Collegium, 1993-95, Internat. Collegium, 1993-95, Univ. Libr. Com., 1993-95. Rsch. grantee Göteborg U., Swedish Dental Assn., Göteborg Dental Soc., Young Rschr. award, 1989, Längmanska Kulturfonden, Fredrika Bremer Förbundet, Lima Linda U. Med. Rsch. Found., Nat. Bd. Health and Welfare, Nat. Bd. Forensic Medicine, Wilhelm och Martina Lundgrens Forskningsfond, Adlerbertska Forskningsfonden, others; Fulbright scholar, 1998. Mem. Internat. Acad. legal Medicine (auditor 1994—), Univ. Tchrs. Assn. (bd. dirs. 1987-2000), Göteborg Dental Soc. (curator 1996—), Internat. Assn. Dental Rsch., Rotary Internat. (bd. dirs. 1997—). Lutheran. Avocations: family, reading, writing poems, friends, embroidery. E-mail: borrman@odontologi.gu.se. Home: Berzeligatan 25, S-412 53 Göteborg Sweden Office: Göteborg U, Box 450, SE-40530 Göteborg Sweden

BORRMANS, MAURICE ALBERT CHARLES, priest, Arabic and Islamic studies educator; b. Lille, France, Oct. 22, 1925; s. Jules and Jeanne (Delmarre) B. BA, France, 1943; lic., Algeria, 1954; PhD, U. Paris, 1971. Prof. Arabic and Islamic studies Pontifico Inst. Studi Arabi e Islamistica, Rome, 1964—. Author: Statut personnel et famille au Maghreb de 1940 à nos jours, 1977, Documents sur la famille au Maghreb de 1940 à nos jours, 1979, Orientations pour un dialogue entre Chrétiens et Musulmans, 1981 (translated into Dutch, German, Arabic, Italian, Turkish, and English), Islam e Christianesimo: le vie del dialogo, 1993, Jésus et les Musulmans d'aujourd'hui, 1996 (translated into Italian); co-author: (with Mohamed Arkoun) Islam, religione e società, 1980, (translated into French) 1981, (with Georges C. Anawati) Tendances et courants de l'Islam arabe contemporain, 1982; editor-in-chief (jour.) Islamochristiana. Recipient ordre Nat. du Mérite, France, 1991. Mem. Internat. Acad. Religious Scis., Missionaries of Africa (White Fathers). Fax: (0039) 06 588 2595. E-mail: pisai@flashnet.it. Office: Pontifico Ist Studi Ara-Isl, Viale di Trastevere N 89, I-00153 Rome Italy

BORROMEO, ROMANA GONZALEZ, obstetrician, gynecologist; b. Biñan, Laguna, The Philippines, May 19, 1940; d. Antonio Reyes and Basilia (Garcia) Gonzalez; m. Rafael Custodio Borromeo, Nov. 6, 1995; children: Rita, Ruth, Ricardo, Regina. AA, U. Santo Tomas, The Philippines, 1957, MD, 1962. Instr. ob-gyn. U. Santo Tomas, 1969-75; sr. cons. ob-gyn. Makati Med. Ctr., 1972—, tng. officer, 1994—. Fellow Am. Coll. Ob-Gyn. (affiliate), Philippines Ob-Gyn. Soc. Roman Catholic. Home: 21 Mercury St Bel Air Village, Makati 1209, The Philippines Office: Makati Med Ctr, de la Rosa St, Makati 1200, The Philippines

BORSA, JUDIT, engineering educator, researcher; b. Budapest, Hungary, May 9, 1948; d. Ivan and Ilona (Miko) B.; m. Andras Recski, May 14, 1983; children: Julia, Gabor. Degree in Chem. Engring., Tech. U., Budapest, Hungary, 1971, PhD, 1978; CSc, Hungarian Acad. Scis., 1991. Lectr. Tech. U. Budapest, 1971-78, asst. prof., 1978-94, assoc. prof., 1994-98, prof., 1998—; UNESCO fellow Tokyo Inst. Tech., 1980-81; vis. rschr. Cornell U., Ithaca, N.Y. Contbr. 60 articles to profl. jours. Named Hungarian Prin. investigator Joint USA Hungarian Fund, 1994-97, Hungarian Nat. Sci. Found., 1993-96, 97—. Mem. The Textile Inst., The Fiber Soc., Am. Chem. Soc. Office: Tech Univ of Budapest, Dept Plastics & Rubber Tech, H-1521 Budapest Hungary

BORSDORF, AXEL, geographer, educator, researcher; b. Bad Oeynhausen, Germany, Mar. 8, 1948; s. Fritz and Maxi (Markus) B.; m. Mariana Bartels; children: Falk, Tilman, Malte. PhD, U. Tübingen, Germany, 1976, habilitation, 1984. Asst. prof. geography U. Tübingen, 1974-85, docent, 1985-91; prof. geography U. Innsbruck, Austria, 1991—; meml mem. Austrian Acad. Sci., Vienna, 1995, dir. Inst. Urban and Regional Rsch., 1999—; v.p. Austrian Nat. Com. Internat. Geog. Union, 1996; mem. bd. Austrian L.Am. Inst., Vienna, 1997; mem. bd. Commn. Austrian L.Am. Rsch., Vienna, 1995—; mem. jury State Prize for Sci., Innsbruck, Austria, 1994—. Author: Die Städte Südamerikas, 1985, Chile in Profilen, 1995; editor: (textbook) Kurswissen Geographie, 1985—; editor (jour.) Die Erde, 1994—. Mem. Austrian Geographical Soc. (v.p. 1994), Humboldt Soc. (mem. acad. coun. 1985—). Home: Gaisauweg 11, A-6401 Hatting Austria Office: U Innsbruck Dept Geography, Innrain 52, A-6020 Innsbruck Austria

BÖRSIG, CLEMENS, finance executive; b. Achern, Baden, Germany, July 27, 1948. Diploma kaufmann, Mannheim (Germany) U., 1973; D in Polit. Sci., 1975. Sci. asst. Mannheim and Munich Univs., 1973-77; corp. planner Mannesmann AG, Düsseldorf, Germany, 1977-81; head corp. planning Mannesmann Kienzle GmbH, VS-Villingen, 1981-84; bus. dir. Mannesmann Tally, Eichingen, Germany, 1984-85; head corp. bus. ops. Robert Bosch GmbH, Stuttgart, Germany, 1985-97; mem. sr. mgmt. Robert Bosch GmbH, Stuttgart, 1990-97, mem. RWE AG bd. mgmt., 1997-99; Mng. Dir., Controlling, Taxes, Audit Deutsche Bank, Frankfurt, 1999—. Res. lt. German Mil., 1967-69. Office: Deutsche Bank, 60262 Frankfurt Germany

BORST-EILERS, ELSE, Dutch government official; b. Amsterdam, The Netherlands, Mar. 22, 1932. MD, Amsterdam U., 1958, PhD, 1972. Resident pediatrics Amsterdam U., 1958-60, resident immunohematology, 1960-65; rschr., lectr. immunohematology Utrecht U., 1956-68; head blood bank U. Hosp., Utrecht, 1969-75, med. dir., 1976; dep. chair Health Coun., 1986-94; prof. evaluation rsch. in clin. medicine Amsterdam U., 1992; Min. of Health, Welfare and Sports Dutch Govt., 1994—; chair Blood Transfusion Bd., Ctrl. Com. on Med. Rsch. Ethics; mem. Sci. and Tech. Adv. Coun.; mem. Inst. Medicine, Washington. Co-editor various med. jours. Democrat. Office: Ministry of Welfare Pub Health & Sport, Sir Winston Churchhillaan, 2280 HK Rijswijk The Netherlands Address: Binnenhof 20, 2500 EA 2513AA The Hague The Netherlands Also: PO Box 20001, 2500 EA The Hague The Netherlands*

BØRSTING, HAKON, electrical engineer, researcher; b. Christiansfeld, Denmark, Sept. 18, 1964; s. Richard and Anne (Jensen) B.; m. Mariane Dohm Pedersen, Aug. 3, 1991; children: Louise, Kathrine. BEE, Aalborg (Denmark) U., 1988, MS, 1990, PhD, 1993. Rsch. asst. Aalborg U., 1990-93, lectr., 1993-94, asst. prof. elec. engring., 1994-95; rschr. Grundfos A/S, Bjerringbro, Denmark, 1995-97, project leader motor-control rsch. group, 1997—; chmn. European Conf. on Power Electronics, Tronheim, Norway,

1997; conf. reviewer European Power Electronics Assn., 1997—. Avocations: tennis, sailing. Office: Grundfos A/S, DK-8850 Bjerringbro Denmark

BORTĂ, ELENA, literary researcher; b. Piatra Neamt, Romania, May 21, 1961; d. Elena Gh. Bortă. MA, U. Bucharest, 1984. Ednl. rschr. I.S.E., Bucharest, 1990-94; part-time lectr. U. Bucharest, Romania, 1992—, literary rschr., 1994—; fgn. rels. counselor Hesperus Found., Romania, 1995—. Contbr. articles to profl. jours. Travel grant U. Göteborg/Soros Found., 1995; conf. grant USIA, U. Seville, 1992; study grant Soros Found. U. Edinburgh, 1991. Mem. Amnesty Internat., European Soc. for the Study of English, Poetics & Linguistics Assn. Avocations: foregin languages, travelling, listening to music, domestic life. E-mail: elenaborta@hotmail.com. Home: Str Tineretului 105-115, BL Sahia 1 SC B AP 28, 8350 Oltenita Romania

BORTON, GEORGE ROBERT, retired airline captain; b. Wichita Falls, Tex., Mar. 22, 1922; s. George Neat and Travis Lee (Jones) B.; m. Anne Louise Bowling, Feb. 5, 1944 (dec.); children: Trudie T., Robert B., Bruce M. AA, Hardin Coll., Wichita Falls, 1940. Cert. airline transport pilot, FAA flight examiner. Flight sch. operator Vallejo (Calif.) Sky Harbor, 1947-48; capt. S.W. Airways, San Francisco, 1948-55; check capt. Pacific Airlines, San Francisco, 1955-68, Hughes Air West, San Francisco, 1968-71; capt. N.W. Airlines, Mpls., 1971-82, ret., 1982. Col. USAF, 1943-73, ret. Decorated Air medal. Mem. Airline Pilots Assn.; Res. Officers Assn., Air Force Assn., Horseless Carriage Club, Model T of Am. Club (San Jose, Calif.). Republican. Home: 325 Denio Ave Gilroy CA 95020-9203

BORUAH, ROMESH CHANDRA, research scientist, chemist; b. Galekey, Sibsagar, India, July 1, 1953; Bipin Chandra and Nayantara (Phukan) B.; m. Monideepa Phukan, Mar. 4, 1984; children: Maitrayee, Atrayee. BSc with honors, Sibsagar (India) Coll., 1974; MSc, Dibrugarh (India) U., 1976, PhD, 1980. Postdoctoral fellow Konstanz (Germany) U., 1982-83; postdoctoral assoc. Ariz. State U., Tempe, Ariz., 1992-94; asst. Regional Rsch. Lab., Jorhat, India, 1978-81, scientist B, 1981-84, scientist C, 1984-89, scientist E I, 1989-94, scientist E II, 1994—. Contbr. articles to sci. publs. DAAD fellow, 1982. Mem. Indian Soc. Chemists and Biologists (life), Indian Chem. Soc. (life). Avocations: reading, playing tennis, cricket, driving, jogging. Home: D-5 Regional Rsch Lab, Assam Jorhat 785006, India Office: Regional Rsch Lab, Assam Jorhat 785006, India

BORUCHOWITZ, STEPHEN ALAN, health policy analyst; b. Plainfield, N.J., Sept. 24, 1952; s. Robert and Earla Louise (Sloat) B.; m. Linda Susan Grant, Sept. 16, 1989; 1 child, Grant Stephen. BA in Internat. Affairs, George Washington U., Washington, 1974; MA in Sci., Tech. and Pub. Policy, George Washington U., 1981. Food prog. specialist U.S. Food & Nutrition Svc., Washington, 1978-81; internat. affairs specialist Office Internat. Cooperation & Devel., Washington, 1981-87; legis. analyst Wash. State Senate, Olympia, 1986-89; project dir. Wash. 2000 Project, Olympia, 1989-92; sr. health policy analyst Wash. Dept. Health, Olympia, 1992—; mem. Pew Commn. task force on regulation of health professions, 1994-95. Editor newsletter: Project Update, 1990-92. Study team mem. Gov.'s Efficiency Commn., 1990-91; com. mem. Coun. of State Govts. Strategic Planning Subcom., Lexington, Ky., 1990-92; chmn. Montclair Divsn. IV Neighborhood Assn., 1989-92, Shadywood Homeowner's Assn., 1992-94; bd. dirs. Classical Music Supporters, Seattle, 1987-89. Recipient Superior Performance award, U.S. Dept. Agr., 1986. Mem. World Future Soc., Internat. Health Futures Network, Internat. Soc. of Tech. Assessment in Health Care, Health Svcs. Rsch. Assn. Avocations: writing, travel, cooking, classical music. Office: Wash Dept Health PO Box 47851 Olympia WA 98504-7851

BORWICK, RICHARD, management consultant; b. Elmira, N.Y., Aug. 15, 1908; s. Abram and Phyllis (Gould) B.; m. Lillian Fine, June 22, 1938; 1 child: Anthony Stephen. AB in Classics and Philosophy with honors, Harvard U., 1929. Reporter Brockton Mass. Enterprise, 1928-30; researcher current history N.Y. Times, N.Y.C., 1932; analyst Fairchild Publs., N.Y.C., 1933; sales promotion Quality Group Mags., N.Y.C., 1933; fin. reporter Washington (D.C.) Herald, Washington Times Herald, 1934-42; pub. exec. Phila. Record, 1943; co-founder Newmyer Assocs. Inc., Washington, 1944—, v.p., 1959-83; cons. in oil industry, ins., electric mfg., telephone communications, industries, 1983—. Speech writer, policy adviser Presdl. Candidates Sen. Estes Kefauver, Washington, 1952, Sen. Henry Jackson, Washington, 1960-82. Mem. Nat. Press Club, Harvard Grad. Soc. (chmn. 1983-85). Clubs: International (Washington); Harvard (N.Y.C.). Home: 3301 O St NW Washington DC 20007-2814

BORYSENKO, VALENTIN OLEKSIYOVYCH, scientist, researcher, academic administrator; b. Nizhny Novgorod, Russia, Jan. 8, 1934; s. Oleksiy Sergiyovych and Natalia Stepanivna Borysenko; m. Tamara Ivanivna Morgunova, Jan. 27, 1961; 1 child, Vitaly.; Diploma in mech. engring., Polytech. Inst., Kiev, Ukraine, 1957; PhD, Acad. Scis. Ukraine, Kiev, 1962, DSc, 1980. Engr. Plant Arsenal, Kiev, 1957-59; scientist, sr. scientist Inst. for Problems Materials Sci., Kiev, 1962-66; sr. scientist, head dept., dep. dir., prof. Inst. for Problems of Strength, Kiev, 1966—. Author: Hardness and Strength of Refractory Materials at High Temperatures, 1984; co-author: Strength of Refractory Metals, 1970, Mechanical Testing of Materials at High Temperatures, 1980; editor: Thermal Deformation of Non-Metallic Destructing Materials, 1983; mem. editl. bd. Internat. Jour. Problems of Strength, 1989—. Recipient M.K. Yanhel prize Nat. Acad. Scis. Ukraine, 1990, winner State Prize Ukraine, 1994. Fellow Shevchenko Sci. Soc.; mem. Acad. Engring. Scis. Ukraine, Nat. Com. Theoretical and Applied Mechanics Ukraine. E-mail: nick@ipp.adam.kiev.ua. Office: Nat Acad Scis Ukraine, 2 Timiryazevska Str, 01014 Kiev Ukraine

BORYSKI, JERZY, chemist; b. Poznan, Poland, Mar. 5, 1951; s. Roman and Krystyna B.; m. Maria Nowaczyk, May 13, 1978; children: Olga, Marta, Jan. MSc in Chemistry, Adam Mickiewicz U., Poznan, Poland, 1974, PhD in Chemistry, 1978; DSc in Chem. Scis., Inst. Organic Chemistry, Polish Acad. Scis., Warsaw, 1992. Rsch. asst. Inst. Bioorganic Chemistry, Polish Acad. Scis., Poznan, 1977-79, rsch. assoc., 1979-92, docent, 1992-2000, full prof., 2000—; rsch. assoc. U. Va. Dept. Chemistry, Charlottesville, 1979-80; vis. scientist Japan Soc. Promotion Sci., Faculty Pharm. Scis., Hokkaido U., Sapporo, Japan, 1984-85, Deutscher Acad. Austauschdienst Faculty Chemistry, U. Konstanz (Germany), 1992; dir. sci. affairs Inst. Bioorganic Chemistry, Polish Acad. Scis., Poznan, 1997—. Contbr. articles to profl. jours. Grantee Polish State Com. Sci. Rsch., 1992, 97. Roman Catholic. Avocations: history of arts, swimming, skiing, chess. Office: Polish Acad Scis, Noskowskiego 12/14, Poznan PL-61704, Poland

BORYSYUK, MYKHAYLO DEMIANOVICH, mechanical engineer; b. Kharleevka, Orel Region, Russia, Nov. 21, 1934; s. Demian Timofeevich and Tatiana Kuzminichna (Gheneralova) B.; m. Alevtina Ivanovna Gavrilova, June 30, 1958; children: Sergiy Mykhaylovich, Mykhaylo Mykhaylovich. Mechanist, Coll. for Mechanization Agr., Zadonsk, Russia, 1953, Armor Sch., Saratov, Russia, 1956; Engr., Malinovskiy Mil. Acad. Armor, Moscow, 1964; D Techniques (hon.), Kharkiv State Polytechnic U., Kharkiv, Ukraine, 1993; Prof., Highest Evaluation Com. of, Ukraine, Kharkiv, 1997. Mil. rep., sr. mil. rep. dep. Machine-Building Plant, Cheliabinsk, Russia, 1964-74; head, gen. designer Rotor Design Bur. of Electromashina/Group of Cos., Cheliabinsk, 1974-90; head and gen. designer Morozov KhMDB, Kharkiv, 1990-92; gen. designer for armoured vehicles engring. industry Kharkiv Morozov Machine-Building Design Bur., Kharkiv, 1992—; lectr. State Polytechnic Kharkiv/Ukraine Inst., 1995—; prof. of the Chair for Wheeled and Tracked Vehicles, Kharkiv State Polytechnic U., 1997—. Co-author: (books) Development and Industrial Production of Welded Turrets With Cellular Filler, 1995 (Ukrainian Govt. Sci./Tech. prize 1995), Development and Acceptance for Service of New MSTA Complex, 1990 (Govt. Lenin prize 1990), Automatic Control of Hydrostatic Transmission and Steering Mechanism of Tracked Vehicles, 1995, Parameters Optimizing of Multi-channel Automatic Control Systems, 1995. Lt. gen. Ukrainian Min. of Def, 1956-59, 64—. Decorated Order of Red Banner of Labour, PSS USSR, Moscow, 1976, Order of October Revolution, 1986, Order For Svcs. III Grade, Pres. of Ukraine, Kyiv, 1997, others; named Hero of Ukraine, Pres. Ukraine, Kyiv, 2000. Avocation: hunting. Office: Kharkiv Morozov Machine/Bld, Design Bur/126 Plekhanivska, Kharkiv 61001, Ukraine

BORZYCKI, KRZYSZTOF WACŁAW, communications research engineer, interpreter; b. Warsaw, Poland, Aug. 10, 1959; s. Wacław and Teresa (Sobota) B. BS in Elec. Engring., Warsaw Tech. U., 1982, MS in Elec. Engring., 1982. Design engr. Inst. Telecomm., Warsaw, 1982-83, rsch. asst., 1983-85, sr. rsch. asst., 1985-95, sr. R&D specialist, 1995—, 1997—; tech. cons. Bydgoszcz (Poland) Cable Factory, 1996-97. Contbr. articles to profl. jours.; patentee in field. Bd. mem. Co. Self-Govt., Employees Coun., Warsaw, 1989-90. With Polish Army, 1983. Recipient Meritorious Comm. Employee Silver award Min. Telecomm., Poland, 1995. Roman Catholic. Avocations: photography, trekking, cycling. Office: Inst Telecomm, 1 Szachowa St, 04-894 Warsaw Poland

BOS, ANNEMARIE GERREDINA, geophysicist; b. Emmen, Netherlands, May 24, 1975; d. Corneus and Else (de Kruj) B. VWO, GSG, Emmen, Netherlands, 1993; Docteranders, U. Utrecht, Netherlands, 1997. Geophysicist Geco-Prakla, Gatwick, U.K., 1997—. Recipient scholarship, Princeton U., 1997. Avocations: skiing, reading, music, hiking, riding. Office: Geco-Prakla Ltd, Buckingham Gate, RHG 0142 Gatwick UK

BOS, LUITE, plant virologist, researcher, retired; b. West-Stellingwerf, The Netherlands, Mar. 22, 1928; s. Jelte and Popkjen (Bijker) B.; m. Geertje Wierda, Mar. 4, 1954; children: Jannie, Jelte. D of Agrl., Agrl. U., 1957. Tchg. asst. plant taxonomy Agrl. U., Wageningen, The Netherlands, 1952-57; plant virologist DLO Rsch. Inst. Plant Protection, Wageningen, 1957-93, ret., 1993; cons. in field; vis. scientist dept. botany Mont. State U., Missoula, 1960. Editor, chmn. Netherlands Jour. Plant Pathology, 1968-77; author: Symptoms of Virus Diseases in Plants, 1963, 3d edit. 1978, Virussen en Planten, 1965, Introduction to Plant Virology, 1983 (with Indonesian translation 1990), Research on Viruses of Legume Crops, 1996, Plant Viruses Unique and Intriguing Pathogens, 1999. Kellogg Found. fellow, 1960, Fulbright fellow, 1960; named Order of Orange-Nassau Queen Netherlands, 1992. Mem. Royal Soc. of Agrl. Sci., Royal Netherlands Soc. of Plant Pathology, Netherlands Cir. of Plant Virologists. Avocations: philosophy, natural sciences, history, sports. Home: Sprengerlaan 13, 6703 GA Wageningen The Netherlands

BOSANAC, MIROSLAV, physicist, researcher; b. Ohrid, Yugoslavia, June 24, 1951; s. Dusan and Roza (Mitkova) B.; m. Zdravka Susilovic, Sept. 18, 1982; children: Lana, Rosana. BSc, U. Split, Yugoslavia, 1975; MSc, U. Zagreb, Yugoslavia, 1982; PhD, U. Ljubljana, Yugoslavia, 1987. Tchr. grammar sch., Split, 1975-76; rschr. Solar Energy Lab., Split, 1976-87; asst. prof. U. Split, 1987-91; scientist Ludwig Maximillians U., Munich, 1991-94; sr. rschr. Danish Technol. Inst., Copenhagen, 1994—; scientific coord. Regional Activity Ctr. for Priority Activities on Renewably Energy Sources, UN Environ. Program-Mediterranean Action Plan, 1988-93; referee Jour. Solar Energy, Internat. Solar Energy Soc., Elsevier Sci., Pubs., N.Y.C., 1995—, mem. editl. bd. materials com. Internat. Jour. Solar Energy North Holland Physics Pub. divsn., 1988-93; expert project team for preparation European Std. for Test of Thermal Solar Energy Sys., European Commn. Orgn. for Standardization, Brussels, 1994-99, cons. to industry, 1994—; expert evaluator for call for proposals for projects on integration renewable energies in bldgs. thermie com. Directorate Gen., European Comm., Brussels, 1996; mem. German expert team Internat. Energy Agy., 1992-93, mem. Danish expert team, 1994; mem. expert com. Danish Std. Orgn., 1994—. Author: Scientific Series of the International Bureau of Research Center Juelich, 1989; contbr. articles to Jour. Solar Energy; inventor dynamic test method for collector arrays characterization. Fellow German Ministry for Rsch., 1986. Mem. Internat. Solar Energy Soc. Avocations: photography, bicycling. Fax: 45-35397942. E-mail: mbosanac@hotmail.com. Home: Vodroffsvej 56 B/2, 1900 Frederiksberg C, Denmark Office: Danish Technol Inst, PO Box 141, 2630 Taastrup Denmark

BOSBACH, FRANZ, historian, educator; b. Germany, Jan. 11, 1952. Prof. early modern history U. Bayreuth, Germany, 1989—. Author: Monarchia Universalis, 1986. Life mem. Clarehall, Cambridge. Mem. Prinz-Albert Gesellschaft (pres. 1995). Home: Wacholderweg 33, D-95445 Bayreuth Germany Office: U Bayreuth, Early Modern History, D-95440 Bayreuth Germany

BOSCH, ANNA, property manager; b. Barcelona, Spain, June 20, 1956; d. Lorenzo Bosch and Montserrat Rovira; m. Jose Manuel Ferrer, Jan. 19, 1980 (div. 1995); children: Marc, Anna, Cristina. Chemist engring., I.Q.S., Barcelona, 1978, PhD in Chem. Engring., 1982; organic chemist, U. Barcelona, 1990; law grad., UNED, Madrid, 1999. Sr. chemist Chemichron, Barcelona, 1982; process chemist Lab. Vita, Barcelona, 1982-88; medicinal chemist Vita-Invest, Barcelona, 1988-95, indsl. property mgr., 1995—; chemist. cons. Derfesa, Sant Coloni, Spain, 1982-85; patent translator Rafal, Barcelona, 1994-98. Mem. AQIQS, AIPPI, LES-Espana. Achievements include over 30 patents in field. Avocations: sports, literature, horticulture. Home: Cami Vell de Sta Creu, d'Olorda a Vallvidrera 4, 08017 Barcelona Spain Office: Labs Vita, Avda Barcelona 69, 08970 Sant Joan Despi Spain

BOSCHETTI, PHILIP JOHN, oil company executive; b. Yonkers, N.Y., Apr. 11, 1944; s. Anthony and Santina (Taccetta) B.; m. Linda Marie Liggio, June 11, 1966; children: Keith Philip, Scott Alan. BBA in Mktg., Iona Coll., 1966. Sales mgr. Firestone Tire and Rubber Co., N.J., 1966; fin. adminstr. William S. Paley & Co., N.Y.C., 1969-91; v.p., CFO Burnett Oil Co., Inc., Ft. Worth, 1991—; asst. sec., treas. The Greenpark Found., Inc., N.Y.C., 1978-91, William S. Paley Found., Inc., N.Y.C., 1978-91; v.p. Burnett Ranches, Inc., Ft. Worth, 1991—, Burnett Aviation Co., Inc., Ft. Worth, 1991—, Exec. Protective Systems, Ft. Worth, 1991—; v.p., CFO Burnett Ranches, Ltd., Ft. Worth, 1992—; v.p., dir. Burnett Svcs., Inc., Ft. Worth, 1992—, Burnett Security Systems, Inc., Ft. Worth, 1994—; v.p. AJJM Capital Corp., Ft. Worth, 1996—; treas., dir. K&M, Inc., Ft. Worth, 1998—, Cookworks of Santa Fe, Inc., 1998—, Cookworks, Tex., Inc., Ft. Worth, 1998—; pres., dir. CW Beverages, Inc., Ft. Worth, 1999—, Addison Warehouse Beverages, Inc., Ft. Worth, 1999—. Bd. dirs., v.p., treas. Westwood Baseball Assn., 1977-88; v.p. Westwood Babe Ruth, 1985-88; treas. Tommy League, 1984-86; dir. Westwood Recreation Youth Football, 1984-86; mem. Westwood Inds. Club, 1976-80. Decorated Bronze star, Air medal with oak leaf cluster, Vietnamese Honor medal, Vietnamese Svc. medal, Vietnamese campaign medal w/four svc. stars, Nat. Def. Svc. medal. Mem. River Crest Country Club. Office: Burnett Oil Co Inc 801 Cherry St Ste 1500 Fort Worth TX 76102-6869

BOSCHI, ENZO, physicist, educator; b. Arezzo, Toscana, Italy, Feb. 27, 1942; s. Alfredo Boschi and Natalina (Boschi) Carli; m. Giovanna Pettini, May 23, 1971; 1 child, Lapo. Grad. in Physics, U. Bologna, Italy, 1968. Chair prof. seismology U. Ancona, Italy, 1975-77, U. Bologna, 1977—; mem. sci. coun. Targeted Geodynamics Project, 1975-80; pres. Istituto Nazionale di Geofisica, Rome, 1982—, Seimsmic Bd. of Coun. for Great Natural Hazards, 1986—, Nat. Geophysics Coun., Ministry of Univ. Italy, 1989—; advisor seismology Dept. Emergency Relief Italy, 1982—; mem. NATO's Adv. Panel Advanced Rsch., Belgium, 1989—; mem. Italian nat. com. Internat. Decade Reduction Natural Hazards, 1991—; vice. pres. com. E. Majorana Ctr., Erice, Italy, 1984—. Author: Physics of the Earth's Interior, 1980, Earthquakes/Observation, Theory and Interpretation, 1983, L'Ira Di Poseidone, 1988, Mednet: The Very-Broad Band Seismic Network for the Mediterranean, 1991. Corr. mem. Accademia Naz. Lincei, Rome, 1982—; dir. Internat. Sch. on Solid Earth and Geodesy-Centro Majorana, Erice. Recipient A. Feltrinelli prize for geophysics, 1981, Glzxo award for dissemination sci., 1988, Gold medal for sci., culture and art, 1988, Universum prize for geophysics, Potenze, Italy, 1991; named Grand Officer of Order of Merit of Italian Republic, 1991. Fellow Am. Geophys. Union; mem. Inst. Nat. Geofisica (pres. 1982—), Academia Europaea U.K. Avocations: cinema, literature. Fax: 0039-06-5041287. Home: Via de'Griffoni 5, 40123 Bologna BO, Italy Office: Inst Nazionale Geofisica, Via Vigna Murata 605, 00143 Rome RM, Italy

BOSCO, ANTHONY GERARD, bishop; b. New Castle, Pa., Aug. 1, 1927; s. Joseph M. and Theresa (Pezone) B. BA, St. Vincent Sem., Latrobe, Pa.; juris canonici licentiatus, Lateran U., Rome; LLD (hon.), Duquesne U., 1971; LHD (hon.), St.Vincent Coll., 1988. Ordained priest Roman Cath. Ch., 1952. Asst. chancellor Diocese of Pitts., 1955-65, vice chancellor, 1965-67, chancellor, 1967-85, aux. bishop, 1970-87; bishop Diocese of Greensburg, Pa., 1987—; chmn. Cath. Comms. Found., 1984—; hon. chmn., trustee Seton Hill Coll., Greensburg, 1987—; ex officio mem., bd. regents St. Vincent Sem., Latrobe, Pa., 1987—. Recipient Leonardo Da Vinci award for Religion Order of Italian Sons and Daughter, 1970; named Pitts.'s Man of Yr. in Religion Pitts. Jaycees, 1975. Mem. Nat. Conf. Cath. Bishops, Christian Assocs. S.W. Pa.

BOSCO, MICHEL FELIX, scientific researcher; b. Nice, France, May 29, 1961; s. Jean P. B. and Rosanna Bosco-Margaria. MS in Engring., Ecole Nat. des Travaux Publics, Lyon, France, 1984; PhD with honors, Ecole Nat. de l'Aeronautique, Toulouse, France, 1988. Rsch. engr. Cete Mediterranee, Aix, France, 1984-88; sci. officer European Commn., Brussels, 1990-98, head internat. cooperation, info. soc. tech. program, 1999—; vis. prof. U. Mass., Amherst, 1988-90; adj. prof. U. Aix, 1986-88. Contbr. articles to profl. jours. NATO grantee, 1989. Mem. IEEE, Assn. Computing Machinery, Assn. Francaise C.E.T. Achievements include design of schemes for scientific cooperation between European Commission and organizations in the U.S.A., Japan and several other industrialized or developing countries; research in database and software engineering. Avocations: horseback riding, chess. Office: European Commn, Rue De La Loi 200, 1049 Brussels Belgium

BOSCOVIC, DRAGAN MILOS, electrical engineer; b. Arandjelovac, Serbia, Yugoslavia, Jan. 6, 1959; arrived in Eng., 1988; s. Miloš Z. and Marija R. (Marković) B.; m. Vesna M. Radosavljevic, Dec. 21, 1985; children: Simonida, Katarina, Igor. Diploma in engring., U. Belgrade (Yugoslavia), 1983, MSEE, 1988; PhD, U. Bath (Eng.), 1991. Chartered engr., Eng. Rsch. assoc. Inst. of Applied Physics, Belgrade, 1983-88; rsch. asst. U. Bath, 1988-91; cons. Wessex Electronics, Bristol, Eng., 1989-91; sr. staff engr. Motorola, Basingstoke, Eng., 1991-96; dep. dir. lab. Motorola, Paris, 1996—. Patentee in field (Inventor of Yr. 1994, 97). Mem. IEEE (jour. reviewer 1995). Avocations: science of chaos, evolution, computers, chess. Office: Motorola Ctr of Rsch, St Aubiu, 91193 Gif-sur-Yvette Cedex, France

BOSE, JAYANTA KUMAR, oil and gas company executive; b. Kotma, India, Oct. 29, 1959; s. Rabindra Nath and Rekha (Palit) B.; m. Tandra Nandy, Feb. 7, 1987; 1 child, Soumik. BE (Mech.), Govt. Engring. Coll., Rewa, India, 1981. Asst. exec. engr. Oil & Natural Gas Corp. Ltd., Dehradun, India, 1982; asst. exec. engr. Oil & Natural Gas Corp. Ltd., Calcutta, 1983-86, exec. engr., 1987-91; dep. superintending engr. Oil & Natural Gas Corp. Ltd., Silchar, 1992-95; superintending engr. drilling Oil & Natural Gas Corp. Ltd., Rajahmundry, 1996—. Mem. Soc. Petroleum Engrs., Oil and Natural Gas Corp. Ltd. Officers Club. Avocations: sports, games. Home: Flat F4 Laxmi Apt 2, Rajahmundry 533103, India Office: Oil & Natural Gas Corp DBG, 4th Fl Shiva Twr Danavaipet, Rajahmundry 533103, India

BOSE, KINGSHUK, research engineer; b. Calcutta, India, Aug. 5, 1968; came to U.S., 1988; s. Kulada Prasad and Bina Bose; m. Minakshi Bose, July 4, 1991; 1 child, Shounak. B in Tech., Indian Inst. Tech., Kharagpur, 1988; MS, Johns Hopkins U., 1990; PhD, U. Pa., 1995. Rsch. asst. Johns Hopkins U., Balt., 1988-90, U. Pa., Phila., 1990-94; sr. rsch. engr. Hibbitt, Karlsson & Sorensen, Inc., Pawtucket, R.I., 1994—. Contbr. articles to profl. jours. Avocation: travel. Office: Hibbitt Karlsson & Sorensen Inc 1080 Main St Pawtucket RI 02860-4847

BOSE, SUBASH CHANDRA, dermatologist; b. Engandiyur, Kerala, India, May 10, 1943; arrived in United Arab Emirates, 1979; parents Ponnamchery Sankaran Kunhunny and Thayyil Kanda Kalliani; m. Kuzhiparambil Madhavan Pushpam; children: Priya, Maya. MB BChir, Med. Coll., Calicut, Kerala, 1966; diploma in venereology and dermatology, Med. Coll., Calcutta, India, 1976. Asst. surgeon Health Svcs., Kerala, 1967-79; specialist Ministry of Health, Ras Al Khaimah, United Arab Emirates, 1979-81, Al Salam Clinic, Sharjah, United Arab Emirates, 1982—. Mem. Indian Relief Com., Dubai, United Arab Emirates, 1995—; mem. World Wide Fund, Gland, Switzerland, 1998—. Fellow Am. Acad. Dermatology (non-resident); mem. Indian Assn. Dermatologists (life), Planetary Soc., Dermatology Club (pres. 1999-00). Fax: 9716-5612448. E-mail: supriyam@emirates.net.ae. Office: Al Salam Clinic, Al Arooba, Sharjah 1640, United Arab Emirates

BOSE, SUBHASIS, physicist, researcher; b. Calcutta, India, July 8, 1957; s. Shyamal Kumar and Anima (Deb Roy) B.; 1 child, Saptaparni. BSc, U. Calcutta, 1977; MSc, Indian Inst. Tech., Kharagpur, 1981, MPhil, 1982, PhD, 1990. Rsch. assoc. Indian Assn. for Cultivation of Sci., Calcutta, 1991-93, scientist dept. solar energy, 1995—; sr. scientist Ankur Sci., Baroda, India, 1994; cons. solar thermal and solar photovoltaic activities in India. Contbr. articles to profl. jours.; inventor in field. Organizer adult literacy program SELF, Dum Dum, Calcutta, 1993; founder ednl. instn. MERIT, Dum Dum; coord. solar cells for power applications in distant villages, West Bengal, India, 1995-97. Fellow Ministry of Non-Conventional Energy Sources, India, 1991-93, Dept. Sci. and Tech. Govt. of India, 1995. Mem. Materials Rsch. Soc. of India, Solar Energy Soc. of India. Hindu. Avocations: light classical music, devotional songs, Rabindrasangeet. Home: 257 Dr Meghnadsaha Rd, Calcutta 700074, India Office: Indian Assn Cultivation Scis Energy Rsch Ctr, 2A & B S C Mullick Rd, Calcutta 700032, India

BOSEKER, BARBARA JEAN, education educator; b. Milw., Dec. 2, 1944; d. Edward Herbert and Alice Margaret (Maas) B.; m. Dale Leslie Sutcliffe, Aug. 8, 1975. Student, U. Nigeria, Nsukka, 1966; BS (hon.) in secondary edn., U. Wis., Milw., 1968; MA in Anthropology, U. Wis., 1971, PhD in edn., 1978. cert. intermediate and secondary English tchr. Wis. Chemistry lab. technician Allen-Bradley Corp., Milw., 1963; coordinator Neighborhood Youth Corps., Madison, 1970; program devel. specialist Tchr. Corps., Madison, 1976-77; asst. prof. edn. Occidental Coll., 1978-80; asst. prof. edn. Moorhead State U., 1980-86, assoc. prof., 1986-90, prof., 1990-95; prof. Winona State U., 1995—; adv. bd.: Annual Editions: Teaching English as a Second Language, 1999—; cons. Inst. Latin Am. Studies U.Tex, Austin, 1980. Grant writer Fargo-Moorhead (N.D.) Indian Center, 1980; evaluator Indian edn. grant Fargo Pub. Schs., 1985-90; contbr. articles to profl. jours. Elks Nat. and State Youth scholar U. Wis.; fellow Ford Found., 1968-69, NDEA, 1970-71, 78. Mem. NEA, Minn. Edn. Assn., Nat. Women's Studies Assn., Mortar Bd., Phi Kappa Phi, Pi Lamda Theta, Kappa Delta Pi, Sigma Tue Delta, Sigma Epsilon Sigma. Democrat. Christian Scientist. Home: 1317 Ridgewood Dr Winona MN 55987-5421 Office: Winona State U Winona MN 55987

BOSERUP, ESTHER MALLING, editor; b. Odder, Denmark, Aug. 10, 1943; m. Niels Boserup, 1967; children: Caroline, Johan. Degree in occupational therapy, U. Aarhus, 1967. Editor Danish Jour. Occupational Therapists Ergoterapeuten, Copenhagen, 1968—. Author: At Blive Slank, 1994; contbr. articles to profl. jours. Bd. dirs. Danish Rheumatoid Assn., 1992—. Mem. Danish Journalist Union, The Assn. Danish Specialised Press (bd. dirs. 1998—). Office: Ergoterapeutforeningen, NR Voldgade 90, 1358 Copenhagen Denmark

BOSIO, ANGELO, pharmacologist, psychiatrist, scientific advisor; b. Brescia, Italy, Jan. 18, 1955; s. Giulio and Teresa (Macetti) B.; m. Barbara Casa, July 1, 2000. MD, Milan U., 1980, degree in pharmacology, 1982, degree in psychiatry, 1988. Intern Milan U. Med. Sch., 1984-88, cons. psychiatrist, 1988—; dir. pharmacological dept. St. Anne Clinic, Brescia, 1987—; dir. neurol. dept. St. Anne Clinic, Brescia, Italy, 1996—; cons. Internat. Pharm. Cos., 1983—, WHO, 1988, others; dir. A.A.N. Drug Monitoring Svc., N.Y.C., 1994—. Author: Handbook of Reaction Time Evaluation, 1991; editor Jour. Percorsi Sanitari, 1986—, Neuroscis. Collection, 1988, H & W in Medicine, 1992—; editor videotapes Neurotransmission, 1988, Axolytic Drugs: An Up to Date, 1989, The Metamorphosis, 1991, Mioclonus and Piracetam, 1991, The Living Proof, 1991, Video Minds Series, 1995, Depression, 1995, Epilepsy, 1996; journalist Sci. and Med. Press, 1982—; mng. dir. A.A.N., 1992—. Recipient Nutrition Found. award, Italy, 1982. Fellow AAAS, N.Y. Acad. Scis., Internat. Psychogeriatric Assn., Italian Psychiat. Soc.; mem. Assn. Advancement Neurosci. (pres. Brescia chpt. 1987-92, Internat. chpt. 1990—). Roman Catholic. Office: Assn Advancement Neurosci, Via Vivanti 9, Brescia 25133, Italy also: AAN 575 Madison Ave Ste 1006 New York NY 10022-2511

BOSL, GEORGE JOSEPH, physician, oncologist; b. Cleve., Oct. 19, 1948. BS in Biology, John Carroll U., 1969; MD, Creighton U., 1973.

Diplomate Am. Bd. Medicine, Am. Bd. Oncology. Intern N.Y. Hosp., 1973-74, resident in medicine, 1974-75; resident in medicine Sloan-Kettering Cancer Ctr., 1974-77; fellow in med. oncology U. Minn. Hosp., 1977-79; oncologist Meml. Sloan Kettering Cancer Ctr., N.Y.C., 1979—, dir. oncology, hematology fellow program, 1986-94, head divsn. solid tumor oncology, 1989-97, assoc. physician-in-chief, 1994-97, chmn. dept. medicine, 1997—; prof. medicine Cornell U., N.Y.C., 1991—. Mem. AMA, Am. Assn. Cancer Edn., Am. Assn. Cancer Rsch., Am. Soc. Clin. Oncology, Alpha Omega Alpha. Office: Meml Sloan Kettering Ctr New York NY 10021

BOSLER, CHARLES WALTER, JR., retired military officer, engineer; b. Phila., May 14, 1949; s. Charles Walter Bosler Sr. and Rosemary (Flynn) Toomey; m. Elizabeth Louise Wagner, Jan. 22, 1977; children: Marc Anthony, Charles Walter III. Degree in fgn. langs., U. Md., Iwakuni, Japan, 1972; AAEE, Johnson County Community Coll., Overland Park, Kans., 1975; Cert. Advanced Studies EE, USN Electronics, Memphis, 1983; BS in Physics, Worcester State Coll., 1988. Avionics supr. USMC, various locations overseas, 1969-78; recruiting officer USMC, Levittown, N.Y., 1978-82; avionics chief USMC, Yuma, Ariz., 1983-87, retired, 1987; program mgr. U.S. Navy programs F/A-18C/D electronic warfare Tech. Resources, Inc., Milford, N.H., 1989-93; mgmt. cons. Bosler Cons., 1993-95; pres., CEO Svcs. and Tech. Group, Inc., 1995—; cons. Stafford Industries, Worcester, Mass., 1987-88, Computer Profls. Unltd., Stowe, Mass., 1987-88; chmn. Project Mgmt. Inst. Risk Mgmt. SIG, 1998—; mem. Am. Project Mgmt. Forum, Global Project Mgmt. Forum. Author computer programs, 1985-87. Coach Yuma Boys Baseball League, 1983-86, mem. exec. bd., 1986-87; coach Yuma Intramural Football League, 1985-86; counselor Ariz. Law Enforcement Acad., Tucson, 1986, St. Patricks Ch., Milford, N.H. Recipient Vol. Action award Pres. U.S., Washington, 1987, Gerald C. Thomas award Sec. Navy, Washington, 1987, Inspirational Leadership award Navy League U.S., Washington, 1987. Mem. Am. Legion (life, fin. officer, adjutant, MSM award 1985, 86, 87, Legionnaire of Yr. award 1987), VFW (life, chaplain 1986-88), Disabled Am.Vets (life), MC Assn. (chartered life, Quantico, Va.), Assn. Old Crows, Elks. Roman Catholic. Avocations: woodworking, gardening, fishing, sports. Home: 42 Falconer Ave Milford NH 03055-4104

BOSLER, LAWRENCE M., III, retired manufacturing engineer; b. Phila., Nov. 21, 1940; s. Lawrence M. Jr. and Emma M. (Weber) B.; m. Carol M. Rankin, Dec. 4, 1965; children: John Lawrence, Robert Lawrence. Diploma, Cleve. Inst. Electronics, 1964. Engring. tech. Philco-Ford Corp., Phila., 1958-71, Optical Scanning Corp., Newtown, Pa., 1971-73, Terak Corp., Scottsdale, Ariz., 1979-81; mgr. ops. Micor Internat., Inc., Tempe, Ariz., 1974-79; sr. mfg. engr. Sundstrand Aviation, Phoenix, 1981-96; sr. mfg. engr. Boeing Aircraft Co., Phoenix, 1997-99, ret., 2000; gen. mgr. Ponderosa, Inc., Warminster, Pa., 1962-76; cons. Computer Consoles, Syracuse, N.Y., 1969. Coach YMCA Soccer Program, Tempe, 1977-82, 86-90. Mem. Am. Vecturist Assn., East Penn Traction Club. Avocations: model tractioneering.

BOSLEY, KAREN LEE, English and journalism educator; b. Beech Grove, Ind., Sept. 23, 1942; d. Lowell Holmes and Kathryn Gertrude (Drake) Foley; m. Norman Keith Bosley, Dec. 21, 1964; children: Mark Harold, Rachael Kathryn, Keith Lowell, Sidney Clark. AB in Lang. Arts summa cum laude, U. Indpls., 1965; MA in English, Northwestern U., 1967; MA in Journalism, Ball State U., 1984; postgrad. (Newspaper Fund fellow), U. Mo., 1973; postgrad., Ohio U., 1977. Copy editor, reporter Indpls. News, 1963-65; English tchr., yearbook adviser Beech Grove (Ind.) Jr. H.S., 1965-66; English tchr. So. Regional H.S., Manahawkin, N.J., 1967-68; prof. humanities, journalism, and English Ocean County Coll., Toms River, N.J., 1971—, student newspaper adviser, 1971—; part-time reporter Daily Times-Observer, Toms River, 1972-77, part-time copy editor, 1993. Contbr. articles to publs. in field. Trustee Long Beach Island Hist. Assn., Friends of Island Libr., 1975-79; pres. Long Beach I PTA; chmn. Long Beach Twp. Dem. Mcpl. Com., 1971-78; Dem. committeeman Long Beach Twp. Dist. 2, 1971-78, 85—; mem. Long Beach Twp. Recreation Commn., 1972-75; bd. dirs. Ocean County Red Cross, 1972-78, Ocean County Family Planning, Inc., 1972-78, Student Press Law Ctr., 1987—, sec., 1994-2000; chmn. Cub Scout pack 32, Ocean County Coun. Boy Scouts Am.; founder, bd. dirs. Long Beach I Hist. Assn., Island Dems., Inc.; mem. adminstrv. bd. First United Meth. Ch. Beach Haven Terrance (N.J.); So. Regional H.S. Band Parent Orgn., 1995-96, pres., 1996-97, corr. sec. Mem. AAUW (pres., dir. Barnegat Light Area br.), NEA, N.J. Edn. Assn., Ocean County Edn. Assn., Faculty Assn. Ocean County Coll. (v.p. 1984-85), Coll. Media Advisers, Inc. (disting. newspaper adviser for U.S. 2-yr. colls. 1978, dir., sec.), Assn. Edn. in Journalism and Mass Comms., C.C. Journalism Assn. (dir., v.p.), Soc. Profl. Journalists, Sigma Delta Chi. Home: 9 E Old Whaling Ln Lg Beach Township NJ 08008-2930 Office: Ocean CC PO Box 2001 College Dr Toms River NJ 08754-2001

BOSMA, ANNE ADRIAAN, electrical engineer; b. Harlingen, The Netherlands, Oct. 12, 1952; arrived in Sweden, 1983; s. Gerlof and Uldrika (Vellinga) V.; m. Johanna M.M. Lodewijks, Oct. 1, 1990. M, Eindhoven U. Tech., The Netherlands, 1979. Rsch. asst. Eindhoven U. Tech., 1979-83; design engineer ABB Switchgear, Ludvika, Sweden, 1983-92; tech. sales support ABB Switchgear, Ludvika, 1993—; application specialist ABB Inc., Varennes, Can., 1992-93; tech. sales support ABB Switchgear AB, Ludvika, Sweden, 1993-99, specialist high voltage switching equipment, 1999—; sec. IEC TC17 & SC 17A, Geneva, 1993—. Mem. IEEE (sr.), CIGRE. Home: Röbacksvägen 67, 77160 Ludvika Sweden

BOSMA, ROEL HERMAN, animal husbandry scientist; b. Finkebourren, Netherlands, May 8, 1953; s. Eelke Rudolphus and Yfke Maria (Dijkstra) B.; m. Alice Toe, Nov. 22, 1986; children: Eelke, Laetitia. BSc, Agrl. U., Wageningen, Netherlands, 1975, MSc, 1979. Extension officer SNV (Dutch Peace Corps), Markoye, Burkina Faso, 1980-82; mgr. livestock ctr. SNV (Dutch Peace Corps), Toma, Burkina Faso, 1982-85; animal scientist U. Groningen, Ouagadougou, Burkina Faso, 1985-90, Royal Tropical Inst. of Amsterdam, Sikasso, Mali, 1990-95; cons. animal prodn. Dutch Ministry Fgn. Affairs, Koudougou, Burkina Faso, 1996-99; rsch. animal prodn. sys. Wageningen U., 2000—. Editor, author: L'elevage en voie d'intensification, 1996. Avocations: carpentry, cycling, bridge. Home: Roghorst 363, 6708 KX Wageningen Netherlands

BOSMAN, MICHAEL JOHN, business executive; b. South Africa, Nov. 13, 1960; s. Jan Christoffel John and Kathleen May Bosman; s. Sabine Mathilde Thien. B in Commerce with honors, LLM. Lic. airline transport pilot, comml. pilot. Articled clk. then audit supr. Coopers & Lybrand, CT, 1983-86; cons. corp. and project fin. Investec Bank, 1988-89; fin. mgr. Kaytrad Commodities Group of Coys, 1989-92; mng. dir. Bosman Johnson FCB, CT, 1992-97; chair, group CEO FCB South Africa, 1998—; chair Electric Ocean, 1994—, The Flying Co., 1994—, FCB Bosman Johnson, 1997—, FCB Lindsay Smithers Bond, 1998—, FCB Lindsay Smithers, 1998—, FCB Jonssons Advt., 1999; bd. dirs. Foote, Cone & Belding Worldwide, 1998—. Capt. South African Air Force, 1986-88. Mem. South Africa Inst. Chartered Accts., IMM, Airline Pilots Assn. South Africa, Comml. Aviation Assn. So. Africa Jhb (pres. 1998-99), Assn. Advt. Agys. (dir. 1997-2000), Aero Club South African (dir. 1997-2000, Gold Wings), Royal Cape Yacht Club. Avocations: flying, classical piano, wine. Office: 150 E 42nd St New York NY 10017

BOSNJAK, MARIJAN, biotechnologist, retired; b. Lovrec, Imotski, Croatia, Dec. 2, 1934; s. Jakov and Andja (Petricevic) B.; m. Nada Kovacic, Mar. 10, 1962; children: Kresimir, Zeljana. BChemE, Zagreb U., 1959, MSc in Biotech., 1961, PhD in Biotech., 1973. Rschr. Pliva Co. Rsch. Inst., Zagreb, 1960-61; fermentation plant mgr. Pliva-Antibiotics, Zagreb, 1962-68; sr. rschr. Pliva-Rsch. Inst., Zagreb, 1969-2000; ret., 2000; governing bd. Rudjer Boskovic Inst., Zagreb, 1995-2000; prof. math. model biochem. engring. Faculty Biotechnol., Zagreb, 1984—; assoc. instr. org. chem. exercises Faculty of Technol., Zagreb, 1964-67. Contbr. articles to profl. jours.; patentee in field. Mem. Croatian Cultural Soc.-Matrix Croatica. Recipient Sci. award Ministry Sci. of Croatia, 1988. Mem. Croatian Soc. Biotech. (chmn. 1990-96), Croatian Soc. Chem. Engring. (chmn. 1988), Croatian Acad. Tech. Sci. Roman Catholic. Avocation: temporary charitable activities. Home: Slovenska 19, HR-10000 Zagreb Croatia

BOSS, WALTER HANS, lawyer; b. Berne, Switzerland, June 6, 1952; s. Hans W. and Lisa (von Kaenel) B.; m. Francesca L. Sadis, June 20, 1987; children: Gianluca, Carolina. Law degree, U. Berne, 1980; LLM in Taxation Law, NYU, 1988. Bar: Zurich and all Swiss Bars, Supreme Ct. Berne, 1980. Legal counsel Fed. Tax Adminstrn., Berne, 1980-84; v.p. Fidinam Fiduciaria SA, Lugano, Switzerland, 1984-86, Arthur Young, Zurich, Switzerland, 1986-87; ptnr. Ernst & Young, N.Y.C., 1988-90, Pestalozzi Gmuer & Patry, Zurich, 1991—; del. OECD Com. on Fiscal Affairs; chmn. GE Capital AG, Zurich, 1993—; dir. Time Life AG, Schaffhausen, Switzerland, 1994—. Author: (legal commentary) Di Eidgenössische Mehrwertsteuer, 1994, (nat. report) Non-Discrimination Rules in International Taxation, 1995; coauthor: (legal commentary) Double Tax Treaty Switzerland-Germany, 1983, Double-Tax Treaty Switzerland-USA, 1997; contbr. articles as sr. corr. to Tax Notes Internat., 1994—. Mem. fin. com. FDP, Berne, 1995—; chmn. tax chpt. bd. Swiss-Am. C. of C. Mem. Internat. Bar Assn., Internat. Fiscal Assn., Bar Assn. Zurich. Mem. FDP. Avocations: art, music, historic cars. Office: Pestalozzi Gmuer & Patry, Löwenstrasse 1, 8001 Zurich Switzerland

BOSSER, STEVEN JOHN, prosecutor; b. Yonkers, N.Y., Dec. 27, 1952; s. John Joseph and Margaret Frances (Flanagan) B.; m. Susan Virginia Coggins, Oct. 17, 1981; children: Timothy, Katharine. BA in Econ., SUNY, Albany, 1977; JD, St. John's U., Jamaica, N.Y., 1984. Bar: N.Y. 1985, N.J. 1985, U.S. Dist. Ct. N.J. 1985, Tex. 1986, U.S. Dist. Ct. (no. dist.) Tex. 1988, U.S. Supreme Ct. 1989, DC Ct. Appeals, 1989. Asst. city atty. City Atty's. Office, Ft. Worth, 1986-87; asst. criminal dist. atty. Tarrant County Dist. Atty's. Office, Ft. Worth, 1987—; lectr. Tex. Dept. Pub. Safety, Austin, 1993-97, Tarrant County Auto Theft Task Force, Ft. Worth, 1994-97. Com. chair Boy Scouts Am., 1994-96, various other positions, 1995—. With U.S. Army, 1973-76. Recipient Prosecutor Yr. award Tex. Assn. Vehicle Theft Investigators, 1994; named to Outstanding Young Men of Am., 1987. Mem. Tex. State Bar Assn., Tex. Dist. and County Attys. Assn., D.C. Bar Assn. Republican. Avocations: camping, hiking, computers. Office: Tarrant County Dist Atty 401 W Belknap St Fl 4 Fort Worth TX 76102-1913

BOSSUYT, XAVIER ANDRE ANNA, pathologist; b. Kortrijk, Belgium, June 14, 1963; s. Guy Bossuyt and Marthe David; m. Rita Maria-Leonia Derua, Sept. 24, 1967. MD, Cath. U., Leuven, Belgium, 1988, PhB, 1991, PhD, 1994, med. specialist in clin. pathology, 1996; M in Informatics, Free U., Brussels, 1990. Doctor U. Hosp., Leuven, 1988-90; rschr. U. Leuven, 1990-93, U. Zürich, 1993-95; Fogarty fellow NIH, Bethesda, Md., 1995-96; clin. pathologist U. Hosp., Leuven, 1996—; presenter in field. Contbr. chpt. to book and articles to profl. jours. Recipient Young Investigator award Cytometry Soc., 1996; grantee Belgian Nat. Fund for Sci. Rsch., 1991-96, D. Collen Rsch. grant, 1993-95. Home: Mechelsveldstraat 24, 2800 Mechelen Belgium Office: Clin Pathology, Univ Hosp, 3000 Leuven Belgium

BOST, JOHN ROWAN, retired manufacturing executive, engineer; b. Spartanburg, S.C., May 9, 1922; s. John Rowan and May Netta (Swink) Bost-McDaniel; m. Martha Angela Simmons, June 8, 1963; children: John Rowan III, Warren Vincent. Aircraft fabrication grad., Anderson Airplane Sch., 1941-42; student spl. courses, USN, 1942-60. Assembler, leadman Goodyear Aircraft, Akron, Ohio, 1942; aviation chief metalsmith USN, 1942-46; v.p., sec., supt. Greenwood (S.C.) Meml. Gardens, 1950-56; owner, pres., engr. B & H Industries, Laurens, S.C., 1959-62; engr. The Torrington Co., Clinton, S.C., 1961-75; engr. and developer Byars Machine Co., Laurens, S.C., 1979-86; pres., engr. Downey Bost Corp., Fountain Inn, S.C., 1986-94; ret., 1994; owner, organizer NIFTI Industries Corp., Laurens, 1994-96; instr. Greenville (S.C.) Tech. Coll., 1962-82; instr. numerous cos., 1962—. Inventor and patentee in field. Baptist. Home: PO Box 902 Laurens SC 29360-0902

BOST, PIERRE-ETIENNE, research scientist; b. Lyon, France, Aug. 3, 1945; s. Georges Louis and Hélène Lucie (Laurent) B.; m. Claude Caroline Bougarel, Feb. 20, 1971; children: Laurence, Emmanuelle, Charles. Degree in chemical engring., Ecole Supérieure de Chimie Industrielle de Lyon, Lyon, 1967; PhD, U. Paris, 1971; MS, MIT. Researcher Inst. Pasteur, Paris, 1967-71; engr. Rhône Poulenc, St. Fons, France, 1971-72; from dept. head to dept. mgr. Rhône Poulenc, France, 1976-81; assoc. researcher MIT, 1973-75; sci. mgr. Rhône Poulenc Group, Paris, 1981-82; from dir. rsch. projects to dir. rsch. Rhône Poulenc Sante', Paris, 1983-90; sr. v.p. drug devel. and R&D planning Rhône Poulenc Rorer, Vitry Sur Seine, France, 1990-94, sci. dir. biochemistry, food ingredients R&D dir., 1995—; mem. Coun. Sci. l'Agence du Medicament, France, 1993—. Editor: The Future Antibiotherapy and Antibiotic Research, 1980. Mem. Com. Applications Acad. Sci. Assn. Office: Rhone Poulenc Chimie, 25 Quai Paul Doumer, 92408 Courbevoie Cedex France

BOSTIC, MARY JONES, librarian; b. Durham, N.C., June 20, 1939; d. Isaac William and Jennie Mae (Edwards) Jones; m. Charles Thomas Bostic Sr., Aug. 4, 1970; 1 child, Precious Jennifer Bostic-Conklin. BA, N.C. Ctrl. U., 1964, MLS, 1969; MS, L.I. U., 1975, cert. advanced studies, 1980. Sec. Randolph County Home Econs. Agt., Asheboro, N.C., 1958-60; adminstrv. asst. chief libr. N.C. Ctrl. U., Durham, 1964-69; asst acquisitions libr. L.I. U., Bklyn., 1969-75, acquisitions libr., 1975—. Contbr. articles to profl. jours. Active Coun. Bd. #13, Queens, 1975—. Mem. Assn. Coll. and Rsch. Librs., N.Y. Tech. Svcs. Librs., N.C. Libr. Assn., N.C. Ctrl. U. Sch. Lib. Sci. Alumni Assn., Palmer Grad. Libr. Sch. Alumni Assn., L.I. U. Faculty Fedn., Beta Phi Mu (Beta Mu chpt.), United Block Assn., Dem. Club (Queens). Baptist. Avocations: reading, writing, theater, bowling, walking. Home: 10416 198th St Jamaica NY 11412-1216 Office: Long Island Univ 1 University Plz Brooklyn NY 11201-5372

BOSTICK, ROBERD MANER, epidemiologist, family physician; b. Beaufort, S.C., Aug. 21, 1951; s. Maner Lawton and Nelrae (Truesdale) B.; m. Rita Thetford, June 17, 1973; children: Sarah Elizabeth, Benjamin David. BS, Wofford Coll., 1973; MD, U. S.C., 1976; MPH, U. Minn., 1990. Diplomate Am. Bd. Family Practice. Physician East Cooper Family Practice, Mt. Pleasant, S.C., 1979-82, Beaufort (S.C.) Family Medicine, PA, 1982-88; fellow acad. medicine U. Minn., Mpls., 1988-90, asst. prof. family practice, cmty. health and epidemiology, 1990-94; assoc. prof. pub. health scis., family and cmty. medicine Wake Forest U., Winston-Salem, N.C., 1994-98; prof. family/preventive medicine, epidemiology, biostats. U. S.C., Columbia, 1998—, dir. divsn. population studies S.C. Cancer Ctr., 1998—; program leader cancer epidemiology and prevention Comprehensive Cancer Ctr. of Wake Forest U., 1994—. Contbr. articles to profl. jours.; mem. editl. adv. bd. Cancer Epidemiology Biomarkers and Prevention, 1995—, Archives of Family Practice, 1994—. Fellow Am. Acad. Family Practice; mem. Am. Soc. Preventive Oncology (chair chemoprevention group 1996—), Am. Assn. Cancer Rsch., Soc. for Epidemiological Rsch. (Merck/SER Clin. Epidemiology Fellowship award 1994), Soc. Tchrs. of Family Medicine (New Faculty award 1992), Phi Beta Kappa, Alpha Omega Alpha, Delta Omega. Democrat. Methodist. Achievements include findings of association of decreased risk of colon cancer with higher intakes of calcium, vitamin E, and increased risk with higher intakes of sucrose. Avocations: fishing, backpacking, gardening, reading. Office: SC Cancer Ctr U SC Ste 301 15 Richland Medical Park Dr Columbia SC 29203-6863

BOSTON, WILLIAM CLAYTON, lawyer; b. Hobart, Okla., Nov. 29, 1934; s. William Clayton and Dollie Jane (Gibbs) B.; m. Billie Gail Long, Jan. 20, 1962; children: Kathryn Gray, William Clayton III. BS, Okla. State U., 1958; LLB, U. Okla., 1962; LLM, NYU, 1967. Bar: Okla. 1961. Assoc. Mosteller, Fellers, Andrews, Snider & Baggett, Oklahoma City, 1962-64; ptnr. Fellers, Snider, Baggett, Blankenship & Boston, Oklahoma City, 1968-69, Andrews, Davis, Legg, Bixler, Milsten & Murrah, Oklahoma City, 1972-86; pvt. practice Boston & Boston PLLC, Oklahoma City, 1986—. Contbr. articles to profl. jours.; mem. adv. bd. The Jour. of Air Law and Commerce, 1995—. Past pres. and trustee Ballet Okla.; past v.p., bd. dirs. Oklahoma City Arts Coun.; past trustee Nichols Hills (Okla.) Methodist Ch.; past trustee, chmn. Okla. Found. for the Humanities; past trustee, vice-chmn., sec. Humanities in Okla., Inc., 1992-95. With U.S. Army, 1954-56. Mem. ABA (former chmn. subcom. on aircraft fin., former chmn. aircraft fin. and contract divsn. forum on air and space law), FBA, Internat. Bar Assn., Inter-Pacific Bar Assn., Okla. State Bar Assn., Oklahoma County Bar Assn. Home: 1701 Camden Way Oklahoma City OK 73116-5121 Office: 4005 NW Expressway St Oklahoma City OK 73116-1691

BOSTRÖM, ANDERS EINAR, mechanics educator; b. Stockholm, Nov. 2, 1951; s. Lennart Lars and Ulla Catarina (Cassel) B.; m. Eva Eleonore Magnusson, May 16, 1985; children: Malte, Emma. MSc in Engring. Physics, Chalmers U. Tech., Göteborg, Sweden, 1975, PhD in Math. Physics, 1980, Docent Math. Physics, 1982. Rsch. asst. Chalmers U. Tech., 1980-85, prof. mechanics, chmn. dept., 1985—, head dept. theoretical and applied mechanics, 1988-97, vice dean Sch. Mech. and Vehicular Engring., 1993-97. Contbr. over 50 articles to sci. jours., including Jour. Acoustical Soc. Am., Wave Motion. Mem. Acoustical Soc. Am. Avocation: running. Home: Mellbyvägen 38, SE-43330 Partille Sweden Office: Chalmers U Tech, Dept Mechanics, SE-41296 Göteborg Sweden

BOSTWICK, JANET, Bahaman government official; b. Nassau, Oct. 30, 1939; m. John Henry Bostwick; 4 children. Stenographer, 1957-67; pvt. sec. Atty. Gen., 1961-67; legal apprentice, 1966-71, adminstrv. officer legal dept., 1967-71; sec. gen. Bahamas Pub. Svc. Union, 1967-71, Crown Counsel, 1971-74; ptnr. Bostwick and Bostwick, 1975—; min. social svcs., nat. ins. housing Govt. of Bahamas, Nassau, 1993-97, min. fgn. affairs, 1994—, atty. gen., 1994-97, 99—. Senator, 1977-79; pres. Bahamas Bar Assn., 1980-82, Internat. Caribbean Women Democracy, 1986—; mem. Bahamian House Assembly, 1982—. Office: Ministry Fgn Affairs, East Hill St POB N-3746, Nassau Bahamas

BOSWELL, ANGELA, history educator; b. Jacksonville, Fla., Dec. 12, 1965; d. Buford Melvin and Wyma Boswell. BA, Southwestern U., Georgetown, Tex., 1987; MA, Rice U., 1995, PhD, 1998. Instr. Del Mar C.C., Corpus Christi, Tex., 1996; asst. prof. history Henderson State U., Arkadelphia, Ark., 1997—. Contbr. articles to profl. jours. Exec. dir. Tex. Women's Polit. Caucus, Austin, 1988-92; sec., bd. dirs. Abused Women & Children, Inc., Arkadelphia, 1998—. Fellow Rice U., 1992-96; P.E.O. scholar, 1996-97. E-mail: boswela@hsu.edu. Office: Henderson State U PO Box 7754 Arkadelphia AR 71999-7754

BOSWELL, GARY TAGGART, investor, former electronics company executive; b. Fr. Worth, Dec. 24, 1937; s. David W. and Marjory (Taggart) B.; m. Margaret Ruth Yelvington, Sept. 8, 1957 (dec. Jan. 1997); m. Tommie Jean Horn, Dec. 19, 1998; children: Michael David, Margaret McQuiston, Susannah Ruth. BA, Tex. Christian U., 1958, MS, 1965; postgrad., San Diego State Coll., 1960-61. Scientist U.S. Govt. White Sands (N.Mex.) Missile Range, 1958-59; rsch. engr. Gen. Dynamics, San Diego, 1959-60; programmer Bell Helicopter, Hurst, Tex., 1960-63; sect. head Collins Radio Co., Dallas, 1963-68; mgr. software devel. Tex. Instruments, Inc., Austin, 1968-72; mgr. ASC (Advanced Sci. Computer) Mktg., 1973-75, mgr. ASC divsn., 1975-76, mgr. computer sys., 1976-80, mgr. global positioning sys., 1980-81, mgr. TI engring. sys., 1981-83, v.p. equipment group, mgr. intelligent sys. divsn., 1983-86; pres. Aydin Monitor Sys., Ft. Washington, Pa., 1987-88; pres. Aydin Computer and Monitor, Horsham, Pa., 1988-95, investor, 1995—; Mem. Am. Nat. Fortran Standards Com., 1970-74. Designer several Fortran Compliers. Winner Western Hemisphere Snipe championship, 1970, also other maj. regattas. Mem. Snipe Classs Internat. Racing Assn. Home and Office: 107 Clubhouse Dr Lakeway TX 78734-4608

BOSWELL, GEORGE MARION, JR., orthopedist, health care facility administrator; b. Dallas, May 12, 1920; s. George Marion and Viola (Scarbrough) B.; m. Veta M. Fuller, Oct. 30, 1958; children: Brianna Boswell Brown, Kama Boswell Koudelka, Maia Boswell. BS, Tex. Tech U., 1940; MD, U. Tex., Southwestern Dallas, 1950. Diplomate Am. Acad. Orthopaedic Surgery. Intern Parkland Hosp., Dallas, 1950-51; resident gen. surgeryand orthopedic surgery Parkland, Baylor and Scottish Rite Hosps., Dallas, 1951-55; practice medicine specializing in orthopedics Dallas, 1955—; v.p. med. affairs Baylor Health Care System, Dallas, 1982-86; dir. orthopaedic clin. studies Baylor U. Med. Ctr., 1995—; owner Bee Aviation Inc., Dallas, 1968—, Boswell Realty Inc., Dallas, 1971—; lectr., cons. on health care delivery. Contbr. articles to profl. jours. Prof. George M. Bowell, Jr. chair in orthopaedic surgery named in his honor Baylor U. Med. Ctr. Fellow ACS; mem. AMA, Am. Acad. Orthopaedic Surgery (Key Man U.S. Congress 1980—), Am. Hosp. Assn., Tex. Hosp. Assn. (Key Man Tex. Legislature 1980—, council on hosp. staffs), Flying Physicians (pres. Tex. 1960-64). Republican. Methodist. Club: Cresent (Dallas). Avocations: flying, photography, fishing, saddle making. Home: 7249 Wabash Cir Dallas TX 75214-3535 Office: Baylor U Med Ctr Dept Orthopaedic Surgery 3500 Gaston Ave Dallas TX 75246-2096

BOSWELL, WILLIAM PARET, lawyer; b. Washington, Oct. 24, 1946; s. Yates Paret and Mary Frances (Hyland) B.; m. Barbara Stelle Schroeder, Sept. 6, 1969; children: Susan Anne, Sarah Mary, Christina Catherine. BA cum laude, Cath. U., 1968; JD, U. Va., 1971. Bar: Va. 1971, D.C. 1972, U.S. Ct. Mil. Appeals 1972, U.S. Supreme Ct. 1975, Pa. 1978. Atty. Peoples Natural Gas Co., Pitts., 1978-82, asst. sec., gen. atty., 1982-85, sec., gen. counsel, 1985-88, v.p., gen. counsel, sec., 1989-99; gen. counsel Hope Gas, Inc., Pitts., 1998-2000; dep. gen. counsel Consol. Natural Gas Co., Pitts., 1999-2000, Dominion Resources, Inc., Pitts., 2000; ptnr. McGuire Woods LLP, Pitts., 2000—; mem. exec. com. Gas Industry Stds. Bd., 1994-97, bd. dirs., 1998—, vice chmn., 1998—. Pres. Borough Coun., Osborne, Pa., 1984-97, mayor, 1998—; bd. dirs. Mendelssohn Choir Pitts., 1996—, pres. 1997-98; trustee Laughlin Found., 1995—. Capt. JAGC, USAF, 1971-78, col. USAFR, 1978-98, ret. Decorated Legion of Merit. Mem. ABA (chair gas com. 1995—), Pa. Bar Assn., D.C. Bar Assn., Va. Bar Assn., Am. Gas Assn. (chair regulatory com. 1996-98), Pa. Gas Assn. (chmn. 1989-90), Am. Corp. Counsel Assn. (pres. Pa. chpt. 1991-92, Excellence in Corporate Practice award 1998), Am. Soc. Corp. Secs., City Club Pitts., Army and Navy Club D.C. Republican. Roman Catholic. Avocations: reading, walking. Home: 405 Hare Ln Sewickley PA 15143-2050 Office: CNG Tower 23 Fl 625 Liberty Ave Fl 23D Pittsburgh PA 15222-3110

BOSWORTH, ALBERT BRIAN, classics educator; b. Mansfield, U.K., Mar. 21, 1942; s. Albert Killick Henry and Madge (Allcock) B. MA, Oxford U., 1965, MPhil, 1967. Prof., personal chair U. Western Australia, 1967—; mem. Sch. Hist. Studies Inst. for Advanced Studies, Princeton, N.J., 1975, 91; fellow Australian Acad. of the Humanities, 1982—; vis. prof. Harvard U., Cambridge, 1980-81; vis. fellow All Souls Coll., Oxford, 1998. Author: (book) Historical Commentary on Arrian's History of Alexander, Vol. I, 1980, II, 1995, From Arrian to Alexander, 1988, Conquest and Empire: The Reign of Alexander the Great, 1988, Alexander and the East, 1996. Office: U Western Australia, Dept Classics and History, Western Australia WA 6907, Australia

BOSWORTH, HAYDEN BARRY, health science educator; b. Huntington, N.Y., Apr. 21, 1970; m. Rebecca Ann Essinger, Sept. 7, 1997. BA, Brandeis U., 1992; MS, Pa. State U., 1994, PhD, 1996. Postdoctoral fellow Duke U., Durham, N.C., 1997, asst. prof., 1997—; health scientist Durham VA Med. Ctr., 1997—. Contbr. articles to profl. jours. Recipient award Nat. Cancer Inst., 1998—. E-mail: hboswort@acpub.duke.edu. Office: Durham VA Med Ctr 508 Fulton St Durham NC 27710-0001

BOSWORTH, STEPHEN WARREN, ambassador; b. Grand Rapids, Mich., Dec. 4, 1939; s. Warren Charles and Mina (Phillips) B.; m. Christine Holmes, June 7, 1984; children—Andrew, Allison. A.B., Dartmouth Coll., 1961; LLD, Darmouth Coll., 1986. Joined U.S. Fgn. Service; service in Panama, Colon, Madrid and Paris; dep. asst. sec. state, 1976-79, ambassador to Tunisia, 1979-81, dep. asst. sec. Inter-Am. affairs, 1981-82; dir. policy planning staff coun. U.S. Fgn. Svc., 1983-84; ambassador Manila, Philippines, 1984-87; pres. U.S.-Japan Found., 1988-96; exec. dir. Korean Energy Devel. Orgn., 1995-97; amb. to Republic of Korea Seoul, 1997—; adj. prof. Columbia U., 1990—. Trustee Dartmouth Coll., 1992—, chmn. bd. trustees, 1996-99. Recipient Dept. State Disting. Honor award, 1976, 86, Arthur S. Flemming award, 1976; named Diplomat of Yr., Am. Acad. Diplomacy, 1986. Office: Am Embassy Seoul South Korea Dept State Washington DC 20521-0001

BÖSZÖRMÉNYI, MIKLÓS, physician, pneumonologist; b. Budapest, Hungary, Jan. 29, 1914; s. Jenö and Ilona (Lèvai)ůB.; m. Éva Milhelffy; children: Catherine, Leslie; m. Maria Hernadi, 1996. Grad., Med. U., Budapest, Hungary, 1938, pneumonologist, 1942; tchr., Acad Music, Budapest, Hungary, 1938. Intern Nat. Inst. for Lung Diseases, Budapest, 1939-48, head physician, 1948-57, dir., 1957-70; prof. U. for Med. Postgrad. Tchg., Budapest, 1964-83, prof. emeritus, 1983—; cons. Nat. Inst. for Pulmonary Diseases, Budapest, 1983—. Author: Drug Treatment of

Tuberculosis, 1964, Lung Diseases in Adulthood, 1968; author and editor: Lung Cancer, 1988. Recipient of Markusovszky prize, Med. Jour., 1964, State prize, Health Ministry, 1970, Pro Urbe, Budapest Coun., 1974; named Hon. Citizen Budapest, Budapest Coun., 1998. Avocations: chamber music, piano. Home: Ábel Jenő 5, 1113 Budapest Hungary

BOTELLO CORTE, RICARDO, information specialist, administrator; b. Mexico City, June 2, 1945; s. Tomas Botello Gasca and Maria Teresa Corte Ramirez; m. Josefina Diaz Sanchez, Sept. 10, 1970; children: Norma Laura, Zaira Veronica, Karla Josefina, Jose Ricardo. MLS, UNAM, Mexico City, 1984, degree in vet. sci., 1969. Tchr. Vet. Sch. Chiapas U., Tuxtla Gutiérrez, Mex., 1978-83, head pub. svcs. Ctrl. Libr., 1985-89, head acad. librs. coord. of libr. sys., 1989-90; trainer Gen. Direction Pub. Librs. of Pub. Edn., Mexico City, 1984-85; head info. svcs. Nat. Inst. Nuc. Rsch., Mexico City, 1990-94, head info. ctr., 1994—; liaison officer Internat. Nuc. Info. Sys. of IAEA, Mexico City, 1995—. Avocations: gardening, travel, reading, social events. Home: Casa Blanca, 107 Perales Apt 3, 52140 Metepec Mexico Office: Nat Inst Nuc Rsch, Km 36.5 Carretera Mex-Toluc, 52045 Salazar Mexico

BOTHA, ANTON DIRK, investment company executive; b. Springs, Gauteng, South Africa, Sept. 1, 1953; s. Theunis Jacobus and Theunsina Johanna (Raubenheimer) B.; m. Brenda Pienaar, Dec. 4, 1976; children: Minante, Antonnet, Jolandie. B in Commerce, U. Pretoria, 1974; JD, U. South Africa, 1981; B in Commerce, Rand Afrikaans U., 1982; postgrad., Stanford U., 1993. Various Esso Std., Johannesburg, South Africa, 1975-78; investment mgr. Gencor Ltd., Johannesburg, 1981-86; chief exec. Genbel Securities, Ltd., Johannesburg, 1987—; bd. dirs. U. Pretoria, South Africa, Genbel SA Ltd. Mem. Investment Analyst Soc. South Africa (chmn. 1987-88), Afrikaanse Handels Inst. Avocations: travel, golf, reading. Office: Genbel Securities Ltd 3A Summit Rd, Dunkeld W PO Box 411420, Graighall Johannesburg Gauteng 2196, South Africa

BOTHMER, DIETRICH FELIX VON, museum curator, archaeologist; b. Eisenach, Thuringia, Oct. 26, 1918; came to U.S., 1939, naturalized, 1944; s. Wilhelm Friedrich Franz Carl and Marie Julie Auguste Karoline (Freiin von und zu Egloffstein) von B.; m. Joyce de la Bégassière, May 28, 1966; children: Bernard Nicholas, Maria Elizabeth Villalba. Student, Friedrich Wilhelms U., Berlin, 1937-38, Wadham Coll., Oxford, 1938-39; diploma classical archaeology, Oxford U., 1939; Ph.D. in Classical Archaeology, U. Calif., Berkeley, 1944; DPhil (hon.), U. Trier, 1997. Asst. curator Greek and Roman art Met. Mus. Art, 1946-51, assoc. curator, 1951-59, curator, 1959-73, chmn., 1973-90, Disting. rsch. curator, 1990—; adj. prof. NYU, 1966—. Book rev. editor: Am. Jour. Archaeology, 1950-57; assoc. editor, 1970-76; author: Amazons in Greek Art, 1957, Ancient Art from New York Private Collections, 1961, An Inquiry into the Forgery of the Etruscan Terracotta Warriors, 1961, Corpus Vasorum Antiquorum, USA fasc. 12, 1963, Greek Vase Painting: An Introduction, 1972, Corpus Vasorum Antiquorum, USA fasc. 16, 1976, Greek Art of the Aegean Islands, 1979, A Greek and Roman Treasury, 1984, The Amasis Painter and His World, 1985, Greek Vase Painting, 1987, Glories of the Past, Ancient Art from the Shelby White and Leon Levy Collection, 1990, Euphronios, Peintre á Athènes au VI siècle avant Jesus Christ, 1990. Mem. Chancellor's Ct. of Benefactors, Oxford U. With AUS, 1943-45. Decorated Bronze Star, Purple Heart; Rhodes scholar Wadham Coll., 1938-39; Internat. House fellow U. Calif., Berkeley, 1940, Alfred B. Jordan fellow, 1940-41, Univ. fellow, 1941-42; Martin Ryerson fellow U. Chgo., 1942-43; Guggenheim Meml. Found. fellow, 1966, hon. fellow Wadham Coll.; Chevalier Légion d'Honneur, 1997. Mem. Archaeol. Inst. Am. (benefactor), Soc. Promotion Hellenic Studies (hon.), Deutsches Archaeol. Inst., Vereinigung der Freunde Antiker Kunst (Basle, Switzerland), Archaeologische Gesellschaft zu Berlin, Institut de France, Académie des Inscriptions et Belles-Lettres (fgn. assoc.), Piping Rock Club, Lyford Cay Club. Home: 401 Centre Island Oyster Bay NY 11771-5011 Office: Met Mus Art Fifth Ave at 82nd St New York NY 10028-0198

BOTKA, FERENC, historian, educator; b. Szabadka, Voivodina, Yugoslavia, Mar. 18, 1929; arrived in Hungary, 1944; s. Ferenc and Ilona (Szabados) B.; m. Eva Lakatos, Dec. 18, 1971; children: Tibor, Attila, Zoltán, Ferenc. Diploma, Eötvös Loránd U., Budapest, Hungary, 1953; PhD, U. Govt., Moscow, 1970; Dr. Lit. Studies, Hungarian Acad., Budapest, 1990. Tchr. Kossuth Lajos Gimnázium, Cegléd, Hungary, 1952-57; chief of libr. Petőfi Lit. Mus., Budapest, 1970-78, dep. dir., 1978-83, gen. dir., 1983-93; prof. lit. history Acad. Fine Arts, Budapest, 1993-2000; mem. Com. of Lit. Studies, Budapest, 1978-93. Author: Captivity and Literature, Hungarian Writers in Russia 1914-1921, 1986; editor: Bibliography of the Hungarian Literary History 1900-1945, 1945-1970, 3 vols., 1982, 89, 91, Contemporaries About Tibor Déry, 1994; author (monograph) Tibor Déry in Berlin, 1994; editor: Dery Archive, 7 vols., 1995-2000. Recipient Prize of Lit., Trade Union Coun., Budapest, 1986, Déry Found., 1992. Mem. Hungarian Soc. Lit. History (pres.). Home: Sas 1 V 10, 1051 Budapest Hungary Office: Magyar Kepzomuveszeti Foisk Hungarian Acad Fine Arts, Petofi Lit Mus, Karolyi 16, 1053 Budapest Hungary

BOTKIN, DANIEL BENJAMIN, biologist, environmental scientist, writer; b. Oklahoma City, Aug. 19, 1937; s. Benjamin Albert and Gertrude (Fritz) B.; m. Ellen Chase, Dec. 22, 1962 (div. 1976); children: Nancy, Jonathan; m. Erene Victoria Youngberg, Apr. 7, 1978 (dec. Mar. 1994). BA, U. Rochester, 1959; MA, U. Wis., 1962; PhD, Rutgers U., 1968. From asst. to assoc. prof. Yale U., New Haven, 1968-76; assoc. scientist Marine Biol. Lab., Woods Hole, Mass., 1976-78; prof. biology U. Calif., Santa Barbara, 1978-92, chmn. environ. studies program, 1978-85; dir. program on global change biology dept. George Mason U., Fairfax, Va., 1993-97; prof. biology George Mason U., Fairfax, 1993-99; pres. The Ctr. for the Study of the Environment, 1992—; rsch. prof. biology U. Calif., Santa Barbara, 1999—. Author: Discordant Harmonies: A New Ecology for the 21st Century, 1990, Forest Dynamics: An Ecological Model, 1993, Our Natural History: The Lessons of Lewis and Clark, 1995, Passage of Discovery: The American Rivers Guide to the Missouri River of Lewis and Clark, 1999, No Man's Garden: Thoreau and a New Vision for Civilization and Nature, 2000; (software) JABOWA, 1970, Timber: model of forest growth, 1983, 87, JABOWA-II, 1992, JABOWA-3 for Windows, 1999; co-author: Forest Succession, 1981, Environmental Studies, 1982, 87, Changing the Global Environment, 1989, Environmental Science: Earth as a Living Planet, 1995, 3d edit., 1999, The Blue Planet, 1999; contbr. articles to profl. jours., popular mags. and newspapers. Trustee Santa Barbara Bot. Garden, 1987-93. Recipient Fernow prize for Internat. Forestry, 1995, First Prize, Mitchell Internat. Prize for Sustainable Devel., 1991; named to Environ. Hall of Fame, Calif. Polytechnic U., 1995; fellow Rockefeller Bellagio (Italy) Inst., 1985, East-West Ctr., Honolulu, 1985-87, Woodrow Wilson Internat. Ctr. for Scholars, Washington, 1977-78; grantee EPA, NSF, NASA, NOAA, Mellon Found., Pew Charitable Trusts, W. Alton Jones Found., World Wildlife Fund, SOHIO Alaska Corp. Fellow AAAS; Cosmos Club, Sigma Xi (lectr. 1981-83). Avocations: aircraft piloting, photography, hiking, music. Office: Ctr in Study of Environment PO Box 30700 Santa Barbara CA 93130-0700

BOTKIN, JAMES W., knowledge business executive; b. Long Branch, N.J., May 15, 1943; s. Harold M. and Julia (Bishop) B.; m. Karin S. Bartow, Aug. 20, 1999; m. Rosvita Botkin; children: Alexander, Christopher. BA, Harvard U., 1965, MBA, 1968, DBA, 1973. Pres. InterClass, Cambridge, Mass., 1990—; fellow U. Tex., Austin, 1985—; internat. advisor New Horizons for Learning, Seattle, 1986—; mem. adv. bd. Cambridge Learning Design, 1999—; internat. recognized pub. spkr. Author: (with M. Elmandjra dn M. Malitza) No Limits to Learning: A Report to the Club of Rome, 1979; (with D. Dimancescu and R. Stata) Global Stakes: The Future of High Technology in America, 1982, The Innovators: Rediscovering America's Creative Energy, 1984; (with D. Dimancescu) The New Alliance: Industry-University Partnerships, 1986; (with J. Matthews) Winning Combinations: Entrepreneurial Partnerships Between Large and Small Companies, 1992; (with Stan Davis) The Monster Under the Bed: How Business is Mastering the Opportunities of Knowledge for Profit, 1994; Smart Business: How Knowledge Communities Can Revolutionize Your Company, 1999. Named Hon. Citizen, Salsburg, Austria, 1977; recipient Innovator award Rausing Fund, Lund, Sweden, 1990, Alliance award Carnegie Corp., N.Y.C., 1986. Mem. Club of Rome. Avocations: hiking, fishing, travel. E-Mail: jbotkine@interclass.com. Office: InterClass 30 Jfk St Cambridge MA 02138-4909

BØTNER, ANETTE, virologist, researcher; b. Solbjerg Sogn, Denmark, May 8, 1954; m. Allan Bøtner; children: Line, Jesper. DVM, Royal Vet. & Ag. U., Copenhagen, Denmark, 1979, PhD, 1984. In practice Nysted, Denmark, 1979-81; rsch. asst. Danish Vet. Lab., Copenhagen, Denmark, 1984-87, Danish Vet. Inst. for Virus Rsch., Lindholm, Denmark, 1987-94; sr. rsch. officer Danish Vet. Inst. for Virus Rsch., 1994—. Home: Geddebakken 2, 4760 Vordingborg Denmark Office: Danish Vet Inst Virus Rsch, Lindholm, 4771 Kalvehave Denmark

BOTREL, JACQUES, science administrator; b. Saint-Malo, France, Mar. 3, 1926; s. Henry Botrel and Suzanne Gautier; m. Christiane Paule Janton, Jan. 25, 1955. M in Chemistry, degree in chem. engring., U. Rennes, France, 1949; D of Pharm. Sci., U. Montpellier, France, 1979; D of Pub. Law, U. Paris XII, France, 1990. Chem. engr. Soc. Anonyme de Traitement Indsl. des Algues, Paris, 1952-56, Rhône-Poulenc, Paris, 1956-89; sec. gen. Sty Chem. Experts, Paris, 1991—; cons. UN Orgn., Vienna and Geneva, 1979-96, European Econ. Cmty., 1991-94; tchr. univs., Montpellier, Reims, Paris; lectr. Pa. State U., Tex. U., Calif. U., Davis, U. Md., Purdue U., West Lafayette, Ind. Author: (books) Agro-food International Organization, 1980, Polymers, Chemistry and Packaging Regulation, 1982, Food Packaging French Regulation, 1986, Packaging, Socio-economical and Legal Statute, 1991; co-author 11 books; contbr. numerous articles to tech. publs. Soldier French Liberation Forces, 1944. Decorated Chevalier Nat. Order of Merit, French Govt., 1978. Fellow French Soc. for Industry (Silver medal 1982, Fauler medal 1988); mem. Nat. Coun. Pub. Health, French Com. Custom Expertise (assessor 1970-86). Home: 30 Rue Ernest-Renan, 75015 Paris France Office: Soc Experts Clim France, 23 Commandant Jean Duhail, 94210 Fontenay-sous-Bois France

BOTSAI, ELMER EUGENE, architect, educator, former university dean; b. St. Louis, Feb. 1, 1928; s. Paul and Ita May (Cole) B.; m. Patricia L. Keegan, Aug. 28, 1955; children: Donald Rolf, Kurt Gregory.; m. Sharon K. Kaiser, Dec. 5, 1981; 1 dau., Kiana Michelle. AA, Sacramento Jr. Coll., 1950; AB, U. Calif., Berkeley, 1954; D of Architecture, U. Hawaii, 2000. Registered architect, Hawaii, Calif. Draftsman, then asst. to architect So. Pacific Co., San Francisco, 1953-57; designer H.K. Ferguson Co., San Francisco, 1955; project architect Anshen & Allen Architects, San Francisco, 1957-63; prin. Botsai, Overstreet & Rosenberg, Architects and Planners, San Francisco, 1963-79, Elmer E. Botsai FAIA, Honolulu, 1979—; of cousnel Groupe 70 Internat., 1998—; chmn. dept. architecture U. Hawaii, Manoa, 1976-80, dean Sch. Architecture, 1980-90, prof., 1990-99, prof. emeritus, 2000—; lectr. U. Calif., Berkeley, 1976, dir. Nat. Archtl. Accrediting Bd., 1972-73, 79; adminstrv. and tech. cons. Wood Bldg. Rsch. Ctr., U. Calif., 1985-90, mem. profl. preparation project com. at U. Mich., Ann Arbor, 1986-87; co-author water infiltration seminar series for Bldg. Owners and Mgrs. Rsch. Ctr., 1986-87; chief investigator effects of Guatemalan earthquake for NSF and AIA, Washington, 1976; steering com. on structural failures Nat. Bur. Standards, 1982-84; chmn., dir. gen. svcs. Adv. Com. State of Calif. Co-author: Architects and Earthquake, Research Needs, 1976, ATC Seismic Standards for National Bur. of Standards, 1976, Architects and Earthquakes: A Primer, 1977, Seismic Design, 1978, Wood-Detailing for Performance, 1990, Wood as a Building Material, 2d edit., 1991; contbr. articles and reports to profl. jours.; prin. works include expansion of Nuclear Weapons Tng. Facility at Lemoore Naval Air Sta., Calif., LASH Terminal Port Facility Archtl. Phase, San Francisco, Incline Village (Nev.) Country Club, 1365 Columbus Ave. Bldg., San Francisco, modernization Stanford Ct. Hotel, San Francisco; monument area constrn. several Calif. ceneteries. With U.S. Army, 1946-48. Recipient Cert. Honor Fedn. Archtl. Colls. Mex. Republic, 1984; named to Wisdom Hall of Fame, 1998; NSF grantee for investigative workshop project, San Diego, 1974-80. Fellow AIA (bd. dirs., 1966-71, treas. No. Calif. chpt. 1968-69, pres. 1971, nat. v.p., 1975-76, nat. pres. 1978, pres. Hawaii 1985); hon. fellow Royal Can. Inst. Architects, N.Z. Inst. Architects, Royal Australian Inst. Architects, La Societed de Arquitectos Mexicano; mem. Archtl. Secs. Assn. (hon.), Soc. Wood Sci. and Tech., Internat. Conf. Bldg. Ofcls. Home: 321 Wailupe Cir Honolulu HI 96821-1524 Office: 925 Bethel St Fl 5 Honolulu HI 96813-4393

BOTSARIS, PANTELIS, electrical engineer; b. Athens, Greece, Aug. 20, 1968; s. Nikolaos and Harry (Karakozi) B.; m. Katerina Nikolaidou, Nov. 20, 1996. MSc, Democritus U., 1991, PhD, 1996. Educator, dir. computer studies Fasma Computer Ctr., Xanthi, Greece, 1992—. Mem. Tech. Chamber of Greece. Home: 46 Adrianoupoleos, 67100 Xanthi Greece

BOTSEAS, DIONYSIOS SOTIRIOS, surgeon; b. Samothrace Island, Evrou, Greece, 1928; s. Sotirios G. and Zoe S. (Vythoulka) B.; m. Calliope D. Pastis; 3 children. BS, Wayne State U., Detroit, 1953; MD, Ind. U., 1954. Diplomate Am. Bd. Surgery. Intern King County Hosp., Seattle, 1955-56, resident, 1955-56; resident Virginia Mason Hosp., Seattle, 1956-59, fellow, 1959-60; sr. resident Roswell Park Meml. Cancer Hosp., Buffalo, 1960-61; assoc. surgeon Pireus (Greece) State Hosp., 1963-64; surgeon Geniki Kliniki Athinon, Hygeia Hosp., Athens, Greece, 1968—; assoc. clin. instr. surgery Athens State Hosp., 1967-73; cons. USAF Hosp., Athens, 1961-86; prof. State Sch. Nurses, 1985—, Internat. Seminars, Athens, 1993-95; pub. spkr. cancer prevention and lifestyle and health for youth, lay groups, student and profls. Author: Inhibition of V2 Carcinoma in Rabbits, 1961 (prize ACS 1961), How to Win Over Cancer, 1970 (award Athens Med. Soc. 1970); co-author: (chpt.) Cancer Therapeutics; contbr. articles, papers to profl. jours. 2nd lt. M.C., Greek mil., 1973. Fellow ACS; mem. Greek Surg. Soc., Greek Am. Med. Soc. (exec. gen. sec. 1972-73). Avocations: watercolors, swimming, public speaking, writing. Office: 8 Marni St, 10433 Athens Greece

BOTSFORD, BETH, swimmer, Olympic athlete; b. Timonium, Md., May 21. Swimmer Pan Pacific Team, 1995, U.S. Olympic Team, Atlanta, 1996. Named Spring Nationals Rookie of the Meet, 1994; 1st place 200 meter backstroke, 1995, 200 meter backstroke Summer Nationals, 1995; recipient Gold medals 100 meter backstroke and 4x100 meter medley relay Olympic Games, Atlanta, 1996, 1st 200m on back, 1st 100m on back 1997 Spring Nats., 1st 400m MRP 1999 World Trials; rep. USA Swimming Nat. A Team Sydney 2000 Olympics. Mem. North Balt. Aquatic Club. Office: US Swimming Inc 1 Olympic Plz Bldg 2A Colorado Springs CO 80909-5770

BOTSHON, LISA, English language educator; b. N.Y.C.. BA, Brandeis U.; PhD, Columbia U. Asst. prof. English U. Maine, Augusta. Home: 28 Windemere Rd Brunswick ME 04011-8131

BOTSIS, JOHN, science and engineering educator; b. Kyriaki, Greece, Jan. 16, 1955; arrived in Switzerland, 1996; s. Loukas and Aikaterini B.; m. Maria Seinfeld, June 16, 1991; children: Katerina, Sofia. Diploma in engring., U. Patras, Greece, 1979; MS, Case Western Res. U., 1981, PhD, 1984. Rsch. asst. Rsch. Ctr. Nat. Defense, Athens, Greece, 1984-86; asst. prof. U. Ill., Chgo., 1986-91, assoc. prof., 1991-95, prof., 1995-96; prof. Swiss Fed. Inst. Tech., Lausanne, 1996—; program dir. UASF Basic Rsch. Office, Washington, 1991-92, 94; cons. in field. Contbr. articles to profl. jours. With Greek Mil., 1984-86. Acad. excellence fellow Nat. Hellenic Found., Athens, 1978, fellow Case Western Res. U., Cleve., 1981-84. Mem. ASME, Soc. Exptl. Mechanics, Soc. Plastics Engrs. Greek Orthodox. Avocations: music, sports, hiking. Office: Swiss Fed Inst Tech, Ecublens, CH-1015 Lausanne Switzerland

BOTT, ANDREAS BENNO, meteorologist, educator; b. Bad Kreuznach, Germany, May 10, 1956; s. Josef and Brigitte (Schmitt) B.; m. Doris Theiss, Oct. 9, 1981; children: Christian, Alexander, Johanna. Diploma in meteorology, U. Mainz, 1982, PhD, 1986. Rsch. assoc. Max-Planck-Inst., Mainz, Germany, 1983-86; rsch. assoc. U. Mainz, 1987-91, rsch. asst., 1992-93, sr. scientist, 1994-99; prof. Theoretical Meteorology U. Bonn, Germany, 2000—. Mem. German Meteorol. Soc. Home: Tongesstr 91, D-55129 Mainz Germany Office: U Bonn Inst Meteorology, Auf dem Hügel 20, D-53121 Bonn Germany

BOTTACCIOLI, FRANCESCO, medical writer, journalist, consultant, educator; b. Umbertide, Italy, Feb. 25, 1949; s. Gaetano Bottaccioli and Giuseppa Ciocchetti; m. Annagloria Simonucci, Dec. 19, 1974 (div. 1991); 1 child, Michele; m. Antonia Carosella, May 23, 1992; 1 child, Anna Giulia. MD, 1996. Editor-in-chief Radiocittafutura, Rome, 1982-85, Quotidiano Dei lavoratori, Rome, 1980-82; regional dep. Consiglio Regionale, Lazio, Italy, 1985-90; editor in chief Notizie Verdi, Rome, 1991-97; prof. Scuola Medicina Naturale, Urbino, Italy, 1997—; sci. dir. Centro Medicina Naturale, Aprilia, Italy, 1997-99; prof. Cath. U., Rome, 1997-99; sci. dir. Scuola Internat. Medicine Integreta, Perguvia, Italy, 1999—; cons. RAI Pub. TV, Rome, 1996—, RED Pub. House, Como, Italy, 1993-97. Author: Psiconeuroimmunologia, 1995, Giovani Piu a Lungo, 1996, Vincere il Cancro, 1998, Meute inquieta, 2000; translation editor numerous English lang. books. Mem. AAAS, N.Y. Acad. Scis., Free Radicals Assn. Home: Via Ofanto, I-04010 Aprilia Italy

BOTTERMAN, JACKY A., oncologist; b. Ghent, Belgium, Aug. 20, 1957; s. Maurice A. and Adriana G. (De Clercq) B.; children: James, Lynn. MD, State U. Ghent, 1983; radiation oncologist, Brussels, 1989. Registrar dept. oncology Free U. Brussels-Univ. Hosp., 1989-90; radiation oncologist St. Lucas Hosp., Ghent, 1990—, med. dir. palliative care unit, 1992—; cons. oncologist Palliative Home Care Team, Ghent, 1989-97. Contbr. articles to profl. jours. Bd. dirs. Belgian Works Against Cancer, Ghent, 1990-98, Palliative Home Care Team, Ghent, 1989, Palliative Care Unit St. Lucas, Ghent, 1992. Recipient award Ednl. Community Fgn. Med. Grads., U.S., 1985. Fellow Coll. of Chest Physicians; mem. Belgian Soc. Radiation Oncology, European Soc. Therapeutic Radiation Oncology, Belgian Soc. Senology, European Palliative Care Assn. Roman Catholic. Avocations: motor biking, oenology. Home: Langerbrugestraat 128, B-9940 Evergem Belgium Office: St Lucas Hospital, Groene Briel 1, 9000 Ghent Belgium

BOTTI, JOHN LAWRENCE, author; b. Jersey City, June 13, 1919; s. Anthony and Gertrude Elizabeth (Moriarty) B.; m. Jacqueline Marie Chick, May 30, 1951; children: Richard Stephen (dec.), Mary Elizabeth Kelly, Melanie Therese Bock, Timothy Martin. BA cum laude, St. Peter's Coll., Jersey City, 1941; MA, Seton Hall U., South Orange, N.J., 1961; LLB, Fordham U., N.Y.C., 1949, JD, 1968. Bar: N.Y. 1995. Admissions officer, registrar St. Peter's Coll., Jersey City, 1941-42, 46-49; registrar, admissions dir. city hall divsn. Fordham U., N.Y.C., 1949-53; dir. pub. rels N.Y. Province, Soc. Jesus, N.Y.C., 1953-56; admissions officer, registrar Paterson (N.J.) Coll. Seton Hall U., 1956-62; dir. alumni rels. Seton Hall U., South Orange, N.J., 1962-67, spl. asst. to pres., 1967-68, asst. to v.p.'s, 1968-72, assoc. prof. bus. law, 1972-87; author, cons. Neptune City, N.J., 1987—; cons., condr. seminars Am. Mgmt. Assn., Nat. Assn. Purchasing Mgmt., Corp. Purchasing Execs. and Depts., 1971—; pres. Orbit Seminars, Inc., 1981—. Author: Law and the Purchasing Professional, 1997, WWII Svcs., 1942-46. Investigator, spl. investigations USAF Res., 1946-78. Col. USAF, 1942-78. Decorated Legion of Merit. Mem. USAF Office Spl. Investigations Former Agts. (life), Bar State N.Y., Nat. Assn. Scholars (life), Ret. Officers' Assn. (life). Roman Catholic. Avocation: travel. Home and Office: Orbit Seminars Inc 7 Steiner Ave Neptune City NJ 07753-6715

BÖTTIGER, HANNA MARGARETA, virologist, educator; b. Sweden, July 29, 1927; d. Olle Westerlund and Rut Sohlman; m. Lars Erik Böttiger, 1948; children: Blenda, Disa, Ylva. MD, Karolinska Inst., Stockholm, 1954, PhD in Medicine, 1966. Rschr. in virology Karolinska Inst., Stockholm, 1957-71, assoc. prof. virology, 1966—; assoc. prof. epidemiology Nat. Bacteriology Lab., Stockholm, 1971-76, prof. and nat. epidemiologist, 1976-93; mem. adv. group on immunizations Swedish Nat. Bd. of Health and Welfare, 1972-93; Swedish rep. on epidmiology group AIDS Rsch. Program of European Union, 1985-93; mem. AIDS Commn. Swedish Govt., 1985-93, European Regional Commn. of Certification of Poliomyelitis Eradication, 1996—; mem. bd. Swedish Data Inspection; expert adviser to Swedish Food Adminstrn., and to WHO at meetings of Expanded Program on Immunizations held by global adv. Group or European adv. group. Contbr. 250 sci. papers to profl. jours. and sci. confs. E-mail: bottiger@swipnet.se. Home: Gransäter, S132 36 Saltsjö-Boo Sweden

BOTTINI, EGIDIO, medical educator; b. Civitella Casanova, Pescara, Italy, Mar. 10, 1931; s. Nunzio Bottini and Margherita Sablone; m. Fulvia Gloria, Oct. 16, 1971; children: Nunzio, Massimo. MD, U. Rome, 1956. Medical diplomate. Asst. prof. U. Italy, 1959-70; chief of rsch. Nat. Rsch. Coun., Italy, 1962-76; prof. genetics U. Italy, 1976-83, prof. peds., 1983—, dept. dir., 1976-83, 85, dir. PhD Sch. of Pediats., 1986—; Italian rep. Coun. of Europe Commn. for the Study of Metabolic Diseases, Strasbourg, 1970-72; Lincei prof. genetics Accademia Nazionale dei Lincei, Interdisciplinary Ctr. for Applied Maths., 1979-85; fellow U. Coll. Hosp. Medical Sch., London, 1960-61; invited rschr. Yale U., 1968-71. Contbr. articles to profl. jours. Grantee NATO, 1972. Mem. European Soc. Pediat. Rsch., Assn. Genetics Italiana. Avocation: gardening. Office: Univ di Roma Tor Vergata, Via Ricerca Scientifica, 00133 Rome Italy

BOTTOMLEY, F. DAVID, advertising executive; b. Barkisland, Yorkshire, Eng., July 28, 1931; s. Frank and Alice (Buchanan) B.; m. Irene Jean Allan, Apr. 14, 1962; children: Bruce, Ruth, Kate. MA with honors, U. Edinburgh, Scotland, 1956. Account exec. Osborne Peacock, Ltd., London and Manchester, Eng., 1956-57, T.B. Browne, Ltd., London, 1957-58; advt. exec. John Mackintosh & Sons, Ltd., Norwich, Eng., 1958-61, advt. mgr., 1961-69; advt. mgr. Europe Rowntree Mackintosh, Norwich and York, Eng., 1969-87; internat. advt. mgr. Rowntree PLC, York, 1987-89; visual communications mgr. confectionery Nestlé, York, Eng., 1989-90; freelance internat. advt. cons., 1990—. Mem. council Brafferton Parochial Ch., 1984—; chmn. Brafferton Parish Coun., 1996—. Served to capt. Royal Artillery Territorial Army, 1950-70. Mem. Internat. Advt. Assn., Inst. Mktg. (chartered). Avocations: history, traveling.

BOTTOMLEY, VIRGINIA HILDA BRUNETTE MAXWELL, government official; b. Eng., Mar. 12, 1948; d. W. John Garnett; m. Peter Bottomley; 3 children. BA, U. Essex; MSc, London Sch. Econs. and Polit. Sci. M.P. from Surrey South-West Ho. of Commons, since 1984; min. for health, 1989-91; co-chmn. Women's Nat. Commn., 1991-92; sec. state for health London, 1992-95; sec. state for Nat. Heritage, London, 1995-97; mem. Ho. Commons, London, 1997—, Ct. Govs. L.S.E., 1985—, Brit. Coun., 1997—; mem. select com. on fgn. affairs Ho. Commons, 1997-99. Vice chmn. Nat. Coun. Carers and Their Elderly Dependents, 1982-88; bd. dirs. Mid South Water Co., 1987-88; freeman City of London; gov. Ditchley Found. Industry Parlt. Trust fellow, 1987. Mem. Ct. of Govs., London Sch. of Econs. Avocation: family. Office: Dept Nat Heritage, House of Commons, London SW1A 0AA, England

BOTTOMS, STEPHEN JAMES, educator; b. Cambridge, Eng., May 1, 1968; arrived in Scotland, 1993; s. Anthony Edward and Janet Freda (Wenger) B. BA with honors, U. Bristol, Eng., 1989; PhD, U. East Anglia, Norwich, Eng., 1995. Lectr. U. Glasgow, Scotland, 1993—; external examiner Manchester (Eng.) Met. U., 1999—. Author: The Theatre of Sam Shepard, 1998; contbr. articles to profl. jours. Avocations: directing, performing and writing for theatre.

BOTTONE, JOANN, health services executive; b. Bklyn., June 20, 1943; d. Anthony and Claire (Bisesti) B.; m. William Recevuto, Feb. 12, 1989; children: Matthew, Sandra. RN, Kings County Hosp. Ctr., Bklyn., 1963; BS, St. Francis Coll., Bklyn., 1980; MPA, Russell Sage Coll., Albany, N.Y., 1986; PhD in Pub. Adminstrn. magna cum laude, Kensington U., 1995. Bd. cert. Health Care Mgmt. Am. Coll. Health Care Execs., 1997. From staff nurse, head nurse, quality assurance coord. Victory Meml. Hosp., Bklyn., 1961-81; instr. infection control Community Hosp. Bklyn., 1981-82; dir. quality assurance Profl. Stds. Rev. Orgn., Bklyn., 1982-85; devel. and coord. HIV post-test counseling program Greater N.Y. Blood Ctr., N.Y.C., 1985-88; dir. HIV/AIDS programs Health Sci. Ctr. SUNY, Bklyn., 1988—; tchr. SUNY Coll. Health Related Professions; mem. working group to develop statewide policies and procedures for health care workers involved in potential HIV exposures N.Y. State Health Commr., 1990; mem. tech. adv. group to develop guidelines for OSHA's bloodborne pathogen standard Greater N.Y. Hosp. Assn., 1992, N.Y.C. Mayor's HIV and Human Svcs. planning coun., 1999; lectr. in field. Contbr. articles to profl. jours. Mem. Am. Coll. Health Care Execs. (diplomate), Greater N.Y. Hosp. Assn. (tech. adv. group).

BOTTU, GUY, chemist; b. Mechelen, Belgium, Mar. 17, 1956; s. Joseph Paul and Anny (Frazelle) B. Licentie scheikunde, Free U., Brussels, 1977, DS, 1984. Rsch. fellow Nat. Found. Sci. Rsch., Sint Genesius Rode, Belgium, 1977-82; asst. Vrije U., Brussels, 1985-91; sci. collaborator U. Libre Brussels, 1992—. With Belgian armed forces, 1980-81. Recipient Stas prize

Royal Acad. for Scis., Arts and Fine Arts. Mem. Former Student Union U. Brussels, Belgian Soc. for Biochemistry and Molecular Biology, Royal Flemish Chem. Soc. Home: Pareipoelstraat 94, 2800 Mechelen Belgium Office: U Libre Brussels, Rue des Chevaux 67, 1640 Rhode-Saint-Genese Belgium

BOTWAY, LLOYD FREDERICK, computer scientist, consultant; b. Flushing, N.Y., June 18, 1947; s. Albert Harold and Alice Rebecca (Halpern) B. BS, Tufts U., 1968; MS, U. Colo., 1970. Programmer Anaconda Co., Butte, Mont., 1970-72; systems analyst U. Mo., Columbia, 1972-77; tech. dir. Dataphase Systems, Inc., Kansas City, Mo., 1977-80; pres. Liberty Logic Corp., Pasadena, Md., 1980-84; computer scientist Computer Sci. Corp., Balt., 1984-86; dir. MIS Internat. Clin. Labs., Nashville, 1986-88; dir. info. systems Nat. Health Labs., Nashville, 1988-94; v.p., chief arch. Quest Diagnostics, San Juan Capistrano, Calif., 1994-2000; actor, writer, musician San Clemente, Calif., 2000—; Cons. Internat. Clin. Labs., Nashville, 1981-85; grad. asst. Dale Carnegie. Contbr. articles to profl. jours., co-author: (reference pamphlet) Latex Command Summary, 1985. Libertarian candidate for U.S. Ho. of Reps. from 5th Tenn. Dist., 1994. Mem. Toastmasters. Avocations: composing music, flying, foreign languages, electronics, acting.

BOTZ, GERHARD, historian, educator; b. Schaerding, Austria, Mar. 14, 1941; s. Anton and Maria (Parzer) B.; children: Aurel, Daniel, Fabian. Student, U. Vienna, Austria, 1959-67; PhD, U. Vienna, 1967. Archivist Chamber of Labour, Vienna, 1966-68; asst. prof. U. Linz, Austria, 1968-79; assoc. prof. U. Linz, 1979-80; prof. history U. Salzburg, Austria, 1980-97; prof. contemporary history U. Vienna, 1997—; dir. Ludwig-Boltzmann Inst. Social Sci. History, Vienna, 1982—; vis. prof. U. Minn., Mpls., 1985, Stanford U., 1986, 87, Ecole des Hautes Etudes en Scis. Sociales, Paris, 1989. Author: Die Eingliederung Oesterreichs in das Deutsche Reich, 1972, 76, 88, Wohnungspolitik und Judenueportation in Wien, 1938-45, 1975, Gewalt in der Politik, 1976, 83, Wien vom Anschluss zum Krieg, 1978, 80, 88, Krisenzonen einer Demokratie, 1987; editor: M. Glas-Larsson: Ich will reden, 1982, Am. translation: I Want to Speak, 1990; co-editor: Jews, Antisemitism and Culture in Vienna, 1987, (German Translation) Eine zerstoerte Kultur, 1990, Kontroversen um Oesterreichs Zeitgeschichte, 1994; series editor Studien zur Historischen Sozialwissenschaft; co-author, editor numerous books; contbr. articles to profl. publs. Alexander von Humboldt Found. grantee, 1976-77, 94-95. Mem. Quantum Working Group Austrian History, Dokumentationsarchiv des oesterreichischen Widerstands (trustee), Naturfreunde Club (Vienna). E-mail: Gerhard.Botz@univie.ac.at. Office: Inst für Zeitgeschichte, Spitalgasse 2-4 1 Hof, A-1090 Wien Austria

BOUAS-LAURENT, HENRI CLAUDE, chemist, educator; b. Bordeaux, France, Nov. 26, 1933; s. Fernand Jean and Antoinette Marthe (Peguet) Bouas; m. Genevieve Marie Castan, July 30, 1964; children: Etienne, Cecile, Olivier. Lic.es Sc.Phys., U. Bordeaux, 1956, Diplôme Pharmacie, 1958, DSc, 1964; D (hon.), Saarbruc U., Germany, 1999. From asst. to maitre de conf. Faculté des Sciences, Bordeaux, 1957-68, prof., 1968-70, titulaire prof. 1st class, 1970-90, prof. class exceptionnelle, 1990-98, prof. emeritus, 1998, head dept. chemistry, 1989-92; mem. Nat. Com. for Univs., Paris, 1984-88; coord. Exch. of Students between European Univs., Bordeaux, 1984—. Co-author, co-editor: Photochromism Molecules and Systems, 1990. Recipient Bronze medal Centre Nat. de la Recherche Scientifique, 1964, prize Vant'Hoff Found., Amsterdam, 1972, Grammaticakis Neuman prize French Acad. Scis., 1986, Alexander von Humboldt Rsch. prize, Bonn, Germany, 1991. Mem. French Chem. Soc. (sec. local sect. 1969-71, chmn. 1971-73), Royal Soc. Chemistry (London), European Photochem. Assn. (sec. exec. com. 1984-88), Am. Chem. Soc. Office: Photochimie Organique, Univ Bordeaux 1, Talence 33405, France

BOUCHAL, ZDENEK, physicist, educator; b. Přerov, Czech Republic, Mar. 23, 1958; s. Bohumil and Jindřiška (Adolfová) B.; m. Ludmila Pospišilová, May 5, 1984; children: Lydie, Petr., Pavlina. Grad., Palacky U., Olomouc, Czech Republic, 1982, PhD, 1993; postgrad. studies, U. Tech., Brno, Czech Republic, 1987, Charles U., Prague, Czech Republic, 1989. Rschr. Meopta, Přerov, Czech Republic, 1982-89; lectr. Palacky U, Olomouc, 1990—, assoc. prof., 1997—. Inventor laser optical scanning system patented 1988; contbr. articles to optical jours. Grantee: Agy. Czech Republic, 1994-95, Ministry of Edn., Czech Republic, 1996—. Mem. Internat. Soc. for Optical Engring., Photonics. Avocations: sport, nature, history. Home: Vetrná 13, 750 00 Prerov Czech Republic Office: Palacky U Dept Optics, 17 listopadu 50, 772 07 Olomouc Czech Republic

BOUCHAREINE, PATRICK, retired physics educator; b. Suresnes, France, July 25, 1939; s. René and Hélène (Frinault) B.; children: Sophie, Laurent, Xavier, Anne, Pascal, Odile. Diploma, Ecole Normale Supérieure, 1958. Asst. Orsay (France) U., 1962-63; agrégé préparateur Ecole Normale Supérieure, Paris, 1963-66; maitre asst. Orsay U., 1966-70; prof. Conservatoire Nat. Arts Métiers, Paris, 1970-88, Orsay U., 1988-99; ret.; chief length lab. Inst. Nat. Metrologie, Paris, 1970-88; sci. advisor Inst. Physics Publ., Bristol, Eng., 1992-98. Editor Jour. Optics, 1984-92. Mem. French Soc. Optics (treas. 1983-91, bd. dirs.). Achievements include a field compensated interferometer for optical wavelength metrology. Home: 14 Allée Descartes, 91400 Orsay France Office: Inst Optique, BP 147, F-91403 Orsay Cedex, France

BOUCHER, BRUCE AMBLER, art historian, art critic; b. Birmingham, Ala., Nov. 5, 1948; arrived in Eng., 1970; s. John Walter and Louise Ambler (Kean) B.; m. Gillian Moore, Aug. 3, 1974 (div. 1981); m. Isabel Ruth Carlisle, Feb. 13, 1982 (div. 1996); children: Venetia, Miranda; m. Diane Michaels, Apr. 17, 1999. AB, Harvard U., 1970; BA, Oxford (Eng.) U., 1972; MA, U. London, 1974, PhD, 1987. Lectr. U. Coll., U. London, 1976-92, reader, 1992-98, prof. art history, 1998—; fellow Villa Itatti, Florence, Italy, 1984-85, Humboldt Found. Bonn, Berlin, 1989-90, 94. Author: Sculpture of Jacopo Sansovino, 1991 (Salimbeni prize 1992), Andrea Palladio, 1994, Italian Baroque Sculpture, 1998. Mem. Internat. Assn. Art Critics, Athenaeum. Anglican. Office: Univ London Univ Coll, Dept History Art Gower St, London WC1E 6BT, England

BOUCHER, WAYNE IRVING, policy analyst; b. Bay City, Mich., Dec. 12, 1934; s. Harold Oscar and Mildred Christine (Born) B.; m. Donna Lou Collins, June 12, 1961 (div. 1972); children: Michèle Annette, Robert Alain. BA in English Lang. and Lit., U. Mich., 1956, MA in English Lang. and Lit., 1960; postgrad. in philosophy, U. Mo., 1959-61. Instr. English U. Mo., Columbia, 1958-63; asst. to pres. Rand Corp., Santa Monica, Calif., 1963-69; rsch. assoc. Inst. for the Future, Middletown, Conn., 1969-71; co-founder, v.p. The Futures Group, Glastonbury, Conn., 1971-76; dept. dir., dir. rsch. Nat. Commn. on Electronic Fund Transfers, Washington, 1976-78; sr. rsch. assoc. Ctr. for Futures Rsch., U. So. Calif., Los Angeles, 1978-84; exec. v.p. Benton Internat., Torrance, Calif., 1984-93; pres. The Ark. Inst., Little Rock, 1993-94; pres., chief ops. officer Electronic Funds Transfer Assn., Herndon, Va., 1994-95; mng. dir. Strategic Futures Internat., Harpers Ferry, W.Va., 1995—; adj. prof. U. Mo., St. Louis, 1962-63, UCLA, 1964, Grad. Sch. Bus. U. Conn., 1973, Sch. Pub. Adminstrn. U. So. Calif., 1979-80; mem. adv. panel on electronic funds transfer Office of Tech. Assessment U.S. Congress, 1979-81; mem. Task Force on Electronic Benefits Transfer, Electronic Funds Transfer Assn., 1990-92. Author: (with J.L. Morrison and W.L. Renfro) Futures Research and Strategic Planning, 1984; Spinoza in English, 1991, 2d edit., 1999, Spinoza: 18th and 19th Century Discussions, 6 vols., 1999; editor: (with J.L. Morrison and W.L. Renfro) Applying Methods and Techniques of Futures Research, 1983; author, editor: The Study of the Future, 1977; editor (with E.S. Quade) Systems Analysis and Policy Planning, 1968; mem. editorial bd. Technol. Forecasting and Social Change, 1978-82, Futures Rsch. Quar., 1984—; contbr. articles to profl. jours. Home: RR 2 Box 667 Harpers Ferry WV 25425-9414 Office: Strategic Futures Internat Shannodale Lake 3 Lakeside Dr Harpers Ferry WV 25425-9414

BOUCHEREAU, JEAN-LUC MARCEL, educator, researcher; b. Beni-Mellal, Morocco, Oct. 29, 1949; s. Claude Leon and Marcelle Yvonne (Roman) B.; m. Francoise Brigitte Joly, Mar. 15, 1975; children: Florent, Thomas, Perrine, Laetitia. DEA in Oceanography, Univ. Marseille, France, 1975; M of Oceanography, Univ. Nice, France, 1974; PhD, U. Marseille, France, 1994. Rschr. ORSTOM, Pointe-Noire, Congo, 1975-77; educator, rschr. Univ., Oran, Algeria, 1977-86; prof. Univ., Montpellier, France, 1986-99. Contbr. articles to profl. jours. Recipient Jacques Poutiers prize, St. Nazaire, France, 1995. Mem. French Soc. Ichthyology, French Assn. Halieumetry. Avocations: philately, collecting post cards, photos, diving, travel. Home: 10 Meridienne St, F-34830 Clapiers France Office: U Montpellier, Eugene Bataillon Pl, 34095 Montpellier France

BOUCHET, ALAN, vascular surgeon; b. Domene, Isere, Feb. 3, 1926; s. Henry Bouchet and Suzanne Nicolet; m. Annik Ingels, June 23, 1960 (div.); children: Estelle, Fabrice; m. Axelle Mathias, July 6, 1967; children: Ariane, Elodie, Mathis. Grad., Notre Dame Sch., Grenoble, France. Intern Hosp. of Lyon, 1952; Dr. of Medicine Lyon, 1959, fellow prof. of anatomy, 1961; surgeon various hosps., Lyon, 1964; titul prof. of anatomy Lyon, 1971; head of vascular surgery Hosp., Lyon, 1986; emeritus prof., Faculty Laennec, Lyon, 1994; hon. surgeon Hosps. of Lyon, 1994. Contbr. articles to profl. jours.; editor: (4 vols.) Treaty of Topographic Anatomy, 1983-91, (monograph/1 vol.) Lab. Rolland Hepatrol, 1999, others. Mem. French Soc. of History of Medicine (past pres. 1985-86), Acad. of Lyon (past pres. 1996). Avocations: skiing, mountaineering, history of medicine. Office: Faculty of Med Laennec, G Paradin St, 69372 Lyon Cedex 08, France

BOUCHEZ, JEAN-ANTOINE PIERRE, magazine publisher; b. Strasbourg, France, Oct. 31, 1937; s. Pierre and Madeleine (Conrad) B. Civil and Aero. Engr., Ecole Nationale Superieure, Paris, 1963; Lic es Sci Economiques, Faculty Law, Paris, 1964. Proupe mieuxvivre Mieux-Vivre, Paris, 1979—. Office: Mieux-Vivre, Groupe Mieux-Vivre 32, rue Notre Dame desVictoures, 75002 Paris France

BOUCHILLON, JOHN RAY, education coordinator; b. Covington, Ga., Sept. 3, 1943; s. John Ray and Mary Edith (Death) B.; m. Martha Jo Logue, Dec. 18, 1965; children: Trey, Monica, Beth. BA, LaGrange Coll., 1965; MEd, Ga. Coll., 1969. Tchr. chemistry Baldwin County, Milledgeville, Ga., 1965-71, career coord., 1971-72; dir. career edn. Liberty County, Hinesville, Ga., 1972-75; career edn. cons. Ga. Dept. Edn., Atlanta, 1975-86, quality basic edn. field adminstr., 1986-87, coord. local strategic planning, 1987-92, sch. support team leader, 1992-98, ret., 1998; asst. dir. sch. improvement and tng. divsn., 1997-98; dir. sch. support svcs., asst. dir. sch. improvement and tng. divsn. Ga. Dept. Edn., 1996-98; chmn. career edn. adv. com. Ga. So. Coll., Statesboro, 1972-73; dir.-at-large guidance div. Ga. Vocat. Assn., Atlanta, 1976; sec.-treas. Ga. Vocat. Guidance Assn., 1976, pres., 1979. Co-editor: (newsletter) Ga. Pupil Personnel, 1975; editor: (newsletter) Ga. Personnel and Guidance, 1977-78; mem. editl. bd. Jour. Career Edn., 1978-80, Future Mag., 1978, Chronicle Guidance Corp., 1987-89. Mem. Ga. Sch. Counselors Assn. (Gov.'s award for Govt. Svc.), Internat. Soc. Ednl. Planners (bd. dirs. 1987-91). Democrat. Methodist. Avocations: photography, woodworking. Home: 4276 Village Green Cir Conyers GA 30013

BOUDA, JAROMÍR, physician; b. Bratislava, Slovakia, July 19, 1929; s. Josef and Bozena (Kvasnicková) B.; m. Zora Brychtová, Sept. 26, 1959; children: Bouda Jan, Bouda Jiri. MD, Masaryk Univ., Brno, Czechoslovakia, 1953. Ob/gyn Hosp., Topolčany, Czechoslovakia, 1954-55, Nitra, Czechoslovakia, 1955-60; asst. prof. Medical Faculty, Plzeň, Czechoslovakia, 1960-69, assoc. prof., 1969-90, prof. ob/gyn, 1990—; head of dept. ob/gyn Charles Univ., Plzeň, 1990; mem. pres. Czech Gyn Ob Soc., 1992, pres. Oncologic section Cz ob/gyn Soc., 1993. Author: Compendium of Gynecological Surgery. Fellow European Soc. Gynecological Oncology; mem. European Fedn. gynecol. oncology (mem. steering com.). Avocations: music, opera, theater, sports. Home: Klatovská 192, 320 08 Plzeň Czech Republic Office: Dept Ob Gyn, Čapkovo nam 1, 307 08 Plzeň Czech Republic

BOUDA, VÁCLAV FRANTIŠEK, engineering educator; b. Úvaly, Prague, Czech Republic, Oct. 9, 1939; s. Josef and Alžběta (Pechová) B.; m. Lea Letošniková, Oct. 12, 1967; children: Denisa Haluzíková, Václav. MS in Engring., Czech Tech. U., Prague, 1963, PhD of Tech. Scis., 1972. Asst. prof. faculty elec. engring. Czech Tech. U., Prague, 1966-85, assoc. prof. materials sci. faculty elec. engring., 1986—, prof. materials electrotech. faculty elec. engring., 1995—; rsch. worker dept. phys. chemistry Rijks U., Leiden, The Netherlands, 1969-70; expert for edn. Mil. Tech. Coll., Cairo, 1974-75; rsch. worker State Rsch. Inst. Materials Sci., Prague, 1984-85; acad. visitor Imperial Coll., London, 1991, Tech. U., Berlin, 1991, Tech. U., Munich, 1994. Contbr. articles to profl. jours.; patentee in field. Grantee European Commn., 1991, 94, Czech Ministry Edn., 1993-94, Grant Agy. Czech Republic, 1998-2000. Mem. European Materials Rsch. Soc., Instn. Materials, Soc. Rheology. Avocations: touring, hiking, culture. E-mail: bouda@feld.cvut.cz. Home: Bělehradská 120, 120 00 Praha 2, Czech Republic Office: Czech Tech U Faculty Elec Engring, Technická 2, 166 27 Prague 6, Czech Republic

BOUDART, YVES HENRY, banker; b. Haine-Saint-Paul, Belgium, Sept. 29, 1948; s. Gustave and Nelly (Dehon) B.; m. Marie-Christine Blariau, Apr. 10, 1976; children: Xavier, Aurelie, Vincent. Grad. tchr., Inst. Notre Dame de Bonne Espérance, Braine le Comte, Belgium. Jr. clk. Banque de Brussels, 1970-71, asst. dealer, 1971-73; dealer Banque Brussels Lambert SA, 1973-74, corp. asst. dealer, 1974-75, corp. dealer, 1976-2000. Treas. Cath. Youth Assn., 1976-79; sec. scholastic com. Sch. Christian Bros., Binche, Belgium, 1986—. Mem. Folk Soc. Gilles, Les Jeunes Independants. Roman Catholic. Home: Rue de la Resistance 67D, 7131 Waudrez Belgium

BOUDIN, MICHAEL, federal judge; b. N.Y.C., Nov. 29, 1939; s. Leonard B. and Jean (Roisman) B.; m. Martha A. Field, Sept. 14, 1984. B.A., Harvard Coll., 1961, LL.B., 1964. Bar: N.Y. 1964, D.C. 1967. Law clk. U.S. Ct. Appeals, 2d cir., 1964-65, U.S. Sup. Ct., 1965-66; assoc. firm Covington & Burling, Washington, 1966-72, ptnr., 1972-87; dep. asst. atty. gen. Anti-trust div. Dept. Justice, Washington, 1987-90; judge U.S. Dist. Ct. of D.C., Washington, 1990-92, U.S. Ct. Appeals, Boston, 1992-98; vis. prof. Harvard Law Sch., 1982-83, lectr., 1983-98; lectr. U. Pa. Law Sch., 1984-85. Contbr. revs. to law jours. Mem. ABA, Am. Law Inst. Office: US Ct Appeals 1st Cir 1 Courthouse Way Ste 7710 Boston MA 02210-3009

BOUDJENAH, YASMINE, foreign diplomat; b. Paris, Dec. 21, 1970. Diplome d'etudes approfondis, Paris VII Univ., 1996, postgrad. Mem. European Parliament, 1999—, mem. com. on devel. and coop., substitute com. on industry, external trade, rsch. & energy; mem. Confederal Group of the European United Left/Nordic Green Left; mem. delegation for relations with the Maghreb countries and the Arab Maghreb Union. Active exec. coll. French Communist Party, 2000—. Mem. French Communist Party.

BOUDON, RAYMOND, sociologist, educator; b. Paris, Jan. 27, 1934; s. Raymond Boudon and Hélene Millet; m. Rosemarie Riessner, Apr. 22, 1962; 1 child, Stephane. PhD, Sorbonne, Paris, 1967; D (hon.), U. Cluj (Romania), 1992, U. Antwerp (Belgium), 1995. Prof. U. Bordeaux, France, 1964-67, Sorbonne, Paris, 1967—. Author: Inequality, Opportunity and social Inequality, 1973 (Acad. Sci. Morales 1973), The Art of Self Persuasion, 1995 (Acad. Française 1995), The Origin of Values, 2000. Mem. AAAS, Acad. Europaea, Acad. Scis. Morales, Brit. Acad., L'Année Sociologique (pres., jour.), Rationality Society (jour.). Office: Maison Sci Homme, 75006 Paris France

BOUDOUVIS, ANDREAS G., engineering educator, researcher; b. Pyrgos, Greece, Jan. 28, 1959; s. George A. and Maria E. (Yannakopoulou) B. Diploma, Nat. Tech. U. Athens, 1982; PhD, U. Minn., 1987. Lectr. Nat. Tech. U. Athens, Greece, 1991-94, asst. prof., 1994-2000; assoc. prof. Nat. Tech. U. Athens, 2000—. Contbr. articles to profl. jours. Recipient 1st prize, Hellenic Math. Soc., Athens, 1976; fellowship Latsis Found., 1976-81, U. Minn., 1984. Mem. Am. Inst. Chemical Engrs., Soc. Indusl. and Applied Math., Internat. Assn. Hydromagnetic Phenomena & Applications. Home: 33 Ithomis St, 11475 Athens Greece Office: Nat Tech U Athens, Zografou Campus, 15780 Athens Greece

BOUDRANT, JOSEPH MARIE ANDRÉ, biotechnologist, researcher; b. Issoudun, France, Feb. 3, 1946; s. Pierre Henri and Louise Marie Antoinette (Champenier) B.; m. Anne Louise Marie Blondel, July 24, 1971; children: Elisabeth, Emmanuel, Guillaume, Edouard, Louise. Licence, Coll. Stanislas, Paris, 1966; Ingr., Ensia Coll., Massy, France, 1969; DSc, U. Montpellier II, France, 1976. Teaching asst. U. Montpellier, 1970-76; rsch. assoc. MIT, Cambridge, Mass., 1976-78; rsch. engr. Rhône-Poulenc, Paris, 1978-82; indsl. engr. Eurolysine, Amiens, France, 1982-86; dir. rsch. Ctr. Nat. Recherche Sci., Vandoeuvre les Nancy, France, 1986—. Editor: Capteurs et Mesures en Biotechnologie, 1994, Agitation et Melange en Biotechnologies Alimentaire et Industrielle, 1994, Strategie Experimentale et Procedes Biotechnologiques, 1995, Eaux residuaires: braitements biologiques et physiochimique, 1996, Materiaux divisés et poudres en industries alimentaires, 1999, Integration des membranes dans les procedes, 2000; contbr. articles to profl. jours. Mem. Am. Soc. Microbiology, Soc. Francaise Microbiology, Groupe Francais de Genie des Procedes (chmn. working party). Roman Catholic. Avocations: gardening, antiques, fine arts. Home: 82 Rue Stanislas, 54000 Nancy France Office: CNRS BP172, 2 Ave de la Foret de Haye, 54505 Vandoeuvre les Nancy France

BOUDVILLE, RODNEY JOHN, manufacturing administrator, general manager; b. Johor Bahru, Malaysia, June 21, 1975; s. Alleyne John Boudville and Puay Min Lim. Diploma in tourism, Reliance Sch. Tourism, Kuala Lumpur, Malaysia, 1993. Ops. asst. P&E Travel, Petaling Jaya, Malaysia, 1994; asst. disc jockey Music Scene, Petaling Jaya, 1994; resident disc jockey Betelnut Fun Pub, Petaling Jaya, 1994-95, Musictheque, Istana Hotel, Petaling Jaya, 1995, Top-Up Fun Pub, Petaling Jaya, 1995-96; chief disc jockey Citadel Discotheque, Sunway Lagoon Club, Petaling Jaya, 1996-97; acct. exec. UDS Direct (M) Sdn Bhd, Petaling Jaya, 1997-98; mktg. dir., gen. mgr. AT Printing and Packaging Industries, Kuala Lumpur, 1998—. Avocations: soccer, swimming, reading, badminton. E-mail: atplast@pd.jaring.ny. Fax: 96414610. Home: Jalan PJS8/9 Taman Sri Subang, 208 Bl B Makmur Apt 1, Petaling Jaya 46000, Malaysia Office: No 2 Jln 1/7 Tmn Indsutri, Jaya Off Jalan Balakong, Balakong 43300, Malaysia

BOUFFETTE, PATRICK PIERRE, oncologist, hematologist; b. Engkien, France, Sept. 24, 1950; s. Jean Georges and Josette (Muller) B.; m. Marina Sanardazic; 1 child: Selena. MD, U. Paris, 1976. Intern, resident Am. Hosp. of Paris, mgr. Oncology Unit, 1988—; cons. St. Louis Hosp., Paris, 1980—. Col. French Army. Mem. Am. Soc. Clinical Oncology, European Soc. Medical Oncology, Paris Soc. Oncology. Avocations: horseback riding, tennis. Office: Am Hosp of Paris, 63 Bld Victor Hugo, 9220 Neuilly France

BOUFFORD, JO IVEY, health and human services administrator; b. Durham, N.C., July 2, 1945. BA in Psychology magna cum laude, Wellesley Coll., 1965; MD with distinction, U. Mich., 1971; DSc(hon.), SUNY, Bklyn., 1992. Diplomate Nat. Bd. Med. Examiners, Am. Bd. Pediats. Resident in social pediats. medicine Montefiore Hosp. and Med. Ctr., Bronx, N.Y., 1971-74, asst. attending physician, 1975-97, co-dir. Inst. for Health Team Devel., 1975-82, dir. residency program in social medicine, 1975-82; adminstrv. dir. Valentine Lane Family Practice, Yonkers, N.Y., 1975-82; v.p. med. ops. N.Y.C. Health and Hosps. Corp., 1982-83, v.p. med. and profl. affairs, 1983-85, exec. v.p., 1985, acting pres., 1985, pres., 1985-89; internat. fellow in comparative health sys. mgmt. King's Fund Coll., London, 1989-91, dir., 1991-93; prin. dep. asst. sec. for health Dept. Health and Human Svcs., Washington, 1993-97; dean Robert F. Wagner Grad. Sch. of Pub. Svc., New York Univ., 1997—; prof. pub. admin., clin. prof. peds. New York Univ., 1997—; asst. prof. dept. pediats. Albert Einstein Coll. of Medicine, Bronx, N.Y., 1976-87, assoc. prof. dept. cmty. health, 1981-82, clin. assoc. prof. dept. pediats., 1987-94, clin. assoc. prof. dept. epidemiology and social medicine, 1982-94; adj. prof. Lehman Coll. Nursing, Bronx, 1974-80; mem. Nat. Adv. Coun. for Health Professions Edn. US-DHHS, 1976-80; mem. tech. panel on the ednl. environ. Grad. Med. Edn. Nat. Adv. Coun., 1979-80; cons. on manpower programs divsn. medicine bur. Health Professions Edn. HRSA-DHHS, 1980-88; mem. N.Y. State Coun. on Grad. med. Edn., 1987-89, N.Y. State Commn. on Grad. Med. Edn., 1985-86; mem. adv. bd. residency program in gen. preventive medicine and occupl. health Mt. Sinai coll. Medicine, 1986-89; mem. Nat. Vis. Coun. for the Health Scis. Faculty Columbia U., N.Y.C., 1988-90; mem. vis. faculty The New Sch. for Social Rsch., 1989; rep. of U.S. on exec. bd. WHO, 1994-97; mem. joint coordinating com. for Radiation Health Effects Rsch., 1994-97; U.S. staff dir. Gore-Chernomyrdin Commn. Health Com., 1994-97; various consulting positions. Mem. editl. bd. Jour. Med. Edn., 1980-86; mem. editl. adv. bd. The New Physician, 1979-89; contbr. articles to profl. jours.; presenter in field. Fellow Am. Acad. Pediats.; mem. APHA, NAS Inst. Medicine (Robert Wood Johnson health policy fellow 1979-80), Am. Med. Women's Assn., Ambulatory Pediats. Assn., Soc. for Health and Human Values, Soc. Med. Adminstrs., Med. Adminstrs. Conf. Office: NYU Robert F Wagner Grad Sch Pub Svc 4 Washington Sq N New York NY 10003-6671

BOUGAS, EFTHEMIOS, occupational health specialist; b. Strand, South Africa, Mar. 3, 1929; arrived in Greece, 1983; s. Panayiotis and Susanna Alexandra (Marais) B.; m. Johanna Christina van den Worm, Dec. 15, 1951 (div. Jan. 1965); 1 child, Philip; m. Marjorie Elsie Dixon, May 1, 1965; children: Peter Henry, Nicholas, Jason. MB ChB, U. Cape Town, South Africa, 1952; diploma in indsl. health, Soc. Apothecaries, London, 1967; cert. in indsl. health, U. St. Andrews, Scotland, 1967; cert. primary aviation medicine, Mil. Med. Inst., Pretoria, South Africa, 1969. Gen. med. practitioner Bonnievale, South Africa, 1953-59; asst. factory med. officer AECI, Umbogintwini, Natal, South Africa, 1959-65, Modderfontein, Transvaal, South Africa, 1965-72; chief med. officer AECI, Johannesburg, Transvaal, 1974-83; regional med. officer Brit. Telecom, London, 1989-93; apptd. physician for examination for certification of pvt. pilots, South Africa, 1969-83, for certification of profl. deep sea divers, 1971-83; part-time hon. sr. lectr. in occupl. toxicology for post grad. students Pretoria U. Med. Sch., 1979-83. Co-author: Agricultural Pesticides, 1972. Chmn. Transvaal chpt. South African Soc. Occupational Health, Johannesburg, 1974-81; councillor for pub. health and ambulance svcs. Modderfontein Municipality, 1973-82, hon. med. officer of health, 1974-80. Fellow Royal Soc. Health, Royal Soc. Medicine, Am. Occupational Med. Assn.; mem. Royal Coll. Physicians of London (occupational medicine faculty), Royal Coll. Physicians of Ireland. Greek Orthodox. Achievements include being a pioneer in the practice of occupational medicine in the chemical and explosives industry in South Africa. Avocations: playing the bouzouki, philately, piano, Greek dancing, tap dancing. Home: Villa Oiantheia, GR 33052 Galaxidi Greece

BOUGAS, JAMES ANDREW, physician, surgeon; b. Bismarck, N.D., Jan. 25, 1924; s. Andrew James and Mary (Psaltiras) B.; m. Tiina Parlin, June 27, 1953; children: Karen Louise, Tiina Maria. MD, Harvard U., 1948. Diplomate Am. Bd. Surgery, Am. Bd. Thoracic Surgery. Intern Columbia U. Svc., Bellevue Hosp., N.Y.C., 1948-50, chief resident in surgery, 1952-53; resident Presbyn. Hosp., N.Y.C., 1950-52, chief resident surgery, 1953; fellow Overholt Clinic, Boston, 1953-55, assoc., 1955-65; chief thoracic surgery U. Hosp., Boston, 1965-70; assoc. prof. surgery Boston U. Sch. Medicine, 1965—; lectr. Tufts U. Sch. Medicine, Boston, 1965-70; chmn. Gordon Rsch. Confs., 1967-68. Contbr. articles to profl. jours. Pres. Heart Assn., Boston, 1967-69; chmn. Mass. Rehab. Commn. Adv. Com.; trustee Boston Tb Assn. With U.S. Army, 1942-44. Fellow AAAS; mem. ACS, Am. Coll. Cardiology, Am. Assn. Thoracic Surgeons, Soc. Thoracic Surgeons, Am. Coll. Cardiology, Mass. Med. Soc. (legis. com., coun.), Norfolk Dist. Med. Soc. (pres. 1989-90, Tri-State regional planning com.). Achievements include development of combined cardiac catheterization; porous metal prostheses fabrication and cardio-pulmonary biology. E-mail jbougas@nebh.caregroup.harvard.edu. Office: NE Bapt Hosp 125 Parker Hill Ave Boston MA 02120-2847

BOUGEARD, DANIEL ROGER A.M., chemistry researcher; b. Pléchatel, Britanny, France, Mar. 14, 1948; s. Ange and Marie (Louvel) B.; m. Beatrix Hövekenmeier, Apr. 13, 1974; children: Dominique, Natalie. Degree in chem. engring., Insa Lyon, Villeurbanne, France, 1969; dr. rer. nat., U. Dortmund, Fed. Republic Germany, 1972; doctor in sci., U. Pierre and Marie Curie, Paris, 1976; habilitation, U. Essen, Fed. Republic Germany, 1978. Rsch. fellow Inst. Angewandte Spektroskopie, Dortmund, 1969-72, LASIR-CNRS, Thiais, France, 1973-77; asst. prof. U. Essen, 1977-89; prof. U. Reims, France, 1989-90; rsch. dir. LASIR-CNRS, Lille, France, 1990—; dir. LASIR, 1997—. Contbr. articles in profl. jours. Office: LASIR-CNRS, Batiment C5 Univ de Lille 1, F 59655 Villeneuve d'Ascq Cedex, France

BOUGHTON, GEOFFREY NEVILLE, forestry educator, civil engineer, consultant; b. Cooma, Australia, May 15, 1954; s. Neville Oliver and Audrey (Jurd) B.; m. Jennie Elizabeth Dufty, July 1, 1978; children: Anthony

Neville, Amanda Patrice, Kendal Thomas. B in Engring. with honors, U. Western Australia, Perth, 1976, M in Engring. Sci., 1980; PhD, James Cook U., Townsville, Australia, 1989. Design engr. Pub. Works Dept., Perth, 1976-78; constrn. engr. Pub. Works Dept., Narrogin, Australia, 1978-81; rsch. fellow James Cook U., 1981-84; cons. Water Authority of Western Australia, Perth, 1984-86; sr. lectr. Curtin U., Perth, 1986-91, 92-95; vis. prof. U. B.C., Vancouver, Can., 1991; dir. timber edn. Forest & Wood Products R & D Corp., Perth, Australia, 1996—; cons. UNIDO, Manila, The Philippines, 1986-91; mem. ISO Stds. Com., Geneva, 1996—, Stds. Australia coms., 1982—; mem. Internat. Commn. Baitment CIB W18, 1988—. Author: Steel Design to AS 4100, 1994, Introduction to Timber Engineering, 1997, Timber, The Material, 1996, Timber Design Handbook, 1998. Recipient Boeing Excellence commendation Assn. Australian Engring. Educators, 1998. Fellow Instn. Engrs. Australia (medal 1975, O.F. Blakey medal 1978), Timber Structures Inst. Australia. Office: PO Box 30, Glengarry PO, Perth WA 6023, Australia

BOUGHTON, ROSS BYRON, composer, television producer; b. Northampton, Mass., Aug. 6, 1960; s. Walter Leroy and Georgia Dagmar (Aune) B. Student, Roger Williams Coll., 1978-80, Berklee Sch. Music, 1980-82. Touring musician, 1985-88; filmmaker Cable TV, N.Y.C., 1988—; freelance composer, arranger N.Y.C., 1988—. Composer, author mus. works. Activist Save the Bandshell, Cen. Park, N.Y.C., 1992. Recipient Excellence in Music award Madrigal Soc. We. Mass., 1983, Promoting Chamber Music award Chamber Orch. Greenfield Mass., 1984. Mem. ASCAP (Popular Music award 1993-94). Republican. Episcopalian. Avocations: collecting antique stringed instruments, philately, sports memorabelia. Home: 48 W 68th St Apt 2C New York NY 10023-6015

BOUGIE, JACQUES, aluminum company executive; b. Montreal, Que., Can., 1947. BABA, Ecole des Hautes Etudes Commerciales; JD, U. Montreal. Mgr. Beauharnois Works (a part of Alcan Smelters and Chems. Ltd.), Montreal, 1979-81; dir. devel. Aluminium Co. of Can., Manitoba, Que., 1981-82, asst. to v.p. planning and adminstrn. N.Am. and W.I., 1982-84; v.p. planning and adminstrn. Alcan Can. Products, 1985-88; pres. Alcan Extrusions, 1988-89; pres., COO Alcan Aluminium Ltd., Cleve., 1989-93, pres., CEO, 1993—; vice chmn. Bus. Coun. on Nat. Issues. Decorated officer Order of Can. Office: Alcan Aluminium Ltd, 1188 Sherbrooke St W, Montreal, PQ Canada H3A 3G2

BOUHDIBA, ABDEL WAHAB, sociologist, philosopher, educator, researcher; b. Kairouan, Tunisia, Aug. 13, 1932; s. Baccar Bouhdiba and Douja M'Rabet; m. Aïcha Mrabet, Sept. 12, 1956; children: Saber, Olfa, Sofiane. Degree, Janson de Sailly, Paris, 1955, Sorbonne U., Paris, 1959; D, Sorbonne U., Paris, 1972. Prof. Alaoui de Tunis, Tunisia, 1959-61; maitre de confs. U. Tunis, 1964-72, prof., 1972-97; permanent expert UNESCO, 1967-72; dir. Ctr. d'Etudes et Recherches Econs. et Sociales, U. Tunis, 1972-91; pres. Tunisian Acad. Sci., Arts and Letters "Beït Al-Hikma", 1995—; mem., pres. Internat. Com. for Info. and Documentation of Social Scis., 1967-83. Author: Criminalité et changements sociaux en Tunisie, 1965, Les préconditions sociales de l'industrialisation dans la région de Tunis, 1968, Les conditions de vie des mineurs de la région de Gafsa, 1968, La sociologie du développement africain, 1968, Public et Justice, 1971, A la Recherche des Normes Perdues, 1973, La sexualité en Islam, 1975, L'Imaginaire maghrebin: dix contes tunisiens pour enfants, 1975, Culture et société, 1978, Dialogue et politique, 1979, Raisons d'être, 1980, L'exploitation du travail des enfants, 1982, Les droits de l'enfant en Tunisie, 1992, Li Afhama-Etudes sur la société et la religion, 1993, Quêtes sociologiques. Continuités et ruptures au Maghreb, 1996; contbr. articles to books, profl. jours.; mem., co-founder Tunisian Rev. Social Scis., 1962, dir., 1971-91; mem. editl. com. Bibliographies Internats. des Scis. Sociales, 1965-83, Internat. Rev. Social Scis., Jour. Arab Affairs, others. Mem., co-founder Universal Movement for Sci. Responsibility, Paris and Geneva, 1974—; founder Tunisian League of Human Rights, Tunis, 1978-87; mem., pres. UN Human Rights Commn., N.Y. and Geneva, Switzerland, 1971-72; mem. ctrl. com. RCD Party, Tunis, 1988-92; mem. Econ. and Social Coun. of Tunisia, 1970-74, 80-85; permanent human rights expert UN, 1971—, mem. sub-com. against racial discrimination and protection of minorities, 1972-82, pres., 1978-79, spl. rapporteur for studies of violations of human rights in Kampuchea, 1978-80, spl. rapporteur for study on worldwide exploitation of child labor, 1980-82; pres. Permanent Arab Commn. for Human Rights, 1983-85. Recipient Nat. prize for humanities and social scis., 1991. Moslem. Home: Rue Doctor Burnet, 1082 Tunis Tunisia Office: Acad Beït Al Hikma, Ave De La Republique, Carthage Tunisia

BOUILLON, RAYAN GABRIEL, development economist, international consultant; b. Montpellier, Languedoc, France, May 12, 1947; s. Henri and Rayan Germaine B. Degree in Gen. Econs., U. Montpellier, France, 1969; Lic. in Internat. Econs., Paris IX Dauphine, 1970, M Econs. and Mgmt. Sci., 1971, PhD, 1973. Mgmt. orgnl. cons. Paris, 1968-73; mgr. Inforga, France, 1974-75; sales mgr. IBM Corp., France, 1976-80; exec. mgr. regional devel. BRL, France, 1981; team leader, assoc. prof. FAO, France and Burkina, 1983-85; cons. UN, World Bank and European Union, 1981-2000; govtl. advisor, governance-local devel. program evaluator missions in 50 developing countries, including, Tanzania, Senegal, Sri Lanka; internat. cons., UN; team leader regional program European Union, 1996-98; chief economist UNDP, Cape Verde, Vietnam, 1991-93; sr. adviser adjustment structural plan World Bank, Madagascar, Burundi, Guinea, 1986-89; sci. economist Mundo Maya program, Mexico and Cen. Am., 1974-75; UNCED Bio 92 Earth Summit editl. conf. proceedings in field, World Conf. on Sustainable Tourism, Spain, 1995. Adviser Panafest Arts, Ghana, 1994, Paris Jazz Festival, 1969; mgr. Bach Music Festival, France, 1979-80, IPA Cooperation Mission, Japan, Russia, 1968, Somalia, 1982, other humanitarian missions. Mem. Medecins Sans Frontieres, WCV, TES, Internat. Assn. Bus. Economists, Assn. Internat. Experts Scientifiques du Tourisme, Graufe de Recherche et Echanges Technologiques (France). Avocations: music, wine grower, humanitarian aid, ecotourism. Home: 9 rue Jacques Draparnaud, 34000 Montpellier France

BOUILLY, FREDERIC C., sales executive; b. Lyon, Rhone, France, July 4, 1967; s. Claude C. and Chantal P. (Vuillaume) B.; m. Julie M. Delamaye, Mar. 30, 1997; 1 child, Philippine. Degree in law, Assas U., Paris, 1987; MBA, ISG, Paris, 1997. Sales engr., 1993-95; sales mgr. Thomson CSE, 1995—. Author: Java a Dsakarta, 1995. Capt. res. French Navy, 1991-93. Home: 1 Rue Bosio, 75016 Paris France

BOUJU, PHILIPPE PIERRE MICHEL A., anesthesiologist; b. Bois-Colombes, France, Apr. 22, 1957; s. Pierre and Jacqueline (Landré) B.; m. Hélène Marie Francoise Henriette Dreux-Boucard; 1 child, Cyrielle. MD, Lariboisiere-St. Louis, Paris, 1983; Specialist Anesthesiology & CriticalCare, Faculte Rene Descartes, Paris, 1989. Cert. d'etudes Speciales d'anesthesie reanimation. Anaesthesia tng. Hosp. Henri Mondor/Creteil Hosp. Tenon, Paris; medecin des hopitaux C.H. Robert Ballanger, Aulnay Sous Bois, France, 1991—, pres. Com. de Lutte Contre la Douleur, 1995—; pres. Assn. de Lutte Contre la Douleur 93; mem. Coll. Francais des Anesthesistes Reanimateurs, Coll. des Praticiens de la Douleur. Contbr. articles to profl. jours. Pres. ALCD 93, non-profit orgn. for promotion pain treatment. Mem. Internat. Assn. for Study Pain, European Soc. Anaesthesiology, European Soc. Regional Anaesthesia, Soc. Francaise de la Douleur, French Coll. Anesthesiologists, Nat. Coll. Pain Practitioners. Home: 32 Bld du General de Gaulle, 93250 Villemomble France Office: C H Robert Ballanger, Bld Robert Ballanger, 93602 Aulnay-sous-Bois France

BOUKARAOUN, HACENE, economist; b. Algiers, Algeria, Apr. 5, 1950; s. Arezki and Messaouda (Ouali) B.; m. Meryam Maza, Aug. 20, 1983; children: Nadia, Nassim. BA of Fin., Nat. Inst. of Fin., 1975; MBA, Doshisha U., Kyoto, Japan, 1989; PhD in Restructuring/Privatisation, Ritsumeikan U., Kyoto, Japan, 1992. Fin. mgr. Pub. Corp., Algiers, 1975-85; researcher Japanese Sogo-shosha, Kyoto, Tokyo, 1985-89, Nippon Telephone & Telegraph Japanese Nat. Railways, Kyoto, Tokyo, 1989-92; sr. cons. Bernard Krief Cons. Group, Paris, 1992—; chmn. fin. restructuring com. of Algerian State Corp., Ministry of Pub. Works, Algiers, 1982-85; active privatisation of NTT and JNR, Japan, 1985-92, privatisation/restructuring of Russian complex, Lipetsk, 1992-93. Contbr. articles to profl. publs. Rsch. grantee Monbusho, Tokyo, 1985, 92, Marubeni, Tokyo, 1990, Kyoto Shimbun, Kyoto, 1991, Komatsu, Tokyo, 1992. Avocations: jogging, Japanese caligraphy. Home: 59 Avenue du Lac, Villiers sur Marne 94350, France Office: Investment & Project Fin, 3 rue Germain Nouveau, 93000 Saint Denis France

BOULAUD, DENIS GEORGES, physicist, researcher; b. Villeparisis, France, Jan. 15, 1947; s. Roger and Madeleine (Schenk) B.; m. Marie Claude Ravizy, Sept. 20, 1970 (dec. Aug. 1990); m. Sophie Marie Payet, Nov. 14, 1992; children: Romain, Gabrielle. MSc, U. Paris, 1970, Doctor 3d cycle, 1973, DSc in Physics, 1977. Asst. prof. U. Paris, 1977-81; asst. head of lab. AEC, Far, France, 1981-85, head of lab., 1985-98; head of svc. AEC, Saclay, France, 1998—, rsch. dir., 1995—; prof. Inst. Nuc. Scis., Saclay, 1994—. Author: The Aerosols: Physic and Metrology; contbr. over 50 articles to profl. jours.; patentee in field of aerosol methodology. Home: 6 allee de l'etang, 91190 Gif Yvette France Office: AEC, Bat 389, 91191 Gif Yvette France

BOULEAU, NICOLAS ANDRE, mathematician; b. Paris, May 20, 1945; s. Charles and Wanda (Rabaud) B.; m. Sylvie Berline, May 31, 1968 (div. 1993); 4 children. Diploma in engring., Ecole Poly., Paris, 1967; degree in engring., Ecole Ponts et Chaussees, Paris, 1970; govt. diploma in architecture, Ecole des Beaux Arts, Paris, 1972; Thèse d'Etat, U. Paris VI, 1980, Habilitation, 1987. Cert. math., civil engring., architecture. Civil engr. Pub. Urban Planning, Torcy, France, 1970-75; rschr. Ecole Polytechnique, Palaiseau, France, 1975-81; rschr., prof. Ecole des Ponts, Paris, 1981—; dir. Rsch. Ctr. Applied Math., Noisy, 1984-93; mem. sci. coun. Nat. Geog. Inst., 1986. Author: Probabilites de l'Ingenieur, 1986, Processus Stochastiques et Applications, 1988, Martingales et marchés Financiers, 1998, Philosohies des Mathématique et de la Modélisation, 1999; co-author: Dirichlet Forms and Analysis on Wiener Space, 1991, Numerical Methods for Stochastic Processes, 1994; editor in chief Annales des Ponts, 1993—. Adminstrn. bd. Ecole Nat. des Ponts et Chaussees, Paris., 1994. 2nd lt. French Inf., 1967-68. Recipient Montyon prize French Acad. Sci., Paris, 1994. Mem. Laplace-Gauss Assn. (treas. 1992—), Civil Engring. Rsch. Com., Math. Soc. France (sec. 1985-89). Avocations: philosophy, history of science, economics, epistemology. Office: Ecole des Ponts, 28 rue des Saint Pères, 75007 Paris France

BOULEY, JOSEPH RICHARD, pilot; b. Fukuoka, Japan, Jan. 7, 1955; came to U.S., 1955; s. Wilfrid Arthur and Minori Cecelia (Naraki) B.; m. Sara Elizabeth Caldwell, July 6, 1991; children: Denise Marie, Janice Elizabeth, Eleanor Catherine. BA in English, U. Nebr., 1977; MAS, Embry Riddle Aeronautical U., 1988. Commd. 2d lt. USAF, 1977; F-117A Stealth Fighter pilot USAF, Persian Gulf, 1991; ret. lt. col. USAFR, 2000; pilot United Airlines, 1992—. Ct. apptd. spl. advocate Office of Guardian Ad Litem, Salt Lake City, 1996-99. Decorated Disting. Flying Cross, Def. Meritorious Svc medal, 4 Air medals, 3 Meritorious Svc. medals, 2 Aerial Achievement medals, Joint Svc. commendation medal, 3 Air Force Commendation medals, Air Force Achievement medal; recipient Alumni Achievement award U. Nebr., 1998. Mem. VFW, Am. Legion, Disting. Flying Cross Soc., Airline Pilots Assn., Red River Valley Fighter Pilots Assn., Aircraft Owners & Pilots Assn. Roman Catholic. Avocations: flying, golf, running, photography. Home: 952 E Springwood Dr North Salt Lake UT 84054-3043

BOULEZ, PIERRE, composer, conductor; b. Montbrison, nr. Clermont-Ferrand, France, Mar. 26, 1925; s. Leon and Marcelle (Calabre) B. Student, recipient 1st prize, Olivier Messiaen at Paris Conservatory. Apptd. dir. music Jean-Louis Barrault's Theater Co., 1948; tchr., lectr., condr.; musical adviser, prin. guest condr. Cleve. Symphony Orch., 1970-71; chief condr. BBC Symphony Orch., 1970-75; musical dir. N.Y. Philharmonic Orch., 1971-77; prof. Coll. de France, 1976-95; dir. Inst. de Recherche et de Coord. Acoustique/Musique, 1976-91; apptd. prin. guest condr. Chgo. Symphony Orch., 1995; pres. The Ensemble Intercontemporain, 1976. Toured Orient, Europe, North and South Am., (with Barrault), conducting appearances include, Edinburgh Festival, 1965, Bayreuth Festival, 1966, 76-80; compositions include Sonatina for flute and piano, 1946, Three Piano Sonatas, 1946, 50, 57, Le Soleil des Eaux for voice and orchestra, 1947, Structures, 1952, Le Marteau sans maitre, 1955, Deux improvisations sur Mallarme, 1957, Doubles for orchestra, 1958, Tombeau (on text of Mallarmé), 1959, Pli selon pli, 1960, Structures II, 1962, Eclat, 1964, Domaines, 1968, Multiples, 1970, Cummings ist der Dichter, 1970, Explosante/Fixe, 1973, Rituel, 1975, Messagesquisse, 1976, Notations, part I, 1980, Répons, 1981, Dialogue de l'Ombre double, 1986, Mémoriale, 1985, Visage Nuptial, 1989, Dérive I, 1985, Anthèmes pour violin solo, 1992, Explosante/Fixe for large ensemble and electronics, 1993, Anthèmes for Violin Solo and Electronics, 1997, Sur Incises, 1998, Notations VII, 1999; author: Relevé, 1966, Points de Repère, 1981, le pays fertile-Paul Klee, 1989, Jalon-10 ans d'enseignement au Collège de France, 1989; musical criticism and analysis, including Penser la Musique d'Aujourd'hui, 1963. Recipient Praemium Imperiale of Japan Art Assn., 1989, Grosses Verdienstkreuz RFA, 1990, Polar Music prize, Sweden, 1996. Office: Inst Recherche Coord Acoustique Musique, 1 place Igor Stravinsky, 75004 Paris France

BOULIER, JEAN-FRANCOIS, bank executive, researcher; b. Caen, Normandy, France, Mar. 14, 1956; s. Michel Maurice Boulier and Marie-Joseph Germaine LeMaitre; m. Marianne Blanche Denis, Apr. 2, 1963; children: Thomas, Marion, Louise. Degree in engring., Poly. U. Paris, 1980, Engref, Paris, 1982; PhD in Fluid Mechanics, U. Grenoble, France, 1985. Engr. Ministry of Agriculture, Grenoble, 1982-85; researcher Nat. Ctr. Sci. Rsch., Grenoble, 1985-87; researcher Credit Comml. France, Paris, 1987-89, head of rsch., head market risk control, 1989-99; pres., chief investment officer SINOPIA Asset Mgmt., Paris, 1999—; chmn. Advanced Asset Allocation-Credit Comml. France-Advisors, Paris, 1990-2000; chmn. Sinopia Soc. de Gestion, 1999—; prof. fin. U. Dauphine, Paris. Editor: (periodical) Quants, 1991-2000; contbr. rsch. articles to sci. jours. Mem. Internat. Statis. Inst., French Assn. Gestion Actif-Passif (bd. dirs. 1993—, chmn. 1999—), French Assn. Fin. (bd. dirs. 1992—, chmn. 1998—), Inquire Europe (rsch. com. 1992—, bd. dirs. 1995—). Avocations: tennis, botany, geography. Home: 5 Quai de l'Orme de Sully, 78230 Le Pecq France Office: Credit Comml France, SINOPIA, 66 rue de Chaussee d'Antin, 75009 Paris France

BOULIS, ZOSER FOUAD, radiologist, consultant; b. Khartoum North, Sudan, Jan. 1, 1944; arrived in Eng., 1971; s. Fouad and Irene Grais (Wassif) B.; m. Afaf Hanna Ayoub, July 12, 1974; children: Michael, Sandra. MB, BS, U. Khartoum, Sudan, 1965. Clin. asst. gen. surgery St. Bartholomew's Hosp., London, 1971-73; registrar gen. surgery Barking Hosp., Essex, England, 1974-76; sr. registrar radiology The Royal Free Hosp., London, 1976-83; cons. in radiology Bromley (United Kingdom) Hosps. Nat. Health Svc. Trust, 1983—. Contbr. articles to profl. jours. Recipient Hamilton Bailey's prize in radiology Royal No. Hosp., London, 1980. E-Mail: zoserboulis@freeule.com. Office: Farmborough Hosp Ultrasound Dept, Farmborough Common, Orpington Kent BR6 8ND, England

BOULTE, PATRICK, consultant; b. Feurs, France, Nov. 13, 1939; s. Andre and Suzanne (Ducreux) B. Auditor C de Saint-Gobain, Paris, 1965-68; controller Le Nickel, Paris, 1969-71; fin. mgr. Servair, Paris, 1971-74, Sodello, Paris, 1976-82; v.p. Finansder, Paris, 1983-88; cons. Intervenance, Paris, 1988—. Author: Diagnostic Des Organisations Applique Aux Associations, 1991, Indiridus En Friche, 1995. Roman Catholic. Home: 49 rue de Richeleieu, 75001 Paris France Office: Intervenence, 13/14 rue de L'Eglise, 75015 Paris France

BOULTON, IAN CHARLES, microbiologist; b. Edinburgh, Scotland, Nov. 15, 1922; came to U.S., 1997; s. Charles Edward and Jean Alison Boulton. BSc with honors, U. Edinburgh, 1994; PhD, U. London, 1997. Dir. Imago Design Graphics, Toronto, Ont., Can., 1994—; rsch. fellow Va. Commonwealth U., Richmond, 1997-99, U. Toronto, 1999—; dir. Thousand Yard Stare, 1999—. Contbr. articles to profl. jours. Mem. Inst. Biology, Biochemistry Soc., New Paradigm Workshop. Libertarian. Avocations: photography, design, athletics, nutrition. E-mail: ian.boulton@utoronto.ca. Home: 66 Spadina Rd, Toronto, ON Canada MB3 2TA

BOULTON, THOMAS BABINGTON, anesthesiologist, educator; b. Bishop Auckland, Eng., Nov. 6, 1925; s. George Babington and Mary Emily (Worboys) B.; m. Helen Currey Brown, Aug. 30 1952; children: Angela Mary, Thomas Adam Babington, Anthony James Babington. BA, Cambridge U., 1946, MB BChir, 1949, MA, 1949, MD, 1999; MA, Oxford U., 1983. Tng. appts. St. Bartholomews Hosp., London, 1950-56; hon. cons., 1961-73; instr. anesthesiology U. Mich., Ann Arbor, 1956-57; cons. Royal Berkshire Hosp., Reading, Eng., 1958-61; cons., lectr. Oxford U., 1975-90; anesthesiologist Barski plastic surgery unit, Saigon, South Vietnam, 1969. Editor Jour. Anaesthesia, 1973-82, asst. editor, 1964-73; assoc. editor Survey of Anesthesiology, 1984-90; contbr. articles to profl. jours. Served to maj. M.C. Brit. Army, 1950-52. Fellow Faculty of Anaesthetists (mem. bd.), Royal Coll. Surgeons Eng., Royal Soc. Medicine (pres. sect. anaesthetics 1983-84); mem. Assn. Anaesthetists Great Britain and Ireland (pres. 1984-86). Conservative. Anglican. Avocations: household carpentry, gardening. Home: Townsend Farm, Streatley RG8 9JX England

BOULYJENKOV, VICTOR EDMUNDOVICH, geneticist; b. Ufa, Russia, Mar. 21, 1948; s. Edmund Davidovich Widicker and Zoya Nicolaevna Boulyjenkova; m. Natalia Petrovna Moussina, Dec. 18, 1975; children: Ludmilla, Igor. Degree in gen. medicine, State Med. Inst., Ufa, 1971; PhD in Med. Scis., Inst. Med. Genetics, Moscow, 1975, DSc, 1984. Rschr. Inst. Med. Genetics, 1976-85; scientist human genetics programme WHO, Geneva, 1986—; mem. permanent com. Internat. Congress of Human Genetics, 1986. Mem. editl. bd. Gene Therapy newsletter, 1994; contbr. over 100 articles to sci. jours.; co-author 5 books in field, including Genetic Approaches for Coronary Heart Diseases and Hypertention, 1991; editor numerous documents and articles in field. Mem. N.Y. Acad. Scis., Russian Soc. Med. Geneticists, European Soc. Human Genetics, Internat. Neurofibromatosis Assn. (mem. editl. bd. 1992, Internat. Pub. Svc. award 1992). Office: WHO, Human Genetics Programme, CH-1211 Geneva 27, Switzerland

BOUMEDIENE-THIERY, ALIMA, foreign diplomat; b. Argenteuil, France, July 24, 1956. Mem. European Parliament, 1999—, mem. com. on citizens' freedoms/rights, justice/home affairs, substitute com. on devel. and coop., substitute com. on petitions; mem. Group of the Greens/European Free Alliance; mem. delegation for relations with the Mashreq countries and the Gulf. *

BOUND, JOHN PASCOE, pediatrician, consultant; b. Redhill, Surrey, England, Nov. 13, 1920; s. George William and May Irene (Emsley) B.; m. Gwendoline Iris Taylor, May 15, 1944; children—Anne, Sarah. M.B., B.S., U. Coll. Hosp., London, 1943, M.D., 1950. House physician Univ. Coll. Hosp., London, 1943; asst. med. officer Alder Hey Childrens Hosp., Liverpool, 1943-44; registrar, sr. registrar in pediatrics Hillingdon Hosp., Middlesex, 1948-53; first asst. dept. pediatrics Univ. Coll. Hosp. Med. Sch., London, 1954-56; cons. pediatrician Victoria Hosp., Blackpool, 1956-83, hon. cons. pediatrician, 1983—; mem. expert group on spl. care for babies Dept. Health and Social Security, London, 1969-70. Contbr. articles on perinatal mortality and congenital malformations to profl. jours. Served to capt., M.C., Royal Army, 1944-47. Mem. British Med. Assn., British Paediatric Assn. (mem. acad. bd. 1972-75), Royal Coll. Physicians. Conservative. Mem. Ch. of England. Avocations: fell-walking. Home: 48 St Annes Rd E, Lytham, St Annes, Lancashire FY8 1UR, England

BOUNDOUKOU-LATHA, PAUL, diplomat; b. Mafoungui, Gabon, Apr. 23, 1952. M in Sociology, U. Tours, France, 1978; cert. Advanced Tng. in Diplomacy, I.I.A.P., Paris, 1981; D in Politics and Devel. Law, U. Poitiers, France, 1982; postgrad., Acad. Internat. Law, The Hague, The Netherlands, 1982; postgrad. in Diplomacy, Paris Sch. Law, 1986; cert. Advanced Studies in Nat. Defense, Inst. Advanced Studies in Nat. Defense, Paris, 1988. Dir. European affairs Gabon Ministry Fgn. Affairs, 1983, head divsn. EEC and We. Europe, 1984, dir. internat. orgns. and multilateral coop., 1984-86, amb. and dir. European affaris, 1986-87, 1st asst. sec. gen., abm., 1987-89; amb. to Morocco Govt. Gabon, 1989-93; amb. to U.S. Govt. Gabon, Washingotn, 1993—. Author: Syndication of Immigrant Workers from Black Africa in France, 1978, Contribution to the Study of a Single African Party: The Gabonese Democratic Party, 1979. Named Officier l'Etoile Equatoriale Govt. Gabon, Officier l'Ordre Nat. de Merit, Govt. France, Commdr. l'Ordre d'Ouissam Alaouite, Govt. Morocco. Office: Embassy Of Gabon 2034 20th St NW Washington DC 20009-5001

BOURANIS, DEMETRIOS LAMBROS, plant physiologist, educator; b. Pireus, Greece, Dec. 8, 1958; s. Lambros and Nota Bouranis; m. Marianna John Glykou, May 28, 1989; children: Lambros, John. Agronomist, Agrl. U. Athens, 1981; Chem. Engr., Nat. Tech. U., Athens, 1986; PhD in Plant Physiology, Agrl. U. athens, 1986. Rsch. fellow Vioryl S.A., Greece, 1986, Nat. Tech. U. Athens, 1989-92; lectr. Agrl. U. Athens, 1992-96, asst. prof. plant physiology, 1997—. Contbr. articles to profl. jours. Mem. Soc. Exptl. Biology U.K., Soil Plant Analysis Coun., Japanese Soc. Plant Physiology, Japanese Soc. Soil Sci. Plant Nutrition. Avocation: electronic organ. Home: Marathonos 30, 15343 Aghia Paraskevi Athens, Greece Office: Agricultural Univ Athens, 75 Iera Odos, 11855 Athens Greece

BOURAOU, NADEJDA IVANOVNA, engineering educator; b. Iskrovka, Ukraine, Oct. 1, 1958; d. Ivan Makarovich and Mariya Antonovna (Ochkas) L.; m. Konstantin Yurievich, Aug. 3, 1979; 1 child, Anastasiya. MSc with honors, Nat. Tech. U., 1981, PhD, 1991. Engr. Nat. Tech. U., Kiev, Ukraine, 1981-86, jr. rschr., 1986-87, rschr., 1987-92, asst. prof., 1992-96, assoc. prof., 1996—; selection bd. chmn. Nat. Tech. U., Kiev, 1995-96. Contbr. articles to profl. jours. Mem. Acoustical Soc. of Am., Ukraine Soc. of Mech. Engring. Avocations: psychology, model designing, traveling. Home: PO Box 117, Kiev 254070, Ukraine Office: Nat Tech Univ, 37 Peremogy pr, Kiev 252056, Ukraine

BOURASSEAU, SERGE, physicist; b. Saint Leger de Montbrun, France, Sept. 21, 1946; s. Joseph and Marcelle (Aubry) B.; m. Brigitte Laverdant, May 26, 1984; children: Laure, Arnaud. B in Chemistry, U. Lyon, 1968, M in Physics, 1969, D of Chem. Kinetics, 1972, DSc, 1973. Prof. physics Santo Domingo U., Dominican Republic, 1973-75; rschr. chem. engring. Laval U., Quebec City, 1975-77; prof. physics Royal Air Acad., Marrakech, Morocco, 1977-79; rsch. engr. Energetics dept. Nat. Office Aerospace Studies and Rsch., France, 1979-87; rsch. engr. Materials dept. Nat. Office Aerospace Studies and Rsch., 1987-93, rsch. engr. Physics dept., 1993-97, rsch. engr. physics dept., 1998—, rsch. engr. dept. mechanics of solid and damage, 1998—. Achievements include studies in heterogeneous photocatalysis, liquid propellant gun studies, general theoretical method for the prediction of performances of propellants and high explosives, smart materials and structure studies. Office: ONERA, PO Box 72, 92322 Chatillon France

BOURCHIER, CHRISTOPHER PAUL, agricultural estates manager; b. Bakewell, Eng., June 15, 1958; s. Cecil and Dorothy (Beaumont) B.; m. Julie Margaret Huntlea, Aug. 10, 1985; children: Oliver Paul, Jonathan James. BSc, U. Nottingham, 1979. From regional specialist to head agr. Agrl. Devel. and Adv. Svc., Oxford and London, 1985-96; head agr., minerals and forestry The Crown Estate, London, 1996-2000, head rural estates, 2000—. Mem. Brit. Soc. Animal Sci., Farmers Club. Mem. Ch. of England. Avocations: running, golf, country sports. Office: The Crown Estate, 16 Carlton House Terrace, SW1Y 5AH London England

BOURCIER, CATHERINE ELIZABETH T., communications company executive; b. London, Mar. 3, 1971; d. Jacques Adair and Elizabeth Beatrice (Ward-Jackson) B. Student, Malvern Coll., 1988-91. Pers. asst. to prodn. dir. Vogue House, The Condé Nast Publs., London, 1991-93; pers. asst. to account dir. J. Water Thompson Co. Ltd., London, 1993-94; press asst. to editor Internat. Press Europe, London, 1994-95, pers. asst. to chmn. bd., then chmn. bd., 1995—; bd. dirs. Universal-PA. Bd. dirs. Elm Lodge Gallery. Conservative. Roman Catholic. Office: Internat Press Europe, 1 Hay Hill Berkeley Sq, London W1J 6DH, England

BOURDEAU, PHILIPPE, environmental scientist; b. Rabat, Morocco, Nov. 25, 1926; s. Michel Edgard and Lucienne (Imbrecht) B.; m. Flora E. Gorirossi; 3 children. Cert. in Agrl. Engring., Sch. Agrl. Scis., Gembloux, Belgium, 1949; PhD, Duke U., 1954. Cert. forestry engr. Asst. prof. N.C. State U., Raleigh, 1954-56, Yale U., New Haven, 1956-58, 60-62; prof. U. Belgian Congo, Butare, Rwanda, 1958-60; head biology svc. Euratom Joint Rsch. Ctr., Ispra, Italy, 1962-71; div. head, dir. environ. rsch. Commn. European Communities, Brussels, 1971-91; spl. adviser Commn. European Communities, 1991-94; chmn. sci. com. European Environment Agy.,

1994—; prof. U. Brussels, 1971—; sec. gen. Sci. Problems of Environment, Internat. Coun. Sci. Unions, Paris, 1992, pres., 1995-98. Editor, co-editor books, reports on ecotoxicology; contbr. over 100 articles on plant ecology, radioecology, ecotoxicology and environ. scis. to profl. publs. Named comdr. Order of Couronne, Belgian Govt. Fellow AAAS, Belgian Am. Ednl. Found.; mem. various sci. socs. Achievements include design, implementation and management of research programs regarding the environment. Office: Universite Libre de Bruxelles, avenue FD Roosevelt 50, B 1050 Brussels Belgium

BOURDIEU, PIERRE FELIX, sociology educator; b. Denguin, France, Aug. 1, 1930; s. Albert and Noémie (Duhau) B.; m. Marie Claire Brizard, 1962; 3 children. Student, Lycée Louis le Grand, Paris, Faculté des lettres, Paris, Ecole Normale Supérieure, 1951-54, Agrégation de Philosophie, 1956. Prof. Lycée de Moulins, 1954-55; asst. Faculté des lettres, Algeria, 1958-60, Paris, 1960-61; maitre de conférences Faculté des lettres, Lille, France, 1961-64; chargé de cours Ecole Normale Supérieure, Paris, 1964-84; directeur d'études Ecole en Scis. Sociales des Hautes Etudes, Paris, 1964—; prof.-titulaire Coll. de France, Paris, 1981—; dir. Centre de sociologie de l'edn. et de la culture, 1964-84, Centre de sociologie européenne, 1985-98, Centre European Soc. Dir. Coll. Le sens commun, 1964-92, Liber, 1997—, (revue) Actes de la recherche en sciences sociales, 1975—, Liber, 1989. Mem. Am. Acad. Arts and Scis. Office: Coll de France, 52 rue du Cardinal Lemoine, 75005 Paris France

BOURÈNE, MAURICE LOUIS, diplomat; b. Tourcoing, Nord, France, Feb. 20, 1939; s. André Françoise and Andrée Eugénie (Fagayet) B.; m. Marie-Héléne Coustaury, July 2, 1966; children: Frédéric, Denis. BA, Lycée du Parc, Lyon, France, 1958; license in Scis., Univ. Marseille, France, 1962, D. in Scis., 1964; license in Japanese, U. Paris, 1981. Rsch. asst. U. Marseilles, France, 1963-64; rschr. French Commissariat a L'energie Atomique, France, 1966-82; attaché Delegation European Commn., Tokyo, 1986—; 1st counselor Delegation European Commn., 1990. Contbr. articles to profl. jours. Ensign French Marine Corps., 1964-66. Recipient Order of the Sacred Treasure, Govt. of Japan, 1986, Ordre Nat. du Merite, French Govt., 1998. Avocations: hiking, jogging, tennis. Home: 5-15-8 Higashi Nakano, Nakano-ku Tokyo 164-0003, Japan

BOURET, ALAIN, publisher; b. Gisors, Eure, France, Nov. 20, 1945; s. Jean Bouret and Mauricette Chaineux; m. Katherine Queysanne, Nov. 4, 1967; 1 child, Sophie. Student, Ecole Francaise des Attaches de Presse, Paris, 1963-66, Studio Serge Holz, Paris, 1966-69. Pub. Edits. Agentzia, Paris, 1968-72; photographer Bur. Etudes Économiques & Sociales, Paris, 1969-75; pub. Edits. Les Loges, Paris, 1976-82, Edits. Hubschmid et Bouret, Paris, 1977-83; pub., owner Edits. Ides et Calendes, Neuchatel, Switzerland, 1981—; dir. Lasercut, Neuchatel, 1981-87; tech. dir. Sereg, Paris, 1969-80. Editor: Dictionnaire des Peintres Paysagistes Francais au XIX eme, 1987 (Aigle d'Or award), Manuel de L'Amateur des Livres Illustres Modernes 1875-1975, 1992 (Livre Expert 1992), L'Ecole de Paris 1945-1965 (prize Acad. Beaux Arts 1993), Catalogue Raisonne Nicolas De Stael, 1996, Encyclopedie Internationale des Photographes, 1997, Catalogue Raisonné, Bissière. Mem. various artists' socs. Avocations: skiing, fishing, electronics, old books, fine arts. Home: 12 Rue de Tournon, 75006 Paris France Office: Ides et Calendes, Evole 19, 2001 Neuchatel Switzerland

BOURGAT, ROBERT MICHEL, educator, curator; b. Perpignan, Pyrenees-Orientales, France, June 6, 1936; s. Marcel and Marie-Louise (Pouches) B.; m. Anne-Marie Gensac, Sept. 13, 1958; children: Nathalie, Sebastien. Licence, U. Montpellier, France, 1959, diplome etudes supérieure, 1963, doctorat, 1969. Prof. Saint Denis, 1959-67; maitre-asst. U. Tananarive, Madagascar, 1967-71; prof. U. Lomé, Togo, 1971-78, U. Perpignan, France, 1978; conservateur Mus., Perpignan, 1982. Contbr. over 100 articles to profl. publs. Corr. Academie de la Reunion, Saint-Denis, Reial Acad. de Drs. de Barcelona. Named Officer Palmes Acadmiques, 1990, Ordre du Mono, 1990. Mem. Rotary Club (Paul Harris fellow), Societe Francaise Parasitologie, Societe Suisse Zoologie. Home: 11 Jean de Noguer, 66100 Perpignan France Office: Univ Perpignan, 52 Ave de Villeneuve, F-66860 Perpignan France

BOURGEAU, JEAN-PAUL LEONCE, pediatrician; b. Nouvelle Calédonie, France, Apr. 30, 1939; s. Jan and Lucienne (Beurnier) B. B, Mathematiques Elementaires, Versailles, 1957; MD, U. Paris, 1966. Externe Hosp. de Paris, 1961; specialist pediatrician Paris, 1969; attaché à la Consultation ds Adolescents Hosp. Necker Enfants Malades, Paris, 1988-94, 96—; pediatrician for children with behavioral disturbances Hosp. for the Deaf, Paris, 1985-96. Mem. du Bur. de la Commn. Musicale de l'Assn. Culturelle de Larchant, 1983-96; pres. Assn. ds Proprietaires du Moulin à Vent à Larchant, 1986, Medecin de la Marine, 1966-67. Mem. Soc. Française Pediatrie (mem. Ile de France com. 1999, nat. com. 1999). Office: 181 rue Legendre, 75017 Paris France

BOURGEAULT, JEAN-JACQUES, air transportation executive; b. Montreal, Que., Can., Feb. 2, 1943; s. Henri M. and Jeanne C. (Cloutier) B.; m. Gilberte C. Tremblay, Sept. 26, 1964 (div. Jan. 1990); m. Manon C. Surprenant, Feb. 2, 1994; 1 child, Martin J. B in Commerce, U. Montreal, 1964. Mgr. pers. Dominion Textile, Montreal, 1964-67; dir. human resources Que. Air, Montreal, 1967-71; dir. labor rels. U. Montreal, 1972-73; from mgr. labor rels. to exec. v.p., COO Air Can., Montreal, Que., 1973—; apptd. sr. exec. v.p. Air Can., Montreal, 1996—; v.p. devel. and recreational tourism Soc. Gen. de Financement, Montreal; chmn. Can. Korea Bus. Coun.; bd. dirs. Centre Internat. de recherches et d'études en mgmt., Internat. Aviation Mgmt. Tng. Inst., Galileo Can. Bd. dirs. World Film Festival. Mem. Air Transport Assn. Can. (bd. dirs.), Club St. Denis. Avocations: jazz, cinema. Office: SGF-Recreational Tourism, 600 de la Gauchetiere West, Montreal, PQ Canada H3B 4L8*

BOURGEOIS, CLAUDE FERNAND, science lab manager; b. Hanoi, Vietnam, Dec. 26, 1938; s. Maurice Elise and Yvette Louise (Gayon) B.; m. Francoise Lemoulan, May 14, 1977. Baccalaureat Math., Cannes, France, 1958; Chem. Engr., INSA, Lyon, France, 1962; MS, Wayne State U., 1968; PhD, INSA and U. Lyon, 1984. Rsch. trainee Zschimmer and Schwarz, Lahnstein/Rhein, Germany, 1962-63; mgr. biochem. & foodtech. lab. Produits Roche divsn. F. Hoffmann-LaRoche, Fontenay sous Bois, France, 1969—; vis. chemist F. Hoffmann-La Roche, Basle, Switzerland, 1968-69; chmn. Assn. des Responsables de la Qualite et Fiabilite Analytique, Cachan, 1987—; mem. exec. com. AOAC Internat. Europe Sect., Washington, 1989—. Author: (book) Determination of Vitamin E: Tocopherols and Tocotrienols, 1993; contbr. articles to profl. jours. and publs.; developer of a method to determine Vitamin C in Food (1976 medal for analytical chemistry Soc. Chimie Indsl.). Brigadier Artillery, 1963-65.. Mem. Soc. de Chimie, AOAC Internat., Assn. Responsables Qualité et Fiabilité Analytique. Roman Catholic. Office: Produits Roche, 52 Marcel & Jacques Gaucher, 94120 Fontenay-Sous-Bois France

BOURGEON, JEAN-MARC VICTOR PIERRE, sales executive; b. Paris, Oct. 18, 1948; s. Gilbert and Danyele (Plein) B.; children: Sylvain, Audrey. Grad. in Gen. Econs., U. Pantheon, Paris, 1970, M of Econs., 1972; grad., Internat. Commerce Inst., Paris, 1977. Educator Nat. Edn., Paris, 1965-74; comml. attache French Trade Comml. Show, Toronto, Can., 1974-75; area export mgr. DuBuit, Paris, 1977-83, internat. sales mgr., 1983—; v.p. DuBuit Far East, Bangkok, Thailand, 1985—. Office: DuBuit, 10/12 rue du Ballon, 93161 Noisy le Grand Cedex, France

BOURGERY, MARC EDMOND CLEMENT, advertising executive; b. Tientsin, China, May 8, 1941; came to France, 1952; s. Edmond Marc and Marjorie Phyllis (Pearson) B.; m. Chantal Anne Bregeault, June 6, 1986; 1 child, Luc. Diploma, Hautes Etudes Commerciales, Paris, 1966. Rschr. Secodip, Paris, 1966-69, CEGOS, 1969-72; group head Feldman Calleux Assocs., Paris, 1972-74, comml. mgr., 1974-75, mng. dir., 1975-90, exec. vice-chmn., 1990-96; chmn. Inst. Media and Advt. Rsch., 1992; v.p. dir. gen. FCA!BMZ, 1994—; pres. French Supervisory Bd. for Media Rsch., 1995-99, IREP, 1992-95, CESP, 1996—; consumer advocate dir. McCann Erickson, 1996-99, regional European strategic planning dir., 1998; exec. v.p. Havas Advt., Levallois-Perret, France, 1999—. Chmn. Inst. for Med. Advt. Rsch., 1992—. Avocations: golf, skiing, theater. Office: Havas Advt, 84 rue de Villiers, 92683 Levallois Perret France

BOURGET OF HORWOOD, CLAUDE P., government official; b. Valence, France, Mar. 20, 1956; s. Maurice L. Bourget and Genevieve C. de Mirabel de Chambaud; m. Anne de Puybonnieux, July 4, 1994. Grad., Lycée Vernet, Valence, France, 1974. Lord of Horwood Devonshire, Eng. Editor Quipos jour., 1989-93. Mem. Assn. Gastronomique, Assn. Historique, Mensa. Avocations: wine, genealogy, yachting, numismatics.

BOURI, MICHAEL, civil servant; b. Maghnia, Algeria, May 5, 1943; s. Hamida and Zoulikha (Senhadji) B.; m. Janet Elizabeth Powell, Feb. 1, 1965 (div. Mary 1, 1973); children: Leila, Hamid; m. Naima Bouri, Mar. 1, 1994. BA, U. Algiers, 1973; MA, Am. U., Washington, 1978. Diplomatic attache Min. of Fgn. Affairs, Algiers, 1967-71; adminstr. Min. of Fgn. Affairs, Washington, 1972-79; asst. prof. U Algiers, 1979-81; civil servant City of Miami, Fla., 1988—. Mem. Acad. of Arts and Scis., Assn. of Govt. Economists, Inst. of Polit. Sci. Democrat. Muslim. Avocations: reading, travel. Home: 750 NE 199th St # H107 Miami FL 33179-3070

BOURILKOV, DIMITRI TODOROV, physicist; b. Sofia, Bulgaria, Apr. 27, 1954; s. Todor Dimov and Liliana Yordanova (Mechkarova) B.; m. Michaela Ilieva Strbanovova, Aug. 30, 1984; children: Alexander, Denis. MS in Nuclear Physics, Sofia U., 1978; PhD in Physics, Inst. Nuclear Rsch., Sofia, 1986. Rsch. assoc. Inst. for Nuclear Rsch., Sofia, 1978-91, Joint Inst. for Nuclear Rsch., Dubna, Russia, 1979-81; sci. rschr. Cath. U., Nijmegen, The Netherlands, 1991-93; rsch. scientist Swiss Fed. Inst. Tech., Zurich, 1993—; vis. scientist ETH, Zurich, 1988-89; coord. Fermion-Pair Group L3 Experiment, Geneva; mem. rsch. team LEP Elecroweak Working Group, CERN, Geneva. Contbr. more than 170 articles to profl. jours. including Jour. High Energy Physics, Physics Letters B. Mem. European Phys. Soc., Am. Phys. Soc. Avocations: bridge, hiking, swimming. E-mail: dimitri.bourilkov@cern.ch. Office: Swiss Fed Inst Tech, EP, CH-1211 Geneva Switzerland

BOURIN, MICHEL SYLVAIN, pharmacology educator; b. Tours, France, Apr. 29, 1944; s. Victor Bourin and Marcelle Mery; m. Monique Sylvaine Derruau, June 14, 1980; children: Veronique, Juliette. BS, Lycee Descartes, Tours, 1963; degree in pharmacy, U. Tours, 1970, MD, 1979. Asst. in analytical chemistry U. Tours, 1971-76, asst. pharmacology, 1976-81; asst. pharmacology U. Nantes, France, 1981-85, prof. pharmacology, 1985-94, full prof. pharmacology, 1994—; psychiatrist French Med. Bd., 1997. Author: Antidepressants, 1983, Hypolipaemic Drubs, 1987, Les Benzodiazepines, 1989, Les Imaos, 1993, General Pharmacology, 1994, 3d edit., 1999. With French mil. svc., 1970-71. Mem. European Coll. Neuropsychopharmacology (hon. treas. 1995—), French Assn. Phrmacologists, French Assn. for Biol. Psychiatry, Brit. Assn. for Psychopharmacology, Collegium Internat. Neuropsycho-pharmacologicum. Avocations: tennis, literature. Home: 98 rue Joseph Blanchart, 44100 Nantes France Office: Dept Pharmacology, 1 Rue Gaston Veil, 44035 Nantes France

BOURKINE, SERGUEI PAVLOVICH, metallurgist, educator; b. Verkhni Ufalei, Russia, July 19, 1941; s. Pavel Vailievich Bourkine and Tatiana Akimovna Erofeenko; m. Vera Grigorievna Valentinova, June 15, 1967 (div. June 1990); 1 child, Nadesgda; m. Elena Anatolievna Andrukova, Sept. 20, 1990. PhD, Urals State Tech. U., Ekaterinburg, Russia, 1972. Engr. Urals State Tech. U., Ekaterinburg, Russia, 1965-70, postgrad. fellow, 1970-72, sr. rsch. scientist, 1972-75, prof., 1979—; prof. L'univ. d'Annaba, Algeria, 1975-79; mem. acad. bd. Urals State Tech. U., 1992. Author: (with A.N. Levanov and V.L. Kolmogerov) Contact Friction in Metal Forming, 1976, (with S.I. Parshakov and V.L. Kolmogerov) Solution of Technological Tasks for Metal Forming by Personal Computer, 1993; contbr. articles to profl. jours.; patentee in field. Recipient medal of 20 years Victory Against Facism, 1965, Gold medal Nat. Econ. Exhbn., 1968, grant Sandie Nat. Labs., 1994. Mem. Internat. Union of Rollermans, Union of Steelmakers Russian Fedn., N.Y. Acad. Scis., Acad. Engring. Scis. Russian Fedn. (acad. counselor 1997). Avocation: submerged swimming. Home: off 69 7 Krasnyth Bortsov, 620012 Ekaterinburg Russia Office: Urals State Tech U, 19 Mira St, 620002 Ekaterinburg Russia

BOURLANGES, JEAN-LOUIS, foreign diplomat; b. Neuilly, France, July 13, 1946. Mem. European Parliament, 1999—, mem. com. on budgets, substitute com. on budgetary control; mem. Group of the European People's Party (Christian Democrats) and European Democrats; mem. delegation to the EU-Poland Joint Parliamentary Com. Union for French Democracy. Office: Parlement européen, Rue Wiertz ASP 13E142, B-1047 Brussels Belgium*

BOURMAYAN, CLAUDE VAHAN, cardiologist; b. Paris, July 27, 1944; s. Vahé and Arpiné (Tatikian) B.; m. Lydie Hrpsimé Bakerdjian, Dec. 7, 1970; children: Asdrig-Carine, Vahé Olivier. MD, U. Paris, 1975, specialization in cardiology, 1976. Intern Hosps. Paris, 1972-76, sr. registrar, 1976-82; tchr. cardiology Med. U. Paris, 1976-82; pvt. practice Boulogne, France, 1982—; cardiologist Boucicaut Hosp., Paris, 1982—. Contbr. articles to profl. jours. including Am. Jour. Cardiology, European Heart Jour., others. 2d lt. French Airforce, 1971-72. Avocations: jogging, cycling, tennis. Office: Pierre Grenier Ave, 92100 Boulogne France

BOURN, ALAN MICHAEL, accounting educator, computer company executive; b. London, June 10, 1934; s. Ernest James and Frances Mary (Fones) B.; m. Karoline Sigrid Hegmann, Apr. 4, 1960 (div. 1986); children: Alexander James Hamilton, Jeremy Robert Stuart; m. Eileen Dorothy Richmond, Aug. 21, 1998; 1 stepchild, Sarah Jane Richmond. BSc in Econs., London Sch. Econs., 1955. Various acad. and profl. posts, 1954-69; prof. indsl. adminstrn. U. Canterbury, Christchurch, New Zealand, 1969-72; prof. bus. studies U. Liverpool, Eng., 1972-80; chmn. Liverpool U. Press, 1976-80; prof. acctg. U. Southampton, Eng., 1980-99, prof. emeritus, 1999—; dep. vice chancellor U. Southampton, 1986-90; chmn. Multicosm Ltd. (now Active Navigation Ltd.), Eng., 1994-97, fin. dir., co. sec., 1997-99; vis. prof. Queen's U., Belfast, Northern Ireland, 2000—; cons. Burnett, Swayne, Southampton, 1994—, Dept. Trade and Industry, London, 1992—, State Bur. of Fgn. Experts, Beijing, 1999—; reviewer UK HE Quality Assurance Agy., 2000—; assoc. Roland Smith Assocs., Eng., 1966-82. Author 5 books and reports, contbr. to 10 books, over 50 articles to acad. and profl. jours. 2d lt. Brit. Army, 1959-60. Fellow Inst. Chartered Accts. in Eng. and Wales (examinerships 1978-99); mem. Southampton Jazz Soc. (chmn. 1990-92, treas. 1992-94, funding officer 1994-96). Avocations: trumpet player and leader of Mardi Gras Dixieland jazz band, squash, tennis. Home: 2 Heatherdene Rd, Chandlers Ford, Eastleigh Hampshire SO53 5BN, England Office: Multicosm Ltd Chilworth Sci, Delta House Enterprise Rd, Chilworth SO16 7NS, England

BOURNAZEL, JEAN PIERRE CHRISTIAN, civil engineer, educator; b. Amiens, Picardie, France, Oct. 17, 1962; s. Christian and Yvonne (Hoornaert) B.; m. Christine Lemaitre, Nov. 21, 1987; children: Martial, Audrey. Maitrise, ENS Cachan, France, 1986, agregation, 1987; PhD, U. Paris VI, 1992, U. Marne la Vallee, France, 1997. Rsch. engr. Electricité de France, Chambery, 1988-89; rschr. Nat. Sci. Rsch. Ctr., Cachan, 1989-92; tchr. civil engring. ENS Cachan, 1992-93, assoc. prof., 1993-97; rsch. dir. Laboratoire d'Etudes et de Recherches sur les Materiaux, Arles, France, 1998—; cons. in field; sci. counselor LERM, Bagnolet, France, 1995-97. Editor: Concrete: From Material to Structure, 1998, also chpts. to books. With Engr. Corps., French Army, 1987-88, Strasbourg. Mem. Assn. Universitaire de Génie Civil, Materials Rsch. Soc. Roman Catholic. Avocations: music, bull fighting, equitation, photography. Home: 9 Impasse des Fauvettes, 13200 Arles Provence, France Office: LERM BP 136, 23 rue de la Madeleine, 13631 Arles Provence, France

BOURNE, ANTHONY JOHN, paediatric pathologist; b. Adelaide, Australia, Aug. 24, 1946; s. Donald John and Mary Veronica (Boylan) B.; m. Jennifer Anne Shepherd, Dec. 30, 1969; children: Andrew, David. MB, BS, U. Adelaide, 1969; Grad. Diploma in Bus., U. So. Australia, 1993. Resident med. officer Queen Elizabeth Hosp., Australia, 1970-71, asst. histopathologist, 1972-76; cons. pathologist Adelaide Children's Hosp., 1977-90, dir. histopathology, 1990-95; dir. histopathology Adelaide Women's and Children's Hosp., 1995—; also bd. dirs.; sec./treas. Australian and New Zealand Paediatric Pathology Group, 1987—. Fellow Royal Coll. Pathologists Australasia (state com. 1985-93, treas. 1987-92, sec. 1990-92); mem. Internat. Paediatric Pathology Assn. (treas. 1990-96, mem. coun. 1996—). Avocations: music, golf, orienteering. Home: 3 Judith Pl, Grange 5022, Australia Office: Women's and Children's Hosp, 72 King William Rd, North Adelaide 5006, Australia

BOURNE, FREDERICK JOHN, veterinary medicine educator, researcher; b. Evesham, Eng., Jan. 3, 1937; s. Sydney John and Florence Beatrice (Craven) B.; m. Mary Angela Minter, Aug. 12, 1959; children: Stephen John, Nigel William. B Vet. Medicine, Royal Vet. Coll., London, 1961; PhD, U. Bristol, Eng., 1972. Pvt. practice, Gloucestershire, Eng., 1961-66; lectr. animal husbandry U. Bristol Vet. Sch., 1966-74, reader, 1974-80, prof. vet. medicine, 1980-88, prof. animal health, 1988—; prof. animal health U. Reading, Eng., 1988-97; dir. rsch. Agrl. and Food Rsch. Coun. Inst. for Animal Health, Compton, Eng., 1988-94, Biotech. and Biol. Scis. Rsch. Coun., 1994-97; chmn. ind. sci. group advising U.K. govt. in control of bovine tuberculosis, 1998—. Contbr. over 200 articles to sci. jours. Decorated comdr. Brit. Empire. Mem. Royal Coll. Vet. Surgeons, Polis Acad. Scis. (fgn. mem.). Avocations: gardening, fishing, golf, music.

BOURNEUF, HENRI JOSEPH, JR., librarian; b. Beverly Farms, Mass.; s. Henri and Elizabeth (McKean) B.; m. Susan Peterson, June 19; 1 child, Anne Peterson. BA, Harvard U., 1969; MLS, Simmons Coll., Boston, 1980. Ref. libr. Widener Libr., Harvard U., Cambridge, Mass., 1980—, head ref. libr., 1995—. Democrat. Home: 119 Huron Ave Cambridge MA 02138-1366 Office: Widener Library Harvard Univ Cambridge MA 02138

BOUROVA, TATIANA GENNADIEVNA, physics educator; b. Saratov, Russia, Sept. 11, 1959; d. Gennadyi Nikolayevich and Nataliya Dmitrievna (Kulagina) Shvedov; m. Vladimir Alexandrovich Bourov, June 30, 1978; children: Elena, Anastasiya. Master Degree, State U., Saratov, 1978, Bachelor Degree, 1981, Doctorate Degree, 1987. Cert. physicist and physics educator. Engr. Inst. Radiotechnics, Saratov, 1981-83; candidate Polytechnical Inst., Saratov, 1983-87; lectr. Mil. Inst., Saratov, 1987-91; lectr. Pedagogical Inst., Saratov, 1991-97, prof., 1997—. Contbr. articles to profl. jours. Named Soros lectr., 1997. Mem. N.Y. Acad. Sci. Avocations: books, music. Home: Lermontov Str 25/1 12, 410002 Saratov Russia Office: Saratov State Pedag Inst, Michurin Str 92, 410028 Saratov Russia

BOUSFIELD, EDWARD LLOYD, biologist; b. Penticton, B.C., Can., June 19, 1926; s. Reginald H. and Marjorie F. (Armstrong) B.; m. Barbara Joyce, June 20, 1953 (dec. Apr. 1983); children: Marjorie Anne, Jessie Katherine, Mary Elizabeth, Kenneth Lloyd; m. Joyce Burton, Feb. 11, 1994. BA, U. Toronto, 1948, MA, 1948; PhD, Harvard U., 1954. Invertebrate zoologist Nat. Mus. of Natural Sci., Ottawa, Ont., Can., 1950-64, chief zoologist, 1964-74, sr. scientist, 1974-86; curator emeritus Nat. Mus. of Natural Sci., Ottawa, 1986-90; rsch. assoc. Royal Ont. Mus., Toronto, 1984—, Royal B.C. Mus., Victoria, 1990-95. Author: Canadian Atlantic Sea Shells, 1960, Shallow-water Gammaridean Amphipoda of New England, 1973, History of the Canadian Society of Zoologists: The First Decade, 1974, Cadborosaurus, Survivor from the Deep, 1995; mng. editor: Amphipacifica, 1994-98, 2000—; contbr. articles to profl. jours. Recipient Outstanding Achievement award Civil Service Can., 1985. Fellow Royal Soc. Can.; mem. Ottawa Field Naturalists Club (hon., pres. 1959-61), Can. Soc. Zoologists (hon., pres. 1979-80, archivist 1971-91, hon. mem. 1993—), Crustacean Soc., New Eng. Estuarine Rsch. Soc., RA Curling Club (pres. 1972-73) (Ottawa), Victoria Curling Club, Highland Park Lawn Bowling Club (pres. 1978-79, 89-90), Victoria Lawn Bowling Club, Granite Curling Club, Sigma Xi. Mem. Alliance Party Can. Avocations: musical instruments (Victoria Melody Makers Orch.), lawn bowling, curling. E-mail: elbousf@magma.ca. Home: 1710-1275 Richmond Rd, Ottawa, ON Canada K2B 8E3

BOUŠKA, VLADIMÍR JAN, geochemist, mineralogist; b. Horusice, Tábor, Czech Republic, Apr. 11, 1933; s. Václav and Marie (Adámková) B.; m. Petra Letošníková; children: Petra, Pavla. Degree in geology, Charles U., Prague, 1955; candidate of Sci., Charles U., 1962, D of Natural Scis., 1966, DSc, 1979. Asst. prof. Charles U., 1954-73, assoc. prof., 1973-90, prof. geochemistry, 1990—; chief of geochemistry Charles U., 1974-94. Author: Precious Stones Around Us, 1979, Geochemistry of Coal, 1979, English edit., 1981, Pierres Précieuses et Pierres Fines, 1985, Moldavites, 1994, many others; author, editor: Geochemistry, 1980, Natural Glasses, 1987, English edit., 1993; co-author: Minerals of the North Bohemian Lignite Basin, 1997; contbr. articles to profl. jours. Grantee Czech Literary Fund, Prague, 1977. Fellow Mineral. Soc. Am. (life, commemorative coun. pin 1997); mem. Czech Geol. Soc., Meteritical Soc., Internat. Mineral. Assn. (working group for organic minerals 1972—). Avocations: natural glasses, precious stones, gardening, classical music. Office: Faculty of Sci Charles U, Albertov 6, 128 43 Prague 2, Czech Republic

BOUSSAGOL, CLAIRE REINE, public affairs specialist; b. Bordeaux, France, May 15, 1963; arrived in Belgium, 1990; d. Pierre and Maguy (Gervès) B. Lic. en droit, U. Bordeaux, 1986, M Bus. Law, 1988; cert. in English law, Warwick U., Eng., 1987; postgrad. degree in European Cmty. Law, U. Strasbourg, France, 1990. Asst. mgr. European Cons. Co., Brussels, 1990-91; dir. European Strategy, Brussels, 1991-95, Apco Europe, Brussels, 1995-99; mng. dir. APCO France, Paris, 1999—. Avocations: walking, singing. Office: APCO France, 48 r Faubourg St Honore, F-75008 Paris France

BOUSSARD, JEAN-MARC, research director; b. Orleans, France, Oct. 23, 1937; s. Jacques and Renée (Morette) B.; m. Isabel Decaris, June 25, 1964; children: Marie Caroline, François-Xavier. Ingenieur agronome, Paris, 1961; DSc, Economiques Faculte de Droit, Paris, 1968. Asst. INRA, Paris, 1961-65, chargé de recherche, 1965-74, dir. 2nd class, 1974-87, dir. rsch. 1st class, 1987; assoc. prof. U. Paris, 1991-92; prof., cons. Inst. Nat. Agronomique, Paris, 1993—. Editl. bd. European Rev. of Agrl. Econs., 1976-93; author: Economie de l'Agriculture, 1987; contbr. articles to profl. jours. Sub-lt. French Army, 1961-62. Mem. Soc. Française d'Economie Rural (pres. 1993-97), Acad. of Agrl. de France. Home: 3 Quai Malaquais, 75006 Paris France Office: INRA-CIRAD, 45 bis Ave belle Gabrielle, 94736 Nogent sur Marne France

BOUSTANY, FADI NABIL, real estate developer; b. Debie, Chouf, Lebanon, Nov. 10, 1967; s. Nabil Majid and Arlette (Bahri) B. BSc with honors, Brighton U., 1989; MBA, Cambridge U., 1994. Contract mgr. Bechtel Internat. Co., Va., 1989-91; CEO Metropole Real Estate S.A.M., Monaco, 1994—; co-owner, v.p. Metropole Palace Hotel, 1993—; bd. dirs. Monafinances, Monaco; pres. Tany Hols, Lebanon, 1999—; dir. Portemilio Summer Resort, Lebanon, 1999—; pres. Metrpole Group, Monaco, 1999—. Mem. Oxford and Cambridge U. Club. Avocations: swimming, tennis. Office: SCI Du Metropole, 1 Av Des Citronniers, Monte Carlo Monaco

BOUTAGY, GEORGE, tourism executive; b. Beirut, June 10, 1948; s. Salim and Jamal Helayel B.; m. Jamal Bedo, Dec. 29, 1979; children: Roy, Carlo. Baccalaureat, Coll. des Freres, Beirut, 1965, Coll. des Freres, Beirut, 1966; Bus. Adminstrn. Diploma, Ctr. Belge, Beirut, 1971. Gen. mgr. Chrysler Cars, Alkhobar, Saudi Arabia, 1975-78; mng. dir. The Traveller's, Alkhobar, Saudi Arabia, 1978—, Al Suwaiket & Ptnrs., Al Khobar, 1992—; pres. Boutagy Investments, Inc., Montreal, Can., 1986—, Boutagy Travel, Montreal, 1986—, Auto Passion, Inc., Montreal, 1987—, Advision Group, Paris, 1991—; bd. dirs. Saudi-Soimi, Alkhobar. Co-establisher Charity Funds for Orphelins, France, 1991, Lebanon, 1989. Mem. Ferrari Club/Monaco, Automobile Club/Monaco, Rotary. Avocations: car racing, hunting, charity. Office: Alsuwaiket Trading & Contra, PO Box 654, 31932 Dhahran Airport, Saudi Arabia

BOUTARIC, JEAN-JOSE ETIENNE, physician, writer; b. Tours, France, Jan. 11, 1938; s. Philippe Louis and Marthe Marie Julie (Dou) B.; m. Michele Annick Salaun; Nov. 5, 1966; children: Anne, Jean-Philippe, François. MD, U. Lyon, 1962, Laureat, 1963; cert. specialized study in anesthesiology, U. Paris, 1971; Diplôme d'Etudes Approfondies d'Histoire et Philosophie des Scis., U. Paris-Sorbonne, 1987. Physician French Air Force, 1964-69; anesthesiologist Hopitaux de l'Assistance Pub., Paris, 1969-71; anesthesiologist at pvt. clinic Paris, 1971-80; gen. practice medicine Brunoy, France, 1980—. Author essays, novels, case studies, short stories. Capt. French Health Svc., 1966-69. Recipient Cesare Pavese prize, 1987, 88, 98. Mem. Groupement des Ecrivains Medecins (adj. sec. gen. 1987—, v.p. 2000), de l'Assn. Medicine Melomanes Europeans. Roman Catholic. Avocations:

piano, writing song lyrics. Home and Office: 17 Rue de Cercay, 91800 Brunoy France

BOUTAUD, OLIVIER GILLES, biochemistry research educator; b. Sartrouville, France, Dec. 24, 1966. BS, U. Louis Pasteur, Strasbourg, France, 1990, MS, 1991, PhD, 1994. Postdoctoral fellow Vanderbilt U., Nashville, Tenn., 1994-98, rsch. instr. biochemistry, 1998—. Contbr. articles to sci. jours. E-mail: oliver.boutaud@mcmail.vanderbilt.edu. Office: Vanderbilt Univ Dept Pharmacology Nashville TN 37232-0001

BOUTCHER, DAVID JOHN, solicitor; b. Derby, Eng., July 24, 1957; s. John and Pauline Margaret Boutcher. Degree in law and econs., U. Kent, 1978. Assoc. Bennetts & Ptnrs., London, 1981-85; ptnr. Richards & Butler, London, 1988. Mem. The Law Soc. Office: Richards Butler Beaufort House, 15 St Botolph St, London EC3A 7EE, England

BOUTEVILLE, ANNE, physicist, educator; b. Angers, France, Oct. 12, 1954; d. Lionel and Raymonde (Chevillotte) Richard; m. Jean-Noël Bouteville, Oct. 6, 1976; children: Pierre Noël, Charles Noël. Thèse de 3emè cycle, U. Nantes, France, 1982; Thèse d'Etat, U. Angers, France, 1987. Asst. U. Sci. Angers, 1982-87, maître de conférences, 1987-93; maître de conférences Ecole Nat. Supérieure d'Arts et Métiers-LPMI, Angers, 1993—. Avocation: horse riding (jumping). Office: ENSAM, 2 Bd du Ronceray, 49035 Angers France

BOUTHET, CATHERINE FRANCOISE, cell biologist; b. Metz, Lorraine, France, Aug. 31, 1961; d. Bernard and Blanche (Depoit) B.; m. Alain Christian Dufour, May 26, 1995; children: Helene, Thomas. PhD, U. Clermont-Ferrand, France, 1991. Postdoctoral fellow U. Tex. Health Sci. Ctr. San Antonio, San Antonio, Tex., 1991-93; lab. mgr. Aloecorp, Dallas, 1993-95; rsch. assoc. U. Cambridge, U.K., 1995-96. Avocation: cinema.

BOUTHILLER, RUSSELL LEE, writer; b. Springfield, Mass., Nov. 30, 1958; s. Norman Alcide Bouthiller and Doris Monica Shaw. BA, Fordham U., 1985. Reader Barr-Woodward Assn., N.Y.C., 1986; freelance prodn. coord. N. Lee Lacy & Assocs., N.Y.C., 1987-90; newswriter, assoc. prodr. Broadway Beat, N.Y.C., 1989—; literary agts. asst. Jay-Garon Brooke Assn., N.Y.C., 1993-94. Author: (screenplays) The Family Tree, 1995, A Voice in the Hollow, 1996, Majesty, 1997 (Bluecat award 1999), Dragula, 1999. Republican. Roman Catholic. Avocations: history, skiing, genealogy. E-mail: rustyinny@aol.com. Home and Office: 134 9th Ave Apt 3R New York NY 10011-4947

BOUTON, DANIEL, banker. Chmn., co-CEO, Societe Generale, Paris. Office: Societe Generale, 70 Cours Valmyan, 92972 Paris France*

BOUTON, MARSHALL MELVIN, academic administrator; b. N.Y.C., Aug. 8, 1942; s. Percy Marshall and Mary Fuller (Melvin) B.; m. Barbara Elizabeth Linn, Sept. 14, 1968; children: Christopher, Alexander. BA cum laude in History, Harvard Coll., 1964; MA in South Asian Studies, U. Pa., 1968; PhD in Polit. Sci., U. Chgo., 1980. Exec. sec., program dir. The Asia Soc., N.Y.C., 1975-77; spl. asst. to amb. U.S. Embassy, New Delhi, India, 1977-80; dir. policy analysis, internat. security affairs Dept. Def., Near East, South Asia,, Africa, 1980-81; dir. contemporary affairs The Asia Soc., N.Y.C., 1981-87, v.p. pres. program planning external affairs, 1987-90, exec. v.p., 1990—; tng. project dir. Peace Corps, Sacramento, summer 1967, tng. coord., Estes Park, Colo., summer 1968; tng. assoc. in internat. devel. The Ford Found., New Delhi, 1968-69; lectr. divsn. of social scis. U. Chgo., 1973-75; vis. scholar So. Asian Inst. Columbia U., 1975-77; cons. World Bank, 1980-81. Author: Agrarian Radicalism in South India, 1985, India's Problem is not Politics, 1998, Foreign Affairs, May/June 1998; co-author: Korea at the Crossroads: Implications for American Strategy, 1987; editor, co-editor: India Briefing; contbr., editor numerous articles to profl. jours. NSF Dissertation Rsch. fellow, 1972-74, U.S. Agy. on Internat. Devel. grantee, 1974-77, Rockefeller Found. travel grantee, 1977. Mem. Coun. on Fgn. Rels., Assn. for Asian Studies, Am. Polit. Sci. Assn., Harvard Club. Office: Asia Society 725 Park Ave New York NY 10021-5088

BOUTROS, ANTOINE EDWARD, journalist, writer; b. Aleppo, Syria, Mar. 10, 1938; arrived in Lebanon, 1956; s. Edward Mihran and Alexandra Helen (Khordoupoulou) B.; m. Constance Spiro Chronis; children: Sandra, Nadine. Editor-in-chief Al Computer, Comm., Electonics, Beirut, Lebanon, 1973—; dir. rsch. ctr. Dar Assayad, 1973—; dir. Inst. Palestine Studies, Beirut, 1967-72; cons. UNDP, 1990-91, UN/ESCWA, 1981-83. Author: Major Scientific Revolutions of the 20th Century, 1994, Encyclopedia of Computer Science, 1991, Information at the Eve of the 21st Century, 1987, The Secret of the Great Pyramid, 1998; contbr. numerous articles to publs. Recipient Svc. award Kuwait Found., 1991. Mem. Inst. Devel. Studies, Ctr. for Study of Japanese Experiences, Bahrain Computer Soc. Avocations: manuscripts, pyramidology, renaissance art, music, horticulture. Office: Dar Assayad Publ House, Beirut Lebanon also: 3 Park Pl-12 Lawn Ln, Vauxhall London SW8 1UA, England

BOUTROS-GHALI, BOUTROS, former United Nations official; b. Cairo, Nov. 14, 1922. LLD, Cairo U., 1946; Diploma of Higher Studies in Pub. Law, Paris U., 1947, Diploma of Higher Studies in Econs., 1948, Diploma of Polit. Sci. Ins., 1949, PhD in Internat. Law, 1949; dr. h.c., René Descartes U., Paris, 1980, Uppsala (Sweden) U., 1986. Prof. internat. law, internat. rels., head dept. polit. scis. Cairo U., 1949-77; min. state Fgn. Affairs, Egypt, 1977-91, dep. prime min., 1991; sec.-gen. UN, N.Y.C., 1992-96, Francophonie, 1997—; assoc. dir. First Dag Hammarskjold Seminar, Netherland, 1963; dir. Ctr. Rsch. The Hague Acad. Internat. Law, 1963-64, mem. study group, 1965-66, mem. external program group, 1968-71, mem. curatorium adminstrv. coun., 1978—; vis. prof. faculty of law Paris U., 1967-68; co-dir. first session external program Acad. Internat. Law, Rabat, 1969; dir. first session of the sr. diplomats Union of the Abu Dhabi, 1973; lectr. internat. law, internat. rels. various univs. Author: (books) Contribution à l'Etude des Ententes Régionales, 1949, Cours de Diplomatie et de Droit Diplomatique et Consulaire, 1951, (with Youssef Chlala) Le Problème de Suez, 1957, Egypt and the United Nations: Carnegie Endowment for International Peace, 1957, Le Principe d'Egalité des Etats et les Organisations Internationales, 1961, Contribution à une Théorie Générale des Alliances, 1963, L'Organisation de l'Unité Africaine, 1969, Le Mouvement Afro-Asiatique, 1969, Les Difficultés Institutionelles du Panafricanisme, 1979, La Ligue des Etats Arabes, 1972, Les Conflits de Frontières en Afrique, 1973; co-author: Foreign Policies in a World of Change, 1983, Will We Survive?, 1989; founder, editor Al Ahram Al-Iktisadi, 1960-75, Al Siyassa Ad-Dawliya; mem. editl. bd. Egyptian Rev. Internat. Law, Yearbook of the Assn. of the Attenders, Alumni of the Hague Acad. of Internat. Law. Mem. Com. application of convs. and recommendations Internat. Labour Orgn., 1971-79; mem. cen. com. Polit. Bur. of the Arab Socialist Union, 1974-77; pres. Ctr. for Polit. and Strategic Studies, Al-Ahram, 1975—; mem. Internat. Commn. Jurist, Geneva, 1975-77; mem. Commn. Internat. Law of the UN, 1979—; mem. secretariat Nat. Dem. Party, 1980-91. Decorated Order of the Nile (Egypt), Grand Croix de l'Ordre de la Couronne (Belgium), Cavaliere di Gran Croce (Italy), Gran Cruz de la Orden de Boyaca (Colombia), Gran Cruz de la Orden de Antonio José de Irisarri (Guatemala), Grand Croix de la Légion d'Honneur (France), Gran Cruz de la Orden Nacional Al Merito (Ecuador), Gran Cruz de la Orden del Liberation San Martin (Argentina), Tishakti Patta (Nepal), Grand Croix de l'Ordre du Mérite du Niger, Grand Officer de l'Ordre du Mérite du Mali, La Condecoracion De Agulia Azteca (Mex.), Grand Croix de l'Ordre Pro Merito Melitensi de l'Ordre Souverain Militaire et Hospitalier de St. Jean de Jerusalem de Rhodes de Malte, Grand Cordon de l'Ordre du Phoenix de Grèce, Grand Cordon du Mérite du Chili, Order of the Crown of Brunei, Grand Cross of the Order of Merit (Germany), Gran Cruz del Sol del Peru, comdr. de l'Ordre du Mérite Nat. de la Côte d'Ivoire, Grand Croix de l'Ordre du Danebrog, Grand Officer Cross of the Order of the Polar Star (Sweden), The Order of Diplomatic Svc. Merit (Gwanghwa, Korea); Fulbright Rsch. scholar Columbia U., 1954-55. Mem. African Soc. Polit. Studies (pres. 1980—), Egyptian Soc. Internat. Law (v.p. 1965—), Inst. Pub. Internat. Law and Internat. Rels. Thessaloniki (curatorium 1976—), Acad. des Scis. morales et politiques (assoc. 1989—), Inst. Internat. Law (pres. 1985-87), Inst. Affari Internazionali (assoc. 1979—), Acad. Mondiale pour la Paix (sci. com. 1975—), Internat. Inst Human Rights (mem. coun., exec. com. 1975—), Assn. Colombiana de Estudios de Politica Internacional Y Diplomacia (hon. 1980—), Malgache Acad., Academia Mexicana de Dir. Internacional. Home: 2 Avenue El-Nil Giza, Cairo Egypt

BOUTTERIN, EMMANUEL, public relations executive; b. Paris, Sept. 19, 1957. Degree, U. Aix-Marseille II, 1987. Journalist Le Meridional, Marseilles, France, 1984-86, Ouest-France, Cherbourg, Caen, 1986-88; dir. radio Frequence Mistral, Sisteron, France, 1988-89; dir. communication Jausiers Vacances Timeshare RCI, Marseilles, 1989-93; dir. gen. Agence Intermedia, Phototelem, Marseilles, 1993—. Lt. French Marines, 1983. Mem. Union Nat. des Anciens Eleves des Ecoles de Journalisme (pres. 1990—). Office: Intermedia, 2 rue Grignan, 13001 Marseille France

BOUVET, JACQUES, mining company executive; b. Versailles, France, Mar. 15, 1934; m. Daniele Grillot, July 21, 1959; children: Franz, Carine, Muriel, Pierre Gilles. Student, Sch. Mines Paris, 1955, Ecole Poly., Paris, 1959. Mining engr. Bur. Mines, Algeria, 1959-62; from tech. advisor to chief mining engr. Ministry of Industry, Paris, 1962-67; from asst. to dir. Dunkirk steel plant to dir. gen. USINOR, Paris, 1971-86; pres. dir. gen. L'Agence Francaise pour la Maitrise de l'Energie, 1987-91; pres. Eco Emballages, 1992-94; pres., dir. gen. Charbonnages de France, Rueil Malmaison, 1992-95; dir. gen., pres. Port autonome de Dunkirque KSB SA, Guillain, 1996-99, pres., 1996—. Office: KSB SA, KSB SAe des Barbanniers, 4 Alle de Barbonniers, 92635 Gennevilliers France

BOUVIER, ALAIN JEAN, mathematics educator; b. Mar. 29, 1943; s. Rene and Georgette (Tastavin) B.; m. Claudine Cauchemont, July 22, 1965; children: Florence, Fabrice. Lic. in Sci., U. Lyons, 1966, D of Splty., 1971, DSc, 1982. Mem. faculty U. Lyon, France, 1966-84; prof. math. U. Lyon, 1984—; vis. prof. Rome U., 1977, Queen's U., Can., 1979, 80, 82, U. Tenn., 1984; others; presenter seminars. Author: La theorie des ensembles, 1969, 3d edit., 1982 (transl. into German, Japanese, Portuguese), Theorie elementaire des series, 1971, Groupes-Observation, theorie, practique, 1974, 2d edit., 1979, Management et projeb des ibablissemarks scolaires, 1994, (with others) Dictionnaire des Mathematiques, 1979, 2d edit., 1983 (transl. into Spanish, English), La mystification mathematique, 1981, Manuel de Didactique-Action, 1986; contbr. numerous papers to profl. publs. Named Chevallier de la Legion d'Honour. Mem. Counseil Scientifique des Irem, Irem de Lyon (dir.), Société Mathematique de France, Assn. des Professeurs Math. (pres. 1972-75, 80-84). Avocations: tennis, piano, touring, reading, theater. Office: IUFM Lyon, 5 rue Anselme, 69317 Lyon Ceden 04, France

BOUVIER, CHRISTIAN RENÉ, audit manager, administration educator; b. Paris, Nov. 13, 1940; s. Raymond and Charlotte (Mirault) B.; m. Jacqueline Boulard, Nov. 4, 1968; children: Romuald, Aldric, Thibault, Astrid. Capitaine au long Cnurs, 1967; CPA, France. Mate and first mate Mcht. Navy, 1960-68; with mktg. dept., then fin. dept. IBM, Paris, 1969-84; audit dir. Hiutchinson then Nouvelles-Galeries, 1984-88; CPA mgr. Author: Audit and Computer Purchasing Audit, 1983. Served with French Navy, 1961-62. Mem. Inst. Internal Auditors. Roman Catholic. Home: 68 Rue de l'Ermitage, 95320 Saint-Leu-la-Forêt France Office: 38 Rue du Chateau d'Eau, 75010 Paris France

BOUVRY, BRIGITTE, economics educator; b. Ath, Belgium, May 18, 1947; d. Robert and Madeleine (Bouton) B.; m. Jean-Paul Pottiez, July 15, 1971; 1 child. Lic., agregation in Econs., F.U.C.A.M., Mons, Belgium. Econ. tchr. Couvin, Belgium, 1969, Pesche, Belgium, 1969, Koekelberg, Belgium, 1970, Leuze, Belgium, 1970, Peruwelz, Belgium, 1970, Tournai, 1971, Chatelineau, 1972, La Louviere, 1973—. Mem. Assn. des eludionts de la FUCAM, Assn. des frofeneus scis. econ., Caisse Sociale ecole (pres. 1987). Roman Catholic. Avocations: narration, lectures, concerts, voyage. Home: Rue du Bois, Blaton 7321, Belgium

BOUWER, JOHAN STEFAAN, otolaryngologist; b. Pretoria, Gauteng, South Africa, Sept. 10, 1954; s. Johannes Jeremia and Dulcie le Claire (Gauché) B.; m. Feléne Maartens, Dec. 16, 1978; children: Rouan, Tamara. M.B.B.Ch., Wits, South Africa, 1978; F.C.S. (Otol et L), Wits, 1987. Pvt. practice, 1987—; dir. Ear, Nose and Throat Mgmt. Co., South Africa, 1997—. Co-author: SAAF at War, 1987. Capt. South African Med. Corps, 1980-81. Recipient Honoris Crux South African Def. Force, 1981, Pro Patria, 1981, So. Africa medal, 1984. Mem. Internat. Plastic Modelling Soc., Ear, Nose and Throat Soc. (exec., tarif com. 1997—). Avocations: military modelling, cycling, militaria collecting, scuba diving. Office: PO Box 1011, Ferndale 2160, South Africa

BOUZAT, CECILIA BEATRIZ, biochemist; b. Bahia Blanca, Argentina, Nov. 10, 1961; d. Jorge Anibal and Beatriz Helena (Argonz) B.; m. Damian Walter Fabiani, Jan. 6, 1989; children: Camila, Mateo. BS in Biochemistry, U. Nacional del Sur, Bahia Blanca, 1985, PhD, 1990. Fellow Inst. of Biochem. Rsch., CONICET, Bahia Blanca, 1986-91, rsch. asst., 1992-97; rsch. fellow Mayo Clinic, Rochester, Minn., 1993-94; tchg. asst. in pathological biochemistry U. Nacional del Sur, 1988-99, prof. pharmacology, 1997—; Mem. Nat. RSch. Coun. Argentina. Contbr. articles to profl. jours., including Biochem. Jour., Pflugers Arch., NeuroReport, Lipids, Molecular Neuropharmacology, Receptors and Channels, Neuron, Proc. Nat. Acad. Scis., others. Vol. Girl Scouts, Bahia Blanca, 1969-78. Mem. Argentinian Neurochem. Soc., Argentinian Soc. for Biochem. Rsch., Argentinian Soc. Achievements include rsch. on the major determinants of the change from fetal to adult nicotinic receptor kinetics that occurs during development of the motor endplate, first spontaneous mutation detected in human muscle nicotinic receptor which leads to altered channel activity and is the cause of a congenital myasthenic syndrome, modulation of nicotinic receptor function. Home: 19 de Mayo 537, 8000 Bahia Blanca Argentina Office: Inst Investigaciones Bioquimicas, Camino La Carrindanga km 7, 8000 Bahia Blanca Argentina

BOUZIANI, AMMAR, pathologist, consultant, educator; b. El Felta, Kef, Tunisia, July 3, 1955; s. Mohamed and Iljia (Chaieb) B.; m. Saida Trabelsi, Sept. 4, 1982; children: Aimen, Amani, Arwa, Miriem. MD, U. Medicine, Sousse, Tunisia, 1982; diploma in Medicine, E.A.S.S.M., Toulon, France, 1983; M of Human Biology, U. Sci., Paris, 1986. Diplomate French Bd. Pathology. Physician in family practice Dept. Def., Tunis, Tunisia, 1982-83; observer tng. St. Anne Hosp., Toulon, France, 1983-84; resident in pathology St. Antoine Hosp., Paris, 1984-88; observer/tng. in pathology Armed Forces Inst. Pathology, Washington, 1991-92; assoc. prof. Med. U., Tunis, 1989—; cons. pathologist Mil. Hosp. Tunis, 1988-96; dir. pathology lab. Mil. Hosp. Gabes, Tunisia, 1996-99, cons. pathologist, Dept. Pathology, Military Hosp. of Tunis, 1999—. Contbr. articles to profl. jours. Lt. Col. Tunis Dept. Def., 1987-89. Mem. Tunisian Med. Soc., Internat. Acad. Pathology (Arab divsn.), N.Y. Acad. Scis. Avocations: tourism, history, movies, books. Office: Mil Hosp of Tunis, 1008 Mont Fleury, Tunis Tunisia

BOVA, VINCENT ARTHUR, JR., lawyer, consultant, photographer; b. Pitts., Apr. 25, 1946; s. Vincent A. and Janie (Pope) B.; m. Breda Murphy, Mar. 20, 1971; 1 child, Kate Murphy Bova. BA in Bus. Adminstrn., Alma (Mich.) Coll., 1968; MPA, Ohio State U., 1972; JD, Oklahoma City U., 1975. Bar: Okla. 1975, N.Mex. 1976, U.S. Dist. Ct. 1976, U.S. Tax Ct., 1976, U.S. Ct. Appeals (10th cir.) 1976, U.S. Supreme Ct. 1979. Mktg. and systems rep., computer systems div. RCA, 1968-70; research analyst Research Atlanta, 1972-73; assoc. Threet, Threet, Glass, King & Maxwell, 1976-78; ptnr. Lill & Bova, P.A., 1978-81; sole practice Albuquerque, 1981—; past pres. Bare Bulls Investment, 1982, Fumilan Investment, 1983, Toastmasters; rsch. analyst urban affairs Ohio Dept. Urban Affairs, Columbus, 1971; panel mem. N.Mex. Med. Rev. Commn., 1981—, N.Mex. Legal/Dental/Osteopathic Podiatry Com., 1981—; prof. Contbr. articles on organizational behavior and mgmt. to profl. jours. Bd. dirs. Rio Grande Nature Ctr.; pres., v.p. spl. projects S.W. Arts and Crafts Festival, Albuquerque, 1986-89; pol. cons. Nov. Group; mem. N.Mex. Estate Planning Coun., 1978—; sec.-treas., vice-chmn. adv. bd. Salvation Army, 1987—; contbr. Ctr. for Home for Prevention of Domestic Violence, 1984-85, Ronald McDonald House, 1984; past chmn. N.Mex. Workers' Compensation Monthly; mem. advt. com. Supreme Ct. Panel; pres. Salvation Army Adv. Bd., Albuquerque; mem. Edn. Forum. With Air N.G., 1969-75. Recipient Pacesetters award Ohio State U., 1972; named one of Outstanding Young Men of Am., 1975, 76. Mem. ATLA (advanced grad. Nat. Coll. Advocacy), Ct. Practice Inst. (advanced diplomate), ABA, N.Mex. Bar Assn. (pres. small firm and solo sect.), State Bar N.Mex. (mem. med. legal panel, med.-dental podiatry legal panel, rep. probate, wills and trusts ann. report), Nat. Def. Lawyers, Assn. (staff chmn. 1986), N.Mex. Trial Lawyers Assn., Internat. Assn. Fin. Planners, Nat. Assn. Social Security Claimants Reps. (past state chmn.), Business Round Table, Albuquerque Bar Assn., N.Mex. Fin. Planning Assn., Sole Practitioners Assn., Internat. Credit Assn. (lectr.), Ohio State U. Alumni Assn. of N.Mex. (pres.), Image Profls. of the S.W. (bd. dirs., print chmn. 1996—), Image Profls. S.W. (photography award 1996, Best of Show 2000, 10 others, 14 awards 1999), Profl. Photography Assn., Photog. Soc. Am. (pres. chpt.), Toastmasters (past pres., v.p., edn. chmn., Able Toastmaster award), Millionaires Tip Club, Enchanted Lens Camera Club (pres.), Profl. Photographers Am. (8 awards 1999), Albuquerque Knife and Fork (pres., v.p., sec.-treas., bd. dirs.), Inn of the Ct., Zia Scuba Club, Phi Alpha Delta, Sigma Tau Gamma. Democrat. Presbyterian. Avocations: flower gardening, photography - video and still, computers, investing, reading. Office: 5716 Osuna Rd NE Albuquerque NM 87109-2527

BOVÉ, ROBERT CHARLES, editor, writer, educator; b. Hackensack, N.J., July 13, 1951; s. Donald Paul and Maryanna (Evers) B. BA in English Lang. and Lit., U. Va., 1974; MFA with hons. in Creative Writing, Bklyn. Coll., 1998. Freelance writer, editor Washington, 1978—; news dir. Sta. WXVA/WZFM Radio, Charles Town, W.Va., 1979-80; sr. writer Office of News and Pub. Affairs George Washington U., Washington, 1980-83; assoc. editor Tng. and Devel. Jour., Alexandria, Va., 1983-87; ptnr. Loco-motive Press, Washington, 1987-91; adj. lectr. English, Pace U., 1998—. Contbg. editor: GRIST On-Line, 1995—; author: Cubesteak Canapés, 1990, Nectar, 1991, Nine from Metronome, 1995; editor: Brooklyn Rev. #15, 1997; designer Edmund Wilson Website, Pace U., 2000. Recipient Eagle Scout award Boy Scouts Am., 1966, Good Citizen citation Dept of N.J. Am. Legion, 1966. Avocations: canoeing, camping, swimming. Home and Office: 139 Joralemon St Brooklyn NY 11201-4070

BOVEE, COURTLAND LOWELL, business educator; b. Red Bluff, Calif., Oct. 4, 1944; s. Courtney Van and Shirley Patricia (Safford) B. AA, Shast Coll., 1965; BS, U. N.D., 1967; MS, U. Tenn., 1968. Mem. faculty Grossmont Coll., El Cajon, Calif., 1968—, now prof. business; prin. Bovee & Thill L.L.C., Las Vegas, Nev., 1997—. Co-author: (textbooks) Business Today, 9th edit., 1999, Excellence in Business Communication, 1999, Business in Action, 2000, Business Communication Today, 6th edit., 2000. Mem. Assn. for Bus. Comm. Avocations: photography, travel. E-mail: bovee@home.com. Office: Bovee & Thill LLC 2950 E Flamingo Rd Las Vegas NV 89121-5208

BOVEN, KATIA, pediatric immunologist, nephrologist; b. Gent, East Flanders, Belgium, Dec. 21, 1960; d. Roland and Jenny (Maebe) B.; m. Gerard Eestermans, Aug. 16, 1977 (div. 1988); children: Thomas, Caroline; m. Luc Truyen; children: Eva, Ben, Sam, Gilles. MD, U. Antwerpen, Belgium, 1985. Lic. pediatric immunologist, nephrologist. Pediatrician in tng. U. Hosp. Antwerpen, Belgium, 1985-90, pediatric staff mem., 1990-95, sr. pediatric staff mem., 1995—; immunology fellow Children's Hosp., Utrecht, The Netherlands, 1990-92; nephrology, immunology cons. Children's Hosp., Antwerpen, Belgium, 1996—. Contbr. articles to profl. jours. Mem. Internat. Soc. for Peritoneal Dialysis, Belgian Pediatric Nephrologists, Belgian Transplantation Soc., Belgian Soc. Nephrology, Belgian Soc. Pediat., Belgian Working Group on Immunodeficiency, Flemish Soc. Nephrology, Flemish Soc. Pediat. Office: Univ Hosp Antwerpen, Wilrijkstraat 10, 2650 Edegem Belgium

BOVEY, LEONARD, physicist; b. Cardiff, Wales, May 9, 1924; s. Alfred and Gladys (Brereton) B.; m. Constance Hudson, Nov. 11, 1943; children: Christopher, Jennifer. BA, Cambridge (Eng.) U., 1943, MA, 1947, PhD, 1950. Chartered physicist. Rsch. physicist Dunlop Rubber, Birmingham, Eng., 1943-46; postdoctoral fellow Nat. Rsch. Coun., Ottawa, Ont., Can., 1950-52; chief scientific officer Atomic Energy Rsch. Establishment, Harwell, Eng., 1952-65; dir. regional office Midlands Ministry of Tech., Birmingham, 1966-70; dir. regional office Yorkshire Dept. Trade and Industry, Leeds, Eng., 1970-73; scientific counselor High Commn., Ottawa, 1974-77; head technol. requirements Dept. Industry, London, 1977-84; editor Materials Jours., 1984-94; ret., 1994. Editor: Spectroscopy in the Metallurgical Industry, 1963; contbr. articles to scientific jours., including Jour. Optical Soc. Am., Spectrochimica Acta, and Jour. Phys. Soc. Chmn. Residents' Assn., Chelsea, Eng., 1990—; sec. Inst. Physics (Spectroscopy), London, 1960-65. Fellow Inst. Physics; mem. Civil Svc. Club, London Diplomatic Sci. Club. Home: 32 Radnor Walk, London SW3 4BN, England

BOVINGDON, MICHAEL EDWARD, pharmacology educator; b. Chalfont Saint Peter, U.K., Sept. 13, 1950; s. Edward Arthur and Vera Elizabeth (Edwards) B.; m. Diane Margaret Hussey, July 25, 1952; children: Elinor Jayne, Clair Josephine. BSc in Physiology/Biochemistry (hons), U. Reading, U.K. Scientific asst. Amersham (U.K.) Internat., 1969-71; project leader Wiggins Teape, High Wycombe, U.K., 1974-76; sr. technician U. Coll., London, 1976—; safety convenor Mfg. Sci. and Fin. Trade Union U. Coll., 1977-2000, Joint Trade Union convenor Safety Com. U. Coll. London, 1997-2000. Parent gov. Secondary Sch., Chesham, U.K., 1995-99. Avocations: woodworking, motorcycling, cricket, philosophy, history of engineering. Office: U Coll Pharmacology Dept, Gower St, London WC1E 6BT, England

BOWD, RONALD GREGORY, information systems executive, statistician; b. Coolah, Australia, Jan. 19, 1949; s. Alan Thomas and Nancy Margaret (Nelson) B.; m. Therese Frances Egan (dec. Aug. 1998), June 5, 1982; children: Kate, Daniel, Leah. Mng. dir. Info Corp., Sydney, Australia, 1978-97, Strategy By Design, Sydney, Australia, 1997—. Mem. Am. Mktg. Assn., Mkt. Rsch. Soc. Australia. Office: Strategy By Design, 7 Help St Ste 201A, Chatswood 2067, Australia

BOWDEN, ELBERT VICTOR, banking, finance and economics educator, author; b. Wrightsville, N.C., Nov. 25, 1924; s. James Owen and Dovie Ellen (Phelps) B.; m. Mary Rose Mariani (div.); m. Doris Adele Fales (div.); children: Elbert V. Jr., Richard Ashley, Doris Ellen, Jack Bryson, William Austin, Joyce Leigh; m. Judith Louise Holbert; children: Kristen R., Amy L. BA in Econs. and Polit. Sci. with high distinction, U. Conn., 1950; MA in Econs., Duke U., 1952, PhD in Econs., 1957. Grad. asst. dept. econs. Duke U., Durham, N.C., 1950-53, instr. dept. econs., 1953-54, 55-56; rsch. assoc. Bur. Bus. Rsch. U. Ky., Lexington, 1954-55; assoc. prof. Norfolk (Va.) Coll. of William and Mary (name now Old Donimion U.), 1956-59, prof., chmn. dept. econs., 1959-63; prof. econs. Elmira (N.Y.) Coll., 1963-64, SUNY, Fredonia, 1970-75; exec. dir. Upper Peninsula Com. for Area Progress, Escanaba, Mich., 1964-65; chief economist, chief of mission Robert R. Nathan Assocs. Trust Terr. Econ. Devel. Team, Saipan, Mariana Islands, 1965-67; assoc. prof., rsch. economist Tex. A&M U., 1967-70; chief econ. adviser, project mgr. Fiji Regional Planning Project UN, Suva, 1975-77; prof. econs. and fin., chair banking Appalachian State U., Boone, N.C., 1977—, Alfred T. Adams disting. prof., 1992—; dir. Houston-Galveston (Tex.) Area Project Fed. Water Pollution Control Adminstrn. and Tex. Water Quality Bd., 1967-69; testifier Interstate Commerce Commn., U.S. Senate Pub. Works Com., U.S. Senate Com. on Interior and Insular Affairs, 1964-66; asst. Blue Ridge Electric Membership Corp.; speaker Olean (N.Y.) Bus. Inst., 1979; adj. prof. Warsaw Sch. Social Econ. Studies, 1998—; cons., presenter seminars, workshops in field. Author: Economics, 1960, rev. edit., 1969, Economics in Perspective, 1974, 7th rev. edit., 2000, Economics: The Science of Common Sense, 1974, 9th edit., 2000, Money, Banking and the Financial System, 1989; co-author: (with Judith Holbert) Revolution in Banking: Regulatory Changes, The New Competitive Environment and the New World for the Financial Services Industry in the 1980s, 1980, rev. 1984, American-Polish Academic Textbook of Macro- and Microeconomics of the Warsaw School of Social and Economic Studies, 2000; contbr. articles, papers, book revs. to profl. publs. and orgns. Mem. fin. com. City of Seven Devils, N.C., 1982-85; asst. N.C. Dept. Marine Fisheries; adv. bd. N.C. Statewide Taxpayers Ednl. Coalition. With U.S. Mcht. Marine, 1943-46, ATO and PTO. Ford Found. fellow, 1960. Mem. AAAS, AAUP, Nat. Assn. Bus. Econs. (U.S. and Carolinas chpts.), Am. Bus. Communication Assn., Am. Econ. Assn., Am. Fin. Assn. (com. 1960-61), Atlantic Econ. Soc., Community Colls. Social Scis. Assn., Ea. Fin. Assn., Fin. Mgmt. Assn., N.Am. Econs. and Fin. Assn., Regional Sci. Assn., So. Econ. Assn., So. Fin. Assn., So. Regional Sci. Assn., Southwestern Social Sci. Assn. (chmn. interdisciplinary symposium on urban and regional problem solving 1970),

Western Econ. Assn., Western Regional Sci. Assn. (program planning com.). Avocations: skiing, surfing, guitar playing, singing, fishing, boating, reading. Home: PO Box 1461 Boone NC 28607-1461 Office: Appalachian State U Coll Bus Banking Chair Boone NC 28608-0001

BOWDEN, GEORGE NEWTON, judge; b. East Orange, N.J., Nov. 21, 1946; s. W. Paul and Catherine A. (Porter) B. BA, Bowdoin Coll., 1971; JD, U. Maine, 1974. Bar: Wash. 1974, Maine 1975, U.S. Dist. Ct. (we. dist.) Wash. 1978, U.S. Ct. Appeals (9th cir.) 1980, U.S. Supreme Ct. 1982. Asst. county atty. Lincoln County, Wiscasset, Maine, 1974; dep. pros. atty. Grays Harbor County, Montesano, Wash., 1974-76, King County, Seattle, 1976, Snohomish County, Everett, Wash., 1976-79; ptnr. Senter & Bowden, Everett, Wash., 1979-97; judge Snohomish County Superior Ct., Everett, Wash., 1997—. Bd. dirs. Everett Symphony Orch. 1993—, pres. 1996-98; v.p. Driftwood Players, Edmonds, Wash., 1978. Sgt. USMC, 1966-68. Mem. ATLA, NADCL, Wash. State Bar Assn. (CLE com., fee arbitration bd., legal aid and pro bono com.), Wash. Assn. Criminal Def. Lawyers (bd. govs., sec. 1993), Wash. State Trial Lawyers Assn., Snohomish County Bar Assn. (pres. 1995), Rotary. Avocations: scuba diving, skiing, bicycling. Office: Snohomish County Courthouse Superior Ct 3000 Rockefeller Ave M/S502 Everett WA 98201-4046

BOWDEN, HOWARD KENT, accountant; b. New Bern, N.C., 1955; s. Paul Franklin and Virginia Belle Bowden; m. Laiad Jitrak; 1 child, Kirk Adam. BSS in Acctg. and Math. summa cum laude, Campbell U., 1976. CPA, Va., N.C. Staff acct. Arthur Andersen & Co., Greensboro, N.C., 1976-78; mgr. McGladrey & Pullen, Fayetteville, N.C., 1978-85; assoc. prin. Thompson, Greenspon & Co., P.C., Fairfax, Va., 1985-91; sr. audit mgr. U.S. Gen. Acctg. Office, Washington, 1991-94, asst. dir., 1994—. Treas. Vander Area Crime Watch, Fayetteville, 1980. Mem. AICPA, Va. Soc. CPAs (chmn. mems. in industry and govt. com. 1993-95, chmn. acctg. and auditing procedures com. 1990-92, Chpt. Pres.'s award 1989-90, Outstanding Mem. in Bus., Industry, and Govt. award 1995-96, chpt. pres. award, 1997-98), N.C. Assn. CPAs, Inst. Mgmt. Accts. (coord. tax symposium 1982, bd. dirs. 1978-84), Assn. Cert. Fraud Examiners (cert.), Assn. Govt. Accts. (cert. govt. fin. mgr.), Lions (bd. dirs. Fairfax club 1986-90, bd. dirs. Fayetteville club 1982-85), Phi Beta Lambda, Phi Kappa Phi. Presbyterian. Avocations: baseball, tennis, softball, other sports. Home: 4337 Farm House Ln Fairfax VA 22032-1613

BOWDEN, KEITH, chemistry educator; b. London, Feb. 1, 1936; s. Henry Bowden; m. Ruby Clark, Aug. 22, 1959; 1 child, Peter Michael. BS, U. Hull, 1959, PhD, 1962, DSc, 1973. Postdoctoral fellow U. B.C., Vancouver, Can., 1962-63; lectr. chemistry U. Salford, Eng., 1964-65; lectr. chemistry U. Essex, Colchester, Eng., 1965-73, sr. lectr., 1973-76, reader, 1976-92, prof., 1992—; Contbr. articles to numerous profl. jours. including Jour. Chem. Soc., Jour. Med. Chemistry, Organic Chemistry, others. Contbr. articles to profl. jours. including Jour. Chem. Soc., Jour. Med. Chemistry, Can. Jour. Chemistry, Jour. Am. Chem. Soc., Prog. in Phys. Organic Chemistry, Advances in Phys. Organic Chemistry. Fellow Royal Soc. Chemistry (chartered). Avocations: natural history, genealogy, history. Home: 10 Redmill, Essex Colchester C03 4RT, England Office: Univ Essex, Wivenhoe Park, Essex Colchester C04 3SQ, England

BOWDRE, PAUL REID, protective services official, consultant; b. N.Y.C., Aug. 27, 1958; s. Philip Ross and Inge Elenore (Eckert) B. BS, Western Carolina U., 1981; cert. in Social Gerontology, U. N.C.-Asheville, 1981; MPS in Gerontology, Coll. Boca Raton, Fla., 1988; PhD, Nova Southeastern U., 1994. Cert. fraud examiner. Rsch. asst. Mo. Gerontology Inst., Columbia, 1981-83; asst. swim coach U. Mo., Columbia, 1981-83, teaching asst. Dept. Sociology, 1982-83; pub. safety officer North Palm Beach Dept. Pub. Safety, Fla., 1983-85; nat. and olympic swim coach Federcion Nacional de Natacion, Guatemala, May-Aug. 1984; police officer ops. div. Town of Palm Beach, 1985, field tng. officer, 1985-86, detective organized crime, vice and narcotics unit, 1986-91, sgt. patrol div., 1991, organized crime, vice and narcotics unit, 1991-93, profl. standards unit, 1993, capt. law enforcement divsn., 1994-95; sr. inspector Inspector Gen.'s Office Fla. Dept. Corrections, 1995—; cons. in field. Author: (with others) Death & Dying: In-Home Care-A Teaching Curriculum, 1983, Safety: In-Home Care-A Teaching Curriculum, 1983; contbr. articles to profl. publs. Asst. scoutmaster Troop 132 Gulf Stream coun. Boy Scouts Am., 1981-84; trustee North Palm Beach Police and Fire Pension Bd., 1984-85. Research grantee Sigma Xi, 1981. Mem. Acad. Criminal Justice Scis., Am. Soc. Law Enforcement Trainers, So. Criminal Justice Assn., Nat. Eagle Scout Assn., Am. Soc. Criminology, Midwest Sociol. Soc. (student dir. 1981-82), Am. Sociol. Assn. (regional newsletter reporter 1982-83), Gerontol. Soc. Am. (Biol. scis. sect. com. member 1983), The Catamount Club, Alpha Kappa Delta, Sigma Phi Omega. Democrat. Baptist. Home: 1145 Duncan Cir Apt 104 West Palm Bch FL 33418-6865 Office: Fla Dept Corrections Inspect Gen's Office 189 SE 3rd Ave Ste 1 Delray Beach FL 33483-4541

BOWELL, ROBERT JOHN, geochemist, consultant; b. Manchester, Lancashire, Eng., Aug. 18, 1966; s. Ronald and Margaret Elsie (Shaw) B.; m. Catherine Ann De Hauteville-Bell, July 15, 1989; children: Hannah, Christopher, Alice, Esther. BS (honors) in Chemistry and Geology, U. Manchester, Eng., 1988; PhD in Geochemistry, U. Southampton, Eng., 1991. Chartered chemist. Geologist A. Mine Corp., Ghana, 1988-91; mineralogist Nat. History Mus., London, 1991-94; cons. BHP, U.K. and W. Africa, 1994-95; chemist Fawley Tech. Svcs., Southampton, Eng., 1995; sr. geochemist Steffen Robertson and Kirston, Cardiff, Wales, 1995—. Author, editor: An Atlas of gold grains, 1999, Solutions to Acid Rock Drainage, 1999, Contbr. articles to books. Local preacher, United Reform. Mem. Soc. Econ. Geology (short course com. 1994-97), Internat. Assn. of Geochemists, Royal Soc. Chemistry (cert.). Achievements include work in exploration and environmental geochemistry, biogeochemistry, process chemistry and mineralogy on metal ores. Avocations: Aikido, guitar, climbing, tai-chi, swimming, mineral collecting. Office: Steffen Robertson & Kirsten, 9/10 Windsor Pl Summithouse, Cardiff CF10 3SR, Wales

BOWEN, CHARLES JOHN, executive; b. Dec. 11, 1941; s. John and Millicent B.; m. Naomi Stevens, 1965; 2 children. BA in Econs. and Statistics, Exeter U., Eng. Mkt. rsch. mgr. ICI Paints Divsn., 1965-67; product mgr. Unilever, 1967-73; mktg. mgr., dir. Gen. Foods UK, 1973-78; gen. mgr. Gen. Foods P.R., 1978-82; v.p. Gen. Foods Corp., U.S.A., 1982-88; exec. dir. Hillsdown Holdings, 1988-93; ceo Booker plc, London, 1993-98; director Legal & General Grp plc, London, 1998S. Fellow Royal Statistical Soc. Home: Isington Mill, Hants GU34 4PW, England Office: Legal & General Group Plc, Temple Court 11 Queen Victoria Street, London EC4 N4TP, England*

BOWEN, CLOTILDE MARION DENT, retired career officer, psychiatrist; b. Chgo., Mar. 20, 1923; d. William Marion Dent and Clotilde (Tynes) D.; m. William N. Bowen, Dec. 29, 1945 (dec.). BA, Ohio State U., 1943, MD, 1947. Intern Harlem Hosp., N.Y.C., 1947-48; resident and fellow in pulmonary diseases Triboro Hosp., Jamaica, L.I., 1948-50; resident in psychiatry VA Hosp., Albany N.Y., 1959-62; asst. resident in psychiatry Albany Med. Ctr. Hosp., 1961-62; pvt. practice N.Y.C., 1950-55; chief pulmonary disease clinic N.Y.C., 1950-55; asst. chief pulmonary disease svc. Valley Forge Army Hosp., Pa., 1956-59; chief psychiatry VA Hosp., Roseburg, Oreg., 1962-66, acting chief of staff, 1964-66; ast. chief neurology and psychiatry Tripler Gen. Hosp., Hawaii, 1966-68; psychiatr. lcons. and dir. Rev. Br. Office Civil Health and Med. Program Uniform Svcs., 1968-70; commd. capt. U.S. Army, 1955, advanced through ranks to col., 1968; neuropsychiat. cons. U.S. Army, Vietnam, 1970-71; chief dept. psychiatry Fitzsimons Army Med. Ctr. U.S. Army, 1971-74, chief dept. psychiatry Tripler Army Med. Ctr., 1974-75; assoc. clin. prof. psychiatry U. Hawaii, 1974-75; comdr. Hawley Army Clin. U.S. Army, Ft. Benjamin, Harrison, Ind., 1977-78; chief dept. primary care and cmty. medicine U.S. Army, 1978-83, chief psychiat. consultation svc. Fitzsimons Army Med. Ctr., 1983-85; chief psychiatry svc. med./regional office ctr. VA, Cheyenne, Wyo., 1987-90; staff psychiatrist Denver VA Satellite Clin., Colorado Springs, Colo., 1990-96; ret., 1996; Locum Tenens practice psychiatry, 1996—; surveyor Joint Commn. on Accreditation Healthcare Orgns., 1985-92; assoc. clin. prof. psychiatary U. Colo. Med. Ctr., Denver, 1971—. Decorated Legion of Merit, several other medals; recipient Colo. Disabled Am. Vets. award, 1994-95, Pres.'s 300 Commencement award Ohio State U., 1987, Profl. Achievement award Ohio State U. Alumni Assn., 1998, Cert. of Appreciation, VFW, 2000. Fellow Am. Psychiat. Assn. (life), Acad. Psychosomatic Medicine; mem. AMA, Nat. Med. Assn., Menninger Found (charter), Ctrl. Neuropsychiatric Assn. (councilor at-large). Home: 1020 Tari Dr Colorado Springs CO 80921-2257

BOWEN, DAVID R., science and technology educator, consultant; b. N.Y.C., Sept. 13, 1939; s. Lewis Howard and Nancy (Nichols) B.; m. Joyce Helen Blades, Mar. 12, 1966; children: Peter Scott, Amy Elizabeth Bowen Herhold. BS in Physics, Haverford Coll., 1961; PhD in Physics, U. Pa., 1966. Rsch. assoc. U. Pa., 1967; rsch. assoc., instr. Cornell U., Ithaca, N.Y., 1967-70; asst. prof. Northeastern U., Boston, 1970-73; asst. prof. Nathaniel Hawthorne Coll., Antrim, N.H., 1973-74, assoc. prof., 1974-75; assoc. prof. Wayne State U., Detroit, 1975—; cons. Ford Motor Co., Dearborn, Mich., 1989—. Contbr. chpts. to books, numerous articles to profl. jours. Recipient numerous grants and rsch. awards. Quaker. Avocations: Internet and computers, sailing, windsurfing. Home: 4704 Elmhurst Ave Royal Oak MI 48073-1780 Office: Wayne State U 2311 A/AB Detroit MI 48202

BOWEN, GILBERT WILLARD, minister; b. Muskegon, Mich., Dec. 30, 1931; s. Bruce Oliver and Beatrice Lillian (Sibley) B.; m. Marlene Mary Michell, July 31, 1954; children: Kathryn Leigh, Mark Kevin, Stephen James. BA, Wheaton Coll., 1955; MDiv, McCormick Theol. Sem., 1957, PhD in Ministry, 1976; cert., Ctr. for Religion and Psychotherapy, 1976; DLL (hon.), Nat. Coll. Edn., 1987. Ordained to ministry Presbyn. Ch., 1956. Minister 1st United Presbyn. Ch., Blue Earth, Minn., 1956-63, Faith United Presbyn. Ch., Tinley Park, Ill., 1963-65, Community Presbyn. Ch., Mt. Prospect, Ill., 1965-70, Kenilworth (Ill.) Union Ch., 1970—; exchange minister Johanneskirche, Neuwied, Fed. Republic Germany, 1961-62; pres. bd. Ctr. for Religion and Psychotherapy; bd. dirs. McCormick Theol. Sem., Chgo., Anatolia Coll., Thessaloniki, Greece, Presbyn. Home, Evanston. Mem. adv. com. North Shore Sr. Ctr., Winnetka, Ill.; bd. dirs. Hospice of North Shore, Wilmette, Ill., Shelter for Battered Women, Evanston; chmn. Instl. Rev. Bd., Evanston. Mem. Am. Assn. Pastoral Counselors, Acad. Parish Clergy, Am. Waldensian Aid Soc. Republican. Club: Indian Hill. Avocations: tennis, golf, vocal music. Home: 909 Westerfield Dr Wilmette IL 60091-1810 Office: Kenilworth Union Ch 211 Kenilworth Ave Kenilworth IL 60043-1299

BOWEN, JONATHAN PETER, computer scientist, researcher; b. Oxford, Eng., Mar. 14, 1956; s. Humphry John Moule and Ursula Hill (Williams) B.; m. Jane Sarah Margaret Horsfall, July 21, 1979; children: Alice Mary, Emma Jane. BA with honors, Oxford (Eng.) U., 1977, MA in Engring. Sci., 1981. Software engr. Marconi Instruments, St. Albans, Eng., 1977-79; programmer Logica, London, 1979; rsch. asst. Imperial Coll., London, 1979-84; rsch. officer Oxford U., 1985-89, sr. rsch. officer, 1989-95; lectr. U. Reading, England, 1995-2000; prof. computing South Bank U., London, 2000—; cons. Sci. Mus. and Nat. Mus. of Photography, Film and TV, London and Bradford, 1979-84, Oxford U. Press, 1987-90; visitor Silicon Graphics, Inc., Mountain View, Calif., 1983-84; chmn. Z User Group, 1992—; vis. rsch. fellow UN U./Internat. Inst. for Software Tech., Macau, 1999. Editor: Towards Verified Systems, 1994, Applications of Formal Methods, 1995, Industrial-Strength Formal Methods in Practice, 1999; author: Formal Specification and Documentation Using Z, 1996, High-Integrity System Specification and Design, 1999; contbr. articles to profl. jours. Mem. IEEE Computer Soc. (tech. segment com. 1994—), IEE (Charles Babbage Premium award 1994), Assn. for Computing Machinery. Avocations: art, museums, photography, walking, World Wide Web. Home: Oak Barn, Sonning Eye, Reading RG4 6TN, England Office: Univ Reading, South Bank Univ, Borough Rd, London SE1 0AA, England

BOWEN, MARY LU, ecumenical developer, community organizer; b. Wheeling, W.Va., Feb. 14, 1930; d. Walter Philip and Helen Elizabeth (Luthy) Wagenheim; m. Robert Edward Bowen, June 13, 1953; children: Jeanne, Thomas, Robert, David. BS in Edn., Wittenberg U., 1952; MA in Social Scis., SUNY, Binghamton, 1989. Cert. tchr., Ohio, W.Va., Tex., N.Y. Various teaching positions, 1952-80; coord. ministry with the aging Coun. of Chs., Broome County, N.Y., 1979-82; adminstrv. asst. Coun. of Chs., Broome County, 1982-83, asst. dir., 1984-86; assoc. for ecumenical devel. N.Y. State Coun. of Chs., Albany, Syracuse, N.Y., 1990-94; regional dir. southern tier N.Y. State Coun. of Chs., Albany, 1995-96; dir. of pub. policy N.Y. State Cmty. of Churches, 1997-98, exec. dir., 1998—; mem., sec. exec. cabinet N.Y. State Coun. Chs., Albany, Syracuse, 1986-91; synodical lay rep. Evang. Luth. Ch. in Am. Region VII Coun., Phila., 1987-91, churchwide leadership team Social Min. Project, Chgo., 1990-91, sec. constituting conv. Upstate N.Y. Synod, Syracuse, 1987. Author: Reclaiming Christianity's Feminist Heritage: Reflections on Patriarchal Teachings and Women's Problems, 1989, Handbook for Clergy on Child Abuse and Neglect, 1995. Active Broome County Coordinating Coun. Child Abuse and Neglect, 1986-88, 96-98, treas. 1997; active Luth. Statewide Advocacy, Albany, 1982-90, 2000—, chmn. exec. com., 1991-99; regional adv. bd. Citizen Action N.Y., Binghamton, 1994-98; co-chmn. Interreligious Health and Justice Coalition, N.Y. Ctrl. So. Tier Region, chair, 1998—; Evangelical Luth. Ch. in Am. Coalition for Mission in Appalachia, 1996—, chair, 2000—. Recipient Citizen Action N.Y. Phoenix award, 1998, Upstate N.Y. Synod Lay Discipleship award, 1999. Mem. Nat. Assn. Ecumenical Staff. Democrat. Lutheran. Avocations: travel, reading. Home: 14 Overbrook Dr Apalachin NY 13732-4234 Office: NY State Cmty Chs Main Office 362 State St Albany NY 12210-1202

BOWEN, MICHAEL GEORGE, archbishop; b. Apr. 23, 1930; s. C.L.J. Bowen and Lady Makins. Student, Trinity Coll., Cambridge, Gregorian U., Rome. Ordained priest Roman Cath. Ch., 1958. With wine trade, 1951-52; with English Coll., Rome, 1952-59; curate at Earlsfield and Walworth London, 1959-63; tchr. theology Beda Coll., Rome, 1963-66; chancellor Diocese of Arundel and Brighton, 1966-70; coadjutor bishop, 1970-71, bishop of Arundel and Brighton, 1971-77, archbishop and metropolitan of Southwark, 1977—; v.p. Bishop's Conf. of Eng. and Wales, 1996-99, pres., 1999-2000. 2d lt. Irish guards Army, 1948-49. Avocations: golf, tennis. Office: Archbishop's House, 150 St George's Rd, Southwark London SE1 6HX, England

BOWEN, PAUL L., information systems and accounting educator; b. Knoxville, June 9, 1951; arrived in Australia, 1993; s. W. L. Paul and Helen (Duboise) B.; m. Christina Wong, Nov. 27, 1999. BS, Ga. Tech., 1973; MBA, U. Tenn., 1976, M of Accountancy, 1990, PhD, 1992, MS in Computer Sci., 1995. CPA. Asst. br. mgr. Valley Fidelity Bank, Knoxville, 1973-76; asst. v.p. 3d Nat. Bank, Knoxville, 1976-80; project mgr. Oak Ridge (Tenn.) Nat. Lab., 1980-88; grad. tchg. asst. U. Tenn., Knoxville, 1988-92; asst. prof. Auburn (Ala.) U., 1992-93; sr. lectr. U. Queensland, Brisbane, Australia, 1993—. Mem. editl. bd. Jour. Info. Sys., 1994—; contbr. articles to profl. jours. Treas. Gideons Internat., Brisbane, 1994—. Am. Assn. of Collegiate Schs. of Bus. doctoral fellow, 1988. Mem. IEEE, Australian Computer Soc., Assn. for Info. Sys., Am. Acctg. Assn., Beta Alpha Psi, Beta Gamma Sigma. Baptist. Avocations: farming, bush walking, cooking. Office: U Queensland, Dept Commerce, Brisbane 4072, Australia

BOWEN, PETER GEOFFREY, arbitrator, investment advisor, business educator; b. Iowa City, Iowa, July 10, 1939; s. Howard Rothmann and Lois Berntine (Schilling) B.; m. Shirley Johns Carlson, Sept. 14, 1968; children: Douglas Howard, Leslie Johns. BA in Govt. and Econs., Lawrence Coll., 1960; postgrad., U. Wis., 1960-61, U. Denver, 1963-64; cert. expert witness, Denver Dist. Ct., 1987. Dir. devel. Mobile Home Communities, Denver, 1969-71; v.p. Perry & Butler, Denver, 1972-73; exec. v.p., dir. Little & Co., Denver, 1973; pres. Builders Agy. Ltd., Denver, 1974-75, The Investment Mgmt. Group Ltd., Denver, 1975-87; independent investor, writer Vail, Colo., 1987—; arbitrator NASD Regulation, Inc., 1996—, Am. Arbitration Assn., 1996—; gen. ptnr. real estate ltd. ptnrships.; adj. prof. bus. Colo. Mt. Coll., 1994—; continuing legal edn. lectr. on real estate syndications, 1983. Contbr. articles to profl. publs. Mem. Colo. Coun. Econ. Devel., 1964-68; vice-chmn. Greenwood Village (Colo.) Planning and Zoning Commn., 1983-85; mem. Vail Planning and Environ. Commn., 1992-96; dir. Vail Partnership Environ. Edn. Programs, Inc., 1993—; elected mem. City Council Greenwood Village, 1985-86, also mayor pro tem, 1985-86; trustee Vail Mountain Sch. Found., 1987-88; bd. dirs. Colo. Plan for Apportionment, 1966; speaker Forward Metro Denver, 1966-67. Mem. Rotary Club (bd. dirs. Vail chpt., named Rotarian of Yr. 1992), Lawrence U. Alumni Assn. (bd. dirs. 1966-72, 82-86). Home: 16006 Double Eagle Dr Morrison CO 80465-9617

BOWEN, RICHARD ANTONY, retired computer engineer; b. Oxford, England, Aug. 18, 1935; s. Edward Alfred and Freda Agnes Cynthia (Kimbrey) B.; m. Patricia Rose Mason; children: John Timothy, Peter Robert. BSc, U. Birmingham, England, 1954. Chartered engr., Eng. Computer engr. U.K. Atomic Energy Authority, Sellafield, England, 1959-61, Dounreay, Scotland, 1961-63; computer engr. British Railways, Derby, England, 1963-65, CentreEuropéene de Recherche Nucléaire, Geneva, 1965-71, European Space Operations Ctr., Darmstadt, Germany, 1975-96. Mem. Brit. Computer Soc. Mem. Ch. of England. Avocations: industrial railways, hill walking, photography. Home and Office: Industriestrasse 1, 63419 Pfungstadt Germany

BOWEN, RICHARD LEE, architect; b. Canton, Ohio, Nov. 1, 1935; s. Raymond Leed and Lillian E. (White) B.; m. Robin Herrington (div.); children: Richard Lee, David Herrington, Laurel Ann, Sean Andrew, Scott Edward; m. Gail Audrey; children: Tabitha Erin, Colin Leed. BA, Case Western Res. U., 1959. Registered architect 50 states, D.C., P.R., Eng., Can., Australia, Nat. Coun. Archtl. Registration Bds., Archtl. Registration Coun. U.K. Founder, pres. Richard L. Bowen & Assocs. Inc., archtl. engrs. and planners, Cleve., Richard L. Bowen & Assocs. Inc., Cleve., 1963—, Richard L. Bowen, Inc., Cleve., 1976—; pres. Enerwaste, Inc., 1992-99; mng. ptnr. ComDel, 1970; pres. Richard L. Bowen & Assocs. of Fla., Pompano Beach, 1969—. Prin. works include Western Campus, Cuyahoga C.C., Akron State Office Bldg., West Jr. High Sch., Cleve. Cen. Police Hdqs., Cleve. Hopkins Internat. Airport, FAA Regional Office Bldg., classroom and libr. bulds. Ashtabula Campus, Kent State U., Wade Park VA Hosp., Westerly Sewage Treatment Facility for Cuyahoga Regional Sewer Authority, Cuyahoa C.C. Manpower Skills Ctr. for Ohio; also others. Mem. Leadership Cleve.; mem. exec. com. Cuyahoga County Rep. Com., Cleve., 1963—; trustee St. Luke's Hosp. Assn., Cleve. Internat. Air Show; mem. adv. bd. Cleve. Inst. Art. Recipient energy conservation design award Fla. Power Winter Garden Shopping Ctr., 1986, merit award Cleve. Restoration Soc., 1992. Mem. AIA (design award of excellence 1976, award 1979), Architects Soc. Ohio (honor award 1988), Nat. Assn. Indsl. and Office Parks (awards 1985, 89), Royal Archtl. Inst. Can., Royal Inst. Brit. Architects, Am. Soc. Ch. Architecture, Soc. Archtl. Historians, Guild for Religious Architecture, Internat. Coun. Shopping Ctrs., Constrn. Specifications Inst., Bldg. Ofcls. Coun. Am., Am. Assn. Planners, Urban Land Inst., Am. Arbitration Assn., Rowfant Club, Cat Cay Club, Ft. Lauderdale Yacht Club, Useppa Island Club, Phi Gamma Delta, also others. Avocations: sailing, skiing, fly and deep sea fishing. E-mail: rbowen@RLB.com. Home: 14926 Hillbrook Dr Chagrin Falls OH 44022-2634 Office: 13000 Shaker Blvd Cleveland OH 44120-2063

BOWEN, WILLIAM GORDON, economist, educator, foundation administrator; b. Cin., Oct. 6, 1933; s. Albert A. and Bernice (Pomert) B.; m. Mary Ellen Maxwell, Aug. 25, 1956; children: David Alan, Karen Lee. BA, Denison U., 1955; PhD, Princeton U., 1958. Mem. faculty Princeton (N.J.) U., 1958-88, prof. econs., 1965-88, dir. grad. studies Woodrow Wilson Sch. Pub. and Internat. Affairs, 1964-66, provost, 1967-72, pres., 1972-88; pres. Andrew W. Mellon Found., N.Y.C., 1988—; bd. dirs. Merck and Co., Inc., Am. Express Co., Univ. Corp. for Advanced Internet Devel. Internet2; bd. overseers Tchrs. Ins. and Annuity Assn.-Coll. Ret. Equities Fund.; chmn., bd. dirs. JSTOR. Author: The Wage-Price Issue: A Theoretical Analysis, 1960, Wage Behavior in the Postwar Period: An Empirical Analysis, 1960, Economic Aspects of Education: Three Essays, 1964, (with W. J. Baumol) Performing Arts: The Economic Dilemma, 1966, (with T. A. Finegan) The Economics of Labor Force Participation, 1969, Ever the Teacher, 1987, (with J. A. Sosa) Prospects for Faculty in the Arts and Sciences, 1989, (with Neil L. Rudenstine) In Pursuit of the PhD, 1992, Inside the Boardroom: Governance by Directors and Trustees, 1994, (with T. Nygren, S. Turner, E. Duffy) The Charitable Nonprofits, 1994, (with Derek Bok) The Shape of the River: Long-Term Consequences of Considering Race in College and University Admissions, 1998. Trustee Ctr. for Advanced Study in Behavioral Scis., 1978-84, 89-92, Denison U., 1992-2000; regent emeritus Smithsonian Instn. Recipient Joseph Henry medal Smithsonian Instn., 1996. Mem. Am. Econs. Assn., Indsl. Rels. Rsch. Assn., Coun. on Fgn. Rels., Phi Beta Kappa. Office: Andrew W Mellon Found 140 E 62nd St New York NY 10021-8124

BOWER, BARBARA JEAN, nurse; b. Akron, Ohio, Aug. 25, 1942; d. William Howard and Maxine (Goodykoontz) Sturm; m. Howard Bower, Aug. 25, 1961 (dec. 1989); children: Nancy, Janet; m. Richard Chavez, Dec. 24, 1993. BA, Elmhurst Coll., 1974, postgrad., 1987—; diploma, Evang. Sch. Nursing, 1970; PhD, U. Chgo., 1993. RN. Supr. nursing Med. Ctr.; nurse critical care Loyola U., Maywood, Ill., 1970-78, Med. Staffing Services, Oak Park, Ill., 1978-84; pres. Heart Care Unltd., Oakbrook, Ill., 1982—; one of first ind. nurse contractors in Ill. Creator ednl. programs for cardiac patients, families and staff, 1971—. Stephen min. Christ Ch. of Oak Brook, Ill. Mem. AAUW, Am. Nurses Assn., Am. Assn. Critical Care Nurses, Am. Heart Assn., Elmhurst Coll. Alumni Assn., U. Chgo. Alumni Assn. Avocations: rose gardening, cooking, candymaking. Office: Heart Care Unltd PO Box 3275 Oak Brook IL 60522-3275

BOWER, MARVIN, management consultant; b. Cin., Aug. 1, 1903; s. William J. and Carlotta (Preston) B.; m. Helen M. McLaughlin, Aug. 17, 1927 (dec. Jan. 31, 1985); children: Peter Huntington (dec.), Richard Hamilton, James McKinsey; m. Clothilde de Véze Stewart, Jan. 22, 1988 (dec. Aug. 1999). Ph.B., Brown U., 1925; JD, Harvard U., 1928, M.B.A., 1930. Bar: Ohio, 1928, Mass. 1928. Assoc. Jones, Day, Reavis & Pogue, Cleve., 1930-33; assoc. McKinsey & Co., 1933-35, ptnr., 1935-50, mng. ptnr., 1950-56, mng. dir., 1956-67, dir., 1956—; cons. to USAF, AUS (Bur. Budget), 1941-43. Author: The Will to Manage, 1966, The Will to Lead, 1997; Editor: Development of Executive Leadership, 1949; Contbr. to various mags. Trustee bd. edn., Bronxville, 1945-48; hon. trustee Nat. Com. Econ. Devel.; former trustee Brown U., Case-Western Res. U.; chmn. Nat. Coun. on Econ. Edn., 1967-76. Named to U.S. Bus. Hall of Fame, 1989. Fellow Internat. Acad. Mgmt.; mem. Delray Beach (Fla.) Club, Harvard Club (N.Y.C.), Alpha Tau Omega, Tau Beta Pi.

BOWER, PHILIP JEFFREY, cardiologist; b. Kenmore, N.Y., Nov. 23, 1935; s. Philip Graydon and Evelyn (McLoney) B.; children: Elizabeth Ann, Susan Lynn. BA, U. Va., 1957; MD, Johns Hopkins U., 1961; MBA, Tulane U., 1998. Diplomate Am. Bd. Internal Medicine with supspecialty in cardiology. Intern in medicine U. N.C., Chapel Hill, 1961-62; resident in medicine Johns Hopkins U., Balt., 1962-63; resident in medicine Mayo Clinic, Rochester, Minn., 1965-66, fellow in cardiology, 1966-68; staff physician Ochsner Clinic, New Orleans, 1964-78; dir. cardiology, dir. catheterization lab. East Jefferson Gen. Hosp., Metairie, La., 1978-98; cardiologist Togus VAH, Maine, 1998—, acting chmn. dept. medicine, 1999—; instr. medicine U. Ga. Sch. of Medicine, Augusts, 1963-65; clin. asst. prof. medicine La. State U., New Orleans, 1974—p clin. prof. medicine Tulane U., New Orleans, 1983—; former mem. bd. dirs. Found. East Jefferson Gen. Hosp. Found., Metairie; cons. in field. Contbr. articles to profl. jours.; presenter in field. Capt. U.S. Army, 1963-65. Fellow ACP, Am. Coll. Cardiology, Am. Coll. Chest Physicians, Coll. Clin. Cardiology, Soc. Cardiac Angiography and Interventions; mem. AMA, Am. Heart Assn. (bd. dirs. 1979-83), So. Med. Assn. Avocations: walking, wine, food, travel. Home: 95 Pumpkin Cove Rd New Harbor ME 04554-4912

BOWER, RUTH LAWTHER, retired mathematics educator; b. Bellaire, Ohio, Nov. 17, 1917; d. James Hood and Mary Blanche (Studebaker) Lawther; (widowed); 1 child, Bruce Alan. BA, Wooster (Ohio) Coll., 1939; EdS, Fla. Atlantic U., 1974, EdD, 1976. Cert. tchr., Fla. Cost acct. Peasley Constrn., New London, Conn., 1942-43; with Palm Beach County Sch. System, West Palm Beach, Fla., 1964-74, 74-85, chmn. math. dept., 1974-78, maths. cons., 1978-85; prof. maths. Palm Beach Atlantic Coll., West Palm Beach, 1985-94; adj. prof. math. Fla. Atlantic U., Boca Raton, 1965-85; prin. summer sch. Palm Beach County Schs., West Palm Beach, 1971, 72; speaker in field. Developer math. games Equivo, NOC, Add-In and others, 1971—; co-author: Individualizing Mathematics Series, 1970-71. Trustee Admiralty

Bank, Juno Beach, Fla. Named Tchr. of the Yr., Fla. Math. Tchrs. Assn., 1977. Mem. Nat. Coun. Tchrs. of Maths., Math. Assn. Am., Phi Delta Kappa, Fibonacci Assn. Address: #315 11381 Prosperity Farms Rd Palm Beach Gardens FL 33410-3459

BOWER, SHELLEY ANN, business management consultant; b. Catskill, N.Y., Jan. 31, 1954; d. Edward Philip and Antoinette (Post) B.; m. Richard D. Connors, Aug. 28, 1976 (div. Mar. 1984); m. Paul Allan Benfatto, Oct. 2, 1999. BA, Mich. Technol. U., 1977; JD, Detroit Coll., 1984. Bar: N.Y. Coord. Cadillac Motorcar, Detroit, 1980-84, employee in tng., 1984-85, supr. EEO, 1985-86; divsn. mgr. property profl. Saugerties, N.Y., 1986-88; engrng. tech., dir. corp. tng. and program adminstrn. Troy, Mich., 1988-92; cons. Electronic Data Syss., Southfield, Mich., 1992-95; dir. planning & devel., corp. counsel C.T. Male Assocs., PC, Latham, N.Y., 1995-96; prin. Oracle Corp., 1996-97; sr. cons., prin. IBM Global Cons. Svcs. Mfg. Industries, White Plains, N.Y., 1997—, cons., 1999. Mem. NAFE, N.Y. State Bar Assn. Avocations: skiing, hiking.

BOWERING, GEORGE HARRY, writer, English literature educator; b. Penticton, B.C., Can., Dec. 1, 1936; s. Ewart Harry and Pearl Patricia (Brinson) B.; m. Angela May Luoma, Dec. 14, 1962; 1 dau., Thea Claire. Student, Victoria Coll., 1953-54; BA, U. B.C., 1960, MA, 1963; postgrad., U. Western Ont., 1966-67. Asst. prof. Am. lit. U. Calgary, 1963-66; writer in residence Sir George Williams U., Montreal, Que., 1967-68; asst. prof. Sir George Williams U., 1968-71; prof. Simon Fraser U., Burnaby, B.C., 1972—. Author: Mirror on the Floor, 1967, Autobiology, 1972, Flycatcher and Other Stories, 1974, Concentric Circles, 1977, A Short Sad Book, 1977, Protective Footwear, 1978, Another Mouth, 1979, Burning Water, 1980, A Place to Die, 1983, Caprice, 1987, Harry's Fragments, 1990, The Rain Barrel, 1994, Shoot!, 1994, Parents From Space, 1994, Piccolo Mondo, 1998, Diamondback Dog, 1998; poetry Points on the Grid, 1964, The Man in Yellow Boots, 1965, The Silver Wire, 1966, Rocky Mountain Foot, 1968, The Gangs of Kosmos, 1969, Touch, 1971, In the Flesh, 1973, The Catch, 1976, Particular Accidents: Selected Poems, 1981, Smoking Mirror, 1984, Kerrisdale Elegies, 1984, 71 Poems for People, 1985, Delayed Mercy, 1986, Sticks & Stones, 1989, Quarters, 1991, Urban Snow, 1992, George Bowering Selected, 1993, The Moustache, 1993, Blonds On Bikes, 1997; (poetry) His Life: A Poem, 2000; (essays) The Mask in Place, 1982, A Way with Words, 1982, Craft Slices, 1985, Errata, 1988, Imaginary Hand, 1988, (history) Bowering's B.C., 1996, Egotists and Autocrats, 1999; editor Taking the Field: The Best of Baseball Fiction, 1990, 92, Likely Stories: A Postmodern Sampler, 1992. Served with RCAF, 1954-57. Mem. Assn. Can. TV and Radio Artists. Home: 2499 W 37th Ave, Vancouver, BC Canada V6M 1P4

BOWERS, BRIAN PETER, engineering historian, researcher; b. Hitchin, Hertfordshire, Eng., Sept. 3, 1938; s. Thomas Henry and Margaret Mary (Edgely) B.; m. Faith Wendy Clark, Oct. 13, 1962; children: Keith Henry, Richard Paul. BSc in Engring., U. London, 1962, PhD, 1974. Chartered engr. Examiner Patent Office, London, 1962-67; curator Sci. Mus., London, 1967-98, sr. rsch. fellow, 1998—. Author: Sir Charles Wheatstone, 1975, A History of Electric Light and Power, 1982, Lengthening the Day: A History of Lighting Technology, 1998; joint editor: Curiosity Perfectly Satisfied-Faradays Travels in Europe, 1813-15, 1991. Fellow IEE (editor hist. books 1979—, chmn. history profl. group 1975-78, 91-94, chmn. London Ctr. 1998—). Baptist. Avocations: family, grandchildren, travel. Home: 89 Brockenhurst Ave, Worcester Park, Surrey KT4 7RH, England

BOWERS, CHRISTOPHER D., lawyer; b. Beeville, Tex., Oct. 31, 1963; s. David Rynning and Mary Helen (Fairly) B.; m. Veronica Angelina Cuadra, Aug. 20, 1997. BS, Tex. A&M U., 1986; JD, Cornell U., 1989. Bar: Tex. 1989, U.S. Dist. Ct. (no. dist.) 1991, U.S. Ct. Appeals (5th cir.). Asst. city atty. City Dallas, 1990—. Author: Alliance Review, 1995, The Urban Lawyer, 1998. Recipient Cert. Black Dall. Remembered, 1991. Mem. ABA (silver key award law student divsn. 1989), Nat. Alliance Preservation Commns. (pres. 1999—), Dall. Bar Assn. Republican. Presbyterian. Office: City Dall 1500 Marilla St Rm 7bn Dallas TX 75201-6390

BOWERS, EDNA REECE, underwriter; b. Greenville, S.C., June 13, 1962; d. Richard Henry and Nancy Elizabeth (Brown) Reece; m. Randall Eugene Bowers, Dec. 10, 1983. AS, Greenville Tech. Coll., 1981. Personal lines customer svc. rep. Fuller Douglas Agy., Greenville, 1983-84; personal lines customer svc. rep. C. Douglas Wilson Co., Greenville, 1984-91, comml. lines customer svc. rep., 1991-98; comml. lines underwriter Jardine So. Risk, Sumter, S.C., 1998-2000, So. Risk LLC, Sumter, 2000—. Named Ins. Woman of Yr., Greenville Assn. Ins. Women. Mem. Sumter Assn. Ins. Women (sec. 1999—, editor newsletter 1999-2000, web page designer 1999-2000), Ins. Women of S.C. (state dir.-elect 1999-2000). Office: So Risk LLC 20 W Wesmark Ct Sumter SC 29150-1996

BOWERS, KAY MARGOT, English educator; b. Manning, Iowa, Mar. 5, 1944; d. Clarence Raymond and Mercedes Catherine Bowers. BS in Edn., U. Nebr., Omaha, 1967; MS in Guidance Counseling, Creighton U., 1977; ESL Cert., U. Nebr., Omaha, 1996. Tchr. social studies Lewis Ctrl. Pub. Schs., Council Bluffs, Iowa, 1967-70, Iowa Sch. for the Deaf, Council Bluffs, Iowa, 1972-77; ESL tchr. Intensive Lang. U. Omaha, 1978-80; ESL tchr., ESL program dir. Millard Pub. Schs., Omaha, 1983—. Recipient Kiewit Nebr. Tchr. Achievement award, 1999. Mem. NEA, TESOL, Middle Tchrs. English to Spkrs. of Other Langs. (conf. presenter), Phi Delta Kappa. Lutheran. Avocations: travel, culture, cooking, reading. E-mail: kbowers@esu3.esu3.k12.ne.us.

BOWERSOCK, GLEN WARREN, historian; b. Providence, Jan. 12, 1936; s. Donald Curtis and Josephine (Evans) B. AB, Harvard U., 1957; BA, Oxford U., Eng., 1959, MA, DPhil, 1962; Dr h.c., U. Strasbourg, 1990, Ecole Pratique Hautes Etudes, Paris, 1999. Lectr. ancient history Oxford U., 1960-62, vis. lectr., 1966; instr. Harvard U., 1962-64, asst. prof., 1964-67, assoc. prof. classics, 1967-69, prof. Greek and Latin, 1969-80, chmn. dept. classics, 1972-77, assoc. dean faculty arts and scis., 1977-80; prof. hist. studies Inst. Advanced Study, Princeton, N.J., 1980—; sr. fellow Dumbarton Oaks Ctr. for Byzantine Studies, Washington, 1984-93; cons. Ednl. Services, Inc., 1964, NEH, 1971—; sr. fellow Center for Hellenic Studies, Washington, 1976-90; sci. com. Scuola Normale Superiore di Pisa, Italy; chmn. sci. com. Maison de l'Orient Méditerranéen, Lyon, France; mem. Internat. Colloquium on the Classics in Edn., 1964-66; vis. prof. Australian Nat. U., 1972, Princeton U., 1986-87, Coll. France, 1997; Sather prof. U. Calif., Berkeley, 1991; Jerome lectr. U. Mich. and Am. Acad. in Rome, 1989; syndic Harvard U. Press, 1977-81; lect. Thompson Lectures, Pomona, 1993, Wiles Lectures, Queens U., Belfast, Ireland, 1993, Coll. de France, 1997. Author: Augustus and the Greek World, 1965, Pseudo-Xenophon, Constitution of the Athenians, 1968, Greek Sophists in the Roman Empire, 1969, Julian the Apostate, 1978, Roman Arabia, 1983, Hellenism in Late Antiquity, 1990, Fiction as History From Nero to Julian, 1994, Studies on the Eastern Roman Empire, 1994, Martyrdom and Rome, 1995; editor: Philostratus' Life of Apollonius, 1970, Approaches to the Second Sophistic, 1974, (with J. Clive and S. Graubard) Edward Gibbon and the Decline and Fall of the Roman Empire, 1977, (with C.P. Jones) L. Robert-Martyre de Pionios, 1994, (with T.J. Cornell) Momigliano-Studies on Modern Scholarship, 1994, (with P. Brown and O. Grabar) Late Antiquity-A Guide to the Postclassical World, 1999; mem. editl. bd. Arabian Archaeology and Epigraphy (Copenhagen), Ancient Civilizations from Scythia to Siberia (Russian Acad. Scis.), Berytus, Am. Jour. Philology, 1987-95, Am. Scholar, 1981-93; gen. editor: Revealing Antiquity. Trustee Am. Schs. Oriental Rsch., 1984-90; bd. dirs. Met. Opera Guild; adv. dir. Met. Opera Assn; mem. nat. coun. Glimmerglass Opera. Rhodes scholar, 1957-60; recipient James H. Breasted prize Am. Hist. Assn., 1992. Fellow Am. Acad. Arts and Scis., Am. Numis. Soc. (coun. 1983-96); mem. Am. Philos. Soc. (coun. 1992-98), Am. Philol. Assn., Leschetizky Assn. Am., Soc. Promotion Roman and Hellenic Studies (hon. Am. sec. of Roman Soc.), German Archaeol. Inst. (corr.), Russian Acad. Scis. (fgn.), Acad. des Inscriptions et Belles-Lettres, Johnsonians, Knickerbocker Club (N.Y.C.), Century Club (N.Y.C.), Phi Beta Kappa. Office: Inst Advanced Study Sch Hist Studies Princeton NJ 08540

BOWES, DONALD RALPH, geologist, educator; b. Brighton, SA, Australia, Sept. 9, 1926; arrived in U.K., 1952; s. Theodore Burton and Dorothy Evelyn (Redman) B.; m. Annie Mary Morris, Apr. 4, 1953; children: Ian James Robert, Gillian Margaret Bowes Borthwick, Alan John Richard. BSc, U. Adelaide, Australia, 1945, BSc with honors, 1946, MSc, 1948; PhD, U. London, 1950; diploma in geology, Imperial Coll., 1950; DSc, U. Glasgow, Scotland, 1968. Lectr. geology U. Adelaide, 1950-52, U. Coll. Swansea, Wales, 1953-56; sr. lectr. geology U. Glasgow, 1956-72, reader geology, 1972-75, prof. geology, 1976-91, emeritus prof., 1991—. Editor: Crustal Evolution in North Western Britain and Adjacent Regions, 1978, Encyclopedia of Igneous and Metamorphic Petrology, 1989; editor Transactions of Royal Society of Edinburgh: Earth Scis., 1978-85; internat. consulting editor Am. Jour. Indsl. Medicine, 1980—. Recipient Gold medal Charles U., Prague, Czech Republic, 1998; Fulbright scholar Columbia U., N.Y.C., 1966; sr. rsch. fellow U. St. Andrews, Scotland, 1986-87. Fellow Royal Soc. Edinburgh (v.p. 1980-83), Geol. Soc. London, Geol. Soc. Am., Mineraol. Soc. Liberal Democrat. Methodist. Avocations: gardening, photography, reading, walking, music. Home: 7 Bute Crescent, Bearsden Glasgow G61 1BS, Scotland Office: Divsn Earth Scis, Univ Glasgow, Glasgow G12 8QQ, Scotland

BOWIE, ALEXANDER GLEN, minister, military chaplain; b. Stevenston, Ayrshire, Scotland, May 10, 1928; s. Alexander and Annie Robertson (Mc Ghie) B.; m. May Mckillop, Mar. 15, 1952 (dec. July, 1991); children: Alexandra, Jenifer. BSc, Glasgow (Scotland) U., 1951, Diploma in Theology, 1954; BA, Open U., 1977. Ordained minister Ch. of Scotland, Dec. 28, 1954. Inducted chaplain RAF, 1954-75, advanced through grades to col., 1975, asst. prin. chaplain, 1975-80, prin. chaplain, 1980-84, ret., 1984. Editor: Scottish Forces Bulletin, 1985-95. London chaplain to moderator Ch. of Scotland, 1985-99; pres. Scottish Chaplains Assn., 1987-88; moderator Presbytery of Eng., 1988-89; hon. chaplain Royal Scottish Corp., London, 1981—. Decorated Cmmdr. British Empire, 1984; named hon. chaplain to H.M. Queen Elizabeth, 1980-84. Avocations: leading holy land pilgrimages, painting, travel. Home: 16 Weir Rd, Hemingford Grey, Huntingdon PE18 9EH, England

BOWIE, JOHN HAMILTON, chemistry educator; b. Melbourne, Victoria, Australia, July 16, 1938; s. William Hamilton and Alice Maud (Boyce) B.; m. Patricia Gwendoline Wright, Aug. 10, 1963; children: Andrew William, Susan Ellen. BSc with honors, U. Melbourne, 1960, MSc, 1961; PhD, U. Nottingham, U.K., 1964; DSc, U. Adelaide, South Australia, Australia, 1969. Postdoctoral fellow U. Cambridge, U.K., 1964-66; lectr. U. Adelaide, 1966-68, sr. lectr., 1968-69, reader, 1969-82, prof. organic chemistry, 1983—, dean faculty of sci., 1981-82, pro-vice chancellor, 1989-92, head chemistry dept., 1993-94; mem. various coms. in field, South Australia, 1985—. Contbr. some 450 articles and revs. to internat. jours.; mem. editl. bd. 4 internat. jours. Fellow Royal Australian Chem. Inst. (pres. South Australian sect. 1978-79, Rennie medal 1969, H.G. Smith medal 1975), Chem. Soc. London; mem. Am. Soc. Mass Spectrometry, South Australian Cricket Assn., Essendon Football Club, Univ. Club. Avocations: walking, music. E-mail: john.bowie@adelaide.edu.au. Home: 21 Bushland Dr, Bellevue Heights South Australia 5050, Australia Office: U Adelaide, Dept Chemistry, Adelaide South Australia 5005, Australia

BOWLBY, LEYMOND AMBROSE, linguist, translator; b. Oklahoma City, June 5, 1922; s. Leymond Leroy and Victoria Maria (Bradshaw) B.; m. Eunice Jacquelyn Kelley, Apr. 17, 1949 (div. June 1958); children: Linda Ley, Victoria Lynn. BA in Journalism/Edn., Oklahoma City U., 1950; MEd, Okla. U., 1960; PhD in Applied Linguistics, Pacific Western U., L.A., 1986. Cert. tchr., Conn.; cert. tchr., media specialist, Okla. Tchr. Mansfield (Conn.) Ctr. Pub. Schs., 1950-51; tchr. Oklahoma City Pub. Schs., 1952-57, audio-visual film libr., 1957-61, instrnl. media cons., 1963-74; grad. asst. Okla. U., Norman, 1961-62; owner, operator nursery Trees 'n Things, Tuttle, Okla., 1975-87; intl. lang. translator Tuttle, 1987—. Author: Audio-Visual: A Manual for Teachers, 1965; photo illustrator: Social Studies for Today's Children, 1964; text contbr. various pamphlets, 1961-73; translator: Disorder and Early Sorrow, 1988. Sgt. U.S. Army, 1942-45, ETO. Decorated French Liberation medal. Mem. Nat. Coalition Ind. Scholars (assoc.), Am. Lit. Translators Assn., Nat. Assn. Scholars; mem. Okla. State Retired Tchrs. Assn., Soc. for Preservation Poultry Antiquities, Normandy Vets. Assn. of Gt. Britain (life), Phi Delta Kappa (local v.p.). Republican. Lutheran. Avocations: genealogy, mycology, horticulture, arboriculture, culinary arts. Home and Office: 4907 E Highway 37 Tuttle OK 73089-8452

BOWLBY, RICHARD ERIC, retired computer systems analyst; b. Detroit, Aug. 17, 1939; s. Garner Milton and Florence Marie (Russell) B.; m. Gwendoline Joyce Coldwell, Apr. 29, 1967. BA, Wayne State U., 1962. With Ford Motor Co., Detroit, 1962-65, 66-94, now computer sys. analyst, ret. 1994; pres. 1300 Lafayette East-Coop., Inc., 1981-82. Mem. Antiquaries, Friends Detroit Pub. Libr., Detroit Symphony Orch. Vol. Coun., Founders Soc. Club (Detroit).

BOWLEG, LISA INGRID, education educator; b. Nassau, Bahamas, Oct. 17, 1965. BS, Georgetown U., 1988, MA, 1991, 97, PhD, 1997. Rsch. asst. AIDS Policy Ctr./Intergovtl. Health Policy Project, Washington, 1988-90, rsch. assoc., 1990-92, dir., 1993-95; sr. rsch. cons. Ctr. for Women Policy Studies, Washington, 1997-98; asst. prof. psychology U. R.I., Kingston, 1988—; adj. prof. women's studies program, Georgetown U., 1994-98; cons. Leadership Coun. for Women-Focused AIDS Policy, Ctr. for Women, Washington; vis. scholar Afro-Am. Studies Program, Brown U., Providence; vis. prof. Collaborative HIV Prevention Rsch. in Minority Communities Program, Ctr. for AIDS Prevention Studies, U. Calif. San Francisco, 1999-2001. Contbr. articles to profl. jours.; contbg. author: (books) Teaching a Psychology of People: Resources for Gender and Sociocultural Awareness, 2000, Sexual Identity in Sociocultural Context: Clinical Implications of Multiple Marginalization, 1998, Teaching Introduction to Women's Studies: Expectations and Strategies, 1999. Bd. dirs. Women's Coun. on AIDS, Washington, 1995-96; mem. Women of Color Leadership Coun., Washington, 1992-94. Recipient Louise Kidder Early Career award Soc. for Psychol. Study of Social Issues, 1999, grants-in-aid award 1996-97. Mem. Am. Psychol. Assn. (Sci. Directorate Rsch. award 1996), Assn. for Women in Psychology. E-mail: bowleg@uri.edu. Office: Dept Psych/Univ Rhode Islan 10 Chaffee Rd Ste 8 Kingston RI 02881-2017

BOWLES, DAVID CHRISTOPHER, finance executive, economist; b. Charleston, W.Va., May 25, 1953; s. Paul Nathan and Martha Jane (Fleming) B.; m. Elizabeth Ann Blizzard, Aug. 23, 1975; children: Hannah E., David C., Andrew P. BA, Johns Hopkins U., 1975; MA, Duke U., 1977, PhD, 1980. Instr. U. Notre Dame, South Bend, Ind., 1979-81; asst. prof. Clemson (S.C.) U., 1981-83; fin. economist Bank of Montreal, Toronto, 1984-85, internat. economist, 1985-86; corp. economist BellSouth Corp., Atlanta, 1986—, sr. economist, 1986-88; dir. competitive analysis BellSouth Telecom., Atlanta, 1997-99, sr. dir. fin., 1999—. Editl. bd. Can. Banker, 1984-86; contbr. articles to profl. jours., books. Chmn. Johns Hopkins U. Alumni Schs. Com., S.C., 1982-83. Mem. Internat. Telecom. Soc., Am. Econ. Assn. Avocations: golf, swimming, tennis, basketball, hiking. E-mail: David.Bowles@bellsouth.com. Office: BellSouth Corp 1155 Peachtree St Atlanta GA 30309

BOWLES, NEWTON ROWELL, United Nations executive; b. Chengdu, Szechuan, China, Dec. 4, 1916; Canadian citizen.; s. Newton Ernest and Muriel Olive (Wood) B.; m. Augusta Davis, Mar. 29, 1946 (div. July 1969); m. Jean Presley Vaudrin, Dec. 4, 1970 (dec. July 1996). BA, U. Toronto, Ont., Can., 1939, MA, 1940; postgrad., Johns Hopkins U., 1941-42. Chief China desk United Nations Relief Rehab. Adminstrn., Washington, 1945-46; dept. dir. programs China Mission United Nations Relief Rehab. Adminstrn., Shanghai, 1946-48; chief China desk UNICEF, N.Y.C., 1948-50, chief Asia sect., 1951-60, dir. program divsn., 1961-76, chief program policy, 1977-85, sr. policy cons., 1986—; mem. UN Task Force for Child Survival Force, Atlanta, 1986-98, UN rep. Canadian United Nations Assn., rep. Sci. for Peace Internat. Peace Bur. Economists Against Arms Race, NGO Disarmament Com. Mem. Soc. for Internat. Devel., Arms Control Assn. Office: UNICEF 3 United Nations Plz New York NY 10017-4486

BOWLIN, LYLE LEWIS, educator; b. Hedrick, Iowa, Mar. 6, 1953; s. Evan John and Irene Doak B.; m. Linda Kay Herman, Sept. 23, 1972; 1 child, Amy Lynn. BLS, U. Iowa, 1982, MA in Fin., 1985. Asst. prof. U. No. Iowa, Cedar Falls, Iowa, 1987-92; pres., founder Positively You, Inc., Cedar Falls, Iowa, 1997-99; dir. UNI Sml. Bus. Devel. Ctr., Cedar Falls, 1992-99; asst. dir. John Pappajohn Entrepreneurial Ctr., Cedar Falls, Iowa, 1999; bd. dirs. Black Hawk Econ. Devel. Corp., Waterloo, Iowa, 1992-99, Cedar Falls C. of C. Author: (book) Mom&Pop.com., 2000. Dist. govt. Lions, Cedar Falls, 1995. Methodist. Avocations: golf, bowling, reading. Office: Univ No Iowa Coll Bus Adminstrn Cedar Falls IA 50614-0001

BOWLIN, MICHAEL RAY, oil company executive; b. Amarillo, Tex., Feb. 20, 1943; m. Martha Ann Rowland; 1 child, John Charles. BBA, North Tex. State U., 1965, MBA, 1967. Scheduler prodn. and transp. A. Brant Co., Ft. Worth, 1965-66; mktg. rep. R.J. Reynolds Tobacco Bo., 1967-68; personnel generalist Atlantic Richfield Co., Dallas, 1969-71; coll. relations rep. Atlantic Richfield Co., Los Angeles, 1971-72, mgr. internal profl. placement, 1973, mgr. corp. recruiting and placement, 1973-75, mgr. behavioral sci. services, 1975, sr. v.p. ARCO resources adminstrn., 1985, sr. v.p. ARCO internat. oil and gas acquisitions, 1987; sr. v.p. Atlantic Richfield Co., L.A., 1987—; employee relations mgr. Atlantic Richfield Co., Alaska, 1975-77; v.p. employee relations Anaconda Copper Co. (divsn. Atlantic Richfield Co.), Denver, 1977-81; from v.p. employee rels. to v.p. fin. planning and control ARCO Oil & Gas (div. Atlantic Richfield Co.), Dallas, 1981-84, v.p. fin. planning and control, 1982-84; sr. v.p. Atlantic Richfield Co., 1985-92; pres. ARCO Coal Co., 1985-87, ARCO Internat. Oil & Gas Co., 1987-92; CEO Atlantic Richfield Co., 1994—, chmn., CEO, 1998—; pres., COO ARCO Internat. Oil & Gas Co., 1993, pres., CEO, 1994-95, chmn., CEO, 1995—. Office: Atlantic Richfield Co 333 S Hope St Los Angeles CA 90071-1406

BOWMAN, BRUCE, art educator, writer, artist; b. Dayton, Ohio, Nov. 23, 1938; s. Murray Edgar Bowman and Mildred May (Moler) Elleman; m. Julie Ann Gosselin, 1970 (div. 1980); 1 child, Carrie Lynn. AA, San Diego City Coll., 1962; BA, Calif. State U.-Los Angeles, 1964, MA, 1968. Tchr. art North Hollywood Adult Sch., Calif., 1966-68; instr. art Cypress Coll., Calif., 1976-78, West Los Angeles Coll., 1969—; tchr. art Los Angeles City Schs., 1966—; seminar leader So. Calif., 1986—. Author: Shaped Canvas, 1976; Toothpick Sculpture and Ice Cream Stick Art, 1976; Ideas: How to Get Them, 1985, (cassette tape) Develop Winning Willpower, 1986, Waikiki, 1988. Contbr. articles to profl. jours. One-man shows include Calif. State U.-Los Angeles, 1968, Pepperdine U., Malibu, Calif., 1978; exhibited in group shows McKenzie Gallery, Los Angeles, 1968, Trebor Gallery, Los Angeles, 1970, Cypress Coll., Calif., 1977, Design Recycled Gallery, Fullerton, Calif., 1977, Pierce Coll., Woodland Hills, Calif., 1978, Leopold/Gold Gallery, Santa Monica, Calif., 1980. Served with USN, 1957-61. Avocation: karate (black belt Tang Soo Do). Home: 28322 Rey De Copas Ln Malibu CA 90265-4463

BOWMAN, CATHERINE MCKENZIE, lawyer; b. Tampa, Fla., Nov. 10, 1962; d. Herbert Alonzo and Joan Bates (Baggs) McKenzie; m. Donald Campbell Bowman, Jr., May 21, 1988; children: Hunter Hall, Sarah McKenzie. BA in Psychology and Sociology, Vanderbilt U., 1984; JD, U. Ga., 1987. Bar: Ga. 1987, U.S. Dist. Ct. (so. dist.) Ga. 1987. Assoc. Ranitz, Mahoney, Forbes & Coolidge, P.C., Savannah, Ga., 1987-91; ptnr. Forbes and Bowman, 1991—. Bd. dirs. Greenbriar Children's Ctr., 1994-98, exec. com. 1995, pres. 1996-98; active Jr. League Savannah; mem. Leadership Savannah, 1994-96. Mem. Am. Employment Law Coun., Ga. Def. Lawyers Assn., Savannah Young Lawyers Assn. (pres. 1996-97), 2000 Club (membership chair 1990-91, pres. 1992), South Atlantic Found. (bd. dirs. 1992). Home: 21 Jameswood Ave Savannah GA 31406-5219 Office: Forbes and Bowman PO Box 13929 7505 Waters Ave Ste D-14 Savannah GA 31406-3824

BOWMAN, DONALD EUGENE, investment counselor; b. Dayton, Ohio, July 9, 1930; s. John Peter and Delia Francis (Sink) B.; m. Mary Louise, Jan. 20, 1984; children: Clark Woodford, Marylouise Chalfant. BA, U. Wis., 1952; MBA, Loyola Coll., Balt., 1982; postgrad., Harvard U., 1974, Stanford U., 1976. Chartered investment counselor. CEO, pres. T. Rowe Price Assn., Balt., 1956-79, Bowman Fin. Mgmt. Co., Balt., 1978—. Bd. dirs. Roland Park Girls Sch., 1969-75, U. Wis. Found., Madison, 1978-95, U. Balt. Found., 1978—, 4-H Found., Washington, 1988—, Wis. Alumni Assn., 1995-2000; chmn., bd. dirs. Towson U. Found., Balt., 1989-95; exec. MBA bd. dirs. Loyola Coll., Balt., 1985—, Balt. Opera Co., 1996—; chmn. bd. St. Pauls Sch. for Girls, 1992-95; mem. adv. coun. ERISA, 1972-75. Capt. USNR, 1952-90. Republican. Avocations: tennis, fitness. Office: Bowman Fin Mgmt Co Inc 1013 N Calvert St Baltimore MD 21202-3823

BOWMAN, LARRY WAYNE, investigator, English and criminal justice educator; b. Mansfield, Ohio, Feb. 8, 1952; s. Ted L. Bowman and Mary Lou (Devore) Dessenberg. B in Criminal Justice, U. Md., 1978, M in Criminal Justice, 1980, MA English Lit., 1980, PhD in Psychology, 1998; PhD in ESL, Am. Internat. U., 1999. Lic. pvt. investigator. Pvt. investigator Ohio and Mont., 1974—; English and criminal justice prof. Yeung Jin Coll., Taegu, South Korea, 1992-97; prof., investigator, guidance counselor Kwajalein Police Dept.; drug awareness educator, 1974-92; prof./investigator, counselor Kwajalein Police Dept., Republic of Marshall Islands, 1997—. Mast. USAF, 1970-74, with Res. ret., 1992. Named Outstanding Young Man of Am., 1988. Mem. VFW (life), NRA, Air Force Assn. (life), Air Force Security Police Assn., Am. C. of C. (Korea), Am. Legion (life), Amvets (life), Lions, Optimist, Elks. Democrat. Presbyterian. Avocations: hunting, fishing, trapping. Home: PO Box 576, Apo AP 96555, Marshall Islands

BOWMAN, RAYMOND DEARMOND, SR., writer, music critic; b. Rockingham, Va., Sept. 4, 1917; s. Rawleigh David and Vesta Virginia (Ratliff) B.; m. Lita Salgado Santos, June 1, 1960; children: R. Christian Anderson, Leslieanne Dreith, Raymond DeArmond Jr. Student in History, Columbia U., 1945-47. Classical violinist Calif. Jr. Symphony, Long Beach Symphony, 1936-38, Long Beach Jr. Coll. Trio-Broadcasts, 1938-40; enlisted Calif. N.G., 1939; advanced through grades to master sgt. U.S. Army, 1955; lit. critic Daily Mirror News, L.A., 1949-50; classical impresario mgr./dir. West Coast Artists, Hollywood, Calif., 1954-75; co-owner Bowman-Mann Art Gallery, Beverly Hills, Calif., 1963-66; impresario "Ice House" Monday Night Concerts, Pasadena, Calif., 1966-83; writer, music critic South Bay Daily Breeze News, Torrance, Calif., 1969-87. Violinist (movie) They Shall Have Music, 1939; contbr. articles to newspapers, books and mags. Adminstr. Hollywood Am. Legion, 1953-60; coord. Civilian Def., L.A., 1950s; vol. L.A. Philharmonic Promotion, 1966-87. Recipient Eistedford medal, 1927, numerous art awards. Mem. Pearl Harbor Survivors Assn. (life). Avocations: painting, writing, book collector, reading, sports. Home: Country Club Estates 2024 Fuerte Ln Escondido CA 92026-1640

BOWMAN, REBECCA ANNE, lawyer; b. Charleston, Ill., Sept. 17, 1957; d. Raymond Louis and Carolyn Anne (Miller) Fischer; m. Jeffrey Lee Bowman, Dec. 27, 1982; children: Eric Steven, Joshua Samuel. BSCE, U. N.D., 1976; MBA, Okla. U., 1980; JD, Duquesne U., 1986. Bar: Pa., 1986; registered profl. engr., Pa.; cert. woman bus. owner, Pa., N.Y., N.J., Mass., Ally County, PennDOT, Pt. Authority of Ally County. With procurement/design dept. Westinghouse Electric, Norman, Okla., 1977-80; with contracts/human resources depts. Westinghouse Electric, West Mifflin, Pa., 1980-88; real estate counsel 84 Lumber, 84, Pa., 1988-89; pvt. practice McMurray, Pa., 1986—; officer Vanadium Enterprises, Bridgeville, Pa., 1990-98, gen. counsel, 1990—; officer KTA Tator, Inc., Pitts., 1986—, Penalty Box, Inc., Glenshaw, 1994—, T3, Pitts., 1999—. Contbr. articles to profl. publs. Event chair Wesley Inst., Pitts., 1987—; mem. adv. bd. Habitat for Humanity, Washington, Pa., 1988—; pres. Hospice Washington County, 1988-97; mem. event com. Interfaith Hospitality Network, 1992—; mission coord. United Way, 1983—. Named Woman of Yr., YMCA, Washington, 1995, S Hills Citizen of Yr., Pitts. Area C. of C., 1997, one of 50 Best Women in Bus., Governor of Pa., Harrisburg, 1999. Mem. ABA, NSPE, Am. Arbitration Assn. (arbitrator/mediator), Women Organized for Mentoring, Empowerment and Networking. Presbyterian. Avocations: piano, needlework, jellies/jams, mission work. Fax: (724) 941-3934. E-mail: rbowmanesq@aol.com. Office: Rebecca A Bowman Esq PE 114 Aston Ct Mc Murray PA 15317-2745

BOWMAN, SHERIDAN GAIL ESTHER, archaeological scientist; b. Westlock, Alta., Can., Mar. 11, 1950; arrived in Eng., 1955; d. Otto Michael Bowman and Eva McKnight Bowman Woodburn. BA in Physics, St. Anne's Coll./Oxford U., 1971, MA, 1973, DPhil in Physics, 1976; MSc in

Math., Chelsea Coll./London U., 1981; Diploma in Archaeology, London U., 1985. Sci. officer Dept. Sci. Rsch., British Mus., London, 1976-89, keeper, 1989—. Author: Radiocarbon Dating, 1990; editor: Science and the Past, 1991. Fellow Soc. Antiquaries of London (v.p. 1993-96). Avocations: walking, theatre, gardening. Office: British Museum, Great Russell Street, London WC1B 3DG, England

BOWMAN, WILLIAM SCOTT (SCOTTY BOWMAN), professional hockey coach; b. Montreal, Sept. 18, 1933; s. John and Jane Thomson (Scott) B.; m. Suella Belle Chitty, Aug. 16, 1969; children—Alicia Jean, David Scott, Stanley Glen, Nancy Elizabeth and Robert Gordon (twins). Student, Sir George Williams Bus. Sch., 1954. Scout exec. Club de Hockey Canadien, Montreal, 1956-66; coach Club de Hockey Canadien, 1971-79; coach, gen. mgr. St. Louis Blues Hockey Club, 1966-71; coach, gen. mgr., dir. hockey ops. Buffalo Sabres Hockey Club, 1979-86; TV analyst Hockey Night in Can., 1987-90; dir. player devel. Pitts. Penguins Hockey Club, 1990-91, interim head coach, 1991-92, head coach, 1992-93; head coach Detroit Red Wings Hockey Club, 1993—, dir. player pers., 1993—. Recipient Jack Adams award, 1977, 96, Victor award for NHL Coach of Yr., 1993, 96, Stanley Cup Championship, 1997; named NHL Exec. of Yr. Sporting News, 1979-80, NHL Coach of the Yr. Sporting News, 1995-96, NHL Coach of the Yr. Hockey News, 1976, 77, 93-97, NHL Exec. of the Yr. Hockey News, 1996-97, NHL Coach of the Yr., 1967-68, Hockey News Coach of Yr., 1968, 76, 95-96, Exec. of Yr., 1997; inducted into Hockey Hall of Fame, 1991; holder NHL career regular season records for wins (1,144) and winning percentage (.658); holder NHL career playoffs records for wins (205) and games (324); recipient Stanley Cup as head coach Montreal Canadiens, 1973, 76, 77, 78, 79, Pitts. Penguins, 1992, Detroit Red Wings, 1997, 98; only coach in HHL history to win Stanley Cup with 3 different teams. Office: Detroit Red Wings Joe Louis Arena 600 Civic Center Dr Detroit MI 48226-4419

BOWNESS, RT. HON. LORD (SIR PETER SPENCER BOWNESS), solicitor; b. Cardiff, Wales, May 19, 1943; s. Hubert Spencer and Doreen Blundell (Davies) B.; m. Marianne Hall, July 26, 1969 (div. 1983); 1 child, Caroline; m. Jane Cullis, June 6, 1984; 1 stepchild, William R. Cook. Student, Whitgift Sch., Croydon, U.K., 1954-61. Solicitor Supreme Ct. Ptnr. Weightman Sadler, Purley, Surrey, Eng., 1970—. Leader coun. London Borough of Croydon, 1976-79, 80-94, leader opposition, 1994-96; mem. Audit Commn. Eng. & Wales, 1983-95; mem. Congress Regional and Local Authorities of Europe (Coun. of Europe), 1990-98; mem. Com. of Regions European Union, 1993-98; conservative frontbench spokesman environ. transp. and regions House of Lords, 1997-98; nat. parliament rep. to European Union Charter of Fundamental Rights Drafting Conv., 1999—. Hon. col. Transport Regiment Royal Corps. of Transport (vol.), 1988-93. Decorated comdr. Order Brit. Empire; created knight, 1986; created life peer, 1995; named dept. lt. Greater London, 1981. Mem. Croydon Law Soc. (past pres.). Conservative. Avocations: travel, gardening. Office: Weightman Sadler, 1 The Exch, Purley Rd, Purley CR8 2YY, England

BOWSER-NOTT, CAROLE ANN, editor; b. Glenelg, Australia, Oct. 21, 1942; d. Colin James and Ninette Verna (Francis) Dew; m. Brian Clamp, June 30, 1962; 1 child, Desiree Juliette. BA with honors, Flinders U., South Australia, 1973, PhD, 1995; MA, U. Adelaide, South Australia, 1977. Piano tchr. Glenelg, South Australia, 1960-70; libr., info. officer State Libr., Adelaide, 1960-62, 68-70; tutor in English U. Adelaide, 1974-76; libr. Edn. Dept. Music, South Australia, 1981; editor Dept. for Edn. and Child Svcs., Adelaide, 1982-96. Australian Govt. scholar, 1969, 74. Avocations: oil painting, classical piano, writing. Home: 23 Berrima St, Glenelg North 5045 South Australia, Australia

BOWSHER, DAVID RICHARD, neurologist; b. Amesbury, England, Feb. 23, 1925; s. Reginald and Marion (Scott) B.; m. Anna Meryl Reid, Sept. 25, 1952 (div. 1960); 1 child, Julian Michael; m. Doreen Arthur, Apr. 1, 1969. BA, Univ. Cambridge, 1947, MA, 1950, MB BChir, 1950, MD, 1960; PhD, Liverpool U., 1961. From asst. lectr. to lectr. U. Liverpool, England, 1956-72, reader, 1972-90; prof. Faculte des Scis., Marseille, France, 1984; prof. Faculte des Scis., Paris, 1963-64; dir. rsch. Pain Rsch. Inst., Liverpool, 1980—; cons. neurologist Walton Hosp., Liverpool, 1974-93. Author 5 books, more than 200 articles, book chpts. and symposia. Nat. Acad. Sci. Rsch. fellow, 1954-55. Fellow Royal Coll. Pathologists, Royal Coll. Physicians (Edinburgh); mem. Internat. Assn. Study of Pain (Brit. and Irish chpt. pres. 1984-89), North England Neurol. Assn. (pres. 1987-88), Br. Med. Assn. (pres. Liverpool divsn. 1983-84. Avocations: languages, linguistics, travel, music, history, uxoriousness. Office: Pain Rsch Inst, Pain Rsch Inst, U Hosp Aintree, Liverpool L9 7AL, England

BOX, VERNON GEORGE S., experimental and theoretical organic chemist, educator, researcher; b. Montego Bay, Jamaica, June 20, 1946; s. Lester and Julia Mae (Blake) B.; m. Lynda Lynette Box, July 3, 1976; children: Samantha Nalini, Ananda Shaula. BSc, U. West Indies, Kingston, Jamaica, 1967, PhD, 1971. From asst. lectr. to sr. lectr. U. West Indies, 1969-82; scientist Schering-Plough Corp., Bloomfield, N.J., 1982-84; assoc. prof. CCNY, 1984-91, prof., 1992—. Author: (molecular modeling computer program) STR3D1, 1989, Molecular Mechanics Force Field, 1994; contbr. articles to profl. jours. Fellow Am. Inst. Chemists, Am. Chem. Soc., Inter-Am. Photochem. Soc., N.Y. Acad. Scis. (chmn. 1990-91, asst. chmn. 1989-90), Masons. Home: 4 Wakefield Dr Edison NJ 08820-1654 Office: CCNY Dept Chemistry Convent Ave at 138th St New York NY 15031

BOXILL, EDITH HILLMAN, music therapist, educator, writer; b. Providence, Nov. 8, 1916; d. Maurice and Lillian Hillman; m. Roger Evan Boxill, 1965; children by previous marriage: Paul R. Epstein, Emily H. Duby. Bd. cert. music therapist. Music instr., composer, performer N.Y.C., 1954-71; dir. music therapy Manhattan Devel. Ctr., N.Y.C., 1974-87, clin. supr. music therapy interns, 1975—; lectr. music therapy dept. NYU, N.Y.C., 1976—, prof., 1979—; musc. therapy confs.; participant profl. confs.; present UN Conf., Internat. Yr. Disable Persons, 1981, World Congress Music Therapy, Genoa, Italy, 1985, III Congreso Mundail del Niñ0 Aislado, Buenos Aires, 1987, Conf. Can. Assn. for Music Therapy, Vancouver, 1988; participant UN Internat. Day of Peace for Children, 1988, World Summit for Children, 1988, Music Therapists for Peace presentation Nat. Conf. of Peacemaking, Montreal, Can., 1989, UN Pacem in Terris Soc., 1989; conducted Plenary Session at IV World Congress of Music Therapy, Spain, 1993; originator Annual Universal Music therapists For Peace Day Worldwide, 1990-95, World Congress of Music Therapy, Rio de Janeiro, 1990, Vitoria, Spain, 1993, 9th World Congress of Music Therapy, Washington, 1999, Music Therapists for Peace presentation and continuing edn. tng. course, Golden Anniversary of Music Therapy Conf., St. Louis, 2000, Joint N.Am. Music Therapy Conf., Toronto, 1993; Peace Sch. Curriculum Through Music Therapy, 1993; music therapy workshops for "Teach for America" at UCLA, 1993, 94, adj. faculty, 1994; music therapy workshops; Edith Hillman Boxill Scholarship Fund for music therapy students; Music Therapy Lifetime Achievement award, 1995, V World Congress on Isolated Child, Buenos Aires, 1994, Creative Arts Therapies Conf., St. Petersburg, Russia, 1994; founder, dir. Music Therapists for Peace, Inc., Students Against Violence Everywhere-S.A.V.E.-Through Music Therapy; originator of Music Therapists for Peace, UN project, Music Therapy for War-Traumatized Children, 2000. Archives of audiocassettes of music therapy sessions at NYU; composer, arranger, prodr. album: Music Therapy for the Developmentally Handicapped, Folkway Records, 1976, issued on cassette by The Smithsonian Inst./Folkways Cassette Series, 1993; editor (jour.) Music Therapy, PeaceNotes; author: (book) Developing Communication with the Autistic Child Through Music Therapy, 1977, A Continuum of Awareness: Music Therapy with the Developmentally Handicapped, 1981, The Miracle of Music Therapy, 1997; (textbook) Music Therapy for the Developmentally Disabled, 1985 (translated into Italian, Japanese, and Korean), Manual: Students Against Violence Everywhere-S.A.V.E.-Through Music Therapy, 1998; co-author: Basic Music Therapy Competencies, 1981; videotape: A Continuum of Awareness: Music Therapy with Developmentally Handicapped, 1979; monograph: Music Therapy for Living: Principle of Normalization Embodied in Music Therapy, 1987; co-prodr. Earth Concert 1989, N.Y.C.; contbr. articles to profl. jours. Originator of Ann. Universal Music Therapists for Peace Day, celebrated UN Ch. Ctr., 1990-94; adv. bd. Potential Unltd. Prodns.; bd. dirs. Symphony for UN, dir., coord. music therapy treatment war-traumatized children. Recipient Peace and Cooperation award for Citizens of the World internat. anthem UN, 1998. Mem. ASCPA, Am. Music Therapy Assn. (hon., bd. dirs., chmn. legis. com., editor Music Therapy Jour. 1987-88, conf. of music therapy 1989), Nat. Assn. Music Therapy, Am. Assn. Mental Deficiency (chair creative arts therapies), Nat. Soc. Autistic Children, Coun. Exceptional Children, Assn. Musicians Greater N.Y., Music Therapists for Peace, Inc. (founder-dir., bd. dirs. 1988), Students Against Violence Everywhere (SAVE)-Through Music Therapy (founder, bd. dirs. 1995). E-mail: ehb2@nyu.edu. Home: 375 Riverside Dr New York NY 10025-2180

BOYADJIEV, LYUBOMIR IVANOV, mathematics educator; b. Pleven, Bulgaria, Sept. 29, 1952; s. Ivan Dimitrov and Tinka Vassileva (Ilova) B.; m. Anna Spasova Pavlova, May 7, 1977; children: Radostina, Janina. M of Math., U. Sofia, Bulgaria, 1977; PhD in Math., Sofia U., 1987. Mathematician Ctrl. Inst. Tech., Sofia, Bulgaria, 1977-82; rsch. assoc. II CICTT, Sofia, Bulgaria, 1982-84, rsch. assoc. I, 1984-88; asst. prof. Tech. U., Sofia, Bulgaria, 1988-94, assoc. prof., 1994—; exec. sec. dept. Tech. U., 1989-91, deputy head dept., 1992-94; vis. prof. Graceland Coll., Iowa, 1994-95, U. Karlsruhe, 1999-2000; lectr. in field. Contbr. articles to profl. jours. Capt. Bulgarian Mil., 1970-72. Recipient scholarship U. Karlsruhe, 1997. Mem. Union Bulgarian Math., Union Scientists Bulgaria, Am. Math. Soc. Avocations: history, travel, soccer. Home: jk Strelbiste Trayanovi Vrata str, 1408 Sofia Bulgaria Office: Tech U, PO Box 384, Sofia Bulgaria

BOYADZHIEV, KHRISTO NONEV, mathematician, educator, researcher; b. Sofia, Bulgaria, Sept. 4, 1948; came to U.S., 1989; s. Nonio Christoff and Maria I. (Doneff) Boyajieff; m. Irina Assenova Dimitrov, May 8, 1982; children: Marinella, Alexandra M. MS in Math., Sofia U., 1972, PhD in Math., 1978. Sr. rsch. fellow Inst. Math. Bulgarian Acad. Scis., Sofia, 1978-90; prof. math. Ohio No. U., Ada, 1990—; reviewer Math. Revs., Ann Arbor, Mich., 1980—, Zentralblatt fur Mathematik, Berlin, Germany, 1988—. Contbr. articles to profl. jours. Recipient Badge of Honor, Sofia U., 1971. Mem. Am. Math. Soc., Math. Assn. Am. Achievements include research and theorems in functional analysis and operator theory. Home: 625 W Lima Ave Ada OH 45810-1615 Office: Ohio No Univ Dept Math Ada OH 45810

BOYAN, A. STEPHEN, JR., political science educator; b. Teaneck, N.J., Apr. 18, 1938; s. Ara Stephen and Deilyle Madden Boyan; m. Catherine Stein, June 27, 1965; 1 child, Justin Andrew. BA, Brown U., 1959; MA, Tufts U., 1961; PhD, U. Chgo., 1966. Prof. Pa. State U., University Park, 1966-71, U. Md. Baltimore County, Balt., 1971—. Co-author: Ecology and the Politics of Scarcity Revisited, 1992; editor: Constitutional Aspects of Watergate, 6 vols., 1976-86. Bd. dirs. Carroll County Dem. Club, Westminster, Md., 1997-2000, v.p., 1999-2000; chmn. Friends of the Watershed, Balt., 1997—. Mem. ACLU (bd. dirs. Md. chpt. 1971—, bd. dirs. 1984-90, v.p. Md. chpt. 1995-98), Am. Polit. Sci. Assn. Avocations: skiing, tennis, hiking, web surfing, backgammon. E-mail: steve@boyan.com. Home: 2715 Bevridge Dr Marriottsvl MD 21104-1153 Office: U Md Baltimore County Polit Sci Dept 1000 Hilltop Cir Baltimore MD 21250-0001

BOYANOV, KIRIL LUBENOV, computer scientist, educator; b. Sofia, Bulgaria, Feb. 22, 1935; s. Luben Kirilov and Darina Jordanova (Kalcheva) B.; m. Vera Isaac Djerassi, Mar. 21, 1960; 1 child, Luben. MS, Tech. U., Sofia, Bulgaria, 1958; PhD, State U., St. Petersburg, Russia, 1966, DSc, 1975; cert. prof., High U. Econ., Sofia, 1985. Sr. rschr. Inst. Math.; head lab. Inst. Computer Tech., Sofia, 1966-82, head dept., 1982-86; dir. Inst. Microprocessor Technology, Sofia, 1986-92, Ctr. Informatic and Computer Technology, Sofia, 1993-96; dir. lab. Bulgarian Acad. Scis., Sofia, 1985—; corr. mem. Bulgarian Acad. Scis., 1989; prof. High U. Econ., Sofia, 1985—; gov. Internat. Coun. Computer Communication, Washington, 1995-99; mem. Fifth Framework Programme, Expert Adv. Group (ISTAG) European Commn.; chmn. UNICOM-B, Sofia, 1992—; academician Internat. Info. Acad., 1995; vice chmn. High Commn. Accreditation, Sofia, 1995-96; vis. prof. Helsinki U. Tech., 1999-2000. Editor: Network Information Processing Systems, 1988, 93, 97; mem. adv. bd. Jour. New Generation Computer Systems, 1987-92, Computing Technique, 1978-86; editor (jour.) Automatics and Informatics, 1978-98, chief editor, 1998—. Sr. lt. radiotechnique, Bulgarian Mil. Res., 1958-95. Recipient Cyril and Methodius medal Bulgarian Govt., 1985. Mem. Computer Soc. of IEEE, Internat. Fedn. Inof. Processing (rep. 1974—, Silver Core 1992), Trans European Rsch. and Edn. Networking Assn. (rep. 1990-99). Orthodox. Avocations: music, literature. Home: Angel Kanchev str No 15, 1000 Sofia Bulgaria Office: Bulgarian Acad Sci, Acad G Bonchev str Bl 25A, 1113 Sofia Bulgaria

BOYAR, JAY MITCHELL, film critic; b. Bklyn., Nov. 19, 1953; s. Samuel and Louise (Jay) B.; m. Deborah E. Beckman, Apr. 9, 1989; 1 child, Evan Paul. BA in English Lit. with honors, SUNY, Buffalo, 1975. Staff mem. New York Post, 1976-77; film critic and feature writer Buffalo Courier-Express, 1977-82; film educator SUNY and Medaille Coll., Buffalo, 1979; film critic E! Entertainment TV, 1992, WMFE-FM, Orlando, Fla., 1993—, MSNBC, 1996—, News channel 13, Orlando, 1997—, The Orlando Sentinel, 1982—; film faculty Rollins Coll., Orlando, 1994, U. Ctrl. Fla., 1999—; panelist, program spkr. Ft. Lauderdale Internat. Film Festival, 1990, 96; journalism workshop leader Orlando Sentinel, 1989, 95, 97, 99. Author: Be a Magician, 1981. Recipient Criticism award Buffalo Newspaper Guild, 1980, Feature Writing award AP, 1981, Criticism award Fla. Soc. Newspaper Editors, 1985, 86, Soc. Profl. Journalists, 1986; Pulitzer Prize nominee, 1981. Mem. Southeastern Film Critics Assn., Fla. Film Critics Cir. (chmn. 1996—), Phi Beta Kappa. Avocation: conjuring. Office: The Orlando Sentinel 633 N Orange Ave # Mp-6 Orlando FL 32801-1325

BOYARCHUK, ALEXANDER A., astronomer; b. Grozny, Russia, June 21, 1931; s. Alexei and Maria (Shiyan) B.; m. Margarita Kropotova, Apr. 27, 1955; 1 child, Cirill. PhD, Pulkovo Obs., Leningrad, USSR, 1958, DSc, 1967. Minor scientist Crimean Astrophys. Obs., Crimea, USSR, 1956-62, sr. scientist, 1962-70, dep. dir., 1970-87; dir. Inst. Astrolomy, Moscow, 1987—; mem. Bur. of Cospar. Editor jour. Astronomy Reports, 1987; contbr. over 200 articles to profl. publs. Recipient State award Govt. of USSR, 1983. Mem. Russian Acad. Scis. (full mem. 1987, presidium 1989, academician-sec. divsn. gen. physics and astronomy), Internat. Astron. Union (pres. 1991-94), Am. Astron. Soc., Am. Phys. Soc., Royal Astron. Soc., Internat. Astron. Acad. Office: Inst Astronomy, 48 Pyatnitskaya St, 109017 Moscow Russia

BOYARCHUK, KIRILL ALEXANDROVICH, physicist, researcher; b. St. Petersburg, Russia, Dec. 23, 1959; s. Aiexandr and Margaret B.; m. Julia Vladimirovna Jacovleva, Mar. 28, 1980; children: Anastasia, Olga. MSc in Physics, St. Petersburg U., Russia, 1983; PhD, Gen. Physics Inst., Moscow, 1987. Rsch. fellow Physics Tech. Inst., St. Petersburg, Russia, 1980-83; rschr. Gen. Physics Inst., Moscow, 1983-98, prof. seismo-ionospheric coupling, 1998—; head of lab. Inst. Terrestrial Magnetism, Ionosphere and Radiowave Propagation Russian Acad. Scis. (IZMIRAN). Achievements include expert in remote sensing of radioactivity contamination and ecol. situations on earth. Office: IZMIRAN, 142190 Troitsk Moscow, Russia

BOYARSKY, TERRY LINDA, music educator; b. Nuremburg, Germany, Aug. 17, 1949; came to the U.S., 1950; d. Saul and Rose Sophie Eisman Boyarsky; m. Robert Watson Alcorn, May 14, 1982; 1 child, Vera Clare. BA in Psychology, Reed Coll., 1970; BA in Eurhythmics, Cleve. Inst. Music, 1977; MA in Ethnomusicology, Kent State U., 1998. Freelance pianist, 1970—; Dalcroze eurhythmics tchr. Cleve. Inst. Music, 1976-86; Dalcroze specialist Cleve. Inst. Dance, 1977-86; vis. faculty Chautauqua (N.Y.) Inst., summers 1988-92; music and movement faculty Hathaway Brown Sch., Shaker Heights, Ohio, 1990-94; artist-in-residence Young Audiences of Greater Cleve., 1999—; presenter in field. Mem. adv. bd., spl. rhythmic cons. Shalhevet Folk Ensemble, Cleve., 1991-95; program rev. com. Young Audiences Greater Cleve., 1997—. Mem. Am. Orff Schulwerk Assn. (cert. levels I and II), Dalcroze Soc. Am. (chmn. nat. conf. 1996, 2000, bd. mem., treas. 1996—, webmaster 1996—), Cleve. Bot. Gardens. Avocations: sewing, gardening, singing. E-mail: touizers@aol.com.

BOYCE, DANIEL HOBBS, financial planning company executive; b. Flint, Mich., Oct. 19, 1953; s. James Edward and Alice Marilyn (Hobbs) B.; m. Suzanne Kay Williams; children: Kenneth C., Geoffrey A., Stephen J. BA, U. Mich., 1974, MA, 1979. Cert. fin. planner; cert. investment mgmt. cons. Rep. Mut. Svc. Corp., Detroit, 1982-87; br. mgr. Investment Mgmt. & Rsch. Inc., Atlanta, 1987—; treas., chief fin. officer Ctr. Fin. Planning Inc., Southfield, Mich., 1988-90; v.p. Southworth, Boyce & McFawn Planning Corp., Troy, Mich., 1982-85; owner, fin. planner Daniel H. Boyce Fin. Adv. Svcs., Birmingham, Mich., 1985-88; mem. adj. faculty Coll. Fin. Planning, Denver, 1985-90; mem. adv. coun. cert. program in personel fin. planning Oakland U., Rochester, Mich., 1987—; edn. cons. Nat. Ctr. for Fin. Edn., Denver, 1985—. Bi-weekly columnist Money Matters, Legal News newsletter, 1984-86; monthly columnist Personal Fin. for suburban Detroit newspaper chain, 1987-93. Bd. dirs. Great Lakes Chamber Music Festival, 1996-98; choir dir. Birmingham Unitarian Ch., 1976—. Cited by Money Mag. and Worth Mag. as One of top 200 fin. planners in U.S., 1987, 96, 97, 98. Mem. Internat. Assn. Fin. Planning (bd. dirs. S.E. Mich. chpt. 1984-87, 89-91), Inst. for Investment Mgmt. Cons., Detroit Soc. Inst. CFPs (pres. 1986-87, chmn. 1987-88), Detroit Chamber Winds (bd. dirs., chmn. 1995-98). Office: Ctr Fin Planning Inc 26211 Central Park Blvd Ste 604 Southfield MI 48076-4164

BOYCHUK, LEONID MIKHAILOVICH, control theory and system analysis explorer and educator; b. Bila-Tserkva, Kyïv, Ukraine, May 17, 1934; s. Mikhail Dmitrievich and Rivka Shmul-Leizerovna (Reiziss) B.; m. Olga Nikolayevna Skirtskova, June 26, 1962; children: Oleg, Nina. DSc, Kyïv Poly. Inst, 1957; Candidate Engrng. Scis., Cybernetics Inst., Kyïv, 1967. Cert. sr. engrng. scientist, Kyïv. Sr. engr. Indsl. Plant, Kyïv, 1957-63; sr. engr. Cybernetics Inst., Ukrainian Acad., Kyïv, 1963-70, sr. scientist control theory, 1970-97; prof. control theory Internat. Sci. Ctr., Ukrainian Acad., Kyïv, 1997—; advisor Natl. Com. Ukrainian Assn. Automatic Control, Kyiv, 1994. Author: Optimal Control Systems, 1965, Method of Structure Synthesis of Nonlinear Control Systems, 1971, Synthesis of Coordination Control Systems, 1991. Mem. Metrological Acad. Russian Fedn. (fgn.). Home: Apt 33, Vladimirskaya Str 51-53, 01034 Kyiv Ukraine

BOYD, DARRELL WAYNE, electrical engineer; b. Rosebud, Ark., Aug. 2, 1948; s. Edgar J. and Lester E. Boyd; m. Sandra E. Guisinger, Mar. 5, 1980; children: Derek J., Jason R. AA, Ind. U./Purdue, Indpls., 1970; BEE, Purdue U., 1972. Project engr. Pub. Svc. Co. Ind., Plainfield, 1972-77; engr. IV Aramco Svcs. Co., Houston, 1977-80; engr. III Abqaiq (Saudi Arabia) Producing Ops. Engrng., 1980, engr. II, 1980-81; engr. I Abqaiq Khurais Aindar Shedgum, 1981-85, supt. so. area power divsn., 1985-89; coord. planning tech. svcs. divsn. Abqaiq Khurais Aindar Shedgum, Dhahran, 1989-90; supt. II oil ops. area III Abqaiq Khurais Aindar Shedgum, Dhahran, Saudi Arabia, 1990-91, coord. planning tech. svcs. power distbn., 1991-93, coord. relay ops. engrng. divsn. power divsn., 1993-94, cons. distbn. tech. support unit, 1994-95, gen. supr. engrng. tech. support divsn., 1995-96, mgr. distbn. tech. support dept., 1996-99; ret., 1999. Contbr. articles to Jour. Tech. Pres. Abqaiq Tennis Assn., 1982-85, Abqaiq Basketball Assn., 1982-89, Ain Nakhl Golf Club, 1985-88; mgr. Dhahran Little League, 1989-96. Mem. IEEE (sr.), Am. Businessman's Assn. Republican. Methodist. Address: 8 Surf Scoter Rd Hilton Head Island SC 29928-5610

BOYD, DAVID GERALD, technologist; b. Columbus, Ohio, May 25, 1947; s. Max Wesley and Wanda Louise Boyd; m. Carol Faye Boyd, June 7, 1969; children: David, Jennifer, Ty, Trevor. BA, U. Ill., 1969; MBA, Golden Gate U., 1974; MA, U. Ill., 1978; PhD, Walden U., 1999. Cert. by Sr. Exec. Svc., U.S.; lic. comml. pilot, master parachute rigger FAA; comml. radiotelephone engr., 2d class comml. radiotelegraph FCC. Commd. 2d lt. U.S. Army, 1969, advanced through grades to lt. col., 1987; ret., 1992; dep. dir. Nat. Inst. Justice U.S. Dept. Justice, Washington, 1992—; mem. White House Nat. Sci. and Tech. Coun., Washington, Nat. Security Coun. Working Group on Weapons of Mass Destruction Preparedness, Washington, 1998; chair Gordon Rsch. Conf. on Illicit Substance Detection, Salve Regina R.I., 1998, Tech. Policy Coun., U.S. Dept. Justice, Washington, 1996—. Author: (book) Public Relations Handbook, 1987; editor: (jour.) European Resource Mgmt., 1988-89; contbr. articles, papers, and reports to profl. jours. and procs. Asst. scoutmaster Boy Scouts of Am., Ft. Sheridan, Ill., 1983-84, camp counselor, Kondersteg, Switzerland, 1986, 87, camp counselor, Va., 1991; boy's soccer coach Youth Assn., Ft. Leavenworth, Kans., 1984; guest tchr. history Heidelberg (Germany) Am. H.S., 1988; vol. examiner Am. Radio Relay League, Va., 1988-95; guest tchr. 4th grade Maryville (Ill.) Elem. Sch., 1999; commencement spkr. U. Cen. Fla., Orlando, 1999. Decorated Bronze Star medal, Purple Heart, Def. Meritorious medal. Mem. Am. Corrections Assn. (chair tech. com. 1998—), Am. Soc. for Pub. Adminstrn., Nat. Assn. Scholars, Am. Radio Relay League (ofcl. observer, coord. 1982-84, ofcl. relay sta. 1978-84, Brass Pounder's League award 1979, 80), Pentagon Amateur Radio Club (pres. 1988-92), Masons (Alt Heidelberg 821, Am. Can. Grand Lodge, master 1985-88, Silver medal 1988, chmn. pub. rels. 1987-88), Supreme Grand chpt. Royal Arch Masons of Germany (grand chaplain 1987-88). Avocations: amateur radio, photography, woodworking. E-mail: k9mx@erols.com. Home: 625 Salvington Rd Fredericksburg VA 22405-3459 Office: Nat Inst Justice 810 7 St NW Washington DC 20531-1000

BOYD, DAVID PRESTON, business educator; b. N.Y.C., Oct. 19, 1943; s. David Preston and Mignon (Finch) B.; m. Sally Sparks, Sept. 9, 1989. BA in English Lit., Harvard U., 1965; DPhil in Behavioral Scis., Oxford U., 1973. Asst. headmaster Dedham (Mass.) Country Day Sch., 1965-69; co-owner the Old Cambridge (Mass.) Co., 1973-77; instr. coll. bus. adminstrn. Northeastern U., Boston, 1977-78, asst. prof., 1978-82, assoc. prof., 1982-87, Patrick F. and Helen C. Walsh rsch. prof., 1985-86, chmn. human resources mgmt. dept., 1986-87, prof., 1987—, acting dean, 1987, dean coll. and grad. sch. bus. adminstrn., 1987-94. Author: Elites and Their Education National Foundation for Educational Research, 1973; mem. editl. bd. Internat. Jour. Value-Based Mgmt., Cross-cultural Mgmt.; contbr. articles to profl. jours. Trustee Pine Manor Coll.; corporator Brookline Savs. Bank. Recipient Excellence in Teaching award Northeastern U., 1980; Northeastern U. grantee, 1982-84, Control Data Corp., 1983, NYU, 1985. Fellow Mass. Hist. Soc.; mem. Soc. Colonial Wars, S.R., Oxford Soc., Tennis and Racquet Club, Somerset Club, Mass Hort. Soc. (trustee), Comml. Club, Beta Gamma Sigma, Phi Kappa Phi. Home: 14 Bristol Rd Wellesley Hills MA 02481-2727 Office: Northeastern U 304 Hayden Hall Boston MA 02115-5000

BOYD, DEREK RAYMOND, organic chemistry educator; b. Portrush, Northern Ireland, Mar. 31, 1941; s. Charles Albert and Kathleen Mary (Heron) B.; m. Doreen Lillian Douglas, Oct. 28, 1967; children: Deborah Karen, Stephen Andrew Samuel, Peter Derek, Jonathan Nicholas Alexander. BSc, Queens U. Belfast, Northern Ireland, 1962, BSc with honors, 1963, PhD, 1966, DSc, 1977. Chartered chemist. Sci. Rsch. Coun. (SRC) postdoctoral fellow Queen's U., Belfast, 1966-67, lectr., 1967-78, reader in chemistry, 1978-89, Nuffield Found. sr. rsch. fellow, 1979-80, prof. organic chemistry, 1989—, head rsch., chair rsch. divsn. Sch. Chemistry, 1996—; vis. scientist NIH, Bethesda, Md., 1968-69, MIT, Cambridge, 1977-88; bd. govs. Meth. Coll., Belfast, 1986-90; mem. Biotech. and Biol. Scis. Rsch. Couns. (BBSRC)Project Mgmt. Com., Link Programme in Applied Biocatalysis, 1995—; cons. in field. Mem. editl. bd. Chirality, 1992-96; contbr. chpts. to books and articles to profls.; patentee in field. Pres. Andrews Club, Queen's U., 1980-81, 94-95, Staff Squash Club, Queen's U., 1981-82. Grantee BBSRC, U.K., 1994, 96, 98, Wellcome Trust-Nuc. Magnetic Resonance (NMR) Spectrometer, U.K., 1995. Fellow Royal Soc. Chemistry; mem. Golf Club. Presbyterian. Avocations: golf, squash, music. E-mail: dr.boyd@qub.ac.uk. Office: The Queens Univ Belfast, Belfast BT9 5AG, Northern Ireland

BOYD, DONALD EDGAR, artist, educator; b. Sparta, Ohio, Feb. 20, 1934; s. Charles William Boyd and Correl Augusta Downing; m. Joyce Martha Hite, June 28, 1964 (div. Mar. 1982); children: Bentley Gale, Laura Dawn, Jonathan Ashley. BFA cum laude, Ohio State U., 1956; MA in Tchg., Harvard U., 1961; MFA in Sculpture, U. Iowa, 1966. Asst. prof. Kenyon Coll., Gambier, Ohio, 1966-72; artist-in-residence S.C. Arts Coun., Walterboro, 1973-74; asst. prof. S.D. State U., Brookings, 1974-86; vis. artist Ohio State U., Columbus, 1986-87; adj. prof. Mt. Vernon (Ohio) Nazarene Coll., 1994-97; assoc. prof. U. S.D., Vermillion, 1997-98; asst. prof. Muskingum Coll., New Concord, Ohio, 1998-2000; adj. prof. art Mt. Vernon (Ohio) Nazarene Coll., 2000—; dir. Fluxus West, 1975—; curator S.D. Exptl. Artists, 55 Mercer St. Gallery, N.Y.C., 1982, Fluxus Columbus, Geoffrey Taber Gallery, 1987. Exhibited works at Boston Arts Festival, 1962, 64, Dayton Art Inst., 1968 (first prize), Venice Biennale, 1976, Young Fluxus, Artists Space, N.Y.C., catalog, 1982, ArtReach Exptl. Art Gallery, Columbus, 1988, Tulsa U., 1989, Wexner Ctr. for the Arts, 1994. Recipient

Nat. First prize in slides, Buffalo, N.Y., 1970, Best of Show, ArtReach Gallery, Columbus, 1987, 1st prize Mansfield Art Ctr., 1990, 2nd prize Zanesville Art Ctr., 1999; grantee NEA, 1975, S.D. Arts Coun., 1981. Mem. Internat. Sculpture Soc., Internat. Conf. on Cast Iron Art, Ohio Designer Craftsmen, Ohio Art League, Mansfield Art Ctr., Zanesville Appalachian Art Group. E-mail: dboyd56@hotmail.com. Home: PO Box 349 Fredericktown OH 43019-0349

BOYD, H. GLENN, missionary agency executive; b. Wewoka, Okla., Mar. 5, 1930; s. Homer G. and Ethel Mae (Carruth) B.; m. Shirley Catherine, Dec. 19, 1952; children: Janet Lynne Boyd Reinhardt, John Kelley, Jayson Glenn. Diploma, U. Heidelberg, 1971, 72; MA in Bible, Harding U., 1953; MA in Missiology, Fuller Theol. Sem., Pasadena, Calif., 1982; D in Missiology, Trinity Evang. Divinity Sch., Deerfield, Ill., 1988. Preacher Ch. of Christ, South Point, Ohio, 1953-58; missionary preacher Gemeinde Christi, Karlsruhe, Germany, 1958-73; dir. "year in Europe" Pepperdine U., Malibu, Calif., 1966-81, prof. German, 1973-81; pres. Internat. Health Care Found., Searcy, Ark., 1981-2000, pres. emeritus, spl. programs dir., 2000—; bd. dirs. Haitian Christian Found., Abilene, Tex., Truth for Today World Mission Sch., Searcy, Zambia Christian Schs., Abilene; mem. pres.'s coun. Harding U., Searcy. Mem. Coll. C. of C. (elder). Avocations: travel, tennis, reading, sports fan. E-mail: gboyd@cswnet.com. Office: Internat Health Care Found 102 N Locust St Searcy AR 72143-5411

BOYD, IAN WILLIAM, research engineer, educator, consultant; b. Peebles, Scotland, Oct. 24, 1958; s. William and Muriel (Fraser) B.; m. Georgina Ann Ellis, June 30, 1979; children: Alan, Fiona. BSc with 1st class honors, Heriot-Watt U., Edinburgh, Scotland, 1979, PhD, 1982. Research scientist U. North Tex., Denton, 1983-84; lectr. U. Coll. London, 1984-89, sr. lectr., 1989-91, reader, 1991-94, prof., 1994—; cons. GEC, England, 1985-88; BICC, England, 1990, Brit. Aerospace, Eng., 1991. Author: Laser Processing of Thin Films, 1987; editor: 8 books; assoc. editor: Materials Rsch. Bull., 1989—, Materials Sci. & Engring., 1991—; contbr. 250 articles to profl. jours. Fellow Inst. Physics, Inst. Elec. Engring.; mem. European Materials Rsch. Soc. (v.p. 1991-96, pres. 1996-97), Internat. Union Materials Rsch. Socs. (com. mem. 1990—), Materials Rsch. Soc., Brit. Assn. Crystal Growth. Avocations: history English lang., coins. Home: 3 Nunnery Stables, Saint Albans AL1 2AS, England Office: U Coll London, Torrington Plz, London WCIE 7JE, England

BOYD, JOHN ADDISON, JR., civil engineer; b. Kansas City, Mo., Dec. 20, 1930; s. John Addison and Sara Frances (Burger) B.; m. Rosemary Kennedy, Jan. 31, 1953; children: Mary Boyd Winter, John K., Thomas K., Christopher K., William K. BSCE, U. Kans., 1952, MSCE, 1960. Registered profl. engr., Mo. Constrn. engr. T.F. Marbut Constrn., Emporia, Kans., 1956-58; engring. instr. U. Kans., Lawrence, 1958-60; engr. Howard, Needles, Tammen & Bergendoff, Kansas City, Mo., 1960-66; pres. Boyd, Brown, Stude & Cambern, Kansas City, 1966—; chmn. Engrs. Joint Documents Com., 1990—, Engring. Adv. Bd., U. Mo., 1986—, U. Kans., 1985—; peer reviewer Am. Cons. Engrs. Coun., Washington, 186—. Bd. dirs. St. Joseph Health Ctr., Kansas City, 1985—; exec. bd. St. Lawrence Ctr., 1984-88; chmn. Mayor's Adv. Bd., Kansas City, 1983-88. Capt. USN, 1952-56. Recipient Claycomb Cup, Phi Delta Theta, 1982, Disting. Svc. award, NSPE, 1986, Cert. of Appreciation, ASCE, 1989, Disting. Engring. Svc. award U. Kans., 1998. Fellow Cons. Engrs. Coun. Mo. (pres. 1982), Am. Cons. Engr. Coun. (nat. dir. 1983), Soc. Am. Mil. Engrs. (pres. 1972, nat. dir. 1975); mem. Mo. Soc. profl. Engrs., Nat. Soc. Profl. Engrs. (vice chmn. exec. bd. 1984-86), ASCE (pres. 1982, nat. dir. 1986-89), Midwest Concrete Industry Bd. (pres. 1974). Roman Catholic. Avocations: tennis, golf, flying. Home: 8101 El Monte St Shawnee Mission KS 66208-5052 Office: Boyd Brown Stude & Cambern 800 W 47th St Kansas City MO 64112-1251

BOYD, KATIE, medical consultant; b. England, July 7, 1953; d. John and Julia (Hancock) Gilbert; m. Andrew Peter Boyd, Feb. 6, 1979; childre: William, Rachel. MB ChB with honors, U. Bristol, England, 1976. Cons. cytopathologist Poole Hosp., England, 1988—. Fellow Royal Coll. Pathologists; mem. Assn. Clin. Pathologists, British Soc. Clin. Cytology (hon. sec. 1998—). Office: Poole Hosp, Longfleet Rd, Poole BH15 2JB, England

BOYD, LAURI LOUISE, lawyer, judge; b. Bremerton, Wash., Oct. 10, 1958; d. Eugene L. Gunkel and Valdi Lee Johanson; m. Mark Lawrence McIntire, Nov. 3, 1978 (div. Jan. 1984); 1 child, Cameron Caid; m. Donald Allen Boyd, Aug. 20, 1988; 1 child, Elena Christine. BA cum laude, Western Wash. U., 1982; JD, Seattle U., 1986. Bar: Wash. 1987, U.S. Supreme Ct. 1999. Assoc. Frderick W. Fleming & Assocs., Tacoma, Wash., 1985-88; asst. city atty. City of Yakima, Wash., 1991-95; mcpl. ct. judge City Selah, Wash., 1995—; appellate atty. Yakima County Prosecutor's Office, Yakima, 1989-91, 95—. Mem. Wash. State Bar Assn. (mem. mandatory CLE bd. 1992-95, chair ct. rules and procedures com. 1995-99, mem. law examiner's com. 1999—). Avocations: skiing, foreign films, opera. Office: Yakima County Prosecuting Atty 128 N 2d St Yakima WA 98901

BOYD, LINDA WHARTON, federal agency administrator; b. Balt., Apr. 21, 1961; d. Frank Arthur and Thelma Kirby Wharton; m. M. Harrison Boyd. BA, U. Pitts., 1972, MA, 1975, PhD, 1979; cert. pub. mgr., George Washington U., 1999. Pres., CEO Wharton Group, Washington, 1988; with HHS, Washington. Choreographer Stairway to Heaven, 1982. Bd. dirs. Hillcrest Children's Ctr., Washington, 1990-93, Mt. Bapt. Ch., 1987—; artistic dir. Mt. Gilead Cultural and Performing Arts. Recipient Mary McLeod Bethune Legacy award Nat. Coun. Negro Women, 1985. Mem. Black Pub. Rels. Soc. (bd. dirs., 1st. v.p., Communicator of the Yr. 1999), Delta Sigma Theta. Avocations: dancing, choreography, music. Office: HHS 2700 MLK Jr Ave SE Washington DC 20032

BOYD, LIONA MARIA, musician; b. London; d. John Haig and Eileen (Hancock) B.; m. John B. Simon, Feb. 1992. BMusic, U. Toronto, 1972; hon. doctorate, 1981, 89, 91, 96. CBS and PolyGram rec. artist and composer; found. Moston Records. Classical guitarist appearing in concert tours in Can., China, England, U.S.A., Europe, Japan, C. Am., S.Am., N.Z., India, Russia, the Caribbean; appeared on numerous TV variety shows, The Life and Times of Liona Boyd (CBS), 1999; recs. include The Guitar, 1975, The Guitar Artistry of Liona Boyd, 1976, Miniatures for Guitar, 1977, The First Lady of the Guitar, 1978, Liona Boyd, Andrew Davis, English Chamber Orch, 1979, First Nashville Guitar Quartet, 1979, Spanish Fantasy, 1980, A Guitar for Christmas, 1981, The Best of Liona Boyd, 1982, Virtuoso Liona Boyd, 1983, Liona Live in Tokyo, 1984, The Romantic Guitar of Liona Boyd, 1985, Persona, 1986, Encore, 1988, Highlights, 1989, Christmas Dreams, 1989, Paddle to the Sea, 1990, Dancing On The Edge, 1991, Classically Yours, 1995, Baroque Favourites, 1998; The Spanish Album, 1998, Whispers of Love, 1999; author 5 music books, autobiog., In My Own Key-My Life in Love and Music, 1998. Decorated officer Order of Can., 1982, Order of Ont., 1991; recipient Juno award for instrumentalist of yr. Can. Music Industry, 1978, 81, 82, 84, 96, Vanier award Can., 1979; voted internat. poll Top Classical Guitarist in Guitar Player mag., 1985, 86, 87, 88, 93; inducted into Hall of Fame Gallery of Greats. Mem. Am. Fedn. Musicians, AFTRA, SOCAN. •

BOYD, LYNNE KAPLAN, software company executive; b. Willimantic, Conn., June 17, 1951; d. Joseph and Rebecca Kaplan; m. William Randolph Boyd, Aug. 18, 1973; 1 child, Joel. Honors exch. student, U. Mich., 1970-71; BS with honors, Vassar Coll., 1973; grad., Stanford U., 1999. Dist. mgr. Xerox Corp., Rosslyn, Va., 1973-85; dir. fed. sales Telic Corp., Rockville, Md., 1985-88; dir. sales Contel Fed. Sys., Fairfax, Va., 1988; sr. v.p. Uniplex Integration Sys., Inc., Dallas, 1988-93, pres., 1993-94; sr. v.p. Jetform Corp., Ottawa, Ont., Can., 1994-99; v.p. worldwide sales Silanis Tech., Inc., Montreal, Que., Can., 1999—. Mem. NAFE, Armed Forces Comms. and Elec. Assn., Bus. Forms Mgmt. Assn., Assn. for Info. and Image Mgmt. Avocations: youth soccer, gardening, sailing. Home: 512 Janneys Ln Alexandria VA 22302-4004 Office: Silanis 2010 Corporate Rdg Mc Lean VA 22102-7838

BOYD, MILES FARRIS, minister; b. Memphis, July 19, 1953; s. Miles Farris and Ruth (Gamble) Boyd; m. Sandra Long Boyd, Dec. 17, 1977; children: Miles III, Matthew. Student, Memphis State U., 1971-74; BS, Union U., 1976; MDiv, Southwestern Bapt. Sem., 1979, D. Ministry, 1990. Ordained to ministry So. Bapt. Ch., 1976. Pastor New Prospect Bapt. Ch., Olive Branch, Miss., 1979-81, Blvd. Bapt. Ch., Memphis, 1982-88, North Trenholm Bapt. Ch., Columbia, S.C., 1988-97, Wallace Meml. Bapt. Ch., Knoxville, 1997—; mem. religion adv. bd. Union U., Jackson, Tenn., 1987-88, Charleston (S.C.) So. U., 1990—; mem. jour. com. Tenn. Bapt. Convention, Nashville, 1985-88; chmn. Memphis ACTS Newtork, 1987; mem. TV ministry KRBB-Knoxville, 1999—; guest TV spkr. Ukraine, 1996; spkr. in field. Author seminar Tng. in Ecclesiology, 1989. Named Chaplian of Day, Memphis City Coun., 1983, Hon. Dep. Sheriff, Shelby County (Tenn.), 1984, Gov.'s Palmetto Svc. award, 1997. Mem. Columbia Metro Assn. (pres. com. 1989—, chmn. orgn. study com. 1989—). Home: 220 Stonecastle Ln Powell TN 37849-3051 Office: Wallace Meml Bapt Ch 701 Merchants Dr Knoxville TN 37912-3807

BOYD, RICHARD ALFRED, school system administrator; b. Coshocton, Ohio, July 4, 1927; s. Lester Stephenson and Opal Irene (King) B.; m. Marye Joanne McPherson, Aug. 29, 1953; children: Lynne, Julie, Michael, Stephanie. BS in Edn., Capital U., 1951, DHL (hon.), 1984; MA, Ohio State U., 1958; EdD, U. Akron, 1970; LHD (hon.) Cleve. State U., 1997, Baldwin-Wallace Coll., 1997. Research assoc. U. Akron, Ohio, 1968-70; asst. supt. Warren City Schs., Ohio, 1970-71, supt., 1971-75; project dir. Commn. Pub. Sch. Personnel Policies of Ohio, Warren, 1971; supt. Warren Pub. Schs., 1971-75, Lakewood Pub. Schs., Ohio, 1975-84; state supt. edn. Miss. Dept. Edn., Jackson, 1984-89; exec. dir. Martha Holden Jennings Found., Cleve., 1990-95; supt. Cleve. Pub. Schs., 1995-97; interim state supt. State of Miss., 1998, prof. Ednl. Leadership, U. Miss., 1999—; mem. steering com. Edn. Commn. of the States, 1987-90; mem. evaluation panel U.S. Dept. Edn., 1987-89; chmn. Nat. Assessment Governing Bd., 1990-92. Contbr. articles to profl. jours. Trustee Jr. Achievement of Warren, Cleve. and Jackson; pres. Trumbull County Community Chest, Warren, 1973-75; bd. dirs. Bar Assn. Greater Cleve., 1983-84. Served with USN, 1945-46. Recipient Outstanding Educator award Ohio PTA, 1979; Educator of Yr. award Coun. Exceptional Children, 1981; Outstanding Contbn. to Adult Edn. award Ohio Assn. Adult Educators, 1983; Exec. Educator 100 award N.Am.'s Top 100 Sch. Execs., 1984; named to Coll. Edn. Hall of Fame, Ohio State U., 1995. Mem. Am. Assn. Sch. Adminstrs. (exec. com. 1983-86), Buckeye Assn. Sch. Adminstrs. (pres. 1981-82), Nat. Coun. for Accreditation Tchr. Edn. (exec. com. 1984-89), Coun. Chief State Sch. Officers (bd. dirs. 1989), So. Assn. Colls. and Schs. (bd. dirs. 1988-89), Southeastern Ednl. Improvement Lab. (pres. 1987-89). Episcopalian. Home: 404 Cherokee Dr Oxford MS 38655-2700

BOYD, ROBERT DAVID, pediatrician; b. Cambridge, Eng., May 14, 1938; s. J.D. and A.C. Boyd; m. Meriel Cornelia Talbot; children: Thomas, Diana, Lucy. MA, Cambridge U, 1959, MB, 1962; MSc (hon.), U. Manchester, Eng., 1981. Vis. prof. Oreg. Health Sci. U., 1988; prof. Manchester U., 1980-96; dean Manchester Med. Sch., 1989-93; chair Nat. Ctr. for R&D in Primary Care, 1994-96, Manchester Health Authority, 1994-96; prin. St. George's Hosp. Med. Sch., London, 1996—; pro-vice chancellor U. London, 2000—; chair coun. Heeds U.K. Med. Schs., 2000—; asst. registrar Royal Coll. Physics, London, 1979-81; chair acad. bd. Brit. Pediatric Assn., 1987-90; mem. Standing Med. Adv. Com., 1989-92; mem. Med. Adv. Com., Higher Edn. Funding Couns., 1993-99; vis. prof. U. Manchester, U. Salford, 1996—, Gov. Kingston U., Coun. Royal Vet. Coll. Author books in pediatrics and fetal physiology; editor Placenta, 1989-95; contbr. articles to profl. jours. Goldsmiths traveling fellow, 1972-73. Fellow Royal Coll. Physicians, Royal Coll. Pediat. and Child Health, Acad. Med. Sci. (U.K.), Faculty of Pub. Health Medicine. Office: St Georges Hosp Med Sch, Cranmer Ter, London SW17 0RE, England

BOYD, THEOPHILUS BARTHOLOMEW, III, publishing company executive; b. Nashville, May 15, 1947; s. Theophilus B. Jr. and Mable (Landrum) B.; m. Yvette Jean Duke, May 5, 1984; children: Theophilus B. IV, LaDonna Yvette, Shalae Shantel, Justin Marriel. BS, Tenn. State U., 1969; DD, Shreveport Bible Coll., 1980; LittD (hon.), Easonian Bapt. Sem., 1983. Pers. dir. Nat. Bapt. Pub. Bd., Nashville, 1969-79, pres., chief exec. officer, 1979—; chmn. Citizens Bank, Nashville, 1982—. Vice chair Meharry Med. Coll. bd. trustees, Nashville, 1989—; trustee Fla. Meml. Coll., Miami, 1984-86; bd. dirs. Nashville Symphone Assn., 1986-87, Nashville cpt. March of Dimes, 1986—; past pres. 100 Black Men of Mid. Tenn.; v.p. fin., treas. 100 Black Men Am., 1992-94. Named Hon. Citizen, City of Dallas, 1980, Man of Yr., 1990; recipient Key to the City, Denver, 1985, New Orleans, 1986, Great Seal of U.S. award; named man of the yr. 1990 March of Dimes. Mem. Nashville Area C. of C. (exec. bd.), Kappa Alpha Psi, Sigma Pi Phi, Richland Country Club, Maryland Farms Country Club. Democrat. Baptist. Avocations: boating, marathon running. Office: RH Boyd Publishing Corp 6717 Centennial Blvd Nashville TN 37209-1017

BOYD, THOMAS JAMES MORROW, physicist; b. Larne, Antrim, Northern Ireland, June 21, 1932; s. Thomas James and Isobel Cameron (Morrow) B.; m. Marguerite Bridget Snelson, Sept. 5, 1959; children: Rebecca Siobhan, Marguerite Isobel. BSc in Physics, Queens U., Belfast, Ireland, 1953, BA in Math., 1954, PhD in Theoretical Physics, 1957. Rsch. fellow U. Birmingham, Eng., 1957-59; cons. in physics Gen. Dynamics Corp., San Diego, 1959-60; asst. prof. U. Md., College Park, 1960-62; sr. rsch. assoc. Culham Lab. UKAEA, Culham, Eng., 1962-65; sr. lectr. U. St. Andrews, Scotland, 1965-68; prof. applied maths.and computation U. Wales, Bangor, 1968-82, dean of sci., 1981-85, prof. theoretical physics, 1982-90; prof. physics U. Essex, Colchester, Eng., 1990-99; mem. U.K.-Austrian Mixed Commn., London and Vienna, 1977-86; vis. prof. U. B.C., Vancouver, Can., 1975, Indian Acad. of Sci., Delhi, 1980, Dartmouth Coll., Hanover, N.H., 1987-88, U. Essex, Colchester, England, 1999—. Author: Plasma Dynamics, 1969; co-author: Electricity, 1979, Physics of Plasmas, 2000; contbr. numerous articles to profl. jours. Ford Found. fellow Princeton (N.J.) U., 1962, Fulbright Commn. fellow, 1987. Fellow Inst. Physics (chmn. plasma group 1975-77); mem. Am. Phys. Soc., N.Y. Acad. Scis. Avocations: climbing, skiing, traveling, choral singing, gardening. Home: 6 Frog Meadow, Brook St, Dedham CO7 6AD, England Office: U Essex Dept of Physics, Wivenhoe Pk, Colchester CO4 3SQ, England

BOYD, WILLARD LEE, academic administrator, museum administrator, lawyer; b. St. Paul, Mar. 29, 1927; s. Willard Lee and Frances L. (Collins) B.; m. Susan Kuehn, Aug. 28, 1954; children: Elizabeth Kuehn, Willard Lee, Thomas Henry. BS in Law, U. Minn., 1949, LLB, 1951; LLM, U. Mich., 1952, SJD, 1962. Bar: Minn. 1951, Iowa 1958. Assoc. Dorsey & Whitney, Mpls., 1952-54; from instr. to prof. law U. Iowa, Iowa City, 1954-64, assoc. dean Law Sch., 1964, v.p. acad. affairs, 1964-69, pres., 1969-81, pres. emeritus, 1981—; pres. The Field Mus., Chgo., 1981-96, pres. emeritus, 1996—; chmn. Nat. Mus. Scis. Bd., 1988-96. Bd. dirs. Nat. Arts Stabilization; chair bd. dirs. Harry S. Truman Libr. Inst., 1997—; past mem. Nat. Coun. on Arts, Ill. Arts Alliance; adv. bd. mem. Met. Opera; past adv. com. Getty Ctr. for Edn. in Arts, Ill. Humanities Coun., Ill. Arts Coun., Chgo. Cultural Affairs Bd. Recipient Charles Frankel prize Nat. Endowment for Humanities, 1989. Mem. ABA (mem. sect. legal edn. and admission to bar chmn. 1980-81, coun. mem. 1975-82, com. social labor and indsl. legislations 1963-65, chmn. 1965-66, chmn. coun. of sect. on legal edn. and admission), Am. Assn. Univs. (chmn.), Nat. Commn. Accrediting (pres.), Iowa Bar Assn., Am. Acad. Arts and Scis. Home: 620 River St Iowa City IA 52246-2433 Office: Univ Iowa Law Sch Iowa City IA 52242-1113*

BOYD, WILLIAM HARLAND, historian; b. Boise, Idaho, Jan. 7, 1912; s. Harland D. and Cordelia (Crumley) B.; m. Mary Kathryn Drake, June 25, 1939 (dec. Aug. 1997); children; Barbara A. Boyd Voltmer, William Harland, Kathryn L. Boyd Nemeyer. AB, U. Calif., Berkeley, 1935; MA, U. Calif., 1936, PhD, 1942. cert. Am. Assn. State and Local History, 1997. Tchr. Fall River H.S., McArthur, Calif., 1937-38, Watsonville (Calif.) H.S., 1941-42, San Mateo (Calif.) H.S., 1942-44; prof. history Bakersfield (Calif.) Coll., 1946-73, chmn. social sci. dept., 1967-73. Author: Land of Havilah, 1952; co-author: (with G.J. Rogers) San Joaquin Vignettes, 1965, (with others) Spanish Trailblazers in the South San Joaquin, 1957, A Centennial Bibliography on the History of Kern County, California, 1966, A California Middle Border, 1972, A Climb Through History, 1973, Bakersfield's First Baptist church, 1975, Kern Country Wayfarers, 1977, Kern Country Tall Tales, 1980, The Shasta Route, 1981, Stagecoach Heyday in the San Joaquin Valley, 1983, Bakersfield's First Baptist Church A Centennial History, 1989, Lower Kern River County, 1997; contbr. articles to profl. jours. Pres. Kern County Hist. Soc., 1950-52; adv. com. Kern County Mus., 1955-60; chmn. Ft. Tejon Restoration Com., Bakersfield, 1952-56, sec., 1955-60; mem. Kern County Hist. Records Commn., 1977—, Bakersfield Hist. Perservation Commn., 1984-87. Recipient Merit award Kern County Bd. Trade, 1960, Doctor-Waddingham award Conf. Calif. Hist. Socs., 1996, commendation Kern County Bd. Suprs., 1982, 76, 78. Mem. Calif. Tchrs. Assn., Am. Hist. Assn., Phi Alpha Theta. Republican. Baptist. Home: 1301 New Stine Rd Apt 216 Bakersfield CA 93309-3501

BOYD-KJELLEN, GIA, social services administrator; b. Vasteras, Sweden, Jan. 3, 1943; d. Gosta M. and Marta E. (Eriksson) Ronngren; m. John Boyd, Jan. 27, 1968 (div. 1977); children: Jonathan, Emily; m. Bo J. Kjellen, Aug. 9, 1980; children: Johan, Fredrik. BA, Stockholm U., 1984. Adminstr. Ministry Fgn. Affairs, Sweden, 1964-77; social worker Geriatric Med. Social, London, 1978-80, Sigtuna Mcpl., Sweden, 1984-86; adminstr. OECD, Paris, 1986-91; advisor Ctr. Handicap Rsch. Uppsala U., Uppsala, Sweden, 1992; sr. adminstr. Nordic Coun. Ministers, Sweden, 1994-97; cons. programme office European Union, Stockholm, 1998; project leader Aral Sea Conf., 1998; sr. adminstr. Baltic Sea 2008 Found., 1998-99; clin. social worker Sigtuna Municipality, 2000—; cons. in field. Author: Disabled Youth: From School to Work, 1991, European Union, Women and Welfare, 1993; editor: Transition of Disabled Youth: The Genua Experience, 1992; author articles. Vice chmn. Swedish Unifem, Stockholm, 1991-98, pres. 1998—; mem. Coop. Orgn. Swedish Women, Stockholm, 1997; chair Home and Sch., Sweden, 1980-85; parent gov. Bessmer Grange Sch., London, 1977-80. Avocations: travel, literature, theatre, music, trekking. Home: Storgatan 22A, 75331 Uppsala Sweden

BOYEN, MARIAN DE See HOUTZAGER, MARIANNE JOHANNA

BOYER, LESTER LEROY, JR., architecture educator, consultant; b. Hanover, Pa., Apr. 6, 1937; s. Lester Leroy and Ruth Florence (Kessler) B.; m. Patricia Barbara Hayes, Dec. 28, 1958; children: Douglas Lester, Blane Edward, Darla Mae. B of Archtl. Engring., Pa. State U., 1960, MS in Archtl. Engring, 1964; PhD in Architecture, U. Calif., Berkeley, 1976. Registered profl. engr., Pa., Mass., Okla. Instr. archtl. engring. Pa. State U., 1960-64; rsch. engr. Armstrong Cork Co., Lancaster, Pa., 1964-68; course dir. Nat. Soc. Profl. Engrs., 1964-74; sr. cons. acoustics and noise control Bolt Beranek and Newman Inc., Cambridge, Mass., 1968-70; faculty Okla. State U., Stillwater, 1970-84; dir. environ. control program Okla. State U., 1970-84, prof. architecture, 1979-84; prof. architecture Tex. A&M U., College Station, 1984-99, chmn. div. design tech. Coll. Arch., 1988-90, prof. emeritus, 1999—; Fulbright scholar U. N.S.W. and U. Queensland, Australia, 1982, Tech. U., Delft, The Netherlands, 1992; dir. daylighting rsch. NSF, 1985-88; vis. researcher Solar Energy Rsch. Inst., Colo., summer 1985; cons. acoustics, environ. comfort and passive energy design, 1970—; dir. earth-sheltered bldg. rsch. Control Data Corp. and U.S. Dept. Energy, 1979-81; chair energy rsch. rev. panel on fenestration Office Energy Rsch., U.S. Dept. Energy, Washington, 1988; gen. chmn. Internat. Conf. Earth Sheltered Bldgs., Sydney, Australia, 1983; tech. chmn. Internat. Conf. Earth Sheltered Bldgs., Mpls., 1986; vis. prof., chair dept. arch. Kuwait U., 1997-98; mem. design team Benham Blair & Affiliates, Oklahoma City. Author: Earth Shelter Technology, 1987; editor: Building Design for Environmental Hazards, 1973, Earth Sheltered Building Design Innovations, 1980, Earth Shelter Performance and Evaluation, 1981, Earth Shelter Protection, 1983, Design in Geotecture, 1986, Proceedings of 5th Internat. Conf. on Underground Space and Earth Sheltered Structures, Tech. Univ. Delft, The Netherlands, 1992; contbg. author Simulating Daylight with Architectural Models, 1987. Recipient 1st Pl. Design award Nat. Energy Design competition Calif. State Office Bldg., Sacramento, 1983. Mem. ASHRAE (nat. daylighting symposium organizer 1988), Am. Solar Energy Soc. (nat. coord. passive earth cooling program 1981), Am. Underground Space Assn. (bd. dirs. 1989-92), Illuminating Engring. Soc. Lutheran. Home: HC 68 Box 19 Fort Garland CO 81133-9702

BOYER, PAUL D., biochemist, educator; b. Provo, Utah, July 31, 1918; s. Dell Delos and Grace (Guymon) B.; m. Lyda Mae Whicker, Aug. 31, 1939; children: Gail Anne (Mrs. Denis Hayes), Marjorie Lynne, Douglas. B.S., Brigham Young U., 1939; M.S., U. Wis., 1941, Ph.D. in Biochemistry, 1943; D.Sc. (hon.), U. Stockholm, 1974. Asst. rschr. biochemistry U. Wis., 1939-43; Instr., research assoc. Stanford, 1943-45; from asst. prof. to prof. biochemistry U. Minn., 1945-56; Hill research prof. U. Minn. Med. Sch., 1956-63; prof. chemistry UCLA, 1963-89, dir. Molecular Biology Inst., 1965-83, dir. biotech. program, 1985-88, 1985-89, prof. emeritus, 1989—; chmn. biochemistry study sect. USPHS, 1962-67; mem. U.S. Nat. Com. for Biochemistry, 1965-71. Editor: Ann. Rev. of Biochemistry, 1965-71, assoc. editor, 1972-88; editor Biochemical and Biophysical Research Communications, 1969-79, The Enzymes, 1970—; Mem. editorial bd.: Biochemistry, 1969-76, Jour. Biol. Chemistry, 1978-83, 87—; Contbr. articles to profl. jours. Recipient McCoy award chem. rsch., 1976, Tolman award, 1984, Rose award Am. Soc. Biochem. and Molecular Biology, 1989; co-recipient Nobel prize for chemistry, 1997; Guggenheim fellow, 1955-56. Fellow AAAS (council, v.p. biol. scis. 1985-88); mem. Nat. Acad. Sci., Am. Soc. Biol. Chemists (past pres., council mem.), Am. Chem. Soc. (past div. chmn., enzyme chemistry award 1955), Biophys. Soc. Home: 1033 Somera Rd Los Angeles CA 90077-2625 Office: Dept Chem-Biochem Rm 200-A 607 Charles B Young Dr E Los Angeles CA 90095-0001

BOYER, RÉGIS RAYMOND EMILE, humanities educator; b. Reims, France, June 25, 1932; s. Robert and Odette (Beaufort) B.; m. Marie-Rose Bronner, July 21, 1960; children: Claire, Odile, Christine, Remi, Blandine, Bertrand, Severine. LLD, Paris U., Nancy, 1955. Lectr. U. of Lódź, Poland, 1959-61, U. of Reykjavik, Iceland, 1961-63, U. of Lund, Sweden, 1963-64; lectr., dir. de la Maison de France U. of Uppsala, Sweden, 1964-70; prof. Scandinavian langs., lit. and civilization U. Paris, Sorbonne, 1970—, head of inst., 1980—. Contbr. articles to profl. jours. Mem. Acad. Scis. Lund, Acad. Scis. Upsala, Danish Acad. Copenhagen. Roman Catholic. Avocation: music. Home: 36 rue Marceau, 94210 La Varenne St Hilaire France Office: Université Paris-Sorbonne, 1 Rue Victor-Cousin, 7500 Paris France

BOYER, TYRIE ALVIS, lawyer; b. Williston, Fla., Sept. 10, 1924; s. Alton Gordon and Mary Ethel (Strickland) B.; m. Elizabeth Everett Gale, June 9, 1945; children: Carol, Tyrie, Kennedy, Lee. BA, U. Fla., 1953, LLB, JD, 1954. Bar: Fla. Atty. Crawford, May & Boyer, Jacksonville, Fla., 1954-58, Boyer Law Offices, Jacksonville, 1958-60; judge Civil Ct. of Record, Jacksonville, 1960-63; cir. judge 4th Jud. Cir. of Fla., Jacksonville, 1963-67; atty. Dawson, Galant, Maddox, Boyer, Sulik & Nichols, Jacksonville, 1967-73; appellate judge 1st Dist. Ct. Appeal, Tallahassee, 1973-79; chief judge 1st Dist. Ct. Appeals, Tallahassee, 1975-76; atty. Boyer, Tanzler, Blackburn & Boyer, Jacksonville, 1979-84, Boyer, Tanzler & Boyer, Jacksonville, 1984—; adj. prof. Fla. Coastal Sch. Law, Jacksonville, 1996—, U. North Fla., 1998—; chmn. Supreme Ct. Com. on Standard Conduct Governing Judges, Tallahassee, 1976-79. Contbr. articles to profl. jours. Chmn. Duval County Hosp. Authority, Jacksonville, 1970-73, Jacksonville Bldg. Fin. Authority, 1980-81; pres. Jacksonville Legal Aid Assn., 1954-61; bd. dirs. Jones Coll., Jacksonville, 1978-85; bd. advs. Fla. Coastal Sch. Law, 1996—; adj. prof. U. North Fla., 1998—. With USN, 1942-45, PTO. Mem. ABA, Am. Judicature Soc., Fla. Bar, Amer. Bar Assn., Jacksonville Bar Assn., Fla. Acad. Trial Lawyers, Am. Bd. Trial Advs., SCV (comdr.), Mil. Order Stars and Bars (comdr.), Masons, dir., Safari Club Internat., Fla. Blue Key, Order of Coif, Phi Beta Kappa, Phi Kappa Phi. Methodist. Avocation: big game hunting. Home: 3966 Cordova Ave Jacksonville FL 32207-6019 Office: Boyer Tanzler & Boyer 210 E Forsyth St Jacksonville FL 32202-3320

BOYER, VINCENT LEE, engineering executive; b. Dallas, Oct. 16, 1956; s. Donald Boyer and Patricia Carolyn (Bills) Bloodsworth; m. Sandra Kay Mayo, Feb. 26, 1974 (div. 1992); children: John Vincent, Donald Lee, Vincent Lee Jr., Whitney Alexandra; m. Vanessa Bradbury, Nov. 7, 1992. AS, Eastfield Coll., Mesquite, Tex., 1980; BS, Abilene Christian U., 1983; MS summa cum laude, Amber U., 1988, MBA, 1988, PhD, 1989. Cert. quality analyst, quality auditor; registered ISO assessor; lic. pvt. investigator, Tex. Engring. mgr. STL Electronics, Dallas, 1977-79, TEC Electronics, Dallas, 1979-80; quality engr. Boeing Electronics, Irving, Tex., 1980-82; systems engr. Searle Optical Lab., Dallas, 1982-83; sr. engr. E-Systems, Inc., Garland, Tex., 1983-88; dir. quality assurance UTL Corp., Dallas, 1988-92; engring. documentation mgr. Electrocom Automation, Arlington, 1992—, documenation dir., 1996-97; dir. quality assurance Peak Corp., 1997—; founder, owner P-C-Coach.com., 1999; cons. The Carmen Group,

Inc., Plano, Tex., 1990—. Author: Software Quality Manual, 1994. Precinct rep. Collin County Reps., Plano, 1990; com. mem. Cub Scout Pack 285, Plano, 1991; v.p. St. Paul's Sports Assn., Richardson, Tex., 1988. With U.S. Army, 1973-76. Mem. IEEE (book rev. author, standards com. mem. 1984-86), Am. Soc. Quality Control (sr., chmn. policy com. 1990—, assoc. newsletter editor 1991-96). Republican. Roman Catholic. Avocations: research, writing, photography. Home: RR 1 Box 124F Monticello FL 32344-9717 Office: Peek Traffic Transyt Corp 2910 Ave F Tallahassee FL 32303

BOYER, YVES MAURICE, aerospace company executive; b. Chateaudun, France, Aug. 29, 1943; s. Paul C. and Madeleine E. (Hermelin) B.; m. Elisabeth Barritault, Apr. 21, 1965; children: Christophe, Pierre-Yves. Diploma in aero. engring., French Air Force Officers Sch., 1969; MBA, Inst. Adminstrn. Enterprises, Paris, 1984. Commd. officer French Air Force, 1969, advanced through grades to capt., 1976, engring. officer, flight testing officer, 1971-78, resigned, 1978; quality engr. Seca Group Aerospatiale, Le Bourget, France, 1979-84; purchasing mgr. Seca Group Aerospatiale, 1985-88, dir. ops., 1989-90, dep. gen. mgr. ops., 1990-96, CEO, 1996—. Avocation: golf. Office: SECA Group Aerospatiale, Aeroport, 93350 Le Bourget France

BOYETT, JOAN REYNOLDS, arts administrator; b. L.A., May 2, 1936; d. Clifton Faris Reynolds and Jean Margaret (Howard) Hauck; m. Harry William Boyett, Oct. 5, 1956; children: Keven William, Suzanne Marie Boyett Liebherr. Student, Occidental Coll., 1954-55, Pasadena Playhouse, 1955-57. Mgr. youth activities L.A. Philharm. Orch., 1970-79; dir., founder edn. divsn. Performing Arts Ctr. L.A. County, 1979—, v.p. edn., 1988—; mem. supt.'s task force on arts edn. Calif. State Dept. Edn., 1997; cons. NEA, Washington; chmn. arts edn. task force Calif. Arts Coun., Sacramento, 1993-95; arts edn. mem. Nat. Working Group, Washington, 1992-95; mem. U.S. Sec. of Edns. Com. on Am. Goes Back to Sch. Active various coms. and task forces, L.A., Sacramento. Named Woman of Yr. L.A. Times, 1976; recipient Labor's award of honor County Fedn. Labor, L.A., 1984, Susan B. Anthony award Bus. and Profl. Women, 1986, Gov.'s award Calif. Arts Coun. and Gov., 1989, R.O.S.E. Outstanding Svc. to Edn. award, U. So. Calif., 1999. Mem. Calif. Art Edn. Assn. (Behind the Scenes award 1985), Calif. Dance Educators Assn. (Svc. award 1985), Calif. Ednl. Theatre Assn. (Outstanding Contbn. award 1990, nominated for Nat. Medal Arts 1996, 97). Republican. Presbyterian. Avocations: reading, attending arts events, gardening, swimming. Home: PO Box 1805 Studio City CA 91614-0805 Office: Performing Arts Ctr LA County 717 W Temple St Ste 300 Los Angeles CA 90012-2655

BOYKIN, ARLETHA FAYE, speaker, publisher; b. Brewton, Ala., Jan. 9, 1960; d. Arthur Lee and Zenobia Alice Dale; 1 child, Joseph Anthony Cater III. BSW, Tuskegee U., 1981. Liaison cons. Bank of Am., Irving, Tex., 1984-95; publ., author, spkr. Always Finding A Way Concepts, Mesquite, Tex., 1995—; site-base mgmt. mem. Mesquite Ind. Sch., 1997-99. Author: Been Through The Fire But Didn't Get Burned 100%, 1995 (One of Tex. Black Women Writer's award 1996). Received Key to City '96 City of Birmingham. Mem. Toastmaster's Internat. (named Best Spkr. 1997), Tuskegee Alumni Club (2d v.p. 1997-99), Alpha Kappa Alpha. Democrat. Avocations: traveling, reading, writing, baking, public speaking. Office: Always Finding A Way Concepts PO Box 871222 Mesquite TX 75187-1222

BOYKIN, WILLIAM EDWARD, retired principal, state legislator; b. Clarendon, Tex., June 27, 1932; s. Garland Lester and Lucy Edna (Matthews) B.; m. Bobby Jo Irving, July 26, 1958 (dec. Apr. 1992); children: Martha Anne, Douglas Irving, Kenneth Garland; m. Jane Ellen Larson, Mar. 1, 1996; stepchildren: Mike, Todd, Phillip Woods. BA in Journalism, N.Mex. State U., 1954, MA in English, 1964, ednl. adminstr., 1976. Tchr., coach, adminstr. Las Cruces (N.Mex.) H.S., 1958-70; asst. football coach N.Mex. State U., Las Cruces, 1970-73; agt., state dir. Fidelity Union Life Ins. Co., Albuquerque, 1973-76; vice-prin., prin. Farmington (N.Mex.) H.S., 1976-86; adminstr. Mesilla Valley Christian Sch., Las Cruces, 1996-98; ret., 1998; mem. N.Mex. Ho. of Reps., 2000—; bd. trustees Mesilla Valley Christian Sch. Author: The Principal of the Thing, The Journal of a High School Principal; edited: The End of the Pillow Slip, Emily Clair Watson, As Told To Edna Matthews Boykin; contbr. articles to profl. jours. Elected to N.Mex State Ho. of Reps., 2000. Capt. USAF, 1954-64. Recipient Secondary Adminstr. of Yr. N.Mex. Adminstrs. Assn., 1986, Leadership award, 1986. Mem. NRA, Am. Legion, Aggie Scholarship Assn., N.Mex. State U. Alumni Assn. (life), People for the West, Phi Delta Kappa, Tau Kappa Epsilon. Republican. Methodist. Avocations: travel, fishing, reading, do-it-yourself, writing. Home: 3035 Hillrise Dr Las Cruces NM 88011-4703

BOYKO, VITALIY, judge. Chmn. Supreme Ct., Ukraine. Office: vul P Orlyka 4, 252601 Kyiv Ukraine*

BOYLAN, BRIAN RICHARD, author, historian, director, photographer, literary agent; b. Chgo., Dec. 11, 1936; s. Francis Thomas and Mary Catherine (Kane) B.; children: Rebecca, Gregory, Ingrid. Student, Loyola U., 1954-58; DD, Universal Ch., 1969. CEO Otitis Media Lit. Agy.; prodr. OTM Prodns.; dir., prodr. Media Medica. Editor: Jour. AMA, Med. World News, Modern Medicine, 1956-77; author: The New Heart, 1969, Infidelity, 1971, The Legal Rights of Women, 1973, Benedict Arnold: The Dark Eagle, 1973, From An Art to a Science, 1975, A Hack in a Hurry, 1980, Final Trace, 1983; works include 16 books, 3 plays, 3 screenplays; book reviewer, critic, 19525; photographer, 19625; theatre dir., 19705; directed works include 31 plays, videotapes and films. Office: 1926 Dupont Ave S Minneapolis MN 55403-3035

BOYLE, DAVID COURTNEY, journalist, writer, editor; b. London, May 20, 1958; s. Richard Adrian and Diana Betty (Evelegh) B. MA, Trinity Coll., Oxford, 1980. Arts editor Oxford Star, Oxford, England, 1982-85; editor Town & Country Planning, London, 1985-88; head of devel. Rapide Prodns., London, 1988-92; freelance writer London, 1992—; editor: Liberal Democrat News, London, 1992-98, New Economics, 1987—, New Democrat, London, 1988-91. Author: Building Futures, 1989, Funny Money, 1999. Trustee Self-Esteem Network, London, 1993-96, Town & Country Planning Assn., London, 1989-91; assoc. New Econs. Found., 1999—. Recipient Churchill fellow CHurchill Trust, 1996. Fellow Royal Soc. of Arts. Home: 23 Camden Hill Rd, Se191NX London England

BOYLE, GREGORY JOHN, psychology educator, research consultant; b. Melbourne, Victoria, Australia, Feb. 20, 1950; s. Douglas Vivian and Joan Margaret (Smith) B.; m. Dolores Mary Bartolo, Mar. 7, 1970; children: Tracy, Linda, Andrew, Michael. BS with honors, U. Melbourne, 1973, MEd, 1978, PhD, 1985; MA, U. Del., 1982, PhD, 1983. Registered psychologist. Math and sci. tchr. State Edn. Dept. Victoria, 1974-75; lectr. in psychology Inst. Cath. Edn., 1976-85; lectr. in ednl. psychology U. Melbourne, 1985-89; sr. lectr. in psychology U. Queensland, 1990-92; assoc. prof. Bond U., Queensland, 1993-95, full prof., 1995—; rsch. cons. Australian Army Psychology Corps., Canberra, ACT, 1987—; part-time pvt. practice in psychology, 1978—; cons. psychologist Larmenier Spl. Sch., Melbourne, 1976-77. Assoc. editor Australian Jour. Psychology, 1990—; contbr. numerous articles to internat. publs. including Multivariate Exptl. Clin. Rsch., Brit. Jour. Ednl. Psychology, Behavior Rsch. and Therapy, Internat. Jour. Sport Psychology; contbr. book chpts.: Handbook of multivariate experimental psychology, Personality psychology in Europe, Vol. 4, International handbook of personality and intelligence, International Review of Professional Issues in Selection and Assessment. Mem. core skills test steering com. Queensland Govt., Brisbane, 1991-92. Recipient Tchg. citation CAUT, 1995; hon. fellow Cattell Rsch. Inst., U.S., 1987. Mem. Australian Psychol. Soc. Avocations: spending time with family, bagpipes, motorbikes, physical fitness, international travel. Office: Bond Univ, 4229 Gold Coast Australia

BOYLE, JOHN BERNARD, artist; b. London, Ont., Can., 1941. One-man shows include 20/20 Gallery, 1967, Rodman Hall Arts Ctr. St. Catharines, 1971, Nancy Poole's Studio, 1972-76, 77, 78, 81, 83, 84, 85, 89, 91-98, London Regional Gallery, 1974, 91, Saidye Bronfman, 1977, Latcham Gallery, 1982; Tom Thomson Meml. Gallery, 1983, 94, Susan Whitney Gallery, Regina, 1986; group exhbns. include London Regional Gallery, 1984, Concordia U., 1984, Art Space Peterborough, 1986, Nancy Poole's Studio, 1988, McIntosh Pub. Gallery, 1989, Tom Thomson Gallery, Owen Sound, 1989, U. Waterloo, 1991, others; represented in permanent collections Can. Coun. Art Bank, Nat. Gallery Can., Art Gallery Ont., Montreal Mus. Fine Arts, London Regional Art Gallery, U. Western Ont., Corp. of the City of Toronto, Clarkson Gordon Coll., Tom Thomson Meml. Art Gallery, Rodman Hall Arts Ctr., CIL Coll., Brock U., Norcen Coll., Dalhouseie U. Coll., Confedn. Gallery P.E.I., East York Bd. Edn., Beaverbrook Art Gallery, Woodstock Pub. Gallery; author: No Angel Came, 1994. Can. Coun. A grantee, 1987. Office: c/o Nancy Pooles Studio, 16 Hazelton Ave, Toronto, ON Canada M5R 2E2

BOYLE, PETER HOWARD, chemistry lecturer; b. Dublin, Ireland, Aug. 1, 1938; s. Richard Henry and Ellen Emily (Barrett) B.; m. Dorathea Elizabeth Mollan, Aug. 22, 1963; children: Wendy May, Richard Charles. BA, Trinity Coll., Dublin, 1960; PhD, 1965. Lectr. in Chemistry Trinity Coll., Dublin, 1961-66; rsch. fellow Syntex Inst., Palo Alto, Calif., 1966-67; lectr. in Chemistry Trinity Coll., Dublin, 1967-72; fellow, 1972-75; Humboldt fellow U. Konstanz, Germany, 1975-76; fellow Trinity Coll., Dublin, 1976-87, sr. dean, 1987-92, fellow, sr. lectr., 1992—. Author: Comprehensive Heterocyclic Chemistry, 1996; contbr. articles to profl. jours. Fellow Inst. Chemistry of Ireland; mem. Royal Soc. Chemistry. Mem. Ch. of Ireland. Avocations: music, singing, travel. Home: Edenville 18 Terenure Rd W, Dublin 6W, Ireland Office: Chemistry Dept, Trinity College, Dublin 2, Ireland

BOYNE, WALTER JAMES, writer, former museum director; b. East St. Louis, Ill., Feb. 2, 1929; s. Walter William and Emily (Campbell) B.; m. Jeanne Quigley, Dec. 26, 1952; children: Mary Louise, Katherine Elizabeth, William James, Margaret Ann. BBA, U. Calif., Berkeley, 1958; MBA, U. Pitts., 1963; PhD (hon.), Salem Coll., 1985. Commd. 2d lt. USAF, 1952, advanced through grades to col., 1971, ret., 1974; asst. curator Nat. Air and Space Mus., Washington, 1974-75, curator, 1975-78, exec. officer, 1978-80, asst. dir., 1980-82, acting dir., 1982-83, dir., 1983-86; ret., 1986; chmn. bd. dirs. Wingspan TV Channel. Author: Boeing B-52, 1981, Messerschmitt Me-262, 1980, Treasures of Silver Hill, 1982, Flying, 1979, Jet Age, 1979, De Havilland DH-4, 1983, McDonnell Douglas F-4, 1983, Vertical Flight, 1983, Leading Edge, 1986, (novel) The Wild Blue, 1986, The Smithsonian Book of Flight, 1987, The Power Behind the Wheel, 1988, Trophy for Eagles, 1989, Weapons of Desert Shield, 1991, Gulf War, 1991, Eagles of War, 1991, Air Force Eagles, 1992, Classic Aircraft, 1992, Art in Flight, 1992, Silver Wings, 1993, Clash of Wings, 1994, Clash of Titans, 1995, Beyond the Wild Blue, 1997, Beyond the Horizons, 1998, Brassey Air Combat Reads, 1999; prodr., writer: (video) Beyond the Wild Blue; author, host, narrator: (video) Clash of Wings, 1998, The Sculptures of John Safer, 1998. Recipient Best Fgn. Book award Aero Club de France, 1982, Robert A. Brooks award Smithsonian Instn., 1980, Best Fiction and Non-Fiction awards Aviation Space Writers, 1987, Thomas McKean Meml. Cup, 1989, Cliff Henderson Trophy 1986, Gil Robb Wilson award AIA, 1997; named Elder Statesman of Aviation Nat. Aviation Assn., 1998. Mem. Daedalians, Am. Aviation Hist. Soc. (nat. advisor), Author's Guild, Sons of the Desert, Cosmos Club. Home: 21028 Starflower Way Ashburn VA 20147-4700

BOYSANOGLU, ERHAN, construction executive; b. Ankara, Turkey, Jan. 16, 1947; s. Ibrahim and Ayse (Edibe) B.; m. Nese Sarkaya, Jan. 9, 1974; children: Mert, Yigit. Architect, Middle East Tech U., Ankara, 1971. Lic. architect. Constrn. mgr. Mesa Housing Industries, Inc., Ankara, 1976-80, asst. gen. mgr., 1980-91; pres. bd. Mesa Mass Housing Industries, Inc., Ankara, 1991—. Recipient Appreciation Letter for Contbns. to Economy, Tansu Giller, Prime Min., Ankara, 1994, Appreciation Letter for successful completion housing units Mr. Lustig, Brigadier Gen., USAF, Incirlik, Adana, Turkey, 1995, award Govt. Dept. Treasury, Ankara, 1995. Mem. Union Internat. Contractors, Union Turkish Contractors, Union Turkish Developers. Avocations: scuba diving, model planes. Home: Me-Sa Korusitesi Kizilcam, Sok No 15, Ankara Turkey Office: Mesa Housing Industrie Inc, Abidin Daver Sok No 12, 06550 Cankaya Ankara, Turkey

BOYSEN, GUDRUN MARGRETHE, neurologist, educator, researcher; b. Utterslev, Lolland, Denmark, Apr. 5, 1939; d. Nis Peter and Ingeborg S. (Olsen) B.; m. Troels Kardel, May 15, 1964; children: Maria Sukuri, Nina Sakina. MD, Copenhagen U., 1966, DMSc, 1973. Specialist in neurology. Resident Mayo Clinic, Minn., 1973-74; cons. Rigshospitalet, Copenhagen, 1980-93; prof. Hvidovre Hosp., Copenhagen, Denmark, 1993-97, Bispebjerg Hosp., Copenhagen, 1998—. Contbr. articles to profl. jours. Chairwoman EFNS Congress, Copenhagen, 2000. Mem. Internat. Stroke Soc. (mem. exec. com. 1996). Avocation: painting. Home: GL Holtevej 117B, 2840 Holte Denmark

BOZBUĞA, MUSTAFA, neurosurgeon, educator, consultant; b. Niğde, Turkey, Nov. 10, 1959; s. Hakki and Fatma (Gürbüz) B.; m. Nilgün Ulusoy, Oct. 15, 1985; 1 child, Mustafa Can. MD, Istanbul U., 1983, PhD in Anatomy, 1998. Gen. practitioner Ministry of Health, Giresun, Turkey, 1983-85; resident dept. neurosurgery Istanbul U., 1985-91, neurosurgeon, 1991-92; staff neurosurgeon Kartal Rsch. and Tchg. Hosp., Istanbul, 1993—; assoc. prof. neurosurgery U. Ankara, 1999—; observer Neurosurg. dept. Zurich U. Hosp., 1988, 89; fellow George Washington U. Med. Ctr., Washington, 1993-94, Osaka City U. Sch. Medicine, 1994. Contbr. articles to profl. jours.; translator: Handbook of Neurosurgery, 3d Edit. (author Mrk S. Greenberg), Neurology and Neurosurgery Illustrated, 3d Edit. (authors Kenneth W. Lindsey, Ian Bone, Churchill Livingstone); mem. editl. bd. Turkish Jour. Trauma and Emergency Surgery. Mem. Turkish Neurosurg. Soc., Istanbul Chamber of Medicine. Avocations: symphonies, opera, philosophy, literature, poetry, history. Home: Alidede Caddesi Disbank, Sitesi B-Blok 15 Kosuyolu, 81020 Istanbul Turkey Office: Ankara Caddesi, #50 Cagaloglu, 34410 Istanbul Turkey

BOZEMAN, ROSS ELLIOT, engineering executive; b. New Orleans, Feb. 16, 1967; s. Robert Ray and Rita (Findley) B. BS cum laude, La. Tech. Inst., 1990. Registered profl. engr., Tex., 1998, La. 1999. Assoc. vessel engr. Litwin Engrs. and Constructors, Houston, 1990-94, vessel engr., 1994-96; engring. mgr. Bergaila Engring. Svcs., Inc., Houston, 1996-99; engring. mgr., owner Bozeman Engring., Houston, 1999—. Mem. ASME (assoc.), Tau Beta Pi. Avocations: country and western dancing, drag racing, study of vehicle dynamics, finite element analysis. Fax: 713-278-0405. E-mail: ross@bozemanengineering.com. Home: Ste 408 7979 Westheimer Rd Houston TX 77063-4517 Office: 2640 Fountain View Dr Ste 212 Houston TX 77057-7610

BOZHILOV, NIKOLAI TZVETANOV, entrepreneur; b. Sofia, Bulgaria, Sept. 4, 1951; s. Tzvetan Yosifov and Stefana Koleva (Ivanova)B.; married 1974 (div. 1983); 1 child, Tzveten; m. Kate Shtereva Karapeneva, May 26, 1984; 1 child, Plamena. Navigating officer, Naval Acad., Varna, Bulgaria, 1974, master mariner, 1989; MSc, Economics U., Varna, 1984. Ship's officer Navibulgar, Varna, Bulgaria, 1974-79; mktg. mgr. Navibulgar, Varna, 1979-81, gen. mgr. Bulcon Container Svc., 1982-85, chief officer, capt., 1985-90; founder, owner, pres., CEO Unimasters Logistics Ltd., Varna, 1990—; chief exec. Unimasters Ferry Ltd., Varna, 1993—, Intermodal Ltd., Varna, 1993—, Unimasters Logistics Group Ltd., Varna, 1993—, Varna Stock Exch., Varna, 1994—; pres., CEO Unidata Ltd., Varna, 1994—, Universal Surveys Ltd., Varna, 1994—, Trademasters Ltd., Varna, 1994-96, Unico Investment Ltd., Varna, 1994-95, Unimasters Air Ltd., 1995. Pres. Union Pvt. Econ. Enterprise, Varna, 1991-93. Fellow Inst. Freight Profls. (London), Inst. of Dir. (London), Varna C. of C. (pres. 1992—); mem. Rotary Club (pres.- elect Varna Dist., pres. 1995—), Bulgarian Shooting Assn. (pres. 1995—), World Trade Ctr. Varna (pres. 1996—), Inst. of Logistics and Transport (Corby), Hotel World Bulgaria (chmn. 1997—), Varna City Promotion Coun. (chmn. 1998-2000), Bulgarian Bus. Leaders Forum (mgmt. bd. mem. 1998—); hon. consul UK, Varna, 2000. Avocations: hunting, fishing, architecture. Office: Unimasters Logistics Group Ltd, 40 Graf Ignatiev St PO Box 229, BG-9000 Varna Bulgaria

BOŽIČEVIĆ, KATICA, environmental engineer; b. Kutina, Moslavina, Croatia, Nov. 28, 1947; d. Alojz and Marija (Tonković) Repić; m. Josip Božičević; children: Silvija, Valerija, Irena. BSc in Chem. Tech., U. Zagreb, Croatia, 1971. Cert. internal quality auditor, environ. mgmt. sys. auditor. Quality control asst. INA-Petrokemija, Kutina, 1971-76, chief gas lab., 1976-84, sr. engr. R&D, 1984-89, lab chief R&D, 1989-93, chief dept. environment, 1993-95, sr. environ. engr., 1995—. Contbr. rsch. articles to sci. jours. Mem. Croatian Air Pollution Prevention Assn., Croatian Water Pollution Control Soc. Roman Catholic. Avocations: gardening, pets, walking. Home: Miroslava Krleže 96, 44320 Kutina Moslavina, Croatia Office: Petrokemija dd, Aleja Vukovar 4, 44320 Kutina Moslav, Croatia

BOZSIK, BELA PAL, retired physician; b. Budapest, Hungary, Sept. 9, 1942; head lab. serology Johan Bela Nat. Inst. Hygiene, 1980.; s. Pal Bozsik and Maria Klinga; m. Marta Schleer, Dec. 4, 1968; children: Bela, Andras Pal, Attila Peter. MD, Semmelweis Med. U., Budapest, 1966. Worker Lenin Metall. Works, Miskolc, Hungary, 1960-61; pathologist St. Istvan Mcpl. Hosp., Budapest, 1966-74; rschr. Nat. Inst. Hygiene, Budapest, 1974-99; head Lyme ctr. St. Rokus Hosp., Budapest, 1999; ret., 1999; head lab. serology Johan Bela Nat. Inst. Hygiene, 1980-99. Author: (in Hungarian) Rules of Ticks, 1995, Advice on Ticks Diseases, 1997. Founder, med. sec. bd. Lyme Borreliosis Found., Budapest. Mem. N.Y. Acad. Scis. Roman Catholic. Achievements include proposing the worldwide accepted technical termfor Lyme Disease and Related Disorders that is Lyme Borreliosis in 1985 at the 2nd World Conference, proposing a diagnostic and therapeutic scheme for Lyme borreliosis seronegativa. Home: Tetenyi St 98 Bldg B, H-1119 Budapest Hungary Office: Lyme Borreliosis Found, Gyali St 2-6, H-1097 Budapest Hungary

BOZTAS, SERDAR, mathematician, educator; b. Limassol, Cyprus, Jan. 3, 1962; s. Hulus and Binnaz (Sadik) B.; m. Leslyn Thompson. BS, MIT, 1983; MS, U. So. Calif., L.A., 1986, PhD, 1990. Rsch. engr. Telecom Australia Rsch. Labs., Melbourne, Australia, 1991-92; lectr. Monash U., Melbourne, Australia, 1992-94; lectr. Royal Melbourne Inst. Tech., 1995-97, sr. lectr., 1998—, dir. postgrad. program on info. security, 2000—; cons. various cos. Contbr. articles to profl. jours. Mem. IEEE (jour referee, cert. of appreciation 1986—). Office: RMIT Dept Math, GPO Box 2476V, Melbourne 3001, Australia

BRAAKSMA, JOHANNA, information specialist, researcher; b. The Netherlands, Apr. 15, 1956. Student, State U. Groningen, The Netherlands, 1984. Rschr. RION, Groningen, The Netherlands, 1984-85, U. Amsterdam, 1985-88; ref. libr., information specialist U. Twente, The Netherlands, 1988—; mem. examination com. GO, 1990-93; chair adv. com. NVB, The Netherlands, 1992-98; mem. adv. com. Sch. for Librs., Deventer, 1998—. Recipient Victorine van Schaick award Stichting Victorine van Schaick Fonds, The Hague, 1996, 97. Office: U Twente, Box 217, 7500 AE Enschede The Netherlands

BRAAM, BEN C., mechanical engineer; b. S. Heerenberg, The Netherlands, Oct. 15, 1949; s. Karel and Doortje (Mulder) B.; m. Renée Marion Moize de Chateleux, Mar. 31, 1988; children: Naomi, Japie, Melati. MSc, Delft Tech. U., The Netherlands, 1981. Scientist Cmty. Rotterdam, The Netherlands, 1982-84, Delft Tech. U., 1984-86; engr. TNO Inst. Applied Physics, Delft, 1986-92, sr. engr., 1992—. Patentee in field. Mem. Am. Soc. Precision Engring., European Soc. Precision Engring. and Nanotech. Office: TNO Inst Appl Physics, Stieltjesweg 1, 2600 AD Delft The Netherlands

BRAASCH, BARBARA LYNN, banker, consultant; b. Santa Monica, Calif., Apr. 14, 1958; d. C. Duane and René Barbara (Siegel) B. Student, Golden Gate U., 1989-91. Ops. officer Bank of Am., Fresno, Calif., 1976-87; v.p., mgr. Wells Fargo Bank, San Fransisco, 1987-96; v.p., mgr. fin. MIS Bank of Am., San Fransisco, 1996-2000, catalyst bus. cons., owner, 2000—; mentor Jr. Achievement, L.A., 1980-83. 1st class scout Girl Scouts Am., 1976, leader, asst. leader, 1976-79, 84-87; vol. Open Hand, San Francisco, 1991-92, San Francisco AIDS Found., various women's groups, 1989—. Mem. Am. Compensation Assn., Bay Area Compensation Assn. Democrat. Jewish. Avocations: music, movies, theatre. Office: Bank of Am 185 Berry St Fl 3 San Francisco CA 94107-1729

BRAASCH, HELEN, biologist; b. Leipzig, Saxony, Germany, Aug. 10, 1936; d. Arthur and Hildegard (Oehme) Stephan; m. Dietrich Braasch, Oct. 30, 1959; children: Rainulf, Heide. Diploma in biology, U. Leipzig, Germany, 1959, PhD, 1966. Scientist Neubrandenburg, Leipzig, 1959, Orgn. for Distbn. of Scientific Knowledge, 1960-61; aspirant Inst. for Tropical and Subtropic Agrl. U. Leipzig, Germany, 1962-66; scientist Ctrl. Plant Protection Svc., Quarantine Lab., Potsdam, Germany, 1967-71; leader Ctrl. Quarantine Lab. of GDR in Ctrl. Plant Protection Svc., Potsdam, 1971-90; scientist/nematologist Fed. Biol. Rsch. Ctr. for Agrl. and Foresty, Kleinmachnow, Germany, 1991—; expert EPPO, 1993—, EU-Commn., Brussels, 1995—, EU Mission to Portugal, Lisbon, 1999. Author: Aus der Wildnis entführt, 1972, Methodische Untersuchungen Attr. Repellents, 1969; contbr. articles to profl. jours. Recipient Lessing medal Govt., 1954. Mem. European Soc. of Nematologists, Deutsche Phytomedizinisch Gesellschaft, Russian Soc. of Nematologists. Avocations: travelling, writing, reading, nematology. Home: Kantstr 5, 14471 Potsdam Germany Office: Fed Biol Rsc Ctr Agr/Forest, Stahnsdorfer Damm 81, 14532 Kleinmachnow Germany

BRAATHEN, LASSE ROGER, dermatologist, educator; b. Oslo, Sept. 14, 1942; s. Erling and Gudrun (Eriksen) B.; m. Kirsten Moe (div. 1991); children: Thomas Alexander, Christer Andreas; m. Marianne König, Mar. 19, 1992. MD, U. Freiburg, 1969; PhD, U. Oslo, 1980, MS in Health Adminstrn., 1988. Physician various orgns., Norway, 1969-75; various positions Nat. Hosp., Dept. Dermatology, Oslo, 1975-80, assoc. prof., 1980-85, prof., 1985-89; prof. U. Berne (Switzerland) Dermatology Clinic, 1989—; dep. chmn. rsch. ethics com., U. Oslo, 1989-90; bd. dirs. Inselspital U. Hosp., Berne; pres. Exec. Com. Interallied Confedn. Med. Res. Officers of NATO, 1998—, sec. gen., 1993-96, com. mem. 1983—. Contbr. articles to profl. jours. Lt. col. Norwegian Army Res. Recipient Gold medal French Ministry of Def., 1996. Mem. The Physicians Collegium (pres. 1990-97), The Norwegian Dermatol. Soc. (pres. 1982-86), Polish Dermatol. Soc. (hon.), Assn. Mil. Surgeons of U.S. (hon.), Finnish Dermatol. Soc. (hon.). Avocations: outdoor sports, skiing. Office: Inselspital U Hosp, Dermatol Clinic, CH-3010 Bern Switzerland

BRABECK-LETMATHE, PETER, food products company executive; b. Villach, Austria, Nov. 13, 1944. Degree in Econs., U. World Trade, Vienna. New products specialist Nestlé S.A., Findus, Austria, 1968-70; nat. sales and mktg. dir., head of mktg. Nestlé S.A., Savory, Chile, 1970-75; frozen food and ice cream specialist Nestlé S.A., Vevey, Switzerland, 1975-76; divsn. mgr. mktg. and sales Nestlé S.A., Chiprodal, Chile, 1976-80; asst. to regional mgmt. for South Am. Nestlé S.A., 1980-81; mng. dir. Nestlé S.A., Ecuador, 1981-83, Venezuela, 1983-87; sr. v.p., head culinary products divsn. Nestlé S.A., Vevey, 1987-92, exec. v.p., head strategic bus. group, 1992-97, group CEO, 1997—. Office: Nestle SA, Ave Nestlé 55, 1800 Vevey Switzerland

BRABON, DAVID LAWRENCE, plastic reconstructive surgeon; b. Medellin, Antioquia, Colombia, Aug. 6, 1947; s. Harold Arthur and Margaret Balfour (Round) B.; m. Gloria Patricia Martinez, Sept. 1, 1990; children: Daniel, Harold. BA, Asbury Coll., Wilmore, Ky., 1969; MD, U. Louisville, 1973. Resident gen. surgery Wayne State U., Detroit, 1973-76; staff physician Good Samaritan Hosp., Lexington, Ky., 1976-80; fellow plastic surgery Straith Hosp., Southfield, 1980-82; staff physician Garrard Meml. Hosp., Lancaster, Ky., 1982-84; rural physician Hosp. Simon Bolivar, Bogotá, Colombia, 1984-85, chief clinics, 1985-96; chief plastic, reconstructive surgery and burn unit Hosp. Simon Bolivar, Bogotá, 1993-96; staff physician Rockcastle Hosp., Mt. Vernon, Ky., 1996—. Recipient Alumni A award Asbury Coll., Wilmore, Ky., 1994. Mem. Am. Coll. Emegency Physicians, Am. Sci. Affiliation, N.Y. Acad. Sci. Methodist. Avocations: history, philosophy, art, music.

BRABOURNE, LORD, film and television producer; b. Nov. 9, 1924; s. 5th Baron and Lady Doreen Geraldine Browne; m. Lady Patricia Edwina Victoria Mountbatten, 1946; seven children. Diploma, Eton, Oxford; DCL (hon.), U. Kent. Prodr.: Harry Black, 1958, Sink the Bismarck, 1959, HMS Defiant, 1961, Othello, 1965, The Mikado, 1966, Romeo and Juliet, Up the Junction, 1967, Dance of Death, 1968, Tales of Beatrix Potter, 1971, Murder on the orient Express, 1974, Death on the Nile, 1978, Stories from a Flying Trunk, 1979, The Mirror Crack-d, 1980, Evil Under the Sun, 1982, A Passage to India, 1984, Little Dorrit, 1987; TV series include: National Gallery, 1974, A Much-Maligned Monarch, 1976, Leontyne, 1988; dir. Thames TV, 1975-93, chmn., 1991-95, Ch. North Downs Cable, Ltd., 1990-

93; dir. Thorn EMI, 1981-86; fellow Brit. Film Inst., 1979, gov., 1979-94, Nat. Film and TV Sch., 1981-96. Mem. Brit. Screen Adv. Coun., 1985-97; trustee Brit. Acad. Film and TV Arts, 1988, Sci. Mus., 1983-94, Nat. Mus. of Photography Film and TV, 1983-94; pres. Kent Trust for Nature Conservation, 1958-98; mem. coun. Caldecott Cmty., 1969-93; chmn. bd. govs. North Knatchbull Sch., 1955-95, gov., 1947; bd. govs. Wye Coll., 1955-2000, chmn. govs., 1994-2000, fellow, 2000; bd. govs. Gordonstown Sch., 1964-94, United World Coll., 1965-96; pro-chancellor U. Kent, 1993-98, mem. coun., 1968-98. Fax: 01233 50224. E-mail: b@knatchbull.com. Office: New House, Mersham, Ashford Kent TN25 6NQ, England

BRACE, C. LORING, anthropologist, educator; b. Hanover, N.H., Dec. 19, 1930; s. Gerald Warner and Huldah (Laird) B.; m. Mary Louise Crozia, June 8, 1957; children: Charles L., Roger C., Hudson H. BA, Williams Coll., 1952; MA, Harvard U., 1958, PhD, 1959. Instr. U. Wis., Milw., 1960-61; asst. prof., then assoc. prof. U. Calif., Santa Barbara, 1961-67; assoc. prof. anthropology U. Mich., Ann Arbor, 1967-71, prof., 1971—, curator phys. anthropology Mus. Anthropology, 1967—. Author: Human Evolution, 1965, 2d edit., 1977, Stages of Human Evolution, 1967, 2d edit., 1995, Atlas of Human Evolution, 1971, 2d edit., 1979, Evolution in an Anthropological View, 2000. With U.S. Army, 1954-56. Fellow AAAS (chmn. sect. H); mem. Am. Ahthrop. Assn., Am. Assn. Phys. Anthropology, Dental Anthropology Assn. (pres. 1988-90), History of Sci. Soc. E-mail: clbrace@umich.edu. Home: 1020 Ferdon Rd Ann Arbor MI 48104-3631 Office: U Mich Mus Anthropology 1109 Geddes Ave Ann Arbor MI 48109-1079

BRACEWELL-MILNES, JOHN BARRY, economic consultant, writer; b. Wallington, U.K., Dec. 29, 1931; s. John Henry and Kathleen Mary (Hill) B-M.; m. Ann Jacqueline Cowley, June 25, 1977; children: Diane Christina, Timothy James Julian. MA, New Coll., Oxford, Eng., 1958; PhD, King's Coll., Cambridge, Eng., 1959. Mem. Iron and Steel Bd., London, 1960-63, Fedn. Brit. Industries, London, 1964-65; mem. Confederation Brit. Industry, London, 1965-68, econ. dir., 1968-73; prin. sci. collaborator Erasmus U., Rotterdam, The Netherlands, 1973-78; econ. adviser Inst. Dirs., London, 1973-96; mem. permanent sci. com. Internat. Fiscal Assn., 1970-93. Author: The Measurement of Fiscal Policy: An Analysis of Tax Systems in Terms of the Political Distinction Between 'Right' and 'Left', 1971, Is Capital Taxation Fair? The Tradition and Truth, 1974, Economic Integration in East and West, 1976, Tax Avoidance and Evasion: The Individual and Society, 1979, The Economics of International Tax Avoidance: Political Power versus Economic Law, 1980, The Taxation of Industry: Fiscal Barriers to the Creation of Wealth, 1982, Land and Heritage: The Public Interest in Personal Ownership, 1982, The Wealth of Giving: Every One in His Inheritance, 1989, (with Ranjit S. Teja) Earmarking in Britain: Theory and Practice in The Case for Earmarked Taxes: Government Spending and Public Choice, 1991, False Economy: The Losses from High Capital Gains Tax Rates, 1993, (with Robert Carnaghan) Testing the Market: Competitive Tendering for Government Services in Britain and Abroad, 1993, A Disorderly House: UK Excise Duties on Alcohol and Tobacco, 1993, Will to Succeed: Inheritance Without Taxation, 1994, A Pool of Resources: Creating Wealth Through the National Lottery, 1996, The Hidden Costs of Inheritance Taxation in Is Inheritance Legitimate?, 1997. Lt. Queen's Own Royal West Kent Regiment, Malaya, 1950-51. Fellow Inst. Statisticians, Soc. Bus. Economists; mem. Reform Club, Inst. Dirs., Montpelerin Soc., Soc. Authors. Conservative. Mem. Ch. of Eng. Avocations: music, travel. Home and Office: 26 Lancaster Ct, SM7 1RR Banstead Surrey England

BRACEY, EARNEST NORTON, political science educator; b. Jackson, Miss., June 8, 1953; s. Willard and Odessa Manola (Ford) B.; m. Atsuko Konuma, Apr. 2, 1995; children: Dominique, Princess, Omar. MPA, Golden Gate U., 1979; MA, Cath. U., Washington, 1983; D of Pub. Adminstrn., George Mason U., 1993; PhD in Edn., Capella U., 1999. Commd. 2d lt. U.S. Army, 1975, advanced through grades to lt. col., 1992; ret., 1995; prof. polit. sci. C.C. of So. Nev., Las Vegas, 1996—; adj. prof. Ctrl. Tex. Coll., Camp Zama, Japan, 1993-95; mem. Nev. faculty alliance C.C. of So. Nev., Las Vegas, 1996—. Author: Choson, 1994, Prophetic Insight, 1999. Mem. NAACP, Am. Soc. of Mil. Comptrs., Assn. of the U.S. Army, Retired Officer Assn. Avocations: jazz trumpeter, marathon runner, writing, poetry, American historian.

BRACHMAN, MALCOLM K., oil company executive; b. Ft. Worth, Dec. 9, 1926; s. Solomon and Etta (Katzenstein) B.; m. Minda Fay Delugach, Sept. 4, 1951; children: Lynn, Malcolm K. Jr., Lisa. BA, Yale U., 1945; MA, Harvard U., 1947, PhD, 1949. CLU. Asst. prof. So. Meth. U., Dallas, 1949-50; assoc. physicist Argonne Nat. Lab., Chgo., 1950-53; rsch. staff Tex. Instruments, Inc., Dallas, 1953-54; v.p. Pioneer Am. Ins. Co., Ft. Worth, 1954-61, pres., 1961-73, chmn. bd., CEO, 1973-79; pres. N.W. Oil Co., Dallas, 1956—; chmn. adv. coun. Econ. Growth Ctr. Yale U. Capt. USAAF, 1950-57. Recipient Yale Presdl. medal, Hon. Alumnus award, Tex. Christian U., 1999. Fellow Am. Phys. Soc., Soc. Petroleum Engrs., Am. Math. Soc.; sr. mem. IEEE, Soc. Exploration Geophysics; mem. Dallas Petroleum Club, Century Assn. (N.Y.C.). Jewish. Avocation: bridge. Home: 3510 Turtle Creek Blvd Apt 16F Dallas TX 75219-5545 Office: NW Oil Co 3232 Mckinney Ave Ste 770 Dallas TX 75204-8588

BRACIALE, VIVIAN LAM, immunologist; b. N.Y.C., June 5, 1948; d. Wing Ching and Wai Ching (Li) Lam; m. Thomas J. Braciale Jr., Aug. 5, 1972 (div. Apr. 1996); children: Kara, Michael Stephen, Laura. AB, Cornell U., 1969; PhD, U. Pa., 1973. Postdoctoral fellow U. Pa., Phila., 1974-75; postdoctoral fellow Washington U. Med. Sch., St. Louis, 1975-76, rsch. instr. pathology, 1978-83, rsch. asst. prof. pathology, 1983-89, asst. prof. pathology, 1989-91; assoc. prof. microbiology Beirne Carter Ctr. Immunology Rsch. U. Va. Health Scis. Ctr., Charlottesville, 1991-98; assoc. prof. microbiology and immunology U. Tex. Med. Br., Galveston, 1998—; mem. clin. scis. study sect. NIH, 1985-89, reviwers res., 1989-93; vis. fellow Australian Nat. U., Canberra, 1976-78. Assoc. editor Jour. of Immunology, 1989-94, sect. editor, 1985-99; sect. editor Jour. Leukocyte Biology, 1997—; contbr. articles in immunology to profl. jours. N.Y. State Regent scholar; NIH Rsch. Svc. awardee. Mem. Am. Assn. Immunologists, Am. Soc. for Microbiology, Soc. for Leukocyk Biology. Office: U Tex Med Br Beirne Carter Ctr 301 University Blvd Galveston TX 77555-5302

BRACK, O. M., JR., English language educator; b. Houston, Nov. 30, 1938; s. O. M. and Olivia Mae (Rice) B.; m. Gay Wilson Stampler, Nov. 27, 1991; 1 child, Matthew Rice; stepchildren: Suzette Richardson, Christopher Luebkin. Student, U. Houston, 1956-57; B.A., Baylor U., 1960, M.A., 1961; Ph.D., U. Tex., Austin, 1965. Asst. prof. William Woods Coll., 1964-65; asst. prof. English lit. U. Iowa, Iowa City, 1965-68; assoc. prof. U. Iowa, 1968-73, dir. center textual studies, 1967-73; prof. English lit. Ariz. State U., Tempe, 1973—; chmn. 18th Century Short Title Catalogue Com., 1970-73; pres. Arete Publs., Ltd., 1976-81; Albert H. Smith Meml. lectr. bibliography Birmingham (Eng.) Bibliog. Soc., 1983 vis. fellow U. Oxford Wolfson Coll., 1986-87. Author: Bibliography and Textual Criticism, 1969, Samuel Johnson's Early Biographers, 1971, Hoole's Death of Johnson, 1972, Henry Fielding's Pasquin, 1973, A Catalogue of the Leigh Hunt Manuscripts, 1973, The Early Biographies of Samuel Johnson, 1974, American Humor, 1977, Twilight of Dawn, 1987, Writers, Books and Trade, 1994, Samuel Johnson in New Albion, 1997; textual editor: Works of Tobias Smollett, 1966—; gen. editor: Works of Tobias Smollett, 1973-86; editor: English Literature in Transition, 1981-82, mem. editl. com., 1982—; editor: Studies in Eighteenth Century Culture, 1981-86; mem. editl. com.: Yale edit. Works of Samuel Johnson, 1977—; editl. cons. The Literature of England, Scott, Foresman & Co., 1977-79, Works of David Hume, Princeton U. Press, 1990-91, Oxford U. Press, 1995—; asst. editor: Eighteenth-Century Bibliography, 1964-73, Books at Iowa, 1966-73; editor: Eighteenth Century: A Current Bibliography, 1983-90 ; mem. editl. com.: Age of Johnson, 1985—, Rocky Mountain Rev. of Lang. and Lit., 1980-98, Clarissa Project, 1987—; mem. adv. bd. 18th-Century Brit. Periodical Subject Index, 1996—, Soc. for Textual Scholarship, 1998; bd. dirs. 18th-Century Short-Title Catalogue, Inc., 1993—. Mem. Salvation Army Coun., South Mountain Corps, 1996—, chair, 1999—. Recipient Grad. Coll. Disting. Rsch. award, 1981-82, Rocky Mountains MLA Huntington Libr. award, 1986, Humanities Rsch. award, 1989-90, Faculty Achievement award Ariz. State U. Alumni Assn., 1991; Am. Philos. Soc. grantee, 1967, NEH grantee, 1993-95, 95—; Phi Kappa Phi Disting. scholar, 1975; Huntington Libr. fellow, 1978, 96, 97, Am. Coun. Learned Soc. fellow, 1979-80, fellow Newberry Libr., 1982, Andrew W. Mellon Fund fellow, Huntington Libr., 1994. Mem. Am. Soc. 18th Century Studies, South Central 18th Century Soc. (pres. 1982-83), Western Soc. for 18th Century Studies, 1991-93, Rocky Mountain MLA, Bibliog. Soc. Am., Bibliog. Soc. U. Va., Bibliog. Soc. (London), Printing Hist. Soc., Am. Printing History Assn., Samuel Johnson Soc. So. Calif. (bd. dirs. 1989—, pres. 1994-95). Roman Catholic. Clubs: Grolier, The Johnsonians. Office: Ariz State U Dept English Tempe AZ 85287-0302

BRACKENRIDGE, KAREN MICHELLE, college math educator; b. Berea, Ohio, Apr. 2, 1969; d. Paul Andrew and Betty Kramer; m. Keith William Brackenridge, July 27, 1996. BS in Edn., Math., Miami U., 1991, MS in Math., 1993. Licensed tchr. secondary math. Coll. math. instr. Miami U., Oxford, Ohio, 1993-98, Wright State U., Fairborn, Ohio, 1998—; adj. instr. Miami U., Hamilton, 1993-99; cons. Richard D. Irwin, Inc., Ill., 1995-97. Math. Assn. Am. Avocations: volleyball, broomball, golf, softball, hockey. E-mail: kbracken@math.wright.edu. Office: Wright State Univ Dept Math and Statistics Colonel Glenn Hwy Fairborn OH 45435

BRACKENRIDGE, N. LYNN, public relations and development specialist; b. Youngstown, Ohio, Sept. 9, 1957; d. John Bruce Brackenridge and Mary Ann Rossi; m. Harry Lee Carrico, July 1, 1994. BA, Lawrence U., 1978; MS, Georgetown U., 1980. Tchg. asst. Georgetown U., Washington, 1979-81, admissions officer, 1984-85, editor, writer devel., 1985-87, asst. dir. devel., 1987-89; dir. devel. Cath. Charitic. U.S.A., Washington, 1989-91, Johns Hopkins U. Bologna (Italy) Ctr., 1991-92; dir. devel. and pub. rels. Nat. Ctr. for State Cts., Williamsburg, Va., 1993-97; v.p. for devel. Gateway Homes Greater Richmond (Va.), Inc., 1998-99, exec. dir., 1999—. Vol. Richmond Ballet, 1993-95, Leukemia Soc. Am., Hampton, Va., 1996—. Georgetown U. fellow, 1979-81; recipient diplome d'etudes Inst. d'Etudes Francaises de Touraine, 1976. Mem. Nat. Soc. Fund Raising Execs. (cert. fund raising exec., chmn. program com., pres. 1997). Democrat. Avocations: flying small aircraft, running, reading, films, languages. Home: 9303 Cragmont Dr Richmond VA 23229-7610 Office: Gateway Homes Greater Richmond Inc PO Box 11303 Richmond VA 23230-1303

BRACKETT, COLQUITT PRATER, JR., judge, lawyer; b. Norfolk, Va., Feb. 24, 1946; s. Colquitt Prater Sr. and Antoinette Gladys (Cacace) B.; m. Pamela Susan Colwell, Oct. 11, 1969 (dec. Aug. 1978); 1 child, Susan Elizabeth; m. Frances Sybil Langford, Jan. 1, 1982 (div. Aug. 2000). BS, U. Ga., 1966, MA, 1968, JD, 1973, LLM, 1976. Bar: Ga. 1973, U.S. Dist. Ct. (so. dist.) Ga. 1974, U.S. Dist. Ct. (mid. dist.) Ga. 1977, U.S. Supreme Ct. 1980, Tenn. 1987. Assoc. Surrett & CoCroft, Augusta, Ga., 1972-74; ptnr. Surrett & Brackett, Augusta, 1974-76; faculty Sch. Law, U. Ga., Athens, 1977-82; mng. ptnr. Brackett, Prince & Neufeld, Athens, 1982-90; adminstrv. law judge Ga. Dept. Med. Assistance, Athens, 1990—; hearing officer Ga. State Bd. Edn., 1979-91; v.p. Mus. Dolls & Gifts, Inc., Pigeon Forge, Tenn., 1983—; pres. Bear Country Lodge and Conf. Ctr., Pigeon Forge, Tenn., 1996—, chmn. bd. Advenutres in Toy Land. Author: Court Administration, 1972; (musical play) Americanization of Mary Poppins, 1995. Pres. Athens Clarke Mental Health Assn., 1985; chmn. bd. dirs. N.E. Ga. Mental Health Assn., 1989-90; bd. dirs. Coalition for The Blue Ridge Pkwy., 1994—, Oconee Cultural Arts Found., 1995-97, Blue Ridge Pkwy. Assn., 1997—. Mem. ABA, Ga. State Bar Assn., Ga. Assn. Adminstrv. Law Judges (bd. dirs. 1990-91), Ga. Trial Lawyers Assn., Western Cir. Bar Assn., Internat. Platform Assn., S.E. Tourism Soc., Rotary Internat., Ea. Nat. Parks Assn., Sevier County Bar Assn., Soc. Am. Poets, Soc. Magna Carta Barons. Episcopalian. Avocations: reading, music, golf, cross-country skiing. Home: 636 Middle Creek Rd Ste 4 Sevierville TN 37862-5013 Office: 2884 Parkway Pigeon Forge TN 37863-3316

BRACKETT, EDWARD BOONE, III, orthopedic surgeon; b. Jan. 5, 1936; s. Edward Boone and Bessie Lee (Hudgins) B.; m. Jean Elliott, July 11, 1959; children: Bess E., Geoffrey, Elliott Mencken, Edward Boone IV, Anneke Gail; m. Andrea Inman, Jan. 30, 1992; children: Amelia, Louisa Jo. Student, Tex. Tech. Coll., 1957; MD, Baylor U., 1961; JD, Ill. Inst. Tech., 1993. Bar: Ill. 1993; diplomate Am. Bd. Orthopaedic Surgery, Am. Bd. Neurol. Orthopaedic Surgeons; cert. flight instr. single and multi-engine land, single engine sea and airline transport pilot, designated med. examiner FAA. Intern Cook County Hosp., Chgo., 1961-62; resident Northwestern U., Chgo., 1962-66; pvt. practice Oak Park, Ill., 1966—, Westgate Orthopaedics Ltd., Oak Park, 1969—; mem. staff Loyola U., Oak Park Hosp., Loretto Hosp., Hinsdale Hosp., Gottlieb Hosp., Westlake Hosp., Rush Med. Sch.; chmn. dept. orthopaedics West Suburban Hosp., pres. med. staff, 1982-84; clin. assoc. prof. orthopaedics Loyola U.; chmn. bd. Chgo. Loop Mediclinic, 1973-75; cons. orthopaedic surgery City Svc. Oil Co., 1970. Cons. orthopaedic editor: Jour. Indsl. Medicine, 1966-67; mem. editl. bd.: Jour. Clin. Orthopaedics. Guarantor Lyric Opera Chgo., 1971-84; guest condr. Chgo. Symphony Orch., 1979, gov. mem., 1992, Chgo. Chamber Orch., 1980; trustee Music of the Baroque; nat. patron Met. Opera Co., N.Y.C.; mem. humanities adv. coun. Triton Coll., 1983-84; charter mem. vis. com. Northwestern U. Sch. Music, 1982—; chmn. Friends of WFMT, Inc. Lt. comdr. USNR, 1967-69, Vietnam. Recipient Outstanding Tchr. award Dept. Orthopaedic Surgery, West Suburban Hosp., 1978, 79. Fellow ACS, Am. Acad. Orthopaedic Surgeons, Inst. of Medicine of Chgo., Am. Acad. Neurol. and Orthopaedic Surgeons, Am. Assn. for Hand Surgery, Internat. Coll. Surgeons; mem. AMA, Am. Trauma Soc. (founder), Royal Soc. Medicine, Ill. Orthopaedic Soc., Chgo. Orthopaedic Soc., Chgo. Med. Soc. (alt. councilor, chmn. ethical rels. com., mem. book rev. panel), Clin. Orthopaedic Soc. (chmn. membership com., libr. historian, 1994, 2d pres.-elect 1997, pres. 1999-2000), Internat. Platform Assn., Civil War Round Table, Friends Chgo. Symphony Orch. (governing mem.), Chgo. Chamber Orch. Assn. (dir., v.p.), Symphonia Musicale (dir.), Sigma Alpha Epsilon, Phi Eta Sigma, Phi Chi, Alpha Epsilon Delta, Phi Alpha Delta. Home: 25333 W Il Route 60 Grayslake IL 60030-9542 Office: 1125 Westgate St Oak Park IL 60301-1007

BRACKETT, PRILLA SMITH, artist, educator; b. New Orleans, Nov. 8, 1942; d. Wilson Fitch and Hannah Balch (Coffin) Smith; m. George Conrad Brackett, Sept. 28, 1968; children: Ethan Samuel, Matthew Aaron. BA in Psychology and Sociology, Sarah Lawrence Coll., 1964; MA in Sociology, U. Calif., Berkeley, 1967; MFA in Painting and Drawing, U. Nebr., 1981. Grad. tchg. asst. U. Nebr., Lincoln, 1979-81; adj. prof. Simmons Coll., Boston, 1989; instr. DeCordova Mus. Sch., Lincoln, 1992-93; adj. prof. U. Mass. Harbor Campus, Boston, 1993, Salem (Mass.) State Coll., 1993; instr. landscape workshops Arts Pro Tem, Hancock, N.H., 1993-95, 97, West Yellowstone, Mont., 1993-95; panel coord., moderator Nat. Women's Caucus for Art, San Francisco, 1989, 95, Boston, 1996; panelist Coll. Art Assn. Nat. Conf., Chgo., 1992; guest lectr. and spkr. in field. One-woman shows include Winfisky Gallery, Salem (Mass.) State Coll., 1989, Gallery 57, Cambridge, 1989, The Bunting Inst., Radcliffe Rsch. and Study Ctr., Cambridge, 1990, Soho 20 Invitational Space, N.Y.C., 1990, Wessell Libr., Tufts U., Medford, Mass., 1990, DeCordova Mus. and Sculpture Park, Lincoln, Mass., 1993, Gallery 57, Cambridge, Mass., 1994, UMF Gallery, Farmington, Maine, 1999, duPont Gallery, Washington and Lee U., Lexington, Va., 1999, Soc. for the Protection of N.H. Forests, Concord, 2000, Berman Mus. Art, Ursinus Coll., Collegeville, Pa., 2000, Watson Gallery, Wheaton Coll., Norton, Mass., 2000, Housatonic Mus. Art, Bridgeport, Conn., 2000, others; group exhbns. include Portland (Maine) Mus. Art, 1998, Creiger-Dane Gallery, Boston, 1998, Fitchburg (Mass.) Art Mus., 1998, St. Lawrence U., Canton, N.Y., 1998, U. Oreg., Eugene, 1998, Berkshire Art Mus., Pittsfield, Mass., 1996, others. Co-pres. Boston chpt. Amigos de las Americas, Boston, 1993-95. Recipient fellowship in painting Bunting Inst., Radcliffe Rsch. and Study Ctr., Cambridge, 1989-90, The Francine Frank fellow residency MillAy Colony of the Arts, Austerlitz, N.Y., 1994, residency at Ragdale Found., Lake Forest, Ill., 1997, 98, 2nd place cash award Lancaster Mus., 1997, Lois Neelie Gill award and residency Ucross Found., Clearmont, Wyo., 1998; Vision Fund grantee, Boston Found., 1998. Mem. Coll. Art Assn., Women's Caucus for Art (coord. for exhbns. nat. conf. 1986, co-chair Boston chpt. 1987-88). Avocations: vegetable and flower gardening, hiking, going to opera, theater, dance and chamber music concerts. Home: 171 Lake View Ave Cambridge MA 02138-2131 Office: 75 Richdale Ave Ste 11 Cambridge MA 02140-2608

BRACKETT, RONALD E., investment company executive, lawyer; b. Rockford, Ill., May 10, 1942; s. F. Earl Brackett and Anne (Christenberry) Townsend; m. Susan Catherine Stichnoth, May 31, 1975; 1 child, Charles William. BA, Trinity Coll., 1964; JD, U. Mich., 1967. Bar: N.Y. 1968. Assoc. Rogers & Wells, N.Y.C., 1968-74, ptnr., 1974-91, mng. ptnr., 1984-85, cons., 1992-94; founder, prin. Associated Growth Investors, L.P., Manhasset, N.Y., 1992—; bd. dirs. King Kullen Grocery Co., Inc., Westbury, N.Y., Heuer Time & Electronics Corp., Springfield, N.J. Mem. ABA, N.Y. State Bar Assn., Phi Beta Kappa. Office: Associated Growth Investors LP PO Box 1399 Manhasset NY 11030-6399

BRACKNER, JAMES WALTER, accounting educator, consultant; b. Selma, Ala., Aug. 6, 1934; s. James Oscar and Ruby Belle (Langston) B.; m. Gayle Linton, Sept. 11, 1959; children: James L., Betsy, Joseph L., David L., Susan, Daniel L., Nancy. BS in Acctg., Brigham Young U., 1961, MS in Acctg., 1962; PhD in Accountancy, U. Ala., 1984. CPA; cert. mgmt. acct., cert. in fin. mgmt.; cert. fraud examiner. Staff acct. Arthur Andersen, L.A., 1962-65; controller, asst. sec. Teledyne-WIW, L.A., 1965-68; CFO Phaostron Electronics, South Pasadena, Calif., 1968-69; instr., asst. prof. Brigham Young U., Provo, Utah, 1969-78; CFO Deseret Mgmt. Corp.-Farms Divsn., Salt Lake City, 1978-81; from asst. prof. to assoc. prof. Utah State U., Logan, 1981-93, prof., 1993-99, Inst. Mgmt. Accts. prof. in residence, 1999—, ALCOA prof. acctg.; cons., expert witness Richards Brandt Miller Nelson, Salt Lake City, 1988-91; cons. Latvian and Russian Fin. Ministries, 1993, Ministry of Labour and Social Welfare, Govt. of Thailand, 1998-99. Author: Management Accounting/Manufacturing Excellence, 1996; contbr. more than 40 articles to profl. jours., chpt. to book. Scout leader, merit badge counselor Boy Scouts Am., Logan, 1982—. With U.S. Army 1954-56. Mem. AICPA, Inst. Mgmt. Accts. (nat. v.p. 1996-97, bd. regents 1995-96, edn. com. 1994-95, ethics com. 1991-94, acad. rels. com. 1998, 99, bd. dirs. 1997—), Am. Acctg. Assn., Nat. Contract Mgmt. Assn., Utah Assn. CPAs (chpt. pres. 1995-96), Assn. Cert. Fraud Examiners. Republican. Mormon. Avocations: fishing, travel, genealogy. Home: 760 Stewart Hill Dr Logan UT 84321-5690 Office: Utah State Univ Sch Accountancy Logan UT 84322-0001

BRACONS I CLAPES, JOSEP, art history educator; b. Barcelona, Spain, July 19, 1957; s. Joan Maria Bracons and Josefina Clapès; m. Maria Rosa Font, Nov. 20, 1986; children: Gabriel, Marta. BA, U. Barcelona, 1981. Medieval art asst. tchr. U. Barcelona, 1981-85; art history tchr. Llotja Fine Arts and Design Sch., Barcelona, 1986-99; art history cons. UOC Barcelona, 1998—; museology tchr. ESCRBCC, Barcelona, 1999—; curator art exhbns.; freelance art critic. Author: The Keys to Gothic Art, 1990. V.p. Cercle Artistic de Sant Lluc, Barcelona, 1993—. Fellow ACCA, Catalan Assn. Art Critics; mem. AICA, Internat. Assn. Art Critics. E-mail: jbracons@campus.uoc.es. Home: Mandri 19, E 08022 Barcelona Spain Office: ESCRBCC, Aiguablava 109-113, E 08033 Barcelona Spain

BRADA, JAROSLAV, economist; b. Usti N Labem, Czechoslovakia, July 25, 1964; s. Jaroslav and Ruzena (Donalova) B. Econ. engr., Prague Sch. Econ., 1987; econometrics dipl., London Sch. Econs., 1992. Rsch. fellow Prague Sch. Econs., Czech Republic, 1987-91; lectr. Prague Sch. Econs., 1991—. Contbr. articles to profl. jours. Mem. Czech Econ. Assn., Czech Econometric Assn. Avocations: history, philosophy. Office: Econ U Prague, W Churchill Sq 4, 13067 Prague Czech Republic

BRADBURN, ROBERT EASTON, economics educator; b. Redondo Beach, Calif., Mar. 13, 1961; s. David Denison and Bertha Stout Bradburn; m. Susan Marie Cravello, Nov. 11, 1986; children: Forrest Easton, Laura Amy. BA in Econs., U. So. Calif., 1983; MDiv, Biola U., 1987. Ordained to ministry Bapt. Ch., 1988. Data control analyst Hughes Aircraft Co., Fullerton, Calif., 1983-86; ch. planter, field chmn. C. B. Internat., Taiwan, China, 1987-95; quality and adminstrv. mgr. Transcend Info. Inc., Orange, Calif., 1995-99; econs. instr. Sunny Hills H.S., Fullerton, 1999—; adj. faculty U. Phoenix, Diamond Bar, Calif., 1999—. Office: 1801 Warburton Way Fullerton CA 92833-2235

BRADBURY, JAMES HOWARD, chemistry educator, researcher; b. Bendigo, Australia, Sept. 7, 1927; s. Joseph Ayrton and Lucy Augusta B.; m. Ruth Marian McComb, Sept. 13, 1952; children: Joanne Ruth, Annette Lyn, Meredith Gaye. BSc, Melbourne (Australia) U., 1948, MSc, 1950, DSc, 1968; PhD, Birmingham (Eng.) U., 1953; DSc, Australian Nat. U., 1981. Overseas research study Birmingham U., Eng., 1951-53; postdoctoral fellow Harvard U., Cambridge, Mass., 1953-54; sr. research officer Commonwealth Scientific and Indsl. Research Orgn., Geelong, Australia, 1954-60; sr. lectr. Australian Nat. U., Canberra, 1961-65, reader in phys. chemistry, 1965-88, vis. fellow, 1989—; sr. fellowship European Molecular Biology Orgn., Oxford, Eng., 1972; vis. prof. Cornell U., Ithaca, N.Y., 1964-65; project leader Australian Centre for Internat. Agrl. Research, Canberra, 1983-88, 91—; aid assignment Australian Devel. Assistance Bur., Canberra, 1979, mem. com., 1985-88. Author: Chemistry and Nutrition of Tropical Root Crops, 1988; contbr. 200 articles to profl. jours.; editorial bd. Journal of Applied Polymer Science, N.Y.C., 1976-88; editor Bulletin of Magnetic Resonance, 1979-82. Mem. coun. Burgmann Coll., Australian Nat. U., Canberra, 1970-80; area organiser Australian Red Cross Soc., Canberra, 1977-99; coord. Asia Pacific Food Analysis Network, 1989-99; Lay Preacher of Uniting Ch. of Australia. Recipient Fulbright Travel award Australian-Am. Edn. Found., Canberra, 1965, David Syme Research prize Melbourne U., 1970. Fellow Royal Australian Chem. Inst. (pres. Canberra br. 1979-80; mem. nat. exec. coun., 1980-82; chmn. 7th nat. conv. 1982, chmn. nat. polymer divsn. 1973-74; recipient Rennie Meml. medal 1957, H.G. Smith Meml. medal 1975), Australian Fulbright Assn. (treas. 1990—); mem. Australian and New Zealand Assn. for Advancement of Sci. (chmn. Canberra sect. 1985-86). Mem. Uniting Ch. of Australia. Avocation: gardening. Home: 118 Vasey Crescent, Campbell 2612, Australia Office: Australian Nat U, Divsn Botany & Zoology, Canberra 0200, Australia

BRADBURY, SIR MALCOLM STANLEY, scriptwriter, educator, author; b. Sheffield, Yorks, Eng., Sept. 7, 1932; s. Arthur and Doris Ethel (Marshall) B.; m. Elizabeth Salt, 1959; 2 sons. Ed., Univ. Coll., Leicester, Eng., Queen Mary Coll.; MA, U. London; PhD, U. Manchester; DLitt (hon.), U. Leicester, 1987, Birmingham U., 1989, U. Hull, 1994, U. Nottingham, 1996. Staff tutor in lit. and drama dept. adult edn. U. Hull, 1959-61; lectr. in English, lang. and lit. U. Birmingham, 1961-65; lectr., later sr. lectr. and reader Sch. English and Am. Studies, U. East Anglia, Norwich, Norfolk, Eng., 1965-70; prof. Am. studies Sch. English and Am. Studies, U. East Anglia, Norwich, 1970-95, prof. emeritus, 1995—; vis. prof. U. Zurich, 1972, Washington U., St. Louis, 1982, U. Queensland, 1983; sr. rsch. fellow St. John's Coll., Oxford, 1994. Author: Eating People is Wrong (novel), 1959, Evelyn Waugh, 1962, E.M. Forster: A Collection of Critical Essays (editor), 1965, Stepping Westward (novel), 1965, What is a Novel?, 1969, A Passage to India: A Casebook, 1970, A Penguin Companion to Literature: Vol. III, American Literature (with E. Mottram), 1971, The Social Context of Modern English LIterature, 1972, Possibilities: Essays on the State of the Novel, 1973, (novel) The History Man, 1975 (Royal Soc. Lit. prize), Modernism (with J.W. MacFarlane), 1976, Who Do You Think You Are? (short stories), 1976, The Novel Today (editor), 1977, An Introduction to American Studies (editor) (with H. Temperley), 1981, The After Dinner Game (TV plays), 1982, Saul Bellow, 1982, All Dressed Up and Nowhere to Go, 1982, (novel) Rates of Exchange (Shortlisted, Booker prize), 1982, The Modern American Novel, 1983, Why Come to Slaka?, 1986, (novel) Cuts, 1987, Mensonge, 1987, Doctor Criminale, 1992, The Modern British Novel, 1993, (collected essays) No, Not Bloomsbury, 1987, Unsent Letters, 1988, The Modern World: Ten Great Writers, 1988, (with Richard Ruland) From Puritanism to Postmodernism: A History of American Literature, 1991, The Modern British Novel, 1993, Present Laughter: An Anthology of Modern Comic Fiction, 1994, Dangerous Pilgrimages Trans-Atlantic Mythologies and the Novel, 1995, Class Work, 1995, The Atlas of Literature, 1996, (stage play) Inside Trading, 1996, (novel) To the Hermitage, 2000, (TV and Film Adaptations) Alison Lurie, Imaginary Friends, Tom Sharpe, Porterhouse Blue (Internat. Emmy award 1987), Kingsley Amis, The Green Man, Stella Gibbons, Cold Comfort Farm, Mark Tavener, In The Red; (TV dramas) A Touch of Frost (4 episodes 1997-98), Dalziel and Pascoe (5 episodes), 1996-2000, Kavanagh QC (1 episode) 1998, Inspector Morse (1 episode), 1998; original TV drama series including Anything More Would Be Greedy, 1989, The Gravy Train (Monte Carlo award 1990), The Gravy Train Goes East, 1991. Decorated comdr. Order of the Brit. Empire, 1991, knight bachelor,

2000; hon. fellow Queen Mary Coll., London, 1984. Office: Curtis Brown Literary Agents, Haymarket House, Haymarket London W1, England

BRADDOCK, DAVID LAWRENCE, health science educator; b. Glendale, Calif., Mar. 10, 1945; s. Mark Perry and Christina Bain Braddock; m. Laura Stanlye Haffer, May 1, 1976; children: Gabriel, Autumn, Adam. BA, U. Tex., 1967, MA, 1970, PhD, 1973. Spl. asst. to dir. sec.'s com. on mental retardation HEW, Washington, 1972; prin. investigator Coun. for Exceptional Children, Reston, Va., 1973-77; cons. White House Conf. on the Handicapped, Washington, 1977-78; rsch. prof., program dir. Inst. Study Devel. Disabilities U. Ill., Chgo., 1979-88, prof. cmty. health scis. Sch. Pub. Health, 1985—, prof. human devel., head dept. Disability & Human Devel., 1988—, assoc. dean for rsch., 1997-98; cons. U.S. Dept. HHS, Washington, 1972—. Author: Federal Policy Toward Mental Retardation, 1987, Residential Services and Developmental Disabilities in U.S., 1992, The State of the States in Developmental Disabilities, 5th edit., 1997; contbr. numerous articles to profl. jours. Cons. Pres.'s Com. on Mental Retardation, Washington, 1973—, Joseph P. Kennedy Jr. Found.; active in promoting civil and human rights of people with mental retardation and other disabilities. Grantee U.S. Dept. Health and Human Svcs., U.S. Dept. Edn.; Nat. Inst. on Disability and Rehab. Rsch. fellow U.S. Dept. Edn., 1988-89; sr. univ. scholar U. Ill., 1998—. Fellow Am. Assn. on Mental Retardation (pres. 1993-94, editor books and monographs 1997—, Career Rsch. award 1998), Delta Omega; mem. AAAS, Assn. for Retarded Citizens of U.S. (mem. sci. adv. bd. 1987—, Disting. Rsch. awrd in Mental Retardation 1987), Am. Assn. Mental Retardation (disting. lectr. 1999, Career Rsch. award 1998). Office: U Ill Chgo Dept Disability & Human Dev 1640 W Roosevelt Rd Chicago IL 60608-1316

BRADDOCK, JOSEPH VINCENT, physicist; b. Hoboken, N.J., Dec. 10, 1929; s. Ralph and Rose (Rago) Braddock; m. Teresa Marquez, June 24, 1961 (dec. Nov. 1961); m. Bertha Soto, Jan. 30, 1965; children: J. Anthony, Robert T. BS in Physics, St. Peter's Coll., 1951; MS in Physics, Fordham U., 1952, PhD in Physics, 1958. Asst. prof. Iona Coll., New Rochelle, N.Y., 1958-60; co-founder, exec. BDM Internat., McLean, Va., 1960-93; trustee Potomac Found., McLean, 1988—; cons. Dept. Def., Washington, 1975—, Dept. Army Sci. Bd., Washington, 1977-83, 93—; adv. bd. Nat. Security Agy., Ft. Meade, Md., 1977-85. Trustee Inova Hosp. Found., McLean, 1996—, Aztec Found., Alexandria, Va., 1988—, Alexandria Symphony Orch., 1990—; bd. dirs. Shrine of Immaculate Conception, Washington, 1995—. Mem. IEEE, Am. Phys. Soc. Roman Catholic. Avocations: travel, architecture, history of science and technology. Home: 1101 Saint Stephens Rd Alexandria VA 22304-1728 Office: Potomac Found 1311 Dolley Madison Blvd Ste 2A Mc Lean VA 22101-3925

BRADEN, SARAH ERGLE, financial aid manager; b. Birmingham, Ala., Mar. 13, 1974; d. Tex Lee and Regina Warren; m. Kevin R. Braden, Aug. 17, 1996. AA, So. Union State C.C., 1994; BS, Birmingham-So. Coll., 1996. Asst. dir. fin. aid Aurora (Ill.) U., 1996-99; fin. aid mgr. Waubonsee C.C., Sugar Grove, Ill., 1999—. Methodist. E-mail: bamalovr@aol.com. Office: Waubonsee Cmty Coll Rte 47 at Harler Rd Sugar Grove IL 60554

BRADETICH, ROBERT WILLIAM, advertising executive; b. Milw., June 1, 1957; s. William Alban Bradetich and Audrey Ruth Hornaday. Student in advt., design, mktg., Milw. Area Tech. Coll., 1975-79. Travel agt. Your Main Tours, West Allis, Wis., 1979-80; advt. rep. Liturgical Publs., New Berlin, Wis., 1980-89; restaurateur 19th Hole Country Club, New Berlin, Wis., 1989-95; pres. Publ. Concepts, West Allis, Wis., 1995-99; parish svcs. Liturgical Publs. St. Louis, 99—; cons. Willies Sports & Spirits, Franklin, Wis., 1998-99, New World Newspaper, Chgo., 1997-99; dir. Promotion Products, Oconomowoc, Wis., 1999. Editor, author sales manual, 1996-99. Mem. Reform Party. Avocations: music, reading, art, boating, travel. Home and Office: Promotional Concepts N27w29960 Maple Ave Pewaukee WI 53072-4202

BRADFORD, BARBARA TAYLOR, writer, journalist, novelist; b. Leeds, Eng.; came to U.S., 1964; d. Winston and Freda (Walker) Taylor; m. Robert Bradford, Dec. 24, 1963. Student pvt. schs., Eng.; D of Letters (hon.), Leeds (Eng.) U., 1990, U. Bradford, West Yorkshire, Eng., 1995; D of Humane Letters (hon.), Teikyo Post U., Waterbury, Conn., 1996. Women's editor Yorkshire (Eng.) Evening Post, 1951-53, reporter, 1949-51; editor Woman's Own, 1953-54; columnist London Evening News, 1955-57; exec. editor London Am., 1959-62; editor Nat. Design Center Mag., 1965-69; syndicated columnist Newsday Spls., L.I., 1968-70; nat. syndicated columnist Chgo. Tribune-N.Y. (News Syndicate), N.Y.C., 1970-75, Los Angeles Times Syndicate, 1975-81. Author: Complete Encyclopedia of Homemaking Ideas, 1968, A Garland of Children's Verse, 1968, How to Be the Perfect Wife, 1969, Easy Steps to Successful Decorating, 1971, Decorating Ideas for Casual Living, 1977, How to Solve Your Decorating Problems, 1976, Making Space Grow, 1979, Luxury Designs for Apartment Living, 1981; (novels) A Woman of Substance, 1979, Voice of the Heart, 1983, Hold the Dream, 1985, screen adaptation, 1986, Act of Will, 1986, To Be the Best, 1988, The Women in His Life, 1990, Remember, 1991, Angel, 1993, Everything to Gain, 1994, Dangerous to Know, 1995, Love in Another Town, 1995, Her Own Rules, 1996, A Secret Affair, 1996, Power of a Woman, 1997, A Sudden Change of Heart, 1999, Where You Belong, 2000. Recipient Dorothy Dawe award Am. Furniture Mart, 1970, 71, Matrix award N.Y. Women in Comms., 1985, Spl. Jury prize for body of lit. Deauville Festival of Am.Film, 1994. Mem. Coun. Authors Guild, Nat. Soc. Interior Designers (Disting. Editl. award 1969, Nat. Press award 1971), Authors Guild Am. (mem. coun. 1989—), Am. Soc. Interior Designers. Office: Bradford Enterprises 450 Park Ave New York NY 10022-2605

BRADFORD, DAVID PAUL, legal assistant; b. Lynwood, Calif., Mar. 23, 1955; s. William H. and Barbara E. (O'Leary) Johnson. AA, Citrus Coll., Azusa, Calif., 1975; BA in Polit. Sci., UCLA, 1978; postgrad., Calif. State U., L.A., 1984-85, U. West L.A., 1990-91. Prin. clerk UCLA Brain Rsch. Inst., 1977-81; adminstrv. asst., supr. UCLA Hosp. and Clinics, 1977-81; dep. to atty. in residence matters office of registrar UCLA, 1981-85; office of clerk L.A. County Bd. Suprs., L.A., 1987-88; judicial asst., ct. clerk L.A. Superior Ct., L.A., 1988—; founder Bradford & Assocs., L.A., 1987—; rsch. dir. citizens Protection Alliance, Santa Monica, 1992—. Active L.A. County Domestic Violence Coun. Recipient Cert. of Appreciation, Domestic Violence Coun., 1990, commendation Los Angeles County Bd. Suprs., 1993, L.A. Police Dept. and Assn. Threat Assessment Profls. award, 1994. Mem. N.Y. Acad. Scis., Los Angeles County Superior Ct. Clks. Assn. (local 575 AFSCME pres. 1993, 94), N.Y. Acad. Polit. Scis. Office: Bradford and Assocs PO Box 26507 Los Angeles CA 90026-0507

BRADFORD, HENRY FRANCIS, neurochemistry educator; b. London, Mar. 9, 1938; s. Henry and Rose Ethel (Harper) B.; m. Helen Caplan, Mar. 28, 1964 (dec. Mar. 1999); children: Sonya Helen, Daniel Benjamin Alexander; m. Mary-Thérèse Nazareth, Sept. 4, 1999. MB BS, U. Coll. Hosp. Med. Sch., London, 1958; BS in Biochemistry with honors, U. Birmingham (England), 1961; PhD in Neurochemistry, U. London, 1964, DS in Neurochemistry, 1976. Lectr. biochemistry Imperial Coll., U. London, 1965-74, reader biochemistry, 1974-78, prof. neurochemistry, 1979—; mem. U.K. Med. Rsch. Coun., 1973-82. Author: Chemical Neurobiology, 1986; editor: Biochemistry and Neurology, 1976, Neurotransmitters Interaction and Compartmentation, 1981, Excitatory Amino Acids, 1986. Mem. U.K. Brains Rsch. Assn., U.K. Biochem. Soc. (hon. archivist 1988-95, hon. sec. 1973-81), Internat. Soc. Neurochemistry (coun. mem. 1988-91). Avocations: music, natural history, history of science. Office: Imperial Coll U London, Imperial Coll Rd, London SW7 2AZ, England

BRADFORD, JUDITH LYNNELL, journalist, artist; b. Denver, Jan. 27, 1946; d. Robert Benjamin and Frances Mildred (Wolfe) B.; m. Gary Paul Zimmerman, Jul. 5, 1985; 1 child, Katherine. BA, East Carolina Univ., 1972. Columnist Keynoter, Fla., 1996—; freelance, 1988—; editor Fgn. Broadcast Info. Svc., 1994-95; weekly arts columnist Solares Hill Newspaper, Key West, 1968-96; ptnr., sec. Guild Hall Gallery, 1987-98; adminstrv. asst., vol. coord. Durham Arts Coun., 1975-76; ind. tchr. painting at Images Art Camp, East Martello Mus., Key West, 1996-97; taught painting and drawing classes, 1991—; tchr. painting Audubon Ho. & Gardens, Key West, 2000—. Invented Lizard Licks, 1979; exhibits paintings at Gallery on Greene, Key West. Coord. Fantasy Fest Parade, 1995—; founded Pathfinders Bicycle Advocacy Group, 1992, Key West, coord. Street Arts Fair, Hemingway Days St Fair, 1994; bd. dirs. Waterfront Playhouse, Last Stand Environ. Group, Montessori Children's Sch., 1991-96. Named Mem. of Yr., Last Stand Environ. Group Key West Cultural Preservation Soc., 1995, Artist of Yr., 1985. Mem. AAUW, Am. Mensa. Home and Office: PO Box 1844 Key West FL 33041-1844

BRADFORD, LOUISE MATHILDE, social services administrator; b. Alexandria, La., Aug. 3, 1925; d. Henry Aaron and Ruby (Pearson) B. BS, La. Poly. Inst., 1945; cert. in social work, La. State U., 1949; MS, Columbia U., 1953; postgrad., Tulane U., 1962, 64, La. State U., 1967; cert., U. Pa., 1966. Diplomate NASW, Am. Bd. Clin. Social Work; cert. social worker Acad. Cert. Social Workers. With La. Dept. Pub. Welfare, Alexandria, 1945-78; welfare caseworker La. Dept. Pub. Welfare, Alexandria, La., 1950-53; children's caseworker La. Dept. Pub. Welfare, Alexandria, 1957-59, child welfare cons., 1959-73, social svcs. cons., 1973-78, state cons. day care, 1963-66; dir. social svcs. St. Mary's Tng. Sch., Alexandria, 1978-2000; adoption splst. Vols. of Am., 2000—; del. Nat. Day Care Conf., Washington, 1964; mem. early childhood edn. com. So. States Work Conf., Daytona Beach, Fla., 1968; mem. La. adv. com. 1970 White House Conf. on Children, also del.; mem. So. region planning com. Child Welfare League Am., 1970-73; mem. profl. adv. com. Cenla chpt. Parents Without Partners, 1970-95; adj. asst. prof. sociology La. Coll. Pineville, 1969-85; lectr. Kindergarten Workshop, 1970-72; mem. La. 4-C Steering Com.; social svcs. cons. La. Spl. Edn. Ctr., Alexandria, 1980-86; del. Internat. Conf. on Social Welfare, Nairobi, 1974, Jerusalem, 1978, Hong Kong, 1980, Brighton, 1982, Montreal, 1984. Bd. dirs. Cenla Cmty. Action Com., Alexandria, 1966-68; mem. kindergarten bd. Meth. Ch., 1967-87, ofcl. bd., 1974-75, 77-81, 83-85, 96-98. Recipient Social Worker of Yr. award Alexandria br. NASW La. Conf. Social Welfare, 1984, Hilda C. Simon award, 1987, George Freeman award, 1987, Meritorious Contbn. award La. Assn. Mental Retardation, 1999. Mem. NASW, Acad. Cert. Social Workers, La. Bd. Cert. Social Workers, So. La. Assn. Children Under Six, La. Conf. Social Welfare (George Freeman award 1987, Hilda C. Simon award 1987), Internat. Coun. on Social Welfare, Am. Pub. Welfare Assn. (S.W. region planning com. 1965), Am. Assn. on Mental Retardation (La. social work chair 1989-94, Meritorious Contbn. to field of mental retardation/devel. disabilities in the 20th century 1999), DAR, Ctrl. La. Pre-Sch. Assn. (dir. 1967-70), Alexandria Golf and Country Club, Lions. Home: 5807 Joyce St Alexandria LA 71302-2510 Office: PO Box 7768 Alexandria LA 71306-0768

BRADFORD, MARK ANDREW, civil engineer, educator; b. Sydney, Australia, Dec. 12, 1955; s. Kenneth Ernest and Maureen (Wallace) B.; m. Suzanne Levy, Feb. 12, 1994. BSc, U. Sydney, 1977, B in Engring., 1979, PhD, 1984; DSc, U. New South Wales, 1998. Chartered profl. engr. Engr. Wholohan Grill & Ptnrs., Australia, 1983; postdoctoral fellow U. Sydney, 1984, U. Warwick, England; from lectr. to prof. civil engring. U. New South Wales, 1998—; rsch. officer Standards Australia, 1983-85; cons. Unisearch Ltd., Australia, 1986—. Fellow Inst. Engrs. Australia; mem. ASCE, Inst. Structural Engrs. Office: U NSW, Sch Civil/Environ Engring, Sydney 2052, Australia

BRADFORD, SUSAN ANNE, broadcast journalist; b. Pasadena, Calif., Dec. 2, 1969; d. Wesley Gene and Nancy Cornelia (Dixon) B. Student, Coll. Cevenol, Le Chambon Sur Lignon, France, 1985, St. Andrews U., Scotland, 1989-90; BA in English, U. Calif., Irvine, 1992; MA in Internat. Rels., Essex U., Eng., 1996, postgrad. Editor-in-chief Gandalf's Gazette, Irvine, Calif., 1987-88; news editor New Univ., Irvine, Calif., 1987-88; intern Sta. CBS-TV News, L.A., 1989; host, exec. producer Witness the News TV show, Irvine, 1990-92; prodn. asst. PBS Red Car Film Project, L.A., 1992-93; intern in news writing Sta. KNX News, L.A., 1993; reporter City News Svc., L.A., 1994-95; founder/editor European Review, 1995-98; sr. rsch. fellow, polit. cons. Atlantic Coun. of the U.K., 1996-98; speechwriter UK Shadow Fgn. Sec. Michael Howard, 1998; prodn. asst. Fox-TV News, 2000—; pres. SAB Consulting & Svcs., 2000—; sr. councillor Atlantic Coun. of U.S., 1999—. Author poems; contbr. articles to profl. jours.; founding editor: European Rev., 1995-98. Bd. dirs. HWPC Scholarship Found., Hollywood, Calif., 1992-93; mem. NATO Univs. Adv. Com., 1996-99. Recipient Writing awards Palos Verdes Nat. Bank, 1987, AFL-CIO, 1987, 3d Pl. award Nat. Fedn. Press Women, 1992. Mem. Calif. Press Women (pub. rels. chair 1991-92), Hollywood Women's Press Club (bd. dirs. 1989-94), European Movement (com./London strategy group media coord.1995-98), Irvine Women's Crew (founder, pres.). Mem. United Ch. of Christ. Avocation: student of history, travel, nature, classical music. Home: 5850 Cameron Run Ter Apt 1112 Alexandria VA 22303-2728

BRADFORD, TUTT SLOAN, retired publisher; b. Apr. 30, 1917; s. Tutt S. and Zula (Bowen) B.; m. Elizabeth Hendley, June 30, 1941 (dec.); children: Nancy, Debbie. Student, Wofford Coll., 1934; LLD, Maryville Coll., 1987. Pub. Cleve. Daily Banner, 1948-51; asst. to pres. Gen. Newspapers, 1951; pub. Bristol (Va.) Herald Courier, 1951-55, Maryville (Tenn.) Alcoa Daily Times, 1955-85; bd. dir. humanities, Tenn., 1971-73; mem. devel. coun. U. Tenn., 1980-83; bd. dirs. Maryville Coll., 1974-79, 81-96, Knoxville Symphony, Knoxville Mus. of Art, Thompson Ctr. for Cancer Survival, Lakeshore Mental Hosp., Tenn. Tech. Found.; Tenn. Resource Valley, 1988-91, 92-95, East Tenn. Found.; pres. Blount Meml. Hosp. Found., Boy's Club Found., Blount Hearing and Speech Found., 1991, Blount County Libr. Found., 1999. Pres. Blount County Indsl. Devel. Bd., 1970-72. With 9th AF AUS, 1943-45, ETO. Recipient Disting. Svc. award Bristol Jr. C. of C., 1952, Maryville-Alcoa Jr. C. of C., 1958, 73, Sequoyah Literacy award Tenn. Hist. Com., 1995; named to East Tenn. Hall of Fame, Jr. Achievement, 1990; named Vol. Yr., U. Tenn., 1994, Outstanding Philanthropist Nat. Soc. Fund Raising Execs., 1991. Mem. So. Newspaper Pubs. Assn. (bd. dirs. 1968-70), Tenn. Press Assn. (pres. 1974), Knox Arts Coun. (award 1988), Blount County C. of C. (pres. 1960), Kiwanis (pres. Maryville 1967). Home: 1901 E Westwood Dr Maryville TN 37803-6359

BRADFORD, WESLEY LAMONT, environmental scientist, consultant; b. Morgantown, W.Va., May 9, 1944; s. Ralph Miller and Martha Ward (Ogilvie) B.; m. Pamela Lynn Jones, Mar. 17, 1968; children: Zachary Roberts, Emily Kuxhaus. BS in Chemistry, W.Va. U., 1966; MS in Chem. Oceanography, Oreg. State U., 1968; PhD in Earth and Planetary Scis., Johns Hopkins U., 1972. Cert. profl. hydrologist, Am. Inst. Hydrology. Summer student rschr. Westinghouse Corp., Pitts., 1962-66; rschr. Johns Hopkins U., Balt., 1968-72; postdoctoral fellow U.S. Geol. Survey, Menlo Pk., Calif., 1972-73; hydologist, water quality specialist U.S. Geol. Survey, Menlo Pk., 1975-80; sr. hydrologist, water quality U.S. Geol. Survey, Reston, Va., 1980-85; water quality engr. URS Rsch. Co., San Mateo, Calif., 1973-75; program mgr., dept. head Versar, Inc., Springfield, Va., 1985-90; mgr., environ. programs Los Alamos (N.Mex.) Tech. Assocs., 1990—; chief scientist product devel. MIDX Corp., Albuquerque, 1994—. Contbr. (with others) more than 50 rsch. papers to profl. jours., also 100 rsch. reports; patentee in field. Mem. Los Alamos Choral Soc., 1992—. Nominee N.Mex. Inventor of Yr. N.Mex. Entrepreneurs Assn., 1995. Mem. AAAS, Am. Chem. Soc., Nat. Ground Water Assn., Internat. Water Assn., Am. Water Works Assn., Phi Beta Kappa. Achievements include devel. of early versions of rapid discharge Ni-Cd batteries, flat-flexible cable, anodic stripping voltammetry; research and invention of M10X water treatment process. Avocations: singing, mountain hiking, skiing, travel, home repair. Home: 1015 Los Pueblos Los Alamos NM 87544-2657

BRADING, ALISON FRANCES, physiologist, educator; b. Bexhill-on-Sea, Sussex, Eng., Feb. 26, 1939; d. Norman Baldwin and Helen Margaret (Gatey) B. BSc in Zoology, Bristol (Eng.) U., 1962, PhD in Zoology, 1965; MA, Oxon U., 1968. Rsch. asst. U. Dept. Pharmacology, Oxford, Eng., 1965-71; dept. demonstrator U. Dept. Pharmacology, Oxford, 1971-72, univ. lectr., 1972—, prof., 1996—; fellow, tutor Lady margaret Hall, Oxford, 1968—; cons. Xeneca/U.S.A., Wilmington, Del., 1991-94, Wyeth Ayerst, Princeton, 1993-96, Glaxo-Wellcome, N.C., 1998—, Abbott Pharms., Chgo., 1998—. Editor: Smooth Muscle, 1981, Women Physiologists, 1994; editor Jour. Physiology,1978-84, Brit. Jour. Pharmacology, 1988-94, Nanyn Schmiedeberg's Archives Pharmacology, 1994—, Brit. Jour. Urology, 1994—; contbr. articles to profl. jours. Grantee Med. Rsch. Coun., Action Rsch., The Wellcome Inst. Office: Univ Dept Pharmacology, Mansfield Rd, Oxford OX1 3QT, England

BRADING, DAVID ANTHONY, education educator; b. Ilford, Essex, Eng., Aug. 26, 1936; s. Ernest Arthur and Amy Mary (Driscoll) B.; m. Celia W. Brading, Jan. 27, 1966; 1 child, Christopher. BA, U. Cambridge, 1960, MA, 1965, LittD, 1991; PhD, U. London, 1965. Asst. prof. U. Calif., Berkeley, 1965-71; assoc. prof. U. Yale, New Haven, 1971-73; univ. lectr. U. Cambridge, 1973-92, univ. reader, 1992-99; fellow Clare Hall, Cambridge, 1995—, prof. Mexican history, 1999—. Author: (books) Miners and Merchants in Bourbon Mexico, 1971 (Bolton prize 1973), Haciendas and Ranchos in the Mexican Bajio, 1979, The First America, 1991, Church and State in Bourbon Mexico, 1994. Fellow Brit. Acad. Roman Catholic. Avocations: music, walking. Office: History Faculty Bldg, West Rd, CB3 9EF Cambridge England

BRADLEY, BARBRA BAILEY, musician, educator, accompanist; b. Windsor, Ont., Can., Dec. 27, 1944; d. Charles David Bailey and Alice Mary Calow; m. Joseph Patrick Bradley, Sept. 19, 1981. BA in Honours Music Edn., U. Western Ont., London, Can., 1967; A of Music in Piano, West. Ont. Conservatory Music, London, 1967; MM in Piano, Ind. U., 1969. Freelance performer, adjudicator Ont., 1974-81; tchr. piano, performer Brigham Young U., Provo, Utah, 1973-74; accompanist concert tour Mu Phi Epsilon Found., various cities, 1974-76; tchr. piano, performer St. Clair divsn. Royal Hamilton Coll. Music, Windsor, Ont., 1975-79; tchr. piano, performer music dept. St. Clair Coll., Windsor, 1979-81; freelance performer Washington, 1981—; tchr. piano, performer Leidzen Sch. Music, Fairfax, Va., 1987-88, Nat. Cathedral Sch., Washington, 1988—. Composer: (music for children's theater) Cricket on the Hearth, 1989, Goldilocks and the Christmas Bears, 1991. Can. Coun. doctoral fellow for grad. study Ind. U., The Can. Coun., 1970. Mem. Am. Fedn. Musicians, Friday Morning Music Club (chamber music performer 1986—), Mu Phi Epsilon (internat. officer, alumni adviser 1996—, pres. Washington alumni chpt. 1990-94, dist. dir. Atlantic-2 dist. 1994-96, Sterling Staff Internat. Competition winner 1974). Mormon. Avocations: ballet, photography, long-distance walking, genealogy. E-mail: barbra bradley@cathedral.org. Office: Nat Cathedral Sch Mount St Albans Washington DC 20016

BRADLEY, BILL, former senator; b. Crystal City, Mo., July 28, 1943; s. Warren W. and Susan (Crowe) B.; m. Ernestine Schlant, Jan. 14, 1974; 1 dau., Theresa Anne. BA, Princeton U., 1965; MA, Oxford (Eng.) U., 1968. Player N.Y. Knickerbockers Profl. Basketball Team, 1967-77; U.S. senator from N.J., 1979-96, mem. fin., energy coms., spl. com. on aging; Disting. leadership scholar, chair U. Md., College Park; Payne Disting. prof. Inst. for Internat. Studies, Stanford U., 1997-98; campaigned for Dem. Presdl. Nomination, 1999-2000; bd. advisors acad. leadership U. Md., College Park; chair advt. couns. adv. com. on pub. issues; essayist CBS TV Weekend Evening News; sr. advisor, vice chair internat. coun. J.P. Morgan and Co., Inc.; vis. prof. pub. affairs Univ. of Notre Dame, 1998; bd. trustee Princeton U.; mem. Coun. Fgn. Rels. Author: Life on the Run, 1976, The Fair Tax, 1984, Time Present, Time Past, 1996, Values of the Game, 1998. Chmn. Nat. Civic League, Ams. Promise (co-chmn. task force on safe spaces, structured activities). Served with USAFR, 1967-78. Rhodes scholar, 1965-67; named three-time basketball All-Am.; recipient Sullivan award as the country's outstanding amateur athlete. Democrat. Achievements include being a mem. NBA championship team, 1970, 73, gold medal team Tokyo Olympics. Address: Bill Bradley for Pres Inc 395 Pleasant Valley Way West Orange NJ 07052-2998

BRADLEY, CHARLES MACARTHUR, architect; b. Chgo., Sept. 26, 1918; s. Harold Smith and Helen Francis (MacArthur) B.; m. Joan Marie Daane, July 27, 1946; children: Mary Barbara, Nancy Ann, Sally Joan, William Charles (dec.). BS in Architecture, U. Ill., 1940. With Holabird & Root, architects, Chgo., 1940-41, Giffels & Vallet, architects and engrs., Detroit, 1941-44; ptnr., corp. pres. Bradley & Bradley, architects and engrs., Rockford, Ill., 1947—; pres. Bradley Bldg. Corp., 1962—. Prin. works include North Sheboygan (Wis.) High Sch. and addition, 1960-68, J.F. Kennedy Middle Sch., Rockford, 1968, Singer Health Clinic, Rockford, 1964, Jacobs H.S., Algonquin, Ill., 1976, Atwood plant, Rockford, 1977, Admiral Home, Chgo., 1978, Bushnell (Ill.) Jr. H.S., 1980, Bloom H.S., 1983, Evenglow Lodge, 1984, East Aurora H.S. addition, 1992, Erie H.S., 1994; author papers on life cycling old schs., roofing procedures. Active Blackhawk coun. Boy Scouts Am. Served with C.E., U.S. Army, 1945-46. Decorated Bronze Star; recipient Meritorious Svc. award Ill. Assn. Sch. Bds., 1976. Mem. AIA (pres. No. Ill. chpt. 1962, treas. Ill. coun. 1973-74), Ill. Soc. Architects (pres. 1974), Edn. Facilities Planners Inst., Ill. Assn. Sch. Bd. Officers, Rotary, Union League, Univ. Club, Midday Club (Chgo.), Shriners, Moose. Republican. Congregationalist. Office: Bradley & Bradley Inc 924 N Main St Rockford IL 61103-7061 also: 4901 Gulf Shore Blvd N Naples FL 34103-2223

BRADLEY, CHARLES WILLIAM, podiatrist, educator; b. Fife, Tex., July 23, 1923; s. Tom and Mary Ada (Cheatham) B.; m. Marilyn A. Brown, Apr. 3, 1948 (dec. Mar. 1973); children: Steven, Gregory, Jeffrey, Elizabeth, Gerald. Student, Tex. Tech., 1940-42; D. Podiatric Medicine, Calif. Coll. Podiatric Medicine U. San Francisco, 1949, MPA, 1987, D.Sc. (hon.). Pvt. practice podiatry Beaumont, Tex., 1950-51, Brownwood, Tex., 1951-52, San Francisco, San Bruno, Calif., 1952—; assoc. clin. prof. Calif. Coll. Podiatric Medicine, 1992-98; chief of staff Calif. Podiatry Hosp., San Francisco; mem. surg. staff Sequoia Hosp., Redwood City, Calif.; mem. med. staff Peninsula Hosp., Burlingame, Calif.; chief podiatry staff St. Luke's Hosp., San Francisco; chmn. bd. Podiatry Ins. Co. Am.; cons. VA; assoc. prof. podiatric medicine Calif. Coll. Podiatric Medicine. Mem. San Francisco Symphony Found.; mem. adv. com. Health Policy Agenda for the Am. People, AMA; chmn. trustees Calif. Coll. Podiatric Medicine, Calif. Podiatry Coll., Calif. Podiatry Hosp.; mem. San Mateo Grand Jury, 1989. Served with USNR, 1942-45. Mem. Am. Podiatric Med. Assn. (trustee, pres. 1983-84), Calif. Podiatry Assn. (pres. No. div. 1964-66, state bd. dirs., pres. 1975-76, Podiatrist of Yr. award 1983), Nat. Coun. Edn. (vice-chmn.), Nat. Acads. Practice (chmn. podiatric med. sect. 1991-96, sec. 1996—), Am. Legion, San Bruno C. of C. (bd. dirs. 1978-91, v.p. 1992, bd. dir. grand jury assoc. 1990), Olympic Club, Commonwealth Club Calif., Elks, Lions. Home: 2965 Trousdale Dr Burlingame CA 94010-5708 Office: 560 Jenevein Ave San Bruno CA 94066-4408

BRADLEY, DONAL DONAT CONOR, physics educator, consultant; b. Windsor, Eng., Jan. 3, 1962; s. Daniel Joseph and Winefride Marie-Therese (O'Connor) B.; m. Beverley Diane Hirst, Apr. 15, 1989; children: Amelia Charlotte, Conor Eliot, Eliza Marie. BSc, Assoc. Royal Coll. Sci., Imperial Coll., London, 1983; PhD, Cambridge (Eng.) U., 1987. Mem. Inst. Physics, Chartered Physicist, Fellow Royal Soc. Arts. Postdoctoral asst. Cambridge U., 1987, Unilever rsch. fellow, Corpus Christi Coll., 1987-89; Toshiba rsch. fellow Toshiba Corp., Kawasaki, Japan, 1987-88; asst. lectr., Cavendish Lab. Cambridge U., 1989-93; reader in physics U. Sheffield, Eng., 1993-95, prof. physics, 1995-2000, warden Tapton Hall, 1994-99; prof. experimental solid state physics Imperial Coll., London, 2000—; Royal Soc. Amersham Internat. sr. rsch. fellow, 1996-97; cons. Dow Chem. Co., Midland, Mich., 1996—, Cambridge Display Tech. Ltd., Cambridge, 1995—, Sci. Generics, Cambridge, 1996, Avecia, Manchester 1998, 99; external rep. on rsch. com. Edgehill U. Coll., Ormskirk, Eng., 1995-99; dir. Ctr. Molecular Materials, U. Sheffield, 1995-2000; mem. functional materials Coll. Engring. and Phys. Scis. Rsch. Coun., 1995—; presenter 14 plenary and 110 invited lectures and seminars. Author 15 patents in field, 1988—; contbr. over 250 articles to sci. jours.; co-inventor conjugated polymer electroluminescence. Holder numerous rsch. grants Sci. and Engring. Rsch. Coun./Engring. and Phys. Scis. Rsch. Coun., Higher Edn. Funding Coun. Eng., Royal Soc., Nat. Econ. Devel. Office, Toshiba Corp., European Cmty., 1990—; recipient Silver medal Royal Soc. Arts, 1983, Daiwa Anglo-Japanese award for rsch. collaboration Daiwa Found., London, 1994, Leverhulme rsch. fellowship Leverhulme Trust, London, 1996, Nat. Econ. Devel. Office (Japan) Internat. Joint Rsch. Program, 1994—. Mem. Am. Inst. Physics, Optical Soc. Am., European Optical Soc., European Phys. Soc. Roman Catholic. Avocations: 20th century history, carpentry, watching rugby, air travel. Office: Blackett Laboratory Imperial Coll, Prince Consort Rd, London SW7 2B7, England

BRADLEY, EDWARD WILLIAM, sports foundation executive; b. Milltown, N.J., Aug. 12, 1927; s. William Ernest and Hilda (Schwendeman) B.; m. Eleanor A Massing, Apr. 12, 1952; children: Scott Richard, Gail Sharon Bradley Klewsaat, Lisa June Bradley LaMarca. BE, Panzer Coll.,

1950. Dir. athletics, supr. phys. edn. and health Milltown Pub. Schs., 1951-69; owner, pres. The Exec. Health Club, East Brunswick, N.J., 1965-84; apptd. by Gov. Florio chmn., CEO N.J. Fitness and Sports Found., Milltown, 1984—; writer Middlesex County Govt., North Brunswick, N.J., 1985—; dir. activities Playboy Club Resort Hotel at Great Gorge, 1972; founder first sch. bicycle safety edn. program curriculum State of N.J., 1996; apptd. exec. coun. Cancer Rsch. Inst. Am. Cancer Soc., 1998. Apptd. by Gov. Kean chmn. CEO Gov.'s Coun. on Phys. Fitness and Sports, 1983—; chmn. CEO Middlesex County Coun. on Phys. Fitness and Sports divsn. Pres.' Coun. on Phys. Fitness, 1992, N.J. Youth Fitness Coalition; chmn. N.J. Olympic XXIII Torch Relay Com., 1984; asst. torch relay U.S. Olympics XXVI, N.J. and Atlanta, 1996; dist. coord., cons. Nat. Assn. Disabled Athletes; founder, chmn. Gov.'s Blue Ribbon Panel on Fitness and Sports, N.J. Health Am. Fitness Leaders Award Program; mem. State of N.J. Blue Ribbon Com. for Baseball in N.J.; dir. Phys. Fitness and Sports for U.S. Job Corp., Edison, N.J.; state-county coord. Nat. Park Svc., N.J. Trails Relay, 1996; mem. Mission Possible task NEA-AAPERD; supt. recreation Borough of Milltown, 1951-64; active Pres.' Coun. on Phys. Fitness and Sports, 1964—; cons. Pres. Kennedy, Johnson, Carter, Nixon, Ford, Reagan, Bush; master cons., adv. Pres.' Coun. the White House, 1988; nat. dir., founder sch. Stay Way project Gen. Jones (Pentagon); meeting with Pres. Clinton (invitation by the White House) nat. project Stay Way, 1994; nat. dir. U.S. Army and NFL, 1993; Chief of Staff Colin Powell meeting at the White House; founder sch. bicycle safety edn. prog. curriculum, N.J., 1996, nat. dir. No-Shows for Charities Shows, 1996-97; VIP del. Pres.' Summit, White House, 1997; VIP del. Pres.' Summit, Washington, 1997; N.J. chmn. Nat. Network on Volunteerism, 1997; mem. Nat. Com. for George W. Bush Pres. Recipient U.S. Outstanding Phys. Leadership award Pres.' Coun. on Phys. Fitness and Sports by Pres. Kennedy and U.S. Jaycees, The White House, 1962, U.S. Healthy Am. Fitness Leaders award Pres.' Coun., U.S. Jaycees and Allstate, 1985, Svc. in Phys. Fitness and Sports award Montclair State Coll., 1988, Phys. Edn. award for Excellence Panzer Coll., Svc. Award Ea. Dist. AAHPERD, N.J. Award for People to Watch, 1984, Jerseyan of Week award Newark Star Ledger, 1988, Honor Fellow award N.J. Assn. Health, Phys. Edn. and Recreation, 1964, Young Man of Yr. award Milltown Jaycees, 1962, Sports Master award by Pres. Reagan, 1987, Svc. to the Cmty., State and Nation Award, Pres. Bush, 1992, Pres. Clinton, 1997, Pub. Svc. award State N.J. and Pres.' Summit, 1997, Daily Point of Light award The White House and Point of Light Found., 1999, Pres.'s Svc. award, The White House, 2000, Outstanding Alumni award Montclair State Coll., 2000, Outstanding Gov.'s award Vol. Svc., Trenton, N.J., 2000, Outstanding Gov.'s award Vol. Svc., Raleigh, N.C., 2000; honored guest Pres. Nixon, 1975, Pres. Reagan, 1987, Richard Nixon Libr., 1990, Pres. Reagan Libr., Pres. Bush-the White House, 1991, 92, State of N.J., Pres.' Historic Summit for 53 Yrs. Pub. Svc., Pres. Clinton, The White House, 1947-2000, Govs. N.J. Leadership award Gov. Whitman, 2000, Govs. Vol. award N.C. Govt. Hunt, 2000, Outstanding Alumni award Montclair State U., 2000; named Leader of N.J. State of N.J., 1998. Mem. VFW (N.C., N.J.), Outstanding Phys. Fitness Leadership Congress, U.S. Jaycees, Nat. Fitness Leadership Assn., Internat. Assn. Approved Basketball Officials, Am. Legion, N.J./N.C. Youth Fitness Coalition, Pres.' Club, Court Club, Amblers Walking Club. Avocations: bicycling, reading, sports, volksmarch programs. Fax: (828) 628-9398, 828 628-2656, 828 628-4328. E-mail: 1gilliam@buncombe.main.NC.us. Office: NC Fitness & Sports Foundation Lambeth Walk Complex Pinkerton Corner Fairview NC 28730 also: PO Box 2510 Wachovia Bank Complex Asheville NC 28802 also: PO Box 2145 Fairview NC 28730-2145 also: NJ Fitness & Sports Found 35 Pinkerton Cor Fairview NC 28730-7737 also: Nat Office Vols PO Box 1253 Asheville NC 28802-1253 also: NC Fitness & Sports No-Shows for Charity-Shows PO Box 2510 Asheville NC 28802-2510 also: NJ Found Office PO Box 311 Whiting NJ 08759-0311

BRADLEY, JAMES MICHAEL, novelist; b. Adelaide, Australia, May 15, 1967; s. Michael Charles and Denise Irene (Haren) B. BA with honors, U. Adelaide, 1990, LLB, 1991; grad. diploma in legal practice, U. South Australia, 1993; cert., Australian Film TV and Radio Sch., 1994. Solicitor Supreme Ct., South Australia, Supreme Ct. NSW. Author: Wrack, 1997 (fellow Australian Writers Lit. award 1998, Kathleen Mitchell Lit. award 1998), The Deep Field, 1999 (Age Fiction Book of Yr. 1999), (poetry) Paper Nautilus, 1994; editor: (anthology) Blur, 1996. Mem. Australian Soc. Authors. Address: 61 Union St, Paddington 2021, Australia

BRADLEY, JOHN, immunology educator, pathologist, physician; b. Bangor, North Wales, July 9, 1933; arrived in Australia, 1975; s. John and Doris (Whitehouse) B.; m. Brenda Mary Whitehouse, Apr. 27, 1961; children: Katherine A.L., Alexandra Lucy, David P.J. (dec.), Paul J.W. BS with honors, U. Birmingham, Eng., 1954, B of Surgery, B of Medicine, 1957, MD, 1967. Cert. med. specialist: internal medicine and pathology. Rsch. fellow dept. exptl. pathology U. Birmingham, 1964-67; USPHS internat. postdoctoral fellow Sch. Medicine U. Tex., Dallas, 1967-68; lectr., sr. lectr. dept. medicine U. Liverpool, Eng., 1969-73, dir. dept. immunology, 1973-75; prof., chmn. dept. immunology, allergy and arthritis Flinders U., Adelaide, Australia, 1975-99, dep. dean, 1979-81, 83-85; emeritus prof., 1999—; hon. prof. Clin. Immunology Centre Shanghai, 1991—; hon. prof. and advisor in immunology Ministry of Health, Viet Nam, 1998—; cons. internat. devel. program to Australian univs. Author: Clinical Immunology; contbr. 140 sci. papers to profl. publs. Capt. Royal Army Med. Corps, 1961-62. Fellow Royal Coll. Physicians (London), Royal Coll. Physicians (Edinburgh, Scotland), Royal Australasian Coll. Physicians, Royal Coll. Pathologists of Australasia (chief examiner immunology 1988—, chmn. immunology quality assurance program 1988—), Australasian Coll. Tropical Medicine. Home: 27 Denning St, Hawthorn SA 5062, Australia Office: Flinders U, Bedford Pk PO Box 2100, Adelaide 5001, Australia

BRADLEY, JOHN M(ILLER), JR., forestry executive; b. Birmingham, Ala., Mar. 20, 1925; s. John Miller and Frances Watkins (Davis) B.; m. Isabella Elmore, Feb. 14, 1953; children: John M. III (dec.), I. Jocelyn. Student, U. Ala., Tuscaloosa, 1941-42, 46-47; BS in Math., Samford U., 1948; BS in Forestry, U. Calif., Berkeley, 1949; MF, Yale U., 1950. Lic. real estate broker, Ala. Laborer, smoke chaser U.S. Forest Svc., 1941, 47; foreman, project supt. U.S. Park Svc., Yellowstone and Glacier Nat. Parks, 1947-49; founder, pres. So. Timber Mgmt. Svc., Birmingham, 1950-63; chmn., pres. Resource Mgmt. Svc., Birmingham, 1963-90, chmn., 1991—; mem. adv. com. on state and pvt. forestry Sec. Agr., Washington, 1972-76; U.S. del. 8th World Forestry Congress, Jakarta, Indonesia, 1975; mem. univ. coun. com. on forestry and environ. studies Yale U., 1985-89. Contbr. articles on forestry to profl. jours. Pres., dir. Search Found., Washington, 1971-99; bd. dirs. Red Mountain (Sci.) Mus. Soc., Birmingham, 1976-84, pres., 1976-78; bd. dirs. Birmingham Hist. Soc., 1975-84, pres., 1977-79; bd. dirs. Red Mountain Mus., Birmingham, 1976-84, chmn., 1978-83; past deacon Briarwood Presbyn. Ch., Birmingham; mem. adv. bd. Birmingham Area coun. Boy Scouts Am., 1992-98; dir. YMCA Camp Cosby, 1988-91. Elected to Wisdom Soc. Hall of Fame, 2000. Mem. Soc. Am. Foresters (chmn. nat. conv. 1986), Assn. Cons. Foresters (sr. v.p. 1972-74, pres. 1974-76, pres. Profl. Forestry Inst. Trust 1986-89, dir. 1986-92), Ala. Forestry Assn. (bd. dirs. 1985-88, named to Hall of Fame 1984), Ala. Com. So. Timber Study, Newcomen Soc. U.S., Birmingham Country Club, Inverness Country Club, The Club, Rotary, Tau Beta Pi. Home: 5006 Applecross Rd Birmingham AL 35242-3916 Office: Resource Mgmt Svc Inc 100 Corporate Ridge PO Box 380757 Birmingham AL 35238-0757

BRADLEY, JONATHAN, economics educator; b. London, July 9, 1951; s. John Anthony and Joan (Belfitt) B.; m. Anne Veronica Greasley, Dec. 27, 1975; children: Sarah, John. BA (hons.), U. Bristol, Eng., 1972. Rsch. grad. Exeter Coll., Oxford, Eng., 1973-76; investment mgr. Morgan Grenfell & Co., Ltd., London, 1976-80; dir. Tyndall Group PLC, London, 1980-86, Aetna Life Ins. Co. (U.K.) Ltd., London, 1986, Tyndall Holdings PLC, London, 1986-90; sr. lectr., dep. chmn. faculty of econs. U. of the West of Eng., Bristol, 1990—; chmn. Perpetual European Investment Trust PLC, London, 1989—; bd. dirs. Regent Pacific Corp. Fin. Ltd., London, 1991—, Pacific Arbitrage Co. Ltd., Cayman Islands, 1992—, Undervalued Assets Fund Ltd., Cayman Islands, 1992—. Author: Privatisation: Themes and Perspectives, 1996. Anglican-Catholic. Avocations: music, butterflies, writing verse. Office: Faculty Econs and Social Sci U West of Eng, Cold Harbour Ln, Bristol BS16 1QY, England

BRADLEY, LEON CHARLES, musician, educator, consultant; b. Battle Creek, Mich., Sept. 8, 1938; s. Leon Harvey and Sigrid Pearl (Anderson) B.; m. Mary Elizabeth, Dec. 23, 1968; children: Kyle Newman, Shannon Sigrid, Karl Norman, Charles Nathan. BA, Mich. State U., 1961; MM Brass Splst., 1967; postgrad., U. Okla., summer 1974, U. Wis., summer 1975. Band dir. Owosso-St. Paul, Mich., 1958-61, Hopkins (Mich.) Pub. Schs., 1961-62, Cedar Springs (Mich.) Pub. Schs., 1962-65; grad. asst. music theory-aural harmaony Mich. State U., East Lansing, 1965-67; asst. prof., asst. dir. bands Minot (N.D.) State Coll., 1967-69; assoc. prof. instrumental music, music edn., dir. bands. Coll. of the Ozarks, Point Lookout, Mo., 1969-93; dept. chmn., 1987-89, ret., 1993; clinician low brass instruments Selmer, Inc., 1979—; founder instrumental ensembles including Am. Concert Band, Xian Conservatory of Music, China, fall 1995; vis. prof. S.W. Bapt. U., fall 1998. Performed with Springfield (Mo.) Symphony Orch., 1969-72, 81-98, Springfield Regional Opera Orch., 1981-98, Branson Brass Quintet, 1982—, Coll. of the Ozarks, others; dir. Abou Ben Adhem Shrine Band, 1978-80; contbr. articles to profl. jours. Condr. Republic (Mo.) Cmty. Band, 1999. Mem. Coll. Band Dir.'s Nat. Assn. (nat. chmn. Sacred Wind Music commn.), Music Educators Nat. Conf., Internat. Assn. Jazz Educators (state treas. 1980—), Nat. Assn. Wind and Percussion Instrs. (new music reviewer, assn. jour. 1968-71), Mo. Music Edn. Assn., Mo. Bandmasters Assn., Am. Fedn. Musicians (local 150), Ducks Unltd. (mem. com. 1978-81, chmn. 1981), Masons (Scottish rite), Lions (pres. 1983-84), Phi Mu Alpha. Home: 119 South Dr Branson MO 65616-3708

BRADLEY, MARILYNNE GAIL, advertising executive, advertising educator; b. Rockford, Ill., Apr. 12, 1938; d. Sherwin S. and Lillian (Leopold) Gersten; m. Charles S. Bradley, 1959 (div. Feb., 1994); children: Suzanne, Scott. BFA, Washington U., 1960; MAT, Webster U., St. Louis, 1975; MFA, Syracuse U., 1981; postgrad., St. Louis Tchrs. Acad., 1990. With Essayons Studio, St. Louis, 1968-69; tchr. Webster Groves (Mo.) H.S., 1970-98; instr. Webster Univ., Webster Groves, 1973-82, 97-99, U. Mo., 1980—, St. Louis U., 1978-99, Washington U., St. Louis, 1984-87; sec. Mo. Art Edn., State of Mo., 1986-87; mem. Tchrs. Acad. 1990-92. Author, illustrator: Arpens and Acres, 1976, Packets on Parade, 1980; illustrator: St. Louis Silhouettes, 1977; editor: (videos) 12 Water Color Lessons, 1987, Techniques of American Watercolor, 1990, The Santa Fe Trail Series, 1993, Over Gauguin's Shoulder, 1994, Aboriginal Art Techniques, 1994, City of Century Homes, 1995, Australian Dreamings, 1996, Aboriginal Art - Past, Present and Future, 1996, Drawing and Painting Techniques, 1997, Line, Shape, Value, 1998, Molas, Snip and Sew: The Kuna Indians, Molas: Panamanian Traditions, 1999. Bd. govs. Webster Groves Hist. Soc., 1965-72, 94—; mem. St. Louis Philharm. Soc., 1956-72; commr. City of Webster Groves, 1995—. Named Tchr. of Yr., 1987. Mem. So. Watercolor Soc. (sec. 1978-80), St. Louis Woman Artists, St. Louis Artist Guild (sec. 1985-86, pres. 1989-92, Disting. Woman 1987, v.p. pres.'s coun. 1995—), Monday Club (chmn. 1979-83). Avocations: music, art, travel. Home and Office: Bradley & Assocs 817 S Gore Ave Saint Louis MO 63119-4023

BRADLEY, MICHAEL JOHN, Cayman Islands government consultant; b. June 11, 1933; s. Joseph and Catherine (Cleary) B.; m. Patricia Elizabeth Macauley, 1965; 1 child. LLB with honours, Queen's U., Belfast, No. Ireland. Solicitor No. Ireland, 1964; atty. Supreme Ct. Turks and Caicos Island 1980; barrister-at-law Ea. Caribbean Supreme Ct. 1982, created Queen's counsel Cayman Islands 1983. Solicitor, No. Ireland, 1964-67; state counsel, Malawi, 1967-69; vol. editor Halsbury's Laws, 1970; sr., later chief, parly draftsman, Botswana, 1970-72; UN legal adviser to the Govt. of Antigua, 1973-76; regional legal draftsman Govts. of East Caribbean Brit. Devel. Div., Fgn. and Commonwealth Office, U.K. Govt., 1976-82; atty. gen. Brit. V.I., 1977-78, Turks and Caicos Islands, 1980, Cayman Islands, 1982-87; gov. of Turks and Caicos Islands, 1987-93; law revision commr. for Cayman Islands Grand Cayman, 1994—. Appointed Companion of Most Disting. Order of St. Michael and St. George, 1990. Mem. Royal Commonwealth Soc., Royal Overseas League, Civil Svc. Club, Meridian Club. Avocations: reading, philately, travel, good wine. Office: Cayman Islands Govt Legal Dept, PO Box 907, Georgetown Grand Cayman, Cayman Islands

BRADLEY, NOLEN EUGENE, JR., personnel executive, educator; b. Memphis, Nov. 29, 1925; s. Nolen Eugene and Anice Pearl (Luther) B.; m. Eloise Mullins, Jan. 7, 1947; children: Sharon (Mrs. Edward W. Vanderpool), Diana (Mrs. Wiley M. Rutledge), Nolen Eugene III, David Lee. BS, Memphis State U., 1951, MA, 1952; EdD, U. Tenn., 1966. Instr. polit. sci. Memphis State U., 1951-52; tchr. English Messick High Sch., Memphis, 1952-56; asst. dean admissions Memphis State U., 1956-64; dir. State Agy. for Title I, Higher Edn. Act, 1965, Div. Continuing Edn., U. Tenn., 1966-70; dean instrn. Vol. State Community Coll., Gallatin, Tenn., 1970-78; tutor, ednl. cons., 1978-79; pers. asst. Hoeganaes Corp., Gallatin, 1979-80; pers. mgr. Hoeganaes Corp., 1980-82; dir. pers. Music Village U.S.A., Hendersonville, Tenn., 1984—. Contbr. articles to profl. jours. Deacon Bapt. ch., 1966—. With AUS, 1944-46, ETO. Mem. Am. Assn. Sch. Adminstrs., Tenn. Adult Edn. Assn., Tenn. Edn. Assn., Omicron Delta Kappa, Pi Delta Epsilon, Phi Delta Kappa, Phi Kappa Phi. Democrat. Lion. Avocations: writing, travel, movies, reading. Home: 907 Harris Dr Gallatin TN 37066-3462

BRADLEY, PATRICIA ELLEN, professional golfer; b. Arlington, Mass., Mar. 24, 1951; d. Richard Joseph and Kathleen Maureen (O'Brien) B. Assoc. in Phys. Edn, Miami-Dade North Jr. Coll., 1971; B.S., Fla. Internat. U., 1974. Mem. Sun-Star Japan-U.S. Team Matches, 1975-76, All-Am. Collegiate Team, 1971, U.S.A. Com., 1974, 76, Golf Mag.'s All Am. Team, 1976, 77-78, 79-81; qualified for Colgate Triple Crown Tournament, 1975, 76, 77, 78; staff mem. Dunlop Golf Co.; under contract with Nabisco. Winner N.H. Womens Amateur Championship, 1967, 69, Fla. Collegiate Championship, 1970, Mass. Womens Amateur Championship, 1972, New Eng. Amateur Championship, 1972, 73, Colgate Far East Tournament, 1975, Girl Talk Classic Tournament, 1976, Bankers Trust Classic Tournament, 1977, Lady Keystone Open, Hoosier Classic, Rail Charity Classic, 1978, 91, J.C. Penny Classic, 1978, 89, Balt. Classic, Peter Jackson Classic, 1980, U.S. Womens Open, 1981, Du Maurier Classic, 1985, LPGA Pro-Am, 1985, Rochester Invitational, 1985, Turquoise Classic, 1990, Centel Classic, 1991, Safeco Classic, 1991, MBS Classic, 1991, HEALTHSOUTH Inaugural, 1995; recipient Most Improved Player award Golf Digest, 1976; named Player of Yr., 1986, Mazda Series, 1986, Vare Trophy, 1986; named to Ladies Profl. Golf Hall of Fame, 1991; mem. U.S. Solheim Cup Team, 1990, 92, 96, named capt., 2000. Mem. Ladies Profl. Golf Assn. Roman Catholic. Achievements include playing exhbn. golf match with Pres. Ford, Vail, Colo., 1976; first woman golfer to win all four USGA Womens Open, LPGA Championship, Du Maurier Classic and Nabisco/Dinah Shore Tournaments; leading money winner PGA, 1986, 91.

BRADLEY, PATRICK JAMES, otolaryngologist; b. Thurles, Ireland, May 10, 1949; s. Gerard and Nan (O'Leary) B.; m. Sheena Josephine Kelly, May 19, 1973; children: Paula, Darragh, Cormac, Eoin, Caitriona. MB, BChir, U. Coll. Dublin, 1973, Diploma in Child Health, 1975. Cert. surgeon in diseases of the ear, nose and throat. Intern St. Vincents Hosp., Dublin, 1973-74; registrar, sr. house officer Royal Coll. Surgeons, Dublin, 1974-77; S.H.O. Royal Victoria Eye/Ear Hosp., Dublin, 1977; registrar Royal Liverpool Hosp., 1979-82; cons. surgeon U. Hosp., Nottingham, Eng., 1982—; faculty mem. Internat. Sisson's Head and Neck Oncology Workshop, 1989—, Second World Meeting Laryncol. Cancer, Sydney, 1994; vice chmn. ENT Adv. Group, Trent Regional Health Authority, 1990-96; clin. dir. dept. otolaryngology/audiology U. Hosp. Nottingham, 1991-96, clin. dir. audit and risk, 1996-2000. Contbr. chpts. to books and articles to profl. jours. Fellow Royal Coll. Surgeons Dublin (examiner), Royal Coll. Surgeons Edinburgh (examiner); mem. Otorhinolaryngological Rsch. Soc. (coun. 1993-96, pres.-elect 2001—), Royal Soc. Medicine (coun. sect. laryngology/rhinology 1990-2000, pres. sect. laryngology/rhinology 1998-99), Br. Assn. Otorhinology/Head and Neck Surgery (chmn. edn. & tng. com. 1999). Roman Catholic. Avocations: golf, skiing, travel, golfing, scuba. Fax: 0115-993-2008. Office: Nottingham Naffield Hosp, 748 Mansfield Rd Woodthorpe, Nuffield NG5 3F2, England

BRADLEY, PHILIP STEPHEN, management consultant; b. Blackburn, Lancashire, England, Aug. 22, 1949; s. Robert and Hilda (Whalley) B.; m. Anne Hill, May 21, 1993; children from previous marriage: Richard Guy, Alexander Robin. Articled clerk Waterworth Rudd & Hare, Blackburn, 1967-71; audit sr. Price Waterhouse, Manchester, 1971-75; consultancy ptnr. Price Waterhouse, Nairobi, Kenya, 1980-84, London, 1987-98; consultancy ptnr. Pricewaterhouse Coopers, London, 1998—. Fellow Inst. Chartered Accts. in England & Wales, Inst. Mgmt. Consultants, Inst. Logistics. Home: Castle Hill Stables, Pembury Rd, Tonbridge Kent TN11 0QG, England Office: Pricewaterhouse Coopers MCS, 1 Embankment Pl, London WC2N 6NN, England

BRADLEY, WILLIAM BRYAN, cable television regulator; b. Charleston, W.Va., Feb. 12, 1929; s. Floyd England and Florence Clara (O'Bryan) B.; m. Virginia Vanderhoof Logan, Oct. 27, 1951; children: Christopher, Thomas, Michael, John, Mary Clare (dec.), Mary Ellen, Ann. BA in Journalism cum laude, U. Notre Dame, 1950. Supr., indsl. engr. Martin Co., Denver, 1958-61, 62-65; cons. Reynolds, Ward & Carey, Denver, 1961-62; analyst Denver City Coun., 1965-69, staff dir., 1969-82; dir. Office of Telecommunications, Denver, 1982-94; sr. assoc. Media Mgmt. Svcs., Inc., 1994-99; co-founder, dir., vice-chmn. Greater Metro Cable Consortium, 1992; initiated joint city-industry cable TV Tech. Stds., 1987, adopted by FCC, 1992. Participant Japanese-Am. conf. on Globalization and Cable TV, Suwa, Japan, 1991. Co-founder Nat. Assn. Telecomm. Officers and Advisors, Washington, 1980, bd. dirs., 1983-88, pres., 1985-87; chmn. telecomm. subcom. Colo. Mcpl. League, Denver, 1985-86; bd. dirs. Denver Cmty. TV, 1996-98. Line Officer USN, 1950-53. Roman Catholic. Avocations: chess, books.

BRADSHAW, ALEXANDER MARIAN, chemical physicist; b. Bushey, Eng.; m. Cornelia Bradshaw. BSc, Univ. London, 1965, PhD, 1968; Dr habil, Univ. Munich, 1973. Scientific dir. Bessy Storage Ring, 1981-85, 88-89; dept. head. Fritz Haber Inst. der Max-Planck-Gesellschaft, Germany, 1980-99; sci. dir. Max-Planck Inst. für Plasmaphysik, Garching, 1999—; adj. prof. chem. Free Univ., 1981—, hon. prof. physics Tech. Univ. Berlin, 1997—. Contbr. over 350 articles to sci. jours. Recipient Max Planck Rsch. prize, 1994. Mem. German Phys. Soc. (pres. 1998-2000). E-mail: amb@ipp.mpg.de. Home: Hirtbacher Weg 18a, 12249 Berlin Germany Office: Max-Planck Inst Plasmaphysik, 85748 Garching bei Munich Germany

BRADSHAW, ANTHONY DAVID, plant ecologist, biology educator; b. Richmond, Surrey, Eng., Jan. 17, 1926; s. Harold Chalton and Mary Lupton (Taylor) B.; m. Betty Margaret Alliston, Sept. 3, 1955; children: Jane, Penelope, Sarah. BA, MA, U. Cambridge, Eng., 1944; PhD, U. Wales, 1959. Lectr. U. Wales, Bangor, 1950-64, reader, 1964-68; prof. U. Liverpool, Eng., 1968-88, emeritus prof., 1988—; mem. Natural Environ. Rsch. Coun., London, 1969-74, Nature Conservancy Coun., London, 1968-73; v.p. Sports Turf Rsch. Inst., Bingley, Eng., 1982—. Author: (with M.J. Chadwick) Restoration of Land, 1980, 5 other books on land reclamation, 1980-90, (with B. Hunt and T. Walmsley) Trees in the Urban Landscape, 1995; contbr. over 250 sci. articles to profl. jours. Chmn., pres. Merseyside Environ. Trust, Liverpool, 1984—. Fellow Linnean Soc., Royal Soc. (hon.), Indian Nat. Acad. Sci. (hon.), Brit. Ecol. Soc. (hon., pres. 1982-84), Bot. Soc. Am. (hon.); mem. Inst. Ecology and Environ. Mgmt. (prs. 1991—). Liberal Democrat. Avocations: sailing, gardening, walking. Home: 58 Knowsley Rd, Liverpool L19 0PG, England Office: U Liverpool, U Liverpool, Sch Biol Scis, Liverpool L69 3BX, England

BRADSHAW, BRIAN ALLEN, lawyer; b. St. Louis, Nov. 13, 1968; s. Mickey Joe Bradshaw and Doris Ann Yohe; m. Cherish Ann Reyes, Feb. 20, 1999; 1 child, Alexandra Makena Reyes Bradshaw. AB, Washington U., 1991; JD, MBA, U. Houston, 1995. Atty. Vinson & Elkins, LLP, Dallas, 1995-97, Skadden, Arps, Slate, Meagher & Flom, LLP, Houston, 1997—. Editor Houston Law Rev., 1992-95. Mem. ABA, Tex. Bar Assn., Houston Bar Assn., U. Houston Alumni (com. mem. 1999—), Washington U. Alumni Club. Avocations: travel, golf, languages. E-mail: bbradshaw@skadden.com. Home: 3510 Pickering Ln Pearland TX 77584-7056 Office: Skadden Arps Slate Meagher LLP 1600 Smith St Ste 4460 Houston TX 77002-7367

BRADSHAW, HAYDON LEIGH, food products executive, consultant; b. London, Feb. 9, 1934; s. Haydon Dorman and Doreen Olive (Blay) B.; m. Gillian Fenwick Rook, Apr. 23, 1960; children: Marcus Haydon, Justin Henry, Francis Alexander. Tea buyer J. Lyons, London, 1954-56; tea broker Wilson Smithett & Co., London, 1956-59; tea buyer Nestle Co., London, 1960, coffee mfg. specialist, mgr. company tasting, 1960-92; coffe cons. Bath, Avon, Eng., 1992—; instr. econs. and philosophy, 1956—. Author: The International Coffee Trade, 1995. Mem. Ch. of England. Avocations: philosophy, economics, arts, plants. E-mail: HaydonB@aol.com. Home and Office: Dunkirk Mill Rosemary Ln, Freshford Bath BA3 6DD, England

BRADSHAW, JAMES EDWARD (JIM BRADSHAW), consultant; b. Waco, Tex., Aug. 18, 1940; s. Leo Herman Sr. and Eleanor Rose (Cogdell) B.; m. Ouida P. Massey; children: Robin Louise, Dorenda and Dorette (twins), James E. Jr., Cogdell O'Neal. BBA in Mktg. and Fin., Baylor U., 1963. Ptnr. Cogdell's Westview, Waco, 1960-64, Kennedy-David & Assocs., Waco, 1966-68; sales rep. Fed.-Mogul Corp., Detroit, 1964-66; pres. Cogdell Auto Supply Co., Inc., Ft. Worth, 1968-77; chmn. bd. dirs. Auto Supply Co., Inc., Ft. Worth, 1979-91; mayor pro tem City of Ft. Worth, 1976-79; cons. pvt. practice, Fort Worth, Tex.; bd. dirs. Sr. Transp. Network, Geriatric Ctr. of Excellence; adv. bd. Betty Ford Ctr., Tarrant County Coun. on Alcoholism and Drug Abuse. Former bd. dirs. Big Bros./Big Sisters Tarrant County, United Way, Jr. Achievement, Tex. Mcpl. League, Austin, 1976-78; mem. adv. bd. dirs. Betty Ford Ctr.; mem. cmty. devel. steering com. Nat. League Cities, 1978-79; chmn. Tarrant County March of Dimes, Ft. Worth, 1979, Future Pres. Orgn., Kansas City, Mo., 1974; councilman City of Ft. Worth, 1975-79, mayor pro tem 1976-79, mem. zoning commn., 1974-75; Republican. candidate 12th Congl. Dist., 1980. Named to Ten to Watch, D mag., 1977. Mem. Colonial Country Club, Masons. Methodist. Avocations: golf, reading, astronomy. Home: 4613 Briarhaven Rd Fort Worth TX 76109-4609 Office: PO Box 100338 Fort Worth TX 76185-0338

BRADSHAW, JEAN PAUL, II, lawyer; b. May 12, 1956; married; children: Andrew, Stephanie. BJ, JD, U. Mo., 1981. Bar: Mo. 1981, U.S. Dist. Ct. (we. dist.) Mo. 1982, U.S. Dist. Ct. (so. dist.) Ill. 1988, U.S. Ct. Appeals (8th cir.) 1986, U.S. Supreme Ct. 1987. Assoc. Neale, Newman, Bradshaw & Freeman, Springfield, Mo., 1981-87, ptnr., 1987-89; U.S. atty. we. dist. Mo. U.S. Dept. Justice, Kansas City, 1989-93; of counsel Lathrop & Gage, Kansas City, 1993-99, mem., 2000—; named Spl. Asst. Atty. Gen. State of Mo., 1985-89; mem., chmn. elect U.S. Atty. Gen.'s adv. com., office mgmt. and budget subcom., sentencing guidelines subcom. Chmn. Greene County Rep. cen. com., 1988-89; pres. Mo. Assn. Reps., 1986-87; bd. dirs. Greene County TARGET, 1984-89; mem. com. on resolutions, family and community issues and del. 1988 Rep. Nat. Conv.; mem. platform com. Mo. Reps., 1988; chmn. Greene County campaign McNary for Gov., 1984, co-chmn. congl. dist. Dole for Pres., 1988, regional chmn. Danforth for Senate, 1988, co-chmn. 7th congl. dist. Webster for Atty. Gen., 1988; county chmn. U. Mo.-Columbia Alumni Assn., 1985-87; bd. dirs. Springfield Profl. Baseball Assn., Inc.; past mem. Mo. Adv. Coun. for Comprehensive Psychiat. Svcs., former bd. dirs. Ozarks Coun. Boy Scouts Am.; pres. bd. trustees St. Paul's Episcopal Day Sch., 1997—. Named Outstanding Recent Grad. U. Mo.-Columbia Sch. Law, 1991. Mem. ABA, Mo. Bar Assn., Kansas City Met. Bar Assn., U. Mo.-Columbia Law Sch. Alumni Assn. (v.p. 1988-89, pres. 1990-91), Law Soc. U. Mo.-Columbia Law Sch. Office: 2345 Grand Blvd Ste 2800 Kansas City MO 64108-2612

BRADSHAW, JOHN ROBERT COVINGTON, III, internet service company executive; b. Carthage, N.Y., Aug. 4, 1942; s. John Covington and Selma Pauline Bradshaw; children: Sean C., Heather Hodgson. BS, U. Mo., 1968, MBS, 1970. Pres., CEO UniGlobe Fin. Inc., Clearwater, 1998—, UniGlobe Leasing., UniGlobe Multimedia; pres., owner ATM Nat. Svcs., Clearwater, Fla., 1989—. Mem. Clearwater C. of C. (chmn. resource com.), Rotary, SCORE. Avocations: boating, travel, model trains.

BRADSHAW, LINDA JEAN, English language educator; b. Beth Page, N.Y., Nov. 15, 1961; d. Howard Richard and Amy Elaine (Jennings) Corry and Jacque Dolores (Wheat) (stepmother) Corry; m. David Scott Waychoff, May 18, 1985 (div. Apr. 4, 1991); 1 child, Skyler Nicole Waychoff; m. Walter Claburn Bradshaw, Dec. 13, 1991; 1 child, Richard Claburn Bradshaw; 1 stepson, Benjamin Robert Bradshaw. BS in Elem. Edn., S.W. Tex. State U., 1984, MA in English, 1989. Cert. elem. tchr. and secondary tchr., Tex.

Learning lab. specialist S.W. Tex. State U., San Marcos, 1984-89; tchr. Judson Ind. Sch. Dist., San Antonio, 1990; project dir. The Psychol. Corp., San Antonio, 1990-91, lang. arts cons., writer, 1991-96; instr. English, lectr. II Sinclair C.C., Dayton, Ohio, 1991-96; dir. ednl. assessments Riverside Pub., Chgo., 1996-2000; spkr. in field, 1983—. Acting mng. editor: (jour.) Family Relations: Journal of Applied Family and Child Studies, 1993-94. Instr. New Braunfels (Tex.) Ind. Sch. Dist. Cmty. Edn., 1986-88. Recipient Future Tchr. scholarship, 1980. Mem. Nat. Coun. Tchrs. English, Coun. of Coll. Tchrs. of English, Internat. Reading Assn. Avocations: writing, reading, crafts. Office: 425 Spring Lake Dr Itasca IL 60143-2076

BRADSHAW, PHYLLIS BOWMAN, historian, historic site staff member; b. Cumberland, Ky., June 19, 1929; d. Lawrence David and Ann Rees Bowman; m. Glenn Lewis Bradshaw, June 30, 1949 (dec. Feb. 2000)); children: Charles Lewis, David Bowman. Student, Ctr. Coll., Danville, Ky., 1947-50, N.Y Sch. Speed Writing, 1967. Sec. to dir. and asst. dir. Shakertown, Pleasant Hill, Ky., 1967-68, asst. food dir., 1968-70, mus. dir. dept. interpretation, 1970-72; mus. hist. interpreter Old Fort Harrod State Pk., Harrodsburg, Ky., 1993-98. Mem. Harrodsburg Hist. Soc., Ky. Hist. Soc., Girl Scouts Am., Nat. Trust, Libr. Congress, Washington; tchr. Sunday sch. Harrodsburg Presbyn. Ch.; life mem. Women's Soc., Burgin Meth. Ch., bd. dirs., tchr./leader H.S. group; pres., sec. Burgin PTA; den mother cub scouts Boy Scouts Am.; life mem. Ky. PTA, Shakertown at Pleasant Hill; founding mem. Harlan (Ky.) Musettes; active Mercer County Blood Bank; assisted in creation of The Ky. Classic Sauces-Bluegrass Trade Assn. Mem. DAR (Jane McAfee chpt.), Lewis and Clark Assn., N.W. Territory Assn., Hite Family Assn., Ky. History Tchrs. Assn., Colonial Dames Ct. of Honor (Ky. chpt.), Ctr. Coll. Alumni Assn., Lions Club. Home: PO Box 304 350 Bradshaw Rd Burgin KY 40310

BRADSHAW, RICHARD JAMES, conductor; b. Rugby, england, Apr. 26, 1944; s. Alfred James and Florence Mary B.; m. Diana Hepburne-Scott, June 30, 1977; children: Jenny Alexandra, James Edward Merton. BA with honors, U. London, 1965. Dir. Music at Higham, 1967-77, New London Ensamble, 1972-77; internat. freelance condr. symphonies & operas, 1972—; chorus dir. Glyndebourne Festival Opera, 1975-77; resident condr. San Francisco Opera, 1977-89; chief condr., head music Can Opera Co., Toronto, 1989—, artistic & music dir., 1994—, gen. dir., 1998—; disting. vis. faculty music U. Toronto, 1999. Conducting fellow Royal Liverpool (England) Philharmonic Orch., 1972; assoc. fellow Massey Coll., U. Toronto, 1995—, sr. fellow 1998—. Office: Can Opera Co, 227 Front St E, Toronto, ON Canada M5A 1E8

BRADSHAW, TONY KERRY, chemistry educator; b. Liverpool, England, Feb. 12, 1946; s. Terence Cecil and Violet Francis (Dawe) B.; m. Christine Margaret Mercer, Nov. 27, 1969 (div. Nov. 1976); m. Julie Sharon Hadlow, Aug. 24, 1991; 1 child, Anna. BSc, U. Adelaide, 1969, BSc (hon.), 1970; PhD, Flinders U., 1973. MRC Rsch. fellow U. Warwick Dept. Biol. Scis., Coventry, Eng., 1974-78; sr. scientist Shell Rsch. Ltd., Sittingbourne, Kent, Eng., 1978-91; sr. lectr. in biol. chemistry and molecular biology Oxford (Eng.) Brookes U., 1991—. Contbr. articles to profl. jours. Sec. Elizabeth West br. Australian Labour Party, Adelaide, 1968. Mem. Genetical Soc., Soc. Gen. Microbiology, The Environ. Mutagen Soc. (meetings organizer 1983), Fabian Soc. Mem. Labour Party. Avocation: golf, writing. Office: Oxford Brookes U, Sch of Biol Scis, OX3 0BP Headington Oxford England

BRADSTOCK, ELEANORE MARGARET, English language educator, poet; b. May 18, 1942; d. Stanley Gordon and Una Mavis Capel (King) Fussell; m. Richard Keith Bradstock, Dec. 28, 1963 (seperated); children: Catherine Margaret, Michael Keith Gordon, Stephanie Elizabeth. BA with hons., Sydney U., Australia, 1962, Dip.Ed, 1963; MA with hons., Macquarie U., Sydney, 1973, PhD, 1985. High sch. tchr. New South Wales Edn. Dept., Australia, 1964-65; tutor Macquarie U., 1971-73; tutor New South Wales, Sydney, 1974-76, lectr. in English, 1977—. Co-author: Small Rebellions, 1984, Rattling the Orthodoxies: A Life of Ada Cambridge, 1991; author poem: The Voyage of St. Brendan, 1984 (Henry Lawson prize 1984, Wesley Michel Wright prize 1999); also articles numerous book revs., poems. Co-editor: Edge City On Two Different Plans, 1983, Words From The Same Heart, 1987, Ada Cambridge's Thirty Years in Australia, 1990, Beyond Blood, 1995, Midday Horizen, 1996, Ada Cambridge's Fidelis, 1997. Lit. Bd. grantee, 1983, 84. Mem. Australian Univs. Lang. and Lit. Assn., Soc. Women Writers, Australian Soc. Authors. Office: U New South Wales Sch English, PO Box 1, Sydney 2033, Australia

BRADSTREET, BERNARD FRANCIS, computer company executive; b. Framingham, Mass., Feb. 17, 1945; s. Franklin Hosea and Kathryn M. (Carragher) B.; m. Carol M. McKenna, Dec. 27, 1968; children—Joshua Franklin, Barret Francis, Kenley Anne. A.B. (NROTC scholar), Harvard U., 1967, M.B.A., 1974. Asst. v.p. Boston regional office 1st Nat. Bank Chgo., 1974-79; v.p., treas. Prime Computer Co., Prime Park, Natick, Mass., 1979-85; v.p. fin. and adminstrn., chief fin. officer Kurzweil Applied Intelligence, Waltham, Mass., 1985-88, pres.; chief exec. officer, 1988-94; pres., CEO Primus Systems, Inc., 1994-99; CEO BCB Cons., 1998—. Served with USMC, 1967-72. Mem. Fin. Execs. Inst. (bd. dirs.), Harvard Bus. Club Boston. Club: Harvard (Boston). Home: 51 Richards Rd Southborough MA 01772-1928

BRADY, BRUCE MORGAN, lawyer; b. Oakland, Calif., Oct. 9, 1950; s. Alfred Foster and Anne Felton (Hazlewood) B.; m. Barbara Jean Gehrett, June 8, 1974; children: Morgan G., Evan L.G. BA in Anthropology, Columbia Coll., 1972; JD, Boston U., 1975. Asst. dist. atty. King's County Dist. Atty., Bklyn., 1975-81, dep. chief criminal ct., 1980-81; assoc. Gabrini & Scher, P.C., N.Y.C., 1981-84, ptnr., 1984-90; sr. ptnr. Callan, Regenstreich, Koster & Brady, LLP., N.Y.C., 1990—. legal adv., exec. com. Children's Aid & Family Svcs., Paramus, N.J., 1990—; pres. Ridgewood (N.J.) Lacrosse Assn., 1993-99. Mem. N.Y. State Trial Lawyers Assn., N.Y.C. Med. Def. Bar Assn. (charter mem.). Avocations: golf, snow sports, theatre, personal computing. Office: Callan Regenstreich Koster & Brady LLP 1 Whitehall St New York NY 10004-2109

BRADY, CONOR PATRICK, newspaper editor; b. Dublin, Ireland, Apr. 24, 1949; s. Conor and Amy (MacCarthy) B.; m. Ann Byron, 1991; children: Neil, Conor. BA, Univ. Coll., Dublin, 1969, MA, 1975. Reporter The Irish Times, Dublin, 1969-73; editor Garda Rev., Dublin, 1974; reporter, presenter RTE, Dublin, 1974-75; editor The Sunday Tribune, Dublin, 1980-82; feature writer The Irish Times, Dublin, 1975-77, asst. editor, 1978-80, dep. editor, 1982-85, dir., 1985—, editor, 1986—; chmn. World Editors Forum, Paris, 1994-98. Author: Guardians of the Peace, 1975. Avocations: swimming, reading, history. Office: The Irish Times, 11/15 d'Olier St, Dublin 2, Ireland

BRADY, DONALD MARIAN, librarian; b. Cavan, Ulster, Ireland, May 3, 1954; s. Donald and Maura (Boland) B. BA, Nat. U. Ireland, Maynooth, 1974, diploma in librarianship, 1975. Asst. libr. Longford/Westmeath Joint Libr. Com., Ireland, 1975-81; exec. libr. Clare County (Ireland) Coun., 1981-82; county libr. Waterford County Coun., Lismore, Ireland, 1982—. Contbg. author: Waterford History and Society, 1992; editor: The Famine in Waterford, 1995, Hansard's History of Waterford, 1997, Comhairle Chontae Phortlairge 1899-1999, 1999. Chmn. West Waterford Heritage Week, 1991-92. Mem. Libr. Assn. Ireland (assoc.), County Librs. Group Impact (chmn. 1982-98). Roman Catholic. Avocations: skiing, local history. Home: 17 Seapark, Abbeyside, Dungarvan Co Water, Ireland Office: Waterford County Libr, Libr Hqrs, Lismore Co Water, Ireland

BRADY, JOAN, writer; b. San Francisco, Dec. 4, 1939; arrived in Eng., 1966; d. Robert Alexander and Mildred Edie Brady; m. Dexter Masters, Sept. 23, 1963 (dec. 1989); 1 child, Alexander. BS, Columbia U., 1965; postgrad., Open U., Milton Keynes, 1992—. Dancer San Francisco Ballet, 1955-58, N.Y.C. Ballet, 1960. Author: (novels) The Impostor, 1979, Theory of War, 1993 (Whitbread novel award 1993, Whitbread Book of Yr. award 1993), paperback edits. U.S. and U.K. 1994, The Netherlands 1995, Germany, France, hardcover edits. France, Germany, Spain, Sweden, Denmark, Norway, Korea, Poland and The Netherlands), Death Comes for Peter Pan, 1996, U.K., The Netherlands, France, The Emigre, 1999; (autobiography) The Unmaking of a Dancer, 1982, Prologue 1994, UK, The Netherlands; contbg. author Harpers, London Times, Telegraph, Independent. NEA grantee, 1986; recipient Prix du Meilleur Livre Etranger, 1995. Mem. Authors Guild, Soc. Authors, Phi Beta Kappa.

BRADY, LAWRENCE PETER, lawyer; b. Jersey City, July 26, 1940; s. Lawrence Peter and Evelyn (Mauro) B.; div; children: Deegan, Tara, Kerry, Melissa, James; m. Mary Helen Reynolds, Mar. 28, 1984. BS in Acctg., St. Peters Coll., 1961; JD, Seton Hall U., 1964; LLM, Bklyn. Law Sch., 1966. Bar: N.J. 1964, U.S. Dist. Ct. N.J. 1964, U.S. Supreme Ct. 1969, U.S. Ct. Appeals (3rd cir.) 1972, N.Y. 1991; cert. civil trial atty. State of N.J. 1982; cert. Nat. Bd. Trial Advocacy 1989. Asst. prosecutor Hudson County, Jersey City, 1964-70; prosecutor Town of Kearny, N.J., 1971-74; sr. ptnr. Doyle & Brady, Kearny, 1974—; dir. and founding incorporator Growth Bank, New Vernon, N.J. Mem. ATLA, Nat. Bd. Trial Advocacy, N.J. State Bar Assn., Hudson County Bar Assn., West Hudson Bar Assn. (sec. 1980, treas. 1981, v.p. 1982, pres. 1983), Am. Trial Lawyers N.J. (bd. govs.), Roxiticus Golf Club (Mendham, N.J.), Sandalfoot Country Club (Boca Raton, Fla.), Ocean Reef Club (Key Largo, Fla.), Ocean Reef Yacht Club. Roman Catholic. Avocations: golf, tennis, travel, fishing, boating. Office: Doyle & Brady 377 Kearny Ave Kearny NJ 07032-2600

BRADY, SHEILA ANN, manufacturing company executive; b. Connersville, Ind., Dec. 11, 1935; d. Francis Elmer and Mary Eleanor (Underwood) B. BS, Ball State U., 1958; postgrad., Rutgers U., 1959-60. Art tchr. various N.J. schs., 1959-68; head dept. art Wardlaw Pvt. Boys Sch., Edison, N.J., 1968-72; asst. to pres. F.E. Brady Products, Inc., Clearwater, Fla., 1972-73; pres., treas. Brady Products, Inc., Clearwater, 1973—, chmn. bd., 1976—; pres., treas. Brady Air Controls, Inc., Muncie, Ind., 1975-84, Mountain Meadow Farms, Lake Toxaway, N.C., 1993—. Co-author: Water Systems Handbook, 5th edit. Recipient Art award City of Dunnellon, N.J., 1972; named Ky. Col., 1989. Mem. Water Systems Coun., Nat. Water Well Assn., RV Women, Carefree Club (Ft. Myers, Fla.). Avocations: composing, art, raising exotic animals. Office: Brady Products Inc 2151 Logan St Clearwater FL 33765-1312

BRADY, STEPHEN R.P.K., physician; b. New London, Conn., Oct. 13, 1955; s. Richard Harris and Jeanne Margaret (Halpin) B.; m. Marsha Anne Erickson, June 18, 1978 (div. Jan. 1993); 1 child, Ericka Anuhea; m. Elizabeth Ada Rewick, Dec. 27, 1994. AB cum laude, Harvard U., 1977; MPH, U. Hawaii, 1978, postgrad., 1979; MD, U. Pa., 1982. Diplomate Am. Bd. Internal Medicine. Intern U. Hawaii, 1982-83, resident in internal medicine, 1983-85, clin. instr. Sch. Medicine, 1986-99, clin. asst. prof. Sch. Medicine, 1999—; co-chair dept. continuing med. edn. Sch. Medicine U. Hawaii, Honolulu, 1993—; physician Kaiser Clinics, Honolulu, 1985-86; physician, med. dir. Kokua Kalihi Valley, Honolulu, 1986-95; physician Waianae (Hawaii) Coast Health Svc., 1989-94; asst. med. dir., physician Am. Hawaii Cruises, Honolulu, 1989-95; physician Straub Clinic & Hosp., Honolulu, 1984—; founding chair Hawaii Consortium for Continuing Med. Edn. U. Hawaii Sch. of Medicine, 1993—. Host weekly Ask the Dr. program KHON-Fox 2 News, Hawaii, 1996—. Cubmaster Boy Scouts Am., Kailua, Hawaii, 1995-2000. Comdr. U.S. Merchant Marine, 1989—. Recipient Po'okela awards, 1991, 93, 95, 99, Guy Milnor award for cmty. svc., 1999; Cub Scouter award Aloha coun. Boy Scouts Am., 1999, Cubmaster award, 2000; rsch. grantee Kuakini Med. Rsch. Inst., Honolulu, 1971, Pacific Health Rsch. Inst., Honolulu, 1972-78, Children's Hosp., Phila., 1979; Paul Harris fellow, 1995; named Scot of Yr., State of Hawaii, 1999. Mem. AMA, ACP, APHA, Am. Soc. Internal Medicine, Am. Statis. Assn., Hawaii Soc. Internal Medicine, Hawaii Med. Assn. (chair continuing med. edn. com. 1987—), Soc. Epidemiologic Rsch., Rotary, Soroptimist (pres.), Aumoana Cmty. Assn., (v.p. 1996—), Kaneohe Yacht Club, Plaza Club, Delta Omega. Congregationalist. Avocations: singing, running, sailing, scuba diving, music. Home: 758 Kapahulu Ave PMB 309 Honolulu HI 96816-1196 Office: Straub Clinic & Hosp 888 S King St Honolulu HI 96813-3083

BRAEHLER, ELMAR, psychology and medical sociology educator; b. Fulda, Germany, Mar. 3, 1946; s. Franz and Karolina (Goldbach) B.; m. Christa Schwab, Aug. 1984; children: Boris, Jan. Dipl-Math, U. Giessen, Germany, 1970; DrRerBiolHum, U. Ulm, Germany, 1976; DrRerBiolHumHabil, U. Giessen, Germany, 1991. Head med. psychology and med. sociology U. Leipzig, Germany. Author: (with J.W. Scheer) Der Giessener Beschwerdebogen, 1983, (with Beckmann and Richter) Der Giessen-Test, 1991, with E. Wirth) Entsolidarisierung, 1995; editor: Body Experience, 1988. Mem. German Soc. for Med. Psychology (prs. 1996—), Polish Soc. for Psychosomatic medicine (hon.). Office: Dept Med Psych/Med Sociol, Liebigstrasse 21, D-04103 Leipzig Germany

BRAEKMAN, WILLY LOUIS, retired educator; b. Sint-Lievens-Houtem, Belgium, Oct. 4, 1931; s. Georges and Suzanne (De Schaepmeester) B.; m. Andrée Marie-Rose Devolder, Dec. 30, 1961; children: Martine, Luc. Doctor Germanic Philology, State U. of Ghent, 1967. Asst. lectr. State U., Ghent, 1963-69; univ. prof. Cath. U., Brussels, 1969-92, ret., 1992. Author: Middelnederlandse Geneeskundige Recepten, 1970, Medische en Technische Middelnederlandse Recepten, 1975, Hier Heb Ik Weer Wat Nieuws In D'Hand, 1990, Spel en Kwel in Vroeger Tyd, Verkenningen van Charivari, Exorcisme, Tovery, Spot en Spel in Vlaanderen, 1992, Middeleeuwse witte en Zwarte Magie in het Nederlands Taalgebied, 1997; chief editor Scripta; editor Zeldzame Volksboeken uit de Nederlanden; editl. bd. Volkskunde, others; contbr. articles to profl. jours. Recipient Provincial award Folklore Province of East Flanders, 1994, Award for Cultural History Royal Flemish Acad. for Lang. and Lit., 1969, 97, Leonard Willems award, 1981, Olbrechts award, 1996. Mem. Royal Belgian Commn. for Folklore, Koninklijke Belgische Commissie Voor Volkskunde, others.

BRAENDLIN, CHRISTOPHER, business development administrator; b. Fergus Falls, Minn.; s. Carlo and Marguerite Braendlin. BA, U. N.D., 1988, MA, 1991. V.p. Rapid City (S.D.) Devel., 1992-95; rep. Gov.'s Office Econ. Devel., Pierre, S.D., 1995-98, dir., 1998—. Pres. S.D. Young Reps., Pierre, 1994—. Presbyterian. Office: Govs Office Econ Devel 711 E Wells Ave Pierre SD 57501-3335

BRAESE, STEFAN, chemistry researcher, educator; b. Kiel, Germany, Nov. 30, 1967; s. Uwe Bruno and Heide Klara (Drenkelfort) B.; m. Katharina Voigt, Aug. 14, 1998. BS, U. Goettingen, Germany, 1991, MS, 1992, PhD, 1995. Post-doctoral fellow U. Uppsala, Sweden, 1995-96, Scripps Rsch. Inst., La Jolla, Calif., 1996-97; habilitand, lectr. Rheinisch-Westfaelische Technische Hochschule Aachen, Germany, 1997—. Author: (books) Metal-Catalyzed Cross-Coupling Reactions, 1998, Chemistry of the 21st Century, 1998. Lt. Pioneer Troops, Germany, 1986-88. Named pre-doctoral fellow Fonds der Chemischen Industrie, Goettingen, Germany, 1993-95, Liebig fellow, Aachen, Germany, 1997-99, post doctoral fellow Deutscher Akademischer Austauschdienst, La Jolla, Calif., 1996-98, Deutsche Forschungsgemeinschaft fellow, 1999—; recipient Richard-Zsigmondy prize U. Goettingen, Germany, 1995, ORCHEM prize Gesellschaft Deutscher Chemiker, 2000. Home: Peliserker Str 55, 52068 Aachen Germany Office: RWTH Aachen, Professor-Pirlet-Str 1, 52074 Aachen Germany

BRAEUTIGAM, RONALD RAY, economics educator; b. Tulsa, Apr. 30, 1947; s. Raymond Louis Braeutigam and Loys Ann (Johnson) Henneberger; m. Janette Gail Carlyon, July 27, 1975; children: Eric Zachary, Justin Michael, Julie Ann. BS, U. Tulsa, 1969; MSc, Stanford U., 1971, PhD, 1976. Petroleum engr. Standard Oil Ind., Tulsa, 1966-70; staff economist Office of Telecom. Policy, Exec. Office of Pres., Washington, 1972-73; from asst. to prof. econs. Northwestern U., Evanston, Ill., 1975—; dir. bus. instns. program, 1995—; Harvey Kapnick prof. Bus. Instns. dept. econs. Northwestern U., Evanston, Ill., 1990—, Charles Deering McCormick prof. tchg. excellence, 1997—; vis. prof. Calif. Inst. Tech., Pasadena, 1978-79. Co-author: The Regulation Game, 1978, Price Level Regulation for Diversified Public Utilities, 1989; assoc. editor Jour. Indsl. Econs., Cambridge, Mass., 1987-90; mem. editorial bd. MIT Press Series on Regulation, Cambridge, 1980—, Jour. Econ. Lit., 1987-91, Rev. Indsl. Orgn., 1991—. Coach Skokie (Ill.) Indians Little League, 1985-91, Evanston Youth Baseball Assn., 1991-96. Grantee, Dept. Transp., NSF, Ameritech, Sloan Found., Mellon Found., others; sr. rsch. fellow Internat. Inst. Mgmt., Berlin, 1982-83, 91. Mem. Am. Econ. Assn., Econometric Soc., Internat. Telecommunications Soc. (bd. dirs. 1990-97), European Econ. Assn., European Assn. for Rsch. in Indsl. Econs. (exec. com. 1992—, pres. 1997-99), Soc. Petroleum Engrs. Avocations: travel, music, German lang., French lang. Home: 731 Monticello St Evanston IL 60201-1745 Office: Northwestern U Dept Econs Evanston IL 60208-0001

BRAFMAN, LIONEL, finance company executive; b. Paris, Oct. 5, 1971; s. Alain and Rachel (Wajsberg) B.; m. Lydia Journo, June 23, 1996; 1 child, Jeremy. Ingenieur Civil des Mines, Ecoles Mines, Nancy, France, 1994; M in Internat. Fin., Hautes Etudes Commerciales, Paris, 1996. Fin. engr. ABF Capital Mgmt., Paris, 1997-98, fund mgr., 1998-99, head fixed income and asset allocations, 1999—, mem. exec. coun., 2000—. Contbr. articles to profl. jours. Scientifique de contingent Ministere Def., 1994-95. Mem. Club Haute Etudes Commerciales Fin. Avocations: tennis, soccer, American literature. Home: 119 rue de Longchamp, 75116 Paris France Office: ABF Capital Mgmt, 46 ave Kleber, 75116 Paris France

BRAGA DE MACEDO, JORGE AVELINO, economics educator; b. Lisbon, Dec. 1, 1946; s. Jorge and Branca Rosa (Mendonca Braga) B.d.M.; m. Luiza S. Almeido Ribeiro, Nov. 30, 1972; children: Joao, Ana. LLB, Faculty of Law, Lisbon, 1971; MA, Yale U., 1973, PhD, 1979. Prof. econs. Nova U., Lisbon, 1987—; pres. OECD Devel. Ctr., Paris, 1999—; pres. Parliament European Affairs Com., Lisbon, 1994-95; min. of finance, Lisbon, 1991-93; dep. dir. gen. European Commn., Brussels, 1991—, dir. nat. econs., 1988-91; dir. Inst. for Tropical Scis. Rsch., Lisbon, 1985—; rsch. assoc. Nat. Bur. Econ. Rsch., Cambridge, Mass., 1980—; rsch. fellow Ctr. for Econ. Policy Rsch., London, 1983—; mem. exec. com. Trilateral Commn. Europe, Paris, 1995. Editor: Currency Convertibility, 1996, Unity with Diversity in the European Economy, 1990. Pres. Coun. European Cmtys., Brussels, 1992. Jr. lt. Portuguese Army, 1973-75. Social Democrat. Roman Catholic. Avocations: jogging, movies. Office: OECD Devel Ctr, 94 rue Chardon-Lagache, 75016 Paris France

BRAGANÇA, MARIA DA LUZ DE CAMPOS PEREIRA DE, editor, public relations professional; b. Lisboa, Portugal, Aug. 23, 1942; d. José Pedro and Maria Emília De Castro de Campos Pereira; m. Dom Duarte de Bragança, Oct. 10, 1966 (dec. May 1994); children: Miguel, Filipa. Student, ISLA, Lisbon, 1965, Getulio Vargas Found., Brazil, 1976. Adminstrv. asst. Cimianto, Lisbon, 1966-69; dir. Diprove Art Galerie, Lisbon, 1973-74; exec. sec., projects supr. Finep, Brazil, 1976-77; specialized techic, pres. asst. Nuclebras, Rio de Janeiro, 1977-80; cordenation-info. office dir. Grao Para, Portugal, 1981-82; mng. dir. Gabinete 1, Lisbon, 1982—. Dir., editor (mags.) Eles & Elas, 1982—, Manchete, Interempresas. Avocations: gardening, writing, horses. Office: Gabinete 1, Rua das Flores 105-1o Esq, 1200-194 Lisboa Portugal

BRAGASON, PALL, executive; b. Reykjavik, Iceland, Mar. 24, 1948; s. Bragi and Marta (Lakner) Olafsson; m. Gudbjorg Kristin Do, July 8, 1972; children: Hinrik, Hjorleifur, Bragi, Vidar. Cand. Oecon., U. Iceland, 1974. Dept. head Falkinn HF, Reykjavik, Iceland, 1971-75, exec. dir., 1975-86, mng. dir., 1986—. Bd. dirs. Stjarnan Football Club, Gardabaer, 1987-92, The Football Assn., Reykjavik, 1992-94. Mem. Icelandic Wholesalers Assn. (bd. dirs. 1983-89, wage negotiations bd. 1995—), Icelandic Employers Assn. (exec. bd. 1986-89). Lutheran. Home: Haedarbyggd 14, 210 Gardabaer Iceland Office: Falkinn HF, Sudurlandsbraut 8, 128 Reykjavik Iceland

BRAGG, ALBERT FORSEY, retired airline captain; b. Providence, Oct. 25, 1932; s. Horatio Frederick Roy and Olive Lavinia (Bardsley) B.; m. Anne Dana Bernard, Mar. 22, 1955 (div. 1977); children: Steven Keith, Gail Marie; m. Anita Bürki, Aug. 6, 1983. Student, Duke U., 1950-53. Lic. air transport pilot, flight engr., FAA. First officer-capt. N.Y. Airways, Inc., N.Y.C., 1959-64; flight ops. instr. United Air Lines, Denver, 1964-65; flight engr. United Air Lines, Chgo., 1965-66; co-pilot United Air Lines, N.Y.C., Denver, 1967-83; capt. United Air Lines, 1983-92; check airman United Air Lines, Denver, 1984-85, 86-89, flight check mgr., 1985-86; internat. capt. United Air Lines, N.Y.C., 1991-92; aerospace edn. officer Civil Air Patrol, Boonton, N.J., 1972-74, Denver, 1974-79; ret. United Air Lines, N.Y.C., 1992. Designer, builder dome for astronomic obs., Sheep Hill Obs., Boonton, N.J., 1973. Mem. sch. bd. Town of Boonton, 1972-75; active Colo. Motor Sports Coun. Comdr. USN, 1954-59. Recipient Life Saving award Civil Air Patrol, Denver, 1977, First place short take off contest Nat. Stearman Fly-In, Galesburg, Ill., 1992-94, 96-97. Mem. Exptl. Aircraft Assn. (safety lectr., tech. counselor Rocky Mountain Builder Forum, instr. Young Eagles program; v.p. chpt. 301 1995-97), Tail Hook Assn., Am. Navion Soc., Antique Aircraft Assn., Stearman Restorers Assn., Mercedes Benz Club (bd. dirs. 1989—, treas. 1992-94, pres. 1994-97, Mem. of Yr. 1991, Otto Saborsky award 1994, Officer of Yr. 1996), Ret. United Pilots Assn., Colo. Mus. Natural History, U.S. Coast Guard Sea Vets., The Eastwind Assn. Republican. Avocations: building, restoring and flying sport, classic and antique aircraft, autoshow judge, track steward. Home: 2509 Elmhurst Pl Longmont CO 80503-2356

BRAGG, BERNARD, actor, educator; b. Gallaudet Coll., 1952; M.A., San Francisco State Coll., 1959. Acad. and drama instr. Calif. Sch. for the Deaf, Berkeley, 1952-67; star weekly TV program The Quiet Man, KQED, San Francisco, 1960-63; tchr. mime Actors' Lab, San Francisco, 1959-61; star What's New, 1961-68; one-man shows throughout America and Europe, 1957-66; founder Nat. Theatre of the Deaf, 1966-67, performed throughout U.S. and Europe, 1967-77, actor, tchr., dir., lectr., adminstr., 1967-77; founding mem., actor Little Theatre of the Deaf, 1968-71; artist-in-residence Moscow Theatre of Mimicry and Gesture, 1973; tchr. mime Nat. Theatre Inc., O'Neill Theater Ctr., 1972-74; tchr. sign mime Nat. Theatre of the Deaf, Waterford, Conn., 1967-79; artist-in-residence Harvard U., 1974; guest actor Sign Me Alice, Chgo. Theater of Deaf, 1975; tchr. total communication Mont. State U., 1973, 74, 75; lectr., performer around the world, 1977-78; vis. prof. Gallaudet Coll., Washington, 1978, artist-in-resident, 1979, asst. prof. theatre arts dept., 1980—; tech. advisor An Your Name is Jonah, 1978; tchr. drama of visual lang. grad. liberal studies program Wesleyan U., Middletown, Conn., 1979; actor appearing in The White Hawk, 1981, Caption Marvelous, 1981, The Disabled Genius, 1981, Can Anybody Hear Me?, 1982, The White Hawk, 1981, Second City, 1983, Disabled Genius, 1983, Sleuth, 1994, A Christmas Carol, 1995; producer videotape Take Makes Two of Us, 1981; drama instr. summer program for gifted hearing impaired youth Boys Town, Omaha, 1982; cons. pub. relations div. Gallaudet Coll., Washington, 1982—; producer, dir. film It's Your Choice, 1983, Gallaudet College is Ready for You, 1983. Author plays: (with Eugene Bergman) Tales From a Clubroom, 1979; That Makes Two of US, 1980; (with Roz Rosen A Handful of Stories, 1981, Lessons in Laughter 1990, (with Eugene Bergman) Meeting Halfway in ASL, 1990; contbr. articles to profl. jours. Bd. mem. Nat. Com. Arts for the Handicapped; cons. World Fedn. of Deaf on Theatre Arts, Nat. Theatre of Deaf on Theatre Arts. Recipient Teegarden award, 1952; Knight of Flying Fingers award Nat. Assn. Deaf, 1967; Plaque, Gallaudet Coll. Theatre, 1971; Plaque, The Deaf of San Diego, 1973; la Decoration au Merite Social Internat.-Premiere Classe, World Fedn. Deaf, 1975; Edward Miner Gallaudet award, 1978, hon. doctorate Gallaudet U., 1988; Spl. Tony award Nat. Theatre Deaf; Plaque-Commendation, Pres.'s Com. on Employment of Handicapped, 1979; named Alumnus of Yr., Kappa Gamma, 1972; Man of Yr., Alpha Sigma Pi, 1978. Office: Gallaudet Coll Kendall Green Washington DC 20002

BRAGG, WILLIAM DAVID, film producer, screenwriter; b. Phila., Sept. 13, 1962; s. D. Gordon and Shirley Marie (Dutcher) B.; m. Kathleen Rose Dressler, Dec. 24, 1980; children: Amanda Lee, Holly Christine, William David, Joseph Edward, Jeff Allen. Student, Mastbaum Area Vocat. Tech. Sch, Phila., 1977-80, The Learning Annex, N.Y.C., 1987. Ind. agt. Mr. Bear Enterprises, North Brunswick, N.J., 1987-89; founder, adminstrv. consul Out House Prodns., Inc., North Brunswick, 1988-90, exec. producer spl. projects, 1989-90, pres., chief exec. officer, 1989—. Producer/screenwriter film Sugar Mountain, 1990; screenwriter films including Army/Navy Games, 1976, Witch Way to Salem, 1977, Skitso, 1986, Babywolf of Manville, 1986, Free, 1989; plays include The Christmas Dog, 1978, Mandi's Room, 1979; author children's series The Adventures of Fat One, 1970. Tng. specialist Raritan Valley workshop Easter Seals, North Brunswick, 1989-90; mem. Indep. Feature Project 2000. Recipient Multi-Svc. Rd. Vehicle Triple A award (Driver of Yr., 1995. Mem. SAG (signatory), Am. Film Inst., Internat. Soc. Dramatists. Methodist Christian. Avocations: soccer, softball, rock and roll music, family activities. Office: OutHouse Productions Inc 14 Easton Ave New Brunswick NJ 08901-1918

BRAGMAN, MICHAEL J., state legislator; b. Cicero, N.Y., Aug. 11, 1940; m. Suzanne M. Collier; children: Michael J. Jr., (twins) Heather, Leslie. BA, Syracuse U., 1963. Mem. N.Y. State Assembly, Albany, 1980—, majority leader, also ex officio mem. standing coms., 1993—; mem. dist. 3 Onondaga County Legislature, 1969-81, minority leader, 1972-75, chmn., 1978-79; former chmn. transp., agr., vol. firefighters and wildlife mgmt. coms., former mem. environ. conservation, local govts., tourism, arts and sports devel., edn., and rules coms., chmn. Dem. campaign com., 1990-92. Chmn. Cicero Dem. Com., 1965-68; del. Dem. Nat. Conv., 1976, 84, 92, 96. Recipient Cmty. Team Spirit award Salvation Army, lifetime achievement award Empire Friends N.Y. Libr. Assn., Citizen of Yr. award Vietnam Vets. Am., legis. award NY. State Conf. Mayors, Legislator of Decade award N.Y. State Conservation Coun., Lifetime Achievement award N.Y. State STOP DWI Coords. Assn., Legislator of Yr. award N.Y. State Assn. for Pupil Transp.; named to N.Y. State Outdoorsmen Hall of Fame. Office: 305 S Main St N Syracuse NY 13212-3119

BRAGUINSKY, SERGUEY, economist; b. Moscow, Nov. 27, 1959. M in Econ. and Oriental Studies, Moscow State U., 1982; cand. of econ. scis., USSR Acad. Sci, Moscow, 1986; D of Econ Scis., Keio U., Tokyo, 1997. Rschr. Inst. of Oriental Studies USSR Acad. Scis., Moscow, 1985-91; assoc. prof. Yokohama (Japan) City U. Faculty Econ. and Bus. Adminstrn., 1991—; cons. Salomon Bros. Asia Ltd., Tokyo, 1991-96; adv. Nat. Inst. Rsch. Advancement, Tokyo, 1997; vis. scholar, U. Chgo., 1998; J.M. Olin fellow in law and econs. U. Chgo., 2000—. Author, editor: Industrial Change in China and Russia, 1996; author: Monetary Policy in Japan, 1989, Incentives and Institutions, 2000; contbr. articles to profl. jours. Fax: 81 45 787 2096. E-mail: serguei@yokohama-cu.ac.jp. Office: Yokohama City Univ, 22 2 Seto Kanazawa Ward, Yokohama 236, Japan

BRAH, SHAUKAT A., business educator; b. Lahore, Punjab, Pakistan, Oct. 26, 1958; parents Abdul Latif and Waheeda Khan; m. Aliya Shaukat Tufail, Dec. 27, 1990; children: Nabeel A. Khan, Shayan A. Khan. BSME, U. Engring. & Tech., Lahore, 1980; MS, Iowa State U., 1983; PhD, U. Houston, 1988. Registered profl. engr., Pakistan. Mech. engr. Packages Ltd., Lahore, 1980-82; rsch. asst. U. Houston, 1984-89; asst. prof. Lahore U. Mgmt. Scis., 1989-91; lectr. faculty bus. adminstrn. Nat. U. Singapore, 1991-96, sr. lectr. faculty bus. adminstrn., 1996—. Mem. Inst. Ops. Rsch. and Mgmt. Scis. Fax: 65 7792621. E-mail: fbabrahs@nus.edu.sg. Office: Nat U Singapore Fac Bus Adm, 15 Law Link, Singapore 117591, Singapore

BRAHA, THOMAS I., business executive; b. Austin, Tex., Sept. 3, 1947; s. Jacob and Valentine (Capone) B.; m. Nancy Elizabeth Rowe, Mar. 31, 1973 (div.); children: Nancy Elizabeth, Jeanne Valentine, Travis Ian. BSME, U. Tex., 1969; MBA, Temple U., 1971; postgrad., NYU, 1971-73. Engr. Davis Electronics, Inc., Austin, 1967, Whirlpool Corp., Evansville, Ind., 1968; project engr. ITE Imperial Corp., Phila., 1969-71; sr. supply analyst Mobil Oil Corp., N.Y.C., 1971-74; pres. Western Hemisphere Bulk Oil (U.S.A.), Inc., N.Y.C., 1974-75; pres., CEO Braha Holding Corp., Braha Oil Corp. and Subs., Braha Estates, Inc., Braha Farms, Braha Profit and Pension Trusts; lectr. The Wharton Sch., U. Pa., 1997. Active Bryn Mawr Presbyn. Ch. Mem. ASME, Am. Mgmt. Assn., Am. Petroleum Inst., Inst. Petroleum (U.K.), Nat. Petroleum Refining Assn., Phila. Country Club. Office: Braha Holding Co PO Box 787 Bryn Mawr PA 19010-0787

BRAHAM, DELPHINE DORIS, supervisory government accountant; b. L'Anse, Mich., Mar. 16, 1946; d. Richard Andrew and Viola Mary Aho; m. John Emerson Braham, Sept. 23, 1967 (div. Aug. 1988); children: Tammy, Debra, John Jr. BS summa cum laude, Drury Coll., 1983; M in Mgmt., Webster U., St. Louis, 1986. Bookkeeper Cmty. Mental Health Ctr., Marquette, Mich., 1966-68; acctg. technician St. Joseph Hosp., Parkersburg, W.Va., 1972-74; material mgr. U.S. Army, Ft. Leonard Wood, Mo., 1982-86; acct., 1986-92; supervisory acct. Dept. Def. Indpls., 1992—; instr., adj. faculty Columbia Coll., 1987-92, Park Coll., 1988-92. Leader Girl Scouts U.S., Williamstown, W.Va., 1972-74, Hanau, Germany, 1977-79. Mem. AAUW (treas. Waynesville br. 1986-90), Am. Soc. Mil. Comptrs., NAFE, Assn. Govt. Accts., Waynesville Bus. and Profl. Women's Orgn. Home: 2752 Pawnee Dr Indianapolis IN 46229-1418

BRAID, IAN CHARLES, software company executive; b. Melbourne, Australia, Dec. 18, 1942; s. Ian Leslie and Lorna (Candy) B.; m. Judith Slater, Nov. 23, 1973; two children. B in Engring., U. Melbourne, 1964; diploma in computing, U. Cambridge, 1969, PhD, 1973. Software developer English Elec. Computers Ltd., 1967-68; leader CAD rsch. group U. Cambridge, 1975-80; founder, dir. Shape Date Ltd., Cambridge, 1974-85, Three-Space Ltd., Cambridge, 1985—; vis. prof., Tech. U. Denmark, 2000; hon. prof. U. Wales, Cardiff, 2000-2005. Author: Designing with Volumes, 1973. Mem. Instn. Mech. Engrs., Br. Computer Soc. Office: Three Space Ltd, Park House Castle Park, Cambridge CB3 0DU, England

BRAILLON, ALAIN LEOPOLD HENRI, health facility administrator; b. Amiens, Somme, France, Mar. 22, 1953; s. Philippe J.M. and Monique (Damade) B.; m. Brigitte M.T. Charrier, Sept. 9, 1978; children: Aymeric P.J., Aurore S.Y., Alexis R.H. MD, U. Amiens, France, 1982; MS, U. Paris, 1984, 86. Cert. in gastroenterology. Resident Amiens (France) U. Hosp., 1978-84, chief fellow in gastroenterology, 1984-86; postdoctoral fellow U. Iowa, 1986-87; assoc. dir. rsch. INSERM, Paris, 1987-90; biomed. rsch. adminstr. Paris Pub. Hosp. Authority, 1990—. Philippe Found. grantee, 1986, French Fgn. Office grantee, 1986. Office: AP-HP Rsch Clinic, 3 Ave Victoria, 75004 Paris France Office: Hopital St Louis, 10 ave Claude Vellefaux, 75010 Paris France

BRAILOVSKY, VICTOR LVOVICH, computer scientist, educator, politician; b. Moscow, Dec. 27, 1935; arrived in Israel, 1987; s. Lev and Debora (Weinstein) B.; m. Irina Fefer, Aug. 1, 1959; children: Leonid, Dalia. MSc, Inst. Energy, Moscow, 1959; PhD, Acad. Sci., Moscow, 1965; D (hon.), U. de Picardie, Amiens, France, 1981, Cath. U. Louvain, Belgium, 1982, Tel Aviv U., 1984, Open U., 1984, Weizmann Inst., Rehovot, Israel, 1987. Rschr. Inst. Computers, Moscow, 1959-72; prisoner Butizskaya Prison, Moscow, 1980-81, Internal Exile, Kazahstan, Russia, 1981-84; rschr., assoc. prof. Tel Aviv U., 1987—; Mem. Israeli Parliament (Knesset), 1999—. Editor Jews in USSR, 1977-80; inventor in field; contbr. articles to profl. jours. and newspapers. Office: Dept Computer Sci, Tel Aviv Univ, 69978 Ramat Aviv Tel Aviv Israel

BRAIM, PAUL FRANCIS, history educator, writer; b. Phila., May 31, 1926; s. Paul Reed and Anna Kathryn (McAvoy) B.; m. Barbara Ann Redline, July 2, 1982 (div. Dec. 1990). AB, Shepherd Coll., 1949; MA, U. Del., 1956, PhD, 1983. Enlisted U.S. Army, 1943, advanced through grades to col., 1968, ret., 1977; pres. Mil. History and Strategy Inc., Daytona, Fla., 1980—; prof. history Embry-Riddle U., Daytona Beach, Fla., 1987-99; lectr. Army, Navy, and Air Force War Colls., 1966-99; strategic planner Offices of Joint Chiefs of Staff, Washington, 1970-74. Author: Revolutionary Warfare, 1966, The Test of Battle, 1998, The Will to Win, 2000, Fighting to Win, 1999; co-author: Military Heritage of America, 1992; editor: How to Defeat Saddam H., 1991. Decorated Silver Star with 2 oak leaf clusters, Bronze Star with 4 oak leaf clusters, Legion of Merit with 2 oak leaf clusters, D.F.C., Purple Heart with 2 oak leaf clusters, Meritorious Svc. medal. Mem. AAUP, The Strategic Inst., Assn. of U.S. Army, Ret. Officers Assn., Mil. Order World Wars. Republican. Avocation: hiking. Office: Embry-Riddle Aero U Daytona Beach FL 32114 Address: 121 Sweetwater Oaks Ln Daytona Beach FL 32114-1162

BRAIMBRIDGE, MARK VINEY, cardiothoracic surgeon; b. London, Feb. 10, 1924; s. Clifford Viney and Jane (Southwell) B.; m. Barbara Alison Cormie, June 10, 1955 (div. 1979); children: Fiona Louise, Nicholas Viney, Laura Lucie, Sophie Elizabeth; m. Elizabeth Jean Boyd Harvey, Feb. 12, 1979. BSc, Rhodes U., Grahamstown, 1941; MA, MB BChir, Cambridge (Eng.), 1949. Registrar St. Bartholomews Hosp., London, 1954-55; Heller fellow Stanford U. Hosp., San Francisco, 1956-57; registrar Hammersmith Hosp., London, 1958; sr. registrar Brompton Hosp. and London Chest Hosp., London, 1959-63; sr. lectr. St. Thomas' Hosp. Med. Sch., London, 1963-65; cons. cardiac surgeon St. Thomas' Hosp., London, 1965—. Author: Lecture Notes on Cardiology, Postop Cardiac Intensive Care, Protection of the Ischemic Myocardium; contbr. articles to profl. jours. Med. advisor Internat. Help for Children, London, 1970—. Lt. Royal Artillery, 1942-45. Recipient Brackenbury scholarship surgery St. Bartholomews Hosp., London, 1951. Fellow Royal Coll. Surgeons England; mem. Am. Assn. for Thoracic Surgery, Soc. Cardiothoracic Surgeons Asia, Soc. Cardiothoracic Surgeons Great Britian and Ireland, British Cardiac Soc., Marylebone Cricket Club (London), Garrick Club (London). Conservative. Anglican. Avocations: English literature, beagling, cricket, opera. Home: 22 Upper Park Rd, London NW3 2UP, England Office: Rayne Inst St Thomas Hosp, Westminster Bridge, London SE1 7EH, England

BRAIN, PAUL FREDRIC, zoology educator; b. Manchester, Eng., July 1, 1945; s. Frederick Ernest and Ada (Squirell) B.; m. Sonja Strijbos, July 4, 1975; children: Fulke, Ilka, Vincent Fredric, Daniel Robert. BS with 1st class honors, U. Hull, 1967, PhD, 1971. Postdoctoral fellow U. Sheffield (Eng.), 1970-71; lectr. zoology U. Wales, Swansea, 1971-78, sr. lectr., 1978-83, reader, 1987-95, personal chair, 1987-95, head biol. scis., 1995-98, accreditor and chair 10B animal user's courses; specialist reviewer organismal bioscis., mem. bioscis. benchmarking team Quality Assurance Agy. Editor: Alcohol and Aggression, 1986; assoc. editor Aggressive Behavior, 1974, Behavioural Processes, 1984; co-editor: The Biology of Aggression, 1981, Ethopharmacology in..., 1987. Recipient internat. prize for medicine UNESCO/WHO, 1980; project grantee Med. Rsch. Coun., 1976—, Brit. Coun., 1985—. Fellow Inst. Biology; mem. Internat. Soc. Rsch. Aggression (pres. 1982-84), Assn. Study Animal Behavior, Lab. Animal Sci. Assn. (v.p. 1992-96), Nat. Conv. Univ. Profs. (mem. com. sec. 1997—), Heads of Univ. Biol. Scis. (pres. 1999—). Avocations: travel, road running and cross-country, reading, music, photography. Home: 8 Landor Dr, SA4 2GL Loughor Nr Swansea Wales Office: Univ Wales-Swansea, Sch Biol Scis, Swansea SA2 8PP, Wales

BRAINARD, CHARLES R., lawyer; b. Jersey City, N.J., Apr. 12, 1933; s. William Everitt and Eleanor Holston; m. Susan Stephenson, Apr. 18, 1962 (div. Oct. 4, 1974); children: Jennifer B. Cunningham, Laura Brainard. BA in Physics, Haverford Coll., 1955; JD, U. Chgo., 1958. Bar: N.Y. 1959. Assoc. Kenyon & Kenyon, N.Y.C., 1958-65, ptnr., 1966—; past examiner U.S. Patent Office; lectr. in field. Contbr. chpts. to books, articles to profl. jours. Trustee, past sec.-treas. The Found. of the Open Eye; adv. bd. The Joseph Campbell Found.,The Laban-Bartenieff Inst. Movement Analysis, Bus. Incubation Ctr. Stevens Inst. Tech., 1990-93. Mem. ABA, Am. Arbitration Assn. (Nat. Panel Arbitrators), Am. Intellectual Property Law Assn. (chmn., com. copyright matters, 1975-77), N.Y. Patent Trademark and Copyright Law Assn. (chmn. com. copyrights and designs 1972-73), Assn. Bar City of N.Y. (past lectr., sec. com. patents 1968-71), Licensing Execs. Soc. (tech. transfer com.),. Office: Kenyon & Kenyon One Broadway New York NY 10004

BRAINE, RAYMOND GERMAINE MARIE HENRI, chemistry educator; b. Liege, Belgium, Sept. 7, 1926; s. Jean A. and Raymonde Braine; m. Jacqueline Ramakers, Nov. 10, 1959; 1 child, Emanuel R. Licencie Scis. Chimiques, U. de l'Etat de Liege, 1950; DSc, Groupe des Scis. Chimiques, 1954. Prof. Ecole Normale Moyenne de Liege, 1950-69; prof. indsl. chemistry Hautes Etudes Commerciales Liege, 1969-91, emeritus, 1991—. Contbr. articles to profl. jours. Decorated chevalier Ordre des Palmes Academiques (France); chevalier Order of Crown, grand officier Ordre Leopold II (Belgium). Mem. Belgian Chem. Soc., Belgian Assn. Profs. Chemistry and Physics, Assn. des Chimistes Sortis de U. Liege. Home: Quai Churchill 19, 4020 Liege Belgium

BRAININ, CONSTANCE SPEARS, psychotherapist, educator, social worker, counselor; b. Princeton, N.J., Feb. 21, 1932; d. Alexander Joseph and Anna (Stuttman) Spears; m. Norman Herbert Brainin, May 29, 1955; children: Kenneth, Risa, Alissa. BA, Northeastern Ill. U., 1975, MA, 1979; PhD, Southeastern U., 1981. Lic. social worker, Ill.; cert. clin. mental health counselor; lic. clin. profl. counselor, Ill. Supr. counseling staff Park Med. Ctr., Chgo., 1980-83; pvt. practice Chgo., 1982—; adj. faculty Oakton C.C., Des Plaines, Ill., 1982—, Northeastern Ill. U., 1984-88; governing bd. Theatre 219, Skokie, Ill., 1984-88; v.p. Edgebrook/Sauganash chpt. Am. Cancer Soc., 1988-93; lectr. Edgebrook C. of C., Chgo., 1985, Am. Cancer Soc., Chgo., 1984. Workshop leader Hope Ctr., Long Grove, Ill., 1984. Mem. APA, Am. Orthopsychiat. Assn., Nat. Acad. Cert. Clin. Mental Health Counselors, Ill. Psychol. Assn. Avocations: tennis, golf, bridge.

BRAININA, KHIENA ZALMANOVNA, chemistry researcher; b. Volgograd, Russia, May 26, 1930; d. Zalman Solomonovich Brainin and Mariya Zinov'evna Gladnikova; m. Boris Abramovich Vidrevich, Jan. 31, 1954; 1 child, Vidrevich Marina. Degree in chemistry, Ural State U., Ekaterinburg, Russia, 1953, PhD in Chemistry, 1959; PhD in Sci., Moscow State U., 1967. Cert. chemist. Engr. Sc.-Rsch. Inst. Oil, Ufa, Russia, 1953-55, Ural State Factory for Chem. Reagents, Ekaterinburg, 1955-56; chief lab. scientist Sci.-Rsch. Inst. Chems., Donetsk, Ukraine, 1959-68; prof. chemistry Ural State Econ. Univ., Ekaterinburg, 1968—. Author: Stripping Voltammetry in Chemical Analysis, 1972, (with E. Neyman) Electroanalytical Stripping Methods, 1993; contbr. articles to profl. jours. Recipient Honored Scientist of Russia award, 1995. Mem. Russian Acad. Engring. Sci. Avocation: traveling, electroanalytical chemistry, environmental monitoring. Fax: 7-3432-222415. E-mail: baz@usue.ru. Home: A Valek St 12-11, 620077 Ekaterinburg Russia Office: Ural State Econ Univ, 8th of March St 62, 620219 Ekaterinburg Russia

BRAITENBERG, VALENTINO, scientist; b. Bolzano, Italy, June 18, 1926; s. Carl von Braitenberg and Ida von Walther; m. Elisabeth Hanna, Feb. 14, 1955; children: Margareta, Carla, Zeno. Md, U. Rome, 1951; libero docente, U. Naples, Italy, 1961; hon. prof., U. Tübingen, 1970; hon. doctor, U. Salzburg, Austria, 1994. Rsch. fellow Yale Med. Sch., New Haven, 1955-57; lectr. U. Naples, 1958-68; dir. Max Planck Inst., Tübingen, 1968-94; pres. Lab. di Sci. Cognitive, U. Trento, Rovereto, Italy, 1998. Author: Texture of Brains, 1971, Vehicles, 1984, Il Gusto Della Lingua, 1996, Ill Oder Der Engel und Die Philosophen, 1999. Home: Madergasse 5, 72070 Tübingen Germany Office: Max Planck Inst, Spemannstr 38, 72076 Tübingen Germany

BRAITHWAITE, WILFRED JOHN, physics educator; b. Ferndale, Wash., Apr. 11, 1940; s. John Alfred and Joyce Elinor (Gunderson) B.; m. Wanda Pearl Chism, June 3, 1961 (div. 1974). BS in Physics with honors, Seattle Pacific U., 1962; MS in Physics, U. Wash., 1965, PhD in Physics, 1971; postgrad., U. Tex., 1988-89. Instr. physics Princeton (N.J.) U., 1970-72; asst. prof. physics U. Tex., Austin, 1972-79, rsch. scientist faculty, 1979-81; tech. and sci. cons. Austin, 1981-89; assoc. prof. physics U. Ark., Little Rock, 1989-95, prof. physics, 1995—; vis. staff mem. Los Alamos (N.Mex.) Nat. Lab., 1975-76, 78-79; vis. scientist Ind. U., Bloomington, 1990-96; affiliate prof. physics U. Wash., Seattle, 1991-95; sci. assoc. PPE divsn. CERN, Geneva, Switzerland, 1992-95; guest scientist Brookhaven Nat. Lab., Upton, N.Y., 1992—; grant referee Ark. Sci. and Tech. Authority, 1990—. Numerous unedited contbns.; jour. referee Phys. Rev. C and Phys. Rev. Letters, 1970—, Found. Physics Assoc. Ed. Ark. Acad. Sci., 2000—. U.S. Dept. Energy rsch. grantee, 1992-95, 99—, Ark. Sci. and Tech. Authority rsch. grantee, 1993-94, 96-98; numerous grants from NSF, Dept. of Energy, Robert A Welch Found. Mem. IEEE, Am. Phys. Soc., Nat. Assn. for Rsch. in Sci. Teaching, N.Y. Acad. Sci., Ark. Acad. Sci. Achievements include tests of time reversal invariance; high excitation neutron particle-hole states; charge-dependent matrix elements in light nuclei; method for determining rotational symmetries of nuclear states using heavy ions; multiply-excited atomic states in helium-like and lithium-like oxygen; strength of the 3-alpha process in stellar helium burning; method for identifying antimatter stars; large isospin mixing in light nuclei via scattering comparisons of positive and negative pions near the pion-nucleon resonance; measurement limits on source sizes formed in symmetric collisions of ultra-relativistic heavy nuclei; method for separating charged kaons and pions in Time Projection Chambers via in-flight decays; instrument design for high-energy nuclear physics. Avocations: astronomy and astrophysics, science education, high-speed computing with 3-D visualizations, sailing, water sports. E-mail: wibraithwait@ualr.edu. Home: 1 Broadmoor Dr Little Rock AR 72204-4818 Office: Univ of Ark at Little Rock Dept Physics and Astronomy 2801 S University Ave Little Rock AR 72204

BRAKE, CECIL CLIFFORD, retired diversified manufacturing executive; b. Ystrad, Mynach, Wales, Nov. 14, 1932; came to U.S., 1967; s. Leonard James and Ivy Gertrude (Berry) B.; m. Vera Morris, Aug. 14, 1954; children—Stephen John, Richard Colin, Vanessa Elaine. Chartered engr.; B.Sc. in Engring., U. Wales, 1954; M.Sc., Cranfield Inst., Bedford, Eng., 1957; grad. A.M.P., Harvard U. Sch. Bus., 1985. Mgr. research and devel. Schrader Fluid Power, Wake Forest, N.C., 1968-70, engring. mgr., 1970-75; mng. dir. Schrader U.K. Fluid Power, 1975-77; v.p., gen. mgr. Schrader Internat., 1977-78; group v.p. Schrader Bellows, Fluid Power, Akron, Ohio, 1978-82; exec. v.p. Scovill, Inc., Waterbury, Conn., 1982-86; pres. Yale Security, Inc. subs. Scovill, Inc.; group exec. Eagle Industries, Inc., Chgo., 1986—; retired, 1997; chief oper. officer Mansfield (Ohio) Plumbing Products Inc., Hart and Cooley Inc., Holland, Mich., Caron Internat., Inc., Rochelle, Ill., Caron Internat., Inc., Rochelle, Ill., Chemineer Inc., Dayton, Ohio, Pulsafeeder Inc., Rochester, N.Y., Clevaflex Inc., Cleve., Equality Specialties Inc., N.Y.C., De Vilbiss Co., Toledo, Hill Refrigeration, Trenton, N.J., Air-Maze Corp., Bedford Heights, Ohio, Burns Aerospace Corp., Winston Salem, N.C., Atlantic Industries, Inc., Nutley, N.J., Stimsonite Products, Niles, Ill.; ptnr., owner Prince of Wales Inc.; bd. dirs. CFI Industries. Avocations: sailing; golf. Office: Eagle Industries Inc 2 N Riverside Plz Chicago IL 60606-2600 also: 17 Harborview Rd Westport CT 06880-5061

BRAKEL, CORNELIUS, retired publishing executive. Past chmn. Wolters Kluwer NV, Amsterdam, The Netherlands, 1995-99. Office: Elsevier Wolters Kluwer NV, Postbus 818, Amsterdam AV 1000, The Netherlands*

BRAKSICK, LESLIE, academic administrator; b. Ellenville, N.Y., Feb. 21, 1965; d. Herb and Connie Wilk; 1 child, Madeleine; m. Matthew Braksick, May 10, 1991; 1 child, Austin. BA in English & Psychology, St. Bonaventine U., Olean, N.Y., 1986; MA in Indsl. Psychology, Western Mich. U., 1987, PhD in Orgnl. Behavior, 1990. Internat. cons. Western Mich. U., Kalamazoo; cons. U. Mich., Ann Arbor, sr. cons.; v.p. performance consulting Century Bus. Svcs., Pitts.; pres., CEO, co-founder Continuous Learning Group, Pitts.; adj. instr. W.Va. U., Mortgantown; sr. cons. Ctr. Entrepreneurial Studies, Morgantown. Author: Unlock Behavior, Unleash Profits, 2000; contbr. articles to profl. jours. Bd. dirs. Heart Ctr. Children's Hosp., Pitts.; v.p. missions Presbyn. Ch. Sewickley, Pa. Mem. Assn. Behavior Mgmt. (bd. dirs.), Orgn. Behavior Mgmt. Network (awards coord.). Avocations: piano, violin, bass, tennis. Home: Backbone Rd Sewickley PA 15143 Office: Continuous Learning Group 500 Cherrington Corp Ctr Coraopolis PA 15108

BRAMAN, HEATHER RUTH, technical writer, editor, consultant, antiques dealer; b. Wilmington, Ohio, Apr. 27, 1934; d. William Barnett and Violet Ruth (Davis) Hansford; m. Barr Oliver Braman, June 29, 1957 (div.); children: Sean Robert, Heather Paige. BA, Hiram Coll., 1956; postgrad., Sinclair Community Coll., Dayton, Ohio, 1977-85, Wright State U., Dayton, 1986. Pers. clk. USAF, Wright-Patterson AFB, Ohio, 1956, specifications editor, 1956-57, publs. editor, writer, 1957-63; vol. Children's Med. Ctr., 1963-67, 995, Dayton Pubs. Schs., 1969-87; tchr. Gloria Dei Montessori Sch., Dayton, 1973-77; asst. mgr., acting mgr., mgr. tennis club USAF, Wright-Patterson AFB, Ohio, 1977-81; tech. writer Miclin, Inc., Alpha, Ohio, 1982, Indsl. Design Concepts, Dayton, 1982-83; tech. writer, cons. Belcan Corp., Cin., 1984-89; tech. cons. Piqua (Ohio) Engring., 1990; owner Chimney Sweep Antiques Shoppe, Arcanum, Ohio, 1991-99; real estate investor; tech. editor Project Mercury Candidate Evaluation Program, 1957-58. Founder, bd. dirs. Trotwood (Ohio) Women's Open Tennis Tournament, 1976-81; mem. Harrison Twp. Parks Bd., 1980-82; ballpersons coord. Dayton Pro Tennis Classic, 1977-80; pres. Dayton Tennis Commn., 1978-80; mem. parents exec. com. Hiram (Ohio) Coll., 1985-91; ct.-appointed Spl. Advocate/Guardian Ad Litem (CASA GAL), 1988-92; tutor English as a second lang. citizenship classes, 1991-93; attendee Ginghamsburg United Meth. Ch.; tutor Meadowdale H.S., Dayton, 2000—. Mem. NOW, NAACP, Dayton Pub. Schs. Orgns., Dayton Tennis Umpires Assn., Mothers Against Drunk Drivers., AARP, WWF, HALT, Sigil of Phi Sigma. Democrat. Mem. Soc. Friends. Avocations: tennis, antiques, reading, property investment. Home: 320 Elm Hill Dr Dayton OH 45415-2943 Office: Belcan Corp 10200 Anderson Way Cincinnati OH 45242-4718

BRAMSEN, INGE, psychologist, researcher; b. The Hague, The Netherlands, Aug. 23, 1964; d. Johan Pieter and Hendrika (Van der Horst) B.; m. Robert Jan Willem, Aug. 10, 1995; children: Tim, Micha. Grad., Leiden (The Netherlands) U., 1990, PhD, 1995. Rschr. Vrye U., Amsterdam, The Netherlands, 1994-96, tchr., 1996—. Mem. Internat. Soc. Traumatic Stress Studies. Office: Vrye U Dept Med Psychology, Van der Boechorststr 7, 1081 BT Amsterdam The Netherlands

BRAMWELL, MARVEL LYNNETTE, nurse, social worker; b. Durango, Colo., Aug. 13, 1947; d. Floyd Lewis and Virginia Jenny (Amyx) B. Diploma in lic. practical nursing, Durango Sch. Practical Nursing, 1968; AD in Nursing, Mt. Hood Community Coll., 1972; BSN, BS in Gen. Studies cum laude, So. Oreg. State Coll., 1980; cert. edn. grad. sch. social work, U. Utah, 1987, cert. counselor alcohol, drug abuse, 1988, MSW, 1992. RN, Utah, Oreg., Ind., Nev.; cert. social worker, Utah, Ind., Nev.; cert. clin. social worker, Ind. Staff nurse Monument Valley (Utah) Seventh Day Adventist Mission Hosp., 1973-74, La Plata Cmty. Hosp., 1974-75; health coord. Tri County Head Start Program, 1974-75; nurse therapist, team leader Portland Adventist Med. Ctr., 1975-78; staff nurse Indian Health Service Hosp., 1980-81; coord. village health services North Slope Borough Health and Social Svc. Agy., Barrow, Alaska, 1981-83; nurse, supr. aides Bonneville Health Care Agy., 1984-85; staff nurse LDS Adolescent Psychiat. Unit, 1985-86; coord. adolescent nursing CPC Olympus View Hosp., 1986-87, 91; charge and staff nurse adult psychiatry U. Utah, 1987-88; nurse MSW Cmty. Nursing Svc., Salt Lake City, 1989-90, Willow Springs Ctr., Reno, Nev., 1996—; resident scvs. coord., dir. nursing Arden Cts., Reno, 1998-99—; med. social worker Meth. Home Health, Indpls., 1994-96; psychiat. nurse Willow Springs Ctr., 1996—; DON, resident svc. coord. Arden Cts., Reno, 1998-99; per diem nurse Reno VA Med. Ctr.; assisted with design and constrn. 6 high tech. health clinics in Alaska Arctic, 1982-83; psychiat. nurse specialist Cmty. Nursing Svc. Contbr. articles to profl. jours. Active Mothers Against Drunk Driving, Program U. Alaska Rural Edn., 1981-83. Recipient cert. of appreciation Barrow Lion's Club, 1983, U.S. Census Bur., Colo., 1970, other awards and scholarships. Mem. NOW, Nat. Assn. Social Workers, Assn. Women Sci. Avocations: water color painting, photography, hiking, horseback riding. E-mail: marvel@BHR.reno.nv.us. Home: 600 Smithridge Park Reno NV 89502-5782

BRANAGH, KENNETH, actor, director; b. Belfast, Northern Ireland, Dec. 10, 1960; m. Emma Thompson, Aug. 1989 (div.). Grad., Royal Academy of Dramatic Art, 1981; LittD (hon.), Queens U., Belfast, 1990. Co-founder Renaissance Theater Co., England. For Renaissance Theater Co. authored play Public Enemy, dir. Twelfth Night, King Lear, A Midsummer Night's Dream, Uncle Vanya, acted in Romeo and Juliet, Hamlet, Much Ado About Nothing, As You Like It, Look Back in Anger, Midsummer Night's Dream, King Lear, Coriolanus, other roles; West End stage debut in Another Country, London; film appearances include High Season, 1987, A Month in the Country, 1987, Swing Kids, 1993, Othello, 1995, Looking for Richard, 1996, Hamlet, The Theory of Flight, 1998, The Gingerbread Man, 1998, The Dance of Shiva, 1998, Love's Labour Lost, 1999, Celebrity, 1998, The Proposition, 1998, The Betty Schimmel Story, 1999, Alien Love Triangle, 1999, Wild Wild West, 1999, others; actor, dir., script adaptation, producer: Henry V, 1989 (B.A.F.T.A. award Best Dir., 1990, Acad. award nominee Best Actor, Best Dir.), Much Ado About Nothing, 1993; actor, dir.: Dead Again, 1991, Peter's Friends, 1992, Hamlet, 1996 (Acad. award nominee Best Screenplay); dir., co-prodr., actor: Mary Shelley's Frankenstein, 1994, Betty Schimmel Story, 1999, Love's Labour Lost, 1999, How to Kill Your Neighbors, 2000, The Road to El Dorado (voice), 2000; dir., writer In the Bleak Midwinter, 1995; TV work includes The Boy in the Bush, Billy, Maybury, To the Lighthouse, Coming Through, Ghosts, The Lady's Not for Burning, (mini-series) Fortunes of War, (series) Thompson, Galapagos: The Enchanted Voyage (voice), 1999, Walking With Dinosaurs (voice), 1999; TV guest appearance Play for Tomorrow, 1982, (narrator) The Cold War, 1998, Great Composers, 1999. Decorated French Order of Arts and Letters, 1994.

BRANAN, JOHN MAURY, psychology educator, counselor; b. Tallahassee, Fla., Oct. 25, 1933; s. Roger Leo and Lala Marian (Crapps) B.; m. Mar. 23, 1957; children: John Maury Jr., Penny Michelle. BA, U. Fla., 1955, M in Rehab. Counseling, 1957, EdD, 1965. Lic. counselor, Ga. Rehab. counselor

State of Fla., Gainesville, 1956-61; asst. prof. psychology Berry Coll., Mt. Berry, Ga., 1962-66; dir. counseling, asst. prof. psychology Valdosta (Ga.) State Coll., 1966-67, prof. psychology, dept. head, 1967-72, prof. psychology, counseling and guidance, 1972—. Author: The Future Makers, 1971; contbr. articles to profl. jours. Mem. Am. Psychol. Assn., Southeastern Psychol. Assn., Am. Assn. Marriage and Family Therapy (clin.), Am. Assn. for Counseling and Devel., Am. Assn. Clin. Hypnosis (clin.), Internat. Club (pres. Valdosta chpt. 1973-74), Kiwanis, Phi Kappa Phi. Home: 1217 W Park Ave Valdosta GA 31602-2719 Office: Valdosta State U Dept Psychology Valdosta GA 36182

BRANCA, JOHN GREGORY, lawyer, consultant; b. Bronxville, N.Y., Dec. 11, 1950; s. John Ralph and Barbara (Werle) B. AB in Polit. Sci. cum laude, Occidental Coll., 1972; JD, UCLA, 1975. Bar: Calif. 1975. Assoc. Kindel & Anderson, Los Angeles, 1975-77, Hardee, Barovick, Konecky & Braun, Beverly Hills, Calif., 1977-81; ptnr. Ziffren, Brittenham, Branca & Fischer, L.A., 1981—; cons. N.Y. State Assembly, Mt. Vernon, 1978-82, various music industry orgns., L.A., 1981—. Editor-in-Chief UCLA-Alaska Law Rev., 1974-75; contbr. articles to profl. jours. Cons., bd. trustees UCLA Law Sch. Com., UCLA Athletic Dept., Occidental Coll., Musician's Assistance Program, 1995. Recipient Bancroft-Whitney award; named Entertainment Lawyer of Yr. Am. Lawyer mag., 1981. Mem. ABA (past trademark and copyright law sect.), Calif. Bar Assn., Beverly Hills Bar Assn. (entertainment law sect.), Phi Alpha Delta, Sigma Tau Sigma. Avocations: art, antiques, music, real estate. Office: Ziffren Brittenham Branca & Fischer 1801 Century Park W Fl 9 Los Angeles CA 90067-6406

BRANCALEONE, SALVATORE JOSEPH, nutritionist, consultant; b. N.Y.C., Oct. 29, 1943; s. Joseph and Julia (Vitale) B.; m. Rebecca Diann Thornburg; children: Dina, Debra. AS, U. Fla., 1963; BS, Fla. Atlantic U., 1966, MEd, 1976. Cert. nutritionist Agy. for Health Care Admin. Bd. Medicine Dept. of Health. Tchr. H.S. and Broward C.C., Hollywood & Coconut Creek, Fla., 1966-82; pres., clin. nutritionist Palm Lakes Natural Food Market, Margate, Fla., 1980-99; nutritional cons. Parkland, Fla., 1999—; radio talk show host WDJA-850, West Palm Beach, Fla., WWNN 1470, Boca Raton, Fla., 1991-99; clin. nutritionist specializing in treatment of degenerative diseases, such as cancer, heart disease, arthritis, diabetes, immune system disfunction, etc.; lectr. in field. Contbr. articles to profl. jours. Bd. dirs., v.p. Cypress Head Homeowners Assn. Mem. Nat. Nutritional Edn. Assn., Nat. Health Fedn., Nat. Counselors Assn. Democrat. Roman Catholic. Avocations: tennis, weight training, jogging, swimming. Home and Office: 7600 Marblehead Ln Parkland FL 33067-2336

BRANCH, DAVID ALAN, business development executive; b. Brentwood, Eng., Oct. 19, 1962; arrived in France, 1992; s. Alan Edward and Kathleen Mary (Debenham) B. BSc in Monetary Econs., London Sch. Econs., 1985; MBA, Internat. Inst. Mgmt. Devel., Lausanne, Switzerland, 1991. Exec. mergers and acquisitions Baring Bros. & Co. Ltd., London, 1985-87; asst. mgr. investment banking S.G. Warburg Securities, London, 1988-91; charge de mission Club Mediterranee, Paris, 1992-93, asst. dir. devel., acquisitions and spl. projects, 1994-96, internat. mktg., 1997—, project mgr.-distbn./tour operating, 1997-2000, regional v.p. devel., 1998—; v.p. internat. ImmoStreet.com, Paris, 2000—. Avocation: tennis, cricket, music. Office: ImmoStreet.com, 131 rue Damrémont, 75018 Paris France

BRANCH, JOHN WELLS (JACK TWIG), lawyer; b. Rochester, N.Y., May 1, 1912; s. John W. and Luna H. (Howell) B.; m. Caroline Wilbur, May 29, 1937 (dec. 1990); m. Margaret Zutterman, May 25, 1991. BA, Cornell U., 1934; J.S.D., 1937; MA in Econs., U. Rochester, 1937. Bar: N.Y. 1937, U.S. Ct. Appeals (2nd cir.) 1958. Assoc. Mann, Strang, Bodine & Wright, Rochester, N.Y., 1937-42; chief price atty. OPA, Rochester Dist., 1942-44; ptnr. and now of counsel Branch, Wise and Dewart, Rochester, 1945—; dir., legal advisor Hawthorne Villages, Inc., Asheville, N.C., 1998—; pres. Nat. Planning Data Corp., Ithaca, N.Y., 1970-76; co-founder, pres. The Branch-Wilbur Fund, Inc., 1967—, Eldergard Svcs., Inc., 1988-94; co-founder Genesee-Volkhov Connection, Inc., 1994—. Recipient Civic award Rochester, N.Y 1995. Mem. N.Y. State Bar Assn., Monroe County Bar Assn., Estate Planning Coun. Monroe County, Rotary, Phi Beta Kappa. Democrat. Orthodox Christian. Avocations: composing, helping foreign students, reciting light verse. Home and Office: 34A Larkspur Ct Asheville NC 28805-1368

BRANCH, MICHAEL ARTHUR, academic administrator; b. Langley, Kent, England, Mar. 24, 1940; s. Arthur Frederick and Mahala (Parker) B.; m.Ritva-Riitta Hannele Kari, Aug. 11, 1963; children: Jane Varpu, Jean Raili, Ann Päivi. BA, U. London, 1963, PhD, 1967; PhD honoris causa, U. Oulu, Finland, 1983. Asst. lectr. in Finno-Ugrian studies Sch. Slavonic and E. European Studies, U. London, 1967-70, lectr. in Finno-Ugrian studies, 1970-72, lectr. in Finnish, 1972-77, reader in Finnish, 1977-86, coll. pres., 1980—, full prof. Finnish, 1986—. Author: A.J. Sjögren-Studies of the North, 1973, (with others) Finnish Folk Poetry: Epic, 1977, Student's Glossary of Finnish, 1980, The Great Bear, 1993 (Finnish Non-fiction Work of Yr. 1993), Uses of Tradition, 1994, Finland and Poland in the Russian Empire, 1995, National History and Identity, 1999. Gov. Britain-Russia Ctr., London, 1980—, British Assn. Ctrl. and Ea. Europe, London, 1986—. Decorated Companion of Order of St. Michael and St. George, comdr. Finnish Lion; comdr. Polish Order of Merit; Terra Mariana cross (Estonia). Mem. Athenaeum Club. Avocations: gardening, walking. Office: Sch Slavonic/E European Std, Malet St Senate House, London WC1E 7HU, England

BRANCH, WILLIAM TERRELL, urologist, educator; b. Paragould, Ark., Dec. 7, 1937; s. William Owen and Mary Rose (Dempsey) B.; m. Mary Fletcher Cox, Dec. 11, 1965; children: Ashley Tucker, William T., Steven K. BS, Ark. State U., 1964, MD, 1971. Diplomate Am. Bd. Urology. Adminstrv. asst. mental retardation planning project State of Ark., Little Rock, 1964-66; intern U. South Fla. Sch. Medicine Affiliated Hosps., Tampa, 1971-72, resident in surgery, 1972-73, resident in urology, 1973-75, chief resident in urology, 1975-76, clin. prof. urology, chmn. dept. surgery, 1976—; practice medicine specializing in urology Tampa, 1976—; mem. staff, sec. urology Tampa Gen. Hosp., 1976-78, vice chief urology, 1978-80, chief urology, 1980-82; mem. staff, co-chief surgery Meml. Hosp., Tampa, 1978-80, vice chief med. staff, 1980-82, chief med. staff, 1982-84, trustee, 1983-88, bd. dirs.; mem. adv. bd. Suncoast Ednl. Telecommunications Systems, 1982; vice chmn., bd. dirs. Meml. Hosp., 1987-88; cons. in urology James A. Haley VA Hosp., Tampa, 1978—; mem. staff St. Joseph's Hosp., Tampa, 1976—, Tampa Gen. Hosp.; cons. staff Women's Hosp., Tampa; adv. bd. Glendale Fed. Savs., 1983-85, Beneficial Harbour Island Savs. Bank, 1985-87, South Trust Bank, 1988—, also bd. dirs., exec. com., chair audit com.; chief urology, bd. mem. Tampa Outpatient Surgery Facility, 2000—; chmn. vol. faculty com. Dept. Surgery U. South Fla. Coll. Medicine; bd. dirs. Shriners Hosp. for Children, Tampa. Author: (with others) Mental Retardation in Arkansas, 1964-66; A Demographic Study, 1966; cons. editor Jour. Fla. Med. Assn., 1978-93. Bd. dirs. Tampa Ballet, 1980, Tampa Charity Horse Show Bd. Dirs. Assn., 1985-87, Shriners Hosp. for Children, Tampa, 2000, Tampa Outpatient Surg. Facility; United Way, Tampa, 1983-90, mem. exec. com., 1984-88; mem. med. adv. bd. Nat. Kidney Found. of Fla., Inc., 1983-90; mem. Tampa Bay Super Bowl Task Force, Super Bowl XXXV Task Force; mem. adv. bd. dirs. Salvation Army; founding chmn. Kettle com., vice chmn. adv. bd. dirs., chmn., 1998—. Recipient Disting. Alumnus award Ark. State U., 1986. Fellow ACS (credit com. region IV, Fla. chpt. 1982—, exec. com. Fla. chpt. 1985—, sec., treas. 1987-88, pres.-elect 1989-90, pres. 1990-92, gov. 1990-96, bd. gov. chpt. activities com. 1991-96, alt. 1993, chmn. nomination com. 1995, chmn. applications com. region IV); mem. Am. Urol. Assn., Royal Soc. Medicine (affiliate), Fla. Med. Assn. (del. 1983, 88-96), Fla. Urol. Soc. (Milton Copeland award 1976, exec. com. 1978-82), Hillsborough County Med. Assn. (exec. com. 1978-81, treas. 1981-82, sec. 1983-84), Fla. Quality Med. Assurance, Inc. (bd. dirs., treas., chmn. exec. com. 1995, chmn. bd. govs.), Southeastern Surg. Congress, Greater Tampa C. of C. (dir. 1982-86, 87-90, chmn. med. meetings task force 1983-84, Super Star award 1983), Tampa Bay Surg. Soc. (founding mem., sec., bd. dirs. 1998, pres. 1999—), Tampa Hist. Soc., Hillsborough County Med. Soc. (pres. polit. action com. 1986-87, 88-89), Tampa Yacht and Country Club (gov. 1984-87), Centre of Tampa Club (founding mem. 1988-93, bd. dirs., chmn. mem. com.), Univ. Club (treas. 1998—, sec. 1999—, bd. dirs. 1998-99), Ye Mystic Krewe of Gasparilla (bd. dirs. 1991—, 1st lt. 1988-89, lord chamberlain 1994-95, chmn. exec. com. 1995-96, capt. 1996-98), King Gasparilla LXXXVI. Home and Office: 2919 W Swann Ave Ste 303 Tampa FL 33609-4051

BRANCO, PAULO JOSÉ COSTA, electrical engineer; b. New Lisbon, Angola, Portugal, Oct. 11, 1965; s. José Manuel and Maria Ernestina (Costa) B.; m. Margarita Filgueira Coelho, Feb. 22, 1992. BSEE, Fed. U. of Rio de Janeiro, 1989, MSEE, 1991; PhD in Elec. Engring., IST/Lisbon, 1998. Elec. engr. Coppe-Eléctrica/UFRJ, Rio de Janeiro, 1989-91; elec. engr. Lab. de Mecatrónica DEEC Inst. Superior Técnico, 1998—; asst. prof. Inst. Superior Técnico, Lisbon, 1998—, rschr. mechatronics lab., 1998—. Contbr. articles to profl. jours. Mem. IEEE, Ordem Dos Engenheiros. Avocations: swimming, reading science fiction books, poetry. Home: Estrada Sassoeiros 2 2F, 2775 Carcavelos Cascais, Portugal Office: Inst Superior Tecnico, DEEC/SMEEP Av Rovisco Pais, 1049-02 Lisbon Portugal

BRANCO, VASCO NOVAIS, real estate executive; b. Almeirim, Portugal, Sept. 7, 1949; s. Adelino Novais and Amelia (Pinheiro) B.; m. Madalena Morais, June 7, 1986; children: Vera, Vasco. Grad., Lisbon U. of Econs., 1973; postgrad., U. Navarra, lisbon, 1984. Dep. contr. ITT/Imprimarte, Lisbon, 1972-73; dir. Centrel, Lisbon, 1974-78, Vale de Lobo, Algarve, Portugal, 1978-80, Planal/Quinta do Lago, Algarve, Portugal, 1983-87; dep. chmn. Cofipsa, 1996—, Lusotur, Vilamoura, 1996—; fin. cons. Conselho, Lisbon, 1980-82; dir. S.P.C., Lisbon, 1981-89, Invesplano, Lisbon, 1987—, Planbelas, Belas-Clube de Campo, Lisbon, 1990—; chmn. fiscal com. TV Cabo Tejo, Lisbon, 1995—. Treas. Santa Casa Misericórdia, Almeirim, 1993—. Avocations: gardening, reading. Home: Trav da Palmeira 31A, 1200 Lisbon Portugal Office: Planbelas SA, Av Marques de Tomar 35-2 DT, 1050 Lisbon Portugal

BRAND, CLIVE MAURICE, law educator, solicitor; b. London, Sept. 22, 1950; s. John Gordon Holmes and Betty Ada (Goodey) B. LLB, U. Newcastle-on-Tyne, 1972. Articled clk. Mayor Aldermen and Burgesses of the Borough of Aldershot, Eng., 1973-75; lectr. law U. Aberdeen, Scotland, 1975-80, U. Liverpool, Eng., 1980-95. Author: Planning Law for Conveyancers, 1983, Notes on the Need for Planning Permission, 1984, Handbook of Business Tenancies, 1985, Mobile Homes and the Law, 1986; editor: Encyclopedia of Compulsory Purchaase and Compensation, 1987—, Practical Financial Management, 1987—, Essential Law for Accountants, 1995—. Mem. Law Soc., Liverpool Law Soc. Avocation: horseracing. Home: 225 Mather Ave, Liverpool, Merseyside L18 9UB, England

BRAND, JOHN WILLIAM DANIEL, lawyer, mediator; b. Johannesburg, South Africa, Feb. 26, 1949; s. John Charles and Iris Lily (Austin) B.; m. Jennifer Ann Leslie, Dec. 2, 1972; children: Edward John, James Austin, Emma Jane, Sarah Ann. BA, U. Witwatersrand, Johannesburg, 1972, LLB, 1976. Bar: South Africa. Judges registrar High Ct., Johannesburg, 1972-73; acticled clk. Webber Wentzel, Johannesburg, 1974-75; profl. asst./assoc. Bowman Gilfillan, Johannesburg, 1976-79, dir., 1980-90; dir. John Brand & Assocs. Inc., Johannesburg, 1990—, Conflict Dynamics, Johannesburg, 1996—; founding trustee Ind. Mediation Svc. South Africa, 1984, vice chair bd. trustees, 1988-94, mediator, arbitrator, trainer conflict resolution; lectr. in field; mem. multinat. team of experts to design mediator tng. Internat. Labor Orgn., Geneva, 1995. Author: Labour Dispute Resolution, 1997; editor-in-chief Employment Law, 1984-94. Trustee Urban Tng. Project, Johannesburg, 1977-79, Family Life Ctr., Johannesburg, 1985-89, Ctr. Applied Legal Studies, U. Witwatersrand, 1987-92. Mem. Law Soc. South Africa, South African Soc. Labor Law, South African Inst. Race Rels., Indsl. Rels. Assn. South Africa (mem. coun. 1995-99). Avocations: running, cycling, swimming, music, bird watching. Office: John Brand and Assocs, PO Box 785812, Sandton Gauteng 2146, Republic of South Africa

BRAND, KENNETH ROGER, small business owner; b. Beverly, Mass., Aug. 24, 1961; s. Roger Gray and Susanne L. B.; m. Mary Isabel, Sept. 6, 1997; children: Christopher, Josh, Craig, Amanda. Grad., Hamilton-Wenham Regional H.S., Mass., 1979. Svc. mgr. Sawtelle Bros., Lawrence, Mass., 1981-84; pres., founder Brand Co., Hamilton, 1984—. Office: Brand Co PO Box 2292 South Hamilton MA 01982-0292

BRAND, MARK, lawyer; b. Sauk Centre, Minn., Feb. 1, 1952; s. Milton A. and Margaret (Kay) B.; m. Margrit B. Kuehn, Sept. 4, 1982; children: Peter, Erik, Natalie. BA cum laude, Concordia Coll., 1974; JD, U Notre Dame, 1979. Bar: Wash. 1979, U.S. Dist. Ct. (we. dist.) Wash. 1979, U.S. Ct. Appeals (9th cir.) 1979, Tex. 1981, U.S. Dist. Ct. (so. dist.) Tex. 1981, U.S. Ct. Appeals (5th and 11th cirs.) 1981, Ill. 1988, U.S. Dist. Ct. (no. dist) Ill. 1988, U.S. Ct. Appeals (7th cir.) 1988, U.S. Dist. Ct. (ea. dist.) Mich. 1992, U.S. Dist. Ct. (cent. dist.) Ill. 1996. Assoc. George, Hull & Porter, Seattle, 1979-80; atty. Gulf Oil Corp., Houston, 1980-85; assoc. Hutcheson & Grundy, LLP, Houston, 1985-87; ptnr. Phelan Pope & John Ltd., Chgo., 1987-93, Brand & Novak Ltd., Chgo., 1993—; spkr., chair various seminars and trial practice, 1986—. Mem. ABA, Chgo. Bar. Assn. Office: Brand & Novak Ltd 135 S La Salle St Ste 3700 Chicago IL 60603-4101

BRAND, OSCAR, folksinger, writer, educator; b. Winnipeg, Man., Can., Feb. 7, 1920; s. Isadore and Beatrice (Shulman) B.; m. Rubyan Saber (div.); children: Jeannie, Eric, James; m. Karen Lynn Grossman, June 14, 1970; 1 child, Jordan. BA, Bklyn. Coll., 1942; Polit. Sci. Laureate, Fairfield U., 1972; PhD (hon.), U. Winnipeg, 1987. Host, performer Folksong Festival, Sta. WNYC-AM-FM, N.Y.C., 1945—; pres. Harlequin Prodns., Inc., Gypsy Hill Music, Inc.; trustee Newport Festival Found.; mem. faculty Hofstra U., New Sch., 1970-80; music adviser nat. bd. YWCA; mem. creative bd. Sesame Street, Pres.'s Com. on Nutrition; cons. Bill Moyers, PBS-TV, 1983; curator Songwriters Hall of Fame. Host: (TV show) World of Folkmusic, H.E.W., 1962-82, Oscar Brand's Am. Odyssey, 1970-72, Treasure Chest, The First Look, 1965-68, (radio show) Voices in the Wind, 1974-80, 13 of Segovia, First Person Am.; star: (TV series) Let's Sing Out, Can., 1962-68, Brand New Scene, Can., 1966; artistic dir. Project America, 92d St. Y, 1998-2000; music dir. (TV series) Nat. Geog. Bicentennial, 1974, Sunday, Exploring; music advisor: (TV series) Nuclear Age, 1986-87, (PBS) Liberty, 1998; writer, dir.: (TV spl. and show) Sing, America, Sing, Kennedy Ctr. Bicentennial Celebration, 1975; composer, lyricist: (broadway show) Joyful Noise, 1966, HYMAN KAPLAN, 1967, (off-broadway show) In White America, 1965, How to Steal an Election, 1968, It's a Jungle, Bridge of Hope for lit. conf., 1969, Celebrate for N.Y. Presbytery, 1970, (off broadway show) Thunder Bay, Fun and Games, Protest, 1999, Ready Aim Sing, 1999, Ballads and Ballots, 2000, Me and Woody, 2000, (songs for film) The Fox, Sybil, The Long Riders, Blue Chips, 1994; author: Singing Holidays, 1957, Bawdy Songs, 1960, Folksongs for Fun, 1961, The Ballad Mongers, 1964, Songs of '76, 1974, When I First Came to This Land, 1975, Party Songs, 1983; rec. artist 96 albums; performer (video) At Home, 1988, Campaigns for Smithsonian, 1999; editor: Words About Music, 1980—. Program coord. Nat. Hadassah, 1989-98; trustee BMI Found., 1995—; music dir. Rukeyser Guide, 1996. Served as sgt. M.C. AUS, 1942-45. Recipient Radio Pioneers of Am. award, 1986, Venice, Edinburgh, Valley Forge, Golden Reel and Cannes Film Festival awards for documentary and ednl. films, 1946, numerous other awards include Emmy, Peabody, Freedoms Found., Scholastic, Edison, Golden Lion for radio, TV and films, 1962-86, Lifetime Achievement award World Folk Music Assn., 1996, Peabody Personal award, 1996; honoree Coalition Against Domestic Violence (adv. bd. 1993—), United Cmty. Fund, 1997. Mem. Nat. Acad. Popular Music (bd. dirs. 1969—), N.Y. Folklore Soc., Sheet Music Soc. Avocations: sailing, carpentry. E-mail: oscarbrand@oscarbrand.com. Office: Gypsy Hill Music PO Box 1362 Manhasset NY 11030-6362

BRAND, STEWART, editor, writer; b. Rockford, Ill., Dec. 14, 1938. BS in Biology, Stanford U., 1960. Formerly with Merry Pranksters; founder Am. Needs Indians; spl. cons. to Gov. Edmund G. Brown, Jr., Calif., 1976-78; rsch. scientist Media Lab, MIT, 1986; vis. scholar Royal Dutch/Shell, 1986. Author: Two Cybernetic Frontiers, 1974, The Media Lab, 1987, How Buildings Learn, 1994, The Clock of The Long Now, 1999; editor/pub.: The Last Whole Earth Catalog, 1968-71 (Nat. Book award), Whole Earth Epilog, 1974, The Next Whole Earth Catalog, 1980-81, The Co-Evolution Quar., 1974-85; editor-in-chief: Whole Earth Software Catalog, 1983-85; writer, presenter: How Buildings Learn, 1997. Founder The WELL teleconf. system, 1984—; co-founder Global Bus. Network, 1988—, The Long Now Found., 1996—; trustee Santa Fe Inst., 1989—. Address: 3E Gate 5 Rd Sausalito CA 94965-1401

BRANDÃO, ANA PAULA LIMA PINTO, political science educator, researcher; b. Braga, Portugal, June 8, 1965; d. Armando Domingos L. and Olga Maria Estelita G. Oliveira; m. Afonso Manuel Cunha de Almeida Brandão, June 20, 1992; children: João Paulo, Pedro Afonso, Ines, Leonor. Degree in internat. rels., U. Minho, Braga, Portugal, 1987, M in European Studies, 1992, PhD in Internat. Rels., 1999. Prof. polit. sci. U. Minho, Braga, 1987-92, lectr. polit. sci., 1992—. Contbr. articles to profl. jours. E-mail: abrandao@eeg.uminho.pt. Home: R Dr João Antunes Guimarães, Rua da Fabrica 259, 4710 Braga Portugal Office: U Minho Sch Econs and Mgmt, Campus of Gualtar, 4710-057 Braga Codex Portugal

BRANDELL, SOL RICHARD, electrical power and control system engineer, research mathematician. Studied piano with Norman Masloff, Juilliard Sch. Music, 1932-41; studied with Sir John Barbirolli, La Follette Sch. Music, N.Y.C., 1939; student, U. Cin., 1943-44, U. Paris, 1945; BEE, CCNY, 1949; postgrad., Poly. Inst. Bklyn., 1952, CCNY, 1954-58. Registered profl. elec. engr. and control systems engr., Calif.; lic. profl. engr., N.Y.; registered profl. engr., N.D. Elec. field engr., designer, estimator Rao Elec. Equipment Co., N.Y.C., 1947-50; elec. designer Edward E. Ashley, P.E., N.Y.C., 1950-51; elec. design engr. Wearn, Vreeland, Carlson, and Sweatt, N.Y.C., 1951-52; sr. elec. engr. Bechtel Assocs., N.Y.C., 1952-57; chief elec. engr. Am. Hydrotherm Corp., N.Y.C., 1957-76; supervising elec. engr. Heyward-Robinson Co., N.Y.C., 1976-77; prin. mem. tech. staff Ralph M. Parsons Co., Pasadena, Calif., 1977-91; pvt. cons., electric power rsch. engr., mathematician Alexandria, Va., 1991—. Co-author: Analysis of Harmonic Pollution on Power Distribution Systems, 1989; author: Recollections of a World War II Infantryman, 1994; contbr. rsch. papers to Am. Hydrotherm Corp. With U.S. Army, 1942-46, ETO. Decorated Bronze Star medal, Purple Heart medal, ETO Campaign medal with 2 bronze campaign stars; N.Y. State War Vet. scholar, 1949. Mem. IEEE (life, sr.), VFW, DAV, Vets. Battle of the Bulge, Combat Infantrymen's Assn., Soc. of 89th Inf. Divsn., U.S. Holocaust Meml. Mus. (hon. charter), Am. Math. Soc., N.Y. Acad. Scis., Sigma Xi. Achievements include patents in electric power applications; engineering and design of electrical supervisory control systems for the first atomic reactor prototype power generating station in U.S. for GE Corp., 1955; research in solid state electronic annunciators, analog to discrete variable conversion system for chemical process temperature control, extremely reliable low-voltage electrical power generating stations for the uninterruptible supply of large-scale FAA air-route traffic control center operations, mathematical modeling and computational harmonic analysis of nonsinusoidal energy flow in electrical power systems, on the decomposition of harmonic distortion power, in various applications of Bessel's equation including experimental work in low frequency eddy-current heating of process liquids in pipes and vessels.

BRÄNDÉN, CARL IVAR, research scientist; b. S. Bergnäs, Lappland, Sweden, May 14, 1934; s. Henry Mauritz and Greta Margot (Nilsson) B.; m. Lisbet Wikander, May 28, 1957 (div. 1991); children: Henrik, Per; m. Malin Åkerblom, Feb. 15, 1992. BSc, Uppsala (Sweden) U., 1957, PhD, 1964. Rsch. asst. Med. Rsch. Coun., Cambridge, Eng., 1962-63; assoc. prof. Swedish U. Agrl. Sci., Uppsala, 1964-70, prof., 1979—; prof. Sci. Rsch. Coun., Uppsala, 1970-79; rsch. dir. European Synchroton Radiation Facility, Grenoble, France, 1992-97; chmn. Chemistry Com., Swedish Sci. Rsch. Coun., 1983-86, EMBO Fund Com., Heidelberg, Germany, 1985-88, Chemistry Class, Swedish Acad. Scis., 1986-90. Author: Introduction to Protein Structure, 1991, Molecules of Life, 1992; editor Structure, 1993—. Mem. City Coun. Health Orgn., Uppsala, 1975-81; mem. rsch. adv. coun. Swedish Govt., Stockholm, 1986-89. Recipient Arrhenius medal Swedish Chem. Soc., 1976, Celcius medal Royal Soc. Scis., Uppsala, 1990, Björkénska prize Uppsala U., 1992. Mem. European Molecular Biology Orgn. (bd. dirs. 1973—), Royal Swedish Acad. Sci. (mem. Nobel com. 1987-93), Academia Europea. Social Democrat. Avocations: art, skiing. Home: Sveddvägen 9B, S-75652 Uppsala Sweden Office: Karolinska Inst Box 280, Micro/Tumor Biol Ctr, S-17177 Stockholm Sweden

BRANDENBERG, ALIKI LIACOURAS See ALIKI

BRANDENBURG, ALBRECHT, physicist, researcher; b. Braunschweig, Germany, Jan. 11, 1960; s. Martin and Rosemarie (Koch) B.; m. Ursula Lehmann, 1989; children: Sophia, Leonard. Diploma in Physics, U. Münster, Germany, 1983; Dr.Ing., Tech. U., Clausthal, Germany, 1989. Head dept. biophotonics and integrated optics Fraunhofer-Inst. Phys. Measurement Techniques, Freiburg, Germany, 1984—. Contbr. numerous articles to profl. jours.; patentee on optical sensor, 1990. Home: Ludwig-Reithmeyer Str, D-79232 March Germany Office: Fraunhofer-Inst Phys Measurement Techniques, Heidenhofstr 8, D-79110 Freiburg Germany

BRANDENSTEIN, HARTMUT, electrical engineer; b. Wonfurt, Bavaria, Germany, July 26, 1965; s. Herbert and Irene Brandenstein; m. Olga Bendikova, Apr. 18, 1997; 1 child, Konstantin. Univ. diploma in engring., U. Erlangen-Nurnberg, Germany, 1992, D in Engring., 1999. Cert. in engring. With U. Erlangen-Nurnberg. E-mail: bra@late.e-technik.uni-erlangen.de. Office: U Erlangen-Nurnberg, Cauerstr 7, Erlangen 91058, Germany

BRANDES, TOBIAS, theoretical physicist; b. Braunschweig, Germany, Mar. 5, 1966; s. Manfred and Heidi (Jaikowski) B. PhD in Physics summa cum laude, U. Hamburg, Germany, 1994; degree in Japanese lang. proficiency, Tokyo, 1996. Sci. asst. U. Hamburg, 1993-95; fellow European Union, Tokyo, 1995-97; scientist Tokyo U., 1997; sci. asst. Univ. Hamburg, 1998-2000; lectr. UMIST, Manchester, UK, 2000—. Contbr. articles to sci. jours.; book editor; workshop organizer. U.S. travel fellow U. Hamburg, 1995. Mem. Japanese Phys. Soc., German Phys. Soc. Avocations: music, literature, cello, Japanese culture.

BRANDIS, TILO, librarian, retired researcher in German studies; b. Hamburg, Germany, Jan. 21, 1935; s. Brandis Günther and Gerda (Hanne) B.; m. Ute Tartsch, Mar. 25, 1966; children: Markus, Christoph, Veronika, Julian. PhD, U. Hamburg, 1964. Libr. Staatsbibliothek, Hamburg, 1962-73; head of manuscript dept. Staatsbibliothek Preussischer Kulturbesitz, Berlin, 1973-00; tchr. U. Hamburg, 1968-73; tchr./prof. Freie U., Berlin, 1973—; cons. Deutsche Forschungsgemeinschaft, Bonn, Germany, 1971-00. Author: Der Harder, 1964, Manuscript Catalogue: S. Petri Hamburg, 1967, Minnereden. Catalogue of Manuscripts and Prints, 1968, Manuscript Catalogue: Codices in scrinio Hamburg, 1972, Catalogue of Nachlässe in German Libraries, 1981, Manuscript Catalogue: Theologische Handschriften Berlin, 1985, Handbuch der Handschriftenbestände Deutschland, 1992, Scrinium Berolinense. Festschrift in honour of Tilo Brandis, 2 vols., 2000, others. Evangelical-Lutheran. Avocation: chamber music. Home: Nachodstrasse 20, D10779 Berlin Germany

BRANDL, HEINZ, research scientist, consultant, educator; b. Znaim, Austria, June 29, 1940; s. George and Elisabeth (Rohrer) B.; m. Annerose Poguntke, Sept. 9, 1966; children: Therese, Peter, Georg. MSc, Tech U., Vienna, Austria, 1963, D Tech., 1966. Rsch. asst. Tech. U., Vienna, 1963-66, asst. prof., 1966-71, head soil lab., 1969-72, assoc. prof., 1971-77, prof., head inst., 1978-81; prof. Tech. U., Vienna, Austria, 1981—; chmn., gen. reporter, keynote lecr., discussion leader numerous internat. confs. Author 15 books, 310 sci. papers. Recipient numerous sci. awards. Mem. Europa Internat. Soc. for Soil Mechanics and Geotech. Engring. (pres. 1997—), Austrian Soc. for Soil Mechanics and Geotech. Engring (pres. 1973—), Belgian Royal Acad. Scis. Avocations: philosophy, fine arts, literature, sports. Home: Nussberggasse 7A/23, A-1190 Vienna Austria Office: Tech U, Karlsplatz 13, A-1040 Vienna Austria

BRANDL, RICHARD, vascular surgeon, consultant; b. Munich, Aug. 3, 1956; s. Rudolf and Maria Wolf; m. Ulrike Bachmann, Aug. 1, 1984; children: Simon, Susanne, Anna-Sophia. Dr.med., LMU, Munich, 1982; privatdozent, TUM, 1998. Asst. prof. vascular surgery Tech. U. of Munich. Home: Aurikelstr 4, 81377 München Germany Office: Tech U of Munich, Ismaningerstr 22, 81675 Münich Germany

BRANDMEIR, CHRISTOPHER LEE, hotel and tourism management educator; b. Seattle, Mar. 6, 1950; s. Jack W. and Betty G. (Lyman) B. BA, U. San Francisco, 1972. Dir. coll. rels. Cogswell Coll., San Francisco, 1983-86; exec. dir. San Lorenzo (Calif.) Village, 1986-88; owner Inn Sight, Seattle, 1996—; pres., co-owner HBH Mgmt., Lopez Island, Wash., 1993-96, Inn at Swifts Bay, Lopez Island, 1988-96; instr., program mgr. hotel and tourism mgmt. Highline C.C., Des Moines, 1998—. Chair San Juan Islands Tourism Resource Coun.; bd. dirs., past chair San Juan Islands Visitor Info. Svc.; bd. dirs., fundraiser Lopez Island Cmty. Ctr.; pres. Lopez Island Chamber. Recipient Lyons Club Svc. award. Mem. Internat. Assn. Culinary Profls. Republican. Roman Catholic. Avocations: cooking, sailing, international studies, politics. E-mail: clb0563@aol.com. and cbrandme@hcc.ctc.edu. Home: 3543 Hampton Way Kent WA 98032-7027 Office: Highline CC 2400 S 240th St MS 18-1 Des Moines WA 98198-2714

BRANDO, MARLON, JR., actor; b. Omaha, Apr. 3, 1924; s. Marlon and Dorothy Pennebaker (Myers) B.; m. Anna Kashfi, 1957 (div. 1959); 1 son, Christian; m. Movita Brando (div.); 1 child. Student, Shattuck Mil. Acad., 1939-41. Actor: N.Y. plays, including Streetcar Named Desire; motion pictures include The Men, 1950, Streetcar Named Desire, 1951, Viva Zapata, 1952 (Best Actor, Cannes Internat. Film Festival), Julius Caesar, 1953, The Wild One, 1953, Desirée, 1954, On the Waterfront, 1954 (Acad. award for best actor), Guys and Dolls, 1955,Teahouse of the August Moon, 1956, Sayonara, 1957, The Young Lions, 1958, The Fugitive Kind, 1960, One Eyed Jacks (also dir.) 1960, Mutiny on the Bounty, 1962, The Ugly American, 1963, Bedtime Story, 1964, The Saboteur, 1965, The Chase, 1966, The Appaloosa, 1966, A Countess from Hong Kong, Reflections in A Golden Eye, 1967, Candy, The Godfather, 1972 (Acad. award for best actor), Last Tango in Paris, 1972, Missouri Breaks, 1976, Superman, 1978, Apocalypse Now, 1979, The Formula, 1980, A Dry White Season, 1989, The Freshman, 1990, Jericho, Christopher Columbus: The Discovery, 1992, Don Juan DeMarco, 1995, The Island of Dr. Moreau, 1996, The Brave, 1997, Free Money, 1998, Autumn of the Patriarch, 1999; TV appearance in Roots: The Next Generations, 1979; author: (with Robert Lindsey) Brando: Songs My Mother Taught Me, 1994.

BRANDON, GARY KENT, physician, health facility administrator; b. Pueblo, Colo.; s. Vernon Charles and Eva M. (Hachey) B.; m. D.J. Harris, May 21, 1976; children: Terry, Belinda, John, Tracye, Sherry, Kimberly. BA, U. So. Colo., 1968; MS, N.Mex. Highlands U., 1969; DO, U. Health Scis., 1973; MPH, Johns Hopkins U., 1979; postgrad., Nat. War Coll., 1989-90. Diplomate Am. Bd. Preventive Medicine, Am. Bd. Med. Mgmt. Intern Lake Side Hosp., Kansas City, Mo., 1973-74; resident Johns Hopkins, 1978-79, USAF Sch. Aerospace Medicine, 1979-80; commd. capt. USAF, 1976, advanced through grades to col., 1986; hosp. comdr. Barksdale AFB, Shreveport, La., 1987-89, MacDill AFB, Tampa, Fla., 1990-93; dir. med. inspection USAF, Albuquerque, 1993-95; ret. USAF, 1995; med. dir. Valley Wide Health Svc., Alamosa, Colo., 1995-97; pres. Brandon Consulting, Grand Junction, Colo., 1997-98; occupl. assoc. med. dir. Occumed Corp. Health Svcs., Freeman Hosps. and Health Sys., Joplin, Mo., 1998—; sr. examiner Malcolm Baldridge Nat. Quality Award, Washington, 1993-97. Author: Aviation, Space and Environmental Medicine, 1980, co-author 2d edit., 1983. V.p. Rocky Mountain HMO, Grand Junction, Colo., 1975, Western Colo. Physicians, Inc., Grand Junction, 1975; pres. Mesa County Osteo. Assn., Grand Junction, 1976. Recipient Med. Leadership award Strategic Air Command USAF, Aboline, Tex., 1986, USAF award for profl. excellence, Washington, 1994. Fellow Am. Coll. Preventive Medicine; mem. APHA, Am. Coll. Occupl. and Environ. Medicine, Am. Soc. Quality Control, Nat. Assn. Managed Care Physicians. Avocations: flying, scuba diving, photography, horseback riding. Office: Occumed Corp Health Svcs 3201 Mcclelland Blvd Joplin MO 64804-3524

BRANDON, PETER SAMUEL, academic administrator, civil and structural engineer; b. Writtle, Essex, Eng., June 4, 1943; s. Samuel and Doris Eileen Florence (Downing) B.; m. Mary Ann Elizabeth Canham, Sept. 14, 1968; children: Samantha, Juliette, Robin. Student, Bournemouth (Eng.) Coll. Tech., 1961-64; MSc in Architecture with commendation, Bristol (Eng.) U., 1978; DSc, Salford Eng.) U., 1996. Chartered Surveyor, Eng. Pvt. practice London, 1963-67; surveyor local govt. Kent, 1968-70; lectr. Portsmouth (Eng.) Polytech., 1969-73, head of surveying dept., 1981-85; prin. lectr. Bristol (Eng.) Polytech., 1973-81; head of surveying dept. Salford (Eng.) U., 1985-93, pro-vice chancellor, 1993—; chmn. rsch. com. Royal Instn. Chartered Surveyors, London, 1987-91, mem. gen. coun., 1989-93, mem. exec. bd., 1991-94; chmn. constrn. com. Sci. and Engring. Rsch. Coun., Eng., 1990-94; chmn. higher edn. funding coun. rsch. assessment and panel for Built Environment and Planning, 1996—; mem. coun. Parliament Univ. Group, 1995-98. Author: (with G. Moore) Microcomputers in Building Appraisal, 1983, (with J. Kirkham) An Integrated Database for Quantity Surveying, 1989, (with DJ Ferry) Cost Planning of Bldgs. rev. 7th edit., 1999; Author: (with others) Computer Programs for Building Cost Appraisal, 1985, Expert Systems: The Strategic Planning of Construction Projects, 1988; editor: Building Cost Techniques: New Directions, 1983, Quality and Profit in Building Design, 1984, Building, Cost Modelling and Computers, 1987, Quantity Surveying Techniques: New Directions, 1990, Investment, Procurement & Performance in Construction, 1991, Management, Quality and Economics in Building, 1991, Integrated Construction Information, 1995, Client Centred: An Approach to Knowledge Based Systems, 1995, Evaluation of the Built Envrionment for Sustainability, 1994, Cities and Sustainability: Sustaining of Cultural Heritage, 2000. Named hon. mem. Assn. S. African Quantity Surveyors, 1993. Fellow Royal Inst. Chartered Surveyors; mem. Design Rsch. Soc., Royal Overseas League. Avocations: mountain biking alongside canals, travel, modern art, swimming. Office: Univ Salford, Rsch and Grad Coll, Salford M5 4WT, England

BRANDRUP, DOUGLAS WARREN, lawyer; b. Mitchel, S.D., July 11, 1940; s. Clair L. and Ruth M. (Wolverton) B.; m. Patricia R. Tuck, Dec. 20, 1986; children: Kendra, Monika, Peter. AB in Econs., Middlebury Coll., 1963; JD, Boston U., 1966. Bar: N.Y. 1969, U.S. Dist. Ct. (so. dist.) N.Y. 1970, U.S. Ct. Appeals (2d cir.) 1970. Assoc. Donovan, Leisure, Newton & Irvine, N.Y.C., 1968-72; ptnr. Griggs, Baldwin & Baldwin, N.Y.C., 1972-80, sr. ptnr., 1980—; chmn. Equity Oil Co.; bd. dirs. Ardshiel, Inc. Mem. Govs. Security Adv. Com., State of N.J., 1975-90. Capt. U.S. Army, 1966-68. Recipient Ellis Island medal of Honor, 1999. Mem. ABA, N.Y. County Bar Assn., N.Y. State Bar Assn., Met. Club (N.Y.C., pres.), Mashomack Preserve Club. Republican. Episcopalian. Office: Griggs Baldwin & Baldwin 27 E 65th St Apt 7D New York NY 10021-6556

BRANDS, TOM, Olympic athlete; b. Omaha, Apr. 9, 1968. BS in Phys. Edn., U. Iowa, 1992. asst. coach U. Iowa. Recipient Gold medal 136.5 pounds freestyle wrestling Atlanta Olympics, 1996; winner U.S. Nats., 1993-95, World Team Trials, 1993-95, Krasnoyarsky Tournament, 1993, Cerro Pelado Tournament, 1994, World Cup, 1994-95, Pan Am. Games, 1995; named USA Wrestling Athlete of Yr., 1993, John Smith Outstanding Freestyle Wrestler, 1993, Amateur Wrestling News Man of Yr., 1993. Office: USA Wrestling 6155 Lehman Dr Colorado Springs CO 80918-3439*

BRANDSTADT, ANDREAS, computer science educator; b. Arnstadt, Germany, Jan. 17, 1949; s. Wilhelm and Charlotte (Baumgarten) B. Diploma, U. Jena, Germany, 1976. Asst. U. Jena, Germany, 1976-91; prof. U. Duisburg, Germany, 1991-94, Y. Rostock, Germany, 1994—. Home: Wakenitz str 36A, 23564 Lübeck Germany Office: U Rostock, A Einstein Str 21, 18059 Rostock Germany

BRANDSTÄTTER, EDUARD JOHANN, psychology educator, researcher; b. Wels, Austria, May 19, 1965; s. Ernst and Erika (Grillnberger) B. MS, U. Innsbruck, Austria, 1992; Dr Rer. Nat., U. Vienna, Austria, 1997. Asst. prof. U. Linz, Austria, 1993—; vis. scholar U. Mich., Ann Arbor, 1996-97. Contbr. articles to profl. jours. With Austrian Army, 1992. Mem. APA (affiliate), Deutsche Gesellschaft für Psychologie, Internat. Assn. Rsch. in Econ. Psychology, Soc. for Judgment and Decision Making, European Assn. for Decision Making, Am. Psychol. Soc. Avocations: sports, arts. Office: U Linz Johannes Kepler, Altenbergerstr 69, A-4040 Linz Austria

BRÄNDSTRÖM, ARNE ELOF, retired chemist; b. Luleå, Sweden, July 26, 1925; s. Karl Elof Vilhelm and Eleonora (Sundgren) B.; m. Margit Elisabet Westerberg Brändström, Aug. 31, 1947; children: Lars, Peter, Margareta, Mats. PhD, U. Uppsala, Sweden, 1954. Asst. U. Uppsala, Sweden, 1948-52; rsch. chemist Pharmacia, Uppsala, Sweden, 1953-59; rsch. dir. chemistry Hässle, Gothenburg, Sweden, 1959-67; sr. scientist Hässle, Mölndal, Sweden, 1967-72; guest prof. Chemistry U. Aarhus, Denmark, 1972-73; sr. scientist Hässle, Mölndal, Sweden, 1973-96; ret. Inventor: Alprenolole, 1965, Metoprolole, 1970, Omeprazole, 1978; author: Preparative Ion Pair Extraction, 1976. Recipient Inventor prize The Swedish Bd. Tech. Devel., 1987, Oscar Carlsson Gold medal The Swedish Chem. Soc., 1988; Gold medal The Royal Swedish Acad. Engring. Scis., 1988, Nauta European Fedn. Medicinal Chemistry, Basel, 1992, Wilhelm Westrups Kingl. Fysiografiska Sällskapet, Lund, Sweden, 1993. Home: Karlsborg 193, Ystad Sweden

BRANDT, ANDREAS, artist; b. Halle, Germany, Dec. 29, 1935; s. Heinrich and Eva-Maria (Gerhardt) B.; div.; 1 child, David; m. Kristina Welin. Meisterschueler, Hochschule fuer bildende Künste, Berlin, 1961. Freelance artist Berlin, 1961-82; prof. textile design Hochschule fuer bildende Künste, Hamburg, Germany, 1982-01. Recipient Emil Nolde award, 1962, Berliner Kunstpreis, 1977, Camille Graeser prize, Zurich, 1990, Fred Thieler prize, Berlin, 1995; USA-Stipendium grantee, 1975-76. Home: Gotteskoogstrasse 22, D-25899 Niebuell Germany

BRANDT, GENE STUART, fundraising consultant; b. N.Y.C., Aug. 29, 1950; s. Eugene Charles and Elsie Virginia (Williams) B.; m. Elizabeth Holland, July 20, 1991; children: Cameron Elizabeth, Christopher Holland. AB in Polit. Sci., Knox Coll., 1972. Asst. dir. admission Knox Coll., Galesburg, Ill., 1972-74; dir. alumni affairs Knox Coll., Galesburg, 1974-76; dir. univ. devel. U. Nev., Reno, 1976-79; dir. devel. Lake Forest (Ill.) Coll., 1979-81, v.p. devel., 1981-86; v.p. external affairs Mus. Sci. and Industry, Chgo., 1986-91; pres. sci. and tech. Mus. of Atlanta, 1991-97; prin., cons. TerMolen Bran, Atlanta, 1997—. Bd. dirs., vice-chmn. Pub. Broadcasting Atlanta; mem. Coun. for Advancement and Support of Edn. Named 1 of Outstanding Young Men of Am., 1981. Mem. Am. Assn. Mus., Nat. Soc. Fundraising Execs., Econ. Club Chgo., Ansley Golf Club, Lahinch Golf Club (Ireland), Univ. Club Chgo. Office: TerMolen Brandt & Assocs 500 N Dearborn St Ste 726 Chicago IL 60610-4997

BRANDT, JOHN ASHWORTH, fuel company executive; b. Chgo., Oct. 3, 1950; s. William W. and Joan V. (Ashworth) B.; m. Debbie M. Fico, June 2, 1984; children: Briana Ashley, Bryan Ashworth. Student, U. Colo., 1969-72. Mgr. co. accounts Lincoln Wood Commodities, Chgo., 1972-74; pres. Lafayette Coal Co., Burr Ridge, Ill., 1974—, Hoosier King Coal Co., 1993—, Ind. Farms, Inc., 1996—; pres. Chgo. Coal Shippers, 1984—; pres. Hoosier King Coal Co.; dir. Muliganeers Non-Profit Orgn. Office: Lafayette Coal Co 200 S Frontage Rd Ste 310 Hinsdale IL 60521-6953

BRANDT, OLIVER, physicist; b. Offenbach/Main, Germany, Mar. 24, 1962; s. Herbert and Rosemarie (Hahn) Schlabbach; m. Christine, Aug. 22, 1988 (div. Oct. 1995); m. Chiyoko Takayama, Apr. 29, 1997. Dipl.phys., U. Regensburg, Germany, 1989; Dr.rer.nat., U. Stuttgart, Germany, 1992. Asst. lectr. U. Regensburg, Germany, 1989-92; rschr. Max-Planck Inst., Stuttgart, Germany, 1992; cons. Mitsubishi Elec., Osaka, Japan, 1992; group leader Paul-Drude Inst., Berlin, 1994—; guest scientist Mitsubishi Elec., 1992-94. Author: (chpts.) III-V Quantum Research, 1995, Physics and Applications of Group III Nitrides Semiconductor Compounds, 1997. Mem. Material Rsch. Soc. Office: Paul Drude Inst, Hausvogteiplatz 5-7, 10117 Berlin Germany

BRANDT, ROBERT BARRY, lay worker; b. Lebanon, Pa., Nov. 13, 1948; s. Marlin Jay Brandt and Arlene Hilda (Bowman) Gable; m. Ruth Ann Peterson, June 6, 1970; 1 child, Matthew Scot. BA in Sociology, Lebanon Valley Coll., 1971; postgrad., United Theol. Sem., Dayton, Ohio, 1973. Lic. to ministry Meth. Ch., 1968. Min. Ea. Pa. United Meth. Ch., Harrisburg, Pa., 1968-72; deacon Ea. Pa. United Meth. Ch., Valley Forge, Pa., 1972-76; local ch. lay leader Ridgewood (N.J.) United Meth. Ch., 1985-87; dist. lay leader no. dist. North N.J. Conf. United Meth., Paramus, N.J., 1986-89; lay leader ann. conf. North N.J. Conf. United Meth., Madison, N.J., 1989-96; chair No. N.J. Bd. of Laity, Madison, 1989-96; chair coun. on ministries Ridgewood United Meth. Ch., 1988-89; mem. bishop's task force No. N.J. United Meth., Madison, 1989, 96-99; mem. Walk to Emmaus Community, 1987—, Disciplined Order of Christ, Nashville, 1988—; v.p. tech. and corp. svcs. Matrix Info. Consulting, Inc., Rochelle Park, N.J., 1987—; mem. gen. coun. on Ministries United Meth. Ch., 1992-96; lay dir. Skylands Walk to Emmaus Cmty., 1996-97. Mem., sec. gen. com. on gen. conf. United Meth. Ch., 1992-2000, del. gen. conf., 1992, 96, 2000; mem. Episcopacy com., N.E. jurisdiction United Meth. Ch., 1991-99; N.E. regional rep. for Internat. Walk to Emmaus, 1998—, internat. steering com., 1998—. Named Layperson of Yr. Northern N.J. Conf., United Meth. Ch., 1993, Man of Yr. Ridgewood United Meth. Ch., 1996. Mem. Nat. Assn. Ann. Conf. Lay Leader. Democrat. Home: 28 Hoitsma Ct Fair Lawn NJ 07410-2760 Office: Matrix Info Cons Inc 365 W Passaic St Rochelle Park NJ 07662-3017

BRANDT, WILLIAM ARTHUR, JR., consulting executive; b. Chgo., Sept. 5, 1949; s. William Arthur and Joan Virginia (Ashworth) B.; m. Patrice Bugelas, Jan. 19, 1980; children: Katherine Ashworth, William George, Joan Patrice, John Peter. BA with honors, St. Louis U., 1971; MA, U. Chgo., 1972, postgrad., 1972-74. Asst. to pres. Pyro Mining Co., Chgo., 1972-74; commentator Sta. WBBM-AM, Chgo., 1977; with Melaniphy & Assocs., Inc., Chgo., 1975-76; pres., cons. Devel. Specialists, Inc., Chgo., 1976—; mem. adv. bd. Sociol. Abstracts, Inc., San Diego, 1979-83. Contbr. articles to profl. jours. Trustee Fenwick H.S., 1991-2000, Comml. Law League of Am., Internat. Coun. Shopping Ctrs., Nat. Assn. Bankruptcy Trustees, Ill. Sociol. Assn., Midwest Sociol. Soc., Urban Land Inst.; mem. Fla. del. to Dem. Nat. Conv., 1996, also mem. Dem. Party 2000's Platform Com. LaVerne Noyes scholar, 1971-74. Mem. Am. Bankruptcy Inst., Am. Sociol. Assn., Amelia Island Plantation Club, Union League Club Chgo., City Club of Miami, gov. mem. Chicago Symphony, Clinton/Gore '96 Natl. Finance Bd., mnging. trustee Democratic Natl. Comm., maj. trust mem. Democratic Senatorial Campaign Comm., life mem. Zoological Soc. of the Miami Metro Zoo. Democrat. Roman Catholic. Home: 2000 S Bayshore Dr Apt 39 Coconut Grove FL 33133-3251 also: Amelia Island Plantation 6518 Beachwood Rd Amelia Island FL 32034-6512 also: 1134 Sheridan Rd Winnetka IL 60093-1538 also: 23 Sea Colony Dr Santa Monica CA 90405-5321 Office: 3 First Nat Plz Ste 2300 Chicago IL 60602 also: 200 S Biscayne Blvd Ste 900 Miami FL 33131-5344 also: Devonshire House, 60 Goswell Rd, London EC1M 7AD, England also: Wells Fargo Ctr 333 S Grand Ave Ste 2010 Los Angeles CA 90071-1524 also: Two Oliver St 11th Fl Boston MA 02109-4901 also: 485 Metro Place S Ste 120 Dublin OH 43017

BRANGE, JENS J.V., biopharmaceutical scientist; b. Vejle, Denmark, Sept. 20, 1940; s. Georg W.V. Jorgensen and Else A. Rasmussen; m. Helle R. Nielsen, Aug. 7, 1962 (div. June 1973); 1 child, Birgitte; m. Lotte Langkjaer, Dec. 20, 1975; children: Sorine L.B., Kristoffer L.B. BSc, Royal Danish Sch. Pharmacy, Copenhagen, 1961, MSc, 1964, DrSci, 1994. Rsch. chemist Novo Industri A/S, Copenhagen, 1966-73, mgr. R&D, 1973-74, dir. R&D, 1974-84; rsch. dir. Novo Rsch. Inst., Copenhagen, 1984-89; dir. pharm. rsch. Novo Nordisk A/S, Copenhagen, 1989-91; vis. prof. U. Calif., San Francisco, 1991-92; sr. scientist Novo Nordisk, Copenhagen, 1993-99; pres. Brange Consult, Advanced Solutions for Proteins, Klampenborg, Denmark, 1999—. Author: Galenics of Insulin, 1987, Stability of Insulin, 1994; mem. editl. bd. Diabetes Tech. and Therapeutics; contbr. articles to profl. jours.; inventor in field. Mem. AAAS, Controlled Release Soc., Am. Assn. Pharm. Scientists, Am. Diabetes Assn., European Assn. for Study of Diabetes, Fedn. Internat. Pharmaceutique. Avocations: history, sports, music, oenology, golf. Home: Kroyersvej 22C, Klampenborg DK-2930, Denmark

BRANGER, HUBERT VINCENT, oceanography researcher; b. La Rochelle, France, Aug. 6, 1959; s. Michel and Liliane (Mothu) B.; m. Dominique France Figarella, Sept. 1, 1984; children: Marine, Frederic, Nicolas, Damien. M, Inst. Polytech Grenoble, France, 1982; PhD, Inst. Mecanique Grenoble, France, 1985. Rschr. CNES, Marseille, France, 1985-87; sr. ingenior SIMINEX, Marseille, France, 1987-91; rschr. CNRS Deg 2, Marseille, France, 1991-95, CNRS Class 1, Marseille, France, 1995—. Contbr. papers to profl. jours. With French Air Force. Mem. AAAS, Rsch. Acad. Scis. Avocation: sailing. Home: Ave Mozart 11 Les Cigales, 13009 Marseille France Office: IRPHE-IOA, Parc Sci Luminy Case 903, 13288 Marseille France

BRANHAM, C. MICHAEL, lawyer; b. Columbia, S.C., Nov. 6, 1957; s. Mack C. and Jennie Louise (Jones) B.; m. Teresa Barrett; children: Anthony, Mark. BS, Auburn U., Montgomery, Ala., 1979; JD, U. S.C., 1983. Bar: S.C.; cert. tax law specialist; CPA. Acct. Wilson, Price, Barranco & Billingsley, CPAs, Montgomery, 1979-80; law clk. Atty. Gen.'s Office, State of S.C., Columbia, 1981-82; acct. Price, Waterhouse, Columbia, 1983-86; tax lawyer Young, Clement, Rivers & Tisdale, LLP, Charleston, S.C., 1986—, chmn. tax, estate planning and probate group, 1999—, firm mgmt. com., asst. mng. ptnr., 1999—; chmn. taxation law specialization adv. bd. S.C. Supreme Ct., 1995-97; mem., pres. Charleston Tax. Coun., 1993-94; mem. dean's adv. bd. Med. U. S.C. Nursing Sch., Charleston, 1994-97; chmn. MUSC Planned Giving adv. coun., 1993-97; mem. exec. com. Roper Found. Planned Giving Coun., Charleston; S.C. case reporter ABA sect. real property, probate and trust law, 1997—; mem. Bishop Gadsden Estate Planning Adv. Coun., Charleston, 1998—. Soccer coach Hungryneck Internat. Soccer Assn., Mt. Pleasant, S.C., 1989-99, James Island/Trident United Soccer Assn., Charleston, 1999—; mem. Charleston Estate Planning Coun. Recipient Am. Jurisprudence award, 1983. Mem. ABA, AICPA, S.C. Assn. CPAs, S.C. Bar Assn., Charleston Breakfast Rotary, S.C. Youth Soccer Assn. (sec. 2000—). Avocations: soccer coaching, weight lifting. Home: 829 Detyens Rd Mount Pleasant SC 29464-5181 Office: Young Clement Rivers & Tisdale LLP 28 Broad St Charleston SC 29401-3070

BRANHAM, MELANIE J., lawyer; b. Kansas City, Mo., Nov. 22, 1960; d. John Francis II and Annette (Bowers) B. BA, U. Kans., 1983, MUP, 1985; JD, We. New Eng. Coll., 1994. Bar: Kans. 1994, Mo. 1995, U.S. Ct. Appeals (10th cir.) 1994, U.S. Ct. Appeals (8th cir.) 1995, U.S. Supreme Ct. 1997. Grad. planner City of Lawrence, Kans., 1984; city planner City of Overland Park, Kans., 1984-85; asst. dir. planning and inspections City of Merriam, Kans., 1985-87; city adminstr. City of Westwood, Kans., 1987-89; town adminstr. Town of Sheffield, Mass., 1989-91; law clk. We. Mass. Legal Svcs., Springfield, Mass., 1992-93; atty./law clk. Kans. Legal Svcs., Olathe, 1993-94; assoc. Johnson County Dist. Atty.'s Office, Olathe, 1994; pvt. practice Olathe, 1994-99; atty. Cohen, McNeile, Pappas & Shuttleworth, P.C., Leawood, Kans., 2000—. Active Nelson-Atkins Mus. of Art, Kansas City, Mo., 1986—; mem. ACLU of Kans. and We. Mo., Kansas City, Mo., 1992—. With CAP Aux., lt. col. USAF, 1972-76. Named to Outstanding Young Women of Am., 1987; recipient Am. Jurisprudence award, 1993. Mem. ABA, Kans. Trial Lawyers Assn., Johnson County Bar Assn., Kans. Bar Assn., Mo. Bar Assn. Episcopal. Office: Cohen McNeile Pappas & Shuttleworth PC Leawood Exec Ctr 4601 College Blvd Ste 200 Leawood KS 66211-1650

BRANIGAN, KEITH, archaeologist, educator; b. Slough, Buckinghamshire, Eng., Apr. 15, 1940; s. Arthur Allan and Constance Gladys (Saunders) B.; m. Kuabrat Sivadith, June 21, 1965; children: Alun Pitchalya, Holly Parima, Tania Anin. BA in Archaeology with honors, U. Birmingham, Eng., 1963, PhD in Archaeology, 1966. Rsch. fellow dept. archaeology U. Birmingham, 1965-66; lectr. dept. classics U. Bristol, Eng., 1966-76; prof. dept. archaeology U. Sheffield, Eng., 1976—, dean Faculty of Arts, 1990-92; chmn. British Univs. Archaeology Com., 1978-84. Author: Foundations of Palatial Crete, 1970, The Tombs of Mesara, 1970, Aegean Metalwork, 1974, The Catuvellauni, 1986, Dancing With Death, 1993, other books. Chmn. Hallam Liberal Assn., Sheffield, 1980-82. Soc. Antiquaries fellow, 1970. Mem. Prehistoric Soc. (v.p. 1982-84). Liberal Democrat. Baptist. Avocations: cricket, football, philately, rock and roll music. Office: U Sheffield, Dept Archaelolgy, Sheffield S10 2TN, England

BRANKOVICH, MARK J., restaurateur; b. Rijeka, Yugoslavia, Mar. 4, 1922; came to U.S., 1951; s. Joseph M. and Rose (Haydin) B.; m. Marilyn J. Severin, Jan. 4, 1957; children: Mark, Laura. BA in Philosophy, U. Zurich, 1944; student, U. Geneva, 1945, U. Padua, Italy, 1947. Owner The Golden Deer, Chgo., 1953-55; mgr. Gaslight Club, N.Y.C., 1955-57; gen. mgr., exec. v.p., dir. Gaslight Club, Chgo., 1959-63; owner, mgr. Franchise Gaslight Club, L.A., 1963-66; owner Monte Carlo Italian Deli, Burbank, Calif., 1969—, Pinocchio Restaurant, Burbank, 1970—, Pinocchio West, Santa Monica, 1972—, Pinocchio Westwood (Calif.), 1978, Italia Foods Wholesale, Burbank, 1972. Mem. Presdl. Task Force, Washington, 1980—, Rep. Senatorial Inner Circle, 1986. Mem. Internat. Platform Assn. Serbian Orthodox. Home: 1250 Hilldale Ave West Hollywood CA 90069-1826 Office: Monte Carlo Italia Foods Inc 3103 W Magnolia Blvd Burbank CA 91505-3046

BRANN, CONRAD BENEDICT, linguist, educator; b. Rostock, Germany, July 20, 1925. MA, Oxford U., 1953; postgrad., Hamburg U., 1952-57, Coll. Europe, Bruges, Belgium, 1957-58. Cert. tchr. Lectr. in English Hamburg U., 1952-57; cultural rels. & reports officer UNESCO, Paris, 1958-65; sr. lectr. in lang. edn. U. Ibadan, Nigeria, 1966-77; prof. applied linguistics U. Maiduguri, Nigeria, 1978—; cons. in field. Contbr. articles to profl. jours. Founder, bd. dirs. Libr. Lang. in Edn. & Soc. Decorated Order of Merit (Germany). Mem. Internat. Sociol. Assn. (rsch. com.), N.Y. Acad. Scis., St. Johns Coll. Club, Oxford Club, Coll. of Europe Club, Brugers Club, Unesco Club. Roman Catholic. Avocations: travel, reading, lectures. Home and Office: Univ Maiduguri, PO Box 2001, Maiduguri Nigeria

BRANN, DONALD LEWIS, JR., school superintendent; b. L.A., Nov. 1, 1945; s. Donald Lewis and Shirley June (Scott) B.; m. m. Sari Ellen Donohoe, June 17, 1967; children: Shannon, Rebecca. AA in BUs. Adminstrn., El Camino Coll., 1966; BSBA, U. So. Calif., L.A., 1968, EdD in Ednl. Adminstrn., 1982; MA in Elem. Edn., Calif. State U., L.A., 1972. Cert. tchr., sch. adminstr., Calif. Tchr. El Segundo (Calif.) Unified Sch. Dist., 1970-72, reading specialist, 1972-76, program coord., 1976-79; prin. Wilsona Sch. Dist., Lancaster, Calif., 1979-81, supt., 1981-84; supt. Old Adobe Union Sch. Dist., Petaluma, Calif., 1984-91, Mother Lode Union Sch. Dist., Placerville, Calif., 1992-93, Wiseburn Sch. Dist., Hawthorne, Calif., 1993—; bd. dirs. Schs. Committed To Reducing Utility Bills, Sacramento, 1983—; mem. State Supts. Small Sch. Adv. Com.; coord. El Segundo Jr. Olympics, 1972; bd. dirs. Antelope Valley Fedn. Tchrs. Credit Union, Lancaster, 1983; v.p., bd. dirs. Friends of Antelope Valley Indian Mus., Lancaster, 1982. Named One of Top 100 Sch. Execs. in N.Am., Exec. Educator, 1985. Mem. Am. Assn. Sch. Adminstrs., Sonoma County Supts. Gang of 13, Assn. Calif. Sch. Adminstrs., Small Sch. Dist. Assn. (founder, pres., treas. 1983—), Alpha Kappa Psi. Home: 640 California St El Segundo CA 90245-3216 Office: Wiseburn Sch Dist 13530 Aviation Blvd Hawthorne CA 90250-6498

BRANNAN, CLEO ESTELLA, retired elementary education educator; b. Turon, Kans., Feb. 22, 1924; d. Jesse Logan and Nancy Elma (Cox) Zink; m. Raymond Eugene Brannan, Aug. 4, 1946 (deceased); children: Raymond Eugene Jr., Nancy Estelle, Tricia Elaine. BS, Ft. Hays State U., 1964. Cert. elem. edn. educator, Kans. Elem. tchr. Pretty Prairie (Kans.) Schs., 1943-45, Meade (Kans.) Elem. Sch., 1945-48, 58-60, 61-87; substitute secondary sch. tchr. Meade (Kans.) Elem. Sch., 1987; ret., 1987. Contbr. articles to Meadowlark mag. Trustee Meade Pub. Libr., 1961-65, trustee, treas., 1990—; state bd. dirs. Friends of Kans. Librs., 1990-96; silver haired legislator, 1999—. Mem. AAUW (local pres. 1985-86), Kans. Ret. Tchr. Assn. (bd. dirs. 1991—, state pres. 1996-97), Silver Haired Legis., Delta Kappa Gamma. Avocations: collecting China, traveling, reading, arranging flowers. Home: PO Box 13 Meade KS 67864-0013

BRANNAN, DAVID ALEXANDER, mathematics educator; b. Cowdenbeath, Fife, Scotland, Sept. 15, 1942; m. Margaret Philomena McAuley, Apr. 1, 1970; children: David, Joseph, Michael. BSc, Glasgow (Scotland) U., 1964; PhD, U. London, 1967. Asst. prof. U. Md., 1967-68; lectr. Glasgow U., 1968-70, U. London, 1970-78; prof. Open U., 1979—, dean math. and computing faculty, 1996—. Author: Geometry, 1999; author, editor: Aspects of Contemporary Complex Analysis, 1980. Chmn. govs. St. Gregory's Roman Cath. Middle Sch., Bedford, Eng., 1985-87. Mem. London Math. Soc. (gen. sec. 1971-81, publs. sec. 1986-96), Am. Math. Soc., European Math. Soc. (sec. 1999—). Roman Catholic. Office: Open U, Walton Hall, Milton Keynes MK7 6AA, England

BRANNEN, GEORGE ELSDON, surgeon; b. Jan. 14, 1943. BA, Dartmouth Coll., 1965; MD, Northwestern U., Chgo., 1969; Bd. Cert. Urologist, Johns Hopkins Hosp., 1975. Diplomate Nat. Bd. Med. Examiners, Am. Bd. Urology. Surg. intern Duke U. Hosp. - Duke U. Med. Ctr., Durham, N.C., 1969-70; surg. resident Duke U. Hosp., 1970-71;

urology resident James Buchanan Brady Urol. Inst. - Johns Hopkins Hosp., Balt., 1971-75; rsch. fellow dept. urology and divsn. oncology Johns Hopkins Hosp., Balt., 1972-73, sr. asst. resident, 1973-74, chief resident, 1974-75, fellow American Cancer Soc., 1973-74; fellow kidney transplant U. Colo. Med. Ctr., Denver, 1977-78; staff urologist and dir. kidney transplantation Va. Mason Med. Ctr., Seattle, 1978-91, staff urologist, dir. kidney transplantation, 1978-91; urologist and gen. surgeon, physician Shisong Mission, Cameroon, W. Africa, 1991-94; prof. clin. urology, chmn. clin. faculty U. Wash., Seattle, 1994—, 98—; staff urologist, bd. dirs. MultiCare Health Svcs., Kent, Wash., 1994—; staff urologist Kent Med. Ctr. - MultiCare Health Systems, Valley Med. Ctr., 1994—; with Gen. Med. Missionary Svc., Cath. Med. Mission Hosp., Shisong, W. Africa, 1991-94;. Contbr. numerous articles to profl. jours. Bd. dirs., med. dir. YMCA Camp Orkila; bd. dirs. YMCA of Greater Seattle, 1998; trustee MultiCare Med. Group; mem. St. Brendan's Cath. Ch. Human Concerns Commn.; regional rep. United Network for Organ Sharing; first aid instr., vol. physician U.S. Forest Svc./ Nat. Ski Patrol; presenter slide lectr. series on personal wilderness experience in the Klondike to various civic and med. groups, others. With med. corps. U.S. Army, 1975-77. Grantee in field. Fellow Am. Coll. Surgeons, Seattle Surg. Soc.; mem. Am. Urol. Assn. (1st prize Joseph McCarthy contest 1979), Northwest Urol. Soc. (2nd prize scientific presentation 1978), Wash. State Med. Soc., Transplantation Soc., Am. Soc. Transplant Surgeons, Northwest Renal Soc., Northwest Transplant Soc., Nat. Renal Adminstrs.' Assn., Am. Fertility Soc. (Weck Urology Rsch. prize 1974), Am. Soc. Andrology, Am. Assn. Clin. Urologists, others. Office: Covington MultiCare Clinic Multi-Care Urology Svcs 17700 SE 272nd St Ste 260 Kent WA 98042-4951

BRANNEY, JOSEPH JOHN, lawyer; b. Casper, Wyo., Aug. 22, 1938; s. John J. and Frances M. (Stanko) B.; m. Sheryl Ann Branney; children: Scott W., John J., Sean W. BA, U. Colo., 1960; JD, U. Denver, 1962. Bar: Colo. 1963, Wyo. 1963. Assoc. Myrick, Criswell & Branney, Englewood, Colo., 1963-69; sole practice Englewood, 1969-72; ptnr. Branney, Hillyard, Ewing & Barnes, Englewood, 1982-85, Branney, Hillyard, Kudla & Lee, Englewood, 1986-95, Branney, Hillyard & Barnhart, Englewood, 1995—; prof. law U. Denver, 1964—. Mem. Wyo. Bar Assn., Arapahoe County Bar Assn., Assn. Trial Lawyers Am., Colo. Trial Lawyers Assn. (pres. 1966-67), Nat. Bd. Trial Advocacy (cert. civil trial adv. 1983), Internat. Soc. of Barristers. Republican. Home: 2416 County Rd 430 PO Box 859 La Veta CO 81055-0859 Office: Branney Hillyard & Barnhart LLP 7887 E Belleview Ave Ste 1200 Englewood CO 80111-6027

BRANNON, DAVE LEE, lawyer; b. Danville, Ill., May 8, 1953; s. Louis Marion and Barbara Jean (Addams) B.; m. Pamela Tarquino, Feb. 21, 1986. BS with honors, USCG Acad., 1975; JD, U. Miami, Coral Gables, Fla., 1980. Bar: Fla. 1980, U.S. Dist. Ct. (so. dist.) Fla. 1982, U.S. Dist. Ct. (mid. dist.) Fla. 1988, U.S. Ct. Appeals (11th cir.) 1986. Commd. ensign USCG, 1975, advanced through grades to lt., 1979; navigator, deck watch officer USCG, Long Beach, Calif., 1975-77; asst. legal officer USCG, Miami, Fla., 1980-84, intelligence officer, 1984-86; resigned USCG, 1986; asst. fed. pub. defender U.S. Dist. Ct. (so. dist.) Fla., West Palm Beach, 1986—; adj. prof. Fla. Atlantic U., Boca Raton, 1990—. Mem. Nat. Mil. Intelligence Assn., U.S. Naval Inst. (life), Craig Barnard Inn of Ct. Office: Fed Pub Defender 400 S Australian Ave Ste 300 West Palm Beach FL 33401-5040

BRANSFORD, RICHARD SAMUEL, physician, missionary; b. Long Beach, Calif., Sept. 3, 1940; s. Richard Jackson and Rubye Irene (Davis) B.; m. Mildred Babb; children: Christopher Shelton, Richard Jackson, Bethany Else Densham, Jonathan Mark, Susan Kathleen, Joshua Moses, Philip James. BA, UCLA, 1962; MD, Johns Hopkins U., 1967; DTM, Prince Leopold Sch. of Tropical Medicine, Antwerp, Belgium, 1976. Diplomate Am. Bd. Surgery. Intern, surg. resident W.Va. U. Med. Ctr., Morgantown, 1967-69; surg. resident U. Nebr. Med. Ctr., Omaha, 1969-72; chief of surgery and obstetrics El Maarouf Hosp., Moroni, Corona Islands, 1976-77; surgeon Kijabe Hosp., Kenya, 1977—; med. dir., chmn. bd. Bethany Crippled Children's Ctr., Kijabe, 1997—; cons. in rehab. surgery Internat. Rescue Com., Kakuma Refugee Camp, Kenya, 1999. Med. cons. Safe Harbor, So. Sudan, 1996-98. Maj. USAF, 1972-74. Recipient Smith, Kline & French fellowship Kijade, 1966. Fellow Am. Coll. Surgeons, Assn. Surgeons of E. Africa. Mem. Christian and Missionary Alliance. E-mail: richard bransford@aimint.org. Office: AIC Bethany Crippled Chldns, Ctr/PO Box 52, Kijabe Kenya

BRANSKI, DAVID, pediatrician, educator; b. Tel Aviv, Israel, Jan. 8, 1944; s. Chaim S. and Yaffa (Krawchinski) B.; m. Effrath Y. Landau; children: Shmuel, Yonatan, Sara, Ehud. MD, Hebrew U., 1972. Resident Bikur Cholim Hosp., Jerusalem, 1972-76, chief physician, 1978-89, dir. pediat. dept., 1989-91; fellow Buffalo Children's Hosp., 1976-78; dir. pediat. dept. Shaare Zedek Med. Ctr., Jerusalem, 1991—; sr. lectr. Hebrew U., Jerusalem, 1983-86, clin. assoc. prof., 1986-89, assoc. prof., 1989-97, prof., 1997—; chmn. pediat. bd. Med. Coun. Israel, 1992—. Series editor: (8 vols.) Pediatric and Adolescent Medicine, 1989—, Pediatric Neurology, 1991, The Obese Child, 1992, Gluten Sensitive Enteropathy, 1992; contbr. more than 140 articles to profl. jours.; editl. mem. Jour. of Pediatric Gastroenterology and Nutrition, 1998. Bd. dirs. Alin Hosp., Jerusalem, 1996—, Jerusalem Coun. for Children, 1996—. Mem. European Soc. for Pediat. Gastroenterology and Nutrition (coun. 1996-99), Israeli Pediat. and Gastroenterology Soc., Israel Pediatric Assn. (pres. 2000). Jewish. Avocation: classical music. Office: Shaare Zedek Medical Ctr, 91031 Jerusalem Israel

BRANSON, FRANK LESLIE, III, law corporation executive; b. Deport, Tex., Feb. 10, 1945; s. Frank Leslie B. Jr.; m. Debbie Dudley; children: Frank IV, Jennifer. BA, Tex. Christian U., 1967; JD, So. Meth. U., 1969, LLM, 1974. Bar: Tex. 1969. Assoc. Watson & Parkhill, Grand Prairie, Tex., 1969; assoc. Bader, Wilson, Menaker, Cox & Branson, Dallas, 1970-75, ptnr., 1975-77; pvt. practice Dallas, 1978—; lectr. personal injury topics State Bar Tex., Am. Trial Lawyers Assn.; mem. adv. com. Tex. Supreme Ct., 1985-86. Contbr. over 20 articles on personal injury litigation to profl. jours.; four arguments to Million Dollar Argument tapes, (with Matthew Bender) Malpractice video tape series, 1982. Mem. Dallas Dem. Fin. Council, 1985-86; bd. dirs. Garland (Tex.) Community Hosp., 1981, 82-84. Mem. Internat. Assn. Trial Lawyers, Internat. Soc. Barristers, Am. Bd. Trial Advs. (pres. Dallas chpt. 1982), Dallas Trial Lawyers Assn. (pres. 1976-77), Tex. Trial Lawyers Assn. (bd. dirs. 1972-94), Am. Trial Lawyers Coll. Med. Malpractice (dean 1985), Med. Malpractice Com. (chmn. 1974-75, 79), So. Trial Lawyers Assn. (pres. 1988-89), Royal Oaks Country Club, Chapparal Club, 2001 Club, ATLA (bd. govs., 1988—), Lochinvar Country Club. Office: 4514 Cole Ave Ste 1800 Dallas TX 75205-4185*

BRANSON, HARLEY KENNETH, finance executive; b. Ukiah, Calif., June 10, 1942; s. Harley Edward and Clara Lucile Branson; 1 child, Erik Jordan. BS in Acctg. and Fin., San Jose State U., 1965; JD, Santa Clara U., 1968. Bar: Calif. 1969-98. Law clk. to judge U.S. Ct. Appeals (9th cir.) San Diego, 1968-69; pvt. practice San Diego, 1969-78; div. counsel Ralston Purina Co., San Diego, 1978-83; group gen. counsel Castle & Cooke, Inc., San Diego, 1983-85; exec. v.p., gen. counsel, corp. sec. Bumble Bee Seafoods, Inc., San Diego, 1985-89; pres., CEO Flying Palms LLC, San Diego, 1995—; bd. dirs. Wind and Weather, Inc., SOPHIA Comm., Inc.; gen. ptnr. Hankins Ptnrs., LLC, 1997—, CEO, Meteor Pics., LLC, 2000—. Exec. prodr. (feature motion picture) Love Always, 1997, Love Unlimited Orchestra, 2000. Bd. dirs. U. C. Univ. Art Gallery, 1995—. Avocations: reading, collecting contemporary art, travel. Office: PO Box 500308 San Diego CA 92150-0308

BRANSTAD, TERRY EDWARD, former governor, lawyer; b. Leland, Iowa, Nov. 17, 1946; s. Edward Arnold and Rita (Garl) B.; m. Christine Ann Johnson, June 17, 1972; children: Eric, Allison, Marcus. BA, U. Iowa, 1969; JD, Drake U., 1974. Bar: Iowa. Sr. ptnr. firm Branstad-Schwarm, Lake Mills, Iowa, until 1982; farmer Lake Mills; mem. Iowa Ho. of Reps., 1973-78; lt. gov. State of Iowa, 1979-82, gov., 1983-99; Bd. dirs. Am. Legion of Iowa Found. With U.S. Army, 1969. Mem. Nat. Govs. Assn. (past chmn.), Rep. Govs. Assn. (task chair), Midwestern Govs. Assn., Am. Legion, Farm Bur. Republican. Roman Catholic. Lodges: Lions, KC. Office: Regency West 2 1401 50th St Ste 325 West Des Moines IA 50266-5924

BRANTLEY, LEE REED, chemistry educator; b. Herrin, Ill., Sept. 23, 1906; s. Homer L. and Blanche R. (Reed) B.; m. Audrey Ryan, June 25, 1930 (dec. 1983); m. Ruth Thomas, Aug. 21, 1984. AB, UCLA, 1927; MS, Calif. Inst. Tech., 1929, PhD, 1930. Registered profl. engr., Calif.; registered chem. engr., Calif. Instr. physics and chemistry Occidental Coll., L.A., 1930-36, asst. prof. chemistry, 1936-40, assoc. prof., 1940-42, prof., 1942-67, head dept. chemistry, 1940-62, prof. emeritus, 1967—; rsch. fellow physics Calif. Inst. Tech., 1936-42; rsch. asst., cons. chemistry Nat. Def. Rsch. Coun. Contract, 1942-44; vis. prof. Lehigh U., 1958-59; prof. chemistry U. Hawaii, Honolulu, 1962-63; vis. prof. chemistry U. Hawaii, 1965-66, rsch. prof. edn. Curriculum R & D Group, 1966-72, emeritus prof., 1972—, phys. sci. dir. Found. Approaches in Sci. Tchg., 1966-72, cons., 1972—, rsch. prof. dept. chemistry, 1985—, cons. chemistry Sch. Architecture, 1986-88; emeritus prof. Occidental Coll., L.A., 1967—; dir. contract Office Naval Rsch. on Principles of Adhesion, 1949-58, Q.M. Rsch. and Devel. Environ. Protection, 1953-58; dir. Corn Industries Rsch. Found. Adhesion Contract, 1957-59; cons. on protective coatings Nat. Bur. Standards, 1951-53; writer Commn. on Sci. Edn., AAAS. Author: Chemistry for Architects, 1986, Chemistry of Building Materials, 1986, Building Materials Technology: Structural Performance and Environmental Impact, 1996; contbr.: Standard Handbook for Civil Engineers, 4th edit., 1996, Time-Saver Standards for Architectural Design Data, 7th edit., 1997; contbr. articles to profl. publs. Past chmn. environ. health adv. com. Am. Lung Assn. Hawaii, 1968-93; past chmn. air com. Oahu chpt. Conservation Council of Hawaii.; Served as sr. gas officer Glendale (Calif.) Citizens Def. Corps, 1943-45. Recipient Petroleum Research award for advanced study Am. Chem. Soc., 1958-59; John R. Kuebler award Alpha Chi Sigma, 1973. Fellow AAAS; mem. Pacific S.W. Assn. Chemistry Tchrs. (past pres.), Calif. Acad. Sci., Am. Chem. Soc. (pres. So. Calif. sect. 1947-48, chmn. Hawaii sect. 1970-71, 50-year emeritus mem.), Electrochem. Soc. (emeritus), Nat. Ret. Tchrs. Assn., Hawaii Acad. Sci., Rotary, Sigma Xi, Alpha Chi Sigma (pres. 1958-60), Kappa Sigma. Home: 2908 Robert Pl Honolulu HI 96816-1720

BRANTON, JAMES LAVOY, lawyer; b. Albany, Tex., Apr. 19, 1938; s. George Lyndon Branton and Oletha Imogene (Westerman) Johnson; m. Molly Branton, May 18, 1968; children: Christina, Victoria, Claudia. BA, U. Tex., 1961, LLB, 1962. Bar: Tex., U.S. Dist. Ct. (we., so, ea. and no. dists.) Tex., U.S. Ct. Appeals (5th cir.). Ptnr. Hardberger, Branton & Herrera, Inc., San Antonio, 1974-78, Branton & Mendelsohn, Inc., San Antonio, 1978-83, Branton, Hall, Warncke & Gonzales, P.C., San Antonio, 1983-88, Branton & Hall, P.C., San Antonio, 1988—; bd. dirs. Tex. Lawyers' Ins. Exch. Co-author: Trial Lawyer's Series, 1981-91. Capt. USAF, 1962-65. Fellow Am. Coll. Trial Lawyers (state com. 1993-95, chair 1996-98), Internat. Soc. Barristers, Internat. Acad. Trial Lawyers, Tex. Bar Found. (chair 1989-90); mem. Tex. Trial Lawyers Assn. (pres. 1975-76), State Bar Tex. (pres. 1994-95), Am. Bd. Trial Advocates (pres. San Antonio chpt. 1990-91, Tex. Trial Lawyer of Yr. 1994). Avocations: flying, scuba diving. Home: 403 Evans Ave San Antonio TX 78209-3725 Office: Branton & Hall PC 711 Navarro St Ste 737 San Antonio TX 78205-1787

BRAOUDE, VADIM BORISOVICH, radio engineer, educator; b. St. Petersburg, Russia, Nov. 27, 1945; s. Boris and Ekaterina (Grigoryeva) B.; m. Nina Ivanovna Andreeva, Mar. 24, 1978 (div. Nov. 1989); 1 child, Olga. MSc, State U. Telecomms., 1968, PhD, 1975. From rschr. to prof. State U. Telecomms., St. Petersburg, 1968—. Author: Matching Techniques in Antennas Design, 1977; contbr. articles to profl. jours. Mem. IEEE, A.S. Popov Soc. Electronics and Comms. Engrs. Russia. Avocation: classical music. Home: PO Box 314, 199406 Saint Petersburg Russia

BRASH, DONALD THOMAS, bank executive; b. Wanganui, New Zealand, Sept. 24, 1940; s. Alan A. and Eljean I. B.; m. Erica Beatty, 1964; m. Je Lan Lee, 1989; 3 children. BA in History and Econs., Canterbury U., MA in Econs. with honors; PhD in Econs., Australian Nat. U.; Doctorate (hon.), U. Canterbury, 1999. Gen. mgr. Broadbank Corp. Ltd., 1971-81; gen. mgr. fin. and computer sect. Fletcher Challenge Ltd., 1981-82; mng. dir. New Zealand Kiwifruit Authority, 1982-86, Trust Bank Group, 1986-88; gov. Res. Bank of New Zealand, Wellington, 1988—; mem. New Zealand Monetary and Econ. Coun., 1974-78, Com. Enquiry into Inflation Accounting, 1976, Auckland C. of C. Coun., 1976-82, New Zealand Planning Coun., 1977-80; chmn. Econ. Monitoring Group, 1978-80; dir. Cavalier Corp. Ltd., 1978-86; dir. Westpac Merchant Fin., 1983-86. Author: New Zealand's Debt Servicing Capacity, 1964, American Investment in Australian Industry, 1966. Bd. mem. Presbyn. Support Svcs., 1978-86. Recipient NZIER-Qantas Econs. award, 1999. Avocation: growing kiwifruit. Office: Reserve Bank New Zealand, 2 The Terrace PO Box 2498, Wellington New Zealand

BRASHEAR, JERRY PAUL, management consultant; b. Oklahoma City, Aug. 25, 1979; s. Henry Paul and Bonnie Genung Brashear; m. Judith Caroline Brinkley, Dec. 29, 1967 (div. 1976); children: Judith Corbin, Regan Pretlow; m. Pamela Ann Newton, Aug. 25, 1979. AB magna cum laude, Princeton U., 1967; MBA, Harvard U., 1969; PhD in Urban, Tech.-Environ. Planning, U. Mich., 1975. Project mgr. Cmty. Sys. Found., Ann Arbor, Mich., 1967-72, Riverside Rsch. Inst., N.Y.C., 1972-75; v.p. Lewin & Assocs., Inc., Washington, 1975-87, bd. dirs., 1980-87; sr. v.p. ICF Kaiser Internat., Inc., Fairfax, Va., 1987-96; 0mng. dir. The Brashear Group LLC, Potomac, Md., 1996—; bd. dirs., mem. exec. com. ICF Resources, Inc., Fairfax, 1987-96. Mem. editl. bd. Jour. Petroleum Scis. and Engring., 1987-91. Usher Cedar Lane Unitarian Universalist Ch., Bethesda, Md., 1998—. Mem. Soc. Petroleum Engrs., Am. Assn. Petroleum Geologists, Internat. Assn. for Energy Econs., Phi Beta Kappa. Avocations: movies, symphony. E-mail: jpb@brashear-group.com. Office: The Brashear Group LLC 10121 Donegal Ct Potomac MD 20854-4340

BRASHER, CHRISTOPHER WILLIAM, journalist, business executive; b. Georgetown, Guyana, Aug. 21, 1928; s. William Kenneth and Katie (Howe) B.; m. Shirley Juliet Bloomer, Apr. 28, 1959; children: Kate, Hugh, Amanda. MA, St. John's Coll., Cambridge U., 1951; Dr (hon.), Stirling U., Scotland, 1989, Kingston U., Surrey, Eng., 1996. Mgmt. trainee Mobil Oil Co., Eng., 1951-57; sports editor The Observer, London, 1957-61, columnist and Olympic corr., 1961-91; reporter/producer BBC TV, London, 1961-81, head gen. features, 1969-72; mng. dir. Fleetfoot Ltd., Lancaster, Eng., 1979-96; chmn. Reebok U.K. Ltd., Eng., 1990-93; founder, chief exec. London Marathon, 1980-95; chmn. Berghaus, Ltd., Washington, Eng., 1993-98, Brasher Boot Co. Ltd., Lancaster, 1993—; Author: Sportsmen of our Time, 1962, Tokyo, 1964, A Diary of the XVIIIth Olympiad, 1968, A Diary of the XIXth Olympia, 1972, (with Sir John Hunt) The Red Snows, 1960. Trustee John Muir Trust, 1983-92, 96—; chmn. Chris Brasher Trust, 1988—, The Petersham Trust, 1999—. Decorated officer Order St. John, comdr. Brit. Empire; recipient Nat. Medal of Honour, Finland, 1975; named Sports Writer of Yr., Brit. Press Awards, 1968, 76. Mem. Racehorse Owners Assn. (coun. 1996—). Avocations: mountains, horse racing, fishing, orienteering, social running. Home and Office: The White House, Chaddleworth, Berks RG20 7DY, England

BRASINGTON, DYAN LINGLE, association executive; b. St. Petersburg, Fla., Jan. 10, 1952; d. Martin Anthony and Dorothea Loos; children: Meghan, David Brasington. Econ. Devel. Cert., U. Okla., 1983; BS, Fla. State U., 1974, MA, 1976. Indsl. rep. Fla. Dept. Commerce, 1977-83; dir. econ. devel. Prince William County, Va., 1983-87, Montgomery County, Md., 1987-91, Howard County, Md., 1991-92; exec. dir. W.Va. Devel. Office, Charleston, W.Va., 1992-94; pres. High Tech. Coun. Md., Rockville, 1994—. Bd. dirs. Reginald Lourie Ctr., Rockville, 1995—, Balt. br. Fed. Res., 2000, Leadership Md., 2000; mem. pres.'s adv. coun. U. Md., 2000; bd. vis. Bowie (Md.) State U., 2000; mem. found. bd. Shady Grove Adventist Hosp., Rockville, 1997—. Named Md. Topp 100 Women Daily Record, 1996, 99. Fellow Am. Econ. Devel. Coun. (mem. exec. com. 1995-98); mem. Am. Soc. Assn. Execs. Office: High Tech Coun Md 9700 Great Seneca Hwy Rockville MD 20850-3308

BRASSINGTON, FREDERICK CHARLES, hydrogeologist, consultant; b. Skegness, Eng., May 22, 1946; s. Frederick Thomas and Kathleen (Suter) B.; m. Sandra Carson; children: David, Elizabeth. BS, U. Liverpool, 1967; MS, U. Birmingham, 1974. Chartered geologist; chartered civil engr. Hydrology asst. Lothians River Purification Bd., Edinburgh, Scotland, 1967-68; hydrogeologist Severn River Auth., Malvern, Eng., 1968-74; sr. hydrogeologist Tyne & Wear County Coun., Newcastle, Eng., 1974-76; prin. hydrogeologist North West Water, Warrington, Eng., 1976-86, hydrogeological svcs. mgr., 1986-88; regional water resources mgr. Nat. River Auth., Warrington, Eng., 1988-91; mng. dir. Hydrotechnics, Shrewsbury, Eng., 1991-93; no. regional dir. So. Sci., Manchester, Eng., 1993-97; tech. dir. Stanger Sci., Manchester, 1997-98; prin. Rick Bassington Cons. Hydrogeologist, Warrington, 1998—; visiting sr. fellow dept. earthsciences U. Liverpool, 1990—. Author: Finding Water, 1983, 2d edit., 1995, Field Hydrogeology, 1988, 2d edit., 1998; editor: The Geologist's Directory, 1980, The Geologist's Directory, 1982. Fellow Geol. Soc. (coun. mem. 1991—), Inst. Geologists (coun. mem. 1978-83, hon. sec. 1980-83, medal 1988), Inst. Water and Environ. Mgmt. (mem. editorial panel 1990, Publ. award 1989); mem. Inst. Civil Engrs.

BRASWELL, PAULA ANN, artist; b. Decatur, Ala., May 6, 1955; d. Andrew Leon and Dorothy Faye (Fretwell) B.; m. Roger Armand Robichaud, June 22, 1990. BA, Jacksonville State U., 1978; postgrad., New Orleans Acad. Fine Arts, 1987, U. New Orleans, 1987-88; MFA, Fla. State U., 1990. Instr. art Butler Sch., Marrero, La., 1984, Fla. Keys Coll., Tavernier, 1985; grad. instr. Fla. State U., Tallahassee, 1989-90; adj. prof. Calhoun Coll., Decatur, Ala., 1990, Chattanooga State Coll., 1991, Cleveland (Tenn.) State Coll., 1991; studio artist Knoxville, Tenn., 1991-96, Toronto, Ont., Can., 1996—. Artist (video sculpture) Museum of Fine Arts, 1998, Fla. State U., Museum of the Ams., Washington, 1997, ARC Gallery, 1997, New American Talent, 1996, Transforming Tradition, 1996, Combined Talents Fla. Nat., 1995, Knoxville (Tenn.) Mus. Art, 1994-95, Contemporary Arts Ctr., New Orleans, 1992, Mus. of the Ams., Washington, 1997, Points of Compass show FSU Mus., 1998, Paula Braswell: Works from 1994 to 2000 ProPeller Gallery, Toronto, 2000, Soul Ecology Exhibit, Toronto, 2000, Propeller Ctr. for the Visual Arts Exhibit, Toronto, 2000; represent Can. in OAS exhibit at The Mus. of the Ams., Washington, 1997. Nat. Endowment Arts grantee, 1991, Ontario Arts Coun. grantee, 1997, 2000—. Mem. AAUW, NOW, Women's Caucus for Arts (exhibitor), Knoxville Mus. Art (exhibitor), Knoxville Arts Coun. (exhibitor), Coll. Art Assn., Contemporary Arts Ctr. (exhibitor), People for Protection of Animals, Humane Soc. U.S. Democrat. Mem. Ch. of Christ. Avocations: gardening, environmental concerns, animal care, skiing, camping. Address: 326 Carlaw Ave Ste 230, Toronto, ON Canada M4M 3N8

BRASZKO, JAN JOZEF, pharmacologist, educator; b. Latyczyn, Poland, Feb. 15, 1947; s. Jan and Genowefa (Wylupek) B. MD, Med. Acad. Bialystok, Poland, 1970, PhD in Pharmacology, 1975, PhD in Neurosci., 1989. Asst. Med. Acad. Bialystok, 1970-72, sr. asst., 1973-78, asst. prof., 1979-90, assoc. prof., 1991-96, prof., 1997—; pres. senate didactic commn. Med. Acad. Bialystok, 1989-92, prorector for sci., 1993-99, head dept. clin. pharmacology, 1994—, pres. senate commn. for fgn. collaboration, 1999—. Contbr. articles to profl. jours. and books. Local sec. Solidarnosc Trade Union, 1981-89. Recipient Ann. Prize Polish Acad. of Scis., 1987, Ministry of Health, 1989, 91, 96. Mem. N.Y. Acad. Sci., Soc. Neurosci. Africa, European Behavioural Pharmacology Soc., Polish Pharmacological Soc., Polish Neurosci. Soc. Avocations: fine arts, swimming, jogging, futurology. Office: Med Acad Bialystok, Waszyngtona 17, 15274 Bialystok Poland

BRATCHER, JUANITA, journalist; b. Columbus, Ga.; d. Benjamin Pickens and Tommie (English) Forte; m. Neal Archie Bratcher; children: Pamela, Angela, Sonya, Neal Jr. AA, Olive Harvey Coll.; BA in Journalism, Columbia Coll., 1976. News reporter South End Rev., Chgo., Roseland Rev., Chgo., Chgo. Defender; editor, publ. Southeast Alliance, Chgo., Copyline Mag., Chgo., 1990—; bd. dirs. Provident Found.; host cable talk show One on One. Author: Harold: The Making of a Big City Mayor, 1993, I Cry for a People: In Their Struggle for Justice, 1996, Crooked Curves: The Last of the Red Hot Mamas, 1999, works appear in Nat. Libr. of Poetry Best Poems of 1997, 98, A Celebration of Poets, 1998, Internat. Libr. of Poetry; recordings include Too Many Memories, 1996, Everything But Love, 1996, I'm Here for You, 1997, You've Been Gone Too Long, 1997, God Can Ease the Pain, 1999, Glorious Day in Heaven, 1999, America, The Land of Freedom, 1999, Freedom, Our Birthright, 1999, Crooked Curves: The Last of the Red Hot Mamas, 1999, (CD) God Can Ease the Pain, 1999, A Glorious Day in Heaven, 1999 (album) America, The Land of Freedom, 1999, Freedom, Our Birthright, 1999; mem. editl. com. One City, Chgo. Coun. Urban Affairs; guest, panelist, guest host numerous TV and radio programs. Mem. Regional Aux. Coun. Atlas Ctr.; press aide Cook County bd. campaign John S. Stroger. Recipient certs. of merit Chgo. Pub. Schs., everyday hero award Ill. Sec. State George Ryan, 1993, Kizzy award The Kizzy Found., 1983, Probation Challenge Portraits of Achievers award, 1983, 87, Editor's Choice award (6) Nat. Libr. Poetry, svc. award Boy Scouts Am., U.S. Dept. Edn. Region V, Outstanding Support of Human Rights award Ill. Dept. Human Rights, 1985, Cmty. Svc. award Ada Park Adv. Coun., 1990, exemplary civic svc. award Dorcas Care Ctr., 1988, Excellence in Achievement award Zeta Phi Beta, Oustanding Svc. in Media and Telecomm. award Delta Sigma Theta, press award Chgo. and No. Dist. Assn. of Club Women, Inc., Par Excellence Journalism award Coalition for United Cmty. Action, 1987, Dedicated Svc. to Cmty. award Firefighters for Justice and Equality, 1987; named black bus. woman of yr. Parkway Cmty. House, Chgo., 1993; inductee Internat. Poetry Hall of Fame, Probation Challenge's Hall of Fame, 1991. Mem. Internat. Soc. Poets. Baptist. Home: 9026 S Cregier Ave Chicago IL 60617-3533

BRATHWAITE, ALFRED FITZGERALD, pathologist; b. Carriacou, Grenada, Apr. 22, 1941; s. Charles and Sophia (McLeod) B.; m. Vivian Albertha Isaacs, Jan. 9, 1971; children: Nanika, Ricio, Chandre. MBBS, U. London, 1967; MD, U. Surinam, 1978. Pathologist Govt. Grenada, 1974-76; head pathology U. Surinam, 1976-78; pathologist Govt. Bahamas, 1978-81; project mgr. WHO, Dominica, 1982-85; med. dir. Govt. Bahamas, 1986—. Fellow Am. Coll. Pathologists, Am. Soc. Clin. Pathologists; mem. Caribbean Assn. Lab. Medicine, Freeport Rugby Club. Mem. Anglican Ch. Avocations: travel, reading, music, sports. Home: Hawaii Ave PO Box F41575, Freeport Bahamas Office: Rand Meml Hosp, E Atlantic Dr PO Box F40071, Freeport Bahamas

BRATMAN, VLADIMIR L'VOVICH, radiophysicist, physics educator; b. Chirchik, USSR, Mar. 26, 1945; s. Lev Girshevich and Roza Zalmanovna (Chaikin) B.; children: Helen, Julia. MS, Nizhny Novgorod State U., USSR, 1967, PhD, 1977; DSc in Physics, Math., High Current Electronics Inst., Tomsk, Russia, 1992. Cert. radiophysicist, rschr. Engr. Rsch. & Devel. Inst. Salyut, Nizhny Novgorod, USSR, 1970-74; jr. rschr. rsch. & devel. Radio-Physics Inst., Nizhny Novgorod, USSR, 1974-77; jr. rschr. rsch. & devel. Inst. Applied Physics Russian Acad. Scis., Nizhny Novgorod, USSR, 1977-80, sr. rschr. rsch. & devel. Inst. Applied Physics, 1980-86, head of lab. rsch. & devel. Inst. Applied Physics, 1986—; assoc. prof. Nizhny Novgorod Poly. Inst., 1986-90, Nizhny Novgorod State U., 1990-92, prof. 1992—. Mem. editorial bd. (collection of reviews) Relativistic High Frequency Electronics, 1981-91. Office: Inst Applied Physics, 46 Ulyanov St, 603600 Nizhny Novgorod Russia

BRATT, OLA, urological surgeon, researcher; b. Lund, Sweden, Sept. 16, 1963; parents Helge Johan Viktor and Ingar (Nilsson) B.; m. Bodil Margareta Persson, May 21, 1988; children: Björn, Tor. MD, U. Hosp., Lund, Sweden, 1991; postgrad., Lund U., 1995—; PhD, Lund Univ., 1999. Resident in urology U. Hosp., Lund, 1991-92, 95-99, resident dept. oncology, 1992-93, rschr. dept. urology, 1995-99; resident County Hosp., Helsingborg, Sweden, 1993-95; res. urological surg., 1999—. Contbr. articles to profl. jours. Mem. European Soc. Residents in Urology (sec. 1996-97), Swedish Soc. Residents in Urology (sec. 1996-2000, chmn. 2000—), South Swedish Prostate Cancer Group (sec. 1996—). Avocations: chess, literature. Home: Lidängsgatan 25, SE-25271 Råå Sweden Office: County Hosp, Dept Surgery, SE-25187 Helsingborg Sweden

BRATTON, WILLIAM EDWARD, electronics executive, management consultant; b. Dallas, Oct. 25, 1919; s. William E. and Edna (Walker) B.; m. Betty Thume, May 30, 1942; children: Dale, Janet, Donna. AB in Econs., Stanford U., 1940; MBA, Harvard U., 1945. From v.p. to pres. Librascope, Glendale, Calif., 1947-63; v.p., gen. mgr. Ampex, Culver City, Calif., 1963-66; pres. Guidance Tech., Santa Monica, Calif., 1967-68; v.p. electronics div. Gen. Dynamics, San Diego, 1969-72; pres. Theta Cable T.V., Santa Monica, 1974-82; pres., chief exec. officer Stagecoach Properties, Salado, Tex., 1959-99; ret. Stagecoach Properties, Salado, 1999. Served to lt. (j.g.) USNR, 1944-46. Republican. Episcopalian. Club: El Niguel Country (Laguna, Calif.) (pres. 1978-79). Avocations: golf, skindiving.

BRATTSTRÖM, STIG, retired ambassador; b. Helsinki, Mar. 11, 1931; m. Mona Forsberg; children: Christina, Marc. LLB, Stockholm U., 1955. With fgn. svc. Ministry Fgn. Affairs, Stockholm, 1956; attaché Ministry Fgn. Affairs, Helsinki, 1957; 3d sec. Ministry Fgn. Affairs, London, 1960; 1st sec., head of sect. Ministry Fgn. Affairs, Stockholm, 1964-68; 1st sec. Swedish Del., Geneva, 1968-71; counsellor Swedish Del., 1972; asst. under sec. Ministry Fgn. Affairs, Stockholm, 1976-78; amb. to Algeria, Swedish Embassy, Algiers, 1979-82; amb. N.Y.C., 1982-83; amb., head del. to European Cmtys., Brussels, 1983-92; amb. to France, Swedish Embassy, Paris, 1992-96; ret., 1996; on spl. missions for Ministry Fgn. Affairs; cons. European Affairs, E.V. Fellow CFIA Harvard U., 1978-79.

BRATVOLD, THOMAS ERIK, physicst; b. Seattle, July 17, 1968; s. Owen Gerald and Bodil Alma (Petersen) B.; m. Melissa Charlene Finch, June 25, 1994; 1 child, Thomas Erik II. BS in Physics, Wash. State U., 1993. Health physicist Westinghouse Hanford Co., Richland, Wash., 1993-96, advanced health physicist, 1996; health physicist II Fluor Daniuel Hanford Co., Richland, Wash., 1996-98; mgr. Duke Engring & Svcs. Hanford Co., Richland, Wash., 1998-99, Fluor Daniel Hanford Co., Richland, Wash., 1999—. Mem. Am. Acad. Health Physics, Health Physics Soc. (mem. lab. accreditation com.), Columbia chpt. Health Physics Soc. Home: 706 Taylor St Richland WA 99352-2927 Office: Fluor Hanford Inc PO Box 1000 Richland WA 99352-1000

BRATZLER, MARY KATHRYN, desktop publisher; b. Albuquerque, Sept. 16, 1960; d. William James and Nancy Jane (Hobbs) Colby; m. Zim Emig, May 30, 1987 (div. Nov. 1990); 1 child, Aeriel Kaylee Emig; m. Steven James Bratzler, Mar. 16, 1996, 1 child, Cody Benjamin. B of Univ. Studies, U. N.Mex., 1995. Comml. artist Modern Press, Albuquerque, 1978-80; asst. composition supr. Graphic Arts Pub., Albuquerque, 1980-84, composition supr., 1984-85, asst. plant mgr., 1985-86; typesetter Universal Printing and Graphics, Albuquerque, 1986-87, Bus. Graphics, Albuquerque, 1988-90; office asst. UNM Gen. Honors, Albuquerque, 1992-93; desktop pub., 1990—; computer specialist NEDA Bus. Cons., Inc., 1996-98; cons. Mary Kay Cosmetics, 1991-96. Participant N.Mex. Pub. Utilities Commn., Santa Fe, 1993; coord. clothing bank PTA, Zia Elem. Sch., 1995-96; parent rep. Unified Student Centered Classroom, 1996-98. Mem. Golden Key, Phi Beta Kappa. Avocations: piano playing, bicycling, hiking, camping.

BRAUCH, HILTRUD BEATRIX, research scientist, consultant; b. Heidersbach, Germany, Mar. 13, 1955; s. Theodor B. and Maria E. Brauch. Diploma in chemistry, U. Fridericiana zu Karlsruhe, Germany, 1981; PhD, Ruprecht-Karl U. Heidelberg, Germany, 1985; habilitation, Tech. U. Munich, 1996. Rsch. asst. Inst. Immunology U. Heidelberg, 1981-85; vis. fellow Frederick (Md.) Cancer R&D Facility Nat. Cancer Inst., 1985-89; scientist Lab. Immunology Program Resource Inc., Frederick, 1989-90; scientist German Cancer Rsch. Ctr., Heidelberg, 1990-92; head lab. molecular pathology Inst. Pathology Tech. U. Munich, 1992-96; head rsch. lab. Womens Hosp. Eppendorf U. Hamburg, Germany, 1996-99; oncology rsch. coord. Bosch-Inst. Clin. Pharmacology, Stuttgart, Germany, 1999—; cons. EPA, Washington, 1998-99, German Mak Commn., Bonn, 1998-99. Contbr. articles to profl. jours. Fogarty Internat. fellow NIH, 1985-89. Mem. Am. Soc. Human Genetics, Am. Assn. Cancer Rsch. (corr.). Roman Catholic. Avocations: arts, literature, music, swimming. Fax: 01149-711-859295. Office: Bosch Inst Clin Pharm, Auerbachstrasse 112, Stuttgart 70376, Germany

BRAUER, HARROL ANDREW, JR., broadcasting executive; b. Oct. 17, 1920; s. Harrol Andrew and Bertie (Gregory) B.; m. Elizabeth Anne Hill, May 18, 1946; children: Harrol Andrew III, William Lanier, Gregory Hill. BA, U. Richmond, 1942; LLD, Christopher Newport U. Chief announcer, program dir., account exec. various radio stas. in Va., 1939-42, 45-49; v.p. Sta. WVEC Radio, Hampton, Va., 1949-80; v.p., dir. sales Sta. WVEC-TV, Hampton, 1953-82; v.p. Peninsula Cable Corp., 1966-82; chmn. Wyatt Bros., 1983-90. Pres. Hampton Cmty. Chest, 1951-52; crusade chmn. Peninsula unit Am. Cancer Soc., 1960—; mem. Hampton Sch. Bd., 1963—, vice-chmn., 1964-68, chmn., 1968-70; pres. Hampton Parking Authority, chmn., 1988—; bd. dirs. YMCA, Va. USO; bd. dirs., vice-chmn. Va. Pub. Telecomms. Bd., chmn., 1985—; chmn. Soc. Founders of Mace Christopher Newport U., 1989—; chmn. bd. trustees Hampton Roads Ednl. TV Assn., 1965-70; rector Christopher Newport U., 1976-82; co-chmn. for 375th Anniversary Celebration City of Hampton, 1985. Lt. USNR, 1942-45. Recipient Thomas P. Chisman award Va. Air and Space Ctr., Disting. Svc. medallion Christopher Newport U., NCCJ award, Am. Advt. Fedn. Silver Medal award, Disting. Citizen award City of Hampton, Outstanding Man of Yr. award Peninsula Ad Club, 1993. Mem. Hampton Retail Mchts. Assn. (past pres., bd. dirs.), Chesapeake Acad. Found. (vice-chmn. 1988—), Jamestowne Soc., Peninsula C. of C. (past bd. dirs.), Broadcast Pioneers, James River Country Club, Hampton Yacht Club, Peninsula Exec.'s Club (past pres., bd. dirs.), Town Point Club, Kiwanis (past bd. dirs., pres., lt. gov.), Sigma Alpha Epsilon. Home: 35 N Boxwood St Hampton VA 23669-2401

BRAUER, STEPHEN FRANKLIN, manufacturing company executive; b. Sept. 3, 1945; s. Arthur John, Jr. and Jane (Franklin) B.; m. Camilla Cary Thompson, June 12, 1971; children: Blackford Fitzhugh, Rebecca Randolph. Student, Washington and Lee U., 1963-64; BA, Westminster Coll., 1967; LLD (hon.), 1997. Sales and mktg. ofcl. Hunter Engring. Co., St. Louis, 1971-78, exec. v.p., 1978-81, pres., 1981—; bd. dirs. Boatmen's Trust Co., St. Louis, 1986-96; ptnr. St. Louis Cardinals baseball club, 1996—; pvt. client bd. Bank of Am., 1996—. Civilian aide Sec. Army, 1991-95; pres. Mo. Bot. Garden, 2000—; trustee Washington U., St. Louis, 2000—; mem. Mo. 21st Jud. Dist. Commn., 1992-96; hon. consul Govt. Belgium, 1987—; mem. St. Louis Consular Corps; mem. nat. bd. Smithsonian Instn., Washington, 1993-99. 1st lt. C.E., AUS, 1968-70. Recipient St. Louis Regional Commerce Growth Assn. Tech. award, 1993, Recognition of Outstanding Bus. Leadership award U.S. Ho. of Reps., 1993, Dean's award Washington U. Sch. Engring., 1998, Spirit of Enterprise award Mo. Rep. Party, 1999. Mem. St. Louis Country Club, St. Louis Club, Log Cabin Club. Republican. Episcopalian. Home: 9630 Ladue Rd Saint Louis MO 63124-1311 Office: 11250 Hunter Dr Bridgeton MO 63044-2306

BRAUERS, WILLEM KAREL, economist, educator; b. Antwerp, Belgium, Oct. 2, 1924; s. Jozef Antoine and Maria Gertrude (Nouwen) B.; m. Marie-Josee Van Espen, Aug. 16, 1955; children: Godelieve, Nele. Licentiate with great honors, U. Louvain, 1947, PhD, 1968; MA in Econs. with honors, Columbia U., 1955. Adviser Dept. Fgn.Affairs, Edn. and Econ. Affairs, Brussels, 1949-59; dir. Ctr. Econometrics and Ops. Rsch. Ministry of Def., Brussels, 1959-83, prof. War Coll., 1969-74; prof. Sch. Mil. Adminstrs., Brussels, 1966-69, U. Louvain, Belgium, 1969-74; chmn. bd. dirs. SORCA BMB Cons. to Developing Countries, Brussels, 1978—; prof. Sch. Bus. Administrn., Antwerp, Belgium, 1960—; prof. faculty for developing countries, faculty of econs. U. Antwerp, (RUCA), 1983—; chmn. bd. dirs. Maresco Internat. Market Rsch., Antwerp, 1982—; cons. pvt. firms, study orgns., govts. of developing nations, 1957—; head bd. auditors Electrabel, Antwerp, 1976-82; auditor Flemish Opera, Ghent, Belgium, 1982-88; bd. dirs. Tropical Inst., Antwerp. Author: System Analysis, Planning and Decision Making, 1976, The Belgian Experience in Inter-regional Input-Output Tables, 1980, Development Planning for New Countries, 1987, Project Analysis for D.C., 1987, Economic Theories and Planning in Developing Countries, 1988; contbr. articles to profl. jours. Town counselor, Town of Berchem, Antwerp, 1976-82. Belgian Am. Ednl. Found. fellow, 1970; higher officer Royal Belgian Order of Leopold. Mem. European Strategic Planning Fedn. (bd. dirs. 1976—, edit. bd. Jour. Long Range Planning), Strategic Planning Soc. London, Am. Econ. Assn., Belgian Assn. Strategic Planners. Roman Catholic. Avocations: skiing, swimming, mountaineering. Home: Birontlaan 97, B 2600 Berchem Antwerp Belgium Office: U Antwerp, Middelheimlaan 1, B 2020 Antwerp Belgium

BRAULIK, GEORG PETER, religious studies educator; b. Vienna, June 20, 1941; s. Franz Braulik and Josefa Münich. D in Theology, U. Vienna, 1966; D in Re Biblica, Pontificio Inst. Biblico, Rome, 1973; Habilitation, U. Vienna, 1975. Ordained to Benedictine Order, 1959. Priest, 1965—; univ. asst. Cath. Theol. U., Vienna, 1969-76, ao univ. prof., 1976-89, univ. prof., 1989—; dir. Dept. Old Testament Studies, Vienna, 1989—; vice-dean Cath. Theol. U., Vienna, 1996-99; vis. prof. SK, IL, RSA; rsch. fellow (D). Author of numerous books; editor: Oesterreichische Biblische Studien, 1979—. Mem. Austria Acad. der Wissenschaft (corr.). Roman Catholic. Home: Freyung 6 Schottenabtei, A-1010 Vienna Austria Office: Inst Alttest Bibelwiss, Schottenring 21, A-1010 Vienna Austria

BRAUN, BENNETT GEORGE, psychiatrist; b. Chgo., Aug. 7, 1940; s. Milton L. and Thelma H. (Gimbel) B.; m. Renate E. Deutsch, Sept. 1, 1963 (div. April 1984); children: Eric, Tamara; m. Jane E. Epstein, June 22, 1986; children: Robyn, Alex, Megan. BS, Tulane U., 1963, MS in psychology, 1964; MD, U. Ill., 1968. Diplomate Am. Coll. Forensic Examiners, Am. Bd. Psychiatry and Neurology, Am. Bd. Med. Hypnosis. Rotating med. intern Michael Reese Hosp., Chgo., 1968-69; resident in psychiatry U. Chgo. Hosp., 1969-71, Rush-Presbyterian-St. Lukes Med. Ctr., Chgo., 1982-84; psychiatrist, administrator Assoc. Psychotherapists of Chgo., 1973-75; med. dir. Assn. Mental Health Svcs., Chgo., 1975-95; practice dir. Apogee, Inc., Chgo., 1995-97; med. dir. Assocs. in Behavioral Medicine Ltd., Skokie, Ill., 1997—; dir. Dissociative Disorders Program sect. on psychiat. trauma Rush-Presbyn. St. Luke's Med. Ctr., 1984-98; med. dir. dissociative disorders program inpatient unit Rush North Shore Med. Ctr., 1989-98; cons. in hypnosis Am. Soc. for Clin. Hypnosis. Editor: Treatment of Multiple Personality, 1986, Society for the Study of Dissociation (newsletter) 1984-97, Dissociation (annual abstract book) 1984-95; assoc. editor Dissociation (jour.) 1988-98; asst. editor American Journal Clinical Hypnosis, 1987—; contbr. over 100 articles and book chpts. Asst. scoutmaster Boy Scouts Am. 505, Chgo., 1964-66. Major, US Army, 1971-73. Recipient Army Commendation medal U.S. Army, 1983, Elena D. Benedetto de Sabelli award for achievement in biol. psychiatry, 1984, Cornelia B. Wilbur award, 1987, Pres.' award, 1989, Disting. Svc. award, 1996, Morton Prince award for scientific achievement, Internat. Soc. Study of Dissociation, 1991, Best Doctors in Am. areas of post traumatic stress disorder and dissociative disorder (2 categories), 1992, 93, 94, 95, Best Doctors MidWest, 1996-97, in post traumatic stress disorder, dissociative disorders and affective disorders (3 categories). Fellow Am. Soc. Clin. Hypnosis (1st v.p. 1975-91), Internat. Soc. for Study Dissociation (pres. 1984-96), Am. Orthopsychiatric Assn., Soc. for Clin. and Experimental Hypnosis; mem. Am. Psychiatry Assn., Internat. Soc. Traumatic Stress Studies. Avocations: scubadiving, skiing, horseback riding, skydiving. Office: Assocs in Behavioral Medicine 1602 E Selface Way-263 Post Falls ID 83854

BRAUN, EUNICE HOCKSPEIER, religious order executive, author, lecturer; b. Alta Vista, Iowa; d. George Phillip and Lydia (Reinhart) Hockspeier; m. Leonard James Braun, May 29, 1937. Student, Gates Coll., 1932-34, Coe Coll., 1941-43, Northwestern U., 1944-47. Freelance writer for mags., newspapers, 1947-52; bus. mgr. Baha'i Publishing Trust, Wilmette, Ill., 1952-55, mng. dir., 1955-71; internat. news editor Baha'i News, 1952-70; tchr. Baha'i schs., Alaska, Can., Europe and U.S., 1958—; lectr. Baha i Faith in U.S., Central Am., Europe, Africa, Asia, 1953—; cons. Baha'i Pub. Trust, New Delhi, India, 1972; mem. aux. bd. Continental Bd. Counselors, Baha'i Faith in the Ams., 1972-86. Author: Know Your Baha'i Literature, 1959; The Dawn of World Peace, 1963; Baha'u'llah: His Call to the Nations, 1967; From Strength to Strength, Half Century of the Formative Age of the Baha'i Faith, 1978; A Crown of Beauty, 1982; The March of the Institutions, 1984; A Reader's Guide: The Development of Baha'i Literature in English, 1986; From Vision to Victory, 1993; contbr. essays to Baha'i World, Internat. Record. Mem. Nat. League Am. Pen Women, Baha'i Faith, Iota Sigma Epsilon. Home: 1025 Forestview Ln Glenview IL 60025-4433

BRAUN, HANS-JOACHIM, historian, educator; b. Koenigsberg, Germany, Oct. 6, 1943; s. Walter G. and Gertrud M. Braun; m. Kathleen Iddon, Sept. 17, 1971; children: Bianca, Salina, Christian. PhD, U. Bochum, Germany, 1971, Dr.phil.habil., 1979. Asst. prof. U. Bochum, 1971-78, sr. lectr., 1979-81; prof. U. German Armed Forces, Hamburg, 1982—. Author: Anglo-German Technological Relations, 1974, German Economy 20th Century, 1990, History of Technology, 20th Century, 1992; editor book series Studies in Technology, Economy and Social History, 1985—. Fellow Royal Soc. Arts; mem. Assn. German Engrs. (pres. hist. com. 1992-96), Soc. Hist. Tech. (mem. exec. com. 1993-95), Internat. Com. Hist. Tech. (exec. com. 1981-92, sec.-gen. 1993—), Georg-Agrl. Soc. (pres. sci. coun.). Avocations: jazz and classical music, soccer. Home: Otto Schumannstrasse 13 b, 22926 Ahrensburg Germany Office: U der Bundeswehr, 22039 Hamburg Germany

BRAUN, HARALD W., diplomat; b. Sindelfingen, Germany, Sept. 11, 1952; s. Kuno F. and Anneliese (Foerster) B.; m. Ute K. Schraudolph, Aug. 30, 1980; children: Frederic, Alexandra, Marilena. MA in Econs., SUNY, Stony Brook, 1978, MA in Lit., 1979, PhD, 1980. Mgmt. trainee IBM Germany, Stuttgart, 1973-75; rsch. assoc. Res. Found. for Jewish Immigration, N.Y.C., 1978-79; asst. prof. SUNY, Stony Brook, 1980-81; attache polit. dept. Fgn. Office, Bonn, Germany, 1981-83; first sec. German Embassy, Beirut, Lebanon, 1983-85; press counsellor German Embassy, London, 1985-88; assoc. dir. pers. Fgn. Office, Bonn, 1988-91; German amb. to Burundi, 1991-92; chief of cabinet Fgn. Min. Genscher, Bonn, Germany, 1992-94; head Parliament and cabinet divsn. Fgn. Office, Bonn, 1994-97; min. for polit. affairs German Embassy, Washington, 1997—. Author: German for the Business Minded, 1986. Lt. German Army, 1971-73. Recipient LVO award Queen Elizabeth II, 1987. Avocations: sailing, modern literature, opera. Office: German Emb 4645 Reservoir Rd NW Washington DC 20007-1918

BRAUN, JEROME IRWIN, lawyer; b. St. Joseph, Mo., Dec. 16, 1929; s. Martin H. and Bess (Donsker) B.; children: Aaron, Susan, Daniel; m. Dolores Ferriter, Aug. 16, 1987. AB with distinction, Stanford U., 1951, LLB, 1953. Bar: Mo. 1953, Calif. 1953, U.S. Dist. Ct. (no. dist.) Calif., U.S. Tax Ct., U.S. Ct. Mil. Appeals, U.S. Supreme Ct., U.S. Ct. Appeals (9th cir.). Assoc. Long & Levit, San Francisco, 1957-58, Law Offices of Jefferson Peyser, San Francisco, 1958-62; founding ptnr. Farella, Braun & Martel (formerly Elke, Farella & Braun), San Francisco, 1962—; instr. San Francisco Law Sch., 1958-69; mem. U.S. Dist. Ct. Civil Justice Reform Act Adv. Com., 1991—; spkr. various state bar convs. in Calif., Ill., Nev., Mont.; request moderator/participant continuing edn. of bar programs; past chmn. 9th Cir. Sr. Adv. Bd., past chmn. lawyer reps. to 9th Cir. Jud. Conf.; mem. appellate lawyers liaison com. Calif. Ct. Appeals 1st dist.; jud.conf. U.S. Com. Long Range Planning; founder Jon Samuel Abramson Scholarship Endowment Stanford U. Law. Revising editor: Stanford U. Law Rev.; contbr. articles to profl. jours. Mem. Jewish Community Fedn. San Francisco, The Peninsula, Marin and Sonoma Counties, pres., 1979-80; past pres. United Jewish Community Ctrs. 1st lt. JAGC, U.S. Army, 1954-57, U.S. Army Res., 1957-64. Recipient Lloyd W. Dinkelspiel Outstanding Young Leader award Jewish Welfare Fedn., 1967, Professionalism award 9th cir. Am. Inns of Ct., 1999. Fellow Am. Acad. Appellate Lawyers, Am. Coll. Trial Lawyers (teaching trial and appellate advocacy com.), Am. Bar Found.; mem. ABA, Calif. Bar Assn. (chmn. adminstrn. justice com. 1977), Bar Assn. San Francisco (spl. com. on lawyers malpractice and malpractice ins.), San Francisco Bar Found. (past trustee), Calif. Acad. Appellate Lawyers (past pres., mem. U.S. Dist. Ct. Civil Justice Reform Act adv. com., Calif. Ct. of Appeals 1st Dist. Appellate Lawyers liaison com., jud. conf. of the U.S., com. on long-range planning, panelist 1994), Am. Judicature Soc. (past dir.), Stanford Law Sch. Bd. of Visitors, U.S. Dist. Ct. of No. Dist. Calif. Hist. Soc. (past pres., bd. dirs.), 9th Cir. Ct. of Appeals Hist. Soc. (past pres.), Mex.-Am. Legal Def. Fund (honoree), Order of Coif. E-mail: jbraun@fbm.com.

BRAUN, JOSEPH CHRISTIAN, surgeon; b. Saint Vith, Belgium, May 3, 1951; s. Heinrich and Barbara Angela (Ramscheidt) B.; m. Maria Wiesemes, Aug. 4, 1976; children: Katrin, Christian. MD, U. Liege, Belgium, 1978, U. Aachen, Germany, 1981; PhD, U. Aachen, Germany, 1988. Clin. asst. dept. surgery Univ., Aachen, 1978-86, asst. med. dir. dept. surgery, 1986-88, chief asst. med. dir. dept. surgery, 1988-96; chmn., surgeon in chief dept. surgery Red Cross Hosp., Bremen, Germany, 1996—; assoc. prof. surgery U. Aachen, 1993. Contbr. over 200 articles to profl. jours. Fellow German Assn. Surgery; mem. Belgian Med. Assn., German Med. Assn. Roman Catholic. Avocation: sailing. Office: Red Cross Hosp, St Pauli Deich 24, 28199 Bremen Germany

BRAUN, KARSTEN, physician, researcher; b. Wuerzburg, Bavaria, Germany, Nov. 5, 1968; s. Ludwig and Ingeborg (Werner) B. MD, U. Saarland, 1994. Arzt in praktikum Dept. Traumatology Kreiskrankenhaus, Luedenscheid, Germany, 1994-95; arzt in praktikum Dept. Orthopaedic Surgery Caritas Krankenhaus, Bad Mergentheim, Germany, 1995, assistenzarzt, 1995-96, 98-99; assistenzarzt Sportklinik, Stuttgart, Germany, 1996-98; orthopaedic surgeon Dept. Orthopaedic Surgery Caritas Krankenhaus, Bad Mergentheim, Germany, 1999—. Co-author: Accidents in Horse Sports, 1994, Hip, 1998, Knee, 1999; contbr. articles to profl. jours. Mem. Deutschsprachige Arbeitgemeinschaft Arthroskopie, Gesellschaft Orthopaedisch-traumatologische Sportmedizin, Deutsche Gesellschaft Manuelle Medizin, Berufsverband Aerzte Orthopaedie, Interessensverband Unfallverletzte. Avocations: sailing, ski, bike, music. Office: Rathausgasse 14, D-97877 Wertheim Germany

BRAUN, RETO, computer systems company executive; b. 1941. With Memorex Internat., 1967-83; group pres. Memorex, 1983-84; exec. v.p. Unisys Corp., 1984-91, pres., COO, 1991-93; chmn. bd., pres., CEO Moore Corp. Ltd., Toronto, Ont., Can., 1993-97; CEO Swiss Post, Bern, Switzerland, 1998—, The Fantastic Corp., Zug, Switzerland, 2000—; bd. dirs. Paine Webber Group, Inc. Office: Swiss Post, CH-3030 Bern Switzerland Mailing: The Fantastic Corp, Bahnhofstrasse 12 PO 1350, 6301 Zug Switzerland*

BRAUN, RICHARD FREDRIC, lawyer, judge; b. N.Y.C., Mar. 24, 1947; s. Herbert and Elayne (Weinglass) B. BA, Queens Coll., 1969; JD, Bklyn. Law Sch., 1975. Bar: Pa. 1975, N.Y. 1976, U.S. Ct. Appeals (2d cir.) 1979, U.S. Dist. Ct. (we. dist.) Pa. 1976, U.S. Dist. Ct. (ea. and so. dists.) N.Y. 1977. Tchr. N.Y.C. Bd. Edn., 1969-70; project devel. coord. N.Y.C. Housing and Devel. Adminstrn., 1970-72, 73; staff atty. Legal Svcs., Erie, Pa., 1975-76; sr. and staff atty. Legal Aid Soc., N.Y.C., 1977-80, 81-85; sole practice N.Y.C., 1985-99; clin. instr. Hofstra Law Sch., 1980-81; justice Supreme Ct., State of N.Y. Mem. Democratic County Com., N.Y.C., 1983-85; pres. Village Ind. Dems., 1984-86; bd. dirs. N.Y. State Am. for Dem. Action, 1983-85; mem. Cmty. Bd. 2 Housing Com., N.Y.C., 1983-85. Mem. N.Y. County Lawyers Assn., N.Y. State Trial Lawyers Assn., Assn. of the Bar of the City of N.Y., N.Y. Jewish Lawyers Guild, Judges and Lawyers Breast Cancer Alert. Office: Supreme Ct State NY 111 Centre St New York NY 10013-4390

BRAUN, RUEDIGER WALTHER, physician, virologist; b. Baden-Baden, Germany, Mar. 24, 1954; s. Volker Burkhard and Irene Christine (Hetzel) B.; m. Monika Peter, Sept. 11, 1992; 2 children. MD, U. Heidelberg, Germany, 1979; Dr. Med., Ruprecht-Karls Univ., Heidelberg, 1979, Habilitation, 1985. Scientist German Cancer Rsch. Ctr., Heidelberg, 1979-85; prof. virology Ruprecht-Karls U., Heidelberg, 1986-90; head Inst. of Virology/Bayer AG, Wuppertal, Germany, 1990-93; dir. rsch. Bayer Yakuhin Ltd., Osaka, Japan, 1993-96; mng. ptnr. med. lab. Stuttgart, Germany, 1996—; vis. scientist Emory U., Atlanta, 1984; con. in pharm. bus., 1987-90. Editor-in-chief Intervirology Jour., 1993—, Clin. Lab. Jour., 1987—, European Microbiology Jour., 1992—, Infection Jour., 1996—; contbr. articles to profl. jours. Maj. German Army, 1980-81, Koblenz. Maj. Germany Army, 1980-81, Koblenz. Mem. AAAS, Soc. Virology (bd. dirs. 1990-93), German Soc. for Hygiene and Microbiology, N.Y. Acad. Scis. Avocations: music, squash, skiing, golf. Office: Med Gemeinschaftslabor, Rosenbergstr 85, 70193 Stuttgart Germany

BRAUN, SIMON GEORG, engineering educator; b. Vienna, Austria, Aug. 19, 1933; arrived in Israel, 1945; s. Aron and Anna (Austeritz) B.; m. Miriam Aftergood, Oct. 20, 1965; children: Dalit, Orit, Romit. BSc, Israel Inst. Tech., Haifa, 1958, MSc, 1961, DSc, 1968. Engr. GE R&D, Schenectady, N.Y., 1970-71, Ford Motor Co., Dearborn, Mich., 1976-78; prof. Israel Inst. Tech., Haifa, 1978—. Author: Mechanical Signature Analysis, 1986; editor Mech. Sys. and Signal Processing, 1986—. Sgt. Israeli Army, 1952-55. Recipient Best Paper award Exptl. Soc., Bethel, Conn., 1991. Mem. ASME (assoc. editor Jour. Vibration and Acoustics 1980-87). Home: 7 Zamenhof, 34344 Haifa Israel Office: Israel Inst Tech, Technion City, 32000 Haifa Israel

BRAUN, TIBOR, chemist; b. Lugos, Romania, Mar. 8, 1932; s. Eugene Braun and Cecilia Friedmann; m. Klara Szepesi, Aug. 27, 1934; children: Robert, András. MSc, U. Cluj, Romania, 1954; PhD, Acad. Budapest, 1968, DSc, 1980. Chemist Med. U., Tirgu Mures, 1955-56; rsch. fellow Inst. Atomic Physics, Bucharest, Romania, 1957-63; asst. prof. L. Eötvös U., Budapest, Hungary, 1963-68, assoc. prof., 1968-80, prof. chemistry, 1980—; dir. Info. Sci. and Scientometrics Rsch. Unit, Budapest, 1980—. Editor-in-chief Jour. Radioanalytical Nuclear Chemistry, 1968—, Scientometrics, 1978—; editor Fullerene Sci. and Tech., 1992—; author: Polyurethane Foam Sorbents, 1985, Scientometric Indicators, 1985, The Literature of Analytical Chemistry, 1987, Fullerene Research, 1985-93, 94-96; editor: Nuclear and Radiation Chemical Approaches to Fullerene Science, 2000. Recipient D de Solla Prize internat., 1986, G. Hevesy Prize Internat., 1996, Chemistry Prize Hungarian Acad. Sci., 1980. Achievements include discovery and applications of a new class of polyurethane foam sorbents; development of relative scientometric indicators; new results in radioanalytical chemistry and in fullerene research. E-mail: H1533hra@ella.hu. Home: Gvadányi 109, 1144 Budapest Hungary Office: L Eötvös U Inst Inorganic and Analytical Chemistry, PO Box 123, 1443 Budapest Hungary also: MTAK, Arany János utca 1, 1051 Budapest Hugary

BRAUN, TORSTEN INGO, computer science educator; b. Oberkirch, Germany, Mar. 15, 1964; s. Walter and Margot Ursula (Ruder) B.; m. Ulrike Möglich, Oct. 13, 1990; children: Anna Lena, Laura. Diploma in computer sci., U. Karlsruhe, Germany, 1990, PhD in Computer Sci., 1993. Vis. scientist INRIA, Sophia-Antipolis, France, 1994-95, IBM ENC, Heidelberg, Germany, 1995-97; prof. computer sci. U. Berne, Switzerland, 1998—. Author: High Performance Communication, 1996, IP Next Generation and Virtual Networks, 1999; contbr. articles to profl. jours. Mem. IEEE, Informatics Soc., Assn. Computing Machinery. Avocation: table tennis. E-mail: t.braun@ieee.org. Home: Alpenstr 52, CH-3084 Wabern Switzerland

BRAUNAGEL, ALFRED, research and development company executive; b. Mainz, Germany, Nov. 25, 1946; s. Gotthard and Elsa Maria (Phillip) B.; m. Inge Balbach, Sept. 20, 1974; children: Christoph, Dominik. Diplomingenieur, Coll. Tech., Darmstadt, Germany. Head analytical dept. M. Astor/Benckiser Cosmetics, Mainz, 1970-78, tech. supr. export svcs., 1971-87, sr. devel. mgr., 1978-88, acting R&D mgr., 1988-92, head of R&D, 1992-93, sr. v.p. R&D color devel. activities worldwide, 1993-97; prin. Cosmetic Consulting & Tech., Mainz, 1997—; cosmetic cons. COSCONTEC; mem. COLIPA Task Force, 1995-97, VCI Task Force, 1991-93. Mem. DGK, IKW (ad hoc working group colorants 1992-97, working group skin care/efficacy testing 1995, com. of experts for toiletries 1995-97), Assn. German Chemists. Fax: 49 6131 33 79 32. E-mail: alfred.braunagel@t-online.de. Home: Ulrichstrasse 55, D 55128 Mainz Germany Office: Cosmetic Cons & Tech, Ulrichstr 55, D 55128 Mainz Germany

BRAUNBERGER, ERIC, cardiac surgeon, researcher; b. Paris, Mar. 17, 1966; s. Pierre Braunberger and Gisèle Hauchecorne. MD, U. Paris VII, 1991, DEA in Surg. Sci., 1997, PhD, 1999. Diploma in extra-corporeal circulation, 1992, diploma in pediat. cardiology, 1993. Intern various hosps., Paris, 1991-98; chief of clinic, hosp. asst. Broussais Hosp., Paris, 1999—. Contbr. articles to profl. med. jours. recipient Lian prize Nat. Med. Acad., 1997, Duval-Marjolin prize Nat. Surg. Acad., 1998, Albert Premier de Monaco prize Nat. Med Acad., 1999. Office: HEGP, 20 Rue Leblanc, 75015 Paris France Address: 241 Rue Saint Charles, Paris 75015, France

BRAUNEDER, WILHELM, parliamentarian, law educator; b. Moedling, Austria, Jan. 8, 1943; s. leo and Josefine (Baumberger) B.; m. Senta Koneczny; children: Claudia, Philipp. Doctor's, U. Vienna, 1965; grad., U. Commerce, Vienna, 1972. Asst. prof. U. Austria, 1967-77, assoc. prof., 1977-80, prof. law, 1980—, dean, 1986-90; mem. editl. bd. Fundamina, Pretoria, 1992—. Editor: (jour.) Zeitschrift für Neuere Rechtsgeschichte, 1979—, (legal series) Rechts—u. Sozialwissenschaftliche Reihe, 1991—; co-editor (legal history series) Rechtshistorische Reihe, 1987. Mem. Baden (Austria) Town Coun., 1990-96; mem. Parliament, Vienna, 1994-99, 3d pres., 1996-99. Corp. Austrian Army, 1966-67. Mem. Vereinigung für Verfassungsgeschichte (past pres.), Internat. Commn. for History of Rep. and Parliamentary (pres.), Rotary Club (Baden). Avocations: literature, classical music, railways. Office: Juridicum, Schottenbastei 10-16, 1010 Vienna Austria

BRÄUNINGER, JÜRGEN, composer, music educator; b. Stuttgart, Germany, Sept. 13, 1956; arrived in South Africa, 1985; s. Helmut and Trude (Haag) B.; m. Brigitte Eva Keck, 1985; children: Hannah, Tania. Staatl. Gepr. Musik Lehrer, Musikhochschule, Stuttgart, Germany, 1982; MA, San Jose (Calif.) State U., 1983; DMus, U. Natal, 1999. Lectr. Kunstakademie, Stuttgart, 1984, Musikhochschule, Stuttgart, 1984; lectr. U. Natal, Durban, South Africa, 1985-90, sr. lectr., 1991-96, assoc. prof., 1997—; co-organizer Studio im Planetarium, Stuttgart, 1981-82. Composer: Saxomanie, 1984, D-ART-S, 1984, Bass-Auf, 1984, The Tam Tam Tape, 1982, The Lawnmower Man, 1992, The Dead Pit, 1989, Ahimsa-Ubuntu, 1995, Durban Noise Works, 1998, others; prodr. Songs From Bambatha's Children, 1989, Music for Liberation, 1990, Celebrating Oral Tradition: Bandlululondini, 1992, Art Gecko, 1992, Stories and Songs From the Little Library, 1993 (repub. as The LIttle Library Reading Kit), 1996, Cow Bells and Tortoise Shells, 1993, Gathering Forces II Live in Durban, 1994, The Little Library Maths Kit, 1996; contbr. articles to profl. jours. Mem. exec. bd. Culture and Working Life Project, 1993—; alt. mem. Com. for the Restructuring of the Arts in Natal (Natal Performing Arts Coun./Natal Cultural Congress), 1992-93; mem. Media Workers Assn. of South Africa support com., 1992; exec. mem. Interim Com. for Establishment of Ind. Radio in Natal, 1992; mem. broadcast com. Durban Media Trainers Group, 1991; bd. dirs. Musica Nova-Soc. New Music and New Jazz, 1981-85. Fulbright scholar, 1982-83. Office: U Natal, Dept Music, 4041 Durban KZN, South Africa

BRAUNSTEIN, SAMUEL LEON, physicist; b. Melbourne, Victoria, Australia, Mar. 4, 1961; s. Solomon and Lea (Erdstein) B. BSc, U. Melbourne, 1982, MSc in Physics, 1985; PhD in Physics, Calif. Inst. Tech., 1988. Rsch. assoc. U. Ariz., Tucson, 1988-91; Lady Davis fellow Technion Inst. Tech., Haifa, Israel, 1991-93; Feinberg fellow Weizmann Inst. Sci., Rehovot, Israel, 1993-95; Humboldt fellow U. Ulm, Germany, 1995-96; lectr. U. Wales, Bangor, 1996-99, reader, 1999—; adv. bd. Fortschritte der Physik, 1997—. Mem. Optical Soc. Am. Office: U Wales Bangor Sch Informatics, Dean St, Gwynedd LL57 1UT, Wales

BRAUSE, RÜDIGER W., information systems educator; b. Borna, Germany, Aug. 27, 1950; s. Martin and Irmgard) B.; m. Nicole Sabart; children: Patrick, Pascal. Diploma Physics, U. Tübingen, Germany, 1978, Dr.rer.nat., 1984; Habil., U. Frankfurt, Germany, 1993. Faculty U. Tübingen, 1980-85; rsch. head, prof. U. Frankfurt, 1985—. Author: Neural Networks, 1991, 2d edit., 1995, Operating Systems, 1998, 2d edit., 2000. Mem. EuropEean Neural Network Soc., Gesellschaft f. Informatik. Office: Univ of Frankfurt, FB Informatik, 60054 Frankfurt Germany

BRÄUTIGAM, PETER, physician; b. Achern, Germany, Sept. 18, 1958; s. Hans and Inge (Peters) B. Staatsexamen I, II, U. Freiburg (Germany), 1981, 85; Subintern, U. Vienna, 1983, 84, U. Wash., 1985, 86; Staatsexamen III, Tech. U. Munich (Germany), 1986; postgrad., 1986—. Cert. Bd. Nuclear Medicine. Resident dept. neurology U. Ulm., Germany, 1987-88; fellow, resident dept. nuc. medicine U. Freiburg, Germany, 1988-96; head dept. nuc. medicine Paracelsus Klinik Osnabrück, Germany, 1996-98, Clinique Ste Therese, Luxembourg, 1998—. Contbr. articles to med. jours. Recipient award Deutsche Krebshilfe, 1992, award UGM, 1999. Mem. Soc. German Speaking Lymphologists (bd. dirs. 1992—, treas. 1997—), Soc. Nuclear Medicine, Internat. Soc. Lymphology (Presdl. award 1995), European Assn. Nuclear Medicine (award 2000). Avocations: sailing, bicycling, outdoor activities, flying. Office: Clinique Ste Therese, 36 Rue Ste Zithe, 2763 Luxembourg Luxembourg

BRAVERMAN, DONNA CARYN, fiber artist; b. Chgo., Apr. 4, 1947; d. Samuel and Pearl (Leen) B.; m. William Stanley Knopf, Jan. 21, 1990. Student, U. Mo., 1965-68; BFA in Interior Design, Chgo. Acad. Fine Arts, 1970. Interior designer Ascher Dental Supply-Healthco., Chgo., 1970-72, Clarence Krusinski & Assocs. Ltd., Chgo., 1972-74, Perkins & Will Architects, Chgo., 1974-77; fiber artist Fiber Co-op Fibrecations, Chgo., 1977, Scottsdale, Ariz., 1977—. Exhibited in group shows at Mus. Contemporary Crafts, N.Y.C., 1977, James Prendergast Library Art Gallery, Jamestown, N.Y., 1981, Grover M. Herman Fine Arts Ctr., Marietta, Ohio, 1982, Okla. Art Ctr., 1982, Middle Tenn. State U., Murfreesboro, 1982, Redding (Calif.) Mus., 1983, Tucson Mus. Art, 1984, 86, The Arts Ctr., Iowa City, 1985, The Wichita Nat., 1986; in traveling exhibitions Ariz. Archtl. Crafts, 1983, Clouds, Mountains, Fibers, 1983; represented in permanent collections Phillips Petroleum, Houston, Metro. Life, Tulsa, Directory Hotel, Tulsa, Keys Estate Ariz. Biltmore Estates, Phoenix, Sohio Petroleum, Dallas, Reichold Chem., White Plains, N.Y., Rolm Telecommunications, Colorado Springs, Mesirow & Co., Chgo., Exec. House Hotel, Chgo., Cambell Estate, Ariz., Dictaphone Worldhead Quarters, Stratford, Conn., Davenport Bldg., Boston; contbr. articles to profl. jours. Avocation: photography. Home and Office: 1041 E Glenrosa Ave Phoenix AZ 85014-4435

BRAVERMAN, HERBERT LESLIE, lawyer; b. Buffalo, Apr. 24, 1947; s. David and Miriam P. (Cohen) B.; m. Janet Marx, June 11, 1972; children: Becca Danielle, Benjamin Howard. BS in Econs., U. Pa., 1969; JD, Harvard U., 1972. Bar: Ohio 1972, U.S. Dist. Ct. Ohio 1972, U.S. Supreme Ct. 1975, U.S. Ct. Appeals (6th cir.) 1980, U.S. Ct. Claims 1980. Assoc. Hahn, Loeser, Freedheim, Dean & Wellman, Cleve., 1972-75; sole practice Cleve., 1975-87; ptnr. Porter, Wright, Morris & Arthur, Cleve., 1987-95, Walter & Haverfield, Cleve., 1996—. Councilman Orange Village, Ohio, 1988—, pres., 1998—. Capt. USAR, 1970-82. Fellow Am. Coll. Trust and Estate Counsel; mem. ABA, Ohio Bar Assn., Bar Assn. Greater Cleve. (former chmn. estate planning trust and probate sect.), Suburban East Bar Assn. (pres. 1978-80), Rotary (Cleveland Heights pres. 1980), B'nai Brith (local pres. 1978-84), Wharton Club Cleve. (pres. 1991—), Am. Jewish Congress (Ohio pres. 1992—). Avocations: golf, symphony, reading. Home: 3950 Orangewood Dr Cleveland OH 44122-7406 Office: Walter & Haverfield 1300 Terminal Tower 50 Public Sq Ste 1300 Cleveland OH 44113-2253 also: 23200 Chagrin Blvd Ste 600 Beachwood OH 44122-5402

BRAVERMAN, JORDAN, columnist; b. Boston, July 4, 1936; s. Morris and Molly (Singer) B. BA, Harvard Coll., 1958; MPH, Yale U., 1963; MS of Fgn. Svc., Georgetown U., 1968. Urban planner, economist City Govt. of Quincy, Mass., 1959-61; adminstr. Nat. Blue Cross Assn., Chgo., 1963-65; economist U.S. Dept. Health Edn. and Welfare, Pub. Health Svc., Washington, 1965-67; mgmt. cons. EBS Mgmt. Cons., Washington, 1967-69; asst. to the exec. dir. Am. Pharm. Assn., Washington, 1969-72; dir. pub. policy rsch. Pharm. Mfrs. Assn., Washington, 1972-74; mng. editor Topics in Health Care Financing, Rockville, Md., 1974-75; dir. legis., policy analysis divsn. Health Policy Ctr., Georgetown U., Washington, 1975-77; cons. editor, author Washington, 1978—; appeared numerous TV and radio shows; speech writer, lectr., pub. spkr., jour./mag. book reviewer, cons. editor VA, Washington, 1986-88, FMAS, Inc., Rockville, 1990—, others; columnist The Balt. Sun, 1990, Am. Weekly News, Washington, 1988—, Capital Jester, Washington, 1993, Internat. Med. News Svc., Washington, 1982—, Consumer Health Reporter, Washington, 1983-84, others; manuscript book referee, reviewer U. Press Am., 1982—, Rowman & Littlefield Publs. Inc., 1995—. Author: Pharmaceutical Payment Plans: An Overview, 1973, Crisis in Health Care, 1978, rev. 1980 (nominated Kulp Book award 1978), The Consumer's Book of Health: How to Stretch Your Health Care Dollar, 1982, The Education of the Osteopathic Physician, 1985, Health Maintenance Organizations: New Choices for Paying and Receiving Medical Care, 1986, Nursing Home Standards: a Tragic Dilemma in American Health, 1970, State Health Insurance Plans: Is Anyone Listening?, 1977, To Hasten the Homecoming: How Americans Fought World War II Through the Media, 1996, others; contbr. Echoes of Yesterday, 1994 (anthologies) Best Poems of 1995, Best Poems of the 90s, 1996, Best Poems of 1997, Best Poems of 1998, Thoughts by Candlelight, 1998, Outstanding Poets of 1998, A Celebration of Poets: Showcase Edition, 1998, The Blush of Morning, 1999, Nature's Echoes, 2000 (poetry anthology) The Falling Rain, 2000 (poetry anthology) American at the Millennium: The Best Poems and Poets of the 20th Century (anthology), 2000, (poetry anthology) Poetry's Elite: The Best Poets of 2000, contbr. poetry to Poetry.com, 2000; (cassette) The Sound of Poetry, 1995-2000, (photog. anthologies) Cherished Moments in Time, 1997, photography exhibited World Sci., Washington, 1997, photograph included in Editor's Choice Desk Calendar, Internat. Libr. Photograpy, 1999, Reflections from the Past, 1998, America at the Millennium: The Best Photos of the 20th Century, 1999, The Best Photos of 2000, 2000, Hidden Treasures, 2000 (photographic anthology); contbr. articles to profl and popular jours., govt. publs., univs.; photog. exhibited in Internat. Photo. Hall of Fame Mus., 1997-99; photography featured in Internat. Libr. Photography Desk Calendar, 1999 (Editor's Choice award 1998-99). Column submitted for nomination of Pulitzer Prize, 1994; William Stoughton scholar Harvard U., 1958-59; recipient Editors Choice award N.Am. Open Poetry Contest, 1994, 97; candidate Robert F. Kennedy Journalism award 1994; nominated Pulitzer Prize in Letters, 1996; candidate John H. Dunning prize in U.S. History, Am. Hist. Assn., 1997, Albert J. Beveridge award in Am. History Am. Hist. Assn., 1997, The PEN/Amazon.com Short Story award, 2000. Mem. Internat. Soc. Poets (Poet of Yr. 1996, Internat. Poet of Merit, 1997, 99, 2000, elected Hall of Fame 1997, nomination Poet of Yr. 1999, 2000), Internat. Soc. Photographers (nominated disting. mem.), Harvard Club of Washington, Yale Club of Washington, Georgetown Club of Washington. Avocations: trumpet, old time radio collector, theatre, sports, cmty. affairs. Home: 2401 H St NW Washington DC 20037-2564

BRAVI, JEAN LUC, advertising executive; b. Carcassonne, Avoe, France, Sept. 2, 1959; s. Jean Pierre and Jeanine (Milese) B.; m. Soledad Boutan, Apr. 23, 1993; children: Margot, Lili. Grad. bus. sch., Paris, 1984. Acct. exec. Paris, 1984-86; brand mgr. Havas Ecom, Paris, 1986-89; bd. acct. dir. DDB Needham, Paris, 1989-93; founder, head of strategy Louis XIV Agy., Paris, 1994—. Avocations: share holder of nat. rugby team, mem. racing-bike team. Office: Loius XIV, 10 Ave de Friedland, 75008 Paris France

BRAVINA, SVETLANA LEONIDOVNA, physicist, researcher; b. Kiev, Ukraine, Apr. 16, 1952; d. Leonid Samoilovich and Maria Semerovna (Dubinska) B.; m. Nicholas Vladimirovich Morozovsky, Aug. 1, 1975; 1 chld, Anna Nicholaevna. M of Radioelectronics, Electronics Coll., Kiev, 1970; MSc, Nat. U., Kiev, 1976; PhD, Inst. Semicondrs., Kiev, 1988. Engr. Inst. Physics of Nat. Acad. Sci. of Ukraine, Kiev, 1976-83, sr. engr., 1983-86, jr. rsch. scientist, 1986-89, rsch. scientist, 1989-94, sr. rsch. scientist, 1994—; cons. Inst. Info. Sci., Kiev, 1992-93, Energoproject, Kiev, 1993-97. Contbr. more than 80 articles to profl. jours.; holder 4 patents. Sec., Regional Election Commn., Kiev, 1991, 93, 98. Grantee Ukraine State Com. of Sci., 1993, 94, 96, State Bur. Fgn. Experts of China, 1997. Mem. Internat. Soc. for Optical Engring. Avocations: English literature, tennis, swimming. Home: fl 122, Borshchagovskaya str 2, 03055 Kiev Ukraine Office: Inst of Physics/NASU, Prospect Nauki 46, 03028 Kiev Ukraine

BRAWER, CATHERINE COLEMAN, foundation executive, curator; b. N.Y.C., Feb. 19, 1943; d. Joseph A. and Beatrice R. Coleman; m. Robert A. Brawer, Sept. 7, 1962; children: Christopher Paul, Nicholas Andrew. BA, Sarah Lawrence Coll., 1964; MA in Art History, NYU, 1966. Publicity coord. Evehjem Mus. Art, Madison, Wis., 1970-75, curator Liebman Collection, 1974-75; mktg. mgr. Maidenform, Inc., N.Y.C., 1975-78; ind. curator N.Y.C., 1978; v.p. Ida and William Rosenthal Found., N.Y.C., 1981-90, pres., 1990—; dir. pub. affairs Maidenform Inc., N.Y.C., 1990-97, bd. dirs., 1970-97; curator Maidenform Mus., 1992-97; trustee Katonah (N.Y.) Mus. Art, 1982-2000, Ind. Curators, Internat., N.Y.C., 1989—, vice chmn., 1998—, Inst. Fine Arts, NYU, 1993—, Musica Viva, 1995—; trustee at large Plimoth Plantation, Plymouth, Mass., 2000—. Author: (catalogues) The Auspicious Dragon in Chinese Decorative Arts, 1978, Many Trails: Indians of the Lower Hudson Valley, 1983, Trade Winds: The Lure of the China Trade, 1985; (book) Making Their Mark: Women Artist Move into the Mainstream 1970-85, 1989, Chinese Export Porcelain from the Liebman Porcelain Collection, 1992. Trustee Plymouth (Mass.) Plantation, 2000. Mem. Am. Ceramic Circle, N.Y. Regional Assn. Grantmakers (mem. com. 1990-91), Art Table N.Y., Soc. of Mayflower Descendants (sec. 2000).

BRAY, CHARLES, artist; b. Salford, Lancashire, Eng., Feb. 26, 1922; s. Charles and Minnie (Mather) B.; m. Margaret Ingram, Dec. 26, 1954; children: David, Stephen, Simon, Andrew. Supplementary cert. ceramics & sculpture, Goldsmiths Coll., London, 1954. Tchr.'s cert., 1947. Cert. wood and metal London, City, Guilds, 1949. Woodcarver J. Gough & Co., Manchester, 1936-40; tchr. Salford Edn. Authority, 1947-53, Cumbria Edn. Authority, 1955-62; prin. lectr. Tchr. Tng. Coll., Sunderland, 1962-75, Art Faculty Poly., Sunderland, 1975-82; artist Cumbria, 1982—; former mem. Crafts Panel of No. Arts. Author: Dictionary of Glass, 1995; group exhbns. include Paysage, Galerie d'Amon, Paris, Internat. Glass, Novy Bor and Prague, East Meets West, Arnhem, Sculpteurs Verriers, Espace Marriane Hofsumer, Brussels, Nomades del Vidre, Barcelona, European Glass Sculpture, Luxembourg and Liege; solo exhbns. include The Pilkington Glass Mus., Sunderland U., The Ancrum Gallery, Scotland, Galerie Het Glashuis, Alkmarr, The Netherlands, The Miller Gallery, N.J., Tullie House, Carlisle, Coleridge, Edinburgh and London; collections displayed in The Turner Collection, Sheffield, Shipley Art Gallery, Gateshead, Salford City Art Gallery, Corning Mus. of Glass, N.Y., The Ulster Mus., Belfast, Durham County Coun.; pvt. collectors include Queen Margarethe of Denmark and ex-king Constantine of Greece; contbr. articles to profl. jours. Leading signalman Royal Navy, 1940-46. Recipient U. Sunderland fellowship, 1997. Fellow Soc. Glass Tech., Royal Soc. Arts. Avocations: music, painting. Home and Studio: Prospect House Farlam, Brampton, Cumbria CA8 1LA, England

BRAY, ERIC HANS, English educator; b. Stockton, Calif., Oct. 23, 1954; s. Mark Stanislaus and Norma (Plaskett) B.; m. Mikiko Hirata; 1 child, Christopher. BA, U. Calif., Santa Cruz, 1984; MEd, Temple U., 1993. Cert. tchr. gen. subjects and secondary Spanish. Tchr. Instituto Bi Cultural, Tuxtla Gutierrez, Mexico, 1985-88; from instr. to acad. dir. Kyoto YMCA English Sch., Japan, 1989-94; instr. Doshisha U., Kyoto, 1994-96, Kansai U., Osaka, Japan, 1996-97; assoc. prof. Yokkaichi U., Mie, Japan, 1997—. Mem. Tchrs. English to Spkrs. Other Langs., Japanese Assn. Lang. Tchrs., Japanese Kyudo Assn. Avocations: Japanese Kyudo, guitar, hiking. Office: Yokkaichi U, 1200 Kayo-cho, 512 Yokkaichi Mie-ken, Japan

BRAY, GERALD LEWIS, minister, educator; b. Montreal, Quebec, Can., Nov. 16, 1948; arrived in Eng., 1972; s. Leonard Lewis and Catherine Viola (Garnett) B. BA, McGill U., Montreal, 1969; DLitt, Sorbonne, Paris, 1973. Ordained to ministry Anglican Ch., 1978. Lectr. Oak Hill Coll., London, 1980-92; prof. Samford U., Birmingham, Ala., 1993—. Author: Holiness and the Will of God, 1979, The Doctrine of God, 1993, Documents of the English Reformation, 1994, Biblical Interpretation: Past and Present, 1996, The Anglican Canons 1529-1947, 1998, Ancient Christian Commentary on Scripture: Romans, 1998, 1 & 2 Corinthians, 1999, James-Jude, 2000, Tudor Church Reform, 2000. Mem. Tyndale Fellowship. Avocations: swimming, cycling. Home: 16 Manor Ct, Pinehurst Grange Rd, Cambridge CB3 9BE, England Office: Samford Univ Beeson Divinity Sch Birmingham AL 35229-0001

BRAY, WILLIAM OTIS, IV, diversified electronics company executive; b. Santa Monica, Calif., Sept. 2, 1949; s. Willliam Otis III and Nadine Hope (Sauer) B.; m. Gerda Smit, Aug. 22, 1982; children: William V, Patricia, Alida, Veronica. BS in Computer Sci., Calif. Poly. State U., San Luis Obispo, 1974; MS in Bus. Adminstrn., San Diego State U., 1985. Cert. computer sci. tchr., Calif. Communications developer spl. systems div. NCR Corp., San Diego, 1975-76, communications cons. spl. systems div., 1976-77, modular lodging systems mgr. Systems Engring./Torrey Pines div., 1978-84, system software products mgr. Systems Engring./San Diego div., 1984-86; exec. asst. exec. office NCR Corp., Dayton, Ohio, 1986-87, dir. systems engring. fins. and div. office systems, 1987-89, asst. v.p. systems architecture and systems mgmt. Integrated Systems Group, 1989-90, gen. mgr. engring. and mfg., 1990-92; v.p. managed svcs. worldwide customer svc. NCR Corp., Dayton, 1997—; v.p. gen. software products group Unisys, Minn., 1992-94; with EVP Tech. Integration, Chgo., 1994-97; adj. instr. Palomar Coll, San Marcos, Calif., 1976-82, San Diego State U., 1982-84; adj. prof. Nat. U., San Diego, 1984-86. Served with USAF, 1968-72. Republican. Lutheran. Avocations: racquetball, tennis, skiing. Office: NCR 1700 S Patterson Blvd Dayton OH 45479-0002

BRAYBROOKE, MARCUS CHRISTOPHER ROSSI, vicar; b. Dorking, Surrey, Eng., Nov. 16, 1938; s. Arthur Rossi and Marcia Nona (Leach) B.; m. Mary Elizabeth Walker, june 20, 1964; children: Rachel Hobin, Jeremy. BA, U. Cambridge, 1962, MA, 1965; MPhil, U. London, 1968. Ordained priest, 1965. Curate St. Michael's, London, 1964-67; team vicar Frindsbury, Kent, Eng., 1967-73; rector Swainswick, Somerset, Eng., 1973-79; dir. tng. Wells, Somerset, 1979-84; dir. Coun. Christians & Jews, London, 1984-87; vicar Christ Ch., Bath, Eng., 1984-91; chaplain Magdalene Chapel, Bath, 1991-93; team vicar Dorchester-on-Thames, Oxford, Eng., 1993—; chmn. World Congress of Faiths, London, 1978-83, 92-99; pres. Parliament of the World's Religions, Chgo., 1993; joint pres. World Congress of Faiths, 1998—;m patron Internat. Interfaith Ctr., 2000—. Author: Together to the Truth, 1971, The Undiscovered Christ of Hinduism, 1973, Interfaith Organizations, 1980, Time to Meet, 1990, Wide Embracing Love, 1990, Pilgrimage of Hope, 1992, Children of One God, 1992, Be Reconciled, 1992, Love Without Limit, 1995, Faith in a Global Age, 1995, How to Understand Judaism, 1995, A Wider Vision, 1996, The Explorer's Guide to Christianity, 1998, The Essential Atlas of the Bible, 1999, Christian-Jewish Dialogue, 2000; editor: Stepping Stones to a Global Ethic, 1993, Dialogue With a Difference, 1993; co-editor: All in Good Faith, 1993, Testing in Global Ethics, 1998. Trustee Three Faiths Forum, 1998—, Internat. Peace Coun., 1995—. Avocations: gardening, photography, travel. Home: Marsh Baldon Rectory, Oxford OX44 9LS, England Office: World Congress of Faiths, 2 Market St, Oxford OX1 3EF, England

BRAZDES, LIVIA, medical physicist; b. Oradea, Romania, June 16, 1946; d. Tudorache and Stefania (Lupascu) Andrei; m. Mircea Brazdes, May 27, 1972 (dec. Feb. 1995). BS, U. Bucharest, Romania, 1969, PhD, 1981. Biophysics diplomate; nuclear physics diplomate. Biophysicist Mil. Ctrl. Hosp., Bucharest, 1969-73; rschr. Nat. Inst. Gerontology and Geriatrics, Bucharest, 1973-90, sr. rschr., 1990—, head biophysics dept., 1973—, dep. scientific dir., 2000—. Editor Romanian Jour. of Gerontology and Geriatrics Editing, 1980; patentee in field. Mem. Romanian Soc. Geriatrics. Avocations: painting, sculpture, pet training (cats). Home: Sector 1, Bd Aviatorilor 70, Bucharest Romania Office: Nat Inst Gerontology Geriat, PO Box 2-4 9 M Caldarusani St, 78178 Bucharest Romania

BRAZIER, RODNEY JOHN, lawyer; b. Loughton, Eng., May 13, 1946; s. Eric and Mildred (Davies) B.; m. Margaret Rosetta Jacobs, Apr. 17, 1974; 1 child, Victoria Anne. LLB, U. Southampton, 1968. Asst. lectr. in law U. Manchester, Eng., 1968-70, lectr. in law, 1970-78, sr. lectr. in law, 1978-89, reader in constitutional law, 1989-92, dean of the faculty of law, 1992-94, prof. law, 1992—; additional bencher Lincoln's Inn, 2000—. Author: Constitutional Practice, 3d edit., 1999, Constitutional Reform, 1991, Constitutional Texts, 1990, Ministers of the Crown, 1997; co-author: Constitutional and Administrative Law, 7th edit., 1994. Justice of the peace Greater Manchester, 1982-89. Fellow Royal Hist. Soc. Office: U Manchester Faculty of Law, Oxford Rd, Manchester M13 9PL, England

BRDIČKA, MIROSLAV, retired physicist; b. Dvur Králové, Czechoslovakia, Sept. 12, 1913; s. Jan and Antonie (Kočová) B.; m. Blanka Houbová, Mar. 30, 1946; 1 child, Petr. PhD, Charles U., Prague, Czechoslovakia, 1946. Lectr. Charles U., Prague, 1945-54, assoc. prof., 1954-59, prof., 1959-68; prof. Czech Tech. U., Prague, 1968-81. Author: Continuum Mechanics, 1959; co-author: Theoretical Mechanics, 1987. Home: Janovskeho 14, 17000 Prague Czech Republic

BREAKWELL, GLYNIS MARIE, psychology educator; b. West Midlands, Eng., July 26, 1952; d. Harold and Vera (Woodhall) B. BSc with honors, U. Leicester, 1973; MSc, U. Strathclyde, 1974; PhD, U. Bristol, 1976. Lectr. Sch. Social Analysis, U. Bradford, Eng., 1976-78; Prize fellow, tutor Nuffield Coll., Oxford U., Eng., 1978-82; lectr. dept. external studies U. Oxford, 1978-85; lectr. dept. psychology U. Surrey, Guildford, Eng., 1981-87, sr. lectr., 1987-88, reader in psychology, 1988-91, head of dept. psychology, 1990-95, prof. psychology, 1991—, pro vice chancellor, 1994—, head Sch. of Human Scis., 1997—, warden Hall of Residence, 1981-83; dir. rsch. Econ. and Social Research Council, 1980-82, 86-90, Dept. Employment, 1981-83, Leverhulme Trust, 1984-86. Author: Facing Physical Violence, 1989, Interviewing, 1990, (with C. rowett) Social Work, 1982; The Quiet Rebel, 1985; Coping with Threatened Identities, 1986, (with Foot and Gilmour) Doing Social Psychology, 1988, (with D. Canter) Social Representations, 1988, Managing Violence at Work: Course Leaders' Guide, 1992, Managing Violence at Work: Workbook, 1992, Careers and Identities, 1992, Basic Evaluation Methods, 1995, Coping with Aggressive Behaviour, 1997;. Fellow Brit. Psychol. Soc. (council 1984—, editor Psychologist jour. Social Psychology prize 1978); mem. Soc. for Risk Analysis, Am. Psychological Assn., Internat. Assn. Applied Psychology, European Soc. Opinion and Mktg. Rsch., European Assn. Exptl. Social Psychologists. Clubs: Univ. Women's (London); Bourne (Farnham, Surrey). Avocations: racquet sports, visual arts. Office: Univ Surrey, Dept Psychology, Guildford Surrey GU2 7XH, England

BREALEY, RICHARD ARTHUR, bank official; b. Barnet, Herts, Eng., June 9, 1936; s. Albert Edward and Irene Gwendoline Brealey; m. Diana Cecily Brown-Kelly; children: David, Charles. MA, Oxford (Eng.) U., 1959. Investment dept. Sun Life Assurance Co. of Can., London, 1959-66; computer applications mgr. Keystone Custodian Funds of Boston, 1966-68; prof. fin. London Bus. Sch., 1968-98; spl. adviser to gov. Bank of Eng., 1998—; vis. prof. fin. London Bus. Sch., 1998—. Author: Introduction to Risk and Return from Common Stocks, 2 edit., 1983; (with S. Myers) Principles of Corporate Finance, 6th edit., 2000; (with S. Myers and A. Marcus) Fundamentals of Corporate Finance, 1994, 3d edit., 2000. Avocations: rock climbing, skiing, horse riding. Office: London Bus Sch, Sussex Pl Regents Pk, London NW1 4SA, England

BREAM, JULIAN, classical guitarist and lutanist; b. London, Eng., July 15, 1933; s. Henry G. B. Ed., Royal Coll. Music; hon. degree, U. Surrey, Eng., 1968. First recital, 1947, London debut, 1950, U.S. debut, 1958; formed Julian Bream Consort, 1960; since performed tours in all 5 continents, regular tours to Europe and U.S.A.; performed concerts, recitals, including with Sir Peter Pears, also chamber music, string quartets, duo with John Williams, Julian Bream Consort world tour with Robert Tear, 1988; appeared in festivals and recitals: Aldeburgh , Berlin, Edinburgh, Bath, Paris, Vienna, Tokyo, New York, recital series at Concertgebouw, Amsterdam, 1992-93, 60th birthday concert at the Wigmore Hall, London, 1993; transcriber Romantic and Baroque works; commd. new works from Benjamin Britten, William Walton, Hans Werner Henze, Malcolm Arnold, others; frequent radio and TV appearances including TV biog. film, A Life in the Country, 1976, series of master classes, film of Elizabethan music and poetry with the late Dame Peggy Ashcroft, 1987, all for BBC; producer, performer 8 films on location in Spain on devel. Spanish music for lute and guitar; numerous recs. for RCA; now under exclusive contract with EMI Classics; recordings include Julian Bream Edition Vol. 1-28, Highlights From the Julian Bream Edition, The Baroque Guitar, A Celebration of Andrés Segovia, Guitar Greatest Hits, La Guitarra Romantica, Impressions for Guitar, Popular Classics for Spanish Guitar, The Romantic Guitar, Julian & John/2; subject of book pub. by Macdonald, 1982. Served with Brit. Army, 1952-55. Decorated Comdr. Brit. Empire, 1985; recipient Grammy award for Classical Performance: An Evening of Elizabethan Music, 1963, Villa-Lobos Gold medal, 1976, 6 awards Nat. Acad. Recording Arts and Scis., 2 Edison awards, various awards from Gramophone mag., Gold Silver and Platinum discs. Achievements include research in Elizabethan lute music. Office: care Hazard Chase Ltd, Richmond Hs 16-20 Regent St, Cambridge CB2 1DB, England*

BREARLEY, STEPHEN, surgeon; b. Liverpool, Eng., Mar. 17, 1953; s. Roger and Joyce Mary (Hewitt) B.; m. Margaret Faith Collier, July 12, 1980; chilern: Jonathan Joshua, Samuel Sebastian James. Student, Liverpool Coll., 1962-71; MB, Gonville & Caius Coll., Cambridge, Eng., 1978; MChir, Gonville & Caius Coll., 1991. Surg. registrar Walsgrave Hosp., Coventry, Eng., 1981-83; rsch. registrar Birmingham (Eng.) Gen. Hosp., 1983-84; surg. registrar Birmingham Children's Hosp., 1985-86, Selly Oak Hosp., Birmingham, 1986-87; sr. surg. registrar West Midlands (Eng.) Regional Health Authority, 1988-91; cons. surgeon Whipps Cross Hosp., London, 1992—; chmn. Hosp. Jr. Staff Com., British Med. Assn., London, 1983-84; elected mem. Gen. med. Commn., 1984—, chmn. registration com., 1998—. Contbr. articles to profl. jours. Fellow Royal Coll. Surgeons; mem. Vasc. Surg. Soc. Great Britain Ireland, Assn. Surgeons Great Britain Ireland. Anglican. Avocations: classical music, golf, flying. Office: Whipps Cross Hosp, Leytonstone, London E11 1NR, England

BREATHNACH, CAOIMHGHÍN SEOSAMH, physiologist, medical historian; b. Dunlavin, Wicklow, Ireland, Oct. 13, 1923; s. Padraig Timothy and

Máire Seosaphín (Whittle) B. MB, BCh, BAO, Nat. U. Ireland, 1948, MD, 1960, PhD, 1962. House physician Mater Hosp., Dublin, Ireland, 1948, St. Kevin's Hosp., Dublin, 1949, Fever Hosp., Dublin, 1950-51; asst. med. officer Rialto Chest Hosp., Dublin, 1951-56; lectr. Univ. Coll., Cork, Ireland, 1956; assoc. prof. U. Coll., Dublin, 1957-88; postdoctoral rsch. fellow Yale U., New Haven, 1962-63. Contbr. articles to profl. jours. Rsch. grantee NIH, 1964-66, Med. Rsch. Coun., Ireland, 1967-70, Wellcome Trust, 1996. Fellow Royal Acad. Medicine Ireland; mem. Physiol. Soc. Avocations: gardening, ambling. Office: U Coll, Earlsfort Ter, Dublin 2, Ireland

BREBNER, JOHN MAIN, psychologist, educator; b. Torry, Scotland, May 17, 1935; arrived in Australia, 1969; s. John Main and Lydia (Watts) B.; m. Mary Jill Fawkes, July 29, 1959; children: Candida, David, Anna (dec.), Christine. MA with honors, U. Aberdeen, Scotland, 1957; PhD, U. Exeter, Eng., 1965. Nuffield rsch. asst. U. Exeter, 1959-62; rsch. fellow U. St. Andrews, Scotland, 1962-64; lectr. U. Dundee, Scotland, 1964-69; lectr. U. Adelaide, Australia, 1969-72, sr. lectr., 1972-83, assoc. prof. psychology, 1983—, dean of arts, 1986-88. Author: Environmental Psychology and Building Design, 1992 (Ergonomics Soc. U.K. rsch. award 1984); assoc. editor Australian Jour. Psychology, 1983-95, Personality and Individual Differences, 1988—. Mem. Channel 7 Children's Med. Rsch. Panel, Adelaide, 1984-91; mem. rsch. grant panel Julia Farr Ctr., Adelaide, 1990-94. Officer RAF, 1957-58. Acad. links travel grantee Brit. Coun., 1991; vis. scholar Wolfson Coll., Oxford, Eng., 1991. Mem. Internat. Soc. for Study of Individual Differences (bd. dirs. 1993-99). Office: U Adelaide, Dept Psychology, Adelaide SA 5005, Australia

BRECHER, BERND, management consultant; b. Germany, Oct. 2, 1932; came to U.S. 1940; s. Jacob and Betty (Lewinsohn) B.; m. Helen Edith Casel, Feb. 1, 1959; children: Jacalyn Naomi, Alison Fay, Daniel Evan. BA, Columbia U., 1954, MS in Journalism, 1955. Dir. devel., pub. rels. and alumni affairs Coll. Physicians and Surgeons, Sch. Dentistry, Columbia U., N.Y.C., 1954-57; campaign dir., supr. John Price Jones Co., Inc., N.Y.C., 1958-67; v.p. Hamilton Coll. and Kirkland Coll., Clinton, N.Y., 1967-69; exec. v.p. John Price Jones Internat., Inc., N.Y.C., 1969-71; sr. v.p. Brakeley, John Price Jones, Inc., N.Y.C., 1971-73; pres. Bernd Brecher & Assocs., Inc., N.Y.C. and Scarsdale, 1973-93, Instl. Advancement Programs, Inc., N.Y.C., Tuckahoe, Becket, Mass., 1979—; cons., strategic planner for arts, health, edn., youth, religious, cmty., environ., and other not-for-profit instns.; exec. dir. The Grad. Ctr. Found., N.Y.C., 1994-97; cons. Lilly Endowment, Indpls., 1994—; interim dir. Lehman Coll. Found., 2000—. Pres. Bd. Edn., Greenburgh, N.Y., 1977-78, Woodlands Scholarship Fund, Hartsdale, N.Y., 1965-66, Soc. of Columbia Graduates, 1980-85; mem. exec. com. Columbia Journalism Sch. Alumni, 1981-89; trustee Berkshire Children's Mus., 1998—. With U.S. Army, 1957-58. Recipient alumni medal for svc. Columbia U., 1983, Pres.'s Cup, 1981, Lion Awards, 1979, 80, 94, 99. Mem. Coun. for Advancment and Support of Edn. (Quarter Century Svc. award 1981), Nat. Soc. Fund Raising Execs. (v.p. N.Y. chpt. 1987-89), Am. Assn. Community and Jr. Colls., Am. Hosp. Assn., Am. Assn. Mus., Princeton Univ. Club, Univ. Club of Chgo. Avocations: theatre, tennis, travel, fine dining. Home: 35 Parkview Ave Bronxville NY 10708-2953 Office: Instl Advancement Programs Inc 65 Main St Tuckahoe NY 10707-2908

BRECHER, HOWARD ARTHUR, lawyer; b. N.Y.C., Oct. 18, 1953; s. Milton and Dorothy (Zahler) B. AB magna cum laude, Harvard U., 1975, MBA, 1979, JD cum laude, 1979; LLM, NYU, 1984. Bar: N.Y. 1980, U.S. Dist. Ct. (so. dist.) N.Y. 1983, U.S. Tax Ct. 1981. Assoc. Roberts & Holland, N.Y.C., 1979-82, Chadbourne, Parke, Whiteside & Wolff, N.Y.C., 1982-84; atty. legal dept. N.Y. Telephone Co., N.Y.C., 1984-91, legal counsel, 1991-96; v.p. Value Line, Inc., 1996—; mem. tax com. N.Y.C. C. of C., 1985-88, 94—. Mem. ABA (tax sect.), N.Y. State Bar Assn. (tax sect., com. taxation of affiliated corps., trusts and estates sect.), Assn. of Bar of City of N.Y., Harvard Bus. Sch. Club of Greater N.Y. Democrat. Jewish. Clubs: Harvard (N.Y.C. and Boston). Office: 220 E 42nd St Ste 6000 New York NY 10017-5891

BRECHTEL, UNDA JURKA, library director; b. Riga, Latvia, Mar. 3, 1935; came to U.S., 1951; d. Aleksanders and Irene (Stesingers) Jurka; m. Philipp Jack Brechtel Jr., Sept. 3, 1960 (div. Aug. 1986); children: Philipp Jack III, Peter Kevin. BS in Psychology, St. Thomas Aquinas, 1981; MLS, L.I. U., 1982. Reference librarian Haverstraw (N.Y.) Pub. Libr., 1982-83; libr. dir. Sloatsburg (N.Y.) Pub. Libr., 1983-85, Wanaque (N.J.) Pub. Libr., 1985-88, Oakland (N.J.) Pub. Libr., 1988—. Mem. N.J. Libr. Assn., N.Y. Libr. Assn. Lutheran. Avocations: ballroom dancing, travel, gardening. E-mail: brechtel@bccls.org. Home: 1-16 Lawrence Pk Piermont NY 10968 Office: Oakland Pub Libr 2 Municipal Plz Oakland NJ 07436-1826

BRECK, HOWARD ROLLAND, geophysicist; b. Kenton, Ohio, Nov. 5, 1912; s. Rolland Franklin and Helen Dunn (Snodgrass) B.; m. Martha Ann Forker, Aug. 7, 1942; 1 child, Robert Rolland. A.B. in Geology, U. Mo., 1934. Geophysicist Seismograph Service Corp., Tulsa, 1937-61; asst. v.p., mgr. acoustic well-logging div. Seismograph Service Corp., 1954-59; exec. dir. Soc. Exploration Geophysicists, Tulsa, 1962-79; exec. dir. emeritus Soc. Exploration Geophysicists, 1979—; cons. in assn. mgmt.; mem. exec. com. Offshore Tech. Conf., 1979-82, chmn. awards com., 1981-82. Contbr. articles on acoustic well-logging and synthetic seimograms to profl. jours., 1954-60; gen. mgr.: Geophysics mag., 1962-78. Mem. Soc. Exploration Geophysicists (hon.), Geophys. Soc. Tulsa (hon. life), Am. Soc. Assn. Execs., Phi Gamma Delta. Home and Office: 709 W 29th St Sand Springs OK 74063-5016

BRECK, SYLVIA THORINGTON, historical researcher; b. Roxbury, Vt., Aug. 1, 1922; d. James Wallace and Lucia Madeleine (Sowles) Thorington; m. Richard Winslow Breck Jr., July 7, 1943; children: Mary Young, David Stoddard Greenough. Student, Union Meml. Hosp., Balt., 1940-41; real estate lic., Mister Lister Sch., Duxbury, Mass., 1971. Clk., supr. Camp Holabird Supply Base, Balt., 1941-43; statis. typist Office of Strategic Svcs., Washington, 1944; researcher U.S. Bur. Ships, Washington, 1945; ad placer Humphrey's Advt. Agy., Boston, 1946-47; sec., bookkeeper Better Packaging, Inc., Boston, 1948; pvt. sec. Cornelius Wood, Andover, Mass., 1959-62; sec. Dean of Students Phillips Acad., Andover, Mass., 1964-69; sales, listing John D. Walsh Real Estate, Pembroke, Mass., 1972-74. Contbr. articles to profl. jours.; writer, editor: Eddy Homesteader, 1988—, Eddy Family Bulletin, 1985—; author, editor: Eddyville-Middleboro, Mass., 1961-87. Legis. chmn. LWV, Andover, Mass., 1958-59; v.p. Navy League of U.S.-New England, Andover, 1960-62; invited artisan Duxbury (Mass.) Art Assn., 1988-93; hist. lectr. Middleboro (Mass.) Founders Day Celebrations, 1990-91; leader Girls Scouts Am., Andover, 1957-62, Medfield, Mass., 1954-56; pres. PTA, Andover, 1962-64; active Girl Scouts Am. 50th Anniversary, Duxbury, 1992. Mem. Eddyville Homestead Assn., Inc. (pres. 1990-93, pres. emeritus 1993-98, v.p. 1993-2000), Eddy Family Assn., Inc. (pres. 1980-87, exec. sec. 1987—), Duxbury Art Assn. Republican. Avocations: professional candy making, sewing, gardening, writing, researching. Home: Box 354 570 Washington St Duxbury MA 02332-3856

BREDE, ANDREW DOUGLAS, research director, plant breeder; b. Pitts., Feb. 4, 1953; s. James Faris and Adele Katherine (Konefal) B.; m. Linda Davis Rudd, Jan. 11, 1992; children from previous marriage: Loralee Elizabeth, Michael Douglas. BS, Pa. State U., 1975, MS, 1978, PhD, 1982. Asst. golf course supt. Valley Brook Country Club, McMurray, Pa., 1975-76; grad. rsch. asst. Pa. State U., University Park, 1976-82; assoc. prof. Okla. State U., Stillwater, 1982-86; dir. rsch. Simplot Turf & Horticulture, Post Falls, Idaho, 1986—; v.p. Turfgrass Breeders Assn., Tangent, Oreg., 1989-91; chmn. variety rev. Lawn Inst., Marietta, Ga., 1990-96; bd. dirs. Nat. Turfgrass Evaluation Program; golf course supr. Assn. Am. Rsch. Com., 1996-97. Author: Turfgrass Maintenance Reduction Manual, 2000; assoc. editor Agronomy Jour., 1993-99; contbr. articles to Agronomy Jour., 150 articles to mags.; prodr. 15 ednl. videos; patentee in field. Rsch. grantee, 1983-86. Mem. Am. Soc. Agronomy. Republican. Achievements include organization of 1st turfgrass conf. in People's Republic of China; developer, patentee 60 plant varieties. Avocation: amateur radio operating. Office: Simplot Turf & Horticulture 5300 W Riverbend Rd Post Falls ID 83854-9456

BREDEHOFT, ELAINE CHARLSON, lawyer; b. Fergus Falls, Minn., Nov. 22, 1958; d. Curtis Lyle and Marilyn Anne (Nesbitt) Charlson; children: Alexandra Charlson, Michelle Charlson. BA, U. Ariz., 1981; JD, Cath. U. Am., 1984. Bar: Va. 1984, U.S. Ct. Appeals (4th cir.) 1984, U.S. Bankruptcy Ct. (ea. dist.) Va. 1987, D.C. 1994, U.S. Ct. Appeals (D.C. cir.) 1994. Assoc. Walton and Adams, McLean, Va., 1984-88, ptnr., 1988-91; ptnr. Charlson Bredehoft, P.C., Reston, Va., 1991—; spkr. Fairfax Bar Assn., CLE, 1992—, VB Assn., CLE, 1993—, 12th Ann. Multistate Labor and Employment Law Seminar, 1994, Va. CLE Ann. Employment Law Update, 1993-96, Va. Women's Trial Lawyers Assn. Ann. Conf., 1998, Va. Bar Assn. Labor and Employment Conf., 1994-97, 99, Va. Trial Lawyers Assn., 1995, 97, Va. Law Found., 1995—, Va. Assn. Def. Attys., 1996; mem. faculty Va. State Bar Professionalism Courses, 1997—; invitee 4th Circuit Judicial Conf., 1997-99, permanent mem., 1999—; invitee Graves Conf., 1999—; substitute judge 19th Judicial Dist., 1998—; mem. faculty Va. State Bar Professionalism Courses, 1997—, chair Fairfax Bar Assn. Diversity Taskforce, 1998-99 (Pres. Vol. award 1998). Bd. dirs. Va. Commn. on Women and Minorities in the Legal System, 1987-90, sec., 1988-90. Mem. Va. Bar Assn. (mem. exec. com. young lawyers sect., mem. litigation com., mem. nominating com., chmn. model jud. com., spkr. CLE 1993—), Va. Trial Lawyers Assn. (vice chmn. ann. conv. 1996-98, mem. com. on long-range planning 1996-97, spkr. 1995, 97), Minn. State Soc., Fairfax Bar Assn. co-chair subcom. on minorities, Pres.'s Vol. award 1998, 99), George Mason Inns of Ct. (master 1996—). Office: Charlson Bredehoft PC 11260 Roger Bacon Dr Ste 201 Reston VA 20190-5252

BREDEHOFT, JOHN MICHAEL, lawyer; b. N.Y.C., Feb. 22, 1958; s. John William and Viola (Struhar) B.; children: Alexandra Charlson Bredehoft, Michelle Charlson Bredehoft. AB magna cum laude, Harvard Coll., 1980, JD cum laude, 1983. Bar: D.C. 1983, U.S. Dist. Ct. D.C. 1985, U.S. Ct. Appeals (D.C. cir.) 1985, U.S. Ct. Appeals (1st cir.) 1986, U.S. Supreme Ct. 1987, U.S. Ct. Appeals (9th cir.) 1988, U.S. Ct. Appeals (3d and 5th cir.) 1989, U.S. Tax Ct. 1989, U.S. Ct. Appeals (4th Cir.) 1990, U.S. Dist. Ct. Mont. 1991, Va. 1992, U.S. Dist. Ct. (ea. dist.) Va. 1992. Assoc. Cleary, Gottlieb, Steen & Hamilton, Washington, 1983-91; prin. Charlson & Bredehoft, Fairfax, Va., 1991-98; ptnr. Venable, Baetjer & Howard L.L.P., McLean, Va., 1998—; Contbg. editor Employment Law in Virginia, 1997. Bd. dirs. Falls Brook Assn., Herndon, Va., 1988-91; nat. class 1983 reunion gift chmn. Harvard Law Sch. Fund, Cambridge, 1988, class agt., 1994—; mem. Harvard Debate Centennial Com., 1992. Named Lawyer of Yr., Met. Washington Employment Lawyers Assn., 1996. Mem. ABA (sect. on litigation), Va. Bar Assn. (sect. on labor and employment law, governing coun. 2000—), Va. Trial Lawyers Assn. (founding officer, employment law sect.), Fairfax Bar Assn. (sect. on employment law, vice chmn. 1997-98, chmn. 1998-99), Def. Rsch. and Trial Inst. (appellate advocacy com., co-chair seminar com.), Va. Law Found./Va. CLE (employment law com.), Va. Women Attys. Assn. Office: 2010 Corp Ridge Ste 400 Mc Lean VA 22102-5203

BREDEMEYER, LORETTA JEANE, public relations, vocational and academic consultant; b. Brownwood, Tex., May 29, 1942; d. James Richard Freeman and Zuma Jeanette (Jones) Ford; m. Bobby Wayne Bredemeyer, Dec. 29, 1976 (div. Dec. 1995); children: Shauna Rhiannon, Francesco Bernard. Student, U. Tex., 1960-62, 63; AS in Bus. Adminstrn., Austin C.C., 1999; student, SW Tex. State U., 1999—. Computer operator Draughtman, Hudson Engr., Inc., Austin, Tex., 1966-69; clk. U.S. Postal Svc., Austin, 1969-76; legal sec. Patton and Norris, Austin, 1976; exec. sec. Alderman-Cave Milling & Grain, Winters, Tex., 1977; ops. mgr. Bredemeyer Farm, Ballinger, Tex., 1977-82; exec. mgr. Techno-Graphic Ctr., Austin, 1982-86; coord. Thomas-Darnell Seminars, Austin, 1984-86; vocat. instr. Austin Ind. Sch. Dist., 1985-88; chief exec. officer Advt. Today, Austin, 1987—; cons. pub. rels. Anderson Mill Swim Team, Austin, 1988-89, Williamson County Mcpl. Utilities Dist. 1, 1988-89, Anderson Mill Mcpl. Utility Dist., 1989-91; vocat. instr. Leander Ind. Sch. Dsit., 1988-90; owner C'est Magnifique Candies, 1982—, Bredemeyer Geriatric Svcs., 1985-95, Profl. Acad. Adv. Svcs., 1992-94; legal rschr. Austin Am.-Statesman newspaper, 1994—. Author, editor: (newsletter) TAG-P.S., 1987-88; editor (spl. lang. project) Purple Sage Talented and Gifted, 1987-88 (edn. award, 1988, 89, 90); contbr. articles to newspapers. Tchr. religion St. Thomas More Cath. Ch., Austin, 1982-88, 91-98, min. to the sick, 1991-97, adminstrv. asst. confirmation program, 1995-97; v.p., program chmn. Round Rock Talented and Gifted Assn., 1988-90, pres., 1990-92; chmn. pub. rels. PTA Purple Sage Elem. Sch., 1988-89, spl. edn. projects, 1988-90; project leader 4-H, 1990-92; active Austin area Campfire Group, 1983-86, Austin area Boy Scouts Am., 1989-91, South Austin Youth Soccer Assn., 1992-94, Austin Flyers Soccer Assn., 1994-96. Mem. NAFE, Nat. Writers Club, Bus. Execs. Assn., N.W. Austin Businesswomen, Nat. Assn. of Self-Employed, Inst. of Mgmt. Accts., Phi Theta Kappa, Heart of Tex. Orchid Soc. Home and Office: 19600 Pecos Dr Lago Vista TX 78645-6002

BREDENKAMP, BRIAN VICTOR, forester, educator; b. Benoni, South Africa, Apr. 16, 1948; s. Benjamin and Alrieka Josephina (Tromp) B.; m. Lani Gerber, Jan. 15, 1972; children: Ian, Ryan. BS, U. Stellenbosch, 1974, BS with honors, 1976, MS, 1977; PhD, Va. Poly. Inst. and State U., 1988. Forester Dept. Forestry, South Africa, 1968-76, rsch. officer, 1976-80; project leader South African Forest Rsch. Inst., 1981-90; prof. forest mgmt. U. Stellenbosch, South Africa, 1991—; chmn. Modelling and Mensuration Working Group, South Africa, 1989—; chmn. Tree Adv. Com. of Stellenbosch I.D.P., 1999—. Co-author: Forest Management, 1993; contbr. articles to profl. jours. Mem. Stellenbosch Philatelic Soc. (pres. 1991—). Avocations: philately, arctophily. Home: 16 Hof Ave, Stellenbosch 7600, South Africa Office: Dept Forest Sci, Pvt Bag X1, Matieland 7602, South Africa

BREDENKAMP, JUERGEN, psychologist; b. Hamburg, Germany, Mar. 29, 1939; s. Hans and Anne Liese (Behrmann) B.; m. Karin Spies, Aug. 9, 1968; children: Silke, Birthe. Diploma in Psychology, U. Hamburg, 1963, PhD, 1964. Asst. prof. U. Heidelberg, 1964-72; prof. U. Bonn, 1972, U. Goettingen, 1972-80, U. Trier, 1980-84, U. Bonn, 1984—; dir. Inst. Psychology, Bonn, 1984—. Author: The Test of Significance in Psychological Research, 1972, Psychology of Learning and Memory, 1977, Imagery and Learning, 1979, Theory and Design of Psychological Experiments, 1980, Imagery and Metacognition, 1992, Learning, Remembering and Forgetting, 1998; co-editor 4 vols. German Encyc. Psychology, 1983; co-editor (jour.) Methodika. Mem. German Psychol. Assn. (pres. 1990-92), German Rsch. Coun. (elected surveyor 1988-92). Avocation: music. Office: Inst Psychlogy, Roemerstr 164, D-53117 Bonn Germany

BREDFELDT, JOHN CREIGHTON, economist, financial analyst, retired air force officer; b. Oct. 31, 1947; s. Willis John and Geraldine Elizabeth (Creighton) B.; m. Barbara Elaine Gutow, June 6, 1984; children: Jason Caulter, Bryan Thomas. BBA, Wichita State U., 1969, MA in Econs., 1971; PhD in Pub. Adminstrn., La Salle U., 1995; grad., Air Command and Staff Coll., 1984, Nat. Defense U., 1987. Dir. Brennan Halls Wichita State U., 1969-71; commd. 2d lt. USAF, 1971, advanced through grades to lt. col., 1987, ret., 1993; budget/cost analyst Aero. Sys. Divsn., Dayton, Ohio, 1971-76; insp. Air Force IG, Andrews AFB, Md., 1976-79; chief economist Dir. Programs AF/PRP, Pentagon, Va., 1979-83; chief cost analyst divsn. USAF Europe, 1985-87; dep. dir. program control, engine program office USAF Europe, Dayton, 1987-89; dir. program control spl. ops. forces USAF, 1989-93; project leader for econs./fin. analyst Modern Techs. Corp., Warner Robins, Ga., 1993—; instr. econs. Wichita State U., 1969-71; bus. prof. Bowie State Coll., 1980-83; econs. instr. European divsn. U. Md., Germany, 1985-87, Sinclair C.C., Dayton, 1988-93, Macon (Ga.) State Coll., 1994—; adj. prof. Mercer U., 1996—, Wesleyan Coll., 1998—. Contbr. articles to profl. jours. Rep., Sunday sch. tchr. Ramstein Protestant Parish Coun. Germany, 1984-86; asst. scout master Ramstein Coun. Boy Scouts Am., 1984-87, den leader Weblos, 1998, Troop 550 charter rep., 1999—; v.p. St. Timothy Lutheran Ch., Dayton, 1989-91. Mem. Assn. Govt. Accts., soc. cost Estimating and Analysis, Am. Soc. Mil. Comptrollers, Nat. Eagle Scout Assn.

BREDHOLT, SVERRE, architect; b. Oslo, Norway, Apr. 24, 1944; s. Sverre and Ingrid (Pedersen) B.; m. Karin Buvik, 1968 (div. 1971); m. Tonje Normann, 1980; children: Trude, Ingrid. MS in Arch., U. Trondheim, Norway, 1970. Arch. Architect Mnal Sverre Bredholt, Oslo, 1970-72, Cappelen & Rodahl Archs., Oslo, 1972-74, Gosta Aaberg Arch., Oslo, 1974-76, Constructor T. Brudevold, Oslo, 1976-78; pvt. practice arch. Oslo, 1978—; arch. in collaboration with Stelios Agioustratitis and Doxiades, Athens, Greece, 1978-80; collaboration with civil engr. Brusletto, Oslo, 1987-95. Profl. cartoonist and illustrator, 1968—; author comic strip Dr. RAMbook, 2000. Chair mem. Norwegian Conservative Party, Oslo, 1962. Mem. Norwegian Journalist Orgn. E-mail: bredholt@teleline.es. Home: Calle Cervantes, 29016 Malaga Spain Office: Apartado 15106, 29080 Malaga Spain

BREDIKHINA, NELINA ALEXANDROVNA, bibliographer, library director; b. Novosibirsk, Russia, June 3, 1939; d. Alexander Nikolayevich and Yelena Konstantinovna (Yurieva) Zelentsky; m. Oleg Vsevolodovich, Aug. 8, 1961; 1 child, Maxim Olegovich. Diploma, State Acad. Culture, St. Petersburg, Russia, 1960. Libr. Regional Sci. Libr., Novosibirsk, 1960, sr. libr., 1961, head dept., 1962, chief bibliographer, 1963-65, dep. dir., 1966-70, dir., 1971—; chmn. state exam. com. Coll. Culture, Novosibirsk, 1976-98. Mem. editl. bd. Jour. Darovanije, 1998—. Bd. trustees Jour. Sibirskaya Gornitsa, Novosibirsk, 1994—; mem. presidium Regional Trade Union Com. Culture Workers, Novosibirsk, 1995—. Named Honored Culture worker Russian Fedn. Ministry of Culture, 1979. Mem. Regional Libr. Assn. (pres. 1996—), Leadership Club. Avocations: readings, travel. Office: Regional Sci Libr, Sovetskaya 6, 630007 Novosibirsk Russia

BREDSDORFF, ELIAS LUNN, writer; b. Roskilde, Denmark, Jan. 15, 1912. Student, U. London, 1934; Cand. mag., Copenhagen U., 1938, Dr.phil., 1964. Tchr. lit. and English Vordingborg (Denmark) Tng. Coll., 1939-43; organizer Frit Danmark, 1943-45, editor newspaper, 1945-46; Queen Alexandra lectr. Danish Univ. Coll. U. London, 1946-49; lectr. Danish Cambridge (Eng.) U., 1949-60, reader and head dept. Scandinavian studies, 1960-79. Author: D.H. Lawrence: Et Forsoeg paa en politisk Analyse, 1937, Corsaren, 1941 (expanded version pub. as Goldschmidts "Corsaren" med en udfoerlig redegoerelse for striden mellem Soeren Kierkegaard og "Corsaren" 1962), John Steinbeck, 1943, Danish Literature in English Translation: A Bibliography, 1950, (with others) An Introduction to Scandinavian Literature, from the Earliest time to Our Day, 1951, H.C. Andersen og Charles Dickens: Et Venskab og dets oploesning, 1951, H.C. Andersen og England, 1952, Hans Christian Andersen, 1805-2nd April-1855, 1955, Danish: An Elementary Grammar and Reader, 1956, Drama i Syrakus, 1956, Kinas Vej: Samtaler og rejseindtryk, 1957, Bag Ibsen's maske: To imaginaere interviews med Henrik Ibsen, 1962, Henrik Pontoppidan og Georg Brandes, 2 vols., 1964, Literatura i obschestvo Skandinavii, 1971, Kommer det os ved?, 1971, Den store nordiske krig om seksualmoralen, 1973, Hans Christian Andersen, 1975, Fra Andersen til Scherfig, 1978, Nonsens og bonsens, 1978, Kjeld Abells Billedkunst, 1979, Revolutionaer humanisme, 1982, Min egen Kurs, 1983, Mit engelske liv, 1984, H.C. Andersen: Mennesket og Digteren, 1985; editor: Sir Edmund William Gosse, Correspondence with Scandinavian Writers, 1960, Kjeld Abell, Synskhedens Gave: Prosa og vers, 1962, En bog om Mogens Fog, 1991, Aerkedansk-12 Essays fra Glaenoe, 1992; Kjeld Abell Et Brevportrait, 1993, H.C. Andersen og Georg Brandes, 1994, Medmennesker og Modmennesker, 1994, Syndebukken, En bog om, Oscar Wilde, 1999, Højskolebarnet, 2000; author introduction, supr. translations Contemporary Danish Plays: An Anthology, 1955, author notes, supr. translations Contemporary Danish Prose: An Anthology, 1968; (with C.E. Bay) Henrik Pontoppidaus Breve I-II, 1998; contbr.to Chambers' Ency., Cassell's Ency. of Literature, Ency. Americana, Penguin Compantions to World Literature; editor. Fellow Peterhouse, Cambridge, 1963-79. Fellow Royal Danish Acad. Sci. and Letters. Home: Kronprinsesse Sofies vej 28, 2000 Copenhagen F, Denmark

BREDSDORFF, THOMAS, literary scholar, educator; b. Silkeborg, Denmark, Apr. 1, 1937; s. Morten Lunn and Frida (Brack) B.; m. Lene Nicolaisen, June 10, 1936; 1 child, Nanna Cecilie. PhD, U. Copenhagen, 1972, DPhil, 1976. Asst. prof. U. Copenhagen, 1968-78, prof., chair Scandinavian lit., 1978—. Author ten books including Tristan's Children, 1982 (Georg Brandes prize 1983, Soren Gyldendal prize 1984), The Sudden Transformation, on Sylvia Plath, 1987, The Black Holes, on P.O. Enquist, 1991, In Other Words, on Henrik Nordbrandt, 1996; lit. critic Politiken, Copenhagen; contbr. articles to profl. jours. Harvard U. scholar, 1972-73, U. Calif. Berkeley scholar, 1990; Clare Hall fellow Cambridge U., Eng., 1981. Home: Sortedam Dossering 25, DK 2200 Copenhagen Denmark Office: U Copenhagen, Njalsgade 80, DK 2300 Copenhagen Denmark

BREE, REMCO DE, otolaryngologist; b. Utrecht, The Netherlands, Dec. 5, 1966; s. Piet K. and Willy (van Krimpen) de Bree. MD, U. Utrecht, 1991; PhD, U. Amsterdam, 1995. Resident in ear, nose and throat Free U. Amsterdam Hosp., 1991—. Avocation: running. Office: Free U Amsterdam Hosp, De Boelelaan 1117 Dept Oto, 1081 HV Amsterdam The Netherlands

BREED, HELEN ILLICK, ichthyologist, educator; b. New Cumberland, Pa., Mar. 12, 1925; d. Joseph Simon and Della May (Brotzman) Illick; m. Henry Eltinge Breed, Jr., Nov. 23, 1957; children: Henry E., Joseph I., Brenda E. BS, Syracuse U., 1947, MS, 1949; PhD, Cornell U., 1953. Tchr. sci. Lyons (N.Y.) Cen. High Sch., 1949-50; instr. zoology and physiology Akron (Ohio) U., 1953-54; postdoctoral Ford Found. fellow, instr. physiology Vassar Coll., Poughkeepsie, N.Y., 1954-55; asst. prof. biology Russell Sage Coll., Troy, N.Y., 1955-57; asst. dir. systematic biology NSF, Washington, 1957; assoc. prof. conservation Cornell U., Ithaca, N.Y., 1957-61; rsch. assoc. biology Rensselaer Poly. Inst., Troy, 1964-68; environ. cons. Eltick Rsch. Corp., Troy, 1971-90; enivron. advisor, cons. Women's Environ. and Devel. Orgn., N.Y.C., 1991—; internat. environ. liaison and coord. N.Y. State Summit and Agenda's 21 Program, Albany, 1992—; ichthyology cons. Ichthyological Assocs., Lake George Project, Troy, 1969, Ithaca, 1971-80, Lima, Peru, 1972-73; internat. environ. liaison and coord. N.Y. State Summit and Agenda's 21 Program, Albany, 1992—, Cornell U. Program on Breast Cancer and Environ. Risk Factors in N.Y. State. Contbr. articles to profl. jours. Capital dist. mem. Syracuse U. campaign for excellence, Troy, 1988-90. Nat. Wildlife Fedn. fellow, 1950, Sports Fishing Inst. fellow, 1951-53, Am. Scandinavian Found. fellow, Trondheim, Norway, 1959-60, Fulbright fellow in fisheries rsch., Trondheim, Norway, 1959-60; recipient scholarship in biology Westinghouse, 1942-43. Mem. AAAS, Am. Soc. Zoologists, Soc. Systematic Zoology, Am. Soc. Ichthyologists and Herpetologists, Am. Fisheries Soc., Brunswick Hist. Soc. Democrat. Lutheran. Avocations: travel, photography of ecological environments. Home and Office: 421 Tamarac Rd Troy NY 12180-9687

BREED, RIA, anthropologist; b. Helden, The Netherlands, Feb. 5, 1944; d. Jan Mathys and Maria Arnoldina (Gommans) Trienekens; m. David Scranton Breed, Sept. 5, 1976; children: Christian, Genevieve. Med. technologist Profl. Sch. Venlo (Netherlands), 1962; BA in Social Anthropology, U. Amsterdam, 1972; MA in Phys. Anthropology, NYU, 1977, PhD, 1984. Clin. technologist St. Lambertus Hosp., Helmond, 1962-65, DePaul Hosp., Norfolk, Va., 1965-66; research technician U. Amsterdam, 1968-70; research technician cardiovascular research NYU Med. Ctr., N.Y.C., 1966-68, 72-77; research assoc. NYU, N.Y.C., 1984; head biomechanics dept. Breed Corp., 1984-88; with Automotive Tech. Internat., Denville, N.J. Home: 48 Hillcrest Rd Boonton NJ 07005-9433 Office: Automotive Tech Internat PO Box 8 Denville NJ 07834-0008

BREEDIN, BERRYMAN BRENT, journalist, public relations, historian, consultant; b. Beaufort, S.C., Nov. 3, 1925; s. Berryman Brent Breedin and Jane Cunningham Dixon; m. Allain Crenshaw, Sept. 1959 (div. Jan. 1978); children: David Singleton, Sarah Breedin Chase, Amelia Breedin Twarogowski. BA, Washington and Lee U., 1947. Reporter Caller-Times, Corpus Christi, Tex., 1947-48; sports editor, columnist Daily Mail, Anderson, S.C., 1949-52; publicist, editor Clemson (S.C.) U., 1952-55, 64-66; resident mgr. Hunt Internat. Oil Co., Pakistan, 1955-58, Australia, 1996-97; press sec. U.S. Senator Strom Thurmond, Washington, 1958-59; info. specialist DuPont Co., Wilmington, Del., 1960-63; editor Am. Coll. Pub. Rels. Assn., Washington, 1966-71, Coun. Libr. Resources, Washington, 1972-75; dir. pub. rels. Georgetown U., Washington, 1977-79, Rice U., Houston, 1981-87; pvt. practice Columbia, S.C., 1988—; historian White House Weekly, Washington, 1998—; adv. Washington D.C. Libr., 1972-76, Houston Zoo, 1981-87. Founding mem. Capital Hill Montessori, Washington, 1964, Field Sch., Washington, 1972. With USN, 1944-45. Mem. Nat. Press Club, Sigma Delta Chi. Episcopalian. Avocations: family history, sports history, movie history. E-mail: brent@compuzone.net. Home and Office: 1829 Senate St Apt 4C Columbia SC 29201-3837

BREEDLOVE, FRANCES BURTON, elementary educator; b. Pearisburg, Va., June 6, 1950; d. Preston Bane and Georgie (Hoback) Burton; m. Lewis A. Breedlove Jr., Sept. 3, 1971 (div. May 1990). BS, Radford (Va.) Coll., 1972; MS, Radford U., 1976; AAS summa cum laude, New River C.C., Dublin, Va., 1982. Postgrad. profl. cert., Va. Tchr. Giles County Pub. Sch., Pearisburg, 1972—; owner, operator B and H. Grocery, Pearisburg, 1980-83; pres. bd. dirs. New River Mgmt. Corp.; mem. state com. Standards of Learning Test Item Review, Richmond, Va., 1997—. Mem. Friends of Libr., Pearisburg, 1997—; mem., contbr. New River Valley Econ. Devel. Alliance, 1992—. Mem. Giles Edn. Assn., Pearisburg Women's Club (sec. 1996—), Giles County C. of C. (Pres.'s award 1993), Giles County Hist. Soc., Alpha Delta Kappa. Methodist. Avocations: golf, travel, economic development, museum docent. E-mail: fbreedlove@gva.net. Home: 100 Chapman Dr Pearisburg VA 24134-2076 Office: Narrows Elem/Middle Sch 401 Wolf St Narrows VA 24124

BREEDON, RICHARD, research physicist; b. Akron, Ohio, Nov. 14, 1955; s. Edward A. and Barbara (Leatherman) B.; children: Earl Chira, Franz Chira. BS in Math./Physics, Kent State U., 1977; MS in Physics, U. Rochester, 1980; PhD in Exptl. Physics, Rockefeller U., 1988. Acting dir. pub. affairs Alaska Pacific U., Anchorage, 1978; rsch. asst. dept. physics U. Rochester (N.Y.), 1978-80; praktikant Hahn-Meitner Inst. for Nuclear Rsch., Berlin, 1980; asst. for rsch. Rockefeller U., N.Y.C., 1980-82; grad. fellow CERN, Geneva, 1982-88; rsch. assoc. Rockefeller U., N.Y.C., 1988-89; rsch. physicist U. Calif., Davis, 1989—; fellow KEK (Nat. Lab. for High Energy Physics), Tsukuba, Japan, 1990-94. Contbr. articles to profl. jours. Fellow Japan Soc. for Promotion of Sci., Tokyo, 1990-94. Mem. Am. Phys. Soc., N.Y. Acad. Sci., Nat. Resources Def. Coun., Sierra Club. Avocations: yoga teaching, photography, bicycling, foreign languages. Office: U Calif Dept of Physics Davis CA 95616

BREEN, FAITH FEI-MEI LEE, economist, management consultant; b. Burbank, Calif., Feb. 3, 1951; d. John Quong and Eleanor S.G. Lee; m. George Edward Breen Jr., Nov. 30, 1974; children: Erika Lee, George Edward III. BA, U. Md., 1972; MA, U. Pitts., 1975; PhD, U. Md., 1990; MPA, Harvard U., 1993. Asst. dir. Ctr. for Health Policy Rsch. Am. Enterprise Inst. Pub. Policy, Washington, 1975-77; economist U.S. Dept. Labor, Bur. Internat. Labor Affairs, Washington, 1978, Nat. Gov.'s Assn., Ctr. Pub. Policy Rsch., Washington, 1978-79; expert cons., economist Pres.'s Adv. Com. Women, Washington, 1979-81; polit. econ. cons. Nat. Assn. State and Territorial Solid Waste Mgmt. Ofcls., Washington, 1981-82; expert cons., economist to dep. under sec. mgmt. U.S. Dept. Edn., Washington, 1980-83; adj. faculty dept. econs. Central Mich. U., 1978—; prof. Sch. Bus. and dept. econs. Largo, Md., 1985—; pres. Systems Resources Mgmt., Inc., 1983-99; dep. exec. dir. Gates Millenium Scholars, 2000—; dep. exec. dir. Gates Millennium Scholarship program, 2000—; lectr. in field. Contbr. articles to profl. jours.; exec. prodr. TV program: Saccharin and the Public Interest, 1978. Past pres. Inner Wheel of College Park, 1986-87; chmn. bd. dirs. Orgn. Chinese Am. Women, 1990, del. Women-to-Women Exchange program, 1987; chair fin. com. University Park Rep. Women's Club, 1985. Recipient Nat. Def. Lang. fellow, 1973-75; cert. of appreciation Sec. U.S. Dept. Edn., 1983; Fulbright-Hays Seminar Abroad, 1986. Mem. Am. Econ. Assn., Harvard Club of Boston. Roman Catholic. Avocations: tennis, swimming, bridge. Home: 5525 Surrey St Chevy Chase MD 20815-5523

BREESKIN, MICHAEL WAYNE, lawyer; b. Washington, Dec. 25, 1947; s. Nathan and Sylvia (Raine) B.; m. Frances Cox Lively, May 29, 1982; children: Molly Louise, Laura Rose. BA cum laude, U. Pitts., 1969; JD, Georgetown U., 1975. Bar: D.C. 1975, Colo. 1983, U.S. Dist. Ct. D.C. 1977, U.S. Dist. Ct. Colo. 1983, U.S. Ct. Appeals (D.C. cir.) 1978, U.S. Ct. Appeals (10th cir.) 1984, U.S. Supreme Ct. 1995. Mng. atty. Tobin & Covey, Washington, 1977-79; assoc. Donald M. Murtha & Assocs., Washington, 1979-80; counsel NLRB Office Rep. Appeals, Washington, 1980-83; trial atty. NLRB Denver Regional Office, 1983-88; assoc. Wherry & Wherry, Denver, 1989-91; sr. atty. The Legal Ctr. for People with Disabilities and Older People (formerly The Legal Ctr. Serving Persons with Disabilities), Denver, 1991-98; gen. counsel Assn. Cmty. Living Boulder County, Inc. (formerly the Assn. for Retarded Citizens in Boulder County, Inc.), 1998-2000; counsel Fox & Robertson, PC, Denver, Colo., 2000—; presenter, lectr. in field. Adv. com. Domestic Violence Initiative for Women with Disabilities, 1997—. Recipient Outstanding Work for People with Disabilities acknowledgement Very Spl. Arts Colo., 1996; named Profl. of Yr., The Arc of Adams County, 1997; recipient Adv. of the Year award Assn. Cmty. Living in Boulder County Inc., 1996, Schenkein award Arc of Denver, Inc., 1997, award Disability Ctr. Ind. Living and Colo. Cross-Disability Coalition, 1999. Mem. ABA, Colo. Bar Assn. (disability law forum com.), Arapahoe County Bar Assn. Avocations: bicycling, skiing, reading. Office: 910 16th St Ste 610 Denver CO 80202-2921

BREGLIANO, JEAN-CLAUDE, geneticist, educator; b. Toulon, Provence, France, Sept. 23, 1938; s. Tullo Emilio and Malfise Josephine (Martini) B.; m. Andree Francine Roberjot, Aug. 8, 1961; children: Anne, Serge. Asst. prof. genetics U. Paris XI, Orsay, France, 1960-67; asst. prof. genetics U. Clermont, Ferrand, France, 1967-73, prof. genetics, 1973-90; prof. genetics U. Mediterranée, Marseille, France, 1990—; dir. genetics lab. U. Clermont, Ferrand, 1973-83, biology rsch. unit, 1983-90; dir. post-grad. sch. Inst. Biology Devel., Marseille, 1995—. Author (chpt. in book) Mobile Genetic Elements, 1983; contbr. numerous articles to profl. jours. Fellow French Soc. of Genetics, French Soc. Cellular Biology. Avocations: woodworking, stoneworking. Office: Inst Biol Devel Marseille, 13288 Marseille France

BREGMAN, ARTHUR RANDOLPH, lawyer, educator; b. Phila., Dec. 9, 1946; s. Nathan and Stella (Husock) B.; m. Patrice Rosalie Gancie, May 30, 1980. BA, Columbia U., 1968; MA, Yale U., 1969; JD, Georgetown U., 1985. Bar: D.C. 1985, U.S. Ct. Appeals (D.C. cir.) 1985, U.S. Dist. Ct. D.C. 1985, U.S. Claims Ct. 1985. Treas. Nat. Coun. for Soviet and E. European Rsch., Washington, 1981-83; law clk. Washington Lawyers' Com. for Civil Rights, 1983-84; assoc. Klores, Feldesman and Tucker, Washington, 1985-86; dir. Soviet and E. European Svcs. APCO, Washington, 1988-91; of counsel Steptoe & Johnson, Washington, Moscow, USSR, 1991-92; ptnr. Steptoe & Johnson, Washington D.C. and Moscow, 1992-99; mng. ptnr. Squire, Sanders & Dempsey, Washington, 1999—; adj. prof. Georgetown U. Law Ctr., Washington, 1986-89; program dir. Internat. Law Inst., Washington, 1986-91; chmn. bd. adv. U.S.-Russia Bus. Law Report, 1990—. Editor: U.S.-Soviet Contract Law, 1987. Recipient Civil Procedure prize Lawyers Coop. Pub. Co., Balt., 1982. Mem. ABA (internat. bar sect.), D.C. Bar. E-mail: rbregman@ssd.com. Home: 3059 Porter St NW Washington DC 20008-3272 Office: 1201 Pennsylvania Ave NW Washington DC 20004-2401

BREGMAN, DAVIS, orthopedist, pain management specialist; b. Nov. 21, 1969. BS, MIT, 1990; MD, NYU, 1994. Diplomate Am. Acad. Pain Mgmt. Intern Lenox Hill Hosp., N.Y.C., 1994-95; resident Hosp. U. Pa., Phila., 1996-97; pres. Polo Medgroup, N.Y.C., 1996-98; med. dir. Medplaza Physicians, Huntington, N.Y., 1998—, pres., 1999—; disease prevention editor Medplaza News, Dix Hills, N.Y., 1998-99; host radio show "Your Health with Dr. Bregman," 1999; developer outpatient healthcare facility, 1998; cons. Ambulatory Surgery Ctr. Devel., 1996-97; pub. spkr. on pain mgmt. topics; pioneer in use of non-surgical spinal decompression therapy. Contbr. articles to profl. jours. Recipient Disting. leadership award for outstanding contbns. to contemporary soc., 1999, 2000, Internat. Order Merit for svcs. to orthops. and medicine; named outstanding intellectual of 20th century for achievement in orthops. and pain mgmt; proclamation for community svc. County Exec. Robert J. Gaffney. Fellow Suffolk Acad. Medicine, Am. Biog. Inst., Am. Biog. Inst. Rsch. Assn. (dep. gov.); mem. Internat. Order of Ambs., Med. Soc. State of N.Y. Office: Medplaza Physicians 1786 E Jericho Tpke Huntington NY 11743-5713

BREGNSBO, HENNING, political scientist, researcher; b. Aarhus, Denmark, Jan. 29, 1928; s. Axel and Ane Kirstine (Thomsen) Mortensen; m. Hanne Vita Palmqvist, Sept. 5, 1961; children: Michael, Anne Christine, Peter. Degree in history, U. Aarhus, 1955; degree in polit. sci., U. Copenhagen, 1969. Assoc. prof., chief of sect. U. Odense, 1969-72; assoc. prof. U. Copenhagen, 1972-96, ret., 1996. Author numerous books on policy-making, pressure politics, lobbying and ideology; contbr. articles to profl. jours. Fulbright scholar, HEW, 1959-60. Mem. Scandinavian and Internat. Profl. Assns. Home: No 28 Voldmestergade, DK-2100 Copenhagen Denmark Office: U Copenhagen Inst Polit Sci, No 15 Rosenborggade, DK-1130 Copenhagen Denmark

BREIDBACH, OLAF, historian, neuroscientist, educator; b. Monheim, Germany, Aug. 11, 1957; s. Hans Joseph and Marianne (Kuchenberg) B.; m. Angela Bohwnen, Dec. 11, 1993; ildren: Lukas, Thomas. PhD in Zoology, PhD in Philosophy, habilitation in Zoology. Sci. worker Inst. Applied Zoology U. Bonn, Germany, 1983-85; U. Cologne, Germany, 1985-87; sci. worker U. Bonn, Germany, 1987-94; employee Math. Inst. U. Bochum, Germany, 1994-95; head dept., prof. U. Jena, 1995—; head. Inst. for History of Medicine and Scis., Jena, 1995—; dir. Mus. Ernst Haeckel Haus, Jena, 1995—; coord. dir. Theolab, Jena, 1999. Author: Der Anglogieschluss in den Natur Wissenschaftend, 1987, Die Materialisierung Des Icks, 1997; editor: The Nervous Systems of Invertebrates, 1995, Natur de Aesthetic der Natur, 1997. Advisor Adv. Group for Protection of Animals Thuringian Ministery, Erfurt, 1996. Mem. German Zoological Soc., Soc. History and Theory of Biology. Roman Catholic. Avocation: gardening. Office: Ernst Haeckel Haus, Berggasse 17, D-07745 Jena Germany

BREININ, GOODWIN M., physician; b. N.Y.C., Dec. 10, 1918; s. Louis and Mary (Mirsky) B.; m. Rose-Helen Kopelman, June 22, 1947; children: Bartley James, Constance. B.S., U. Fla., 1939; A.M., Emory U., 1940, M.D., 1943. Diplomate Am. Bd. Ophthalmology (dir., vice chmn., cons.). Intern U.S. Marine Hosp., Stapleton, N.Y., 1944; resident ophthalmology N.Y. U.-Bellevue Med. Center, 1947-51, sr. Heed fellow ophthalmology, 1954, Daniel B. Kirby prof. research ophthalmology, 1957, Daniel B. Kirby prof., chmn. dept. ophthalmology, 1959—, chmn. med. bd., 1975-77; dir. eye service Bellevue and U. Hosps., N.Y.C., 1959—; mem. vision commn. NRC, 1960-65; hon. assoc. U. Coll., London, 1966-67; chmn. vision research tng. com. Nat. Insts. Neurol. Diseases and Blindness, 1963-64; chief cons. Manhattan VA Hosp.; cons. Manhattan Eye, Ear and Throat, St. Vincent's, Beth Israel hosps., Lenox Hills Hosp.; surg. gen. USPHS; chmn. Nat. Res. Rev. Com., 1976-77; vis. prof., cons. Hailie Selassie I Univ. Found., Ethiopia, 1972; lectr. Mem. various adv. coms. relating to field, mem. med. adv. bd. Nat. Council to Combat Blindness; pres. Council for U.S./USSR Health Exchange, 1977; mem. Am. com. Internat. Agy. for Prevention of Blindness, 1980—; pres. 2d Internat. Symposium in Visual Optics, Tucson, 1982. Author: The Electrophysiology of Extraocular Muscle, 1962; editor: Advances in Diagnostic Visual Optics, 1983; mem. editorial bd. Investigative Ophthalmology, Archives of Ophthalmology; Contbr. articles to profl. jours. Mem. nat. coun. for medicine Emory U., Atlanta; mem. coun. visitors Marine Biol. Labs., Woods Hole, Mass. Recipient Knapp medal for contbn. ophthalmology A.M.A., 1957, Edward Lorenzo Holmes lectr. citation and award for contbns. to med. sci. Inst. Medicine Chgo., 1959, Gifford lectr. and award Chgo. Ophthal. Soc., 1970, Heed Ophthalmic Found. award, 1968, Emory U. medal, 1993; Wright lectr. U. Toronto, 1972; Lloyd lectr. Bklyn. Opthal. Soc., 1971; May lectr. N.Y. Acad. Medicine, 1974; guest of honor Australian Coll. Ophthalmologists, 1974, Japanese Cong. Neuro-ophthalmalogy, 1979; Scobee lectr., 1977. Fellow Am. Acad. Ophthalmology and Otolaryngology (v.p. 1979, Sr. Honor award 1984), ACS, N.Y. Acad. Medicine (sec. sect. ophthalmology 1962-63, chmn. sect. 1967-68); mem. AMA (sec. sect. on ophthalmology 1966-69, chmn. 1970-71), Rsch. Ophthalmology, Am. Ophthal. Soc., N.Y. Ophthal. Soc. (pres. 1980), Harvey Soc., AAAS, Am. Commn. for Optics and Visual Physiology (chmn. 1970—), Am. Orthoptic Coun., Assn. Univ. Profs. Ophthalmology, Pan. Am. Assn. Ophthalmology, Sigma Xi, Alpha Omega Alpha. Clubs: Century Assn., Practitioners, Charaka (N.Y.C.). E-mail: gb7@is2.nyu.edu. Home: 912 Fifth Ave New York NY 10021-4159 Office: NYU Med Ctr 550 1st Ave New York NY 10016-6481

BREIPOHL, WALTER EUGENE, real estate broker; b. Ottawa, Ill., Mar. 24, 1953; s. Eugene E. and Margaret L. (Hughes) B. Student, Ill. Valley C.C.; BS, Loyola U., Chgo., 1974. Real estate broker and devel. Breipohl Co., Ottawa, 1975—; bd. dirs. No. Ill. Devel. Corp., Union Banc Corp., Ottawa, Union Bank, Ea. Divsn., Ottawa. Bd. dirs. Greater Ottawa, Inc., 1984—, pres., 1997; bd. dirs. Main Street U.S.A. Program, Ottawa, 1991-93, Cmty. Hosp. of Ottawa Found., 1994-97; chmn. Indsl. Devel. Commn., Ottawa, 1985-88; gov. Cmty. Hosp. Ottawa, 1986-89. Mem. Illini Valley Assn. Realtors (sec.-treas. 1983-85, President's award 1985), No. Ill. Comml. Assn. Realtors, Ill. Assn. Realtors, Nat. Assn. Realtors, Nat. Assn. Real Estate Appraisers, Ottawa Area C. of C. and Industry (chmn. bd. dirs. 1988), Ill. C. of C. (bd. dirs. 1997, Polit. Action Com. dir. 1998), Ill.-Mich. Canal Corridor Assn. (dir. 1997), Internat. Club (Chgo.), Boat Club, Union League Club (Chgo.), Elks, KC. Republican. Roman Catholic. Home and Office: PO Box 1039 Ottawa IL 61350-6039

BREITBART, ARNOLD SOL, plastic surgeon; b. Newark, Sept. 18, 1959; s. Morris and Lucy (Gliklich) B.; m. Viviane Dabbah, Apr. 5, 1986; children: Morris, Charles, Marcelle. AB, Princeton U., 1981; MD, NYU, 1985. Diplomate Am. Bd. Plastic Surgery, Am. Bd. Surgery. Resident in gen. surgery NYU Med. Ctr., N.Y.C., 1985-91, resident in plastic surgery, 1991-93, craniofacial surgery fellow, 1993; microsurgery and breast reconstrn. fellow Meml. Sloan-Kettering Cancer Ctr., N.Y.C., 1994; attending surgeon plastic and reconstructive surgery North Shore U. Hosp., Manhasset, N.Y., 1994—; attending surgeon Columbia-Presbyn. Med. Ctr. N.Y. Hosp., 1999—; asst. prof. clin. surgery Columbia U. Coll. Physicians and Surgeons; adj. asst. prof. surgery Well Cornell U. Med. Coll. Contbr. (book chpt.) Grabb and Smith's Plastic Surgery, 1997, articles to profl. jours. Plastic Surgery Edn. Found. rsch. grantee, 1993. Mem. ACS, Am. Soc. Plastic and Reconstructive Surgeons, Plastic Surgery Rsch. Coun. Avocations: running, skiing, tennis. Office: NY Presbyn Hosp Columbia Presbyn Ctr Divsn Plastic and Reconstructive Surgeon 622 W 168th St Ph 12-126 New York NY 10032-3720

BREITKREUZ, HARTMUT DIETER, English and humanities educator, researcher; b. Mainz, Germany, Feb. 20, 1937; s. Erich and Irmgard (Hett) B.; m. Helga Ducker, Dec. 21, 1963; children: Beate, Elke. 1st State Exam, U. Munster, Germany, 1963, MA, 1965; 2nd State Exam, Studienseminar Kassel, 1966; Dozent, Ednl. Univ., Heidelberg, Germany, 1973. Studienreferendar Kassel, 1964-66; studienassessor Gottingen, Germany, 1966-68; studienrat Max-Planck-Gymnasium, Gottingen, 1969-73; prof. English Ednl. U. Heidelberg, 1974—; dir. of studies Linguaphone Inst., Hamburg, 1975-80; head English dept. Ednl. U., Heidelberg, 1974-75, 80-81, 89-90, 96-97, fgn. rels. rep. of the senate; Ednl. U., Heidelberg rep. for European Credit Transfer System, 1997—; guest prof. Tech. U. Berlin, 1995-96; dep. dir. gen. Internat. Biog. Ctr., Cambridge, 1998. Author: False Friends, 1991, More False Friends, 1992, Studien zur fruhen Fehlerforschung in Deutschland, 2000, others; editor: (book series) Foreign Language Studies, 1977—; contbr. chpts. to books; contbr. more than 80 articles to profl. jours.; festschrift: English in the Modern World, 2000. Rsch. fellow Am. Biog. Inst., Raleigh, N.C., 1997; recipient Great Bus. medal 1st class Grosser Bären-Orden, 1999. Mem. Austrian Acad. Scis., World Edn. Fellowship, German Humboldt Soc., Deutscher Anglistenverband, German Shakespeare Soc. Avocation: tennis. Office: Educational Univ, Im Neuenheimer Feld 561, 69120 Heidelberg Germany

BREITMAN, RICHARD DAVID, historian, educator, writer; b. Hartford, Conn., Mar. 27, 1947; s. Saul Harold and Gloria Pearl Breitman; m. Carol Rose Wax, Sept. 12, 1982; children: David Russell, Marc Eduard. BA, Yale U., 1969; MA, Harvard U., 1971, PhD, 1975; DHL honoris causa, Hebrew Union Coll., 1999. From asst. prof. history to assoc. prof. history Am. U., Washington, 1976-86, prof. history, 1987—, chair history dept., 1995-97; cons. Office of Spl. Investigations, U.S. Dept. Justice, Washington, 1995-98. Author: (books) German Socialism and Weimar Democracy, 1981, The Architect of Genocide, 1991 (Fraenkel prize 1991), Official Secrets, 1998; co-author: (with Walter Laqueur) Breaking the Silence, 1986; editor: (jour.) Holocaust and Genocide Studies, 1996—; mem. editl. bd.: Jour. Contemporary History, 1994—. Mem. Am. Hist. Assn., German Studies Assn., World War II Studies Assn., Conf. Group for Cen. European History. Democrat. Jewish. Avocations: tennis, chess. E-mail: rbreit@american.edu. Office: Am U Dept History 4400 Massachusetts Ave NW Washington DC 20016-8003

BREITWIESER, KARINA MARIA, civil engineer; b. Linz, Austria, Feb. 19, 1963; d. Franz and Elfriede (Lehner) B.; 1 child, Stanislaus. Diploma in engring., Tech. U., Vienna, Austria, 1989; MSC, Imperial Coll., London, 1990. Engr. Fugro McClelland, Hemel Hempstead, Eng., 1988-89, Ove Arup, London, 1990, Mott McDonald, Croyden, Eng., 1991; engr., project mgr. Buro Weiss, Vienna, 1992-93, Austrian Energy and Environment, Vienna, 1993-99; project mgr. Waagner-Biro Stahl-Glas-Technik, 2000—; reader Tech. U., Wien, 1997—. Mem. Oesterr Gesellschaft Erdbeben Ingenieurwesen. Avocations: playing Go, researching history of industrial architecture. Home: Stolberggasse 25/11, A-1050 Vienna Austria Office: Waagner-Biro Stahl-Glas-Tch, Stadlauergasse 54, A-1221 Vienna Austria

BREIVIK, LEIV EGIL, English language educator; b. Haram, Norway, June 6, 1944; s. Peder and Karen (Larsson) B.; children: Per Olav, Kyrre, Margrete. Cand. Philol., U. Bergen, 1971; DPhil, U. Tromsoe, 1982. Rsch. asst. U. Bergen, Norway, 1972-74, U. London, 1974-76; assoc. prof. U. Tromso, Norway, 1976-83, prof., 1984-88; prof. U. Bergen, 1988—, dean faculty of arts, 1993-98. Author: Existential There, 1983, 2d edit., 1990; editor: Language Change, 1989, Essays on English Language, 1989; editor: Internat. Jour. Applied Linguistics, 1994—; mem. editorial bd. three internat. jours., 1983—. Hon. Rsch. fellow U. London, 1991; Rsch. grantee Norwegian Rsch. Coun. Sci. and Humanities, 1974-76, 83-84, 96. Mem. Internat. Assn. Applied Linguistics (mem. internat. com. 1982—), Norwegian Assn. Applied Linguistics (pres. 1982—), Det Norske Videnskaps-Akademi, Det Kongelige Norske Videnskabers Selskab. Home: Nordre Skogvel 11, 5057 Bergen Norway Office: U Bergen Dept English, Sydnesplass 9, 5007 Bergen Norway

BREMER, HOWARD WALTER, consulting patenting and licensing lawyer; b. Milw., July 18, 1923; s. Walter Hugo and Lydia Martha (Schmidt) B.; m. Caryl Marie Faust, May 28, 1948; children: Katharine, William (dec.), Thomas, Timothy, Margaret. BSChemE, U. Wis., 1944, LLB, 1949. Bar: Wis. 1949, U.S. Patent and Trademark Office 1954, U.S. Supreme Ct. 1957, U.S. Ct. Appeals (fed. cir.) 1959, U.S. Dist. Ct. (so. dist.) Ohio 1960. Patent atty. Procter & Gamble Co., Cin., 1949-60; patent counsel Wis. Alumni Rsch. Found., Madison, 1960-88; cons., Madison, 1988—; mem. adv. com. Coun. on Govtl. Rels., Washington, 1975-93; panel mem. Office Tech. Assessment, Washington, 1981-83; mem. Adv. Commn. on Patent Law Reform, Washington, 1991-92. Mem. internat. adv. bd. Industry and Higher Edn. Jour., 1996—; contbr. articles to profl. jours. Pres. Edgewood Campus Sch. PTA, Madison, 1967-69; mem. adv. bd. Edgewood H.S., 1971-80, chmn. adv. bd., 1973-74. With USN, 1944-46. Recipient alumni appreciation award Edgewood H.S., 1990, Award of Distinction, U. Wis. Coll. Agrl. and Life Scis., 2000. Mem. ABA (chmn. com. 1993—), Am. Intellectual Property Law Assn. (chmn. com. 1996-99), State Bar Wis. (chmn. intellectual property sect. 1967-68, 79-80), Wis. Intellectual Property Law Assn. (pres. 1989-90), Assn. Univ. Tech. Mgrs. (trustee 1977-78, 80-82, pres. 1978-80, com. chmn. 1985-93, mem. editl. bd. jour. 1990—, Birch award 1980). Avocations: building furniture, home maintenance, model railroading, travel, reading. Home: 1106 Brookwood Rd Madison WI 53711-3116

BREMER, WILLIAM RICHARD, lawyer; b. San Francisco, Jan. 5, 1930; m. Margaret Herrington; children: Mark Richard (dec.), Karen Elizabeth, William Richard Jr. BS in Bus. Adminstrn., Menlo Coll., 1952; JD, U. San Francisco, 1958. Bar: Calif. 1959, U.S. Dist. Ct. (no. dist.) Calif. 1959, U.S. Ct. Appeals (9th cir.) 1959, U.S. Supreme Ct. 1965, U.S. Ct. Mil. Appeals 1973. Pvt. practice San Francisco Bay area, 1959—; officer, dir. Marshall Hale Meml. Hosp., 1986-88, Childrens Hosp. San Francisco, 1988-91; bd. dirs. Bridgeway Plan for Health, 1988-92. Bd. dirs. Bay Area USO, 1980-89; arbitrator Marin County and San Francisco County Ct., 1977—; city councilman City of Tiburon (Calif.), 1966-70, mayor, 1968-69; v.p., bd. dirs. Tiburon Peninsula Found.; regional v.p. No. Calif. Naval War Coll. Found., 1997—. Lt. USMC, 1952-54, Korea; col. USMC Res. (ret.), 1954-82. Mem. Am. Arbitration Assn. (panel arbitrator 1965—), ATLA, San Francisco Trial Lawyers Assn., San Francisco Bar Assn., San Francisco Lawyers Club, Marin County Bar Assn., Calif. Trial Lawyers Assn., Navy League U.S. (life mem. San Francisco Coun., pres. 1978-80, nat. bd. dirs. 1978-88, no. Calif. state pres. 1981-82, nat. dep. JAG 1997—), Marine Corps Res. Officers Assn. (life), Res. Officers Assn. (life), Naval Order of U.S. (life, San Francisco commandery, comdr. 1982, 83, comdr. gen., nat. pres. 1993-95), Corinthian Yacht (commodore 1986-87), Montgomery St. Motorcycle (pres. 1974-75), Marines Meml. San Francisco (pres. 1985-86), Kiwanis (bd. dirs. San Francisco chpt. 1981-83), The Tiburon Rotary (bd. dirs. 1997—, chair cmty. svc., pres. elect 2000). Office: William R Bremer 120 Taylor Rd Tiburon CA 94920-1061

BREMNER, FION DOMNALL, ophthalmic surgeon; b. Brentwood, U.K., June 22, 1964; s. Malcolm Stuart and Joan Patricia Eimear (Guina) B.; m. Philippa Louise Merriman, Oct. 21, 1995; children: Jessica, Sophie, Imogen. BSc with 1st class honors, London U., 1985, PhD in Neurophysiology, 1988, MBBS, 1991. Rsch. scientist, demonstrator dept. physiology U. Coll., London, 1985-88; sr. ho. officer in ophthalmology St. Thomas' Hosp., London, 1993-96; rsch. fellow dept. neuro-ophthalmology Nat. Hosp., London, 1996—; specialist registrar in ophthalmology St. Bartholomew's Hosp., London, 1998-99, Queen Elizabeth II Hosp., Welwyngarden City, 1999—, Moorfields Eye Hosp., London, 2000—; lectr. Moorfields Eye Hosp., London, 1997—. Author: (with others) Hutchinson's Clinical Methods, 1999, Neuro-Ophthalmology, 1999; contbr. articles to profl. jours. Recipient Aguilonius award The European Neuro-Ophthamological Soc. Fellow Royal Coll. of Ophthalmologists, Royal Soc. of Medicine; mem. The Physiological Soc. (Dale Fund award 1985). Avocations: walking, photography, cooking, music. Office: Dept Neuro-Ophthalmology, Nat Hosp Queen Square, London WC1N 3BG, England

BREMNER, JOHN BARNARD, chemistry educator; b. Perth, Australia, Apr. 16, 1943; s. John Andrew and Gwendoline Florence (Hunt) B.; m. Susan Louise Crawley, Dec. 13, 1965; children: James Andrew, Michael John. BSc with honors, U. Western Australia, 1964; PhD, Australian Nat. U., 1968; diploma in chem. pharmacology, U. Edinburgh, 1975. Rsch. fellow Harvard U., Cambridge, Mass., 1967-68; lectr. U. Tasmania, Hobart, Australia, 1968-73, sr. lectr., 1974-80, reader, 1981-91, head of dept., 1989, 90-91; prof. organic chemistry U. Wollongong, Australia, 1991—, head dept. chemistry, 1994—; adj. vis. assoc. prof. Pa. State U., State College, 1979-80; vis. fellow Australian Nat. U., Canberra, 1983-84; cons. Tasmanian Alkoloids Pty. Ltd., Westbury, Australia, 1986-88, Port Arthur (Australia) Hist. Site Mgmt. Authority, 1990. Author: (with others) Studies in Natural Products Chemistry, 1990; contbr. articles to profl. jours. Sec. Scots Ch., Uniting Ch. in Australia, Hobart, 1982-86. Recipient travel award Internat. Union of Pure and Applied Chemistry, 1971, Brit.Coun., 1974-75. Fellow Royal Australian Chem. Inst. (pres. Tasmanian br. 1981-82), Royal Soc. Chemistry; mem. Am. Chem. Soc., European Photochemistry Assn. Avocations: bushwalking, stamp collecting. Office: U Wollongong Dept Chemistry, Northfields Ave, Wollongong 2522 NSW, Australia

BREMS, DAVID PAUL, architect; b. Lehi, Utah, Aug. 10, 1950; s. D. Orlo and Gearldine (Hitchcock) B.; m. Johna Devey Brems; children: Stefan Tomas Brems, Beret Alla Brems. BS, U. Utah, 1973, MArch, 1975. Registered architect, Utah, Calif., Colo., Ariz., Wyo., N.Mex., Idaho, Mont., Tex., Wash. Draftsman Environ. Assocs., Salt Lake City, 1971-73; draftsman/architect intern Environ. Design Group, Salt Lake City, 1973-76; architect/intern Frank Fuller AIA, Salt Lake City, 1976-77; prin. Edward & Daniels, Salt Lake City, 1978-83; pres. David Brems & Assocs., Salt Lake City, 1983-86; prin. Gillies, Stransky, Brems, Smith P.C., Salt Lake City, 1986—; adj. prof. U. Utah Grad. Sch. Architecture, 1990-93; mem. urban design com. Assist, Inc., Salt Lake City, 1982-85, Salt Lake County Planning Commn., 1991-97, chmn., 1992-96; mem. Emigration Twp. Planning Commn., 1997—, chmn. 1997-99; mem. Emigration Masterplan Adv. Com., 1997-99; invited lectr. Wyo. Soc. Archs., 1992, sch. engring. U. Utah, 1993, 95, Va., 1993, Utah Soc. Archs., 1994, Utah Power and Light, 1994, Utah Soc. Archts., 1994; juror U. Utah Grad. Sch. Architecture, 1975—, Utah Soc. Am. Planning Assn., 1994—, Sunstone Symposium, 1995, Contemporary Arts Group, 1995—; with adv. com. U. Utah Grad. Sch. Architecture, 2000—. Pub. Firm Profile Intermountain Architecture, 1996, Web Mag., 1997; prin. works include solar twin homes Utah Holiday (Best Solar Design award), Sun Builder, Daily Jour., Salt Lake Tribune, Brian Head Day Lodge, Easton Aluminum, Four Seasons Hotel, Gore Coll. Bus., CMF Tooele, utah Regional Corrections Facility, St. Vincents De Paul Ctr., Steiner Aquatic Ctr., U. Utah Football Support Facility, Sports Medicine West, West Jordan

Cmty. Water Park, Utah Nat. Guard Apache Helicopter Hangar & Armory, Kashmitter I Residences, St. Thomas More Cath. Ch., Spanish Fork Cmty. Water Park, Natures Herbs, ABC Office Bldg. Divsn. of Natural Resources Bldg., Kashmitter II Residence, Litton Residence, Elliott Residence, Speed Skating Oval for 2002 Olympics, Vis. Ctr. Grand Staircase Escalante Nat. Monument, and others; ALTA Club mem., Great Salt Lake Yacht Club mem., mem. Leadership Utah; mem. 2002 Olympic Energy and Water sub-com., 1996—; mem. State of Utah Divsn. of Facilities Mgmt. Com. on Energy Efficient Architecture. Active adv. com. Salt Lake City Bus. Advisory. Recipient three awards Am. Concrete Inst., 1993, Chief Engrs. Honor award U.S. Army Corps Engrs., 1994; Bronze medalist Utah Summer Games, 1991, Silver medalist, 1992, Gold medalist, 1994, Design award Dept. Def., 1995, Blue Seal award, 1995, Outstanding Project award U.S. Dept. Def., 1995, Salt Lake County Citizen Vol. of Yr. award, 1995, Western Mountain Region Hon. Mention St. Thomas More, 1996, Solar Today award Sun award, Energy Uses News award Dept. Natural Resources, 1996; named Best Pvt. Project by Intermountain Architecture, 1994, Salt Lake County Vol. of Yr. Salt Lake County Planning Commn., 1995, Best Recreation Project Intermountain Arch., 1995. Mem. AIA (pres. Salt Lake chpt. 1983-84, pres. Utah Soc. 1987, chmn. Western Mountain Region conf., 1986, com. on design 1990—, chmn. com. on environment AIA Utah 1993, chmn. Design for Life Workshop at Sundance 1993, Honor awards 1983, 88, Merit awards 1983, 85, 88, 93, 99, chmn. Western Mountain Regiona honor awards 1983, 88, PCI award 1988, IFRAA award 1988, 94, Juror Colo. West awards 1992, award Utah sect. IES for St. Thomas More), Am. Planning Assn. (juror awards 1994), Acorn Hills Water Assn. (pres.), Black Builder Mesa Water Assn. (sec.), Utah Soc. Architects, Am. Solar Energy Soc., Hobie Fleet 67 (commodre 1985-86), Salt Lake Olympic Com. (environ. adv. com.), Utah Open Lands (so. Utah br.), Illuminating Engring. Soc. (assoc.), Am. Solar Soc. Home: 3497 Little Tree Rd Salt Lake City UT 84108-1601

BRENDEL, ALFRED, concert pianist; b. Wiesenberg, Austria, Jan. 5, 1931; s. Albert and Ida (Wieltschnig) B.; m. Iris Heymann-Gonzala, 1960 (div. 1972); m. Irene Semler, 1975; 1 son, 3 daus. Studied piano under, Sofija Dezelic, Zagreb, Yugoslavia, Ludovika V. Kaan, Graz, Austria, Edwin Fischer, Lucerne, Switzerland, Paul Baumgartner, Basel, Switzerland, Edward Steuermann, Salzburg, Austria; studied harmony under Franjo Dugan, Zagreb; studied composition under A. Michl, Graz, Austria; DMus (hon.), U. London, 1978; DLitt (hon.), Sussex U., 1981; DMus (hon.), Oxford U., 1983, Warwick U., 1991, Yale U., 1992; fellow, Royal No. Coll., Manchester, 1988; Bayer, Akademie der Wissenschaften. First piano recital Graz, 1940, concert tours through Europe, Latin Am. and N.Am., 1963—, Australia, 1963, 66, 69, 76, appeared at many music festivals including Salzburg, 1960—, Vienna, Berlin, Montreux, Lucerne, Edinburg, Aldeburgh, Athens, Granada, P.R.; has performed with most maj. orchs. in Europe and U.S. and others; performed all Beethoven piano sonatas in concert cycle Paris, London, Berlin, Amsterdam, Vienna, Hamburg, Basel, Dusseldorf, Freiburg, Vevey, N.Y.C., 1983, 92—; recording The Alfred Brendel Collection. Recipient Premio Citta de Bolzano Concorso Busoni, 1949; recipient Grand Prix du Disque, 1965, 84, Edison prize, 1973, 81, 84, 87, Brit. Music Trade Assn. award 1973, 78, 81, Grand Prix des Disquaires de France, 1975, Deutscher Schallplattenpreis, 1976, 77, 81, 82, 84, Wiender Flotenuhr, 1976, 77, 79, 82, 84, 87, Gramophone award, 1978, 80, 82, 84, Japanese Grand Prix award, 1977, 78, 80, 82, 84, 87, Franz Liszt prize, 1979, 80, 82, 83, 87, Frankfurt Music award 1984, Busoni Found. award, 1990, Diapason D'Or award, 1992, Preis der deutschen Schallplatten-Kritik, 1992, Orden pour le Merite fur Wissenschaften und Kunste, 1991; decorated knight British Empire, 1989. Fellow Exeter Coll.; mem. Am. Acad. Arts and Scis. (hon.), Royal Acad. Music (hon.), Comdr. des Arts et Letters. Office: care Colbert Artists Mgmt Inc 111 W 57th St New York NY 10019-2211

BRENDER, ANTON, economist; b. Bucharest, Romania, July 16, 1946; arrived in France, 1948; m. Agnes Chevallier, 1978; children: Thomas, Olivia, Anna. Degree in Russian, Nat. Sch. Oriental Langs., Paris, 1968, degree in Chinese, 1978; advanced degree in polit. scis., U. Paris, 1971, PhD in Econs., 1975. Rschr. Centre d'Etudes Prospectives et d'Informations Internat., Paris, 1969-78, dept. head, 1978-82, dep. dir., 1982-90, dir., 1990-92; chief economist CPR, 1992-99; chmn. CPR Gestion, Gestion, 1999—; assoc. prof. U. Paris IX. Author: Socialism and Cybernetics, 1977, Cybernetical Analysis of Financial Intermediation, 1980, A Clash of Nations, 1988, (with Michael Aglietta) The Wage Earner Society's Metamorphoses, 1983, (with P. Gaye, V. Kessler) Post-dollar Years: Analysis and Simulation of the Multi-Currency System, 1986, (with M. Aglietta, V. Coudert, F. Hyafil) Financial Globalization: The Inescapable Experience, 1989, The Solidarity Imperative: France Facing Globalization, 1996, (with Florence Pisani) Interest rates an empirical approach, 1997, The New Age of the American Economy, 1999. Office: CPR, 30 rue St Georges, 75312 Paris Cedes 09, France

BRENDLER, CHARLES BURGESS, urologist; b. Charlottesville, Va., June 20, 1944; s. Herbert and Virginia Burgess B.; m. Lucretia Cattley Rock, June 18, 1966; children: Christopher, Amy, Emily, Peter. AB, Harvard Coll., 1966; MD, U. Va., 1974. Instr. urology Johns Hopkins U., Balt., 1980-81, asst. prof. urology, 1981-85; assoc. prof. urology Johns Hopkins U., 1985-93; chief urology Balt. City Hosps., 1981-84; prof., chief urology U. Chgo., 1994—; mem. surg. exec. com. U. Chgo. Med. Ctr., 1994—, mem. surgery edn. com., 1994—. Assoc. editor: Urologic Surgery, 5th edit., 1998; co-author: Campbell's Urology, 1985, 92, 97, Urologic Surgery, 1983, 91, assoc. editor, 1998; co-author Operative Urology 1990, 97; contbr. articles to profl. jours. Capt. USAF, 1967-71. Mem. Am. Urol. Assn. (2d prize clin. rsch. 1983, 1st prize clin. rsch. Mid-Atlantic sect. 1991, 92), Am. Assn. Genito-Urinary Surgeons, Nat. Urol. Forum, Soc. Basic Urol. Rsch., Soc. Urol. Oncology, Am. Joint Commn. on Cancer (advisor task force on urol. cancer 1997), Alpha Omega Alpha. Democrat. Unitarian. Avocations: skiing, hiking, jogging, travelling. E-mail: ewayte@surgery.bsd.uchicago.edu. Home: 6301 S County Line Rd Burr Ridge IL 60521-4866 Office: U Chgo Sect Urology 5841 S Maryland Ave # Mc6038 Chicago IL 60637-1463

BRENDSEL, LELAND C., mortgage company executive; b. Sioux Falls, S.D.; married. BA, U. Colo., 1967; D in Fin., Northwestern U., 1974. Prof. U. Utah; economist Farm Credit Banks, Fed. Home Loan Bank, Des Moines; exec. v.p., CFO Fed. Home Loan Mortgage Corp., McLean, Va., 1982-85, acting pres., CEO, 1985-87, pres., CEO, 1987-89, chmn., CEO, 1989—; adv. bd. J. L. Kellogg Grad. Sch. Northwestern U.; chmn. bd. Freddie Mac Found.; bd. trustees Nat. Urban League. Named Washingtonian of the Yr., 1991, Children's Champion UNICEF Coun., 1992, Corp. Citizen of the Yr. Nat. Black Child Devel. Inst., 1993, Corp. Advocate of the Yr. Child Welfare League Am., 1995; recipient N.Y. Coun. Adoptable Children's award, 1993, Give Your Heart to Child award Vo. Emergency Families for Children, 1997. Office: Fed Home Loan Mortgage Corp 8200 Jones Branch Dr Mc Lean VA 22102-3107

BRENMAN, STEPHEN MORRIS, lawyer; b. San Francisco, Mar. 25, 1945; s. Irving I. and Vivian H. (Weiss) B.; m. Laura R. Yocum, Aug. 14, 1968; children: Jeremy S., Sara N. BS, Miami U., Oxford, Ohio, 1967; JD with distinction, Valparaiso (Ind.) U., 1970. Bar: Ind. 1970, U.S. Dist. Ct. (no. and so. dist.) Ind. 1970, U.S. Ct. Appeals (7th cir.) 1970, U.S. Supreme Ct. 1973, U.S. Tax Ct. 1973, U.S. Ct. Claims 1973. Assoc. Saul I. Ruman & Assocs., Hammond, Ind., 1970-73; ptnr. Katz & Brenman, Gary and Merrillville, Ind., 1973-78; mng. ptnr. Katz & Brenman, Merrillville, 1978-99; pvt. practice Merrillville, 2000—; lectr. Valparaiso U. Sch. Law, 1970; chief pub. defender Gary City Ct., 1973-78, staff coord., 1973-78; dir. and officer Dunes Volkswagen, Inc., Gary, 1977-80, Len Pollak Buick, Inc., Gary, 1977-83, Merrillville Volkswagen, Porshe-Audi, Inc., Merrillville, 1980-83; lectr. alcoholic beverage laws in Ind., miscellaneous trade orgns., 1980—; temp. probate commr., pro-tem and temp. judge Superior Ct. Lake County, Civil Divsn., East Chicago, Ind., 1980—; lectr. estate planning and right to die Congregation Beth Israel, Inc., Hammond, 1989—, Jewish Fedn., Inc., Highland, Ind., 1989—. Note editor Valparaiso U. Law Rev., 1969-70; contbr. articles to profl. jours. Co-chmn. Ind. Alcoholic Beverage Commn. Study Com., Rules, Regulations and Forms Rev., 1990, 2000—; election judge and commr. Lake County Election Bd., Crown Point, Ind., 1973-78; dir. Munster (Ind.) Little League, 1980-84, umpire and coach, 1980-84; bd. dirs. Munster Youth Athletic Assn., 1980-84; bd. dirs. Jewish Fedn., Inc., Highland, 1980-85, Congregation Beth Israel, Inc., Hammond, 1980-85; dir. Hoosier Boys Town, Inc., Schererville, Ind., 1990-94, dir. and officer Hoosier Boys Town Found., 1990-94; mem. Munster H.S. Booster Club, 1987—; mem., dir., officer Alpha Epsilon Pi Parents Club, Inc., Bloomington, Ind., 1990-94./. Recipient Disting. Svc. award Jewish Fedn., 1980, 83, 84, Red and White Club, Munster H.S. Booster Club, 1989, Mustang Club, 1989; Valparaiso U. scholar, 1968-70. Mem. ABA (sect. bus. law, adminstrv. law and regulatory practice, real property, probate, trust law sects.), Nat. Assn. Estate Planners and Couns., Nat. Assn. Criminal Def. Attys., Ind. State Bar Assn., Fed. Bar Assn., Assn. Trial Lawyers Am., Ind. Trial Lawyers Assn., Lake County Bar Assn. (chmn. legal forms com.), Am. Judicature Soc. (corp. counsel inst. mem.), Phi Alpha Delta, B'nai B'rith, Miami U. Alumni Assn., Valparaiso U. Sch. Law Alumni Assn., Zeta Beta Tau. Democrat. Avocations: racquetball, tennis, boating, motor vehicle racing. Office: 107 West 79th Ave Merrillville IN 46410-5438

BRENNAN, ANDREW ANDERSON, philosopher, educator; b. Kirkcaldy, Fife, Scotland, May 9, 1945; arrived in Australia, 1992; s. John Murnin Brennan and Andrewina Anderson; divorced; children: Cally, Nicky. MA, St. Andrews, Scotland, 1967, U. Calgary, Can., 1968; BPhil, U. Oxford, England, 1970. Lectr. U. Stirling, Scotland, 1970-87, sr. lectr., 1987-89, reader, 1989-92; prof. philosophy U. Western Australia, 1992—; vis. prof. Free U., Brussels, 1991—, U. Oslo, Norway, 1995, 96. Author: Conditions of Identity, 1988, Thinking About Nature, 1988; editor: (rsch. collection) Ethics of the Environment, 1995, (with Nina Witoszek) Philosophical Dialogues, 1999, (book series) Environmental Philosophies, 1993—; mem. editl. bd. Australasian Jour. Philosophy, Jour. Applied Philosophy, Environmental Ethics, Environmental Values. Sec. Labour Party, Scotland, 1975-78. Grantee Carnegie Found., Scotland, 1988, Australian Rsch. Coun., 1993-95, 95-96, 97-99. Mem. Scots Philosophical Club, Mind Assn., Am. Philosophical Assn., Australian Assn. Philosophy, Internat. Soc. Environ. Ethics (founder, bd. dirs.), BioPolitics Internat. (founder, bd. dirs.), PErth Flying Squadron Yacht Club. Avocations: cycling, walking, music. Office: U Western Australia, Dept Philosophy, Perth 6097, Australia

BRENNAN, SIR GERARD, judge; b. Rockhampton, Queensland, Australia, May 22, 1928; s. Justice T. Brennan; m. Patricia O'Hara; 7 children. Student, Christian Bros. Coll., Downlands Coll. Toowoomba; BA, LLB, U. Queensland; LLD (hon.), Trinity Coll., 1988, U. Queensland, 1996, Australian Nat. U., Canberra, 1996; D. U. Tech., Sydney, 1998; DLitt (hon.), Ctrl. Queensland U., 1996; D Univ. (hon.), Griffith U., Queensland, 1996, U. Melbourne, 1998. Bar: 1951. Pres. Bar Assn. Queensland, 1974-76; pres. Australian Bar Assn., 1975-76, adminstrv. review coun., 1976-79, adminstrv. appeals tribunal, 1976-79; mem. Exec. Law Coun. Australia, 1974-76, Australian Law Reform com., 1975-77; additional judge Supreme Ct. A.C.T., 1976-81; judge Australian Indsl. Ct., 1976-81, Fed. Ct. Australia, 1977-81; justice High Ct. Australia, 1981-95, chief justice, 1995-98; prof. of law U. New South Wales, 1998; chancellor U. Tech., Sydney, 1998; judge Supreme Ct. of Fiji Rep., 1999-2000, Hong Kong Ct. Final Appeal, 2000—. Office: Piccadilly Tower Ste 2604, 133 Castlereagh St, Sydney 2000, Australia

BRENNAN, H(AROLD) GEOFFREY, social sciences educator, researcher; b. Sydney, NSW, Australia, Sept. 15, 1944; s. Harold Neville and Jessie (Patterson) B.; m. Margaret Gytha Youngman, Dec. 14, 1968; children: Susan Margaret, Michael Andrew, Philip Alexander, Robyn Elizabeth. BS with honors in Econs., Australian Nat. U., Canberra, 1966; PhD, Australian Nat. U., 1976. Lectr. Australian Nat. U., 1968-72, sr. lectr., 1973-78, prof. Econs. faculty, 1984-88, prof. Rsch. Sch. of Social Scis., 1988—, dir. Rsch. Sch. of Social Scis., 1991-96; prof. Pub. Choice Ctr., Va. Poly. Inst. & State U., Blacksburg, 1978-84. Author: The Power to Tax, 1980, The Reason of Rules, 1985 (with James Buchanan), Democracy and Decision, 1993 (with Loren Lomasky); contbr. articles to profl. jours. Fellow Acad. Social Scis. in Australia. Office: Australian Nat U, Rsch Sch Social Scis, Canberra ACT 0200, Australia

BRENNAN, PATRICK CHRISTOPHER, radiographer, lecturer; b. Bradford, England, Jan. 1, 1965; arrived in Ireland, 1993; s. Kevin Francis and Vera Margaret (McIntyre) B.; m. Elizabeth Christine Nichols; children: John, Beth. Diploma Coll. Radiographers, Ipswich Sch. Radiography, Eng., 1986, higher diploma Coll. Radiographers, 1991, clin. tutor's cert., 1991; PhD, Queen's U., Belfast, Ireland, 1994. Radiographer Colchester (Eng.) Hosp., 1986-88, lectr., 1988-91; scientist, lectr. U. College, Dublin, Ireland, 1993—; dir. rsch. groups at U. Coll. Dublin. Editor-in-chief Radiography Ireland; contbr. articles to profl. jours. Grantee Forbairt, Dublin, 1995, Health Rsch. Bd., Dublin, 1998, 99. Mem. Nat. Qualification's Bd. Ireland, Radiographer Validation Bd., Irish Inst. Radiography. Avocations: reading, swimming, astronomy. Home: Sidmonton Rd, 3 Ellerslie Villas, Bray Ireland Office: Univ Coll Sch Diagnostic Im, Herbert Ave, Dublin 4 Ireland

BRENNAN, TERESA MARY ISABEL, social theory educator, writer; b. Melbourne, Australia, Jan. 5, 1952; came to U.S., 1994; d. Columb Henry Brennan and Joan Marie (Hollingshead) Crosland. BA with honors, Sydney (Australia) U., 1976; MA, Melbourne U., 1986; PhD, Cambridge (Eng.) U., 1989. Affiliated lectr. social sci. Cambridge U., 1990-94; vis. prof. New Sch. for Social Rsch., N.Y.C., 1994-97, Brandeis U., Boston, 1997-98, Harvard U., Cambridge, Mass., 1998; Schmidt Disting. prof. humanities Fla. Atlantic U., 1997—; vis. prof. Philosophy Dept. U. Melbourne, 1994; vis. disting. prof. U. Alta., Can., 1993; spkr. UN World Health Orgn. Working Group in Genetic Engring., 1994, UNESCO, Nat. Inst. Sci., Tech. and Devel. Studies, India, 1994, 96; curriculum designer designer Pub. Intellectuals PhD Program, Fla. Atlantic U. Author: The Interpretation of the Flesh, 1992, History after Lacan, 1993, Jenseits der Hybris, 1997; co-editor: (with Martin Jay) Vision in Context, 1996, Exhausting Modernity: Grounds for a New Economy, 2000. Advisor U.S. Congress, 3d dist. Md., 1981. Mem. MLA, Am. Sociol. Assn., Am. Philos. Assn. Avocations: Egyptology, archaeology. Office: Fla Atlantic U Schmidt Chair in Humanities 777 Glades Rd Boca Raton FL 33431-6424

BRENNAN, THOMAS JOHN, city and state official, consultant, educator; b. Bklyn., Mar. 23, 1923; s. Thomas Joseph and Violet Emma (Jurgens) B.; m. Margaret Karen Jensen, Sept. 18, 1948; children: Debra Gail, Mark Kevin, Laurie Kathleen. AB, Wittenberg Coll., 1949; MGA, Fels Inst. of Local and State Govt., Wharton Grad. Sch., 1950. Dep. sec. for adminstrn. Dept. Welfare, Commonwealth Pa., Harrisburg, 1957-59, dep. sec. for state properties Pa. Dept. Property and Supplies, 1959-64; exec. officer Del. Dept. Mental Health, Dover, 1965-67; v.p. Exec. Mgmt. Svc., Arlington, Va., 1967-76; exec. dir. Gov.'s Justice Commn. and Pa. Commn. on Crime and Juvenile Delinquency, 1976-79; dir. water utility City of New Brunswick, N.J., 1983-91; chief labor negotiator City of New Brunswick, N.J., 1988-91; pers. mgr., 1988-91, exec. officer police dept., 1989-91; pub. mgmt. cons., 1991—; adj. instr. U. Del., 1965-67; adj. assoc. prof. Rider Coll., Lawrenceville, N.J., 1983-84, 84-85; hearing officer N.J. Dept. Civil Svc., Trenton, 1976—, cons. exam. constrn., 1985; cons. to staff com. UN, 1982-84; cons. various municipalities and agys.; presenter papers to profl. orgns. Bd. dirs. Bucks County Opera, Pa., 1975-80, Bucks County Play House, New Hope, Pa., 1970s; active mem. Bucks County Hist. Soc., Doylestown, Pa., 1983—; elected mem. alumni coun. Wittenberg U., 1989—; mem. Merrill's Maurauders, World War II. Decorated Silver Star, Bronze Star with 2 oak leaf clusters, Combat Infantry badge; recipient various plaques; Fels scholar U. Pa., 1948. Mem. VFW (Post #6393), Internat. Personnel Mgmt. Assn., Am. Pub. Works Assn. (dist. rep. Eastern Pa. bldg. and grounds com.), Am. Water Works Assn., Internat. Chiefs of Police Assn., Nat. Conf. State Justice Planning Adminstrn. (regional chmn., mem. exec. com.), Criminal Justice Tng. Inst. (chmn. planning com. 1978, 79). Club: Huntington Valley Hunt (Bucks County) (bd. dirs. 1975-80), Am. Legion (Post #79), Upper Makefield Hist. Soc. (dir.), Wharton Alumni (Phila.), U. Pa. Faculty. Lodge: Fraternal Order of Police. Avocations: fox hunting, pleasure riding. Home: 327 Pineville Rd Newtown PA 18940-3111

BRENNAN, WALTER MATTHEW, JR., construction sales consultant; b. L.A.; s. Walter Matthew and grace Ann (Zoccano) B.; m. Krysten Ann Petersen; 1 child, Reilly Ann. BA, UCLA, 1970, MA, 1973; MA, UCLA, 1974. Terminal mgr. Pacific Intermountain, San Diego, 1978-81; field cons. Tremco Inc., Cleve., 1982-92; field cons. W.P. Hickman Systems, Inc., Solon, Ohio, 1992-98, regional sales mgr., 1998-99, corp. acct. mgr., 1999—. Contbr. articles to profl. jours. Capt. USMC, 1974-78. Mem. Internat. Inst. of Plant Engrs. (bd. dirs. 1999—), Calif. Soc. of Hosp. Engrs., AIA Indland Calif. Democrat. Roman Catholic. Avocations: skiing, hunting, golf, rowing. Office: W P Hickman Systems Inc 30700 Industrial Pkwy Solon OH 44139

BRENNAND-ROPER, DAVID ANDREW, cardiologist, consultant; b. Derbyshire, Eng., Aug. 22, 1946; s. John Hanson and Joyce (Deans) B.; m. Sheila Jane Boswell; children: Tanya Alexandra, Anneka Louise, Alexander James, Giles William. B of Medicine and Surgery, Oxford U., London, 1971, MA, 1971. Rsch. fellow in nuclear cardiology Guy's Hosp., London, 1979-81, registrar in cardiology, 1981-82; cons. cardiologist Guy's Hosp. and St. Thomas Trust Hosp., West Hill Hosp., London, 1982—; vis. cons., Malta, 1982—; hon. cons. Heart Ctr., Calcutta, 1987—. Contbr. articles to profl. jours., chpts. to books. Recipient Gold Medal of British Nuclear Medicine, 1980. Fellow Royal Coll. Physicians; mem. Brit. Cardiac Soc., European Soc. Cardiology, Brit. Med. Assn. Avocations: golf, photography, oenology. Home: Blackheath, 30 Kidbrooke Grove, London SE3 OL9, England Office: Ste 201 Emblem House London Bridge Hosp, 27 Tooley St, London SE1 2PR, England

BRENNECKE, SHAUN PATRICK, obstetrician-gynecologist, educator; b. North Adelaide, Australia, May 8, 1953. B of Med. Sci. with honors, Adelaide U., 1975, MBBS, 1978, BA, 1978; DPhil, Oxford (Eng.) U., 1984. Intern Queen Elizabeth Hosp., Woodville, Australia, 1978; rsch. fellow Nuffield dept. ob-gyn. John Radcliffe Maternity Hosp., Oxford, 1979-82; grad. mem. Wolfson Coll., Oxford, 1979-83; ob-gyn. registrar Queen Elizabeth Hosp. & Flinders Med. Ctr., Adelaide, 1983-85; sr. lectr dept. ob-gyn. Monash U., Clayton, Victoria, Australia, 1986-91, dep./acting chmn. dept. ob-gyn., 1987-89; cons. obstetrician-gynecologist Monash Med. Ctr., Clayton, 1989-91, clin. dir. Monash perinatal unit, 1989-91; prof., dir. dept. perinatal medicine Royal Women's Hosp., Carlton, Victoria, 1992-99; prof. ob/gyn. U. Melbourne, 1999—; founding mem. Inst. Reprodn. and Devel., Monash U., Clayton, 1990—; mem. rsch. adv. com. Royal Children's Hosp., Parkville, Victoria, 1991-98. Contbr. numerous rsch. reports and revs. to biomed. publs. Dr. Davies-Thomas scholar U. Adelaide, 1973, Shell postgrad. sci. scholar Shell Co., 1977; Nicoll's fellow Royal Soc. Medicine, 1981. Fellow Royal Australian Coll. Obstetricians-Gynecologists (Arthur Wilson scholar 1990, 91); mem. Australian Soc. for Med. Rsch., Australian Med. Assn., Australian Perinatal Soc., Australasian Soc. for Study of Hypertension in Pregnancy, Brit. Med. Assn. (Katherine Bishop Harman award 1980). E-mail: s.brennecke@obgyn-rwh.unimelb.edu.au. Office: Royal Women's Hosp, 132 Grattan St, Carlton Victoria 3053, Australia

BRENNER, FREDERIC JAMES, biology educator, ecological consultant; b. Warren, Ohio, Dec. 25, 1936; s. Frederick James and Katherine Louise (Newberry) B.; m. Patricia Elaine Gavin, Aug. 27, 1967; children: Elaine, Cheryl. BS, Thiel Coll., Greenville, Pa., 1958; MS, Pa. State U., 1960, PhD, 1964. Teaching intern Denison U., Granville, Ohio, 1964-65; asst. prof. biology Thiel Coll., 1965-69; asst. prof. biology Grove City (Pa.) Coll., 1969-70, assoc. prof., 1970-86, prof., 1986—; pres. Brenner Ecol. Svc., Grove City, 1974—. Editor: (with others) Species Spl. Concern Pa., 1985, Endangered and Threatened Species Program in Pa., 1986, Environ. Consequences of Energy Prodn., 1987, Wetlands Ecology and Conservation Emphasis in Pa., 1989, Biological Diversity: Problems and Consequences, Environmental Contaminants, Ecosystems and Human Health, 1995, Forests: A Global Perspective; contbr. over 250 articles to profl. jours. Chmn. Mercer County Solid Waste Authority, 1988—; sec.-treas. Mercer County Conservation Dist., 1975—; treas., vice chmn., chmn. Mercer County Regional Planning Commn., 1989-93, sec., 1990; mem. exec. bd. Shenango Conservency; mem. exec. bd. French Creek Coun., Erie, 1972; dir. Woodbadge Course Boy Scouts Am., 1973-89 (Silver Beaver award 1973, Dist. award merit 1976). Recipient Nat. Conservation award DAR, 1989, Grove City United Way Cmty. Svc. award, 1993, Alpha Phi Omega Disting. Alumni Svc. award, 1994. Fellow AAAS, Ohio Acad. Sci.; mem. Ecol. Soc. Am. (exec. coun. 1978-82), Pa. Acad. Sci. (editor newsletter PAS 1966, pres.-elect 1992-94, pres. 1994-96, exec. coun. 1986—, Lifetime Achievement award), Nat. Assn. Acad. Scis. (sec. 1995-98, pres.-elect 1998-99, pres. 1999-2000), Wildlife Soc. (pres. Pa. chpt. 1975-77), Nat. Assn. of Acad. of Sci. (pres. 1999-2000), Beta Beta Beta (v.p. 1993—, Yokley Faculty Svc. award). Republican. Episcopalian. Avocations: hunting, fishing, hiking, camping. Office: Grove City Coll Dept Biol Grove City PA 16127

BRENNER, JANET MAYBIN WALKER, lawyer; b. Arkansas City, KS .; d. D. Arthur and Maybin (Gardner) Walker; children: Margaret Maybin Jones, Theodore Kimball Jones, Amanda Nash Freeman; m. Edgar H. Brenner, Aug. 4, 1979. AB, U. So. Calif.; JD, George Washington U., 1978. Bar: D.C. 1978, U.S. Dist. Ct. (D.C). Sponsor Brenner Women's Leadership com.; mem. women's com. Corcoran Gallery Art, Washington, 1969—, Pres.'s Cir., Planned Parenthood D.C., 1969—, Found. for Preservation of Hist. Georgetown. Mem. D.C. Bar Assn., Sulgrave Club (Washington). Home: 3325 R St NW Washington DC 20007-2310 also: Shadow Ridge Farm Washington VA 22747

BRENNER, MARTIN JOHN, aerospace engineer; b. Chgo., Dec. 27, 1955; s. Richard R. and Delores Harriet B.; m. Maryellen Fisher, Dec. 17, 1983; children: Adrienne, Ross. BS in Aeronaut./Astronaut. Engring., U. Ill., 1979; MS in Systems Sci., U. Calif., San Diego, 1985; MS in Applied Mechs., Calif. Inst. Tech., Pasadena, 1990. Coop. engring. student NASA Dryden Flight Rsch. Ctr., Edwards, Calif., 1975-79; forest maintenance profl. U.S. Forest Svc., Concrete, Wash., 1979; secondary sch. math./sci. tchr. U.S. Peace Corps, Kenya, Africa, 1979-81; aerospace engr. NASA Dryden Flight/Rsch. Ctr., Edwards, Calif., 1982—. Author: (book) Robust Aeroservoelastic Stability Analysis, 1999; contbr. articles to profl. jours. Sci. fair judge Lancaster Sch. Dist., 1996-99. Mem. AIAA, Soc. Indsl. and Applied Math. Avocations: backpacking, cycling, kayaking, mountain biking. E-mail: martin.brenner@dfrc.nasa.gov. Office: NASA Dryden Flt Rsch Ctr MS 4840D/RS Edwards CA 93523-0273

BRENNER, MICHAEL EDWARD, executive search consultant; b. Bklyn., Apr. 30, 1935; s. Arthur Allen and Edythe (Madoff) B.; m. Elsa Ferda Claman, June 23, 1958 (div. July 1974); children: Deborah Ann, Amy Beth, Gabriel Stephen; m. Roberta Lee Gorsky, Apr. 8, 1976; 1 child, Samantha Allyn. SB in Indsl. Mgmt., MIT, 1957; D Engring., Johns Hopkins U., 1963. Mgr. sys. analysis Bell Telephone Labs., 1962-69; assoc. prof. NYU, N.Y.C., 1969-72; prin. Arthur Young & Co., N.Y.C., 1975-80; pres. Michael Brenner Assocs., N.Y.C., 1980-83; sr. v.p. PA Cons., N.Y.C., 1983-86; ptnr. Canny Bowen, N.Y.C., 1986-91; sr. ptnr. LAI Worldwide, N.Y.C., 1991-99; chief resource Brenner Exec. Resources Inc., N.Y.C., 1999—. Pres. N.Y. chpt. Soc. for Human Resource Mgmt., 1983-84; trustee Columbia Grammar & Prep. Sch., N.Y.C., 1989-94; bd. dirs. Fed Cap, N.Y.C., 1999. Capt. U.S. Army, 1957-58. Mem. Soc. for Info. Mgmt., Univ. Club. Democrat. Jewish. Avocations: hiking, roller blading, yoga, opera, travel. E-mail: mbrenner@brennerresources.com. Home: 33 Riverside Dr Apt 4C New York NY 10023-8025 Office: Brenner Exec Resources 1212 Avenue of the Americas New York NY 10036-1602

BRENOWITZ, ELIOT A., neurobiologist, educator; b. Bklyn., June 5, 1953; s. Nathan and Ruth Brenowitz; m. Rebecca A. Brenowitz, Aug. 1, 1998; 1 child, Lilah. BA with distinction, Swarthmore Coll., 1975; PhD, Cornell U., 1982. Prof. U. Wash., Seattle, 1987—. Contbr. over 60 articles to profl. jours.; guest editor Jour. Neurobiology, 1997. Rsch. fellow Alfred P. Sloan Found., N.Y.C., 1989; rsch. scholar Bloedel Hearing Rsch. Ctr., Seattle, 1999. Fellow Animal Behavior Soc.; mem. AAAS, Soc. for Neurosci., Internat. Soc. Neuroethology.

BRENT, HAL PRESTON, sales executive; b. Jackson, Miss., Dec. 30, 1955; s. Mildred (Newman) Brent. BBA, U. Miss., 1978; postgrad., Marine Corps Jet Pilot, 1981. Sales rep. Control Data, Avon, Conn., 1984-87, sales mgr., 1987-89, v.p. sales, 1989-92; v.p. sales & mktg. PC-Excel, 1992-93; dir. ARETE Group, Ltd. Investment Banking, 1994-96; CEO Media Exch. Group, Coconut Creek, Fla., 1996—; v.p. sales and mktg. Smith, Gardner & Assocs., Delray Beach, Fla., 1996-97; v.p. sales SS&C Techs., Atlanta, 1997-99; bd. dirs. PC-Excel Media Exchange Group, 1992-94, Media Exch. Group, Glenwood Sys. Capt. USMC, 1978-84, Korea and CBI. Home: 97 Foxton Ct Beacon Falls CT 06403-4914

BRENT, PAUL LESLIE, mechanical engineering educator; b. Douglass, Okla., July 3, 1916; s. Paul Leslie and Ruth (McKee) B.; m. Aledo Render, May 29, 1938; children: Carolyn J., Paul Richard; m. E. Ferne McCoy, Nov. 19, 1984. BS, Central State U., 1938; MEd, U. Okla., 1949, EdD, 1959. Tchr. math. and sci. public schs. Adair, Okla., 1938-40; prin. Alden Public Schs., Carnegie, Okla., 1940-43; supt. Alden Public Schs., 1950-58; tchr. public schs. Cooperton, Okla., 1946-47; prin. high sch., public schs. Washita, Okla., 1947-48; supt., 1948-50; asst. prof. Calif. State U., Long Beach, 1959-63, assoc. prof. edn., 1963-72, asst. to chmn. div. edn., 1961-67, prof. instructional media, 1972-86, coordinator graphics support sect. dept. mech. engring., 1981-86, prof. emeritus, 1986—; mem. Baptist Edn. Study Task, 1966-67; trustee Calif. Bapt. Coll., 1969-74. Co-Author: Point, Line, Plane and Solid, 1984. Served with USNR, 1943-46. Mem. NEA, Am. Assn. Sch. Adminstrs., Congress of Faculty Assns., Calif. Faculty Assn. (pres. elect), Calif. Media and Libr. Educators, Calif. State U. Emeritus and Ret. Faculty Assn. (pres. Long Beach chpg. 1993-96), Phi Delta Kappa, Kappa Delta Pi, Phi Kappa Phi, Phi Beta Delta. Republican. Baptist. Home: 11112 Bos Pl Cerritos CA 90703-6426 Office: Calif State U 1250 N Bellflower Blvd Long Beach CA 90840-0001

BRENTON, TIMOTHY DEANE, barrister; b. Gillingham, Kent, Eng., Nov. 4, 1957; s. Ronald William and Peggy Cecelia (Biggs) B.; m. Annabel Louisa (Robson) B., Aug. 29, 1981; children: Louisa Elizabeth, Benjamin Alexander. LLB 1st class, U. Bristol, Eng., 1979. Barrister, Eng. Lectr. law King's Coll., U. London, 1980; pvt. practice London, 1982—; apptd. Queen's Counsel, 1998. Editl. bd. mem. Internat. Maritime Law. Midshipman/sub-lt. Royal Navy, 1976-79. Mem. Comml. Bar Assn. Avocations: golf, fishing. Office: 4 essex Ct, Temple London EC4, England

BRERA, GIUSEPPE RODOLFO, physician, psychotherapist, educator, scientist; b. Arona, Novara, Italy, Jan. 7, 1948; s. Francesco and Lydia (Vespignani) B.; m. Rosaria Fissi, Apr. 22, 1978; 1 child, Francesco Emanuele. MD, U. Milan, degree in med. psychology. Cert. psychotherapist. Hosp. asst. Psychiatric Hosp., Pavia, 1973-74; coord. Families of Drug Abusers Family Counselling Svcs., Milan, 1973-74, Lombardia Health Dist., Youth Mental Health Svc., Milan, 1974-77; sci. dir. Italian Ctr. Med. Rsch. on Med. Psychology, 1980—; founder, clin. dir. Medicine and Psychology Adolescence Inst., Milan, 1983—; dir. dept. adolescentology and med. psychology U. Ambrosiana, 1995—; dir. splty. course in adolescentology Medicine and Psychology Adolescence Inst., Milan, 1988-95, dir. master diploma, 1992—; clin. counselor. Editor: Medicine and Mind, 1983, Adolescence, 1996; editor: (newsletter) Adolescentology, 1993; author: Adolescentology, 1991, Health Psychology and Health Education in Adolescence, 1993, The Universal Declaration of Youths Rights and Dutiees, 1993, The Kairos of Existence: Mystery, Possibility and Reality in Adolescence, 1994, A Revolution for the Clinical Method and Bio-medical Research: The Determinate and the Quality Indeterminate RElativity of the Biological Reactions, 1996, International Convention for TV Programmers, 1996, The Epistemological Manifesto of Person-Centred Medicine, 2000. Mem. Med. Coun. Milan, 1973—; founder, rector U. Ambrosiana, Milan, 1995. Mem. Italian Soc. Adolescentology (pres.) and Adolescence Med., Med. Roll of Psychotherapist, Stress and Anxiety Internat. Soc., World Fedn. and Soc. of Adolescentology (founder, pres. 1994-97), Europe, 1998, Internat. Com. for Universal Declaration of Youth Rights and Duties (coord. 1993). Home and Office: Viale Romagna 51, 20133 Milano Italy

BRESKOVSKI, VASSIL STOYTCHEV, lawyer, educator; b. Sofia, Bulgaria, June 11, 1965; s. Stoytcho and Nona (Motekova) B. ML, U. Sofia, 1992, U. Mich., 1993; PhD, European U. Inst., Florence, Italy, 1998. Rsch. fellow U. Mich. Law Sch., Ann Arbor, 1993; fgn. atty. Arnold & Porter, Washington, 1994; rschr. European U. Inst., 1994-98; advocate Petrov & Breskovski, Sofia, 1994—; assoc. lectr. in econ. Sofia U., 1999—; assoc. lectr. in internat. law U. World and Nat. Economy, Sofia, 1999—; cons. UN Secretariat, N.Y., 1994, Ctr. for Study Democracy, Sofia, 1992. Author: After the Cold War: Does International Trade and Financial Law Matter?, 1999; co-author: Martindale Hubbell Internat. Law Digest, 1995, 96, 97, 98, 99, 2000; editor: Ecoglasnost, 1990-91; assoc. editor Survey of East European Law, 1994—; contbr. articles to newspapers and jours. Asst., dep. dir. Internat. Music Festival, Bulgaria, 1992. Sgt. Bulgarian mil., 1983-85. Mem. Sofia Bar Assn. Avocations: classical music, art, swimming, hiking. Address: Iordan Iovkov St Bl 14-2-30, 1408 Sofia Bulgaria

BRESLIN, EILEEN MARY, lawyer; b. N.Y.C.; d. Hugh Edward Breslin Jr. and Eileen Edith Whalen; m. Joseph Amedeo Rocca, Sept. 4, 1983; children: Andrew Amedeo, Adriana Eileen, Stephanie Mary Elizabeth. BA, SUNY, N.Y.C., 1981; JD, Yale U., 1984. Bar: N.Y., U.S. Dist. Ct. (so. dist.) N.Y., U.S. Dist. Ct. (ea. dist.) N.Y. Assoc. corp. and banking dept. Milbank, Tweed, Hadley & McCloy LLP, N.Y.C., 1984-95; ptnr., mem. mgmt. com. Greenberger & Forman, N.Y.C., 1995-97; ptnr. Jaspan Schlesinger Hoffman, LLP, Garden City, N.Y., 1997—. Pro Bono work includes social security, VA benefits, domestic violence cases. Mem. Nat. Assn. Women Bus. Owners. Avocations: young astronauts program. Office: Jaspan Schlesinger Hoffman LLP 300 Garden City Plz Garden City NY 11530-3302

BRESLIN, EVALYNNE LOUISE WOOD-ROBERTSON, retired psychiatric nurse; b. Richmond, Ohio, July 7, 1931; d. Evan P. and Ada Augusta (Huscroft) Wood-Robertson; m. Donald Joseph Breslin, Jan. 30, 1954; children: Lisa Karen, Mark Nathaniel, Paul Andrew Scott. Diploma, Cleve. Met. Gen. Hosp., 1952; student, Case Western Res. U., 1953-55, Akron U.; HHD (hon.), London Inst. of Applied Rsch., 1973. Lic. RN, Ohio, Mass; RN, Ohio, Mass. Head nurse Cleve. Met. Gen. Hosp., 1952-55, Cleve. State Receiving Hosp., 1952-55; cons. mental illness and addictions Mass.; ret. Bd. dirs. Triple Trouble; ret. vol. monitor state hosp. facilities Alliance for Mentally Ill; vol. nursing/psychiat. work with abandoned adolescents, 1968—; vol. tour guide Barefoot Beach Preserve, Inc.; tchr. ESL, 1999—.

BRESLIN, MIKE ALOYSIUS, writer, philosopher; b. Red Bank, N.J., Sept. 21, 1946; s. John Aloysius and Bertha (Conrad) B.; m. Phyllis Margaret Mack, Sept. 30, 1967 (div. Aug. 1973); children: Tara, Dorothy Grace; m. Helena Margaret Rochford, July 30, 1977. AA, Monmouth Coll., 1966; BS, U. Ill., 1974; MS, Columbia U., 1982. Cert. tchr. English, N.J., 1978. Author: The Hairdresser, 1994, 99, A Triptych in Sanity, 1995, The Healer (Just Nuts About Shakespeare!), 1995, The Interpersonal Problem, 1996, Short on Certainty, 1997, Short on Criminality and Insanity, 1997, Short on Meaning, 1998, Short on Ethical Beauty, 1998, Short on Being Resonably Right, 1998, Short on a Sense of Goodness, 1999, Short on a Vision of Worth, 1999, Short on Overcoming the Stigma, 1999. Avocations: oil painting, sculpting, photography, walking. Home and Office: Crescent Lodge, 32 St Mary's Rd, Galway Ireland

BRESLIN, WILBUR F., real estate broker, developer; b. Bronx, N.Y., Nov. 10, 1926; children: Karen Breslin Cooper, Kenneth Breslin. Grad., Hempstead (N.Y.) H.S., 1943. Pres. Breslin Realty Devel. Corp., Garden City, N.Y., 1953—; real estate appraiser; property mgr.; real estate cons.; mem. adv. bd. 1st Am. Title, N.Y.; bd. dirs. Nat. Bank of N.Y.C. Trustee Hofstra U., Uniondale, N.Y.; bd. dirs. Bath & Tennis Corp., West Hampton, N.Y. Named one of L.I. 100 Most Influential Execs., L.I. Bus. News, 1988, 92, 93, 96. Mem. Nat. Assn. Real Estate Bds., Nat. Inst. Real Estate Appraisers, Nat. Assn. Home Builders of U.S., Farm & Land Inst., Nat. Assn. Real Estate Counselors, Nat. Assn. Rev. Appraisers, L.I. Bd. Realtors, Internat. Coun. Shopping Ctrs., Internat. Mortgage Brokers Assn. Republican. Avocations: tennis, music. Office: Breslin Realty Devel Corp 500 Old Country Rd Ste 200 Garden City NY 11530-1995

BRESSLER, BARRY E., lawyer; b. Phila., Apr. 7, 1947; s. Joseph and Shirley M. (Eiseman) B.; m. Risé Sharon Cohen, June 14, 1970 (dec.); children: Allison Ivy, Michelle Amy. AB, Franklin and Marshall Coll., Lancaster, Pa., 1968; JD, U. Pa., 1971. Bar: Pa. 1971, U.S. Dist. Ct. (ea. dist.) Pa. 1973, U.S. Ct. Appeals (3d cir.) 1977, U.S. Supreme Ct. 1988, U.S. Dist. Ct. (mid. dist.) Pa. 1990. Law clk. to judge Superior Ct. Pa., Phila., 1971-73; assoc. Meltzer & Schiffrin, Phila., 1973-79, ptnr., 1979-86; ptnr. Fox, Rothschild, O'Brien & Frankel, Phila., 1987-88; mem., sr. lawyer real estate litigation & creditors' rights Pelino & Lentz, P.C., Phila., 1988-2000; ptnr. Schnader, Harrison, Segal & Lewis, LLP, Phila., 2000—; adj. instr. landlord-tenant law Delaware County C.C., Media, Pa., 1985-96, Montgomery County C.C., Blue Bell, Pa., 1987—. V.p. English Ceramic Study Group, Phila.; v.p., sec. Temple Sinai, Dresher, Pa., 1991-97; mem. Leadership, Inc., Phila. Mem. ABA (litigation sect.), Pa. Bar Assn. (corp. banking and bus. sect.), Phila. Bar Assn. (real property sect.), Bankruptcy Conf. Ea. Dist. Pa. (treas. 1995-2000), Am. Arbitration Assn. Republican. Jewish. Avocations: tennis, ceramics, bridge. Office: Schnader Harrison Segal and Lewis LLP 1600 Market St Ste 3600 Philadelphia PA 19103-7287

BRESSLER, BARRY LEE, theoretical physicist, systems analyst; b. Reading, Pa., Feb. 16, 1936; s. Kenneth Russell and Lillian Mary (Good) B. BS in Physics, Ursinus Coll., 1957; MS in Physics, Va. Poly. Inst. State U., 1979, PhD in Physics, 1986. Tchr., curator insect collection Reading Pub. Mus., 1954-55; data-processing technician Philco Corp., Phila., 1956; jr. engr. Philco Corp., Spring City, Pa., 1957-58; physicist Naval Surface Warfare Ctr., Dahlgren, Va., 1958-94; group leader Naval Surface Warfare Ctr., Dahlgren, 1983-89, fellow, 1983-85, sr. scientist, 1989-94; prin. scientist EG&G Tech. Svcs., Inc., Dahlgren, 1994-95, sr. prin. scientist, 1995—; cons. Windy Knoll Enterprises, Inc., Magnolia, Tex., 1994—; adj. prof. physics Va. Poly. Inst. State U., Blacksburg, 1994—. Bryn Mawr Coll. scholar, 1957. Mem. Am. Phys. Soc., Coleopterists Soc. (jour. referee 1991-95), Sigma Pi Sigma, Sigma Xi. Avocations: ecology, myrmecology, cerambycid taxonomy, Shetland sheepdogs. Home: PO Box 1345 Fredericksburg VA 22402-1345 Office: EG&G Services PO Box 552 Dahlgren VA 22448-0552

BRETON, PAUL CHARLES STANISLAS, retired philosophy educator; b. Gradignan, Gironde, France, June 3, 1912; s. Louis Charles and Marie Eugenie (Drouineau) B. PhD, Angelicum, Rome, 1946; Docteur es Peltzu phil., Sorbonne, Paris, 1959; Docteur Theologie, Inst. Catholique, Paris, 1973; Docteur honoris causa, Univ. Catholique, Louvain, Belgium, 1989. Philosophy prof. Faculté Philosophy, Rome, 1949-56; prof. philosophy Faculté Philosophy, Paris Institut Catholique, 1959-80, Lyon Inst. Catholique, 1956-80; prof. philosophy Ecole Normale Superieure, Paris, 1968-74; philosophy prof. Dept. Philosophy Montreal U., 1961-63; ret., 1982. Author: L' "esse in" et l' "esse ad" in the Metaphysics of Relationships, 1951, Essence and Existence, 1962, Mystique of the Passion, 1962, Saint Thomas Aquinas, 1965, Philosophy and Mathematics According to Proclus, 1969, Foi et raison logique, 1971, Concerning Principle, 1971, Being, World and Imagination, 1971, Toward a Theology of the Cross, 1979, The Word and the Cross, 1981, Two Mystics of Excess: J.J. Surin and M. Eckhart, 1985, Nothing or Something, 1987, Poetry of the Sensible, 1988, Saint Paul, 1988, Erratic Philosophy, 1989, Free Commentaries, 1990, Skethces of Politics, 1991, The Thinking of Nothing, 1992, Matter and Disperson, 1993, The Other and the Otherwise, 1995, Towards the Original, 1995, Philosophy and Mysticism, 1996, the Future of Christianity, 1999, Causality and Project, 2000. Home: 25 rue Pierre Loti, 94500 Champigny-sur-Marne France

BRETON, PHILIP JOSEPH, musician; b. Mutrie, Sask., Can., Mar. 29, 1916; s. Adolphe and Louise (Caron) B. with Breton Orch., Montmartre, Sask., 1929-38, Larry's Swing Band, 1938-39, Walter Palke Orch., Regina, Can., 1939-40. Composer over 800 songs, classical opus, 1929-87; author various books including autobiography, (piano course book) Songs Are Popular Songs 800; debut as pianist, 1927; performer numerous Can. dance bands, 1929-48, Paul Perry Orch., 1948—, Hank Winder Orch., Tony Bradley Orch., Dick Wiekman Orch., N.Y., Chgo., Greg Spevak Orch. With Can. Army Med. Corps., 1942-45. Mem. Omaha Musicians Assn. Home: 2509 Farnam St Omaha NE 68131-3613

BRETT, JAMES CLARENCE, retired journalism educator; b. Watertown, N.Y., July 28, 1931; s. Clarence Richard and Justina Leone (Cleland) B. BA, Notre Dame U., 1953. With Watertown Daily Times, 1955-71, author series on Frederick Exley, 1968; chmn. Times Editl. Assn., 1970; adj. assoc. prof. Oswego (N.Y.) State U. Coll., 1970-71, asst. prof., 1971-96; ret., 1996; mem. organizing com. SUNY Colls. in the North Country, Fort Drum, Watertown, N.Y., 1985; organizer, dir. student internship program New York Times, 1972. Pvt. first class U.S. Army, 1953-55. Mem. Royal Hort. Soc., Am. Hort. Soc., Jefferson County Hist. Soc., Master Gardeners Am., N.Y. State Ret. Tchrs. Assn., Oswego Emeriti Assn., Am. Legion, Ives Hill Country Club. Republican. Roman Catholic. Avocations: gardening, traveling, reading. Home and Office: 146 Ward St Watertown NY 13601-4616

BRETT, JOHN BRENDAN, JR., corporate advertising and public relations executive; b. Mar. 28, 1944; s. John Brendan and Vera Mae (Locke) B.; m. Alyene Maybeth Wales, Apr. 30, 1966; children: Heather Allyson, Sean Timothy. Student, U. Md., 1964-65, U. So. Miss., 1965-66; BS in Advt., U. Fla., 1969. Advt. supr. Armstrong Cork Co., Lancaster, Pa., 1969-72; mgr. advt. K-D Mfg. Co., Lancaster, 1972-75; dir. mktg. comm. Brodart Inc., Williamsport, Pa., 1975-78; mktg. comm. supr. E.I. duPont de Nemours & Co., Wilmington, Del., 1978-80; group mgr. mktg. comm., carpet fibers E.I. duPont de Nemours & Co., Wilmington, 1980-85, mgr. corp. advt., 1985-87, group mgr. mktg. comm. electronics, 1987-91, sr. cons., external affairs, 1991-92; mgr. mktg. commn. and pub. affairs Sontara Tech./Dupont Nonwovens, Wilmington, 1992-99, global brand mgr., 1999—; mem. Idea98 & Idea2001 com. INDA Nonwovens Assn., 1997-99; mem. advt. adv. coun. U. Fla., 1984-87. Mem. editl. sounding bd. Advertising Age mag., 1985-87. Vice chmn. Del. all-star football game com. Del. Found. for Retarded Children, 1982-83, chmn., 1984, trustee, 1989-92; bd. govs. Automotive Advertisers Coun., 1975; mem. vestry St. Thomas Episc. Ch., 1974-75, St. David's Episc. Ch., Wilmington, 1989-92, sr. warden, 1991-92; treas. N.E. Missionary Convocation, Diocese of Mid. Tenn., Diocesesan Conv. Del., 1995; chmn. bldg. com. Country Hills Homeowners Assn., 1994-2000, sec. bd. dirs., 2000—. Recipient Outstanding Advt. Campaign award Am. Bus. Press/Bus.-Profl. Advt. Assn., 1974. Mem. Assn. Nat. Advertisers (corp. advt. com. 1985-86). Avocations: outdoor photography, gardening, antique autos. Home: 119 Spy Glass Way Hendersonville TN 37075-8550 Office: DuPont Co 1002 Industrial Rd Old Hickory TN 37138-3696

BRETTENTHALER, MARTIN STEFAN, wood and forestry products industry executive; b. Salzburg, Austria, Dec. 10, 1970; s. Reiner and Ursula (Karres) B. Student, Polit. Sci. Studies, Paris, 1992-93; Lic Oec, U. St. Gallen, Switzerland, 1996. Cons. Boston Cons. Group, Munich, Germany, 1996-97, Paris, 1997-98; head strategic control HIAG AG, Riehen, Switzerland, 1998-99, chief corp. strategy officer, divsn. gen. mgr., 1999—, also bd. dirs.; bd. dirs. Pannovosges S.A., Rambervillers, France, PISA, Rambervillers, France, Fideris Ag, Switzerland, Pavatex AG, Switzerland, Pavatex Fribourg SA, Switzerland, Nybron Flooring Internat., Switzerland. Served with Austrian Army, 1990. Roman Catholic. Avocations: German and French literature, travel, languages, art. Home: 6 Rue des Haudriettes, 75003 Paris France

BRETT-MAJOR, LIN, lawyer, mediator, arbitrator, educator, lecturer; b. N.Y.C., Sept. 21, 1943; d. B.L. and Edith H. Brett; children from previous marriage: Dania S., David M. BA, U. Mich., 1965; JD cum laude, Nova Law Ctr., 1978; postgrad., Harvard U., 1993. Bar: Fla. 1978, U.S. Ct. Appeals (5th and 11th cirs.) 1981, U.S. Tax Ct. 1981, U.S. Dist. Ct. (so., mid. and no. dist.) Fla. 1982, U.S. Supreme Ct. 1984, U.S. Dist. Ct. (mid., so. and no. dists.) Fla. 1984, U.S. Ct. Mil. Appeals 1990. Internat. communications asst. Mitsui and Co., Ltd., N.Y.C., 1962; with dept. pub. relations and devel. St. Rita's Hosp., Lima, Ohio, 1965-66; reporter The Lima News, 1969-70; honors intern U.S. Atty.'s Office, Miami, 1977; pvt. practice, Ft. Lauderdale, Fla., 1979-93; alternative dispute resolution mediator Conflict Solutions, Boca Raton, Fla., 1993-98; vis. prof. grad. program of dispute resolution Sch. Social and Systemic Studies, Nova Southeastern U., Ft. Lauderdale, 1997-98; participant Gov.'s Conf. on World Trade, Miami and Jacksonville, Fla., 1984, Unidroit Workshop Devel. Pvt. Internat. Comml. Law, 1992; spkr. trial and negotiation Bus. Owner's Conf., Hollywood, Fla., 1986, Nova U. Law Ctr., 1988, ABA Nat. Conv., Toronto, 1988, Fla. Atlantic U., 1989, CPA Club, 1992, ABA Sect. Meeting, Bal Harbor, Fla., 1996, Nova U. Sch. Social & Systemic Studies, 1996. Contbr. articles to profl. jours. on internat. anti-trust law. Bd. dirs. Neurol. Rehab. Ctr., Broward Navy Days, 1992-96; mem. Ft. Lauderdale Opera Soc., 1986, Ft. Lauderdale Mus. Art, 1985, Ft. Lauderdale Opera Guild, 1990-97, Fla. Grand Opera Dance, 1997—; Dept. Def. ESGR Com., 1996—. Recipient Silver Key award ABA, 1977. Mem. ABA, FBA, ATLA, Fla. Bar Assn. (mil. law com. 1989—, chmn. legis. issues subcom. 1990-92, media-law com. 1991-93), U. Mich. Alumni Assn. (Gold Coast pres. 1988-90, S.E. U.S. dist. v.p., sec.-treas. 1992-95, pres. 1995-98, dir. 1998—), U.S. Propeller Club (nat. del. Port Everglades, Fla. 1981). Republican. Avocations: fencing, skeet and trap shooting, tennis, yachting. Home: 242 Seaspray Ave Palm Beach FL 33480-4229

BREUER, GEORG, writer, journalist, peace advocate; b. Vienna, Oct. 24, 1919; s. Ernst and Dora (Fraenkel) B.; m. Eva Brill, Aug. 9, 1943 (div. 1947); 1 child, Emmi; m. Rosa Grossmann, Dec. 10, 1949; children: Hans, Elisabeth. Matura (Abitur), Linz, Austria, 1937; student, Acad. Music, Vienna, 1938. Editor Young Austria, London, 1941-45; journalist Vienna, 1946-57, writer, journalist, 1957—. Author: Could Austria survive?-The consequences of a total war, 1964, Can doomsday be avoided?-Marxism in the nuclear age, 1968, Interview with the future-Our World in 20 years, 1968, Weather modification: prospects and problems, 1976, 80, Air in Danger: Ecological Prespectives, 1978, 80, Energy without fear - How to manage without fast breeders, 1980, The green car (electrocars) - An alternative concept for traffic, 1983; Sociobiology and the human dimension, 1981, 82; chmn. editl. bd. memorandum ind. groups Vienna CSCE conf., 1986; contbr. to Catalogue of Hope, 1990; translator: (Max Nicholson) The Environmental Revolution, 1970, The Family and its Future - Ciba Foundation Blueprint, 1970, (J.R. Ravetz) Scietific Knowledge and its Social Problems, 1971, (Ralph Nader, John Abbotts) The Menace of Atomic Energy, 1977. Sec. Easter Marches for Peace and Disarmament, Vienna, 1963-68, Com. Solidarity with Democracy in Czechoslovakia, Vienna, 1973-90; various functions Communist Party Austria, Vienna, London, 1935-68. Recipient Austrian State award for Scientific Journalists Ministry for Sci. and Rsch., 1981. Avocations: writing music. Home: Birnbaumg 4/3, A-1100 Vienna Austria

BREUER, MORDECHAI MARCUS, retired history educator, musicologist; b. Frankfurt am Main, Germany, Apr. 8, 1918; arrived in Israel, 1936; s. Isaac and Jenny (Eisenmann) B.; m. Fanny Simcha Levy, Aug. 1943; children: Dinah, Shlomo, Miriam, Zipporah, Chava, Tamar, Yizchak. Intermediate BA, London U., 1943; BA, Hebreww U., Jerusalem, 1958, MA, 1960, PhD, 1967. Tchr. elem. and high schs. Horeb, Jerusalem, 1938-48; founder, prin. Kfar Eliyahu, Gedera, Israel, 1949-57, Even Ha'ezer Dist. Sch. (Children's Village Aliyat Hanoar), Naham, Israel, 1958-60; prin. Horeb Schs., Jerusalem, 1961-70; prof. Jewish history Bar-Ilan U., Ramat Gan, Israel, 1971-86; vis. prof. Harvard U., Boston, 1979-80; mem. former chmn. Gen. Archives for History of Jews, Jerusalem, 1980-96; founder, editor Isaac Breuer Meml. Found., Jerusalem, 1947-95. Author: Modernity within Tradition (in German, Hebrew and English), 1986-92; co-author: Deutsch-jüdische Geschichte der Neuzeit (in German and English), 1996; editor: Nizzachon Yashan, 1978, Zemach David, 1983, The Ashkenazic Rabbinate in the Middle Ages, 1976; co-editor: Ha-Ma'ayan,, 1953—; prin. rschr., editor Germania Judaica, 1980—; contbr. articles to profl. jours. including Zion, Ha-ma'ayan, Tarbiz, She'arim, Jewish Action, also Ency. Judaica, Hebrew Ency., Ency. Edn., Bar-Ilan Yearbook, Procs. World Congresses Jewish Studies. Co-founder, prin. Ezra Youth Movement, Jerusalem, 1937-47; mem. Jewish Agy. for Palestine Relief unit to Bergen-Belsen Camp, Germany, 1946-47; mem. Israel Broadcasting Authority, Jerusalem, 1959-72, Oz ve-Shalom, Jerusalem, 1975—. With Haganah, Israel Def. Forces, 1936-70. Recipient Shazar award Shazar Inst., 1992; Rabbi Berman rsch. grantee, Rehovot, Israel, 1971, Wolf Found. rsch. grantee Israel Sci. Acad., 1985. Mem. Israel Hist. Soc. (past pres.), Leo Baeck Inst. (bd. dirs.), Renaissance Soc. Am., Inst. for Sacred Music. Avocation: musicology. Home: 54 Ben-Maimon Ave, 92261 Jerusalem Israel Office: Hebrew U, Merkaz Dinur, Giv'at Ram, Jerusalem Israel

BREUER, ROLF, stock exchange executive. Dep. mem. bd. managing dirs. Deutsche Bank AG, Frankfurt, W. Ger., then dep. chmn. supervisory bd., chmn., mem. supervisory bd. major cos.; chmn. German Stock Exch. AG; Office: Deutsche Börse AG, Taunusanlage 12, 600325 Frankfurt am Main, Germany*

BREVETTI, FRANCINE CLELIA, journalist; b. San Francisco, July 20, 1943; d. Frank Albert and Tecla Puccetti Brevetti. BA in French, U. Calif., Berkeley, 1966; MA in Theater, UCLA, 1969. Staff writer Jour. Commerce, N.Y.C., 1977-85; pvt. practice Hong Kong, 1985-97; bus. writer The Oakland (Calif.) Tribune, 1998—; dir. Francine Brevetti Prodns., 1984—; West Coast corr., past Hong Kong corr. Seatrade Rev., Seatrade Orgn., 1994—; Hong Kong corr. Pensions & Investments, Crain Comm., 1995—; cons. Renwick-McCormick, Hong Kong, 1995-97. Editor ECA China News, 1995—; contbr. Hobson's Publs., 1996—, The Securities Jour., 1996—. Mem. Soc. Profl. Journalists, Women in Pub. (Hong Kong chpt. pres. 1994-96), Hong Kong Journalists' Assn., Fgn. Corr. Club (com. mem. 1987—), N.Y. Fin. Writers Assn. Fax: 510-208-6477. E-mail: francineb@earthlink.net. Office: The Oakland Tribune Oakland CA 94607

BREVIK, J. ALBERT, communications consultant; b. Seattle, Aug. 1, 1920; s. Anton Christian and Olga Elise (Setter) B.; m. Norma Jacquelin Ringman, June 26, 1953 (dec. 1987); children: Jay Christian, Jon Henry; m. Joann Bradford, Jan. 20, 1990. B.A., U. Wash., 1947, M.A., 1951. Guidance counselor music dept. U. Wash., Seattle, 1947-52; entertainment dir. athletic dept. U. Wash., 1947-52; vocal music educator Clover Park High Sch., Tacoma, Wash., 1952-54; television coordinator Pierce County Schs., Tacoma, 1954-59; dir. television edn., gen. mgr. KPEC-TV, Clover Park Schs., Tacoma, 1959-72; dir. communications KPEC-TV, Clover Park Schs., 1972-80; mgr. KPEC-TV, KPEC-FM, 1960-76; also in charge publs. and pub. relations dept., film prodn. unit, new media prodn. and services; gen. mgr. Sta. KCPQ-TV, Tacoma, 1976-80; communications cons., 1980—; pres. Avcom Pacific, Communications Cons., 1981—; assoc. faculty dept. edn. U. Puget Sound, 1955-69; dir. Intermarket Corp., Norwegian Male Chorus, Seattle, 1946-48, Clarion Chorus, Seattle, 1947-52; free-lance radio musician, Seattle, 1938-52; entertainment dir. BC Lions (profl. football club), Vancouver, Can., 1954-55; ednl. TV cons., B.C., Can., 1960-61; v.p. Wash. Ednl. Network, 1978. Mem. Fir Tree, Fircrest Golf Club (Tacoma), Kiwanis (pres. Tacoma club 1963, bd. dirs. 1955-71), Phi Mu Alpha Synfonia, Phi Delta Kappa. Lutheran (v.p., dir. 1959-69). Home and Office: 1920 Day Island Blvd W University Place WA 98466

BREWER, A. BRUCE, university administrator; b. Pasadena, Tex., Oct. 18, 1951; s. Leo Louie and Norma Jane (Nabors) B.; m. Patricia Anne Lumley, Mar. 12, 1977; stepchildren: Frank D. Hollifield III, Patrick C.M.; 1 child, April Bruce. AB in Am. Studies, U. Ala., 1974, MA in Counseling and Guidance, 1975; PhD in Higher Edn. Leadership, Ga. State U., 1988. Coord. Career Devel. Ctr. Auburn U., Montgomery, Ala., 1977-81; coord. cooperative edn. Placement and Cooperative Edn. Office/West Ga. Coll., Carrollton, Ga., 1981-82; dir. dept. career svcs. State U. of West Ga., Carrollton, 1982—; asst. dir. admissions Auburn U., Montgomery, Ala., 1976-79. Pres. Sertoma Civic Club, Carrollton, 1996-97; dist. chmn. Boy Scouts of Am., Carrollton, 1994-95; pres. West Ga. Indsl. Leaders Assn., Carrollton, 1995, West Ga. Pers. Assn., Carrollton, 1992. Mem. Ga. Assn. Colls. and Employees (pres. 2000-01). Baptist. Avocation: music. Office: State Univ West Ga Maple St Carrollton GA 30118-0001

BREWER, BARBARA BAGDASARIAN, nursing administrator; b. Providence, Apr. 18, 1950; d. Bagdasar and Grace (Sarkisian) Bagdasarian; m. Timothy F. Brewer III, May 28, 1983. BSN, U. R.I., 1972; MA in Liberal Studies, Conn. Wesleyan U., 1986; MSN, Yale U., 1988; MBA, Columbia U., 1992; postgrad., Sch. Nursing U. Ariz., 1998—. RN, Ariz., Conn., R.I. Staff nurse Miriam Hosp., Providence, R.I., 1972; head nurse orthopeds. unit Frisbie Meml. Hosp., Rochester, N.H., 1973-76; staff nurse St. Francis Hosp. and Med. Ctr., Hartford, Conn., 1976; clin. coord. continuing care unit Middlesex Meml. Hosp., Middletown, Conn., 1976-86; dir. cardiology svcs. Lawrence and Meml. Hosp., New London, Conn., 1988-92, v.p. ambulatory svcs., 1992-95; adminstrv. leader emergency svcs. Tucson Med. Ctr., 1996-97; rsch. assoc. U. Ariz., Coll. of Nursing, 1998—; predoctoral fellow NIH, 1999—; rschr. in field. Co-author: Improving Your Skills in 12-Lead ECG Interpretation, 1990. Mem. Sigma Theta Tau. Home: 4575 E Blue Mountain Dr Tucson AZ 85718-3560

BREWER, DEREK STANLEY, retired humanities educator; b. Cardiff, Wales, Great Britain, July 13, 1923; s. Stanley Leonard and Winifred Helen (Forbes) B.; m. Lucie Elisabeth Hoole, Aug. 17, 1951; children: Sarah, Michael, Helena, Adrian, Guy. BA, Oxford U., 1948, MA, 1948; PhD, U.

Birmingham, 1956; LittD, Cambridge U., 1980; LLD (hon.), U. Keio, 1982, Harvard U., 1984, Williams Coll., 1990; LittD (hon.), U. Birmingham, 1985; DUniv (hon.), U. York, 1985, U. Paris IV, 1988, U. Liège, 1990. Lectr. Birmingham (United Kingdom) U., 1949-56, sr. lectr., 1958-64; prof. Internat. Christian U., Japan, 1956-58; lectr. Cambridge (United Kingdom) U., 1965-76, reader, 1976-83, prof., 1983-90, emeritus prof., 1990—; founder D.S. Brewer Pub., United Kingdom, 1979—; master Emmanuel Coll., Cambridge, 1977-90. Author: Chaucer, 1953, Proteus, 1958, Chaucer and His World, 1978, Symbolic Stories, 1980; editor: Cambridge Rev., 1981-86, The Parlement of Foulys, 1960, Chaucer in His Time, 1964, Chaucer and Chaucerians, 1966, The Morte Darthur: Parts Seven and Eight, English Gothic Literature, 1983, Studies in Medieval English Romances, 1988, Medieval Comic Tales, 1996, Companion to Gawain-poet, 1997, Seatonian Exercises and Other Verses, 2000, Chaacer's World, 2000; contbr. articles to profl. jours. Trustee, chmn. Brit. Taiwan Cultural Assn., London, 1989-97, SOS Children's Villages, 1992—, Chaucer Heritage Trust, 1992—. Capt. Brit. Infantry, 1942-45. Mem. Japan Acad. (hon.), Medieval Acad. Am. (corr.). Mem. Ch. of England. Avocations: reading, walking, travel. Home: 240 Hills Rd, Cambridge CB2 2QE, England Office: Emmanuel Coll, Saint Andrews St, Cambridge CB2 3AP, England

BREWER, DOMINIC JAMES, economist, researcher, administrator; b. Reading, Eng., May 24, 1966; came to U.S., 1988; s. James Gordon Brewer and Caroline Margaret Sherwood. BA with honors, Oxford (Eng.) U., 1987; MA, U. Wis., Milw., 1989; PhD, Cornell U., 1994. Economist RAND Corp., Santa Monica, Calif., 1994-99, dir. edn., 1999—; vis. prof. econ. UCLA, 1995—. Assoc. editor Econs. of Edn., 1998—; contbr. chpts. to books and articles to profl. jours. Mem. Am. Econ. Assn., Am. Edn. Rsch. Assn. E-mail: dominic brewer@rand.org. Home: 16 19th Ave Venice CA 90291-4113 Office: RAND Corp 1700 Main St Santa Monica CA 90401-3297

BREWER, EDWARD CAGE, III, law educator; b. Clarksdale, Miss., Jan. 20, 1953; s. Edward Cage Brewer Jr. and Elizabeth Blair (Alford) Little; m. Nancy Corr Martin, Dec. 27, 1975 (div. Sept. 1985); children: Katherine Martin, Julia Blair; m. Laurie Carol Alley, June 27, 1993 (div. Dec. 1999); 1 child, Caroline Elizabeth McCarty. BA, U. of the South, 1975; JD, Vanderbilt U., 1979. Bar: Ala. 1980, U.S. Ct. Appeals (5th and 11th cirs.) 1981, U.S. Dist. Ct. (so. dist.) Ala. 1981, Ga. 1982, U.S. Dist. Ct. (no. dist.) Ga. 1982, U.S. Dist. Ct. (so. dist.) Ga. 1988, U.S. Ct. Appeals (3d and 8th cirs.) 1983, U.S. Dist. Ct. (mid. dist.) Ga. 1992, U.S. Supreme Ct. 1996. Law clk. to Hon. Virgil Pittman U.S. Dist. Ct. (so. dist.) Ala., Mobile, 1979-81; law clk. to Hon. Albert J. Henderson U.S. Ct. Appeals (5th and 11th cirs.), Atlanta, 1981-82; pvt. practice Atlanta, 1982-96; instr. Coll. of Law Ga. State U., Atlanta, 1992, 94; adj. prof. legal writing Emory U., Atlanta, 1994-96; asst. prof. law No. Ky. U., Highland Heights, 1996-2000, assoc. prof. law, 2000—. Co-author: Railway Labor Act of 1926: Legislative History, 1988, Georgia Appellate Practice, 1996; contbr. articles to profl. jours. Mem. Phi Beta Kappa, Omicron Delta Kappa. Episcopalian. Avocations: choral music, guitar, motorcycles, hiking, canoeing. Office: No Ky U Salmon P Chase Coll Law Nunn Dr Highland Heights KY 41099

BREWER, NEVADA NANCY, elementary education educator; b. Balt., Jan. 21, 1949; d. Leo and Rebecca (Johnson) B. BS, Coppin State Coll., 1973, MEd, 1974; MEd, Coppin State Coll., 1981; postgrad., C.C. Balt., 1985. Cert. elem. tchr., spl. edn. tchr. Tchr. Balt. County Adult Edn., Towson, Md., 1973-88; coord. just say no to drugs program Balt. City Sch. Sys., tchr., mgr. summer sch., 2000; coord. Heads Up Program, 1980, math-a-thon program for St. Jude Rsch. Ctr., 1993—, 24 Challenge Math. Tournament, 1996—; supr. tchr. for student tchrs. Towson State U., Coll. Notre Dame, Coppin State Coll., 1989—; leadership tchr. STARS sci. program, 1995; participant in Project Future Search Phone-a-Thon to recruit minority students U. Md., College Park., Write to Learn Program, Balt. City Sch. Sys., 1990-91. Coord. Echo Hill Outdoor Sch., 1988—. Recipient Freedom Found. award 1974. Home: 1616 Wentworth Ave Baltimore MD 21234-6125

BREWERTON, TIMOTHY DAVID, psychiatrist; b. Baton Rouge, Mar. 26, 1953; s. John Lee and Helen (Bouy) B.; m. Therese Kathleen Killeen, June 16, 1990. BS, La. State U., 1974; MD, Tulane U., 1978. Diplomate Am. Bd. Psychiatry and Neurology, Am. Bd. Child and Adolescent Psychiatry, Am. Bd. Forensic Psychiatry. Intern, resident in psychiatry U. Calif., San Francisco, 1978-82; staff psychiatrist Hawaii State Hosp., Kaneohe, 1982-84; med. staff fellow NIMH, Bethesda, Md., 1984-87, guest rschr., 1987-95; asst. prof. psychiatry and behavioral scis. Med. U. S.C., Charleston, 1987-90, assoc. prof. psychiatry and behavioral scis., 1990-97, prof. psychiatry and behavioral scis., 1997—, fellow in child and adolescent psychiatry, 1994-96, tenure, 1999—; dir. Eating Disorders Program, Inst. Psychiatry, Charleston, 1987—; med. cons. Nat. Crime Victims Rsch. and Treatment Ctr., 1996—. Contbr. articles to profl. jours. Recipient Award for Creative Achievement Dept. Psychiatry U. Calif. San Francisco, 1982. Fellow Am. Psychiat. Assn.; mem. Soc. Biol. Psychiatry, Am. Acad. Clin. Psychiatrists (Clin. Rsch. award 1989, bd. dirs. 1993-97), N.Y. Acad. Sci., Eating Disorders Rsch. Soc., Acad. Eating Disorders (bd. dirs. 2000—), Am. Acad. Child and Adolescent Psychiatry, Soc. Light Treatment and Biol. Rhythms, Am. Profl. Soc. on Abuse of Children, Internat. Soc. for Traumatic Stress Studies. Office: Med U S C Inst Psychiatry PO Box 250861 67 President St Charleston SC 29425-0001

BREW-GRAVES, SAMUEL HENRY, pediatrician, international health and management consultant; b. Cape-Coast, Ghana, Oct. 11, 1934; s. Christian Rhule Graves and Emma Gyepi Garbrah; m. Charlotte Ampofo, Sept. 18, 1963; children: Emmeline, Christine, Henry. MD, St. Thomas Hosp. Med. Sch., London, 1961; MPH, Johns Hopkins U., 1967. Commd. Ghana Army Med. Corps, 1963, advanced through grades to lt. col., 1971; various clin. and adminstrv. positions in pediats. and pub. health Ghana Army Med. Corps, Accra, Ghana, 1963-74; resident Sick Children's Hosp., Toronto, 1964-66; ret. Ghana Army Med. Corps, 1977; maternal and child health physician WHO, Lusaka, Zambia, 1974-78; advisor, team leader WHO, Seychelles, 1978-80; team leader WHO, Freetown, Sierra Leone, 1980-81; rep. WHO, Entebbe, Uganda, 1981-85, Lagos, Nigeria, 1985-94; cons. chief med. officer Seychelles Ministry of Health, 1978-80; exec. dir. Radmed Cons. Ltd., Accra, 1994—; med. cons. Sports Coun. Ghana, Accra, 1969-71; hon. fellow Commonwealth Hall-U. Ghana, Legon, 1970; hon. lectr. maternal and child health U. Zambia, Lusaka, 1975-80, U. Makerere, Kampala, Uganda, 1982-85, U. Lagos, 1985-94; bd. trustees Otumba Tunwase Nat. Pediat. Found., Lagos, 1992; mem. adv. bd. Eye Found., Lagos, 1992. Decorated Order of Internat. Ambs., 1999; Harriet Lane fellow Johns Hopkins U., 1966-67, Paul Harris fellow Rotary Internat., 1977; Commonwealth Found. scholar Govt. of Can., 1964-66; named Sports Adminstr. of Yr., Sports Coun. Ghana, 1973. Fellow Am. Acad. Tropical Medicine, Royal Soc. Health, West African Coll. Physicians; Post Grad. Med. Coll. Pediats. Avocations: African and classical music, sports medicine, adolescent health activities, swimming. Office: Radmed Consultancy Svcs Ltd, PO Box KA 9492, Airport Accra Ghana

BREWIN, KEITH ALAN FREDERICK, publisher, accountant; b. Birmingham, Eng., Aug. 24, 1933; s. Alfred and Hilda Florence (Moseley) B.; m. Julie Bishop, June 25, 1960; children: Amanda Jane, Stephanie Louise, Alistair James. Diploma in modern langs., King Edward's Sch., Birmingham, 1950. Chartered sec.; inc. practising acct. Trainee acct. metals divsn. I.C.I. Ltd., Birmingham, 1953-54; asst. group sec. Cooper & Co. Ltd., Birmingham, 1954-58; group sec. Component Metal Pressings Ltd., Birmingham, 1958-68; fin. dir. Bar Prodns. Group, Bromsgrove, Eng., 1968-81; group sec. Maxim Investments Ltd., London, 1981-86; mng. dir. Brewin Books Ltd., Studley, Eng., 1981—; bd. dirs. Sutpaprint (Redditch) Ltd., Eng.; sr. ptnr. K.A.F. Brewin & Co. Accts., Studley, 1981—. Author: The Cygnet Players-A Short History, 1976. Lay chmn. Nat. Health Svc. Ind. Rev. Panel, Birmingham, 1996—; mem. pub. practice panel The Inst. Chartered Secs. and Adminstrs., London, 1989-97. Served with Brit. Royal Army Ednl. Corps., 1951-53, Royal Artillery, Territorial Army, 1953-57. Fellow Inst. Co. Accts.; mem. Inst. Chartered Secs. and Adminstrs. (Sir Cuthbert Grundy medal 1968), The Groucho Club (London). Avocations: antiquarian books, country walking. Office: Brewin Books Ltd, Doric House 56 Alcester Rd, Studley B80 7NP, England

BREWKA, GERHARD, information sciences educator; b. Regensburg, Germany, Jan. 23, 1955; s. Gerhard Michael and Elisabeth Charlotte (Huber) B.; m. Anna Hildegard Haarmann, Aug. 28, 1979; children: Kristina, Janna, Alena. Diploma in computer sci., U. Bonn, Germany, 1984; PhD, U. Hamburg, Germany, 1989. Rschr. Gesellschaft fuer Math. and Datenberarbatung, St. Augustin, Germany, 1984-91, sr. rschr., 1992-94; rschr. Internat. Computer Sci. Inst., Berkeley, Calif., 1991-92; prof. T. Univ. Vienna, Austria, 1995-96, U. Leipzig, Germany, 1996—; dir. knowledge representation Doctoral Progam, Leipzig. Author: Nonmonotonic Reasoning, 1991, (with Dix, Konolige) Nonmonotonic Reasoning: An Overview, 1997; editor: Principles of Knowledge Representation, 1996. Mem. Gesellschaft Fur Informatik. Home: Goerreshof 14, 53347 Alfter Germany Office: U Leipzig, Augustusplatz 10-11, 04109 Leipzig Germany

BREWSTER, ROBERT GENE, concert singer, educator; b. Pinson, Ala., July 7, 1938; s. Hubert and Chrisella (Ayers) B.; m. Premala Edwards (div.); 1 child, Ravindra Robert. MusB in Piano Performance with honors, Wheaton Coll., 1958; MusM in Voice with distinction, Ind. U., 1961; PhD in Vocal Performances Practices and Musicology, Washington U., St. Louis, 1967; Konzertreife Diploma, Staatliche Hochschule fuer Musik und Darstellender Kunst, Stuttgart, Fed. Republic Germany, 1970; diploma in Lieder and Opera, Mozarteum, Salzburg, Austria, 1969. Tchr. music and French Westfield (Ala.) High Sch., 1959-60; chmn. dept. music Miles Coll., Birmingham, Ala., 1960-62; chmn. area fine arts Jackson (Miss.) Coll., 1962-63; asst. tchr. voice Washington Univ., 1963-66; touring tenor throughout Europe, 1966-73; chmn. dept. music Dillard Univ., New Orleans, 1974; chmn. dept. voice Univ. Miami, Coral Gables, Fla., 1974-82; past pres. Breff Agy., Inc., N.Y.C.; pres. European Fashion Imports, N.Y.C., 1984-88, Fashion Suite, Inc., 1988—; guest lectr. Stanford U. in, Germany, Beutelsbach, 1968-70; dozent fur gesang Berliner Kirchenmusikschule, 1970-72. Concert tours throughout, Europe, Asia and, The Ams.; rec. artist (album) I See the Stars, 1960. Seely Mudd fellow, 1964-66; Fulbright fellow, 1966-68; Deutsche Akademische Austausch Dienst award, 1968-70. Mem. Nat. Assn. Tchrs. Singing, Coll. Music Soc., AAUP, Am. Musicol. Soc., Fla. Vocal Tchrs. Assn., Nat. Assn. Schs. Music, Nat. Arts Club, Phi Mu Alpha. Democrat. Episcopalian. Home and Office: 475 W 57th St Apt 18A New York NY 10019-1778

BREYER, DETLEV RICHARD HANS, ophthalmologist; b. Weiden, Germany, Feb. 7, 1968; s. Erich Hans Paul and Barbara Amanda (Most) B.; m. Anitra Jsolde Beate Pacurar, Aug. 18, 1999. MD, US Med. Licensing Examination, 1994; PhD, U. Erlangen, Germany, 1996. Resident eye dept. U. Duesseldorf, Germany, 1995-96; priv. Bannen eye dept. U. Witten-Herdecke Klinikum, 1997-99. Mem. Deutsche Ophthalmologische Gesellschaft, Berufsverband Augenaerzte, Forschungsgruppe Akupunktur. Avocations: golf, sailing, art, literature, society. Office: Klinikum Wuppertal GMBH, Augenklin, 42283 Wuppertal Germany

BREYER, HILTRUD, member of the European parliament; b. Saarbrucken, Fed. Republic Germany, Aug. 22, 1957. Mem. European Parliament, Brussels, 1999—; mem. Group of the Greens/European Free Alliance, European Parliament; mem. com. on the environ., pub. health and consumer policy; substitute mem. com. on legal affairs and the internal market, com. on women's rights and equal opportunities; mem. delegation for rels. with the mem. states of ASEAN, South-east Asia and the Republic of Korea. Office: Europaisches Parlament, Rue Wiertz ASP 8G265, B-1047 Bruxelles Belgium also: Regionalburo, Ormesheimer StraBe 3, D-66399 Mandelbachtal Saar Germany*

BREYER, STEPHEN GERALD, United States supreme court justice; b. San Francisco, Aug. 15, 1938; s. Irving G. and Anne R. B.; m. Joanna Hare, Sept. 4, 1967; children: Chloe, Nell, Michael. A.B., Stanford U., 1959; B.A. (Marshall scholar), Oxford U., 1961; LL.B., Harvard U., 1964; LL.D. (hon.), U. Rochester, 1983. Bar: Calif. 1966, D.C. 1966, Mass. 1971. Law clk. Justice Goldberg, U.S. Supreme Ct., 1964-65; spl. asst. to asst. atty. gen. U.S. Dept. Justice, 1965-67; asst. prof. law Harvard U., 1967-70, prof., 1970-81, lectr., 1981—, prof. govt. J.F. Kennedy Sch., 1978-81; asst. spl. prosecutor Watergate Spl. Prosecution Force, 1973; spl. counsel U.S. Senate Judiciary Com., 1974-75, chief counsel, 1979-81; judge U.S. Ct. Appeals (1st cir.), Boston, 1981-90, chief judge, 1990-94; Oliver Wendell Holmes lectr. Harvard Law Sch., 1992; assoc. justice U.S. Supreme Ct., Washington, 1994—; mem. Judl. Conf. of U.S., 1990-94, U.S. Sentencing commn., 1985-89; vis. lectr. Coll. Law, Sydney, Australia, 1975, Salzburg (Austria) Seminar, 1978, 93; Jud. Conf. rep. to Adminstrv. Conf. U.S., 1981-94; vis. prof. U. Rome, 1993. Author: (with Paul MacAvoy) The Federal Power Commission and the Regulation of Energy, 1974, (with Richard Stewart) Administrative Law and Regulatory Policy, 1979, 3rd edit., 1992, Regulation and its Reform, 1982, Breaking the Vicious Circle, 1993; contbr. articles to profl. jours. Trustee U. Mass., 1974-81; bd. overseers Dana Farber Cancer Inst., Boston, 1977—. Mem. ABA, Am. Bar Found., Am. Law Inst., Am. Acad. Arts and Scis., Coun. Fgn. Rels. Office: US Supreme Ct Supreme Ct Bldg 1 1st St NE Washington DC 20543-0001

BREYMEYER, ALICJA IRENA, ecologist; b. Siedlce, Poland, Oct. 20, 1932; d. Franciszek Witold and Stefania (Sliwon) Dabrowska B.; m. Krzysztof Jan Breymeyer, Feb. 1959 (div. 1974); 1 child, Ewa Anna. BAC, Warsaw Univ., Poland, 1955, D, 1964, Docent, 1974; prof., Polish Acad. Sci., 1984. Dept. head Inst. of Ecology, Warsaw, 1955-73; sci. fellow Ga. State Univ., Athens, 1965, Smith Tropical Inst., Balboa, Panama, 1968-69; vis. prof. Univ. Central, Caracas, Venezuela, 1974; dept. head Inst. of Geography, Warsaw, 1984—; vice-chair UNESCO/MAB ICC, Paris, 1992-96; chair Polish MAB/SCOPE Com., Warsaw, 1990—; co-chair SCOPE Program, Paris, 1987-96. Co-editor, co-author: Grasslands, Systems Analysis and Man, 1980, Global Change Effects on Coniferous Forests and Grasslands, 1996; editor and co-author: Managed Grasslands, 1990, Biosphere Reserves in Poland, 1994, 97; inventor in field. Organizer Seminar on Transborder Protected Areas, Carpathians, 1994, Polish Ecological Soc. 1991, pres., 1991-94, 1998—; co-orgn. Solidarity Union, 1981. Fellow Dialogue Univ.; mem. UNESCO-MAB ICC. Avocations: travelling, vacation with grandson, dogs breeding. Office: Inst of Geography PAS, Twarda 51/55, 00 818 Warsaw Poland

BREZEANU, GHEORGHE ION, engineering educator, researcher; b. Ditesti, Prahova, Romania, Oct. 29, 1948; s. Ion and Aurelia (Bucur) B.; m. Doinita Baleanu, Apr. 29, 1978; 1 child, Mihai. Engr., U. Politehnica, Bucharest, 1972, PhD in Microelectronics, 1981. Asst. prof. electronics faculty U. Politehnica Bucharest, Bucharest, 1972-86, lectr. in electronics faculty, 1986-90, assoc. prof. electronics faculty, 1990-92, prof. electronics faculty, 1992—; sci. chair electronics faculty U. Politehnica Bucharest, 1996—; mem. program com. Internat. Semiconductor Conf., Bucharest, 1985—; chair Electron Devices Romania Chpt., Bucharest, 1993-96, 99—. Author: Metal-Semiconductor Contacts in Microelectronics, 1988, Power Diodes and Thyristors, 1989; editor: Microelectronics, 1987, New Research in Microelectronics, 1994, Electron Circuits, 1999; contbr. more than 110 papers in periodicals and conf. proceedings. Recipient award Romanian Acad., Bucharest, 1974. Mem. IEEE, Electron Devices Soc. Avocations: theatre, sports, mountain climbing. Home: Drumul Taberei 64, 77387 Bucharest Romania Office: Electronics/Telecomm Fac, I Maniu 1-2, 77202 Bucharest Romania

BRÉZÍLLON, OLÍVÍER, license company executive; b. Neuilly, France, Feb. 5, 1959; s. Claude and Jacqueline (Desnos de Kerjean) B. M degree, Law U. French mgr. Modi Group, New Delhi, 1982-85; mgr., chief executive officer OIC Sarl License Co. and Svcs., Paris, 1984-86; chmn. bd. Parfums Jean Desprez, Paris, 1987-90, Parfums Jacomo, Paris, 1988-90, Jean D'Aveze Cosmetics, Paris, 1988-90, Daniel Hechter, Paris, 1990—. Roman Catholic. Avocations: horseback riding, tennis, jogging. Home: 9 rue Leverrier, 75006 Paris France Office: Daniel Hechter, 4, Ter Ave Hoche, 75008 Paris France

BREZINKA, WOLFGANG, educator; b. Berlin, June 9, 1928; s. Josef and Hildegard (Kreis) B.; m. Erika Schleifer, Dec. 17, 1954; children: Christoph, Veronika, Thomas. Lic. phil., U. Salzburg, 1949; PHD, U. Innsbruck, 1951. Asst. Inst. Comparative Edn., Salzburg, Austria, 1951-55; lectr. edn. U. Innsbruck, 1954-58; rsch. scholar Columbia U., N.Y.C., 1957-58, Harvard U., Cambridge, Mass., 1957-58; prof. edn. Tchrs. Coll. U. Würzburg, Germany, 1958-60, Inst. Edn., U. Innsbruck, 1960-67; prof. dept. educology U. Konstanz, Germany, 1967-96. Author: Erziehung als Lebenshilfe, 1957, Italian transl., 1972, Persian transl., 1992, Metatheorie der Erziehung, 1971, Italian transl., 1980, Japanese transl., 1990, English transl., 1992, Grundbegriffe der Erziehungswissenschaft, 1974, Italian transl., 1976, Japanese transl., 1980, Spanish transl., 1990, English transl., 1993, Die Pädagogik der Neuen Linken, 1972, Italian transl., 1974, Japanese transl., 1975, Norwegian transl., 1977, Spanish transl., 1988, Erziehungsziele, Erziehungsmittel, Erziehungserfolg, 1976, English transl., 1997, Erziehung in einer wertunsicheren Gesellschaft, 1986, Italian transl., 1989, Spanish transl., 1990, Japanese transl., 1992, Korean transl., 1997, Tüchtigkeit, 1987, Aufkeärung über Erziehungsthedrien, 1989, English transl. 1994, Glaube, Moral und Erziehung, 1992, Italian transl., 1994, English transl., 1994, Japanese transl., 1995, Czech transl., 1996, Pädagogik in Österreich.die Geschichte des Faches an den Universitäten vom 18 bis zum Ende des 20, Jahrhunderts, 2000. Bd. dirs. Austrian Inst. of Youth Affairs, Vienna, 1961-67, Fed. Coun. Youth Affairs, Bonn, 1965-69; cons. Ctrl. Com. German Caths., 1979-83; ednl. cons. Irish Jour. Edn., 1967—. Smith Mundt and Fulbright grantee, 1957; Tiroler Adlerorden in Gold, Govt. Tirol, Austria, 1984. Mem. Comparative Edn. Soc. Europe, Austrian Acad. Scis., Profl. Assn. Austrian Psychologists, German Soc. Educology, Austrian Soc. Philosophy. Mem. Christian Democratic Union. Roman Catholic. Home: Gagers 29, A6165 Telfes im Stubai Tirol, Austria

BREZIS, HAIM, mathematician; b. Riom es Montagnes, France, June 1, 1944; s. Jacob and Rebecca (Kanner) B.; m. Michal Govrin; children: Rachel, Miriam. Doctorat, U. Paris, 1971; Doctorat Honoris Causa, U. Louvain (Belgium), 1996, Technion of Israel, 1998, U. Bucarest, 2000. Prof. maths. U. Paris, 1972—; vis. disting. prof. Rutgers U., N.J., 1988—; hon. prof. Academia Sinica, Beijing, Fudan U., Shanghai. Author: Analyse Fonctionelle, 1983, (with F. Bethuel, F. Helein) Ginzburg-Landau Vortices, 1994. Recipient E. Catalan prize Royal Acad., Belgium, 1990, Grand Prix award Acad. Sci. Paris, 1985. Mem. AAAS (fgn. hon.), Acad. Sci. Paris, Acad. Europaea, Acad. Romana, Royal Acad. Scis. Madrid. Home: 18 Rue de la Glacière, 75013 Paris France Office: Analyse Numerique U Paris 6, 4 pl Jussieu, 75252 Paris Cedex 05, France

BRIAN, A(LEXIS) MORGAN, JR., lawyer; b. New Orleans, Oct. 4, 1928; s. Alexis Morgan and Evelyn (Thibaut) B.; m. Elizabeth Louise Graham, 1951; children: Robert Morgan, Ellen Graham. BA, La. State U., 1949; MS, Trinity U., 1954; JD, La. State U., 1956. Bar: La. 1956, U.S. Supreme Ct. 1971. Assoc. Deutsch, Kerrigan & Stiles, New Orleans, 1956-60, ptnr., 1961-79; sr. ptnr. Brian, Simon, Peragine, Smith & Redfearn, New Orleans, 1979-82, Fawer, Brian, Hardy & Zatzkis, New Orleans, 1982-86; sole practice New Orleans, 1986—; spl. asst. to La. Atty. Gen., 1982-87; spkr. profl. seminars; lectr. Inst. CLE, La. State U. Law Ctr., 1972—. Contbr. articles to profl. jours. Local merit badge counselor Boy Scouts Am., 1963—; bd. dirs. Goodwill Industries New Orleans, 1969-84, v.p., mem. exec. com., 1975-77, mem. adv. bd., 1978, 86—; life deacon, past chmn., trustee, pres., lay preacher, Bible tchr., mem. coms. 1st Bapt. Ch., New Orleans; spkrs. convs., confs. So. Bapt. Conv., 1956—, La. Bapt. Conv., 1956—, Am. Platform Assn.; past pres., trustee New Orleans Bapt. Theol. Sem., 1961-74; bd. dirs. New Orleans Bapt. Theol. Sem. Found., 1972-81, Inter-Varsity Christian Fellowship, 1974—, La. State U. Found., 1976-81; mem. nat. legal adv. coun. Ams. United for Separation of Ch. and State, 1977—. Staff sgt. USAF, 1951-55. Recipient Boss of Yr. award New Orleans Legal Secs. Assn., 1966. Mem. ABA (TIPS fidelity and surety com., forum com. constrn. industry), La. State Bar Assn. (asst. examiner comm. on bar admissions 1968-89, fidelity, surety and constrn. sect. 1991—), New Orleans Bar Assn., Internat. Assn. Def. Counsel (vice chmn. fidelity and surety com. 1978-79, archs., engrs. and constrn. litig. com., advocacy com.), La. Assn. Def. Counsel, Def. Rsch. Inst., Am. Arbitration Assn. (arbitrator 1970—), La. Civil Svc. League, Internat. Ho., La. State U. Alumni Fedn. (life), Trinity U. Alumni Assn., La. State U. Law Ctr. Alumni Assn. (life) Upper Carrollton Neighborhood Assn. (v.p. 1976), Christian Legal Soc., Theta Xi, Phi Delta Phi. Democrat. Fax: (504) 895-4803. E-mail: ambrian@bellsouth.net. Home: 5216 Pitt St New Orleans LA 70115-4107 Office: Box 534 5500 Prytania St New Orleans LA 70115-4237

BRIAN, ROBERT FRANCIS, parliamentary librarian; b. Utrecht, The Netherlands, Nov. 11, 1938; arrived in Australia, 1953; s. Franciscus Antonius and Louisa Johanna (Spierings) B.; m. Maureen Anne Callachor, May 9, 1968; children: Kathryn Louise, Patrick James, Monica Frances. BA, Australian Nat. U., Canberra, 1964; diploma in librarianship, U. New South Wales, Kensington, Australia, 1966. Librarian Nat. Library of Australia, Canberra, 1965-67, High Ct. Australia, Sydney, N.S.W., 1967-70; law librarian U. New South Wales, 1970-91; parliamentary librarian New South Wales Parliament, 1992—; cons. High Ct. Australia, Canberra, 1984, James Cook U., North Queensland, Townsville, 1986, Bond U., Robina, Queensland, Australia, 1988-89, Queensland U. Tech., Brisbane, 1989, Murdoch U., Perth, Australia, 1989, U. Western Sydney, 1990-92. Author: Librarians and Australian Copyright Law: An Exposition of the Law in Simplified Form, 1981. Mem. univ. coun., U. New South Wales, 1981-85; pres., Wunanbiri Aboriginal Pre-Sch. Com., Surry Hills, New South wales, 1985-86; dep. chmn., Cath. Edn. Commn., New South Wales, 1986-88. Mem. Australian Libr. and Info. Assn. (acting exec. dir. 1977), Internat. Fedn. Libr. Assns. and Instns. (mem. standing com. govt. info. and ofcl. publs. sect. 1998—), Internat. Assn. Law Librs. (bd. dirs. 1980-83), Australian Law Librs. Group (founding), Ea. Suburbs Leagues Club. E-mail: Rob.Brian@parliament.nsw.gov.au. Home: 28 Lancaster Rd, Dover Heights 2030, Australia Office: Parliament House, Macquarie St, Sydney 2000, Australia

BRIAND, FREDERIC, environmental scientist; b. Paris, Nov. 1, 1949. BSc, U. Paris, 1969; PhD, U. Calif., Irvine, 1974. Prof. environ. sci. U. Ottawa, Can., 1974-85; vis. prof. Mus. Nat. Natural History, Paris, 1985-86; dir. ecol. programs IUCN World Conservation Union, Switzerland, 1986-89; dir. population programs UNESCO, Morocco, 1989-91; dir. gen. Internat. Commn. Mediterranean Sci., CIESM, Monaco, 1991—; founder, v.p. Internat. Ctr. Alpine Environ.-ICALPE, Trento, Italy, 1988—; adminstr. Monaco Sci. Ctr., 1992—; advisor European Parliament, 1993—; whaling commr. IWC, 1994—. Author: Pollution of the Mediterranean Sea, 1994; co-author: Community Food Webs, 1990, The Alps: A System Under Pressure, 1990; editor: CIESM Mediterranean Science Series, 1995—, CIESM Atlas of Exotic Species in the Mediterranean Sea, 2000. Office: 16 Bd de Suisse, MC98000 Monte Carlo Monaco

BRIASOULIS, EVANGELOS, medical oncologist, consultant; b. Trikala, Greece, Jan. 27, 1953; s. Cristos E. and Alexandra T. (Karamani) B.; m. Smaro Mavroudi, July, 13, 1980; children: Alexandra, Orestis. Degree in theology, U. Athens, Greece, 1975, degree in medicine, 1982; Doctor, U. Ionnina, Greece, 1998. Intern in internal medicine 1st Pub. Hosp., Athens, 1984-89; head med. dept. Pub. Health Ctr., Aliartos, Greece, 1989-90; sr. registrar in med. oncology Ioannina Univ. Hosp., 1990-93, med. oncologist, 1993-94, sr. med. oncologist, 1996-98, cons. head early drug devel. unit, 1998—. Clin. rsch. fellow Ctr. Cancer Therapeutics, ICR and Royal Marsden Hosp., London, 1994-95. Mem. Brit. Assn. Cancer Rsch., European Soc. Med. Oncology, European Assn. Cancer Rsch., Am. Soc. Clin. Oncology, European Orgn. Rsch. Treatment of Cancer, Hellenic Assn. Med. Oncology, N.Y. Acad. Scis. Greek Orthodox. Avocations: climbing, music. E-mail: ebriasou@otenet.gr. Fax: 30-651-99394. Office: Ioannina Univ Hosp, Panepistimiou 1, 450 00 Ioannina Epirus, Greece

BRIBES, JEAN-LUC, chemistry educator; b. Montpelier, France, Apr. 4, 1940; s. Pierre and Louise-Marie (Masson) B.; m. Françoise Boyon, July 30, 1966; children: Marie Sophie, Estelle Bérengère, Pierre-Philippe. Lic. Phys. Sci., U. Montpellier II, 1964, Doctorat de 3 cycle, 1968, Doctorat d'Etat, 1971. Asst. U. Montpellier II, 1966-71, maître-asst., 1971-85, prof. lab. materials and membranes processes, 1985—; pensionnaire Maison Franco-Japonaise, Tokyo, 1972-74; maître de Conf. U. Yaounde, Cameroon, 1976-79. Contbr. articles to sci. jours. Mem. Soc. Française de Chimie. Roman Catholic. Avocation: general aviation VFR pilot. Office: U Montpellier II, Pl E Bataillon, 34095 Montpellier France

BRICE, CHARLES STEVEN, airline executive; b. Columbus, Ohio, Feb. 13, 1951; s. Charles Simonton Jr. and Rita Eva (Kuder) B.; m. Darlene Lynn

Call, Sept. 13, 1978 (div. June 1986); m. Sally Ann Minard, Sept. 20, 1997; children: Marissa Kay and Jessica Victoria (twins). BA, San Francisco State U., 1974. Lic. FAA airframe and power plant. Ops. mgr. Lockheed Aircraft Co., San Francisco, 1979-83; mgr. ramp svcs. Northwest Airlines, San Francisco, 1983-88, mgr. passenger svcs., 1988-92, dir. customer svc. and ground ops., 1992—; vice-chmn. bd. dirs. San Francisco Fgn. Flag Carriers, 1997—; chmn. Sta. Mgrs. Am. Transport/SFO, San Francisco, 1994, chmn. security com., 1995. Bd. dirs. March of Dimes, San Mateo County, Calif., 1994-95; mem., airline advisory bd. Calif. Dept. Agr., Sacramento, 1991-92; mem. adv. bd. San Francisco City Coll., 1988—. Mem. Commonwealth Club. Avocations: skiing, hiking, golf, tennis. Home: 153 N San Mateo Dr Apt 410 San Mateo CA 94401-2775 Office: NW Airlines San Francisco Inter Airport San Francisco CA 94128

BRICEL, MARK LEON, marketing executive; b. Ljubljana, Slovenia, Apr. 11, 1929; s. Ivan John and Ivanka (Kregar) B.; m. Liselotte Ringer, Mar. 10, 1951; children: Gary, Tania. Student, Air Force Acad, Mostar, Bosnia and Herzegovina, 1948, Nautical Acad., Rijeka, Croatia, 1949. Lic. pvt. pilot. Exec. v.p. Toni Sailer Ski Co., Montreal, Que., Can., 1960-64; supr. G.M. Plastic Corp., Granby, Quebec, Can., 1964-66; gen. sales mgr. G.M. Plastic Corp./GMP Sports Ltd., Granby, 1966-70, G.M.P. Sports, Inc., Westport, Conn., 1967-70; exec. v.p. House of Colonial Furniture Ltd., Montreal, 1970-75; gen. sales agt. Arcese Bros. Furniture Ltd., Missisauga, Ont., Can., 1976-96; pres. M.L. Bricel Agys. Ltd., Missisauga, 1984—, M.L Bricel Mktg. and Sales, Inc., Naples, Fla., 1991—, Progressive Mktg., Ltd., Hamilton, Bermuda, 1992—, M.L. Bricel Mktg., & Sales, Ltd., Mississauga, Ont., Can., 1999—; dir. mktg. and sales Arcese Bros. Furniture Ltd., Mississauga, 1991-96, VR Furniture Inc., Brampton, Ont., Can., 1997—. Served to lt. Yugoslav Air Force, 1946-48. Recipient Silver Medal award FIS, 1947. Mem. Can. Owners and Pilots Assn., Royal Can. Flying Clubs Assn. (Blue Seal 1984), Blue Springs Golf Club. Roman Catholic. Avocations: photography, flying, golfing. Office: Unit 2, 2170 Dunwin Dr, Mississauga, ON Canada L5L 5M8 Office: ML Bricel Mktg & Sales Inc 603 Serendipity Dr Naples FL 34108-2829

BRICHON, PIERRE-YVES, cardiothoracic surgeon; b. Annecy, France, Oct. 10, 1954; s. Pierre and Jeannine (Mallinjoud) B.; m. Nathalie Dragone, Sept. 4, 1993. MD, U. Grenoble, 1983. From resident to head dept. cardiothoracic surgery Univ. Hosp., Grenoble, France, 1979—. Mem. European Assn. Cardiothoracic Surgery. Avocations: golf, tennis. Home: 4 place Jean Achard, 38000 Grenoble France

BRICKER, WILLIAM RUDOLPH, organization executive; b. Reading, Pa., May 5, 1923; s. William Theodore and Elsie Elizabeth (Weber) B.; m. Eleanor Schubert, June 9, 1945; children: Cynthia Anne (Mrs. Mark Hilgendorf), William Randall, Suzanne Lee (Mrs. William Sullivan). B.S., Millersville (Pa.) U., 1947; M.A. (Hayden grad. fellow), NYU, 1948; D.H.L., George Williams Coll., 1980. Exec. dir. Boys' Clubs Am., 1948-72, nat. dir., ceo, 1972-89; chmn. Nat. Collaboration for Youth, 1975; mem. U.S. Pres.'s Commn. for Juvenile Justice and Delinquency Prevention, 1975; mem. adv. bd. Nat. Inst. Justice, 1975, U.S. Pres. Commn. Employment, 1978; bd. dirs. U.S. Congl. Award, 1979; trustee Nat. Commn. for Coop. Edn., 1980. Mem. U.S. Pres. Commn. on Pvt. Sector Initiatives, 1982, U.S. Pres. UNESCO Commn, 1984; vice chmn. U.S. Presdl. Commn. on Child Safety, 1986; trustee Freedoms Found., 1986; chmn. U.S. Nat. Panel for Teen Pregnancy, 1987; U.S. Presdl. envoy to UNESCO, 1985, Micronesia, 1987; adv. bd. Cummings Meml. Fund, 1988; vice chmn. Jamestown Philomenian Libr., 1989; bd. dirs. R.I. Facilities Authority, 2000; vice chmn. Nat. PPF Found., 2000. Air group comdr. USN, 1942-45, 50-70. Mem. Soc. Mil. Horologists, (pres. 1995). Avocations: aviation, horology, management.

BRICKEY, SUZANNE M., editor; b. Grand Rapids, Mich., Apr. 4, 1951; d. Robert Michael and Elizabeth (Rogers) Stankey; m. Homer Brickey, Jr. B.A., Ohio U., Athens, 1973; B.J., U. Mo., Columbia, 1977. Editor Living Today, The Blade, Toledo, 1980-82, Toledo Mag., The Blade, 1982-92, Living Today, Toledo, 1992—. Mem. Toledo Press Club, Toledo Rowing Club. Home: 2510 Kenwood Blvd Toledo OH 43606-3601 Office: The Blade 541 N Superior St Toledo OH 43660-0001

BRICKHILL, WILLIAM LEE, international finance consultant; b. Rahway, N.J., Oct. 13, 1937; s. William Welch and Wilma Eloise (Gay) Mumford; m. Margaret A. Stempel, June 16, 1961 (div. 1971); children: William L., Barbara A., Cynthia A., Robert L.; m. Joan Marie Ward, May 19, 1988. Student, U. Ga., 1957, Sophia U., Tokyo, 1958-60; BBA, George Washington U., 1970. Lic. comml. and instrument rated pilot. Internat. specialist Am. Security & Trust Co., Washington, 1960-62; loan officer Export-Import Bank of U.S., Washington, 1962-90, dep. mgr. contract adminstrn., 1990-91, dep. v.p. contract adminstrn., 1991-94, ret., 1994; cons. internat. fin., 1994—. Contbr. articles to profl. jours. With U.S. Army, 1956-58, Germany. Mem. Nat. Capital Bromeliad Soc. (1st v.p. 1991—), Nat. Capital Orchid Soc., Gem, Mineral and Lapidary Soc. (bd. dirs., v.p. 1965-75). Roman Catholic. Avocations: aviation, botany, horticulture, woodworking. Home and Office: 6338 Phyllis Ln Alexandria VA 22312-6402

BRICKL, ROLF STEFAN, pharmacokineticist; b. Munich, Oct. 8, 1944; s. Stefan and Anna (Ostermeier) B.; m. Christl Weigel, Dec. 19, 1969; children: Andreas, Evelyne. Diploma in chemistry, Tech. U. Munich, 1969, PhD in Chemistry, 1971. Group leader Boehringer Ingelheim Pharma Deutschland, Biberach, Germany, 1972—; presenter in field. Contbr. over 30 articles to scientific jours.; patentee n fields of new dermatol. agts. and improved pharm. formulations. Recipient Oscar-Gans prize, Basotherm, 1980. Mem. Drug Info. Assn., Controlled Release Soc., Arbeitsgemeinschaft für Angewandte Humanpharmakologie. Avocations: sports, video. Home: Erlenweg 37, D-88447 Warthausen Germany Office: Boehringer Ingelheim Pharma, Birkendorfer Str 65, D-88397 Biberach Germany

BRICKMAN, LESTER, law educator; b. N.Y.C., Sept. 4, 1940; s. Frank B. and Lillian (Bernstein) B.; m. Miriam Dorf; 1 child, Anna. BS in Chemistry, Carnegie Tech. INst., 1961; JD, U. Fla., 1964; LLM, Yale U., 1965. Bar: N.Y. 1977, U.S. Ct. Appeals (3d and 5th cirs.). Prof. of law U. Toledo, 1965-69, 70-76, Cardozo Law Sch., N.Y.C., 1976—; acting dean Cordozo Law Sch., N.Y.C., 1980-82; cons. Adminstrv. Conf. of U.S., Washington, 1991, U.S. Office of Edn., Washington, 1978-88, NSF, Washington, 1975, Ford Found., N.Y.C., 1970-71. Co-editor: The Role of Research in the Delivery of Legal Services, 1976; co-author monograph: Rethinking Contingency Fees, 1994. Mem. Mayor's Com. on Judiciary, N.Y.C., 1981-82. Mem. Assn. of Bar of City of N.Y. (com. on profl. responsibility 1990-93, com. on profl. and jud. ethics 1994-97), N.Y. State Bar Assn. (com. on profl. ethics 1985-87). Avocation: wine. Office: Cardozo Law Sch 55 5th Ave New York NY 10003-4301

BRIDGE, JOHN WILLIAM, law educator; b. Crewkerne, Eng., Feb. 2, 1937; s. Harry and Rebecca (Lilley) B.; m. Jane Faith Hearn, July 28, 1962; 1 child, Susan Elizabeth. LLB, U. Bristol, Eng., 1959, LLM, 1962, PhD, 1973. Lectr., then sr. lectr. U. Exeter, Eng., 1961-74, prof. pub. law, 1974—, dean of law, 1979-82, head dept. law, 1983-88, 97-99, dep. vice chancellor, 1992-96; vis. prof. Coll. of William and Mary, Williamsburg, Va., 1977-78, 97, U. Conn., Hartford, 1985, 91, U. Mauritius, 1987, U. Fribourg, Switzerland, 1990; chmn. U.K. Nat. Com. on Comparative Law, London, 1992—. Author: European Community Law, 1972-94, European Legislation, 1975, Fundamental Rights, 1975; contbr. articles to profl. pubs. Fulbright Commn. sr. scholar, 1977-78, 91-92; vis. fellow All Souls Coll., Oxford, Eng., 1988-89. Fellow Soc. for Advanced Legal Studies (hon.); mem. Internat. Acad. Comparative Law, Soc. Pub. Tchrs. of Law. Mem. Ch. of England. Avocations: music, gardening, family history. Office: U Exeter, Amory Bldg Rennes Dr, Exeter Devon EX4 4RJ, England

BRIDGE, T(HOMAS) PETER, psychiatrist, researcher; b. Nashville, June 2, 1945; s. Thomas Gale and Hilma Elizabeth (Hartzler) B.; m. Mary L. Matthews, Dec. 15, 1969 (div. Sept. 1974); m. Beth J. Soldo, Sept. 20, 1975. BA, Duke U., 1967; MD, Med. Coll. Va., 1971. Diplomate Am. Bd. Psychiatry and Neurology. Rsch. fellow Duke U., Durham, N.C., 1972-74; clin. staff fellow NIMH, Bethesda, Md., 1977-79; chief unit on geriatrics NIMH, Washington, 1980-83; sci. advisor Alcohol, Drug, and Mental Health Adminstrn., Rockville, Md., 1983-86, AIDS coord., 1986-90; chief clin. trials br. Nat. Inst. on Drug Abuse, Rockville, 1990—. Editor: AIDS Neuropsychiatry, 1989; contbr. more than 75 articles to profl. jours. Named J.D. Lane Outstanding Investigator, USPHS, 1984; recipient New Investigator award Am. Geriatrics Soc., 1985, Sec.'s Disting. Svc. award DHHS, 2000. Fellow Coll. Internat. Neuropsychopharmacology; mem. AAAS, Am. Coll. Neuropsychopharmacology. Achievements include patents for novel pharmacologic treatments for cognitive enhancement, chronic fatigue, and psoriasis. Home: 2910 Brandywine St NW Washington DC 20008-2138 Office: CTB MDD NIDA 11a55 5600 Fishers Ln Rockville MD 20857-0001

BRIDGER, ALISON FRANCES COLVILL, meteorologist, researcher, educator; b. Hove, Sussex, Eng., Feb. 13, 1953; came to U.S., 1975; d. Anthony Paul Colvill and Audrey Dorothy Vera (Whymark) B.; 1 child, Andrew. BSc, Sussex U., Brighton, Eng., 1974; MSc, Reading (Eng.) U., 1975; PhD, Colo. State U., 1981. Postdoctoral fellow Nat. Ctr. for Atmospheric Rsch., Boulder, Colo., 1981-83, McGill U., Montreal, 1983-84; asst. prof. San Jose (Calif.) State U., 1984-88, assoc. prof., 1988-95, prof., 1995—; rschr. NASA Ames, Mountain View, Calif., 1991—. Editor: Fundamentals of Atmospheric Dynamics and Thermodynamics, 1992. Fulbright-Hayes scholar, 1975; recipient Amelia Earhart award Zonta Internat., 1979, 80. Mem. Am. Meteorol. Soc., Am. Geophys. Union, Am. Astron. Soc. Avocations: swimming, biking, watching TV, gardening. Office: San Jose State U Dept Meteorology One Washington Sq San Jose CA 95192-0104

BRIDGES, ALVIN WESLEY, security professional, business owner; b. Rockford, Ala., Oct. 17, 1919; s. Thomas Lafayette and Ola Bea Bridges; widowed; 1 child, Charlene Bridges Myers. Student, Livingston State U., 1938-39. Dept. head, warehouse V.G. Elmore 5 & 10, Clanton, Ala., 1939-41; owner Bridges grocery, Clanton, 1945-62, Dixie Cafe, Clanton, 1949-51, Bridges Clothing, Clanton, 1961-77, Clanton Sales, 1955-81; ad salesman Boone Paper Co., Clanton, 1985-94; with Twin City Security, Clanton, 1994—. With U.S. Mil., 1944-45, PTO. Republican. Avocations: reading, fishing, sports. Home: 107 Shennandoah Dr Clanton AL 35045-9601

BRIDGES, EDWIN MAXWELL, education educator; b. Hannibal, Mo., Jan. 1, 1934; s. Edwin Otto and Radha (Maxwell) B.; m. Marjorie Anne Pollock, July 31, 1954; children: Richard, Rebecca, Brian, Bruce. BS, U. Mo., 1954; MA, U. Chgo., 1956, PhD, 1964. English tchr. Bremen Community High Sch., Midlothian, Ill., 1954-56; asst. prin. Griffith (Ind.) High Sch., 1956-60, prin., 1960-62; staff assoc. U. Chgo., 1962-64, assoc. prof., 1967-72; assoc. dir. Univ. Coun. for Edn. Adminstrn., Columbus, Ohio, 1964-65; asst. prof. Washington U., St. Louis, 1965-67; assoc. prof. U. Chgo., 1967-72; prof. U. Calif., Santa Barbara, 1972-74; prof. edn. Stanford (Calif.) U., 1974—; mem. nat. adv. panel Ctr. for Rsch. on Ednl. Accountability and Tchr. Evaluation, 1990-95; external examiner U. Hong Kong, 1990-92; vis. prof. Chinese U., Hong Kong, 1976, 96; cons. World Bank, China, 1986, 89; dir. Midwest Adminstrn. Ctr., Chgo., 1967-72. Author: Managing the Incompetent Teacher, 1984, 2d edit., 1990, The Incompetent Teacher, 1986, 2d edit., 1991, Problem Based Learning for Administrators, 1992; co-author: Introduction to Educational Adminstration, 1977, Implementing Problem-based Leadership Development, 1995. Recipient of the R.F. Campbell Lifetime Achievement award, 1996; named Outstanding Young Man of Ind., C. of C., 1960; named hon. prof. and cert. of honor So. China Normal U., 1989, Citation of Merit for Outstanding Achievement and Meritorious Svc. in Edn., U. Mo. Coll. Edn., 1999. Mem. Am. Ednl. Rsch. Assn. (v.p. 1974-75). Office: Stanford U Sch Edn Stanford CA 94305

BRIDGES, JULIAN CURTIS, sociologist educator, department head; b. Miami, Apr. 3, 1931; s. Clyde Clifton and Bessie Myrtle (Williams) B.; m. Charlotte Annelle Martin, Aug. 24, 1954; children: Rebecca Ann, Deborah Lea Gil, Esther Marelyn Shedd. AB, U. Fla., 1952; BD, ThD, Southwestern Bapt. Theol. Sem., Ft. Worth, 1956, 61; MA, U. Fla., 1968, PhD, 1973. Cert. family life educator; lic. marriage and family therapist. Pastor So. Bapt. Conv., Dallas, Rhome, Tex., 1953-59; rep. in Mexico Fgn. Mission Bd., Mexico City, 1959-73; prof., dept. head sociology Hardin-Simmons U., Abilene, Tex., 1973—; cons. William Jewel Coll., Liberty, Mo., 1984; prof. sociology and ethics Bapt. Theol. Sem., Madrid, Spain, 1981, Arusha, Tanzania, 1987, Hong Kong Bapt. U., 1991. Editor, sr. author: Sociology: A Pragmatic Approach, 1986; author: Celulas de Companerismo Cristiano, 1965, Expansion Evangelica en Mexico, 1973, Into Aztec Land, 1968; contbr. articles to profl. jours. and encys. Mem. city coun. City of Abilene, 1982-85, mayor pro tem, 1984-85, mem. human rels. com., 1988-96, pres. 1995-96; chair election com. Atty. Gen., State of Tex., Taylor County, 1984; v.p., bd. dirs. Mental Health Mental Retardation, Abilene, 1985-88; pres. bd. Harmony Family Svcs., Abilene, 1992-93, Harmony Family Svcs. Holding Co., 1998—, City Light Cmty. Ministries, 1997—. Recipient Faculty Rsch. award Hardin-Simmons U., 1985, Amigo award Hispanic Heritage Commn., 1996; Lily Found. Teaching fellow, Southwestern Bapt. Theol. Sem., Ft. Worth, 1957-58; named Nat. Def. Edn. Act Title VI fellow U. Fla., 1969-70. Mem. Tex. Coun. on Family Rels. (pres. 1983-84), Southwestern Sociol. Assn., Am. Assn. Marriage & Family Therapists, Abilene Southwest Rotary Club (bd. dirs., pres.-elect 2000—). Baptist. Avocation: community svc. Home: 1526 N Pioneer Dr Abilene TX 79603-4035 Office: HSU PO Box 16216 Abilene TX 79698-0001

BRIDGES, PAUL KENNETH, psychiatrist, consultant; b. London, July 24, 1931; s. Albert Charles and Alice Elizabeth (Paul) B. MB, BS, U. London, 1956, DPM, 1960, MD, 1965, PhD, 1969. Psychiat. registrar, rsch. fellow Royal Free Hosp., London, 1960-63; sr. psychiat. registrar Kings Coll. Hosp., London, 1963-65; sr. lectr. Royal Free Hosp., London, 1965-70; cons. psychiatrist Guys Hosp., London, 1970-96; sr. lectr. United Med. and Dental Schs. Guy Hosp., U. London, 1975-96, Maudsley Hosp., London, 1995—; examiner med. degrees U. London, 1982-86, examiner clin. pharmacology, 1993-96; assessor Nat. Health and Med. Rsch. Coun., Australia, 1984-90. Author: Psychiatric Emergencies, 1971, (with others) Psychiatry for Students, 1989, New Directions in Affective Disorders, 1989, Handbook of Affective Disorders, 1992, Depression: Neurobiological, Psychopathological and Therapeutic Advances, 1997, Clinical Neurology, 1998. Maj. Royal Army M.C., 1957-60. Fellow Royal Soc. Medicine (pres. psychiatry sect. 1983-84), Brit. Assn. Psychopharmacology (hon. treas. 1974-79, hon. sec. 1981-83); mem. Collegium Internationale Neuropsychopharmacologicum, Royal Automobile Club (London). Avocation: British country houses. Office: Guy's Hospital Keats House, 24-26 St Thomas St, London SE1 9RT, England

BRIDGES, ROBERT SEYMOUR, environmental engineer; b. Guildford, Eng., Oct. 15, 1944; s. Wilfrid Edward Seymour and Mary Winifred (Cameron) B.; m. Laraine Olwen, Dec. 7, 1996; children: Ian Paul, Paul Anthony, Michael Philip, David Raymond, David Robert. BSc in Engring. 1st class, U. London, 1968; MSc, MPhil in Biomechanics, U. Surrey, 1977; PhD, Jundi Shapur U., 1978; MBA with distinction, Kingston U., 1988. European engr.; chartered engr., Engring. Coun. Project engr. Westland Helicopters, Somerset, England, 1968-70; lectr. engring. Kingston U., Surrey, England, 1970-74; head biomechanics Jundi Shapur U., Ahvaz, Iran, 1978-79; tech. dir. Applied Dynamics Ltd., Surrey, 1979-82; engring. dir. Portals Holdings plc, Surrey, 1982-88; mng. dir. Normond Environ. Sys. Ltd., England, 1988-92, Micrelec Environ. plc, Surrey, 1992; CEO Thyme Mgmt. Ltd., Surrey, 1992—, MassTech. Internat. Ltd., Fleetwood Mobiles Ltd., The Pensford Consulting Group Ltd.; vis. prof. Kingston U., Surrey, 1994—. Co-author: Organisational Analysis, 1988, Operations Management, 1990; author: The Management of Change, 1992, Management Consultancy, 1997; patentee in field. Lt. Royal British Navy, 1974-78. Decorated Queens Silver Jubilee medal. Fellow Inst. Dirs., Instn. Mech. Engrs. (chmn. selection panel 1989-94), Instn. Elec. Engrs., Inst. Mgmt.; mem. Inst. Petroleum, Engring. Coun. (chmn. 1987-90). Mem. Ch. of England. Home: 20 Pensford Close, Crowthorne RG45 6QR, England Office: MassTech Internat Ltd, 20 Pensford House, Crowthorne RG45 6QR, England

BRIDGES, RONALD CLAUDE, medical records clerk; b. San Antonio, Tex., Dec. 6, 1938; s. Claude Raymond Bridges and Winnie Mae Scott. Enlisted U.S. Army, 1973, advanced through ranks to staff sgt., heavy elec. engr., 1959-62, armour crewman tank comdr., 1965-68, personnel mgmt., 1970-84; med. records clk. South Tex. Vets. Health Care System, Kerrville, 1984—. Decorated Vietnamese Cross of Gallantry with palm Rep. of Vietnam, Grant of Arms, Count de Sare (Umberto II of Italy), Cascals, Portugal, 1966, Cert. of Arms, Cronista Rey de Arms, madrid, 1978, Register Arms, Min. of Justice, Madrid, 1978, Army Commendation medal U.S. Army, Matriculation of Arms, The Ct. of the Lord Lyon, Edinburgh, Scotland, 1991, Register Arms, Hist. Assn. Modling, Austria, 1995. Mem. Nat. Geographic Soc., Royal Asiatic Soc., Heraldry Soc. of Scotland, Clan Scott Soc., Disabled Am. Vets. (life), Scots of the Tex. Hill Country, SAR, Ecumenical Confraternity of St. Sepulchre of Jerusalem. Republican. Avocations: heraldry, heraldic art, collecting books, Korean porcelain, art prints, and coins. Home: PO Box 457 Center Point TX 78010-0457 Office: South Tex Vets Health Care 3600 Memorial Blvd Kerrville TX 78028-5768

BRIDGMAN, HOWARD ALLEN, environmental scientist, geography educator; b. Boston, Nov. 9, 1944; arrived in Australia, 1977; s. Howard Allen and Esther Campbell (Floyd) B.; m. Diana Claire Kozlousky, June 22, 1974; children: Howard Allen, Heather Ann. BA, Beloit Coll., 1966; MA, U. Hawaii, 1968; PhD, U. Wis., 1977. Vis. scientist climate monitoring & diagnostic lab. Nat. Oceanographic & Atmospheric Adminstrn., Boulder, Colo., 1986-87, 92-93; vis. scientist Environ. Can., Toronto, Ont., 1992; assoc. prof. geography U. Newcastle, NSW, Australia, 1977—, chairperson bd. environ. studies, 1980-81, 82-85, coord. environ. sci., 1993—; cons. NSW Dept. State Devel., Newcastle, 1992-93, Cleanaway/Brambles, Newcastle, 1990-91, NSW Dept. Pub. Works, Newcastle, 1983-84; vis. fellow Sch. Environ. Sci. Univ. East Anglia, Norwich, Eng. Author: Global Air Pollution Problems for the 1990s, 1990, Urban Physical Environments, 1996, Climates of the Southern Hemisphere, 1998, contbr. over 70 articles to sci. jours. Founding pres. Newcastle Univ. Choir, 1979-85; air quality advisor Hunter Devel. Bd. and Newcastle City Coun., 1977—; active Hunter Opera Co., Newcastle, 1990—, Hunter Orch. Soc., Friends of the Conservatorium; sec. Wallsend Jr. Soccer Club, 1991-92, past team coach; field asst. Waratah/Mayfield Little Athletics; badge tester Lambton Girl Guides; former coach girls basketball, Newcastle City League. 1st lt. USAF, 1969-71. Recipient Environ. Achievement award Bd. Environ. Studies, 1991. Fellow Clean Air Soc. (Australia and New Zealand chpts.); mem. Am. Geophys. Union, Am. Meteorol. Soc., Assn. Am. Geographers, Austria-New Zealand Assn. for Advancement of Sci., Royal Meteorol. Soc. (mem. founding com. Sydney br. 1978-80), Australian Meteorol. and Oceanog. Soc., Inst. Australian Geographers, Australia-New Zealand Clean Air Soc., Hunter Environ. Inst., Am. Philatelic Soc., Newcastle Philatelic Soc., Sigma Xi. Office: Univ Newcastle, Dept Geography, NSW Newcastle 2308, Australia

BRIDGWATER, JOHN, chemical engineering educator; b. Birmingham, Eng., Jan. 10, 1938; s. Eric and Mary (Thornley) B.; m. Diane Louise Tucker, Dec. 29, 1962; children: Eric, Caroline. BA, U. Cambridge, 1959, PhD, 1973, ScD, 1986; MSE, Princeton (N.J.) U., 1961. Chartered engr. Royal Acad. Engring. Rsch. asst. Princeton U., 1960-61; chem. engr. Courtaulds, Coventry, 1961-64; demonstrator, lectr. U. Cambridge, 1964-71, Shell prof. chem. engring., 1993—, head dept. chem. engring., 1993-98; Esso sr. rsch. fellow, lectr. U. Oxford, 1971-80; prof. chem. engring. U. Birmingham, 1980-93, head dept. chem. engring., 1983-90, dean Sch. Engring., 1989-92; vis. prof. U. B.C., 1970-71, U. Calif., Berkeley, 1992-93; pres. Instn. of Chem. Engrs., London, 1997-98; Lubbock fellow Balliol Coll., Oxford, 1973-80. Author: (with others) Paste Flow and Extrusion, 1993; chmn. editl. bd. Chem. Engring. Sci. Jour., 1984—. Office: Dept Chem Engr U Cambridge, Pembroke St, Cambridge CB2 3RA, England

BRIDGWATER, RODEN JOHN, chemical company executive; b. Stoke, Staffs, Eng., Oct. 19, 1926; s. Edward Roden and Minnie Bridgwater; m. Gladys May Goode; children: Roden, Jacqueline, Katrina, Janet Odette. BS, Nottingham (Eng.) U., 1947; PhD, Swansea (Wales) U., 1951. Demonstrator UNN Swansea, 1948-51; lectr. Guys Hosp. Med. Sch., London, 1951-63; owner Maybridge Chem. Co. Ltd., Tintagel, Cornwall, Eng., 1963-97. Home: Little Manor Widemouth Bay, Bude EX23 0AQ, England

BRIE, ANDRE, member European parliament; b. Schwerin, Fed. Republic Germany, Mar. 13, 1950. Mem. European Parliament, Berlin, 1999—; mem. Confederal Group of the European United Left/Nordic Green Left, European Parliament; mem. com. on fgn. affairs, human rights, common security and def. policy; substitute mem. com. on employment and social affairs, com. on petitions; mem. delegation for rels. with Israel. Office: PestalozzistraBe 37, D-13187 Berlin Germany*

BRIEGER, GEORGE, lawyer; b. Hungary, Apr. 30, 1966; came to the U.S., 1977; s. Jenö and Miriam Brieger. BS in Computer Sci., Bklyn. Coll., 1988; postgrad., Yeshiva U., 1988-90, JD, 1993. Bar: N.Y. 1994, U.S. Dist. Ct. (so. and ea. dists.) N.Y. 1995, U.S. Ct. Internat. Trade, 1999. Internat. counsel Bacher & Ptnrs. Atty. at Law, Budapest, Hungary, 1996-98; atty. Internat. Trade Litigation U.S. Customs Svc., N.Y.C., 1998—; cons. Fin. Svcs. Vol. Corps, N.Y.C., 1996. Editor New Europe Law Rev. Cardozo Sch. Law, N.Y.C., 1992-93; contbr. chpt. to book. Mem. adv. bd. Budapest-N.Y. Sister City Com., N.Y.C., 1996—. Mem. N.Y. City Bar Assn. (ctrl. and ea. European law com. 1996-98). Avocations: reading about linguistics, philosophy, Tai Chi, swimming. E-mail: georgebrieger@yahoo.com. Office: US Customs Svc 26 Federal Plz Ste 258 New York NY 10278-0107

BRIEM, SIGURDUR, personnel director; b. Reykjavik, Iceland, Aug. 25, 1936; s. Gunnlaugur and Halldora M. (Gudjohnsen) B.; m. Thora Gudrun Moeller, Aug. 30, 1969; children: Dora Kristin, Gunnar Jakob, Gunnlaugur Thor. Grad. elec. engring., Royal Inst. Tech., Sweden, 1962. Elec. engr. Reykjavik Elec. Power Works, 1963-66; head dept. electricity Icelandic Aluminum Co. Ltd., Straumsvik, Iceland, 1967-80, head dept. electrolysis, 1981-84, plant engr., 1984-90, pers. mgr., 1991—. Mem. Assn. Chartered Engrs. Iceland, Rotary. Home: Markarflot 27, 210 Gardabaer Iceland Office: Icelandic Aluminum Co Ltd, PO Box 244 Straumsvik, 222 Hafnarfjordur Iceland

BRIERLEY, PETER WILLIAM, charitable foundation administrator; b. London, Oct. 30, 1938; s. Joseph Clifford and Anne Sophia (New) B.; m. Cherry Antoinette Goatman, Apr. 3, 1965; children: Stephen, Timothy, Kim, Michael. BSc in Stats., U. London, 1961, diploma in theology, 1964; DLitt, Greenwich U., 1996. Actuarial clk. Prudential Ins. Co., 1957-58; sr. sci. officer War Office, London, 1961-62; tchr. Edn. Authority, Southampton, Eng., 1965-67; statistician Ministry of Def., London, 1967-70, Cabinet Office, London, 1970-78; program dir. Brit. Fgn. Bible Soc., London, 1978-83; European dir. MARC Europe, London, 1983-93; exec. dir. Christian Rsch. Assn., 1993—; chmn. S.E. Asian Outreach, Gravesend, Eng., 1985-92, vice chmn. 1992-97; mem. fin. com. Evang. Union S.Am., London, 1970-82, Eng. and Wales aux. Leprosy Mission, London, 1970-76, Brit. Inst. Mgmt. Coun., 1985-91, mgmt. com. Evang. Missionary Alliance, 1983-89, 90-99, vice chmn., 1989, exec. com., 1985-89, 90-99; chair Blyk Wood Bank Mgmt. Co., 1993—; chmn. mgmt. and property cos. Blyte Wood Park, 1993—. Author: Mission to London Phase I, II, 1984, 95; editor: U.K. Christian Handbook, 1973, 76, 77, 78, 81, 82, 84, 86, 88, 91, 93, 95, 97, 99, Beyond the Churches, 1984, World Churches Handbook, 1997, UKCH: Religious Trends, 1997, 99, Future Church, 1998; compiler: Vision Bldg., 1989, Christian England, 1991, Act on the Facts, 1992, Priorities, Planning and Paperwork, 1992, Reaching and Keeping Teenagers, 1993, Prospects for the Eighties vol 1, 1980, vol. 2, 1983, Prospects for Wales, 1983, Prospects for Scotland, 1985, Prospects for Scotland 2000, 1995, The Tide is Running Out, 2000, Steps to the Future, 2000, several MARC monographs, 1984-93, Leaders Briefings, 1994—; cons. editor Strategies for Growing Churches mag., 1990—. Mem. Doughty St. Internat. Students Centre Mgmt. Com., 1971-85, treas. 1973-81; mem. gen. and exec. coms. Brit. & Fgn. Bible Soc., 1976-78, staff mem.; rsch. assoc. Lausanne Com. for World Evangelisation, Europe, 1984-92, sr. assoc. for rsch., 1992—; first gov. Bullers Wood Comprehensive Sch. for Girls, 1989-94; dir. mission Christ Ch., 1994-97. EUSA Fin. sub-com., 1971-82, Doughty Street Internat. Students Ctr. Mgmt. Com., mem. Inst. Charity and Fundraising Mgrs. (steering com. 1982-83), Royal Statis. Soc. (social sect. 1980-82), Social Research Assn. (exec. com. 1979-82), Christian Booksellers Assn. (bd. dirs. 1984-88), Spinnaker Trust (coun. of reference 1987—) Crusaders (adv. coun. 1995-99, patron Inn Christian 1990—, coun. reference Monarch Pubs. 1992-99, coun. reference Outlook 1991—), Market Rsch. Soc., Brit. Ch. Growth Assn. (gen. and exec. coun. 1994—), Evangelical Alliance Coun., Assn. Rsch. Ctrs. in Social Scis. (mem. exec. com. 1998—, treas. 2000—). Mem. Anglican. Avocations: reading, making math. models, collecting postmarks and stamps, ch. activities. Home: 37 Blyth Wood Park,

Bromley Kent BR1 3TN, England Office: Christian Rsch/Vision Bldg 4, Footscray Rd, Eltham London SE9 2TZ, England

BRIERLY, MARY CAROL, physician, dermatologist, consultant; b. Harrogate, Eng., Aug. 27, 1918; d. Sydney Clifford and Alice Tolson (Wright) B.; m. John Aitken Holgate, 1949 (div. 1956); children: Sarah, Campbell. MB, ChB, Leeds U., 1949; DSc in Complementary Medicines, Open U., 1995. Cert. hypnotherapist, psychotherapist, Soc. Med. and Dental Hypnotists. Cons. dermatologist Nat. Health Svc., Huddersfield, 1969-73; pres. World Fedn. of Healing, 1985-87; dir. Prometheus Sch. Healing, 1973—; lectr. World Fedn. Healing, Brit. Soc. Dowsing, other schs., Germany and Eng., 1982—. Contbr. articles to profl. jours. Mem. Brit. Soc. Dowsing, Psionic Med. Soc. Coun. Avocations: music, writing, reading. Home: 18 Dam Hill, Shelley Huddersfield HD8 8JH, England

BRIET, PHILIPPE, mathematician, physicist; b. Toulon, France, Sept. 30, 1954; s. Robert and Nathalie (Mouravski) B.; m. Marie Pierre Lapalu, Mar. 31, 1957; children: Nicola, Frederic. DEA in Physics, U. Aix-Marseille II, 1981, These 3 Cycle, 1983; These de Doctorate/Scis., U. Toulon, 1995. Maitre de conf. U. Toulon, France, 1987-91, maitre de conf. 1st class, 1991—. Contbr. articles to profl. jours. Office: CNRS/CPT, Luminy Case 907, F13288 Marseille 09, France

BRIGALDINO, GLENN, social scientist, consultant; b. Regina, SK, Canada, Oct. 19, 1958; s. Klaus Brigaldino and Gisela (Eicher) Bastian; m. Bayush Worku Woldegiorgis, Aug. 12, 1991; children: Jens Worku, Melcamm Worku, Samrawit Worku. MSc in Social Scis., U. Duisburg, Germany, 1986; cert., U. London, 1996, U. Wis., 1996, 98. UN officer UN High Commn. for Refugees, 1988-93; sr. program officer European Ctr. for Devel. Policy Mgmt., Maastricht, The Netherlands, 1993-96; mgr., owner Glenn Brigaldino Cons., Maastricht, 1996-2000; rep. APK Consulting, South Africa, 1999—; assembly mem. Ökobank, Frankfurt, Germany, 1997—; bus. ptnr. Shegaw & Ptnrs., Addis Ababa, Ethiopia. Co-editor: EPO-internet, Bonn, Germany, 1998—; contbr. articles to profl. jours. E-mail: melcamm@yahoo.com. Address: 790 Springland Dr Ste 227, Ottawa, ON Canada K1V 6L7

BRIGGS, BARON OF LEWES (ASA BRIGGS), historian, academic administrator; b. Keighley, Yorkshire, Eng., May 7, 1921; s. William Walker and Jane Briggs; m. Susan Anne Banwell; children: Katharine, Daniel, Judith, Matthew. Degree 1st class history, Cambridge (Eng.) U., 1941; BSc 1st class econs., London U., 1941. Prof. history U. Leeds (Eng.), 1955-61; prof. history, dean of social studies U. Sussex (Eng.), 1961-66, vice-chancellor, 1961-66; provost Worcester Coll., Oxford, Eng., 1976-91; chancellor Open U., Milton Keynes, Eng., 1979-95; chmn. European Inst. of Edn. and Social Policy, Paris, 1975-90, Commonwealth of Learning, Vancouver, Can., 1988-93. Author: Victorian People, 1954, Victorian Cities, 1963, A Social History of England, 1983, revised edit., 1994, Victorian Things, 1988, 5 vols. on history of British broadcasting. Trustee Glyndebourne Arts Trust, 1966-91. Named to Life Peerage, 1976; recipient Marconi Medal for Communication History, 1975, Médaille de Vermeil de la Formation, Fondation de l'Acad. d'Architecture, 1979. Fellow Brit. Acad., AAAS; mem. Social History Soc. (pres. 1976—), Victorian Soc. (pres. 1983—). Home: The Caprons Keere St, Lewes Sussex, England Office: 26 Oakmede Way, Ringmer East Sussex BN8 5JL, England

BRIGGS, ANTHONY DAVID PEACH, retired foreign language eduactor; b. Sheffield, Yorkshire, Eng., 1938; s. Horace and Doris Lily (Peach) B.; m. Pamela Anne Metcalfe, July 28, 1962; children: Fiona, Antonia, Julian. BA, U. Cambridge, Eng., 1961, MA, 1963; PhD, U. London, 1968. Lectr. Russian Queen's U., Kingston, Ont., Can., 1963-65; lectr. to reader Russian U. Bristol, Eng., 1968-87; sr. rsch. fellow U. Bristol, 1999; prof. Russian lang. and lit. U. Birmingham, Eng., 1987-98; ret., 1999. Author: Alexander Pushkin, 1983, 91, Pushkin: Eugene Onegin, 1992; editor: Alexander Pushkin, 1999, (6 vols. poetry) Pushkin, Omar Khayyam, English Sonnets, Shakespeare, Love Poetry, 1997, English Love Poetry, 1997-2000. E-mail: adpbriggs@aol.com. Fax: 01761 462100. Home: Over Moreton Breach Hill, Chew Stoke, Bristol BS40 8YG, England

BRIGGS, GEORGE ANDREW DAVIDSON, materials science educator; b. Dorchester, Dorset, Eng., June 3, 1950; s. John Davidson and Catherine Mary Briggs; m. Diana Margaret Ashley Johnson, July 11, 1981; children: Felicity, Lizzie. BA in Physics, Oxford (Eng.) U., 1971, MA in Physics, 1975; PhD in Physics, Cambridge (Eng.) U., 1976, BA in Theology, 1978. Praktikant Glanstoff AG, Wuppertal, Germany, 1968; tchr. Canford Sch., Dorset, 1971-73; rsch. asst. Cambridge U., 1979; rsch. fellow Oxford U., 1980-82, Royal Soc. rsch. fellow, 1983-84, lectr., 1984-96, reader in materials, 1996-99, prof. materials, 1999—. Author: An Introduction to Scanning Acoustic Microscopy, 1985, Acoustic Microscopy, 1992; editor: The Science of New Materials, 1992, Advances in Acoustic Microscopy, Vol. 1, 1995, Vol. 2, 1996. Acting pilot officer RAF, 1969-70. Recipient Holliday prize Inst. Metals, 1986, Metrology for World Class Mfg. award, 1999. Fellow Royal Microscopical Soc. (hon., treas. 1989-91). Anglican. Avocation: private pilot. Home: 5 Northmoor Rd, Oxford OX2 6UW, England Office: Oxford U, Dept Materials, Oxford OX1 3PH, England

BRIGGS, JAMES HENRY, II, engineering administrator; b. San Francisco, Dec. 25, 1953; s. James Henry and Barbara (Cordes) B.; m. Niwana Alice Page, Sept. 1, 1979; children: Melanie Shannon, James Henry III. AA in Bus. Adminstrn., Albany (Ga.) Jr. Coll., 1976; BS in Computer Sci., U. N.C., Wilmington, 1979; BSEE, So. Tech., Marietta, Ga., 1985. Lic. 1st class radio telephone; registered profl. engr., Calif. Asst. chief engr. WECT-TV, Wilmington, 1978-82; maintenance supr. Cable News Network, Atlanta, 1982-85; mgr. engring. ops. KCOP-TV, L.A., 1985-87; sr. product support engr. Abekas Video Systems, Redwood City, Calif., 1987-92; dir. engring. D.T.S., Union City, Calif., 1991-97; chief engr. Sta. CSUH-TV Calif. State U., Hayward, 1997-98; v.p. Charis Constrn., 1997-99; design engr. Stage Front Presentation Sys., Savannah, Ga., 1999—. Editor: Video Prodn. in the 90's. Mem. Soc. Motion Picture and TV Engrs., Soc. Broadcast Engrs., Greenpeace, Toastmasters Club, Lions. Avocations: biking, model trains, music, camping, sailing.

BRIGGS, PHILIP HAROLD, retired engineer, consultant; b. Boston, Eng., Jan. 22, 1921; s. Charles Lionel and Hilda (Hankinson) B.; m. Barbara Winifred Halliday, June 16, 1949; children: Michael Peter, Richard Jonathan, David Philip. B Tech. Sci., Manchester (Eng.) Victoria U., 1940; M Tech. Sci., U. Manchester, 1964, PhD, 1966; LLB, U. London, 1974. Chartered mech. and elec. engr. Radar lab. engr. Ferranti Ltd., Moston, Manchester, 1940-42, sect. leader indsl. devices, 1947-49, chief design engr. domestic appliances, 1949-51; joint chief engr. indsl. electronics Fielden Electronics Ltd., Wythenshawe, Manchester, 1951-53; joint mng. dir. Dukes & Briggs Engring. Ltd. and Flow Control Ltd., Trafford Park, Manchester, 1953-66; acad. rschr. power systems network analysers U. Manchester Inst. Sci. and Tech., 1964-66, external examiner and postgrad. supr., 1964-67; tchr. math, physics, craft and design, computer advisor Cheshire County Schs., Eng., 1975-85; engring. cons. to small industries, 1966—. Inventor early electronic means of watch regulation, numerous indsl. electronic devices, including automotive wheel balancers, cloth guider, childsafe radiant electric fire. Local authority councillor Wilmslow (Eng.) Urban Dist. Coun., 1962-65, chmn. parks and cemetaries, 1963, chmn. pub. health, 1964; chmn. bd. govs. Hough Boys Secondary Sch., Wilmslow, 1968-75; gov., initiator Engrs. Found. for Christ's Hosp. (Bluecoat) Sch., Horsham, Eng. Capt. Royal Elec. and Mech. Engrs., 1942-47, NATOUSA, MTO. Indsl. fellow Bath (Eng.) U. Tech., 1967-70. Fellow Instn. Elec. Engrs.; mem. Instn. Mech. Engrs., Christ's Hosp. Club. Avocations: cycling, constructing 2 small houses, early computer construction, talking books and newspapers for blind. Home: 59 Broad Walk, Wilmslow Cheshire SK9 5PN, England

BRIGGS, PHILIP JAMES, political science educator, author, lecturer; b. N.Y.C., July 28, 1938; s. Philip Edward and Florence Marie (Fulham) B.; m. Candace Rae Kohn, Jan. 30, 1971; children: Nicola Fulham, Adam Kohn. BS, SUNY, Oswego, 1960; MA, Maxwell Sch. Citizenship and Pub. Affairs, Syracuse U., 1962, PhD, 1969. Asst. prof. social sci. SUNY Coll. Tech., Delhi, 1963-65; admissions counselor Syracuse (N.Y.) U., 1967; assoc. prof. polit. sci. East Stroudsburg (Pa.) U., 1968-72, prof. polit. sci., 1972-99, dept. grad. coord.and chmn., 1977-95, faculty Fulbright adviser, 1981-82, disting. prof. emeritus, 2000—; Foxhowe lectr., 1980; Commonwealth spkr. Pa. Humanities Coun., 1984-86, 96-99, spkr., 2000; invited del. Sci. Rsch. Coun., Acad. Sci. USSR, 1979; invited participant seminar Georgetown U., 1983; invited scholar Presdl. Conf. Com., Hofstra U., 1984, 85, 87; panel co-chair Internat. Polit. Sci. World Congress, Paris, 1985, panel chair, Berlin, 1994. Cons. McGraw-Hill Book Co., N.Y.C., 1981; manuscript referee Armed Forces and Soc., Chgo., 1979, 93; author: Making American Foreign Policy, President-Congress Relations from the Second World War to Vietnam, 1991, 92, Making American Foreign Policy, President-Congress Relations from the Second World War to the Post-Cold War Era, 1994, 95, 97; contbg. author (series): The Congress of the United States, 1789-1989; editor: Politics in America, Readings and Documents, 1972; contbr. articles to profl. publs.; TV appearances on C-Span, 1987, Blue Ridge Cable and Pennarama, 1991, Action News 24, Erie, Pa., 1999. Polit. commentator civic groups, 1991, 92, 94, 97, 98; exec. dir. Rsch. Com. on Armed Forces and Soc. Internat. Polit. Sci. Assn., 1990-99; panel chmn. rsch. com. Fundacion Jose Ortega y Gasset, Madrid, 1990; mem., panel participant Ctr. for Study of Presidency, 1995, 96. With USCG, 1962, USCGR, 1962-70. Mem. Rsch. Com. on Armed Forces and Soc. (exec. sec. 1985-90), Pa. Polit. Sci. Assn. (panel chmn. ann. meetings 1993-99), Can. Polit. Sci. Assn. (panel chair and discussant ann. meeting 1989, panel chair 1998), Pi Sigma Alpha (charter mem. campus chpt.). Democrat. Unitarian.

BRIGGS, STELLA, optometry educator, researcher; b. Calabar, Nigeria, Apr. 1, 1958; arrived in Can., 1997; d. Sunday Tombeama and Vidah B.; 1 child, Donald. BS, Ind. U., 1978, MS, 1979; PhD, U. Wales, U.K., 1987. Cert. advanced contact lens practice, practice of refraction. Lectr. U. Sci. and Technology, Port Harcourt, Nigeria, 1987-91; asst. prof. King Saud U., Riyadh, Saudi Arabia, 1991-99, assoc. prof., 1999-2000. Contbr. articles to profl. jours. Postgrad. scholar Fed. Govt. of Nigeria, 1984-87. Fellow Royal Soc. of Health; mem. Internat. Assn. Contact lens Educators, N.Y. Acad. of Sci. Avocations: reading, music, travel, exercise, dancing. Home: 1530 Reeves Gate Unit 22, Oakville, ON Canada L6M 3I4 Office: King Saud Univ, PO Box 10219, 11433 Riyadh Saudi Arabia

BRIGGS, WARD WRIGHT, classics educator; b. Riverside, Calif., Nov. 26, 1945; s. Ward Wright and Madge Elizabeth (Ravenscroft) B. BA, Washington & Lee U., 1967; MA, U. N.C., 1969, PhD, 1974. Instr. classics U. S.C., Columbia, 1973-74, asst. prof., 1974-80, assoc. prof., 1980-86, prof. classics, 1986—, Carolina disting. prof. classics, 1996—, Louise Fry Scudder prof. humanities, 1996—, interim assoc. provost, 1996-97; vis. prof. U. Va., Charlottesville, 1988, U. Colo., 1988; fellow Inst. for Advanced Study, Princeton, 1999-2000. Author: Narrative and Simile from the Georgics in the Aeneid, 1980; editor: Letters of B.L. Gildersleeve, 1987; editor: Biographical Dictionary of North American Classicists, 1994, Soldier and Scholar, 1998; co-editor: Classical Scholarship, 1990; editor Vergilius, Jour. of Vergilian Soc. Am., 1986-95. Mem. Am. Philol. Assn., Classical Assn. Middle West and South (pres. 1988-89), Cambridge Philol. Soc., Phi Beta Kappa. Episcopalian. Home: 1904 Pendleton St Columbia SC 29201-3906 Office: Dept French and Classics U Sc Columbia SC 29208-0001

BRIGHAM, JOHN ALLEN, JR., financial executive, environmentalist, polititian; b. San Francisco, June 17, 1942; s. John Allen, Sr. and Susan (Endberg) B.; m. Patricia Katherine Carney, Feb. 4, 1968; 1 child, Jennifer. BS in Acctg., San Jose State U., 1967. Acct. Shell Oil Co. Data Ctr., Palo Alto, Calif., 1963-66; asst. plant controller Brown Co., Santa Clara, Calif., 1966-68; budget mgr. Varian Assocs., Palo Alto, 1968-80; cost acctg. mgr. Adac Labs., San Jose, Calif., 1980-86; contr. Crystal Tech., Palo Alto, 1986-90; contr., v.p. fin., CFO GV Custom Modular Constrn., Inc., Healdsburg, Calif.; controller GV Contractors, Heraldsburg, Calif., 1994—; part-time sci. tchr. Insects and Dinosaurs, 1994-96. Del. League Calif. Cities, 1974-78; mem. Saratoga (Calif.) City Council, 1974-78; vice-chmn. Santa Clara County Polity Planning Use Commn., 1975-78; chmn. Santa Clara Com. on Mass Transit, 1976-78; chmn. Open Space Bond Issure, 1976; treas. Calif. State Solar Bond Issue, 1976; mem. Castle Rock State Pk. Com., 1972-74; vice-chmn. Saratoga Hillside Com. 1978-79. Recipient 10 and 25 Yr. Sierra Club Activist awards, 1989, Chpt. Svc. award, 1990, Spl. Achievement award, 1990; Local Outstanding Young Man of Am. award, 1974, Siemens USA Personality of the Month award, Jan. 1990. Mem. Am. Entomol. Soc., Archeol. Inst. Am., Nat. Acctg. Assn., Sierra Club (vice chmn., treas. Loma chpt. 1985-94, treas. Redwood chpt. 1994-97, internat. chmn. 1989-97, Centennial chmn. 1990-92, liaison to USSR and Mex., co-chair Earth Day 1990, taskforce 1989, chmn. fin. commn. 1985-90), Am. Diabetes Soc. (treas., bd. dirs. Santa Clara County chpt.), Nat. Wildlife Fedn., Cousteau Soc., Planetary Soc., Napoleonic Soc., Bromiliad Soc., Am. Diabetes Assn., Sierra Club. Independent. Roman Catholic. E-mail: johnb@gvcm.com.

BRIGHT, GLEN, mechanical engineer, researcher; b. Durban, Natal, South Africa, Apr. 22, 1966; s. William Thomas and Sheila Arin (Goodwin) Bright; m. Lizell Currin, Sept. 9, 1990; 1 child, Tyrone. BSc in Mech. Engring., U. Natal, Durban, South Africa, 1987, MSc in Mech. Engring., 1989, PhD in Engring., 1993. Trainee Natal Roads Dept., 1988; project engr. GEC Elec. Project Ltd. Co., Rugby, England, 1989; from lectr. to sr. lectr. U. Natal, Durban, 1990-95, sr. lectr., 1995—; vis. lectr. Mangosuto Technikon, Durban, 1992; referee IASTED Internat. Conf. Robotics and Mfg., Cancun, Mex., 1995. Inventor in field; contbr. articles to profl. jours. Recipient Excellence award Literati Club MCB Univ. Press, England, numerous awards and grants for rsch. Mem. IEEE. Fax: 027 31 2603217. E-mail: brightg@eng.und.ac.za. Home: 23 Elgie Rd Glenwood, Durbin 4001, South Africa Office: Univ Natal Faculty Engring, Mechanical Engring, Durban 4041, South Africa

BRIGHT, HARVEY R., petroleum corporation executive; b. Muskogee, Okla., Oct. 6, 1920; s. Christopher R. and Rebecca E. (Van Ness) B.; m. Mary Frances Smith, May 27, 1943 (dec. Apr. 1971); children—Carol Bright Hunter, Margaret Bright Vonder Hoya, Christopher R., Clay Van Ness; m. Peggy Braselton, Dec. 15, 1972. B.S., Tex. A&M U., 1943. Ptnr. Bright & Co. (oil producers), Dallas; bd. dirs. State Fair of Tex., Dallas; chmn. bd. dirs. Bright Truck Leasing Corp., Dallas. Chmn. bd. Children's Health Services of Tex., Dallas. Served with AUS, World War II. Home: 4500 Lakeside Dr Dallas TX 75205-3821 Office: 2911 Turtle Creek Blvd Ste 700 Dallas TX 75219-6251

BRIGINO-BUENAVENTURA, EMERITA, immunologist, allergist; b. Quezon City, Manila, The Philippines, Apr. 6, 1957; d. Delfin Santos and Fermina (Natividad) B.; m. Joseph Verne Buenaventura, Dec. 10, 1997. BS in Zoology magna cum laude, U. of the Philippines, Quezon City, Manila, 1979, MD, 1984. Diplomate Am. Bd. Pediats., Am. Bd. Allergy and Immunology. Resident in pediats. Montefiore Med. Ctr., N.Y.C., 1991-93; fellow in allergy and immunology All Children's Hosp.-U. South Fla., St. Petersburg, 1993-95, fellow in clin. lab. immunology, 1995-96; assoc. clin. prof. pediats. Philippine Gen. Hosp.-U. of the Philippines, Manila, 1998—. Contbr. articles to profl. jours. including Clin. Revs. in Allergy and Immunology, Proceedings of the Nat. Acad. Sci., Acta Paediatrica Scandinavia. Mem. Am. Acad. Asthma, Allergy, and Immunology, Am. Coll. Allergy and Immunology, Philippine Pediat. Soc. E-mail: jem@pacific.net.ph. Office: UP-PGH Dept Pediats, Taft Ave, Manila The Philippines

BRIHAT, DENIS, photographer; b. Paris, Sept. 16, 1928; s. Georges and Rose (Guasco) B.; m. Solange Robert, July 8, 1967; children: Anne, Pierre. Profl. photographer, Paris, 1947-52, Biot, France, 1952-56, Provence, France, 1958—; dir. Brihat Ann. Photography Workshops, Provence, 1969—; co-founder, instr. dept. photography Marseille-Provence U., 1975-77; one-man shows Brihat Studio, Biot, 1952, Société Française de Photographie, Paris, 1957, 88, Galerie Montaigne, Paris, 1962, Galerie Pierre Coren, Aixen-Provence, France, 1962, Galerie La Proue, Lyon, France, 1963, Galerie Les Contards, Lacoste, France, 1965, Mus. des Arts Décoratifs, Paris, Mus. Modern Art, N.Y.C., 1967, Artek Gallery, Helsinki, Finland, Orly Airport Gallery, Paris, 1968, Galerie La Lampe à Huile, Marseilles, France, 1971, Galerie La Demeure, Paris, Witkin Gallery, N.Y.C., Art Ctr., Washington, Conn., 1972, Fondation Grand Cachot de Vent, Neuchatel, Switzerland, 1973, Galleria 291, Milan, 1974, Photo-Galerie Fiolet, Ctr. Culturel Toulouse, 1975, Amsterdam Galerie Paule, Pia, Antwerp, 1976, Musé e d'Angouleme, France, 1976, Galerie Agathe Gaillard, Paris, 1977, 82, Galerie Jean Dieuzaide, Toulouse, France, 1977, Musé e Nicephore Niepce, Chalon-sur-Saone, France, 1977, Galerie Photo-Art, Basle, 1978, Mus. des Beaux-Arts, Besançon, Galerie Portfolio, Lausanne, 1979, 82, 86, Galerie Municipale du Chateau d'Eau, Toulouse, 1980, Musé e des Beaux Arts, Neuchatel, Switzerland, 1981, Musé e d'Orange, France, 1982, Galerie de la Salle, St. Paul de Vence, France, 1982, 85, Galerie Photogramme, Montreal, 1982, Espace Canon, Paris, 1982, Galerie L. d'Alessandro, Torino, Italy, 1983, Ctr. for Photography, Santa Fe, 1983, Galerie S. Kuepfer, Bienne, Switzerland, Camera Obscura Gallery, Denver, 1983 Wooster Art Ctr., Danbury, Conn., 1985, Musé e Henri Fabre, Montpellier, France, 1986, Galerie Suisse, Paris, 1986, Maison Valdotaine de la Photographie, Aoste, Italy, 1997, Photographer's Gallery, Palo-Alto, Calif., 1988, 96, 98, Galerie de la Gare, Bonnieux, 1989, 92, 98, Anne Berthoud Gallery, London, 1989-91, Photo-Forum Biehl, Switzerland, 1990, Maison Francaise, NYU, 1991, Palais de Tokyo, Paris, 1993, Musée de Salon de Provence-France, Musée de l'-Elysée-Lausanne, Maison Européenne de la Photographie, 1996, Galerie Gilbert-Albert, Geneva, 1996, Galerie du Forum, Toulouse, France, 1996, Candace Perich Gallery, Katonah, N.Y., 1997, Espace Photographique Montpellier-France, 1999; represented in permanent collections: Bibliothèque Nationale, Paris, Musé e Reattu, Arles, France, Musé e Nicephore Niepce, Chalon-sur-Saone, Musé e d'Angouleme, France, Het Sterckshof Mus., Antwerp, Mus. Modern Art, N.Y.C., Ctr. Creative Photography, U. Ariz., Tucson, Fond Nat. d'Art Contemporain, Paris, Maison europeenne de la Photographie, Paris; Moderna Museet, Stockholm. Recipient Niepce prize Société des Gens d'Images, 1957; medal of Vermeil, Grand Prix de la Ville de Paris, 1987.

BRILEY, MICHAEL, research scientist; b. Romford, England, Sept. 17, 1947; s. Stanley Briley and Eileen Baker; m. Chantal Moret, Apr. 25, 1981; 1 child, Loic. BSc, U. Bath, 1970, PhD, 1973. Rsch. scientist U. Buenos Aires, 1973-74, Pasteur Inst., Paris, 1975-77; project leader Synthelabo Rsch., Paris, 1977-82; head ctrl. nervous sys. rsch. Pierre Fabre Rsch. Ctr., Castres, France, 1982-95; dep. head rsch. Pierre Fabre Rsch. Ctr., Castres, 1995-97, head scientific evaluation, 1997-99; scientific dir. worldwide ops. Pierre Fabre Medicament, Castres, 1999—. Avocations: sailing, skiing, hiking. E-mail: mike.briley@pierre-fabre.com. Office: Pierre Fabre Medicament, Parc Indsl Chartreuse, 81100 Castres France

BRILL, LAWRENCE JOEL, lawyer; b. Washington, Sept. 11, 1945; s. Robert Melvin and Elaine (Friedman) B.; m. Rita Joan Kopit, June 14, 1969; children: Matthew Jason. BS in Bus., Syracuse U., 1968; JD, U. Balt., 1974. Bar: Md. 1975, D.C. 1976. Legis. officer U.S. Dept. Commerce, Washington, 1972-78, spl. asst. to dep. asst. sec. textiles and apparel, 1978-79, internat. trade specialist textiles and apparel, 1979—; atty. Pres.' Task Force on Regulatory Reform, Occupational Safety and Health, 1976. Counsel Harpers Choice Village Assn., Columbia, 1976-79, Kings Contrivance Village Assn., Columbia, 1981-83. Served with USAR, 1969-75. U.S. Dpet. Commerce Sci. and Tech. fellow, 1979-80. Mem. Md. Bar Assn. Home and Office: 9630 W Window Way Columbia MD 21046-2035

BRILL, MICHAEL HENRY, physicist, vision scientist; b. Bay Shore, N.Y., Jan. 26, 1949; s. Henry and Wenonah (Beale) B. BA in English and Physics, Case Western Res. U., 1969; MS in Physics, Syracuse U., 1971, PhD, 1976. Postdoctoral fellow MIT, Cambridge, 1974-77; physicist Perception Tech. Corp., Winchester, Mass., 1977-79; chief scientist Solotest Corp., Framingham, Mass., 1979; sr. scientist Jaycor, Alexandria, Va., 1980-83; sr. staff scientist Sci. Applications Internat. Corp., McLean and Falls Church, Va., 1983-94; mem. tech. staff Sarnoff Corp., Princeton, N.J., 1994—; pres. Inter-Soc. Color Coun., 1998-2000; chmn. tech. com. i-56 improved color matching functions Internat. Illumnination Commn., 1999—. Co-author: Dimensional Analysis through Perspective, 1990; assoc. editor Physics Essays, 1995—; mem. editl. bd. Color Rsch. and Application, 1990—; contbr. some 60 articles to profl. jours. 2d lt. USAF, 1972. Mem. Optical Soc. Am., Am. Soc. for Photogrammetry and Remote Sensing, Soc. for Info. Display, Phi Beta Kappa. Achievements include retina model with adaptive contrast sensitivity and resolution; volumetric theory of color constancy; broken-mirror model of acoustic rough-surface scattering; formulation of theories of perspective invariance in images; four patents on vision modeling. Avocations: poetry writing, table tennis, recreational mathematics. Home: 1 Makefield Rd Apt D130 Morrisville PA 19067-5020 Office: Sarnoff Corp 201 Washington Rd Princeton NJ 08540-6449

BRILLA, CHRISTIAN GEORG, cardiologist, researcher, educator; b. Bytom, Poland, Jan. 9, 1956; s. Josef Georg and Rosa Mathilde (Skolik) B.; m. Sabine Barbara Schmid, Aug. 10, 1979; children: David, Marius, Patrick. MD, Eberhard Karls U., Tübingen, Germany, 1982, PhD, 1985. Resident, fellow dept. medicine U. Tübingen, 1982-88; fellow Michael Reese Hosp. and Med. Ctr./U. Chgo., 1988-90; asst. prof. medicine divsn. cardiology U. Mo., Columbia, 1990-91; fellow divsn. cardiology U. Marburg, Germany, 1991-93, assoc. prof. medicine divsn. cardiology, 1993-98, dir. molecular cardiology lab., 1994- , prof. medicine divsn. cardiology, 1998—; mem. adv. bd. on cardiovascular disease Hoechst, AG, 1995—; mem. sci. com. Am. sect. Internat. Soc. for Heart Rsch., 1992-93; mem. sci. comm. working group on heart failure European Soc. Cardiology, 1996—; rschr. in field. Contbr. 120 articles to profl. jours. German Rsch. Found. grantee, 1988—. Mem. Am. Physiol. Assn., Am. Heart Assn. (award 1990), German Soc. Cardiology (award 1994, mem. sci. com. working group on heart failure 1993—, mem. sci. com. working group on mycardial function and energetics 1994—), German Soc. Internal Medicine, Colegio Panamericano del Endotelio (hon.), Internat. Soc. for Molecular Nutrition and Pharmacotherapy (mem. coun. 1995—), Internat. Aldosterone Coun. (award 1991, 94—, sci. com. European sect. 1997—). Avocations: philosophy, photography, tennis. Office: Philipps U Marburg, Baldingerstr Div Cardiology, 35033 Marburg Germany

BRILMAN, DERK WILLEM FREDERIK, chemical engineer, educator; b. Meppel, Drenthe, The Netherlands, Feb. 19, 1968; s. Gerrit Hendrik and Jannie (Reilink) B. IR, U. Twente, 1991, D in Chem. Engring., 1998. Asst. prof. chem. engring. U. Twente, Enschede, The Netherlands, 1993—. Recipient Hoogewerff Twaio prize Hoogewerff Fund, 1993. Home: Parijsstraat 53, 7559 KP Hengelo The Netherlands Office: Univ Twente, PO Box 217, 7500 AE Enschede The Netherlands

BRILMAN, JEAN FRANS, management consultant; b. Saigon, Vietnam, Sept. 2, 1939; s. Frans Christoffel Brilman and Berthe Magali Herisson; m. Jacqueline C. Batbie, 1964 (div. 1970); children: Sophie J. Michalet, Laurence Brilman; m. Marthe Helene Philippe, Apr. 29, 1972; children: Nathalie de Quelen, Jennifer C. Kouassi. BS, Ecole Polytechnique, Paris, 1959; MBA, Inst. Adminstrn. Entreprises, Paris, 1962; B Engring., Ecole Petroles et Moteurs, Paris, 1962. Fin. analyst Eurofinex, Paris, 1962-64; cons. CEGOS, Paris, 1964-67, sr. cons., 1968-71, ptnr., 1972-73, internat. v.p., 1974—; prof. French Fin. Analysts Soc., Paris, 1976-86. Author: Le redressement d'entreprises en difficulte, 1978, Modeles culturels et performances economiques, 1982, Gestion de crise et redressement d'entreprises, 1986, Gagner la competition mondiale, 1991, Les cles de la relance, 1993, L'enterprise réinventée, 1995, Les meilleures pratiques de Management, 1998; co-author: (with Andre Gaultier) Pratique de l'evaluation et de la negociation des entreprises, 1976, (with Claude Maire) Manuel d'evaluation des entreprises, 1988. Lt. USAF, 1961-62. Office: CEGOS rue René Jacques, 8 rue Jean Jacques Rous René Jac, 92 Issy les Moulineaux France

BRIM, HASSAN, microbiologist, researcher; b. Casablanca, Morocco, Jan. 28, 1968; s. Said Brim and Aicha Azagui; m. Zohra El Mkami, Jan. 26, 1999. Degree Gen. Univ. Studies, Factly of Scis. II, Casablanca, 1987; Lic. es-scis. in molecular biology, Faculty Scis. Fès (Morocco), 1989; M in Molecular Biology and Biotechnology cum laude, Free U. Brussels, 1990, PhD, 1997. Microbiologist pathology dept. Uniformed Svcs. U. Health Scis., Bethesda, Md., 1997—; Spkr., presenter in field. Contbr. numerous articles to profl. jours. Mem. AAAS, Am. Soc. Microbiology, Moroccan Soc. Biology. Muslim. Avocations: sports, music, reading. Home: 4007 Connecticut Ave NW Apt 213 Washington DC 20008-1142 Office: USUHS Pathology Dept 4301 Jones Bridge Rd Bethesda MD 20814-4799

BRIMIOULLE, SERGE, intensive care physician; b. Charleroi, Belgium, 1951. MD, U. Brussels, 1976, specialist in internal medicine, 1981, PhD, 1990. Asst. prof. Erasmus Hosp., Brussels, 1981-90, assoc. prof., 1990—. Recipient Scientific award and grants. Mem. SCCM, ATS, APS. Avocation:

informatics. Office: Erasme U Hosp, Lennik Rd 808, B-1070 Brussels Belgium

BRINCH, NIELS, foreign news correspondent; b. Copenhagen, Oct. 3, 1956; s. Viggo and Jytte (Pedersen) B. Master in Journalism, Danish Sch. Journalism, Århus, 1980. Reporter Frederinsborg Amts Avis, Hilleroed, Denmark, 1980-84, B.T., Copenhagen, 1984-88; reporter/domestic TV 2 Denmark, Odense, 1988-91, corr./fgn., 1991—, mem. bd., 1993—. With Danish Civil Def., 1976. Home: Frederiksborggade 22 LTV, 1360 Kobenhavnk Denmark Office: TV 2 Denmark, Ruggaardsvej 25, 5100C Odense Denmark

BRINCK, ULRICH, pathologist, researcher; b. Hannover, Germany, Sept. 25, 1958; s. Jobst and Lucia (Vonnahme) B. Physician, U. Goettingen, 1985; doctor, U. Wuerzburg, 1987. Asst. doctor Dept. Anatomy, U. Wuerzburg, 1985-86, Dept. of Neuropathology, Duesseldorf, 1987; fellow Max Planck Inst., Goettingen, 1988; asst. doctor Dept. Pathology, U. Goettingen, 1989—. Contbr. articles to profl. jours. Mem. Internat. Soc. of Histochemistry, Internat. Acad. of Pathology, Polish Soc. of Pathology, Deutsche Gesellschaft für Pathologie. Avocations: egyptology, body building, biking. Home: Rohnsweg 12, 37085 Göttingen Germany Office: Dept Pathology, Robert Koch Str 40, 37075 Göttingen Germany

BRIND'AMOUR, ROD JEAN, professional hockey player; b. Ottawa, Ont., Can., Aug. 9, 1970; m. Kelle; 2 children. Grad., Mich. State U. With St. Louis Blues, 1988-91; left wing/center Phila. Flyers, 1991-99, Carolina Hurricanes, 1999—; mem. CCHA All-Rookie team, 1988-89; player NHL All-Star game. Recipient CCHA Rookie of the Year award, 1988-89. Office: Carolina Hurricanes 1400 Edwards Mill Rd Raleigh NC 27607-3624

BRINEGAR, CLAUDE STOUT, retired oil company executive; b. Rockport, Calif., Dec. 16, 1926; s. Claude Leroy Stout and Lyle (Rawles) B.; m. Elva Jackson, 1950 (div.); children: Claudia, Meredith, Thomas; m. Mary Katharine Potter, 1983 (dec. 1993); m. Karen Bartholomew, 1995. BA, Stanford U., 1950, MS, 1951, PhD, 1954; LLD (hon.), Elmira Coll., 1997. V.p. econs. and planning Union Oil (now Unocal), L.A., 1965; pres. Pure Oil divsn. Union Oil (now Unocal), Palatine, Ill., 1965-69; sr. v.p., pres. refining and mktg. Union Oil (now Unocal), L.A., 1969-73; U.S. Sec. of Transp. Washington, 1973-75; sr. v.p. adminstr. Unocal Corp., L.A., 1975-85, mem. exec. com., 1968-73, 75-92, exec. v.p., CFO, 1985-91, also bd. dirs., 1968-73, 75-95, vice chmn. bd., 1990-95; founding dir. Conrail, Inc., 1974-75, 90-98; bd. dirs. Maxicare Health Plans, Inc., 1991-2000, CSX Corp.; vis. scholar Stanford U., 1992-97. Author: monograph on econs. and price behavior, 1970; contbr. articles to profl. jours. on statistics and econs. Chmn. Calif. Citizens Compensation Commn., 1990—; mem. regional selection panel White House Fellows Program, 1976-83, chmn., 1983. Mem. Am. Petroleum Inst. (bd. dirs. 1976-85, 88-91, hon. life dir. 1992), Georgetown Club, Boothbay Harbor Yacht Club, Southport Yacht Club, Phi Beta Kappa, Sigma Xi. Avocation: collecting first editions of Mark Twain. Home and Office: PO Box 20246 Stanford CA 94309-0246

BRINGEL, FRANÇOISE, microbiologist, researcher; b. Mulhouse, Haut-Rhin, France, June 14, 1963; d. Lucien and Monique (Sifferlen) B.; m. Brett Norris Johnson; children: Nathan Arno Johnson, Clara Anne Maya Johnson. PhD, U. Louis Pasteur, Strasbourg, France, 1990; postgrad., Emory U., 1990-92. Rschr. Ctr. Nat. Rsch. Sci., Strasbourg, France, 1992—. Contbr. articles to profl. jours. PhD fellow French govt., 1987-89. Mem. Assn. Française Microbiologie. Avocations: hiking, pottery, cooking, theater, travel. Office: U Louis Pasteur UPRESA 7010, 28 Rue Goethe, 67083 Strasbourg France

BRINGHURST, ROBERT, poet; b. L.A., Oct. 16, 1946; s. George Heber and Marion Jeanette (Large) B.; 1 child, Piper Laramie. Student, MIT, 1963-64, 70-71, U. Utah, 1964-65; BA in Comparative Lit., Ind. U., 1973; MFA, U. B.C., Vancouver, Can., 1975. Vis. lectr. dept. creative writing U. B.C., Vancouver, 1975-77, lectr. dept. English, 1979-80; adj. lectr. Simon Fraser U., Burnaby, B.C., 1983-84; writer-in-residence U. Winnipeg, Man., Can., 1986; Can./Scotland exch. fellow U. Edinburgh, Scotland, 1989-90; Ashley Fellow Trent U., Peterborough, Can., 1994; writer in residence U. Western Ontario, 1998-99; conjunct prof. Trent U., 1998—; Author history and criticism: Visions: Contemporary Art in Canada (with others), 1983, Ocean/Paper/Stone, 1984, Shovels, Shoes and the Slow Rotation of Letters, 1986, Part of the Land, Part of the Water: A History of the Yukon Indians (with others), 1987, the Black Canoe: Bill Reid and the Spirit of Haida Gwaii, 1991, 2d edit., 1992, The Elements of Typographic Style, 1992, 2d edit., 1996, A Story as Sharp as a Knife: The Classical Haida Mythtellers and Their World, 1999; co-author: The Raven Steals the Light, 1984, 2d edit., 1996, A Short History of the Printed Word, 1999; author stage prodns., works for multiple voices. Author books of poetry: Shipwright's Log, 1972, Cadastre, 1973, Deuteronomy, 1974, Eight Objects, 1975, Bergschrund, 1975, Jacob Singing, 1977, Stonecutter's Horses, 1979, Tzuhalem's Mountain, 1982, Beauty of the Weapons: Selected Poems 1972-82, 1982, Tending the Fire, 1985, Blue Roofs of Japan, 1986, Pieces of Map, Pieces of Music, 1987, Conversations with a Toad, 1987, The Calling: Selected Poems, 1970-95, 1995, Elements, 1995, The Book of Silences, 2000, numerous poetry broadsides; editor, translator: Nine Visits to the Mythworld, 2000; contbr. to numerous anthologies. Guggenheim fellow in poetry, 1988. Home: Box 357, 1917 W. 4th Ave, Vancouver, BC Canada V6J 1M7

BRINGMAN, JOSEPH EDWARD, lawyer; b. Elmhurst, N.Y., Jan. 31, 1958; s. Joseph Herman and Eileen Marie (Sheehy) B.; m. Laurie Lynn Cunningham, July 11, 1992; children: Joseph Edward Jr., Elizabeth Grace. BA, Yale U., 1980; JD, Stanford U., 1983. Bar: N.Y. 1984, Wash. 1985, U.S. Dist. Ct. (we. dist.) Wash. 1986, U.S. Ct. Appeals (9th cir.) 1986, U.S. Ct. Appeals (fed. cir.) 1988, U.S. Dist. Ct. (ea. dist.) Wash. 2000. Acting asst. prof. U. Wash. Law Sch., Seattle, 1983-85; assoc. Perkins Coie, Seattle, 1985-91, of counsel, 1992—; dir. Perkins Coie Cmty. Fellowship, Seattle, 1990-96, chair assoc. tng. com., 1997—. Editor: Stanford Jour. Internat. Law, 1980-83. Mem. Yale Alumni Schs. Com., Seattle, 1983—, Palo Alto, Calif., 1980-83. Nat. Merit scholar, 1976; recipient Pro Bono Publico award Trumbull Coll. (Yale U.), 1980. Mem. ABA, Wash. State Bar Assn., King County Bar Assn. (jud. screening com. 1993-96, chair fair campaign practices com. 1997-99). Democrat. Roman Catholic. Office: Perkins Coie LLP 1201 3rd Ave Fl 48 Seattle WA 98101-3029

BRINGMANN, INGRA MONIQUE, resident, researcher; b. Nieuwenhagen, Limburg, The Netherlands, Feb. 19, 1972; d. Bernard Gerhard Joseph Bringmann and Anjes Johanna Rosenboom. MD, Erasmus (The Netherlands) U., 1997. Cert. advanced trauma life support. Resident surgery Groene Hart Hosp., Gouda, The Netherlands, 1997-98, Leyenburg Hosp., The Hague, The Netherlands, 1998, Rynland Hosp., Leiderdorp, The Netherlands, 1998-99; Acad. Hosp. Geiden, 1999—; rschr. Royal Infirmary, Edinburgh, Scotland, 1997, Groene Hart Hosp., Gouda, 1997-98, Rynland Hosp., Leiderdorp, 1998-99. Mem. Dutch Surg. Assn., Dutch Traumatol. Assn. Roman Catholic. Avocations: travel, music, theatre. Office: Univ Hosp Geiden, PO Box 9600, 2300 RC Leiden The Netherlands

BRINK, ANDRÉ PHILIPPUS, author, educator; b. Vrede, South Africa, May 29, 1935; s. Daniel and Aletta (Wolmarans) B.; m. Estelle Naude, Oct. 3, 1959 (div.); 1 child, Anton; m. Salomi Louw, Nov. 28, 1965 (div.); 1 child, Gustav; m. Sophia Albertina Miller, July 17, 1970 (div.); children: Danie, Sonja; m. Marèsa de Beer, Nov. 16, 1990. BA, Potchefstroom U., 1955, MA, 1958; MA, Potchefstroom U., 1959; DLitt, Rhodes U., 1975; DLitt (hon.), Witwatersrand U., 1985, Orange Free State U., 1997; PhD (hon.), Univ. Montpellier. Lectr. Rhodes U., Grahamstown, 1961-73, sr. lectr., 1973-75, asst. prof., 1976-79, prof., 1980-90; prof. U. Cape Town, 1991—. Author: Brandy in South Africa, 1973, Dessert Wine in South Africa, 1974, Die wyn van bowe, 1974, Die klap van die meul, 1974, Die fees van dies malles: 'n keur uit die humor, 1981, Mapmakers: Writing in a State of Siege, 1983, oom Kootjie Emmer en die nuwe bedeling, 1983, The Essence of the Grape, 1993; (fiction) Eindelose Weë, 1960, Lobola vir die lewe, 1962, Die Ambassadeur (File on a Diplomat), 1963, Orgie, 1965, Miskien nooit, 1967, A Portrait of Woman as a Young Girl, 1973, Kennis van die aand (Looking on Darkness), 1973, Die Geskiedenis van oom Kootjie Emmer van Witgatworteldraai, 1973, 'n Oomblik in die wind (An Instant in the Wind), 1975, Gerugte van Reën (Rumours of Rain), 1978, (Central News Agy. awrd for English Lit., 1978), 'n Droë wit seisoen (A Dry White Season), 1979 (Martin Luther King Meml. prize 1980, Prix Médicis ètranger 1980), Houd-den-bek (A Chain of Voices, Ctrl. News Agy. award for English Lit.), 1982; (essays) Die Muur van die pes (The Wall of the Plague), 1984, Loopdoppies: Nog dopstories, 1984, States of Emergency, 1988, An Act of Terror, 1991, Cape of Storms, 1993, On the Contrary, 1993, Imaginings of Sand, 1996 (Premio Mondello 1997), Reinventing a Continent, 1996, Destabilising Shakespeare, 1996, Devil's Valley, 1998, The Rights of Desire, 2000; (plays) Caesar, 1961, Bagasie: Triptiek vir die toneel, 1964, Elders mooiweer en warm, 1965, Die Rebelle: Betoogstuk in nege episodes, 1970, Die Verhoor: Verhoogstuk in drie bedrywe, 1970, Kinkels innie kabel: 'n verhoogstuk in elf episodes, 1971, Afrikaners is plesierig, 1973, Pavane, 1974, Die hamer die hekse, 1976, Die jogger, 1997 (Hertzog prize 2000); (criticism) Orde en chaos: 'n studie oor Germanicus ed die tragedies van Shakespeare, 1962, Aspekte van die nuwe prosa, 1967, Die Poësie van Breyten Breytenbach, 1971, Aspekte van die nuwe drama, 1974, Voorlopige rapport: Beskouings oor die Afrikaanse literatuur van Sewentig, 1976, Tweede voorlopige rapport: Nog beskouings oor die Afrikaanse literatuur van sewentig, 1980, Waarom literatuur?, 1985, Literatuur in die strydperk, 1985, Vertelkunde: 'n inleiding tot die lees van verhalende tekste, 1987, The Novel: Language and Narrative from Cervantes to Calvino, 1998; (travelogues) Pot-pourri: Sketse uit Parys, 1962, Sempre diritto: Italiaanse reisjoernaal, 1963, Olé: Reisboek oor Spanje, 1965 (Central News Agency award for Afrikaans literature 1965), Midi: Op reis deur Suid-Frankryk, 1969, Fado: 'n reis deur Noord-Portugal, 1970, Latynse Reise, 1991; translator: Lewis Carroll's Alice Through the Looking Glass (So. African Acad. Prose Translation prize 1970), others. Decorated Chevalier de Legion d'honneur, France, Commandeur de L'Ordre des arts et des lettres (France); recipient Beina Geerligs prize, 1964. Office: Univ Cape Town, Rondebosch, Cape Town 7701, South Africa

BRINK, DAVID MAURICE, physicist; b. Hobart, Tasmania, Australia, July 20, 1930; s. Maurice Ossian and Victoria May (Finlayson) B.; m. Verena Wehrli, Sept. 11, 1958; children: Anne-Katherine, Thomas David, Barbara Verena. BSc, U. Tasmania, 1951; DPhil, Oxford U. Lectr. Balliol Coll., Oxford, 1954-58, fellow, 1958-93; CUF lectr. Oxford U., 1958-64, lectr., 1965-88, Moseley Reader, 1988-93; prof. Univ. Trento, Italy, 1993-98. Co-author: Angular Momentum, 1961; author: Nuclear Forces, 1961, Semi-Classical Methods, 1985. Rhodes scholar, Oxford, 1951. Fellow Royal Soc. London, Inst. of Physics; mem. Royal Soc. Uppsala. Avocations: bird watching, hiking, cross-country skiing. Home: 34 Minster Rd, Oxford OX4 1LY, England

BRINK, NILS ERIK, ecohydrologist; b. Färila, Sweden, Nov. 27, 1921; s. Jon Olof and Anna Petréa (Hannberg) B.; m. Greta Maria Broborg, Apr. 5, 1947 (div. Aug. 31, 1994); children: Karl Johan, Anna Karin. Agronomist, Agrl. Coll. of Sweden, Uppsala, 1949, Agronomie Licentiate, 1954, DAgrl, 1962, lectr., 1963, prof., 1984. Tchr. Farm Sch., Arbrå, Sweden, 1948-49; asst., 1st asst. Agrl. Coll. of Sweden, Uppsala, 1948-62, rschr., 1962-70, asst. prof., 1970-77; asst. prof. Swedish U. Agrl. Scis., Uppsala, 1977-84; prof., 1984-87, emeritus prof., 1987—, rschr. on composting, 1987—; founder Divsn. Water Protection, Agrl. Coll., 1970; rschr. agro-hydrology, 1948-54, purification of sewage water, 1954-62, on selfpurification in soils and streams, studies on protozooan in sandfilters, 1962-72, on water pollution from agriculture and forests, leaching of nutrients and pesticides, 1972-87, composting, 1975-82, 87-99; tchr. hydrology, wat. prot. Inst. Soil Sci., Agrl. Coll., 1949-87, tchr. math., 1963-70; tchr. Inst. Tech. Stockholm, 1949-56, dept. limnology Uppsala U., 1965-69; cons. in ecohydrology, Uppsala, 1990-98; with Swedish Agr. and Forest Rsch. Coun., Nat. Swedish Environ. Protection Agy., Swedish Acad. Agr. and Forestry, Nordic Agrl. Soc., Scandinavian Coun. Applied Rsch., Swedish Soc. Conservation Nature; lectr. in field. Contbr. articles to profl. jours. and chpt. to books. Chmn. Health Care, Uppsala, 1968-72; active Ekhaga Found. Officer of Res., Infantry, 1945-70, Hort. Exptl. Sta. at Swedish U. Agrl. Scis. Named hon. gov. Swedish Govt., Stockholm, 1984. Fellow The Masonic Order, Red Cross. Achievements include patents in Sewage Water Purification. Home: N Parkvägen 5, 75645 Uppsala Sweden Office: Swedish U Agrl Scis, 75007 Uppsala Sweden

BRINKEN, FRANK, manufacturing executive; b. Duisburg, Germany, Nov. 10, 1948; arrived in Switzerland, 1979; s. Helmut and Hannelore (Dickel) B.; m. Petra Brinken, Aug. 8, 1980; 1 child, Berit. MSc in Engring., U. Aachen, Germany, 1975, PhD in Polymer Processing, 1979; postgrad., U. St. Gallen, Switzerland, 1980. Rsch. assoc. IKV Plastics Processing, Aachen, 1975-79; product mgr. George Fischer, Schaffhausen, Switzerland, 1979-88; v.p. Alusuisse-Airex, Zurich, Switzerland, 1988-94; pres., CEO Maag Textron AG, Zurich, Switzerland, 1995—. Co-author: (book) PVC Handbook, 1985. Home: Lerchenweg 14, 6343 Risch-Rotkreuz Switzerland

BRINKER, THOMAS MICHAEL, finance executive; b. Phila., Sept. 8, 1933; s. William Joseph and Elizabeth C. (Feeley) B.; m. Doris Marie Carlin, Oct. 11, 1958; children: Thomas Michael, James E., Joseph F., Diane M. Student, St. Joseph's U., U. Pa.; MS in Fin. Svcs., Am. Coll., 1980; DBA, Heed U., 1990; BA in Orgnl. Mgmt., Ea. Coll., 1991. Registered investment advisor; CLU, ChFC, CFP, AEP. With Ice Capades, 1951-52, 56; with Casa Carioca, Garmisch, Fed. Rep. Germany, 1954-56; profl. ice skating tchr. and mfrs. rep. Ridley Park, Pa., 1956-60; agt., div. mgr. Prudential Ins. Co., Phila., 1960-65; gen. agt. Mut. Trust Life Ins. Co., 1965-70; pres., founder Fringe Benefits Inc., Havertown, Pa., 1970—, Fin. Foresight Ltd., Havertown, Pa., 1983—; adj. prof. Pa. State U., 1984—, St. Joseph's U., 1985—. Host weekly radio show: Financial Forum, Sta. WWDB-FM, 1982-90, Sta. WCZN-AM, 1990-91, daily report on fin. foresight Sta. WFLN-FM, 1992—, WCZN-AM, 1994—, children's fin. reports on Dr. Tom on Money Matters, WPWA-AM, 1994—, weekly radio program WWCN, Estero, Fla., 1997, others; co-host weekly radio program Fin. Foresight, Sta. WFIL-AM, Phila., 1998—; author: HI, I'm Tom Brinker, You're on WWDB, 1987; columnist: Financially Yours, 1983—, Dollars and $ense, 1999—; ghostwriter: Nat. Assn. Life Underwriter's Fin. Fitness campaign, 1985; columnist Dollars and $ense, 1999—; contbr., author, condr. of seminars on fin. planning; contbr. articles to profl. jours. Pres., Delaware County Estate Planning Coun., 1979-80, Pipeline Inc., Springfield, Pa., 1970-71; dir. nat. coun. Invest-in-Am., 1986; bd. dirs. Pacific Advisors Fund, Inc., 1992—, Cypress Benefit Svcs., Inc., 1997—. Recipient Nat. Quality awards Nat. Assn. Life Underwriters, 1966—, Nat. Sales Achievement awards, 1970—. Mem. CLU (ChFC), Delaware County Life Underwriters (pres. 1975-76, 82-83), Am. Coll. Life Underwriters, Nat. Assn. Life Underwriters, Internat. Platform Assn., Internat. Assn. Fin. Planners (CFP practitioner, v.p. Delaware Valley chpt. 1986-88, pres. 1989—, chmn. 1990—), Million Dollar Round Table (mem. Ct. of the Table 1986—, Top of the Table 1991, 93, 94, 95, Twenty-Five Million Dollar Internat. forum 1992-93), Lake Naomi Club (v.p., mem. bd. govs. 1982, pres. 1986), KC, Manor Club, Tom Brinker's Op. Christmas Baskets (pres.), Kingsport Club, Inc. (bd. dirs., treas. 1997—). Roman Catholic. Home: 115 Locust Ave Springfield PA 19064-1619 Office: 1 N Ormond Ave Havertown PA 19083-5010

BRINKERHOFF, PETER JOHN, manufacturing company executive; b. Hackensack, N.J., Aug. 1, 1945; s. James Walter II and Janet Stole (Mohair) B.; m. Jeannine Teresa Heneault, Aug. 2, 1969; children: Jodie, Peter, Jill. BA in Polit. Sci., Georgetown U., 1967; MBA in Fin., Am. U., 1972. Investment mgr. Am. Security & Trust Co., Washington, 1969-72; ops. exec. ITT, N.Y.C., 1972-75; mgr. corp. devel. Chgo. Pneumatic Tool Co., N.Y.C., 1975-76; v.p. mktg., exec. v.p., pres. Jacobs Mfg. Cos. subs. Chgo. Pneumatic Tool Co., Bloomfield, Conn., 1976-85; founder, chmn., CEO Polestar Group, Inc., West Simsbury, Conn., 1985—, also bd. dirs.; chair, CEO J.H. William Indsl. Products, Inc., Columbus, Ga., 1987-94; COO, Weldotron Corp., Piscataway, N.J., 1995-97; bd. dirs. Am. Supply & Machinery Mfg., Cleve., Allegiance Health Svc., LLC, Lake Success, N.Y., 2000—; Merrill Lynch Interfunding, Inc., N.Y.C., advisor 1987-93; bd. dirs. Scully & Scully, N.Y.C., 1995—; interim COO Shape, Inc., Biddeford, maine, 1988; interim CEO Cannon Ball Industries, Inc., Harvard, Ill., 1989; pres. CEO Aqua Fab Industries, Inc., East Greenwich, R.I., 1990-92; chmn. bd., CEO Gt. Hill Ins. Co., Ltd., Bermuda, 1991-92; founder, CEO Omega Inventory, LLC, 2000—. Bd. dirs. Conn. Bus. Coalition on Health, Hartford, 1984-85; grad., mem. Hartford Leadership Coun., 1982-83; bd. dirs. Simsbury Edn. Enhancement Found., 1994—. Lt. USNR, 1967-69. Mem. Am. Supply and Machinery Mfrs. Assn. (bd. dirs. 1983-85, 89-93), Nat. Spa and Pool Inst. (mfrs. coun. 1991-92), Hand Tool Inst. Inc., Hartford Club (Conn.), World Affairs Coun., Western Hwy Inst., Hartford County Mfrs. Assn. (bd. dirs. 1983-85). Roman Catholic. Avocations: skiing, hunting, reading, racquet sports. Office: Polestar Group Inc 20 N Canton Rd West Simsbury CT 06092-2000

BRINKHOUS, KENNETH MERLE, retired pathologist, educator; b. Clayton County, Iowa, May 29, 1908; s. William and Ida (Voss) B.; m. Frances E. Benton, Sept. 5, 1936; children: William Kenneth, John Robert. Student, U.S. Mil. Acad., 1925; AB, U. Iowa, 1929, MD, 1932; DSc, U. Chgo., 1967, U. N.C., 1995. Asst. in pathology U. Iowa, 1932-33, instr., 1933-35, assoc. in pathology, 1935-37, asst. prof., 1937-45, assoc. prof., 1945-46; prof. pathology U. N.C., Chapel Hill, 1946-61; alumni distinguished prof. U. N.C., 1961-80, emeritus, 1980-93; Mem. Nat. Adv. Heart and Lung Council, 1969-74; chmn. med. adv. council Nat. Hemophilia Found., 1954-73; sec. gen. Internat. Com. Hemostasis and Thrombosis, 1966-78. Bd. editors Perspectives in Biol. Medicine, 1968—; editor Archives Pathology and Lab. Medicine, 1974-83, Yearbook Pathology Clin. Pathology, 1980-91. Served from capt. to lt. col. M.C. U.S. Army, 1941-46; col. Med. Res. Corps 1946—. Co-recipient Ward Burdick award Am. Soc. Clin. Pathologists, 1941, 63, O. Max Gardner award, 1961, N.C. award, 1969, Internat. Heart Rsch. award, 1969, Murray Thelin award Nat. Hemophilia Found., 1972, Disting. Achievement award Modern Medicine, 1973, Maude Abbott award Internat. Acad. Pathology, 1985, Disting. Svc. award AMA, 1986, 50th Yr. Rsch. award NIH, 1992, Landsteiner award Am. Assn. Blood Banks, 1994; named H.P. Smith lectr., 1974. Mem. Nat. Acad. Scis. Inst. of Medicine, Am. Acad. Arts and Scis., Assn. Am. Physicians, Internat. Soc. Thrombosis and Haemostasis (pres. 1971, Robert P. Grant award 1985), Am. Assn. Pathologists and Bacteriologists (sec., treas. 1968-71, pres. 1973, Gold-headed Cane award 1981), Am. Soc. Exptl. Pathology (pres. 1965-66), Fedn. Am. Socs. Exptl. Biology (pres. 1966-67), Univs. Assoc. Research and Edn. Pathology (pres. 1964-68), Assn. Pathology Chmn. (Disting. Svc. award 1989), Acad. Clin. Lab. Physicians and Scientists (Cotlove award 1991). Home: 524 Dogwood Dr Chapel Hill NC 27516-2884

BRINKLEY, DAVID MCCLURE, news commentator; b. Wilmington, N.C., July 10, 1920; s. William Graham and Mary (West) B.; m. Ann Fischer, Oct. 11, 1946; children: Alan, Joel, John; m. Susan Adolph, June 10, 1972; 1 child, Alexis. Reporter Wilmington (N.C.) Star-News, 1938-41; reporter, bur. mgr. United Press Assns., various So. cities, 1941-43; news writer, broadcaster radio and TV NBC, Washington, 1943—; Washington corr. NBC, 1951-81; anchorman ABC This Week, 1981-97; ret., 1997. Recipient duPont award, Peabody award, Sch. Bell award, Pres. Medal of Freedom, 1992, other journalism awards. *

BRINKLEY, SHELIA M., poet; b. Apr. 27, 1949. Acting supr. U.S. Postal Svc., Washington; owner Heart to Heart Splty. Co. Author: Two Sides To A Coin. Mem. Poetry Soc. Am., Soc. for Scholarly Pub. Address: 7900 Anchor St Landover MD 20785-4803

BRISARD, JEAN-CHARLES, business intelligence executive; b. Dijon, France, May 13, 1968; s. Maurice and Bogena (Jerocka) B.; m. Geraldine Lesieur, July 2, 1997; 1 child, Sixtine. BA, Georgetown U., 1990; MD, Sch. Comparative Law, Paris, 1991, Institute Jud. Studies, Paris, 1993; PhD in Internat. Law, U. Law, Paris, 1994. Asst. Senator Timothy E. Wirth, Washington, 1989-90, Mem. Parliament Christian Estrosi, Paris, 1991-93, Mem. Parliament Alain Marsaud, Paris, 1993-95; legal cons. CGE Group, Paris, 1995-97, asst. dep. mgr. water divsn., 1997-98; dep. dir. analysis and prospective Vivendi Group, Paris, 1998—; asst. for intelligence Pierre Lellouche; diplomatic advisor Mayor of Paris, 1992-93; advisor for internat. law of the sea Pres. of French Polynesia, 1993; asst. press sec. Prime Min. Edouard Balladur, Paris, 1995; lectr. Nat. Security Coun., Inst. des Hautes Etudes de Def. Nat., Paris, 1992, Def. and Intelligence, 1992; legal advisor Tuareg Intermediation Com., Paris, 1991-92. Author: Charles Pasqua, Une Force Peu Tranquille, 1995, Enquete Au Coeur Du RPR, 1996; contbr. articles to profl. jours. Mem. Ctr. for Internat. Rels. Rsch. and Info. (pres. 1989—), Soc. of Competitive Intelligence Profls. Office: Vivendi, 42 Ave De Friedland, 75008 Paris France

BRISBY, JOHN CONSTANT SHANNON, barrister; b. London, May 8, 1956; s. Michael Douglas James and Liliana Rada (Daneff) B.; m. Claire Alexander Anne Logan, Apr. 20, 1985. MA, Oxford (Eng.) U., 1977. Barrister, 1978, apptd. Queen's Counsel, 1996. Barrister Chambers of Mr. Philip Heslop QC, London. 2d lt., 5th Royal Inniskilling Dragoon Guards, 1974. Avocations: hunting, tennis, gardening, opera. Office: 4 Stone Bldgs, Lincolns Inn, London WC2A 3XT, England

BRISCOE, JOHN, classical languages educator; b. London, Feb. 10, 1938; s. Emmanuel and Rita Rosie (Simmons) B.; m. Lynden Margaret Moore, Mar. 19, 1966 (div. 1975); children: Celia Patricia, Ivan Terence. BA, U. Oxford, England, 1960, MA, 1963, DPhil, 1965. Lectr. ancient history Corpus Christi Coll., U. Oxford, England, 1967-68; lectr. Greek and Latin U. Manchester, England, 1968-74, sr. lectr. Greek and Latin, 1974-82, reader Latin, 1982-96, hon. rsch. fellow, 1996—. Author: Commentary on Livy, 31-33, 1973, Commentary on Livy, 34-37, 1981; editor: Titi Livi ab urbe condita libri XLI-XLV, 1986, Titi Livi ab urbe Candita libri XXXI-XL, 1991, Valeri Maximi facta et dicta memorabilia, 1998; contbr. articles to profl. jours. recipient Rsch. awards Brit. Acad., 1976, 78-79, 84, 87, 90; jr. rsch. fellow Corpus Christi Coll., U. Oxford, 1962-67, vis. fellow Wolfson Coll., U. Oxford, 1981-82. Mem. Roman Soc. (mem. coun. 1976-79), Classical Assn. (hon. sec. Manchester br. 1974-81, 84-96, chmn. 1983-84, v.p. 1996—), South-west Manchester Cricket Club. Mem. Labour Party. Home: 4 Lisburn Ave, Chorlton-cum-Hardy, Manchester M2i0TQ, England Office: Dept Latin/Classics/History, Univ of Manchester, Manchester M13 9PL, England

BRISEBOIS, MARCEL, museum director; b. Valleyfield, Que., Can., Oct. 25, 1933; s. Marc and Rose-Alma (Emond) B. BA, Coll. Valleyfield, 1954; PhD, La Sorbonne U., Paris, 1967; Lic. in Theology, Grand Seminar, Montreal (Que), 1968; hon. degree in art, McGill U., Montreal, 1999. Prof. French, philosophy Coll. Valleyfield, 1958-61, prof. philosophy, head dept., 1968-71, asst. dir., 1971-79, sec. gen., 1979-85; animator, interviewer Radio-Can., Montreal, 1960—; dir. gen. Mus. of Contemporary Art, Montreal, 1985—. Decorated Legion d'Honneur, Ordre du Canada, Ordre de Malte, Ordre de la Pleiade. Office: Musee d'Art Contemp/Montreal, 185 Rue Ste Catherine Quest, Montreal, PQ Canada H2X 3X5

BRISKIN, MADELEINE, paleo-oceanographer, paleoclimatologist, micropaleontologist; b. Paris, Sept. 4, 1932; came to U.S., 1951, naturalized, 1956; d. Michel and Mina B. BS, CCNY, 1965; MS, U. Conn., 1967; PhD, Brown U., 1973. Prof. geology Geology-Physics Bldg., U. Cin., 1980—. Recipient award Rsch. Support, 1971-72, Support award NSF, 1978. Mem. AAAS, Am. Geophys. Union, Am. Quaternary Assn., Paleontologist Soc., Climap, Cin. Engrs. and Scientists Soc., Woods Hole Oceanographic Instn., Lamont-Doherty Geol. Obs., N.Y. Acad. Scis., Sigma Xi. Achievements include discovery of 430,000 plus years astronomical cycle in deep-sea sediments; development of pulsating earth model. Office: U Cin Dept Geology Cincinnati OH 45221-0001

BRISLAIN, JUDY ANN, psychologist; b. Hawthorne, Nev., Apr. 24, 1947; d. Margaret Johnson; m. Gregory Brislain, July 4, 1976. BA in English Edn., U. Nev., 1969; MA in Spl. Edn., Calif. State U., 1972; EdD in Ednl. and Counseling Psychology, U. Pacific, 1984. Lic. ednl. psychologist, marriage, family child therapist; lic. secondary tchr., Calif., learning handicapped tchg. specialist, Calif., pupil pers. svcs., Calif., C.C. instr., Calif. Tchr. English, forensic coach Placer Joint Union High Sch. Dist., Auburn, Calif., 1969-70; disgnostic clinician Melvin-Smith Sch., Sacramento, Calif., 1970-71, tchr., 1971-74, resource specialist, program coord., 1974-75, program and behavior guidance coord., 1975-77; clin. edn. dir. Brislain Learning Ctr., 1977—; pvt. practice, 1980—; cons. Dept. Grants and Rsch. Devel. Calif. State U., Chico, others. Author: Diagnosis in the Classroom: Program for Success, 1973, Ready, Set Go: A Language Program, 1974. Bd. dirs. Campfire, Inc., 1984, Chico Mus. Found.; co-chair Chico Tomorrow, 1986; mem. steering com. Sch. Bond Election, 1988, Butte County Literacy Coun., 1990; bd. dirs. Chico Community Found., Project Child; mem. steering com. Chico Unified Sch. Dist. Hall of Fame; apptd. by Gov. Pete Wilson to Calif. State Bd. Behavioral Sci. Examiners, 1992, chair, 1994-96. Mem. Am. Assn.

Marriage & Family therapy, P.G. & E. Caribou Group for Women Leaders, Rotary Internat. (bd. dirs., pres. 1998— Chico chpt.), Greater Chico C. of C. (chair edn. com., bd. dirs., chair bus.-sch. partnership subcom., Athena award 1991). Office: Brislain Learning Ctr 1550 Humboldt Rd Ste 3 Chico CA 95928-9115

BRISSENDEN, ALAN (THEO), writer; b. Griffith, Australia, Oct. 13, 1932; s. Arthur Piercy and Nellie (Rogers) B.; m. Elizabeth Jane Irwin King, Oct. 15, 1960; children: Roger James, Piers King, Celia Jane. BA with honors, U. Sydney, 1954, diploma in edn., 1955; PhD, U. London, 1962. Tchr. Edn. Dept. of NSW, Sydney, 1955, rsch. officer, 1956-59; lectr. U. Adelaide, Australia, 1963-67, sr. lectr., 1968-81, reader in English, 1982-94, hon. vis. rsch. fellow, 1995—, chmn. dept., 1985-86; mem. adv. com. for South Australia Australian Broadcasting Commn., 1972-75, com. chmn., 1976-77; dance reviewer ABC-Radio, 1984-88; vis. fellow Wolfson Coll., Oxford, 1987, 92; dance critic Sydney Morning Herald, 1952-55, Advertiser, Adelaide, 1976-84, Dance mag., 1979-83, Dance Australia, 1980—, Australian, 1990—. Author: Rolf Boldrewood, 1972, Shakespeare and the Dance, 1981; co-editor: They Came to Australia, 1961; editor: A Chaste Maid in Cheapside, 1968, Lawson's Australia, 1973, The Drover's Wife and Other Stories by Henry Lawson, 1974, Aspects of Australian Fiction, 1990, As You Like It, 1993; writer TV series Theatre Through the Ages, 1963; gen. co-editor series Studies in Tudor and Stuart Literature, 1973-83; contbr. Spenser Encyclopedia and Reference Guide to English Literature; contbr. to lit. and dance jours. South Australian mem. Nat. Lit. Bd. of Review, 1971-74; mem. exec. com. Arts Coun. South Australia, 1971, chmn. and v.p., 1972-74; bd. govs. Adelaide Festival Arts, 1981-94; chmn. Early Imprints Project in South Australia, 1977—; exec. mem. Early Imprints Project in Australia and New Zealand, 1979—; pres. Friends of State Library S. Australia, 1994—; hon. life mem. Friends of Adelaide Festival, 1996. Decorated Order of Australia, 1996; grantee Australian Rsch. Grants Com., 1968-71, 78-82, Brit. Coun., 1974-75, Ian Potter Found., 1979, 92; fellow Huntington Libr., 1979. Mem. Bibliographical Soc. Australia and New Zealand (pres. 1983-86), English Assn. (chmn. Adelaide br. 1970-73), Bibliographical Soc. (Eng.), Australian and New Zealand Shakespeare Assn. (v.p. 1990-92, pres. 1992-94, hon. life 1998). Office: U Adelaide, Dept English, Adelaide SA 5005, Australia

BRISSON, THERESE, hockey player; b. Dollard-des-Ormeaux, Can., Oct. 5, 1966. PhD in Phys. Activity Sci., U. Montreal. Profl. hockey player Maritime Sports Blades, 1989—; asst. prof. kinesiology U. New Brunswick, 1995—; mem. Ringuette Championship Team, 1990. Recipient ice hockey Silver medal Olympic Games, Nagano, Japan, 1998. Avocations: golf, ball hockey, wine making. Office: Can Olympic Assn Av Pierre Dupuy 2380, Montreal, PQ Canada H3C 3R4*

BRISSOT, PIERRE GABRIEL, physician, medical educator; b. Paris, Sept. 13, 1947; s. Georges Albert and Antoinette Amélia (Devaux) B.; m. Régine Blanche Maillard, Sept. 5, 1970; children: Fabien, Vincent, Eolia, Virginie. MD, Faculty of Medicine, Rennes, France, 1974. Prof. medicine U. Pontchaillou Hosp., Rennes, France, 1979—; head of liver disease unit Pontchaillou Hosp., Rennes, 1987—; vis. assoc. prof. medicine U. Calif., San Francisco, 1983; dir. rsch. group Inserm Rsch. Unit, Rennes, 1985—; vice-dean Faculty of Medicine, Rennes, 1989-96; mem. sci. com. Found. for Med. Rsch., Paris, 1990-94; vis. prof. medicine Harvard Med. Sch., Boston, 1990, U. Calif. San Diego, 1995. Contbr. articles to profl. jours. Avocations: family life, piano. Office: Univ Hosp Pontchaillou, rue Henri Le Guilloux, 35033 Rennes France

BRISTOW, CYNTHIA LYNN, immunologist; b. Altus, Okla., Aug. 19, 1951; d. Robert O'Neil Bristow and Gaylon Eva Walker; children: Charlie, Bo, Rachel, Mary Ann, Rudy. BA, Winthrop U., 1972; MS, Med. U. S.C., Charleston, 1979, PhD, 1986. Postdoctoral assoc. biochemistry Med. U. of S.C., Charleston, 1986-88; postdoctoral assoc. dental rsch. ctr. U. N.C., Chapel Hill, 1988-94; clin. immunologist Pathology and Lab. Medicine U. N.C. Hosps., Chapel Hill, 1999—; rsch. asst. prof. U. N.C., Chapel Hill, 1994-98. Mem. editl. bd. Biotechnology and Applied Biochemistry, 1996; contbr. articles to profl. jours., chpts. to books; patentee in biotechnology. Recipient Elsa Pardee Found. award, 1990; grantee NIH., 1994. Mem. Am. Soc. Microbiology, Am. Assn. Immunologists, Am. Chem. Soc., Sigma Xi. Episcopalian. Avocations: running, music, poetry, art, tennis. Office: UNC Hosps Mclendon Clin Labs Chapel Hill NC 27599-0001

BRISTOW, JAMETT LAGENIA, not-for-profit developer; b. Ft. Dix, N.J., May 22, 1965; d. James Eugene and Davetta Kaie (Florance) B.; m. Lemule V. Mills, Feb. 14, 1984 (div. May 1988). BA in English, Bennett Coll., 1990. Programmer, instr. City of Greensboro (N.C.), 1990-92; programmer Muscular Dystrophy, Greensboro, 1992-93; dir. edn., advtsg. YWCA, Greensboro, 1994-97; exec. dir. Teen Resource Ctr., High Point, N.C., 1997-98, African-Am. Heritage Soc., Pensacola, Fla., 1997-98; dir. bus. devel. nat. office AAUW, Washington, 1998—; owner JB Enterprise, Greensboro, N.C.; cons., com. chair Greensboro C. of C., 1992-96. Author: poems. Mem. Wake-Up Rep. Women, Greensboro, 1997, Escambia County Rep. Women, 1998-99; mem. nat. adv. bd. Women's Sports Found., Greensboro, Pensacola and Herndon, Va., 1995—. Mem. Herndon/Dulles C. of C., Alpha Kappa Alpha, Sigma Tau Delta. Avocations: community advocate for women, writing, community building. Office: AAUW 111 Sixteenth St NW Washington DC 20036

BRISTOW, JOHN LESLIE, science consulting company executive; b. Brisbane, Queensland, Australia, Oct. 22, 1931; s. Joseph Francis and Winifred Mary (Peterson) B.; m. Ruth Helen Bevege, Dec. 7, 1957; children: David Joseph, Helen Elizabeth, Andrew Peter John. BS, U. Queensland, 1955, 1955. Registered profl. engr., Queensland; companion Instn. Engrs. Australia. Indsl. chemist Brisbane City Coun. Water Supply & Sewerage Dept., 1951-62, Intercolonial Boring Co. Pty. Ltd., Brisbane, 1962-64; mgr. IBC/Culligan Pty. Ltd., Brisbane, 1964-69; indsl. chemist M.A. Simmonds Cons. Chem. Engrs., Brisbane, 1970-76; ptnr. M.A. Simmonds & Bristow, Brisbane, 1976-81; mng. dir. Simmonds & Bristow, Brisbane, 1981-95; mng. dir., sci. cons. Bristow Cons. Pty. Ltd., Brisbane, 1995—. Author: Water and Wastewater Treatment Evaluation and Upgrading of Existing Treatment Plants, 1975; contbr. articles to profl. jours. Chmn. Moggill Progress Assn., Brisbane, 1976-78; outings chmn. Nat. Parks assn. Qld. 1997-99; pres. Rural Environ. Planning Assn., 1998-2000. Mem. Australian Water and Wastewater Assn. (life., pres. com., editor Old Branch newsletter Watertalk 1992-95), Australasian Corrosion Assn. (life, mem. com. 1962—, sec. 1970-78, treas. 1990-98, pres. 1993-97), Am. Water Works Assn. (life), Nat. Parks Assn. Queensland (outings chmn. 1997-99), Royal Australian Chem. Inst., Rural Environ. Planning Assn. (pres. 1998-99). Avocations: bushwalking, photography, four wheel driving. Office: Bristow Cons Pty Ltd, 84 Essendon Rd, Anstead Brisbane Queensland 4070, Australia

BRISTOW, LOUISE ALICE, mental health nurse; b. N.Y.C., Mar. 9, 1943; d. Edward Frances and Elinore (Spuler) Leffert; m. Marshall Roger Bristow, May 31, 1970; 1 child, Christopher Darius. BS, Rutgers Coll. Nursing, 1966; MEd, Columbia U., N.Y.C., 1973. Nurse clinician Bellevue Hosp. Ctr., N.Y.C., 1967-69; cmty. mental health nurse South Beach Psychiat. Ctr., Bklyn., 1969-72; sr. psychiat. nurse NYU Med. Ctr., N.Y.C., 1974-79; clin. specialist Beth Israel Med. Ctr., N.Y.C., 1979-84; asst. prof. nursing Dalhousie U., Halifax, N.S., Can., 1973-74, CCNY, 1974-75; ind. med.-legal cons. N.Y.C., 1985-89, cons. ego devel. and child rearing, 1989—; med.-legal cons. Commn. for Human Rights, N.Y.C., 1987-88. Active Dem. Nat. Com., N.Y.C., 1992—, LWV, N.Y.C., 1991—. NIMH scholar, Washington, 1965-72. Mem. ANA, N.Y. Nurses Assn. (mem. dist. 13 coms. 1990—). Roman Catholic. Avocations: orchid raising, painting, community activities. Home: 10 Waterside Plz New York NY 10010-2602

BRISTOW, ROBERT O'NEIL, writer, educator; b. St. Louis, Nov. 17, 1926; s. Jesse Reuben and Helen Marjorie (Utley) B.; children by previous marriage—Cynthia Lynn, Margery Jan Wu, Gregory Scott, Kelly Robert. B.A. in Journalism, U. Okla., 1951, M.A. in Journalism, 1965. Asst. advt. mgr. Altus (Okla.) Times Democrat, 1951-53; free-lance writer Altus, 1951-60; prof. English Winthrop Coll., Rock Hill, S.C., 1960-87, prof. emeritus, 1987—. Author: Time for Glory, 1968, Night Season, 1970, A Faraway Drummer, 1973, Laughter in Darkness, 1974. Served with USNR, 1944-45. Recipient award for lit. excellence U. Okla., 1969, award for novel Friends of Am. Writers, 1974. Mem. Alpha Tau Omega. Home: 613 1/2 Charlotte Ave Rock Hill SC 29730-3648

BRISTOW, WALTER JAMES, JR., retired judge; b. Columbia, S.C., Oct. 14, 1924; s. Walter James and Caroline Belser (Melton) B.; m. Katherine Stewart Mullins, Sept. 12, 1952; children: Walter James III, Katherine Mullins (dec.). Student, Va. Mil. Inst., 1941-43; AB, U. N.C., 1947; LLB cum laude, U. S.C., 1947-50; LLM, Harvard U., 1950. Mem. Marchant, Bristow & Bates, 1953-76, S.C. Ho. of Reps., 1956-58, S.C. Senate, 1958-76; resident judge 5th Cir. Ct. S.C., 1976-88; ret., 1988; nat. pres. Conf. Ins. Legislators, 1974-75. Trustee Elvira Wright Fund for Crippled Children, 1963-76; mem. bd. visitors ex officio The Citadel, Charleston, S.C., 1967-76. Served with AUS, 1943-45; ETO, brig. gen. S.C. Army N.G. Decorated Meritorious Svc. medal; recipient Order of Palmetto, 1999, Order of Cypress, 1999. Mem. ABA, Wig and Robe, S.C. Law Inst., S.C. Coun. on Holocaust, Capital City Club, Cotillion Club, Forest Lake Club, Palmetto Club, Columbia Ball Club, Sertoma, Alpha Tau Omega. Democrat. Office: PO Box 1147 Columbia SC 29202-1147

BRITO, ADELSON SILVA DE, physicist, educator, producer, entertainer; b. Salvador, Bahia, Brazil, Aug. 30, 1954; s. Jandir Cardoso de Brito and Conceicão Silva de Brito; m. Mieko Nagai de Brito, June 29, 1991. Ed., Electro-Mechanics Sch., Salvador, 1972; degree, Fed. U. Bahia, Salvador, 1987. Prof. physics Nat. Svc. for Indsl. Learning, Salvador, 1973-74; mgr. Brito's Car Repair & Parts Ltd., Salvador, 1974-81; maintenance mgr. Agrl. Coop. of Cotia, Sao Paulo, Brazil, 1983-85; sr. technician, cons. Caraiba Copper Mine Corp., Jaguarari, Bahia, 1985-87; gen. supr. Sansuy Plastic Corp., Camacari, Bahia, 1987-88, Co. Valley of Rio Doce, Serrinha, Bahia, 1988-89; with Creation Ho., Hamamatsu, Shizuoka, Japan; cons. Agrl. Coop. of Cotia, 1973-74, Soc. for Study of African Culture in Brazil, Salvador, 1987-90. Contbr. articles to profl. jours. Counselor Olodum Afro-Brazil, Salvador, 1986-87, cons., 1987—; translator Police of Shizuoka, 1997; mem. host com. Congress Nat. Assn., Salvador, 1987. Mem. AAAS, Planetary Soc. Roman Catholic. Avocations: fine arts, foreign languages, musical performances, Afro-Brazilian culture, play writing and producing. Office: Creation Ho, Renjaku-cho 314-36 405, Shizuoka Hamamatsu 430, Japan

BRITO, EMILIO, priest, educator; b. Havana, Cuba, Oct. 8, 1942; arrived in Belgium, naturalized, 1993; s. Emilio Brito and Lucila Lanzada. BA, Fordham U., 1967, MA, 1969; PhD, Louvain (Belgium) U., 1979, Maître-agrégé, 1983. Mem. Jesuits, 1961—; ordained priest Roman Catholic Ch., 1972; cert. univ. prof. dogmatics and philosophy of religion. Prof. Archdiocesan Sem., Santo Domingo, Dominican Republic, 1976-79, Jesuit Theologate, Brussels, 1979-83, Louvain U., 1983—. Author: (books) Hegel's Christology, 2 vols., 1979, 83, Schelling's Doctrine of Creation, 1987, Aquinas and Hegel on Being and God, 1991, Schleiermacher's Pneumatology, 1994, Heidegger and the Holy, 1999; editl. cons. Ephemerides Theologicae Lovanienses, Louvain, 1984—, Revue théologique de Louvain, 1995—. Mem. Theol. Soc. Louvain, Philos. Soc. Louvain. Roman Catholic. Home: Ave de l'Equerre 21 Apt 106, 1348 Louvain-la-Neuve Belgium Office: Faculty Theology, Grand-Place 45, 1348 Louvain-la-Neuve Belgium

BRITO, HECTOR HUGO, aerospace engineer; b. Cordoba, Argentina, May 13, 1944; s. Juan Hector and Elba Angelica (Gomez) B.; m. Maria Cristina Ramallo, Sept. 17, 1971; children: Claude Martin, Veronica Ines, Marcos Alejandro. Ingenieur Civil de L'Aeronautique, Ecole Nat. Supérieure de l'Aéronautique et de l'Espace, Toulouse, France, 1971. Cert. engr. Project engr. Soc. Europeenne de Propulsion, Paris, 1971-74; head propulsion divsn. Instituto de Investigaciones Aeronauticas y Espaciales, Cordoba, Argentina, 1974-80, head system analysis divsn., 1980-84, flight dynamics sci. advisor, 1984-88; space systems sci. advisor Inst. de Investigaciones Tecnologicas de Fuerza Aerea, Cordoba, Argentina, 1988-91; project dir. microsatellite, cons. ops. rsch. Inst. Universitario Aeronautico, Cordoba, Argentina, 1991-99; project mgr. plasma propulsion, 1999—; lectr. Universidad Nacional de Rio Cuarto, Argentina, 1976—, dir. computational mechanics group, 1988—. Contbr. articles to profl. jours.; patentee in field. Com. leader Centro de Estudios Aeroespaciales, Cordoba, 1983. French Govt. scholar, 1968-71; grantee German Govt., 1978, U. Rio Cuarto, 1988-89, Govt. Cordoba, 1991—, award for outstanding achievement in space tech. Govt. Cordoba, Argentine Air Force and tech. assns., 1996, 97. Fellow Brit. Interplanetary Soc.; mem. AIAA, Interplanetary Soc., Interstellar Propulsion Soc., Engrs. and Scientists France. Avocations: playing electric guitar, soccer, chess games, reading. Office: Inst Univ Aeronautico, Ruta 20 Km 6.5, 5022 Cordoba Argentina

BRITO, JOSÉ, planning executive, management consultant; b. Dakar, Senegal, Mar. 19, 1944; s. Máximo Nascimento and Judith (Serrão) B.; m. Gisele Monique Regy, Aug. 23, 1969 (div. Aug. 1986); children: Lydia, Mehdi, Christel; m. Maria de Lourdes Oliveira Santos, June 24, 1988; 1 child, Cristofer Wali. M Physics, U. Abidjan, Ivory Coast, 1967; degree in chem. engring., French Inst. Petroleum, Rueil Malmaison, France, 1969. Tech. dir. SIR, Abidjan, 1969-75; internat. coop. dir. Govt. of Cape Verde, 1975-77, state sec. coop. and planning, 1977-86, min. planning and coop., 1986-91; dir. African futures project UNDP, Abidjan, 1992-96; dir. planning UMC, Malabo, Equatorial Guinea, 1997-99; v.p. govt. rels. Ocean Energy, 1999-2000; ind. strategic mgmt. cons., Ivory Coast, 1996-97; co-chmn. UN Conf. on Less Developed Countries, 1981; negotiator Lomé Convention; chmn. meeting Coords. of European Union and Sahel countries. Editor: Filières Natronales et Marchés Nondiaux de Natières Premières, 1997, African Futures Bull., 1994-96. Mem. Parliament, Govt. of Cape Verde, 1985-90; bd. dirs. Amilcar Cabral Found., 1989-91. Mem. World Future Soc. Mem. African Party for Independence of Cape Verde. Avocations: African politics, professional readings, transcendental meditation, television sports. E-mail: xbrito@aol.com. Office: Ocean Energy 1001 Fannin St Ste 1600 Houston TX 77002-6794

BRITO-CRUZ, CARLOS HENRIQUE, physicist, researcher, science administrator; b. Rio de Janeiro, July 19, 1956; s. Jose Armenio and Helena (Brito) Cruz; m. Cibele Andrade Macchi. Elec. engring. degree, ITA, Sjcampos, Brazil, 1978; MSc, Unicamp, Campinas, Brazil, 1980; PhD, Unicamp, 1983. Prof. Physics Inst. Unicamp, Campinas, 1983-85, 87-91; resident visitor AT&T Bell Labs., Holmdel, N.J., 1986-87; dir. Physics Inst. Unicamp, Campinas, 1991-94, dean of rsch., 1994-98, dir., 1998—. Contbr. tech. articles to profl. jours. Mem. Optical Soc. Am. Office: Cidade Universitaria, Physics Inst Unicamp, 13083-970 Campinas Brazil

BRITT, DAVID PAUL, biomedical sciences educator; b. Beckenham, Eng., Jan. 9, 1939; s. Bertram Stanley and Edith Hannah (Jefferies) B.; m. Shirley Margaret Glenville, Mar. 28, 1964; 1 child, Adam. Tchr.'s Cert., U. Leicester, 1967; BA, Open U., 1973; MSc., Salford U., 1978; PhD, Liverpool U., 1984. Med. lab. sci. officer King's Coll. Hosp., London, 1956-63; sr. med. lab. sci. officer Charing Cross Hosp. Med. Sch., London, 1963-64; asst. master for biology Vale of Catmose Village Coll., Oakham, Eng., 1967-68; lectr. med. lab. sci. North East Liverpool Tech. Coll., 1968-74; adviser Nat. Vet. Research Inst., Vom, Nigeria, 1974-77; researcher/demonstrator vet. preventive medicine Liverpool U., 1979-81; sr. research fellow Liverpool Sch. Tropical Medicine, 1982-86; asst. prof. allied health scis. and nursing Kuwait U., 1986-91; health scis. cons. Brit. Coun., Manchester, Eng., 1992—. Contbr. articles on sci. and animal welfare to profl. jours. Winston Churchill Meml. Trust travelling fellow, 1984. Fellow Royal Soc. Tropical Medicine and Hygiene, Inst. Med. Lab. Scis., Inst. Biology; mem. Freshwater Biol. Assn. (life), Wirral Soc. (exec. com. 1985-86, 92—). Avocation: natural history. Home: Nelson Cottage 15 Station Rd, Parkgate South Wirral, Cheshire CH64 6QJ, England Office: Brit Coun Med Dept, Bridgewater Ho Whitworth, Manchester M1 6BB, England

BRITT, DAVID VAN BUREN, retired educational communications executive; b. Needham, Mass., July 30, 1937; s. Paul Merwyn and Ellen Sibront (Bent) B.; m. Marjorie Joan Hoag, Feb. 15, 1958 (div. 1984); children: Pamela Britt Barr, Barbara B. Schaefer, Paul David; m. Sue Britt Cushman, July 22, 1989. AB, Wesleyan U., 1959; MPA, Harvard U., 1967. Ops. mgmt. staff No. Trust Co., Chgo., 1959-62; legis. chief U.S. AID, Washington, 1962-68; chief programs and plans U.S. EEOC, Washington, 1968-69; dep. dir. policy planning U.S. Overseas Pvt. Investment Corp., Washington, 1969-70; ind. cons. Washington, 1970-71; from v.p. to COO Sesame Workshop, N.Y.C., 1971-90; CEO Children's TV Workshop, N.Y.C., 1990-99. Trustee New World Found., N.Y.C., 1978-86, Wesleyan U., Middletown, Conn., 1989-92, CTW, 1990-99; chmn., bd. dirs. KidsVoing, USA; mem. Coun. on Fgn. Rels. Recipient Disting. Alumnus award Wesleyan U., 1994. Episcopalian. Home: 1598 Regatta Dr Amelia Island FL 32034-5541

BRITT, RONALD LEROY, manufacturing company executive; b. Abilene, Tex., Mar. 1, 1935; s. Elvin Elbert and Lona Helen (Conn) B.; m. Judith Ann Salter, June 29, 1957; children: Brett Gavin, Mark Damon, Melissa Ann. B.S.M.E., Wichita State U., 1963. From product engr. to product planner Hotpoint divsn. G.E. Co., Chgo., 1963-68; product planner Norge Co., Chgo., 1968; product mgr., asst. dir. engirng. Leigh Products Inc., Coopersville, Mich., 1968-74; mgr. rsch. and devel. Miami Carey divsn. Jim. Walter Corp., Monroe, Ohio, 1974-84; sr. v.p. mfg. and engring. Belvedere (Ill.) USA Corp., 1984—; industry rep. for electric fans Underwriters Labs. Acitve Boy Scouts Am., 1970-73, PTA, 1973-78; exec. adviser Jr. Achievement, 1984-85, Boone County chmn., 1968-88; bd. dirs. YMCA, Belvidere, 1990-96, vice-chmn., chmn. fin. com., 1991, v.p., 1992; dir. on adv. bd. St. Joseph Hosp., 1990-95 97-99, chmn. long range planning com., 1991; bd. dirs. Boone County Dist. # 100 Edn. Found., 1991-95. Served with U.S. Army, 1958-60. Recipient Inventor's award Gen. Electric Co., 1967. Mem. ASME, Home Ventilation Inst. (engring. com. 1975-84), Belvidere C. of C. (bd. dirs. 1986-89), No. Ill. Corvette Club, Free Blown Glassblowing, Rotary (v.p. 1999-2000). Republican. Congregationalist. Home: 1628 Riverside Rd Belvidere IL 61008-8655 Office: 1 Belvedere Blvd Belvidere IL 61008-8594

BRITTAN, LEON, former British government official, lawyer; b. London, Sept. 25, 1939; s. Joseph and Rebecca Brittan; m. Diana Peterson, 1980; 2 stepchildren. Ed., Trinity Coll., Cambridge U., Yale U.; DCL (hon.), Newcastle, 1990; LlD (hon.), Hull, 1990; Dr. honoris causa, Edinburgh U., 1991; DL (hon.), U. Bradford, 1991; DCL (hon.), U. Durham, 1992; LLD (hon.), U. Bath, 1995. Called to Inner Temple bar, 1962. Chmn. Bow Group, 1964-65; contested N. Kensington seat Parliament, 1966, 70; vice chmn. govs. Isaac Newton Sch., 1968-71; M.P. for Cleveland and Whitby, 1974-83; M.P. for Richmond Yorkshire, 1983-88; vice chmn. Parliamentary Conservative Party Employment Com., 1974-76, opposition spokesman on devolution, 1976-78, on employment, 1978-79, min. state home office, 1979-81, chief sec. to treasury, 1981-83, home sec., 1983-85, sec. of state for trade and industry, 1985-86; v.p. Commn. of European Cmtys., 1989—; vice chmn. UBS Warburg, 2000—; disting. vis. fellow Policy Studies Inst., 1988. Author: (with others) Millstones for the Sixties, Rough Justice, Infancy and the Law, How to Save Your Schools, A New Deal for Health Care, 1988, Defence and Arms Control in a Changing Era, 1988, Europe: Our Sort of Community, 1989, Discussion on Policy, 1989, Monetary Union: The Issues and The Impact, 1989, European Competition Policy, 1992, Europe: The Europe We Need, 1994; editor Crossbow, 1966-67. Apptd. mem. Privy Coun., com. Brit. Atlantic Group of Young Politicians; apptd. chancellor U. Teesside, 1993. Henry fellow Yale U.; decorated knight, 1989. Mem. Nat. Assn. Sch. Govs. and Mgrs. (vice chmn. 1970-78), Soc. Conservative Lawyers (chmn. 1986-89), Cambridge U. Conservative Assn. (chmn. 1960). Office: UBS Warburg, 1/2 Finsbury Ave, Londonls EC2M 2PP, United Kingdom*

BRITTEN, WILLIAM HARRY, editor, publisher; b. Aug. 25, 1921; s. Harry William and Gertrude Alice (Lehman) B. BA, Western Union Coll., 1943; postgrad., Iowa State Coll., summer 1942; MA, State U. Iowa, 1948. Reporter Worcester (Mass.) Telegram, 1948-55; landscaper John F. Keenen, Leicester, Mass., 1956; sales dept. clk. Reed & Prince Mfg. Co., Worcester, 1957-63, inventory control clk., 1964, chief expeditor, 1965; state editor Marshalltown (Iowa) Times-Rep., 1965-66, staff writer, 1966-67; news editor Denison (Iowa) Bull. and Rev., 1967-68; city editor Boone News Rep., 1968; editor, pub., owner The Tri-County News, Zearing, 1968-89, editor emeritus, 1990—; editor, pub. Hubbard (Iowa) Rev., 1969-72. Sec. Young Men's Rep. Club, Worcester, 1957; corr. sec. Young People's Rep. Club, 1958; mem. Ward 8 Rep. Com., Worcester, 1960-65; Rep. candidate Mass. state legislature, 1960; ward chmn. to elect Edward W. Brooke atty. gen. Mass., 1962, 64; bd. dirs. Story County (Iowa) Cancer Soc., 1976-81; chmn. Story County, Lincoln Twp. Reps., 1992, 94; active Ch. of Christ, United Meth. Ch. With AUS, 1943-45. Mem. Iowa Newspaper Assn., Nat. Newspaper Assn., Am. Legion (post comdr. 1982-83), U. Iowa Alumni Assn. Home: 416 S Pearl St Zearing IA 50278-2009 Office: Custer St Zearing IA 50278

BRITTON, MONICA ENA LOUISE, community health nurse, public health nurse; b. Manchester, Jamaica, July 30, 1933; came to U.S., 1967; d. Horatio Agustus and Advira (Campbell) Green; m. Frank Raphael Britton, Nov. 20, 1955. BSN, CUNY-Hunter Coll., 1977, MS in Cmty. Health Edn., 1982. RN, Fla., N.Y.; State Registered Nurse, State Cert. Midwife, Eng. Staff nurse, then sr. staff nurse N.Y.-Cornel Hosp., N.Y.C., 1967-71; staff nurse Vis. Nurse Svc., N.Y.C., 1971-72; pub. health nurse N.Y.C. Dept. Health, 1972-84, pub. health nurse supr., asst. clinics dir., 1984-92; pub. health nurse educator Renaissance Health Care, N.Y.C., 1992-95; regional nursing dir. Child Health Clinics, N.Y.C., 1995—; mem. bd. occupational rev. N.Y.C. Dept. Health, 1984-88. Travel consult to Kenya, Ch. of God World Tour, Anderson, Ind., 1983, travel consult to Hong Kong, 1987; travel consult to Kenya and Uganda, Med. Missions Task Force, Anderson, 1993. Mem. Caring Ptnrs. Internat. (med. mission, Kenya 1997, 99). Democrat. Avocations: travel, reading, community activities, church activities, theatre. Home: 67 Park Ter E New York NY 10034-1445

BRITTON, PAUL, molecular biologist, researcher; b. Leeds, Yorkshire, Eng., July 22, 1956; s. Thomas and Kathleen (Rothary) B.; m. Sarah Jane Emergy, Oct. 6, 1984; 1 child, James George. BSc, Leeds U., 1977; PhD, Edinburgh U., 1981. Postdoctoral rsch. asst. dept. biochemistry U. Cambridge, 1980-83; rsch. scientist divsn. molecular biology Inst. for Animal Health, Compton, 1983—. Contbr. articles to profl. jours. Mem. Soc. for Gen. Microbiology, Biochem. Soc. Avocations: photography, gardening, traveling. Office: Inst Animal Health, Compton, Newbury RG16 ONN, England

BRITTON, PETER LESLIE, mathematician, physicist, educator; b. London, May 12, 1943; arrived in Australia, 1983; s. Francis Henry and Sylvia Margaret (Kerslake) Baragwnath; m. Hazel Ann Fitzgerald, Feb. 23, 1963; children: Mark Falcon, Paul Falcon. BSc in Math., Birmingham (Eng.) U., 1964; postgrad. cert. in edn., External U. of London, 1965. Cert. tchr. Queensland Bd. of Tchr. Edn. Tchr. math. Balovale (Zambia) Secondary Sch., 1965-67; head dept. math. Sawagongo Secondary Sch., Yala, Kenya, 1968-72; sr. master Shimo-La-Tewa Sch., Mombasa, Kenya, 1973-81; tchr. sr. math. Maidstone Grammar Sch., Eng., 1982; head math. All Souls' & St. Gabriel's Sch., Charters Towers, Australia, 1983-93, head math. and sci., 1994-99; mem. Bd. Sr. Secondary Sch. Studies Panel in math. I, Townsville Dist., 1985-95, math. II, 1985-95, math. C, 1994-99. Editor The Sunbird jour., 1990—; contbr. articles to profl. jours.; author: Breeding Seasons of East African Birds, 1979, Birds of East Africa, 1980, Gulls and Terns in The Birds of Africa, 1985. Avocations: ornithology, bird banding, environmental conservation and management. Home and Office: All Souls' & St Gabriel's Sch, Charters Towers 4820 QLD, Australia

BRITTON, RONALD SKIRROW, psychoanalyst, psychiatrist; b. Lancaster, Eng., June 3, 1932; s. Thomas Skirrow and Mary Margaret (Jackson) B.; m. Ritaclare Garlich, June 17, 1957; children: Mark, Julia, Sophia. MB, BChir, Univ. Coll. Hosp. Med. Sch., London, 1956. Commd. lt. Royal Army Med. Corps, 1957, advanced through grades to lt. col., 1968; asst. ho. physician Nat. Hosp. Nervous Disease Queen Sq., London, 1960-61; registrar Maudsley Hosp. Child Psychiatry, London, 1963-64; prof. psychiatry Royal Army Med. Coll., London, 1968-70; sr. registrar Tavistock Clinic, London, 1970-72, cons. psychiatrist, 1974-84; tng. analyst Inst. Psychoanalysis, London, 1985—; vis. prof. child psychiatry Letterman Gen. Hosp., San Francisco, 1971, 72; cons. to social svcs. Kensington/Chelsea, London, 1972-74, Camden, London, 1974-80; chmn. child and parents dept. Tavistock Clinic, London, 1975-81. Author: The Oedipus Complex today, 1989, Belief and Imagination, 1998; book reviewer Jour. Am. Psychoanalysis Assn., 1997, 98, 99; contbr. articles to profl. jours. Princess Elizabeth scholar Princess Elizabeth Birthday Fund, South Rhodes, Africa, 1950. Fellow Royal Coll. Psychiatrists; mem. Brit. Psycho-Anal Soc. (tng. analyst 1985—, chmn. tng. staff 1995-99). Avocations: English literature, philosophy, cinema, hill walking, jogging. E-mail: RBpsych@aol.com. Fax: 171 794 6318. Home and Office: 24 Hillfield Rd, London NW6 1PZ, England

BRITTON, WESLEY ALAN, English language educator; b. Munich, Sept. 29, 1953; came to the U.S., 1955; s. Royce J. and Betty Ruth (Somers) B. BA in English, Calif. U. Pa., 1977; MA in English, U. North Tex., 1986, PhD, 1990. News dir. Calif. U. Pa., 1975-77; prin. Wes Britton Advt. Agy., Dallas, 1977-79; pub. rels. dir. VISTA, Dallas, 1982-83; teaching fellow U. North Tex., Denton, 1983-90, prof. English, 1990-92; instr. Paul Quinn Coll., Dallas, 1991-93; prof. Bacone C.C., Muskoqee, Okla., Southeast Okla. Coll., Durant Cooke C.C., 1993-94, Grayson C.C., Sherman, Tex., 1994-98; cons. Wentwork Films, Washington, 1991; instr. Cedar Valley C.C., Dallas, 1992, Harrisburg (Pa.) Area C.C., 1998—; bd. dirs. KNON, Dallas, 1992. Contbr. poetry, plays, articles to profl. jours., ency. entries and indices. Trustee Assn. Individuals with Disabilities, Dallas, 1981-83; adv. bd. North Tex. Radio for Blind, Dallas, 1983; writer, producer Sta. KERA-Fm Radio, Dallas, 1978-79. Mem. MLA, North Tex. Interdisciplinary Forum (pres. 1990-91), Grad. Students in English (v.p. 1988-89), Rsch. Soc. Am. Periodicals, Texoma Area Poetry Soc. (program dirs. 1995-98), Mark Twain Circle Am., Friends Mark Twain Ctr., We. Lit. Assn., Sigma Tau Delta. Democrat. Avocations: collecting '60s music, drums, travel. Home: 2439 Penn St Harrisburg PA 17110-1120

BRIZ, JULIAN E., economics educator; b. Cuenca, Spain, Jan. 29, 1942; s. Miguel Briz and Teresa Escribano; m. Isabel Boente Felipe; children: Jaime, Teresa, Carlos. Degree in engring., Etsiagronomos, Madrid, 1968; diplomado, IAMZ, Zaragoza, Spain, 1969; MSc, U. Minn., 1970; PhD, U. Politecnica, Madrid, 1973; merito agricola, MAPA, Madrid, 1977. Asst. prof. Polite U., Madrid, 1971-73, assoc. prof., 1973-82, prof., 1986-89, head mark dept., 1986-89, head res. unit mktg., 1990—; prof. U. Cordoba, Spain, 1982-83; head grain divsn. Mapa, Madrid, 1970-82; vis. prof. U. Fla., 1990-99. Author, editor: Espana Europa Verde, 1979; author: Marketing Aprario, 1993, Food and Agribusiness, 1993, Agrofood Marketing, 1997, Naturacion Urbana, 1999, Comercio Exterior Agrario, 2000, Internet y Comercio Electronico, 2000. Vice chmn. Food Work Group, Brussel, 1989-91; sec. Agricola Editor, Madrid, 1990—; pres. PRONATUR, Madrid, 1996—. Mem. Am. Agrl. Econ. Assn., Spanish Assn. Agrl. Econs. (sec. 1980-83). Avocations: painting, tennis, walking. Office: Polytech U, ETS Ingenieros Agronomos, 28040 Madrid Spain Address: U Politecnica Madrid, Lagasca 87, 28006 Madrid Spain

BRIZUELA, GRACIELA PETRA, chemical physics researcher; b. Comodoro Rivadavia, Argentina, Nov. 11, 1959; d. Marcelo Arturo and Petra (Rodriguez) B.; m. Alfredo Juan, Apr. 12, 1988; 1 child, Julian. Degree in chemistry, U. del Sur, Bahia Blanca, Argentina, 1981, BCE, 1984, MSChemE, 1989, PhD, 1996. Fellow Plapiqui-Conicet, Bahia Blanca, Argentina, 1984-86, prin. fellow, 1986-88; teaching asst. Depto de Fisica-UNS, Bahia Blanca, Argentina, 1986-88; lectr. Dept. Fisica-UNS, Bahia Blanca, Argentina, 1988-97, prof., 1997—. Author: Simple Experiment and Surface Science Studies, 1991, Theoretical Condensed Matter Physics, 1997. Postdoctoral fellow Cornell U., 1997-98. Roman Catholic. Avocations: classic music, science fiction films. Office: Depto de Fisica-UNS, Alem 1253, 8000 Bahia Blanca Argentina

BRIZUELA DE AVILA, MARÍA EUGENIA, financial and insurance company executive, lawyer; b. San Salvador, El Salvador, Oct. 31, 1956; d. Miguel Angel and María Leonor (Boillat) Brizuela; m. Ricardo Antonio Avila Araujo, Mar. 31, 1979; children: José Ricardo, Leonor Eugenia, Roberto Antonio. Diploma in French Lang. and Civilization, U. Paris Sorbonne, 1976; Law Degree, U. Dr. José Matías Delg., San Salvador, 1984; postgrad., Swiss Ins. Tng. Ctr., Zurich, 1990; MBA summa cum laude, INCAE, San Salvador, 1996. Pres., gen. mgr. La Auxiliadora Funeral Co., San Salvador, 1979—; pres. Internat. Seguros Ins. Co., 1996—; min. fgn. rels. Sec. of State, San Salvador, 1999—; bd. dirs. Banco Salvadoreno, San Salvador; treas. U. Dr. José Matías Delgado, 1995—, prof. hereditary law, 1989—; fgn. min. El Salvador, 1999—. Author: Considerations on Salvadorean Hereditary Law, 1984. Mem. directive coun. Salvadorean Social Security Inst., San Salvador, 1994, Social Investment Fund, San Salvador, 1995; mem., former pres. Found. for Devel. of Salvadorean Women, 1992—; bd. dirs. Patronage of the Hospice, San Vicente de Paul, 1986—, Entrepreneurial Found. for Ednl. Devel.; coord. Swiss Alumni for Ins. Tng. in El Salvador, 1991—. Mem. Lawyers Assn. of El Salvador (disting. mem.), Salvadorean Lawyers Assn. (bd. dirs. 1985—), Assn. Internationale de Droit d'Assurances (pres. El Salvador sect. 1995—), Ctr. for Jud. Studies (bd. dirs. 1988), Assn. Am. Sch. Ex-Alumni (bd. dirs. 1990), Young Pres.'s Orgn. Roman Catholic. Office: Min de Relaciones, #5500, San Salvador El Salvador

BRKIĆ, LUKA, political scientist, educator; b. Drenovci, Croatia, Aug. 29, 1956; s. Djuro and Kata (Nekić) B.; m. Nadežda Orlović, Apr. 22, 1986; children: Goran, Igor. Diploa, Faculty Polit. Sci., Zagreb, Croatia, 1984, postgrad., 1989, PhD, 1992; postgrad., Inst. Polit. Sci., Mainz, Germany, 1992. Asst. Faculty Polit. Sci., 1986-92, asst. prof., 1992—. Author: Economic Policy of EC, 1991, Monetary Union of EC, 1992, Industry Policy of EEA, 1993; contbr. articles to profl. jours. Recipient Rector awards U. Zagreb, 1978, Johannes Gutenberg award Govt. of Germany, 1980-82. Mem. Soc. Polit. Scis., Soc. Univ. Profs. Avocations: film, music. Home: Malesnica 46, 41000 Zagreb Croatia Office: Faculty Polit Scis, Lepusiceva 6, 41000 Zagreb Croatia

BRLEK, DARKO, managing and artistic director; b. Ptuj, Slovenia, Dec. 8, 1964. Student, U. Ljubljana, Slovenia, Music Acad., Slovenia, Höchschule för Musik und darstellende Kunst, Graz, Austria. Past dir. Slovene Nat. Theatre, Opera and Ballet, past pres. coun.; past solo clarinet Ljubljana Opera House; founder, mem. Trio Luwigana; past prof. Acad. Music, Ljubljana; dir. Festival of Ljubljana; past mem. jury internat. singing competition, Padova, Italy; prof. Musici Artis Internat. Acad., Italy. V.p. Cultural Chamber Slovenia. Mem. ISPA, European Festivals Assn. (v.p.), Internat. Festivals Assn. Europe, Internat. Musikcentrum Wien Imago, Slovene Music Art Assn. (com. mem.). Avocations: music, opera, skiing. Office: Festival Ljubljana, Trg francoske revolucije 1, 1000 Ljubljana Slovenia

BRLJEVIC, MATKO, diplomat, theater and television director, producer; b. Metkovic, Dalmatia, Croatia, Nov. 29, 1959; s. Ivan and Ana (Obrvan) B.; m. Tihana Skaricic, Feb. 10, 1990; children: Dante Dorian, Dali Anton. MSEE in Automatics, U. Zagreb, Croatia, 1983, MA in Dramatic Arts, 1988. Dir., prodr. theater radio and TV various projects and prodns., Zagreb, Croatia, 1984-88; dir., prodr. Creative Arts Prodns., L.A., 1989-97; first consul pub. and cultural affairs Consulate Gen. Republic of Croatia, L.A., 1997—; bd. dirs. Consular Press Orgn., L.A. Prodr., dir.: (TV documentaries) What is Croatia, Anyway?, 1991 (recognized as best short documentary about background of war), Sunny South of California (part 1), Traveling Through an American Dream (part 2), 1995; author, dir.: (TV documentary) Croatian Fisherman Fleet-Alaska, 1999; dir., prodr.: (theater play) CraftWoMenship, 1997. Mem. Croatian Art, Media and Entertainment Orgn. (founding mem.). Roman Catholic. Avocations: travel, history. Fax: 310 477 1866. E-mail: CroConLA@aol.com. Office: Consulate Gen Republic Croatia 11766 Wilshire Blvd Ste 1250 Los Angeles CA 90025-6538

BROAD, CYNTHIA ANN MORGAN, special education educator, consultant; b. Toledo, Ohio, Apr. 19, 1947; d. James Glenn and Elaine Louise (Morris) Morgan; m. Alan Hugh Broad, Aug. 2, 1975; children: Travis Alan, Trevor Morgan. BS in Edn., Bowling Green State U., 1969, MEd, 1970, Accomplished Grad. (hon.), 1993. Cert. spl. edn. tchr., elem. tchr. Tchr. remedial reading ednl. therapy unit Toledo (Ohio) State Hosp., 1970; spl. edn. tchr. Green Elem. Sch. L'Anse Creuse (Mich.) pub. schs., 1970-81, spl. edn. tchr. Lobbestael Elem. Sch., 1982-95, spl. edn. cons., 1989-95, spl. edn. tchr. Higgins Elem. Sch., 1995—. Contbr. articles to profl. jours.; developer talking animal idea telephone teachng tool, 1978. Fellow Masters Level Bowling Green State U., 1969-70; recipient Tchr. of Yr. State of Mich. Dept. Edn., 1989-90, Nat. Educator award Milken Family Found., 1990, Burger King Disting. Svc. to Edn. award, 1990. Mem. NEA, Mich. Edn. Assn., Mich. Reading Assn., Mich. Assn. Children with Learning Disabilities, Coun. Exceptional Children (Golden Nugget award 1989), Delta Kappa Gamma, Kappa Delta Pi. Avocations: technology, golf, biking, telecommunications, reading. Home: 71 S Deeplands Rd Grosse Pointe MI 48236-2643 Office: L'Anse Creuse Higgins Elem Sch 29901 24 Mile Rd Chesterfield MI 48051-1760

BROAD, ELI, financial services executive; b. N.Y.C., June 6, 1933; s. Leon and Rebecca (Jacobson) B.; m. Edythe Lois Lawson, Dec. 19, 1954; children: Jeffrey Alan, Gary Stephen. BA in Acctg. cum laude, Mich. State U., 1954. CPA, Mich. 1956. Cert. public acct., 1954-56; asst. prof. Detroit Inst. Tech., 1956; co-founder, chmn., pres., CEO SunAmerica Life Ins. Co. (formerly Kaufman & Broad, Inc.), L.A., 1957—; chmn. Anchor Nat. Life Ins. Co., First SunAmerica Life Ins. Co., CalAmerica Life Ins. Co.; chmn. Kaufman and Broad Home Corp., L.A., 1989-93, chmn. exec. com., 1993-95, founder, chmn., 1993—; chmn. Stanford Ranch Co.; mem. exec. com. adv. bd. Fed. Nat. Mortgage Assn., 1972-73; active Calif. Bus. Roundtable, 1986—; co-owner Sacramento Kings and Arco Arena, 1992-99; trustee Com. for Econ. Devel., 1993-95; mem. real estate adv. bd. Citibank, N.Y.C., 1976-81; bd. dirs. Am. Internat. Group, Inc., L.A. Bus. Advisors, Sacramento Kings and ARCO Arena; co-owner Sacramento Kings & Arco Arena, 1992-99. Mem. bd. dirs. L.A. World Affairs Coun., 1988—, chmn., 1994—, DARE Am., 1989-95, hon. mem. bd. dirs. 1995—; founding trustee Windward Sch., Santa Monica, Calif., 1972-77; bd. trustees Pitzer Coll., Claremont, Calif., 1970-82, chmn. bd. trustees, 1973-79, life trustee, 1982—, Haifa U., Israel, 1972-80, Calif. State U., 1978-82, vice chmn. bd. trustees, 1979-80, trustee emeritus, 1982—, Mus. Contemporary Art, L.A., 1980-93, founding chmn., 1980, Archives Am. Art, Smithsonian Instn., Washington, 1985-98, Am. Fedn. Arts, 1988-91, Leland Stanford Mansion Found., 1992—, Calif. Inst. Tech., 1993—, Armand Hammer Mus. Art and Cultural Ctr. UCLA, 1994—; pres. Calif. Non-Partisan Vote Registration Found., 1971-72; chancellor's assoc. UCLA, 1971—, mem. vis. com. Grad. Sch. Mgmt., 1972-90, trustee UCLA Found., 1986—, exec. com. bd. visitors Sch. of the Arts & Architecture, 1997—; assoc. chmn. United Crusade, L.A., 1973-76; chmn. Mayor's Housing Policy Com., L.A., 1974-75; del., spkr. Fed. Econ. Summit Conf., 1974, State Econ. Summit Conf., 1974; mem. contemporary coun. L.A. County Mus. Art, 1973-79, bd. trustees acquisitions com., 1978-81, trustee, 1995—; bd. fellows, mem. exec. com. The Claremont (Calif.) Colls., 1974-79; nat. trustee Balt. Mus. Art, 1985-91; mem. adv. bd. Boy Scouts Am., 1982-85, L.A. Bus. Jour., 1986-88; mem. adv. coun. Town Hall of Calif., 1985-87; trustee Dem. Nat. Com. Victory Fund, 1988, 92, 96; mem. painting and sculpture com. Whitney Mus., N.Y.C., 1987-89; chmn. adv. bd. ART/LA, 1989; bd. overseers The Music Ctr. of L.A. County, 1991-92, mem. bd. govs., 1996—; mem. contemporary art com. Harvard U. Art Mus., Cambridge, Mass., 1992—; mem. internat. dirs. coun. Guggenheim Mus., N.Y.C., 1993—; active Nat. Indsl. Pollution Control Coun., 1970-73, Maeght Found., St. Paul de Vence, France, 1975-80, Mayor's Spl. Adv. Com. on Fiscal Adminstrn., L.A., 1993-94; bd. dirs. UCLA/Armand Hammer Mus. Art And Cultural Ctr., 1994—. Recipient Man of Yr. award City of Hope, 1965, Golden Plate award Am. Acad. Achievement, 1971, Housing Man of Yr. award Nat. Housing Coun., 1979, Humanitarian award NCCJ, 1977, Am. Heritage award Anti Defamation League, 1984, Pub. Affairs award Coro Found., 1987, Honors award visual arts L.A. Arts Coun., 1989; Eli Broad Coll. Bus. and Eli Broad Grad. Sch. Bus. named in his honor Mich. State U., 1991; knighted Chevalier in Nat. Order Legion of Honor, France, 1994; recipient lifetime achievement award L.A. C. of C., 1999, visionary award Harvard Bus. Sch. Assn. So. Calif., 1999. Mem. Beta Alpha Psi, Regency Club, Hillcrest Country Club (L.A.), California Club. Office: SunAmerica Inc 1 Sun America Ctr Los Angeles CA 90067-6121

BROADBENT, EDWARD GRANVILLE, mathematics professor; b. Huddersfield, Eng., June 27, 1923; s. Joseph Charles and Lucetta (Riley) B.; m. Elizabeth Barbara Puttick, Sept. 7, 1949. BA, U. Cambridge, Eng., 1946; MA, U. Cambridge, 1947, DSc, 1975. Chartered engr. Govt. scientist Royal Aircraft Establishment, Farnborough, Eng., 1943-83; vis. prof. Imperial Coll., London, 1983—; cons. London, 1983—. Author: Elementary Theory of Aeroelasticity, 1956; contbr. scientific papers to symposiums and profl. jours. Fellow Royal Aero. Soc. (medals 1956, 60, 91), Inst. of Math. and Applications, Royal Soc. London, Royal Acad. Engring. Anglican. Avocations: gardening, bridge, chess, theatre, concerts. Home: 11 Three Stiles Rd, Surrey Farnham England GU9 7DE Office: Imperial Coll Sci & Tech, Math Dept, Queens Gate, London England SW7 2AZ

BROADBENT, GEOFFREY HAIGH, architecture educator; b. Huddersfield, Yorkshire, Eng., June 11, 1929; s. Albert and Florence Broadbent; m. Anne Barbara, June 25, 1955 (dec. 1985); children: Mark John, Antony James; m. Gloria Camino Maldonado, Aug. 3, 1991. BA, U. Manchester, Eng., 1955; Doctor honoris causa, Tucuman U. Cert. Royal Inst. Brit. Architects. Asst. architect Fairhursts, Manchester, 1956-59; lectr. U. Manchester, 1959-61; sec. IAAS U. York, Eng., 1961-62; lectr. U. Sheffield, Eng., 1963-67; head Sch. Architecture Portsmouth (Eng.) Poly., 1967-88, prof. architecture, 1982-92; prof. architecture U. Portsmouth, 1992-94; mem. faculties of architecture and fine arts Brit. Sch. at Rome, 1981—; Brit. Coun. and other lecture tours to U.S., Can., C.Am., S.Am., Middle East, South Africa, Australia, China, Europe, others. Author: Design in Architecture, 1973, 2d edit., 1988, Emerging Concepts in Urban Space Design, 1990, Tomas Taveira, 1991, Deconstruction: A Student Guide, 1991, Miguel Angel Roca, 1994, Tomas Taveira II, 1994. Chmn. Portsmouth Soc., 1974-88. Recipient several hon. professorships. Mem. Royal Inst. Brit. Architects (mem. some 15 coms. 1966—), Royal Soc. Arts. Anglican. Avocation: music, photography, travel. Home and Office: 11 Hereford Rd Southsea, Portsmouth P05 2DH, England

BROADBENT, J. MICHAEL, wine writer, wine auctioneer; b. Saddleworth, Yorkshire, Eng., May 2, 1927; s. John Fred and Hilary Louise (Batty) B.; m. Daphne Broadbent, June 19, 1954; children: Emma Louise Arbuthnot, Bartholomew. Cert. in architecture, University Coll., London, 1952. Trainee Layton's Wine Merchants, London, 1952-53; retail asst. Saccone & Speed, London, 1953-55; local dir. Harvey's of Bristol, Manchester, Eng., 1955-61; sales dir. U.K. Harvey's of Bristol, London, 1961-66; head wine dept. Christie's, London, 1966-92, chmn. internat. wine dept.; dir. Christie, Manson & Woods Ltd., London, 1967-92, Christie's Fine Art, Ltd., London, 1998-2000. Author: Wine Tasting, 1968, currently 11th edit. and transl. 8 fgn. langs., (le Grand Prix de l'Académie Internat. du Vin 1984, Glenfiddich award 1978, Silver medal Akademie Deutschlands E.V. Gastronomische for new German edit. 1993), The Great Vintage Wine Book, 1980 (le Grand Prix de l'Académie Internat. du Vin 1984, André Simon Meml. award 1981, Glenfiddich award 1981), The Great Vintage Wine Book II, 1991, Pocket Guide to Wine Vintages, 1992; contbr. to Decanter mag. and Falstaff. 2d lt. Royal Artillery, 1945-48. Decorated Chevalier dans l'Ordre National du Mérite (France), Medaille de la Ville de Paris-Echelon Vermeil (France), comdr. Confrérie des Chevalier du Tastevin (France); named Gentilhomme de Fronsac, France, Master of Wine, Inst. Masters of Wine, 1960, Man of Yr., Decanter mag., 1993, Personnalité de l'Année, Internat. Oenology, Paris, 1985; recipient Disting. Svc. award Wine Spectator, N.Y., 1991, Lifetime Achievement award Svc. Bacchus of Am., 1992, Marques de Caceres award, 1987, Alles über Wein Millenium award 2000. Mem. Internat. Wine and Food Soc. (past pres., gold medal), Worshipful Co. of Distillers (past master), Inst. Masters of Wine (past chmn.), Wine and Spirit Trades Benevolent Soc. (past chmn.), l'Académie du Vin Bordeaux (membre d'honneur 1965, pres. Fête de la Fleur 1988), Confrérie St. Etienne (confrère d'honneur), Confraria do Vinho do Porto (cavaleiro). Avocations: classical piano playing, drawing, painting. Home: 87 Rosebank Holyport Rd, London SW6 6LJ, England Office: 88 Rosebank, London SW6 6LJ, England

BROADBRIDGE, PHILIP, mathematics educator; b. Adelaide, Australia, Sept. 7, 1954; s. Edward William and Elsie (Levins) B.; m. Alice Elizabeth Bodnar; children: Matthew, Daniel. BSc with honors, U. Adelaide, 1976, PhD, 1983; diploma in edn., U. Tasmania, Hobart, Australia, 1977. Tchr. Burnie H.S., Tasmania, 1977-78; sr. tutor West Australian Inst. Tech., Perth, 1982-83; rsch. scientist Commonwealth Sci. and Indsl. Rsch. Orgn., Canberra, Australia, 1983-87; sr. lectr. La Trobe U., Melbourne, Victoria, Australia, 1987-90; prof. U. Wollongong, N.S.W., Australia, 1991—, head dept. math., 1993-97. Assoc. editor Jour. Math. Analysis and Applications, 1999—, Math. and Computer Modelling, St. Louis, 1992—, guest editor, 1993; contbr. many articles to sci. publs., including Jour. Math. Physics, Procs. of Royal Soc. London, Jour. of Australian Math. Soc. B, Soil Sci., Transport in Porous Media, Jour. Engring. Math., Internat. Jour. Nonlinear Mechanics, others. Mem. N.Y. Acad. Scis., Internat. Assn. Math. Physics, Australian Math. Soc., Australian Inst. Physics., Amnesty Internat. Avocations: travel, fishing, sports. Office: U Wollongong Dept Math, Northfields Ave, Wollongong NSW 2522, Australia

BROADDUS, JOHN ALFRED, JR., bank executive, economist; b. Richmond, Va., July 8, 1939; s. John Alfred Sr. and Norma (Coleman) B.; m. Margaret C. Lemley, Apr. 16, 1966; children: John Alfred III, Christopher McRae. BA, Washington & Lee U., 1961; diplome, U. Strasbourg, France, 1962; MA, Ind. U., 1970, PhD, 1972; LLD (hon.), Washington and Lee U., 1993. Intelligence rsch. specialist Def. Intelligence Agy., Washington, 1964-66; economist Fed. Res. Bank Richmond, 1970-72, asst. v.p., 1972-75, v.p., 1975-85, sr. v.p., dir. rsch., 1985-92, pres., 1993—; mem. adv. com. U. Richmond Sch. Bus. Author: A Primer on the Fed, 1988; contbr. articles to publs. Chmn. bd. trustees United Way of Greater Richmond, 1990; vice chmn. bd. trustees Health Corp. of Va., 1980s; pres. Richmond Meml. Hosp. Found., 1980-85; chmn. bd. govs. St. Christopher's Sch., 1992-96; mem. Gov.'s Adv. Coun. on Revenue Estimates, Va., 1993—; bd. assocs. Gallaudet U., 1998—; trustee Va. Coun. Econ. Edn., 1994—, Confed. Meml. Lit. Soc., 1995—, E. Angus Powell Endowment Econ. Edn., 1995-99, Bon Secours Richmond Health, 1995-98, Richmond Meml. Found., 1998—; exec. com. Metro Richmond Coalition Against Drugs, 1994-95, Richmond Renaissance, 1998—. 1st lt. U.S. Army, 1962-64. Named Fulbright scholar, 1961. Mem. Am. Econ. Assn., Nat. Assn. Bus. Economists, So. Econ. Assn., Phi Beta Kappa, Omicron Delta Kappa. Avocation: running. Office: Fed Res Bank Richmond 701 E Byrd St PO Box 27622 Richmond VA 23261-7622

BROADHURST, MATTHEW KENYON, research scientist, educator; b. Brisbane, Queensland, Australia, May 25, 1967; s. Peter John Kenyon and Helen Lee (Hinder) B. B Applied Sci., Australian Maritime Coll., Australia, 1987, M Applied Sci., 1994; PhD, U. Queensland, 1997. Tech. asst. N.S.W. Fisheries, Sydney, Australia, 1989-90, sr. tech. officer, 1990-97; sr. rsch. scientist South Australian R & D Inst., Adelaide, Australia, 1997-98, Universidade Fed. Rural de Pernambuco, Recife, Brazil, 1998—; cons. in field; adj. prof. Australian Maritime Coll., 1999. Contbr. 30 articles to profl. jours. Sec. Cronulla (Australia) Youth Orgn., 1995-96. Winston Churchill fellow Winston Churchill Meml. Trust, 1995. Mem. Royal Soc. New Zealand, Winston Churchill Assn. Anglican. Avocations: surfing, weight training, swimming. Home: Apt 708, Rua dos Navegantes 157, Boa Viagem Recife Pernambuco Brazil Office: U Fed Rural Pernambuco, Av Dom Manuel de Medeiros, Dois Irmaos Recife Brazil

BROADHURST, NORMAN NEIL, foods company executive; b. Chico, Calif., Dec. 17, 1946; s. Frank Spencer and Dorothy Mae (Conrad) B.; m. Victoria Rose Thomson, Aug. 7, 1976; 1 child, Scott Andrew. BS, Calif. State U., 1969; MBA, Golden Gate U., 1975. With Del Monte Corp., San Francisco, 1969-76, product mgr., 1973-76; product mgr. Riviana Foods, Inc. divsn. Colgate Palmolive, Houston, 1976-78; new products brand devel. mgr. foods divsn. Coca Cola Co., Houston, 1978-79, brand mgr., 1979-82, mktg. dir., 1982-89; v.p. mktg. Beatrice Foods Co., Chgo., 1983-86; pres., COO, Famous Amos Chocolate Chip Cookie Co., Torrance, Calif., 1986-88; corp. sr. v.p., gen. mgr. Kerr Group Inc., L.A., 1988-92; corp. sr. v.p., pres. Kerr Group Consumer Products, 1992-95; chmn. dir. Double Eagle Holding, Inc., Seal Beach, Calif., 1995—; chmn., CEO, Double Eagle Market Devel. Co., Seal Beach, 1997—; chmn., pres. and CEO Trusted Brands, Inc., 1995-98. Chmn. youth soccer program Cystic Fibrosis Found., Houston, 1982-83; chmn., pres. South Coast Symphony, 1985-88; mem. nat. bd. dirs. Literacy Vols. Am., 1988—, vice chmn., 1993-95, chmn., 1997-99; bd. dirs. Human Options , 1997—. Mem. Assoc. Sales and Mktg. Co., Am. Mktg. Assn., Am. Mgmt. Assn.

BROADHURST, VIOLET ALISON, safety consultant; b. Manchester, U.K.. BA with honors, U. Manchester, Eng.; PhD, Pacific Western U.; Barrister, Inner Temple, London. Univ. lectr. U.S. Internat., Calif., City U., London, U. Strathclyde, Glasgow, Scotland; inspector of factories U.K. Govt.; safety cons. self employed, Christchurch, Dorset, Eng. Author: (book) The Health and Safety at Work: Act in Practice, 1978, Health and Safety, 3d edit., 1996; co-author: (book) Employees' Health and Safety, 1979. Home and Office: 10 Avon Run Close, Christchurch BH23 4DT, England

BROADLEY, KENNETH JOHN, pharmacology educator; b. Orpington, Kent, U.K., May 18, 1943; s. Ronald Charles and Evelyn Mable (Johnson) B.; m. Patricia Marion Prior, Sept. 12, 1964; children: Simon James, Duncan Kenneth. BPharm, U. London, 1964, PhD, 1968, DSc, 1988. FRPharmS. Lectr. U. Brighton, U.K., 1967-71; lectr. U. Wales, Cardiff, U.K., 1971-80, sr. lectr., 1980-89, reader, 1989-97, prof., 1997—; hon. lectr. U. Auckland, New Zealand, 1983; rsch. fellow U. Melbourne, Australia, 1987. Editor-in-chief Jour. of Autonomic Pharmacology, 1982—; author: (book) Autonomic Pharmacology, 1996; contbr. articles to profl. publs. Fellow Can. Heart Found., Vancouver, Can., 1979; grantee British Heart Found., 1980-83, 97—, 2000—, Asthma Rsch. Coun., 1987. Mem. Brit. Pharm. Soc., Brit. Assn. Lung Rsch. Avocations: cycling, renovation, restoration. Office: Welsh Sch Pharmacy, U Wales Cardiff/Cathays, Park Cardiff/Wales CF13XF, United Kingdom

BROADWATER, JAMES E., publisher; b. Tacoma, Nov. 5, 1945; s. Robert L. and June J. B.; m. Diane K. Plummer, Apr. 22, 1967; children: James Tegan, Kelly Diane, Robert Charles, Krista Dawn. BS in Journalism, U. Fla., 1967. Acct. mgr. Young & Rubicam, Inc., Detroit, Kansas City, Kans., N.Y.C. and Houston, 1968-73; assoc. pub. Tex. Monthly Mag., Austin, 1973-78; pres., pub. Saturday Rev. Mag., N.Y.C., 1978-80; regional pub. dir. Baker Publs., Houston, 1980-87; pres. HBC, Inc., Houston, 1982-84; assoc. pub. Tex. Sportsworld Mag., 1985-86; pub. Washington Journalism Rev., 1987-92; pres. The Broadwater Co., Houston, 1993—. Mem. Mag. Pub. Assn., Nat. Press Club, Am. Mgmt. Assn., Direct Mail Mktg. Assn., Lambda Chi Alpha. Baptist.

BROCA, LAURENT ANTOINE, aerospace scientist; b. Nov. 30, 1928; came to U.S., 1957; naturalized, 1963; s. Paul L. and Paule Jeanne (Ferrand) B.; m. Leticia Garcia Guerra, Dec. 18, 1972; 1 child, Marie-There Yvonne. BS in Math., U. Bordeaux, France, 1949; lic. es Scis. in Math. and Physics, U. Toulouse, France, 1957; grad., Inst. Technique Professionnel, France, 1960; PhD in Elec. Engring., Calif. Western U., 1979; postgrad., Boston U., 1958, MIT, 1961, Harvard U., 1961. Tchg. fellow physics dept. boston U., 1957-58; spl. instr. dept. physics N.J. Inst. Tech., Newark, 1959-60; sr. staff engr. advanced rsch. group ITT, Nutley, N.J., 1959-60; examiner math. and phys. scis. univ. Paris and Caen (France) Exam Ctr., N.Y.C., 1959-69; sr. engr. surface radar divsn. Raytheon Co., Waltham, Mass., 1960-62, Hughes Aircraft Co., Culver City, Calif., 1962-64; asst. prof. math. Calif. State U., Northridge, 1963-64; prin. engr. astrionics lab. NASA, Huntsville, Ala., 1964-65; fellow engr. Def. and Space Ctr. Westinghouse Electric Corp., Balt., 1965-69; cons. and sci. adv. electronics, phys. scis. and math. to indsl. firms and broadcasting sats., 1969-80; head engring. dept. Videocraft Mfg. Co., Laredo, Tex., 1974-75; asst. prof. math. Laredo State U., summer 1975; engring. specialist dept. sys. performance analysis ITT Fed. Electric Corp., Vandenberg AFB, Calif., 1980-82; engring. mgr. Ford Aerospace and Comms. Corp., Nellis AFB, Nev., 1982-84, Arcata Assocs., Inc., North Las Vegas, Nev., 1984-85; sr. scientific specialist engring. and devel. EG&G Spl. Projects, Inc., Las Vegas, 1985—. With French Army, 1951-52. Recipient Published Paper award Hughes Aircraft Co., 1966; Fulbright scholar, 1957. Mem. IEEE, Am. Nuclear Soc. (vice chmn. Nev. sect. 1982-83, chmn. 1983-84), Am. Def. Preparedness Assn., Armed Forces Comms. and Electronics Assn., Air Force Assn. Home: 5040 Lancaster Dr Las Vegas NV 89120-1445 Office: EG&G Spl Projects Inc PO Box 93747 Las Vegas NV 89193-3747

BROCH, EINAR, geological engineering educator, administrator; b. Arendal, Norway, May 1, 1938; s. Jens Petter and Signe (Fløystad) B.; m. Ingrid Elise Helgemo, July 20, 1963; children: Jens Petter, Hanna Rachel. Diploma in civil engring., Norwegian Inst. Tech., Trondheim, Norway, 1961; MSc in Engring., Imperial Coll. Sci. & Tech., London, 1971; Dr.Ing., U. Trondheim, 1977. Rsch. asst. Norwegian Inst. Tech., 1962-65, lectr., 1965-72, prof., 1972—; dean Faculty Applied Earth Scis. Norwegian U. Sci. and Tech., Trondheim, 1996-98; mem. panel experts World Bank, Nepal, Lesotho, China, 1990—; cons., adviser tunnel, hydropower projects in 12 countries. Editor: Hydropower '92, 1992, Hydropower '97, 1997, Rock Support, 1997; sr. editor Tunnelling and Underground Space Tech., 1986—; contbr. over 100 sci. articles to profl. jours. Mem. Norwegian Acad. Tech. Scis., Norwegian Soc. Profl. Engrs., Internat. Tunnelling Assn. (pres. 1986-

89). Home: Bjarne Ness v.13, N-7033 Trondheim Norway Office: Norwegian U Sci & Tech, N-7491 Trondheim Norway

BROCHIER, MIREILLE L., cardiologist, educator; b. Algiers, Mar. 23, 1924; arrived in France, 1962; d. Emile B. MD, Univ., Algiers, France, 1953. Chief of dept. cardiology U. Hosp. Tours, 1977-92; pres. French Found. Cardiology, 1981-87, French Soc. Cardiology, 1989-91; emeritus prof. of cardiology Univ., Tours, France, 1993. Recipient Legion d'honneur Chevalier Officer, 1976—, Ordre Nat. merit Commandeur, 1998. Home: 2 alleé François Millet, Tours 37000, France

BROCK, BARRY JAMES, health services administrator, educator, consultant; b. Grove Hill, Ala., Oct. 1, 1953; s. Ben Jones and Doris (Forehand) B.; m. Denise Defant, Aug. 20, 1976; 1 child, Barry Jason. BS, U. Ala., 1976; MPA, U. W. Fla., 1982; EdD, U. Ctrl. Fla., 1993. Cert. healthcare exec.; cert. profl. in human resources. Dir. human resources Hosp. Corp. Am., Nashville, 1978-85; mktg. adminstr. Orlando (Fla.) Regl. Med. Ctr., 1985-88; adminstrv. dir. Rebound Rehab., Orlando and Nashville, 1988-89; v.p. Healthcare Rsch. & Resources, Orlando, 1989—; acad. chair, asst. prof. Barry U., Miami, Fla., 1993—; faculty U. Ctrl. Fla., Orlando, 1992—; coord. Health Profl. Inst., Seminole C.C., Sanford, Fla., 1992-93; adv. bd. Seminole C.C., Sanford, 1992-93, bd. dirs. HR & R, Mt. Dora, Fla., 1993—; exec. officer Naval Res. Naval Hosp., Jacksonville, Fla., 1996—. Author: Analysis of Middle Manager Competencies, 1994. Chmn. United Way, Nashville, 1983-85; advisor Jr. Achievement, Orlando, 1986-87. Lt. Comdr. Med. Svc. Corps, USNR, 1987—. Mem. Am. Acad. Med. Adminstrn., Am. Coll. Healthcare Execs., Commerce Execs. Soc., Assn. Med. Svc. Corps Officers, Assn. Vocat. Edn. and Rsch., Toastmasters (pres., Nashville, 1984-85), Pi Kappa Phi. Avocations: golf, tennis. Home: 887 Bentley Green Cir Winter Spgs FL 32708-4338 Office: Barry U 1650 Sand Lake Rd Orlando FL 32809-7681

BROCK, DAVID ALLEN, state supreme court chief justice; b. Stoneham, Mass., July 6, 1936; s. Herbert and Margaret B.; m. Sandra Ford, 1960; 6 children. AB, Dartmouth Coll., 1958; LLB, U. Mich., 1963; postgrad., Nat. Jud. Coll., 1977. Bar: N.H. 1963. Assoc. Devine, Millimet, McDonough, Stahl & Branch, Manchester, N.H., 1963-69; U.S. atty. State of N.H., 1969-72; ptnr. Perkins, Douglas & Brock, Concord, N.H., 1972-74, Perkins & Brock, 1974-76; spl. counsel to gov. and exec. coun. N.H., 1974-76, legal counsel to gov. N.H., 1976; assoc. justice N.H. Superior Ct., 1976-78; assoc. justice N.H. Supreme Ct., 1978-86, chief justice, 1986—; chmn. State of N.H. Legal Svcs. Adv. Commn., 1977-79; chmn. dist. ct. reform subcom. Gov.'s Commn. for Ct. System Improvement, 1974-75; chmn. N.H. Commn. Ct. Accreditation, 1986—; mem. Select Commn. on Unified Ct. System, 1980-84, chmn. N.H. Supreme Ct. Com. on Jud. Conduct, 1981-89, rules adv. com., 1985-97; mem. State N.H. Jud. Coun., 1979-87; mem. nat. adv. bd. Leadership Inst. for Jud. Edn., 1989-96, Nat. Jud. Coll. long range planning com., 1990-91; mem. Jud. Edn. and Tech. Assistance Consortium, 1989-97; chmn. Interbranch Coun. on Substance Abuse and the Criminal Justice System, 1991-95; bd. dirs. State Justice Inst., 1992-98, vice-chmn., 1994-95, co-chmn., 1995-98; bd. dirs. Conf. Chief Justices, 1993-94, v.p., 1996-97, pres-elect 1997-98, pres., 1998-99; bd. dirs. Nat. Ctr. for State Cts., 1996—, chmn.-elect, 1997-98, chmn., 1998-99. Bd. dirs. Manchester Cmty. Guidance Ctr., 1966-72, pres., 1969-72; chmn. Manchester Rep. Com., 1967-69; vice chmn. N.H. Rep. State Com., 1968-69; Rep. candidate U.S. Senate, 1972; del. N.H. Constl. Conv., 1974: mem. Gov.'s Commn. for Handicapped, 1978-79. Fellow ABA (mem. edn. com. of appellate judges conf. 1981-97, appellate advocacy com. 1982-84, faculty appellate judges' seminar program 1984-89, del. ho. of dels. 1994-96), N.H. Bar Assn. (chmn. constl. revision com. 1976-77), N.H. Bar Found. (hon.). Office: NH Supreme Ct Noble Dr Concord NH 03301

BROCK, JOHN HEDLEY, mining company director; b. Kelly Bray, Cornwall, Eng., Jan. 18, 1912; s. John and Mary (Priest) B.; m. Vera Wonnacott, June 6, 1940 (dec. Feb. 1972); 1 child, John David; m. Ann Laity, Feb. 8, 1973. Student, Callington Sch., Cornwall, Eng. Mgr. Lloyds Bank PLC, Plymouth, Eng., 1950-74; dir. Coverack (Eng.) Harbour Co. Ltd., 1970—; chmn. China Clay Council, St. Austell, Eng., 1972—; exec. Cornish Chamber of Mines, 1985—. Served to lt. comdr. Royal Navy, 1940-46. Decorated Order of the Brit. Empire, Her Majesty The Queen, 1976. Fellow Chartered Inst. Bankers; mem. Cornish Mining Devel. Assn. (pres. 1975—). Conservative. Methodist. Avocation: music. Home: Chy An Mor, Coverack, Helston Cornwall TR12 6SZ, England

BROCK, KERRY LYNN, internet executive; b. Ft. Lewis, Wash., Feb. 4, 1957; d. Frank Harvey and Carol Jean (Carpenter) B.; m. John Michael Seigenthaler, Jan. 4, 1992; 1 child, Jack. BA in Speech, Comms., Wash. State U., Pullman, 1979. Anchor, reporter KNDU TV, Kennewick, Wash., 1979-80, KIVI TV, Boise, Idaho, 1980-81, WOWT TV, Omaha, 1981-83, KOMO TV, Seattle, 1983-93; broadcasting, programming dir. First Amendment Ctr. Vanderbilt U., Nashville, 1993-97; broadcasting and programming dir. Media Studies Ctr., N.Y.C., 1997-99; dir. bus devel. Edifice Rex.com., N.Y.C., 1999—. Moderator (TV program) Freedom Speaks. Bd. dirs. Wash. State Leukemia Soc., Seattle, 1986-93, Sinking Creek Film Festival, Nashville, 1993-97; trustee Wash. State U., Pullman, 1990-97; adv. bd. dirs. Seattle Jr. League, 1992-93. Mem. NATAS (bd. dirs.), Soc. Profl. Journalists, Radio and TV News Dirs. Assn., Internat. Women's Media Found., Nat. Press Club, N.Y. New Media Assn. Office: 200 Park Ave Fl 17 New York NY 10166-1799

BROCK, MICHAEL GEORGE, retired literature educator, writer; b. Bromley, Eng., Mar. 9, 1920; s. Laurence George and Ellen Margery (Williams) B.; m. Eleanor Hope Morrison, July 28, 1949; children: George Laurence, David Michael, Paul Morrison. BA, Oxford U., Eng., 1943, MA with honors, 1948; DLitt (hon.), U. Exeter, Devon, Eng., 1982. Jr. rsch. fellow Corpus Christi Coll., Oxford U., 1948-50, fellow, tutor, 1950-66; v.p. Bursar Wolfson Coll., Oxford U., 1967-76; dir. Sch. of Edn. Exeter U., Eng., 1977-78; warden Nuffield Coll., Oxford U., 1978-88, St. George's House, Windsor Castle, Eng., 1988-93; ret., 1993; jr. proctor Oxford U., 1956-57, pro-vice chancellor, 1980-88. Author: The Great Reform Act, 1973, (chpt.) Britain Enters the War (1914), 1988, (chpt.) The University (Oxford) Since 1970, 1994; editor: (with wife) H.H. Asquith: Letters to Venetia Stanley, 1982, (with M.C. Curthoys) Nineteenth-Century Oxford, Part 1, 1997, Part 2, 2000. Trustee St. Luke's Coll. Found., Exeter, 1977-84, chmn., 1979-82; mem. Ct. and Coun., Reading (Eng.) U., 1977-86, v.p., 1982-86; dir. Williams Coll. Oxford Program, Oxford, 1985-93; chmn. Nat. Primary Trust, Oxford, 1992-97. Served to capt. Brit. Army, 1940-45. Recipient Hon. fellowship Wolfson Coll., 1977, Corpus Christi Coll., 1982, Nuffield Coll., 1988; named Companion of Brit. Empire, Her Majesty the Queen, 1981. Fellow Royal Hist. Soc., Royal Soc. Lit., Soc. for Rsch. into Higher Edn.; mem. Athenaeum Club. Liberal Democrat. Mem. Ch. of Eng. Avocations: walking, gardening. Home: 11 Portland Rd, Oxford OX2 7EZ, England

BROCKENBROUGH, EDWIN CHAMBERLAYNE, surgeon; b. Balt., July 24, 1930; s. Edwin Chamberlayne Sr. and Martha Davis (Coale) B.; m. Jean McClure, May 4, 1968; children: John, Martha, Andrew, Ann, Susan. BA, Coll. William & Mary, 1952; MD, Johns Hopkins U., 1956. Intern Johns Hopkins Hosp., Balt., 1956-57, resident, 1957-59; sr. asst. surgeon Nat. Heart Inst., Bethesda, Md., 1959-61; chief resident surgery U. Wash., Seattle, 1961-64, faculty mem. dept. surgery, 1964-75; pvt. practice Seattle, 1975-98; clin. prof. surgery U. Wash., 1984—; pres. King County Med. Soc., Seattle, 1992; trustee Health Resources N.W., Seattle; med. dir. Pacific Vasc. Inst., 1996—. Contbr. chpt. to book and articles to profl. jours. Sr. asst. surgeon USPHS, 1959-61. Fellow ACS (pres. Wash. State chpt. 1985), Seattle Surg. Soc. (sec. 1972); mem. North Pacific Surg. Assn. (pres. 1995-96), Pacific Coast Surg. Assn., Am. Rhododendron Soc. (pres. 1977-79, Silver medal 1985). Republican. Episcopalian. Avocations: gardening, hybridizing rhododendrons, photography, culinary arts, fishing. Home and Office: 3630 Hunts Point Rd Bellevue WA 98004-1114

BROCKHOUSE, BERTRAM NEVILLE, physicist, retired educator; b. Lethbridge, Alta., Can., July 15, 1918; s. Israel Bertram and Mable Emily (Neville) B.; m. Doris Isobel Mary Miller, May 22, 1948; children: Ann, Gordon, Ian, James, Alice Elizabeth, Charles. BA, U. B.C., 1947; MA, U. Toronto, 1948, PhD, 1950; DSc, U. Waterloo, 1969, McMaster U., 1984, U. Toronto, 1995, U. B.C., Can., 1996; Doctor of Laws, Dalhousie U., 1996; D Arts and Scis, U Lethbridge, 1997. Research officer Atomic Energy of Can., Ltd., Chalk River, Ont., 1950-60; br. head, neutron physics Atomic Energy of Can., Ltd., 1960-62; prof. physics McMaster U., Hamilton, Ont., 1962-84; chmn. dept. physics McMaster U., 1967-70. Contbr. sci. articles on neutron physics and condensed matter physics to profl. jours. Served with Royal Canadian Navy Vol. Res., 1939-45. Recipient Centennial medal of Can., 1967, Queen's Jubilee medal, 1977, Order of Can., 1982, Companion, 1995, Duddell medal and prize Inst. Physics and Phys. Soc., 1963, Nobel Prize in Physics, 1994; Guggenheim fellow, 1970-71; NRC of Can. grantee, 1962-78. Mem. Royal Soc. Can. (Tory medal), Royal Soc. London, Can. Assn. Physicists (medal), Am. Phys. Soc. (Buckley prize), Am. Acad. Arts and Scis. (hon. fgn. mem.), Royal Swedish Acad. Scis. (fgn. mem.). Roman Catholic. Home: PO Box 7338, Ancaster, ON Canada L9G 3N6*

BROCKHURST, PETER JOHN, retired materials scientist; b. Glenelg, Australia, May 18, 1935; m. Heather Fay Harding; children: Lara, Tom, Anna. B of Tech., U. Adelaide, 1959; MS, U. New South Wales, 1964; PhD, Sydney U., 1970. Metallurgist trainee Stewarts & Lloyds, Adelaide, 1952-59; prof., officer dept. metallurgy U. New South Wales, Sydney, 1963-66; tutor Sydney U., Sydney, 1966-70; lectr. RMIT, Melbourne, 1974-76; materials scientist Australian Dental Stands Lab., Melbourne, 1976-91; sr. lectr. dept. dentistry U. Queensland, Brisbane, 1991-2000; ret., 2000; Australian rep. ISO TC 150, 1970, ISO TC 106, 1976—. Contbr. scientific papers to profl. publs. Hon. sr. fellow Sch. Dental Sci., U. Melbourne. Avocations: family, opera, coffee, wine, fishing. Office: PO Box 85, Mt Beauty VIC 3699, Australia

BROCKINGTON, COLIN FRASER, social and preventive medicine educator; b. Worcester, Eng., Jan. 8, 1903; s. William Allport Brockington and Jessie McGeoch; m. Joyce Margaret Furze, Sept. 21, 1933; children—Anne Deirdre, Ian Fraser, Richard Alexander, John David. M.A., M.D., Cambridge U., 1928, B.Chir., 1928, D.P.H., 1928; M.R.C.P., London, 1955; M.Sc. (hon.), Manchester U., 1960; Barrister-at-Law (Mid. Temple), 1939. Med. supr. Sanatorium, Brighton, Eng., 1928; asst. county health office, Worcestershire, Eng., 1929-33; gen. practice medicine, Devon, Eng., 1933-36; med. office health Horsham and Petworth, Sussex, Eng., 1936-39, County of Warwick, Eng., 1939-46, County of West Riding, Eng., 1946-51; prof. social and preventive medicine, Manchester U., 1951-64, prof. emeritus, 1964—; cons. WHO, 1951-71. Author: Health of the Community, 1954, 3d edit., 1965; Public Health in the Nineteenth Century, 1965, World Health, 1958, 3d edit., 1975; Health of the Developing World, 1985. Avocations: book binding; travel. Home: 44 Silverburn,, Ballasalla, Isle of Man, Great Britain

BROCKINGTON, JOHN LEONARD, Indology educator; b. Oxford, Eng., Dec. 5, 1940; s. Leonard Herbert and Florence Edith (Woodward) B.; m. Mary Fairweather, Aug. 2, 1966; children: Anne Mary, Michael John. BA, U. Oxford, 1963, MA, 1966, DPhil, 1968. Lectr. in Sanskrit U. Edinburgh, Scotland, 1965-82, head dept. Sanskrit, 1975-98, sr. lectr., 1982-89, reader in Sanskrit, 1989-98, prof., 1998—, head Sch. of Asian Studies, 1998-99. Author: The Sacred Thread, 1981, Righteous Rama, 1985, Hinduism and Christianity, 1992, The Sanskrit Epics, 1998, Epic Threads, 2000. Recipient Boden Sanskrit prize U. Oxford, 1962. Mem. Internat. Assn. Sanskrit Studies (sec. gen. 2000—). Home: 3 Eskvale Ct, Penicuik Midlothian EH26 8HT, Scotland Office: U Edinburgh Sch Asian Studies, 7 Buccleuch Pl, Edinburgh EH8 9LW, Scotland

BROCKLEBANK, JOHN TREVOR, pediatrician, consultant, educator; b. Sheffield, Yorkshire, Eng., Sept. 25, 1938; s. Henry Pearson and Eva Mary (Wood) B.; m. Susan Hall Kinghorn, Sept. 8, 1969; children: Simon, Emma Hall, Sophie Hall. MB, BChir, Durham U., 1962. Pediat. registrar Royal Victoria Infirmary, Newcastle, U.K., 1968-70; instr. in pediat. Washington U., St. Louis, 1970-76; lectr. U. Leeds, U.K., 1976-78; sr. lectr. U. Leeds, 1978-95, reader, 1995—; cons. pediatrician St. James Hosp., Leeds, 1980—. Author: (textbooks) Clinical Biochemistry and the Sick Child, 1994, Investigations in Pediatrics, 1994, Oxford Textbook of Nephrology, 1997; mem. editl. bd. Archives of Disease in Childhood, 1992-96. Fellow Royal Coll. Physicians London, Royal Coll. Physicians Edinburgh, Royal Coll. Paediatrics and Child Health. Office: St James Univ Hosp, Becket St, Leeds LS9 7TF, England

BROCKMEIER, DIERK, biostatistician, researcher; b. Bad Hersfeld, Hessia, Germany, July 25, 1944; s. Heinrich and Ottilie (Weller) B.; m. Brigitte Beutler, July 23, 1971; children: Tim Sebastian, Kirsten, Daniel. Diploma in Physics, U. Giessen, Germany, 1971, PhD in Human Biology, 1982, Habil., 1991. Rsch. fellow neurology U. Giessen, 1971-74, rsch. fellow in pediatrics, 1975-82; biostatistician/pharmacokineticist Hoechst AG, Frankfurt, Germany, 1982-98, U. Giessen, Germany, 1999—. Recipient Human Medicine Faculty prize U. Frankfurt, 1982, U. Giessen, 1983, Paul Martini prize Paul Martini Soc., 1991. Mem. German Soc. Pharmacology and Toxicology, German Soc. Univ. Lectrs., German Soc. Clin. Pharmacology and Therapy (F.H. Dost prize 1996). Avocations: cooking, trekking, skiing. Office: U Giessen Clin Pharm, Gaffky Strasse 11C OG, D-35385 Giessen Germany

BROCK-UTNE, BIRGIT, education educator; b. Oslo, Norway, May 4, 1938; d. Gerhard and Gertrud Marie Agnes (Hessenberg) B-U.; m. Bard Gaarder, Oct. 1, 1960 (div. Dec. 1973); 1 child, Siri; m. Garbo Brock-Utne, Dec. 22, 1973; 1 child, Gunnar. Tchg. cert., Oslo Coll., 1960, Cand. Polit., 1971, PhD, 1981, DPhil, 1988; DPhil, U. Ill., 1964. Lectr. Tromsø (Norway) Tchr. Coll., 1966-73; rsch. cons. Ministry of Edn., Norway, 1973-77; rschr. Peace Rsch. Inst. Oslo, 1981-82; prof. U. Dar Es Salaam, Tanzania, 1987-92, U. Antioch, Ohio, spring 1992, U. Oslo, 1977—. Author: (books) Ungdomsokderi Utikling, 1980, Educating for Peace—A Feminist Perspective, 1985, Feminist Perspectives on Peace and Peace Education, 1989, Whose Education for All the Recolonization of the African Mind, 2000; co-author: (book) Kunnskap Uten Makt, 1980. Pres. Student Assn. Tromsø, 1966-68; chair Tromsø Social Liberal Party, 1971-72, Tromsø chpt. People's Movement Against Norway's Entry into Common Market, 1971-72; bd. dirs. Norwegian Film Industry, Oslo, 1971-75, UNESCO Inst. Edn., Hamburg, Germany, 1992-00. Scholar Stanford Student Body, Stanford U., 1957-58, Swedish Govt., 1968, DAAD-German Acad. Exch. Program, 1991. Mem. Norwegian Assn. Ednl. Rschrs. (pres. 1974-76), Internat. Peace Rsch. Assn. (bd. dirs. 1983-88), Nordic Assn. for Study of Edn. in Developing Countries (bd. dirs. 1995-99), Comparative and Internat. Edn. Soc. Social-Democrat. Avocations: downhill skiing, cross-country skiing, dancing, walking in woods, bridge. Home: Dalbovn 64, 1458 Fjellstrand Norway Office: U Oslo, PB 1092 Blindern, 0317 Oslo Norway

BROCKWAY, STEPHEN SWIFT, health facility administrator, psychiatrist, addiction medicine specialist; b. Lansing, Mich., Nov. 22, 1949; s. Carl Bernard and Helen Kenney (Smith) B.; children: Ross, R.J., Nicole, Ben. BA, Dartmouth Coll., 1971; MD, Med. Coll. Wis., 1975. Diplomate Am. Bd. Adolescent Psychiatry, Am. Bd. Psychiatry and Neurology, Am. Soc. Additicon Medicine, Am. Assn. Psychiatrist in Addiction. Staff psychiatrist The Med. Ctr. Clin., Pensacola, Fla., 1978-83; dir. alcohol dependency treatment program Prescott (Ariz.) VA Med. Ctr., 1983-84; dir. combat stress program Phoenix VA Med. Ctr., 1984-88; dir. adult & chem. dependency programs Charter Hosp. of East Valley, Chandler, Ariz., 1988-92; dir. chem. dependency program East Valley Camelback Hosp., Mesa, Ariz., 1991-92; med. dir. The Meadows, Wickenburg, Ariz., 1992—; med. dir. Lifegate Adolescent Treatment Ctr., Phoenix, 1990-92, Bethany Cmty. Ch. Counseling Ctr., Mesa, 1990-92. Contbr. articles to profl. jours. Bd. dirs. St. Francis Meth. Ch., Tucson, 1975-78, Yarnell (Ariz.) Fire Dist., 1997-98. Fellow Am. Psychiat. Assn.; mem. Am. Soc. Addiction Medicine (sec. Ariz. chpt. 1996—), Am. Soc. Psychiatrists in Addiction Medicine. Republican. Avocations: horseback riding, cowboy poetry, hiking, writing. Office: The Meadows 1655 N Tegner St Wickenburg AZ 85390-1461

BROCKWELL, PETER JOHN, statistics educator; b. Melbourne, Australia, Oct. 12, 1937; s. Jeck Ellery and Cardia Leo Brockwell; m. Pamela Audrey B., Feb. 6, 1965; children: Anthony Edward, Matthew James, Harold Peter. BA with honors, U. Melbourne, 1960, B in Elec. Engring., 1960, MA, 1962; PhD, Australian Nat. U., Canberra, 1967. Asst. mathematician Argonne Nat. Lab., Chgo., 1967-70; assoc. prof. math. Mich. State U., East Lansing, 1971-73; prof. stats. LaTrobe U., Melbourne, 1973-76, Colo. State U., Ft. Collins, 1976—; prof. stats. U. Melbourne, 1988-89, Royal Melbourne Inst. Tech., 1993-96. Author: Time Series: Theory and Methods, 1987, 91, Introduction to Time Series and Forecasting, 1996; contbr. over 80 articles to profl. jours.; editor Advances in Applied Probability, 1982-89; editl. bd. Stochastic Models, 1984-97, Annals of Stats., 1998-99, Jour. Time Series Analysis, 1997—. Fellow Am. Stats. Assn., Inst. Math. Stats.; mem. Internat. Statis. Inst. E-mail: pjbrock@stat.colostate.edu. Office: Colo State U Dept Statistics Fort Collins CO 80523

BROD, MORTON SHLEVIN, oral surgeon; b. Bklyn., Apr. 19, 1926; s. Joseph and Celina (Fromberg) B.; m. Anne Turville Bigelow, June 3, 1955; children: Brian Seth, Timothy Andrew, Abbe Rena. Student, U.S. Mil. Acad., 1947-48; BA, Adelphi Coll., 1951; DDS, Columbia U., 1955. Diplomate Am. Bd. Oral Surgery, Am. Bd. Forensic Dentistry. Intern oral surgery Columbia Presbyn. Med. Ctr., N.Y.C., 1955-56; resident oral surgery Bronx VA Hosp., N.Y.C., 1956-58; pvt. practice oral surgery Norwalk, Conn., 1958-98; attending oral surgeon chief dental service Norwalk Hosp.; attending oral surgeon Bellevue Hosp.; attending surgeon Seaview Hosp.; cons. Manhattan State Hosp., Bronx State Hosp., Psychiat. Inst. N.Y.; instr. dentistry div. clin. oral physiology Columbia Sch. Dental and Oral Surgery, N.Y.C., 1957-69, asst. prof. dentistry, 1969-72, assoc. prof., 1972-84, research assoc. dept. stomatology, 1968-84; mem. dental mission to Govt. Anguilla, West Indies, 1969, 70, 71; assoc. prof. dentistry NYU; dir. clin. rev.-oral surgery Physicians Health Svcs.; lectr., Eng., Russia, China, Japan. Contbr. articles to profl. jours., textbooks. Sec. Westport Flood and Erosion Control Bd.; capt. CAP Flying Sharks Search and Rescu Squadron, Conn., 1968—; exec. com. Boy Scouts Am., Westport; mem. Westport Rep. Town Meeting, chmn. pub. works com.; trustee Westport-Weston br. Am. Cancer Soc.; bd. dirs. Norwalk Bd. Dental Health Clinic; dir. Westport Transit Dist., Precision Closure Corp., Auto-Grip Corp.; v.p., treas. Riverview E. Assocs. Real Estate, Inc.; mem. Southwestern Regional Planning Agy., Fairfield County adv. bd. Bridgeport Hydraulic Co. With USAF, 1943-47. Fellow Am. Coll. Oral Surgeons, Am. Soc. Oral Surgeons, Internat. Soc. Oral Surgeons, N.Y. Acad. Dentistry, Am. Coll. Forensic Examiners; mem. ADA, New Eng. Soc. Oral Surgeons, Conn. Soc. Oral Surgeons, Am. Soc. Dentistry for Children (pres. Fairfield County sect. 1962-63), Am. Acad. History Dentistry, Fedn. Dentaire Internat., N.Y. Acad. Scis., N.Y. State Dental Soc. (exec. com. 1966-67, pres. 1967-68), Norwalk Dental Soc., Christian Dental Soc., Flying Dentists Assn., Airplane Owners and Pilots Assn., Pilots Internat. Assn., Fairways Homeowners Assn. (mem. fin. and audit com.). Home and Office: 10 Rosewood Dr Lakewood NJ 08701-5709

BRODBECK, FELIX CLAUS, psychology educator; b. Hamburg, Germany, May 31, 1960; s. Werner Heinrich and Bernadine Franziska Clementine (Dieckgers) B.; children: Moritz Zacharias, Noah, Leander. MA in Clin. Psychology, U. Munich, 1987; PhD in Psychology, U. Giessen, Germany, 1993; Habil., U. Munich, 1999. Sci. asst. dept. psychology indsl. and orgnl. psychology U. Munich, 1987-91, assoc. prof. psychology, 1994-00; asst. prof. psychology U. Giessen, 1991-94; prof. social and orgnl. psychology, chair dept. Aston Bus. Sch., Birmingham, Eng., 2000—; mem. working group Internat. Standardization Orgn., 1989-94, coord. team Global Leadership and Orgnl. Behavior Effectiveness Program, 1996—. Author: Komunikation und Leistung in Projektarbeitsruppen, 1993; co-author (computer software, book) Einführung in die Statistik, 1989; co-editor: Produktivität und Qualität in Software-Projekten, 1994. Fulbright scholar CUNY, 1983-84; recipient Software Ergonomics award Am. Assn. Computing and Machinery, 1995. Mem. APA (fgn.), Germany Psychol. Soc. (Heinz-Heckhausen Jr. Scientist award 1994), European Assn. Work and Orgnl. Psychologists. Avocations: family, tennis, hiking, philosophy, lecturing. Office: Inst Psychology, Ludwig Maximilians U, 80802 Munich Germany

BRODE, ANDREW STEPHEN, publisher, accountant; b. Birmingham, Eng., Sept. 2, 1940; s. Heinz Lion and Irene Sophia (Guenther) B.; m. Diane Vida Taylor, Oct. 13,1965; children: Caroline Jane, Alexandra Claire. BA, U. Manchester, Eng., 1962. Chartered acct. Audit mgr. Arthur Andersen & Co., London, 1965-71; asst. dir. Rothschild Intercontinental Bank, London, 1971-75; mng. dir. Croner Pubs., London, 1975-85, Wolters Kluwer, London, 1986-90; chmn., prin. Eclipse Group Ltd, London, 1990-2000; chmn. RWS Group Plc, 1995; bd. dirs. Rage Software plc., RWS Polyglot LLC. Adviser Prince's Youth Bus. Trust, London, 1993—. Fellow Inst. Chartered Accts; mem. Royal Automobile Club, Worshipful Co. Stationers, Newspaper Makers (liveryman). Avocations: golf, tennis. Office: RWS Group plc, Europa House Marsham Way, Gerrards Cross SL9 8BQ, England

BRÖDER, ERNST-GÜNTHER, financial executive, economist; b. Cologne, Germany, Jan. 6, 1927. D in Econs., Cologne U., Mayence U., Freiburg U., Paris U. Mem. corp. staff Bayer AG Leverkusen, Germany, 1956-61; mem. projects dept. World Bank, Washington, 1961-64; head dept. Kreditanstalt für Wiederaufbau, Frankfurt, Germany, 1964-68; dep. mgr. Kreditanstalt für Wiederaufbau, Frankfurt, 1968-69, mgr., 1969-75, mem. bd. mgmt., 1975-84, spokesman bd. mgmt., 1980-84; dir. European Investment Bank, Luxembourg, 1980-84, pres., chmn. bd. dirs., 1984-93, hon. pres., 1993—; active inspection panel The World Bank, Washington, 1996-99, chmn. inspection panel, 1994-96, 98-99; adv. com. Asian Devel. Bank, 1981-82; panel of conciliators Internat. Ctr. Settlement of Investment Disputes, 1976—. Home and Office: 15 Op den Aessen, L-6231 Bech Luxembourg

BRODEUR, MARTIN, professional hockey player; b. Montreal, Que., Can., May 6, 1972. Selected 1st round NHL entry draft N.J. Devils, 1994, goalie, 1991—; named to QMJ Hockey League All-Star 2d team, 1991-92, NHL All-Rookie team, 1993-94; played in NHL All-Star Game, 1996; mem. Stanley Cup Championship team, 1995. Recipient Calder Meml. Trophy, 1993-94. Office: c/o New Jersey Devils 50 Rt 120 N PO Box 504 East Rutherford NJ 07073-0504

BRODEUR, MICHAEL STEPHEN, dean; b. Jacksonville, Fla., Oct. 15, 1949; s. Victor Edward Jr. and Amy (Ropke) B.; m. Deborah Crystal Cazalas, Aug. 9, 1975 (div. Oct. 1979); m. Cheri Anne Winton, Apr. 10, 1982; children: Trey, Aaron, Dana, Margaret. BB in Econs., U. South Fla., 1972, BA in Fin., 1972; MPA, U. North Fla., 1989. Acctg. mgr. Raymond James Fin., St. Petersburg, Fla., 1974-78; asst. OMB dir. Pinellas County, Fla., Clearwater, 1978-79; dir. OMB Alachua County, Clearwater, Fla., 1979-83; treas. City of Orlando, Fla., 1983-84; dir. OMB Orange County, Fla., Orlando, 1984-86; dir. of fin. State of Fla., Gainesville, 1986-91; chief of staff U. Fla. Coll. of Pharmacy, Gainesville, 1994-98, asst. dean fin. and adminstrv. affairs, 1999—. Exec. v.p. COP Faculty Practice Assn., Inc., Gainesville. Recipient Davis Productivity award Davis Found. Fla. Taxwatch, Inc., 1993, 98, Disting. Svc. Alachua County Bd. Commrs., 1983. Mem. Heritage Club Inc., Heritage Links Country Club. Democrat. Presbyterian. Avocations: watch collecting, golf, target shooting. Fax: 352-392-7826. E-mail: brodeur@ufl.edu. Home: 4818 NW 37th Way Gainesville FL 32605-1034 Office: U Fla Coll of Pharmacy PO Box 100484 1600 SW Archer Rd Gainesville FL 32610-0484

BRODEY, WARREN MORTIMER, researcher; b. Toronto, Ont., Can., Jan. 25, 1924; s. Abraham and Blanche (Levy) B.; m. Martha Jane Schlenker Tolsen, Nov. 16, 1956 (div.); children: John, Kim, Lisa, Benjamin, Ivan. MD, U. Toronto, Ont., Can., 1947. Bd. cert. Am. Bd. Psychiatry and Neurology. Rsch. psychiatrist NIMH, 1956-59; pvt. practice, 1959-64; assoc. clin. prof. Georgetown U., 1959-64; cons. NASA Electronics, 1965-66; dir. MII Upward Bd. Project, 1966-68, Environ. Ecology Lab. Inc., Boston, 1968-70; vis. scientist Inst. Tech. Cybernetics Norwegian Tech. U., 1973-74, cons., 1974-75; cons. biomed. instrumentation group U. Tianjin, China, 1980-81; founder, dir. Biomachine Sys. Inc., 1982-88; assoc. prof. Sch. Medicine Meharry Med. Coll., 1992—; cons. Artificial Intelligence Lab., MIT, 1966-67; loyalty pilot Learningship Group, Oslo, 2000—; dir., founder Computouch Inc., 1997—; founder Interactive Arts Tools and Toys Found., 1994. Inventor in field; author: Family Dance, Earth Child; contbr. articles to sci. jours. Leader Com. Against Racism, Oslo, 1977-79. Mem. Am. Bd. Psychiatry and Neurology, Am. Soc. Cybernetics (charter).

BRODHEAD, QUITA, artist. spkr. in field. One woman shows at Salon d'Autonne, Paris, Chez Barbier, Paris, also 8 in N.Y., 7 in Phila.; exhibited in group show at Creuse gallery, Paris; retrospective Pa. Acad. Fine Arts Sch. gallery; represented in permanent collections at Pa. Acad. Fine Arts, Phila. Art Mus., Del. Art Mus., Wilmington, N.J. State Mus., Trenton, Munson-Williams-Proctor, Ithaca, N.Y., Bryn Mawr (Pa.) Coll. Libr., Woodmere

Mus., Phila., Westerdahl Collection C.I. Spain, Ashville (N.C.) Art Mus., Museo des Bellas Artes, Tenerefe, Spain, State Mus. Pa.; also pvt. collections. Past bd. fellows Acad. Fine Arts, Pa.; chmn. exhbn. com. Nat. Exhibits of Blind Artists. Recipient numerous awards for excellence in art; fellow Va. Ctr. for Creative Arts. Mem. Artists Equity, Mus. Modern Art N.Y.C., Phila. Mus. Art, Woodmere Art Mus. Phila., Pa. Acad. Fine Arts. Address: 211 Atlee Rd Wayne PA 19087-3835

BRODIE, ALICE VELMA, health and ethics advocate; b. Akron, Ohio, June 20, 1924; d. Charles Alvin and Lillian Snowden (Twentyman) Keller; m. Milton John Brodie, Dec. 8, 1980 (dec. 1983). Student, U.S. Nurse Cadet Corps, 1944-47; grad., Mt. Sinai Sch. Nursing, Cleve., 1947; BSN in Pub. Health Nursing, Western Res. U., 1952; postgrad., U. Wash., 1963-64, U. Calif., Berkeley, 1969-70, 81, 86, U. San Francisco, 1987-89, Calif. State U., Dominguez Hills, 1997—. RN, Ohio, Calif.; cert. pub. health nurse. Nursing supr. Mt. Sinai Hosp., Cleve., 1952-54; sch. nurse Renton (Wash.) Sch. Dist., 1958-60; pub. health nurse, vis. nurse, sch. nurse King County Health Dept., Seattle; people to people citizen amb. to UN Internat. Red Cross, 1967; with Ministry of Health, England, Ireland, Germany, France, Italy, Switzerland, Netherlands, Can., Mex., 1967; ship nurse numerous voyages to Australia, New Zealand, South Sea Island, Suva, 1968; rschr. No. State Hosp., Wash., 1963-64. Vol. BSF Internat., 1968-74, 93-99, ARC, Seattle, 1958-67, Buck Ctr. for Rsch. in Aging, Marin County, Calif., 1989, 90, Family Radio Tours to China, Hong Kong, Taiwan, 1985, Siberia, Mongolia, 1990s, Argentina, Brazil; mem. Vision for Progress, Vallejo, Calif., 1996—, Calif. Lawyers for Arts, San Francisco, 1996—; amb. People-to People citizen amb. UN Internat. Red Cross Ministry of Health, U.K., Eng., Germany, Italy, Switzerland, Ireland, Holland, Netherlands, France; family radio tours to China, Siberia, Hong Kong, Argentina, Brazil, 1985-94. Mem. APHA, ANA (founding mem. Calif. chpt. 1996), AAUW, Calif. Nurses Assn. (former del. to ANA conv. Detroit), Nat. Coun. for Aging, Calif. Lawyers for Arts, Vallejo C. of C. Avocations: health policy analysis, world travel, education, health legislation.

BRODIE, DAVID ALAN, exercise science educator; b. Hindhead, Eng., June 24, 1946; s. William Dinnell and Margaret (Blackwell) B.; m. Megan Elizabeth Plummer, Aug. 21, 1971; children: Jo-Anne, Tom. BEd, Nottingham (Eng.) U., 1969; MSc, Loughborough (Eng.) U., 1972, PhD, 1980. Dir. phys. welfare Abingdon Sch., Berkshire, 1969-72; lectr. St. Peter's Coll., Birmingham, Eng., 1972-74; rsch. fellow Carnegie Sch., Leeds, Eng., 1974-81; head of dept. mov. sci. Liverpool (Eng.) U., 1981—. Author: Health Matters at Work, 1994, Research Methods for Health Scientists, 1994, Microcomputing in Sport and Physical Education, 1983, Inner City Sport, 1992. Mem. Internat. Soc. Advancement Kinanthropometry (exec. coun.), British Assn. Cardiac Rehabilitation, British Assn. Sport and Exercise Scis. Methodist. Avocations: running, basketball gardening, travel. Home: 19 Oakway, Gayton CH60 3SP, England Office: U Liverpool, Liverpool L69 3BX, England

BRODIE, HARLOW KEITH HAMMOND, psychiatrist, educator, past university president; b. Stamford, Conn., Aug. 24, 1939; s. Lawrence Sheldon and Elizabeth White (Hammond) B.; m. Brenda Ann Barrowclough, Jan. 26, 1967; children: Melissa Verduin, Cameron Keith, Tyler Hammond, Bryson Barrowclough. AB, Princeton U., 1961; MD, Columbia U., 1965; LLD hon., U. Richmond, 1987; LHD (hon.), High Point U., 1992. Diplomate Am. Bd. Psychiatry and Neurology. Intern Ochsner Found. Hosp., New Orleans, 1965-66; resident in psychiatry Columbia-Presbyn. Med. Center, N.Y.C., 1966-68; clin. assoc. intramural research program NIMH, 1968-70; asst. prof. psychiatry, dir. gen. clin. research center Stanford U. Med. Sch., 1970-74; prof. psychiatry, chmn. dept. Duke U. Med. Sch., 1974-82, James B. Duke prof. psychiatry and behavioral scis., 1981—, prof. dept. psychology, prof. law, 1980—; psychiatrist-in-chief Duke U. Med. Center, 1974-82; chancellor Duke U., 1982-85, pres., 1985-93, pres. emeritus, 1993—; mem. Pres. Biomed. Rsch. Panel, 1975; mem. Carnegie Coun. on Adolescent Devel., 1986-97; trustee Com. for Econ. Devel., 1986-93, mem. subcom. on edn. and child devel., 1990; trustee Nat. Humanities Ctr., 1988-93; mem. nat. rev. and adv. panel for improving campus race rels. Ford Found., 1990-94; mem. subcom. on Edn. on Child Devel. Com., 1990; bd. dirs. Inst. of Medicine, Mental Health and Behavioral Medicine, 1981-83, chmn., 1981-82; mem. Com. on Leadership Devel., Am. Coun. on Edn., 1990-93; chmn. Com. on Substance Abuse and Mental Health Issues in AIDS Rsch., 1992-95. Co-author: The Importance of Mental Health Services to General Health Care, 1979, Modern Clinical Psychiatry, 1982; co-editor: American Handbook of Psychiatry, vols. 6, 7 and 8, 1975, 81, 86, Controversy in Psychiatry, 1978, Psychiatry at the Crossroads, 1980, Critical Problems in Psychiatry, 1982, Signs and Symptoms in Psychiatry, 1983, Consultation-Liaison Psychiatry and Behavioral Medicine, 1986, AIDS and Behavior: An Integrated Approach, 1994, Keeping an Open Door: Passages in a University Presidency, 1996; assoc. editor Am. Jour. Psychiatry, 1973-81. Recipient Disting. Med. Alumni award Columbia U., 1985, Disting. Alumnus award Ochsner Found. Hosp., 1984, Strecker award Inst. of Pa. Hosp., 1980, N.C. award for sci., 1990, William C. Menninger Meml. award ACP, 1994. Fellow Royal Soc. Medicine; mem. NAS, Am. Psychiat. Assn. (sec. 1977-81, pres. 1982-83), Inst. Medicine, Royal Coll. Psychiatrists, Soc. Biol. Psychiatry (A.E. Bennet rsch. award 1970). Home: 63 Beverly Dr Durham NC 27707-2223 Office: Duke U Office of Pres Emeritus 205 E Duke Bldg Durham NC 27708

BRODIE, HOWARD, artist; b. Oakland, Calif., Nov. 28, 1915; s. Edward and Anna (Zeller) B. Student, Art Inst. San Francisco, Art Student's League, N.Y.C., U. Ghana, Accra; LHD (hon.), Acad. Art Coll., San Francisco, 1984. Mem. staff Life mag., Yank: the Army Weekly, Collier's, AP, CBS News, 1969-89; freelance artist, journalist, 1990—. Author: (book) Howard Brodie War Drawings, 1963, Drawing Fire, A Combat Artist At War, 1996; art journalist: (major wars) World War II, Korea, French Indo-China, Vietnam, (trials) Jack Ruby, Ray, Sirhan, My Lai, Charles Manson, Chicago Seven, Watergate, John Hinckley, Klaus Barbie in France, (famous people) John Wayne, Pres. Kennedy, James Jones; art at White House, 1946, 48; work represented in permanent collections Calif. Palace of Legion of Honor, San Francisco, Soc. Illustrators, N.Y., Libr. Congress, Washington, Air Force Acad., Colo.; prints, books: U.S. Army Infantry Mus., Ft. Benning, Ga., U.S. Army Mus., Presidio, Monterery, Oreg. Nat. Mil. Mus., The Hoover Instn. on War, Revolution and Peace, Anne S.K. Brown Mil. Collection Brown U. Libr., The Mus. of Books, Lenin Libr., Moscow, Gorky Sci. Libr., Moscow, Admiral Nimitz State Hist. Park, Tex., Henry E. Huntington Libr. (award), San Marina, New Britain Mus. Am. Art, Conn., West Point Libr., N.Y., Brown U. Libr., R.I.; commd. to draw The Contemporary Soldier in Action, Assn. U.S. Army, 1999; guest on Merv Griffin Show, Charles Kuralt Sunday Morning program, Ted Koppel program, Night Line; featured Andy Rooney CBS Sunday Morning program, Nostagia Network, Dennis Wholey Am. Program; featured 1 out of 7 artists (PBS Documentary) They Drew Fire, 2000, (incompanion TV book) They Drew Fire, Combat Artists of World War II, 2000. Sgt., U.S. Army. Decorated Bronze Star; recipient honor medals Freedom Found., 1957, 58, 60, 61. Office: PO Box 221940 Carmel CA 93922-1940

BRODIE, JAMES WILLIAM, marine scientist; b. Bebington, Cheshire, Eng., Oct. 7, 1920; s. James T. Fielding and Isabella (Garner) B.; m. Audrey Jacobsen, 1945 (dec. Jan. 1996); children: James Sheldon, Philip Quentin. BSc, U. New Zealand, 1945, MSc in Geology, 1949. With Dept. Lands and Survey, Wellington, New Zealand, 1937-45; editl. positions Dept. Sci. and Indsl. Rsch., Wellington, 1945-50, adminstr. geophysics divsn., 1951-54; dir. Fisheries Rsch. divsn. Marine Dept., Wellington, 1964-67, New Zealand Oceanographic Inst., Wellington, 1954-77; hist. and biog. rschr., 1993; editor Stockade Karori Hist. Soc., Wellington, 1994—; cons. in marine scis. UNESCO, 1965-79, sci. advisor for S.E. Asia, Jakarta, Indonesia, 1978-79, chair West Pacific Oceanographic Workshop, Tokyo, 1978; mem. devel. team Mus. New Zealand Project, 1985-92. Editor New Zealand Stamp Collector, 1980-85; editor, pub. New Zealand Soc. of Friends hist. publs., 1988—; author books, monographs and jour. articles. on geol. and marine sci. topics and on hist. and biog. subjects. Decorated Order Brit. Empire; recipient Marsden medal New Zealand Assn. Scientists, 1978. Fellow Royal Soc. new Zealand (home sec. 1983-87, v.p. 1986-87). Avocations: archaeology, historical research. Home: 1 Fettes Crescent, Wellington 6003, New Zealand

BRODINE, CHARLES EDWARD, physician; b. Sioux City, Iowa, May 10, 1925; s. Ivar and Dorothy B.; m. Lois Bliss, June 26, 1949; children: Stephanie Kay, Jennifer Leah, Charles Edward. B.S., Iowa State U., Ames, 1948, research fellow malaria project, 1948-49; M.D., Washington U., St. Louis, 1953. Intern St. Louis County Hosp., 1953-54, resident in internal medicine, 1954-55; resident in internal medicine U.S. Naval Hosp., Oakland, Calif., 1957-59; fellow in hematology, clin. instr. medicine U. Cin. and Cin. Gen. Hosp., 1955-57; head hematology svc. U.S. Naval Hosp., Oakland, 1959-61, Bethesda, Md., 1961-62; cons. in hematology U.S. Naval Hosp., 1962-73; head divsn. rsch. hematology Naval Med. Rsch. Inst., Bethesda, 1962-66; chmn. dept. clin. investigation Naval Med. Rsch. Inst., 1966-70, exec. officer, 1970-73; program mgr. Navy frozen blood and trauma rsch. program research div. Bur. Medicine and Surgery U.S. Dept. Navy, Washington, 1962-71; dir. rsch. divsn. Bur. Medicine and Surgery U.S. Dept. Navy, 1973-74; spl. asst. med. rsch. and devel. to Surgeon Gen. U.S. Navy, 1974-77; comdg. officer Naval Med. Rsch. and Devel. Command, Nat. Naval Med. Center, Bethesda, 1974-77; asst. med. dir. environ. health and preventive medicine Office Med. Svcs. Dept. State, Washington, 1977-90; mem. Agt. Orange Working Group, 1982-90; exec. com. Nat. Council Internat. Health, 1982-90; Bd. dirs. Gorgas Meml. Inst. Tropical and Preventive Medicine, 1973-89; mem. Bur. Medicine and Surgery Policy Council, 1974-77; med. adviser ARC, 1975-79; adv. com. Nat. Sickle Cell Disease, NIH, 1974-77; mem. com. on biomed. rsch. U.S.-Egypt Joint Working Group, 1975-77; mem. White House Working Group on Internat. Health, 1977; clin. asso. prof. dept. medicine Georgetown U., Washington, 1971—; Dept. State mem. Nat. Council for Internat. Health, 1978-89. Contbr. articles in field to med. jours. Exec. com. Gorgas Meml. Inst., 1978-88. Decorated Legion of Merit for blood rsch. project, 1968; recipient Meritorious Service medal for work at Naval Med. Rsch. Inst. U.S. Dept. Navy, 1973; Robert Dexter Conrad award for outstanding sci. achievement Sec. of Navy, 1977. Mem. AMA, Assn. Mil. Surgeons (sustaining membership award 1967), Acad. Medicine of Washington (bd. dirs. 1992—), Soc. for Cryobiology (editorial bd. 1964-66), Soc. Fed. Med. Agys., Western Soc. Clin. Investigation, Soc. Med. Cons. Armed Forces. Home: 9213 Friars Rd Bethesda MD 20817-2313

BRODKIN, ADELE RUTH MEYER, psychologist; b. N.Y.C., July 8, 1934; d. Abraham J. and Helen (Honig) Meyer; m. Roger Harrison Brodkin, Jan. 26, 1957; children: Elizabeth Anne Brodkin Brauer, Edward Stuart. BA, Sarah Lawrence Coll., 1956; MA, Columbia U., 1959; PhD, Rutgers U., 1977. Lic. psychologist, N.J. Sch. psychologist pub. schs., River Edge, Norwood, 1961-66, Morristown, Chatham, N.J., 1967-73; cons. psychologist United Hosp. Newark, 1973; assoc. dir. Infant Child Devel. Ctr. St. Barnabas Med. Ctr., Livingston, N.J., 1977-79; clin. asst. prof. dept. psychiatry U. Medicine and Dentistry N.J., Newark, 1979-90, clin. assoc. prof., 1990—; vis. scholar Hasting (N.Y.) Ctr. for Life Scis., 1979; mem. Essex County Mental Health Adv. Bd., Essex County, N.J., 1985-87; sr. child devel. cons.; cons. Scholastic, Inc., 1988—; clin. assoc. prof. psychiatry UMDNJ-N.J. Med. Sch., 1990—. Author: The Lonely Only Dog, 1998, Between Teacher and Parent, Supporting Young Children As They Grow, 1994, (with A.T. Jersild and E. Alina Lazar) The Meaning of Psychotherapy in the Teacher's Life and Work, 1962; author, prodr. (video documentary) Competing Commitments, 1984 (Best Ednl. Videotape award N.J. Cable); co-author, prodr. ednl. videotapes: Passage to Physicianhood, 1985, The Insidious Epidemic, 1986; columnist Between Tchr. and Parent, Pre-K Today mag., 1988-93, Early Childhood Today, 1993—, Scholastic Parent and Child mag., 1994—; child devel. columnist, 1991-92; columnist You and Today's Child, Instr. mag., 1992-93, Kids in Crisis, Instr. mag., 1993-96; columnist Adolescent Devel., Mid. Yrs. mag., 1990-95; columnist Scholastic.com "Ask Dr. Brodkin" 1997—; columnist Scholastic Network, 1995— contbr. articles to profl. jours. Grantee Gannett Found., Cmty. Fund for N.J., Carter-Wallace, Inc., Schering Corp.; Adelaide M. Ayer fellow Columbia U., 1962-63, NIMH fellow, 1962, Louis Bevier fellow Rutgers U., 1976-77. Fellow Am. Orthopsychiat. Assn.; mem. APA, N.J. Psychol. Assn. (Psychol. Recognition award 1982, 86, 90), Am. Sociol. Assn. Avocations: cairn terrier, grandchildren. Home and Office: 2 Trevino Ct Florham Park NJ 07932-2724

BRODLEY, JOSEPH F., law educator, consultant; b. Washington, Sept. 22, 1926; s. Joseph an dBarbara (Gross) B.; m. Angeli B. Brodley, June 4, 1960; children: Barbara Joanna, Carla Elizabeth. BA, UCLA, 1949; LLB, Yale U., 1952; LLM, Harvard U., 1953. Assoc. Dewey, Ballantine, N.Y.C., 1956-61; assoc. ptnr. Richards, Watson & Hemmerling, L.A., 1961-68; prof. law Ind. U., Bloomington, 1968-79; prof. law and econ., Kenison disting. scholar of law, prof. econs. Boston U., 1986—, interim dean Law Sch., 1989-90; cons. Ford Motor Co., Dearborn, Mich., 1984, UN Devel. Project People's Republic of China, Beijing, 1992—, U.S. Dept. Justice, Washington, 1994-95; vis. prof. U. Mich., Ann Arbor, 1982; vis. fellow Wolfson Coll., U. Oxford, Eng., 1985; pub. testifier Senate Jud. Com., Washington, 1986, 87, 90, House Subcom. Monopolies, 1977; life fellow Clare Hall, U. Cambridge, Eng., 1993—. 1st lt. JAG, USAF, 1953-56, Korea. Mem. Harvard Club (Boston), Yale Club (Boston) English Speaking Union. Office: Boston U Sch of Law 765 Commonwealth Ave Boston MA 02215-1401

BRODSKY, ALLEN, radiological and health physicist, consultant; b. Balt., Nov. 5, 1928; s. Nathan Michael and Gertrude Devera (Silberman) B.; m. Paula Fishman, June 17, 1951 (div. 1983); children: Richard, Karen, Jay; m. Phyllis Levin, Mar. 16, 1984. BS in Engring., Johns Hopkins U., 1949, MA in Physics, 1960; ScD, U. Pitts., 1966. Diplomate Am. Bd. Health Physics, Am. Bd. Indsl. Hygiene, Am. Bd. Radiology. Radiol. physics fellow Oak Ridge (Tenn.) Nat. Lab., 1950; head health physics unit U.S. Naval Rsch. Lab., Washington, 1950-52; physicist region 2 FCDA, Olney, Md., 1956-57; health physicist AEC, Washington, 1957-61; rsch. assoc. Grad. Sch. Pub. Health U. Pitts., 1961-71, assoc. prof., 1966—; radiation physicist Mercy Hosp., Pitts., 1971-75; sr. health physicist U.S. Nuclear Regulatory Commn., Washington, 1975-86; cons. CD, NAS, Washington, 1975; adj. prof. sch. pharmacy Duquesne U., Pitts., 1971-75; radiation sci. fellowship bd. Oak Ridge Associated Univs., 1967-70; adj. prof. radiation sci. Georgetown U., Washington, 1986—; sr. scientist Sci. Applications Internat. Corp., 1997—. Editor-in-chief, author: Radiation Measurement and Protection, Vol. I, 1979, Vol. II, 1982, Vol. III 1982, Vol. IV 1986; author: Radiation Risks and Uranium Toxicity, 1996; contbr. regulatory guides, book chpts., articles in field. Pres. Western Pa. Profs. for Peace in Mid. East, Pitts., 1970-71; witness on radiation effects U.S. Ho. of Reps., Washington, 1978, witness on radiation studies U.S. Senate, Washington, 1978-81, expert witness U.S. Dept. Justice, Washington, 1983-84. Lt. C.E., U.S. Army, 1952-54. Named W.H. Langham lectr., U. Ky., 1979, Failla Meml. lectr., Radiol. and Med. Physics Soc., Health Physics Soc. N.Y., N.Y.C., 1987; recipient Leadership and Sci. Contbns. cert. Conf. on Bioassay, Environ., and Analytical Radiochemistry, 1986. Mem. Am. Nuclear Soc. (radiation sci. and tech. award 1993), Am. Assn. Physicists in Medicine, Am. Indsl. Hygiene Assn., Am. Statis. Assn., Health Physics Soc. (chmn. standards com. 1959-61, 67-70, bd. dirs. 1967-70, pres. Western Pa. chpt. 1967-68, Western Pa. chpt. disting. svc. award 1966, pres. Balt.-Washington chpt. 1982-83, sec.-treas. govt. sect. 1988-92, Founder's award 1986, Fellow award 1992, video interviewer for history file 2000, life mem. W.Pa. chpt.). Avocations: tennis, piano, composing songs, singing, political campaigns. Home: 27 Saint Martins Ln Berlin MD 21811-1902

BRODSKY, DAVID MICHAEL, lawyer; b. Providence, Oct. 16, 1943; s. Irving and Naomi (Richman) B.; m. Stacey J. Moritz; children: Peter, Isabel, Nell. AB cum laude, Brown U., 1964; LLB, Harvard U., 1967. Bar: N.Y. 1968, U.S. Dist. Ct. (so. dist.) N.Y. 1969, U.S. Ct. Appeals (2d cir.) 1974, U.S. Dist. Ct. (ea. dist.) N.Y. 1977, U.S. Supreme Ct. 1977, U.S. Ct. Appeals (D.C. cir.) 1981, U.S. Ct. Appeals (3d cir.) 1984, U.S. Tax Ct. 1984, U.S. Dist. Ct. (no. dist.) Tex. 1986. Law clk. to U.S. Dist. judge U.S. Dist. Ct. (so. dist.) N.Y., 1967-69; asst. U.S. atty. So. Dist. N.Y., 1969-73; assoc. Guggenheimer & Untermyer, N.Y.C., 1973-75, ptnr., 1976-80; ptnr., chmn. litig. dept. Schulte Roth & Zabel, N.Y.C., 1980-99; mng. dir., gen. counsel-Ams., Credit Suisse First Boston, 1999—; lectr. in field. Co-author: Federal Securities Litigation: A Deskbook for the Practitioner, 1997. Chmn., bd. dirs. N.Y. Lawyers for Pub. Interest, Inc., 1991-94, vice chair, 1994-96. Recipient Pathways to Justice award. Fellow Am. Coll. Trial Lawyers (mem. access to justice com., mem. downstate N.Y. com.); mem. ABA, (litig. sect., co-chmn. ann. meeting 1998, co-chmn. trial practice com. 1990-94, task force on jury sys. 1995—), Assn. of Bar of City of N.Y., Anti-Defamation League (exec. com., legal com. 1994—), Am. Law Inst., N.Y. County Lawyers Assn., Fed. Bar Coun., Harvard Club, Scarsdale Golf Club. Jewish.

BRODSKY, WESLEY GEORGE, electrical engineer; b. Staten Island, N.Y., May 1, 1950; s. George and Helen (Merrell) B.; m. Elizabeth Dexter, Mar. 16, 1989. B.Engring., NYU, 1971; M.Engring., MIT, 1974. Staff MIT Lincoln Lab., Lexington, Mass., 1974-83; prin. engr. Raytheon Co., Marlboro, Mass., 1983—. Patentee in field. Mem. Medford Cmty. Cable, 1988—. Mem. IEEE, IEEE 802.11 Working Group.

BRODT, BURTON PARDEE, chemical engineer, researcher; b. Evanston, Ill., June 3, 1931; s. Harry Snowden and Marjorie Florence (Pardee) B.; m. Virginia Faye Futch, June 20, 1954; children: Howard A., Stephen R., Cynthia A., Phillip D. BS in Chem. Engring., U. Fla., 1954, MS in Chem. Engring., 1958. Devel. engr. DuPont Elastomers, Louisville, Ky., 1958-62; sr. rsch. engr. DuPont Elastomers, Wilmington, Del., 1962-66; tech. supr. DuPont Elastomers, Deepwater, N.J., 1966-69; rsch. supr. polymers div. E.I. DuPont de Nemours and Co., LaPlace, La., 1969-83; sr. supr. rsch. E.I. DuPont de Nemours and Co., Wilmington, 1983-89; sr. rsch., assoc. E.I. DuPont de Nemours and Co., LaPorte, Tex., 1989-91; tech. fellow E.I. DuPont de Nemours and Co., LaPlace, 1991-96; tchg. fellow, sr. scientist DuPont Dow Elastomers, LLC, LaPlace, 1996-98, ret., 1998; tech. cons. Washington, 1998-99; pres. TechDoc, Inc., Easton, 1998—; tech. cons. Wilmington, Del., 1999—. Author: What They Didn't Teach You in College: How to Succeed (or Fail) in Industry, 1993, also several novels; contbr. to profl. publs. Chmn. Citizens for Goldwater, Wilmington, 1964; founder, pres. Del. Conservative Union, Wilmington, 1965-69; pres. Homeowners Assn., Chadds Ford, Pa., 1988. Lt. USAF, 1954-56. Mem. AIChe. Republican. Achievements include patent for accelerator encapsulation, high-viscosity level control, proprietary processes, powder attrition tester; development of chemical processes now in commercial use, Brodt equation for phase transfer catalysis. Home and Office: 6051 Canterbury Dr Easton MD 21601-8555

BRODY, AARON LEO, food and packaging consultant; b. Boston, Aug. 23, 1930; s. Nathan and Lillian (Gorman) B. m. Carolyn Goldstein, Apr. 11, 1953; children: Stephen, Glen, Robyn. BS, MIT, 1951, PhD, 1957; MBA, Northeastern U., 1970. Head food rsch. labs. Whirlpool Co., St. Joseph, Mich., 1957-61; packaging and product devel. mgr. Mars, Inc., Hackettstown, N.J., 1961-66; packaging coord. Arthur D. Little, Inc., Cambridge, Mass., 1967-73; new ventures mgr. Mead Packaging, Atlanta, 1973-81; mgr. mktg. devel. Container Corp. Am., Oaks, Pa., 1981-85; v.p. strategic studies Schotland Bus. Rsch. Inc., Princeton, N.J., 1985-91; mng. dir. Rubbright/Brody, Inc., Duluth, Ga., 1991—; course dir. Mich. State U., East Lansing, 1959-61; adj. assoc. prof. dept. food sci. U. Del., Newark, 1983-86; instr. Emory U., 1979; vis. prof. St. Joseph's U., Phila., 1990—; adj. prof. Spring Garden Coll., Phila., 1990, U. Ga., 1995—; instr. Keller Grad. Sch. of Mgmt., 1996—. Contbr. articles to profl. jours.; author books; patentee in field. Mem. optimal program for edn. DeKalb County (Ga.), 1975, sec., 1975; mem. food svc. adv. com. USN, 1958-62; active Kerry for Congress campaign, 1972, Levitas for Congress campaign, 1974; mem. legis. subcom. on spl. edn. State of Ga., 1974; mem. Nat. Def. Exec. Res., 1978-88; mem. pres.'s coun. Spring Garden Coll., Phila., 1984-89. Served with AUS, 1952-54. William Underwood fellow, 1955-56; recipient Willis H. Carrier award ASHRAE, 1960, Indsl. Achievement award Inst. Food Technologists, 1964, Braverman meml. award Israel Inst. Tech., 1976, Outstanding Alumnus award Northeastern U., 1982; named Packaging Man of Yr. Nat. Inst. Packaging, Handling and Logistics Engrs.; named to Packaging Hall of Fame, 1995. Fellow AAAS, Packaging Inst., Inst. Food Technologists (Riester-Davis Food Packaging Achievement award 1988, Inds. Scientist award 1994, Nicholas Appert award 2000); mem. Packaging Inst. (v.p. 1973-79), Soc. Packaging Profls., Inst. Packaging Profls. (hon. life, Mem. of Yr. 1994-95; cert.), League Internat. Food Edn., Planning Execs. Inst., N.Y. Acad. Scis., Product Devel. and Mgmt. Assn., MIT Club (pres. 1977-79, exec. com., v.p. ednl. coun.), Toastmasters, Sigma Xi. Home and Office: 4981 Trevino Cir Duluth GA 30096-6072

BRODY, EUGENE B., psychiatrist, educator; b. Columbia, Mo., June 17, 1921; s. Samuel and Sophie B.; m. Marian Holen, Sept. 23, 1944; children: Julie Anne, James Clarke, John Holen. AB, MA, U. Mo., 1941, DSc (hon.), 1991; MD, Harvard, 1944; grad., N.Y. Psychoanalytic Inst., 1957. Resident Yale Med. Sch., 1944-46, 48-49, from instr. to assoc. prof., 1949-57; prof. psychiatry U. Md. Sch. Medicine, Balt., 1957-76; chmn. dept., also dir. Inst. Psychiatry and Human Behavior, 1959-76, prof. psychiatry and human behavior, 1976-87, prof. emeritus, 1987—; sr. assoc. sch. of hygiene and pub. health Johns Hopkins U., 1986—; vis. prof. U. Brazil, 1968, U. W.I., Kingston, Jamaica, 1972, 73, James Cook U., No. Queensland, Australia, 1992; vis. prof. psychiatry Harvard Med. Sch., 1997—; fellow Center for Advanced Studies in Behavioral Scis., Stanford, 1975-76, U. Otago (N.Z.), 1981, Inst. for Advanced Studies, Tel Aviv U., 1986; mem. adv. bd. Inst. Social Psychiatry, U. San Marcos, 1968-70; mem. nat. profl. adv. bd. psychiatry, psychology and neurology service VA, 1963-67; cons. WHO (Pan Am. Health Orgn. and Geneva, Switzerland), 1965—; program dir. Interam. Mental Health Studies Program, 1967-69; mem. exec. bd. World Fedn. Mental Health, 1969-83, adminstrv. mem., 1972-74, mem.-at-large, 1979-81, pres., 1981-83, sec. gen., 1983-99, sr. cons., 1999—; mem. epidemiol. studies rev. com. NIMH, 1975-79, cons. clin. infant devel. program, 1979-81, hosp. rev. com., 1979-86, AIDS grant rev. com. 1987-92; mem. internat. adv. bd. Peruvian Nat. Inst. Mental Health, 1984—, mem. editl. bd. jours., 1985—; mem. adv. coun. Hogg Found., 1986-89; mem. sci. com. Internat. Social Sci. Coun., 1989, exec. com. 1989-91, 92-95; cons. UNESCO, 1986—; sr. advisor in Refugee Trauma, Harvard Program, 1989—. Author: The Lost Ones, Social Forces and Mental Illness in Rio de Janeiro, 1973, Sex, Contraception and Motherhood in Jamaica, 1981, Psychoanalytic Knowledge, 1990, Biomedical Technology and Human Rights, 1993, The Search for Mental Health: A History and Memoir of WFMH, 1948-1997, 1998; editor: (with F.C. Redlich) Psychotherapy with Schizophrenics, 1952, (with R. Monroe and G. Klee) Psychiatric Epidemiology and Mental Health Planning, 1967, Minority Group Adolescents in the United States, 1968, Behavior in New Environments, 1970; cons. editor Jour. Nervous and Mental Disease, 1959-67, editor in chief, 1967—; adv. editor: Tice Med. Ency., 1967-80, Harper & Row Med. Ency., 1980-86; mem. editorial bd. Psychiatry Digest, 1967-71, Mental Hygiene, 1968-70, Social Psychiatry, 1970-81, Internat. Jour. Psychosomatic Obstetrics and Gynecology, 1984-92, Population and Environment, 1987-92; contbr. numerous articles to profl. jours. Chmn. adv. bd. Balt. chpt. Internat. Students Council, ARC, 1964-67; bd. dirs. Md. Partners of Alliance for Progress, 1965-66, Nat. Assn. Mental Health, 1964-66, mem. profl. adv. bd., 1967-71; mem. adv. bd. Inst. for Victims of Trauma, 1988-97. Served to capt. M.C. AUS, 1946-48. Fellow Am. Psychiat. Assn. (life; chmn. com. transcultural psychiatry 1966-68, rep. interam. council 1965-71, trustee 1968-71, chmn. task force family planning 1973-75), Am. Coll. Psychiatrists (charter), Am. Coll. Psychoanalysts (charter); mem. Assn. Behavioral Sci. and Med. Edn. (pres. 1981), Am. Psychoanalytic Assn. (life), Internat. psychoanalytic assns., Internat. Coll. Pediatrics (senate 1978-86), Internat. Assn. Psychosomatic Ob-Gyn (exec. bd. 1977-86), Peruvian Psychiat. Assn. (hon.), Peruvian Assn. Psychiatry, Neurology and Neurosurgery (hon.). Club: Cosmos (Washington), West River Sailing Assn., 14 W. Hamilton St. Club (Balt.). Home: 70 Olmstead Green Ct Baltimore MD 21210-1508 Office: Jour Nervous/Mental Disease care Sheppard & Enoch-Pratt Hosp PO Box 6815 Baltimore MD 21285-6815

BRODY, LAWRENCE, lawyer, educator; b. St. Louis, Aug. 12, 1942; s. Max and Jeannette (Cohen) B.; m. Janice Dobinsky, Dec. 25, 1967; 1 child, Michael Allen. BS in Econs., U. Pa., 1964; JD, Washington U., St. Louis, 1967; LLM in Tax, NYU, 1968. Bar: Mo. Assoc. atty. Husch, Eppenberger, Donohue, Elson & Cornfeld, St. Louis, 1968-74, ptnr., 1974-86; ptnr. Bryan Cave, LLP, St. Louis, 1986—; adj. prof. Washington U. Sch. Law, 1968—. Author: Missouri Estate Planning, 1988; author, editor Life Insurance Counsellor Series, 1990, 91. Fellow Am. Coll. of Trust and Estate Counsel, Am. Coll. Tax Counsel; mem. Adv. Bd. of Tax Mgmt. Office: Bryan Cave LLP 211 N Broadway Ste 3600 Saint Louis MO 63102-2733

BROEKAERT, JOSE ALFONS C., chemistry educator; b. Opbrakel, Belgium, Sept. 7, 1948; s. Joseph and Albertine (Verbeurgt) B.; m. Paula Monique M. Claeys, Apr. 20, 1974; children: Ilse, Sigrid, Carmen. Candidate Scis., U. Gent, Belgium, 1968, Lic. in Chemistry, 1970, PhD in Chemistry, 1976; DS, U. Antwerpen, Belgium, 1985. Univ. asst. U. Gent, 1970-76; rsch. fellow ISAS, Dortmund, Germany, 1977, sr. rschr., 1978-91; univ. prof. (C3) U. Dortmund, 1991-98; univ. prof. (C4) U. Leipzig, 1998—. Co-editor: (book) Metal Speciation in the Environment, 1990; asst. editor:

Sci. Jour. Spectrochimica Acta B., 1981-93; mem. editl. and editl. adv. bds. of various analytical chem. jours.; contbr. articles to profl. jours. Recipient Alexander von Humboldt fellowship, Germany, 1977, NATO collaborative rsch. grant, 1990, 92, 94; Fulbright rsch. scholar Ind. U., 1998. Office: U Leipzig/Inst Analyt Chem, Linnestrasse 3, D-04103 Leipzig Germany

BROGAN, DENIS HUGH VERCINGETORIX, historian, educator; b. Oxford, England, Mar. 20, 1936; s. Denis William and Olwen Phillis Frances (Kendall) B. BA, Cambridge U., England, 1959, MA, 1964. Mem. staff The Economist, London, 1960-62; lectr. history U. Essex, England, 1974-87, sr. lectr., chmn. history dept., 1987-90, R.A. Butler prof. history, 1993-98, rsch. prof., 1998—. Author: Tocqueville, 1973, The Life of Arthur Ransome, 1984, Longman History of the U.S.A., 1985, Mowgli's Sons: Kipling and Baden-Powell's Scouts, 1987, Kennedy, 1996. Harkness fellow Commonwealth Fund, 1962-64, fellow St. John's Coll., Cambridge, 1964-74. Fellow Royal Hist. Soc., Survivors Club (Colchester) (pres. 1984-86), Reform Club London. Avocation: collecting English epitaphs. Office: Univ of Essex, Wivenhoe Park, Colchester England

BROGAN, JOSEPH WILLIAM, JR., safety and health consultant; b. North Arlington, N.J., Aug. 22, 1926; s. Joseph William and Beulah Catherine (Heys) B.; m. M. Jean Taylor, Jan. 27, 1948; children: Joseph William III, John P. BS, Union Coll., 1948; postgrad., Rutgers U., 1948-53; MPA, Nova U., 1978. Registered profl. engr., Calif.; cert. safety profl., indsl. hygienist, hazard material mgr. Chemist Bakelite Div. Union Carbide, Bound Brook, N.J., 1951-53; group leader Callery (Pa.) Chem. Co., 1953-55; sr. project engr. ITT Labs., Nutley, N.J., 1955-66; mem. tech. staff Computer Scis. Corp., Falls Church, Va., 1966-70; mem. sr. staff Martin-Marietta Corp., Washington, 1971; sr. safety engr. OSHA, Dept. Labor, Washington, 1971-89; pres. J. Brogan & Assocs., Ltd., Annandale, Va., 1990—; mem. Interagy. Ad Hoc Com. on Oil Well Safety, Washington, 1986-89; mem. emergency med. response ad hoc com. Fed. Emergency Mgmt. Adminstrn., Washington, 1987-89; mem. interagy. oil spill com. EPA, Washington, 1988-89. Contbr. articles to profl. jours. Mem. Am. Soc. Safety Engrs. (sr.), N.Y. Acad. Scis., Vets. of Safety. Achievements include safety and health rules for oil well work, design and implementation of shipboard meteorological data collection system; demonstration of analysis of complex mixtures using cross correlation techniques on spectral data; construction and implementation of high speed facsimile mail system. Home: 4204 Breezewood Ln Annandale VA 22003-2000 Office: J Brogan and Assocs Ltd PO Box 1284 Annandale VA 22003-9284

BROGARD, JEAN-MARIE, internist, physician; b. Strasbourg, Alsace, France, Dec. 26, 1935; s. Paul and Isabelle (Ganter) B.; m. Christiane Meyer, July 7, 1960; children: Michel, Yves-Francois, Catherine, Anne-Florentine. MD, U. Strasbourg, 1965. Diplomate Bd. Internal Medicine. Extern Civil Hosp. Strasbourg, 1955-58, intern, 1958-65; chief clinic, hosp. asst. Ctr. Hosp., U. Strasbourg, 1965-72, chief of works, 1972-75, prof. internal medicine, 1975—. Served with French Army, 1960-62. Mem. European Assn. Internal Medicine (gen. sec. 1977-85). Home: 17 Rue de l'Observatoire, 67000 Strasbourg France Office: Med Clinic B Hospices Civil, 1 Place l'Hopital, 67091 Strasbourg France

BROGDON, W.M. "ROWE", lawyer; b. Columbia, S.C., Oct. 14, 1953; s. Wallace M. and Helen (Deloach) B.; m. Cynthia S. Brogdon, Feb. 28, 1987; 1 child, Emily Elizabeth. BS in Biology magna cum laude, Ga. So. U., 1976; JD cum laude, Mercer U., 1982. Bar: Ga. 1982. Law clk. to Hon. B. Avant Edenfield U.S. Dist. Ct. (so. dist.) Ga.; ptnr. Smith & Brogdon Attys., Savannah, Ga., 1983-87, Brannan & Brogdon Attys., Claxton, Ga., 1987-93, Franklin, Taulbee, Rushing & Brogdon, P.C., Statesboro, Ga., 1994—. Contbr. articles to profl. jours. Vice chmn. bd. trustees Bulloch Acad. Sch., Statesboro, 1998—; bd. govs. Mercer U. Law Sch., 1979-81. State of Ga. law scholar, 1980. Mem. ATLA, Am. Bd. Trial Advocates, Ga. Trial Lawyers Assn. (chmn. Amicus com. 1996-98, v.p. mid. cir. 1996-97), Atlantic Cir. Bar Assn. (pres. 1991-92), Ogeechee Cir. Bar Assn. (pres. 1996-97), Nat. Bd. Trial Advocacy (cert.), Am. Bd. Trial Advocates, Rotary (treas. 1992-93), Phi Delta Phi. Methodist. Avocation: fishing. Home: 4599 Country Club Rd Statesboro GA 30458-9007 Office: Franklin Taulbee Rushing & Brogdon 12 Siebald St Statesboro GA 30458-1002

BROGLIO, TIMOTHY PAUL, priest, administrator; b. Cleveland Heights, Ohio, Dec. 22, 1951; s. Antonio Secondo and Ruth Norma (Hines) B. AB, Boston Coll., 1973; STB, Gregorian U., Rome, 1976, JCL, 1981, JCD, 1983. Pontifica Accademia Ecclesiastica; cert. diplomat Holy See. Assoc. pastor St. Margaret Mary Parish, S. Euclid, Ohio, 1977-79; sec. Apostolic Nunciature, Abidjan, Ivory Coast, 1983-87; auditor, sec. Apostolic Nunciature, Asuncion, Paraguay, 1987-90; desk officer Secretariat State, Vatican City State, Italy, 1990—, cabinet chief, 1992—; pastoral assistance St. Thérèse Parish, Abidjan, 1984-87, St. Cecile English Lang. Cmty., 1984-87, San Rafael Parish, Asuncion, 1988-90; instr. spiritual theology novitiate Domincans Blessed Sacrament, Asuncion, 1988-90; lectr. theology Notre Dame Coll. Ohio, S. Euclid, 1978-79. Contbr. Quaderni di Diritto Ecclesiale. Named Commdr. Nat. Order, Govt. Ivory Coast, 1987, Commdr. Order Polar Star Govt. Sweden, 1991, Commdr. Order Antonio José de Irisarri, Govt. Guatemala, 1997, Grand Ofcl. Order Bernardo O'Higgins, Govt. Chile, Grand Cross Order Libertador San Martin, Govt. Argentina. Mem. Am. Friends Vatican Libr. (charter). Avocations: tennis, music, history. Home: Secretariat State, 00120 Vatican City Italy

BROHAMMER, RICHARD FREDERIC, psychiatrist; b. Rockford, Ill., Nov. 9, 1934; s. Joseph C. and Marthe Marie (Ringuette) B.; m. Shirley Ruth Noble, June 22, 1956; children: Richard Frederic II, Renee Marie, Rory Christopher. PhB, U. Detroit, 1960; MD, U. Fla., 1964; postgrad. basic tng. diving medicine, Internat. Underwater Explorers Soc., 1973; advanced tng. diving medicine, Internat. Underwater Explorers, 1974. Diplomate Am. Bd. Psychiatry and Neurology, Am. Bd. Forensic Medicine. Rsch. fellow tropical medicine La. State U., Costa Rica, Fla., 1963, 93, Ctrl. Am., Costa Rica, 1963; intern Duval Med. Ctr., Jacksonville, Fla., 1964-65; resident psychiatry U. Fla., 1965-68; practice medicine specializing in psychiatry Imperial Point Med. Ctr., Ft. Lauderdale, Fla., 1968-97; mem. staff Broward Gen. Med. Ctr., 1968—, Imperial Point Med. Ctr., 1974—, Holy Cross Hosp., 1968—; chmn. dept. psychiatry Imperial Point Hosp., 1975-80, Holy Cross Hosp., 1981-83. Served with USAF, 1954-58, Korea. Rsch. fellow tropical medicine La. State U., Costa Rica, 1963, Ctr. Am., 1968, Costa Rica, 1993. Mem. AMA (pres. student chpt. 1961-64), Broward County (Fla.) Med. Assn., Broward County Psychiat. Soc., Undersea Adventures, Internat. Soc. Diving Medicine. Republican. Roman Catholic.

BROK, ELMAR, member European parliament; b. Verl, Germany, May 14, 1946. Mem. European Parliament, Brussels, 1999—; mem. Group of the European People's Party (Christian Democrats) and European Democrats, European Parliament; mem. conf. of com. chmn.; chmn. com. on fgn. affairs, human rights, common security and def. policy; substitute mem. com. on constnl. affairs; mem. delegation for rels. with the U.S. Office: Europaisches Parlament, Rue Wiertz ASP 10E138, B-1047 Brussels Belgium also: Fr.-Verleger-StraBe 3, D-33719 Bielefeld Germany

BROKA, SERGE MAURICE, anesthesiologist; b. Rocourt, Belgium, Oct. 12, 1963; s. Serge Roger and Jacqueline Elisabeth (Vermeiren) B.; m. Anne Thomas, July 2, 1994; children: Coline, Romane, Lisa. MD, Cath. U. Louvain, Brussels, 1989. Resident Cath. U. Louvain, Brussels, 1994; instr. cardiothoracic anesthesiology U. Clinic Mont-Godinne, Yvoir, Belgium, 1994-97, asst. prof. cardiothoracic anesthesiology, 1997—. Contbr. articles to profl. jours. Mem. European Assn. Cardiothoracic Anesthesiologists, European Soc. Anesthesiologists, Am. Soc. Echocardiography, Soc. Cardiovascular Anesthesiologists. Avocation: mountaineering. Home: Trou D'Herbois 6, B5332 Crupet Belgium Office: U Clinic Mont Godinne, Ave Therasse 1, B-5530 Yvoir Belgium

BROKAW, CLIFFORD VAIL, III, investment banker, business executive; b. N.Y.C., Sept. 17, 1928; s. Clifford Vail and Audrey (Stransom Joel) B.; m. Elizabeth Stokes Rogers, June 29, 1960; children: Clifford Vail IV, George Rogers. B.A., Yale U., 1950; JD, U. Va., 1956. Bar: N.Y. 1957. Assoc. White & Case, N.Y.C., 1956-59; assoc. Blyth & Co., Inc., N.Y.C., 1959-61; assoc., then gen. ptnr. W.E. Hutton & Co., N.Y.C., 1961-67; gen. ptnr., sr. v.p. Eastman Dillon Union Securities & Co. and successor firm Blyth, Eastman, Dillon & Co., Inc., N.Y.C., 1967-77; chmn., CEO Invail Capital, Inc., N.Y.C., 1977-95; CEO IRT Corp., San Diego, 1977-95, chmn. bd., 1986-94; bd. dirs., chmn. fin. com. Brazos River Gas Co., Mineral Wells, Tex., 1962-91; chmn. bd. Cayman Resources Corp., Tulsa, 1977-88, bd. dirs., 1992-95. Bd. advisors Marine Mil. Acad., Harlingen, Tex., 1985-91; mem. alumni assn. coun. U. Va. Sch. Law, 1976-79; founder Brokaw chair corp. law U. Va. Sch. Law, 1985, mem. dean's coun., 1990—, bus. adv. coun., 1995—; mem. indsl. adv. com. Sch. Engring and Applied Sch. U. Va., 1987-94; vestryman French Ch. du St. Espirit, 1986-88, treas., 1988-92, warden, 1989-93. Lt. col. USMCR, 1950-73. Decorated Purple Heart. Mem. ABA, Suffolk County Bar assn., Pilgrims U.S., Mil. Order Carabao, Mil. Order World Wars (vice comdr. N.Y. chpt.), Mil. Order Fgn. Wars U.S., Nat. Inst. Social Scis. (bd. dirs. 1991-94, pres. 1992-94), Nat. Gavel Soc., Ends of Earth, Huguenot Soc. Am. (coun. 1974-80, v.p. 1986-89, pres. 1989-92), Am. Soc. Order of St. John, U. Va. Lawn Soc., Burning Tree Club, Lyford Cay Club, The Meadow Club, Bathing Corp. of Southampton, Union Club (N.Y.C.), Masons, Shriners, Yale Club (N.Y.C.). Republican. Episcopalian. Avocation: tennis, golf. Office: PO Box 5002 Southampton NY 11969-5002

BROKAW, THOMAS JOHN, television broadcast executive, correspondent; b. Webster, S.D., Feb. 6, 1940; s. Anthony Orville and Eugenia (Conley) B.; m. Meredith Lynn Auld, Aug. 17, 1962; children—Jennifer Jean, Andrea Brooks, Sarah Auld. BA in Polit. Sci, U. S.D., 1962, hon. degree; hon. degree, Washington U., St. Louis, Syracuse U., Hofstra U., Boston Coll., Emerson Coll., Simpson Coll., Duke U., 1991, Notre Dame U., 1993. Morning news editor Sta. KMTV, Omaha, 1962-65; news editor, anchorman Sta. WSB-TV, Atlanta, 1965-66; reporter, corr., anchorman Sta. KNBC-TV, Los Angeles, 1966-73; White House corr. NBC, Washington, 1973-76; anchorman Sat. Night News, N.Y.C., 1973-76; host Today show, N.Y.C., 1976-82; anchorman, editor NBC Nightly News, 1982—; corr. Exposé NBC, 1991—; corr. NBC coverage U.S. Presdl. elections, 1976, 80, anchor, 1984, 88; mem. adv. com. Reporters Com. for Freedom of Press. Corr. numerous NBC News specials, including To Be A Teacher, 1987, Wall Street: Money Greed and Power, 1987, A Conversation with Mikhail S. Gorbachev (Alfred I. DuPont award), 1987, Home Street Home, 1988, To Be An American (George Foster Peabody award). Trustee Norton Simon Mus. Art, Pasadena, Calif., U. S.D. Found.; adviser Asia Soc. Mem. AFTRA (dir. 1968-72), Sigma Delta Chi. Office: NBC News 30 Rockefeller Plz Fl 3 New York NY 10112-0002

BRÖLMANN, HANS, gynecologist; b. Amsterdam, The Netherlands, Jan. 24, 1951; s. Joop and Gyps (Jansen) B.; m. Martje van Hees; children: Fleur, Jan. MD, U. Groningen, The Netherlands, 1975; BSc, St. Ignatius Coll., Amsterdam, 1969; MD, U. Groningen, The Netherlands, 1975; PhD, U. Utrecht, The Netherlands, 1984. Resident in gynecology Lucas Hosp., Amsterdam, 1975, Onze Lieve Viouwen Hosp., Amsterdam, 1978-83, Andreas Hosp., Amsterdam, 1983-84; gynecologist St. Joseph Hosp., Veldhoven, The Netherlands, 1984—, head resident tng. in gynecology, 1986—; mem. sci. com. Doelen Congress, Rotterdam, The Netherlands, 1990—; dir. Laparoscopic Tng. Ctr., Eindhoven, The Netherlands, 1992—. Author: Transvaginal Ultrasound in Gynecology, 1996; contbr. chpt. to book; inventor laparoscopic deschamps needle. Mem. Dutch Soc. Gynecol. Endoscopy (pres. 2000—), NVOG (chmn. steering group 1995-96), Internat. Soc. Gynecol. Endoscopy (bd. dirs. 1998—). Avocations: cabaret, golf. Home: Ruusbroeclaan 17, 5611 LT Eindhoven The Netherlands Office: St Joseph Hosp, PO Box 7777, 5500 MB Veldhovem The Netherlands

BROMAN, GEORGE ELLIS, JR., retired surgeon; b. Decatur, Ill., Sept. 17, 1932; s. George Ellis Sr. and Cora Roberta (Corder) B.; m. Nancy Claire Rogers, Dec. 21, 1957; children: George E. III, Beth Claire, David Andrew, Rebecca Linde. AB, Washington U., St. Louis, 1954, MD, 1958. Diplomate Am. Bd. Surgery. Intern, resident St. Joseph's Hosp., Denver, 1958-63; pvt. practice Culpeper, Va., 1965-97; team physician Culpeper County High Sch., 1967—. Deacon, elder Culpeper Presbyn. Ch., 1968—. Capt. U.S. Army, 1963-65. Recipient Disting. Svc. award Va. High Sch. Coaches Assn., Culpeper, 1981, Henretty award Culpeper County C. of C., 1980; athletic field named after Culpeper County Sch. Bd., 1992. Fellow ACS; mem. AMA (del. 1986), Med. Soc. Va. (life, vice speaker 1985-88, speaker 1988-91, pres. 1992-93, Disting. Svc. award 1993), Va. Surg. Soc., Southeastern Surg. Assn., House of Delegates of the Virginia Gen. Assembly representing the 30th Dist., 2000—. Avocations: music (vocal and instrumental), running, sports, reading. Home: 570 Greens Ct Culpeper VA 22701-3348

BROMBERG, ALAN ROBERT, law educator; b. Dallas, Nov. 24, 1928; s. Alfred L. and Juanita (Kramer) B.; m. Anne Ruggles, July 26, 1959. A.B., Harvard U., 1949; J.D., Yale U., 1952. Bar: Tex. 1952. Assoc. firm Carrington, Gowan, Johnson, Bromberg and Leeds, Dallas, 1952-56; atty. and cons., 1956-76; of counsel firm Jenkens & Gilchrist, P.C., 1976—; asst. prof. law So. Meth. U., 1956-58, assoc. prof., 1958-62, prof., 1962-83, Univ. Disting. prof., 1983—, mem. presdl. search group, 1971-72; faculty adviser Southwestern Law Jour., 1958-65; sr. fellow Yale U. Law Faculty, 1966-67; vis. prof. Stanford U., 1972-73; mem. adv. bd. U. Calif. Securities Regulation Inst., 1973-78, 79-87; counsel Internat. Data Systems, Inc., 1961-65, sec., dir., 1963-65; mem. Tex. Legis. Council Bus. and Commerce Code Adv. Com., 1966-67. Author: Supplementary Materials on Texas Corporations, 3d edit, 1971, Partnership Primer-Problems and Planning, 1961, Materials on Corporate Securities and Finance—A Growing Company's Search for Funds, 2d edit, 1965, Securities Fraud and Commodities Fraud, Vols. 1-7, 1967-93, 2nd edit., 2000, Crane and Bromberg on Partnership, 1968, Bromberg and Ribstein on Partnership, Vols. 1-2, 1988, Vols. 3-4, 1994-2000, Bromberg and Ribstein on Limited Liability Partnerships and the Revised Uniform Partnership Act, 1997-2000; mem. ednl. publs. adv. bd., Matthew Bender & Co., 1977-95, chmn., 1981-94; contbr. articles and revs. to law and bar jours.; adv. editor: Rev. Securities and Commodities Regulation, 1969—, Securities Regulation Law Jour, 1973—, Jour. Corp. Law, 1976—, Derivatives: Tax, Regulation, Finance, 1995-97. Sec., bd. dirs. Community Arts Fund, 1963-73; gen. atty. Dallas Mus. Contemporary Arts, 1956-63 ; bd. dirs. Dallas Theater Center, 1955-73, sec., 1957-66, fin. com., 1957-65, mem. exec. com., 1957-70, 79-85, life, 1973—, v.p., trustee endowment fund, 1974-85; trustee Found. for the Arts, 1996—; bd. dirs. Found. for the Arts, 1996—. Served as cpl. U.S. Army, 1952-54. Mem. ABA (coms. commodities, partnerships, fed. regulation securities), Dallas Bar Assn. (chmn. com. uniform partnership act 1959-61, libr. com. 1981-83), Tex. Bar Assn. (chmn. sect. corp. banking and bus. law 1967-68, vice chmn. 1965-67, com. corps. 1957—, mem. com. securities 1965—, chmn. 1965-69, mem. com. partnerships 1957—, chmn. 1979-81), Am. Law Inst. (life), Southwestern Legal Found. (co-chmn. securities com. 1982-85), Tex. Bus. Law Found. (bd. dirs. 1988—, co-chmn. legis. com. 1994—). Office: So Meth U Sch Law Dallas TX 75275-0001 also: 1445 Ross Ave Ste 3200 Dallas TX 75202-2785

BROMBERG, MYRON JAMES, lawyer; b. Paterson, N.J., Nov. 5, 1934; s. Abraham and Elsie (Baker) B.; m. Lisa Murtha, Nov. 28, 1987; children—Kenneth Karl, Eric Edward, Bruce Abraham. BA, Yale U., 1956; LLB, Columbia U., 1959. Bar: N.J. bar 1960, N.Y. bar 1981. Law asst. to dist. atty. N.Y. County, 1958; law asst. U.S. atty. So. Dist. N.Y., 1958-59; asso. mem. firm Ralph Porzio, Morristown, N.J., 1960-61; ptnr. Porzio, Bromberg & Newman, Morristown, 1962-77, mng. prin., 1980-96; atty. Morris County Bd. Elections, 1963-64; town atty., Town of Morristown, 1965-67; lectr. trial practice Rutgers Inst. CLE, 1965-94. Chmn. fund and membership Morristown chpt. ARC, 1965; chmn. retail div. Community Chest Morris County, 1963; chmn. Keep Morristown Beautiful Com., 1963; mem. Morris Twp. Com., 1970-72; committeeman Morris County Democratic Com., 1962-63, 72-77; lay trustee Delbarton Sch., Morristown, 1972-75; trustee Morris Mus., 1973-79. Fellow Am. Coll. Trial Lawyers (chmn. com. on admission to fellowship 1986-91, com. on complex litigation 1992-98, com. on tchg. of trial and appellate advocacy 1998—), Am. Law Inst. (cons. group product liability), Am. Bar Found. (life); mem. ABA, Internat. Acad. Trial Lawyers (chair N.J. 1997-99, regional chair 3d jud. cir. 1997—), N.J. Bar Assn. (named outstanding young lawyer 1970, chmn. joint conf. com. with N.J. Med. Soc. 1970-72), Morris County Bar Assn., Am. Judicature Soc., Trial Attys. N.J. (pres. 1976-77, Trial Bar award 1989), Internat. Soc. Barristers (N.J. State chmn., bd. govs., sec.-treas. 1996-97, v.p. 1998-00, pres. 2000—), Internat. Assn. Def. Counsel (chair com. on toxic and hazardous substances 1994-96, dir. Def. Counsel Trial Acad. 1996), Andover Alumni Assn. N.Y.C., Columbia U. Law Sch. Assn. of N.J. (bd. dirs. 1986-95), Yale Club (N.Y.C. and ctrl. N.J.), Park Ave. (N.J.) Club, Merchants Club (N.Y.C.), Chi Phi, Phi Delta Phi. E-mail: mjbromberg@pbn.law.com. Home: 9 Thompson Ct Morristown NJ 07960-6326 Office: 100 Southgate Pkwy Morristown NJ 07960-7324

BROMBERGER, DOMINIQUE JEAN MARIE, journalist, news correspondent; b. Paris, Mar. 24, 1944; s. Hervé G. and Paulette M. (Deschaux) B.; m. Genevieve M.J. Gillio, Apr. 17, 1986; 1 child, Camille. Diploma, Inst. Polit. Studies Paris, 1965; diploma superior studies of pub. right, Paris Faculty of Law, 1966. Parliamentary corr. Radio Monte Carlo, Monaco, 1966-69; anchorman Radio Lebanon, 1969-70; sr. polit. corr. France-Inter, 1971-74; diplomatic editor TFI, 1975-76; corr. TFI, London, 1976-77, Washington, 1977-81; fgn. editor, editor-in-chief, anchorman TV Francaise 1, Paris, 1981-95; anchorman, Paris bur. chief ARTE, Strasbourg, France, 1995-98; anchorman daily radio column Nat. French Pub. Radio, 1996—, editl. editor, 2000—. Author: (novel) Itineraire de Pahran au Chateau d'Alamut, 1978, (essay) Le Grand Manége, 1993; contbr. daily column to l'Independent, weekly column to Investir, Le Telegramme. Decorated knight Nat. Order of Legion of Honor, officer Ordre Nat. du Merite (France); recipient Roland Dorgelès prize, 2000. Mem. French Diplomatic Press Assn. (pres. 1994-98, hon. pres. 1998—), Internat. Inst. for Strategic Studies (London), Franco-Brit. Coun., Press Club de France (v.p. 1998—). Office: ARTE la Sept Video, 116 Ave du Pres Kennedy, 75016 Paris France

BROMLEY, ANNA LUCY, publications executive; b. Monkton Farleigh, Wiltshire, U.K., Mar. 9, 1966; d. Harvey Hans and Hazel Ruth (Ware) B. BSc in Biochemistry with honors, Birmingham (Eng.) U., 1987. Sci. officer Viggo-Spectramed, Eng., 1987-89; sales and mktg. exec. Viggo-Spectramed, 1989-91; asst. city ctr. mgr. Bath (Eng.) City Coun., 1991-94; med. device report writer PJB Publs., London, 1994-96, commissioning mgr. clin. reports, 1996—; pvt. practice shiatsu practitioner, London, 1994—. Author: Patient Monitoring in Critical Care, 1995, Cardiovascular Implants, 1996, Magnetic Resonance Imaging, 1996. Mem. Shiatsu Soc. Avocations: alternative health, shamanic dance, camping, hiking, rock climbing. Home: 26 Brent Ct, Emlyn Gardens, London W12 9UB, England Office: PJB Publs, 18-20 Hill Rise, Richmond Surrey, England

BROMLEY, PAUL DOUGLAS, exercise physiologist, educator; b. London, Mar. 30, 1967; s. John Frederick and Shirley Anne (Waters) B.; m. Lisa Kay Davies, July 17, 1999. MSc, City U., London, 1997; postgrad., Greenwich U., Australia, 1999—. Phys. tng. instr. Royal Navy, 1984-94; lectr., course dir. Premier Tng. and Devel. Ltd., Wiltshire, Eng., 1994; freelance cons. London, 1994-95; dir. tng., mng. dir. Body in Action Tng. and Edn. Ltd., London, 1995-97; sr. health, fitness and rehab. advisor St. Mary's Hosp., London, 1997-98; clin. exercise and phys. activity mgr. South London & Maudsney NHS Trust, London, 1998-99; sr. lectr., dir. human performance lab. Buckinghamshire (Eng.) Chilterns Univ. Coll., 1999—. Co-author: Taming the Hungry Bear — Your Way to Recover From Chaotic Overeating, 1999; contbr. articles to profl. jours. and mags. Recipient NATO medal, 1993. Mem. Royal Instn. Great Britain, Brit. Assn. Sport and Exercise Scis. (mem. exercise sci. spl. com., accredited exercise physiologist), Inst. Biology (chartered biologist), Am. Coll. Sports Medicine. Conservative. Avocations: reading, exercise. Office: Ctr Exercise Health Perform Buckinghamshire Chilters Univ, Kingshill Rd High Wycombe, Buckinghamshire HP13 5BB, England

BROMLEY, STEPHEN C., zoology educator; b. L.A., Aug. 31, 1938; s. Karl F. and Fae Christenson Bromley; m. Wendy McGarry, Oct. 1968 (div. Oct. 1995); children: John Axel, Anna Ruth, Joseph Jacob, James Asa, Jane Alexis, Stephen Calder. BS, Brigham Young U., 1960; AM, Princeton U., 1962, PhD, 1965. Instr. dept. biology Princeton (N.J.) U., 1964-65; asst. prof. dept. zoology U. Vt., Burlington, 1965-69; rsch. assoc. dept. zoology Mich. State U., East Lansing, 1969-70, assoc. prof. dept. zoology, 1970-76, prof. dept. zoology, 1976—, dir. biol. sci. program, 1970-91, dir. The Conservatory, 1988-90. Mem. AAAS. Avocations: handball, wood working, music, athletic conditioning, target shooting. E-mail: sbromley@msu.edu. Home: 1023 Glenhaven Ave East Lansing MI 48823-2622 Office: Dept Zoology Mich State Univ East Lansing MI 48823

BROMWICH, MICHAEL, accounting and finance educator; b. Watford, Eng., Jan. 29, 1941; s. William James and Margery (Townley) B.; m. Christine Margaret Elizabeth Whitehead, Aug. 10, 1972. BSc Econs., London Sch. Econs., 1965; DSc in Econs. (hon.), U. Lund, Sweden, 1992. Acctg. trainee Ford Motor Co., Essex, Eng., 1958-61, acctg. mgr., 1965-66; prof. econs. Univ. Coll., Cardiff, Wales, 1971-77, U. Reading, Eng., 1977-85; lectr. London Sch. Econs., 1966-71, prof. econs., 1985—; mem. com. Social Sci. Rsch. Coun., 1980-84, 91-95, Acctg. Stds. Com., London, 1980-84; head dept. acctg. and fin. London Sch. Econs., 1985-89, 92-96, gov., 1992-96. Author: Economics of Capital Budgeting, 1976, Financial Reporting Information and Capital Markets, 1992, Management Accounting: Pathways to Progress, 1994, Accounting for Overheads: Critique and Reforms, 1997. Fellow Chartered Inst. Mgmt. Acctg. (pres. 1987-88, v.p. 1985-87, mem. coun. 1982-91), Am. Acctg. Assn., European Acctg. Assn. Avocations: working, dining at restaurants. Home: 14 Thornhill Rd, London N1 1HW, England Office: London Sch Econs, Houghton St, London WC2A 2AE, England

BRONAUGH, DEANNE RAE, home health care administrator, consultant; b. Cameron, Mo., Feb. 3, 1952; d. Myron McMillin and Kathryn Marie (Ogden) Bell; m. Richard N. Bronaugh, July 18, 1987; 1 child, Elisabeth Catherine. BSN magna cum laude, Avila Coll., 1974. Cert. nursing adminstr., ANA. Staff nurse Bapt. Meml. Hosp., Kansas City, Mo., 1974-77; nurse clinician North Kansas City (Mo.) Meml. Hosp., 1977-78; asst. dir. Bethany Med. Ctr., Kansas City, 1978-79, spl. projects dir., 1979-80, dir. critical care, 1980-81; DON Lee's Summit (Mo.) Community Hosp., 1981-84; asst. adminstr. Muskogee (Okla.) Regional Med. Ctr., 1984-86; cons. Creative Nursing Mgmt., Mpls., 1986-87; pres. Liberty Cons., Muskogee, 1992-93; state liaison for accreditation affairs ABC Home Health, 1993-94; regional adminstr. 1st Am. Home Care (formerly ABC Home Health), 1994-96; regional dir. clin. svcs. Integrated Health Svcs., Overland Park, Kans., 1996-97; assoc. Corridor Group, Inc., Overland Park, Kans., 1997; sr. assoc. Curran Care, North Riverside, Ill., 1997-98; gen. mgr. VNA Plus, Lenexa, Kans., 1998-99; design cons. Norwalk Furniture, Lenexa, Kans., 1999—; health care cons., 2000—; mem. adv. bd. Am. Heart Assn., Kansas City, Kans., 1979-81. Mem. Rep. Women's Club, Muskogee, 1988, P.E.O., Muskogee, 1992. Mem. Sigma Theta Tau. Home: 11502 W 127th Ter Overland Park KS 66213-3534

BRØNDUM-NIELSEN, TROELS, engineering educator; b. Copenhagen, Aug. 31, 1917; s. Johannes and Frieda (Christensen) B.; m. Hertha Ellen Holm, June 28, 1943; children: Bolette, Malene. Grad. civil engring., Tech. U., 1941. Chief engr. Christiani & Nielsen, Copenhagen, 1957-63; prof. theory of structures Tech. U., Denmark, 1963-87. Author: Structural Concrete, 1973. Decorated Knight Order of Dannebrog, 1971, 1st degree 1979. Fellow Am. Concrete Inst.; mem. Danish Soc. for Structural Sci. and Engring. (hon.), Com. Euro-Internat. du Béton (hon.). Home: Tovesvej 12, 2850 Naerum Denmark Office: Tech U of Denmark, 2800 Lyngby Denmark

BRONFMAN, EDGAR MILES, beverage company executive; b. Montreal, June 20, 1929; s. Samuel and Saidye (Rosner) B.; married. Student, Williams Coll., 1946-49; B.A., McGill U., 1951; LHD (hon.), Pace U., 1982; LLD (hon.), Williams Coll., 1986. Chmn. adminstrv. com. Joseph E. Seagram & Sons, Inc., 1955-57, pres., 1957-71; chmn., CEO, pres. Distillers Corp.-Seagram Ltd., Montreal, 1971-75; now chmn. The Seagram Co. Ltd. and Joseph E. Seagram & Sons Inc.; bd. dirs. Am. Technion Soc. Mem. citizens com. for N.Y.C., U.S.-USSR Trade and Econ. Coun.; chmn. Samuel Bronfman Found.; pres. N. Am. Consortium for Free Market Study, World Jewish Congress; mem. internat. adv. bd. Sch. Internat. and Pub. Affairs, Columbia U.; mem. exec. com. Am. Jewish Congress, Am. Jewish Com.; chmn. Anti-Defamation League N.Y.; bd. dirs. Am. Com. Weizmann Inst. Sci., Israel; mem. Bus. Com. for Arts, United Jewish Appeals; hon. chmn. Fedn. Jewish Philanthropies; bd. dels. Union Am. Hebrew Congregation. Named Chevalier de la Légion d'Honneur French Govt. Mem. Coun. Fgn. Rels., Ctr. Inter-Am. Rels., Hundred Year Assn. N.Y., Com. for Econ. Devel., Fgn. Policy Assn., B'nai B'rith (bd. overseers). Office: Joseph E Seagram & Sons Inc 375 Park Ave New York NY 10152-0002 also: The Seagram Co Ltd, 1430 Peel St, Montreal, PQ Canada H3A 1S9

BRONGE, CHRISTIAN ÅKE OLOF, hydrology and climatology researcher; b. Visby, Gotland, Sweden, July 1, 1949; s. Ingemar and Ingegärd (Nordlander) B.; m. Laine Boresjö, Aug. 19, 1989; children: Erica, Ian. MSc, Royal Inst. Tech., Stockholm, 1974; PhD, Stockholm U., 1989. Engr. Hwy. Dept., Stockholm, 1974-79; course adminstr. Royal Inst. of Tech., Stockholm, 1980-81; rsch. asst. Stockholm U., 1981-86, rsch. fellow, 1990-95, sr. lectr., 1995-96, rschr., 1997—; project leader Australian Nat. Antarctic Rsch. Expedns., Davis Sta., Antarctica, 1987-88, 90-91; chmn. bd. dirs. Birka Air Charter, Stockholm, 1989-90; project leader Swedish Antarctic Rsch. Programme, Svea Sta., Antarctica, 1992-93. Contbr. articles to profl. jours. Travel grantee Rotary, 1967. Mem. Swedish Gen. Aviation Assn./Aircraft Owners and Pilots Assn., Royal Swedish Aero Club, Australian Geographic Soc. Avocations: flying, skating, astronomy, history. Home: Bigårdsvägen 1, S-17832 Ekerö Sweden Office: Unit Paleogeophysics & Geodynamics, Stockholm U, S-10691 Stockholm Sweden

BRONISCH, THOMAS ERNST, psychiatrist; b. Hamburg, Germany, Feb. 13, 1948; s. Otfried and Annemarie (Katter-Gnauth) B.; m. Petra Kohler, May, 1997; 1 child, Anatole Thomas-Benjamin. MD, U. Heidelberg, Erlangen, Germany, 1974, cert. prof., 1998. Med. asst. clinic for internal medicine Nuremberg Max-Planck-Inst. of Psychiatry Clinic of Surgery, Munich, 1973-74; psychiatrist in tng. Psychiat. Hosp., Haar, Munich, 1975-76, Neurol. Clinic, Haar, Munich, 1976-77; psychiatrist in tng. Max-Planck-Inst. of Psychiatry, 1977-80, asst. head out- and in-patient dept., 1981-91, head of outpatient dept., 1991—. Author: Die depressive Reaktion, 1992, Der Suizid, 1995. Mem. Internat. Assn. for Suicide Prevention, German Assn. for Suicide Prevention, Assn. for Rsch. on Personality Disorders, Internat. Soc. for Study of Personality Disorders. Home: Viktoriastrasse 2, 80803 Munich Bavaria, Germany Office: Max Planck Inst Psychiatry, Kraepelinstrasse 10, 80804 Munich Bavaria, Germany

BRONK, J(OHN) RAMSEY, biochemistry educator; b. Phila., Dec. 20, 1929; s. Detlev Wulf and Helen (Ramsey) B.; m. Sylvia Smith, June 6, 1955; children: Richard Anthony Charles, Christopher Ramsey. AB, Princeton U., 1952; DPhil, Oxford U., 1955. Scientist USPHS, Bethesda, Md., 1956-58; asst. prof. zoology Columbia U., N.Y.C., 1958-60, assoc. prof., 1960-65, prof., 1965-66; prof. biochemistry U. York (Eng.), 1966-97, emeritus prof., 1997—. Author: Chemical Biology, 1973, Membrane Adenosine Triphosphatases and Transport Processes, 1974, Human Metabolism, 1999; chmn. European editorial com. Physiol. Revs., 1980-85; editor Clin. Sci., 1987—; contbr. over 75 articles to profl. jours. Rhodes scholar, 1952-54; Guggenheim fellow, 1964-65. Fellow AAAS; mem. Biochem. Soc. (com. mem. 1977-81), Am. Soc. for Biochemistry and Molecular Biology, Physiol. Soc. (editor 1971-78). Avocation: sailing. Office: U York Dept Biology, Heslington, York YO1 5DD, England

BRONKAR, EUNICE DUNALEE, artist, art educator; b. New Lebanon, Ohio, Aug. 8, 1934; d. William Dunham and Helen Kate (Hypes) Connor; m. Charles William Bronkar, Jan. 26, 1957; 1 child, Ramona. BFA, Wright State U., 1971, M in Art Edn., 1983, postgrad. art studies, 1989; postgrad. art studies, Dayton Art Inst., 1972. Cert. art tchr., Ohio. Part time tchr. Springfield (Ohio) Mus. of Art, 1967-77; adjunct instr. Clark State C.C., Springfield, 1974-84, lead tchr., 1984-94, adj. asst. prof., 1998-2000, asst. prof., 1989-94; ret., 1994; artist private practice, Urbana, Ohio, 1995—; edn. chmn. Springfield Mus. Art, 1973-74; image banks participant, Ohio Arts Coun., Columbus, Visual Arts Network, Dayton, Ohio, 1994—; affiliated with The Art Ctr. of St. Augustine, Fla. Art Scene, Little Gallery, Springfield, Ohio, The Wilson Gallery, Sidney, Ohio. One-woman shows include in Springfield, Ohio: Polo Club, Upper Valley Mall Cinema, Security Nat. Bank, Mr. C's Beauty Salon, Lakewood Beach, Springfield Mus. of Art, Clark State C.C.; Dayton, Ohio: Miami Valley Hosp., High St. Gallery, Stoeffer's Restaurant, Wegerzyn Garden Ctr., Meml. Hall, Wright State Univ., Urbana, Ohio: Champaign County Arts Coun., Urbana Cinema; South Charleston, Ohio: Cmty. Park Dedication, Philip Caldwell spl. guest speaker, Chmn. of the Bd. and CEO Ford Motor Co; 4-person show Springfield Mus. Art, 1999, Zanesville (Ohio) Art Ctr., 2000; accepted in over 90 area, state, regional, and nat. juried exhibitions including: Ohio Water Color Soc.'s Annual Traveling shows 1983-84, 86-87, Western Ohio Watercolor Soc., Hon. Mention 1983, Chase Patterson award, 1985, Spl. Merit award, 1990, 1st, 1995, 2000, Merit award 1997, 98; Springfield Mus. of Art: awards 1965, 68; 2d pastel 1972, 2d pastel and 1st drawing 1976, Jurors award pastel 1979, 1st drawing 1986, 3d drawing 1987, 2d drawing 1989, 1st drawing 1990, 1st drawing and 2d painting 1991, 1st drawing 1992, 2d, 1998, 2d pastel 1998, 1st drawing 2000; Dayton Soc. Painters and Sculptors: Best of Show 1974, 2000, 1st painting, 2d painting 3d drawing 1978, Hon. Mention 1979, 3d Graphic 1980, Best of Show drawing and 1st pastel 1981, 1st drawing 1991, 3d painting 1993; Champaign County Fair: Best of show drawing and 1st pastel 1968; drawings and paintings in Am. Artist Renown, 1981, Shades of Gray, 1983, 84, 86, 87, 90, 91, 93, 94, 97; group shows include Wilson Gallery, Sidney, Ohio; represented in six public and numerous private collections. Cleaned and restored art collections at Springfield Pub. Schs., Hist. Soc. in Springfield, Warder Pub. Libr., Foos Manor Bed & Breakfast and the Masonic Temple, Penn House and Mus. of Art in Springfield, 1970-00, Calumet Antiques, Yellow Springs, Ohio, other groups and numerous pvt. collections, 1970—; mem. adv. com. comml. art, Clark County JVS Sch., Springfield, 1991-99; judge more than 10 pub. h.s. art shows, 1970s-90s; judge Logan County (Ohio) Fair Fine Art Show profl. and amateur, 1998. Recipient medal Bicentennial Com. and 4H Found. of Ohio, Springfield, 1976, Outstanding Tchr. award Clark State C.C., 1992, commd. to paint 2 past pres. Generals of the Natl. Soc. Daughters of the Amer. Revolution, which hangs in Continental Hall, Washington. Mem. Western Ohio Water Color Soc, Springfield (Ohio) Mus. of Art, Dayton Soc. Painters and Sculptors, Cin. Art Club, Ohio Water Color Soc., Nat. Mus. Women in Arts, Audubon Artists Soc., Pastel Soc., St. Augustine (Fla.) Art Assn., others. Avocations: swimming, walking, sewing, flower arranging, travel to Europe, Caribbean, Russia, Israel and Ireland. Studio and Home: 5516 S US Highway 68 Urbana OH 43078-9420

BRONKHORST, JOHANNES, Indologist, educator; b. Schiedam, The Netherlands, July 17, 1946; s. Johannes Catharinus Bronkhorst and Adriana Johanna Bouman; m. Joy Manné, Aug. 17, 1987. BSc, Free U., Amsterdam, The Netherlands, 1968; MA, U. Poona, India, 1976, PhD, 1979; PhD, U. Leiden, The Netherlands, 1980. Rschr. U. Leiden, 1981-87; prof. Indology, U. Lausanne, Switzerland, 1987—; guest prof. Practical Sch. Higher Studies, Paris, 1997, U. Calif., Berkeley, 1999. Author 8 books; editor: Handbuch der Orientalistik, Brill's Indological Libr., Asiatische Studien/Études Asiatiques; contbr. over 85 articles to profl. jours. Mem. Royal Netherlands Acad. Sci. (corr.), Swiss-Asia Soc. (coun. 1988—), Swiss Soc. for Sci. Religion (sec. 1988-93). Home: Avenue de Lavaux 26, 1009 Pully Vaud, Switzerland Office: U Lausanne, BFSH 2, 1015 Lausanne Vaud, Switzerland

BRONNER, GARY, science educator; b. Bulawayo, Zimbabwe, June 1, 1961; s. George Bronner and Emma Helena (Dominick) Jenkins; m. Elizabeth De Wet, Nov. 9, 1993. BSc, U. Natal, Durban, South Africa, 1984, BSC with honors, 1985, MSc, 1986, PhD, 1995. Curator mammals Transvaal Mus., Pretoria, South Africa, 1989-91, head curator mammals, 1991-96; sr. lectr. Potchefstroom (South Africa) U., 1996-99, assoc. prof., 1999—; exhbs. chair 8th Intenrat. Theriological Congress, Pretoria, 1998—; founder, chair Gauteng Bat Interest Group, Pretoria, 1995-96; cons. Elec. Supply Commn., Megawat Park, South Africa, 1991, 95, 96—; mem. steering com. Rapid Biodiversity Assessment Workshop, Pretoria, 1995. Contbg. author: The Complete Book of South African Mammals, 1996; co-editor newsletter African Small Mammal Newsletter, 1992-95; contbr. articles to profl. jours. Rsch. grantee Anglo-Am./DeBeers Ednl. Trust, Johannesburg, South Africe, 1997, Found. Rsch. Devel., Pretoria, 1997-98, Nat. Rsch. Found., Pretoria, 1999. Mem. Am. Soc. Mammalogists, Royal Soc. South Africa, IUCN/SSC Working Group. Avocations: gardening, birdwatching, reading non-fiction, philosophy of science. Home: 8 Silver Park, 112 Rissik St, Potchefstroom 2531, South Africa Office: Potchefstroom U, Toms St, Potchefstroom 2531, South Africa

BRONSON, CHRISTOPHER HERBERT, financial service company executive, planner; b. Lajes AFB, Portugal, Sept. 4, 1959; (parents Am. citizens); s. Herbert Everton and Barbara Ann Bronson; m. Nancy Ann Davis, Apr. 23, 1983; children: Andrea Marie, Sean Michael, Jessica Nicole, Michael Geoffrey. Student, Citadel; BA, Rice U., 1983; cert. fin. mgr., Merrill Lynch Inst. Fin. cons. Merrill Lynch, Pierce, Fenner & Smith Inc., Vero Beach, Fla., 1989-90; regional sales mgr. James L. Mitchell & Co., Orlando, Fla., 1990; life agt., registered rep. N.Y. Life Ins. Co., Orlando, 1991; sales mgr. Furniture Man, Vero Beach, 1991-92; stewardship cons. James L. Paris Fins. Svcs., Inc., Longwood, Fla., 1993-94; fin. cons. Mercer Global Advisors, Inc., Tampa, Fla., 1994-99; br. mgr. Mercer Global Advisors, Inc., Bala Cynwyd, Pa., 1999—. Campaign mgr. Rep. Candidate State Rep., Indian River County, Fla., 1989; chmn. parish fin. com. St. Sebastian Parish, Fla., 1991; treas. Cypress Meadows Homeowners Assn., Tampa, 1997; asst. scoutmaster Troop 339 Boy Scouts Am., Tampa, Fla., 1999, asst. scoutmaster Troop 19, Bryn Mawr, Pa., 2000. 1st lt. USAR, 1984-2000. Mem. Fin. Planners Assn. Republican. Avocations: outdoor activities, reading. Fax: 610-747-0277. Office: Mercer Global Advisors Inc 401 E City Ave Ste 720 Bala Cynwyd PA 19004-1128

BRØNS-PETERSEN, OTTO, federal official, educator; b. Glostrup, Denmark, Jan. 8, 1961; s. Bent and Else Gerda (Hansen) Brøns-P.; 1 child, Andreas Brøws-Riise. Candidate in Econs., Copenhagen U., 1989. Asst. editor Finanstidende, Denmark, 1986-89; head sect. Ministry Taxation, Denmark, 1989-92; spl. advisor Ministry Taxation, 1992, dir., 1999—; spl. advisor Ministry Econ. Affairs, 1992-93, dir., 1993-99; lectr. Copenhagen Bus. Sch., 1991-93; assoc. prof. Copenhagen U., 1993—. Mem. Mont Pelerin Soc. Home: Gl Kongevej 84 4 TH, DK 1850 Frederiksberg Denmark Office: Ministry Taxation, Slotholmsgade 12, DK 1216 København Denmark

BROO, ANDERS DAN, systems analyst, chemistry researcher; b. Gothenburg, Sweden, Oct. 18, 1961; s. Åke and Merit (Johnsson) B.; m. Ann Elfström, Jan. 9, 1988; children: Louise, Viktor. BS in Chemistry, U. Gothenburg, 1987, PhD in Chemistry, 1991, docent in phys. chemistry, 1997. Postdoctoral rschr. U. Uppsala, Sweden, 1991-92, U. Fla., Gainesville, 1993-94; asst. prof. Chalmers U. Tech., Gothenburg, 1994-97, assoc. prof., 1997; systems analyst Volvo Car Corp., Gothenburg, 1998-99, Volvo Info. Tech., Göteborg, 1999—. Mem. Am. Chem. Soc. Home: Valkyrianvägen 22, 433 62 Sävedalen Sweden Office: Volvo Info Tech, Dept 9142 PVÖS 21, 40508 Göteborg Sweden

BROOCKS, ANDREAS, psychiatry and psychology educator; b. Soltau, Germany, July 2, 1960; m. Britta Suhr; four children. MD, Georg-August U., Göttingen, Germany, 1986; PhD, Tech. U., Munich, 1990. Intern Guy's Hosp., London, 1983-84, Padhar Hosp., India, 1985; rsch. fellow Max-Planck Inst. Psychiatry, Munich, 1987-89; resident clin. neurology and clin. neurophysiology Neurol. U. Clinic, Göttingen, 1989-92; rsch. fellow lab. clin. sci., sect. clin. neuropharmacology NIMH, Bethesda, Md., 1992-93; resident Psychiat. U. Clinic, Göttingen, 1993-97; clin. cons. dept. psychiatry and psychotherapy Med. U., Lübeck, Germany, 1998—. Recipient Otto-Hahn medal Max-Planck-Soc., 1989; grantee Volkswagenstiftung, 1994, Smith-Kline Beecham, 1997; scholar German Nat. Scholarship Found., 1981-86. Mem. German Soc. of Psychiatry Rsch., German Soc. of Psychiatry, Psychotherapy and Neurology, German Socs. of Behavior Therapy, German Balint Soc. Achievements include research in anxiety disorders, eating disorders, smoking and nicotine addiction, serotonin, cognitive behavioral therapy, religion and mental health, exercise and mental health. E-mail: broocks.a@psychiatry.mu-luebeck.de. Fax: 0451-500 24 58. Office: Psychiat Klinik Med Univ, Ratzeburger Allee 160, D-23538 Lübeck Germany

BROOK, CHARLES GROVES DARVILLE, pediatric endocrinology educator; b. Chilbolton, Hampshire, Eng., Jan. 15, 1940; s. William Arthur Darville Brook and Marjorie Jean (Grant) Hamilton; m. Catherine Mary Hawke, Mar. 16, 1963; children: Charlotte Griselda Mary, Henrietta Diana Darville. MA, MD, Magdalene Coll., 1964. Intern St. Thomas Hosp., 1964-65; resident St. Thomas's Hosp., London, 1964-67; resident and rsch. fellow Hosp. for Sick Children at Ormond St., London, 1967-74; rsch. fellow Kinderspital, Zürich, Switzerland, 1972-73; cons. pediatrician Middlesex and Great Ormond St. Hosp., London, 1974-2000; sr. lectr. Univ. Coll., London, 1983, reader, 1987, prof., 1989, prof. emeritus, 2000. Author: Growth Assessment, 1982; editor: Clinical Paediatric Endocrinology, 1981, 2d edit., 1990, 3rd. edit., 1995. Spl. trustee Middlesex Hosp., London, 1983-95; trustee Richmond (Eng.) Parish Lands Charity, 1988-93; treas. Royal Med. Benevolent Fund, London, 1990-96. Fellow Royal Coll. Physicians, London, 1979. Fellow Royal Coll. Paed. Child Health. Avocations: fishing, walking, gardening, do-it-yourself. Home: Hadspen Farm, Castle Cary, Somerset BA7 7LX, England Office: Middlesex Hosp, Mortimer St, London W1N 8AA, England

BROOK, DONALD, visual arts educator emeritus; b. Leeds, Yorkshire, Eng., Jan. 8, 1927; arrived in Australia, 1962, naturalized, 1974; s. William Sidney and Dorothy Mary (Newton) Brook; m. Nancy Elizabeth Playfair, Jan. 30, 1948 (div. June, 1960); children: Martin Menzies, Janet Mary; m. Phyllis Leadbetter, Nov. 20, 1968. Student, U. Leeds, 1944-46; BA with 1st Class Hons., U. Durham, Newcastle, Eng., 1953; PhD in Philosophy, Australian Nat. U., Canberra, 1965. Sr. lectr. U. Sydney, Australia, 1967-73; prof. visual arts The Flinders U., Adelaide, Australia, 1974-89; prof. emeritus The Flinders U., Adelaide, 1990—; art critic Canberra (Australia) Times, 1964-68, Sydney (Australia) Morning Herald and Nation Rev., 1968-73; Australian adv. editor Leonardo, Paris, 1972-89. Contbr. over 100 articles to learned jours. and jours. of informed opinion including Jour. Aesthetics and Art Criticism, Brit. Jour. Aesthetics, Leonardo, Studio Internat., Mind, Hemisphere, Quadrant, Meanjin, Ednl. Philosphy and Theory, Art Monthly, Jour. Inst. Art Edn., Kodikas/Code, Word and Image, Artlink, AustralAsian Jour. of Philosophy, Overland and others.

BROOK, ELAINE ISABEL, travel guide, writer; b. London, May 23, 1949; d. Alec and Isabel May (Stanley) Turner; m. Lhakpa Sherpa, Apr. 19, 1986. Degree in Art Edn., Loughborough Coll., 1971; degree in Ecology, Leicester U., 1973. Art tchr. Castleton Sch., Derbyshire, Eng., 1973-75; mountain guide Fantasy Ridge Alpinism, Colo., 1975-78; dir. Himalayan Travel Co., Peterchurch, Eng., 1987—. Author: The Windhorse, 1986, Land of the Snow Lion, 1987, A Guidebook to the Festival, 1992, In Search of Shambhala, 1996; contbr. articles to profl. publs. Dir. Buddhist Meditation Ctr., 1993—. Fellow Royal Geog. Soc.; mem. Tibetan Community in Britain. Buddhist. Avocation: meditation. Office: Jonathan Cape Pubs, 20 Vauxhall Bridge Rd, London SW1V 2SA, England

BROOK, STEPHEN, journalist; b. London, June 20, 1947; m. Maria Lonstrup. MA, Trinity Coll., Cambridge U., 1969. Staff editor Atlantic Monthly, Boston, 1972-73; editor David R. Godine, Boston, 1973-75, Routledge & Kegan Paul, London, 1976-80; freelance writer London, 1982—; wine columnist New Statesman, London, 1986-87, Vogue, London, 1988-94, Conde Nast Traveller, 1997—. Author: New York Days, New York Nights, 1983, Honkytonk Gelato, 1985, Maple Leaf Rag, 1987, Liquid Gold: Dessert Wines of the World, 1987, The Double Eagle, 1988, Winner Takes All: A Season in Israel, 1990, Prague, 1991, The Veneto, 1990, The Dordogne, 1985, Los Angeles Days, Los Angeles Nights, 1993, The Penguin Book of Infidelities, 1994, Opera: A Penguin Anthology, 1995, Pauillac, 1998, The Wines of California, 1999, God's Army, 1999. Avocations: opera, wine, travel.

BROOKE, BARON AINSLIE, solicitor; b. London, Dec. 24, 1918; arrived in Australia, 1919; s. Baron and Kathleen Adele (Halloran) B.; m. Lynn Dumbrill, Aug. 7, 1948. Diploma in law, Sydney U.T.S., New South Wales, Australia, 1946. Ptnr. Lightoller, Talty & Brooke, Sydney, 1948-87; cons. Dibbs, Crowther & Osborne, Sydney, 1987-2000. Pres. Old Cranbrookians' Assn., 1960-63. With RAAF, 1940-45. Mem. Royal Australian Air Force Assn. (pres. 1970-2000), Royal Sydney Golf Club, Royal Prince Edward Yacht Club. Avocations: golf, cricket, rugby football, swimming. Home: 14 Leura Rd, Double Bay, Sydney 2028 NSW, Australia

BROOKE, CHRISTOPHER NUGENT LAWRENCE, historian, educator; b. Cambridge, Eng., June 23, 1927; s. Zachary Nugent and Rosa Grace (Stanton) B.; m. Rosalind Beckford Clark, 1951; 3 children (one dec.). BA, Cambridge U., 1948, MA, 1952, LittD, 1973; D (hon.), U. York, Eng., 1984. Fellow Gonville and Caius Coll., Cambridge U., 1949-56, 77—; univ. asst. lectr. Cambridge U., 1953-54, lectr., 1954-56, Dixie prof. ecclesiastical history, 1977-94; prof. mediaeval history U. Liverpool, Eng., 1956-67; prof. history Westfield Coll., U. London, 1967-77. Author: The Dullness of the Past, 1957, From Alfred to Henry III, 1961, The Saxon and Norman Kings, 1963, Europe in the Central Middle Ages, 1964, Time the Archsatirist, 1968, The Twelfth Century Renaissance, 1969, Structure of Medieval Society, 1971, Medieval Church and Society, 1971, Marriage in Christian History, 1978, A History of Gonville and Caius College, 1985, The Church and the Welsh Border, 1986, The Medieval Idea of Marriage, 1989, A History of the University of Cambridge, IV, 1870-1990, 1993, Jane Austen: Illusion and Reality, 1999, Churches and Churchmen in Medieval Europe, 1999; (with W. Swaan) The Monastic World, 1974; (with G. Keir) London, 800-1216, 1975; (with Rosalind Brooke) Popular Religion in the Middle Ages, 1000-1300, 1984; (with A. Morey) Gilbert Foliot and His Letters, 1965, (with R. Highfield, W. Swaan) Oxford and Cambridge, 1988; part editor: The Book of William Morton, 1954; co-editor: The Letters of John of Salisbury, vol. 1, 1955, vol. II, 1979, Carte Nativorum, 1960, The Letters and Charters of Gilbert Foliot, 1967; (with D. Knowles and V. London) Heads of Religious Houses, England and Wales 940-1216, 1972; (with D. Whitelock and M. Brett) Councils and Synods I, 1981; (with R.A.B. Mynors) rev. edit. of Walter Map, De nugis Curialium, 1983; (with M. Brett and M. Winterbottom) Hugh the Chanter, History of the Church of York, 1990; (with R. Lovatt and others) David Knowles Remembered, 1991; (with S. Bendall and P. Collinson) A History of Emmanuel College, Cambridge, 1999; contbg. author: A History of St. Paul's Cathedral, 1957, A History of York Minster, 1977; gen. editor: Oxford (formerly Nelson's) Medieval Texts, 1959-87; contbr. articles and revs. to profl. jours. Mem. Royal Commn. on Hist. Monuments, Eng., 1977-84; mem. rev. com. on Export of Works of Art, 1979-82. Fellow Brit. Acad., 1970. Fellow Royal Hist. Soc., Soc. Antiquaries (pres.), Medieval Acad. Am. (corr.), Monumenta Germaniae Historica (corr.), Bavarian Acad. Scis. (corr.), Societa Internat. Studi Francescani. Office: Gonville and Caius Coll, Cambridge CB2 1TA, England

BROOKE, PETER LEONARD, British government official, former secretary of state for Northern Ireland; b. Eng., Mar. 3, 1934; m. Joan Margaret Smith, 1964 (dec. 1985); 4 sons (1 dec.); m. Lindsay Allinson, 1991. Student, Marlborough; MA, Oxford (Eng.) U.; MBA, Harvard Bus. Sch.; DLitt (hon.), U. Westminster, 1999. Commonwealth Fund fellow, 1957-59; research asst. IMEDE, Lausanne, Switzerland, 1960-61; with Spencer Stuart & Assocs., Mgmt. Cons., 1961-65, dir., 1965-79, chmn., 1974-79; M.P. Ho. of Commons, London, 1977—; asst. govt. whip, 1979-81; lord commr. HM Treasury, 1981-83; Parliamentary under-sec. of state Dept. Edn. & Sci., 1983-85; Minister of State, 1985-87, Paymaster Gen. HM Treasury, 1987-89, chmn. Conservative and Unionist Party, 1987-89, sec. of state for No. Ireland, 1989-92, sec. of state for Nat. Heritage, 1992-94; con mem. for cities of London and Westminster Ho. of Commons; pres. Inc. Assn. of Prep. Schs., 1980-83; trustee Wordsworth Trust, 1976—, Cusichaca Project, 1978-98. Lay advisor St. Paul's Cathedral, 1980-99; chmn. COTAC, 1994-98, Chs. Conservation Trust, 1995-98; pres. Brit. Antique Dealers' Assn., 1995—, Brit. Am. Market Fedn., 1996; mem. coun. U. London, 1995—. Sen. fellow RCA, 1987; Presentation fellow King's Coll., London, 1989. Hon. fellow Queen Mar, Westfield Coll., 1996; clubs: Beefsteak, Brooks's, City Livery, MCC, I Zingari, St. George's (Hanover Sq.) Conservative. Avocations: churches, conservation, cricket, pictures, planting things. Office: House of Commons, London SW1A 0AA, England

BROOKE, ROBERT ZACHARY, stock market strategist; b. Sheffield, Yorkshire, United Kingdom, Apr. 30, 1956; s. Michael Zachary and Hilda (Gillatt) B.; m. Helen Chase Kimball, Apr. 25, 1987; children; Cecilia Zoë, Laura Elizabeth. BA, Cambridge U., Eng., 1978, PGCE, 1979, MA, 1981; postgrad., U. Alta., 1980; MBA, Insead U., Fontainebleau, France, 1984. Analyst W.I. Carr Overseas Ltd., London, 1985-86; assoc. dir. Swiss Bank Corp., London, 1986-89; dir. BZW Internat. Equities Ltd, London, Tokyo, 1989-92; mng. dir. Brooke Rsch., Ltd., London, 1992—. Fellow Royal Soc. Arts; mem. Insead Internat. Alumni, Assn. MBAs, Brit. Inst. Mgmt. Home and Office: 35 Castlebar Rd, London W5 2DJ, England

BROOKE, TAL (ROBERT TALIAFERRO), writer; b. Washington, Jan. 21, 1945; s. Edgar Duffield and Frances (Lea) B. BA, U. Va., 1969; M in Theology/Philosophy, Princeton (N.J.) U., 1986. V.p. pub. rels. nat. office Telecom Inc., 1982-83; pres., chmn. Spiritual Counterfeits Project, Inc., Berkeley, 1989—; guest lectr. Cambridge U., Eng., 1977, 86, 97, 99, Oxford and Cambridge U., 1979, 84. Author: Avatar of Night: Millennial Edition, 1999, Lord of the Air, 1990, When the World Will Be As One, 1989 (best-seller 1989-90), Riders of the Cosmic Circuit, 1986, Avatar of Night, 1987 (bestseller in India 1981-84), 2d edit., 1999, The Other Side of Death, Lord of the Air: The International Edition, 1976, America's Waning Light, 1994, Virtual Gods, 1997, Conspiracy to Silence the Son, 1998, One World, 2000. Mem. Internat. Platform Assn., Authors Guild, Soc. of The Cincinnati. Office: SCP Inc PO Box 4308 Berkeley CA 94704-0308

BROOKE-LITTLE, JOHN PHILIP BROOKE, genealogist, armorist, writer; b. London, Apr. 6, 1927; s. Raymond and Constance Marie (Egan) Brooke-L.; m. Mary Lee Pierce, Apr. 30, 1960; children: Philip, Clare, Leo, Merlin. MA in History, Oxford (Eng.) U., 1957. Sch. master various schs., U.K., 1945-47; rschr. Conservative Party, U.K., 1946; editor Dod's Peerage and Parliamentary Companion, U.K., 1953-60; Bluemantle Pursuivant of Arms Royal Household, U.K., 1957-67, Richmond Herald of Arms, 1967-80, Norroy and Ulster King of Arms, 1980-95, Clarenceux King of Arms, 1995-97; founder, chmn. The Heraldry Soc., U.K., 1947-97, pres., 1997—; chmn. govs. Clayesmore Sch., U.K., 1971-83; chancellor Brit. Assn. of Order of Malta, Rome, 1973-77; registrar Coll. of Arms, Eng., 1974-82, treas., 1978-95, libr., 1974-94. Decorated Comdr., Royal Victorian Order, Her Majesty the Queen, Knight of Justice, Order of St. John, Her Majesty the Queen, Knight Grand Cross of Grace and Devotion, Order of Malta, Rome, Disting. Cruz San Raimundo de Peñaforte, Spain. Fellow Soc. Aniquaries; mem. The Heraldry Soc., Inst. Heraldic and Geneal. Studies, Soc. Genealogists. Roman Catholic. Avocations: writing poetry, painting, antiquities, comparative religion. Home: Heyford House, Lower Heyford, Bicester Bicester, Oxon OX25 5NZ, England

BROOKES, ALAN THOMAS, civil engineer; b. Lichfield, Eng., Nov. 30, 1944; s. William Thomas and Dorothy Brenda (Brown) B.; m. Daphne Mabel Bird, Apr. 2, 1966 (div. Nov. 1984); children: Sarah Jane, Louise Emma; m. Patricia Lilian Bowman, Aug. 1, 1988. M in Philosophy, U. Birmingham, Eng., 1991; PhD, U. Birmingham, 1993. Cert. mine surveyor, 1967. Mine surveyor Nat. Coal Bd., Cannock, Eng., 1961-67; land surveyor City of Birmingham, Eng., 1967-70; staff county minerals office Staffordshire County, Stafford, Eng., 1970-79; devel. mgr. Pioneer, London, 1979-84; civil engr. Cannock Coun., 1984-86; prin. engr. Warsau (Eng.) Coun., 1986-88; head of tech. North Birmingham Coll., 1988—; chief examiner No. Examining Body, Manchester, Eng., 1992—, BTec: London Constn. and Built Environ., AEB: Guildford Built Environ.; cons. Brooklands Survey, Cannock, 1985—. Author: Electronic Surveying, 1990, Calibration, 1993. Mem. Inst. Mining Engrs. (assoc.), Inst. Civil Engrs. and Surveyors, Inst. of Quarrying, Faculty of Architects and Surveyors (Inc. surveyor). Mem. Ch. of Eng. Avocations: playing euphonium in brass band and orchestra. Home: Brookslade House, 498 Pye Green Rd, Cannock WS12 4HT, England Office: North Birmingham Coll, Aldridge Rd, Birmingham B44 8NE, England

BROOKES, HUGH CLIVE, chemistry educator, researcher; b. Cape Town, South Africa, Apr. 21, 1941; s. Hugh J. and Phyllis (Kelleher) B.; m. K. Bridget McMullan, Jan. 8, 1966; children: Kathleen, Suzanne, Virginia. BSc, U. Cape Town, 1961, BSc with honors, 1962, PhD, 1966. Analytical chemist Sea Fisheries, Capt Town, 1966-67; NRC of Can. postdoctoral fellow Toronto U., 1967-69; from lectr. to prof. dept. chemistry Natal U., Durban, South Africa, 1969—; rsch. fellow Southampton (Eng.) U., 1975; rsch. assoc. Imperial Coll., London, 1983; cons. in electrochemistry South African Energy Coun. Contbr. some 55 articles to profl. jours. including South African Jour. Chemistry, Inorganic Chemistry, Jour. Electrochem. Soc., Can. Jour. Chemistry, J.C.S. Faraday, Electrochimica Acta. Mem., chmn. local grade sch. coms., 1975-85. Sr. Fulbright fellow, 1992-93; sr. rsch. visitor Pa. State U., 1995. Mem. South African Chem. Inst., South African Corrosion Inst., Royal Soc. Chemistry (electrochemistry divsn.). Avocations: music, bridge. E-mail: Brookes@che.und.ac.za. Office: Natal U, Dept Chemistry, 4041 Durban South Africa

BROOKES, MURRAY, retired physician, anatomy educator; b. Salford, Lancashire, Eng., Jan. 26, 1926; s. Jack and Julia (Reikan) B.; m. Esther Doreen Levine, Mar. 24, 1957; children: Alison Rosalie, Sally Rebecca, Jocelyn Simon, Max Julian. MB BCh, Oxford (Eng.) U., 1949, MA, 1952,

MD, 1960. Robert Glee fellow Liverpool (Eng.) U., 1957-58, jr. lectr., 1958-60, lectr., 1960-61; sr. lectr. Guy's Hosp., London, 1962-66, reader of anatomy and human morphology, 1966-83; prof. orthopaedic anatomy U. London, 1983-91; prof. embryology St. George's U., Grenada, W.I., 1985-95; mem. faculty Assn. Internat. de la Osteosyntese Dynamique, Strasbourg, France, 1989-97; v.p. European Assn. Internat. pour la Recherche sur la Circulation Osseuse, Toulouse, France, 1989-95; vis. examiner in anatomy U.K. Univs., India, Nigeria, 1970-90. Author: The Blood Supply of Bone, 1971; co-author: (with R. Warwick) Nomina Anatomica, 6th edit., 1989, (with W. Revell) Blood Supply of Bone, 1998, (with A. Zietman) Clinical Embryology, 1998; contbr. more than 80 articles to profl. jours. Capt. Brit. Army of the Rhine, 1953-55. Recipient Otto Aufranc award Hip Soc. Am., 1988, medal Vojnomedicinska Akademija JNA, Yugoslavia, 1988. Mem. Royal Coll. Surgeons. Avocations: translating Latin text, walking. Fax: 0208 371 0941. Home: 68 Lakenheath, Southgate, London N14 4RP, England

BROOKES, PETER T., legislative staff member; b. Peekskill, N.Y., Feb. 10, 1960. BS in Engring., U.S. Naval Acad., 1982; Diploma, Naval War Coll., 1992; MA in Govt., Johns Hopkins U., 1998; Def. Lang. Inst. Diploma, Monterey, Calif. Naval officer USN, Japan, Panama, 1982-89; program mgr. E-Systems, Falls Church, Va., 1989-90; analyst TASC, Reston, Va., 1990-91; fgn. svc. officer U.S. Dept. State, Washington, 1991-94; profl. staff SAIC, Washington, 1994-96; staff/action officer Joint Chiefs of Staff, Pentagon/Washington, 1996; prin. advisor for East Asian Com. on Internat. Rels., Washington, 1997—. Comdr. USN, 1982—. Decorated Joint Svc. Commendation medal, Navy Commendation medal (3 times), Navy Achievement medal; recipient Kellogg award Def. Lang. Inst., Monterey, 1986. Republican. Roman Catholic. Avocations: sports, fitness. Office: Com Internat Rels Us Ho Of Reps 2170 Rayburn Washington DC 20515-0001

BROOKES, PHILIP CHARLES, soil microbial ecologist; b. Berkeley, Eng., Mar. 26, 1951; s. Leonard Charles and Kathleen Mary (Baker) B. BSc in Applied Zoology and Chemistry, Coventry (U.K.) U., 1972, PhD in Forest Ecology, 1976, DSc in Soil Sci., 1998. Prin. sci. officer Rothamsted Exptl. Sta., Harpenden, Herts., U.K., 1976—; hon. lectr. U. Nottingham, U.K., 1991—. Achievements include development of methods to measure soil microbial biomass; new findings of significant leaching of phosphate from soil to water. Home: 161 Strathmore Ave, Luton LU1 3QR, England Office: Rothamsted Exptl Sta, Dept Soil Sci, Harpenden AL5 2JQ, England

BROOKNER, ANITA, writer, educator; d. Newson and Maude B. Ed., King's Coll., 1946-49, U. London, Courtauld Inst., Paris, 1949-53. vis. lectr. U. Reading, 1959-64; Slade prof. U. Cambridge, 1967-68; lectr. Courtauld Inst. of Art, 1964. Author: Watteau, 1968, The Genius of the Future, 1971, Greuze: The Rise and Fall of an Eighteenth Century Phenomenon, 1972, Jacques-Louis David, 1980, (novels) A Start in Life, 1981, Providence, 1982, Look At Me, 1983, Hotel du Lac, 1984 (Booker McConnell prize), Family and Friends, 1985, A Misalliance, 1986, A Friend From England, 1987, Latecomers, 1988, Lewis Percy, 1989, Brief Lives, 1991, Fraud, 1992, A Family Romance, 1993, A Private View, 1995, Altered States, 1996, Visitors, 1997, The Visitors, 1998, Soundings, 1998, Falling Slowly: A Novel, 1999; contbr. articles to mags.

BROOKS, BRIAN WALTER, chemical engineering educator; b. Twickenham, Eng., Oct. 1, 1937; s. Charles Walter and Maggie Georgina (Sears) B.; m. Pamela Winifred Howe, Sept. 1964; 1 child. BS, Leeds U., Eng., 1960; PhD, 1964, DSc, 1984. Chartered engr. Rsch. fellow Carleton U., Can., 1964; rsch. worker Shell Chemical Co., Eng., 1964-66; lectr. Loughborough U., Eng., 1966-73; sr. lectr., 1973-84, reader, 1984-89, prof., 1989—; head of dept. Loughborough U. Chem. Engring., Eng., 1986-92. Contbr. articles to profl. jours. Recipient Polymer prize Soc. Chem. Industry, 1971. Fellow Inst. Chem. Engrs.; mem. Soc. Chemical Industry. Avocations: woodworking, running. Office: Dept Chemical Engring, Loughborough University, Loughborough LE11 3TU, England

BROOKS, EDWARD CHARLES, retired priest; b. Chatham, Kent, Eng., May 19, 1918; s. Edward Thomas and Charlotte Elizabeth (Spells) B.; m. Mary Bettles, June 29, 1946; children: Paul Edward, Anne Mary, Jean Elizabeth. BA with honors, Leeds U., 1942; BD with honors in Theology, U. London, 1950; MA in Theology with distinction, Leeds U., 1957, PhD in Theology, 1972. Apprentice B.T.H., Coventry, Eng., 1931-36; curate Bushey Ch., Hertfordshire, Eng., 1944-46; curate St. Barnabas Ch., Hove, 1946-48, Epsom, 1948-52; rector Elsing Ch., Norfolk, 1952-57; rector, rural dean St. Cuthberts Ch., Thetford, 1957-69; rector Somerleyton Ch., Lowestuft, 1969-83; ret.; lectr., tutor classical studies Open U., Milton Keynes, 1975-93; cons. tutor for stipendiary clergy and lay readers, 1952-83. Author: 1000 Years of Village History, 1979, Sir Samuel Morton Peto Victorian Entrepreneur 1809-1889, 1996, Life of St. Ethelbert, East Anglican King and Martyr, 779-794, 1995, Life and Times of Clement of Rome, 25-101 AD. Dist. commr. Scouts, South Norfolk, 1959-69; hon. chaplain Royal Brit. Legion, Norfolk, 1953-59; sch. gov. City of Norfolk, 1959-80. Mem. bury Clerical Soc. (chmn. 1995—). Ch. of England. Avocations: historical research, gardening, wood crafting, book binding. Home: Wheelwrights, Bury Rd Thorpe Morieux, Bury Saint Edmunds 1P30 0NR, England

BROOKS, GENE (LESLIE GENE BROOKS), cultural association administrator; b. Fletcher, Okla., June 15, 1936; s. Frank and Ethel E. (Spears) B.; m. Nancy E. Carman, Aug. 17, 1970; 1 child, Steven Frank. B of Music Edn., Okla. Bapt. U., 1959; M of Music Edn., U. Okla., 1962, D of Music Edn., 1968; postgrad., U. Colo. Chmn. music dept. Cameron U., Lawton, Okla., 1962-69, Midwestern State U., Wichita Falls, Tex., 1969-75, U. Ark., Little Rock, 1975-77; exec. dir. Am. Choral Dirs. Assn., Lawton, 1977—; sec.-gen. Internat. Fedn. Choral Music, 1982-85; dir. numerous choral internat. festivals and conventions; internat. guest conductor, clinician, adjudicator and spkr.; mem. juries 25th Internat. Choir Competition, Varna, Bulgaria, 38th Internat. Choral Competition, Gorizia, Italy, 1999, 2000 Nat. Choir Competition, New Zealand, 6th Internat. Choral Competition, Riva del Garda, Italy, 2000 World Olympics Choral Music, Linz, Austria and numerous others. Recipient Disting. Alumni award Okla. Bapt. U., 1985, in music, 1996, U. Okla., 1997. Mem. Music Tchrs. Nat. Assn. (chmn. music in higher edn. 1975-77, nat. choral chmn. 1972-75), Music Educators Nat. Conf. (life), Coll. Music Soc. (life), Am. Choral Dirs. Assn. (life). Southern Baptist. Avocations: traveling, snow skiing. Home: 18816 Woody Creek Dr Edmond OK 73003-4108 Office: Am Choral Dir Assn PO Box 6310 Lawton OK 73506-0310

BROOKS, GERALD THOMAS, toxicology educator; b. Mansfield, Eng., Oct. 5, 1931; s. Harry and Edith Alberta (Beason) B.; m. Ann Weatherley, Mar. 29, 1958; children: Peter, Alan, Nicola. BSc, U. London, 1953, PhD, 1957, DSc, 1987. Chartered chemist and biologist, Eng. Civil svc. rsch. fellow Pest Infestation Lab., Slough, Eng., 1956-61, sr. sci. officer, 1961-64, prin. sci. officer, 1964-69; prin. sci. officer ARC Unit of Invertebrate Chemistry and Physiology, Sussex U., Brighton, Eng., 1969-76, sr. prin. sci. officer, 1976-82; head Agrl. and Food Rsch. coun. Insect Chemistry Group, Sussex U., 1982-87; vis. rsch. fellow biochemistry and physiology dept. U. Reading, Eng., 1987—; cons. FAO, Rome, Vienna, 1972—; bd. dirs. Brit. Crop Protection Coun., Farnham, Eng., 1990—; exec., mem. sci. program com. 9th Internat. Congress Pesticide Chemistry, 1994-98. Author: Chlorinated Insecticides, 1974; editor: Pesticide Science, 1990—. Fellow Royal Soc. Chemistry, Inst. Biology (coun. 1985-89); mem. Biochem. Soc., Brit. Toxicology Soc., Agrochem. Div. Am. Soc., Pesticide Sci. Soc. Japan, Soc. Chem. Industry London. Avocations: gardening, golf, tennis. Home and Office: 40 Wykeham Way, Burgess Hill RH15 0HF, England

BROOKS, GWENDOLYN, writer, poet; b. Topeka, June 7, 1917; d. David Anderson and Keziah Corinne (Wims) B.; m. Henry L. Blakely, Sept. 17, 1939; children: Henry L., Nora. Grad., Wilson Jr. Coll., Chgo., 1936; L.H.D., Columbia Coll., 1964. Instr. poetry Columbia Coll., Chgo., Northeastern Ill. State Coll., Chgo.; mem. Ill. Arts Council; cons. in poetry Library of Congress, 1985-86; Jefferson lectr., 1994. Author: (poetry) A Street in Bronzeville, 1945, Annie Allen, 1949 (Pulitzer prize 1950), Maud Martha: (novel) Bronzeville Boys and Girls, 1953; (for children) The Bean Eaters, 1956; poetry, 1960, Selected Poems, 1963, In the Mecca, 1968, Riot, 1969, Family Pictures, 1970, Aloneness, 1971, To Disembark, 1981; (autobiography) Report From Part One, 1972, The Tiger Who Wore White Gloves, 1974, Beckonings, 1975, Primer for Blacks, 1980, Young Poets' Primer, 1981, Very Young Poets, 1983, The Near-Johannesburg Boy, 1986, Blacks, 1987, Gottschalk and the Grande Tarantelle, 1988, Winnie, 1988, Children Coming Home, 1991, Report From Part Two, 1995. Named one of 10 Women of Yr. Mademoiselle mag., 1945; recipient Creative Writing award Am. Acad. Arts and Letters, 1946, Anisfield-Wolf award, 1969, Essence award, 1988, Frost medal Poetry Soc. Am., 1989, Lifetime Achievement award Nat. Endowment for the Arts, 1989, Soc. for Lit. award U. Thessaloniki, Athens, Greece, 1990, Aiken-Taylor award, 1992, Jefferson lectr. award NEH, 1994, Nat. Book Found. medal for lifetime achievement, 1994, Am. Book award Gwendolyn Brooks Jr. H.S., 1995, Nat. medal of arts, 1995; Guggenheim fellow, 1946, 47; named poet laureate of Ill., 1968; inducted into Nat. Women's Hall of Fame, 1988; Gwendolyn Brooks chair in Black Lit. and Creative Writing established in her honor Chgo. State U., 1990; The Gwendolyn Brooks Ctr. established, 1992; Gwendolyn Brooks Elem. Schs. named in her honor, Aurora, Ill., 1995, Harvey Ill., DeKalb Ill. Mem. Soc. Midland Authors. Home: 5530 S South Shore Dr Apt 2A Chicago IL 60637-1921

BROOKS, JOHN SAMUEL JOSEPH, pathologist, researcher; b. Phila., Feb. 2, 1948. BS in Biology, St. Joseph's Coll., Phila., 1970; MD, Thomas Jefferson U., 1974. Diplomate Am. Bd. Pathology. Resident in pathology U. Pa., Phila., 1974-78, chief resident, 1978, asst. prof., 1979-84, assoc. prof., 1984-88, prof., 1988-93; chmn. dept. pathology Roswell Pk. Cancer Inst., Buffalo, 1993—, chmn. dept. lab. medicine, 1997—, pres. med. staff, 1997-98; prof., vice chmn. pathology Med. Sch. SUNY, Buffalo, 1993—; vis. prof. Royal Marsden Hosp./Inst. Cancer Rsch., London, 1987; expert in immunohistochemistry. Author: Pathology, 1989; contbr. articles to New Eng. Jour. Medicine, Jour. of AMA, Jour. Urology, Internat. Jour. Ob.-Gyn. Pathology, Am. Jour. Pathology; editor Internat. Jour. Surg. Pathology, 1993—; mem. bd. editors: Jour. Modern Pathology, Am. Jour. Surg. Pathology, and reviewer; contbr. over 140 articles to profl. jours. Fellow Royal Coll. Pathology; mem. AAAS, Am. Assn. Cancer Rsch., Pathology Soc. Phila. (pres. 1988-90), Ea. Coop. Oncology Group (chmn. sarcoma pathology com. Madison chpt. 1988-95), Internat. Acad. Pathology (edn. com. Atlanta chpt. 1989—), U.S.-Can. Acad. Pathology (coun. mem. 1993-96), Am. Soc. Clin. Pathologists (chair anat. pathology coun. 1995-97, dep. commr. 1997—, bd. dirs. 2000—), Arthur Purdy Stout Soc. for Surg. Pathologists (coun. mem. 1994), Am. Assn. Clin. Rsch., Fedn. Am. Soc. for Exptl. Biology, Medicine Coverage Adv. Com. Lab. Diagnostics Panel, Nat. Internat. Reputation in Diagnostic Surg. Pathology. Democrat. Roman Catholic. Achievements include research in significance of double phenotypes in sarcomas, growth factors in sarcomas, in immunohistochemistry; posthumous diagnosis of Pres. Cleveland's tumor. Home: 34 Deer Run Orchard Park NY 14127-3454 Office: Roswell Pk Cancer Inst Dept Pathology Elm & Carlton Sts Buffalo NY 14263

BROOKS, JOHN SCOTT, county official; b. Ventura, Calif., June 9, 1964; s. John Wilburn and Carolyn Ruth (Hartley) B.; m. Maria Acela Nunez, May 8, 1990; children: Sierra Lynn, Shasta Lee, Jason Scott. AA, Ventura (Calif.) C.C., 1987; BS in Environ. Planning and Comms., Humboldt State U., Arcata, Calif., 1990; MPA, U. So. Calif., 2000. Waste mgmt. specialist Calif. Integrated Waste Mgmt. Bd., Sacramento, 1990-93, assoc. waste mgmt. specialist, 1993-96; program dir. Regional Coun. Rural Counties, Environ. Svcs. Joint Powers Authority, Sacramento, 1996—; apptd. local govt. adv. task force by Gov. Wilson, 1997-98; dep. dir. Regional Coun. Rural Counties, 1999-2000, CFO, 2000—. Co-author, editor: The Rural Cookbook-Recipes for Successful Waste Prevention, 1994. Recipient Customer Svc. award Calif. EPA, Sacramento, 1995, Outstanding Achievement award Calif. Integrated Waste Mgmt. Bd., Sacramento, 1994, Rural County Assistance award Regional Coun. of Rural Counties, Sacramento, 1994. Avocations: genealogy, camping. Office: Regional Coun Rural Counties Environ Svcs Joint Powers 1020 12th St Ste 400 Sacramento CA 95814-3996

BROOKS, LILLIAN DRILLING ASHTON, adult education educator; b. Grand Rapids, Mich., May 27, 1921; d. Walter Brian and Lillian Church; m. Frederick Morris Drilling, 1942 (div. Apr. 1972); children: Frederick Walter, Stephen Charles, Lawrence Alan, Lynn Anne; m. Richard Moreton Ashton, Aug. 25, 1973 (dec.); m. Ralph J. Brooks, May 21, 1994. Student, Grand Rapids Jr. Coll., 1939-41, Wayne State U., 1941-42, Grand Rapids Art Inst., 1945-49, UCLA, 1964-69, Loyola Marymount Coll., Westchester, Calif., 1970-73. Life teaching credential, Calif. Decorator John Widdicomb Furniture Co., 1945-49; tchr. art Inglewood (Calif.) Sch. Dist., 1965-73; tchr. adult edn. art Downey (Calif.) Unified Sch. Dist., 1973-95; lectr. Downey Art League, 1990-92, Whittier (Calif.) Art Assn., 1991, h.s. and mid. sch. lectr., 1994-95; judge Children's Art Exhibit, Downey, 1992; participant Getty Found., San Francisco, 1993, Getty Found., Cranbrook, 1994, Getty Conf. on Aesthetics, 1995, Cin. U., 1992, El Segundo, 1994; mem. state accreditation com. Inglewood and Downey United Sch. Dists., 1966-70, 75-80, 85—; owner A & B Furniture Svc. Ctr., 1995—. One-woman shows include El Segundo Mcpl. Libr., 1965, Pico Rivera Art Gallery, 1978, Downey Art Mus., 1999; exhibited in group shows at Fairlane Show, Dearborn, Mich., 1959, Jane Lessing Art Gallery, 1966, Westchester Mcpl. Libr., 1971, Inglewood City Hall, 1973, Aegina Sch., Greece, 1973, Downey Mus. Art, 1992, 99-2000; represented in permanent collection U. Mich. Pres. bd. dirs. Downey Art Mus., 1998-99, dir. Mus., 1998, vol. dir., 1999, bd. dirs. 1998-2000; art commr. City of Dearborn, Mich., 1954-59; former pres. Dearborn Art Inst., Pacific Art Guild; pres. Downey Art League, 1991-94, Exhbn. Ch., 1995, v.p. 1996-98; vol. dir. Art Mus., 1998-99; lectr. on art as a career local Downey high and mid. schs. Recipient Certs. of Appreciation for contbn. of leadership Coord. Coun. Downey, Downey Governing Bd., Downey Bd. Edn., 1997, Cmty. Svc. award for Outstanding Svc. Downey Rotary, 1994, Cert. of Recognition Calif. State Assembly, 1999, Downey Coord. Coun., 1998-99; named Tchr. of Yr., Masons, Downey, 1986; painting chosen to represent dist. in state capital, 1999. Mem. Calif. Coun. on Art Edn. (parliamentarian Downey 1990-92, Calco Excellence in Tchg. award 1991, various certs.). Avocations: reading, hiking, internat. travel, photography, painting. Home: 9318 Fostoria St Downey CA 90241-4020

BROOKS, MRS. MEL See BANCROFT, ANNE

BROOKS, NICHOLAS PETER, historian, educator; b. Virginia Water, Surrey, Eng., Jan. 14, 1941; s. William Donald Wykeham and Phyllis Kathleen (Juler) B.; m. Chloë Carolyn Willis, Sept. 16, 1967; children: Carolyn Ebba, Crispin Edmund Hartley. BA, Oxford U., Eng., 1962, MA, PhD, 1969. Lectr. medieval history U. St. Andrews, Fife, Scotland, 1964-77, sr. lectr., 1977-85; prof. U. Birmingham, Eng., 1985—, dean faculty arts, 1992-95; adviser Toronto (Univ.) Old English Dictionary, 1982—; bd. dirs. St. Andrews Univ. Excavations. Author: The Early History of the Church of Canterbury, 1984, Communities and Warfare 700-1400, 2000, Anglo-Saxon Myths, 400-1066, 2000; editor: Studies in the Early History of Britain (series), 1977—, Studies in Early Medieval Britain, 2000—; contbr. articles to profl. jours. Trustee St. Andrews Preservation Trust, 1971-85, chmn. 1977-81; active Council for Mus. and Galleries of Scotland, Edinburgh, 1982-85. Fellow Brit. Acad., Royal Hist. Soc., Soc. Antiquaries London. Avocations: squash, golf, gardening, walking. Office: Birmingham U Sch Hist Studies, Edgbaston, Birmingham B15 2TT, England

BROOKS, PETER HEATH, agriculture educator, consultant, researcher; b. Warmington, Eng., July 28, 1945; s. Edgar Perris and Marjorie Eva (Heath) B.; m. Carole Ann Spybey (div. Sept. 1985); children: Annabel, Emily. BS with honors, U. Nottingham, Eng., 1967, PhD, 1970. Lectr. animal prodn. Seale-Hayne Coll., Devon, Eng., 1972-74, head agriculture, 1974-90; head agriculture Seale-Hayne Faculty Poly. S.W., Devon, 1990—, prof., 1991-93; head rsch. Seale-Hayne Faculty U. Plymouth, 1993-96, prof. animal prodn., 1996—; bd. dirs. Carbo Cons., Devon. Contbr. over 50 articles and revs. to profl. jours. Mem. Internat. Soc. Animal Ethology, Brit. Soc. Animal Prodn. Office: U Plymouth, Seale-Hayne Faculty, Newton Abbot TQ12 6NQ, England

BROOKS, TERRENCE MICHAEL, lawyer; b. Monterey, Calif., Dec. 12, 1955; s. James S. and Alice Masa (Yemoto) B. Student, U. Guam, 1976; BS, N.Mex. State U., 1979; JD, Thomas Cooley Law Sch., Lansing, Mich., 1983. Bar; Guam, Hawaii, U.S. Dist. Ct. Guam, U.S. Ct. Appeals (9th cir.). Sports reporter/asst. sport editor Pacific Daily News, Agana, Guam, 1973-75, 79-80; composition mgr. Roundup-N.Mex. State U. Student Newspaper, Las Cruces, 1976-79; law clk./spl. asst. to presiding judge Superior Ct. of Guam, Agana, 1984-85; ptnr. Brooks & Brooks, P.C., Agana, 1985-97, Carbullido Bordallo & Brooks LLP, Hagatma, 1997—. Mem. Guam Interscholastic Athletic Counsel, U. Guam, 1985-89; commr. Guam Pub. Utilities Commn., 1989—, vice chmn., 1993, chmn. 1994. Mem. ABA, Assn. Trial Lawyers Am., Nat. Assn. Regulatory Utility Commrs., Hawaii Bar Assn., Guam Bar Assn. (sec. 1990-94). Avocations: football, golf, basketball, computers. Office: Carbulliao Bordallo Brooks, 251 Martyr St #101, Hagatma Guam 96910

BROOKS, WILLIAM GEORGE, aeronautical engineer; b. Calgary, Alta., Can., June 6, 1940; came to U.S., 1965; s. William Henry Charles and Mary Robertson (Henderson) B.; m. Lynn Chung. BS in Aero. Engring., Wichita State U., 1963, BSME, 1965; MBA, Pepperdine U., 1978. Engr. Sun Oil Co., Estevan, Sask., Can., 1964; design engr. The Carlson Co., Wichita, Kans., 1965-66; engr. United Airlines, San Francisco, 1966-67, aero. engr. B, 1967-70, aero. engr. A, 1970-71, aircraft engr. A, 1971-84, staff engr., 1984-91, sr. staff rep. engring., 1991—. Mem. ASME, Soc. Automotive Engrs. Internat. Avocations: walking, hiking. Home: 1001 Sandhurst Dr Vallejo CA 94591-6881 Office: United Airlines San Francisco Int Airport San Francisco CA 94128-3800

BROOKSBANK, RAY STEPHEN, retired professional society administrator; b. Lymington, Hampshire, Eng., Dec. 14, 1946; s. Barbara Hermione Brooksbank. Nursing diploma, Chelsea & Westminster Hosp., London, Roffey Park Horsham, 1969. Chief exec. internat. divsn. Brit. Nursing Assn., London, 1971-77; mng. dir. Allied Internat. Med. Svcs., London, 1972-77, Euroserv (S.L.), San Pedro Alcantra, Malaga, Spain, 1978-91; staff cons. Canadian Fed./Provincial Govts. Staffing Problems, 1974-77, Iranian Nat. Hosp. Project, United Arab Emirates Hosp. Projects, 1975. Sec. Assn. Concordia Anti Sida, Marbella, Malaga, Spain, 1994-2000. Mem. Lansdown Club (London). Anglican. Avocations: reading, travel, gardening, good wine. E-mail: stephen@mundofree.com. Home: Apartado de Correos 209, San Pedro de Alcántara, 29670 Málaga Spain

BROOKS SHOEMAKER, VIRGINIA LEE, volunteer, librarian; b. Oklahoma City, Sept. 16, 1944; d. Leo B. and Eloise Gilreath; m. Phil Ashley Brooks, Aug. 10, 1972 (dec. Oct. 1982); 1 child, Philip Brooks; m. Gene Darrell Shoemaker, Feb. 16, 1986; children: Rob, Julie, Donna, Gary. Student, Oklahoma City C.C., 1980; BS, U. Ctrl. Okla., 1988, M in Sch. Media, 1991, postgrad., 2000—. With Dept. Human Svcs., Oklahoma City, 1970-75, State Dept. Librs., Oklahoma City, 1980-87; substitute tchr. Oklahoma City Schs., 1989-91; vol. libr. Children's Libr., Children's Hosp., Oklahoma City, 1992—; libr. vol. Corpus Christi Sch. Libr., 1998—; vol. children's sect. First Bapt. Libr.; vol. Libr. for Blind. Sponsor World Vision, Seattle, 1994—; active Cub Scouts; active, life mem. Meth. Ch. of the Servant, women mission groups, Wesley Meth.; vol. Habitat for Humanity; vol. childrens sect. First Bapt. Libr. Recipient Adopt-a-Park awards, Oklahoma City Beautiful, Omniplex Sci. Mus., Oklahoma City, 1986-89. Mem. Coun. for Exceptional Children, Omniplex Sci Mus. Zool. Soc. (Adopt-a-Park award 1986-89), U. Ctrl. Okla. Alumni Assn., Classen Alumni Assn. Baptist. Avocations: piano, children's books to be published and art, reading inspirational biographies, creative writing, dogs as companions.

BROOM, DONALD MAURICE, animal scientist, educator; b. London, July 14, 1942; s. Donald Edward and Mavis Edith (Thompson) B.; m. Sally Elizabeth Riordan, May 31, 1971; children: Oliver Edward, Thomas Charles, Giles Alexander. BA, Cambridge U., 1964, PhD, 1967, MA, 1968. Lectr. U. Reading, Eng., 1967-79, sr. lectr., 1979-82, reader, 1982-86; Colleen Macleod prof. animal welfare U. Cambridge, 1986—; vis. asst. prof. U. calif., Berkeley, 1969; vis. lectr. U. West Indies, Trinidad, 1972; vis. scientist C.S.I.R.O., Perth, 1983; mem. eEC Farm Animal Welfare Expert Group, Brussels, 1981-89; sci. advisor Coun. of Europe Standing Com. of the Conf. on the Protection of Animals Kept for Farming Purposes, Strasbourg, 1987-2000; chmn. sci. vet. com. animal welfare sect. European Union, Brussels, 1990-97; mem. sci. com. on animal health and animal welfare European Union, 1997—. Author: Birds and Their Behaviour, 1977, Biology of Behaviour, 1981; co-author: Farm Animal Behaviour and Welfare, 1990, Stress and Animal Welfare, 1993; contbr. numerous articles to profl. jours. Mem. Farm Animal Welfare Coun., Ministry Agr., U.K. Govt., 1991-99, mem. animal procedures com., 1998—; European Union rep. quadripartite working group on humane trapping stds., 1995-96; mem. N.E.R.C. (U.K. Govt.) Nat. Com. on Seals, 1986-96. George Fleming prize, Brit. Vet. Jour., 1990. Fellow Myerscough Coll. U. Ctrl. Lancashire (hon.); mem. Assn. for Study of Animal Behaviour (hon. treas. 1971-80), Internat. Soc. for Applied Ethology (pres. 1987-89), Internat. Ethological Com., 1976-79. Fellow Zool. Soc. London (animal welfare com. 1986-95). Avocations: squash, water polo, modern pentathlon, ornithology. E-mail: dmb16@cam.ac.uk. Fax: 44-1223-337610. Office: U Cambridge De Clin Vet Med, Madingley Rd, Cambridge CB3 0ES, England

BROOME, JOHN, philosophy educator; b. Kuala Lumpur, Malaysia, May 17, 1947; s. Richard and Tamsin Broome; m. Ann Rowland, Oct. 7, 1970; children: Kitty, Richard. BA in Math. and Econs., Cambridge (Eng.) U., 1968; PhD in Econs., MIT, 1972; MA in Philosophy, London U., 1973. Lectr. in econs. Birkbeck Coll., London U., 1972-78; reader in econs. U. Bristol, U.K., 1979-91, prof. econs., 1991-94; prof. philosophy U. St. Andrews, U.K., 1995-2000, U. Oxford, U.K., 2000—; vis. fellow/vis. prof. U. Va., 1974, Australian Nat. U., 1986, 94, All Souls Coll., Oxford, Eng., 1982-83, Princeton U., 1987-88, U. Wash., 1988, U. B.C., Can., 1994, U. Uppsala, Sweden, 1997-98. Author: Weighing Goods, 1991, Counting the Cost of Global Warming, 1992, Ethics Out of Economics, 1999; editor jour. Econs. and Philosophy, 1994-99. Rsch. grantee Econ. and Social Rsch. Coun., U.K., 1984, 91, 92, 98. Fellow Royal Soc. Edinburgh, Brit. Acad.

BROOME, KATHRYN, secondary education educator; b. Natchez, Miss., Dec. 7, 1950; d. Jackson Daniel and Edna Louise (Barrett) B.; m. John Bridges, Dec. 23, 1997. BS, Miss. State Coll. for Women, 1973; M English Edn., Miss. Coll., 1995. Tchr. Columbia (Miss.) Pub. Schs., 1973-74, Larmar County Schs., Hattiesburg, Miss., 1974-77, Monroe County Schs., Hamilton, Miss., 1977-84, Jackson (Miss.) Pub. Schs., 1984—; real estate agt. Century 21 Eddie Rosamond Realty, Jackson, 1997-98, Re/Max Properties, Jackson, 1998—; student coun. sponsor Powell Middle Sch., Jackson, Miss., 1991—, team leader 8th grade 1991-92; varsity cheerleader sponsor Hamilton H.S., 1979-80, 95. Mem. Jackson pub. schs. supts. orgn. for student coun. Jackson Pub. Schs., 1991-93; rep. Parent/Tchr. Student Assn., Jackson, 1997; supporter United Way. Grantee IBM, 1996, Jackson Pub. Schs., 1997, Entergy, 1997, Tchr. Talk, 1997, Bell South, 1997, Jr. League, 1997. Mem. Miss. Fedn. Tchrs., Jackson Fedn. Tchrs., Jackson Assn. of Realtors, Jr. Beta Club, Sigma Tau Delta. Republican. Baptist. Avocations: people, animals, swimming, painting, cooking. Home: 250 Ina Dr Madison MS 39110-9650 Office: Jackson Public Schs 662 S President St Jackson MS 39201-5601

BROOMFIELD, JOHN PHILIP, corrosion engineer, consultant; b. Surbiton, Surrey, Eng., Sept. 14, 1953; s. Philip Elliot and Olive Margaret (Boxall) B.; m. Amanda Jane Cleary, June 18, 1980 (div. May 1989); m. Veronica June Selio, May 18, 1991. BSc upper 2d class honors, Sussex, Brighton, Eng., 1975; D. Philosophy, Oxford (Eng.) U., 1983. Chartered engr. Rsch. officer Cen. Electricity Rsch. Lab., Leatherhead, Surrey, Eng., 1979-84; sr. corrosion engr. Taylor Woodrow, Southall, Eng., 1984-88; tech. contract mgr. strategic hwy. rsch. program NRC/NAS, Washington, 1988-90; pvt. practice corrosion cons. London, 1990—. Author: Corrosion of Steel in Concrete: Understanding Investigation and Repair, 1997; contbr. articles on surface and corrosion phenomena to profl. jours. Chmn. Transp. Rsch. Bd. Corrosion Com. Fellow Inst. of Corrosion (U.K.), Inst. Materials; mem. Nat. Assn. Corrosion Engrs. (corrosion specialist), Instn. Civil Engrs. (grad.), Am. Concrete Inst. (com. 222), ASTM, Concrete Soc. (U.K.), Savage Club (London). Avocations: swimming, travelling, reading, theatre, classical music. Home: 36 Kingfisher Ct, Bridge Rd, East Molesey KT8 9HN, England Office: 78 Durham Rd, London SW20 0TL, England

BROOTEN, KENNETH EDWARD, JR., retired lawyer, writer, chief counsel United States Congress; b. Kirkland, Wash., Oct. 17, 1942; s. Kenneth Edward Sr. and Sadie Josephine (Assad) B.; m. Patricia Anne Folsom, Aug. 29, 1965 (div. Apr. 1986); children: Michelle Catherine, Justin Ken-

neth. Diploma, Lewis Sch. Hotel, Restaurant and Club Mgmt., Washington, 1963; student, U. Md., 1964-66; AA with honors, Santa Fe C.C., Gainesville, Fla., 1969; BS in Journalism with highest honors, U. Fla., 1971, MA in Journalism and Communications with highest honors, 1972, JD with honors, 1975; law student, U. Idaho, 1972-73; diploma in internat. law, Polish Acad. Scis., Warsaw, 1974; postgrad. in Internat. Law, Cambridge (Eng.) U., Eng., 1974. Bar: Fla., D.C., U.S. Dist. Ct. (no., mid. and so. dists.) Fla., U.S. Dist. Ct. D.C., U.S. Tax Ct., U.S. Ct. Appeals (5th, 9th, 11th and D.C. circs.), U.S. Supreme Ct., Trial Counsel Her Majesty's Govt. of United Kingdom. Asst. to several congressmen U.S. Ho. of Reps., Washington, 1962-67; adminstrv. asst. VA Cen. Office, Washington, 1967; adminstrv. officer VA Hosp., Gainesville, Fla., 1967-72; ptnr. Carter & Brooten, P.A., Gainesville, Fla., 1975-78, Brooten & Fleisher, Chartered, Washington and Gainesville, Fla., 1978-80; pvt. practice, Washington and Gainesville, 1980-86, Washington, 1987-88, Washington and Orlando, Fla., 1988-91, Washington and Winter Park, Fla., 1991-98; ret., 1998; permanent spl. counsel, acting chief counsel, dir. Select Com. Assassinations U.S. Ho. of Reps., 1976-77; counsel Her Majesty's Govt. of U.K. (in U.S.). Author: Malpractice Guide to Avoidance and Treatment, 1987; episode writher TV series Simon and Simon; nat. columnist Pvt. Practice, 1988-90, Physicians Mgmt., 1991-93; commentator Med. News Network, 1993-94; contbr. more than 200 articles to profl. jours.; composer. Served with USCGR, 1960-68. Named one of Outstanding Young Men Am., U.S. Jaycees, 1977. Mem. Fla. Bar Assn., D.C. Bar Assn., Sigma Delta Chi. Roman Catholic. Avocations: writing, marksmanship, dangerous game hunting. Address: The Oxbow Bascom FL 32423-9361

BROPHY, KEVIN THOMAS, writer; b. Castlebar, Ireland, June 17, 1943; s. James and Sarah (Garvey) B.; m. Mary Fergus, Aug. 22, 1967 (div. 1987); children: Adam, Sara, Georgia. BA, Nat. U. Ireland, Galway, 1964, higher diploma in edn., 1970; MA, Leeds U., 1999. Cert. tchr. English as a fgn. lang. Tchr. English various high schs., Ireland and Eng., 1965-72; editl. dir. Sch. & Coll. Pub., Dublin, Ireland, 1972-77; pres. Brophy Ednl., Dublin, 1977-90; freelance writer Galway, 1991—; pub. Irish Univ. Rev., Dublin, 1987 . Author: (autobiography) Walking the Line: Scenes from an Army Childhood, 1994, (novel) Almost Heaven, 1997, In the Company of Wolves, 1999; editor: (anthology) Prayers for Living, 1992; columnist Intercom mag., 1995-98. Avocations: reading, cinema, music, theatre, walking. Home and Office: 31 The Baily Circular Rd, Galway Ireland

BRO-RASMUSSEN, FINN, educator; b. Brenderup, Denmark, Aug. 2, 1928; s. Richard N. and Marie Christophersen (Bro) Rasmussen; m. Kirsten Gundestrup Andreasen, Feb. 3, 1930; children: Thomas, Marie, Mette. MS, Tech. U. Denmark, 1951. Sci. asst. Nat. Vitamin Lab., Denmark, 1952-60; head lab. Nat. Pesticide Lab., Denmark, 1960-68; head dept. Nat. Food Inst., Denmark, 1968-77; prof. Tech. U. Denmark, 1977—; cons. FAO, Zambia, Poland & Burma, 1970-82; mem. chmn. FAO Pesticide Residue Panel, 1972-82, EU Commn. Adv. Com. Toxicity and Ecotoxicity Chems., 1978-97, chmn., 1983-88, 91-96; chmn. Soc. Environ. Sci. Ecotoxicol., 1988-92. Contbr. articles to profl. jours. Recipient Gold medal U. Copenhagen, 1955, Kaskelot prize Danish Biol. Soc., 1984, prize Danish Consumers Assn., 1996. Mem. Danish Acad. Tech. Scis., EU-Sci. (mem. adv. com., pres. 1989-95). Home: Soelleroed Pk 7/6, DK-2840 Holte Denmark Office: Tech U Denmark, Bldg 424, DK-2800 Lyngby Denmark

BRORSON, SVERRE HENNING, biochemist; b. Jevnaker, Oppland, Norway, Sept. 26, 1963; s. Sverre and Berglyot Therese (Olsen) B. MS, U. Oslo, 1993, PhD, 1997. Bioengr., biochemist Ullevål Hosp., Oslo, 1986—. Avocation: computing. Home: Kirkeveien 41, N-0368 Oslo Norway Office: Ullevål Hosp, Kirkeveien 166, N-0407 Oslo Norway

BROSELOW, LINDA LATT, medical office technician, aviculturist; b. Harrisburg, Pa., July 9, 1940; d. Herman and Ricci (Buch) Latt; m. Robert Joel Broselow, Nov. 26, 1966; children: Andrew M., Katherine, Jordan. BS, Pa. State U., 1962; MA, Columbia U., 1965. Vol. Peace Corps, Ankara, Turkey, 1962-64; office mgr. Robert J. Broselow, M.D., Lubbock, Tex., 1984-88, med. office technician, 1990-98. Vol. South Park Hosp., Lubbock, 1986-87, Ronald McDonald House, Lubbock, 1990-92. Mem. ASPCA, Am. Diabetes Assn., Am. Assn. Ret. Persons, Audubon Soc., Arkadashlar, Assn. of Univ. Women, Children Internat. Avocation: reading. Home: 4609 9th St Lubbock TX 79416-4710 Office: 3506 21st St Ste 506 Lubbock TX 79410-1200

BROSKY, JOHN G., judge; b. Scott Twp., Pa., Aug. 4, 1920; m. Rose F. Brosky, June 24, 1950; children: John C., Carol Ann, David J. BA, U. Pitts., 1942, LLB, 1949, JD, 1968; D in Pub. Svc. (hon.), La Roche Coll., Pa., 1996. Bar: Pa. 1950. Asst. county solicitor Allegheny County, Pa., 1951-56; judge County Ct. Allegheny County, 1956-61; adminstrv. judge family divsn. Common Pleas Ct. Allegheny County, 1961-80; judge Superior Ct. Pa., 1980—; mem. faculty Pa. Coll. Judiciary. Chmn. Operation Patrick Henry, Boy Scouts Am.; pres. Scott Twp. Sch. Bd., 1946-56; 1st pres. Chartiers Valley Joint Sch. Dist., Allegheny County; pres. Greater Pitts. Guild for Blind. Served with U.S. Army, 1942-46; maj. gen. (ret.) USAF-Pa. Air N.G. Recipient Disting. Jud. Svc. award Pa., Mason Juvenile Ct. Inst., Man of Yr. award in law Pitts. Jr. C. of C., 1960, Humanitarian award New Light Men's Club, 1960, Loyalty Day award VFW, 1960, Four Chaplains award, 1965, Man of Yr. award Cath. War Vets., 1960, 62, Svc. award Alliance Coll., Disting. citation Mil. Order World Wards, Humanitarian award Variety Club, 1974, Jimmy Doolittle fellow award Aerospace Edn. Found., 1975, Pa. Meritorious Svc. medal Pa. N.G., 1976, State Humanitarian award Domestic Rels. Assn. Pa., 1978, Man of Yr. award Am. Legion, 1978, Pa. Disting. Svc. medal, Disting. Svc. award Pa. N.G., 1980, Exceptional Svc. award USAF, 1982, Gen. Ira Eaker fellow, 1981, Brotherhood of Man award Fraternal Socs. Greater Pitts., 1987, Cmty. Svc. award Chartiers Valley Commn. on Human Rels., 1988, George Washington Honor medal Freedoms Found., 1990; named Pitts. Polonian of Yr., 1988; recipient St. Thomas More award Allegheny County Bar Assn., 1989, Man of Yr. award Kosciuszko Found., 1991, Vectors/Pitts., 1994, Gen. John G. Brosky Day Pride in Pa. award, 1995, Disting. Achievement award Sch. Law and Dept. Edn., U. Pitts., 2000. Mem. ABA, ATLA, Am. Judicature Soc., Pa. Bar Assn. (co-chmn. professionalism com. 1987-88), Inst. Jud. Adminstrn., Inc., Internat. Platform Assn., Air Force Assn. (nat. dir., nat. pres., chmn. bd., presdl. citation 1974, 80, 81), Am. Acad. Matrimonial Lawyers, N.G. Assn. Pa. (pres.), Pa. Conf. State Trial Judges (past pres.), Pa. Joint Family Law Coun., Press Club, Variety Club, Aero Club (past pres.). Office: 2703 Grant Bldg Pittsburgh PA 15219-2302

BROSNAN, CAROL RAPHAEL SARAH, retired arts administrator, musician; b. Paterson, N.J., July 19, 1931; d. Basil Roger and Mary Ellen Carroll (McDonald) B. Student, George Washington U., Washington, 1956-61, U. Va., 1975, U. Oxford (Eng.), 1975; BA in History, George Washington U., 1981, postgrad., 1983-87; piano student of, Iris Brussels, 1940-53. Adminstrv. clk. Dept. of Army, Def., Pentagon, Office of asst. chief of staff intelligence, Washington, 1955-58; clk. fgn. sci. info. program NSF, Washington, 1958-60, adminstrv. clk., 1960-65, adminstrv. fellowship clk. grad. fellowship program, 1965-72; staff asst. to Jane Alexander, chmn. Nat. Endowment for the Arts, Washington, 1972-94; ret., 1994; music tchr. piano, Paterson, N.J., 1945-53; piano recitalist U.S., Heidelberg, W. Ger. Served with WAC, 1953-55. Recipient Young People's Concerts award, 1945. Hon. fellow Harry S. Truman Libr. Inst. Nat. and Internat. Affairs, 1975. Mem. Am. Hist. Assn., Nat. Assn. Uniformed Svcs., Acad. Polit. Sci. (contbg. 1978-81), Am. Classical League, Friends of Bodleian Libr. (Oxford U.), Luther Rice Soc. of George Washington U. (life), Phi Alpha Theta. Home: 6030 Sunset Ridge Ct Centreville VA 20121-3051 Office: Nat Endowment for Arts 1100 Pennsylvania Ave NW Washington DC 20004-2501

BROSS, STEWARD RICHARD, JR., lawyer; b. Lancaster, Pa., Oct. 25, 1922; s. Steward Richard and Katherine Mauk (Hoover) B.; m. Isabel Florence Kenney, May 10, 1943; 1 dau., Donna Isabel Bross Campagna. Student, McGill U., Montreal, Can., 1940-42; LLB, Columbia U., 1948. Bar: N.Y. 1948. Pvt. practice N.Y.C.; ptnr. Cravath, Swaine & Moore, 1958-92, ret., 1992; adv. com. fgn. direct investment program Office of Sec. Dept. Commerce, 1969; adv. com. regulations Office Fgn. Direct Investment, 1968-70. Regent, trustee emeritus The Cathedral Ch. of St. John the Divine, N.Y.C.; warden emeritus Trinity Ch., N.Y.C. Served as officer Canadian Navy, 1942-45. Mem. ABA, N.Y. State Bar Assn., Assn. of Bar of City of N.Y., Pilgrims U.S., Econ. Club N.Y., Union Club, Rockefeller Center Club, Links Club, Univ. Club N.Y. Home: 215 E 68th St New York NY 10021-5718 also: Ashgrove 130 Litchfield Rd Norfolk CT 06058-1252 also: 3200 Wailea Alanui Dr Apt 1101 Kihei HI 96753-7757 Office: Cravath Swaine & Moore 825 8th Ave New York NY 10019-7475

BROSSE, JEAN-CLAUDE, polymer chemistry educator, consultant, researcher; b. Le Mans, France, Oct. 16, 1940; s. Bernard and Simone (Grassin) B.; m. Françoise Dantzer, Mar. 31, 1964; children: Sylvie, Catherine, Claude-Arnaud. Lic. in phys. scis., U. Caen, France, 1963; grad. in engring., Nat. Sch. Chemistry, Caen, 1964; D Phys. Scis., U Maine, Le Mans, 1970. Asst. lectr. chemistry U. Maine, 1964-80, prof., 1981—; cons. Inst. Recherche Appliquée sur Polymères, Le Mans, 1976—, Nat. Soc. Poudres et Explosifs, Paris, 1985—, Textile Inst. France, Lyon, 1989—, Inst. Supérieur Plasturgie, Alençon, France, 1994—; participant over 250 confs., N.Am., Europe, Asia, Africa; expert UN Indsl. Devel. Orgn., 1981, 87, 89. Contbr. over 200 articles to sci. revs., chpts. to books; numerous patents in field. Mem. Nat. Coun. Univs., France, 1995. Mem. French Soc. Chemistry, Am. Chem. Soc. Avocations: competition horse riding, skiing. Home: La Closeraie, 72160 Duneau France Office: U Maine, Ave Olivier Messiaen, 72000 Le Mans France

BROSSMAN, KAREN REBECA, healthcare administrator; b. Caracas, Venezuela, Jan. 9, 1960; came to U.S., 1974; d. Rudolf Franticek and Dagmar Ana Marie Brossman. B of Gen. Studies, U. Southwestern La., 1982, BSN, 1991; MS, U. St. Francis, 1994; postgrad., SUNY, 2000—. RN, La., Ky., Ill., Ind. Staff nurse Lafayette (La.) Med. Ctr., 1990-94; instr. Blue Cliff Sch. Therapeutic Massage, Lafayette, 1993-99; nurse, team leader Our Lady of Lourdes Regional Med. Ctr., Lafayette, 1994-99; dir. patient care svcs. Dialysis Affiliates, LLC, Evansville, Ind., 1999—; weekend supr. Amelia Manor Nursing Home, Lafayette, 1993-99; dir. Dialysis Affiliates, LLC, Evansville; instr. subtle body energetics, therapeutic comm. and HIV, 1993-99. Contbr. articles to profl. jours. V.p., pres. Lafayette Bus. and Profl. Women's Club; pres., rec. sec. Lafayette Rep. Women's Club. Mem. Am. Holistic Nurses' Assn. (networker 1993—, scholar 1998), Alpha Zeta, Sigma Theta Tau, Alpha Rho chpt. Sigma Delta Pi. Republican. Roman Catholic. Avocations: animals, outdoors, charitable healthcare organizations. Home: 5533 Schneider Rd Newburgh IN 47630-9545 Office: Dialysis Affiliates LLC 3900 Washington Ave Evansville IN 47714-0550

BROSSNER, CLEMENS, urologist; b. Oberwart, Austria, Oct. 19, 1959; s. Otto and Margarete (Zettl) B. MD, U. Vienna, 1988. Tng. gen. practitioner Oberwart Hosp., Austria, 1989, resident in urology, 1993-95, 96-98, urologist, 1998—; resident in urology U. Vienna, Austria, 1995-96. Contbr. articles to profl. jours. Recipient Theodor Körner prize Theodor Körner Fonds, 1997. Fellow European Bd. Urology; mem. European Assn. of Urology (reviewer of the European Urology), Austrian Soc. of Urology (prostatarbeitskreis 1998—). Avocation: tennis. E-mail: broessner@yahoo.de. Home: Habichtgasse 6, A-7400 Oberwart Austria Office: Dept Urology Oberwart Hosp, Dornburggasse 80, A-7400 Oberwart Austria

BROTCHI, JACQUES, medical educator, neurosurgeon; b. Liege, Belgium, Aug. 11, 1942; s. Isac and Haia (Ghelburd) B.; m. Rachel Kesselman, June 30, 1967; 1 child, Nathalie. MD, U. Liege, 1967, PhD, 1979. Resident in neurosurgery Baviere Hosp-U. Liege, 1967-73, affiliated neurosurgeon, 1974-79, assoc. prof. neurosurgery, 1979-81; head dept. neurosurgery Erasme Hosp., Brussels, 1982—; prof., chmn. dept. neurosurgery U. Brussels, 1984—. Co-author: (with G. Fischer) Intramedullary Spinal Cord Tumors, 1996; contbr. over 200 articles to sci. publs., also chpts. to books. Bd. gov.'s Hebrew U., Jerusalem; pres. Lions, Seraing, Belgium, 1981-82. Decorated Commdr. of the Order of Leopold, Belgium, Chevalier of the Legion of Honor, France, Chevalier of the Order of Danneborg, Denmark; anoblished by His Majesty King Baudouin of Belgium, 1988. Mem. Belgian Soc. Neurosurgery (pres. 1989-91), French Lang. Soc. Neurosurgery (pres. 1992-94), World Fedn. Neurol. Socs. (treas. 1993-97, chmn. edn. com. 1997—). Office: Dept NeurSurg Erasme Hosp, 808 Rt de Lennik, B-1070 Brussels Belgium

BROTCHIE, JOHN FREDERICK, research scientist; b. Melbourne, Victoria, Australia, July 17, 1929; s. Leslie John and Veronica Evelyn (Dobson) B.; m. Jean Noelle Alford, Sept. 1, 1951; children: Robert John, Susan Janet, Peter Rodney. B in Civil Engring., U. Melbourne, Australia, 1951; D in Engring., U. Calif., Berkeley, 1961. Cert. civil engr. Design engr., supervising structural engr. Australian Dept. Works, 1951-61; sr. rsch. scientist Commonwealth Sci. and Indsl. Rsch. Orgn., Melbourne, 1961-74; chief rsch. scientist CSIRO, Melbourne, 1974-94, cons., 1994—; grad. rsch. asst. U. Calif., Berkeley, 1958-61; vis. assoc. prof. MIT, Cambridge, Mass., 1963-65; mem. internat. panel Harvard Inst. Internat. Devel., Tehran, 1976; pres. Regional Sci. Assn., Australasia, 1977-80, internat. v.p., 1981; mem. Internat. St. Group Land Use Transp., U.K., 1981-85; coord. Internat. Coun. Bldg. Rsch., 1982-94; co-founder, dir. market studies VFT Rail Project Australia, 1984-90. Editor: (procs.) Cities of the 21st Century, 1991, Cities in Competition, 1995; East-West Perspectives, 1999; contbr. articles to profl. jours. Fellow ASCE, Australian Instn. Engrs., Australian Inst. Bldg., Australian Acad. Tech. Scis. and Engring.; mem. Internat. Coun. for Tall Bldgs. and Urban Habitat, N.Y. Acad. Scis., Sigma Xi. Avocations: tennis, swimming, writing. Office: John Brotchie & Assocs, 62 Cascade St, North Balwyn 3104, Australia

BROTHERS, FLETCHER ARNOLD, minister, religious organization founder, director; b. Carthage, N.Y., Mar. 8, 1948; s. Rae L. and Hildred (Weaver) B.; m. Keri L. Ellis; children: Jeremy, Jamie Lynn. Student, Houghton Coll., 1965-66, Utica Coll., 1966-67; HHD (hon.), Freedom Bible Coll., Lakemont, N.Y., 1988. Ordained to ministry Ind. Bible Chs. Am., 1975. Pastor Gates Community Chapel, Rochester and Lakemont, N.Y., 1975—; founder Freedom Village U.S.A., Lakemont, 1981—; chmn. Freedom Bible Coll., 1986—. Author several books; founder Victory Today Radio and TV Programs, 1977—. Bd. dirs. Religious Round Table, Washington, 1979—; pres. Save Am.'s Youth, Washington, 1988—; bd. govs. Coun. for Nat. Policy, Washington, 1989-90; mem. Inner Circle, Rep. Party, 1990-91. Recipient Angels award, 1989. Mem. Ind. Bible Ch. Home and Office: Freedom Village USA RR 14 Lakemont NY 14857

BROTMAN, RICHARD DENNIS, counselor; b. Detroit, Nov. 2, 1952; s. Alfred David and Dorothy G. (Mansfield) B.; m. Debra Louise Hobold, Sept. 9, 1979. AA, East L.A. Jr. Coll., 1972; AB, U. So. Calif., 1974, Ms, 1976. Lic. marriage, family and child counselor, Calif.; cert. counselor, Calif. Instructional media coord. Audiovisual divsn. Pub. Libr., City of Alhambra, Calif., 1971-78; clin. supr. Hollywood-Sunset Cmty. Clinic, L.A., 1976—; client program coord. North Los Angles County Regional Ctr. for Devel. Disabled, 1978-81; sr. counselor Eastern L.A. Regional Ctr. for Devel. Disabled, 1981-85; dir. cmty. svcs. Almansor Edn. Ctr., 1985-87; tng. and resource devel. Children's Home Soc. Calif., 1987-90; program supr. Pacific Clinics-East, 1990-94; dir. clin. svcs. Alma Family Svcs., 1994—; probable cause hearing officer Orange County (Calif.) Healthcare Agy., 1986—. Corp. dir. San Gabriel Mission Players, 1973-75. Mem. Am. Assn. for Marriage and Family Therapy (approved supr.), Calif. Pers. and Guidance Assn., Calif. Rehab. Counselors Assn. (officer), San Fernando Valley Consortium of Agys. Serving Devel. Disabled Citizens (chmn. recreation subcom), L.A. Aquarium Soc. Democrat. E-mail: brieftherapy@compuserve.com. Home: 3515 Brandon St Pasadena CA 91107-4542 Office: Alma Family Svcs 9140 Whittier Blvd Pico Rivera CA 90660-2444

BROUÉ, MICHEL, mathematician, educator; b. Paris, Oct. 28, 1946; s. Pierre Broué and Simone Paulette (Charras) Lemarchand; m. Marie-Claude Cidère, Sept. 10, 1966; children: Isabelle Sandrine, Caroline Séverine. Maitrise/DEA/Doct. 3èc., 1970; Agrégation de Math., École Normale Supér., 1969; Doctorat d'Etat es. Sc., U. Paris 7, 1975. Élève-prof. École Normale Super., Saint-Cloud, France, 1966-70; attachè de recherche CNRS, Paris, 1970-75; prof. U. Paris 7, 1980-83, prof. lère classe, 1983-90, prof. classe exc., 1990—; dir. svc. math. École Normale Supér. de Jeunes Filles, France, 1983-86; dir. math. dept. and Info. École Normale Supérieure, 1986-94; mem. de l'Institut Universitaire de France, Universite Denis-Diderot, 1993—, dir. Inst. Henri-Poincaré. Contbr. numerous articles to profl. jours. Sec. Com. Mathematicians, Paris, 1974—. Mem. Soc. Math. France, Am. Math. Soc. Home: 9 rue Brézin, 75014 Paris France Office: Inst Henri Poincaré, 11 Rue Pierre/Marie Curie, F-75005 Paris France

BROUGHTON, JAMES WALTER, real estate development executive, consultant; b. Atlantic City, Dec. 16, 1946; s. Walter Lennie and Janet Caroline (Mossman) B.; m. Sharon Carter, Mar. 10, 1980; children: Jennifer Christine, Matthew James. Student, U. Colo., Colorado Springs, 1967-68, U. Md., 1968-70, U. Colo., Denver, 1972-73. Asst. regional sales dir. Del E. Webb Corp., Denver, 1972-76; dir. mktg. Interval Internat., Miami, Fla., 1981-82; exec. dir. Time Sharing Inst., Miami, 1981-82; pres. J. Broughton, Inc., Miami, 1976-83, Spectrum Mktg. Group, Denver, 1983-84, Ocean Resourts Devel. Co., Ventura, Calif., 1984-85; sr. v.p. Fairfield Cmtys., Inc., Atlanta, 1985; chmn., pres., CEO, Lexes Enterprises, Inc., Las Vegas, Nev., 1985—; bd. dirs. Consol. Resorts, Inc., PC Cons., Inc., Sea-Shore, Inc., Internat. Cruise and Excursion Gallery; pub. Time Sharing Ency., 1981, Time Sharing Ind. Rev., 1981. Contbr. articles to profl. jours. With USAF, 1964-71. Mem. Am. Resort Devel. Assn. (bd. dirs. 1985—, exec. com. 1988—, chmn. meetings coun. 1991—, resort devel. forum 1993—, treas. 1993—, recruitment award 1983, NTC svc. award 1987, Leader of Yr. award 1991, Industry Visionary Leader of Yr. award 1993), Nat. Time Sharing Coun. (chmn. 1984-86, bd. govs. 1984-92, recruitment award 1984), Interval Internat. (adv. bd. 1982-91), Urban Land Inst. (recreational devel. coun. 1993—). Republican. Office: Lexes Enterprises Inc 3175 Casanova Cir Las Vegas NV 89120-1926

BROUNTZOS, ELIAS NIKOLAOS, radiologist; b. Piraeus, Greece, Nov. 28, 1956; s. Nicholaos and Irene (Strountzi) B. MD, Athens (Greece) U., 1981, PhD, 1986. Cert. radiologist. Gen. practitioner Levadia (Greece) Gen. Hosp., 1983; resident in surgery Patras U., 1983-84, resident in radiology, 1984-88, lectr. radiology, 1989-99; staff radiologist Metaxa Cancer Hosp., Piraeus, Greece, 1989-2000; radiologist Athens U. Sch. Medicine, 1993-99; asst. prof. radiology Athens U., 2000—; rsch. fellow Harvard U., Boston, 1991-92. Contbr. articles to profl. jours. Mem. Cardiovascular Interventional Radiol. Soc. Europe, Soc. Cardiovascular and Interventional Radiology, Hellenic Radiologic Soc., Greek Soc. Interventional Radiology. Avocations: rock climbing, ski mountaineering, ice climbing, wind surfing. Home: 34 Aidiniou St, 16675 Glyfada Athens, Greece Office: Athens U 2d Dept Radiology, 20 Papadiamantopoulou St, Athens 11538, Greece

BROUQUI, PHILIPPE LUCIEN, infectious diseases and tropical medicine educator; b. Marseille, France, June 19, 1958; s. Michel and Sabine (Esteve) B.; m. Natalie Cailles, Apr. 4, 1963; children: Coralie, Laurine. MD, U. Marseille, France, PhD. Fellow Med. Sch., Marseille, 1987, from asst. prof. to assoc. prof., 1991-98; prof. Med. Sch. and Faculty, Marseille, 1998—. Contbr. chpts. to books and articles to profl. jours. Mem. Am. Soc. Microbiology, Am. S. Rickettsiae and Rickettsial Diseases, Am. Soc. Tropical Medicine and Hygiene. Office: chu Hopital Nord, Ch des bourrely, 13015 Marseille France

BROUSE, DEBORAH ELIZABETH, health association executive; b. Buffalo, Oct. 3, 1950; d. Richard William Jr. and Mary (Brewer) B.; m. George Osborn Bergantz, June 7, 1969 (div. 1973); m. Elliott Jan Gilberg, Apr. 11, 1980; children: Stephen Brouse Gilberg, Sarah Brouse Gilberg. BA in Music magna cum laude, Brown U., 1972; MA in Planning and Adminstrn., Antioch U., 1981. Health worker Feminist Women's Health Ctr., Santa Ana, Calif., 1974; program dir. Teen Help, Inc., Fountain Valley, Calif., 1974-75; program coord. Diogenes Youth Svcs., Davis, Calif., 1975-76, program dir., 1976-78; tng. and tech. assistance specialist Ctr. for Community Change, Washington, 1978-84; dir. edn. and outreach Zero Population Growth Inc., Washington, 1985-94; orgnl. assistance dir. Environ. Support Ctr., Washington, 1994-98; exec. dir. Child Life Coun., Rockville, Md., 1998—. Mem. Wilson Sr. High Parent Tchr. Student Assn., v.p. for fundraising, 1999-2000. Mem. Alliance for Environ. Edn. (exec. com. 1987-89, bd. dirs. 1985-89), Lafayette Home & Sch. Assn. (bd. dirs. 1993-95). Democrat. Avocations: music, hiking. Office: Child Life Coun 11820 Parklawn Dr Ste 202 Rockville MD 20852-2529

BROUSE, JOHN AMMON, JR., fiber optics engineer; b. Lewisburg, Pa., Oct. 6, 1948; s. John A. Sr. and Dotty I. Brouse; m. Suzanne Cardenas, Dec. 1, 1979; children: Jesse P., Jason P. BS in Meterology, U. Utah, 1974; MS in Telecom., U.S. Naval Postgrad. Sch., Monterey, Calif., 1984. Mil. officer USN, various locations, 1968-88; sys. engring. mgr. Jones Intercable, Ft. Lauderdale, Fla., 1988-91; sr. engr. Jones Intercable, Denver, 1991-92, mgr. advanced applications, 1992-93, dir. network devel., 1993-95, engring. dir., 1995-96, v.p. engring., 1996-97; v.p. engring. 21st Century, Chgo., 1997—; mem. curriculum adv. bd. U. Denver, 1995-97. Contbr. articles to profl. jours. Mem. Soc. Cable Telecom. Engrs. (chair scholarship com. 1995-97, Polaris award 1996), Internat. Engring. Consortium (exec. advisory bd.). Lutheran. Office: 21st Century 350 N Orleans St Ste 600 Chicago IL 60654-1597

BROUWER, ADRIAAN, financial executive; b. Hilversum, The Netherlands, Feb. 11, 1951; s. Willem and Maria Catharina (Fey) B.; m. Grada Frederika Dierssen, Jan. 18, 1972; children: Mardi, Pieter. Economist, Hogere Economische Sch., Arnheim, The Netherlands, 1971. Registered acct. NIVRA, Amsterdam, 1977. Head statis. divsn. Ctrl. Bank, Antilles, 1971-74; sr. account mgr. Citco, Antilles, 1974-78; mng. dir. Intertrust Amsterdam, 1978-87, Banque Nationale de Paris-Inst., Amsterdam, 1987-89; coord. Europe EMI, Amsterdam, 1989—; mng. dir. Spheric Music Pub., Amsterdam, 1978—. Fin. advisor, Sassenheim, 1987—. Mem. Reformed Ch. Avocations: fishing, diving, golf. Home: Van Goghlaan 4, 2172 DB Sassenheim The Netherlands Office: EMI Group Internat BV, Amsteldijk 166, 1079 LH Amsterdam The Netherlands

BROVCHENKO, VLADIMIR GRIGORIEVICH, nuclear engineering researcher; b. Novocoobansk, Krasnodar, Russia, Dec. 5, 1923; s. Grigori Efimovich and Anna Haritonovna (Peklo) B.; m. Zoia Petrovna Evlampieva, July 12, 1946. Grad. as engr.-physicist, Bauman Tech. U., Moscow, 1951; D Tech. Sci., Lebedev Physics Inst, Moscow, 1971. Cert. in electronic engring. Rschr. Kapitsa Inst., Moscow, 1951-55; leading rschr. Kurchatov Inst., Russian Rsch. Ctr., 1955—. Co-author: (monograph) Electronics for Electrostatic Accelerators, 1969; mem. editl. bd. Instruments and Exptl. Techniques, 1978—; contbr. articles to sci. publs., including Reports Acad. Scis. USSR, Instruments and Exptl. Techniques. Recipient Order of the Red Star 1944, Sign of the Honour, 1984, of the Patriotic War, 1985. Home: Street Acad Bochvar 17-53, 123098 Moscow Russia Office: Russian Rsch Ctr Kurchatov, Inst, Kurchatov Sq 1, 123182 Moscow Russia

BROWDER, FELIX EARL, mathematician, educator; b. Moscow, July 31, 1927; s. Earl and Raissa (Berkmann) B.; m. Eva Tislowitz, Oct. 5, 1949; children: Thomas, William. SB, MIT, 1946; PhD, Princeton U., 1948; MA (hon.), Yale U., 1962; D (hon.), U. Paris, 1990. C.L.E. Moore instr. math. MIT, 1948-51, vis. assoc. prof., 1961-62, vis. prof., 1977-78; instr. Boston U., 1951-53; asst. prof. Brandeis U., 1955-56; from asst. prof. to prof. Yale U., 1956-63; prof. math. U. Chgo., 1963-72, Louis Block prof. math., 1972-82, Max Mason disting. svc. prof., 1982-87, chmn. dept., 1972-77, 80-85; v.p. rsch. Rutgers, The State U. N.J., 1986-91; univ. prof. Rutgers U., New Brunswick, 1986—; vis. mem. Inst. Advanced Study, Princeton (N.J.) U., 1953-54, 63-64; vis. prof. Princeton U., 1968, Inst. Pure and Applied Math., Rio de Janeiro, 1960, U. Paris, 1973, 75, 78, 81, 83, 85; sr. rsch. fellow U. Sussex, Eng., 1970, 76; Fairchild Disting. visitor Calif. Inst. Tech., Pasadena, 1975-76; invited speaker Internat. Congress of Math., 1970, Sci. Bd. Santa Fe Inst., 1986-98. Contbr. theorems to books, including Nonlinear Problems, 1966, Functional Analysis and Related Fields, 1970, Nonlinear Operators and Nonlinear Equations of Evolution in Banach Spaces, 1976, Nonlinear Functional Analysis and Its Applications, 1986. With AUS, 1953-55. Guggenheim fellow, 1953-54, 66-67, Sloan Found. fellow, 1959-63, NSF sr. postdoctoral fellow, 1957-58. Fellow AAAS (chmn. sect. A 1982-83), NAS (coun. mem. 1992-95), Am. Acad. Arts and Scis., Am. Math. Soc. (editor bull. 1959-68, 78-83, mem. coun. 1959-72, 78-83, mng. editor 1964-68, 80, exec. com. coun. 1979-80, colloquium lectr. 1970, pres. 1999—, U.S. Nat. Med. Sci. 1999), Math. Assn. Am., Sigma Xi (pres. chpt. 1985-86). Achievements include development of linear and nonlinear partial differential equations, nonlinear functional analysis and fixed point and mapping theorems.

BROWER, JAMES CALVIN, graphic artist, painter; b. Clarksburg, W.Va., Dec. 30, 1914; s. Leroy Cooper and Margaret Wood (Watkins) B.; m. Elsie Margaret Day, Sept. 19, 1936; children: James Lawrence, Sandra Joan, Margaret, Linda Ann, Beth. Grad. high sch., Charleston, W.Va., 1932. Pvt. practice Huntington, W.Va., 1933-43, Toledo, 1952—; ptnr., art dir. Brower, Brownsberger and Burda, Toledo, 1944-51; dir. art and design Meeks Heit Pub. Co., 1992-99. Illustrator: Education for Sexuality, 1970, Human Sexuality, 1982, Education for Sexuality and HIV/AIDS, 1993; paintings featured in The Creative Artist, 1990, The Best of Watercolor 2, 1997, The Best of Watercolor Composition, 1997. Recipient Pres. award Okla. Watercolor Soc., 1987, Past Pres. award San Diego Watercolor Soc. Internat. Exhbn., 1989. Mem. Ohio Watercolor Soc. (bd. dirs. 1986-92, publicity chmn. 1986-92, Gold medal 1984, Charles Burchfield Meml. award 1991, Exhbn. award 1992), Northwestern Ohio Watercolor Soc. (pres. 1983-84), Nat. Water Color Soc. (Artist's Mag./Liquitex award 1990, Mem.'s Exhbn. awards 1996, 98), Ky. Watercolor Soc. (artist mem.), Ga. Watercolor Soc. (Gold award Nat. Exhbn. 1990), Midwest Watercolor Soc. (signature mem.), Toledo Fedn. Art Soc. (pres. 1987-88), Tile Club Toledo, Toledo Artists Club (gold medal 1998). Republican. Presbyterian. Avocations: chess, bridge. Home and Office: 2222 Grecourt Dr Toledo OH 43615-2918

BROWER, JANICE KATHLEEN, library technician; b. Chgo., July 29, 1952; d. Gerald B. and Emily (Kavicky) B. AA, Lincoln Coll., 1973; BS, Ill. State U., 1975; postgrad., U. Okla., 1984-86. Libr. assoc. Chgo. Pub. Libr., 1975-80, 81-83; libr. technician U. Okla. Biol. Sta., Norman, 1987; libr. technician Jim E. Hamilton Correctional Ctr. Okla. Dept. of Corrections, Hodgen, 1987—. Lutheran. Avocations: reading, walking, visiting historical sites and museums, architecture. Office: Jim E Hamilton Correctional Ctr HC 63 Box 5390 Hodgen OK 74939-9712

BROWN, ALEXANDER, engineering educator; b. Berwick Upon Tweed, Eng., Apr. 6, 1935; s. Alexander and Mary Helen (Dixon) B.; m. Ellen Alice Bennett, Aug. 21, 1954 (div.); children: Wendy Anne Miles, Sandra Elaine Price, Helen Alice Huber. BS with honors in Physics, Nottingham U., Eng., 1956; MME, Nottingham U., 1962, D in Sci., 1987; PhD in Mech. Engring., Queens U., Belfast, No. Ireland, 1967. Tech. asst. Armstrong Siddeley Motors, Coventry, Eng., 1956-60; tech. asst. Bristol Siddeley Motors, Bristol, Eng., 1960-63; lectr. Queens U., Belfast, 1963-70; sr. lectr. UWIST, Cardiff, Wales, 1970-77; reader UWIST, 1977-82; prof., head mech. engring. Royal Mil. Coll. Sci., Shrivenham, Eng., 1982-84, prof., head Sch. Engring. and Applied Sci., 1984—. Contbr. over 60 rsch. papers to profl. jours. Recipient many rsch. grants and contracts from rsch. couns., govt. depts. and industry. Fellow ASME (European membership rep.). Avocations: golf, holidaying in France.

BROWN, ALISTAIR JAMES PETERSEN, microbiology educator; b. Nicosia, Cyprus, Feb. 5, 1955; (parents Brit. citizens); s. Alexander M. and Jean B. (Sylvester) B.; m. Carolyn H. Michie, June 23, 1984; children: Myles C.A., Cameron V.J. BSc with honours, U. Aberdeen, Scotland, 1976, PhD, 1979. Rsch. fellow Brewing Rsch. Found., Redhill, Eng., 1979-81; postdoctoral fellow MIT, Cambridge, 1981-83; lectr. Glasgow (Scotland) U., 1983-89; lectr. microbiology Aberdeen U., 1989-91, sr. lectr., 1992-96, reader, 1996-98, prof., 1998—. Editor: Yeast Gene Analysis, 1998; contbr. over 100 articles to sci. jours. Grantee U.K. Rsch. Couns., European Cmty., Wellcome Trust. Mem. Soc. for Gen. Microbiology (physiology, biochem. & molecular genetics com.), Am. Soc. for Microbiology, Biochem. Soc., Aberdeen Fungal Group. Office: U Aberdeen Inst Med Scis, Foresterhill, Aberdeen AB25 2ZD, Scotland

BROWN, ANN LENORA, community and business development professional; b. Austin, Tex., Aug. 29, 1955; d. William Alley and Ann Dyke (Shafer) B.; 1 child, Dancy Ann Lukeman. BArch, U. Tex., 1983. Main St. project dir. City of Brenham, Tex., 1983-86; owner, cons. TEXANA Cmty. Cons., La Grange, Tex., 1980-91; dir. residential programs and arch. svcs. Galveston Hist. Found., 1988-91; realtor Barney Rapp, Inc. Realtors, Galveston, 1995-96; urban planner City of Galveston, 1996; exec. dir. Colorado City Econ. Devel. Orgn., Inc., 1998-2000; bus. cevel. and mktg. cons., La Grange, 2000—; cmty. devel. cons. hist. neighborhoods and comml. dists., 1991-98; faculty mem. Coll. Arch., U. Houston hist. preservation program, 1991-93. Archtl. illustrator calendar U. Tex. Med. br., Galveston, 1991. Chair Broadway Redevel. Com., Galveston, 1990-93; founder, exec. dir. Galveston Cmty. Devel. Corp., 1991-96; bd. dirs., pres. Galveston Housing Fin. Corp., 1992-97. Recipient Preservation award Tex. Hist. Commn., 1986. Mem. AIA (assoc., tri-chair urban design 1991, chair hist. resources 1990-93), Tex. Cmty. Devel. Assn. Tex. (steering com. Tex. Devel. Inst. 1991-92). Episcopalian. Avocations: antiques, needlework, photography.

BROWN, ANNE SHERWIN, speech pathologist, educator; b. Denver, Oct. 15, 1952; d. John Frederick and Barbara Toft Sherwin; m. Max Dennis Brown, June 15, 1985; childre: Jack Steven, Michael Patrick. BA, Adams State Coll., 1974, MA, 1975. Tchr. Aurora (Colo.) Pub. Schs., 1978—. Author: Adopt-A-Cop, 1994. Bd. mgrs. YMCA, Aurora, 1996-98. Pub. Svc. Co. grantee, Denver, 1996-97, 98-99. Mem. ASCD, Aurora Edn. Assn., Internat. Reading Assn. Avocations: reading, dancing, sewing, guitar, motorcycles. Home: 416 S Victor Way Aurora CO 80012-2447 Office: Aurora Pub Schs 395 S Troy St Aurora CO 80012-2472

BROWN, ARLENE PATRICIA THERESA See RENI

BROWN, ARNOLD, physical therapy consultant; b. N.Y.C., Apr. 8, 1930; s. Murray and Tessie Brown; m. Alice L. Kahn, July 31, 1955; 1 child, Alan. BS in Edn., Panzer Coll., 1951; cert. in phys. therapy, Columbia U., 1952; MA in Psychology, Ball State U., 1972. Lic. phys. therapist, Ind. Staff phys. therapist VA Hosp., East Orange, N.J., 1954-55; sr. phys. therapist Cerebral Palsy Clinic, Union City, N.J., 1955-56; chief phys. therapist Mobility, Inc., New Rochelle, N.Y., 1956-57, Inland Steel Co. Hosp., East Chicago, Ind., 1957-67, Ball Meml. Hosp., Muncie, Ind., 1967-84; dir. phys. therapy Profl. Med. Svc., Clay County, Ind., 1984-86, St. Anthony Hosp., Michigan City, Ind., 1986-93; ret., 1993, cons. physical therapy, 1993-96; cons. Lake County Assn. Retarded Children, Gary, Ind., 1963-67; insvc. instr. Ball Meml., St. Anthony Hosp., 1967-93; instr. Michigan City High Schs., Health Care Practicum, 1987-93; adj. clin. prof. phys. therapy Andrews U., Berrien Springs, Mich., 1987-93; clin. supr. student affiliations Ball State U., 1975-83, clin. instr. Ball State U., 1981-83; clin. supr. student affiliations Ind. U., 1975-83; mem. adv. bd. Vis. Nurse Assn., Muncie, 1972-78; tchr. health care practicum Michigan City H.S.'s, 1987-93. Author: Physiological and Psychological Considerations in Management of Stroke, 1976; author/instr.: Orientation to Physical Therapy, 1979, Body Mechanics, 1987(videotapes); contbr. to profl. jours. Bd. dirs. Nat. Multiple Sclerosis Soc., 1974-77, Easter Seal Soc., Muncie, 1976-78. With U.S. Army, 1952-54. Recipient Vocat. Dirs. award A.K. Smith Career Ctr., Michigan City, 1993. Mem. Am. Phys. Therapy Assn. (mgmt. sect.). Avocations: piano, walking, exercise, reading. Home: 2 Buckingham Ct Apt 2 Michigan City IN 46360-1588

BROWN, ARNOLD, management consultant; b. Boston, Aug. 18, 1927; s. Frank and Frances B.; children: Pamela, Cynthia, Derek. BA with honors, UCLA, 1950. Asst. dir. sales promotion Mut. Benefit Life Ins. Co., Newark, 1957-61; v.p. Inst. Life Ins., N.Y.C., 1961-77; chmn. Weiner, Edrich, Brown, Inc., N.Y.C., 1977—; guest lectr. Harvard Bus. Sch., Duke U., Wharton Sch. Co-author: Supermanaging, 1984, Office Biology, 1993, Insider's Guide to the Future, 1997; mem. editl. bd. MacMillan Encyclopedia of the Future, On the Horizon mag.; contbr. articles to profl. jours. Served with USN, 1944-46. Office: 200 E 33rd St New York NY 10016-4874

BROWN, AUSTIN DUNCAN, research scientist, writer; b. Wellington, New Zealand, May 8, 1925; arrived in Australia, 1928; s. Herbert Duncan and Ruby Evelyn (Dalton) B.; m. Joan Linley Clark, June 10, 1950; children: Diana, Janet. BSc, U. Sydney, Australia, 1946, MSc, 1952; PhD, U. Manchester, Eng., 1958. Rsch. chemist Australian Paper Mfrs., Melbourne, 1947-49; rsch. officer, sr. rsch. officer Commonwealth Sci. and Indsl. Rsch. Orgn., Brisbane, Australia, 1950-56; sr. rsch. scientist divsn. fisheries and oceanography Commonwealth Sci. and Indsl. Rsch. Orgn., Cronulla, 1958-60; ICI fellow U. Manchester, 1957, 58; sr. lectr., assoc. prof. microbiology U. N.S.W., Australia, 1961-74; Found. prof. biology U. Wollongong, Australia, 1974-85; vis. fellow Australian Nat. U., 1992, visitor, 1993—; vis. prof. U. Calif., San Francisco, 1968, U. Cambridge, Eng., 1973, Yale U., New Haven, Conn., 1977, Norwegian Inst. Tech., Trondheim, 1983, U. Tübingen, Germany, 1985; speaker in field. Author: Microbial Water Stress Physiology, 1990; contbr. articles, revs. to profl. jours. Active Social Responsibility in Sci., Sydney, 1969-74, Scientist Against Nuclear Arms, Sydney, 1980-94. Fulbright fellow, 1968, 77; Wellcome Found. grantee, 1973, U.S. Dept. Agr. and Dept. Energy, 1979, Norwegian Fisheries Rsch. Coun., 1983, German Acad. Exch. Svc., 1985. Mem. AAAS, Greenpeace, Australian Conservation Found. Avocations: music, kayaking, bushwalking, cross country skiing, cycling. Home: PO Box 17, Tuross Head NSW 2537, Australia

BROWN, BARRY JOHN, lawyer; b. Wanganui, New Zealand, Oct. 2, 1950; s. Graeme Dudley and Nola (Brighton) B.; m. Janis Margaret Saunders; children: Amy, Julia, Hamish. LLB with honors, Victoria U. of Wellington, New Zealand, 1973. Bar: N.Y. Solicitor Chapman Tripp, Wellington, 1972-75, 78-79, ptnr., 1980—, mng. ptnr., 1992-93, mem. nat. bd., 1991-94, 98—; solicitor J.B. McAlwey & Co., Perth, Australia, 1975, Bragy & Waller, London, 1976-77. Trustee Wellington Girl's Coll., 1995—. Mem. Wellington Dist. Law soc. Presbyterian. Avocations: skiing, golf, tennis, family. Office: Chapman Tripp, AMP Ctr Grey St, 6000 Wellington New Zealand

BROWN, BETTY MARIE, government agency administrator; b. Siler City, N.C., June 11, 1952; d. Ardentries and Emma (Peoples) Mason; m. Tommy E. Brown, Aug. 8, 1968 (dec.); 1 child, Christopher T.; m. Roger L. Cook, June 10, 1973 (dec. Feb. 1981); 1 child, Felicia M. AAS, Phila. Community Coll., 1981; BS, Drexel U., 1986. Cert. early childhood edn. tchr., elem. edn. tchr., Pa. Mgr. Mr. Gourmet Deli, Phila., 1977-80; pres. Parents, Friends and Vols. Community Svc. Orgn., Phila., 1983—; tchr. Phila. Sch. Dist., 1988-89; remittance perfection clk. IRS, Phila., 1990-92; account analyst IRS-Automated Collection Sys., Phila., 1992—; with Censur Bur./Dept. Commerce, 1980; tchr. Mid City YWCA, Phila., 1983-88. Sec. support community outreach project Dept. Human Svcs., Phila., 1990-91. Recipient Community Svc. award Dept. Human Svc., 1988. Baptist. Avocations: reading, swimming, dancing, flying, tennis. Home and Office: Parents of the 39th Dist 1132 Easton Rd Apt B Philadelphia PA 19150-2708

BROWN, BRUCE ANDREW, lawyer; b. Cleve., Oct. 16, 1959; s. Andrew and Ruby Louise (Bishop) B. BA, Brown U., 1981; JD, Columbia U., 1984. Bar: N.Y. 1985, Ohio 1990. Assoc. Proskaver Rose Goetz and Mendelsohn, N.Y.C., 1983-86, Finley, Kumble Wagner Heine Vnderberg Manley Myerson & Casey, N.Y.C., 1986-87; pvt. practice B. Andrew Brown & Assocs., Cleve., 1987—. Mem. NAACP, Urban League (bd. dirs. 1988—), Omega Psi Phi. Democrat. Muslim. Avocation: golf. Office: B Andrew Brown & Assocs 1300 Bank One Ctr 600 Superior Ave E Cleveland OH 44114-2611

BROWN, CHARLES ALEXANDER, retired ophthalmic surgeon; b. Aberdeen, Scotland, July 10, 1915; s. John and Charlotte Jane (Thomson) B.; m. Vera Mary Dingley, Aug. 26, 1943; children: Alison, Rosemary, David, Peter, Angela, Andrew. MA, Aberdeen U., 1935, MB ChB, 1939, MD, 1946. Registrar in ophthalmology Royal Eye Hosp., London, 1946-49, Moorfield's Eye Hosp., London, 1947-49, King's Coll. Hosp., London, 1947-49; cons. ophthalmic surgeon Bristol Eye Hosp., Eng., 1950-80; surgeon Southmead Hosp., Bristol, 1950-80; ret., 1980; coun. mem., Oxford Ophthalmol. Congress, 1964-83, master, 1981-82; coun. mem., Faculty Ophthalmologists, London, 1971-80. Co-author: Congenital Abnormalities in Infancy, 1963, 2d edit., 1971; contbr. papers to profl. publs. Deacon, Westbury Bapt. Ch., Bristol. Maj., ophthalmic specialist Royal Army M.C., 1941-46, ETO, CBI. Fellow Royal Soc. Medicine (London), Royal Coll. Surgeons (Eng.); mem. Ophthol. Soc. U.K., Oxford Ophthal. Congress. Avocations: golf, gardening. Home: Combe House, Winter's Lane, Redhill Bristol BS 405SH, England

BROWN, CHARLES SAMUEL, singer, composer, educator; b. Marianna, Ark., Sept. 26, 1940; s. Carey Brown and Narcisse (Angel) Richards. Student, Morehouse Coll., 1963-66; MusB, U. Mich., 1974, MusM, 1975, postgrad., 1975-77. Asst. prof. music Lincoln U. Mo., Jefferson City, 1977-80; adj. prof. music Borough of Manhattan C.C., N.Y.C., 1980-81, 95-99; tchr. music N.Y.C. Bd. Edn., 1986—; artist, mem. faculty Berkshire Choral Inst., Sheffield, Mass., 1983-85; mus. dir. The Open Eye Inst., N.Y.C., 1991-92; mem. adv. coun. sch. concert series N.Y. Chamber Symphony, 1991-93. Composer: The Barrier, 1974, A Song Without Words, 1977, Calvary, 1972, 5 Spiritual Settings for Chorus, 1991; back-up vocalist Ray Charles, 1988, Cab Calloway, 1988; an arranger for Kathleen Battle and Jessye Norman Spirituals Concert, Carnegie Hall, N.Y.C., 1990. Bd. dirs. Melodious Accord. With U.S. Army, 1966-69, Vietnam. Mem. Nat. Assn. Tchrs. Singing, Music Educators Nat. Conf., Am. Guild Mus. Artists, Am. Choral Dirs. Assn., Music Educators Assn. N.Y.C., Pi Kappa Lambda. Avocations: cooking, photography, reading.

BROWN, CLIFFORD BRYANT, financial consultant; b. Trenton, N.J., Dec. 7, 1970; s. Clifford and Dorothy Mae Brown; 1 child, Bryanna D. AA, So. Calif. Internat. Coll., 1995. Fin. cons. Ind. Capital Mgmt., Huntington Beach, Calif., 1994-95; fin. advisor Prudential, N.Y.C., 1996-98, Manhattan Planning Group, N.Y.C., 1998—. Vol., Hale Ho., N.Y.C. Sgt., USMC, 1989-95; mem. USMCR. Fellow Nat. Assn. Life Underwriters; mem. Harlem C. of C. Baptist. Avocations: travel, golf, basketball. Office: Manhattan Planning Group 60 E 42nd St Fl D49 New York NY 10165-0006

BROWN, DALE SUSAN, government administrator, educational program director, writer; b. N.Y.C., May 2, 1954; d. Bertram S. and Beatrice Joy (Gilman) B. BA, Antioch Coll., 1976. Rsch. asst. Am. Occupational Therapy Assn., Rockville, Md., 1976-79; writer Pres.' Com. on Employment of People with Disabilities, Washington, 1979-82, program mgr., 1982—; program mgr. labor com. Pres.' Com. on Employment of People with Disabilities, 1985, 96-98, program mgr. work environment and tech. com., 1988-94, program mgr. com. on libr. and info. svcs., 1984-86, youth devel com., 1986-88, new products devel. team, 1987-90, agy. rep., 1991-93, with interagy. tech. assistance coordinating team, 1992-94; program mgr. Job Accomodation Network, 1997-99; mgr. Nat. Conf. of Youth with Disabilities, 2000—; cons. in field, gen. assembly speaker nat. conv. Gen. Fedn. Women's Clubs, 1981, mem. Rehab Svcs. Adminstrn. Task Force on Learning Disabilities, 1981-83; mgr. Nat. Conf. of Youth with Disabilities, 2000. Author: Steps to Independence for People with Learning Disabilities, 1980, Pathways to Employment for People with Learning Disabilities, 1991, Working Effectively with People Who Have Learning Disabilities and Attention Deficit Hyperactivity Disorder, 1995, I Know I can Climb the Mountain, 1995, Learning Disabilities and Employment, 1997, Learning A Living Guide to Planning Your Career and Finding A Job for People with Learning Disabilities, Attention Deficit Disorder and Dyslexia, 2000; writer film: They Could Have Saved Their Homes, 1982; dir. videotape Part of the Team People with Disabilities in the Workforce, 1990; editorial bd. Perceptions, 1981-83, Learning Disabilities Focus, 1988-90, In the Mainstream, 1994-98; co-editor Learning Disabilities and Employment; cons. editor Learning Disabilities Rsch. and Practice, 1990—. Pres. Assn. Learning Disabled Adults, Washington, 1979-80, bd. dirs. Closer Look Nat. Info. Ctr., Washington, 1980-83, Am. Coalition fo Citizens with Disabilities, 1985-86, chair 5th ann. conf. on Info. Tech. for User With Disabilities, 1989, spl. asst. for people with disabilities Federally Employed Women, 1991-92, mem. congrl. task force Rights and Empowerment of Ams. with Disabilities, 1988-90, mem. blue ribbon panel on Nat. Telecommunications Access for People with Disabilities, 1989-94, profl. adv. bd. Nat. Attention Deficit Disorder Assn., 1996—; del. Nat. Writer's Union, 1999; rep. com. on fed. govt. as model employer Presdl. Task Force on Employment of Adults with Disabilities, 1999—, rep. com. on youth with disabilities, 1999; bd. mem. The Coun. on Quality and Leadership, 2000. Grantee Found. for Children with Learning Disabilities, 1982; recipient Margaret Byrd Rawson award, 1989, Personal Achievement award Women's Program USDOL, 1989, Individual Achievement award Nat. Coun. on Communication Disorders, 1991, Spl. Acievement award Pres.'s Com. on Employment of People with Disabilities, 1991, Gold Screen award Nat. Assn. Gov. Communicators, 1991, Arthur S. Fleming award, 1992, 94; named One of Ten Outstanding Young Ams. U.S. Jr. C. of C., 1984, Jaycees, 1994. Mem. Nat. Network of Learning Disabled Adults (founder, pres., 1980-81, rep. Inter-agy. com. on computer support handicapped emploees 1998—), Nat. Assn. Govt. Communicators (Blue Pencil award 1986, rep. inter-agy. com. on handicapped employees 1989—), Learning Disabilities Assn. (bd. dirs. 1986-91), ALA. Democrat. Jewish. Office: Pres Com Employment of People with Disabilities 1331 F St NW Washington DC 20004-1107

BROWN, DAVID, motion picture producer, writer; b. N.Y.C., July 28, 1916; s. Edward Fisher and Lillian (Baren) B.; m. Liberty LeGacy, Apr. 15, 1940 (div. 1951); 1 son, Bruce LeGacy; m. Wayne Clark, May 25, 1951 (div. 1957); m. Helen Gurley, Sept. 25, 1959. AB, Stanford U., 1936; MS, Columbia U., 1937. Apprentice San Francisco News and Wall St. Jour., 1936; night editor, asst. drama critic Fairchild Publs., 1937-39; editorial dir. Milk Research Council, 1939-40; assoc. editor Street & Smith Publs., 1940-43; assoc. editor, exec. editor, editor-in-chief Liberty mag., 1943-49; editorial dir. Nat. Edn. Campaign, A.M.A., 1949; assoc. editor, mng. editor Cosmopolitan mag., 1949-52; mng. editor, story editor, head scenario dept. 20th Century-Fox Film Corp. Studios, Beverly Hills, Calif., 1952-56, mem. studio exec. com., 1956-60, producer, 1960-62; v.p., dir. story operation 20th Century Fox Film Corp., Beverly Hills, Calif., 1964-69, exec. v.p. creative operations, 1969-70, dir., 1968-70; exec. v.p. creative operations, dir. Warner Bros., 1971-72; ptnr. Zanuck/Brown Co., N.Y.C., 1972-87; pres. Manhattan Project Ltd., 1987—, Island World, 1990-92; exec. story editor, head scenario dept., editorial v.p. New Am. Library World Lit., Inc., 1963-64; final judge for best short story pub. in mags. Benjamin Franklin Mag. ann. awards, 1955-58. Author: Brown's Guide to Growing Gray, 1987, Let Me Entertain You, 1990, The Rest of your Life is the Best of Your Life, 1991; contbr. articles to Am. mag., Collier's, Harpers, Sat. Evening Post, Reader's Digest, others; editor: I Can Tell It Now, 1964, How I Got That Story, 1967; contbr.: Journalists in Action, 1963; prodr.: (films) The Sting, 1973, The Sugarland Express, 1974, The Eiger Sanction, 1975, Jaws, 1977, MacArthur, 1977, Jaws II, 1978, The Island, 1980, Neighbors, 1981, The Verdict, 1982, Target, 1985, Cocoon, 1985; exec. prodr. Driving Miss Daisy, HBO Women and Men, 1 and 2, 1990, 91, The Player, 1992, A Few Good Men, 1992, Watch It, 1993, The Cemetery Club, 1993, Canadian Bacon, 1994, Kiss The Girls, 1997, The Saint, 1997, Deep Impact, 1998, Angela's Ashes, 1999, Chocolat, 2000. Trustee com. on film Mus. Modern Art, N.Y.C. Served as 1st lt., M.I. AUS, World War II. Mem. Acad. Motion Picture Arts and Scis. (recipient Irving G. Thalberg Meml. award 1991), Producers Guild Am. (David O. Selznick Lifetime Achievement award 1993), Nat. Press Club (Washington), Coffee Ho. Club (N.Y.C.), Bd. of Visitors Columbia U. Grad Sch. of Journalism, Players Club (N.Y.C.), Dutch Treat (N.Y.C.), Century Assn. (N.Y.C.), N.Y. Friars Club. Office: Manhattan Project Ltd 1775 Broadway Ste 410 New York NY 10019-1903

BROWN, DAVID RICHARD, school system administrator, minister; b. Manhattan, Kans., Oct. 22, 1929; s. Marion Arthur and Dorothy (Bailey) B.; m. Jeannette Christine Phoenix, July 28, 1962; children: David M., Mark, Thomas. BA, U. So. Calif., 1951; MDiv, U. Chgo., 1955; postgrad., U. So. Calif., 1956, 57. Ordained minister, Presbyn. Ch. Assoc. pastor Federated Community Ch., Flagstaff, Ariz., 1957-59; minister of edn. Lakeside Presbyn. Ch., San Francisco, 1959-62; pastor of edn. 1st Presbyn. Ch., Medford, Oreg., 1962-69; pastor 1st Presbyn. Ch., Newark, Calif., 1969-75; founder, pastor Community Presbyn. Ch., Union City, Calif., 1975-89; founder, supt. Christian Heritage Acad., Fremont, Calif., 1984—; organizing pastor New Life Presbyn. Ch., Fremont, 1989—; asst. prof. Chabot Coll., Hayward, Calif., 1975-80; moderator Presbytery of No. Ariz., 1959. Dir. various Shakespearian theatrical prodns., 1982-84 (Thesbian award 1984). Pres. Boys Christian League, L.A., 1953-54, Coconino Assn. for Mental Health, Flagstaff, 1958-59; chaplain Mozumdar YMCA Camp, Crestline, Calif., 1952-56; chmn. Tri-City Citizens Action Com., 1986-90. Recipient plaque KC, 1989. Mem. Rotary (chpt. pres. 1988-89, Paul Harris fellow 1989). Avocations: skiing, stamps, choir, drama. Office: Christian Heritage Acad PO Box 7688 Fremont CA 94537-7688

BROWN, DEBORAH ELIZABETH, television producer; b. Aledo, Ill., Nov. 29, 1952; d. Kenneth M. and Mary Esther (Gilmore) B.; m. K. J. Lester, Nov. 28, 1975 (dec. Mar. 1982); children: Rebekah Jean, Aaron Mark, Jonathan Caleb. Student, Letourneau Coll., 1970; BA in Theater Arts, Sterling Coll., 1974; MA in Comm., Wheaton Coll., 1977. Producer, dir. Sta. WCFC-TV, Chgo., 1978-80; sales mgr. SNG Enterprises, St. Charles, Ill., 1980-82; pres., CEO Circle Family Video Stores, Niles, Mich., 1982-87; exec. producer Picture Radio Pictures, Naples, Italy, 1987-93, 98-2000; mgr. Computer Keyboard, Portland, Oreg., 1993-96, Michelle's Piano and Organ Co., Portland, 1996-98; exec. prodr. TV Napoli, Naples, 2000—; vis. prof. comm. Wheaton (Ill.) Coll., 1980; video cons. Spring Arbor Distbrs., Belleville, Mich., 1985, Gospel Films, Muskegan, Mich., 1985. Producer, dir., writer (TV program and book) Crafts With Emilie, 1979 (Spl. Emmy nomination); video contbg. editor Christian Booksellers Assn. jour., 1984-85; set decorator Cindy Williams Comedy Spl., 1993. Corp. sponsor Pregnancy Care Ctr., Niles, 1985-87; producer Four Flags Area Apple Festival, Niles, 1987. Mem. ISGI Internat. (dir. 1998—), Fellowship of Christians in Arts, Media and Entertainment, Christian Video Retailers Assn. (exec. dir. 1985-87). Baptist. Fax: 503-408-1829. Office: TV Napoli, Via R Raone 36, 80026 Casoria NA, Italy

BROWN, DENISE SCOTT, architect, urban planner; b. Nkana, Zambia, Oct. 3, 1931; came to U.S., 1958; d. Simon and Phyllis (Hepker) Lakofski; m. Robert Scott Brown, July 21, 1955 (dec. 1959); m. Robert Charles Venturi, July 23, 1967; 1 child, James C. Student, U. Witwatersrand, South Africa, 1948-51; diploma, Archtl. Assn., London, 1955; M of City Planning, U. Pa., 1960, MArch, 1965, DFA (hon.), 1994; DFA (hon.), Oberlin Coll., 1977, Phila. Coll. Art, 1985, Parsons Sch. Design, 1985; LHD (hon.), N.J. Inst. Tech., 1984, Phila. Coll. Textiles and Sci., 1992; DEng (hon.), Tech. U. N.S., 1991; HHD (hon.), Pratt Inst., 1992; DFA (hon.), U. Pa., 1994; LittD (hon.), U. Nev., 1998; D. Arch.(hon.), U. Miami, 1997. Registered architect, U.K. Asst. prof. U. Pa., Phila., 1960-65; assoc. prof., head urban design program UCLA, 1965-68; with Venturi, Rauch and Scott Brown, Phila., 1967—, ptnr., 1969-89; prin. Venturi, Scott Brown and Assocs. Inc., Phila., 1989—; vis. prof. arch. U. Calif., Berkeley, 1965, Yale U., 1967-70; asst. prof. U. Pa., 1960-65, vis. prof. Sch. Fine Arts, 1982, 83; Eliot Noyes design critic in arch. Harvard U., Cambridge, Mass., 1989-90; mem. visitors com. MIT, 1973-83; mem. adv. com. dept. arch. Temple U., 1980—; cons. to dean search com. Sch. Arch., Washington U., St. Louis, 1992; mem. adv. bd. dept. arch. Carnegie Mellon U., 1992-96; mem. jury Prince of Wales Prize in Urban Design, Grad. Sch. Design Harvard U., Cambridge, 1993; mem. bd. overssers U. Librs. U. Pa., 1995—. Author: Urban Concepts, 1990; co-author: Learning from Las Vegas, 1972, rev. edit., 1977, A View from the Campidoglio: Selected Essays, 1953-84, 85, On Houses and Housing, 1992; contbr. numerous articles to profl. jours.; prin. works include: campus plans U. Mich., Dartmouth Coll., U. Pa., city plans Miami Beach, Memphis, plans for Civic Ctr. Cultural Complex, Denver, Nat. Gallery, London, Hotel du Department de la Haute Garonne, Toulouse, France, Life Scis. Inst., U. Mich. Mem. curriculum com. Phila. Jewish Children's Folkshul, 1980-86; policy panelist design arts program NEA, 1981-83; mem. bd. advisors Architects, Designers and Planners for Social Responsibility, 1982—; mem. capitol preservation com. Commonwealth of Pa., Harrisburg, 1983-87; bd. dirs. Ctrl. Phila. Devel. Corp., 1985—, Urban Affairs Partnership, Phila., 1987-91; trustee Chestnut Hill Acad., Phila., 1985-89. Decorated commendatore Order of Merit (Italy); recipient numerous awards, citations, commendations for designs and urban planning, including Chgo. Architecture award, 1987, U.S. Presdl. award nat. medal of Arts, 1992, Hall of Fame award Interior Design mag., 1992, (with Robert Venturi) The Phila. award, 1993, The Benjamin Franklin medal Royal Soc. for Encouragement of Arts, Mfg. and Commerce, 1993, Am. Coll. Schs. of Architecture/AIA Topaz medallion, 1996, Giants of Design award House Beautiful Mag., 2000, Chevalier del'Ordre des Arts et des Lettres, France, 2000. Mem. Royal Inst. Brit. Archs., Am. Acad. Arts and Scis., Archs. Designers and Planners for Social Responsibility, Am. Planning Assn, Archtl. Assn. London, Internat. Women's Forum, Soc. Coll. and U. Planning, Soc. Archtl. Historians (bd. dirs. 1981-84), Carpenters Co. of City and County of Phila., Athenaeum of Phila., Royal Soc. Encouragement of Arts, Mfr. and Commerce. Democrat. Jewish. Office: Venturi Scott Brown & Assocs Inc 4236 Main St Philadelphia PA 19127-1603

BROWN, DENNIS GEOFFREY, psychoanalyst, psychotherapist, consultant; b. Leeds, England, Sept. 27, 1928; s. Myer and Eva (Myers) B.; m. Dorothy Rose Bookman, June 5, 1965; 1 child, Matthew. MB ChB, Leeds

U., England, 1951, DPM, 1959, MD, 1970. Lectr. psychiatry Leeds U., England, 1961-63; med. asst. Cassel Hosp., Richmond, England, 1966-69; cons. psychotherapist St. Georges Hosp., London, 1969-74, St. Mary's Hosp., London, 1974—; external examiner psychotherapy course Leeds U., 1984—; tng. group analyst Inst. Group Analysis, London, 1977—. Co-author: (with J. Pedder) Introduction to Psychotherapy, 1979, 2d edit., 1991, 3d edit., 2000, (with L. Zinkin) The Psyche and the Social World; contbr. articles to profl. jours., chpts. to books. Flight lt. RAF, 1952-54. Rsch. fellow Middlesex Hosp. Med. Sch., London, 1963-66; Fulbright Travel grantee Cornell U., 1955. Fellow Royal Soc. Medicine, Royal Coll. Physicians Edinburgh, Royal Coll. Psychiatrists; mem. Group-Analytic Soc. (London) (pres. 1983-88), Brit. Psychoanalytical Soc. (assoc.), Inst. Group Analysis. Labour. Jewish. Avocations: gardening, hill walking. Home: 19 Dunstan Rd, London England NW11 8AG Office: Group-Analytic Practice, 88 Montagu Mansions, London England W1H 1LF

BROWN, DEREK JOHN FINLAY, plant nematologist; b. Nairn, Highland, Scotland, May 18, 1950; m. June Thompson, May 2, 1970; children: Derek W.I., Richard A. BA, Open U., 1977, PhD, 1983, DSc, 1999. Asst. sci. officer Scottish Crop Rsch. Inst., Dundee, Scotland, 1970-75, sci. officer, 1975-80, higher sci. officer, 1980-85, sr. sci. officer, 1985-91, prin. rsch. leader, 1991—; vis. prof. Zhejiang Agrl. U., Hangzhou, 1998—. Chief editor Russian Jour. of Nematology, 1993—; editor Nematologia Mediterranea, 1989—, Nematode Morphology and Systematics, Helminthologia, 1998—; co-author: Nematode Vectors of Plant Viruses, 1997, An Introduction to Nematatodes: General Nematology, 2000. Chmn. Letham and Dist. Cmty. Coun., 1995—. Recipient Disting. Svc. award European Soc. of Nematologists, Skryabin 100th Anniversary medal Russian Acad. of Scis., 1996. Fellow Russian Soc. Nematologists, Am. Soc. Nematologists, Inst. of Biology (chartered biologist). Avocations: opera, ballet, music, travel. Office: Scottish Crop Rsch Inst, Invergowrie, Dundee DD2 5DA, Scotland

BROWN, DORIS JANE, nursing aide; b. Mo., Dec. 6, 1934; d. Lowell Emmitt and Lottie Nancy (Downing) Heinrich; m. Thomas B. Brown, Aug. 12, 1958 (div. 1967); 1 child, Doris Ann. AA, Penn Valley Met. C.C., 1982. Accredited nurse aide, Mo. Clk. Western Auto, Kansas City, Mo., 1952-55; acctg. sec. Allied Signal, Kansas City, 1955-58; various positions K.C. Paper Box Co., Kansas City, 1958-61; various positions Winn-Senter Constrn. Co., Kansas City, 1961-90, exec. sec., 1990-92; adminstrv. asst. Miller & Assocs., Lee's Summit, Mo., 1992-93; cert. nurse aide Nat. Health Care, West Plains, Mo., 1994—. Vol. Vista, Kansas City, Mo., 1961. Mem. nat. health care coms. Avocations: volunteer facilitator Project Literacy, sports. Home: 11106 State Route J West Plains MO 65775-5851 Office: 211 Davis Dr West Plains MO 65775-2242

BROWN, E. MERRITT, engineering technician; b. Petoskey, Mich., June 15, 1946; s. Edwin Merritt and Joy (Valentine) B.; m. Mary Elizabeth Brown, Aug. 16, 1975. AS, North Ctrl. Mich. Coll., 1966; BS, Mich. Tech. U., 1978. Sales mgr. Lee's Sports Inc., Kalamazoo, Mich., 1968-71; labor Cushmans Contrn. Inc., Otsego, Mich., 1971-76; pntr./owner Waterfront Specialties, Otsego, 1977-95; instr. Gove Assoc.,Inc., Kalamazoo, 1978-81; engrng. asst. City of Three Rivers, Mich., 1981—; owner Shadetree Enterprise, Schoolcraft, Mich., 1986-95, Wildwood Landscape, Schoolcraft, Mich., 1995-97. Mem. Am. Pub. Works Assn., Mich. Forestry & Parks Assn., Little Traverse Conservancy. Republican. Methodist. Avocations: white water canoeing, cross country skiing, reading, birding, rock collecting. Office: City of Three Rivers 1015 S Lincoln Ave Three Rivers MI 49093-1999

BROWN, EDGAR CARY, retired economics educator; b. Bakersfield, Calif., Apr. 14, 1916; s. Verne Brainard and Ruth (Cary) B.; m. Tomlin Edwards, May 28, 1937 (div.); children: Rebecca, Gretchen; m. Margaret Durham, June 6, 1969 (div.); children: Elizabeth, Robert. B.S., U. Calif., Berkeley, 1937; Ph.D., Harvard U., 1948. Teaching fellow U. Calif. at Berkeley, 1937-39; economist U.S. WPB, 1940-41; teaching fellow Harvard U., 1941-42; economist U.S. Treasury Dept., 1942-47; prof. econs. MIT, Cambridge, 1947-86; head dept. MIT, 1965-83, 84-85, assoc. dean, head fgn. langs. and lits., 1985-86, prof. emeritus, 1986—; vis. prof. econs. Yale U., 1953-54, U. Chgo., 1963-64; cons. various govt. agys., Brookings Instn., N.Y. State Regents Commn. on Higher Edn., 1992-93. Author: Financing Defense, 1951, Depreciation Adjustments for Price Changes, 1952, Studies in Economic Stabilization, 1967, Paul Samuelson and Modern Economic Theory, 1983; acting editor: Nat. Tax Jour, 1958-59; asso. editor: Jour. Pub. Econs, 1972-81. Guggenheim fellow, 1957; Ford Found. Faculty Research fellow, 1956-57. Mem. Nat. Tax Assn., Am. Econ. Assn., Am. Acad. Arts and Scis., Phi Beta Kappa, Beta Gamma Sigma. Home: 39 Cranberry Ln Concord MA 01742-3930 Office: MIT Dept Econs Cambridge MA 02139

BROWN, EDWARD JAMES, SR., utility executive; b. Ft. Wayne, Ind., Sept. 30, 1937; s. William Theodore and Jane Elizabeth (Dix) B.; m. Margaret Bessey, June 17, 1989; children: Edward James Jr., Elena Emily. BA, Yale U., 1959; MA, Fordham U., 1962. Chartered fin. analyst. Fin. writer E.F. Hutton & Co., N.Y.C., 1970-71; economist N.Y. Power Authority, N.Y.C., 1971-74, prin. economist, 1974-80, mgr., customer svcs., 1980-83, mgr. spl. projects, 1983-86, dir. strategic planning, 1986-93, dir. new bus., 1993-94; mem. mgmt. com. Iroquois Gas Transmission System, 1989-94. Pres. Park Ave. Meth. Trust, N.Y.C., 1981—; pres. Friends of the Shakers, Inc., Sabathday Lake, Maine, 1982-84, dir., 1980—, treas., 1995—; trustee United Soc. of Shakers, Sabathday Lake, 1982-84, 95—, John St. Meth. Episcopal Trust Soc., N.Y.C., 1982—; bd. dirs. Meth. Ch. Home for Aged, Riverdale, N.Y., 1995—, mem. investment com., 1983—, co-chmn., 1994—, treas., 1996—; pres. Meth. Ch. Home Fund, 1996-99; bd. dirs., treas. John Wesley Towers, 1999—; bd. dirs. Yorkville Emergency Alliance, N.Y.C., 1982-88; internat. adv. coun. Mus. of Am. Folk Art, N.Y.C., 1988—; dir., chmn. investment com. United Meth. City Soc., N.Y.C., 1999—. Mem. N.Y. Soc. Security Analysts, Assn. Investment Mgmt. and Rsch. Home: 500 E 85th St New York NY 10028-7405

BROWN, EDWARD MAURICE, retired lawyer, business executive; b. Watertown, N.Y., Aug. 22, 1909; s. Ernest E. and Eunice (Lewis) B.; m. Anne Amos, Oct. 2, 1937; children—Edward Dustin, Ernest Amos. AB magna cum laude, Miami U., 1931, LLD, 1972; JD, Harvard U., 1934. Bar: Ohio 1934, N.Y. 1948, U.S. Supreme Ct. 1941. Assoc. Nichols, Wood, Marx & Ginter, 1934-47; asst. to pres. McCall Corp., N.Y.C., 1947-49, v.p., asst. sec., 1949-51, v.p., sec., dir., 1951-57; treas. Sperry Gyroscope Co. div. Sperry Rand Corp., 1958-59, v.p., treas., 1959-60, v.p., adminstr., 1960-65; v.p. Sperry Group, 1965-68; asst. treas. Sperry Rand Corp., 1958-68; group exec. of Teledyne, Inc., 1968-80; chmn. bd. Teledyne Can. Ltd., 1971-81. Trustee Village of Pelham Manor, N.Y., 1961-65, village mayor, 1965-67; mem. bd. govs. Nat. Ctr. for Disability Svcs., 1965-93. Lt. comdr. USNR, 1942-45. Decorated Bronze Star with Combat "V" award for svc. Mem. ABA, Phi Beta Kappa, Phi Eta Sigma, Phi Sigma, Beta Theta Pi. Republican. Episcopalian. Home: 165 Shadowy Hills Dr Oxford OH 45056-1440

BROWN, ELIZABETH ELEANOR, retired librarian; b. Charlotte, Mich., Aug. 29, 1921; d. Delbert Francis and Katherine Eleanor (Griffith) B. AB, Albion Coll., 1943; MLS, Pratt Inst., 1953. Info. specialist Enjay Co., N.Y.C., 1943-50; reports indexer Bakelite Co., Bound Brook, N.J., 1950-52; reference libr. IBM, Poughkeepsie, N.Y., 1953-69, Yorktown Heights, N.Y., 1953-69; info. retrieval specialist, libr. IBM, White Plains, N.Y., 1969-82; ret. IBM, White Plains, 1982. Vol. Nat. Archives Rocky Mountain Region, 1986—; mem. del. spl. librs. to Russia and Czech Republic Citizen Amb. program People to People Internat., 1995. Mem. ALA, DAR, Am. Chem. Soc., Spl. Librs. Assn. (chmn. tech. sci. group N.Y.C. chpt. 1970-71, sec.-treas. engring. divsn. 1968-70, archivist 1970-72, charter mem., past pres. Hudson Valley chpt.), Soc. Mayflower Descendants, Pilgrim John Howland Soc., New Eng. Historic Geneal. Soc., Colo. Geneal. Soc., Colo. Mayflower Soc. (historian 1996-2000), Gwynedd Family History Soc., Columbine Geneal. and Hist. Soc., Welsh-Am. Geneal. Soc., Internat. Soc. Brit. Genealogy and Family History, Colo. Welsh Soc., Wales, Ireland, Scotland and Eng. Family Hist. Soc., Grand Traverse Area Geneal. Soc., Kalamazoo Valley Geneal. Soc., Phi Beta Kappa, Alpha Lambda Delta, Mortar Board, Delta Zeta.

BROWN, ELIZABETH RUTH, neonatologist; b. Washington, Sept. 29, 1946; d. Paul Ambrose and Helene Marie (Kiley) B.; m. William James Pyne, Sept. 28, 1980. BS, Coll. Mt. St. Vincent, Bronx, N.Y., 1968; MD, U. Md., 1972. Diplomate Am. Bd. Med. Examiners, Am. Bd. Pediatrics, sub-board neonatal-perinatal medicine; lic. physician, Mass. Intern McGill U., Montreal (Que., Can.) Children's Hosp., 1972-73, resident in pediat., 1973-75; neonatal rsch. fellow dept. pediat. Harvard Med. Sch. Joint Program in Neonatology, Boston, 1975-78; dir. infant follow-up program, med. dir. project welcome The Children's Hosp., Boston, 1979-85; dir. neonatology Newton (Mass.) Wellesley Hosp., 1984-85; dir. neonatal follow up clinic Boston City Hosp., 1985-88; co-dir. Boston Perinatal Ctr., 1985—; dir. neonatology Boston Med. Ctr. (formerly Boston City Hosp.), 1985—; clin. instr. pediat. Tufts U. Sch. Medicine, Boston, 1987—; summer fellow tng. program in pub. health N.Y.C. Dept. Pub. Health, Met. Hosp., 1969; mem. Kellogg Found. Nat. Fellowship Program, Battle Creek, Mich., 1988-91; assoc. prof. pediat. Boston U. Sch. Medicine, 1987—, assoc. prof. ob-gyn., 1985—; instr. pediat. Harvard Med. Sch., 1979-85, tutor in medicine, 1980-82; lectr. Coll. Pharmacy and Allied Health Professions, Northeastern U., Boston, 1981—; assoc. neonatologist Joint Program in Neonatology, 1979-85; med. dir. Boston Dept. Public Health, 1991-96. Contbr. articles to profl. jours., chpts. to books. Bd. dirs. Boston Inst. for Devel. of Infants and Parents, Inc., 1983-96, NICU Parent Support, Inc., 1980-95; pres. bd. dirs. Coalition Adiction, Pregnancy & Parenting; adv. bd. Children's Hosp. AIDS Program, 1988; bd. dirs. March of Dimes, Mass. chpt., 1989, Coalition on Addiction, Pregnancy and Parenting, 1990. Named Citizen of Yr. Mass. Assn. Retarded Citizens, 1984; recipient Excellence award Boston Inst. for Devel. Infants and Parents, Inc., 1988, Disting. Alumna award Coll. Mt. St. Vincent, 1995. Mem. AMA, Am. Acad. Pediatrics, Mass. Perinatal Assn., Mass. Med. Soc., Aircraft Owners and Pilots Assn. Achievements include research in perinatal effects of maternal substance abuse, perinatal transmission of HIV, early childhood growth and development, prevention of prematurity, infant mortality.

BROWN, ELMIRA NEWSOM, retired elementary school educator; b. Proctor-Crittenden, Ark., May 31, 1907; d. Emanuel Newsom and Tennessee Johnson; m. James Jefferson Brown, Nov. 19, 1942. BS, U. Ark., Pine Bluff, 1950; MS, U. Ark., Fayetteville, 1954. Tchr. Wynoka (Ark.) Elem. Sch., 1930-34, Mildred Jackson Elem. Sch., Hughes, Ark., 1934-42; prin. McCrory (Ark.) Elem. Sch. (now Elmira N. Brown H.S.), 1943-50; tchr. Scipio A. Jones H.S., North Little Rock, Ark., 1950-53, Howard Elem. Sch., Ft. Smith, Ark., 1954-60, Goldstein Elem. Sch., Hot Springs, Ark., 1960-67, Langston H.S., Hot Springs, 1967-68; ret., 1968; interim exec. dir. Coun. Econ. Opportunity, Hot Springs, 1968—. v.p. Woodland Shores Cmty. Action, Royal, Ark., 1983-92; mem. Dem. Nat. Com., Washington, 1992-97; chairperson task force Dem. Congl. Campaign Com., Royal, 1992-96; mem. women's missionary soc. African Meth. Episcopal Ch., dir. connectional skill shops WMS, 1980. Mem. AAUW, LWV, Ch. Women United, U. Ark. Alumni Assn., Zeta Phi Beta. Mem. African Meth. Episcopalian Ch. Avocations: softball, basketball, fishing, boating, gardening.

BROWN, ERIC HERBERT, geography professor; b. Melton Mowbray, Leicestershire, England, Dec. 8, 1922; s. Sammuel and Ada (Hewes) Brown; m. Eileen Reynolds, 1945 (dec. 1984); children: Jane, Megan. BSc, London U., 1947; MSc, U. Coll., Wales, 1949; PhD, U. London, 1955. Lectr. U. Coll., Wales, 1947-49, London, 1950—; prof., reader U. Coll., 1950-88. Author: Relief and Drainage of Wales, 1961; editor: Geography Yesterday and Tomorrow, 1980. Mem. Nat. Environ. Research Council, 1981-83. Served with the British air force, 1941-45. Mem. London Geog., Argentina Geog. Soc. (hon.), Royal Geog. Soc. (hon. sec. 1977-87, Back award 1966, v.p. 1987—), Brit. Nat. Com. for Geography (chmn. 1985), Athenaeum Club. Anglican. Avocations: rugby, opera. Home: Monterey Castle Hill, Berkhamsted Herts HP4 1HE, England Office: U Coll, Gower St, London WC1E 6BT, England

BROWN, ERIC JOSEPH, chemist, educator; b. Grenoble, France, Sept. 2, 1939; s. Douglas William and Lucienne (David) B.; Ingenieur des Industries Chimiques, Ecole Nationale Superieure des Industries Chimiques, Nancy, 1961; Ph.D., Cambridge (Eng.) U., 1964; D.Sc., U. Caen, 1967; m. Françoise Dumas, Apr. 13, 1966 (div. 1982); children: Peggy, Marjorie. Research asst. Nat. Center Sci. Research, Caen, 1966-68; maitre de confs. U. Le Mans, 1968-73, prof. organic chemistry, 1973—; dir. Ecole Nationale Supérieure de Chimie de Rennes, 1980-83; cons. Pharmuka Co., 1975-80. Laureate, French Chem. Soc., 1973, French Acad. Scis., 1977; recipient Protex prize for applied chemistry, 1981. Mem. Chem. Soc. France, Royal Soc. Chemistry (London). Roman Catholic. Lodge: Rotary (Le Mans). Author, patentee in field; inventor trisacryls polymers and other reagts. Home: Le Grand Roux Trange, 72650 La Milesse France Office: Univ du Maine, Route de Laval, BP 535 Le Mans 72017, France

BROWN, ERIC MOITE, economist. Diploma in stats., U. Ghana, 1987, BA in Econs. with honors, 1991. Geog. asst. Census Office, Accra, Ghana, 1980-83; tech. officer grade 2 Census Office, Accra, 1983-87; sr. tech. officer Ghana Statis. Svc., Accra, 1987-92, asst. statistician, 1992-93; acting regional statistician Ghana Statis. Svc., Cape Coast, 1993-94, dep. regional statistician, 1994; dep. regional statistician Ghana Statis. Svc., Wa, 1994-95; economist Electricity Corp. Ghana, Accra, 1995-97, acting tariff mgr., 1997—. Avocations: current affairs, reading, music, chess. Home: PO Box OS 2572, Accra Ghana

BROWN, ERIC N. W., JR., hospital administrator; b. Clarendon, Jamaica, Sept. 2, 1959; s. Eric Sylvester and Muriel (McPherson) B.; m. Serene Brown; m. Cynthia Kornegay, Sept. 1983; 1 child, Keith. BS in Computer Sci., CUNY, 1983. Mgr. John F. Kennedy Med. Ctr., Atlantis, Fla., 1990-98; dir. Plantation (Fla.) Gen. Hosp., Columbia/HCA; com. mem. Health Info. App. Access, Fla. Organizer Am. Heart Walk, 1994-97. Avocations: music, cars. E-mail: eric.brown1@columbia.net. Home: 821 44th St West Palm Beach FL 33407-3729 Office: Plantation Gen Hosp 401 NW 42d Ave Plantation FL 33317

BROWN, FELICIA M. JEFFERSON, academic administrator; b. East St. Louis, Ill., Apr. 11, 1971; d. Lena Lee; m. Johnny M. Brown Sr., Apr. 22, 1992; children: Equangela, Asheli, Johnny. Student, Augusta State U., 1998. Sr. adminstrv. sec. Med. Coll. Ga., Augusta, 1996—. Author: Improper, 1999. Leader Girl Scouts Am., 1997-98. With U.S. Army, 1992-95. Mem. Am. Assn. Med. Assistants, Ga. Writers Inc. Avocation: genealogy.

BROWN, FRANCES LOUISE (GRANDMA FRAN), artist, art gallery owner; b. Indpls., Oct. 19, 1925; d. Harley and Lenore (Spencer) Netherland; m. C.G. Clarkson, July 24, 1943 (div. Aug. 1967); children: James E. Clarkson, John B. Clarkson, Deborah L. Cromis. Thomas L. Currey, June 9, 1972 (dec. May 1978); m. George L. Brown, Jr., Mar. 3, 1982; 1 stepchild, Nancy Snow. BS in Edn., Miami U., 1968; MA in Edn., Ball State U., 1970. Elem. sch. tchr. Liberty (Ind.) Elem. Sch., 1968-71; tchr. Ball State U., Muncie, Ind., 1971-72; instr. Colby (Kans.) C.C., 1972-75; gallery owner, primitive artist Currey Studio Gallery, Berryville, Ark., 1975—. Author: Now Hear This, 1974; works exhibited at Nat. Mus. Am. Art, Washington, Wichita (Kans.) Art Assn. Gallery, Ark. Coll., Batesville, South Ark. Art Ctr., El Dorado, Harding Coll., Searcy, Ark., U. Ark., Fayetteville, Eureka Springs (Ark.) Hist. Mus., Western State Coll. Colo., Gunnison, MacMurray Coll., Jacksonville, Ill., Colby (Kans.) Coll., Claremore (Okla.) Coll., Warren Hall Coutts, III, Meml. Art Gallery, Inc., El Dorado, Kans., Masur Mus. Art, Monroe, La., Nebr. State Hist. Soc. Mus., Lincoln, Ind. State Mus., Indpls., Ozark Folk Ctr., Mountain View, Ark., Ft. Smith (Ark.) Art Ctr., Ctr. for So. Folklore, Memphis, Rogers (Ark.) Hist. Mus., Albrecht Art Mus., St. Joseph, Mo., Shiloh Mus., Springdale, Ark., Intenrat. Ctr. Contemporary Art, Paris, John Judkyn Meml. Mus., Eng., Mykonos (Greece) Folklore Mus., Musees Royaux des Beaux-Arts de Belgique, Brussels, Setagaya Art Mus., Tokyo; represented in permanent collections Smithsonian Instn., Washington, Mus. Am. Folk Art, N.Y.C., Nebr. State Hist. Soc. Mus., Lincoln, Ind. State Mus., Indpls., Ozark Mountain Folk Ctr., Mountain View, Ctr. for So. Folklore, Memphis, others; paintings recognized in various books, newspapers and articles. Avocations: pilot, sewing, reading, fishing, cooking. Home and Office: Currey Studio Gallery 3331 Highway 62 W Berryville AR 72616-8948

BROWN, FREDERICK LEE, health care executive; b. Clarksburg, W.Va., Oct. 22, 1940; s. Claude Raymond and Anne Elizabeth (Kiddy) B.; children: Gregory Lee, Michael Owen-Price. BA in Psychology, Northwestern U., 1962; MBA in Health Care Adminstrn., George Washington U., 1966. Vocat. counselor Cook County Dept. Pub. Aid, Chgo., 1962-64; adminstrv. resident Meth. Hosp. Ind., Inc., Indpls., 1965-66, adminstrv. asst., 1966, asst. adminstr., 1966-71, assoc. adminstr., 1971-72, v.p. ops., 1972-74; exec. v.p., chief operating officer Meml. Hosp. DuPage County, Elmhurst, Ill., 1974-82, Meml. Health Svcs., Elmhurst, 1980-82; pres., chief executive officer Christian Hosp. NW-NW, St. Louis, 1982-89; pres., chief exec. officer CH Health Techs., Inc., St. Louis, 1983-93, Christian Health Svcs., St. Louis, 1986-93, CH Allied Svcs., Inc., St. Louis, 1988-93; pres. BJC Health System, St. Louis, 1993—, CEO, 1993-98, vice-chmn, 1999—; adj. instr. Washington U. Sch. Medicine, St. Louis, 1982—; mem. chancellor's coun. U. Mo., St. Louis, 1990—; bd. dirs. HealthLink, Inc., 1985-92, mem. exec. com., 1986-92, chmn. bd., 1989-91; pres., chief exec. officer Village North, Inc., 1986-93; bd. dirs. Am. Healthcare Systems, Inc., chmn. shareholder communications com., 1985-86, v. chmn. 1992; bd. dirs. Commerce Bank St. Louis, Am. Excess Ins. Ltd.; mem. corp. assembly Blue Cross Blue Shield Mo., 1991—. Contbr. articles to profl. jours. Co-chmn. hosp. div. United Way Greater St. Louis, 1983, chmn., 1984, chmn. health svcs. div., 1985-86, vice chmn. region, 1988—, bd. dirs., 1986, Kammergild Chamber Orch., 1984-88, v.p., 1985-88, Mo. Heart Inst., 1988-92, Alton Meml. Hosp., 1987-91, bd. dirs., 1987-91; mem. exec. bd. St. Louis Area coun. Boy Scouts Am. Northstar chpt., 1989, activities coun. chmn. 1993—, bd. trustees 1990-92, chmn. Friends of Scouting Campaign, 1991-92; communion steward Webster Hills Meth. Ch., 1987—; mem. medicaid budget task force Mo. Dept. Social Svcs., 1990; mem. emergency rn. svcs. task force St. Louis Regional Med. Ctr., 1985; mem. corp. assembly Blue Cross Blue Shield of Mo., 1991; bd. dirs. Sold on St. Louis, 1991-93; St. Louis Reg. Commerce & Growth Assn., 1993—; mem. St. Louis City and County Task Force, 1991—. Fellow Am. Coll. Healthcare Execs. (chmn. credentials com. 1978, task force governance and constituencies 1986-88; mem. Gold Medal award com. 1985, chmn. task force on governance and constituencies 1986-87, com. on ethics 1989-91, chmn. awards & testamonials com., 1992—, bd. regents 1991-93); gov. dist V, mem. Am. Acad. Med. Adminstrs. (life, state dir. 1988—, Health Care Exec. of Yr. 1990, Statesman in Healthcare, 1992), Hosp. Pres.'s Assn., Advt. Club Greater St. Louis, Am. Hosp. Assn. (coun. on mgmt. 1987, alt. del. for healthcare systems 1988-90, del. to ho. of dels. for health care systems 1991, fin. com. chair 1995, chair-elect 1998, chmn. 1999), Am. Pub. Health Assn., George Washington U. Alumni Assn. for Health Svcs. Adminstrn. (preceptor 1975—, Alumnus of Yr. award 1981, Frederick Gibbs award, 1993), Hosp. Assn. Met. St. Louis (bd. dirs. 1984—, chmn. bd. 1988-89, sec. 1985-86, treas. 1987, chmn. coun. on pub. affairs and communications 1985, vice chmn. 1987, various coms.), Greater St. Louis Health Care Alliance (co-chair 1992—), Mo. Hosp. Assn. (mem. coun. on rsch. and policy devel. 1983-88, chmn. coun. on multi-instnl. hosps. 1986-88, mem. dist. coun. pres.'s 1986-89, bd. dirs. 1988-92, chmn. bd. trustees 1990), Cen. Ea. Profl. Rev. Orgn. (bd. dirs. 1982-85, various coms.), St. Louis Met. Med. Soc. (lay advisor 1990-92), Healthcare Execs. Study Soc., Internat. Health Policy and Mgmt. Inst. (bd. dirs. 1988—), Am. Protestant Health Assn. (bd. dirs. 1988-93, chmn. 1992-93), St. Louis Club, Algonquin Golf Club, Arena Club, Stadium Club (St. Louis), Rotary. Republican. Office: BJC Health System 120 S Central Ave Ste 1200 Saint Louis MO 63105-1735

BROWN, GARDNER RUSSELL, engineering executive; b. Sterling, Mass.; m. Sondra Jupin Gillice, Jan. 12, 1980; children: Kevin, Stephen, Thomas. BS in Mech. and Nuclear Engrng., USN, 1955. Project mgr U.S. AEC, Washington, 1953-71; mgr. Northeast Utilities Svc. Co., Berlin, Conn., 1971-73; dept. head Potomac Electric Power Co., Washington, 1971-88; CEO RusSon, Inc., Engrs. and Ind. Power Developers, Arlington, Va., 1981—. Asst. to chmn. Rep. Nat. Com. Conv., Dallas, 1984. Comdr. USN, 1945-70, PTO, Korea. Decorated Purple Hearts. Mem. Am. Nuclear Soc., U.S. Mex. C. of C., Explorers Club, Edgartown Yacht Club, Army Navy Club, Army Navy Country Club. Republican. Episcopalian. Achievements include patent in field. Office: RusSon Inc 1745 Jefferson Davis Hwy Arlington VA 22202-3402

BROWN, GEORGE E., judge, educator; b. Hammond, Ind., July 27, 1947; s. George E. and Violet M. (Matlon) B.; m. Patricia A. Schneider, June 6, 1970; children: Janet M., Elizabeth A. BS, Ball State U., 1969; JD, DePaul U., 1974; grad., Ind. Jud. Coll., 1996. Bar: Ind. 1974, Ill. 1974, U.S. Dist. Ct. (no. dist.) Ind. 1979, U.S. Supreme Ct. 1977, U.S. Tax Ct. 1977. Pvt. practice LaGrange & Lake Counties, Ind., 1974-84; judge LaGrange County Ct., 1984-87, LaGrange Superior Ct., 1988—; part-time chief dep. prosecutor LaGrange County, 1975-77; adj. faculty Tri-State U., Angola, Ind., 1991—. Vol. Jr. Achievement, 1997—. Mem. ABA, Ind. State Bar Assn. (ho. of dels., com. on written pub., com. on legal ethics, com. on legal edn. and admissions to the bar), LaGrange County Bar Assn. (pres. 1978), Ind. Judges Assn., Nat. Conf. State Trial Judges (criminal justice com.), LaGrange Rotary (past dir., v.p. 1999-2000, pres. 2000—). Office: Lagrange Superior Ct Courthouse Lagrange IN 46761

BROWN, SIR GEORGE NOEL, Belize chief justice; b. Gales Point Village, Belize, June 13, 1942; s. Noel Todd and Elma Priscilla (O'Brien) B.; m. Eleanor Marie Williams, June 5, 1962 (div. May 1972); children: Georgia Yvette Marie, Aubrey Noel David, Marsha Elizabeth, Roxanne Patricia; m. Magdalene Elizabeth Bucknor, Aug. 24, 1974. Cert. in pub. adminstrn., Carlton U., Ottawa, Ont., Can., 1970; LLB with 2d class honors, U. W.I., Barbados, 1976; cert. in legal edn., Norman Manley Law Sch., Kingston, Jamaica, 1978; cert. in legis. drafting, Commonwealth Law Sch., Nairobi, Kenya, 1979. Customs examiner Belize Customs and Excise Dept., Belize City, 1960-67; clk. of cts. Belize Magistrates Cts., Belize City, 1967-69; adminstrv. asst. Belize Ministry Trade and Industry, Belize City, 1970-72; lay magistrate, various cities, Belize, 1972-73; crown counsel Atty. Gen.'s Ministry, Belmopan, Belize, 1978-81, solicitor gen., 1981-84; puisne judge Belize Supreme Ct., Belize City, 1984-90, chief justice, 1990-98; law revision commr. Law Revision Office, Belize City, 1998-99; legal cons., 2000—; dep. gov. gen. Gov. Gen.'s Office, Belize, 1986-95; mem. Belize Adv. Coun., 1986-88, sr. mem., 1988—; mem. prison parole bd., 1998—. Mgr., coach primary and secondary sch. soccer teams, Belize City, 1986—, 1st divsn. soccer club, Belmopan, 1981-84; sec., chmn. Belize Harbour Regatta Com., Belize City, 1958-85. Decorated Knight Order of Brit. Empire, 1991. Mem. Belize Bar Assn. (sec. 1979-81). Seventh Day Adventist. Avocations: yachting, soccer, drama, cricket. Home: 6203 Cor Park Ave, Seashore Dr PO Box 236, Belize City Belize Office: Sabido & Co Atty at Law, 5 New Rd, Belize City Belize

BROWN, GERALD JAMES, dentist; b. Houma, La., Mar. 26, 1957; s. Allen M. and Sandra M. Brown; m. Tammy L. Craun; 3 children. BA in Econs., Coll. William & Mary, 1979; DDS, Va. Commonwealth U., 1986. Assoc. dentist Dr. Barry Herbst, Oakton, Va., 1986-87; pvt. practice Winchester, Va., 1987—. V.p. cmty. devel. Jaycees, Winchester, 1988-89; fund-raising chmn. Am. Cancer Soc., Winchester, 1991-92; hospitality chmn. Apple Blossom Festival, Winchester, 1992—; bd. dirs., vol. Free Med. Clinic, , Winchester, 1992—. Master Acad. Gen. Dentistry; mem. ADA, Va. Acad. Gen. Dentistry (state chmn. continuing edn. 1995-98, v.p. 1996-97, pres.-elect 1997-98, pres. 1998-99), Va. Dental Assn. (vice chmn. budget & fin. investment 1995—, mem. history & necrology com. 1995-97, mem. jour. staff 1996-97), No. Va. Dental Study Club, Shenandoah Valley Dental Assn. (del. 1989—, sec., treas. 1995-96, pres.-elect 1996-97, pres. 1997-98), Winchester/ Frederick County Dental Soc. (pres. 1993-98). Avocations: running, travel, cooking. Office: 1871 Amherst St Winchester VA 22601-2801

BROWN, G(LENN) WILLIAM, JR., bank executive; b. Waynesville, N.C., June 9, 1955; s. Glenn William and Evelyn Myralyn (Davis) B.; m. Amy Margaret Moss, Apr. 14, 1984; children: Elizabeth Quinn, Lauren Alexandra. BS in Biology, MIT, 1977, BS in Polit. Sci., 1977; JD, Duke U., 1980. Bar: N.Y., 1980. Assoc. Donovan Leisure Newton & Irvine, N.Y.C., 1980-84; assoc. Sidley & Austin, N.Y.C., 1984-87, ptnr., 1988-89; v.p. Goldman Sachs & Co., N.Y.C., 1990-94; exec. dir. Goldman Sachs Internat. Fin., London, 1994-96; sr. v.p. AIG Internat. Inc., Greenwich, Conn., 1996-97; prin. Morgan Stanley & Co., Inc., N.Y.C., 1997, mng. dir., 1997—. Mem. ABA, Am. Fin. Assn. Presbyterian. Home: 31 Lindsay Dr Greenwich CT 06830-3402 Office: Morgan Stanley Dean Witter & Co 1585 Broadway Frnt 4 New York NY 10036-8200

BROWN, GLORIA VASQUEZ, central banker; b. Alice, Tex., Aug. 7, 1945; d. Mauro and Aurora (Canales) Vasquez; m. Larry R. Brown, July 5, 1986. BA in Math., Tex. Woman's U., 1967; postgrad., U. Tex., San Antonio, 1979. Tchr. math. Corpus Christi (Tex.) Ind. Sch. Dist., 1967-69,

Columbus (Ohio) Ind. Sch. Dist., 1969-70; with Urban Mass Transp., Washington, 1971-77; owner/operator Derma Clinic, San Antonio, 1977-79; field svcs. officer Neighborhood Reinvestment Co., Dallas, 1979-89, spl. projects officer, 1989-91; cmty. affairs officer Fed. Res. Bank of Dallas, 1991-96, v.p. pub. affairs, 1997—; lectr. in field; instr. So. Meth. U./Southwestern Grad. Sch. Banking. Creator: Breaking Ground, 1995 (Merit award 1995); creator/editor Banking and Cmty. Perspectives, 1992. Bd. dirs. Arts Dist. Friends, Dallas, 1991-94, Shared Housing Ctr., 1997—, Dallas Women's Found., 2000—; mem. Region VI adv. coun. U.S. SBA, Dallas, 1992—; mem. program com. Dallas Nonprofit Capacity Bldg. Program, 1994-96; vice chair IMAGE de Dallas, 1993-94; mem. Hispanic 50, Dallas Friday Group. Recipient Women Making a Difference award Minority Bus. News, Dallas, 1995, Key to the City, City Coun. of Lafayette, La., 1980's; Leadership Tex. Found. for Women's Resources, Austin, 1996. Mem. Greater Dallas C. of C. (women's bus. issues adv. coun. 1994—, finalist Athena award 1998), Tex. Woman's U. Alumnae Assn., Hispanic Bankers Assn. Roman Catholic. Avocations: movies, travel, card games, walking. Home: 7107 Judi Ct Dallas TX 75252-6118 Office: Federal Reserve Bank Dallas 2200 N Pearl St Dallas TX 75201-2272

BROWN, GODFREY NORMAN, retired educator, small business owner; b. Farnham, Surrey, Eng., July 13, 1926; s. Percy Charles and Margaret Elizabeth (Weller) B.; m. Freda Bowyer, Jan. 11, 1960; children: Denton Charles, Nigel Willis, Martin Giles. BA, Oxford (Eng.) U., 1950, MA, 1952, DPhil, 1954. Social affairs officer UN, N.Y.C., 1953-54; sr. history master Barking Abbey Sch., Essex, 1954-57; edn. lectr. U. Coll., Ghana, 1958-61; prof. U. Ibadan, Nigeria, 1961-66; prof., dir. Inst. Edn. U. Keele, Eng., 1967-80; dir. Betley Court Gallery, Cheshire, 1980-96; v.p. Coun. for Edn. in World Citizenship, Eng., 1978—, Cmty. Coun. of Staffordshire, 1980—; mem. coun. Rural Bldgs. Preservation Trust, Eng., 1994—; vis. prof. U. Coll. of Rhodesia, 1963; cons. to UNESCO, OECD, among others. Author: An Active History of Ghana, Vol. 1, 1961, Vol. 2, 1964, Stories from the South of Nigeria, 1966, Living History, 1967, Apartheid: A Teacher's Guide, 1974, This Old House: A Domestic Biography, 1987; editor: Towards a Learning Community, 1971, (with J.C. Anene) Africa in the Nineteenth & Twentieth Centuries, 1966, (with M. Hiskett) Conflict and Harmony in Education in Tropical Africa; contbr. more than 60 articles to profl. and cultural jours. Lt. Intelligence Corps, Royal Armoured Corps, 1944-48. Avocations: conservation, writing, art history, traveling, collecting. Home: Betley Court, Betley, Crewe Cheshire CW3 9BH, England

BROWN, GORDON, British government official; b. Feb. 20, 1951; s. John and J. Elizabeth B. MA, Edinburgh U., 1972, PhD, 1982. Rector Edinburgh (Scotland) U., 1972-75, lectr., 1976; lectr. Glasgow (Scotland) Coll. of Tech., 1976-80; journalist, current affairs editor Scottish TV, 1980-83; chmn. Labour Party Scottish Coun., 1983-84; opposition chief sec. Brit. Treasury, 1987-89, opposition trade and industry sec., 1989-92, opposition treas. sec., 1992-97, chanceller of the exchequer, 1997—. Editor: The Red Paper on Scotland, 1975, Scotland: The Real Divide, 1983; author: Maxton, 1986, Where There is Greed, 1989, (with H.M. Drucker) The Politics of Nationalism and Devolution, 1980, (with J. Naughtie) John Smith: Life and Soul of the Party, 1994, (with T. Wright) Values, Visions and Voices, 1995. Avocations: reading and writing, football, tennis. Office: Her Majesty's Treasury, Parliament St, London SW1P 3AG, England also: House of Commons, London SW1A 0AA, England*

BROWN, GORDON STEWART, diplomat, business association administrator; b. Rome, Feb. 24, 1936; s. George Stewart and Helen (Meyer) B.; m. Olivia Collins, Mar. 25, 1961; children: Marian E. Sprague, Louise M., Stewart L. BA, Stanford U., 1957. Intelligence splst. U.S. Army, 1957-60; with fgn. svc. U.S. Dept. State, Tunisia, Saudi Arabia, Egypt, 1961-91; amb. to Mauritania U.S. Dept. State, 1991-94; pres. U.S.-Qatar Bus. Coun., Washington, 1997-2000; cons. Global Bus. Assocs., Ltd., Washington, 1996—. Author: Coalition, Coercion & Compromise, 1997. Served with U.S. Army, 1957-60. Recipient Meritorius Civilian Svc. award U.S. Sec. Def. Avocations: writing, history, tennis. Home: 6225 32nd Pl NW Washington DC 20015-2427

BROWN, HAROLD EUGENE, magistrate; b. Damascus, Ark., Jan. 6, 1935; s. Amos Eugene and Hazel Gladys (Thomas) B.; m. Carolyn Marie Sanders, Aug. 26, 1972; children: James Daryl, Deena Leigh, Cynthia Marie. Student, U. Md. Overseas div. Verdun, France, 1962-64, Germanna Community Coll., 1978-84. Enlisted U.S. Army, 1954, advanced through grades to sgt. maj., 1977; White House liaison Chief of Staff Army, Washington, 1969-73; dep. dir. Def. Coop. Agy., New Delhi, India, 1973-77; post sgt. maj., co. comdr. Fort A.P. Hill, Bowling Green, Va., 1977-81; district chief magistrate 15th dist. Supreme Ct. Va., Fredericksburg, 1982—, apptd. chief magistrate, 1987—. Bd. dirs. Rappahannock Coun. Domestic Violence, Rappahannock United Way. Decorated Cross Gallantry Rep. Vietnam, 1969. Mem. Am. Judges Assn., Va. Magistrates Assn., Va. Cmty. Criminal Justice Assn., Ret. Sgts. Maj. Assn. Avocations: golf, photography, computer programming. Home: PO Box 5431 Fredericksburg VA 22403-0431 Office: 2124 Jefferson Davis Hwy Stafford VA 22554-7264

BROWN, HELEN GURLEY, editor, writer; b. Green Forest, Ark., Feb. 18, 1922; d. Ira M. and Cleo (Sisco) Gurley; m. David Brown, Sept. 25, 1959. Student, Tex. State Coll. for Women, 1939-41, Woodbury Coll., 1942; LLD, Woodbury U., 1987; DLitt, L.I. U., 1993. Exec. sec. Music Corp. Am., 1942-45, William Morris Agy., 1945-47; copywriter Foote, Cone & Belding (advt. agy.), Los Angeles, 1948-58; advt. writer, account exec. Kenyon & Eckhardt (advt. agy.), Hollywood, Calif., 1958-62; editor-in-chief Cosmopolitan mag., 1965-97; editorial dir. Cosmopolitan Internat. Edits., 1972—; editor-in-chief Cosmopolitan Internat. Edits, 1997—. Author: Sex and the Single Girl, 1962, Sex and the Office, 1965, Outrageous Opinions, 1967, Helen Gurley Brown's Single Girl's Cook Book, 1969, Sex and the New Single Girl, 1970, Having It All, 1982, The Late Show, 1993, The Writer's Rules, 1998, I'm Wild Again, 2000. Named 1 of 25 most influential women in U.S., World Almanac, 1976-81; recipient Francis Holmes Achievement award for outstanding work in advt., 1956-59, Disting. Achievement award U. So. Calif. Sch. Journalism, 1971, Spl. award for editl. leadership Am. Newspaper Woman's Club, Washington, 1972, Disting. Achievement award in journalism Stanford U., 1977, Matrix award in matg. category N.Y. Women in Comm., 1985, Henry Johnson Fisher award Mag. Pubs. of Am., 1995; Helen Gurley Brown Rsch. Professorship established in her name Northwestern U. Medill Sch. Journalism, 1986; inducted into Pubs.' Hall of Fame, 1988. Mem. Authors League Am., Am. Soc. Mag. Editors (Hall of Fame award 1996), AFTRA, Eta Upsilon Gamma. Office: Cosmopolitan The Hearst Corp 959 8th Ave New York NY 10019-3737

BROWN, HERBERT CHARLES, chemistry educator; b. London, May 22, 1912; came to U.S., 1914; s. Charles and Pearl (Gorinstein) B.; m. Sarah Baylen, Feb. 6, 1937; 1 son, Charles Allan. AS, Wright Jr. Coll., Chgo., 1935; BS, U. Chgo., 1936, PhD, 1938, DSc (hon.), 1968; hon. doctorate, Wayne State U., 1980, Lebanon Valley Coll., 1980, L.I. U., 1980, Hebrew U. Jerusalem, 1980, Pontificia Universidad de Chile, 1980, Purdue U., 1980; hon. doctorates, U. Wales, 1981, U. Paris, 1982, Butler U., 1982, Ball State U., 1985. Asst. chemistry U. Chgo., 1936-38, Eli Lilly post-doctorate rsch. fellow, 1938-39, instr., 1939-43; asst. prof. chemistry Wayne U., 1943-46, assoc. prof., 1946-47; prof. inorganic chemistry Purdue U., 1947-59, Richard B. Wetherill prof. chemistry, 1959, Richard B. Wetherill rsch. prof., 1960-78, emeritus, 1978—; vis. prof. UCLA, 1951, Ohio State U., 1952, U. Mexico, 1954, U. Calif. at Berkeley, 1957, U. Colo., 1958, U. Heidelberg, 1963, SUNY, Stonybrook, 1966, U. Calif., Santa Barbara, 1967, Hebrew U., Jerusalem, 1969, U. Wales, Swansea, 1973, U. Cape Town, South Africa, 1974, U. Calif., San Diego, 1979; Harrison Howe lectr., 1953, Friend E. Clark lectr., 1953, Freud-McCormack lectr., 1954, Centenary lectr., Eng., 1955, Thomas W. Talley lectr., 1956, Falk-Plaut lectr., 1957, Julius Stieglitz lectr., 1958, Max Tishler lectr., 1958, Kekule-Couper Centenary lectr., 1958, E.C. Franklin lectr., 1960, Ira Remsen lectr., 1961, Edgar Fahs Smith lectr., 1962, Seydel-Wooley lectr., 1966, Baker lectr., 1969, Benjamin Rush lectr., 1971, Chem. Soc. lectr., Australia, 1972, Armes lectr., 1973, Henry Gilman lectr., 1975, others; hon. prof. Organomet Chem., Chinese Acad. Scis., 1994; chem. cons. to indsl. corps; rschr. in phys., organic and inorganic chemistry relating chem. behavior to molecular structure, selective reductions, hydroboration and chemistry of organoboranes. Author: Hydroboration, 1962, Boranes in Organic Chemistry, 1972, Organic Synthesis via Boranes, 1975, The Nonclassical Ion Problem, 1977, (with A.W. Pelter and K. Smith) Borane Reagents, 1988; contbr. articles to chem. jours. Bd. govs. Hebrew U., 1969-90; co-dir. war rsch. projects U. Chgo. for U.S. Army, Nat. Def. Rsch. Com., Manhattan Project, 1940-43. Decorated Order of the Rising Sun, Gold and Silver Star (Japan); recipient Purdue Sigma Xi rsch. award, 1951, Nichols medal, 1959, award Am. Chem. Soc., 1960, S.O.C.M.A. medal, 1960, H.N. McCoy award, 1965, Linus Pauling medal, 1968, Nat. Medal of Sci., 1969, Roger Adams medal, 1971, Charles Frederick Chandler medal, 1973, Chem. Pioneer award, 1975, CUNY medal for sci. achievement, 1976 Elliott Cresson medal, 1978, C.K. Ingold medal, 1978, Nobel prize in chemistry, 1979, Priestley medal, 1981, Perkin medal, 1982, Gold medal award Am. Int. Chemists, 1985, G.M. Kosolapoff medal, 1987, NAS award in chem. scis., 1987, Oesper award Cin. sect.-Am. Chem. Soc., 1990, Herbert C. Brown medal and award for creative rsch. in synthetic methods Am. Chem. Soc., 1998; Hon. fellow U. Wales Swansea, 1994; named One of Top 75 Disting. Contbrs. to Chem. Enterprise Chem. & Engring. News, 1998. Fellow AAAS, Royal Soc. Chemistry (hon.), Indian Nat. Sci. Acad. (fgn.); mem. NAS, Am. Acad. Arts and Sci., Am. Chem. Soc. (chmn. Purdue sect. 1955-56), Chem. Soc. Japan (hon.), Pharm. Soc. Japan (hon.), Ind. Acad Sci., Chinese Acad. Sci. (hon. prof. 1994), Phi Beta Kappa, Sigma Xi, Alpha Chi Sigma, Phi Lambda Upsilon (hon.). Office: Purdue U Dept Chemistry Purdue University IN 47907

BROWN, HERBERT GRAHAM, entrepreneur; b. Opelousas, La., Nov. 22, 1923; s. T.G. and Mamie (Walker) B.; m. Diane Fontenot, Oct. 18, 1953; children: Deborah, Graham, Jared, Greg, Donna. Student, U. So. La., 1944, Eckerd Coll., St. Petersburg, Fla., 1985. Owner, prin. appliance and furniture stores, La. and Fla., 1939-89, rice and cattle farm, La., 1948-89, Browns Thrift City, La., 1961-70; owner, developer shopping ctrs. and apartments, various locations, 1955-89; pres. Am. Bank, La., 1954-63; sr. v.p. Jack Eckerd Corp., Fla., 1970-72; owner, ptnr., developer K-Marts, Mobile Home Parks, shopping ctrs., Fla. and La., 1970-89. Dist. gov., R.I., 1968-69; ; vice chmn. ARC, United Way; pres. Fla. & La. vol. Boy Scouts Am.; trustee, vice chmn. Morton F. Plant Hosp., Clearwater, Fla.; world chmn. R.I. Health Hunger & Humanity Com., 1981-86; U.S. chmn. Polio Plus Campaign Com., 1986-88. Cpl. U.S. Army, 1943-45. Recipient Silver Medallion Brotherhood award NCCJ, Silver Beaver award Boy Scouts Am., Citizen of Yr. award State of La., Humanitarian of Yr. award Fla. Mar. of Dimes, Goodwill Industries, Watson Clinic, Medulla Al Merito Rotario, Columbia, Meritorious Svc. award Rotary Internat., Svc. to Mankind award Sertoma; elected to Tampa Bay BUs. Hall of Fame; named Entrepreneur of Yr., State of Fla. Mem. Heartbeat Internat. (bd. dirs.), La. C. of C. (bd. dirs., pres.), Rotary Internat. (bd. dirs. 1978-80, trustee found., pres.-elect 1994-95, pres. 1995-96, chmn. found. 2000—, Disting. Svc. award 1986-87). Republican. Roman Catholic.

BROWN, IAN COLIN, mathematics educator; b. Chesham, Bucks., Eng., Sept. 28, 1940; s. Alan John and Evelyn Margaret Brown; m. Marion Elizabeth Bird, Mar. 28, 1970; children: Sarah Jane, Julia Lindsey. BA with honours, U. London, 1962, MA with distinction, 1964; PhD, City U., London, 1973. Chartered mathematician, Eng. Rsch. asst. Sir John Cass Coll., London, 1962-64, lectr. math., 1964-67, sr. lectr., 1967-70; sr. lectr. City of London Poly., 1970-93, London Guildhall U., 1993-95; prof. Brit. Am. Coll., London, 1995—; cons. on promoting and stimulating achievement in math.; organizer Royal Instn.—Sir John Cass Master Classes in Math., London, 1985—, math. problem solving competition for young people of inner London; participant internat. confs. on ednl. tech. and math. competitions. Contbr. articles to profl. jours. Elder, preacher Grace Bapt. Chs. Office: London Guildhall U, Brit Am Coll London, Regents Coll/Inner Circle, Regents Park/London NW1 4NS, England

BROWN, IFIGENIA THEODORE, lawyer; b. Syracuse, N.Y., Mar. 14, 1930; d. Gus and Christine Theodore; m. Paul Frederick Brown, Sept. 16, 1956; 1 child, Paul Darrow. BA, Syracuse U., 1951, LLB/JD, 1954. Bar: N.Y. 1956. Acting police justice Village of Ballston Spa, N.Y., 1960-62; sr. ptnr. Brown Brown & Peterson Esqs, Ballston Spa, 1958-2000; of counsel Brown, Peterson and Craig, Ballston Spa, 2000—; chmn. N.Y. State Bd. Real Property Svcs., Albany, 1996—. Mem. Charlton Sch. Bd., 1989-93, Ballston Spa Libr. Bd., 1991-94; founder, pres. Saratoga County Women's Rep. Club; vice-chmn. Saratoga County Rep. Com., 1958-72. Mem. N.Y. State Bar Assn., Saratoga County Bar Assn. (treas. 1983-84, pres. 1984-85), Zonta (pres. Saratoga County 1962, 90), Order Ea. Star. Republican. Greek Orthodox. Avocations: church choir, piano. Home: 42 Hyde Blvd Ballston Spa NY 12020-1608 Office: Brown Peterson and Craig One E High St Ballston Spa NY 12020

BROWN, IVOR JOHN, consulting minerals, land reclamation-planning engineer; b. Eng., Apr. 20, 1937. Mining diploma, Staffordshire U., 1959; PhD, Leicester U., 1975. Chartered engr., U.K. Various mining positions Nat. Coal Bd., Shropshire, Eng., 1952-59, underground mgr., 1959-62; lectr. mining and quarrying Doncaster Coll., Yorks, Eng., 1963-68, Grantham Coll., Lincolnshire, Eng., 1968-71; group engr. for land reclamation Telford Devel. Corps., Shropshire, Eng., 1972-76; county minerals and waste disposal officer West Yorkshire Coun., 1977-86, Leeds City Coun., 1986-91, Staffordshire Coun., 1991-93; minerals, reclamation and planning cons. engr., Wakefield, Eng., 1993—. Dir. Peak Dist. Mining Mus. Ltd., 1992—, Welsh Mines Preservation Trust Ltd., 1994—. Author books; contbr. over 200 articles on mining, engring., minerals planning, waste disposal, and mining history and interpretation to tech. jours. Fellow Inst. Mining Engrs., Inst. Quarrying (vice chmn., chmn. Yorkshire br. 1988-92), Nat. Assn. Mining History Orgns. (vice chmn., chmn. 1985—). Home and Office: 95 Manygates Ln, Sandal, Wakefield WF2 7DL, England

BROWN, JAMES FRANKLIN, political writer, consultant; b. N.Y.C., Mar. 8, 1928; arrived in Eng., 1932 (parents Brit. citizens); s. Josiah Brown and Tabitha Evans; m. Margaret Wood, Aug. 14, 1954; children: Alison, Julia. BA in History with honors, Manchester (Eng.) U., 1949, MA in History, 1951; postgrad., U. Mich., 1951-52. Dir. rsch. dept. Radio Free Europe, Munich, 1969-78, dir., 1978-83; sr. analyst Rand, Santa Monica, Calif., 1987-91, Carnegie Internat. Commn. on the Balkans, Berlin, 1995-96; cons. Rand, Santa Monica, 1974—, Stiftung Wissenschaft und Politik, Ebenhausen, Germany, 1983-85; vis. prof. U. Calif., Berkeley, 1989, UCLA, 1989-91, Am. U. Bulgaria, 2000. Author: The New Eastern Europe: The Khruschev Era and After, 1966, Bulgaria Under Communist Rule, 1971, Eastern Europe and Communist Rule, 1988, Surge to Freedom: The End of Communist Rule in Eastern Europe, 1991, Hopes and Shadows: Eastern Europe After Communism, 1994, The Grooves of Change: Eastern Europe in the New Millennium, 2000; contbr. numerous articles to scholarly jours. Flying officer Royal Air Force, 1952-54. Rsch. scholar Columbia U., 1968-69. Mem. Nat. Liberal Club (London). Mem. Labor Party. Anglican. Avocations: America-watching, walking, cricket, watching soccer. Home: 8 Norham End, Oxford OX2 6SG, England

BROWN, JAMES THOMPSON, JR., computer information scientist, logistics specialist; b. Orange, N.J., Jan. 3, 1935; s. James Thompson and Marjorie (Hale) B.; m. Alice Beasley, Oct. 3, 1959; children—Kathryn, James. B.M.E., Cornell U., 1957; M.S., Stanford U., 1964. Applied sci. rep. IBM Corp., Schenectady, N.Y., 1957-59, corp. staff mem., White Plains, N.Y., 1960-68; cons. Case & Co., Stamford, Conn., 1969-74, dir., 1975-83, pres., 1983-84; pres. Tom Brown & Co., Wilton, Conn., 1985—; advisor Russian Fedn. Customs Svc. Developer inventory mgmt. systems and svc. pricing techniques. Life mem. Rep. Inner Circle. Mem. Internat. Assn. Chain Stores (adviser, speaker 1971—), Nat. Grocers Assn. (adviser 1983—), Am. Inst. Indsl. Engrs. (sr. mem.), Inst. Ops. Rsch. and Mgmt. Scis., Landmark Club, Cornell Club (N.Y.), Capitol Hill Club. Republican. Home: 135 Middlebrook Farm Rd Wilton CT 06897-2019 Office: Tom Brown & Co PO Box 431 Wilton CT 06897-0431

BROWN, J'AMY MARONEY, journalist, media relations consultant, investor; b. Oct. 30, 1945; d. Roland Francis and Jeanne (Wilbur) Maroney; m. James Raphael Brown, Jr., Nov. 5, 1967 (dec. July 1982); children: James Roland Francis, Jeanne Raphael. Student, U. So. Calif., 1963-67. Reporter L.A. Herald Examiner, 1966-67, Lewisville Leader, Dallas, 1980-81; editor First Person Mag., Dallas., 1981-82; journalism dir. Pacific Palisades Sch., L.A., 1983-84; freelance writer, media cons., 1984-88; media dir., chief media strategist Tellem Inc., 1990-92, comm. cons., issues mgr., 1992—; press liaison U.S. papal visit, L.A., 1987; pres., CEO and owner PRformance Group Comm., 1995—; auction chmn. Assn. Pub. Broadcasting, Houston, 1974, 75; vice chmn. Dallas Arts Council, 1976-80; vice chmn. Met. March of Dimes, Dallas, 1980-82; del. Dallas Council PTAs, 1976-80; bd. dirs. Santa Barbara City Coll. Bus. and Industry Coun., Montecito Assn.; mem. core-coun. Santa Barbara Coun. on Self-Esteem; coord. specialist World Cup Soccer Organizing Com. Recipient UPI Editors award for investigative reporting, 1981. Mem. NAFE, Pub. Rels. Soc. Am. (accredited), Women Meeting Women, Women in Comm., Am. Bus. Women's Assn., Goleta Valley Art Assn., Santa Barbara C. of C. (media com.), Montecito Assn. (bd. dirs.). Republicatn. Roman Catholic. Home: 1143 High Rd Santa Barbara CA 93108-2430

BROWN, JANET LEE, defense electronics company executive; b. Elmhurst, Ill., Nov. 3, 1951; d. John Richard and Doris Mae (Corlew) B. B.S.B.A. cum laude, U. Wis., 1982; M.B.A., U. Ill.-Chgo., 1985. Dir. Goodwill Industries, Racine, Wis., 1974-82; supr. U.S. Dist. Ct., Chgo., 1983; fellow, rsch. asst. U. Ill.-Chgo., 1983-84; analyst Northrop Corp. DSD, Rolling Meadows, Ill., 1984-86, contract adminstr., 1986-87, mgr. govt. relations/compliance, 1987-97, mgr. fin., 1994—; cons., trainer numerous orgns. and profl. assns., 1977—. Contbr. poetry to Chime, 1983. Cons., advocate Soc.'s Assets, Inc., Racine, 1976-77; deacon Bellwood P Presbyterian Ch., Ill., 1986-87, tchr., 1982-83, youth fellowship leader, 1982-83, elder, 1988-92. Mem. ASTD, Inst. Mgmt. Accts., Chgo. Coun. Fgn. Rels., Nat. Dev. Indsl. Assn., Women in Def., Nat. Contract Mgmt. Assn., Nat. Assn. Female Execs., Phi Kappa Phi, Alpha Mu Alpha. Democrat. Avocations: poetry, theatre, opera, jazz, professional singing. Home: 209 E Butterfield Rd # 161 Elmhurst IL 60126-5103 Office: Northrop Grumman Corp-DSD 600 Hicks Rd Rolling Meadows IL 60008-1015

BROWN, JANICE ANNE, political organization executive; b. Nov. 13, 1942; d. Rexford S. and Helen L. (Stickel) B.; divorced; 1 child, Kevin Scott Carey. Asst. mgr. front desk Stratosphere Hotel and Casino, Las Vegas; exec. dir. Nev. State Dem. Party. Mem. Carson City Dem. Ctrl. Com., Nev. Dem. State Ctrl. Com., 1986—; mem. Clark County Dem. Ctrl. Com.; bd. dirs. Nev. Common Cause, 1988-94. Mem. Womens Polit. Caucus, Carson City Dem. Women's Club (pres. 1986-89), Clark County Women's Club. Roman Catholic. Office: 1785 E Sahara Ave Ste 496 Las Vegas NV 89104-3712

BROWN, JANIECE ALFREIDA, pilot; b. Ellensburg, Wash., May 23, 1956; d. Don Elmer and LaRhee Deloris (Montgomery) Lewis; m. David E. Brown, Oct. 10, 1993. AA, Big Bend C.C., Moses Lake, Wash., 1980-82; BS, Ctrl. Wash. U., 1982-84. Pilot AAR Western Skyways, Troutdale, Oreg., 1984-87; airline capt. N.P.A., Inc., Pasco, Wash., 1987-89; flight engr. airline pilot Alaska Airlines, Seattle, 1989—, 1st officer Boeing 727 and MD-80, capt. MD-80, 1996—; bus. mgr. David Brown & Assocs., 1994-99; airline capt. MD-80 Alaska Airlines, Seattle, 1996—; pres. Interlachen Inc., 1998—. Lobbyist Save Our Watershed, Roslyn, Wash., 1978-80; pres. Interlachen, Inc., A Homeowners Assn., 1998—. Recipient Scholastic award CleElum (Wash.) High Sch., 1974. Mem. Airline Pilot Assn. (mem. dangerous goods com.), Interlachen, Inc. (pres. 1998—), Alpha Eta Rho (pres. Ctrl. Wash. U. chpt. 1983-84). Avocations: skiing, sewing, backpacking, contractor, remodeler of own home and rental. Home: 20912 NE Interlachen Ln Troutdale OR 97060-8731 Office: Alaska Airlines PO Box 61900 Seattle WA 98178

BROWN, JAY MARSHALL, retired secondary education educator; b. Bklyn., July 26, 1933; s. Sidney and Bertha (Swirsky) B.; m. Merle Thelma Kaminsky, Nov. 4, 1956; children: Sidney Matthew, Ellen Beth Factor. BS in Journalism, NYU, 1955, MA in Am. Civilization, 1960; postgrad., Yeshiva U., 1958-60, U. Conn., West Hartford, 1968-70; 6th yr. profl. diploma, So. Conn. State Coll., 1977. Pub. relations dir, asst. credit mgr. Colonial Sand & Stone Co., N.Y.C., 1955-60; employment counselor N.Y.C. Dept. Welfare, 1960-63; attendance tchr. Bd. Edn., N.Y.C., 1963-65; youth dir. Jewish Community Ctr., Rochester, N.Y., 1965-67; exec. dir. Conn. Valley Regional B'nai B'rith Youth, New Haven, 1967-70; resource tchr. Sheridan Middle Sch., Bd. Edn., New Haven, 1970-72; learning ctr. tchr. Bd. Edn., New Haven, 1972-74; social studies tchr. Troup Middle Sch., Bd. Edn., New Haven, 1974-80; history tchr. Hillhouse High Sch., Bd. Edn., New Haven, 1980-93; U.S. history tchr. New Eng. Acad. for Jewish Studies, New Haven, 1984-85; audio-visual and media specialists Quinnipiac Coll., Hamden, Conn., 1982. Contbr. articles to profl. jour.; editor BBYO Bd. dirs. newsletter, Bklyn., 1961-62; columnist The Luna Spark, Bklyn., 1961-63. Chmn. clear sch. mission com. Hillhouse H.S., 1984, mem. effective sch. steering com., 1984, mem. sch. planning and mgmt. team, 1988-91, coord. teenagers adv. program, 1989-91, mem. faculty senate, 1991-93; bd. dirs. Citizen TV, Inc., 1991-93; acting pres. Alliance for Mentally Ill, 1993-94, pres., 1995—; pres. Brotherhood of Mishkan Israel, 1976-78, 83-84, 88-89, sec., 1997-98, treas., 1998—; asst. treas. Congregation Mishkan Israel, 1983-84, budget chmn., 1987-88, chmn. house and property com., 1979-84, trustee, 1978-84, 86-92, 94—, mem. pers. com., 1996—, mem. abatement com., 1997-98, libr. and archivist, 1981-84, mem. opers. com., 1999—; past chmn. Hamden Cmty. Devel. Action Planning Com. on Youth Svcs.; past sec. Hamden Anti-Drug Task Force; mem. Hamden Dem. Town Com., 1974-76; corr. sec. Jewish Hist. Soc., New Haven, 1980-81; v.p. Regency Hills Condo Assn., 1994-95; active Mental Health Month Com., 1995-99, Family Resource Ctr. com. Consultation Ctr., 1994-98; coord. Mental Health Network Speakers Bur., 1996-97, 98; facilitator Journey of Hope Ednl. Program, 1995-98; mem. Regional Mental Health Bd., Catchment Area 7, 1996-97, vice chmn., 1997—; mem. review and evaluation team State Regional Mental Health Bd. Dist. 2, 1996-2000, vice chmn., 1997-2000; bd. govs. Inst. Learning and Retirement, 1998-2000; treas. Nat. Alliance Mentally Ill, 1998-99; coord. New Haven County's Mental Illness Awareness Week, 1998—, People Helping People Program, 1998—. Recipient Man of Yr. award of merit Congregation Mishkan Israel's Brotherhood, 1978; named Outstanding Profl. in Human Svcs., 1974-75. Mem. New Haven County Ret. Tchr. Assn. (v.p. 1994-95, sec. 1997—), Regency Hills Condo Assn. (pres. 1995-96), Phi Delta Kappa. Democrat. Jewish. Avocations: philately, polit. items, sports items, community svc. Home: 25 Wright Ln Hamden CT 06517-2126

BROWN, JEREMY RONALD COVENTRY, lawyer; b. Durban, Natal, S. Africa, May 2, 1948; s. Kenneth Coventry and Mavis Kathleen (Keal) B. BSc in Chem. Engring., U. Natal, 1970, MSc in Chem. Engring., 1971; B.Iur., U. S. Africa, 1975. Registered patent agt. S. Africa 1974; atty. Supreme Ct. S. Africa, 1976; solicitor Supreme Ct. of Eng. and Wales, 1980. Assoc. Spoor and Fisher, Pretoria, Johannesburg, 1971-78; assoc. Linklaters & Paines, London, 1978-82, ptnr., 1982—. Contbr. articles to profl. jours., chpts. to books. Mem. AIPPI (coun. mem. 1990—), Licensing Exec. Soc. G.B. and Ireland (pres. 1991-92), Licensing Exec. Soc. Internat. (pres. 1995-96). Avocations: tennis, travel, the Arts. Office: Linklaters, One Silk St, London EC24 8HQ, England

BROWN, JESSE, former federal official; b. Detroit, Mar. 27, 1944; married; 2 children. Grad. with honors, Chgo. City Coll.; student, Roosevelt U., Cath. U. Am. Nat. svc. officer Disabled Am. Vets., Chgo., 1967-72; supr. nat. svc. staff and nat. appeals staff Disabled Am. Vets., Washington, chief of claims nat. svc. and legis. hdqrs., dep. nat. svc. dir., exec. asst. to nat. adjutant, exec. dir., 1989-93; sec. Dept. Vets. Affairs, Washington, 1993-97; v.p. Mayor's Com. on Employment of Handicapped, Chgo. With USMC, 1963-65. Decorated Purple Heart, Vietnam Svc. Medal, republic of Vietnam Campaign medal. Mem. AMVETS, DAV, VFW, Am. Legion, Marine Corps League, Mil. Order Purple Heart, Polish Legion Am. Vets., U.S.A. Ret. Enlisted Assn., Jewish War Vets., Vietnam Vets. Am. Inc. Office: DAV 807 Maine Ave SW Washington DC 20024*

BROWN, JOHN FRED, steel company executive; b. Floydada, Tex., May 20, 1941; s. Rex R. Brown and Martha L. (McCleskey) Mayfield; m. Karolyn Kay Robertson, July 31, 1960; children: John Robert, Jonathan David, William Charles. BSME, U. Wis., 1968; MBA, Tex. Tech U., 1978. Staff engr. Continental Oil Co., Houston, 1971-73; sr. buyer Continental Oil Co., Lake Charles, La., 1973-74; v.p. WedgeCor, Inc., Billings, Mont., 1974-76; chmn., CEO Tri-Steel Structures, Inc., Denton, Tex., 1976—, Hawk Industries, Inc., Denton, 1978—; chmn. Tri-Steel Structures, Conyers, Ga., 1989—, R.S.F. Constrn. Inc., Denton, 1994—. Contbg. author: Steel

Homes, 1985. Mem. Rep. Senatorial Inner Circle; active Denton Bible Ch. With U.S. Army, 1968-69, Vietnam. Decorated Bronze Star. Mem. Ctr. for Entrepreneurial Mgmt., CEO Club, Mensa, Presdl. Roundtable, Denton Country Club. Avocations: golf, travel, photography, lic. comml. pilot. Home: RR 1 Box 362E Denton TX 76207-9202 Office: 5400 S Stemmons St Denton TX 76210-2338

BROWN, SIR JOHN (GILBERT NEWTON), publisher; b. July 7, 1916; s. John and Molly B.; m. Virginia Braddell, 3 children. Ed. Lancing Coll., Hertford Coll.; M.A. in Zoology, Oxford U. With Bombay br. Oxford Univ. Press, 1937-40, 46-49, sales mgr., 1949-56, pub., 1956-80; chmn. Univ. Bookshops Ltd., Oxford; dir. Book Tokens Ltd., Willshaw Booksellers Ltd., Manchester, Eng.; chmn. B.H. Blackwell Ltd., dir. Blackwell Group Ltd., 1980-87; pres. Pubs. Assn., 1963-65; mem. nat. libraries com. EDC for Newspapers, Printing and Pub. Industry, 1967-70; mem. Adv. Com. Sci. and Tech. Info., 1969-73; mem. communication adv. com. U.K. nat. com. UNESCO; asst. treas. Royal Lit. Fund; bd. dirs. Brit. Library, 1973-79; mem. Royal Soc. Sci. Info.; past mem. bd. Brit. Council. Commd. Royal Arty., 1941, served, 1941-46, Japanese prisoner of war, 1942-45. Professorial fellow Hertford Coll., Oxford U., 1974-80.

BROWN, JOHN THOMAS, lawyer; b. Ft. Dix, N.J., Dec. 16, 1948; s. Thomas Maurice and India Olean B.; m. Jerilyn Iris Post, June 24, 1972; children: India Claire, Solon Neville. BA with honors and distinction, Calif. State U., Chico, 1975; JD, U. Calif., San Francisco, 1978; grad. diploma in applied fin., Securities Inst. of Australia, 1999. Bar: Calif. 1978, Guam 1982, No. Mariana Islands 1983, NSW, 1999. Vol. VISTA, Gt. Lakes Region, 1968-69; assoc. Belzer & Jackl, Oakland, Calif., 1978-82; gen. counsel Jones & Guerrero Co., Inc., Agana, Guam, 1982—; v.p. Jones & Guerrero Co. Inc., Sydney, Australia, 1989—; instr. Chabot Jr. Coll., Hayward, Calif., 1980-82; prin. broker Rimpac Realty, Agana, 1987—. Bd. dirs. Job Tng. Partnership Coun., Agana, 1987-89; hon. amb.-at-large for Guam. Fellow Australian Inst. Co. Dirs.; mem. ABA, Calif. Bar Assn., Guam Bar Assn. (ethics com.), Bar Assn. No. Mariana Islands, Lawasia Soc., Securities Inst. Australia (assoc.), Guam C. of C. (bd. dirs. 1986-89, chmn. ethics com. 1987-89, chmn. bd. dirs. 1988-89), Sydney Turf Club, Am. Nat. Club, Australia Jockey Club, Law Soc. of NSW. Office: Jones & Guerrero, GPO Box 3539, Sydney New South Wales 2001, Australia

BROWN, JOY ALICE, social services administrator; b. Redmesa, Colo., Mar. 19, 1917; d. Ezra E. and Alice M. (Pinkerton) Walker; m. Clayton Henry Brown, Apr. 9, 1941; children: Kimleigh Clayton, Loraleigh Joy. B.A., Highlands U., 1958; M.A., U. No. Colo., 1967, EdD, 1970. Tchr. La Plata County, Colo., 1936-41; prin. Bayfield (Colo.) pub. schs., 1942-46; tchr. Aztec (N.Mex.) pub. schs., 1946-63; spl. edn. coordinator primary schs. Palmer, Alaska, 1963-67; lab. sch. supr. U. No. Colo., 1967-70; assoc. prof. edn. N.Mex. State U., 1970-75; dir. Open Door Center, Las Cruces, N.Mex., 1975—; cons. Tex. Edn. Service Center, Roswell (N.Mex.) schs.; sec. Dona Ana Human Services Consortium, 1977. Contbr. articles on edn. to profl. jours. Recipient Community Service award Las Cruces Eastside Center, 1972; Outstanding Contribution award N.Mex. Council of Exceptional Children, 1977. Mem. NEA, Council for Exceptional Children, Nat. Assn. Retarded Citizens, Phi Delta Kappa. Home: 34081 Country Rd M Mancos CO 81328 Office: 2325 Nevada Ave Las Cruces NM 88001-3902

BROWN, JUDITH ANN, association executive; b. L.A., Mar. 4, 1944; d. Bertha Marie; m. Paul Anthony Brown, Dec. 30, 1967; children: Hugh Richard, Catherine Marie, Christina Lee. D in Humanities, Valley Christian U., 1985. Pres. Am. Life League, Inc., Stafford, Va., 1999—. Author: Choices in Matters of Life and Death (with Paul Brown), 1987, Veritatis Splendor: A Study Guide, Contraception and Abortion, Abortion Your Risks, Moral and Logical Arguments (with Robert Evangelisto), Exceptions: Abandoning the LEast of These (with Brian Young), Celebrate Life Mag., Life Guide Series: The Facts of Life, The Facts About Birth Control, The Facts About Abortion, The Facts About Title X: The Six Billion Dollar Scam, Reflections on Suffering, Facing the Struggle: Pain Has a Name, Waht Is Mercy Killing?. Recipient Knights of Columbus Svc. award, 1976, Protector award Pro-Life Action LEague, 1982, Most Admired Conservative Women Not In Congress, 1983, 84, Lefe Leader award Greater Pitts. March for Life, 1985, Internat. Human Life award, Human Life Internat., 1990, Friend of the Youth award, Diocese of Monterey, Calif., 1991, Solution of Hope award, Mom's House, 1995. Mem. Fellowship of Cath. Scholars, Citizens United Resisting Euthanasia, World Fedn. of Doctors Who Respect Human Life, Lady of the Equestrian Order of the Holy Sepulchre of Jerusalem, Cardinal Newman Soc., The Intercollegiate Fedn. for Life, Cath. Assn. of Scientists and Engrs., Saints' Stories, Inc., Scholars for Social Justice, Legatus, Nat. Lawyers Assn., Pontifical Acad. for Life, Pro Life Nat. Coordination in Ecuador, EWTN Experts Forum. Roman Catholic. E-mail: jbrown@all.org. Fax: 540-659-4193. Home: 1206 Harbour Dr Stafford VA 22554-1926 Office: American Life League Inc 1179 Courthouse Rd Stafford VA 22554-7106

BROWN, KATHERINE JANE, editor, retired, chamber of commerce executive; b. Corinth, Miss., Jan. 17, 1924; d. William Lloyd and Sara Camille (Ray) Parker; m. Frederic Warren Brown, July 9, 1944; children: Kathy Lee Clementz, Melanie Sue Peters, Robin Eric, Frederic Warren II. Diploma, Palestine Twp. H.S., 1942. Postal clk. U.S. Post Office, Palestine, Ill., 1942; sec. import-export mgr. John Oster Mfg. Co., Genoa, Ill., 1944; owner boutique Jane's in Genoa, Ill., 1961-64; state editor, retired Daily Gazette, Sterling, Ill., 1964-71; sec.-mgr. Genoa C. of C., 1971-78. Editor Parker Pathways newsletter, 1986-98; author: Parker Pathways, 2986. Recipient Hon. Mention award Heart of Am. Geneol. Soc. & Libr. Inc., 1997. Fellow Kishwaukee Valley Heritage Mus. Soc. (sec. 1989-90). Mem. Pentecostal Ch. Avocations: art collection, cooking, geneology, travel in Europe, Israel and U.S. Home and Office: 32785 Genoa Rd Genoa IL 60135-8229

BROWN, KATHRYN LISBETH, secondary education educator; b. Cleve., June 22, 1948; d. Henry Walter and Muriel Ann (Sindelar) Makowski; m. Gary A. Brown, Sept. 27, 1974 (div. June 1988); 1 child, Sarah G. AA, Cuyahoga C.C., 1970; BA, U. Akron, 1988. Cert secondary educator, Ohio. Tchr. English, journalism and history Medina (Ohio) City Schs., 1989—. Coach Cheerleaders of Medina H.S., 1989-96; advisor journalism staff, 1994—, Jr. Class, 1991, Vol. Opportunities for Teens, 1993-94. Mem. Mensa. Avocations: photography, gardening. Home: 500 Pine St Medina OH 44256-2532 Office: Medina H S 777 E Union St Medina OH 44256-1970

BROWN, KEITH LAPHAM, retired ambassador; b. Sterling, Ill., June 18, 1925; s. Lloyd Heman and Marguerite (Briggs) B.; m. Carol Louise Liebmann, Oct. 1, 1949; children: Susan, Briggs (dec.), Linda, Benjamin. Student, U. Ill., 1943-44, Northwestern U., 1946-47; LLB, U. Tex., 1949. Bar: Tex., Okla., Colo. Assoc. Lang, Byrd, Cross & Ladon, San Antonio, 1949-55; v.p., gen. counsel Caulkins Oil Co., Oklahoma City, 1955-70, Denver, 1955-70; founder, developer Vail Assocs., Colo., 1962; pres. Brown Investment Corp., Denver, 1970-87; developer Colo. State Bank Bldg., Denver, 1971; amb. to Lesotho Dept. State, 1982-84; amb. to Denmark Dept. State, Copenhagen, 1988-92; ret., 1992; chmn. Brown Investment Corp., Denver, 1993—; mem. adv. bd. Ctr. for Strategic and Internat. Studies. Chmn. Rep. Nat. Fin. Com., 1985-88; hon. trustee, past pres. bd. Colo. Acad. Served with USN, 1943-46. Mem. Coun. Am. Ambs. (pres.), Denver Country Club, San Antonio Country Club, Univ. Club, Bohemian Club. Presbyterian. Address: PO Box 1172 Edwards CO 81632-1172 also: 11 Auburn Pl San Antonio TX 78209-4739 Office: 1490 Colo State Bank Bldg 1600 Broadway Denver CO 80202-4927

BROWN, KEITH SPALDING, JR., chemistry and ecology educator; b. Chgo., Oct. 1, 1938; arrived in Brazil, 1964; s. Keith Spalding and Katherine (McLennan) B.; m. Kay Fowell (dec.); children: Eric Nelson (dec.), Julia McLennan Brown Petty, George Gardner, Elizabeth Brown Vallim Brisola. BS, Calif. Inst. Tech., 1959; PhD, U. Wis., 1962; Livre Docencia, U. Estadual Campinas, São Paulo, Brazil, 1979. Rsch. asst. Merck, Sharp & Dohme, Rahway, N.J., summer 1959; tchg. asst., Woodrow Wilson and NSF fellow U. Wis., Madison, 1959-62; postdoctoral fellow Stanford U., Palo Alto, Calif., 1963; prof. postgrad. courses U. Brazil/UFRJ, Rio de Janeiro, 1964-73; livre-docente prof. U. Estadual de Campinas, São Paulo, 1974—; vis. prof. Cornell U., Ithaca N.Y., 1979-80; field rschr. Biol. Dynamics of Forest Fragments Project, Manaus, Amazonas, Brazil, 1980-95; pres., rep. in Brazil KMB Charitable Found., Pitts., 1983-2000; vis. rschr. Allyn Mus. Entomology, Sarasota, Fla., 1992-93; cons., invited spkr., vice-chair of Lepidoptera Specialist Group, Species Survival Commn., IUCN, Gland, Switzerland, 1988-97; prin. advisor for 20 masters and 7 doctor's theses. Author: Biogeography and Quaternary History in Tropical America, 1987, 5 others; contbr. articles to profl. jours., chpts. to books. Mem. Internat. Soc. Chem. Ecology (mem. coun. 1984-90), Lepidopterists Soc. (coun. coms., v.p. 1972, Karl Jordan award 1980), Soc. Conservation Biology. Presbyterian. Avocations: singing, discovery travel, hiking, bird watching, reading, animal breeding. Office: Inst Biologia Dept Zoology UNICAMP, CP 6109, 13083970 Campinas SP, Brazil

BROWN, KENNETH JOHN, nuclear engineer; b. Boston, May 15, 1941; s. Thomas James and Mary Elizabeth B.; m. Elizabeth Julia Strasunskas, Aug. 26, 1961; children: Daniel Joseph Brown, Timothy Michael Brown, Donna Marie Allen. BS in Marine Engring., Mass. Maritime Acad., 1961. Registered profl. nuclear engr., Calif. Third asst. engr. Sun Oil Co., Marcus Hook, Pa., 1961-62, Am. Export Lines, Hoboken, N.J., 1961-62; test engr. DeLaval Turbine Co., Trenton, N.J., 1962-63; third asst. engr. Sun Oil Co., Hoboken, N.J., 1962-63; sr. test engr. Gen. Dynamics/Electric Boat, Groton, Conn., 1963-68; ops. mgr. GE, San Jose, Calif., 1968-82; sr. project mgr. Inst. Nuclear Power Ops., Atlanta, 1982-87; nuclear engring. contractors numerous orgns., 1987—. With USNR, 1961-67. Mem. KC. Republican. Roman Catholic. E-mail: kjbrown@dellnet.com. Home and Office: 308 Walking Horse Way Kennesaw GA 30144-1622

BROWN, KENT NEWVILLE, ambassador; b. Oakland, Calif., May 7, 1944; s. Victor B. and Mary E. (Shaver) B.; m. Norma Giorno, Dec. 29, 1995; children from previous marriage: Steven D., Karen E. BA, U. Calif., Davis, 1964, MA, 1966. 3rd sec. U.S. Embassy, Panama, 1967-69; 2nd sec. U.S. Embassy, Prague, Czechoslovakia, 1970-73; watch officer to exec. secretariat U.S. Dept. of State, Washington, 1973-74; fellow Hoover Instn., Stanford, Calif., 1974-75; officer Soviet desk U.S. Dept. of State, Washington, 1976-80; 1st sec. U.S. Embassy, Moscow, 1980-83; sr. advisor U.S. Arms Control Del., Vienna, Austria, 1984-88; office dir. Strategic Nuc. Policy U.S. Dept. of State, Washington, 1989-90; polit. advisor Supreme Allied Comdr. Europe, Belgium, 1990-92; amb. U.S. Embassy, Tbilisi, Georgia, 1992-95; dir. pers. U.S. Dept. of State, Washington, 1995-96; v.p. govt. rels. Ea. Europe J.T. Internat., Geneva, 1996—; bd. dirs. NATO workshop, Menlo Park, Calif. Bd. dirs. U.S.-Russia Bus. Coun. Mem. Internat. Inst. for Strategic Studies. Office: 12 Ch de Rieu, Geneva 17, Switzerland

BROWN, KEVIN, writer; b. Kansas City, Mo., Sept. 3, 1960; s. John and Duane (Nimmons) B. BA, Columbia U., 1988. Author: Romare Bearden, 1994, Malcolm X, 1995; contbg. editor: New York Public Library African-American Desk Reference, 1999; contbr. essays and revs. to literary jours. including London Times Lit. Supplement, Washington Post Bookworld, others. Gen. Studies scholar Columbia U., 1988. Mem. PEN Am. Ctr. Roman Catholic. Avocations: travel, music, fine arts, wines, cooking. Home: 65-60 Booth St Apt 2E Rego Park NY 11374

BROWN, LAMAR BEVAN, lawyer; b. Tooele, Utah, Apr. 26, 1951; s. John B. and Reva M. B.; children: Sean La Mar, Kyle Ross, Ian Lawrence. BA, Utah State U., 1974; JD, We. State U., 1980. Bar: Calif. 1980, U.S. Dist. Ct. (so. dist.) Calif. 1980, U.S. Ct. Appeals (9th cir.) 1986, U.S. Dist. Ct. (no. and ctrl. dist.) 1992. Assoc. Law Offices George Andrews, San Diego, 1980-82, Higgs, Fletcher & Mack, San Diego, 1982-90, Law Offices Craig McClellan, San Diego, 1990-95; ptnr. McClellan & Brown, San Diego, 1995—. Mem. Consumer Attys. Calif., Consumer Attys. San Diego, Western Trial Lawyers Assn., San Diego County Bar Assn. Democrat. Office: McClellan & Brown 1144 State St San Diego CA 92101-3529

BROWN, L(ARRY) EDDIE, tax practitioner, real estate broker, financial planner; b. Aug. 31, 1941; s. Earl and Lois Ovoca (Norrod) B.; m. Lillian Virginia Edwards, Feb. 9, 1965; children: Clifford Bruce, Michael Dwayne, Jennifer Noelle. BBA, Ga. State U., 1974, MBA, 1976. Cert. tax profl.; accredited tax advisor; accredited bus. acct.; enrolled agt. Mgmt. trainee Citizens Bank, Cookeville, Tenn., 1963-65; office mgr. Redisco, Tampa, Fla., 1965-67; methods analyst Delta Air Lines, Atlanta, 1967-83; owner Brown Enterprises, College Park, Ga., 1971—; pres. So. Heritage Properties, Inc., 1984—; instr. Ga. State U., 1976-80. Bd. dirs. Ga. Spl. Olympics, Atlanta, 1983-90; Ga. del. White House Conf. on Small Bus., 1995, Congl. Small Bus. Summit, 1998, 2000. With USAF, 1959-63. Mem. Nat. Soc. Tax Profls. (Ga. state com. 1994-99), Nat. Assn. Tax Practitioners (Ga. bd. dirs. 1994-98), Nat. Soc. Pub. Accts., Ga. Assn. Pub. Accts. (pres. So. Cres. chpt. 1993-95, bd. govs. 1994—, 1st v.p. 1996-97, pres. 1997-99), Internat. Assn. Fin. Planners, Nat. Assn. Securities Dealers, Atlanta Bd. Realtors, Civitan Club (pres. Airport-Southside, Atlanta 1982-83, treas. Airport Area, Atlanta 1979-81, Civitan of Yr. chpt. 1982, bd. dirs. Ga. dist. north 1984-86, trustee Ga. dist. North Found. 1985-88), Masons. Mormon. Office: Brown Enterprises 392 Glynn St N Fayetteville GA 30214-1191

BROWN, LAURENCE BINET, retired psychology educator; b. Wellington, New Zealand, Aug. 13, 1927; s. William Binet Brown and Annie Martha Embury; m. Dorothy Fay Wood, Dec. 12, 1952; children: Roger Binet, Rachel Sheila, Martin Raphael, Thomas Pascal. BA, Victoria U., New Zealand, 1949, MA, 1950; diploma in edn., Victoria U., 1951; PhD, U. London, 1954. Mem. New Zealand Def. Sci. Corps., 1951-55; lectr. U. Adelaide, Australia, 1957-64; prof. Massey U., New Zealand, 1965-66, Victoria U., 1967-74, U. NSW, Australia, 1975-92; dir. Alister Hardy Rsch. Ctr., Oxford, Eng., 1993-96. Author: Psychology in Contemporary China, 1981, Psychology of Religion, 1988, The Woman Side of Prayer, 1994; editor: Advances in the Psychology of Religion, 1985. Fellow Brit. Psychol. Soc., New Zealand Psychol. Soc. Avocation: academic life. Home: 6 Easdale St, Wellington New Zealand

BROWN, LAURENCE DAVID, retired bishop; b. Fargo, N.D., Feb. 16, 1926; s. John Nicolai and Ada Amelia (Johnson) B.; m. Virginia Ann Allen, Sept. 6, 1950; children: Patricia Ann, Julia Louise, Claudia Ruth. BS, U. Minn., 1946; BA, Concordia Coll., 1948; M of Theology, Luther Theol. Sem., 1951. Ordained to ministry Evang. Luth. Ch., 1951. Pastor Our Savior's Luth. Ch., New Ulm, Minn., 1951-55; nat. assoc. youth dir. Evang. Luth. Ch., Mpls., 1955-60; nat. youth dir. Am. Luth. Ch., Mpls., 1960-68; instn. dir. Tchr. Tng., U. Minn., Mpls., 1968-69; exec. dir. Freedom from Hunger Found., Washington, 1969-73; sr. pastor St. Paul Luth. Ch., Waverly, Iowa, 1973-79; bishop Iowa Dist. Am. Luth. Ch., Des Moines, 1979-89, N.E. Iowa Synod, Evang. Luth. Ch. in Am., Waverly, 1989-92; prof. religion Wartburg Coll., Waverly, Iowa, 1992-93; interim sr. pastor Ctrl. Luth. Ch., Mpls., 1994-95, Calvary Luth. Ch., Mpls., 1996-97; ret.; bd. regents Luther Coll., Decorah, Iowa, 1989-92, Wartburg Coll., 1988-92, Wartburg Theol. Sem., Dubuque, Iowa, 1988-91, Self-Help, Inc., 1989-94. Author: Take Care: A Guide for Responsible Living, 1983; contbr. articles to profl. jours. Lt. USN, 1943-46. Lutheran. Avocation: reading. Home: 7201 York Ave S Apt 514 Edina MN 55435-4444

BROWN, LAVEDA PAGE, consultant; b. Madisonville, Tex., Jan. 9, 1956; d. William Sr. and Frankie Bell Hardy; m. Gregory Arnold Page (dec. 1979); children: Gregory D., Bettina D. Student, El Centro Jr. Coll., 1975-77, Abilene Christian U., 1990, Cisco Jr. Coll., 1991-92. Cert. bus. devel. specialist. Owner, mgr. Master' Touch, Dallas, 1988-91; procurement specialist Abilene (Tex.) Christian U. Caruth Small Bus. Devel. Ctr., 1992-94; bus. cons., procurement specialist McLennan C.C., Small Bus. Devel. Ctr., Waco, Tex., 1994—; with Affiliated Computer Svcs., Dallas, 1989-90; advisor Sign of the Times, Waco. Mem. Tex. Econ. Devel. Coun., Austin, 1999-00. Recipient Distinction award Tex. Assn. Minority Bus. Enterprise, 1995, Adv. Yr. Fort Worth Small Bus. Admstrn., 1998. Mem. Am. Bus. Women Assn. (v.p. mktg. 1999-00, top recruiter dist. II award 2000), Nat. Purchasing Assn., Nat. Contract Mgmt. Assn., Svc. Corps Retired Execs. (procurement specialist), Tex. Assn. Procurement Ctrs. (legis. com. 1994-96), Gtr. Waco C. of C. (com. mem. 1999-00). Republican. Mem. LDS Ch. Avocations: reading, ceramic, cross stitching, gardening. E-mail: ljb@mcc.cc.tx.us. Office: McLennan Cmty Coll Small Bus Devel Ctr 401 Franklin Ave Waco TX 76701-2127

BROWN, LAWRENCE PETER, computer science educator; b. Frankston, Victoria, Australia, Nov. 22, 1961; s. Ronald and Roberta (Sandercock) B. BS with honors, Monash U., Melbourne, Victoria, 1983; PhD, U. New South Wales, Canberra, Australia, 1991. Computer systems officer Australian Bur. Stats., Canberra, 1984-85; programmer Australian Def. Force Acad., Canberra, 1985-86, teaching fellow dept. computer sci., 1986-89, rsch. officer Univ. Coll., 1989-90, lectr., 1991—. Co-designer Loki Data Encryption Algorithms, 1989, 91, 97. Recipient Dance Composers award Traditional Social Dance Assn. Victoria, 1990, 93. Fellow Brit. Interplanetary Soc.; mem. IEEE, Internat. Assn. for Cryptologic Rsch., Wireless Inst. Australia. Avocations: ballroom, bush, ceroc and scottish country dancing, amateur radio, skiing. Office: Australian Def Force Acad, Sch Computer Sci, UC UNSW, Canberra ACT 2600, Australia

BROWN, LEE PATRICK, city official, law enforcement educator; b. Wewoka, Okla., Oct. 4, 1937; s. Andrew and Zelma (Edwards) B.; m. Yvonne Carolyn Streets, July 14, 1958 (dec.); children: Patrick, Torri, Robyn, Jenna; m. Frances M. Young, Dec. 29, 1996. BA, Fresno State U., 1960; MA, San Jose State U., 1964; MS, U. Calif., 1968, D in Criminoloy, 1970; D of Pub. Affairs (hon.), Fla. Internat. U., 1982; LLD (hon.), John Jay Coll., 1985; HHD (hon.), Portland State U., 1990; LHD (hon.), Fresno State U., 1994; LLD (hon.), SUNY Brockport, 1995. Officer San Jose (Calif.) Police Dept., 1960-68; prof. Portland (Oreg.) State U., 1968-72; assoc. dir. Urban Affairs Inst. Howard Inst., Washington, 1972-75; sheriff Sheriff's Dept., Mulnomah County, Oreg., 1975-76; dir. Dept. Justice Services, Mulnomah County, 1976-78; commr. Dept. Pub. Safety, Atlanta, 1978-82; chief of police Houston Police Dept., 1982-90; police commr. N.Y.C., 1990-92; prof. Tex. So. Univ., 1992-93; dir. Nat. Drug Control Policy, Washington, DC, 1993-96; mem. Pres. Cabinet, 1993-96; prof. Rice Univ., HOuston, 1996-98; mayor City of Houston, 1998—; adj. prof. U. Houston, U. Tex. Health Sci. Ctr., Houston, Tex. So. U., Houston; cons. U.S. Dept. Justice, Washington, Police Found., Washington, various state and local govts., Houston; chmn. Nat. Minority Adv. Council on Criminal Justice; mem. Nat. Adv. Commn. on Criminal Justice Standards and Goals, Washington, Nat. Commn. on Higher Edn. for Police, Washington, Commn. on Accreditation for Law Enforcement Agencies, Washington, Presdl. Task Force, 1993—. Co-author: Attitudes of Black Police Officers, 1976, Police and Society, 1981; editor: Neighborhood Team Policing, 1976, Violent Crime, 1981; author of numerous articles and book chpts. Bd. dirs. Boy Scouts Am., United Way, Urban League, Blue Bonnet Bowl, "Just Say No", Peoples Workshop for Visual and Performing Arts, Houston, 1987—, Nat. Black Child Devel. Inst., Washington, 1987—, Nat. Alliance Against Violence, N.Y., 1986—, Sheltering Arms, Houston, 1985—; task forcemem. Nat. Ctr. for Missing and Exploited Children, Washington, 1986—; adv. bd. Nat. Inst. Against Prejudice and Violence, Balt., 1987—; mem. Police Activities League, Houston, 1987—; mem. adv. policy bd. Nat. Incident Based Reporting System, 1988—; mem. adv. com. Fannie Mae, Washington, 1999; bd. dirs. Police Found., 2000; mem. U.S. Conf. of Mayors, Mayors and CEOs. Recipient Peace and Justice award Martin Luther King Jr., 1981, Nat. Law Enforcement award Nat. Black Police Assn., 1982, Disting. Alumnus award Fresno State U., 1983, Police Leadership award, Police Exec. Research Forum, 1987, Liberty Bell award Houston Young Lawyers Assn., 1987, August Vollmer award Am. Soc. Criminology, 1988, Cartier Pasha award Cartier Internat., 1992, Exemplary Leader award Am. Leadership Forum, 1994; named to Gallup Hall of Fame by Gallup, Inc., 1993; named Mgr. of Yr., Nat. Mgmt. Assn., Practitioner of Yr., Nat. Assn. of Blacks Criminal Justice, 1984, Communicator of Yr. Washington News Service, 1986, Father of Yr. Nat. Father's Day com., 1991, Politician of Yr. Libr. Jour.; rsch. fellow Harvard U., 1988. Mem. Internat. Assn. Chiefs of Police (past pres.), Nat. Orgn. of Black Law Enforcement Execs. (v.p. 1985, Robert Lamb Jr. Humanitarian award 1987), Police Exec. Research Forum, Internat. Narcotic Enforcement Officers Assn., Nat. Forum for Black Pub. Adminstrs., N.Y. Police Chiefs Assn., Tex. Police Assn., Tex. Criminal Justice Task Force, Nat. Police Athletic League, Mich. State U. (adv. council nat. neighborhood foot patrol ctr.), Nat. Research Council (com. on research on law enforcement and the adminstrn. of justice, com. on status of Black Ams.), Harvard U. (com. exec. session on community policing), Nat. Council on Crime and Delinquency (bd. dirs.), Nat. Acad. Pub. Adminstrn. (Nat. Pub. Svc. award 1988), Am. Soc. Pub. Adminstrn. (Nat. Pub. Svc. award 1988), Am. Leadership Forum, Forum Club of Houston (bd. dirs. 1987—), Calif. Alumni Club of Tex., Houston Bus. and Profl. Men's Club, Alpha Phi Alpha (Award of Merit 2000), Sigma Pi Phi. Democrat. Avocations: travel, reading. Office: City Hall 901 Bagby St Fl 3 Houston TX 77002-2526

BROWN, LEONARD ASHLEIGH, JR., lawyer; b. Newberry, S.C., July 24, 1969; s. Leonard Ashleigh and Sarah Gibson B.; m. Amy Durr, May 16, 1992; 1 child, Courtney. BA in History, Presbyn. Coll., 1991; JD, U. S.C. Sch. Law, 1997. Bar: S.C. Assoc. Welch Law Firm, Greenwood, S.C., 1997—; prosecutor City of Greenwood, 1998—, Lander U., Greenwood, 1999—; radio broadcaster Lander U. baseball, 1999—. Pres. Broken Ridge Homeowner's Assn., Greenwood, 1998—. Mem. ATLA, S.C. Assn. Criminal Def. Lawyers, S.C. Trial Lawyers Assn., Supreme Ct. Hist. Soc., Scotsmans Club, Big Blue Club. Methodist. Avocations: baseball, historical traveling, hunting, reading, scuba diving. Home: 210 Twisted Oak Dr Greenwood SC 29646-7564

BROWN, LESTER B., social work educator; b. Whitmire, S.C., Jan. 11, 1943; s. William Barney and Minnie Eugenia (Vaughn) B. AB in Psychology, U. Chgo., 1969, AM in Social Work, 1971, PhD in Social Treatment, 1980. Sr. child care counselor, therapist Nicholas J. Pritzker Ctr. and Hosp., Chgo., 1964-68, 69; social worker I Ill. Dept. Children and Family Svcs., Chgo., 1967-70, social worker II, 1971; group homes social worker Jewish Children's Bur., Chgo., 1971-73; social worker, field instr. Jackson Park Hosp., Chgo., 1973, clin. dir., 1973-74, cons., 1975-77; cons. SUNY-Albany, 1981, asst. prof. social work, chmn. undergrad. social welfare, 1981-86; prof. social worker Wayne State U., 1986-89; assoc. prof.. social work Calif. State U., Long Beach, 1989-95, prof. social work and Am. Indian studies, dir. studies, 1995—; lectr. U. Wis., Milw., 1977-78, instr., 1978-70; lectr. U. Chgo., 1977-78; guest lectr. Boston Coll., 1981; cons., presenter in field. Author: Two Spirit People: American Indian Lesbian Women and Gay Men, 1997, Aging Gay Men, 1997; contbr. articles to profl. jours., chpts. to books; mem. editl. bd. Health Care Mgmt. Rev., 1981-84. Condr. workshops on ethnic sensitive work Pittsfield Sch. Dist., Mass., 1984; participant workshops on mental health and child welfare; bd. dirs. Capital Dist. Travelers Aid Soc., 1983-86; mem. com. Urban League. Grantee Sch. Social Welfare, 1982, SUNY, 1981, U.S. Dept. HHS, 1981. Mem. NASW, Acad. Cert. Social Workers, Coun. Social Work Edn. Democrat. Avocation: baking/cooking. E-mail: Lbrown2@csulb.edu. Home: 810 Orizaba Ave Long Beach CA 90804-4926 Office: Calif State Univ Long Beach Am Indian Studies and Social Work 1250 N Bellflower Blvd Long Beach CA 90840-0006

BROWN, LESTER RUSSELL, research institute executive; b. Bridgeton, N.J., Mar. 28, 1934; s. Calvin C. and Delia (Smith) B.; m. Shirley Ann Woolington, June 12, 1960 (div.); children: Brian, Brenda. BS in Agrl. Sci., Rutgers U., 1955; MA in Agrl. Econs., U. Md., 1959; MPA, Harvard U., 1962; hon. degree, Dickinson Coll., U. Md., Franklin Coll., Williams Coll., Rutgers U., Glassboro State Coll., Tufts U., Coll. of Wooster, Clark U., Ripon Coll., Otterbein Coll., U. Pisa, McGill U., U. Notre Dame, Northland Coll., St. Lawrence U.; hon. deg., Claremont Coll., Villanova U., Westminster Coll. With Dept. of Agr., 1959-69, adminstr. internat. agr. devel. service, 1966-69; sr. fellow Overseas Devel. Council, 1969-74; pres. Worldwatch Inst., Washington, 1974—; mem. faculty Salzburg Seminar in Am. Studies, summer 1971, 74; guest scholar Aspen Inst., summers 1972-74; project dir., co-author State of the World, 1984-95; adv. com. mem. Population Reference Bur., Inst. for Internat. Econs. Author: Man, Land and Food, 1963, Increasing World Food Output, 1965, Seeds of Change, 1970, World Without Borders, 1972, In the Human Interest, 1974, (with Erik Eckholm) By Bread Alone, 1974 (Christopher award), The Twenty-Ninth Day, 1978 (Ecologia Firenze award), (with Colin Norman and Christopher Flavin) Running on Empty, 1979, Building a Sustainable Society, 1981, State of the World, 1984—, (with others) Vital Signs, 1992—, Full House, 1994, Who Will Feed China?, 1995, Tough Choices: Facing the Challenge of Global Food Scarcity, 1996; editor: (with Ed Ayres) World Watch Reader, 1998, (with Flavin and Sandra Postel) Saving the Planet, 1991, (with Gardner and Halweil) Beyond Malthus, 1999, numerous others; also articles. Mem. adv. com. Inst. Internat. Econs., Com. for Nat. Insts. for Environ., UN Found., Eco-Policy Ctr./Rutgers U.; mem. bd. advisors Internat. Fund for China's Environment; mem. internat. coun. Earth Day 2000; mem. in-

ternat. adv. com. Asahi Shimbun Create 21; bd. dirs. N.W. Environment Watch, Inst. for Sustainable Devel., Poland; mem. adv. coun. Internat. Fund for Agrl. Rsch.; advisor Clean Up the World Project, Australia, Internat. Coun. Earth Day 2000; mem. adv. bd. Ctr. for a New Am. Dream. Recipient Superior Svc. award Dept. Agr., 1965, Arthur S. Flemming award, 1965, A.H. Boerma award UN Food and Agrl. Orgn., 1981, Lorax award Global Tomorrow Coalition, 1985, award World Wildlife Fund for Nature Internat., 1989, UN Environment prize, 1989, A Bizzozero award U. Parma, 1990, Humanist of Yr. award, 1991, Pro Mundo Habitabili award King Carl XVI Gustaf, Sweden, 1991, Delphi Internat. Cooperation award, 1991, Robert Rodale Lectr. award, 1992, Environmentalist of Yr. award Japan Jaycees, 1992, Cert. Spl. Recognition Assn. Am. Geographers, 1993, Blue Planet prize Asahi Glass Found., 1994, J. Sterling Morton Arbor Day award, 1995, Pub. Svc. award Fedn. Am. Scientists, 1995, Disting. Achievement award Heylar House Alumni Assn. Rutgers U., 1995; selected as 100 Who Made A Difference The Earth Times, 1995, 100 Champions of Conservation, Audubon Soc., 1998, Rachel Carson Environ. Achievement award Nat. Nutritional Foods Assn., 2000. Mem. Coun. Fgn. Rels., Zero Population Growth (nat. adv. bd.), World Future Soc., Cosmos Club. Office: Worldwatch Inst Ste 800 1776 Massachusetts Ave NW Washington DC 20036-1995

BROWN, LILLIAN HILL, retired educator; b. Newport News, Va., Nov. 24, 1932; d. Charlie Wyatt and Caroline Melinda (Rowlett) Hill; m. Louis Franklin Brown, June 30, 1956; children: Avery L., Colin H. BS, Va. State Univ., 1955; MS, U. Bridgeport, 1967, profl. diploma advanced study, 1983; post grad., So. Conn. State Univ., 1985. Chmn. guidance and pers. svcs. Wilby H.S., Waterbury, Conn., team mem. student assistance team, coord. natural helpers program, proctor SAT coll. bds. prog.; mem. pres.'s adv. bd. Teikyo Post U.; admission advisor com. Naugatuck Valley Comty.-Tech. Coll.; adv. bd. to bd. govs. for higher edn. in Waterbury; adv. panel Racial Imbalance Regulations of Pub. Schs. in Conn.; regional adv. bd. dirs. Bank Boston. Bd. trustees St. Margaret's-McTernan Sch.; bd. dirs., chmn. nominating com. Waterbury Symphony Orch.; trustee, chair nominating com. The Antiquarian and Landmark Soc.; bd. dirs. Children's Comty. Sch.; chmn. bd. dirs. Waterbury chpt. ARC; bd. trustees, chmn. scholarship com. The Waterbury Found.; bd. mgrs., mem. The Waterbury Club; mem. devel. com. Waterbury Hosp. Health Network, Inc.-Waterbury Hosp.; mem. oral history project African Ams. in Waterbury; co-chair Leavenworth Soc./United Way; vestry bd., chalice bearer St. John's Episcopal Ch.; life mem. NAACP; mem. Waterbury chorale; co-founder In Search of Excellence A Scholarship Fund for African Am. Students; incorporator Child Guidance Clinic; co-chair United Way-Leavenworth Soc.; adv. regional bd. Bank Boston. Recipient Plaque for Outstanding Leadership in Comty., Tribute to Conn. Women, Plaque for Outstanding Leadership in Comty., Alpha Kappa Alpha, Achievement award Nat. Assn. Negro Bus. and Profl. Woman's Clubs, Inc., Comty. Svc. award Waterbury Jaycees, 1991, St. John's Order of the Eagle, 1995, Humanitarian Svc. award Henderson's Boys Club, 1999. Mem. NEA (life), Conn. Edn. Assn., Waterbury Tchr. Assn., Pupil Pers. and Guidance Assn., The Sch. Counselor (Conn. chpt.), Phi Delta Kappa (Plaque for Dedicated Svc. to U. of Conn. chpt. 1993), Delta Sigma Theta (charter mem. New Haven alumnae chpt.), The Links, Inc. (charter mem. Waterbury chpt.). Avocations: domestic and foreign travel, collecting Lladro porcelain, chorale singing, collecting porcelain dolls of color. Home: 59 Timber Ln Waterbury CT 06705-3608

BROWN, LINDA K., secondary education educator, writer; b. Balt., Mar. 23, 1952; d. Jack and Lillie Estelle (Boykin) B. BS in History, Towson U., 1974, MS in Profl. Writing, 1998; MA in Ed. History, U. Md., 1980. Advanced profl. cert. 5-12 history and social studies tchr., Md. Tchr. Balt. City Pub. Schs., 1974-78, 81-82; grad. tchg. and rsch. asst. history dept. U. Md., College Park, 1978-80; tchr. Harford County (Md.) Pub. Schs., 1986-92, St. Paul's Sch. for Girls, Brooklandville, Md., 1991-94; dir. Mid. East project Am. Friends Svc. Com., Balt., 1982-83; prof. English, Nat. Sch. for Engrs. Gabes, Tunisia, 1983-85; tchr. Baltimore County Pub. Schs., Balt., 1994—, corod. internat. baccalaureat program, 1998—, also author in-svc. course for tchrs. on Mid. East. Contbr. essays to profl. publs. Bd. dirs., editor newsletter Beverly Hills Improvement Assn., Balt., 1990-95. Fulbright scholar, 1977, Arabic lang. study scholar Mid. East Inst., 1981-82. Mem. World History Assn., Mid. East Studies Assn. (local arrangements com. ann. conf. 1985).

BROWN, LYNETTE RALYA, journalist, publicist; b. Beloit, Wis., Dec. 15, 1926; d. Lynn Louis and Ethel Clara (Meeker) Ralya; m. Donald Adair Brown, Jr., Dec. 20, 1947; children: Donald Adair III, Alison Laura, Julia Carol. BA in Journalism, Mich. State U., 1948; MA in Journalism, Michigan State U., 1985; MA in Mass Comm., Wayne State U., 1983. Actress, publicist Grand Traverse Playhouse, Traverse City, Mich., 1946 (summer), N.Y. Summer Playhouse, Mackinac Island, Mich., 1947 (summer); writer WILS Radio, Lansing, Mich., 1947-48; writer, performer WJBK Radio, TV, Detroit, 1948-49; editor Denby Ctr. News, Detroit, 1949-51; freelance writer Oakland County, Mich., 1952-78; editor Henry Ford Mus., Dearborn, Mich., 1979-81; writer, reporter Legal Advertiser Newspaper, Detroit, 1983-85; publicist Bloomfield (Mich.) and Birmingham (Mich.) Pub. Librs., 1986-89; freelance writer, publicist Lynette Brown Comm., Birmingham, Mich., 1989—. Columnist: (newspaper) At the Libraries, 1986-89; solo performer Elizabeth Cady Stanton, 1995—. Probation sponsor Dist. Ct. Mich., 1960-70; publicist Oakland County Vol. Bur., 1979-82; leader sr. high/jr. high youth group Drayton Ave. Presbyn. Ch., Oakland County, 1952-54, 62-66, Pine Hill Congl. Ch., Oakland County, 1968-71, Northbrook Presbyn. Ch., Oakland County, 1976-77; polit. campaign worker Rep. candidates and non-partisan jud. candidates, 1952—; Cub Scout leader Royal Oak Emerson Sch., Oakland County, 1961-64; Girl Scout troop leader Bloomfield Twp. Meadow Lake Sch., Oakland County, 1966-71. Grantee N.Y. State's Thanks Be To Grandmother Winifred Found., 1996. Mem. AAUW (chair women's issues, pub. info. dir. 1995-2000, state projects dir. 2000—), Oakland County C. of C. (Athena award 1995), Mich. Women's Studies Assn. (bd. dirs. 1999—). Home and Office: 6120 Westmoor Rd Bloomfield Hills MI 48301-1355

BROWN, MABEL WELTON, lawyer; b. Geneseo, Ill., Dec. 7, 1916; d. Harry E. and Mabel (Welton) B. BA, Oberlin Coll., 1938; JD, U. Chgo., 1941. Bar: Ill. Ptnr. Brown and Brown, Geneseo, 1941-44; sole owner Brown & Brown, Geneseo, 1944-81; sr. ptnr. Brown and Ray, Geneseo, 1981—; atty. Green River Spl. Drainage Dist., Henry and Bureau Counties, Ill.; chmn. Geneseo Planning Commn., 1961-68. Mem. ABA, Ill. Bar Assn., Henry County Bar Assn. (pres. 1973-76). Republican. Methodist. Office: Brown and Ray 115 N State St Geneseo IL 61254-1345

BROWN, MAHLON CARL, social science educator; b. Downsville, N.Y., Dec. 26, 1926; s. Carl and Sarah Elizabeth Brown; m. Thelma Marie Brown, Oct. 22, 1949; children: William, Phillip, Scott. BA, Syracuse U., 1951, PhD in Social Sci., 1959. Prof. Marshall U., Huntington, W.Va., 1955-92, dir. study abroad program, 1974, developer, dir. W.Va. state social studies fair, 1978-82; asst. dir. study abroad program SUNY, Buffalo, 1970. Staff sgt. U.S. Army, 1944-46. Mem. Kiwanis, USCG Auxiliary. Mem. United Ch. of Christ. E-mail: melodee@crosslink.net. Home: 132 Lancaster Dr Apt 711 Irvington VA 22480-9746

BROWN, MELISSA BABBETTE, business owner, actress; b. Vienna, Nov. 11, 1963; arrived in France; d. kurt Adolf Schickelgrubber and Sarah Maria Winkelmein; m. Ruben Moshi Cohen, Feb. 11, 1983 (div. July 1988); children: Simon, Jonathan, Judith; m. John Stearton Brown, March 4, 1999; children: Kurt, Jack, Wilhelm, Artur, Maria, Sally, Elrabien. BA, Oxford U., England, 1981, LLB, 1983; MBA, MIT, 1988. Asst. mgr. ICI, England, 1984-86; v.p. L'Oreal, France, 1986-89; exec. v.p. Carrefour, France, 1989-92; pres. Uniforce, France, 1992—; dir. La-La-oo, France, 1993—; asst. exec. ARC, France, 1996—. Author: Les Oiseaux de dunkirk; dir. theatre Hamlet, 1997.; contbr. articles to profl. jours. Local organizer Front Nat., Nice, 1997—. Recipient medaille noire Front Nat., 1998; Legion d'honneur 3rd classe, 1999. Mem. Athanaeum. Avocations: theatre, dancing.

BROWN, MICHAEL EWART, chemistry educator; b. Johannesburg, South Africa, July 12, 1938; s. Sydney Arthur Ewart and Joan Caroline (Sweeny) B.; m. Cynthia Millicent Aylmeré Kay, Dec. 11, 1965; children: Richard, Linda. BS with honors, U. Witwatersrand, 1960; PhD, Rhodes U., 1966. Jr. lectr. Rhodes U., Grahamstown, South Africa, 1962-65, lectr., 1967-70, sr. lectr., 1971-77, assoc. prof., 1978-85, prof., 1986—; rsch. officer Chamber of Mines, Johannesburg, 1966; Leverhulme fellow Queen's U., Belfast, 1971; vis. fellow Cavendish Lab., Cambridge, England, 1980; vis. rschr. ICI, Scotland, 1989; vis. prof. Queen's U., 1989; dean of sci. Rhodes U., 1986-92. Author: Introduction to Thermal Analysis, 1988, Thermal Decomposition of Ionic Solids, 1999; contbr. articles to profl. jours. Recipient Mettler award for thermal analysis N.Am. Thermal Analysis Soc., 1996. Fellow Royal Soc. South Africa. Home: 3 Frances St Grahamstown 6139, South Africa Office: Rhodes U Dept Chemistry, PO Box 94, Grahamstown 6140, South Africa

BROWN, MICHAEL JOHN, solicitor; b. London, Sept. 23, 1932; s. Stanley Reginald Brown and Ada Phyllis (Evett) B.; m. Margaret Jordan, Sept. 20, 1963 (dec. Nov. 1988); children: Edward Hugh, Thomas Andrew, Robert Michael (dec.), Adam Charles. MA in Jurisprudence, Oxford U., 1954. Ptnr. Denton Hall & Burgin, London, 1959-80; sr. ptnr. Brown Cooper, London, 1981-96; cons. Brown Corp., 1996—; chmn. Urwick Orr & Ptnrs., U.K., 1980-84, Pooh Properties Trust, U.K., 1973-2000. Mem. Soc. English and Am. Lawyers (hon. pres. 1989-92), Law Soc. Gr. Britain, Copinger Soc. (hon. pres. 1992-93), Variety Club Gt. Britain (hon. solicitor 1966-2000), The Pilgrims, The Garrick Club (hon. life mem.). Anglican. Office: Brown Cooper, 7 Southampton Pl, London WD3 5LW, England

BROWN, MICHAEL JOHN, judge; b. Racine, Wis., Sept. 28, 1933; s. John Richard and Evelyn Mary Brown; m. Anna C. Brown, Jan. 21, 1966 (dec. Apr. 1975); children: Brian, Kevin, Michael L. LLB, U. Notre Dame, 1955; JD, U. Ariz., 1959. Bar: Ariz., U.S. Dist. Ct. Ariz., U.S. Ct. Appeals, U.S. Supreme Ct. Pvt. practice Tucson, 1959-61; ptnr. Brown, Finn & Rosenberg, Tucson, 1962-66; chief city prosecutor City of Tucson, 1962-65; ptnr. Brown & Finn, Tucson, 1966-78; pvt. practice Michael J. Brown, P.C., Tucson, 1978-81; superior ct. judge Pima County Superior Ct. Ariz., Tucson, 1981—; presiding judge Superior Ct. Ariz., 1991-99; mem. malpractice com. Supreme Ct. Ariz., 1982, mem. litigation com., 1983—, mem. jury utilization com., 1995—. Pres., bd. dirs. La Frontera Ctr., Tucson, 1975-81. Fellow State Bar Ariz.; mem. Pima County Bar Assn. Avocations: rafting, scuba diving, racquetball. Office: Superior Ct Ariz 110 W Congress St # 450 Tucson AZ 85701-1331

BROWN, MICHAEL STUART, geneticist, educator, administrator; b. N.Y.C., N.Y., Apr. 13, 1941; s. Harvey and Evelyn (Katz) B.; m. Alice Lapin, June 21, 1964; children: Elizabeth Jane, Sara Ellen. BA, U. Pa., 1962, MD, 1966; DSc (hon.), Rensselaer Poly. Inst., 1982, U. Chgo., 1982, U. Pa., 1986, U. Buenos Aires, 1988, U. Paris, 1988, So. Meth. U., 1993, U. Miami, 1996. Intern, then resident in medicine Mass. Gen. Hosp., Boston, 1966-68; served with USPHS, 1968-70; clin. assoc. NIH, 1968-71; asst. prof. U. Tex. Southwestern Med. Sch., Dallas, 1971-74; Paul J. Thomas prof. U. Tex., 1977—; mem. med. adv. genetics, dir. Ctr. for Molecular Genetics, U. Tex., 1977—; mem. med. adv. bd. Scripps Inst.; dir. Pfizer, Inc., Regeneron, Inc. Co-editor: The Metabolic Basis of Inherited Disease, 1983. Trustee Lamplighter Sch. Recipient Pfizer award Am. Chem. Soc., 1976, Passano award Passano Found., 1978, Lounsbery award U.S. Nat. Acad. Scis., 1979; Lita Annenberg Hazen award, 1982, Albert Lasker Med. Rsch. award, 1985, Horwitz prize, 1985, Nobel Prize in Medicine or Physiology, 1985, Nat. Medal of Sci. U.S., 1988. Mem. Nat. Acad. Scis., Am. Soc. Clin. Investigation, Assn. Am. Physicians, Harvey Soc., Royal Acad. Scis. (fgn. mem.). Office: U Tex Health Sci Ctr Dept Molecular Genetics 5323 Harry Hines Blvd Dallas TX 75390-7208

BROWN, MILLIE LOUISE, mental health nurse; b. Boston, Dec. 18, 1937; d. Joseph Francis and Louise Frances (McGunigle) B. RN, Boston City Hosp., 1959; student, Mt. St. Mary, 1964-65, Dean Coll., 1971-76. Head nurse maximum security males Boston State Hosp., 1959-64, Harvard Svc. Boston City Hosp.; head nurse Harvard Surg. Svc. Boston City Hosp., 1965-67; head nurse maximum security males Wrentham (Mass.) State Sch., 1971-73; ret., 1973. Organizer Millie's March for Arthritis; numerous community svc. activities. Recipient Ernie Bock Community Salute Award; named one of Outstanding Young Women of Am., 1972. Mem. Blackstone Valley Writers Guild. Home: 270 Garden Ln Wrentham MA 02093-1366

BROWN, MORRIS JONATHAN, clinical pharmacology educator, physician; b. Edinburgh, Scotland, U.K., Jan. 18, 1951; s. Arnold and Irene (Goodman) B.; m. Diana Phylactou, July 31, 1977; children: Emily Irene Annie, Chrysothemis Celia Margaret, Ophelia Wendy Elizabeth. MA, Cambridge U., 1971, MB BChir, 1974; MSc, U. London, 1980; MD, Cambridge U., 1984. Intern Univ. Coll. Hosp., London, 1974; resident Guy's Hosp., London, 1975, Brompton Hosp., London, 1976, Hammersmith Hosp., London, 1977-79; sr. fellow MRC and Royal Postgrad. Med. Sch., London, 1982-85; prof. clin. pharmacology Cambridge U., U.K., 1985—. Editor: Advanced Medicine, 1985, Clin. Sci., 1983—; contbr. articles on catecholamines and hypertension to profl. jours. Recipient Raymond Horton Smith prize, Cambridge U., 1984; Warren Macdonald fellow Australian Heart Found., 1985. Fellow Royal Soc. Medicine (Alma Edwards prize 1981); mem. Brit. Pharm. Soc., Med. Research Soc., Royal Coll. Physicians. Avocations: violinist, tennis. Office: Clin Pharmacology Unit, Level 6, ACCI Box 110, Cambridge CB2 2QQ, England

BROWN, NAN MARIE, clergywoman; b. Winton, N.C., Jan. 2, 1931; d. Richard and Aberdeen Elizebeth (Clanton) Watford; m. Joseph Linwood Blunt, June 9, 1947 (dec. Sept. 1970); children: Linette, Joseph Linwood Jr., Alvin; m. Frank Coolige Brown, Oct. 2, 1972; stepchildren: Ameedah Ali, Sami Nuridden. BS, D.C. Tchrs. Coll., 1972; MDiv magna cum laude, Va. Union U., 1982, D Ministry in Ch. Adminstrn., 1993. Ordained to ministry Bapt. Ch., 1980. Clk., sec., adminstr. Dept. Commerce and AEC, Suitland, Germantown, Md., 1960-65; program analyst Job Corps, U.S. Office Econs., Washington, 1965-67; licensing asst. U.S. Nuclear Regulatory Commn., Bethesda, Md., 1967-72, pers. mgmt. analyst, 1972-74; mgr. nat. fed. women's program U.S. Dept. Energy, Germantown, 1974-76; nat. dir. fed. women's program U.S. Dept. Interior, Washington, 1979; asst. pastor Pleasant Grove Bapt. Ch., Columbia, Va., 1975-83; pastor Mt. Level Bapt. Ch., Dinwiddie, Va., 1983-87, New Hope Bapt Ch., Esmont, Va., 1987-89; founder, pastor The Way of Cross Bapt. Ch., Palmyra, Va., 1989—; vice moderator, moderator Albemarle Bapt. Assn., 1996-98; moderator Slate River Bapt. Assn., 1997-99; bd. dirs. AIDS Svcs. Group; cons. Nan M. Brown Assocs., bus. cons.; vol. cons., reviewer AIDS proposals for funding Va. Health Dept., Richmond, 1979-89; founder, dir. Children's Saturday Enrichment Program, Palmyra, 1990—; mem. gen. bd. Bapt. Gen. Conv. Va., mem. social concerns com., 1990; vice moderator Slate River Bapt. Assn., 1995—; cert. AIDS trainer; adj. professor, Va. Union U., Samuel Dewitt Sch. of Theology, Evans-Smith Leadership Inst. 1982—; founder, CEO The Way of the Cross Comm. Devel. Corp., Inc., 1998—. Author: (devotionals) The Word in Season, 1986, The Patience To Wait, Vol. I, 1988, Vol. II, 1992; contbg. author: Wise Women Bearing Gifts, 1988, Those Preachin' Women, 1988, Sister to Sister, 1995. Founder, pres. Black Women in Sisterhood for Action, Washington, 1979-82; vol. chaplain Martha Jefferson Hosp., Charlottesville, Va., 1993—; bd. dirs. AIDS Support Group, Charlottesville, 1990; mem. Fluvanna County Minority Health Coalition, 1993—; mem. Fluvanna County Commn. on Youth, 1999—; U.S. del. to Internat. Women's Yr. Conf. on Women, Mexico City, 1975; participant First All-Africa Theol. Conf./Bapt. World Alliance, Zimbabwe; selected by Women's Internat. Dem. Fedn. to represent U.S. as del. to World Congress on Women, Moscow, 1987, others. Named Disting. Black Woman, Black Women in Sisterhood for Action, 1982; recipient recognition for cmty. svc. Interfrat. Coun., Charlottesville, 1993, award for excellence Sister Care Internat., 1995, spl. achievement and cmty. svc. award Charlottesville Tribune, 1996. Mem. NAACP (pres. Fluvanna County chpt. 1979-81, cert. of appreciation 1994), Va. Women in Ministry (founder, pres. 1983-88, chaplain, Founder's award 1986, 90, 95). Avocations: reading, listening to music, sewing, travel, playing piano. Home: PO Box 39 RR 2 Box 1785 Kents Store VA 23084-9731 Office: Way of Cross Bapt Ch State Rt 640 Palmyra VA 23084

BROWN, NANCY CHILDS, marriage and family therapist; b. Butler, Ga., Feb. 17, 1938; d. Preston Bussey and Essie Lou (Jones) Childs; m. Luther Edward Brown (dec. Oct. 6, 1988); children: Melanie B. Ketchum, Catherine B. Tucker, Anthony E. Brown. BA in English with honors, Mercer U., 1960, MS, 1998. Lic. assoc. marriage and family therapist. Stockbroker/sales asst. Evans & Co./Robinson-Humphrey Co., Augusta, Ga., 1961-64; real estate owner/mgr. Macon, Ga., 1975-98; exec. dir. Macon Arts Alliance, 1985-92; assoc. marriage and family therapist in pvt. practice, 1998—; bd. leaders Atlanta Internat. Mus. Art and Design, 1994—; bd. dirs. Ga. Coun. for the Arts (gov. appointee), 1994-97. Treas. Hay House, 1995-96, adv. bd., 1996—; pres. Macon Heritage Found., 1979-80; mem. founding bd. City Club of Macon, 1989-91; v.p. legislation Assocs. to Ga., Soc. Ophthalmology, 1985; chmn. City of Macon Cmty. Devel. Inner City Adv. Com., 1979-82; bd. dirs. tourism devel. com. Macon Conv. and Visitors Bur., 1990-97; mem. MAPS (City of Macon) Policy Com. (mayoral appointee ward 3), 1994-99; former pres. Bibb County Med. Soc. Alliance; choir of Vineville United Meth. Ch., 1988—; bd. dirs. Macon Symphony Orch., 1998—. Recipient Macon Cultural award Macon Arts Alliance and City of Macon, 1992; named Woman of Achievement Career Women's Network, Macon, 1990; winner Algernon Sydney Sullivan award, 1960, Alumni Meritorious Svc. award Mercer U., 1977. Mem. Career Women's Network, City Club of Macon, Ga. Trust for Hist. Preservation, Am. Assn. for Marriage and Family Therapy, Phi Kappa Phi. Avocations: choral singing, golf, culinary arts, piano playing, travel. Home: 937 Walnut St Macon GA 31201-1918

BROWN, NICK, administrator; b. June 12, 1950. BA, Manchester U., England, 1971. Mem. Tyne City Coun., 1980-84; elected mem. Parliament, 1983—; deputy to shadow leader of commons, 1992-94, deputy chief opposition whip, 1995-97, govt. chief whip, 1997-98; min. Dept. Agrl., Fisheries & Food, 1998—. Office: Min Agrl Fisheries & Food, Whitehall Pl, London SW1A 2HH, England*

BROWN, NIGEL LESLIE, research molecular biologist, educator; b. Beverley, Eng., Dec. 19, 1948; s. Leslie Charles and Beryl (Brown) B.; m. Gayle Lynnette Blackah, Aug. 7, 1971; children: Sarah Victoria, Katharine Elizabeth. BS in Biochemistry, U. Leeds, 1971, PhD in Biochemistry, 1974. ICI postdoctoral fellow Lab. Molecular Biology, Med. Rsch. Coun. Ctr., Cambridge, Eng., 1974-76; lectr. in biochemistry U. Bristol, Eng., 1976-81, EPA Cephalosporin Fund sr. rsch. fellow dept. biochemistry, 1981-88; vis. fellow in genetics U. Melbourne, Australia, 1987-88; prof. molecular genetics and microbiology U. Birmingham, Eng., 1989—, head biol. scis., 1994-99, dep. head bioscis., 1999-2000; mem. Leverhulme Trust Rsch. Fellowship, 2000—. Contbr. articles to sci. jours. Fellow Inst. Biology (chartered), Royal Soc. Chemistry (chartered). Avocations: home improvements, wine, science, travel. Office: U Birmingham Sch Biol Scis, U Birmingham Sch Bioscis, Edgbaston, Birmingham B15 2TT, England

BROWN, OTHA NATHANIEL, JR., political official, retired educator; b. DeQueen, Ark., July 19, 1931; s. Otha Brown and Elizabeth Gossitt; m. Marjorie Gay, June 19, 1956 (div. Feb. 1967); m. Lela Evelyn Brown, Dec. 30, 1975; children: Darrick O., Leland K. BS, Ctrl. State U., Wilberforce, Ohio, 1952; MA, U. Conn., 1956; 6th Yr. Profl. Diploma, U. Bridgeport, 1959. Cert. ednl. adminstr., sch. counselor, Conn. Tchr. Bd. Edn., Stratford, Conn., 1957-61; tchr., counselor Bd. Edn., Stamford, Conn., 1961-90; guidance dir., counselor J.M. Wright Tech. Sch., Stamford, Conn., 1990-92; coord. state program Dept. Human Resources, State of Conn., Hartford, 1992-93; dir., CEO regional campus U. Conn., Waterbury, 1994-98; mem. State Jud. Task Force, Hartford, 1987-91; mem. internat. affairs com. Am. Waterworks Assn., Denver, 1992-99; mem. adv. bd. Patriot Nat. Bank, Stamford, 1994—. Author: (poetry) Remembering. . ., 1977; contbr. articles to profl. jours. Mem. Norwalk Common Coun., City of Norwalk, Conn., 1963-69; mem. Conn. Ho. of Reps., Hartford, 1966-72, 77-81; trustee, sec. U. Conn., Storrs, 1975-93; commr. 2d Taxing Dist./Water Dept., South Norwalk, Conn., 1982—; charter mem. Action Housing, Inc., mem. exec. bd., 1970—. 1st lt. U.S. Army, 1952-54. Recipient The Univ. medal U. Conn., 1994; named Young Man of Yr., Jaycees, 1967; named to Hall of Fame, Ctrl. State U., Wilberforce, 1996. Mem. NAACP (pres. 1967-69), Norwalk Area Improvement League (founder, pres. 1976—), Elks, Masons, Alpha Phi Alpha (pres., dir.). Democrat. Avocations: writing, chorale singing, politics, jazz, travel. Home: 21 Shorefront Park Norwalk CT 06854-3752 Office: 2d Taxing Dist 164 Water St Norwalk CT 06854-3739

BROWN, PATRICIA ANN, child health nurse; b. Kokomo, Ind., Apr. 4, 1938; d. John Conrad and Marie L. (Landseadel) B. BSN, Ind. U., 1959, MSN, 1969; Pediatric Nurse Assoc., U. Tenn., 1976. Staff nurse, asst. head nurse Ind. U. Children's Hosp., Indpls., 1960-66; chief nurse Child Devel. Ctr., Memphis, 1966-67; instr., asst. prof. child health nursing Ctr. for Health Scis., U. Tenn., Memphis, 1969-73; asst. prof. child health nursing U. Tenn., Knoxville, 1973-75, U. Tenn. Ctr. for Health Scis., Memphis, 1975-84; child health nursing faculty Holmes Jr. Coll., Grenada, Miss., 1985-89; dir. nursing East Ark. C.C., Forrest City, Ark., 1989-96; chairperson Nursing Faculty Coun., Memphis. Hospice vol. Hospice of Memphis, 1981-84. Mem. Nat. League for Nursing, Tenn. Nurses Assn. (chairperson Maternal Child Health), Ark. State Bd. Nursing, Coun. Nursing Adminstrs. of Nursing Edn. Programs in Ark. (chairperson assoc. degree nursing coun. 1992-94), Ind. U. Alumni, Sigma Theta Tau, Pi Lambda Theta. Methodist. Avocations: needlework, baking, traveling, family, yard work. Home: 7625 Saddlebrooke Dr Knoxville TN 37938-4044

BROWN, PAUL DEAN, microbiologist, researcher; b. Kingston, Jamaica, Feb. 7, 1968; s. Percival and Constance Adelaide (Morgan) B.; m. Audrey Jacqueline Hawthorne, Mar. 22, 1997. BSc, U. West Indies, Mona, Jamaica, 1989, MPhil, 1992; PhD, U. West Indies, Cave Hill, Barbados, 1995. Cert. counseling, human rels. and bus. etiquette, conversational French. Lab. demonstrator U. West Indies, Mona, 1989-92, lab. technician, 1991-92; rsch. fellow U. West Indies, Cave Hill, Barbados, 1995-97; lectr. U. Tech., St. Andrew, Jamaica, 1991; chief forensic officer Jamaica Constabulary, 1997-99; asst. prof. microbiology, grad. program coord. No. Caribbean U., Mandeville, Jamaica, 1999—; chmn. AIDS Care, Edn. & Tng., Barbados, 1995-97, tng. coord., 1995-97. Contbr. articles to profl. jours., chpt. to book. Recipient fellowship Jamaica Flour Mills, 1988, postgrad. fellowship Jamaica Agrl. Devel. Rsch. Program, 1991, 92. Mem. ASCD, Internat. Leptospirosis Soc., Caribbean Biotech. Network. Avocations: reading, athletics, soccer, aerobics, swimming.

BROWN, PAUL SHERMAN, lawyer; b. St. Louis, June 26, 1921; s. Paul Michael and Norma (Sherman) B.; m. Ann Wilson, Feb. 7, 1959; 1 son, Paul S. BS in Commerce, St. Louis U., 1943, JD cum laude, 1951. Bar: Mo. 1951, U.S. Dist. Ct. (ea. dist.) Mo. 1951, U.S. Ct. Appeals (8th cir.) 1951, U.S. Supreme Ct. 1966. Shareholder, Brown & James , P.C., St. Louis, 1980—; instr. St. Louis U. Night Law Sch., 1978—; lectr. in field. Mem. St. Louis Amateur Athletic Assn. (dir. 1974-76, pres. 1976-78); mem. com. on civil pattern jury instructions, Mo. Supreme Ct. Fellow Am. Coll. Trial Lawyers, Internat. Acad. Trial Lawyers, Internat. Soc. Barristers; mem. ABA (vice-chmn. com. consumer products liability 1977-78), Mo. Bar Assn. (bd. govs. 1963-67), Am. Bd. Trial Advocates, Lawyers Assn. St. Louis, Bar Assn. Met. St. Louis (pres. 1970-71), Am. Judicature Soc., Order of Woolsack, Alpha Sigma Nu. Roman Catholic. Contbr. numerous articles to profl. jours. Home: 7331 Kingsbury Blvd Saint Louis MO 63130-4143 Office: Brown & James 705 Olive St Ste 1100 Saint Louis MO 63101-2270

BROWN, PHILIP JOHN, scientific author, publisher, computer consultant; b. Coventry, U.K., Apr. 5, 1948; s. John and Irene (Riley) B.; m. Patricia Ann Adams; 1 child, Kelvin. BSc in Physics with honors, Nottingham (U.K.) U., 1969. Tchr. English Berlitz Schule, Mainz, Germany, 1970-71; tchr. math. various schs., Coventry and Cambridge, U.K., 1971-77; researcher Cambridge U., 1977-80; lectr. Hereward Coll., Coventry, 1980-86; systems analyst GEC Plessey Telecoms, Coventry, 1987-92; author, pub. Penny Press, Coventry, 1992-94; cons. Sharelink, Birmingham, U.K., 1992-94, Mac User Mag., London, 1987-89, Eastern Electricity, U.K., 1996-99, Hewlett Packard, 1999-2000. Author: Hyperdictionary, 1988, Global Vision, 1992; editor: Midlands Computing Newsletter, 1988-97; editor History of the Universe website (www.historyoftheuniverse.com), 1999—. Mem. Brit. Computer Soc. (past holder various offices), History of the Universe Assn. (founder, chmn.). Avocations: classical music, drawing, walking. Email: philip@pennypress.co.uk. Office: Penny Press Ltd, 176 Greendale Rd, CV5 8AY Coventry England

BROWN, RANDALL L., reinsurance company executive; b. Chillicothe, Ohio, May 16, 1956; s. Donald Clair Brown and Lois Mae Daniels; (div. July 1999); children: Casey, Lisa, Tim. BS, Ohio State U., 1978. Comml.

underwriter Royal Ins., Chgo., 1978-84; 2nd v.p. Nat. RE, Stamford, Conn., 1984-93; exec. v.p. CNA RE, Chgo., 1993-99; chmn. Continental Nat. Ind., Cin., 1999—. Republican. Lutheran. E-mail: RBrown6242@aol.com.

BROWN, RICHARD COLIN, physicist; b. Swaffham, Eng., July 25, 1944; s. George Alfred and Hilda Emma (Bennington) B. BSc, U. Sheffield, Eng., 1967; PhD, U. Sheffield, 1970, D of Tech. Sci., 1994. Chartered physicist, chartered engr., Eng. Sr. prin. scientist Health and Safety Lab., Sheffield, 1992—. Author: Air Filtration, 1993; patentee in field; contbr. articles to profl. jours. Mem. Royal Soc. for Protection of Birds, Campaign for Preservation of Rural Eng., Woodland Trust, Rambler's Assn. Fellow Inst. of Physics; mem. Worshipful Co. of Spectaclemakers of London (freeman). Avocations: music, ancient Greek literature, country-walking, swimming. Office: Health & Safety Lab, Broad Ln, Sheffield S3 7HQ, England

BROWN, RICHARD HARRIS, information technology executive; b. New Brunswick, N.J., June 3, 1947; s. Harris Ransford and Winifred (Clelland) B.; Christine Demler, Sept. 27, 1969; children: Ryan, Allison. BS in Communications, Ohio U., 1969. Comml. rep. Ohio Bell, Columbus, 1969-71, comml. mgr., 1971-74; dist. comml. mgr. Ohio Bell, Toledo and Cleve., 1974-80; div. mgr. Ohio Bell, Cleve., 1980-81; v.p. engring. & ops. United Telephone System, Inc. subs. United Telecommunications, Inc., Westwood, Kans., 1981-82; v.p. ops. United Telephone Co. of Midwest, Overland Park, Kans., 1982-83; v.p., COO United Telephone Co. of Fla., Apopka, 1983-87; sr. v.p. human resources & adminstrn. United Telecommunications, Inc., Shawnee Mission, Kans., 1987, sr. v.p. ops., 1987-89, exec. v.p., chief info. & planning officer, 1989; vice chmn., bd. dirs. Ameritech, 1993-95, Chgo., 1993-95; pres., CEO H&R Block, Inc., Kansas City, Mo., 1995-96; CEO, bd. dirs. Cable and Wireless PLC, London, 1996-99; chmn., ceo EDS (Elec. Data Systems), Plano, TX, 1999—; bd. dirs. The Seagram Co. Ltd.; chmn. Hong Kong Telecomm., bd. dirs., The Seagram Co., Ltd. Trustee, vice-chmn. Ohio U. Found., Athens, 1989—; vice chmn. Chog. United Way Campaign, 1994. With USNG, 1969-74. Named Outstanding Alumnus, Coll. of Interpersonal Comms., Ohio U., 1988. Mem. Chgo. Club, Shoreacres Country Club, Coml. Club, Econ. Club, Northwestern U. Assocs. Execs. Club, The Bus. Roundtable, 1999. Office: EDS 5400 Legacy Dr Plano TX 75024-3199

BROWN, RICHARD LAWRENCE, lawyer; b. Evansville, Ind., Dec. 8, 1932; s. William S. and Mildred (Tenbarge) B.; m. Alice Rae Costello, June 14, 1957; children: Richard, Catherine, Vanessa, Mary, James. AA, Vincennes U., 1953; BA, Ind. State U., 1957; JD, Ind. U., 1960. Bar: Ind., 1960, U.S. dist. ct. (so. dist.) Ind., 1961, U.S. Ct. Apls. (7th cir.), 1972, U.S. Sup. Ct., 1972. Mng. ptnr. Butler, Brown, Hahn and Little, and predecessor firms, Indpls., 1961-85, Butler, Brown and Blythe, Indpls., 1985-92; city atty. City of Beech Grove, Ind., 1967—; pvt. practice Beech Grove, Ind., 1992—; of counsel Blythe & Ost, Indpls., 1994-96, Holwager, Byers & Caughy, Beech Grove, 1996—; sec., treas. Internat. Bus. Inst., Dayton, Ohio, 1987—, Internat. Pub. Inst., Dayton, 1987-96; bd. dirs. Vincennes U. Found. Editor: Indiana Municipal Lawyers Assn. Newsletter, 1985—. Chmn. bd. zoning appeals small cities and towns Marion County, Ind., 1965-66; gen. counsel Habitat for Humanity Greater Indpls., 1985-95; parish chmn. St. Jude's Ch. With U.S. Army, 1953-55. Fellow Indpls. Bar Assn.; mem. ABA, Ind. Bar Assn., Ind. Mcpls. Lawyers Assn. (co-editor newsletter, bd. dirs., pres. 1987-88), Vincennes U. Alumni Assn. (pres., bd. dirs. 1990-92), KC, Delta Theta Phi. Roman Catholic. Avocation: golf. Office: 1818 Main St Beech Grove IN 46107-1418

BROWN, RICKY, medical consultant; b. New Brunswick, N.J., Jan. 21, 1948. MD, Harvard U., 1963. Med. dr. RWJ Hosp. and St. Peter's Hosp., New Brunswick, 1962-63; cons. Assissi Bonopart Moves, New Brunswick, 1990—. Mem. Dem. Congl. Campaign Commn., 1992; Rep. Presdl. Task Force, 1997. Pilot U.S. Army, 1963. Mem. Am. Mus. Nat. History, Am. Inst. Aeronautics and Astronomy, Libr. Democrat. Roman Catholic. Avocations: football, wrestling, track, swimming. Home: 118 Joyce Kilmer Ave Apt C3C New Brunswick NJ 08901-2925

BROWN, ROBERT FREDERICK, industrial systems engineer, technology applications, industrial systems and management systems consultant; b. N.Y.C., Nov. 8, 1944; s. Robert Joseph and Ruth Mildred (Mueller) B.; children: Dana Marguerite, Cristina Ruth. BS, Kans. State U., 1970, MS, 1971; MBA, U. Richmond, 1976. Cert. master hazardous materials mgr., cert. plant engr.; reg. profl. engr., Tenn. Indsl. engr. Philip Morris USA, Richmond, Va., 1972-77; mgr. indsl. engring. Consolidated Aluminum, St. Louis, 1977-78; mgr. system engr. System Devel. Corp., Oak Ridge, Tenn., 1978-84; project dir. Roy F. Weston Inc., West Chester, Pa., 1984-86; project mgr. Systematic Mgmt. Svcs., Inc., Oak Ridge, Tenn., 1986-88; v.p. Systematic Mgmt. Svcs., Inc., Oak Ridge, 1988-91; mgr. Tenera, L.P., 1991-92; regional dir. Pragmatics Inc., Oak Ridge, 1992-95; ind. cons., 1996-99; ops. mgr. Cambridge Mgmt. Cons., 1999—. Pres. Crestwood Farms Resident Assn., Richmond, 1976; coun. chmn. Knoxville Ctr. Kairos Found. With U.S. Army, 1966-69, Vietnam. Mem. NSPE, Am. Soc. Engring. Mgmt., Inst. Indsl. Engrs. (cert. sys. imtegration, chpt. pres. 1969—), Am. Soc. Cost Engrs., U.S. Power Squadron (comdr. 1984-85), Nat. Contract Mgmt. Assn., Project Mgmt. Inst. (cert. project mgmt. profl.), Nat. Corvette Restorers Soc., Am. Soc. Quality Control, Soc. Am. Value Engrs., Am. Nuclear Soc., Nat. Coun. Sys. Engring., Order of Engr., Am. Mensa, Rotary. Avocations: scuba, sailing, skiing, racquetball, auto restoration. Office: 71-75 Uxbridge Rd, Ealing London W5 5SL, England

BROWN, ROBERT G., lawyer; b. Boston, Apr. 29, 1956; s. Roger Ellis and Ida Margaret (Roherty) B.; m. Margaret H. Brown Dec. 11, 1991. AA, Cape Cod C.C., 1976; BA, Northeastern U., 1979; JD, Suffolk U., 1982. Counsel Barnstable Conservation Found., Inc., 1983-1990, Hyannis (Mass.) Fire Dist., 1985-93, Cotuit (Mass.) Fire Dist., 1985-88, West Barnstable (Mass.) Fire Dist., 1987—, Old King's Hwy Region Hist. Dist. Com., 1984—, Mass. Dept. Correction, Boston, 1989-95; dir. Barnstable Conservation Found. Inc., 1983-85. Mem. Barnstable Town Meeting, 1975-87, Barnstable Planning Com., Barnstable Charter Com., 1976-77, Barnstable Planning Bd., 1979-85. Mem. Mass. Bar Assn. (small firm mgmt. sect. coun. 1991-93), Mass. Acad. Trial Attys., Barnstable County Bar Assn., Phi Alpha Delta. Office: 86 Willow St Yarmouth Port MA 02675-1758

BROWN, ROBERT STEPHEN, JR., physician; b. N.Y., Sept. 14, 1963; s. Robert Stephen and Judith (Kaufman) B.; m. Susan M. Wilson, June 26, 1993; children: Jacqueline Rachel Wilson Brown, Robert Dylan. AB, Harvard Univ., 1985; MD, N.Y.Univ., 1989; MPH, Univ. Calif., 1996. Attending physician Univ. Calif., San Francisco, 1995-96; medical dir. liver transplant Univ. N.C., Chapel Hill, 1996-98; medical dir. for liver disease Columbia Univ., N.Y. Presbyterian, N.Y., 1998—; pres., bd. dirs. Centerspan, Washington, 1999—. Contbr. articles to profl. jours. Recipient Young Investigator award Am. Soc. Transploration, 1996. Mem. Am. Coll. Physicians, Am. Assn. Study Liver Disease, Am. Gastroenterological Assn., Am. Soc. Transplantation. E-mail: rb464@columbia.edu. Office: Ctr for Liver Disease N Y Presbyterian 622 W 168th St Fl 14 New York NY 10032-3720

BROWN, ROBERT THORSON, retired forest ecology educator, researcher; b. Rochester, Minn., Sept. 29, 1923; s. Lloyd Kent and Alma Idso Brown; m. Viola Jarvenpaa, Sept. 1, 1953; children: Linda Anne, Cynthia Ellen, Lisa Linnea, Erik Thorson. BSChE, U. Wis., 1947, BS in Botany, 1948, MS in Botany, 1949, PhD in Botany, 1951. Prof. Mich. Technol. U., Houghton, 1951-83, Tianjin (China) Inst. Tech., 1992-93; Fulbright prof. Helsinki (Finland) U., 1971-72, Cukurova U., Adana, Turkey, 1980-81, U. West Indies, St. Augustine, Trinidad, 1986-87; USAID prof., Gorakhpur (India) U., 1968; lectr. Soviet Acad. Sci., Kiev, 1972. Contbr. numerous articles to profl. jours., including Ecology, Forest Sci., Soil Pollution, Acta Forestalia Fennica, Water, Air & Soil Pollution, others. Mem. sch. bd., Houghton, 1962-65; pres. Mich. Tech Credit Union, Houghton, 1962-68. Recipient medal of Forestry, Finnish Forestry Soc., 1979. Fellow AAAS. Democrat. Presbyterian. Avocations: photography, gardening. Home: 500 Garnet St Houghton MI 49931-1421

BROWN, RONALD DRAYTON, chemistry educator; b. Melbourne, Australia, Oct. 14, 1927; s. William Harrison and Linda Grace (Drayton) B.; m. Florence Catherine Mary Stringer, July 10, 1950; children: Ronald Drayton, David Drayton, Penny. BS, Melbourne U., 1946, MS, 1948; PhD, U. London, 1952. Asst. lectr. chemistry dept. London U., 1952-53; sr. lectr. gen. chemistry Melbourne U., 1953, reader theoretical chemistry, 1959; prof. chemistry dept. Monash U., Clayton, Victoria, Australia, 1959-92; bd. dirs. Centre for High-Resolution Spectroscopy and Optoelectronic Tech., Melbourne. Author: Manual of Elementary etc., 1955, 63, 66, 75, Valency, 1979. Fellow Australian Acad. Sci. (v.p. 1972-74, sec. phys. scis. 1976-80), Internat. Union of Pure and Applied Chem. (mem. bur.), Internat. Astron. Union (pres. commn. 51). Avocations: golf, skiing, tennis. Office: Monash U Chemistry Dept, Wellington Rd, 3168 Clayton Australia

BROWN, RONALD ERIK, lawyer; b. Phila., Sept. 26, 1954; s. Ernest Warren and Betty Lee Brown; m. Mary Ellen Jeanette, July 11, 1987; children: Hannah Mackenzie, Sarah Frances (dec.), Meredith Jeanette. BS in Nuclear Engring., Pa. State U., 1975; MS, Rensselaer Poly. Inst., 1980; JD, U. Conn., 1985. Bar: Conn. 1985, U.S. Patent and Trademark Office 1986, U.S. Ct. Appeals (fed. cir.) 1987, U.S. Dist. Ct. Conn. 1987, U.S. Dist. Ct. (so. and ea. dists.) N.Y. 1987, N.Y. 1988, D.C. 1988, U.S. Supreme Ct. 1999. Physicist nuclear engring. dept. Combustion Engring., Windsor, Conn., 1975-80, engr. instrumentation and control engring. dept., 1980-86; assoc. Kane, Dalsimer, Sullivan et al, N.Y.C., 1987-98, ptnr., 1999; ptnr. Pitney, Hardin, Kipp & Szuch, LLP, N.Y.C., 2000—. Mem. ABA, IEEE, Conn. Bar Assn., N.Y. Intellectual Property Law Assn., Conn. Patent Law Soc., Mensa. Office: Pitney Hardin Kipp & Szuch LLP 711 3rd Ave New York NY 10017-4014

BROWN, RONALD LAMING, lawyer; b. Springfield, Mass., Aug. 26, 1944; s. Douglas Seaton and Elizabeth Ruth (Stover) B.; m. Barbara Jo Roesler Moher, June 13, 1967 (div. Mar., 1987); children: Kimberly Lynn, Kathryn Jo, Karen Elizabeth, Kristine Ann, John Paul; m. Susan Janet Toth, Jan. 2, 1988; 1 child, Megan Christina. Chapman Col., 1968-70; JD, Creighton U., 1972. Bar: Neb. 1973, U.S. Dist. Ct. Neb. 1973, U.S. Ct. Appeals (8th cir.) 1974, U.S. Dist. Ct. Wyo. 1974, U.S. Ct. Appeals (10th cir.) 1976, Colo. 1987, U.S. Dist. Ct. Colo. 1987. 2d v.p., comml. loan counsel Omaha Nat. Bank, Omaha, 1973-74; prosecuting atty. Natrona County Atty., Casper, Wyo., 1974-75; partner Brown, Drew, Apostolos, Massey & Sullivan, Casper, Wyo., 1975-83; shareholder Burke & Brown, Casper, Wyo., 1983-86; pvt. practice Casper, Wyo., 1986-88, Ft. Collins, Colo., 1987—; bd. dirs. Tooke Internat., Inc.; trustee Brown Investment Trust, Ventura, Calif., 1996—; lectr. Casper (Wyo.) Col., 1980. Mem. sch. bd. St. Anthony's Sch., Casper, Wyo., 1979-82, Ft. Collins (Colo.) Connections, 1995—. Sgt. USMC, 1964-68. Mem. Neb. Bar Assn., Wyo. Bar Assn., Colo. Bar Assn. Republican. Avocations: golf, motor cycling, auto restoration, reading, home repair. Home: 1400 Wildwood Rd Fort Collins CO 80521-4026 Office: 425 W Mulberry St Ste 105 Fort Collins CO 80521-2864

BROWN, RONALD MALCOLM, engineering corporation executive; b. Hot Springs, S.D., Feb. 21, 1938; s. George Malcolm and Cleo Lavonne (Plumb) B.; m. Sharon Ida Brown, Nov. 14, 1964 (div. Apr. 1974); children: Michael, Troy, George, Curtis, Lisa, Brittney. AA, Southwestern Coll., 1970; BA, Chapman U., 1978. Commd. USN, 1956, advanced through grades to master chief, 1973, ret., 1978; engring. mgr. Beckman Inst., Fullerton, Calif., 1978-82; mfg. engring. br. mgr. Northrop Corp., Hawthorne, Calif., 1982-83; dir. of ops. Transco, Marina Del Rey, Calif., 1983-85; v.p. ops. Decor Concepts, Arcadia, Calif., 1985-87; design dir. Lockheed Aircraft Corp., Ontario, Calif., 1987-97; v.p. engring. and program mgmt. Ducommon Inc., Carson, Calif., 1997—. Mem. Soc. Mfg. Engrs., Inst. Indsl. Engrs., Nat. Trust for Hist. Preservation, Fleet Res. Assn., Am. Film Inst., Nat. Mgmt. Assn. Avocations: golf, running, racquetball.

BROWN, RONALD WILLIAM, airline executive; b. Perth, Australia, Apr. 14, 1951; s. William Harrison and Norma Mavis (Kinghorn) B.; m. Ramona Concita Masiello, Sept. 2, 1977; children: Tracey Louise, Matthew Christopher, Elissa Claire. Grad. high sch., Perth. Traffic officer MacRobertson Miller Airlines, Karratha, Australia, 1971-74; traffic officer MacRobertson Miller Airlines, Paraburdoo, Australia, 1974-75, sr. traffic officer, 1975-76; br. mgr. Tom Price, Australia, 1976-77, Kununurra, Australia, 1977-81; br. mgr. Airlines Western Australia, Kununurra, 1984; mgr. Ansett Western Australia Airlines, Kununurra, 1984-87; field sales mgr. Ansett Airlines, Perth, 1987-90; mgr. Ansett Airlines, Alice Springs, 1990-92; mgr. customer svcs. Ansett Australia Melbourne Airport, 1992-94, mgr. ramp svc., 1994-95; gen. mgr. Indonesia Ansett, Australia, Jakarta, Indonesia, 1995-96; mng. dir. Ron Brown & Assocs., Perth, Austrailia, 1996—; comml. dir. APS Airline Mgmt., Jakarta, Indonesia, 1996-97, Perth, Australia, 1997-98, New Delhi, India, 2000—; mgmt. cons. Internat. Divsn. Merpati Nusantara Airlines, Jakarta, 1996-97; dir. mktg. Classic Cars Australia, Perth, 1999, joint mng. dir., 2000—; mgmt. cons. Sahara India Airlines, New Delhi, 2000—. Contbr. articles to profl. jours. Hon. treas. Kununurra Visitors Ctr., 1977-87; pres. Kununurra C. of C., 1979-80; founding chmn. Celebrity Tree Park Mgmt. Commn., Kununurra, 1983-87; councillor Shire of Wyndham/East Kimberley, Kununurra, 1985-87. Named Citizen of Yr. City of Kununurra, 1987, Agt. of Yr. Perth Bldg. Soc., 1978, 82; recipient Internat. Best Exec. award, Jakarta, 1996, ASEAN Devel. award Jakarta, 1996. Lodge: Rotary (pres.-elect 1986-87, Youth Leadership award 1969). Avocations: genealogy, numismatics. Home: 41 Harrison St, Balcatta, 6021 Perth Australia

BROWN, ROXANNE (JERENE ROXANNE BROWN), sales executive; b. L.A., July 5, 1947; d. John Phillip and Margaret Leona (Dalrymple) Ortiz; m. Terry Lee Wood, May 7, 1966 (div. Sept. 1969); 1 child, Tiffany Christine Wood Suraco; m. Christopher Corey Brown, July 17, 1984 (dec. Sept. 1984); children: Jason Michael and John Charles (twins); m. Richard L. Gibbs, Apr. 18, 1996 (dec. Feb. 2000). Student, Casper Coll., 1977. Info. operator Gen. Telephone, Baldwin Park, Calif., 1965-67; long distance operator Gen. Telephone, Santa Maria, Calif., 1967-69; office mgr. Monroe Calculator, Las Vegas, Nev., 1972-74; mgr. Exch. Club, Salt Lake City, 1977-81, Pouches Inc., Salt Lake City, 1981-82; asst. producer KSTU TV 20, Salt Lake City, 1982-84; sec. ADVO - Sys., Inc., Orange, Calif., 1984-85, terr. sales rep., 1985-88; major account exec. ADVO - Sys., Inc., Garden Grove, Calif., 1988-95; v.p. JRB & Assocs., Long Beach, Calif., 1995—; cons. Rice - Urmana Advt., Huntington Beach, Calif., 1989-91. Bd. dirs. ACLU, Salt Lake City, 1977; precinct worker Voter Registrar, Huntington Beach, 1988, Long Beach, Calif., 1990; bd. dirs., sec. Alamitos Bay Beach Peninsula Preservation Group, 1996-98. Mem. ACLU, Platform Speakers Assn., Alamitos Bay Garden Club (v.p., ways and means com. 1996-98). Avocations: sculpting, photography, sailing. Home: 77 Ximeno Ave Long Beach CA 90803-3056

BROWN, SARAH M., artist, gallery owner, educator, publisher; b. Longview, Tex., Jan. 30, 1935; d. Phil Uhls and Fannie Belle (Keating) B. BFA, U. Chgo. and Art Inst. Chgo., 1957; student, Tulane U., 1960, Odyssey Studio, Atlanta, 1978, Nat. Watercolor Seminar, 1980. Tchr. ceramics Pensacola Fla. Jr. Coll., 1958; dir. art dept. Pensacola Fla. Adult Vocat. Sch., 1958-59; owner S. Brown Studio-Gallery, New Orleans, 1959-63, Atlanta, 1963-89, Roswell, Ga., 1986-89; owner Sarah Brown Studio-Gallery, Atlanta, 1989—; founder Sarah Brown Art Tours, 1973—, The Little Brown Press, 1976—; conductor seminars in field. One-woman shows include Longview (Tex.) Art Assn., Pensacola Art Assn., Douglasville Cultural Arts Ctr., 1995; exhibited in group shows Nat. Western Small Painting Exhbn., 1982 (Best of Show, 1st pl.), Palm Beach Galleries (3d pl. show, 1st pl. Western category), NLAPW Ga. State Competition (1st pl. oils), Midwest Armory Art Exhbn., Chgo., Johnson Galleries, Chgo., Three Arts Club, Chgo., Southside Arts Festival, Chgo., Delgado Mus., New Orleans, Pensacola Quadricentennial, Royal Orleans Hotel, New Orleans, Piedmont Art Festival, Berman Lipton Interiors, Atlanta Artists Group Show, Jr. C. of C., Am. Painters in Paris, Winter Pk. (Fla.) Outdoor Art Festival, Festival of the Masters, Lake Buena Vista, Fla., Knickerbocker Artists 31st Annual, N.Y.C., Catherine Lorillard Wolfe Art Club Exhibit, N.Y.C., Nat. Western Small Painting Exhbn., Bosque Farms, N.Mex., Palm Beach Galleries, New Orleans, ABC Art and Frame Show, Atlanta, Ga. Wildlife Fedn., 1994, Safari Internat. Exhbn., Galleria Mall, Atlanta, 1995; commissions include A.H. Stephens Meml., Crawfordville, State of Ga., Dept. Natural Resources, Warm Springs Lodge, Elijah Clarke Mus., New Echota Historic Site, Hofwyl Plantation, Savannah, Ga.; represented in numerous pvt. and pub. collections including Reynolds Plantation and Great Waters, Eatonton, Ga.; contbr. art to mags. Founder Mitzi Brown Drama Fund, Shamrock H.S., Atlanta, 1974. Mem. Nat. League Am. Pen Women, Nat. Mus. Women in the Arts (charter), Portrait Soc. Am., Inc., Atlanta High Mus., Atlanta Zool. Soc., Ga. Wildlife Fedn. Office: Sarah Brown Studio-Gallery 2947 Lookout Pl NE # 2 Atlanta GA 30305-3217

BROWN, SEYOM, international relations educator, government consultant; b. Hightstown, N.J., May 28, 1933; s. Benjamin I. and Sarah E. (Sokolow) B.; m. Vanda Felbabova; children: Lisa, Steven, Elliot, Nell, Benjamin, Matthew, Jeremiah. B.A., U. So. Calif., 1955, M.A., 1957; Ph.D., U. Chgo., 1963. Social scientist Rand Corp., Santa Monica, Calif., 1962-69; cons. Dept. Def. and Dept. State, Washington, 1967-68; sr. fellow Brookings Instn., Washington, 1969-76; program dir. Carnegie Endowment, Washington, 1976-78; vis. prof. Harvard U., summers 1979—; acting dir. Univ. Consortium for Rsch. on N.Am., Harvard U., 1983-84; assoc. Harvard Ctr. Internat. Affairs, 1985-94; prof. Brandeis U., 1978—, chair dept. politics, 1987-93; vis. fellow Brookings Instn., Washington, 1999-2000. Author: New Forces in World Politics, 1974, The Crises of Power, 1979, The Faces of Power, 1994, New Forces, Old Forces, and the Future of World Politics, 1995, International Relations in a Changing Global System, 1996, Human Rights in World Politics, 2000. Mem. Internat. Studies Assn. (Harold and Margaret Sprout award 1980). Office: Brookings Instn Foreign Policy Studies 1775 Massachusettes Ave NW Washington DC 20036

BROWN, SHIRLEY MARGARET KERN (PEGGY BROWN), interior designer; b. Ellensburg, Wash., Mar. 30, 1948; d. Philip Brooke and Shirley (Dickson) Kern; m. Ellery Kliess Brown, Jr., Aug. 7, 1970; children: Heather Nicole Coco, Rebecca Cherise, Andrea Shirley Serene, Ellery Philip. BA in Interior Design, Wash. State U., 1973. Apprentice then interior designer L.S. Higgins & Assocs., Bellevue, Wash., 1969-72; interior designer ColorsPlus Interiors, Inc., Bellevue, Wash., 1972, Strawns Office Furniture & Interiors, Inc., Boise, 1973-75, Empire Furniture, Inc., Tulsa; owner Inside-Out Design Co., Ltd., Boise, 1973-82; interior designer Architekton, Inc., Tulsa, 1984-86, Johnson Brand Design Group, Inc., 1986-87, Ellery Brown & Assocs. Arch., 1987—, Seattle Design Ctr.-Visions & Studio Programs, Scottsdale, Ariz., 1998—, Mehagian's Fine Furniture, Scottsdale, Ariz.; lectr. in field. Contbr. articles to profl. jours. Pres. PTA, co-chair capital bond prin. sel. com., enrollment rev. com., 1989-95; bd. dirs. Paradise Valley Young Life. Recipient Seattle Design Ctr. Marjorie Siegel award, 1997. Mem. AAUW, Am. Soc. Interior Designers (Wash. state presdl. citation 1995, 96, 97, presdl. citation Oreg. chpt. 1977, 95-96, dir. chpt. 1976-77, chmn. Boise subchpt. 1977-79, sec. 1980-81, chmn. Wash. chpt. step workshop chmn. 1993-97, NCIDQ chmn. 1993-97), Nat. Soc. Interior Designers, Idaho Hist. Co., Wash. State U. Alumni Assn., Jr. League Seattle, Jr. League Phoenix, Zonta, Alpha Gamma Delta. Republican. Presbyterian. Office: 16227 N 50th St Scottsdale AZ 85254-9652

BROWN, STEPHANIE C., credit and collections manager; b. N.Y.C., July 1, 1951; d. Hubert Robert Beatty and Mercedes Lenor Dawson; m. Jimmy Brown, Aug. 31, 1974 (div. Feb. 1986); 1 child, Rashan J. AAS in Nursing, Kingsborough C.C., Bklyn., 1974; BA in Psychology, York Coll., 1978. Credit asst. Schenley Industries, N.Y.C., 1978-79; credit supr. North Am. Philips, N.Y.C., 1980; credit mgr. Julius Wile & Sons, Great Neck, N.Y., 1980-82; collector Greenville (S.C.) Hosp. Sys., 1982-83; credit adminstr. Showtime/The Movie Channel, N.Y.C., 1983-84; credit mgr. Times Mirror, N.Y.C., 1985-89; mgr. credit & collections Reed Elsevier, New Providence, N.J., 1989-2000; spkr. in field. Film critic Courier News, 1995-98; editor, co-pub. Directory Mary Mother of God Ch., 1999. Vol. United Cancer Soc., Workforce N.J.-Transition Ctr., United Way, project blue print grad., 1998, cmty. problem solving com., 1999, compass 2.0 steering com., 1999; mem. Hillsborough (N.J.) Neighbors of Color, 1990-98. Mem. NACM (edn. com., bd. govs.), Fin. Women Internat., Twin Women in Mgmt. (bd. dirs.). Democrat. Roman Catholic. Avocations: travel, music, the arts, books, philately. E-mail: sbrown6627@aol.com. Home: 2305 Tudor Ct Somerville NJ 08876-5540

BROWN, SIR STEPHEN, judge; b. Oct. 3, 1924; s. Wilfrid and Nora Elizabeth B.; m. Patricia Ann Brown, 1951; 5 children. Student, Malvern Coll., Queens Coll., Cambridge (Eng.) U.; LLD, U. Birmingham, Eng., 1985, U. Leicester, Eng., 1997. Bar: Inner Temple, 1949, Bencher, 1974, Treas., 1994. Dep. chmn. Staffs Quarter Session, 1963-71; recorder West Bromwich, 1965-71, 72-75; judge family divsn. High Ct., 1975-77; judge Queen's Bench Divsn., 1977-83; presiding judge Midland and Oxford Cir., 1977-81; lord justice of appeal, 1983-88, pres. family divsn., 1988-99; active Parole Bd. Eng. and Wales, 1967-71; mem. Butler Com. on Mentally Abnormal Offenders, 1972-75; mem. adv. coun. Penal Sys., 1977; chmn. adv. com. Conscientious Objectors, 1971-75. Chmn. coun. Malvern Coll., 1976-94. Lt. Royal Naval Res., 1943-46; pres. Edgbaston H.S. Girls, 1989—. Mem. Garrick Club. Avocation: sailing. Office: 78 Hamilton Ave, Harborne, Birmingham B17 8AR, England

BROWN, STEPHEN FREDERICK, civil engineering educator; b. Worthing, Eng., Sept. 29, 1939; s. Francis Maurice and Ruth Audrey (Swallow) B.; m. Maryse La Hausse de Lalouviere, Apr. 27, 1963; children: Andrew, Timothy, Christopher, Michelle. BSc, U. Nottingham (Eng.), 1960, PhD, 1967, DSc, 1982. Chartered engr. Jr. engr. Sir R. McAlpine, Newport, Eng., 1960-61; jr. asst. engr. Dormon Long (Africa), Durban, Republic of South Africa, 1961-62, Scott Wilson Kirkpatrick, London, 1962-63; sr. rsch. asst. U. Nottingham, 1963-65, lectr., 1965-74, sr. lectr., 1974-78, reader, 1978-83, prof., 1983—, head dept. civil engring., 1989-94, dean engring., 1992-94, pro vice-chancellor, 1994-98, head sch. civil engring., 1999—; bd. dirs. SWK Pavement Engring. Ltd., Nottingham, pres. SW Pavement Engring., Inc., N.J. Contbr. numerous tech. articles to profl. jours. Fellow Inst. Civil Engrs., Inst. Hwys. & Transp., Inst. Asphalt Tech., Royal Acad. of Eng.; mem. U.S. Assn. Asphalt Pavement Tech., Brit. Geotech. Soc. (chmn. 1987-89). Office: U Nottingham Civil Engring, University Park, Nottingham NG7 2RD, England

BROWN, STEPHEN HAYZE, JR., human services caseworker; b. Chgo., Sept. 7, 1954; s. Stephen Hayze Brown and Barbara Elizabeth Grandpré; m. Judith Eileen McCain, Mar. 5, 1997; 1 child, Javon. BS in Biology, Chgo. State U., 1981; diploma hematology and phlebotomy, Med. Careers Inst. Rsch. asst. Chgo. State U., 1980; instr. anatomy U. Ill. Coll. Dentistry, Chgo., 1982; ind. landscaping contractor, 1982-86, 87-89; tchr. Chgo. Bd. Edn., 1986-87; case mgr. Ill. Dept. Human Svcs., Chgo., 1999—. Assemblyman 44th Ward Assembly, Chgo., 1976-77. Ill. State scholar, 1972, Nat. Merit/Achievement scholar, 1972. Mem. Nat. Space Soc., The Planetary Soc. Roman Catholic. Avocations: music, science fiction, philosophy, comparative religion, astronomy.

BROWN, STEVEN BRIEN, radiologist; b. Ft. Collins, Colo., Jan. 18, 1952; s. Allen Jenkins and Shirley Irene (O'Brien) B.; m. Susan Jane DiTomaso, Sept. 10, 1983; children: Allison Grace, Laura Anne. BS, Colo. State U., 1974; MD, U. Calif., San Diego, 1978. Diplomate Am. Bd. Radiology with cert. of added qualifications in Neuroradiology and Vascularand Interventional Radiology. Intern U. Wash., Seattle, 1978-79; resident in radiology Stanford (Calif.) U., 1979-82; fellow in interventional and neuro-radiology Wilford Hall, USAF Med Ctr., San Antonio, 1982-83; staff radiologist Wilford Hall, USAF Med Ctr., 1983-86; staff radiologist Luth. Med. Ctr., Wheat Ridge, Colo., 1986—, chief angiography and interventional radiology, 1987-96; pres. Luth. Med. Ctr. Joint Venture, 1992-95; mem. bd. mgrs. Primera HealthCare LLC, 1995-97; pres. HealthCare Select Inc., 1995—. Contbr. articles to profl. jours. Mem. Rep. Nat. Com., Washington, 1984—, Nat. Rep. Senatorial Com., 1985—, Rep. Presdl. Task Force, 1986—; bd. dirs. The Health Care Initiative. Maj. USAF, 1982-86. Fellow Radiol. Soc. N.Am., Am. Coll. Radiology (exec. com. intersoc. commn. 1996—); mem. Colo. Radiol. Soc. (pres. 1995-96), Rocky Mt. Radiol. Soc. (pres. 1994-95), Soc. Cardiovasc. and Interventional Radiology, Western Neuroradiol. Soc., Am. Soc. Neuroradiology, Colo. Preferred Physicians Orgn. (bd. dirs. 1987—), World Wildlife Orgn., Colo. Angio Club. Republican. Presbyterian. Avocations: skiing, sailing, gardening. Office: Luth Med Center 8300 W 38th Ave Wheat Ridge CO 80033-6005

BROWN, TEION O'DELL, engineering executive; b. Chgo., Aug. 29, 1974; m. Sandra E. Brown; 1 child, McHale Campbell Brown. B in Engring., U. Ill., Chgo., 1997; M in Fin., Brown U., 1999. Pres., CEO Brown, Inc., Chgo., 2000—. Bd. dirs. Off St. Club, Chgo., 1992, 93, 95; chmn. bd. dirs.,

CEO ALU Found., N.Y.C., 1997-00. Avocations: reading, writing, baketball. Home and Office: 1521 S Wabash Ave Chicago IL 60605-2919

BROWN, THOMAS CHRISTOPHER KENNETH, anesthesiologist; b. Tumutumu, Kenya, Dec. 9, 1935; arrived in Australia, 1966; s. William Monteith B. and Jessie Catherine McMaster; m. Janet Patricia Penfold, July 8, 1961; children: Catherine, Maryann, Fraser, Kester, Kenneth. MBChB, St. Andrews U., Scotland, 1960; MD, U. Melbourne (Australia), 1980. Intern Victoria Hosp., London, Ont., 1960-61; gen. practitioner Yellowknife, N.W. Terr., Can., 1961-62; resident in anesthesia U. B.C. (Can.), 1963-65, Hosp. for Sick Children, Toronto, Can., 1965; registrar Royal Melbourne (Australia) Hosp., 1966; med. officer intensive care Royal Children's Hosp., Melbourne, 1967, anaesthetist, 1968-74, dir. anesthesia, 1974—, divsn. dir., 1979-96; convenor sci. programme com. World Congress of Anaesthesia, 1996. Author: Anaesthesia and Patient Care, 1984; main author, editor: Anaesthesia for Children, 1979, 2nd edit., 1992; contbr., editor: Acute Pain Management in Children; contbr. chpts. to books. Recipient Robert Orton medal Australian and New Zealand Coll. Anaesthetists, 1992, gold medal Royal Childrens Hosp., 1995. Fellow Royal Coll. Anaesthetists London, Faculty Anaesthetists, Royal Australasian Coll. Surgeons (state edn. officer 1970-75, chmn. 1975-77), Royal Australian and New Zealand Coll. Anaesthetists; mem. Australian Soc. Anaesthetists (life; convenor sci. program com. 1972-96, mem. overseas aid com. 1984-95, Gilbert Brown award 1984, Ben Barry medal 1996), Assn. pediatric Anaesthetists (Eng.), World Fedn. Socs. Anaesthesiology (mem. edn. com. 1984-92, chmn. 1987-92, mem. exec. com. 1992-2000, chmn. exec. com. 1996-2000, pres. 2000—), Order of Australia. Avocations: painting, photography, tennis, hockey. Office: Royal Children's Hosp, Anesthesia Flemington Rd, 3052 Parkville Victoria, Australia

BROWN, THOMAS HUNTINGTON, neuroscientist; b. N.Y.C., June 13, 1945; s. Thomas Huntington and Elvira R. (Crandall) B. BA in Molecular Biology, Calif. State U.-San Jose, 1972, MA in Psychology, 1972; PhD in Neurosci., Stanford U., 1977. Postdoctoral fellow Stanford U., Calif., 1977-79; asst. rsch. scientist Beckman Rsch. Inst., Duarte, Calif., 1979-82, assoc. rsch. scientist, 1982-86; rsch. scientist Beckman Rsch. Inst., Duarte, 1986-88; prof. dept. psychology Yale U., New Haven, 1988—; mem. joint appt. dept. cellular molecular physiology Yale U., 1992—, dir. Ctr. for Theoretical and Applied Neurosci., 1992-96; adviser NIH, NIMH study sects., 1982-83, 89-94, 94-98, mem. NIH-IFCN5 study sect., IFCN1 study sect., 1998—. Mem. editl. bd. Behavioral Neurosci. Jour., 1983-89, Network: Computation in Neural Systems, 1990-92, Synapse, 1990—, Hippocampus, 1990-93, Psychobiology, 1997—; contbr. articles to sci. jours., 1976—. Recipient Epilepsy Found. Am. award, 1980, McKnight Found. Scholar's award, 1981, McKnight Found. Career Devel. award 1984, Muscular Dystrophy Found. fellow, 1977, NIH fellow, 1978; grantee in field, 1980—. Mem. AAAS, Am. Psychol. Soc., N.Y. Acad. Sci., Conn. Acad. Sci. Engring., Soc. Neurosci., Internat. Neurol. Network Soc. Office: Yale U Dept Psychology PO Box 208205 New Haven CT 06520-8205

BROWN, THOMAS PHILIP, III, lawyer; b. Washington, Dec. 18, 1931; s. Raymond T. and Beatrice (Cullen) B.; m. Alicia A. Sexton, July 28, 1955; children: Thomas, Mark, Alicia, Maria, Beatrice. B.S., Georgetown U., 1953, LL.B., 1956. Bar: D.C., Md. Pvt. practice law, 1958—. Author monograph and articles on legal malpractice. Pres. Cath. Youth Orgn. of Washington, 1972. Served to 1st lt. USMCR, 1955-58. Mem. Bar Assn. D.C. (pres. 1986, bd. dirs. 1987), Barristers Club, Columbia Country Club. Home: 5210 Norway Dr Chevy Chase MD 20815-6672 Office: 4948 Saint Elmo Ave Bethesda MD 20814-6013

BROWN, TOD DAVID, bishop; b. San Francisco, Nov. 15, 1936; s. George Wilson and Edna Anne (Dunn) B. BA, St. John's Coll., 1958; STB, Gregorian U., Rome, 1960; MA in Theology, U. San Francisco, 1970, MAT in Edn., 1976. Dir. edn. Diocese of Monterey, Calif., 1970-80, vicar gen., clergy, 1980-82, chancellor, 1982-89, vicar gen., chancellor, 1983-89; pastor St. Francis Xavier, Seaside, Calif., 1977-82; bishop Roman Catholic Diocese of Boise, Idaho, 1989-98; appointed and installed bishop Roman Cath. Diocese of Orange, Calif., 1998; mem. subcom. on laity, mem. 3d millenium com. Nat. Conf. Cath. Bishops, chmn. com. on ecumenism and interreligious affairs, past mem. com. on mission, pastoral practices, past chair laity com.; mem. episcopal bd. govs. N.Am. Coll. Named Papal Chaplain Pope Paul VI, 1975. Mem. Cath. Theol. Soc. Am., Cath. Biblical Assn., Canon Law Soc. Am., Equestrian Order of the Holy Sepulchre in Jerusalem. Avocations: films, travel, reading, exercise. Office: Diocese of Orange Marywood Ctr 2811 E Villa Real Dr Orange CA 92867-1932

BROWN, TREVOR ERNEST, environmental risk consultant; b. Cheviot, Canterbury, New Zealand, Oct. 31, 1939; s. Ernest Carl and Helen Farely (Dickinson) B.; m. Joyce Burnett, Mar. 10, 1964 (div. Apr. 1984); children: Ross Trevor, Lenaire; m. Kerrie Therese Conant, Jan. 7, 1985; 1 child, Brett. Diploma in med. tech., U. Otago, New Zealand, 1962; B Applied Sci., U. Otago, 1964. Chief technologist Med. Labs., Napier, New Zealand, 1964-75; sect. leader Cockburn Sound Study, Perth, Australia, 1975-78; environ. supt. Pancon Mining Ltd., Jabiluka, Australia, 1978-80, Rundle Oil Shale Project, Gladstone, Australia, 1980-81, CSR Ltd., Sydney, Australia, 1981-83; tech. mgr. Brown Coal Liquefaction, Morwell, Victoria, Australia, 1983-85; dir. environment Tasmania Dept. Environ., Hobart, Australia, 1985-89; prin. Dames & Moore, Sydney, 1989-91, AGC Woodward-Clyde, 1991-98; dir. environment divsn. Hyder Consulting (Australia) Pty Ltd., St. Leonards, NSW, 1998—. Contbr. articles to profl. jours. Bd. dirs. Marineland New Zealand, Napier, 1968-72; chmn. Litter Control Assn., Hobart, 1985-89, State Oil Pollution Com., Hobart, 1985-89, Australian Environ. Coun., 1988-89. Mem. Royal Australian Chem. Inst., Australian Soc. Microbiology (assoc.), Australia Med. Lab. Scientists Inst., Environ. Inst. Australia (assoc.), Am. Chem. Soc. Presbyterian. Avocations: golf, computing, bush walking.

BROWN, VALERIE KATHLEEN, ecologist; b. Farnborough, Hampshire, U.K., May 11, 1944; d. Reginald Herbert and Kathleen Nora (Southerton) B.; m. Clive Wall, Sept. 2, 1970. BSc in Zoology, Imperial Coll., London, 1966, PhD in Entomology, 1969. Lectr. Royal Holloway Coll., London, 1969-74; lectr. Imperial Coll., London, 1975-84, sr. lectr., 1984-89, reader, 1989-94; dir. Internat. Inst. Entomology sub. CAB Internat., London, 1994-97; dir. environment CABI Biosci., 1998-2000; dir. Ctr. Agri-Environ. Rsch. U. Reading, 2000—. Author: Grasshoppers, 1983, editor: Insect Life History Strategies, 1983, Multitrophic Interactions in Terrestrial Systems, 1997, Herbavores: Between Plants and Predators, 1999; contbr. over 100 articles to profl. jours. Fellow Royal Entomol. Soc. London (editorial officer 1978-84, v.p. 1995-97); mem. Ecol. Soc. Am., British Ecol. Soc. (v.p. 1993-95). Mem. Ch. of England. Achievements include research on insect development and life cycles, experimental community ecology especially interactions between the effects of climate change and habitat disturbance on insects and plants, agroecology and effects of changing agricultural practice on biodiversity. Office: CABI Bioscience, Silwood Park Ascot, Berks SL5 7TA, England

BROWN, WALTER CREIGHTON, biologist; b. Butte, Mont., Aug. 18, 1913; s. D. Frank and Isabella (Creighton) B.; m. Jeanette Snyder, Aug. 20, 1950; children: Pamela Hawley, James Creighton, Julia Elizabeth. AB, Coll. Puget Sound, 1935, MA, 1938; PhD, Stanford U., 1950. Chmn. dept. Clover Park High Sch., Tacoma, Wash., 1938-42; acting instr. Stanford U., Calif., 1949-50; instr. Northwestern U., Evanston, Ill., 1950-53; dean sci. Menlo Coll., Menlo Park, Calif., 1955-66, dean instrn., 1966-75; rsch. assoc., fellow Calif. Acad. Sci., San Francisco, 1978—; lectr. Sillman U., Philippines, 1954-55, dir. rsch. Program on Ecology and Systematics of Philippine Amphibians and Reptiles, 1958-74; rschr. rels. of amphibian faunas of Philippines & Indo-Australian Archipelago; vis. prof. biology Stanford U., 1962, 64, 66, 68, Harvard U., Cambridge, Mass., 1969, 72. Author: Philippine Lizards of the Family Gekkonidae, 1978, Philippine Lizards of the Family Scincidae, 1980, Lizards of the Genus Emoia (Scincidae) with Observations of Their Evolution and Biogeography, 1991, Philippine Amphibians: An Illustrated Field Guide ; contbr. over 80 articles to profl. jours. Served with U.S. Army, 1942-46. Fellow AAAS; mem. Am. Soc. Ichthyologists and Herpetologists, Am. Inst. Biol. Scis., Sigma Xi. Office: Calif Acad Scis Dept Herpetology Golden Gate Park San Francisco CA 94118

BROWN, WENDY JOAN, physical education educator; b. Rotherham, Yorkshire, Eng., Apr. 23, 1950; arrived in Australia, 1978; d. Neil McKechnie and Joan (Lander) Barron; m. Peter Richard Brown, July 25, 1975; children: Andrew James, Alasdair Peter. BSc in Biol. Scis. with honors, U. Birmingham, Eng., 1972; MSc in Human Biology, U. Loughborough, Eng., 1976; PhD in Human Physiology, U. Newcastle, NSW, Australia, 1984. Mgr. Hunter Centre for Health Advancement, NSW, 1991-95; dir. Rsch. Inst. for Gender and Health U. Newcastle, 1996-99; prof. human movement studies U. Queensland, St. Lucia, 2000—; prin. investigator Australian Longitudinal Study on Women's Health, 1995, mgr., 1996-99; presenter in field. Contbr. articles to profl. jours. Mem. nat. com. Commonwealth Dept. Health and Aged Care Australia, 1996—; mem. Nat. Heart Found., nat. adv. com. on phys. activity, 1996—; mem. Queensland Phys. Activity Task Force, 1999—. Recipient commendation Prime Min. Women and Sports awards, 1993, Excellence award Good Practice in Women's Health, Commonwealth Secretariat (London), 1993, Best Paper award Nat. Sci. Conf. Australian Sports, 1990; recipient numerous grants. Mem. Australian Coun. Health, Phys. Edn., and Recreation, Australian Assn. for the Study of Obesity, Australian Behavioural Medicine Assn., Pub. Health Assn. Australia. Office: U Queensland, Sch Human Movement Studies, Saint Lucia QLD 4072, Australia

BROWN, WILLIAM HILL, III, lawyer; b. Phila., Jan. 19, 1928; s. William H. Jr. and Ethel L. (Washington) B.; m. Sonya Morgan Brown, Aug. 29, 1952 (div. 1975); 1 child, Michele D.; m. D. June Hairston, July 29, 1975; 1 child, Jeanne-Marie. BS, Temple U., 1952; JD, U. Pa., 1955. Bar: Pa. 1956, D.C. 1972, U.S. Ct. Appeals (3d cir.) 1959, U.S. Ct. Appeals (4th cir.) 1978, U.S. Dist. Ct. (ea. dist.) Pa. 1957, U.S. Ct. Appeals (10th cir.) 1986, U.S. Ct. Appeals (5th cir.) 1988, U.S. Dist. Ct. D.C. 1994, U.S. Ct. Appeals (D.C. cir.) 1994, U.S. Ct. Appeals (fed. cir.) 1997. Assoc. Norris, Schmidt, Phila., 1955-62; ptnr. Norris, Brown, Hall, Phila., 1962-68; ptnr. Schnader, Harrison, Segal & Lewis, Phila., 1974—, mem. exec. com., 1983-87; chief of frauds Dist. Atty.'s Office, 1968, dep. dist. atty., 1968; commr. EEOC, Washington, 1968-69; chmn. EEOC, 1969-73; lectr. S.W. Legal Found., Practising Law Inst., Nat. Inst. Trial Advocacy; bd. dirs. United Parcel Svc., Inc., 1983—, Lawyers Com. Civil Rights Under Law; chmn. Phila. Spl. Investigation Commn. MOVE; pres. Nat. Black Child Devel., Inc., 1986-90; bd. dirs. Cmty. Legal Svcs., 1986—; mem. exec. com. Schnader, Harrison, Segal & Lewis, 1983-87; bd. dirs., mem. exec. com. Lawyers Com. Civil Rights Under law, 1977—, co-chair, 1991-93; mem. Commn. on Comml. Operation of U.S. Customs Svc., 1994-98. Contbr. articles to profl. jours. Bd. dirs. Mid. States Colls. and Secondary Schs., 1983-89, Main Line Acad., 1982—, Nat. Sr. Citizens Law Ctr., 1988-94; mem. nat. bd. govs. Am. Heart Assn., 1994-96, mem. audit com., mem. pub. affairs policy com., bd. dirs., 1986-94, mem. audit com., mem. pub. affairs policy com.; mem. adv. com. on appellate ct. rules Supreme Ct. Pa., 1989-95. With USAF, 1946-48. Recipient award of merit Fed. Bar Assn., Columbus, 1971, NAACP award, 1971, Dr. Edward S. Cooper award Am. Heart Assn., 1995, Whitney M. Young Jr. Leadership award Urban League, 1996, Whitney North Seymor award Lawyers Com. for Civil Rights Under Law, 1996, Champions for Social Justice and Equality award Black Law Students Assn. Rutgers-Camden, 1997, Earl G. Harrison Pro Bono award, 1998, law alumni award U. Pa., 2000. Fellow Internat. Acad. Trial Lawyers, Am. Law Inst.; mem. ABA, Phila. Bar Assn. (Fidelity award 1990), D.C. Bar Assn., Pa. Bar Assn., Fed. Bar Assn., Nat. Bar Assn., Inter-Am. Bar Assn., World Assn. Lawyers (founding mem.), Am. Arbitration Assn. (past bd. dirs.), Barrister's Assn. Phila., Inc. (J. Austin Norris award 1987), Citizens Commn. on Civil Rights, NAACP (bd. dirs. legal def. and ednl. fund), Alpha Phi Alpha (Recognition award 1969). Republican. Episcopalian. Office: Schnader Harrison Segal & Lewis 1600 Market St Ste 3600 Philadelphia PA 19103-7287

BROWN, WILLIAM L., banker; b. Hendersonville, N.C., Feb. 1, 1922; s. William W. and Sarah (Maxwell) B.; m. Helen Presbrey, August, 1947; children: Kathryn H., Richard P., Steven J., Melissa M. Student, Mars Hill Coll., Newbury Coll.; M.B.A., Harvard, 1947. With First Nat. Bank Boston/Bank of Boston Corp., 1949-89, asst. v.p., 1949-59, v.p., 1959-66, sr. v.p., 1966-69, exec. v.p., 1969-71, bd. dirs., 1969-92, dir. of corp., 1970-92, pres., COO, 1971-83, chmn., CEO, 1983-87, ret., 1989; bd. dirs. Gen. Cinema Corp., Chestnut Hill, Mass., Ionics, Inc., Watertown, Mass., N.Am. Mortgage Co., Santa Rosa, Calif.; trustee Bradley Real Estate Trust, Boston. Hon. life overseer Children's Hosp. Med. Ctr., Boston; trustee assoc. Boston Coll., Marine Biol. Lab., Woods Hole, Mass.; trustee, mem. corp. Mus. Sci.; bd. dirs. Jobs for Mass., Inc., John F. Kennedy Libr. Found., Ret. Artery Bus. Com., Ret. Friends of Post Office Sq.; mem. corp. Northeastern U. Lt. USNR, World War II. Office: Bank of Boston MS/01-28-02 100 Federal St Fl 8 Boston MA 02110-1898

BROWN, WILLIAM MICHAEL, scientist, consultant, writer, editor, lawyer; b. Poole, Dorset, England, Nov. 17, 1965; came to U.S., 1991, naturalized, 1999; s. Michael C. and Shirley L. (Rowney) B. BSc in Biochemistry summa cum laude, U. Southampton, England, 1988, PhD in Molecular Biology & Biochemistry, 1991; MBA, Fairleigh Dickinson U., 1997; JD magna cum laude, N.Y. Law Sch., 1998. Bar: N.Y., N.J., U.S. Ct. Appeals (fed. cir.), U.S. Patent Office; chartered chemist, biologist; cert. regulatory affairs. Awdrsch. fellow in neurology Ctr. Neurol. Diseases Harvard Med. Sch. and Brigham and Women's Hosp., Boston, 1991-92; fellow Johnson & Johnson's Skin Biology Rsch. Ctr., Raritan, N.J., 1992-93; rsch. fellow Meml.-Sloan Kettering Cancer Ctr., N.Y.C., 1993-94; sci. cons. Sills, Cummis, Zuckerman, Radin, Tischman, Epstein and Gross, Newark, N.J., 1994-96, Whitman, Breed, Abbott & Morgan, N.Y.C., 1996-97; sci. advisor/assoc. Kaye, Scholer, Fierman, Hays & Handler, N.Y.C., 1997-99; patent counsel Taro Pharms., USA, Inc., 1999—; vis. fellow NIH, Balt., 1991-92; freelance sci. cons., writer, editor, 1993—; hon. rsch. fellow dept. physiology and anatomy U. Tasmania, Hobart, Tasmania, Australia, 1995—; reviewer/evaluator Current Drugs, 1997—, Fin. Times Pharms. Publ., 1998—. Author: Alzheimer's Disease: Current Treatments and Future Prospects, 1999; co-author: Fetuin, 1995, Transcription, 2000; articles editor N.Y. Law Sch. Law Rev., 1996-97; contbr. numerous articles to profl. jours. Recipient Brit. Assn. for Advancement of Sci. award, 1987, G. A. Kerkut prize, 1988, Maxwell Found. award, 1987, Woodrow Wilson Constl. Law award, 1998, Otto L. Walter Disting. Legal Writing award, 1998; Wellcome Trust rsch. scholar, 1987, Irving Mariash scholar N.Y. Law Sch., 1994-98; Vis. Rsch. fellow NIH, 1991-92. Fellow Royal Soc. Encouragement of Arts, Mfg. and Commerce; mem. AAAS, Am. Assn. Pharm. Scientists, Royal Soc. Chemistry, Inst. Biology, N.Y. Acad. Scis., Regulatory Affairs Profl. Soc., Federalist Soc., Sigma Xi, Epsilon Pi Tau, Delta Mu Delta. Achievements include cloning of the human tau gene with Dr. A. Andreadis; cloning of bovine, ovine and porcine fetuin cDNAs with Dr. K.M. Dziegielewska and Prof. N.R. Saunders; research in Alzheimer's disease. Office: Taro Pharms USA Inc 5 Skyline Dr Hawthorne NY 10532-2155

BROWN, WYN, physical chemist, educator, researcher; b. Bristol, Eng., Oct. 18, 1934; arrived in Sweden, 1969; s. Donald Henry and Vera May (Stock) B.; m. Karin Elisabet Groop, July 17, 1960; children: Anna, Carolina. BSc, U. London, 1957; PhD, U. Uppsala, Sweden, 1961. Rschr. Med. Rsch. Coun., Cambridge, Eng., 1964-66, Westvaco Corp., S.C., 1966-67; assoc. prof. N.C. State U., Raleigh, 1967-69; assoc. prof. U. Uppsala, 1969-96, prof., 1996—; cons. Westvaco Corp., Charleston, S.C., 1966-70. Editor: Dynamic Light Scattering, 1993, Light Scattering, 1996, Scattering in Polymeric & Colloidal Systems, 1999. Home: Örentuna, Östa, 74391 Storvreta Uppsala, Sweden Office: U Uppsala, Dept Phys Chemistry, 75121 Uppsala Sweden

BROWNE, AIDAN FRANCIS, lawyer; b. Dublin, Ireland, Apr. 24, 1955; came to the U.S., 1986; s. Terence J. and Eileen (Dowling) B.; m. Jill Whitney, June 6, 1981; children: Jessica, Sam, Caoimhe. B in Commerce, U. Coll., Dublin, 1979; JD, Suffolk U., 1989. Bar: Ireland, Mass. Ptnr. Hickey Beauchamp Kirwan O'Reilly, Dublin, Dublin, 1981-87; of counsel Sullivan & Worcester, Boston, 1987—; dir. Pacific Internat. Inst., Lewiston, Idaho; trustee Maruzen Coll., Antrim, N.H., 1989-92; bd. dirs. North Atlantic Trade Group, Boston, Univ. Coll. Dublin in N.Am., Boston. Fin. dir. Paul Harold for Congress, Boston, 1992; active Clinton/Gore Campaign, Boston, 1992, Friends of Fianna Fail, Boston, 1990. Mem. Irish Bar Assn., English Bar Assn., Welsh Bar Assn., Asian Pacific Bar Assn., Boston Bar Assn., Royal Dublin Golf Club, Lansdown Rugby Club (sec. 1986). Roman Catholic. Avocations: art, golf, soccer, rugby, snooker. Home: 80 Woodmere Dr Sudbury MA 01776-1776 Office: Sullivan & Worcester 1 Post Office Sq Ste 2300 Boston MA 02109-2129

BROWNE, BENJAMIN CHAPMAN, solicitor; b. Linton, U.K., May 18, 1953; s. Benjamin Chapman and Marjorie Grace (Hope-Gill) B.; m. Sara Katharine Pangbourne, July 28, 1979; children: Benjamin, Edward, Rebecca. BA, Cambridge U., 1975, MA (hon.), 1977. Qualified as solicitor, 1978. Articled clk. Lovell White & King, London, 1976-78, asst. solicitor, 1978-79; asst. solicitor Morrell Peel & Gamlen, Oxford, U.K., 1979-81; asst. solicitor Clyde & Co., Guildford, U.K., 1981-85, ptnr., 1985—; specialist in shipping and marine ins. law. Avocations: walking, gardening. Office: Clyde and Co, Beaufort House Chertsey St, Guildford GU1 4HA, England

BROWNE, DENIS GEORGE, Roman Catholic bishop; b. Auckland, New Zealand, Sept. 21, 1937; s. Neville Joseph and Catherine Anne (Moroney) B. Student, Holy Cross Coll., 1959-62; DD, Holy Cross Coll., Rome, 1977. Bishop Rarotonga, Cook Islands, 1977-83; bishop Auckland, New Zealand, 1983-94, Hamilton, New Zealand, 1994—. Capt. med. corps. New Zealand Army, 1970-75. Office: Chanel Ctr, 51 Grey St PO Box 4353, Hamilton East Hamilton, New Zealand

BROWNE, JOHN (PHILLIP) (EDMUND BROWNE), oil company executive; b. Hamburg, Germany, Feb. 20, 1948; s. Edmund and Paula Browne. MA in Physics, Cambridge U., Eng., 1969; MS in Bus., Stanford (Calif.) U., 1980; DEng (hon.), Heriott Watt U.; DTech (hon.), Robert Gordon U. Registered profl. engr., U.K. Petroleum engr. Brit. Petroleum Co., London, N.Y., Calif. and Alaska, 1969-79; regional petroleum engr. Brit. Petroleum Co., London, 1979-80, comml. mgr., 1981-83, group treas., 1984-86; mgr. forties field Brit. Petroleum Co., Aberdeen, Scotland, 1983-84; exec. v.p., CFO, CEO Standard Oil Co. of Ohio, Cleve., 1986-87; CEO Standard Oil Prodn. Co., 1987-89; chief fin. officer BP America, Inc., Cleve., 1987-89; mng. dir., chief exec. officer BP Exploration, London, 1989-95; mng. dir., bd. The Brit. Petroleum Co., PLC, 1991-98, group chief exec., 1995-98; group chief exec. BP Amoco, 1998—; nonexec. dir. Redland PLC, 1992-96, Smithkine Beecham, 1995-99, Intel Corp., 1997—, Goldman Sachs; mem. supervisory bd. Daimler-Chrysler AG, 1997—. Emeritus chmn. adv. bd. Stanford Grad. Sch. Bus., 1997; trustee Brit. Mus., 1995—, Conf. Bd., Inc.; mem. governing body London Bus. Sch., 1996—; v.p., bd. dirs. Prince of Wales Bus. Leaders Forum; hon. fellow St. John's Coll., Cambridge. Knighted, 1998; Trevelyan open scholar. Fellow Royal Acad. Engring., Inst. Mining and Metallurgy, Inst. Chem. Engrs. (hon.); mem. Athenaeum Club (London). Avocations: ballet, opera, photography, pre-Columbian art.

BROWNE, JOSEPH PETER, retired librarian; b. June 12, 1929; s. George and Mary Bridget (Fahy) B. AB, U. Notre Dame, 1951; STL, Pontificum Athenaeum Angelicum, Rome, 1957, STD, 1960; MS in L.S., Cath. U. Am., 1965. Joined Congregation of Holy Cross, Roman Cath. Ch., 1947, ordained priest, 1955. Asst. pastor Holy Cross Ch., South Bend, Ind., 1955-56; libr., prof. moral theology Holy Cross Ch., Washington, 1959-64; mem. faculty U. Portland, Oreg., 1964-73, 75—, dir. libr., 1966-70, 76-94, dean Coll. Arts and Scis., 1970-73, assoc. prof. libr. sci., 1967-95, prof. emeritus, 1995—, regent, 1969-70, 77-81, chmn. acad. senate, 1968-70; prof., head dept. libr. sci. Our Lady of Lake Coll., San Antonio, 1973-75; chmn. Interstate Libr. Planning Coun., 1977-79. Mem. Columbia River chpt. Huntington's Disease Soc. Am., 1975-90, pres., 1979-82; pastor St. Birgitta Ch., Portland, 1993—; chmn. Archdiocesan Presbyteral Coun., 1994-98; mem. coll. of cons. Archdiocese of Portland, 1995-2000. Recipient Culligan award U. Portland, 1979. Mem. ALA, Cath. Libr. Assn. (life, pres. 1971-73), Cath. Theol. Soc. Am., Pacific N.W. Libr. Assn. (pres. 1985-86), Oreg. Libr. Assn. (life, pres. 1967-68), Nat. Assn. Parliamentarians, Oreg. Assn. Parliamentarians (pres. 1985-87), Mensa Internat., All-Ireland Cultural Soc. Oreg. (pres. 1984-85), Ancient Order of Hibernians, KC. Democrat. Home: 11820 NW Saint Helens Rd Portland OR 97231-2319

BROWNE, PAUL, banker; b. Croydon, Eng., Apr. 3, 1959; s. Eric Wilfred Browne and Ann Margaret (Notley) Burton; m. Nicola Matthews, July 18, 1987; children: William, Morgan, Owen, Christiana. MA with honors, Oxford (Eng.) U., 1981; MBA, Manchester (Eng.) U., 1987. Mem. internat. staff Std. Chartered Bank, Bahrain and Qatar, 1981-85; mgr. group strategy Std. Chartered Bank, London, regional head corp. and instnl. banking Africa; mgmt. cons. Bain & Co., London, 1987-89; strategic planning mgr. Abbey Nat., London, 1989-91; dir. E-Commerce. Avocations: strategy games, rugby, music. Office: Std Chartered Bank, 1 Aldermanbury Sq, London EC2V 7SB, England

BROWNE, PERRY JAMES, electrical engineer, mathematician; b. Winchester, Eng., Feb. 26, 1948; s. Bernard James and Fay Harriet (Johnson) B. BSc, Leeds (Eng.) U., 1969; BSc in Math., Brighton (Eng.) Poly., 1991; PhD in Math., Sussex U., Brighton, 1996. Chartered engr. Engr. W.S. Atkins & Ptnrs., Epsom, Eng., 1969-78; pilot Dan Air Svcs., Newcastle, Eng., 1978-81; project engr. APV, Crawley, Eng., 1981-84; sr. engr. Electrowatt, Horsham, Eng., 1984-89, Brit. Aerospace, Farnborough, Eng., 1989—; vis. rsch. fellow Sussex U. Author: Kybernetika V30, 1994; co-author: (with J.A. Bather) Bayesian Sampling Schemes for Auditors, 1993; contbr. articles to profl. jours. Mem. Inst. Elec. Engrs., Royal Aero. Soc. Anglican. Avocations: classical music, aviation. Home: 4 Wenlock Close, Crawley RH11 8NH, England

BROWNE, ROGER MICHAEL, oral pathology educator, consultant; b. Birmingham, U.K., June 19, 1934; s. Arthur Leslie and Phyllis Maud (Baker) B.; m. Lilah Hilda Manning, May 31, 1958; children: Nicola Jane, Andrew Manning. BS, U. Birmingham, 1954, B of Dental Sci., 1957, PhD, 1960, DDS, 1974. Rsch. fellow U. Birmingham, 1958-60, lectr. in conservative dentistry, 1961-64, lectr. in dental pathology, 1964-67, sr. lectr. in oral pathology, 1967-77, prof. oral pathology, 1977-96, prof. emeritus, 1997—; vis. prof. U. Lagos, Nigeria, 1969; postgrad. advisor in dentistry U. Birmingham, 1977-82, dir. Sch. Dentistry, 1986-89. Author: Colour Atlas of Oral Histopathology, 1975, Radiological Atlas of Diseases of the Teeth and Jaws, 1983, Atlas of Dental and Maxillofacial Radiology and Imaging, 1995; editor: The Investigative Pathology of Odontogenic Cysts, 1991, Self-assessment Picture Tests - Oral Radiology, 1997. Fellow Royal Coll. Pathologists, Dental Surgery Royal Coll. Surgeons (Charles Tomes medal 1995); mem. Internat. Assn. for Dental Rsch. (Disting. Scientist award in pulp biology 1991), Brit. Soc. Oral Pathology (pres. 1985-86, 91-94), Brit. Dental Assn. (pres. hosps. group 1986-87). Avocations: rugby football, tennis, walking. Office: Dental School, St Chads Queensway, B4 6NN Birmingham United Kingdom

BROWNE, THOMAS REED, neurologist, researcher, educator; b. Lakewood, N.J., Aug. 10, 1943; s. Thomas Reed and Margaret (King) B.; m. Lynne Van Beuren, Mar. 27, 1969; children: Hilary Katherine, David Gerard. BA cum laude, Princeton U., 1965; MD with honors, U. Rochester, 1969. Diplomate Am. Bd. Psychiatry and Neurology, Am. Bd. Clin. Neurophysiology. Intern in medicine Cornell U. Med. Ctr., N.Y.C., 1969-70; staff assoc. epilepsy NIH, Bethesda, Md., 1970-72; resident in neurology Mass. Gen. Hosp., Boston, 1972-75; fellow in epilepsy Childrens Hosp., Boston, 1975-76; asst. prof. neurology Boston U. Sch. Medicine, Boston, 1976-80, assoc. prof. neurology, 1980-84, prof. neurology, 1984—, vice-chmn. dept. neurology, 1987—; clin. instr. in neurology Harvard Med. Sch., 1976-86; lectr. neurology Harvard Med. Sch., Boston, 1987—; assoc. chief neurology svc. VA Med. Ctr., Boston, 1987-97, chief neurology svc., 1997—. Editor: Epilepsy: Diagnosis and Management, 1983, 5th Frontiers of Pharmacology Symposium, Stable Isotopes in Pharm. Res., 1987, Handbook of Epilepsy, 1997, 2d edit. 1999, Stable Isotopes in Pharmaceutical Research, 1997; sect. editor Jour. Clin. Pharmacol., 1987—, Pharmacotherapy, 1982—, Am. Jour. Therapeutics, 1994—; contbr. 180 articles to profl. jours. Recipient Ciba Geigy award Internat. League Epilepsy, 1985. Fellow Am. Coll. Clin. Pharm. (regent 1985-90, McKeen Cattell award 1993), Am. Acad. Neurology, Am. EEG Soc.; mem. Am. soc. Clin. Pharmacol. Therapy, Mass. Epilepsy Soc. (profl. adv. bd.). Achievements includes development of stable isotope tracer methods for human pharmacology studies. Avocations: sailboat racing, model railroading.

BROWNE, WILLIAM JAY, JR., operations administrator; b. Detroit, Feb. 19, 1956; s. William Jay and Helen L. (Viau) B.; m. Barbara Ann Kobrin, June 22, 1986; children: William Scott, Stephanie Lauren. BS in Engring.,

Mich. State U., 1979; MBA, U. Detroit, 1985. Mfg. engr. Detroit Diesel-GM, 1979-85; advanced mfg. engr. CPC group GM, Pontiac, Mich., 1986-87; mgr. mfg. engring. Kelsey-Hayes Co., Brighton, Mich., 1987-88; engring. mgr. TRW Technar Inc., Rochester Hills, Mich., 1988-92; dir. mfg. engring. Mattel Toys Hong Kong Ltd., Hong Kong, 1992-96; dir. quality assurance and product integrity Mattel Power Wheels, Ft. Wayne, Ind., 1996-98; dir. ops. Bretford Mfg. Inc., 1998—. Mem. Am. Soc. for Quality Control, Am. Mgmt. Assn., Soc. Mfg. Engrs., Mich. State U. Alumni Assn., Beta Theta Pi. Republican. Methodist. Achievements include reseach disclosure for piston installation, device utilized as a partial vacuum with self aligning pick and place device to automatically install pistons into a cylinder block. Home: 2631 Saddlebrook Dr Naperville IL 60564-4616 Office: Bretford Mfg Inc 11000 Seymour Ave Franklin Park IL 60131-1230

BROWNHILL, H. BUD, small business owner, canine behavior therapist; b. Fort Erie, Ont., Can., May 22, 1941; came to U.S., 1958; s. Charles V. and June M. (Ott) B. Student, Fullerton (Calif.) Coll., 1960-62, Fanshaw Coll., London, Ont. Can., 1971-73, Brock U., Ont., Can., 1977. Cert. canine behavior therapist in aggression solving, trainer, Calif.; registered certifier of svc. dog qualications. Owner Brownhill Basics Dog Tng., N.Y., Ariz., Calif., Can., Dogs-Calif. Tng., Anaheim, 1988—; internat. chmn. tng. and spl. projects heart therapy svc. Dogs Internat., 1998—; presenter seminars to dog tng. assns. in U.S. and Can., on dog tng. and safety to pub. schs.; spkr. on dog-bite prevention to various orgns.; puppy expert, gen. problem solving trainer, specialist in competition tng.; instr. other profl. dog trainers for pvt. bus. and govt.; legal cons. dog aggression, expert witness in and out of ct. lectr. seminars on dog tng. anti-aggression to tng. assns. and pvt. industry, U.S. A. and Can.; contbr. articles to profl. jours. Active Smithsonian, Habitat for Humanity, Nat. Found. for Animals and Therapy Dogs Internat. Recipient Highest Scoring Dog in Trials awards Am. Kennel Club, Can. Kennel Club, Bermuda Kennel Club, Mex. Kennel Club; winner High in Trial U.S. Chesapeake Obedience Nat., 1989, Shuffle Bd. Champion, 1980; 1st pl. Gaines Western U.S. Obedience Championship, 1985, 3d pl. tie World Series Obedience Competition, 1985; recipient Calif. State award, Golden State award. Mem. NRA, Am. Assn. Ret. Persons, Calif. Handlers Advanced Obedience Soc., Internat. Platform Assn., Am. Amateur Trap-Shooting Assn. (class winner 1977, 78, 79, 80, 83, 84, 85), Long Beach German Shepherd Dog Club (obedience chmn. 1985-90, 94-95), Nat. Fishing Assn., Nat. Hunting Assn., Dog Owners Internat. Travel (founder, internat. chmn. 1987-90, 94), Doberman Club (Santa Ana, obedience cons. 1984-86), Orange Coast Obedience Club (program dir. 1984), Can. Nat. Assn. (provincial rep. 1980). Avocations: target shooting, fishing, hunting, sufffleboard, auto racing. Home and Office: 2147 W Avon Cir Anaheim CA 92804-4306 also: RR #1 Southwold, Ontario, Canada N0L 2G0

BROWNING, DON SPENCER, religious educator; b. Trenton, Mo., Jan. 13, 1934; s. Robert Watson and Nelle Juanita Browning; m. Carol LaVeta Browning, Sept. 28, 1958; children: Elizabeth Dell, Christopher Robert. AB, Ctrl. Meth. Coll., Fayette, Mo., 1956; BD, U. Chgo., 1959, PhD, 1964; DDiv, Christian Theol. Sem., Indpls., 1990; DDiv (hon.), U. Glasgow, Scotland, 1998. Asst. prof. Phillips U., Enid, Okla., 1963-65; instr. Div. Sch., U. Chgo., 1965-66, asst. prof., 1966-69, assoc. prof., 1969-77, prof., 1977-79, Alexander Campbell prof. of ethics and social sci., 1979—. Author: Atonement and Psychotherapy, 1966, Generative Man: Society and Good Man in Philip Rieff, Norman Borwn, Erich Fromm and Erik Erikson, 1973, The Moral Context of Pastroal Care, 1976, Pluralism and Personality: William James and Some Contemporary Cultures of Psychology, 1980, Religious Ethics and Pastoral Care, 1983, Religious Thought and the Modern Psychologies, 1987, A Fundamental Practical Theology, 1991, From Culture Wars to Common Ground: Religion and the American Family Debate, 1997. Recipient Oskar Pfister Award Lecture, Am. Psychiat. Assn., 1999; Cadbury Lectr., U. Birmingham, Eng., 1998; Guggenheim fellow, 1975-76; Lilly Endowment grantee, 1991-97, 97. Home: 5513 S Kenwood Ave Chicago IL 60637-1713 Office: Univ of Chicago Divinity Sch Chicago IL 60637

BROWNING, KEITH ANTHONY, meteorology educator; b. Sunderland, Eng., July 31, 1938; s. James Anthony and Amy Hilda (Greenwood) B.; m. Ann Muriel Baish, Aug. 4, 1962; children: Michelle, Jacqueline, Julian. BS in Physics, Imperial Coll., London, 1959, PhD in Meteorology, 1962. Rsch. atmosphere physicist Air Force Cambridge Rsch. Labs., Sudbury, Mass., 1962-66; prin., then chief meteorol. officer Met Office Radar Rsch. Lab, Royal Signals & Radar Est., Malvern, Eng., 1966-74, 75-85; chief scientist Nat. Hail Rsch. Experiment Nat. Ctr. for Atmospheric Rsch., Boulder, Colo., 1974-75; dep. dir. phys. rsch. Meteorol. Office, Bracknell, Eng., 1985-89; dir. rsch. Meteorol. Office, Bracknell, 1989-91; dir. Joint Ctr. for Mesoscale Meteorology, Reading, 1992—; prof. meteorology U. Reading, 1995—; chair meteorology and atmospheric physics subcom. Brit. Com. for Geodesy and Geophysics, 1985-89; mem. Natural Environment Rsch. Coun., 1984-87; vis. prof. dept. meteorology U. Reading, Eng., 1988-94; mem. Joint Sci. Com. World Climate Rsch. Program, 1992-94; chair Global Energy & Water Cycle Experiment Cloud Sys. Sci. Panel, 1992-96; mem. World Weather Rsch. Program, 1998—. Editor Nowcasting, 1982; co-editor: (with R.J. Gurney) Global Energy and Water Cycles, 1999; contbr. numerous articles to books and profl. jours. Fellow Royal Meteorol. Soc. (chartered meteorologist, pres. 1988-90, chair accreditation bd. 1994-99, L.F. Richardson prize 1968, Buchan prize 1972), Am. Meteorol. Soc. (Meisinger award 1974, Jule G. Charney award 1984), The Royal Soc.; mem. Academia Europaea, U.S. Nat. Acad. Engring. (fgn. assoc.). Office: U Reading, Joint Ctr Mesoscale Meteor, Reading RG6 6BB, England

BROWNING, PETER CRANE, packaging company executive; b. Boston, Sept. 2, 1941; s. Ralph Leslie and Nancy (Crane) B.; m. Carole Ann Shegog, Dec. 14, 1963 (div. 1974); children: Christina, Jennifer; m. Kathryn Anne Klucharich, July 27, 1974; children: Kimberly, Peter. AB in History, Colgate U., 1963; MBA, U. Chgo., 1976. Salesman, mktg. mgr. White Cap div. Continental Can, Northbrook, Ill., 1964-75; mgr. mktg. Conally Venture div. Continental Can, 1975-79; gen. mktg. and sales mgr. Bondware div. Continental Can, 1979-81, v.p., gen. mgr., 1981-84; v.p. gen. mgr. White Cap. div. Continental Can, 1984-86, exec. v.p., oper. officer, 1987-89; pres. Gold Bond Bldg. Products div. Nat. Gypsum Co., Charlotte, N.C., 1989-90; pres., CEO Nat. Gypsum Co., Dallas, 1990-93, Aancor Holdings Inc., Dallas, 1990—; chmn. bd. dirs., CEO Nat. Gypsum Co. parent co. Aancor Holdings, Inc., 1991-93; exec. v.p. Sonoco Products Co., Hartsville, S.C., 1993-96, pres., COO, 1996-98, pres., CEO, 1998-2000; chmn. bd. dirs. Nucor Corp., 2000—, Wachovia Corp., Lowe's Cos., Inc., Phoenix-Home Life. Mem. bd. visitors McColl Sch. Bus./Queens Coll.; mem. coun. on Grad. Sch./U. Chgo. Mem. Quail Hollow Country Club, DeBordieu Country Club. Republican. Episcopalian. Avocations: mountain climbing, running, reading. Home: 1400 W Carolina Ave Hartsville SC 29550-4902 Office: Sonoco Products Co 1 N 2nd St Hartsville SC 29550-3305

BROWNING, WILFRID ROBERT, Anglican clergyman; b. London, May 29, 1918; s. Charles Robert and Mabel Elizabeth (Chaney) B.; m. Mary Elizabeth Browning, July 31, 1948; children: Hilary, Sarah, Simon, Timothy. BA, U. Oxford, 1940, MA, 1944, BD, 1949. Lectr. Cuddesdon Coll., Oxford, 1951-59, 65-70; residentiary canon of Christ Ch. Cathedral Ch. of Eng., Oxford, 1965-87, hon. canon, 1987—; tutor Westminster Coll., Oxford, 1992—. Author: Dictionary of the Bible, 1996; contbr. articles to profl. jours. Mem. Labor Party. Avocation: public transport. Home: 33 Dunstone Rd Plymstock, Plymouth PL 9 8RJ, England

BROWN-JONES, VALERIE, economist; b. N.Y.C., Apr. 12, 1969; d. Frank Edward and Claudia Roberta Brown; m. Jose Juan Padilla, July 15, 1992 (div. Apr. 1996); 1 child, William; m. Dennis Charlesworth Jones, Sept. 19, 1997; 1 child, Zachary. BS, N.C. Agrl. and Tech. State U., 1991, MS, 1996. Intern to the pres. DeLashmet Ogilvy & Wicks, Greensboro, N.C., 1990-91; intern U.S. Agy. for Internat. Devel., Sri Lanka, 1993; adminstrv. apointee, intern USDA, Washington, 1995, coop student Internat. Trade Policy Divsn., 1995, economist, mktg. specialist Domestic Outreach, 1996, internat. trade show coord. AgExport Svcs., 1997—. Vol. Big Bros. and Sisters, Greensboro, 1996; vol. Martha's Table, Washington, Boys & Girls Club, Upper Marlboro, Md. Grantee 2000 New Leader Program, USDA, Washington, 2000; recipient Adminstr.'s Spl. award for Disting. Contbn. to Fgn. Agrl. Svc., 1998, others. Mem. Gamma Sigma Delta, Alpha Kappa Alpha. Roman Catholic. Avocations: reading, writing fiction, working with the homeless. E-mail: brownvr@fas.usda.gov. Office: USDA/SW Stop 1052 1400 Independence Ave SW Washington DC 20250-0002

BROWN LEATHERBERRY, THOMAS HENRY, gospel music company executive, clergy member; b. Wilmington, Del., June 24, 1930; s. Glenn Ford and Rita (Leatherberry) Brown; m. Grace L. Wilson, Mar. 1, 1950 (div. 1978); children: Linda Henry, Patricia Williams, Lucinda Brown, Martha Baccus, Tommy Jr. (dec.), Jason James. Student, Carnegie Hall Sr. Drama Sch., N.Y.C., 1961; A. in Engring. Comms., N.Y. Sch. Announcing, N.Y.C., 1968; BA in Behavioral Sci. and Bibl. Edn., U. Del.; M Bibl. Theology, Ea. Bapt. U.; DD (hon.), Trinity Coll., Knoxville, Tenn., 1970. Artist, comedian Mantan Moreland, N.Y.C., 1959-62; road mgr., negotiator Langston Hughes Prodns., N.Y.C., 1963-66; dir. music Chs. of God in Christ, Bklyn., 1968-78; dir. arts Gospel Arts Coalition, Inc., Wilmington, 1978—; pastor Bible Way House of Prayer Worldwide Inc., Wilmington, 1989—; minister of music Bibleway Mid-Atlantic Diocese, Balt., 1990—; dir. asst. Alvin Ailey Dancers, N.Y.C., 1963; disk jockey Sta. WWRL, N.Y.C., 1969, tchr. Christina Cultural Arts, Wilmington, 1983-89; music dir. World Christian Fellowship, 1989—. Dir. recs. Rite Enterprise Rec. Co., 1954; actor Prodigal Son, 1963, Black Nativity, 1964; asst. to producer (TV) MD, 1967; stage dir., program mgr. Gospel Music shows, CBS-TV, 1967; author (radio) America Calls, 1967, Israel Radio Calls, 1967; dir., engr. RCA Inst. TV, Sta. ABC-TV, 1968. Program dir. Y.M.C.A., Wilmington, 1978-81; entertainer for Gov. Dupont, State of Del., 1980; dir. gospel music coun. 6602, City of Wilmington, 1983. With U.S. Army, 1950-53. Named State Leader, African Am. Proclamation Inc., Phila., 1983; recipient Attestation Pilgrimage award, Minister of Courison, Jerusalem, 1983, award of Grand Performance, Jewish Community Rels. Com., Wilmington, 1988. Mem. BMI, Am. Guild Authors and Composers, Trinity Coll. Alumni Assn., Am. Legion (chaplain Brandywine, Del.), VFW (life), Masons (grand music dir. 1989—, past worshipful master, illustrious master, imperial dep. chaplain 1997—), Masons (past grand high priest, 33 degree), Order Ea. Star (past worthy patron), Shriners, Elks (Appreciation award Paul Lawrence Dunbar lodge #106 1981), Heroines of Jericho (grand Joshua), Honor Guard Assn. (lt. col.), Del. Phylaxis Soc. (pres.), Epsilon Delta Psi (life). Democrat. Avocations: football, basketball, movies, playing organ and piano. Office: NOW Gospel Arts Singers PO Box 824 Wilmington DE 19899-0824

BROWNLEE, DONALD EUGENE, II, astronomer, educator; b. Las Vegas, Nev., Dec. 21, 1943; s. Donald Eugene and Geraldine Florence (Stephen) B.; m. Paula Szkody. B.S. in Elec. Engring, U. Calif., Berkeley, 1965; Ph.D. in Astronomy, U. Wash., 1970. Research assoc. U. Wash., 1970-77, asso. prof. astronomy, 1977-89; asso. geochemistry Calif. Inst. Tech., Pasadena, 1977-82; prof. astronomy U. Wash., 1989—; cons. NASA, 1976—. Author papers in field, chpts. in books. Grantee NASA, 1975; recipient J. Lawrence Smith medal Nat. Acad. of Sciences, 1994. Mem. AAAS, Internat. Astron. Union, Am. Astron. Assn., Meteoritical Soc. (Leonard medal 1996), Com. Space Rsch. Dust, NAS (NASA PI stardust mission). Office: U Wash Dept Astronomy Seattle WA 98195-0001*

BROWNLEE, JUDITH MARILYN, priestess, psychotherapist, psychic; b. Beaumont, Tex., May 16, 1940; d. Alvin Maurice and Juanita M. (Whittington) B.; m. Theodore Blakey Peak, Apr. 12, 1974 (div. 1981); 1 child, Daniel David Brownlee Peak; m. Floyd S. Bond, Aug. 18, 1996. BA, Lamar U., Beaumont, Tex., 1962; postgrad., U. Denver, 1971; MA, Avalon Inst., Boulder, Colo., 1992; student, Our Lady Perpetual Responsibility, The Silent Cir., 1975-79. Wiccan priestess; cert. master tarot reader Am. Tarot Assn. Tchr. Deer Trail (Colo.) H.S., 1963-64, Lutcher Stark H.S., Orange, Tex., 1967-69; libr. technician Denver Pub. Libr., 1970-73; bus. exec. Weight Watchers Rocky Mtn., Denver, 1974; mail order divsn. mgr. Mile High Comics and Books, Denver, 1975-81; religious tchr. The Silent Cir., Denver, 1979-83; gov. employee Colo. Atty. Gen. Office, Denver, 1983-92; minister Fortress Temple, Denver, 1984-96; psychotherapist, 1992—; pub. spkr. Spring Mysteries Festival, Seattle, 1988-92; counselor Profl. Psychic Counselors Network, 1993-96, Morningstar Inc., 1997, Oracle Tree New Age Mall, 1997—; pub. spkr. Denver, 1988—; workshop leader Spring Mysteries Festival, Seattle, 1988, 92, Dragonfest Pagan Festival, Denver, 1987-92; lectr. Isis Metaphys. Ctr., workshop leader, 1985—; lectr. Raven & Rose Bookstore, Ft. Collins Colo., 1992-93, Enchanted Chalice Bookstore, 1994-2000, Herbs & Arts Bookstore, 1996, Spirit Ways Bookstore, 1998; organizer Front Range Pagan Festival, 1985; guest spkr. Greeley (Colo.) Unitarian Fellowship, 1992; spkr. Rocky Montain Fiction Writers Conv., 1993; creator, dir. Edn. for Pagan Youth com. Pagan Sch., 1990-94, 96-97; spkr. in field. Author: Pagan Parenting, 1987, The Wheel of the Year, 1988; contbr. articles to profl. jours.; participant Dedication to Faith, Images and Voices, 1999, Roundtable Discussions with Artist and Spiritual Leaders, 1999. Interviewee KOA Radio, 1984, 92, 95, 96, KNUS and KYBG, 1992, KUSA Channel 9, 1987, 90, Rocky Mountain News, Denver, 1992, 96; cmty. prodr. Mile High Cablevision, 1987; tel. counselor Lifeline of Colo., Denver, 1988; field tng. supr. Iliff Sch. Theology, Denver, 1995-96; bd. dirs. Inst. for Interfaith and Mulicultural Studies and Social Concerns U. Denver, 1999—. Recipient Hart and Crescent Disting. Youth Svc. award Covenant of the Goddess, 1995. Mem. Colo. Assn. Psychotherapists, Assn. Past Life Rsch. and Therapy, Women's Spiritual Leadership Alliance (bd. dirs. 1992—), Daus. of New Moon (founder, facilitator), Soc. for Creative Anachronism (Colo. founder, CEO 1970-73, treas. 1981-83), Denver Area Sci. Fiction Assn. (editor 1969-70, dir. 1974-75, conf. chmn. 1970-75), Denver Area Interfaith Clergy Conf., Covenant Unitarian Universalist Pagans. Avocations: reading, theatre, films, science fiction, internet. E-mail: judith1152@aol.com. Office: PO Box 172271 Denver CO 80217-2271

BROWNSON, ANNA LOUISE HARSHMAN, publishing executive, editor; b. Indpls., May 4, 1926; d. Walter W. and Jennie Andrea Harshman; m. Charles B. Brownson (dec.); children: Dwight, Bruce, David, Catharine, Scott. BA, Butler U., 1949, postgrad., 1950-51. Asst. biochemistry lab. Ind. U. Med. Sch., Indpls., 1944-47; grad. asst. Butler U., Indpls., 1949-51; adminstrv. asst. to U.S. congressman from 11th Dist. Ind. Indpls., 1951-58; assoc. editor, treas. Congl. Staff Directory, Ltd., 1959-79, pres., 1980-96, pub. emeritus, 1996—; pub., owner, editor Advance Locator for Capitol Hill, 1963-82, Election Index Congl. Staff Directory, 1966-82, Fed. Staff Directory, 1982-96, Jud. Staff Directory, 1987-96; gen. ptnr. Brownson Partnership Corr. sec. Fusaliers; past pres. Former Mem. U.S. Congress Aux.; exec. com., trustee George C. Marshall Found. Bd. dirs. Madison Coun. The Libr. of Congress, Accokeek Found., Nat. Colonial Farm; v.p. Nat. Capitol area Boy Scouts Am. (silver Beaver award); active Mt. Vernon Life Guard, Gunston Hall, World Affairs Coun. Washington, Fairchild Gardens, Mount Vernon 100, Gunston Hall. Recipient Ann L. Brownson award Va. Assn. Museums, 1999. Mem. Internat. Palm Soc., Eisenhower World Affairs Inst., Potomac River Basin Consortium, Capitol Hill Club, U.S. Capitol Hist. Soc., Va. Assn. Mus. (sec., Professionalism in Mus. award 1999), Kappa Alpha Theta (treas. Zeta Iota House Corp.). Presbyterian. Home: 1261 S Alhambra Cir Coral Gables FL 33146-3104 Office: PO Box 17 Mount Vernon VA 22121-0017

BROWNSON, KENNETH C., university dean; b. Hazleton, Pa., Apr. 16, 1945; s. Kenneth George and Mary Louise (Dennion) B. AAS in Nursing, Del. Tech. and C.C., 1978; BS in Profl. Arts, St. Joseph's Coll., Standish, Maine, 1984; MS in Mgmt., The Am. Coll., 1986; MS in Psychology, Calif. Coast U., 1989; EdD in Adult and Nontraditional Edn., Newport U., 1991; Cert. in Cmty. Health Edn., Calif. Coll. Health Sci., 1999. RN, Del., Pa. Evening supr., asst. head nurse intensive/critical care unit Riverside Hosp., Wilmington, Del., 1980-83; staff RN, nurse/counselor crisis svc. unit Crozer-Chester Med. Ctr., Chester, Pa., 1983-94; pres. Adult Edn. Resource, New Castle, Del., 1987—; dean undergrad. studies Greenwich U., Australia, 1989—; mem. adv. bd. Insvc. Tng. Inst.; bd. dirs. Brandywine Counseling, Wilmington. Mem. editl. bd. Health Care Mgr. With USN, 1965-69, Vietnam. Home and Office: 33 W 4th St New Castle DE 19720-5092

BROWNWOOD, DAVID OWEN, lawyer; b. L.A., May 24, 1935; s. Robert Scott Osgood and Ruth Elizabeth (Bellamy) B.; m. Sigrid Carlson, Mar. 3, 1956 (div. 1972); children: Jeffrey Owen, Kirsten, Scott David, Daniel Stuart; m. Susan Sloane Jannicky, July 4, 1975; 1 child, Mary Ruth Bellamy; stepchildren: Bradbury, Stephanie Ellington. AB with distinction, Stanford U., 1956; LLB magna cum laude, Harvard U., 1964. Bar: Calif. 1965, N.Y. 1969. Law clk. Ropes & Gray, Boston, 1963; assoc. McCutchen, Doyle, Brown & Enersen, San Francisco, 1964-66; lectr. law U. Khartoum, Sudan, 1966-67, Kenya Inst. Adminstrn., Lower Kabete, 1967-68; assoc. Cravath, Swaine & Moore, N.Y.C., 1968-72, ptnr., 1973—, recruiting ptnr., 1978-82, mng. ptnr. for legal staff, 1983-86; ptnr. in charge London office, 1995—; treas. N.Y. Law Inst., 1978-83, chmn. exec. com., 1983-88, pres., 1988-93. Mem. editorial bd. Harvard U. Law Rev., 1963-64. Dir. Literacy Assistance Ctr., N.Y.C., 1983-94, co-chmn. bd. dirs. 1987-94; trustee Greenwich (Conn.) Country Day Sch., 1985-92, v.p., 1986-88, pres., chmn. bd. trustees, 1988-92; co-chmn. Harvard U. Law Sch. 25th Reunion Gift, 1988-89; nat. chair Harvard U. Law Sch. Fund, 1991-93; N.Y. regional com. campaign for Harvard Law Sch., 1991-95; com. on univ. resources Harvard U., 1991—, mem. Harvard law sch. vis. com., 1995—; keystone regional vice chair centennial campaign Stanford U., 1986-92; exec. com. Stanford U. N.Y. Coun., 1992-95; vice chmn. Stanford U. N.Y. Major Gifts Com., 1993-95; co-chair Stanford U. Ea. Coun., 1993; bd. govs. Stanford Assocs., 1993-95, pres., chmn. bd. govs., 1994-95; bd. advisors Stanford Trust (U.K.), 1995—; mem. nat. adv. bd. Outward Bound USA, 1993-96. 1st lt. USAF, 1956-61, fighter pilot Air Def. Command, capt. USAFR, Mass. Air N.G., 1961-66. Recipient Centennial medallion Stanford U., Stanford Assocs. award. Fellow Am. Bar Found., N.Y. State Bar Found.; mem. ABA, Internat. Bar Assn., N.Y. State Bar Assn., Assn. Bar City N.Y., Round Hill Club (Greenwich), Field Club (Greenwich), Sankaty Head Club (Nantucket), Siasconset Casino Assn. (Nantucket), Harvard Club (N.Y.C.). Home: 19 Pelham Crescent, London SW7 2NR, England also: 39 Baxter Rd Siasconset MA 02564 Office: Cravath Swaine & Moore, City Point One Ropemaker St, London EC2Y 9HR, England also: Cravath Swaine & Moore 825 8th Ave Fl 46 New York NY 10019-7416

BROX, GEORG ALEXANDER, consultant histopathologist, researcher; b. Leipzig, Germany, Mar. 12, 1949; arrived in Eng., 2000; s. Georg Anton and Carola Anna (Walther) B. A-level exams., Hanover, Germany, 1969; primary clin. exams., U. Kiel, Germany, 1972; MD magna cum laude, U. Mainz, Germany, 1976. Gen. med. lic.; gen. practitioner lic.; full registration as gen. practitioner in Gen. Med. Coun. U.K.; lic. cons. histopathologist; lic. cons. of accident and emergency; registered specialist Gibraltar Health Authority, U.K. Cons. accident and emergency Deputizing Dr. Svc., Wiesbaden, Germany, 1978-99; sr. house officer, registrar Sch. Human Medicine Johann Wolfgang Goethe U., Frankfurt, 1979-86; dir., owner, mgr. Histopathol. Lab., Wiesbaden, Germany, 1986-2000; cons. histopathologist, cytopathologist Surrey and Sussex Health Care Nat. Health Svc. Trust, Crawley, U.K., 2000—; cons. accident and emergency Internat. Patient Recovery Svc., Gen. Automobile Assn. Germany, 1981-99; mgr. accreditation process of lab. Coll. Am. Pathologists, 1991-99, inspector list, 1991-99; mem. Com. for Diagnostic Quantitative Pathology, 1987—. Contbr. articles to profl. jours. Med. capt. Nat. Mil. Svc., Germany, 1978-79. Fellow Royal Soc. Medicine; mem. Internat. Acad. Pathology, Nat. Assn. Primary Care, Brit. Assn. Dermatologists, Brit. Soc. Clin. Cytology, Brit. Assn. Med. Mgrs., Assn. Clin. Pathologists, Pathol. Soc. Gt. Britain and Ireland.

BROYLES, MICHAEL LEE, geophysics and physics educator; b. Corpus Christi, Tex., Apr. 3, 1942; s. Ned Lee and Marion (Richardson) B.; m. Laura Ruth Ferguson, July 30, 1983; 1 child, William Matthew. BA in Phys. Sci., San Francisco State U., 1965; MST in Physics, U. Wis., Superior, 1972; MS in Geophysics, U. Hawaii, 1977; EdD in Higher Edn., Tex. A&M U., Commerce, 1999. Cert. sec. sch. tchr. Tchr. sci. and math. Upper Lake and Sonoma (Calif.) Pub. Schs., 1966-72; geophys. rschr. Hawaii Inst. Geophysics, Honolulu, 1973-79; rsch. geophysicist Amoco Prodn. Co., Tulsa, 1979-80; exploration geophysicist Mobil Oil Corp., Dallas, 1980-86; prof., chmn. dept. physics and astronomy Collin County C.C., Plano, Tex., 1986—. Mem. editl. bd.: UFO Phenomena Mag., Bologna, Italy, 1976-79; contbr. Sci. Ency., 1979-96; contbr. articles to profl. jours. Grantee NSF, 1991—. Mem. Am. Assn. Physics Tchrs., Tex. Jr. Coll. Tchrs. Assn., Mutual UFO Network (state dir. Hawaii 1975-79, state sect. dir. Dallas County 1987-92). Methodist. Achievements include geothermal research and developing teaching methodologies for elementary particle physics. Office: Collin County CC 2800 E Spring Creek Pky Plano TX 75074-3300

BROYLES, RUTH RUTLEDGE, principal; b. Sullivan County, Tenn., July 15, 1912; d. Floyd Lylburn and Ethel Sally (Gross) Rutledge; m. David Lafayette Broyles, Aug. 15, 1937 (dec. Oct. 1980); children: Nancy Ann Broyles McCracken, Edwin Joseph, Dava Lee Broyles Russell. BS, East Tenn. State U., 1934, MA, 1968. Cert. English and biology tchr., Tenn., elem. edn. supr., supt. cert. Tchr. English Jonesborough (Tenn.) High Sch., 1934-38; tchr. 3d and 4th grades Telford (Tenn.) Elem. Sch., 1956-57; tchr. 3d grade Midway Elem. Sch., Jonesborough, 1957-62; tchr. 5th grade Jonesborough Elem. Sch., 1962-67; supr. tchr. corp. program East Tenn. State U., Johnson City, 1967-69; prin. Cherokee Elem. Sch., Johnson City, 1969-78, ret., 1978. County commr. Washington County Ct., 1980-90; chair Jonesborough Civic Trust, 1982-85, Watauga Regional Libr. Bd., Washington County, 1982-87, Washington County/Jonesborough Mus., Jonesborough, 1984—, Tenn. Homecoming 1986, 1985-86; mem. Washington County Libr. Bd., 1991—; mem. expansion com. Washington County/Jonesboro Libr., 1997—; mem. Washington County Oak Hill Sch. Edn. Project, 1998—; mem. fin. com. Washington County Bd. Edn., 1991-95; historian Washington County, 1991—; elder, Sunday sch. tchr., chair Christian edn. com. Jonesborough (Tenn.) Presbyn. Ch., 1989-91; moderator Presbyn. Women, chair adminstrv. com. Holston Presbytery, Kingsport, Tenn.; historian Synod of Living Waters Presbyn. Women, Brentwood, Tenn.; mem. Synod of Living Waters Ministry Divsn., Brentwood; mem. ch. coun. Tusculum Coll., Greenville, Tenn.; mem. Bicentennial com. for Washington County State of Tenn., 1993-97; mem., vice-chmn. Appalachian Christian Village Resident Coun., 1998—, chair, 1999—; mem. Washington County Mus. Com. on Oak Hill sch. project, 1998—; mem. expansion com. Jonesborough Libr., Washington County, 1998—. Recipient E. Harper Johnson Human Rels. award for edn. Tenn. Edn. Assn., 1997; named Woman of the Yr., Bus. and Profl. Women, Jonesborough, Tenn. 1975, Hon. Col., State of Tenn., 1989; Ruth Rutledge Broyles Scholarship Fund for tng. tchrs. named in her honor, 1994. Mem. Tenn. Ret. Tchrs. (state pres. 1985-86, Nashville 1978—, legis. asst. East Tenn. 1991-95, Plaque 1985-86), N.E. Tenn. Tourism Coun. (chair, Silver Tray 1989, Outstanding Svc. award 1993), Tenn. Congress Parents and Tchrs. (v.p. Nashville 1948-69), Tenn. Libr. Assn. (trustee Nashville 1984-85), Washington County Ret. Tchrs. (life, chmn. scholarship com. 1991—), Tenn. Ret. Tchrs. Assn., Washington County Hist. Soc. (pres. 1994-96). Presbyterian. Avocations: traveling, historian, preservationist. Home: Appalachian Christian Vill 2020 Sherwood Dr Apt 324 Johnson City TN 37601-3274

BROZOVIC, DALIBOR, former Croatian vice president, Slavic languages educator; b. Sarajevo, Bosnia & Herzegovina, July 28, 1927; s. Andrija and Olga (Čabrajic) B.; m. Nevenka Košutic, Nov. 26, 1952; children: Lada, Dunja, Hrvoje. BA, U. Zagreb, Croatia, 1951, Dr. Sc., 1957. Teaching asst. Acad. Theater Art, Zagreb, 1952-53; lectr. Slavic U. Ljubljana, Slovenia, 1953-56; teaching asst. Slavic dept. U. Zadar, Croatia, 1956-58, asst. prof., 1958-62, assoc. prof., 1962-67, prof., 1967-90; v.p. Republic of Croatia, Zagreb, 1990; gen. dir. Lexicographic Inst., Zagreb, Croatia, 1991—; vis. prof. U. Mich, Ann Arbor, 1969, U. Regensburg, Fed. Republic Germany, 1971; guest Chinese Acad. Scis., 1979, Govt. Austria, Vienna U., 1982, Govt. Norway, U. Oslo, 1982. Author: Standard Language, 1970, The Vocabulary of the Language, 1969, (with P. Ivic) Serbo-Croatian/Croato-Serbian Language, 1988, The Kuna and the Lipa, 1994; mem. editl. bd. All Slavic Linguistic Atlas, 1964—, Atlas Linguarum Europae, 1982—; contbr. more than 300 studies to internat. jours. V.p. Croation Dem. Union, 1989-93; M.P. Fgn. Policy Com.; v.p. State Monetary Commn. Mem. Croatian Acad. Scis. Arts, Macedonian Acad. Scis. Arts, Acad. Europaea, Matica Hrvatska, Matica Srpska. Roman Catholic. Avocation: numismatics. Home: Stjepana Radica 2, 57000 Zadar Croatia also: Koranska 1 A, 41000 Zagreb Croatia Office: Lexicographic inst, Frankopanska 26, Zagreb Croatia

BRUCE, CHRISTOPHER, artistic director; b. Leicester, U.K., Oct. 3, 1945; s. Alexander and Ethel (Parker) B.; m. Marian Meadowcroft, Nov. 24, 1967; 3 children. Student, Rambert Sch., London. Dancer Ballet Rambert, London, 1963-80, assoc. dir., 1975-79, assoc. choreographer, 1979-87; artistic dir. Rambert Dance Co., London, 1994—; assoc. choreographer English Nat. Ballet, London, 1986-91; resident/assoc. choreographer Houston Ballet, 1989—. Choreographer (ballets) George Frideric, 1969, Wings, 1970, for these who die as cattle, 1971, There was a time, 1972, Weekend, 1974, Unfamiliar Playground, 1974, Ancient Voices of Children, 1975, Black Angels, 1976, Cruel Garden, 1977, Night with Waning Moon, 1979, Dancing

Day, 1981, Ghost Dances, 1981, Cantata, 1981, Village Songs, 1981, Berlin Requiem, 1982, Concertino, 1983, Curses and Blessings, 1983, Intimate Pages, 1984, Sergeant Early's Dream, 1984, Land, 1985, Ceremonies, 1986, The World Again, 1986, The Dream is Over, 1987, Swansong, 1987, Gautama Buddha, 1989, Symphony in Three Movements, 1989, Journey, 1990, Rooster, 1991, Nature Dances, 1992, Kingdom, 1993, Moonshine, 1993, Waiting, 1993, Crossing, 1994, Meeting Point (for United We Dance Internat. Festival to celebrate 50 yrs. of UN), 1995, Quicksilver, 1996, Stream, 1996, Four Scenes, 1998, God's Plenty, 1999; (musicals) Joseph and the Amazing Technicolour Dreamcoat, 1972, Mutiny, 1985, (opera) Venus and Adonis, 1980; choreographer/prodr. (operas) Il Ballo delle Ingrate, 1980, Combattimento di Tancredi e Clorinda, 1981; co-prodr. (opera) Agrippina, 1982. Decorated comdr. Brit. Empire; recipient Inaugural Dance award Evening Standard, 1974, 97, Internat. Theatre Inst. award, 1993. Office: Rambert Dance Co, 94 Chiswick High Rd, London W4 1SH, England

BRUCE, GEORGE JOHN DONE, portrait painter; b. London, Mar. 28, 1930; s. George John Gordon and Dorothy Violet (Done) B. Student, Byam Shaw Sch. Drawing and Painting. Exhibited portraits, landscapes, still life and flowers in U.K.; numerous one-man shows; portrait commns. include the Right Hon. Lord Butler of Saffron Walden, Master Trinity Coll., Cambridge, 1970, Viscount Tonypandy, Speakers Chambers, House of Commons, 1979, Arthur Michael Ramsey, Lord Archbishop of Canterbury, Lambeth Palace, London, 1982, Annabel Etkind, 1985, Mrs. Charles Dent, Ribston Hall, 1992. Mem. Royal Soc. Portrait Painters (elected mem., hon. sec. 1970-84, v.p. 1985-90, pres. 1991-94), Soc. Tchrs. Alexander Technique. Avocations: windsurfing, skiing. Home and Studio: 6 Pembroke Walk, London W8 6PQ, England

BRUCE, IAN JAMES, biochemist, researcher; b. London, Aug. 14, 1956; s. Alwyn and Tessa (Groom) B.; m. Antonella Antimiani, Dec. 18, 1982; children: Caterina Jane, Marco James, Francesca Giulia. BS, U. London, 1978; MS, U. Kent, Eng., 1980; PhD, U. London, 1982. Postdoctoral fellow Univ. Coll., London, 1982-84; sr. postdoctoral fellow Guys Hosp., U. London, 1984-85; lectr. to prof. U. Greenwich, London, 1985-93, dir. biol. scis. rsch. ctr.; mng. dir. Molecular Scis. Ltd., London, 1993—; cons. Hybaid Ltd., London, 1985-94, Hercules Ltd., London, 1987—, Techne Ltd., Cambridge, 1991-99, Whatman Internat. Ltd., 1996-99. Author: Yeast Genetics, 1989; contbr. articles to profl. jours. Fellow Royal Soc. Medicine, Inst. Biology. Office: Norwood Labs U Greenwich, Wellington St, London SE18 6PF, England

BRUCE, IAN WAUGH, health science association administrator; b. Southampton, Eng., Apr. 21, 1945; s. Thomas Waugh and Una Nellie (Eagle) B.; m. Tina Rowland; children: Hannah, Tom. B Social Sci. with honors, U. Birmingham, Eng., 1968, D Social Sci. (hon.), 1995. Engring. trainee Courtaulds, Coventry, Eng., 1964-65; mktg. mgr. Unilever, London, 1968-70; asst. dir. Age Concern, London, 1970-74; dir. Vol. Ctr. U.K., Herts, Eng., 1975-81; asst. chief exec. London Borough of Hammersmith and Fulham, 1981-83; dir. gen. Royal Nat. Inst. for the Blind, London, 1983—; dir. VOLPROF, City U. Bus. Sch., London, 1991—; cons. UN div. Social Affairs, Europe, 1970-72; vis. prof., dir. Ctr. for Non Profit Mgmt., City U., London. Author: Public Relations in the Social Services, 1972, Patronage of the Creative Artist, 1974, Blind and Partially Sighted Adults in Great Britain, 1991, Successful Charity Marketing, 1994, 2d edit., 1998. Mem. Nat. Coun. for Voluntary Orgns., U.K., 1978-81, Exec. Com. Age Concern Eng., 1986, Nat. Coun. on Employment for Disabled People, 1987; chmn. Nat. Disability Benefits Consortium, 1988—. Recipient Sir Raymond Priestley Expeditionary award, U. Birmingham, 1968. Mem. Brit. Inst. Mgmt. (companion), Inst. of Contemporary Arts. Avocations: arts, countryside. Home: 54 Mall Rd, W6 9DG London England Office: Royal Nat Inst for Blind, 224 Great Portland St, W1 London England

BRUCE, JOHN ANTHONY, artist; b. L.A., Apr. 8, 1931; s. Merle VanDyke and Katherine Mary (Butler) B.; children: Marsha Lee, Margaret Lorren, James Cole, Glenn Allen, Mark Corwin, Leslie Ann. BA in Psychology and Art, Calif. State U., L.A., 1965. Design engr. N.Am. Aviation Corp., Downey, Calif., 1952-57; comml. artist Aerojet Gen. Corp., Sacramento, 1957-59; advt. mgr. Flow Equipment Co., Santa Fe Springs, Calif., 1959-63; art dir. Barnes-Champ Advt., Santa Ana, Calif., 1963-66, Long Beach (Calif.) Ind. Press Telegram News, 1970-73; freelance art cons. Epcot project Walt E. Disney Enterprises, Glendale, Calif., 1976-77. Permanent collections Smithsonian Inst., Washington, D.C.; one man shows Ghormley Gallery, L.A., 1966, Les Li Art Gallery, L.A., 1970, Upstairs Gallery, Long Beach, Calif., 1973, El Prado Gallery, Sedona, Ariz., 1987; group shows Newport Beach Invitational, Newport Beach, Calif., 1964, Laguna Beach Art Festival, Laguna Beach, Calif., 1962, 63, 64, 65, Butler Inst. Am. Art, Youngstown, Ohio, 1970, Allied Artists, N.Y.C., 1988; currently exhibiting with Bartfield Gallery, N.Y.C., New Masters Gallery, Carmel, Calif. With U.S. Army, 1949-52, Korea. Recipient John B. Grayback award Am. Profl. Artists League, 1988, Best of Show award Gene Autry Mus. AICA Show, 1996, San Dimas Festival of Western Art, 1996, Best of Show Chgo. Windy City Artists, 1999, numerous others. Republican. Studio: 5394 Tip Top Rd Mariposa CA 95338-9609

BRUCE, MICHAEL IAN, chemistry educator; b. London, Nov. 17, 1938; arrived in Australia, 1973; s. Alfred Herbert and Ivy Winifred (Peeke) B.; m. Jennifer Ann Harding, Sept. 23, 1961 (div. 1994); children: David Michael Robert, Timothy Edmund Gregory, Louise Anne-Marie. BA with honours, U. Oxford, Eng., 1961, MA, 1976; PhD, U. Bristol, Eng., 1967, DSc, 1976. Exptl. officer Plant Industry divsn. Commonwealth Sci. and Indsl. Rsch. Orgn., Canberra, Australia, 1961-65; jr. fellow U. Bristol, 1966-67, lectr. inorganic chemistry, 1967-73; prof. inorganic chemistry U. Adelaide, Australia, 1973-82, Angas prof. chemistry, 1982—; lectr. Royal Soc. Chemistry, 1986. Contbr. numerous articles to profl. jours. Recipient H.G. Smith medal Royal Australian Chemistry Inst., 1986, Burrows medal, 1989. Fellow Australian Acad. Sci. Avocations: photography, music, reading, bush walking, traveling. E-mail: michael.bruce@adelaide.edu.au. Office: U Adelaide, Chemistry Dept, Adelaide 5005, Australia

BRUCE, RIITTA PIA KAARINA, chemist; b. Karhula, Finland, Nov. 29, 1959; d. Pertti Johannes and Eila Anneli (Turunen) B.; m. Mika Rikhart Inkeroinen, June 20, 1980 (div. 1985); m. Lasse Allan Koskinen, Aug. 26, 1994; 1 child, Tom Bruce. BS, U. Helsinki, Finland, 1982, MS in Organic Chemistry, 1985, postgrad., 1988—. Rschr. The Ministry for Fgn. Affairs, Helsinki, 1984-86; rschr. Orion Pharmaceutica-Orion Corp. Ltd., Espoo, Finland, 1986-88, lab. mgr., 1988-89; group leader Cultor Ltd. Tech. Ctr., Kirkkonummi, Finland, 1989-92, HPLC devel. mgr., 1992-93, project mgr., 1993-94; head lab. Orgn. for Prohibition of Chem. Weapons, The Hague, The Netherlands, 1994-99, sr. external rels. officer, website coord., 1999—. Co-author: Air Monitoring as a Means for Verification of Chemical Disarmament, C.3. Field Tests, Part I, 1985, Part II, 1986; contbr. articles to profl. jours. Mem. Assn. Official Analytical Chemists, Assn. Finnish Chem Socs., Finnish Chemists Soc. Avocations: aerobics, bicycling, gardening. Office: OPCW, Vohan de Wittlaan 32, The Hague The Netherlands

BRUCE, THOMAS ALLEN, physician, philanthropist, educator; b. Mountain Home, Ark., Dec. 22, 1930; s. Rex Floyd and Dora Madeline (Fee) B.; m. Dolores Fay Montgomery, May 28, 1960; children: T.K. Montgomery, Dana Fee Thomas. B.S.M., M.D., U. Ark., 1955, DSc (hon.), 1995. Intern Duke Hosp., 1956-57; resident medicine Bellevue Hosp., N.Y.C., 1957, Meml. Center Cancer and Allied Diseases, N.Y.C., 1958, Parkland Meml. Hosp., Dallas, 1958-59; cardiopulmonary trainee Southwestern Med. Sch. of U. Tex., 1959-60; cardiac research fellow Hammersmith Hosp. and U. London Postgrad. Med. Sch., London, 1960-61, Harvard Bus. Sch., 1974; from instr. to prof. medicine Wayne State U., 1961-68, also asst. dean Sch. of Medicine; prof. medicine, head cardiovascular sect. U. Okla. Med. Center, 1968-74; prof. medicine, dean Coll. Medicine, U. Ark. Med. Scis., 1974-85, emeritus prof., 1997—; med. dir. Barton Research Inst., 1974-85; coordinator Sino-Am. Med. Exchange Program, 1979-85; mem. research support rev. com. NIH, 1983-85; program dir. in health W.K. Kellogg Found., 1985-97, program cons. and advisor, 1997—; bd. dirs. Grantmakers in Health, 1986-94; co-chair session 312 Salzburg Seminar, Austria; mem. nat. adv. com. Native Am. Substance Abuse Prevention Initiative, Robert Wood Johnson Found., History of Medicine Assocs.; nat. adv. bd. cmty. health leadership program Robert Wood Johnson Found.; mem. policy adv. bd. Ctr. for Health Improvement U. Ark. for Med. Scis.; mem. program adv. com. Found. for the Midsouth; advisor group XVI Kellogg Nat. Leadership Program, Coalition for Healthier Cities and Communities in U.S.; founding mem. MidSouth Leadership Alliance; bd. dirs. Ctr. Advancement of Cmty.-Based Pub. Health, Founder's Soc., U. Ark. Coll. Medicine, Watershed Human Svcs. Agy., Heifer Project Internat., Ark. Grantmakers Assn.; adj. staff Ark. Cmty. Found. Bruce Soc. Am. Rsch. and publs. on cardiovascular disease including left ventricular function in cardiac denervation, coronary heart disease, myocardial metabolism relating to phospholipids in graded cardiac ischmia, med. edn. with particular reference to rural health care, health promotion and disease prevention, primary health care, community-based pub. health. Master gardener, chmn. garden docents, mem. adj. staff Wildwood Pk. Performing Arts; mem. adv. com. Ark. Advocates for Children and Families; mem. policy adv. com. Ark. LWV. Recipient Ark. Gov.'s Meritorious Achievement award, Lugene Chilcote award, 1999. Fellow ACP, Am. Coll. Cardiology; mem. APHA, AMA, Assn. Am. Med. Colls., Am. Rhododendron Soc., Garvon Woodland Gardens, Founder's Soc., Ark. Caduceus Club, Leila Arboretum Soc. (pres. 1989-92), Sigma Xi, Alpha Omega Alpha. Home: 6 Spy Glass Ln Little Rock AR 72212-4418

BRUCH, CAROL SOPHIE, lawyer, educator; b. Rockford, Ill., June 11, 1941; d. Ernest and Margarete (Willstätter) B.; m. Jack E. Myers, 1960 (div. 1973); children: Margarete Louise Myers Feinstein, Kurt Randall Myers. A.B., Shimer Coll., 1960; J.D., U. Calif.-Berkeley, 1972. Bar: Calif. 1973, U.S. Supreme Ct. 1980. Law clk. to Justice William O. Douglas U.S. Supreme Ct., 1972-73; acting prof. law U. Calif.-Davis, 1973-78, prof., 1978—, chair doctoral program in human devel., 1996—; acad. vis. law dept. U. Munich, 1978-79, 92, U. Cologne, 1990, U. Cambridge, 1990, London Sch. Econs. and Polit. Sci., 1991, Kings Coll., London, 1991; vis. prof. U. Calif., Berkeley, 1983, Columbia U., 1986, U. Basel, 1994, vis. Fulbright prof. Hebrew U., Jerusalem, 1996-97; vis. fellow Fitzwilliam Coll., Cambridge, Eng., 1990, U. Calif. Humanities Rsch. Inst., Irvine, 1999, vis. scholar, London Sch. Econs., King's Coll. (London) & Inst. for Advanced Legal Studies (Univ. London), 1991; cons. to Ctr. for Family in Transition, 1981, Calif. Law Revision Commn., 1979-82, NOW Legal Def. and Edn. Fund, 1980-81; lectr., legis. drafting and testimony, 1976—; mem. U.S. del. 4th Inter-Am. Specialized Conf. on Pvt. Internat. Law, OAS, 1989. Contbr. articles to legal jours. Editor Calif. Law Rev., 1971; editorial Bd. Family Law Quar., 1980-87; Representing Children, 1995—; lectr. in field. Mem. adv. com. child support and child custody Calif. Commn. on Status of Women, 1981-83, child support adv. com. Calif. Jud. Coun., 1991-94, adv. com. on private internat. law U.S. Dept. State, 1989—, internat. child abduction steering com. Internat. Ctr. for Missing and Exploited Children (London); host parent Am. Field Service, Davis, 1977-78. Max Rheinstein sr. rsch. fellow Alexander von Humboldt Found., Fed. Republic Germany, 1978-79, 92, Fulbright fellow, Western Europe, 1990, Israel, 1997, rsch. fellow Univ. Calif. Humanities Rsch. Inst., 1999, Fulbright Sr. Scholar Awd., The Hebrew Univ. of Jersualem, 1997, Disting. Pub. Svc. award U. Calif. Davis Acad. Senate, 1990. Mem. ABA, Calif. State Bar Assn. (inactive), Am. Law Inst., Internat. Soc. Family Law (exec. coun. 1994—), Order of Coif. Democrat. Jewish. Office: U Calif Sch Law 400 Mrak Hall Dr Davis CA 95616-5201

BRUCK, DANIEL STEPHEN, producer, director; b. Los Angeles; s. Leon Bruck and Rose Mary Stevens. BA, Loyola Marymount U., L.A., 1979. Videographer KNBC-TV News, Burbank, 1980-84; media dir. City of Beverly Hills, Calif., 1984-88; dir. ABC's Home Show, 1989-90; supr. prodr. Home R&R, 1990-91; creative dir. Xerox Media West, L.A., Calif., 1991—. Named one of Top 100 AV Video Multimedia Prodr., Video & Multimedia Producer Magazine, 1998, 99. Avocations: bicycling, backpacking. Office: 5152 Sepulveda Blvd # 201 Sherman Oaks CA 91403-1154

BRUCKER, PETER JOACHIM SIEGFRIED, mathematics educator; b. Berlin, Germany, Jan. 3, 1942; s. Siegfried and Ursel (Schwarze) B.; m. Gisela Aschan, Dec. 21, 1970; two children. PhD, Free Univ., 1969. Sr. tchg. asst. Free U., Berlin, 1967-69; asst. prof. U. Regensburg, Germany, 1969-74; assoc. prof. U. Oldenburg, Germany, 1974-80; prof. U. Osnabrueck, Germany, 1980—. Author: Theory of Matrix Algorithms, 1974, Proceedings of the 9th Symposium on Operations Research, 1984, Scheduling Algorithms, 1995. Mem. Gesellschaft für Ops. Rsch., Informs. Office: U Osnabrueck FB6, Albrechtstr 28, 49069 Osnabrück Germany

BRUCK LIEB PORT, LILLY, retired consumer advisor, broadcaster, columnist; b. Vienna, Austria, May 13, 1918; came to U.S., 1941, naturalized, 1944; d. Max and Sophie M. Hahn; m. Sandor Bruck, Mar. 7, 1943; 1 child, Sandra Lee (Mrs. John David Evans III); m. David L. Lieb, Dec. 7, 1985; m. Charles S. Port, Nov. 22, 1998. PhD in Econs., U. Vienna; postgrad., Sorbonne, Paris, Sch. of Econs., London, Sch. of Bus., Columbia U., 1941-42, Sch. of Social Work, NYU, 1964-66. Dir. consumer edn. Dept. Consumer Affairs, City of N.Y., 1969-78; project dir. Am. Coalition of Citizens with Disabilities, 1977-78; consumer advisor, broadcaster In Touch Networks, N.Y.C., 1978-90; consumer affairs commentator Nat. Pub. Radio, 1980-82; ret. Author: Access, The Guide to a Better Life for Disabled Americans, 1978; contbr. articles to disability and rehab. to books, ency. and mag. Presid. Scarsdale Hadassah, 1960-68. Chmn. Westchester county, Bonds for Israel, 1960-68; trustee Kol AMI-JCC, White Plains, N.Y.; assoc. Jewish Mus.; sponsor Lilly Bruck Lieb Creative Writing Program, Purchase Coll., SUNY; mem. pres.'s coun. White Plains (N.Y.) Hosp. Recipient Woman of Yr. award Anti Defamation League, 1972. Democrat. E-mail: lblone@aol.com. Home: 25 Murray Hill Rd Scarsdale NY 10583-2829

BRUCKNER, JOHN JOSEPH, patent lawyer, materials engineer; b. Bronxville, N.Y., Jan. 13, 1960; s. John H. and Judith B. (Egan) B. AA, Union County Coll., 1986; BS, Rutgers U., 1989; JD, George Mason U., 1994; postgrad., Argonne Nat. Lab., 1995-96; MS, U. Wis., 1997; postgrad., Oak Ridge (Tenn.) Nat. Lab., 1996-98. Student technician Ctr. for Ceramic Rsch., Piscataway, N.J., 1988-89; patent examiner U.S. Patent and Trademark Office, Arlington, Va., 1989-92; patent agt. Wegner, Cantor, Mueller & Player, Washington, 1992-94; patent atty. Nilles & Nilles, Milw., 1994-97, Wilson, Sonsini, Goodrich & Rosati, Palo Alto, Calif., 1997—. Mem. Materials Rsch. Soc., Am. Vacuum Soc., Am. Intellectual Property Law Assn., Am. Radio Relay League. Avocation: horticulture. Office: 650 Page Mill Rd Palo Alto CA 94304-1001

BRUCKNER, THOMAS JOHANN CHRISTIAN, physicist, researcher; b. Furth im Wald, Bavaria, Germany, Jan. 6, 1966; s. Johann and Rosa (Mühlbauer) B.; m. Sabine Franz, Sept. 4, 1992; children: Tobias, Simon. MS in Physics, U. Würzburg, 1992, PhD in Theoretical Physics, 1997. Rsch. asst. U. Würzburg, 1992-96; rsch. scientist Potsdam (Germany) Inst. Climate Impact Rsch., 1996—. Contbr. articles to profl. jours. Cusanuswerk scholar, Bonn, 1988-92. Roman Catholic. Office: Potsdam Inst Climate Impact Rsch, Telegrafenberg C4, 14412 Potsdam Germany

BRUDERL, JOSEF, sociologist; b. Fridolfing, Germany, Aug. 26, 1960; s. Josef and Aloisina (Maier) B.; m. Christine Lenz, Oct. 25, 1997. Diploma in sociology, U. Munich, 1986, diploma in econs., 1988, Dr.rer.pol, 1990. Asst. prof. U. Munich, 1987-97; prof. U. Mannheim, 1998—. Author: Mobility in Firms, 1991, The Success of Newly Founded Firms, 1996; contbr. articles to profl. jours. Office: U Mannheim, A 5, 68131 Mannheim Germany

BRUDVIG, GLENN LOWELL, retired library director; b. Kenosha, Wis., Oct. 14, 1931; s. Lars L. Brudvig and Anna Elizabeth (Hillesland) B. Lovejoy; m. Myrna Winifred Michael, Oct. 1, 1953; children—Gary Wayne, Lee Anthony, James Lowell, Kristin Elizabeth. BA in Edn., U. N.D., 1954, MA, 1956; MALS, U. Minn., 1962. Tchr. pub. schs. Mahnomen and Herman, Minn., 1954-55, 56-58; librarian, archivist U. N.D., Grand Forks, 1958-62; asst. librarian U. N.D., 1962-63; supr. dept. libraries U. Minn., Mpls., 1964; dir. bio-med. libr. U. Minn., 1964-83; dir. librs. Calif. Inst. Tech., Pasadena, 1983-95, ret., 1995; instr. library sci. U. N.D., Grand Forks, 1962-63; asst. dir. for research and devel. U. Minn., Mpls., 1968-79, instr. library sci., 1968-71, dir. Inst. Tech. Libraries, 1982-83; cons. Nat. Library of Medicine, Bethesda, Md., 1971-75. Contbr. articles to profl. jours. Served with U.S. Army, 1951-52. Nat. Library of Medicine grantee, 1967-79. Home: 15 Eagle Ridge Rd Saint Paul MN 55127-6411

BRUE, THIERRY CHRISTIAN, endocrinology educator; b. Toulon, France, Dec. 4, 1959; s. Philippe and Jacqueline (LaForest) B.; m. Catherine Fabre, Sept. 3, 1988; children: Clara, Thomas, Heloise. MD, Faculty Medicine Marseille, France, 1990; PhD, U. La Mediterranee, Marseille, 1995. Resident Hops. Marseille, France, 1984-90, sr. registrar, 1990-93, practitioner, 1993-94, prof. endocrinology, 1994—. Co-author: La Sante et Lavie, 1986; contbr. articles to profl. jours. Mem. French Soc. Endocrinology, Endocrine Soc. Home: 10 Impasse Bonnasse, 13012 Marseille France Office: Hosp Timone Svc D Endocrinologie, 13385 Marseille France

BRUECKNER, ROLF ALBERT OTTO, materials science educator, researcher; b. Urnshausen, Thueringen, Germany, Mar. 10, 1928; s. Fritz and Gertrud (Nennstiel) B.; m. Elisabeth Barbara Doepke, July 14, 1956; 1 child, Gerd. Grad. in physics, U. Würzburg, Germany, 1955; PhD in Physics, Teh. U., Clausthal-Zellerfeld, Germany, 1961. Rschr. Max Planck Inst., Würzburg, 1955-70, Fraunhofer Inst., Würzburg, 1971-73; assoc. prof. Tech. U., Clausthal-Zellerfeld, 1971-73; prof. materials sci. Tech. U., Berlin, 1973—, dir. Inst. Nonmetallic Materials, 1974-78, 90-92. co-editor jour. Glass Science and Technology; editor: Glastechnische Fabrikationsfehler, 1980; regional editor Jour. Non-Crystalline Solids, 1981-91; contbr. about 250 articles to sci. jours. Mem. German Glass Soc. (hon. mem.; chmn. sci. sect. 1986-95, bd. dirs. 1987—, industry award 1969, Golden Gehlhoff Ring 1987, Otto Schott Memory award 1994), German Ceramic Soc., Sci. Soc. Berlin. Avocations: tennis, swimming. Home: Fritz Mueller Strasse 57, 82467 Garmisch-Partenkirch Bavaria, Germany Office: Tech U Inst Nonmetallic Mat, Englische Strase 20, 10587 Berlin Germany

BRUEMMER, RUSSELL JOHN, lawyer; b. Decorah, Iowa, Apr. 23, 1952; s. John William and Marion Jean (Wartinbee) B. BA, Luther Coll., 1974; JD, U. Mich., 1977. Bar: Minn. 1978, D.C. 1980, U.S. Dist. Ct. D.C. 1981, U.S. Supreme Ct. 1990. Law clk. to judge U.S. Ct. Appeals (8th cir.), 1977-78; spl. asst. to the dir. FBI, Washington, 1978-80, chief counsel congl. affairs, 1980-81; assoc. Wilmer, Cutler & Pickering, Washington, 1981-84, ptnr., 1985-87, 90—, counsel to dir. of cen. intelligence, 1987-88; gen. counsel CIA, 1988-90; speaker numerous profl. seminars. Editor-in-chief U. Mich. Jour. of Law Rev.; mem. editl. adv. bd. Electronic Banking Law and Commerce Report; contbr. articles to law and banking jours. Recipient Disting. Intelligence medal Order of the Coif, 1977. Mem. ABA (banking law com. 1982—, subcom. on bank holding cos. and nonbanking activities, chmn. 1985-87, chmn. subcom. on securities activities 1994-96, 98-99, mem. standing com. on law and nat. security 1995-98), Am. Law Inst., Coun. on Fgn. Rels. Republican. Lutheran. Home: 4024 40th St N Arlington VA 22207-4608 Office: Wilmer Cutler & Pickering 2445 M St NW Ste 500 Washington DC 20037-1487

BRUEN, JAMES A., lawyer; b. South Hampton, N.Y., Nov. 29, 1943; s. John Francis and Kathryn Jewell (Arthur) B.; m. Carol Lynn Heller, June 13, 1968; children: Jennifer Lynn, Garrett John. BA cum laude, Claremont Men's Coll., 1965; JD, Stanford U., 1968. Bar: Calif. 1968, U.S. Dist. Ct. (no., ea., so. and cen. dists.) Calif. 1970, U.S. Ct. Claims 1972, U.S. Tax Ct. 1972, U.S. Ct. Appeals (9th cir.) 1972, U.S. Supreme Ct. 1973, Ariz. 1993. Atty. FCC, Washington, 1968-70; asst. U.S. atty. criminal div. Office of US. Atty., San Francisco, 1970-73, asst. U.S. atty. civil div., 1973-75, chief of civil div., 1975-77; ptnr. Landels, Ripley & Diamond, San Francisco, 1977—; mem. faculty Nat. Jud. Coll. ABA; lectr. Am. Law Inst. Am. Bd. Trial Advocates, Practising Law Inst. Def. Rsch. Inst., others. Co-author: Pharmaceutical Products Liability, 1989; contbg. editor: Hazardous Waste and Toxic Torts Law and Strategy, 1987-92; contbr. numerous articles to profl. jours. Mem. ABA (vice chmn. environ. quality com. nat. resources sect. 1989-93, co-chmn. enforment litigation subcom. environ. litigation com. litigation sect. 1990-92), Am. Inn of Ct. (master-at-large), Internat. Soc. for Environ. Epidemiology. Avocations: scuba diving, travel. Office: Landels Ripley & Diamond Ste 208 60 E Sir Francis Drake Blvd Larkspur CA 94939-1713

BRUEN, MICHAEL PATRICK, civil engineer, researcher; b. Sligo, Ireland, June 17, 1953; s. William Stanislaus and Mary Philomena (Emmett) B.; m. Anne Elizabeth Bacon, Aug. 10, 1991; children: Benen, Liam, Tomás. BE in Civil Engring., Univ. Coll. Dublin, 1975, PhD, 1985. Lectr. Univ. Coll. Galway, Ireland, 1980-85; project leader U. Dar es Salaam, Tanzania Irish Dept. Fgn. Affairs, Tanzania, 1985-90; dir. water resources engring. U. Dar es Salaam Grad. Programme, Tanzania, 1985-90; lectr. Univ. Coll. Galway, 1990-92; dir., lectr. water engring. Univ. Coll. Dublin, 1991-97; dir. Ctr. for Water Resources Rsch., Dublin, 1997—; cons. UNESCO, Zimbabwe/France, World Meteorol. Orgn., Zimbabwe, 1985, various engring. firms. Co-author: Education Systems for Hydrology Technicians, 1993, Applied Hydrology for Technicians, 1995, ELECTRE and Decision Support-Methods and Applications in Engineering and Infrastructure Investment, 1999; contbr. articles to profl. jours. Recipient bronze medal Cuman na Mire Gaile, Dublin, 1996. Fellow Inst. Math. & Its Applications; mem. ASCE, Instn. Engrs. Ireland. Avocations: scuba diving, sailing. Home: 27 Strand Rd Sandymount, Dublin 4, Ireland Office: Univ Coll Dublin, Earlsfort Ter, Dublin 2, Ireland

BRUEREN, MARK MATTHEUS, general practice physician; b. Venlo, Limburg, The Netherlands, Mar. 11, 1954; s. Joseph John and Catrine (Driessen) B.; m. Anne Maria Buijs; children: Pim, Pauke, Kasper. MD, U. Niumegen, The Netherlands, 1982, degree in gen. practice, 1985; PhD, Maastricht U., The Netherlands, 1998. Rschr. Maastricht U., The Netherlands, 1990—, asst. prof., 1995—; gen. practice medicine Helmond, The Netherlands, 1994—; mem. com. guidelines depression Dutch Coll. Gen. Practitioners, Utrecht, The NEtherlands, 1992-94. Contbr. articles to profl. jours. Mem. Netherlands Coll. Gen. Practice. Avocations: reading, playing piano. Office: U Maastricht Dept Gen Pract, PO Box 616, 6200 MD Maastricht The Netherlands

BRUESEWITZ-LOPINTO, GAIL C., marketing professional; b. N.Y.C., May 17, 1956; d. Arthur George and Blanche Juliana (Dobos) Bruesewitz; m. Joseph LoPinto, Sept. 1990; children: Frank Joseph, Joseph Arthur. BA in Eng. Lit., SUNY, Binghamton, 1978. Mem. promotion and artist devel. staff Columbia Records/CBS Records, Inc., N.Y.C., 1979-82, dir. nat. dance music mktg., 1982-89; coord. promotion/artist devel. Ear Candy Records, 1990-91; prodn. coord. AIG Risk Mgmt., Inc. divsn. Am. Internat. Group, Inc., N.Y.C., 1991-96, Swiss Reins. Am. Alternative Risk Transfer Div., N.Y.C., 1996-98; meeting and event specialist corp. comm. Swiss Re New Markets, N.Y.C., 1999-2000; rep. record div. Women's Orgn. Coun. CBS, Inc., N.Y.C., 1980-82; adv. bd., dance/music, New Music Seminar, N.Y.C., 1989—. Editor newsletter Brueser's Boogie Backpage, 1983-90. Bd. dirs. Mt. Tremper (N.Y.) Lutheran Camp and Retreat Ctr., 1976-78, Camp Wilbur Herrlich, Pawling, N.Y., 1990; active Big Sisters, Binghamton (N.Y.) Social Svcs. dept., 1975-78. Named N.Y. rep. for Mademoiselle mag., 1975. Democrat. Lutheran. Avocations: sailing, dance (jazz and ballet). E-mail: gail lopinto@swissre.com. Office: Swiss Re New Markets 55 E 52d St New York NY 10055

BRUETON, MARTIN JOHN, pediatrician; b. Bristol, Eng., Feb. 2, 1944; s. Neville Frederick William and Nancy Rushton (Baldwin) B.; m. Patricia Ann May; children: Nicola, Mark, Catherine. BS, MB, U. London, 1967, MD, 1978; MSc in Immunology, U. Birmingham, 1978. Fellow Royal Coll. of Physicians, Royal Coll. Pediat. and Child Health. Intern, resident, registrar St. Bartholomew's Hosp., London, 1968-70; sr. registrar Ahmadu Bello U., Zaria, Nigeria, 1971-73; lectr. U. Birmingham, Eng., 1973-78; sr. lectr. Charing Cross Westminster Med. Sch., U. London, London, 1979-88, reader, 1989—; clin. dir. women and children's directorate Chelsea and Westminster Healthcare Trust, 1992-95; examiner in pediatric medicine U. London, 1981—, U. Birmingham, 1989-91, U. Sci. and Tech., Kumasi, Ghana, 1987. Editor: Practical Paediatric Therapeutics, 1990, Diseases of Children in the Tropics and Sub-Tropics, 1990; contbr. chpts. to books and articles to profl. jours. Fellow Royal Soc. Physicians (examiner 1995), Royal Coll. Pediat. and Child Health (coun., chmn. higher specialist tng. com.); mem. Brit. Soc. Gastroent., Brit. and European Soc. for Pediatric Gastroent. and Nutrition (pres. 1998—), Brit. Soc. Immunology. Avocations: tennis, theatre, music, family. Home: 40 Furze Ln, Purley Surrey CR8 3EG, England Office: Acad Dept Child Health, Chelsea Westminster Hosp 369 Fulham Rd, London SW10 9NH, England

BRUGGEMAN, LEWIS LEROY, radiologist; b. N.Y.C., Sept. 9, 1941; s. Louis LeRoy and Edwina Jane (Mickel) B.; m. Ann Margaret Kayajan, May 28, 1966; children: Gretchen Ann, Kurt LeRoy. AB, Dartmouth Coll., 1963, B in Med. Sci., 1965; MD, Harvard U., 1968. Intern Los Angeles County Harbor Gen. Hosp., Torrence, Calif., 1968-69; resident in diagnostic radiology Columbia Presbyn. Med. Ctr., N.Y.C., 1969-72; chief dept. radiology Bremerton (Wash.) Naval Regional Med. Ctr., 1972-74; pvt. practice diagnostic radiology South Coast Med. Ctr., South Laguna, Calif., 1974-96, dir. dept. radiology, 1983-95, hosp. bd. trustees, 1985-87; pvt. practice diagnostic radiology Saddleback Cmty. Hosp., Laguna Hills, Calif., 1974-95; pres., chmn. bd. dirs. South Coast Med. Group Inc., South Laguna, Calif., 1983-95; gen. ptnr. Jovian Ptnrs., L.P., a Hedge Fund, 2000—; pres. Bruggeman Capital Mgmt., Inc., Dana Point, Calif., 2000—; pres. So. Coast Radiol. Med. Group Inc., South Laguna, 1986-95; vice-chmn. and bd. trustees South Coast Med. Ctr. Found., 1993—. Lt. comdr. M.C., USN, 1972-74. Mem. Am. Coll. Radiology, Dartmouth Club Orange County. Avocations: golf, skiing.

BRUGGER, HANS JOHANN GEORG, engineer; b. Marktoberdorf, Germany, Jan. 11, 1956; m. Barbara Brugger; children: Lisa, Simon. Diploma, Tech. U., Munich, 1983, PhD, 1987. Mem. faculty Walter-Schottky Inst., Munich, 1987-88; postdoctoral fellow IBM Rsch. Lab., Zurich, 1988-89; mgr. R&D Daimler Benz Ag Rsch. Ctr., Ulm, 1989-96; mng. wafer fab ops. UMS GmbH, Ulm, 1996—. Patentee in field. Avocations: sports, mountain biking and hiking, skiing, house and garden. Office: United Monolithic, Semiconductors GmbH, D-89081 Ulm Germany

BRUGGER, HERMANN, physician; b. Brunico, Bolzano, Italy, Dec. 30, 1951; s. Alfons and Elisabeth (Walter) B.; m. Elfriede Gangl, Apr. 29, 1978; children: Franz, Johanna. MD, U. Vienna, Austria, 1978. Med. asst. Hosp. Sisters of Charity, Linz, Austria, 1979-83; gen. practitioner Nat. Health Svc., Brunico, Italy, 1984—; emergency physician Nat. Red Cross, Brunico, 1984—; mountain rescue physician Mountain Rescue Orgn., Brunico, 1984—; cons. Assn. Mountain Guides, Bolzano, 1984—, U. Padua, 1995—. Contbr. articles to profl. jours. Recipient Eduard Wallnöfer prize Tyrolean Industry, 1992, Georg Grabner prize U. Vienna, 1995, Medal of Merit, Govt. Tyrol, 1994. Mem. N.Y. Acad. Scis., Internat. Commn. Alpine Emergency Medicine, Italian Soc. Mountain Medicine (exec. bd.), Austrian Soc. Alpine and High Altitude Medicine (exec. bd.). Roman Catholic. Avocations: mountaineering, downhill skiing, photography. Home: Via Europa 17, I-39031 Brunico Italy

BRUGHA, TRAOLACH SEAN, psychiatrist; b. Dublin, Jan. 6, 1953; s. Ruairi and Maire (MacSweeny) B.; m. Maire Nic Eoghain, Apr. 3, 1976; children: Rossa, Lia, Cillian. MB, BChir, BA in Obstetrics, U. Coll. Dublin, 1977, MD, 1987. Rsch. worker Medico Social Rsch. Bd., Dublin, 1976, ho. officer; registrar in psychiatry St. Vincent's Hosp., Dublin, 1978-80, Bethlem & Maudsley Hosp., London, 1980-82; clin. scientist Med. Rsch. Coun., London, 1982-87; sr. lectr. psychiatry U. Leicester, 1986—; sr. med. officer Dept. Health, London, 1995-97; hon. cons. psychiatrist Leicester Health Authority, 1987—; hon. sr. registrar Maudsley Hosp., 1982-86; lectr. Inst. Psychiatry U. London, 1984—; prof. psychiatry U. Leicester, 2000—. Assoc. editor Psychol. Medicine, 1995—; mem. editl. bd. Internat. Jour. Methods in Psychiat. Rsch., 1990-96. Rsch. grantee Irish Med. Rsch. Coun., Dublin, 1979-82. Mem. Royal Coll. Psychiatrists London. Roman Catholic. Office: U Leicester Dept Psychiatry, Section Social & Epid Psych, Leicester LE5 4PW, England

BRUGIONI, DINO ANTHONY, writer, lecturer, consultant; b. Bevier, Mo., Dec. 16, 1921; s. John and Frances (Fraulini) B.; m. Theresa Harich, Jan. 29, 1949; children: Theresa, John. BA, George Washington U., 1947, MA, 1978. Liaison officer Tenn. Valley Authority, Washington, 1945-48; officer CIA, Washington, 1948-55; sr. officer, aerial reconnaissance, photo interpretation expert Nat. Photog. Interpretation Ctr., Washington, 1955-82; cons. CIA, 1982—, Nat. Imagery and Mapping Agy., Washington, 1995-97; lectr. in field, Harvard, MIT, U. Calif., Berkeley, Nat. War Coll., Def. Intelligence Coll., State Dept. Fgn. Svc. Sch., Smithsonian Instn. Author: The Holocaust Revisited: A Retrospective Analysis of the Auschwitz-Birkenau Extermination Complex, 1979, The Civil War in Missouri: As Seen from the Capital City, 1987, Eyeball to Eyeball: The Inside Story of the Cuban Missile Crisis, 1991, From Balloons to Blackbirds, 1993, Photo Fakery: The History and Techniques of Photographic Deception and Manipulation, 1999; contbr. over 80 articles to profl. jours.; appeared on numerous TV shows, U.S., Germany, France, Japan. Recipient commendation for performance during Cuban Missile Crisis, Pres. Kennedy, 1962, award for best scholarly article Nat. Intelligence Study Ctr., 1970, Sherman Kent award for outstanding contbns. to lit. of intelligence, 1973, 79, Disting. Alumnus award Jefferson City Pub. Schs. Alumni Assn., 1980, Pioneer in Space medal, 1986. Mem. Medmenham Club, VFW, DAV, Purple Heart Assn. Roman Catholic. Avocations: writing, travel. Home and Office: 301 Storck Rd Fredericksburg VA 22406-4731

BRUHNS, ERIKA LUISE (HAZMUKA), ethologist, horse educator; b. Wien, Austria, Nov. 20, 1932; d. Bruno and Hildegard Nunnenmacher (Edle von Rollfeld) Hazmuka; m. Walter Bruhns, July 17, 1953; children: Markus, Ingo, Iris, Heimo. Tchr., Tchr. Tng. Sch., Wien, 1952. Freelance journalist Wien, 1955—, freelance pedagogue, 1972-95, tchr. horse edn., 1995—; founder Hippagogic Sta., 1974; mgr. Haflinger Cup, Niederösterreich, Austria, 1980-96. Author, editor: Wer Denkt Mit, 1971; author, editor Haflingersport, 1986—, Kartenspiele fur Kinder, 1999, Mit Pferden spielen, 1999, So sage ich es meinem Pferd, 1999, Handbuch Offenstall, 2000, Pferdeerziehung vom Fohlenalter an, 2000; video: So sage ich es meinem Pferd, 1999. Mem. Zentrum für Artgerechte und Gewaltfreie Pferdeerziehung (founder, pres. 1995—). Avocation: horses. Office: Haflingersport, Haymogasse 19, A-1238 Wien Austria

BRUHNS, OTTO TIMME, mechanics educator; b. Durnkrut, Austria, Sept. 26, 1942; s. Gustav Otto and Elfriede (Beitl) B.; m. Edda Hilker, Aug. 30, 1969; children: Imke, Maike. Diploma in Civil Engring., Tech. U., Hannover, 1967, D Engring., 1969; D Engring. Habil., Ruhr U., Bochum, 1974. Rschr. Tech. U., Hannover, 1968-69; sr. engr. Ruhr U., Bochum, 1969-75, lectr., 1975-76, prof. mechanics, 1976-80; full prof. Ruhr U., 1987—, U. Kassel, 1980-87; cons. Interatom Gmbh, Berg. Gladbach, 1979-90. Author: (books) Elemente der Mechanik I, II, III, 1993, 94, Aufgabensammlung Technische Mechanik 1, 2, 3, 1996, 97, 99; co-editor books in field; contbr. articles to profl. jours. Mem. Soc. Applied Math. and Mechanics, Hochschulverband. Office: Lehrstuhl Tech Mechanik, Ruhr U/Universitatsstr 150, D-44780 Bochum Germany

BRULAND, TRYGVE, investment company executive; b. Trondheim, Norway, June 10, 1967; s. John and Anne Marie (Loftingsmo) B. MS in Econs., Norwegian Sch. Econs. & Bus., Bergen, 1991; MBA, INSEAD, Fountainbleau, France, 1994. Assoc. Boston Cons. Group, Stockholm, 1991-92; sr. assoc. Boston Cons. Group, Munich, Germany, 1992-93; assoc. McKinsey & Co., Oslo, Norway, 1994-96; v.p. Orkla Enskilda Securities, Oslo, Norway, 1996—; dir. Farder Kapital, Oslo, 1998—. Sgt. Norwegian Army, 1986-87. Office: Orkla Finans AS, Tordenskioldsgt 8-10, 0121 Oslo Norway

BRULL, SORIN JOSEPH, educator, physician; b. Romania, June 25, 1956; s. Dosolo and Ana Brull; m. Leslie E. Brull; children: Alex, Evan, Sara. BS, Brandeis U.; MD, W.Va. U., 1984. Instr. anesthesiology Yale U. Sch. Medicine, New Haven, 1987-88, asst. prof. anesthesiology, 1988-93, assoc. prof. anesthesiology, 1993-98; prof., chmn. dept. anesthesiology U. Ark. for Med. Scis., Little Rock, 1998—; anesthesiologist in chief Univ. Hosp. of Ark., Little Rock; cons., sci. rev. NIH, Bethesda, Md., 1994, 95, cons. spl. rev. group on nursing rsch., 1994, 95; assoc. examiner Am. Bd. Anesthesiology, 1994. Author: Physiology of Spinal Anesthesia, 1993, Manual of Anesthesia and Critical Care, 2000; mem. editl. bd. sci. jours., 1994—; contbr. numerous articles to profl. jours. Mem. Com. on Physician Resources, Park Ridge, Ill., 1998—, Com. on Quality Improvement, Park Ridge, 1997, Com. on Residents and Med. Students, Park Ridge, 1998; co-chair Anesthesia Patient Safety Found.; mem. sci. papers com. ASA, Park Ridge. Recipient 23 grants, 1988—. Mem. Am. Soc. Anesthesiology (teller Ho. of Dels. 1996-98, chair com. on local anesthesia and pain), Royal Coll. Surgeons in Ireland (sci. dir. 1990, 93, 97). Avocations: tennis, oenology. E-mail: sorin.brull@exchange.UAMS.edu. Office: U Ark for Med Scis Dept Anes/Coll Medicine 4301 W Markham St # 515 Little Rock AR 72205-7101

BRULLO, ROBERT ANGELO, chemical company executive; b. Chgo., Aug. 20, 1948; s. Ralph V. and Vicky M. (Santapa) B.; m. Kathleen M. Peltier, Feb. 27, 1993; children: Jennifer, Amy, Dawn. BSChemE, Ill. Inst. Tech., 1970; MBA, U. St. Thomas, 1976. Sr. analyst corp. mktg. 3M Co., St. Paul, 1977-78, supr. market devel. comml. chems. divsn., 1978-80; sr. account rep. comml. chems. divsn. 3M Co., Detroit, 1980-82; mgr. market devel. comml. chems. divsn. 3M Co., St. Paul, 1982-86, global mktg. mgr. indsl. chem. products divsn., 1986-88, global bus. mgr. indsl. chem. products divsn., 1988-92, dept. gen. mgr. specialty fluoropolymers dept., 1993-96; pres., CEO, Dyneon LLC (3M Hoechst Enterprise), 1996-2000; mng. dir. 3M U.K.-Ireland region, Berkshire, 2000—; bd. dirs., vice chmn. Alventia LLC (Dyneon/Solvay JV 1998-2000). Patentee in field. Mem. Rubber Mfrs. Assn., Am. Chem. Soc. (bd. dirs. rubber div. area 1986-88), Twin Cities Rubber Group (sec. 1979-80), Ft. Wayne Rubber Group, Soc. Plastics Industry (fluoropolymers div.), Chem. Mfrs. Assn. Lutheran. Home: 23 Albury Rd, Burwood Park Surrey KT12 5DY, England Office: 3M UK PLC, 3M House PO Box 1 Market Pl, Bracknell Berkshire RG12 1JU, England

BRUMEN, VLATKA, occupational and environmental health educator; b. Zagreb, Croatia, Sept. 12, 1958; d. Vladimir and Stanka (Djurovic) B.; m. Robert Mahović, May 19, 1984 (div. Oct. 1990); twins: Roberta and Lav. Med. diplomate, U. Zagreb, 1982, Masters Degree, 1987, PhD, 1988. Intern Clin. Hosp. Sisters of Mercy, Zagreb, 1982-83; physician Cmty. Med. Ctr., Duga Resa, Croatia, 1984; rsch. fellow Inst. for Med. Rsch. and Occupl. Health, Zagreb, 1984-87, rsch. asst., 1987-98; univ. lectr., asst. prof. Sch. Medicine, U. Zagreb, 1998—; non-ionizing radiation expert group mem. Ministry of Health Republic of Croatia, Zagreb, 1996—; chief investigator several project health risk assessment in non-ionizing radiation exposures. Contbr. articles to profl. jours. Mem. European Environ. Mutagen Soc., Croatian Med. Assn., Croatian Radiation Protection Soc. Avocations: gardening, swimming. E-mail: vlatka.brumen@snz.hr. Home: 49 Zvonigradska St, 90000 Zagreb Croatia Office: Sch Med U Zagreb, 4 Rockefellerova St, 10000 Zagreb Croatia

BRUMMER, ALEXANDER, editor; b. Brighton, Eng., May 25, 1949; s. Michael and Hilda (Caplin) B.; m. Patricia Lyndsey Magrill, Oct. 26, 1975; children: Jessica, Justin, Gabriel. BSc in Social Sci., U. Southampton, 1970; MSc in Mgmt., U. Bradford, 1972. Mgmt. trainee De La Rue, London, 1972-73; reporter Haymarket Pub., London, 1973-74; fin. journalist, then fin. corr. The Guardian, London, 1974-79; Washington corr. The Guardian, 1979-84; bur. chief The Guardian, Washington, 1984-89; fin. editor The Guardian, London, 1989-99; city editor Daily Mail, London, 1999—. Office: Associated Newspapers, Northcliffe House Derry St, London WE 5TS, England

BRUN, BERNARD, editor, researcher; b. Avesnes upon Helpe, France, Oct. 25, 1949; m. Jeanine Rovet, 1974 (div. 1982); children: Etienne, Marianne. Student, Ecole Normale Supérieure, 1969-74; PhD, U. Sorbonne, Paris, 1986. Rschr. CNRS, Paris, 1974—; editor, Bulletin d'Information Proustiennes Presses de L'Ecole Normale Superieure, Paris, 1975—. Co-editor: Dining at Princess of Guermantes, 1982, Remembrance of Things Past; contbr. articles to profl. jours. Home: 1 Ave des Quatre-Chemins, 92330 Sceaux France Office: ITEM, 45 rue l'Ulm, 75230 Paris Cedex 05, France

BRUN, GEORGES HARRIS, gynecologist; b. St. Cyr, Dordogne, France, Oct. 29, 1931; s. Emile and Marie Therese (Golfier) B.; m. Anquetil Suzanne, Dec. 31, 1960. BS In Physics, Chemistry, Biology, U. Scis. Poitiers, France, 1951; MD, Faculté de Medicine, Bordeaux, 1966. Cert. gynecologist. Intern, 1953-62; physician, chef de clinique CHR, Bordeaux, France, 1962; prof. Agregé Coop., Marroco, France, 1966-70; chmn. gynecology Nat. Edn. Health Service, Bordeaux, 1970—, emeritus prof., 2000—. Contbr. articles on gynecology to profl. jours. Mem. French Soc. Gynecol. Oncology (adminstrv. coun.), Order of Academic Palms. Avocations: gardening, history.

BRUN, THEOBALD TSOE ZIU, lawyer; b. Lucerne, Switzerland, Aug. 29, 1962; s. Hans and Lifang (Lee) B.; m. Stefania Brun. LLB, Zurich (Switzerland) U., 1986; LLM, U. San Diego, 1992; LLD, Zurich U., 1995. Lawyer Tettamenti-Spiess, Lugano, Switzerland, 1986-88; in-house counsel NESTLE, Vevey, Switzerland, 1988-90; lawyer Bär & Karrer, Lugano, 1992-98. Author: The Seizure of Banking Documents in International Legal Assistance in Criminal Matters, 1996; co-author: Cross-Border Mergers in Europe, 1989. Sec. Swiss-Chinese C. of C., Ticino (Switzerland) chpt., 1995—. Achille Isella scholar, Ministry Edn., 1982, Baker McKenzie scholar, Chgo., 1991. Mem. Ticino Bar Assn., Ticino Notary Assn. Avocations: art, Asian art and culture. Office: Brun Studio Legalee, Notarile, Via Anosto 6, 6901 Lugano Ticino, Switzerland

BRUNA, JOSEF, radiology educator; b. Lukanad Jihlavou, Czech Republic, Jan. 3, 1938; s. Josef and Marta (Hrodkova) B.; m. Eva Zivna, Mar. 24, 1937 (dec. 1985); children: Jan, Dana; m. Jana Valderova, Dec. 17, 1951. MD, U. Brno, Czech Republic, 1961; PhD, Charles U., Prague, 1974, DrSc, 1982; Dr honoris causa, Valenca U., 1995. Named titular prof. Czech and Slovak Republic. Asst. prof. biophysics UJEP, Czech Republic, 1959-61; registrar Hosp. Kromeriz, Czech Republic, 1961-65, radiologist, 1965-69; asst. prof. Postgrad. Inst., Prague, 1969-74; assoc. prof. Charles U., Prague, 1974-86, prof. radiology, 1986-92; cons. OFS U., Bloemfontein, 1992—. Author: (books) Clinical Lymphography, 1977, Xeroradiography of Lymphatic System, Whole Body Computed Tomography, CT of Bones and Joints. Mem. European Radiol. Assn., N.Y. Acad. Scis., Czechoslovakian/Czech Med. Soc., Internat. Soc. Lymphology, South African Radiol. Soc., Italian Med. Ctr. (hon.), China Med. Soc. (hon.), Brazilian Med. Soc. (hon.), others. Avocations: tennis, skiing, classical music, history. Office: Dept Diagnostic Radiology, 9300 Bloemfontein South Africa

BRUNALE, VITO JOHN, aerospace engineer; b. Mt. Vernon, N.Y., July 2, 1925; s. Donato and Antoinette (Wool) B.; m. Joan Florence Montuori, Apr. 23, 1949; 1 child, Stephen. AAS, Stewart Aero. Inst., 1948; BSAE, Tri-State U., 1958; MSME, U. Bridgeport, 1966; DSc, Nev. Inst. Tech., 1973; PhD (hon.), Internat. U., Spain, 1987; DSc, Pacific Western U., 1984. Rsch. engr. Norden Labs., White Plains, N.Y., 1948-55; instr. Tri-State U., Angola, Ind., 1955-58; engring. cons. Norden Div. United Aircraft, Norwalk, Conn., 1958-67; chief engring. cons. Singer-Kearfott Corp., Pleasantville, N.Y., 1967-73; chief engr. Diagnostic/Retrieval Systems, Mt. Vernon, N.Y., 1973-76; tech. problem mgr. Fairchild Republic Co., Farmingdale, N.Y., 1977-87; sr. tech. expert Sikorsky Aircraft, 1987—; cons. in field; engring. tutor to coll. students; v.p. Lithoway, Inc., 1969-73; lectr. in field; tech. guest speaker numerous tech. soc. meetings.; participant engring. exchange program, USSR, People's Republic China. Contbr. articles to profl. jours. including Product Engring., Aviation Week, Environ. Scis. Participant U.S.A. Citizen Amb. Program. Served with USAAF, 1943-45. Decorated Purple Heart (3), Air medals, D.F.C. Tri-State U. tcht. fellow, 1955-58; NSF grantee; recipient Aircraft Design award, 1948, Inst. Aero. Sci. Lecture award, 1948, Norden Rsch. award, 1963, Cost Reduction award, 1965, Singer Engring. award, 1970, 72, Fairchild outstanding achievement award, 1985, 86, 87, Fairchild award of excellence, 1984, Am. Biographical Inst. and Research Assn. Outstanding Performance award, 1989, Aircraft Recognition award, 1986, citation N.Y. State Assembly, 1988, Conspicuous Service Cross N.Y. State, 1988, Prisoner of War medal, 1988, others; honoree Nat. Air and Space Mus.; named to Wisdom Hall of Fame, 1998. Mem. AIAA (award 1973, Aviation award 1994, Sr. Mem. award 1994, Merit award 1998, membership award 1998, award 1998), VFW, DAV, K.C., U.S. Naval Inst., Air Force Assn., Am. Ordnance Asssn., Inst. Environ. Sci., Nat Space Inst., Newman Club, Internat. Students Assn., Internat. Platform Assn., World Inst. of Achievement. Roman Catholic. Achievements include patent (with others) for Bearing Spin Rail Test; development of method of discriminate displacement for equilibrium of structures, of the position point vibration isolation technique, of the vapress vibration system, of advanced techniques for structural and vibration analyses, of the Doppler-Inertial-Loran system, of state of the art mathematical and structural analyses techniques, of Mars Doppler Lander system, computer time studies, anti-corrosion methods; resolution of 140 technical problems on the Fairchild A-10 aircraft, of more than 30 technical problems with the Saab-Fairchild 340; solution of Grumman A-6A radar tracking problem in Vietnam; elimination of technical problems on LEM inertial guidance; rsch. in mfg. productivity, co-planer structural analyses. Home: 459 Bronxville Rd Bronxville NY 10708-1102 Office: Main St Bridgeport CT 06606

BRUNDA, DANIEL DONALD, retired aerospace engineer, consultant, inventor; b. Lansford, Pa., Oct. 22, 1930; s. Michael Theodore and Ella (Jurba) B. BSME, Lehigh U., 1952, MSME, 1953; postgrad., Johns Hopkins U., 1955, Princeton U., 1958-65, Drexel U., 1983. Registered profl. engr., N.J. Engr. Bell Aircraft aerodynamicist Glenn L. Martin, Balt.; devel., test, evaluation and performance propulsion engr. Bell Aircraft Glenn L. Martin & Curtiss Wright, Princeton, N.J., 1953-57; aerospace engr. rsch. U.S. Naval Air Propulsion Ctr., Ewing, N.J., 1957-72, local mgr. ind. R&D, 1972-83; powerline radiation energy engring. cons. Ewing, N.J., 1978—. Contbr. more than 20 articles to profl. jours. Fellow Bioelectromagnetic Soc. (assoc.); mem. ASME (life), AIAA. Achievements include research, patents, and copyrights on powerline radiation, which determined the molecular weight, radiation limits, inductive impedance of average adult human beings; proved that powerline radiation is a cause of cancer; explained mathematically Volta's electrophonic effect 1800 A.D.; discovered Brunda's Absorbance Law and the Absorbance of DNA. Home and Office: Powerline Radiation Energy Engring Cons 106 W Upper Ferry Rd Ewing NJ 08628-2724

BRUNDAGE, GERTRUDE BARNES, pediatrician; b. Neptune, N.J., May 13, 1941; d. John Holt and Mary Downey (Chatham) B. BS in Chemistry, Marietta Coll., 1964; MD, Jefferson Med. Coll., 1971. Diplomate Am. Bd. Pediatrics. Chemist Lederle Labs., Pearl River, N.Y., 1964-67; intern pediatrics Harrisburg (Pa.) Polyclinic Hosp., 1971-72; resident pediatrics Wilmington (Del.) Med. Ctr., 1972-74; pediatrician East Orange, N.J., 1974—; chief dept. pediatrics Hosp. Ctr. at Orange, 1990-98. Moderator Presbytery of Newark, 1996. Mem. AMA, N.J. Med. Women's Assn., Am. Med. Women's Assn., Essex County Med. Soc., Med. Soc. N.J., Alpha Gamma Delta, 1st Presbyn. Ch. (elder, trustee 1982-87, 89-92). Republican. Presbyterian. Avocations: choral singing, needlework, gardening. Home: 18 Farrington St West Caldwell NJ 07006-7716 Office: Gertrude B Brundage MD 572 Park Ave East Orange NJ 07017-1904

BRUNDTLAND, GRO HARLEM, prime minister of Norway; b. Oslo, Apr. 20, 1939; d. Gudmund and Inga (Brynolf) Harlem; m. Arne Olav Brundtland, 1960; children: Knut, Kaja, Ivar, Jorgen. M.D., Oslo U., 1963; M.P.H., Harvard Sch. Pub. Health, 1965. Med. officer Nat. Directorate of Pub. Health, Oslo, 1965-67; asst. med. dir. Sch. Health Services, Oslo, 1968-74; minister of environment Norwegian Govt., 1974-79, M.P. from Oslo, 1977-79, mem. standing com. on fin., chmn. standing com. on fgn. and constitutional affairs, 1979-81, dep. leader Labour Party's parliamentary group, 1979-81, leader Labour Party and parliamentary group, 1981-92, standing com. on fgn. and constl. affairs, 1981-86; chmn. standing com. on fgn. and constnl. affairs; prime minister of Norway Norwegian Govt., 1981, 86-89, 90-96; dir.-gen. WHO, Geneva, 1998—. Contbr. scientific work in child growth and devel. Mem. Ind. Commn. on Disarmament and Security Issues, UN, 1980; chmn. World Commn. on Environment and Devel., 1983; bd. dirs. Better World Soc., 1985. Recipient Third World prize Third World Found., 1989, Indira Gandhi prize, 1990, Onassis Found. award, 1992.

BRUNE, DAG KRISTEN, publishing executive; b. Oslo, Aug. 1, 1931; s. Johannes and Arna (Ørum) Brune; m. Hanne Kristin Langeland, Oct. 16, 1982; children: Eli Kathrine, Synne. MSc in Civil Engring., Chalmers U. Tech., Gothenburg, Sweden, 1956; PhD, Royal Inst. Tech., Stockholm, 1962. Rsch. assoc. Swedish Nuclear Energy Rsch. Ctr., Studsvik, 1956-76; head divsn. physics, chemistry Scandinavian Inst. Dental Materials, Oslo, 1976-85; environ. cons. Eureka, Oslo, 1985-93; pub. Scandinavian Sci. Pub., Oslo, 1993—; guest rschr. Ctr. Etudes Nucleaires, Grenoble, France, 1968, Mayer-Leibnitz Inst., 1969, Mössbauer Inst., Garching, Munich, 1969; advisor Internat. Atomic Energy Agy., Colombia, Peru, Ecuador, 1970-78. Author, editor 7 books; mem. editl. bd. Sci. Total Environ., 1972-95; contbr. over 120 articles to profl. jours.; patentee in field. Chmn. Arna & Johannes Brune's Meml. Found., Oslo; mem. Congl. Coun. Bakkehaugen Parish, Oslo. Mem. Norwegian Engring. Soc., Swedish Physics Soc., Swedish Chem. Soc., Swedish Engring. Soc. Lutheran. Avocations: mountaineering, skiing, theater, literature. Home and Office: Scandinavian Sci Pub, Bakkehaugveien 16, 0873 Oslo Norway

BRUNEEL, DIRK, bank executive; b. Diksmuide, Belgium, June 20, 1950; s. Joseph and Suzanne (Gurdebeke) B.; m. Christianne Buyse, Mar. 22, 1974; children: Karolien, Katrijn, Jan. Licentie Econ. Sci., Ghent State U., 1972; M of Fin. Mgmt., Vlekho, Brussels, 1982. With ASLK-CGER-Bank, Brussels, 1973-93, attaché econ. studies dept., contr., auditor, asset liability mgmt. mgr., mng. dir., 1992-93, also bd. dirs.; mng. dir. BACOB-Bank, Brussels, 1993—, also bd. dirs., chmn. mgmt. bd., 1995—; with Artesia Bank, Brussels, 1997—; bd. dirs. Artesia Bank, Brussels, 1997—, chmn. mgt. bd., 1998—; chmn. mgt. bd., bd. dirs. Artesia Banking Corp., 1999—. Christian Democrat. Roman Catholic. Avocations: jogging, film, music. Office: Artesia Banking Corp, Blvd du Roi Albert II 30 B2, B-2000 Brussels Belgium

BRUNEL, OLIVIER, dermatologist; b. Colombes, France, Jan. 18, 1952; s. Louis and Micheline (Rambault) B. MD, St. Antoine U., 1977. Resident Am. Hosp., Paris, 1976-80, Hosp. St.-Michel, France, 1980-84; pvt. practice Paris, 1984—; music critic various newspapers and mags., including Le Quotidien du Médecin, Classica. With French Army, 1979-80. Roman Catholic. Avocations: music, yoga. Home: 5 Place des Ternes, 75017 Paris France Office: 174 Rue de la Pompe, 75116 Paris France

BRUNEL, PIERRE DENIS, education educator; b. Moutardon, France, July 17, 1939; s. Julien and Madeleine (Deschamps) B.; m. Françoise Verguet, Apr. 12, 1962; children: Laurence, Sophie, François-Marie. Doctorat D'Etat, Ecole Normale Superieure, Paris, 1970. Prof. Sorbonne, U. Paris IV, 1970—; prof. Institut Universitaire de France, 1995. Author: Claudel et Shakespeare, 1971, Vincenzo Bellini, 1981, Mythocritique, 1992, Forms Baroqus in Théâtre, 1996. Home: 17 Rue de l'Annonciation, 75516 Paris France Office: U Paris IV Sorbonne, 47 Rue des Écoles, 75005 Paris France

BRUNELL, GERARD ARTHUR, disability consultant; b. Sacramento, Dec. 28, 1941; s. George A. Brunell and Glendeen Ome Davis. PhD in Behavioral Scis., Behavioral Sci. Inst., 1988, M in Behavioral Scis., 1988; D in Clin. Hypnotherapy, AIH, 1992. Cert. Am. Bd. Hypnotherapy. Pvt. practice pain mgmt. and bio-feedback Sacramento, 1982—; disability cons. Disability Cons. Group, Sacramento, 1986—. Author: Deep Scars Never Heal, 1992. Mem. Am. Inst. Clin. Hypnotherapy, Nat. Assn. Social Security Reps., Nat. Assn. Disability Examiners (bd. mem. 1986—), Free and Accepted Masons. Democrat. Jewish. E-mail: gabrun@pacbell.net. Office: Disability Cons Group PO Box 163723 Sacramento CA 95816-9723

BRUNELLI, ALESSANDRO, thoracic surgeon; b. Ancona, Italy, Jan. 29, 1967; s. Gianfranco and Paola Maria (Matarante); m. Grazia Scutti, Oct. 11, 1997. MD, Med. Sch. Ancona, Italy, 1992. Thoracic surgeon bd. cert., Italy, 1998. Gen. surgeon intern U. Ancona, Italy, 1993-94, thoracic surgery fellow, 1996-99; staff surgeon Ancona, Italy, 1999—; clin. rschr. dept. thoracic surgery, Ancona, 1996-99. Contbr. articles to profl. jours. Grantee Found. Biancalana Masera, Ancona, 1999, rsch. award 1994. Fellow Am. Coll. Chest Physicians, N.Y. Acad. Scis. Avocations: travel, reading, music, sports. Home: Via S Margherita 23, 60179 Ancona Italy

BRUNELLO-MCCAY, ROSANNE, sales executive; b. Cleve., Aug. 26, 1960; d. Carl Carmello and Vivan Lucille (Caranna) B.; m. Walter B. McCay, Feb. 26, 1994 (div. 1998); 1 child, Angela Breanna. Student, U. Cin., 1978-81, Cleve. State U., 1981-82. Indsl. sales engr. Alta Machine Tool, Denver, 1982; mem. sales./purchases Ford Tool & Machine, Denver, 1982-84; sales/ptnr. Mountain Rep. Enterprises, Denver, 1984-86; pres., owner Mountain Rep. Ariz., Phoenix, 1986—; pres. Mountain Rep. Oreg., Portland, 1990—, Mountain Rep. Wash., 1991—; pres. Mountain Rep.

Calif., Sunnyvale, 1997—, San Clemente, 1998—, Port Clinton, Ohio, 1999—, Milford, Ohio, 1999—; sec. Computer & Automated Systems Assoc., 1987, vice chmn., 1988, chmn., 1989. Active mem. Rep. Party, 1985—; mem. Phoenix Art Mus., Grand Canyon Minority Coun., 1994; vol. Make-A-Wish Found. fund raiser, 1995—. Named Mrs. Chandler Internat., Mrs. Ariz. Internat. Orgn., 1996, Mrs. East Valley U.S., 1997; finalist Mrs. Ariz. Internat., 1996, Ms. Ariz. 2000, Ms. U.S. Continental Pageant. Mem. NAFE, Soc. Mfg. Engrs. (pres. award 1988), Computer Automated Assn. (sec. 1987, vice chmn. 1988 chmn. 1989), Nat. Hist. Soc., Italian Cultural Soc., Tempe C. of C., Vocat. Ednl. Club Am. (mem. exec. bd., pres. 1987—). Roman Catholic. Avocations: sports, aerobics, dancing, skiing, golfing, tennis. E-mail: rosanne@mtnrep.com. Office: Mountain Rep Ariz 410 S Jay St Chandler AZ 85225-6253

BRUNER, ROBERT FRANK, business educator; b. Chgo., Oct. 31, 1949; s. Henry P. and Marjorie (Williamson) Bruner; m. Barbara McTigue, July 29, 1978; children: Jonathan E., Alexander W. BA, Yale U., 1971; MBA, Harvard U., Boston, 1974, D Bus. Adminstrn., 1982. Asst. prof. bus. U. Va., Charlottesville, 1982-87, assoc. prof., 1988-93, Vandell rsch. prof. bus. adminstrn., 1993-96, disting. prof. bus. adminstrn., 1996—. Author: Case Studies in Finance, 1990, 3d edit., 1999; co-author: (CD-ROM tutorial software) Finance Interactive, 1997, (tradebook) The Portable MBA, 1998; contbr. numerous articles to profl. jours. Elder 1st Presbyn. Ch., Charlottesville, 1995—. Recipient Disting. Prof. award U. Va. Alumni Assn., 1995, Outstanding Faculty award Va. Coun. Higher Edn., 1996; named Master of MBA Classroom, Bus. Week mag., 1994. Avocations: canoeing, scripophily, music. Fax: 804-243-7678. E-mail: rfb9k@virginia.edu. Office: U Va Darden Grad Bus Sch PO Box 6550 Charlottesville VA 22906-6550

BRUNER, WILLIAM EVANS, II, ophthalmologist, educator, researcher; b. Cleve., Oct. 10, 1949; s. Clark Evans and Pauline (Schrenk) B.; m. Susan Lee Fraser, June 7, 1975; children: Amanda Lee, Andrew Evans. BA, Wesleyan U., 1971; MD, Case Western Res. U., 1975. Diplomate Am. Bd. Ophthalmology. Intern in surgery Univ. Hosps., Cleve., 1975-76, resident in ophthalmology, 1976-79; fellow in cornea and anterior segment surgery Johns Hopkins Hosp., Balt., 1979-81; asst. prof. ophthalmology Case Western Res. U., Cleve., 1981-89, assoc., 1989-93, assoc. clin. prof., 1993-96, clin. prof., 1996—. Sr. editor; manual of Corneal Surgery, 1987; contbr. chpts. to med. textbooks and articles to profl. jours. Trustee Case Western Res. U, Cleve., Hawken Sch., Gates Mills, Ohio. Recipient Alfred S. Maschke award Case Western Res. U. Sch. Medicine, 1975. Fellow Am. Acad. Ophthalmology; mem. ARVO, Wilmer Residents Assn., cleve. Acad. Medicine, Alpha Omega Alpha, Tavern Club, Cleve. Skating club, The Kirtland Club. Avocations: snow skiing, tennis, golf, music, art. Home: 2906 Weybridge Rd Shaker Hts OH 44120-1874 Office: 1611 S Green Rd Cleveland OH 44121-4128

BRUNER, WILLIAM GWATHMEY, III, lawyer; b. Gadsden, Ala., Nov. 29, 1951; s. William G. and Nicolette A. (Diprima) B.; m. Eloisa Fernandez, Aug. 7, 1976; children: Nicolette, Virginia, William, Weston. BSE, U. Mich., 1973; JD, U. Va., 1976. Bar: Ind., Pa. Assoc. Bingham, Summers, Indpls., 1976-78; corp. counsel Scott Paper Co., Phila., 1978-86; group counsel Emhart Corp., Farmington, Conn., 1986-89; corp. counsel Black & Decker, Towson, Md., 1989-93, sr. corp. counsel, 1994—. Mem. ABA (EEO com. labor and employment law sect., taxation sect.). Republican. Roman Catholic. Office: Black & Decker Corp 701 E Joppa Rd Baltimore MD 21286-5502

BRUNETTE, HERVE, business executive; b. Rouen, France, May 15, 1954; s. Armand and Denise (Leseigneur) B.; m. Betti Braunstein; children: Benjamin, Celine, Alexandre. Hautes etudes commls., Paris, 1979. Account dir. Saatchi, Paris, 1979-84; dep. gen. mgr. BDDP, Paris, 1984-90; pres. BDDP Milan, 1990-94; exec. v.p. Europe BDDP/TBWA, Paris, 1994—. Office: TBWA Internat, 162 rue Billancourt, 92100 Boulogne France

BRUNETTI, MAURIZIO, international lawyer; b. Milan, Italy, Sept. 10, 1957; s. Franco and Afra Margherita (Agnetti) B. Licentiatus iuris magna cum laude, U. Zurich, Switzerland, 1982. Bar: Canton of Ticino, Switzerland, atty.-at-law, 1987, civil law notary, 1987. Acad. asst. ETH, Zurich, 1983-84; law clerk Pretura di Lugano, Switzerland, 1985; articles atty. Bolla & Bonzanigo, Lugano, Switzerland, 1985-87, assoc., 1987-88; legal adviser Iran-U.S. Claims Tribunal, The Hague, The Netherlands, 1989-95, dep. sec.-gen., 1995—; instr. LL.M. program Leiden U., The Netherlands, 1997; arbitrator in field. Contbr. articles to law jours. Mem. ABA (assoc.), Am. Soc. Internat. Law, Swiss Arbitration Assn. Avocations: running, fitness, skiing, cooking. Office: Iran-US Claims Tribunal, Parkweg 13, 2585 JH The Hague The Netherlands

BRUNHAMMER, YVONNE SUZANNE, curator; b. Belfort, France, Oct. 22, 1927; d. Fernand E. Brunhammer and Marie-Louise Arbeit. Diploma, Ecole du Louvre, Paris, 1954. With Mus. Decorative Arts, Paris, 1950—, asst. curator, 1963-69, curator, 1969-85, chief curator, 1986-89, dir., chief curator, 1989-91; dir., chief curator Mus. of Fashion, Paris, 1991—, gen. curator museums, 1991-93, gen. curator du patrimoine emeritus; cons. Musée des Arts Décoratifs, Montreal, Que., Can., 1994—. Decorated chevalier Arts and Letters, Legion of Honor, Officer Nat. Order of Merit, 1995; sr. fellow CASVA Washington Gallery Art, 1993-94.

BRUNHES, BERNARD, executive; b. Parame, France, Mar. 22, 1940; s. Julien and Francoise (Arnoux) B.; m. Annick Henry, July 4, 1963; children: Frederic, Sylvie, Anne-Laure, Marion. Diploma, Ecole Polytechnique Inst. Etudes Politiques, Paris, 1963. Adminstr. INSEE, Paris, 1963-73; asst. dir. Bur. Statis., UN, N.Y.C., 1973-75; chef du svc. Affaires Sociales Commissariat du Plan, Paris, 1975-81; conseiller Premier Min., Paris, 1981-83; pres. Groupe Caisse Depots Devel., Paris, 1983-86, Bernard Brunhes Cons., Paris, 1987—. Author: Les Habit Neufs De L'Emploi, 1996, Eurothérapies de l'emploi, 1999. Lt. French Army, 1960-61. Home: 10 Rue Erard, 75012 Paris France Office: Bernard Brunhes Cons, 89 Rue Du Faubourg St Antoine, 75011 Paris France

BRUNIE, CHARLES HENRY, investment manager; b. N.Y.C., July 17, 1930; s. Charles Henry and Olivia (Swanston) B.; m. Jean Isbell Corley, June 23, 1965; stepchildren: William Corley, Jean Corley Yankus, Ellen Corley. B.A., Amherst Coll., 1952; M.B.A., Columbia, 1956. Analyst N.Y. Life Ins. Co., N.Y.C., 1956-60, Faulkner, Dawkins & Sullivan, 1960-63, Oppenheimer & Co., N.Y.C., 1963-65; gen. ptnr. Oppenheimer & Co., 1965-82, mem. exec. com., 1969-82; chmn. Oppenheimer Capital, 1969-96, chmn. emeritus, 1996—; trustee Manhattan Inst., 1978—, chmn. bd., 1980-1990, chmn. emeritus, 1990—. Served with AUS, 1952-54. Mem. N.Y. Soc. Security Analysts, Chartered Financial Analysts, Mont Pelerin Soc., Delta Upsilon. Clubs: Knickerbocker (N.Y.C.), Doubles (N.Y.C.), Annabell's (London), Bronxville Field, Siwanoy Country (Bronxville). Home: 21 Elm Rock Rd Bronxville NY 10708-4202 Office: Oppenheimer Capital 1345 6th Ave New York NY 10102-0001

BRUNKWALL, JAN SIGGE, vascular surgeon, consultant, educator; b. Stockholm, Jan. 14, 1954; s. Sigge L. and Marianne S. (Anderson) B.; m. Birgitta M. Koopmann, Feb. 25, 1984; children: Frederik, Andreas. MD, Lund (Sweden) U., 1980, cert. specialist in gen. surgery, 1985, PhD, 1990. Intern County Hosp., Halmstad, Sweden, 1979-80, resident, 1980-84; resident Univ. Hosp., Malmö, Sweden, 1984-86, sr. resident, 1987-90, cons., 1990-99, assoc. prof. surgery, 1990—, prof. surgery, 1999—; rsch. fellow U. Mich., Ann Arbor, 1986-87. Author chpts. to books; contbr. articles to profl. jours. Mem. European Soc. for Vascular Surgery, Internat. Union Angiology, Internat. Soc. Endovascular Surgery, Swedish Soc. Medicine, Swedish Surg. Soc., Nordic Surg. soc., Soc. Internat. de Chirurgie, N.Y. Acad. Sci. Home: Am Stadtwald 17, D-53177 Bonn Germany Office: Dept Vascular/Visceral Surgery, U Cologne, D-50923 Cologne Germany

BRUNNER, JANET LEE, physician assistant; b. Milw., Sept. 15, 1955; d. Donald Edward and Carol Louise (Radtke) B. BA in Biology, Luther Coll., 1977; MA in Edn., Ctrl. Mich. U., 1984; BS in Physician Assistance, U. Iowa, 1989. Cert. physician asst., Pa. Nat. Commn. on Certification of Physician Assts; registered med. technologist. Staff med. technologist St. Joseph's Hosp., Milw., 1977-79, 81-87, Hosp. Castañer (P.R.), 1979-81; physician asst. med. oncology Med. Coll. Wis., Milw., 1989-92; physician asst. bone marrow transplant Med. Coll. Wis., 1992-94, sr. coord. bone marrow transplant program, 1993-94; physician asst., sr. coord. bone marrow transplant program Thomas Jefferson U. Hosp., Phila., 1995—; lab. cons. Am. Immediate Care, Chgo., 1984; guest lectr. Allentown Coll., Center Valley, Pa., 1996-99. Sec. bd. dirs. Wis. Interfaith Com. on Ctrl. Am., Milw., 1992-94; election observer U.S. Citizens Election Observer Mission, El Salvador, 1994; mem. coun. Prince of Peace Luth. Ch., 1997-99. Fellow Am. Acad. Physician Assts.; mem. Pa. Soc. Physician Assts. Avocations: aerobics, travel, bicycling. Home: 47 Lavister Dr Mount Laurel NJ 08054-2642 Office: Thomas Jefferson U Hosp 130 S 9th St Ste 400 Philadelphia PA 19107-5233

BRUNNER, KIRSTIN ELLEN, pediatrician, psychiatrist; b. Allentown, Pa., July 26, 1959; d. John Wilson and Ingrid Ulla Brita (Arvide) B. BS, Muhlenberg Coll., Allentown, Pa., 1981; DO, Phila. Coll. Osteo. Medicine, 1986. Diplomate Am. Bd. Pediatrics, Am. Bd. Psychiatry and Neurology in child and adolescent psychiatry and adult psychiatry. Resident U. Ky., 1992; dept. dir. Integra Health Family Devel. Ctr., Cedar Rapids, Iowa, 1993-98; with Hamot Inst. for Behavioral Health, Erie, Pa., 1998—; med. dir. Hamot Child and Adolescent Psychiat. Unit, Erie, 1999—. Fellow Am. Acad. Pediatrics; mem. AMA, Am. Acad. Child and Adolescent Psychiatry, Am. Psychiat. Assn. Avocations: cross country skiing, soccer (outdoor and indoor). Office: Hamot Inst Behavioral Health 118 E 2d St Erie PA 16507-1507

BRUNNER, PAUL HANS, science educator; b. Zürich, Switzerland, Oct. 31, 1946; arrived in Austria, 1991; s. Hans Paul and Margarete (Gadmer) B.; m. Sandra Gabriela Stössel, Oct. 11, 1978; children: Andrea, Christian. Diploma in nat. sci., ETH-Zürich, Switzerland, 1972, DSc, 1976. Cert. civil engr. Resident assoc. Internat. Reference Ctr. IRC/WHO, Dübendorf, Switzerland, 1977-78; rsch. affiliate Stanford (Calif.) U., 1979; sr. res. assoc. EAWAG, Dübendorf, Switzerland, 1980-88, dep. dept., 1988-91; sr. lectr. ETH, Zürich, Switzerland, 1981-90; prof. U. Tech., Vienna, Austria, 1991—; vis. scientist, adj. prof. Carnegie-Mellon U., Pitts., 1990-91. Author: Metabolism of the Anthroposphere, 1991; editor and author: Umwelt und Unternehmen, 1995; editor (jour.) Waste Mgmt. and Rsch., 1991-95. 1st lt. with Swiss Army, 1968-91. Am. Field Svc. scholar, 1964-65; Swiss Nat. Rsch. Found. grantee, 1978. Mem. European Environ. Rsch. Orgn., Am. Chem. Soc., Austrian Water and Waste Mgmt. Assn. (dep. head), Internat. Solid Waste Assn. Avocations: skiing, hiking, photography, movies. Home: Franz Schubert Str 6, A-2371 Hinterbrühl Austria Office: U Tech, Karlsplatz 13/226.4, A-1040 Vienna Austria

BRUNNER, SAM AAGE, radiologist; b. Copenhagen, Feb. 18, 1920; s. Aage and Sigrid (Hansen) B.; m. Kirsten Randbøll Petersen, Nov. 5, 1948; children: Bente, Nils, Lars. MD, U. Copenhagen, 1947, PhD, 1964. Radiologist Dept. Radiology, Borås, Sweden, 1948-51; sr. resident Dept. Surgery, Varberg, Sweden, 1951-53; fellow dept. ear-nose-throat Sundby Hosp., Copenhagen, 1953-57; radiologist U. Rigshosp., Copenhagen, 1957-59, Gentofte U. Hosp., Copenhagen, 1959-64; chmn., prof. dept. radiology Gentofte U. Hosp., 1964-90. Author: Modern Thin-Section Tomography, 1973, Advances in Oto-Rhino-Laryngology, 1974, Diagnostic Radiology; editor: Early Detection of Breast Cancer, 1984, Breast Cancer, 1986, Advances in Breast Cancer Detection. Recipinet Flemming Møller prize, 1965, King Christian Memory award, 1970. Mem. Danish Soc. Diagnostic Radiology (hon.), Scandinavian Soc. Diagnostic Radiology (hon.). Avocations: golf, hunting. Home: 79 Kvaedevej, 2830 Copenhagen Denmark

BRUNO, GUGLIELMO, physician, educator, consultant, researcher; b. Bari, Puglia, Italy, June 25, 1946; s. Concetto and Natalia (Pierro) B.; m. Maria Teresa De Nitto, Apr. 26, 1975; children: Giulia, Alessandra. MD, La Sapienza U., Rome, 1972. Intern Instituto Patologia Medica La Sapienza U., 1975-78, adj. Instituto Malattie Tropicali e Infettive, 1978-79, asst. Istituto I Clinica Medica, 1979-85, assoc. prof. internal medicine, 1985-88, prof. medicine, 1989—; asst. prof. sch. of allegology and clin. immunology La Sapienza U., 1975—; asst. prof. internal medicine, 1988—; asst. prof. hygiene and preventative medicine, 1990—; asst. prof. clin. pharmacology, 1993—; mem. prevention and treatment of allergic diseases Com. of Italian Health Inst., 1984-86. Contbr. articles to profl. jours. 2d lt. Italian Air Force, 1973-74. Recipient rsch. grants. Mem. European Acad. of Allergology and Clin. Immunology, Italian Soc. of Allergology and Clin. Immunology (chmn. Lazio-Abruzzo regional sect. 1998—), Eleonora Lorillard Spencer Cenci Found. Avocations: swimming, travel, bridge. E-mail: guglielmo.bruno@uniroma1.it. Home: Via Antonio Serra 62, 00191 Rome Italy Office: La Sapienza U, Viale del Policlinico, 00161 Rome Italy

BRUNO, SHERRYL LYNN, county official; b. Detroit, Sept. 5, 1951; d. James Marzion and Carol Louise Kerr; m. Ronald James Bruno, Dec. 26, 1971 (dec. Sept. 1993). BA, U. Ark., Little Rock, 1989. Office supply buyer Internat. Graphies, Little Rock, 1973-80; clk. Erga Income Tax, Little Rock, 1980-84; editor, designer Leisure Arts, Maumelle, Ark., 1984-86; bookkeeper Bruno & Assocs., Little Rock, 1986-92, Pulaski County Tax Collector, Little Rock, 1992-94; supr. civil/criminal dept. Pulaski County Cir. Clk., Little Rock, 1994—. Active Pulaski County Dem. Com., Little Rock. Mem. North Little Rock Sertoma Club (bd. mem. 1991-95, sec.). Avocations: gardening, painting, stained glass. E-mail: slbruno@aristote.net. Home: 927 Garland Ave North Little Rock AR 72116-8213 Office: Pulaski County Cir Clk 401 W Markham St Ste 102 Little Rock AR 72201-1428

BRUNOLD, AXEL MANFRED, mechanical engineer, consultant; b. Ludwigshafen/Rhein, Germany, Dec. 17, 1965. MA in Engring., U. Karlsruhe, Germany, 1994; PhD in Engring., Martin Luther Univ., Halle-Wittenberg, Germany, 1998. Registered profl. engr. Scientist Inst. fur Werkstofftechnologie, Halle/Saale, Germany, 1995-98; scientific asst. Fraunhofer Patentstelle, Munich, Germany, 1998—. Contbr. articles to profl. jours. Mem. Verein Deutscher Ingenieure. Office: Fraunhofer Patentstelle, Leonrodstrasse 68, D-80636 Munich Germany

BRUNORI PAGLIANO, PEDRO ALBERTO, priest, media executive, consultant; b. Buenos Aires, July 18, 1951; s. Hilario E. Brunori Ducret and Francisca Y. Pagliano Donadio. D in Indsl. Engring., Argentina Cath. U., Buenos Aires, 1974, Licentiate in Operational Rsch., 1981; STD, Pontifical U. of the Holy Cross, Rome, 1995. Ordained priest Roman Cath. Ch., 1999. Sys. and info. cons. Buenos Aires, 1974-78; rector's cons. U. Buenos Aires, 1976; cons. gen. program activities Argentina Color TV, Buenos Aires, 1977; cons. math. Rio de la Plata Bank, Buenos Aires, 1977-80; cons. stats. Argentina Nat. Grain Coun., Buenos Aires, 1978-80; pres. Rectumsa Svcs. Co., Buenos Aires, 1980-85; dir. Vatican Info. Svc., Vatican City, Italy, 1989-98; v.p. Internat. Univerisitary Coll Rome, 1992-98. Author documentaries for radio and TV programs, 1994-99. Decorated knight comdr. Pontifical Order of St. Gregory; recipient Premio Estate Domenico Silverj. Mem. Knights of Malta. Roman Catholic. Home and Office: Vicente López 1950, 1128 Buenos Aires Argentina

BRUNS, BILLY LEE, electrical engineer, consultant; b. St. Louis, Nov. 21, 1925; s. Henry Lee and Violet Jean (Williams) B.; m. Lillian Colleen Mobley, Sept. 6, 1947; children: Holly Rene, Kerry Alan, Barry Lee, Terrence William. BA, Washington U., St. Louis, 1949; postgrad., Sch. Engring., St. Louis, 1959-62; EE, ICS, Scranton, Pa., 1954. Registered profl. engr., Mo., Ill., Wash., Fla., La., Wis., Minn., N.Y., N.C., Iowa, Pa., Miss., Ind., Ala., Ga., Va., R.I., Wyo. Supt., engr., estimator Schneider Electric Co., St. Louis, 1950-54, Ledbetter Electric Co., St. Louis, 1954-57; tchr. indsl. electricity St. Louis Bd. Edn., 1957-71; pres. B.L. Bruns & assocs. Cons. Engrs. Inc., St. Louis, 1963-72; v.p., chief engr. Hosp. Bldg. & Equipment Co., St. Louis, 1972-76; pres., prin. B.L. Bruns & Assocs. Cons. Engrs., St. Louis, 1976—; tchr. elec. engring. U. Mo. St. Louis extension, 1975-76. Tech. editor The National Electrical Code and Blueprint Reading, Am. Tech. Soc., 1959-65. Mem. Mo. Adv. Coun. on Vocat. Edn., 1969-76, chmn., 1975-76; leader Explorer post Boy Scouts Am., 1950-57. Served with AUS, 1944-46, PTO, Okinawa. Decorated Purple Heart. Mem. NSPE, Mo. Soc. Profl. Engrs., Profl. Engrs. in Pvt. Practice, Am. Soc. Heating, Refrigeration and Air Conditioning Engrs., Illuminating Engrs. Soc., Am. Mgmt. Assn., Nat. Fire Protection Assn. (health care divsn., archtl./engr. divsn.), Masons. Baptist. Home: 1243 Hobson Dr Ferguson MO 63135-1422 Office: 400 Brookes Dr Ste 203 Hazelwood MO 63042-2745

BRUNSDON, GEOFFREY NORMAN, investment company executive; b. Sydney, NSW, Australia, Jan. 3, 1958; s. Norman Keith and Ruth (Legg) B.; m. Jillian Joyce Taylor, Nov. 3, 1984; children: Madeleine Kate, Angus Geoffrey Lloyd. B in Comms., U. NSW, Sydney, 1978. Chartered acct., NSW. Acct. Touche Ross & Co., Sydney, 1979-81; exec. Martin Corp., Ltd., Sydney, 1981-83; dir. Baring Bros., Sydney, 1983-88, Warburg Dillon Read, Sydney, 1988-99, Winstar Partnership, 2000—; non-exec. dir. Simsmetal Ltd., Mercantile Mut. Ltd., ING Bank Ltd.; mem. listing com. Australian Stock Exch., 1993—. Mem. fin. com. St. Vincent's Hosp., Sydney, 1994. Mem. Inst. Chartered Accts. Australia (assoc.), Securities Inst. Australia (assoc.), Australian Club, Mid. Harbor Yacht Club Sydney. Avocations: ocean racing, skiing, music. Office: Warburg Dillon Read, 1 Farrer Pl Level 25, NSW Sydney 2000, Australia

BRUNSON, KENNETH WAYNE, cancer biologist; b. Chico, Tex., Sept. 18, 1936; s. George Starr and Gwendolyn Laverne (Mount) B.; m. Myrna Marquerite Lapré, Jan. 26, 1963; children: Gregory Sean, Geoffrey Gordon. BA in Biology, Chemistry, U. N. Tex., 1964, MA in Biology, Chemistry, 1966; PhD in Microbiology, Biochemistry, U. Minn., 1973; postdoctoral Tumor Biology, The Salk Inst., San Diego, Calif., 1974-77. Lectr. U. Calif., Riverside, 1974-75; rsch. assoc. The Salk Inst., La Jolla, Calif., 1974-77; asst. specialist U. Calif., Irvine, 1977-79; asst. prof. Sch. Medicine Ind. U., Indpls., Gary, 1979-84; assoc. mem. grad. sch. Ind. U., Bloomington, 1979-84; sr. rsch scientist Pfizer Inc, Groton, Conn., 1984-91; assoc. prof. Sch. Medicine U. Pitts., 1991-99; affiliate mem. U. Pitts. Cancer Inst., 1991-94, mem., 1994-99, dir. Tumor Model Lab., 1995-99, dir. in vivo preclin. rsch. for health scis., 1996-99; dep. dir. Inst. for Cancer Rsch. U. North Tex. Health Sci. Ctr., Fort Worth, 1999—; adj. prof. dept. molecular biology and immunology U. N.Tex. Health Sci. Ctr., 2000—; bd. dirs. Am. Cancer Soc., Merrillville, Ind., 1981-84, Pa. Soc. for Biomed. Rsch., 1997-99; mem. expert panel workshop Exptl. Metastasis: Designing New Strategies, 1988; founding mem. sci. edn. com., Pfizer, Inc. Groton, Conn., 1987-91. Sci. advisor 10-vol. treatise Cancer Growth and Progression, 1986-89; editor: (book) Local Invasion and Spread of Cancer, 1989; contbr. (jour.) Current Opinion in Oncology, Jour. Nat. Cancer Inst., Cancer Rsch., In Vivo. Mem. planning com. Regional Health Adminstrn. Conf., Ind., 1984, exec. bd. Shadyside Action Coalition, Pitts., 1993-96, chmn. parking and transp. com., 1993-95. With U.S. Army, 1958-61. Recipient XVI Internat. Cancer Congress award Internat. Union Against Cancer, New Delhi, India, 1994. Mem. Am. Assn. for Cancer Rsch., Am. Assn. Immunologists, Am. Soc. Cell Biology, Metastasis Rsch. Soc., Am. Soc. for Microbiology, (chmn. edn. com., Ind. br.), Am. Inst. Biol. Scis., Pa. Soc. Biomed. Rsch. (bd. dirs. 1997-99). Achievements include pioneering research in cancer metastasis models, some of which has been described in Sci. Am., Mar., 1979, Proceedings of Nat. Acad. of Sci. , 1980, Cancer Growth and Progression, 1989, and Biologic Therapy of Cancer, 1995. Home: 6266 Salem Cir Apt 222 Fort Worth TX 76132-3070 Office: U North Tex Health Sci Ctr Inst Cancer Rsch 3500 Camp Bowie Blvd Fort Worth TX 76107-2644

BRUNT, MANLY YATES, JR., psychiatrist; b. Winston-Salem, N.C., Nov. 7, 1926; s. Manly Yates and Jessie Corina (Evans) B.; M.D., Wake Forest U., 1948; m. Jacklyn Beatrice Bray, Dec. 2, 1961; children—Diane Strachan, William Bray, Douglas Evans, Kenneth Sherman. Intern, Grad. Hosp. U. Pa., 1949-50; exec. med. officer Inst. of Pa. Hosp., Phila., 1952-62, mem. sr. attending staff, 1968—, prin. investigator Behavior Research Lab., 1957-61; mem. faculty U. Pa., 1953-68; dir. emeritus dept. psychiatry Bryn Mawr (Pa.) Hosp., past pres. staff and chmn. exec. com. Pres. Community Nursing Bur. Met. Phila., 1961-64; bd. dirs. Main Line Health Care Group, Inc. Served with M.C., AUS, 1950-52. Diplomate Am. Bd. Psychiatry and Neurology. Mem. AMA, Am. Psychiat. Assn., Am. Psychoanalytic Assn., Phila. Coll. Physicians and Surgeons, Wake Forest U. Med. Alumni Assn. (pres. 1985), Alpha Omega Alpha. Republican. Presbyterian. Clubs: Merion Cricket, Phila. Skating and Humane Soc., Little Egg Harbor Yacht. Home: 633 Malin Rd Newtown Square PA 19073-2612 Office: 864 County Line Rd Bryn Mawr PA 19010-2516

BRUNTON, DANIEL WILLIAM, mechanical engineer; b. Ft. Wayne, Ind., Sept. 25, 1956; s. Paul Edward and Margaret Alice (Rice) B.; m. Carol Marie Pryor, Feb. 19, 1994; children: Edward Daniel, Ann Marie. BS, UCLA, 1978, MS in Engring., 1980, M of Engring., 1986. Mem. tech. staff Hughes Missiles Group, Canoga Park, Calif., 1978-89, dept. mgr., 1989-93; mech. engr. dept. mgr. Litton Itek, Lexington, Mass., 1993-94; sr. engr. Raytheon Missile Sys., Tucson, 1994-97, engring. fellow, 1997—. Mem. Soc. Photonic Instrumentation Engrs., Tau Beta Pi. Achievements include 4 patents filed on cryogenics, optical material testing, and mechanisms. Office: Raytheon Missile Sys PO Box 11337 Tucson AZ 85734-1337

BRUS, WLODZIMIERZ, retired economics educator; b. Plock, Poland, Aug. 23, 1921; s. Abram and Helena (Askanas) Zylberberg; m. Irena Stergien, Apr. 15, 1945 (div. June 1955); children: Helena, Janina; m. Helena Wolinska-Brus, May 5, 1956; 1 child, Tomek. MA in Econ. Planning, Planning Inst., SARATOV, USSR, 1942; PhD in Polit. Economy, Main Sch. of Planning and Statistics, Warsaw, 1951. Asst. prof. Main Sch. of Planning and Statistics, Warsaw, 1949-52, assoc. prof., 1952-54; prof. polit. economy U. Warsaw, 1954-68; rsch. assoc. Inst. of Housing, Warsaw, 1968-72; sr. rsch. fellow St. Antony's Coll., Oxford, Eng., 1973-76; lectr. U. Oxford, 1976-85, prof., 1985-88, prof. emeritus, 1988—; dir. Rsch. Bur., Polish Planning Commn., Warsaw, 1956-58; vice chmn. Econ. Coun. Poland, Warsaw, 1957-63; cons. to World Bank, Washington, Beijing, 1980, 82, 84. Author: General Problems of Functioning of the Socialist Economy, 1961, Socialist Ownership and Political Systems, 1975, Economic History of Eastern Europe, 1983; Co-author: From Marx to the Market, 1989. Active mem. Polish United Workers' Party, Warsaw, 1948-67. Recipient Isaac Deutscher Meml. prize, London, 1976. Avocations: walking, swimming. Office: Wolfson Coll, Linton Rd, Oxford England OX2 6UD

BRUSH, MARTYN THOMAS, bank executive; b. London, Jan. 18, 1963; s. Paul Thomas and Jean Brush. European head non ferrous derivatives Mocatta Group, London, 1984-87; European head fgn. exch. and precious metal derivatives Republic Nat. Bank N.Y., London, 1987-95; global head fx derivatives HSBC Group, London, 1995—; dir. InnovativeSolutions, London, 1999. Avocation: sailing. Office: HSBC Bank plc, 10 Queen Street Pl, London EC4R 1BQ, England

BRUSILOVSKIJ, BORIS ARKADJEVICH, physicist; b. Kiev, Ukraine, July 2, 1928; s. Arkady Grigorjevich and Bella Kivovna (Guzman) B.; m. Tamara Borisovna Novoselskaya, Aug., 22, 1957; 1 child, Leonid Borisovich. MS, Poly. Inst., Donetsk, Ukraine, 1966; DS, Tech. U., Donetsk, Ukraine, 1995; specialization in physics of metals, Kiev U. Engr. Novo-Kramatorsk, Kramatorsk, Ukraine, 1952-67; asst. prof. Indsl. Inst., Kramatorsk, 1967-96; prof. Donbass State Engring. Acad. (formerly Indsl. Inst.), Kramatorsk, 1996—, sci. advisor, 1967—, rsch. assoc., 1967—. Contbr. numerous articles to profl. pubs.; inventor in field. Mem. N.Y. Acad. Scis. Avocations: jogging, swimming, playing chess, growing cacti. Home: 15/3 B Chmelnitsky Str, 343913 Kramatorsk Donetsk, Ukraine Office: Donbass State Acad, Shkadinov Str 72, 343913 Kramatorsk Donetsk, Ukraine

BRUSKEWITZ, FABIAN W., bishop; b. Milw., Sept. 6, 1935. Ordained priest Roman Catholic Ch., 1960. Ordained priest, 1960; bishop Diocese of Lincoln, Nebr., 1992—. Office: Chancery Office PO Box 80328 Lincoln NE 68501-0328

BRUSKI, PAUL STEVEN, marketing executive; b. Kansas City, Mo., Mar. 10, 1949; s. Paul and Elizabeth Ann (Cravens) B.; m. Mary Margaret Williams, May 3, 1980. BS in Journalism, U. Berlin, 1972. With engring. mgmt. Storage Tech. Corp., Louisville, Colo., 1973-77; dir. tech. svcs. Internat. Mktg. Communications, Denver, 1977-79; ptnr. Flack and Bruski Advt., Denver, 1979-80; pvt. practice advt. cons. Schenectady, N.Y., 1981-82; dir. tech. Services D. J. Moore Advt., Guilderland, N.Y., 1983-84; dir. mktg. Enable Software, Inc., Ballston Lake, N.Y., 1984-86; dir. corp. commnications Innovative Software Inc., Lenexa, Kans., 1986-89, Informix Software. Inc. (formerly Innovative Software, Inc.), Lenexa, 1988-89; pres. Market Rels. Cons., Olathe, Kans., 1989—, Am. Ednl. Resources, Inc., Olathe, Kans., 1989-91, MRC Cons., Olathe, 1992—; dir. Corp. Comms. & Spl. Sys. sect. Long Data Sys., Inc., Lenexa, Kans., 1992-96; v.p. mktg. and

sales Visual Applications, Inc., Kansas City, Mo., 1996-97; pres. Images That Sell, Olathe, Kans., 1997; cons. publ. Brodock Press Inc., Utica, N.Y., 1983-86; computer cons. and freelance journalist, 1974—; mktg. cons. Security Benefit Group, Topeka, 1997-99. Author: Collected Works, 1977. With U.S. Army, 1968-72. Mem. Pub. Rels. Soc. Am. (accredited, Prism award 1989). Avocations: race car design, ski racing. Office: Market Rels Cons 15404 W 152nd St Ste F Olathe KS 66062-3085

BRUSKIN, LEONID GREGORY, physicist, researcher, educator; b. Vsolie-Sibirskoe, Russia, May 24, 1962; s. Gregory Zorohovich and Raisa Naumovna (Dashevskaya) B.; m. Irina Romanovna Safonova, Sept. 27, 1962; 1 child, Svetlana. MS in Radio Physics, Irkutsk (Russia) State U., 1984; PhD in Geophysics, Inst. Solar-Terrestrial Phys., Irkutsk, 1989; PhD in Physics, Tsukuba (Japan) U., 1996. Rsch. assoc. Inst. Applied Physics, Irkutsk, 1984-85, rschr., 1985-87; lectr. Irkutsk State Tech. U., 1987-90, assoc. prof. physics, 1990-96; rsch. assoc. U. Tsukuba, 1996-99; software developer Electronic Co. New Zealand, 1999—. Contbr. articles to profl. jours., chpt. to book. Mem. Soviet youth orgn. Komsomol, Irkutsk, 1976-83. Officer in Res., Irkutsk Mil. Dept., 1984—. Mem. Plasma Physics and Nuc. Fusion Soc. Avocations: tennis, karate. Home: 24 Cutler St, New Lynn Auckland New Zealand Office: Electronic Co New Zealand, 19 Newton Rd, Auckland New Zealand

BRUSOV, PAVEL GEORGIEVICH, surgeon, researcher; b. Nygniy Tagil, Sverdlovsk, Russia, Jan. 23, 1938; s. Georgiy Sergeevich and Nina Gavrilovna (Garkunova) B.; m. Irina-Christina Boguslavovna Levitskaya, Mar. 4, 1961; children: Gleb, Georgiy, Ludmila. Physician, Med. Instn., Lvov, Russia, 1961; MD, U. Moscow, 1986. Intern Khabarovsk Mil. Hosp., 1961; resident in surgery Mil. Med. Acad., St. Petersburg, Russia, 1968-70; thoracic surgeon Main Mil. Clin. Hosp., Moscow, 1971-78, chief surgery, 1987-89; surg., cons. Main Mil. Hosp., Moscow, 1976-84; main oncologist, 1984-86, 1984-86, head hosp., 1986-87; chmn. surgery Mil. Inst. Postgrad. Med. Edn., Moscow, 1990—; surgeon gen. Russian Army, 1989-98; surgeon, cons. Main Mil. Hosp., Moscow, 1978-84, main oncologist, 1984-86, head hosp., 1986-87. Author, editor: Organization of Medical Care to the Injured with Mechanical Traumas, 1994, Forecasting in Disaster Medicina, 1995, Course of Lections for Military-Field Surgery, 1996, Military-Field Surgery, 1996, Trauma of the Extremities in Combat, 1996. With Russian mil., 1961-67, gen. maj., 1989—. Recipient Laureate of State award of USSR, 1989, Laureate of State award of Russia, 1997. Mem. Internat. Surg. Soc., European Thoracic Surg. Soc., Soc. Surgeons Moscow (chmn. sect. mil.-field surgery 1990—). Office: Main Mil Hosp, 3 Hospitalnaya Ploshad, 105229 Moscow Russia

BRUSS, DAGMAR, physicist; b. Bad Pyrmont, Germany, Nov. 8, 1963; d. Helmut and Ingrid (Siedschlag) B. Diploma, U. Aachen, Germany, 1989; MSc, U. Edinburg, Britain, 1990; Dr.rer.nat., U. Heidelberg, Germany, 1994. European rsch. fellow U. Oxford, U.K., 1996-97, Inst. for Scientific Interchange, Torino, Italy, 1998; rschr. U. Hannover, Germany, 1999—. Contbr. articles to profl. jours. Grantee German Scholarship Found., 1986-90, Landesgraduiertenforderung Baden-Württemberg, 1992-94. Office: Inst Theoretical Physics, Appelstr 2, D-30167 Hannover Germany

BRUST, EDWIN H., automotive executive; b. Dearborn, Mich., July 16, 1944. BS in Engring., U. Mich., 1967; MBA, Wayne State U., 1968, MS in Engring., 1973. With Ford Motor Co., 1967-84; mgr. advanced product programs Chrysler Can. Ltd., Windsor, ON, Can., 1984; chief long range product strategy Chrysler Can. Ltd., Windsor, 1984-86, exec. long range product plans program, 1986, dir. specialty car and Mex. planning, 1987, gen. product mgr. Eagle, 1988, gen. mgr. new platform planning, 1989-91, gen. product mgr. large car, 1991-93, gen. mgr. Jeep and Eagle divsn., 1993-96, v.p. Latin Am., Middle East and Africa ops., 1996-99; pres., CEO Chrysler Can. Ltd. (now called Daimler Chrysler Can. Inc.), Windsor, 1999—. Office: Chrysler Can, 2450 Chrysler Ctr, Windsor, ON Canada N9A 4H6*

BRUSTEIN, MICHAEL LABE, lawyer; b. May 13, 1949; s. Louis and Flora Eva (Forman) B.; m. Joan Lorraine Goldfrank; 1 child, Tess. BA cum laude, NYU, 1971; MD, U. Conn., 1974. Bar: Conn. 1974. Chief adult and vocat. edn. br. Office Gen. Counsel HEW, Washington, 1974-79; legal cons. Dept. Edn. Transition Team, Washington, 1980; ptnr. Brustein & Manasevit, Washington, 1980—; legal cons. Nat. Assn. Workforce Bds., Nat. Inst. Edn., State Edn. Agencies of N.Y., Calif., N.Mex., Tenn., Fla., R.I., Wyo., Ga., La., N.C., Mich., W.Va., Ark., P.R.; lawyers com. Civil Rights Under Law; gen. counsel Nat. Assn. Partnerships in Equity. Author: School-to-Work User's Guide: Understanding Federal Cost Principles and Avoiding Audit Liability, 1997, The AVA Guide to the School-to-Work Opportunities Act, 1994, The AVA Guide to Federal Funding for Tech-Prep, 1993, The AVA Audit Handbook: Avoiding Liability Under the 1990 Perkins Act, rev. edit., 1992; contbr. articles to profl. jours. Mem. Nat. Assn. Fed. Fin. Adminstrs. (gen. counsel), Nat. Assn. State Couns. Vocat. Edn. (gen. counsel), Nat. Coordinating Coun. Vocat. Student Orgns. (gen. counsel), D.C. Bar Assn., Conn. Bar Assn., N.Y. Bar Assn., Phi Beta Kappa, Phi Sigma Alpha. Home: 3726 Van Ness St NW Washington DC 20016-2226 Office: 3105 South St NW Washington DC 20007-4419

BRUSTEIN, WILLIAM IRVING, sociology educator; b. Fairfield, Conn., July 13, 1947; s. Louis I. and Flora Eva Brustein; m. Yvonne Christine Ramey, Feb. 14, 1981; children: Arielle Lauren, Maximilian Samuel. BA, U. Conn., 1969; MA, John Hopkins U., 1971; PhD, U. Wash., 1981. Asst./assoc. prof. sociology U. Utah, Salt Lake City, 1981-88; assoc. prof. sociology U. Minn., Mpls., 1989-94, prof., Morse Alumni Disting. Tchg. prof. sociology, 1994—, adj. prof. polit. sci., 1994—, dir. Ctr. for European studies, 1992-95, chair dept. sociology, 1995-98; Disting. McKnight Univ. prof., 2000—; panelist sociology program NSF, Washington, 1998-2000; vis. scholar London Sch. Econs. and Polit. Sci., 1999; dir. Univ. Ctr. Internat. Studies, 2001—, UCIS Prof. Internat. Studies, U. Pitts., 2001—. Author: The Social Origins of Political Regionalism: France, 1849 to 1981, 1988, The Logic of Evil: The Social Origins of the Nazi Party, 1925-1933, 1996 (James S. Coleman Disting. Contbn. to Rational-Choice scholarship 1997); editor: Nazism as a Social Phenomenon, 1998; cons. editor Am. Jour. Sociology, 1998-2000. Bd. dirs. Jewish Family Svc., St. Paul, 1991-95, Hillel, Mpls., 1998—; exec. bd. Student Project for Amity Among Nations, Mpls., 1998-2000. Grantee NSF, Washington, 1999. Mem. Am. Sociol. Assn. (coun. mem. polit. sociology and comparative hist. sociology 1987-90, 88-91, sec.-treas. rational choice sect. 1995-97, chair PhD granting depts. 1996-98), Am. Polit. Sci. Assn., Phi Beta Kappa. Democrat. Avocations: coaching boys soccer, reading, international travel, skiing. E-mail: brustein@atlas.socsci.umn.edu. Fax: 612-624-7020. Home: 4053 Deerwood Trl Eagan MN 55122-1885 Office: Office of Dir U Pitts Univ Ctr Internat Studies 4G40 Wesley W Posvar Hall Pittsburgh PA 15260

BRÜSTLE, OLIVER, neuropathologist, researcher; b. Ulm, Germany, Oct. 7, 1962; s. Rudolf and Herta (Geiger) B.; m. Lucia Johanna Steinhauser, May 16, 1985; children: Isabel, Ruben, Johanna, Fabian. MD, U. Ulm, 1989. Neuropathologist U. Zurich (Switzerland), 1989-91; neurosurgeon U. Erlangen, Germany, 1991-93; vis. assoc. NIH, Bethesda, Md., 1993-97; neuropathologist U. Bonn (Germany), 1997—. Dep. receiving editor: European Jour. Neurosci., 1996; mem. editl. bd. Brain Pathology, 1999; contbr. articles to profl. jours., chpts. to books. Recipient Stipent DFG, 1993, Jr. Rsch. award State of Nordhein-Westfalen, 1998. Mem. German Soc. Neuropathology, Gesellschaft Deutscher Naturforscher Ärzte, Soc. Neurosci. Avocations: playing French horn and piano, biking. Office: U Bonn Med Ctr, Sigmund-Freud-Str 25, 53105 Bonn Germany

BRUSTMANN, HERMANN, pathologist, researcher; b. Vienna, Austria, Dec. 2, 1955; s. Hermann and Rosalia (Taurer) B.; m. Rebecca Poquita, Dec. 18, 1985; children: David, Sarah. PhD, U. Vienna, 1981, MD, 1983. Registrar dept. pathology Austrian Med. Assn., Moedling, Vienna, 1984-90; sr. med. officer, 1990—. Contbr. articles to profl. jours. Recipient award Med. Assn. Lower Austria, 1998. Mem. Internat. Acad. Pathology, Intenrat. Soc. Preventive Oncology. Methodist. Avocations: karate, bulldogs, aquariums. Home: Willergasse 59/14, A-1230 Vienna Austria Office: Landeskrankenhaus-Pathology, Sr Maria Restitutagasse 12, A-2340 Moedlina Vienna, Austria

BRUTIAN, GEORG ABEL, philosopher, researcher, science educator, science administrator; b. Sevkar, Armenia, Mar. 24, 1926; s. Abel Michael and Mariam Arshak (Khachatrian) B.; m. Hranoush Ara Markarian, May 26, 1955; children: Lilit, Narine, Ara. Degree in engring., Poly. Inst., Yerevan, Armenia, 1947; degree in history internat. rels., Yerevan U., 1950; PhD in Logic, Moscow U., 1951, D ScD in Philos. Scis., 1962. Assoc. prof. Yerevan U., 1951-62, chmn. philosophy, logic, 1970-86; chmn. philosophy Yerevan Brussov Inst., 1962-70; academician sec. Nat. Acad. of Scis., Republic of Armenia, 1977-94, v.p., 1994—. Author: Logic, 1957, 4th rev. edit., 1987, Theory of Knowledge of General Semantics, 1959, Critical Analysis of Semantic Philosophy, 1962, Philosophical Introduction to Mathematical Logic, 1968, Sapir-Whorf Hypothesis, 1968, Philosophy and Language, 1972, Philosophy by Dialogue, vol. 1, 1975, 78, 85, vol. 2, 1981, 86, Outline of the Analysis of Philosophical Knowledge, 1979, David the Invincible's Study on Logic, 1980, Transformational Logic, 1983, 95, Argumentation, 1984, Outline of a Theory of Argumentation, 1992, Concise Course of Logic, 1993, Logic, 1998, Logic, Language and Argumentation in Projection of Philosophical Knowledge, 1998, Armenology and Metaarmenology, 1999, The Subject-Matter to Armenology and Its Methods, 1999, numerous others; edtl. bd. Philos. Scis., Moscow, 1972-87, Philosophy and Rhetoric, Pa. U., 1970-72, 89-98, Argumentation, Belgium, the Netherlands, 1989—, Communication and Cognition, Belgium, 1989—, Informal Logic, Can., 1989—, Newsletter, the Netherlands, 1990—, Society and Economics, 1996, Armenian Mind, 1997—, others. Founder, pres. Armenian Philos. Acad., 1987—, Internat. Inst. Argumentation, 1991—; v.p. Internat. Assn. Informal Logic and Critical Thinking, U.S., 1989—; senator Internat. Parliament for Safety and Peace, Italy, 1991-96; mem. internat. sci. coun. Black Sea U., Rumania, 1996—; bd. dirs. Ansted U., Malaysia, 2000—. Recipient Order of Friendship of Peoples award Presidium Supreme Soviet of USSR, Moscow, 1986, Kamenski medal Univ. Bratislava, 1971, Sign of Honour 1st Class medal, Czechoslovakia, 1971, Veteran of Labour medal, 1983, Vavilov medal, 1986, 50th Anniv. Victory (1941-45) Great Patr. War, 1995; named hon. citizen Masterton Borough Coun., New Zealand, 1966. Mem. Nat. Acad. Scis., Armenia (corr. mem. 1971-82), World Lit. Acad., Eng., Ararat Internat. Acad. Scis, Paris, London Diplomatic Acad., World Inst. Achievement, U.S., European Ctr. Study of Argumentation, Belgium, Internat. Soc. Comm. and Cognition, Belgium (editl. bd.), Internat. Soc. Study Argumentation, the Netherlands (adv. bd.). Achievements include: finding Prin. of Linguistic Complementarity, which world philos. and linguistic lit. is named after him, transformational logic, has created a synthetic theory of argumentation, a model of discourse, and exposes the specifity of philosophical argumentation. The development of the investigation of argumentation in the Soviet Union is connected first of all with Brutian's name. His students and followers from a number of newly independent countries, as well as from some other countries investigated the conceptions of argumentation on the basis of his ideas. The Yerevan School of Argumentation was formed which is known in the world centers for investigations of argumentation.contbr. to Armenian philos. and logical thought. He has great authority in international philosophical circles, the evidence of which are the letters to him of many famous philosophers and logicians such as Bertrand Russel, Kurt Godel, Rudolf Carnap, Alfred Tarsky, Alfred Aeyer, and others. E-mail: brut@sci.am. Home: Pushkin St 40 Apt 90, Yerevan 375010, Armenia Office: Nat Acad Scis, Marshal Baghramian Ave 24, Yerevan 375019, Armenia

BRUTON, ERIC MOORE, author, publisher, diamond consultant; b. London, Aug. 5, 1915; s. James Eli and Flora Elizabeth (Moore) B.; widower. Qualified mech. engring., Chelsea Poly. and RAF Officers, Sch., 1939-41; Dipl. in Gemmology, Gemmological Assn. G.B., 1950. Asst. tech. editor Motor Transport and Bus & Coach, London, 1936-38; feature writer Practical Motorist and Practical Mechanics, London, 1938-40; founder, editor Farm Machinery, London, 1946, Travel, and Tools and Equipment, London, 1947; editor Horological Jour., Goldsmiths Jour., Gemmologist, Indsl. Diamond Rev., London, 1947-62; founder, pub. Retail Jeweller, Thomson Internat., London, 1961-86; founder Diamond Boutique, Maidenhead, Eng., 1965—; cons. Thomson Internat., London, 1987-94; owner N.A.G. Press Ltd., East Anglia, Eng., 1983-93; organizer study tours to world's gem mines, 1965-88; founder, diamond grading course Sir John Cass Coll., London, 1965. Author 15 tech., antiquarian and reference books, 11 mystery novels, including The Devil's Pawn, 1962, The Laughing Policeman, 1963, The Finsbury Mob, 1964, The Smithdield Slayer, 1965, The Wicked Saint, 1965, The Fire Bug, 1967, Diamonds, 1970, Antique Clocks and Clock Collecting, 1974, The History of Clocks and Watches, 1979, Dating English Antique Clocks, 1981, Legendary Gems, 1986, Collectors Dictionary of Clocks and Watches, 2000. Freeman, City of London, 1955—. With RAF, 1940-46, CBI. Recipient award Am. Watchmakers Inst., 1968, Hanneman award, 1981. Fellow Gemmological Assn. Gt. Britain (pres. 1994-96, Gold medal 1996), Brit. Horological Inst., Nat. Assn. Goldsmiths (pres. 1983-85), Soc. Jewelry Historians, Crime Writers Assn., Worshipful Co. Clockmakers (liveryman), Worshipful Co. Turners (liveryman), Worshipful Co. Goldsmiths (freeman). Avocations: travel, horseback riding.

BRUTON, JOHN, Irish government official; b. Dublin, Ireland, 1947; married; 4 children. BA, Clongowes Wood Coll., Kildare; LLB, UCD Kings Inns, Dublin. Mem. Dail, 1969; parliamentary sec. to min. for edn. Govt. of Ireland, 1973-77, parliamentary sec. to min. for industry and commerce, 1975-77, min. for fin., 1981-82, 86-87; leader of the house Dail, 1982-86; min. for industry trade, commerce and tourism Govt. of Ireland, 1983-86; front bench spokesperson on industry and commerce Fine Gael, 1987-89, front bench spokesperson on edn., 1989-90, dep. leader, 1987-90, leader, 1990—; prime min. Govt. of Ireland, Dublin, 1994-97. Office: Office of Taoiseach, Fine Gael 51 Upper Mount Street, Dublin Ireland*

BRUTON, JOHN MACAULAY, trade association executive; b. Mexico City, Nov. 13, 1937; s. Edmund Macaulay and Byrd (Grant) B.; m. Frances McMillan Marks, Nov. 25, 1960; children: Alexander, Macaulay, Brinley. BA, Duke U., 1959. Pres., gen. mgr. Grant Advt. de Panama, Panama City, 1970-72, Mexico City, 1972; comm. dir. Am. C. of C. of Mex., Mexico City, 1972-74, gen. mgr., 1974-77, exec. v.p., CEO, 1977—; v.p. exec. mgmt. Assn. Am. C. of C. in Latin Am., L.A., Washington, 1985-88, v.p. membership svc., 1988—. Bd. dirs. Am. Benevolent Soc., Mex., 1964-68, Am. Soc. Mex., 1975-78, 80-84; adv. bd. Jr. League Mexico City, 1978—; founder, bd. dirs. Jr. Achievement Mex., 1977—; bd. trustees Fomento Educacional A.C., 1988—, treas., 1993—. Mem. Univ. Mex. (bd. dirs. 1979-83, pres. 1981-82). Episcopalian. Home: Ameyalcali, Ocotepec 80, 10200 Mexico City Mexico Office: Am C of C Mex, Lucerna 78, 06600 Mexico City Mexico

BRUWIER, M.W., internist; b. Crisnee, Deliege, Belgium, Sept. 23, 1930; s. Georges and Renee (DeFalle) B.; m. Jenny Christoffel, Sept. 7, 1957. MD, St. Louis Coll., Liege, 1957. Gen. practice medicine Louveigne, Belgium, 1957-71; practice medicine specializing in internal medicine Hosp. Valvor, U. Liege, 1977—. Contbr. articles to profl. jours. Roman Catholic. Address: 12 Route des Fawes, 4960 Louveigne Belgium

BRUYN, KIMBERLY ANN, public relations executive; b. Grand Rapids, Mich., Jan. 25, 1955. BA in English, Calvin Coll., Grand Rapids, 1977; MS in Journalism, U. Kans., 1979. Advt. copywriter, acct. exec. Mendenhall, Jones & Leistra Advt., Grand Rapids, 1979-81; advt. copywriter Johnson & Dean Advt., Grand Rapids, 1981-82; pub. rels. analyst Amway Corp., Ada, Mich., 1982-84, sr. pub. rels. analyst, 1984-85, sr. pub. rels. specialist, 1986-87, pub. rels. supr., 1987-88, pub. rels. mgr., chief corp. spokesperson, 1988-93, sr. mgr. pub. rels., chief corp. spokesperson, 1993-98; v.p. comms. The Windquest Group, Grand Rapids, 1998-2000; exec. dir. Straightline Pub. Rels., 2000—. Mem. pub. rels. and mktg. com. Grand Rapids Symphony Orch., 1992; mem. planning com. Spl. Olympics Festival of Trees, Grand Rapids, 1990-92, Gerald R. Ford Presdl. Mus. 10th Anniversary Celebration, Grand Rapids, 1992; bd. dirs. Celebration on the Grand, 1989-96, co-chair, 1993, 94; co-chair pub. rels. Heart Ball, Am. Heart Assn., 1996-2000; chair pub. rels. Van Andel Arena Grand Opening, 1996, Presdl. Tribute to Gerald R. Ford, 1997. Mem. PRSA (Spectrum award 1990-98), Direct Selling Assn. (chair comm. com. 1997-98). Office: The Windquest Group 25 Ionia Ave SW Grand Rapids MI 49503-4179

BRUYNES, EDUARD, urologist; b. Amsterdam, June 18, 1950; s. Antonie and Pietje (Stom) B.; m. Astrid Knaap, Sept. 30, 1977; children: Vincent Antonie John, Roderick Laurens Olivier. MD, U. Amsterdam, 1978, Urologist, 1985. Scientist, exptl. surgery U. Amsterdam Acad. Hosp., 1977-85; urologist Ziekenhuis Gooi Noord, Blaricum, The Netherlands, 1985—; dir. E.B. Bruynes B.V., Blaricum, 1989—; dir. med. info. and adv. ctr. Laren, The Netherlands, 1992—; bd. dirs. Pro Urologica Found., Blaricum, De Prostaatstichting Found., Blaricum. Editl. bd.: Urology Digest, 1978-99; contbr. articles to profl. jours. Mem. Dutch Urol. Occpl. Interests Bd. (pres. 1999—), Dutch Urol. Assn. (bd. dirs. 1999—), Dutch Cen. Union of Cooperations of Ind. Med. Cons. (sec. 1977—), Cooperation of Ind. Med. Cons. (sec.), Bd. of Med. Strategy Ziekenhuis Gooi Noord (pres. 1989-96), European Urol. Assn., European Soc. Surg. Oncology, Dutch Soc. Gen. Surgeons, European Soc. Pediatric Urology, Soc. Internat. d'Urologie, others. Avocations: skiing, cycling, swimming, music, investment. Office: Ziekenhuis Gooi Noord, Ryksstraatweg 1, 1261 An Blaricum The Netherlands

BRUYNSERAEDE, YVAN JULIEN, physics educator; b. Oostende, Belgium, Feb. 2, 1938; m. Henrotte Myriam; children: Christophe, Isabelle, Valerie, Alexane. Degree Physics, Katholieke U. Leuven (Belgium), 1961, PhD in Physics, 1967. Rsch. asst. Fonds Kollektief Fundamenteel Wetenschappelyk Onderzoek, Belgium, 1961-63; rsch. asst. Katholieke U., Leuven, Belgium, 1963-64, 66-67, head asst., 1967-68, 70-72, asst. prof., 1972-76, assoc. prof., 1976-78, prof. physics, 1978—; rsch. fellow, assoc. European Orgn. Nuclear Rsch., Switzerland, 1968-70, vis. scientist, summer 1971, 72; vis. scientist Kernforschungszentrum Karlsruhe (Germany), Technische Hochschule Clausthal-Zellerfeld (Germany), Argonne (Ill.) Nat. Lab., U. Calif., San Diego, U. Nice (France); mem. com. thin film div. IUVSTA, 1983-94; mem. Solid States Physics Commn., Belgian Nat. Sci. Found., 1984-94; chmn. Rsch. Coun. Katholieke U. Leuven, 1990-95; mem. sci. adv. coms. Belgian Study Ctr. for Nuclear Energy, 1987—; mem. Coun. European Synchrotron Radiation Facility, Grenoble, France, 1988-98. With Belgian mil., 1964-66. Fellow Am. Phys. Soc.; mem. Belgian Phys. Soc. (pres. 1989), European Phys. Soc. (chmn. low temperature physics sect. condensed matter div. 1988—), Am. Vacuum Soc., Am. Materials Rsch. Soc., European Materials Rsch. Soc., Flemish Coun. Rsch. Policy, European Phys. Soc. (bd. dirs. 1977—), Royal Flemish Acad. Belgium for Scis. and Arts (pres. 1999—). E-mail: yvan.bruynseraede@fys.kuleuven.ac.be. Home: Jachthoorn 11, B 3210 Linden Belgium Office: U Leuven, Lab Solid-State Phys & Magn, Celestijnenl 200D, B 3001 Heverlee Belgium

BRUZZONE, RAUL ALBERTO, engineer, manufacturing executive; b. Mar Del Plata, Argentina, Oct. 26, 1954; s. Julio Florentino Bruzzone and Lidia Urdiales; m. Laura Beatriz Perez, July 5, 1954; children: Paula Marcela, Leticia Andrea. BS in Engring., U. Montevideo, Uruguay, 1976, degree in engring., 1986; degree in indsl. engring., U. Madrid. Mobile comms. chief engr. UTE, Montevideo, 1983-90; mobile comms. sys. group leader Alcatel, Madrid, 1990-93, rwys. comms. sys. mgr., 1993-95, wireless local loop project mgr., 1995-96; wireless sys. mgr. Philips, Le Mans, France, 1996—; sr. tech. officer Philips Consumer Comm., 2000; mem. conf. U. Lille, France, 1998-99, Philips Rsch. Labs., The Netherlands, 1999, U. Erlangen, Germany, 1999. Patentee antenna direction finding in mobile phones, power control in mobile phones, mobile with indication of stds. availability, radio signal direction finding. Mem. IEEE. E-mail: raul.bruzzone@philips.com. Office: Philips Consumer Comms, Rte d'Angers, 72081 Le Mans France

BRYAN, A(LONZO) J(AY), retired service club official; b. Washington, N.J., Sept. 17, 1917; s. Alonzo J. and Anna Belle (Babcock) B.; m. Elizabeth Elfreida Koehler, June 25, 1941 (div. 1961); children: Donna Elizabeth, Alonzo Jay, Nadine; m. Janet Dorothy Onstad, Mar. 15, 1962 (div. 1977); children: Brenda Joyce, Marlowe Francis, Marilyn Janet. Student. Retail florist Washington, N.J., 1941-64. Fund drive chmn. ARC, 1952; bd. dirs. Washington YMCA, 1945-55, N.J. Taxpayers Assn., 1947-52; mem. Washington Bd. Edn., 1948-55. Mem. Washington Grange, Sons and Daus. of Liberty, Soc. Am. Florists, Nat. Fedn. Ind. Businessmen, Florists Telegraph Delivery Assn., C. of C., Masons, Tall Cedars of Lebanon Club, Jr. Order United Am. Mechanics, Kiwanis (pres. Washington N.J. 1952, lt. gov. internat. 1953-54, gov. N.J. dist. 1955, sec. 1957-64, sec. S.E. area Chgo. 1964-74, editor The Jersey Kiwanian 1958-64, internat. staff 1964-85, sec.-treas. Rocky Mountain dist. 1989, pres. South Denver 1990-91, editor Rocky Mountain Kiwanian 1990-96), Breakfast Club (Chgo., pres. 1981-82). Methodist. Home: 8115 S Poplar Way B 203 Englewood CO 80112-3174

BRYAN, FELICITY ANNE, literary agent; b. Sowerby Bridge, Yorkshire, Eng., Oct. 16, 1945; d. Paul E. and Betty M. (Hoyle) B.; m. Alex Duncan. BA, U. London, 1967. Journalist Fin. Times, London, Washington, 1968-70, Economist, London, 1970-73; literary agt. Curtis Brown, London, 1973-88, Felicity Bryan Literary Agy., Oxford, 1988—. Author: (book) The Town Gardener's Companion, 1979, A Garden for Children, 1985, Nursery Style, 1989. Office: Felicity Bryan Literary Agy, 2A North Parade/Banbury Rd, Oxford OX26LX, England

BRYAN, FRANK LEON, microbiologist, consultant, researcher; b. Indpls., Aug. 29, 1930; s. Frank Leslie and Marie Georgia (Vogt) B.; m. Ruth Ann McDonald, Aug. 30, 1952; children: Steven Harris, Sharryl Ann. B.S., Ind. U., 1953; M.P.H., U. Mich., 1956; Ph.D., Iowa State U., 1965. Instr. U. Mass., Amherst, 1956-58; also tng. officer New Eng. Field Tng. Sta.; tng. officer in environ. health Communicable Disease Ctr., Atlanta, 1958-63; research in salmonella Communicable Disease Ctr., Ames, 1963-65; chief foodborne disease activity and scientist dir. Ctrs. for Disease Control, Atlanta, 1965-85; cons. in food safety and tng. Ctrs. for Disease Control, Lithoria, Ga., 1985—; mem. WHO adv. panel food safety, Internat. Commn. on Microbiol. Specifications for Foods, mem. com. Nat. Research Council, Nat. Acad. Scis., lectr. foodborne disease epidemiology and control. Author: (with Riemann) Foodborne Infections and Intoxications, 2d edit., 1979; (with others) Microorganisms in Foods 1, 1978, Microbiological Ecology for Foods, Vol. 1 and 2, 1980; Diseases Transmitted by Foods, 1982, Microorganisms in Foods, 1986, Hazard Analysis Critical Control Point Evaluations, 1992; manuals or investigation of foodborne, waterborne and vector-borne illnesses, and hazard analyses critical control point systems; contbr. articles to profl. jours. Served to 1st lt. U.S. Army, 1953-55, to capt. USPHS, 1956-85. Recipient Norbert Sherman award, 1979, 82, 86, 91; Meritorious Service medal USPHS, 1981. Fellow Internat. Assn. Milk, Food and Environ. Sanitarians (life, award 1991); mem. Am. Soc. Microbiology, Inst. Food Technologists, World Assn. Veterinary Food Hygienists (v.p.), Am. Pub. Health Assn., Nat. Assn. Sanitarians, Sigma Xi, Phi Tau Sigma, Gamma Sigma Delta.

BRYAN, GERALD JACKSON, retired British government administrator; b. Belfast, Northern Ireland, Apr. 2, 1921; s. George and Ruby Evelyn (Jackson) B.; m. Georgiana Wendy Cockburn Hull, Oct. 4, 1947; children: Diana Evelyn, Mary Georgiana, Caesar Michael Pollexfen. Attended, Wrekin Coll., Shropshire, Eng., 1934-39, Royal Mil. Coll., Woolwich, Eng., 1939, New Coll., Oxford, Eng., 1948-49. Asst. dist. commr. H.M. Colonial Svc., Swaziland, 1944-50; asst. colonial sec. H.M. Colonial Svc., Barbados, 1950-54; establishment sec. H.M. Colonial Svc., Mauritius, 1954-59; adminstr. H.M. Colonial Svc., Brit. V.I., 1959-62, St. Lucia, 1962-67; govt. sec. Govt. Isle of Man, 1967-69; gen. mgr. Londonderry (Northern Ireland) Devel. Corp., 1969-73, Bracknell Devel. Corp., Eng., 1973-82; ind. inquiry inspector Lord Chancellor, Eng., 1982-91; non-exec. dir. Lovaux Engring. Ltd., Berkshire, 1982-90, MDSL Estates Ltd., 1990—, Hampshire; sec. gen. Assn. Contact Lens Mfrs., 1983-88. Mem. Berkshire County Coun., 1983-85. Maj. Royal Engrs., 1939-44, Middle East. Decorated Companion Order St. Michael and St. George, Comdr. Royal Victorian Order, Officer Order. Brit. Empire all by Her Majesty the Queen, Mil. Cross by His Majesty the King; knight Order of St. John of Jerusalem. Fellow Inst. Mgmt. Conservative. Mem. Ch. of Eng. Avocation: swimming. Home: Whitehouse, Murrell Hill Ln Binfield, Bracknell Berkshire RG42 4BY, England

BRYAN, JOHN HENRY, food and consumer products company executive; b. West Point, Miss., 1936. BA in Econs. and Bus. Adminstrn, Rhodes Coll., Memphis, 1958. Joined Bryan Foods, 1960; with Sara Lee Corp. (formerly known as Consol. Food Corp.), Chgo., 1960—; from exec. v.p. to pres. Sara Lee Corp. (formerly known as Consol Food Corp), Chgo., 1974, chief exec. officer, 1975—, chmn. bd., 1976—, also bd. dirs.; bd. dirs. Gen.

Motors Corp., Amoco Corp., 1st Chgo. Corp., 1st Nat. Bank Chgo. Chmn. bus. adv. coun. Chgo. Urban League; bd. govs. Nat. Women's Econ. Alliance, Chgo.; trustee, vice-chmn., exec. com. U. Chgo., Rush-Presbyn.-St. Luke's Med. Ctr.; trustee Com. Econ. Devel.; trustee, treas. Art Inst. Chgo.; chmn. Catalyst; bd. dirs. Bus. Com. for Arts; chmn. Chgo. com. Chgo. Coun. on Fgn. Rels.; mem. trustee's coun. Nat. Gallery Art, Washington; mem. pres.'s com. on the arts and humanities; dir. bus. com. for the arts. Decorated Legion of Honor (France), Order of Orange Nassau (The Netherlands), Order of Lincoln Medallion; recipient Nat. Humanitarian award NCCJ, William H. Albers award Food Mktg. Inst., Man of Yr. award Harvard Bus. Sch. Club Chgo.; named Exec. Yr. Crain's Chgo. Bus., 1992, Jr. Achievement Chgo. Bus. Hall of Fame, 1992, Miss. Hall of Fame, 1992. Mem. Grocery Mfrs. Assn. (sr., past. chmn. bd.), Bus. Coun., Bus. Roundtable. Office: Sara Lee Corp 3 1st Nat Plz 70 W Madison St Ste 4500 Chicago IL 60602-4260*

BRYAN, JOHN RODNEY, management consultant; b. Berkeley, Calif., Dec. 29, 1953; s. Robert Richard and Eloise (Anderson) Putz; m. Karen Nelson, Jan. 20, 1990. BA in Chemistry, U. Calif., San Diego, 1975; MBA, Rutgers U., 1985. Agt. Prudential, San Diego, 1975-79; sales mgr. Herman Schlorman Showrooms, L.A., 1980-83; pvt. practice mgmt. cons. Basking Ridge, N.J., 1983-85; mgmt. cons. The Brooks Group, Hollywood, Fla., 1985-99; pvt. practice San Diego, 1988—; with Western Productivity Group, 1990-95; pres. eProcesses Consulting, Inc., 1999—. Elder La Jolla Presbyn. Ch., 1991—. Mem. Inst. Indsl. Engring., Rutgers Club So. Calif., Beta Gamma Sigma. Avocations: singing, golf. Address: 6265 Hurd Ct San Diego CA 92122-2917 Office: 5230 Carroll Canyon Rd Ste 318 San Diego CA 92121-1781

BRYAN, LAWRENCE DOW, college president; b. Barberton, Ohio, Jan. 30, 1945; s. W. Richard and Celia A. (Evans) B.; m. Marjorie Napier, June 15, 1968; children: Mark Evans, Alexa Marie. BA, Muskingum Coll., 1967; MDiv., Garrett Theol. Sem., 1970; PhD, Northwestern U., 1973. Tchg. asst. Nat. Coll. Edn., Evanston, Ill., 1969-71; biog. rsch. fellow Garrett Theol. Sem., Evanston, 1972-73; asst. prof. religious studies, chaplain McKendree Coll., Lebanon, Ill., 1973-77, asst. v.p. acad. affairs, 1977-78, dean, 1978-79, assoc. prof., 1978-79; prof. philosophy and religion, v.p., dean Franklin (Ind.) Coll., 1979-90; pres. Kalamazoo Coll., 1990-96, MacMurray Coll., Jacksonville, Ill., 1997—; trustee Parkstone Group of Funds. Mem. Forum for Kalamazoo County, 1990-94, Kalamazoo Symphony Orch. Bd., 1990-96; pres. Heyl Found., Kalamazoo, 1990-96; bd. dirs. Bronson Hosp., 1991-96; trustee Interlochen Ctr. for Arts, 1994-97. Mem. Internat. Bonhoeffer Soc., Rotary, Phi Sigma Tau, Delta Sigma Rho-Tau Kappa Alpha, Alpha Psi Omega, Theta Alpha Phi. Methodist.

BRYAN, ROBERT FESSLER, former investment analyst; b. New Castle, Pa., Jan. 19, 1913; s. Harry A. and Nell (Fessler) B.; m. Elaine A. Norwood, Sept. 7, 1940; children: Diane Elaine Bryan Lyon, Barbara Norwood Bryan Bardo; m. Dorothy Darr MacKenzie, Aug. 11, 1961; m. Gertrude B. Bruneau, Feb. 10, 1978. AB summa cum laude, Oberlin Coll., 1934; PhD, Yale, 1939. Instr. econs. Yale U., 1935-36, 37-39, Princeton U., 1936-37; economist Lionel D. Edie & Co., Inc., N.Y.C., 1939-40; asst. v.p. Lionel D. Edie & Co., Inc., 1943-45, v.p., 1946-48; price exec., rubber br. OPA, 1941-42; economist Goodyear Aircraft Corp., Akron, Ohio, 1943; with J.H. Whitney & Co., N.Y.C., 1948-50; partner J.H. Whitney & Co., 1951-59; financial v.p., treas., dir. Whitney Communications Corp., 1959-69; ret., 1969; ptnr. Whitcom Investment Co., 1967-69. Mem. exec. com. Yale Grad. Sch. Council, 1969-73; trustee Oberlin Coll., 1960-70. Mem. Am. Mgmt. Assn. (fin. coun. 1952-55), Gulfstream Golf Club, Gulfstream Bath and Tennis Club, Ocean Club, Ekwanok Country Club, Phi Beta Kappa. Home: 200 N Ocean Blvd Delray Beach FL 33483-7126

BRYAN, THELMA JANE, university administrator, English language educator; b. Scotland, Md., Aug. 21, 1945; d. Joseph Webster and Mary Gertrude (Holley) B.; m. David George Preston, Mar. 17, 1980; 1 child, Bryan David Preston. BA, Morgan State Coll., 1970, MA, 1975; PhD, U. Md., 1982. Instr. English Coppin State Coll., Balt., 1979-82, asst. prof., 1982-87, assoc. prof., 1987-90; prof., 1990—; chair lang., lit., journalism, and philosophy Coppin State Coll., Balt., 1987-90, dean honors divsn., 1990-98, dean Coll. Arts and Scis., 1991-98; acting assoc. vice chancellor for acad. affairs U. System of Maryland, 1998-99, assoc. vice chancellor for acad. affairs, 1999—; coun. mem. preparing future faculty Assn. Am. Colls. & Univs., Washington, 1994-97; steering com. mem. Alliance for Success, Urbana-Champaign, Ill., 1989-97; dean's com. mem. Africa-Am. Inst., N.Y.C., 1994—; scholarship com. mem. Md. Paper Box Co., Linthicum, 1984-90. Contbr. articles, poetry to profl. jours. Adv. coun. mem. campus prism Nat. Coun. Christians and Jews, Balt., 1984-85; bd. trustees Stella Maris, Inc., Towson, Md., 1996-97. Recipient Governor's Citation award State of Md., Annapolis, 1992. Mem. MLA, Am. Assn. Higher Edn., Coll. Lang. Assn., Nat. Coun. Tchrs. English, Nat. Collegiate Honors Coun., Northeast Nat. Collegiate Honors Coun. (faculty rep. 1984-95), Alpha Kappa Mu (dir. 1989-95, Outstanding Advisor award 1989, 91, Outstanding Regional Dir. award 1990-91). Democrat. Roman Catholic. Avocations: jogging, aerobic dancing, body building, reading, creative writing.

BRYANT, DENNIS MICHAEL, publisher, educator; b. Austin, Tex., June 30, 1947; s. L.D. and Mildred (Perkins) B.; m. Nancy Louthan, Apr. 17, 1976; children: Michael, Sarah. BS, Trinity U., 1970. Sales mgr. Southland Equipment Co., Houston, 1973-74; mgr., equipment specialist Briggs Weaver Co., San Antonio, 1974-81; life ins. specialist N.Y. Life Ins. Co., San Antonio, 1981-85; territorial ins. specialist Merrill Lynch Life Agy., San Antonio, 1985-86; life and group ins. mgr. Cen. Fin. Ins. Svcs., San Antonio, 1986—; owner Bryant Agy./Trinity Fin. Concepts, San Antonio, 1988-92; chmn. Focus on Growth, 1993—; chmn. Focus on Growth, Inc. Active Project Any Baby Can, San Antonio, 1983-88, pres. 1984-85. 1st lt. U.S. Army, 1971-73. Republican. Avocations: skiing, running, flying. Home: 110 Skyvue Ave New Braunfels TX 78132-4635

BRYANT, EDWARD ARNOT, geoscience educator; b. Hamilton, Ontario, Canada, Sept. 28, 1948; arrived in Australia, 1973; s. Robert Oliver and Mabel Jane (Skewes) B.; m. Dianne Charlotte Gray, June 8, 1981; children: Kate, Mark. BA, McMaster U., 1970, MS, 1972; PhD, Macquarie U., 1977. Tutor Dunmore Lane Coll, Sydney, 1975-77; postdoctoral fellow Bedford Inst. Oceanography, Halifax, N.S., 1977-78; rschr. Tech. Field Surveys, Sydney, 1978-79; univ. lectr. Wollongong (New South Wales) U., 1979—, head dept. geography, 1992-93, head sch. geoscis., 1999—. Author: Natural Hazards, 1991, Climate Process and Change, 1997. Nat. Rsch. Coun. scholar, 1970, Brit. Commonwealth scholar, 1974; grad. fellow Govt. of Ont., 1972. Mem. Am. Geophys. Union, Australian Quaternary Assn., Co. Dunmore Lane Coll. Mem. Ch. of England. Office: Sch Geoscis U Wollongong, Northfields Ave, Wollongong NSW 2522, Australia

BRYANT, JAMES MITCHELL, electronic engineer, consultant; b. Liverpool, Eng., Dec. 5, 1942; s. James Jackson and Margaret Elise (Mitchell) B.; m. Felicity Ann Roe, Aug. 26, 1964 (div. Aug. 1989); children: James Nigel, Rosemary Ann. BS in Physics, Philosophy, U. Leeds, Eng., 1964. Engr. Smiths Industries, Cheltenham, Eng., 1964-68; salesman Plessey Semiconductors, Swindon, Eng., 1968-70, integrated circuit designer, 1970-72, applications mgr., 1972-81; spl. projects mgr. Voxson Audio, Abingdon, Eng., 1981-82; head European applications Analog Devices, Newbury, Eng., 1982-99, Bath, Eng., 1999, Hasselt, Belgium, 1999—; tech. advisor ad-hoc parliamentary All-Party Citizens' Band Radio com., London, 1978-85. Contbr. articles to profl. jours. Pres. Citizens' Band Assn., Cheltenham, Eng., 1976-85. Fellow Brit. Interplanetary Soc., European Engrs.; mem. FEANI, Inst. Elec. Engrs., Radio Soc. Gt. Britain (corp. mem.), Polite Soc. (life.). Roman Catholic. Avocations: amateur radio G4CLF, hypnotism, science fiction, travel, cooking. E-mail: jbryant@iee.org. Home: Burgemeester Bollenstr 9 #2, B-3500 Hasselt Belgium

BRYANT, JAMES WILLIAM, management educator, consultant; b. Torquay, Eng., Oct. 29, 1946; s. Willie Ruberry and Ruth (Corcos) B.; m. Pauline Ann Leader, Aug. 7, 1971 (div. Sept. 1982); m. Hazel Sinfield, May 14, 1988; children: Abigail, Peter. BSc, Durham (Eng.) U., 1967; MA, Lancaster (Eng.) U., 1968, PhD, 1973; BA, Open U., Eng., 1975. Chartered engr. Operational rsch. analyst TAC Constrn. Materials, Ltd., Manchester, Eng., 1972-74; lectr. U. Sussex, Brighton, Eng., 1976-81; prin. lectr. Sheffield (Eng.) City Poly., 1981-89; prof. mgmt. Sheffield Hallam U., 1989—. Author: Problem Management, 1989; editor: Financial Modelling in Corporate Management, 1982. Mem. Brit. Computer Soc., Operational Rsch. Soc., Conflict Rsch. Soc.

BRYANT, JOHN, author, publisher; b. Washington, Oct. 26, 1943. Student, Antioch Coll., 1963; BA in Math., Am. U., 1968; postgrad. in philosophy of logic, Union Grad. Sch., Yellow Springs, Ohio, 1978-79. Founder, mgr. Socratic Press, St. Petersburg, Fla., 1986—, 701 Advt., St. Petersburg, 1986—. Author: The Mortal Works of J.B.R. Yant and Other Irritations, 1987, The Most Powerful Idea Ever Discovered, 1987, Success in Marriage Guaranteed, 1987, Bryant's Law and Other Broadsides, 1989, Systems Theory and Scientific Philosophy, 1991, Mortal Words Special Topics Series, 25 vols., 1994-97, others; creator Mortal Words Birds cartoon feature; columnist and cartoonist, Nationalist Times, 1994-98; editor, pub. Birdman's Weekly Internet Letter, 1998—; contbr. articles to profl. jours.; editor, pub. (internet) Birdman's Weekly Letter, 1998—. Founder, dir. extended family program Unitarian Soc. Germantown, Phila. Mem. Mensa. Avocations: computers, tennis, futures trading, pigeons.

BRYANT, JOHN ALLEN, biology educator, researcher, consultant; b. Croydon, Surrey, Eng., Apr. 14, 1944; s. Joseph Samuel and Beatrice Maud Patricia (Wallace-Page) B.; m. Marjorie Joan Hatch, July 27, 1968; children: Jonathan Mark, Simon James Fraser. BA with honors, Cambridge (Eng.) U., 1965, MA, 1969, PhD, 1969. Fellow Inst. Biology; Chartered Biologist; Fellow Royal Soc. Arts, Manufacture and Commerce. Rsch. fellow U. East Anglia, Norwich, Eng., 1969-70; lectr. U. Nottingham, Eng., 1970-74; lectr. U. Wales, Cardiff, 1974-77, sr. lectr., 1977-82, reader, 1982-85; prof. biology U. Exeter, Eng., 1985—; dir., chair Biotech. South West Ltd., U.K., 1988—; various consultancy/advisory activities in plant sci. and biotech. Editor, co-editor, or author of 8 books; contbr. 70 rsch. and tech. articles to profl. jours. Chair local br. Liberal Democratic Party, 1992—. Nuffield Found. sci. rsch. fellow, Cardiff, 1980-81; recipient several rsch. grants. Mem. Soc. Exptl. Biology (mem. coun. 1981-87, 92—, hon. sec. 1983-87), Biochem. Soc. (com. 1993-96), Internat. Soc. Plant Molecular Biology. Liberal Democrat. Church of England. Avocations: competitive road- and cross-country running, birdwatching, hill and mountain walking. Office: U Exeter, Dept Biological Scis, Exeter EX4 4QG, England

BRYANT, JOSEPHINE HARRIET, library executive; b. Oshawa, Ont., Can., Dec. 3, 1947; d. Donald Joseph and Margaret Mary (Quilty) B.; children: David Joseph, Michael Andrew. BA, U. Toronto, Ont., 1969, BLS, 1970, MLS, 1974; diploma in Pub. Adminstrn., U. Western Ont., London, 1988. Libr. Ont. Hydro, Toronto, 1970-74; libr. supr. Brampton (Ont.) Pub. Libr. and Art Gallery, 1974-77, branch head, 1977-79; regional dir. Fairview North York (Ont.) Pub. Libr., 1983-85, mgr. cen. libr., 1986; dep. dir. North York (Ont.) Pub. Libr., Ont., 1986-88; CEO North York (Ont.) Pub. Libr., 1988-98; city libr. Toronto Pub. Libr., Ont., Can., 1998—; co-chair faculty info. sci. fundraising com. and dean's adv. com. U. Toronto. Co-chair U. Toronto Faculty Info. Sci. Fundraising com.; mem. U. Toronto Dean's Adv. com. Mem. ALA, Can. Libr. Assn., Ont. Libr. Assn., Inst. Pub. Adminstrn., Urban Librs. Coun., Bertelsmann Found., Can. Inst. for Hist. Micro-reprodns. Avocation: golf. Office: Toronto Pub Libr, 789 Yonge St, Toronto, ON Canada M4W 2G8

BRYANT, PAUL T., electronics engineering manager; b. Washington; s. Herbert Arnold and Lucy Mae Bryant; m. Sharon Lynn Wilson; children: Matthew Paul, Andrew Paul. BS in Elec. Engring., U. Md., 1964; Program Mgmt. Cert., Def. Sys. Mgmt. Coll., 1981. Engr. Value Engring., Alexandria, Va., 1964-66; electronic design engr. White Electromagnetics Inc., Rockville, Md., 1966-68; sys. engring. dept. head Litton Industries, College Park, Md., 1968-76; electronic warfare program mgr. Naval Electronic Sys. Command, Washington, 1976-84; advanced concepts sect. head Naval Rsch. Lab., Washington, 1984-91; engring. sect. head NASA, Greenbelt, Md., 1991-97, engring. br. head, 1997—. Patentee in field. Chmn. Bowie Postal Customer Adv. Coun., Md., 1994-98; bd. mem. Takoma Park Cmty. Svc. Ctr., Md., 1994-98. Recipient letter of appreciation U.S. Postal Svc., 1994, Joint Spl. Ops. Com., 1988. Home: 16306 Alderwood Ln Bowie MD 20716-1511 Office: NASA-Goddard Space Flight Ctr Code 565 Greenbelt MD 20771-0001

BRYANT, RICHARD TODD, lawyer; b. Kansas City, Mo., Sept. 3, 1952; s. Francis Todd and Marion Audrey (Weum) B.; m. Carol H. Olsen, Mar. 24, 1979. A.A., Longview Community Coll., 1972, A.A.S., 1972; B.B.A., U. Mo.-Kansas City, 1974, M.P.A., 1975, J.D., 1978. Bar: Mo. 1978, D.C. 1995, U.S. Dist. Ct. (we. dist.) Mo. 1978, D.C. 1995, U.S. Dist. Ct. (ea. dist.) Mo. 1995, Kans. 1996, Territorial Ct. of the Virgin Islands 1999. Assoc. Harding & Copilevitz P.C., Kansas City, Mo., 1978-85; ptnr. Copilevitz, Bryant, Gray & Jennings, P.C., Kansas City, 1985-95; bailiff ct. Overland Park, Kans., 1974-84; ptnr. Richard T. Bryant & Assocs. PC, Kansas City, 1995-98, mng. shareholder, 1998—. Contbr. articles to legal jours. cons. Westwood & Lenexa (Kans.) Police Dept., 1977-78; adminstrv. hearing officer Housing Authority of Kansas City, 1988—; chmn. ad hoc com. Kansas City (Mo.) City Coun., 1992. Mem. ABA (liaison standing com. assn. standards criminal justice 1978, com. adminstrn. criminal justice 1977-78), Am. Arbitration Assn. (bd. of arbitrators, bd. of mediators), Kansas City (Mo.) Bar Assn. (mcpl. ct. com., vice chmn. 1991-94, chmn. 1994-95), First Amendment Lawyers Assn., Phi Delta Phi, Omicron Delta Kappa, Phi Theta Kappa. Office: 804 Bryant Bldg 1102 Grand Blvd Kansas City MO 64106-2316

BRYANT, ROBERT JOHN, consultant; b. Chingford, Essex, U.K., Oct. 22, 1948; s. Robert John and Patricia Kathleen (Robertson) B.; m. Michelle Francoise Dupas, Aug. 31, 1970; children: Johann, Susie Natasha (dec. Nov. 1998), Melissa. BA in Natural Scis. with honors, Cambridge U., 1971, MA, PhD, 1974. Postdoctoral asst. U. Heidelberg, Fed. Republic Germany, 1974-75, Ecole Superieure de Chimie Industrielle de Lyon, Lyon, France, 1975-76, Univ. Coll., North Wales, U.K., 1976-78; sr. scientist Sterling Organics, Fawdon, U.K., 1978-84; tech. mgr. Orsynetics Ltd., Consett, U.K., 1984-86; head of R & D Macfarlan Smith (Glaxo Group), Edinburgh, Scotland, 1986-88; ind. cons. fine chems. Edinburgh, 1988; sr. cons. Chem Systems Ltd., London, 1988-91; prin. Chem. Sys. Ltd., London, 1991-92, Brychem, 1992—, Agranova, 1998—. Patentee for Aromatic Chemistry. Henry Hawkins scholar Peterhouse, Cambridge, 1971; Deutsche Akadmeische Austauch Dienst scholar Coun. of Europe, Heidelberg, 1974. Mem. Royal Soc. Chemists, Soc. Chem. Industry, Am. Chem. Soc.

BRYANT, ROLAND WARWICK, dentist, educator; b. Sydney, NSW, Australia, Mar. 2, 1944; m. Moira Leonie Fisher, 1970. BDS, U. Sydney, 1966, MDS, 1969, PhD, 1983. Pvt. practice London, 1969-70; lectr. U. Birmingham, Eng., 1971-74; from lectr. to assoc. prof. U. Sydney, Australia, 1974-92; prof. U. Sydney, 1992—; pvt. practice, Sydney, 1974—. Contbr. articles to dental jours. Fellow Royal Australian Coll. Dental Surgeons. Fellow Internat. Coll. Dentists, Pierre Fauchard Acad.; mem. Internat. Assn. Dental Rsch., Soc. Endodontology, Prosthodontic Soc., Australian Dental Assn. Office: Westmead Hosp Dental Sch, Westmead 2145, Australia

BRYANT, STEWART JAMES, pathologist; b. Maryborough, Queensland, Australia, June 3, 1939; s. James Dudley and Jean McVittee (Cunningham) B.; m. Lynette June Maskell, Sept. 7, 1963; children: Peter, Jonathan, Nicholas. MB, BS, Univ. Queensland, Brisbane, 1963. Intern Royal Brisbane Hosp., 1963-64, pathology registrar, 1965-69, chem. pathologist, 1970-72, dir. chem. pathology, 1973-82, dir. pathology svcs., 1982—, 1992-95; gen. mgr. Southpath St. George Hosp., Australia, 1995-99; dir. pathology svcs. So. Cross Pathology Monash Med. Ctr., Clayton, Australia, 1999—; assoc. mem. commn. on quantities and units Internat. Union of Pure and Applied Chemistry., London, 1989—; del. commn. on world standards World Assn. Societies of Pathology., Northfield, Ill., 1990—. Contbr. articles to profl. jours. Fellow Royal Coll. Pathologists Australasia (bd. censors 1978-85, chmn. quality assurance and sci. edn. com. 1988—, rsch. grantee 1979); mem. Australian Assn. Clin. Biochemists, Am. Assn. Clin. Chemistry, Coll. Am. Pathologists (assoc.), Tattersal's Club, Untied Svcs. Club. Avocations: sailing, farming. Home: Hill-Side Smalls Rd, Highvale, Queensland 4520, Australia Office: So Cross Pathology, Monash Med Ctr, Clayton VIC 3168, Australia

BRYANT, TIMOTHY CLARK, investment brokerage executive; b. Akron, Ohio, Apr. 11, 1943; s. Alan Willard and Clara Sherman (Clark) B.; m. Mary Esther Snell, Jan. 17, 1981. AB, Dartmouth Coll., 1967; MBA, U. Chgo., 1971; MS in Taxation, DePaul U., 1975. CPA, Ill. Dir. fin. and adminstrn. Fibre Box Assn., Chgo., 1975-77, Akers Packaging Co., Middletown, Ohio, 1977-78; dir., sec., treas. CompuShop, Inc., Dallas, 1978-80, dir., 1980-85; v.p. fin., dir. Rubicon Corp., Richardson, Tex., 1980-82, Automated Mgmt. Inc., Dallas, 1982-83; v.p. fin., dir. Avian Corp., Clearwater, Fla., 1983-85, pres., bd. dirs., 1985-87; v.p. investments A.G. Edwards and Sons, 1990—; chmn. bd. dirs. Adventures Away, Inc., Chgo., 1983-87; pres., treas., bd. dirs. Talk2 Corp., Clearwater, 1987-90; cons. Nevada Brake Corp., 1985-91, So. Conf. Bur., Inc., 1987-90, Innovative Products Group, Inc., 1987-90. With U.S. Army, 1965-66, Korea. Mem. AICPA, Chgo. Yacht Club, Vinoy Club. Home: 307 Brightwaters Blvd NE Saint Petersburg FL 33704-3709 Office: A G Edwards & Sons 3170 3rd Ave N Saint Petersburg FL 33713-7684

BRYANTSEV, ALEKSANDR MIKHAYLOVICH, energy plant executive, educator; b. Kondopoga, Karelia, Russia, June 13, 1951; s. Mikhail Grigorievich Bryantsev and Nina Georgievna Donskikh; m. Lioudmila Gennadievna Titova, Aug. 28, 1971; children: Natalia, Mikhail, Maria. MSc, Alma-Ata (Kazakhstan) Poly., 1973; Postgrad. Diploma, Alma-Ata Power Inst., 1978, DTechScis, 1992. Cert. in engring. splty. electric machines. Prorector for sci. work, dean, docent, prof., chair dept. Alma-Ata Power Inst., 1973-93; dep. chief engr. Moscow Electrotech Plang, 1993-95; prof., chair electromechanics Moscow Power Inst., Smolensk, 1997—; vice gen. dir. Energia Electrotech. Plant, Ramenskoe, Moscow, 1997—; cons. magnetic-flux-controlled electric shunt reactors Alma-Ata Power Inst., 1980-93, All-Russian Elec. Engring. Inst., Toliatty, 1995—; cons. devel. and preparation of elec. reactor mfg. facilities Moscow Electrotech Plant, 1993-95; postgrad. referee, chmn. State Exam. Com., Moscow Electromechanics Inst. Contbr. numerous articles to profl. jours.; patentee in field. Dep., Alma-Ata City Coun., 1990-93. Laureate, Kazakhstan Nat. Econ. Achievements Exhbn., 1976, USSR Nat. Econ. Achievements Exhbn., 1991; recipient award Energia Electrotech. Plant, Ramenskoe, 1998. Mem. Acad. Elec. Scis. of Russia, N.Y. Acad. Scis., United Energy Sys. Russia. Avocation: mountaineering. E-mail: ambryantsev@cerc-reactors.com. Home: House 38 Flat 10, Chougunov St, 140105 Ramenskoye, Moscow Russia Office: Ramensky Electrotech Plant, Levasheva Str House 21, 140106 Ramenskoye, Moscow Russia

BRYCE, WILLIAM DELF, lawyer; b. Georgetown, Tex., Aug. 7, 1932; s. D. A. Bryce and Frances Maxine (Wilson) Bryce Bakke; m. Sarah Alice Riley, Dec. 20, 1954; children: Douglas Delf, David Dickson. BA, U. Tex., 1955; LLB, Yale U., 1960. Bar: Tex. 1960, U.S. Dist. Ct. (we. dist.) Tex. 1963, U.S. Ct. Claims 1964, U.S. Supreme Ct. 1971. Briefing atty. Tex. Supreme Ct., Austin, 1960-61; sole practice, 1961—; lectr. U. Tex., 1965-66. Editor Tex. Supreme Ct. Jour. Served to 1st lt. USAF, 1955-57. Fellow Tex. Bar Found. (sustaning, life); mem. ABA, Travis County Bar Assn., Williamson County Bar Assn., State Bar Tex., Rotary Internat. (dist. 5870 gov. 1999-2000), Headliners Club (Austin), The Argyle (San Antonio). Home: 308 E University Ave Georgetown TX 78626-6813 also: 511 S Main St Georgetown TX 78626-5609

BRYDEN, HOWARD DESMOND, computer system and database administrator; b. Brisbane, Australia, Oct. 17, 1957; s. Harold Desmond and Elizabeth Dyer (Scott) B. BS, U. Queensland, Brisbane, 1977, BS (hon.), 1979, Diploma in Computer Sci., 1987. Geologist Mt. Isa Mines, Queensland, Australia, 1980; programmer Mt. Isa Mines, Brisbane, 1981-83; pvt. contract programmer Australia, 1985-87; computer adminstr. Comalco, Weipa, Australia, 1988—. Mem. IEEE, Australian Computer Soc., Assn. Computing Machinery. Avocation: golf. Office: Comalco Minerals & Alumina, Prodn Bldg, Weipa Queensland 4874, Australia

BRYDEN, WILLIAM DONALD, JR., manufacturing executive, retired military officer; b. Phila., May 6, 1935; s. William Donald and Georgia Elizabeth (Sherry) B.; m. Mary Lou Pursell, Aug. 5, 1959; children: Donald Christopher, William Scott. BS in Metull. Engring., U. Pa., 1962. Cert. Master Navigator, USAF. Commd. 2d lt. USAF, 1959, advanced through grades to lt. col., 1977, ret., 1985; instr. navigator USAF, James Connally AFB, Tex., 1962-65; chief materials tech. Space and Missiles Systems USAF, L.A., 1966-69; weapons system officer 18th spl. ops. squadron USAF, Udorn, Thailand, 1970-71; chief navigator, flight test wing USAF, Wright Patterson, Ohio, 1971-74; chief engr. A-10 flight test program USAF, Edwards AFB, Calif., 1974-78; dir. test policy USAF, Andrews AFB, Md., 1978-81; comdr. Ascension Aux Air Field USAF, Ascension Island, 1981-83; dep. program mgr. data system modernization USAF, Sunnyvale, Calif., 1983-85; mgr., FAA Tower Systems IBM Advanced Automation Systems, Rockville, Md., 1985-96, Lockheed Martin Internat. Air Traffic Mgmt., London and Swanwick, Eng., 1997-2000. Bd. dirs. Signal Hill Home Assn., Burke, Va., 1979-81, Flints Grove Homeowners' Assn., North Potomac, Md., 1986-90; mem. KWV, Ascension Island, 1981-83; instr. U.S. Power Squadron, Rockville, Md., 1988-98. Decorated Air medal with one silver, three bronze clusters, DFC, Legion of Merit. Mem. Air Force Assn., Met. Stained Glass Assn. (pres.). Republican. Episcopalian. Avocations: boating, model railroads, stained and etched glass, woodworking. Office: Lockheed Martin Air Traffic 9210 Corporate Blvd Rockville MD 20850-4608 also: 805 Gull Point Rd Wilmington NC 28405-5264

BRYDON, DONALD HOOD, investment management executive; b. May 25, 1945; s. James Hood and Mary Duncanson (Young) B.; children: Fiona, Angus. Degree in Math. Sci., U. Edinburgh, 1970. Dep. mng. dir. Barclays Investment Mgrs., London, 1981-86; dir. BZW Investment Mgmt., London, 1986-88, mng. dir., 1988-91, chief exec., 1991-94, chmn., 1994-95; dep. chief exec. BZW Holdings, London, 1994-96; bd. dirs. London Stock Exch., 1991-98, Edinburgh Inca Trust PLC, 1995—; chmn., chief exec. AXA Investment Mgrs. S.A., 1997—; dir. Allied Domecq, Nycomed Amersham, Sun Life and Provincial; v.p. Nat. Assn. Pension Funds, 1988-91; chmn. Inst. Shareholders Com., 1988-91, FT-SE Actuaries FTSE Indices Steering com., 1992-94. Co-author: Economics of Technical Information Services, 1977. Recipient OBE award, 1993. Mem. Fund Mgrs. Assn. (chmn. 1999—), European Asset Mgmt. Assn. (pres. 1999—).

BRYE, GARY MELVIN, chief of police, personnel consultant; b. Concord, Calif., Nov. 10, 1958; s. Trygve Martinez and Claire (Johnson) B. BA, Tex. A&M U., 1980; MS, Sam Houston State U., 1991. Cert. Master Police Officer, Tex. Commn. Law Enforcement Officer Stds. and Edn. Police officer Tex. A&M U., College Station, 1980, City of West Univeristy Place, Houston, 1980-81; sgt. to cpl. City of West Univeristy Place Police Dept., Houston, 1981-94, capt. to lt., 1994-98, chief of police, 1998-99; chief of police Memorial Villages Police Dept., Houston, 1999—; pers. cons. Brye & Ure Consulting Group, Stafford, Tex., 1994-99. Com. mem. Houston Livestock Show & Rodeo, 1996, com. capt., 1997-98, com. vice chmn., 1999; mem. Harris County Area Chiefs of Police, 1996—; active Tex. Spl. Olympics, Houston, 1989-91. Mem. Gtr. Southwest Houston C. of C. (chmn. crime prevention com. 1998). Avocations: hunting, building, cycling, archery, horses. E-mail: mvpd@wt.net. Home: 12419 Fern Meadow Dr Stafford TX 77477-2214 Office: Memorial Villages Police Dept 11981 Memorial Dr Houston TX 77024-6231

BRYER, ANTHONY APPLEMORE MORNINGTON, Byzantine studies educator; b. Southsea, Eng., Oct. 31, 1937; s. Gerald Mornington and Joan Evelyn (Grigsby) B.; m. Elizabeth Lipscomb, Aug. 2, 1961 (dec. Dec. 1995); children: Theodora Jane, Anna Caroline, Sarah Katherine; m. Jennifer Ann Banks, July 11, 1998. Diploma, Sorbonne U., Paris, 1955; MA, Balliol Coll., Oxford, Eng., 1967, DPhil, 1967. Rsch. fellow Athens U., Greece, 1962-63; rsch. fellow to prof., dir. Ctr. Byzantine, Ottoman & Greek U. Birmingham, Eng., 1964-93, prof. Byzantine studies, 1980-99, emeritus, 1999—, pub. orator, 1991—; vis. fellow Dumbarton Oaks, Harvard U., 1969—; vis. Byzantinist, Medieval Acad. Am., 1987; Wiles lectr. Queen's U., Belfast; vis. lectr. Australian Nat. U., 1989; chmn. Brit. Nat. Com. of Internat. Byzantine Assn., 1988-95. Author books on Byzantine studies; contbr. articles to profl. jours. Served with Royal Air Force, 1955-58. Fellow Soc. Antiquaries, Royal Hist. Soc. Avocations: travel, cooking. Home: 33 Crosbie Rd, Harborne, Birmingham B17 9BG, England Office: U Birmingham, Ctr Byzantine Ottoman Greek, Birmingham B15 2TT, England

BRYKNAR, ZDENEK, physics educator; b. Roskopov, Czech Republic, Mar. 11, 1944; s. Josef and Marie (Podzimkova) B.; m. Ladislava Lauerova, June 23, 1967; children: Natalie, Pavlina. MS in Solid State Physics, Czech Tech. U., 1967, PhD in Exptl. Physics, 1976. Rschr. Inst. of Comm. Technology, Prague, 1967-68; tchg. asst. Czech Tech. U., Prague, 1968-71, asst. prof., 1971-90, assoc. prof., 1990—; mem. scientific coun. Inst. of Physics of Czech Acad. of Scis., Prague, 1996—, nat. Optical Lab., Prague, 1994—, faculty senate, Czech Tech. U., 1990-91; mem. editl. bd. Fine Mechanics and Optics, 1993—; guest investigator U. Stuttgart, Germany, 1978, U. Giessen, Germany, 1990; vis. prof. Fritz-Haber Inst. of Max Planck Soc., Berlin, 1993, 95, 96. Author: (textbook) Physics of Dielectrics, 1983 (award of Chancellor 1984); co-author: (book) New Materials, 1991; inventor in field; contbr. articles to profl. jours. Fellow Assn. of Czech Mathematicians and Physicists, Czech Spectroscopic Soc.; mem. SPIE. Avocations: skiing, basketball, lit., woodworking. Office: Czech Tech Univ, V Holesovickach 2, CZ-18000 Prague 8, Czech Republic

BRYLD, CLAUS, modern history educator; b. Frederiksberg, Copenhagen, Denmark, May 29, 1940; s. Børge Michael Bering and Alice Elisabeth (Sidney-Møller) B.; m. Tine Begtrup, Oct. 11, 1961 (div. 1971); m. Clara Elisabet Thaning, May 27, 1972; children: Esben, Lea, Cecilie, Alice, Clara. PhD, U. Copenhagen, 1969; Dr.Habil, U. Roskilde, Denmark, 1993. Sr. fellow U. Copenhagen, 1972-73; lectr. U. Roskilde, 1973-88, docent, 1988-95, prof. modern history, 1995—; external examiner U. Denmark Sys., 1974—; reviewer Daily INfo., 1995—. Author: The Emergence of Democratic Socialism in Denmark, 1884-1916, 1992, (autobiography) Which Liberation, an Account From A Childhood in the Shadow of Nazism and the Judicial Purge, 1995, (with Anetta Warring) The Period of Occupation as Collective Memory, 1998. Home: Frederiksberg Allé 47, 1820 Frederiksberg Denmark Office: Roskilde U Ctr Inst. Hist, Samfundsforhold Postbox 260, 4000 Roskilde Denmark

BRYNER, PETER, chiropractor; b. Auckland, New Zealand, Dec. 16, 1955; arrived in Australia, 1976; s. Hans Jakob and Hedi Heidi (Schaufelberger) B.; m. Janice Helen Bryner, Sept. 1, 1978. BS in Applied Sci., Chiropractic Phillip Inst., 1981; grad. diploma, RMIT, 1991, M in Chiropractic Sci., 1999. Pvt. practice Upwey Chiropractic Ctr., Melbourne, Australia, 1981-85, Causeway Chiropractic Ctr., Perth, Australia, 1994-98, Burswood Health Profls., Perth, Australia, 1998—; lectr. Phillip Inst., RMIT, Melbourne, 1982-94; convenor sect. meeting Assn. for History of Chiropractic Internat. Chiropractic Congress, 1988. Editor: Chiropr Assoc Web Page; mem. editl. bd. Jour. Chiropractic Technique, Chiropractic Jour. Australia. Grantee ASRF, 1994, 89. Mem. Australian Spinal Rsch. Found. (mem. rsch. com.), Australian Pain Soc., Internat. Assn. for Study of Pain. Avocations: tennis, skiing, research. Office: Burswood Health Profls, 21 Harvey St, Burswood Perth 6100 WA, Australia

BRYNJOLFSSON, ERIK, management educator, researcher; b. Roskilde, Denmark, Apr. 14, 1962; m. Martha Pavlakis. AB, Harvard U., 1984, SM, 1984; PhD, MIT, 1991. Ptnr., co. founder Foundation Technologies, Cambridge, Mass., 1986-90; instr. Harvard U.; asst. prof. MIT Sloan Sch., Cambridge, Mass., 1990-95, assoc. prof., Douglas Drane chair, 1995—; vis. prof. Stanford (Calif.) U., 1996-98. Contbr. numerous articles to profl. jours. Office: MIT Sloan Sch 50 Memorial Dr Rm E53-313 Cambridge MA 02142-1347

BRYSKIER, ANDRÉ JULIEN, physician, microbiologist; b. Paris, Dec. 10, 1947; s. Boleslas Bryskier and Helen Szymanska; m. Marie-Therese A. Labro, Feb. 24, 1978; children: Marie-Isabelle, Jean-Marie. MD, Faculty Medicine, Paris, 1974. Asst. in parasitology U. Paris XI, 1971-74; asst. prof. U. Paris VI, Paris, 1974-78; dep. clin. microbiology labs. Versailles hosp., 1978-79; head clin. microbiol. lab. Hosp. Charleville-Mézières, Paris, 1979-81; cons. Hosp., Argenteuil, 1982—; med. advisor Roussel-UCLAF, Paris, 1981-83, internat. med. project leader, 1983-85, med. dir., 1985-90, head clin. rsch., 1990-92, head clin. pharmacology anti-infectives, 1992—. Editor four books in field; contbr. articles to profl. publs. Mem. Brit. Soc. Antimicrobial Chemotherapy, Japan Soc. Chemotherapy, French Soc. Microbiology, Am. Soc. Microbiology, Paul Ehrlich für Chemotherapy, Infectious Disease Soc. Am., N.Y. Acad. Sci. Office: 102 Rt de Noisy, 93230 Romainville France

BRYSON, NIGEL ROBERT, veterinarian, researcher; b. Chatham, Kent, Eng., Sept. 3, 1950; s. Robert Walker and Honor (Bridges) B.; m. Janine Carol Bryce, Dec. 21, 1985; children: Mark, Danielle. BSc, Natal U., Pietermaritzburg, South Africa, 1972; BSc with honors, Rhodes U., Grahamstown, South Africa, 1975; BVSc, Pretoria U., 1981, MMedVet in Parasitology, 2000. Asst. Tick Rsch. Unit, Grahamstown, 1975-76; asst. various vet. pvt. practices in South Africa, 1981-82, vet. locum, 1983-84, 85-99; sr. lectr. Med. U. So. Africa, 1999—; sr. lectr. vet. tropical diseases U. Pretoria. Contbr. articles to profl. jours. including South African Jour. Vet. Rsch., Vet. Record. Mem. South African Vet. Assn., Parasitol. Soc. South Africa. Mem. Democratic Party. Avocations: trout fishing, bird watching. Home: 12 Rubida St, Lynnwood Ridge, Pretoria Gauteng 0081, South Africa Office: U Pretoria/Dept Vet Dis, Fac Vet Sci, Pretoria Gauteng 0110, South Africa

BRYSON, VERN ELRICK, nuclear engineer; b. Woodruff, Utah, May 28, 1920; s. David Hyrum and Luella May (Eastman) B.; m. Esther Sybil de St Jeor, Oct. 14, 1942; children: Britt William, Forrest Lee, Craig Lewis, Nadine, Elaine. Commd. 2d lt. USAAF, 1941; advanced through grades to lt. col. USAF, 1960, ret., 1961; pilot, safety engr., civil engr., electronic engr., nuclear engr., chief Aeronaut. Systems div., Aircraft Nuclear Propulsion Program, Wright-Patterson AFB, Ohio, 1960-61; chief Radiation Effects Lab., also chief Radiation Effects Group Boeing Airplane Co., Seattle, 1961-65; nuclear engr. Aerospace Corp., San Bernardino, Calif., 1965-68; service engr., also head instrumentation lab., Sacramento Air Logistic Ctr. USAF, McClellan AFB, Calif., 1968-77; owner, mgr. Sylvern Valley Ranch, Calif., 1977—; Mem. panel Transient Radiation Effects on Electronics, Weapon Effects Bd., 1959-61. Contbr. research articles on radiation problems to profl. pubs. Decorated D.F.C. with oak leaf cluster, Air medal with 12 oak leaf clusters. Mem. IEEE. Mem. Ch. Jesus Christ of Latter-day Saints. Home: 1426 Caperton Ct Penryn CA 95663-9515

BRZOSKO, WITOLD JOZEF, physician, medical educator, researcher, scientist; b. Warsaw, Poland, May 16, 1929; s. Roch and Katarzyna (Kruszewska) B.; m. Hanna Maria Siedlanowska, July 17, 1952; children: Magdalena, Katarzyna. MD, Acad. Warsaw, 1952, PhD, 1959. Asst. prof. Med. Acad. Warsaw, 1952-59, prof., 1975-83; assoc. prof. State Inst. Hygiene, Warsaw, 1963-73, prof., 1973-75; prof. Communicable Disease Hosp., Warsaw, 1985-90; dir. Centuria and Beluland Ltd. Cos., 1990-94, Centuria and Tymoform Ltd. Cos., 1994—. Contbr. articles to profl. jours.; patentee prodn. of hepatitis B vaccine. Mem. Polish Immunology Soc., N.Y. Acad. Scis., Polish Pathology Soc. E-mail: biuro@tymofarm.pl. Office: Tymofarm, Willowa 8/10, 00-790 Warsaw Poland

BRZOZOWSKA-RYCZER, MALGORZATA, management consultant; b. Olsztyn, Poland, June 1, 1967; d. Czeslaw Zbigniew Brzozowski and Józefa Czaja; m. Jerzy Wojciech Ryczer, Oct. 11, 1997; 1 child, Wojciech Aleksander. MA in Applied LInguistics, U. Warsaw, Poland, 1992; diploma in mktg. & mgmt., Main Sch. Commerce, Warsaw, 1997. Bus. analyst Co. Assitance, Warsaw, 1991-92; cons. Co. Asstistance Ltd., Chem. Bank, Warsaw, London, N.Y.C., 1993-95; project mgr. CAL Co. Assistance, Warsaw, 1996-99, dir. strategic reports & market studies, 1999-2000; dir. Internet Info. Svc., 2000; dir. E-commerce Easy Net S.A., 2000—. Editor: Industry Overviews, 1992-94; contbr. articles to profl. jours. Roman Catholic. Avocations: languages, psychology, skiing, tennis. Fax: 48-22-633-1706. Office: ul Panska 77/79, 00-834 Warsaw Poland

BRZOZOWSKI, KENNETH CHARLES, artist, artistic studio executive; b. Amsterdam, N.Y., Feb. 11, 1959; s. Charles H. and Maryellen Cooper Brzozowski; m. Kathleen Mary Vanselow, Dec. 16, 1960; children: Dylan C., Frances Judy. Pres. VectorTech Inc., Brant Lake, N.Y., 1989—; v.p. Scenic Outlook Studios Inc., Riparius, N.Y., 1994—. Office: Scenic Outlook Studios Inc 440 Riverside Station Riparius NY 12862

BUADU, LAWRENCE DANSO, physician, researcher; b. Accra, Ghana, July 2, 1963; s. Albert Addo and Grace Dumaa (Appiah) B.; m. Annemarie Adwoa, Amoa-Forson, Jan. 2, 1993; 1 child, Adwoa Adumea. MB ChB, U. Ghana Med. Sch., 1992; PhD, Kyushu U., 1997. With nat. svc. personnel Cmty. Improvement Unit, Accra, 1983-84; house officer Korle-Bu Tchg. Hosp., Accra, 1992-93; rsch. fellow Kyushu U., Fukuoka, Japan, 1994-97; resident physician dept. gen. surgery Mich. State U., Kalamazoo, 1997-98; resident physician dept. radiology U. Rochester (N.Y.) Med. Ctr., 1998—; presenter in field. Contbr. articles to profl. jours. Mem. Fukuoka Internat. Ch., 1996, Kyushu U. Fgn. Students Assn., 1994. Rsch. fellowship grant Ministry of Edn., 1993. Mem. AAAS, Radiol. Soc. of N.Am., Japanese Breast Cancer Soc. Avocations: jazz music collector, swimming, badminton, walking. Office: U Rochester Med Ctr Dept Radiology 601 Elmwood Ave Rochester NY 14642-0001

BUALLAY, JASSIM MUHAMMAD, Bahrain diplomat; b. Muharraq, Bahrain, 1942; m. Safiya Buallay, 1969; 4 children. BBA, Am. U. Beirut, Lebanon, 1963. Supt. bursaries and UNESCO sects. Min. Edn., 1961-70; program specialist divsn. higher edn. UNESCO, Paris, 1970-74; 1st sec. Min. Fgn. Affairs, Bahrain, 1974-75; chargè d'affaires Bahrainian Embassy, France, 1975-76; amb. of Bahrain to France Bahrain, 1976-79; dir. econ. affairs directorate Min. Fgn. Affairs, Manama, Bahrain, 1979-87; amb. to Tunisia Govt. of Bahrain, 1987-94; permanent rep. of Bahrain UN, N.Y.C., 1994—. Bd. dirs. UNICEF, 1983-85. Decorated Nat. Order Merit, France, Alawite First Degree, Morocco, Republic First Degree, Tunisia. Mem. Chaine des Rotisseurs (Bailli d'Honneur), Alumni Club, Tennis Club (Tunis). Avocations: music, theatre, tennis, swimming. Office: Permanent Mission Bahrain to UN 866 2d Ave 14th-15th Fls New York NY 10017-4403*

BUANES, TROND ARNULF, surgeon, researcher; b. Drammen, Norway, July 28, 1950; s. Alf and Marit (Wengaard) B.; m. Tove Soerensen, June 30, 1973; children: Marita, David. MD, U. Oslo, 1975; PhD, 1988. Pvt. practice, 1975-83, specialist, gen. surgery, 1983-92; specialist, gastroent. surgery Ulleval Hosp., Oslo, 1992—; prof. surgery, 1998—; cons., 1990—; head of dept., 1993—. Office: Surgical Dept, Ulleval Hosp, N 0407 Oslo Norway

BUBÁN, TAMÁS, horticultural engineer, researcher; b. Nyiregyháza, Hungary, Aug. 2, 1938; s. József and Józsefné Erzsébet (Erdei) B.; m. Tamásné Irén Tatár, Aug. 7, 1963 (div. Feb. 1988); children: Tamás, Andrea; m. Ágota Princzinger, Apr. 7, 1990. Degree in Hort. Engring., U. Horticulture, Budapest, 1960; PhD, Hungarian Acad. Sci., Budapest, 1977, DSc, 1992. Asst. rsch. worker Rsch. Sta. for Fruitgrowing, Ujfehértó, Hungary, 1960-63, rsch. fellow, 1964-77, sr. rsch. fellow, 1978-91, sci. counsellor, 1992—; titular prof. hort. Coll. of the Gödöllö, U. Agrl. Scis., Nyiregyháza, Hungary, 1993—. Author: Chemical Treatments to Ensure Regular Bearing in Fruit Trees, 1979; co-author: Floral Biology of Fruit Trees and Small Fruits, 1996, Handbook for the Integrated Apple Production, 1995; co-inventor in field. Recipient Honor for sci., Coun. of Province Szabolcs-Szatmár-Bereg, 1995. Mem. Internat. Soc. Hort. Scis., Hungarian Acad. Scis. (mem. hort. com. 1993—, mem. regional com. 1992—). Avocations: photography, literature. Home: 1/8, Szántó Kovács J 20, H-4400 Nyiregyháza Hungary Office: Rsch Exten Ctr Fruitgrowing, Vadastag 2, H-4244 Ujfehértó Hungary

BUBENÍK, JAN, cancer researcher, biology educator; b. Brno, Czech Republic, Apr. 23, 1940; s. Jan and Terezie (Klimentová) B.; m. Dana Wustingerová, Mar. 24, 1976. MD, Charles U., Prague, Czechoslovakia, 1962; PhD, Acad. Scis., Prague, 1965, DSc, 1973. Sr. investigator Acad. Scis., Prague, 1965-72, chief dept., 1972—; dep. dir. Inst. Molecular Genetics, Prague, 1990—; assoc. prof. Charles U., 1992-95, Komenius U., Bratislava, Slovakia, 1993—; vis. scientist Stockholm U., 1969-70, Cancer Ctr., Houston, 1992-93; vis. prof. Fibiger Inst., Copenhagen, 1985, 92; prof. cellular and molecular biology, Charles U., 1995—. Contbr. over 180 articles to sci. jours.; mem. editl. bd. Internat. Jour. Oncology, Neoplasma, Gene Therapy, Jour. Cancer Rsch. and Clin. Oncology, Microbiologica, Jour. Exptl. and Clin. Cancer Rsch., others. Recipient State prize in medicine Czechoslovakia, 1985, Yamagiwa-Yoshida award Internat. Union Against Cancer, 1991, E. Nuti prize for cancer rsch. Assn. Promozione Study Immunology of Tumor, Rome, 1992. Mem. European Cytokine Soc., Internat. Endotoxin Soc. (charter mem.), N.Y. Acad. Scis., European Assn. for Cancer Rsch. (exec. com. mem.). Roman Catholic. Avocations: sport fishing, scuba diving. Office: Czech Acad Sci, Flemingovo nám 2, 166 37 Prague 6, Czech Republic

BUBLIKOV, IGOR ALBERTOVICH, engineering educator; b. Sakmara, Russia, Jan. 9, 1959; s. Albert Ivanovich and Nina Fedorovna (Zaharova) B.; m. Larisa Koravai, June 4, 1988; two children. Degree in engring., Novocherkask Poly. Inst., 1982; MSc, Moscow Energy Inst., 1991. Engr. Vniam, Volgodonsk, Russia, 1982-83, Ignalinskay NPS, Snechkus, Lithuania, 1983-84; tchr. Novocherkassk Tech. U., Voldogonsk, 1984-96, mgr., chair dept., 1996—. Mem. Euro-Asian Phys. Soc., N.Y. Acad. Scis. Avocations: literature, horticulture. Office: Novocherkassk Tech U, 73 Lenina St, 347340 Voldogonsk Russia

BUBNICKI, ZDZISLAW, computer science and engineering educator; b. Lvov, Poland, June 17, 1938; s. Franciszek and Stefania Bubnicki. MSc, Silesian Tech. U., Gliwice, Poland, 1960; PhD, Wroclaw (Poland) U. Tech., 1964, DSc, 1967. Asst. prof. control and systems engring. Wroclaw U. Tech., 1960-68, assoc. prof. control and systems engring., 1968-73, full prof. control and systems engring., 1973—; dir. Inst. Control and Systems Engring., Wroclaw, 1981—; pres. Wroclaw br. Polish Acad. Scis., 1991—, chmn. scientific coun. of Systems Rsch. Inst., 1989—, pres. automation com., 1988—; mem. Gen. Assembly of Internat. Fedn. for Info. Processing, 1988—; chmn. Internat. Confs. on Systems Sci., Wroclaw, 1973—. Author: Divergence of Approximation Processes in Discrete Systems, 1966, Identification of Control Plants, 1980, Introduction to Expert Systems, 1990, Foundations of Management Information Systems, 1993; editor-in-chief (internat. jour.) Systems Sci., 1975—. Recipient award for Outstanding Scientific Achievements, Ministry Rsch. and High Edn., Poland, 1992; recipient Silver Core award Internat. Fedn. Info. Processing, 1998. Mem. N.Y. Acad. Scis., 1999—. Office: Inst Control and Sys Eng, Wyspianskiego 27, 50-370 Wroclaw Poland

BUBNOV, SERGEY IGOREVICH, financial analyst; s. Igor Dmitrievich and Alla Evseevna (Mogilevskaya) B. Diploma, Inst. Internat. Rels., Moscow, 1989; MA, U. Chgo., 1992, MBA, 1994. From assoc. to v.p. CS First Boston/Credit Suisse First Boston, 1994-99; assoc. European Bank Reconstrn. & Devel., 1999-2000; v.p. Merrill Lynch, Pierce, Fenner & Smith Ltd., 2000—.

BUC, HENRI CHRISTOPHE, molecular biologist; b. Paris, Nov. 20, 1934; s. Charles E. and Marie Henriette (Depoux) B.; m. Marie Helene Caron; children: Philippe, Guillaume. Engr., ESPCI, Paris, 1957; PhD, U. Paris, 1965. Engr. ESPCI, Paris, 1953-57; rsch. assoc. CNRS, Paris, 1957-67, dir. rsch., 1967—; Fulbright fellow Harvard U., Cambridge, Mass., 1963-65, vis. scientist, 1980-81; head of unit Inst. Pasteur, Paris, 1971—, prof., 1986—; chmn. sci. adv. com. EMBL, 1980-94. Contbr. articles to profl. jours. Recipient Prize A. Lacassagne, Acad. Scis., Paris, 1973, prize M.Th.Lebrasseur Fond. de France, Paris, 1988, Rapkine medal, 1992. Mem. EMBO, EMBL (pres. sci. adv. com. 1980-84). Home: 35 rue François Bonvin, 75015 Paris France Office: Inst Pasteur, 25 rue du Docteur Roux, 75724 Paris France

BUC, MILAN, medical educator, researcher; b. Slovenska Lupca, Slovakia, Dec. 14, 1944; s. Jozef and Anna (Pavlovská) B.; m. Mária Žalkovicová, Feb. 4, 1989; children: Veronika, Miroslav; m. Zlatica Nemcová, Dec. 9, 1970 (div. 1985); 1 child, Eugénia. MD, Comenius U., Bratislava, Slovakia, 1968, PhD, 1976, DSc, 1987. Physician Hosp., Krupina, Slovakia, 1968-69; asst. prof. Faculty Medicine, Bratislava, 1969-80, assoc. prof., 1981-88, prof., 1988—; head dept. faculty medicine, Bratislava, 1992—. Author: HLA System in Medicine, 1989 (Slovan Literature Fund award 1990), Immunogenetics, 1994, Clinical Immunology, 1997 (SLF award 1998); mem. editl. bd. Warsaw, 1995—, Prague, 1991—, Paris, 1991—; contbr. over 150 articles to profl. jours. Recipient award Ministry of Health, Bratislava, 1979. Mem. Slovak Immunol. Soc. (vice chmn. 1991—), European Fedn. Immunogenetics. Office: Comenius Univ Medicine, Dept Immunol Sasinkova 4, 811 08 Bratislava Slovakia

BUCALA, RICHARD, biochemistry educator, immunologist; b. New Britain, Conn., Sept. 15, 1957; m. Anne, Sept. 1, 1983. BS summa cum laude, MS, Yale U., 1979; PhD, Rockefeller U., 1985; MD, Cornell U., 1986. Asst. prof. Rockefeller U., N.Y., 1990-91; assoc. prof. Picower Inst. Med. Rsch., N.Y., 1991-93, prof., head Lab. Med. Biochemistry, 1993—; mem. scientific adv. bd. Alteon, Inc., N.J., Am. Diabetes Assn., Va.; dir. Picower Inst. for Med. Rsch., 1999—. Contbg. editor: Molecular Medicine. Mem. Am. Soc. Clin. Investigation, Am. Soc. Biochemistry and Molecular Biology, Am. Chem. Soc., Molecular Medicine Soc., Phi Beta Kappa. Office: Picower Inst Med Rsch 350 Community Dr Manhasset NY 11030-3849

BUCCAFUSCO, JERRY JOSEPH, pharmacologist, educator; b. Jersey City, Aug. 20, 1949; s. Dominick A. and Rose N. B.; m. Regina N. Neilan, Dec. 22, 1973; children: Christopher, Martin. BS, St. Peter's Coll., 1971; MS, Canisius Coll., 1973; PhD, U. Medicine & Dentistry N.J., Newark, 1978. Postdoctoral fellow Roche Inst. Molecular Biology, Nutley, N.J., 1977-79; rsch. pharmacologist VA Med. Ctr., Augusta, 1985—; prof., dir. animal behavioral ctr., Alzheimer's Rsch. Ctr. Med. Coll. Ga., Augusta, 1979—. patentee in field. Mem. Am. Soc. Pharmacology & Exptl. Therapeutics, Soc. Neurosci., Behavioral Toxicology Soc., Sigma Xi. Office: Med Coll Ga 1120 15th St Augusta GA 30912-0006

BUCCI, REGINALDO, engineering company administrator, educator; b. Orlandia, Brazil, Sept. 24, 1947; s. Roque and Genny (Lima) B.; m. Sandra Onofre, Dec. 17, 1977; children: Cintia, Rafael. Degree in indsl. engring., Poly. U. São Paulo, Brazil, 1971; degree in adminstrn., Escola Adminstrn. Empresas São Paulo, 1977. Sys. analyst Prodam/SP, São Paulo, 1973-77, sys. coord., 1978-84; sys. mgr. Copersucar/União, São Paulo, 1985-95, chief info. officer, 1996—; tchr., faculty tech. U. Paulista/São Paulo, 1985—. Office: Copersucar/União, R Borges de Figueiredo 237, 03110900 São Paulo Brazil

BUCCIERO, JOSEPH MARIO, JR., executive consultant; b. Phila., Mar. 27, 1948; s. Joseph Mario Sr. and Carmela (Biscari) B.; m. Nancy Louise Arnquist, Aug. 19, 1972; children: Paul Joseph, Mark Benjamin. BS, Villanova U., 1969. Software programmer, project software engr. Leeds and Northrup Co., North Wales, Pa., 1969-72; applications engr. Leeds and Northrup Co., North Wales, 1972-74; systems cons. Macro Corp., Horsham, Pa., 1974-76; consulting engr. Macro Corp., Horsham, 1976-82, sr. consulting engr., 1982-89; strategic bus. unit mgr. Alstom ESCA, Bellevue, Wash., 1989-90; prin. cons. KEMA-ECC, Fairfax, Va., 1990—; bus. area mgr. KEMA Consulting, Fairfax, 1991—; v.p. KEMA Consulting, Inc., Fairfax, 1992-98; sr. v.p. KEMA Cons., Horsham, Pa., 1999—. Contbr. articles to profl. jours. Ch. coun. pres. Little Zion Luth. Ch., Telford, Pa., 1980-85. Mem. IEEE (sr. mem.). Avocations: bowling, down hill skiing, traveling. Home: 43 Radcliff Dr Doylestown PA 18901-2654

BUCCINO, DANIEL L., psychotherapist, consultant; b. Chgo.; s. Alphonse and Estelle Buccino. BA, Johns Hopkins U., 1987, MA, 1987; MSW, Smith Coll., 1989. Diplomate NASW. Student coord. cmty. psychiatry, psychotherapist Johns Hopkins Bayview Med. Ctr., Balt., 1989—; pvt. practice psychotherapy Balt., 1992—; co-founder, co-dir. Balt.-Washington Brief Therapy Inst., Inc., Balt., 1994—; asst. prof. psychiatry Johns Hopkins U. Sch. Medicine, Balt., 2000—; clin. asst. prof. U. Md. Sch. Social Work, Balt., 1996—; faculty field instr. Smith Coll. Sch. Social Work, Northampton, Mass., 1998—; presenter and cons. in field. Editor: Maryland Social Work Legal Handbook, Vol. 1, 1994, Vol. 2, 1996; contbr. articles to profl. jours. and newspapers. Fellow Am. Orthopsychiat. Assn.; mem. Clin. Social Work Fedn. Avocations: family, film, music, fitness. Office: 711 W 40th St Ste 456 Baltimore MD 21211-2199

BUCH, TOMAS, chemical physicist; b. Berlin, July 7, 1931; arrived in Argentina, 1938; s. Alfons and Annie (Schuck) B.; m. Lilian Genoveva Canova, Feb. 5, 1963; children: Esteban M., Natalia I., Alfonso D. License in physics, U. Buenos Aires, 1955; PhD in Chem. Physics, Northwestern U., 1960. Prof. U. Buenos Aires, 1961-66, U. Chile, Santiago, 1966-69, 73, U. Paris VI, 1969-72, U. Comahue, Bariloche, 1973-76; project leader INVAP, Bariloche, Rio Negro, Argentina, 1973-85, mgr. prospective, 1985-91, mgr. human resources, 1991-92; ind. cons., 1992—; mem. cons. com. Nat. Coun. Sci. and Tech., Argentina, 1984-89. Contbr. articles to profl. jours. Avocations: sculpture, writing. Home: Michay 151, 8400 S Carlos Bariloche Argentina Office: INVAP, F P Moreno 1089, 8400 Bariloche Argentina

BUCHALA, ANTONY JOSEPH, plant biology educator; b. Aberdeen, Scotland, Oct. 31, 1946; arrived in Switzerland, 1971; s. Stefan Josef and Anne (Dick) B. BS in Chemistry (hon.), Aberdeen (Scotland) U., 1968, PhD in Chemistry, 1971. Fellow dept. plant biology Royal Soc. European, U. Fribourg, Switzerland, 1971-73, rsch. asst. dept. cardiology, 1973-77, rsch. asst. dept. plant biology, 1977—, lectr. dept. plant biology, 1982—; part time cons. various chem. companies in Switzerland, 1977—; adv. bd. mem. Jour. Experimental Botany, Eng., 1994—. Co-author more than 50 articles. Rsch. grantee Swiss Nat. Sci. Found., 1983-93, Roussel/Uclaf (France), 1981-84. Fellow Royal Soc. Chemistry; mem. Swiss Soc. Plant Physiology, Am. Soc. Plant Physiologists, Japanese Soc. Plant Physiologists, Am. Phytopathol. Soc., Soc. Exptl. Biology, Phytochem. Soc. Europe. Avocations: hill walking, gardening, computers. Office: Univ Fribourg, 3 rue A Gockel, CH-1700 Fribourg Switzerland

BUCHAN, CRAIG NORMAN, technical officer; b. Perth, Australia, Mar. 14, 1955; s. Norman Malcom and Muriel Lucre (Davenport) B.; m. Margaret Ann Butler, Mar. 9, 1985 (div. Jan. 1996). Telecom technician Postmasters Gen. Dept., Perth, Australia, 1971-76, 76-80; telecom tech. officer Telecom Australia, Perth, 1980-88; leading hand Commonwealth Indsl. Gasess, Perth, 1988-90; tech. officer Dept. Transp. & Communications, Perth, 1991-93, Spectrum Mgmt. Agy., Perth, 1993-95; field test officer Visionstream Pty Ltd., Malaga, Australia, 1995-97; sr. broadband specialist TELSTRA, Perth, 1997—. Avocations: amateur radio, astronomy, photography, model planes, electronics. E-mail: cnbuchan@telstra.com. Home: 8 Malu Close, Ballajura WA 6066, Australia Office: TELSTRA BCO, 98 Pier St 4th Fl, Perth WA 6000, Australia Mailing: PO Box 343, Mt Hawthorn WA 6915, Australia

BUCHAN, JOHN, physician; b. Aberdeen, Scotland, Apr. 20, 1954; s. Alexander and Frances Lawrie (Craig) B.; m. Patricia Anne Reilly, Apr. 1, 1978; children: Emma Jane, Jonathan Michael, Nicholas Alexander James. M.B.Ch.B., Aberdeen U., 1977; diploma in Practical Dermatology, U. Wales, 1990. Diplomate Royal Coll. Obstetricians, Faculty Family Planning. House officer Woodend Hosp. and City Hosp., Aberdeen, 1977-78; sr. house officer Sick Children's Hosp., Aberdeen, 1978-79, Maternity Hosp., Aberdeen, 1979, Kingseat Hosp., Aberdeen, 1979-80; gen. practice trainee Aboyne (Scotland) Practice, 1980-81; prin. Rhayader (Wales) Practice, 1981—; divsn. surgeon St. John's Ambulance, Wales, 1981—; med. officer Royal Brit. Legion Home, Rhayader, 1985—; sec. Powys L.M.C., 1992-95. Contbr. articles to profl. jours. Serving bro. Order of St. John, Wales, 1984. Mem. Royal Coll. Gen. Practitioners, Primary Care Dermatology Soc. (founder, treas. 1994—). Avocations: thinking, listening, writing, speaking. Home: Upper Mill Cumdauddwr, Rhayader LD6 5EY, Wales Office: Rhayader Surgery, Caeherbert Ln, Rhayader LD6 5ED, Wales

BUCHAN, RONALD FORBES, internal and preventive medicine physician; b. Concord, N.H., Sept. 24, 1915; s. Robert and Mary Jean (Forbes) B.; m. Maureen O'Regan, June 17, 1940; children: Robert Bruce, Joan Dallas (Mrs. Fleming), Ian Forbes Morgan. A.B., U. N.H., 1936; M.D., C.M., McGill U., 1942; postgrad., Princeton U., 1958. Diplomate Nat. Bd. Med. Examiners, Am. Bd. Preventive Medicine. Reporter Concord Daily Monitor, 1936; asst. exec. sec. Unemployment Compensation Commn., N.H. Dept. Labor, 1937; sanitarian City of Concord and Eastern Health Dist. N.H., 1938; chief, med. unit Bur. Indsl. Hygiene, Conn. Dept. Health, 1943-46; dir. Hartford Small Plant Indsl. Med. Svcs., 1946; clin. dir., asst. prof. indsl. medicine Yale U. Inst. Occupational Medicine and Hygiene, 1946-48; assoc. clin. prof. indsl. medicine N.Y.U. Bellevue Post Grad. Med. Sch., 1948-57; assoc. med. dir. Prudential Ins. Co. Am., 1948-49, dir. employee health, 1949-57; med. dir., v.p. med. svcs. Prudential Ins. Co. Am., Boston, 1957-74, cons. occupational medicine, environ. medicine, toxicology, 1974—; chief med. dir., v.p. Mediscreen, 1974-87; propr. Portsmouth (N.H.) Athenaeum; assoc. clin. prof. preventive medicine Tufts U. Sch. Medicine, 1958-74; vis. lectr. numerous med. schs., 1948-89. Narrator (audio hist. tour) The

Freedom Trail, Boston, (audio visual hist. survey) Shipbuilding on the Kennebec-Maine Maritime Mus.; author: Industrial Toxicology; contbr. Oxford Medicine, Current Therapy, Occupational Medicine, Encyclopedia-Medico-Chirurgicale (Paris); also numerous articles to profl. and lit. jours. Chmn. rsch. adv. com. Brattleboro (Vt.) Retreat, 1960-70; mem. sci. adv. bd. Office Chief Staff USAF, chmn. life scis. human factors facilities, 1960-65, protocol rank, lt. gen.; cons. R.I. Group Health Assn., 1973-75, Harvard Community Health Plan, 1972-75; bd. dirs. Met. Boston chpt. ARC, 1971-73, chmn. com. on safety, 1972-74; founding mem. Challenger Space Ctr., 1987; trustee Miles Meml. Hosp., Damariscotta, Maine, 1988-91. Sr. asst. surg., USPHS, 1943-46; surgeon-lt. York (Maine) Militia-Gov.'s Footguard, 1971—. Recipient Honor award Wisdom Soc., 1970. Fellow Am. Coll. Occupl. and Environ. Medicine (past pres.), Am. Coll. Preventive Medicine (chmn. com. on clin. procedures 1972-74), Am. Acad. Occupl. Medicine (past pres.), Acad. Medicine N.J. (past pres.); mem. AAAS, Am. Indsl. Hygiene Assn., Am. Acad. Ins. Medicine, AMA (assoc. editor Archives Environ. Health), Assn. Internationale Pour La Medicine Du Travail (permanent commn. 1965-74), Mass. Med. Soc., Ramazzini Soc., Academie Europeene des Arts, Sciences et des Lettres, Am. Assn. Sr. Physicians, N.Y. Acad. Scis., Nat. Trust Hist. Preservation, Soc. for Preservation of New Eng. Antiquities, John Buchan Soc. (Edinburgh), Osler Libr. (patron McGill U., Montreal), Soc. for Protection of N.H. Forests, North Country Authors and Scientists League (past pres.), Newcomen Soc. N.Am., St. Andrew's Soc. of Maine, Can. Hist. Soc., Clan Buchan U.S.A., Clan Forbes U.S.A., U.N.H. Alumni Assn. (gen. awards com. 1987-90, sec. U.N.H. class of '36, 1981—), McGill U. Alumni Assn., Friends of Bowdoin Coll., Friends of Mt. Holyoke Coll., Friends of Middlebury Coll. Home: Mount St Mary # 308 1701 Hooksett Rd Hooksett NH 03106-1644

BUCHANAN, ANN HERMIONE, social studies educator; b. Winchester, Hampshire, U.K., May 21, 1941; d. Raymond Alexander and Peggy (Campbell-Preston) Baring; m. Alistair John Buchanan, July 20, 1993; children: Katie, Tessa, Helen. Diploma in Social Studies, U. London, 1968, U. Bath, Eng., 1980; PhD in Social Studies, U. Southampton, Eng., 1990; MA (hon.), U. Oxford, Eng., 1994. Cert. of qualification in social work. Psychiat. social worker Berkshire County Coun., Reading, Eng., 1980-89; lectr. Bracknell Coll., Berkshire, Eng., 1989-91, U. Southampton, 1991-94; lectr. U. Oxford, 1994—, fellow St. Hilda's Coll., 1994—. Author: Children Who Soil, 1993, Partnership in Practice, 1994, Cycles of Child Maltreatment, 1996, What Happened When They Were Grown Up, 1997, Parenting, Schooling and Children's Behavior, 1998, What Works for Troubled Children, 1999. Avocations: gardening, walking. E-mail: ann.buchanan@socres.ox.ac.ua. Home: Hillbarn House, Great Bedwyn, Marlborough Wilts, England Office: U Oxford Dept Social Policy & Social Work, Barrett House Wellington Sq, Oxford OX12 2ER, England

BUCHANAN, JAMES MCGILL, economist, educator; b. Murfreesboro, Tenn., Oct. 2, 1919; s. James McGill and Lila (Scott) B.; m. Anne Bakke, Oct. 5, 1945. BS, Middle Tenn. State Coll., 1940; MA, U. Tenn., 1941; PhD, U. Chgo., 1948; D honoris causa, U. Giessen, 1982, U. Zurich, 1984, George Mason U., U. Valencia, New U. Lisbon, 1987, Ball State U., 1988, City U., London, 1988, Lycoming Coll., 1992, Free U., Rome, 1993, U. Bucharest, 1994, Acad. Econ. Studies, Romania, 1994, U. Catania, 1994, U. Porto, 1995, U. Valladolid (Spain), 1996. Assoc. prof. U. Tenn., 1948-50, prof. econs., 1950-51; prof. Fla. State U., 1951-56; prof. U. Va., 1956-62, Paul G. McIntyre prof. econs., 1962-68, chmn. dept., 1956-62; prof. UCLA, 1968-69; Univ. Disting. prof. Va. Poly. Inst., 1969-83; Univ. Disting. prof. George Mason U., 1983-99, prof. emeritus, 1999—; adv. dir. Ctr. for Pub. Choice, 1969—; Fulbright rsch. scholar, Italy, 1955-56; Ford Faculty rsch. fellow, 1959-60; Fulbright vis. prof. Cambridge U., 1961-62. Author: (with C.L. Allen and M.R. Colberg) Prices, Income and Public Policy, 954, Public Principles of Public Debt, 1958, The Public Finances, 1960, Fiscal Theory and Political Economy, 1960, (with G. Tullock) The Calculus of Consent, 1962, Public Finance in Democratic Process, 1966, The Demand and Supply of Public Goods, 1968, Cost and Choice, 1969, (with N. Devletoglou) Academia in Anarchy, 1970; Editor: (with R. Tollison) Theory of Public Choice, 1972, (with G.F. Thirlby) LSE Essays on Cost, 1973, The Limits of Liberty, 1975, (with R. Wagner) Democracy in Deficit, 1977, Freedom in Constitutional Contract, 1978, What Should Economists Do?, 1979, (with G. Brennan) The Power to Tax, 1980; (with G. Brennan) The Reason of Rules, 1985; Liberty Market and State, 1985, Economics: Between Predictive Science and Moral Philosophy, 1987, Explorations in Constitutional Economics, 1989, Economics and Ethics of Constitutional Order, 1991, Better than Plowing, 1992, Ethics and Economic Progress, 1994; editor: (with Yong Yoon) Return to Increasing Returns, 1994, Post-Socialist Political Economy, 1997, (with R. Congleton) Politics By Principle, Not Interest, 1998, Collected Works of James Buchanan, Vols. I-X, 2000; contbr. articles to profl. jours. Lt. USNR, 1941-46. Decorated Bronze Star; recipient Seidman award, 1984, Nobel Prize in Econs., 1986. Fellow Am. Acad. Arts and Scis.; mem. Am. Econ. Assn. (exec. com. 1966-69, v.p. 1971, dist. fellow 1983—), So. Econ. Assn. (pres. 1963), Western Econ. Assn. (pres. 1983), Mt. Pelerin Soc. (pres. 1984-86). Home: PO Box G Blacksburg VA 24063-1021 Office: George Mason U Buchanan House Mail Stop 1 E6 Fairfax VA 22030-4443

BUCHANAN, JOHN GRANT, chemistry educator; b. Dumbarton, Scotland, Sept. 26, 1926; s. Robert Downie and Mary Hobson (Wilson) B.; m. Sheila Elena Lugg, July 14, 1956 (dec. Sept. 1996); children: Andrew, John, Neil. BA, Cambridge (Eng.) U., 1947, MA, 1951, PhD, 1951, ScD, 1966. Rsch. fellow U. Calif., Berkeley, 1951-52; rsch. asst. Lister Inst. Preventive Medicine, London, 1952-54; lectr. King's Coll., U. Durham, Newcastle upon Tyne, Eng., 1955-62; sr. lectr. U. Newcastle upon Tyne, 1962-65, reader, 1965-69; prof. organic chemistry Heriot-Watt U., Edinburgh, Scotland, 1969-91; professorial fellow U. Bath, U.K., 1991—; mem. editl. adv. bd. Nucleosides and Nucleotides, Dekker Jour., 1982—. Mem. editl. bd. Carbohydrate Rsch., Elsevier Jour., 1966—, editor, 1992-96; contbr. articles to profl. publs. Fellow Royal Soc. Edinburgh (mem. coun. 1980-82), Royal Soc. Chemistry (mem. coun. 1982-85); mem. European Carbohydrate Orgn. (pres. 1989-93). Avocation: golf. Office: U Bath Dept Chemistry, Claverton Down, Bath BA2 7AY, England

BUCHANAN, JOHN G.S., oil industry executive. Group treas., CEO BP Fin., to 1996; group CFO, mng. dir. Brit. Petroleum P.L.C., 1996—, Brit. Petroleum P.L.C. (now BP Amoco plc); bd. dirs. Boots; mem. U.K. Acctg. Stds. Bd. Office: BP Amoco plc Britannic Ho, 1 Finsbury Circus, London EC2M 7BA, England*

BUCHDAHL, GERD, history and philosophy of science educator; b. Mainz, Germany, Aug. 12, 1914; s. Max and Emmy (Bendix) B.; m. Nancy Miriam Wann, July 2, 1925; children: Roger Martin, Christopher Miles, Joseph Matthew. Higher Nat. Diploma, Brixton Poly., London, 1936; BA with honors, Melbourne U., Melbourne, Australia, 1945; MA first class, Melbourne U., 1953; MA Cantab., Cambridge U., Cambridge, Eng., 1958. Licentiate Inst. of Builders Eng. Structural design engr. H. John Paton, London, 1937-38, Messrs. Mouchel & Ptnrs., London, 1938-40; sr. lectr. U. Melbourne, 1947-57; lectr. U. Cambridge, 1958-66, reader, 1966-81, emeritus reader, 1981—. Author: Metaphysics and the Philosophy of Science, 1969, Kant and the Dynamics of Reason, 1992. Fellow, Darwin Coll., Cambridge, 1964—. Mem. Acad. Internat. de Philosphie des Sciences. Anglican. Avocation: music. Home: The Lodge Horningsea, Cambridge CB5 9JD, England Office: Cambridge U, Dept History & Philosophy, of Science Free School Ln, Cambridge CB2 3RH, England

BÜCHEN-OSMOND, ULLA MARIA CORNELIA, biologist, consultant; b. Waldshut, Baden, Germany, Oct. 22, 1943; d. Wilhelm and Christiana (Deckwer) B.; m. Eckard Gauhl (dec. 1978); m. Charles Barry Osmond. Diploma in biology, Univ. Frankfurt, 1971, PhD MED, 1980. With Wissenschaftlicher Mitarbeiter, U. Frankfurt, Germany, 1972-83; postdoctoral fellow Australian Nat. U., Canberra, 1984-87, rsch. officer, 1991—; cons. Am. Type Culture Collection, Manassas, Va., 1991—; database mgr. Internat. Comm. Taxonomy of Viruses, 1993—. Contbr. articles to prof. jours. Recipient Netwatch citation Sci. Mag., 1999, citation ICTV 12th Internat. Cong. Virology, 1999. Mem. Am. Soc. Microbiology. Avocations: gardening, cooking. Office: Rsch Sch Biol Scis Box 475, Australia Nat U, Canberra ACT 2601, Australia

BUCHER, STEFAN JOHANNES, linguist, educator; b. Karlsruhe, Germany, May 31, 1960; arrived in Taiwan, 2000.; s. Diethelm and Rosemarie (Kramer) B.; m. You-Kyong Kim, July 9, 1993. PhD magna cum laude, Westfälische Wilhelms U., 1989. Rsch. asst. Arbeitsbereich Linguistik U. Münster, Germany, 1985-86, Ehrenpreis Ctr. U. Münster, Germany, 1987-89; instr. Dolmetscher Inst. Münster, 1989; vis. asst. prof. German lang. pedagogy and linguistics Kyongbuk Nat. U., Korea, 1990-96; asst. prof. Chinese U. of Hong Kong, 1997-99, Tamkang U., Taipei, Taiwan, 2000—; instr. Daegu U., Korea, 1992; lectr. in philosophy Keimyong U., Korea, 1992-94; instr. Ednl. Broadcasting System, Seoul, 1992-93. Author: Zwischen Phänomenologie und Sprachwissenschaft: Zu Merleau-Pontys Theorie der Sprache, 1991; editor: Fehler und Lernerstrategien, 1997; co-editor: Deutsch nebenher. Ist-Stand und Aussichten des Fachs Deutsch als zweite Fremdsprache in Ostasien; contbr. articles to profl. jours. Mem. Gesellschaft für Angewandte Linguistik, Hong Kong Examinations Authority. Roman Catholic. Avocations: foreign languages and cultures, hiking, water sports. Office: Tamkang U German Dept, 151 Yin-Chuan Rd Tamshui, 251 Taipei Hsien, Taiwan

BUCHERRE, VERONIQUE, environmental company executive, writer, translator, interpreter; b. Casablanca, Morocco, Nov. 20, 1951; came to U.S., 1967; d. Maurice Daniel Bucherre and Lucette Jaqueline Piani; m. Douglas Lee Frazier; 1 child, Marc-Andrew. Diploma Para Profesores, Gregorio Maranon, Madrid, 1972; MA, San Francisco State U., 1974; PhD in Latin Am. Affairs, U. Paris-Sorbonne, 1980; diploma in conf. interpreting, London Sch. of Poly., 1983. Lic. real estate broker, Md. Instr. French Peace Corps, Baker, La., 1968; editl. asst. Newsweek mag., San Francisco, 1970-72; faculty San Francisco State U., 1972-74, 77; conf. interpreter-translator France and U.S., 1974-85, rural developer, 1976-86; pres. Bucherre & Assocs., Washington, 1985-88; inventor The Rainbank System, 1985; bd. dirs. Rainbank System; CEO, pres. Rainbank Group Ltd., 1988—; vis. prof. Am. U., Washington, 1992-93, Seoul U. Fgn. Studies, 1996-97; student body rep. IHEAL Sorbonne, Paris, 1974-75; mem. bd. mgmt. Inst. des Hautes Etudes de l'Amerique Latine, Paris, 1975-76; mem. Lab III, Ctr. Nat. de Rsch. Sci., Paris, 1975-77; civilian pers. rules editing com. Inter-Am. Def. Bd., 1991-94, pres. internat. civilian staff, 1987-92; pres. Translations 2000, 1999—. Author: Florence, 1979, Uruguay, 1980; co-author: Civilian Personnel Rules of the Inter-American Defense Board, Relief Ops. Manual. Named Hon. Citizen City of Mobile, Ala. Mem. Le Droit Humain (Paris), Droit Humain Club (Paris), Georges Washington Union, Lodge Liberty #3. E-mail: bucherre@aol.com. Office: 15 Highland Blvd Kensington CA 94707-1029

BUCHERT, THOMAS, cosmology educator; b. VS - Schwenningen, Germany, Aug. 18, 1959; s. Helmut and Walburga (Glatz) B. Diploma in Theoretical Physics, Ludwig-Maximilians U., Munich, 1984; Dr in Theoretical Physics, Ludwig-Maximillians U., Munich, 1988, Dr in Astronomy, 1994. Rsch. assoc. Max-Planck-Inst. Astrophysics, Garching, Germany, 1984-95; rsch. assoc., pvt. docent and rsch. assoc. Ludwig-Maximilians U., Tech. U., Munich and Garching, 1995-98; project rep. Sonderforschungsbereich 375, Munich, 1995-2000; assoc. mem. personnel, CERN, Geneva, Switzerland, 1998-99; Tomalla vis. prof. U. Geneva, 1999; Ctr. Excellence rschr. Nat. Astron. Observatory, Tokyo, 1999-2000. Contbr. articles to profl. jours. Grantee DM, Munich, 1988-94, 95-2000. Mem. European Cosmology Network. Office: Ludwig-Maximilians U, Theresienstrasse 37, Munich 80333, Germany

BUCHHEIM, LOTHAR-GÜNTHER, publisher, writer; b. Weimar, Germany, Feb. 6, 1918; m. Diethild Wickboldt, 1955; 2 children. Student, Dresden Acad., Art Acad., Munich. Owner, pub. Buchheim Verlag, Feldafing, Germany. Author: Tage und Nächte steigen aus dem Strom, 1941, Die Künstlergemeinschaft Brücke, 1958, Graphik des deutschen Expressionismus, 1959, Max Beckmann, 1959, Otto Mueller, 1963, Das Boot, 1973, U-Boot-Krieg, 1976, Staatsgala, 1977, Mein Paris, 1977, Die Tropen von Feldafing, 1978, Staatszirkus, 1978, Der Luxusliner, 1980, U 96, 1981, Der Film-Das Boot, 1981, Das Segelschiff, 1982, Die U-Boot-Fahrer, 1985, Das Museum in den Wolken, 1986, Zu Tode gesiegt-Der Untergang der U-Boote, 1988, Malerbuch, 1988, Ehrenbürger von Chemmitz, 1992, Ernst-Hoferichter-Preis München, 1993, Die Festung, 1995, Grosses Verdienstkreuz mit Stern des Verdienstordens der Bundesrepublik Deutschland, 1996, Jäger im Weltmeer, 1997, Bayer Maximilianorden, 1998, Max-Pechstein-Ehrenpreis der Stadt Zwickau, 1999. With German Navy. Office: Buchheim-Verlag, Biersackstr 23, 82340 Feldafing Germany

BUCHHEIT, MARCELLUS, software designer; b. Homburg, Saar, Germany, Aug. 16, 1962; s. Hubertus and Anne-Lise (Dupré) B. Dipl.-Informatiker, U. Karlsruhe, Germany, 1987. Pres., exec. WIBU-Systems GmbH, Karlsruhe, 1989-95, dir. bd., v.p. rsch. & devel., 1996—; ind. regional dir. Microsoft, 1996—. Author: Windows Programmierbuch, 1992; contbr. articles to profl. jours. Mem. Assn. Computing Machinery. Roman Catholic. Home: Kronenstrasse 30, D-76133 Karlsruhe Germany Office: WIBU-Systems AG, Rüppurrer Strasse 54, D-76137 Karlsruhe Germany

BUCHIN, STANLEY IRA, educator, management consultant; b. N.Y.C., Sept. 7, 1931; s. K. and Bertha (Handman) B.; m. Jacqueline Thurber Chase, Sept. 14, 1957; children: Linda C., David L., Gordon T. SB, MIT, 1952; MBA, Harvard U., 1956, DBA, 1962. Asst. to treas. Bay State Abrasives, 1956-58; rsch. asst. Harvard Bus. Sch., 1958-59, rsch. assoc., 1959-60, instr., 1960-61, lectr., 1961-62, asst. prof., 1962-66, assoc. prof., 1966-69; pres. Applied Decision Sys., Wellesley, Mass., 1969-78; v.p. Temple, Barker & Sloane, Inc., Lexington, Mass., 1975-80; sr. v.p. Temple, Barker & Sloane, Inc., Lexington, 1980-90; prin. Arthur D. Little, 1991-99; pres. Boston-Bermuda Cruising Ltd., 1992-97, Gen. Ship Cruising Corp., 1994-97; vis. lectr. Templeton Coll. Oxford (Eng.), 1991-93; prof. Arthur D. Little Sch. Mgmt., 1992—; assoc. prof. Boston U., 1997—. Trustee Mass. Sch. Profl. Psychology. Served in Chem. Corps, U.S. Army, 1952-54. IBM fellow, 1962-63; George F. Baker scholar, 1956. Mem. Am. Mktg. Assn., Inst. Mgmt. Sci., Fin. Mgmt. Assn., Harvard Club Boston, Tau Beta Pi. Republican. Congregationalist. Home: Union Wharf # 304 Boston MA 02109-1206 Office: 808 Commonwealth Ave Boston MA 02215-1206

BUCHMANN, RAINER, periodontology educator, researcher; b. Dortmund, Germany, Apr. 20, 1960; s. Hermann H. and Ursula B.; children: Anina, Swantje, Lilli, Greet. Dentist, Westfalian Wilhelm U., Münster, Germany, 1984; DMD, 1985, specialist in periodontology, 1988, pvt. dozent, 1999. Pvt. practice periodontology, Osnabrück, Germany, 1988-90; rsch. assoc. dept. periodontology U. Münster, 1990-96, sr. lectr., 1996-99, assoc. prof., 1999—; asst. prof. Boston U. Goldman Sch. Dental Medicine, 2000—; cons. Dental Chamber Münster, 1990—. Contbr. articles to dental jours., including Jour. Clin. Oral Implants Rsch., Jour. Periodontology. Recipient ann. award German Soc. for Periodontology, 1987, 92, 94, W.D. Miller Sci. award, 1998; travel grantee German Fedn. Periodontology, 1991, 93, 94, 97, German Rsch. Soc., 1993, 95, 96, 99, Butler, 1997. Mem. German Soc. for Tooth, Mouth and Jaw Med. Sci., Am. Acad. Periodontology, Internat. Assn. for Dental Rsch. Avocations: sailing, hiking, living nature, his 4 daughters. Office: Boston U Goldman Sch Dental Medicine 100 E Newton Street G108 Dept Periodontology and Oral Biology Boston MA 02118

BUCHNER, AMOS, oral pathologist, educator and researcher; b. Tel Aviv, Mar. 12, 1939; s. Arie and Esther Buchner; m. Bruria Atzmoni, Aug. 16, 1961; children: Tzeela, Iris. DMD, Hebrew U., Jerusalem, 1962; MSD, U. Wash., 1968. Dir. dental svcs. Israel Def. Forces, 1969-73, head forensic identification, 1975-93; chmn. dept. oral pathology Tel-Aviv U., 1969—, head Sch. Dental Medicine, 1980-87, prof. oral pathology, 1981—, Incumbent of Ed and Herb Stein chair in oral pathology, 1989—; cons. Internat. Dental Fedn., 1972—; mem. internat. expert com. WHO Classification of Odontogenic Tumors, 1981; mem. dental adv. com. Ministry of Health, Israel, 1992-94; chmn. sci. coun. Israel Dental Assn., 1992-95, chmn. com. for accreditation of dept. specialty tng., 1995—; vis. prof. oral pathology SUNY-Stony Brook, U. Calif.-San Francisco, U. Pacific, San Francisco; mem. Internat. Dental Fedn. Expert Network on Oral Cancer, 1998—. Editor Israel Jour. Dental Medicine, 1963-66; contbr. more than 160 articles to profl. jours. Fulbright awardee, 1966. Fellow Acad. Internat. Dental Studies (hon.), Israel Dental Assn. (hon., mem. sci. coun., chmn./mem. coms. for specialties tng. of oral surgery, oral pathology and oral medicine, sci. coun. 1980—); mem. Am. Acad. Oral Pathology, Am. Acad. Oral Medicine, Internat. Assn. Oral Pathology, Brit. Soc. Oral Pathology, Internat. Assn. Dental Rsch., Internat. Coll. Dentists, Internat. Dental Fedn. Jewish. Avocations: music, stamps. Office: Tel Aviv Univ, Sch Dental Medicine, 69978 Tel Aviv Israel

BÜCHSEL, ELFRIEDE ELISABETH, retired secondary education educator, researcher; b. Rostock, Germany, Aug. 21, 1922; d. Friedrich and Marie-Louise (Hoppe) B. Student, U. Rostock, 1940; diploma in edn., U. Strassbourg, Germany, 1944; grad., U. Göttingen, Germany, 1953. Tchr. Hannover (Germany) H.S., 1947-84. Author: Bibisches Zeugnis und Sprachgestalt bei J.G. Hamann, 1953, Über den Ursprung der Sprache, 1963; contbr. articles to profl. jours. Mem. Synode der Evang. Ch. Germany, 1966-78. Mem. Eugen Rosenstock Huessy Soc. Lutheran.

BUCHSTAB, GÜNTER, historian, archivist; b. Lauchheim, Germany, Feb. 20, 1944. PhD, U. Bonn, 1974. Dir. reference and rsch. svcs. Konrad-Adenauer-Stiftung, Sankt Augustin, Germany. Editor: Forschungen und Quellen zur Zeitgeschichte, Historisch-Politische Mitteilungen. Vorsitzender der Fachgruppe der Partei-und Parlamentsarchivare im Verein Deutscher Archivare. Mem. Internat. Coun. on Archives (pres. sect. of archives and archivists of parliaments and polit. parties). Office: Konrad-Adenauer-Stiftung, Rathausallee 12, 53757 Sankt Augustin Germany

BUCHWALD, ART, columnist, writer; b. Mt. Vernon, N.Y., Oct. 20, 1925; s. Joseph and Helen (Kleinberger) B.; m. Ann McGarry, Oct. 11, 1952; 3 children. Student, U. So. Calif., 1945-48. Syndicated columnist, 550 newspapers throughout world; columnist Los Angeles Times Syndicate. Author: Paris After Dark, 1950, Art Buchwald's Paris, 1954, The Brave Coward, 1957, A Gift From the Boys, 1959, More Caviar, 1958, Un Cadeau Pour Le Patron (Prix de la Bonne Humeur 1958), Don't Forget to Write, 1960, Art Buchwald's Secret List to Paris, 1963, How Much Is That in Dollars?, 1961, Is It Safe to Drink the Water?, 1962, I Chose Capitol Punishment, 1963, And Then I Told the President, 1965, Son of the Great Society, 1966, Have I Ever Lied to You, 1968, The Establishment Is Alive and Well in Washington, 1969, Counting Sheep, 1970, Getting High in Government Circles, 1971, I Never Danced at the White House, 1973, The Bollo Caper, 1974, I Am Not a Crook, 1974, Irving's Delight, 1975, Washington is Leaking, 1976, Down the Seine and Up the Potomac, 1977, The Buchwald Stops Here, 1978, Laid Back in Washington, 1981, While Reagan Slept, 1983, You CAN Fool All of the People All the Time, 1985, I Think I Don't Remember, 1987, Whose Rose Garden Is It Anyway?, 1989, Lighten Up, George, 1991, Leaving Home: A Memoir, 1994, I'll Always Have Paris, 1996. Served as sgt. USMCR, 1942-45. Recipient Pulitzer prize for outstanding commentary, 1982. Mem. Am. Acad. Arts and Scis., Am. Acad. Humor Columnists. Office: 200 Pennsylvania Ave NW Washington DC 20006*

BUCHWALD, NAOMI REICE, judge; b. Kingston, N.Y., Feb. 14, 1944. BA cum laude, Brandeis U., 1965; LLB cum laude, Columbia U., 1968. Bar: N.Y. 1968, U.S. Ct. Appeals (2d cir.) 1969, U.S. Dist. Ct. (so. and ea. dists.) N.Y. 1970, U.S. Supreme Ct. 1978. Litigation assoc. Marshall, Bratter, Greene, Allison & Tucker, N.Y.C., 1968-73; asst. U.S. atty. So. Dist. N.Y., N.Y.C., 1973-80, dep. chief civil divsn., 1976-79, chief civil divsn., 1979-80; U.S. magistrate judge U.S. Dist. Ct. (so. dist.) N.Y., N.Y.C., 1980-99, chief magistrate judge, 1994-96, U.S. dist. judge, 1999—. Editor Columbia Jour. Law and Social Problems, 1967-68. Recipient spl. citation FDA Commrs., 1978, Robert B. Fiske Jr. Assn. William B. Tendy award, Outstanding Pub. Svc. award Seymour Assn., Columbia Law Sch. Class of 1968 Excellence in Pub. Svc. award, 1998. Mem. Fed. Bar Coun. (trustee 1976-82, 97-2000, v.p. 1982-84), N.Y. State Bar Assn., Assn. of the Bar of the City of N.Y. (trademarks and unfair competition com. 1988-89, mem. long range planning com. 1993-95, litigation com. 1994-96, ad hoc com. on jud. conduct 1996-99), Phi Beta Kappa, Omicron Delta Epsilon. Office: US Ct House Foley Square New York NY 10007-1316

BUCIO, ESPINOZA MIGUEL ANGEL, microbiologist, researcher; b. Morelia, Michoacan, Mex., Sept. 8, 1966; s. Garcia Higinio Bucio and Santacruz Imelda Espinoza; m. Mendoza Flora Beatriz Macias, Oct. 21, 1995; 1 child, Miguel Angel Bucio Macias. Grad. in chem. pharm. biology, U. Michoacana, Uruapan, Mex., 1989. Asst. Lab. Clin. Lab., Morelia, Mex., 1989-90, leader, 1990-91; lab. leader Procesadora de Aguacate y Frutas, Uruapan, Mex., 1992-94, quality control mgr., 1994-96, plant mgr., 1997-99, quality assurance mgr., 1999—; cons. quality assirance programs HACCP; owner Micro Bac Labs.; internal cons. Fresh Directions Mexicana HACCP Programs, 1999. Mem. Am. Soc. for Microbiology, Inst. Food Technologists, AOAC Internat. Roman Catholic. Avocations: reading books, playing soccer and tennis, running, television. Home: 5 de Mayo Apt 20, 60 000 Uruapan Mexico Office: Fresh Directions Mexicana, Paseo Lazaro Cardenas 10-C, 60050 Uruapan Mexico

BUCK, EARL WAYNE, insurance investigator, private detective; b. La Porte City, Iowa, Jan. 15, 1939; s. Edwin Earl and Uleta Pearl (Purdy) B.; m. Maxine E. Parker, Oct. 19, 1969; children: Brian, Douglas. LLB, La Salle U., 1969. Asst. mgr. Chgo. br. Atwell, Vogel & Sterling, Scarsdale, N.Y., 1965-70; pvt. detective, Sioux City, Iowa, 1968-74; mgr. Milw. br. Atwell, Vogel & Sterling, Scarsdale, N.Y., 1970; sr. auditor Comml. Union Ins. Co., Chgo., 1970-74; police chief McHenry Shores (Ill.) Police Dept., 1973-79; self-employed ins. investigator McHenry, Ill., 1980-88, Rapid City, S.D., 1988—; owner Corral Motel, Rapid City, 1988—; liquor liability investigator for various ins. cos., 1980-88; farm owner, 1986-96; owner High Plaines Detective Agy., 1990—; ptnr. Juke Boxes, Western Fla. Chmn. McHenry Shores (Ill.) Zoning Commn., 1972, Police Support Subcom., C. of C. Pub. Safety Com.; key contact Help Abolish Legal Tyranny; active Rapid City Police Res., 1989-90, North Rapid Civic Assn., 1991-94, pres., chmn. bd., 1993-94; active Pennington County Air Quality Bd., 1990-93, chmn., 1992-93. With U.S. Army, 1957-61. Recipient Police Meritorius Service award Vill. of McHenry Shores, 1979. Mem. Midwest Ins. Auditors Assn., McHenry County Police Chief's Assn., Rapid City Police Officers Assn., Rapid City Area Hospitality Assn. (bd. dirs.), Rapid City Area C. of C. (safety com. 1989-91), Black Hills Badlands & Lakes Assn., Fed. Weed and Seed Program Rapid City (steering com.), NRA, Moose. Republican. Lutheran. Avocations: flying, amateur archaeology, photography, fishing, hunting.

BUCK, PITMAN AUGUST, JR., writer; b. Houston, Aug. 1, 1929; s. Pitman August, Sr. and Katherine W. Kaule B.; m. Nellwyn Angela B., Dec. 21, 1957; children: Kevin Dwayne, Phillip Warren, Eric David. Student, Stephen F. Austin State Coll., 1951-52, U. Houston, 1955-57. Chem. technician, ret., 1984. Author: American Freedom and Zionist Power, 1977, The Colossal Fraud of Involuntary Perjury, 1996; editor: Torah, Zionism and Palestine, 1983; contbr. numerous articles to publs. Del. Nat. Conf. Great Decisions in U.S. Fgn. Policy, 1975, testified before U.S. Senate subcom.; pres. Ams. for Middle East Peace, Houston, 1982-83; v.p. Gulf Coast Coun. Fgn. Affairs, Texas City, Tex., 1976-77. Home and Office: 2525 Sunnycrest Dr Texas City TX 77590-5018

BUCK, RICHARD PIERSON, chemistry educator, researcher; b. L.A., July 29, 1929; s. Richard Maurice and Lucile Frances (Pierson) B.; m. Mary Ann Kenney, May 23, 1959; children: Nancy Elizabeth Buck McKenna, Pierson Kenney, Margaret Ruth. BS, Calif. Inst. Tech., 1950, MS, 1951; PhD, MIT, 1954. Teaching asst. MIT, Cambridge, 1951-52, NSF fellow, 1952-53, Dupont teaching fellow, 1953-54; rsch. chemist Chevron Rsch. Corp., Richmond, Calif., 1954-61, asst. to gen. mgr., 1956-58; prin. rsch. chemist Bell & Howell Rsch. Ctr., Pasadena, Calif., 1961-65; sr. scientist Beckman Instrument Co., Fullerton, Calif., 1965-67; assoc. prof. chemistry U. N.C., Chapel Hill, 1967-75, prof., 1975—, adj. prof. biomed. engring. and math. Sch. Medicine, 1990—, prof. emeritus, 1998—; Kenan prof.-on-leave U. Bristol, Eng., 1976-77; vis. prof. Imperial Coll., London, 1987, Bundeswehr U. Munich, 1989-91; cons. Eastman Kodak, Rochester, N.Y., 1969-77, E.I. duPont de Nemours & Co., Wilmington, Del., 1979-84; mem. adv. bd. I-Stat Corp., Princeton, N.J., 1984-90, HemoSense, Inc., San Jose, Calif., 1998—, NIH resource at Case Western Res. U., Cleve., 1977-84, Ctr. for Solid State Sensors, U. Pa. Moore Sch. Engring., Phila., 1980-84; chmn. A Nomenclature Commn., Internat. Union Pure and Applied Chemistry, 1991—. Author: (with V.V. Cosofret) Pharmaceutical Applications of Membrane Sensors, 1992; mem. editorial bd. 4 internat. chemistry jours.; contbr. over 350 articles to sci. jours. Recipient C.N. Reilley award Soc. Electroanalytical Chemistry, 2000; Von Humboldt grantee, Bonn, Germany,

1989-91, grantee Advanced Rsch. Projects Agy., 1967-71, NSF, 1971—, N.C. Biotech. Ctr., 1990-94. Fellow Electrochem. Soc. (div. chmn., outstanding achievement award sensor divsn. 1996); mem. Am. Chem. Soc., Internat. Soc. Electrochemistry (bd. dirs. 1988-91), Bohemian Club (San Francisco). Avocations: performing chamber music, solo piano playing. Home: 101 Creekview Cir Carrboro NC 27510-4111 also: 139 Elliott Dr Menlo Park CA 94025-2622 Office: U NC Dept Chemistry Cb 3290 Venable Hl Chapel Hill NC 27599-0001

BUCKAWAY, WILLIAM ALLEN, JR., lawyer; b. Bowling Green, Ky., Dec. 3, 1934; s. William Allen and Kathryn Anne (Scoggin) B.; m. Bette Joan Cross, July 27, 1963; 1 child, William Allen III. AB, Centre Coll. of Ky., 1956; JD, U. Louisville, 1961. Bar: Ky. 1961, U.S. Dist Ct. (we. dist.) Ky. 1981, U.S. Dist. Ct. (ea. dist.) Ky. 1986, U.S. Supreme Ct. 1975. Assoc. Tilford, Dobbins, Caye & Alexander, Louisville, 1961-78; ptnr. Tilford, Dobbins, Alexander, Buckaway & Black, Louisville, 1978—; atty. Masonic Homes of Ky., Louisville, 1985—; gen. counsel Kosair Charitites. Elder 2d Presbyn. Ch., Louisville, 1975; emeritus mem. bd. govs. Lexington (Ky.) unit Shriners Hosp. for Cripled Children, 1986, sec., 1989-94; mem. children's oper. bd. Kosair Children's Hosp., 1986-99; mem. bd. govs. Norton Health Care, Louisville, 1999—. With USNR, 1956-58. Named Disting. Alumnus U. Louisville Sch. Law, 1986, Centre Coll., 1986. Mem. SAR (pres. Ky. soc. 1999-2000), Nat. Eagle Scout Assn., Soc. of the Cin. in State of Va., Sons Confederate Vets. (adj. John Hunt Morgan Camp 1993-96), Masons (33 deg., past master Crescent Hill lodge 1967, chmn. jurisprudence and law com. imperial coun. Shrine of N.Am. 1989-91), Kosair Shrine Temple (potentate 1986), Rotary, Soc. Colonial Wars (Ky. coun.), Soc. War of 1812 (pres. Ky. soc. 1998-2000), Sigma Chi, Phi Alpha Delta. Home: 1761 Sulgrave Rd Louisville KY 40205-1643

BUCK-EMDEN, RUEDIGER, software company executive, computer scientist; b. Stade, Germany, Nov. 21, 1955; s. Walter Peter and Christine Agathe (Ryborz) B.-E.; m. Hilka Bagung, Oct. 26, 1984; children: Franziska, Alexander. Dipl.Inform., U. Braunschweig, Germany, 1983, DrRerNat, 1988. Computer scientist U. Braunschweig, 1983-88; group leader Nixdorf Computer AG, Munich, Germany, 1988-90; tech. mgr. SAP AG, Walldorf, Germany, 1990-96, program dir., 1997—, v.p., 1998; lectr. computer sci. Adult Coll., Braunschweig, 1984-86, univ. lectr. computer sci., 1997—. Author: The SAP R/3 System, 1994; contbg. author: Client/Server Architecture, 1993; founding editor Addison-Wesley's Edition SAP, 1996; contbr. articles to profl. jours.; speaker, conf. presenter. Mem. IEEE Computer Soc., Assn. Computing Machinery, Gesellschaft Informatik. Avocations: windsurfing, sailing, tennis. Office: SAP AG, Neurottstrasse 16, D-69190 Walldorf Germany

BUCKHOLTZ, THOMAS JOEL, computer and telecommunications executive; b. L.A., Sept. 19, 1945; s. Joel and Sylvia Lee (Joseph) B.; m. Helen Chu, Nov. 22, 1973; 1 child, Catheryne M. BS in Math., Calif. Inst. Technology, 1967; PhD in Physics, U. Calif., Berkeley, 1971. Scientist, engr. aerospace, def. and rsch. orgns., 1963-72; physicist Lawrence Livermore (Calif.) Nat. Lab., 1972-77; v.p. Ins. Tech. Co., 1976-78, Berkeley (Calif.) Tech. Assocs., 1978-81; software mgr. Friends Amis, 1981-82; sr. analyst Pacific Gas & Electric Co., San Francisco, 1982-89; commr. GSA, Washington, 1989-93; lectr. George Washington U., Washington, 1993; sr. prin. cons. Oracle Corp., 1997-98; exec. v.p. Enter Net Devel. Corp., 1998—; mem. working group Pres.'s Coun. on Competitiveness, 1990-91; mem. Mil. Comm. Electronics Bd., 1991-93, Interagency Com. for Fed. Lab. Tech. Transfer, 1991-93, Computer Sys. Tech. Adv. Bd., U.S. Dept. Commerce, Washington, 1989; mem. Calif. Info. Tech. Commn., 1996-99; mem. telecom. program adv. bd. U. San Francisco, 1994—; mem. adv. bd. Goldman Sch. Pub. Policy, U. Calif., Berkeley, 1999—; mem. corp. rels. com. World Affairs Coun. No. Calif., 1999—; chmn. web tech. adv. bd. Rep. Nat. Com., 2000—. Author: Information Proficiency: Your Key to the Information Age, 1995; contbr. various articles on computer sci., physics and math. to profl. jours. Life mem. The Assocs. of the Calif. Inst. Technology, Pasadena, 1979—; regional chmn. Caltech Alumni Fund, 1988-89, class chair, 1999; county co-chmn. Bush-Quayle '88, Piedmont, Calif., 1988; mem. Wilson coun. Woodrow Wilson Internat. Ctr. for Scholars, Smithsonian Instn., 2000—; bd. trustees Com. Econ. Devel., 2000—. Recipient Grad. fellowship NSF, 1967-71. Mem. Am. Phys. Soc., Soc. for Info. Mgmt. Republican.

BUCKINGHAM, AMYAND DAVID, chemistry educator; b. Sydney, NSW, Australia, Jan. 28, 1930; s. Reginald Joslin and Florence Grace (Elliot) B.; m. Jillian Bowles, July 24, 1965; children: Lucy Elliot, Mark Vincent, Alice Susan. BSc with honors, Sydney U., 1951, MSc, 1953; PhD, Cambridge U., Eng., 1956, ScD, 1985. Cert. chemist; cert. physicist. Lectr., tutor Christ Ch., Oxford, Eng., 1955-65; lectr. Oxford U., 1958-65; prof. theoretical chemistry Bristol (Eng.) U., 1965-69; prof. chemistry Cambridge (Eng.) U., 1969-97, prof. emeritus, 1997—; fellow Pembroke Coll., Cambridge, 1970-97, emeritus fellow, 1997—. Author: Laws and Applications of Thermodynamics, 1964; editor: Organic Liquids, 1978, Principles of Molecular Recognition, 1993; editor Molecular Physics, 1968-72, Internat. Revs. in Phys. Chemistry, 1981-89, Chem. Physics Letters, 1978-99. Trustee Henry Fund, 1976—. Decorated comdr. Brit. Empire. Fellow Royal Soc. (Hughes medal 1996), Royal Soc. Chemistry, Inst. of Physics, Optical Soc. Am., Am. Phys. Soc., Royal Australian Chem. Inst.; mem. AAAS (hon.), NAS (fgn. assoc.), Am. Chem. Soc., Internat. Acad. Quantum Molecular Sci., Royal Swedish Acad. Scis. (fgn. mem.). Avocations: cricket, tennis, travel. Office: Univ Chem Lab, Lensfield Rd, Cambridge CB2 1EW, England

BUCKINGHAM, JOHN MICHAEL, surgeon; b. Melbourne, Victoria, Australia, July 19, 1947; s. Donald James and Joyce Olive (Craven) B.; m. Susan Margaret Mary Brady, June 10, 1972; children: James, Peter, Kathryn, Michael. MB, BS, Sydney (Australia) U., 1971; MS in Surgery, U. Minn., 1977. Resident St. Vincent's Hosp., Sydney, 1971-72; fellow Mayo Clinic, Rochester, Minn., 1972-77; asst. prof. surgery Loyola U., Maywood, Ill., 1978; vis. med. officer gen. surgery Calvary Hosp., Bruce, ACT, Australia, 1979—; chmn. med. staff assn. Calvary Hosp., Bruce, Australia, 1986-88, 91-93. Fellow ACS, Royal Australian Coll. Surgeons (chmn. ACT com. 1993-95); mem. Royal Australian Coll. Med. Administrs. Roman Catholic. Avocation: travel. Office: Calvary Clinic Ste 9, Bruce ACT 2617, Australia

BUCKINGHAM, JULIA CLARE, pharmacology educator; b. Devizes, Wiltshire, Eng., Oct. 18, 1950; d. Jack William Harry and Barbara Joan (Baker) B.; m. Simon James Smith, Nov. 29, 1974. BSc, Sheffield (Eng.) U., 1971; PhD, London U., 1974, DSc, 1987. Rsch. fellow Royal Free Hosp. Sch. Medicine, London, 1974-80, sr. lectr. pharmacology, 1980-87; prof., head pharmacology dept. Charing Cross & Westminster Med. Sch., London, 1987-97, asst. dean preclin., 1992-97; prof. pharmacology, head dept. neurendocrinology, dep. head divsn. neurosci. and psychological medicine Imperial Coll. Sch. Medicine, London, 1997—. Mem. editl. bd. Brit. Jour. Pharmacology, 1978-84, 96—, Jour. Endocrinology, 1986-91, 2000—, Jour. Neuroendocrinology, 1988-99, Toxicology and Ecotoxicology News, 1993-96; assoc. editor Pharmacology Communications, 1991—, Pharmacology and Therapeutics, 1993-99. Mem. Soc. Endocrinology (mem. com. 1990-93, treas. 1996—), Brit. Pharmacol. Soc. (mem. com. 1988-91), Physiol. Soc., Internat. Soc. Neuroendocrinology, European Soc. Endocrinology, Brain Rsch. Assn., Brit. Neuroendocrine Group (trustee 1998—), Biochem. Soc. Avocations: music, sailing, skiing, tennis, reading. Office: Imperial Coll Sch Medicine, Fulham Palace Rd, London W6 8RF, England

BUCKINGHAM, MICHAEL JOHN, oceanography educator; b. Oxford, Eng., Oct. 9, 1943; s. Sidney George and Mary Agnes (Walsh) B.; m. Margaret Penelope Rose Barrowcliff, July 15, 1967. BSc with hons., U. Reading (Eng.), 1967, PhD, 1971. Postdoctoral rsch. fellow U. Reading, 1971-74; sr. sci. officer Royal Aircraft Establishment, Farnborough, Eng., 1974-76; prin. sci. officer Royal Aircraft Establishment, 1976-82; exchange scientist Naval Rsch. Lab., Washington, 1982-84; vis. prof. MIT, Cambridge, 1986-87; sr. prin. sci. officer Royal Aircraft Establishment, 1983-86, 1987-90; prof. oceanography Scripps Instn. of Oceanography, La Jolla, Calif., 1990—; vis. prof. Inst. Sound and Vibration rsch., Southampton, Eng., 1990—; UK nat. rep. Commn. of European Communities, Brussels, Belgium, 1989-92; dir. Arctic rsch. Royal Aerospace Establishment, Farnborough, 1990-94. Author: Noise in Electronic Devices and Systems, 1983; editor: Sea Surface Sound '94, Proceedings of the III Internat. Mtg. on Natural Phys. Processes Related to Sea Surface Sound; editor-in-chief Jour. Computational Acoustics; editor Phys. Acoustics; contbr. articles to profl. jours.; patentee in field. Recipient Clerk Maxwell Premium, Inst. Electronic and Radio Engrs. London, 1972, A.B. Wood Medal, Inst. Acoustics, Bath, Eng., 1982, Alan Burman Pub. award, Naval Rsch. Lab., 1988, Commendation for Disting. Contbns. to ocean acoustics Naval Rsch. Lab., 1986. Fellow Inst. Acoustics (U.K.), Inst. Elec. Engrs. (U.K.), Acoustical Soc. Am. (chmn. acoustical oceanography tech. com. 1991—, Sci. Writing award for profls. in acoustics 1997), Explorers Club; mem. Am. Geophys. Union, N.Y. Acad. Scis., Sigma Xi. Avocations: photography, squash, flying gliders. Home: 7921 Caminito Del Cid La Jolla CA 92037-3404 Office: Scripps Inst Oceanography Marine Phys Lab La Jolla CA 92093-0238

BUCKLER, JOHN MICHAEL, retired medical educator; b. Sutton Coldfield, Eng., July 13, 1935; s. Thomas Arnold and Dorothy (Hargreaves) B.; m. Janet Brimley Spong, May 21, 1966; children: Andrew, Timothy, Mark. MB, Oxford (Eng.) U., 1959, MA, 1960, DM, 1970, DSc, 1992. Intern and resident St. Bartholomew's Hosp., London, 1960; asst. chief resident Children's Hosp., Phila., 1966-67; rsch. asst. Great Ormond St. Hosp., London, 1967-70; sr. lectr. child health U. Leeds, 1970-95; hon. cons. pediatrician U. Leeds Hosps., 1972-95; ret., 1995. Author: A Reference Manual of Growth and Development, 1979, 2nd edit., 1997, The Adolescent Years, 1987, A Longitudinal Study of Adolescent Growth, 1990, Growth Disorders in Children, 1994. Fellow Royal Soc. Medicine, Royal Coll. Physicians (coun. 1991-95), Royal Coll. Pediatrics and child health (regional pediatric adviser 1989-95); mem. Brit. Med. Assn. Anglican. Avocations: classical music, reading, ornithology, meteorology, walking. Home: 4 Grosvenor Ter, Grosvenor Rd, Leeds LS6 2DY, England Office: Leeds Gen Infirmary Dept Pediats, D Fl Clarendon Wing, Leeds LS2 9NS, England

BUCKLEY, ADRIAN ARTHUR, finance educator; b. Poole, Dorset, Eng., Dec. 28, 1938; s. Arthur Penketh and Beatrice Maisy (Bailey) B.; m. Jennifer Rosalie Moyse, Aug. 6, 1966 (dec. Aug. 1977); children: Peter James Scott Buckley, David John Scott Buckley. Diploma, Sheffield U., Eng., 1966; MSc, Bradford U., Eng., 1968; BA, Open U., Eng., 1983; PhD, Free U., Amsterdam, The Netherlands, 1995. Mgr. Wood Albery & Co., London, 1958-64; acct. Guinness, London, 1964-65; mgmt. cons. Merrett Cyriax, London, 1966-70; merchant banker Charterhouse, London, 1970-73; treas. Redland PLC, Reigate, Eng., 1973-80; prof. Cranfield (Eng.) U., 1980—; dir. PMC, Aldbury, Eng., 1987—. Author: Multinational Finance, 1986, 4th edit., 2000, The Essence of International Money, 1990, 2d edit., 1996, From Domestic to International Investment With Real Operating Options, 1995, International Capital Budgeting, 1996, Corporate Finance Europe, 1998, International Investment—Value Creation and Appraisal. A Rela Options Approach, 1998. Fellow Inst. Chartered Accts. Eng. and Wales, Assn. Corp. Treasurers. Avocations: skiing, cricket, theatre. Office: Cranfield U, Sch Mgmt, Bedford Cranfield MK4 30AL, England

BUCKLEY, BRIAN BURKE, artist, educator; b. Schenectady, Feb. 25, 1956; s. Robert Joseph and Mary Dee Buckley; m. Susan Frances Buckley, June 25, 1988; children: Olivia Frances, Madeline Burke. BA in Studio Art, Wesleyan U., Middletown, Conn., 1978; MAT in Ceramics, Printmaking, Carnegie-Mellon U., 1983, MFA in Ceramics, 1985. Art instr. Sewickley (Pa.) Acad., 1979-85; chmn. dept. art Roxbury Latin Sch., West Roxbury, Mass., 1986—; cons. Allegheny Internat., Pitts., 1985-86; artist in residence North Allegheny H.S., Pitts., 1985. Sculptures include: Yahday, 1985, Tuesday, 1985, Sculpting Clay, 1992. CCD tchr. St. James the Great Parish, Wellesley, Mass., 1996—. Mem. New Eng. Sculptors Assn. (bd. dirs. 1999—), Wellesley Soc. Artists. Roman Catholic. Avocations: reading, soccer, drawing. Office: The Roxbury Latin Sch 101 Saint Theresa Ave West Roxbury MA 02132-3496

BUCKLEY, EDGAR, political organization worker; b. London; m. Jacqueline Buckley; 5 children. BA with honors, London U., 1967, PhD, 1974. Tchr. London; pvt. sec., vice chief air staff UK Mil., London, 1976-78, prin., civilian mgmt. specialist, 1978-80, asst. dir. strategic sys. fin., 1980-84, asst. dir. nuclear policy, 1984-85, head navy resources and programs, 1985-89, head def. arms control unit, 1991-92, asst. under sec. home and overseas, 1996-99; def. counsellor UK del. to NATO, 1992-96; asst. sec. gen. def. planning and ops. NATO, Brussels, 1999—. Office: NATO Hdqtrs, Blvd Leopold III, 1110 Brussels Belgium

BUCKLEY, FREDERICK JEAN, lawyer; b. Wilmington, Ohio, Nov. 5, 1923; s. William Millard and Martha (Bright) B.; m. Josephine K. Buckley, Dec. 4, 1945; children: Daniel J., Fredrica Buckley Elder, Matthew J. Student, Wilmington Coll., 1941-42, Ohio State U., 1942-43; AB, U. Mich., 1948, LLB, 1949. Bar: Ohio 1950, U.S. Dist. Ct. (so. dist.) Ohio 1952, U.S. Supreme Ct. 1978, U.S. Ct. Appeals (6th cir.) 1981, Fla. 1982, U.S. Dist. Ct. (mid. dist.) Fla. 1991; cert. cir. ct. mediator, Fla.; cert. arbitrator Fla. state and fed. cts. Assoc. G.L. Schilling, Sr., Wilmington, 1951-52; ptnr. Schilling & Buckley, Wilmington, 1953-56; sole practice Wilmington, 1956-62; sr. ptnr. Buckley, Miller & Wright, Wilmington, 1962—; chmn., counsel The Wilmington Savs. Bank, 1971—, also dir.; solicitor City of Wilmington, 1954-63. Contbr. articles in field. With AUS, 1943-46, ETO. Joint program Mich. Inst. Pub. Adminstrn. fellow, 1948. Fellow Am. Coll. Trial Lawyers; mem. ABA, Am. Arbitration Assn. (comml. panel), Fed. Bar Assn., Ohio State Bar Assn., Clinton County Bar Assn., Selden Soc., Fla. Bar, Fla. Acad. Profl. Mediators, Soc. Profls. in Dispute Resolution, Collier County Bar Assn., Ohio State Bar Found. Republican. Methodist. Office: 145 N South St Wilmington OH 45177-1646

BUCKLEY, JOHN JOSEPH, JR., health care executive; b. Evanston, Ill., Oct. 5, 1944; s. John Joseph and Mary Ruth (Smith) B.; m. Sarah Amelia Puceloski, May 16, 1970; children—Ruth Mary, Patricia Kimberly, John Joseph III. A.B., Kenyon Coll., 1966; M.B.A., George Washington U., 1969. Asst. adminstr. Maricopa County Gen. Hosp., Phoenix, 1969-71; asst. adminstr. St. Joseph's Hosp. and Med. Ctr., Phoenix, 1971-74, assoc. adminstr., 1974-76, v.p., 1976-79, pres., 1984-88; pres. St. Anthony's Hosp., Amarillo, Tex., 1979-84, St. Anthony's Devel. Corp., Amarillo, 1982-84; chief operating officer Harrington Cancer Ctr., Amarillo, 1982-84; sr. v.p. Mercy Health System, Cin., 1988-91; pres. So. Ill. Healthcare Enterprises, Carbondale, Ill., 1992—; pres. So. Ill. Hosp. Svcs., Health Svcs. of So. Ill., Regional Health Plan, 1992-99. Active Amarillo Alliance of Cmty. Svc. Execs., Amarillo Area Acad. Health Ctr. Corp., Amarillo Area Hosp. Home Care, Amarillo Found. Health and Sci., Panhandle chpt. Tex. Soc. to Prevent Blindness, Amarillo Jr. League, Children's Oncology Svcs. of Tex. Panhandle; Amarillo diocesan coord. health affairs; mem. adminstrv. com. Amarillo; pres. Mercy Svcs. Corp., 1984-88; bd. dirs. Greater Phoenix Affordable Health Care Found., 1984-88; trustee Kenyon Coll., Gambier, Ohio, 1991-95, mem. alumni coun., 1998—; mem. SI Edge, 1995—. Fellow Am. Coll. Healthcare Execs. (regent Ariz. 1984-88, regent So. Ill. 1998—); mem. Tex. Hosp. Assn. (trustee 1983-84), Ill. Hosp. & Health Sys. Assn. (trustee 1995—, chmn. 2000), Cath. Health Assn. U.S. (bd. dirs., svcs. com., trustee 1985-91), Ariz. Kidney Found., Ariz. Hosp. Assn., Alumni Assn. of George Washington U. Health Svcs. Mgmt. and Policy (pres. 1995-97), Delta Phi (Phi chpt. Kenyon Coll. chpt., pres. alumni assn. 1988—). Republican. Roman Catholic. Office: So Ill Health Care Enterprises PO Box 3988 Carbondale IL 62902-3988

BUCKLEY, PETER JENNINGS, economics educator; b. Ashton-under-Lyne, Lancashire, Eng., July 11, 1949; s. Robert and Florence (Jennings) B.; m. Ann Patricia Kelland; children: Alice Louise, Thomas Robert. BA in Social Scis. with honors, U. York, Eng., 1970; MA, U. East Anglia, Norwich, Eng., 1971; PhD, U. Lancaster, Eng., 1975. Esmee Fairbairn rsch. asst. U. Reading, Eng., 1973-74; lectr. internat. bus. U. Bradford (Eng.) Mgmt. Ctr., 1974-80, sr. lectr., 1980-84, prof. econs., 1984-94; prof. internat. bus. U. Leeds, 1995—; vis. prof. U. Reading, U. Paris I, Pantheon-Sorbonne, 1993-96, U. Rennes, 1995-99, U. Groningen, 1998—, U. Lancaster, 2000—; hon. prof. U. Internat. Bus. and Econs., Beijing, China, 1998. Author: The Future of the Multinational Enterprise, 1976, others; editor Handbook of Internat. Trade, 1983; contbr. numerous articles to profl. jours. Fellow Acad. of Internat. Bus. (v.p. 1991-92, chmn. U.K. region 1985-91), Brit. Acad. Mgmt., Brit. Royal Soc. for Encouragement of Arts, Manufactures and Commerce; mem. Royal Econ. Soc., Shibden Valley Soc. (vice chmn. 1983-89). Anglican. Avocations: walking, history, conversation, reading, collecting books on economics. Office: U Leeds, Ctr Internat Bus, Leeds LS2 9JT, England

BUCKLEY, RALF CHRISTOPHER, research scientist; b. Bishop's Castle, England, Apr. 13, 1954; arrived in Australia, 1975; s. Franklin Barry and Jane Patience Poole (Allsebrook) B. BA with honors, Cambridge U., 1973, MA, 1975; PhD, Australian Nat. U., 1978. Chief environ. scientist Australian Mineral Devel. Labs., Adelaide, 1982-86; prof. environ. mgmt. Bond U., Gold Coast, Australia, 1989-90; prof. engring. & applied sci. Griffith U., Gold Coast, Australia, 1991-95, chair ecotourism, 1995—; dir. Wet Tropics Queensland World Heritage Mgmt. Authority, 1990, Ctr. Environ. Mgmt., Gold Coast, 1989—, Internat. Ctr. Ecotourism Rsch., Australia, 1993—, Nature and Adventure Tourism, CRC Tourism, Australia, 1997—; adj. prof. bus. Bond U., 1990—; dean engring. and applied sci. Griffith U., 1996-97; rsch. program leader Coop. Rsch. Ctr. Sustainable Tourism, 1996—. Author: Handbook for Environmental Audit, 1980, Environmental Planning Techniques, 1987, Perspectives in Environmental Management, 1993, others; editor: Ant-Plant Interactions in Australia, 1982, International Trade, Investment & Environment, 1994, Tourism Ecolabelling, 2000; contbr. over 150 articles to profl. jours. Australian Inst. Marine Sci. fellow, Townsville, 1979, Waite Inst. fellow Adelaide U., 1979, Rothmans rsch. fellow Australian Nat. U., Canberra, 1980-81, U. New England fellow, Armidale, Australia, 1987, sr. rsch. fellow Australian Nat. U., 1988, sr. Fulbright fellow, 1994. Mem. Australian Marine Sci. Assn., Assn. Tropical Biology, Ecol. Soc. Australia, Ecotourism Assn. Australia, Internat. Assn. Impact Assessment, Inst. Arid-Zone Rsch., Internat. Ecol. Assn., The Ecotourism Soc., Nat. Environ. Law Assn., Worldwide Fund Nature, Australian Conservation Found. Avocations: surfing, sailboarding, kayaking, snowboarding. Office: Griffith U, Parklands Dr, Southport 4217, Australia

BUCKLEY, RICHARD GEORGE, architect, educator; b. Urbana, Ill., Feb. 25, 1953; s. George and Madeline (Murad) B.; m. Diane Joy Stone, Feb. 14, 1987. BArch magna cum laude, U. Wash., 1980; MArch, U. Pa., 1982. Registered architect, Idaho, Wash., Nev., N.Y., Alaska, Hawaii, N.C., Pa., Ala., Ariz., Colo., Fla., Ill., Kans., La., Mich., Miss., Mont., N.H., NMex., S.C., Tenn., D.C., W.Va., Wyo. Instr. Phila. Inst. Art, 1982-84, U. Pa., Phila., 1983-84; architect Venturi, Rauch and Scott Brown, Phila., 1981-84; ptnr. in charge of design, architect NBBJ Architecture, Design and Planning, Seattle, 1984—; vis. prof. Coll. Arch. and Urban Planning U. Wash., Seattle, 1984—; bd. dirs. dept. arch. profl. adv. bd. U. Wash., 1995—; guest critic Cornell U., 1999. Prin. works include Samsung Kang Buk Hosp., Seoul, Sun Mountain Lodge (Interiors Mag. ann. internat. design awards best in hospitality award 1991), Market Pl. Tower (AIA Hon. Mention award 1988), Fluke Hall (AIA Honor award 1987), Microsoft Conf. Ctr. Chmn. Pioneer Sq. Hist. Preservation Bd., Seattle, 1992-95; bd. dirs. Seattle Zool. Soc., Mayor's Pine St. Task Force, Seattle, 1995; mem. Patrons of N.W. Civic, Charitable and Cultural Orgns., Seattle, 1995—; mem. Seattle Art Mus. Young Leaders Orgn., 1996. E. Lewis Dales traveling fellow, 1981; Narramore scholar, 1981-82, Aurhur Spayd Brooke Gold Medal in Design. Mem. AIA. Avocations: travel, collecting wine, history. E-mail: rbuckley@nbbj.com. Home: 915 37th Ave Seattle WA 98122-5226 Office: NBBJ Arch Design Planning 111 S Jackson St Seattle WA 98104-2820

BUCKLEY, ROBERT JOHN, academic research administrator; b. N.Y.C., Jan. 12, 1949; s. John Patrick and Mary Elizabeth (Carroll) B.; m. Lillian Perez, Apr. 28, 1973. BA, Fordham U., 1970; MBA, NYU, 1976. Asst. dir. devel. Hunter Coll. CUNY, 1970-72, asst. to dean programs in edn., 1972-77, dir. office research adminstrn., 1977—; chair coun. grants officers CUNY, 1984-86, 88—. Mem. Nat. Coun. Univ. Rsch. Adminstrs., Soc. Rsch. Adminstrs., Assn. Univ. Tech. Mgrs. Office: CUNY Hunter Coll 695 Park Ave New York NY 10021-5024

BUCKMASTER, CHRISTOPHER MEREDITH, business association executive; b. Liverpool, Eng., Oct. 29, 1938; s. John Meredith and Helen (Bass) B. BA with honours in Politics-Philosophy, Oxford (Eng.) U., 1960, MA (hon.), 1985. Various positions in W.I. and Africa, Booker McConnell Ltd., London, 1960-72; mng. dir. Stevenson & Howell Ltd., London, 1972-74; various directorships Dalgety Group, London, 1974-90; chief exec. Ea. Africa Assn., London, 1990—. Mem. London regional coun. Confedn. Brit. Industry, 1987-90; bd. govs. Holland Park Sch., London, 1994—; chmn. East Africa com. Bd. Overseas Trade, London, 1994-96; councillor Royal Borough Kensington and Chelsea, London, 1994—; chmn. edn. and librs. com. Royal Borough Kensington and Chelsea. Mem. Travellers Club. Mem. Conservative Party. Anglican. Avocations: food, wine, travel, skiing, music. E-mail: cmbuckm@btinternet.com. Fax: 020-7727-2683. Home: 23 Kensington Pl, London W8 7PT, England

BUCKNALL, CLIFFORD ADRIAN, cardiologist; b. Sale, Eng., Feb. 25, 1956; s. Eric and Elsie Constance (Whittaker) B.; m. Sarah Anne Topp, July 30, 1983 (div. 1996); children: Samuel Clifford, Thomas Adrian; m. Clare Collis, Nov. 22, 1997. Degree, Leamington (Eng.) Coll., 1967-74; MB BS, Westminster Med. Sch., London, 1979; MD, London U., 1987. House surgeon Warwick (Eng.) Hosp. Nat. Health Svc., 1979-80; house physician Westminster Hosp. Nat. Health Svc., London, 1980; sr. house physician Nottingham (Eng.) Hosp. Nat. Health Svc., 1980-82; rsch. fellow in cardiology Guys Hosp., London, 1982-84; sr. registrar Guy's Hosp., London, 1987-89, dir. cardiology, 1992-93; registrar Brighton (Eng.) Hosp., 1984-85, King's Coll. Hosp., London, 1985-86; sr. registrar King's Coll. Hosp., 1986-87, cons. cardiologist, 1989-92; dir. cardiology and cardiothoracic Guys & St. Thomas' Hosp. (NHS) Trust, 1996-97, dir. cardiac svc. and thoracic surgery, 1996-97; cons. cardiologist King's Coll., Dulwich Hosp., London Bridge Hosp., Sloane Hosp., London, 1989—, Guys and St. Thomas Hosp.; chief med. officer Royal and Sun Alliance, 1997-2000. Contbr. papers, chpts. to med. publs. Fellow Royal Soc. Medicine, Royal Coll. Physicians, European Soc. Cardiology; mem. Royal Coll. Surgeons, Brit. Cardiac Soc., Brit. Med. Assn. Anglican. Avocations: hockey, tennis, swimming. Office: St Thomas Hosp Cardiothoracic Ctr, Lambeth Palace Rd, London SE1 7EH, England also: Emblem House Ste 302, 27 Tooley St, London SE1 2PR, England

BUCKNELL, KATHERINE, writer; b. Saigon, Vietnam, June 11, 1957; d. John Addison Cobb Bucknell and Louise Wolcott (Devine) Carter; m. James Robert Maguire, Jr., Aug. 11, 1984; children: James Robert III, Lucy Wolcott, John Edward Carter. BA summa cum laude, Princeton U., 1979; BA, Oxford (Eng.) U., 1981, MA, 1986; MPhil, Columbia U., 1984, PhD, 1987. Jr. rsch. fellow Worcester Coll., Oxford, 1986-88; freelance writer, editor. Editor: W.H. Auden: The Map of All My Youth, 1990, W.H. Auden, Juvenilia: Poems 1922-1928, 1994, W.H. Auden: The Language of Learning and the Language of Love, 1994, W.H. Auden: In Solitude, For Company, 1995, ChristopherIsherwood Diaries Volume One 1939-1960, 1996, Christopher Isherwood Lost Years: A Memoir 1945-51, 2000. Nicolson fellow Columbia U., 1981-84, Newcombe fellow Woodrow Wilson Found., 1984-85, fellow Mrs. Giles Whiting Found., 1985-86. Mem. W.H. Auden Soc. (founding, bd. dirs. 1987—). Avocations: squash, tennis, skiing, running, swimming. Home: 78 Clarendon Rd, London W11 2HW, England

BUCKNER, MELVIN DANIEL, artist-designer, educator; b. Washington, Mar. 28, 1915; s. Jack Houston and Anne (Garfinkle) B.; m. Ruth Samuel, May 1, 1937 (div. May 1942). Conditional degree Carnegie-Mellon U., 1939; B.A., George Washington U., 1941. Artist U.S. Govt., Washington, 1938-41, artist-designer, 1946-56, 72-77; artist U.S. Army Air Force, Washington, 1941-44; artist-designer U.P.R., Santurce, 1944-46; mem. faculty U. D.C., 1956-58; tchr. pub. schs., Washington, 1971-72; pres. Soc. Washington Artists, 1957-61; sec. Artists Equity, Washington, 1964. One-man shows Georgetown Gallery, 1940, 41, Bader Gallery, 1947, Chelsea Gallery, N.Y.C., 1955, Corcoran Gallery Art, 1969; exhibited in 37 group shows throughout U.S., 1930-77; represented in permanent collection Phillips Gallery, Washington. Served with USAAF, 1941-44. Recipient Gold and Silver medals Soc. Washington Artists, 1940, 47, 56, 61, Brit. Biennial award, 1982. Avocations: photography; cooking. Home and studio: 33 Bridewell St, Clare Sudbury Suffolk C010 8QD, England

BUCKNER-REITMAN, JOYCE, psychologist, educator; b. Benton, Ark., Sept. 25, 1937; d. Waymond Floyd Pannell and Willie Evelyn (Wright) Whitley; m. John W. Buckner, Aug. 29, 1958 (div. 1970); children: Cheryl, John, Chris; m. Sanford Reitman, Aug. 13, 1994. BA, Ouachita Bapt. Coll., 1959; MS in Edn., Henderson State U., 1964; PhD, North Tex. State U.,

1970. Lic. psychologist, Tex., marriage and family therapist; cert. Nat. Registry Health Svc. Providers in Psychology; master trainer in imago relationship therapy. Assoc. prof. U. Tex., Arlington, 1970-80, chmn. dept. edn., 1976-78; pvt. practice psychology, Arlington, 1974—; dir., chief profl. officer Southwest Inst. Relationship Devel., Weatherford, Tex.; author, profl. speaker; appeared on internat. TV shows, including Oprah Winfrey Show. Mem. APA, Nat. Assn. for Imago Relationship Therapy (pres.), Nat. Speakers Assn., Am. Assn. Marital and Family Therapy. Avocations: dancing, travel, art. Home: 2208 Farmer Rd Weatherford TX 76087-6964

BUCKWALTER, ROGER JEROME, editor, columnist, TV interviewer; b. New Britain, Conn., Aug. 14, 1946; s. Benjamin Irving and Harriet Hoskins Buckwalter; m. Karen Ruth Adelson, June 8, 1974. BS in Broadcasting, U. Fla., 1968, MA in Journalism, Comm., 1969. Columnist The Jupiter (Fla.) Courier, 1978—, editorial page editor, 1982—; guest lectr. Palm Beach C.C., Lake Worth, Fla., 1992, 98, Fla. Atlantic U. Jupiter, Fla., 2000; guest interviewer WPTV, Channel 5, W. Palm Beach, Fla., 1994-99; polit. forum moderator Jupiter (Fla.)-Tequesta-Juno Beach C. of C., 1995—; mem. Fla. Atlantic U. Honors Coll. Adv. Bd., 1999—, Wal-mart Scholarship Selection bd., 2000. Vice chmn. Charter Rev. Com., Juno Beach, Fla., 1973-74; pres. Jupiter-Tequesta (Fla.) Unit Am. Cancer Soc., 1997-2000. 1st lt. U.S. Army, 1969-71, Vietnam. Recipient Best News Story award Surburban Newspapers Am., 1976. Mem. Nat. Conf. Editl. Writers, Fla. Press Assn. (Best Serious Column awards 1987, 96, Best Editl. awards 1989, 90, 93, 96), Fla. Press Club (Opinion and feature writing awards 1997). Avocations: painting, theater, writing. Office: The Jupiter Courier 800 W Indiantown Rd Jupiter FL 33458-7501

BUCKY, PETER STERN, psychologist; b. Berlin; naturalized U.S. citizen, 1942; s. Franz and Ellen (Bucky) Stern; children: Debra A., Janet L. BA, NYU, 1955, PhD (fellow), 1972. Psychologist various N.J. public schs., 1960-72; dir., mgr., psychologist Meridian Learning Ctr., 1972-75; psychologist and psychotherapist in pvt. practice North Bergen and Fort Lee, N.J., 1960—; instr. Rutgers U., 1968-69, Fairleigh Dickinson U., 1970-71; Staff and chief psychologist U.S. Air Force, Dayton, Ohio, 1957-60. Served to capt. USAF, 1957-60. Mem. Am. Psychol. Assn. Home and Office: 5 Horizon Rd Apt 2002 Fort Lee NJ 07024-6641

BUCOVE, ARNOLD DAVID, psychiatrist; b. Toronto, Sept. 22, 1934. BA, Columbia U., 1956; MD, NYU, 1961. Diplomate Am. Bd. Psychiatry and Neurology. Intern Lenox Hill Hosp., N.Y.C., 1961-62; resident in psychiatry Bellevue Hosp., N.Y.C., 1962-63, St. Luke's Hosp., N.Y.C., 1963-65; chief psychiatry 36th Tactical Hosp., Bitburg, Germany, 1965-67; pvt. practice psychiatry Pleasant Valley, N.Y., 1967-92, Poughkeepsie, N.Y., 1992-93; pvt. practice Oneonta, N.Y., 1993-99; attending staff Craig House, Beacon, N.Y., 1977-93; asst. dir. Dutchess County Mental Health Clinic, Poughkeepsie, N.Y., 1967-68; chief psychiatry Fox Meml. Hosp., Oneonta, 1993-99, sec.-treas. med. staff, 1997-98, pres.-elect, 1998-99, pres., 1999; pvt. practice Millbrook, N.Y., 1999—; staff psychiatrist St. Francis Hosp. Counseling Ctr., Poughkeepsie, N.Y., 1999—; cons. psychiatrist Greer Children's Cmty., Millbrook, N.Y., 1968-77; mem. courtesy staff Sharon (Conn.) Hosp., 1967-90; cons. IBM, Poughkeepsie, 1968. Contbr. articles to profl. jours. Bd. dirs. Town of Washing Civic Assn., Millbrook, 1986-93, Millbrook Music Assn., 1986-92; mem. vestry Grace Ch., Millbrook, 1971-74, mem. vestry St. Peter's Ch., Millbrook, 1989-92. Capt. USAF, 1965-67. Fellow Am. Psychiat. Assn. (pres. Mid-Hudson chpt. 1977-79); mem. N.Y. State Med. Soc., Dutchess County Med. Soc., Millbrook Hunt (bd. govs. 1968-71), Millbrook Golf and Tennis Club, Poughkeepsie Tennis Club. Avocations: riding, skiing, tennis. Office: St Francis Hosp Counseling Ctr 20 Manchester Rd Poughkeepsie NY 12603-2412

BUCSKY, PETER PAL, pediatrician; b. Budapest, Hungary, June 22, 1946; arrived in Germany, 1984; s. Sandor and Maria Terezia (Fayl) B.; m. Györgyi Gizella Kovács Bucsky, July 29, 1972; children: Beata, Peter, Bence. Med. diploma, Semmelweis Med. U., Budapest, Hungary, 1971, specialist in Pathology, 1974, specialist in Pediatrics, 1983; PhD, Med. U. Lübeck, Germany, 1994. Asst. prof. dept. pathology Semmelweis Med. U., Budapest, Hungary, 1971-80, asst. prof. clinic of pediatrics, 1980-84; rschr. Med. U. Ulm, Germany, 1984-86; asst. prof. Med. Sch. Hannover, Germany, 1986-90; head dept. pediatric oncology, hematology, immunology Med. U. Lübeck, Germany, 1990—; prof. peds., 1999; chmn. Malignant Histiocytosis Study Group of Histiocyte Soc., 1989—, Lübeck Hilfe für Krebskranke Kinder e. V, LÜbeck, Germany, 1991—, Therapy Trial for Malignant Endocrine Tumors in Children in Germany, 1996—. Co-author: Hodgkin's Disease in Children, 1989, Cancer in the First Year of Life, 1990, Hematology/Oncology Clinics of North America, 1998. Lutheran. Avocations: music, fine arts, theater. Office: Med U Lübeck, Ratzeburger Allee 160, D-23538 Lübeck Germany

BUCUR, ROMULUS VASILE, chemist; b. Padua, Italy, Mar. 19, 1928; s. Vasile and Elda (Fabbroni) B.; m. Doina Motiu, May 19, 1943; 1 child, Ioana-Rodica. Grad. in chemistry, U. Cluj, Romania, 1955; PhD, U. Bucharest, Romania, 1970. Head lab. Solvay Factory, Ocna Mures, Romania, 1955-56; sci. rschr. Inst. Atomic Physics, Cluj, Romania, 1956-58; prin. sci. rschr. Inst. Isotopic & Molecular Technology, Cluj, 1958-87, head lab., 1974-87; rsch. inorganic chemistry Uppsala U., Sweden, 1988-93; rsch. assoc. Ångström Lab. Uppsala U., 1993-98. Avocations: gardening, computer painting. E-mail: rvbucur@swipnet.se. Home: Näktergalsv 5, 352 42 Växjö Sweden

BUCURESCU, DOREL AMEDEU, nuclear physicist; b. Rasvani, Romania, Mar. 7, 1944; s. Amedeu and Dora (Diaconu) B.; m. Irina Stanculescu, June 21, 1970; 1 child, Iuliana. Diplomate, U. Bucharest, Romania, 1966; PhD in Nuclear Physics, Inst. Atomic Physics, Bucharest, 1972. Physicist Inst. Atomic Physics, Bucharest, 1967-70, rschr., 1970-73, sr. rschr., 1973-83, 85—; physicist I.A.E.A., Vienna, Austria, 1983-85; vis. scientist N.R.C. Demokritos, Athens, U. Koln, I.P.N. Orsay, I.S.N. Grenoble, L.N. Legnaro, J.I.N.R., Dubna, Tech. U., Munich, U. Tokyo, RIKEN Tokyo, U. Yale. Editor: Nuclear Collective Dynamics, 1983, Recent Advances in Nuclear Structure, 1991; contbr. articles to profl. jours. Mem. Romanian Phys. Soc., European Phys. Soc. Greek Orthodox. Avocations: travel, mountain hiking, classical music. Home: 73 Sandu Aldea, 71338 Bucharest Romania Office: Nat Inst Physics & Nucl Engring, PO Box MG-6, Bucharest Romania

BUCY, J. FRED, JR., retired electronics company executive; b. Tahoka, Tex., July 29, 1928; s. J. Fred and Ethel (Montgomery) B.; m. Odetta Greer, Jan. 25, 1947; children: J. Fred, Roxanne, Diane. B.Physics, Tex. Tech. U., 1951; M.Physics, U. Tex., 1953; DSc (hon.), Tex. Tech U., 1994. With Tex. Instruments, Inc., Dallas, 1953-85, engr. 53-63, corp. v.p. mil. sys., 1963-67, corp. group v.p. microchips, 1967-72, exec. v.p., 1972-75, exec. v.p., chief operating officer, dir., 1975-76, pres., chief operating officer, dir., 1976-84, pres., chief exec. officer, dir., 1984-85; cons. Tex. Instruments, Inc., 1985-97; dir. Thomas Group, Inc., Optical Data Systems, Inc., Hypres, Inc., Southwest Rsch. Inst., Rectractable Tech. Inc., Intrusion.com; cons., chmn. Tex. Nat. Rsch. Lab. Com. Patentee in field. Mem. Tech. Assessment of U.S. Congress; mem. Comptroller Gen.'sPanel, Pres.'s Commn. for Nat. Agenda for 80's,; comm. chmn. Nat. Rsch. Coun., Washington, Def. Sci. Bd. Dept. Def.; mem. bd. regents Tex. Tech U., Health Sci. Ctr. Tex. Tech U., 1973-91; chmn. bd. regents Tex. Tech U. and Health Sci. Ctr., 1980-82, 89-90; mem. adv. com. rsch. Tex.Higher Edn. Coordinating Bd.; external adv com. Arnold O. and Mabel M. Beckman Inst. Advanced Sci. Tech., U. Ill.; adv. coun. Woodrow Wilson Internat. Ctr. for Scholars, Washington; chmn. Tex. Sci. Adv. Coun.; nat. chmn. Enterprise Campaign Tex. Tech U.; mem. vis. com. Russian Rsch. Ctr., Harvard U.; mem. physics vis. com. MIT. Recipient Disting. Engr. award Tex. Tech U., 1972, Disting. Alumnus award, 1991. Fellow IEEE; mem. NAE, Am. Inst. Physics, Soc. Exploration Geophysicists, Conf. Bd., Sigma Pi Sigma, Tau Beta Pi, Cosmos Club (Washington), Dallas Petroleum Club. Address: PO Box 780929 Dallas TX 75378-0929

BUDAEV, VLADIMIR MICHAILOVICH, architect, designer; b. Moscow, Oct. 25, 1955; s. Valentina Vasilievna Budaeva; m. Olga Ivanovna, May 5, 1979; 1 child, Liza. Degree architecture, Moscow Archtl. Inst., 1984. Head architecture Artistic Planning Inst., Moscow, 1990—. Prin. works include Meml. of Victory, Pobedy Park at Poklonnaya Gora, Moscow, Ctrl. Mus. of Great Patriotic War, Cathedral of Georgiy Pobedonosetz, Synagogue Meml., Monument of Peter the Great, Moscow Zoo, also mcpl. bldgs.; contbr. articles to profl. jours. Recipient medal Holy Sergiy Radonezsky Russian Orthodox Ch., Honored architect Pres. of Russia, 1995. Office: Petrovka 26-28, 103051 Moscow Russia

BUDD, THOMAS MATTHEW, solicitor; b. Murwillumbah, NSW, Australia, Sept. 12, 1958; arrived in U.K., 1984; s. Derek Knight and Gwenda Molly (Gregor) B.; m. Gillian Susan Grendale, June 27, 1992; children: Matthew Charles Hamilton, Rory Edward Andrew. B Comm., U. Queensland, Brisbane, Australia, 1980, LLB, 1982; LLM, U. Cambridge, Eng., 1985. Cert. solicitor, Queensland, New South Wales, Eng., Wales. Articled clk. Morris, Fletcher & Cross, Brisbane, 1982-84, solicitor, 1984; solicitor Slaughter and May, London, 1985-92; ptnr. Gouldens, London, 1992—. Mem. Internat. Bar Assn. Office: Gouldens, 10 Old Bailey, London EC4M 7NG, England

BUDDE, THOMAS, cardiologist, educator; b. Essen, Germany, Feb. 11, 1957; s. Heinz and Renate (Herold) B.; m. Ute Stoermer; children: Sebastian, Adrian. MD, U. Düsseldorf, Germany, 1961; Habil., U. Münster, 1994. Lic. physician in internal medicine, cardiology and intensive care medicine, Germany. Resident U. Düsseldorf, 1981-88; jr./sr. attending physician U. Münster, 1988-95, sr. lectr., 1994—; head rsch. group Interventional Studies Inst. for Rsch. in Arteriosclerosis, Münster, 1991-95; head dept. internal medicine/cardiology Alfried Krupp Krankenhaus, Essen, 1995—, vice med. dir., 1998—; prof. U. Münster, 2000—. Author, editor: Experimental Studies on the Function of Subcutaneous-transvenous Defibrillators, 1995; co-author: Clinician's Manual on Management of Patients with Coronary Heart Disease, 1998; contbr. articles to profl. jours. Fellow European Soc. Cardiology; mem. German Soc. Cardiology, Rotary. Avocations: sailing, skiing. Home: Vossbergring 37, D-45259 Essen Germany Office: Alfried Krupp Hosp, Alfried-Krupp-Strasse 21, D-45117 Essen Germany

BUDDENSIEK, VOLKER WILHELM HANS DIETER, conservationist, journalist; b. Krebshagen, Schaumburg, Germany, Oct. 5, 1955; s. Friedrich and Christa (Grond) B.; m. Dorothee Wohlers, Dec. 29, 1987; children: Malte-Florian, Arne Sebastian. Cert. secondary tchr. biology, chemistry, U. Hannover, Germany, 1982, PhD in Zoology, 1991. Landscape engr. Schmal & Ratzbor, Hannover, 1991-95; pvt. rschr., 1996—. Author: (CD) The Succulent Euphorbia, 1998. Grantee Norddeutsche Naturschutz Acad., 1993. Mem. Euphorbiaceae Study Group. Avocations: plant propagation, photography. Home and Office: Kampstr 23, D 31655 Staothagen Germany

BUDDINGTON, PATRICIA ARRINGTON, engineer; b. Takoma Park, Md., Dec. 25, 1950; d. Warren and Elsie (Miller) B. BS, Northrop Inst. Tech., 1973; MS, Fla. Inst. Tech., 1986. With Air Force Systems Command, Edwards AFB, Calif., 1973-78; various positions Boeing Def. & Space Group, Huntsville, Ala., 1978-81, test engr. reaction control system inertial upper stage, 1981-86, lead engr. microgravity material processing facility, 1986-88, task leader advanced civil space systems, 1988—. Mem. AIAA (assoc. fellow). Office: Boeing Spl Projects PO Box 240002 (JN-04) 499 Boeing Blvd SW Huntsville AL 35824-3001

BUDGE, IAN, political science educator; b. Leeds, U.K., Oct. 21, 1936; s. John Elder and Elizabeth (Barnett) B.; m. Judith Beatrice Ruth Harrison, July 17, 1964; children: Gavin Elder, Eileen Elizabeth. MA, U. Edinburgh, Scotland, 1959; PhD, Yale U., 1967. Lectr. U. Strathclyde, Glasgow, Scotland, 1963-66; lectr. U. Essex, Colchester, U.K., 1966-68, reader, 1968-76, prof., 1976—; vis. prof. U. Wis., Madison, 1969-70, European U. Inst., Florence, Italy, 1982-85, U. Calif., Irvine, 1989, U. Autonoma, Barcelona, Spain, 1991; rsch. fellow Netherlands Inst. for Advanced Studies, Wassenaar, 1995-96. Co-Author: American Political Science Review, 1990, also over 50 others; author: The New Challenge of Direct Democracy, 1996; contbr. articles to profl. jours. Exec. dir. European Consortium for Polit. Rsch., Colchester, 1979-83; mem. polit. sci. com. Soecon. and Social Sci. Coun. U.K., London, 1980-83. Fellow Royal Soc. Arts and Mfrs. London; mem. Polit. Sci. Assn. U.K. (membership dir. 1974-77). Avocations: walking, gardening, theatre, Scotland, Italy. Home: 4 Oxford Rd, Colchester Essex C03 3HW, England Office: Univ Essex, Dept Govt, Colchester Essex C04 3SQ, England

BUDHIRAJA, SHASHI BHUSHAN, management consultant; b. Patiala, Punjab, India, Mar. 23, 1931; s. Kashmiri Lal and Sushilla (Batra) B.; m. Manorama Lal, Jan. 23, 1957; children: Sudeep, Rajeev. BS with honors, St. Stephens Coll., Delhi, India, 1949; BME with honors, U. Roorkee, India, 1952. Cert. mgmt. cons. Sr. staff Burmah-Shell, Bombay, 1952-67; mgmt. svcs. mgr. Indian Oil, Bombay, 1967-70; mng. dir. IBP Ltd., Calcutta, India, 1970-74, Balmer Lawrie, Calcutta, India, 1972-74, Indian Oil Corp., Bombay, 1974-78; overseas dir. Al Futtiam Group, Dubai, United Arab Emirates, 1978-82; fellow Harvard U. Ctr. for Internat. Affairs, Cambridge, Mass., 1982-83; mng. dir. Indian Oxygen Ltd., Calcutta, 1984-89; exec. dir. Mgmt. Devel. Inst., Gurgaon, India, 1990-93; chmn. Gunin Cons. Network Pvt. Ltd., Delhi, 1993—; pres. Inst. Mgmt. Cons. India, Bombay, 1993-95; chmn. Confederation India Industry Eastern Region, Calcutta, 1988-89. Co-editor: Cases in Strategic Management, 1996; contbr. articles to profl. jours. Pres. Jaycees, New Delhi, 1965, Indian C. of C., Calcutta, 1989-90. Named Mktg. Man of Yr. Inst. Mktg. and Mgmt., 1978. Fellow Inst. Mgmt. Cons. India, All India Mgmt. Assn.; mem. Willingdon Club, Bengal Club, Delhi Gymkhana, Rotary. Hindu. Avocations: travel, bridge, photography. Office: Gunin Cons Network, 3 Sukhchain Marg DLF Qutab, 122002 Gurgaon India

BUDININGSIH, YUSTY, petroleum engineer; b. Yogyakarta, Diy, Indonesia, May 22, 1963; came to U.S., 1993; B (PE), UPN Vet., Yogyakarta, 1992; MS in Petroleum Engring., N.Mex. Inst. Mining and Tech., 1995. Sec. Mada Ctr. Tropical Medicine U. Gadjah, Yogyakarta, 1996; reservoir engr. Conoco Indonesia Inc., Jakarta, 1996—. Pertamina PSC scholar, 1993-95. Mem. Soc. Petroleum Engrs., Soc. Indonesian Petroleum Engring., Indonesian Petroleum Assn.

BUDISAN, NICOLAE ILIE, electrical and control engineering educator, consultant; b. Cuvin, Arad, Romania, July 21, 1927; s. Ilie Dumitru and Maria Gheorghe (Cicirean) B.; m. Liliana Ioan Pantea, Oct. 24, 1953; children: Trica Lia, Stern Sorina. Student, Poly. Sch., Timisoara, Romania, 1946-48; Elec. Engr., Poly. Inst., Leningrad, Russia, 1953; PhD in Tech. Scis., Energetical Inst., Moscow, 1959. Ast. prof. Tech. Inst., Craiova, Romania, 1953-56; rschr. Romanian Acad., Timisoara, 1959-71; assoc. prof. Poly. U., Timisoara, 1959-71, prof., 1971—; vis. assoc. prof. Purdue U., Hammond, Ind., 1994; head br. Inst. for Automation, Timisoara, 1985-87; cons. Hidrotim S.A., Timisoara, 1991-94; rschr., sci. cons. Ctr. for Aeroenergetics, Timisoara, 1994—. Author: Systems Theory, vols. 1-3, 1986, 87, Systems Theory for Advanced Students, 1980, Automation and Telecommunication, 1968; contbr. articles to profl. jours.; patentee in field. Mem. Romanian Scientists Assn., Romanian Wind Energy Assn. Achievements include research in problems of automatic induction generator systems at unconventional hydro/wind/diesel/biogas energetical groups. Home: 6 Paciurea Sc B Apt 7, 1900 Timisoara Romania Office: U Politechnica, 2 Vasile Parvan Blvd, 1900 Timisoara Romania

BUDNIAKIEWICZ, THERESE, writer; b. Mons, Belgium, Sept. 28, 1948; came to U.S., 1961; naturalized, 1967; d. Tadeusz Eugeniusz and Janina Antonina (Więckowska) B.; m. Bart S. Ng, July 6, 1972. BA in Math., U. Chgo., 1971; MA in Comparative Lit., U. Mich., 1972, PhD in Comparative Lit., 1986. Lectr. in English Ind. U.-Purdue U., Indpls., 1987-92. Author: Fundamentals of Story Logic, 1992; contbr. Ency. of Semiotics, 1998. Recipient 20th Century award for achievement Internat. Biog. Ctr., Cambridge, Eng. Mem. MLA, Semiotic Soc. Am., Can. Semiotic Assn., Internat. Assn. for Semiotics of Law, Internat. Assn. for Semiotic Studies. Avocation: publishing technologies. Home and Office: 5823 Dapple Trace Indianapolis IN 46228-1698

BUDNICK, THOMAS PETER, social worker; b. Ludlow, Mass., Feb. 16, 1947; s. Henry F. and Mildred Mary (Killian) B. BS, Am. Internat. Coll., 1972, MA, 1975. Lic. cert. profl. social worker. Mailhandler U.S. Postal Svc., Springfield, Mass., 1970-72; substitute tchr. Pub. Schs. Dept., Ludlow, Mass., 1973-74; social worker Mass. Dept. Pub. Welfare, Springfield, 1975—; pres. Am.'s Manifest Destiny Soc., Inc., West Harwich, Mass., 1979—; bd. dirs. Mass. Astronomy Club, Boston, 1988—. Contbr. numerous articles to jours. V.p. Local 509, Boston, 1989. Democrat. Home: 19 Harding Ave Ludlow MA 01056-2327

BUDNIKOV, HERMAN CONSTANTINOVICH, chemistry educator, researcher; b. Moscow, USSR, Oct. 8, 1936; s. Constantin Petrovich and Seraphima Matveevna (Tovstyko) B.; m. Tatyana Victorovna Troepol'skaya, Aug. 13, 1936; children: Yulia, Victor. MSc in Chemistry, Kazan State U., 1959, PhD in Chemistry, 1963, DrSc in Analytical Chemistry, 1976. Lab. asst. Inst. of Chemistry/Acad. of Scis. of USSR, Kazan, 1958-60, jr. sci. worker, 1960-66; asst. prof. Kazan State U., 1966-67, assoc. prof., 1967-76, prof. analytical chemistry dept., 1976-86, head analytical chemistry dept., 1986—, dir. analytical rsch. group, 1986—. Author: Voltammetry Oscillographic Polarography, 1975, Electrochemistry of Metal Chelates in Nonaqueous Solutions, 1980; co-author: Basic Principles of Electroanalysis, 1986, Chemically Modified Electrodes for Voltammetry, 1994. Mem. Russian Acad. Natural Scis. (corr.), Internat. Acad. Higher Sch., Russian Ecol. Acad. (corr.). Orthodox. Avocations: gardening, shooting. Home: 40 Karbyshev Str, 420087 Kazan Russia Office: Kazan State U, 18 Kremlyovskaya, 420008 Kazan Russia

BUDO, CAMILLE JEAN RAYMOND, ophthalmologist, researcher; b. Horpmaal, Limburg, Belgium, July 7, 1947; s. Joseph M. Budo and Mia J. Ralet; m. Françoise M. Montanus; children: Valérie, Christophe, Gauthier. MD, U. Liege, Belgium, 1972. Tng. in ophthalmology U. Liege, 1972-76; pvt. practice, Sint Truiden-Melveren, Belgium, 1976—. Contbr. articles on ophthalmology to med. jours. Grantee Am. Soc. Cataract and Refractive, 1985-95, European Soc. Cataract and Refractive Surgeons, 1996. Home: Hasseltsesteenweg 40, 3800 Sint Truiden Belgium Office: Sint Godfriedstraat 8, 3800 Sint Truiden Melveren, Belgium

BUDOFF, PENNY WISE, physician, author, researcher; b. Albany, N.Y., July 7, 1939; d. Louis and Goldene Wise. BA, Syracuse U., 1959; MD, SUNY-Upstate Med. Sch., 1963. Intern St. Luke's Meml. Hosp., Utica, N.Y., 1963-64; practice medicine specializing in family practice, women's health, Woodbury, N.Y., 1964-85; clin. assoc. prof. family medicine SUNY, Stony Brook, 1980—; founder, dir. emeritus North Shore U. Hosp. Women's Healthcare (formerly Penny Wise Budoff Women's Health Svcs.), Bethpage, N.Y., 1985, ground-breaking women's health care facility; attending dept. ob/gyn. North Shore U. Hosp., 1992-97; asst. prof. ob/gyn. Cornell U. Med. Coll., 1993-96, pres. Bonne Forme Vitamins and Skin Care, divsn. Vitamins for Women, Farmingdale, N.Y., 1983—; prin. investigator pilot study to determine heavy metals in breast cancer tissue for patients residing on L.I. 10 yrs. or more, North Shore Hosp. and Brookhaven Nat. Lab., 1994; lectr., TV guest on women's medicine and health issues; mem. panel menopause NIH, 1993; clin. rsch. on menstrual pain, premenstrual syndrome, menopause, breast cancer and osteoporosis. Author: No More Menstrual Cramps and Other Good News, 1980, No More Hot Flashes and Other Good News, 1983, No More Hot Flashes and Even More Good News, 1998, World Book Health and Medical Annual, 1994; med. reviewer Jour. JAMA; contbr. articles to profl. jours. Bd. dirs. Coalition Against Domestic Violence. Named Woman of Yr. C.W. Post Coll., 1981; recipient Nat. Consumers League award, 1983, Max Cheplove award Erie chpt. N.Y. State Acad. Family Physicians, 1983, Women of Distinction award Soroptimist Internat. of Nassau County, L.I., 1990, award for promoting better understanding of menopause N.Am. Menopause Soc., 1999; honoree Nassau County Coalition Against Domestic Violence, 1992. Fellow Nassau County Med. Soc., Am. Acad. Family Physicians (nat. com. on pub. rels.); mem. NOW (Equality award in Health 1988, Unsung Heroine award), Am. Med. Women's Assn. (co-chmn. nat. women's health com., liaison), Nassau Acad. Family Physicians (past pres.).

BUDRUGEAC, PETRU, chemist, researcher, educator; b. Caransebes, Caras-Severin, Romania, June 30, 1949; s. Constantin and Elena Iuliana (Candus) B.; m. Ana Sanda Tatoli, July 31, 1970; children: Andreea, Raluca. Diplomat in Chemistry, U. Faculty Chemistry, Bucharest, Romania, 1972; PhD in Chemistry, Inst. Physical Chemistry, Bucharest, Romania, 1981. Chemistry rschr. Inst. Physical Chemistry, Bucharest, 1972-84; prof. chemistry Gheorghe Sincai Coll., Bucharest, 1984-86; sr. rschr. Rsch. and Design Inst. for Elec. Engring., Bucharest, 1986-95, Eurotest S.A., Bucharest, 1995-97, ICPE-Rsch. and Design Inst. for Elec. Engring., Bucharest, 1998—. Author: Problems of Chemistry, 1986, Elastomer Technology Handbook, 1993; patentee in field; contbr. articles to profl. jours. Recipient Nicolae Teclu premium Romanian Acad., 1990. Mem. N.Y. Acad. Sci., Romanian Thermal Analysis Group. E-mail: icpe.sa@icpe.ro. Home: Stoian Militaru 101 Bl3 #48, Sector 4 Bucharest 75349, Romania Office: ICPE-Res & Design Inst, Splaiul Unirii 313, Sector 3 Bucharest 74204, Romania

BUDZIKIEWICZ, HERBERT M. A., organic chemistry educator; b. Vienna, Feb. 20, 1933; arrived in Germany, 1965; s. Alfred and Maria (Hoffmann) B.; m. Renate Metzker, Apr. 1, 1970; children: Christine, Peter. PhD, U. Vienna, 1959. Asst. U. Vienna, 1957-60; sr. rsch. assoc. U. Stanford, Calif., 1960-65; dozent U. Braunschweig, Germany, 1965-69; prof. U. Koeln, Germany, 1970-98, prof. emeritus, 1998—; head of inst. U. Koeln, 1970-98, dean faculty of sci., 1972-74, 80-91, 88-89; head of inst. Rsch. Inst., Stoeckheim, 1966-69. Contbr. numerous articles to profl. jours. Mem. German Soc. Chemistry, Royal Soc. Chemistry, Am. Soc. Mass Spectrometry, German Soc. Mass Spectrometry. Avocations: skiing, mountain climbing, opera. Fax: 49-221-470-5057. E-mail: h.budzikiewicz@uni-koeln.de. Office: Inst for Organic Chemistry, Greinstr 4, Cologne D-50939, Germany

BUDZINSKI, ELISABETH, English language educator; b. Vienna, Austria, May 5, 1954; d. Alfred and Maria Kowarz; (div. 1988); 1 child, Eric. Teaching cert., Paedagogische Akademie, Baden, Austria, 1976; MEd, U. Ill., 1979; Magister Philosophy, U. Vienna, 1985; PhD, UCLA, 1992. Cert. C.C. counselor, instr., Calif. Cert. tchr., Austria. Adminstrv. asst. Am. Assn. Tchrs. of German, 1981-83; program coord. Goethe Inst., L.A., 1983-87; PhD student, articles editor UCLA, 1985-90; tchr. ESL Perchtoldsdorf, Austria, 1990—. Author: Looking for Paradise, 1993; (poetry) American Poetry Anthology, 1989. Recipient UCLA fellowship for doctoral students, 1988-89, stipend from Austrian govt. to study in U.S., 1976-77; rep. Austrian youth at Olympic Games, Munich, 1972; participant in Europeade, Spain, 1969. Avocations: philosophy, esoteric works, spiritual development, mind-body interaction. Home: Eggendorferg 12/1/4, A 2353 Guntramsdorf Austria

BUECHLEIN, DANIEL MARK, archbishop; b. Jasper, Ind., Apr. 20, 1938; s. Carl and Rose (Blessinger) B. BA, St. Meinrad Coll., 1961; student, St. Meinrad Sch. Theology, 1961-64; Licentiate Sacred Theology, Benedictine U. Sant' Anselmo, Rome, 1966. Ordained priest Roman Cath. Ch., 1964, consecrated bishop, 1987, archbishop, 1992. Asst. dean students St. Meinrad Coll., 1966-68, dir. spiritual formation, 1968-71; pres., rector St. Meinrad Sch. Theology, 1971-82, St. Meinrad Sch. Theology and St. Meinrad Coll., 1982-87; bishop Diocese of Memphis, Tenn., 1987-92; installed archbishop of Indpls., 1992—; chmn. divsn. religion St. Meinrad Coll., 1967-71, mem. Archabbey Coun., 1967-87; dir. First Nat. Conf. for Sem. Spiritual Dirs., summer 1971; mem. formation com. Conf. of Major Superiors of Men of USA, 1971-78; mem. nat. steering com. for follow-up of 1983 Nat. Assembly Sem. Rectors and Ordinaries; chmn. com. on proestly formation Nat. Conf. Cath. Bishops, 1990-93, mem. adminstrv. com. 1990-93, com. on marriage and family life, 1987, advisor doctrine com., 1989-93, mem. com. on doctrine, 1989-93, adminstrv. com., 1990-93, budget com., 1990-92, bishop's emergency relief com., 1990-92, chmn. ad hoc com. to oversee use of Catechism of Cath. Ch., 1994—, mem. subcom. on pastoral message in abortion, 1994—; peritus Internat. Synod on Priestly Formation, Rome, 1990; bd. dirs. S.E. Regional Office for Hispanics Afairs and S.E. Pastoral Inst.; co-pres. Disciples of Christ-Roman Cath. Internat. Dialogue, 1995—. Co-author: (with Bleichner and Leavitt) Preparing a Diocesan Priest: The Holistic Experience, 1987; Celibacy for the Kingdom, 1990; Commentary on a Survey of Priests Ordained Five to Nine Years, 1991; contbr. articles to profl. jours. Bd. dirs. Southeast Regional Office for Hispanic Affairs and Southeast Pas-

toral Inst., 1987—. Hon. chaplain KC, State of Tenn., 1987. Mem. Nat. Assn. Sem. Spiritual Dirs. (founding coord. 1972), Midwest Assn. Sem. Spiritual Dirs. (founding coord. 1971), Midwest Assn. Theol. Schs. (sec.-treas. 1972-74, ptrd. 1974-75), Theol. Edn. Assn. Mid-Am. (sec. 1972-74, 80-82, v.p. 1974-76, pres. 1976-78, 82-84), Nat. Cath. Edn. Assn. (chmn. exec. com. of sem. divsn. 1984-85, 85-86), Nat. Conf. Catholic Bishops (mem. com. on marriage and family life 1987-89, com. on priestly formation 1987-89, adminstrv. com. 1988—, bd. dirs. 1988—, budget and fin. com. 1990-92). Office: Archdiocese of Indpls PO Box 1410 D.BUECHLEIN Indianapolis IN 46206

BUECKMANN, DETLEF GEORG, biologist, educator; b. Helgoland, Germany, Nov. 4, 1927; s. Adolf Otto and Hildegard Eugenie (Thomae) B.; m. Erika Hedwig Stahl, Aug. 26, 1959; children: Elisabeth, Rudolf. DS, U. Hamburg; Dr.rer.nat., U. Mainz, 1952. Asst. U. Mainz, Germany, 1953-58; dozent, prof. U. Goettingen, Germany, 1958-65; prof. U. Giessen, Germany, 1965-69, U. Ulm, Germany, 1969-96; prof. emeritus U. Ulm, 1996, rector, 1979-83. Co-author: Physiologie der Insekten, 1995; contbr. articles to profl. jours. Recipient Wissenschaftspreis Stadt Ulm, 1972, Bundesverdienstkreuz am Bande 1983. Mem. Deutsche Zoologische Gesellschaft (v.p. 1974-76); Verband Deutscher Biologen (v.p. 1996), European Soc. Comparative Endocrinology. Office: Univ Ulm, Albert Einstein Allee 11, D 89081 Ulm Germany

BUEHLER, EVELYN JUDY, poet; b. Chgo.; d. Marzell William and Ida Mae Rubbia (Fields) Regulus; m. Henry Eric Buehler, Aug. 23, 1985; children: Ashley Leonard, Evelyn Judy. Student, Harold Washington Coll., Chgo. Author: Tales of Summer, 1998; contbr. short stories to Daring to Dream, 1995, Tears of Fire, 1995, A Moment to Remember, Wisdom of the Ages, 1997, Mortal Thoughts, 1997, Calm Winds, 1997, To Have and to Hold, 1997, A Writer's Season, 1995, The Best Writers of 1995, Wordly Thoughts and Lyrics of Poetry, 1995, Millennium The Alpha The Omega, Silver Words and Golden Thoughts, Where Words Haven't Spoken; contbr. poetry to Today's Greatest Poems, Our Twentieth Century's Greatest Poems, Our World's Best Loved Poems, Our World's Most Beloved Poems, Night Skies in Winter, Worldly Thoughts, Lyrics of Poetry, Am. Poetry Anthology, Best New Poets of 1987, Poems That Will Live Forever, The Best Poems of the 90's, Whispers in the Wind, Outstanding Poets of 1994, The Songs of Poetry, At Day's End, Calm Fires, 1995, Mortal Words, 1995, Words of the Soul, 1996, Beginning of a New Dawn, 1996, A Time to Remember, 1996, The Best Writers of 1996, Tears of a Soul, 1997, The Isle of View, 1997, The Other Side of Midnight, 1997, Diamonds and Pearls, 1997, Today, Tomorrow and Beyond, 1997, Masquerade of Words, 1997, The Best Writers of 1997, Endless Skies of Blue, 1998, The Best Poems of 1998, 2000 Outstanding People of the 20th Century, 1998, Outstanding Poets of 1998, 1998, others; contbr. chpts. to books, poetry to books and articles to profl. publs. Elected to Internat. Poetry Hall of Fame; named Internat. Woman of Yr. 197-98, 98-99, Internat. Woman of Millennium; recipient Twentieth Century Achievement award, 1999. Mem. Internat. Soc. Poets (life). Democrat. Baptist. Avocations: gardening, bicycle riding, hiking, art, camping. Home: 5658 S Normal Blvd Chicago IL 60621-2966

BUEHLER, JENNIFER SUE, English educator; b. Plymouth, Ind., July 16, 1945; d. Loren D. and Phyllis Elizabeth Waltz; m. Rance V. Buehler, Aug. 22, 1965 (dec. 1998); children: Elizabeth J., Aaron R. BA in English, U. Ill., 1967; MA in Curriculum and Instrn., Concordia U., River Forest, Ill., 1999. Tchr. Cmty. Consol. Sch. Dist. 15, Palatine, Ill., 1967-76, 88-99; instr. parent edn. Baxter Labs, Round Lake, Ill., 1986-88. Presenter Nat. Middle Sch. Conf., Denver, 1998. Mem. sch. bd. Cmty. Unit Sch. Dist. 220, Barrington, Ill., 1983-88; mem. Barrington Jr. Women's Club, 1978-88; bd. dirs. Barrington Area Hist. Soc., 1980-84, Barrington Area Devel. Coun., 1998—; mem. supt.'s comm. coun. Cmty. Consol. Sch. Dist. #15, 1997—. Methodist. E-mail: ejandr1@aol.com. Home: 204 W Lincoln Ave Barrington IL 60010-4268 Office: Sundling Jr HS 1100 N Smith St Palatine IL 60067-2606

BUEHLER, MARTIN, hotel executive; b. Berne, Switzerland, May 24, 1947; s. Ernst Jakob and Marie (Studer) B.; m. Rosemarie Eugster, Feb. 29, 1968 (div.); children: Christiane, Mark. BBA, U. Berne, Switzerland, 1967; postgrad., Tufts U., 1978. Cert. travel agt., internat. mktg. auditor. Mgr. Tourist Office, Berne, 1972-75; exec. v.p. Inter-Europe-Hotels, Berne, 1979-84; pres. Dial Europe Inc., Miami, Fla., 1984-85; v.p. Europe Choice Hotels, Berne, 1985-88; exec. v.p. Hotel & Touristik Expert Inc., Berne, 1988-91; area pres., CEO Europe and Mid. East Park Plz. Hotels & Resorts Internat., Montreux, Switzerland, 1991-98; chmn. Boutique Hotels & Resorts Internat., Scottsdale, Ariz., 1999, First Capital Hosp. Fin. Group, Miami, 1999—; guest prof. Hosta, Lexsin, Switzerland, 1988-91, Ritz Hotel Sch., Switzerland, 1993, Fairleigh Dickinson U., 1994; adminstr. Internat. Jazz Festival, Berne, 1976-85. Author textbook: Hotel Marketing, 1989. Fellow Internat. Mktg. Audit Assn. Office: 1221 Brickell Ave Fl 9 Miami FL 33131-3224

BUEHLER, THOMAS, psychotherapist, expressive therapist; b. Zurich, Switzerland, Aug. 9, 1943; came to U.S 1989.; s. Adolf and Margrit (Gredig) B.; m. Marina Schmidheiny, July 27, 1969 (div. 1986); m. Rosemarie Schiller, Apr. 19, 1995. MS, Med. Sch. U. Zurich, 1970. Cert. psychotherapist, Switzerland. Intern Accredited Swiss Hosp., 1969-75; multimedia artist Switzerland, 1973—; psychotherapist and expressive therapist, 1979—; co-founding, training therapist Internat. Sch. of Interdisciplinary Studies, 1982-85, advisory bd. Swiss Assocs. of Psychotherapists, 1984-85; founding chmn. Cardon Found., 1991—, Cirio Found., N.Y., 1993—;. Author: Der Vulkan ist aufgebrochen, 1976; one man performance Roter Stadtkriecher, 1985, Red Broadway Crawler, 1985, one man show, 1999. Mem. Internat. Assoc. of Artist Therapists, Nat. Expressive Therapy Assn., Swiss Assoc. of Psychotherapists. Avocations: piano, guitar, travel, wilderness, foreign cultures. Home: 140 Grand St #3WR New York NY 10013-3127 Office: Cirio Found 853 Broadway Ste 1708 New York NY 10003-4703

BUEMI, GIUSEPPE, chemist, educator; b. Novara di Sicilia, Italy, Nov. 26, 1940; s. Antonio and Alfia Rosa (Sofia) B.; m. Rosalba Concetta Floridia, Aug. 10, 1966; children: Agata, Carla, Antonio. Degree in indsl. chemistry, U. Catania, 1966. From rschr. to assoc. prof. physical chemistry U. Catania, Italy, 1966—. Author of more than 100 papers pub. in internat. scientific jours. Mem. Italian Soc. Chemistry. Avocations: gardening, jokes. Home: Via F Ciccaglione nr 15-D, 95125 Catania Sicily, Italy Office: U Catania, Viale Andrea Doria nr 6, 95125 Catania Sicily, Italy

BUENO, GRACIELA, computer science researcher; b. Mexico City, May 26, 1950; d. Jose and Aurora (Aguilar) B.; m. Enrique Arjona, Apr. 25, 1975; children, Saul, Andres. BS in Actuary, Nat. Autonomous U. of Mex., 1973; MSc in Stats., Postgrad. Coll., Mex., 1974; MSc in Computer Sci., U. Wis., 1977; DSc in Math., Nat. Politechnic Inst., Mex., 1999. Rschr. Internat. Ctr. for Corn and Wheat Improvement, Mex., 1973-74; prof. Autonomous U. Chapingo, Mex., 1986—; rsch. prof. Postgrad. Coll., Mex., 1974—, publs. supr., 1996—; cons. to several cos., Mex., 1980—. Author: (book) Introduction to Linear Programming and Sensibility Analysis, 1987, (book chpt.) Business in Less Developed Capital Markets, 1991; contbr. articles to profl. jours. Rsch. grantee Nat. Coun. Sci. and Tech., 1985, 94, 97. Mem. Soc. Computer Simulation Internat. Avocations: singing, swimming. Office: Postgrad Coll, Km 35 5 Carr Mexico-Texcoco, 56230 Montecillo Mexico

BUENZ, ALEXANDER PETER, chemical engineer, consultant; b. Hamburg, Germany, July 13, 1963; s. Peter Ingeborg (Schulz) B.; m. Tatiana Kutschera, Dec. 3, 1999. Diploma, Tu Hamburg-Harburg, Germany, 1990, PhD, 1995; student, TSM Bus. Sch., Enschede, The Netherlands. Registered profl. engr. Post-doctoral fellow U. Calif., Berkeley, 1995-96; group leader physical properties Degussa-Huels, Marl, Germany, 1996-99, knowledge process cons., 1999—. Author: Fortshrittsberichte VDI, 1995; contbr. articles to profl. jours. with German Army, 1983-84. Recipient Ernest-Solvay stipend, Stifterverband Deutsche Wissenschaft, 1989, NATO stipend DAAD, 1994, TSM & VDI, 1998. Mem. AIChe, VDI, Dechema. Avocations: swimming, furniture design, painting. Office: Degussa-Huels AG, Paul Baumann Str 1, 43764 Marl Germany

BUERGENTHAL, THOMAS, lawyer, educator, international judge; b. Lubochna, Czechoslovakia, May 11, 1934; came to U.S., 1951, naturalized, 1957; s. Mundek and Gerda (Silbergleit) B.; children: Robert, John, Alan; m. Marjorie J. Bell, 1983; stepchildren: Sebastian, Cristina. B.A., Bethany Coll., 1957, LL.D., 1981; J.D., N.Y. U., 1960; LL.M., Harvard U., 1961, S.J.D., 1968; Dr. Jur. (hon.), U. Heidelberg, 1986; Dr.Jur. (hon.), Free U. of Brussels, 1994; LLD, SUNY, Buffalo, 2000. Bar: N.Y. State 1961, D.C. 1983, U.S. Supreme Ct. 1982. Instr. law U. Pa., 1961-62; asst. prof. SUNY, Buffalo, 1962-64; assoc. prof. SUNY, 1964-67, prof., 1967-75; vis. prof. U. Tex.-Austin, 1975-76, prof., 1976-77, Fulbright and Jaworski prof., 1977-80; judge Inter-Am. Ct. Human Rights, 1979-91, pres., 1985-87; dean, prof. law Am. U., Washington, 1980-85; disting. prof. law and human rights Emory U. Sch. Law, 1985-86, I.T. Cohen prof. of human rights, 1987-89; Lobinger prof. of comparative law and jurisprudence George Washington U., Washington, 1989-2000, Lobinger prof. emeritus, 2000—; judge Adminstrv. Tribunal, Inter-Am. Devel. Bank, 1989-94, pres., 1993-94; mem. UN Human Rights Com., 1995-99; mem. Claims Resolution Tribunal for Dormant Accts. in Switzerland, 1998-2000, vice-chmn., 1999—; judge Internat. Ct. of Justice, 2000—; mem. adv. com. Restatement (3d) of the Fgn. Rels. Law of U.S.; chmn. human rights com. U.S. Nat. Commn. for UNESCO, 1976-79; U.S. rep. UNESCO Human Rights Working Group, 1977-78; U.S. expert UN Interregional Expert Meeting on Crime Prevention and Control, 1978; mem. adv. bd. Pres. Holocaust Commn., 1978-80; v.p. UNESCO Congress on Tchg. of Human Rights, 1978; mem. UN Truth Commn. for El Salvador, 1992-93; mem. U.S. Holocaust Meml. Coun., 1996—, chmn. com. on conscience, 1997-2000. Author: Law-Making in the International Civil Aviation Organization, 1969, (with L.B. Sohn) International Protection of Human Rights, 1973, (with J.V. Torney) International Law and the Helsinki Accord, 1977, (with R.E. Norris) Human Rights: The Inter-Am. System, 1982, (with Norris and Shelton) Protecting Human Rights in the Americas, 1982, 4th edit., 1995, (with H. Maier) Public International Law in a Nutshell, 1985, 2d edit., 1990, International Human Rights in a Nutshell, 1988, 2d edit., 1995, (with Grossman and Nikken) Manual Internacional de Derechos Humanos, 1990, (with Kiss) La Protection Internationale des Droits de l'Homme, 1991; contbr. articles to profl. jours. Recipient Pro-Humanitas Ring, West-Ost Kulturwerk, Fed. Republic of Germany, 1978, Disting. Svc. in Legal Edn. award NYU Law Sch. Assn., 1987, Wolfgang Friedmann Meml. award Columbia U. Law Sch., 1989. Mem. Am. Law Inst., Am. Soc. Internat. Law (v.p. 1980-82, Goler T. Butcher medal for excellence in internat. human rights 1997), Coun. Fgn. Affairs, Inter-Am. Inst. Human Rights (pres. 1980-92, hon. pres. 1992—). Office: George Washington U, Internat Ct Justice Peace Palace, The Hague The Neherlands*

BUERMANN, WERNER, retired engineering educator; b. Hilden, Germany, Feb. 17, 1934; s. Wilhelm and Else (Backhaus) B.; m. Renate Weber, July 31, 1965; 1 child, Philipp. Diploma in engrng., U. Karlsruhe, Germany, 1965, D in Engrng., 1972. Cert. in mech. and civil engrng. Sci. worker U. Karlsruhe, 1965-77, sci. employee, 1977-93, asst. prof., 1993-99; ret., 1999; project mgr. U. Karlsruhe, 1969-93, sec. diploma exam. commn., 1989-95. Author: (book) Waste Management Internationa, 1992; contbr. numerous papers to profl. jours. Mem. Assn. German Engrs., Karlsruhe U. Assn., Alumin KaTH. Roman Catholic. Avocations: literature, music, family research, sailing, tennis. Home: Bulacher Strasse 23C, 76275 Ettlingen Germany

BUFF, MARGARET ANNE, psychiatric nurse practitioner; b. Hanover, N.H., Nov. 2, 1955; d. Kenneth Andrew and M. Irene (Pender) Le Clair; m. James Steve Buff, Jan. 2, 1982; children: Jennifer, Steven, J. Thomas. BSN, BA in Psychology, RN, U. N.H., 1979; MA in Counselor Edn., U. N.Mex., 1985; MSN in Psychiat./Mental Health Nursing, Rivier Coll., 1997. RN, N.H., Mass.; ARNP, 1998. Staff nurse Vista Sandia Hosp., Albuquerque, 1980-81; charge nurse Los Lunas (N.Mex.) Hosp. and Tng. Sch., 1981-82; child devel. specialist Pueblo Infant Parent Edn. Project, Bernalillo, N.Mex., 1985-86; nurse, therapist Heights Psychiat. Hosp., Albuquerque, 1986-87; charge nurse Meml. Hosp., Albuquerque, 1987-88; staff nurse So. N.H. Regional Med. Ctr., Nashua, N.H., 1990-98; with Greater Lawrence (Mass.) Mental Health Ctr., 1998-2000; psychiatric nurse practioner Boston Rd. Clinic, Worcester, Mass., 2000—. Roman Catholic. Avocations: swimming, tennis. Home: 28 Hillside Dr Brookline NH 03033-2123 Office: Boston Road Clinic 324 Grove St Worcester MA 01605-3936

BUFFELAN-LANORE, JEAN-PAUL RAYMOND, lawyer; b. Toulouse, Haute-Gar., France, Apr. 12, 1931; s. Joseph Buffelan and Renée Jouhate; m. Yvaine Lanore, July 25, 1961; children: Isabelle, Marie-Aude, Marie-Axelle, Pierre, Olivier. PhD in Law, U. Toulouse and Paris Inst., Polit. Studies; JD, U. Paris; Diploma Pub. Law, Engrng. Sch. Scientific, Orgn. and Work. Laywer Ct. of Appeals, Toulouse, 1952-54, sec.-gen., 1954-60; fellow Fondation Thiers, Paris, 1960—; rschr. Ctr. Nat. de la Recherche Scientifique, Paris, 1960-68; dir. Ctr. de Documentation de l'Inst. de Recherche d' Info., 1968-71; prof. Nat. U. of Gabon, 1974-85, Nat. U. of Madagascar, 1985-87; dir. Inst. de Rsch. d'Info. Juridique, U. Parix VIII, 1987—; founder Jurindex, 1971. Author: (books) Les Institutions Municipales a Toulouse Sous L'Ancien Regime, 1961, le Complot Du 13 Mai 1958 Dans Le Sud-Ouest, 1966, Introduction a l'informatique Juridique, 1975, Communication, Documentation Juridique Et Traitement Informatique, 1977, Théorie de la Communication Juridique, 1984, la Noblesse des Capitouls de Toulouse, 1986, Informatique Juridique Documentaire, 1992, Vocabulaire de l'Admin. 1996, Droit Admin. gene rel, 1995, Contentieux Admin., 1996, Administration Citoyenne et cyberdroit, 1997, Le langage du cyberdroit, 1998. Decorated chevalier Nat. Order Merit, chevalier Order Palmes Academiques (France); recipient Gold medal City of Paris, Faculty of Law Laureat, Acad. Legis.; Citoyen d'honneur de la ville de Mazeres, France. Mem. Acad. de Langue doc des Ariegeois de Paris (pres.). Avocation: swimming. E-mail: jpbl@cybercable.fr. Office: U Paris VIII, 2 Rue de la Liberte, Saint-Denis 93526, France

BUFFET, MARIE-GEORGE, government official; b. Sceaux, France, May 7, 1949; married; 2 children. Degree in history & geography. Chari French fedn. Univ. Halls of Residence, 1970-72; mcpl. councilor, then deputy mayor Chetenay-Malabry, 1977-83; mem. ctrl. com. PCF, 1987—; nat. assembly deputy Seine-Saint-Denis, 1997; min. Ministry Youth & Sports, Paris, 1997—. Office: Ministry Youth & Sports, 78 rue Olivier de Serres, 75739 Paris France*

BUFFETT, WARREN EDWARD, entrepreneur; b. Omaha, Aug. 30, 1930; s. Howard Homan and Leila (Stahl) B.; m. Susan Thompson, Apr. 19, 1952; children: Susan, Howard, Peter. Student, U. Pa., 1947-49; B.S., U. Nebr., 1950; M.S., Columbia, 1951. Investment salesman Buffett-Falk & Co., Omaha, 1951-54; security analyst Graham-Newman Corp., N.Y.C., 1954-56; gen. partner Buffett Partnership, Ltd., Omaha, 1956-69; now chmn. Berkshire Hathaway Inc., Omaha, 1970—, also CEO; chmn. bd. Berkshire Hathaway, Inc., Nat. Indemnity Co., Nat. Fire & Marine Ins. Co., See's Candy Shops, Inc., Columbia Ins. Co., Buffalo Evening News; bd. dirs. Capital Cities/ABC, Salomon, Inc., Coca-Cola Co., Gillette Co., Fechheimer Bros. Co., Associated Retail Stores, Scott and Fetzer Co., Home & Auto Ins. Co., Omaha World Herald, Precision Steel Warehouse, Inc. Life trustee Grinnell Coll., 1968—, Urban Inst. Office: Berkshire Hathaway Inc 1440 Kiewit Plz Omaha NE 68131

BUFON, MILAN, geographer, educator; b. Trieste, Italy, May 28, 1959; s. Dusan and Tea (Berger) B.; m. Xenia Majovski, June 29, 1985; two children. BSc, U. Ljubljana, 1984, MSc, 1993, PhD, 1995. Rschr. Slovene Rsch. Inst., Trieste, 1985-95; sr. rschr. Sci. & Rsch. Ctr. Republic, Koper, Slovenia, 1996—; from asst. to assoc. prof. U. Ljubljana, 1986—. Author: Ethnicity and Territoriality: The Slovenes in Italy and Their Regional Identity, 1992, Space, Borders, Peoples, 1995, Schools and Lesser Used Languages: The Slovenes in Italy, 1996. Mem. Internat. Geographic Union. Office: U Ljubljana, Askerceva 2, 1000 S Ljubljana Slovenia

BUFORD-BAILEY, TONJA YEVETTE, track and field Olympic athlete; b. Dayton, Ohio, Dec. 13, 1970; d. Georgianna B.; m. Victor Bailey, Oct. 28, 1995. Grad., U. Ill., 1993. Mem. U.S. Olympic Team, Barcelona, Spain, 1992, Atlanta, 1996. Recipient 16 individual Big Ten championships U. Ill., 9 relay Big Ten championships, conf. title indoor awards for 55 and 200 dashes, 55 hurdles, conf. title outdoor awards for 100, 200, 400 and both hurdles, bronze medal Pan Am. Games, Havana, Cuba, 1991, silver medal Pan Am. Games, Argentina, 1995, silver medal World Championships, Gothenburg, 1995, bronze medal 400 meter hurdles Olympic Games, Atlanta, 1996; participant Olympics, Barcelona, 1992; ranked 7th in world for 400 meter hurdles, 1992, ranked 5th, 1993, ranked 2nd, 1995, ranked 3rd, 1996, ranked 6th, 1997. Office: USA Track and Field PO Box 120 Indianapolis IN 46206-0120

BÜGER, MATTHIAS, mathematician; b. Giessen, Hessen, Germany, May 3, 1969; s. Rüdiger and Ulrike Doris (Knoche) B.; m. Ariane Petra Warnat, July 25, 1997. Abitur, Herderschule, Giessen, Germany, 1988; diploma in math., J. Liebig U., Giessen, Germany, 1994, PhD, 1995. Rschr. J. Liebig U., Giessen, 1996—. Contbr. articles to profl. jours. Chmn. Junge Liberale, Giessen, 1991-98, treas., Hessen, 1993—. Named Best Young Scientist in Math., Jugend Forscht, Darmstadt, Germany, 1989. German Free Democratic Party. Home: Helgebachstrasse 3, D-35578 Wetzlar Germany Office: Math Inst J Liebig Univ, Arndtstrasse 2, D-35392 Giessen Germany

BUGGLE, FRANZ, psychology educator; b. Freiburg, Germany, Aug. 18, 1933; s. Hans and Ida (Löffler) B.; children: Anja Friederike, Birgit Ulrike Woglo. Diplma in psychology, U. Freiburg, Germany, 1958, PhD, 1963. Asst. lectr. U. Freiburg, 1961-63, prof., 1974—; asst. lectr. U. Hamburg, Germany, 1963-70; prof. U. Regensburg, Germany, 1970-74; dir. Psychol. Inst., U. Freiburg, 1974-98, dean philos. faculty, 1980-81. Author: Heutige Deutsche Universitats Studenten, 1965, Psychologie Gegenstand, Methodir, Soziale Raimenbedingungen, 1974, Die Entwicklungs Psychologie Jean Piagets, 1985, 3rd edit., 1997; Denn Sie Wissen Nicht, Wassie Giauben, 1992, 97. Mem. Deutsche Gesellscaft für Psychologie. Office: Psychol Inst U Freiburg, Beltortstr 18, Freiburg Germany

BUGHIN, JACQUES RENE, business executive, educator; b. Montigny, Belgium, Mar. 31, 1964; s. Guy and Mary-Therese (Wouters) B. B of Econs., U. Namur, Belgium, 1986, M of Econs., 1987; MS in Ops. Rsch., U. Pa., 1987; PhD in Ops. Rsch. and Econs., U. Louvain, Belgium, 1992. Cons. Andersen Consulting, Belgium, 1987, McKinsey & Co., various locations, 1992—; ptnr. McKinsey & Co., Belgium, 1998—; lectr. econs. U. Brussels, 1992—; lectr. NYU. Author: European Economic Review, 1999; contbr. articles to profl. jours. Mem. UNICEF. Recipient awards EARIE, CEPR, World Econ. Congress. Mem. Internet Soc. Office: McKinsey & Co, Ave Louise 480, 1050 Brussels Belgium

BUHAC, IVO, gastroenterologist; b. Dubrovnik, Croatia, Sept. 4, 1926; s. Ivan and Blazenka (Dulcic) B.; m. Susanne Rossband, Sept. 14, 1963; 1 child, John. MD, U. Med. Sch., Zagreb, Croatia, 1952, ScD, 1963; MD, U. Med. Sch., Erlangen, Germany, 1962. Staff physician Hosp. O. Novosel, Zagreb, 1957-68; resident in gastroenterology VA Hosp., Richmond, Va., 1968-70; asst. prof. medicine Albany (N.Y.) Med. Coll., 1970-74, assoc. prof. medicine, 1974-82, prof. medicine, 1982-88, chief of gastroenterology, 1970-88. Contbr. articles to Gastroenterology, Hepatology, N.Y. State Jour. Medicine, Deutsche Medizinische Wochenschrift. Mem. Am. Gastroenterology Assn., Am. Assn. for Study of Liver Diseases, N.Y. Acad. Scis. Achievements include research on the pathophysiology of ascites formation in liver cirrhosis, diagnosis of disease causing death of Herod the Great. Home: 64 Spruce St Clifton Park NY 12065-1145

BUHALIS, DIMITRIOS, tourism and hospitality educator, consultant; b. Athens, Greece, Aug. 18, 1967; arrived in Eng., 1990; s. Theodoros and Stella (Dounia) B. BBA, U. Aegean, Chios, Greece, 1989; MSc in Tourism, U. Surrey, Guildford, Eng., 1991, PhD in Tourism, 1995. Cert. tourism mgmt., hospitality mgmt. Chief photographer Photomat/Club Med, Greece, 1984-89; rschr. U. Aegean, Chios, Greece, 1986-90; cons. Enalme SA, Athens, Greece, 1989-90; rschr. U. Surrey, Guildford, 1991-96; cons. Surrey Rsch. Group, Guildford, 1991-96; sr. lectr. U. Westminster, London, 1995—; adj. prof. Cornell U.-ESSEC, Paris, 1997—; cons. Phare/European Union, Romania, 1984, World Tourism Orgn., Ivory Coast, 1996; dir. tourism rsch. U. Westminster, London, 1995—. Editor: Information Technology and Tourism, 1998, 99; asst. editor Progress in Tourism and Hospitality Jour., 1996—; contbr. articles to profl. jours., chpts. to books. Mem. Assn. Tourism Tchrs. and Trainers (chmn. 1997—), Tourism Soc., Internat. Fedn. for Info. Tech. and Tourism, Trinet. Avocations: photography, travel, swimming, walking. Fax: 44 1483 574463. Home: 173 Walnut Tree Close, Guildford GU1 4UB, England Office: Dept Tourism U Westminster, 35 Marylebone Rd, London NW1 5LS, England

BUHL, CYNTHIA MAUREEN, foreign policy educator and advocate; b. Los Angeles, Apr. 14, 1952; d. Albert Buhl and Dorothy Jane (Loth) Henry. BA, Lewis & Clark Coll., 1974. Dir. Resource and Counseling Ctr., Portland Youth Advs., Oreg., 1971-72; resource coordinator S.E. Youth Service Ctr., Portland Action Coms. Together, 1975-77; sec., asst. Human Rights Office Nat. Council Chs. Christ, N.Y.C., 1977-78; human rights coordinator Coalition for a New Fgn. and Mil. Policy, Washington, 1978-85; cons. Fgn. Policy Edn. Fund, Washington, 1986; nat. adv. bd. Caribbean Basin Info. Project, 1983-85; bd. dirs., legis. dir. Pax Am.'s/Priorities-PAC, 1986-90; legis. dir. Ctrl. Am. Working Group, 1990-93; dir. Indigenous Peoples Program, Bank Info. Ctr., 1994-96; legis. dir. U.S. Rep. James A. McGovern, 1997—. Author: Citizen's Guide to the Multilateral Development Banks and Indigenous Peoples: The World Bank, 1994, Spanish transl., 1995, Bahasa transl., 1996, Russian transl., 1996; co-editor: Central America 1985: Basic Information and Legislative History on U.S.-Central American Relations, 1985. Contbr. articles to various jours., mags. Co-chmn. Human Rights Working Group, Washington, 1978-81, chmn., 1982-85; chmn. Central Am. Lobby Group, 1983-85; mem. Commn. on U.S.-Central Am. Relations, 1983-85.

BUHLER, JILL LORIE, editor, writer; b. Seattle, Dec. 7, 1945; d. Oscar John and Marcella Jane (Hearing) Younce; 1 child, Lori Jill Moody; m. John Buhler, 1990; stepchildren: Christie Reynolds, Cathie Zatarian, Mike. AA in Gen. Edn., Am. River Coll., 1969; BA in Journalism with honors, Sacramento State U., 1973. Reporter Carmichael (Calif.) Courier, 1968-70; mng. editor Quarter Horse of the Pacific Coast, Sacramento, 1970-75, editor, 1975-84; editor Golden State Program Jour., 1978, Nat. Reined Cow Horse Assn. News, Sacramento, 1983-88, Pacific Coast Jour., Sacramento, 1984-88, Nat. Snaffle Bit Assn. News, Sacramento, 1988; pres., chief exec. officer Communications Plus, Port Townsend, Wash., 1988—; campaign mgr. N.W. Maritime Ctr., 2000—; mag. cons., 1975—; campaign mgr. N.W. Maritime Ctr., 2000—. Interviewer Pres. Ronald Regan, Washington, 1983; mng. editor Wash. Thoroughbred, 1989-90. Mem. 1st profl. communicators mission to USSR, 1988; bd. dirs. Carmichael Winding Way, Pasadena Homeowners Assn., 1985-87; mem. scholarship com. Thoroughbred Horse Racing's United Scholarship Trust; mem. governing bd. Wash. State Hosp. Assn., 1996-2000, mem. legis. com., 1999—, hosp. commr. Jefferson Gen. Hosp., 1995—, chair bd. dirs. 1997-2000; mem. Jeferson County Bd. Health, 1997, vice chair, 1998; vice-chair Jefferson County Bd. Health, 1998—. Recipient 1st pl. feature award, 1970, 1st pl. editorial award Jour. Assn. Jr. Colls., 1971, 1st pl. design award WCHB Yuba-Sutter Counties, Marysville, Calif., 1985, Photography awards, 1994, 95, 96. Mem. Am. River Jaycees (Speaking award 1982), Am. Horse Publs. (1st Pl. Editl. award 1983, 86), Port Townsend C. of C. (trustee, v.p. 1993, pres. 1994, officer 1996, 97, 98), Mensa (bd. dirs., asst. local sec., activities dir. 1987-88, membership chair 1988-90), Kiwanis Internat. (chair maj. emphasis program com., treas. 1992—), 5th Wheel Touring Soc. (v.p. 1970). Republican. Roman Catholic. Avocations: sailing, photography. Home: 440 Adelma Beach Rd Port Townsend WA 98368-9280

BÜHLER, NICOLAS, financial executive; b. Beziers, France, Feb. 18, 1950; s. Jean Bühler and Marcelle Arnaud; m. Muriel Gauch; children: Fabrice, Vincent, Florent. Degree in acctg. and commerse, ESC, Marseille, France, 1972; D Mgmt. Scis., U. Grenoble, 1974. Cons., ptnr., then sr. ptnr. Bossard Cons., 1980-95; v.p. Leroy Cons., 1995-96; sr. ptnr. Coopers & Lybrand, 1996-98, Pricewaterhouse Coopers, Paris, 1998—. Co-author: Sociodynamics of Change, 1992, Le Travail au xxi Siecle, 1995. Avocations: sailing, jazz, piano, tennis. Office: Pricewaterhouse Coopers, 34 Place de Corolles, 92908 La Defense Cedex Paris, France

BUHOLTE, AGNESE, library director; b. Ligatne, Cēsis, Latvia, June 5, 1952; d. Jānis Dancis and Rasma (Timermane) Dance; m. Jānis Buholts, Sept. 7, 1974; children: Jānis, Inese. Diploma in Lib. Scis., U. Latvia, Riga, 1974. Diplomated librarian and bibliographer. Librarian Patent and Tech. Lib. of Latvia, Riga, 1974-75, chief librarian, 1975-76, head methodics dept.,

1976-85, dir., 1985—. Mem. Lib. Assn. Latvia (bd. dirs. 1990—), Latvian Academic Lib. Assn. (v.p. 1998—). Avocations: gardening, sewing, knitting, travel, music. Home: 14 Upes St Apt 11, Riga Latvia LV-1013 Office: Patent and Tech Libr of Latvia, Skunu Iela 17, 1974 Riga Latvia

BUI, HUONG QUOC, neuropsychiatrist; b. Bac-Kan, Vietnam, Aug. 31, 1924; arrived in France, 1970; s. Tuong Phat and San Thi (Han) B.; m. Marie Thuc Thi Vu, July 16, 1954; children: Claude Hinh, Phillipe Hung, Pierre-Andre Hien. MD, Faculty of Medicine, U. Hanoi, Vietnam, 1952; cert. neuropsychiatry, diploma malariology, Faculty of Medicine, U. Paris, 1957, agregation in neuropsychiatry, 1962. Clinic chief Faculty of Medicine, Hanoi U., 1953, asst. prof., 1953-54; asst. prof. Faculty of Medicine, Paris, 1954-56; assoc. prof. Faculty of Medicine, Saigon, Vietnam, 1957-63, maitre de conference, 1963-65, prof. neurology and psychiatry, 1965-69; practice medicine specializing in neuropsychiatry Paris, 1977—; vis. prof. Georgetown U. Hosp., Washington, 1969, researcher, 1970-76. Contbr. articles to profl. jours. Recipient Nat. Sci. Research prize Ministry Culture Vietnam-Unesco, 1966. Mem. World Fedn. Neurology, Soc. Francaise de Neurology (fgn. hon. 1964, assoc. 1987). Confucian. Avocations: violin, classical music, history, travel. Home: 7 Rue Nicolas Roret, Gobelin, 75013 Paris France Office: 14 Rue Pirandello, 75013 Paris France

BUI, KHOI TIEN, college counselor; b. Binh Dinh, Vietnam, Dec. 23, 1937; came to U.S., 1975; naturalized, 1982; s. Luu and Quang Thi (Tran) B.; m. Yen Kim Nguyen, Dec. 7, 1962; children: Khanh, Huy, Huan. BS in Agri., Agrl. Coll., Vietnam, 1962; BS, Law U., Vietnam, 1965; MS, Polit. and Bus. Mgmt. U., Vietnam, 1972; PhD, Polit. and Bus. Mgmt. U.; DLitt (hon.), London Inst. for Applied Rsch., 1991. With Ministry Agri., Republic of Vietnam, 1962-75; counselor Houston C.C., 1976—, chmn. Indochinese Culture and Refugee Info. Ctr., 1981—; Nat. Planner Tng., Taiwan, 1963, Philippines, 1965, Australia, 1968, Japan, 1970, Thailand, 1971. Author: (poetry books) America My First Feelings, 1981, 20 Poems and 1000 Thoughts, 1994; contbr. to other poetry books, novel and textbook in Vietnamese. Founder, moderator radio sta. The Voice of Free Vietnam, Houston, 1980—; chmn. Indochinese and Refugee Info. Ctr., Houston Community Coll. Recipient Nat. Lit. prize Republic Vietnam, 1966, Houston's Poet Laureate award, 1984, Golden Poet award World of Poetry, 1985, Edn. award, 1985, Men of Achievement award, 1989, Medal of Honor, 1990, One-in-a-Million Medal, 1991, Most Admired Man of the Decade award, 1992, Twentieth Century award for Achievement, 1992, various medals Govt. of the Republic of Vietnam; named Man of Yr., 1990, Internat. Man of Yr., 1992. Mem. Leadership Houston Assn., Pen Am. Ctr. Avocations: writing poetry, reading, swimming. Home: 13715 Towne Way Dr Sugar Land TX 77478-1652 Office: Houston CC 1300 Holman St Houston TX 77004-3834

BUI, LONG VAN, church custodian, translator; b. Cao Xa, Vietnam, May 1, 1940; came to U.S., 1985; s. So Van and Ninh Thi (Nguyen) B.; m. Dung Thi Le, May 14, 1970; children: Van Thanh Bui, Long Ba Bui. Student, U. Dalat, Vietnam, 1960; AA, Houston C.C., 1991. H.S. tchr. Vietnam, 1964, mil. svc., 1965-75, detainee, 1975-81; grocery store cashier Houston, 1986; custodian Spring Branch Cmty. Ch., Houston, 1986—. Editor: Holy Family newsletter of Youth Better Found., Houston, 1993—; translator Medjugorie The Message into Vietnamese, 1993, Fatima the Great Sign into Vietnamese, 1994, Testimony of Father Robert DeGrandis, S.S.J., 1998, Healing the Father Relationship, 1998, Failure in Your Life, 1998, The Ten Commandments of Prayer into Vietnamese, 1998, Multiplication des Apparitions de la Vierge Aujourd'hui into Vietnamese, 1998. Capt. Vietnamese Army, 1965-75. Mem. Youth Better Found. Roman Catholic. Avocations: reading, translating. Home: Apt 2303 8801 Hammerly Blvd Houston TX 77080-6507 Office: Youth Better Found 11906 Drummond Park Dr Houston TX 77044-5002

BUILLARD, MICHEL, mayor; b. Papeete, French Polynesia, Sept. 9, 1950; married; 2 children. Lic. in law. Former dir. Territorial Office Social Action and Solidarity; mcpl. counselor City of Pirae, Tahiti; min. work, employment, profl. tng. and housing, 1984-86, min. youth, sports, and housing, 1986-87, coun. Territorial Assembly French Polynesia, dist. Iles du Vent, 1991; v.p., min. health, solidarity, housing, and rsch. Govt. French Polynesia, 1991, v.p., min. health, housing, and rsch., 1991, v.p., min. health and housing, 1994, min. health and culture, 1995—, min. youth, social involvement youth in sports and city politics, 1996—; mayor City of Papeete, 1995—. Office: City of Papeete, Minister Youth, Sports & Local Govt, Papeete French Polynesia*

BUILO, SERGEY IVANOVICH, physicist; b. Rostov-on-Don, Russia, June 17, 1948; s. Ivan Builo and Irina Mogilina. Grad., Rostov-on-Don State U., 1972, MSc in Physics, 1972, PhD, 1984. From rschr. to head solid body acoustics dept. Rostov-on-Don State U., Russia, 1972—. Author: Acoustic Emission: Physical and Mechanical Aspects, 1986; contbr. articles to profl. jours. Home: pr Stachki 193/2 app 61, 344058 Rostov-on-Don Russia

BUIS, PATRICIA FRANCES, geology educator, researcher; b. Jersey City, Dec. 29, 1953; d. George Herman Buis and Marie Agnes Fitzsimmons. BA in Geology, Rutgers U., 1976; MA in Geology, Queens Coll., 1983; PhD in Geology, U. Pitts., 1988; MS in Mining Engring., Mich. Tech. U., 1994, PhD in Mining Engring., 1995. Coal quality geochemist Pa. Geologic Survey, Harrisburg, 1989-91; asst. prof. U. Miss., Oxford, 1994-96, Japanese Sci. and Tech. Mgmt. Program scholar, 1996-97; vis. asst. prof. mining engr. dept. U. Alaska, Fairbanks, 1997-98; vis. lectr. earth sci. dept. N.E. Ill. U., Chgo., 1998-99; cons., reviewer of sci. textbooks prior to pub. Winston-Rinehart, Austin, Tex., 1994—. Dept. Edn. doctoral fellow in mining Mich. Tech. U., 1991-95, Provost Predoctoral fellow U. Pitts., 1988; Dept. Edn. grantee Mich. Tech. U., 1993; nat. merit scholar Schering-Plough, Rutgers U., 1971-75. Mem. Soc. Exploration Geochemistry, Nat. Water Wells Assn., Am. Mineralogist, Sigma Xi.

BUIST, RICHARDSON, corporate executive, retired banker; b. Bklyn., Aug. 8, 1921; s. George Lamb and Adelaide (Richardson) B.; m. Jean Mackerley, Oct. 2, 1948; children: Peter Richardson, Jean Morford Buist Earle, Mary Elizabeth Buist Leach. Student, Yale U. Advt. copywriter Ecloss Co., Sparta, N.J., 1946-48; advt. mgr. Sussex County Ind., Newton, N.J., 1948-50, Dover (N.J.) Advance, 1950-53; bus. mgr. N.J. Herald, Inc., Newton, 1953-70, dir., v.p., 1958-70, pub., 1967-70; dir. N.J. Press Assn., 1966-70; asst. sec., asst. treas. Morford Conservation Co., Hamburg, 1965-72, pres., 1986-95, v.p., 1995—; trust officer Midlantic Nat. Bank/Sussex & Mchts., Newton, 1971-88, Midlantic Nat. Bank, Edison, N.J., 1972-86, cons. 1986-90, dir. Newton Cemetary Co., 1989-2000, v.p., 1998-2000. Pres. Sussex County chpt. Am. Cancer Soc., 1956-58, Sussex County Music Found., 1959-61; mem. Morris-Sussex Area Health Facilities Planning Coun., 1965-68; v.p. Sussex County Coun. Arts, 1971-73; chmn. pub. rels. Morris-Sussex Area Coun. Boy Scouts Am., 1986-88; trustee Sussex County Music Found., 1955-75; v.p., chmn. fin. devel. com. Newton Meml. Hosp., 1966-68, bd. govs. 1962-88, 93-95, emeritus 1995—, pres. bd. govs., 1968-71, chmn., 1971-73; founding incorporator, trustee NW Jersey Health Care, 1971-76; trustee, mem. exec. com. regional health planning coun. Health Systems Agy., 1976-83, 1984-87, v.p., 1978-79; trustee United Way of Sussex County, 1984-90, spl. gifts chmn., 1984-88, mem. allocations com. 1990-93; dir. North Jersey Health Care Corp., 1988-95, dir. emeritus, 1995—, asst. treas., 1991-93; dir. Prime Care, Inc., 1989-95, chmn. bd. trustees, 1989-92; mem. Sussex County Arts and Heritage Coun., chmn. hist. house tour, 1993-95; steering com. N.J. Highlands Coalition, 1993—. Mem. N.J. Vet. Med. Soc. Aux. (del. 1979-82, 88-91, 2d v.p. 1990-91), Am. Vet. Med. Soc. Aux. (nat. chmn. legis. com. 1986-88, long-range planning com. 1990-95, chmn. 1992, mem. constitution, by-laws coms. 1993-95), Morristown (N.J.) Club, Rotary (pres. 1967-68, Paul Harris fellow 1988, Svc. Above Self award 1993, Meritorious Svc. award 1998), Vernon Civic Assn. (dir. 1996-2000, v.p. 1997-98). Home: 4123 Fellowship Rd Basking Ridge NJ 07920

BUJARRABAL, VALENTIN, astronomer; b. Madrid, Aug. 23, 1954; s. Luis Bujarrabal and Maria Fernandez; m. Concepcion Dueso, Dec. 15, 1983; children: Alejandro, Arturo. Grad. in Math., U. Complutense, Madrid, 1977, Grad. in Physics, 1976; PhD in Physics, U. Paris VII, 1981. Prof. U. Complutense, Madrid, 1976-77; assoc. prof. U. Complutense, 1983—; fellow Observatoire de Meudon, Paris, 1978-81, Nat. Radioastronomy Observatory, Green Bank, 1979; astronomer Observatorio Astronomico Nacional, Madrid, 1982—; cons., referee Millimeter Radio Astronomy Observatory, Europe, 1985—, European Space Agy., Europe, 1994—, European VLBI Network, Europe, 1995-97, Direccion Gen. de Ciencia y Tecnologia, Spain, 1989—. Contbr. articles to profl. jours. Mem. Internat. Astron. Union. Office: Observatorio Astron Nac, Apartado 1143, 28800 Alcala de Henares Spain

BUJDOSÓ, GEORGETTE, biochemist, researcher, actor; b. Budapest, Hungary, Apr. 8, 1939; d. József Bujdosó and Ibolya Dèsi; m. Károly Mècs. Diploma, U. Budapest, 1968, D, 1972; PhD, Acad. Scis., Budapest, 1982. Sci. mem. Inst. Forensic Medicine, Semmelweis U. Medicine, Budapest, 1968, sr. mem., 1983, sci. cons., 1991, head lab. human genetics, 1991—; cons. in field. Co-author: Gammopathy, 1993, Klinikai Genetika, 1995, Advances in Forensic Sciences, vol. 6, 1995, Genetischer Atlas des Authropologie und Zrblielogie, 1999; author (album) Antropomorphgenetik, 1995. Mem. Assn. Environ. Edn. (bd. dirs. 1992), European Soc. Human Genetics, European Soc. Mutagenesis, N.Y. Acad. Scis. Roman Catholic. Avocations: writing, swimming. Office: Sommelweis U Medicine Inst Forensic Medicine, Üllöi ut 93, 1091 Budapest Hungary

BUJ-FLORES, H.E. ENRIQUE, Mexican diplomat; b. Mexico City, Aug. 26, 1942; s. Enrique Buj-Requena and Maria Helena Flores; m. Marina Cabezas, Aug. 30, 1976; children: Valentina, Marietta. Student, U. Mex., El Colegio de Mex., U. Nebr. Cultural attache Mexican Embassy, El Salvador; sec. Mexican Embassy, Havana, Cuba; counselor Mex. Embassy, Washington; dept. perm. rep. Mex. Mission to UN, N.Y.C.; amb. Mex. Embassy, Kenya, Africa; consul gen. Mex. Consulate, El Paso, Tex.; internat. orgns. dep. Ministry Fgn. Affairs, Mex.; consul gen. Mex. Consulate, Sydney, Australia; amb. Mex. Embassy, Australia, Turkey, 1996—. Mem. Rotary. Avocations: music, swimming, cinema. Home and Office: Embassy of Mexico, Rabat Sokak 16, GOP, 06700 Ankara Turkey

BUJON DE L'ESTANG, FRANCOIS, diplomat; b. Neuilly sur Seine, France, 1940; m. Anne de Margerie; four children. Grad., Inst. Politique Paris, Ecole Nat. Adminstrn. Joined Ministry Fgn. Affairs, 1966, staff mem. office of the permanent sec., 1966, spl. advisor, dep. to pres. diplomatic advisor, 1966-69, from second to first sec. French Embassy in the U.S., 1969-73, first sec., second counselor French Embassy in London, 1973-75; advisor on internat. affairs to del. gen. for energy Ministry Industry, Paris, 1975-78; dir. internat. rels. Atomic Energy Commissariat, 1978-80; chief of staff Min. Industry, 1980-81; creator, pres., CEO COGEMA, Inc., Washington, 1982-86; sr. advisor for diplomatic affairs, def. and cooperation French Govt., 1986-88, amb. of France to Can., 1989-91; sr. v.p. Compagnie de Navigation Mixte and Via Banque, Paris, 1991-92; chmn., CEO S.F.I.M., 1991-92; founder FBE Internat. Cons., 1992-95; amb. of France to the U.S. Washington, 1995—; French rep. bd. govs. Internat. Atomic Energy Agy., 1979—; bd. dirs. SOFRATOME, TECHNICATOME, EURODIF, Inst. Francais des Rels. Internat. Mem. editl. bd. Revue des Deux Mondes. Pres. Harvard Bus. Sch. Club France. Named Knight of the Order of the Legion of Honor, Officer of the Nat. Order of Merit. Office: 4101 Reservoir Rd NW Washington DC 20007-2186

BUKENYA, REMIGIUS ZIRABA, biology educator; b. Masaka, Buganda, Uganda, Nov. 25, 1953; s. Peter Batobewa Matovu and Pelagia Ndagire; m. Mary Nampijja Bukenya (Aug. 1988); children: Anne, Christine, Ronald. BS, Makerere U., Uganda, 1977, PhD, 1993; MS, U. Ghana, 1980. Spl. asst. botany Makerere U., 1977-79, lectr. in botany, 1981-86, sr. lectr. in botany, 1986-96, assoc. prof. botany, 1996—, head dept. botany, 1994—; tchg. asst. botany U. Ghana, 1979-80. Contbr. articles to profl. jours. Coord. The Uganda Group of the African Network of Ethnobotany/Ethnoecology, 1997—. Recipient Dennis Stanfield award, Linnaean Soc., London, 1990, DAAD award German Govt., Bonn, 1992, UNESCO award, Paris, 1992. Mem. Assn. Taxonomic Study Flora of Tropical Africa, Internat. Biometric Soc., N.Y. Acad. Sci., Internat. Soc. Ethnobiology. Avocations: playing chess, music, travel.

BUKHKALO, SERGEY PETROVICH, biologist, researcher; b. Kharkov, Ukraine, May 1, 1952; s. Petr Zakharovich Bukhkalo and Alexandra Avtonomovna Nechyporenko; m. Albina Alexandrovna Tchvetkova, Apr. 1, 1987. B, Kharkov State U., 1974; PhD, Russian Acad. Scis., 1989. Sch. tchr. Kharkov, 1974-77; sci. worker Inst. Biol. Problems of the North Russian Acad. Scis., Magadan, 1977—; head rsch. sta. "Contact", 1986—; tchr. No. Internat. U., Magadan, 1996—. Author: The Terrestrial Invertebrate Communities of the Contact Station, 3 vols., 1995, 96, 97; editor: Complex Ecological Research on Contact Station, 1993. Avocation: coin collecting. Office: Inst Biol Problems of North, Portovay 18, 685000 Magadan Russia

BUKIN, KIRILL VICTOROVICH, geophysicist, educator; b. Krasnoyarsk, USSR, Oct. 25, 1965; s. Victor Ivanovich Bukin and Maya L'vovna Nechaeva; m. Margarita Anatol'evna Bezmaternykh, Dec. 30, 1988 (div. July 1993); 1 child, Philippe. MS, State U., Leningrad, Russia, 1988; PhD, State U., St. Petersburg, Russia, 1997. Jr. rsch. assoc. State U., Leningrad, 1988-91; sr. lectr. State U., St. Petersburg, 1991-97, assoc. prof. geophysics, 1997-99. Contbr. articles to profl. jours. Lt. topogeodetic svc. Soviet Army, 1984-88. Avocations: basketball, sport fishing, hunting. Home: Magazeynaya ul 29/52, Pushkin, 196620 St. Petersburg Russia

BUKOVICS, CHRISTIAN EDUARD, oil company executive; b. Vienna, Austria, July 6, 1951; s. Erich and Brigitte (Radon) B.; m. Birgit Heiller, June 4, 1977; children: Edith, Ingrid. PhD, U. Vienna, Austria, 1979. Exploration geophysicist Norske Shell Exploration and Prodn., Stavanger, Norway, 1980-84; ops. geophysicist NAM, Assen, The Netherlands, 1984-88; head of exploration Shell Todd, New Plymouth, New Zealand, 1988-91; sr. staff geophysicist Shell Western Exploration and Prodn., Houston, 1991-93; exploration team leader Shell UK Exploration and Prodn., London, 1993-94, subsurface coord., 1994-95, head exploration evaluation, 1995-96; mgr. new bus. devel. Ctrl. North Sea unit Shell UK Exploration and Prodn., 1996-99; gen. mgr. Shell Temir Petroleum Devel., Kazakhstan, 1999-2000, Shell Tech. Svcs. Iran, Teheran, 2000—. Contbr. articles to profl. jours. Chmn. Soc. Supporting the Found. of Nat. Pk., Niedere Tauern, Vienna, 1980—. Lancecorp. Austrian Army, 1969-70, Vienna. Mem. EAEG. Lutheran. Avocations: running, skiing, mountaineering. Office: Shell Temir Petrol Devel BV, PO Box 60, NL-2280 AB Rijswijk Netherlands

BUKRINSKY, ANATOLI MATVEEVICH, nuclear engineer, consultant; b. Illintsi, Ukraine, June 16, 1926; arrived in Russia, 1941; s. Matvey Minaevich Bukrinsky and Fenia Minaevna Frumina; m. Engelina Lukjanovna Efremenko, Sept. 10, 1950; children: Irene, Aleksey. Degree in mech. engring., Moscow Aviation Inst., 1950; DSc, Leningrad Ship-industry Inst., 1962. Engr., sr. rschr. Leningrad Ship-industry Inst., Moscow, 1950-62; head of divsn. All Union Heat Engring. Inst., Moscow, 1962-87; head of divsn. Nuclear Radiation Safety Sci. Engring. Ctr. RF GOSATOMNADZOR, Moscow, 1987-99, prin. scientist nuclear radiation safety sci. engring. ctr., 1999—, cons., 1999—. Co-author numerous books including Safety Culture, 1991, The Safety of Nuclear Power, 1992, Defense in Depth in Nuclear Safety, 1996, General Provision for Ensuring Nuclear Power Plant Safety, 1998; author: Accidents on Nuclear Power Plants with WWER, 1982; editor, co-author: Accidents Localization on Nuclear Power Plants, 1987; patentee in field; contbr. articles to profl. jours. Mem. N.Y. Acad. Scis. Home: prospect Vernadskogo, 117571 Moscow Russia Office: RF GOSATOMNADZOR nuc radiat, 14/23 Avtozavodskaya St, 109280 Moscow Russia

BUKRY, JOHN DAVID, geologist; b. Balt., May 17, 1941; s. Howard Leroy and Irene Evelyn (Davis) Snyder. Student, Colo. Sch. Mines, 1959-60; BA, Johns Hopkins U., 1963; MA, Princeton U., 1965, PhD, 1967; postgrad., U. Ill., 1965-66, De Anza Coll., 1995-96. Geologist U.S. Army Corp Engrs., Balt., 1963; research asst. Mobil Oil Co., Dallas, 1965; geologist U.S. Geol. Survey, La Jolla, Calif., 1967-84, U.S. Minerals Mgmt. Svc., La Jolla, 1984-86, U.S. Geol. Survey, Menlo Park, Calif., 1986-96; scientist emeritus U.S. Geol. Survey, La Jolla, 1996-98, Menlo Park, 1998—; rsch. assoc. Geol. Rsch. Divsn. Scripps Instn. Oceanography-U. Calif., San Diego, 1970—; cons. Deep Sea Drilling Project, La Jolla, 1967-87; lectr. Vetlesen Symposium, Columbia U., N.Y.C., 1968, 3d Internat. Planktonic Conf., Kiel, Fed. Republic Germany, 1974, Brit. Petroleum Exploration Seminar on nannoplankton biostratigraphy, Houston, 1989; shipboard micropaleontologist on D/V Glomar Challenger, 5 Deep Sea Drilling Project cruises, 1968-78; mem. stratigraphic correlations bd. NSF/Joint Oceanographic Instns. for Deep Earth Sampling, 1976-79. Author: Leg I of the Cruises of the Drilling Vessel Glomar Challenger, 1969, Coccoliths from Texas and Europe, 1969, Leg LXIII of the Cruises of the Drilling Vessel Glomar Challenger, 1981; editor: Marine Micropaleontology, 1976-83, mem. edtl. bd. Micropaleontology, 1985-90. Mobil Oil, Princeton U. fellow, 1965-67; Am. Chem. Soc., Princeton U. fellow, 1966-67. Fellow AAAS, Geol. Soc. Am., Explorers Club; mem. NSTA, Hawaiian Malacological Soc., Paleontol. Rsch. Inst., Am. Assn. Petroleum Geologists, Soc. Econ. Paleontologists and Mineralogists, Internat. Nannoplankton Assn., Ecol. Soc. Am., European Union Geoscis., Oceanography Soc., U. Calif.-San Diego Ida and Cecil Green Faculty Club, San Diego Shell Club, Princeton Club No. Calif., Sigma Xi. Avocations: basketball, photography, shell and mineral collecting. Achievements include research in stratigraphy, paleoecology and taxonomy for 300 new species of marine nannoplankton used in ocean history studies. Office: US Geol Survey 910 345 Middlefield Rd Menlo Park CA 94025-3591

BUKVIC, NENAD, physician, researcher, educator; b. Sarajevo, Bosnia and Herzegovina, Apr. 22, 1965; arrived in Italy, 1992; s. Miroslav and Suhreta (Bakal) B.; m. Natasa Gojkovic, Mar. 8, 1995. BS, U. Sarajevo, 1989, MSc in Extpl. Medicine, 1992; PhD in Reprodn. Biology, U. Bari, Italy, 1996; postdoc., U. Bari, 1997-99; Dr. Med. Sci., U. Sarajevo, 2000. Physician Ctr. for Human Genetics, Sarajevo, 1989-92, Pediat. Clinic, Sarajevo, 1990-92; rschr. med. genetics U. Bari, 1992—, prof. med. genetics, 1996—; cons. Ctr. for Prenatal and Postnatal Cytogenetics Diagnosis, Bari, 1993-96; vis. prof. medicine U. Sarajevo, 1996—. Editor: Voice of Medical Doctor, 1989; contbr. articles to profl. jours. Grantee Soros Open Soc., 1995-96. Mem. European Cytogenetists Assn., Nat. Geog. Soc. Avocations: tennis, skiing, basketball, swimming. Office: U Bari DIMIMP, Piazza G Cesare-Policlin, 70100 Bari Italy

BULANOV, SERGEI VLADIMIROVICH, physicist, physics educator; b. Kuljab, Tadjikistan, USSR, Aug. 16, 1947; s. Vladimir Antonovich and Vera Yakovlevna (Potapova) B.; m. Nadezhda Alexandrovna Bobrova, July 26, 1974; children: Stepan, Vadim. MS, Moscow Inst. Physics and Tech., Dolgoprudnyi, 1971, PhD, 1974; DSc, Acad. Scis. USSR, Moscow, 1990. Jr. rsch. scientist theoret. dept. P.N. Lebedev Phys. Inst., Acad. Scis. USSR, Moscow, 1974-83, sr. rsch. scientist plasma physics dept., 1983-85, leading rsch. scientist, 1985-86; head lab. Gen. Physics Inst. Russian Acad. Scis., Moscow, 1986—; asst. prof. Moscow Inst. Physics and Tech., 1978-83, prof., 1992—; vis. prof. Turin (Italy) U., 1995, Ruhr U., Bochum, Germany, 1996, Scuola Normale Sueriore, Pisa, Italy, 1998; inst. laser engr., Osaka U., Japan, 1998-99. Co-author: Astrophysics of Cosmic Rays, 1990; mem. editl. bd. Plasma Physics Reports, 1989—; contbr. 165 articles to profl. jours. Fellow Japan Soc. Promotion Scis., 1997-98; recipient USSR State prize on scis. and tech. State Com. USSR, 1982. Avocations: cross-country and downhill skiing, tennis, fishing, hunting. Fax: 007 (095) 135 80 11. E-mail: bulanov@fpl.gpi.ru, bulanov@orc.ru. Home: apt 193, Leningradskyi Prospekt 28, Moscow 125040, Russia Office: Gen Physics Inst, Vavilov St 38, Moscow 117942, Russia

BULATOVIC, MOMIR, president of Republic of Montenegro; b. Belgrade, Yugoslavia, 1956. Grad., U. Montenegro. Former mem. League of Communists Montenegro; leader Rep. League of Communists; chair Dem. Party Socialists, 1990—; pres. Presidium of Montenegro, 1990-92, Republic of Montenegro, 1992-97; prime min. Govt. Yugoslavia, 1998—. Office: Office of Prime Minister, Bulevar Lenjina 2, 11070 Belgrade Yugoslavia*

BULAVAS, VLADAS, library director; b. Kaunas, Lithuania, Oct. 24, 1936; s. Juozas and Vanda (Mikolaityte) B.; m. Stanislava Grazina Bigelyte, July 4, 1959; children: Gediminas, Viktoras. BE, Polytech. Inst., Kaunas, 1959, D in scis., 1974; docent, Vilnius (Lithuania) U., 1994. Registered profl. engr. Engr., dept. head Electricity Bd., Vilnius, 1959-74; inst. dir. Electricity Network Inst., Kaunas, 1974-82; libr. dir. Nat. Libr. Lithuania, Vilnius, 1982—; lectr. Kaunas Polytech. Inst., 1974-82, Vilnius U., 1982—; head consortium Lithuanian Rsch. Librs., 1993-97. Deputy City Municipality Kaunas, 1974-82, City Municipality Vilnius, 1990-95. Mem. Lithuanian Libr. Assn. Office: Nat Libr Lithuania, Gedimino pr 51, LT 2600 Vilnius Lithuania*

BULBULYAN, MARIANA ANTONOVNA, physician, researcher; b. Batumi, Adjaria, Georgia, Mar. 12, 1938; arrived in Russia, 1956; d. Anton Ivanovich Bulbulyan and Ashkhen Georgievna Nacharyan; m. Leonidovich Iatsko, Mar. 15, 1963 (dec. Apr. 1995); children: Michael, Veronika. D of Med. Scis., Blokhin Cancer Rsch. Ctr., 1984. Sanitary inspector Sanitary and Epidemiologic Sta., Moscow, 1963-67; rschr. Blokhin Cancer Rsch. Ctr., Moscow, 1967-73, scientific worker, 1973-81, leading scientific worker, 1981-92, chief lab. occupl. cancer epidemiology, 1993—; cons. postgrad. students Blokhin Cancer Rsch., Ctr., 1992—; mem. scientific counsel Inst. of Carcinogenesis, Moscow, 1999. Contbr. articles to profl. jours. Grantee Soros Fund, 1995-96, Nat. Priorities in Medicine, 1996-98, Russian Fund of Fundamental Investigations, 1997-98. Avocations: reading Russian literature, voyages. Home: Valovaya St 6/8 flat 11, 113054 Moscow Russia Office: RAMS Oncol Scientific Ctr, 24 Kashirskoye shosse, 115478 Moscow Russia

BULGIN, SALLY ANN, publisher, editor; b. Ashford, Kent, Eng., Nov. 8, 1957; d. Ernest Arthur and Patricia Joy (Aldrich) B. BA with honours in Fine Art-Art History, Reading (Eng.) U., 1981; MA in History of Art, London U., 1982, PhD in History of Art, 1992. Publishing editor The Artist Mag., Tenterden, Eng., 1985—; pub. Leisure Painter Mag., Tenterden, Eng., 1985—. Author: Acrylics Master Class, 1994, Oils Master Class, 1996; commissioning editor: Drawing and Painting Made Easy, 1994; co-author: Lucy Willis: Light in Watercolour, 1997, Ken Howard--Inspired by Light, 1998; editor Brush Strokes Mag., 2000—; cons. editor ArtClass, 1999. Mem. Nat. Acrylic Painters Assn. (v.p. 1993-95), Royal Birmingham Soc. Artists (hon. v.p. 1993—), Assn. Internat. Critics Art. Avocations: squash, circuit training, skiing, badminton, reading. Office: The Artist Mag, The Artist Pub Co Ltd, 63-65 High St, Tenterden TN30 6BD, England

BULIGESCU, LUCIAN E. D., gastroenterologist, hepatologist, educator; b. Ploeshti, Prahova, Romania, Oct. 17, 1929; s. Emil Er. and Alice-Florica Al. (Dobrescu) B.; m. Lia-Maria N. Goia, Aug. 22, 1952; 1 child, Sorin George. MD, U. Cluj, Romania, 1953; DMS, U. Bucharest, Romania, 1957, DScis, 1974. Candidate masterate Colentina Hosp., Bucharest, 1953-54; asst. prof. internal medicine C. Davilla Hosp., 1954-65; univ. asst., 1965-67, lectr., 1976-79, asst. prof., 1979-81, prof. intenal medicine hepatology, 1981—; mem. staff Fundeni Hosp., Bucharest, 1965—; vis. prof. U. Medicine Bichat, Paris, 1972, U. Medicine Toulouse, Rangueil, France, 1978-90, U. Medicine Royal Free Hosp., London, 1975. Author: Exocrine Pancreas, 1971, Chronic Hepatitis, 1971, Diseases of the Liver, Biliary Tract and Pancreas, 1981; author, editor: Treatise of Hepato-Gastroenterology, 2 vols., 1997-99; mem. editl. bd. Gastroent. Clin. Biology, 1972—, Jour. Hepatology, 1990-96; contbr. over 600 articles to profl. jours. Mem. com. study dept. Christian and Dem. Party, Bucharest, 1997; com. mem. Forum for Sci. and Reform, Bucharest, 1997. Mem. Romanian Assn. for Study Liver (pres. 1990), European Assn. Internal Medicine, European Assn. for Study Liver, Internat. Assn. for Study Liver, French Assn. for Study Liver, French Gastroenterology Soc., Belgium Gastroenterology Soc. (hon.). Orthodox. Avocations: literature, travel. Home: Precupetii Vechi Str 23, 72154 Bucharest Romania Office: Fandeni Hosp, Chaussee Fundeni 258, 72437 Bucharest Romania

BULKELEY, THOMAS FOSTER RIVERS, retired military officer; b. Albrighton, Eng., Mar. 15, 1916; arrived in France, 1968; s. Frederick Rivers and Elizabeth Muriel (Lyon) B.; m. Bridget Pattinson, Apr. 27, 1944 (div. 1963); 1 child, John Edward Rivers; m. Rose Marie De Lestrac, Oct. 19, 1963. Grad., Royal Mil. Coll., Sandhurst, Eng., 1935, Imperial Def. Coll., 1965. Commd. 2d lt. Brit. Army, 1944, advanced through grades to brig. gen., 1960; brigade maj. Guards Brigade, 1944-45; with Mil. Ops. Br. War Office, 1953-54; directing staff Staff Coll., Camberley, 1948-50; comdr. 1st Br. Scots Guards, 1954-57, 51 Highland Brigade, Scotland, 1960-62; brig. gen. staff to Gen. Lemnitzer-Shape, Paris, 1962-64; insp. intelligence U.K., 1966-68. Contbr. articles to profl. jours. Mem. Brit. Empire. Avocations: amateur steeple chase rider, squash (rep. Brit. Army), lawn tennis (rep. Brit.

Army), cricket, training shooting dogs (silver medalist Vets. French Ski Championship).

BULKIN, BERNARD JOSEPH, oil industry executive; b. Trenton, N.J., Mar. 9, 1942; s. Jacob and Beatrice Bulkin; m. Susan H. Lees, Dec. 31, 1975; children: Anna, Noah, David. BS, Poly Inst. Bklyn., 1962; PhD, Purdue U., 1966. Postdoctoral fellow Eidg. Tech. Hochschule, Zürich, Switzerland, 1966-67; prof. chemistry CUNY, 1967-75, chmn. chemistry dept., 1973-75; dean arts and sci. Poly. Inst. N.Y., Bklyn., 1975-82, v.p., 1982-85; dir. downstream oil R&D Sohio Corp., Cleve., 1985-88; mgr. products div. Brit. Petroleum, London, 1988-90, head oil rsch., 1991-93; head oil tech. and mfg., supply and distbn. BP Oil Internat., London, 1993-97; v.p. environ. affairs BP Amoco, 1997—; bd. dirs. Viscon Internat., N.Y.C.; cons. numerous cos., 1970-85. Author: Chemical Application of Raman Spectroscopy, 1983, Raman Spectroscopy, 1991; contbr. articles to profl. jours. Bd. dirs. Cleve. Edn. Fund, 1986-88. Recipient medal N.Y. Soc. Applied Spectroscopy, 1978. Fellow Royal Soc. Chemistry, Royal Soc. Arts; mem. Soc. Applied Spectroscopy (numerous coms.), Am. Chem. Soc., Coblentz Soc. (Coblentz award 1975), Sigma Xi (Rsch. award 1982). Office: Britannic House, 1 Finsbury Circus, London EC2M 7BA, England

BULL, DENNIS LEE, counselor; b. Iowa City, Nov. 28, 1946; s. Ivan O. and Dorris Lucille (O'Neal) B.; m. Patricia Ann Price, Sept. 7, 1968; children: Matthew Ryan, Kathryn Colleen. BA, U. Wis., 1968; ThM, Dallas Theol. Sem., 1972; MA, Chapman Coll., 1974; PhD, U. North Tex., 1983. Family counselor Green Acres Bapt. Ch. Pine Cove Ctr., Tyler, Tex., 1974-76, Dallas Christian Counseling Svc., Richardson, Tex., 1977-79; minister of counseling N.W. Bible Ch., Dallas, 1979-89; pvt. practice Richardson, 1979—; assoc. prof. pastoral ministries Dallas Theol. Seminaries, 2000—. Mem. Am. Assn. for Marriage and Family Therapy, Christian Assn. for Psychol. Studies, Tex. State Bd. Examiners Profl. Counselors, Incest Recovery Assn. (founder), Tyler Mental Health Assn. (bd. dirs.), Tex. State Bd. of Examiners Marraige and Family Therapists, Am. Soc. Clin. Hypnosis, Internat. Soc. for the Study of Dissociation. Home: 502 S Lois Ln Richardson TX 75081-4219 Office: Gateway Counseling 1701 Gateway Blvd Ste 391 Richardson TX 75080-3546

BULL, HELEN MAY, artist, writer; b. Sweet Springs, Mo., Apr. 20, 1920; d. John Theodore Langewisch and Ethel Henrietta (Von Berkelo) Butemeyer; widowed; children: Jan Emerson Bull, Guy William Bull. BFA, Otis Art Inst., L.A., 1971; advanced certification Indsl. Rels., UCLA, 1983. Dir. Brazilian Primitive Painting Exhbn., L.A., 1972; pres. Bay West Assn. of Comty Assistance to Homeless Youngsters, L.A., 1973-74; artist, represented by Agora Art Gallery, N.Y.C.; panelist Inst. for Study of Women in Transition, 1976; nursing career devel. con., San. Antonio, Tex., 1978-80. Artist: Spl exhbn. of canvasses in Vista Rm., Faculty Ctr. UCLA, 1973, Art in Permanent Collections includes KTSC-TV, Pueblo, Colo, and framed mural of St. Luke, St. Luke's Luth. Ch., (Gold award 1993); one-person show Agora Gallery, 1999; exhibited group show at Agora Gallery, 1998. Recipient Cert. of merit, UCLA Juried Faculty Exhibit, 1960. Lutheran. Avocations: travel, hiking, numismatics. Office: Agora Art Gallery 560 Broadway New York NY 10012-3938

BULL, KENNETH WINSON, retired rancher; b. Bangs, Tex., Dec. 4, 1930; s. Malta Willis Bull and Lessie D. Conklin; m. Barbara Louise Bell, June 28, 1952; children: Karen Camille, Kenneth Lewis. BSME, Okla. State U., 1958; M in Nuclear Physics, Tex. A&M, 1965; M in Radiol. Physics, U. Tex. Health Sci. Ctr., Dallas, 1973. Self-employed McCulloch County, Tex., 1974—; radiation cons. Brady, Tex., 1974—; asst. prof. U. Tex. Health Sci. Ctr., Dallas, 1973-74; physicist USAF, Washington, 1965-71; engr. USAF, Dayton, 1958-63; radar observer USAF, Eglin AFB, Fla., 1952-61; control tower operator USAF, Almagordo, N.Mex., 1951-52. Contbr. articles to profl. jours. County Chmn., McCulloch County Rep. Party, 1976—; dir. Richland Spl. Utility Dist., Tex., 1988—; pres. Cen. Tex. Taxpayers Assn., Brady, 1990—; mayor pro tem City of Brady, 1978-82. Lt. col. USAF, 1951-71. Decorated Legion of Merit, USAF. Mem. McCulloch County Crime Stoppers (pres. 1988-92), Nat. Cattlemens Assn., McCulloch County Ind. Cattlemens Assn. (pres. 1976-77), Civil Def. for Emergency mgmt. (bd. dirs., dept. 1982-84). Republican. Methodist. Avocations: golf, fishing, poetry, crafts. Office: RR 1 Box 57A Rochelle TX 76872-9715

BULL, MATTHEW JAMES, radiologist; b. London, Aug. 10, 1957; s. Albert Graham and Beryl Lexey (Cope) B.; m. Amanda Bownes, Oct. 9, 1982; children: Charlotte, Emily, Lydia. MB, BChir, U. Sheffield, Eng., 1980. House physician, surgeon Nat. Health Svc., Sheffield, 1980-81; med. intern Nat. Health Svc., Coventry, Eng., 1981-89; trainee radiologist Nat. Health Svc., Sheffield, 1989-90; cons. radiologist Sunderland (Eng.) Hosps., 1990-91, No. Gen. Hosp., Sheffield, 1991—; clin. dir. Diagnostic Imaging, No. Gen. Hosp., Sheffield, 1995—. Contbr. articles to profl. jours. Fellow Royal Coll. Radiologists (clin. tutor 1991-95, mem. fellowship examination multiple choice Yorkshire com. 1992—), Assn. Chest Radiologists. Anglican. Avocations: swimming, skiing, cycling. Home: 263 Dobcroft Rd, Sheffield S11 9LG, England Office: No Gen Hosp, Herries Rd, Sheffield S5 7AU, England

BULL, NIGEL RUSSELL, bank executive; b. Farnborough, Kent, Eng., Nov. 27, 1960; s. Carl Leonard and Helen (Totsky) B. Credit adminstr. Citibank NA, London, 1980-82; head credit adminstrn. Citibank AB, Stockholm, 1984-88; from head credit adminstrn. to fin. contr. Citibank Oy, Helsinki, Finland, 1982-84, 88-94; mgmt. assoc. to relationship mgr. fin. instns. Finland br. Citibank Internat. PLC, Helsinki, 1994—. Mem. Ch. of Eng. Avocations: music, golf, figure skating.

BULL, PETER JOSEPH, retired economic consultant; b. Devon, Eng., Jan. 19, 1929; s. Frank Reginald and Teresa (Rooney) B. Alternate exec. dir. for U.K. Internat. Monetary Fund, Washington, 1972-76; adv. European monetary affairs Bank of Eng., London, 1977-83; dep. head Bank of Eng., 1983-85; econ. cons. SGST Securities, Ltd., London, 1986—. Mem. Royal Inst. Internat. Affairs, Soc. Bus. Economists, European-Atlantic Group, Lombard Assn., Overseas Bankers Club. Home: 38 Radnor Walk, London SW3 4BN, England Office: SGST Securities Ltd, 3 Moorgate Pl, London EC2 R6HR, England

BULL, PETER TOWNLEY, consultant anesthetist; b. Wrexham, U.K., Nov. 23, 1943; s. Mervyn Robert and Ethel (Lloyd) B.; m. June 26, 1968 (div. 1980); 1 child, Jeremy; m. Elayne Salter, Sept. 2, 1981; children: Andrew, Suzanna. MB, BChir, Liverpool U., 1967. Commd. surg. lt. Royal Navy, 1968, advanced through grades to surgeon comdr., 1980, med. officer, 1968-83; med. officer HMS Ark Royal, 1976-77; hon. sr. registrar anesthetics Cambridge (Eng.) U., 1978-79; sr. anesthetist South Atlantic Hosp. Ship, Uganda, 1982; cons. anesthetist Trent Regional Authority, Mansfield, Nottinghamshire, 1983—; sr. med. officer HMS Sherwood, Nottingham, 1984-88. Recipient Pask Cert. Honor, Assn. Anesthetists, London, 1983. Fellow Coll. Anesthetists; mem. Med. Defence Union. Conservative. Mem. Ch. of England. Avocations: gardening, reading, cricket, golf, bridge. Home: Kota Tinggi, Mansfield Rd, Farnsfield NG22 8HG, England Office: Kings Mill Hosp, Sutton-in-Ashfield, Notts NG17 4JL, England

BULL, PHILIP JAMES, history educator; b. Adelaide, Australia, July 24, 1942; s. Leslie Wallace and Lillian Trevenen (Richards) B.; m. Linley Anne Jackson, June 11, 1966 (div. 1988); m. Sheridan Palmer, Nov. 25, 1989; children: Alexandra, Lilian. BA with honors, U. Adelaide, 1968; PhD, U. Cambridge, Eng., 1972. Tchr. Modbury H.S., Adelaide, 1965-67; tutor in history U. Adelaide, 1968; asst. Bodleian Libr., Oxford, Eng., 1971-74; lectr./sr. lectr. history La Trobe U., Melbourne, Australia, 1975—. Author: Land, Politics and Nationalism, 1996; contbr. articles to profl. jours. Mcpl. councillor City of Fitzroy, Melbourne, 1977-82. Office: La Trobe Univ, Dept History, Melbourne VIC 3083, Australia

BULL, SANDY (ALEXANDER BENJAMIN BULL), musician, composer; b. N.Y.C., Feb. 25, 1941; s. Harry and Daphne (Bayne) B.; m. Candice Ann Marks, June 20, 1979; children: Cassandra, Jesse, Jackson. Studied banjo with Eric Darling, 1955-57; student in music, Boston U., 1959-61; studied percussion with Billy Higgins, 1961-64, studied oud with Hamza El Din, 1963-68, studied sarod with Ali Akbar Khan, 1976-77. Multi-instrumentalist on guitar, keyboards, bass, banjo, pedal steel, percussion, oud and sarod, also engr., composer, arranger, prodr.; host/prodr. The Music of Man/ WNCN-FM, N.Y.C., 1963; compositions include Blend, Gospel Tune, No Deposit No Return Blues, Carnival Jump, Moodswing Salsa, Serious City, Alligator Wrestler, Rain Forest, Sanctified Steel, Love is Forever; recordings include The Samplers in Person, 1960, The Folksingers of Washington Square, 1962, Fantasias, 1963, Inventions, 1965, E. Pluribus Unum, 1969, Demolition Derby, 1972, Jukebox Sch. of Music, 1988 (Best Liner Notes award Nat. Assn. Ind. Record distbr. 1989, 20 Best Albums of 1988 Nat. Pub. Radio), Vehicles, 1991, Steel Tears, 1996 (nominated best folk album Nashville Music Awards 1997), Sandy Bull: Re-inventions: The Best of the Vanguard Yrs., 1999; arrangements include L. Bonfa's Manha de Carnival for oud, two movements of Carl Orff's Carmina Burana for 5 string banjo, excerpt from J.S. Bach's Brandenburg Concerto # 5 for Fender guitar, strings and Fender Rhodes; instrumental arrangement of C. Berry's Memphis. Mem. NARAS, ASCAP, Audio Engring. Soc. Avocation: learning Bach chorales on keyboard, skiing, soaring. Office: Timeless Rec Soc PO Box 1177 Franklin TN 37065-1177

BULL, SIR GEORGE, food service executive. Dir. Internat. Distillers and Vintners, 1962-84; chief exec. drinks sector Grand Met. plc, London, 1984-92, chmn. grandmet food sector, 1992-93, also bd. dirs.; group chief exec. Grand Met. plc, 1994-96, chmn., 1996-97; joint chmn. Diageo plc, 1997-98; chmn. J. Sainsbury plc, London, 1998—. Office: J Sainsbury plc, Stamford House Stamford St, London SE1 9LL, England

BULLARD, RICKEY HOWARD, podiatric physician, surgeon; b. Corinth, Miss., Aug. 9, 1954; s. Herman A. and Bonnie Ruth (Gurley) B.; m. Carolyn Jean Strickland, June 6, 1981. BS in Biology, Millsaps Coll., Jackson, Miss., 1975; BS in Med. Sci., Ill. Coll. Podiatric Medicine, Chgo., 1980, DPM, 1980. Diplomate Am. Bd. Podiatric Orthops. and Primary Podiatric Medicine. Mem. courtesy med. staff Iuka (Miss.) Hosp., 1980—; pvt. practice Tupelo and Iuka, 1980—; assoc. med. staff North Miss. Med. Ctr., Tupelo, 1992—; cons. Miss. State Bd. Med. Licensure, Jackson, 1982—, Tighomingo Manor Health Ctr., Iuka, 1981—, Cedars Health Ctr., Tupelo, 1983—, Lee Manor Health Ctr., Tupelo, 1984—, Alcorn Care Inn, Corinth, 1985—; bd. dirs. Diabetes Treatment Ctr., Tupelo, 1994—. Watkins scholar Millsaps Coll., 1973. Fellow Am. Assn. Hosp. Podiatrists, Am. Coll. Foot and Ankle Orthops. and Medicine, Internat. Acad. Podiatric Medicine; mem. Am. Podiatric Med. Assn. (del. 1984, 87, 89), Miss. Podiatric Med. Assn. (pres. 1984-86, sec., treas. 1987—), SAR, Christian Med. Soc., Gen. Soc. War of 1812. Methodist. Avocations: golf, fly fishing, military history, gardening. Home: 2381 Amelia Ln Tupelo MS 38801-7203 Office: 1904 W Main St Tupelo MS 38801-3228

BULLARD, ROGER PERRIN, artist; b. N.Y.C., July 2, 1913; s. Roger Harrington and Annie Adams (Sturges) B.; m. Georgie Genevieve Hosford, Nov. 15, 1944; 1 child, Virginia Anne. Student, Art Students League, N.Y.C., 1934-37, Universal Photographers Inc., N.Y.C., The Bullard Haven Tech. Sch., Bridgeport, Conn., 1946. Freelance artist Fairfield, Conn., 1937-40; machinist Heime Co., Fairfield, 1947-50, Exide Battery, Fairfield, 1950-52, Dictaphone, Bridgeport, Conn., 1952-55; draftsman Aircraft Drafting, Bridgeport, 1955-57, Sikorski Aircraft and Valve Corp., Bridgeport, 1955-56; airbrush artist Poly Photo, Bridgeport, 1957; freelance photographer Fairfield, 1958-77. Contbr. pen and ink drawings to Prof. Henry Fairfield Osborn's book, Probosidea Memoirs Mus. Natural History, N.Y.C., 1933-35. With U.S. Army, 1940-45, WWII. Republican. Episcopalian. Avocations: photography, art research, tennis, writing. Home: c/o Mary Rouseau 449 Mill Plain Rd Fairfield CT 06430-5047

BULLARO, GRACE RUSSO, literature, film and foreign language educator, speaker, book reviewer; b. Salerno, Italy, July 11, 1949; came to the U.S., 1958; d. Salvatore and Carmela (Paciello) Russo; m. Frank John Bullaro, Sept. 19, 1971; children: Christian, Adrian Alexander. BA magna cum laude, CCNY, 1971; MA, SUNY, Stony Brook, 1989, PhD in Comparative Lit., 1993. Grad. tchg. asst. SUNY, Stony Brook, 1988-92; adj. asst. prof. SUNY-Nassau C.C., Garden City, N.Y., 1990—; adj. asst. prof. CUNY-Lehman Coll., Bronx, N.Y., 1991—; adj. asst. prof. CUNY-Lehman Coll., Bronx, 1998, adj. assoc. prof., 2000—; substitute asst. prof. Lincoln Ctr., N.Y.C., 1997, 2000, collaborative educator, 1999-2000, adj. assoc. prof., 2000—; mem. libr. com. CUNY senate, mem. acad. senate, 1999—; Faculty Exec. Com. Lehman Coll., Bronx, N.Y., 1999—; book reviewer in field. Contbr. chpts. to books and articles to profl. jours. Acad. senate CUNY, Lehman Coll., 1997-99, CUNY, 1998—, mem. Faculty Exec. Com., 1999—. Recipient Chancellor and Pres.'s award for Excellence in Tchg., SUNY-Stony Brook, 1991. Mem. MLA, Nat. Coun. Tchrs. English, Inst. Français, Soc. Profs. Français, Phi Beta Kappa. Avocations: fitness trainer, tennis, travel, swimming, horseback riding. E-mail: gracerbullaro@msn.com. Office: CUNY Lehman Coll English Dept Bedford Park Blvd W Bronx NY 10468

BULLECER, EDGAR LADERA, agriculturist; b. Salay, Philippines, Aug. 5, 1953; s. Ventura Gumahin and Vilma (Ladera) B.; m. Rebecca Vivares, Sept. 18, 1977; 4 children. Student, Cagayan de Oro, 1975; acct., Philippines Sch. Bus., 1976. CPA. Mgr., dir. Western Pacific Aqua, Bohol, The Philippines, 1985-89; mgr. Bukidnon (The Philippines) Resources Co., Inc., 1990-97, La Frutera, Inc., Datu Paglas, The Philippines, 1997—; mgr., sr. adviser Paglas Corp., Datu Paglas, 1999—; v.p., dir. Mountain Springs Devel., Bukidnon, 1983—, Agriman Cons., Makati, The Philippines, 1985-88; v.p. Northern Foods, Ilocos, The Philippines, 1984-87; chmn., pres. Langit Ray Nasayud, Makati, 1987—; dir. Gamma Sages, Makati, 1990—, Windsor Pacific, Davao, The Philippines, 1996—; cons. Tokwan Ltd., Cabanatuan, The Philippines, 1987—; founding trustee Kaduma Devel. Found., Inc., Bukidnon, 1997—. 4th rep. UN Office, Geneva, Switzerland for Pan African Islamic Soc., The Gambia, West Africa, 1998—. Mem. Rotay Club (bd. dirs.), C. of C., Oxford Club (life). Avocations: reading, nature trekking, skygazing. Office: 2/F SJRDC Bldg, Insular Village Comm Area, Lanang Davao City Philippines

BULLIER, ANTOINE JEAN, law educator, political scientist; b. Paris, Oct. 26, 1946; s. Paul Alfred and Marie-Rose (Watin) B.; m. Françoise Jeanne Picard, Jan. 7, 1984. LLM, U. Mich., 1974; D 3e Cycle, U. Paris Sorbonne, 1977, D d'Etat Paris 3, 1977; LittD, U. Paris Sorbonne Nouvelle, 1987. Lectr. U. Potchefstroom, Republic of South Africa, 1975-77, U. of Witwatersrand, Republic of South Africa, 1977-78, U. Natal, Durban, Republic of South Africa, 1978-81; maître asst. U. Réunion, St. Denis Réunion, France, 1981-86; maître de Conférences U. Panthéon-Sorbonne, Paris, 1986-89, prof., 1989—. Author: Géopolitique de l'Apartheid, 1982, Le Parler franco-mauricien au Natal, 1983, Partition et Répartition, 1988; contbr. more than 40 articles to various internat. acad. jours. Brit. Coun. scholar, 1970, Franco-Am. scholar, 1973, South African Govt. scholar, 1976. Avocations: swimming, reading. Office: U Pantheon Sorbonne, 12 place du Panthéon, 75231 Cédex 05 Paris France

BULLINGTON, GAYLE ROGERS, writer, researcher; b. Watsonville, Calif., May 17, 1923; d. Manley Duane and Gladyce Thelma (Horton) Rogers; m. Keith Charles Brown, Nov. 26, 1944 (div. Mar. 30, 1962); children: Kendall Keith, Kevin Doran, Manley Duane; m. Jack William Bullington, Dec. 23, 1978. BA, UCLA, 1946, secondary sch. cert., 1947; postgrad. studies, Calif. Luth. U., Northridge U., 1962-65; MA, Calif. Luth. U., 1974. Cert. tchr., Calif. Tchr. Southgate (Calif.) Jr. H.S., 1947-48, Virgil Jr. H.S., L.A., 1948-50, North Hollywood (Calif.) H.S., 1950-52, Van Nuys (Calif.) H.S., 1953-54, Thousand Oaks (Calif.) H.S., 1963-79. Author: The Second Kiss, 1972, Nokoa's Woman, 1975-81, Gladyce With a C, 2000. Mem. ACLU, Pub. Citizen, Common Cause, Nation Assocs. Home: 23119 19th Ave NE Arlington WA 98223-7631

BULLMANN, HANS UDO, member of European parliament; b. Giessen, Fed. Republic Germany, June 8, 1956. Mem. European Parliament, Frankfurt, 1999—; mem. Group of the Party of European Socialists, European Parliament; mem. com. on econ. and monetary affairs; substitute mem. com. on employment and social affairs, mems. from European Parliament to the Joint Assembly of the Agreement between the African, Caribbean and Pacific States and the European Union (ACP-EU). Office: SPD Europaburo Hessen-Sud, Fischerfeldstrasse 7-11, D-60311 Frankfurt Germany

BULLOCK, ALAN LOUIS CHARLES, English educator; b. Dec. 13, 1914; s. Frank Allen Bullock; m. Hilda Yates, 1940; 4 children. MA, Oxford U., Eng. Raleigh lectr. Brit. Acad., 1967; Stevenson meml. lectr. LSE, 1970; Leslie Stephenson lectr. Cambridge U., Eng., 1976; with St. Catherine's Coll., Oxford. Author: Hitler: A Study in Tyranny, , 1952, rev. edit., 1964, The Liberal Tradition, 1956, The Life and Times of Ernest Bevin, vol. 1, 1960, vol. 2, 1967; editor: (with Oliver Stallbrass) Dictionary of Modern Thought, 1977, new edit. (with S. Trombley), 1988, new edit., 1999, The Faces of Europe, 1980, (with B.R. Woodings) Fontana Dictionary of Modern Thinkers, 1983, The Humanist Tradition in the West, 1985, Hitler and Stalin: Parallel Lives, 1991, rev. edit., 1993, Building Jerusalem: A Portrait of My Father, 2000; gen. editor: (with Sir William Deakin) The Oxford History of Modern Europe. Trustee Aspen Inst. Home: Gable End 30 Godstow Rd, Oxford OX2 8AJ, England Office: St. Catherine's Coll, Oxford OX1 3UJ, England

BULLOCK, DONALD WAYNE, elementary education educator, educational computing consultant; b. Tacoma Park, Md., Mar. 24, 1947; s. B.W. and Margaret (Harris) B.; m. Pamela Louise Hatch, Aug. 7, 1971. AA in Music, L.A. Pierce Coll., Woodland Hills, Calif., 1969; BA in Geography, San Fernando Valley State Coll., 1971; Cert. Computer Edn., Calif. Luth. U., 1985, MA in Curriculum-Instrn., 1987. Tchr. music Calvary Luth. Sch., Pacoima, Calif., 1970-71; elem. tchr. Ist Luth. Sch., Northridge, Calif., 1971-73; elem. tchr. Simi Valley (Calif.) Unified Sch. Dist., 1973—, computer insvc. instr., 1982-85, computer mentor tchr., 1985-87, mentor tchr. ednl. tech., 1992-95; lectr. Calif. Luth. U., Thousand Oaks, 1985-92; ednl. computer cons. DISC Ednl. Svcs., Simi Valley, 1985—; speaker profl. confs. Contbr. articles to profl. publs. Pres. Amen Choir, Van Nuys, Calif., 1981-83. Recipient Computer Learning Month grand prize Tom Snyder Prodns., 1988, Computer Learning Found., 1990, Spl. Commendation of Achievement, Learning mag. profl. best tchr. excellence awards, 1990, Impact II Disseminator award Ventura County Supt. of Schs. and Ventura County Econ. Devel. Assn., 1995; grantee Tandy-Radio Shack, Inc., 1985, Calif. Dep. Edn., 1985. Mem. NEA, ASCD, Internat. Soc. Tech. in Edn., Computer Using Educators Calif., Gold Coast Computer Using Educators (bd. dirs. 1988-89, 95-96), Basset Hound Club am., Basset Hound Club So. Calif. (bd. dirs. 1994-95, 98-99, pres. 1995-98), Western Hound Assn. So. Calif. (newsletter editor 2000—). Avocations: singing, travel, photography, writing, woodworking. Home: 2805 Wanda Ave Simi Valley CA 93065-1528 Office: Garden Grove Elem Sch 2250 Tracy Ave Simi Valley CA 93063-2753

BULLOCK, FRANCIS JEREMIAH, pharmaceutical research executive; b. Brookline, Mass., Jan. 14, 1937; s. Jeremiah Francis and A. Grace (Vitali) B.; m. Lorraine Marie Littig, Aug. 26, 1961; children: Christine, Gregory. BS, Mass. Coll. Pharmacy, 1958; AM, Harvard U., 1961, PhD, 1963. Rsch. assoc. Harvard Med. Sch., Boston, 1963-64, Chem. Biodynamics Lab. U. Calif., Berkeley, 1964-65; sr. project staff Arthur D. Little, Inc., Cambridge, Mass., 1965-72; mgr. medicinal chemistry Abbott Labs., North Chicago, Ill., 1972-79; v.p. new drug discovery Schering-Plough Pharm. Co., Bloomfield, N.J., 1979-81, sr. v.p. rsch. ops., 1981-93; sr. cons. Arthur D. Little, Inc., Cambridge, 1993—; lectr. MIT, Cambridge, 1971-72, Northeastern U., Boston, 1971-72; bd. dirs. TSI Corp., Genzyme Transgenics Corp, Neogenesis, Array BioPharma; bd. govs. Union County Coll., N.J.; mem. com. on young investigators in biol. scis. NRC, 1991-92, com. on nat. needs for biomed. and behavioral rsch. pers., 1993-94. Editor jour. Drug Metabolism and Distbn., 1970-73; contbr. numerous rsch. papers to profl. jours., 1964-75. Fellow NIH, 1961-65. Mem. AAAS, Am. Chem. Soc., Royal Soc. Chemistry, Fedn. Am. Socs. Exptl. Biology, Am. Soc. Pharmacology and Exptl. Therapeutics, Am. Soc. for Microbiology, Assn. Harvard Chemists, Harvard Club (Boston and N.Y.C.). Republican. Roman Catholic. Avocation: airplane pilot. Office: Arthur D Little Inc 35 Acorn St Cambridge MA 02139-4722

BULLOCK, PETER, soil scientist; b. Bridgnorth, Shropshire, Eng., July 6, 1937; s. Cecil Richard and Alice (Jackson) B.; m. Patricia Margaret Standidge, Aug. 17, 1963; children: Martin (dec.), Alison Clare. BA, Birmingham (Eng.) U., 1958; MSc, Leeds (Eng.) U., 1964; PhD, Cornell U., 1968. Sci. officer Soil Survey Eng. and Wales, Harpenden, U.K., 1957-64, sr. sci. officer, 1968-72, prin. sci. officer, 1972-85, dir., 1985-87; dir. Soil Survey and Land Rsch. Ctr., Silsoe, U.K., 1987-97; prof. land resource mgmt. Cranfield U., Silsoe, U.K., 1989—; chmn. commn. soil micromorphology Internat. Soc. Soil Sci., 1978-85; gov. Inst. Grasslands Environ. Rsch., U.K., 1997—; chmn. adv. com. European Soil Bur., 1989, 98—; spl. advisor Royal Commn. on Environ. Pollution, 1994-95. Author, editor 8 books; contbr. over 80 articles to profl. jours. Fulbright travel scholar, 1964. Fellow Inst. Profl. Soil Scientists; mem. Brit. Soc. Soil Sci. (v.p. 1994-96, 98-2000, pres. 1996-98). Avocations: sports, decorative and fine arts, theater, walking. Office: Cranfield U, Sch Agrl, Food, Environ, Silsoe Bedfordshire MK45 4DT, United Kingdom

BULLOCK, PETER BRADLEY, company director; b. Tipton, Eng., June 9, 1934; s. William Horace Bradley and Catherine (Garner) B.; m. Joyce Rea, Nov. 1, 1958; children: Claire Elizabeth Bradley, Penelope Jane Bradley. BSc, U. London. Chartered engr., U.K. With Nat. Coal Bd., 1959-65, Thomas Potterton Ltd., 1966-67, Fibreglass Ltd., 1965-66, 67-69; pres., mng. dir. Flymo Ltd.; dir. Electrolux Ltd.; joint mng. dir. Electrolux Group UK, 1976-83; group chief exec. James Neill Holdings PLC, 1983-89, Spear & Jackson Internat. PLC, 1986-90; chmn. Neill Tools Ltd., 1983-90; pres dir., gen. AMV (France), 1986-90; chmn. London & Geneva Securities Ltd., 1990—, James Dickie Pub. Ltd. Co., 1995-98, Scala Collections Ltd., 1997—; bd. dirs. 600 Group Pub. Ltd. Co., Syltone Pub. Ltd. Co. With Brit. Army, 1956-58. Mem. Inst. Energy, Inst. Mktg., Inst. Dirs. Mem. Ch. of Eng. Clubs: Leander, Phyllis Court, Henley-on-Thames. Home: The Cottage Queenwood, Christmas Common Watlington, Oxford OX9 5HW, England

BULLOCK, WELDON KIMBALL, health facility administrator, pathologist, pathology educator; b. Vernal, Utah, Jan. 6, 1908; s. John Kimball and Adelaide (Arnold) B.; m. Dosia Opal Newton, Dec. 26, 1931; children: John, Jim. BA, U. Utah, 1930; MD, Northwestern U., 1934, MSc in Pathology, 1942. Diplomate Am. Bd. Pathology; lic. MD, Calif., Idaho, Utah. Intern Alameda County Hosp., 1933-34; resident in medicine Cook County Hosp., 1940-41; resident in pathology L.A. County-U. So. Calif. Med. Ctr., 1946-47; head surg. pathology LAC-U. So. Calif. Med. Ctr., 1949-69; instr. pathology Sch. Medicine U. So. Calif., 1947-48, asst. prof., 1955-62, clin. prof., 1963-74, clin. prof. emeritus, 1974—; exec. dir. Calif. Tumor Tissue Registry, various locations, 1955-95; dir. emeritus Calif. Tumor Tissue Registry, 1995—; chief pathology svc. Orthop. Hosp., 1956-63; assoc. pathologist St. Luke Hosp., 1963-70, chief pathologist, 1970-77, assoc. pathologist, 1977-81; clin. prof. pathology Sch. Medicine Loma Linda U., 1992—; James Ewing fellow in pathology Meml. Hosp. for Cancer and Allied Disease, 1948-49; cons. Calif. Assn. Cytotechnologists, 1962—, So. Calif. Acad. Oral Pathology, 1963—, Orthop. Hosp., 1963—; mem. Am. Joint Com. Cancer Staging and End Result Reporting, 1963-69, chmn. audio-visual task force, 1966-69, mem. exec. com., 1969; mem. rev. com. clin. cancer tng. grants Nat. Cancer Inst., 1965-68; mem. cancer planning com. Calif. Regional Med. Program, Area V, U. So. Calif., 1967-69; mem. pub. health svc. spl. project rev. com. HEW, State of Calif., 1967-69; meml. lectr. Arthur Purdy Stout Soc. Surg. Pathologists, 1979. Author: Oral Cancer & Tumors of the Jaws, 1956; contbr. articles to profl. jours. Lt. Col. U.S. Army Res., 1941-45, PTO. Decorated Bronze Star. Mem. AMA, Coll. Am. Pathologists (mem. com. cancer 1965-70), Am. Soc. Clin. Pathologists, Soc. Surg. Oncology, Calif. Med. Assn., Calif. Soc. Pathologists (mem. exec. com. 1960-62, sec.-treas. 1962-65, pres.-elect 1965-66, pres. 1966-67), L.A. County Med. Assn. (chmn. com. med. examiner 1968-72), L.A. Soc. Pathologists (past pres. exec. com. 1961-62), Soc. Grad. Pathologists-L.A. County-U. So. Calif. Med. Ctr., Soc. Grad. Surgeons-L.A. County-U. So. Calif. Med. Ctr. E-mail: cttr@linkline.com. Home: 1000 Cordova St Apt 106 Pasadena CA 91106-2917 Office: Calif Tumor Tissue Registry 11021 Campus St # 335 Loma Linda CA 92354

BULLOCK, WILLIAM HENRY, bishop; b. Maple Lake, Minn., Apr. 13, 1927; s. Loren W. and Anne C. (Raiche) B. B.A., Notre Dame U., 1948, M.A., 1962; Ed.S., St. Thomas Coll., St. Paul, 1969; HHD (hon.), St. Ambrose U., Davenport, Iowa, 1989. Ordained priest Roman Catholic Ch., 1952, ordained bishop Roman Catholic Ch., 1980. Assoc. pastor Ch. of St.

Stephens, Mpls., 1952-55, Ch. of Our Lady of Grace, Edina, Minn., 1955-56, Ch. of Incarnation, Mpls., 1956-57; instr. St. Thomas Acad., Mendota Heights, Minn., 1957-61, headmaster, 1968-71; pastor Ch. of St. John the Baptist, Excelsior, Minn., 1971-80; former pastor Ch. of Our Lady of Perpetual Help, Mpls., from 1980; aux. bishop Archdiocese of St. Paul and Mpls., 1980-87; apptd. bishop Diocese of Des Moines, 1987, installed, 1987-93; apptd. bishop Madison, Wis., 1993—; v.p. Wis. Cath. Conf.; mem. Cath. Relief Svcs. Bd. Trustee St. Francis Sem. Mem. U.S. Bishops-Region II, Nat. Conf. Cath. Bishops (NCCB/USCC com. evangelization), KC (4th degree), Knights of Holy Sepulchre, Cath. Relief Svcs. (exec. com., Africa com., com. overseas programs and ops.). Lodges: KC; Knights of Holy Sepulchre. Office: Diocese of Madison Cath Pastoral Ctr PO Box 44983 Madison WI 53744-4983

BULLOUGH, RONALD, research consultant; b. Farnworth, Lancashire, Eng., Apr. 6, 1931; s. Ronald and Edna (Morrow) B.; m. Ruth Corbett, July 31, 1954; children: David Andrew, Timothy John, Mark Adrian, Neil Philip. BSc, Sheffield (Eng.) U., 1952, PhD, 1955, DSc, 1972. Chartered engr.; chartered physicist. Rsch. scientist Associated Electrical Industries Lab., Eng., 1955-63; divsn. head Harwell Lab., Eng., 1963-88; chief scientist, rsch. dir. U.K. Atomic Energy Authority, Eng., 1988-93; bd. dirs. Nat. Phys. Lab., Eng.; vis. prof. U. Ill., 1964-65, U. Surrey, Eng., 1969-73; cons. Rolls-Royce Assn., Eng., 1997—. Contbr. rsch. articles to profl. jours. including Advances in Physics, Trans. Royal Soc., Procs. Royal Soc. Fellow Royal Soc., Inst. Physics, Inst. Materials. Avocations: golf, walking, reading. Home: 4 Long Meadow Manor Rd, Goring Reading RG8 9EQ, England

BULLOUGH, WILLIAM ALAN, mechanical engineering educator, consultant; b. Bolton, Lancashire, Eng., May 22, 1939; s. John and Maggie (Townley) B.; children: Oliver William, Charles. BS, Strathclyde U., U.K., 1962; MSc, Birmingham U., U.K., 1963. Chartered engr., U.K. Various positions to sys. analyst de Havilland Propeller Co/Hawker Siddley Dynamics at Lostock, Hatfield, U.K., 1954-64; rsch. assoc. Osbourne Reynolds Hydraulics Lab., U. Manchester, U.K., 1964-67; from lectr. to reader dept. mech. engring. U. Sheffield, U.K., 1967—; chmn. Smart Machines, Materials and Related Techs., U. Sheffield, 1991, head thermodynamics and fluids groups, 1995-2000. Author chpts. to books and over 150 articles to profl. jours. Fellow Instn. Mech. Engrs.; mem. Royal Aeronautical Soc. (assoc.), Royal Instn. Gt. Britain. Avocation: golf.

BULMAHN, EDELGARD, government official; b. Minden, Germany, Mar. 4, 1951. B. Edn., U of Hanover, Germany, 1972-1980. Dist. councillor Hanover-Linden, 1981-86; mem. Bundestag, Germany, 1987—; SPD Dep. Spokesperson on rsch. & tech. policy Bundestag, 1990-1994; mem. SPD caucus parliamentary exec. com., 1991-98, SPD nat. exec. com., 1993—; chmn. Bundestag Com. on Edn., Sci., Rsch & Tech., 1995-96, Sci. Forum for Soc. Democracy, 1995; parliamentary spokesperson on edn. & rsch., 1996-98; federal minister of edn. and rsch. Govt. of Germany, 1998—. mem. Soc. Democratic Party (SPD), 1969—. Office: Ministry Edn & Rsch, Heinemannstr 2, D-53175 Bonn Germany

BULMAN PAGE, PHILIP CHARLES, chemistry researcher; b. Erith, Kent, Eng., Dec. 28, 1955; s. Henry Charles and Doris (Bulman) Page; m. Patricia Rosina Howard, June 19, 1980. BSc, Imperial Coll., London, 1978, PhD, 1981. Lectr. U. Liverpool, 1983-90, sr. lectr., 1990-94, reader, 1994-96; prof. Loughborough (Eng.) U., 1996—. Contbr. over 140 articles to profl. jours. Fellow Royal Soc. of Chemistry; mem. Am. Chem. Soc., Soc. of Chem. Industry. Office: Dept Chemistry, Loughborough U, Loughborough Leicestershire LE11 3TU, England

BULMER, MARTIN, sociologist, educator; b. Newcastle-on-Tyne, England, Aug. 25, 1943; s. Charles Philips Trevelyan and Edith Bulmer; m. Joan Boer, Aug., 1966; children: Michael, Georgina. BSc in Sociology, London Sch. Econs., 1967; PhD, U. London, Eng., 1981. Lectr. U. Durham, Eng., 1970-74; statistician Brit. Govt., London, 1975; from lectr. to reader London Sch. Econs., 1975-93; vis. prof. U. Chgo., 1987; prof. sociology Southampton (Eng.) U., 1993-95; Found. Fund prof. U. Surrey, Guildford, Eng., 1995—; vice-chair Rsch. Resources and Methods Com. Econ. and Social Rsch. Coun., 1985-87; editor Ethnic and Racial Studies, Acad. Jour., 1992—. Author: The Chicago School of Sociology, 1984; co-editor: (essays) The Social Survey in Historical Perspective, 1991, (lectures) Citizenship Today, 1996; (reader) Social Research in Developing Countries, 1993, Racism, 1999. Mem. Brit. Sociol. Assn., Am. Sociol. Assn., Internat. Sociol. Assn. Mem. Soc. of Friends. Avocations: cinema, walking. Office: U Surrey, Dept Sociology, Guildford GU2 7XH, England

BULT, HIDDE, pharmacologist; b. Kerkrade, The Netherlands, July 15, 1948; m. Lucie Constance M. Van Wersch, Oct. 8, 1971; children: Merel, Wouter. BSc, State U. Utrecht, 1973; PhD, Erasmus U., 1977; DSc, U. Antwerp, 1991. Asst. dept. pharmacology U. Rotterdam, The Netherlands, 1973-77; from asst. divsn. pharmacology to assoc. prof. U. Antwerp, Belgium, 1978—. Mem. Internat. Soc. Applied Vascular Biology, Br. Pharmacol. Soc., Dutch Pharmacol. Soc., Belgian Soc. Fundamental and Clin. Physiology and Pharmacology, N.Y. Acad. Scis. Avocations: bird census work, bird watching, traveling. Office: U Antwerp, Divsn Pharmacology, B 2610 Wilrijk Belgium

BUMAGIN, NIKOLAY ALEXANDROVICH, chemist; b. Dzerzhinskii, Russia, June 11, 1951; s. Alexander Alexandrovich and Tatyana Romanovna Proshkina B.; m. Irina Grigor'evna Brodskaya, Dec. 4, 1975. BS, Moscow State U., 1975, PhD, 1979, DS in Chemistry, 1986. Sci. rschr. Moscow State U., 1979-86, sr. sci. rschr., 1987-89, leading sci. rschr., 1990—; cons. Organic Semi-Products and Dyes Inst., Moscow, 1986-94; lectr. Moscow State U., 1986—. Contbr. articles to profl. jours. Recipient Nesmeyanov award Russian Acad. Scis., Moscow, 1991, Soros Prof. Soros Internat. Sci. Found., Moscow, 1994. Office: Lomonosov Moscow State Univ, Vorob'evy Gory, 119899 Moscow Russia

BUMBRY, GRACE, soprano; b. St. Louis, Jan. 4, 1937; d. Benjamin and Melzia (Walker) B. Student, Boston U., 1954-55, Northwestern U., 1955-56, also fgn. countries, Music Acad. West, 1956-59; studied with, Lotte Lehmann, 1956-59; HHD (hon.), St. Louis U.; hon. doctorates in humanities, Rust Coll., Holly Spring, Miss., U. St. Louis, U. Mo.; MusD (hon.), Rockhurst Coll. Operatic debut, Paris Opera, 1960; debut Basel Opera, 1960, Bayreuth Festival, 1961, Vienna State Opera, 1963, Royal Opera House, Covent Garden, 1963, Salzburg Festival, 1964, Met. Opera, 1965, La Scala, 1964, Les Troyens, Paris, 1990, Turandot, Wembley Arena, 1991; has appeared all major opera houses worldwide, S.Am., Japan, U.S.; command performances The White House; recs. for Deutsche Grammophon, Angel, London and RCA. Recipient John Hay Whitney award, Richard Wagner medal, 1963, Grammy award, 1979, Royal Opera House medal, 1988, Puccini award, 1990, Commandeur de l'Ordre des Arts et Lettres, France, 1996. Mem. Zeta Phi Beta, Sigma Alpha Iota. Office: J F Mastroianni Assocs 161 W 61st St New York NY 10023-7400

BUMGARDNER, CLOYD JEFFREY, school principal; b. Lorain, Ohio, Feb. 4, 1964; s. Cloyd Otis and Lois Christina (Todd) B. BS, Eastern Ky. U., 1987, MS, 1990. Cert. sch. adminstr., Ky. Sci. tchr. Pulaski County Schs., Somerset, Ky., 1990-93; asst. prin. Calloway County Schs., Murray, Ky., 1993-94; prin. Calloway County Mid. Sch., Murray, 1994—; adj. faculty U. Ky., 1990-93, Somerset C.C., 1990-93, Ea. Ky. U., Richmond, 1992-93; environ. cons. Am.-Russian Eco-bridge Team, Murray, 1994—; content adv. bd. mem. Ky. Dept. Edn., Frankfort, 1994-96; mem. Beline Sci. Expd., 1996, Nat. Energy Edn. Devel. Project, Washington, 1996—. Contbr. articles to profl. jours. Fundraiser Am. Heart Assn., Murray, 1995-98, Internat. Assn. Lions Clubs, Murray, 1994—; mem. Ky. Col. Commn., Gov. State of Ky., 1995. Named Hon. Capt. of Ky. Lake, Judge Exec. of Calloway County, 1995. Mem. NEA, Nat. Alliance for Restructuring Edn., Nat. Assn. Secondary Sch. Prins., Nat. Sch. Leaders Network, Ky. Assn. Environ. Edn., Internat. Assn. Lions Clubs, Ky. Acad. Scis., Phi Delta Kappa. Republican. Avocations: woodworking, golf. Office: Calloway County Middle School 2108A College Farm Rd Murray KY 42071-8805

BUMGARNER, MARLENE ANNE, writer, editor, educator; b. Yorkshire, Eng., Nov. 6, 1947; came to U.s., 1949; naturalized, 1965; d. Rowland and May (Whittaker) Skirrow; m. John Owen Bumgarner, June 17, 1967 (div. 1992); 1 child, Deborah Ann. AA, Coll. San Mateo, 1967; BA, San Diego State Coll., 1970; MA, San Jose (Calif.) State U., 1982; EdD, Nova U., 1992. Tech. editor electronics firms, 1967-70; coordinator Peer Counseling Center, Las Cruces, N.Mex., 1970-72; tchr. elem. sch., 1974-76, 82-84; owner, mgr. Morgan Hill (Calif.) Trading Post natural food store, 1976-80; editor Natural Living Newsline, 1979-81; mgr. Natural Living Assocs., 1979-82; dir. Morgan Hill Country Day Sch., 1980-82; prof. child devel., chair social sci. Gavilan Coll., 1979—, coord. child devel. programs, 1985—, chair social sci. dept., 1999—; new products editor Classroom Computer Learning mag., 1980-82. Author: Book of Whole Grains, 1976, (contbr.) The People's Cookbook, 1977, Organic Cooking for (not-so-organic) Mothers, 1980, (contbr.) Real Food Places to Eat, 1981, Working With School-Aged Children, 1999; food columnist San Jose Mercury, 1977-80, Gilroy Dispatch, 1984-86; sr. tech. writer Boole and Babbage, Inc., 1983-85; contbg. editor Mothering mag., 1981-87; contbr. articles to Mother's Manual, Baby Talk, Am. Baby, McCalls, Family Computing and others. Leader, founder La Leche League of Morgan Hill, 1977-85; supt. Sunday sch. St. John's Episc. Ch., 1982-85, sr. warden, 1992—; coord. Morgan Hill Cmty. Garden, 1982-84; participant Leaders for the 80's, 1987; bd. dirs. Calif. Sch. Age Consortium, 1998—. Named Woman of Achievement Santa Clara County, 1987. Mem. AAUW, Nat. Assoc. for Edn. of Young Children, Rotary Internat.

BUMIN, MUSTAFA, judge. Judge Constitutional Ct. Turkey, Ankara, Turkey, 1992—; pres., 2000—. Office: Anayasa Mah Kemisi, Selanik Cad 37, Yenisehir Ankara, Turkey*

BUMP, REBECCA RUTH, financial analyst, accountant; b. Portland, Oreg., Apr. 15, 1967; d. Edwin Albert Bump and Emily Catherine Kadi. BA in Acctg., Western Wash. U., 1990; MSc in Finance, Seattle U., 1994; MSc in Internat. Acctg., Finance, London Sch. Econs., 1995. Acct. Eagle Ins. Group, Seattle, 1992-94; financial analyst Spaint PCS, Pleasanton, Calif., 1995-97; staff financial analyst NEC Electronics, Santa Clara, Calif., 1997-99; sr. financial analyst eBay, San Jose, Calif., 1999—; adv. com. eBay Found., San Jose, 1999. Mem. Inst. Mgmt. Accts. (dir. cmty. svc. 1996-97).

BUNCE, JILLIAN MARGERY, therapy educator; b. Newcastle-Upon-Tyme, Eng., Mar. 28, 1949; s. William and Edna Margery (Sidebotham) Breese; m. David Maurice Bunce; children: Michael Joseph, Emily Anne. BA in Theology with honors, U. Birmingham, Eng., 1991; MA in Dance Movement Therapy, Laban Ctr., London, 1995. Registered dance movement therapist. Asst. tchr. Southland Sch., New Romney, Eng., 1970-71, Harcourt Secondary Sch., Folkstone, Eng., 1971-72; head remedial edn. Pent Valley Sch., Folkstone, 1972-75; head slow learners unit Canonfrome, Eng., 1975-76; supply tchr. Staffs Edn., 1992-94; part-time lectr. Derby (Eng.) U., 1994-98, sr. part-time lectr., 1998—; pvt. practice dance movement therapy, 1991—; hon. mem. Staffs Neurol. Unit, Stafford, 1991-98; support tchr. Staffordshire Edn., 1994-95; lectr. in field. Stood for Councillor Green Party, 1987,. Avocations: painting on silk, gardening, interior design. Home: 28 The Crescent, Eccleshall Stafford ST21 6AZ, England

BUNCH, RICHARD ALAN, writer, educator; b. Honolulu, June 1, 1945; s. Thornton Carlisle and DeLores (Veal) B.; m. Rita Anne Glazar, Aug. 11, 1990; children: Katharine, Richard Jr. AA, Napa Coll., 1965; BA in Comms., Stanford U., 1967; MA in History, U. Ariz., 1969, MDiv, 1970, DD, 1971; postgrad., Vanderbilt U., 1972-75, Temple U., 1975-76; JD, U. Memphis, 1980. Tchg. asst. philosophy Vanderbilt U., Nashville, 1973-74; instr. philosophy Belmont U., 1973-74; law clk. Cir. Ct. Shelby County, Tenn., 1979-81; atty. Horne and Peppel, Memphis, 1981-83; law clk. Tenn. Ct. Appeals, 1983; instr. philosophy Chapman U., 1986-87; instr. law Sonoma State U., 1986-87, instr. philosophy, 1990-91; lectr. U. Calif., Berkeley, 1995; adj. humanities faculty Napa Valley Coll., 1985—; instr. history and humanities Diablo Valley Coll., 1991-94, 97. Author: Summer Hawk, 1991, Night Blooms, 1992, Wading the Russian River, 1993, Santa Rosa Plums, 1996, A Foggy Morning, 1996, South By Southwest, 1997, Sacred Space, 1998, Rivers of the Sea, 1998; contbr. Hawai'i Rev., Black Mt. Rev., The Plaza, Black Moon, Xavier Rev., European Judaism, The Windsor Rev., FUGUE, Poetry Nottingham, The Alembic, others; assoc. news editor, reporter, feature writer Napa Valley Times, 1985. Mem. staff Nashville Human Rights Forum, 1974-75; chair housing authority-bldg. authority bd. City of Napa, 1985-89. Recipient Grand prize Ina Coolbrith Nat. Poetry Day Contest, 1989, Jessamyn West creative writing prize, 1990, nominated for Pushcart Prize, 1988, 97. Mem. Acad. Am. Poets, Ina Coolbrith Cir. Home: 248 Sandpiper Dr Davis CA 95616-7546

BUNDA, STEPHEN MYRON, political advisor, consultant, lawyer, classical philosopher; b. Jersey City, N.J., Oct. 5, 1949; s. Stephen and Anna (Yaschak) B. BA summa cum laude, St. Peter's Coll., Jersey City, 1971; MA with honors, New Sch. Grad. Faculty, N.Y.C., 1976; JD, Rutgers Law Sch., Newark, N.J., 1987. Bar: N.J. Pol. cons. Democratic Party, N.J., 1977-92; pol. adv. Govt. of Ukraine, 1991—; counsellor-at-law Bunda & Co., Lyndhurst, N.J., 1994—; advisor on Ukraine to U.S. Congress, Office of the Pres., Nat. Security Coun., Washington, 1991—. Mem. Nat. Honor Soc., Am. Hist. Assn., Am. Philos. Assn., Ukrainian-Am. Bar Assn., N.J. Bar Assn., Soc. for Ukrainian-Jewish Rels., Ukrainian Nat. Assn., Lawyers Com. for Human Rights. Democrat. Mem. Ukrainian Catholic Ch. Avocations: reading philosophy and history, educational travel and sight-seeing, music, art, literature, theatre. Home: 691 Union Ave Lyndhurst NJ 07071-2815 Office: Stephen Myron Bunda Esquire PO Box 461 Lyndhurst NJ 07071-0461

BUNDER, MARTIN WICHER, mathematics educator, researcher, dean; b. The Hague, The Netherlands, Dec. 13, 1942; came to Australia, 1951; s. Adriaan Theodoor Visser and Anna Cornelia (Doppenberg) Bunder; m. Simonette Johanna Visser, Mar. 22, 1969; children: David, Judith, Miriam, Mark, Rachel. BSc, U. New South Wales, 1962; MA, U. New Eng., Armidale, 1966; PhD, U. Amsterdam, 1969. Tutor, tchg. fellow U. New Eng., 1963-66; grad. asst. U. Amsterdam, 1966-69; lectr., sr. lectr., reader U. Wollongong, N.S.W., Australia, 1969—, dean faculty math. scis., found. dean, 1989-90; dean faculty informatics U. Wollongong, N.S.W., 1990-92. Author: Set Theory Based on Combinatory Logic, 1969. Mem. Australian Math. Soc., Am. Math. Soc., Assn. Symbolic Logic, Australian Assn. Logic (pres. 1979-80). Roman Catholic. Avocations: table tennis, squash, stamp collecting, reading. Home: 22 Cedar Grove, Keiraville New South Wales, Australia Office: Math Dept U Wollongong,, Wollongong, New South Wales 2500, Australia

BUNDITJAROENPUN, SOMCHET, information systems specialist; b. Bangkok, Jan. 2, 1962; s. Somjai and Dhanormsri (Isarankura) B. BS in Gen. Sci., Chulalongkorn U., Bangkok, 1984; MBA in Info. and Computer Sci., Greenwich U., 1998; PhD in Internat. Bus. Admin., Kennedy-Western U., Thousand Oaks, Calif., 2000. Programmer Toyota Motor (Thailand) Co., Ltd., Bangkok, 1984-88, Triumph Internat. Thailand Ltd., Bangkok, 1988-90; asst. MIS mgr. Cosmo Group of Cos., Bangkok, 1990-2000, MIS mgr., 2000—; cons. Forward Group of Cos., Bangkok, 1997—. mem. Asian Inst. Tech. (AIT), Thailand. Avocations: music, internet. Fax: 603.215.2713; 66.2.259-8510. E-mail: somchet@loxinfo.co.th. Home: 253/7 Moo 5 Soi Kusolsong 1, Old Railway Rd Samrong Prapradaeng, 10130 Samutprakarn Thailand also: Forward Group Cos, 1/47-49 Soi 39 Sukhumvit Rd, Wattana Bangkok 10110, Thailand

BUNDRED, NIGEL JAMES, surgeon; b. Sunderland, Durham, Eng., July 17, 1957; s. James and Georgina Bundred; m. Sara Michelle Prize, Mar. 18, 1969. MBBS, Newcastle U., Eng., 1980; MD, U. Newcastle-Upon-Tyne, Eng., 1990. Lectr. U. Edinburgh, Scotland, 1982-84, U. Birmingham, Eng., 1989-91; surg. registrar Leicester (Eng.) Area Health Authority, 1985-87; postfellowship registrar U. Hosp. of Wales, 1988-89; sr. lectr. U. Manchester, Eng., 1991-96, reader in surg. oncology, 1996—; cons. surgeon U. Hosp. South Manchester, 1991—, Christie Hosp., Manchester, 1991—; dir. Manchester Surg. Rsch. Fund, Eng., 1991—. Author: Wolfe Atlas of Breast Diseases, 1994. Fellow Royal Coll. Surgeons London (Hunterian prof. 1994), Royal Coll. Surgeons Edinburgh; mem. Surg. Rsch. Soc. (Patey prize 1991, 94, 99, mem. nat. com.), Brit. Assn. Surg. Oncology (mem. nat. com., breast care campaign sci. com.). Avocations: soccer, tennis, contemporary music. Fax: 961-291-3846. E-mail: bundredn@fs1.with.man.ac.uk. Office: U Hosp South Manchester, Dept Surgery Nell Ln, Manchester M20 8LR, England

BUNDSCHUH, BERNHARD OSKAR, electrical engineering and communications educator; b. Amorbach, Bavaria, Germany, Mar. 7, 1957; s. Werner Gottfried and Emilie (Konz) B.; m. Iris Susanne Dick, June 16, 1989; 1 child, Matthias. Diploma in engring., U. Siegen, Germany, 1983, PhD, 1990. Engr. ANT, Backnang, Germany, 1983-84; rschr. U. Siegen, 1985-91, postdoctoral scientist, 1991-94; prof. elec. engring., sys. theory and telecom. U. Merseburg, Germany, 1994—; co-founder, co-owner Sentec, Siegen, 1989-94. Author: Laseroptische 3D-Konturerfassung, 1991. With German Army, 1976-77. Avocations: bicycling, science in general. Home: Dürerweg 4, D-57290 Neunkirchen Germany Office: U Merseburg, Geusaer Strasse 88, D-06217 Merseburg Germany

BUNDSCHUH, MANFRED OTTO, insurance company executive, educator; b. Frankfurt, Germany, May 21, 1946; m. Ursula Lisbeth Grabowski, July 5, 1974; children: Gunhild Ursula, Meinhard Erik. Diploma in math., U. Frankfurt, 1975. Operator, customer attendant IBM Frankfurt, 1968-72; sch. tchr. Meschede, 1975-77; info. tech. cons. Hamburg, 1977-83; info. tech. methods planner Cologne, 1983—; appt. prof. U. Hamburg, 1983; apptd. prof. Fachhoch Schule Cologne, 1983—; examiner C. of C., Cologne, 1983-94, mgr. exams., 1986-94; pres. DASMA e.V., Cologne, 1996—. Author: Objektorientierte Software-Entwicklung, 1993, Praxis der Entscheidungstechnik, 1994, Dialog Design, 1994, Aufwandschaetzung von it-projekten, others. Mem. Assn. Computing Machinery, Deutsche Gesellschaft fuer Projektmanagement, World Future Soc. Avocations: astronomy, archeology, futurology, cybernetics, knowledge organization. Home: Sander Hoehe 5, D-51465 Bergisch Gladbach Germany Office: CNV AG House 4 1 4, Colonia Allee 10-20, D-51067 Cologne Germany

BUNGER, ROLF, physiology educator; b. Hamburg, Germany, Oct. 19, 1941; came to U.S., 1979; s. Heinz Johannes Albert and Helga (Franz) B.; m. Margriet Akkerman, Dec. 14, 1973; children: Nils, Frank. MD, U. Hamburg, 1969, U. Heidelberg, Germany, 1970; MD habil., U. Munich, 1979. Intern Heidberg Infirmary, Hamburg, 1970; asst. of physiology U. Aachen, Germany, 1970-75, U. Munich, 1975-79; asst. prof. dept. physiology F. E. Hebert Med. Sch., USUHS, Bethesda, Md., 1979-82, assoc. prof., 1983-92; prof. USUHS, Bethesda, Md., 1992—; prof. of molecular and cellular biology US Univ. Health Svc., Bethesda, Md., 1994—; prof. anesthesiology US Univ. Health Svc., Bethesda, 2000—; cons. U. Buffalo, 1983, U. Ala., 1986-89, U. Tex., Ft. Worth, 1990—, AAALAC, 1997—; referee, editl. reviewer domestic and fgn. sci. med. rsch. jours. and instns., including NIH, VA, NSF, HFSP, Dutch Heart Found., MRC, 1994—; vis. prof. Erasmus U., Rotterdam, 1992; lectr. in field. Mem. editorial bd. Internat. Jour. Purine and Pyrimidine Rsch., 1989-93, Internat. Jour. Angiology, 1991-95, Am. Jour. Physiology, 1999—; licensed patentee in field. Webelo leader Boy Scouts Am., McLean, Va., 1986-87, packmaster, 1987-89. Capt., German Air Force Med. Corp. Grantee Uniformed Svcs. U. Health Scis., 1979—, NIH, 1982—, Dept. of Def., 1995—. Fellow Am. Heart Assn.; mem. Am. Physiol. Soc., Deutsche Physiol. Gesellschaft. Achievements include clarification of adenylate compartments in myocardium; demonstration of energy-linked and work dependence of myocardial pyruvate dehydrogenase flux, of interstitial free AMP in myocardium; research in substrate enhancement of isolated and in-situ preischemic and postischemic heart preparations; metabolic protection of cytosolic phosphorylation potential by pyruvate and adenosine during myocardial reperfusion, adenylate-related theory of metabolic coronary control, energy-linked control of sarcoplasmic reticulum Ca 2+ - ATPase, pyruvate protection against apoptosis and hemorrhagic shock, Redox control of NADH oxidase. Home: 1922 Kenbar Ct Mc Lean VA 22101-5321 Office: USUHS Dept Physiology 4301 Jones Bridge Rd Bethesda MD 20814-4799

BUNIN, MIKHAIL ALEKSEEVITCH, physicist, researcher, educator; b. Rostov-on-Don, Russia, May 20, 1951; s. Alexey Mikhailovitch and Anna Petrovna (Gurasheva) B. MS in Physics and Computer Applications, Rostov State U., 1973, PhD in Physics and Math., 1981. Jr. rschr. Rostov State U., Rostov-on-Don, 1977-80, sr. rschr., 1980—, lectr., 1984—, supr. grads. and postgrads., 1975-89; reviewer Inst. Info. (VINITI), Moscow, 1982—. Contbr. articles to profl. jours. Recipient diploma Ministry of Edn. USSR, 1972; grantee Ctr. Fundamental Problems, 1994-95. Avocations: gardening, sports, tennis. Office: Rsch Inst Physics, 194 Stachky Ave, 344090 Rostov-on-Don Russia

BUNKER, BERYL H., retired insurance executive, community volunteer; b. Chelsea, Mass., Aug. 18, 1919; d. Albert Crocker and Eva Agnes (Norris) Hardacker; m. John Wadsworth Bunker, Oct. 31, 1942. Student, Simmons Coll., 1936-38, Boston Coll. Law, 1948-49; grad., Bentley Sch. Acctg., Boston, 1958; BBA with highest honors, Northeastern U., 1962, MBA, 1967. CFA. Legal rsch. clerk Frank Shepard Co., N.Y.C., 1938-43; cost acct. Johns Manville Corp., Pittsburg, Calif., 1943-46; studio mgr. Wheelan Studios, Boston, 1946; clerical supr. Columbian Purchasing Group, Boston, 1946-48; office mgr. Wellesley (Mass.) Coll., 1948-51; statistician Eastman Kodak Co., Rochester, N.Y., 1951-53; investment officer John Hancock Mut. Life, Boston, 1953-74; sr. v.p. John Hancock Advisers, Boston, 1974-84. Nat. bd. dirs. YWCA of the U.S.A., 1988-94, hon. bd. dirs., 1998—, mem. World Svc. Coun., 1992—; pres. bd. dirs. Boston YWCA, 1985-87, active 1977-96; chair bd. Vis. Nurses Assn. Cape Cod Found., South Dennis, Mass., 1995; bd. dirs. Old South Meeting House Mus., Boston, 1989-92; corporateor Simmons Coll., 2000—; trustee Simmons Coll., 1994-2000, chair centennial com. 1999-2000, corporator, 2000—; mem. women's coun. exec. com. Pine St. Inn, 1992—; bd. visitors Women's Edn. and Ind. Union, 2000—; mem. acad. outreach com. Boston Women's Fund, 2000—; mem. adv. com. On The Rise, 1997—; mem. Ctr. for Women in Politics and Public Policy, Assocs. of the Boston Pub. Libr. Bd., The Coll. Club of Boston, 1998—, Cambridge YWCA, Neighborhood Assn. of the Back Bay; honoree Pine St. Inn Women's Coun., 2000. Recipient Philanthropy award Women in Devel., 1990, Disting. Alumni award Bentley Coll., 1994; named Woman of Achievement, Cambridge YWCA, 1991, Lifetime Service to Women award, On The Rise, 1998, Lifetime Achievement award, College Club, 1998. Mem. AARP, LWV, NOW, AAUW, Assn. Investment Mgmt. Rsch., Mass. Action for Women, Mass. Women Polit. Caucus, Boston Security Analysts Soc. (treas. 1973-76), Mass. Women's State Wide Legis. Network (dir. 1987), Simmons Coll. Alumnae Assn. (pres. 1989-91, Alumnae Svc. award 1984, Planned Giving award 1993), Older Women's League, The Internat. Alliance, Harwich Hist. Soc., Project Vote Smart, Women's Ednl. & Indsl. Union, Friday Forum, Network for Women in Politics and Pub. Policy, Eire Soc., Wellesley Ctrs. for Women. Avocations: fundraising, theater, reading. Home: 790 Boylston St Apt 22F Boston MA 02199-7921 also: 22 Cross St Harwich Port MA 02646-1813

BUNKER, DONALD HARRY, lawyer, sole proprietor, educator; b. Montreal, Que., Can., Aug. 31, 1940; s. Harry James and Anne (Roberts) B.; m. Pamela Mary Mockridge, Sept. 24, 1960; children: Kenneth, Thomas, Stephen, Christy. BA in Econs., Sir George Williams U., 1967; BCL, McGill U., 1971, LLM, 1985, DCL, 1988. From law clk. to ptnr. Ogilvy Renault, Montreal, 1963-95; lawyer Donald H. Bunker & Assocs., Dubai, United Arab Emirates, 1995—; adj. prof. law McGill U. Author: The Law of Aerospace Finance in Canada, 1988, Canadian Aviation Finance Legislation, 1989, Plunder: The Looting of Canada by the Welfare State, 1993. Fin. advisor Internat. Civil Aviation Orgn. Fellow Royal Aero. Soc.; mem. ABA, Internat. Bar Assn., Acad. Transport. Russia, Chartered Inst. Transport N.Am., Que. Bar Assn. Office: Ste 1606 AlReem Tower, PO Box 29726, Dubai United Arab Emirates

BUNKER, TIMOTHY DAVID, orthopaedic surgeon; b. Nairobi, Kenya; arrived in U.K., 1956; s. Derek and Molly (Hunt) B.; m. Sue Wilson, June 21, 1975; children: Simon, Christopher. BS with honors, St. Barts, London, 1973, MB BChir with honors, 1976; MCh in Orthopaedics, U. Liverpool, Eng., 1987. Sr. registrar Nottingham, Eng., 1985-90; cons. surgeon Princess Elizabeth Orthopaedic Hosp., Exeter, Eng., 1990—. Author: Pathology of Frozen Shoulder, 1995; co-author: Shoulder Arthroscopy, 1990, Clinical Challenges in Orthopaedics—The Shoulder, 1997; editor: Frontiers in Fracture Management, 1989. Recipient Hampson prize S. W. Orthopaedic Surgeons, 1996. Fellow Royal Coll. Surgeons Eng. (Hunterian prof. 1996-97, G. B. Ong Gold medal 1980-81), Royal Coll. Surgeons Edinburgh (Gold medal 1981), Brit. Shoulder and Elbow Surgeons (treas., coun. mem. 1992-95), Am. Shoulder and Elbow Surgeons (corres.); mem. European Shoulder and Elbow Surgeons. Avocations: classic cars, sailing.

BUNKOV, YURIY MICHAILOVICH, physicist; b. Stavropol, Russia, Aug. 29, 1950; s. Michail and Klavdiya (Barkovskaya) B.; m. Olga Dmitrievna Timoteevskaya, Oct. 5, 1974; children: Svetlana, Elena. BSc, Moscow Phys. Tech. Inst., 1974; PhD, Kapitza Inst., 1979, DSc, 1986. From rschr. to leading scientist Kapitza Inst., Moscow, 1974-95; dir. rsch. CRTBT-CNRS, Grenoble, France, 1995—. Recipient Russia State prize for science & technology, 1993. Office: CRTBT-CNRS, 25 ave des Martyrs BP 166, 38042 Grenoble France

BUNKŠE, EDMUNDS VALDEMĀRS, geographer, educator, consultant; b. Liepāja, Latvia, July 29, 1935; came to U.S., 1950; s. Jēkabs Bunkše and Anna Leontine Bucholts Birznieks; m. Moira Daly (div.); Elizabeth Murray Sutherland, Feb. 9, 1988 (div.); m. Grizelda Astrida Liepins, Oct. 15, 1995; children: Andrejs, Margarita. AB, Syracuse U., 1962; MA, U. Calif., Berkeley, 1966, PhD, 1973; D honoris causa, U. Latvia, 1991. Tchg. asst. U. Calif., Berkeley, 1963-65; instr. Coll. Holy Names, Oakland, Calif., 1965-67; cartographer Assn. Bay Area Govts., Berkeley, 1965; instr. U. Del., Newark, 1969-73, asst. prof., 1973-80, assoc. prof. dept. geography, 1980—, dir. London program, 1991; vis. Fulbright prof. U. Latvia, Riga, 1990, adj. prof., 1995—; assoc. prodr. Latvian TV, Riga, 1992-95. Editor GeoJour. Baltic Peoples, 1994; contbr. articles to profl. jours. and book. Mem. com. CIES-Fulbright Selection, Washington, 1992-95, Danish-Latvian Coop., 1990-95; in edn. reform U. Latvia, Riga, 1992—; mem. promotion and Dr. Habilis com. U. Latvia. Fulbright awardee, 1983-84, 90. Mem. Latvian Acad. Sci. (fgn.), Fulbright Alumni Assn., Assn. Am. Geographers, Ea. Hist. Geog. Assn., Assn. Latvian Geographers, Lidums. Mem. Evang. Luth. Ch. Avocations: sailing, skiing, sketching, chess. E-mail: ebunkse@udel.edu. Office: U Del Dept Geography Newark DE 19716

BUNNELL, GEORGE ELI, lawyer; b. Miami, Fla., Apr. 28, 1938; s. George A. and Lillian E. (Hurley) B.; Dianne Railton, Dec. 1, 1990; children: Kelley, Courtney. BA, U. Fla., 1960, LLB, 1962. Bar: Fla. 1963, U.S. Dist. Ct. (so. dist.) Fla. 1963, U.S. Ct. Appeals (11th cir.) 1982, U.S. Supreme Ct. 1970. Assoc. Nicholson, Howard & Brawner, Miami, 1963-64; assoc. Dean, Adams, George & Wood, Miami, 1964-67, ptnr., 1968-71; officer, dir. Huebner, Shaw & Bunnell, P.A., Fort Lauderdale, Fla., 1972-77; pres., dir. Bunnell, Woulfe, Kirschbeum, Keller Cohen & McIntyre, P.A., Fort Lauderdale, 1977—. Mem. advance staff White House, 1974-76; mem. City of Fort Lauderdale Marine Adv. Bd., 1974-76, City of Fort Lauderdale Civil Svc. Bd., 1977-79; bd. dirs., sec. Fort Lauderdale Mus. Art, 1990—. Fellow Am. Coll. Trial Lawyers; mem. Internat. Assn. of Def. Counsel, Am. Bd. Trial Advs. (pres. Ft. Lauderdale chpt. 1992), Def. Rsch. inst., Fla. Def. Lawyers Assn., Broward County Bar Assn., Fla. Acad. of Hosp. Attys., Am. Health Lawyers Assn., Lauderdale Yacht Club. Republican. Office: Bunnell Woulfe Kirschbaum Keller & McIntyre PA 888 E Las Olas Blvd Fl 4 Fort Lauderdale FL 33301-2272

BUNNER, PATRICIA ANDREA, lawyer; b. Fairmont, W.Va., Sept. 16, 1953; d. Scott Randolph and Virginia Lenore (Keck) B. AB in History & English magna cum laude, W.Va. U., 1975, JD, 1978; postgrad., Trinity Theol. Sem., 1995—, W.Va. U., 1996—. Bar: W.Va. 1978, N.Y. 1981, D.C. 1981, U.S. Dist. Ct. (so. dist.) W.Va. 1978, U.S. Dist. Ct. (no. dist.) W.Va. 1985, U.S. Ct. Claims 1990, U.S. Supreme Ct. 1989; cert. Christian counselor, 1986—. Mem. staff Dem. Nat. Com., Washington, 1978-79; assoc. Gailor, Elias & Matz, Washington, 1979-81, N.Y. State Bankers Assn., N.Y.C., 1981-83; ptnr. Bunner & Bunner, Fairview, W.Va., 1984-94; exec. dir. N.Y. State Consumer Mortgage Rev. Bd.; chmn. dist. VIII Consumer Mortgage Rev. Com., N.Y.C., 1982-83; cons. atty. Energy Cons. Assocs., Spring Harbor, N.Y., 1981; of counsel Monongahela (W.Va.) Soil Conservation Dist., 1985; vis. scholar Pitts. Theol. Sem., 1997—. Author: How Charley Metheney Broke the Four Minute Mile, 1971, Across the Bennefield Prong, 1973, German Anti-Semitism, Bismarck Through Weimar, 1973, N.Y. State Bankers Assn. Legis. Directory, 1983, Through a Glass Darkly, A Compendium of Film Noir, 1996, The Influence of the Seventeenth Century Scientific Revolution on Anglo-American Law, 1996, Rene Descartes, Phenomenologist, 1996, Psychology of Thomas Aquinas, 1997, John Locke's Influence on Modern Science, 1998, Conceptions of Property in Early America, 1787-1801, 1999, John Locke's Influence on Thomas Jefferson's View of Property, 1999, Thomas Jefferson as Reformer of Property Law, 1999, Plato's Influence As Seen In Environmental Traditions, 2000, Nietzches Influence on Modern Environment Thought, 2000, Islamic Cities, 2000, Newtonian Science in Colonial America, 2000, Thomas Jefferson's Land Ethic, 2000, Progress and Property, 1945-1970, 2000; presenter in field. Pres. Monongalia County Dem. Women, 1987-89; sec. Monongalia County Devel. Authority, 1984-91; pres. United Taxpayers Assn., Inc., W.Va., 1985-88; bd. dirs. W.Va. U. Morgantown, 1974-75; active W.Va. State Dem. Exec. Com., 1990, 94. Recipient WVU Canaga prize in Am. History, 1999-2000; Rilla Moran Woods fellow Nat. Fedn. Dem. Women, Washington, 1978. Mem. ATLA, ABA (vice chmn. legal econs. and new lawyers coms. 1986-87, litigation sect., 1st amendment rights and media law com., gen. practice com., corps. and banking com.), W.Va. Bar Assn. (com. econs. of law practice 1987—, com. corps. and banking 1987—), W.Va. Trial Lawyers Assn., N.Y. State Bar Assn., Monongalia County Bar Assn., Marion County Bar Assn., W.Va. Criminal Def. Lawyers Assn., Women's Info. Ctr. (founding), LWV, NAFE, W.Va. Alliance for Women's Studies (founding), Bus. and Profl. Women (bd. dirs.), Climates, Inc., Monongalia County Hist. Soc., W.Va. Brain Injury Assn., Clay-Battelle Alumni Assn., W.Va. Coll. Law Alumni Assn., Nat. Rifle Assn. (life), Nature Conservancy, Nat. Arbor Day Found., World Wildlife Fund, Am. Farmland Trust, AAUW, Sierra Club, Audobon Soc., Young Dems. Club W.Va. (sec. 1976), Phi Alpha Theta (chpt. pres. 1974-75), Phi Beta Kappa, Zeta Phi Eta, Alpha Rho (chpt. pres. 1974), Phi Kappa Phi. Baptist. Club: Woman's (bd. dirs. Morgantown chpt. 1986—). Avocations: clothing design, cooking, creative writing, piano, swimming. Address: PO Box 86 Fairview WV 26570-0086

BUNNER, WILLIAM KECK, lawyer; b. Fairmont, W.Va., Sept. 2, 1949; s. Scott Randolph and Virginia Lenore (Keck) B. BS in Secondary Edn. magna cum laude, W.Va. U., 1970, MA in History, 1973, ABD in History, 1975, JD, 1978, postgrad., 1998—. Bar: W.Va. 1978, U.S. Dist. Ct. (so. dist.) W.Va. 1978, U.S. Dist. Ct. (no. dist.) W.Va. 1985. Tchr. Monongalia County Bd. Edn., Morgantown, W.Va., 1970-78; contract lawyer dept. fin. and adminstrn. State of W.Va., Charleston, 1978-79; pvt. practice law Fairview, W.Va., 1979-84; pres. Farm Home Svc., Inc., 1983—; ptnr. Bunner & Bunner, Morgantown and Fairview, 1984-92; pres. Climates, 1988—; presenter History of Barn Dance in U.S.A., Rush D. Holt History Conf., W. Va. U., 1999. Author: Planting Churches: A Case Study of Western Monongalia County, West Virginia, 2000, Anxiety, Alienation and Adjustment: Filmnoir and the Returning Warriorfrom WWII, 2000. Pres. Monongalia County Young Dems., 1974; parliamentarian Monongalia County Dem. Exec. Com., 1982-94; counsel, parliamentarian Young Dem. Clubs W.Va., 1974-77; bd. dirs., supr. Monongahela Soil Conservation Dist., 1982—; advisor West Run Watershed Improvement Dist., 1983—; mem. W.Va. Commn. on Rural Abandoned Mines, Rural Alliance, Monongalia County Solid Waste Auth., 1989—, also chmn., 1990-92. Mem. ABA, Monongalia County Bar Assn., Assn. Rural Conservation, Soil Conservation Soc. Am., United Taxpayers' Assn. (counsel), Monongalia County Hist. Soc., Marion County Hist. Soc., Marion County Bar Assn., W.Va. Trial Lawyers Assn, Phi Alpha Delta, Phi Alpha Theta. Democrat. Avocations: music, politics, farming, videos, regional history and genealogy. Home and Office: 109 Lamesa Vlg Morgantown WV 26508-6243

BUNNING, RICHARD LESLIE, management consultant; b. Buffalo, Wyo., Apr. 22, 1945; arrived in U.K., 1991; s. Harold William and Jean Marjorie (Eder) B.; m. Kathleen Elizabeth Powers, Jan. 22, 1970 (div. Sept. 1980); children: Bridget Kathleen, Melinda Coleen. BA, U. Wyo., 1967, MA, 1970; PhD, Ariz. State U., 1976. Dir. adult edn. Morgan C.C., Ft. Morgan, Colo., 1970-73; dir. tng. and devel. Samaritan Health Svc., Phoenix, 1973-79; exec. dir. Ariz. Consortium for Edn./Ariz. State U., Tempe, 1979-81; spl. asst. to pres. Good Samaritan Med. Ctr., Phoenix, 1981-83; orgn. devel. cons. Pilkington, St. Helens, Eng., 1983-96; mgmt. cons. Phoenix Assocs. (U.K.) Ltd., St. Helens, 1996—; adj. faculty Ariz. State U., Phoenix, 1986-89, U. Phoenix, 1984-89, Sonoma (Calif.) State U., 1990-91, Durham (Eng.) U., 1997—; accreditation panelist Assn. MBAs, London, 1997—. Contbr. articles to profl. jours. Sgt. U.S. Army, 1967-69. Mem. Chartered Inst. Pers. and Devel. Democrat. Roman Catholic. Avocations: biking, running, reading, travel, writing. Home and Office: 57 Higher Ln, Rainford WA11 8AY, England

BUNT, MARION ADAMS, retired administrative secretary/coordinator; b. Port Huron, Mich., Oct. 21, 1916; d. Lewis Richard and Gladys (Wakeham) Adams; m. Floyd Walter Gordon Bunt, Aug. 16, 1941 (dec. Dec. 22, 1999); children: Floyd Walter Gordon Jr., Mary Elizabeth Adams Bunt, Theodore James, Terrence Lewis. BA, Oakland U., 1982. Adminstr., sec. Oakland U., Rochester, Mich., 1962-80, coord., 1980-89; ret. Oakland U., 1989. Pres. Women of Oakland U., 1987-89; founding mem., bd. dirs. Oakland Sail; active numerous coms. and offices Cranbrook House and Gardens Aux., including bd. dirs., sec. 1992—, joint exec. bd.; active Cranbrook Ednl. Community; founder Cranbrook Ice Skating Club, Cranbrook Tennis Club; mem. founding com. Cranbrook Music Guild. Recipient Thistle award for meritorious svc., Cranbrook House and Gardens Aux. Mem. LWV, Oakland U Alumni Assn. (sec. bd. dirs. 1991-93, v.p. 1993-94, various other coms., Alumni Spirit award 1994), Altrusa Club (various coms., ofcl. positions). Avocations: gardening, volunteering, genealogy. Home: 4536 Middleton Ct West Bloomfield MI 48323-3633

BUNTROCK, DEAN LEWIS, retired waste management company executive; b. Columbia, S.D., June 6, 1931. BA, St. Olaf Coll., Northfield, Minn., 1955. Founder Waste Mgmt. Inc., Oak Brook, Ill., 1968—; chmn. bd., dir. Waste Mgmt. Inc. (changed to WMX Technologies in 1993), Oak Brook, Ill., 1968—; also chmn. bd., bd. dirs. WMI Internat., until 1997; bd. dirs. Wheelabrator Techs., Inc., First Nat. Bank Chgo., Waste Mgmt. Internat., Plc. Trustee Chgo. Symphony Orch.; mem. adv. bd. J.L. Kellogg Grad. Sch. Nortwestern U., Evanston, Ill. Named Outstanding CEO, Fin. World Mag., Wall St. Transcript; appointed to Pres.'s Coun. on Environ. Quality. Mem. Am. Pub. Works Assn., Environ. Industries Assn. (co-founder, past pres., sec.-treas., dir.), Bus. Roundtable. Office: Oakbrook Terrace Tower One Tower Ln Ste 2242 Oakbrook Terrace IL 60181-4636

BUNTROCK, ROBERT E., information consultant, organic chemist; b. Mpls., Nov. 19, 1940; s. Eric Frank and Louise Ada (Intorf) B.; m. Gloria Carolyn Kral, June 24, 1961; children: Stephen Robert, Christine Louise Selby. BS in Chemistry, U. Minn., 1962; MA, Princeton U., 1964, PhD, 1967. Rsch. chemist Air Products & Chem., Allentown, Pa., 1967-70, Amoco Oil Co., Whiting, Ind., 1970-71; rsch. info. scientist Amoco Corp., Naperville, Ill., 1971-80, sr. rsch. info. scientist, 1980-85, rsch. assoc., 1985-95; pres. Buntrock Assocs., Inc., Naperville, 1995—; mem. adv. bd. Derwent Ltd., London, 1980-86, Chem. Abstracts Svc., Columbus, Ohio, 1985—, Questel Orbit, McLean, Va., 1989-93. Contbr. articles to Database, Online, Jour. Chem. Info. and Computer Sci., 1975—; patentee in field. Bd. dirs. Naperville Area Transcribing for the Blind, 1973-80. Mem. Am. Chem. Soc. (chmn. divsn. chem. info. 1981, bd. dirs. Chgo. sect. 1985—), Assn. Ind. Info. Profls., Sigma Xi. Lutheran. Avocations: reading, recorders, cross-country skiing, bicycling. Office: Buntrock Assocs Inc 11335 300th Ave NW Princeton MN 55371-3349

BUNT SMITH, HELEN MARGUERITE, lawyer; b. L.A., Oct. 8, 1942; d. Alan Verbanks and Nettie Virginia (Crandall) Bunt; m. Charles Robert Smith, Jan. 12, 1974; children: John, Sharon. BS, U. Calif., L.A., 1964; JD, Southwestern U., 1972. Bar: Calif. 1972; cert. secondary tchr., Calif. Tchr. L.A. City Schs., 1965-72; pvt. practice Pasadena, Calif., 1973—; Law Day chmn. Pasadena Bar Assn., 1980, sec., 1981. Editor (newsletter) Lawyer's Club, 1984-85. Sunday sch. tchr. Lake Ave. Congrl. Ch., Pasadena, church choir; sec. Pasadena Sister Cities Com., 1994-96; Law Day chmn. Pasadena Bar Assn., 1980, sec., 1981. Mem. San Gabriel Bar Assn. (bd. dirs. 1999—). Avocations: jogging, singing, stained glass. Office: 465 E Union St Ste 102 Pasadena CA 91101-1783

BÜNTZEL, JENS, physician, researcher, oncologist; b. Mühlhausen, Germany, Nov. 8, 1964. Diploma in Medicine, U. Leipzig, Germany, 1987, MD, 1989. Intern Bad Berka Hosp, Weimar, 1989; res. internal medicine ENT, 1990-96; physician Zentralklinik, Bad Berka, Germany, 1989-92, HNO-Klinik, Suhl, Germany, 1992—. Contbr. articles to profl. jours. Mem. German Soc. ENT, German Soc. HNS, Multinat. Assn. Supportive Care Cancer, German Cancer Soc., Am. Soc. Clin. Oncology, Head and Neck Surgery, N.Y. Acad. Scis., Deutsche Krebsgesellschaft. Avocations: literature, history. Office: HNO Klinik am Klinikum Suhl, A-Schweitzer-Str 2, Suhl D-98527, Germany

BUNUS, FLORIN TEODOR, chemical engineer; b. Teaca, Romania, Jan. 9, 1928; s. Teodor Ioan and Aurelia (Margineanu) B.; m. Geta Grancerov, Apr. 30, 1963; 1 child, Paul Florin. MS, U. Durham, England, 1962; PhD, Tech. U. Bucharest, 1965. Rsch. worker Inst. Chem. Rsch., Bucharest, Romania, 1952-65; head dept. Inst. Uranium, Bucharest, Romania, 1965-70; sr. rsch. worker Inst. Atomic Physics, Bucharest, 1970-80; head dept. Chimneneg Inst., Craiova, Romania, 1980-94, advisor, 1994—; prof. Tech. U., Bucharest, Romania, 1999—. Author: Radioisotopes, 1970, Nuclear Chemistry, 1976, Actinides, 1981; co-author: Pollution Control in Fertilizer Production, 1994; contbr. over 150 papers to profl. pubs.; inventor infield. Mem. N.Y. Acad. Scis. Home: str Baba Novac 19 G 12, apt 38, Bucharest Romania

BUNYAN, S. WYANNE, arbitrator, mediator; b. St. Petersburg, Fla., 1945. BA, Calif. State U., San Francisco, 1967; JD, Georgetown U., 1971; LLM, London Sch. Econs., London, 1997. Bar: Calif. 1971, D.C. 1972, Alaska 1976, U.S. Ct. Claims, U.S. Supreme Ct. Faculty, adminstr. Hastings Coll. Law U. Calif., San Francisco, 1971-76; chief coun. to Calif. Sec. State Calif. State Govt., Sacramento, 1976-77; asst. atty. gen. State Ala., Juneau, Anchorage, 1978-83; gen. coun. Bering Straits Native Corp., Nome, Anchorage, 1983-84; pvt. practice, 1984—. Office: PO Box 445 Hanalei HI 96714-0445

BUON, TONY, mental health services professional, educator; b. Hellenburgh, Scotland, Dec. 22, 1960; arrived in Australia, 1971; m. Caitlin Buon. Grad. with honors, Sydney Inst. Tech., Australia, 1984; BA in Behavioral Scis., Macquarie U., Sydney, 1988, MA with honors, 1993, cert. in Higher Edn., 1996. Cert. employee assistance profl. Spare parts mgr. Wilson Morgan, Sydney, 1976-79; sr. rsch. asst. Media Monitors, Australia, 1979-81; counselor, youth worker Careforce, Sydney, 1981-85; nat. mgr. Employee Assistance Internat. Psychol. Svcs., Sydney, 1988—, co. dir. employee assistance, 1994—, gen. mgr. for China, 1999—; casual lectr., tutor U. Western Sydney, 1993-95; casual lectr. Macquarie U. Australia, 1993-96, part-time lectr., 1996—. Contbr. articles to profl. jours. Postgrad. scholar Australian Govt., 1991-93; recipient Youth Leadership award Rotary Internat., 1981. Mem. Australian Med. Soc. Alcohol & Other Drugs, Devel. Youth Svcs. Assn. (life), City U. Hong Kong MBA Alumni Assn. (hon. advisor), Mazda MX-5 Club (captl 1995-96, pres. 1996-98). Avocations: car racing, communications, reading, computing. Office: IPS Employee Assistance, Level 3, 85 Castlereagh St, Sydney NSW 2000, Australia

BUOTE, ROSEMARIE BOSCHEN, special education educator; b. Jamaica, N.Y., Nov. 13, 1939; d. George Frederick and Mary (Bernadich) Boschen; m. Victor Roy Buote, June 27, 1964; children: Kristine, Alissa. BA, Barrington (R.I.) Coll., 1962; MEd, R.I. Coll., Providence, 1985, Fitchburg (Mass.) State Coll., 1991. Cert. spl. edn. and elem. tchr. Elem. tchr. Town of Barrington, 1962-68, 69-70; resource rm. instructional aide Town of Rehoboth (Mass.), Mass., 1983-84; spl. edn. tchr., behavior mgmt. specialist dept edn. Dept. of Edn. Tri-County Dist., Ednl. Svcs. in Instnl. Settings, Taunton, Mass., 1985—. Sec. Conservation Commn., Town of Dighton, 1971-74; lay eucharistic minister Pastoral Outreach Commn., Episcopal Diocese Mass.; bd. dirs. Gordon Coll. Alumni Bd., Wenham, Mass., 1989-92, Am. Cancer Soc. S.E. Mass., Taunton area; sec. Friends of the Taunton Libr. Bd. Mem. AAUW (sec., Taunton area br. past pres.), Nat. Marine Educators Assn., Mass. Marine Educators, Coun. Exceptional Children, Coun. Children with Behavioral Disorders, Coun. for Children with Learning Disabilities, Mass. Computer Using Educators, Dighton Garden Club (pres. 1979-82), Delta Kappa Gamma. Avocations: reading, writing, gardening, theater. Home: 1690 Wellington St Dighton MA 02715-1000 Office: Dept of Edn-Tri-County Dist 60 Hodges Ave Taunton MA 02780-3034

BURACZEWSKI, ADAM TADEUSZ, mathematician, educator; b. Zimodry, Poland, Apr. 14, 1926; s. Adam Buraczewski and Zofia Buraczewska; m. Janina Theodora Komorowska, Sept. 18, 1965 (div. 1976); children: Martha, Monika; m. Anna Krefft Buraczewska, Sept. 29, 1983; 1 child, Silvia. Cert. in math., Physical Lyceum, Luban Slaski, Poland, 1946-48; MS, Warsaw U., Poland, 1953; PhD, Math. Inst., Warsaw, 1961; DSc, Warsaw Tech. U., 1975. Cert. math. tchr. Asst. Warsaw Tech. U., 1952-62; sr. lectr. U. Sci. and Tech., Kumasi, Ghana, 1962-64, assoc. prof., 1964-65, prof., 1965-75; assoc. prof., dept. head Higher Pedagogical Inst., Olsztyn, Poland, 1976-80; prof., dept. head U. Papua New Guinea, Port Moresby, 1980-83; prof. Sebha U., Libya, 1983-86; assoc. prof. Higher Pedagogical Inst., Olsztyn, 1986-91, prof., 1991-99, dept. head, 1987-96; prof. U. Warmiá & Mazury, Olsztyn, 1999—; vis. prof. U. Nairobi, Kenya, 1972. Contbr. numerous articles to profl. jours. Served as cpl. artillery, 1944-46, ETO. Decorated Gold Cross of Merit (Warsaw); recipient Higher Edn. Minister's awards research achievements 1980, ednl. achievements, 1978, medal of honour Nat. Edn. Com., 1989. Mem. Polish Math. Soc., Am. Math. Soc., N.Y. Acad. Scis., Assn. Combatants. Roman Catholic. Avocations: chess, traveling, fishing. Office: U Warmia & Mazury Inst Math Informatics and Physics, Zolnierska 14 a, 10-561 Olsztyn Poland

BURAK, MARKUS RENÉ, communications executive; b. Hamburg, Germany, Apr. 25, 1963; s. Rudolf Gerhard and Ellen-Karla (Panek) B. Diploma, Tech. U., Berlin, 1991. Sci. employee Gesellschaft fur Math. und Deuten. (GMD) MD Fokus, Berlin, 1991-96; project mgr. Deutsche Telekom Berkom, Berlin, 1996—; dep. leader ATM Test and Conformance Ctr. GMD Fokus, Berlin, 1994-96; cons. TLG, Berlin, 1996. Contbr. articles to profl. jours. Mem. IEEE (program co-chmn. 1996, program com. 1997), Assn. Computing Machinery, N.Y. Acad. Scis. Office: Deutsche Telekom Berkom, Goslarer Ufer 35, D-10589 Berlin Germany

BURANAKARN, VIRA, architect; b. Supanburi, Thailand, May 15, 1935; s. Udom and Salee (Chutikul) B.; m. Uneklarb Sunee, Jan. 23, 1967; children: Vorasun, Vorawat, Peerakarn. BArch with honors, Chulalongkorn U., Bangkok, 1959; MArch with distinction, Iowa State U., 1965; PhD in Architecture, Pacific Western U., 1995. Registered architect Assn. Siamese Architects. Lectr. architecture Chulalongkorn U., 1959, asst. prof. architecture, 1964, assoc. prof. architecture, 1969-95, assoc. dean Fac. architecture, 1987-90, head dept. architecture, 1991-95, chair grad. program architecture, 1991-95; advisor AEP Architects LP, Bangkok, 1967, sr. advisor, 1970-80; sr. v.p. AEP Internat Co., Ltd., Bangkok, 1973-85, pres., owner, 1990—; v.p. Thai Group Cons. Co. Ltd., Bangkok, 1985—; bd. dirs. Thai Group Cons. Ltd. Author: Information System Planning and Management, 1990 (award 1991); prin. works include Nat. Bank of Thailand (1st prize 1966), Fishery, Sci. and Forestry Blds. Kasetsart Campus, 1979 (Internat. World Bank 1st prize), Acad. Resource Ctr., Chulalongkorn U., 1980 (Princess Sirinthorn award 1982). Chair subcom. Civil Svcs. Comms. Office of Prime Min., Bangkok, 1993; mem. subcom. pvt. univ. com. State U. Ministry, Bangkok, 1992; mem. subcom. planning and devel. com. Bangkok Municipality Office, 1991. Lt. Royal Thai Air Force, 1959. Recipient award Fulbright Found., 1964, Acad. award Office of Prime Min., 1990. Mem. Assn. Siamese Architects (life, sec. gen.-treas. 1982-83), Royal Navy Golf Club, Royal Army Golf Club, Royal Bangkok Sports Club. Buddhist. Avocations: golf, jogging, table tennis, weight lifting. Home: Wachiratam 32, 938 938/1 Sukumvit 101/1, Bangkok Prakanong 10260, Thailand Office: AEP Internat Co Ltd, Sukumvit 101/1 Ste 954/7, Bangkok Prakanong 10260, Thailand

BURANELLI, FRANCESCO, archaeologist, museum director; b. Rome, Mar. 26, 1955; s. Raffaele and Maria Adelaide (d'Amelio) B.; m. Susanna Le Pera, Oct. 4, 1982; children: Tommaso, Giacomo. Degree in Letters, U. Rome, 1979, PhD in Archaeol. Rsch., 1987. Dir. Gregorian Etruscan Mus. Vatican Mus., 1982-96; acting dir. gen. Monumenti Musei e Gallerie Pontificie, Vatican City, 1996—; mem. internat. com. Corpus Speculorum Etruscorum, Vatican City State, 1988, 99, pontifical nomination to represent Holy See in Comitato Internazionale di Storia dell Arte and Centro Internazionale di Studi per la Conservazione ed il Restauro dei Beni Culturali. Author: La necropoli villanoviana Le Rose di Tarquinia, 1983, L'urna Calabresi di Cerveteri, 1985, La tomba François di Vulci, 1987, Le urne a capanna rinvenute in Italia, 1987, La raccolta Giacinto Guglielmi, 1989, Gli scavi a Vulci della società V.Campanari--Governo Pontificio, 1992, The Etruscans--Legacy of a Lost Civilization from the Vatican Museums, 1992, Ugo Ferraguti: l'ultimo archeologo-mecenate, 1994. Decorated Cavalier Ordine Costantiniano di S. Giorgio, cavlier Ordine dei Santi Maurizio et Lazzaro (Italy); named Hon. Citizen of Memphis, 1992, Hon. Citizen of Dallas, 1992. Mem. Inst. German Archaeology, Etruscan Acad. Cortona, Pontifical Acad. Roman Archaeology, Nat. Inst. Etruscan Studies. Home: Via Giovanni Nicotera 8, 00195 Rome Italy Office: Monumenti Musei e Gallerie, Pontificie, 00120 Vatican City Vatican City

BURASELIS, KOSTAS, historian; b. Athens, Greece, Nov. 28, 1950; s. Nikolaos and Aikaterini Buraselis; m. Anastasia Plakas; 1 child, Nikolaos. Diploma, U. Athens, 1973; PhD in Ancient History, U. Marburg, Germany, 1979. Rsch. fellow Acad. Athens, Rsch. Ctr. for Antiquity, 1980-95, dir., 1985-89; assoc. prof. ancient history U. Athens, 1989-2000, prof. ancient history, 2000—; dir. hist. libr. U. Athens, 1991-96, 98—. Author: (books) Das hellenistische Makedonien und die Ägäis (Hellenistic Macedonia and the Aegean), 1982, Divine Donation, 1989, Between Hellenism and Rome, 2000; editor: (book) Unity and Units of Antiquity, 1994. Recipient Corr. Mem. award German Archaeol. Inst., 1995. Mem. Soc. for Promotion of Hellenic Studies (London), Soc. for Promotion of Roman Studies, Am. Assn. Ancient Historians. Avocations: jogging, swimming. Office: U Athens, Dept History, GR-15784 Athens Greece

BURAS-ELSEN, BRENDA ALLYNN, retired public affairs executive; b. New Orleans, May 1, 1954; d. Allen Anthony and Gloria Violet (Short) B. BA in Commerce, Loyola U., New Orleans, 1976, MBA, 1984. Stenographer Texaco Inc., New Orleans, 1974-76, engr.'s asst., 1976-78, natural gas contracts analyst, 1978-80, pub. affairs asst., 1980-83, pub. and govt. affairs coord. S.E. region, 1983-89; banking officer, mgr pub. rels. and mktg. promotion, asst. v.p., community reinvestment act officer Alerion Bank, New Orleans, 1990; pub. affairs advisor Mobil Oil Corp., Chalmette, La., 1990-92, rep. western region Multi-Quest Internat., Inc., 1992; cert. lectr. Silva Method Mind Devel. and Stress Control. Loaned exec. United Way Greater New Orleans, 1978, mem. speakers bur., 1979-83, vol. leadership devel. program, 1987; voting commr. St. Bernard Parish, 1976-80; chmn. subcom. United Way Corp. Recognition/Thank-You, 1988-89; vice chairwoman United Way Yr.-Round Communication Com., 1989-90, United Way External Communication Com., 1990; mem. cen. svc. budget com. United Way, 1990; host, media com. for Rep. Conv. 1988; chairwoman pub. rels. com., mem. grants and membership coms., bd. dirs. New Orleans Food Bank for Emergencies, 1989; bd. dirs., vice-chair comm. com., mem. edn. svcs. com.; bd. dirs. Met. Area Com., 1991, Jefferson Performing Arts Soc., 1992, Friend of 4-H, St. Bernard Parish, 1992; mem. St. Bernard adv. coun. United Way Greater New Orleans, 1991-92, producer Saints Pre-game Show, 1991; mem. adv. coun. Family Svc., 1991-92. Producer Bringing Out the Best Awards Show, 1988. Named Outstanding Communication Com. Vol., United Way, 1988. Mem. Assistance League. Republican.

BURATTI, MARCO, mathematician; b. Rome, Aug. 7, 1959; s. Armando and Laura Maria (Fiorioli Della Lena) B.; m. Evelina Vincenza Doronzo, Oct. 17, 1992; 1 child, Andrea. Degree math., U. La Sapienza, Rome, 1985. Math tchr. secondary sch. Liceo Scientifico Ettore Majorana, Guidonia, Italy, 1987-91; rschr. in math. U. L'Aquila, Italy, 1991-99; prof. math. U. Di Perugia, Italy, 1999—. Editl. bd. various jours.; contbr. articles to profl. publs. Scholarship Istituto Nazionale Di Alta Matematica, 1985. Fellow Unione Hatematica Italiana, Inst. of Combinatorics and its Applications (Hall medal 1998). Avocation: chess player. Office: Dept Elec Engring, U De L'Aquila, I-67040 Poggio di Rolo Italy

BURBANK, ROBINSON DERRY, crystallographer; b. Berlin, N.H., Oct. 3, 1921; s. Paul William and Hazel Louise (Robinson) B.; m. Jeannette Murielle Bisson, July 14, 1945 (div. 1975); children: Paul Robinson, Claudia Olive. BA, Colby Coll., 1942; PhD, MIT, 1950. Rsch. asst. Manhattan Project, MIT, Cambridge, 1942-45, Lab. Insulation Rsch., MIT, 1945-50; sr. physicist Gaseous Diffusion Plant, Oak Ridge, Tenn., 1950-53; group leader, crystallography Olin Industries, New Haven, Conn., 1953-55; tech. staff Bell Telephone Labs., Murray Hill, N.J., 1955-86; U.S. del. Internat. Union Crystallography, Stony Brook, L.I., N.Y., 1969, Amsterdam, 1975; mem. U.S.A. Nat. Com. Crystallography, 1968-76. Contbr. technical papers to profl. jours. Bd. dirs. Chester Twp. Taxpayers Assn., N.J., 1961-65, 70-74,

pres. 1973. Mem. AAAS, Am. Crystallographic Assn. (treas. 1965-68, v.p. 1974, pres. 1975), Com. Sci. Soc. Presidents, Phi Beta Kappa, Sigma Xi. Achievements include X-ray crystallography of inorganic compounds, interhalogen compounds, noble gas compounds, phase transformations, thin films. Home: 45 Woodland Ave Summit NJ 07901-2141

BURCH, FRANCIS FLOYD, clergyman, educator; b. Balt., May 15, 1932; s. Thaddeus Joseph and Frances Fidelis (Greenwell) B. BA, Fordham U., 1956, MA, 1958; PhL, Woodstock Coll., 1957, STL, 1964; postgrad., Tronchinnes, Belgium, 1964-65; Docteur, U. Paris, Sorbonne, 1967. Joined Soc. of Jesus, 1950, ordained priest Roman Catholic Ch., 1963. Tchr. Gonzaga H.S., Washington, 1957-60; asst. prof. English St. Joseph's U., Phila., 1967-71, assoc. prof., 1971-76, prof., 1976—, asst. acad. dean, 1972-74, bd. dirs., 1971-76, sec. bd. dirs., 1971-75; artist-scholar-in-residence Millersville U., Pa., 1978. Author: Tristan Corbiere: l'originalite des "Amours jaunes" et leur influence sur T.S. Eliot, 1970; editor: (with P.O. Walzer) Tristan Corbiere: Oeuvres completes, 1970, Sur Tristan Corbiere: lettres inedites adressees au poete et premieres critiques le concernant, 1975; translator: The Path to Transcendence: From Philosophy to Mysticism in Saint Augustine (Paul Henry), 1981, The Personalist Challenge: Intersubjectivity and Ontology (Maurice Nedoncelle), 1984; contbr. articles to profl. jours. Recipient Merit award St. Joseph's U., 1980, 83. Mem. MLA, Internat. Soc. Neoplatonic Studies, Alpha Epsilon Delta, Alpha Sigma Nu. Home and office: 5600 City Ave Philadelphia PA 19131-1308

BURCH, G. DAVID, sculptor; b. Charlottesville, Va., Oct. 31, 1925; s. Paul Randolph Burch and Doris Katherine Fisher; m. Mary Alma Crawford, Mar. 29, 1947 (div. Sept. 1976); children: Tina Marie, David Randolph, Anthony Bayard. Grad., Radford H.S., 1943. With Thiokol Corp.; now ret.; instr. photography Cecil C.C., North East, Md., 1974-84; guest lectr. Cecil County Arts Coun.; artist-in-residence Prince George's C.C. One-person shows at Cecil County Arts Coun., Elkton, Md., 1990, Arnold & Porter, Washington, 1992, Art Gallery, Essex (Md.) C.C., 1993, Cecil County C.C., 1993, Md. Fedn. Art, Annapolis, 1995, Sullivan County Mus. Art, Hurleyville, N.Y., 1997, INSA Gallery, Seoul, Korea, 1997, Gallery B.A.I., N.Y.C., 1997, 98; exhibited in group shows at Haltzman Gallery, Towson (Md.) State U., 1991, 92, Md. Fedn. Art, Annapolis, 1991, Washington Sq., 1992, Greensboro (N.C.) Artist League Gallery, 1992, CAA Galleries, Chautauqua (N.Y.) Instn., 1992, Artshowcase Gallery, Balt., 1992, Dundalk (Md.) C.C., 1992, Internat. Sculpture Ctr., Washington, 1993, Fairfax County Coun. of Arts, Annandale, Va., 1993, Isospin Two South, Balt., 1993, Art Gallery, Essex C.C., Md., 1992, 94, Ward-Nasse, N.Y.C., 1992-94, 2000, Epilepsy Soc. N.Y., N.Y.C., 1994, AAAS, Washington, 1993, 95, Am. Ctr. Physics, College Park, Md., 1994, 95, Marlboro Gallery, Prince George's County C.C., Largo, Md., 1992, 93, 96, Perry House Galleries, Alexandria, Va., 1993, 96, Columbia (Md.) Art Ctr., 1996, 2000, Mill River Art Ctr. Gallery, Ellicott City, Md., 1996, 2000, Liriodendron Mansion, Bel Air, Md., 1995, 97, Pa. State U., Media, 1994, 96, 97, Gallery Art Club 21, Seoul, 1995, Lancashire U., Preston, Eng., 1995, St. Helens (Eng.) Coll. Art and Design, 1996, Gallery B.A.I., Barcelona, Spain, 1996, Pratt Libr., Falls Point, Balt., 1996, Sharjah (United Arab Emirates) Internat. Art Biennial, 1997, Forum Artis Mus., Modena, Italy, 1997, Cecil County Arts Coun., Elkton, Md., 1998, Md. Ho. Dels., Annapolis, 1997-2000, Acad. of Arts, Easton, Md., 1998, Cecil C.C., Md., 1999, West Md. Coll., Westminster, 1999, Towson (Md.) U., 1999, Grounds for Sculpture, Hamilton, N.J., 2000. With USMC, WWII. Recipient Sculpture award Towson State U., 1992, 1st Pl. Sculpture award Epilepsy Soc., 1994, Perry House Galleries, Alexandria, 1996. Home and Studio: 1585 Tome Hwy Port Deposit MD 21904

BURCH, JOHN THOMAS, JR., lawyer; b. Balt., Feb. 22, 1942; s. John T. and Katheryn Estella (Peregoy) B.; m. Linda Anne Shearer, Nov. 1, 1969; children: John Thomas, Richard James. BA, U. Richmond, 1964, JD, 1966; LLM, George Washington U., 1971. Bar: Va. 1966, U.S. Supreme Ct. 1969, D.C. 1974, Mich. 1983, Md. 1993. Pvt. practice Richmond, 1966, Washington, 1974-77; pres. Burch, Kerns and Klimek, 1977-82, Burch & Assocs., Washington, 1982-95, Burch & Bennett, P.C., Washington, 1983-85; ptnr. Alagia, Day, Marshall, Mintmire & Chauvin, Washington, 1985-90, Maloney & Burch, Washington, 1990-96; pres. Burch & Cronauer, P.C., Washington, 1995—, Burch & Assocs., Washington, 1982-95; Rep. committeeman, City of Alexandria, Va., 1975-92; aide-de-camp Brigadier Gen. to gov., State of Va., 1976—; alt. del. Rep. Nat. Conv., 1988, 94. Decorated Bronze Star, Meritorious Svc. medal, others; named Ky. Col. Mem. ABA (sec. pub. contract law sect. 1976-77), Fed. Bar Assn. (nat. coun., dep. sec. 1982-83), Am. Arbitration Assn., Am. Legion, VFW (dep. comdr. 1986-87), Spl. Forces Assn., Nat. Vietnam and Gulf War Vets. Coalition (nat. chmn. 1983—), Va. War Meml. Found. (trustee), Va. Soc. SAR (pres. 1975-76, Patriots medal 1978, Good Citizenship award 1970), Sons of Confederate Vets., Soc. of the War of 1812; Cheveliar, Order of St. Constantine Magna, Scabbard and Blade, Phi Alpha Delta, Phi Sigma Alpha. Republican. Episcopalian. Home: 1015 N Pelham St Alexandria VA 22304-1905 Office: Burch & Cronauer PC 1660 L St NW Ste 205 Washington DC 20036-5603

BURCHARD, ELLEN WILLIAMS, actress, producer, artist, writer; b. Newport, R.I., June 13, 1913; d. Clarence Raymond and Mary Christine (Stewart) Williams; m. John Church Burchard, Feb. 6, 1943; 1 child, John Church. studied acting U. Wis., 1944, Stella Adler Studio, 1954-56, Herbert Berghof Studio, 1957-65, Harold Clurman's Profl. Acting Classes, N.Y.C., 1960-62. Actress on Broadway, films and TV, also in Rome and London; founder Carriage House Theatre, Little Compton, R.I., 1958, producer, artistic dir., actress Pro Summer Repertory Co., 1958-76; off-Broadway producer, N.Y.C., 1958-76; producer, artistic dir. Actors Repertory Co., Little Compton, 1959-94; actress R.I. Playwrights Theatre Summer Festival, Providence, 1985; lyricist Morning Song, 1979; playwright Marguerite, 1978, Scenes from the Past, 1979; off-Broadway roles include Journey to Endor, 1987-88, Ashen Victors, 1993-94, Love Letters, 1994; films include Mr. North, The Buccaneers, The Fitzgeralds and the Kennedys, True Lies, Ashen Victors, 1996, Amistad, 1997; editor (poetry) To Diana, 1985. Founder, pres. Young Women's Rep. Club, Newport, 1935-37, 46-54, Little Compton Rep. Club, 1946-57, Newport Players Guild, 1936-42, 46-52; founder, 1st v.p. New Eng. Council Young Reps., 1932-37; Young Rep. Nat. Committeewoman from R.I., 1932-43. Mem. Actors Equity Assn., Screen Actors Guild, AFTRA, R.I. Short Story Club (pres. 1982-85), R.I. Water Color Soc., Newport Art Mus., Westport Art Club, Bus. Womens Club (charter, Newport). Congregationalist. Club: Mosaic (charter mem.) (Newport).

BURCHARDT, JØRGEN, ethnologist, consultant; b. Copenhagen, Dec. 10, 1946; s. Kaj-Henning and Ketty (Sørensen) B.; m. Anne-Grethe Andersen; 1 child, Mikkel. PhD, U. Copenhagen, 1993. Dir. Musik Og Lys, Copenhagen, 1970-73, rsch. leader, 1974-83; mus. asst. Faaborg Kulturhistoriske Museer, Faaborg, Denmark, 1984-91; mus. planner Arbejdermuseet, Copenhagen, 1992-93; dir. Danmarks Vejmuseum, Farø, Denmark, 1994, rschr., 1995—; mgr. Kulturbøger, Ringe, Denmark, 1980—. Author: Provinsindustri, 1984, Industri and Håndvaerk, 1993, Arbejdsliv Og Ny Teknologi, 1995, NKT 100 ÅR, 1998, Historiens Lange Tråd, 1999; author, editor: De Nye Tider, 1978, 81, Vi laerte At Arbejdoe, 1981, Arbejderliv, 1981, Grav Hvor Du Står, 1982, Fabrik, 1982; editor Nord Nytt, 1978-97, Bok Nytt, 1982-94, Nyt om Arbejdermuseet, 1988-93, Mantim Bibliografi, 1976-86, Tidsskrift for Arbejdsliv, 1999—. Avocations: bicycling, music, nature. Home: Nyborgvej 13 Sødinge, DK-5750 Ringe Denmark

BURCHELL, BRENDAN JOSEPH, social and political science educator; b. Surrey, Eng., Sept. 21, 1958; s. Charles Kasper and Bernadette (O'Connor) B.; m. Lynda Joy Carney, Sept. 6, 1985; children: Josephine, Sarah. BSc in Psychology, Birmingham (Eng.) U., 1981; PhD in Social Psychology, Warwick (Eng.) U., 1986. Lectr. City U., London, 1984-85; rsch. officer dept. applied econs. U. Cambridge, Eng., 1985-88, lectr. social and polit. sci. faculty, 1988—; teaching fellow Magdalene Coll., Cambridge, 1990—. Editor Cambridge Jour. Econs., 1990—, Gender, Work and Organization, 1995—; contbr. articles to learned publs., chpts. to books. Mem. Internat. Working Party on Labour Market Segmentation. Avocations: walking, woodcraft, family, cycling. Office: Univ Cambridge, SPS 8-9 Jesus Ln, Cambridge CB5 8BA, England

BURCHELL, ROBERT ARTHUR, historian, educator; b. Plymouth, Eng., Mar. 31, 1941; s. Arthur Thomas and Mary Leonora (Symons) B. BA, U. Oxford, 1960, MA, 1967, LittB, 1969. Asst. lectr. Am. history and instns. U. Manchester, Eng., 1965-68, lectr., 1968-80, sr. lectr., 1980-91; prof., 1991-96; dir. Eccles Ctr. for Am. Studies, Brit. Libr., 1991—; Author: Westward Expansion, 1974, San Francisco Irish, 1979. Author: San Francisco Irish, 1980, End of Anglo America, 1991, Harriet Martineau and America, 1996. Fellow Royal Soc. Arts; mem. Brit. Assn. for Am. Studies (treas. 1979-84, sec. 1984-89, chair 1989-92), Orgn. Am. Historians, St. Anselm Hall Assn. (chmn. 1987-89), European Assn. for Am. Studies (sec. 1986-90, editor Am. Studies in Europe 1992—), Am. Studies Network (pres. 1996-98). Avocations: travel, squash, swimming, walking, entertaining. Office: The Brit Libr Eccles Ctr, 96 Euston Rd, London NW1 2DB, England

BURCHENAL, JOAN RILEY, science educator; b. N.Y.C., Dec. 11, 1925; d. Wells Littlefield and Bertha Barclay (Fahys) Riley; m. Joseph Holland Burchenal, Mar. 20, 1948; children: Elizabeth Payne Burchenal Paul, Joan Littlefield Burchenal Nycum, Barbara Fahys Burchenal Landers, Caleb Wells, David Holland, Joseph Emory Barclay; 1 stepchild, Mary Holland Burchenal Nottebohm. BA, Vassar Coll., 1946; MAT, Yale U., 1971; MA, Fairfield U., 1981. Sci. tchr. New Canaan (Conn.) Country Sch., 1968-69, Low Heywood Sch., Stamford, Conn., 1968-69, The Thomas Sch., Rowayton, Conn., 1972-73; sci. tchr. Darien Bd. Edn., Conn., 1973-91, ret.; mem. panel on grants for tchrs. enhancement program NSF, 1987, 92. Bd. dirs., chmn. standards com. A Better Chance, Darien, 1985-99; bd. dirs. Darien Nature Ctr., 1975-91, Darien Audubon Soc., 1978-86, Darien LWV, 1951-62; hon. chmn. Darien Sci. Fair, 1986; mem. steering com. Holly Pond Saltmarsh Conservation Com., 1968-71; mem. acad. courses com. Darien Cmty. Assn., 1964-71, chmn., 1971; trustee Garrison Forest Sch., 1959-62; bd. dirs. Alumnae and Alumni Vassar Coll.; rep. Town Meeting of Darien, 1993—, mem. edn. com., 1993—, chair edn. com. 1995-97; cmty. rep. K-12 Sci. Curriculum Com., 1994—; elder First Presbyn. Ch. of New Canaan, 1994-97, Stephen min., 1994—. Recipient Presdl. award for excellence in sci. teaching Nat. Sci. Tchrs. Assn., NSF, Washington, 1985. Mem. AAAS, N.Y. Acad. Sci., Nat. Assn. Biology Tchrs., Nat. Sci. Tchrs. Assn., Assn. Presdl. Awardees in Sci. Teaching (nominating com. 1987-90), Cosmopolitan Club, Ausable Club, Noroton Yacht Club, Phi Beta Kappa. Republican. Presbyterian. Avocations: grandchildren, reading, travel, trekking, birding. Home: 18 Juniper Rd Darien CT 06820-5707

BURCROFF, RICHARD TOMKINSON, II, economist; b. Ticonderoga, N.Y., Nov. 10, 1939; s. Richard Tomkinson and Anna (Gonyea) B.; m. Maria-Clara Soberano Roldan, June 9, 1974; children: Kevin, Ana; children from a previous marriage: Kirsten, Trevor. BS in Econs., Rensselaer Polytechnic Inst., 1961; PhD in Econs., U. Wash., 1972; postgrad. in Law & Econs., Yale U., 1973. Asst. prof. U. Hawaii, Honolulu, 1968-73; visiting prof. U. Philippines, Quezon City, 1973-74; sr. economist Asian Devel. Bank, Manila, 1974-79; prin. economist World Bank, Washington, 1979-97; pres. Crown Point Cons., Inc., 1997—; cons. State of Hawaii Legal Svcs. Office, Honolulu, 1969-71, U. Hawaii Sch. Edn., 1970, U.S. AID, Washington, 1970-72; vis. rsch. assoc. Inst. Philippine Culture Ateneo de Manila, Quezon City, 1973-75; advisor Rsch. Ctr. Rural Devel., Beijing, 1987-89; dir. transition in socialist agr. project World Bank, 1994-97; rsch. advisor Rural Asia update Asian Devel. Bank, Manila, 1997. Author: Turkey-Opportunities for Agricultural Growth with Exports, 1982, China-Managing an Agricultural Transformation, 1991, (with others) Options for Food Policy and Agricultural Sector Reform in the former U.S.S.R., 1992, (with others) Rural Asia: Challange & Opportunity, 1988; contbr. World Development Report, 1996. Active Lincolnia Park Civic Assn., Annandale, Va., 1981-96, Burgundy Farms Country Day Sch., Alexandria, Va., 1985-92; fin. advisor Lincolnia Park Recreation Assn., Annandale, 1989-90. Lt. USN, 1961-65. Rsch. grantee Yale U. Found., 1973, Asia Found., 1973, Rockfeller Found., 1973-74, Ford Found., 1994. Mem. Am. Econs. Assn., Soc. Internat. Devel. Democrat.

BURCZYK, BOGDAN WOJCIECH, chemist, educator; b. Przesławice, Pomerania, Poland, July 25, 1930; s. Bolesław and Jadwiga (Kaminska) B.; m. Krystyna Maria Kaminska, July 11, 1955; children: Ewa Krystyna, Wojciech Bolesław. MSc in Chemistry, Wrocław U. Tech., 1955, PhD, 1962, DSc, 1970. Asst., adj., docent Faculty of Chemistry, Wrocław U. Tech., 1955-76, prof. chemistry, 1976—; head divsn. chem. tech. Inst. of Organic and Polymer Tech., Wrocław, 1972-96, dep. dir., 1972-81, dir., 1991-96; mem. com. of chemistry Polish Acad. Scis., Warsaw, 1993-95; mem. Ctrl. Commn. for Sci. Title and Degrees, Warsaw, 1994—. Contbr. articles to profl. jours.; editl. bd. Chem. News, 1978—; patentee in field. Decorated Golden Cross of Merit, Pres. Polish Republic, 1972, Knight's Cross, Order of Polonia Restituta, 1977, Officer's Cross, 1990; recipient Rsch. awards Min. Nat. Edn., 1971, 81, 86, 98, Edn. award, 1978, medal Commn. Nat. Edn., 1983. Mem. Polish Chem. Soc., Am. Oil Chemists Soc., Internat. Assn. Colloid and Interface Scientists, Kolloid-Gesellschaft. Avocations: classical music, sight-seeing. Office: Wrocl Univ of Tech, Wybrzeze Wyspianskiego 27, 50-370 Wrocław Poland

BURD, GENRICH ISRAEL, microbiologist; b. Moscow, Russia, Aug. 20, 1939; s. Israel Chaim and Sarah Yechiel (Shapiro) B.; m. Elena Dimitryi Vanyakina, Oct. 14, 1971 (div. 1989); children: Ilya, Genrich; m. Irina Zak, Apr. 6, 1990; children: Daniel, Genrich. MSc in Pharm., 1st Med. U., 1962; PhD in Biochemistry, Gamaleya Inst., 1967, DSc in Microbiology, 1978. Sr. rschr. lab. biochem. genetics Gamaleya Inst. Epidem. Microbiology, Moscow, 1968-82; head of lab. Inst. Genetics of Indsl. Microorganisms, Moscow, 1983-90; rsch. prof. dept. molecular microbiology/biotech. Tel-Aviv U., 1991-92; rsch. prof. dept. biology U. Waterloo, Can., 1983—. Recipient Metchnikoff Prize Russian Acad. Med. Sci., 1980, Gamaleya prize, 1982. Mem. N.Am. Soc. Indsl. Microbiology, Russian Soc. Microbiology, Russian Soc. Biochemistry. Jewish. Achievements include patents in the field of industrial microbiology and medical microbiology; discovery role of bacterial sugar transport system (PTS system) in the regulation catabolic genes expression. Home: 350 Erb Str West #15, Waterloo, Canada N2L 1W6 Office: Dept Biology Univ Waterloo, 200 University Str West, Waterloo, ON Canada N2L 3G1

BURD, STEVE, food service executive; b. 1949. BS, Carroll Coll., 1971; MA in Econs., U. Wis., 1973. With fin. and mktg. So. Pacific Transp. Co., San Francisco; with Arthur D. Little, N.Y.C., 1982-87; mgmt. cons., 1986-91; cons. Stop & Shop Cos., Boston, 1988-89, Fred Meyer Inc., Portland, Oreg., 1989-90, Safeway Inc., Oakland, Calif., 1986-87, 91—; pres., CEO Safeway Inc., 1992—, chmn. bd. dirs. Office: Safeway Inc 5918 Stoneridge Mall Rd Pleasanton CA 94588-3229

BURDA, HYNEK, zoologist, researcher; b. Chlumec nad Cidlinou, Czech Republic, Nov. 27, 1952; arrived in Germany, 1986; s. Frantisek and Jitka (Kovandová) B.; m. Jana Provaznikova, Dec. 1, 1978; children: Tomas, Jan. Diploma in biology, Charles U., Prague, Czech Republic, 1976, D of Natural Sci., 1977, PhD, 1981. Rsch. assoc. Inst. Exptl. Medicine, Prague, 1977-84; sr. lectr. dept. biology U. Zambia, Lusaka, 1984-86; vis. rschr. Inst. Zoology Goethe U., Frankfurt, Germany, 1986-88; rsch. assoc. Goethe U., Frankfurt, 1988-89, rsch. assoc. med. sch., 1989-94; prof., head of dept., chair U. Essen, Germany, 1995—; vis. prof. South Bohemian U., Ceske Budejovice, Czech Republic, 2000—. Author: Swahili-Czech Dictionary, 1980; co-editor 2 books; contbr. over 120 articles to jours. in field. Fellow Alexander von Humboldt Found., Bonn, Germany, 1984-86. Mem. German Zool. Soc., German Ethological Soc., German Mammalogical Soc., Am. Mammalogical Soc. Roman Catholic. Avocations: painting, photography, travel, languages. Home: Im Rosengärtchen 2, D-61440 Oberursel Germany Office: Dept Gen Zoology, U Essen, D-45117 Essen Germany

BURDA, RENATE MARGARETE, biologist, researcher; b. Munich, Jan. 14, 1960; d. Wilhelm Eduard and Margarete (Oppold) B. Degree in biology, Ludwigs-Maximilians U., 1993. Sci. worker chem. engring. Tech. U., Munich, 1985-2000, Lehrstuhl of Anthropology, Munich, 1993; sci. rschr. Inst. Clin. Chemistry Hosp. Bogenhausen, Munich, 1994-95; lab. worker urology Dr. Kuetgens/Dr. Ehlers, Munich, 1995, 98, 2000; tech. asst. nuclear medicine Klinikum Rechts d. Isar, Munich, 1996, chief sec. orthopady, 1997-98, 99; med. diplomate SmithKline Beecham, Munich, 1996-97, 2000—; asst. EVAX Techs., Munich, 1998; clin. svc. Bayer Diagnostic, 1999-2000; with nuclear medicine, x-ray dept. Hosp. Harlachins, Munich, 2000; chief asst. Venomous Spider Working Group, Weissenburg, 1995—; lector Jour. Latrodecta, 1995—; leader bio-tech. co. AbiTec, 1999—. Organizer sci. exhbns., 1995—. Judge trampoline sports. Avocations: sports, carnivorous plants, puzzles, travel. Home: Eichenstrasse 17, 82054 Sauerlach Germany

BURDACH, STEFAN E.G., pediatrics educator; b. Berlin, Apr. 12, 1952; s. Erich A.G. and Gerda Elisabeth (von Reuss) B.; 1 child, Severin Maximilian Etienne. MA, Friedrich-Wilhelm Coll., Cologne, Germany, 1971; MD, Albertus-Magnus U., Cologne, Germany, 1980; PhD, Heinrich-Heine U., Düsseldorf, Germany, 1989. Diplomate European cert. pediatrician. Resident and fellow Children's Hosp. Med. Ctr., Cologne, Germany, 1978-83; rsch. fellow Stanford (Calif.) U., 1984-87; primary care physician Fred Hutchinson Cancer Rsch. Ctr., Seattle, 1986; attending physician Children's Hosp. Med. Ctr., Düsseldorf, 1988—; chmn. dept. pediatrics, dir. cell and gene therapy program Martin Luther U., Halle-Wittenberg, 1998. Author: Cytokine Knockouts in Contemporary Immunology, 1997, Cytokine and Cytokine Gene Transfer in Therapy of Childhood Diseases, 1997, Hematopoietic Stem Cell Transplantation Principles and Practice, 1996, Immunoregulation of Blood Cell Production, 1992; contbr. articles to sci. jours. Grantee German Cancer Aid Agy., 1988, 95, German Rsch. Coun., 1984, 88, 95. Mem. AAAS, Internat. Soc. Pediatric Oncology, Internat. Soc. Exptl. Hematology, European Soc. Paediatric Hematology and Immunology, Am. Soc. Hematology, Am. Fedn. Med. Rsch. Avocations: snow-boarding, music, poetry, philosophy. Office: Martin-Luther U Halle-Wittenberg Klinik und Poliklinik, Ernst Grube Str 40, 06097 Halle Germany

BURDEAU, GENEVIEVE BASTID, international law educator; b. Lyon, Rhône, France, Apr. 10, 1946; d. Paul and Suzanne (Basdevant) Bastid; m. Michel Burdeau, May 3, 1969; children: Christine, Laurent, Beatrice. Diploma d'etudes superieures, Faculty of Law, Paris, 1969; diploma, Inst. Polit. Studies, Paris, 1968; D d'Etat, U. Paris II, 1976. Asst. Faculty of Law, Paris, 1969-72; prof. Faculty of Law, Dijon, France, 1976-92, U. Pantheon Sorbonne, Paris, 1992—; sec. gen. Hague Acad. Internat. Law. Contbr. articles to law jours. Mem. Internat. Law Assn., French Soc. for Internat. Law (mem. coun. 1974—), Annuaire Francais de Droit Internat. (bd. editors 1991—), Am. Soc. Internat. Law, Institut de Droit Internat. (assoc.). Home: 19 rue du Petit Potet, 21000 Dijon France Office: U Paris I, 12 Place du Pantheon, 75005 Paris France

BURDEN, CEDRIC JEROME, English educator; b. Mobile, Ala., Nov. 6, 1969; s. Andrew O'Neal and Juanita (Coleman) B.; m. Teresa Ballard, Mar. 26, 1995; 1 child, Jasmine Renee. AS, S.D. Bishop State Coll., 1989; BA, Univ. Montevallo, 1991, M, 1992. English prof. Lawson State Cmty. Coll., Birmingham, Ala., 1993—. Editing cons. Writing Voyage, 1996, Fictions, 1997. Sec. Alabaster Parks & Rec. Adv. Bd., 1997—. Mem. Ala. Assn. for Developmental Edn., Nat. Assn. for Devel. Edn., Nat. Coun. of Tchrs. of Eng., Alabaster Lions Club (sec.-treas. 1997-98), Alpha Phi Alpha. Avocations: model car building, pets, playing saxophone. Home: 620 Park Forest Ln Montevallo AL 35115-8994 Office: Lawson State Cmty Coll 3060 Wilson Rd SW Birmingham AL 35221-1717

BURDEN, JAMES EWERS, lawyer; b. Sacramento, Oct. 24, 1939; s. Herbert Spencer and Ida Elizabeth (Brosemer) B.; m. Kathryn Lee Gardner, Aug. 21, 1965; children: Kara Elizabeth, Justin Gardner. BS, U. Calif., Berkeley, 1961; JD, U. Calif., Hastings, 1964; postgrad., U. So. Calif., 1964-65. Bar: Calif. 1965, Tax Ct. U.S. 1969, U.S. Supreme Ct. 1970. Assoc. Elliott and Aune, Santa Ana, Calif., 1965, White, Harbor, Fort & Schei, Sacramento, 1965-67; assoc. Miller, Starr & Regalia, Oakland, Calif., 1967-69, ptnr., 1969-73; ptnr. Burden, Aiken, Mansuy & Stein, San Francisco, 1973-82, James E. Burden, Inc., San Francisco, 1982—; of counsel, Aiken, Kramer & Cummings, Oakland and San Francisco; bd. dirs. IP Floor Products, Inc., San Leandro, Calif., Denver; underwriting mem. Lloyds of London, 1986-93; instr. U. Calif., Berkeley, Merritt Coll. 1968-74; prin. Dorset C apital LLC; founder, dir. Info4cars.com., Inc., Asheville, N.C., Landmkt.com., Inc., San Francisco. Contbr. articles to profl. jours. Mem. ABA, Claremont Country Club, Commonwealth of Calif., Inst. Dirs. (London), The Univ. Club. E-mail: jeburden@compuserve.com. Office: One Maritime Plz 4th Fl San Francisco CA 94111-3407

BURDEN, JEAN (PRUSSING), poet, writer, editor; b. Waukegan, Ill., Sept. 1; d. Harry Frederick and Miriam (Biddlecom) Prussing; m. David Charles Burden, 1940 (div. 1949). BA, U. Chgo., 1936. Sec. John Hancock Mutual Life Ins. Co., Chgo., 1937-39, Young & Rubicam, Inc., Chgo., 1939-41; editor, copywriter Domestic Industries, Inc., Chgo., 1941-45; office mgr. O'Brion Russell & Co., Los Angeles, 1948-55; adminstr. pub. relations Meals for Millions Found., Los Angeles, 1955-65; editor Stanford Research Inst., South Pasadena, Calif., 1965-66; propr. Jean Burden & Assocs., Altadena, Calif., 1966-82; lectr. poetry to numerous colls. and univs., U.S., 1963—; supr. poetry workshop Pasadena City Coll., Calif., 1960-62, 66, U. Calif. at Irvine, 1975; also pvt. poetry workshops. Author: Naked as the Glass, 1963, Journey Toward Poetry, 1966, The Cat You Care For, 1968, The Dog You Care For, 1968, The Bird You Care For, 1970, The Fish You Care For, 1971, A Celebration of Cats, 1974, The Classic Cats, 1975, The Woman's Day Book of Hints for Cat Owners, 1980, 84, Taking Light from Each Other, 1992; poetry editor: Yankee Mag, 1955—; pet editor: Woman's Day Mag, 1973-82; contbr. numerous articles to various jours. and mags. MacDowell Colony fellow, 1973, 74, 76; Recipient Silver Anvil award Pub. Relations Soc. of Am., 1969, 1st prize Borestone Mountain Poetry award, 1963, Gold Crown award for lit. achievement, 1989. Mem. Poetry Soc. Am., Acad. Am. Poets, Authors Guild. Address: 1129 Beverly Way Altadena CA 91001-2517

BURDETT, BARBRA ELAINE, biology educator; b. Lincoln, Ill., Mar. 18, 1947; d. Robert Marlin and Klaaska Johanna Baker; m. Gary Albert Burdett, Sept. 27, 1968; children: Bryan Robert, Heather Lea, Amanda Rose. AA, Lincoln Coll., 1981; postgrad., Ill. State U. Edn. Core, 1982-83; BS, Millikin U., 1985; postgrad., Western U., 1994-95, U. Ill., Springfield, 1997, Quincy (Ill.) U., 1998. Cert. tchr., Ill. Tchr. advanced placement biology, botany and human physiology Brown County H.S., Mt. Sterling, Ill., 1985-95; tchr. zoology, botany, environmental sci. Pleasant Plains (Ill.) H.S., 1995-97; tchr. biology Quincy (Ill.) H.S., 1997-98; owner Wild Winds Pub. Co., 1999—; dir. Drama Club, Brown County H.S., 1988-90, dir. sci. fairs; ednl. advisor Nat. Young Leaders Conf. Author: Misty White, 1991, Possums Sing, 1994; co-author: The Last Button on Gabe's Coat, 1999, Derthro—Meet Mrs. Claus, 1999. Sponsor Children, Inc., Richmond, Va., 1985—, Internat. Wildlife Coalition, North Falmouth, Mass., 1991—; commdr. club, silver leader., 1988—. Mem. ASCD, Nat. Assn. Biology Tchrs. (Biology Tchr. of Yr. in Ill. 1994), Ill. Sci. Tchrs. Assn., Phi Delta Kappa (newsletter editor 1990), Phi Theta Kappa. Episcopalian. Avocation: classical guitar.

BURDETTE, JANE ELIZABETH, nonprofit association executive, consultant; b. Huntington, W.Va., Aug. 17, 1955; d. C. Richard and Jewel Kathryn (Wagner) B. AAS, Parkersburg (W.Va.) C.C., 1976; BA, Glenville State Coll., 1978; MA, W.Va. U., 1984. Fund raiser, recruiter Muscular Dystrophy Assn., Charleston, W.Va., 1973, 74, 75; sec., bookkeeper Nationwide Ins. Co., Parkersburg, 1975; v.p. Burdette Funeral Home, Parkersburg, 1976-85; intake and referral specialist Wood County Sheltered Workshop, Parkersburg, 1985-91; cons. in field, 1991—. Bd. dirs. Sheltered Workshop, Parkersburg, 1982-86, Western Dist. Guidance Ctr., Parkersburg, 1984-94; vol. St. Joseph's Hosp., 1991-96; mem. W.Va. Coun. Ind. Living, 1992-94; mem. W.Va. Muscular Dystrophy Assn. task force on disability issues, 1992—; bd. advisors, vice chmn. Parkersburg C.C., 1980-89, Domestic Violence Interdisciplinary Adv. Com., 1987, Just Say No, 1987-91; past chmn. Wood County Commn. on Crime, Delinquency and Corrections, Parkersburg, 1985—; chmn. Mid Ohio Valley United Fund Agy., 1986 Heads; v.p. Jr. League of Parkersburg, 1989—; mem. Sanctuary Soc., 1991—, All Saints Guild, 1991-95, St. Margaret Mary Parish Coun., 1992-97; bd. dirs. Cmty. Svc. Coun., 1985—, Parkersburg Transit Authority, 1994-98; mem. W.Va. Statewide Rehab. Adv. Cou., 1998—; liaison Gov. Commn. on Disabled Persons, Charleston, W.Va., 1981-85; mem. Career Adv. Network, 1987-91; treas. W.Va. Women's Conf., 1987, Children's Discovery Ctr. Mus., 1998—; exec. com. W.Va. chpt. Muscular Dystrophy Assn., 1987—; mem. We've Been There Parent Support Group, 1987-90; v.p. A Spl. Wish Found., 1988-98; mem. Parkersburg Consumer Adv. Group; mem. founding com. Banquet of Wealth, 1988-91; bd. dirs. Horizon's Ind. Living Ctr., 1990-98; past transition plan team leader Wood County Bd. Edn.; past liason Internat. Yr. Disabled Persons; past treas., program chmn.

Gov.'s Conf.; former pres. Y Teen Club, YWCA; former adv. com. Mountwood Pk. White Oak Village, Organ Donor Com., 1989; mayoral candidate City of Parkersburg, 1997. Named Miss Wheelchair W.Va., 1981, Outstanding Young Woman of Yr. for W.Va., 1981, Outstanding Young Woman of the Yr., 1986; recipient Kenneth Hieges award Muscular Dystrophy Assn., 1982, Outstanding Citizen award Frat. Order of Police, 1984, Cmty. Svc. award Moose Lodge, 1995, Cert. Appreciation, State W.Va., Gov. Jay Rockefeller, Cert. Appreciation, Am. Legion Aux., Trail of New Beginning award Banquet of Wealth Trail Blazer award YWCA/Altrusa, 1989, Personal Achievement award for W.Va., MDA, 1993, 94, 97, Mary Harriman Cmty. Leadership award Jr. League Internat., 1994, Jennings Randolph award W.Va. Rehab. Assn., 1996, Good Neighbor award Supermarket Comm./Big Bear, 1997, Jefferson award Sta. WCHS-TV, 1998; named W.Va.'s Disabled Profl. Woman of Yr. Pilot Internats., 1989, Hometown Hero Sta. WSAZ-TV, 1993, One Who Makes a Difference, Sta. WTAP, 1994, Profl. and Bus. Woman's Internat. Hall of Fame, 1995, Nat. Hall of Fame for Persons with Disabilities, 1998, W.Va. Women Hall of Fame, 1999, Cover Girl Women At their Best award, 1999. Mem. NAFE, Toastmasters (Comm. and Leadership award 1989). Democrat. Roman Catholic. Avocation: designing. Home: 2500 Brooklyn Dr Parkersburg WV 26101-2913

BURDETT-SMITH, PETER, emergency physician; b. Sale, Eng., June 6, 1959; s. Barry and Gillian (Winterburn) B.-S.; m. Katherine Jane Lee, June 23, 1984; children: Anna, Sarah, Rachel, Alexander. B Medicine, Charing Cross Hosp., London, 1983, B Surgery, 1983; diploma, royal Coll. Anaesthetists, London, 1990. Sr. house officer Tamerside Hosp., Manchester, Eng., 1986-87, Sunderland (Eng.) Hosps., 1989-90; registrar Royal Victoria Infirmary, Newcastle, Eng., 1987-89, 90-91; sr. registrar Yorkshire Health Authority, Leeds, Eng., 1991-94; cons. A/E medicine Royal Liverpool (Eng.) U. Hosp., 1994—; treas.-sec. Hosp. Med. Bd., Liverpool, 1997—. Mem. coun. Liverpool Med. Inst., 1998—. Rsch. grantee N.W. Region R&D, Manchester, 1998-99. Fellow Royal Coll. Physicians, Royal Coll. Surgeons, Faculty Accident and Emergency Medicine; mem. Brit. Assn. for Accident and Emergency Medicine (treas. 1999—), ATLS (N.W. regional rep. 1998—). Home: Royal Liverpool U Hosp, Prescot St, Liverpool L7 8XP, England

BURDICK, CLAUDE OWEN, pathologist; b. Oconomowoc, Wis.; s. Lawrence Theodore and Florence (Owens) B.; m. Margaret Huiskamp, June 18, 1955; children: Katherine, Roberta, Lawrence, Jack (dec.). BS in Med. Sci., U. Wis., 1955, MD, 1958. Diplomate Am. Bd. Pathology, Am. Bd. Dermatopathology. Intern Letterman Army Med. Ctr., San Francisco, 1958-59, resident, 1959-63; pathologist, chief hematology Berkshire Med. Ctr., Pittsfield, Mass., 1968-70; pathologist, dir. labs. Valley Care Health Sys., Livermore/Pleasanton, Calif., 1970-98; chmn., bd. dirs. Valley Care Health Sys., 1993-96; med. dir., cons. Spectra Labs., Inc., Fremont, Calif., 1994—; pres. Livermore Alameda Valley Med. Group, 1972-76. Lt. col. U.S. Army, 1957-68. Fellow Am. Soc. Clin. Pathology, Coll. Am. Pathologists; mem. AMA, Calif. Med. Assn., Calif. Soc. Pathologists (bd. dirs. 1983-86), Alameda Contra Costa Med. Soc., Am. Soc. Blood Banks, South Bay Pathology Soc. (pres. 1981). Democrat. Presbyterian. Avocation: choral music (Ohlone College Chamber Singers). Office: Western Labs Med Group 2945 Webster St Oakland CA 94609-3496

BURDICK, WILLIAM MACDONALD, biomedical engineer; b. Providence, R.I., Apr. 24, 1952; s. Franklin Pierce and Lola Alice (Cook) B. BS, Ind. U. Pa., 1975; M of Engring., Tex. A&M U., 1981; postgrad., U. Tex., 1982-86. Engring. analyst FDA, Winchester, Mass., 1988-90; reviewer neurological devices FDA, Rockville, Md., 1990-94; reviewer, gen. hosp. and personal use devices FDA, Rockville, 1994—. Inventor in field; contbr. articles to profl. jours.; contbr. poem to: Dance on the Horizon (Editor's Choice award Nat. Libr. Poetry), America at the Millennium. Active Native Am. Rights Fund. With USAF, 1976-78. Mem. Biomed. Engring. Soc., Nature Conservancy, Humane Soc. U.S., Am. Assn. Med. Instrumentation, Nat. Multiple Sclerosis Soc., World Wildlife Fund. Congregationalist. Avocations: reading, writing (poetry, songs, fiction), gardening, sports. Office: HHS/PHS/FDA/ODE/GHDB 9200 Corporate Blvd Rockville MD 20850-3229

BURDON, DOUGLAS WILLIAM, medical microbiologist; b. Newcastle-upon-Tyne, Eng., June 28, 1937; s. Robert William and Elizabeth Raine (Claughan) B.; m. Minnie Elizabeth de Villiers, May 5, 1962; children: James Robert Claughan, David Louis de Villiers, William Leonard Gilbey. MB BS, London U., 1962. Cons. Gen. Hosp., Birmingham, 1972-95, Univ. Hosp., Birmingham, 1995—. Author: Antimicrobial Prophylaxis in Surgery, 1979. Fellow Royal Coll. Pathologists; mem. Pathol. Soc. Gt. Britain and Eire. Avocations: history, genealogy, music, gardening. Home: 186 Rosemary Hill Rd, Sutton Coldfield B74 4HP, England Office: Queen Elizabeth Hosp, Microbiology Dept, Birmingham B15 2TH, England

BURDON, IAN, electrical and electronic design engineer; b. Sunderland, Eng., Feb. 2, 1958; s. Edward Pollen and Muriel (Mitchinson) B. BSc in Elec. and Electronic Engring., Newcastle Poly., Eng., 1981. Apprentice Mullard, Durham, Eng., 1974-81; grad. engr. Brit. Aerospace, Stevenage, Eng., 1982; design engr.-cons. Modus Sys. Ltd., Baldock, Eng., 1983-84; design engr., office mgr. Vernon Gauging Sys. Ltd., Hitchin, Eng., 1984-95; EMC design leader Xerox Ltd. Design Ctr., Welwyn Garden City, Eng., 1995—. E-mail: i burdon@lineone.net and ian.burdon@gbr.xerox.com. Home: 19 Shott Ln, Letchworth, Hertfordshire SG6 1SD, England Office: Xerox Ltd, Bessemer Rd, Welwyn Garden City AL7 1HE, England

BURDUS, JULIA ANN, marketing researcher; b. Alnwick, Eng., Sept. 4, 1933; d. Gladstone and Julia Wilhelmina (Booth) Beaty; m. Ian Buchanan Robertson. BA in Psychology, St. Mary's, Durham, Eng., 1956. Research exec. O&M, London, 1961-67; dir. research Garland Compton, London, 1967-71; dir. research McCann Erickson, London, 1971-77, N.Y.C., 1977-79; chmn. McCann & Co., London, 1979-81; dir. strategic planning I.P.G., N.Y.C., 1981-83; dir. AGB Research, London, 1983-86; sr. v.p. mktg. and comms. divsn. Olympia & York Canary Wharf, Ltd., London, 1989-92; part-time dir. Civil Aviation Authority, 1993-97; non-exec. dir. Dawson Internat., 1992-98, Safeway Plc, 1992-99, Next Plc, 1992—, Prudential Plc, 1992—; mem. com. Autobobile Assn., 1992-99. Dep. chmn. Health Edn. Authority, London, 1987-90. Fellow Inst. Practitioners Advt.; mem. Advt. Assn. (chmn. 1981-82). Club: WACL.

BURDYUZHA, VLADIMIR VLADIMIROVICH, astrophysicist; b. Krasnodar, USSR, Aug. 10, 1942; s. Vladimir Vasilyevich and Ekaterina Andreevna B.; m. Genrietta Afanasevna Selivanova, Sept. 4, 1965 (div. Sept. 1981); children: Elena Vladimirovna, Svetlana Vladimirovna. Diploma of Engring., Moscow Aviation Inst., 1966; DSc, Moscow State U., 1987, prof. astrophysics, 1996. Engr. Mil. Inst., near Moscow, 1966-67; engr. Inst. Nuclear Rsch. Moscow State U., 1967; engr. Astronomical Inst. Moscow U., 1968-69; scientific worker Inst. Space Rsch., 1973-91; leading scientific worker Lebedev Phys. Inst. Russian Acad. Scis., Moscow, 1991—; head All Moscow Astrophys. Seminar, 1991, Russian br. Antarctic Rsch., 1993-95; chmn. conf. memory Ya B. Zeldovich, 1992, The Future of the Universe and the Future of Our Civilization, 1999. Contbr. 75 articles to profl. jours. Grantee in field. Mem. Russian Phys. Soc., Russian Astronom. Soc. (v.p. 1991-93), European Astronom. soc., Eurosci., Internat. Astronom. Soc., Running Club. Avocations: alpinism, running. Office: Astro-Space Ctr Lebedev Phys Inst, Profsoyuznaya 84/32, 117810 Moscow Russia

BURE, PAVEL, professional hockey player; b. Moscow, Mar. 31, 1971. Wing Fla. Panthers, Sunrise, 1998—. Recipient Calder Meml. trophy, 1991-92; NHL regular season and playoff Top Goal Scorer, 1993-94. Office: Fla Panthers One Panthers Pkwy Sunrise FL 33323

BURELLO, JOSEPH MATTHEW, publishing executive; b. June 11, 1976. BA in Polit. Sci., Ariz. State U., 1999. Rsch. adminstr. Snell & Wilmer, Phoenix, 1997-99; CEO, founder Burello Publs. Inc., Tempe, Ariz., 1997—. Author: Liar! a critique of lies and the act of lying, 1998, Tribal Civil Ordinance Violations: Measures of Civil Regulatory Power Over Non-Indians, 1999, Screenplay Formatting, 1999; exec. editor AIDS Law and Policy Reporter, 1998—. Office: Burello Publs Inc 700 E Mesquite Cir Ste Q119 Tempe AZ 85281-1939

BUREŠ, STANISLAV, ornithologist, educator; b. Olomouc, Czech Republic, Mar. 26, 1958; s. Stanislav and Marie (Dolénková) B.; m. Jana Klimešová, Mar. 17, 1984; 1 child, Michal. PhD, Mendel Agrl. U., Brno, Czech Republic, 1990. Tchr. Šternberk (Czech Republic) Secondary Sch. Forestry, 1983-90; zoologist Litovelské Pomoraví Natural Park Adminstrn., Olomouc, 1991; asst. prof. ornithology Palacky U., Olomouc, 1992-96, assoc. prof. ornithology, 1996—, head dept. zoology, 1996—, head Lab. Ornithology, 1997—. Editor-in-chief ornithol. jour. Zprávy MOS, 1992-96; contbr. numerous articles to profl. jours., including Ibis, Jour. Avian Biology, Nature, etc. Mem. Internat. Ornithol. Com., Czech Soc. Ornithology (mem. com. 1995-97), Moravian Ornithol. Soc. (chmn. 1992), Internat. Soc. Behavioral Ecology, Slovak Ornithol. Soc. Avocations: photography, mountain trekking, canoeing. E-mail: bures@prfnw.upol.cz. Home: Na zahrádkách 476, 783 14 Bohuňovice Czech Republic Office: Palacky U Dept Zoology, tř Svodoby 26, 771 46 Olomouc Czech Republic

BURG, BRENT LAWRENCE, lawyer; b. Houston, Mar. 2, 1940; s. Abner Danford and Bess (Levin) B.; m. Patricia S. Petitt, 1980; 1 child, Brook Lawrence. BA, U. Tex., 1962; JD, 1966. Bar: Tex. 1966, U.S. Dist. Ct. (so. dist.) Tex. 1966, U.S. Ct. Appeals (5th cir.) 1966, U.S. Supreme Ct. 1970, U.S. Ct. Appeals (4th cir.) 1976, U.S. Dist. Ct. Md. 1976, U.S. Ct. Appeals (11th cir.) 1981. Dist. judge 309th Dist. Ct., Harris County, Tex., 1981-82; assoc. mcpl. judge City of Piney Point Village, 1990-98, City of Bunker Hill Village, 1991-98; ptnr. Rentz, Burg and Assocs., Houston, 1983-95; pvt. practice Brent Burg, Houston, 1995-97; assoc. judge 312th Dist. Ct., Houston, 1999—; of counsel Fouts & Moore, L.L.P., 1997-98. Chairperson Houston Vol. Lawyers Program, Inc., 1988-89, 89-90. Fellow Tex. Bar Found.; mem. Houston Bar Found., State Bar Tex. (grievance com.), Houston Bar Assn. (family law sect. treas. 1978-79, chairperson elect 1980-81, dir. 1982-83, chairperson 1984-85; mem. Supreme Ct. of Tex. child support and visitation guidelines adv. com. 1986-87, 96-97), Phi Alpha Delta. Office: 312th District Ct 1115 Congress St Houston TX 77002-1927

BURGA, LUISA R., marketing researcher; b. Lima, Peru, Sept. 7, 1959; d. César C. Burga and Rosa F. Rivera; m. Carlos N. Cabala; 1 child, Ignacio. BA, U. Pacífico, Lima, 1982; MS in Mgmt., Arthur D. Little Sch. Mgmt., Mass., 1989. Mktg. asst. Parera, Lima, 1982-83; asst. to dir. U. Pacífico, 1983-86, prof., 1987-93, project mgr., 1989-93, chmn. bus. dept., 1995-97; project dir. Apoyo, Lima, 1997—. Office: Apoyo, Republica Panamá 6380, Lima 18, Peru

BURGANOS, VASILIS NIKOLAOS, researcher; b. Athens, Attica, Greece, Mar. 3, 1960; s. Nikolaos and Vaia (Triantafillou) B.; m. Maria I. Kati, June 18, 1988; 1 child, Vayana. Diploma, Nat. Tech. U., Athens, 1983; MSc, U. Rochester, 1986, PhD, 1988. Cert. chem. engring. Rsch. asst. U. Rochester, 1983-88, tchg. asst., 1983-87; post-doctoral fellow Inst. Chemical Engring. & High Temp. Chem. Processes, Patras, Greece, 1988-90; rsch. assoc. Inst. Chemical Engring. & High Temp. Chem. Processes, Patras, 1990-94, prin. rschr., 1995-99, rsch. dir., 1999—; adj. lectr. U. Patras, 1992-93, 94-97; sci. cons. IRC Help Forward, Greece, 1993-95; R&D proposal evaluator Gen. Secretariat of Rsch. and Tech., Greece, 1993-94; scientist-in-charge European, Nat. and Indsl. R&D Projects, Greece, 1994—; referee Chem. Engring. Sci., U.K., 1994—, Transport in Porous Media, The Netherlands, 1998—. Editor: Computational Methods in Water Resources, 1998; guest editor Materials Rsch. Soc. Bull., 1998; contbr. articles to profl. jours. Airman first class Greek Air Force, 1990-91. Elon Huntington Hooker fellow U. Rochester, N.Y., 1986-87. Mem. AAAS, Combustion Inst. (Greek br.), Technical Chamber of Greece. Avocations: tennis, photography, track and field. Office: ICE/HT-FORTH, PO Box 1414, GR 26500 Patras Greece

BURGARD, RALPH, cultural/education planner; b. Buffalo, June 22, 1927; s. Willard Henry and Elise (Waite) B.; m. Cecily Ward, Mar. 17, 1956 (div. Apr. 1985); m. Elaine Johansen Hawk, Apr. 8, 1989 (div. Dec. 1994); m. Marjorie Dean Martin, Aug. 8, 1998; children: Christopher, Timothy, Nadia. BA in Philosophy, Dartmouth Coll., 1949. Mgr. R.I. Philharm. Orch., Providence, 1952-54; assoc. mgr. Buffalo Philharm. Orch., 1954-55; dir. Winston-Salem (N.C.) Arts Coun., 1955-57, St. Paul Coun. Arts and Scis., 1957-65; exec. dir. Am. Coun. for Arts, N.Y.C., 1965-70; pres. Burgard Assocs., N.Y.C., Cambridge, Mass., Kittery Point, Maine, 1970—; founder St. Paul Chamber Orch., 1958, A+ Schs. Program, 1987, Spectra Schs., 1998. Author: Arts in the City, 1968. former sec. N.Am. Assembly of State and Provincial Arts Agys.; former mem. adv. panel Nat. Endowment for Arts, N.Y. State Coun. on Arts, N.Y.C. Cultural Coun.; mem. Nat. Coun. Amenity Planners. Recipient 10th Yr. Tribute, Hartford Arts Coun., 1981, Merit award Assn. Coll., Univ., Cmty. Arts Adminstrs., 1982, Tribute, Nat. Assembly Cmty. Arts, 1987, Chancellor's award N.C. Sch. Arts, 1997, Selina Roberts Ottum award Ams. for Arts, 2000; Ralph Burgard Day, City of St. Paul, 1986. Mem. Century Assn. Avocations: rowing, books, nature, ballooning. Office: Burgard Assocs PO Box 251 Kittery Point ME 03905-0251

BURGDOERFER, JERRY, lawyer; b. Jeffersonville, Ind., May 3, 1958; s. Jerry Jack and Barbara Jean (Hofherr) B. BS, Ind. U., 1980, MBA, 1983, JD cum laude, 1983. Bar: Ill. 1984, U.S. Dist. Ct. (no. dist.) Ill. 1984, U.S. Tax Ct. 1984. Assoc. Adams, Fox, Adelstein, Rosen & Bell, Chgo., 1983-88, ptnr., 1988-89; assoc. Jenner & Block, Chgo., 1989-90, ptnr., 1991—, co-chair corp., tax and bus. transactions, 1999—; with Mori Sogo Law Offices, Tokyo, 1991-93. Author articles. Vol. United Cerebral Palsy Assn., 1995—, dir., 1999—. Named 2d Benton Nat. Moot Ct. Competition, 1982. Mem. ABA, Internat. Bar Assn., Inter Pacific Bar Assn., Ill. Bar Assn., Chgo. Bar Assn. (chairperson '34 Act Com. 1996-98, reporter, Securities Com. 1997-98, vice chair 1998-99, chair 1999—), Japan Am. Soc. Chgo., Ind. U. Alumni Club Chgo. (vol. 1988-89), Econ. Club Chgo., Execs. Club Chgo., Chgo. Coun. on Fgn. Rels., Japan-Am. Soc. of Chgo., Phi Eta Sigma, Phi Delta Phi, Phi Delta Theta (sec. chpt. 1977-78, co-founder, steering com. Chgo. alumni club 1988-89). Avocations: bicycling, water skiing, Japanese language. Office: Jenner & Block 1 E Ibm Plz Fl 4000 Chicago IL 60611-7603

BURGE, LARRY BRADY, artist; b. Fayetteville, N.C., Feb. 2, 1948; s. Billie Dixie and Elma Leigh (Westbrook) B.; m. Lori Jo Shepard, June 17, 1995. Student, Coll. of the Albemarle, Elizabeth City, N.C., 1972, Art Instrn. sch., Mpls., 1976. One man shows include Village Smith Galleries, Winston-Salem, N.C., 1982, Kinston (N.C.) Arts Coun., 1983, Ballantyne Art Gallery, New Bern, N.C., 1984, Collector's Gallery, Raleigh, N.C., 1986, N.C. Maritime Mus., Beaufort, N.C., 1986, 91, World Art Gallery, Jacksonville, N.C., 1995, Art Masters Gallery, Beaufort, 1998, Arts and Things, Morehead City, N.C., 1999; group exhibits include Coll. of the Albemarle Art Ctr., Elizabeth City, 1972, Riverside Gallery, New Bern, 1978, Fairfield Harbor Art Exhibit, New Bern, 1978, Weyerhaeuser Art Exhibit, Grifton, N.C., 1981, 7th Ann Realist Invitational Remarque Gallery, High Point, N.C., 1983, Remarque Gallery, High Point, N.C., 1984, Spartanburg (S.C.) Arts Ctr., 1985, Snyder Gallery, Charlotte, N.C., 1987, Wilkes Art Gallery, North Wilkesboro, 1990, Mid-Town Gallery, Winston-Salem, 1993, Hampton House Gallery, Winston-Salem, 1997, N.C. Seafood Festival, Morehead, N.C., 1999, Core Sound Decon Festiveal, Harker's Island, N.C., 1999; works in corp. collections at Wachovia Bank and Trust Co., Winston-Salem, RJR Nabisco, Winston-Salem, Trotman's Gallery, Winston-Salem, Marine Fed. Credit Union, Jacksonville, N.C., Core Sound Waterfowl Mus., Harker's Island, Onslow Meml. Hosp., Jacksonville, N.C. Seafood Festival; prodr. ltd.-edit. prints of maj. paintings Salem Graphics, Inc., 1990—; listed in Ency. Living Artists, 1990, Am. Artists-A Survey of Leading Contemporaries, 1991. Home and Office: PO Box 623 927 Church St Newport NC 28570-9679

BURGE, LEGAND L., III, computer science educator, consultant; b. Stillwater, Okla., Feb. 5, 1972; s. Legand L. and Gwenetta V. (Patterson) B. Jr. BS summa cum laude in Computer Sci., Langston (Okla.) U., 1992; MS in Computer Sci., Okla. State U., 1995, PhD in Computer Sci., 1998. Grad. asst. Okla. State U., Stillwater, 1992-98; adj. prof. Langston U., 1993-98; asst. prof. Howard U., Washington, 1998—; cons. Mercury Marine, Stillwater, 1994-96, Teubner & Assocs., Inc., Stillwater, 1995; founder, CEO Mecca Rsch., Inc., Dallas, 1999—. Recipient NSF grant, 1996, USENIX rsch. grant, 1997. Mem. IEEE, Assn. for Computing Machinery, F&AM Prince Hall Affiliation, Sigma Xi, Alpha Phi Alpha, Phi Kappa Phi. Democrat. Mem. A.M.E. Ch. Avocations: piano, swimming, bowling, computer programming, traveling. E-mail: blegand@howard.edu. Home: 5901 Mount Eagle Dr Alexandria VA 22303-2503 Office: Howard U 2300 6th St NW Washington DC 20059-0001

BURGE, PETER SHERWOOD, internist, consultant; b. London, July 8, 1944; s. Graham Mowbray and Anne Elizabeth (Batt) B.; m. Anne Willard, Aug. 17, 1969; children: Cedd, Chad. MB, BChir, Royal Free U., London, 1969; MSc in Occupl. Medicine, London Sch. Hygiene/Trop. Med., 1978; MD, London U., 1984, Diploma of Indsl. Health. Registrar U. Coll. Hosp., London, 1972-76; lectr. in clin. immunology Cardiothoracic Inst., London, 1976-80; cons. physician Birmingham (Eng.) Heartlands Hosp., 1980—. Contbr. chpt. to book, articles to profl. jours. Fellow Royal Coll. Physicians U.K.; mem. Acad. Indoor Air Sci., European Respiratory Soc. Anglican. Avocations: punting, skiing, dongoling. Office: Birmingham Heartlands Hosp, Bordesley Green East, Birmingham B9 5SS, England

BURGE, RONALD EDGAR, physics educator, consultant; b. Cardiff, Glamorgan, Wales, Oct. 3, 1932; s. John Henry and Edith Beatrice (Thompson) B.; m. Janet Mary Pitts, Dec. 26, 1953; children: Andrew John, Peter Ronald. BSc, U. London, 1953, PhD, 1957, DSc, 1975. Asst. lectr. physics Kings Coll. U. London, 1954-58, lectr., 1958-62, reader in biophysics, 1962-63, prof. physics, dept. head, 1984-89, vice prin., 1987-91, Wheatstone prof. physics, 1989—; rsch. dir. Leverhulme Trust grant Cambridge (Eng.) U., 1994—; dept. head Kings Coll. U. London, 1989-92; prof., dept. head Queen Elizabeth Coll. U. London, 1963-84; cons. Min. of Def., U.K., 1975—; vis. fellow U. Cambridge, 1992, life mem. Author rsch. papers in field. Recipient Rodman medal Royal Photographic Soc., 1993, Daiwa award for x-ray lasers, 1994; King's Coll. fellow, 1988; grantee EEC, Min. Def. King's Coll. London, Sci. and Engring. Rsch. Coun., Med. Rsch. Coun. Mem. Royal Instn. (Davy Faraday rsch. com.), Royal Soc., Leverhulme Trust. Avocations: gardening, walking. Office: Physics Dept King's Coll, Strand, London WC2R 2LS, England also Office: Cavendish Lab, Madingley Rd, Cambridge CB3 0HE, England

BURGEL, HANS DIETMAR, management educator, researcher; b. Radeberg, Germany, Apr. 22, 1935. Diploma, U. Cologne, Germany, 1960; Dr. rer. pol., U. Cologne, 1964. Rschr. U. Cologne, 1956-62; lectr. U. Stuttgart, Germany, 1980-92, prof., 1992—; fin. analyst Ford Werke AG, Cologne, 1962-65; head planning dept. Boehringer, Ingelheim, Germany, 1965-72; contr. Standard Electric Lorenz AG, Stuttgart, 1972-92. Author: R&D Controlling, 1989, R&D Management, 1994, R&D Project Management, 1979, Management of Science, 1998. Home: Lessingstr 8, 71263 Weil der Stadt Germany Office: U Stuttgart Abt VIII F&E, Breitscheidstr 2C, 70174 Stuttgart Germany

BURGEN, SIR ARNOLD, pharmacologist; b. London, Mar. 20, 1922; s. Peter and Elizabeth (Wolfers) B.; m. Judith Browne, Aug. 4, 1946; children: Andrew, Jennifer, Stephen; m. Olga Kennard, Dec. 5, 1993. MB, BS, London U., 1945, MD, 1959; MA, Cambridge (Eng.) U., 1962; DSc (hon.), Leeds U., 1973, McGill U., 1973; MD (hon.), U. Utrecht, 1983, U Zurich, 1983; DUniv (hon.), U. Surrey, 1983; DSc (hon.), U. Liverpool, 1989. Intern Middlesex Hosp., London, 1946-47; prof. physiology McGill U., Montreal, 1949-62; prof. pharmacology Cambridge U., 1962-71; dir. Nat. Inst. for Med. Rsch., London, 1971-82; master Darwin Coll., Cambridge, 1982-89; pres. Academia Europaea, 1988-94; dir. Amersham Internat. plc. Contbr. articles to sci. jours. Deocrated knight bachelor. Fellow Royal Soc. London (v.p. 1980, fgn. sec. 1981); mem. NAS, Oxford and Cambridge Club (London). Avocation: sculpture. E-mail: asvb@cam.ac.uk. Home: 8A Hills Ave, Cambridge CB1 4XA, England Office: Downing Coll, Tennis Court Rd, Cambridge CB2 1DQ, England

BURGER, ANNA, agricultural and geographical economics educator; b. Újpest, Hungary, May 19, 1931; d. Imre Gimes and Piroska Reinhard; m. Kálmán Burger, Nov. 24, 1953; children: Gábor, Zsuzsanna. MD, U. Agr., Gödöllö, Hungary, 1953; PhD, U. Econs., Budapest, Hungary, 1964; DSc, Hungarian Acad. Scis., Budapest, 1970. Ofcl. Planning Office, Budapest, 1954-57; rschr. Econ. Inst. Acad., Budapest, 1959-68; chief editor Kossuth Pub. House, Budapest, 1968-72; prof., head dept. U. Horticulture, Budapest, 1972-84, Ctr. Mgmt. Edn., Budapest, 1984-88; prof. econ. geography U. Szeged, Hungary, 1988—. Author: Some Economic Problems of Consumer's Services, 1970, Food Economics, 1985, The Agriculture of the World, 1994, others; contbr. over 120 articles to profl. publs. Mem. Internat. Assn. Agrl. Economists, European Assn. Agrl. Economists, Internat. Soc. Hort. Sci. (v.p. 1979-87), Acad. Scis. (pres. com. econs. 1990-99). Office: Univ Szeged, Egyetem u 2 6701, PF 650 Szeged Hungary

BURGER, HENRY GEORGE, endocrinologist; b. Vienna, Austria, May 23, 1933; s. George Emanuel and Claire Hildegard (Schroth) B.; m. Jennifer Anne Treyvaud, Sept. 19, 1959; children: Martine, Mark, David, Anna, Louisa. MBBS, U. Melbourne, Australia, 1956, MD, 1960. Dir. Prince Henry Med. Rsch. Ctr., Melbourne, Australia, 1972-90, Prince Henry's Inst. Med. Rsch., Melbourne, Australia, 1990-99; unit head, dir. endocrinology dept. Monash Med. Ctr., Melbourne, Australia, 1992-99. Contbr. numerous articles to profl. jours. Fellow Australian Acad. Scis.; mem. U.S. Endocrine Soc. (Disting. Physician 1999), Endocrine Soc. Australia (past pres.), Internat. Menopause Soc. (pres. 1996-99), Order of Australia (officer 1993). Avocations: tennis, skiing, music. Home: 36 Berry St, Melbourne 3002, Australia Office: Prince Henry's Inst Med Rch, 246 Clayton Rd, Victoria 3168, Australia

BURGER, WERNER CARL, retired art educator; b. Pforzheim, Germany, Dec. 27, 1925; came to U.S., 1926; s. Karl Frederick and Helen Rosalie (Schlaefle) B. BS, NYU, 1950, MA, 1951. Cert. secondary tchr., N.J. Fine arts tchr. Westfield (N.J.) H.S., 1951-56; chmn. art dept. West Morris H.S., Chester, N.J., 1956-60; prof. painting and drawing Kean U., Union, N.J., 1961-92, prof. emeritus, 1993—; cons. Hunterdon Mus., Clinton, N.J., 1960. Exhibited in Newark Mus., 1996, N.J. State Mus., Trenton, 1997, Hunterdon Mus. Art, 2000. Cpl. U.S. Army, 1944-46. Recipient Grumbacher Outstanding Svc. to Arts award, 1990. Mem. N.J. Watercolor Soc. (bd. dirs. 1970—), Phi Delta Kappa. Avocations: working out, body building, gardening.

BURGERS, MARTHINUS STEPHANUS, government official; b. Utrecht, South Africa, Aug. 6, 1940; s. Jacob Philippus and Anna Magdalena (Erasmus) B.; m. Annemarie Vorster, Dec. 18, 1965; children: Jacob Philippus, Barend Jacobus. BSc in Agr., U. Pretoria, South Africa, 1963, MSc in Agr. cum laude, 1966, DSc in Agr., 1982. Rsch. officer Dept. Agr., South Africa, 1965-69; lectr. agronomy U. Pretoria, 1970-80; sr. lectr. agronomy U. of North, South Africa, 1980-82; prof., head dept. plant prodn., dean faculty agr. U. of North, 1983-94; mem. provincial legislature, mem. exec. coun. portfolio Northern Province Govt., Pietersburg, South Africa, 1994-97; mem. prov. legislature Northern Province Govt., 1997—; chairperson portfolio com. on health & welfare, 1999—; dir. Lebowa Agrl. Corp., South Africa, 1984-94. Mem. African Nat. Congress. Avocations: hiking, squash. E-mail: drtienne@mweb.co.za. Home: 1 Anton St, Bendorpark, Pietersburg 0699, South Africa Office: Dept Agr Land & Environ, 66 Biccard St, Pietersburg 0700, South Africa

BURGESS, ANTHONY REGINALD FRANK, consultant; b. London, Jan. 27, 1932; s. Beatrice Burgess; m. Carlyn Shawyer, May 21, 1960; 1 child, Paul. BSc in Econs., U. London, 1953. Journalist London, 1955-62; editor European Cmty. Info. Svc., Luxembourg, 1962-65; with Her Majesty Diplomatic Svc., London, 1966-67; first sec. Brit. High Commn., Dhaka, Pakistan, 1967-69; first sec. S.E. Asia Fgn. Commonwealth Office, London, 1970-72; first sec. econs. Br. High Commn., Ottawa, Can., 1972-76; H.M. consul Brit. Embassy, Bogota, Colombia, 1976-79; first sec. Rhodesia Dept. FCO, London, 1979-80, asst. head info., 1980-82; dep. high commr. Br. High Commn. Dhaka, Bangladesh, 1982-86; counsellor Brit. Embassy, Havana, 1986-89. Co-author: The Common Market and the Treaty of Rome Explained, 1967. Lt. Royal Army Ordnance, 1953-55. Named Comdr. Royal Victorian Order, Her Majesty the Queen, 1983. Avocations: travel, photography, shooting. Home: c/o Brooks', St James' St, London SW1A 1LN, England

BURGESS, DAVID, lawyer; b. Detroit, Nov. 30, 1948; s. Roger Edward and Claire Theresa (Sullivan) B.; m. Rebecca Culbertson Stuart, 1985 (dec. Dec. 1988); m. Catherine Mounteer, 1993; children: Jalil Riahi, Leila Riahi, Bryan Valentine, Grace Catherine. BS in Fgn. Svc., Georgetown U., 1970, MS in Fgn. Svc., 1978, JD, 1978. Bar: D.C. 1978, U.S. Dist. Ct. D.C. 1979, U.S. Ct. Appeals (D.C. cir.) 1979, U.S. Ct. Appeals (fed. cir.) 1988, U.S. Ct. Internat. Trade 1988. Rsch. asst. Georgetown U. Sch. Bus. Adminstrn., Washington, 1975, asst. to dean, 1975-76; rsch. assoc., prof. Acad. in the Pub. Svc., Washington, 1976-79; asst. editor Securities Regulation Law Report, Washington; legal editor Internat. Trade Reporter Bur. Nat. Affairs, Washington, 1978-79; atty. Cadwalader, Wickersham & Taft, Washington, 1979-81; mng. editor Bur. Nat. Affairs, Washington, 1981-82; dir. U.S. Peace Corps, Niamey, Niger, 1982-84, Rabat, Morocco, 1984-85; dir. policy planning, mgmt. Peace Corps, Washington, 1985-87; dir. Bur. Human Rights and Humanitarian Affairs U.S. Dept. State, Washington, 1987-92; regional dir. Lawyers for Bush-Quayle Re-Election Campaign, 1992; chief party Rwanda Dem. and Governance Project, 1994, Russia NGO Sector Project, Moscow, 1994; dir. democracy and civil soc. program, sr. advisor World Learning, Washington, 1995 (dir. U.S. Democracy Fellows program, Washington, 1995—); spkr. workshops Minority Legis. Edn. Program, Ind. Assn. Cities and Towns, Georgetown U. Continuing Edn. Program, Comms. Workers Am., Colo. State U., U. Wis. Alumni rep. Internat. Sch. Bangkok, 1972-74. Author: Financing Local Government, 1977, 2d edit., 1978, Preparation of the Local Budget, 2 vols., 1976, 2d edit., 1978, Local Government Accounting Fundamentals, 2d edit., 1977, Understanding Federal Assistance Programs, 2d edit., 1978, The POW/MIA Issue: Perspectives on the National League of Families, 1978; contbr. articles to publs. Adv. com. Arlington County Fiscal Affairs, 1993-94; mem. pres. coun. Mary Washington Coll.; mem. Rep. Nat. Com.; vol. G.W. Bush Campaign, 1999—. Mem. D.C. Bar Assn., Washington Fgn. Law Soc., Hoyas Unltd. (pres. 1992-94), Federalist Soc., Georgetown U. Alumni Assn. (bd. govs. 1975-00, class rep. 1971-91, mem. alumni senate 2000—), Rep. Nat. Lawyers Assn., Pachyderm Club No. Va. (pres. 1992-93), Pres.'s Club, RNC Eagle Club. Republican. Roman Catholic. Home: 3115 1st Pl N Arlington VA 22201-1037 Office: 1015 15th St NW Ste 750 Washington DC 20005-2605

BURGESS, IAN GLENCROSS, insurance company executive; b. Sydney, Australia, Nov. 26, 1931; m. Barbara J. Hastie, 1957. Grad., U. New South Wales. Dir., chmn. CSR Ltd., 1987—, 1997—, Australian Mut. Providence Soc., Sydney, 1989-98, 1994-98; chmn. AMP Ltd., 1998—; dir., chmn. Western Mining Corp., 1993—, 1999—; dir. Pacific Dunlop Ltd., 1993-98; Bd. dirs. Pacific Dunlop., Western Mining co., Atlas Copco, trustee, Walter & Eliza Hall Trust. Avocations: reading, golf. Office: Australian Mut Provident Ltd, 33 Alfred St, Sydney NSW2000, Australia also: CSR Ltd, 9 Help St Level 1, Chatswood NSW 2067, Australia*

BURGESS, JOHN RICHARD, endocrinologist; b. Devonport, Tasmania, 1965; s. Richard and Deda B.; m. Jennifer, 1992; children: James, William, Matthew. B Med. Sci., U. Tasmania, 1986, MBBS, 1989, MD, 1998. Resident, registrar Royal Hobart Hosp., Tasmania, Australia, 1990-95; registrar St. Vincent's Holsp., Melbourne, Australia, 1996; cons. endocrinologist Royal Hobart Hosp., 1997—. Fellow Royal Australasian Coll. Physicians; mem. Australian Med. Assn., Endocrine Soc. Avocation: sailing.

BURGESS, MARVIN FRANKLIN, human resources, management specialist, consultant; b. Heathsville, Va., Mar. 18, 1932; s. Marvin Judson and Emma Elizabeth (Bradberry) B.; m. Beatrice Ione Hildahl, Feb. 7, 1932; children: Michael Marvin, Linda Ione. BA in Math. and Physics, U. Richmond, 1953; postgrad., Va. Tech., 1953-54; MA in Sociology and Psychology, Duke U., 1962. Commd. USCGR, 1956, advanced through grades to capt., dist. insp., port security, adminstr., ret., 1992; NASA engr., admin., mgmt., tech. pub. Langley Rsch. Ctr., Hampton, Va., 1954-84; cons. outplacement Career Dynamics II, Virginia Beach, Va., 1984—; adj. prof. sociology Christopher Newport Coll., Newport News, 1970-72; mgmt. tng., human resources orgn. analyst, efficiency and planning cons. U.S. Dept. Transp., Washington, 1972-80; funding, human resources mgmt., productivity cons. NASA, 1965-84; spkr., rschr. in field. Author: Rebuilding Downtrodden Job Market and Madhouse Society, 1996. Post comdr. Am. Legion, Yorktown, Va., 1978-82; chmn., pres. PTA Yorkshire Acad., York County, Va., 1968-69; mgr. Little League and Am. Legion Baseball, York County, 1970-80; player Chesapeake League semi-pro baseball, Northern Neck, Va., 1951-56; mem. govt. com. Kiwanis, Yorktown, 1966-68. Methodist. Avocations: politics, writing, speaking, restoring old houses, sports. Home: 130 Mill Ln Yorktown VA 23692-3214 Office: Career Dynamics II 1 Columbus Ctr Ste 673 Virginia Beach VA 23462-6722

BURGESS, ROBERT GEORGE, academic administrator; b. Sherborne, Eng., Apr. 23, 1947; s. George and Olive Mary (Andrews) B.; m. Hilary Margaret Mary Joyce, Aug. 3, 1974. BA, U. Durham, 1971; PhD, U. Warwick, 1981; DLitt (hon.), Staffordshire U., 1998. Cert. tchr., Eng. Lectr. U. Warwick, 1974-84, sr. lectr., 1984-88, dir. Ctr. Edni. Devel. Appraisal & Rsch., 1987-99, prof. sociology, 1988-99, chair faculty social studies, 1988-91, founding chair grad. sch., 1991-95, sr. pro vice-chancellor, 1995-99; vice chancellor U. Leicester, 1999—. Author: Experiencing Comprehensive Education, 1983, In the Field, 1984, Research Methods, 1994; coauthor: Implementing In-Service Education and Training, 1993. Mem. Brit. Sociol. Assn. (pres. 1989-91), Brit. Ednl. Rsch. Assn., Assn. Tchrs. Social Scis. (pres. 1991-93), U.K. Coun. Grad. Edn. (founding chair 1993-99), Coun. Econ. & Social Rsch. Coun. (chair tng. bd. 1997-2000). Office: U Leicester, Vice Chancellors Office, Leicester LE1 7RH, England

BURGESS, ROBERT RONALD, human resources executive; b. Memphis, Dec. 2, 1943; s. Doyle Eugene Burgess and Mildred Burgess (Sparks) Hamill; m. Suzie Strong, June 28, 1985; 1 child, Mary Weldon. BS in Psychology, Memphis State U., 1967, MEd, 1975, EdD (ABD), 1979. Dir. Teen Challenge, Vienna, Austria, 1971-73; religious affairs coord. Memphis State U., 1973-80; dir. human resources The Peabody, Memphis, 1980-81, GE/RCA, Memphis, N.Y.C., 1981-86; exec. dir. The Promus Companies, Memphis, 1986-99; v.p. human resources Argosy Gaming Co., Alton, Ill., 1999—; chmn. coord. coun. Profl. Religious Assn. in Higher Edn., N.Y.C., 1978-79. Editor: Dialogue on Campus, 1978. Fund raiser WKNO Edn. T.V., Memphis, 1989, United Way, Memphis, 1988. With U.S. Army, 1969-71. Recipient Disting. Svc. award U.S. Army, Berlin, 1971. Mem. Human Resources Assn., Human Resources Planning Soc. (corp. sponsor 1989—), St. Louis Club. Avocations: antique restoration, gardening, fatherhood. Home: 50 Berkshire Dr Saint Louis MO 63117-1046 Office: Argosy 219 Piasa St Alton IL 62002-6232

BURGESS, RUTH LENORA VASSAR, speech and language educator; b. Pune, India, Aug. 6, 1939; d. Theodore R. and F. Estelle (Barnett) Vassar; m. Stanley Milton Burgess, Feb. 26, 1960; children: John Bradley, Stanley Matthew, Scott Vassar, Heidi Amanda Elizabeth, Justin David. BS in Edn., Tex. Tech. U., 1960; MA, U. Mo., 1968, PhD, 1979. Speech therapist Inkster (Mich.) Pub. Schs., 1961-62; mid. sch. tchr. Strafford (Mo.) Pub. Schs., 1962-63; speech therapist Fulton (Mo.) Pub. Schs., 1967-68; speech-lang. clinician Springfield (Mo.) Pub. Schs., 1963-66; asst. prof. Evangel Coll., Springfield, 1968-76; prof. Sch. Tchr. Edn. S.W. Mo. State U., Springfield, 1976—, dir. Ctr. Rsch. and Svc., 1990-97; mem. sci. adv. bd. Internat. Ctr. Enhancement of Jerusalem, Israel, 1993—; field reviewer Dept. Edn., Washington, 1993-96, U.S. Vocat. Rehab., Washington, 1993, 94, 96, 99; mem. evaluation team Title I Springfield Schs., 1994. Author: The Status of the Educational Resource Teacher, 1981; editor The Learner in the Process, 1978-80; contbr. articles to profl. jours. Ex-officio bd. dirs. Orphanage Assn., Pune, 1968—; mem. Kodaikanal-Woodstock Alumni Assn., Atlanta, 1956—; mem. Women Issues Network, Springfield, 1993—. Grantee Dept. Edn., 1978-83, 90-92, Dept. Elem. and Secondary Edn., 96, Mellon Found., 1988-90. Mem. AAUW, ASCD, Am. Speech, Lang. and Hearing Assn. (cert.), Internat. Assn. for Cognitive Edn. (field editor 1990-94). Avocations: literary group, hiking, creative writing, travel, advocacy. Office: SW Mo State U 901 S National Ave Springfield MO 65804-0088

BURGESS, STEVEN MICHAEL, marketing professional, educator; b. Columbus, Ohio, Feb. 11, 1954; s. Richard Edgar and Rita Ursula (Douglas) B.; m. Colleen Anne Wright, Aug. 5, 1994; children: Ariel Shai, Alethe Soraya, Richard Douglas, Jonathan Blackwell, Thandiwe Bahia. BSBA, Ohio State U., 1977; PhD, U. Witwatersrand, Johannesburg, South Africa, 1990. Sales and mktg. mgr. Glicks Furniture Rental Inc., Columbus, 1977-81; regional sales mgr. Johnson & Johnson Ltd., Johannesburg, 1981-84; pres. Leonard Burgess Group Ltd., Durban, South Africa, 1984-86; sr. product mgr. Johnson & Johnson, East London, South Africa, 1986-89; sr. lectr., faculty coord. U. Witwatersrand, 1989-94; exec. dir. Steve Burgess and Assocs. Closed Corp., Johannesburg, 1989—; mng. dir. Autopage Cellular (Pty.) Ltd., Johannesburg, 1994-95; dir. Autopage Holdings Ltd., Johannesburg; prof. bus. adminstrn. in mktg. Grad. Sch. Bus. U. Cape Town, South Africa; part-time faculty MBA program Grad. Inst. Mgmt. and Tech., Johannesburg, 1990-97; Assoc. Marketers prof. mktg. U. Witwatersrand. Author: The New Marketing, 1998; contbr. articles to profl. jours. mem. organizing com. South African Nat. Coun. Child and Family Welfare, Johannesburg, 1986-93; mem. task group Nat. Telecomm. Forum, Johannesburg, 1995-96. Sgt. USAR, 1973-79. Recipient Internat. Alumni award Ohio State U. Coll. Bus., 1999. Mem. So. African Mktg. Rsch. Assn., Acad. Mktg. Sci., Am. Mktg. Assn., European Mktg. Acad., Inst. Mktg. Mgmt., Assn. Consumer Rsch., Soc. Consumer Psychology. Avocations: scuba diving, road running, golf. Home: 13 Singer St, Woodmead Sandton South Africa Office: Graduate Sch Business, Breakwater Campus Portswood Rd, Greenpoint Cape 8000, South Africa

BURGGRAF, FRANK BERNARD, JR., landscape architect, retired educator; b. N.Y.C., Nov. 13, 1932; s. Frank Bernard and Johanna (Verbaan) B.; m. Jane Martin Rannenberg, June 25, 1955 (div. 1997); children: Helen Marguerite, Frank Bernard, John Christian; m. Margaret Goff, Oct. 31, 1998. BS, SUNY-Syracuse, 1954; MLA, U. Pa., 1958. Registered landscape architect, N.Y. Asst. prof. U. Ga., Athens, 1958-63; assoc. prof., dir. regional planning grad. program Pa. State U., University Park, 1963-70; chief planning analyst N.Y. State Pub. Service Commn., Albany, 1970-80; cons. landscape architect, planner Delmar, N.Y., 1980-84; prof. landscape architecture U. Ark., Fayetteville, 1984-97, dir. program in landscape architecture, 1984-87, emeritus prof. landscape architecture, 1997—; mem. N.Y. State Bd. Landscape Architecture, 1977-84, chmn., 1979-81. Contbr. articles to profl. jours. Served to lt. col. USAFR, 1954-81. Fellow Am. Soc. Landscape Architects; mem. Am. Planning Assn., Elks (exalted ruler local lodge, 1990), Delta Upsilon (chpt. faculty advisor 1984-90). Democrat. Avocations: sailing; handball. Home: 18665 Brentwood Mountain Rd Winslow AR 72959-9755

BURGHARDT, ANDRZEJ ANTONI, chemical engineer; b. Falenica, Warsaw, Poland, Dec. 9, 1928; s. Stanisław and Maria (Stefańska) B.; m. Aleksandra Joanna Sanetra, July 12, 1956; 1 child, Jacek. MSc, Tech. U., 1954, PhD, 1962, DSc, 1965. Reader Tech. U., Gliwice, Poland, 1954-66; dep. dir. Inst. Chem. Engring., Gliwice, 1966-70; dir. Inst.Chem. Engring., Gliwice, 1970—; mem. ctrl. qualifying com. for acad. degrees, 1994—. Author: Fundamentals of Chemical Engineering, 1977, 83, Mass Transfer in Multicomponent Systems, 1980, Kondensation von Mehrstoffgemischen, 1991, 94, 97, English translation, 1993, Dynamics of Processes in a Porous Catalyst Pellet, 1996. Recipient Golden Cross of Merit, knight's cross Order of Polonia Restituta, officer's cross Order of Polonia Restituta, comdr.'s cross Order of Polonia Restituta (Poland). Mem. Polish Acad. of Scis. (chmn. chem. engring. com. 1991—, scientific sec. br. 1994—). Avocations: medieval history, skiing, climbing. Home: Curie-Skłodowskiej 12/7, 44-100 Gliwice Poland Office: Polish Acad Scis, Inst Chem Eng Bałtycka 5, 44-100 Gliwice Poland

BÜRGI, HANS-BEAT, crystallography educator; b. Münsterlingen, Switzerland, Jan. 20, 1942; s. Johann Paul and Gertrud (Akermann) B.; m. Verena Schmid, Apr. 6, 1984. Diploma in Chemistry, ETH, Zurich, Switzerland, 1965, D Natural Sci., 1969, D Habilitation, 1975. Asst. ETH, Zurich, 1967-69, Oberasst., 1971-79; rsch. assoc. U. Mich., Ann Arbor, 1969-71; prof. crystallography U. Bern, Switzerland, 1979—; vis. prof. Princeton U., 1981, Technion, Haifa, Israel, 1991, Caltech, Pasadena, 1994-95, Tokyo Inst. Tech., 1996, U. Calif., San Diego, 2000; vis. fellow Australian Nat. U., Canberra, 1986. Author, editor: Structure Correlation, 1994. Recipient Alfred Werner award Swiss Chem. Soc., 1975. Mem. Am. Crystallography Assn., Switzerland Gesellschaft Kristallographie, Gesellschaft Deutscher Chemiker. Office: U Bern Lab Crystallography, Freiestr 3, 3012 Bern Kt Bern, Switzerland

BÜRGI-SCHMELZ, ADELHEID HILDEGARD, software company executive, computer scientist; b. Bottrop, Germany, Oct. 12, 1957; m. Rudolf Walter Burgi, Oct. 13, 1984; children: Felicitas Adelheid Onida, Constantin Rudolf Salomo. MA, Bonn U., Germany, 1981; MS, Rensselaer Poly. Inst., Troy, N.Y., 1983; PhD, Berne U., Switzerland, 1995. Tech. staff mem. Bellcore, Livingston, N.J., 1984-85; R&D sector mgr. Schindler Aufzüge AG, Ebikon, Switzerland, 1986-91; rsch. fellow Berne U., 1990-93; head European Coop. Dept. Berne (Switzerland) U., 1993-96; chief tech. officer Ascom Infrasys AG, Solothurn, Switzerland, 1996-98; CEO quality of svc. Ascom Infrasys AG, Solothurn, 1998—; cons. Schindler Mgmt., Ebikon, Switzerland, 1991-92; mng. dir. Contec, Berne, Switzerland, 1991-95; sec. gen. ING-Paed CH Register, Berne, Switzerland, 1994-96; founder BSV, Bätterkinden, Switzerland, 1996—; mem. Working Group of Swiss Coun. of Sci., Berne, Switzerland, 1988-92; rapporteurship European Telecomms. Standardization Inst., 1997-99. Editor, author, pub.: Eurocor-Schriftenreihe (series of books) Vol. 1-5, 1994-96, Erfolgsfaktoren bei der Entwicklung und Einführung Wissensbasierter Systeme, 1996; author: Bulletin SEV/VSE, 1988, 90, 93, 96, Futura FER, 1990, 91. Recipient Gold medal Internat. Soc. for Engring. Edn., 1996. Mem. ACM, IEEE, AAAI, Informs. Office: ASCOM Infrasys AG, Glutz-Blotzheim Str 1-3, CH-4503 Solothurn Switzerland

BURGOYNE, GRANT THOMAS, lawyer; b. Ketchikan, Alaska, Aug. 9, 1953; s. Richard Thomas and Florence Marjorie Burgoyne; m. Christina Lea Burgoyne, May 20, 1978; children: Crystal Lea, Katherine Ann. BA, U. Idaho, 1975; JD, U. Kans., 1988. Bar: Idaho 1988, U.S. Dist. Ct. Idaho 1988, U.S. Ct. Appeals (9th cir.) 1991. Intern Idaho Gov. Cecil Andrus, Boise, 1975; asst. Idaho Sec. of State, Boise, 1976-77; child support enforcement officer Idaho Dept. Health and Welfare, Boise, 1978-79; adminstrv. hearing officer Idaho Dept. Employment, Boise, 180-86; atty. Moffatt, Thomas, Barrett, Rock & Fields, Boise, 1988-95; mng. ptnr. Mauk & Burgoyne, Boise, 1996—. Co-author: Idaho Employment Policies Handbook, 1998, The Idaho Tort and Insurance Law Deskbook, 1989. Bd. dirs. Human Resources Assn. of Treasure Valley, Boise, 1998-2000; chmn. Ada County Dem. Ctrl. Com., Boise, 1992-94; platform com. chmn. Idaho State Dem. Party, 1992. Mem. Idaho State Bar Assn. (chmn. employment and labor law sect. 1997-98), Vandal Boosters. Democrat. Methodist. Office: Mauk & Burgoyne 515 S 6th St Boise ID 83702-7634

BURGOYNE, LEIGH ALEXANDER, biology educator; b. Adelaide, Australia, Sept. 22, 1939; s. William Alexander and Thelma Doreen (Parker) B.; m. Judith Leslie Watson, Dec. 23, 1967; children: Mark William, Laura Leeanne, Kirsten Leslie. PhD, Adelaide U., 1967. Postdoctoral fellow Yale U., New Haven, 1967-68; lectr. Flinders U., Adelaide, 1969—. Fulbright scholar, 1967. Fellow Fulbright Assn.; mem. Australia New Zealand Forensic Soc., Genetics Soc. Australia. Avocation: ancient history. Home: 18 Broughton Ave, Mitcham SA, 5062 Adelaide Australia Office: Sch Biol Scis, GPO Box 2100, 5001 Adelaide SA, Australia

BURHAN, HALIS, career military officer; b. Trabzon, Black Sea, Turkey, Sept. 1, 1933; s. Dursun and Zekiye (Yilmaz) B.; m. Firkat Ayse Inal, Sept. 16, 1957; children: Murat L., Nejat. Diploma, Air War Coll., Izmir, Turkey, 1955, Air War Acad., Istanbul, 1967, Joint Mil. Acad., Istanbul, 1969, Indsl. Coll. of the Armed, Forces, USA, 1972. Chief of staff Turkish Air Force, Ankara, 1986-88; commdr. 1st TAF Turkish Air Force, Eskisehir, 1988-90; dep. commd. officer Turkish Air Force, Ankara, 1991-92, commdr., 1992-95, chmn. exec. bd. air war history and strategic study group, 1995—; served to gen. Turkish Air Force, 1990-95. Columnist "Turkey" newspaper. Bd. dirs. Traffic Found. Recipient King Abdulaziz medal Bin Fadh Bin Abdulaziz, Al-suud, 1993. Mem. of Air War History and St. Study Group, Ankara Club, Anadolli Club. Office: TUAF Hdqtrs, Bakanliklar, 06100 Ankara Turkey

BURINI, SONIA MONTES DE OCA, apparel manufacturing and public relations executive; b. Havana, Cuba, Apr. 28, 1935; d. Francisco and Nilda (Diaz) Montes de Oca; m. Franco Burini, Apr. 5, 1959. Student, U. Havana, 1954-57, Georgetown U., 1958; BA in History cum laude, U. Miami, Coral Gables, Fla., 1971. Adminstr. Roma Fashions, Inc. D/B/A Franco B., Coral Gables, 1976-95; entrepreneur, pub. rels. exec., 1995—. Founder Nat. Parkinson Found., 1986—; v.p. Vizcayans Fund Raising Orgn., 1990—, chmn. fine arts events, 1993-95; co-chmn. 1st annual fund raising event Am. Cancer Soc. Winn-Dixie Hope Lodge Ctr.; mem. women with heart group Heart Assn. Greater Miami, Fla., 1981—; founder, bd. dirs. Cancer Link program U. Miami Comprehensive Cancer Ctr., 1987; chmn. spring fantasy luncheon Am. Cancer Soc., 1988; founding chmn. Rose Group, Am. Lung Assn., chmn. Rose Ball, 1989; amb. Mercy Hosp. Found., 1987-95; bd. dirs. Newborn program U. Miami, 1978, bd. dirs., 1982-87, amb. category years; vol. guide Viscaya Mus., Dade County, Fla., 1972-79, chmn. various coms., 1979—, found. bd. dirs., steering com., mem. com. of 100; bd. dir., Young Patroness of the Opera, 1979-87; grand patron Greater Miami Opera, 1986-95, bd. dirs., 1978—, chmn. opera gala, 1987, mem. opera guild, 1988; founding bd. mem. Ears Dears U. Miami, 1986—, chmn. 1990 gala; mem. Dade County Performing Art Ctr. Trust, 1993—; spl. chmn. fine arts events Vizcayans, 1993—; mem. sister cities com. Cities of Miami, Fla. and Nice, France, 1994—, Nat. Trust Hist. Preservation, 1997—. Named Oustanding Woman of Yr. Mayor of Dade County, 1986, Woman of Yr. Heart Assn. Greater Miami, 1986, named to Miss Charity Biscayne Bay Marriott Hotel and Marina, 1987, One of the Leading Ladies for the March of Dimes, 1998. Mem. Nat. Trust Historic Preservation, Ballet Soc. Miami (bd. dirs. 1979-80, named one of Miami's Oustanding Women 1986), Confrerie de la Chaine des Rotisseurs. Home: 700 Coral Way Coral Gables FL 33134-4880 Office: Roma Fashions Inc 3311 Ponce De Leon Blvd Coral Gables FL 33134-7210 also: Corregidor Aguirre 21, Las Palmas de Canaria Spain also: Burini Enterprises, Inc PO Box 347558 Coral Gables FL 33234-7374

BURIONI, ROBERTO, immunologist, virologist, medical educator; b. Pesaro, Italy, Dec. 10, 1962; s. Gaetano and Elvira (Bovicelli) B. MD, Cath. U., Rome, 1987; PhD, U. Genova, 1992. Attending physician A. Gemelli Hosp., Rome, 1987-90, asst. physician, 1990-94, med. dir., 1995-99; postdoctoral fellow U. Calif., San Diego, 1989; vis. investigator Scripps Rsch. Inst., La Jolla, Calif., 1991-94; asst. prof. Cath. U., Rome, 1995-99, Med. Sch. U. Ancona, Italy, 1999—; med. dir. virology Torrette Hosp, Anacona. Office: Servizio Virologia Ospedale, Torrette, Via Conca, 60020 Ancona Italy

BURISCH, MATTHIAS, psychologist, educator. Psychologist, U. Hamburg, 1969, PhD, 1976. Wiss. asst. Universiteaetsklinik Hamburg, Germany, 1970; Wiss. angestellter U. Hamburg, 1971—; cons. in field. Author: The Burnout Syndrome, 1994; contbr. chpt. in book and articles to profl. jours. E-mail: burisch@uni-hamburg.de. Office: Dept Psychology, von Melle Park 5, D-20146 Hamburg Germany

BURJA, ADAM MARTIN, marine microbiologist, epidemiologist; b. Melbourne, Australia, June 27, 1974; s. Peter Zvonko Emil and Cathleen Mary (Martin) B. BS, Melbourne U., Victoria, Australia, 1995; postgrad., Heriot-Watt U., Edinburgh, Scotland. Cert. comml. diver, level 1; sci. scuba diver; first aid and advanced CPR; nucleic acid analyst; recombinant DNA proficient. Tech. officer CSIRO: Australian Animal Health Lab., Geeolong, 1995-96, rsch. officer, 1997; exptl. scientist Australian Inst. Marine Sci., Townsville, 1997-99; organizer Microbial Aquatic Symbiosis Conf., Townsville, 1999—; invited rsch. scientist Russian Acad. Sci., Lake Baikal, 1999. Contbr. articles to profl. jours. Lab. safety officer Australian Inst. Marine Sci., 1997-99. Mem. AAAS, Australian Soc. Microbiology (convenor 1999—), Am. Soc. Microbiology. Roman Catholic. Avocations: scuba diving, golf, Tae Kwon Do. Office: Heriot Watt Univ, Dept Biol Scis, Edinburgh EH14 4AS, Scotland

BURKARD, RAINER ERNST, mathematician, educator; b. Graz, Austria, Jan. 28, 1943; s. Otto Michael and Herta (Waidbacher) B.; m. Heidemarie Knobloch, 1969; children: Michael, Reinhild, Thomas. Dr.phil., U. Vienna, 1967. Asst., U. Graz, Austria, 1967-73; full prof. applied math. U. Cologne, Fed. Republic Germany, 1973-81; prof. math. Tech. U. Graz, Austria, 1981—, dean faculty scis., 1993-96. Author: Methoden ganzz. Optimierung, 1972; (with U. Derigs) Assignment and Matching Problems, 1980. Contbr. articles to profl. jours. Recipient Forderpreis, Austrian Math. Soc., 1971, Sci. prize Soc. Math. Econs. and Ops. Rsch., 1997 Euro Gold medal. Mem. Austrian Ops. Research Soc., Hungarian Acad. of Scis., others. Office: Institut für Mathematik, TU Graz Steyrergasse 30, A-8010 Graz Austria

BURKE, AL, publisher, editor; b. Elizabeth, N.J., Feb. 9, 1943; s. Roland Edward and Edna Marian (Owen) B. MA, Rutgers U., 1969, MPhil, 1972. Lectr. sociology various univs., U.S., 1968-73; editor, pub. Tsitika Publs., Victoria, B.C., Can., 1974-78; owner Sea Otter Prodns., Seattle, 1978-88; freelance writer, translator, Sweden, 1989-92; editor, pub. Nordic News Network, Stockholm, 1993—. Author: Misery in the Name of Freedom, 1988; contbr. articles to profl. jours. and popular publs. Founder Bainbridge-Nicaragua Assn., Bainbridge Island, Wash., 1985-88. Office: Nordic News Network, Box 1181, S-181 23 Lidingö Sweden

BURKE, FRANK DESMOND, orthopedic surgeon, educator; b. Newcastle Upon Tyne, Eng., Mar. 23, 1944; s. Frank and Jay (Fox) B.; m. Linda Margaret Poole, July 18, 1970; children: Richard, Sarah, Timothy. MBBS, U. Newcastle, 1967. Ho. physician, surgeon Royal Victoria Infirmary, Newcastle, 1967-68; surg. fellow registrar rotation U. Newcastle, 1971-73; mem. orthopedic tng. program Oswestry, Eng., 1973-78; hand fellow Derbyshire (Eng.) Royal Infirmary, 1975, cons. hand surgeon, 1978—; hand fellow Derbyshire (Eng.) Royal Infirmary, Louisville, 1976, Iowa City, 1977. Co-author: Principles of Hand Surgery, 1990, Caring for the Hand, 1991. Fellow Royal Coll. Surgeons; mem. Brit. Assn. Hand Therapists (hon., inaugural pres. 1988), Brit. Soc. Surgery of the Hand (sec. 1989-91, pres. 1997), Am. Soc. Surgery of the Hand, Brit. Soc. for Surgery of the Hand. Office: Pulvertaft Hand Ctr, Derbyshire Royal Infirmary, London Derby, England

BURKE, GAY ANN WOLESENSKY, lawyer; b. Crete, Nebr., Apr. 16, 1954; d. Robert Melvin and Camille Mary (Fountain) Wolesensky; m. Richard Donald Crosier, May 12, 1973 (div. 1981); 1 child, Joshua Jay; m. Kenneth John Burke, June 4, 1983; 1 child, John Tynan. BS, Nebr. Wesleyan U., 1975; JD with high distinction, U. Nebr., 1981. Bar: Colo. 1982, Nebr. 1987, U.S. Dist. Ct. Colo. 1983, U.S. Tax Ct. 1987, U.S. Ct. Appeals (10th cir.) 1987. Assoc. Holme Roberts & Owen, Denver, 1982-86, Otten, Johnson, Robinson, Neff & Ragonette, Denver, 1986; ptnr. Burke & Burke, Denver, 1986-88, Massey Burke & Showalter, Denver, 1988-90; sole practice Denver, 1990—; gen. counsel, exec. v.p. E.J. Renner & Assocs. Inc. (dba Malott Peterson Renner Inc.), 1991-93; lectr. U. Denver Coll. Law, 1988-97. Pres., CEO, bd. dirs. Pumpkin Ltd. dba Pumpkin Masters, Inc. 1993—; bd. dirs. Mackintosh Acad. Mem. ABA, Colo. Bar Assn., Nebr. Bar Assn., Order of Coif. Democrat. Presbyterian. Avocation: fly fishing. Office: 1905 Sherman #1000 Denver CO 80203

BURKE, JAMES EDWARD, consumer products company executive; b. Feb. 28, 1925; s. James Francis and Mary (Barnett) B.; m. Alice Eubank, Apr. 27, 1957 (dec.); children: Mary Clotilde, James Charles; m. Diane W. Burke, Nov. 7, 1981. BS in Econs., Holy Cross Coll., 1947; MBA, Harvard U., 1949. Sales rep., then asst. brand mgr., brand mgr. Procter & Gamble, 1949-52; product dir. Johnson & Johnson, 1953-54, dir. new products, 1954-57, dir. advt. and merchandising, 1958-62, gen. mgr. Baby Products Co. divsn., 1962-64, exec. v.p. mktg., 1964-65, gen. mgr. Johnson & Johnson Products Co. divsn., 1965-66, pres., 1966-70, chmn. bd., 1970-71, corp. dir., mem. exec. com., 1973-76, dir., mem. exec. com. parent co., 1965-89, former vice-chmn. exec. com., from 1971, CEO, chmn. bd. parent co., 1976-89. Chmn. Partnership for Drug-Free Am. Ensign USN, WWII, PTO. Office: Johnson & Johnson 100 Albany St Ste 200 New Brunswick NJ 08901-1227

BURKE, JAMES JOSEPH, JR., investment banker; b. Wilmington, Del., Dec. 19, 1951; s. James Joseph and Kathleen Gertrude (Nauss) B.; m. Jeanne Elizabeth Burke, Aug. 6, 1977; children: James III, Jennifer, Brian. AB in Psychology, Brown U., 1973; MBA with distinction, Harvard U., 1979. 2d v.p. Chase Manhattan Bank, N.Y.C., 1973-77; assoc. Merrill Lynch, N.Y.C., 1979-83, v.p., 1983-85, mng. dir., 1985-94; pres., CEO Merrill Lynch Capital Ptnrs., N.Y.C., 1987-94; mng. ptnr. First Capital Ptnrs., N.Y.C., 1994—, Stonington Ptnrs., Inc. (formerly First Capital Ptnrs.), N.Y.C., 1995—; bd. dirs. Ann Taylor Stores Corp., N.Y.C., Burns Internat. Svcs., Chgo., United

Artists Theatre Circuit Inc., Englewood, Colo., Brown U. Third Century Fund, Edn. Mgmt. Corp., Pitts. Pres. In-Sch. Divsn. Boy Scouts Am., N.Y.C.; trustee Seton Hall Prep. Sch., West Orange, N.J.; chmn. Eerie Entertainment, LLC, N.Y.C. Office: Stonington Ptnrs 767 5th Ave New York NY 10153-0023

BURKE, JOHN PATRICK, internist, educator; b. Marshalltown, Iowa, Mar. 19, 1940; s. Raphael Eggleston and Marjorie N. (Busch) B.; m. Andrea Marie Keane, May 9, 1970; children: Paul, Matthew, Edward, Erin. BA, U. Iowa, 1961, MD, 1964. Diplomate Am. Bd. Internal Medicine, Am. Bd. Infectious Disease. Intern Yale-New Haven Hosp., 1964-65, resident in medicine, 1965-67; rsch. fellow Harvard med. unit Boston City Hosp., 1968-70; chief infectious disease sect. Latter-day Saints Hosp., Salt Lake City, 1970—; asst. prof. medicine U. Utah, Salt Lake City, 1970-75, assoc. prof., 1975-83, prof., 1983—, Mark Presdl. endowed chair in medicine, 1999—; spl. reviewer NIH, Bethesda, Md., 1978, 80; mem. tech. panel on infections within hosps. Am. Hosp. Assn., 1996; cons. Inst. Medicine, NAS, 1998—, Ctrs. for Disease Control and Prevention, 1994, 99, Nat. Patient Safety Found., 1999; co-founder, med. dir. TheraDoc.com, Inc., 1999. Mem. editl. bd. Am. Jour. Infection Control, 19805, Infection Control and Hosp. Epidemiology, 1979-88; contbr. numerous articles to med. jours., chpts. to books. Surgeon USPHS, 1967-70. NIH-Nat. Inst. Allergy and Infectious Disease grantee, 1974-79, 79-82, 83-85, 86-89, FDA, 19995. Fellow Infectious Disease Soc. Am., ACP; mem. Soc. for Healthcare Epidemiology Am. (councillor 1981-82, treas. 1985-88, pres. 1992), Am. Med. Info. Assn., Utah Med. Assn. (del. 1975-77), Am. Epidemiol. Soc. Mem. Christian Ch. Home: 1966 Yale Ave Salt Lake City UT 84108-1827 Office: LDS Hosp Med Office Bldg Ste 204 370 9th Ave Salt Lake City UT 84103

BURKE, MICHAEL DESMOND, pathologist; b. Galway, Ireland, May 25, 1935; came to U.S., 1959; s. James and Margaret (McKee) B.; m. Joan Long, June, 1960 (div. Apr. 1966); children: James Niall, Richard Joseph; m. Maria Sperazi, June 19, 1966; children: Marina, Claudia. MB, BCh., BAO, Nat. U. of Ireland, Galway, 1959. Diplomate Am. Bd. of Pathology in Clin., Chem. and Anatomical Pathology. Assoc. pathologist Mt. Sinai Hosp., Mpls., 1969-81; from asst. prof. to prof. pathology U. Minn., Mpls., 1971-81; prof. pathology and dir. clin. pathology U. Hosp. SUNY, Stony Brook, N.Y., 1981-95; prof. pathology, vice chmn. lab. medicine, dir. clin. labs. N.Y. Presbyn. Hosp./Weill Cornell Med. Ctr., N.Y.C., 1996—; Faculty of Pathology fellow Royal Coll. Physicians of Ireland, 1993; trustee Am. Bd. Pathology, Tampa, Fla., 1997; edtl. cons. clin. pathology Stedman's Med. Dictionary 25th edit., 1990. Editor Clinical Decisions and Laboratory Use, U. Minn. Press, 1982; adv. editor Lab. Medicine, 1985; assoc. editor Am. Jour. of Clin. Pathology, 1990-2000. Capt. USAR, 1961-63. Fellow Am. Soc. Clin. Pathologists (pres. 1995-96, Disting. Svc. award 1984, Ward Burdick award 1998), Coll. of Am. Pathologists; mem. AMA, Am. Assn. for Clin. Chemistry (Outstanding Speaker award 1991), Acad. Clin. Lab. Physicians and Scientists (pres. 1993-94, Gerald T. Evans award 1997, Cotlove Lectureship award 1998). Office: NY Presbyn Hosp Cornell Med Ctr 525 E 68th St New York NY 10021-4870

BURKE, PAUL EDMUND, social scientist, activist; b. N.Y.C., June 28, 1948; s. Mack and Patricia Anne (Gill) B. AB in Math., Brown U., 1970, AM in Urban Studies, 1972; postgrad., Johns Hopkins U., Washington, 1974-75. Tchr., adminstr. Apam (Ghana) Secondary Sch., 1970-72; program evaluator HUD, Washington, 1973-78, social scientist, 1978-98; ind. edn. rschr. Washington, 1987—. Author: Senate Guidebook, How to Get Laws You Can Live With, 1991; editor: Researcher's Guide to HUD Data, 1982, American Housing Survey Database, 1978-98; contbr. articles on math. edn., survey design, housing and internat. trade to profl. publs. Chmn. survey com. Group Health Assn. Coop., Washington, 1979; candidate for Washington Bd. Edn., 1987; sponsor contest to describe young adults' experiences after high sch., 1988; coord. for Washington pub. schs. Washington Stats. Soc., 1992-95; bd. dirs. PB, Home Owner Coalition, Shepherdstown Music & Dance. Avocations: sailing, contra dancing. Home: PO Box 1320 Shepherdstown WV 25443-1320

BURKE, (ULICK) PETER, history educator, author; b. Stanmore, Middlesex, Eng., Aug. 16, 1937; s. John Patrick and Jennie (Colin) B.; m. Susan Patricia Dell, 1972 (div. 1983); m. Maria Lucia Garcia Pallares, Mar. 3, 1989. BA, Oxford (Eng.) U., 1960. Lectr., reader history U. Sussex, Brighton, Eng., 1962-78; lectr., reader, then prof. history Cambridge (Eng.) U., 1979—. Author: The Renaissance Sense of the Past, 1969, Culture and Society in Renaissance Italy, 1972, 2nd edit., 1974, ed. edit., 1986, reprinted, 1988, 91, 93, 94, Venice and Amsterdam: A Study of Seventeenth-Century Elites, 1974, Popular Culture in Early Modern Europe, 1978, reprinted, 1979, 83, 88, Dutch Popular Culture in the 17th Century: A Reconnaissance, 1978, Sociology and History, 1980, Montaigne, 1981, reprinted, 1994, Vico, 1985, Historical Anthropology of Early Modern Italy: Essays on Perception and Communication, 1987, reprinted, 1989, 94, The Renaissance, 1987, reprinted, 1989, 90, 92, 93, 2d edit., 1997, Küchenlatein, 1989, Language and Identity in Early Modern Italy, 1989, The French Historical Revolution: The Annales School, 1929-89, 1990, reprinted 1999, The Fabrication of Louis XIV, 1992, paperback edit., 1994, History and Social Theory, 1992, reprinted 1994, 95, 96, 98, O Mundo como Teatro: Estudos de Antropologia Histórica, 1992, Antwerp, A Metropolis in Europe, 1993, The Art of Conversation, 1993, The Fortunes of the Courtier: The European Reception of Castiglione's Cortegiano, 1995, The European Renaissance, 1998; books translated into numerous langs. With Brit. Army, 1955-57. Fellow Royal Hist. Soc. (coun. 1981-84), Brit. Acad., Acad. Europe. Avocation: travel. Home: 14 Warkworth St, Cambridge CB1 1EG, England Office: Cambridge U, Emmanuel Coll, Cambridge CB2 3AP, England

BURKE, PHILIP GEORGE, mathematical physics educator; b. London, Oct. 18, 1932; s. Henry and Frances Mary (Sprague) B.; m. Valerie Mona Martin; children: Helen Frances, Susan Valerie, Pamela Jean, Alice Charlotte. BSc, U. Coll. Southwest Eng., Exeter, Eng., 1953; DSc (hon.), Exeter U., 1981; PhD, U. Coll., London, 1956; DSc (hon.), Queens U., 1999. Rsch. fellow U. Coll., 1956-57; lectr. London U. Computer Unit, 1957-59; rsch. fellow Alvarez bubble chamber group, theory group Lawrence Radiation Lab., Berkeley, Calif., 1959-62; rsch. fellow, sr. prin. sci. officer Ukaea Harwell, Eng., 1962-67; prof. Queens U., Belfast, N. Ireland, 1967-98, emeritus prof., 1998—; head div. theory and computational sci. Joint Appointment with Serc Daresbury Lab., Cheshire, U.K., 1977-82; mem. U.K. Sci. and Engring. Rsch. Coun., Swindon, 1989-94, Joint Policy com. Advanced Rsch. Computing, London, 1988-90, ABRC Supercomputing Sub-Com., 1991-94; chmn. Serc Supercomputing Mgmt. Com., 1991-94. Author 6 books; contbr. articles to profl. jours.; editor numerous jours. Fellow U. Coll. London, 1986. Fellow Royal Soc. (mem. coun. 1990-92), Inst. Physics (Guthrie Medal and Prize 1994), Am. Phys. Soc.; mem. Royal Irish Acad., European Phys. Soc. (CBE 1993). Home: Brook House Norley Ln, Crowton, Northwich CW82RR, England Office: Queens U, Dept Applied Math/Theor Phys, Belfast BT7 1NN, Northern Ireland

BURKE, RANDY SCOTT, psychologist; b. New Bedford, Mass., June 8, 1970; s. Gerald Douglas and Marilyn Linda B. BS, U. Mass., Amherst, 1992; MS, Va. Polytech. Inst., Blacksburg, 1995; PhD, Va. Polytech. Inst., 1999. Doctoral trainee VAMC, Martinsburg, W.V., 1997; adj. instr. Randolph-Macon Woman's Coll., Lynchburg, Va., 1997; psychology resident VAMC/U. Miss. Med. Ctr., Jackson, 1998-99, psychology post-doctoral fellow, 1999—. Reviewer: (jour.) The Journal of Behavioral Health Services and Research; contbr. articles to profl. jours. Recipient Rsch. Travel award, Va. Polytech. Inst., 1998. Mem. APA, Miss. Psychol. Assn., Phi Beta Kappa, Phi Kappa Phi, Golden Key Honor Soc. Independent. Avocations: reading, computers. Fax: 601-984-5857. E-mail: randy.burke@med.va.gov. Home: 16 N Hill Pkwy # D Jackson MS 39206-5563

BURKE, ROBERT HARRY, surgeon, educator; b. Cambridge, Mass., Dec. 22, 1945; s. Harry Clearfield and Joan Rosalyn (Spire) B.; m. Margaret Cauldwell Fisher, May 4, 1968; children: Christopher David, Catherine Cauldwell. Student, U. Mich. Coll. Pharmacy, 1964-67; DDS, U. Mich., 1971, MS, 1976; MD, Mich. State U., 1980. Diplomate Am. Bd. Oral and Maxillofacial Surgery, Am. Bd. Cosmetic Surgery. Pvt. practice cosmetic and reconstructive surgery Ann Arbor, Mich.; house officer oral and maxillofacial surgery U. Mich. Sch. Dentistry, U. Mich. Hosp., Ann Arbor, 1973-76; clin. asst. prof. dept. oral surgery U. Detroit Sch. Dentistry, 1976-77; adj. asst. rsch. scientist Ctr. Human Growth and Devel. U. Mich., 1976-77, adj. rsch. investigator, 1982-85; clin. asst. prof. Mich. State U., East Lansing, 1978-80, 1987—; house officer surg. emphasis St. Joseph Mercy Hosp., Ann Arbor, 1980-81; adj. rsch. investigator dept. anatomy U. Mich. Med. Sch., 1982-85; clin. asst. prof. oral and maxillofacial surgery U. Mich., 1984-86; lectr. U. Detroit Sch. Dentistry, 1986, assoc. clin. prof. oral and maxillofacial surgery, 1987-90; cons., lectr. dept. occlusion U. Mich. Sch. Dentistry, 1986; head sect. dentistry and oral surgery dept. gen. surgery St. Joseph Mercy Hosp., 1982-87, mem. exec. com. dept. gen. surgery, 1984-87; chmn. com. emergency care rev. Beyer Meml. Hosp., Ypsilanti, Mich., 1986, also active, 1987, 1990-2000; active staff St. Joseph Meml. Hosp.; courtesy staff Saline (Mich.) Cmty. Hosp., 1978-88; Chelsea (Mich.) Med. Ctr., 1978-88, 90-92, McPherson Cmty. Hosp., Howell, Mich., 1984-87, Herrick Meml. Hosp., 1998—, Bixby Hosp., 1998—; dir. Mich. Ctr. Cosmetic Surgery. Mem. editl. bd. Topics in Pain Mgmt., 1985—; contbg. editor Am. Jours. Cosmetic surgery, 1990-91; sect. editor Internat. Jour. Aesthetic and Restorative Surgery, 1992-95, 96—. Campaign chmn. med. and dental sects. United Way Washtenaw County, Ann Arbor, 1982, dental sect. 1983; profl. adv. com. March of Dimes Genesee County Valley Chpt., Flint, 1979; pres. Huron Pkwy. Pla. Condominium, 1984—. Fellow ACS, Internat. Coll. Surgeons (bd. dirs. Mich. chpt., vice regent), Am. Coll. Oral and Maxillofacial Surgeons (v.p. 1987-88, pres.-elect 1989-90, pres. 1991-93), Am. Acad. Aesthetic and Restorative Surgery (trustee 1997-99); mem. AMA, Am. Assn. Cosmetic Maxillofacial Surgeons (chmn. bd. dirs. 1997-99), Am. Assn. Craniomaxillofacial Surgeons (pres. 1992—, chmn. bd. dirs. 1997-99), Internat. Soc. Cosmetic Laser Surgeons (trustee 1992-93, sec. 1992), British Soc. for Oral and Maxillofacial Surgeons (assoc.), European Soc. Aesthetic Surgery and Liposuction, Chalmers Lyons Acad. Oral Surgery, European Assn. for Cranio-Maxillofacial Surgery (assoc.), Washtenaw County Med. Soc. (exec.com. sec. 1987-88, pres. 1990), Inst. Study Profl. Risk (bd. dirs. 1985-90), Victor's Club, Pres.'s Club, Omicron Kappa Upsilon. Congregationalist. Avocations: triathlon, chang moo kwan, tae kwon do. Home: 5207 Red Fox Run Ann Arbor MI 48105-9364 Office: 2260 S Huron Pky Ann Arbor MI 48104-5151

BURKE, THOMAS JOHN, communications executive; b. Appleton, Wis., Jan. 23, 1947; s. John George and Rosella Sally (Vanderlois) B.; m. Barbara Jean Koth, June 13, 1970; children: Bradley John, Michael James. BSME, Purdue U., 1970; MBA, Fairleigh Dickinson U., 1979. Registered profl. engr., N.J. Salesman Am. Air Filter, Louisville, 1970-72; product mgr. Polycon, Ramsey, N.J., 1972-74; sales engr. Joy Mfg., N.Y.C., 1974-75; sr. sales engr. Joy Mfg., Chgo., 1975-88; publ. Node News, 1986; pres. Burke Ventures Ltd./Burke Communication Systems, Oak Park, Ill., 1988—; publ. Node News, 1996; pres. Phone Svcs. Internat., Chgo., 1998—; CEO, chmn. bd. dirs. ProCom Network Svc. Inc., 2000—; Jaycee trainer Life Dynamics, Chgo., 1983-86; lectr. Leadership Tng., Chgo., 1983-87; cons. Time Mgmt., Chgo., 1983-87; co-owner Minou Cafe & Bakery, Oak Park, Ill., 1986-92; chmn. bd. ProCom Network Services, 2000. Author: Dream Genesis, 1986, History of Imperial Hotel and Frank Lloyd Wright, 1987; co-pub. Chic Menu Guide. Pres. Oak Park Austin Coun. for Community Rels., 1983-87; mem. edn. com., pub. speaker Frank Lloyd Wright Home and Studio, 1986—; officer Oak Park Mall Merchants Assn., 1988-92; cub master Boy Scouts Am., Oak Park, 1985-89. Mem. Oak Park C. of C. (Athena judge Best Bus. Women of Yr. 1988—), Friends of Small Bus., Entrepreneurial Coun., Jaycees (v.p. 1983-86, Oak Park Jaycee of Yr. 1983), TLC Book Club (co-counder). Achievements include development of whole new generation of telecommunication services under the product name Magi Call, which is the first two-way prepaid phone card. Avocations: sailing, reading, bicycling, art. E-mail: tomburke@magicallone.com. Home: 742 N Taylor Ave Oak Park IL 60302-1750

BURKE, THOMAS JOSEPH, civil engineer; b. Grosse Pointe Park, Mich., Sept. 1, 1927; s. Cyril Joseph and Marie Estelle (Sullivan) B.; BCE, Villanova U., 1949; m. Elaine Kiefer, Nov. 10, 1951; children: Judy Lee Burke Brooks, Kathleen Marie Harness, Maureen Elaine Beck, Thomas P. Chmn., Burke Rental Service, Sterling Heights, Mich., 1949—, Cyril J. Burke, Inc., Sterling Heights, Mich., 1949—. Trustee Villanova U., 1980—. Served to lt. USAF, Korea. Mem. ASCE, Detroit Builders Exchange (v.p. 1976-78, dir. 1975-78), Associated Equipment Distbrs. (dir. 1955-58, 75-78), Associated Underground Contractors (dir. 1965-68), Mich. Ready Mix Concrete Assn. (dir. 1960-65), Villanova U. Alumni Assn. (nat. v.p. 1978-79, nat. pres. 1980), Detroit Engring. Soc. Roman Catholic. Clubs: Grosse Pointe Yacht, Otsego Ski, Ocean Reef, Detroit Athletic, Villanova U. of Detroit (pres. 1955-65). Home: 578 Shelden Rd Grosse Pointe MI 48236-2640 also: 688 N Lakeshore Rd Port Sanilac MI 48469-9713 Office: PO Box 8010 36000 Mound Rd Sterling Heights MI 48311-8010

BURKEE, IRVIN, artist; b. Kenosha, Wis., Feb. 6, 1918; s. Omar Lars and Emily (Quardokas) B.; m. Bonnie May Ness, Apr. 12, 1945; children: Brynn, Jill, Peter (dec.), Ian (dec.). Diploma, Sch. Art Inst. Chgo., 1943, postgrad., 1944-45. Owner, silversmith, goldsmith Burkee Jewelry, Blackhawk, Colo., 1950-57; painter, sculptor, Aspen, Colo., 1957-78, Cottonwood, Ariz., 1978-92, Pietrasanta, Italy, 1978—; instr. art U. Colo., 1946, 50-53, Stephens Coll., Columbia, Mo., 1947-49. John Quincy Adams travel fellow, Mex., 1945. Executed copper mural of human history of Colo, 1st Nat. Bank, Englewood, 1970, of wild birds of Kans., Ranchmart State Bank, Overland Park, 1974, copper, bronze and silver mural of Rocky Mountain wild birds for Aspen Ctr. Environ. Studies, 2000; exhibited in group shows Art Inst. Chgo., Smithsonian Instn. (award 1957), Milw. Art Inst., Krannert Mus., William Rockhill Nelson Gallery, St. Louis Art Mus., Denver Art Mus.; represented in southwestern galleries, also pvt. collections throughout U.S.; work illustrated in books Design and Creation of Jewelry, Design through Discovery, Walls. Rocky Mountain Coll. Sculpture grantee, 1972. Mem. Nat. Sculpture Soc., Sedona Chamber Music Soc. (painter yearly festival poster 1989—). Address: PO Box 5361 Lake Montezuma AZ 86342-5361

BURKE-FANNING, MADELEINE, artist; b. New Orleans, Feb. 12, 1941; d. Henry Raymond Burke Sr. and Ella Mae Falgout-Burke; children: Denise Angele Duizend-Glenn, Michele Renee Duizend-Meyer, Jeanne Monet Duizend-Fillman; m. Joel Cornell Fanning, Mar. 28, 1981. Student, Pensacola (Fla.) Jr. Coll., 1988-96. coord. New Orleans World Trade Ctr., Pensacola Cultural Ctr.; adj. prof. advanced watercolor Pensacola Jr. Coll.; tchr., workshops; instr. advanced watercolor City of Pensacola, Vickrey Ctr., Fla. One-woman shows include Michele Dion Gallery, 1994, Soho Gallery, 1994, Wise Choice Gallery, 1996, The Wright Place, 1997, Awakenings, Gulf Breeze, Fla., 1997-98, The Shoppe Gallery, 1998, Pensacola Mus. Art, 1998, Adams Street Gallery, 1998, Ducks Unltd., Pensacola, 1998, Right Angles Gallery, Pensacola, 1999, Kate Holmes-Branton Gallery, Pensacola, 1999, 2000, The Art Market, Gulf Breeze, Fla., 2000, Art and Design Soc. Ft. Walton Beach, Fla., 2000, White Cloud Gallery and Gifts, Pensacola, 2000, Sam Houston Racetrack, Houston, 2000; exhibited in group shows including Pensacola Jr. Coll., 1988-96, Gnu Zoo, 1995, 96, Eastern Shore Mus. Art, Fairhope, Ala., 1994, 95, 96, Pensacola Regional Airport, 1996, World Trade Ctr., 1996, Schmidt's Gallery, 1996, Pensacola Cultural Ctr., 1997, Adams Street Gallery, 1998, Artel Gallery, 1999, Right Angles Gallery, Pensacola, 1999, ARTEL, Inc., 1998, Art with an Edge; host TV show Art and Healing, 1997; TV feature Inside Scope, New Orleans, 1993; TV show Art Vision, 1994, Cultural Center BLAB TV, 1996. Art judge Just Say No Program, 1996-97, PTA Reflective Program, 1997-98; art chairwoman Pensacola chpt. Ducks Unltd., 1998; instr. Ctr. Ind. Living, Pensacola, 1998-2000, Vickery Ctr., Pensacola, 2000—, Pensacola Jr. Coll., 2000—. Recipient Rockport Pubs. award of distinction for inclusion in Best of Watercolor: Painting Texture, 1997. Mem. Am. Soc. Portrait Artists, Nat. Mus. Women in Arts, Fla. Watercolor Soc., La. Watercolor Soc., Tallahassee Watercolor Soc., Pensacola Mus. Art, Woodbine Figure Painters, Bay Cliff Watercolor Soc. (founder), Artel.Art with an Edge. Avocations: gardening, reading, travel, sailing, photography. Home and Studio: Palm Cottage Studio 4160 Rommitch Ln Pensacola FL 32504-4490

BURKE-KENNEDY, DESMOND B., marketing executive; b. Dublin, Ireland, Nov. 11, 1942; s. Bernard E. and Esther (Nagle) B.; m. Mary Patricia Finnegan, Aug. 15, 1969; children: Wendy, Sam. BBS, Trinity Coll., Dublin, Ireland, 1968, MA, 1994. Mng. dir. Chloride Ltd., Dublin, 1981-87, Advance Tyre Co., Dublin, 1988—; mng. dir. D'Orlan Ltd., London, 1986. Mem. Inst. Mktg., Internat. Waterski Fedn. (world media chmn. 1998, 99, chmn. Irish chpt., chmn. Golden Falls chpt. 1988—). Avocations: waterskiing, motor racing. Home: Mount Salus Knocknacree Rd, Dublin Ireland Office: Advance Tyre Co Ltd, Advance House JFK Drive, Dublin 12, Ireland

BURKERT, WALTER, Greek language educator, historian; b. Neuendettelsau, Germany, Feb. 2, 1931; arrived in Switzerland, 1969; s. Adolf and Luise (Grossmann) B.; m. Maria Bosch, Aug. 1, 1957; children: Reinhard, Andrea, Cornelius. PhD, U. Erlangen, Fed. Republic Germany, 1955; LLD (hon.), U. Toronto, Ont., Can., 1988; PhD (hon.), U. Fribourg, Switzerland, 1989, Oxford (Eng.) U., 1996. Dozent U. Erlangen, 1961-65; jr. fellow Ctr. Hellenic Studies, Washington, 1965-66; prof. Tech. U. Berlin, 1966-69, U. Zürich, Switzerland, 1969-96; Sather prof. U. Calif., Berkeley, 1977. Author: Lore and Science in Ancient Pythagoreanism, 1972, Homo Necans, 1983, Greek Religion, 1985, Greek Mystery Cults, 1987, The Orientalizing Revolution, 1992, Creation of the Sacred, 1996; contbr. numerous articles to scholarly publs. Decorated Orden Pour le Mérite; recipient C.F. Gauss medal Braunschweigische Wissenschaftliche Gesellschaft, 1982, Balzan prize, 1990, Ingersoll prize, 1992. Mem. Heidelberger Akademie der Wissenschaften, Bayerische Akademie der Wissenschaften, Oesterreichische Akademie der Wissenschaften, Berlin-Brandenburgische Akademie der Wissenschaften, Brit. Acad., Am. Philos. Soc., Am. Acad. Arts and Scis. Home: Wildsbergstrasse 8, CH-8610 Uster Switzerland Office: Klassisch-Philologisches Seminar, Rämistrasse 68, CH-8001 Zurich Switzerland

BURKE-SMITH, KATRIN KANDEL, investment bank executive; b. Balt.; d. Nelson Robert and Brigitte (Kleemaier) Kandel; m. Andrew Jon Burke-Smith, Apr. 16, 1991; children: Alexandra, Peter. Student, U. Munich, 1979-80; BA, U. Pa., 1980; MA, Johns Hopkins U., 1983; student, Cambridge (Eng.) U., 1984; JD, U. Balt., 1986; student Kings Coll. Law Faculty, U. London, 1986-87. Analyst German, Citicorp Scrimageour Vickors, London, 1988-90; mng. dir. SAL:Oppenheim Jr. & Cie Securities (U.K.) Ltd., London, 1991—. Tchg. fellow Johns Hopkins U., 1980-83. Mem. German Honor Soc. Office: SAL Oppenheim Securities, Saddlers Ho Gutter Lane, London EC2V 6BR, England

BURKETT, GERALD ARTHUR, lawyer, musician; b. Oklahoma City, Apr. 23, 1939; s. Francis Gerald and Leta Carey (Weaver) B.; m. Carolyn Ruth Hicks, Aug. 7, 1960; 1 child, Debora Lynne Burkett Nutt. BA, David Lipscomb U., 1962; MA, Peabody Coll., 1967; JD, Nashville Sch. of Law, 1974. Bar: Tenn. 1975, U.S. Dist. Ct. (mid. dist.) Tenn., 1976, U.S. Ct. Appeals (6th cir.), 1977, U.S. Tax Ct., 1981, U.S. Supreme Ct. 1993. Leader Fritz's German Band, Nashville, 1972-97; pvt. practice law office Nashville, 1975—; jud. commr. Met. Nashville/Davidson County, Tenn., 1999—; adj. instr. Vol. State Community Coll., Gallatin, Tenn., 1979-93, Nashville State Tech. Inst., 1984-89; band leader Strohaus, 1982 World's Fair, Knoxville, 1982. Conductor of German band for commls. and concerts including Monday Night Football, 1994-2000, Super Bowl, 1995, Oktoberfest Concert, Soldier Field, Chgo., 1995. Accordionist Charlie Rich's Bi-Centennial Album, 1976, film soundtrack Sweet Dreams, 1983. Mem. Nashville Assn. Musicians, Alliance Francaise (treas. 1985-86), Nashville Bar Assn., Tenn. Assn. of Spanish Spkg. Attys., Phi Delta Kappa (treas. 1967-68). Mem. Ch. of Christ. Avocations: travel, foreign languages. Office: PO Box 8566 Hermitage TN 37076-8566

BURKETT, HELEN, artist; b. Washington, Feb. 15, 1942; d. Harding Theodore and Helen Louise (Torris) B.; m. J.D. Collins, Sept. 1, 1961 (Apr. 16, 1975); children: Mark W. Collins, Donna L. Collins; m. Charles Talbot Marshall, Dec. 24, 1975; 1 child, Gabrielle T. Marshall. Student, Strayer Sch. of Bus., 1960-61, Corcoran Sch. of Art, 1968-69, Md. U., 1970-73, Hilton Leech Studio-Gallery, 1976-80, Ringling Sch. Art, 1980-81. Asst. to dir. Hilton Leech Studio, Sarasota, Fla., 1975-80, workshop organizer, figure study coord., 1978-80; demonstrator, tchr., artist, owner/operator Helen Burkett Studios, Sarasota, Fla., 1975—; juror Ann Arbor St. Art Fair, 1998. One person show at Manatee Jr. Coll., 1984, Ctrl. Fla. C.C., Ocala, 1987, State Capitol, Tallahassee, Fla., Divsn. Cultural Affairs, Sec. State Offices, 1997; exhibited in group show at WNat. atercolor Soc. Show, Thousand Oaks, Calif., 1999; permanent exhibits include Ctrl. Fla. C.C., Ocala, Epsom Clinic, Orlando, Fla., Orlando Sentinel, Winter Park (Fla.) Meml. Hosp., Polk Mus., Lakeland, Fla., The Disney Corp., The Ford Motor Co., The Amoco Corp., Fla. Dept. State, Hayfield Mansion, Louisville, The Former Duchess of Winsor; exhibitor numerous art festivals, 1987—; subject of periodical The Artist Mag., 1992, The Am. Artist Mag., 1996, also newspaper article Ann Arbor News, 1998. Tchr. Vis. Artist Program, Coconut Grove, Fla., 1990—; artist, tchr. Donne Bitner Studio, Cocoa Beach, Fla., 1996. Recipient 2d prize in watercolor U. Tampa, 1991, 93, 1st prize in watercolor Lowe Art Mus./U. Miami, 1992, Purchase award Festival of the Masters-Disney Corp., 1995, Purchase award Wayne State U.-Ford Motor Co., 1995. Mem. ACLU, NOW, Am. Watercolor Soc. (assoc.), Nat. Watercolor Soc. (assoc.), Nat. Assn. Ind. Artists, Sarasota Art Assn. (bd. dirs. 1980-82), Fla. Watercolor Soc. (life, Award of Distinction 1985, 92), So. Watercolor Soc., Mich. Guild Artists. Avocations: photography, reading, hiking, bicycling. Home and Studio: Helen Burkett Studio 2988 Oak St Sarasota FL 34237-7346

BURKHALTER, SUSAN SHIVELY, music educator, organist; b. Washington, Apr. 16, 1946; d. William Mays and Thelma Louise (Kanatzer) B.; m. Curtis Allen Shively, Feb. 5, 1977; children: Rachel Mirabel, Stuart William. MusB, Coll. Wooster, 1970. Organist, choir dir. Olivet Episcopal Ch., Springfield, Va., 1976-77; children's choir dir. Our Savior Lutheran Ch. and Sch., Arlington, Va., 1997-1998; pvt. piano tchr., freelance organist, 1976—; advisor music majs. Coll. Wooster, Ohio, 1995—. Contbr. mags. and newspapers including Washington Post, American Organist, Psychology Today, and more; performer in various concerts. Vol. Carderock Springs Elem. Sch., Bethesda, Md., 1988-95, Pyle Middle Sch., 1994-2000, Walt Whitman High Sch., 1997—; mem. Sierra Club, ASPCA, World Wildlife Fund, African Wildlife Fund; mem. Gen. Fedn. Women's Clubs, Suburban Women's Club of Montgomery County, Md., 1999—. Mem. Music Tchrs. Nat. Assn., Am. Guild Organists, Carderock Springs Swim and Tennis Club. Democrat. Avocations: cats, sewing, gardening, art, writing poetry. Home: 7504 Hamilton Spring Rd Bethesda MD 20817-4542

BURKHANOV, GENNADII SERGEEVICH, metallurgical engineer; b. Moscow, Sept. 18, 1932; s. Sergei Fedotovich and Nina Ivanovna (Kirillova) B.; m. Kalinina Lyubov Viktorovna; 1 child: Elena Gennadievna. BS, Moscow Inst. Steel and Alloys, 1955; PhD, Baikov Inst. Metallurgy, 1961, DSc, 1975. Rsch. scientist Baikov Inst. Metallurgy, Acad. Scis. Russia, Moscow, 1958-63, sr. rsch. scientist, 1963-84, head lab. pure refractory and rare metals/alloys, 1984—; cons. Plant of refractory and High Temp. Metals, Chirchik, Uzbekistan, 1960—, Soyuztverdosplav, Moscow, 1960—, Magneton, Vladimir, Russia, 1970—, Inst. Chemistry of High-Purity Substances of Acad. Sci., N. Novgorod, 1970—; disting. prof. Baikov Inst. Metallurgy, Russian Acad. Scis., 1986; mem. sci. spel. coun. Inst. Chemistry of High-Purity Substances, 1987—. Co-author: Physical Metallurgy of Refractory Metals and Alloys, 1971, Properties of Elements, 1985, High-Purity Refractory and Rare Metals, 1997, others; patentee in field; contbr. over 250 articles to profl. jours.; editl. adv. bd. Inorganic Materials, 1985—. Mem. Acad. Nature Scis. Russia (corr., sci. coun. on problem of chemistry of high-purity inorganic materials 1985—), N.Y. Acad. Scis. Avocation: popular and sci. literature. Fax: (095) 135-15-70. Home: ul Akd Anokhina 38-1-77, 117602 Moscow Russia Office: Baikov Inst Metallurgy/Matl, Leninskii pr 49, 117911 Moscow Russia

BURKHARD, DOROTHEE J. M., geology educator; b. Friedberg, Hessen, Germany, May 9, 1956; d. Wolfgang and Marietheres (esser) B. Arbitur, Goethe Gymnasium, Dortmund, Germany, 1975; diploma, U. Zürich, Switzerland, 1982; PhD, U. Heidelberg, Germany, 1987; Habilitation, U. Marburg, Germany, 1995. Rschr. U. Melbourne, Australia, 1988-90; docent U. Utrecht, The Netherlands, 1990-94; tchr., rschr. U. Marburg, 1995—. Recipient award Studienstiftung des Deutschen Volkes, 1984-97; Heisenberg fellow, 1995-98. Home: Hinterfeld 20, 35043 Marburg Germany Office: Univ Marburg, Inst For Mineralogy, 35032 Marburg Germany

BURKHARDT, EDWARD ARNOLD, railway executive; b. N.Y.C., July 23, 1938; s. Edward Arnold Burkhardt Sr. and Kathryn C. (Pfister) Dow; m. Sandra Kay Schwaegel, June 9, 1967; 1 child, Cynthia Kay. BS Indsl. Adminstrn., Yale U., 1960. Various operating positions Wabash R.R., St. Louis, 1960-64, Norfolk and Western Rlwy., St. Louis, 1964-67; asst. to gen.

mgr. Chgo. Northwestern Transp. Co., 1967-68, gen. supt. transp., 1968-70, asst. v.p. transp., 1970-76, v.p. mktg., 1976-79, v.p. transp., 1979-87; bd. dirs., chmn., pres., CEO Wis. Ctrl. Transp. Corp., Chgo., 1987-99, also bd. dirs.; chmn. Tranz Rail Ltd., 1993-99; pres. Algoma Ctrl. Rlwy. Inc., 1995-99; pres./CEO Rail World, Inc., 1999—; pres. RailPolska, 1999—; bd. dirs., chmn., CEO English, Welsh and Scottish Ry. Ltd., 1995-99; bd. dirs., chmn. Australian Transport Network, 1997-99; pres. CargoCentral Europe, 2000—; chmn. Baltic Rail Svc., 2000—. Trustee Village of Kenilworth, Ill., 1984-93; bd. dirs. Wheeling & Lake Erie Rlwy. Co., Nat. Transport Mus., York, England, Lake Superior Mus. Transp., Duluth, Minn., John W. Barringer R.R. Libr., St. Louis, U.S./New Zealand Coun., Washington. Hon. consul New Zealand, Chgo. Mem. Am. Assn. R.R. Supts., Western Ry. Club, Kenilworth Club, Union League Club. Republican. Episcopalian. Home: 573 Earlston Rd Kenilworth IL 60043-1014 Office: Rail World Inc 8600 W Bryn Mawr Ave Chicago IL 60631-3579

BURKHARDT, FREDERICK HENRY, editor; b. Bklyn., Sept. 13, 1912. BA, Columbia U., 1933; LittB, Oxford U., 1935; PhD, Columbia U., 1940, LLD (hon.), 1974; LLD (hon.), Mich. U., 1968, Ball State U., 1976. Instr., asst. prof. philosophy U. Wis., Madison, 1937-43, assoc. prof. philosophy, 1946-47; pres. Bennington (Vt.) Coll., 1947-57, Am. Coun. Learned Socs., N.Y.C., 1957-74; gen. editor The Works of William James, 19 vols. Harvard Press, 1975-88; editor The Corr. of Charles Darwin, 11 vols. sponsored by ACLS and Cambridge U. Libr., 1985—; rsch. analyst Office of Strategic Svcs., 1943-45; acting chief Divsn. Rsch. for Europe, Dept. State, 1945-46; dep. dir. Office Pub. Affairs, U.S. High Commr. for Germany, 1950-51; mem. N.Y.C. Bd. Higher Edn., 1966-73, chmn., 1969-71; trustee N.Y. Pub. Libr., 1970-71, chmn., 1974; chmn. Nat. Commn. on Librs. and Info. Sci., 1971-78. Editor, translator: J.G. Herder: God, Some Conversations [on Spinoza's System], 1940, 62; editor: Cleavage in Our Culture, 1952; contbr. The Comparative Reception of Darwinism, 1975. Lt. USNR, 1944-46. Recipient Alumni award for excellence Columbia U., 1987, Morton N. Cohen award for disting. edition of letters MLA, 1991. Mem. Am. Philos. Soc., Am. Acad. Arts and Scis., Century Assn. E-mail: fhb@sover.net. Home and Office: PO Box 1067 Bennington VT 05201-1067

BURKHARDT, MARTIN, design engineer; b. Berlin, Oct. 23, 1963; arrived in The Netherlands, 1998; s. Peter and Lilo Burkhardt. Diploma in engring., Tech. U. Berlin, 1988; PhD, MIT, 1995. Mem. tech. staff Tex. Instruments Inc., Dallas, 1995-98; sr. designer ASML, Eindhoven, The Netherlands, 1998—. Mem. IEEE, SPIE, Sigma Xi. Home: Stationsweg 22, 5611 BX Eindhoven The Netherlands

BURKHARDT, THOMAS DIRK RALF, finance educator; b. Saarlouis, Germany, Mar. 8, 1965; s. Heinz and Anita (Fonck) B. Diploma in physics, U. Göttingen, Germany, 1990, diploma in bus. adminstrn. and econs., 1992, Dr.rer.pol., 1994. Rsch. asst. Inst.Betriebswirtschaftliche Geldwirtschaft/U. Göttingen, 1990-94; postdoctoral fellow UCLA, 1994-95; asst. prof. fin. U. Freiberg, Germany, 1995—. Author: Down-and-Out Optionen, 1994; contbr. articles to profl. jours. Mem. AEA, DGF, Verein für Socialpolitik. Office: TU Bergakademie Freiberg, Lessingstr 45, D-09596 Freiberg Germany

BURKIEWICZ, KRYSTYNA, plant physiologist; b. Gdynia, Poland, Oct. 27, 1952; d. Henryk Jerzy and Maria Wiesława (Leszczyszyn) Kluszczynska; m. Adam Mikołaj Burkiewicz, Jan. 21, 1978 (div. Mar. 1986); 1 child, Mikołaj Michał. BSc, Gdańsk U., Gdynia, 1976, PhD, 1985. Student asst. Gdańsk U., 1977-78, asst. lectr., 1978-85; prof.'s asst., 1985—, asst. head dept. plant physiology, 1986-87, tutor, 1994-96; pres. specialistic group Ctr. of Tchr. Edn., Gdańsk, 1994—; pres. Reg. Com. of biol. Olympiad, Gdynia, 1996—. Contbr. articles to profl. jours. Recipient Rector's award Gdańsk U., 1979, 81, 83, 88, grant for sci. rsch., 1994, 95, 97, 99, 00, Pres.'s award Ctrl. Com. of biol. Olympiad, 1993, 99, medal Nat. Edn. Commn., 1997. Fellow Polish Bot. Soc. (bd. dirs.), Fedn. European Socs. Plant Physiology. Avocations: books, gardening, walking. Office: Gdańsk U Dept Plt Phys, Al Piłsudskiego 46, 81-378 Gdynia Poland

BURKIN, ALFRED RICHARD, extractive metallurgy educator; b. London, Sept. 23, 1923; s. Alfred William and Theodora Kathleen (Specht) B.; m. Ruth May Partridge, July 5, 1949. BSc in Chemistry, U. London, 1943, MSc, 1945, PhD, 1949. Chartered chemist, chartered engr. Rsch. chemist Ilford Ltd., London, 1943-46; lectr. chemistry Univ. Coll., U. Southampton (Eng.), 1946-52; lectr. mineral tech. Royal Sch. Mines, Imperial Coll., London, 1952-60, lectr. hydrometallurgy, 1960-66, reader hydrometallurgy, 1966-82, prof. hydrometallurgy, 1982-88; emeritus prof. hydrometallurgy Imperial Coll., London, 1988—; cons. in field, London, 1966-86; bd. dirs. Consort Rsch. Ltd., London, 1986-97. Fellow Royal Soc. Chemistry (hon.), Instn. Mining and Metallurgy (hon.); mem. Soc. Chem. Industry (chmn. CRAC, editorial bd. 1989-96). Conservative. Office: Imperial Coll, Imperial Coll/TH Huxley Sch, RSM Bldg, London SW7 2BP, England

BURKINA, ROSA SEMYONOVNA, physics educator; b. Zaporozarje, Ukraine, Dec. 9, 1950; d. Semyon Lazarevich and Vera Maksimovna (Karaulova) Goldman; m. Viktor Vladimirovich Burkin, Feb. 19, 1974; 1 child, Maksim. Degree in engring. and physics, Tomsk (Russia) State U., 1974, PhD, 1982. Asst. Tomsk State U., 1974-83, asst. prof., 1983—. Co-author: (textbook) Asymptotics of Combustion Problems, 1982. Mem. Combustion Inst. of Inst. of Mechanics Problems (Russian sect.). Avocation: chess. E-mail: roza@ftf.tsu.ru. Office: Phys Tech Fac Tomsk State U, 36 Lenin Ave, 634050 Tomsk Russia

BURKOV, ILYA VLADIMIROVICH, mathematician educator; b. Leningrad, Russia, June 30, 1962; s. Vladimir A. and Olga A. (Terent'eva) B.; m. Olga A. Zhidkova, 1987 (div. 1997); 1 child, Ekaterina. Diploma in math., Leningrad U., 1984; PhD in Math., St. Petersburg (Russia) U., 1993; diploma in mgmt., U. Mich., 1997. Engr. St. Petersburg Tech. U., 1984-87, 90-91, asst. prof., 1991-98, assoc. prof., 1999—. Contbr. articles to profl. jours. Grantee Russian Found. Fundamental Rsch., Moscow, 1993-96, German Office Acad. Exch., Bonn, 1996, Ford Rsch. Lab., Detroit, 1997. Avocations: skiing, swimming. E-mail: burkov@osipenko.stu.neva.ru. Office: St Petersburg Tech U, Politehnicheskaya St 29, 195251 St Petersburg Russia

BURKS, JACK D., investment executive; b. San Antonio, Apr. 1, 1951; s. D.C. and Inez M. (Lyons) B.; m. Pamela Kay Bowen. BA, Ind. U., 1972, MBA, 1979. V.p. Pitts. Nat. Bank, 1973-84; mgr. dir. Offitbank, N.Y.C., 1984—. Bd. dirs. Alzheimers Assn., N.Y.C., 1994-98. Avocations: travel, military history, wine.

BURKS, ROCKY ALAN, independent living center executive, consultant; b. San Bernardino, Calif., June 12, 1952; s. Lloyd Jackson and Vivian Elnora B.; m. Nikki Ann Stone (div. 1974); 1 child, Gannon LeRoy; m. Lydia Ann Deatherage, Aug. 20, 1983. BA in Social Welfare, Calif. State U., Chico, 1979, BA in Sociology, 1979. Instrument flight instr. USAF, Del Rio, Tex., 1971-75; dir. outreach and recruitment, Office of Vets. Affairs Calif. State U., Chico, 1976-81; exec. dir. Easter Seal Soc. of Butte County, Chico, 1981-82, No. Calif. Ind. Living Program, Chico, 1982-85; soc. worker Butte County (Calif.) Welfare Dept., 1985-87; exec. dir. Ind. Living Svcs. of N. Calif., Inc., Chico, 1988—; bd. dirs. Calif. Coalition of Ind. Living Ctrs., Sacramento, Calif., pres., 1991-94; bd. dirs. Pub. Interest Ctr. on Long-term Care, Sacramento, treas., 1994-98; mem. disability access adv. bd. Divsn. of the State Arch., Sacramento, 1995-99, Disabled Access Bd. of Appeals, Butte County Building Divsn., Oroville, 1994—; mem. disability access code adv, com. Calif. Bldg. Stds. Commn., 1999—; bd. dirs. Nonprofits' Ins. Alliance of Calif., Santa Cruz, 1999—. Editor: (newsletter) Independent Life, 1988—, Voice, 1976-81. Mem. Transp. Adv. Commn., Butte County Assn. Govts., Oroville, 1992—; mem. Californians for Disability Rights. Recipient Cert. of Congl. Recognition, Congressman Wally Herger, Chico, 1993, 96, Disability Advocate award Calif. Assn. Persons with Handicaps, 1994, Region IX Disability Advocate award Nat. Coun. Ind. Living, 1998, Master Instr. award Air Tng. Command, USAF, 1975; named citizen Chickasaw Indian Nation. Mem. Am. Legion, Vietnam Vets. Am., Masons, Shriners, Scottish Rite, Chico Breakfast Lions (pres. 1991-92, Lion of Yr. award 1990, Melvin Jones fellow), Lions Eye Found. Calif. and Nev. (life). Avocations: scuba diving, boating, reading, art. Home: 4135 Keefer Rd Chico CA 95973-8956 Office: Ind Living Svcs No Calif 1161 East Ave Chico CA 95926-1018

BURLACU, CONSTANTIN, journalist, educator; b. Botosani, Romania, Jan. 20, 1949; came to U.S., 1980; s. Petru and Elena (Matei) B.; m. Elisabeta Busaga, Apr. 4, 1974; children: Monica, Johnny. BS, U. Nicolas Doubloway, Santiago, Chile, 1994; MA, Pacific Western U., 1996; D (hon.), U. Nicolas Doubloway, 1994; PhD, Pacific Western U., 2000. Chmn. The League of Nat. Def., N.Y.C., 1985—; pub. The New Right Mag., N.Y.C., 1985—; dep. mem. assembly Internat. Parliament for Safety and Peace, Sicily, Italy, 1993—; consul gen. Oceanus Govt., Miami, Fla., 1996—; prof. U. Nicolas Doublaway, 1996—. Author: The History of Nationalism in Eastern Europe: A Study of Its Origins and Background in Romania, 1996, History of Moldova and its Connection with Political and Social Circumstances from the Earlist Time to the Present Day, 1998. Mem. Rep. Nat. Com., Washington, 1985—, Rep. Presdl. Legion of Merit, Washington, 1993—, Rep. Presdl. Task Force, Washington, 1989—, Am. Fedn. Police, Miami, 1990—, N.Y. State Fraternal Order Police, N.Y.C., 1998—. Named Knight, Sovereign Noble Religious Order of St. Tatjana, Belgium, 1994; recipient Presdl. Order of Merit, Nat. Rep. Senatorial Com., 1991, Citizen of Yr. award Principality of Hutt River Province, Australia, 1995, Polish Patriotic Eagle Freedom award, Salem, Mass., 1989; diplomate of honor The League of Romanian Freedom Fighters, Brasov, Romania, 1989, diploma of honor Anticomunist Revolutionary Movement, Brasov, 1997. Mem. NRA, Nat. Rep. Senatorial Com., Nat. Rep. Congl. Com., Freedom Army, Amnesty Internat. USA, Am. Defense Com., Am. Security Coun., Liberty Lobby, Reform Party, Populist Action Com., New Iron Guard. Avocations: reading, swimming, hunting, keeping up with current events. E-mail: dacialan@aol.com. Fax: 718-381-3804. Home: 464 Woodward Ave Ridgewood NY 11385-1533 Office: League of Nat Def PO Box 292 Brooklyn NY 11237-0292

BURLAKA, DMYTRO PETROVYCH, experimental oncologist, researcher; b. Village of Dmytroushky, Ukraine, Jan. 4, 1952; s. Petro Vlasovych and Nadiya Terentiyivna (Bardakova) B.; m. Halyna Mykolayivna Tarnovs'ka, Aug. 14, 1982; children: Oleg, Marina. Grad. in biology, physiology, Shevtshenko State U., Kyiv, Ukraine, 1978; med. radioelect. diploma, 1980; candidate in biol. scis., Inst. Exptl. Pathology, Oncology, Radiobiology, Kyiv, Ukraine, 1992. Mem. faculty med. radioelectronics Kyiv People U. Tech. Progress, 1978-80; sr. lab. worker R.E. Kavetsky Inst. Pathology, Oncology & Radiobiology, 1978-84, jr. rschr., 1984-92, rschr., 1992-95, sr. rschr., 1995—. Contbr. articles to profl. jours. Mem. Eurosci. Avocations: radio-engineering, photography. Office: Inst Exptel Pathology Oncol, Vasylkivs'ka 45, 03022 Kyiv Ukraine

BURLAND, BRIAN BERKELEY, novelist, poet, painter, scenarist; b. Paget, Bermuda, Apr. 23, 1931; s. Gordon Hamilton and Honor Alice Croydon (Gosling) B.; m. Charlotte Ann Taylor, 1952 (div. 1957); children: Susan, Anne, William; m. Edwina Ann Trentham, 1962 (div. 1979); 1 child, Benjamin; m. Isabella Petrie, 1990 (div. 1999). Grad., Aldenham Sch., Elstree, Eng., 1948; student, U. Western Ont., Can., 1948-51. Mng. dir. Burland Estates, Ltd., Gosling Estates, Ltd.; 1st v.p. G.H. Burland & Co., Ltd., 1951-56; assoc. editor Bermudian Mag., 1957; lectr. Am. Sch., London, 1974, Washington and Lee U., Va., 1973; writer in residence So. Sem., Va., 1973, Bermuda Writers Conf., 1978, U. Hartford, Conn., 1981-82; guest fellow Yale U., 1982-83; vis. prof. Conn. Coll., 1986-87; judge P.E.N. Syndicated Fiction Project, 1985; narrator stories and poems BBC, 1968—; condr. poetry and fiction readings Yale U., Washington and Lee U., U. Hartford, U. Mass., Amherst, Arts Coun. Princeton, 1990-93; founder Princeton Writers Group, 1990, 91, 92, Poetry Arts Coun. at Princeton, 1990-91, Fiction and Film, Arts Coun. at Princeton, 1990-02; writer, painter-in-residence Melville Coll., 1992, Shotts (Scotland) Prison; lectr. Bermuda Coll., 1995-96. Author: A Fall from Aloft, 1968, A Few Flowers for St. George, 1969, Undertow, 1970, The Sailor and the Fox, 1973, Surprise, 1975, Stephan Decatur, 1976, The Flight of the Cavalier, 1980, Love is a Durable Fire, 1985 (children's book), St. Nicholas the Tub, 1964; (poetry) To Celebrate a Happiness That is America, 1971, For My Beloved Bermuda, 1998; represented in various pvt. collections worldwide. Mem. Princeton Arts coun. Served with Brit. Mcht. Svc., 1944. Recipient Lifetime Achievement award Bermuda Arts Coun., 1993. Fellow Royal Soc. Lit., Acad. Am. Poets; mem. PEN, Poetry Soc. Am., Authors Guild, Am. Ctr. Soc., Princeton Writers Group (founder), Royal Bermuda Yacht Club, Chelsea Arts Club (London). Mem. Bah'ai World Faith.

BURLAND, JOHN BOSCAWEN, civil engineering educator, consulting engineer; b. Little Chalfont, Eng., Mar. 4, 1936; s. John Whitmore and Margaret Irene (Boscawen) B.; m. Gillian Margaret Miller, Mar. 30, 1963; children: David, Timothy, Tamsin. BSc, U. Witwatersrand, South Africa, 1959, MSc, 1961, DSc, 1982; PhD, U. Cambridge, Eng., 1967; DEng (hon.), Heriot-Watt U., Scotland, 1994; DSc (hon.), Nottingham (Eng.) U., 1998. Engr. Ove Arup and Ptnrs., Eng., 1961-63; prin. sci. officer Bldg. Rsch. Establishment, Eng., 1966-72, head geotechnics divsn., 1972-79, asst. dir., 1979-80; prof. soil mechanics Imperial Coll. Sci., Tech. and Medicine, London, 1980—; vis. prof. U. Strathclyde, Scotland, 1973-82. Contbr. articles to profl. jours. Chmn. Churches Together, Wheathampstead, 1990-98; mem. Italian Prime Min.'s Commn. on Stabilizing Leaning Tower Pisa, 1990—. Fellow Royal Acad. Engring., Royal Soc., Instn. Civil Engrs. (Kelvin medal 1989), Geol. Soc.; mem. Instn. Structural Engrs. (Kevin Nash gold medal 1994). Mem. Anglican Ch. Avocations: golf, sailing, painting. Office: Imperial Coll Sci Tech Medicine, Imperial College Rd, London SW7 2BU, England

BURLATCHUK, LEONID FOKICH, philosophy educator; b. Leningrad, Russia, Jan. 1, 1947. Student, U. Leningrad; MA in Philosophy, Kiev U., USSR, 1970; PhD in Psychology, Leningrad Sci. Rsch. Psychoneurol. Inst., 1975; DSc, Kiev U., 1991. Lectr. Kiev U., 1970, chief dept. social and pedagogical psychology, 1991-92, head sci. coun., 1991—, prof., 1992—, chief psychodiagnostics and med. psychology dept., 1992—; sci. rschr. Sci. Rsch. Inst. Psychology Acad. Pedagogical Scis. of Ukraine, 1991—. Mem. editl. coun. jour. Psychosomatic Medicine; mem. internat. com. jour. Psychologie Clinique et Projective, Paris; contbr. over 140 articles to profl. publs. Mem. Acad. Pedagogical Scis. Ukraine (corr.), Internat. Acad. Acmeological Scis., N.Y. Acad. Scis. Address: Lesnoi Prospekt 6 ap 94, 253166 Kiev Ukraine

BURLAUD, ALAIN JEAN, management educator, consultant; b. Paris, Jan. 30, 1946; s. Paul Andre and Odile Aimee (Schouller) B.; m. Genevieve Huguette Imbert, July 12, 1967; children: Sophie, Denis. Docteur d'Etat es scis de gestion, U. Paris, Sorbonne, 1976. Asst. prof. Ecole Supèrieure de Commerce de Paris, 1969-72; secondary sch. tchr. Lycee Paul Langevin, Suresnes, France, 1972-73; asst. Inst. U. de Tech., Villetaneuse, France, 1973-74, U. Paris, Sorbonne, 1974-80; prof. U. Tours, France, 1980-83, U. Paris Val de Marne, 1984-94, Conservatoire Nat. des Arts et Metiers, 1994—; chmn. exam. bd. Diplome d'expertise comptable, 1985-95; pres. Conseil Nat. des Univs., 2000—. Author: Comtabilitè et Inflation (Prix de l'Acad. de Comptabilitè 1979), 1978; (with R. Laufer) Public Management, 1980, (with C. Simon) Couts/Controle, 1981, controle de Gestion, 1997, (with Raimbault and Saussois) Approche Systèmique des relations Etat-industrie: la relation d'aide, 1984, (with C. simon) Comptabilitè de Gestion, 2000; mem. editl. bd. Politiques et management Public, 1982—, Sciences de gestion, 1984—, Comptabilite, Controle, Audit, 1995—, Finance, Controle, Strategie, 1998—, Zeitschrift fur Betriebswirtschaft, 1999—; editl. advisor Accounting Education, 1998—. Fellow Assn. Française de Comptabilitè (pres. 1997-98); mem. Compagnie des Commissaires aux Comptes, Ordre des Experts Comptables, Internat. Fedn. Accts. (edn. com., French rep. 1985-97), Internat. Fedn. Scholarly Assns. Mgmt. (pres.-elect 1993-94, pres. 1995-96, past pres. 1997-98), Internat. Assn. Acctg. Edn. adn Rsch. (v.p. 1993-97). Home: 19 Allee Courbet, F 93190 Livry-Gargan France Office: CNAM/INTEC, 292 Rue Saint Martin, 75003 Paris France

BURLEIGH, A. PETER, ambassador; b. L.A., Mar. 7, 1942; s. Ralph Wendell and Margaret (McKenney) B. AB, Colgate U., 1963; postgrad., U. Pa., 1965-66. Vol. Peace Corps, Nepal, 1963-65; joined Fgn. Svc., 1967; various positions Dept. State, Washington, 1967-85, dir. No. Gulf Affairs, 1985-87, dep. asst. sec. for Near Eastern and South Asian Affairs, 1987-89, dep. asst. sec. for intelligence and rsch., 1989-91, coord. for counter-terrorism, amb., 1991-92, dep. asst. sec. for pers., 1992-95; amb. Dem. Socialist Republic Sri Lanka, Republic Maldives, 1995-97; dep. U.S. rep. to UN, 1997-99; ret. Recipient Presdl. Svc. award U.S. Govt., 1990, 93. Office: 2300 Riverlane Ter Fort Lauderdale FL 33312-4762

BURLESKI, JOSEPH ANTHONY, JR., information technology executive; b. Poughkeepsie, N.Y., June 30, 1960; s. Joseph Anthony Burleski Sr. and Fredeline Cyr; m. Judith Ann Lezon, June 10, 1989; children: Joseph Anthony III, Jessica Ann. BSBA, Marist Coll., 1982; MBA Mktg., U. Phoenix, 1992; grad. in human rels. and effective speaking, Dale Carnegie, 1990. Cert. project mgmt. profl. Project Mgmt. Inst.; IBM cert. sr. project mgr. Computer operator IBM, Poughkeepsie, 1982-83, lead/sr. computer operator, 1983-84, systems programmer, 1984-85, assoc. systems programmer, 1985-86, mgr. offshift computer ops., 1986-87; mgr. info. processing IBM, Boulder, Colo., 1987-88, mgr. MVS systems programming, 1988-91; mgr. location and field svcs. devel. Integrated Systems Solutions Corp. subs. IBM, Boulder, 1991-93, mgr. location and field svc. devel. ind. test, 1992-93; mgr. VM/VSE svcs. Integrated Sys. Solutions Corp. subs. IBM, Boulder, 1993-94, account mgr., 1994-96; delivery project exec. IBM Global Svcs., Boulder, 1997-98; delivery exec. IBM Global Svcs., St. Louis, 1998—; cert. sr. project mgr. IBM, 1999—, chair cert. bd., 2000—; mentor IBM, 1987—; mem. IBM Data Processing Ops. Coun., Poughkeepsie, 1983-92, Project Mgmt. Inst., 1995—; grad. asst. Dale Carnegie Inst., Boulder, 1990-98. Coach Spl. Olympics, 1987-98; mem. Order of the Arrow Hon. Soc., chpt. sec., editor, 1976-77, chpt. pres. 1977-78, chpt. treas. 1980-81. Mem. Am. Mgmt. Assn., Am. Assn. Individual Investors, Marist Coll. Alumni Assn. (contbr.), Vigil Nat. Honor Soc. Roman Catholic. Avocations: running, reading, camping, hiking, raising tropical fish. Office: 800 Lindbergh Blvd Saint Louis MO 63167-0001

BURLEY, PETER CAMPBELL, urban economist, researcher; b. Palo Alto, Calif., Aug. 26, 1952; s. Clarence Augustus Burley and Shirley Bowman Albertson; m. Ellen F. Schamberg, July 14, 1974 (dec. Oct. 1983); 1 child, Katherine; m. M. Penelope Clark, Oct. 6, 1988; 1 child, Tallant. BA, U. Calif., Santa Barbara, 1974, U. Calif., Santa Barbara, 1979; MA, U. Calif., Santa Barbara, 1981. Lifetime credential coll. instr., Calif. Lectr. in geography U. Calif., Santa Barbara, 1981; cartographer Def. Mapping Agy., St. Louis, 1982-83; dir. Washington U., St. Louis, 1983-84; sr. rschr. Allstate Rsch. Ctr., Menlo Park, Calif., 1985-95; dir. rsch. Amstar Group, Ltd., Denver, 1995—; acad. advisor U. Calif., Santa Barbara, 1980-82, coord. office of dean, 1982; cons. Regional Analytics, &c., Calif. and Colo., 1995—. Contbr. articles to profl. jours.; editor Notes on the Economy, 1997-99. Officer Episcopal Diocese of Calif., San Francisco, 1989-95. Mem. Urban Land Inst. (assoc.), Nat. Assn. Bus. Econs. (policy panelist 1996—), Assn. Am. Geographers, Am. Planning Assn., Population Assn. of Am., Am. Real Estate and Urban Econs. Assn. Democrat. Avocations: writer, antique collecting, sheep ranching. Home: 5042 N Blazingstar Trl Castle Rock CO 80104-9449 Office: Amstar Group Ltd 1050 17th St Ste 1200 Denver CO 80265-2050

BURLINGAME-SMITH, JUNE, English language educator, administrator; b. Barrington, N.J., June 1, 1935; d. Leslie Grant and Esther (Bellini) Burlingame; m. Gregory Lloyd Smith, July 6, 1963 (dec. July 1997); children: Gilia Cobb Smith, Cyrus Comstock Smith. BA, Reed Coll., 1956; MS, Ind. U., 1959; MA, Calif. State U., Dominguez Hills, 1986. Prof. English L.A. C.C.-Harbor Coll., Wilmington, 1986—, pres. acad. senate, 1997-2000. Mem. exec. bd. Harbor Interfaith Shelter, San Pedro, Calif., 1993-2000; mem. task force Recreation and Pks. L.A., San Pedro, 1999; mem. Cabrillo Marine Aquarium Vol. Neighborhood Oversight Com., 2000—. Mem. AAUW (legis. chair 1988—), Nat. Coun. Tchrs. of English. E-mail: burling102@aol.com. Office: Harbor Coll 1111 Figueroa Pl Wilmington CA 90744-2311

BURMAZ, JOHN DAMIAN, engineering educator, consultant; b. Benoni, Gauteng, South Africa, Oct. 11, 1931; s. Ante and Stefe (Cikara) B.; m. Neda Domijan, Oct. 9, 1960. Diploma in mech. engring., Croatia, 1952; engrs. cert. of competency, South Africa, 1957; BA, U. South Africa, 1982; MTech, Wits Technikon, South Africa, 1989. Mech. engr. Mandy Engring., South Africa, 1954-66; indsl. engr. Rand Mines Ltd., South Africa, 1967-73; officer edn. Eskom Utilites, South Africa, 1974-79; lectr. WITS Technikon, South Africa, 1980-84, head dept., 1985-96, cons., 1997—. Fellow South Africa Production and Inventory Control Soc. (v.p. edn. 1991-92); mem. South Africa Production Engrs. (pres. 1987-88), South Africa Bd. Pers. Practice. Roman Catholic. Avocations: lawn bowling, chess, personal effectiveness/development. Home: Orange Grove, 46 3rd St, Johannesburg 2192, South Africa Office: WITS Technikon, Bunting Rd Auckland Park, Johannesburg 2092, South Africa

BURMEISTER, HELMUT, museum director, secondary education educator; b. Kassel, Hesse, Germany, July 7, 1940; s. Heinrich-August and Annemarie (Steinbach) B.; m. Gudrum Gross, Mar. 12, 1966; children: Thorsten, Heike, Arne. Abitur Albert Schweitzer Sch., Kassel, Germany, 1960; grad. Philipps U., Marburg, Germany, 1967; Cert. secondary edn. teacher. Author, editor: Die Geschichte unserer Heimat, 1988—; editor (essays/yearbook) Zeitschrift fur Hessische Geschichte und Landeskunde, 1984-99 (Golden Shield of Honor award), 1986, Jahrbuch des Landkreises Kassel, 1972— (Silver Shield award 1992, Golden Needle of Honor 1997). Dir. Town of Hofgeismar Mus., 1977—; pres. Hofgeismar Parliament Social Democrat Party, 1991-97; active various Hessian cultural orgns. Decorated Fed. Order of Merit (Germany); recipient Ehrenbrief award Land Hessen, 1985, Forderpreis zum Kulturpreis, 1992, Paul Dierichs Stiftung prize, HNA newspaper, 1982, others. Lutheran. Avocations: reading, gardening, dogs, birds, Danish paintings. Home: 8 Arensberg, 34369 Hofgeismar Hesse, Germany Office: Stadtmuseum Hofgeismar, 2 Petriplatz, Hesse Hofgeismar 34369, Germany

BURMEISTER, MARGIT, research scientist, educator; b. Hamelin, Germany, Aug. 6, 1958; d. Hans-Jürgen and Edith (Kostmann) B.; m. Michael Hortsch, Apr. 9, 1983; children: Ruthi, Natania. Student, Free U., Berlin, 1977-82, Weizmann Inst. Sci., Rehovot, Israel, 1982-83; diploma in biochemistry, Free U. Berlin, 1983; PhD, U. Heidelberg, Germany, 1987. Postdoctoral fellow U. Calif., San Francisco, 1987-91; asst. prof., asst. rsch. scientist U. Mich., Ann Arbor, 1991-97, assoc. prof., sr. assoc. rsch. scientist, 1997—; vis. prof. Max-Planck-Inst. Molecular Genetics, Berlin, 1999-2000; mem. rev. com. Nat. Inst. Deafness and Comm. Disorders, 1998—; chair mouse chromosome com. Mammalian Genome Orgn., 1997-99. Editor (with L. Ulanovsky): Pulsed-Field Gel Electrophoresis, 1992; mem. editl. bd. Mammalian Genome, 1997—; contbr. over 50 articles to profl. jours. Klingenstein fellow in neuroscis., 1995-98; recipient Young Investigator award Nat. Alliance for Rsch., 1993, 96; Humboldt Found. fellow, 1999—. Mem. Am. Soc. Human Genetics, Human Genome Orgn., Internat. Mammalian Genome Soc. Office: U Mich MHRI 205 Zina Pitcher Pl Ann Arbor MI 48109-0720

BURMEISTER, PAUL FREDERICK, farmer; b. Great Bend, Kans., June 11, 1938; s. Ferdinand Frederick Adam and Gertrude Nellie (Hanson) B. BA in Chemistry and Agr., Ft. Hays State U., 1960; postgrad., U. Kans., 1961. Farmer Claflin, Kans., 1952-61, 64—; farmer coop. Kans. Agrl. Experiment Sta., Ft. Hays Br. Sta., Hays, Kans., 1970, Kans. Rural Ctr., Whiting, 1991, 92; panel mem. Kans. Sustainable Agr. Conf., Great Bend and Salina, 1991, 92; mem. Kans. Natural Resource Coun., Topeka, 1975—, Nat. Resources Def. Coun., N.Y.C., 1975—; participant,U. Akron Nat. Energy Forum, 1976, Nat. Low-Level Radioactive Waste Mgmt. Strategy Rev. Workshop, Washington, 1981; participant pub. forum on radioactive wastes Office Radiation Programs, EPA, Denver, 1978; guest speaker, Rapid City, S.D., 1993; mem. Kans.-Okla. Conf. Coun., 1999—. Contbr. articles to environ. and agrl. jours. Vol. Am. Peace Corps, Ludhiana, India, 1961-63; local organizer campaign Union of Concerned Scientists, Cambridge, Mass.; lobbyist on environ. protection and conservation issues, Topeka, 1976-80; mem. Renew Am., Washington, 1980—; mem. The Menninger Found., Topeka, 1989—, Environ. Action, 1982—; lay mem. ad hoc task force on ecology Christian lifestyle United Ch. of Christ, 1977-78, commn. on out-reach Kans.-Okla. conf., 1988-96, 98-99, network environ. and econ. responsibility; participant Kans. Citizens Forum Com. for Humanities, Topeka, 1987; mem. farmer adv. com. Sunshine Farm Project, Land Inst., Salina, Kans., 1995—. With USNG, 1963-69. Recipient Bankers award Banks of Barton County, Kans. and U.S. Soil Conservation Svc., 1990. Mem. Nat. Wildlife Fedn. (life), Nat. Coun. Returned Peace Corps Vols., Nat. Arbor

Day Found., World Wildlife Fund (charter), Am. Wind Energy Assn., Am. Solar Energy Soc. (life), Midwest Renewable Energy Assn., 1998—, Kans. Assn. Wheat Growers, Kans. Farmers Union, Kans. Organic Prodrs., Inc., Friends of the Earth, Cousteau Soc. (founding yr. mem.), Kans. State Hist. Soc. (life), Kans. Wildlife Fedn., Sierra Club (life), Native Forest Coun., Ducks Unlimited Inc., Environ. Def., Wilderness Soc., Friends of India, Tau Kappa Epsilon (sec. 1958-59, scholar 1959), Nature Conservancy, Phi Eta Sigma (historian 1958-59), Phi Kappa Phi, Delta Epsilon. Avocations: photography, hiking, exploring. Address: 1332 NE 180th Rd Claflin KS 67525-9219

BURMESTER, GERD RÜDIGER, medical educator, physician; b. Hannover, Germany, Nov. 30, 1953; s. Willi and Helga (Thiel) B.; m. Ilona Inge Ria Gehrig, Sept. 26, 1977; children: Annika, Kristin. MD, Hannover Med. Sch., 1978; prof. rheumatology, Erlangen Med. Sch., Germany, 1990; prof. medicine, Humboldt U., Berlin, 1993. Diplomate German Bd. Internal Medicine, Bd. Rheumatology. Postdoctoral fellow Rockefeller Y., N.Y.C., 1980-82; resident U. Erlangen-Nuremberg, Germany, 1982-88, sr. registrar, 1988, prof. rheumatology, clin. immunology, 1990; prof. medicine Charité Univ. Hosp. Humboldt U., 1993—, vice dean, 1995-97; vis. scholar Hosp. Joint Diseases Mt. Sinai Sch. Medicine, 1980-82; mem. nat. rev. com. internal medicine German Sci. Found., 1996—; mem. nat. rev. com. rehab. German Min. Edn., Rsch. & Tech., 1996—. Assoc. editor Annals Rheumatic Diseases; editl. bd. Arthritis & Rheumatism, 1992-95, Jour. Rheumatology, Clin. Rheumatology, Zschr. of Rheumatol.; guest editor Rheumatology Internat. nos. 305, vol. 9, 1989. physician German mil., 1978-80. Recipient German Therapy Cong. award, 1991, Jan-van-Breemen medal Dutch Soc. Rheumatology; German Sci. Found. scholar. Mem. German Soc. Immunology, German Soc. Rheumatology (bd. dirs. 1992—, pres.-elect, Bruno Schuler award 1992), German Soc. Internal Medicine, German Soc. Advancement Internal Medicine, German Cancer Soc., Am. Coll. Rheumatology, Berlin-Brandenburg Acad. Sci. Avocations: theater, music, sports. Office: Charite Univ Hosp, Schumannstr 20-21, 10098 Berlin Germany

BURN, JOHN PHILIP, neurologist; b. Bristol, Eng., Aug. 19, 1956; s. Andrew Southerden and Elizabeth June (Norbury) B.; m. Susan Catherine Bremer, Jan. 1986; children: Laurel, Katie May, Elinor, Nicholas, Hester. BA, U. Cambridge, 1977; BMBch, U. Oxford, 1980, DM, 1993. Diplomate European Bd. Phys. Medicine and Rehab. Rsch. fellow Oxfordshire Cmty. Stroke Project, 1987-90; sr. registrar Dept. Rehab. Medicine, Southampton, 1991-94; cons. Brain Injury Svc., Poole, Eng., 1994—. Contbr. articles to profl. jours. Mem. Soc. Rsch. into Rehab., Brit. Stroke Rsch. Group, Brit. Soc. Rehab. Medicine (regional coord. 1994—). Avocations: choral, recorder. Office: Poole Hosp Brain Injury Svc, Longfleet Rd, Poole Dorset BH15 2JB, England

BURNETT, ALFRED DAVID, librarian; b. Edinburgh, Scotland, Aug. 15, 1937; s. Alfred Harding and Jessie Miller (Scott) B. Scottish Leaving Cert., George Watson's Boys' Coll., Edinburgh, 1955; MA with honors in English lang. and lit., U. Edinburgh, 1959; Associateship of Library Assn., U. Strathclyde, Glasgow, 1964. Library asst. U. Glasgow Library, 1959-64; asst. librarian Durham U. Library, 1964-90; Author numerous poems; contbr. articles to profl. jours. Recipient Patterson Bursary in Anglo-Saxon award U. Edinburgh, 1958, Kelso Meml. prize in bibliography U. Strathclyde, 1964, Sevensma prize Internat. Fedn. Library Assns., 1971. Mem. Libr. Assn. (com. Internat. and Comparative Librarianship Group 1973-88, Essay prize, 1966) Pvt. Librs. Assn., Colpitts Poetry Club (com. mem. Durham, 1975-87). Socialist. Presbyterian. Avocations: reading, walking. Home: 33 Hastings Ave, Merry Oaks, Durham DHI 3QG, England Office: Durham U Library, Palace Green, Durham DH1 3RN, England

BURNETT, DAVID GRANT, curator, writer; b. Lincoln, Eng., Oct. 2, 1940; s. Wilfred Brunett; children: Charles, Wenham, Emma; m. Marilyn Schiff, 1983. BA, U. London, 1965; MA, Courtauld Inst. Art, 1967, PhD, 1973. Lectr. history of art U. Bristol, Eng., 1967-70; assoc. prof. art history Carleton U., 1970-80, chmn. dept., 1974-77, 78-79; curator contemporary Can. art Art Gallery Ont., 1980-84; dir. Drabinsky Gallery, Toronto, 1990-2000; chief curator The Art Vault, 2000—; com. mem. Can. Coun. Awards to Artists, Assn. Univs. and Colls. Scholarship Bd.; com. mem., sec.-treas. Univ. Art Assn. Can.; com. mem. Acad. Com. on Art Policy Discipline Force, chmn., 1979-80. Exhbns. and catalogues include A Tribute to Paul Klee 1879-1940, Nat. Gallery Can., 1979, Guido Molinari Drawings, Agnes Etherington Art Ctr., Kingston, 1981, Robert Bourdeau and Phillip Pocock, Art Gallery Ont., 1981, Gershon Iskowitz, Art Gallery Ont., 1982, Alex Coville, Art Gallery Ont., 1983, Noel Harding, Art Gallery Ont., 1982, Oscar Cahén, Art Gallery Ont., 1983, Toronto Painting, Art Gallery Ont., 1984, Harold Town Retrospective, Art Gallery Ont., 1986; catalogues Guido Molinari: Quantificateur Musée d'art Contemporain Montreal, 1979, Jeremy Smith Mira Godard, 1985, Jack Chambers Retrospective, London Regional Art Gallery, 1988; author: (with M. Schiff) Contemporary Canadian Art, 1983, Alex Colville, 1983, Town, 1986, Anton Cétin, 1986, Jeremy Smith, 1988, Cineplex Odeon: The First Ten Years A Celebration of Contemporary Canadian Art, 1989, Masterpieces of Canadian Art from the National Gallery of Canada, 1990; contbr. articles to profl. jours. Can. Coun. grantee, 1974, 80. Mem. Internat. Assn. Art Critics. Avocations: flying, scale modeling.

BURNETT, DAVID HENRY, banker; b. Isleworth, Middlesex, England, Dec. 16, 1951; s. George Dawson and Ferdinanda Anna (Van Den Brandeler) B. BA, Cambridge (Eng.) U., 1974, MA, 1978. Dir. Orion Royal Bankers Ltd., London, Eng., 1976-88; mng. dir. bus. ops. HSBC Investment Bank PLC, London, Eng., 1988—. Office: HSBC Investment Bank PLC, Thames Exchg 10 Queen St Pl, London EC4R 1BL, England

BURNETT, FRANCES, concert pianist, music educator; b. Centralia, Ill., Dec. 3, 1920; d. Bernard Baumheuter and Ollie Dee Burnett; m. Hinton Joseph Baker, June 24, 1943 (div. 1956); children: Eve Baker Street, Celeste Baker Simonds. MMus, Cin. Conservatory Music, 1942; studied with David Saperton, Karin Dayas; Gina Bachauer, Ilona Kabos, N.Y.C., London, Switzerland; studied with Guido Agosti, Siena and Rome; diploma di merito, Acad. Musicale Chigiana, Siena. Piano faculty Longy Sch. Music, Cambridge, Mass., 1955-64; piano faculty Coll. Mus. Arts Bowling Green (Ohio) State U., 1964-91, mem. piano staff Coll. Mus. Arts, tchr. creative arts dept., 1991—. Appeared as recitalist, ensemble artist and soloist with orchs. throughout U.S., Europe and Mex.; pub. appearances include concerts at Town Hall and Merkin Hall in N.Y.C., Jordan Hall and the Gardner Mus., Boston, Abraham Goodman House, N.Y.C., Carnegie Recital Hall, N.Y.C., Phillips Gallery and Nat. Gallery, Washington, Toledo Mus. Art, Cleve. Inst., Wigmore Hall, London, Broadcast BBC, London, Musikrerein, Vienna, Hamburg, Berlin, Amsterdam; played on 3 CDs, 1994; recording of a concerto written for her by William Thomas McKinley with Seattle Symphony, 2000; contbr. book chpt.: Gina Bachaner, A Pianists Odyssey, 1999; contbr. articles to Clavier Mag. Mem. Toledo Piano Tchrs., Monday Musicale, Ohio Music Tchrs. Assn., Music Tchrs. Nat. Assn. Democrat. Roman Catholic. Avocation: swimming. Home: 23 Georgetown Dr Bowling Green OH 43402-9373

BURNETT, JEAN BULLARD (MRS. JAMES R. BURNETT), biochemist; b. Flint, Mich., Feb. 19, 1924; d. Chester M. and Katheryn (Krasser) Bullard; B.S., Mich. State U., 1944, M.S., 1945, Ph.D. (Council fellow), 1952; m. James R. Burnett, June 8, 1947. Research assoc. dept. zoology Mich. State U., East Lansing, 1954-59, dept. biochemistry, 1959-61, acting dir. research biochem. genetics, dept. biochemistry, 1961-62, assoc. prof., asst. chmn. dept. biomechanics, 1973-82, prof. dept. anatomy, 1982-84, prof. dept. zoology, Coll. Natural Sci. and Coll. Osteo. Medicine, 1984—; assoc. biochemist Mass. Gen. Hosp., Boston, 1964-73; prin. research assoc. dermatology Harvard, 1962-73, faculty medicine, 1964-73, also spl. lectr., cons., tutor Med. Sch.; vis. prof. dept. biology U. Ariz., 1979-80. USPHS, NIH grantee, 1965-68; Gen. Research Support grantee Mass. Gen. Hosp., 1968-72; Ford Found. travel grantee, 1973; Am. Cancer Soc. grantee, 1971-73; Internat. Pigment Cell Conf. travel grantee, 1980; recipient Med. Found. award, 1970. Mem. AAAS, Am. Chem. Soc., Am. Inst. Biol. Sci., Genetics Soc. Am., Soc. Investigative Dermatology, N.Y. Acad. Scis., Sigma Xi (Research award 1971), Pi Kappa Delta, Kappa Delta Pi, Pi Mu Epsilon, Sigma Delta Epsilon. Home: PO Box 805 Okemos MI 48805-0805 Office: Mich State Univ Dept Zoology Natural Sci Bldg East Lansing MI 48824

BURNETT, JUDITH JANE, public relations consultant; b. Muncie, Ind., Aug. 21, 1947; d. Albert Ward and Jane M. (Collins) Burnett. Grad., Ind. U. Svc. dir., ops. mgr. Indiana Homemakers, Inc., Indpls., 1975-80, exec. v.p., 1980-83, dir.; corp. sec. Mgmt. Alternatives, Inc., Indpls., 1984-85; exec. v.p., dir. Three-I Homemakers, Inc., Illini Homemakers, Inc., 1980-83; dir. Home Care Med. Products Co., 1980-82; adminstrv. Extended Svcs., 1988-92; owner Projects & Promotions, 1988—, Lab Plus, Inc., 1989-93; exec. dir. Ryan White Found., 1994-97. Named One of Indpls.'s Influential Woman, 1999. Mem. adv. coun. Marion County Step Ahead, 1999—, U.S. Tennis Writers Assn. Home and Office: 9992 Estep Dr Indianapolis IN 46280-1588

BURNETT, PATRICIA HILL, portrait artist, author, sculptor, lecturer; b. Bklyn.; d. William Burr and Mimi (Uline) Hill; m. William Anding Lange, 1944 (div. 1947); 1 child, William Hill; m. Harry Albert Burnett III, , Oct. 9, 1948 (dec. 1979); children: Harry Burnett III, Terrill Hill, Hillary Hill; m. Robert L. Siler, 1989. Student, U. Toledo, 1937-38, Goucher Coll., 1939-41, MA program Inst. D'Allende, Mex., 1967, Wayne State U., 1972; pvt. studies with, John Carroll, Detroit, 1941-44, Sarkis Sarkisian, Detroit, 1956-60, Wallace Bassford, Provincetown, Mass., 1968-72, Walter Midener, Detroit, 1960-63. Actress Long Ranger and Green Hornet prgrams, Radio Blue Network, 1941-46; tchr. painting and sculpture U. Mich. Extension, Ann Arbor, 1965—; lectr. N.Y. Speakers Bur., 1971—; propr. Burnett Studios, Detroit, 1962-88, mgr., 1962—. Numerous one-woman shows of paintings and sculptures include Scarab Club, Detroit, 1971, Midland (Mich.) Art Ctr., Wayne State U., Detroit, The Gallery, Ft. Lauderdale, Fla., Agra Gallery, Washington, Salon des Artes, Paris; numerous group shows include: Palazzo Pruili Gallery, Venice, 1971, Detroit Inst. of Arts, 1967, Butler Mus., Cleveland, 1972, Windsor (Ont., Can.) Art Ctr., 1973, Weisbaden (Germany) Gallery, 1976, Retrospective Show: Birmingham Bloomfield Art Assn., 1997; represented in permanent collections: Detroit Inst. Arts, Wayne State U., Wooster (Ohio) Coll., Ford Motor Co., Detroit, Bloomfield Art Assn., Bloomfield Hills, Mich., Henry Ford Hosp. Collection, Fed. Ct. Appeals in Washington, City-County Bldg., Detroit, Mich. State Capitol Bldg., Royal Acad. of Art, London, Moscow Mus., Moscow, Russia, Mich. State Capital, Lansing, Mich., Royal Palace of India, New Delhi, Palace of The Philippines, Manila, Mansion of Prime Minister, Greece; also pvt. collections: numerous portrait paintings including Indira Ghandi, Benson Ford, Joyce Carol Oates, Mrs. Edsel Ford, Betty Ford, Mayor Roman Gribbs, Princess Olga Mrivani, Lord John Mackintosh, Marlo Thomas, Viveca Lindfois, Betty Freidan, Gloria Steinem, Congresswoman Martha Griffiths, Margaret Papandreou, Valentina Tereshkova, Barbara Walters, Margaret Thatcher, Corazon Aquino, Violetta Chamarra, Jackie Joyner Kersee, Mayor Dennis Archer, Wayne U. pres. David Adamany, author Kate Millett, Michele Engler and triplets, Patricia Ireland, Rosa Parks, others; mem. editl. bd. Am. Portrait Soc.; author: True Colors: An Artist's Journey from Beauty Queen to Feminist. Chairwoman of Mich. Women's Commn., 1972—; pres. Detroit House of Correction Commn., 1975—; treas. Rep. Dist. 1 of Mich., 1973—; mem. Issues com., Rep. State Ctrl. Com., 1975-76; sec. Rep. State Ways and Means com., 1975—, Detroit Libr. Commn., 1980-85, Detroit Human Rights Comn., 1976-80, Detroit City Planning Commn., 1985-90; mem. Mich. State Adv. Coun. vocat. Edn.; mem. Mich. Arts in Edn. Coun., 1978—; mem. New Detroit Arts Com., 1979—; chmn. World Feminist Commn., 1974—; life mem. NAACP. Recipient Silver Salute award Mich. State U., 1976, Most Popular award San Diego Sculpture Show, 1971, First prize award Cape Cod Artists Show, 1968, State of Mich. award for creativity Gov. John Engler, 1999; named Disting. Woman of Mich., Bus. and Profl. Women's Orgn., 1974, Disting. Woman Northwood Inst., 1977, Artist of Yr., Mich. Art Train, 1989, Disting. woman award Mich. Bus. and Profl. Women Internat.; named to Ohio Hall of Fame, 1987, Mich. Women's Hall of Fame, 1988, one of Most Outstanding Women in Mich., Women in Advt., 1998, one of 10 People with Most Clout Outside of County, Detroit Free Press, 1998. Mem. Mich. Women's Forum (founder 1989, bd. dirs. 1989-99, Internat. Women's Forum, bd. dirs. 1989-99), Detroit Inst. Arts (dir. membership com. 1958—), Nat. Assn. Commns. for Women (pres. 1976-78), Mich. Acad. of Arts, Detroit Soc. Women Painters and Sculptprs, Women in the Arts, Scrab Club (dir. 1962-63), Ibex Club (pres. 1951), NOW (nat. bd. 1971-75, del. UN conf. Mex., 1975, Feminist of Yr.), Coun. Leading portrait Painters (elect), Women's Econ. Club, N.Y. Portrait Club (nat. adv. bd. 1977—), French-Am. C.of C. (v.p.), Alpha Phi, Zonta, Detroit Econ. Club (bd. dirs.). Episcopalian. Home and Studio: 13 Oaks Ct Bloomfield Hills MI 48304-2120

BURNETT, RAYMUND CARMI, retired rancher, agricultural researcher; b. Sydney, Australia, Dec. 8, 1926; s. Carmi and Irene May (Smythe) B.; m. Lucille Caroline Harvey, May 26, 1951; children: Peter, Ann, Fiona. Engring. Degree, Ultimo, Sydney, 1950; student, Sydney U., 1967, 68-70. Design draftsman Cockatoo Docks & Engring., Sydney, 1952-54; lead draftsman A.C. Willard Chem. Engrs., Sydney, 1954-55; asst. group engrs. Lewis Berger & Sons, Sydney, 1955-57; tech. advisor Nestlé, Sydney, 1957-71; ptnr. R.C. & L.C. Burnett, Byabarra, Australia, 1971-96; ret., 1996; cons. North Coast Rural Producers Consultative Com., Grafton, Australia, 1992-94. Mem., chmn. Byabarra Hall Trust, 1973-89, Wachore Show Soc., 1982-88; mem. Hstings Catchment Com., Wauchope, 1993-94; chmn. water resources divsn. Wauchope Econ. Forum, 1994-95. Mem. NSW Farmers Assn. (chmn.), N.Y. Acad. Sci. Avocations: computers, electronics, reading, fishing, surfing. Home: 102 Settlement Point Rd, Port Macquarie 2444, Australia Office: RC & LC Burnett, 702 Comboyne Rd, Byabarra 2446, Australia

BURNETT, ROBERT ADAIR, university administrator, history educator; b. Spartanburg, S.C., Jan. 25, 1934; s. Wendell and Curtiss Catherine (Adair) B.; m. Mary Maude Vaughan, July 26, 1958; children: Dorothy Catherine Autin, Wendy Jo. AB in Econs., Wofford Coll., 1956; MA in History, U. N.C., 1959, PhD in History, 1968. Asst. prof. Pfeiffer Coll., Misenheimer, N.C., 1960-63; instr. U. N.C., Chapel Hill, 1963-66; asst. prof. U. Louisville, 1966-69, assoc. prof., 1969-74, prof., 1974-78, chmn. history dept., 1968-71, univ. ombudsman, 1974-76; prof. Armstrong State Coll., Savannah, Ga., 1978—, dean arts and scis., 1978-80, acad. v.p., 1980-82, acting pres., 1982-84, pres., 1984—. Editor: Marshall's World War II Encyclopedia, 1979; contbr. articles to profl. jours. Mem. Savannah Arts Commn., 1985-90; trustee Ga. Coun. on Econ. Edn., Atlanta, 1984—, Candler Gen. Hosp., Savannah, 1985—; bd. dirs. Boy Scouts Am., Savannah, 1982—; mem. bd. Savannah Econ. Devel. Authority, 1987—. 1st lt. U.S. Army, 1956-58. Mem. Am. Assn. State Colls. and Univs. (various coms.), So. Assn. Colls. and Schs. (cons. 1983—), NCAA (Pres.' commn.), Phi Beta Kappa, Phi Alpha Theta. Episcopalian. Office: Armstrong Atlantic State U Office of Pres 11935 Abercorn St Savannah GA 31419-1989

BURNEY, MARY ANN, mental health nurse; b. Feb. 19, 1947; d. William R. and Mary E. (Welborn) Pickett. ADN, Alvin Community Coll., Houston, 1984; LVN, Community Sch. Vocat., Houston, 1981; BSN, U. Tex., 1992, MSN in Psychiatric, 1994. Clin. specialist psychiat.-mental health nurse CS, neuro-linguistic programmer. Staff nurse Spring Shadows Glen Psychiat. Hosp., Houston, 1984, DePelchin Children's Ctr., Houston, 1985-88; nursing supr. DePelchin Children's Ctr., Houston, 1989-92; primary care nurse geriatric unit Harris County Psychiat. Ctr., Houston, 1992-94, supr., 1994-97; pvt. practice, asst. DON Gulf Pines Hosp., 1997—; asst. nurse mgr. Ben Taub Gen. Hosp., 1997-98; nurse mgr./dist. psychiatric inpatient svcs. Harris Co. Hosp., 1998—; Cons. in field. Producter tng. videos, audio visual aids in field; contbr. articles to profl. jours. Mem. ANA, Am. Psychiat. Nursing Assn., Phi Theta Kappa, Sigma Theta Tau.

BURNHAM, DANIEL PATRICK, manufacturing company executive; b. Birmingham, Mich., Nov. 28, 1946; s. Edward Francis and Helen Cecilia (Keane) B.; m. Mary Margaret Cavanaugh, June 8, 1968; children—Daniel, Amy, Peter, Ellen. B.S. in Econs., Xavier U., 1968; M.B.A. in Fin., U. N.H., 1970. Corp. controller Carborundum Corp., Niagara Falls, N.Y., 1976-78, dir. strategy devel., 1979-80, dir. abrasives mktg., 1980-81, gen. mgr. insulation div., 1981-82; v.p., controller Allied Corp., Morristown, N.J., 1982-84, v.p., gen. mgr. engineered plastics, 1984-86; pres. Plastics and Performance Matls. div. Allied-Signal Inc., Morristown, N.J., 1986-88, pres. fibers div., 1988-90; pres. AiResearch Group, Torrance, Calif., 1990-91, Allied-Signal Aerospace Co., Torrance, Calif., 1991-2000; chmn., CEO Raytheon Co., Lexington, Mass., 2000—; chmn. Internat. Turbine Engine Co.; bd. dirs. Light Helicopter Turbines Engring. Co., Normalair Garrett Ltd. (U.K.); bd. govs. Aerospace Ind. Assn. Served to capt. U.S. Army, 1970. Republican. Roman Catholic. Home: 66 Charles St # 541 Boston MA 02114-4604 Office: Raytheon Co 141 Spring St Lexington MA 02421-7899*

BURNHAM, J. V., sales executive; b. Pascagoula, Miss., May 23, 1923; s. George Luther and Eli Vashti (Hough) B.; m. Patti Lauri Latham, May 18, 1946; children: James Steven, Jon Douglas, Richard Scott, Bruce Edward, Vernon Alan. AA, Jones County (Miss.) Jr. Coll., 1946; AS, Rochester Inst. Tech., 1948; BS, U. Houston, 1951, MEd, 1953. Mgr. The Progress-Item, Ellisville, Miss., 1948-50; asst. prof., asst. mgr. U. Houston Journalism and Printing Plant, 1950-57; estimator, product supt. purchasing Chas. P. Young Co., Houston, 1957-67, asst. sec.-treas., 1967-69, v.p. sales, 1969-91, sr. v.p., 1991—. Assoc. editor Am. Oceanography, 1968-71; southwest corr. Inland Printer and Nat. Lithographer, 1952-60. Pres. Printing Industries of Gulf Coast, Houston, 1971-73; chmn. emeritus, bd. dirs. Tex. Printing Edn. Found., Houston; treas./bd. dirs. Mus. of Printing History, Houston; mem. Rep. Presdl. Task Force, Nat. Rep. Senatorial Com. Order of Merit, Nat. Rep. Congl. Com., Rep. Nat. Com. (life, chmn.'s adv. bd.), Rep. Party of Tex., Rep. Nat. Candidate Trust, The Heritage Found., Gramm Senate Club, The Concord Coalition; active Houston Mus. Natural Sci., Adm. Nimitz Found., Am. Air Mus., Am. Farmland Trust, Nat. Wildflower Rsch. Ctr. Lt. USNR, 1943-46. Recipient Scouters award Boy Scouts Am., 1960, Scouters Key award, 1965, Wood Badge award, 1964; named Man of Yr., Houston Graphics Soc., 1968, Printing Industry of Gulf Coast, 1970. Mem. NRA (life), Am. Fedn. Police, Gun Owners Am., Second Amendment Found. (charter), Second Amend Task Force, USS Constitution Mus. Found., Pres's. Club of Chas. P. Young Co. (charter, Outstanding Sales Achievement award), Houston Lithographic Club, U.S. Hist. Soc. (life), Nat. Eagle Scout Assn. (life), Tex. State Rifle Assn. (life), Tex. Police Officers Assn., Naval Airship. Assn., Rep.-Presdl. Legion of Merit, Bush Presdl. Libr. (assoc.), Am. Legion (life), U. Houston Alumni (life), Jones County Jr. Coll. Alumni (life), Rochester Inst. Tech. Alumni Assn., U.S. Golf Assn., Houston Golf Assn., 100 Club Houston, Braeburn Country Club, Hummel Collecters Club (Houston), The Landing at Seven Coves (Conroe, Tex.), NRA Whittington Ctr. Founders Club, Santa Fe Trail Gun Club (life), Houston Craftsmens Club (hon. life., past pres., Ben Franklin award 1971), Crime Stoppers of Houston (gold cir. mem.), Pinto Horse Assn. Am., Ducks Unltd., U.S. Navy Meml. Found., Naval Aviation Mus. Found., U.S. Navy Pub. Affairs Alumni Assn. (life), VFW (life), Houston Public TV, United Srs. Assn., WWII Meml. Found., Claremont Inst., BAMPAC, High Frontier, Citizens Against Govt. Waste, Nat. Arbor Day Found., Am. Kidney Fund, Am. Diabetes Assn., Juvenile Diabetes Fedn., PGA Ptnrs. Club (charter, life), Nat. Home Gardening Club (life). Republican. Methodist.

BURNHAM, LEM, psychologist; b. Winter Haven, Fla., Aug. 30, 1947; s. John L. and Lillie Belle B.; m. Barbara J. Mackin, Sept. 8, 1981; children: Shannon LeeAnne, Lewis, Kara, Bryan. Diploma, N.Am. Sch. Conservation, Irvine, Calif., 1969; BA in Psychology, U.S. Internat. U., 1974; MS in Counseling Psychology, Minn. State U., 1978; PhD in Psychoednl. Processes, Temple U., 1984. Diplomate Am. Bd. Forensic Examiners, Am. Bd. Psychol., Am. Psycholtherapy Assn. Specialties; cert. forensic clin. psychology, psychol. assessment, evaluation and testing, substance abuse psychology. Profl. football player World Football League, Honolulu, 1974-75, Can. Football League, Winnipeg, Can., 1976, NFL Phila. Eagles, 1977-80; cross-cultural community planner City and County of Honolulu, 1975; sr. counselor Pa. Prison Soc., Phila., 1982; pres. bd. Career Transition Inst., Inc., Phila., 1981-83; psychologist, health care adminstr. West Jersey Health System, 1984-87; pvt. practice cons., 1988—; pres., chief exec. officer Athletic Motivation, Inc., 1989-92; team psychologist for Balt. Orioles, 1989-94, Phila. Eagles, 1988-92, Phila. 76ers, 1986-92; lectr. in field; dir. player programs NFL, 1992-97, v.p. employee and player devel., 1997—; bd. dirs. YMCA of Greater N.Y. Mem. Nat. Adv. Coun. on Violence Against Women, chmn. sports subcom., 1995—; bd. dirs. Corp. Alliance to End Ptnr. Violence, 1995—. Served with USMC, 1965-69, Vietnam. Decorated Vietnamese Service award, Vietnamese Commendation award; recipient cert. of appreciation Kiwanis Club, Ramon, Calif., 1979, Del. Valley Med. Ctr., Phila., 1980, Community Service award Com. on Alcohol and Drug Abuse Crozer Chester Hosp., 1981. Mem. Am. Psychol. Assn., Am. Psychotherapy Assn., N.Y. Acad. Scis., Am. Coll. Forensic Examiners, World Fedn. Mental Health, NFL Alumni Assn. (bd. dirs. Phila. Eagles chpt. 1986-98), Maxwell Football Club (life, v.p. community rels. 1990—, bd. govs.). Office: NFL Hdqs 280 Park Ave New York NY 10017-1216

BURNHAM, PATRICIA WHITE, consultant advocate, writer, business executive; b. Omaha, July 30, 1933; d. William Max and Berniece Irene (Shockey) Orr; m. William L. White, June 18, 1955 (div. Nov. 1979); children: Lucinda, Christopher, Duncan; m. Robert A. Burnham, Feb. 23, 1980. BA in English, DePauw U., Greencastle, Ind., 1955; MA in English, Ill. State U., 1966, PhD in Adminstrn., 1977. Tchr. Morton Grove (Ill.) and Evansville (Ind.) pub. schs., 1955-60; instr. Ill. State U., Normal, 1963-71, dir. Nat. Student Exchange, 1971-74, dir. continuing edn., 1974-76, asst. dean, 1976-79; assoc. dir. Ill. Bd. Higher Edn., Springfield, 1979-80; assoc. vice provost Ohio State U., Columbus, 1980-81; specialist bus. ins. Nationwide Ins. Co., Columbus, 1981-83; v.p. pvt. banking Chase Manhattan Bank, N.A., N.Y.C., 1983-88; pres. Transitions Group, Inc., East Burke, Vt., 1986—; adj. prof. U. Vt., 1997—. Author: Life's Third Act, 1994; contbr. articles to publs. and seminars on successful aging, adult policies and programs. Pres. bd. dirs. Northeastern Vt. Hosp., St. Johnsbury, 1995—; bd. dirs. Vt. Cmty. Loan Fund, Vt. Coun. on Humanities, Vt. Assn. Nonprofit Orgns., 1998—; pres. Coun. Vt. Elders, 1994-99. Mem. Gerontol. Assn., Phi Beta Kappa, Phi Delta Kappa. Congregationalist. Avocations: hiking, literature, computers. Office: Transitions Group Inc PO Box 239 East Burke VT 05832-0239

BURNIE, JAMES PETER, medical microbiologist, educator; b. Rotherham, Yorkshire, Eng., Aug. 17, 1956; s. James Peter and Margaret Mark (Reid) B.; m. Ruth Christine Matthews, May 30, 1987; children: James Richard, Andrew Peter. BA, Cambridge (Eng.) U., 1977, MA, 1980, MB BChir, 1980, MD, 1986, DSc, 1998. Lectr. Royal London Hopss., 1983-86; sr. lectr. St. Bartholomew's Hosp., 1986-89; prof. med. microbiology Manchester U., 1989—, dir. clin. svcs., 1991—, head of dept. pathol. scis., 1994—; med. dir. NeuTec Pharma PLC, 1996—. Contbr. more than 100 articles to profl. jours. including Jour. Clin. Microbiology, Infection and Immunity, among others. Mem. Royal Coll. Physicians, Royal Coll. Pathologists (examiner 1996-97). Avocation: entomology. Home: 1 Greystoke Dr, Alderley Edge, Cheshire SK9 7PY, England Office: Manchester Royal Infirm, Oxford Rd, Manchester M13 9WL, England

BURNLEY, JUNE WILLIAMS, secondary school educator; b. St. Augustine, Fla., Mar. 13, 1936; d. Marcellus Henry Gilford and Ella (Broadus) Williams. BS, N.C. Agrl. and Tech. U., 1958; MA, Villanova U., 1975, St. John's Coll., Annapolis, Md., 1993; student, Oxford U., London, 1996. Cert. English tchr., counseling psychologist. Grade sch. tchr., 1958-59; lang. arts supr. Wharton Ctr., Phila., 1967-68; English/French lang. tchr. Hatch. Jr. H.S., Camden, N.J., 1962-68; English lang. tchr. George Washington H.S., Phila., 1968-93, secondary counseling intern, 1975; mem. English Club, Phila., 1968-95, Pa. State Coun. English Tchrs., 1968-93, Educators to Africa, Phila., 1993-97; tutor Temple-New Career Ladders, 1975-76; Commonwealth partnership Bryn Mawr Coll., 1985. Mem. Germantown Civic League, Phila., 1993, West Mt. Airy Neighbors, Phila., 1968—, Social Action Com., Phila., 1993-95, Germantown Hist. Soc., Unitarian Soc. Germantown; vol. guide in tng. Phila. Mus. Art, 1996—. Pa. State Bd. Edn. fellow, 1985, Arco & Exxon fellow, 1991, St. John's Coll. fellow, 1992-93. Fellow Commonwealth Partnership; mem. Nat. Coun. English Tchrs. (Svc. award 1972), Eleanor Trailor Readers (co-founder), Literary Group (founder), Literati (founder), Amnesty Internat., Phi Delta Kappa, Delta Sigma Theta. Avocations: reading, travel, knitting, sewing, word games. Home: 700 Elkins Ave Apt E3 Elkins Park PA 19027-2315

BURNOUF, THIERRY PIERRE, pharmaceutical executive; b. Pontoise, France, Mar. 8, 1955; came to U.S., 1983; s. Roger Jules and Therese (Martin) B.; m. Julia Miryana Radosevich; children: Sylvie, Pierre-Alain. B. Sci. U., Lille, France, 1976; MS, Sci. U., 1977, PhD, 1981; postdoc. degree, No. Regional Rsch. Ctr., Peoria, Ill., 1984. Postdoc. rsch. asst. USDA, Peoria, 1981-84; head rsch. and devel. CRTS, Lille, 1984-86, dir. plasma fractionation, 1986-94; scientific dir. LFB, Paris, 1994-95; v.p. Haemonetics, Braintree, Mass., 1996-98; pres. Biotrust Internat. Corp., Taipei, Taiwan,

1999—; cons. World Bank, Washington, 1991, Coun. Europe, Strasbourg, France, 1992-96, European Commn., Luxembourg, 1992-97. Editor: Plasma Fractionation in Developing Countries, 1999; contbr. numerous articles to profl. jours.; patentee in field. Rotary fellow, 1981-82. Mem. Internat. Soc. Blood Transfusion, World Fedn. Hemophilia, European Soc. Biochromatography. Avocations: hiking, reading. Office: HPPS, 18 Rue Saint-Jacques, 59800 Lille France

BURNS, BONNIE, educator; b. Oak Park, Ill.; d. Albert and Irene Zanzi; 1 child, Julia Burns. BA, Northeastern Ill., 1967, MA, 1976; EdD, Loyola U., 1990. Tchr. Elk Grove (Ill.) Schs., 1967-70, River Grove (Ill.) Schs., 1972-79; reading lab. specialist Plainfield (Ill.) Schs., 1979-81; adminstrv. intern River Forest (Ill.) Schs., 1981-82; prin. Sauk Village (Ill.) Schs., 1982-85; tchr. River Forest Schs., 1988-2000, Dominican U., River Forest, 2000—; cons., state trainer Ill. Assessment, 1990-2000; instr. Triton Coll., River Grove, 1993-94; instr./facilitator Skylight/St. Xavier, Chgo., 1994-2000; nat. presenter Skylight Profl. Growth, Tenn., N.J., N.Y., Ill., 1995-2000. Author: How to Teach Balanced Reading and Writing, 1999; contbr. articles to profl. jours. Mem. Ill. Reading Coun., Phi Delta Kappa, Phi Sigma (sec. 1994-2000).

BURNS, BRENT EMIL, electrical engineer; b. Wynnewood, Okla., Dec. 3, 1952; s. Frank Brent and Dorothy Esther (Westberg) B. BSEE, U. Okla., 1978, MSEE, 1979; PhD of Elec. Engring., Stanford U., 1987. Mgr. Northrop Grumman Integrated Micro Sensors Group, Palos Verdes, Calif., 1985-98; prod. R and D mgr. Integrated Micromachines Inc., Pasadena, Calif., 1998—. Patentee on micro-electro-mechanical systems/silicon micromachining. With U.S. Army, 1972-74. Scholarship NSF 1979-82. Mem. IEEE, Electrochem. Soc., Tau Beta Pi, Eta Kappa Nu. Achievements include 4 U.S. patents in micro-electro-mechanical sys., silicon micromachining. Avocations: racquetball, bicycling, outrigger canoeing. Home: 26566 Basswood Ave Rancho Palos Verdes CA 90275-2269

BURNS, CASSANDRA STROUD, prosecutor; b. Lynchburg, Va., May 22, 1960; d. James Wesley and Jeanette Lou (Garner) Stroud; m. Stephen Burns; children: Leila Jeanette, India Veronica. BA, U. Va., 1982; JD, N.C. Cen. U., 1985. Bar: Va. 1986, N.J. 1986, U.S. Dist. Ct. (ea. dist.) Va. 1987, U.S. Ct. Appeals (4th cir.) 1987, U.S. Bankruptcy Ct. (ea. dist.) Va. 1987; cert. in criminal law. Law clk. Office Atty. Gen. State of Va., Richmond, summer 1984; law intern Office Dist. Atty. State of N.C., Durham, 1985; staff atty. Tidewater Legal Aid Soc., Chesapeake, Va., 1987-89; asst. atty. Commonwealth of Va., Petersburg, 1989-90; assoc. atty. Bland and Stroud, Petersburg, 1990; asst. pub. defender City of Petersburg, 1990-91; Commonwealth's atty. City of Petersburg, Va., 1991—; founder BED Task Force on Babies Exposed to Drugs, 1991, Buddies of Petersburg Program, 1997—. Sec. Chesapeake Task Force Coun. on Youth Svcs., 1987-89; ch. directress and organist; mem. NAACP; chair Petersburg-Dinwiddie Cmty. Criminal Justice Bd. Mem. Va. Bar Assn. (mem. coun. 1993—), Old Dominion Bar Assn., Va. Assn. Commonwealth Attys. (bd. dirs., mem. coun. 1993—), Legal Svcs. Corp. Va. (bd. dirs.), Nat. Bd. Trial Advocacy (cert.), Soutside Va. Legal Aid Soc. (bd. dirs.), Petersburg Bar Assn., Nat. Black Prosecutors Assn. (regional dir.), Petersburg Jaycees, Order Eastern Star, Peterburg C. of C., Kiwanis, Internat., Buddies Club, Phi Alpha Delta, Alpha Kappa Alpha. Democrat. Baptist. Avocations: piano, organ, volleyball, needlework, pets. Home: 326 N Park Dr Petersburg VA 23805-2442 Office: Commonwealth's Atty 39 Bollingbrook St Petersburg VA 23803-4568

BURNS, DAN W., manufacturing company executive; b. Auburn, Calif., Sept. 10, 1925; s. William and Edith Lynn (Johnston) B.; 1 child, Dan Jr. Dir. materials Menasco Mfg. Co., 1951-56; v.p., gen. mgr. Hufford Corp., 1956-58; pres. Hufford div. Siegler Corp., 1958-61; v.p. Siegler Corp., 1961-62, Lear Siegler, Inc., 1962-64; pres., dir. Electrada Corp., Culver City, Calif., 1964; pres., chief exec. officer Sargent Industries, Inc., L.A., 1964-85, chmn. bd. dirs., 1985-88; now chmn. bd. dirs., CEO Arlington Industries, Inc.; bd. dirs. Gen. Automotive Corp., Dover Tech. Internat., Inc., Kistler Aerospace Corp. Bd. dirs. San Diego Aerospace Mus., Smithsonian Inst., The Pres.'s Cir., Nat. Acad. Scis., Atlantic Coun. of U.S., George C. Marshall Found. Capt. U.S. Army, 1941-47; prisoner of war Japan; asst. mil. attache 1946, China; adc to Gen. George C. Marshall 1946-47. Mem. OAS Sports Com. (dir.), L.A. Country Club, St. Francis Yacht Club, Calif. Club, Conquistador del Cielo, Cosmos Club Washington. Home: 7400 Bryan Canyon Rd Carson City NV 89704-9588

BURNS, DOUGLAS ALAN, hydrologist; b. Worcester, Mass., Dec. 15, 1956; s. Richard Fosdick and Marilyn (Carlson) B.; m. Karen Marie Pirozzi, Jan. 19, 1992 (div. Mar. 9, 1999). BA, Hope Coll., 1978; MS, U. Va., 1982; PhD, SUNY, Syracuse, 1999. Instr. Washington and Lee U., Lexington, Va., 1982-83; tchr. Charles E. Smith Jewish Day Sch., Rockville, Md., 1983-84; hydrologist U.S. Geol. Survey, Reston, Va., 1984-87, Troy, N.Y., 1987—; vis. scientist Nat. Inst. Water and Atmospheric Rsch., Hamilton, New Zealand, 1999. Contbr. articles to profl. jours. Mem. Geol. Soc. Am., Am. Geophys. Union. Ecol. Soc. Am., Soil Sci. Soc. Am., New Zealand Hydrological Soc., Sigma Gamma Epsilon. E-mail: daburns@usgs.gov. Office: US Geol Survey 425 Jordan Rd Troy NY 12180-8349

BURNS, JAMES MILTON, retired educator; b. Coal City, Ind., Feb. 22, 1922; s. Ray L. and N. Eugenie (Pickett) B.; m. Thomasina Ciofalo, Aug. 22, 1970. MusB, Manhattan Sch. Music, 1949, MusM, 1953; EdD, Fairleigh Dickinson U., 1984. Tchr. music Atlantic City Bd. Edn., 1968-92; researcher acoustics of band instruments. With USAAF, 1942-46. Mem. over 20 profl. assns.

BURNS, JOHN F., reporter; b. 1944. Fgn. corr., New Delhi bur. chief N.Y. Times, 1994-98, spl. corr. Islamic affairs, 1999—; bur. chief N.Y. Times, Johannesburg, Moscow, Peking, Toronto, Sarajevo, New Delhi. Recipient Pulitzer Prize for internat. reporting, 1993, 97, George Polk award for Fgn. Corr., 1979, 97. Office: NY Times 229 W 43rd St New York NY 10036-3959

BURNS, NEAL MURRAY, advertising agency executive; b. Chgo., July 16, 1933; s. Jack Arnold Burns and Esther (Dinitz) Rosenberg; m. Sandra Greenberg, 1958 (div. 1973); children: Marc Hillel, Scott Zachary; m. Martha Garrett Russell, 1988; 1 child, Alison Russell. Student, U. Chgo., 1951; BS, U. Ill., 1955; MSc, McGill U., 1955; PhD, Mcgill U., 1959. Lic. cons. psychol.;. Instr. McGill Univ., Montreal, 1956-58; chief environ. stress br. Air Crew Equipment Lab. USN, Phila., 1959-62; dir. mktg. Honeywell, Inc., Mpls., 1962-71; assoc. exec. dir. Higher Edn. Coord. Commn., St. Paul, 1971-74; pres. chief exec. officer The Burns Group, Inc., Mpls., 1974-86, pres., chief exec. officer, 1983-86; sr. v.p. Carmichael Lynch, Inc., Mpls., 1986-97, dir. rsch. and acct. planning; adj. prof. advt. U. Minn., 1987-97; prof. dept. advt. U. Tex., Austin, 1997—. Author, editor Unusual Environ. and Human Behavior, 1964. William Randolph Hearst fellow U. Tex., 1995. Mem. N.Y. Acad. Sci., Bus. Profl. Advt. Assn., Am. Acad. Advt. Avocations: traveling, theater. Office: CMA 7142 U Tex Austin TX 78712

BURNS, PAT ACKERMAN GONIA, information systems specialist, software engineer; b. Birmingham, Ala., July 16, 1938; d. Richard Lee and Hattie Eugenia (Bragg) Ackerman; m. Robert Edward Gonia, June 4, 1957 (div. Jan. 1973); children: Deborah Hayes, Junita Grantham, Ronald Gonia; m. James Clayton Burns, June 23, 1984 (dec. Dec. 1989). BS in Math., U. Ala., 1970, postgrad., 1971-77. Cert. secondary tchr., Ala. Missionary United Meth. Bd. of Missions, Sumatra, Indonesia, 1961-64; homebound tchr. Huntsville (Ala.) City Schs., 1970-75; mem. tech. staff Gen. Rsch. Corp., Huntsville, 1975-79; rsch. scientist Nichols Rsch. Corp., Huntsville, 1979-84, mgr. personnel div., 1984-87, mgmt. info. systems dept. head, 1987-90, dir. info. systems div., 1990-95; program mgr. MIS and tech. MIS U.S. Army Space and Strategic Defense Systems, 1990-93; dir. info. sys. Trinity United Meth. Ch., Huntsville, 1996-98; exec. dir. Trinity Personal Growth Ctr., Huntsville, 1999—; mem. adv. com. Drake Tech. Sch., Huntsville, 1988-94; program mgr. USASDC MIS//TMIS, 1990-94. Mem. PTA, Huntsville, 1994, Ch. Women United, Huntsville, Cmty. Chorus, Huntsville; bd. dirs. United Meth. Children's Home, 2000—. Mem. IEEE, NAFE, Data Processing Mgmt. Assn., Assn. Pers. Adminstrs., Am. Computer Soc., Huntsville C. of C. (spkr. 1986-95). Democrat. Methodist. Avocations: travel, music, old movies. Office: Trinity United Meth Ch 607 Airport Rd SW Huntsville AL 35802-1310

BURNS, PAUL YODER, forester, educator; b. Tulsa, Okla., July 4, 1920; s. Paul Patchin and Mary Emily (Knowles) B.; m. Kathleen Iola Chase, Dec. 4, 1942; children: Virginia B. Belland, Margaret B. Feierabend, Nancy B. McNeill. BS, U. Tulsa, 1941; M in Forestry, Yale U., 1946, PhD, 1949. Asst., assoc. prof. U. Mo., Columbia, 1948-55; prof. forestry La. State U., Baton Rouge, 1955-86, prof. emeritus of forestry, 1986-96; dir. sch. forestry La. State U., Baton Rouge, 1955-76; commr. La. Forestry Commn., Baton Rouge, 1955-76. Editor: Forest Management in Plan & Practice, 1956, Southern Forest Soils, 1959; co-editor: Southern Forestry in Practice, 1977, Christmas Tree Production & Marketing, 1983. Pres. bd. dirs. La. State U. YMCA-YWCA, Baton Rouge, 1957-59; mem. La. Conf. Ch. Bd., Baton Rouge, 1967-73; pres. La. Coun. Human Rels., Baton Rouge, 1987-89; chair bd. dirs. The FISH Good Samaritans, Baton Rouge, 1996. Recipient Disting. Alumnus award U. Tulsa, 1974, Humanitarian award Baton Rouge Coun. Human Rels., 1984, Peacemaking award, Bienville House Ctr. for Peace, Baton Rouge, 1991, Brotherhood award Baton Rouge chpt. NCCJ, 1995. Fellow Soc. Am. Foresters, La. Soc. Am. Foresters (chmn. 1990, Disting Svc. to Forestry 1989), Phi Kappa Phi, Sigma Xi, Xi Sigma Pi. Presbyterian. Avocations: tennis, piano. Home: 2137 Cedardale Ave Baton Rouge LA 70808-2810 Office: La State Univ Sch Forestry Wildlife And Fi Baton Rouge LA 70803-0001

BURNS, RICHARD GORDON, retired lawyer, writer, consultant; b. Stockton, Calif., May 15, 1925; s. Earl Gordon and Alberta Viola (Whale) B.; m. Eloise Estelle Beil, June 23, 1951 (div. May 25, 1985); children: Kenneth Charles, Donald Gordon. AA, U. Calif., Berkeley, 1948; AB, Stanford U., 1949, JD, 1951. Atty. Clausen & Burns, San Francisco, 1951-61; cons. Wyo. Pacific Oil Co., L.A., 1956—; pvt. practice Corte Madera, Calif., 1961-86; cons. Wyo. Pacific Oil Co., L.A., 1986—; pub. Good Book Pub., Kihei, Hawaii, 1991—; bd. dirs. Clean Fuels Hawaii. Author (as Dick B.): New Light on Alcoholism: God, Sam Shoemaker and A.A., 1999, The Akron Genesis of Alcoholics Anonymous, 1998, (with Bill Pittman) Courage To Change, 1998, Anne Smith's Journal, 1998, Dr. Bob and His Library, 1998, The Good Book and The Big Book: AA's Roots in the Bible, 1998, The Oxford Group and Alcoholics Anonymous, 1998, That Amazing Grace, 1996, The Books Early AAs Read for Spiritual Growth, 1999, Good Morning! Quiet Time, Morning Watch, Meditation, and Early A.A., 1998; Turning Point: A History of Early A.A.'s Spiritual Roots and Successes, 1997, Hope!: The Story of Geraldine D., 1998, Utilizing A.A.'s Spiritual Roots for Recovery Today, 1999, The Golden Text of A.A., 1999, By the Power of God, 2000; case editor Stanford Law Rev., 1950. Dir. Almonte Sanitary Bd., Marin County, Calif., 1962-64; v.p./sec. Lions Club, Corte Madera, 1961-64; pres. Almonte Improvement Club, Mill Valley, Calif., 1960, Cmty. Ch., Mill Valley, 1971, C. of C., Corte Madera, 1972, Corte Madera Ctr. Merchant Co., 1975, Redwoods Retirement Ctr., Mill Valley, 1980; dir. Clean Fuels Hawaii, 2000. Sgt. U.S. Army, 1943-46. Mem. Am. Hist. Assn., Authors Guild, Maui Writers Guild, Christian Assn. for Psychol. Studies, Phi Beta Kappa, Delta Tau Delta, Phi Delta Phi. Avocations: travel, Bible study, swimming, walking. Office: PO Box 837 Kihei HI 96753-0837

BURNS, RICHARD RAMSEY, lawyer; b. Duluth, Minn., May 3, 1946; s. Herbert Morgan and Janet (Strobel) B.; Jennifer, Brian; m. Elizabeth Murphy, June 15, 1984. BA with distinction, U. Mich., 1968, JD magna cum laude, 1971. Bar: Calif. 1972, U.S. Dist. Ct. (no. dist.) Calif. 1972, U.S. Ct. Appeals (9th cir.) 1972, Minn. 1976, U.S. Dist. Ct. Minn. 1976, Wis. 1983, U.S. Tax. Ct. 1983. Assoc. Orrick, Herrington, Rowley & Sutcliffe, San Francisco, 1971-76; ptnr. Hanft, Fride, P.A., Duluth, 1976—; gen. counsel Evening Telegram Co., Superior, Wis., 1982—, Murphy TV Stas., Madison, Wis., 1982—. Chmn. Duluth-Superior Area Cmty. Found., 1988-90; chair United Way of Greater Duluth, Inc., 1998-99; bd. dirs. Miller Dwan Found., Duluth Airport Authority, Northland Coll., Ashland, Wis. Fellow Am. Coll. Trust and Estate Counsel; mem. Calif. Bar Assn., Wis. Bar Assn., Minn. Bar Assn. (exec. com. bd. govs., past chmn. probate and trust coun.), 11th Dist. Bar Assn. (past pres., past chmn. ethics com.), Arrowhead Estate Planning Coun. (pres. 1980), Northland Country Club (pres. 1982), Boulders Club, Kitchi Gammi Club, Mpls. Athletic Club. Republican. Avocations: travel, golf, tennis, fishing. Home: 180 Paine Farm Rd Duluth MN 55804-2609 Office: Hanft Fride PA 1000 First Bank Pl 130 W Superior St Ste 1000 Duluth MN 55802-2056

BURNS, ROBIN C(AROL), mathematics theoretician, accountant; b. L.A., Mar. 18, 1948; d. Kenneth and Jeanne C. (Murray) B.; m. Philip L. Benedict, Aug. 25, 1966 (dec. 1968); m. Terrance R. Fuchek, Sept. 5, 1969 (div. 1988); children: Tracy, Bryan, Conni, Loren, Allan; m. William E. Pavone, July 6, 1991 (div. June 1993). Owner Math Pro Bus. Svcs., Tacoma, Wash., 1992—. Creator/producer pub. TV series: 9 Patch Palace, 1979-83, Robin's Nest, 1983-86; creator/owner WWW.MOMWIZ.COM; writer/producer songs: Cry on My Shoulder, Nothin' Average About Him, 1992-93; inventor in field; contbr. articles to profl. jours. Mem. Math. Assn. Am., Am. Assn. Profl. Bookkeepers, Alpha Sigma Lambda. Avocations: ethnic dance choreography, camping, songwriting, internet publishing. Home and Office: 2522 N Proctor St Tacoma WA 98406-5338

BURNS, TONI ANTHONY, artist; b. L.A., Sept. 6, 1937; d. Earle Francis and LaVerne Myrtle (Holmberg) Anthony; m. George Orin Burns, May 14, 1965; children: Robert Anthony, James Randolph. BA in Fine Arts, Calif. State U., Long Beach, 1959, postgrad., 1960. Cert. secondary tchr., Calif. Interior decorator Ruth Connor Interiors, Downey, Calif., 1960-62; tech. illustrator N.Am. Rockwell Corp., Downey, 1962-64, McDonnell-Douglas Aircraft, Long Beach, Calif., 1964-65; graphic layout artist Beckman Instruments, Fullerton, Calif., 1968-70; owner, creator Original Art Rock Owls, San Juan Capistrano, Calif., 1970-78; custom jewelry designer Jewelry by Toni Burns, San Juan Capistrano, 1979-98; jewelry designer, ptnr. SuperNatural Art, San Juan Capistrano, 1999—; wholesale exhibitor L.A. Gift Show, 1971-78, Beckman Handcrafts, L.A., 1982. Juried shows include Village West Gallery, Laguna Beach, Calif., summers 1971-75, Art-A-Fair Festival, Laguna Beach, 1984-86, Downey Art Mus., 1992, Fine Arts Pavillion, 1993. Recipient 1st pl. San Clemente Art Gallery, 1984, 99. Mem. Am. Craft Coun., Metal Arts Soc. So. Calif. Avocations: family genealogy, travel, photography. Office: SuperNatural Art 31412 Windsong Dr San Juan Capistrano CA 92675-2788

BURNSTEIN, DANIEL, lawyer; b. Hartford, Conn., Oct. 12, 1946; s. Lawrence J. and Margaret (Le Vien) B. AB, U. Calif., Berkeley, 1968; JD cum laude, New Eng. Sch. Law, 1975. Bar: Mass. 1975, U.S. Dist. Ct. Mass. 1976, U.S. Ct. Appeals (1st cir.) 1976. Pres. Beacon Expert Systems, Inc., 1989-99; dir. Interactive Video Project Harvard Law Sch., Cambridge, 1985-89, clin. instr.; lectr. Clark U., 1997—; pres. Ctr. for Atomic Radiation Studies, Acton, Mass., 1982—; advisor Am. Mgmt. Assn. for Negotiation Curriculum to Mgrs., 1993; pres.-COO BuzzIT.com, 1999—. Editor: The Digital MBA, 1995. Mem. ABA, Mass. Adv. Coun. on Radiation Protection. Office: 35 Gardner Rd Brookline MA 02445-4512

BURNTON, STANLEY JEFFREY, high court judge; b. London, Oct. 25, 1942; s. Harry and Fay (Levy) B.; m. Gwenyth Frances Castle, Sept. 2, 1971; children: Abigail, Simon, Rebecca. MA, U. Oxford, 1964. Barrister Mid. Temple, 1965-82; Queen's counsel, 1982-2000, high court judge, 2000—; Queen's Counsel; Bencher Mid. Temple. Avocations: travel, theatre, music, food, wine. Office: Royal Cts of Justice, Strand, London WC2A 2LL, England

BURR, BROOKS MILO, zoology educator; b. Toledo, Aug. 15, 1949; s. Lawrence E. and Beverly Joy (Herald) B.; m. Patti Ann Grubb, Mar. 5, 1977 (div. July 1987); 1 child, Jordan Brooks. BA, Greenville Coll., 1971; MS, U. Ill., 1974, PhD, 1977. Cert. scuba diver, Nat. Assn. Underwater Instrs. Lab. instr. dept. biology Greenville (Ill.) Coll., 1971-72; rsch. asst. Ill. Natural History Survey, Champaign, 1972-77; affiliate scientist Ctr. for Biodiversity Ill. Natural History Survey, Urbana, 1989—; from asst. prof. to prof. dept. zoology So. Ill. U., Carbondale, 1977—; mem. adv. panel U.S. Fish and Wildlife Svc., 1990—; adj. prof. dept. biology U. N.Mex., Albuquerque, 1991—; adj. prof. dept. ecology, ethology and evolution U. Ill., 1993—. Co-author: A Distributional Atlas of Kentucky Fishes, 1986, A Field Guide to Fishes, North America North of Mexico, 1991 (selected as one of Outstanding Acad. Books of 1992 by Choice Mag.); contbr. more than 90 articles to profl. jours. Recipient Paper of Yr. award Ohio Jour. Sci., 1986. Mem. AAAS, Am. Soc. Ichthyologists and Herpetologists (sec., mem. exec. com. 1990-94, pres.-elect 2000—), Soc. Systematic Zoology, Biol. Soc. Washington, Assn. Systematic Collections, Sigma Xi (Leo M. Kaplan award 1990). Achievements include the discovery and description of 9 species of fish new to science from North American fresh waters. Home: 203 S Wedgewood Ln Carbondale IL 62901-2147 Office: So Ill Univ Dept Zoology Carbondale IL 62901-6501

BURR, NORMAN JOHN, journalist, researcher, technical writer; b. Ilford, Essex, Eng., July 6, 1949; s. Edgar Charles and Ethel Kathleen (Deacon) B.; m. Wendy Holbrook, May 5, 1978; children: Thomas Alan, Jocelyn Frances. BSc in Engring., Bath (Somerset, Eng.) U., 1971, MS in Engring., 1973. Asst. editor Morgan-Grampian Ltd., London, 1974; staff writer Thomas Telford Ltd. New Civil Engr. Mag., London, 1974-78; chief sub editor Morecambe Press Ltd., Trial & Motocross News, 1978-79; editor Peter Fieldhouse & Co., N.W. Indsl. Rev., Manchester, Eng., 1978-79; tech. writer Lonsdale Tech. Svcs., Seconded to Vickers Shipbuilding, Barrow, Eng., 1979-80; asst. editor Textile Horizons, The Textile Inst., Manchester, 1980-82; freelance and editor Microlight Flying, Lancaster, Eng., 1982-95—; dir. Pagefast Ltd. (Design and Print), Lancaster, 1989—; cons. editor, 1995—. Co-author: (books) Ultralight and Microlight Aircraft of The World, Edit. 1, 1983, Rev. Edit. 2, 1985, 32 Days to Beijing, 1994, Living With Speed, 1997. Recipient Ashley Doubtfire trophy for svcs. to microlight aviation, 1995. Mem. Nat. Union of Journalists (br. treas. 1987-95). Avocations: motoring, history, travel, politics. Home: Bankfield House, Priest Hutton Carnforth, Lancashire LA6 1JL, England Office: PageFast Ltd, 4-6 Lansil Way, Lancaster LA1 3QY, England

BURRELL, E. WILLIAM, retired university adminstrator, educator; b. Providence, Apr. 28, 1927; s. Edward John and Helene Agnes (Kelly) B.; m. Barbara Mary O'Connor, Apr. 18, 1953; children: Jason Edwin, Mary Elizabeth. Student, Providence Coll., 1945-47; AB, Fordham U., 1949; MA, Boston U., 1959; EdD, Harvard U., 1964; HLD honoris causa, Salve Regina U., 1996. Tchr. Providence Sch. Dept., 1957-65; prof. English and edn. Salve Regina U., Newport, R.I., 1965-96, chmn. dept. edn., 1967-73, dean of coll., 1974-77, v.p., dean of faculty and grad. studies, 1977-95, emeritus prof., 1996—; mem. accreditation team, sometime chmn. New Eng. Assn. Schs. and Colls., Winchester, Mass., 1975-86. Mem. allocations panel United Way Southeastern New Eng., Providence, 1976-93; bd. dirs. Samaritans of R.I., Providence, 1985-90. Mem. R.I. Coun. Tchrs. English (life; founder 1959, pres. 1965-67), Barnard Club (pres. 1971-72), Phi Delta Kappa. Home: Pinard Cottages Apt H Newport RI 02840 also: The Abbey F202 1223 Commonwealth Cir Naples FL 34116-3626

BURRELL, JOEL BRION, neurologist, researcher, clinician; b. Orange, N.J., Nov. 27, 1959; s. Robert and Barbara (Miller) B. BS in Biology, Rutgers U., 1982, grad. student, 1983; MD, Temple U., 1987. Diplomate Am. Bd. Med. Examiners. Intern Abington (Pa.) Meml. Hosp., 1987-88; neurology resident The Mt. Sinai Med. Ctr., N.Y.C., 1988-91; neuroimmunology fellow Cleve. Clin. Found., 1991-93; attending physician with pvt. clin. practice, 1993—; asst. clin. prof. Med. Coll. Ohio, 1993-98. Presenter in field. Recipient Pinnacle award Being Single Mag., 1995; named to Outstanding Young Men of Am., 1998. Fellow Stroke Coun. of Am. Heart Assn., Internat. Biog. Assn. (named one of 2000 outstanding people of 20th century); mem. AMA (Physician's Recognition award 1992—), Am. Acad. Clin. Neurophysiology, Am. Acad. Neurology, Nat. Med. Assn., Acad. Medicine Cleve., Ohio Acad. Sci., Med. Alumni Assn. Temple U., Temple U. Gen. Alumni Assn., Huron County Med. Soc. (treas./sec. 1996-97), Am. Assn. Physicians and Surgeons. Avocations: tennis, skiing, ice skating, golf, travel. E-mail: Burrell@dnamail.com. Fax: (440)365-2903. Office: 511 S Abbe Rd Ste C Elyria OH 44035-6301

BURRELL, MARGARET ANN, French educator; b. Lower Hutt, New Zealand, May 19, 1947; d. Hughie Gilbert and Mary Alicia (Baker) B.; m. Malcolm Gordon Laird, Apr. 5, 1975; children: Tamsin Eleanor, Marion Islay, Fiona Beatrice. BA, U. Canterbury, New Zealand, 1968; MA with honors, Victoria U. of Wellington, New Zealand, 1969; PhD, U. Toronto, Can., 1974. Lectr. U. Canterbury, 1972-79, sr. lectr., 1979—; mem. Canberbury Opera. Editor jour. Australasian Univs. MLA, 1975-88, 91-98; founding editor U. Canterbury Press, 1988-91; contbr. articles to profl. jours. V.p. Kindergarten Com., Christchurch, 1986; mem. com. Christchurch Ballet Soc., 1987-88, Burnside H.S. PTA, Christchurch, 1997, Friends of Canterbury Opera, 1997. Commonwealth scholar Can. Govt., 1969; summer fellow U. Toronto, 1971, vis. fellow HRC, Australian Nat. U., 1978. Mem. Univ. Bd. Mgmt. Inco., Internat. Arthurian Soc., Soc. for Study of Medieval Langs. and Lit. Avocations: choral singing, gardening. Office: U Canterbury Dept French, Pvt Bat 4800, Christchurch New Zealand

BURRELL, MICHAEL PHILIP, actor, writer; b. Harrow, Eng., May 12, 1937; s. Frederick Albert and Dora Edith (Jones) B. BA, Peterhouse, Cambridge U., 1961, MA, 1965. Mem. Royal Shakespeare Co., 1961-64; dir. King's Lynn Festival, 1965, Chichester Festival Co., 1966, 68; assoc. dir. Royal Lyceum Theatre, Edinburgh, Scotland, 1966-68, Derby Playhouse, 1974-76; dir. Wells Ctr. Ltd., 1982-86; chmn. KBE Ltd., 1983-89; dir. TieBreak Ltd., 1988—; dir. Theatre Royal, Bury St. Edmunds, 1994-2000; dir., chief exec. Angles Theatre, Wisbech, 1995-2000; artistic adviser King's Lynn Festival, 1997-98; chmn. Wisbech Events Forum, 1998—. Star theatrical prodn. and TV adaptation Hess, London, 1978, N.Y.C., 1979 (Bronze award for TV version N.Y. Film Festival 1986, Capital Critics citation as best actor-stage version, Ottawa, Ont., Can. 1986); stage appearances in 40 countries and numerous TV appearances, 1963—; author: (plays) Hess, 1978, Love Among the Butterflies, 1984, Borrowing Time, 1986, The Man Who Lost America, 1989, My Sister Next Door, 1989, Funker Rauch, 1992, Lord of the Fens, 1999, others. Served with Brit. Army, 1956-58. Recipient Obie award, 1980, Best Actor and Best Show awards Edmonton Theatre Festival, Can., 1984, Best Actor award for Burrell on the Bard, Edmonton, 1985. Office: care Richard Stone Ptnrship, 2 Henrietta St, London WC2E 8PS, England

BURRI, BETTY JANE, research chemist; b. San Francisco, Jan. 23, 1955; d. Paul Gene and Carleen Georgette (Meyers) B.; m. Kurt Randall Annweiler, Dec. 1, 1984. BA, San Francisco State U., 1976; MS, Calif. State U., Long Beach, 1978; PhD, U. Calif. San Diego, La Jolla, 1982. Research asst. Scripps Clinic, La Jolla, 1982-83, research assoc., 1983-85; research chemist Western Human Nutrition Rsch. Ctr., USDA, San Francisco, 1985-99, Davis, Calif., 1999—; adj. prof. nutrition dept. U. Nev., 1993-98, U. Calif., 2000—; mem. steering com. Carotenoid Rsch. Interaction Group, 1994-97. Co-editor Carotenoid News; contbr. articles to profl. jours. Grantee NIH, 1982, 85, USDA, 1986-2000, Spinal Cord Rsch. Found., 1998; affiliate fellow Am. Heart Assn., 1983, 84. Mem. Assn. Women in Sci. (founding dir. San Diego chpt.), N.Y. Acad. Sci., Carotenoid Rsch. Interaction Group, Internat. Carotenoid Soc., Am. Chem. Soc. Office: Western Human Nutrition Rsch Ctr Mailstop U000 1 Shields Ave Davis CA 95616-5270

BURRIDGE, RICHARD ALAN, college dean; b. Bath, Eng., June 11, 1955; s. Alan and Iris Joyce (Coates) B.; m. Susan Morgan, Sept. 1, 1979; children: Rebecca, Sarah. BA in Literae Humaniores, Oxford (Eng.) U., 1977, MA, 1981; PGCE, Nottingham (Eng.) U., 1978, diploma in theology, 1983, PHD, 1989. Ordained minister Ch. of England, 1985. Classics master Sevenoaks Sch., Kent, Eng., 1978-82; curate St. Peter & St. Paul, Bromley, Kent, 1985-87; chaplain, lectr. U. Exeter, Devon, Eng., 1987-94; dean King's Coll. London, 1994—; rep. for U. London to Gen. Synod, 1994—; lic. reader St. Mary's Ch., Kippington, Sevenoaks, Eng., 1979-82, St. Helen's Ch., Stapleford, 1982-85; convenor Ctr. Bromley Ministers' Fraternal, 1986-87; mem. coun. mgmt. St. John's Coll., Nottingham, 1986-99; tutor St. John's Coll., 1985-90; lectr., acad. tutor South West Ministry Tng. Course, 1987-94; chaplain Northcott Theatre, Exeter, 1987-94; mem. coun. reference Monarch Publs., Tunbridge Wells, Eng., 1992-99; mem. bd. studies North Thames Ministry Tng. Course, 1994—; theol. adviser (film) Miracle Maker, 1995-2000; mem. comm. com. Ch. of Eng., 1995-99, chmn. ednl. validatory panel, 1995—; adviser, writer New Millennium Experience Co., 1998-2000. Author: Sex Therapy: Some Ethical Consideration, 1985, What are the Gospels? A Comparison with Graeco-Roman Biography, 1992, paperback edit., 1995, Four Gospels, One Jesus? A Symbolic Reading, 1994, Where Shall We Find God?, 1998, John: The People's Bible Commentary, 1998, Faith

Odyssey, 2000; contbr. articles to profl. publs. and regular contbr. and spokesman on TV, radio and other media. Commissary for the bishop of High Veld Ch. of the Province So. Africa, 1997—. Mem. Soc. for Study of Theology, Soc. Bibl. Lit., Studiorum Novi Testamenti Societas, Christian Evidence Soc. Mem. Ch. of Eng. Avocations: reading, cycling, golf. Office: King's Coll, London Strand, London WC2R 2LS, England

BURRIDGE, SIMON ST. PAUL, advertising executive; b. London, Mar. 20, 1956; s. James Dugdale B. and Anne Henrietta Maria St. Paul (Butler) Younger; m. Camilla Rose Barkes, Sept. 13, 1986; children: Facility, Laura, Katie. MA, Oxford U., 1977. Grad. trainee Auerbarker Negoman, London, 1979; acct. exec. Minden Luby & Assocs., London, 1979-80; acct. dir. Dewt Rogerson, London, 1980-84, bd. dir., 1984-87; bd. dir. JWT, London, 1987-94; sr. bd. dirs. AMV BDBO, London, 1994-96; mnd. dir. JWT, 1996—. Home: 26 Herndon Rd, London SW18 2DG, England Office: J Walter Thompson, 40 Berkcley Sq, London W1X 6AD, England

BURRIEL, RAMON, physicist, researcher; b. Zaragoza, Spain, May 7, 1950; s. Roman Burriel and Pascuala Lahoz; m. Juliana Lopez, July 20, 1974; children: Marta, Monica, Isabel. B of Physics, U. Zaragoza, 1974, PhD in Physics, 1979. Postdoctoral scholar U. Mich., Ann Arbor, 1980-81; rsch. assoc. U. Ill., Chgo., 1981-83; asst. prof. U. Zaragoza, 1983-87; rsch. scientist Consejo Superior de Investigaciones Cientificas, Zaragoza, 1987-93, prof., head dept., 1993—; assoc. rsch. dir. Nat. Ctr. Sci. Rsch., Grenoble, France, 1992; vis. prof. U. Ill., Chgo., 1988; rsch. assoc. Argonne (Ill.) Nat. Lab., 1988. Contbr. numerous papers to sci. jours. Officer Spanish Mil., 1973-74. Doctoral grantee Ministry of Edn., 1975-78, postdoctoral grantee, 1980-83. Mem. European Physics Soc., Spanish Physics Soc. Avocations: mountaineering, squash, music, reading. Home: Ruisenores 22, 50006 Zaragoza Spain Office: Inst Materials Scis Aragon, Plaza San Francisco, 50009 Zaragoza Spain

BURRIS, B. SHANE, economist; b. Oak Ridge, Tenn., June 6, 1960; s. Charlie Benjamin Burris and Gloria Fay Harmon. BSBA, U. Tenn., 1982. Cert. economist. Loan officer Capitol Credit Corp., Knoxville, Tenn., 1983-86; loan officer collection mgr. and asst. mgr. Security Pacific Fin. Co., Knoxville, 1986; account officer FDIC, Knoxville, 1986-87; state loan officer State of Tenn., Nashville, 1988-92; dir. Monroe County Econ. Devel., Madisonville, Tenn., 1992—. 0em. So. Indsl. Devel. Coun., Knoxville, 1993—, Tenn. Indsl. Devel. Coun., 1993—; sec./treas. East Tenn. Indsl. Coun., 1996, v.p., 1997, pres., 1998. Mem. Kiwanis, Monroe County C. of C. Baptist. Avocations: hunting and fishing, golf, racquetball, water-skiing. Office: Monroe Cty Econ Devel 103 College St Ste 5 Madisonville TN 37354-1462

BURRIS, BOYD LEE, psychiatrist, psychoanalyst, physician, educator; b. Knoxville, Tenn., Jan. 28, 1930; s. Fred Roosevelt and Mildred Blanche Burris. BS, U. Tenn., Knoxville, 1951; MD, U: Tenn., Memphis, 1952. Diplomate in psychiatry Am. Bd. Psychiatry and Neurology; cert. in psychoanalysis. Tng. and supervising analyst Balt.-Washington Inst. for Psychoanalysis, Washington, 1974—, co-dir., 1980-86; clin. prof. psychiatry and behavioral scis. George Washington U. Sch. Medicine, Washington, 1983—; clin. prof. psychiatry Georgetown U. Sch. Medicine, Washington, 1990—; dir., pres. bd. trustees Ctr. for Advanced Psychoanalytic Studies, Princeton, N.J., Aspen, Colo., 1994—; pvt. practice psychiatry and psychoanalysis Washington, 1960—; active staff George Washington U. Hosp., 1963-96; cons. Potomac Found. for Mental Health, Bethesda, Md., 1969-78, St. Elizabeth's Hosp., Washington, 1969-88. Contbr. chpt. to book, articles to profl. jours. Lt. comdr. M.C., USN, 1954-56. Mem. Am. Psychiat. Assn. (chair tellers com. 1987-88), Am. Psychoanalytic Assn. (bd. on profl. standards 1982-86, 2000-2002), Balt./Washington Soc. for Psychoanalysis (pres. 1978-79). Home: 3100 Rolling Rd Chevy Chase MD 20815-4038 Office: 4545 42nd St NW Ste 310 Washington DC 20016-4623

BURRIS, CRAVEN ALLEN, retired college administrator, educator; b. Wingate, N.C., Sept. 11, 1929; s. Craven Cullom and Virginia Neulin (Currie) B.; m. Jane Russell Burris, June 19, 1955; children: Christa Cullom, David Allen. AA, Wingate Coll., 1949; BS, Wake Forest U., 1951; BDiv, Southeastern Bapt. Sem., Wake Forest, N.C., 1958; MA, Duke U., 1959, PhD, 1964. Prof. history and govt. Gardner-Webb U., Boiling Springs, N.C., 1958-66; prof. history, govt. and interdisciplinary studies St. Andrews Presbyn. Coll., Laurinburg, N.C., 1966-69; v.p., dean of coll., prof. history and politics Meredith Coll., Raleigh, N.C., 1969-98, ret., 1998, acting pres., 1971. Contbr. articles to profl. jours. Precinct ofcr. State Conv. del., N.C. Dem. Party, 1969, 71; pres., dir. Tammy Lynn Found./Retarded Children, Raleigh, 1980—; chmn. Raleigh Hist. Dists. Commn., 2000-2001. Lt. USNR, 1951-55, Italy and Atlantic Fleet. Recipient Disting. Alumni award Wingate U., 1983, Fulbright Study Trip, U.S. Govt., Pakistan, 1973, Study Trip USSR, 1988, Rsch. Brit. Mus. and Libr., 1963, 97. Mem. Civitan Internat. (v.p. bd. dirs. 1970—), Lions Club (editor 1965), Masons. Baptist. Avocations: choral singing, tennis, racquetball, golf, sailing, gardening. Home: 1322 Duplin Rd Raleigh NC 27607-3721 Office: Meredith Coll 3800 Hillsborough St Raleigh NC 27607-5237

BURRIS, KENNETH WAYNE, biologist, educator; b. Salisbury, N.C., Nov. 22, 1941; s. Ira J.B. and Dorothy Virginia (Rodgers) B.; m. Peggy Rogister Whitt, June 7, 1964; children: Kenneth Wayne Jr., Susan M. BS, High Point U., 1964; MA, East Carolina U., 1968; postgrad., N.C. State U., 1973-75. Specialist environ. health Moore County Health Dept., Carthage, N.C., 1964-65; instr. biology Mitchell Coll., Statesville, N.C., 1967-68; assoc. prof. biology Louisburg (N.C.) Coll., 1968-75; prof. biology Sandhills C.C., Pinehurst, N.C., 1975—. Author: Laboratory Exercises for Microbiology, 1985; co-author: Diseases of Fish, 1974; contbr. articles to profl. jours. Grantee NSF, 1969, 71. Mem. AAUP, Human Anatomy and Physiology Soc., Phi Theta Kappa (Horizon award 1995, advisor 1991—). Democrat. Avocations: sailing, sailboat racing, gardening. Home: 530 North Seven Lakes NC 27376 Office: Sandhills Cmty Coll 2200 Airport Rd Pinehurst NC 28374-8283

BURRONI, LUCA, nuclear medicine physician; b. Siena, Tuscany, Italy, Feb. 6, 1961; s. Graziano and Luciana (Periccioli) B.; m. Lucia Monti, Sept. 23, 1995. MD, U. Siena, 1987. Med. diplomate; cert. of specialization in nuclear medicine and radiology. Nuclear medicine physician U. Siena, 1992-95, head nuclear medicine, 1995—. Contbr. articles to profl. jours. Pres. Assn. Blood Donors, Siena, 1992—. With Italian Army, 1989-91. Mem. Internat. Soc. Radiolabelled Blood Elements, European Assn. Nuclear Medicine, Italian Assn. Nuclear Medicine, Automotor Club Storico Italiano. Roman catholic. Office: U Siena Policlinico Scotte, Viale Bracci, 53100 Siena Tuscany, Italy

BURROUGH, PETER ALAN, physical geographer; b. Wimborne, Eng., Aug. 26, 1944; s. Reginald Valentine and Lilian Abia (Peatey) B.; m. Josephine Pauline Barbara Mira Boenisch, June 5, 1971; children: Alexander Jan, Nicholas Peter. BSc with 1st class honors, U. Sussex, 1965; PhD, U. Oxford, 1969. Jr. lectr. phys. geography U. Oxford, 1968-69; sr. sci. officer U.K. Land Resources divsn. Ministry of Overseas Devel., U.K., 1970-73; lectr. in soil sci. U. N.S.W., Australia, 1973-76; sr. lectr. dept. soil sci. and geology Wageningen Agrl. U., 1980-84; prof. geographic info. systems and phys. geography U. Utrecht, The Netherlands, 1984—, dir. Utrecht Ctr. for Environment and Landscape Dynamics, 1998—; vis. rsch. scientist Soil Survey Inst., Wageningen, 1976-80; chmn. bd. Nexpri-Dutch Inter Univ. Ctr. for Spatial Info., 1988—, numerous others; chmn. sci. bd. European Geog. Info. Confs., 1990-94; chmn. rev. bd. U.K. Econs. and Social Rsch. Coun. GIS Labs., 1990-91; mem. exec. com. European Umbrella Orgn. for Geog. Info., 1994-98. Author: Principles of Geographical Information Systems, 1986, 2d edit., 1998; contbr. 40 books and book chpts.; contbr. over 140 articles to profl. publs.; mem. editl. bd. Internat. Jour. Geographical Info. Systems, Transactions in GIS, GIS Europe and Computers, Environment and Urban Systems. Grantee Dutch Nat. Sci. Found., European Union, others. Mem. British Soc. of Soil Sci., Dutch Soc. of Soil Sci., Dutch Remote Sensing Soc. Achievements include development, application and teaching of methods and tools of geographical information analysis for environmental monitoring and modelling. Office: U Utrecht Faculty Geogaphical Sci, Heidelberglaan 2, Utrecht The Netherlands

BURROUGHS, ANDREW KENNETH, internist, hepatologist, consultant; b. Beckenham, Kent, Eng., May 26, 1953; s. Kenneth Douglas and Vidia (Sfredda) B.; m. Rajesvarie Nulliah, Aug. 19, 1978 (div. Aug. 1991); 1 child, Natasha; m. Clare Constantine Davey, Nov. 27, 1993; children: James, Helena. MB, ChB with honors, Liverpool (Eng.) U., 1976. House physician Walton Hosp., Liverpool, 1976-77; sr. house officer Broadgreen Hosp., Liverpool, 1977-78; registrar in medicine Royal Free Hosp., London, 1978-81, clin. rsch. fellow, 1981-83; lectr. medicine Royal Free Hosp. Sch. Medicine, 1983-88, sr. lectr., 1988-93; cons. physician and hepatologist Royal Free Hampstead Nat. Health Svc. Trust, London, 1993—. Contbr. more than 200 articles to profl. jours. Decorated cavalier ufficiale Ordine del Merito (Italy). Fellow Royal Coll. Phyicians (London); mem. Internat. Assn. for Study Liver, Am. Assn. for Study Liver, European Assn. for Study Liver (sci. sec. 1997-99), Brit. Soc. Gastroenterology (coun. 1982-85). Methodist. Avocations: travel, philately, Italian. Office: Royal Free Hampstead NHS Tr, Pond St, Hampstead NW3 2QG, England

BURROUGHS, OLIVE JAMES, telephone company executive, city official; b. Owensboro, Ky., Sept. 24, 1950; d. Leroy Hayes and Minnie L. James; m. Jimmy L. Burroughs, Oct. 19, 1968; children: Yager Burroughs Lewis, Courtney, Kris Crawford. Student, Owensboro Bus. Coll., Brescia Coll. Telephone operator BellSouth, Owensboro, 1977—. Commr. City of Owensboro; city rep. to bd. dirs. O-DC C. of C., 1997; mem. Owensboro Youth Coun., 1997, Urban Charter Commn., Owensboro, 1989, African-Am. Heritage Commn., Ky., 1995; mem. human devel. bd. Ky. League of Cities, 1996, mem. human devel. commn., 1991; bd. dirs., pres. H.L. Neblett Cmty. Ctr., 1993—; mem. instnl. rev. bd. Owensboro Mercy Health Systems, 1996—; treas. Owensboro Human Rels. Commn.; v.p. Boys and Girls Club Coun., 1987; mem. Free Clinic of Owensboro, 1994-97; mem. Longfellow Edn. Adv. Coun., 1997—. Recipient Ky. Girl Scouts Woman of Distinction award Girl Scouts U.S., 1995, Svc. to Youth award Boys and Girls Club of Am., 1996, Outstanding Alumni award Govt. Leadership Owensboro Alumni Assn., 1997. Mem. Comm. Workers of Am. (sec. 1985). Democrat. Baptist. Avocations: jogging, cooking, reading, swimming. Office: City of Owensboro PO Box 10003 101 E 4th St Owensboro KY 42302-9003

BURROUGHS, SUSAN MARIE, psychologist, professor; b. Des Plaines, Ill., Dec. 16, 1969; d. James Edward and Dorothy Ann (Luszcz) B. BA with honors, Eastern Ill. U., 1992; MA with honors, Roosevelt U., 1995; PhD with honors, U. Tenn., 2000. Intern Human Rsch. and Data, Palatine, Ill., 1991; HR dept. Eastern Ill. U., Charleston, Ill., 1992, London House, Rosemont, Ill., 1994-95; cons. psychologist to industry, tchr., 1994—; Asst. Prof. mgmt. Roosevelt U., Chgo./Schaumburg, Ill., 2000—. Author: J of Org Beh (with M. Bing), 2001, J of Mgmt (with J. Bishop and K.D. Scott), 2000, J of Community Psychology (with L.Eby), 1998, J of Vocational Behavior (with T. Allen and M. Poteet), 1997, Plant Svs. (with J. Jones), 1995, Occupational Health/Safety (with J. Jones), 1995; chpt. in book, numerous presentations in field, papers under jour. review. Recipient: Am. Psychological Assn. Dissertation Rsch. award, 2000, Walter Melville Bonham Meml. Endowment award, 1999, Scholarly Rsch. Grant, 1999, Bus. Admin./Finance Fellowship award, 1998, Student Travel awards, 1997-00, Roosevelt U. Grad. Scholarship, 1994, Community/Econ. Devl. Assn. Scholarship, 1990-91, James J. McGrath Humanities Endowment Scholarship, 1990, Faculty Senate Scholarship, 1990, Honors: Outstanding Tchg. Award Nominee, 1999, Doctoral Consortium Rep., 1999, Ctr. for Advancement of Rsch. Methods/Analysis Junior Scholar, 1998, Internat. Personnel Mgmt. Assn. Assessment Coun. Paper Finalist, 1997, Psi Chi Honor Soc. Outstanding Psychology Student of the Year, 1992. Member: APA, Acad. Mgmt., Soc. Human Resource Mgmt., Soc. Indsl./Organizational Psychology, So. Mgmt. Assn. Committee svc. and participant in other activities. Roman Catholic. Avocations: theater, museums, drawing, music. Fax: 847-619-4852. E-mail: susanmburr@aol.com. Home: 707 N Prospect Manor Ave Mount Prospect IL 60056-2051 Office: Roosevelt Univ Coll Business Adminstrn 1400 N Roosevelt Blvd Schaumburg IL 60173-4377

BURROW, JOHN WYON, history educator, writer; b. Southsea, Hants, Eng., June 4, 1935; s. Charles Wyon and Alice Amy (Vosper) B.; m. Diane Margaret Dunnington, Nov. 10, 1958; children: Laurence Patrick, Francesca Mary. BA, Christ's Coll., Cambridge, 1957, PhD, 1961; D Polit. Sci. (hon.), U. Bologna, Italy, 1988. Rsch. fellow Christ's Coll., 1959-62; fellow Downing Coll., Cambridge, 1962-65; reader U. East Anglia, Norwich, 1965-69; reader U. Sussex, Brighton, 1969-81, prof., 1981-94; prof. U. Oxford, Eng., 1995-2000. Author: Evolution and Society, 1966, A Liberal Descent, 1981, Gibbon, 1985, Whigs and Liberals, 1988, The Crisis of Reason, 2000. Recipient Wolfson prize Wolfson Found., 1981; fellow Balliol Coll. Oxford, 1995-2000.. Fellow Brit. Acad., Royal Hist. Soc. Office: Arts Bldg, U Sussex, Falmer, Brighton BN1 9QN, England

BURROWS, CLIFFORD ROBERT, mechanical engineering educator; b. Shoeburyness, Eng., July 20, 1937; s. Edward Stephen and Edith Mable (Aspland) B.; m. Margaret Evelyn Mathews, July 8, 1961; children: Stephen Peter, Paul Robert, John Alastair, Rachel Elizabeth. BScME with 1st class honours, U. Wales, Swansea, 1962; PhD in Automotic Control, U. London, 1969, DSc in Engring., 1989; Dr-IngEh, U. Aachen, 2000. With borough treas.' dept. Southend Borough Coun., 1953-55; indsl. trainee Thames Board Mills Ltd., 1955-58; rsch. asst. Univ. Coll., Swansea, 1962-63; lectr., sr. lectr., then prin. lectr. West Ham Coll. Tech., 1963-69; lectr. U. Sussex Sch. Engring. and Applied Scis., 1969-80, reader, 1980-82; prof. dynamics and control U. Strathclyde, Scotland, 1982-87; prof. sys. engring., dir. Ctr. for Power Transmission and Motion Control U. Bath., Eng., 1987—, head Sch. Mech. Engring., 1990-95; dean of engring. and design U. Bath., 1996—; vis. rsch. assoc. U. Waterloo, Eng., 1976; dir. Engring. Design Ctr. in Fluid Power Sys., 1992—; vis. prof. Monash U., Melbourne, Australia, 1993; guest prof. Tokyo Inst. Tech., 1995; cons. to major cos. and govt. depts., U.K., 1975—. Editor Research Studies Press Fluid Power Series, 1988-97; contbr. more than 160 articles to profl. jours. Non-stipendiary priest Ch. of Eng., 1977—. Recipient O. Hugo Schuck best paper award Am. Automatic Control Coun., 1976. Fellow Royal Acad. Engrs., Instn. Elec. Engrs., Instn. Mech. Engrs. (editor Jour. Sys. and Control Engring. 1991—, mem. coun. 1995-98, mem. qualifications bd. 1995-96, chmn. machine sys., computing and control group com. 1994-96, William Sweet Smith prize 1990, Joseph Bramah medal 1993, Donald Julius Groen prize 1994), Inst. Mech. Engrs. (83rd Thomas Hawksley lectr.). Anglican. Avocation: rugby. Office: U Bath Fac Engring/Design, Claverton Down, Bath BA2 7AY, England

BURROWS, ELIZABETH MACDONALD, religious organization executive, educator; b. Portland, Oreg., Jan. 30, 1930; d. Leland R. and Ruth M. (Frew) MacDonald. Certificate, Chinmaya Trust Sandeepany, Bombay; PhD (hon.), Internat. U. Philosophy and Sci., 1975; ThD, Christian Coll. Universal Peace, 1992. Ordained to ministry First Christian Ch., 1976. Mgr. credit Home Utilities, Seattle, 1958, Montgomery Ward, Crescent City, Calif., 1963; supr. Oreg. dist. tng. West Coast Telephone, Beaverton, 1965; pres. Christ Ch. of Holy Chalice, Seattle, 1971—; prof. religion Christ Ch. of Holy Chalice, also bd. dirs.; pres. Archives Internat., Seattle, 1971—; v.p. James Tyler Kent Inst. Homeopathy, 1984-95; sec. Louis Braille Inst. for the Blind, 1995—. Author: Crystal Planet, 1979, Pathway of the Immortal, 1980, Odyssey of the Apocalypse, 1981, Maya Sangh, 1981, Harp of Destiny, 1984, Commentary for Gospel of Peace of Jesus Christ According to John, 1986, Seasons of the Soul, 1995, Voyagers of the Sand, 1996, The Song of God, 1998, Hold the Anchovies, 1996, Pilgrim of the Shadow, 1998, The Song of God, 1998; author of poetry (Publisher's Choice award Poets of the New Era, Disting. Poets of Am.). Recipient Pres. award for literary excellence CADER, 1994, 95, 97, Diamond Homer award Famous Poets Soc., 1998. Mem. Internat. Speakers Platform, Internat. New Thought Alliance, Cousteau Soc., Internat. Order of Chivalry, The Planetary Soc. Home: 10529 Ashworth Ave N Seattle WA 98133-8937

BURROWS, JOHN PHILIP, atmospheric research scientist, educator; b. Liverpool, England, Aug. 16, 1954; s. William Frederick and Kathleen Mary (Farley) B.; m. Brigitte Holtkotte, Apr. 20, 1990; 1 child Jan Drechsel. BA with honors, Trinity Coll., Cambridge U., 1975, MA, 1979, PhD, 1978. Rsch. scientist Smithsonian Astrophysical Obs., Cambridge, Mass., 1978-79; HSO UKAEA, 1979-82; visitor PCL Oxford U., 1979—; rsch. scientist Max-Planck-Inst. for Chemistry, Mainz, Germany, 1982-92; prof. atmospheric physics Bremen (Germany) U., Bremen, Germany, 1992—; vis. NASA-GSPC, Greenbelt, Md., 1995—; lead scientist GOME-ESA, 1988—; prin. scientist SCIAMACHY, 1988—. Mem. AGU, ACS. Roman Catholic. Home: Benquestrasse 47, 28209 Bremen Germany Office: Inst Environ Physics, U Bremen, 28334 Bremen Germany

BURROWS, MALCOLM, zoology educator; b. Luton, Eng., May 28, 1943; s. William Roy and Jean Jones (Brincklow) B.; m. Christine Joan Ellis, Jan. 1, 1966; children: Mark Callum, Gwynne Ruth. BA, Cambridge (Eng.) U., 1964, DSc, 1983; PhD, St. Andrews U., Scotland, 1967; MA, Oxford (Eng.) U., 1972. Postdoctoral fellow U. Oreg., Eugene, 1967-70; rsch. fellow Oxford (Eng.) U., 1970-74; lectr. Cambridge (Eng.) U., 1974-76, reader, 1983-86, prof. neurosci., 1986-96, prof. zoology/dept. head, 1996—; Cornelius Wiersma prof. Caltech, Pasadena, Calif., 1991; disting. vis. prof. U. Calif., Davis, 1992. Editor: Jour of Expl. Biolgoy; contbr. more than 100 articles to profl. jours. Recipient sci. medal Zool. Soc., 1980, Preistrager award Alexander von Humboldt, 1993. Fellow Royal Soc. London, Wolfson Coll. Cambridge; mem. Academia Europaea, Bayeriske Akademie du Wissenschaften, Munich, Germany. Avocations: modern jazz, cricket, gardening. Office: Cambridge U Dept Zoology, Downing St, Cambridge CB2 3EJ, England

BURROWS, MICHAEL DONALD, lawyer; b. Oak Park, Ill., May 23, 1944; s. Milford Denton and Helen Jean (Spitali) B.; m. Sandi Miller, Feb. 6, 1982; 1 child, Matthew Denton. BA, Williams Coll., 1967; JD, N.Y. Law Sch., 1973. Bar: N.Y. 1974, U.S. Dist. Ct. (ea. and so. dists.) N.Y. 1974, U.S. Ct. Appeals (2d cir.) 1978, U.S. Supreme Ct. 1981. Assoc. Baker & McKenzie, N.Y.C., 1973-80, ptnr., 1980-95, of counsel, 1995-99, mem. internat. exec. com., 1986-88; ptnr. Winston & Strawn, N.Y.C., 1999—. Co-author: The Practice of International Litigation, 1992. Served with USMC, 1968-70. Mem. ABA, Assn. Bar City N.Y. Office: Winston & Strawn 200 Park Ave New York NY 10166-0005

BURROWS, PHILIP NICHOLAS, physicist, researcher; b. Chorley, Eng., July 22, 1964; came to U.S., 1989; s. Nicholas Charles Burrows and Winefred Grace (Coyle) Hart. BA with honours, Oxford (Eng.) U., 1985, MA, DPhil, 1988. Chartered physicist, Eng. Rsch. assoc. Rutherford Lab., Eng., 1988; physicist Stanford (Calif.) Linear Accelerator Ctr., 1989—; rsch. assoc. MIT, Cambridge, 1989-91, rsch. scientist, 1991-95, prin. rsch. scientist, 1995-98; fellow particle physics and astronomy rsch. U. Oxford, Eng., 1998—. Contbr. articles to profl. jours. including Zeitschrift fü4 Physik C, Physics Letters B, Phys. Rev. D., Phys. Rev. Letters. Mem. Am. Phys. Soc., U.K. Inst. Physics, Sierra Club. Avocations: tennis, swimming, hiking, the arts, travel. Office: Stanford Linear Accelerator Ctr PO Box 4349 Stanford CA 94309-0450

BURROWS, ROBERT PAUL, optometrist; b. Chehalis, Wash.; s. Fremont O. and Pauline A. (Kostick) B.; m. Marilyn Burrows. BS in Visual Sci., Pacific U., 1979, OD, 1981. Assoc. optometric physician L.E. Hedgen, O.D. & Assocs., Chehalis, 1981-86; ptnr. Lewis County Eye & Vision Assocs., Chehalis, 1986—. Active United Way, 1981—. Rsch. grant PTU, 1980. Mem. Am. Optometric Assn. (charter contact lens sect., recognition award 1984-2000), Wash. Assn. Optometric Physicians, Kiwanis (dir. 1984-85, 89-90, 2000—), Twin City C. of C., Omega Epsilon Phi. Methodist. Office: 1179 S Market Blvd Chehalis WA 98532-3427

BURSA, MILAN, geodesist educator; b. Bojanov, Bohemia, Czech Republic, July 4, 1929; s. Josef and Berta (Dobiasova) B.; m. Danuse Hrubesova, Nov. 30, 1957 (div. Feb. 1981); 1 child, Milan. Astrogeodesy Engr., Moscow Geodetic Inst., 1956; Candidatus Scienciarum, Czech Tech. U., Prague, 1959; D Scienciarum, Czech Acad. Scis., Prague, 1973. Cert. space geodesy, astrogeodesy. Sr. scientist Rsch. Inst. Geodesy, Prague, 1956-74; head dept. solar sys. dynamics Astron. Inst. Acad. Sci., Prague, 1974-90, sr. scientist emeritus, 1994—; prof. space geodesy Czech Tech. U., Prague, 1987—; pres. Spl. Commn. IAG Astrogeodetic Constants, 1991-95; mem. adv. bd. Acta Geodaetica et Geophysica Hungarica, 1995—. Co-author: Gravity Field and Dynamics of the Earth, 1993, Dynamics of Artificial Satellites, 1993; contbr. articles to profl. jours., patentee in field. Recipient state prize for sci. Govt. Czech Republic, 1977. Fellow Internat. Assn. Geodesy (v.p. 1983-87); mem. Internat. Astron. Union, Astron. Soc. Czech Acad. Sci. (hon.), Czech Acad. Scis. (corr.). Avocation: science. E-mail: bursa@ig.cas.cz. Home: Donska 19/168, 11000 Prague Czech Republic Office: Astron Inst Czech Acad Scis, Bocni II/1401, 14131 Prague Czech Republic

BURSTEIN, STEPHEN DAVID, neurosurgeon; b. Bklyn., Apr. 10, 1934; s. Moe and Anna (Bloch) B.; m. Ronnie Sue Deutsch, Oct. 8, 1972; 1 dau., Alissa Aimee. B.A. with distinction, U. Mich., 1954; M.D., SUNY-Bklyn., 1958; M.S. in Neurosurgery, U. Minn.-Rochester, 1965. Diplomate Am. Bd. Neurol. Surgery. Surg. intern Johns Hopkins Hosp., Balt., 1958-59; neurosurgery fellow Mayo Clinic, Rochester, 1961-65; chief dept. neurosurgery South Nassau Community Hosp., Oceanside, N.Y., 1980—, pres. med. staff, 1980-82; chief dept. neurosurgery Franklin Gen. Hosp., Valley Stream, N.Y., 1980—; prin. Neurol. Surgery & Neurology, P.C., Freeport, N.Y., 1965—. Contbr. articles to med. jours. Bd. dirs. South Nassau Community Hosp., 1978—. Served to lt. USNR, 1959-61. Recipient Neurosurg. Travel award Mayo Found., 1966. Fellow ACS; mem. L.I. Hearing and Speech Soc. (bd. dirs.), N.Y. State Neurosurgeons Soc. (bd. dirs.), N.Y. State Neurosurg. Soc. (pres. 1981-82), Sigma Xi, Alpha Omega Alpha. Hebrew. Avocations: theatre; travel. Home: PO Box 752 Freeport NY 11520-0752 Office: Neurol Surgery & Neurology 88 S Bergen Pl Freeport NY 11520-3510

BURSTEN, STUART LOWELL, physician, biochemist; b. L.A., Jan. 19, 1953; s. Leo and Goldie (Zeff) B.; m. Colleen Sue Thompson, May 4, 1980; children: Elisa Michelle, Shawna Mariel, Tiana Marie. BS in Biology, Stanford U., 1975, AB Psychology, 1975; MD, Yale U., 1980. Diplomate Am. Bd. Internal Medicine, Am. Bd. Nephrology. Intern Boston City Hosp., 1980-81; resident internal medicine U. Wash., Seattle, 1981-83, fellow nephrology, 1983-85, postdoctoral rsch. fellow, nephrology, 1985-86; acting instr. U. Wash. Sch. Medicine, 1986-88, asst. prof. medicine, 1988-92, clin. asst. prof. medicine, 1992-94, clin. assoc. prof. medicine, 1994—; co-dir., second messenger protein chemistry divsn. Cell Therapeutic, Inc., 1992-95, prin. scientist, lipid biology and biochemistry, 1995-2000. Contbr. articles to profl. jours.; patentee. Rsch. dir. Friends of Snoqualmie Valley, Wash., 1986-89. Nat. Merit Found. scholar 1971, Nat. Grocers Assn. scholar, 1971, S&H Green Stamps Assn. scholar 1971; grantee NIH, 1975-78; recipient Northwest Kidney Found. Rsch. award, 1988-89, Nat. Inst. Arthritis, Diabetes, Digestive, and Kidney Diseases fellowship, 1985-86, others. Mem. AAAS, Am. Heart assn., Am. Fedn. Med. Rsch., N.Y. Acad. Scis., Am. Soc. Nephrology, Am. Chem. Soc., Am. Stats. Assn. Achievements include discovering that theobromine-based alkyl chains with patentable substitutions result in modulation of fatty acid and lipid peroxidative metabolism in mammalian cells, which in turn results in profound protection against acute inflammation and oxidant injury - this has introduced or is introducing an entire new class of compounds for treatment of a broad range of human diseases, incuding renal and liver disease, and protection against acute immune damage and the side effects of radiation; in addition, related compounds have been found to have potent anti-tumor activity based on interaction with lipid-directed enzymes. Home: PO Box 1870 Issaquah WA 98027-0077

BURSTIN, FRANCIS ERIC, political speaker, public relations consultant; b. Brussels, Belgium, Mar. 15, 1945; s. Octav and Marguerite (Piermont) B.; m. Danielle Toussaint, May 12, 1973; 1 child, Veronique. Lic. polit. and diplomatic scis., Free U. Brussels, 1970. Journalist La Libre Belgique, Brussels, 1968-80; dep. chief of cabinet dep. Prime Min., Min. Justice, Brussels, 1981-88; gen. dir. l'Institut Belge d'Information et de Documentation, Brussels, 1982-91; bd. mem. Sabena S.A., Brussels, 1984-92; spokesman Parti Reformateur Liberal, Brussels, 1992-99; vice chmn. Radio-TV (RTBF) de la Communaute 'française de Belgique, 1995-99; dep. head cabinet dep. Prime Minister Minister Fgn. Affairs, Brussels, 1999—; hon. mem. bd. S.A. Sabena, 1992—. Author: Maurice Cauwe, une revolution dans la distribution, 1972. Chmn. La Pense Liberale, Brussels. Officier de l'Ordre de Léopold II. Home: Avenue Penelope 63, 1190 Brussels Belgium Office: Ministry Fgn Affairs, rue des Petits Carmes 15, 1000 Brussels Belgium

BURT, ALASTAIR DAVID, medical researcher; b. Dunfermline, Scotland, Mar. 9, 1957; s. George Hoggan and Iris Helen Forrest (Young) B.; m. Alison Carol Tweedlie, Dec. 29, 1980; children: Jennifer, Stuart. BSc with 1st class honors, U. Glasgow, Scotland, 1979, MBChB with Commendation, 1981, MD with honors, 1991. Registrar Western Infirmary, Glasgow, 1982-85, sr. registrar, 1986-89; Peel traveling fellow Free U. Brussels, 1985-86; sr. lectr. pathology Newcastle (Eng.) Med. Sch., 1989-95; postgrad. sub-dean U. Newcastle, 1994-98; prof. hepatopathology Newcastle (Eng.) Med. Sch., 1995-98, head acad. dept. pathology, prof. pathology, 1998—; cons. Newcastle upon Tyne Hosps. Trust, Newcastle, 1989—. Author, editor: Pathology of Liver, 1994; editor Jour. Pathology, 1993-98, Hepatogastroenterology, 1994-98; editor-in-chief Liver, 1998—. Recipient Bellahouston medal U. Glasgow, 1992, Canterbury Med. Found. award Christchurch Med. Sch., 1993. Mem. Internat. Acad. Pathologists, Internat. Assn. for Study of Liver, Am. Assn. for Study of Liver Diseases, Royal Coll. Pathologists, Path. Soc. (Oakley lectr. 1993). Avocations: chamber and contemporary classical music, Indian cooking. Office: U Newcastle Dept Pathology, Royal Victoria Infirmary, Newcastle Upon Tyne NE1 4LP, England

BURT, PAUL ALEXANDER, oncologist; b. White Haven, U.K., Nov. 3, 1956; s. William Donald and Joan Hannah (Asquith) B.; m. Susan Frances Coster, Apr. 29, 1989; children: Jenna Natalie Rowena, Lauren Bethany Rebecca. MB, ChB, U. Birmingham, Eng., 1980. Sr. house officer radiotherapy Christie Hosp., Manchester, 1986, registrar radiotherapy, 1986-87, sr. registrar radiotherapy, 1987-89, cons. clin. oncologist, 1990—; registrar radiation oncology Westmead Hosp., Sydney, Australia, 1989-90; vis. clin. oncologist Leighton Hosp., Crewe, Eng., 1990—. Contbr. articles to profl. jours. Fellow Royal Coll. Radiologists, Royal Coll. Physicians London, Lancashire County Cricket Club, 1951 Radiotherasy Traveling Club. Avocations: cricket, gardening, wine, food, Stockport County Football Club. Office: Christie Hosp, Wilmolow Rd Withington, Manchester M20 4BX, England

BURTI, CHRISTOPHER LOUIS, lawyer; b. Muroc, Calif., Oct. 15, 1950; s. Louis Burti and Johanna Renate (Schmidt) Landa; m. Linda Carol Pipkin, Sept. 15, 1973; children: Christopher Louis Jr., Erika Pipkin. BSBA, East Carolina U., 1975; JD, U. N.C., 1979. Bar: N.C. 1979, U.S. Dist. Ct. (ea. dist.) N.C. 1983. Assoc. Lewis, Lewis & Lewis, Farmville, N.C., 1979-82; ptnr. Lewis & Burti, Farmville, 1982-94; v.p., legal counsel Statewide Title, Inc., Greenville, N.C., 1994—; atty. Town of Farmville, N.C., 1982-94, Town of Falkland, 1989—. Bd. dirs. Farmville Child Devel. Ctr., 1983-84, 2000—, Farmville Cmty. Arts Coun., 1983-84, Farmville Charitable Svcs., 1987-89; cubmaster Farmville Troop 25 Boy Scouts Am.; sec. N.C. Land Title Assn., 1999-00. With U.S. Army, 1970-72. Mem. N.C. Bar Assn., N.C. Mcpl. Attys. Assn. (bd. dirs. 1988-89, chmn. cable comm. com. 1991), Pitt County Bar Assn., Nat. Inst. Mcpl. Law Officers (mcpl. utilities com.), Farmville C. of C. (bd. dirs. 1982-83), Farmville Country Club, Masons (past master, past dist. dep. grand master), Phi Kappa Phi, Beta Gamma Sigma, Phi Sigma Pi. Democrat. Episcopalian. Avocations: sailing, skiing, woodworking, photography. Office: Statewide Title Inc 110 E Arlington Blvd Greenville NC 27858-5012

BURTLEY, CALVIN, painter, educator, publisher; b. Cairo, Ill., Feb. 28, 1945; s. Brooks Jr. and Gustava (Robinson) B. Cert., Famous Artist Sch., Conn., 1973; AA, L.A. Trade Tech. Coll., 1982; BFA, U. So. Calif., 1992. Ordained elder, Presbyn. of Pacific. Graphic artist U. So. Calif., L.A., 1982-92; art cons. L.A., 1992-95; pub. rels. adminstr. Cultural Affairs, L.A., 1995-96; pres. Burtley Fine Arts, L.A., 1997—; tchr. Jr. Art Ctr., L.A., 1999. Exhbns. include Palms Westminster Presbyn. Ch., L.A., 1995, L.A. Mcpl. Art Gallery, 1996, St. Andrews Abbey, Valyermo, Calif., 1997, The Presbytery of the Pacific, L.A., 1997, Hollywood Digital, L.A., 1998, City of Brea Gallery, 1998, Palos Verdes Art Ctr., 1999, Nat. Art Program City of L.A., 1999. V.p. Palms Westminster Presbyn. Ch., L.A., 1996—; mem. Cmty. Coalition, L.A., 1999; vol. Cir. of Friends, Easter Seals, After Sch. Programs, L.A., 1999. With USN, 1965-69. Named Person of Yr., Palms Westminster Woman's Assn., 1996. Mem. Am. Legion. Democrat. Avocations: painting, reading, languages, classical music. E-mail: art-brush@email.com.

BURTON, ALAN HARVEY, city official; b. Chgo., Mar. 26, 1952; s. Harvey C. and Lois (Fitzpatrick) B.; (div. Oct. 1987); children: Douglas Alan, Marla Joy. Bs, Western Ill. U., 1974, MS, 1986. Recreation supr. Park Ridge (Ill.) Park Dist., 1974-75; dir. parks and recreation York Ctr. Park Dist., Lombard, Ill., 1975-78; dir. parks and recreation City of Berwyn, Ill., 1978-82, adminstr., 1982-86; dir. parks and recreation Norridge (Ill.) Park Dist., 1986-93; recreation bur. chief City of Orlando, Fla., 1993-96; dir. leisure svcs. City of Ormond Beach, Fla., 1996—; chmn. Berwyn Bus. Commn., 1984-86; cons. Berwyn Devel. Corp., 1986-88. Mem. Suburban Cook County Spl. Olympics, Franklin Park, Ill., 1983; hon. EMT Ill. Dept. Pub. Health, 1984; mem. at large Boy Scouts Am., La Grange, Ill., 1986, chmn. dist. nominating com.; rep. West Cen. Mcpl. Conf., Western Springs, Ill., 1987; pres. United Way of Harwood Heights (Ill.)/Norridge, 1990; active Fla. Conservation Corps., 1994, Birthplace of Speed Centennial Com., 2000; bd. dirs. Ormond Art Mus.; bd. mem. Ormond Meml. Art Mus. Recipient Arbor Day award Ill. Assn. Park Dists., 1977, Individual Merit award, 1986, Gold Medal finalist Nat. Sporting Goods Found., 1991, 92, 93, Faculty award FRPA, 1999. Mem. Nat. Park and Recreation Assn. (U.S. del. to Japan, youth at risk sect., so. regional rep.), Nat. Soc. Fundraising Execs., Fla. Recreation and Park Assn., Ill. Park and Recreation Assn. (issues com., long-range planning com., Meritorious Svc. award 1990), Northeastern Ill. Planning Commn. (open space com. 1991-92), Fla. Park and Recreation Assn., West Suburban Spl. Recreation Assn. (bd. dirs. 1991), Berwyn Hist. Soc., Kiwanis Club of Ormond Beach. Lutheran. Avocations: backpacking, theater, genealogy, biking, science fiction. Home: 915 Ocean Shore Blvd Apt 707 Ormond Beach FL 32176-8307

BURTON, ANTHONY DAVID, environmental education consultant, writer; b. Stonnall, Eng., Feb. 21, 1953; s. Richard Anson and Renee Elisabeth (Gyles) B.; m. Gwen Annette Chan, Mar. 28, 1988; children: Marisa Ta-Li, Trevor Anthony. MA, Cambridge U., 1973. Head of geography Basseterre H.S., St. Kitts, 1974-77; geography master King's Sch., Bruton, U.K., 1977-79; head of geography Greengates Sch., Mexico City, 1979-82, dep. head, 1982-86; dir. Odisea Mexico, Jocotepec, Mexico, 1986-97; regional rep. Traveler's Guide to Mex., 1987-97; adv. bd. Aero Mag., Mex., 1994-97. Editor Lloyd's Mexican Econ. Report, 1993—; author: Islands in the Sun, 1976, Western Mexico-A Traveller's Treasury, 1993; contbr. numerous articles to profl. jours. Bd. dirs. Amigos del Lago, Chapala, Mex., 1996-97. Fellow Royal Geographical Soc.; mem. Hawk's Club, Roosters. Avocations: golf, travel, reading, philately, hiking. Office: Box 4, Ladysmith, BC Canada V9G 1A1

BURTON, BARRY LAWSON, librarian, educator; b. Ulverston, Cumbria, Eng., Dec. 30, 1942; s. William Lawson and Runah (Sandwell) B.; m. Wendy Fay Monks, Dec. 4, 1970 (dec. Oct. 1997); children: Jodi, Nigel Robin, Simon Lawson. BA, U. Keele, 1965. Reference office Flinders U., Australia, 1966-67; chief libr. Salisbury Coll. Advanced Edn., 1968-71; dep. univ. libr. Makerere U., Uganda, 1972; libr. Hong Kong Polytechnic U., 1973—; pres. Internat. Fedn. for Info. and Documentation, Commn. for Asia and Oceania, 1981-88. Editor Directory of Professional Associations and Learned Societies in Hong Kong, 1988—; contbr. articles to profl. jours. Mem. Hong Kong Libr. Assn. (chmn. 1975), Libr. Assn. Australia (assoc.), Brit. Inst. Mgmt., Inst. Info. Scientists, Hong Kong Wine Soc. (chmn. 1983—), Hong Kong Jockey Club. Avocations: wine tasting, horse racing. Home: 1811 Convention Plaza, 1 Harbour Rd, Wanchai Hong Kong Office: Hong Kong Polytechnic U, Univ Librarian, Kowloon Hong Kong

BURTON, BERNARD OTTWAY, lawyer; b. Axton, Va., May 12, 1916; s. John Washington and Annie Kate (Harvey) B.; m. Ruby Francis Brown, June 22, 1946; children: Amanda Brown Burton McCartney, Benjamin Randolph, Molly Harrison. BA in Commerce, U. N.C., 1941; IA, Harvard U., 1943; JD, U. N.C., 1945. Bar: N.C. 1945, U.S. Dist. Ct., 1948. Counsel Randolph County Airport Commn., Asheboro, N.C., 1948-50; spl. right-of-way N.C. Hwy. Commn., Asheboro, N.C., 1965-68; sole-practice Ottway Burton PA, Asheboro, N.C., 1945—. Dir. N.C. R.R. Co., 1964-68. With Med. Svc. Corps., 1934-37. Mem. ABA, N.C. Acad. Trial Lawyers (charter mem.), N.C. State Bar Assn., Randolph County Bar Assn. (pres. 1958-59), Oasis Temple. Democrat. Methodist. Avocations: gardening, photography, golf, history. Office: Ottway Burton PA 115 Worth St Asheboro NC 27203-5517

BURTON, DAN L., congressman; b. Indpls., June 21, 1938; m. Barbara Jean Logan, 1959; children: Kelly, Danielle Lee, Danny Lee II. Mem. Ind. Ho. Reps., Indpls., 1967-68, 77-80, Ind. State Senate, 1969-70, 81-82; owner ins. and real estate firm, 1968—; mem. 98th-106th Congresses from 6th Ind. dist., 1983—; mem. internat. rels. com.; chmn. govt. reform and oversight com. Pres. Vols. of Am.; pres. Ind. Christian Benevolent Assn., Com. for Constl. Govt., Family Support Ctr. Served with U.S. Army, 1957-58. Republican. Office: US Ho of Reps 2185 Rayburn Ofc Bldg Washington DC 20515-0001

BURTON, DANIEL G., insurance executive; b. N.Y.C., Mar. 12, 1935; s. Herbert Edward and Leabelle (Bigelman) Goodstein; m. Roberta Rosenbaum, Dec. 25, 1957 (div. Mar. 1980); children: Marc, Lisa, Paul; m. Anita Jurrist, Nov. 28, 1982. BSBA, NYU, 1960; D of Commerce Sci., London Inst. Applied Sci., 1973; CFP cert., Adelphi U., 1982. Registered investment adviser; cert. fin. planner, cert. sr. advisor. Nat. sales mgr. Bernardi Originals, NYU, 1958-68; agt. New Eng. Life Ins. Co., 1968-77; gen. agt. U.S. Life Ins. Co., 1978-98; pres., CEO Burton Security and Investigation, Rockville Centre, N.Y., 1986—, Innovative Monetary Designs Group, Rockville Centre, N.Y., 1979-98; CEO Life Assocs. Inc., 1998—; mem. Nassau County Police Res., 1990—; lectr. in field. Contr. articles to profl. jours. Pres. bd. mgrs. Lido Beach (N.Y.) Towers Condominium, 1990-98. Sgt. U.S. Army, 1954-56. Mem. Inst. CFPs, Nat. Assn. Ins. and Fin. Advisors. (bd. dirs. 1987-88, cert. sr. advisor), Soc. Fin. Planners Adelphi U. (pres. 1983-85), Soc. Cert. Sr. Advisors, Million Dollar Round Table (life), Shriners, Masons. Avocation: fishing. Home: 5058 Windsor Parke Dr Boca Raton FL 33496-1637 Office: 100 Merrick Rd Rockville Centre NY 11570-4800 also: 5030 Champion Blvd Ste G6 Boca Raton FL 33496-2496

BURTON, DEON (NEON DEON BURTON), soccer player; b. Reading, Eng., Oct. 25, 1976. Forward Derby County (Eng.) Football Club, 1997. Office: Derby County Football Club, Pride Park Stadium, Derby DE24 8XL, England*

BURTON, JOHN JACOB, retired real estate company executive appraiser; b. N.Y.C., Dec. 31, 1912; s. Fannie (Rosenfeld) Burton; m. Sylvia R. Carlin, Oct. 12, 1940 (dec. 1981); children: Frances Lee, Barbara, Spencer, Gerald K. BS in Physics with honors, L.I. U., 1935, DSc (hon.), 1987; MAI, Columbia U., 1937. Lic. real estate broker, Fla. With Manpower Commn. Sci. and Specialized Personnel, N.Y., N.J., 1942-46; owner, mgr. John J. Burton Real Estate, Mortgages & Appraisals, Boston, 1946-50, John J. Burton Gen. Real Estate & Appraisals, Hollywood, Fla., 1950-92; ptrn. Am. Title Corp.; ret., 1995; personal aide col. to gov. State of Mass., 1966-68; trustee Broward County Investment Trust, Dania, Fla.; co-founder Technion, Israel. A founder Jewish Chapel at U.S. Mil. Acad. West Point, N.Y.; mem. exec. com. Broward County Rep. Com., 1958-74; mem. Presdl. Commns., 1986, 92. Recipient Presdl. Medals of Merit, 1985, 90, 93, Rep. Presdl. Legion of Merit, 1985, 94, U.S. Presdl. Commn., Pres. Ronald Reagan, 1986, U.S. Presdl. Commn., Pres. George Bush, 1992; commd. col. by Pres., 1986. Mem. AAAS, Internat. Orgn. Real Estate Appraisers (sr.), Nat. Assn. Real Estate Appraisers (cert.), Fla. Assn. Cert. Real Estate Appraisers, U.S. Navy League Commodore, Security and Intelligence Fund. (founder), Naval Intelligence Profls., Mil. Order of the World Wars (life mem.), Masons (32 degree), Shriners, B'nai B'rith. Jewish. Avocations: science, philanthropy. Home: 2470 N Park Rd Apt 328S Hollywood FL 33021-3753

BURTON, JOHN LLOYD, dermatologist, author; b. Buxton, Derbyshire, Eng., Aug. 29, 1938; s. Lloyd and Dorothy (Pacey) B.; m. Patricia Anne Crankshaw, Sept. 12, 1964; children: Jane Mary, Benjamin John, Helena Catherine. BS, Manchester U., 1961, MB, ChB, 1964, MD, 1970; student, FRCP, London, 1976. FRCP (London). Intern Manchester Royal Inf., 1964; resident Hammersmith Hosp., London, 1965; with Edinburgh Royal Inf., 1966-68; sr. registrar Newcastle Royal Inf., Eng., 1969-73; sr. lectr. Bristol U., Eng., 1973-82; prof. dermatology Bristol U., 1993; Parkes-Weber lectr., examiner Royal Coll. Physicians, 1983. Author: Aids to Postgraduate Medicine, 6th edit., 1994, (with B.J. Burton) Aids to Undergraduate Medicine, 6th edit., 1996, Essential Medicine, 2d edit. 1981, Essentials of Dermatology, 3rd edit., 1990; co-editor: Rook's Textbook of Dermatology (4 vols.), 4th edit. 1986, 6th edit. 1998; editor: Brit. Jour. Dermatology, 1980-85; contbr. about 350 articles to profl. jours., chpts. to books. Recipient Dickson Rsch. prize N.E. Regional Health Authority, 1971. Fellow Royal Coll. Physicians London; mem. Royal Soc. Medicine (pres. dermatology sect. 1994, Dowling Orator 1980); mem. Brit. Assn. Dermatologists (pres. 1996), Brit. Soc. investigative Dermatology. Avocation: fine book binding. Office: Norland House, 33 Canynge Rd, Bristol BS8 3LD, England

BURTON, JOHN PAUL (JACK BURTON), lawyer; b. New Orleans, Feb. 26, 1943; s. John Paul and Nancy (Key) B.; m. Anne Ward; children: Jennifer, Susanna, Derek, Catherine. BBA magna cum laude, La. Tech. U., 1965; LLB, Harvard U., 1968. Bar: N.Mex. 1968, U.S. Dist. Ct. N.Mex. 1968, U.S. Ct. Appeals (10th cir.) 1973, U.S. Supreme Ct. 1979. Assoc. Rodey, Dickason, Sloan, Akin & Robb, Albuquerque, 1968-74, dir., 1974—, chmn. comml. dept., 1980-81; mng. dir. Rodey, Dickason, Sloan, Akin & Robb, Santa Fe, 1986-90. Co-author: Boundary Disputes in New Mexico, 1992, Unofficial Update on the Uniform Ltd. Liability Co. Act, 1994. Mem. Nat. Coun. Commrs. on Uniform State Laws, 1989—, drafting com. UCC Article 5, 1990-95, UCC Article 9, 1993-95, UCC Articles 2 and 2A, 1999—, Power-of Sale Foreclosure Act, 1999—, Uniform Ltd. Liability Co. Act, 1993-95, Legis. Coun., 1991-99, divsn. chair, 1993-95, 99—, chair legis. com., 1995-99, exec. com., 1995-99; joint editl. bd. Uninc. Bus. Orgns., 1994-95, Trust and Estates Acts, 1999—; pres. Brunn Sch., 1987-89. Fellow Am. Coll. Real Estate Lawyers, Lex Mundi Coll. Mediators; mem. ABA, Am. Law Inst. (rep. to UCC Article 5 drafting com. 1992-95), Am. Coll. Mortgage Attys., Am. Arbitration Assn. (mem. panel arbitrators), N.Mex. State Bar Assn. (chmn. comml. litig. and antitrust sect. 1985-86). Office: Rodey Dickason Sloan Akin & Robb PA PO Box 1357 Santa Fe NM 87504-1357

BURTON, RICHARD IRVING, orthopedist, educator; b. Providence, Sept. 18, 1936; s. Kenneth Gould and Edith Irving (Vayro) B.; m. Margaret Ann Leaman, Apr. 5, 1961; children: Thomas Kenneth, Douglas Leaman. BA, Amherst Coll., 1958; MD, Harvard U., 1962. Diplomate Am. Bd. Orthopaedic Surgery (examiner 1980—, bd. dirs. 1989-98). Intern U. Rochester, N.Y., 1962-63, resident in surgery, 1963-64; resident in orthopedic surgery Harvard U., 1966-70; fellow in hand surgery Roosevelt Hosp., N.Y.C., 1970-71; asst. prof. Cleve. Clinic Found., 1971-72, head sect. surgery of hand, 1971-74, assoc. prof., 1973-74; mem. faculty U. Rochester Med. Sch., 1974—, head sect. surgery of hand, 1974—, prof. orthopedics, 1979—, Marjorie Strong Wehle prof. orthopedics, 1995-2000, assoc. chmn. dept. orthopedics, 1981-88, chmn., 1987-2000; sr. assoc. orthopedist Strong Meml. Hosp., Rochester, 1974-79, orthopedist, 1979—; Chmn. cert. of added qualifications com. Am. Bd. Orthopaedic Surgery, 1994-98. Assoc. editor Jour. Hand Surgery, 1980-84; contbr. articles to profl. jours., chpts. to books. Mem. exec. com. Monroe County chpt. Am. Arthritis Found., 1983-86; elder Presbyn. Ch. Buswell Disting. Svc. fellow, U. rochester, 1980-81. Recipient Exec. of Yr. award Profl. Secs. Internat., Flower City chpt., 1981. Mem. ACS, AAAS, Am. Acad. Orthopedic Surgeons (chmn. hand and wrist com. 1986-89, orthopedic resources com. 1989-91), Am. Bd. Med. Specialties (voting rep. 1995-98), Am. Soc. Surgery of the Hand (coord. divsn. edn. 1982-85, coun. 1985-89, chmn. membership com. 1991, v.p. 1990, pres.-elect 1991, pres. 1992), Am. Orthopedic Assn. (exec. com. 1986, resident rsch. conf. com. 1987-89, chair 1989, membership com. 1989-92, chmn. 1992, exec. com. 1992, forward planning com. 1996-99), Interurban Orthopedic Soc., Am. Rheumatism Assn., Eastern Orthopedic Assn., Monroe County Med. Soc., N.Y. State Med. Soc., Rochester Acad. Medicine, Rochester Orthopedic Soc., Soc. N.Y. State Orthopedic Surgeons, J. William Littler Soc., Amherst Alumni Assn., Harvard U. Med. Sch. Alumni Assn. Home: 7869 Hidden Oak Pittsford NY 14534-9607 Office: U Rochester Med Ctr Dept Orthopedics 601 Elmwood Ave Rochester NY 14642-0001

BURTON, RICHARD JAY, lawyer; b. N.Y.C., May 4, 1949; s. Melvin F. Burton and Shirley (Burton) Silber; m. Truly Demetra Dourdis, June 11, 1972; 1 child, Marc Aaron. BA, George Washington U., 1971; JD, U. Miami, 1974. Bar: Fla. 1974, D.C. 1976, U.S. Supreme Ct. 1979. Founder Med. Commn. on Human Rights, Washington, 1969-71; adminstrv. aide Fla. Legis., 1973-74; gov. affairs liaison Dade County Fla. Legis., 1974; assoc. Richard H.W. Maloy and Assocs., Coral Gables, Fla., 1974-76; atty., advisor FAA, Washington, 1976-77; assoc. Pompan, Rumizen & Reynolds, Washington, 1978-79, Donald M. Murtha and Assocs., Washington, 1978-79; ptnr. Schoninger, Siegfried, Kipnis, Burton & Sussman PA, Miami, Fla., 1979-82; sole practice Miami, 1982—; gen. counsel Rexall Sundown Inc., 1982-90; guest lectr. U. Miami Sch. of Law, Coral Gables, 1982. Mem. Am. Arbitration Assn. Constr. law panel, 1974—, Builders Assn. S. Fla., legis. com. 1980—, Builder Industry Polit. action com.; fire commr. Met. Dade County, 1988, 92, vice chmn., fire commr., 1989-90. Mem. ABA, D.C. Bar Assn., Fed. Bar Assn., Fla. Bar Assn. (constr. law com.). Democrat. Jewish. Avocations: skiing, scuba diving, tennis. Home: 1000 W Island Blvd Apt 1109 N Miami Beach FL 33160-4973

BURTON, ROBERT CHARLES, public health physician; b. Melbourne, Victoria, Australia, Sept. 23, 1943; s. Charles Wilson and Clélie Frances (Coles) B.; children: Craig Alexander, Bridget Jane, Daniel James. MBBS, Melbourne U., Australia, 1967; B Med. Sci., Melbourne U., 1971, PhD, 1977, MD, 1978; BA, Newcastle U., Australia, 1992. Med. and surgical residen Royal Melbourne and Royal Childrens Hosps., Melbourne, Australia, 1968-72; cardiac surgery fellow Green Lane Hosp., New Zealand, 1973; post grad. scholar Walter & Eliza Hall Inst., Australia, 1974-77; Nat. Health and Med. Rsch. Coun. fellow Harvard U., Boston, Mass., U.S., 1977-80; asst. prof. Harvard U., Boston, 1981; prof. surgical sci. Newcastle U., Australia, 1981-95; dir. Anti Cancer Coun. of Victoria, Australia, 1995—; prof. surgery Monash U., 1997—; prof. pub. health U. Melbourne, 1997%; mem. regional grant interview com. Nat. Health and Med. Rsch. Coun., Australia, 1986-88, 89-91, 94; chmn. of surgery John Hunter Hosp., Australia, 1989-92; vis. scientist Internat. Agy. for Rsch. on Cancer, France, 1992-93, Oxford U., 1986-87; bd. dirs. Nat. Breast Cancer Ctr., 1999—; bd. dirs. Nat. Cancer Control Initiative, 1997—, chair, 1997-99. Author: (book) Health, Solar UV Radiation and Environmental Change, 1993; contbr. many articles to profl. jours. including, New Eng. Jour. Medicine, Nature, Jour. Exptl. Medicine, and others, also chpts. to med. and sci. books. Mem. Hunter Valley Cancer Appeal, Newcastle, 1982-85; advisor NBN Telethons, Newcastle, 1984-92; chmn. Mater Hosp. Oncology Com., Newcastle, 1982-85. Fellow Royal Australasian Coll. Surgeons (John Mitchell Crouch fellowship 1980, Alan Newton prize 1981), Royal Australasian Coll. Physicians, Australasian Faculty Pub. Health Physicians; mem. Hunter Surg. Soc. (pres. 1994-95), Melbroune Club, Melbourne Cricket Club. Avocations: aerobics, opera, drama, French, lit. Office: Anti Cancer Coun Victoria, 1 Rathdowne st, Victoria South Carlton 3053, Australia

BURTON, SANDRA JEAN, journalist; b. Long Beach, Calif., Dec. 21; d. Charles Orrin and Helen Burton. BA, Middlebury Coll., 1963. Reporter, photographer Hunterdon County Dem., Flemington, N.J., 1963-64; sec. Time Inc., N.Y.C., 1964-66; researcher Time Mag., N.Y.C., 1967-70; corr. Time Mag., L.A., 1970-73, Paris, 1977-82; bur. chief Time Mag., Boston, 1973-76, Hong Kong, 1982-86, Beijing, 1988-90; sr. corr. Time Mag., Hong Kong, 1990-97; contbr. Time Mag., 1998—; mem. exec. com. Hong Kong affiliate Coun. Fgn. Rels. Author: Impossible Dream--The Marcoses, The Aquinos and The Unfinished Revolution, 1989; co-author: Massacre in Beijing, 1989. Edward R. Murrow fellow Coun. on Fgn. Rels., 1986-87. Mem. Fgn. Corrs. Club Hong Kong (v.p. 1984), Royal Hong Kong Yacht Club. Presbyterian. Avocations: writing, photography, oil painting, scuba diving.

BURTON, TIM, film director; b. Burbank, Aug. 25, 1958. Student Calif. Inst. Arts (Disney Fellowship). Cartoon artist Disney Prodn., apprentice animator. Film dir. Pee-Wee's Big Adventure, 1984, Beetlejuice, 1988, Batman, 1989, Edward Scissorhands, 1990, Batman Returns, 1992, Ed Wood, 1994, Mars Attacks, 1996, Sleepy Hollow, 1999; others include: Frankenweenie, Vincent; prodr. The Nightmare Before Christmas, 1993, Cabin Boy, 1994, Batman Forever, 1995, James and the Giant Peach, 1996; dir. TV film Aladdin, Faerie Tale Theatre series; appeared in film Singles, 1992; author: My Art & Films, 1993, The Melancholy Death of Oyster Boy and Other Stories, 1997. Office: Chapman Bird & Grey 1990 S Bundy Dr Ste 200 Los Angeles CA 90025-5240

BURTON, WILLIAM JOSEPH, engineering executive; b. Gaffney, S.C., Mar. 22, 1931; s. Emory Goss and Olivia (Copeland) B.; m. Joan Holland Burton, Sept. 26, 1987. BSME, U. S.C., 1957, MSME, 1964; PhDME, Tex. A&M U., 1970. Registered profl. engr., Tenn., Fla. Sr. dynamics engr. Lockheed-Ga. Co., Marietta, 1957-62; sr. project engr. Allison div. GM Corp., Indpls., 1964-67; asst. prof., researcher Tex. A&M U., College Station, 1968-70; asst. prof. U. Tenn., Knoxville, 1970-74; projects mgr. Tenn. Valley Authority, Chattanooga, 1974-79; program mgr. Dept. Navy, Washington, 1979-94; cons. engr. Ocean and Power Applications, Lakeland, Fla., 1993—; chmn. equal employment opportunity com. Chesapeake div. Naval Facilities Engring. Command, Washington, 1982-83. Author: On the Heating Surface Effects of Nucleate Boiling Data Correlation, 1964, The Effects of Surface Roughness on the Wave Forces on a Circular Cylindrical Pile, 1970; author more than 50 articles on ocean engring., power and propulsion, aircraft structures, planning and economics, ethics. Secretary, mem. hospitality com. Exch. Club, Knoxville, 1975, bd. dirs., 1976; coord. charitable campaign Naval Facilities Engring. Com., Washington, 1982. With U.S. Army, 1951-53. Recipient Occupation medal and Nat. Def. Svc. medal U.S. Army, Antarctic Svc. medal U.S. Dept. of Navy, 1962, Wisdom award of honor, 2000; Eminent Wisdom fellow Scroll of Wisdom Hall of Fame, 2000. Fellow ASME (chmn. exec. com. ocean engring. divsn. 1985, mem.-at-large energy resources bd. 1986-92, chmn. com. honors & awards energy resources bd. 1992-98, com. on tech. planning coun. on engring. 1992-94, fellow peer rev. bd. 1992-97, rep. energy resources bd. to nat. nominating com. 1998—, Golden Cert. ocean engring. divsn. 1989), Va. Soc. Profl. Engrs. (no. Va. regional coun. 1988); mem. AAAS, NSPE (pres.-elect Fairfax chpt. 1988), Soc. Mfg. Engrs., Soc. Naval Architects and Marine Engrs., S.C. Hist. Soc., Nat. Trust for Historic Preservation, Polk County (Fla.) Hist. Assn., VFW, Marine Tech. Soc., The Univ. South Caroliniana Soc., Sigma Xi. Baptist. Avocations: travel, bicycling, classic guitar, golf, tennis. E-mail: wmburton@hotmail.com. Home: 307 Miramar Dr Lakeland FL 33803-2633 Office: Naval Facilities Engring Svc Ctr E Coast Detachment 901 E M St SE 218 Wash Navy Ya Washington DC 20374-0001

BURTT, LARICE A.R., artist; b. Phila., June 22, 1928; d. Milo A.J. Roseman and Anna Sterling; m. James C. Burtt, June 25, 1960; childen, James M., Kyleann S. BS in Biology, Bucknell U., 1950; MS in Nursing, Yale U., 1955; studied art with Dr. Selma Burke, studied with William A. Smith; cert., Katherine Gibbs Sec. Sch., 1951. Med. clinical instr. Jefferson Hosp., Phila., 1956-57; med. surgical instr. Rowan Meml. Hosp., Salisbury, N.C., 1958-59; workshop leader Yale, New Haven Hosp. Pain Mgmt. Ctrs., New Haven, Ct., 1996, Attleboro Nursing Home, Langhorne, Pa., Chandler Hall, Newtown, Pa.; instr. Delaware Valley Schs., Pa., 1979—; profl. demonstrator in field, 1977—. Painter (three-dimensional stone painting), many locations, 1976-99; one person exhbns. at Arnot Art Mus., Elmira, N.Y., 1987, Grand Canyon Nat. Park Mus. piece in permanent collection, Utah, 1991, Cannon Bldg., Washington, 1995, Yale Univ. Sch. Nursing, New Haven, Conn., 1996, Immaculata Col Group Exhibitions, 1996-99, many area group exhbns., 1977—. Mem. AAUW, Heritage Conservatory Bucks County, Northhampton Hist. Soc., Middletown Grange, Childrens Cultural Ctr., Pa. & Bucks County Guild Craftsman (exhbn. at Franklin and Marshall Coll. 1979-96), James Michener Art Mus., Doylestown (Pa.) Art League, Ctrl. Bucks C. of C., Arts bridge. Avocations: tennis, piano, visual/performing arts. Home: 31 Beth Dr Richboro PA 18954-1901

BURUKHIN, SERGEY BORISOVITCH, chemistry educator; b. Severodvinsk, Russia, Apr. 17, 1955; s. Boris Nikolaevitch and Maria Nikolaevna (Medvedeva) B.; m. Galina Aleksandrovna Kurbatova, Aug. 20, 1977; 1 child, Maria. Degree in engring., Mendeleev Inst. Chem. Tech., Moscow, 1978; PhD, Karpov Phys. Chem. Inst., Moscow, 1990. Sr. rschr. Karpov Phys. Chem. Inst., Moscow, 1978-96; assoc. prof. Obninsk Inst. Nuclear Power Engring., Studgorodok, 1996—. Author: Radiation Chemical Methods Providing Improvement in Barrier Properties of Plastics, 1987; contbr. articles to profl. jours. Mem. N.Y. Acad. Sci. Avocations: psychology, pedagogics, philosophy. Home: 21 Gagarin Str Apt 20, 249020

Obninsk Russia Office: Obninsk Inst Nuclear Power, Engring, 249020 Studgorodok Russia

BURWOOD, RICHARD JOHN, nuclear medicine physician; b. Lowestoft, Suffolk, Eng., Jan. 13, 1939; s. William John and Vera Joan (Porter) B. BA, Trinity Coll., Dublin, Ireland, 1962, MB, BCh, BAO, 1963, MA, 1970; MD, Bristol (Eng.) U., 1970. Asst. Ctrl. Sys., Tromsø, Norway, 1965; lectr. in radiology Bristol (Eng.) U., 1966-71; sr. lectr. in radiology Ahmadu Bello U., Nigeria, 1971; med. dir. Sussex Diagnostic Clinic, Brighton, Eng., 1972—; cons. Royal Sussex County Hosp., Brighton, 1972—; chmn. British Med. Ultrasound, Brighton, 1987. Hon. cons. Chailey Heritage Hosp., 1972—. Mem. British Nuclear Medicine Soc. (coun. 1991—), Royal Coll. Radiologists, British Med. Ultrasound Soc., British Inst. Radiology. Roman Catholic. Avocations: contract bridge, aviculture, gardening. Office: Royal Sussex County Hosp, Eastern Rd Dept Radiology, Brighton East Sussex BN2 5BE, England

BURY, JO B.J., research institute administrator; b. Ghent, Flanders, Belgium, July 28, 1958; s. Leon and Anne (Vanparys) B.; m. Els Coopman, May 18, 1985; children: Eva, Pieter-Jan, Alexander. Pharmacist, Ghent U., 1981, PhD, 1986. Rsch. fellow Ghent U., Brugge, Belgium, 1981-86; hosp. pharmacist A.Z. ST-JAN, Brugge, 1986; postdoctoral fellow U. Libre Brussels, 1986-87; sci. advisor Fed. Inst. Scientific Rsch. Industry & Agrl., Brussels, 1987-91; 1st sci. advisor Flanders Inst. Sci. & Tech. Industry, Brussels, 1992-95; dir.-gen. Flanders Interuniv. Inst. Biotech., Zwijnaarde, Belgium, 1995—; mng. dir. Flanders Action Programme in Biotech., Brussels, 1990-95; reviewer Clin. Chemistry, Brussels, 1985-86; rep. European Commn., Brussels, 1993-95; asst. Ghent U., 1980-81. Author: HDL Function in Metabolism of TGRL, 1986, Reviews of Immunoassay Technology, 1989; contbr. articles to profl. jours. Pres. pharmacy students Ghent U., 1978-80. Lt. Belgian Army, 1984-85. Grantee IRSIA, 1981-85. Mem. AAAS, Belgian Bioindustries Assn., Biotech. Industry Orgn. Office: VIB, Rijvisschestraat 120, B-9052 Zwijnaarde Flanders, Belgium

BURY, STEPHEN JOHN, librarian, lecturer; b. Blackburn, Eng., May 12, 1954; s. Edwin and Ethel (Gregson) B. BA in Modern History with honours, Oxford U., 1975; Diploma in Librarianship, Univ. Coll., London, 1977; MA in Victorian Studies, Birkbeck Coll., London, 1986, PhD, 1990. Asst. libr. Chelsea Sch. Art, London, 1978-85, libr., 1985-89; head of learning resources Chelsea Coll. of Art & Design, London, 1989-2000; head modern English collections The Brit. Libr., London, 2000—; cons. Mus. of Modern Art, Oxford, 1993—. Author: Brian Chalkley: New Work, 1990, Artists' Books, 1995, ARtists' Multiples, 2000; contbg. author: Dictionnaire de l'Art Moderne, 1993. Recipient H.W.C. Davis prize U. Oxford, 1973. Fellow Libr. Assn.; mem. Art Librs. Soc. (U.K.) (chair cataloguing com. 1986-89), Chelsea Arts Club, Inst. Contemporary Artists (London). Avocations: madrigals, opera, swimming. Home: 28 Argyle Pl, London W6 0RQ, England Office: The Brit Libr, 96 Euston Rd, London NW1 2DB, England

BURYAN, PETR, chemical technology educator; b. Pudlov, Karviná, Czechoslovakia, Jan. 6, 1947; s. Josef and Anna Szymeczková (Buryanová) B.; m. Irene Mackiewicz, July 14, 1979; children: Petr, Šimon. Engr., Inst. Chem. Tech., Prague, Czech Republic, 1971. Engring. diplomate. Rsch. worker Dept. Gas and Coke Tech., Prague, 1972-94, assoc. prof., 1994-97, head dept. gas, coke and atmosphere protection tech., 1994—, prof., 1997—; dir. Lab. Emission Metrology related to faculty of environ. protection tech., faculty environ. technology, Prague; cons. Inst. Chem. Tech., Dept. Gas Tech., Coking Chem. and Dir. Project, Prague, 1975—. Author, co-author 18 monographs and books; contbr. articles to profl. jours.; patentee in field. Grantee Ministry Edn. Czech Republic, 1995, 96, European Union, 1996. Mem. Czechoslovak Sci. Soc. (mem. ctrl. com. gas 1972-89), Czech Gas and Oil Assn. (mem. exec. com. 1989—), Czech Carbon Soc. (exec. com. 1990—). Home: Šaldova 16, 186 00 Prague 8, Czech Republic Office: Inst Chem Tech, Technická 5, 166 28 Prague 6, Czech Republic

BURYLEV, BORIS PETROVICH, chemist, educator; b. Omsk, Russia, Jan. 5, 1934; s. Petr Ivanovich and Efrosinija Agafonovna (Sterhova) B.; m. Tamara Samuilovna Alecsandrovich, Jan. 7, 1957; children: Kritskaja Ekaterina, Kostenko Natal'ja. Grad., Siberian Metall. Inst., Novokuznetsk, Russia, 1957; Candidate Tech. Scis., U. Sverdlovsk, Russia, 1963, D Tech. Scis., 1968. Crt. engring.-metallurgist. Asst. Siberian Metall. Inst., Novokuznetsk, 1957-62, asst. prof., 1962-67, prof. phys. chemistry, 1967-70; prof. phys. chemistry Krasnodar (Russia) Politecnic Inst., 1970-76; chair analytical chemistry Kuban State U., Krasnodar, 1976-92; sr. prin. rschr. Joint Stock Co. NIIMontaz, Krasnodar, 1992—. Author: Thermodynamics of Metallic Interstitial Solutios, 1984; (with L. Moysov) Phisico-Chemical Bases Formtion New Welding materials, 1993; (with I Sryvalin, V. Korpachev) Theory of Solution, V I-2, 1979-80 (regional adminstrn. award 1994); editor Chemistry and Thermodynamic Transitional Metals and Their Combinations, 1977, 79, 82, 85, 89. Recipient awards Scandium, Jour. Chemistry and Life, 1993, Internat. Sci. Found., 1993. Mem. Meritorious Sci. and Tech. Worker Russian Fedn., N.Y. Acad. Scis., Fourth Sci. Coun. Avocations: science work, symphony concerts, art exhibitions, walking with grandchildren. Fax: (8612) 550229. Home: Korpus I, kv 117, Moskovskaja No 2, 350042 Krasnodar Kuban, Russia Office: Joint Stock Co NIIMontaz, Rashpilevskaja No 148, 350020 Krasnodar Kuban, Russia

BUSARD, HUBERTUS LAMBERTUS, neuro-psychiatrist, consultant, researcher; b. Margarten, Holland, Mar. 15, 1953; s. Hubertus Lambertus and Yvonne Maria (Bollen) B.; m. Ingrid Patricia ten Hoedt, May 31, 1981; children: Tom, MiLou, Celine. Grad., KU U., Nymegen, Holland, 1979, diploma in neuropsychiatry, 1984, diploma in psychotherapy, 1984, diploma in neurophysiology, 1987. Psychiatrist KU U., Nymegen, 1985; neuropsychiatrist De Weezerlanden, Zwolle, Holland, 1985—, cons., 1993—. Author: Lafora's Disease, 1992. Mem. ISPSO. Avocations: sports, music. Home: Boomkensdiep 15, 8032 XZ Zwolle Holland Office: De Weezenlanden, Groot Wezenland 20, 8011 JW Zwolle Holland

BUSBY, MORRIS D., former ambassador; b. Memphis; married; 2 children. BA, Marshall U.; MS, George Washington U.; postgrad., U.S. Naval Destroyer Sch., Def. Intelligence Sch., Naval War Coll. With USN, various locations including Vietnam, 1971-73; mem. staff Office of Coord. of Ocean Affairs, dir. Office Oceans and Polar Affairs, dep. asst. sec. ocean affairs, amb. oceans and fisheries affairs Dept. of State, 1973-81; alt. rep. to conf. on disarmament Dept. of State, Geneva, Switzerland, 1981-83; dep. chief of mission Dept. of State, Mexico City, 1984-87; founder, office head assistance program for Nicaraguan resistance Dept. of State, 1987-88, prin. dep. asst. sec. inter-Am. affairs, 1987-88, spl. envoy to C.Am., sr. dep., 1988-89; head counter-terrorism Dept. State, 1989-91; amb. to Colombia Dept. of State, Bogota, 1991-94; pres. BGI, Internet. Cons. Svcs., 1994—; bd. dirs. InVision Techs., Newark, Calif., 1998—. Decorated Bronze Star; recipient 3 Presdl. Meritorious Svc. awards Govt. Colombia Gran Cruz de Boyaca. Office: BGI Inc 1800 K St NW Ste 716 Washington DC 20006-2228

BUSCAGLIA, ADOLFO EDGARDO, economist, educator; b. Buenos Aires, Jan. 10, 1930; s. Adolfo Angel and Francisca (Summa) B.; m. Maria Teresa Reyna Vila, Apr. 10, 1955; children: Edgardo Adolfo, Mariano Jorge, Teresita Sofia. BA in Econs., Nat. U. La Plata, Argentina, 1956; MA in Econs, Stanford U., 1965, PhD, 1966. Diplomate economist and academic. From economist to dir. econ. rsch. div. Cen. Bank Argentina, Buenos Aires, 1956-69; gen. dir. Analysis and Programming Inc., Buenos Aires, 1970-81, 83—; pres., chmn. Bank of Province of Buenos Aires, 1982—; prof. econs. Cath. U. Buenos Aires, 1967-76, U. Buenos Aires, 1977-98; bd. dirs. Bagley SA, 1979-81, Salto Grande's Hydroelectric Multipurposes Project, Buenos Aires, 1969-71, Ctr. Market, Buenos Aires, 1972-73, Martin Garcia's Island Devel. Plan, Buenos Aires, 1971-72; prof. money, credit and banking, U. Buenos Aires, 1976-97, hon. prof. monetary theory, 1991-97, hon. prof. advanced econ. theory, 1998—; advisor gen. in econs. and fin. Nat. Congress' Gen. Comptroller Bur., 1995-99, councillor Govt. of the City of Buenos Aires, 1998—. Author: Hacia una Argentina Posible, 1983; author, editor: Dinero, Inflación e Incertidumbre, 1985, Com. Internacional Integracion y Estabilidad Monetarid, 1996; contbr. articles to profl. jours. Founder Club of Argentina's Nat. Constn., Buenos Aires, 1988—. With Argentina infantry, 1951. Fellow Argentine Assn. Fiscal Legis.; mem. Nat. Acad. Econ. Sci. Argentina (hon., life, dep. pres., 1st v.p.), Am. Econ. Assn., Argentine Econ. Assn., Info and Ops. Rsch. Assn., Nat. Acad. Moral and Polit. Scis. (life), Buenos Aires Stock Exch. Roman Catholic. Avocations: golf, fishing. E-mail: buscalla@interserver.com.ar. Office: Gen Pueyrredon 1269, 1641 Acassuso, 1049 Buenos Aires Argentina

BUSCH, AUGUST ADOLPHUS, III, brewery executive; b. St. Louis, June 16, 1937; s. August Anheuser and Elizabeth (Overton) B.; m. Susan Marie Hornibrook, Aug. 17, 1963 (div. 1969); children: August Adolphus IV, Susan Marie II; m. Virginia L. Wiley, Dec. 28, 1974; children: Steven August, Virginia Marie. Student, U. Ariz., 1957-58, Siebel Inst. Tech., 1960-61. With Anheuser-Busch, Inc., St. Louis, 1957—, pres., 1974-75; chmn. bd., pres. Anheuser Busch Cos., Inc., St. Louis; bd. dirs. SBC Comms., GenAmerica, Emerson Electric Co. Exec. bd. St. Louis Boy Scouts Am.; bd. dirs. United Way Greater St. Louis. Mem. St. Louis Country Club, Log Cabin Club. Office: Anheuser-Busch Cos Inc 1 Busch Pl Saint Louis MO 63118-1852

BUSCH, C. THOMAS, fundraising executive; b. Champaign, Ill., Feb. 2, 1945; s. Harold Carl and MaryJane Shafer B.; m. Deborah Ann Lindrud, Aug. 16, 1980; children: Jennifer Marie Lindrud Busch, Christopher Thomas Lindrud Busch. BA, So. Ill. U., 1971. Cert. assn. exec. Am. Soc. Assn. Execs.; cert. fundraising exec. Nat. Soc. Fundraising Execs. Acting dir. Student Ctr. So. Ill. U., Carbondale, 1975-76, asst. to v.p. for student affairs, 1976-81, asst. to pres., 1981-85; exec. dir. Alumni Rels. U. System of Md., Adelphi, 1988-91; exec. dir. The Md. 4-H Found., Inc., College Park, Md., 1991-96; mng. ptnr. Lindrud Busch & Assocs., Columbia, Md., 1996—; dir. of devel. Nat. Tooling Found., Ind., Ft. Washington, Md., 1998—; v.p. bd. dirs., Consultants Consortium, Washington, 1997—; trustee Assn. Leadership Found., Greater Washington Soc. of Washington, D.C., 1996-99. Bd. dirs. Student Cmty. Svc. Found., Md., 1995-97, Md. Horse Coun., 1992-96, Columbia Forum, 1990-93, OMNI House, Glen Burnie, Md., 1990-92. With USNR, 1966-68. Mem. Am. Soc. Assn. Execs., Greater Washington Soc. Assn. Execs., Assn. Found. Group, Nat. Soc. Fundraising Execs., Phi Delta Kappa. Avocations: golf, reading, gourmet cooking, antique sports cars. Office: Nat Tooling & Machining Fnd 9300 Livingston Rd Fort Washington MD 20744-4905

BUSCH, JOHN A., sociologist; b. Mpls., Mar. 13, 1943; s. John V. Busch and Marlys Mae Ellis; m. Gladys Masih Busch, Nov. 28, 1968; children: Kanti L., John Vijay. MA, Ind. U., 1968, PhD in Sociology, 1974. Prof. U. Louisville, Ky., 1974—. Editor: Issues in Sociocybernetics, 1984; author: Sociocybernetics, 1992; contbr. articles to profl. jours. Office: U Louisville Lutz Hall 103 Louisville KY 40292-0001

BUSCH, MARTIN, radio oncologist, consultant; b. Göttingen, Germany, Oct. 21, 1957. Privat dozent, U. Munich, MD, D Med. Habilitation. Bd. cert. gynecology, obs., radiotherapy, radio oncology. Cons. Clinic Radiotherapy and Oncology, Ludwig Maximilian U., Munich; head dept. radiation oncology St. George's Hosp., Hamburg, Germany; Contbr. more than 100 articles to sci. jours. Mem. Am. Soc. Therapeutic Radiology and Oncology, Degro, DRG, European Soc. Therapeutic Radiology and Oncology. Office: St George's Hosp Dept Rad, Oncology, Lohnmuehlen Str 5, D-20099 Hamburg Germany

BUSCH, NANCY ELIZABETH, artist, educator; b. Manitowac, Wis., Sept. 7, 1944; d. Edgar Wilhelm and Dorothy Janette (Blust) Putz; m. Charles Nels Busch, Aug. 21, 1965; 1 son, Alexander. BA in Journalism, U. Mich., 1966; student, Birmingham Bloomfield Art Assn, 1978-88, Ctr. for Creative Studies, 1985; postgrad., U. Mich., 1987-88; MFA, Wayne State U., 1990. Sales rep. Grosse Pointe News, Mich., 1966-68; pres. Nels Advt. Co., Birmingham, Mich., 1968-75, Busch & Morris, Birmingham, 1975-80, Busch & Assocs., Birmingham, 1980-88; prof. Instituto Federico Brandt, Caracas, Venezuela, 1991-93; cons. U. Mich. Devel. Bd., Ann Arbor, 1973-80. One-woman shows include Wayne State U., Mich., 1990, Sala Mendoza, Caracas, 1991, 93, Galeria Diners, Bogota, 1993-94, Galeria Ruth Benzacar, Buenos Aires, 1996, Centro Cultural Borges, Buenos Aires, 1996, Joseph Borges Museo, Caracas, Venezuela, 1998; group shows include Creative Arts Ctr., Pontiac, Mich., 1990, Wayne State U., Mich., 1990, Willis Gallery, Detroit, 1990; pvt. collections include Aco Corp. Collection, Caracas, Univ. de los Andes, Bogota, Columbia, Museo de Arte Contemporaneo, Bogota. Recipient award of Excellence Nat. Pub. Rels. Soc. am., 1975-80, Design awared Internat. Graphics, 1980. Mem. Econs. Club of Detroit, Adcraft Club of Detroit, Am. Mktg. Assn., Southeastern Mich. Hosp. Assn. (awards for concept and creative devel. in reports, brochures and other collateral materials 1975-80), Am. Hosp. Assn., Mich. Hosp. Assn. (awards for reports, brochures and othe materials 1975-80).

BUSCH, PAUL, mathematical physicist; b. Bergisch Gladbach, Germany, Feb. 15, 1955; arrived in Eng., 1995; m. Elke Hildegard Fetzer; 4 children. Diploma in Physics, U. Cologne, Germany, 1979, Dr.rer.nat., 1982, Habilitation, 1988. Rsch. asst. U. Cologne, 1979-87; rsch. assoc. MPI, Göttingen, Germany, 1987-88; docent in theoretical physics U. Cologne, 1988-95; lectr. applied math. U. Hull, Eng., 1995-96, reader, 1996—; vis. assoc. prof. math. Fla. Atlantic U., Boca Raton, 1986; vis. scholar physics Harvard U., Cambridge, Mass., 1994-95; external docent dept. physics U. Turku, Finland, 1991—. Editl. bd. Found. of Physics Letters Jour., 1995—; co-author: (book) The Quantum Theory of Measurement, 1991, 2d edit., 1996, (monograph) Operational Quantum Physics, 1995; contbr. articles to profl. jours. Feodor Lynen fellow Alexander von Humboldt Found., 1994. Mem. Internat. Assn. Math. Physics, Internat. Quantum Structures Assn. (councillor 1996—). Office: Univ of Hull Dept Math, Cottingham Rd, Hull HU6 7RX, England

BUSCH, SALLY J., librarian, accounting clerk; b. Columbus, Ohio, Sept. 25, 1918; d. Homer Denison and Lela (Wyatt) Holler; m. Charles Edward Busch, Aug. 2, 1943; children: David Wyatt, Chase III, Suzie, Carol, Mary, Dale. AA in Edn., Kellogg C.C., Battle Creek, Mich., 1967; BS, Western Mich. U., 1973, M in Libr. Sci., 1976. Acctg. clerk U.S. Steel, Homestead, Pa., 1941-43, weighmaster-open hearth, 1943-45; acctg. clerk Am. Bridge, Pitts., Pa., 1947-49; libr. Galesburg (Mich.) Meml. Libr., 1969-75; antique dealer Augusta, Mich., 1975—. Mem., pres. Friends of Richland Libr., 1983-2000; mem. League of Women Voters, 1998-2000. Mem. Seedlings Garden Club, Sierra Club. Democrat. Methodist. Avocations: investments, Dixieland music, Girl Scouts. Home: 15834 D Ave Augusta MI 49012

BUSCHIAZZO, DANIEL EDUARDO, agronomist; b. Bahia Blanca, Buenos Air, Argentina, Oct. 10, 1951; s. Eduardo and Elsa (Monteoliva) B.; m. Julia Eulalia Llanes, June 17, 1977; children: Marina, Emilio. BS, Nat. U., Bahia Blanca, 1969; Ingeniero Agronomo, U. Nat. Sur, Bahia Blanca, 1976, MS, 1982; PhD in Agronomy, German U., Hohenheim, 1985. Fellow Conicet, Argentina, 1977-84; prof. Univ. Nat. La Pampa, Santa Rosa, Argentina, 1977—; technician Inst. Nat. Tech. Agropecuaria, 1988—. Author: Labranzas en la region semiarida Argentina, 1996, Siembra Directa, 1998; editor Argentinian Soil Sci. Soc., 1998—; contbr. articles to profl. jours.; author 2 books. Mem. Internat. Soil Sci. Assn., Am. Soil Sci. Soc., Argentinian Soil Sci. Soc. Home: Liniers 231, 6300 Santa Rosa La Pampa, Argentina Office: INTA, CC11, 6320 Anguil Argentina

BUSCH-VISHNIAC, ILENE JOY, mechanical engineering educator, researcher; b. Phila., Jan. 28, 1955; d. Leonard and Ruth (Rudnick) Busch; m. Ethan Tecumseh Vishniac, June 13, 1976; children: Cady Anne, Miriam Rachel. BA in Math. magna cum laude, U. Rochester, 1976, BS in Physics magna cum laude, 1976; MSME, MIT, 1978, PhD in Mech. Engring., 1981. Mem. tech. staff acoustics rsch. dept. Bell Labs., 1980-82; asst. prof. mech. engring. U. Tex., Austin, 1982-86, assoc. prof., 1986-91, prof., assoc. chmn. mech. engring. for acad. affairs, 1991-95, Harry H. Power prof., 1994-98; dean Whiting Sch. of Engring. Johns Hopkins U., 1998—; Cons. AT&T Bell Labs., 1982-84, Nat. Inst. Justice, 1988, Body, Vickers, Daniels, 1989-93, to Tex. atty. gen., 1989-95; also others; mem. vis. com. dept. mech. engring. MIT, 1993-99; presdl. young investigator NSF, 1985; numerous presentations to profl. soc. mtgs., workships, confs.; numerous invited lectures; chmn. session on micro-automation, sensing and hardware issues Internat. Symposium on Robotics and Mfg., 1992, mem. mfg. program com., 1994; numerous others. Author: Electromechanical Sensors and Actuators, 1999; contbg. author: Handbook of Acoustics, 1992; contbr. numerous articles to sci. jours. Program mentor YWCA, 1989; speaker Tex. Energy Sci. Symposium for H.S.'s, 1989, Austin Sci. Acad., 1989, 90; speaker, session chmn. Expanding Your Horizons Workshop, 1991. Recipient Curtis McGraw rsch. award Am. Soc. for Engring. Edn., 1994, best paper award in mfg. Internat. Symposium on Robotics and Mfg., 1994; fellow Fannie and John Hertz Found., MIT, 1976-80, GM Found. Centennial tchg. fellow in mech. engring., 1985; grantee NSF, 1983—, Univ. Rsch. Inst., 1983-85, U. Tex. Bur. Engring. Rsch., 1983-85, Office Naval Rsch., 1985-87, Bosque Found., 1986-88, Semicondr. Rsch. Corp., 1987-90, GM, 1988-89, Tex. Instruments, 1989, Tex. Dept. Transp., 1994—; others. Fellow Acoustical Soc. Am. (v.p. 1997-98, tech. com. on engring. acoustics 1982—, tech. com. on noise 1982—, exec. com. 1988-91, com. on status of women in the Soc. 1992—, chmn. Austin chpt. 1986, nominating com. 1989, Lindsay award 1987); mem. ASME (micro-mech. sys. panel dynamic sys. and control div. 1992—, Outstanding Mech. Engring. Faculty Advisor award 1983), Inst. Noise Control Engring. (assoc.), Soc. Women Engrs. (achievement award 1997), AAUW, Golden Key, Phi Beta Kappa. Achievements include patent on electret transducer with a selectively metallized backplate, with a variably charged electret foil, with a variable electret foil thickness, with a variable effective air gap, with a variable actual air gap; integrated capacitive microphone, electret transducer for blood pressure monitoring, six degree-of-freedom optical sensor. Office: Johns Hopkins U NEB 120 3400 N Charles St Baltimore MD 21218-2680

BUSCK, OLE ARNOLD, publishing company executive; b. Copenhagen, Aug. 12, 1937. MBA, Copenhagen Sch. Econs./Bus. Adminstrn., 1966. Pres. Nyt Nordisk Forlag Arnold Busck Inc., Copenhagen, 1969—; lectr. Copenhagen Sch. Econs. and Bus. Adminstrn. Served to col. Danish Army. Mem. Internat. Pubs. Assn. (exec. com. 1990-96), Danish Pubs. Assn. (pres. 1984-96). Office: Nyt Nordisk Forlag Arnold Busck, Købmagergade 49, DK-1150 Copenhagen Denmark

BUSFIELD, ROGER MELVIL, JR., retired trade association executive, educator; b. Ft. Worth, Feb. 4, 1926; s. Roger Melvil and Julia Mabel (Clark) B.; m. Jean Wilson, Mar. 26, 1948 (div. Oct. 1960); children: Terry Jean, Roger Melvil III, Timothy Clark; m. Virginia Bailey, Dec. 1, 1962 (dec. July 1991); 1 child, Julia Lucille; m. Addie Howard Davis, June 17, 1995. Student, U. Tex., 1943, 46; BA, Southwestern U., 1947, MA, 1948; PhD, Fla. State U., 1954. Asst. prof. Southwestern U., 1947-49; instr. U. Ala., 1949-50, Fla. State U., 1950-54; asst. prof. speech Mich. State U., 1954-60; editl. svcs. specialist Oldsmobile divsn. Gen. Motors Corp., Lansing, Mich., 1960; gen. publs. supr. Consumers Power Co., Jackson, Mich., 1960-61; assoc. dir. Mich. Hosp. Assn., Lansing, 1961-73; exec. dir. Ark. Hosp. Assn., Little Rock, 1973-81, pres., 1981-94, pres. emeritus, 1994—; adj. prof. health svcs. mgmt. Webster U., 1979-97. Author: The Playwright's Art, 1958, Arabic transl., 1964, (with others) The Children's Theatre, 1960; editor Theatre Arts Bibliography, 1964; contbr. articles to profl. jours.; author profl. motion picture scenarios. Trustee Ctrl. Mich. U., 1967-73, chmn., 1970; mem. Mich. Gov.'s Commn. on Higher Edn., 1972-74; mem. Ark. Gov.'s Emergency Med. Svcs. Adv. Coun., 1975-94, chmn., 1978-84; mem. Ark. Gov.'s Task Force on Rural Hosps., 1988-89, Ark. Dept. of Health Long Range Planning Com., 1988-89; chmn. AIDS adv. com. Ark. Dept. Health, 1990-97; mem. Ark. Gov.'s Task Force Health Care Reform, 1993-96; chmn. Health Data Task Force, Ark. Resources Comm., 1994-95; mem. adv. bd. Ark. Pediat. Facility, 1995-96. Served with USMC, 1943-46. Named Tex. Outstanding Author, Theta Sigma Phi, 1958; recipient Disting. Alumnus award Southwestern U., 1971, Senate-House Concurrent Resolution of Tribute, Mich. Legis., 1973, Bd. Trustees award Am. Hosp. Assn., 1994, Merit award Ark. Hosp. Assn., 1994. Mem. Am. Soc. Assn. Execs., Ark. Soc. Assn. Execs. (pres. 1981-82), Pub. Rels. Assn. Mich. (pres. 1966), Speech Comm. Assn., Am. Coll. Health Care Execs., State Hosp. Assn. Exec. Forum (sec., treas. 1989, pres. 1991), Am. Hosp. Assn. (coun. legis. 1975-77, coun. allied and govtl. rels. 1983-86), San Gabriel Writers League (pres. 2000), Rotary (Little Rock). Methodist. Home: PO Box 2267 Georgetown TX 78627-2267

BUSH, ARTHUR JOE, mining engineer, educator; b. Washington, Mar. 27, 1922; s. Arthur Edward and Cassie (Rice) B.; m. Margaret Elizabeth Strausser, Dec. 25, 1956; children: Beryl Candice, Diane Denise. BS in Mining Engring., Mo. Sch. Mines, 1947, MS, 1963; MS in Urban Planning, Transp., Purdue U., 1970. Registered profl. engr., Mo., Ind., Ky. Asst. mining engr. Fredericktown (Mo.) Lead Co., 1947-49; mining engr. solvay process divsn. Allied Chem. & Dye Corp., Prairie du Rocher, Ill., 1949-53, acting asst. quarry supt., 1950-53; mining engr. Internat. Salt Co., Retsof, N.Y., 1953-55; engr. Frazier-Davis Constrn. Co., Morgantown, Pa., 1955-56; chief engr. baroid divsn. Nat. Lead Co., Malvern, Ark., 1956-60; instr. engring. graphics U. Mo., Rolla, 1962-65; asst. prof. civil engring. Tri-State U., Angola, Ind., 1965-72; city coord., city engr. City of Kendallville, Ind., 1972-73; assoc. prof. engring. tech. Western Ky. U., Bowling Green, 1974-87; cons. in field. Co-author: Black Powder to Black Gold. 1st lt., U.S. Army, 1943-46. Decorated Silver Star with oak leaf cluster; recipient Silver Beaver award Boy Scouts Am., 1997. Mem. AIME, ASCE, Soc. Engring. Edn., Am. Rd. Builders Assn., Ky. Soc. Profl. Engrs., Nat. Soc. Profl. Engrs., Mammoth Cave chpt. Profl. Engrs., Am. Fencers Assn., Hobson House Assn., Am. Soc. Explosives Engrs., Steuben County Hist. Soc. Sertoma (Lewis B. Hershey chpt.), Rolla Arts Group, Arts Alliance Bowling Green, So. Ky. Past-Finders, Sigma Xi, Pi Kappa Alpha, Sigma Gamma Epsilon, Tau Beta Pi. Achievements include rsch. in explosives and dynamic creep. Home: 1927 Price Ave Bowling Green KY 42104-3329

BUSH, BARBARA PIERCE, volunteer, former First Lady of the United States; b. Rye, N.Y., June 8, 1925; d. Marvin and Pauline (Robinson) Pierce; m. George Herbert Walker Bush, Jan. 6, 1945; children: George Walker, John Ellis, Neil Mallon, Marvin Pierce, Dorothy Walker. Student, Smith Coll., 1943-44; hon. degrees, Stritch Coll., Milw., 1981, Mt. Vernon Coll., Washington, 1981, Hood Coll., Frederick, Md., 1983, Howard U., Washington, 1987, Judson Coll., Marion, Ala., 1988, Bennett Coll., Greensboro, N.C., 1989, Smith Coll., 1989, Morehouse Sch. Medicine, 1989. Oper. & facilities div. Dept. Administration, Washington, 1992; with Office of George Bush, Washington, 1992—. Author: C. Fred Story; Millie's Book; Barbara Bush: A Memoir, 1994. Hon. chair adv. bd. Reading is Fundamental; hon. mem. Bus. Coun. for Effective Literacy; mem. adv. coun. Soc. of Meml. Sloan-Kettering Cancer Ctr.; hon. mem. bd. dirs. Children's Oncology Svcs. of Met. Washington, The Washington Home, The Kingsbury Ctr.; hon. chmn. nat. adv. coun. Literacy Vols. of Am., Nat. Sch. Vols. Program; sponsor Laubach Literacy Internat.; nat. hon. chmn. Leukemia Soc. of Am.; hon. mem. bd. trustees Morehouse Sch. of Medicine; hon. nat. chmn. Nat. Organ Donor Awareness Week, 1982-86; pres. Ladies of the Senate, 1981-88; mem. women's com. Smithsonian Assocs., Tex. Fedn. of Rep. Women, life mem., hon. mem.; hon. chairperson for the Nat. Com. on Literacy and Edn. United Way, Barbara Bush Found. for Family Literacy, Washington Parent Group Fund, Girls Clubs of Am., 10th anniversary Harvest Nat. Food Bank Network; hon. chmn. Nat. Com. for the Prevention of Child Abuse and Childhelp U.S.A.; hon. pres. Girl Scouts U.S; hon. chair Nat. Com. for Adoption; mem. bd. trustees Mayo Clinic Found.; hon. chair Read Am., Boarder Baby Project; mem. bd. visitors M. D. Anderson Cancer Ctr.; hon. chair Leukemia Soc. Am., Children's Literacy Initiative; hon. mem. Reading is Fundamental; ambassador at large Americares; honorary mem. Barbara Bush Found. for Family Literacy. Recipient Nat. Outstanding Mother of Yr. award, 1984, Woman of Yr. award USO, 1986, Disting. Leadership award United Negro Coll. Fund 1986, Disting. Am. Woman award Coll. Mt. St. Joseph, 1987, Free Spirit award Freedom Forum, 1995. Mem. Tex. Fedn. Rep. Women (life), Internat. II Club (Washington), Magic Circle Rep. Women's Club (Houston), YWCA. Episcopalian.

BUSH, EUGENE NYLE, pharmacologist, research scientist; b. McKeesport, Pa., Apr. 14, 1952; s. Nyle E. and Rosalia M. (Merlino) B.; m. Janet Rosemary Ruscitto, May 7, 1977; children: Stephen Michael, Rebecca Renee, Timothy George. BS in Pharmacy, U. Pitts., 1977, PhD in Pharmacology, 1981. Registered pharmacist, Pa., Ill. Tchg. asst. U. Pitts., 1978-81; staff pharmacist Western Pa. Hosp., Pitts., 1977-81; pharmacologist II Abbott Labs., 1981-84, pharmacologist I, 1984-87; sr. rsch. sci. Abbott Labs., Abbott Park, Ill., 1986-88, rsch. investigator, 1988-89, group leader, endocrine pharmacol., 1989-91; sr. group leader endocrine pharmacol. Abbott Labs., 1991-97, assoc. Volwiler rsch. fellow, 1996—. Co-author numerous publs.; contbr. articles to profl. jours. Mem. Endocrine Soc., Am. Pharm. Assn., Am. Diabetes Assn., Nat. Eagle Scout Assn., Sigma Xi. Republican, Roman Catholic. Avocations: gardening, photography, com-

puters, bicycling. Home: 816 Bedford Ct Libertyville IL 60048-3002 Office: Abbott Labs 100 Abbott Park Rd Abbott Park IL 60064-3502

BUSH, GAIL, secondary school educator, librarian, consultant, writer; b. Chgo., May 2, 1952; d. George William and Norma T. Fish; m. Robert K. Bush, Sept. 7, 1978; children: Matthew Thomas, Claire Anne. BA in Anthropology magna cum laude, U. Ill., 1973, MS in Libr. Sci., 1977; PhD in Ednl. Psychology, Loyola U., Chgo., 2000. Cert. libr. media, Ill. Head libr. Nat. Coll. Edn. (now Nat.-Louis U.), Chgo., 1977-79; corp. libr. mgr. Heidrick & Struggles, Chgo., 1979-82; grad. rsch. instr., ref. libr. Nat. Coll. Edn., Wilmette, Ill., 1982-92; curriculum libr. Maine Twp. H.S. West, Des Plaines, Ill., 1992—; goals 2000 cons. Loyola U. Chgo., 1997—, lectr., 1998—; pub. cons. Greenwood Press, Westport, Conn., 2000—; info. lit. cons. Great Plains Network, Lincoln, Nebr., 1999—. Mem. editl. bd. Am. Assn. Sch. Librs., 1997-2000; contbr. articles to profl. jours. including Ednl. Leadership, Knowledge Quest, Sch. Libr. Jour., NASSP Bull., Emergency Libr., Voice Youth Advocates, Ill. Reading Coun. Jour. Named Sch. Libr. of Yr. North Suburban Libr. Sys., 1999. Mem. ALA, ASCD, Am. Assn. Sch. Librs. (Nat. Sch. Libr. Media Program of Yr. 1996), Internat. Reading Assn., Am. Ednl. Rsch. Assn., Freedom to Read Found., Beta Phi Mu. E-mail: gbush@maine207west.k12.il.us. Office: Maine Twp HS West 1755 S Wolf Rd Des Plaines IL 60018-1923

BUSH, GEORGE HERBERT WALKER, former President of the United States; b. Milton, Mass., June 12, 1924; s. Prescott Sheldon and Dorothy (Walker) B.; m. Barbara Pierce, Jan. 6, 1945; children: George W., John E., Neil M., Marvin P., Dorothy W. Koch. BA in Econs., Yale U., 1948; numerous other hon. degrees. Co-founder Bush-Overbey Oil Devel. Co., 1951; Co-founder, dir. Zapata Petroleum Corp., Midland, 1953-59; pres. Zapata Off Shore Co., Houston, 1956-64; chm. bd. Zapata Off Shore Co., 1964-66; mem. 90th-91st Congresses from 7th Dist. Tex., 1967-71, Ways and Means com.; U.S. amb. to UN, 1971-73; chmn. Rep. Nat. Com., 1973-74; chief U.S. Liaison Office Peking, People's Republic China, 1974-75; dir. CIA, 1976-77; adj. prof. adminstrv. sci. Rice U., Houston, 1978; V.P. of U.S., 1981-89, Pres. of U.S., 1989-93; chmn. Eisenhower Exch. Fellowships; bd. visitors M.D. Anderson Cancer Ctr., Houston. Del. Rep. Nat. Conv., 1964, 69; Rep. candidate U.S. senator from Tex., 1964, 70. Lt. (j.g.), pilot USN, WWII. Decorated D.F.C., Air medals (3). Office: 10000 Memorial Dr Houston TX 77024-3422

BUSH, LARRY DON, communications company administrator; b. Sulphur Springs, Tex., June 8, 1945; s. Robert Lawson and Margret Laverne (Davis) B.; m. Opal June Chamberlain, Jan. 15, 1965 (div. Nov. 1969); 1 child, Laura Michelle; m. Kathleen Ann Merkel, May 4, 1974; children: Angela Dawn, Andrea Danielle. BBA summa cum laude, Dallas Bapt. U., 1993. Engring. technician Tex. Instruments, Richardson, 1962-65; sys. engr. Sci. control Corp., Carrollton, Tex., 1965-69; course developer Southwestern Bell, St. Louis, 1972-74; ctrl. office technician Southwestern Bell, Dallas, 1969-72, transmission specialist, 1974-79, network mgr., 1977-86, sr. design cons., 1986-89, area mgr. tech. support, 1989-95; area mgr. Integrated Svc. Ctr. Southwestern Bell, 1995-99, competitive analyst, 1999—. Tchr. New Covenant World Outreach, 1997-99; dir. Ministries New Covenant World Outreach Wylie, Tex., 1999—. Mem. Soc. Competitive Intelligence Profls., Tex. Soc. Telephone Engrs., Tex. Telephone Pioneers, Alpha Chi, Alpha Sigma Lambda, Delta Mu Delta. Republican. Avocations: woodworking, digital electronics. Home: 1096 Midnight Pass Rockwall TX 75087-7200 Office: Southwestern Bell Telephone Four Bell Plz Rm 1830 07 Dallas TX 75202-5398

BUSH, MARILYN WOLIN, software engineer, management consultant; b. Phila., Dec. 2, 1948; d. Louis and Minnie (Goldsmith) Wolin; m. Ronald Bush, Dec. 14, 1969; 1 child, Charles Max. BSEE, U. Pa., 1969. Rsch. asst. Cavendish Labs. Cambridge (Eng.) U., 1970; electronic engr. Dept. Def., 1970-75; project mgr. Trans. Sys. Ctr., Cambridge, Mass., 1975-82; software product assurance mgr. NASA Jet Propulsion Lab. Calif. Inst. Tech., Pasadena, 1982-92; internat. lectr., cons. Pasadena and Phila., 1992—; vis. scientist Software Engring. Inst., Carnegie Mellon U., Pitts., 1992-94, 95-96; tutor Winthrop House, Harvard U., Cambridge, Mass. Co-author: The Capability Maturity Model: Guidelines for Improving the Software Process, 1995; contbr. articles to profl. jours. Mem. Mass. High Tech. Coun., Boston. Recipient awards NASA, 1991. Mem. IEEE (nat. adv. com. on edn., program com. internat. conf.), IEEE Computer Soc. (nat. exec. com. tech. com.), Boston Profl. Coun. (founding pres. 1981-82). Avocations: jogging, travel. Home and Office: 39 St Giles, Oxford OX1 3LW, England

BUSH, MITCHELL LESTER, JR., retired federal agency administrator; b. Syracuse, N.Y., Feb. 1, 1936; s. Mitchell Bush and Sarah (Skenandore) Gonyea. Grad. H.S., Lawrence, Kans. Tribal enrollment specialist Bur. Indian Affairs, Washington, 1962, 66; area tribal enrollment officer Bur. Indian Affairs, Anadarko, Okla., 1964-65; acting chief Bur. Tribal Enrollment Svcs., Washington, 1982, chief, 1983, ret., 1991. Co-editor: American Indian Society Cookbook, 1974, 2d edit., 1984. Vice-chmn. Va. Coun. on Indians, Richmond, 1989-95. With U.S. Army, 1958-61. Recipient Points of Light cert., award for Outstanding Pub. Svc. to U.S.A., U.S. Sec. of Interior, Washington, 1990, Maharishi award Maharishi U., Washington, 1985. Mem. Am. Indian Soc. (founder, pres. 1966-91, editor newsletter 1991—, Disting. Svc. award 1971, 90, Outstanding Elder/Advisor award 1996). Methodist. Avocations: raising ornamental fowl, collecting Native American artwork, travel, collecting coins. Home: 22230 Cool Water Dr Ruther Glen VA 22546-3309 Office: AIS Newsletter 22258 Cool Water Dr Ruther Glen VA 22546-3309

BUSH, RAYMOND GEORGE, lawyer; b. Phila., Mar. 27, 1952; s. Raymond George and Florence Dorothy (Glassman) B.; children: Katherine Elizabeth, James Crisfield, Margaret Lindsley, Abigail Josephine. BA, Widener U., 1975; MPA, Temple U., 1980, postgrad., 1981-83, JD, 1988. Bar: Pa. 1988, N.J. 1989, U.S. Ct. Appeals (3d cir.) 1988, U.S. Ct. Appeals (fed. cir.) 1989, U.S. Ct. Mil. Appeals 1989, U.S. Dist. Ct. (ea. dist.) Pa. 1989, U.S. Dist. Ct. (mid. dist.) Pa. 1991, U.S. Supreme Ct. 1993, U.S. Dist. Ct. N.J. 1995; cert. estate practitioner. Employee rels. specialist regional office U.S. Dept. Health and Human Svcs., Phila., 1980-83; labor rels. officer U.S. VA, Coatsville, Pa., 1983; paralegal Office Gen. Counsel U.S. Dept. Health and Human Svcs., Phila., 1984; labor rels. specialist Fed. Labor Rels. Authority, Phila., 1984-88; mgmt. rep. U.S. Dept. Navy, Phila., 1988-89; assoc. Duane, Morris and Heckscher, Phila., 1989-90, Tallman, Hudders & Sorentino, Allentown, Pa., 1990-91; pvt. practice Bethlehem, Pa., 1991—; lectr. at profl. meetings and confs.; adj. asst. prof. Widener U., Chester, Pa., 1988-89, instr. paralegal program; adj. faculty Nat. Bus. Inst.; adj. instr. Cedar Crest, Allentown, Pa., 1996-99, Muhlenberg Coll., Easton, Pa., 1999—. Contbr. numerous articles to profl. publs. Bd. dirs. Community Dispute Settlement of Delaware County, Media, Pa., 1988-89; community mediator, bd. dirs. Common Ground, Bethlehem, Pa., 1989-90; personnel com. Cathedral Ch. of Nativity, Bethlehem, 1990, also vestry and solicitor; fundraising capt. Minsi Trail coun. Boy Scouts Am., 1990; active Leadership Lehigh Valley, 1991. Mem. ABA (labor and employment law sect., com. on fed. svc. labor and employment law), Pa. Bar Assn. (labor and employment law sect.), Phila. Bar Assn. (labor com.), Indsl. Rels. Rsch. Assn. (planning com. Phila. chpt. 1986-88, v.p. programming 1991—, mem. adv. bd., past pres. NE chpt.), Soc. Fed. Labor Rels. Profls. (pres. Mid-Atlantic chpt. 1981-88, exec. dir. 1988-89, nat. exec. bd. 1986-87), Northampton County Bar Assn. (chair labor rels. com. 1990-94, mem. pers. com. 1994—), Pi Gamma Mu, Phi Delta Phi. Republican. Episcopalian. Avocations: sailing, cross-country skiing, golf, photography, classical music. Home: 226 E Wall St Bethlehem PA 18018-6118 Office: 65 E Elizabeth Ave Ste 901 Bethlehem PA 18018-6516

BUSH, STANLEY GILTNER, secondary school educator; b. Kansas City, Mo., Nov. 4, 1928; s. Dean Thomas and Sallie Giltner (Hoagland) B.; m. Barbara Snow Adams, May 23, 1975 (dec. Mar. 1994); stepchildren: Deborah Gayle Duclon, Douglas Bruce Adams. BA, U. Colo., 1949, MA, 1959, postgrad., 1971; postgrad., U. Denver, 1980, 85, 90. Tchr. Gering (Nebr.) Pub. Schs., 1949-51, 54-57, Littleton (Colo.) Pub. Schs., 1957-91; emergency plan dir. City of Littleton, 1961—; safety officer Littleton Pub. Schs., 1968—; founder, chief Arapahoe Rescue Patrol, Inc., Littleton, 1957-92, search mission coord., 1975—; pres. Arapahoe Rescue Patrol, Inc., 1957—, Expedition, Inc., Littleton, 1973—; owner Emergency Rsch. Cons., 1990—. Contbr. chpts. to Boy Scout Field Book, 1984; co-author: Managing Search Function, 1987; contbr. articles to profl. jours. Safety advisor South Suburban Parks Dist., Littleton, 1985—; advisor ARC, Littleton, 1987—, Emergency Planning Com., Arapahoe County, Colo., 1987—; coord. search and rescue Office of Gov., Colo., 1978-82; state judge Odyssey of the Mind, 1996-97. Sgt. U.S. Army, 1951-54. Shell Oil Co. fellow, 1964; recipient Silver Beaver award Boy Scouts Am., 1966, Vigil-Order of Arrow, 1966, Award of Excellence Masons, 1990, Service to Mankind award Arapahoe Sertoma, 1999. Mem. Nat. Assn. for Search and Rescue (life, Hall Foss award 1978), Colo. Search and Rescue Bd., NEA (life). Methodist. Avocations: mountaineering, wilderness emergency care, emergency services. Home: 2415 E Maplewood Ave Littleton CO 80121-2817 Office: Littleton Ctr 2255 W Berry Ave Littleton CO 80165-0001

BUSH, WILLIAM ARDEN, internal revenue agent; b. Ogallala, Nebr., Feb. 1, 1948; s. James L. and Phyllis M. (Sullivan) B.; m. Carol L. Jensen, June 14, 1970; 1 child, Daniel Arden. A in Bus. Adminstr., Northeastern Jr. Coll., 1969; BSBA, Kearney (Nebr.) State Coll., 1972, MBA, 1981; MS in Acct., Okla. City U., 1987. CPA, Okla. Gen. mgr., controller Sullivan-Bush Dept. Store, Ogallala, 1972-73, ptnr., 1973-79; grad. teaching asst. in acctg. Kearney State Coll., 1980-81; job office mgr. South Prairie Constrn. Co., Oklahoma City, 1981; agt. IRS, Enid, Okla. and Oklahoma City, 1981-87; supr. IRS, Oklahoma City, 1987—; prin. W.A. Bush Investment Advisor, Ogallala, 1974-75; instr. supplemental acctg. Rose State Coll., 1990; adj. prof. Rose State Jr. Coll., Oklahoma City, 1988, Oklahoma City C.C., 1990. Chmn. bd. trustees Congl. Ch., Ogallala, 1974; wrestling coach, Ogallala Jaycees, 1975; leader Cub Scouts Am., Ogallala, 1976. Republican. Club: Big Mac Sports (Ogallala) (com. chmn. 1978-79). Lodge: Rotary (1st v.p. 1979), Masons. Avocations: studying, reading, travel. Home: 11321 N Shannon Ave Oklahoma City OK 73162-2149 Office: IRS 55 N Robinson Ave Ste A Oklahoma City OK 73102-9237

BUSHNAQ, ABDUL RAUOF ABDULLAH, agricultural engineer; b. Ommer, Palestine, 1944; s. Kathkuda and Shafiqa (Hussain) B.; m. Essam Zakout, 1956; children: Sanaad, Saif, Saji, Bassam, Mirna. BA, U. Skopke, 1979. Pub. security Jordanian Police; agrl. engr. Aida Estate Trading & Agriculture, Jeddah, Saudi Arabia. Home: PO Box 1462, Jeddah 21431, Saudi Arabia

BUSHNELL, GEORGE EDWARD, JR., lawyer; b. Detroit, Nov. 15, 1924; s. George E. and Ida Mary (Bland) B.; children: George Edward III, Christopher Gilbert Whelden, Robina McLeod Bushnell Hogan. Mil. student, U. Kans., 1943; BA, Amherst Coll., 1948; LLB, U. Mich., 1951; LLD, Detroit Coll. Law, 1995. Bar: Mich. 1951, D.C. 1980, U.S. Dist. Ct. (ea. dist.) Mich. 1951, U.S. Dist. Ct. (we. dist.) Mich. 1971, U.S. Ct. Appeals (6th cir.) 1955, U.S. Ct. Appeals (fed. cir.) 1995, U.S. Ct. Appeals for the Armed Forces 1995, U.S. Supreme Ct. 1971, U.S. Ct. Internat. Trade 1995. From assoc. to sr. ptnr. Miller, Canfield, Paddock and Stone, Detroit, 1953-77, of counsel, 1989—; sr. ptnr. Bushnell, Gage, Doctoroff & Reizen, Southfield, Mich., 1977-89; commr. Mich. Jud. Tenure Comm., 1969-83, chmn., 1978-80; pres. State Bar Mich., 1975-76; bd. dirs. Nat. Jud. Coll., 1985-89; mem. Mich. Atty. Discipline Bd., 1990-96; lectr. in field. Elder Grosse Pointe Meml. Ch.; moderator Detroit Presbytery, United Presbyn. Ch. U.S.A., 1972, pres. program agy. bd., 1972-76; bd. dirs. Econ. Devel. Corp. of Detroit, 1976—, Econ. Growth Corp. of Detroit, 1978-96, Tax Increment Fin. Authority, Detroit, 1984—, Econ. Devel. Authority, Detroit, 1988-98; bd. trustees New Detroit, Inc., 1972—, chmn., 1974-75, Mich. Ptnrship Prevent Gun Violence, 1995—, pres.-elect, 1999-2000. Served with USAR, 1942-56. Decorated Bronze Star, Army Commendation medal. Mem. NAACP (life, co-chmn. fight for freedom fund dinner 1968), ABA (ho. of dels. 1976—, chmn. ho. of dels. 1988-90. pres.-elect 1993-94, pres. 1994-95, past pres. 1995-96, others, Trial Attys. of Am. (pres. 1971-89), State Bar Mich. . bd. of bar commrs. 1970-76, pres. 1975-76, John Hensel award for svcs. to the arts 1990, Roberts P. Hudson award for spl. svcs. to the bar and the people of Mich., 1979, 85, Cooley Law Sch. Louis A. Smith (disting. jurist award 1995), Detroit Bar Assn. (bd. dirs. 1958-65, pres. 1964-65, past pres. com. 1980—, bench & bar award for svc. to the judicial sys., the legal profession and the cmty. 1989), Nat. Conf. of Bar Pres. (pres. 1984-85), 6th Jud. Cir. Conf. (life), Am. Law Inst., Am. Arbitration Assn. (bd. dirs. 1970-82), Am. Coll. Trial Lawyers, Am. Bar Found. (life), Am. Judicature Soc. (bd. dirs. 1977-82), Can. Bar Assn. (hon.), Internat. Soc. Barristers, Fed. Bar Assn., Masons (33 deg.), Met. Club (N.Y.C.) Phi Delta Phi, Psi Upsilon. Democrat. Office: Miller Canfield Paddock & Stone 150 W Jefferson Ave Ste 2500 Detroit MI 48226-4416

BUSHNELL, RODERICK PAUL, lawyer; b. Buffalo, N.Y., Mar. 6, 1944; s. Paul Hazen and Martha Atlee Bushnell; m. Suzann Yvonne Kaiser, Aug. 27, 1966; 1 child, Arlo Phillip. BA, Rutgers U., 1966; JD, Georgetown U., 1969. Bar: Calif. 1970, U.S. Supreme Ct. 1980.; cert. Civil Trial Advocate, Nat. Bd. Trial Advocates. Atty. dept. water resources Sacramento, 1969-71; ptnr. Bushnell, Caplan & Fielding, San Francisco, 1971—; adv. bd. dirs. Bread & Roses, Inc., Mill Valley, Calif. Mem. ATLA, San Francisco Bar Assn. (labor and employment sects.; arbitrator), San Francisco Superior Ct. (arbitrator), Fed. Ct. Early Neutral Evaluator, Calif. Bar Assn. (labor and employement sects.), Consumer Attys. Calif., San Francisco Trial Lawyers Assn., No. Calif. Criminal Trial Lawyers Assn., Nat. Employment Lawyers Assn., Calif. Employment Lawyers Assn. Office: Bushnell Caplan & Fielding 221 Pine St Ste 600 San Francisco CA 94104-2705

BUSHUE, SHERLYN JEAN, wallpapering group executive, writer; b. Kansas City, Kans., Mar. 5, 1950; d. Robert and Gwyanetha June (Stockton) Norton Hicks; m. Carl James Bushue, Feb. 14, 1997; children: Chad Josef, Tara Jonet, Brittany Lynn. BS, Drury Coll., 1972. Lic. realtor; lic. social worker; approved foster care mother. Real estate saleswoman Gaslight Realtors, Gladstone, Mo., 1974-77; social worker Vis. Nurse Assn., Kansas City, Mo., 1979-82; owner Touch of Class Wallpapering Group, Olathe, Kans., 1982—. Baptist. Avocations: softball, soccer, swimming, volleyball, arts and crafts. Home: 9002 W 121st Ter Shawnee Mission KS 66213-1531

BUSHUEV, VLADIMIR ALEKSEEVICH, physics researcher; b. Moscow, May 13, 1947; s. Aleksey Efimovich and Nadezhda Trofimovna (Malaya) B.; m. Olga Andreevna Zamura, Apr. 10, 1970; 1 child, Andrew. Grad., Moscow State U., 1971, postgrad., 1971-74. Jr. rsch. worker Moscow State U., 1974-86, rsch. worker, 1986-88, sr. rsch. worker, 1988-93, prof. phys. dept., 1993—. Author: (books) Secondary Process in X-Ray Optics, 1990, Physical Principles of X-Ray Diffractometry Analysis of the Finding Parameters of Real Multilayer Structure of Epitaxial Layers, 1996, Secondary Process in X-Ray Optics, 1990. Sr. lt. Russian mil., 1968-71. Democrat. Avocations: popular music, kayaking. Office: Physics Dept, Moscow State U/Vorobjovi Go, 119899 Moscow Russia

BUSJAHN, ANDREAS, psychologist; b. Berlin, Dec. 10, 1958; s. Harald and Christa (Schönborn) B.; m. Dorothea Maass, June 9, 1979; children: Christoph, Teresa. Diploma psychology, Humboldt U., 1985; Dr.rer.nat., Acad. of Scis., 1989. Scientist Inst. for Cardiovascular Rsch., Berlin, 1985-91, Max Delbrück Ctr. for Molecular Medicine, Berlin, 1992-96, Franz-Volhard Clinic, Berlin, 1996—; rsch. fellow Ind. U., 1995. Rsch. award Leopoldina, 1995; recipient Internat. Young Rsch. award Ctr. for Study of Multiple Birth, 1996. Mem. Behavior Genetics Assn., Internat. Soc. for Twin Studies, Am. Soc. Human Genetics, German Soc. for Human Genetics. Office: Franz-Volhard Clinic, Wiltbergstr 50, 13125 Berlin Germany

BUSS, GERALD VERE AUSTEN, educator, clergyman; b. Canterbury, Kent, Eng., May 17, 1936; s. Humphrey Austen and Angela (Horne) B.; m. Vivian Margaret Buss; children: Celina Lucie, Sofie Maria, Chloe Susanna Austen. Diploma in theology, St. Stephen's House, Oxford, Eng., 1963; PhD, Cambridge U., 1987. Trader messrs. Holiday, Cutler, Bath and Co., Singapore, 1956-59; asst. priest St. Peter's Ch., Petersham, Surrey, Eng., 1963-66, Holy Trinity Ch., London, 1966-70; sr. chaplain, lectr. modern history Hurstpierpoint Coll., Hassocks, Eng., 1970-96; mem., part-time researcher Keston Coll., Kent, 1980—. Author: The Bear's Hug: Religious Belief and the Soviet State 1917-86, 87. Served to lt. inf. Brit. Army, 1954-56. Airey Neave Meml. scholar Ho. of Commons, 1984; fellow-commoner Corpus Christi Coll., Cambridge, 1986. Mem. Nat. Assn. Soviet and East European Studies. Club: Nikaean (London). Home: Souches The Street, Albourne BN6 9DJ, England

BUSS, MARTIN, electronic engineer; b. Darmstadt, Germany, Aug. 19, 1965; s. Herbert and Ingeborg (Zehnter) B.; m. Yuko Murata, July 24, 1996. Diploma, Tech. U. Darmstadt, 1990; DSc, U. Tokyo, 1994. Postdoctoral rschr. Australian Nat. U., Canberra, 1994-95; sr. rsch. asst., lectr. Tech. U. Munich, Germany, 1995—. Mem. IEEE, Robotics Soc. Japan, Japanese Soc. Instrument & Control Engrs. Office: Inst Automatic Control Eng, Tech U Munich, 80290 Munich Germany

BUSSINO, MELINDA HOLDEN, human services administrator; b. Boston, Apr. 20, 1946; d. Sharon Virtulan and Grace (Fitzgerald) Holden; m. Louis Logue Doyle, Feb. 14, 1974 (dec. Oct. 1980); children: Sarah, Joseph; m. Fred John Bussino, Sept. 22, 1998 (dec. Jan. 2000). BA in Psychology, U. N.H., 1968. Dir. outreach and tng. Stratford County Cmty. Action, Somersworth, N.H., 1968-73; trainer, cons. New Eng. Regional Commn., Boston, 1971-73; office mgr. Beacon Banjo Co., Westminster, Vt., 1980-88; asst. to pastor United Meth. Ch., Brattleboro, Vt., 1985-89; exec. dir. Brattleboro Area Drop In Ctr., 1989—; cons. Putney, Vt., 1994—. Chmn. Brattleboro Human Resource Coun., 1990—; bd. dirs., past pres. Vt. Affordable Housing Coalition, 1990—, Vt. Campaign to End Child Hunger, 1991-99; housing commr. Windham Regional Commn., Brattleboro, 1995—; organizer, bd. dirs. N.H. Low Income Advocacy Coun., 1972-73, Operation Low Income People, N.H., 1969-73; adv. coun., bd. mem. Vt. Protection Advocacy, Montpelier, Vt., 1995—. Recipient Vt. Woman of Distinction award, 1996. Democrat. Methodist. Avocations: gardening, cooking, grandchildren, skiing. Home: PO Box 387 Putney VT 05346-0387 Office: Brattleboro Area Drop In Ctr PO Box 175 Brattleboro VT 05302-0175

BUSSMANN, RAINER WILLI, vegetation ecologist; b. Leutkirch, Germany, May 30, 1967; s. Wilhelm Theodor and Karin Rosa (Geigle) B. BSc, U. Tuebingen, 1989, MSc, 1993; PhD, Dr.rer.nat., U. Bayreuth, 1994. Rsch. scientist U. Bayreuth, 1993-94, rsch. assoc., 1994—; sci. dir. Estacion Cientifica San Francisco, Loja, Ecuador, 1996—, v.p. 1996—; dir. for nature conservation D.A.V., Leutkirch, Germany, 1992-93; v.p., dir. Fundacion Cientifica San Francisco, Del Mar, Calif., 1997—; dir., spkr. Internat. Network for Cultural and Biol. Diversity, Munich, 2000—. Contbr. articles to profl. jours. Pfc German Mountain Divsn., 1986-87. Rsch. fellow San Diego Mus. of Man, 1995—. Avocations: climbing, hiking, skiing. E-mail: ceja.andina@t-online.de. Home: Boosstr. 17, 81541 Munich Germany Office: U Bayreuth, Universitaetsstr 30, 95440 Bayreuth Germany

BUSSON, GEORGES, geology educator; b. Algiers, France, Apr. 5, 1929; s. Armand and Mathilde (Dillinger) B.; m. Andrée Pons, Oct. 8, 1955; children: Pierre, Michel, Marie. BS, U. Algiers, 1952; Doctorat ès Sci., U. Paris, 1971. From tech. to maitre asst. U. Algiers, 1950-62; maitre asst. U. Nancy, France, 1962-63; from sous. dir. to prof. Mus. Nat. Histoire Naturelle, Paris, 1964-98; Pres. Mus. 2000, Paris, 1992-94. Author: Le Mésozoique saharien, part 1, 1967, part 2, 1970, Principes méthodes et résultats d'une étude stratigraphique du Mésozoique saharien, 1972; editor, co-editor: Evaporites et hydrocarbures, 1988, Evaporite deposits, 1980, Evaporite sequences vol. 1 et vol. 2, 1994, Sedimentary deposition in rift and foreland basins in France and Spain, 1997. Served to 2d lt. French infantry, 1953-54, 55-56. Mem. Am. Assn. Petroleum Geology, N.Y. Acad. Sci., Comité National Francais de Géologie. Avocation: hiking. Home: 10 Bd Diderot, 75012 Paris France Office: Mus Nat Histoire Naturelle, 43 Rue de Buffon, 75005 Paris France

BUSTAMANTE, ACONA MANUEL, architect, consultant; b. Mexico City, Aug. 22, 1943; s. Manuel and Josefina (Acuna) B.; children: Cecilia, Jose M.; m. Lourdes Linares, Apr. 24, 1990. Grad. in Arch., Iberoamericana U., Mexico City, 1968. Exec. mgr. Fioscer, Mexico City, 1976-80; ptnr. Bustamente, Carrcon y Asociados, S.A., Mexico City, 1981-85; dir. Inst. Capacitacion Industria Construccion, Mexico City, 1985-86; gen. mgr. Prod. Flex, S.A., Mexico City, 1992-96; titular prof. dept. arch. and urbanism UIA, Mexico City, 1990-95; dean dept. arch. and urbanism Iberoamericana U., 1996—; cons. Diseno Arquitectonico A.P., Mexico City, 1966-72; ptnr. Habit S.A., Mexico City, 1971-74; mem. coun. arts divsn. U. Iberoamericana, 1996, chmn. Acad. Assn., 1995—. Author: Shape and Space, 1994; editor (drawings collection) Dibujos Jose Ma. Velasco, 1978. Chmn. Mex. Montessori Assn., Mexico City, 1979-81, Comunidad Educativa Montessori A.C., Mexico City, 1983-85. Mem. UIA Archs. Assn., Convivium Musicum Choir. Avocations: music, painting. Office: Iberoamericana Univ, Prolongacion Reforma 880, 01210 Mexico City Mexico

BUSTAMANTE, DONALD D., information systems administrator, consultant; b. Las Vegas, Aug. 11, 1953; s. Pete J. and Mary M. Bustamante. BS in Chemistry summa cum laude, N.Mex. State U., Las Cruces, 1975, MBA, 1981. Dir. Computer Ctr., Luna Vo-Tech Inst., Las Vegas, N.Mex., 1981-87; project mgr. N.Mex. State U., 1987—; mgmt. cons., 1981—; info. sys. cons., 1981—; session chair 1st Internat. Conf. on Multi-Sensor Multi-Source Data Fusion; sci. program com. Internat. Conf. on Data Fusion. Contbr. numerous articles to profl. jours. Mem. IEEE, IEEE Computer Soc., Am. Meteorol. Soc. (sci. and tech. adv. bd. on artificial intelligence 1998—), Mensa. Office: NMex State U PO Box 30002 Las Cruces NM 88003-8002

BUSTAMANTE, NESTOR, lawyer; b. Havana, Cuba, Apr. 20, 1960; came to the U.S., 1961; s. Nestor and Clara Rosa (Sanchez) B.; m. Marilyn Gonzalez, Sept. 20, 1986; children: Tiffany Alexandra, Nestor C. AA, U. Fla., 1980, BS in Journalism, 1982, JD, 1985. Bar: Fla. 1986, U.S. Dist. Ct. (so. dist.) Fla. 1989, U.S. Supreme Ct. 1991. Asst. state atty. State Atty.'s Office 11th Cir., Miami, 1986-88; juvenile serious offender prosecutor State Atty.'s Office, Miami, 1987-88, spl. prosecutor, gang prosecutor, 1987-88; asst. divsn. chief State Atty.'s Office-11th Jud. Cir., Miami, 1987-88; of counsel Fernandez-Caubi, Fernandez & Aguilar et al., Miami, 1988-89; atty. Ferencik, Libanoff, Brandt and Bustamante PA, Ft. Lauderdale, Fla., 1989—, ptnr., 1996—; mem. code and rules of evidence com. The Fla. Bar, 1989-90, judicial evaluation com., 2000; adj. faculty dept constrn. mgmt. Fla. Internat. U. Contbr. articles to newsletters. Mem. Miami-Dade Constrn. Trades Qualifying Bd. Named Hon. mem. Quien es Quien Publs., Inc., N.Y.C., 1990. Mem. ATLA (scoring judge nat. finals student trial advocacy competition 1994, 95), Fed. Bar Assn., Dade County Bar Assn. (mem. juvenile divsn. com. 1988-92, mem. media and pub. rels. com. 1989-91, mem. constrn. law com. 1990-91), Phi Delta Phi, U. Fla. Alumni Assn. Office: Ferencik Libanoff Brandt & Bustamante PA 150 S Pine Island Rd Ste 400 Fort Lauderdale FL 33324-2667

BUSTAMANTE, PILAR, pharmaceutics educator; b. Cadiz, Spain, July 22, 1950; d. Fernando Bustamante and Pilar Martinez; m. Joaquin Bosque, July 3, 1973. BS in Pharmacy, U. Granada, Granada, Spain, 1974; PhD, U. Granada, 1979. Instr. U. Granada, 1976-78; asst. prof. U. Alcala, Spain, 1981-82, assoc. prof., 1982-84, prof. pharmaceutics, 1984—; rschr. SEFIG, Spain, 2000. Co-author: (with A. Martin) Problem Solving: Physical Pharmacy, 1993, Physical Pharmacy, 4th edit., 1993; contbg. author: Tratado de Farmacia Galenica, 1994, Tecnologia Farmaceutica, 1998; contbr. articles to profl. jours. Mem. UNICEF, Spain. Rsch. grantee Fondo Investigaciones Sanitarias, Spain, 1988, Comision Interministerial Ciencia y Tecnologia, Spain, 1989, Comunidad Autonoma Madrid, Spain, 1995. Mem. AAAS, N.Y. Acad. Sci. Avocations: guitar, classical music, walking. Home: Goiri 30 5D, 28039 Madrid Spain Office: U Alcala de Henares, Dept Pharmacy/Tech Pharm, 28871 Madrid Spain

BUSTANI, MYRNA, business executive; b. Beirut, Lebanon, Dec. 20, 1937; d. Emile and Laura Bustani; m. Fouad el Khazen, 1958 (div. 1970); children: Jamil, Laura. Degree, Coll. Protestant Francais, Beirut, 1954; license es lettres psychology/philosophy, Ecole Superieure des Lettres, Beirut, 1958. Mem. Lebanese Parliament, 1963-64; ptnr. C.A.T. Contracting Co.; mem. bd. C.A.T. Holding, Luxemburg; dir. Société Hotelière de Tourisme, Beirut, Banque de L'Industrie et du Travail, Beirut, Banque de Financement et d'Investissement, Geneva. Trustee Am. U. Beirut, 1980; founder, mem. Centre Lebanese Studies, Oxford; pres. Al Bustan Internat. Festival Music and the Arts, 1994—. Mem. Mid. East Assn. (London), Brit. Lebanese Assn. (London). Mem. Christian Ch. Office: PO Box 11-1036, Beirut

Lebanon also: care Incotes Ltd, Wickfield House, 18-22 Disney Pl, London SE1 1HJ, England

BUSTIN, DUŠAN, chemistry educator, academic administrator; b. Martin, Slovakia, Sept. 12, 1937; s. Martin and Alzbeta (Kysely) B.; m. Ludmila Duchácek, Aug. 24, 1946; children: Helena, Martina. Diploma in engring., Slovak Tech. U., Bratislava, Slovakia, 1960, DrSc, 1986; PhD, Czech Acad. Scis., Prague, Czech Republic, 1966. Asst. lectr. Faculty Chem. Tech. Slovak U. Tech., Bratislava, 1960-73, assoc. prof., 1973-87, prof., 1987—; postdoctoral fellow Georgetown U., Washington, 1966-67; vice-chmn. Slovak Nat. Com. Pure & Applied Chemistry, Bratislava, 1993—; nat. rep. Commn. Electroanalytical Chemistry, Oxford, U.K., 1994—. Author: Analytical Chemistry, 1987; contbr. articles to profl. jours. Grant Agy. Sci. grantee, Bratislava, 1990, Slovak Grant Agy. Sci., Bratislava, 1993, 96. Mem. Am. Chem. Soc., Slovak Chem. Soc., N.Y. Acad. Scis. Evangelic. Avocation: music. Home: Nezabudkova 8, 82101 Bratislava Slovakia Office: Slovak U Tech, Radlinskeho 9, 81237 Bratislava Slovakia

BUSTIN, GEORGE LEO, lawyer; b. Perth Amboy, N.J., Feb. 10, 1948; s. George and Agnes W. (Bulvanoski) B.; m. Halina Orestovna Kaniuka, July 9, 1979; children: Michael G., Alexander G. AB summa cum laude, Princeton U., 1970; JD magna cum laude, Harvard U., 1973. Bar: N.Y. 1973, U.S. Dist. Ct. (so. dist.), U.S. Ct. Appeals ((2nd cir.), 1974. Assoc. Cleary, Gottlieb, Steen & Hamilton, N.Y.C., 1973-81, ptnr., 1982-84; vis. prof. Princeton (N.J.) U., 1991; ptnr. Cleary, Gottlieb, Steen & Hamilton, Brussels, 1984-90, 1992—; chair Brussels chpt. Internat. divsn. N.Y. State Bar Assn., 1996—; chair Princeton Alumni Schs. Com., Belgium, 1998—; mem. Ctr. for European Policy, Brussels, 1988—, European Cmty. Studies Assn., N.Y.C., 1991—; dir. Sabre Found. (Europe) S.p.r.l. Author: Business Transactions with the USSR, 1975, International Business Transactions, 1980, International Financial Law Review, 1990, Insights, 1990. Mem. Cercle Gaulois Artistique et Litteraire, Harvard Law Sch. Assn. (sec. Brussels 1989-92), Am. European Union Assn. (pres.'s group), Am. and Common Market Club, N.Y. State Bar Assn., Ordre Francais du barreau de Bruxelles, Brussels Sports Assn. (bd. dirs. 1996-98). Home: 39 Rue de La Gendarmerie, 1380 Lasne Belgium Office: Cleary Gottlieb Steen & Hamilton, 23 Rue de La Loi, 1040 Brussels Belgium

BUSTOS, EDUARDO, civil engineering consultant, international trader; b. Buenos Aires, Dec. 19, 1936; s. Juan Carlos and Alicia (Paz) B.; m. Maria A. Ruga, Dec. 21, 1960 (div. 1978); children: Maria Andrea, Eduardo Daniel, Carla Valeria, Juan Manuel, Sebastian; m. Sara Rosa Beraldi, May 8, 1982. Grad in Civil Engring., U. Buenos Aires, 1963; MS in Civil Engring., Century U., L.A., 1983. Cert. civil engr. Field supt. Juan Carlos Bustos S.C.A., Buenos Aires, 1962-71; internat. mktg. mgr. E.B. Eximport, Buenos Aires, 1972-75; tech. asst. to chmn. Direccion Vialidad Prov. Buenos Aires, La Plata, 1975-79, dir. updating tech. programs, 1976-79; spl. projects designer Fed. Hwy. Dept. Direccion Nacional de Vialidad, Buenos Aires, 1979-80, dir. tng. programs, 1980, supr. lab. testing programs, 1980; chief engr. Ebudese S.A., Buenos Aires, 1980—; founder Tecnologia Vial Aplicada S.A., cons., 1985—. Author: (handbook) Asphalt Pavement Recycling, 1980; (manual) Recycling Guide for Designer, 1982; co-author rsch. report. Mem. Internat. Road Fedn., Asphalt Recycling Reclaiming Assn., Internat. Bridge Tunnel Turnpike Assn., Centro Argentino de Ingenieros, Jockey Club, San Andres Club. Avocations: golf, private pilot, guitar, squash, fly fishing. Home: Laprida 183, 1642 San Isidro, Buenos Aires Argentina Office: Ebudese SA, Suipacha 612 1 Deg C, Buenos Aires 1425, Argentina

BUSUOLI, GILBERTO, Italian environmental official; b. Finale Emilia, Modena, Italy, Aug. 12, 1937; m. Marisa Tartarini, Aug. 4, 1962; children: Massimo, Barbara. BSc in Physics, U. Bologna, 1961. Head health physics lab. Nat. Agy. New Tech., Energy and Environ., Bologna, Italy, 1978-83; head environ. sci. divsn. Nat. Agy. New Tech., Energy and Environ., Cascaccia (Rome), Italy, 1988-95, head environ. monitoring sect., 1991-93; head environ. sci. sector Nat. Agy. New Tech., Energy and Environ., Cascaccia (Rome), 1993-95, dep. dir. environ. dept., 1995—; mem. editl. bd. Radiation Protection Dosimetry Jour., UK, 1984—; bd. dirs. Gran Sasso Rsch. Consortium, L'Aquila, Italy, 1995—. Mem. Italian Radiation Protection Assn. (sec. 1977-83, pres. 1983-93, hon. mem. 1997). Home: Viale R Belloni 11, 00061 Anguillara Sabazia Italy Office: Nat Agy Tech Energy Environ, Via Anguillarese 301, 00060 Rome San Maria Di Galeria, Italy

BUSYGINA, IRINA MARKOVNA, geographer, educator; b. Moscow, Russia, Mar. 29, 1964; d. Tatiana Sergevna and Viotor Naumovich (Vasilicva) B.; m. Oleg Anatolievich Busygin, Sept. 24, 1987; 1 child, Elizaveta; m. Alexander Barnewitz, May 25, 1998; 1 child, Sophia-Leonore. Magister, State U. Moscow, 1988; PhD, Inst. Europe, Moscow, 1993. Rschr. Inst. Europe, Moscow, 1989-93, sr. rschr., 1993-97, head divsn., 1997—; prof. Inst. Internat. Relations, Moscow, 1999—. Author: (book) Regions of Germany, 1999. Recipient State prize of Russian Federation, Moscow, 1997, Prize of European Acad., Paris, 1996. Office: Inst Europe, ul Mokhovaya 11-3B, 103873 Moscow Russia

BUSZKO, HENRYK BRONISLAW, architect; b. Lwow, Poland, Sept. 3, 1924; s. Jan and Henryka (Luczek) B.; m. Jozefa Brzoza, July 17, 1948; children—Marta Maria, Jan Pawel. M.Arch., Tech. U., Cracow, Poland, 1949. Architect, town planner, Katowice, Poland, 1949-58; mem. leading team Archtl. Atelie, Katowice, 1958—; interior and exhbn. designer Fine Art Studios, Katowice; asst. to prof. Sch. Architecture, Wroctaw, Poland, 1949-50; lectr. Tech. U., Gliwice, Poland, 1970-78; mem. Cons. Commn. Architecture, Katowice, 1954—; mem. com. State awards Archtl. sect., Warsaw, 1969—; mem. cons. Ctrl. Commn. for Town Planning, Warsaw, 1982—; mem. juries numerous archtl. competitions. Archtl. works include: Trade Unions Centre House, Regional Theatre, Rybnik, Poland, 1000-Year Urban Housing Devel., Mt. Health Resort Ustron Zawodzie, Roman Cath. Ch. in Katowice, Polish Cath. Ch. in Częstochowa, many others; author: My Meditations About Housing, 1982. Recipient awards Com. of Architecture and Town Planning 1959, 61, 62; Archtl. award Ministry of Bldg, 1969, 73; Sci. award Sci. and High Schs. Ministry, 1973; Tech. award Fedn. Engrs. Assn., 1973; Artistic award of Silesia region. Mem. Assn. Polish Architects (pres. 1965-75, hon. award 1975), AIA (hon.), Mexican Architects Assn., Counsel of Internat. Union Architects, Polish Acad. Sci. (com. for architecture and urbanism). Roman Catholic. Office: Prac Projektow Budown Ogoln, Misjonarzy Oblatow 19, P-40-129 Katowice Poland also: SARP, ul Foksal 2, Warsaw Poland

BUTCHER, JACK ROBERT (JACK RISIN), manufacturing executive; b. Akron, Ohio, Dec. 10, 1941; s. William Hobart and Marguerite Bell (Dalton) B.; m. Gloria Jean Hartman, June 1, 1963 (dec. July 1995); children: Jack R. II, William H. (dec. 1970), Charlotte Jean. BA in Math., Jacksonville U., 1964; cert. mgmt. consulting, Akron U., 1979; cert. paralegal, CCT Inst., 1990; cert. radio broadcasting, Chaffey Coll., 1994. Pres. Portableacher Corp., Hesperia, Calif., 1977—; v.p. Nice Day Products, Hesperia, 1980-85; pres. The Mark of Profl. Mgmt. and Design Co., Hesperia, 1983—, Nice Day Products, Hesperia, 1985—; owner The Movie Funding Without Risk Co., 1996—; bd. govs. Internat. Platform Assn., 1996—; co-owner JB Scale Co., Hesperia, Calif., 1991—; acting, voice-overs and commls. Film Industry Workshop Sch. of Acting, 1995—; pres. Vallivue Prodns. Author: (poems) Something Good, 1978, Forever My Valentine, 1996; patentee in field. Mem. Internat. Platform Assn. (bd. govs. 1996—, Silver Bowl award 1995), Screen Actors Guild, Masons, Shriners, Royal Order of Jesters. Avocations: hunting, travel, designing, acting, commercial voice-overs. Office: PO Box 402540 Hesperia CA 92340-2540

BUTCHER, RUSSELL DEVEREUX, author, photographer; b. Bryn Mawr, Pa., Feb. 8, 1938; s. Devereux and Mary Frances (Taft) B.; m. Pamela Richards, Apr. 12, 1967 (div. 1993); children: Pamela Marie (dec.), Neill Devereux, Wendy Nan; m. Karen T. Black, Nov. 29, 1997. BA, U. Colo., 1960; postgrad., U. Mich., 1960-61. Rsch. editor Sierra Club, San Francisco, 1961-65; editl. writer N.Y. Times, 1963-79; publicity writer Save-the-Redwoods League, San Francisco, 1963-65; conservation specialist Nat. Audubon Soc., N.Y.C., 1965-66; chief pub. rels. and publs. Mus. of N.Mex., Santa Fe, 1967-69; freelance writer, photographer, author, 1969-80; conservation zoning cons. Town of Mount Desert (Maine), 1978-79, S.W. and Calif. rep. Nat. Parks and Conservation Assn., 1980-90, Pacific S.W. regional dir., 1990-93. Author: Maine Paradise, 1973, New Mexico: Gift of the Earth, 1975, The Desert, 1976, Field Guide to Acadia National Park, Maine, 1977, Exploring Our National Parks and Monuments, 9th edit., 1995, Exploring Our National Historic Parks and Sites, 1997; author, compiler: Guide to National Parks (8 regional guides), 1999; mem. editl. bd. Audubon mag.; manuscript editor KC Publs., 1985-88; contbr. articles to environ. jours. Mem. Ariz. Strip Dist. adv. coun. U.S. Bur. Land Mgmt., 1983-90; bd. dirs. Friends Saguaro Nat. Park, 1997—. Nat. Parks and Conservation Assn. fellow, 1993-99. Mem. Save-the-Redwoods League (life), Nat. Parks and Conservation Assn., Maine Audubon Soc. (pres. Down East chpt. 1978-80, trustee 1979-80), Friends of Lake Dist. Eng. (life), Sierra Club (life). Episcopalian (vestryman 1978-81). Address: 5948 N Misty Ridge Dr Tucson AZ 85718-3438

BUTEL, YVES, foreign diplomat; b. Abbeville, France, Nov. 1, 1948. Mem. European Parliament, 1999—, mem. com. on industry, external trade, rsch. and energy, substitute com. on regional policy, transport and tourism; mem. Group for a Europe of Democracies and Diversities; mem. delegation for relations with the Maghreb countries and the Arab Maghreb Union; substitute delegation to the EU-Estonia Joint Parliamentary Com. *

BUTERA, ANN MICHELE, consulting company executive; b. Bayside, N.Y., Apr. 27, 1958; d. Gaetano Thomas and Josephine (Inserro) B. BA, L.I. U., 1979; MBA, Adelphi U., 1982. Dept. mgr. Abraham & Straus Stores, Huntington, N.Y., 1978-80; mgmt. cons. Chase Manhattan Bank N.A., Lake Success, N.Y., 1980-83, Nat. Bankcard Corp., Melville, N.Y., 1983-84; pres. Whole Person Project, Inc., Elmont, N.Y., 1984—. Bd. dirs. Nassau County coun. Girl Scouts U.S., 1985-95. Recipient Bus. Achievement award Women on the Job, 1990. Mem. NAFE, ASTD, Fin. Women Internat., L.I. Networking Entrepreneurs (pres. 1984-91), Inst. Internal Auditors, Assn. Govt. Auditors, L.I. Ctr. for Bus. and Profl. Women, World Futurists Soc. Republican. Roman Catholic. Avocations: tennis, dancing, gardening. Home and Office: Whole Person Project Inc 82 Cerenzia Blvd Elmont NY 11003-3631

BUTHELEZI, PRINCE MANGOSUTHU GATSHA, government official; b. Mahlabatini-Lilundi, KwaZulu, South Africa, Aug. 27, 1928; s. Inkosi Mathole and Princess Magogo Constance (Zulu) B.; m. Princess Irene Audrey Thandekile, July 2, 1952; 8 children. BA in History, U. Forthare; LLD (hon.), U. Zululand, 1976, U.C.T., 1978, Tampa U., Fla., 1985, Boston U., 1986. CEO Zululand Territorial Authority, Nongoma, South Africa, 1970-72; chief exec. councilor KwaZulu Legis. Assembly, Ulundi, South Africa, 1972-76, chief min., 1976-94; pres. Inkatha Freedom Party, South Africa, 1975—; chmn. South Africa Black Alliance, 1980-83; min. home affairs Govt. of Nat. Unity, South Africa, 1994—; traditional prime min. Zulu People; sr. traditional advisor to His Majesty King Goodwill Zwelithini ka Bhekuzulu, Inkosi Guthelezi Tribe, 1953—; chair external rels. Inkatha Freedom Party, South Africa Black Alliance. Columnist South Africa Newspapers, 1974-75. Named Newsmaker of Yr., South Africa Soc. Journalists, 1973, Knight Commdr. of Star of Africa for Outstanding Leadership, Pres. Tolbert, Liberia, 1975, Apostle of Peace, Pandit Satyapal Sharma of India, 1983, Fin. Mail Man of Yr., Indian Acad. South Africa, 1985, Newsmaker of Yr., Pta. Press Club, 1985, Man of Yr., I.P.M., 1986; recipient Citation for Leadership, D.C. Coun., 1976, French Nat. Order of Merit, 1981, George Meany Human Rights award AFL/CIO, 1982, Nadaraja award Indian Acad. South Africa, 1985, Hon. Freedom of City of Pinetown award, 1986, Man of Yr. award Inst. Mgmt. Cons. South Africa, 1986, Freedom of Ngwelezana award, 1988, Unity, Justice & Peace award Inkatha Youth Brigade, 1988, Magna award for Outstanding Leadership, Hong Kong, 1988. Anglican. Avocation: music. Home: P/Bag X01, 3838 Ulundi South Africa Office: P/Bag X741, Petronia 0001, South Africa*

BUTKEVICH, IRINA PAVLOVNA, physiologist, researcher; b. Leningrad, USSR, Aug. 3, 1950; d. Pavel Ivanovich Butkevich and Galina Mikhailovna Bashmakova. MSc, U. Leningrad, 1974; PhD, Russian Acad. Sci., Leningrad, 1981. Asst. Pediat. Med. Inst., Leningrad, 1974-76; rsch. scientist I.P. Pavlov Physiol. Inst. Russian Acad. Sci., 1976-77, 80-87, sr. rsch. scientist, 1987—. Contbr. articles to profl. jours. Named laureate of All-Union prize Russian Govt., 1981; travel grantee IBRO, 1992, Russian Fond Acad. Med. Sci., 1995, grantee Stephen Batory Found., 1997; travel grantee IASP, 1999. Mem. IASP, Pavlov Physiol. Soc., Internat. Brain Rsch. Orgn., Soc. for Neurosci. Office: IP Pavlov Inst Physiol, Nab Makarova 6, 199034 Saint Petersburg Russia

BUTKEVIČIENĖ, BIRUTE, librarian; b. Joniškis, Lithuania, Aug. 20, 1938; d. Juozas and Sofija (Boreikaitė) Lipeika; m. Antanas Kuzminskas, Dec. 14, 1963 (dec. Jan. 19, 1969); 1 child, Arvydas; m. Boleslovas Butkevičius, May 25, 1975 (dec. Nov. 7, 1993). Librarian, Vilnius U., 1962. Head regional libr. Varniai (Lithuania) Regional Libr., 1962-63; libr. Vilnius U. Libr., 1963-66, head dept., 1966-67, bibliographer, 1968-70, head dept., 1971-77, dep. dir., 1978-85, acting dir., 1985-91, dir., 1991—. Mem. Assn. Lithuanian Librs., Women Assn. of Lithuanian Univs., Club of M. Mažvydas, Lithuanian Acad. Librs. Assn. Avocation: gardening. Office: Vilniaus Univ Biblioteka, Universiteto 3, 2633 Vilnius Lithuania

BUTLER, ANN BENEDICT, neuroscientist, educator; b. Wilmington, Del., Dec. 2, 1945; d. Thomas Harold and Arlene Benedict; m. Thomas Parke Butler, June 8, 1967; 1 child. BA, Oberlin Coll., 1967; PhD, Case Western Res. U., 1971. From asst. prof. to assoc. prof. anatomy Georgetown U., Washington, 1973-84; dir. Ivory Tower Neurobiology Inst., Arlington, Va., 1988-97; rsch. prof. Krasnow Inst. Advanced Study George Mason U., Fairfax, Va., 1994—, prof. psychology, 1997—. Author: Comparative Vertebrate Neuroanatomy, 1996; mem. editl. bd. Jour. Comparative Neurology, 1998—; contbr. articles to profl. jours. Mem. Soc. Neuroscience, Am. Assn. Anatomists, J. B. Johnston Club. Avocation: neuroscience. Office: George Mason U Krasnow Inst Advanced Study MSN2A1 Fairfax VA 22030

BUTLER, DAVID DALRYMPLE, screenwriter, actor; b. Larkhall, Lanarkshire, Scotland, Nov. 12, 1927; s. James and Mary (Dalrymple) B.; m. Norma Ronald; m. Kathleen Mary McPhail, May 31, 1969; children: Alexandra Katrina, Miranda Henrietta. Student, St. Andrews U., Scotland, 1946-50; Rada diploma, Royal Acad. Dramatic Art, London, 1953. Appeared for several yrs. in revues and West End prodns. including The Quare Fellow; TV shows include Emergency Ward 10; TV credits include The Strauss Family, Edward VII, Lillie, Disraeli, Within These Walls, The Further Adventures of Oliver Twist, Duchess of Duke Street, Black Beauty (Writers Guild award 1972), Countercrime, Dame of Sark; films include Voyage of the Damned (Oscar award nomination for Best Screenplay), Jesus of Nazareth, Adventures of Marco Polo, The Scarlet and the Black; plays include Person Unknown, Legend; books include Lusitania, Edward VII (2 vols.), Disraeli, Lillie, Mountbatten, The Last Viceroy. Mem. Am. Acad. Motion Picture Arts and Scis., Writers Guild Great Britain. Home: 10 Highgate W Hill, London N6 6JR, England

BUTLER, GEORGE FRANK, editor, literary historian; b. Bridgeport, Conn., 1962; s. Stanley M. and Wanda F. Butler. AB, Lafayette Coll., 1984; MA, U. Conn., 1985, PhD, 1988. Cert. Inst. for Effective Teaching, Conn. Teaching asst. U. Conn., Storrs, 1984-88; acquisitions editor Greenwood Pub. Group, Westport, Conn., 1990-93, assoc. editor acquisitions, 1993-99, sr. editor, 1999—; invited spkr. mid-winter conv. ALA, Denver, 1993, panelist, Phila., 1995, San Antonio, 1996. Contbr. articles and revs. to profl. jours. Predoctoral fellow U. Conn., 1984; State of Conn. scholar, 1980; Francis A. March fellow Lafayette Coll., 1984. Mem. MLA, Renaissance Soc. Am., Milton Soc. Am. (life). Roman Catholic.

BUTLER, GILLIAN, clinical psychologist, consultant; b. Longparish, Eng., Apr. 13, 1942; d. Christopher Payan and Patricia (Wake) Dawnay; m. Ian Christopher Butler, June 25, 1966; children: Sophie Rosalind, Josephine Laura. BA in Politics, Philosophy & Econ., Oxford (Eng.) U., 1965, BA in Experimental Psychology, 1974, MS in Abnormal Psychology, 1976; PhD, Open U., Eng., 1990. Clin. psychologist Nat. Health Svc., Oxford, 1976-78, prin. clin. psychologist, 1989-92, cons., 1992—; rsch. assoc. Psychol. Treatment Rsch. Unit, Oxford U., 1979-85, U. Oxford, 1986-89; mem. steering group Cognitive Therapy in Oxford, 1991—; treas., mem. sci. com. World Congress Cognitive Therapy, Oxford, 1989. Co-author: Manage Your Mind: The Mental Fitness Guide, 1995, Psychology: A Very Short Introduction, 1998; author: Overcoming Social Anxiety and Shyness, 1999. Grantee Med. Rsch. Coun., Oxford, 1986-89. Fellow British Psychol. Soc. (assoc., chartered clin. psychologist, European liaison officer divsn. clin. psychology 1991-92), Brit. Assn. of Behavioral and Cognitive Psychotherapy, Soc. for Exploration of Psychotherapy Integration. Avocations: walking, music, reading, gardening, tennis. Office: Warneford Hosp Headington, Dept Psychology, Oxford OX3 7JX, England

BUTLER, GWENDOLINE WILLIAMS (JENNIE MELVILLE), writer; b. London; d. Alfred Edward and Alice (Lee) Williams; m. Lionel Butler, Oct. 16, 1949 (dec.); 1 child, Lucilla. MA, Lady Margaret Hall, Oxford (Eng.) U., 1948. Writings include: Receipt for Murder, 1956, Dead in a Row, 1957, The Dull Dead, 1958, The Murdering Kind, 1958, The Interloper, 1959, Death Lives Next Door, 1960, Make Me a Murderer, 1961, Coffin in Oxford, 1962, Coffin for Baby, 1963, Coffin Waiting, 1963, Coffin in Malta, 1964, A Nameless Coffin, 1966, Coffin Following, 1968, Coffin's Dark Number, 1969, A Coffin from the Past, 1970, A Coffin for Pandora, 1973 (Silver Daggar award Crime Writers Assn. 1973), A Coffin for the Canary, 1974, The Vesey Inheritance, 1975, The Brides of Friedberg, 1977, The Red Staircase, 1980 (Romantic Novelists Assn. prize 1980), Albion Walk, 1982, Coffin the Water, 1986, Coffin in Fashion, 1987, Coffin Underground, 1988, Coffin in the Black Museum, 1989, Coffin and the Paperman, 1990, Coffin in the Museum of Crime, 1990, Coffin on Murder Street, 1992, Cracking Open a Coffin, 1992, Coffin for Charley, 1993, Coffin Tree, 1994, A Dark Coffin, 1995, A Double Coffin, 1996, The Butterfly, 1996, Let There Be Love, 1997, Coffin's Game, 1997, A Grave Coffin, 1998, Coffin's Ghost, 1999, The King Cried Murder, 2000; (as Jennie Melville) Come Home and Be Killed, 1962, Burning Is a Substitute for Loving, 1963, Murderers' Houses, 1964, There Lies Your Love, 1965, Nell Alone, 1966, A Different Kind of Summer, 1967, The Hunter in the Shadows, 1969, A New Kind of Killer, An Old Kind of Death, 1970, Ironwood, 1972, Nun's Castle, 1973, Raven's Forge, 1975, Dragon's Eye, 1976, Axwater, 1978, Murder Has a Pretty Face, 1981, The Painted Castle, 1982, The Hand of Glass, 1983, Listen to the Children, 1986, Death in the Garden, 1987, Windsor Red, 1988, A Cure for Dying, 1989, Witching Murder, 1990, Footsteps in the Blood, 1990, Dead Set, 1992, Whoever Has the Heart, 1993, Baby Drop, 1994, The Morbid Kitchen, 1995, The Woman Who Was not There, 1996, Revengeful Death, 1997, Stone Dead, 1998, Dead Again, 1999. Fellow Royal Soc. Arts, hon. sec., Detection Club, 1992-95.

BUTLER, IAN JOHN, neurologist; b. Adelaide, Australia, Sept. 19, 1941; came to U.S., 1972; s. John Alfred and Susan Pearl (Matters) B.; m. Patricia Mary Gordon, Feb. 28, 1969; children: Sarah, Katherine, Philip. MBBS, U. Adelaide, 1964. Diplomate Am. Bd. Psychiatry and Neurology. Resident Adelaide (Australia) Childrens Hosp., 1966-67; med. registrar Royal Childrens Hosp., Victoria, Australia, 1968; fellow neurology U. Melbourne, Victoria, 1969; sr. house officer Hosp. for Sick Children, London, 1970; registrar U. Wales Hosp., Cardiff, 1971; resident neurology, asst. prof. Johns Hopkins Univ. Hosp., Balt., 1972-76; assoc. prof. neurology U. Tex., Houston, 1976-79, prof. neurology and pediatrics, 1979—; prof. pediatrics dept. M.D. Anderson Cancer Ctr., Houston, 1980—; assoc. prof. Grad. Sch. Biomed. Scis., U. Tex. Health Sci. Ctr., Houston, 1978—; cons., dir. neuromuscular clinic Shrine Hosp., Houston; lectr. in field. Mem. editl. bd. Jour. Child Neurology, 1987—, assoc. editor, 1990—; contbr. articles to profl. jours. Chmn. prof. adv. com. Ctr. for Retarded, Inc., 1981—, bd. govs. mem., 1981—. Grantee Huntington Chorea Found., 1977-79, NSF, 1978, March of Dimes, 1978-80, Am. Parkinson Disease Assn., 1980-83, Epilepsy Ctr. Baylor Coll. Medicine, 1984-86, 88-93, Brandt Family Found., 1986, Meadows Found., 1986-91, Muscular Dystrophy Assn., 1988-90, 90-91, 91-93, NIH, 1989-94, 91-94, Shriner Hosp. for Crippled Children, 1990-93, 93-94, 95-97, 96-99, NASA, 1991-93. Fellow Royal Soc. Medicine, Royal Australasian Coll. Physicians; mem. AAAS, Am. Neurol. Assn., Assn. Rsch. in Nervous and Mental Disease, Am. Acad. Neurology, Soc. Neurosci., Internat. Child Neurology Assn., Child Neurology Soc., N.Y. Acad. Scis., Tex. Med. Assn., Harris County Med. Soc., Houston Pediatric Soc., Houston Neurol. Soc., Alpha Omega Alpha. Episcopalian. Avocations: music, reading, tennis. Home: 2200 Glen Haven Blvd Houston TX 77030-3606 Office: Univ Tex Dept Neurology 6431 Fannin St Ste 7044 Houston TX 77030-1501

BUTLER, JAMES ROBERTSON, JR., lawyer; b. Cleve., May 29, 1946; s. James Robertson and Iris Davis (Welborn) B. AB magna cum laude, U. Calif., Berkeley, 1966, JD, 1969. Bar: Calif. 1970, U.S. Tax Ct. 1977, U.S. Supreme Ct. 1980, Nev. 1997. Chmn. real estate devel. and Global Hospitality Group Jeffer, Mangels, Butler & Marmaro, LLP, L.A. and San Francisco, 1982—; founder, chmn. JMBM Global Hospitality Group Briefing Series, 1991—; expert panelist on hospitality industry topics NYU Hospitality Industry Investment Conf., UCLA Hospitality Investment Conf., Calif. Soc. CPAs ann. hospitality confs., 1992, 93, 94, 95; spkr., panelist Robert Morris Assocs. Nat. Conf., Chgo., 1989, nat. ann. conf. Ind. Bankers Assn. Am., 1992; frequent guest expert securities, real estate and banking various TV programs, 1985—; participant comml. real estate workouts workshop FDIC & RTC Nat. Tng. Conf., San Antonio, 1989, San Diego, 1990; adv. bd. Bur. Nat. Affairs, Washington. Author: Arbitration in Banking, A Robert Morris Associates State of the Art Book, 1988, Lender Liability: A Practical Guide, A BNA Special Report, 1987; editor Global Hospitality Advisor 1991—, Banking Law Report Capital Adequacy series, 1985, Global Hospitality Advisor, 1991—, Calif. Law Rev.; co-chmn. adv. council Money and Real Estate: The Jour. of Lending, Syndication, Joint Ventures, and the Third Market; contbr. chpt., Mapping the Minefield--Lender's Liability, The Workout Game, Solutions to Problem Real Estate Loans, 1987; contbr. over 100 articles to profl. jours, chaps. to books. Mem. Am. Arbitration Assn., Comml. Arbitration Panel; founding dir. Liberty Nat. Bank; Charter Adv. bd. dirs., Adv. Council of the Banking Law Inst. Recipient Kraft Prize U. Calif., 1966; Bartley Cavenaugh Crum scholar U. Calif. Sch. Law, 1969. Mem. ABA (corp., banking and bus. law sect., taxation sect.), Internat. Soc. Hospitality Cons., L.A. County Bar Assn., Century City Bar Assn. (chmn. fin. instn. sect. 1990-91), Beverly Hills Bar Assn., Calif. League of Savs. Instns. (chmn. arbitration com. 1987, 88), Order of Coif, Phi Beta Kappa, Pi Sigma Alpha. Avocations: personal computers (beta reviewer for various software developers including, Microsoft). E-mail: jbutler@jmbm.com. Office: Jeffer Mangels Butler & Marmaro LLP 2121 Avenue Of The Stars Los Angeles CA 90067-5010

BUTLER, LESLIE WHITE, epidemiologist; b. Huntington, N.Y., July 22, 1954; d. John B. and Inez M. (Montecalvo) W.; m. Thomas Butler, 1997. BS, Mary Washington Coll., 1976; MPH, Johns Hopkins U., 1990; postgrad., U. Md., 1993-95. Microbiologist II Am. Type Culture Collection, Rockville, Md., 1980-83; analyst InterAm. Assocs., Rockville, Md., 1984-86; sr. assoc. Triton Corp., Washington, 1986-87; health analyst Row Scis., Inc., Rockville, 1987-88; rsch. analyst Nat. BioSystems, Rockville, 1988-90; sr. assoc. Clement Internat., Fairfax, Va., 1990-92; project dir. epidemiology Consultants in Epidemiology and Occupational Health, Washington, 1992-93, 99—; dir. epidemiology Scis. Internat., Inc., Alexandria, Va., 1993-94; pres. Epidemiology and Health Rsch., Inc., Bethesda, Md., 1994—, Dist. Nuskin/IDN Internat., Bethesda, 1996—; realtor Weichert Realtors, Potomac, Md., 1997—; cancer epidemiologist Lombardi Cancer Ctr. Georgetown U., 1998-99; sr. epidemiologist Birch & Davis Assoc. Inc., Falls Church, Va., 1999; sr. epidemiologist, cons. in epidemiology and occupl. health Washington, 1999—. Mem. APHA, U.S. Tennis Assn., Soc. Epidemiologic Rsch., Am. Indsl. Hygiene Assn., Montgomery Assn. Realtors, Nat. Assn. Realtors, Bethesda Country Club. Avocations: tennis, ballet, reading, public health. Office: Epidemiology & Health Rsch Inc PO Box 34319 West Bethesda MD 20827-0319

BUTLER, MARILYN SPEERS EVANS, college rector; b. London, Feb. 11, 1937; d. Trevor and Margaret (Gribbin) Evans; m. David Edgeworth Butler, Mar. 3, 1962; children: Daniel, Gareth, Edmund. BA, St. Hilda's Coll., Oxford, Eng., 1958, DPhil, 1966; hon. degree, U. Leicester, Eng., 1992, U. Birmingham, Eng., 1993, Oxford Brookes, 1994, Williams Coll., Mass., 1995, U. Lancaster, Eng., 1997, U. Surrey, Eng., 1997, U. Kingston, Eng., 1998. Prodr. BBC, London, 1960-62; coll. tutor, univ. lectr. St. Hugh's, Oxford, 1973-86; King Edward VII prof. English lit. Cambridge (Eng.) U., 1986-93; rector Exeter Coll., Oxford, 1993—. Author: Maria Edgeworth, 1972 (Crawshay prize Brit. Acad. 1973), Jane Austen and the War of Ideas, 1975, Romantics, Rebels and Reactionaries, 1981, Wollstonecraft's Works, 1989, Edgeworth's Castle Rackrent and Ennui, 1992; editor: Frankenstein,

the 1818 Edition, 1993, Northanger Abbey, 1995, Collected Works of Maria Edgeworth, 1999-2000. Mem. Royal Soc. Lit., Royal Soc. Arts, Am. Acad. Arts and Scis. (fgn. hon.). Avocations: films, plays, books, people. Home and Office: Rector's Lodgings, Exeter Coll, Oxford OX1 3DP, England

BUTLER, MICHAEL GREGORY, German language and literature educator; b. Nottingham, Eng., Nov. 1, 1935; s. Maurice Gregory and Winifred (Barker) B.; m. Jean Mary Griffith, Dec. 31, 1960; children: Julian Michael, Emma Catherine. BA, Cambridge U., 1957, MA, 1960; diploma in edn., Oxford U., 1958; PhD, Coun. Nat. Acad. Awards, England, 1974; LittD, Cambridge U., 1999. Asst. master The King's Sch., Worcester, U.K., 1958-61, Reuchlin Gymnasium, Pforzheim, Germany, 1961-62; head German Ipswich (U.K.) Sch., 1962-70; from lectr. German to head dept. German studies U. Birmingham, U.K., 1970—; prof. modern German lit., U. Birmingham, 1986, head sch. modern lang., 1988-93, pub. orator, U. Birmingham, 1998—. Recipient Cross of the Order of Merit, Germany. Fellow Inst. Linguists; mem. Conf. Univ. Tchrs. of German of Great Britian and Ireland (v.p. 1994-96, pres. 1996-99). Roman Catholic. Home: 45 Westfields, Catshill Bromsgrove B61 9HJ, England Office: U Birmingham, Dept German Studies, Birmingham B15 2TT, England

BUTLER, MICHAEL WARD, economics educator; b. Great Bend, Kans., June 11, 1939; s. George Ward and Mary Jane (Lambert) B.; m. Regina Ann Hammond, Sept. 8, 1995; 1 child, Alexander Ward. BSBA, Fort Hays State U., 1963, MS in Econs., 1964; PhD in Econs., U. Ark., 1974. Diplomate Am. Bd. Forensic Examiners. Data processing sales rep. IBM, Wichita, Kans., 1964-66; instr. econs. Butler County C.C., El Dorado, Kans., 1964-70; asst. prof. econs. U. North Ala., Florence, 1973-75, assoc. prof. econs., 1975-78, prof. econs., 1978-97, dean coll. bus., 1997—; referee Jour. Forensic Econs., Kansas City, Mo., 1988—; editl. adv. Ark. Bus. Econs. Rev., Fayetteville, Ark., 1976-99; editl. bd. Am. Bd. of Forensic Examiners, Springfield, Mo., 1995-98; mem. mgmt. adv. com. Wise Alloys, L.L.C., 1999—; bd. dirs. Avalon Aluminum, Inc., 1998-99; pres. Region 3, Assn. of Collegiate Bus. Schs. and Programs, 1999-2000. Editor: Jour. Legal Econs., 1991—. Recipient Outstanding Achievement award Am. Higher Ed., 1985; Distinguished Serv. award Ala. C. of C., Montgomery, 1976. Mem. Assn. Collegiate Bus. Schs. and Programs (pres. region 3 1999-00), Nat. Assn. Forensic Economists, Am. Coll. Forensic Examiners, Am. Rehab. Econs. Assoc. (adv. bd. 1992-94), MidSouth Acad. Econs. and Fin. (pres. 85-86), Am. Acad. Econ. Fin. Experts (pres. 1994-96, svc. award 1995), Am. Econs. Assn., Am. Statis. Assn., C. of C. of the Shoals (bd. dirs. 1999-00). Avocations: wine collecting, boating. Home: 462 Ridgecliff Dr Florence AL 35634-2322 Office: U North Ala PO Box 5013 Florence AL 35632-0001

BUTLER, NICHOLAS JONES, economist; b. Amersham, United Kingdom, Nov. 22, 1954; s. Frank and Jessie Butler; m. Rosaleen Hughes, Aug. 1, 1987; children: Julia, James. BA with honors, Trinity Coll., 1977. Econ. Brit. Petroleum, London, 1977-81; sr. investment analyst Brit. Petroleum, various cities, 1984-92; mgr. govt. and pub. affairs Brit. Petroleum, London, 1992-95, group policy advisor, 1995—; rsch. fellow RIIA, London, 1981-84; chmn. Ctr. for European Reform, 1996—; adviser to Prime Mins. Policy Unit, 1999—. Author: The IMF-Time for Reform, 1982, The Plongshares War, Foreign Affairs, 1983, The International Grain Trade, 1985, Working for Common Security, 1988; editor: The Economic Consequences of Mrs. Thatcher, 1983. Hon. treasurer Fabian Soc., London, 1982—; candidate for parliament Labour Party, Lincoln, United Kingdom, 1987, 92; mem. fin. com. Royal Inst. Internat. Affairs, London, 1994—. Mem. Inst. Strategic Studies, Pacific Coun., World Econs. Forum (mem. global policy issues group 1999—). Avocations: theater, opera. Home: 28 Rodenhurst Rd, London SW4 8AR, England Office: BP Britannic House, 1 Finsbury Circus, London EC2, United Kingdom

BUTLER, ORTON CARMICHAEL, education educator; b. Millersburg, Ohio, June 9, 1923; s. Maxon Henry Butler and Atossa Ruth Carmichael; m. Betty Ellen Johnson, Sept. 15, 1951; children: Marilyn Jean, Kathryn Ellen. BA, Oberlin Coll., 1948; MA, Clark U., 1951; PhD, Ohio State U., 1969. Rsch. analyst U.S. Army Engr. Strategic Intelligence, Washington, 1951-60; prof. Memphis State U. (now U. Memphis), 1960-81; prof. emeritus U. Memphis, 1981. Author: (book) An Introductory Soils Laboratory Handbook, 1979, other publs. Cpl. U.S. Army, 1942-46, PTO. Mem. Masons. Republican. United Ch. of Christ. Avocations: tree farming, gardening, golf.

BUTLER, PETER MARK, barrister, solicitor; b. Geelong, Australia, Oct. 5, 1952; arrived in Eng., 1998; s. Barry L. and Patricia M. (Nicholson) B.; m. Jill Keys, 1977; children: Kate, Jane, Sarah. LLB, U. Melbourne, 1977. Bar: Victoria, New South Wales and High Ct. of Australia. Ptnr. Freehills, 1983; dep. chamn. Freehills, Melbourne, 1990-98, nat.practice ptnr., 1997-98; pres. Berry St. Inc., Melbourne, 1995-98, PILCH, Melbourne, 1996-98, spec. couns. to bd., 1998-2000, head of Compliance, Reuters, 1998-2000; head Nat. Litigation of Freehills, 2000—. Maj. Australian Army, 1982. Recipient Res. Force decoration, 1996, Order of Australia medal, 1998. Mem. Melbourne Club, Melbourne Cricket Club. Avocations: farming, reading, charities.

BUTLER, ROBERT ANTHONY, lawyer; b. Akron, Ohio, Feb. 24, 1932; m. Elda Celli Butler, June 19, 1954 (div. 1976); children: Debra Zahara, Michael C., Dorothy Brundige; m. Carole Cronin Berry, 1976 (div. 1992); 1 child, Beth Ann Butler. JD, Ohio State U., 1955. Bar: Ohio 1956, U.S. Dist. Ct. Ohio 1956, U.S. Ct. Mil. Appeals, 1959; cert. specialist in worker's compensation. Ptnr. William J. Ahern, Columbus, 1960-63; founder, sr. ptnr. Butler, Cincione, DiCuccio & Barnhart, Columbus, 1963—; dir. spl. and continuing legal edn. Capital U. Law Sch.; preceptor Ohio State U. Coll. of Medicine; presenter in field. Contbr. articles to profl. jours. 1st lt. USAF, 1957-60. Mem. Columbus Bar Assn. (former pres., Award of Merit), Franklin County Trial Lawyers Assn. (former pres.). Democrat. Avocations: fiction writing, water colors, calligraphy. Office: Butler Cincione DiCuccio & Barnhart 50 W Broad St Ste 700 Columbus OH 43215-3337

BUTLER, ROBERT MOORE, JR., podiatrist; b. Camp Lejeune, N.C., Mar. 21, 1949; s. Robert Moore and Virginia Lee (Keen) B. BA in Anthropology, U. Calif., Santa Barbara, 1971; BS in Med. Scis., Calif. Coll. Podiatric Medicin, San Francisco, 1975; DPM, Calif. Coll. Podiatric Medicin, 1976. Diplomate Am. Bd. Podiatric Surgery, Am. Bd. Podiatric Orthop. and Primary Podiatric Medicine (examinations com. 1993-95). Pvt. practice San Diego, 1977-78, U.S. Army Reynolds Army Med. Ctr., Ft. Sill, Okla., 1978-80, U.S. Army 97th Gen. Hosp., Frankfurt, Germany, 1980-83; cons. in podiatry to commdg. gen. 7th Med. Command, 1980-83; with U.S. Army Walter Reed Army Med. Ctr., Washington, 1984-85, VA Med. Ctr., Alexandria, La., 1985—; clin. instr. Calif. Coll. Podiatric Medicine, San Francisco, 1978-80. Maj. USAR, ret. Decorated Army Commendation medal. 1981; recepient Expert Field Med. badge 3d Bat., U.S. Army, 1984. Fellow Am. Coll. Foot and Ankle Surgeons, Am. Coll. Foot and Ankle Orthop. and Medicine, Am. Acad. Pain Mgmt. (diplomate, bd. cert., Am. Podiatric Med. Assn. (del. ho. of dels. 1985-96, budget com. 1994-96). Avocation: snow skiing. Office: VA Med Ctr Alexandria LA 71306

BUTLER, THOMAS FREDERICK, bishop; b. Birmingham, Eng., Mar. 5, 1940; s. Thomas John and Elsie (Bainbridge) B.; m. Barbara Joan Clark, Aug. 1964; children: Nicholas, Anna. BSc, U. Leeds, Eng., 1961, MSc, 1962, PhD, 1972; LLD (hon.), U. Leicester, Eng., 1995; DSc (hon.), U. Loughborough, 1998. Curate St. Augustine's, Wisbech, Eng., 1964-66, St. Saviour's, Folkestone, Eng., 1966-68; lectr., chaplain U. Zambia, 1968-73; acting dean Holy Cross Cathedral, Lusaka, Zambia, 1968-73; chaplain U. Kent, Canterbury, Eng., 1973-80; archdeacon Northolt, Eng., 1980-85; bishop Willesden, Eng., 1985-91, Leicester, 1991-98, Southwark, 1998—. Co-author: (with B. Butler) Just Mission, 1993, Just Spirituality in a World of Faiths, 1996. Mem. Ch. of Eng. Avocations: reading, mountain walking. Home and Office: Bishops House, 38 Tooting Bec Gardens, London SW16 1QZ, England

BUTLER, WALTER, investment executive; b. Rio de Janeiro, Aug. 16, 1956; s. Walter Burnett Butler and Vera Cecile de Almelda de Roux; m. Laetitia Gerard, June 20, 1992; children: Eléonore, Henry. Inspecteur des fin., ENA, Paris, 1983; M Law, U. Bordeaux, France. Inspector fin. French Treasury, Paris, 1983-86; advisor Minister of Culture and Comm., Paris, 1986-88; exec. dir. Goldman Sachs, N.Y.C., 1988-91; chmn. WB Fin. et Ptnrs., Paris, 1991—, Butler Capital Ptnrs., Paris, 1991—, AFIZ, Paris, 1997—. Co-author: Cutting Taxes: Foreign Countries Experience, Economics, 1985, Privitization: Foreign Countries Experiences, Economics, 1986. Recipient Chevalier des Arts et Lettres, Paris, 1976. Mem. Nouveau Circle de l'Union Internatallie, Golf de St.-Clorets, Maxoru's Bus. Club. Avocation: golf. Office: Butler Capotal Ptnrs, 30 Cours Albert Ier, 75008 Paris France

BUTLER, WILLIAM ELLIOTT, comparative law educator, lawyer; b. Mpls., Oct. 20, 1939; came to Eng., 1970; s. William Elliott and Maxine Swan (Elmberg) B.; m. Darlene Mae Johnson, Sept. 2, 1961 (dec. Nov. 23, 1989); children: William III, Bradley; m. Maryann Elizabeth Gashi, Dec. 6, 1991. AA, Hibbing Jr. Coll., 1959; BA, Am. Univ., Washington, 1961; MA, Johns Hopkins U., 1963; JD, Harvard U., 1966; PhD, Johns Hopkins U., 1970; LLD, London U., 1979; LLM, Russian Acad. Scis., 1997. Bar: D.C. 1967, U.S. Supreme Ct. 1970, Uzbekistan 1996, Russia 1997. Rsch. asst. Johns Hopkins U., Washington, 1966-68; rsch. assoc. Harvard Law Sch., Cambridge, Mass., 1968-70; reader in comparative law U. London, 1970-76, prof. comparative law, 1976—; ptnr. White & Case, London, 1994-96; resident ptnr. PricewaterhouseCoopers CIS Law Firm, Moscow, 1997—; dir. The Vinogradoff Inst., Univ. Coll. London; dean and M.M. Speranskii prof. internat. and comparative law, Moscow Sch. Social and Economic Scis., 1995—. Editor Bookplate Internat., 1994—, Sudebnik, 1996—, Russian Law: Theory and Practice, 2000—; contbr. numerous articles to profl. jours.; author more than 100 books. Rsch. fellow Leverhulme Trust, London, 1991, FSA. Mem. Internat. Fedn. Ex-Libris Socs. (exec. sec.), Russian Acad. Natural Sci. (academician 1992—), Nat. Acad. Scis. Ukraine (academician 1992—), Russian Acad. Legal Scis. Avocations: book collecting, bookplate collecting. Home: Stratton Audley Park, Bicester, Oxon OX27 9AB, England Office: Univ Coll London, 4/8 Endsleigh Gardens, London WC1H 0EG, England

BUTOR, MICHEL, author, educator; b. Sept. 14, 1926; s. Emile Butor and Anne Brajeux; m. Marie-Josephe Mas, Aug. 22, 1958; children: Cècile, Agnès, Irène, Mathilde. Degree, U. Paris. Tchr. Sens, France, 1950, Minieh, Egypt, 1950-51, Manchester, Eng., 1951-53, Salonica, Greece, 1954-55, Geneva, 1956-57; vis. prof. Bryn Mawr Coll. and Middlebury Coll., 1960, Northwestern U., Evanston, Ill., 1965, U. N.Mex., Albuquerque, 1969-70, Nice and Geneva, 1974-75; assoc. prof. Vincennes, 1969, Nice, 1970-73; prof. modern French U. Geneva, 1975—. Author: (novels) Passage de Milan, 1954, L'Empoi du temps, 1956 (Prix Felix Fènèon 1957), La modification, 1957 (Prix Theophraste Renaudot 1957), Degrès, 1960, Portrait de l'artiste en jeune singe: capriccio, 1967, Intervalle, 1973, Matière de rêves, 1975, Second Sous-sol, 1976, Troisième Dessous, 1977, La Rêve d'Irènèe, 1979, Vanitè: conversation dans les Alpes-Maritimes, 1980, Quadruple Fond, 1981, Explorations, 1981, Mille et un plis, 1985, L'Embarquement de la Reine de Saba: d'après le tableau de Claude Lorrain, 1989, (plays) Rèseau aerien, 1962, Votre Faust, 1962, 6 810 000 Litres d'eau par seconde, 1965, Elseneur: Suite dramatique, 1979, (poetry) Cycle sur neuf goaches d'Alexandre Calder, 1962, Illustrations (4 vols.) 1964-1976, Litanie d'eau, 1964, Dans les Flammes, 1965, Comme Shirley, 1966, La Banlieue de l'aube à l'aurore, 1968, Tourmente, 1968, Travaux d'approche, 1972, Envois, 1980, Brassée d'Avril, 1982, Exprès, 1983, Liminaires et prèliminaires, 1983, Herbier lunaire, 1984, Victor Hugo ècartelè, 1984, Hors d'oeuvre, 1985, Les Jouets du vent, 1985, Roberte et Gulliver, 1987, Ailes, 1987, Zone Franche, 1989, La Forme courte, 1990, (other) Zanartu, 1958, Le Genie du lieu, 1958, Rèpertoire 1-5 (5 vols.), 1960-82 (Grand Prix de la Critique Litteraire Assn. de Critiques Litteraire 1960), Histoire extraordinaire, 1961, Mobile, 1962, Description de San Marco, 1963, Hèrold, 1962, Essais sur les modernes, 1964, Le Masque, 1966, Entretiens avec Michel Butor, 1967, Dialogues des Règnes, 1967, Paysage de Rèpons, 1968, Essais sur Les Essais, 1968, Inventory: Essays, 1968, Essais sur le roman, 1969, Les Mots dans la peinture, 1969, La Rose des vents, 1970, O, 1971, Dialogue avec 33 variations de Ludwig van Beethoven sur une valse de Diabelli, 1971, Les Sept Femmes de Gilbert le Mauvais, 1972, Rabelais: ou, C'était pour rire, 1972, Boomerang, 1978, Filaments sensibles, 1981, Treize à la douzaine, 1981, Sept à lè demi-douzaine, 1982, Naufragès de l'arche, 1982, Vieira da Silva: peintures, 1983, Problèmes de l'art contemporain à partir des travaux d'Henri Maccheroni, 1983, Rèsistances, 1983, La Vision de Namur, 1983, Loisirs et brouillons, 1984, Le Chien roi, 1984, Alechinsky dans le texte, 1984, Dimanche matin, 1984, L'Office des mouettes, 1984, La Quinte major, 1984, Frontière, 1985, Chantier, 1985, La Famille Grabouillage, 1985, Avant-goût (4 vols.), 1985-90, Le Congrès des cuillers, 1986, Menace intime, 1986, ABC de correspondance, 1986, Cartes et lettres, 1986, D'un Jour à l'autre, 1987, Angkor silencieux, 1988, Le Retour du Boomerang, 1988, Au Jour le jour, 1989, Alechinsky: Frontières et bordures, 1989, De la Distance, 1990, Andre-Pierre Arnal: progrès du jeu assez lent, 1990, Transit, 1992, L'utilite poètique, 1994, Le Japon depuis la France, 1994, A la Frontière, 1995, Curriculam Vitae, 1996, Gyroscope, 1996, Ici et là, 1997, Pour tourner la page, 1997; Improvisations sur Balzac (3 vols.), 1998, Entretiens (3 vols.); editor: Essais by Montaigne, 1964. Decorated chevalier Ordre National du Mèrite: Ordre des Arts et des Lettres. Address: 216 Place de l'Eglise, F-74380 Lucinges France

BUTORAC, FRANK GEORGE, librarian, educator; b. Crosby, Minn., Feb. 12, 1927; s. Frank and Mary (Paun) B.; m. Mary Regis McGowan Ratigan, Apr. 8, 1972; stepchildren: Helen Elizabeth, Nicholas. AB, U. Mich., 1950, AM, 1956, AMLS, 1958; postgrad., Cornell Law Sch., 1950-51, Harvard U., 1953; postgrad. in philosophy, U. Notre Dame, 1959, 60-62; postgrad. in theology, Holy Cross Coll., 1962-66; postgrad., Cath. U., 1963, Georgetown U., 1965, NYU, 1968-70, 79-81, Cambridge U., 1975, Oxford U., 1989, 95, Trinity Coll., Dublin, 1990. With exec. tng. program U.S. Rubber, Mishawaka, Ind., 1952-53; tchr. 6th grade Jefferson Sch., Wayne, Mich., 1953-54; tchr. social studies Slauson Jr. H.S., Ann Arbor, Mich., 1954-55; supervising tchr. social studies Lincoln Consol. H.S., Ea. Mich. U., Ypsilanti, 1955-57; circulation libr., engring. libr. U. Mich., Ann Arbor, 1958-59; joined Congregation of Holy Cross, 1959; postulant U. Notre Dame, 1959; seminarian and temporary profession, 1959-66; novice Sacred Heart Novitiate, Jordan, Minn., 1959-60; registrar Mercer C.C., Trenton, N.J., 1966-68; asst. dir. cmty. and ext. svcs. Mercer C.C., Trenton, 1968-70, dir. evening and ext. ops., 1970-71, dir. spl. programs, 1971-74, dir. libr. svcs., 1974-84, chmn. libr. tech. program, 1974-84, dir. libr. devel., 1984-87, libr., 1987—; cons. libr. edn., libr. mgmt. Pres. U. Mich. Clubs Coun. 2d Dist., 1991-93; chmn. U. Mich. Newman Ctr. Fund Drive, 1958; professed Secular Franciscan Order Monastery of St. Clare, Bordentown, N.J., 1984. Bd. dirs. U. Mich. Alumni Assn., 1995-98; chmn. Anna B. Stokes Found., Trenton, 1972; dean's adv. com. Cornell Law Sch., 1972-73; mem. N.J. State Adv. Com. on Aging, 1971; mem. Mich. State Ctrl. Com. Young Democrats, 1949-50. Served with USN, 1944-47. Recipient Tall Cedars of Lebanon award for Cmty. Svc., Trenton, 1974. Mem. ALA, N.J. Libr. Assn. (exec. bd. 1977-78), Purnell Sch. Parents Assn., Cornell Law Assn., Bennington Coll. Parents Assn., Pine Manor Coll. Parents Assn., U. Mich. Ctrl. N.J. (pres. 1987-91), Mensa, English Speaking Union, Nassau Club (Princeton, N.J.), Princeton Club (N.Y.C.), Trenton Lions Club (pres. 1972), Trenton Torch Club (pres. 1972), Cornell Club Ctrl. N.J. (pres. 1977-78), Marines' Meml. Club (San Francisco), Cath. Alumni Club Trenton (pres. 1968), Theta Delta Chi, Phi Delta Phi, Phi Delta Kappa, Kappa Delta Pi, Alpha Phi Omega. Republican. Roman Catholic. Home: 6 Mercer St Princeton NJ 08540-6808 Office: 1200 Old Trenton Rd Princeton Junction NJ 08550-3407

BUTROUS, GHAZWAN S., cardiologist, researcher; b. Allepo, Syria, Oct. 7, 1952; arrived in U.K., 1981; s. Saleem and Elvier (Jarjour) B.; m. Mouna El-Hajjar, Aug. 18, 1984; children: Paul Alfred, Elsa Madonna. MB, ChB, Sch. of Medicine, Baghdad, 1976; PhD, U. London, 1989. Rsch. fellow St. Bartholomew's Hosp., London, 1981-84, lectr. in cardiology, 1984-88; dir. Electrophysiology Lab. St. George's Med. Sch., London, 1988-91, hon. sr.lectr., 1991—; sr. clin. project mgr. Pfizer U.K., London, 1991—; vis.prof. cardiology U. Padua, Italy, 1996. Editor, author: Clinical Aspects of Ventricular Repolarization, 1989; mem. editl. bd. European Jour. Pacing and Electrophysiology, others; contbr. chpts. to books, numerous articles to profl. jours. Fellow European Soc. Cardiology; mem. Brit. Cardiac Soc., N.Am. Soc. Cardiol. Pacing and Electrophysiology. Roman Catholic. Avocations: history of art, computing, Medieval history, history of dogma, illuminated manuscripts. Office: Pfizer Ctrl Rsch, Ramsgate Rd, Kent CT13, England also: St George's Hosp/Med Sch, Cranmer Terrace, Tooting, London SW17, England

BUTTERFIELD, BONNIE SUE, psychology educator, librarian, researcher, university webmaster; b. Covina, Calif., Dec. 31, 1942; d. Robert David and Marjorie Helen (Vosberg) Berry; m. David Charles Butterfield, Dec. 4, 1965; children: Stacie Ann Butterfield Cruz, Devin David. BA, Calif. State U., 1965; MA, Immaculate Heart Coll., 1968; MA in Neuroscience, Calif. State U., 1997. Libr. Los Angeles County Pub. Libr., Baldwin Park, Calif., 1968-78; neurosci. rschr. U. Calif., Riverside, 1990-93; computer libr. Calif. State U., San Bernadino, 1993—, prof. psychology, 1993—, univ. home page webmaster, 1998—, dir. univ. libr., 2000—. Contbr. articles to profl. jours. Rsch. grantee Calif. State U., 1996. Mem. Cherokees Calif. Democrat. Avocations: poetry, writing, oil paintings. Office: Calif State U Palm Desert CA 92260

BUTTERWECK, HANS JUERGEN, electrical engineering educator; b. Gevelsberg, Germany, June 23, 1932; arrived in Netherlands, 1964; s. Hans and Anny (Schaefer) B.; m. Hannelore Bachmann, Feb. 11, 1960; children: Ute, Christoph. Diploma in engring., Aachen Inst. Tech., Fed. Republic Germany, 1956; D of Engring., Aachen Inst. Tech., 1959. Lectr. Aachen Inst. Tech., 1958-64; rsch. fellow Philips Rsch., Eindhoven, Netherlands, 1964-67; prof. elec. engring. Eindhoven U. Tech., 1967—. Author: Mikrowellenband-filter, 1959, Elektrische Netwerken, 1974. Mem. IEEE, Verein Deutscher Elektrotechniker, European Assn. Signal Processing. Avocations: music, walking, history. Home: Akert 148, 5664 RL Geldrop The Netherlands Office: Eindhoven U, Den Dolech, Eindhoven The Netherlands

BUTTERWORTH, DAVID, engineering consultant; b. Denton, England, Oct. 24, 1943; s. John and Annie May (Claugton) B.; m. Pauline Patricia Morgan, Aug. 2, 1966; 1 child, Richard David. BS in Engring., U. Coll., London, 1962. With UKAEA, Harwell, England, 1965-76, group leader, 1977-89, dir., 1980-95; cons. pvt. practice, Abingdon, England, 1995—; vis. engr. MIT, Cambridge, Mass., 1976-77; vis. prof. Aston U., Birmingham, England, 1997—, Cranfield, England, 1996—, Bristol U., England, 1993—; gen. sec. Aluminum Plate-Fin Heat Exch. Mfrs. Assn., 1997—. Author: Introduction to Heat Transfer, 1977; co-editor: Two Phase and Heat Transfer, 1977, Design and Operation of Heat Exchangers, 1992, New Developments in Heat Exchangers, 1996. Fellow Royal Acad. Engring., Royal Soc. Encouragement Arts, Mfg. & Commerce, Inst. Chem. Engrs. Avocations: cooking, landscape, painting. Home and office: 29 Clevelands, Abingdon OX14 2EQ, England

BUTTERWORTH, BARON JOHN BLACKSTOCK, barrister; b. Nottingham, Eng., Mar. 13, 1918; s. John William and Florence (Blackstock) B.; m. Doris Crawford Elder, Mar. 4, 1948; children: Anna, John, Laura. MA, Queen's Coll. Oxford, 1939; D in Civil Law (hon.), U. Liena Leone, 1976; DSc (hon.), U. Aston, Birmingham, Eng., 1985; LLD (hon.), U. Warwick, Eng., 1986. Barrister at law. Fellow New Coll., Oxford, 1946-63, bursar, 1956-63; 1st vice chancellor U. Warwick, 1963-85; mng. trustee Nuffield Found., 1964-85, trustee, 1985—. Justice of the Peace, Coventry, Eng., 1963-88; pres. Found. for Sci. and Tech., 1998; bd. govs. Royal Shakespeare Theatre, 1964—; hon. bencher Lincoln's Inn, 1989; dep. lt. West Midlands, 1974—. Decorated comdr. Brit. Empire; named Life Peer, House of Lords, 1985. Conservative. Anglican. Home: The Barn Barton, Guiting Power GL54 5US, England also: 727 Nell Gwynn House, London SW3 3AX, England

BUTTERWORTH, MARTIN PAUL, software systems research and development manager; b. Wegburg, Germany, July 31, 1964; s. Robert James and Patricia Anne (Hawley) B. BSc in Elec. Engring. with honors, Leeds (Eng.) U. Rsch. asst. Leeds (Eng.) U., 1985-88; sci. MMARL, Cambridge, Eng., 1989, project leader, 1989-91; prin. systems engr. Marconi Underwater Systems, Waterlooville, Eng., 1991-92; devel. mgr. Micromise Plc., London, 1992-95; sys. devel. cons. Micromuse Plc., London, 1995-96; tech. dir., Network Media Comm. Ltd., 1996—; mng. dir. NETmc Group Ltd. Mem. IEEE. Home and Office: 13 Spring Cottages, Horsham Rd, South Holmwood RH5 4LU, England Office: Media House, 260 High St, Dorking RH4 1QT, England

BUTTIN, GÉRARD, science educator; b. Chambéry, Savoie, France, Oct. 21, 1931; s. Albert and Jeanne (Vullierme) B.; m. Claudette Vanmaele, July 29, 1959 (dec. Aug. 1972); 1 child, Dominique; m. Michelle Debatisse, Mar. 31, 1978; 1 child, Florence. Teaching Degree in Natural Sci., Ecole Normale Supérieure, Paris, 1956; DSc, U. Paris, 1963. Rsch. assoc. Ctr. Nat. Sci. Rsch., Paris, 1958-63, head lab cellular genetics, inst. rsch. molecular biology, 1970-81; Rockefeller fellow Stanford (Calif.) U., 1963-65; asst. dir. lab. cellular genetics Collège de France, Paris, 1965-70; prof. U. Pierre et Marie Curie, Paris, 1970—, Pasteur Inst., Paris, 1984-99; dir. unit somatic cell genetics Pasteur Inst., 1983-99, mem. sci. coun., 1992-95; mem. sci. coun. Dept. Life Scis., Ctr. Nat. Sci. Rsch., 1991-95; dir. unité 361 Ctr. Nat. Sci. Rsch., 1983-95; trustee Pasteur Inst., 1994-2000; mem. sci. coun. Pasteur-Weizman. Contbr. over 100 rsch. and rev. articles to profl. jours. Lt. French Artillery, 1956-58. Mem. AAAS, European Molecular Biology Orgn., French Soc. Biochemistry and Molecular Biology (v.p.), Internat. Cell Rsch. Orgn. (mem. coun., treas.), French Soc. Cellular Biology (mem. coun.), French Soc. Genetics, Nat. Coun. Univs. Home: 63 rue Croulebarbe, 75013 Paris France Office: Pasteur Inst Somatic Genetics, 25 rue du Dr Roux, 75724 Paris Cedex 15, France

BUTTNER, JEAN BERNHARD, publishing company executive; b. New Rochelle, N.Y., Nov. 3, 1934; d. Arnold and Janet (Kinghorn) Bernhard; m. Edgar Buttner, Sept. 13, 1958 (div.); children: Janet, Edgar Arnold, Marianne. BA, Vassar Coll., 1957; cert. bus. adminstrn., Harvard-Radcliffe program, 1958; Montessori diploma, Coll. Notre Dame, Belmont, Calif., 1967; D Bus. Adminstrn. (hon.), U. Bridgeport, 1994. Past v.p. Buttner Cos., Oakland, Calif.; pres. Value Line Inc. (subs. Arnold Bernhard & Co.), N.Y.C., 1985, chmn., pres., CEO, 1988—; chmn., CEO, pres. Arnold Bernhard & Co., Inc., 1988; chmn., pres. Compupower, 1988—, Valve Line Securities, Inc., 1988—, Value Line Distbn. Ctr., 1994; chmn., pres. Value Line Mutual Funds. Editor-in-chief The Value Line Investment Survey, The Value Line Mut. Fund Survey, The Value Line No-Load Fund Advisor, The Value Line Options Survey, The Value Line Convertible Survey, The Value Line Spl. Situations Service, Value Line Select, Value Line Investment Survey for Windows, Value Line Mut. Fund Survey for Windows, Value Line Daily Options, Convertibles DataFile, DataFile and DataFile II, Estimates and Projections, Value Line on Microfiche; web editor: www.ValueLine.com. Trustee Skidmore Coll.; past pres. Piedmont Sch. Bd.; past dir. Berkeley Montesorri Sch.; mem. N.Y.C. Partnership, Com. of 200; past mem. adv. coun. Stanford Bus. Sch.; past mem. The Presdl. Roundtable; past vis. com. for bd. overseers Harvard Bus. Sch.; past bd. dirs. Harvard Bus. Sch. Club Greater N.Y.; past west coast admissions rep. Vassar Coll., Radcliffe Coll., Harvard U., Harvard Bus. Sch; past trustee, Williams Coll., Emma Willard Sch., Coll. Prep. School, comm. for econ. devel. Named one of N.Y.'s 75 Most Influential Women in Business, Crain's, 1996, One of N.Y.'s 100 Most Influential Women in Business, Crain's, 1999; recipient Alumni Achievement award, Harvard U. Grad. Sch. Bus. Adminstrn., 1995, Alumnae award Choate Rosemary Hall, Wallingford, Conn., 1995, Emma Lazarus award Associated Builders and Owners of N.Y., Inc., 1996; Life Achievement award Emma Willard Sch., 1998. Mem. Harvard Bus. Sch. Club Greater N.Y. Republican. Congregationalist. Avocations: reading, swimming, biking, tennis, skiing. Office: Value Line Inc 220 E 42nd St Fl 6 New York NY 10017-5891

BUTTON, GLENN MARSHALL, aeronautical engineer; b. L.A., June 26, 1958; s. Albert Ronald Button and Laurel Lang (Bluske) Ratkay; m. Mary Josephine Puetzer, May 16, 1981; children: Nichole Elisabeth, Jessica Sarah, Laura Marie. BS in Physics, Ariz. State U., 1980. Counselor Adventure Unlimited Ranches, Buena Vista, Colo., 1977; aerodynamics engr. aircraft divsn. Northrop Grumman Corp., Hawthorne, Calif., 1980-82, structures rsch. engr. aircraft divsn., 1982-85, engring. specialist aircraft divsn., 1986-91; database application software developer B-2 divsn. Northrop Grumman Corp., Pico Rivera, Calif., 1991-92, lead configuration specialist, design application software aircraft divsn.; prin. GMB Assocs. Mktg., Cypress, Calif., 1988—; electronic process devel. prin. engr., scientist Long Beach (Calif.) Divsn., The Boeing Co., Long Beach, Calif., 1996-98; supplier integration mgr. Long Beach (Calif.) Divsn., The Boeing Co., Long Beach, 1998—; aerodynamics cons. Kachina Racing, Tempe, Ariz., 1977-93; software cons.

Aeromax, Cypress, 1989—. Contbr. articles to sci. jours. Pres. Villas Figueroa Homeowners Assn., Carson, Calif., 1983; tchr. Grace Ch., Cypress, Calif., 1990—. Mem. Soc. Automotive Engrs., Boeing Long Beach Mgmt. Assn. Republican. Mem. Christian Ch. Avocations: cycling, teaching, skiing, reading, mountain climbing. Home: 10441 Santa Elise St Cypress CA 90630-4234 Office: The Boeing Co D801-0011 3855 N Lakewood Blvd Long Beach CA 90846-0003

BUTUZA, OCTAVIAN, radio producer, journalist; b. Baia Mare, Romania, June 2, 1957; s. Ioan and Samfira-Anastasia (Breban) B. Student, Gheorghe Sincai Coll., Baia Mare, 1979, Babes-Bolyai, Cluj, Romania, 1984; journalist, Romanian Journalists Assn., Bucharest, 1992, Found. for Pluralism, Bucharest, 1994. Tchr. h.s. Baia Mare, 1985-87; inspector Cultural Inspectorate, Baia Mare, 1987-89; journalist newspapers Baia Mare, 1989-91; chief editor TV Cinemar, Baia Mare, 1992-99, Clipa Daily, Baia Mare, 1993-94; prodr. talk show Radio Galaxia, Baia Mare, 1998—; shows organizer Theatre, Baia Mare, 1990-92; artistic cons. Folklore Group, Baia Mare, 1992; editl. counselor ad. Din Nord-Vest Weekly, Satu Mare, Romania, 1999—; editor, dir. Everything for Us, 2000—. Author: (books) In the Heart of the Fortress, 1996, Happiness Like a Wound, 1997 (Best Book of Yr. in Town 1997), Pain Like a Cure, 1998 (Best Book of Year in Town 1998), Searching for the Light, 1999. Hon. pres. Pro Union Cultural Soc., Baia Mare, 1998; founder mem. Ora Pro Nobis, Baia Mare, 1995; founder pres. Octavian Butuza Social-Cultural Found., Baia Mare, 1999; hon. mem. Romanian Assn. Fighting Against Corruption, Bucharest, 1998. Sgt. Romanian Army, 1978-79. Recipient Spl. award of Jury, Nat. Festival of Poetry, 1987. Mem. Romanian Journalists Assn. Orthodox. Avocations: music, reading, writing poems, theater, cars. Home: Nicolae Iorga 1/12, 4800 Baia Mare Romania

BUTZ, LORI GAIL, nursing administrator; b. Allentown, Pa., Nov. 4, 1967; d. Adam Stephen and Janet Jane Butz. Assoc., Lehigh Carbon C.C., Sohnecksville, Pa., 1987; BS in Nursing, Cedar Crest Coll. cum laude, Allentown, Pa., 1996. Nurse Comprehensive Pain Ctrs., Allentown, Pa., 1997-98; nurse rep. Medtronic Neurol. Inc., Malvern, Pa., 1998-99; nurse Pa. Pain Mgmt., Allentown, 1999; practice mgr., nurse, physician extender Jay E. Kloin, Emmaus, Pa., 1999—; nurse physician extender Lehigh Valley Hosp., Allentown, 1998-99, Sacret Heart Hosp., Allentown, 1998-99. Mem. Sigma Theta Tau. Office: 431 Chestnut St Emmaus PA 18049-2401

BUTZ, OTTO WILLIAM, political science educator; b. Floesti, Romania, May 2, 1923; came to U.S., 1949, naturalized, 1959; s. Otto E. and Charlotte (Engelmann) B.; m. Velia DeAngelis, Sept. 13, 1961. B.A., Victoria Coll., U. Toronto, 1947; Ph.D., Princeton, 1953. Asst. prof. polit. sci. Swarthmore Coll., 1954-55; asst. prof. politics Princeton U., 1955-60; asso. editor Random House, N.Y.C., 1960-61; prof. social sci. San Francisco State Coll., 1961-67; academic v.p. Sacramento State Coll., 1967-69, acting pres., 1969-70; pres. Golden Gate U., 1970-92; pres. emeritus, 1992—. Author: German Political Theory, 1955, The Unsilent Generation, 1958, Of Man and Politics, 1960, To Make a Difference—A Student Look at America, 1967. Recipient Calif. State Colls. Outstanding Tchr. award, 1966. Mem. Am. Polit. Sci. Assn. Home: Wolfback Rdg Sausalito CA 94965 Office: 536 Mission St San Francisco CA 94105-2921

BUTZER, GARY WILLIAM, mural artist; b. Morton, Minn., Mar. 19, 1945; s. Walter and Rachel B. Grad. h.s., Morton, Minn. Owner Butzer Art Studio, Morton, 1963—. Prin. works include over 200 permanent exterior murals in rural So. Minn., 1963—. Bd. dirs. Southwest Minn. Arts & Humanities Coun. Home and Studio: 171 N Quarry Dr Morton MN 56270-0027

BUVAT, JACQUES ALAIN, endocrinologist; b. Oignies, Pas de Cal, France, July 12, 1945; s. Emile and Rolande (Caullet) B.; m. Michele Herbaut, 1976 (div. 1996); 2 children. MD, Lille U., France, 1970. Qualified specialist in neuropsychiatry, internal medicine, endocrinology, sexology. Intern Hosp. Lille, 1970-74, asst. dept. internal medicine/endocrinology, 1973-75; dir. Ctr. d'Etude Traitement de la Pathologie de l'Appareil Reproducteur et de la Psychomatique, Lille, 1974—; head sect. human reprodn. dept. gynecol. surgery Centre Hospitalier Regional, Lille, 1981-86; head Ctr. Assistance Reprodn., Clinique du bois, Lille, 1987—. Sci. dir. book series: Progress in Andrology; founder, chief editor Andrologie; coord. 4 French books: Iatrogenic Erectile Dysfunction, Ejaculation and Its Disturbances, Reproductive and Sexual Functions of Diabetics, Induction and Stimulation of Ovulation; contbr. over 200 articles to profl. jours. Medicine commandant French Army Res., 1982-96. Mem. Internat. Soc. for Impotence Rsch. (sec.-gen.), Internat. Soc. Andrology, Am. Fertility Soc., Soc. Sexologie des Univ. Belges, French Speaking Soc. Andrology (pres. 1991-93), Assn. Pour l'Etude de la Pathologie de l'Appareil reproductive et de la Psychomatique (pres. 1982—), Assn. pour le Devel. de l'Info. et de la Rsch. sur la Sexualité (pres. 1999—). Avocations: travel, game and bird watching, pheasant breeding. Office: Centre Etparp, 3 rue Carolus, 59000 Lille France

BUXTON, ANDREW ROBERT FOWELL, bank executive; b. Apr. 5, 1939; m. Jane Margery Grant, 1965; 2 children. Student, Winchester Coll., Pembroke Coll., Oxford, Eng. With Barclays Bank Ltd., 1963-78; dir. Barclays Bank UK Ltd., 1978-80; gen. mgr. Barclays Bank PLC, 1980-84, mng. dir., 1988-92, CEO, 1992-93, chmn., 1993-99; mem. Ct. of Bank of England. Mem. British Bankers Assn. (pres.), Royal Automobile Club. Office: Barclays Bank PLC, 54 Lombard St, London EC3P 3AH, England*

BUXTON, BARRY MILLER, museum director, historical author, educator; b. Blowing Rock, N.C., Aug. 5, 1949; s. Augustin Kinnard and Carrie (Miller) B.; m. Deborah Keyes, June 15, 1984; children: Loren Augustin, Peter I. BS, Appalachian State U., 1971, MA, 1973; PhD, U. Nebr., 1976. Cert. tchr., N.C. Dean Southeast C.C., Lincoln, Nebr., 1977-81; exec. dir., dir. press Appalachian Consortium, Boone, N.C., 1982-90; exec. dir. Health Adventure Mus., Asheville, N.C., 1991-95; dir. Mus. Health and Med. Sch., Houston, 1995-98; pres., CEO Eighth Air Force Heritage Mus., Savannah, Ga., 1998-2000; v.p. for instnl. advancement Savannah Coll. Art and Design, 2000—; cons. Howard Hughes Med. Inst., Chevy Chase, Md., 1993-95, Girl Scouts U.S., N.Y.C., 1984; prin. rschr. Nat. Park Svc., Asheville, 1987-90; project dir. Nat. Humanities Coun., Washington, 1986-87. Author: (history) A Village Tapestry, 1989, Moses H. Cone, 1987, Mabry Mill Historic Study, 1989, The Brenegar Cabin, 1988. Trustee Tex. A&M U., Inst. Bioscis., Houston, 1996-98, YMCA, Savannah, Ga., 1998-99; mem. policy coun. Tex. Med. Ctr., Houston, 1995-98; bd. dirs. Conv. and Visitors Bur., Savannah, 1998-99; bd. dirs. N.C. Health Alliance, 1993-95, Savannah Econ. Devel. Authority, 1998-99; v.p. Project ASSIST, 1994-95. Recipient Cmty. Historian of Yr. award N.C. Soc. Historians, 1989, Disting. Svc. award N.C. Soc. Historians, 1987; named Outstanding Fund Raiser, Nat. Soc. Fundrising Execs., 1996; Lovill fellow Appalachian State U., 1971. Mem. Houston Museums Assn. (v.p., 1996-98), N.C. Sci. Museums (v.p. 1993-95). Republican. Episcopalian. Avocations: tennis, bicycling, hiking, landscape architecture, history. Home: 114 W Gaston St Savannah GA 31401-4903 Office: PO Box 3146 201 W Charlton St Savannah GA 31402-3146

BUYDENS, WALTER, environmental engineer; b. Opbrakel, Belgium, Aug. 21, 1958; s. Georges and Christiane (Maroye) B.; m. Christine Van Borm, Aug. 23, 1986; children: Laila, Louella. BS in Bioengring., Cath. U., Louvain, 1981; MS, Delft U., 1983; PhD, Cornell U., 1992. Hydrographic asst. Ministry of Environ., Oostende, Belgium, 1981-82; mem. scientific staff IHE Delft (The Netherlands) U., 1983-84; assoc. expert World Meteorological Orgn., Niamey, Niger, 1984-87; rschr. Cornell U./Ford Found., Ithaca, N.Y., 1987-92; cons. The World Bank, Washington, 1989-92; dir. Aries Environment, Brussels, Belgium, 1992-94; mng. dir. Environ. Resources Mgmt.-ERM France-Benelux, Brussels, Belgium, 1994—; guest lectr. Delft U., 1994—. Mem. ASCE, Warande. Achievements include development of early warning drought river Niger at Niamey, Niger in 1995, improved irrigation management system, Puna, India. Home: Lierenhoek 26, 9572 Lierde Belgium Office: Environ Resources Mgmt, Visverkopersstraat 13, 1000 Brussels Belgium

BUYER, STEVE EARLE, congressman, lawyer; b. 1958; m. Joni Buyer; children: Colleen, Ryan. BS in Bus. Adminstrn., The Citadel, 1980; JD, Valparaiso U., 1984. Officer Med. Svc. Corps U.S. Army, 1980; spl. att to U.S. Atty. U.S. Army, Va., 1984-87; atty., 1988—; dep. atty. gen. Ind., 1987-88; legal counsel 22nd Theater Army, Saudi Arabia, 1990-91; legal advisor U.S Armed Forces/Western Enemy Prisoner of War Camps/War Crimes Interrogations, Saudi Arabia, 1991; mem. 103d Congress from 5th Ind. Dist., 1993—; com. mem. mil. forces personnel, vets. affairs; mem. oversight and investigations subcom. VA Com.; subcom. chmn. on mil. pers., mem. mil. installations and facilities Armed Svcs. Com. Decorated Bronze Star. Republican. Office: US Ho Reps 227 Cannon St Washington DC 20515-0001

BUYOYA, PIERRE, president of Burundi; b. 1949. Student, Royal Mil. Acad., Brussels. Min. def. Burundi, 1987-92, pres., 1987-93, 96—; mem. cen. com. Union pour le progrès national, 1982-87; past chief oper. officer Ministry Nat. Def.; chmn. Mil. Com. for Nat. Salvation, 1987—. Address: Office of President, Bujumbura Burundi*

BUYSSE, PAUL HENRI, trading company executive; b. Mar. 17, 1945; s. Eugene and Germain (Van Hecke) B.; children: Frank, Pia, Ann, Sophie, Thomas. Asst. to mng. dir., gen. mgr. Brit. Leyland, Antwerp, 1976-79; gen. mgr. Poclain Belgium, Aartselaar, 1979-81; mng. dir. Tenneco Belgium N.V., Aartselaar, 1981-88; regional dir. J I Case Benelux, Aartselaar, 1984-86, J I Case Europe North, 1986-88; group mng. dir. Hansen Transmissions Internat., Edegem, 1988—; group chief exec. BTR Industries Ltd., 1989, regional chief exec. 1994-98; dir. BTR Internat. Ltd., 1991; CEO Vickers Place, 1998-2000; chmn. Bekaert N.V., 2000. Decorated Knight in the Order of Leopold, 1988; knighted by King Boudouin I, 1993; named Commdr. of the British Empire (Baron) King Albert II, 1998. Home: Sparrendreef 104, 8300 Knokke Belgium Office: Bekaert N V Diamant Bldg, A Reyerslaan 80, 1030 Brussels Belgium

BUYST, ERIK CESAR, economic history educator; b. Schoten, Belgium, July 2, 1960; s. Adhemar D. and Eveline A. (Kerremans) B.; m. Helga A. De Doncker, Aug. 29, 1997. PhD in History, U. Leuven, Belgium, 1988; MA in Econs., Northwestern U., 1989. Sr. economist Kredietbank-Brussels, 1989-93; assoc. prof. U. Leuven, 1993-95, prof. econ. history, 1995—; cons. in field. Author: An Economic History of Residential Building in Belgium, 1992; contbr. articles to profl. jours. Laureate, Belgium Royal Acad. Arts and Scis., Brussels, 1989. Mem. Fondation Univ. Brussels. Office: U Leuven Ctr Econ Studies, Naamsestraat 69, B-3000 Leuven Belgium

BÜYÜKÜNAL, CENK S.N., pediatric surgeon, pediatric urologist, educator; b. Istanbul, Turkey, Dec. 3, 1952; s. Salahaddin and Ayhan (Sayinald) B.; m. Evin Togay, Oct. 22, 1976; 1 child, Burcu. Degree, Med. Faculty Cerrahpasa, Istanbul, 1976; degree in gen. surgery, Cerrahpasa Med. Sch., Istanbul, 1980, degree in pediat. surgery, 1983. Resident in gen. surgery Cerrahpasa Med. Sch., 1976-80, chief resident, 1980-81, resident in pediat. surgery, 1981-83; asst. prof. dept. pediat. surgery Cerrahpasa Med. Sch., 1985-88, assoc. prof., 1988-90, prof., 1990-2000; cons. prof. Am. Hosp., Istanbul, 1990-2000. Contbr. articles to profl. jours. Recipient Eczacibasi Med. prize, Istanbul, 1987, 89, History prize Brit. Assn. Pediat. Surgeons, 1988. Mem. Am. Acad. Pediat., Turkish Assn. Pediat. Surgeons (sec. 1998-2000), Brit. Assn. Pediat. Surgeons (coun. 1986—), Internat. Soc. Pediat. Oncology. Avocations: studying history of pediatric surgery, collecting medical antique pieces, puppets. Office: Pediat Surgery & Urology Ct, Valikonagi Cad 173 D:12/3, Istanbul 80220, Turkey

BUYYA, RAJKUMAR, research scholar; b. Bidar, Karnataka, India, June 1, 1970; s. Eshwarappa and Parwathi Buyya; m. Smrithi R. Konagurthu, Feb. 13, 1997; 1 child, Soumya. B in Engring., Mysore U., Karnataka, 1992; M in Engring., Bangalore (India) U., 1995. Software engr. Applied Computer Techs., Bangalore, 1992-94; scientist Ctr. for Devel. of Advance Computing, Bangalore, 1995-98; rsch. scholar Queensland U. Tech., Brisbane, Australia, 1998, Monash U., Melbourne, Australia, 1999—. Author: Microprocessor x86 Programming, 1995, Mastering C++, 1997; editor: High Performance Cluster Computing: Vol. 1-Architectures and Systems, Vol. 2-Programming and Applications, 1999. Recipient Dharma Ratnakara Meml. Trust gold medal for acad. excellence in computer sci. and engring. Kuvempu U., India, 1992; Overseas Postgrad. Rsch. scholar Australian Govt., 1998—; grantee Sun Microsystems, Compaq, Monash U., Distribute Sys. Tech. Ctr., Asian Tech. Info. Ctr. Mem. IEEE (spkr. Computer Soc. 1998—, chmn. task force on cluster computing 1999, Richar E. Merwin award 1999), Assn. for Computing Machinery, Unix Users Assn.: The Advanced Computing Sys. Assn. Avocation: cricket. E-mail: rajkumar@ieee.org. Fax: 61-3-9903 2863. Home: 4/56 Grange Rd Carnegie, Melbourne VIC 3168, Australia Office: Monash U, Sch Computer Sci Caulkfield, Melbourne VIC 3168, Australia

BUZAK, EDWARD JOSEPH, lawyer; b. Jersey City, Apr. 20, 1948; s. Edward and Nellie (Scalone) B.; m. Gail Marie Capizzi, July 24, 1971; children: Craig E., Lindsay T. BA, Union Coll., 1970; JD, Georgetown U., 1973. Bar: N.J. 1973, D.C. 1974. Assoc. Villoresi & Flanagan, Boonton, N.J., 1973-75; ptnr. Villoresi & Buzak, Boonton, N.J., 1976-82; owner Edward J. Buzak, Montville, N.J., 1983—; trustee Housing Partnership of Morris County, Morristown, N.J., 1992—. Contbr. articles to profl. jours. Chmn. affordable housing com., asst. counsel N.J. State League of Municipalities, Trenton, N.J., 1986—; asst. counsel N.J. Planning Ofcls., 1998—. Mem. Assn. Environ. Authorities (legis. com. chair 1986—), N.J. Inst. Mcpl. Attys. (2d v.p.), N.J. State Bar Assn. (local gov. com. chair 1985-87). Roman Catholic. Avocations: running, skiing, music, reading. Office: 150 River Rd Ste N4 Montville NJ 07045-8920

BUZARD, DAVID ANDREW, lawyer; b. Evanston, Ill., Dec. 8, 1961; s. Clifford Howard and Mary Louise (Dole) B.; m. Véronique Elisabeth Marie Ravisé-Noël, Nov. 25, 1985; children: Clémentine, Victor. Student, Carleton Coll., 1980-82; BA in Linguistics, Northwestern U., 1984; JD, Tulane U., 1990. Bar: Ill. 1991, Va. 1997, U.S. Ct. Mil. Appeals 1991, U.S. Ct. Appeals (4th cir.) 1991, U.S. Dist. Ct. (ea. dist.) Va. 1997, U.S. Dist. Ct. (no. dist.) Ill. 1998, U.S. Supreme Ct. 1998. Law clk. U.S. Atty.'s Office, New Orleans, 1988-90; judge advocate U.S. Navy, 1990-97; assoc. Glasser & Glasser, PLC, Norfolk, Va., 1997-98, Bennett & Zydron, P.C., Virginia Beach, Va., 1998—; v.p., counsel Alliance Française Chapitre de Grasse, Norfolk, Va., 1996—; judge Jessup Internat. Law Moot Ct. Competition, 1998. Contbr. articles to profl. jours. Lt. USN, 1990-97; lt. comdr. USNR, 1998—. Nat. Merit scholar. Mem. ATLA (vice chair fed. tort liability and mil advocacy sect., nursing homes litigation group), Va. Bar Assn. (bd. govs. mil. law sect.), Va. Trial Lawyers Assn., Norfolk and Portsmouth Bar Assn. (founder, chair mil. law and lawyers com. 1997—), Judge Advocates Assn., Disabled Am. Vets., Naval Res. Assn., Pan European Orgn. Personal Injury Lawyers. Avocations: helping people, travel. Office: Bennett & Zydron PC 120 S Lynnhaven Rd Virginia Beach VA 23452-7419

BUZASH, MICHAEL D., Romance languages educator; s. Mike and Flora (Urden) B. Student, U. Mex., Mexico City, 1952; BA in French and Spanish, Ind. State U., 1953; MA in Romance Langs., U. Western Res., 1960; postgrad., U. Wis., 1963-69; Cert. de Stage, Purdue U., 1984, 86, U. Wis., 1993; postgrad., Mich. State U., 1994; cert. attendance, U. Ill., 1995. Cert. superior rating Am. Coun. on Tchg. of Fgn. Langs. Tchr. French, Spanish, English Lawrence H.S., 1954-59; dir. pilot program in French and Spanish Lawrence Jr. H.S., 1956-57; tchr. French Ind. State U., summers 1980-97, assoc. prof. Romance langs., 1959-98; del. internat. symphonies; presenter in field; leader symposia and workshops. Author: Exercices Pratiques de Français Oral, 1983-90, Repetition et Acquisition Pratique, 1989-95, Revision Pratique de Français, 1990-96, honors edit., 1981, 89-90, 94-96; contbr. chpt. to book: From Third World to One World, 1988, Proceedings of Black Studies Conferences, 1989-91; contbr. papers and book revs. to procs. and profl. jours.; contbr. poetry to anthologies. Mem. Friends of Cunningham Libr., Ind. State U., Terre Haute Symphony Assn., Swope Art Mus., Indpls. Art Mus.; hon. mem. Hoosiers for Econ. Devel., 1982. Mem. AAUP, MMLA, Internat. Book Distbr. Ltd., Am. Translators Assn., Am. Assn. for Advancement of Core Curriculum, Am. Assn. Romanian Studies, Am. Assn. Tchrs. of French (Ind. chpt.), Am. Coun. on Tchg. of Fgn. Langs. (25-Yr. pin 1995), Ind. Fgn. Lang. Tchrs. Assn., European Studies Conf., Vigo County Ret. Tchrs. Assn. (treas. 2000), Cen. States Conf. of Tchg. of Fgn. Langs., Univ. Club, Ind. State U., Masons, Blue Key (faculty advisor 1979-95), Phi Sigma Iota (life, nat. v.p. 1971-75), Kappa Delta Pi, Theta Alpha Phi. Avocations: reading, traveling, gardening. E-mail: flbuza@scifac.indstate.edu.

BUZEA, CALIN GHEORGHE, physicist, researcher; b. Iasi, Romania, Apr. 8, 1966; s. Theodor and Iuliana (Cocirta) B. B, D Cantemir Lyceum, Iasi, 1984; diploma, Al.I.Cuza Univ., Iasi, 1989, PhD, 1998. Tchr. Cenei, Timisoara, Romania, 1989-90; engr. Radio-TV, Iasi, 1990-91; rschr. Inst. Tech. Physics, Iasi, 1991—. Author: Fundaments of Space-Time Theory, 1997, Nonlinear Phenomena in Materials Science, 1999; contbr. articles to profl. jours. Participant Cancer League, Iasi, 1997-99. Lt. artillery, Bacau, Romania, 1984-85. Avocations: fashion, modelling, photography, landscapes, computers. Office: Inst Tech Physics, D Mangeron No 47, 6600 Iasi Iasi, Romania

BUZEK, JERZY, prime minister of Poland; married; 1 child. Grad., Silesian Tech. U., Gliwice, Poland. Chem. engring. prof. Chem. Engring. Inst. Polish Acad. Scis., Gliwice, 1997—; prime min. Poland; pres. Social Movement Solidarity Election Action, 1999—; mem. Solidarity Trade Union, 1980, chair 1st nat. congress, 1981. Contbr. numerous articles to profl. jours.; co-author Solidarity Election Action eco. program. Office: Office Chancellory Prime, Min Aleje Ujazdowskie 1/3, 00-583 Warsaw Poland*

BUZINKAY, GÉZA, historian, curator; b. Budapest, Hungary, June 21, 1941; s. Gyôrgy and Katalin (Ney) B.; m. Krisztina Rozsnyai; 1 child, Gyôrgy Ferenc. MA, Budapest U., 1971, PhD, 1973; postgrad., Hungarian Acad. Scis., 1983. Libr. Semmelweis Mus. for History of Medicine, Budapest, 1969-71, head of dept., 1971-77; editor Corvina Pub. House, Budapest, 1977-85, sr. editor, 1985-89; rsch. fellow Inst. of History, Budapest, 1990-91; dir. Budapest Hist. Mus., 1992-95, sr. curator, 1996—; lectr. history of journalism Budapest U., 1994—. Author: History of Comic Journals, 1983; co-author: History of the Hungarian Press, 1985, 94, A Short History of the Hungarian Press, 1993, The Budapest History Museum, 1995, An Illustrated History of Budapest, 1998; editor (quar.) Communicationes de Historia Artis Medicinae, 1972-88; editor-in-chief Magyar Média, 2000. Recipient J. Pulitzer Commemorative prize, 1995. Mem. Internat. Coun. Mus., Assn. Hungarian Journalists. Home: Bartók B u 36, H-2000 Szentendre Hungary Office: Budapest Torteneti Museum, Szent György tér 2, H-1014 Budapest Hungary

BUZO, ALEXANDER JOHN, writer; b. Sydney, NSW, Australia, July 23, 1944; s. Zihni Joseph and Elaine Winifred (Johnson) B.; m. Merelyn Elizabeth, Dec. 21, 1968; children: Emma, Laura, Genevieve. BA, U. NSW, Sydney, Australia, 1966. Profl. writer Sydney, NSW, Australia, 1968—; resident playwright Melbourne Theatre Co., Victoria, Australia, 1972-73. Author: (play) Norm and Ahmed, 1968, Pacific Union, 1994, (book) Tautology, 1980, The Longest Game, 1990. Recipient Gold medal Australian Lit. Soc., 1973, Alumni award U. NSW, 1998. E-mail: ajbu@ozemail.com.au. Home: 14 Rawson Ave, Queens Park, Sydney 2022, Australia

BUZOV, IAN, physician; b. Mirlović, Croatia, June 12, 1947; s. Ivan and Filomena (Negodić) B.; m. Milka Dražić, Nov. 28, 1980; children: Filip, Ivana. MD, Zagreb U., Croatia, 1973, MScMed, 1980, DrScMed, 1985. Psychiatrist Clinic for Med. Psychology, 1978-80, psychiatrist, psychotherapist, 1980—. Author: Personality Disorders, Psychoanalysis of Mourning, Mourning, Freud and Croatia; editor: Dreams in Psychotherapy; contbr. articles to profl. jours. Home: Klekovačka, 10040 Zagreb Croatia

BUZUNOV, VLADIMIR AFANASIYEVICH, epidemiologist, researcher; b. Kirovgrad, Sverdlovsk, USSR, Oct. 17, 1937; s. Afanasy Y. and Maria K. Buzunov; m. Yulia A. Litvinova; 1 child, Liubov A. MD, Med. Inst. Sverdlovsk, Russia, 1961; DMS, Inst. Occpl. Medicine, Kiev, Ukraine, 1984. Head physician Sanitary Epidemiologic Station, Nakhodka, 1961-64; rsch. worker Inst. Occpl. Medicine, Kiev, 1964-78, lab. head, 1978-88; dir. Epidemiologic Inst. Radiation Injury, Kiev, 1988—. Co-author: Hygiene and Physiology of Work at Thermal Power Plants, 1982, Hygiene of Training Teenagers for Main Agricultural Activities, 1982, Production Factors and Age Working Capacity, 1991. Fellow Ukrainian Soc. Hygienists. Avocations: fishing, gardening, philosophy, history. Office: Radiation Med Rsch Ctr, 53 Melnikova St, 253050 Kiev Ukraine

BUZZELLI, CHARLOTTE GRACE, educator; b. Mar. 21, 1947; d. Edmund Albert and Sarah Agnes (Russo) Buzzelli. BS, U. Akron, 1969, MS in Edn., 1976. Tchr. St. Anthony Sch., Akron, 1969-76; program coord., tchr. Akron Montessori Sch. Continuing Edn. Program, Eastwood Ctr., Akron, 1976-77; dir. edn. Fallsview Psychiat. Hosp., Cuyahoga Falls, Ohio, 1977-92, developer job tng. partnership grant program and spl. needs handicapped grant program, 1992-97; tng. coord. N.E. regional & program education children svcs. Ohio Dept. Mental Health State Operated Svcs., 1992-97; spl. edn. svcs. developer and educator cmty svcs. div. North Coast Behavioral Healthcare Sys., 1997—; part-time tchr. adult basic edn. program Akron City Sch. Dist., 1992—; cons. in field; pioneered first spl. edn. program in Ohio for adult state psychiat. hosp.; developed 1st community-based adult basic edn. program in state instn. in Ohio; program cons. state operated svcs. State of Ohio; participant U. Hawaii Study Tours Rsch. Projects, Internat. Edn. and East Asia Pi Lambda Theta Orient Study Tour, Manoa campus, 1990, spl. edn. rsch. U. Ark., 1976. Gospel Meets Symphony choral mem. Akron Symphony Orch. Gospel Choir, 1996—, Diocese of Cleve., St. John's Cathedral, Mass of Jubilee Gospel Choir, 1998, 2000. Named Ohio Tchr. of Yr., 1979; recipient A Key award U. Akron, Cmty. Svc. Achievement award Italian Am. Socs. Mem. CEC (coun. pres.), ASCD, Assn. Children with Learning Disabilities, Internat. Reading Assn., U. Akron Alumni Assn., Univ. Club, Akron Women's City Club, Pi Lambda Theta (pres.), Phi Delta Kappa, Delta Kappa Gamma, Gamma Beta (pres.). Avocations: pet therapy to children and adults with disabilities, reading, travel, writing, singing, creating community resources for spl. edn. students and mental health clients. Home: 662 Dayton St Akron OH 44310-2301 Office: Ohio Dept Mental Health NorthCoast Behav HealthCare 157 W Cedar St Akron OH 44307-2564

BUZZELLI, DENNIS KEVIN, mechanical engineer; b. Jersey City, Apr. 8, 1946; s. Albert F. and Mildred G. (Corrado) B. B of Engring., Stevens Inst. Tech., 1969; MME, Poly. Inst. N.Y., 1973. Propulsion engr. Grumman Aero. Corp., Bethpage, N.Y., 1969-70; project engr. Ducon Co. divsn. U.S. Filter Corp., Mineola, N.Y., 1970-77, Metco Inc. divsn. Perkin-Elmer, Westbury, N.Y., 1977-83, East/West Ind., Farmingdale, N.Y., 1983-84, Airborn Instruments Lab. divsn. Eaton Corp., Farmingdale, N.Y., 1984-89, Radiation Dynamics, Inc., Farmingdale, N.Y., 1989—. Patentee plasma spray nozzle, electronic module locking mechanism. Mem. ASME (Stevens chpt. v.p. 1968-69), AIAA. Roman Catholic. Home: 38 Fairway Dr Old Bethpage NY 11804-1740

BYCHKOV, SEMYON, conductor; b. Leningrad, Russia, Nov. 30, 1952; came to U.S., 1975; s. May and Doroteya (Kreizberg) B.; m. Tatiana Rozina, July 3, 1973; children: David, Elizabeth Rachel. Diploma of honor, Clinka Choir Sch., 1970; student, Leningrad Conservatory, 1970-74; diploma, Mannes Coll. Music, N.Y.C., 1976. Music dir. Bonch-Bruyevich Inst. Chorus, Leningrad, 1970-72; condr. Leningrad Conservatory Symphony and Opera Orch., 1972-74; assoc. condr., then music dir. Mannes Coll. Music Orch., 1976-80; music dir., condr. Grand Rapids (Mich.) Symphony, 1980-85; assoc. condr. Buffalo Philharm. Orch., 1979—, music dir., 1985-89, prin. guest condr., 1985—; music dir. Orch. de Paris, 1989—; prin. guest condr. Cmty. Theater Florence, Italy, 1993; guest condr. Berlin Philharm., London Philharm., Philharmonia, Vienna Symphony, Bayerische Rundfunk, NDR Hamburg, Bamberg Symphony, Boston Symphony, Phila. Orch., Toronto Symphony, Montreal Symphony, Balt. Symphony, BBC Symphony, Royal Philharm. Orch. de Suisse Romande, Israel Chamber Orch., N.Y. Philharm., Spoleto Festival, Concertebouw Orch., Art Park Festival, Cin. Symphony, San Remo Symphony, Aix-en-Provence Music Festival, Tivoli Symphony, Indpls. Symphony, Bournemouth Symphony, Chautaqua Symphony, Colombus Symphony, Lyon Opera, Seattle Symphony, L.I. Philharm., Minn. Orch., CBS Chamber Orch., Syracuse Orch., Can. Art Ctr. Orch., Detroit Symphony, summers 1981-83, N.Y.C. Opera, fall 1981, Monte Carlo Philharm., Strasbourg Philharm.; recs. for Philips Records. Music dir. Bonch-Bruyevich Inst. Chorus, Leningrad, 1970-72; condr. Leningrad Conservatory Symphony and Opera Orch., 1972-74; assoc. condr., then music dir., Mannes Coll. Music Orch., 1976-80; music dir./condr., Grand Rapids (Mich.) Symphony, 1980-85; assoc. condr., Buffalo Philharm. Orch., 1979—, prin. guest condr., 1985—, music dir., 1985-89; music dir. Orchestra de Paris,

1987—; guest condr. Berlin Philharm., London Philharm., Philharmonia, Vienna Symphony, Bayerische Rundfunk, NDR Hamburg, Bamberg Symphony, Boston Symphony, Phila. Orch., Toronto Symphony, Montreal Symphony, Balt. Symphony, BBC Symphony, Royal Philharm. Orchestre de la Suisse Romande, Israel Chamber Orch., N.Y. Philharm., Spoleto Festival, Concertebouw Orch., Art Park Festival, Cin. Symphony, San Remo Symphony, Aix-en-Provence Music Festival, Tivoli Symphony, Indpls. Symphony, Bournemouth Symphony, Chautaqua Symphony, Columbus Symphony, Lyon Opera, Seattle Symphony, L.I. Philharm., Minn. Orch., CBS Chamber Orch., Syracuse Orch., Can. Nat. Arts Center Orch., Detroit Symphony, summers 1981-83, N.Y.C. Opera, fall 1981, Monte Carlo Philharmonic, Strasbourg Philharmonic; recordings for Philips Records. Recipient 1st prize Rachmaninoff Conducting Competition, 1973, Franco Abbiati prize, 1994, 96, Musa Polinnia prize Acad. Internat. Le Muse, Florence, 1995, Abbiati prize for prodn. Fierrabras (Schubert), 1996. Mailing Address: care Ms P McCormick #336, Stratford Wkshps Burford Rd, London E15 2SP, England also: Kunstlermanagement Internat, Mitarbeiterin: Ursula Groos, D-80331 Munich Germany*

BYE, ERIK, scientific advisor; b. Oslo, Sept. 13, 1945; s. Martin Johansen and Nelly (Andersen) B.; m. Kirsten Offenberg, Aug. 1, 1970; children: Tonje, Synne. MSd in Chemistry, U. Oslo, Norway, 1972, PhD, 1976. Rsch. asst. U. Oslo, Norway, 1972-78; sr. scientist Statens arbeidsmiljøinstitutt, Oslo, 1979-96, sci. advisor, 1997—; postdoctoral fellow Eidgenössiche Technische Hochschule, Zürich, 1977; rsch. fellow Senter for Industriforskning, Oslo, 1987. Mem. editl. bd. Scandinavian Jour. Work and Environ. Health, 1982-96; contbr. articles to profl. jours. Mem. Norsk Kjemisk Selskap, Norsk Yrkeshygienisk Forening, Norsk Forskerforbund. Avocation: trumpet playing. E-mail: Erik.Bye@stami.no. Office: Nat Inst Occupl Health, PO Box 8149, N-0033 Oslo Norway

BYE, KARYN, Olympic hockey athlete; b. River Falls, Wis., May 18, 1971. Degree in Phys. Edn., U. N.H., 1993; grad. diploma, Concordia U., Montreal, 1995. Hockey player U. N.H., 1989-93, Concordia U., Montreal, 1993-95; capt. IIHF Pacific Women's Hockey Championship, 1996; mem. U.S. Women's Select Teams, 1993, 95, 96,97, U.S. Women's Nat. Team, 1992, 94, 95, 96, 97; mem. U.S. Women's Tng. Program, 1996-97. Named Rookie of Yr. Eastern Coll. Athletic Conf., 1989-90, All-Eastern Coll. Athletic Conf. accolates, 1991-93, Most Valuable Player Concordia U., 1994-95, Fittest Female Athlete Concordia U., 1994; recipient Sportswoman of Yr. award Sports Found., 1995, Outstanding Performance award Women's World Championship, 1994, U.S. Hockey Women's Player of Yr., 1995. Office: USA Hockey Inc 1775 Bob Johnson Dr Colorado Springs CO 80906-4090*

BYEFF, PETER DAVID, hematologist, oncologist; b. Nov. 27, 1948; s. Herbert Isaac and Ruth Helen (Wolfe) B.; m. Gail Schneider, Apr. 2, 1982. BA, U. Pa., 1970; MD, Johns Hopkins U., 1974. Diplomate Am. Bd. Internal Medicine (subcert. in med. oncology and hematology), Nat. Bd. Med. Examiners. Intern Georgetown U. Hosp., Washington, 1974-75, resident in internal medicine, 1975-77; vis. fellow in hematology and oncology Columbia-Presbyn. Med. Ctr., N.Y.C., 1977-81, Damon Runyon-Walter Winchell oncology fellow, 1977-81; instr. Coll. Physicians and Surgeons, Columbia U., N.Y.C.; assoc. prof., attending physician U. Conn.; attending physician Bradley Meml. Hosp., Southington, Conn., New Britain (Conn.) Gen. Hosp., med. dir. George Bray Cancer Ctr.; sr. investigator Gynecologic Oncology Group; prin. investigator Eastern Cooperative Oncology Group, Nat. Surg. Bowel and Breast project. Office: Bradley Med Bldg 55 Meriden Ave Ste 1-a Southington CT 06489-3237 also: 40 Hart St New Britain CT 06052-1743

BYEON, JONG HEON, education educator; b. Chongwon, Chungbuk, South Korea, Jan. 16, 1966; s. Hong-Kyoo Byeon and Jong-Duk Rhee; m. Yon-Mi Kim, Mar. 15, 1997; 1 child, Jeong-Hyeon. BA, Seoul Nat. U., 1987, ME with honors, 1989, PhD with honors, 1995. Cert. in edn. Tchg. asst. Seoul Nat. U., 1987-89; tchr. Muhak Girls' H.S., Seoul, 1989-96; instr. Seoul Nat. U., 1995-97, Myongji U., Seoul, 1996-97, Seowon U., Chongju, Korea, 1996-97; asst. prof. Cheju (Korea) Nat. U. Edn., 1997—. Author: (books) Systems Science and National Policy, 1997, Modern Society and Ideology, 2000, Ethics and Moral Education II, 2000; contbr. articles to profl. jours. Seoul Nat. U. scholar, 1987. Fellow Korea Assn. No. Studies, Korean Soc. for Sys. Scis.; mem. Internat. Soc. for Sys. Scis., Korean Ethics Studies Assn. Avocations: calligraphy, haedonggumdo, tennis, hiking. Fax: 82-64-755-5061. E-mail: byjh@ns.cheju-e.ac.kr. Office: Cheju Nat U Edn, 4810 Whabuk 1 Dong, Cheju 690-061, South Korea

BYER, THEODORE SCOTT, accountant; b. Trenton, N.J., Oct. 2, 1957; s. Fred and Norma (Handis) B.; m. Marcy Pam Steier, Aug. 8, 1981; children: Sarah, Tara, Hallie. BA, Muhlenberg Coll., 1979; MBA, Rider Coll., 1986. CPA. Auditor State of N.J., Trenton, 1979-80; staff acct. Louis H. Linowitz and Co., Trenton, 1980-82; supr. Amper, Politzner & Mattia, Flemington, N.J., 1982-88; tax mgr. Price Waterhouse, N.Y.C., 1988-90; sr. mgr. Salomon & Co., P.C., N.Y.C., 1990-94; ptnr. Mintz, Rosenfeld & Co., Fairfield, N.J., 1994—. Co-author: Taxation of Foreign Nationals in the United States, 1990; editor: Selecting and Installing Medical Practice Computer Software, 1996. Fellow N.J. State Soc. CPAs (co-founder Hunterdon-Warren chpt.); mem. AICPA, N.Y. State Soc. CPAs. Avocations: avid reader, music, computers. Home: 87 Cedar Ln Berkeley Heights NJ 07922-2400 Office: Mintz Rosenfeld & Co 60 Route 46 E Fairfield NJ 07004-3007

BYFIELD, BERT A., novelist; b. Lansing, Mich., Mar. 9, 1943; s. Virgil Albert and Frances Mary Pitts; m. Theresa Anne Baldassare, Dec. 2, 1972 (div. Dec. 1996); children: Cyndee, Maria, Catherine, Charity; m. Barbara Lloyd Scott, May 16, 1998. Author Caravela Books, Henrietta, N.Y., 1995—. Author: Rage of the Bear, 1995, Scream of the Eagle, 1999, Last Stand at Perekop, 2000, Father Gregory, 2000. Organizer Computer People for Peace, 1968-70. With USN, 1960-64. Russian Orthodox. Avocations: computer programming, computer games. E-mail: bbww@caravelabooks.com. Office: Caravela Books 134 Goodburlet Rd Henrietta NY 14467-9503

BYINGTON, MARY, artist, designer; b. Loup City, Nebr., June 24; arrived in Australia, 1987; d. E.C. and C.T. Baillie; children: Ann, Robert. BA in History, U. Nebr., 1968, MS in Edn., 1970, MS in Design with honors, 1978. Tchr. pub. schs., Lincoln, Nebr., San Jose, Calif., 1970-78; instr. European and Asian art history Santa Barbara (Calif.) C.C., 1978-85; owner, mgr. Byington Gallery, Santa Barbara and Sydney, Australia, 1978-96; artist-in-residence, opera costume designer U. Nebr., Lincoln, 1974-83. One-woman shows Haymarket Gallery, Lincoln, 1980-88, Los Llanos Gallery, Santa Fe, 1984, Denver Art Mus., 1986; represented in permanent collections at Julie Noyes, Sheldon Art Gallery, Lincoln, R. Maniktatz and Assocs., Dr. E. Eugene Baillie, Rick Franz Assocs., others. Recipient Marimekko textile award, 1981, purchase award Maniktala & Assocs., 1986, William E. White award for textile, 1981, juried art prize, Santa Barbara, 1985-88. Mem. Omicron Nu, Kappa Kappa Delta. Home: PO Box 448, Paddington 2021, Australia

BYINGTON, S. JOHN, retained search executive, lawyer; b. Grand Rapids, Mich.; children: Nancy, Barbra. B.Phar., Ferris State U., Big Rapids, Mich., 1959; hon. doctorate, Ferris State U., 1986; postgrad., U. Mich. Law Sch.; J.D., Georgetown U., 1963; hon. doctorate, Albany Sch. Pharmacy, 1977. Bar: Mich. 1963, D.C. 1978. Dir. pub. rels. Am. Pharm. Assn., 1961-64; asst. pros. atty. Kent County, Grand Rapids, 1964-65; exec. asst. Gov. George Romney State of Mich., 1965-68; sr. exec. Synercom Communications Corp., 1969-72; practice law Oakland County, Mich., 1969-72; dir. Detroit Office, 1972; dep. dir., field ops. and nat. export mktg. dir. U.S. Dept. Commerce, Washington, 1972-74; dep. dir. Office Consumer Affairs HEW, Washington, 1974-76; dep. spl. asst. for consumer affairs to Pres. Ford White House, Washington, 1974-76; chmn. U.S. Consumer Product Safety Commn., 1976-78; mng. ptnr. Washington office Bushnell, Gage, Reizen & Byington, Detroit, 1978-81; ptnr. Rogers Hoge & Hills, N.Y.C. and Washington, 1981-83, Pillsbury Madison & Sutro, San Francisco and Washington, 1983-92; pres., CEO Synthecell/Vega Biomolecules Corp., Columbia, Md., 1992-94; exec. v.p., COO Buckner & Co., Dallas, 1994-97; mng. ptnr. Page-Wheatcroft & Co., Ltd., Dallas, Washington, N.Y., London, 1997—; bd. dirs. Light Stream Techs., Inc., Wild Goose Brewery; chmn. esqNetwork.com Inc.; founder, mem. Interagy. Regulatory Liaison Group, Washington, 1976-78; mem. Pres.'s Aviation Safety Commn., 1987-88. Mem. D.C. Bar Assn., Mich. Bar Assn., Univ. Club, City Club. Home: 414 S Fayette St Alexandria VA 22314-5905

BYK, CHRISTIAN JACQUES, judge, law educator; b. Paris, May 5, 1955; s. Albert and Micheline (Kimel) B.; m. Dominique Patricia Dolcet, Oct. 4, 1982; 1 chld, Elena. LLM, U. Paris, 1979, PhD in Law, 1991. Accreditation to supervise rsch. Judge Superior Ct., Creteil, France, 1979-81, Beauvais, France, 1981-83; legal adviser Dept. Justice, Paris, 1983-91; spl. adviser for bioethics Coun. of Europe, Strasbourg, France, 1991-93; sr. legal adviser Internat. Law Office, Dept. Justice, Paris, 1993-98; prof. law U. Poitiers, France, 1993—; dep. chief justice Paris North Superior Ct., 1998—; sec.-gen. Dept. of Justice Fgn. Law Com., Paris, 1989—; mem. exec. bd. French Ctr. Comparative Law, Paris, 1989—; sec.-gen. Internat. Assn. Law, Ethics and Sci., Paris, 1989—; v.p. Coun. Internat. Orgns. Med. Scis., Geneva, 1993-99; cons. in field. Author: (book) The Gardens of Provence & the French Riviera, 1988, Ethics Committees and the Law, 1996; editor: (book) The New Reproductive Technologies: What's About Ethics & Law, 1989; gen. editor Internat. Jour. Bioethics, 1990—; co-author: Dictionary of Bioethics and Bioetechnology, 1993, Bioethics and Culture, 1996. Recipient M. Rapin prize for med. ethics, 1995. Mem. AAMS, European Acad. Sci., Art and Humanities, Czech Ctrl. Ethics Commn., Internat. Coun. on Monuments and Sites, Rumanian Acad. Med. Scis., Internat. Pvt. Law Com. Paris, Bar Assn. Paris (bioethics com.), Mexican Acad. Bioethics, Fgn. Law Soc., N.Y. Acad. Scis., Humane Genome Orgn. Avocations: garden history, history of art, photography. Home: 19 Rue Carpeaux, 75018 France Office: Dept of Justice, 13 pce Vendome, 75001 Paris France

BYNES, FRANK HOWARD, JR., physician; b. Savannah, Ga., Dec. 3, 1950; s. Frank Howard and Frenchye (Mason) B.; m. Janice Ratta, July 24, 1987; children: Patricia, Frenchye. BS, Savannah State Coll., 1972; MD, Meharry Med. Coll. Resident gen. surgery Staten Island (N.Y.) Hosp., 1978-82; resident internal medicine N.Y. infirmary Beekam Downtown Hosp., N.Y.C., 1983-86; dir. medicine USAF Sheppard Regional Hosp., Sheppard AFB, Tex., 1986-87; pvt. practice internal medicine N.Y.C., 1987-90; attending physician Bronx (N.Y.) Lebanon Hosp., 1990-93; pvt. practice internal medicine Savannah, Ga., 1994—. Maj. USAF, 1986-87. Mem. AMA, AAAS, ACP, N.Y. Acad. Scis., Assn. Mil. Surgeons of U.S., Alpha Phi Alpha.

BYRD, ANDREW WAYNE, investment company executive; b. Nashville, Apr. 16, 1954; s. Benjamin F. and Allison (Caldwell) B.; m. Marianne Menefee; children: Marianne, Valere, Andrew Jr. BA, Vanderbilt U., 1976, JD, 1979; LLM, Georgetown U., 1981. Bar: Tenn., 1979, U.S. Dist. Ct. (mid. dist.) Tenn. 1979. Atty. Stokes & Bartholomew, Nashville, 1981-84; exec. v.p. Gen. Cap Am. Inc., 1987-94; exec. v.p. Gen. Capital Corp., Nashville, 1984-89, pres., 1989-94; pres. Andrew W. Byrd & Co., LLC, 1994—; chmn., bd. dirs. Multi-Link, Inc., Lexington, Ky., Albertville Quality Foods, Inc., Albertville, Ala. Mem. Leadership Nashville, 1984-85; deacon 1st Presbyn. Ch., 1982-92; bd. dirs. Tenn. divsn. Am. Cancer Soc., 1982-88, 92-97, Cheekwood, 1987-93; bd. dirs. Boy Scouts of Am., Mid. Tenn. Coun., 1995—; bd. dirs. Vanderbilt Children's Hosp., 1987-93, chmn., 1991-93. Mem. ABA, Tenn. Bar Assn., Nashville Bar Assn., Nashville C. of C., Cumberland Club Nashville, Exch. Club (pres. 1993-94). Democrat. Avocations: tennis, gardening, travel. Home: 4419 Harding Pl Nashville TN 37205-4530 Office: Andrew W Byrd & Co LLC 201 4th Ave N Ste 1250 Nashville TN 37219-2092

BYRD, BENJAMIN FRANKLIN, JR., surgeon, educator; b. Nashvillle, May 18, 1918; s. Benjamin Franklin and Ida (Brister) B.; m. Allison Caldwell, Feb. 6, 1950; children: Benjamin Franklin, Barney Duncan, Damon Winston, Andrew Wayne, Evelyn Hope, John W. Thomas. A.B., Vanderbilt U., 1938, M.D., 1941. Intern, Nashville Gen. Hosp., 1941-42, asst. resident, 1942; asst. resident Vanderbilt U. Hosp., 1945-47, resident, 1947-48; practice medicine, specializing in surgery Nashville, 1948—; chief surgery St. Thomas Hosp., 1964-70, pres. staff, 1977-79; mem. staff Baptist Hosp.; instr. surgery Vanderbilt U., Nashville, 1947-54; assoc. clin. prof. surgery Vanderbilt U., 1954-71, clin. prof. surgery, 1971-99; chmn. bd. of overseers Vanderbilt U. Cancer Ctr., 1993—; assoc. clin. prof. surgery Meharry Med. Coll., Nashville, 1951-69; prof. clin. surgery Meharry Med. Coll., 1969—, clin. prof. surgery emeritus, 1999—; dir., mem. trust bd. Commerce Union Bank, 1974-80, 82-91; dir. NLT Corp. Pres. Tenn. divsn. Am. Cancer Soc., 1963, nat. bd. dirs., 1965—, nat. exec. com., 1970-80, chmn. med. and sci. exec. com., 1973—&, nat. pres., 1975-76; pres., mem. exec. bd. Tenn. Bot. Gardens and Fine Arts Ctr., 1971-73; trustee Sr. Citizens, Hermitage Assn.; bd. dirs. Cumberland Mus., Univ. Sch., 1985-91. Lt. col. M.C., AUS, 1941-45. Decorated Bronze Star with 2 oak leaf clusters, Silver Star, Purple Heart; named Nashvillian of Yr., Nashville Kiwanis, 1986; recipient Human Rels. award Nat. Fellow ACS (gov. 1973-79, chmn. commn. on cancer); mem. Am. Surg. Assn., So. Surg. Assn., Nashville Surg. Soc. (pres. 1962-63), Soc. Surg. Oncology, Tenn. Med. Assn. (mem. council, Disting. Service award, Physician of Yr. 1986), So. Med. Assn. (mem. council), Société International de Chirurgie, Southeastern Surg. Congress (mem. council, pres. 1968-69, Disting. Service award 1977), Nashville Acad. Medicine (pres. 1980, chmn. 1981), Nashville C. of C. (bd. govs. 1967-70, 82—, pres. 1985), Vanderbilt U. Med. Alumni (pres. 1979-81), Sigma Xi. Club: Nashville Exchange. Home: 400 Ellendale Ave Nashville TN 37205-3402 Office: PO BOx 380 4220 Harding Rd Nashville TN 37202

BYRD, ELLEN STOESSER, dermatology nurse; b. Dayton, Tex., Dec. 10, 1941; d. Edward Joseph and Nina Mae (Cannon) Stoesser; m. C. Robert Byrd, June 6, 1964; children: Byron, Preston, Aaron, Robyn. BSN, Baylor U., 1964. RN, Tex. Nurse Parkland Hosp., Dallas, 1964-65; nurse gyn. svcs. Baylor U. Med. Ctr., Dallas, 1965-66; charge nurse med./surg. Collin Meml. Hosp., McKinney, Tex., 1967-68; nurse newborn nursery St. Paul Hosp., Dallas, 1972; pvt. duty nurse Dist. 4 Tex. Nurse Assn., Dallas, 1976; sch. nurse Dallas Ind. Sch. Dist., 1989-90; home health nurse Rehab Home Care, DeSoto, Tex., 1994-98; dermatology nurse, 1999—; mem. adv. bd. Baylor U. Sch. Nursing, Dallas, 1994—, chmn. adv. bd. 1999—; advisor Baylor U. Woman's Coun., Dallas, 1995—, pres., 1994-95. Author: History of Dallas CPA Wives, 1983, Biography of Mae Stoesser, 1988, Byrd Family 25 Years, 1990. Program chmn. Freedom Found. Valley Forge, Dallas, 1986-89; centennial circle chmn. Dallas County Heritage Soc., Dallas; deacon Cliff Temple Bapt. Ch., 1988; v.p. DeSoto Svc. League, 1990; pres. Dallas CPAs Wives Club, 1984-85; mem. Richardson Jr. League. Recipient W.T. White Meritorious Svcs. award Baylor U. Alumni Assn., 1996. Mem. Richardson Jr. League, Richardson Newcomers Club. Repubican. Baptist. Avocations: European travel, grandchildren. Fax: 972-234-8448. E-mail: EllenByrd@aol.com. Home: 304 Prince Albert Ct Richardson TX 75081-5059

BYRD, GARY ELLIS, lawyer; b. Dothan, Ala., Mar. 8, 1957; m. Emily Marie Reid; children: Elizabeth, Virginia and Victoria (twins). BS in Pre-Law and Am. History summa cum laude, Troy State U., 1979; JD, U. Ala., 1982. Bar: Ga. (no. and middle dists.) 1983, U.S. Dist. Ct. (no. and so. dists), Ga., U.S. Ct. Appeals. Pntr. Bishoff & Byrd, Talbotton, Ga., 1982-86; assoc. Bunn & Kirby, Hamilton, Ga., 1993—, 1993-96; ptnr. Bunn & Byrd, Hamilton, Ga., 1996—; city atty. Woodland, Ga., 1986—, Geneva, Ga., 1988—, Shiloh, Ga., 1994—; chmn. bd. dirs. Talbot County Law Libr., Talbotton, 1992-2000; bd. dirs. Harris County Law Libr., Hamilton, 1998-2000. Contbr. numerous articles to newspapers and profl. jours., chpt. to book; author City of Woodland city code, 1986. Bd. dirs. Chattahoochie-Flint RESA, Americus, Ga., 1986-87, Pine Mountain Regional Arts Coun., Manchester, Ga., 1986-88; pres., chmn. exec. com. Talbot County 2000 Group, Talbotton, 1987-88; coach debate team dept. social studies Manchester (Ga.) H.S., 1982; chmn. appropriations com. Harris County YMCA, Hamilton, 1994, 95, 96, 97, 98, 99, bd. dirs. 1994, 95, 96, 97, 98, 99, 2000; mem. budget com. City of Talbotton, 1989-92, councilman, 1985-92, mem. policy adv. com., 1986-92, vol. fireman, 1982-93; ct. apptd. administr. City of Geneva, Ga., 1992; mem. adv. com. Am. Security Coun., Washington, 1976-82; dir. Harris County Indigent Def. Program, 1999-2000. Recipient Outstanding Svc. award Talbot County Jaycees, 1983,. Mem. Ga. Bar Assn., Ga. Mcpl. Assn. (atty.'s sect.), Talbot County C. of C. (chmn. membership com. 1992-93, bd. dirs. 1993), Harris County C. of C. (bd. dirs. 2000), Troy State U. Alumni Assn. (membership com. East Ala./West Ctrl. Ga. chpt. 1993-99, Rotary, Phi Kappa Phi, Phi Alpha Theta (State Hist. Rsch. award 1979). Avocations: model trains, stock car racing, antique car restoration. Home: PO Box 119 Hamilton GA 31811-0119 Office: 103 N College St PO Box 489 Hamilton GA 31811-0489

BYRD, MARC ROBERT, florist, designer; b. Flint, Mich., May 14, 1954; s. Robert Lee and Cynthia Ann (Poland) B.; m. Bonnie Jill Berlin, Nov. 25, 1975 (div. June 1977). Student, Ea. Mich. U., 1972-75; grad., Am. Floral Sch., Chgo., 1978. Gen. mgr., dir. flowers shop; designer Olive Tree Florist, Palm Desert, Calif., 1978-79, Kayo's Flower Fashions, Palm Springs, 1979-80; owner, designer Village Florist, Inc., Palm Springs, 1980-85; pres. Mon Ami Florist, Inc., Beverly Hills, 1986-87; gen. mgr. Silverio's, Santa Monica, 1987; gen. mgr., hotel florist, creative dir. Four Seasons Hotel, Beverly Hills, 1988-90; pres. Marc Fredericks, Inc., Beverly Hills, 1990-97; event florist Marc Byrd of Floral Works, L.A., 1997—. Author: Celebrity Flowers, 1989. Del., Dem. County Conv., 1972, Dem. County Conv., 1972, Dem. State Conv., 1972, Dem. Nat. Conv., 1972. Mem. Soc. Am. Florists, So. Calif. Floral Assn., Desert Mus., Robinson's Gardens. Republican. Mem. Dutch Reformed Ch. Avocations: skiing, tennis, community service. Fax: (323) 962-9275. Office: Floral Works 2415 Creston Dr Los Angeles CA 90068-2203

BYRDWELL, WILLIAM CRAIG, chemist, educator; b. New Orleans, Oct. 10, 1961; s. James Hewitt and Ila Jean (Beck) B.; divorced; children: Matthew, Heather. BS, U. Louisville, 1987, PhD, 1994. Postdoctoral rschr. Nat. Ctr. Agrl. Utilization Rsch. Agrl. Rsch. Svc., Peoria, Ill., 1994-95, rsch. chemist, 1995-99; asst. prof. Fla. Atlantic U., Boca Raton, 1999—; co-chair symposium Am. Oil Chemist's Soc., Champaign, Ill., 1998, 99. Mem. Am. Chem. Soc. Democrat. Avocations: scuba diving, aquarist. e-mail: byrdwell@fau.edu. Office: Fla Atlantic U 777 Glades Rd Boca Raton FL 33431-6424

BYRES, MARSHALL HENRY, financial executive; b. Aberdeen, Scotland, UK, May 25, 1951; s. Henry Findlay and Hilda (Shand) B.; m. Dorothy Agnes Richards, Jan. 27, 1984; children: Melvin Stuart, Lyndsay Kathryn, Harrison Duncan, Heather Louise. BS, Aberdeen U., Scotland, 1973. Insp. of taxes U.K. Inland Revenue, Aberdeen, 1974-79; dist. insp. in chg. London Provincial Dist. 23, Edinburgh, 1980-81; tax cons. Ernst & Whinney, Hong Kong, 1981-85, tax ptnr., 1986-89; tax ptnr. Ernst & Young, Hong Kong, 1990-99; COO, Ernst & Young China, Hong Kong, 2000—; chmn. Far East tax com. Ernst & Whinney, Singapore, 1986-89, mem. internat. tax com., N.Y.C., 1986-89, chmn. tax svcs. Hong Kong and Far East, 1990—, mem. internat. tax com., 1990-99. Editor Taxation in Hong Kong; contbr. articles to profl. jours. Mem. Joint Liaison Com. on Taxation, Hong Kong, 1988—, dep. chmn., 1992—; chmn. Com. on Double Taxation, 1987. Named Top Tax Cons., Tax Rev. Internat., 1994, 95, 96, 98, 99. Mem. Hong Kong Soc. Accts. (chmn. tax 1987-91), Internat. Fiscal Assn. Amsterdam, Hong Kong Gen. C. of C. (tax and econ. svcs. coms. 1991—, coalition svc. industries com. 1998—), Brit. C. of C. in Hong Kong (econ. svcs. com. 1991-94), Hong Kong Football Club (treas. 1984), Royal Hong Kong Jockey Club, Aberdeen U. of Hong Kong Assn. (pres. 1990—). Avocations: soccer, rugby, photography, writing, reading. Home: 15 Kotewall Rd, Flat 2A Hatton House, Hong Kong Hong Kong Office: Ernst & Young, 15/F Hutchison House, Hong Kong Hong Kong

BYRNE, BRENDAN JOSEPH, theology educator, priest; b. Melbourne, Victoria, Australia, Oct. 12, 1939; s. Francis Patrick and Mary Alice (Flanagan) B. BA with honors, U. Melbourne, Australia, 1966; MA, U. Melbourne, 1972; BD with honors, Melbourne Coll. Divinity, 1972; PhD, Oxford (Eng.) U., 1977. Joined S.J., 1957. Lectr. Corpus Christi Coll., Werribee, Australia, 1971; prof. new testament united faculty theology Jesuit Theol. Coll., Parkville, Australia, 1977—; prin. Jesuit Theol. Coll., Parkville, 1992-97; rector Campion Coll., Kew, Australia, 1979-84; v.p. Melbourne Coll. Div., 1998-2000, pres. 2000—. Author: Sons of God-Seed of Abraham, 1979, Reckoning with Romans, 1986, Paul and the Christian Woman, 1988, Romans (Sacra Pagina), 1996, The Hospitality of God, 2000. Mem. Soc. for New Testament Studies, Cath. Bibl. Assn. Am., Australian Cath. Bibl. Assn. (pres. 1997-98). Avocations: reading, cycling. Home: 175 Royal Pde, Parkville VIC 3052, Australia Office: Jesuit Theol Coll, 175 Royal Parade, Parkville VIC 3052, Australia

BYRNE, GRANVILLE BLAND, III, lawyer; b. San Antonio, Jan. 26, 1952; s. Granville Bland and Mary (Dowling) B.; divorced; children: Peyton Smith, Fulton Buckner; m. Monique Renée Wise, 1999. AB, U. N.C., Chapel Hill, 1974; JD, Harvard U., 1978. Bar: Ga. 1978, U.S. Dist. Ct. (no. dist.) Ga. 1978, U.S. Ct. Appeals (5th cir.) 1978, U.S. Ct. Appeals (11th cir.) 1981. Assoc. Swift, Currie, McGhee & Hiers, Atlanta, 1978-84, ptnr., 1984-94; prin. Byrne, Eldridge, Moore & Davis, P.C., Atlanta, 1994-99, Byrne, Moore & Davis, P.C., Atlanta, 1999—; bd. dirs. Compeer Atlanta, Inc., chmn., 1996—; bd. dirs. Cagle's, Inc. Elder, mem. session 1st Presbyn. Ch. Atlanta, 1993-96, 99—. Mem. ABA, Ga. Bar Assn., Atlanta Bar Assn. Democrat. Presbyterian. Home: 3555 Castlegate Dr NW Atlanta GA 30327-2601 Office: Byrne Moore & Davis PC 3340 Peachtree Rd NE Atlanta GA 30326-1000

BYRNE, KATHARINE CRANE, lawyer; b. Chgo., Dec. 31, 1958; d. William Patrick and Jane M. (Burke) B.; 1 child, William Byrne Vogt. BA, St. Mary's Coll., Notre Dame, Ind., 1980; JD, Loyola U., 1988. Bar: Ill. 1988, U.S. Dist. Ct. (no. dist.) Ill. 1988, U.S. Ct. Appeals (7th cir.) 1991, Fed. Trial Bar (no. dist.) Ill. 1992. Event planner Gaper's Caterers, Chgo., 1980-84; coord. Jane Byrne Campaign Com., Chgo., 1985-87; law clk. Cooney & Conway, Chgo., 1987-88, atty., 1988—; lectr. Andrews 8th Ann. Asbestos Litigation Conf., 1996, 97, 99. Author: Premises Liability, 1994. Lectr. Ill. Inst. for Continuing Legal Edn., Chgo., 1991; pres. Beautiful Chgo. (Ill.) Commn., 1994. Mem. ATLA, Ill. Trial Lawyers Assn. (lectr. seminar 1995, 97, 98, 2000, bd. mgrs. 1998—), Celtic Lawyers. Democrat. Roman Catholic. Home: 111 E Chestnut St Chicago IL 60611-2051 Office: Cooney & Conway 120 N La Salle St Chicago IL 60602-2424

BYRNE, MARTHA F.C., education association executive; b. Shelbyville, Tenn., June 20, 1952; d. John Peyton Crigler and Frances Bramblett; m. Donald J. Byrne, June 21, 1975. BA, Stephens Coll., 1973. Account exec. Weightman Advt., Phila., 1975-79; advt. mgr. Phila. Savs. Fund Soc., 1979-83; dir. mktg. and sales Am. Fedn. Info. Processing Socs., Reston, Va., 1983-87; dir. mktg. Coun. for Exceptional Children, Reston, 1987-88; sr. v.p., gen. mgr. Montgomery County Assn. Realtors, Rockville, Md., 1989-93; v.p. Career Coll. Assn., Washington, 1995—. Mem. Am. Soc. Assn. Execs. Office: Career Coll Assn 10 G St NE Ste 750 Washington DC 20002-4258

BYRNE, NOEL THOMAS, sociologist, educator; b. San Francisco, May 11, 1943; s. Joseph Joshua and Naomi Pearl (Denison) B.; m. Dale W. Elrod, Aug. 6, 1989. BA in Sociology, Sonoma State Coll., 1971; MA in Sociology, Rutgers U., 1975, PhD in Sociology, 1987. Instr. sociology Douglass Coll., Rutgers U., New Brunswick, N.J., 1974-76, Hartnell Coll., Salinas, Calif., 1977-78; from lectr. to assoc. prof. dept. mgmt. Sonoma State U., Rohnert Park, Calif., 1978-94, chmn. dept. of mgmt., 1990-91, from. assoc. prof. to prof. sociology dept., 1994—, chmn. dept. sociology, 1997—; cons. prof. Emile Durkheim Inst. for Advanced Study, Grand Cayman, B.W.I., 1990-93. Contbr. articles and revs. to profl. lit. Recipient Dell Pub. award Rutgers U. Grad. Sociology Program, 1976, Louis Bevier fellow, 1977-78. Mem. AAAS, Am. Sociol. Assn., Pacific Sociol. Assn., N.Y. Acad. Sci., Soc. for Study Symbolic Interaction (rev. editor Jour. 1980-83), Soc. for Study Social Problems, Commonwealth Club. Democrat. Home: 4773 Ross Rd Sebastopol CA 95472-2114 Office: Sonoma State U Dept Sociology Rohnert Park CA 94928

BYRNE, ROBERT EUGENE, chess columnist; b. N.Y.C., Apr. 20, 1928; s. Frank and Elizabeth Eleanor (Cattelier) B.; m. Florence Mary Dolley, Sept. 8, 1954 (div. Feb. 1971); children: Benjamin (dec.), Thomas Edward; m. Ursula Maria von Krebs, Sept. 11, 1971. BA, Yale U., 1952; postgrad., Ind. U., 1952-60. Chess reporter N.Y. Daily News, N.Y.C., 1971-72; chess columnist N.Y. Times, 1972—; mem. U.S. Olympiad teams U.S. Chess Fedn., New Windsor, N.Y., 1952-84, capt., 1984, U.S. chess champion, 1972, quarter finalist world chess championship; world chess champion Internat. Chess Fedn., Geneva, 1974; U.S. Open champion U.S. Chess Fedn., New Windsor, 1960, 63, 66; cons. for IBM on Deep Blue chess computer project.

Author: Beginning Chess, 1972, Both Sides of the Chessboard, 1972, The Road to the World Championship, 1976, (calendar) The Chess Calendar, 1998, 99, 2000, N.Y. Times Book of Great Chess Victories and Defeats, 1990. Mem. U.S. Chess Fedn., Manhattan Chess Club (hon. bd. dirs. 1980—). Avocations: opera, ballet, archaeology, tennis. Home and Office: 16 Rockledge Ave Scarborough NY 10510

BYRNE, ROSS LEON, accountant; b. Oatlands, Tasmania, Australia, Sept. 2, 1953; s. Donald Francis and Jean Elsie (Young) B.; m. Claire Elizabeth Goodwin, Feb. 12, 1977 (div. 1991); children: Allyson, Scott, Rachel; m. Jennifer Leonie Cordwell, May 8, 1999; stepchildren: Nathan, Justin. B in Econs., U. Tasmania, 1978. Chartered acct.; cert. fin. planner. Acct. Wiselord & Ferguson, Hobart, Australia, 1972-74, Garrott & Garrott, Hobart, 1976-78; resident mgr. Coopers & Lybrand, Hobart, 1979-83; ptnr. Moore Dobson Woods & Byrne, Hobart, 1983-88, Moore Robsons, Hobart, 1988—; bd. dirs. St. John Ambulance Australia, Tasmania. Col. Australian Army, 1972—. Decorated RFD, Order of St. John. Fellow Inst. Chartered Accts., Australian Inst. Mgmt. (assoc.). Avocations: trout fishing, rowing.

BYRNE, SHAUN PATRICK, law enforcement officer; b. Atlantic City, Aug. 22, 1963; s. Warren Patrick and Donna Mae (Curlott) B. Student, Nat. Acad. Paralegals, Egg Harbor, N.J., 1991; AS, Cumberland County Coll., Vineland, N.J., 1994; BA in Criminal Justice, Stockton State Coll., Pomona, N.J., 1995; grad., Widener U. Sch. Law, 2000. Police officer Atlantic City Police Dept., 1984-85; with trade union, 1986-91; sr. detective Jamesway Corp., Secaucus, N.J., 1991-95; law clk. Atlantic County Pub. Def. Office, 1999—; security advisor P.S.I., Inc.; paralegal, 1991-92; mediation counselor Criminal Justice Inst., 1995—; deputy gen. dir. Internat. Biog. Ctr., 1999; mediator U.S. Post Office, 1999—. Martial arts trainer/demonstrator Fighting Dragons Dojo, Atlantic City, 1980—; high sch. presentations on violence/drugs, Vineland, 1995. Named Outstanding Person 20th Century Internat. Biog. Ctr., 1997; Am. Biog. Inst. fellow, 1998. Republican. Roman Catholic. Avocations: martial arts, kick boxing, scuba diving, weight training. Home: PO Box 1081 Absecon NJ 08201-5081

BYRNE-DEMPSEY, CECELIA (CECELIA DEMPSEY), journalist; b. L.A., Aug. 7, 1925; d. John Joseph and Margaret Agnes (Frakell) B.; m. John Dempsey, Mar. 25, 1951 (dec. June 1981); children: Margaret, Elizabeth, John, Cecelia, Cathrine, Patricia, Bridget, Charles, Mary Teresa. Student, Immaculate Heart Coll., 1944; BA in Psychology, Calif. State U., Northridge, 1975, BA in Journalism, 1978, MA in Mass Communication, 1992. Staff Lockheed Aircraft Corp., Burbank, Calif., 1943—, Office Naval Rsch., San Francisco, 1947—; with Sisters of Mercy, Burlingame, Calif., 1945—, Sisters of Presentation, San Francisco, 1949—; mem. staff Calif. State U., Calif., 1976—; rschr., journalism historian early Am. newspapers, 1978—. Author: The Meaning Index: A Model for Early American Newspaper Indexing, 1992. Mentor 4-H Club; past mem. Urban Corp., L.A. Mem. Mensa, Kappa Gamma Delta. Republican. Jewish. Avocations: poetry, gardening, philosophical meditation.

BYRNES, PAUL DAVID, software engineer, consultant; b. Mpls., Jan. 27, 1962; s. Ferdinand F. and Rosemary (Abrams) B.; m. Laurie S., May 20, 1989. BS in Engring., USAF Acad., 1984; MBA in Fin., Bentley Coll., 1988; postgrad., Air Force Inst. Tech., 1989. Commd. 2d lt. USAF, 1984, ret. capt., 1990; mgr. software engring. program Carnegie Mellon U., Pitts., 1990-94, project mgr. Software Engring. Inst., 1992-94; prin., mng. dir. Integrated System Diagnostics, Inc., Pocasset, Mass., 1994—; presenter in field. Contbr. articles to profl. jours. Vol. Meals on Wheels, Boston, 1984-88, Northland Pub. Libr., McCandless, Pa., 1990—, WQED Pub. Rels., Pitts., 1994—. Capt. USAFR, 1990—. Mem. IEEE, Am. Assn. Individual Investors, Assn. Computing Machinery, Tech. Transfer Soc., USAF Acad. Assn. Grads. Democrat. Roman Catholic. Avocations: sports, weightlifting, music, investing. Home: 112 Washington Pl Apt 7A Pittsburgh PA 15219-3504 Office: Ste 230 Two Chatham Ctr Pittsburgh PA 15219

BYRON, E. LEE, real estate broker; b. Gt. Falls, Mont., Oct. 1, 1945; d. Chase and Mary Lee (Evans) Kimball; m. H. Thomas Byron Jr., May 18, 1966; children: H. Thomas Byron III, Chase K., Lee-Hayes. AB, Smith Coll., 1967; MA, Monterey Inst. Fgn. Studies, 1971; Montessori cert., St. Nicholas. Ctr., London, 1971. Lic. real estate broker, Fla. Lectr. Monterey (Calif.) Inst. Fgn. Studies, 1971-72; founder, dir., owner Children's Sch. and Summer Dynamics, Auburn, Ala., 1975-79; instr. Child Study Ctr. Auburn U., 1973-79; hosp. dir. Fruitville Vet. Clinic, Sarsasota, Fla., 1980-93; broker assoc. Michael Saunders & Co., Sarasota, 1993—; founder, adv. bd. mem. Guaranty Bank, North Port, Fla., 1987-99; owner, ptnr. Lee Ventures Real Estate Partnership, Sarasota, 1984-99; presenter in field, organizer various discussion panels. Co-author: Preschool Theme Lesson Plans, 1975. Bd. dirs. Jr. League, Sarasota, 1981-90; bd. dirs. Pine View Assn. PTA, 1981-90, chmn., 1984-85; bd. dirs. Teen Ct., Sarasota, 1990—, Fla. Sch. Bd. Assn., cert., 1993; bd. dirs. Taxpayers Assn. Sarasota County, 1995-99, pres., 1996-97; bd. dirs. Civic League Sarasota, 1995-2000, 2nd v.p., 1997-98, 1st v.p., 1998-99, pres., 1999-2000; chmn. Sarasota County Exceptional Student Edn. Sch. Adv. Bd., 1984-90; mem. Pine View Sch. Adv. Com., 1994-98, chmn., 1994-97; bd. dirs. Consortium for Children and Youth, Sarasota, 1986—, pres., 1993-97; vice chair Action Task Force Venice (Fla.) 20/20, 1995-97, Children and Youth Svcs. Adv. Com., 1993—, chair, 1996-98, vice chair, 1999-2000; co-chmn. Pres.'s Spl. Com. Exceptional Edn. Fla. Sch. Bd. Assn., 1992-93; mem. Bishop's Com. Sexual Misconduct Cath. Diocese, Venice, 1994-95, Multi-Stakeholder's Group (Future Land Planning East Sarasota County), 1995-99; mem. adv. com. Fla. House Inst., 1998—; mem. Sarasota County Sch. Bd., 1990-94; bd. govs. Big Bros./Big Sisters of the Suncoast, 1998—, Fla. Women's Alliance, 1994—; eucharistic minister St. Patrick's Ch., 1995—. Recipient Sustainer of Yr. award Sarasota Jr. League, 1993, Cmty. Svc. award, 1995; Women of Power award Nat. Coun. Jewish Women, 1997; named One of 100 Vols. for 100th birthday, Internat. Assn. Jr. Leagues, 1996. Mem. Sarasota Assn. of Realtors (program com. 1995-99), Nat. Assn. Realtors (Grad. Realtor Inst. 1996). Republican. Roman Catholic. Avocations: reading, swimming, skiing. Home: 653 Sinclair Dr Sarasota FL 34240-9367 Office: Michael Saunders & Co 5100 Ocean Blvd Sarasota FL 34242-1693

BYRON, H. THOMAS, JR., veterinarian, educator; b. Troy, N.Y., Feb. 13, 1944; s. Henry Thomas and Mary Katherine (Hayes) B.; m. E. Lee Kimball, May 18, 1966; children: H. Thomas III, Chase Kimball, Lee Hayes. BS, Stonehill Coll., 1965; MS, U. Fla., 1973; DVM, Auburn U., 1977. Intern Animal Med. Clinic, Lakeland, Fla., 1977; resident in radiology, instr. Auburn (Ala.) U., 1977-79; chief staff Ctrl. Animal Hosp., Tampa, Fla., 1979-80; founder Fruitville Vet. Clinic, Sarasota, Fla., 1980-94; chief vet., dir. animal programs Circus World, Haines City, Fla., 1981-83; bus. broker Bus. Resource Group, Sarasota, Fla., 1994—; owner Pet Wellness, 1996-2000, Moore Animal Clinic, Venice, Fla., 1998-2000; liasion S.W. Fla. Vet. Med. Assn., Humane Soc., 1984-92; cons. Ringling Bros., Barnum and Bailey Circus, Venice, Fla., 1986—, Busch Gardens, Tampa, 1984—, Roberts Bros. Circus, Hanneford Circus, Coronas Circus, Hoxie Bros. Circus, Sarasota, 1979—, Circus Vargas Internat., L.A., 1984—, Parc Safari, Hemingford, Que., Can., 1993; lectr. U. Fla. Vet. Sch., 1989—, mem. adv. coun. Coll. Vet. Medicine, 1991—. Contbr. articles to profl. jours. Troop leader Boy Scouts Am., Auburn, Sarasota, 1977-81, scoutmaster, packmaster; vet. chmn. Sarasota United Way, 1980—; lectr., vol. Sarasota County Schs., 1980—; mem. Sarasota County rabies control com. Pub. Health Dept., 1980-92; founding mem. Sarasota County Animal Welfare Adv. Com., 1992; bd. dirs. Sarasota Girls' Choir, 1987-89, Pine View Sch. Parents' Assn. Bd., 1990-94; bd. dirs., pres. Sunset Royale Condominium Assn., Siesta Key, Fla., 1988-89, 91-93. Lt. USNR. Recipient Aux. award AVMA, 1977, recognition award Sarasota County Commrs., 1993; Alexander Hamilton scholar Stonehill Coll., 1964-65; fellow NAS, 1972-73, Ger aldine Page wildlife fellow Tufts U., 1987. Mem. Fla. Pub. Health Assn., Fla. Vet. Medicine Assn. (fin. com. 1982-86, bd. dirs. 1986-92, chmn. legis. com. 1982-90, Gold Star award 1988), S.W. Fla. Vet. Med. Assn. (bd. dirs., sec.-treas., v.p., pres. 1980-85), Aquatic Animal Vet. Assn., Zoo Animal Vet. Assn., Sarasota C. of C. (legis. com. 1986-91), Phi Zeta. Republican. Roman Catholic. Avocations: water skiing, fishing, scuba diving. Home and Office: 653 Sinclair Dr Sarasota FL 34240-9367

BYRON, JULIE ANNE, author; b. Sydney, NSW, Australia; d. Kenneth William and Stella Mavis (Sullivan) B. Grad. h.s., Canberra, Australia. Author: Amazing Psychic Experiences of the Famous, 1993, Japanese translation, 1995, Portuguese translation, 1998; contbr. articles to profl. publs. Avocations: research, writing. Home: PO Box 3068, Canberra ACT 2611, Australia

BYRSKOG, SAMUEL PER-ERIK, theology educator; b. Filipstad, Värmland, Sweden, Mar. 13, 1957; s. Erik and Sonja (Bolander) B.; m. Angela Franca Resenterra, June 18, 1983; children: Michael, Jessica. ThM, Lund (Sweden) U., 1986, ThD, Docent of N.T., 1994. Instr., asst. Lund U., 1988-93; ast. prof. Bapt. Theol. Sem., Rüschlikon, Switzerland, 1994-95; rsch. fellow Humboldt Found., Tübingen, Germany, 1996; assoc. prof. dept. religious studies Göteborg (Sweden) U., 1997—. Author: Jesus the Only Teacher, 1994, Story as History-History as Story, 2000; contbr. articles to religious jours., including Zeitschrift für N.T. Wissenschaft, Jour. for Study N.T., Revue Biblique. Rsch. grantee Humanistisk-samhällsvetenskapliga forskningsrådet, 1995, 2000—; rsch. scholar Humboldt Found., 1996, Göteborg U., 1997-2000. Mem. Studiorum Novi Testamenti Societas. Home: Handbollsvägen 2, SE 24741 Södra Sandby Sweden Office: Goteborg U Dept Religious, Studies, PO Box 200, SE 40530 Göteborg Sweden

BYSTRAND, FREDRIK VILHELM, information systems executive; b. Flen, Sweden, Dec. 24, 1936; s. David V. and Stina E. (Svensson) B.; m. Laila Hjelm, Dec. 26, 1960; children: Clara, Jeanna. Programmer Swedish Bd. of Computing Machinery, Stockholm, 1959; analyst programmer Quantum Chemistry Group, U. Uppsala, Sweden, 1960-63; systems mgr. Mathema AB, Stockholm, 1964-65; owner Programmeringskonsult AB, Stockholm, 1966-67; mgmt. cons. Parsons & Williams, Copenhagen, L.A., 1968-69; info. sys. mgr. Sandvik AB, Sandviken, Sweden, 1970-83; pres. Sandvik Info. Sys. Inc., Fair Lawn, N.J., 1984-85; v.p. Sandvik Coromant Inc., Fair Lawn, N.J., 1986-87; mgr. global info. sys. Sandvik Coromant AB, Sandviken, 1988-92; corp. v.p. ABB Asea Brown Boveri Ltd., Zurich, Switzerland, 1993—; mem. bd. dirs. Digital Equipment (India) Ltd., Bangalore, India, 1999—; adv. bd. Lotus Inc., Cambridge, Mass., 1995—, Hewlett Packard, Palo Alto, Calif., 1994-99, Digital Equipment, Boston, 1995-98, BMC, Houston, 1997-99; mem. exec. roundtable Microsoft Corp., Redmond, Wash., 1999—, Compaq Computer Corp., Houston, 2000—. Home: Parkweg 4, 8800 Thalwil Switzerland Office: Asea Brown Boveri Ltd, Affolternstrasse 44, 8050 Zurich Switzerland

BYSTRITSKY, ALEXANDER, psychiatry educator; b. St. Petersburg, Russia, Jan. 12, 1954; came to the U.S., 1979; s. Stanislav Bystritsky and Irina Oberstein; m. Marina Schmidt, Dec. 16, 1978; two children. MD, St. Petersburg U., 1977. Resident NYU, N.Y.C., 1981-85; Robert Wood Johnson clin. scholar UCLA, 1985-87, asst. clin. prof., 1987-93, assoc. clin. prof., 1993-98, clin. prof., 1998—, dir. anxiety disorder program, 1987—. Contbr. articles to profl. jours. Fellow Am. Psychiat. Assn.; mem. Coll. Internat. Neuropsychopharmacology. E-mail: abystrit@ucla.edu. Office: UCLA/NPI 300 Ucla Medical Plz Los Angeles CA 90095-8346

BYSTRÖM, BENGT-OLOV, wood processing equipment company executive; b. Örnköldsvik, Sweden, Sept. 5, 1942; m. Yvonne Nordin, Aug. 7, 1968; 3 children. D Economy, U. Umeå (Sweden), 1971. Tchr. U. Umeå (Sweden), 1966-72; mgmt. cons. Devel. Fund., Härnösand, Sweden, 1972-90; mng. dir. Logosol, Härnösand, 1990—. Inventor, designer Logosol sawmill. Office: Logosol AB, Industrigatan 13, 87153 Härnösand Sweden

BYSTRYN, MARCIA HAMMILL, city program administrator; b. Louisville, Dec. 17, 1947; d. William Arthur and Jane Lind (Krieger) Hammill; m. Jean-Claude Bystryn, May 14, 1972; children: Anne, Alexander. BA, NYU, 1969, PhD, 1977. Asst. prof. sociology Northeastern U., Boston, 1977-81; program officer The Twentieth Century Fund, N.Y.C., 1981-84, asst. dir., 1984-88, acting dir., 1988-89; exec. dir. N.Y. State Moreland Act Commn. on the Returnable Container, N.Y.C., 1989-90; asst. commr. Bur. of Waste Prevention, Reuse and Recycling N.Y.C. Dept. Sanitation, 1990-94; chief environ. officer Port Authority of N.Y. and N.J., N.Y.C., 1994-99; exec. dir. N.Y. League of Conservation Voters, N.Y.C., 1999—. Contbr. articles to Social Rsch., Am. Jour. Sociology, Sociol. Quar. NEH fellow, 1979-80. Mem. Mcpl. Waste Mgmt. Assn. (exec. com. 1992-93). Office: NY League Conservation Voters 130 William St Rm 801 New York NY 10038-3806

BYTH, SIMON HAROLD, marketing analyst, consultant; b. Brisbone, Queensland, Australia, July 15, 1958; s. Leonard Lindsay and Pauline (Pope) B.; m. Kerrie Anne Lee, Feb. 10, 1990; children: Rosemary Christine, Stephen Murray. BA (hons), Australian Nat. U., Canberra, 1987; MBA, Royal Melbourne Inst. Tech., Australia, 1990. Sales and mktg. mgr. Pergamon Press Australia, Sydney, 1984-87; mktg. mgr. Vision Control Australia, Melbourne, 1987-90, Mintel Australia, Melbourne, 1990-94; mng. dir. Bus. Info. Focus Pty Ltd., Melbourne, 1994—.

BYUL-BYUL, POLAD, government official; b. Baku, Azerbaijan, 1945. Grad., Azerbaijan Nat. Conservatory, 1968. Composer, singer Azerbaijan folk music and pop music; dir., artistic mgr. Nat. Philharmonic; min. culture Govt. of Azerbaijan, Baku, 1988—; rep. of Azerbaijan culture worldwide. Named Honored Artist of Azerbaijan, 1973, Azerbaijan People's Artist, 1982, many other awards. Office: Ministry of Culture, Azadlyt Meidany 1, 370016 Baku Azerbaijan*

BYUN, JOON HYUNG, mechanical engineer, researcher; b. Pusan, Korea, Mar. 9, 1957; s. Dong Hae and Bo Saeng (Jung) B.; m. Jung Soon Jung, Dec. 26, 1987; 1 child, Deborah. BS, Hanyang U., Seoul, 1980; MS, Korea Advanced Inst. Sci. and Tech., Seoul, 1982; PhD, U. Del., 1992. Rschr. Korea Inst. Sci. and Tech., Seoul, 1982-86; rsch. asst. U. Del., Newark, 1987-92, postdoctoral fellow, 1992-93; prin. rschr. Korea Inst. Machinery and Materials, Changwon, Korea, 1993—. Mem. Am. Soc. for Composites, Soc. Mfg. Engrs., Korean Soc. for Mech. Engrs., Korean Soc. for Composite Materials. Achievements include research on process, microstructure and performance relationships of three-dimensional textile composite materials; development of automated 2-step and multi-step braiding machines; process and mechanical models of three-dimensional textile composites, Processing of thermoplastic composites. Office: Korea Inst Machinery/Materials, 66 Sangnam-Dong, 641-010 Changwon Republic of Korea

CAAN, ALBERT WOODBURN, psychologist; b. N.Y.C., Apr. 8, 1954; arrived in Eng., 1966; s. Albert Joseph Zijdenstad and Esther Sutherland (Terpenning) C. BA, Cambridge (Eng.) U., 1975, MA, 1979; PhD, Oxford U., 1983. Rsch. asst. Exptl. Psychology, Oxford, Eng., 1978-81; lectr. Royal London Hosp., London, 1983-86; rsch. fellow Sch. of Pharmacy, London, 1987-88; lectr. (rsch. and evaluation) St. George's Hosp., London, 1988-91; rsch. coord. Bethlem Royal and Maudsley Hosps., London, 1991-94; head of rsch. and devel. Lifespan Healthcare, Cambridge, Eng., 1994-99; pub. health specialist in R&D Barking and Havering Health Authority, U. Coll. London, 2000—; hon. lectr. Royal London Hosp., 1989—, ICD-10 PHC project Inst. of Psychiatry, London, 1992—; cons. on drug rsch. Dept. Health, Malta, 1991-92; regional coord. psychiat. audit Anglia & Oxford Regional Health Authority, Cambridge, 1994-95, regional coord. primary care rsch., 1995-99; conf. organizer Mental Health, 1991, 92, 93. Contbr. articles to profl. jours.; creator of plays and skits for hosps. and colls. Mem. various coms. Psychiat. Rsch. Trust, Nat. Schizophrenia Fellowship, Motor Neurone Disease Assn., Help in Need Assn., London. Recipient award for rsch. in gen. practice Syntex, Croydon, Eng., 1991. Mem. Soc. for Study of Addiction, Brain Rsch. Assn., Brit. Soc. for Mental Health and Deafness (founding mem.), Royal Coll. of Psychiatrists Philosophy Group, Acad. Learned Socs. for the Social Scis. (academician 2000). Avocations: writing plays and poetry, painting seascapes, church history. Office: Barking & Havering Health, The Clock House East St, Barking IG11 8EY, England

CABADA, ALBERTO, mathematics educator; b. Sarria, Spain, July 4, 1966; s. Eliseo Cabada and Dolores Fernandez; m. Marina Armada, Aug. 14, 1989. Degree in math., U. Santiago, Spain, 1989, D of Math., 1992. Assoc. prof. math. U. Santiago, 1989-92, asst. prof., 1992-94, prof., 1994—. Contbr. articles to profl. jours. Mem. Internat. Fedn. Nonlinear Analysts. Office: Dept Analise Math, U Santiago, 15706 Santiago Spain

CABAHUG, SUSANA BARING, educational administrator, consultant; b. Lapulapu, Cebu, The Philippines, Aug. 11, 1935; d. Isidro Remulta Baring and Casimira Ceniza (Suico) C.; m. Vicente Alinsug Cabahug, Dec. 23, 1961; children: Omar, Waldo, Jason, Gladys. BS in Edn., U. Visayas, Cebu City, Philippines, 1956, MA in Edn., 1959, AB, 1963; PhD in Edn., U. San Carlos, Cebu City, 1972. Career exec. svc. officer. Secondary sch. tchr. U. Visayas, 1956-59, coll. instr., 1959-61, prof. Grad. Sch., 1961-76, dean Coll. Liberal Arts., 1972-73, deal Coll. Commerce., 1975-76; prof., chmn. grad. edn. U. San Carlos, 1978-83; asst. schs. divsn. supt. Divsn. of Mandaue City, Philippines, 1976-85, schs. divsn. supt., 1985-86, 86-90; asst. regional dir. Dept. Edn., Culture and Sports, Cebu City and Davao City, Philippines, 1991-94; regional dir. Dept. Edn., Culture and Sports, Davao City, 1995—. Editor Philippine Guidance and Pers. Jour., 1985-90, Philippine Assn. Schs. Supts. Jour., 1985-86. Pres. Girl Scouts of the Philippines, Cebu City, 1994-95; pres. Cultural, Hist., Edn., Sports and Tourism Found., Mandaue City, 1993-94; bd. dirs. Philippine Nat. Red Cross, Davao City, 1995-97. Named One of Ten Outstanding Citizens of Mandaue City, 1987, Woman of Achievement in Edn., Women In Travel, 1994. Mem. Assn. Regional Execs. of Nat. Agys. (dir.), Assn. DECS Dirs., Phi Delta Kappa. Roman Catholic. Avocations: newswriting, orchid growing, reading, computer. Home: Abellana St, Pagsabungan 6014 Mandaue City Philippines Office: Dept Edn Culture and Sports, Torres St, 8000 Davao City Philippines

CABALLERO, FRANCISCO MANUEL, aerospace engineer; b. Melilla, Spain, Nov. 27, 1943; s. Francisco Caballero and Ana Requena; m. Maria Paz Tocino, Apr. 8, 1978; children: Barbara, Alicia. Aeronaut. Engr., U. Polit., Madrid, 1976, D Aero. Engring., 1993. Range safety engr. INTA, Huelva, Spain, 1977-90, head ops. unit, 1990-94, head control/flight safety, 1994-97, head ops. control area, 1997-98; ground segment engr., dept. space programs and sys. INTA Hdqrs., Madrid, 1998—; tech. adviser steering com. for Transmediterranean Balloons, Italy, France, Spain, 1982—, sec. steering com., 1995—. Contbr. to profl. publ. Mem. AIAA, Spanish Aeronaut. Engrs. Assn. Office: INTA/Spanish Inst Aero Rsch, Hdqrs 28850 Torrejon Ardoz, Madrid Spain

CABALQUINTO, LUIS CARRAZCAL, freelance writer; b. Magarao, Camarines Sur, Philippines, Jan. 31, 1935; came to U.S., 1968; s. Geminiano and Irene (Carrazcal) C. BA in Journalism, U. Philippines, 1967; postgrad., Cornell U., 1968-71, NYU, 1982-84. Editor Office Philippine Pres., Manila, 1960-66; editor, instr. U. Phillipines, Los Baños, 1966-75; customer svc. rep. Pfizer Inc., N.Y.C., 1980-90; pvt. practice N.Y.C., 1990—. Author: The Dog-eater and Other Poems, 1989, The Ibalon Collection, 1991, Dreamwanderer, 1992. Recipient Dylan Thomas Poetry award New Sch. Social Rsch., 1979, Poetry prize Acad. Am. Poets, 1985, fiction prize Philippine Graphic Mag., 1992; fellow N.Y. Found. Arts, 1989. Mem. Poetry Soc. Am., Poets Writers, Writers Cmty., Am. PEN. Avocations: fishing, movies, gardening, sports, travel. Home and Office: 1 Stuyvesant Oval New York NY 10009-2101

CABAÑAS BRAVO, MIGUEL, art historian, educator; b. Madrid, Feb. 19, 1963; s. Godofredo and Alfonsa (Bravo) C.; m. Teresa Engenios, Dec. 18, 1993; children: Inés, Gloria. Lic., U. Complutense, Madrid, 1987, D in Art History, 1991. Postdoctoral grantee CONACYT-UNAM, Mexico City, 1992-93, CCHNCCE-NYU, 1993; assoc. prof. art history U. Autónoma, Madrid, 1995-96; assoc. prof. U. Complutense, Madrid, 1996-98; predoctoral grantee Higher Ctr. Sci. Rsch., Madrid, 1988-91, investigator, 1993-96; sci. titular Instituto de Historia, Madrid, 1998—. Author: El Ocaso de la Política Artística Americanista, 1995, Artistas Contra Fanco, 1996, Política Artística del Franquismo, 1996; contbr. articles to prof. publs. Fellow Madrid Assn. Críticos de Arte, Assn. para el Estudio de los Exilios, Assn. Amigos Museo Ruiz de Luna. Office: CSIC Instituto de Historia, Duque de Medinaceli 6, E-28014 Madrid Spain

CABATIC, ED, accountant; b. The Philippines, Nov. 5, 1955; came to U.S., 1985; s. Cirilo R. and Catalina C. Cabatic; m. Janene Lynette Eighmey, Sept. 14, 1966; 1 child, Tyler Howard. BSBA in Acctg., U. of the East, The Philippines, 1976; M Profl. Acctg., Strayer U., 1989. Comptr. Strayer U., Washington, 1985-94; audit mgr. Mynit & Buntua CPAs, Arlington, Va., 1994-97; revenue control mgr. Colonial Parking-GMU, Fairfax, Va., 1997-98; sr. acct. Am. Assn. Marriage and Family Therapy, Washington, 1998—. Mem. Am. Soc. Assn. Execs., Washington Assn. Fin. Mgmt. Roundtable. Avocations: reading, basketball, golf, table tennis, bowling. E-mail: ccabatic@aamft.org. Home: 6401 Cranston Ln Fredericksburg VA 22407-8374 Office: AAMFT 1133 15th St NW Ste 300 Washington DC 20005-2710

CABEZA, FRANK D., insurance executive; b. Camaguey, Cuba, Apr. 16, 1932; came to U.S., 1962; s. Francisco and Maria Cabeza; m. Victoria M. Cabeza, Nov. 14, 1976; children: Ana Q. Bunnasar, Vicky. Degree in bus., U. Havana, 1954. Cert. estate planner Liberty Inst., 1999—. Mem. Rotary (pres. Miami Granada chpt. 1999—). Democrat. Roman Catholic. Address: 1143 Alhambra Cir Miami FL 33134-3529

CABEZA, JAVIER ANGEL, chemistry educator; b. Soria, Castilla, Spain, July 18, 1958; s. Eleuterio C. and Segunda De Marco; m. Ana Beatriz Antuña, Oct. 5, 1996. BSc in Chemistry, U. Zaragoza, Spain, 1980, PhD in Chemistry, 1983. Rsch. fellow U. Sheffield, Eng., 1983-85, U. Zaragoza, Spain, 1985-87; lectr. in chemistry U. Oviedo, Spain, 1987—; dir. rsch. U. Oviedo, 1990—. Contbr. numerous rsch. articles to profl. jours. including Inorganic Chemistry, Organometallics, Jour. of Organometallic Chemistry, Jour. Chem. Soc. Mem. Royal Soc. Chem. (Eng.), Spanish Chem. Soc., Am. Chem. Soc. Avocations: sailing, trekking, mountain climbing. Office: U Oviedo Facultad Quimica, Inst Quimica Organometalica, E-33071 Oviedo Asturias, Spain

CABEZA, MARISA, reproductive biochemist, educator; b. Mexico City, Sept. 26, 1949; d. Luis and Ernestina Cabeza; m. Jose Luis Duarte, Jan. 20, 1973; children: Jose, Juan. Degree in biology, Univ. Nacional Autonoma de Mexico, 1973, MSc in Physiology of Reproduction, 1974, MSc in Biomed. Scis., 1991, PhD, 1995. Assoc. prof. chemistry U. Nacional Autónoma de Mexico, 1972-75; from assoc. prof. to prof. dept. biol. sys. U. Autónoma Metropolitana, Mexico City, 1976—; mem. Dictamination Com. for Acad. Pers., 1985-96; chief Pharmacokinetic and Pharmacodinamic Investigation Area, 1998. Author: Hormones and Reproduction, 1990; patentee in field; contbr. articles to profl. jours. Recipient award best sci. article published Mex. Pharm. Assn., 1984. Mem. AAAS, Mex. Assn. Clin. Biochemistry, Western Pharmacology Soc. Avocations: reading, writing, painting. Fax: 52-5 5724-52-37. E-mail: marisa@cueyatl.uam.mx. Office: U Autonoma Met Dept Biol Sy, Calzada del Hueso #1100, Mexico City 04860, Mexico

CABEZAS, HERIBERTO, chemical engineer, researcher; b. La Esperanza, Las Villas, Cuba; s. Heriberto and Ana Rosa C.; m. Isaura Vazquez. BSChemE, N.J. Inst. Tech., Newark, 1980; MSChemE, U. Fla., 1981, PhD in Chem. Engring., 1985. Rsch. asst. U. Fla., Gainesville, 1980-85; asst. prof. chem. engring. U. Ariz., 1985-93; leader simulation and design team, sustainable tech. divsn. EPA Nat. Risk Mgmt. Rsch. Lab., Cin., 1994-2000; acting chief sustainable environ. br. sustainable tech. div. EPA Nat. Risk Mmgt. Rsch. Lab., Cin., 2000—; cons. Nat. Inst. Stds. and Tech., Gaithersburg, Md., 1986-93, rschr. biotech. divsn., 1993-94. Contbr. articles in profl. jours. Mem. AIChE, Am. Chem. Soc., Tau Beta Pi, Omega Chi Epsilon. Roman Catholic. Achievements include development of Paris II solvent design software, waste reduction algorithm for chemical process design. Office: US EPA 26 W Martin Luther King Dr Cincinnati OH 45268-0001

CABIBBO, NICOLA, scientific academy executive, physicist, educator; b. Rome, Apr. 30, 1935. Degree in physics, La Sapienza U. Rome. Rschr. INFN Frascati Nat. Labs.-CERN, Lawrence Radiation Lab., Berkeley, Calif., 1965-66; prof. theoretical physics U. L'Aquila, 1966-82, La Sapienza U. Rome, 1982; prof. theoretical physics faculty math., physics Vergata U., Rome, 1993—; pres. Pontificia Acad. Scientiarum, Vatican City, Tor Vergata U. Rome, 1983-93; chmn. Istituto Nazionale di Fisica Nucleare, 1983; chmn. Italian Nat. Agy. New Technologies, Energy and Environ. Recipient award Pres. Italian Republic, 1979, Sakurai prize Am. Phys. Soc., 1989, Spl. prize for sci. rsch. Pres. Coun. Mins., 1989, European Phys. Soc. prize, 1991. Office: U Rome Tor Vergata Physics, Via Ricerca Scientifica 16, I-00133 Rome Italy*

CABLE, RICHARD CHARLES, education administrator, educator, consultant; b. Waterbury, Conn., Aug. 21, 1943; s. Harry Arthur and Eunice Lavina (Smith) C.; m. Nancy Jayne Dittbrenner, Aug. 22, 1976; children: Jared W., Jordan D.; stepchildren: Sigrid B. Stang Beaton, Jonathan A. Stang. BS, Ctrl. Conn. State U., 1965, MS, 1972; cert. advanced grad. studies, Fairfield U., 1981. Cert. profl. educator State Conn., aerobics and fitness instr. Aerobics Fitness Assn. of Am., pers. trainer, Am. Coun. on Exercise. Tchr. Sharon (Conn.) Schs., 1965-68, Tarsus Amerikan Koleji, Turkey, 1968-71, New Britain (Conn.) Schs., 1972-83, Nangatuck Valley Cmty. Tech. Coll., 1972—, Litchfield (Conn.) Schs., 1983-84; adminstr. Waterbury (Conn.) Pub. Schs., 1985-99; prof. U. New Haven, West Haven, 1994—, Teikyo Post U., Waterbury, 1997—; workshop presenter Nat. Youth at Risk Conf., Savannah, Ga., Nat. Parent Coalition Confs., Kansas City, Mo., Charlotte, N.C., Balt., others; cons. in field. Contbr. articles to profl. jours. Mem. Conn. Assn. Supervision and Curriculum Devel., Conn. Assn. for Gifted, Theta Alpha Phi. Democrat. Avocations: theatre, skiing, mountain and road biking, backpacking, aerobics. Home: 68 Wilson Ave Apt 423 Torrington CT 06790-6447

CABO MONTES DE OCA, ALEJANDRO, physicist; b. Lahabana, Cuba, Sept. 19, 1947; s. Juan Luis Cabo and Maria Julia Montes de Oca; m. Milagros Bizet; children: Nana Geraldine, Alejandro. BS in Physics, Havana U., 1970; PhD, Lebedev Physical Inst., Moscow, 1983. Prof. physics Havana U., 1970-76; rschr. Inst. Cybernetics Maths. and Physics, Havana, 1977-79, sr. rschr., 1984-2000; vis. rschr. Lebedev Phys. Inst., 1980-83; vis. prof. Inst. Physics U. Guanajuato, Leon, Mexico, 1996-98; fellow CERN, Geneva, Switzerland, 1992; affiliate rschr. Ctr. Theoretical Studies of Phys. Sys., Clark Atlanta U., 1999—. contbr. articles to profl. jours. Recipient The Ann. Cuban Acad. of Sci. award, 1990, 98. Sr. mem. Internat. Ctr. Theoretical Physics, 1997—. Avocations: movies, drawing. Home: Calle 5 e/2 y 4 #551 Apt 3, Vedado Havana Cuba Office: Inst Cybernetics Math/Phys, Calle E #309 e/13 y 15, Vedado Havana Cuba

CABOT, HUGH, III, painter, sculptor; b. Boston, Mar. 22, 1930; s. Hugh and Louise (Melanson) C.; m. Olivia P. Taylor, Sept. 8, 1967; student Boston Museum, 1948, Ashmolean Mus., Oxford, Eng., 1960, Coll. Ams., Mexico City, 1956, San Carlos Acad., Mexico City. Portrait, landscape painter; sculptor in bronze; one-man shows: U.S. Navy Hist. and Recreation Dept., U.S. Navy Art Gallery, The Pentagon, Nat. War Mus., Washington, La Muse de la Marine, Paris; group shows include: Tex. Tri-state, 1969 (1st, 2d, 3d prizes), Starmont Vail Med. Ctr. Topeka, Kans., Tucson Med. Ctr. Ariz., Harwood Found. Taos, N.Mex., Washburn U. Topeka, Kans., U. Ariz. Tucson, Ariz. Served as ofcl. artist USN, Korean War. Named Artist of Yr., Scottsdale, Ariz., 1978, 30th ann. Clubs: Salmagundi (N.Y.C.). Author, illustrator: Korea I (Globe).

CABOT, LEWIS PICKERING, manufacturing company executive, art consultant; b. Sept. 6, 1937; s. John Moors and Elizabeth (Lewis) C.; m. Judith Ogden, July 1, 1960 (div. 1974); children: Elizabeth Lewis, Edward Ogden, Timothy Pickering; m. Susan Knight, July 15, 1978; children: James Eliot, Alexander Lee. AB, Harvard U., 1961, MBA, 1964. Trainee F.S. Moseley & Co., Boston, 1961-62; analyst John P. Chase, Inc., Boston, 1964-68; prin. Gardner & Preston Moss, Boston, 1968-73; chmn., pres. Artcounsel, Inc., Portland, Maine, 1973—; chmn., CEO Southworth Internat. Group, Inc., Portland, Maine, 1977—; pres. ZY-AX Realty, Portland, Maine, 1977—; chmn. Shellback Corp., 1984-93; pres., chmn. Maine Art Leasing, 1988—; bd. dirs. Material Handling Roundtable; trustee NE Pooled Common Fund, Princeton, N.J., 1972-94. Trustee, pres. Soc. Arts and Crafts, Boston, 1962-66; trustee Phila. Maritime Mus., 1963-68, Mus. Fine Arts, Boston, 1966-90, Mus. Am. Folk Art, N.Y.C., 1973-77, Maine Coll. Art, 1982-91, Portland (Maine) Mus. Art, 1994—, Storm King Art Ctr., Mountainville, N.Y., 1961-72, Maine Maritime Mus., 1997—. Mem. com. Harvard U. Art Mus., Cambridge, Mass., 1982-88; bd. dirs. Maine State Music Theater, 1996—. Mem. Met. Club (Washington), Somerset Club (Boston), N.Y. Yacht Club (N.Y.C.), Portland Yacht Club. Office: Southworth Internat Group 11 Gray Rd Falmouth ME 04105-2027

CABRAL, ALFREDO LOPES, ambassador; b. Dakar, Senegal, 1946; married. Chief of cabinet Guinea-Bissau Fgn. Ministry, 1973-75, dir. Afro-Asian divsn., 1975-79; 1st counsellor Permanent Mission to UN, N.Y.C., 1979-83, permanent rep. to UN, 1986-90, 96—; amb. to Algeria and M.E., 1983-86; amb. to U.S. Embassy of Guinea-Bissau, Washington, 1990-96. Office: Permanent Mission Republic of Guinea-Bissau to UN 211 East 43d St Rm 704 New York NY 10017*

CABRERA, ARTURO, diplomat; b. Quito, Ecuador, Aug. 9, 1967; s. Arturo Efrén Cabrera and Elba Hidalgo. Diploma, Diplomatic Acad. Ecuador, Quito, 1992; JD, Cath. U., Quito, 1995; M in Pub. Adminstrn. and Govt., Harvard U., 1999. Cert. diplomacy, law and pub. adminstrn. Fgn. svc. officer Ministry Fgn. Affairs Ecuador, Quito, 1988-93; alt. rep. Mission Ecuador to the O.A.S., Washington, 1993-95; cónsul of Ecuador Gen. Consulate Ecuador, Washington, 1995-96; cultural and polit. attache Embassy of Ecuador in Washington, 1996-98; chief of staff Undersecretariat Adminstrv. Affairs, Ministry Fgn. Affairs, Quito, 1999—; vis. fellow U. Cambridge, Eng., 1993; lectr., rschr. Cath. U., Quito, 1999—; lectr. Nat. Acad. War, Quito, 1999—; conf. presenter. Edward Mason fellow Kennedy Sch. Govt., Harvard U., 1999. Mem. Ecuadorian Bar Assn., The Hague Acad. Internat. Law Alumni Assn. Avocations: fencing, music. E-mail: arturocabrera@hotmail.com.

CABRERA, EDUARDO M., diversified financial services company executive; b. Matanza, Cuba, Nov. 28, 1959; came to U.S., 1962; s. Eddy and Isa C.; m. Maria Luisa, June 13, 1983; children: Melissa, Audrey, Edward, William. BS in Engring. Econs., U. Fla., 1983; MBA, Harvard U., 1987. Cert. fin. analyst, profl. engr. Mfg. mgr. GE, Tamaulipas, Mex., 1983-84; plant mgr. GE, Burlingtin, Vt., 1984-85; equity analyst Raymond James & Assocs., St. Petersburg, Fla., 1987-89; environ. svc. equity analyst Painewebber, Houston, 1989-90; CEO Atlas Waste Systems, Houston, 1990-91; Mex. analyst HSBC/James Capel, N.Y.C., 1991-92; mgr. L.Am. rsch. Merrill Lynch, N.Y.C., 1992—; instl. investor All-American Rsch. Team, 1992-98; mem. adv. bd. World Trade Exec., Inc., Concord, Mass., 1993—. Pres. PTA, Houston, 1990, Cir. Rd. Assn., Scarsdale, N.Y., 1996. Recipient #1 Ranked Strategist Greenwich Survey, 1997. Mem. Kiwanis, Scarsdale Sports Assn. Avocations: adventure racing, sailing, triatholon. Home: 10 School Ln Scarsdale NY 10583-5608

CABRERA, ELIZABETH FRASER, educator, consultant; b. Fayetteville, N.C., July 27, 1968; d. Lewis Keith and Mary Lynn (McBryde) Fraser; m. Angel Cabrera, Mar. 19, 1994; children: Alex, Emily. BA, Rhodes Coll., Memphis, 1990; MS, Ga. Inst. Tech., 1993, PhD, 1995. Prof. Universidad Carlos III, Madrid, 1995—. Contbr. articles to profl. jours. Mem. APA, Acad. Mgmt. Assn., Soc. Indsl. and Orgnl. Psychology. Office: Econom Empresa/U Carlos III, c/Madrid 126, 28093 Getate, Madrid Spain

CABRERA, KATHERINE E., health facility administrator; b. Bklyn., Oct. 22, 1949; d. Peter Thomas and Diana Beatrice C. AAS, N.Y.C. C.C., Bklyn., 1969; BA, Bklyn. Coll., 1988; MPH, Hunter Coll., 1993. Asst. to dir. N.Y. Meth. Hosp., Bklyn., 1969-80, adminstr. coord., 1980-90; v.p. Radiation Therapists Assocs. PC, Bklyn., 1990—. Contbr. article to profl. jour. Office: Radiation Therapists Assoc PC 506 6th St Brooklyn NY 11215-3609

CABRERA, LUIZ CARLOS DE QUEIRÓS, executive search consultant; b. Sao Paulo, Mar. 5, 1944; s. Luiz da Silva and Celina Mascarenhas (Queirós) C.; m. Maria Christina Pereira da Rosa, June 28, 1969; children: Christiano, Luciana, Alexandre. Degree in metall. engring., Escola de Engring. Mauá, Sao Paulo, 1967; BBA, Sao Paulo Bus. Sch.-FGV, 1973; ext., U. So. Calif., 1976. Engr. Estrela Toys Mfg., Sao Paulo, 1969; asst. to cons. Execs. S.A., Sao Paulo, 1971-75; ptnr. PMC Amrop Internat., Sao Paulo, 1975—; tchr. Fundação Getulio Vargas, Sao Paulo, 1980—; bd. dirs. Amrop Internat. Author: (book) Transição 2000, 1993, (video) Human Resources Management, 1990. Home: Rua 31 de Março 440, 05657-030 Sao Paulo Brazil Office: PMC Amrop Internat, Rua do Rocio 220 conj 82, 04552000 Sao Paulo Brazil

CABRERA-FEBOLA, WALTER, ecologist, natural structuralist; b. Lima, Peru, Sept. 18, 1945; s. Isaias Cabrera and Angelica Febola. BS, U. San Marcos, 1978; postgrad., U. Wash., 1987-89. Practitioner Imarpe, Lima, Peru, 1977-78; tchg. asst. U. San Marcos, Lima, 1976-80; biologist Imarpe, 1980-81; asst. prof. U. San Marcos, 1982—. Bd. editor Jour. Biol. Systems, 1993; author papers in field and 10 books of poems. Grantee UNESCO, 1983, Br. Coun., 1986, OAS, 1987-89, others. Mem. Soc. Math. Biology, Ecol. Soc. Am., Am. Soc. Naturalists, Brit. Ecol. Soc., Assn. Sci. Study of Consciousnes, Latin Am. Assn. Biomath., British Soc. for the Philosophy of Sci. Avocations: soccer, music, poetry. Office: U San Marcos, Apt 170090 Oficina 29, Lima 17, Peru

CABRERA-GOMEZ, JOSE ANTONIO, neurologist researcher; b. Sagua la Grande, Cuba, Jan. 29, 1950; s. Gregorio Urbano and Onelia Antonia (Gómez) C.; m. Yolanda Eugenia Nuñez, Dec. 2, 1972 (div. 1985); children: Juan Cristóbal, José Antonio, Anelis, Analis. MD, Havana (Cuba) U., 1971; Internship Neurology, Inst. of Neurology, Havana, Cuba, 1972; aux. prof. neurology, 1999, PhD, 2000. Cert. by the Clin. Neurology Bd., 1978, 87. Postgrad. med. dr. Palmira Policlinica, Palmira, Cuba, 1972-73; MD Cienfuegos (Cuba) Hosp., 1973-74; resident Villa Clara (Cuba) Hosp., 1974-75, Inst. Neurology, Havana, Cuba, 1975-78; neurologist Cienfuegos (Cuba) Hosp., 1979—; dir. Palmira Policlinica, Palmira, 1972-73; vice-dir. Cienfuegos (Cuba) Hosp., 1973-74, vice dir. chief neurological svc., 1979—; mem. exec. com. Latin Am. Com. for Treatment and Rsch. in Multiple Sclerosis, 1999. Co-author: (book) Temas de Geronto-Geriatria, 1990 (First award 1990); inventor: Biotherapy, 1994 (First award 1994), Revista Finlay, 1993 (First Prize 1993); contbr. articles to profl. jours. Mem. Cuban Com. Against Nuclear War, 1987—. Recipient Best Med. Sci. Rsch. First award, 1982, 1995, 1st award Provincial Ann. prize, 1993, 94, 95, 96, 97, 98, 99, 1st award Best Sci. Work, 1993, 94, 95, 96, 98, 99, Outstanding prize VII Forum Ciencia y TÉcnica, 1994, 1st Del. prize for poster 4th Congress of European Fedn. of Neurol. Socs., 1999. Fellow Am. Acad. Neurology (corr.); mem. Internat. Brain Rsch. Orgn., Multiple Sclerosis Group of Cuba, Alzheimer's Nat. Group, Internat. League Against Epilepsy (Cuban chpt. 1993), Cuban Soc. Neurosciences Havana, Am. Acad. Neurology, World Fedn. Neurology, European Fedn. Neurol. Socs., Consortium of Multiple Sclerosis Ctrs., Nat. Group Neurology Cuba (pres. demyelinating sect. 1999). Achievements include research in clinical trials with interferons, immunoglobulins in Multiple Sclerosis, Alzheimer's disease and schizophrenia, researches in epidemiological, genetical, clinical trials, natural history of multiple sclerosis. Avocations: basketball, baseball. Fax: 53-432-451375/451392. E-mail: cabrera@jagua.cfg.sld.cu. Home: Edif 25 Apart 11 Calle 101, %72y74, 55100 Cienfuegos Cuba Office: Servicio de Neurologia, Hosp. Gustavo Aldereguia, Avenida 5 de Septiembre, 55100 Cienfuegos Cuba

CABRIJAN, TOMISLAV VIKTOR, internist, endocrinologist, educator; b. Oct. 22, 1934; s. Viktor and Zora (Pelčić) C.; m. Ivanka Tušek, Mar. 30, 1962; children: Zeljko, Snježana. MD, U. Zagreb, Croatia, 1959; Internal Medicine specialist, U. Zagreb Med. Clinic, Croatia, 1968; PhD, U. Zagreb, Croatia, 1975, full prof. Internal Medicine, 1987. Ward internist, endocrinologist Sisters of Mercy U. Hosp., Zagreb, 1968-70, head of ctr. for diabetes, dept. endocrinology, 1970-90, head dept. endocrinology, diabetes and metabolic diseases, 1990—; consulting endocrinologist and diabetes expert, Ministry of Sci. and Tech., Zagreb, Croatia, 1987—; acting dir. Sisters of Mercy Univ. Hosp., Zagreb, Croatia, 1990. Editor: (book) Obesity and Apnea Syndrome, 1992, (translation) Taking Care of Your Diabetes, 1995, Urgent States in Endocrinology, 1996; contbr. articles to profl. jours. including: Jour. of Pathology, Jour. Cancer Rsch. and Clin Oncology, Progress in Cancer and Therapy, Anticancer Rsch. Recipient yearly award for sci. Parliament of Republic of Croatia, 1999, 2000; fellow Alexander Von Humboldt Found., Bonn, Germany, 1972, 75, 78, 82, 89. Mem. Acad. Med. Scis. (Croatia chpt.), German Diabetes Assn., European Assn. Study Diabetes, Am. Endocrine Soc. Roman Catholic. Avocations: swimming, skiing. Home: Petrova 110, 10 000 Zagreb Croatia Office: Sisters of Mercy Univ Hosp, Vinogradska Str 29, 10 000 Zagreb Croatia

CABRISAS RUIZ, RICARDO, Cuban government official; b. Jan. 21, 1937. BA in Social Scis. Amb. to Japan Cuban Embassy, Tokyo, 1971-73; vice min. fgn. trade Govt. of Cuba, Havana, 1973-80, min. of fgn. trade, from 1980, now min. without portfolio. Communist. Office: Plaza de la Revolacion, Havana Cuba*

CABROL, CHRISTIAN EMILE, cardiologist; b. Chezy sur Marne, Aisne, France, Sept. 16, 1925; s. Roger and Lucienne (Gratiot) C. MD, Paris Sch. Medicine, 1954. Intern, resident, surgeon Parisian Hosp., 1948-67; chief outpatient surg. clinic Hosp. La Pitie, Paris, 1967-72, chief dept. noma thoracic surgery, 1972—; dir. Sch. Surgery Paris, 1973-93; pres. France Transplant, 1988-94. Editor: Don De Soi, 1996, Parole De Medecin, 1992, Manger Vrai, 1997, Histoire de Coeur, 1999; contbr. articles to profl. jours. Pres. coun. Nat. Alimentation, 1994-99; mem. European Parliament, 1996-99; dep. mayor, Paris. Recipient Gruntzig award European Soc. Cardiology, 1989, Claude Bernard award De La Ville, 1986, Grimbaum prize Inst. de France, 1956, Litteraire prize Acad. France, 1996; named Officier e Legion of Honor, Ordre du Merite. Mem. Internat. Soc. Cardiovascular Surgery, Internat. Soc. Heart Transplantation (pres. 1986), Am. Assn. Thoracic and Cardiovascular Surgery, Acad. Nat. de Medecine. Roman Catholic. Avocations: bicycling, sailing. Office: Hosp La Pitie, 87 B De L'Hospital, 75013 Paris France

CACCAMISE, GENEVRA LOUISE BALL (MRS. ALFRED E. CACCAMISE), retired librarian; b. July 22, 1934; d. Herbert Oscar and Genevra (Green) Ball; m. Alfred E. Caccamise, July 7, 1974. BA, Stetson U., 1956; MLS, Syracuse U., 1967. Tchr. grammar sch. Sanford, Fla., 1956-57; tchr. elem. sch. Longwood, Fla., 1957-58; tchr., libr. Enterprise (Fla.) Sch., 1958-63; libr. media specialist Boston Ave. Sch., DeLand, Fla., 1963-83; head media specialist Blue Lake Sch., DeLand, 1983-87; ret., 1987. Author: Volusia County manual Instructing the Library Assistant, 1965, Echoes of Yesterday: A History of the DeLand Area Public Library, 1912-1995, 1995, A Quest for Beauty: A History of the Garden Club of DeLand, Florida, 1927-97, 1997. Charter mem. West Volusia Meml. Hosp. Aux., DeLand, 1962-81; leader Girl Scouts U.S., 1955-56; area dir. Fla. Edn. Assn., Volusia County, 1963-65; bd. dirs. Alhambra Villas Home Owners Assn., 1972-75; trustee DeLand Pub. Libr., 1977-86, sec., 1978-80, v.p., 1980-82, pres., 1982-84; v.p. Friends of DeLand Pub. Libr., 1987-88, 98—, bd. dirs., 1987—, pres., 1989-90, 95-97, newsletter editor 1992-95, 99—; charter mem. Guild of the DeLand Mus. Art, 1988—, v.p., 1990, pres., 1991-92, co-rec. sec., 1997-98, mus. bd. dirs., 1991-95; co-orgn. chmn. Friends DeLand Mus. Art, 1993. Mem. AAUW (2d v.p. chpt. 1965-67, rec. sec. 1961-65, 78-80, pres. 1980-82, parliamentarian 1982-84), Assn. Childhood Edn. (1st v.p. 1965-66, corr. sec. 1963-65), DAR (chpt. registrar 1969-80, asst. chief page Continental Congress, Washington 1962-65), Fla. Libr. Assn., Bus. and Profl. Women's Club (corr. sec. DeLand 1968-71, 2d v.p. 1969-70), Stetson U. Alumni Assn. (class chmn. for ann. fund dr. 1968), Volusia County Assn. Media in Edn. (treas. 1977), Volusia County Ret. Educators Assn. (pres. Unit II 1988-90, scholarship chmn. 1992-95), Soc. of Mayflower Descendants (lt. gov. Francis Cook Colony 1988-90), Pilgrim John Howland Soc., Colonial Dames XVII Century, Magna Carta Dames, Nat. Soc. New Eng. Women (v.p. Daytona Beach Colony 1990-91), Nat. League Am. Pen Women (corr. sec. 1996-98, 2000—, pres. 1998-2000), Hibiscus Garden Cir. (treas. 1988-89, v.p. 1990-93, 96-97, pres. 1997-99), Nat. Soc. U.S. Daus. of 1812 (rec. sec. Peacock chpt. 1989-90), West Volusia Hist. Soc. (sec. 1996, libr. 1993—, v.p. 2000—, bd. dirs.), Fla. Hist. Soc., DeLand Garden Club (corr. sec. 1993-95, editor newsletter 1993-95, v.p. 1997-99), Delta Kappa Gamma (pres. Beta Psi chpt. 1982-84, treas. 2000—). Address: PO Box 241 Deland FL 32721-0241

CACCIARI, MASSIMO, philosophy and aesthetics educator; b. Venice, Italy, June 5, 1944; s. Pietro and Gilda (Momo) C. Laurea, U. Padua, Italy, 1967. Asst. U. Padua, 1967-71; assoc. prof. Inst. of Architecture, Venice, 1971-85; prof. aesthetics U. Venice, 1985—; mem. European Parliament, Brussels, Belgium. Author: Krisis, 1976, Icone della Legge, 1985, l'Angelo Necessario, 1986, Dell Inizio, 1990, Geo-Filosofia Dell' Europa, 1994, L'Arcipelago, 1997. Dep., Parliament, Rome, 1976-83; mayor Municipality of Venice, 1993-2000. Home: S Polo 2872, 30125 Venice Italy Office: Municipality Rialto, 30100 Venice Italy

CACCIAVILLAN, AGOSTINO, archbishop; b. Vicenza, Italy, Aug. 14, 1926. JCD, Pontifical Lateran U.; JD, State U., Rome. Ordained priest Roman Cath. Ch., 1949, archbishop, 1976. Joined diplomatic svc. Holy See, Rome, 1959; served The Philippines, Spain, Portugal in Vatican Secretariat of State, until 1976; apostolic pro-nuncio Kenya, 1976-81, India, 1981-90; joint appointment to Nepal, 1985-90; apptd. Apostolic pro nuncio to U.S. and Permanent Observer of the Holy See to O.A.S., 1990-98; pres. adminstrn. of Patrimony of the Apostolic See, 1998—.

CACCOMO, JEAN-LOUIS, economist, consultant; b. Carcassonne, France, June 23, 1963; s. Louis and Simone (Andre) C.; m. Pascale Rinaldi; children: Robin, Tom. Lic., U. Aix-Marseille, France, 1983, M in Econs., 1984, DEA, 1985, PhD in Econs., 1995, habilitation of rsch. direction, 1996. Rschr. U. Mediterranean, Aix, France, 1990-95; lectr., economist U. Perpignan, France, 1995—; supr. rsch. team econs. of tourism U. Perpignan; cons. World Tourism Orgn., Madrid, 1997-98. Author: Les Defis Economiques de l'information, 1996; contbr. articles to profl. jours. Mem. Internat. Schumpeter Soc. Avocation: music. Home: 1 rue des Jonquilles, F-66280 Saleilles France Office: U Perpignan, 52 Ave de Villenneuve, F-66680 Perpignan France

CACHALIA, GHALEB KAENE, management consultant; b. Johannesburg, South Africa, Nov. 12, 1956; d. Yusuf and Amina (Asvat) C.; m. Jo-Anne Isaacs, 1980; children: Luiza, Chiara. BA with honors, London U., 1979. Mng. dir. Snapper Group, Johannesburg, 1994—, Genrho, Johannesburg, 1994-97, Dicke & Wicharz Cachalia & Mothupi, Johannesburg, 1997-98; global account mgr. Monitor Co., Johannesburg, 1998—; dir. CTN TV, Johannesburg, 1997—. Contbr. articles to profl. jours. Bd. mem. United World Colls., 1997—; past chmn., com. mem. 1926 Club, South Africa, 1992—. Mem. United World Colls. Trust South Africa (trustee 1985—), India/South Africa Rotary Trust (trustee 1997—), Rand Club (past com. mem.). Avocation: fly fishing. Home: Forest Town 2193, 12 Birnam Rd, Johannesburg South Africa Office: PO Box 3265, Johannesburg 2000, South Africa

CACHIA, ADRIAN RALSTON, anatomical pathologist; b. Sydney, NSW, Australia, May 6, 1966; s. Catherine Mary (Purcell) C. MB BChir, Sydney U., 1989. Resident med. officer Westmead Hosp., Sydney, 1989-90; registrar St. George Hosp., Sydney, 1991-95; clin. rsch. fellow Edinburgh (Scotland) U., 1996; staff specialist Inst. Clin. Pathology and Med. Rsch.-Westmead Hosp., Sydney, 1997—; cons. dermatologist, Skin and Cancer Found., Sydney, 1999—. Contbr. articles to profl. jours. Fellow Royal Coll. Pathologists Australia; mem. Internat. Acad. Cytology. Avocations: film, information technology, tennis, scuba diving. Office: Westmead Hosp, Dept Tissue Pathology, 2145 Sydney NSW, Australia

CACHIN, HERVÉ, insurance company executive; b. Paris, Feb. 10, 1939; s. Marcel and Anne-Marie (Delaage) C.; m. Marie-Françoise Chassin, June 25, 1962; children: Christophe, Delphine. Grad., Ecole Poly., Paris, 1960, Inst. Polit. Studies, Paris, 1963. Examiner ins. dept. Min. Fin. Econ., 1963-69; mgr. SCOR, Paris, 1970-80, dpe. gen. mgr., 1981-87; dpe. gen. mgr. SAFR, Paris, 1988-89, gen. mgr., 1989-94; chmn., CEO SAFR, Paris, 1994—. With. French Mil., 1958-61. Recipient Offcer Dans L'Ordre Nat. Mérite, 1990, Chevalier Palmes Acad., 1996. Mem. French Inst. Actuaries (hon.). Office: SAFR, 153 Rue De Courcelles, 75017 Paris France

CACIC, MIRJANA, surgical pathologist; b. Zagreb, Croatia, Mar. 8, 1950; d. Franck and Ana (Maras) C.; m. Petar Pilipovic, July 24, 1985 (div. 1987); 1 child. MD, Med. Sch. Zagreb, Croatia, 1974, MS, 1983, PhD, 1992. Chief urological pathology Clin. Hosp. Rebro, Zagreb, Croatia, 1992—. Mem. Croatian Soc. Pathology, European Soc. Pathology. Roman Catholic. Avocation: reading. Home: Novotnijeva 10, 10000 Zagreb Croatia Office: Clin Hosp Rebro, Kispaticeva 12, 10000 Zagreb Croatia

CACKOVIC, HINKO, physicist, researcher, artist; b. Zagreb, Croatia, Aug. 27, 1930; arrived in Germany, 1970; s. Walter Victor and Emma (Habermann) C.; m. Jasna Loboda, July 28, 1962. Diploma in physics, U. Zagreb, Croatia, 1962, MSc in Solid State Physics, 1964, PhD, 1970; postgrad., Fritz-Haber Inst. der Max-Planck-Gesellschaft, Berlin, 1970-72. Scientist Inst. Physics U. Zagreb, 1962-65, Atom Inst. Ruder Boskovic, Zagreb, 1967-71, Fritz-Haber-Inst. der Max-Planck-Gesellschaft, Berlin, 1970-80, Tech. U. Berlin, 1980-95. Contbr. over 55 articles to profl. jours.; contbr. art to jours. including Kunstblatt No. 1 and 2, 1995, Kunst-aktuell No. 2, 1995, 99, Kunst-aktuell Art-Frankfurt, 1996; contbr. art to books including Dokumenta Artis, 1995, 99, Modern Artists 3D Art, 1996, Allgemeines Lexikon der Kunstschaffenden in der Bildenden und Gestaltenden Kunst des Ausgehenden XX Jahrhunderts, Band 4, 1996, Meisterwerke Zeitgenossischer Kunst, 1998, Meister Bildender Künstler, 1999, Meisterwerke-Küunstler unserer Zeit, 1999, also numerous catalogues; work included in Cyber Mus. wwwART channel, Internet Gallery of Forschungs-Inst. Bildender Künste, Nürnberg, Germany. Recipient Euro Hon. prize Dresden exhbn., Germany, 1994, Baden-Baden exhbn., Germany, 1995, graphic prize Offener Kunstpreis, 1995, 98; grantee Tech. U. Berlin, 1965-67, Alexander von Humboldt Stiftung, 1970-72, Max-Planck-Gesellschaft, 1972-73. Fellow Internat. Biog. Assn. Avocations: literature, music, astrophysics. Home and Studio: Im Dol 60, 14195 Berlin Germany

CADBURY, SIR DOMINIC, food products executive; b. May 12, 1940; s. Laurence John and Joyce C.; m. Cecilia Sarah Symes, 1972; 3 children. Student, Eton Coll., Eng., Trinity Coll., Eng., Cambridge (Eng.) U.; MBA, Stanford U. CEO Cadbury Schweppes plc, London, 1984-93, chmn., 1993-2000; with The Wellcome trust, London, 2000—; bd. dirs., chmn. Economist Group; mem. Stanford Adv. Coun., 1989-95; mem. advt. com. Royal Mint, 1986-94; bd. dirs. EMI, dep. chmn., 1999—. V.p. Edgbaston H.S. for Girls, Birmingham, Eng., 1987—; gov. Tudor Hall Sch., 1993—; mem. Nat. Adv. Coun. for Edn. and Tng. Targets; dep. chmn. Qualifications and Curriculum Authority, 1997—. Fellow Charted Inst. Mktg.; mem. Confedn. Brit. Industry (mem. pres.'s com. 1989-94, chmn. edn. and tng. affairs com. 1993-97), Food Assn., Brit. Inst. Mgmt. (companion 1984), Food and Drink Fedn. (pres. 1998-99). Avocations: tennis, golf, shooting. Office: The Wellcome Trust, 183 Euston Rd, London NW1 2BE, England

CADIET, LAURENT, psychiatrist, anthropology researcher; b. St. Nazaire, Brittany, France, May 27, 1966; s. Claude and Sylviane (Le Cerf) C. Degree in philosophy, U. Rennes, France, 1996; degrees in psychoanalysis, human scis., U. St. Denis, Vincennes, France, 1997; D, U. Nantes, France, 1997. Intern Regional and Univ. Hosp., Nantes, 1992-97, specialist-asst. gen. hosp., 1997-99, hosp. psychiatrist, 1999—. Author: Psychiatric Emergencies, 1997. Avocations: sailing, riding. Office: Gen Hosp, Casualty Dept BP 414, 44606 Saint-Nazaire Cedex, France

CADOGAN, CHARLES CAMPBELL, mathematics educator; b. St. Peter, Barbados, Oct. 8, 1935; s. Conrad Cyril Leacock and Ila Amanda (Cadogan) Whitehead; children: Kathy, Sophia, Konrad. BS, London U. Coll. West Indies, Jamaica, 1960; PhD, U. West Indies, Jamaica, 1969. Tchr. Govt. Barbados, 1956, 60-65; teaching asst. U. West Indies, Jamaica, 1965-67, asst. lectr., 1967-69; lectr. U. West Indies, Barbados, 1970-72; sr. lectr. U. West Indies, Batbados, 1972-79, prof., 1979—, head dept. computer sci., math. and physics, 1996-99. Author: Elements of Mathematical Structures, 1987; editor-in-chief Jour. Math. and Computing Scis., 1990—. Postdoctoral fellow U. Waterloo, Can., 1969-70; Fulbright scholar, MIT, 1982. Mem. Am. Math. Soc., Soc. Indsl. and Applied Math. Anglican. Avocations: jogging, weight-training, cricket. Office: Dept Computer Sci Math & Physics, PO Box 64, Bridgetown Barbados

CADOGAN, PETER WILLIAM, retired educator, activist; b. Whitley Bay, Eng., Jan. 26, 1921; s. Archibald Douglas and Audrey (Wannop) C.; m. Joyce Stone (div. 1969); 1 child, Claire. BA in History with honors, U. Newcastle, Newcastle Upon Tyne, Eng., 1950, diploma in edn., 1951. Tchr. Kettering (Eng.) Secondary Modern Sch., 1951-53, Chesterton Sch., Cambridge, Eng., 1953-65; nat. sec. Com. of 100, London, 1965-68; gen. sec. Save Biafra Campaign, London, 1968-70, South Place Ethical Soc., London, 1970-81; lectr. Birkbeck Coll., U. London, Workers Ednl. Assn., 1981-93; founder, convenor Values & Vision, London, 1991—. Author: Early Radical Newcastle, 1973, Direct Democracy, 1975; contbr. articles to profl. jours. Sec.

No. Ireland Project, The Gandhi Found., London, 1988—. Cpl. Royal Air Force, 1941-46. Mem. The William Blake Soc. (chmn. 1988-94, v.p. 1994—), Kilburn 2000 (co-founder), London Alliance (chmn. 1999—). Avocations: community regeneration, history, social invention. Home: 3 Hinchinbrook House, Greville Rd, London NW6 5UP, England

CADWALDER, HUGH MAURICE, psychology educator; b. Mt. Ayer, Iowa, July 1, 1924; s. Hugh M. and Mary (Crouch) C.; m. Melba Atwood, May 22, 1944 (div. 1975); children: Mark M., Mindy M.; m. Dianna Renfro-Reeves, May 15, 1980. MA, Baylor U., Waco, Tex., 1955, PhD, 1962; DD, Houston Bible Coll., 1963; ArtsD (hon.), Inst. Applied Rsch., London, 1970. Cert. compulsive gambling specialist, Tex.; master addictions counselor; ordained to ministry Bapt. Ch., 1944; diplomate Am. Bd. Med. Psychotherapists. Instr. psychology Baylor U., Waco, Tex., 1955-62; acad. dean Southwestern Agrl. Coll., Waxahachie, Tex., 1962-64; sr. minister Christian Life Community Ch., Dallas, 1964-69, 1st Assembly of God Ch., Corpus Christi, Tex., 1969-74; mem. faculty dept. psychology San Jacinto Coll., Pasadena, Tex., 1974—; seminar dir. Cadwalder Behavioral Ctr., Houston, 1982-90; staff psychologist Charter Hosp., Sugar Land, Tex., 1990-95; full staff mem. Bellaire (Tex.) Gen. Hosp., 1993-98, Forest Springs Hosp., Houston, 1988-95; seminar dir. Sharpstown Christian Singles, Houston, 1975-92; v.p. 1st Colony Mcpl. Utility Dist. 6, Sugar Land, 1988-96; host radio talk show Sta. KTEK. Author: Some Psychological Determinants Involved in Religious Attitudes, 1965, The Spiritual Dimension of Recovery from Addiction, 1988, Emotional Adhesions and Their Cure, 1989, Some Current Trends in the Mental Health Field, Or What To Do until the Psychiatrist Arrives with the Paramedics, 1995, How to be Happier Though Married, 1998, Spirituality: Horrible Hoax or an Honest, Holy Hologram?, 1999. Pres. bd. Community Ednl. TV Network, 1989-92; bd. dirs. Cadwalder Behavioral Ctr.; mem. Rep. Presdl. Task Force. Fellow Am. Bd. Med. Psychotherapists (diplomate, cert. criminal justice specialist); mem. NASW, Am. Assn. Coll. Profs., Am. Pub. Health Assn., Community Coll. Humanities Assn., Am. Assn. Retired Persons, Tex. Jr. Coll. Tchrs. Assn., Am. Assn. Christian Counselors, Am. Coun. on Alcoholism, Am. Assn. Coll. Profs., Community Coll. Humanities Assn., Harris County Sheriff's Deputies Assn. (cert. hon. membership 1985), Nat. Mental Health Assn., N.Y. Acad. Sci., Ind. Bus., Forum Club Houston, Phi Delta Kappa. Office: Cadwalder Counseling 7324 Southwest Fwy Ste 850 Houston TX 77074-2018

CAEN, JACQUES PHILIPPE, physician; b. Metz, France, Mar. 11, 1927; s. Lucien and Renee (Levy) C.; m. Genevieve Francou, Feb. 2, 1951; children: Remi, Anne-Sophie. MD, U. Paris, 1951. Resident U. Lausanne, Switzerland, 1949-50; chief of lab. faculty medicine U. Paris, 1956-65; assoc. prof. medicine U. Paris VII, 1966-78, prof., 1978-95; chief rsch. dept. hemostasis and thrombosis med. rsch. coun. U. Paris, 1971; mem. faculty Caius and Gonville Coll., Cambridge (Eng.) U., 1976-77; assoc. prof. U. Sydney, 1983. Contbr. articles to profl. jours. Decorated officer Legion of Honor, 1989, Commdr. of Merit, 1992, Honoris Causa Suzhou, 1985, Maastricht, 1986, Shanghai, 1988. Fellow Royal Coll. Pathologists London; mem. Internat. Soc. Thrombosis and Hemostasis (sec.-gen. 1976, Robert S. Grant medal 1979), European Thrombosis Rsch. Orgn. (pres. 1972), Internat. Soc. Hematology, French Acad. Sci. (corr.), French Acad. Medicine. Home: 32 Ch Floquet, 75007 Paris France

CAEN, JEAN-BERNARD, financial executive; b. Suresnes, France, July 23, 1956; m. Fabienne Rouge Caen, June 11, 1988 (div. 2000); children: TimothéE, Barthelemy, Thomas. Degree in civil engring., Ecole Spéciale Travaux Pub., Paris, 1979; MS in Tech. and Policy, MIT, 1980. Info. sys. cons. McDonnell Info. Sys., Paris, 1982-84; banking and ins. dir. Comshare Inc., Paris, 1984-90; mng. dir. Fin. & Tech. Mgmt. S.A., Paris, 1990—; mem., presenter at numerous confs. on risk mgmt.; pres. Eurosilver SAS, 2000—. Fellow Assn. Française des Gestionnaires Actif Passif, Assn. Française des Controleurs de Gestion de Banques; mem. Global Assn. Risk Profls. (mem. exec. com. French, Luxembourg and Belgium chpt.). Avocations: skiing, yachting, golf. Home: 69 rue de Tureune, 75003 Paris France Office: FTM, 112 Bd Haussmann, 75008 Paris France

CAETANO, RAUL, psychiatrist, educator; b. São Paulo, Brazil, May 5, 1945; came to U.S., 1978; s. Silvestre Vieira and Vera Vieira (Barbosa) C.; m. Patrice Vaeth, Sept. 30, 1995; children: Izabel, Lauren, Helena. MD, U. Rio de Janeiro, 1969, diploma in psychiatry, 1971; MPH, U. Calif., Berkeley, 1979, PhD, 1983. Psychiatrist Pine Hosp., Rio de Janeiro, 1969-73; asst. prof. State U., Rio de Janeiro, 1969-73; rsch. psychiatrist Inst. Psychiatry U. London, 1973-76; asst. prof. Inst. Psychiatry, Rio de Janeiro, 1976-78; vis. scholar Alcohol Rsch. Group, Berkeley, 1978-83, assoc. scientist to sr. scientist, 1983-94, dir., 1992—; adj. prof. Sch. Pub. Health, U. Calif., Berkeley, 1991-98; assoc. dir. Calif. Pacific Med. Ctr. Rsch. Inst., San Francisco, 1992-93; prof., asst. dean Sch. Pub. Health, U. Tex., 1998—. Contbr. numerous sci. papers to profl. jours. WHO fellow, 1973-76; rsch. grantee Nat. Inst. Alcohol Abuse and Alcoholism, 1985—. Mem. APHA, Am. Coll. Epidemiology, Rsch. Soc. Alcoholism. Roman Catholic. Office: V8112 5323 Harry Hines Blvd Dallas TX 75390-7208

CAFARO, PHILIP JUSTIN, philosophy educator; b. N.Y.C., Feb. 27, 1962; s. Ralph Anthony and Claire June Cafaro. BA, U. Chgo., 1984; MA, U. Ga., 1988; PhD, Boston U., 1997. Asst. prof. S.W. State U., Marshall, Minn., 1997-99; asst. prof. dept. philosophy Colo. State U., Ft. Collins, 1999—. Contbr. articles to profl. jours., including Ethics and the Environment, Borderlines, others. Lobbyist Sierra Club, Boston, 1994-96, mem. exec. com., 1988-90, 95-96; lobbyist Wilderness Soc., Washington, 1990. Presdl. fellow Boston U., 1990-93; grantee Otto Bremer Found., Marshall, 1998. Mem. Am. Philos. Assn., Internat. Soc. Environ. Ethics. Democrat. Avocations: hiking, birdwatching. E-mail: cafaro@lamar.colostate.edu. Home: 1402 Laporte Ave Fort Collins CO 80521-1905 Office: Colo State U Dept Philosophy Fort Collins CO 80523-0001

CAFÉ FILHO, ADALBERTO CORREA, plant pathologist; b. Rio de Janeiro, May 25, 1960; s. Adalberto Correa and Maria da Conceicao Flores (Arruda) C.; m. Patricia Motta, Feb. 1, 1986; children: Renata Motta, Debora Motta. BSc, U. Brasilia, Brazil, 1982, MSc, 1984; PhD, U. Calif., 1993. Rschr. Embrapa, Brasilia, 1985-87; postgrad. rschr. U. Calif., 1992-93; asst. prof. U. Brasilia, 1987-93, prof., 1993—, dept. head dept. plant pathology, 1997—; rsch. fellow NRC, Brazil, 1994—. Assoc. editor Jour. Fitopatologia Brasileira 1993-99; contbr. articles to profl. jours. Mem. Am. Phytopath. Soc., Soc. Fitopatologia do Brasil. Home: SQS 202-L-202, 70232120 Brasilia Brazil Office: U Brasilia, Dept Plant Pathology, 70910900 Brasilia Brazil

CAFFARELLI, ARTURO JORGE, commercial executive; b. Buenos Aires, Aug. 2, 1951; s. Jorge Caffarelli and Renata Ellena; m. Norma Biano, Dec. 3, 1976 (div. Mar. 1988); children: Mariana, Sebastian; m. Silvia LÓpez, Nov. 9, 1990. Degree, U. Buenos Aires, 1976. Cert. indsl. engr. Asst. cons. Arthur Andersen & Co., Buenos Aires, 1976-79; brand mgr. Gillette Co., Buenos Aires, 1979-80; comml. mgr. Econs. Lab., Buenos Aires, 1980-82; mktg. mgr. Pelikan SA, Buenos Aires, 1982-87; comml. mgr. Ink and Paper SA, Buenos Aires, 1987-92, Rio Platense Meat Packer, Buenos Aires, 1992-94; gen. mgr. Argentina office Mattel Toys, 1994-95; assoc. Global Outsourcing Consultants in Mgmt., Buenos Aires, 1995&; prof. mktg. Buenos Aires U., 1976-79, Del Salvador U., 1987-90. Mem. Mktg. Assn. (assoc., bd. dirs. 1982-87). Roman Catholic. Avocations: squash, boating. Office: Juncal 655 3-A, 1062 Buenos Aires Argentina

CAFFERATA, LAZARO F.R., chemistry educator, organic chemistry researcher; b. Gualeguaychu, Argentina, Sept. 1, 1933; s. Lazaro J. and Rosa Loreta (Morena) C.; m. Nelly Bergamin, Feb. 11, 1966; 1 chld, Maria Lorena Cafferata Bergamin. BS, U. Nacional La Plata, Argentina, 1951, PhD in Chemistry, 1960. Demonstrator U. Nacional La Plata, 1957-58, rsch. asst., 1958-66, lectr., 1958-72, prof. chemistry, 1972—; head of rsch. UNLP, La Plata, 1976—; rsch. cons. for govt. Author: Gas Chromatography, 1981; patentee in field. Roman Catholic. Avocations: playing guitar, home renovation, yachting. Home: Calle 15 N-2924, 1897 MB Gonnet, Buenos Aires Argentina Office: Laboratorio Ladecor (UNLP), Calles 47 y 115, 1900 La Plata Argentina

CAFFREY, JAMES F., industrial engineer; b. Cork, Ireland, Sept. 7, 1970; s. James Joseph Caffrey and Marie Alice Roche. B Engring., U. Limerick, Ireland, 1992; M Engring., U. Limerick, 1994; MBA, Henley (Eng.) Mgmt. Coll., 1998—. Trainee engr. Kromberg & Schubert, Ireland, 1990; rsch. engr. U. Dortmund, Germany, 1992-94, U. Limerick, 1992-94; product engr. Betatherm Ireland, Galway, 1994-96; applications engr. Bourns, Frankfurt, Germany, 1996-98; mgr. worldwide automotive product Bourns Electronics Ireland, Cork, 1998-99, market devel. mgr., 1999-2000; mktg. mgr. Analog Devices, Limerick, Ireland, 2000—. Contbr. articles to profl. jours., including Internat. Jour. Ops. and Prodn. Mgmt. Erasmus scholar European Union, 1993. Mem. Assn. German Elec. Engrs. (chmn. stds. working group 1998-2000). Achievements include patent for Positive Temperature Coefficient fuse box. Avocations: walking, taek-won-do (qualified instructor, black belt), swimming. Office: Analog Devices, Raheen Indsl Estate, Limerick Ireland

CAFRITZ, ROBERT CONRAD, art historian, critic, consultant; b. July 5, 1953; s. Conrad B. Cafritz and Jennifer (Stats) Phillips; 1 child, Nicholas H. BA, Columbia U., 1977, MA, 1978. Asst. curator Phillips Collection, Washington, 1978-82, assoc. curator, 1982-87, curator 19th Century Art, 1987-88; fine arts advisor, critic and historian, 1989—. Author: Georges Braque, 1981; contbg. author: Master Paintings from the Phillips Collection, 1981; co-author: Places of Delight: The Pastoral Landscape, 1988; editor exhbn. catalogs Three Pioneers of Japanese Painting, 1979, Leon Spilliaert, 1980, Sam Francis, 1980, Georges Braque: Late Paintings, 1982, Howard Hodgkin, 1984, Odilon Redon: The Ian Woodner Collection, 1988; contbr. to scholarly jours. Overseer Phillips Collection, Washington, 2000—. Home and Office: 3044 O St NW Washington DC 20007-3107

CAGANDAHAN, SABINO MAGNO, accountant; b. Iloilo City, The Philippines, July 8, 1964; arrived in Saudia Arabia, 1995; s. Jose Carmince Cagandahan and Angelina Guillaran Magno. BS in Commerce-Acctg. cum laude, Ctrl. Philippine U., Iloilo City, 1986. Lic. Philippine Inst. CPAs. Gen. acct. Fortune Republic Cement Corp., Manila, 1987-94; acctg. supr. Express Telecomms. Co., Manila, 1994-95; sr. acct., fin. analyst Hewlett Packard divsn. Modern Electronics Establishment, Riyadh, Saudi Arabia, 1995—. Pres. Youth Civic Action Program, Leon, Iloilo, 1981, Math. and Sci. Club, Leon, 1981. Mem. Philippine Inst. CPAs (Riyadh chpt.). Avocations: swimming, reading, Internet surfing. Office: MEE-HP Divsn, PO Box 22015, Riyadh 11495, Saudi Arabia

CAGIANO DE AZEVEDO, RAIMONDO, demographer, educator; b. Rome, Dec. 6, 1942; s. Michelangelo and Marilena (Campanari) Cagiano de A.; m. Letizia Norci, May 5, 1970; children: Elena, Alessandro, Michele, Chiara. D of Econs., U. La Sapienza, Rome, 1965. Prof. Faculty of Econs., Rome, 1985—, dean, 1996; pres. Centro Italiano Formazione Europea, Nice, Paris, 1973—; cons. Coun. of Europe, Strasbourg, France, 1973—. Dir. European Federalist Movement, Pavia, Italy, 1966—. Mem. Internat. Union Scientific Study of Population, European Assn. Population Studies. Office: Faculty of Econs, Via Castro Laurenziano 9, 00161 Rome Italy

CAGINALP, GUNDUZ, mathematician, educator, researcher; b. Ankara, Turkey, July 20, 1952; came to U.S., 1959; s. Nejat Tahsin and Munire Feyma (Deniz) C; m. Eva Keller, Aug. 14, 1992; children: Carey Allen, Reginald Jarrett. AB cum laude with distinction in all subjects, Cornell U., 1973, MA, 1976, PhD, 1978. Postdoctoral fellow Cornell U., Ithaca, N.Y., 1978; rsch. assoc. Rockefeller U., N.Y.C., 1978-80; Zeev Nehari rsch. asst. prof. Carnegie-Mellon U., Pitts., 1980-83, vis. asst. prof., 1983-84; asst. prof. math. U. Pitts., 1984-85, assoc. prof., 1985-90, prof., 1990—, group leader applied math., 1988-90; reviewer Math. Revs., Ann Arbor, Mich., 1981-90. Mem. editl. bd. Applied Math. Fin.; contbr. articles to profl. jours. Cornell U. grad. fellow, 1973; grantee NSF, 1980—, NIST, 1990-92, Dreman Found., 1997—; disting. vis. rsch. scholar Internat. Found. for Rsch. in Exptl. Econs., 1999. Mem. Am. Math. Soc., Am. Phys. Soc., Soc. for Indsl. and Applied Math., Econs. Scis. Assn., Phi Beta Kappa. Achievements include proof of theorems on existence and properties of surface free energy; studied connections between statistical mechanics and quantum field theory; developed phase field methods for studying free boundary problems; research on applying renormalization group methods to differential equations; analyzed experimental economics using differential equations and time series; established that price patterns in financial markets have predictive value. Home: 12 Rosemont Ln Pittsburgh PA 15217-3161 Office: U Pitts Dept Math Pittsburgh PA 15260

CAGLAYAN, NEVZAT, chemical engineer, consultant; b. Merzifon, Amasya, Turkey, Nov. 22, 1954; s. Muzaffer and Fatima (Keskin) G.; m. Dilek Yakin, Oct. 2, 1982; children: Sevgi, Utku. BS, Ankara U., 1977, MS, 1980, PhD, 1996. Lt. Turkish Land Forces Command, Ankara, 1978, advanced through grades to col., 1980, gen. chemistry tchr. War Sch., 1980-89, project officer, chief divsn., 1989-98, ret., 1998; tech. cons. gen. mgr. Roketsan Missiles Industries Inc., Elmadag, 1998—. Mem. N.Y. Acad. Scis. Avocations: walking, listening to music, reading. Office: Roketsan Missiles Indus Inc, PO Box 30, Elmadag 06780 Ankara, Turkey

CAGLIOTI, GIUSEPPE, physicist, researcher; b. Naples, Aug. 19, 1931; s. Vincenzo and Adriana (Stolfi) C.; Elena Bonanni, July 25, 1956; children: Vincenzo, Maria Clara, Livia; m. Tatiana Tchouvieva, Dec. 3, 1994. Laurea, U. Rome, 1953, postgrad., 1955; Diploam, Sch. Nuclear Sci. and Engring., 1956. Researcher U. Rome, 1953-56, ENEA, Rome, 1955-64; dir. activities ENEA, Ispra, Italy, 1964-72; prof. solid state physics Poli. Milan, 1972—; former prest. Gruppo Italiano Frattura. Author: The Dynamics of Ambiguity, 1992, Introduzione alla Fisica dei Materiallli, 1994, Eidos e Psiche, 1995, Casanova e la Scienza, 1998. Recipient Gold Medal Accademia Nazionale dei XL, 1978. Mem. Inst. Accademico de Roma (mem. acad. coun. 1985—), Accad. Sci. e Lettere (mem. Istituto Lommardo), Soc. Italiana Fisica. Office: Poli Milano, Via Ponzio 34/3, 20133 Milan Italy

CAGNEY, WILLIAM ROBERT, psychologist; b. Pitts., Oct. 7, 1937; s. Edward Patrick and Pearl Barbara (Sebastian) C.; m. Vivian Antoinette Tartaglia, June 26, 1965; children: Lori Anne, Julie Alissa, Melissa Beth. BS, Duquesne U., 1960, MA, 1965, PhD, 1968. Lic. psychologist, Pa.; cert. Nat. Register Health Svcs.; cert. diplomate in clin. hypnotherapy NBCCH, Nat. Bd. cert. clin. Hypnotherapists. Psychology intern, staff psychologist Dixmont State Hosp., Glenfield, Pa., 1962-68; staff psychologist South Hills Child Guidance Ctr., Pitts., 1968-69; asst. dir., psychol. svcs. Woodville State Hosp., Carnegie, Pa., 1968-70; chief psychologist Counseling Ctr. of South Hills, Pitts., 1970-72; clin. dir. Chartiers MH/MR Ctr., Bridgeville, Pa., 1972-79; pvt. practice Pitts., 1971—; cons. Outreach South, Mt. Lebanon, Pa., 1976—, South Hills Interfaith Ministries, Bethel Park, Pa., 1969—, Crisis Addiction Recovery Edn., Inc., Washington, Pa., 1984-88, YMCA South Hills, Pitts., 1977-78; field supr. dept. psychology U. Pitts., 1970-73, W.Va. U., Morgantown, 1973-78; resident psychologist Sta. KDKA-TV Pitts. Today, 1978-79; presenter seminars and workshops to profl. and cmty. groups, 1972—. Cons. Twp. Upper St. Clair Adminstrn., Police, Schs., Family Resource Program, Upper St. Clair, Pa., 1986-89. Fellow Pa. Psychol. Assn.; mem. APA, Greater Pitts. Psychol. Assn., Am. Group Therapy Assn. Avocations: fitness activities, art and music appreciation. Office: 1725 Washington Rd Ste 509 Pittsburgh PA 15241-1207

CAGNOL, JOHN, mathematics educator; b. Jan. 9, 1973. BS, U. Nice-Sophia Antipolis, Nice, France, 1994, MS, 1995; PhD in Math., U. Nice-Sophia Antipolis, Sophia-Antipolis, France, 1998. Rschr. Ecole des Mines de Paris, Sophia Antipolis, 1995-98; lectr. U. Nice-Sophia Antipolis, 1998-99, U. Va., 1999—. Mem. Internat. Fedn. for Info. Processing. Fax: 630-214-6198. E-mail: john.cagnol@sophia.inria.fr. Office: Pole Univ Leonard De Vinci, Der Calcul Scientifique, 92916 Paris France

CAHANA, ALEX, anesthesiologist, pain specialist; b. Jerusalem, Apr. 4, 1964; s. Yeshaiahu and Lydia (Käss) C.; divorced; 1 child, Noa. MD, Tel-Aviv U., 1988. Diplomate Am. Acad. of Pain Mgmt. Battalion marine physician Med. Corps Israel Def. Force, 1990-91, regiment marine physician, 1991-93; comdr. trauma instr. Mil. Sch. of Medicine, 1993-94; resident dept. anesthesiology Sheba Med. Ctr., 1994-97; fellow Pain Control Ctr. Vanderbilt U., Nashville, Tenn., 1997—; instr. Advanced Trauma Life Support, Israel, 1993, Advanced Pediatric Life Support, Israel, 1994, Advanced Cardiac Life Support, Israel, 1994; dir. Sheba Multidisciplinary Analgesia Ctr., Israel, 1999—. Exch. student Youth for Youth, Germany, 1981; mentor Tel-Aviv U., Israel, 1983. Maj. Surgeon Gen. Hdqrs., 1989-94. Scholarship Am. Physician Fellowship, 1997. Mem. Internat. Assn. Study of Pain, Am. Pain Soc., Urological Pain Interest Group. Jewish. Avocations: reading, yoga, piano. Office: Dept Anesthesiology, Sheba Med Ctr, 52621 Sheba Israel

CAHANA, MICHAEL, quality assurance and engineering consultant; b. Bucharest, Romania, Mar. 17, 1953; arrived in Israel, 1970; s. Aharon and Iosefina (Grünstein) C.; m. Hannah Miedzinski, Mar. 8, 1979; children: Nir, Zvi, Gil. BSEE, Technion, Haifa, Israel, 1979. R&D engr. Rafael, Haifa, Israel, 1979-88, quality engr., 1988-93; quality engr. Cvalim Ltd./Thermofil, Maalot, Israel, 1994-95; quality cons. Mgmt. Sys., Nahariya, Israel, 1996—. Sgt.-maj. Israeli Air Force, 1973-76. Mem. Am. Soc. for Quality (cert. quality engr.), Israel Soc. for Quality. Avocations: listening to music, stamps. Mailing Address: PO Box 281, Nahariya 22102, Israel

CAHEN, DAVID, materials chemist, educator; b. Vught, The Netherlands, Aug. 14, 1947; arrived in Israel, 1966; s. Max. and Henriette (Elion) C.; m. Geula-Pimentel-Meruk, July 13, 1983; children: Anat Meruk, Maya Meruk, Yair, Yael. BS, Hebrew U., 1969; PhD, Northwestern U., 1973. Weizmann fellow Weizmann Inst. of Sci., Rehovot, Israel, 1973-74; Bogen fellow Hebrew U. of Jerusalem, Israel, 1974-75; scientist Weizmann Inst. of Sci., Rehovot, 1975-78, sr. scientist, 1978-93, assoc. prof., 1993-98, prof., 1998—, head electron microscopy unit, 1995-97, head chemistry Feinberg Grad. Sch.; mem. editl. adv. bd. Marcel Dekker Pub. Co., 1991-96, Solar Cells, 1984-91, Applied Physics Comm., 1990-95, Solar Energy Materials Solar Cells, 1992-99; chair Recanati Career Devel., 1978-85; vis. prof. insts. U.S.A., Europe, Australia, South Am., 1979—. Contbr. more than 275 articles to sci. publs.; holder 16 patents in field. Adv. U.S.-Israel Binat. Sci. Found., 1984-96. Recipient E.D. Bergmann prize Weizmann Inst., 1980, Jewish Polish Soldiers prize for novel devices, 1998. Mem. IEEE (sr.), Israel Chem. Soc., Israel Vacuum Soc. (sec. 1994-96, pres. 1996-98), Am. Phys. Soc. Achievements include patents in materials, semiconductors, devices and energy conversion. Avocations: history, travel. Office: Weizmann Inst Sci, Dept Materials & Interfaces, Rehovot 76100, Israel

CAHILL, KEVIN MICHAEL, physician, educator; b. N.Y.C., May 1936; s. John and Genevieve (Campion) C.; m. Kathryn M. McGinity; children: Kevin, Sean, Christopher, Brendan, Denis. AB cum laude, Fordham U., 1957; MD, Cornell U., 1961; DTM&H, London Sch. Tropical Medicine, 1963; LLD (hon.), Iona Coll., N.Y., LeMoyne Coll., N.Y.; DSc (hon.), N.Y. Med. Coll., St. John's U., N.Y.; LHD (hon.), Villanova U., Pa.; LittD (hon.), Fordham U.; LLD (hon.), Niagara U., N.Y., U. Liverpool; HHD (hon.), U. Ctrl. Am., Nicaragua; LHD (hon.), Marymount Coll., Coll. Boca Raton, Am. Coll. Switzerland, Geneva, Georgetown U.; MD (hon.), Nat. Autonomous U. Nicaragua, Managua; DSc (hon.), Seton Hall U., Dominican Coll., N.Y. Diplomate Am. Bd. Microbiology, Am. Bd. Preventive Medicine. Dir. clin. tropical medicine, head dept. epidemiology U.S. Naval Med. Rsch. Unit, Cairo, 1963-65; assoc. prof. microbiology, clin. medicine N.Y. Med. Coll., N.Y.C., 1965-67; clin. prof. pub. health, preventive medicine U. N.J., Newark, 1971-95; pres. Ctr. Internat. Health Coop., N.Y.C.; dir. tropical disease ctr. Lenox Hill Hosp., N.Y.C.; pvt. practice N.Y.C.; prof. tropical medicine NYU Sch. Medicine; prof. internat. humanitarian affairs City U. N.Y.; mem. scientific adv. coun. Am. Found. Tropical Medicine, 1966-74; med. adv. African-Am. Inst., N.Y.C., 1967-77, Will Rogers Meml. Fund, N.Y., 1970-87; mem. com. pub. health N.Y. Acad. Medicine, 1974-80; advisor on health Govt. N.Y. State, 1975-81, chmn. health planning commn., 1975-81, chmn. health rsch. coun., 1975-81; sr. mem. N.Y. Bd. Health, 1981-93; sr. cons. UN Med. Svc., 1970-97; Alfred Gellhorn prof. CUNY, 1980-81; clin. prof. tropical medicine, parasitic diseases, medicine NYU; prof. chmn. dept. internat. health, tropical medicine Royal Coll. Surgeons, Dublin, Ireland; clin. prof. medicine Seton Hall U., N.J.; cons. tropical diseases St. Vincent's Hosp. and Health Ctr., N.Y.C.; med. adv. Cath. Relief Svc., Balt., Cath. Med. Mission Bd., N.Y.; spl. advisor to spkr. and health com. chmn. N.Y. City Coun.; impartial specialist tropical medicine N.Y. State, Workmen's compensation Bd.; prof., dir. Internat. Humanitarian Affairs Hunter Coll. CUNY. Author: Tropical Diseases in Temperate Climates, 1964, Health on the Horn of Africa, 1970, Medical Advice for the Traveler, 1970, 3d edit., 1977, Clinical Tropical Medicine Vol. 1, 170, 2d edit., 1972, The Untapped Resource: Medicine & Diplomacy, 1973, Clinical Tropical Medicine Vol. 11, 1973, Teaching Tropical Medicine, 1973, Tropical Diseases: A Handbook for Practitioners, 1975, 2d edit., 1976, Health and Development, 1975, Health in New York State, 1977, Irish Essays, 1980, Somalia: A Perspective, 1980, Threads for a Tapestry, 1981, Famine, 1982, The AIDS Epidemic, 1983, The American-Irish Revival, 1984, A Bridge to Peace, 1988, Un Pont Vers La Paix, 1989, Un Puente Tendido Hacia La Paz, 1989, Imminent Peril: Public Health in Declining Economy, 1991, A Framework for Survival, 1993, Clearing the Fields: Solutions to the Global Land Mines Crisis, 1994, Silent Witnesses, 1995, Preventive Diplomacy, 1996; co-author: (with W. O'Brien) Pets and Your Health, 1987, Tropical Medicine: A Clinical Text, 1989, 2d edit., 1990, The Open Door: Health and Foreign Policy, 1999; Medicine Tropicale: Precis Clinique, 1990; contbr. over 215 articles to profl. jours. Trustee Fordham U., N.Y.C., 1968-74, Mt. St. Vincent Coll., N.Y.C., 1968-74. Lt. U.S. Navy, 1962-65. Lehman fellow, 1959, Royal Free Hosp. fellow, 1960-61, Hosp. Tropical Diseases fellow, 1962-63; recipient Highest Order, Govt. Sudan, Govt. Somalia, 1968, with sash, 1972, Colles medal Royal Coll. Surgeons, Xavier award Jesuit Order, Pres.'s medal Niagara U., Miguel Larenega Order, Order of Miguel Ramirez Goyena, Govt. Nicaragua, Internat. award Pan Am. Med. Assn., Health Scis. award SUNY, Assn. Retarded Children medal, Order of Merit, Knights of Malta, Disting. Svc. award Am.-Jewish Congress, Grand Crall Pro Merito Melitensi, The Vatican, Bicentenial medal Georgetown U., Order of Carlos Finlay, Havana. Fellow Am. Coll. Chest Physicians, Am. Coll. Preventive Medicine; Am.-Irish Hist. Soc. (pres.-gen.), Royal Coll. Physicians Ireland; mem. N.Y. Soc. Tropical Medicine (pres. 1990-92), Hist. Soc. of Kerry/Cork. Office: 850 5th Ave New York NY 10021-5802

CAHILL, NEIL, economics educator, chaplain; b. Woonsocket, S.D., May 5, 1923; s. Neil and Mollie (Miller) C. BSc, Creighton U., 1943, MDiv in Counseling, 1977; AB, St. Louis U., 1948, MA in Econs., Licentiate in Philosophy, 1950, Licentiate in Sacred Theology, 1958; MDiv in Counseling, Creighton U., 1977; D in Ministry, San Francisco Theol. Sem., 1991. Ordained priest Jesuit Order, 1956. Instr. Campion Jesuit H.S., Prairie du Chien, Wis., 1950-53; asst. prof. Coll. Bus. Adminstrn. Creighton U., Omaha, 1962—, chaplain, 1963—. Author: Creighton University, College of Business Administration: The First 75 Years, 1996. Mem. AAUP, Am. Econ. Assn., KC, Beta Gama Sigma, Omicron Delta Epsilon, Alpha Sigma Nu, Delta Sigma Pi, Beta Alpha Psi, Phi Kappa Psi (adivsor 1962—). Republican. Roman Catholic. Avocations: geneaology, classical music. Home and Office: Creighton U Coll Bus Adminstrn 2500 California Plz Omaha NE 68178-0001

CAHILL, RICHARD FREDERICK, lawyer; b. Columbus, Nebr., June 18, 1953; s. Donald Francis and Hazel Fredeline (Garbers) C.; m. Helen Marie Girard, Dec. 4, 1982; children: Jacqueline Michelle, Catherine Elizabeth, Marc Alexander. Student, Worcester Coll., Oxford, 1973; BA with highest honors, UCLA, 1975; JD, U. Notre Dame, 1978. Bar: Calif. 1978, U.S. Dist. Ct. (ea. dist.) Calif. 1978, U.S. Dist. Ct. (cen. dist.) Calif. 1983, U.S. Dist. Ct. (so. dist.) Calif. 1992, U.S. Ct. Appeals (9th cir.) 1992. Dep. dist. atty. Tulare County Dist. Atty., Visalia, Calif., 1978-81; staff atty. Supreme Ct. of Nev., Carson City, 1981-83; assoc. Acret & Perochet, Brentwood, Calif., 1983-84, Thelen, Marrin, Johnson & Bridges, L.A., 1984-89; ptnr. Hammond Zuetel & Cahill, Pasadena, Calif., 1989-98, Pivo, Halbreich, Cahill & Yim, Irvine, Calif., 1999—. Mem. Pasadena Bar Assn., Los Angeles County Bar Assn., Assn. So. Calif. Defense Counsel, Notre Dame Legal Aid and Defender Assn. (assoc. dir.), Phi Beta Kappa, Phi Alpha Delta (charter, v.p. 1977-78), Pi Gamma Mu, Phi Alpha Theta (charter pres. 1973-74), Phi Eta Sigma, Sigma Chi. Republican. Roman Catholic. Avocation: tennis. Home: 201 Windwood Ln Sierra Madre CA 91024-2677 Office: Pivo Halbreich Cahill & Yim 1920 Main St Ste 800 Irvine CA 92614-7227

CAHN, ANDREW THOMAS, diplomat; b. Henley, Berkshire, Eng., Apr. 1, 1951; s. Robert Wolfgang and Patricia (Hanson) C.; m. Virginia Zachry Beardshaw, Nov. 26, 1976; children: Jessica Marion, Thomas Pierre Robert,

Lawrence Zachry. BA with honors, U. Cambridge, Eng., 1973. Asst. prin. Ministry Agr., Eng., 1973-76; 2d sec. Fgn. Office, Eng., 1976-77; 1st sec. Fgn. Office, Belgium, 1982-85; prin. Ministry Agr., Fisheries and Food, Eng., 1978-82; v.p. cabinet of Lord Cockfield Commn. of European Communities, Brussels, 1985-88; asst. sec. Ministry Agr., Fisheries and Food, 1988-92; prin. pvt. sec. Chancellor of Duchy of Lancaster, 1992-95; dep. head European secretariat Cabinet Office, 1995-97; chef de cabinet Rt. Hon. Neil Kinnock, Commr. for Transport, V.P. E.C., 1997-2000; dir. Brit. Airways, 2000—. Trustee Gatsby Charitable Trust, 1996—. Fellow Royal Soc. Arts. Home: 91 Patshull Rd, London NW5 2LE, England Office: European Commn, 200 Rue De La LO1, 1049 Brussels Belgium

CAHN, ROBERT WOLFGANG, physical metallurgist; b. Fuerth, Germany, Sept. 9, 1924; s. Martin Max and Else (Heinemann) C.; m. Patricia Lois Hanson, Aug. 9, 1947; children: Martin, Andrew, Judith, Alison. BA, Cambridge (Eng.) U., 1945, PhD, 1950, ScD, 1963. Sr. rsch. officer Atomic Energy Rsch., Harwell, Eng., 1947-51; lectr., sr. lectr., reader Birmingham (Eng.) U., 1951-62; prof. matl. tech. U. Coll. North Wales, Bangor, 1963-64; prof. mater. sci. Sussex U., Brighton, 1965-81; prof. metallurgy U. Paris-Sud, Orsay, 1981-83; vis. rsch. fellow GE, Schenectady, N.Y., 1985; Fairchild disting. fellow Calif. Inst. Tech., Pasadena, 1985-86; disting. rsch. fellow dept. materials sci. Cambridge U., 1986—; material sci. corr. Nature jour., 1968—. Author: The Coming of Materials Science, 2001; editor-in-chief: (book series) Materials Science and Technology, 1987-99; editor: Physical Metallurgy, 1965, 4th edit., 1996; exec. editor Advances in Materials Sci. and Engring., 1986-92; sr. editor Cambridge Solid State Sci. Soc., 1972-92; editor Pergamon Materials Series, 1993—; joint editor-in-chief Ency. of Materials, 1998—; contbr. articles to profl. jours. Recipient A.A. Griffith medal, Materials Sci. Club, London, 1983, Medaille Ste. Claire-Deville, French Metall. Soc., 1975, Heyn medal German Materials Soc., 1996; recipient numerous research grants. Fellow Royal Soc. of London, Am. Soc. Materials Internat., Inst. Metals London (v.p. 1975-77), Inst. Physics London, Indian Nat. Sci. Acad. (fgn.), The Minerals, Metals and Materials Soc.; mem. AIME, Acad. Arts and Scis. Göttingen, Academia Europaea London, Royal Acad. Exact Sci. (Madrid), Chinese Acad. Sci. Conservative. Jewish. Avocations: music, mountaineering, alpine plants, theatre, literature. E-mail: rwc12@am.ac.uk. Home: 6 Storey's Way, Cambridge CB3 0DT, England Office: Cambridge U Dept Materials Sci, Pembroke St, Cambridge England CB2 3QZ

CAHUZAC, GEORGES, research aerospace engineer; b. Labastide de Lévis, Tarn, France, Aug. 10, 1947; s. Pierre and Paulette (Déléris) C.; m. Monique Saube; children: Olivier, Sophie. M Tech., U. Toulouse, France, 1971; grad. in aerospace engring., ENSICA, Toulouse, 1972; Lic. accélérée in econs., U. Bordeaux, France, 1973. Rsch. jr. engr. Aerospatiale Matra Lanceurs, Saint Médard en Jalles, France, 1974-88, sr. engr., 1988—. With French Air Force, 1972-73. Mem. European Soc. Composite Materials, N.Y. Acad. Scis., Amis de Robert Alkan (award 1987). Achievements include numerous patents in field; inventor 3D weaving processes for carbon-carbon rocket nozzles, thick fabric named 2.5D used for reentry shields, industrial parts in silicon industry and evaluated for jet motor fan blades; efficient fiber placement machinery used for airbus struts, tricky way for linking composite fabrics by a one-face stitching used for airbus parts; multilayer braiding loom named 3.5D. Home: 14 Ave Ausone, 33110 Le Bouscat Gironde, France Office: Aerospatiale Matra Lanceurs, BP 11 Issac, 33165 Saint Médard en Jalles France

CAI, BAOLI, molecular biology educator; b. Xinglong, Hebei, China, Jan. 23, 1945; s. Dehuai Cai and Cuiying Zhang; m. Fuguo Zhang, Sept. 15, 1971; 1 child, Xiang yu. BS, Nankai U., 1969. Tchr. Nankai U., Tianjin, China, 1969-78, lectr., 1979-87, assoc. prof., 1990-93, prof., 1998—; hon. fellow U. Minn., Mpls., 1988-89, sr. fellow, 1994-96; cons. Acad. of Environtl. Scis., Tianjin, China, 1998—. Author: Molecular Biology of Plasmids, 1999; contbr. articles to profl. jours. Mem. The Soc. of Chinese Biochemistry. Avocations: reading, music, touring. Office: Inst Molecular Biology, Nankai Univ, Tianjin 300071, China

CAI, DE FU, information systems educator; b. Shanhai, China, July 8, 1935; s. Jun Ji Cai and Han Zhao Wei; m. Li Hui Liu; children: Song-Yun, Ling-Han, Shuda. Grad., Jiao-Tong U., Shanghai, 1956. Asst. prof., lectr. Inst. Electronics Chinese Acad. Sci., Beijing, 1965-68; sr. engr. China Ministry Aerospace, Xi'an, 1968-78; dir. dept. Inst. Electronics Chinese Acad. Sci., 1978-95, prof., 1981—; vis. rsch. Heinrich-Hertz Inst., Berlin, 1982, Inst. Indsl. Sci., Tokyo, 1989—; cons. City of Fuzhou (China), 1984-92, City of An'Shan (China), 1992—, City of Yu'Yao (China), 1996—. Fellow China Assn. Imagery and Graphics (vice-chmn. 1990-98), Computer Vision & Intelligent Control/China Assn. Artiicial Intelligence, Soc. Signal Processing/Chinese Inst. Electronics. Avocations: classical music, competetive sports. Office: Inst Electronics Chinese Acad Sci, 17 Zhong-Guan-Cun Rd, Beijing 100080, China

CAI, ER FU, engineering executive; b. Shanghai, China, Mar. 22, 1939; s. Jia Lu and Li Juan (Zhou) C.; m. Shi Lin Gong, May 1, 1972; children: Zheng Ted, Rong Jack. BS, Tung Ji U., Shanghai, 1963; postgrad., U. Toronto, 1980. Engr. Beijing Chem. Design Inst., 1963-72, Yanshan Petrochem. Design Inst., Beijing, 1972-79; vis. engr. Lummus Can., Toronto, 1979-82; dept. mgr. Beijing Petrochem. Engring. Co., 1982-84; v.p. Sino Fluor Engrs., Beijing, 1984-89; asst. gen. mgr. Keystone Valve China, Shenzhen, Guangdong, China, 1989-93; chief rep. Keystone Beijing Rep. Office, 1993-96; chief rep., China sales mgr. Durco Valtek (Asia Pacific) Pte. Ltd., Beijing, 1996-98; sr. advisor Jing Shing Ltd., 1998—. Author: Petrochemical Piping Design, 1986, Chemical Plant System Design, 1992; co-author: The Application of TI-59 Program for Piping and Pressure Vessel Calculation, 1985, Petrochemical Automated Control Design Manual, 3d edit., 2000. Mem. ASME, Chinese Inst. Chem. Industry, Chinese Mech. Engring. Soc., Western Returned Students Assn. Office: Jing Shing Ltd 1313, 3A Chongwenmenenwai St, Beijing 100062, China

CAI, JIN-XING, electrical engineer; b. Gaocheng, China, Oct. 11, 1967; came to U.S., 1995; m. Yi Yang. BS, Tsinghua U., Beijing 1988, MS, 1994; PhD, U. So. Calif., 1999. Rsch. asst. State Key Lab. of Transient Optics and Tech., Xian, China, 1988-90, Tsinghua U., 1990-94, Jt. Lab. Advanced Tech. in Measurements, Beijing, 1994-95, U. So. Calif., L.A., 1995-99; sr. mem. tech. staff Tyco Submarine Systems, Ltd., 1999—. Contbr. articles to profl. jours. Home: 1429 Rustic Dr Apt 7 Asbury Park NJ 07712-7459

CAI, KHIEM VAN, technologist, researcher, administrator; b. Phu Cat, Binh Dinh, Viet Nam, Sept. 10, 1954; s. Trang Van and Chi Thi (tran) C.; m. Thuy T. Ha (dec. Dec. 1988); children: Kim Thien, Dan Van; m. Tuyet Hong Bui-Tran. BEE, Viet Nam Poly. U., 1975; MEE, Purdue U., 1978, PhD, 1981. Rsch. assoc. Radar Lab. Purdue U., West Lafayette, Ind., 1976-81; sr. staff engr., head advanced data link and analysis group Hughes Aircraft Co., Fullerton, Calif., 1982—; divsn. chief scientist, mgr. sys. engring. operation Raytheon Sys. Co., Torrance, Calif., 1996—; mem. adv. com. Tay Son Binh Dinh Assocs., So. Calif., 1990—. Contbr. tech. papers to profl. jours.; patents in communications and signal processing. Co-founder Vietnamese Student Assn., 1981, Vol. Svc. Group, 1981; instr. Vietnamese Youth Ctr., Garden Grove, Calif., 1982. Recipient Disting. Patent award in comms. Hughes Aircraft Co., 1990; David Ross scholar Purdue U., 1978. Mem. IEEE, N.Y. Acad. Sci., Tau Beta Pi, Eta Kappa Nu, Sigma Xi. Avocations: photography, skiing, volleyball, writing. Home: 2151 Clear Springs Rd Brea CA 92821-4390 Office: Hughes Aircraft Co NS 231/2011 3100 Lomita Blvd Torrance CA 90505-5177

CAI, MINGJIE, scientist; b. Lianyungang, Jiangsu, China, Nov. 14, 1953; parents Jianhua Cai and Ci Zheng; m. Liping Zhu, Jan. 1, 1981 (div. Nov. 1990); 1 child, Hong; m. Gekmui Ho, Jan. 9, 1999. BS, Nanjing (Jiangsu) U., 1977; MSc, Inst. Biochemistry, Shanghai, 1981; PhD, Stanford U., 1990. Chem. analyst Anti-epidemic Sta., Lianyungang, 1977-78; asst. prof. Shanghai Inst. Biochemistry, 1981-83, Nanjing U., 1983-85; postdoctoral fellow dept. genetics U. Wash., Seattle, 1990-92; prin. investigator Inst. Molecular and Cell Biology, Singapore, 1992—; cons. Clontech Labs., Inc., Palo Alto, Calif., 1990-92. Contbr. rsch. publs. to sci. jours. China-U.S. Biochem. Examination & Application Program predoctoral fellow Govt. of China, 1985, Markey Found. predoctoral fellow Stanford U., 1986, Damon-Runyon-Walter Winchell Cancer Rsch. Fund postdoctoral fellow, 1990.

Avocations: poetry, music. Fax: 65-7791117. E-mail: mcbcaimj@imcb.nus.edu.sg. Office: Nat U Singapore, 30 Medical Dr, Singaproe 117609, Singapore

CAI, WEIPING, physicist, material scientist; b. Ninghai, China, Apr. 28, 1959; s. Zhizhen Cai and Yuemei Chu; m. Ping Lu, Sept. 23, 1988; 1 child, Xuguang. BS, Northeast U., 1982, MS, 1984; PhD, Huazhong U. Sci. & Technology, 1994. From asst. to assoc. prof. Wuhan Iron & Steel U., China, 1984-95; prof., doctoral supr. Inst. Solid State Physics/Academia Sinica, Hefei, China, 1997—; prof. U. Sci. and Tech. China, Hefei, 1997—. Avocations: reading, travel, fishing, sports. Office: Inst Solid State Physics, Academica Sinica, 230031 Hefei Anhui, China

CAI, XIAOQIANG, engineering educator, researcher; b. Suixi, China, July 9, 1961; s. Zhi Cai and Xuezhen Huang; m. Yu Chang, Aug. 8, 1988; children: Yulong, Yuqi. BEng, Harbin (China) Shipbldg. Inst., 1982; MEng, Tsinghua U., Beijing, 1985, PhD, 1988. Lectr. Tsinghua U., 1988-89; postdoctoral scholar U. Cambridge, Eng., 1989-90; vis. fellow Queen's U., Belfast, No. Ireland, 1990-91; lectr. dept. math. U. Western Australia, Perth, 1991-92; lectr. dept. sys. engring. and engring. mgmt. The Chinese U. Hong Kong, 1993-96, sr. lectr., 1996—, chmn. dept., 1996—. Mem. editl. bd. IIE Transactions on Scheduling and Logistics, 1996—; Jour. of Scheduling, 1997—; contbr. numerous articles to profl. jours. Grantee Rsch. Grant Coun., Hong Kong, 1994, 96, 97, 99, Industry and Tech. Devel. Coun., Hong Kong, 1994. Mem. INFORMS, N.Y. Acad. Scis. Avocation: reading. Office: Dept Sys Engring Eng Mgmt, Chinese U Hong Kong, Shatin NT HK, China

CAI, XUAN SAN (HSUAN SAN TSAI), electrical engineering educator; b. Shanghai, People's Republic of China, Apr. 24, 1929; s. Zhen and Hui Fang (Bao) Tsai; m. Wen Hua Lee, Jan. 19, 1957; children: Rong, Lucy, Yue. B of Engring., Tsinghua U., Beijing, 1950. Teaching asst. Tsinghua U., Beijing, 1950-55, lectr., 1955-61, assoc. prof., 1961-85, prof. dept. elec. engring., 1985—; bd. dirs. electromagnetic automation equip. lab. Tsinghua U., Beijing, 1959-66, power conversion lab., 1989-93; hon. prof. Hebei Inst. Tech., Tianjin, China, 1993—. Author: Magnetic Amplifiers, 1961, Optimization and Optimal Control, 1983, Transient Analysis of Circuits, 1986, High Frequency Power Electronics, 1993, Principle and Design of Switching Power Supply, 1998. Recipient Spl. Contbn. award State Coun. China, 1992, Advance of Sci. awards Govt. Beijing City, 1986, 96, Achievement award China Electro-Tech. Found., 1991, Advance of Sci. award Edn. Ministry China, 1993, Advance of Sci. award Province HeBei, China. Fellow IEEE (vice chmn. Beijing sect. 1989-93, chmn. 1993-94, exec. com. 1994-98, chmn. edn. activities Asia-Pacific Region com. 1995-97, chmn. fellow nomination com. Beijing sect. 1999—), China Power Supply Soc. (chmn. 1993-97), Power Electronics Soc., China Power Electronics Soc. (vice chmn. 1995-99). E-mail: xscai@unet.net.cn. Office: Tsinghua Univ, Elec Engring Dept, Beijing 100084, China

CAI, ZHIGANG, physics educator, researcher; b. Xiamen, Fujian, China, Nov. 14, 1962; s. Rongcheng and Chunzhi Cai; m. Juan Lin, Jan. 27, 1995; 1 child, Yang(Lin). MSc, U. Bucharest, Romania, 1985, PhD, 1989. Postdoctoral fellow Inst. Laser and Spectroscopy, Zhongshan (Sun Yat-Sen) U., Guangzhou, China, 1989-92, lectr. physics, 1992, assoc. prof., 1992—; assoc. dir. State Key Lab. Ultrafast Laser Spectroscopy, Guangzhou, China, 1996-2000; assoc. dir. Inst. Laser and Spectroscopy Zhongshan (Sun Yat-Sen) U., Guangzhou, China, 1996-2000. Recipient award Ma Yingbiao Found., 1996, Natural Sci. award Guangdong Province, 1999. Mem. Physics Soc. China, Optics Assn. China. Avocations: Falun Gong, laser spectroscopy, nonlinear optics, polymers, computers. E-mail: zgcai@china.com. Office: Zhongshan U Inst Laser, Ultrafast Laser Spectr Lab, Guangzhou 510275, China

CAILEANU, CORNELIU M., engineering educator; b. Iasi, Romania, May 9, 1963; s. Mihai and Maria (Macovei) C. BSc, Poly. Inst., Iasi, 1987; PhD, Tech. U., Iasi, 1997. Sys. engr. IEPAM, Bârlad, Romania, 1987-90, Tech. Physics Inst., Iasi, 1990-91; asst. prof. Tech. U., Iasi, 1991-94, lectr., 1994—. Author: Control Algorithms for AC Drives, 1998; co-author: Real World Applications of Intelligent Technology, 1996; contbr. over 30 articles to profl. jours. With Romanian Army, 1981-82. Mem. IEEE, Internat. Fedn. Automatic Control, N.Y. Acad. Sci. Avocations: music, literature, sports. E-mail: ccailean@ee.tuiasi.ro. Home: Aleea Decebal 1, 6600 Iasi Romania Office: Tech U Iasi, St D Mangeron 53, 6600 Iasi Romania

CAILLIEZ, JEAN-CHARLES, biologist; b. Lille, France, Sept. 8, 1962; s. Patrick and Michèle (Straetmans) C.; m. Nancy Poret; children: Thomas, Romain. Lic. of scis., U. Lille, 1984, MSc, 1985, PhD, 1990, HDR, 1998. Lectr. Free Faculty of Scis., Lille, 1992-95, assoc. prof., 1995-99, prof., 1999—. Contbr. articles to profl. jours. Sgt. Artillery, 1985-86. Recipient Wicar and Hagelstein award Soc. of Scis., 1996. Avocations: tennis table, marathons, ski, mountain biking. E-mail: jean-charles.cailliez@pasteur-lille.fr. Office: Pasteur Inst of Lille, 1 Rue Professeur Calmette, 59019 Lille France

CAIN, FRANCIS MICHAEL, historian, educator; b. Warracknabeal, Victoria, Australia; s. Francis Michael and Beatrice Monica (Dolley) C.; m. Elaine Beryl Lokan, Aug. 13, 1960; children: Penelope, Felicity. BA, U. Adelaide, South Australia, 1961, BA with honors, 1964, MA, 1972; PhD, Monash U., Victoria, 1980. Lectr. Australian Air Force Acad., Point Cook, Victoria, 1966-73, sr. lectr., 1973-80; vis. fellow U. New South Wales, Sydney, Australia, 1981-82, sr. lectr. dept. history, 1983—. Author: Origins of Political Surveillance in Australia, 1983, The Wobblies at War: A History of the IWW and the Great War in Australia, 1993, ASIO: An Unofficial History, 1994; editor: Menzies of War and Peace, 1997, Arming Australia: A History of Defence Science and Technology, 1999; contbr. articles on Australian polit. history to profl. publs. Avocation: re-building and driving vintage motor cars. Home: 8 Goldsworthy Pl, 2617 South Bruce Australia Office: U New South Wales, 2600 Campbell Australia

CAIN, MICHAEL DEAN, research forester; b. Pascagoula, Miss., Nov. 9, 1946; s. Thomas R. and Bennie (Gleghorn) C. AS, Perkinston (Miss.) Jr. Coll., 1966; BS, Miss. State U., 1969; MS, La. State U., 1973. Registered forester, Miss. Rsch. forester So. Rsch. Sta., Pineville, La., 1975-78, Crossett, Ark., 1978-87, Monticello, Ark., 1987—. Contbr. articles to Forest Sci., So. Jour. Applied Forestry, Forest Ecology and Mgmt., Internat. Jour. Wildland Fire, New Forests, Nat. Areas Jour., Can. Jour. Forest Rsch., Am. Midland Naturalist, Jour. of the Torrey Bot. Soc., Wildlife Soc. Bull., The Cons., Tree Planters Notes, Fire Mgmt. Notes, Soc. Am. Foresters Conf. Procs., Procs. of the So. Weed Sci. Soc., univ. rsch. publs., USDA Forest Svc. rsch. publs., Ont. Forest Rsch. Inst. publ. With U.S. Army, 1969-71. Mem. Soc. Am. Foresters, Weed Sci. Soc. Am., So. Weed Sci. Soc., Ecol. Soc. Am., Internat. Assn. Wildland Fire, Soc. for Conservation Biology, Torrey Bot. Soc. Office: So Rsch Sta PO Box 3516 Monticello AR 71656-3516

CAIN, MICHAEL HANEY, lawyer; b. Chicoutimi, Que., Can., Mar. 26, 1929; s. Murray Vincent and Anna Marie (Feeney) C.; children: Murray, Evelyn. B.A., McGill U., 1950, B.C.L., 1953. Called to bar Que., 1954. Sr. ptnr. firm Cain Lamarre Casgrain Wells and predecessors, Chicoutimi, 1954-71, 72—; judge Mcpl. Ct., Chicoutimi North, 1965-70; justice Superior Ct. Que., Chicoutimi, Quebec City, 1971-72; mem. Canadian Inst. for Adminstrn. of Justice; mem. Adv. Com. Nomination Fed. Jud. Appointments Que., 1994-99. Founding pres. Found. U. Quebec at Chicoutimi Inc., 1969; bd. dirs. Found. Roland Saucier Inst.; dir., Bar of Que. Ins. Fund, 1986, v.p., 1991-96; dir. Sta. CJPM-TV, Inc. Founding mem. Que. Human Rights Commn., 1976-83; pres. com. on discipline Order of Nurses of P.Q.; pres. arbitration bd. Ministry of Edn. P.Q. Mem. Que. Bar Assn. (Forest medal 1993, 96), Can. Bar Assns. (v.p. Que. 1973-74, pres. 1974-75), Am. Coll. Trial Lawyers, Bar of Saguenay (batonnier 1969-70, 70-71), Found. Pierre & Gisele Laberge Inc., Found. Jercy & Phillida Brochocki. Home: 1786 Des Maristes, Chicoutimi, PQ Canada G7H 7M2 Office: 255 Racine St E, Chicoutimi, PQ Canada G7H 6J6

CAIN, THOMAS WILLIAM, judge; b. June 1, 1935; s. James Arthur Cain and Mary Edith Cunningham Lamb; m. Felicity Jane, 1961; 3 chil-

dren. Student, Marlborough Coll.; BA, Worcester Coll., Oxford, 1958, MA, 1961. Bar: Eng. 1959, Isle of Man, 1961. Atty. gen. Govt. of Isle of Man, Douglas, 1980-93, deemster (judge), 1993—. Chmn. Manx Wildlife Trust. 2d lt. RAC, 1953-55. Avocation: sailing. Home: Ivie Cottage, Kirk Michael 1M6 1AU, Isle of Man Office: Cts of Justice, Douglas Isle of Man

CAINE, MICHAEL, actor; b. London, Mar. 14, 1933; s. Maurice and Ellen Frances Marie Micklewhite; m. Patricia Haines, 1954; children: Dominique, Natasha; m. Shakira Baksh, 1973. Asst. stage mgr. Westminster Repertory, Horsham, Sussex, England, 1953; actor Lowestoft Repertory, 1953-55, Theatre Workshop, London, 1955. Author: What's It All About?: An Autobiography, 1993; numerous TV appearances, 1957-63; appeared in play Next Time I'll Sing for You, 1963; films include A Hill in Korea, 1956, How to Murder a Rich Uncle, 1958, Zulu, 1964, The Ipcress File, 1965, Alfie, The Wrong Box, Gambit, 1966, Hurry Sundown, Woman Times Seven, Deadfall, 1967, The Magus, Battle of Britain, Play Dirty, 1968, The Italian Job, 1969, Too Late the Hero, 1970, The Last Valley, Get Carter, 1971, Zee & Co., Kidnapped, Pulp, 1972, Sleuth, 1973, The Black Windmill, Marseilles Contract, The Wilby Conspiracy, 1974, Fat Chance, The Romantic Englishwoman, The Man Who Would Be King, Harry and Walter Go to New York, 1975, The Eagle Has Landed, A Bridge Too Far, Silver Bears, 1976, The Swarm, 1977, California Suite, 1978, Beyond the Poseidon Adventure, 1979, Dressed to Kill, The Island, 1980, The Hand, Victory, 1981, Deathtrap, 1982, Educating Rita, 1983, Beyond the Limit, 1983, The Jigsaw Man, The Holcroft Covenant, Blame It On Rio, 1984, The Whistle Blower, 1985, Hannah and Her Sisters, 1986 (recipient Acad. award for best supporting actor, 1987), Water, Sweet Liberty, Mona Lisa, Half Moon Street, 1986, Jaws The Revenge, Surrender, The Fourth Protocol (also co-exec. prodr.), 1987, Without a Clue, Dirty Rotten Scoundrels, 1988, Shock to the System, 1989, Bullseye!, Jekyll and Hyde, Mr. Destiny, 1990, Noises Off, 1991, The Muppets Christmas Carol, 1992, On Deadly Ground, 1994, Bullet to Beijing, 1995, Blood and Wine, 1996, Curtain Call, 1997; (TV miniseries) Jack the Ripper, 1988, World War II: When Lions Roared, 1994 (Emmy nominee for Lead Actor in a Miniseries, 1994, (TV movie) Blue Ice, 1993, Midnite in St. Petersburg, 1995, Mandela and Deklerk, 1996, (ABC-TV) 20,000 Leagues Under the Sea, 1996, Curtain Call, 1997, Shadow Run, 1997, Little Voice, 1998, Debtors, 1999, Cider House Rules, 1999, Quills, 1999, Shiner, 2000, Get Carter, 2000, Miss Congeniality, 2000. Office: care Pam PR Inc 4401 Wilshire Blvd Los Angeles CA 90010-3728 also: Chelsea Harbour, London England

CAINE, PHILIP DAVID, retired military officer, author; b. Chadron, Nebr., July 3, 1933; s. Clifford M. Caine and Eulah Ann Robertson; m. Doris E. Caine, Aug. 1, 1954; children: Barbara, Virginia, Jennifer. BA, U. Denver, 1955; MA, Stanford U., 1963, PhD, 1966; grad., Air War Coll., 1972, Nat. War Coll., 1978. Tchr. Denver Pub. Schs., 1955; commd. 2nd lt. USAF, 1955, advanced through grades to brig. gen., 1992, pilot, 1956-61; prof. history USAF Acad. USAF, Colo., 1963-69, 1970-78; head project CHECO 7th Air Force USAF, Saigon, Vietnam, 1969-70; prof. Nat. Def. U. USAF, Washington, 1978-80; dep. comdt. cadets USAF Acad. USAF, Colo., 1980-92; ret. USAF, 1992; sr. fellow Nat. Def. U., Washington, 1987; sr. Mil. Sch. Rev. Bd., Washington, 1987. Author: Eagles of the RAF, 1991 (Blue Line award 1992), American Pilots in the RAF, 1993 (Mil. Book Club selection 1993), Spitfires, Thunderbolts and Warm Beer, 1995 (Mil. Book Club selection 1995), Aircraft Down!, 1997 (Mil. Book Club selection 1997). Dir. Woodmoor Improvement Assn., Monument, Colo., 1972-74; trustee Falcon Found., USAF Academy, Colo., 1996—; sec. Friends of the Acad. Libr., USAF Academy, 1998—. Decorated Commendation medals USAF, 1968, 87, Bronze star USAF, 1970, Meritorious Svc. medals USAF, 1980, 87, Legion of Merit USAF, 1992. Mem. Air Force Assn., Sertoma Internat., Order of Daedalians. Avocations: travel, woodworking, writing, art. E-mail: PhilDCI@aol.com. Home: 19060 Pebble Beach Way Monument CO 80132-8931

CAIRE, JEAN-PIERRE, chemical engineering educator; b. St-Etienne, France, Mar. 24, 1947. Doctorate, Nat. Inst. Polytech. Grenoble, France, 1985. Registered chem. engr. Maitre-de-conf. Nat. Inst. Poly. Grenoble, 1978—. Office: Enseeg, Rue-de-la-Riscine, F38402 Saint Martin D'Here France

CAIRNS, MARGOT BERESFORD, business writer, leadership expert; b. Newcastle, Australia, Jan. 29, 1954; d. Allan Beresford and Joan (De Mestre) C.; m. Niel Simpson, Apr. 12, 1973 (div.); children: Lisa, Andrew; m. Christian B. Muzard, Jan. 12, 1991. B Edn., Sydney U.; MBA, AGSM, Sydney, Australia. CEO Darwin Family Peulies, Australia, 1981-83; lectr. U. No. Territory, Australia, 1982-84, Sydney U., Australia, 1985—; asst. dean AGSM, 1985-86; leadership columnist, 1985—; chair The Chande Dynamic Pty Ltd., 1986—; pub. spkr. Saxton's Speakers Bur., Australia, 1998—. Author: (books) Peacful Chaos, 1992, Reaching For The Stars, 1994, Approaching The Corporate Heart, 1998. Anglican. Avocations: sailing, walking, art. Office: The Change Dynamic, PO Box 21, 2092 Seaforth Australia

CAIRNS, ALAN JOSEPH, transportation executive; b. Newcastle, Northumberland, Eng., Jan. 12, 1933; s. Frank and Mary (McGlen) C.; m. Zena Constance Smith, Apr. 1, 1959; children: Gerrard, Trudie, Angela, Richard. Grad. high sch., Surrey, Eng. Traffic officer Britavia Group, London, 1953-56; cargo officer KLM Royal Dutch Air, London, 1956-59; mgr. cargo sales Brit. Caledonia Air, London, 1959-74, Europe Air New Zealand, London, 1974-90, Cairns Mktg., 1990—. Author: Ceramics 1890, 1980, Bastards Aye Have Known, 1982, New Zealand-The Boring Land, 1990, Transport Marketing, 1995. Served with Royal Air Force, 1951-53. Mem. United Kingdom Air Cargo Assn., Thames Valley Exporters. Club: Hartleys (London). Avocations: riding, ceramics, art research. Office: Firlands House Church Rd, Mortimer West End, Reading Berks RG7 2HO, England

CAIRNS, DIANE PATRICIA, motion picture executive; b. Fairbanks, Alaska, Mar. 2, 1957; d. Dion Melvin and Marsha Lala (Andrews) C. BBA, U. So. Calif., 1980. Literary agt. Sy Fischer Agy., L.A., 1980-85; sr. v.p. Internat. Creative Mgmt., L.A., 1985-96; sr. v.p. prodn. Universal Pictures, L.A., 1996-97. Mem. NOW, NARAL, Acad. Motion Picture Arts and Scis., Women's Action Coun., Amnesty Internat., L.A. County Mus. of Art, Mus. of Contemporary Art (L.A.), Mus. TV and Radio (L.A.)

CAIVANO, JOSE LUIS, architect; b. Junin, Argentina, Mar. 26, 1958; s. Abel Luciano and Alba Argentina (Acedo) C.; m. Marcela Fiorillo, June 22, 1985 (div. 1997); m. Mabel A. López, Feb. 24, 1998; 1 child. BA, Nat. Coll., Junin, 1977; Nat. Prof. Music, Nat. Conservatory, Buenos Aires, Argentina, 1979; Architect, Buenos Aires U., 1984. Architect diplomate. Rsch. fellow Buenos Aires U., 1986-89, prof., 1993—; rsch. assoc. Ind. U., Bloomington, Ind., 1989, 94; rsch. fellow Nat. Coun. of Rsch., Argentina, 1990-94; postdoctoral rsch. fellow Nat. Coun. Rsch., 1995-97; practicing architect Argentina, 1984-86; rschr. Nat. Coun. Rsch., 1997—; dir. program rsch. Buenos Aires U., 1997—; adj. prof. Buenos Aires U., 1988-93; lectr. various univs., Argentina, 1990—. Editor of publs. School Architecture, Buenos Aires U., 1994—; editor of proceedings Argentine Color Group, 1992—; author: (book) Guide to Do, Write and Publish Research Papers (in Spanish) 1995, others; contbr. articles to profl. jours. Grantee Buenos Aires U., 1993, 95, 96, 97, 99. Mem. Argentine Color Group (pres. 1994—), Internat. Assn. Interdisciplinary Study of Symmetry (adv. bd.), Internat. Assn. for Semiotic Studies, Internat. Assn. Semiotics of Space, Internat. Assn. for Visual Semiotic, Internat. Color Assn. Study Groups on Environmental Color Design and Visual Illusions (chmn. 1997—), Semiotic Soc. of Am., Argentine Assn. for Semiotics, Soc. for Computational Modelling of Creative Processes, N.Y. Acad. Scis., Found. for Vision Rsch. "F. Mattiello" (v.p.), Jour. of Internat. Assn. for Visual Semiotics (mem. edtl. com.). Avocations: classical music, photography, book binding. Home: Ciudad de La Paz 3485, 1429 Buenos Aires Argentina Office: Secretaria Investigacion Facultad Arquitectura, U Buenos Aires Piso 4, 1428 Buenos Aires Argentina

CAIXIA, TU, dermatologist, educator; b. Dalian, Liaoning, China, Jan. 5, 1956; p. Changqing and Guimei (Wang) T.; m. Shiming Liu, Sept. 16, 1984; 1 child, Kecheng. B Med, China Med. U., Shenyang, 1983; MD, Dalian Med. U. 1990. Resident 1st Affiliated Hosp. of Dalian Med. U., 1983-89, vis. staff, 1989-93, assoc. prof., 1993-98, prof. dermatology, 1998—, vice

chmn. dept. dermatology, 1996. Editl. mem. Jour. Practical Nursing, 1995; contbr. articles to profl. jours. and books. Recipient Sci. and Tech. Promoting prizes Nat. Edn. Commn., 1991, Dalian Mcpl. Govt., 1998. Avocations: swimming, stamp collecting. Office: 1st Affil Hosp Dalian Med U, 222 Zhongshan Lu Dept Derm, Dalian 116011, China

CAJUEIRO, MARCELO SANTOS DE, communications company executive, correspondent; b. Ribeirão de Pinhal, Paraná, Brazil, Jan. 25, 1967; s. Sergio Cajueiro and Lia Santos de (Brandão) C.; m. Paula Ferreira Machado, Jan. 10, 1999. Cert. in English proficiency, U. Mich. and Mich. State U., 1986; grad. cum laude, Fed. U. Rio de Janeiro, 1989; MS in Journalism, Columbia U., 1992. Registered journalist, Brazil. Tchr. English, Fait English Course, Rio de Janeiro, 1985-87; staff writer Conn. Post, Bridgeport, 1991-92; corr. Reuters New Agy., Rio de Janeiro, 1992-94; CEO, Diagrama Comunicações Ltda., Rio de Janeiro, 1993—; Rio de Janeiro corr. Variety, 1994—, Variety/Deal Memo, 1994—, LatinCom, 1999—, Multichannel News Internat., 1999—;. Contbr. numerous articles to newapapers and mags. Human rights activist, newsletter editor Grupo Tortura Nunca Mais, Rio de Janeiro, 1985—; environ. and human rights activist Amanaka, N.Y.C., 1990-92. Avocations: cinema, reading, soccer, travel. E-mail: cajueiro@centroin.com.br. Home: Rua São Clemente 28/1003, 22260000 Rio de Janeiro Brazil Office: Diagrama Comunicações, Av Pres Vargas 583/914, 20071003 Rio de Janeiro Brazil

CAKMAKOGLU, SABAHATTIN, Turkish government official. Min. of nat. def. Ankara, Turkey. Office: Milli Savunma Bakaligi, Ankara Turkey*

CALABRESI, GUIDO, federal judge, law educator; b. Milan, Oct. 19, 1932; s. Massimo and Bianca Maria (Finzi Contini) C.; m. Anne Gordon Audubon Tyler, May 20, 1961; children: Bianca Finzi Contini, Anne Gordon Audubon, Massimo Franklin Tyler. BS in Analytical Econs., Yale U., 1953, LLB, 1958, MA (hon.), 1962; BA in Politics, Philosophy and Econs., Oxford U., 1955, MA in Politics, Philosophy and Econs., 1959; LLD (hon.), Notre Dame U., 1979, Villanova U., 1984, U. Toronto, 1985, Boston Coll., 1986, Cath. U. Am., 1986, U. Chgo., 1988, Conn. Coll., 1988, Chgo.-Kent-I.T.T., 1989, William Mitchell Coll. Law, 1992, Princeton U., 1992, Skidmore Coll., 2000, Detroit Mercy Sch. Law, 1994, Seton Hall U., 1995, Albertus Magnus Coll., 1995, Lewis and Clark Coll., 1996, St. John's U., 1997, Pace U., 1998, Iona Coll., 1998, Roger Williams U., 1999, Hofstra U., 1999, N.Y. Law Sch., 1999, Skidmore Coll., 2000; Dott. Ius SD (hon.), U. Turin, Italy, 1982; JD (hon.), U. Pavia, Italy, 1987, U. Stockholm, 1993; PhD (hon.), U. Haifa, Israel, 1988; DPhil, U. Tel Aviv, 1998; LHD (hon.), U. New Haven, 1989, Williams Coll., 1991, Quinnipiac Coll., 1993; DSc in Politics (hon.), U. Padua, Italy, 1990; Dott. Jur. (hon.), U. Bologna, Italy, 1991, U. Milan, 1998; LLD (hon.), Skidmore Coll., 2000. Bar: Conn. 1958. Asst. instr. dept. econs. Yale U., New Haven, Conn., 1955-56; law clk. to Hon. Hugo Black U.S. Supreme Ct., Washington, 1958-59; asst. prof. Yale U. Law Sch., 1959-61, assoc. prof., 1961-62, prof., 1962-70, John Thomas Smith prof. law, 1970-78, Sterling prof. law, 1978-95; prof. emeritus, lectr. Yale U., 1995—; dean Yale U. Law Sch., 1985-94; Sterling prof. law emeritus, lectr. Yale U. Law Sch., New Haven, 1995—; judge U.S. Ct. Appeals 2d cir., New Haven, 1994—; fellow Timothy Dwight Coll., 1960—; vis. prof. Harvard U. Law Sch., 1969-70, Japan Am. Studies Seminar, Kyoto-Doshisha Univs., summer 1972, European U. Inst., Florence, Italy, 1979; Arthur L. Goodhart prof. legal sci. Cambridge U., also fellow St. John's Coll., 1980-81. Author: The Costs of Accidents: A Legal and Economic Analysis, 1970; (with P. Bobbitt) Tragic Choices, 1978; A Common Law for the Age of Statutes, 1983 (ABA citation of merit, Order of Coif Triennial Book award); Ideals, Beliefs, Attitudes and the Law: Private Law Perspectives on a Public Law Problem (Silver Gavel award ABA), 1985; contbr. articles to profl. jours. Hon. trustee Hopkins Grammar Sch., pres. 1976-80; trustee St. Thomas More Chapel, Yale U.; vice-chmn. bd. trustees Carolyn Found., Minn. Rhodes scholar, 1953; named one of Ten Outstanding Young Men Am., U.S. Jaycees, 1962; recipient Laetare Medal, U. Notre Dame, 1985, Marshall-Wythe medal Coll. William and Mary, 1985, award for outstanding rsch. in law and govt. Fellows of Am. Bar Found., 1998, Thomas Jefferson medal in law Jefferson Found./U. Va. Law Sch., 2000. Fellow Am. Acad. Arts & Scis., Associazione Italiana di Diritto Comparato, Brit. Acad. (corr.), Royal Swedish Acad. Scis. (fgn.), Nat. Acad. dei Lincei (fgn.), Acad. delle Sci. di Torino (fgn.); mem. Conn. Bar Assn., Assn. Am. Law Schs. (exec. com. 1986-89), Am. Philos. Soc. Home: 639 Amity Rd Woodbridge CT 06525-1206 Office: US Ct Appeals 2d Cir 157 Church St New Haven CT 06510-2100

CALAIS, JOSETTE, mathematics educator; b. Monsols, France, July 5, 1931; d. Adrien and Marcelle (Tabernier) C. Degree in Math., U. France, 1954; D in Math., U. Paris, 1964. Prof. dept. math. U. Reims, France, 1967-99; prof. emeritus U. Reims, 1999—. Author: Elements de Théorie des Groups, 1984. Recipient Palmes Academiques award Grad de Commandeur, 1990. Mem. Soc. Math. France, Soc. Agregisde Umounts, Assn. Profs. Math. Office: Univ Reims Dept Math, Moulin de la Housse, 51062 Reims France

CALANDRI, CESARE, hematologist; b. Rome, Italy, Feb. 27, 1953; s. Alessandro and Anna (Cornelio) C.; m. Yvette Kathleen Cooper, Dec. 26, 1985; children: Robin Devon, Lucia Gabriella, Terry Ann, Alex. MD, U. La Sapienza, Rome, 1983. Diplomate Am. Bd. Internal Medicine, 1987; Hematology, U. La Sapienza, Rome, 1988. Resident Episcopal Hosp., Phila., 1984-87; fellow Mt. Sinai Hosp., N.Y., 1987-90; mgr. oncology rsch. Bristol-Myers-Squibb, Rome, 1991-92; assoc. physician internal medicine Civil Hosp., Orvieto, Italy, 1992-98; assoc. physician med. oncology Bellaria Hosp., Bologna, Italy, 1998—. Office: Ospedale Bellaria Med Onc, Via Altura 3, 40100 Bologna Italy

CALÇADO, ANTONIO CELSO, pediatric gastroenterology administrator, educator; b. Rio de Janeiro, Apr. 9, 1952; s. Celso Da Rocha and Maria Delphina (Teixeira) C.; m. Jacqueline Coelho de Oliveira, Sept. 15, 1995; children: Luiz Felippe Fontoura de Souza, Ricardo Augusto, Fernanda Luiza Valladares, João Lucas Oliveira, Maria Clara Oliveira. Physician, Fed. U. Rio de Janeiro, 1975, MSc, 1979, PhD in Pediats., 1992; MBA in Mktg., Fundacão Getulio Vargas, Rio de Janeiro, 1999. Lic. physician, pediatrician. Cons. physician Ministry of Health, Rio de Janeiro, 1977—; prof. pediats. Fed. U. Rio de Janeiro, 1980—, coord. pediat. edn., 1986-87, co-coord. postgrad. in pediats., 1990-92, chief of dept. of pediats., 1994-96, head of pediat. gastroenterology unit, 1989—; hon. sr. lectr. King's Coll. Hosp., U. London, 1988; cons. diarrhea diseases control program Ministry of Health, Brasilia, Brazil, 1991-94, cons. dept. drug adminstrn., 1995-97; cons. to pharm. industry; presenter in field. Author: (book) Digestive Tract in Pediatrics, 1986; editor: (books) Topics in Pediatric Gastroenterology, 1993, Handbook of Pediatric Gastroenterology, 1995; contbr. numerous articles to profl. jours. and chpts. to books. Rsch. grantee in pediat. gastroenterology Nat. Coun. for Rsch., 1976-77, 82-83; recipient prize Fed. U. Rio de Janeiro, 1975. Mem. Internat. Soc. for Pediat. Gastroenterology and Nutrition (co-pres. 1995-97, Honor Cert. 1995), Brazilian Soc. Pediats. (specialist in pediats. 1979, coord. bd. for concession of the cert. of pediatrician 1991-93, 1st sec. 1992-95), N.Y. Acad. Scis. Roman Catholic. Avocations: traveling, football. E-mail: acalcado@gbl.com.br. Office: Praia de Botafogo, 210 Sala 308, 22250040 Rio de Janeiro Brazil

CALCATERRA, JEFFREY RONALD, aerospace engineer; b. Detroit, May 31, 1970; s. Ronald and Cecilia (Denomme) C.; m. Melanie Ann Bain, Mar. 19, 1994; 1 child: Bobby. B in Aerospace Engring., Ga. Inst. Tech., 1992, MS in Aerospace Engring., 1993, PhD in Aerospace Engring., 1996. Tchg. asst. Ga. Inst. Tech., Atlanta, 1992-93, rsch. asst., 1993-96; post doctoral rsch. assoc. Air Force Inst. Tech., Dayton, Ohio, 1996-98; aerospace engr. Air Force Inst. Tech., Dayton, 1998-99, USAF 46th Test Wing, Dayton, 1999—; tech. chmn. Space and Air Survivability Workshop 2000, Denver; integrating concept leader spacecraft survivability USAF 46th Test Wing, Dayton, 1999—. Contbr. articles to profl. jours. Mem. tech. com. Holy Angels Ch., Dayton, 1998-99. Mem. AIAA, ASTM. Roman Catholic. Avocations: building furniture, restoring old cars, playing football, basketball and softball. Home: 400 Monteray Ave Dayton OH 45419-2653 Office: 2700 D St Bldg 22B Wright Pat OH 45433-7403

CALDA, PAVEL, obstetrician-gynecologist, consultant; b. Prague, Czechoslovakia, Jan. 7, 1957; s. Pavel and Žofie (Zimmermannová) C.; m. Dana Somolíková, July 11, 1987; children: Denisa, Barbara. MD, Charles U., Prague, 1983, PhD, 1994. Resident, fellow dept. ob-gyn. Charles U., Prague, 1984-90, cons. dept. ob-gyn., 1990-94, head Ctr. Fetal Medicine, 1994—, assoc. prof., 1998. Editor in chief Jour. Modern Gynecology, 1999. Mem. Czech Ob-Gyn. Soc. (sec. sci.). Office: Charles U Dept Ob-Gyn, Apolinarska 18, 128 51 Prague Czech Republic

CALDAS, CARLOS M., physician, researcher; b. Oliveira de Frades, Portugal, June 27, 1960; s. Carlos and Isilda (Simaõ) C.; m. Maria Isabel Andrade Sousa, May 7, 1988; children: Carlos, Madalena. MD, U. Lisbon, Portugal, 1984. Diplomate Am. Bd. Internal Medicine, Am. Bd. Med. Oncology. Intern, resident U. Tex. S.W. Med. Sch., Dallas, 1988-91; sr. clin. fellow Johns Hopkins Oncology Ctr., Balt., 1991-94; rsch. fellow Inst. Cancer Rsch., London, 1994-96; mem. faculty dept. oncology U. Cambridge, Eng., 1996—. Fellow Am. Coll. Physicians; me. Am. Assn. Cancer Rsch. (corr.). Office: Dept Oncology, U Cambridge, Cambridge CB2 2QQ, England

CALDECOTT, KEITH WILLIAM, science educator; b. Crewe, Cheshire, Eng., Mar. 16, 1965; s. William James and Dorothy Iris (Boulton) C.; m. Rachel Marie Warke, Oct. 25, 1990; children: Alice Charlotte, Richard James. BSc with honors, Sheffield (Eng.) U., 1987; PhD, Nat. Inst. Med. Rsch., London, 1990. Postdoctoral fellow U. Calif., San Francisco, 1990-93, ICRF, London, 1993-95; sr. rsch. fellow, lectr. U. Manchester, Eng., 1995—; cons. Astrazeneca Pharms., Eng., 1995—. Contbr. articles to profl. jours.; patent pending molecular DNA damage sensor. Grantee Govt. Med. Rsch. Coun., 1996, 98, 99. Office: U Manchester, Stopford Bldg Oxford Rd, Manchester M13 9PT, United Kingdom

CALDEIRA, ALEXANDRE DAVID, nuclear engineer; b. Rio de Janeiro, Brazil, Oct. 27, 1958; s. Gilberto Da Silveira and Suely (David) C.; m. Leila Magalhaes Brito, July 24, 1981; children: Igor, Caio. Degree in electronic engring., GamaFilho U., 1980; MSc in Nuclear Engring., Mil. Inst. Engring., Rio de Janeiro, 1983; PhD in Nuclear Engring., Inst. Energy and Nuclear Rsch., 1999. Electronics tchr. EstaciodeSa High Edn. Soc., Rio de Janeiro, 1982-84; rchr., head nuclear data subdivsn. Aerospace Tech. Ctr., Sao Jose dos Campos, Brazil, 1984—. Avocations: soccer, indoor soccer, fishing. E-mail: alexdc@ieao.cta.br. Fax: 55 12 347-5495. Home: Rua Antares 125 Apto 307, 12230904 Sao Jose dos Campos Brazil Office: Aerospace Tech Ctr, Rodovia dos Tamoios Km 5,5, 12231970 Sao Jose dos Campos SaoPaulo, Brazil

CALDENTEY, JAVIER, biochemist, researcher; b. Barcelona, Spain, May 3, 1954; s. Miguel Caldentey and Maria-Cinta Otero; m. Kirsi-Marja Oksman, July 3, 1982; 1 child, Tania Maria. MSc in Chemistry, U. Barcelona, 1977; M Molecular Biology, U. Basel, Switzerland, 1982, PhD in Biochemistry, 1986. Rschr. Sandoz Ltd., Basel, 1979-80, U. Basel, 1981-86; rsch. scientist VTT, Espoo, Finland, 1986; rsch. assoc. dept. med. chemistry U. Helsinki, Finland, 1987-88, rsch. assoc. dept. genetics, 1988-93, docent, 1992—, sr. scientist Inst. Biotech., 1993—; expert Nat. Acad. Medicines, Helsinki, 1977—. Contbr. articles to profl. jours., chpts. to books. Cpl. Spanish Army, 1978-79. Embo fellow, 1991; Spanish Ministry Edn. grantee, 1992-93. Mem. Finnish Biochem. Soc. Roman Catholic. Avocations: music, books, travel, railroading. Office: U Helsinki Inst Biotech, PO Box 56 Viikinkaari 5, 00014 Helsinki Finland

CALDER, KENT EYRING, political science educator, diplomat; b. Salt Lake City, Apr. 18, 1948; s. Grant H. and Rose (Eyring) C.; m. Toshiko Matsuura; children: Mari, Ryan. BA with honors, U. Utah, 1970; AM, Harvard U., 1972, PhD, 1979. Staff mem. U.S. Ho. of Reps., Washington, 1968-69; teaching fellow Harvard U. Dept. of Govt., Cambridge, Mass., 1972-74; rsch. economist U.S. Fed. Trade Commn., Washington, 1974-78; visiting fellow U. Tokyo, Japan, 1977-78; exec. dir. U.S.-Japan Program Harvard U., Cambridge, 1979-80, lectr., 1979-83; asst. prof. Woodrow Wilson Sch. Princeton (N.J.) U., 1983-89, assoc. prof., 1989—, dir. U.S.-Japan program, 1990—; internat. adv. bd. Japanese Ministry of Fin., Inst. of Fiscal and Monetary Policy, Tokyo, 1987-96; Japan chair Ctr. for Strategic and Internat. Studies, Washington, 1989-91, 96; spl. advisor to U.S. Amb. to Japan, 1996—. Author: Crisis and Compensation, 1988 (Ohira and Arisawa Meml. prizes 1990), Japan's Changing Role in Asia, 1992, Strategic Capitalism, 1993, Pacific Defense, 1996 (Mainichi Asia-Pacific Grand prize 1997); co-author: The Eastasia Edge, 1982. Instr. Japan Soc. U.S.-Japan Leadership Program, N.Y.C., 1988-91, U. Pa. Wharton Sch. Internat. Forum, 1990—; trustee Princeton in Asia, 1987—; mem. Coun. on Fgn. Rels., 1990—, internat. adv. bd. Waseda U. Sch. Asia-Pacific Studies, 1998—, World Econ. Forum East Asia Summits, 1998—. 1st lt. U.S. Army, 1975-76. Named Fulbright Faculty Fellow and Doctoral Fellow, 1985-86, 75-76, Faculty Research Fellow The Japan Found., 1984, Graduate Prize Fellow Harvard U., 1970-74. Mem. Am. Polit. Sci. Assn., Assn. for Asian Studies, Phi Beta Kappa, Phi Kappa Phi (Sparks Fellow 1970-71, Gibbs Fellow 1970), OECD Tide 2000 Club. Avocations: stamp collecting, collecting classic African musical instruments, tennis. Home: 197 Shadybrook Ln Princeton NJ 08540-4135 Office: US Embassy Tokyo Unit 45004 Box 200 APO AP 96337-5004

CALDER, MARTIN CHARLES, social welfare administrator; b. Preston, Eng., Sept. 21, 1962; s. Walter Hornby and Rita (McDermott) C.; m. Janet Fairclough, Aug. 20, 1988. BA with honors, U. Bradford, U.K., 1985; diploma in child protection, U. Lancaster, 1990, MA in Child Protection, 1992. Social worker Berkshire County Coun., U.K., 1985-87; specialist in protection, social worker Cheshire County Coun., U.K., 1987-93; child protection coord. City of Salford Coun., U.K., 1993—; mem. Baspcan, York, 1989—, NOTA, 1999—; presenter in field. Author: Juveniles and Children Who Sexually Abuse: A Guide to Risk Assessment, 1997, Working With Young People Who Sexually Abuse: New Pieces of the Jigsaw Puzzle, 1999, Assessing Risk in Adult Male Sex Offenders, 1999, A Practice Guide to Sexual Abuse Assessment, 2000; co-author: Working for Children on the Child Protection Register; contbr. articles to profl. jours. Avocations: reading, writing, eating, sports, sleeping. Home: 11 Hanwell Close Pennington, Leigh WN7 3NU, U.K. Office: City of Salford Social Svcs, Avon Close Worsley, Salford M28 OLA, United Kingdom

CALDER, NIGEL DAVID RITCHIE, freelance writer; b. London, Dec. 2, 1931; s. Peter Ritchie and Mabel (McKail) C.; m. Elisabeth Palmer, May 22, 1954; children: Sarah, Penelope, Simon, Jonathan, Katharine. MA, Cambridge (Eng.) U., 1954. Editor New Scientist mag., London, 1962-66; freelance sci. writer Crawley, Eng., 1966—; mem. initiative group Found. Sci. Europe, Maastricht, The Netherlands, 1986-88; cons. public info. European Space Agy., 1994—. Author: Einsteins Universe, 1979, The Comet Is Coming!, 1980, Timescale, 1983, The English Channel, 1986 (Book of the Sea award), Spaceship Earth, 1991, Giotto to the Comets, 1992, Beyond this World, 1995, The Manic Sun, 1997; scriptwriter for TV programs. Recipient Kalinga prize UNESCO, 1972; AAAS fellow, 1985; Rochester Mus. fellow, 1985. Mem. Assn. Brit. Sci. Writers (chmn. 1962-64), Royal Astron. Soc., Royal Geog. Soc., Cruising Assn. (v.p. 1981-84). Avocation: sailing. Home and Office: 26 Boundary Road, Northgate Crawley RH10 2BT, England

CALDERON, MOISES, cardiothoracic transplant surgeon; b. Mexico City, Mex., May 25, 1961; s. Salomon and Yael (Abbo) C.; m. Susan Lombroso, Apr. 1, 1990; children: Samantha, Alexa. MD, Met. Autonomous U., 1986; postgrad. specialist in surgery, Nat. Autonomous U. of Mex., 1989; PhD in Health Care Mgmt., LaSalle U., 1995. Staff surgeon dept. cardiac surgery La Raza Med. Ctr., Mexico City, 1992-96; dir. dept. circulatory support Laraza Med. Ctr., Mexico City, 1993-96, dir. thoracic transplant program, 1993-96, surgeon in chief, all cardiac surgery depts., 1996—; dir. Mex. artificial heart project Mex. Inst. for Social Security, Mexico City, 1993—; founder, chmn. Circulatory Support Inc., Mexico City, 1995—; chmn. sch. of extracorporeal tech. LaRaza Med. Ctr., Mex. Inst. for Social Security, Mexico City, 1993—, head prof. cardiothoracic surgery LaRaza Med. Ctr., Nat. Autonomous U. of Mex., 1996—, head prof. of thoracic transplantation, 1997—; med. dir., founder Mex. Cardiovascular Inst., 1999. Author: Epistemology, Insights on Transplantation and Artificial Organs, 1996, Images of the Heart, 1996, Cardiac Transplantation, 1997, El Sueno Guajiro, 1998, patient Manual After Cardiac Surgery, 1999; editor: Circulatory Support and Thoracic Transplantation, 1994; inventor in field. Founder, pres. Mex. Cardiovascular Found., Mexico City, 1996—; mem. Friends of Fine Arts, Mexico City, 1997—. Postgrad. fellow in cardiothoracic surgery Tex. Heart Inst. U. Tex., Houston, 1991; recipient Medal of Honor Med. Sch. Autonomous Met. U., 1988. Mem. Ose Mex. Charitable Soc. (surgeon 1992—), MD Charitable Soc. (surgeon 1994—), Mex. Soc. of Cardiac Surgery (founder), Internat. Soc. for Heart and Lung Transplantation, Soc. of Thoracic Surgeons. Jewish. Home: Paseo de la Soledad 69, 53920 La Herradurn Mexico Office: Bufete Medico, Federico T de 12 Chila 2103, 53100 Satelite Mexico

CALDERON, REYNA OLGA, science educator, researcher; b. Cordoba, Argentina, July 17, 1939; d. Ramon Felipe Calderon and Matilde Rodriguez; m. Bruno Maggio. Secondary tchr. degree, A Carbo, Cordoba, 1957; tchr. of music degree, Conservatorio Prvincial, Cordoba, 1956; biochemist degree, U. Nat., Cordoba, 1963, PhD in Biochemistry, 1981. Instr., rsch. asst. Nat. U. Cordoba, 1963-73; rsch. assoc. U. Coll. U. London, 1974-76; rsch. assoc. Nat. U. Cordoba, 1976-88, asst. prof., 1980-88; postdoctoral rsch. assoc. dept. chemistry Yale U., New Haven, Conn., 1984-85; postdoctoral sr. rsch. assoc. dept. biochemistry Med. Coll. Va., 1989-94; dir. undergrad. courses Faculty Chemistry, Cordoba, 1980-88; prof. admission for med. practitioners Nat. U. Cordoba, 1979-88, dir. rsch. project, 1985-88; with IDEM, 1994—. Contbr. articles to profl. jours. Recipient Nat. Rsch. Svc. award NIH, 1993. Mem. Biology Soc. Cordoba. Office: Sch Med, Ciudad U, 5000 Cordoba Argentina

CALDERWOOD, STANFORD MATSON, investment management executive; b. Scottsbluff, Nebr., Nov. 6, 1920; s. Herbert Merle and Hazel Emjore (Matson) C.; m. Norma Jean Smith, Mar. 17, 1942. B.A., U. Colo., 1942. Reporter-photographer Manchester (N.H.) Union-Leader, 1946-48; staff corr. U.P.I., 1948-51, bus. rep., 1951-52; pub. relations writer Eastern Gas & Fuel Assos., Boston, 1952-53; with Polaroid Corp., Cambridge, Mass., 1953-70; v.p. advt. Polaroid Corp., 1960-62, v.p. sales and advt., 1962-66, v.p. marketing, 1966-69, exec. v.p., 1969-70; pres., dir. Polaroid of Japan, 1962-70, Polaroid Overseas, 1962-70, Polaroid Can., 1962-70, Polaroid France, 1965-70; pres. Polaroid GmbH, 1965-70, Polaroid (Italia) S.p.A., 1965-70; gen. mgr. dir. Polaroid (Nederlands), N.V., 1962-70; gen. mgr. Polaroid (Internat.) N.V., 1965-70; pres. WGBH Ednl. Found., Boston, 1970-71; cons. Corp. Pub. Broadcasting, 1971-72; vice chmn., dir. Endowment Mgmt. & Research Corp., Boston, 1972-77; pres. Trinity Investment Mgmt. Corp., Boston, 1978-85, chmn., chief exec. officer, 1985-99, chmn. emeritus, 1999—; lectr. econs. Wellesley Coll., 1972-73, vis. prof., 1974-85; trustee Ea. Enterprises, 1977-93. Bd. dirs. Internat. Student Assn., 1965-69; bd. dirs. MacDowell Colony, also treas., 1973-78; bd. overseers Old Sturbridge (Mass.) Village; trustee Radcliff Coll., 1960-72, Boston Inst. Contemporary Art; corporator Boston Mus. Sci.; vis. com. Center for Internat. Affairs, Harvard, 1976-83. Served to lt. USNR, 1942-46. Recipient Norlin award for Disting. Achievement U. Colo., 1986. Mem. Pi Gamma Mu. Home: 136 Fletcher Rd Belmont MA 02478-2019 Office: 75 Park Plz Boston MA 02116-3934

CALDIZ, DANIEL OSMAR, plant physiology educator; b. La Plata, Argentina, June 19, 1955; s. Osmar Fermin and Irma (Coltrinari) C.; m. Adriana Ethel Marino, Mar. 18, 1982; children: Gonzalo, Agustina, Rocío, Felipe. BS, Nat. Coll., 1973; degree in agrl. engring., La Plata Nat. U., 1978; PhD, Wageningen U., 2000. Asst. prof. faculty of agronomy La Plata Nat. U., 1979-92, adj. prof. faculty agrl. and forestry scis., 1992—; asst. researcher Nat. Rsch. Coun., Buenos Aires, 1985-90, adj. rschr., 1990-98; ind. rsch. Nat. Rsch. Coun., La Plata, 1999—; cons. Ministry Fgn. Affairs, Dominican Republic, 1994, various agrochem. cos., Buenos Aires, 1987-97. Contbr. scientific papers to profl. publs. Sci. Rsch. Bd. fellow, La Plata, 1979-82, Nat. Rsch. Coun. fellow, 1983-85, Netherlands Govt. fellow, Wageningen, 1981, Wageningen Agrl. Univ., 1994—; recipient Camara Latinoamericana do Parana award, 1995. Mem. Nat. Soc. Plant Physiology (sec. 1983-85, 87-89), Latin Am. Soc. Plant Physiology, N.Y. Acad. Scis., Internat. Allelopathy Soc. (v.p. 1994-96, regional coord. Ctrl. and S.Am. 1996-99), Malaysian Soc. Plant Physiology. Avocations: paddle tennis, camping, fishing. E-mail: dacaldiz@ceres.agro.unlp.edu.lar. Office: La Plata Nat U, CC 327, 1900 La Plata Argentina

CALDWELL, CLAUD REID, lawyer; b. Augusta, Ga., Sept. 18, 1909; s. John Mars and Ethel (Bennett) C.; student Acad. Richmond County, 1922-26; m. Josephine F. Clarke, June 30, 1940; children: Claud R., Kathryn C., James W. Bar: Ga. 1932, U.S. Supreme Ct. Ga. 1949, Ga. Ct. Appeals 1949, U.S. Dist. Ct. 1934, U.S. Ct. Appeals (5th cir.) 1953, U.S. Ct. Appeals (11th cir.) 1981, U.S. Supreme Ct. 1968. Pvt. practice, Augusta, 1934-95; ret. 1995; judge Mcpl. Ct., City of Augusta, 1948-49. Pres., Richmond County Ind. Party, 1950-51; bd. dirs. Augusta chpt. ARC, YMCA; chmn. Augusta council Boy Scouts Am., 1949-50. With AUS, 1941-45; ETO; col. USAR (ret.). Recipient Distinguished Pistol Marksman award U.S. Army, 1965. Mem. ABA, Ga. State Bar. Assn., Augusta Bar Assns., Ga. Sport Shooting Assn. (dir., past pres.), Augusta-Richmond County Hist. Mus., Mil. Order World Wars, Nat. Sojourners, Heroes of '96 (Gen. Oglethorpe chpt.), Res. Officers Assn. (Augusta chpt.), Am. Legion, Sons of Confederacy, Assn. U.S. Army, Masons, Augusta Country Club. Presbyn. (deacon). Home: 343 Hemlock Hill Rd Augusta GA 30909-3635

CALDWELL, DAN EDWARD, political science educator; b. Oklahoma City, May 12, 1948; s. John Edward and Hester Evelyn (Kiehn) C.; m. Lora Jean Ferguson, Mar. 21, 1970; children: Beth Christine, Ellen Claire, John Ferguson. BA in History, Stanford U., 1970, MA in Polit. Sci., PhD in Polit. Sci., 1978; MA in Internat. Rels., Tufts U., 1971. Staff mem. Office Emergency Preparedness, Exec. Office of Pres., Washington, 1972; rsch. and teaching fellow Stanford (Calif.) U., 1975-78; assoc. dir. Ctr. for Fgn. Policy Devel., Brown U., Providence, 1982-84; prof. polit. sci. Pepperdine U., Malibu, Calif., 1978-82, 84—, pres. faculty orgn., 1980-81, 89-90; dir. Forum for U.S.-Soviet Dialogue, Washington, 1984—, pres., 1989-91. Author: American-Soviet Relations, 1981, The Dynamics of Domestic Politics and Arms Control, 1991, World Politics and You, 2000; editor: Henry Kissinger, 1985. Elder Pacific Palisades (Calif.) Presbyn. Ch. With USN, 1971-74. Named Prof. of Yr., Pepperdine U. Student Alumni Assn., 1992.; rsch. fellow U.S. Inst. Peace, 1987, Pew faculty fellow Harvard U. Kennedy Sch. Govt., 1990. Mem. Internat. Inst. Strategic Studies (London), Am. Polit. Sci. Assn., Internat. Studies Assn. (sect. exec. com. 1982-87, dir. sect. on Am.-Soviet rels. 1984-86, fellow 1977), Coun. on Fgn. Rels. Avocations: tennis, skiing. Home: 654 Radcliffe Ave Pacific Palisades CA 90272-4331 Office: Pepperdine U Social Sci Divsn 24255 Pacific Coast Hwy Malibu CA 90263-0002

CALDWELL, JOHN WINSTON, III, petroleum engineer; b. Gainesville, Fla., Nov. 21, 1955; s. John Winston Jr. and Barbara T. (Thostenson) C.; m. Melissa Ann Myers, June 26, 1981; children: Graham Colin, Alexandra Alyssa, Evan Benjamin. BSCE, U. Idaho, 1977. Registered profl. engr., Okla. Prodn. engr. Texaco, Inc., Hobbs, N.Mex., 1978-80; drilling/prodn. engr. Southland Royalty Co., Farmington, N.Mex., 1980-82; reservoir engr. Southland Royalty Co., Oklahoma City, Okla., 1982-84, Houston, Tex., 1985; sr. reservoir engr. Meridian Oil Inc., Billings, Mont., 1986, regional joint interest engr., 1987; regional reservoir engr. Meridian Oil Inc., Farmington, N.Mex., 1988-89, regional drilling engr., 1990-95, regional planning engr., 1996-97, divsn. team leader, 1997-2000, divsn. prodn. mgr., 2000—; expert witness on reservoir issues in Okla., Tex., Colo., N.D., Mont., N.Mex., Ark. State Oil Commns. Mem. Soc. of Petroleum Engrs. Achievements include leading drilling team in engineering horizontal wells in San Juan Basin, use of geoservice measurement while drilling, N2 membrane drilling, slimhole horizontal R/C, and leading team in exploiting shale gas in San Juan Basin. Home: 4109 Saint Michaels Dr Farmington NM 87401-0806 Office: Burlington Resources Oil and Gas Inc 3401 E 30th St Farmington NM 87402-8807

CALDWELL, RONALD DEWITT, SR., industrial engineer, consultant; b. Dayton, Ohio, Dec. 9, 1958; s. James Edward Jr. and Mary Alice (Watson) C.; m. Yvonne Desiree Brown, Mar. 21, 1981; children: Ronald DeWitt, Danielle Nicole, Nia Denise. BS in Indsl. Engring., U. Cin., 1982; MS in Engring., Wright State U., 1996. Material pricing analyst McDonnell Douglas Corp., St. Lois, 1983-85; advanced mfg. engring. supr. B.F. Goodrich Co., Troy, Ohio, 1985-91; assoc. prof. Sinclair C.C., Dayton, Ohio, 1988-98; pres., CEO Future Systems Internat. Corp., Trotwood, Ohio, 1994—; pres., co-owner, founder Superior Cuts of Trotwood Barber Shop,

1997—; mem. drafting adv. com. Patterson Co-op H.S., Dayton, 1992-95; mem. adv. coun. Broadmoor Acad. Elem., Dayton, 1992-95. Contbr. tech. articles to profl. jours. Pres. Gifted Child Assn., Trotwood-Madison Sch. Dist., 1994-95; v.p. Trotwood Wee Rams Football, 1994; team mgr. YMCA Youth Basketball Program, Trotwood, 1992-94. Mem. Inst. Indsl. Engrs. (sr. mem.; bd. dirs. Dayton chpt. 1996), Human Factors and Ergonomics Soc., Soc. Mfg. Engrs. (sr. mem.), Avraham Y. Goldratt Inst. (Acad. Jonah). Achievements include patent pending for an innovative automatic U.S. postal box. Avocations: physical fitness through weight lifting, youth coaching of softball and track. Office: Future Systems Internat Corp PO Box 26043 Trotwood OH 45426-0043

CALDWELL, ROSSIE JUANITA BROWER, retired library service educator; b. Columbia, S.C., Nov. 4, 1917; d. Rossie Lee and Henrietta Olivia (Irby) Brower; m. Harlowe Evans Caldwell, Aug. 6, 1943 (dec. 1983); 1 adopted dau., Rossie Laverne Caldwell Jenkins. BA magna cum laude, Claflin U., 1937; MS, S.C. State Coll., 1952; MSLS, U. Ill., 1959. Tchr. libr. Reed St. H.S., Anderson, S.C., 1937-39, Emmett Scott H.S., Rock Hill, S.C., 1939-42; tchr. libr. Wilkinson H.S., Orangeburg, S.C., 1942-43, libr., 1945-57; civilian pers. War Dept., Tuskegee Army Air Field, 1943-45; asst. prof., then assoc. prof. libr. svc. dept. S.C. State U., Orangeburg, 1957-83. Contbg. author book in field; author articles. Life mem. NAACP; trustee, Christian advocate United Meth. Ch. in S.C., 1978-86; assoc. mem. Orangeburg Regional Hosp. Aux,; coord. comms. Trinity United Meth. Ch. Recipient Presdl. citation Claflin Coll., 1989, Links award for cmty. achievement, 1998, numerous ann. vol. work citations; Founders Day honoree, 1994; named to Claflin Coll. Hall of Fame, 1997. Mem. NAACP, ALA (continuing life mem.), ALA Black Caucus (emeritus), AAUP (emeritus), VFW Aux. (life), S.C. Libr. Assn. (hon.), AAUW (editor Orangeburg br. bull.), Friends of the Libr. (Orangeburg County), Palmetto Med. Dental Pharm. Assn. Aux. (historian, state pres., Woman of Yr. 1972), Links Club (archivist, historian), As You Like It Bridge Club, Daus. of Isis, Claflin Univ. Forerunners Club (coord., founder), Golden Scholarship Club (co-founder), Sigma Pi Phi (archousa, Claflin queen 1935-37, emeritus queen 1999), Phi Delta Kappa (emeritus mem.), Alpha Kappa Alpha (life mem.), Omega Psi Phi (Omega Lambda Sigma chpt. Scroll of Honor), Beta Phi Mu (mem. internat. Libr. hon. soc., mem. libr. sci. soc.). Home: 1320 Ward Ln NE Orangeburg SC 29118-1342

CALDWELL, THOMAS HOWELL, JR., accountant, financial management consultant; b. Wichita Falls, Tex., Feb. 5, 1934; s. Thomas Howell and LaVerne Louise C.; m. Bernell Irons, Apr. 12, 1968 (div. Jan. 1979); 1 child, Thomas Howell III (dec.). BA in Religion, Baylor U., 1956; postgrad., Tex. Christian U., 1958-63, North Tex. State U., 1973-75; LLD (hon.), London Inst. Applied Rsch., 1994. Cert. internal auditor. Tech. writer Gen. Dynamics, Ft. Worth, 1956-60; asst. dir. pers. Harris Hosp., Ft. Worth, 1960-62; with fiduciary tax sect. 1st Nat. Bank, Ft. Worth, 1962-64; jr. acct. various CPA's, Dallas, 1964-65; auditor Def. Contract Audit Agy., Dallas, 1965-74; tax appraiser, mcpl. acct. City of McKinney, Tex., 1974-75; systems acct. USDA, Dallas, 1975-83; auditor U.S. Army C.E., Dallas, 1983-86; acct. rep. IRS, Dallas, 1986-87; systems acct. Def. Fin. & Acctg. Svc., Dallas, 1987-93; fin. mgmt. cons. Caldwell Fin. Mgmt. Cons., Dallas, 1993—; airport amb. vol. program Dallas Ft. Worth Internat. Airport, 1999—; mem. Airport Amb. Vol. Program, Dallas Ft. Worth Internat. Airport, 1999—. Mem. jr. bd. 1st Bapt. Ch., Dallas. With USAFR, 1957-63. Mem. Descs. Vets. Mexican War, (bd. dirs., treas.), Baylor U. Ex-Students Assn., Masons, Shriners, Scottish Rite. Republican. Avocations: flying, dogs, watching football, church. Home and Office: 10822 Pagewood Dr Dallas TX 75230-4468

CALDWELL, WALLACE CAUGHEY, physicist, engineer; b. Britt, Iowa, Sept. 9, 1918; s. Harry Vincent and Julia Leona Caldwell; m. Beth Caldwell, Feb. 8, 1948 (dec. Dec. 6, 1995); children: Linda R. Caldwell Gahring, Gregory G.; m. LaVaune Wood, Aug. 1, 1998. BS in Physics, Iowa State U., 1939, MS in Physics, 1940; PhD in Physics, Cornell U., 1948. Student aide Iowa State U., Ames, 1935-39, tchg. asst., 1939-41; tchg. asst. Cornell U., Ithaca, N.Y., 1941-43; computation cli. Met. Life Ins. Co., N.Y.C., summer 1941; student engr. Western Electric Co., summer 1942; staff mem. radiation lab. MIT, 1943-46; tchg. asst. Cornell U., 1946, NRC predoctoral fellow, 1946-48; asst. prof. Iowa State U., Ames, 1948-51; cons. The Bendix Corp., Teterboro, N.J., 1951-52; chief engr. The Bendix Corp., Eatontown, N.J., 1952-55; mgr. The Bendix Corp., Holmdel, N.J., 1955-62; dir. Collins Radio Co., Cedar Rapids, Iowa, 1962-70; budget officer Bd. Regents, Des Moines, Iowa, 1970-83; adj. prof. Iowa State U., 1983-93, adj. prof. emeritus, 1993—. Co-author: Microwave Duplexers, 1946, Physics-The Root Science, 1995. Del. Rep. Party, 1980. Mem. Kiwanis (treas. 1980-97), Pi Mu Epsilon, Phi Kappa Phi, Sigma Xi. Methodist. Avocations: music, skiing, ice skating, boating, traveling. E-mail: walcldwl@netins.net. Home: 3524 Grand Ave Des Moines IA 50312-4300 Office: Iowa State Univ 2229 Lincoln Way Ames IA 50011-0001

CALDWELL, WILLARD E., psychologist, educator; b. Flushing L.I., N.Y., July 10, 1920; s. Howard Eugene and Lillian (Warner) C. AB in Psychology, U. Fla., 1940, MA in Psychology, 1941; PhD in Psychology, Cornell U., 1946; postgrad., Washington Sch. Psychiatry, 1948-53. Lic. psychologist, D.C. Grad. asst. psychology U. Fla., Gainesville, 1940-41; teaching asst. Psychology Dept. Cornell (N.Y.) U., 1943-46; prof. psychology, dept. chmn. Mary Baldwin Coll., Staunton, Va., 1947-48; asst. prof., assoc. prof., prof. psychology The George Washington U., Washington, 1948-85, prof. emeritus psychology, 1985—; psychotherapist. Editor, contbg. author: Principles of Comparative Psychology, 1960; contbr. over 50 articles to profl. jours. Pvt. U.S. Army, 1941-42. Mem. APA, Am. Psychol. Soc., D.C. Psychology Assn., Internat. Soc. Biometerology. Republican. Episcopalian. Avocations: swimming, gardening, traveling. Home: Apt 316 1101 New Hampshire Ave NW Washington DC 20037-1509

CALDWELL, WILLIAM EDWARD, educational administration educator, arbitrator; b. Providence, Aug. 18, 1928; s. James E. and Eva E. (Barker) C.; m. Doris E. Parlee, June 17, 1950; children: William E., Donna E., Allen E. BA in Math., Ea. Nazarene Coll., 1950; MEd in Secondary Edn., U. N.H., 1957; PhD in Ednl. Adminstrn., NYU, 1968. Cert. prin., supt., arbitrator. Tchr. math., dir. music, coach pub. schs. Berwick, Maine, 1950-54; tchr. math., supr. pub. schs. Valley Stream, N.Y., 1954-61; guidance counselor, prin. pub. schs. Manchester, Conn., 1961-67; dir. secondary tchr. tng. U. Hartford, Conn., 1967-69; exec. dir. Pa. Sch. Study Coun., University Park, 1970-78; prof. ednl. adminstrn. Pa. State U., University Park, 1969—, pres. faculty coun., 1985-86, ombudsman Coll. Edn.,, 1986-90, chmn. edn. adminstrn. program, 1987-90, chmn. adminstrn., policy, founds. and internat. edn., 1990-93, prof. emeritus, 1993—; state dir. mediation Commonwealth of Pa., Harrisburg, 1979-80; conciliator, fact finder Pa. Labor Rels. Bd., Harrisburg, 1971—; arbitrator AAA, FMCS, Pa. Labor Rels. Bd., 1971—. Author: Collective Negotiation in Public Education, 1970, Agreement, Policy for Principal/Supervisor, 1983; mem. editl. bd. Jour. Individual Employment Rights, 1993—; contbr. articles to profl. jours., chpts. to books, author reports. Nat. del. Am. Assn. Sch. Adminstrs., Washington, 1976, 77, 79; bd. dirs. Fed. Credit Union, Manchester, Conn., 1963-67, Appalachian Ednl. Lab., Charleston, W.Va., 1970-78; examiner Pa. Civil Svc. Commn., Harrisburg, 1972-79. Lt. col. USMCR, ret. 1988. Recipient Commendation award Pa. Sch. Bds. Assn., 1980, Acad. Achievement award NYU, 1969, Outstanding Svc. award Commonwealth Pa., 1973, Outstanding Svc. award Pa. Dept. Labor, 1987, Excellence in Instrn. award Pa. Sch. Study Coun., 1994, William E. Caldwell Excellence in Adminstrn. award Pa. Sch. Study Coun., 1997—. Mem. Am. Ednl. Rsch. Assn. (presenter), Pa. Assn. Secondary Sch. Prins. (rsch. chmn., Commendation award 1983, Excellence in Edn. award 1986).

CALDWELL, WILLIAM MACKAY, III, business executive; b. L.A., Apr. 6, 1922; s. William Mackay II and Edit Ann (Richards) C.; m. Mary Louise Edwards, Jan. 16, 1946 (dec. 1980); children: William Mackay IV, Craig Edwards, Candace Louise; m. Jean Bledsoe, Apr. 27, 1985. BS, U. So. Calif., 1943; MBA, Harvard U., 1948. Mgr. spl. projects U. Southern Calif., L.A., 1948-49; asst. to pres. Pacific States Corp., Pasadena, Calif., 1949-50; purchasing agt. C.F. Braun & Co., Alhambra, Calif., 1950-53, mgr. gen acctg., 1953-57; sec., treas., dir. Photo Color Corp., Glendale, Calif., 1957-60, Drewry Bennetts Corp., Glendale, Calif., 1957-60; sr. v.p., CFO Am. Cement Corp., L.A., 1960-69, dir., 1960-69; dir. Hawaiian Cement Corp., 1960-69, Am. Cement Properties, L.A., 1960-69, Am. Cement Internat., L.A., 1960-69, Graham Levingston Co., L.A., 1960-69; chmn., pres. Van Vorst Corp., L.A., 1970-81, Seattle, 1970-81; chmn., pres. Southern Cross Industries, Atlanta, 1977-84; chmn. Englander Co., 1979-82, King Koil Licensing Co., 1979—; chmn., pres. Kyco Industries, Inc., 1979—; cons. prof. U. So. Calif.; mem. men's com. L.A. Med. Ctr.; bd. dirs. Commerce Assocs., Calif. Mus. Sci. and Industry, U. So. Calif. Assocs., Pres.'s Cir., Am. Cement Found. Mem. Friends Huntington Libr. Served to lt. USNR, 1943-46. Mem. Newcomen Soc., Harvard Bus. Sch. Soc. Calif. (dir. 1960-63), Kappa Alpha, Alpha Delta Sigma. Clubs: L.A. Country Club, Town Hall Club, Calif. Club (L.A.), Trojan Club, Annandale Golf Club, Eldorado Country Club, Chaparral Golf Club. Office: PO Box 1151 Pasadena CA 91102-1151

CĂLEANU, CĂTĂLIN DANIEL, electronics engineer, educator; b. Timisoara, Timis, Romania, June 30, 1971; s. Ghedrehe and Lucia Florica (Georgevici) C.; m. Malvina Stefana Suru, June 11, 1998; 1 child, Iulian Alexandru. Engring. diploma, U. Poly. Timisoara, 1995, MSE, 1996, postgrad., 1996—; PhD, N.Y. Acad. Scis., 1997. Cert. in engring. Rsch. asst. U. Poly. Timisoara, 1995-98, tchg. asst., 1998—; cons. Computerland, Timisoara, 1998. Co-author: (book) Neural Networks, 1999. Grantee Tempus, U. Cen. Lancashire, Eng., 1996, U. Strathclyde, Glasgow, Scotland, 1999. Mem. IEEE (assoc.). Orthodox. Avocations: artificial life, neural networks, genetic algorithms, UFOs. Home: Str Constanta Nr 2, 1900 Timisoara Timis, Romania Office: U Poly Timisoara, B-Dul V Pârvan Nr 2, 1900 Timisoara Romania

CALENDA, EMILE, anesthesiologist; b. Battinaglia, Naples, Italy, Apr. 1, 1955; arrived in France, 1961; s. Mario and Anna Maria (Albano) C.; m. Patricia Lenoir, Feb. 3, 1979; children: Vanessa, Dorian, Auriance. MD, U. Pierre et Marie Curie, 1983; anesthesiologist, Hosp. Foch, Suresnes, France, 1987. Anesthesiologist Ctr. Hosp. U., Rouen, France, 1987—. Contbr. articles to profl. jours. Mem. Syndicat Nat. Praticiens Anesthesistes Reanimateurs, Soc. French Anesthesia. Avocations: swimming, running, Judo, walking. Home: 27b rue Poussin, 76000 Rouen France Office: Ctr Hosp Univ, 1 rue de Germont, 76031 Rouen France

ČALFA, MARIÁN, lawyer, government official; b. Trebišov, Czechoslovakia, May 7, 1946. Grad. in Law, Charles U., Prague, Czechoslovakia, 1970. Lawyer Czechoslovak News Agy.; with Office Govt. Presidium at the Legis. Dept., 1972-83, with dept. econ. law, 1983-86, head, 1986-88; sec. Legis. Coun. Czechoslovak Govt., 1986-88; dep. head Office Govt. Presidium, 1987-88; min. without portfolio Govt. of Czechoslovakia, 1988-89, first dep. premier, 1989-90, premier, 1989-92, advisor, 1992; ptnr. CTL Cons., Prague, 1992, Čalfa, Bartošík A Partneri, Prague, 1992-94, Calfa, Bartošík A Pertneri, Attys. at Law, Prague, 1994—; mem. supr. bd. dirs. I.C. Banka. Editor-in-chief Judiricial Counsellor, 1992-95, chmn. editl. bd., 1995-99. Office: Karlovo nám 24, Prague Czech Republic

CALHOUN, JOHN ALFRED, social services administrator; b. Phila., Dec. 1, 1939; s. John Alfred and Helen Fordham (Webster) C.; m. Ottilia Klenota, May 29, 1971; children: Byron, Hollis. BA, Brown U., 1962; M in Div., Episcopal Div. Sch., Cambridge, Mass., 1965; MPA, Harvard U., 1986. Tchr. Phila. pub. schs., 1965-66; program adminstr. Action for Boston Community Devel., 1966-70; v.p. Tech. Devel. Corp., Boston, 1970-73; exec. dir. Justice Resource Inst., Boston, 1973-76; commr. Mass. Dept. of Youth Svcs., Boston, 1976-79, U.S. Adminstrn. for Children, Youth and Families, Washington, 1979-81; dir. Ctr. for Govtl. Affairs Child Welfare League, Washington, 1981-83; pres., CEO Nat. Crime Prevention Coun., Washington, 1983—; pres. bd. dirs. Nat. Ctr. for Youth as Resources; v.p. Internat. Ctr. for the Prevention of Crime; bd. dirs. Nat. Funding Collaborative on Violence Prevention, Ctr. for Internat. Leadership, D.C.; bd. dirs. Pacific Ctr. for Violence Prevention, The Nat. Assembly of Voluntary Health and Social Welfare Ags., Childrens Trust Neighborhood Initiative; assoc. in edn. Harvard U., 1978; moderator Aspen Inst., 1980—; founder Pre-trial Diversion Programs, Mass., Urban Ct. Mediation Cmty. Sentencing, Mass., Cmty. Responses to Drug Abuce, 10 Sites Across the U.S.; mem. U.S. Atty. Gen.'s Coordinating Coun. on Juvenile Justice; founder Youth as Resources., Mass. and Ind.; adv. bd. Nat. League of Cities Children and Youth subcom. Author: What, Me Evaluate?, 1986; editor: Crime in Urban Communities, 1986, Making a Difference, 1985, Reaching Out: School-based Community Service Programs, Teen Crime and the Community, National Service and Public Safety: Partnerships for Safer Communities, Taking the Offensive: How Seven Cities Did It; contbr. articles to profl. jours. Coach McLean (Va.) Youth; tchr. confirmation class Louisville Presbyn. Ch., McLean; state chmn. Mass. Adolescent Task Force, 1978; chmn. Mass. State of the Family Task Force, 1979; pres. Franklin Flaschner Found., 1978; treas. Met. Beaverbrook Area Mental Health Bd.; bd. advisors U. Mass. Coll. Cmty. Pub. Svc., 1979; bd. dirs. Edna Stein Acad., Boston, Pekinese Island Sch., Woods Hole, Mass. Littauer fellow Harvard U. Kennedy Sch. of Govt., 1986; recipient award of Recognition Am. Arbitration Assn., 1978, award of Recognition, U.S. Office Juvenile Justice and Delinquency Prevention. Mem. Am. Probation/ Parole Assn. (prevention com.). Democrat. Episcopalian. Avocations: photography, tennis, gardening, coaching, skiing. Home: 921 Mackall Ave Mc Lean VA 22101-1617 Office: Nat Crime Prevention Coun Office Pres & CEO 13th Fl 1000 Connecticut Ave NW Washington DC 20036-5302

CALHOUN, THOMAS C., sociology and African American studies educator; b. Crystal Springs, Miss., Aug. 31, 1946; s. Walter Lee and Earnestine (Abney) C. BA in Sociology, Tex. Wesleyan Coll., 1970; MA in Sociology, Tex. Tech U., 1971; PhD in Sociology, U. Ky., 1988. Instr. sociology Mt. Union Coll., Alliance, Ohio, 1971-74, Old Dominion U., Norfolk, Va., 1974-78, Western Ky. U., Bowling Green, 1984-88; asst. prof. Ohio U., Athens, 1988-96; assoc. prof. sociology and African Am. stidoes U. Nebr., Lincoln, 1996—, dir. Inst. for Ethnic Studies, 1998—; bd. mem. Sociol. Focus, 1997—. Co-editor Sociol. Spectrum, 1997-99; dep. editor Jour. Contemporary Ethnography Sociology, 1998—. Bd. dirs. Planned Parenthood, Lincoln; mem. bd. United Campus Ministries, Lincoln. Mem. Assn. Social and Behavioral Scis. (pres. 2000-01), North Ctrl. Sociol. Assn. (v.p. 1996-97), Mid-South Sociol. Assn. (v.p. 1989-99). Methodist. Avocations: travel, reading. Fax: 402-472-0531. E-mail: tcalhoun1@uni.edu. Office: U Nebr Dept Sociology 711 Oldfather Lincoln NE 68502

CALIGARI, PETER DOUGLAS SAVARIA, geneticist, researcher; b. Rinteln, Germany, Nov. 10, 1949; (parents British citizens); s. Kenneth Vane Savaria and Mary Annetta (Rock) C.; m. Patricia Ann Feeley, June 23, 1973; children: Louise Rebecca Vane, Helena Rachel Vane. BSc, U. Birmingham, Eng., 1971; PhD, U. Birmingham, 1974, DSc, 1989. Sr. scientific officer Scottish Crop Rsch. Inst., Edinburgh, 1981-84, prin. scientific officer, 1984-86; prof. agrl. botany U. Reading, Eng., 1986—; head dept. U. Reading, 1987-98; rsch. asst., U. Birmingham, 1971-74, rsch. fellow, 1974-81; mem. gov. bd. Plant Scis. Rsch. Ltd., Norwich, Eng., 1991-94, John Innes Ctr., Norwich, 1994-99; mng. dir. BioHybrids Ltd., Reading, 1996—, Biomarkers, Ltd., 1997—. Co-author: Selection Methods in Plant Breeding, 1995; coeditor: Compositae: Biology and Utilization, 1996; editor: Plant Breeding, 1993-99, Heredity, 1988-91. Royal Soc. Arts fellow, 1990. Fellow Inst. Biology (v.p. 1999—, chmn. sci. policy bd. 1999—); mem. Genetical Soc. (mem. com. 1985-91), Eucarpia, European Assn. Potato Rsch., Potato Assn. Am., Internat. Lupin Assn. Avocations: writing poetry. Office: U Reading Whiteknights Dept Agri Bot, PO Box 221, Reading RG6 6AS, England

CALIGARIS, LUIGI, foreign affairs and defense consultant; b. Torino, Italy, Oct. 4, 1931; s. Valentino and Carolina (Voli) C.; m. Paola Chiaramello, June 10, 1961; children: Valentina, Enrico. Degree, Scoola di Guerra, Italy, 1967, Staff Coll., U.K., 1969. Army appts. Italian Army Cavalry, 1951-82; ret. brig. gen. Italy, 1982; military attache Italian Embassy, London, 1974-77; dir. polit. mil. affairs Min. Def., Rome, 1978-82; columnist, def. corr. Republica Newspaper, 1983-84, Corriere Della Sera, Italy, 1984-91, Italy, 1984-94, Giornale, Italy, 1993-94; def. commentator State TV, Italy, 1986-90, 91-92, 95-96, Giorno-Resto del Carlino, Nazione; prof. strategy State U., Bologna, Italy, 1986, Scuola di Guerra, Army, Italy, 1986-90; European parliamentarian, Brussels, Belgium, 1996-99; lectr. security policies in Europe, U.S., Can. Co-author: I Nuovi Militari, 1983, Obiettivo Difesa, 1986; author: Paura Di Vincere, 1995; editor: Difesa Europea Proposte e sfide, 1990. Co-founder Forza Italia Party, 1994. Mem. Def. Analysis, IISS, RUSI. Avocations: sports, arts. Home and Office: via Paisiello 26, 00198 Rome Italy

CALIN, ANDREI, rheumatologist, consultant; b. Andover, U.K., Jan. 7, 1944; s. Frederick and Felicia (Grad) C.; m. H. Jane Weller, Aug. 11, 1973; children: Tara, Sasha, Marisa. MB, BChir, Cambridge U., London, 1968, MA, 1969, MD, 1979. Diplomate Bd. Internal Medicine, Bd. Rheumatology. Intern, resident Guy's Hosp., Hammersmith Hosp., Brompton Hosp.; house physician, house surgeon, sr. house officer Guy's Hosp., London, 1968-69, from registrar to sr. registrar, 1971-74; sr. house officer Hammersmith Hosp., London, 1969, Brompton Hosp., London, 1970; assoc. prof. medicine Stanford (Calif.) U., 1974-83; consulting rheumatologist Bath, U.K., 1983—. Editor: Spondylarthritis, 1984, 2d edit., 1997; contbr. over 200 articles to profl. jours. Fellow Royal Coll. Physicians. Avocations: theatre, walking, travel. Home: Holmpatrick Weston Rd, Bath BA1 2XU, England Office: Royal Nat Hosp for, Rheumatic Diseases, Bath England

CALKINS, EVAN, physician, educator; b. Newton, Mass., July 15, 1920; s. Grosvenor and Patty (Phillips) C.; m. Virginia McC. Brady, Sept. 9, 1946; children: Sarah Calkins Oxnard, Stephen, Lucy McCormick, Joan, Benjamin, Hugh, Ellen Rountree, Geoffrey, Timothy. Grad., Milton Acad., 1939; AB, Harvard U., 1942, MD, 1945. Intern, asst. resident medicine Johns Hopkins, 1946-47, 48-50; chief resident physician Mass. Gen. Hosp., 1951-52, mem. arthritis unit, 1952-61; NRC fellow med. scis. Harvard, 1950-51, instr., asst. prof. medicine, 1952-61; practice medicine, specializing in rheumatology Boston, 1951-61, Buffalo, 1961—; prof. medicine SUNY, Buffalo, 1961-94, prof. emeritus, 1994—; chmn. dept. medicine SUNY, 1965-77; head dept. medicine Buffalo Gen. Hosp., 1961-68; dir. medicine E.J. Meyer Meml. Hosp., 1968-78; head gerontology sect. Buffalo VA Med. Ctr., 1978-90; head div. geriatrics/gerontology SUNY-Buffalo, 1978-90; founder, pres. Network in Aging of Western N.Y., Inc., 1980-83; cons. Nat. Inst. Arthritis and Metabolic Diseases Tng. Grants Com., 1958-62, Program Project Com., 1964-68, Nat. Instn. Spl. Study Sect. for Health Manpower, 1969-77, for Behavioral Medicine, 1978-79; mem. acad. awards com. Nat. Inst. on Aging, 1979-80, mem. nat. adv. coun., 1985-88; dir. Western N.Y. Geriatric Edn. Ctr., 1983-88, co-dir., 1988-90; dir. Multidisciplinary Ctr. on Aging SUNY-Buffalo, 1989-90, prof. family medicine, 1987-94; sr. physician and coord. geriatric programs Health Care Plan, 1990-97; ptnr. Promedicus Health Group, 1998—, co-dir. WNY/Rochester Osteoporosis Ednl. Resource Ctr., 1999. Editor: Handbook of Medical Emergencies, 1945, Geriatric Medicine, 1983, Practice of Geriatrics, 1986, 2d edit., 1991, New Ways to Care for Older People: Building Systems Based on Evidence, 1998; contbr. articles to profl. jours. Pres. Nat. Assn. Geriatric Edn. Ctrs., 1992-93. Capt. M.C. AUS, 1943-45, 46-48. Recipient Presdl. citation for Community Service, 1983. Fellow ACP (master 1989, Laureate award N.Y. Upstate chpt. 1998), Am. Coll. Rheumatology (founder, pres. 1967-68, master 1986), Gerontol. Soc. Am. (chair clin. med. sect. 1989, Freeman award 1991), Am. Geriatrics Soc. (Milo D. Leavitt award 1986); mem. Am. Clin. and Climatological Assn. (v.p. 1987), Am. Soc. Clin. Investigation, Assn. Am. Physicians, Soc. Medicine Argentina (hon.), Argentine Soc. Gerontology and Geriatrics (hon.), Soc. Fellows John Hopkins U., Alpha Omega Alpha. Home: 3799 Windover Dr Hamburg NY 14075-6338 Office: Mosher Med Bldg 899 Main St Buffalo NY 14203-1109

CALKINS, NOEL CLIFTON, retired industrial engineer; b. Alhambra, Calif., July 29, 1931; s. Leon Clifton and Alma Dorothy (Ray) C.; m. Lillian Archuleta, Sept. 20, 1997; 1 child, Kirk Clifton. BS in Indsl. Engring., Tex. Tech U., 1957. Project engr. Cameron Iron Works, Houston, 1957-60; design group leader ACF Industries (now GE), Albuquerque, 1960-65; asst. plant mgr. Denver Equipment Co. (now Joy), Colorado Springs, Colo., 1965-66; mgr. process engring. Coors Porcelain (now Coors Ceramics), Golden, Colo., 1966-69; devel. engr. Cabot Machinery Divsn., Pampa, Tex.; plant mgr. Selas Corp., Baxter Springs, Kans.; chief engr. Algas Industries, Dallas; design and devel. engr. Los Alamos (N.Mex.) Nat. Lab., 1980-93; CEO, pres. cons. and metal fabrication Calkins R&D, Inc., Albuquerque and Ruidoso, N.Mex., 1991—. Contbr. articles to profl. publs. Sgt. USAF, 1951-55, Korea. Mem. Soc. Mfg. Engr., Nat. Srs. Coalition. Presbyterian. Achievements include patents for ultrasonic impact grinder feed system, constrained ceramic filled polymer armor, glass matrix armor, propane motor fuel thermostat, all metal vacuum tight valve, heat pipe to exhaust manifold heat source, impact implantation of particulate material into polymer surfaces, advanced steam generator. Avocations: physical workouts, automobiles, prototyping patents. Home and Office: PO Box 4515 Ruidoso NM 88355-4515

CALLAGHAN, LEONARD JAMES, British government official; b. Portsmouth, Eng., Mar. 27, 1912; s. James and Charlotte G. (Cundy) C.; m. Audrey Elizabeth Moulton, 1938; children: Margaret Ann (Baroness Jay of Paddington), Julia Elizabeth (Mrs. Ian Hubbard), Michael James. Student elem. sch., Portsmouth; LLD (hon.), U. Wales, 1976, 95, Sardar Patel U., Gujarat, India, 1978, U. Birmingham, 1981, U. Sussex, 1988, U. Westminster, 1992, Open U., Milton Keynes, Eng., 1996, U. Liverpool, 1996; PhD (hon.), Meisei U., Tokyo, 1984; hon. bencher, Inner Temple, 1976. Tax officer Inland Revenue Dept., 1929-36; br. asst. sec. Inland Revenue Staff Fedn., 1936-47; parliamentary pvt. sec. to undersec. state dominion affairs, 1945; chmn. def. and svcs. com. Labour Pary, 1945-47; mem. youth del. to USSR, 1945, parliamentary del. to West Africa, 1947; substitute rep. Consultative Assembly Coun. Europe, 1949, rep. 2d session, 1950; rep. 2d session Consultative Assembly Coun. Europe, Strasbourg, France, 1954; parliamentary sec. to Ministry Transport, 1947-50; parliamentary and fin. sec. to Admiralty, 1950-51; chmn. adv. com. on oil pollution of sea, 1952-63, pres. adv. com. on protection of sea, 1963—; attended 6th Unofcl. Commonwealth Rels. Conf., Royal Inst. Internat. Affairs, New Zealand, 1959; dep. chmn. Parliamentary Assn. del. to Ctrl. Africa; mem. parliamentary del., Zanzibar, Mauritius, Madagascar, 1961; chief spokesman Colonial Affairs, 1956-61; attended Conf. African Socialism, Senegal, 1962-63; pres. U. Wales Swansea, 1986-95; hon. fellow U. Swansea, 1992; mem. nat. exec. com. Labour Party, 1957-80, treas., 1967-76, chmn., 1974; chief spokesman on treasury affairs, 1961-64; privy councillor, 1964; chancellor of Exchequer, 1964-67; sec. of state for home dept., 1967-70; sec. of state for fgn. and commonwealth affairs, 1974-76; prime min. and 1st lord of Treasury, 1976-79; Labour M.P. for Cardiff SS.E., 1945-87. Author: A House Divided: the dilemna of Northern Ireland, 1973, (authbiography) Time and Chance, 1987. Lt. Royal Navy, 1942-45. Decorated Knight of Garter (Eng.); hon. life fellow Nufield Coll., Oxford U.; hon. freeman City of Cardiff, 1975, City of Sheffield, 1979, City of Portsmouth, 1991, City of Swansea, 1993; hon. mem. Ct. Govs., University Coll., Cardiff, 1978; hon. fellow Univ. Coll., Cardiff, 1978, Cardiff Inst. H.E., 1991, Portsmouth U., 1981, Liverpool U., 1996, Open U., 1996; recipient Hubert H. Humphrey award for Internat. Statesmanship, 1978. Mem. U.K. Pilots Assn. (pres. 1973-76), Internat. Maritime Pilots Assn. (hon. pres. 1971-76). Office: House of Lords, London SW1A 0PW, England

CALLAGHAN, PAUL TERENCE, physicist, researcher; b. Wanganui, New Zealand, Aug. 19, 1947; s. Ernest Edward and Mavis Eileen (Hogg) C.; m. Susan Audrey Roberts, Jan. 18, 1969; children: Catherine Eileen, Christopher James. BSc with honors, Victoria U., Wellington, New Zealand, 1970; DPhil, Oxford U., 1974, DSc, 1995. Lectr. in physics Massey U., New Zealand, 1975-84, prof. physics, 1984—. Author: Principles of Nuclear Magnetic Resonance Microscopy, 1991; contbr. numerous articles to profl. jours. Recipient Mechaelis medal Otago U., 1994. Fellow Royal Soc. New Zealand (Cooper medal 1998, Hector medal 1998).

CALLAHAN, ALSTON, physician, author; b. Vicksburg, Miss., Mar. 16, 1911; s. Neil and Effie (Alston) C.; m. Eivor Holst, Feb. 23, 1941; children: Kristina Alice, Patrick Alston, Michael Alston, Timothy Alston, Karin Eivor, Kevin (dec. 1961). AB, Miss. Coll., 1929; MD, Tulane U., 1933, MS in Ophthalmology, 1936; RSM, Tulane U., London, 1990. Diplomate Am. Bd. Ophthalmology. Intern Charity Hosp., New Orleans, 1933-35, resident in ophthalmology, 1936-37; hon. mem. emeritus Eye Found. Univ. Hosps., Birmingham, Ala., 1959—; also founder Callahan Eye Found. Hosp., Birmingham, Ala., 1964; co-developer Rsch. and Profl. Office Bldg. E.F. Hosp., 1985-87; founder Internat. Retinal Rsch Found., Inc., Birmingham, 1997. Author: Surgery of the Eye, Injuries, 1950, Surgery of the Eye, Diseases, 1956, Reconstructive Surgery of the Eyelids and Ocular Adnexa, 1966, (with M. Callahan) Ophthalmic Plastic Surgery, 1979; contbr. articles to profl. jours. Served to capt. M.C., AUS, 1944-46. Recipient award Ala.

Acad. Honor, 1996; named Tulane Alumnus of Yr., 1997, to Ala. Healthcare Hall of Fame, 1998. Fellow ACS, Royal Australian Coll. Ophthalmology (hon.); mem. Am. Acad. Ophthalmology, So. Med. Assn. (emeritus), Am. Soc. Ophthal. Plastic Surgery, Alpha Omega Alpha, Sigma Alpha Epsilon. Clubs: Mountain Brook, The Club, Metropolitan, Explorers. Home: 2020 Warwick Dr Birmingham AL 35209-1360 Office: 711 29th St S Birmingham AL 35233-2809 also: Internat Retinal Rsch Found Inc 700 18th St S Ste 511 Birmingham AL 35233-3802

CALLAHAN, DANIEL JOSEPH, surgeon, consultant; b. Balt., Sept. 28, 1945; s. Thomas Daniel and Mary Catherine C.; m. Barbara Joan Danahy, Nov. 24, 1979; 1 child, Daniel Joseph, Jr. BA, LaSalle Coll., 1967; MD, Thomas Jefferson U., 1971. Asst. prof. plastic and reconstructive surgery St. Louis U., 1977-80, founder, divsn. hand clinic; chief surgery, vice chief of med. staff St. Petersburg (Fla.) Gen. Hosp., 1992; chief plastic surgery Sunrise Med. Ctr., Freeport, Bahamas, 1995-97; clin. cons. Isla Mujeres, Q-Roo, Mex., 1997—. Contbr. articles to profl. jours. Mem. AMA, AAAS, N.Y. Acad. Scis. Achievements include first successful multi-digit microvascular reimplantation in Missouri, 1977.

CALLAHAN, JAMES ROBERT, retired agricultural products administrator; b. Frankfort, Ind., Apr. 19, 1935; s. CEcil Charles and Olive Naomi C.; m. Julia Ann Callahan, Dec. 20, 1953; children: Kevin, Maureen. Student pre-vet., U. Ill., 1953-54; BS in Agr., Purdue U., 1957. Farm mgr. Murray (Callahan, Frankfort, 1957-68; field rep. Del Monte Foods, Stevens Point, Wis., 1968-73; field supt. Del Monte Foods, Tampa, Fla., 1973-80; project leader Del Monte Foods, Rochelle, Ill., 1980-81; area field supt. Del Monte Foods, DeKalb, Ill., 1981-89, raw product mgr., 1990-91; dir. agr. Del Monte Foods, Irapuato, Mex., 1991-92; ret. Author: Melungeon Colony of Newman's Ridge, 1999. Lay tchr. 1st Presbyn. Ch., Frankfort, 1958-68, deacon, 1965-68; projects leader Jaycees, Frankfort, 1966-68; bd. dirs. Brown County Literacy Coalition, 1998-2000; mem. adminstrv. bd. Nashville (Ind.) United Meth. Ch., 1998-2000. Mem. Lions. Republican. Methodist. Avocations: taxidermy, photography, Bonsai and bromeliads, writing, travel. E-mail: melungo@ail.com. Home: 696 Freeman Ridge Rd Nashville IN 47448-8872

CALLAHAN, LOUGH, investment management consultant; b. Dayton, Ohio, Jan. 18, 1948; s. John G.P. and Marie Bernadette (Loughlin) C.; m. Mary Bernadette Reilly, May 5, 1973; children: Christopher, Denise. BA with honors, Holy Cross Coll., Worcester, Mass., 1969; JD cum laude, Harvard U., 1972. Lawyer Davis Polk & Wardwell, N.Y.C., 1972-80; dir. S.G. Warburg & Co. Ltd., London, 1980-86, S.G. Warburg Securities, London, 1986-92; dir. Mercury Asset Mgmt. Ltd., London, 1992-98, mng. dir., 1998-99; dir. Tribune Trust plc; cons. Ernst & Young, 1999—; chmn. European Tech. and Income Co. Ltd. Mem. ABA. Roman Catholic. Avocations: art, music, theater, tennis. Home: 7 Spencer Hill, London SW19 4PA, England Office: Ernst & Young, 7 Rolls Bldgs Fetter Ln, London EC4A 1NH, England

CALLAHAN, MICHAEL THOMAS, lawyer, construction consultant; b. Kansas City, Mo., Oct. 7, 1948; s. Harry Leslie and Venita June (Yohn) C.; m. Stella Sue Paffenbach, Mar. 21, 1970; children: Molly Leigh, Michael Kroh. BA, U. Kans., 1970; JD, U. Mo., 1973, LLM, 1979; postgrad., Temple U., 1976-77. Bar: Kans. 1973, N.J. 1975, Mo. 1977. V.p. T.J. Constrn., Inc., Lenexa, Kans., 1973-74; sr. cons. Wagner-Hohns-Inglis, Inc., Mt. Holly, N.J., 1974-77; v.p. Wagner-Hohns-Inglis, Inc., Kansas City, Mo., 1977-86; exec. v.p. CCL Constrn. Cons., Overland Park, Kans., 1986-88, pres., 1988—; adj. prof. U. Kans., Iowa State U.; arbitrator, lectr. in field, author; chmn. CCL Pacific Corp.; pres. Handcrafted Wines Kans., Inc. Home: 9011 Delmar St Shawnee Mission KS 66207-2343 Office: CCL Constrn Cons 4600 College Blvd Ste 104 Overland Park KS 66211-1606

CALLAN, TERRENCE A., lawyer; b. San Francisco, Sept. 20, 1939; s. Harold A. and Viola A. (Briese) C.; m. Gail R. Raine, Apr. 20, 1968; 1 child, Ryan T. BA, U. San Francisco, 1961; JD, U. Calif., San Francisco, 1964. Bar: Calif. 1965, U.S. Dist. Ct. (no. dist.) Calif. 1965, U.S. Ct. Appeals (9th cir.) 1965, U.S. Dist. Ct. (cen. dist.) Calif. 1970, U.S. Supreme Ct. 1975, U.S. Dist. Ct. (so. dist.) Calif. 1981, U.S. Dist. Ct. (ea. dist.) Calif. 1996. Rsch. asst. Pillsbury, Madison & Sutro, San Francisco, 1964-65, assoc., 1965-72, ptnr., 1973—. Dir. sec., gen. counsel Presidio Soc., 1981-94; dir., sec., legal counsel Ft. Point and Presidio Hist. Assn., 1984—; bd. trustees 1066 Found., Mildred E. Stearns Found. Mem. ABA, Calif. State Bar Assn. (past chmn., exec. com. antitrust and trade regulation sect.), San Francisco Bar Assn. (past mem. judiciary com., antitrust, 9th cir. no. dist. merit screening com. for bankruptcy judgeships), Lawyers Club San Francisco (bd. govs.), U. Calif. Alumni Assn., Hastings Coll. of the Law Annual Campaign (nat. chair), U. San Francisco Alumni Assn. (bd. govs.), Order of Coif, Green and Gold Club (chmn. bd. dirs.), U. San Francisco Club, Phi Alpha Delta. Roman Catholic. Office: Pillsbury Madison Sutro LLP PO Box 7880 San Francisco CA 94120-7880

CALLANAN, MARGARET MARY, clinical psychologist; b. Cork, Ireland, Feb. 3, 1960; arrived in England, 1972; d. Denis Joseph and Winifred Monica (McDermot) C.; m. Keith Kelsey, Sept. 24, 1988; children: Ruari, Cormac, Caoive. BA, Hull U., 1981; MSc, Univ. East London, 1984; PhD, Inst. Neurology U. London, 1990. Rsch. clin. psychologist Inst. Neurology, London, 1984-87; prin. clin. psychologist Bethlem & Maudsley Health Auth., London, 1987-99; hon. lectr. Inst. Psychiatry, London, 1990-99; from clin. rsch. organizer to cons. dir. Salomons Ctr., Kent, England, 1990-2000; dir. practice consultancy, 2000—; external examiner Queens U., Belfast, Ireland, 1995—; rsch. examiner Br. Psychol. Soc., 1992-95, chair com. on tng. 1998-2000. Roman Catholic. Avocations: family life, reading, walking, singing. Office: Salomons, Broomhill Rd, TN3 0TG Kent UK

CALLANDER, KAY EILEEN PAISLEY, business owner, retired gifted talented education educator, writer; b. Coshocton, Ohio, Oct. 15, 1938; d. Dalton Olas and Dorothy Pauline (Davis) Paisley; m. Don Larry Callander, Nov. 18, 1977. BSE, Muskingum Coll., 1960; MA in Speech Edn., Ohio State U., 1964, postgrad., 1964-84. Cert. elem., gifted, drama, theater tchr., Ohio. Tchr. Columbus (Ohio) Pub. Schs., 1960-70, 80-88, drama specialist, 1970-80, classroom, gifted/talented tchr., 1986-90, ret., 1990; sole prop. The Ali Group, Kay Kards, 1992—; coord. Artists-in-the Schs., 1977-88; cons., presenter numerous ednl. confs. and sems., 1971—; mem., ednl. cons. Innovation Alliance Youth Adv. Coun., 1992—. producer-dir., Shady Lane Music Festival, 1980-88; dir. tchr. (nat. distbr. video) The Trial of Gold E. Locks, 1983-84; rep., media pub. relations liason Sch. News., 1983-88; author, creator Trivia Game About Black Americans (TGABA), exhibitor of TGABA game at L.A. County Office Edn. Conf., 1990; presenter for workshop by Human Svc. Group and Creative Edn. Coop., Columbus, Ohio, 1989. Benefactor, Columbus Jazz Arts Group; v.p., bd. dirs. Neoteric Dance and Theater Co., Columbus, 1985-87; tchr., participant Future Stars sculpture exhibit, Ft. Hayes Ctr., Columbus Pub. Schs., 1988; tchr. advisor Columbus Coun. PTAs, 1983-86, co-chmn. reflections com., 1984-87; mem. Columbus Mus. Art, Citizens for Humane Action, Inc.; mem. supt.'s adv. coun. Columbus Pub. Schs., 1967-68; presenter Young Author Seminar, Ohio Dept. Edn., 1988, Illustrating Methods for Young Authors' Books, 1986-87; cons. and workshop leader seminar/workshop Tchg. About the Constitution in Elem. Schs., Franklin County Ednl. Coun., 1988; sponsor Minority Youth Recognition Awards, 1994. Named Educator of Yr., Shady Lane PTA, 1982, Columbus Coun. PTAs, 1989, winner Colour Columbus Landscape Design Competition, 1990; Sch. Excellence grantee Columbus Pub. Schs.; Commendation Columbus Bd. Edn. and Ohio Ho. of Reps. for Child Assault Prevention project, 1986-87; first place winner statewide photo contest Ohio Vet. Assn., 1991; recipient Muskingum Coll. Alumni Disting. Svc. award, 1995. Mem. ASCD, AAUW, Assn. for Childhood Edn. Internat., Ohio Coun. for Social Studies, Franklin County Ret. Tchrs. Assn., Nat. Mus. Women in the Arts, Ohio State U. Alumni Assn., U.S. Army Officers Club, Navy League, Liturgical Art Guild Ohio, Columbus Jazz Arts Group, Columbus Mus. Art. Nat. Coun. for Social Studies, Columbus Art League, Columbus Maennerchor (Damen sect.). Republican. Avocations: painting, photography, swimming, golfing, playing piano and organ. Home: 2323 Colts Neck Rd Blacklick OH 43004-9003 Office: The Ali Group Kay Kards PO Box 13093 Columbus OH 43213-0093

CALLANS, DAVID JOHN, cardiologist; b. Joliet, Ill., Sept. 15, 1960; s. John David and Yvonne (Vogrin) C.; m. Linda Elinor Skinner, Aug. 20, 1988; children: Christopher, Lauren. AB, U. Chgo., 1982; MD, Johns Hopkins U., 1986. Intern then resident in internal medicine Hosp. U. Pa., Phila., 1986-89; fellow in cardiology and cardiac electrophysiology U. Pa. Hosp., Phila., 1988-93; dir. heart sta., clin. asst. prof. medicine Phila. Heart Inst., U. Pa., 1993-95; assoc. prof. medicine Med. Coll. Pa.-Hahnemann Sch. Medicine, Phila., 1996-98; co-dir. electrophysiology lab., assoc. prof. medicine U. Pa., Phila., 1999—. Mem. ACP, AHA, Am. Coll. Cardiology, N.Am. Soc. Pacing and Electrophysiology. Office: Hosp U Pa Cardiology Divsn 3400 Spruce St Philadelphia PA 19104-4206

CALLAOS, NAGIB CHARLY, systems engineering educator; b. Aleppo, Syria, July 9, 1943; s. Georges Nagib and Leonida (Farra) C.; m. Bekis Margarita Sanchez, Mar. 30, 1979; children: Leonisol Liliana, Belkis Helena, Jorge Emeterio. B of Elec. Engring., Ctrl. U. Venezuela, 1968; MSEE, U. Tex., 1970, PhD, 1976. Instr. Ctrl. U. Venezuela, Caracas, 1968-69, asst., 1971-73, chmn. dept., 1977-78; assoc. titular prof. U. Simon Bolivar, Caracas, 1977-94; gen. mgr. Fund for Tech. Innovation, Caracas, 1981-83; dean U. Simon Bolivar, 1984-86, prof., 1994—; pres. Systemica, Caracas, 1984-89, Rsch. & Devel. Found. U. Simon Bolivar, 1989-90, Callaos and Assocs., Caracas, 1990—, World Multiconf. on Systemics, Cybernetics and Informatics, 1996-98; dir. Profl. Improvement Inst. Venezuelan Coll. Engring., Caracas, 1993-96; elected dir. Int. Soc. Systems Scis., 1994-95; chmn. Internat. Inst. Infomaticsa and Systemics. Co-author: Comprehensive Systems Design, 1990, Praxeology, 1994. Gen. sec. engring. Christian Dem. Party, 1965-68, nat. young coord., 1971-74, nat. sec. info., 1983-90; cons. Inst. Christian Dem. Edn., Venezuela, 1992. Inter-Am. Bank Devel. grantee, 1975-76; UNESCO scholar, 1969-71; recipient Outstanding Achievement award in sys. rsch. Internat. Inst. Sys. Rsch. and Cybernetics Can., 1994. Mem. IEEE/Computer Soc. (chmn. Venezuelan chpt. 1996—), Internat. Systems Inst. (rsch. fellow, bd. dirs. 1993—), Internat. Soc. Systems Scis., Venezuelan Systems Assn. (pres. 1982—), Assn. Computing Machinery, Venezuelan Exec. Assn., Venezuelan Chpt. Tech. Transfer Execs. (pres. 1983-85), Venezuelan Acad. Engring. (life). Roman Catholic. Avocation: jogging. Home: Calle Union Parque Union, # 37 Lomas de la Lagunita, Caracas Venezuela Office: U Simon Bolivar, Sartenejas A P 89000, Caracas Venezuela

CALLAWAY, CLIFFORD WAYNE, physician; b. Easton, Md., May 28, 1941; s. Charles Herschel and Anna Agnes (Stradley) C.; 1 child, David Wayne; m. Jackie Chalkley. BA, U. Del., 1963; MD, Northwestern U., 1967. Diplomate Am. Bd. Internal Medicine, Am. Bd. Endocrinology, Diabetes and Metabolism, Am. Bd. Nutrition. Resident internal medicine Northwestern U. Med. Ctr., Chgo., 1967-69, Mayo Grad. Sch. Medicine, Rochester, Minn., 1971-73; advanced clin. resident endocrinology Mayo Grad. Sch. Medicine, 1973-75; assoc. cons. Mayo Clin., Rochester, 1975-78; cons. endocriminology Mayo Clin., 1978-85, dir. nutrition and lipid clins., 1980-85; rsch. assoc. Harvard Med. Sch., Boston, 1976-78; dir. ctr. clin. nutrition George Washington U., Washington, 1986-88; sr. sci. cons. Food & Ntrition Bd., NRC/NAS, Washington, 1987-88; pvt. practice Washington, 1988—. Author 4 books; contbr. articles to profl. jours. Acting exec. sec. nutrition coordinating office HHS, Washington, 1980. Mayo Found. scholar, 1976-78. Mem. Am. Soc. Clin. Nutrition (treas. 1988), Am. Bd. Nutrition (mem. bd. dirs. 1983-89, 95-98, sec.-treas. 1984-86, v.p. 1986-88), Am. Inst. Nutrition (chair and various coms.), Am. Osler Soc. (bd. dirs.), Am. Assn. Clin. Endocrinologists (bd. dirs. 1992-95), Cen. European Ctr. for Health and Environment (bd. dirs. 1993—). Achievements include development and writing of dietary guidelines for Americans(USDA/DHHS). Office: 2311 M St NW Ste 301 Washington DC 20037-1468

CALLEBAUT, PIWNICA CAROLE, lawyer; b. Brussels, Belgium, Feb. 12, 1958; d. Pierre and Nicole (Dierickx) C.; m. Emmanuel Piwnica, Oct. 14, 1988; children: Eve, Pierre, Charles. Bar: N.Y. Assoc. various law firms N.Y., 1985-87; assoc. Shearman & Sterling, Paris, France, 1987-92; gen. counsel Societe Centrale D'Investissements et Associes, Paris, 1991-94; various mgmt. positions Anylum Group, Paris, 1994—; chmn. Anylum Group, 1996; dir. Anylum, N.V., Belgium, 1991, Tunnel Refineries, Ltd., England, 1991, Cip, 1996, Tate & Lyle, 1997, Toepfer, 1997, Spa Nonopoues, 1999. Office: Anylum, 43/47 Ave de la Grande, 75782 Armee Paris Cedex 16, France

CALLEO, DAVID PATRICK, history educator, political economy and international relations educator; b. Binghamton, N.Y., July 19, 1934; s. Patrick and Gertrude (Crowe) C.; m. Avis Thayer Bohlen. BA, Yale U., 1955, MA, 1957, PhD, 1959. Instr. polit. sci. Brown U., Providence, 1959-60; from instr. to assoc. prof. polit. sci. Yale U., New Haven, 1961-67; cons. to undersec. for polit. affairs U.S. Dept. of State, Washington, 1967-68; sr. Fulbright lectr. Fed. Republic Germany, 1975; assoc. fellow Jonathan Edwards Coll, Yale U., New Haven, 1972—; v.p. Lehrman Inst., N.Y.C., 1972-87; project dir. The Twentieth Century Fund, N.Y.C., 1981-85; pres. and trustee Washington Found. for European Studies, Washington, 1987—; prof., dir. European studies Nitze Sch. Advanced Internat. Studies, Johns Hopkins U., Washington, 1968—; project dir. The 20th Century Fund, N.Y.C., 1993-99; assoc. Centre d'Etudes et de Recherches Internationales, 1993-94; enseignant invité Institut d'études politiques de Paris, 1993-94, Institut universitaire de hautes études internationales, Geneva, 1999; Dean Acheson chair Nitze Sch. Advanced Internat. Studies, Washington, 1988—. Author: America and the World Political Economy, 1973 (Gladys M. Kammerer award Best Book Analyzing Am. Nat. Policy, Am. Polit. Sci. Assn. 1973), The German Problem Reconsidered, 1978, The Imperious Economy, 1982, Beyond American Hegemony, 1987, The Bankrupting of America, 1992. Trustee, Jonathan Edwards Trust; pres. Washington Found. for European Studies. Rsch. fellow Nuffield Coll., Oxford U., 1966-67. Mem. Am. Polit. Sci. Assn., Coun. on Fgn. Rels., Internat. Inst. for Strategic Studies, Brooks' (London), Met. Club Washington, Century Assn. (N.Y.C.), The Literary Soc. (Washington). Avocations: gardening, squash, opera.

CALLIER, FRANK MARIA, applied mathematics educator, researcher; b. Antwerp, Belgium, Nov. 27, 1942; s. Pierre Andréc and Henriette Marie-Jeanne (Mazurelle) C.; m. Nicole Maria De Sloovere, Mar. 28, 1969; children: Ann, Mike. Diploma of Elec. Engring., State U. Ghent, Belgium, 1966; Cert. in Nuclear Engring., Swiss Fed. Inst. Tech., Zurich, 1967; MSc in Elec. Engring. and Computer Sci., U. Calif., Berkeley, 1970, PhD, 1972. Asst. in automatic control State U. Ghent, 1968-69; asst. prof. elec. engring. U. Calif., Berkeley, 1972-73; rsch. assoc. in automatic control Belgian Nat. Fund of Sci. Rsch., Brussels, 1973-74; chargé de cours in applied math. Facultés Universitaires N.D. de la Paix, Namur, Belgium, 1974-80, prof., 1980-86, full prof., 1986—, dir. dept. math., 1992-94; vis. prof. U. Calif., Berkeley, 1981. Co-author: Multivariable Feedback Systems, 1982, Linear System Theory, 1991; assoc. editor Systems and Control Letters, North Holland, 1984-90, Automatica, 1995-99; contbr. more than 65 publs. to the profl. lit. Served to cpl. Belgian Mil., 1967-68. Belgian Am. Ednl. Found. grad. fellow, 1969; U. Calif. Berkeley rsch. grantee, 1975, 77, 79, 81, 84, 86. Fellow IEEE; mem. Belgian Am. Ednl. Found., Royal Soc. Flemish Engrs., Belgian Inst. Regulation and Automation. Roman Catholic. Avocations: reading history, walking, music (playing the recorder). Home: 66 Ave du Petit Sart, B 5100 Namur Belgium Office: Facultes Univ ND de la Paix, 8 Rempart de la Vierge, B 5000 Namur Belgium

CALLIESS, JÖRG, historian, educator; b. Berlin, June 10, 1941; s. Curt and Gisela (Weiland) C.; m. Gretl Schede, Sept. 22, 1972; children: Franca, Tilman. MA, Ludwig Maximilian U., Munich, 1968; PhD, Tech. U. Braunschweig, Germany, 1974. Lectr. Ludwig Maximilian U., 1968-69, Tech. U. Braunschweig, 1970-77; mem. ednl. staff Internationales Hans Sonnenberg, St. Andreasberg, Germany, 1977-79; dir. studies Evangelische Akademie Loccum, Germany, 1979—; lectr. Tech. U. Braunschweig, 1977-99, hon. prof., 1999. Author: Militär in der Krise. Die bayerische Armee in der Revolution 1848/49, 1976, Strukturen und Probleme der Säkularisierungsprozesse in Europa, erschein in englischer und in arabischer Sprache in El Albeit-Stiftung, 1997; author numerous handbooks, including Praxis der Umwelt- und Friedenserziehung, vols. 1 and 2, 1987, vol. 3, 1988; contbr. numerous chpts. to books and articles to profl. jours., including IFDT, Die Friedenswarte, others. Chmn. German Platform for Conflict Prevention and Conflict Resolution. Capt., German Engrs., 1960-63, Germany. Mem. Informationsstelle Wissenschaft und Frieden, Bonn (mem. bd. 1987—), Forschungsstätte der Evangelische Studiengemeinschaft, Heidelberg (mem. bd. 1995—, Verband der Historiker Deutschlands. Lutheran. Avocations: opera, symphony, tennis, soccer. E-mail: Joerg.Calliess@evlka.de. Home: Am Scheibenstand 1, D-31547 Loccum Germany Office: Evangelische Akad Loccum, P.O. Box 2158, Loccum Germany

CALLMEYER, FERENC, architect; b. Apr. 3, 1928; s. Ferenc and Ilona (Zachar) C.; m. Eva Szep, Jan. 30, 1953; children: Judith, Laszlo. Architect, Poly. U., Budapest, 1951; MArch, Hungarian Assn. Architects, 1953. Architect-designer Mezoterv, Budapest, 1951-55; head dept. Iparterv, Budapest, 1955-63; architect-designer Sheppard, Robson Pts., London, 1963-65; head office TTI, Budapest, 1965—; prof. H.C. Tech. U., Budapest, 1990—; chmn. Archtl. Examining Bd., Budapest, 1978—, Creative Coun., 1986. Author: Holyday Homes, 1972, Family Houses (award 1978), 1974, Habitate for Humanity Internat. Hungarian Affiliate, 1992-96. Mem. bd. DLA Tech. U. Recipient prize Coun. of Ministers, Budapest, 1957, Silver medal of Labor, 1981; Best Bldg. Yr. award Min. of Bldg, Budapest, 1978; U.S. Govt. grantee, 1984. Fellow Hungarian Assn. Architects (v.p. 1986—), AIA (hon.); mem. World Assn. Hungarian Engrs. and Architects (pres. 1989-93), Hungarian Chamber of Architects (pres. 1997-99, European Engrs., Townplanning Com. City of Budapest. Office: Callmeyer & PTS Architects, Orgona U 134, 2089 Telki Hungary

CALLO, KATHLEEN ELIZABETH, media executive; b. N.Y.C., Aug. 25, 1958; d. Joseph Francis and Susan Catherine (Jones) C.; m. Peter Wilson-Smith, Sept. 14, 1991; children: Henry John Wilson-Smith, Benedict Lucas Wilson-Smith. BA, SUNY, Purchase, 1981; MS, Columbia U., 1985; MSc, London Bus. Sch., 1999. Corr. Reuters, London, Brussels, Manila, Hong Kong, Hanoi, 1985-93; advt. editor Reuters, London, 1995-98; dir. strategic bus. devel. Reuters, 1999-2000, v.p. pictures, 2000—. Mem. The Royal Inst. Internat. Affairs. Roman Catholic. Avocations: skiing, scuba diving, tennis. Office: Reuters Ltd, 85 Fleet St, London EC4P 4AJ, England

CALLOW, KEITH MCLEAN, judge; b. Seattle, Jan. 11, 1925; s. Russell Stanley and Dollie (McLean) C.; m. Evelyn Case, July 9, 1949; children: Andrea, Douglas, Kerry. Student, Alfred U., 1943, CCNY, 1944, Biarritz Am. U., 1945; BA, U. Wash., 1949, JD, 1952. Bar: Wash. 1952, D.C. 1974. Asst. atty. gen. Wash., 1952; law clk. to justice Supreme Ct. Wash., 1953; dep. pros. atty. King County, 1954-56; ptnr. Little, LeSourd, Palmer, Scott & Slemmons, Seattle, 1957-62, Barker, Day, Callow & Taylor, 1964-68; judge King County Superior Ct., 1969-71, Ct. of Appeals Wash., Seattle, 1972-84; presiding chief judge Ct. of Appeals Wash., 1985-90; justice State Supreme Ct. Wash., Olympia, 1985-90, chief justice, 1989-90; cons. Prior-Martech, 1998—; 2d v.p. Conf. of Chief Justices; Booneville Power Admin. Rate Hearings Officer, 1995-96; lectr. bus. law U. Wash., 1956-62, Shefelman Disting. lectr., 1991; faculty Nat. Jud. Coll., 1980, Seattle U. Environ. Law, 1992, 94-95; co-organizer, sec. Coun. of Chief Judges of Cts. of Appeals; Rep. of Estonia, 1993-96, advisor Nat. Ct. and Ministry of Justice; advisor Kyrgyzstan, Kazakhstan, Georgia, Armenia, 1997; presenter in field. Editor-in-chief Commercial Law Desk Book, 1992-95; editor works in field. Chief Seattle coun. Boy Scouts Am.; adviser Gov. Health Care Commn. State of Washington, 1991-92; pres. Young Men's Rep. Club, 1957. With AUS, 1943-46. Decorated Purple Heart; recipient Brandeis award Wash. State Trial Lawyers Assn., 1981, Douglas award, 1990. Fellow Am. Bar Found.; mem. ABA (chmn. com. on judiciary 1984-90), Wash. State Bar Assn. (mem. exec. com., appellate Judges Conf.), D.C. Bar Assn., Seattle-King County Bar Assn., Estate Planning Coun., Navy League, Rainier Club (sec. 1978, trustee 1989-92), Forty Nine Club (pres. 1972), Masons, Rotary, Psi Upsilon, Phi Delta Phi.

CALLUS, ASHLEY, Olympic athlete; b. Brisbane, Queensland, Australia, Oct. 3, 1979. Recipient Gold medal 4 x 100m freestyle relay Commonwealth Games, Kuala Lumpur, 1998; 2d 100m freestyle Qantas World Cup, Sydney, 2000, 3d 50m freestyle Telstra Australian Short Course Championships, 1999, 4th 100m freestyle World Short Course Championships, Athens, 2000, 3d 50m and 100m freestyle 2000 Telstra Selection Trials, 2000; mem. 1st Olympic team. Mem. Redlands Club (Queensland). Avocation: surf lifesaving. Office: Australian Swimming Inc, PO Box 940, Dickson ACT 2602, Australia*

CALNAN, ARTHUR FRANCIS, ophthalmologist; b. Boston, Mar. 11, 1926; s. Augustine Francis and Mary Ellen (Callahan) C.; m. Jeanne Elizabeth Faber, Nov. 27, 1954; children: Kathleen, Diane, Barbara, Jeffrey, Douglas, David. BS, Tufts U., 1946, MD, 1950; MS, U. Pa., 1954. Diplomate Am. Bd. Ophthalmology, Am. Bd. Med. Examiners. Rotating intern St. Louis City Hosp., 1950-51; resident ophthalmology, rsch. fellow Wills Eye Hosp., Phila., 1954-55, resident, 1955-57; preceptorship Trygye Gundersen MD, Boston, 1957-65; chair ophthamology dept. Lahey Clinic, Boston, 1965-70; sr. mem. South Suburban Ophthalmology, Hingham, Mass., 1970—; clin. instr. ophthalmology Tufts U. Sch. Medicine, 1958; mem. active staff ophthalmology South Shore Hosp., Weymouth, Mass., 1960—; jr. assisting surgeon ophthalmology Carney Hosp., Dorchester, Mass., 1963—; asst. ophthalmology Milton (Mass.) Hosp., 1973—. Mem. Plymouth County Rep. Club. Served to capt. USAF, 1950-53. Recipient Humanitarian of Yr. award Vis. Nurse Assn., 1992. Mem. AMA, Internat. Assn. Ocular Surgeons, Am. Acad. Ophthalmology, Am. Intra-Ocular Implant Soc., New Eng. Ophthalmol. Soc., Mass. Soc. Ophthalmic Physicians and Surgeons, Mass. Med. Soc., Norfolk-South Med. Soc., Am. Soc. Cataract and Refractive Surgeons, Am. Soc. Contemporary Ophthalmology, Contact Lens Assn. Ophthalmologists, Mass. Eye and Ear Infirmary Alumni Assn., Wills Eye Hosp. Alumni Assn., Erie Soc., Clan Gillean Assn., South Shore C. of C., Air Force Assn., Guild St. Luke. Roman Catholic. Avocations: travel, gardening, music. Home: 170 Old Oaken Bucket Rd Scituate MA 02066-4435 Office: S Suburban Ophthalmology 31 Derby St Hingham MA 02043-3706

CALÒ, PIETRO GIORGIO, surgeon, researcher, educator; b. Cagliari, Sardinia, Italy, July 7, 1966; s. Isidoro Antonio and Viviana (Binelli) C. MD, U. Cagliari, 1990. Diploma in surgery and surg. oncology. Intern Surgery and Oncology Inst. U. Cagliari, 1990-92, rschr., 1992-95, confirmed rschr., 1995—, tchr. geriatric surgery, 1996—; cons. Sardinian Assn. Assistance Mamopathic, Cagliari, 1991—, Italian Assn. Tumors, Cagliari, 1992—; rsch. bd. adv. Am. Biographical Inst. Contbr. articles to Minerva Chirurgica, Jour. of Chemotherapy, Tumori, British Jour. of Surgery, Anti-Cancer Drugs, European Jour. of Cancer, European Jour. of Surg. Oncology, Annals of Oncology, British Jour. of Radiology, Jour. of Balkan Union of Oncology, Chirurgia, Gastroenterology Internat. Govt. of Malta scholar, 1988. Mem. AAAS, Italian Soc. Surgery, Italian Soc. Surg. Oncology, Italian Soc. Day Surgery, Italian Assn. Stoma Patients (attachè), Aistom Data Processing Working Team (attachè), Italian Polispecialistic Soc. of Young Surgeons, European Soc. of Surg. Oncology. Avocations: football, music, reading, cinema, walking. Home: Via Dei Colombi 38, 09126 Cagliari Sardinia, Italy Office: U Hosp Bomed Scis/Biomed, Viale Marconi 160, 09045 Quartu S Elena Cagliari, Italy

CALODNY, ALAN LEE, retired pharmacist; b. Bklyn., Feb. 27, 1934; s. Benjamin Lewis and Rose C.; m. Akie Luckhoo (dec. May 1990). BS in Pharmacy, Bklyn. Coll. Pharmacy, 1955; MS in Hosp. Pharmacy Adminstrn., L.I. Univ., 1973. Pharmacist Whelan Drug Stores, N.Y.C., 1956-57, C&M Pharmacy, Bklyn., 1957-58; asst. chief pharmacist L.I. Jewish Hosp., Glen Oaks, N.Y., 1958-59; chief pharmacist Parsons Hosp., Flushing, N.Y., 1959-84; pharmacist N.Y. State Dept. Corrections, 1984-90, Bronx-Lebanon Hosp., N.Y., 1989-93. Life mem. Cancer Care, Inc., Flushing, 1977. Mem. Am. Pharm. Assn., N.Y. State Coun. Health Sys. Pharmacists, L.I. Soc. Health Sys. Pharmacists, Rho Chi.. Democrat. Jewish. Avocations: philately, study of outer space/UFOs, study of animals and natural history, geography. Home: 82-59 268th St Floral Park NY 11004

ČALOGOVIĆ, MARKO, engineering educator; b. Zagreb, Croatia, May 12, 1915; s. Milan and Hinka (Marač) C; m. Eleanora Huml, June 19, 1943 (dec. Oct. 1993); children: Vladimir, Milan. Diploma in engring., U. Zagreb, 1939. Civil engr. Alpen Elektrowerke, Wien, Austria, 1943-45, Elektroprojekt, Zagreb, 1948-63; dir. Geotechnical Inst., Zagreb, 1963-66; prof. statics, hydrotech. structures, dams U. Zagreb, 1966-82, prof. emeritus, 1982—; cons. Elektroprojekt, Zagreb, 1949—. Home: Rokova 9, 10000 Zagreb Croatia

CALOOY, SONYA RENEE, advertising executive, consultant; b. Verdun, France, Feb. 6, 1961; naturalized U.S. citizen, 1961; d. Rudy A. and Frances (Rosales) C. BFA in Advt. Design with honors, North Tex. State U., 1983. TV studio mgr. Tex. Dept. of Mental Health/Mental Retardation, Denton, Tex., 1983-85; prodn. coord. Kim Dawson Agy., Dallas, 1983-91; art dir., owner Image by Design Group, Dallas, 1986-89; sr. art dir. The Promotion Network, Dallas, 1989-90; art dir., prin., founder, owner Calooy & Co., Dallas, 1990—; creative dir., prin., founder The Lucky Seven Project, Dallas, 1997-99; pres., CEO Creative Showcase, Inc., Dallas, 1998—; founder, pres. WebMacster.com, 1999—; creative svcs. cons. Pepsico Creative Pool, Plano, Tex., 1995-98; vis. scholar, adj. faculty internet pub. and e-commerce techs. program El Centro C.C., Dallas, 2000—. Choral musician The Women's Chorus of Dallas, 1991—; mem. Dallas/Ft. Worth Minority Bus. Devel. Coun. Mem. North Tex. Women's Bus. Coun., Greater Dallas C. of C., Gamma Beta Phi. Democrat. Avocations: choral musician, jazz musician, fine artist.

CALORE, EDENILSON EDUARDO, physician, researcher; b. Rio Claro, Sao Paulo, Brazil, June 1, 1960; s. Evaristo Rafael and Antonia do Carmo Rodrigues Calore; m. Nilda Maria Perez, Dec. 19, 1995; children: Thais, Eduardo Augusto. MD, Med. Sch. Mogidas Cruzes U., Mogi Das Cruzes, 1983; pathologist, São Paulo U., 1989, PhD, 1997; asst. étranger, Marseille Medicine Sch., France, 1992. Med. diplomate. Asst. étanger Faculty Medicine de Marseille, 1990-92; med. doctor, rschr. Adolfo Lutz Inst., São Paulo, 1992-94, Emilio Ribas Inst., São Paulo, 1994—; prof. pharmacology dept. Vet. Medicine Sch., Biomed. Inst., Sao Paulo U.; mem. Nat. Comn. Toxicology Evaluation of Agrotoxic Products, Brasilia, Brazil, 1999; cons. CNPq, Brasilia, 1999. Contbr. articles to profl. jours. Mem. Brazilian Pathology Soc., Brazilian Soc. Neurosci., Brazilian Soc. Toxicology. Avocation: music. E-mail: calore@sti.com.br. Fax: 55-011-37511811. Office: Emmlio Ribas Inst, Av Dr Arnaldo 165 Patologia, 01246902 Sao Paulo Brazil

CALOVSKI, NASTE, diplomat. Macedonia rep. to UN, N.Y.C. Office: UN 866 U N Plz Rm 517-518 New York NY 10017-1822

CALOW, PETER, biology educator; b. Chesterfield, Derbyshire, Eng., May 23, 1947. BSc, U. Leeds (Eng.), 1969, PhD, 1972, DSc, 1984. Chartered biologist. Lectr. U. Glasgow (Scotland), 1972-81, reader, 1981-84; prof. U. Sheffield (Eng.), 1984—, dir., 1991—; pres. SETAC-Europe, 1991-92. Founding editor Functional Ecology, 1986—, Integrated Environ. Mgmt., 1991—; author: Biological Machines, 1976, Invertebrate Biology, 1981, Evolutionary Principles, 1983; editor: (book series) Functional Biology, 1983; contbr. over 130 articles to profl. jours. Chmn. Brit. Govt. Adv. Com. on Hazardous Substances. Grantee Rsch. Couns. Industry, European Commn.; decorated officer Order of the Brit. Empire. Home: 4 Daleside, Riverdale Rd, Sheffield S10 3FA, England

CALTABIANO, MARIE LOUISE, psychologist; b. Innisfail, Australia, Oct. 17, 1959; d. Alfio and Rosetta (Finocchiaro) C. BA in Psychology, James Cook U., Townsville, Australia, 1980, BA with honors, 1981, PhD, 1989. Registered psychologist, Queensland. Rsch. asst. James Cook U., Townsville, 1980-83, from tutor to lectr., 1984-96, assoc. dean faculty arts, 1995—; tchr. Italian Consulate, Townsville, 1982; exec. com. Nat. Tertiary Edn. Industry Union, Townsville, 1994-96; arts faculty com. James Cook U., Townsville, 1995—, treas. acad. staff assoc., 1994-96; cons., lectr. and presenter in field. Co-editor: Achieving Inclusion: Exploring Issues in Disability, 1997; co-author: Menopausal Health and the Family, 1997, Influences of Healthy Eating Patterns in Ethnic Communities, 1998; mem. editl. bd. Ctr. for Social & Welfare Rsch., 1995—, Northern Australia Social Rsch. Inst., 1995—; contbr. articles to profl. jours. Travel scholar U. N.S.W., 1984; Merit Rsch. grantee James Cook U., 1990, Rsch. grantee Rotary, 1995. Mem. AAAS, Am. Psychol. Soc., Australian Psychol. Soc. (sci. affairs divsn. 1986-96, exec. com. North Queensland br. 1995—, newsletter editor 1995), Internat. Fedn. Univ. Women, Pub. Health Assn. Australia, Amnesty Internat., Dante Alighieri Soc. (com. mem. 1980-84). Mem. Australian Labour Party. Roman Catholic. Avocations: travel, reading, ceramics, music. Office: James Cook U Sch Psychology, Smithfield, 6811 Cairns 6811, Australia

CALUDE, CRISTIAN, mathematician, computer scientist; b. Galati, Romania, Apr. 21, 1952; s. Constantin and Jeanette (Bobulescu) C.; m. Elena Anghel, Oct. 21, 1978; 1 child, Andreea. B.A. in Math. and Computer Sci. with honors, U. Bucharest, Romania, 1975, Ph.D. in Math., 1977. Prof. U. Bucharest, 1975—, U. Auckland, 1992—; dir. COMTCS, 1995—; assoc. mem. Solvay Insts., 1998—; Mombusho vis. prof. JAIST, 1999. Author: Theories of Computational Complexity, 1988, Information and Randomness, 1994, People and Ideas in Theoretical Computer Science, 1999, Computing with Cells and Atoms, 2000; contbr. numerous articles to sci. publs. Mem. New Zealand Math. Soc., Am. Math. Soc., New Zealand Royal Soc., European Assn. Computer Sci. Avocation: lawn tennis. Office: Univ Auckland Dept Computer Sci, Private Bag 92019, Auckland New Zealand

CALVAER, ANDRE, electrical engineering educator, consultant; b. Brussels, Belgium, July 4, 1921; s. John B. and Flore M. (Romain) C.; m. Cecile G. Mahaux, Sept. 2, 1953; children: Myriam M., Yves F., Sophie M. B in Civil and Mining Engring., State U. Liege, Belgium, 1946; PhD, State U. Liege, 1957. Lic. elec. engr., Belgium. Chief engr. Nat. Elec. Coordn. Co. CPTE, Brussels, 1947-66; adviser to bd. Nat. Elec. Coordn. Co., Brussels, 1966-86; assoc. prof. U. Liege, 1961-63, full prof., 1964-86, head dept. elec. engring., 1968-74, dean faculty of engring., 1972-75, bd. dirs., 1975-79; cons. Laborelec and Tractebel, Brussels, 1986-95; mem. Internat. Conf. on Large Elec. Systems (CIGRE), Paris, 1954-90; mem. Internat. Electrotech. Commn., Geneva, 1962-88. Author: Electricite Theorique (5 vols.), 1963; contbr. numerous papers to sci. and tech. publs. Decorated comdr. Order of Crown, grand officer Order of Leopold II (Belgium), Comdr. Order Palmes Academiques (France); recipient internat. Montefiore prize, 1960, Lamme medal IEEE, 1997. Fellow IEEE (life), N.Y. Acad. Scis., Soc. Electriciens et Electroniciens (emeritus); mem. Assn. Engrs. U Liege (chmn. sci. com. 1978-82, gold medal 1982), Belgian Royal Acad. Coun. for Applied Scis. Avocations: abstract painting, modern art history. Home: Ave Blonden 23/091, B 4000 Liège Belgium

CALVERLEY, PETER MARTIN ANTHONY, respiratory physician; b. Blackburn, U.K., Nov. 27, 1949; s. Peter and Jennifer (Taylor) C.; m. Margaret Elizabeth Tatam, June 28, 1973; children: Adam, James, Robert, Thomas. MB, BChir, U. Edinburgh, Scotland, 1973. House staff City Hosp. Edinburgh, Scotland, 1973-74; sr. house officer Lothian Hosp., Edinburgh, 1974-75, Dept. Medicine, U. Leicester, Eng., 1975-76; MRC clin. fellow Dept. Medicine, U. Edinburgh, Scotland, 1976-79, sr. registrar, 1979-85; cons. physician Aintree Hosps., Liverpool, Eng., 1985—; prof. of pulmonary and rehab. medicine Univ. Liverpool, Liverpool, 1995—; travelling fellow Meakins-Christie Lab., Montreal, Can., 1982-83. Editor: Chronic Obstructive Pulmonary Disease, 1994; assoc. editor (med. jour.) Thorax, 1990-95, European Respiratory Jour., 2000—; contbr. articles to profl. jours. Fellow Royal Coll. Physicians (London), Royal Coll. Physicians (Edinburgh, Croom lectr. 1980); mem. Am. Coll. Chest Physicians, Am. Thoracic Soc., Brit. Thoracic Soc. (exec. 1992-95, chmn. sci. meetings com. 1992-95), Brit. Lung Found. (vice chmn. grants com. 1992-95, chmn. 1995—). Anglican. Avocations: travel, conversation, skiing, sailing. Office: Aintree Chest Ctr, Aintree Chest Ctr, Longmoor Ln U Hosp Aintree, Liverpool L9 7AL, England

CALVERT, PETER ANTHONY RICHARD, political science educator; b. Islandmagee, Ireland, Nov. 19, 1936; s. Raymond and Irene (Earls) C.; m. Sue Ann Milbank, 1987. BA, U. Cambridge, Eng., 1960, MA, PhD, 1964; AM, U. Mich., 1961. Vis. lectr. U. Calif., Santa Barbara, 1966; research fellow Harvard U., Cambridge, 1969-70; lectr. U. Southampton, Eng., 1964-71, sr. lectr., 1971-74; reader, 1974-83; prof. comparative and internat. politics U. Southampton, Eng., 1984—. Author: The Mexican Revolution, 1910-1914: The Diplomacy of Anglo-American Conflict, 1968, Latin America: Internal Conflict and International Peace, 1969, Study of Revolution, 1970, Mexico, Nation of the Modern World, 1973, The Mexicans: How They Live and Work, 1975, Emiliano Zapata, 1979, The Concept of Class, 1982, The Falklands Crisis: The Rights and The Wrongs, 1982, Politics Power and Revolution, 1983, Boundary Disputes in Latin America, 1983, Revolution and International Politics, 1984, Guatemalan Insurgency and American Security, 1984, Guatemala, A Nation in Turmoil, 1985, The Foreign Policy of New States, 1986, (with Susan Calvert) Political Culture and Instability, 1989, Revolution and Counter-Revolution, 1990, (with Susan Calvert) Latin America in the Twentieth Century, 1990, 93, (with Susan Calvert) Sociology Today, 1992, An Introduction to Comparative Politics, 1993, The International Politics of Latin America, 1994, (with Susan Calvert) Politics and Society in the Third World, 1996, The North, the South, and the Environment, 1999; editor: The Process of Political Succession, 1987, The Central American Security System, 1988, (with Peter Burnell) The Resilience of Democracy, 1999. Mem. Cambridge City Coun., 1962-64, Dorset (Eng.) edn. com., 1985-89. Ford Found. grantee, Southampton, 1984-88. Fellow Royal Hist. Soc.; mem. Polit. Studies Assn., Soc. Latin Am. Studies. Office: U Southampton, Southampton S017 1BJ, England

CALVEZ, JEAN YVES, political science and theology educator; b. Saint Brieuc, France, Feb. 3, 1927; s. Jean Marie and Claire Marie (Lemaire) C. Diploma in Polit. Sci., U. Paris, 1953; MTh, U. Lyons, France, 1958. Joined Soc. of Jesus, 1943. Dir. Social Inst. Cath. U., Paris, 1960-67; gen. asst. Soc. Jesus, Rome, 1971-83; editor in chief Rev. Etudes, France, 1984-95; prof. Centre Sèvres, Paris, 1995—; bd. dirs. Georgetown U., Washington. Author: La Pensée de Karl Marx, 1956, The Church and Economic Society, 1965, Politique, 1995, Nécessité du travail, 1997, Socialismes et marxismes Inventaire pour demain, 1998. Mem. Internat. Assn. Polit. Sci. (chmn. study group religion and politics). Roman Catholic. Home: 35 bis Rue de Sèvres, 75006 Paris France

CAL-VIDAL, JOSÉ, food scientist, educator; b. Pontevedra, Galicia, Spain, July 16, 1945; arrived in Brazil, 1958; Degree in chem. engring., U. Fed. Ceará, Recife, Brazil, 1970; MSc in Food Sci., U. Calif., Davis, 1971-73; D of Chem. Engring., U. São Paulo, Brazil, 1982. Registered chem. engr.; cert. univ. prof. Postdoctoral in food engring. U. Karlsruhe, Germany, 1983; U. B.C., Vancouver, Can., 1990; chem. engr. Nestlé Co., São Paulo, 1970-71; rsch. asst. U. Calif., Davis, 1972-73; tech. asst. Nestlé Alimentana S.A., Orbe, Switzerland, summer 1972; asst. prof. ESAL-Escola Superior Agr., Lavras, Brazil, 1976-82; assoc. prof. U. Fed. Lavras, Brazil, 1982-92; prof. U. Fed. Lavras, 1992—; sci. dir. Grad Program Food Engring., 1991—; prin. rschr. Lab. Microstructure and Food Arch., 1990—; founder pres. ALIMENTAR-Estudos & Projetos, Lavras, 1990—. Patentee cool-drying process; contbr. sci. articles to profl. jours. including Food Engring. and Process Applications, Devels. in Food Engring., Jour. Food Sci., Internat. Jour. Food Sci. and Tech. Founder, pres. Green Cross Found., Vancouver, 1990; founder 1st pres. CODEMA-Coun. for Environ. Protection, 1981. Recipient Student award SOS/70 Internat. Congress Food Sci. & Tech., Washington, 1970; fellow Orgn. Am. States, Washington, 1972-74, Latin Am. tchg. fellow Tufts U., Boston, 1976, rsch. fellow Nat. Rsch. Coun., Brasilia, Brazil, 1977—, fellow Deutscher Akademischer Austauschdienst, Bonn, Germany, 1982-83. Fellow Inst. Food Sci. and Tech. (London); mem. Inst. Food Technologists (profl. mem.), Brazilian Soc. Food Sci. and Tech. Roman Catholic. Avocation: nature exploration. Office: Univ Fed Lavras, Dept Ciécias dos Alimentos, 37200000 Lavras Brazil

CALVIÉ, LUCIEN, humanities educator; b. Béziers, France, Mar. 14, 1946. Student, Ecole Normal Supérieure, Paris, 1966-71; lic. d'allemand, Sorbonne, 1967, maîtrise d'allemand, 1968; agrégation d'allemand, France, 1970; Doctorat d'Etat ès Lettres, U. Paris III, 1979. Lectr. U. Nancy II, France, 1971-74, U. Montpellier III, France, 1974-83; prof. U. Grenoble III, France, 1983-99, U. Toulouse II, 1999—; dir. Rsch. Ctr. CERAAC, dir. yearbook Chroniques allemandes. Author: Le Renard et les raisins-La Révolution française et les intellectuels allemands 1789-1845, 1989; co-author: (with Francois Furet) Marx et la Révolution française, 1986; contbr. articles to profl. jours. Mem. Soc. des Etudes romantiques et dix-neuviémistes, Soc. des études robespierristes. Home: la Pleiade Rte de Grezac, 34700 Lodéve France Office: Dept d'Etudes Germaniques, Section d'allemand, Univ Toulouse II, Le Mirail France

CALVIN, ALLEN DAVID, psychologist, educator; b. St. Paul, Feb. 17, 1928; s. Carl and Zelda (Engelson) C.; m. Dorothy VerStrate, Oct. 5, 1953; children—Jamie, Kris, David, Scott. B.A. in Psychology cum laude, U. Minn., 1950; M.A. in Psychology, U. Tex., 1951, Ph.D. in Exptl. Psychology, 1953. Instr. Mich. State U., East Lansing, 1953-55; asst. prof. Hollins Coll., 1955-59, assoc. prof., 1959-61; dir. Britannica Center for Studies in Learning and Motivation, Menlo Park, Calif., 1961; prin. investigator grant for automated teaching fgn. langs. Carnegie Found., 1960; USPHS grantee, 1960; pres. Behavioral Research Labs., 1962-74; prof., dean Sch. Edn., U. San Francisco, 1974-78; Henry Clay Hall prof. Orgn. and leadership, 1978—; pres. Pacific Grad. Sch. Psychology, 1984—. Author textbooks. Served with USNR, 1946-47. Mem. Am. Psychol. Assn., AAAS, Sigma Xi, Psi Chi. Home: 1645 15th Ave San Francisco CA 94122-3523 Office: Pacific Grad Sch Psychology 935 E Meadow Dr Palo Alto CA 94303-4233

CALVIN, DOROTHY VER STRATE, computer company executive; b. Grand Rapids, Mich., Dec. 22, 1929; d. Herman and Christina (Plakmyer) Ver Strate; m. Allen D. Calvin, Oct. 5, 1953; children: Jamie, Kris, Bufo, Scott. BS magna cum laude, Mich. State U., 1951; MA, U. San Francisco, 1988; EdD, U. San Francisco, 1991. Mgr. data processing. Behavioral Rsch. Labs., Menlo Park, Calif., 1972-75; dir. Mgmt. Info. Systems Inst. for Prof. Devel., San Jose, Calif. 1975-76; systems analyst, programmer Pacific Bell Info. Systems, San Francisco, 1976-81; staff mgr., 1981-84; mgr. applications devel. Data Architects Inc., San Francisco, 1984-86; pres. Ver Strate Press, San Francisco, 1986—. Instr., Downtown C.C., San Francisco, 1980-84, Cañada C.C., 1986-92, Skyline Coll., 1988-92, City Coll. of San Francisco, 1992—; mem. computer curriculum adv. coun. San Francisco City Coll., 1982-84. V.p. LWV, Roanoke, Va., 1956-58; pres. Bulliss Purissima Parents Group, Los Altos, Calif., 1962-64; bd. dirs. Vols. for Israel, 1986-87. Mem. NAFE, Assn. Computing Machinery, IEEE Computer Soc., Assn. Systems Mgmt., Assn. Women in Computing, Phi Delta Kappa. Democrat. Avocations: computing, gardening, jogging, reading. Office: Ver Strate Press 1645 15th Ave San Francisco CA 94122-3523

CALVO, JULIO CESAR, forestry educator; b. San Jose, Costa Rica, Feb. 25, 1958; s. Antonio and Hilda (Alvarado) C.; m. Maria Elena Rodriguez, Oct. 26, 1960; children: Cesar, Natalia, Sofia. BS, Inst. Tecnologico Costa Rica, Cartago, 1979; MSc, SUNY, Syracuse, 1982; PhD, N.C. State U., 1991. Prof., rschr. Inst. Tecnologico de Costa Rica, Cartago, 1980—; cons. Tropical Sci. Ctr., San Jose, Costa Rica; chmn. Sch. of Forestry Inst. Tecnologico de Costa Rica, Cartago, 1983-86; exec. dir., Tropical Scis. Ctr., 1997—; directorship Tropical Sci. Ctr., San Jose, 1991-93, Orgn. for Tropical Studies, San Jose, 1993—. Contbr. articles to profl. jours. Recipient PhD Fulbright fellowship N.C. State U., 1987-91. Mem. Internat. Soc. Tropical Forest, Internat. Assn. Hydrological Scis., Sigma Xi, Gamma Sigma Delta, Xi Sigma Pi. Roman Catholic. Office: Inst Tecnologo Costa Rica, PO Box 8-3870-100, San Jose Costa Rica

CALVO, VÍCTOR JOSÉ, thoracic surgeon; b. Malaga, Spain, Nov. 30, 1962; s. Victoriano Calvo and Maria Victoria Medina; m. Guadalupe Gil, Dec. 18, 1993. Degree in medicine, U. Malaga, 1986; MD, Valencia (Spain) U., 1999. Physician Servicio Andaluz de Salud, Malaga, 1986-89; resident in family practice Servicio Andaluz de Salud/Hosp. Puerta Del Mar, Cadiz, Spain, 1990-92; resident in thoracic surgery Servicio Valenciano de Salud/Hosp. La Fe, Valencia, Spain, 1993-97; thoracic surgeon Servicio Valenciano de Salud, 1998—, lung transplant coord., 1998—; coord. Valencia Lung Transplant Group, 1998-99. Mem. Soc. Española de Neurologia y Cirugia Toracica. Roman Catholic. Avocations: computers, multimedia, graphic design. Home: C/Eolo No 4 Pta 5, 46021 Valencia Spain Office: Hosp U La Fe, Av Campanar No 21, 46009 Valencia Spain

CALVO DE DIOS, JUAN JOSE, pulp and paper manufacturing executive; b. Havana, Cuba, Nov. 19, 1942; s. Juan Antonio and Francis America (De Dios) Calvo Gonzalez del Campillo; B.Sc.E.E., MIT, 1963, B.Sc. in Indsl. Mgmt., 1962, postgrad. Sloan Sch., 1963; Advanced Mgmt. Program, Harvard U., 1986; m. Mariá Valentina Perez Ramirez, Feb. 10, 1984; children: Juan Antonio, José; children by previous marriage: Gilda Maria, Maria Helena. Systems engr. IBM, Atlanta, 1963; with IBM Venezuela, 1963-73, br. mgr. govt. and petroleum accounts, 1968-73; ops. support mgr. IBM Latin Am.-Western region, 1974-75; v.p. NCR-Summa Sistemas, Caracas, Venezuela, 1976-77; gen. mgr. Moldeados Andinos, C.A., Caracas, 1977-81; gen. mgr. C.A. Venezolana de Pulpa y Papel, Venepal, Caracas, 1981-88, dir., 1984—; exec. v.p. Venepal, 1988-92, pres., ceo, 1992, first vice chm., 1993—; v.p. Chilena de Moldeados, Santiago, 1978-82; asst. prof. info. systems U. Simon Bolivar, Caracas, 1976-84 . Contbr. articles to profl. jours. Recipient Top Performer's Mktg. award IBM, 1969, 72, Orden al Merito En El Trabajo, 1987, Orden Francisco de Miranda, 1996. Pres. Confederacion Venezolana de Industriales., Assn. Venezolana de Ejecutivos, Assn. Productores de Pulpa Papely Carton (v.p. 1989—), Fundacion Eu genio Mendoza (mem. exec. com. 1989—), Venezuelan-Am. C. of C., Camara Venezolana del Envase, Lagunita Country Club, Harvard Club of Boston. Roman Catholic. Office: Apartado Postal 2075, Caracas Venezuela

CAMACHO, CÉSAR LEOPOLDO, mathematician, researcher; b. Lima, Peru, Apr. 15, 1943; arrived in Brazil, 1971; s. Leopoldo Alberto and Filomena (Manco) C.; m. Maria Izabel Tavares, Aug. 21, 1971; children: Fernando, Priscila. Engr., UNI, Peru, 1965, Dr honoris causa, 1998; MSc, Math. Inst., Brazil, 1968; PhD, U. Calif., Berkeley, 1971; Prof. honoris causa, Cath. U., Peru, 1998. Prof. Instituto de Matematica Pura e Aplicada, Rio de Janeiro, Brazil, 1971—. Recipient Nat. prize in Sci., Brazilian Govt., 1996, Third World Acad. Scis. award, 1996. Mem. Brazilian Math. Soc. (pres. 1991-93, 95-97). Office: IMPA/Estrada Dona Castorina, 119 Jardim Botanico, Rio de Janeiro 22460, Brazil

CAMACHO, LUIS HERNANDO, oncologist; b. Bogotá, Colombia; s. Luis Hernando Camacho and Alba Lucia Guerrero; m. Maria Emilia Acosta, Nov. 20, 1992; 1 child, Mateo. MD, U. Mil. Nueva Granada, Bogotá, 1988; MPH, George Washington U., 1998. Intern internal medicine George Washington U., 1998; fellow hematology and med. oncology Cornell U. Med. Sch./Meml. Sloan Kettering Cancer Ctr., N.Y.C., Jill and Weill Sanford fellow medicine. Avocations: soccer, sailing. E-mail: lhcamacho@hotmail.com and camachol@mskcc.org. Fax: 212-639-7900. Home: 504 E 63rd St Apt 15-0 New York NY 10021-7919 Office: Meml Sloan Kettering Cancer Ctr Dept Medicine 1275 York Ave # 8 New York NY 10021-6094

CAMARA, MAHAWA BANGOURA, diplomat. Amb. for Guinea U.N., N.Y.C., 1995—. Office: Perm Mission Republic of Guinea to UN 140 E 39th St New York NY 10016-0914

CAMARGO, IVAN MARQUES DE TOLEDO, electrical engineering educator; b. Resende, Brazil, June 26, 1960; s. Jose Maria de Toledo and Isis Marques de Toledo Camargo; m. Gisele Ribeiro de Toledo Camargo, June 22, 1984; children: Natalie, Laura, Felipe. Elec. Engr., U. Brasilia, Brazil, 1982; D, Inst. Nat. Poly., Grenoble, France, 1988. Registered elec. engr. Cons. Themag, Brazil, 1982-84; prof. U. Brasilia, 1989—, chmn. engring., 1996—. Mem. IEEE (sr.). Home: SQS 309 F-404, 70362060 Brasilia Brazil Office: U Brasilia, ENE-FT, 70910900 Brasilia Brazil

CAMBEL, ALI B., engineering educator; b. Merano, Italy, Apr. 9, 1923; came to U.S., 1943, naturalized, 1951; s. H. Cemil and Remziye (Hakki) C.; m. Marion dePaar, Dec. 20, 1946; children: Metin, Emel, Leyla, Sarah. BS, Robert Coll., Istanbul, Turkey, 1942; postgrad., U. Istanbul, 1942-43, MIT, 1943-45; MS, Calif. Inst. Tech., 1946; PhD, U. Iowa, 1950. Registered profl. engr. Instr. State U. Iowa, 1947-50, asst. prof., 1950-53; from assoc. prof. to prof. mech. engring. Northwestern U., 1953-61, Walter P. Murphy disting. prof., 1961-68, dir. gas dynamics lab., 1955-66, chmn. dept. mech. engring. and astronautical scis., 1957-66; from dir. research and engring. support divsn. to v.p. rsch. IDA, 1966-68; dean Coll. Engring., Wayne State U., Detroit, 1968-70; exec. v.p. for acad. affairs Wayne State U., 1970-72; v.p., dir. system rsch. divsn. Gen. Rsch. Corp., 1972-74; dep. asst. dir. for sci. and tech. NSF, 1974-75; prof. engring. and applied sci. George Washington U., Washington, 1975-88, prof. emeritus, 1988—; chmn. dept. civil, mech. and environ. engring. George Washington U., 1978-80, dir. energy programs, 1976-88; cons. in field; staff dir. Pres.'s Interdeptl. Energy Study, 1963; engring. scis. adv. com. USAF Office Sci. Research, 1961-63; mem. Commn. Engring. Edn., 1966-68, Army Sci. Advisory Panel, 1966-72; nat. lectr. Sigma Xi, 1961-62. Author: Plasma Physics and Magnetofluidmechanics, 1963; co-author: Gas Dynamics, 1958, Real Gases, 1963, Plasma Physics, 1965, Applied Chaos Theory: A Paradigm for Complexity, 1993; co-editor: Transport Properties in Gases, 1958, The Dynamics of Conducting Gases, 1960, Magnetohydrodynamics, 1962, Second Law Analysis of Energy Devices and Processes, 1980, Dissipative Structures in Integrated Systems, 1989; co-editor AIAA Jour., Jet Propulsion, 1955-60, Energy, The Internat. Jour., 1975-95; mem. editl. bd., Energy, Environment, Economics, 1991; contbr. articles to profl. jours. Bd. dirs. YMCA. Recipient leadership award YMCA, 1953; citation for solar satellite power system evaluation Dept. Energy/NASA, 1981; cert. for patriotic service Sec. of Army; award for excellence NSF/RANN; award for contbns. to sci. and edn. U.S. Immigrants League.; Washburn scholar, 1938. Fellow AIAA (J. Edward Pendray award 1959, nat. dir.), AAAS; mem. Am. Soc. Engring. Edn. (Curtis McGraw award 1960, George Westinghouse award 1966, chmn. engring. and pub. policy divsn. 1986-87), ASME (founding chmn. energy systems analysis tech. com. 1980-82), Cosmos Club (Washington), Sigma Xi, Pi Tau Sigma, Tau Beta Pi. Mem. Soc. of Friends. Home: 6155 Kellogg Dr Mc Lean VA 22101-3120

CAMBON-THOMSEN, ANNE M., medical researcher; b. Toulouse, France, Nov. 9, 1949; d. Theophile F.L. and Agnes (Delclaux) Cambon; m. Jacques De Mouzon, Dec. 18, 1971 (div. Mar. 1981); 1 child, Olivier; m. Mogens Gruner Thomsen, Dec. 30, 1982. Baccalaureat, Lycee St. Sernin, Toulouse, 1967; Med. qualification, U. Toulouse III, 1974, M in Biochemistry, 1974, M in Human Biology, 1975. Med. doctor, 1978; cert. immunologist. Asst. rsch. fellow U. Toulouse III, 1973-75; postdoctoral fellow U. Copenhagen, Denmark, 1981-82; rsch. fellow INSERM, France, 1976-88; dir. rsch. CNRS, France, 1988—; dir. INSERM U 100, Toulouse, 1985-90, CNRS, UPR 8291, Toulouse, 1987-97; mem. rsch. team on population genetics, ethics and decision on pub. health INSERM, 1998—. Editor two books in field of population genetics; author/co-author 70 chpts. in specialized books on immunology, histocompatibility, human genetics; contbr. 100 articles to profl. jours. Mem. French Soc. Genetics, Human Genome Orgn., Internat. Genetics Epid. Soc., Internat. Soc. Transplants, others. Roman Catholic. Avocations: music, road-runner, mountain walks, children's lit., theater. Office: INSERM U518 Fac Medicine, 37 allees Jules Guesde, 31073 Toulouse Cedex, France

CAMDESSUS, MICHEL (JEAN), international organization executive; b. Bayonne, France, May 1, 1933; s. Alfred and Madeleine (Cassembon) Camdessus; m. Brigitte d'Arcy, Dec. 7, 1957; children: Francois, Marie-Odile, Christine, Thibaut, Claire, Marie-Genevieve. Licencie en Droit, U. Paris; Diplome d'etudes superieures d'economie politique et de sciences economiques, Diplome de l'Institut d'etudes politiques, Ancien eleve de l'Ecole Nationale d'Administration (promotion Alexis de Tocqueville). With Ministry of Fin. and Econ. Policies French Treasury, 1960—, asst. dir., 1971-74, dep. dir., 1974-82, dir., 1982—; chief bur. indsl. affairs Treasury, French Ministry Econs. and Fin., 1969-70, dep. dir. treasury, 1974-82, dir. Treasury, 1982-84, gov. Bank of France, Paris, 1984-87; fin. attache Permanent Representation, EEC, Brussels, 1966-68, mem. monetary com. EEC, 1978-84, pres. monetary com., 1982-84; mng. dir. Internat. Monetary Fund, Washington, 1987-2000. Chmn. Paris Club, 1978-84. Decorated chevalier Nat., chevalier Légion d'Honneur, Order Merit, Cross of Mil. Valor.

CAMELIA-ROMER, SUSANNE, Netherlands Antilles prime minister. Prime min. Govt. of Netherlands Antilles. Office: Office Prime Min, Ft Amsterdam 17 Willemstad, Curacao Netherlands Antilles*

CAMERON, JAMES, film director, screenwriter, producer; b. Kapuskasing, Ont., Can., Aug. 16, 1954; m. Gale Ann Hurd (div.); m. Katheryn Bigelow (div.); 1 child with Linda Hamilton, Josephine Archer. Grad. in Physics, Calif. State U., Fullerton. Head Lightstorm Entertainment, Burbank, Calif., 1992—; CEO Digital Domain, 1993—. Film industry experience includes art dir.: Battle Beyond the Stars, 1980; prodn. designer: Galaxy of Terror, 1981; creator spl. effects: Escape from New York, 1981; film dir.: Piranha II: The Spawning, 1981; dir., screenwriter: The Terminator, 1984, Aliens, 1986, The

Abyss, 1989; screenwriter: Rambo: First Blood Part II, 1985; dir., prodr., screenwriter: Terminator II: Judgement Day, 1991, True Lies, 1994; exec. prodr.: Point Break, 1991; dir., Terminator 2 3-D, 1996, Titanic, 1997; writer: Strange Days, 1995. Office: Lightstorm Entertainment 919 Santa Monica Blvd Santa Monica CA 90401-2704

CAMERON, JAMIE DIARMID, publisher; b. Poona, India, Nov. 12, 1935; s. Stuart Stillingfleet and Edna (Carpenter) C.; m. Katharine Mabel Bate, Oct. 13, 1962 (div. 1992); children: Stuart, Ruth; m. Patricia Harriet Jarvis, Sept. 17, 1994; children: Charles, Olivia. BA, Oxford (Eng.) U., 1958, MA, 1961. Tchr. Falcon Coll., Zimbabwe, 1958-61; editor J. Wiley & Sons Ltd., Chichester, Eng., 1962-80; dir. pub., dep. mng. dir. J. Wiley & Sons Ltd., Chichester, 1980-86; mng. dir. Springer Verlag, London, 1987-90, L.A. Pub., London, 1990-92, Profl. Engring. Publ. Ltd., London, 1995—; chmn. serials com. Internat. Assn. Sci. Technical and Med. Publishers , Amsterdam, The Netherlands, 1978-85. Serials com. Publishers Assn., London, 1975-83. Mem. Oxford-Cambridge Club. Avocations: agriculture, classical music, outdoor activities, history. Home: Upper Norwood Farm, Graffham, Petworth GU28 0QG, England Office: Instn Mech Engrs, 1 Birdcage Walk, London SW1H 9JJ, England

CAMERON, JANICE CAROL, executive assistant; b. Pitcairn, N.Y., Feb. 16, 1940; d. Lawrence Baird and Alice Irene (Manchester) Morgan; m. Albert A. Cameron, III, June 11, 1960 (div. Oct. 26, 1967); children: Albert A. IV, Richard D. AA, Jefferson C.C., Watertown, 1978; BA in Mgmt., St. Mary's Coll., Moraga, Calif., 1984. Nat. dir. Howard Ruff cmty. forums Target, Inc., 1982-86; sr. mktg. adminstr. IPF divsn. The Pacific Bank N.A./ Providian Bancorp, San Francisco, 1989-96; with legal dept. Nat. IPF, Mesa, Ariz., 1996-97; notary public. Contbr. articles to profl. jours. Founder, chair First Support Group for Parents of Gay Mormons LDS, Social Svcs. Divsn., Fremont, Calif., 1986-94, Utah Gen. Authorities for Soc. Svcs. Program; 1st chpt. dir. Parents, Families and Friends of Lesbians and Gays, Danville-San Ramon chpt., Calif., 1993-94. Democrat. Home: 9200 Alcosta Blvd Apt E-4 San Ramon CA 94583-4130

CAMERON, KEITH COLWYN, foreign language educator; b. Cwmbran, Gwent, United Kingdom, Apr. 1, 1939; s. Leonard George and Ethel (Booth) C.; m. Marie-Edith Briens, Aug. 4, 1962; children: Anne, Cécilia, Virginia. BA, U. Exeter, United Kingdom, 1961; cert. in edn., U. Cambridge, United Kingdom, 1962; degree, U. Rennes, France, 1964, doctorate, 1964. Lectr. in French U. Aberdeen, U.K., 1964-66; lectr. U. Exeter, 1966-76, sr. lectr., 1976-88, reader, 1988-94, prof. French and Renaissance studies, 1994—; dir. Elm Bank Publs., 1972—. Author: Agrippa D'Aubigné, 1976, Maligned or Malignant King? - The Satirical Iconography of Henri de Valois, 1978, Montaigne and His Age, 1981, René Maran, 1985, From Valois to Bourbon, 1989, The Nation, Myth or Reality?, 1994, Concordance of J. du Bellay's Poetic Works, 1988, Louise Labé, 1990, Humour and History, 1993, Literary Portrayal of Passion, 1996, Call: Media, Design and Applications, National Identity, 1999, Concordance of Philippe Desportes' Poetic Works, 2000; editor: Exeter French Texts, 1970—, Exeter Tapes, 1972—, Computer Assisted Lang. Learning, 1990—, Europa, 1994—, European Studies (Intellect), 1993—. Chmn. Devon br. European Movement, 1985—. Decorated Chevalier dans l'ordre des Palmes académiques. Fellow Royal Hist. Soc.; mem. Soc. Renaissance Studies, Soc. French Studies, Soc. des Seizièmistes. Avocations: theatre, walking, travel. Office: Univ Exeter, Queens Bldg, Exeter EX4 4QH, England

CAMERON, LOLITA ANN, writer; b. Rice Lake, Wis., Oct. 21, 1943; d. William Angus and Lolita Bessie (Lofgren) C.; m. Charles Stewart Harvey, June 21, 1969 (div. Mar. 1975); m. William Thomas Cherry, Jr., Nov. 2, 1990; stepchildren: Angela Cherry Falcone, Cristi Cherry. BA with honors, Harvard U., 1965; MFA, U. Iowa, 1972. Author: The Stories Julian Tells, 1981 (Irma Simonton Black award 1983), More Stories Julian Tells, 1986, The Most Beautiful Place in the World, 1988 (Jane Addams award 1989), The Stories Huey Tells, 1995; adapter The Kidnapped Prince: The Life of Olaudah Equiano, 1995, More Stories Huey Tells, 1997, The Secret Life of Amanda K. Woods, 1998 (finalist Nat. Book award, 1998), Gloria's Way, 2000. Vol. dir. Biblioteca Popular, Panajachel, Guatemala, 1993—. Grantee Nat. Endowment for the Arts, Washington, 1974; recipient Irma Simonton Black award Bank Street Coll., 1982, Jane Addams Award for Peace and Freedom, 1989. Mem. Authors' Guild. Democrat. Avocations: reading, swimming, fundraising for local library. Home: Calle Principal, Panajachel Sololá, Guatemala

CAMERON, NICHOLAS ALLEN, diversified corporation executive; b. Phila., Jan. 6, 1939; s. Nicholas Guyot and Katherine (Rogers) C.; m. Leslie Wood, Dec. 14, 1974; children: Christopher Wilson, Pamela Wilson. BS, Yale U., 1960. Treas. Allied Corp., Morristown, N.J., 1979-81, v.p. and treas., 1981-82, v.p. fin., 1982-83, v.p. planning and devel., 1983-85; sr. v.p. planning, devel. and adminstrn. Allied-Signal Inc., Morristown, N.J., 1985-86; sr. v.p. tech. and bus. devel. Bendix Aerospace-Allied-Signal, Inc., Arlington, Va., 1986-87; group pres. Allied-Signal Aerospace, 1988; sr. v.p. ops. svcs. Allied-Signal, Inc., Morristown, N.J., 1988-90, sr. v.p., gen. mgr. chem. intermediates, 1990-95. Bd. dirs. Morristown Meml. Health Found., 1996—, United Way of Morris County, Morristown, N.J., 1980-86, 90-98, campaign chmn., 1991, chief vol. officer, 1993-95, bd. chmn., 1996-98; bd. dirs. Morris 2000, 1990, chmn., 1993-96; mem. adv. bd. Morristown Hosp., 1998—; commr. Morris County Park Commn., 1999-2004. Mem. Morris County C. of C. (bd. dirs. 1975-86, 1990-98), Tau Beta Pi. Republican. Episcopalian. Clubs: St. Elmo Soc. (New Haven); Morris County Golf. Home and Office: 37 Barkman Way Chester NJ 07930-2222

CAMERON, RONDO, economic history educator; b. Linden, Tex., Feb. 20, 1925; s. Burr S. and Annie Mae (Dalrymple) C.; m. Claydean Zumbrunnen, July 26, 1946; children: Alan, Cindia. AB, Yale U., 1948, AM, 1949; PhD, U. Chgo., 1952. Instr. Yale, 1951-52; asst. prof. U. Wis., Madison, 1952-56, assoc. prof., 1957-61, prof. econs. and history, dir. grad. program econ. history, 1961-69; William Rand Kenan prof. Emory U., 1969-93, prof. emeritus, 1993—; vis. prof. U. Chgo., 1956-57, U. Glasgow, 1962-63, U. Chile, 1965-67, Keio U., Tokyo, 1987, U. Augsburg, Fed. Republic Germany, 1988-89, Fed. U. Rio de Janeiro, 1990; spl. field rep. Rockefeller Found., S.A., 1965-67. Author: France and the Economic Development of Europe, rev. edit., 1966, trans. to French and Spanish, 1971, Banking in the Early Stages of Industrialization, 1967, trans. to Japanese, 1973, Spanish, Italian, The European World, 2d edit., 1970, Civilizations: Western and World, 1975, A Concise Economic History of the World from Paleolithic Times to the Present, 3d rev. edit., 1997, trans. into Spanish, French, German, Dutch, Italian, Polish, Finnish, Hungarian, Czech, Japanese, Korean and Chinese; editor: Essays in French Economic History, 1970, Civilization Since Waterloo, 1971, Banking and Economic Development, 1972, International Banking, 1870-1914, 1991, Financing Industrialization, 1992; Am. rev. editor jour. Econ. History, 1968-69, editor, 1975-81; Econ. History Rev., 1960-65, rev. editor; contbr. articles to profl. jours. Chmn. Council Research Econ. History, 1967-69; bd. dirs. Albert Schweitzer Fellowship. Fulbright scholar France, 1950-51; Guggenheim fellow Europe, 1954-55, 70-71; fellow Center Advanced Study Behavioral Scis., 1958-59; Fulbright prof. U. Glasgow, 1962-63, Fed. U. Rio de Janeiro, 1990; Fellow Woodrow Wilson Internat. Center for Scholars, 1974-75. Mem. Am. Hist. Assn. (co-chmn. program com. 1983), Internat. Econ. Hist. Assn. (exec. com., v.p. 1986-90), Am. Econ. Hist. Assn. (pres. 1974-75), Brit. Econ. Hist. Assn., French Econ. Hist. Assn. Home: 885 Barton Woods Rd NE Atlanta GA 30307-1305

CAMERON, SHAWN DEE, artist, cattle rancher; b. Phoenix, Ariz., Mar. 17, 1950; d. Louis Henry and Billie Burke (Osborne) Wingfield; m. Dean Grant Cameron, Feb. 14, 1970; children: Dee Ann, Brooks, Kacie. B in Edn., Prescott Coll., 1989. Tchr.'s cert. Exhibited in group shows including Mountain Oyster Club Show, Tucson, 1991-98, Phippen Western Art Show, Prescott, Ariz., 1991-94, 96, Internat. Enterprises, Orlando, Fla., 1992-94, Cowboy Classics, Phoenix, 1992-97, 99, Wickenburg (Ariz.) Gallery, 1994-00, Women Artists of the West, Tucson, 1994-96, Venture Fine Arts, Tucson, 1994-98, Jackson-Kirkland Fine Arts, Santa Fe, N.Mex., 1998-2000, Cattlemen's Western Art Show, San Luis Obispo, Calif., 1998-99, Beyond the 98th Meridian, Sedona, Ariz., 1999, Trailside Gallery, Scottsdale, Ariz., 1999-00, Trailside Gallery, Jackson Hole, Wyo., 2000; illustrator: (cookbook) Country Cookin', 1986, (poetry book) His Place Or Mine, 1993. Adv. person Mayer Schs., Yavapai County, 1977-91; scholarship chmn. Yavapai Cowbelles, 1979-80, sec., 1980; cmty. 4-H leader Lonesome Valley 4-H Club, Yavapai, 1980-91; bd. dirs. Ariz. Cowpuncher's Crisis Fund, 2000. Recipient Phippen Family Art award George Phippen Art Show, 1993, 2d pl. Art award, 1993; named Artist on the Rise, Art Talk, 1997. Mem. Nat. Cattlemen's Assn., Yavapai Cattle Growers Assn., Ariz. Cattle Growers Assn. Avocations: poetry writing, hiking, horseback riding. Home and Studio: 13990 N Spotted Eagle Dr Prescott AZ 86305-4532

CAMERON, WILLIAM DUNCAN, plastics company executive; b. Harrell, N.C., June 14, 1925; s. Paul Archiebald and Atwood (Herring) C.; m. Betty Gibson, Oct. 3, 1953; children: Phillip MacDonald, Colleen Kay. Student, Duke U., 1945-49. Chmn. emeritus Reef Industries, Inc., Houston. Pres. bd. trustees Trinity Epsicopal Sch., Galveston, Tex., 1981-82; trustee William Temple Found., 1987-90. Served with U.S. Army, 1943-45. Mem. Houston C. of C. (chmn. mfg. com. 1967), Rotary, Galveston Artillery, Bob Smith Yacht Club. Home: 3614 Acorn Wood Way Houston TX 77059-3741 Office: Reef Industries Inc 9209 Almeda Genoa Rd Houston TX 77075-2339

CAMERY, JOHN WILLIAM, computer engineer; b. Cin., Feb. 5, 1951; s. Donald Otis and Mary Lynne (Edgington) C. BA, U. Cin., 1972; MS, Carnegie-Mellon U., 1974. Mathematician U.S. Army Material Systems Analysis Agy., Aberdeen Proving Grounds, Md., 1973; student asst. engring. spectrum analysis task force Fed. Comms. Commn., Park Ridge, Ill., 1974; mathematician U.S. Army Comms. Electronics-Engring. Agy., Washington, 1975-83; computer specialist U.S. Army Mgmt. Systems Analysis Agy., Washington, 1983; mathematician Def. Comms. Agy., Washington, 1983-86; programmer, analyst Gen. Scis. Corp., Laurel, Md., 1986-87; software engr. Sygnetron Protection Systems, Timonium, Md., 1987-88, Automation Cons., Inc., Balt., 1988-89, RDA Logicon, Leavenworth, Kans., 1989—; cons. Martin Marietta Ocean Systems Ops., Glen Burnie, Md., 1988—. Carnegie-Mellon U. fellow, 1972-73. Mem. Am. Math. Soc., Societe Mathematique de France, Soc. for Indsl. and Applied Math., European Math. Soc., Internat. Platform Assn., Imperial Hawaii Vacation Club, Greater Cin. Amateur Radio Club. Republican. Mem. Christian Ch. Avocations: music, dancing, swimming, electronics, traveling. Home: 655 Sheridan Ct Leavenworth KS 66048-4449 Office: RDA Logicon PO Box 681 Leavenworth KS 66048-1098

CAMFIELD, RONALD FREDERICK, manufacturing and engineering company executive; b. London, May 6, 1946; s. Arthur Henry and Francis Helen (Cooper) C.; m. Carol Patricia Brown, June 8, 1968; children: Neil David, Paul Barry, Ian Andrew. Area mgr. York Trailer Co., Barking, England, 1973-76; mng. dir. AI Internat. Motor Engring. Ltd., Maldon, England, 1976-86; dir. C.T.R., 1986-98; chmn. AI Internat. Ltd., 1998—; dir. Moorhall Devels., Maldon, Hadleigh Indsl. Holdings, Ipswich; cons. in field. Sgt. Brit. Army, 1964-73. Mem. Brit. Inst. Mgmt., Inst. Road Transport Engrs. Conservative. Anglican. Avocations: badminton, gardening. Office: AI Internat Motor Engring Ltd, Pillar Box Corner, Mundon Maldon CM9 6NS, England

CAMHY, SHERRY WALLERSTEIN, painter; b. N.Y.C., Nov. 12, 1940; d. Abraham and Irene Kronen Wallerstein; children: Abraham, Caroline. M of Art Edn., Columbia U., 1970; postgrad., NYU. Med. sch. tchr. anatomy Montclair Art Mus., Montclair, N.J., 1987, 88; tchr. painting and drawing Rockland Ctr. for the Arts, N.Y., 1989-93; tchr. Tisch Sch. Arts N.Y. Univ., 1998—; tchr. anatomy Sch. of Visual Arts, N.Y.C., 1999—; tchr. anatomy and life drawing Art Students League, N.Y.C., 1999—. Author: The Art of the Pencil, 1997; one-person shows Pace U., N.Y.C., 1993, Nat. Arts Club, N.Y.C., West Hampton Beach Libr., L.I.; groups shows include Santa Barbara Mus. of Natural History, 1990, Frank Caro Gallery, Santa Barbara, Calif., 1992, Nat. Art Club, 1996, Faculty Sch. of Visual Arts and Art Students League, 1994-97, Prince Street Gallery, 1994, Hammond Mus., 1993, So. Alleghenies Mus. Art, Aldrich Mus. Ridgefield, 1999, numerous others; work collected at Isreal Mus., The Internat. Fin. Group, Atlantic Levenson Internat., Inc., Art Student's League, others. Mem. Nat. Arts Club. Office: Studio 819 West Chelsea Art Ctr 526 W 26th St # W New York NY 10001-5517

CAMICAS, JEAN-LOUIS, entomologist; b. Agen, France, Apr. 5, 1940; s. André and Paule (Bagau) C.; m. Mireine Cassagne, July 21, 1962; 1 child, Maxime. Veterinarian, Ecole Nat. Vet. d'Alfort, France, 1962, Dr. Veterinary, 1963. Entomologist trainee ORSTOM, 1964-66; sr. scientist ORSTOM, Montpellier, France, 1992—; med. entomologist Inst. Pasteur, Dakar, 1967-86, sr. scientist, 1986-92; chief ORSTOM med. zoology lab. Inst. Pasteur, Senegal, 1986-92. With French Army, 1962-63. Mem. West African Soc. Parasitology (bd. dirs. 1985-92). Home: 22 Rue de Verdun, 34000 Montpellier France Office: IRD/Dept Sante BP 5045, 911 Ave Agropolis, 34032 Montpellier France

CAMILLI, CARLO, management consultant; b. Rome, Jan. 4, 1946; s. Luigi and Marta (Carosi) C.; m. Robinia Quarta, July 1993; 1 child, Luigi. BSIE, Rutgers U., 1973, MBA, 1974. Rsch. assoc. Rutgers U., Newark, 1973-74; mgmt. analyst Blue Cross/Blue Shield, Newark, 1974-75; brand mgr. Internat. divsn. Procter & Gamble, Cin., 1975-78; mktg. dir. Seagram's Italia, Milan, 1978-82; gen. mgr. Gruppo Gafin, Milan, 1982-84; dept. head mktg., sales mgmt. IFAP-IRI Group, Inst. for Mgmt. Rsch. and Tng., Rome, 1985-94; pres., ptnr., mgmt. cons. Team Corp. S.r.l., Rome, 1985—; faculty Mgmt. Ctr. Europe, Brussels, 1987-88; mktg. prof. Boston U. in Rome, 1992-93. Author: Il manager delle Vendite Pirola Editore, 1993; contbr. articles to profl. jours.; patentee in field. Office: Via Boncompagni 79, Rome Italy 00187

CAMLIBEL, DIZDAR, marketing professional, advertising consultant; b. Ankara, Turkey, July 9, 1950; came to U.S., 1996; s. Nuri and Mubahat (Acikgoz) C.; m. A. Canan Ucer, June 6, 1981; children: Zeynep, Nazli. BA, Schiller Coll., Heidelberg, Germany, 1978; BS, San Diego State U., 1980. Specialist in fgn. banking Pamukbank, Istanbul, Turkey, 1981-83; dep. gen. mgr. Gama Mktg., Ankara, 1983-86; mng. dir., owner C&D Mktg. Ltd., Ankara, 1986—, Scala Advt. Co., Ankara, 1991-95, C&D World Mktg., Chevy Chase, Md., 1996—. Mem. Ankara Coll. Sports Club (pres. 1994-96). Avocations: skiing, travel, soccer. Home: 5610 Wisconsin Ave Apt 18C Chevy Chase MD 20815-4415 Office: C ve D 1C Dis Ticaret, Koza Sokak 63/4, G101P Ankara Turkey

CAMLITEPE, YILMAZ, biologist, researcher; b. Giresun, Turkey, Dec. 20, 1962; parents Yusuf and Emine Camilitepe. BSc, Hacettepe (Turkey) U., 1984; MSc, Trakya U., Edirne, Turkey, 1987; PhD, Exeter (Eng.) U., 1996. Cert. biologist. Tchg. assistantship Exeter U., 1992-96; rsch. asst. Trakya U., Edirne, 1985-90, asst. prof. dr., 1996-98, assoc. prof. dr., 1999—; dir. Trakya Univ. Edirne Vocat. Coll., 1999—. Bd. dirs. Lectr.'s Assn., Trakya U., Edirne, 1999. State scholar Higher Edn. Assn. Turkey, 1990. Fellow Royal Entomol. Soc. (London); mem. Am. Behavior Soc., Brit. Internat. Union for Study of Social Insects. Avocations: reading, tennis, swimming, football. Fax: 90 284 2120927. E-mail: yilmazc@trakya.edu.tr. Home: Trakya U Tip Fak, Lojmanlari B-17, Edirne 22030, Turkey Office: Trakya U Dept Biology, Fen-Edeb Fak, Edirne 22030, Turkey

CAMMAS, THIERRY, media company executive; b. Montreuil, France, June 6, 1965; s. Gabriel and Marie Paule C. MBA, ESSEC Bus. Sch., Paris, 1988; MPhil, Sorbonne, Paris, 1988. Fin. analyst CSA Fin., Paris, 1989-91; mktg. contr. BIS, Paris, 1991-93; fin. and devel. mgr. MCM/MUZZIK, Paris, 1993-98, gen. mgr., 1998—. Avocations: guitar, diving. Office: MCM/MUZZIK, MCM/MUZZIK, 109 rue du Faubourg St Honore, 75008 Paris France

CAMMENGA, HEIKO KARL, chemist, educator, consultant; b. Bremen, Germany, July 30, 1938; s. Karl and Henriette (Müller) C.; m. Ingrid Potthoff, July 8, 1965; children: Anne, Jörg. MSc, Tech. U., Braunschweig, Germany, 1964; DSc, Tech. U., 1967. Resident asst. Tech. U., Braunschweig, 1967-69, prof., 1977—; asst. prof. U. Rochester, N.Y., 1970-71. Author: Evaporation Mechanisms of Liquids, 1980, Methods of Thermal Analysis, 1989; editor: Chemistry of Construction Materials, 1996; inventor in field. Recipient award Swiss Soc. Thermal Analysis and Calorimetry, 1987. Mem. German Chem. Soc., Bunsen Soc., Internat. Confedn. Thermal Analysis and Calorimetry, Internat. Union Pure and Applied Chemistry (pers. mem.). Avocations: scientific photography, sailing. Home: Johannisterstr 7A, 38104 Braunschweig Germany Office: Tech U, Hans-Sommer-Str 10, 38106 Braunschweig Germany

CAMMISA, FRANK P., JR., surgeon, educator; b. Waterbury, Conn., Jan. 18, 1956; m. Gail McGovern; children: Anne Katherine, Frank P. III, John Patrick. BS summa cum laude, Tufts U., 1978; MD, Columbia U., 1982. Diplomate Nat. Bd. Med. Examiners, Am. Bd. Orthopaedic Surgery. Resident in gen. surgery The Presbyn. Hosp., Columbia-Presbyn. Med. Ctr., N.Y.C., 1982-83; resident in orthopaedic surgery The Hosp. for Spl. Surgery, N.Y.C., 1983-87; fellow in spinal surgery U. Miami (Fla.)-Jackson Meml. Med. Ctr., 1987-88; asst. scientist rsch. divsn. The Hosp. for Spl. Surgery, N.Y.C., 1988-99, asst. attending surgeon, 1988-99, chief spine svc., 1995—, assoc. scientist rsch. divsn., assoc. attending surgeon, 2000—, dir. spine care Inst., 1999—; vis. clin. fellow surgery Coll. of Physicians and Surgeons, Columbia U., N.Y.C., 1982-83; clin. assoc. surgery Cornell U. Med. Coll., N.Y.C., 1983-87, instr. orthopaedic surgery, 1988-89, asst. prof. orthopaedic surgery, 1990-99, assoc. prof. clin. orthopaedic surgery, 2000—; attending surgeon VA Hosp., Miami, 1987-88; asst. attending surgeon The N.Y. Hosp., N.Y.C., 1988-99; attending surgeon spinal cord injury svc. Burke Rehab. Ctr., White Plains, N.Y., 1988—; attending surgeon VA Hosp., Bronx, N.Y., 1988—; assoc. attending surgeon N.Y. Presbyn. Hosp., 2000—; presenter in field; cons. Meml. Sloan Kettering Cancer Ctr., N.Y.C., 1988—; spinal cons. St. John's U. Athletic Teams, 1988—, N.Y. Knights World League of Am. Football, 1991-92, Phoenix Alliance, 1993, N.Y. Racing Assn., 1993. Editorial bd.: Orthopaedic Product News, 1990-91; contbr. chpts. to books and articles to profl. jours. Grantee The Hosp. for Spl. Surgery, 1986, Acromed Corp., 1988, Orthopaedic Rsch. and Edn. Found., 1991-92; recipient Harvard Book prize Harvard Club So. Conn., 1974, Tufts Psychology Soc. Rsch. award Tufts U., 1978, Resident award N.Y. Acad. Medicine, Sect. Orthopaedic Surgery, 1986, 87, Lewis Clark Wagner award Hosp. for Spl. Surgery, N.Y.C., 1986; N.Am. Traveling fellowship Am. Orthopaedic Assn., 1989; Ofcl. citation Gen. Assembly State of Conn., 1992. Mem. ACS, ACP, Am. Acad. Orthopaedic Surgeons, Internat. Coll. Surgeons, Am. Coll. Spine Surgery; mem. AMA, N.Am. Spine Soc., Am. Spinal Injury Assn., Internat. Soc. for Study of Lumbar Spine, Cervical Spine Rsch. Soc., Scoliosis Rsch. Soc., Med. Soc. State N.Y., N.Y. State Soc. Orthop. Surgeons, N.Y. County Med. Soc., Alumni Assn. The Hosp. for Spl. Surgery, Assn. of the Alumni, Coll. Physicians and Surgeons, Columbia U., The Irish-Am. Orthop. Soc., Ea. Orthop. Assn. (Fellow scholar award 1988, Spinal Rsch. award 1989), Groupe Internat. Cotrel-Dubousset, N.Y. Athletic Club, Winged Foot Golf Club, Phi Beta Kappa, Psi Chi, Alpha Omega Alpha, Delta Tau Delta. Office: Hosp for Spl Surgery 535 E 70th St New York NY 10021-4898

CAMNER, HOWARD, author, poet; b. Miami, Fla., Jan. 14, 1957; s. Edward I. and Ida (Puldy) C.; Susan Clara, July 29, 2000. BA in English, Fla. Internat. U., 1982; LittD (hon.), London Sch. Applied Rsch., 1995. Cert. English tchr., Fla. Editor Southwind Mag., Miami, Fla., 1976-78; performance poet Writers' Exch., N.Y.C., 1979-81; freelance writer various publications, Miami, 1982-84; screenwriter Harris Prodns., L.A., 1985-89; TV prodr., host Century Cable, L.A., 1986-88; writing instr. Dade County Schs., Miami, 1990—. Author: (poems) Notes from the Eye of a Hurricane, 1979, Transitions, 1980, Scattered Shadows, 1980, Road Note Elegy, 1980, A Work in Progress, 1981, Poetry from Hell to Breakfast, 1981, Midnight at the Laundromat, 1983, Hard Times on Easy Street, 1987, Madman in the Alley, 1989, Stray Dog Wail, 1991, Banned in Babylon, 1993, Jammed Zipper, 1994, Bed of Nails, 1995, Brutal Delicacies, 1996; contbr. to anthology: Florida in Poetry, 1995, also over 100 lit. collections. Mem. Nat. Writers Assn., Acad. of Am. Poets, Poets and Writers, Inc., Poetry Soc. of Am., So. Fla. Poetry Inst., Authors Guild. E-mail: hcamner@sol.com. Home: 10440 SW 76th St Miami FL 33173-2903

CAMNER, PER JONAS HILDING, environmental medicine educator; b. Stockholm, Sweden, Oct. 5, 1938; s. Gunnar Hilding and Märta Lovisa Adolfina (Hofsten) C.; m. Jane Christine Wadelius, Oct. 10, 1941; children: Christina, Elisabeth, Anna, Gunnar. MSc, U. Stockholm, 1965; MD, Karolinska Inst., Stockholm, 1968, PhD, 1972. Lab. physician Nat. Inst. Environ. Medicine, Stockholm, 1968-76, assoc. prof. environ. medicine, 1976-88; prof. Karolinska Inst., 1988—. Home: Värmdövägen 226, SE-13142 Nacka Sweden Office: Inst Environ Medicine, Karolinska Inst, Box 210, SE-17177 Stockholm Sweden

CAMOMOT, OSCAR LLANOS, priest; b. Sibonga, Cebu, The Philippines, Feb. 21, 1937; s. Vicente Quijano Camomot and Esperanza Diez Llanos. PhB, San Carlos Sem., Cebu, 1956; B in Canon Law, U. Santo Tomas, Manila, 1963; Licentiate in Canon Law, Cath. U. Am., 1965. Ordained priest San Carlos Sem., 1960. Cmty. organizer St. Angela Merlol Parish, N.Y.C., 1968-69; coadjutor Pap do Parish, Cebu, 1970-74; priest Faina (Brazil) Parish, 1975-81, Curaca (Brazil) Paris, 1974-81; exec. dir. Labor Apostolate, Cebu, 1988—; founder Kamasi, Sibunga, The Philippines, 1981; chairperson Clear, Cebu, 1993-2000, Forge, Cebu, 1996-98; prof. San Carlos Seminary, Cebu, 1994—; cons. KMKB, Bagtic, The Philippines, 1994-2000. Translator, editor: Christian Community Bible, 1991-93; editor: Revised Edition-Bible, 1999; translator (pamphlets) Rute and Dez Mandamentos, 1990. Organizer Kamania, Cebu City, 1996, Workers Party, Cebu, 1998; coord. Claretian Ctr., Cebu, 1990, Feeding Edn., Cebu, 1998. Mem. Seminary Formators. Office: Kamama Found, 06 Villanueva St, Cebu 6000, The Philippines

CAMORO, SIMEON FERNANDEZ, human resources and public relations executive; b. Polomolok, Philippines, May 25, 1954; s. Ariston P. and Leonarda Somcio (Fernandez) Camoro; m. Josephine Moscoso Tandog, Dec. 30, 1979; children: Rosejanne, Josim Kristoffer. BSE in Biology, Notre Dame of Marbel Coll., Koronadal, Philippines, 1975. Cert. KT program leader; cert. team bldg. facilitator. Fish technician aide Dole Seafoods, Calaumpang, Philippines, 1980-82; tng. and publs. asst. Dole Philippines, Polomolok, 1982-87, tng. supr., 1987-93; sr. mgr. human rels. RD Group of Cos., Gen. Santos City, Philippines, 1997-99, asst. v.p., corp. human rels., 1999—; project cons. local govt. unit Autonomous Region of Muslim Mindanao, Philippines, 1996, Malalag Municipality, Philippines, 1995; judge Search for Most OUtstanding Quality Circle Projects, 1999; spkr. in field. Vice chmn. RD Cmployees Credit Coop., 1999—, San Lorenzo Ruiz Transport Coop., 1999—; chmn. Dolefil Employees Coop. Complex, 1995-96; assoc. mem. Dolefil Multi-Purpose Coop., 1980—. Mem. Productivity Improvement Circles Assn. So. Mindanao (v.p. 1992—, dir. 1992—), Pers. Mgmt. Assn. Philippines (tng. dir. 1999—). Roman Catholic. Avocations: basketball, billiards, bowling, chess. Home: Polotana III, 9504 Koronadal, Polomolok Philippines Office: RD Group of Cos, 1st Rd, Calumpang, 9500 Gen Santos City Philippines

CAMP, CRAIG CHARLES, financial analyst; b. Swarthmore, Pa., Apr. 18, 1958; s. George Herbert and Barbara Marie (Hiddemen) C.; m.Joyce Elizabeth Cianciulli, Feb. 11, 1984; children: Chelsea Margaret, Alana Georgeanna. BS in Biology, Pa. State U., 1980, MBA in Fin., 1982; MS in Taxation, Widener U., 1988. Project supr. Am. Health Mgmt. and Cons., Wayne, Pa., 1980-81; fin. mgr. Am. Health Resources, West Chester, Pa., 1982-83; tax acct. Sun Co., Radnor, Pa., 1983-84, fin. analyst, 1984-86; mgr. fin. analysis Claneil Enterprises, Inc., Plymouth Meeting, Pa., 1986-92; v.p. Wings Aviation, Blue Bell, Pa., 1990-92; v.p., CFO Resource Holdings, Ltd., Exton, Pa., 1992-98; CFO Genetics Inst. Alfigon, Pasadena, Calif., 1998—; adviser fin. bd. Sun Fed. Credity Union, Radnor, 1985-86; v.p. Pa. Aviation, Inc., 1990-92. Bd. dirs. and treas. Planned Parenthood, 1987-95. Avocations: scuba diving, photography, golf. Office: Alfigon 11 W Del Mar Blvd Pasadena CA 91105-2505 Address: 11202 Bentcreek Rd Moorpark CA 93021-3746

CAMP, DELPHA JEANNE, counselor; b. Yakima, Wash., Apr. 20, 1937; d. George Emerson and Emilie Loraine (Rivard) Stevens; m. George Ernest Mills, Aug. 13, 1960 (dec. 1975); children: Adriene Phillips, Stacey Harcus, Ryan, Tiffany; m. James Clell Camp, June 24, 1978; children: Catherine Thompson (dec.), Wayne (dec.), Darla Coolman, John, Janna Barnes. BEd, Gonzaga Univ., 1959; MS, Univ. Oreg., 1977. Lic. profl. counselor; cert. grief counselor and death educator. Tchr. Riverside Sch. Dist., Milan, Wash., 1959-61, Cheney (Wash.) Sch. Dist., 1968-70; asst. prof. Univ. Oreg., Eugene, 1979-92; pvt. practice Eugene, 1992—; mem. faculty Marylhurst (Oreg.) U., 1992—. Mem. Assn. for Death Edn. and Counseling (bd. dirs.

1990-93, co-chair conf. 1994, 1st v.p. 1998-99, pres. 1999-00, Svc. award 1990), Am. Mental Health Counselors Assn., Oreg. Counseling Assn., Oreg. Mental Health Counselors Assn. Avocations: reading, classical music. Home: 440 E 39th Ave Eugene OR 97405-4722 Office: 317 W Broadway Ste 217 Eugene OR 97401-2890

CAMPAGNOLI, CARLO, endocrinologist, gynecologist; b. Ivrea, Turin, Italy, Sept. 4, 1940; s. Luigi and Maddalena Vittoria (Migone) C.; m. Paola Dagna, Apr. 23, 1968; children: Giorgio, Maria Francesca. MD cum laude, U. Turin, 1965. Intern Sant Anna Gynecologic Hosp., Turin, 1970-78, asst. head dept. endocrinologic gynecology, 1978-89, head dept. endocrinologic gynecology, 1989—; prof. endocrinologic gynecology Postgrad. Sch. Ob-Gyn., Turin, 1971—. Contbr. articles to profl. jours. Chmn. sci. bd. Osteoporosis Found. Piemonte, Turin, 1995; sci. dir. Postgrad. Sch. Endocrinologic Gynecology, Confalonieri-Ragonese Found., 1998. Mem. European Menopause Andropause Soc., Italian Soc. Third-Age Gynecology (vice-chmn. 1997-2000, chmn. 2000—), Italian Menopause Soc. (gen. sec. 1999—), Italian Fertility-Sterility Soc. (vice chmn. 1983-88), Internat. Menopause Soc., Internat. Soc. Gynecological Endocrinology, European Progestin Club, Rotary. Roman Catholic. Avocations: reading, hiking. Home: Via Principe Amedeo 12, 10123 Turin Italy Office: St Anna Gynecology Hosp, Dept Endocrinol Gynecology, Corso Spezia 60, 10126 Turin Italy

CAMPANELLI, GIAMPIERO, surgeon; b. Rome, Aug. 3, 1960; s. Augusto and Mariarosaria (Visconti) C.; m. Marina Lodi, Apr. 22, 1990; children: Camilla, Vittorio. MD, U. Naples, 1985; postgrad. in surgery, U. Milan, 1990. Int. Policlinico Hosp., Milano, 1985-90; asst. prof. dept. surgery U. Milan, 1988-98; coord. day surgery unit Policlinico - Beretta Est-Milan, 1992; assoc. prof. surgery U. Costanza, Romania, 1994; cons., sec., day surgery, Italian Soc., 1992-99, Italian Fedn. of Day-Surgery, Rome, 1997, Minerva Chirurica Editor, Torino, 1990. Author: Ambulatory Surgery of Inguinal Hernia, 1994, Recurrent Inguinal Hernia: Principles of Technique and Indication, 1996, contbr. numerous articles to profl. jours. Recipient Young Investigators award Internat. Coll. of Surgeons, 1990. Fellow Italian Soc. of Surgery; pres. Italian Soc. of Young Surgeons (pres. 1997—). Roman Catholic. Avocations: winter and water skiing, tennis, golf, literature. Home: Via S Francesco, Policlinico 11, 20122 Milan Italy Office: U Milan Policlinico Beretta, Est-Via F Sforza 35, 20122 Milan Italy

CAMPBELL, A. KIM, diplomat; b. Port Alberni, B.C., Can., Mar. 10, 1947; d. George thomas and Lissa (Vroom) C.; m. Nathan J. Divinsky, Sept. 15, 1972 (div. 1984); m. H. Hershey Felaer, Sept. 1, 1997. BA (hons.), U. B.C., 1969, LLB, 1983; postgrad., London Sch. Econs., 1970-73; LLD (hon.), Law Soc. Upper Can., Toronto, 1992, Brock U., St. Catherine's, Ont., 1997; DPS (hon.), Northeastern U., Boston, 1999. Lectr. polit. sci. U. B.C., Vancouver, 1975-79; lectr. polit. sci. and history Hangara Coll., Vancouver, 1979-82; atty. Ladner Downs, Vancouver, 1983-85; exec. dir. Office of Premier, Victoria, B.C., 1985-86; mem. Legis. Assembly, Victoria, 1986-88, Parliament, Ottawa, Ont., 1988-93; consul gen. of Can. Govt. of Can., L.A., 1996—; radio host CKNW, Vancouver, 1995; vis. com. Ctr. for Internat. Affairs, Harvard U., Cambridge, Mass., 1995—; sr. fellow, adv. bd. Sch. Pub. Policy, UCLA, 1996-98, 99—. Author: (memoir) Time and Chance, 1996; lyricist: (musical) Noah's Ark, 1997. Mem. bd. trustees Thunderbird Am. Sch. Internat. Mgmt., Phoenix, 1999—; trustee, chmn. Vancouver Sch. Bd., 1980-84; min. of state Indian affairs and northern devel. Gulf of Can., Ottawa, 1989-90; min. justice, atty. gen. Govt. of Can., Ottawa, 1990-93, min. of nat. def. and vets. affairs, 1993, prime minister, 1993. Named Woman of the Yr., Chatilaine Mag., Toronto, 1993, Woman of Distinction, YWCA, Vancouver, 1994, Woman of the Yr., Hollywood Bus. and Profl. Women, L.A., 1999; London Sch. Econs. Hon. fellow, 1994. Mem. Internat. Women's Forum (v.p. global membership 1999—), Women's Fgn. Policy Group, Coun. of Women World Leaders (chair 1999—). Progressive Conservative. Avocations: piano, cello, painting. Office: Canada Consulate Gen 550 S Hope St Los Angeles CA 90071-2627

CAMPBELL, ANDREW EUSTACE CLAVERING, business strategy educator; b. Muir of Ord, Scotland, Aug. 3, 1950; s. Alastair E. H. and Catherine A. (Leatham) C.; children: Alastair, Lucy; m. Amanda A. Hailes, Apr. 29, 1989; children: Duncan, Flora, Connie. MA, U. Edinburgh, Scotland, 1973; MBA, Harvard U., 1978. Contr. Investors in Industry, Edinburgh, 1973-76; cons. McKinsey & Co., L.A., 1978-80, London, 1980-84; fellow London Bus. Sch., 1984-87; dir. Ashridge Strategic Mgmt. Ctr., London, 1987—. Author: (Scottish dance guide) The Swinging Sporran, (with Michael Gould) Strategy and Styles, 1987, A Sense of Mission, 1990, Do You Need a Mission Statement? 1990, Mission and Business Philosophy, 1990, Strategic Synergy, 1992, (with Michael Goold and Marcus Alexander) Corporate Level Strategy, 1994, Breakup! Why Large Companies Are Worth More Dead than Alive, 1997, Synergy, 1998; contbr. numerous articles on multi-bus. cos. to profl. jours., chpts. to books. Dir. Capstone fellowship selection com. Ft. Harkness Ch. Fellow Royal Soc. of Arts and Mfrs. Avocations: family, tennis, Scotland, skiing, jam making. Office: Ashridge Strategic Mgmt Ct, 17 Portland Pl, London WIN 3AF, England

CAMPBELL, BERT LOUIS, lawyer, mediator, arbitrator; b. Tyler, Tex., Aug. 11, 1939; s. Bert M. and Jocelyn M. (Day) C.; m. Mary Ann Suatoni, July 17, 1965; children: Stephen, Brian, Rebecca. BA, U. Tex., 1961, B in Journalism, 1970, JD, 1970. Ptnr. Vinson & Elkins, Houston, 1970—; writer, lectr. in field. Trustee Cullen Found. Lt. (j.g.) USN, 1963-66. Mem. ABA, Tex. Bar Assn., Houston Bar Assn., Am. Health Lawyers Assn. (atty.-mediators mediation panel), Am. Arbitration Assn., Atty.-Mediators Assn. Office: Vinson & Elkins 1001 Fannin St Ste 2500 Houston TX 77002-6706

CAMPBELL, BRUCE DONALD, biologist, researcher; b. Christchurch, New Zealand, June 13, 1957; s. Kevin James and Glennys Winifred (McLean) C.; m. Philippa Mary Joll, May 22, 1982; children: Victoria Alice, Rebecca Emily, James Bruce. B Agrl. Sci. with 1st class honors, Massey U., New Zealand, 1980; PhD, U. Sheffield, U.K., 1988. Rsch. asst. Massey U., 1979; scientist Dept. Sci. and Indsl. Rsch., New Zealand, 1980-92; sr. scientist Agresearch, Palmerston North, New Zealand, 1992-96, asst. sci. leader, 1997-99, sci. leader, 1999—; mem. Nat. Sci. Strategy Com. for Climate Change, 1994—; mem. New Zealand IGBP Com., 1995—; leader Internat. Geosphere-Biosphere Programme-Global Change and Terrestrial Ecosystems Pastures and Rangelands, 1992—. Contbr. articles to profl. jours. Nat. Rsch. Adv. Coun. postgrad. rsch. fellow, 1985. Mem. New Zealand Grassland Assn., Internat. Assn. Vegetation Sci., Brit. Ecol. Soc. Avocations: golf, flying. Office: Agresearch, Pvt Bag 11008, Palmerston North New Zealand

CAMPBELL, CASSIE, hockey player; b. Richmondhill, Can., Nov. 22, 1973. Degree in sociology and nutrition with honors, U. Guelph, Ont., Can. Hockey player N.Y. Aeros, 1980—. Recipient gold medal World Championship, Lake Placid, N.Y., 1994, gold medal Pacific Rim, San Jose, Calif., 1995, Richmond, B.C., 1996, 3 Nations Cup, 1996, 3 Nations Cups and World Championship, Kitchener, Ont., 1997, ice hockey Silver medal Olympic Games, Nagano, Japan, 1998. Avocations: guitar, soccer, basketball. Office: Can Assn Advancement Women & Sports, 1600 James Naismith Dr, Gloucester, ON Canada K1B 5N4*

CAMPBELL, SIR COLIN MURRAY, university vice chancellor; b. Dec. 26, 1944; m. Elaine Campbell, 1974 (div. 1999). LLB with honors, U. Aberdeen. Lectr. U. Dundee, 1967-69, U. Edinburgh, 1969-73; prof. jurisprudence Queen's U. of Belfast, 1974-88, dean Faculty of Law, 1976-79, pro vice-chancellor, 1983-87; vice chancellor U. Nottingham, England; standing Adv. Com. Med. Workforce Planning, Food Advisory Com.; non-exec. dir. Swiss Re GB. Editor: Do We Need a Bill of Rights?; co-editor: Law and Society; contbr. articles to profl. jours. Former mem. Higher Edn. Funding Coun. for Eng.; former chmn. Human Genetics Adv. Commn., Lace Market Devel. Co., No. Ireland Econ. Coun., Human Fertilization and Embryology Authority; former mem. Standing Adv. Commn. on Human Rights for No. Ireland, Mental Health Legislation Rev. Com., Legal and Adv. Com. for No. Ireland, Univs. Funding Coun., Inquiry into Police Responsibilities and Rewards, Trent RHA. Avocations: music, reading, sports. Office: U Nottingham, Nottingham NG7 2RD, England

CAMPBELL, CRAIG JOHN, podiatrist; b. S.I., N.Y., Feb. 12, 1963; s. John Joseph and Florence Elizabeth (Tromer) C.; m. Awilda Garcia, Dec. 4, 1999; 1 child, Catherine Judith. BA in Bus. Adminstrn., Muhlenberg Coll., 1985, BA in Psychology, 1985; D in Podiatric Medicine, N.Y. Coll. Podiatric Medicine, 1990. bd. cert. in foot surgery. Resident N.Y. Cornell Med.-Wyckoff Heights Divsn., Bklyn., 1990-91; resident in podiatric surgery Little Neck Cmty. Hosp. divsn. Wyckoff Heights Med. Ctr., Bklyn., 1991-92, clin. asst., 1992—; clin. asst. Little Neck (N.Y.) Cmty. Hosp., 1992-98, The Bklyn. Hosp. Ctr., 1993—, Doctors' Hosp. S.I., N.Y., 1993—; chief podiatry Doctors' Hosp. S.I., 1997—; clin. asst. Bayley Seton Hosp., S.I., 1993—, St. Vincent's Med. Ctr., S.I., 1994—; founder Forest Foot Care Group, 1994—. Mem. Country com. Dem. Party of Richmond, profl. adv. panel Autism Found. S.I. Fellow Am. Coll. Foot Surgeons; mem. Am. Podiatric Med. Assn., Am. Bd. Podiatric Opthopaedics (assoc.), Am. Bd. Primary Podiatric Medicine, N.Y. State Podiatric Med. Assn., Ancient Order Hiberians (chmn. standing com. S.I. 1996-99, sentinel divsn. I 1999—), Pi Mu Delta. Democrat. Roman Catholic. Avocations: photography, swimming, sports. Fax: (718) 981-6792. Office: Forest Foot Care Group 827 Forest Ave Staten Island NY 10310-2410

CAMPBELL, DAVID GEORGE, ecologist, researcher, author; b. Decatur, Ill., Jan. 28, 1949; s. George Robert and Jean Blossom C.; m. Karen S. Lowell; 1 child, Tatiana Claire. BA, Kalamazoo Coll., 1971; MS, U. Mich., 1973; PhD, Johns Hopkins U., 1984. Exec. dir. Bahamas Nat. Trust, Nassau, 1974-77; ecologist N.Y. Bot. Garden, Bronx, 1984-88, leader Amazon Expdns., 1974-92, research fellow, 1989—; prof. biology, Henry R. Luce prof. nations-global environ. Grinnell (Iowa) Coll., 1991—; adj. prof. U. Nanjing, China, 1993—; prof. Semester at Sea, 1997; prof. Grinnell-in-London, 1999; cons. Internat. Union for Conservation of Nature, 1978-79, leader Maya forest project, Belize, 1993-96; biologist and lectr. M.V. World Discoverer in Amazon and Antarctic, 1981-87, I.B. Yamal to North Pole, 1995; biologist Brazilian Antarctic Expdn., 1987-88. Author: The Ephemeral Islands, 1978, The Crystal Desert, 1992, Islands in Space and Time, 1996; editor: Floristic Inventory of Tropical Countries, 1989; contbr. articles to profl. jours. Recipient Fulling award Soc. Econ. Botany, 1987, Houghton Mifflin Lit. fellow, 1992, Pen/Martha Albrand award for nonfiction, 1993, John Burroughs medal, 1994; Guggenheim fellow, 1989. Fellow Linnean Soc. London, Royal Geog. Soc. London. Office: Grinnell Coll Dept Biology Grinnell IA 50112

CAMPBELL, DAVID GWYNNE, petroleum executive, geologist; b. May 2, 1930; s. Lois Raymond Henager and La Vada (Ray) Henager Campbell; m. Janet Gay Newland, March 1, 1958; 1 child, Carl David. BS, Tulsa U., 1953; MS, U. Okla., 1957. Geologist Lone Star Producing Co., Okla. City, 1957-65; dist. geologist, geol. cons. Tenneco Oil Co., Okla. City, 1965-77; exploration mgr. Leede Exploration, Okla. City, 1977-80; pres. Earth Hawk Exploration, Inc., Okla. City, 1980—; divsn. exploration mgr. PetroCorp., Inc., Okla. City, 1983-92, divsn. gen. mgr. 1992-96; cons. Jr. Achievement, Okla. City, 1996—; active U. Okla. Sch. Geology and Geophysics Alumni 1985—, bd. dirs. adv. coun. 1988-90, sec. 1990-91, vice chmn., 1991-92, chmn., 1992-93. Contbr. articles to Jour. Cherokee Studies. Active Last Frontier Coun. Boy Scouts Am., 1960-73, edn. chmn. Eagle Dist. 1963-67. Recipient Certificate of Appreciation award Nat. Exchange Club, Okla. City, 1999. Mem. AAAS, Internat. Assn. Energy Economists, Soc. Ind. Profl. Earth Scientists (pres. Okla. chpt. 1988, chmn. 1989, chmn. polit. affairs com. 1991), Soc. Profl. Well Log Analysts, Am. Assn. Petroleum Geologists (hon. mem. 1995, chmn. house of dels. 1981-82, house of dels. mem.-at-large 1982—, exec. com. 1981-82, 90-91, found. trustee assoc. 1993—, corp. mem. Am. Assn. Petroleum Geologists Found. 1996—, mem. adv. coun. 1984-87, councillor mid-continent sect. 1984-87, nominating com. 1984-85, 86-87, astrogeology com. 1984—, mem. liaison subcom. astrogeology com. 1984, honors and awards com. 1984-85, 85-86, adv. bd. Treatise of Petroleum Geology 1986-91, nat. membership adv. coun. 1987-90, membership com. chmn. mid-continent sect. 1987-90, Disting. Svc. award 1989, nat. v.p. 1990-91, cand. nat. pres.-elect. 2000-2001, mid-continent councillor energy minerals divsn. 1992-94, chmn. com. of coms. 1992-98, mem. com. of coms. 1992—, charter mem. divsn. Environ. Geoscis. 1992), Okla. City Geol. Soc. (hon. life mem. 1992, pub. rels. chmn. Spkrs. Bur. 1963-64, chmn. stratigraphic code com. 1967-68, presdl. appointee 1969-70, advt. mgr. Shale Shaker 1969-71, rep. to AAPG Ho. of Dels. 1980-86, bylaws and incorp. rev. com. 1986), Okla. City Geol. Found. (founding pres. 1993-98, bd. dirs. 1993—), Ind. Petroleum Assn. Am. (Okla. chpt. regulatory affairs com. 1991-93), Okla. City Assn. Petroleum Landmen, Houston Geol. Soc., Tulsa Geol. Soc., Petroleum Exploration Soc. Great Britain, Okla. City Petroleum Club (bd. dirs. 1987-90, 1995-98, sec. 1989, 2d v.p. 1990, chmn. membership com. 1988-. Home: 6109 Woodbridge Rd Oklahoma City OK 73162-3220 Office: Earth Hawk Exploration Inc PO Box 25396 Oklahoma City OK 73125-0396

CAMPBELL, DAVID REED, financial services executive; b. Memphis, Dec. 9, 1957; s. Donald Broughton and Dorothy (Reed) C.; m. Patricia Keating, Aug. 6, 1983; children: Daniel, Sarah, Nathan, Olivia, Zachary, Elisha. BA in Math., Bowdoin Coll., 1980. Mgr. consulting Arthur Andersen & Co., Cleve., 1980-86; sr. v.p. tech. & ops. BancSystems Assoc., Westlake, Ohio, 1986-89, EDS, Westlake, 1989-90; sr. v.p. info. systems Society Corp., Cleve., 1990-94; sr. v.p. card svcs. Key Corp., Cleve., 1994-95; exec. v.p payment svcs. Key Corp., 1995-98, exec. v.p. strategic mgmt., 1998-99, exec. v.p. credit card svcs., 1999—; Mem. U.S. Deposit Access Com., Mastercard Internat., Purchase, N.Y., 1997-99, Maestro U.S. bd. dirs., Mastercard Internat., 1995-96, bd. dirs. Key Merchant Svcs., Atlanta, 1998. Pres. Continue Life, Inc., Cleve., 1996—; bd. dirs. Fellowship of Christian Athletes, Cleve., 1999—; mem. Union Club, Hermit Club, 1992-95. Mem. The Club at Key Ctr. Avocations: ice hockey, sailing. Office: Key Corp 127 Public Sq Cleveland OH 44114-1306

CAMPBELL, EDWARD ADOLPH, judge, electrical engineer; b. Boonville, Ind., Jan. 16, 1936; s.Revis Allen and Sarah Gertrude (Hunsaker) C.; m. Nancy Colleen Keys, July 26, 1957; children: Susan Elizabeth Campbell Frisse, Stephen Edward, Sara Lynne. BEE, U. Evansville, 1959; JD, Ind. U., 1965; grad. Nat. Coll. Dist. Attys., U. Houston, 1972; grad. Nat. Jud. Coll., U. Nev., 1978; grad. Am. Acad. Jud. Edn., U. Va., 1979; grad. Ind. Grad. Program for Judges, Ind. Jud. Ctr., 1999. Bar: Ind. 1965, U.S. Dist. Ct. (so. dist.) Ind. 1965, U.S. Ct. of Customs and Patent Appeals 1967, U.S. Supreme Ct. 1973, U.S. Ct. Appeals (fed. cir.) 1982. Patent examiner U.S. Patent Office Digital Computer Divsn., Washington, 1959-60; patent adv. U.S. Naval Avionics, Indpls., 1960-65; patent atty. Gen. Elec. Co., Ft. Wayne, Ind., 1965-66; ptnr. Weyerbacher & Campbell, attys., Boonville, Ind., 1966-71; pros. atty. 2nd Jud. Cir., Warrick County, Ind., 1971-77; judge Warrick Superior Ct. No. 1, 1977—. Fellow Ind. Bar Found.; mem. IEEE, Ind.State Bar Assn., Evansville Bar Assn., Warrick County Bar Assn., Ind. Judges Assn., Nat. Coun. Juvenile and Family Ct. Judges, Ind. Coun. Juvenile and Family Ct. Judges, Warrick County C. of C. (bd. dirs. 1978-84, 97—), Lions Club, Kiwanis Club, Sigma Pi Sigma, Phi Delta Phi. Democrat. Methodist. Home: 911 Julian Dr Boonville IN 47601-9556 Office: Warrick Superior Ct No 1 Warrick Jud Ctr Ste 300 PO Box 666 Boonville IN 47601-0666

CAMPBELL, ELEANOR ELIZABETH BRYCE, chemical physicist, educator; b. Rothesay, Scotland, Apr. 13, 1960; arrived in Germany, 1985, arrived in Sweden, 1998; d. William A. and Isobel M. (Bryce) Cowan; m. Iain Campbell, Apr. 21, 1984 (div. 1990). BSc, Edinburgh (Scotland) U., 1982, PhD, 1985. Rsch. fellowship Free U., Berlin, 1985-86; rsch. fellowship U. Freiburg, Germany, 1986-87, asst. prof., 1988-93; dept. head Max-Born-Inst., Berlin, 1993-98; prof. atomic and molecular physics U. Göteborg, Sweden, 1998—. Co-editor: Applied Physics A, 1998—; contbr. chpts. to books and articles to profl. publs.; patentee in field. Mem. EPS, Deutsche Physikalischen Gesellschaft, Swedish Phys. Soc. Office: Göteborg U & Chalmers, Dept Exptl Physics, Göteborg S-41296, Sweden

CAMPBELL, ELLA O., botanist; b. Dunedin, New Zealand, Oct. 28, 1910; d. Orr and Agnes Campbell. MA, U. Otago, New Zealand, 1934, DSc, 1976. Botany lectr. Victoria U., Wellington, 1936, U. Otago, 1937-44; sr. lectr. Massey Agrl. Coll., 1945-76, hon. rsch. assoc., 1976—; study leave Cambridge (Eng.) U., 1958, U. Mich., 1968, U. Cin., 1968. Co-author: (with J.S. Yeates) Agricultural Botany; contbr. articles to profl. jours. including Transactions of Royal Soc. New Zealand, Agrl. Botany, Tuatara, The Mich. Botanist, Proplasma, New Zealand Bot. Soc. Newsletter. Recipient Disting. Svc. medal Massey U., 1992; named Dame Companion New Zealand, Order of Merit. Office: Massey U, Pvt Bag 11222, Palmerston North New Zealand

CAMPBELL, EUGENE PAUL, physician, retired public health administrator; b. St. Paul, July 22, 1907; s. Eugene Paul and Fan (Berry) C.; m. Reba Lowe, Oct. 3, 1936; 1 child, Marilyn Joyce. BA in Zoology, UCLA, 1929; MD, Johns Hopkins U., 1933; MPH, U. Pa., 1942. Intern Balt. City Hosp., 1933-34, asst. resident in medicine, 1935; practice medicine specializing in preventive medicine, 1939—; ward officer Communicable Disease sect. Walter Reed Hosp., Washington, 1935-39; asst. prof. epidemiology U. Pa. Sch. Pub. Health, Phila., 1939-42; chief of Coop. Health Program Guatemala, 1942; field dir. South Am. Coop. Health Programs, 1943-45; chief Coop. Health Program Brazil, 1945-55; dep. chief pub. health divsn. ICA, Washington, 1955-57; dir. Office of Pub. Health, Washington, 1959-62; chief pub. health divsn. AID, New Delhi, 1962-65; health attache Am. Embassy, India, 1962-65; chief pub. health divsn. AID, Brazil, 1966-70; ret., 1970, now cons.; v.p. Internat. Environ. Services, Inc., 1985—; mem. U.S. del. WHO Gen. Assembly, 1957, 58, 60. Bd. dirs. Am. Sch., Rio de Janeiro, Brazil, Strangers Hosp., Rio de Janeiro. Decorated grand ofcl. Order Med. Merit, Brazil, 1955; recipient Meritorious Service citation U.S. Govt., 1956, Merit citation Nat. Civil Service League, 1958. Fellow Am. Pub. Health Assn., ACP; mem. Royal Acad. Tropical Medicine and Hygiene, Am. Soc. Tropical Health and Hygiene, Indian Assn. Advancement Med. Edn., Royal Soc. Health, Brazilian Soc. Hygiene, Washington Soc. for History of Medicine (pres. 1979-80), Antarctican Soc. U.S.A. Home: 1001 Middleford Rd Seaford DE 19973-3638

CAMPBELL, F(ENTON) GREGORY, college administrator, historian; b. Columbia, Tenn., Dec. 16, 1939; s. Fenton G. and Ruth (Hayes) C.; m. Barbara D. Kuhn, Aug. 29, 1970; children: Fenton H., Matthew W., Charles H. AB, Baylor U., 1960; postgrad., Philipps U., Marburg/Lahn, Germany, 1960-61; MA, Emory U., 1962; postgrad., Charles U., Prague, Czechoslovakia, 1965-66; PhD, Yale U., 1967; postgrad., Harvard U., 1981. Rsch. staff historian Yale U., New Haven, 1966-68, spl. asst. to acting pres., 1977-78; asst. prof. history U. Wis., Milw., 1968-69; asst. prof. European history U. Chgo., 1969-76, spl. asst. to pres., 1978-87, sec. bd. trustees, 1979-87, sr. lectr., 1985-87; pres., prof. history Carthage Coll., Kenosha, Wis., 1987—; fellow Woodrow Wilson Internat. Ctr. for Scholars, Smithsonian Instn., Washington, 1976-77; participant Japan Study Program for Internat. Execs., 1987; bd. dirs. AAL Mut. Funds, Johnson Family Mut. Funds., Praire Sch., United Health Systems, Wis. Author: Confrontation in Central Europe, 1975; joint editor Akten zur deutschen auswartigen Politik, 1918-1945, 1966-96; contbr. articles and revs. to profl. jours. Fulbright grantee, 1960-61, 73-74; Woodrow Wilson fellow, 1961-62; U.S.A.-Czechoslovakia Exch. fellow, 1965-66, 73-74, 85. Mem. Mid-Day Club (Chgo.), Kenosha Country Club, Phi Beta Kappa, Omicron Delta Kappa. Home: 623 17th Pl Kenosha WI 53140-1360 Office: Carthage Coll Kenosha WI 53140-1360

CAMPBELL, GEORGE, JR., physicist, administrator; s. George Washington and Lillian (Britt) C.; m. Mary Schmidt, Aug. 24, 1968; children: Garikai, Sekou, Britt. BS, Drexel U., 1968; PhD, Syracuse U., 1977; postgrad., Yale U., 1988; hon. doctorate, Drexel U., 2000. Sr. faculty Nkumbi Internat. Coll., Kabwe, Zambia, 1969-71; staff scientist AT&T Bell Labs., Holmdel, N.J., 1977-83; third level mgr. AT&T Bell Labs., Holmdel, 1983-89; pres., CEO Nat. Action Coun. for Minorities in Engring., Inc., N.Y.C., 1989-2000; Porth disting. lectr. U. Mo.-Rolla, 1993, 99; pres. Cooper Union for the Advancement of Sci. and Art, N.Y.C., 2000—; adv. bd. U.S. Sec. of Energy, Washington, 1990-93, NRC Com. on Women in Sci. and Engring., 1991-95, Coll. Engring. Cooper Union, Sta. WGBH-TV Discovering Women series, 1993-94, Merck Inst. Sci. Edn., 1993-99; mem. nat. commn. Ill. Inst. Tech., 1994; pres. Coalition for Equity and Access to Sci., Tech., Engring. and Math., 1996-97. Contbr. chpts. to books, articles to profl. jours. including Phys. Rev. D, Jour. Math. Physics, Issues in Sci. and Tech., Procs. IEEE Globecom, Black Issues in Higher Edn., Black Collegian, Chronicle of Higher Edn., NACME Rsch. Letter, AAAS Sci. and Tech. Policy Yearbook, 1995; commentator Nightly Bus. Report, 1993—. Bd. dirs. N.Y. Hall of Sci., 1994—, Oak Ridge Assoc. Univs., 1993-99, Crossroads Theater Co., 1990-95, Consolidated Edison, Inc., 2000—; mem. NSF adv. bd. Comprehensive Regional Ctr. for Minorities, N.Y. chmn., 1990-93; trustee, mem. exec. com. Rensselaer Poly. Inst., Troy, N.Y., 1991—; chmn. N.Y.C. Chancellor's Task Force on Sci. Edn., 1992-93; task force on minorities in sci. Nat. Inst. Environ. Health Scis./AAAS, 1994; bd. govs. All Nations Alliance for Minority Participation in Sci. and Engring., 1995—; trustee Poly. U., Bklyn., 1997—; mem. Pres.' Info. Tech. Adv. Com. Socio-Econ. and Workforce Panel, 1998—; mem. Congl. Commn. on Advancement of Women and Minorities in Sci. and Tech., 1999-2000. Recipient George Arents Pioneer medal in physics Syracuse U., 1993, Drexel U. Centennial medal, 1992, Presdl. award for excellence in math., sci. and engring. mentoring, 1996, EPIC award U.S. Dept. Labor, 1998, Disting. Svc. award for sci. and tech. Poly. U., 1999; named Black Achiever in Industry, YMCA, N.Y.C., 1987; Simon Guggenheim scholar Guggenheim Found., Phila., 1963-67. Fellow AAAS (com. on sci., engring. and pub. policy 1990-96), N.Y. Acad. Scis. (pres. coun. 1991—), ; mem. Am. Phys. Soc. (pres. cir. 1997—), Nat. Acad. Scis., Nat. Acad. Engring. and Inst. Medicine, Sigma Pi Sigma. Achievements include extending bootstrap model to SU(4)-symmetric strong interaction physics; responsible for third generation satellite 3 power system development. Office: The Cooper Union Empire State Bldg 30 Cooper Sq Fl 3 New York NY 10003-7125

CAMPBELL, GEORGE EMERSON, lawyer; b. Piggott, Ark., Sept. 23, 1932; s. Sid and Mae (Harris) C.; m. Anna Claire Janes, June 22, 1960 (dec. Mar. 1971); children: Dianne, Carole; m. Joan Stafford Rule, Apr. 7, 1973. J.D., U. Ark., Fayetteville, 1955. Bar: Ark. 1955, U.S. Supreme Ct. 1971. Law clk. to judge Ark. Supreme Ct., 1959-60; mem. Rose Law Firm, P.A., Little Rock, 1960—; Del. 7th Ark. Constl. Conv., 1969-70; regional v.p. Nat. Mcpl. League, 1974-86; mem. Ark. Ednl. TV Commn., 1976-92, chmn., 1980-82, 88-91; bd. dirs. Ark. Ednl. TV Found., 1984-92, chmn., 1988-91. Chmn. bd. Pulaski County Law Libr., 1980—; bd. dirs. Ark. Arts Ctr., 1991-95, sec. 1992-93), Ark. Symphony Orch. Soc., 1982-87, Ark. Capital Corp., Ark. Cert. Devel. Corp., Downtown Partnership; bd. dirs. Youth Home Inc., 1986-92, pres., 1991-92. With USNR, 1955-77, ret.. Fellow Am. Bar Found.; mem. ABA, Ark. Bar Assn., Pulaski County Bar Assn., Am. Law Inst., Am. Judicature Soc., Nat. Assn. Bond Lawyers. Office: Rose Law Firm PA 120 E 4th St Little Rock AR 72201-2893

CAMPBELL, HEATHER JOY, environmental and safety professional; b. Winton, New Zealand, Mar. 3, 1967; d. James and Helen Judith (McDonald) C. B in Engring. (hon.), U. Melbourne, 1989, M in Engring., 1995; grad. diploma occupl. hygiene, Deakin U., 1997. Process engr. Conoflex Packaging, Melbourne, 1989-91, prodn. engr., 1991-94; environ. coord. Amcor, Melbourne, 1996-98; mgr. environ. engring. Containers Packaging, Melbourne, 1994-98; mgr. environment and safety Amcor Packaging, Melbourne, 1998-2000; gen. mgr. workplace risk mgmt. Amcor, Melbourne, 2000—. Sec. Internat. House Students Club, U. Melbourne, 1986, Internat. House Coun., 1986. Mem. Australian Industry Group, Instn. of Engr., Clean Air Soc. of Australia and New Zealand. Avocations: playing bagpipes, hiking. Office: Amcor, 679 Victoria St, Abbotsford VIC 3067, Australia

CAMPBELL, IAIN DONALD, minister, editor; b. Stornoway, Isle Lewis, Scotland, Sept. 20, 1963; s. John Norman and Lily Maciver (Mackenzie) C.; m. Anne Macsween Davidson, July 31, 1984; children: Iain Gordon, Stephen John, Emily Anne. MA, U. Glasgow, Scotland, 1985; BD, U. London, 1988; Diploma in Theology, Free Ch. of Scotland Coll., Edinburgh, 1988; MTh, Ctrl. Sch. Religion, London, 1997. Minister Snizort Free Ch., Isle of Skye, 1988-95, Back Free Ch., Isle of Lewis, 1995—. Author: (book) In Thy Likeness, 1990; editor (book) The Heart of the Gospel, 1995; editor (Free Ch. of Scotland mags.), The Instructor, 1990-96, The Monthly Record, 1996-2000, The Doctrine of Sin, 1999. Avocations: reading, computing. Home and Office: Free Ch of Scotland Manse, Vatisker, Lewis HS2 OLN, Scotland

CAMPBELL, IAN DAVID, opera company director; b. Brisbane, Australia, Dec. 21, 1945; came to U.S., 1982; m. Ann Spira; children: Benjamin, David. BA, U. Sydney, Australia, 1967. Prin. tenor singer The Australian Opera, Sydney, 1967-74; sr. music officer The Australia Council, Sydney,

1974-76; gen. mgr., stage dir. The State Opera of South Australia, Adelaide, 1976-82; asst. artistic adminstr. Met. Opera, N.Y.C., 1982-83; gen. dir. San Diego Opera, 1983—; guest lectr. U. Adelaide, 1978; guest prof. San Diego State U., 1986—; cons. Lyric Opera Queensland, Australia, 1980-81; bd. dirs. Opera Am., Washington, 1986-95, 97—; chmn. judges Met. Opera Auditions, Sydney, 1989, Masterclasses, Music Acad. of the West, 1993-96. Producer, host San Diego Opera Radio Program, 1984—, At the Opera with Ian Campbell, 1984—; stage director La Boheme, 1981, The Tales of Hoffmann, 1982 (both in South Australia), Falstaff (San Diego Opera), 1999, Cavalleria Rusticana/Pagliacci (Santa Barbara Grand Opera), 1999, Il Trovatore (San Diego Opera), 2000. Mem., bd. dirs. San Diego Conv. and Visitors Bur., 1997—. Recipient Peri award Opera Guild So. Calif., 1984; named Headliner of Yr., San Diego Press Club, 1991, Father of Yr., San Diego, 1997. Fellow Australian Inst. Mgmt.; mem. Kona Kai Club, Rotary, San Diego Pres Club (Headliner award 1991). Avocations: squash, golf, tennis. Office: San Diego Opera 1200 3rd Ave Fl 18 San Diego CA 92101-4112

CAMPBELL, IAN GARTH, medical educator; b. Harvey, Australia, July 22, 1959; s. Ronald Hay and Sheila Agnes (Wickham) C.; m. Catherine Barbara Ann Fudge, Sept. 21, 1991; 4 children. BSc with honors, U. Western Australia, 1980, PhD, 1986. Tutor U. Western Australia, 1986-88; rsch. fellow Imperial Cancer Rsch. Fund, Eng., 1988-93; lectr. U. Southampton, Eng., 1993-99; assoc. prof. Peter MacCallum Cancer Inst., Melbourne, Australia, 1999—. E-mail: i.campbell@pnci.ummelb.edu.au. Office: PEter MacCallum Cancer Inst, St Andrews Pl, Melbourne 3002, Australia

CAMPBELL, JAMES R., transportation executive; b. July 16, 1941; s. Ray E. and Anne Louise (Wooten) C. BS, U. Houston, 1965; postgrad., Case Western Res. U., 1967-68, Yale U., 1990. Personnel asst. The Standard Oil Co., Cleve., 1966-68; dir. equal opportunity programs Turner Constrn. Co., Cleve., 1968-73; employment project dir. Nat. Assn. Drug Abuse Problems, N.Y.C., 1973-74; exec. dir. The Cuyahoga Plan Ohio, Cleve., 1974-77; dir. EEO compliance and cmty. activities the continental Group, Inc., Stamford, Conn., 1978-85; cons. human resources James Campbell & Assocs., Inc., 1985-88; asst. v.p. strategic human resource planning MTA N.Y.C. Transit, Bklyn., 1988-96, acting dep. v.p. employee resources, 1993-96, asst. v.p. employee resources, 1988-90; v.p. adminstrn. MTA Long Island Bus, 1996—; expert witness HUD, 1970, U.S. Ho. of Reps. subcom., 1972. Contbr. articles to profl. jours. Task Force chmn., mem. steering com. Cleve. Fedn. Cmty. Devel. Manpower Planning & Devel. Commn., 1971-73; mem. cmty. adv. bd. Cleve. Press, 1972; mem. Pres.'s Com. Employment of People with Disabilities, 1985-91. With USAF, 1958-62, Japan. Recipient key to city Cleve., 1970, Outstanding Cmty. Svc. award, Urban League Cleve., 1972. Mem. ASTD, Am. Soc. Tng. & Devel., Human Resource Assn. N.Y., N.Y. Caledonian Club, Inc. (chieftan 1999, trustee 2000—), The Congregation St. Saviour Cathedral Ch. St. John The Divine, N.Y.C., The Clan Campbell Soc. (N.Am. chpt., trustee 2000—, dep. commr. N.Y.C. 1998—, pres.), Clan Campbell Edn. Assn. Inc. (trustee 2000—), Soc. Human Resources Mgmt. (life-time profl. cert. advanced level), Personnel Accreditation Inst., N.Y. Human Resources Planning Soc., Omicron Delta Kappa (circle v.p. 1965, Gold Key 1965). Home: 504 W 110th St Apt 8-d New York NY 10025-2008 Office: MTA LI Bus 700 Commercial Ave Garden City NY 11530-6410

CAMPBELL, JAMES ROBERT, banker; b. Rochester, Minn., May 24, 1942; s. Donald William and Alice Marie (Gray) C.; m. Carmen Dawn Starkson, July 11, 1964; children: Peter Ian, Kathryn Ann. B.S. in Bus, U. Minn., 1964. Comml. banking officer Norwest. Nat. Bank Mpls., 1964-67, asst. v.p., 1967-71, sr. v.p. nat. dept., 1976-79, pres., chief operating officer, 1984-86; pres., dir. Lease Northwest, Inc., Mpls., 1971-75, Norwest Bank Omaha N.A., Omaha, 1979-82; regional pres. Norwest Corp.-Norwest Banks, 1982-84; pres., CEO Wells Fargo Bank, Mpls., 1986-95, chmn. bd. dirs., 1995—; chmn. bd. Norwest Bank Minn. N.A., Mpls., 1995-98; group exec. v.p. Wells Fargo & Co., 1998—; exec. v.p. Norest Corp.; bd. dirs. Allianz U.S.A. Bd. dirs. Mpls. Inst. Arts, U. Minn. Found., Abbott-Northwestern Hosp., Viking coun. Boy Scouts Am., United Way Mpls. Mem. Minn. Exec. Orgn., World Press Orgn., Minikahda Club, Mpls. Club, Bankers Round Table, Spring Hill Golf Club, Bay Colony Golf Club. Republican. Presbyterian. Home: 5521 Woodcrest Dr Minneapolis MN 55424-1651

CAMPBELL, JEANNE MARIE, government relations executive; b. Chgo.; d. John and Wilhelmina Evelyn (Powers) Kruzic; widowed; children—Keith Maclean, Scott McElroy. B.A., B.S., No. Ill. U., 1966; M.S. in Edn., 1971; M.A., Loyola U., Chgo., 1975; postgrad. Am. U., Washington. Mem. faculty Am. U., Washington, Loyola U., Chgo., 1973-77, George Washington U.; speechwriter Congressman Dan Rostenkowski, 1977-79; press sec. Congresswoman Margaret Heckler, 1979-80; v.p. New Eng. Council, Inc., Washington, 1981-85; sr. assoc. Martin Haley Cos., 1981-85; pres. Campbell Crane & Assocs., Washington, 1985—. Vol. tutor Laubach Lit. Assn., Ill. and Washington, 1965—. Mem. Tax Coalition, Am. League Lobbyists (sec. 1983, bd. dirs.), Women in Govt. Relations. Avocation: writing. Office: Campbell Crane and Assocs 1010 Pennsylvania Ave SE Washington DC 20003-2142

CAMPBELL, JOAN VIRGINIA LOWEKE, secondary school educator, language educator; b. Detroit, Nov. 8, 1942; d. George Paul and Lolamae (Weians) L.; m. James Bachelder Campbell, July 26, 1975; 1 child, James Bachelder Loweke. BA in German, French, Hope Coll., 1965; student, U. Cologne (Germany), 1964, U. Salzburg (Austria), 1968, U. Stuttgart (Germany), 1970-71, Sampere Inst., Madrid, 1982, Millersville (Pa.) State U., 1983, 84, 90, Va. Poly. Inst. and State U., 1976-77, 80-84, U. Va., 1996-97, 98-99. Cert. secondary tchr., Mich., Kans., Va. Tchr. French and German I, II Grand Haven (Mich.) Jr. H.S., 1965-69; asst. instr. elementary and intermediate German U. Kans., Lawrence, 1969-70, 71-72; tchr. German I, II Ctrl. Jr. H.S., Lawrence, Kans., 1972-74; tchr. French I, II, sr. English Oskaloosa (Kans.) H.S., 1974-75; tchr. German I-IV Highland Park H.S., Topeka, 1975-76; tchr. French I-V, Spanish I and II Blacksburg (Va.) H.S., 1977—; tchr. French, Spanish YMCS, YMCA evening courses, Blacksburg, Va., 1976-80; mem. audio visual com. Montgomery County Fgn. Lang. Collaborative Group, Blacksburg, 1984-87; chaperone Am. Inst. Fgn. Study, Germany, France, Spain, 1968-82, area adminstr. summer and winter programs abroad, We. Mich., 1968-69; chaperone Ednl. Adventures, Quebec City, Montreal, 1984, 90-91, 93-94, 98, Montgomery County Schs.; presenter in field. Author: The Gothic Cathedral, 1995. Mem. Internat. Host Family Orgn. Va. Poly. Inst. and State U., Blacksburg, 1977—;. Fulbright exch. fellow U. Kans., 1970-71, Fulbright fellow Goethe Insts., 1976, Rockefeller fellow Rockefeller Assn. and Nat. Endowment Humanities, 1986, NDEA fellow, 1966; recognized as Va. Gov.'s Sch. Outstanding Educator, 1990. Mem. Am. Assn. Tchrs. French (state and region IV U.S. Recognition effort, dedication and high scores on nat. French exams, 1988, 96, 97, founder La Soc. Hon. de Français for Outstanding Students in French Blacksburg chpt. 1977, state com., dist. adminstr. Le Grand Concours-Nat. French Exams 1980—), Am. Assn. Tchrs. Spanish and Portuguese, Am. Assn. Tchrs. German (Va. exec. com. sec. 1977-83, co-chmn. nat. German exams Va. chpt. 1984-87, state nominating com. 1984-87, chmn. 1984-85), Nat. Assn. Edn. (Blacksburg H.S. rep. 1980-82), Va. Assn. Edn., Montgomery County Assn. Edn., Assn. Supervision and Curriculum Devel., Fgn. Lang. Assn. Va. (life). Republican. Presbyterian. Avocations: flower gardening, hiking, mountain climbing, visit art history. Home: 3003 Mclean Ct Blacksburg VA 24060-8110 Office: Blacksburg HS 520 Patrick Henry Dr Blacksburg VA 24060-3106

CAMPBELL, JOHN GAVIN, securities exchange executive; b. Lautoka, Fiji, Nov. 19, 1935; s. William Arthur and Isabel Ruth Campbell; m. Angela Gay Daly, Feb. 1967; children: Garth, Raewyn, Erica. B in Chem. Engring., U. Sydney, NSW, Australia, 1958, B in Econ., 1965. Various positions with CSR Ltd., Sydney, 1953-86, exec. dir. ops., 1986, exec. dir. fin., 1986-87; mng. dir. Australian Stock Exch., Sydney, 1988-94; chmn. Victorian Power Exch., 1994-97; dir. Cable & Wireless Optus, 1997—; dir. NECA, 1999—. *

CAMPBELL, JOHN HONE FITZGERALD, diplomat; b. Dublin, Ireland, June 23, 1936; s. Ernest Henry Fitzgerald and Bertha (Willan) C.; m. Nicole Lafon, Sept. 1, 1964; children: Marc, Jonathan. BA, Trinity Coll., Dublin, 1958; MA, Yale U., 1960. With Irish Dept. Fgn. Affairs, 1961—; minister London, 1975-80; amb. to People's Republic of China Beijing, 1980-83; amb. to Fed. Republic of Germany Bonn, 1983-86; permanent rep. Ireland to European Communities, Brussels, 1986-91; amb. to France, 1991-95; permanent rep. of Ireland UN, N.Y.C., 1995-98; amb. to Portugal, 1998—. Office: Embassy of Ireland, Imprensa da Estrela 1, Lisbon 1200, Portugal

CAMPBELL, JOHN RICHARD, pediatric surgeon; b. Pratt, Kans., Jan. 16, 1932; s. John Ross and Laura (Harkrader) C.; m. Susan Charlotte Baker, June 9, 1962; children: Kathryn, John Richard, George Ridgway. B.A., U. Kans., 1954, M.D., 1958. Diplomate Am. Bd. Surgery with cert. of spl. qualifications in pediatric surgery. Rotating intern Hosp. U. Pa., 1958-59; resident in gen. surgery U. Kans. Hosp., 1959-63; resident in pediatric surgery Children's Hosp. of Phila., 1965-67; asst. instr. U. Pa. Med. Sch., 1965-67; mem. faculty U. Oreg. Health Scis. Ctr., Portland, 1967-2000, prof. surgery and pediat., 1972-2000, prof. surgery and pediatrics emeritus, 2000—, chief pediatric surgery, prof. emeritus surgery and pediats., 2000—; surgeon-in-chief Doernbecher Children's Hosp., Portland, 1967-99; cons. VA, Shriners Crippled Children's hosps., Alaska Native Med. Ctr., Anchorage. Served to lt. comdr. M.C. USNR, 1963-65. Mem. A.C.S., Soc. Acad. Surgeons, Am. Acad. Pediatrics, Am. Pediatric Surg. Assn., Pacific Assn. Pediatric Surgeons, North Pacific Pediatric Soc., North Pacific Surg. Assn., Pacific Coast Surg. Assn., Portland Acad. Pediatrics, Portland Surg. Soc. Presbyterian. Office: Oreg Health Scis Univ 745 SW Gaines St # Cdw7 Portland OR 97201-2901

CAMPBELL, JOHN STEPHEN, agricultural consultant; b. London, Apr. 4, 1923; came to U.S., 1963; m.; 3 children. BSc, Reading U., Eng., 1943; postgrad., Cambridge U., 1946-47; diploma in tropical agriculture, Imperial Coll. T. A., 1948; advanced mgmt. program diploma, Harvard U., 1972. Agrl. officer Dept. Agriculture, Nigeria, 1948-50; sr. lectr. Imperial Coll. Tropical Agriculture, Trinidad, 1950-61; lands devel. officer Tate & Lyle Sugar Corp., Trinidad, 1961-63; v.p. Imperial Tobacco Ltd., Wilson, N.C., 1963-80; cons. Wilson, 1980—. Contbr. numerous papers to profl. jours. Chmn. Tobacco Quality com., Tobacco Assn. U.S., 1967-89; dir. N.C. Tobacco Found., Inc., 1975-80, 82-86, 87-91; chmn. Agri-Bus. com., Wilson, N.C., 1975; dir. Wilson County Red Cross, 1975-79, 80; dir. Wilson County C. of C., 1976, v.p., 1977, pres., 1978, dir., 1981-84, chmn. Cmty. Devel. Dept., 1982, 83; chmn. Leadership Wilson, 1981-90; mem. Food and Agriculture com., U.S. C. of C., 1978-80, Wilson Indsl. Air Ctr. adv. commn., 1987-93; dir. Wilson County Interfaith Svcs. Bd., Hope Sta., 1987-97, treas., 1992-96, chmn., 1996; mem. City of Wilson Appearance Commn., 1996—, chmn., 1998-99. Sub-lt. Royal Navy, 1943-46. Recipient Tobacco Econs. award Tobacco Merchants Assn., N.Y.C., 1979, Tobacco Great award N.C. State U., 1979, Disting. Svc. award S.C. Tobacco Warehouse Assn., Inc., 1980. Mem. Rotary (Paul Harris fellow 1993), Gamma Sigma Delta. Home: 1001 Parkside Dr NW Wilson NC 27896-1537

CAMPBELL, JONATHAN WESLEY, astrophysicist, aerospace engineer; b. Alexander City, Ala., Sept. 1, 1950; s. Harry Underwood and Sarah Ruth Campbell; children: Jason Jonathan, Christopher Sanders, Benjamin Robert. BS disting. mil. grad., Auburn U., 1972, MS, 1974; MS, U. Ala., 1988, PhD, 1992. Cert. flight instr. Coop. engr. Pratt & Whitney Aircraft, West Palm Beach, Fla., 1968-70; instr. physics Auburn U., 1972-74; astrophysicist, aerospace engr. Missile and Space Intelligence Ctr., Huntsville, Ala., 1978-80; space scientist, supervisory aerospace engr. propulsion, exec. asst. to dir., lead engr. space telescope fine guidance sensor NASA/Marshall Space Flight Ctr., Huntsville, Ala., 1980—; pres. Redstone Aerospace Inc.; cons. Starflight Assocs. Part-time pastor United Meth. Ch.; sheriff's dep. Sheriff's Res. Recipient Eagle Scout award. Mem. AIAA, Air Force Assn., Res. Officer Assn., Aircraft Owners and Pilots Assn., Scabbard and Blade, Tau Beta Pi, Sigma Gamma Tau, Sigma Pi Sigma. Home: PO Box 295 Harvest AL 35749-0295 Office: NASA E51 Marshall Space Flight Ctr Huntsville AL 35812

CAMPBELL, JOSEPH JOHN, financial services executive; b. Harrisburg, Pa., May 24, 1947; s. John Patrick and May (Murray) C.; m. Susan Jane Ott, Jan. 28, 1966; children: John William, Allison Susan. BA in Econs., Allentown Coll. of St. Francis, de Sales, Center Valley, Pa., 1970; Advanced Mgmt. Cert., U. Pitts., 1980. Computer and systems profl. Gen. Acceptance Corp., Allentown, Pa., 1968-70; v.p. sys. planning and devel. Fin.Am. Corp. (Bank Am. Corp.), 1970-83; v.p. sys. devel. and strategic planning Chrysler First, 1983-87; sr. v.p., chief info. offier Dollar Dry Dock Bank, N.Y.C., 1987-90; sr. v.p., retail bank opers. and tech. Citicorp/Citibank, N.Y.C., 1990-91; sr. v.p. mortgage opers. and tech. Citicorp/Citibank, St. Louis, 1991-93; exec. v.p. Home Ins. Co., N.Y.C., 1993-95; exec. v.p., chief info. officer Zurich Risk Mgmt. Svcs./Zurich Fin. Group, N.Y.C., 1995—; mem. Pres.'s Coun. Allentown Coo. of St. Francis de Sales, 1988—; owner Breakthrough Fitness Ctr., Hilton Head Is., S.C. Inventor computer system in fin. field. Mem. Allentown Coll. of St. Francis de Sales Alumni Assn. (pres. 1981-85, Alumnus of Yr. award 1986). Avocations: golf, tennis, raquetball. Home: 54 Deer Hill Rd West Redding CT 06896-2331 Office: Zurich Risk Mgmt Svcs 59 Maiden Ln New York NY 10038-4502

CAMPBELL, LEWIS B., aerospace technology executive; b. 1946. BS in Mech. Engring., Duke U. Various mgmt. positions Gen. Motors, 1968-88, v.p., gen. mgr. Flint automotive divsn. Buick-Oldsmobile-Cadillac group, 1988-91, v.p., gen. mgr. GMC truck divsn., 1991-92; exec. v.p., COO Textron Inc., 1992-94, pres., COO, 1994-98, chmn., CEO, 1998—; exec. v.p., COO Avco Corp.; pres., COO Davidson Textron Inc., 1994-98; chmn./CEO Textron, 1998—. Office: Textron Inc 40 Westminster St Providence RI 02903*

CAMPBELL, MAGDA, child psychiatrist, researcher, educator; b. Subotica, Yugoslavia, Jan. 22, 1928; came to U.S., 1957; d. Bela and Marija (Lipoženčic) Pijukovic; m. Francis P. Campbell, July 2, 1961; children: Maria D., John F. MD, U. Belgrade, Yugoslavia, 1953. Diplomate in psychiatry and child psychiatry Am. Bd. Psychiatry and Neurology. From tchg. asst. to prof. psychiatry NYU, N.Y.C., 1963-95, prof. emeritus, 1995—; dir. divsn. child adolescent psychiatry, 1987-91, dir. tng. edn., 1990-91. Co-author: Child and Adolescent Psychopharmacology, 1985, Clinical Evaluation of Psychotropic Drugs for Psychiatric Disorders, 1993; contbr. over 225 articles to profl. jours., chpts. to books. Grantee NIMH, 1973-95. Fellow Am. Psychiatric Assn. (Blanche Ittleson award 1986, Agnes Purcell McGavin award 1990), Am. Acad. Child Adolescent Psychiatry (Rieger award 1989, The George Tarjan award 1997), Am. Coll. Neuropsychopharmacology. Office: NYU Med Ctr Dept Psychiatry 1st Ave New York NY 10016

CAMPBELL, MARY LORIMER, writer, broadcaster; b. Carlisle, Cumbria, Eng.; d. James William and Catharina Johana (Lorier) Barnes; m. Bobby Campbell, Oct., 1968 (div. 1978). LittD, Salford U., Eng., 1996, Oxford Brookes U., 1998, Open U., 1999. Journalist Morning Star, London, 1967-76, Time Out, London, 1979-81, City Limits, London, 1981-88; freelance broadcaster and writer, 1988—. Author: (with Anna Coote) Sweet Freedom, 1981; Wigan Pier Revisited, 1984, The-Iron Ladies, 1987 (Fawcett Soc. prize), Diana Princess of Wales, How Sexual Politics Shook the Monarchy, 1993, Unofficial Secrets, The Cleveland Child Abuse Controversy, 1998. Home and Office: 5 Heaton Grove, Newcastle Upon Tyne NE0 5NN, England

CAMPBELL, NAOMI, model; b. London; d. Valerie Campbell. With Elite Model Mgmt., N.Y., 1987-93, Elite Premier, London; with Ford Models, Inc., Paris, 1991—, N.Y., 1993—; with Women Model Mgmt., N.Y.C. appearances include (T.V. series) The Fresh Prince of Bel Air, The Cosby Show, (videos) George Michael's Freedom, Michael Jackson's In the Closet, (book) Madonna's Sex, 1992, (films) Ready to Wear, 1994, Miami Rhapsody, 1995, Unzipped, 1995, To Wong Foo, Thanks for Everything, Julie Newmar, 1995, Catwalk, 1995, Girl 6, 1996, Invasion of Privacy, 1996, An Alan Smithee Film: Burn Hollywood Burn, 1997, Beautopia, 1998, Trippin, 1999, Prisoner of Love, 1999, Destinazione Verna, 2000, (TV film) Naomi Conquers Africa, 1998; author: Swan, 1994; album: Love and Tears, 1994. Achievements include first black model to appear on the cover of French Vogue. Office: Women Model Agy 2nd Fl 107 Greene St Fl 2 New York NY 10012-3803*

CAMPBELL, NEAL FRANKLIN, music educator; b. Pittsboro, N.C., Jan. 27, 1953; s. Owen Riley and Aline Grey (Mangum) C.; m. Gwynn McLaurine Callis, May 13, 1996. MusB, Manhattan Sch. Music, 1983, MusM, 1985, D of Mus. Arts, 1996. Asst. organist All Saints' Ch., Chevy Chase, Md., 1973-76; organist, choirmaster St. Peter's Ch., Phila., 1976-77, St. George's By the River, Rumson, N.J., 1977-80, Christ Ch., Bloomfield, N.J., 1980-85, St. Stephen's Ch., Richmond, Va., 1985—; adj. asst. prof. music U. Richmond, 1997—. Author: Music and Life of Harold Friedell, 1996; performer recordings, radio and TV. Recipient Bronson Ragan award Manhattan Sch. Music, 1983. Mem. Am. Guild Organists (dean 1989-90, chair recital com. 1995-96, nat. coun. 2000—), Assn. Anglican Musicians, Organ Hist. Soc., Royal Coll. Organists (London), Ch. Club N.Y. Episcopalian. Office: 6000 Grove Ave Richmond VA 23226-2601

CAMPBELL, PAUL, III, lawyer; b. Chattanooga, Feb. 1, 1946; children: Paul IV, Kolter M. BA, Vanderbilt U., 1968; MA, Middlebury Coll., 1972; postgrad., So. Meth. U., 1971-72, Emory U., 1972-73; JD, U. Tenn., 1975. Bar: Tenn. 1976, Ga. 1977. Tchr. English St. Mark's Sch., Dallas, 1968-72; ptnr. Campbell & Campbell, Chattanooga, 1976-98; mem. Witt, Gaither & Whitaker, Chattanooga, 1998—; adj. prof. English, U. Tenn., Chattanooga, 1976, adj. prof. law, 1979-81, adj. prof. pre-trial litigation, Knoxville, 1996; mem. Tenn. Ct. of Judiciary, 1995—; mem. Tenn. Jud. Evaluation Guidelines Commn., 1994-95. Author: Tennessee Admissibility of Evidence in Civil Cases, 1987; co-author: Tennessee Automobile Liability Insurance, 1986, 95, 96, 99; editor-in-chief Tenn. Law Rev., 1975; contbr. articles to profl. jours. Bd. mgrs. YMCA Youth Residential Ctr., 1977-80; mem. McCallie Sch. Alumni Coun., 1987-93, U. Tenn. Dean's Alumni adv. coun. law coll., 1979—; trustee, Harbison Found., 1994-96. Recipient Am. Jurisprudence award U. Tenn., 1974, U. Ten. Coll. Law Pub. Svc. award, 1995; Alumni Achievement award McCallie Sch., 1994. Mem. ABA, Am. Bar Found., Tenn. Bar Assn. (bd. govs. 1985-94, pres. 1992-93), Tenn. Bar Found., Chattanooga Bar Found., Chattanooga Bar Assn. (bd. govs. 1983-85), State Bar Ga., Fed. Bar Assn. (dir. chpt. 1983-88), Fed. Ins. and Corp. Counsel, Def. Rsch. Inst., Internat. Assn. Def. Counsel, Order of Coif, Phi Kappa Phi. Office: Witt Gaither & Whitaker 736 Market St Ste 1100 Chattanooga TN 37402-4856*

CAMPBELL, PETER NELSON, biochemist; b. Dartford, Eng., Nov. 5, 1921; s. Alan and Nora Campbell; m. Mollie Winifred Manklow, Jan. 3, 1946; children: Alastair, Julia. BSc, U. London, 1943, PhD, 1949, DSc, 1960. Production chemist Standard Telephones and Cables, London, 1942-46; asst. lectr. Univ. Coll. London, 1947-49; mem. staff Nat. Inst. for Med. Research, Hampstead and Mill Hill, 1949-54; with Courtauld Inst. Biochemistry Middlesex Hosp. Med. Sch., 1954-57, sr. lectr., 1957-64, reader, 1964-67; dir., 1976-87; now prof. emeritus U. of London; prof., biochemistry dept. head Leeds U., Eng., 1967-75. Author: Biochemistry Illustrated; editor-in-chief Biotechnology and Applied Biochemistry, 1981-95. Fellow Inst. Biology, Univ. Coll. London; mem. Biochem. Soc. (hon.), Fedn. European Biochemistry Socs. (diplome d'honneur). Home: 1 Hillside Gardens, Highgate, London N6 5SU, England Office: U Coll London/Biochem & Mol, Gower St, London WC1E 6BT, England

CAMPBELL, RAMSEY, writer; b. 1946. Film critic BBC, Liverpool; tax officer Liverpool, 1962-66; libr. asst. Liverpool Pub. Librs., 1966-73. Author: The Inhabitant of the Lake and Less Welcome Tenants, 1964, Demons by Daylight, 1973, The Height of the Scream, 1976, The Doll Who Ate His Mother, 1976, The Face That Must Die, 1979, To Wake the Dead, 1980, The Nameless, 1981, Dark Companions, 1982, Night of the Claw, 1983, Incarnate, 1983, Obsession, 1985, Cold Print, 1985, The Hungry Moon, 1986, Scared Stiff, 1986, The Influence, 1987, Dark Feasts, 1987, Ancient Images, 1989, Midnight Sun, 1990, Needing Ghosts, 1990, The Count of Eleven, 1991, Waking Nightmares, 1991, Alone with the Horrors, 1993, Two Obscure Tales, 1993, Strange Things and Stranger Places, 1993, The Long Lost, 1993, The One Safe Place, 1995, The House on Nazareth Hill, 1996, Far Away and Never, 1996, Ghosts and Grisly Things, 1998, The Last Voice They Hear, 1998, Silent Children, 2000; (with Charles L. Grant) Black Wine, 1986, (with Lisa Tuttle and Clive Barker) Night Visions 111, 1986; editor: Superhorror, 1976, New Terrors, 2 vols., 1980, New Tales of the Cthulhu Mythos, 1980, The Gruesome Book, 1983, Stories That Scared Me, 1987, Uncanny Banquet, 1992; co-editor: Best New Horror, 1990. Mem. Brit. Fantasy Soc. (pres. 1976—). Office: 31 Penkett Rd, Wallasey Merseyside CH45 7QF, England

CAMPBELL, RICHARD JAMES, philosopher; b. Sydney, Australia, Jan. 18, 1939; s. Albert Tebbutt and Eileen Beryl (Saunders) C.; m. Mathilda Wilhelmina Jeannetta Van Wijk, Aug. 13, 1960 (div. Sept. 1980); children: Peter Malcolm, Michael Ian; m. Petronella Bernardina Maria Kuhnapfel, June 25, 1989. BA, U. Sydney, 1959, BD, 1963, MA, 1964; DPhil, U. Oxford, Eng., 1972. Min. Presbyn. Ch., Glebe, Australia, 1961-65; tchg. fellow U. Sydney, 1965; tutor Magdalen Coll., Oxford, U.K., 1966-67; lectr. philosophy Australian Nat. U., Canberra, 1967-72, sr. lectr. philosophy, 1972-79, reader philosophy, 1980-93, dean faculty of arts, 1990-94, prof. philosophy, 1993—, pro-vice chancellor, 1994-98. Author: From Belief to Understanding, 1976, Truth and Historicity, 1992, Philosophy and the Turn to History, 1993. Chmn. Australian Capital Terr. Schs. Authority, Canberra, 1979-85, mem. working com. on Australian Capital Terr. Coll. Proposals, Canberra, 1971-73; mem. Australian Capital Terr. Interim T.A.F.E. Authority, Canberra, 1975-76. Installed as Mem. Order of Australia, Her Majesty the Queen, 1986. Fellow Australian Coll. Edn. Home: 12 Morphett St Dickson, Canberra 2602, Australia Office: Australian Nat Univ, Dept Philosophy and Arts, Canberra 0200, Australia

CAMPBELL, ROBBI ELIZABETH MARGARET, counselor, educator; b. Ballymoney, Northern Ireland, May 31, 1952; d. Robert and Joan Elizabeth (Rea) C.; m. Mostafa Kamel Ali El-Sayed, Mar. 17, 1980 (div. 1988); 1 child, Sara. BA in Fine Arts with honors, Ulster Coll. Art & Design, Belfast, No. Ireland, 1975; diploma in teaching English fgn. lang., Chichester (Eng.) Coll., 1983; postgrad. diploma in counselling, Brighton (Eng.) U., 1990; MA in Counselling Psychology, Sussex (Eng.) U., 1993. Registered ind. counselor U.K. Register of Counselors. Graphic design asst. Saintfield, No. Ireland, 1973-76; mother's helper, nanny Pink Floyd, 1976-78, The King's Singers, Monty Python Films, 1979; tchr. English as fgn. lang. various locations, 1978-90; tchr. English and life skills to Vietnamese refugees, 1982-83; women's counselor Brighton Mosque, Eng., 1983-85; freelance counselor, cons. supr. Worthing, Eng., 1988—; dir. Arun Counselling Ctr., 2000—; qounseling project mgr. Sussex Eye Hosp., Brighton, 1990-92; vis. lectr., various orgns., Eng., 1991—; lectr. in counseling Crawley (Eng.) Coll., 1992-93, sr. tutor, course dir. diploma in therapeutic counseling, 1993-99; external examiner Fareham Coll., 1997—; complaints mediator West Kent Coll., 1998—; affiliate counselor Ind. Counseling and Adv. Svcs., various locations, Eng., 1993-99, course dir. diploma in therapeutic counseling; ICAS assoc. counsellor, 1993—; writer, checker Readers Digest, London, 1994-95; reader, reviewer Routledge Ltd., London, 1994—, Sage Publs., Ltd., 2000—; co-editor: European Jour. of Psychotherapy Counselling and Health, 1996-98. Mem. editl. bd. Psychotherapy, Counselling and Health; reviewer Sage Publs.; contbr. articles to profl. jours. Fellow Brit. Assn. for Counseling (trustee 1994-98, dep. chair 1994-96, mem. bus. com. 1999—, profl. accreditation 1991, 96); mem. European Assn. for Counseling, Lead Body for Advice, Guidance Counselling and Psychotherapy (segment chair 1992-96), Counselling in Med. Settings Divsn. (chair 1991-94). Avocations: writing, poetry, fine art, painting, craft work.

CAMPBELL, ROBERT DAVID, minerals and metals executive; b. Teaneck, N.J., May 5, 1947; s. Robert Wesley and Phyllis May Julich; m. Elizabeth I. Young, June 15, 1978; 1 child, Ariel. BS, Syracuse U., 1969. Trader C. Tennant Sons & Co., N.Y.C., 1969-73, Cargill, N.Y.C., 1974-75; mng. dir. Amalgamated Metal Corp., Zug, Switzerland, 1975-79; pres. Amalgamet Inc., N.Y.C., 1978-80; v.p. Samincorp Inc., N.Y.C., 1980-84; pres. RST Resources, Inc., N.Y.C., 1984-93; pres., CEO Global Minerals & Metals Corp., N.Y.C., 1993—. Mem. N.Y. Copper Club, Metropolitan Club, Cannon Point South (dir. 1983-95). Avocations: tennis, scuba, sailing, skiing. Home: 45 Sutton Pl S New York NY 10022-2444

CAMPBELL, ROBERT H., retired oil company executive; b. Pitts., June 11, 1937; children: R. Douglas, Heather; m. Nancy Wertz, Feb. 27, 1976. B in ChemE, Princeton U., 1959; M in ChemE, Carnegie Mellon U., 1961; M in Mgmt., MIT, 1978. Various engring. positions Sun Co., Phila., 1960-75; mgr. refinery ops. Sun Co., Corpus Christi, Tex., 1975-77; v.p. human

resources Sun Ship, Inc., Chester, Pa., 1978-80, pres., 1980; pres. Sun Refining and Mktg. Co., Phila., 1983-89; exec. v.p. Sun Co. Inc., Radnor, Pa., 1988-91, pres., CEO, 1991, CEO, chmn., 1991-00, also chmn. bd.; ret., 2000; bd. dirs. The Phila. Nat. Bank, Elwyn Insts. Apptd. mem. by Dep. Sec. of Energy W. Henson Moore to Alternative Fuels Coun., 1990. Mem. Am. Petroleum Inst. (bd. dirs. 1988). Republican. Office: Sunoco 1801 Market St Ste Sl Philadelphia PA 19103-1699*

CAMPBELL, ROBIN, primary education educator; b. Hornchurch, Eng., May 15, 1937; s. John Brodie and Myra Anderson (McLauchlan) C.; m. Ruby Elisabeth Pettit, Oct. 31, 1937; children: Robert, Mary. Diploma in Child Devel., U. London, 1968; BA, Open U., Eng., 1975, MPhil, 1982; PhD, U. London, 1985. Cert. tchr., Eng. Primary sch. tchr. Essex (Eng.) Schs., 1961-71; head tchr. Tanys Dell Sch., Essex, 1971-74; lectr. in edn. Hatfield Poly. Sch., 1975-89; reader in primary edn. U. Hertfordshire, Eng., 1990-92, prof. primary edn., 1992—. Author: Hearing Children Read, 1988, Reading Together, 1990, Reading Real Books, 1992, Miscue Analysis in the Classroom, 1993, Reading in the Early Years Handbook, 1995, Literacy in Nursery Education, 1996, Facilitating Preschool Literacy, 1998, Literacy From Home to School: Reading With Alice, 1999. Mem. U.K. Reading Assn. (Donaly Moyle award 1991, rev. editor Reading 1988—), Internat. Reading Assn. Avocations: running, foreign travel, reading. Office: U Hertfordshire, Wall Hall, Watford WD2 8AT, England

CAMPBELL, RUSSELL DRUMMOND, filmmaker, educator; b. Wellington, New Zealand, Aug. 27, 1944; s. Ian Drummond and Emily Helen (Kennedy) C.; 1 child: Camille Wrightson. BA, Victoria U., Wellington, 1965; MA, U. Wis., Madison, 1972; PhD, Northwestern U., Ill., 1978. Project officer New Zealand Film Commn., Wellington, 1979-80; lectr., sr. lectr. in film Victoria U., 1981—; ptnr. Vanguard Films, Wellington, 1979—; freelance film and TV cons., 1980—. Editor: Photographic Theory for the Motion Picture Cameraman, 1970, Practical Motion Picture Photography, 1970; author: Cinema Strikes Back: Radical Filmmaking in the United States, 1930-1942, 1982; contbr. articles to profl. jours.; editor, pub. Backtrack: A Journal of Film Criticism, 1968, The Velvet Light Trap: Review of Cinema, 1971-73; editor: Illusions: A New Zealand Magazine of Film, Theatre, and Television Criticism, 1986-90; co-dir.: (films) A Century of Struggle, 1981, Wildcat, 1981, Kinleith '80, 1982, Islands of the Empire, 1985 (Peace Media award); dir.: Rebels in Retrospect, 1991; prodr.: A Grasp of Wind, 1982; editor: Kasama, 1988. Knapp fellow U. Wis., 1970, Univ. fellow Northwestern U., 1975, 76, 77; Fulbright travel grantee, 1975. Mem. New Zealand Fedn. Film Socs. (mgmt. com. 1980-95), Assn. Univ. Staff (mem. edn. com. 1997-98), New Zealand Writers Guild, Friends Film Archive (mem. com. 1996—). Mem. New Labour Party. Avocations: crime fiction, travel. Home: 39 Holloway Rd Aro Valley, Wellington 6002, New Zealand Office: Victoria U Wellington, Sch English Film & Theatre, PO Box 600 Wellington New Zealand

CAMPBELL, SIMON JOHN, public company director; b. Manchester, Lancashire, U.K., Jan. 9, 1958; s. Joseph and Joyce (Leech) C.; m. Angela Mary Casson, May 8, 1982; children: James, Joseph. BSc in Chemistry, Salford U., Manchester, U.K., 1980. Salesman Royal Ins., Manchester, 1982-83, Estridge and Powell Ltd., Manchester, 1983-87; gen. mgr. Wigwam Acoustics Ltd., Manchester, 1987-90; mng. ptnr. Angela Campbell Opticians, Manchester, 1990-95, Angela Campbell Opticians, Ltd., Manchester, 1995-99, Felix Corp., 1996—, Angela Campbell Group plc, 1996-99; chmn. Erskine Corp. Ltd., Clitheroe, Eng., 1996—; chmn. Jigsaw IT Sys. Mgmt. Ltd., 1996-99. Mem. Inst. of Dirs. Avocations: guitarist, food and wine lover, classic cars, travel. E-mail: simon@erskinecorp.com. Office: Erskine Corp Limited, PO Box 19, Clitheroe, Lancs BB7 4GJ, England

CAMPBELL, STEWART CLAWSON, retired sales executive, artist; b. Salt Lake City, Aug. 18, 1903; s. Alexander Stewart and Alice Young (Clawson) C.; m. Mary M. McIntyre, June 27, 1942 (dec. July 1983); children: Stewart, Jeffrey, David (dec.), James, Scott, Judith. Student, U. Utah, 1928-31. Pres. Mormon Mission Conf., Dresden, Germany, 1924-28; surveyor Wasatch Gas Co., Salt Lake City, 1928-31, United Gas Sys., Houston, 1931-32; warehouse supr. Maceys Dept. Store, N.Y.C., 1932-35; overseer Alaska Rural Rehab. Corp., Palmer, 1935-39; regional adminstr. Nat. Youth Adminstrn., Cleve., 1939-41; spl. asst. Fed. Civil Def. Emergency Adminstrn., Washington, 1941-42; pres. Utah Wonderland Stages, Salt Lake City, 1946-51; regional adminstr. Fed. Civil Def. Adminstrn., 1952-56; gen. sales mgr. O.C. Tanner Co., Salt Lake City, 1956-75; ret., 1975. One-man shows include Wilma Wayne Gallery, London; maker Petrohlyphs replicas (ancient Indian images in stone), Galerie Royal, Paris, 1984; conceived (new art form) Tower-Mosaic for Human Rights Space Movement and Tower: Mosaic; proposed meml. to Am.'s ten pioneer astronaut heroes; originator of painting with fire art form. Lt. col. USAF, 1942-46. Named to Hon. Order of Ky. Colonels, 1953; accepted by NASA for consideration in next selection of astronauts for aging rsch. in space. Mem. LDS Ch. Avocations: reading, alpine skiing, ice skating, ballroom and contemporary dancing. Home: Apt 10 A 777 E South Temple Salt Lake City UT 84102-1274

CAMPBELL, STEWART FRED, foundation executive; b. St. Louis, June 29, 1931; s. Archibald Stewart and Charlotte (Ehrmann) C.; m. Ann Abbey Hudson, Dec. 18, 1954; children: Karen Ann, Deborah Ann. B.S., Lehigh U., Bethlehem, Pa., 1954; M.B.A., NYU, 1961. With Mfrs. Hanover Trust Co., N.Y.C., 1958-64; asst. sec. Mfrs. Hanover Trust Co., 1962-64; with Duke Endowment, N.Y.C., 1964-79, asst. treas., 1967-73, treas., 1973-79; sec.-treas. Alfred P. Sloan Found., N.Y.C., 1979-86, fin. v.p., sec., 1986—; treas. Doris Duke Trust, 1973-79, Angler B. Duke Meml., Inc., 1973-79, Nanaline H. Duke Fund, 1973-79; asst. treas. Duke Power Co., 1968-75; bd. dirs. Skytop Lodge, Inc., 1992—, v.p., 1993-95, chmn. bd., 1995-2000. Treas. Essex unit N.J. Assn. Retarded Children, 1967-72, trustee, 1966-74; trustee Meml. Home of Upper Montclair, 1987-96, pres., 1990-95. Mem. Delta Phi. Clubs: Rockefeller Center (N.Y.C.); Montclair Golf; Skytop (Pa.). Home: 3 Wendover Rd Montclair NJ 07042-3031

CAMPBELL, SUSAN D., engineer; b. Winter Haven, Fla.. AA, Polk C.C., Winter Haven, 1977; BS in Engring., U. Ala., Huntsville, 1986, MS in Engring., 1993. Producibility engr. U.S. Army Missile Command, Rsch., Devel. and Engring., Huntsville, 1987-92, configuration mgmt./prodn. engr., 1992-93; sys./interfaces engr. Nat. Missile Def. Ground Based Radar Project Office, Huntsville, 1993-95, hardware-in-the-loop test-bed project leader, 1995-98; models and simulations devel. lead Nat. Missile Def. X-Band Radar Project Mgmt. Office Def., Huntsville, 1998—. Contbr. articles to profl. jours. Troop leader Girl Scouts U.S., Huntsville, 1995-97; treas. Toastmasters Internat., Huntsville, 1996-98. Mem. AIAA. Avocations: running, snow skiing, hiking, ballroom dancing. Fax: (256) 722-1339. E-mail: susan.campbell@gbr.redstone.army.mil. Office: Space and Missile Def Command PO Box 1500 Huntsville AL 35807-3801

CAMPBELL, THOMAS DOUGLAS, lawyer, consultant; b. N.Y.C., Jan. 5, 1951; s. Edward Thomas and Dorothy Alice (Moore) C.; m. Mary Anne Makin, Dec. 22, 1978; 1 child, Kristen Anne. BA, U. Del., 1972; JD, U. Pa., 1976. Bar: Del. 1977. Law clk. Law Offices Bayard Brill & Handleman, Wilmington, Del., 1974-77; govt. affairs rep. Northeastern U.S. Std. Oil Co. Ind., 1977-78; Washington rep. Std. Oil Co., Ind., 1978-85; pres. Thomas D. Campbell and Assocs., Inc., Alexandria, Va., 1985—; govt. affairs rep. Northeastern U.S., Std. Oil Co. Ind., 1977-78. With U.S. Army, 1968-69, Del. Air N.G., 1969-77. Mem. ABA, Del. Bar Assn., Congl. Awards Found. (chmn. bd. dirs.), Phi Beta Kappa, Phi Kappa Phi, Omicron Delta Epsilon, Omicron Delta Kappa. Republican. Episcopalian. Home: 517 Queen St Alexandria VA 22314-2512 also: 300-30 Great Cruz Bay Rd Saint John VI 00830

CAMPBELL, THOMAS DOUGLAS, law educator; b. Glasgow, Scotland, Mar. 3, 1938; s. Sidney and Bessie (Barrow) C.; m. Ailsa Morag Davidson, Jan. 3, 1969 (div. 1983); children: Flora Marion, Alexander Magnus; m. Lisbeth Ellen Mitchell, Apr. 20, 1991; 1 child, Emily Katherine. MA, U. Glasgow, 1962; BA, U. Oxford, 1964; Phd, U. Glasgow, 1969. Lectr. U. Glasgow, Scotland, 1964-73; prof. philosophy U. Stirling, UK, 1973-79; prof. law U. Glasgow, 1979-90; prof. law Australian Nat. U., Canberra, 1990—, dean law, 1994-97. Author: Adam Smith's Science of Morals, 1971, The Left and Rights, 1976, Justice, 1988, Mental Illness: Prejudice, Discrimination and the Law, 1991, The Legal Theory of Ethical Positivism, 1996. Fellow Royal Soc. Edinburgh, Australian Acad. Social Scis. Avocation: golf. Office: Australian Nat U, Faculty Law, 0200 Canberra Australia

CAMPBELL, TROY DAVID, officer; b. Kendallville, Ind., July 26, 1964; s. Jerry L. and Marsha Ann (Henney) C.; m. Dawn Suzanne Krumwiede, Aug. 2, 1986; children: Meaghann Michelle, Trevor Scot. BS in aerospace tech., Ind. State Univ., 1986; MS in aerospace tech., Embry-Riddle Aeronautical Univ, 1997. Lic. comml./instrument pilot. FB-111 radar navigator 393 BMS, Pease AFB, N.H., 1989-90; F111F weapon systems officer,radar stike officer 492 Tactical Fighter Squadron, RAF Lakenheath, U.K., 1990-92; F 15E Weapon Systems Officer/training officer 492 Fighter Squadron, RAF Lakenheath, 1992-94; 48 FW Strike Plans officer/F 15E weapon systems officer 48 Operational Support Squadron, RAF Lakenheath, 1994-96; F 15 Tactical electronic warfare Suite Program mgr. 36 Engineering & Test Squadron, Eglin AFB, Fl., 1996-98; major US Air Force, Seymour Johnson AFB, N.C., 1998—; chief 4 FW operational plans.F 15E weapons systems officer 4 Fighter Wing Plans and Evaluations, Seymour Johnson AFB, NC, 1998—. pastor Parrish Rels Com., Salem United Methodist Ch., Goldsboro, N.C., 2000—. Named U.S. Air Force in Europe Bowling champion Ramstein Air Base, Germany, 1995. Mem. Air Force Assn., Aircraft Owners and Pilot Assn., Moose Lodge, Gideons Internat. Methodist. Avocations: bowling, sports, flying, SCUBA diving. Office E-mail: troy.campbell@seymourjohnson.af.mil; Home E-Mail: 100410.3447@compuserve.com. Office: 4 FW/XP 1510 Wright Brothers Ave Sjafb NC 27531-2456

CAMPBELL, VINCENT BERNARD, judge, lawyer; b. Rochester, N.Y., Nov. 1, 1943; s. Paul and Lucy (Tarricone) C.; m. Geraldine Miceli, July 4, 1970; children: Dina, Tracy. BS, Syracuse U., 1965, LLD, 1968. Bar: N.Y. 1969. Lawyer Goldman and Shinder, Rochester, N.Y., 1970-74, Vincent B. Campbell Law Firm, Rochester, N.Y., 1974—; businessman Flower City Builders Supply Corp., Rochester, N.Y., 1974—; real estate developer V.R.J.D. Devel. Inc., 40 West Ave. Properties, Rochester, N.Y., 1970—; judge Town of Greece, N.Y., 1994—. V.p. Monroe County Legislature, Rochester, 1976-88; N.Y. state committeeman Rep. Party, Rochester, 1988-93; town councilman Town of Greece, 1990-94; bd. trustees N.Y. Chiropractic Coll., Seneca Falls, N.Y., 1992; econ. devel. com. Nazareth Coll., Rochester, 1991-93. Recipient Robert Roantree award Syracuse Credit Mfrs. Assn., 1965, Am. Jurisprudence award Lawyers Coop., 1969; named Legislator of the Yr., Monroe County Conservative Party, 1983-84. Mem. ABA, N.Y. State BarAssn., Monroe County Bar Assn., N.Y. State Magistrate's Assn., Rochester Yacht Club. Avocations: sailing, golfing, hunting, winemaking. Office: 1577 Ridge Rd W Ste 203 Rochester NY 14615-2511

CAMPBELL, WILLIAM IAN, physician, consultant; b. Belfast, U.K., May 30, 1952; s. John Charles and Georgina Sarah (McEndoo) C.; m. Anna Elizabeth Martin Campbell, May 18, 1978; children: John, Martin, Anne. MBBch, Queens U., Belfast, Ireland, 1976, MD, 1989, PhD, 1997. Chmn. anaestic divsn. Ulster Hosp., Belfast, Ireland, 1986-88; convenor Northern Ireland Pain Soc., 1988-95; personal tutor Northern Ireland Sch. Anaesthesia, 1989-96; clin. dir. Anaesthetics & Intensive Therapy, Belfast, Ireland, 1990-95; examiner primary fellowship in anaesthetics Royal Coll. Surgeons, Dublin, Ireland, 1993—; coord. in anaesthesiology Ulster Hosp., Belfast, Ireland, 1995—, lead clinician in chronic pain, 1996—; coll. tutor Ulster Hosp., Belfast, 1996-99, dir. intensive therapy, 1996-99, vice chmn., 1998-2000, chmn. med. staff, 2000—; hon. asst. treas. The Pain Soc. of Great Britain and Ireland, 1999—. Contbr. articles to profl. jours. Recipient Dundee medal Northern Ireland Soc. Anesthetists, 1983, Bronze Medallion Cmty. Med. Award, Assn. British Insurers, Northern Ireland, 1991; assoc. Royal Photographic Soc. Great Britain, 1999. Mem. Assn. Anaesthetists, Ulster Med. Soc., Pain Soc. Great Britain and Ireland, Internat. Assn. for Study of Pain, World Soc. of Pain Clinicians. Avocations: photography, art, hill walking, amateur radio. Office phone: 02890 484511. Office: Ulster Hosp Dundonald, Upper Newtownards Rd, Belfast BT16 1RH, United Kingdom

CAMPBELL, WILLIAM STEEN, publishing executive, writer, speaker; b. New Cumberland, W.Va., June 27, 1919; s. Robert N. and Ethel (Steen) C.; m. Rosemary J. Bingham, Apr. 21, 1945 (dec. Dec. 1992); children: Diana J., Sarah A., Paul C., John W. Grad., Steubenville (Ohio) Bus. Coll., 1938. Cost acct. Hancock Mfg. Co., New Cumberland, 1938-39; cashier, statistician Weirton Steel Co., W.Va., 1939-42; travel exec. Am. Express Co., N.Y.C., 1946-47; adminstr., account exec. Good Housekeeping mag., 1947-55; pub. Cosmopolitan mag., 1955-57; asst. dir. circulation Hearst Mags., N.Y.C., 1957-61; gen. mgr. Motor Boating mag., 1961-62; v.p., dir. circulation Hearst Mags., 1962-85; pres. Internat. Circulation Distbrs., 1978-81, Mags., Meetings, Messages, Ltd., 1986—; with Periodical Pubs. Svc. Bur., subs. Hearst Corp., Sandusky, Ohio, 1964-85, v.p., chief exec., 1964-69, pres., chief exec., 1970-85; dir. Audit Bur. Circulations, 1974-86, Periodical Pubs. Svc. Bur., 1964-85, Nat. Mag. Co., Ltd., London, Randolph Jamaica Ltd., Omega Pub. Corp. Fla., Hearst Can. Ltd., 1964-85; former chmn. Ctrl. Registry, Mag. Pubs. Assn.; chmn. bd trustees Hearst Employees Retirement Plan, 1971-85; mem. pres.'s coun. Brandeis U., 1974-94; chmn. nat. corp. and found. com. U. Miami, 1979-85; dir. Broadway Assn., 1985-90, v.p., 1988-90; keynote spkr. Fifth Ann. Hospitality Industry Luncheon, Santa Barbara, Calif., 1996. Bd. dirs. Santa Barbara Rep. Club, 1993-94, Lobero Theatre Found., 1994-96, v.p., 1995-96. Lt. col. USAF, 1942-46, ETO. Recipient Lee C. Williams award Mag. Fulfillment Mgrs. Assn.; Torch of Liberty award Anti-Defamation League, 1979. Mem. Campbell Clan Soc., Mil. Order of World Wars (chaplain), Masons, Cosmopolitan Club (chaplain). Home and Office: 1150 Coast Village Rd Santa Barbara CA 93108-2740

CAMPBELL, WILLIAM YATES, investment banker; b. Rochester, N.Y., Sept. 30, 1953; s. Frederick William and Marjorie (Smith) C.; children: Courtney, Elizabeth, Yates. BA, Albion (Mich.) Coll., 1976; MBA, Bowling Green (Ohio) State U., 1977. Registered investment advisor, SEC, registered securities prin. Credit analyst Mich. Nat. Bank of Detroit, Troy, 1978; loan rev. officer Mich. Nat. Bank of Detroit, Clawson, 1978-79; mgr. credit adminstrn. Mich. Nat. Bank of Detroit, Troy, 1979; v.p. comml. lending Mich. Nat. Bank of Detroit, 1979-82; group head spl. lending Mich. Nat. Bank of Detroit, Clawson, 1982-83; v.p., head comml. lending Standard Bank, Troy, 1983; v.p. investment banking First Mich Corp., Detroit, 1983-84, s.v.p., 1984-85; sr. v.p., co-mgr. investment banking First Mich. Corp., Detroit, 1985-88; chmn., mng. dir. W.Y. Campbell & Co. Investment Banking, Detroit, 1988—; chmn. Peninsula Capital Ptnrs., Detroit, 1995—; pres. Comerica Capital Markets Corp., Detroit, 1995—; mng. dir. Huron Capital Ptnrs. LLC, Detroit, 1999—. Mem. Detroit Zool. Soc., Friends of Detroit Pub. Libr.; Founders Soc. of Detroit Inst. Arts; dir. Grosse Pointe Farms/City Little League. Mem. U. Liggett Sch. Alumnae Assn., Grosse Pointe Club, Country Club of Detroit, Les Cheneaux Club, Yondotega Club, St. Clair Flats Shooting Co. Avocations: fly fishing, hunting, golf, tennis, antique boats.

CAMPBELL DAVIS, TREVOR FRASER, communications company executive; b. Bangor, Ireland, July 16, 1950; s. Thomas Campbell and Elizabeth Mary Evelyn (Fraser) Davis; m. Anne Eperon. BSc in Communications Engring./Mgmt Scis, U. Manchester (Eng.), 1971. Cert. engring., acctg., mgmt. Acct. Coopers & Lybrand, London, 1971-76; fin. dir. W.H. Allen and Co., London, 1976-80, McGraw-Hill Book Co., Maidenhead, Eng., 1980-84; mng. dir. McGraw-Hill Internat. Tng. Co., Maidenhead, 1984-87; co. chmn. European Communications Group, London, 1987—; chmn. Parkside Health-Nat. Health Svc. Trust, London, 1991-98, St. Mary's NHS Trust, London, 1998-2000; CEO Whittington Hosp., London, 2000—; bd. dirs. The Not So Silly Tng. Co., Marlow, Eng., 1990—. Fellow Inst. Dirs., Inst. Mgmt., Inst. Fin. Accts., Royal Soc. Arts; mem. Inst. Elec. Engrs. (assoc.), U. Manchester Inst. Sci. and Tech. (assoc.). Avocations: opera, travel, skiing, literature. Office: Parkside Health The Med Ctr, Woodfield Rd, London W9 3XZ, England

CAMPIONE-PICCARDO, JOSÉ ALFONSO DOMINGO, virologist, educator; b. Montevideo, Uruguay, May 3, 1945; s. José Campione Tomassino and Adela Piccardo Zappetini; m. Martha Ruben Barreto, Dec. 30, 1977; children: Nicolas, Sofia, Alejandro. MD, State U., Uruguay, 1974; PhD in Med. Scis., McMaster U., 1981. Reg. microbiologist specialist Can. Coll. Microbiologists; med. lic. Coll. Physicians and Surgeons New Brunswick. Asst. dept. bacteriology State U. Uruguay, 1969-72, adj. instr. dept. bacteriology, 1972-75, asst. dept. basic scis., 1970-75; rsch. fellow Med. Rsch. Coun., Can., 1978-83; rsch. scientist Lab. Ctr. Disease Control, Can., 1985-90, med. officer 3, 1990-95; adj. prof. microbiology U. Ottawa, Can., 1985—; virologist, cons. Pan Am. Health Orgn. Caribbean Epidemiology Ctr., Port-of-Spain, Trinidad, 1995-98; head molecular virology unit LCDC, 1985-90, chief nat. lab. viral oncology, 1990-95, scis. and lab. advisor, 1998—. Contbr. over 100 articles to profl. jours. Mem. Am. Soc. Microbiology, Am. Soc. Virology, Can. Soc. Microbiologists. Avocation: sailing. Office: Ctr for Infectious Disease, PL-0601E2, Ottawa, ON Canada K1A OL2

CAMPLIN, JAMIE ROBERT, publisher; b. Bishop's Stortford, England, Apr. 27, 1947; s. Norman Arthur and Alma Sybil (Farmer) C.; m. Beryll Patricia Stirk, June 25, 1971 (div. Dec. 1996); children: Beth Louise, Hal Dominic Jamie, Maximilian Aldous. BA, Corpus Christi Coll., Cambridge, England, 1968; MA, Cambridge U., 1971. Mng. editor Thames & Hudson, London, 1976-77, assoc. dir., 1977-79, editl. dir., 1979—. Author: The Rise of the Plutocrats: Wealth and Power, 1978. Mem. Hist. Assn. E-mail: j.camplin@thameshudson.co.uk. Home: 10 Church Ln, London SW19 3PD, England Office: Thames & Hudson Ltd, 181A High Holborn, London WC1V 7QX, England

CAMPMAN, CHRISTOPHER KULLER, consulting company executive; b. Bryn Mawr, Pa., May 25, 1949; s. Curtis Oscar Campman and Agnes R. (Kuller) Baberick; m. Sarah Ann Gladish, July 15, 1972; 1 child, Kurt Christopher. AS in Bus. Administrn., Montgomery County C.C., 1987. Asst. dir. solid waste Montgomery County, Norristown, Pa., 1970-84; owner, pres. C.K. Campman, Inc., Cons., Lansdale, Pa., 1984—; nat. mktg. mgr. Gannett Fleming Engrs., Inc., Camp Hill, Pa., 1998—. Chmn. bd. dirs. park and recreation adv. bd. Upper Gwynedd Twp., Pa., 1986—. Mem. Am. Pub. Works Assn. (assoc.), Nat. Solid Waste Mgmt. Assn. (dir. landfill divsn., mem. internat. bd.), Montgomery County Pub. Works Assn. (sec. 1978—), Solid Waste Assn. N.Am. (tech. dir. Swana). Republican. Lutheran. Avocations: golf, skiing, fresh-water fishing, hunting. Home: 934 Patriot Dr Lansdale PA 19446-5529 Office: GAnnett Fleming Inc PO Box 30794 Valley Forge PA 19484

CAMPO, JAIME, information technology administrator, researcher; b. Cali, Valle, Colombia, Oct. 7, 1956; s. Honorio and Glafira (Rodriguez) C. BS, Pacific Western U., Cali, Colombia, 1989; Specialist, Eafit U., Medellin, Colombia, 1991, Javeriana U., Cali, 1991; Masters, U. Valley, Cali, 1993; MS, Pacific Western U., L.A., 1995, PhD with honors, 1998; Specialist, U. Valley, 1998. Sys. analyst CIAT, Cali, 1979-91; chief rsch. info. sys. EMCALI, Cali, 1991-92, dir. info. tech., 1992—; prof. S/Buenaventura U., Cali, 1994—; mem. conflict resolution com. EMCALI, 1995-96, 98. Recipient Outstanding Rschr. award Enterprise/400, Mex., 1997. Home: Avenida 2G no 52A-77, Apt 303C Santa Margarita, Cali Valle Colombia Office: EMCALI, Cam Torre Emcali Piso 2o, Cali Valle Colombia

CAMPOLETTANO, THOMAS ALFRED, international contract manager; b. Long Island City, N.Y., Feb. 13, 1946; s. Barney and Mary (Felner) C.; m. Kathy Lee Clemons, Mar. 19, 1989; 1 stepchild, Christopher; children by previous marriage: Lisa, Jennifer, Tricia. AAS, Nassau Coll., 1971; BA, U. South Fla., 1977; postgrad., Am. Grad. U., 1980-85, Touro Coll., 1980-85; internat. contracting cert., George Washington U., 1998. Cert. profl. contract mgr. Cost/price analyst Grumman Aero. Corp., Bethpage, N.Y., 1963-70; sr. cost/price analyst Potter Instrument Co., Plainview, N.Y., 1970-73; prin. fin. analyst, govt. liaison Space Systems div. Honeywell, Inc., Clearwater, Fla., 1973—; prof. Honeywell Fed. Contracting Tng. program (recipient 1992 Honeywell Fin. Achievement award). Author: Profit Proposal Initiatives, 1990; co-author: Weighted Guidelines Profit, 1984. With USN, 1963-66, Vietnam. Recipient Apollo Space Program commendation, NASA, 1969. Mem. Nat. Contract Mgmt. Assn., Fin. Exec. Inst. (mem. com. on govt. bus. 1985), Def. Industry Offset Assn., U.S. Track & Field, Road Runners Club Am. Republican. Roman Catholic. Avocation: long-distance and marathon running, golf. Office: Honeywell Inc 13350 Us Highway 19 N Clearwater FL 33764-7290

CAMPORINI, VINCENZO, air force officer; b. Como, Italy, June 21, 1946; s. Carlo and Maria (Ricci) C.; m. Silvana Alemanno; 1 child, Marta. BS, Liceo Ferraris, Varese, Italy, 1965; grad., Air Force Acad., Pozzuoli, Italy, 1969; postgrad., Jr. War Coll., Florence, 1973, Sr. War Coll., Florence, 1982. Commanding officer 28 squadron Italian Air Force, Villafranca, 1979-80; commanding officer test ctr. Italian Air Force, Pratica di Mare, 1988-90; chief R&D air staff Italian Air Force, Rome, 1991-93, chief ops. air staff, 1993-96; inspector aviation for the Navy Italian Navy, 1996-97; inspector flight safety Italian Air Force, 1997-98; dir. mil. policy Italian Min. Def., Rome, 1998—; major gen. Italian Air Force, 1996—; Italian nat. rep. adv. group aerospace rsch. devel., aerospace applications studies com. NATO, Paris, 1988-93; Italian nat. dir. AEW project mgmt. orgn. NATO, Brunssum, The Netherlands, 1991-93. Contbr. articles to profl. jours.; editor Sicurezza del Volo, 1997-98. Decorated Santos Dumont medal Rep. of Brazil, 1996, Commandeur Ordre Merit, Rep. of France, 1998; recipient Paul Tissandier diploma Fedn. Aeronautics Internat., 1996. Mem. Aeroclub of Italy (exec. com. 1993-96, probi viri com. 1997—). Home: Via Claudia 51, 00062 Bracciano Rome, Italy Office: Stato Maggiore Difesa, Via XX Settembre 11, 00187 Rome Italy

CAMPOS, FÁBIO, electronics company executive; b. Recife, Brazil, June 29, 1967; s. Ryam Paulo and Hermínia Terezinha (Lopes) C. Degree in elec. engring., U. Pernambuco, Recife, 1989; cert. in indsl. automation, CEFET-PR, Curitiba, Brazil, 1991; M Electronics, U. Fed. Pernambuco, Recife, 1990-91. Trainee Cobra S.A., Recife, 1985, maintenance technician, 1986; trainee U. Pernambuco, Recife, 1988-89; prof. Escola Técnica Federal de Pernambuco, Recife, 1990—; dir. R&D Innovatec Eletrônica Ltd., Recife, 1992—; cons. U. Fed. Pernambuco, 1990-91; bus. developer Innovatec, Porto, Portugal, 1994; lectr. Encontro Nat. Fisica da M.C. Caxambu, Brazil, 1991, 92; expositor Hannover (Germany) Fair, 1994. Patentee in field; contbr. articles to profl. jours. Mem. Abinee, Recife, 1992, Associação Pernambucana Empresas Base Tecnológica, Recife, 1993. Mem. IEEE, N.Y. Acad. Scis., Soc. Brasileira Física, Soc. Brasileira Automática, Consumer Electronics Soc. Avocations: reading, motorcycling, videos, films. Home: Apt 404, Rua Joao Sales Menezes 338, 50740110 Recife Brazil Office: Innovatec, Rua Antonio Figueiredo 172, 51011510 Recife Brazil

CAMPOS, HAROLDO EURICO BROWNE DE, poet, educator; b. São Paulo, Brazil, Aug. 19, 1929; s. Eurico and Elvira (Prado Browne)de C.; m. Carmen de Paula Arruda, May 8, 1954; 1 child, Ivan Persio. LLB, U. São Paulo, 1952, PhD, 1972; DLitt (hon.), U. Montreal, Can., 1996. Vis. lectr. Tech. Hochschule, Stuttgart, Germany, 1964; advanced scholar NAS, U.S., 1968; allocation DGRC, Paris, 1969; vis. prof. U. Tex., Austin, 1971, E.L. Tinker vis. prof., 1981; vis. prof. Pontifical Cath. U., São Paulo, 1971-72, asst. prof., 1973-78, assoc. prof., 1979-81, prof., 1982-89, prof. emeritus, 1990—; vis. prof. Yale U., New Haven, 1978; founder, promoter Concrete Poetry Movement, São Paulo, 1953-56. Author: (poetry) Auto do Possesso, 1950, Servidão de Passagem, 1962, Xadrês de Estrelas, 1976, Signantia: Quasi Coelum, 1979, Galáxias, 1984 (Roger Caillois award 1999), A Educação dos Cincos Sentidos, 1985, Finismundo: A Última Viagem, 1990, Os Melhores Poemas, 1992 (Jabuti prize 1993), Yugen, Cuaderno Japonês, 1993, Koncrét Versek, 1997, Crisantempo, 1998 (Jabuti prize 1999), A Méquina do Mundo Repensada, 2000; (essays) O Arco-Íris Branco, 1997; (anthology) Oswald de Andrade, 1967; co-author: (with A. De Campos) Revisão de Sousândrade, 1964, Sousândrade-Poesia, 1967, Os Sertões Dos Campos, 1997, Guimarães Rosa em Três Dimensões, 1970, (with A. De Campos and D. Pignatari) Teoria da Poesia Concreta, 1965; translator: Dante: Seis Cantos do Paraiso, 1976, Qohélet (Eclesiastes), 1990 (Jabuti prize 1991), Bere'Shith, 1993, Mênis: A Ira de Aquiles, 1994, Hagoromo de Zeami, 1994 (Jabuti prize 1994), Escrito Sobre Jade, 1996, Pedra e Luz Na Poesia de Dante, 1998, Os nomes E Os navios, 1999, (with O. Paz) Transblanco, 1994; contbr. numerous essays to books. Recipient Jabuti prize Câmara Brasileira do Livro, São Paulo, 1992, Chevalier dans L'Ordre des Palmes Academiques, Republique Francese, 1995, Octavio Paz prize Octavio Paz Found., 1999; fellow John Simon Guggenheim Found., 1972, Fulbright Hays Found., 1978. Home: Rua Monte Alegre 635, 05014000 São Paulo Brazil

CAMPOS, LUÍS MANUEL BRAGA DA COSTA, mathematics, physics, acoustics and aeronautics educator; b. Lisbon, Portugal, Mar. 28, 1950; s. Elmano Neves and Francelina (dos Reis Braga) da Costa Campos; m. Maria Isabel Carreira de Vila-Santa, Aug. 8, 1978; children: Nuno Luis, Ana Isabel. Diploma Mech. Engring., Inst. Superior Tecnico, Lisbon Tech. U., 1972, ScD, 1982; PhD, Cambridge U., 1977. Lectr. applied mechanics and math. Inst. Superior Tecnico, Lisbon Tech. U., 1972-78, aux. prof., 1978-80, assoc. prof., 1980-85, prof., 1985—, coord. aerospace engring., 1992—; counsellor Nat. Inst. Sci. Rswch., 1985—. Author: Funcoes Complexas e Campos Potenciais, Forms of Existence, Aircraft Design Integration and Affordability; contbr. articles to profl. jours. and aerospace sects. of Encyclopedia Verbo. Fellow AIAA (assoc.), Cambridge Philos. Soc.; mem. ASME, Am. Math. Soc., Am. Astron. Soc., European Astron. Soc. (founding mem.), European Math. Soc., London Math. Soc., Soc. Indsl. and Applied Math., Internat. Astron. Union, Adv. Group for Aerospace Rsch. and Devel. (chmn. Flight mechanics panel), Rsch. and Tech. Orgn. (vice chmn. sys. concepts and integration panel), Acoustic Soc. Am., European Sci. Found. (mem. space sci. com.), NSF (liaison mem. space sci. bd.), Societe Francaise d'Acoustique, Internat. Coun. for Aero. Scis., Aero. Rsch. and Tech. (v.p., mgmt. com. European Community Aero. program), Portuguese Acad. Engring. (bd. dirs.). Avocations: classical music, plastic arts, photography, swimming. Office: Inst Superior Tech, Av Rovisco Pais, 1049-001 Lisbon Portugal

CAMPOS, PAULO CAMPANA, health services executive; b. Dasmarinas Cavite, Philippines, July 27, 1921; s. Jose Sayoto Campos and Luisa (Matro) Campana; m. Lourdes R. Espiritu, Dec. 9, 1951; children: Jose, Paulo, Enrique. AA, U. Philippines, 1940, MD, 1945, DSc (hon.), 1990; postgrad. various, including, Johns Hopkins Sch. of Medicine, 1951-53, 58; Nat. Scientist, 1989; MD, U. Philippines, 1990. Pres. Univ. Physicians' Svcs., Inc., 1967-98; prof. medicine Coll. Medicine/Emilio Aguinaldo Coll., 1979-86; pres. Yaman Lahi Found., Inc., 1980-93; prof. Coll. of Medicine/Univ. Philippines, 1952-82, prof. emeritus, 1989; pres. emeritus De La Salle U./Emilio Aguinaldo Coll., 1991; fellow Third World Acad. Scis.; pres. emeritus Nat. Rsch. Coun. of Philippines, 1984—; mem. various governing couns. including Governing Coun. of Philippine Coun. for Health Rsch. and Devel., 1982-89, Governing Coun. of the Pacific Sci. Assn., 1983-89; pres. Nat. Acad. Sci. and Tech., 1978-89; mem. UNESCO Nat. Commn. of Philippine Tech. Group on Sci. and Tech., 1983-88; investigator various projects; mem. bd. of regents Univ. Philippines, 1995—; del. internat. confs. in field, other. Editorial bd.: The Medicial Jour. of Emilio Aguinaldo Coll., 1984-86, Acta Medica Philippines, 1961-73, Jour. of Philippine Med. Assn., 1963-71, The Family Physician, Asian Jour. of Medicine, others. Trustee Gota de Leche, 1963—, Joaquin P. Roces Found., Inc., 1989—; trustee Jose P. Rizal Meml. Found., Inc., 1967—, 1st v.p., 1987—. Fulbright grantee, 1952; recipient U.P. fellowship, 1958, Internat. Atomic Energy Agy. Travel grant, 1965, Rockefeller grant, 1966, IAEA fellowship, 1971, WHO travel grant, 1978, 79, NAST travel grant, 1982, ICSU travel grant, 1983, others. Fellow Am. Nuclear Soc., Philippine Assn. Advancement of Sci. (pres. 1966-68), Philippine Coll. Physicians, Philippine Heart Assn., Third World Acad. Scis.; mem. Philippine Med. Assn., N.Y. Acad. Scis., Ermita Sci. Community, WHO (expert adv. panel on health manpower 1980-83), Philippine Fulbright Assn., Philippine Music Found., Philippine Internat. Friendship Orgn., Am. Numismatic Soc., Manila Med. Soc., Philippine Diabetes Assn. (bd. dirs.), Rotary, Phi Kappa Phi, others. Home: Pasong Lawin, Dasmarinas, Cavite The Philippines Office: 1122 General Luna St, Ermita The Philippines

CAMPOS-CHRISTO, MARCELO, surgeon, educator; b. Belo Horizonte, Brazil, June 7, 1929; s. José Carlos and Maria Lourdes Campos Christo; m. Magda Lucia Figueiredo, Dec. 29, 1955; children: Adriana, Marcelo, Cláudia, Sérgio, Sylvia, Marco Antônio, Roberto. MD, Fed. U. Minas Gerais, 1952, D in Medicine, 1956; postgrad., U. São Paulo, 1962-64. Med. diplomate. Resident in gen. surgery Hosp. Joao XXIII, Belo Horizonte, 1953-54; tng. in thoracic and cardiovascular surgery Univ. Hosp. Med. Sch., State U. Sao Paulo, 1962-64; assoc. prof. exptl. surgery faculty of medicine Fed. U. Minas Gerais, Belo Horizonte, 1961-66, assoc. prof. clin. surgery, 1966-78, full prof., 1978-90; dir. postgrad. course surgery Fed. U. Minas Gerais, 1978-81, prof. thoracic surgery postgrad., 1990—; chief thoracic and cardiovascular surgery Hosp. Felício Rocho, Belo Horizonte, 1967—; spkr. in field. Author: Partial Splenectomies: Sistematization of partial Splenectomies, 1959, Lienectomies Parciales, 1959, Splenectomies Reglees, 1959, Segmental Resections of the Spleen, 1962, Anatomical and Experimental Basis of Planned Partial Splenec, 1963, Partial Splenect in Hematologic Diseases, 1993; contbr. chpt. to book, articles to profl. jours. Lt. Brazilian Army, 1948-49. Fellow ACS, Brazilian Coll. Surgeons (emeritus); mem. AAAS, Acad. Medicine of Minas-Gerais, N.Y. Acad. Scis. Achievements include development of pioneer techniques for partial resection of the spleen; pioneer in conservative surgery of the spleen. Fax: (031) 295-2242. Home: Rua Dias Toledo 76, 30380670 Belo Horizonte Brazil Office: Rua Uberaba 370-10o andar, 30180080 Belo Horizonte Brazil

CAMPO SIEN, CARLOS, nephrologist; b. Dec. 6, 1962; s. Mariano Campo and Florencia Sien; m. Maria Victoria Zabala; 1 child, Virginia. MD, U. Complutense de Madrid, 1986, postgrad., 1990-91. Fellow nephrology Hosp. 12 de Octubre, 1988-91, physician hypertension unit, 1992—; physician dialysis unit La Luz Clinic. Contbr. articles to profl. jours., chpts. to books. Address: C/Dinamarca 7 ESC 2 6 ctro, Leganés, 28916 Madrid Spain

CAMPS, PETRUS HENRICUS J.M. (ARNULF CAMPS), retired religious studies educator, researcher; b. Eindhoven, The Netherlands, Feb. 1, 1925; s. Lodewijk A.L. and Catharina A. (Rutten) C. BTh, U. Nijmegen, The Netherlands, 1951; MA in Theology, U. Fribourg, Switzerland, 1952, DD, 1957. Ordained priest Roman Cath. Ch., 1950. Prof. Regional Sem., Karachi, Pakistan, 1957-61; mission sec. Franciscan Order, Weert, The Netherlands, 1961-63; prof. missiology Cath. U. Nijmegen, The Netherlands, 1963-90; cons. Papal Coun. Dialogue, Vatican City, 1964-79; bd. dirs. Sta. WCRP, N.Y.C. Author: Jerome Xavier S.J., 1957, Partners in Dialogue, 1983, The Sanscrit Grammar of H. Roth S.J., 1988 (Book of Yr. 1988), The Third Eye, 1990, The Friars Minor in China (1294-1955), especially the years 1925-55, 1995, Studies in Asian Mission History, 1956-1998, 2000. Decorated knight Order of Dutch Lion (The Netherlands). Mem. Deutsche Gesellschaft fur Missionswissenschft, Am. Soc. Missiology, Internat. Assn. for Missiology, Soc. European Theologians. Mem. Christian Dem. Party. Home and Office: Helmkruidstaat 35, NL-6602 Cz Wijchen The Netherlands

CAMPTON, DAVID, writer; b. 1924. Clk. dept. edn. City of Leicester, Eng., 1941-49; clk. East Midlands Gas Bd., Leicester, 1949-56. Author: Going Home, 1951, Honeymoon Express, 1951, Change Partners, 1951, Sunshine on the Righteous, 1952, The Laboratory, 1955, The Cactus Garden, 1955, Doctor Alexander, 1956, Cuckoo Song, 1956, The Lunatic View: A Comedy of Menace, 1960, Roses Round the Door, 1958, Frankenstein: The Gift of Fire, 1959, Little Brother, Little Sister, 1960, Four Minute Warning, 1960, Funeral Dance, 1960, Passport to Florence, 1961, Silence on the Battlefield, 1961, Usher, 1962, Incident, 1962, On Stage: Containing Seventeen Sketches and One Monologue, 1964, Resting Place, 1964, The Manipulator, 1964, Split Down the Middle, 1965, Little Brother, Little Sister and Out of the Flying Pan, 1966, Two Leaves and a Stalk, 1967, Angel Unwilling, 1967, More Sketches, 1967, Ladies Night: Four Plays for Women, 1967, The Right Place, 1969, Laughter and Fear: 9 One-Act Plays, 1969, On Stage Again: Containing Fourteen Sketches and Two Monologues, 1969, The Life and Death of Almost Everybody, 1970, Now and Then, 1970, Timesneeze, 1970, Gulliver in Lilliput, 1970, Gulliver in the Land of the Giants, 1970, The Wooden Horse of Troy, 1970, Jonah, 1971, The Cagebirds, 1971, Us and Them, 1972, Carmilla, 1972, Come Back Tomorrow, 1972, In Committee, 1972, Three Gothic Plays, 1973, Modern Aesop, 1976, One Possessed, 1977, The Do-It-Yourself Frankenstein Outfit, 1978, What Are You Doing Here?, 1978, Zodiac, 1978, After Midnight: Before Dawn, 1978, Parcel, 1979, Everybody's Friend, 1979, Pieces of Campton, 1979, Who Calls?, 1980, Attitudes, 1980, Freedom Log, 1980, Dark Wings, 1981, Look-Sea, 1981, Great Whales, 1981, Who's A Hero Then?, 1981, But Not Here, 1984, Dead and Alive, 1983, Mrs. Meadowsweet, 1986, Singing in the Wilderness, 1986, Our Branch in Brussels, 1986, Cards, Cups and Crystal Ball, 1986, The Vampyre, 1986, Can You Hear the Music?, 1989, The Winter of 1917, 1989, Smile, 1990, Becoming a Playwright, 1992, Who's Been Sitting in My Chair?, 1992, Eskimos & Provisioning, 1993, The Evergreens, 1994, Permission to Cry, 1996. Office: 35 Liberty Rd, Glenfield Leicester LE3 8JF, England

CAMUS, MICHEL, writer, poet, philosopher; b. Namur, Belgium, Oct. 20, 1929; arrived in France, 1957; s. Lucien Camus and Gabrielle Marcq. Fondé de pouvoir C.S.F., Paris, 1957-69; rédacteur, fondateur Revue Lettre Ouverte, Paris, 1960-62; sec. gen. Sigma Constructeur, Paris, 1969-71; dir. adjoint Galerie Anspach, Paris, 1972-73; rédacteur Encyclopédie Internat. de Criminologie, Lausanne, Switzerland, 1973-75; rédacteur-en-chef Revue Obliques, Paris, 1976-83; dir. littéraire Editions Lettres Vives, Paris, 1981—; producteur délégúe Radio France France Culture, Paris, 1984—; rédacteur, fondateur Revue L'autre, Paris, 1990-92; rédacteur en chef Revue Mémoire du XXI Siecle, Paris, 1998—. Author: Hymne à Lilith, 1993, L'Enjeu du Grand Jeu, 1994, Entretiens avec Christian Bobin, 1995, Antonin Artaud Une Autre Langue du Corps, 1996, Aphorismes Sorciers, 1996, L'arbre de vie du vide, 1998, Les avatars du regard, 1999, Adonis Le Visionnaire, 2000. Chercheur Associu Paleocorsu, Corsica, 1985. Recipient Grand prize Internat. de Poésie Lucian Blaga, Roumanie, 1995. Mem. Internat. Found. for Edn. and Culture (coun. mem.), Ctr. Internat. Rsch. et Etudes Transdisciplinaires (adminstr.), Tango Nomade (v.p., treas.), d'Honneur de L'Union des Écrivains Roumains. Fax: 0142783761.

CAMUS, PHILLIPPE, aerospace company executive; b. Paris, June 28, 1948. Grad., Inst. d'Etudes Politques Paris, 1970, Ecole Normale Supérieure, Paris, 1971; agrégation degree in physics, Ecole Normale Supérieure, 1971. Spl. projects mgr. Caisse des Depots et Consignations, 1972-82, dir. sr. mgmt. chmn. of the fin. com., 1982-92; chmn. supervisory bd. Banque Arjil, 1987-93; gen. ptnr., chmn., CEO ARCO, 1992—; co-pres., chmn. fin. com. Lagardère Group, 1993-98, co-chief exec. officer, 1998—; CEO Aerospatiale Matra, 1999—, chmn. mgmt. bd., 1999—; co-chief exec. officer European Aeronautic Def. and Space Co., 2000—; mem. bd. govs. Institut d'Expertise et de Prospective, Avaiation Week Aerospace Laureate, 1989. Office: Aerospatiale Matra, 37 Blvd de Montmonency, 75781 Paris France*

CANAHUATI, JUDY, lactation consultant; b. Phila., July 17, 1941; d. Max and Bessie S. (Creshkoff) Weiner; m. Pedro Felipe Canahuati, Sept. 6, 1969; children: Emilia, Pedro Cesar. BA, U. Pa., 1963; MPhil in Anthropology, Columbia U., 1974. Internat. bd. cert. lactation cons. Cmty. organizer Planned Parenthood, N.Y.C., 1966-67; instr. U. Nacional Honduras, San Pedro Sula, 1970-72; import-export mgr. Contessa Indsl., San Pedro Sula, Honduras, 1978-82; tech. adv. USAID, Tegucigalpa, 1982-85, Mgmt. Scis. for Health, Boston, 1986-88; bd. dirs. La Leche League Internat., Schaumburg, Ill., 1986, project dir., 1989-91; cmty. adv. Wellstart Internat., Washington, 1991-96; cons. Centro de Apoyo a la Lactancia Materna, San Salvador, 1981-83, Ednl. Devel. Ctr., Boston, 1985, UNICEF, N.Y.C., Tegucigalpa, 1989, China, 1997; researcher Inst. Reproductive Health Georgetown U., Washington, 1990-92; cons. Wellstart Internat., Washington, 1996, World Relief, Tegucigalpa, Honduras, 1994, Catholic Relief Svcs., San Salvador, El Salvador, 1996, Project Hope, Managua, Nicaragna, 1996, CARE, Honduras, 1997, Acad. Ednl. Devel., 1997, others; dir. project to improve basic edn. World Bank, Honduras, 1998; supt. Escuela Internacional Sampedrana, Honduras, 1999-00. Co-author: Community-based Breastfeeding Support: A Planning Manual, 1996; contbr. articles to profl. jours.; co-prodr.: (video) Investing in the Future: Women, Work, and Breastfeeding, 1995. Bd. dirs. Escuela Internacional Sampedrana, San Pedro Sula, Honduras, 1980-85, spt., 1999; bd. dirs. Soc. Pro-Musica, San Pedro Sula, 1975-76. Fellow Nat. Inst. Mental Health, 1968-69. Mem. Internat. Lactation Cons. Assn., Consumer's Edn. and Protective Assn., La Leche League Internat., World Alliance for Breastfeeding Action, Phi Beta Kappa. Avocations: reading, writing, cooking. Home: PO Box # 512, San Pedro Sula Honduras

CANAS, JOSÉ ANTONIO, physics educator; b. Granada, Spain, Jan. 6, 1949; s. José and Dolores (Torres) C. MSc, St. Louis U., 1977, PhD, 1980; D in Physics, Barcelona (Spain) U., 1978. Jr. specialist seismology Calif. U., Berkeley, 1977-78; assoc. prof. geophysics U. C. Madrid, 1980-81; rschr. U. Nacional Autonoma, Mexico City, Mex., 1981-83; assoc. prof. geophysics Politech. U. Cataluna, Barcelona, 1983-88; prof. geophysics Politech. U. Cataluña, Barcelona, 1988-96; gen. dir. Geographical Inst., Madrid, 1996—; dept. dir. physics Politech. U. of Catalonia, 1984-87, dept. dir. geotech., 1994-96; pres. Nat. Geographical Inf. Ctr., Madrid, 1996—, Nat. Astronomical Commn., Madrid, 1996—, Nat. Geodesy and Geophysics Commn., Madrid, 1996—, Nat. Seismoresistent Normative, Madrid, 1996—; v.p. Geographical Superior Coun., Madrid, 1996—. Contbr. articles to profl. jours. Mem. adminstrv. coun. AUXINI, Madrid, 1996-97, HOLSA, Barcelona, 1997—, ENTE Publico Retevision, Madrid, 1996—. Mem. Rel. Soc. Española Fisica Quimica, Am. Geophys. (regional adv. com. to Europe 1991—), St. Louis U. Alumni Associated. Roman Catholic. Avocations: music, reading, movies, soccer. Office: Geograph Inst of Spain, Gen Ibanez Ibero 3, 28003 Madrid Spain

CAÑAS MURILLO, JESÚS, Spanish literature educator; b. Madrid, Apr. 25, 1951; s. José María Cañas and Josefa Murillo González; m. Magdalena Álvarez Franco, Aug. 3, 1984; 1 child, Magdalena. PhD in Hispanic Philology, U. Autónoma de Madrid, 1978. Prof. Spanish literature U. Autónoma de Madrid, 1973-79, U. de Extremadura, Spain, 1979-2000; dir. Spanish literature dept. U. de Extremadura, 1986, dir. dept. Spanish philology, 1986-89, dir. dept. Hispanic philology, 1991-95. Author, editor: Libro de Alexandre, 1988, Blas Nasarre Disertacion, 1992, La comedia Sentimental, 1994, Honor en Lope de Vega, 1995; editor: La Petimetra, 1989. Mem. Soc. Medieval Hispanic Literature, Sociedad Española de Estudios del Siglo XVIII, Asociación Escritores Extremeños. Avocation: books. Office: U de Extremadura, Avda de la Universidad S/N, 10001 Cáceres Spain

CANAT, JEAN FRANCOIS, lawyer; b. Millau, France, Sept. 17, 1947; s. Charles and Francoise (Pechdo) C.; children: Charlotte, Olivia. LLB, Paris U., 1972. Bar: Paris. Gen. mgr. Canat SA, Millau, 1971-72; assoc. Gide-Loyrette, Paris, 1972-75, Bell & Campbell, Paris, 1976-78; ptnr. Lefevre & Co., Paris, 1978-91, Berlioz & Co., Paris, 1991-93; founding ptnr. UGGC, Paris, 1993—. Avocations: golf, tennis, modern painting. Office: UGGC, 47 Rue De Monceau, 75008 Paris France

CANAVESI RIMBAUD, MARIE LISSETTE E., anthrologyst; b. Montevideo, July 23, 1956; arrived in Bolivia, 1986; d. Hebert José Canavesi and Elba Esther Rimbaud; children: Cristian Daniel Sahonero, Diana Ximena Sahonero. BS, U. Republica, Uruguay, 1985; MS, U. Mayor de San Andres, La Paz, 1993; PhD, LaSalle U., 1994—. Coord., dir. Regional Programme Indigenous, Bolivia and Venezuela, 1987-93; chief, coord. U. May San Andres, Bolivia, 1990-92, dir. pres. univ., 1991, dir. anthropol. carreer, 1992; coord. Indigenous Program PNVD, Bolivia, 1993; jr. cons. Ohio Univ., Bolivia, 1987, UNICEF, Bolivia, 1991; sr. cons. CAF, Bolivia and Ecuador, 1993—, IFAD, Bolivia, Peru and Rome, 1993—, PNUD/UN Devel. Program, LaPaz, 1991—; resources human chief BID/FNDR, 1995-97; univ. prof. U. Mayor de San Andres, Bolivia, 1986—, U. Católica Bolinana, Bolivia, 1986-91; nat. and regional coord. Programa Nacional de Gobenabilidad-Pronagob-subprogrma and descentralization-BID/Min Presidencia; nat. coord. to proyecto gestion Indigena local UNESCO/DONIDA JAIPO, 1999-2000. Contbr. articles to profl. jours. Avocations: playing guitar, painting, writing poetry. Office: UN-UNDP Mcal Sta Cruz 1350, 12612 Almeda Bldg Rm 1204 B, 15080 La Paz Bolivia

CANCINO, JAVIER, art director; b. Santiago, Chile, May 21, 1961; s. Raul Cancino and Marta Díaz; m. Catalina Santa Cruz, Mar. 14, 1992; children: Tomas, Elisa. Student, U. Catolica Valparaiso (Chile), 1980-81, U. Catolica Valparaiso (Chile), 1981-84. Art dir. Porta (Advtsg. Agy.), Santiago, 1985-86, BBDO Chile, Santiago, 1987-90, Tiempo BBDO, Madrid, 1988, Leo Burnett, Santiago, 1991-94, Paula Mag., Santiago, 1994-96; exec. creative dir. Ogilvy & Mather Direct, Santiago, 1996-97; creative and art dir. Editl. Avellaneda, Santiago, 1997—. Recipient 1st prize Nat. Advt. Festival, 1988, 90, 91, Grand Prix Internat. de l'Affichage Paris, 1989, Outdoor Advt. Internat. Grand Prix, 1989, 2nd Prize Nat. Advt. Festival, 1991, Spl. Prize Mus. Nacional Bellas Artes, 1991, Ambulance 2nd prize Nat. Film and TV Festival, 1991, Finalist award Ambulance Internat. Film and TV Festival of N.Y., 1991, Ambulance Spl. prize, 1991, Gaucho de Oro prize, 1992; named Best Art Director Nat. Film and TV Festival, 1998. Mem. Old Mackayans Rugby Football Club, John Jackson XV 1980 Rugby Selection of Brit. Schs. in Chile, Granadilla Country Club. Avocation: golf. Office: Editl Avellaneda Of 21, Av Isidora Goyenechea 3356, Santiago Chile

CANDA, EDWARD R., social work educator; b. Dec. 8, 1954; s. Frank W. and Anne R. C.; m. Hwi-Ja Canda, Aug. 5, 1977. BA in Anthropology summa cum laude, Kent State U., 1976; MA in Religious Studies, U. Denver, 1979; PhD in Social Welfare, Ohio State U., 1986. Edn. coord. and counselor unaccompanied minor refugee pgm. Luth. Social Svcs. of Cen. Ohio, Columbus, 1982-83, supr. unaccompanied minor refugee program, 1983; cons. Transcultural Family Inst., Columbus, 1982-86; grad. tchg. fellow Sung Kyun Kwan U., Seoul, 1976-77; asst. prof. social welfare U. Iowa, Iowa City, 1986-89; asst. prof. social welfare U. Kans., Lawrence, 1989-92, assoc. prof. social welfare, 1992-99, prof. social welfare, 1999—; cons. editor Social Work jour., Washington, 1997—. Author: Contemporary Human Behavior Theory: A Critical Perspective for Social Work, 1998, Spiritual Diversity in Social Work Practice, 1999; editor: Spirituality in Social Work: New Directors, 1998; editor spl. issue Reflections: Narratives of Profl. Helping, 1995. Bd. dirs. Kans. Friends of Religious Studies, Lawrence, 1998—, exec. bd. 1999—; dir. for Internat. Course on Spirituality and Social Work, Inter-Univ. Ctr., Dubrovnik, Croatia, 1998—. Mem. Soc. for Spirituality and Social Work (founder, bd. dirs. 1990—), NASW, Coun. on Social Work Edn. Avocation: world percussion. Office: Univ Kans Sch Social Welfar Twente Hall Lawrence KS 66045-7587

CÂNDEA, VASILE, cardiovascular surgeon; b. Lisa Vanatori, Teleorman, Romania, May 24, 1932; s. Vasile and Anica (CÂlin) C.; m. Ana Tudor, Aug. 30, 1961; children: Bogdan Teodor, Dragos Octavian. Med. lic., Faculty Gen. Medicine, Bucharest, Romania, 1957; specialist surgeon in gen. surgery, Univ. Sch. Medicine, Bucharest, 1971, cardiovasc. surgeon, 1976, prof. cardiovasc. surgery, 1993. Specialist surgeon in gen. surgeon Cen. Mil. Hosp., Bucharest, 1964-71; asst. dr., chair in anatomy Univ. Sch. Medicine, Bucharest, 1972-74; chief cardiovasc. surgery dept. Cen. Mil. Hosp., Bucharest, 1976-90; dir. Cardiovasc. Diseases Ctr. of Army, Bucharest, 1990-95; prof., chief 2d Clinic of Cardiovasc. Surgery Univ. Sch. Medicine, Bucharest, 1993—; dir. Prof. C.C. Iliescu Inst. Cardiovasc. Disease, Bucharest, 1995—; hon. prof. Ovidius U. Author: (monograph) Limphatic System in Shock, 1983; co-author: (monograph) The Shock and Phisiopatology Clinic and Treatment (Romanian Acad. award 1975). Dep. Social Dem. Party Romania, Teleorman, 1996. Gen. mil. medicine divsn., 1989-95, ret. Recipient award Romanian Cineasts Union for Sci. Films. Mem. Romanian Scientists Acad. (pres. 1994), Med. Balkanik Union (gen. sec. 1995), Romanian Acad. Med. Scis. (mem. med. scis. leadership presidium 1996). Social Democrat. Orthodox. Avocations: painting, music, touring. Home: BD Primăverii 37, 71207 Bucharest Romania Office: Prof Dr CC Iliescu Inst Cardiovascular Disease, 258 Fubndeni, 72435 Bucharest Romania

CANDIA, RENE CONTRERAS, architecture educator; b. La Paz, Bolivia, Jan. 26, 1942; s. Celso Contreras Gutierrez and Mercedes Candia Tapia; m. Gaudelia Sigler Cabañas, Sept. 30, 1966; children: Anahi, Celia, Alberto. BS, Ayacucho, La Paz, 1959; postgrad., Havana (Cuba) U., 1970-78, San Andres U., La Paz, 1998; magister, San Andres U., La Paz, 1998. Sector responsible Urban Corp., Santiago, Chile, 1971-72; gen. architect Bldg. Ministry, Havana, 1973-76; specialist Enterprise # 5, Havana, 1977-80, Enterprize # 4, Havana, 1981-85, Enterprise # 2, Havana, 1986-91; dept. chief San Andres U., La Paz, 1991-92; prof. Havana U., 1988-90, San Andres U., La Paz, 1991—; planning chief Arch. Faculty, La Paz, 1996—. Prin. works include farmer's typical home (1st prize Bldg. Min. Cuba 1981), turistic bungalo (hon. mention), meml. (1st prize Nat. Union of Writers and Artists of Cuba 1988). Mem. Friendship Instn., La Paz, 1992-96; electoral del. Nat. Electoral Ct., La Paz, 1998. Mem. Architects Coll. Avocations: crafts, music, literature, swimming, travel. E-mail: Renecons@ceibo.entelnet.bo. Home: Juan Pinto No 214, PO Box 7516, La Paz Bolivia Office: San Andres U, 6 de Agosto Ave No 2170, La Paz Bolivia

CANDIANI, CARLOS LUIS, electronics executive; b. Buenos Aires, Jan. 19, 1948; s. Jose Lorenzo and Yolanda Marina (Meza) C.; m. Carlota Monica Marcuzzi, Dec. 28, 1973; children: Ana Carolina, Silvana Patricia. Degree in elec. engring., Cordoba, Argentina. Maintenance supr. Renault Agrl., Cordoba, q, Argentina, 1970-78; rschr. U. Stuttgart, Germany, 1980-82; tech. mgr. CCCConsultores, Cordoba, 1982-86, Controles Automation SRL, Cordoba, 1986-96; dir. U. Tech., Cordoba, 1985-97; gen. mgr. Controles Autmoation, Cordoba, 1996—; prof. U. Tech., Cordoba, 1985—; cons. in field. Author: Balanced Systems. Mem. IEEE, AADECA. Home: Pan de Azucar 137, 5009 Cordoba Argentina Office: Controles Automaticos, Para La Industria, 5009 Cordoba Argentina

CANDIDO, A. MICHAEL, contracting company executive, real estate manager; b. Falls Church, Va., June 23, 1953; s. Albert Babbitts and Rose Marie (Naturale) C.; m. Joyce Mary Baratta, Sept. 27, 1975; children: Rosalie, Elizabeth, Jacqueline, Allison. BA in Acctg., William Paterson U., 1975. Office mgr. J. Moore & Co., Livingston, N.J., 1973-79; v.p. J. Moore & Co., Livingston, 1979-95, pres., 1995—; pres. Essex Realty Co., Cedar Grove, N.J., 1991—; adj. prof. Kean U. N.J., Union, 1988-93. Mem. Essex Fells (N.J.) Zoning Bd., 1995—; trustee Steamfitters Local 475, Warren, N.J., 1995—; chmn. bldg. and grounds com. Notre Dame Ch., No. Caldwell, N.J., 1997—; active MCAA Industry Fund, Washington, 1999—; mem. MCA Legis. Com., 2000—. Mem. ASHRAE, Internat. Soc. Pharm. Engrs., Mech. Contractors Assn. (polit. action com. treas. 1998, legis. com. 2000—), Mech. Contractors Assn. N.J. (treas. 1998-2000, v.p. 2000—), Essex Fells Country Club, Bay Head Hist. Soc. Roman Catholic. Avocations: golf, photography, books, music, fishing. Office: J Moore & Co 118 Naylon Ave Livingston NJ 07039-1006

CANE, LOUIS PAUL JOSEPH, sculptor; b. Beaulieu, France, Dec. 13, 1943; s. Albert and Andree (Pasquier) C.; m. Nicole Rondinella, Oct. 12, 1970; children: Cecile, Florence. Exhbns. include Hall des Remises en Question, Nice, 1967, Galerie Givaudan, 1969, Galerie Yvon Lambert, Paris, 1971, 72, Galerie Daniel Templon, Milan, and Paris, 1971, 73, 77, 78, 79, 81, 84, 85, Galerie Francoise Lambert, Mileu, 1971, London ICA, 1973, Galerie Lia Rumma, Naples, 1973, Galerie Rudolf Zwirner, Cologne, 1974, Galerie del Cortile, Rome, 1974, Galerie Fischer, Dusseldorf, 1975, Galerie Bischofberger, Zurich, 1976, Humlebaeck La. Mus. Modern Art, 1976, Montreal Mus. Contemporary Art, 1976, 1976, Frankfurter kunstverein, Frankfort, 1977, Galerie Leo Castelli, New York, 1977, 82,, Galerie Arnessen, Copenhagen, 1977, Nat. Mus. Modern Art, Paris, 1977, Galerie del Milione, Milan, 1978, Israel Mus., Jerusalem, 1978, Bâle Art 9 '78, 1978, Kunsthalle, Bielefeld, 1978, Galerie Art in Progress, Dusseldorf, 1979, Galerie Art Line, The Hague, 1979, 80, Galerie Charles Krivine, Brussels, 1979, Mus. Modern Art, Strasbourg, 1979, Galerie Mantra, Turin, 1979, Galerie Art in Progress, Munich, 1980, 81, 82, Galerie Ressle, Stockholm, 1981, FIAC, Paris, 1981, 84, 95, Galerie Beanbourg, 1982, Maeght Found., St Paul de Vence, 1983, City of Paris Mus. Modern Art, 1983, Galerie de France, Paris, 1985, Galerie Beaubourg, Paris, 1986, Galerie Reckerman, Cologne, 1986, 90, 93, Mus. Modern Art, Toulon, 1987, Galerie des Ponchettes, Nice, 1988, Galerie Okada, Tokyo, Galerie San Andrea, Savone, 1989, Galeria Edurne, Madrid, 1989, Chapelle St. Louis de la Salpêtrière, Paris, 1990, Espace Fortant de France, Sète, 1990, Musée de l'Hospice St. Roch, Issoudun, 1990, Casa de Monte, Madrid, 1990, Museo Municipal de Bellas Artes, Santander, 1991, Galeria Ambiante Cero, Valence, 1991, Galerie Bjorn Olsson, Stockholm, 1991, Mus. Modern Art, St. Etienne, 1992, Galerie Hélène Trintignan, Montpellier, 1992, Galerie Beaubourg, Vence, 1993, Musée de l'Orangerie, Paris, 1994, Inst. Français, Athens, 1994, galerie Bonomo, Bari, 1994, 1995, Mus. Chiba, Japan, 1995, Mus. Modern Art, Hokkaido, Japan, 1995, Mcpl. Mus., Faensa, 1995, Galerie Patricia Dorfman, Paris. Home: 184 rue St Maur, 75010 Paris France Office: Galerie en Esclusivite, 17 rue Bonaparte, 75006 Paris France

CANE, REGINALD FRANK, chemical engineer, educator; b. Hobart, Tasmania, Australia, Apr. 22, 1917; s. Frank Byron and Margaret Grace (Ellis) C.; m. Ruth Mathias, Apr. 27, 1941; children: Susan Margaret, Jennifer Marie, Hiliary Vivienne. BS with honors, U. Tasmania, Australia, 1937, DS, 1945. Lectr. applied chemistry U. Melbourne, Australia, 1959-61; reader chemistry U. Tasmania, 1963-68; prof. chem. engring. U. West Indies, Trinidad, B.W.I., 1968; head dept. chemistry Queensland U. Tech., Brisbane, Australia, 1968-79, dean applied sci., 1977-79; hon. rsch. assoc. U. Tasmania, 1979—; adj. prof. U. Utah, Salt Lake City, 1979—, E.E. Clyde prof., 1979, Stirling McMurrin Disting. prof., 1981; mem. chemistry com. U. NSW, 1957-66; chmn. petroleum and fuels com. NATA, 1963-68; mem. com. Dept.

Indsl. Devel., Tasmania, 1966-68; mem. acad. bd. Queensland U. Tech., 1963-79; mem. com. Tasmanian Energy Coun., 1980-83. Contbg. author: Oil Shale, 1978 (Archebald Olle prize Royal Australian Chem. Inst. 1978); mem. editl. bd. The Geochem. Jour. (Japan), 1978-82, Fuel Processing Tech., 1978-88; contbr. over 60 articles to profl. jours. Commonwealth Rsch. fellow U. Tasmania, 1937/39; Murphy lectr. U. NSW, 1958; Sr. Fulbright scholar Australian-Am. Edn. Found., 1979. Fell0w Royal Australian Chem. Inst. (state com. 1951-77, fed. com. 1952-54, editl. bd. 1965-68), Instn. Chem. Engrs. U.K.; mem. Nat. Assn. Testing Authorities (chemistry com. 1949-62), Oil and Colour Chemists Assn., Instn. Chem. Engrs. Queensland (state com. 1970-75). Achievements include initial elucidation of the mechanism of the thermal decompositon of oil shale. Home: 7 Talune St, Lindisfarne Tasmania Australia Office: Univ Tasmania, Dept Chemistry GPO Box 252C, Hobart 7001, Australia

CANEL, SERVANE MARIE, energy company executive; b. Pau, Pyrenees, France, June 11, 1972; d. Pierre-Franck and Rose-France (Pineau) C. French Baccalaureat in Math. and Sci., 1990; diploma, Grad. Sch. Bus. Adminstrn., Nantes, France, 1994; MBA, Madrid U., 1995; diploma, Dauphine U., Paris, 1996. Acctg. analyst Elf Petroleum Norge, Stavanger, Norway, 1993; corp. account officer Credit Comml. de France, Paris, 1996; cons. Cambridge Energy Rsch. Assocs., Paris, 1996—. Mem. UNESCO Choir, 1997—, chair Orch. Philharmonique Internat., 1997—. Home: 75 Rue du Commerce, 75015 Paris France Office: Cambridge Energy Rsch Assoc, 21 Blvd de la Madeleine, 75038 Paris France

CANEPA, GIACOMO GIOVANNINI, architect; b. Chiavari, Genoa, Italy, May 3, 1937; arrived in Peru, 1948; s. Agostino Canepa Sanguineti and Gemma Giovannini Mezzofanti; m. Ive Beusan Roković, June 2, 1962; children: Giuseppina, Carla, Agostino, Fabrizio, Gemma. Degree in Arch., U. Nacional de Ingenieria, Lima, 1959. Ptnr. Balli & Canepa Architects, Lima, 1962-71; owner Giacomo Canepa Architects, Lima, 1972—. pres. Italian Assn. Peru, Lima, 1984-85; coun. mem. Municipio de La Molina, Molina, Lima, 1980-83; pres. Comitato Italiani All'estero Comites, 1988-98; delegato Al Consiglio degli Italiani All'estero, 1992—. Decorated cavaliere and ufficiale Italian Orders; recipient awards for Best Architecture, Pueblo Libre, 1966, Peru, 1970, La Molina, 1974, San Isidro, 1975, La Punta, 1984, others. Mem. Alleanza Nazionale (Italy). Roman Catholic. Avocations: footing, squash, tennis. Office: Giacomo Canepa Architects, Los Rosales 180, Lima 27, Peru

CÁNEPA, JAVIER DARÍO, lawyer, consultant, writer; b. San Martín, Argentina, Sept. 15, 1969; s. Juan Dionisio Cánepa and Edda Argentina Santini C. B Polit. Sci., U. del Salvador, Argentina, 1990, Lic. in Internat. Rels., hon. diploma, 1993, Broker in Internat. Trade, 1995, Lic. Law, 1996; M. Polit. Sociology, Acad. Scis., Czech Republic, 1995; MBA, U. de Deusto/Agostini, 1998; PhD in Polit. Sci., Marlborough U., 1999; LittD in Polit. Sci., St. Clements Australian Nat. U., 2000. Bar: Argentina 1996. Founder Chanetonsa, Argentina, 1994; cons. Maicasa, Argentina, 1992-97, Tomisa, Argentina, 1995-97; asst. in instnl. rels. CEVETRE, 1990-94, chief of instnl. rels., 1994-99; CEO Red Link Hering, 1999-2000; project mgr. Dehave Cons. BIVO, 2000—; cons. in polit. and internat. law C&A Inc., 1996-98; sr. cons. East West Consulting Group, 2000—; cons. mem. No. Ireland Ctr. for Health Coop. and Devel., 2000—. Author: The Fall of Communism and its Consequences for the Social Science Theory, 1995, Social Change in East Central Europe, 1996. Searching for a New Model of Social Policy, 1996, Post Commuist Transformation, 1997, Comprehending the Politics, 1999. Mem. The Citizen's Power Found., Am. Sociol. Fund, Fund for Advancement of Discipline, Minority Fellowship Program. Recipient awards in internat. trade, 1996, PRAGMA prize, 1996, Simón Bolivar grant, 1997. Mem. AAAS, Carb Club, Readers Club, Ctr. for Study of the Presidency U.S.A., Acad. Polit. Sci. U.S., Acad. Internat. Mgmt. U.K., Am. Sociol. Acad., N.Y. Acad. Scis., U.S. Planetary Soc, Nat. Geog. Soc., Am. Ednl. Rsch. Assn., Am. Polit. Sci. Assn., Ctr. State of Presidency, Am. Hist. Assn., Am. Assn. Polit. Cons., Am. Soc. Internat. Law. Home: LaPlata 3551, (1676) Santos Lugares Argentina

CANER, ALP, structural engineer; b. Ankara, Turkey, Apr. 10, 1970; s. Arif Ihsan and Hacer Gunes Caner; m. Nur Asena, May 18, 1994; 1 child, Kaan. BS with high honors, Mid. East Tech. U., Ankara, 1991; MS, N.C. State U., 1994, PhD, 1996. Summer intern Ankara Sheraton, 1989, Izmir (Turkey) Hilton, 1990; tchg. asst. Mid. East Tech. U., 1991-92; rsch. asst. N.C. State U., Raleigh, 1992-96; structural engr. Parsons Brinckerhoff, N.Y.C., 1996—. Mem. Am. Concrete Inst., Prestressed Concrete Inst., Structural Engrs. N.Y. Avocations: reading, tennis, music. E-mail: caner@pbworld.com. Office: Parsons Brinckerhoff 1 Penn Plz Fl 2 New York NY 10119-0021

CANESSA, FRANCESCO, theatre administrator, music critic; b. Island of Capri, Naples, Italy, Sept. 19, 1927; s. Guglielmo Canessa and Anna Canessa Papale; m. Italia Carloni, Nov. 9, 1953; children: Riccardo, Bruno, Susanna. Ed., Scuola di Musicologia; LLD. newspaper music critic La Patria, Milan, Italy, Roma, Naples, Il Mattino, Naples; former supt., artistic dir. Arena Sferisterio Teatro di Tradizione, Macerata; supt. Teatro di San Carlo, 1990—. Decorated commendatore al merito Della Repubblica Italiana. Mem. Rotary. Office: Teatro San Carlo, Via San Carlo 93-F, I-80132 Naples Italy*

CANESTRI, FRANCO, biophysicist, researcher; b. Novi Ligure, Alessand., Italy, Dec. 17, 1955; arrived in Germany, 1984; s. Lorenzo Canestri and Maria Ferreretto; m. Britta Wegner, May 21, 1988; children: Fabrizio, Riccardo. Bachelor, Sci. Sch., Novi Ligure, 1974; degree, Physics Inst., Genoa, Italy, 1979; PhD, Biophysics Inst., Milan, 1983. With R&D, IBM, Milan, 1982-84; bus. mgr. Hewlett Packard, Germany, 1984-85; with European/Mid. East mktg. support Hewlett Packard Med., Böblingen, Germany, 1985-87, clin. specialist, tng. program mgr., 1987-95; bus. devel. mgr. Asia/Pacific Hewlett Packard Fiberoptic, Böblingen, 1995—. Author: Experimental LCA Algorithm (Prediction of Laser's Crater Shape), 1987, Mathematical Formulation of LCA, 1992, New Techniques in Computer-Controlled CO2 Lasers Applications in Medicine, 1999; contbr. articles to profl. jours. Sgt. Alpine Mt. Troops, Italy, 1980. Vis. fellow Nat. Cancer Inst., Milan, 1979-83, Sackler Med. Sch., Tel Aviv, 1994. Office: Hewlett-Packard, Herrenberger Str 130, 71034 Böblingen Germany

CANGELARIS, PANAYOTIS D., Greek diplomat; b. Alexandria, Egypt, Mar. 14, 1951; s. Dimitri P. and Angelique I. (Kyriakou) C.; m. Diana Macris, Nov. 19, 1989; children: Dimitri, Marina. JD, U. Athens, 1976, Diploma Pub. Law and Polit. Scis., 1977. Acct. Nat. Bank of Greece, Athens, 1970-73; jr. barrister and barrister-at-law Athens Ct. of Justice, 1976-77; attaché later 3d Sec. and Head of Desks Hellenic Min. of Fgn. Affairs, Athens, 1977-79, 79-81, 89-91, 93-95; 2d to 1st sec. and head of consular sect. Embassy of Greece, Berlin, G.D.R., 1981-85; first sec. later counsellor Greek Permanent Mission/UN Office and Other Internat. Orgns., Geneva, 1985-89; consul gen. Consulate Gen. of Greece, Alexandria, Egypt, 1991-93; first counsellor then min. counsellor Embassy of Greece, Islamabad, Pakistan, 1995-2000; consul gen. Consulate Gen. Greece, Hannover, Germany, 2000—; mem. Cavafy Internat. Com., Alexandria, 1991-93; rep. Hellenic Min. of Fgn. Affairs, Hellenic Red Cross Cen. Adminstrv. Coun., Athens, 1994-95. Author: (book) Athanasios Lefkaditis 1872-1944, Founder of the Greek Scout Movement, 1972, 94, Dictionary of Greek Philatelists, 1982, Reflections Upon Greek Contemporary Painting, The Cangelaris Collection, vol. I, 1991, vol. II, 1999. Scout leader, leader trainer Scout Assn. of Greece, Athens, 1969-81, 74-81; rep. Hellenic Philatelic Fedn., Youth Commn. of the Internat. Philatelic Fedn., Zurich, 1974-81; Baden-Powell fellow World Scout Found., Geneva, 1986—; mem. internat. rels. com. Scout Assn. of Greece Found., 1990—, mem. emeritus, 1994—. Decorated St. Mark's Cross, 1st Class, Patriarchate of Alexandria, 1985, St. Daniel's medal, Patriarchate of Moscow, 1991; recipient Disting. Svc. medals Scout Assn. of Greece, 1994, Hellenic Red Cross, 1985, Long Svc. medal Scout Assn. Greece, 1980.

CANHAM, PRUELLA CROMARTIE NIVER, retired educator; b. Statesboro, Ga., Dec. 4, 1924; d. Esten Graham and Mary Lee (Jones) Cromartie; m. Robert E. Niver June 4, 1946 (div. 1965) m. David L. Canham July 26, 1985; 1 child, Peddy Niver Hayhurst Moran; grandchild, Matthew William Hayhurst. BS in Bus. and Music, Ga. So. U., 1944; post-grad., various univs. tchr. voice, piano, chorus and bus. career maths. North Ft. Myers H.S., Fla.; former sec. Statesboro Air Base, Ga., Warner Robbins Air Base, Macon, Ga.; former tchr. Westside Sch., Bulloch County, Ga., Southside Sch., Opelika, Ala. Mem. Singers Club of L.I.; guest spkr., panelist various cultural orgns. in Fla. and so. states; soloist various chs. and schs.; music cons. local theater groups; mem. Fla. State Secondary Music Instructional Materials Coun. Nominee Gannett Found. Heart of Gold Humanatarian award, 1981; named Vocal Solo. Lit. Music Specialist State of Florida, Lee County Florida Tchr. of the Year, 1987, nominee Nat. Tchr. Hall of Fame, 1998; recipient Nat. Libr. Poet's Editor's Choice award, 1994; cert. Appreciation Nat. Park Trust, 1995, Lee County Sch. Dist. Fla., 1991. Mem. AAAS, Am. Ch. Dirs. Assn., Fla. Music Educator Assns., Music Educator's Nat. Conf., Lee County Alliance of the Arts (charter), Fla. Vocal Assn. (past coord., state bd.), Nat. Assn. of Tchrs. of Singing in Am. and Cand., So. Fla. Symphony and Chorus Assn., Am. Guild of Organists, Fla. League of the Arts (past pres. and bd. dirs., hon. life, 1998—), Lee County Retired Tchrs. Assn., Fla. Vocal Assn., Am. Choral Assn., Internat. Soc. Poets (disting. mem. 1994, merit award, 1995), others. Home: 1271 Burtwood Dr Fort Myers FL 33901-8711

CANIVET, M. GUY, judge. 1st pres. Cour de Cassation, Paris, 1999—. Office: Cour de Cassation, 5 Quai de l'Horloge, 75055 Paris RP, France*

CANIVEZ, GARY LYNN, psychologist, educator; b. Chgo., Nov. 17, 1960; s. Lynn and Carol (Busser) C. BS, Bemidji State U., 1982; MS in Edn., So. Ill. U., 1985, PHD, 1987. Lic. psychologist, Ariz.; cert. sch. psychologist, nat., Ariz., Ill. Sch. psychologist Deer Valley Unified Sch. Dist. #97, Phoenix, 1987-90, Tempe (Ariz.) Sch. Dist. #3, 1990-95; asst. prof. Ea. Ill. U., Charleston, 1995-98, assoc. prof., 1998—; adj. prof. No. Ariz. U., Flagstaff, 1988-95; sport psychologist Ea. Ill. U., Charleston, 1995—; sport psychologist, cons. Apex Sport Psychology Svcs., Charleston. Contbr. articles to profl. jours. Recipient Past Pres. award Ariz. Assn. Sch. Psychologists, Phoenix, 1993, Max Jones Meml. Rsch. award Ariz. Assn. Sch. Psychologists, Phoenix, 1993. Mem. APA, Nat. Assn. Sch. Psychologists, Ill. Sch. Psychologists Assn. (trainer rep. 1997-99). Home: 921 Williamsburg Dr Charleston IL 61920-4331 Office: Ea Ill Univ 600 Lincoln Ave Charleston IL 61920-3011

CANJAR, PATRICIA MCWADE, psychologist; b. Pitts., Mar. 14, 1932; d. Robert Malachai McWade and Lillian Kathryn (Seidenstricker) Robb; m. Lawrence N. Canjar, Aug. 4, 1951 (dec. Nov. 1972); 1 son, R. Michael; m. James M. McDonald, Sept. 24, 1977. A.A., Carlow Coll., 1951; B.A., U. Detroit, 1973, M.A., 1975. Lic. psychologist, Mich. Psychologist, Robinwood Clinic, Detroit, 1973-77, Psychol. Resources, Birmingham, Mich., 1977-80, Realistic Living Ctr., Warren, Mich., 1983-85, Behavior Ctr., Birmingham, 1980-84; with Eastwood Cmty. Clinic, Big Beaver, Mich., 1984-94; ret. 1994. Mem. Nat. YWCA Spl. Commn., Boston, N.Y.C. and Washington, 1967; bd. dirs. YWCA, Pitts., 1961-65, Detroit, 1965-67; asst. coordinator United We Sing, Pitts. Music Festival, 1955-65; pres. Carnegie Mellon Women's Club, Pitts., 1963-65, U. Detroit Faculty Wives' Club, 1968-70; mem. State of Mich. Fair Campaign Practices Commn., 1968-70; treas. Grandview Beach Assn., 1982-84, pres., 1984-87. Fellow Am. Psychol. Assn.; mem. Mich. Assn. Profl. Psychologist, Mich. Assn. Alcohol and Drug Abuse Counselors. Democrat. Roman Catholic.

CANNADAY, KENNETH D., retired federal agency administrator; b. Canalou, Mo., Jan. 22, 1927; s. Daniel Elijah and Ola Blanche (Buckner) C.; m. Anna Kathleen Barnes, Dec. 16, 1946 (div. June 1966); children: Marinelle, Kathy Ann (dec.), Heidi Lynn, Heather Lee; m. Lois Annette McCormich, Sept. 21, 1985. AB, U. Mo., Columbia, 1950; STB, Boston U., 1955; cert., St. Christopher's, London, 1976. Dept. chief Vets. Med. Ctr., Wichita, Kans., 1976-84, VA Med. Ctr., 1984-90; ret., 1990. Editor, coauthor: Working with Dying Patients, 1978 (award); editor Rotary Newsletter. Chair United Meth. Ch., Waukesha, Wis., 1955-59, sr. pastor, 1959-62; pres. ARC, Bath, N.Y., 1987; pres. Ministerial Assn., Cape Coral, Fla. With USN, 1944-45. Grantee Fed. Govt., 1990-98, 95; named Hometown Hero, C. of C., 1997; recipient commendation Gov. of Iowa, 1959, Spl. award County Fund Raisers Com., 1979; Ken Cannaday Day named in his honor. Mem. Gulf Coast Soc. Fundraising Execs., Masons (Grand Prelate 1964-65, Grand Comdr. 1965), Rotary (hon.). Avocations: reading, fishing. E-mail: KC1927@aol.com. Home: 721 Dean Way Fort Myers FL 33919-2517

CANNADY, WALTER JACK, lawyer; b. Alameda, Calif., July 9, 1942; s. Jack Stephen and Marie E. (Schmalenberger) C.; m. Shirley Padovan, June 26, 1966 (div. June 1980); 1 child, Amber L. BS in Polit. Sci., Calif. State U., Hayward, 1964; JD, Lincoln U., San Francisco, 1969. Bar: Calif. 1970, U.S. Dist. Ct. (no. dist.) Calif. 1970. Pvt. practice Oakland, Calif., 1970-79; ptnr. Cannady & Whitehorn, Oakland, 1979-82; of counsel Moore Clifford Wolfe et al, Oakland, 1982-85; pvt. practice San Leandro, Calif., 1985-96, Emeryville, Calif., 1996—. Office: 2200 Powell St Ste 680 Emeryville CA 94608-1876

CANNIFF, BRIAN P., lawyer; b. Phila., Apr. 24, 1967; s. Paul J. and Arlene P. C.; m. Mary C., Apr. 23, 1999. BA in Philosophy, BS in Computer Sci., Villanova U., 1989, JD, 1992. Pvt. practice Phila., 1993-95; assoc. Elman & Assoc., Phila., 1995-00, White and Williams, Phila., 2000—. Mem. Am. Intellectual Property Law Assn., Ben Franklin Am. Inn of Ct., Ultimate Player's Assn. (dir. jrs. nat. tournament 1999, 00).

CANNING, ELIZABETH URSULA, zoologist; b. Redruth, England, Sept. 29, 1928; d. Miles Howell and Winifred (Jenkin) C.; m. Christopher Maynard Wilson, Aug. 15, 1953; children: Victoria Jane, Catherine Alexandra, Miles Richard Guy. BSc, Imperial Coll., 1951; PhD, London Sch. Hygiene, 1955; DSc, U. London, 1976; Dr. (hon.), U. Blaise Pascal, France, 1995. From lectr. to prof. to sr. rsch. fellow Imperial Coll., London, 1955—. Mem. Soc. Protozoologists (hon.), Royal Soc. Tropical Medicine and Hygiene, Soc. Invertebrate Pathology, Br. Soc. Parasitology (hon.). Avocations: bridge, golf, crossword puzzles. Office: Imperial Coll Silwood Park, Buckhurst Rd, Ascot SL5 7PY, England

CANNON, DAVID C., aquaculture company executive, mechanical engineer; b. Raleigh, N.C., Sept. 27, 1937; s. Doyle L. and Katherine C. (Coker) C.; m. Patsy Sturgeon, Feb. 12, 1977; children: Patricia, Mary, Ann, Katherine, John, Ben. BSME, Clemson U., 1959; MSME, Case Inst., 1965. Registered profl. engr., S.C. Sr. project engr. Sonoco Products Co., Hartsville, S.C., 1965-87; pres. Edisto Shrimp Co., Edisto Island, S.C., 1987-92, Edisto Seafarms, Inc., Edisto Island, 1993—. Chmn. Darlington County Rep. Party, Darlington, S.C., 1968. 1st lt. Ordnance Corps, U.S. Army, 1960-68. Mem. ASME (chpt. pres. 1979-80), World Aquaculture Soc., S.C. Aquaculture Assn., S.C. Shrimp Growers Assn. (bd. dirs. 1989-2000). Methodist. Achievements include patents for square column form, die cutter feeder, disposable beer keg. E-mail: dcannon@dycon.com. Home: PO Box 370 Edisto Island SC 29438-0370 Office: Edisto Seafarms Inc PO Box 39 Edisto Island SC 29438-0039

CANNON, FRANCIS V., JR., former academic administrator, electrical engineer, economist; b. Poughkeepsie, N.Y., Nov. 1, 1935; s. Francis Vincent and Marietta Elizabeth (Yerry) C.; m. Margaret Ann Klisart; children: JoAnn, John, Joseph. BSEE, Milw. Sch. Engring., 1963; MSEE, Marquette U., 1969; PhD, U. Wis.-Milw., 1987. Registered profl. engr., Wis. Technician Oster Mfg. Co., Milw., 1959-60, AC Sparkplug div. Gen. Motors Corp., Milw., 1960; instr. Milw. Sch. Engring., 1963-70, acad. dean, 1970-79, v.p. acads., 1979-85, exec. v.p., provost, 1985-89, chancellor, 1989-92; pres. DeVry Inst. Tech., Dallas, 1992-99; cons. engr. Systems Design Co., Milw., 1964-75; adj. prof. U. Wis.-Milw., 1987. Contbr. articles to profl. jours. Officer East Side Community Coun., Milw., 1965-79; chmn. East Side Transit Study Com., Milw., 1975; mem. Gov.'s Coun. on Econ. Issues, 1990-92. Named Disting. Tchr. Milw. Sch. Engring., 1969, Outstanding Tchr. Salgo-Noren Found., N.Y.C., 1970. Mem. IEEE (sect. officer 1965-73, edn. award 1974), Am. Soc. Engring. Edn. (com. chmn. 1976-79), Engrs. and Scientists Milw. (pres. 1978-79), Wis. Econ. Edn. Coun. (bd. dirs.), Wis. Soc. Profl. Engrs. (chpt. pres. and officer 1976-82), Am. Legion (exec. com. 1987-90), Irving C. of C. (bd. dirs. 1993—, chmn. 1999-2000), Irving Symphony Orch. Assn. (bd. dirs., pres. 1996—), Rotary. Republican. Roman Catholic. Avocations: golf, cross-country skiing, fishing, camping. Home: 7706 Brookview Ct Irving TX 75063-3177 Office: DeVry Inst Tech 4800 Regent Blvd Irving TX 75063-2439

CANNON, HUGH, lawyer; b. Albemarle, N.C., Oct. 11, 1931; s. Hubert Napoleon and Nettie (Harris) C.; m. Jo Anne Weisner, Mar. 21, 1988. AB, Davidson Coll., 1953; BA, Oxford U., 1955, MA, 1960; LLB, Harvard U., 1958. Bar: N.C. 1958, D.C. 1978, S.C. 1979. Mem. staff U. N.C. Inst. Govt., Chapel Hill, 1959; mem. firm Sanford, Phillips, McCoy & Weaver, Fayetteville, N.C., 1960; asst to Gov. of N.C., Raleigh, 1961; dir. adminstrn. State of N.C., 1962-65, state budget officer, 1963; mem., mng. ptnr. Sanford, Cannon, Adams & McCullough, Raleith, 1965-79; pvt. practice Charleston, S.C., 1979—; mem. Everett, Gaskins, Hancock and Stevens attys., Raleigh, 1990—; v.p. fin. Palmetto Ford, Inc., Charleston, 1979—. Author: Cannon's Concise Guide to Rules of Order, 1992. Parliamentarian NEA, 1965—; mem. nat. adv. coun. Am. Inst. Parliamentarians; pres. Friends of Coll., Raleigh, 1963; alt. de. Dem. Nat. Conv., 1964, chief parliamentarian, 1976, 80, 84, 88, 92, 96; bd. govs. U. N.C., 1972-81; trustee Davidson Coll., 1966-74, N.C. Sch. Arts, 1963-72. Rhodes scholar, 1955. Mem. Phi Beta Kappa, Omicron Delta Kappa, Phi Gamma Delta. Episcopalian. Home: PO Box 31820 Charleston SC 29417-1820 Office: 1625 Savannah Hwy Charleston SC 29407-2236

CANNON, J. TIMOTHY, psychology educator, neuroscientist; b. Scranton, Pa., Aug. 26, 1949; s. Thomas F. and Nancy (Culkin) C.; m. Brooke J. Szuhay, Nov. 17, 1984; children, Jaye A., Linnea F.; children from previous marriage: Christina M., Sean T., Michael R. BS, U. Scranton, 1971; PhD, U. Maine, 1977. Postdoctoral fellow UCLA, 1977-81; prof. psychology U. Scranton, 1981—, dir. neurosci., 1987—, assoc. chair, 1987-2000; chair IACUC, Scranton, 1985—. Contbr. articles to profl. jours. Named State of Pa. Prof. of Yr., Coun. for Advancement and Support of Edn., 1995; NSF ILI grantee, 1992. Mem. Internat. Assn. for Study of Pain, Soc. for Neurosci., Am. Psychol. Soc. Office: U Scranton Dept Psychology Alumni Meml Hall Scranton PA 18510-4596

CANNON, JOHN, III, lawyer; b. Phila., Mar. 19, 1954; s. John and Edythe (Grebe) C. BA, Denison U., 1976; JD, Dickinson Sch. Law, 1983. Bar: Pa. 1983, Hawaii 1986, U.S. Dist. Ct. (ea. dist.) Pa. 1983, U.S. Ct. Appeals (3d cir.) 1985. Account exec. PRO Services, Inc., Flourtown, Pa., 1976-79; br. officer mgr. PRO Services, Inc., Pitts., 1979-80; law clk. Montgomery County Ct. of Common Pleas, Norristown, Pa., 1983-84; assoc. Rawle & Henderson, Phila., 1984-88; comml. litigation counsel CIGNA Corp., Phila., 1988-90; counsel CIGNA Internat. Fin. Svcs. Divsn., Phila., 1990-93; sr. counsel CIGNA Internat., Phila., 1993-95, v.p., sr. counsel, 1995-97, sr. v.p., chief counsel, 1997—; sr. v.p., chief counsel CIGNA Healthcare, Bloomfield, Conn., 1999—, Conn. Gen. Life Ins. Co., Bloomfield, Conn., 1999—; bd. dirs. CIGNA Stu Zychie, Warsaw, Poland, INA Himawari Life Ins. Co. Ltd., Tokyo; v.p. Life Ins. Co. N.Am.; trustee U.S.-China Legal Coop. Fund, Washington, 1998—. Comments editor Dickinson Internat. Law Ann., 1983. Mem. ABA, Pa. Bar Assn., Hawaii State Bar Assn., Kappa Sigma (pres. 1975-76), Gamma Xi (v.p., trustee 1982-86). Republican. Episcopalian. Office: Cigna Cos PO Box 7716 2 Liberty Pl Philadelphia PA 19192

CANNON, JUNE A., social worker; b. Columbus, Ohio, Nov. 16, 1963; d. Richard M. and Dorothy M. Stoughton; m. James K. Cannon, Oct. 15, 1988; children: Michael K., Caleb J., Kyle M. BA, Miami U., 1985; MA, U. Dayton, 1988. Lic. social worker, registered play therapist. Dir., therapist foster care, asst. dir. cmty.-based svcs. St. Joseph Children's Treatment Ctr., Dayton, Ohio, 1987-98; exec. dir. Miami County Children's Svcs. Bd., Troy, Ohio, 1998—. Mem. Play Therapy Assn. Office: Miami County Children's Svcs Bd 1695 Troy Sidney Rd Troy OH 45373-9794

CANO, KRISTIN MARIA, lawyer; b. McKeesport, Pa., Oct. 27, 1951; d. John S. and Sally (Kavic) C. BS in Biochemistry, Pa. State U., 1973; MS in Forensic Sci., George Washington U., 1975; JD, Southwestern U., 1978; LLM in Securities Regulation, Georgetown U., 1984. Bar: Calif. 1978, U.S. Dist. Ct. (cen., no. and so. dists.) Calif. 1984, U.S. Dist. Ct. Ariz., 1988, U.S. Supreme Ct. 1988, U.S. Ct. Appeals (9th cir.) 1992. Assoc. Yusim, Cassidy, Stein & Hanger, Beverly Hills, Calif., 1979-81, Walker and Hartley, Newport Beach, Calif., 1981-82, Milberg, Weiss, Bershad, Spethrie & Lerach, San Diego, 1984; pvt. practice Newport Beach, 1984—. Bd. dirs., v.p. Sandcastle Community Assn., Corona del Mar, Calif., 1987-97; active Leadership Tomorrow Class of 1994. Mem. Orange County Bar Assn., Balboa Bay Club. Democrat. Roman Catholic. Avocations: ballet, ice skating, bicycling, photography, golf. E-mail: cano@securities-law.com. Office: 1 Corporate Plaza Dr Ste 110 Newport Beach CA 92660-7924

CANSECO, JOSE, professional baseball player; b. Havana, Cuba, July 2, 1964; s. Jose and Barbara (dec.) C.; m. Esther Haddad, October 25, 1988. With Oakland (Calif.) Athletics, 1982-92, 97-98, Tex. Rangers, 1992-94, Boston Red Sox, 1994-96; outfield/designated hitter Toronto Bluejays, 1997-98; with Tampa Bay Devil Rays, 1999—. Appeared in instructional video, Jose Canseco's Baseball Camp, 1989. Named Minor League Player of Yr. The Sporting News, 1985, MVP So. League, 1985, Am. League Rookie of Yr. The Sporting News, 1986, Baseball Writers' Assn. Am., 1986, Sporting News Am. League All-Star Team, 1986, 88-92, Sporting News Am. League Silver Slugger Team, 1988, 90-91, Am. League MVP Baseball Writers' Assn. Am., 1988, Sporting News Comeback Player of Yr., 1994, MVP Am. League, 1988; first player to have 40 home runs and 40 stolen bases in same season, 1988; mem. Championship Team, 1989. Mem. Am. League All-Star Team, 1986, 88, 89, 90, 92. Office: Tampa Bay Devil Rays One Tropicana Dr Saint Petersburg FL 33705

CANTARELLA, PAOLO, automotive executive. Pres., CEO Fiat S.p.A., Turin, Italy. Office: Fiat, Via Nizza 250, 10136 Turin Italy*

CANTA YOY, CARLOS ANDRÉS, business executive, trade consultant; b. Montevideo, Uruguay, Dec. 27, 1939; s. Andres Canta Alba and Maria Concepcion Yoy; div.; children: Patricia Elizabeth, Andres Eduardo, Eduardo Francisco Antonio. Ed., Uruguayan U., 1968. Exec. Cenci-Uruguay, Montevideo, 1964-71, Cenci Iberoamericana, Buenos Aires, 1971-75, CENRA, Buenos Aires, 1975—; cons. Centro Despachantes Aduana, Buenos Aires, 1987—, Camara Comercio Industria y Produccion, Buenos Aires, 1982—; prof. Instituto Capacitacion Aduanera, Buenos Aires, 1992—. Editor some 100 books on external trade. Mem. Spanish C. of C., Am. C. of C., Chamber Commerce and Prodn. Baptist. Avocations: reading, astronomy, soccer, classical music. Home: Avenida de Mayo 953, 10o, G, 1084 Buenos Aires Argentina

CANTELL, CARL-ERIK, zoologist; b. Visby, Sweden, Nov. 6, 1938; s. Carl-August and Gunborg Katarina (Gustavsson) C.; m. Jadwiga Sobolewska, Nov. 4, 1989. BA, Uppsala U., Sweden, 1961, MA, 1962, DPhil, 1972. Asst. Uppsala U., Sweden, 1962-71, lectr. zoology, 1974-79, sr. lectr., 1971-74, 80—, assoc. prof., 1993—; vis. lectr. U. Dinköping, Sweden, 1973-79. Contbg. author: Reproductive Biology of Invertebrates, Vol. IV, 1989. Avocations: gardening, skiing, travel. Achievements include rsch. on morphology, devel. and biology of phylum Nemertea (Rhynchocoela). Home: Tennisvägen 5A, 19277 Sollentuna Sweden Office: EBC Dept Animal Devel, Norbyvägen, 75236 Uppsala Sweden

CANTERBURY-COUNTS, W. DOUGLAS, psychologist; b. Lancaster, Pa.; s. William L. Jr. and Marion E. (Winters) Counts; m. Belinda Jaya Canterbury, Mar. 12, 1977; 1 child, William Andrew Hanuman. BA, So. Calif. Coll., 1979; MDiv, Ea. Bapt. Theol. Sem., 1983; PhD, Temple U., 1989. Pvt. practice roofing contractor Calif. & Pa., 1976-88; counselor Pathways Counseling Svc., Swarthmore, Pa., 1985-86; psychotherapist, clin. coord. dept. medicine Temple U., Phila., 1985-88; pvt. practice clin. psychologist Lake Worth and Sebastian, Fla., 1989—; lectr. Temple U., Coll. Edn., Phila., 1983-86; adj. prof. Fla. Atlantic U., Boca Raton, 1990—; cons. Goodwill Industries, Inc., West Palm Beach, Fla., 1995—, River Sch., Sebastian, 1995—; founder, pres. Ctr. for Sacred Psychology, 1992. County del. Delaware County Crisis Intervention and Suicide Prevention, Media, Pa., 1981-83; chairperson bereavement com. Fla. chpt. NAMES Project AIDS Meml. Quilt, Sebastian, 1997—; bd. dirs. River Fund, Sebastian, 1997—; mem. Coun. Interfaith Call, World Tibet Day Found. Sgt. USMC, 1969-75.

Mem. APA, Nat. Acad. Neuropsychology, Fla. Psychol. Assn., Ctr. for Jungian Studies SE Fla, Inc. (v.p. 1990-96). Democrat. Avocations: T'ai Chi Ch'uan, Tae Kwon Do, camping, white water rafting. E-mail: sacredp-syc@aol.com. Fax: 561-388-3323. Office: PO Box 1365 Roseland FL 32957-1365

CANTILLI, EDMUND JOSEPH, safety engineering educator, translator, writer, consultant; b. Yonkers, N.Y., Feb. 12, 1927; s. Ettore and Maria (deRubeis) C.; m. Nella Franco, May 15, 1948; children: Robert, John, Teresa. AB, Columbia U., 1954, BS, 1955; cert., Yale Bur. Hwy. Traffic, 1957; PhD in Transp. Planning and Engrng., Poly. Inst. Bklyn., 1972; postgrad. in urban planning and pub. safety, NYU, 1968-71. Registered profl. engr., N.Y., N.J., Calif.; profl. planner, N.J.; bd. cert. safe ty profl. (BCSP); bd. cert. planner (AICP); bd. cert. forensic engr. (BCFE). Supervising engr. safety rsch. and studies Port Authority of N.Y. & N.J., 1955-69; prof. transp. and safety engrng. Poly. U., N.Y.C., 1969-90; pres. Urbitran Assocs., 1973-81; exec. dir., chmn. bd. Internat. Inst. for Safety Trans., Inc., 1977—; pres. EJC Safety Assocs., Inc., 1989—; tchr. Italian, algebra, traffic engrng., urban planning, transp. planning, urban and transp. geography, land use planning, aesthetics, environment, indsl., traffic and transp. safety engrng., human factors engrng., ethics for engrs.; cons. transp. and traffic safety engrng., community planning, traffic engrng., transp. planning, accident reconstrn., environ. impacts, 1969—; vis. prof. transp. safety engrng. Inst. Superior Técnico, Lisbon, 1987-97; advisor to doctorate students Poly. U., CUNY, 1969-94, Politecnico di Milano, U. Trieste, Italy, 1980—; consulting forensic engr., accident reconstructionist, expert witness transp. accident litigation including hwy. traffic, railroad, rail rapid transit, pedestrian accidents, 1969—. Translator (Italian-English autobiog. Joseph Tusiani): The Difficult Word; The New Word; The Ancient Word, 1988; author: Programming Environmental Improvements in Public Transportation, 1974, Transportation and the Disadvantaged, 1974, Transportation System Safety, 1979; editor: Transportation and Aging, 1971, Pedestrian Planning and Design, 1971; editor, contbr.: Traffic Engineering Theory and Control, 1973; editor and calligrapher There Is No Death That Is Not Ennobled by So Great A Cause, 1976; contbr. over 200 articles to profl. jours. and trade jours.; developer daylight running lights, methods of severity evaluation of accidents, identification, priority-setting and treatment of roadside hazards, transp. system safety methodology; expert systems for improving traffic safety; introduced diagrammatic traffic signs, collision energy-absorption devices. With U.S. Army, 1945-49, 50-51. Fellow ASCE, Inst. Transp. Engrs., Nat. Acad. Forensic Engrs.; mem. NSPE, Am. Planning Assn. (charter), Am. Inst. Cert. Planners (cert.), Am. Soc. Safety Engrs., N.Y. Acad. Scis., Nat. Assn. Profl. Accident Reconstrn. Specialists, Internat. Assn. for Accidents and Traffic Medicine, Human Factors Soc., N.Y. Acad. Scis., System Safety Soc., Sigma Xi. Home: 134 Euston Rd West Hempstead NY 11552-1024 Office: PO Box 63 Franklin Square NY 11010-0063

CANTLEY, MARK FLETT, biotechnology adviser; b. Belfast, No. Ireland, Dec. 30, 1941; s. Benjamin G. and Margaret N. (Flett) C.; m. Elizabeth K. Kirby, Aug. 24, 1963; children: Kathryn, Heather, James, Rosemary, Elizabeth-Julia, Patrick, Ross. BA in Math. with honors, Cambridge (Eng.) U., 1963; diploma in ops. rsch., MS in Econs., U. London, 1965; cert. diploma in acctg. and fin., 1973. Grad. apprentice, sr. sci. officer Brit. Iron and Steel Rsch. Assn., Eng., 1963-67; sr. lectr. ops. rsch. U. Lancaster, Eng., 1967-77; strategic planning advisor Scienta S.A., Luxembourg, 1970-77; fellow Internat. Inst. for Applied Systems Analysis, Laxenburg, Austria, 1978-79; mem. Forecasting and Assessment in Sci. and Tech. team Commn. of European Coms., Brussels, 1979-83, head Concertation Unit for Biotech. in Europe, 1984-92; head biotech. unit Orgn. for Econ. Coop. and Devel., Paris, 1992-98; adviser life scis. directorate gen. rsch. European Commn., 1999—. Contbr. numerous papers to profl. jours. County councillor Lancashire (Eng.) County Coun., 1974-78. Recipient Bronze medal Operational Rsch. Soc., 1969. Avocations: history of ideas, studying societies. Home: 131 rue Verbist, B-1030 Brussels Belgium Office: European Commn SDM, 200 rue de la Loi, B-1049 Brussels Belgium

CANTONI, LOUIS JOSEPH, psychologist, poet, sculptor; b. Detroit, May 22, 1919; s. Pietro and Stella (Puricelli) C.; m. Lucile Eudora Moses, Aug. 7, 1948; children: Christopher Louis, Sylvia Therese. AB, U. Calif., Berkeley, 1946; MSW, U. Mich., 1949, PhD, 1953. Personnel mgr. Johns-Manville Corp., Pittsburg, Calif., 1944-46; social caseworker Detroit Dept. Pub. Welfare, 1946-49; counselor Mich. Div. Vocat. Rehab., Detroit, 1949-50; conf. leader, tchr. psychology, coordinator family and community relations program Gen. Motors Inst., Flint, Mich., 1951-56; from assoc. prof. to prof., dir. rehab. counseling Wayne State U., Detroit, 1956-89. Author books and monographs including: The 1939-1943 Flint Michigan Guidance Demonstration, 1953, Marriage and Community Relations, 1954; (with Mrs. Cantoni) Counseling Your Friends, 1961, Supervised Practice in Rehabilitation Counseling, 1978, Writings of Louis J. Cantoni, 1981, Essays, Theses and Projects in Rehabilitation Counseling, 1989; (with Mrs. Cantoni) Theoretical Underpinnings of Practice in Family Service Agencies, 1990; (poetry) With Joy I Called to You, 1969, Gradually The Dreams Change, 1979, A Festival of Lanternes, 1994; editor: Placement of the Handicapped in Competitive Employment, 1957; poetry editor Cathedral Digest, 1973-75; co-editor: Preparation of Vocational Rehabilitation Counselors Through Field Instruction, 1958; prin. editor: (poetry) Golden Song Anthology, 1985; editor jours. Mich. Rehab. Assn. Digest, 1961-63, Grad. Comment, 1963-64; bibliography, books and reprints placed in Reuther Libr. Archives Wayne State U., Detroit; contbr. articles, revs., poems, comments, abstracts, and illustrations to jours. Judge Mich. regional and nat. essay and poetry contests, 1965-77; bd. dirs. Mich. Rehab. Assn., 1962-64, 78-79, Mich. Rehab. Counseling Assn., 1985-87. 2d lt. AUS, 1942-44. Recipient award for leadership and service Mich. Rehab. Assn., 1964, Mich. Rehab. Counseling Assn., 1985, 87, 88, Outstanding Service award Mich. State Bd. Edn., 1989, South and West ann. poetry award, 1970, Meritorious Service award Wayne State U., 1971, 81, 86, 87, 89, Excellence in Poetry award Pig's Wing Press, 1997, Edizioni Universum Author of the Yr. award, 2000. Fellow AAAS; mem. AAUP, APA, Coun. of Rehab. Counselor Educators (sec. 1957-58, chmn. 1965-66), Nat. Rehab. Assn., Nat. Congress of Orgns. of the Physically Handicapped, Nat. Assn. of the Physically Handicapped, Nat. Alliance for the Mentally Ill, Am. Inst. Econ. Rsch., Poetry Soc. Am., Mich. Rehab. Assn. (pres. 1963-64), Detroit Rehab. Assn. (pres. 1958), Mich. Counseling Assn., Mich. Career Devel. Assn., Mich. Assn. for Humanistic Edn. and Devel. (Outstanding Svc. award 1997), Mich. Employment Counselors Assn., Mich. Assn. for Marriage and Family Counseling, Internat. Inst. Met. Detroit, World Poetry Soc. (Edwin A. Falkowski Meml. award 1990), Acad. Am. Poets, Detroit Inst. Arts, Friends of Detroit Pub. Libr., Friends of Marshall M. Fredericks Sculpture Gallery, Soc. for Study of Midwestern Lit., U.S. Hist. Soc., Italic Studies Inst., USN Meml., Internat. Sculpture Ctr., Nat. Sculpture Soc., Sculptors Guild Mich., Lladro Collectors Soc., Birmingham-Bloomfield Art Assn., Psychology and the Arts, Poetry Soc. Mich. (Outstanding Svc. award 1984), Detroit Film Soc., Detroit Zool. Soc., Poetry Resource Ctr. Mich., Univ. Club, Scarab Club (Detroit), Phi Kappa Phi, Phi Delta Kappa. Democrat. Episcopalian. Achievements include research in theory and practice of counseling and psychotherapy, psychosocial aspects of disabling conditions, therapeutic and vocational counseling with disabled persons, workplace accommodation for the disabled, vocational rehabilitation of the severely disabled. Home: 2591 Woodstock Dr Detroit MI 48203-1062

CANTOR, ALAN BRUCE, management consultant, computer software engineer; b. Mt. Vernon, N.Y., Apr. 30, 1948; s. Hoaward and Muriel Anita C.; m. Judith Jolanda Szrka, Mar. 1, 1987; 1 child, Alec Brandon. BS in Social Scis., Cornell U., 1970; MBA, U. Pa., 1973. Mgmt. cons. M & M Risks Mgmt. Svcs., N.Y.C., 1974-78; nat. svcs. officer spl. projects divsn. Marsh & McLennan Risk Mgmt. Svcs., L.A., 1980-81; sr. v.p. sr. cons. prin. Warren, Mc Veigh & Griffin, Inc., 1981-82; founder, pres. Cantor & Co., 1982—; co-mgr. Air Travel Rsch. Group, N.Y.C., 1977-79; instr. risk mgmt. program Am. Mgmt. Assn.,; lectr. Risk and Inst. Mgmt. Soc. Conf., 1975-87; seminars How to Use Spreadsheets in Risk Mgmt., 1986-89, How to Use Computers in Risk Mgmt., 1989-93. Copyright airline industry model; contbr. articles to profl. jours.; creator, developer, copyright RISKMAP risk mgmt. software products, 1982-2000, Exposure Base Mgmt. System (EBMS), 1985, 86, patient care monitoring system, 1985-92, Med. Quality Mgmt. Systems Plus, 1991-2000, MQMS Plus Windows version, 1997-00, COLTS corp. overal legal tracking system, 1984, 86, 87, 89, 90, 91, 93, 94, RISKMAP ins. schedules system, 1989. Cons., vol. Urban Cons. Group, N.Y.C.; elder Beverly Hills Presbyn. Ch., 1991—; co-project dir. East European Orphans Toy Ministry, 1999—. Mem. Cornell Alumni Assn. N.Y.C. (bd. govs., program chmn.), Cornell Alumni Assn. So. Calif., Wharton Bus. Sch. Club (N.Y.C., chmn., mem. adv. com. L.A.), L.A. Athletic. Office: Cantor & Co 9100 Wilshire Blvd Beverly Hills CA 90212-3415

CANTOR, BERNARD JACK, patent lawyer; b. N.Y.C., Aug. 18, 1927; s. Alexander J. and Tillie (Henzeloff) C.; m. Judith L. Levin, Mar. 25, 1951; children—Glenn H., Cliff A., James E., Ellen B., Mark E. B. Mech. Engrng., Cornell, 1949; J.D., George Washington U., Washington, 1952. Bar: D.C. 1952, U.S. Patent Office 1952, Mich. 1953; registered patent atty. U.S., Can. Examiner U.S. Patent Office, Washington, 1949-52; pvt. practice Detroit, 1952-88; ptnr. firm Harness, Dickey & Pierce, Troy, Mich., 1988—; lectr. in field. Contbr. articles on patent law to profl. jours. Mem. exec. council, legal officer Detroit Area Boy Scouts Am., 1972—. Served with U.S. Army, 1944-46. Recipient Ellsworth award patent law George Washington U., 1952, Shofar award Boy Scouts Am., 1975, Silver Beaver award, 1975, Disting. Eagle award, 1985. Fellow Mich. State Bar Found.; mem. ABA, Mich. Bar Assn. (dir. econs. sect., arbitrator State of Mich. grievance com.), Detroit Bar Assn., Oakland Bar Assn., Mich. Patent Law Assn., Am. Arbitration Assn. (arbitrator), Cornell Engrng. Soc., Am. Technion Soc. (bd. dirs. Detroit 1970—), Pi Tau Sigma, Phi Delta Phi, Beta Sigma Rho. Home: 5685 Forman Dr Bloomfield Hills MI 48301-1154 Office: Harness Dickey & Pierce 5445 Corporate Dr Troy MI 48098-2617

CANTOR, BRIAN, engineering educator; b. Manchester, Eng., Jan. 11, 1948; s. Oliver Horace and Gertrude Mary (Thompson) C.; m. Margaret Elaine Parkes Pretty (div. 1979); Matthew, Oliver Charles; m. Anne Catherine Sharry (dec. Jan. 1993). BA, Christ's Coll., Cambridge, Eng., 1968, PhD, 1972. Chartered engr. Rsch. fellow, lectr. Sch. Engrng. Sussex U., Brighton, Eng., 1972-81; lectr., reader dept. materials Oxford U., Eng., 1981—, prof., 1995—, head dept materials, 1995-2000, head divsn. math. and phys. scis., 2000—; indsl. fellow GE, 1982; sr. rsch. fellow Jesus Coll., Oxford, 1986-95; professorial fellow St. Catherine's Coll., Oxford, 1995—; head divsn. Math. and Phys. Sci. Oxford U., Eng., 2000—; cons. IOP Press, Bristol, Eng., 1984—, Alcan, Banbury, Eng., 1988-93, Rolls-Royce, Derby, Eng., 1996—. Editor: Rapidly Quenched Metals III, 1978; co-editor: A Tribute to J.W. Christian, 1992; co-author: Stability of Microstructure in Metallic Systems, 1997; editor Progess in Materials Sci., Elsevier, Eng., 1988—; co-editor Jour. Materials Synthesis and Processing, 1994—. Named hon. prof. Northeastern U., Shenyang, China, 1996. Fellow Royal Acad. Materials, Inst. Materials (Rosenhain medal 1993), Inst. Physics Royal Microscopical Soc.; mem. Am. Inst. Metall. Engrs., Materials Rsch. Soc. India (hon.), Acad. Europaea (mem. coun. Oxford U.). Avocations: mountain climbing, guitar. Office: Oxford U Div Math/Phys Scis, 9 Parks Rd, Oxford OX1 3PH, England

CANTOR, HAL, biomedical engineer, research scientist; b. Farmington Hills, Mich., Aug. 14, 1963. BSChemE, U. Mich., 1984, MS in Biol. Scis. and Biomed. Engrng., 1986, PhD in Biomed. Engrng., 1994. Dept. head Cybernet Sys. Corp., Ann Arbor, Mich., 1996-97; pres. Advanced Sensor Techs., Inc., Farmington Hills, Mich., 1997—. Grantee Small Bus. Innovation Rsch., Nat. Inst. Health, Nat. Inst. Neural Disorders and Stroke, Defense Advanced Rsch. Projects Agy.; recipient New Investigator award Soc. Study Reproduction, 1993. E-mail: hal@bizserve.com. Fax: 248-539-0869. Office: Advanced Sensor Techs Inc 27970 Orchard Lake Rd Farmington Hills MI 48334-3767

CANTOR, HERBERT I., lawyer; b. N.Y.C., Dec. 10, 1935; s. David and Ethel C.; m. Lynn Hardie, July 8, 1972; children: David, Susan. BA in Chemistry, NYU, 1965; JD, Cath. U. Am., 1970. Bar: Md. 1970, U.S. Dist. Ct. Md. 1970, D.C. 1971, U.S. Dist. Ct. D.C. 1971, U.S. Ct. Appeals (5th, D.C. and fed. cirs.) 1971, U.S. Supreme Ct. 1974, U.S. Ct. Appeals (4th cir.) 1981, U.S. Ct. Claims 1987. Patent examiner U.S. Patent Office, Washington, 1965-67; agt. Jacobi, Davidson & Jacobi, Washington, 1967-68; pvt. practice Washington, 1968-70; with Kraft, Cantor & Singer, Cantor & Lessler, Washington, 1971-85; ptnr. Cantor & Lessler, Washington, 1982-85, Wegner, Cantor, Mueller & Player, Washington, 1985-94; Evenson, McKeown, Edwards & Lenahan, Washington, 1994—; adj. prof. Law Ctr. Georgetown Univ., Washington, 1988-89. Assoc. editor Cath. U. Law Rev., 1969-70. Mem. Am. Chem. Soc., Fedn. Internat. des Conseils Propriete Industrielle, Am. Intellectual Property Assn. Office: Evenson McKeown Edwards & Lenahan 1200 G St NW Ste 700 Washington DC 20005-6703

CANTOR-GRAAE, ELIZABETH REVA, psychologist; b. N.Y.C., Oct. 17, 1945; arrived in Sweden, 1972; d. Louis and Ida Diane (Banks) C.; m. Klavs Graae, Nov. 2, 1973 (div. 1981); 1 child, Nikolai. BA cum laude, Harvard U., 1967; MA, U. Calif., Berkeley, 1968, U. Lund, Sweden, 1988; PhD, U. Lund, Sweden, 1995. Prof. ceramic artist Sweden, 1979-87; lab. tech. U. Lund (Sweden), 1989-91, rsch. psychologist dept. psychiatry, 1991-96, rsch. psychologist dept. cmty. medicine, 1997—, assoc. prof. psychiatric epidemiology Faculty of Medicine, 1999—. Author: Neurodevelopmental Aspects of Schizophrenia, 1995; contbr. articles to profl. jours. Mem. Internat. Soc. Neuroimaging Psychiatry. Avocations: painting, creative writing, Japanese ceramics. Home: Iliongrand M:210, 22471 Lund Sweden Office: U Hosp MAS Dept Cmty Medicine, ing 59, 20502 Malmö Sweden

CANTRELL, CAROL KAY, English and Latin educator; b. Dallas, Sept. 12, 1938; d. Walter A. Gatlin and Peggy Joan Harris Gatlin Elrod; children: James Lee, Gary Don, Calvin Dean, Sherry Kay. BA, Baylor U., 1961; MA, U. Tex., Arlington, 1985. Tchr. English and Latin Irving (Tex.) H.S., 1961-62; tchr. English and Latin Grand Prairie (Tex.) H.S., 1963-67, 73-99, part-time tchr., 1999—; tchr. English Jackson Jr. H.S., Grand Prairie, 1968-69; proof reader Ct. Reporters, Arlington, 1990-99. Mem. Grand Prairie Fedn. Tchrs., Order Ea. Star, Order of Rainbow Girls (advisor 1988-89). Democrat. Baptist. Avocations: reading, movies, geneology, travel. Home: 721 Blueberry Ln Grand Prairie TX 75052-5007 Office: Grand Prairie High Sch 101 Highschool Dr Grand Prairie TX 75050-3798

CANTRELL, SHARRON CAULK, principal; b. Columbia, Tenn., Oct. 2, 1947; d. Tom English and Beulah (Goodin) Caulk; m. William Terry Cantrell, Mar. 18, 1989; 1 child, Jordan; children from previous marriage: Christopher, George English, Steffenee Copley. BA, George Peabody Coll. Tchrs., 1970; MS, Vanderbilt U., 1980; EdS, Mid. Tenn. State U., 1986. Tchr. Ft. Campbell Jr. High Sch., Columbia, Tenn., 1970-71, Whitthorne Jr. High Sch., Columbia, Tenn., 1977-86, Spring Hill (Tenn.) High Sch., 1966—. Mem. NEA, AAUW (pres. Tenn. divsn. 1983-85), Maury County Edn. Assn. (pres. 1983-84), Tenn. Edn. Assn., Assn. Preservation Tenn. Antiquities, Maury Alliance, Friends of Children's Hosp., Rotary (bd. dirs.), Phi Delta Kappa. Mem. Ch. of Christ. Home: 5299 Main St Spring Hill TN 37174-2495 Office: Spring Hill High Sch 1 Raider Ln Columbia TN 38401-7346

CANTRIL, ALBERT H(ADLEY), public opinion analyst; b. N.Y.C.; s. Hadley and Mavis Katherine Cantril; m. Susan Bradford Davis. AB, Dartmouth Coll., 1962; PhD, MIT, 1966. Asst. to Bill Moyers The White House, Washington, 1965-67; cons. to dir. Bur. of the Budget, Washington, 1967; spl. asst. to asst. sec. East Asian and Pacific affairs Dept. of State, Washington, 1967-69; exec. sec., com. on def. social sci. rsch. Nat. Acad. Scis., Washington, 1969-70; cons. Dem. Nat. Com. and candidates, Washington, 1971-74; dir. rsch. Commn. Op. of U.S. Senate, Washington, 1975-76; pres. Nat. Coun. on Pub. Polls, Washington, 1976-81, Bur. Social Sci. Rsch., Inc., Washington, 1981-86; fellow and rsch. fellow Inst. of Politics Harvard U., Cambridge, Mass., 1986-88; cons. ABA, 1989-96; cons. pub. opinion rsch. with Susan Davis Cantril ACLU Found., 1991-93, Woodrow Wilson Internat. Ctr. for Scholars, 1996-2000; mem. editl. adv. bd. Pub. Opinion Quar., 1985-89; trustee Nat. Coun. on Pub. Polls, 1982-94; adj. prof. internat. politics Fletcher Sch. Law and Diplomacy, Tufts U., Medford, Mass., 1991-94. Author: The Opinion Connection: Polling, Politics and the Press, 1991, Agenda for Access: The American People and Civil Justice, 1996; co-author: Hopes and Fears of the American People, 1971, Polls: Their Use and Misuse in Politics, 1972, 2d edit., 1980, Live and Let Live: American Public Opinion about Privacy at Home and at Work, 1994, Reading Mixed Signals: Ambivalence in American Public Opinion About Government, 1999; editor: Polling on the Issues, 1980, Psychology, Humanism and Scientific Inquiry: The Selected Essays of Hadley Cantril, 1988. Recipient Mecklin award Dartmouth Coll., 1962. Mem. Am. Assn. Pub. Opinion Rsch. Avocations: jazz, tennis.

CANTWELL, CHRISTOPHER WILLIAM, artist; b. Atwater, Calif., Dec. 24, 1960; s. Donald Byron and Ann Louise Cantwell; m. Susan Rebecca Moore, Sept. 19, 1982 (div. 1997); children: Claire Elyse Moore, Katie Lynn Moore. Owner, artist Christopher W. Cantwell Woodworks, Modesto, Calif., 1979-82, Oakhurst, Calif., 1982—; cons. Internat. Union for conservation of Natural Resources, Cambridge, Eng., 1991—. Contbr. art book Jewelry Boxes, 1996; exhibited at Del Mano Gallery, 1990, 98, 99, Furniture Soc. Conf., San Francisco, 1998, Del Mano, 1999, Laguna Art Mus., 1999; represented in permanent collections Irving Lipton Collection, White House Ornament Collection. Youth advisor Oakhurst Luth. Ch., 1992-96. Mem. Am. Craft Coun., World Wildlife Fund, Program for Belize, Good Wood Alliance (CITES Liaison 1994—), Box Art Soc. (pres. 1999—). Democrat. Avocations: rock climbing, skiing, fishing. Home and Office: PO Box 1736 Oakhurst CA 93644-1736

CAO, BIAO, engineering researcher; b. Yuanjiang, Hunan, China, Oct. 1, 1963; s. Zhengcai and Huifeng (Fang) C.; m. Ping Hou, Feb. 1990; 1 child, Yi. Bachelor, Beijing U. Sci. and Tech., 1983, Master, 1986; PhD, Ctrl. South U. Tech., Changsha, China, 1998. Lectr. Ctrl. South U. Tech., 1986-98; sr. engr. Metallic Materials Inspection Ctr., Guangdong Entry-Exit Inspection and Quarantine Bur., Guangzhou, China, 1998—. Avocations: bridge, Weiqi, tennis. Office: Metallic Materials Insp Ctr, 66 Huacheng Ave Zhujiang Xincheng, 510623 Guangzhou Guangdong, China

CAO, BISONG, physics educator, researcher; b. Taixing City, China, Oct. 26, 1946; s. Deming and Xiaozhen (Hu) C.; m. Xiuzhi Yan, Jan. 22, 1972; 1 child, Yan. Diploma, Tsinghua U., Beijing, 1970, MSc, 1981; PhD, Tokyo U., 1989. Asst. Tsinghua U., Beijing, 1970-78, lectr., 1981-85, assoc. prof., 1990-94, prof., 1995—; chmn. 10th Internat. Conf. on Positron Annihilation, Beijing, 1994. Author: Application of Nuclear Technology on Material Science, 1986; editor procs.; contbr. articles to profl. jours.; patentee temperature controlling apparatus. Recipient Progress in Sci. and Tech. award State Edn. Commn. China, 1989, 94. Mem. Chinese Soc. Electronics (sr.), N.Y. Acad. Sci. Office: Tsinghua U Dept Physics, 100084 Beijing China

CAO, CHANG QING, physiologist, researcher; b. Jiaozhou, Shandong, China, May 9, 1953; s. Gui Xiang and Xi Qin (Chen) C.; m. Xiu Fen, Dec. 24, 1980; 1 child, Rui. B Vet. Sci., Changchun (China) Vet. Coll., 1978, MSc, 1982; PhD, China Acad. Chinese Medicine, Beijing, 1990. Med. diplomate. Rsch. asst. Vet. Coll., Changchun, 1981-83, lectr., 1984-90; vis. rsch. fellow U. Edinburgh, Scotland, 1991-92; rsch. fellow U. Bristol, Eng., 1992-95, sr. rsch. fellow, 1996—; rsch. fellow U. Coll. London, 1996; sr. rsch. scientist AstraZeneca R&D, Montreal, 1997—. Author: Physiology of Domestic Animal, 1986 (Chinese 3d prize 1987). Recipient internat. fellowship Wellcome Trust, London, 1990. Mem. Internat. Brain Rsch. Orgn. (travel grant 1991), N.Y. Acad. Sci., Brit. Pharmacological Soc., Soc. for Neurosic., Internat. Assn. of Pain. Avocations: collecting, swimming, travel, walking. Office: AstraZeneca R&D Montreal, 7171 Frederick-Banting, Saint Laurent, PQ Canada H4S 1Z9

CAO, FU TIAN, physicist, educator; b. Jilin, China, July 24, 1924; s. An Kui and Cao (Hou) C.; m. Fung Pu Jia, Dec. 20, 1943 (dec. 1955); children: Wei Guang, Hang; m. Shu Lin Yang, Aug. 2, 1956; children: Hua, Xiao Hong. Student, Jianguo U., Changchun, China, 1945; Degree in Physics, Changchun U., 1948. Vis. tchr. Tsinghua U., Beijing, 1954-55; elec. engrng. lectr. Northeastern U., Shenyang, China, 1956-73; assoc. prof. Tianjin Normal U., 1979-88, prof. physics, 1988-90, 92—; vis. scholar Waseda U., Tokyo, 1990-92. Contbr. articles to profl. jours. Home: Hexiqu Wujiayo St, Tianjin 300074, China Office: Tianjin Normal Univ, Balitai, Tianjin 300074, China

CAO, HEPING, biologist, researcher; b. Pingxiang, Jiangxi, China, Feb. 15, 1964; came to U.S., 1991; s. Shengwen Cao and Shuzhen Huang; m. Rin Lin, June 28, 1991; 1 child, Nancy L. BS in Agr., Jiangxi Agrl. U, Nanchang, China, 1984; MS in Agr., Southwestern Agrl. U., 1987; PhD, Pa. State U., 1994. Instr. physiology and biochemistry of plant steriod hormone Jiangxi Agrl. U., 1987-88; grad. asst. molecular biology plant devel. rsch. Chinese Acad. Scis., Beijing, 1988-91; grad. asst. physiology, genetics, biochemistry rsch. Pa. State U., Univ. Pk., 1991-94; vis. rsch. assoc. biochemistry and molecular biology Mich. State U., East Lansing, 1994-95; postdoc. rsch. assoc. biochemistry and molecular biology Tex. Tech U., Lubbock, 1996-97, Iowa State U., Ames, 1997-2000; postdoctoral fellow Nat. Inst. Environ. Health Scis., 2000—. Contbr. articles to Jour. Protein Chemistry, Jour. Plant Physiology, Plant Physiology, Physiologia Plantarum, Nature Jour., Arch. Biochem. Biophy., Jour. Plant Growth Regulation, Plant Growth Regulation, Chinese Sci. Bull. Recipient Creative Student award Jiangxi Province, 1986, Hon. Mention award Pa. State U., 1993, 94, Wilton R. Earle award Soc. for In Vitro Biology,1994. Mem. AAAS, Am. Soc. Plant Physiologists. Achievements include discovery of a critical factor important in crop yield; designed cloning method for a gene critical to crop protein quality; rsch. in expressing a gene important for resisting insects by crops and a gene for crop yield and quality. E-mail: cao2@niehs.nih.gov. Home: 5803 Tattersall Dr Apt 21 Durham NC 27713-9024 Office: Nat Inst Environ Health Sci Lab Signal Transduction Research Triangle Park NC 27709

CAO, JIA-DING, mathematics educator; b. Shanghai, Republic of China, Sept. 14, 1940; s. Cao An Shi and Shen Xi Fen. Grad. in dept. math., Fudan U., Shanghai, 1962. Asst. dept. math. Fudan U., Shanghai, 1962-85, lectr. dept. math., 1985-88, prof. dept. math., 1988—; participant Tex. Conf., 1989, Memphis Conf., 1991, three Indsl. Applied Math. Soc. Confs., 1994-95; advisor Hong Kong Acad. Scis. Reviewer editl. Office Math. Revs., U.S., 1991—, editl. Office Math Abstracts, Germany, 1996—; contbr. articles and abstracts to profl. jours. Mem. Am. Math. Soc., Am. Planetary Soc., N.Y. Acad. Scis. Home: Feng Yang Rd 376 No 13, Shanghai 200003, China Office: Fudan U Dept Math, Han Dan Rd No 220, Shanghai 200433, China

CAO, JIE-YUAN, electronics engineer, researcher; b. Shanghai, July 24, 1944; s. Zong-Quan and Pei-Li (Zheng) C.; m. Ai-Yu Lu, Dec. 8, 1973; 1 child, Wei-Wei. BS, Beijing Poly. Inst., 1966; MSc, Shanghai Jiao Tong U., 1981. Engr. Microwave Tech. Rsch. Inst., Du Yuan, 1966-78; lectr. Shanghai Jiao Tong U., 1981-87, rsch. fellow, 1990-95; vis. scientist Internat. Ctr. Theoretical Physics, Trieste, Italy, 1988-89; sr. scientist EXB Tech. Inc., Sunnyvale, Calif., 1995-97, Kaifa Tech. Inc., Sunnyvale, 1998-99, Oplink Comm. Inc., San Jose, 1999—. Co-author: Optical Fiber Transmission Technology, 1988; patentee in field. Mem. IEEE, Chinese Comm. Soc., Internat. Soc. Optical Engrng., Optical Soc. Am. Achievements include work on a novel manufacturing method for plastic optical fiber star couplers. Avocations: photography, stamp collecting. Home: 3076 San Juan Ave Santa Clara CA 95051-1640 Office: Oplink Comm Inc 3475 N 1st St San Jose CA 95134-1801

CAO, JIN DE, mathematician; b. Anhui, China, Nov. 8, 1963; s. Shang Ping and Shan Yun (Zhou) C.; m. Qiong Li, Sept. 8, 1988; 1 child, Yang. BS, Anhui Normal U., Wuhu, China, 1986; MS, Yunnan U., Kunming, China, 1989; PhD, Sichuan U., Chengdu, China, 1998. From lectr. to assoc. prof. Yunnan U., Kunming, 1992-96, prof., 1996—. Contbr. articles to profl. jours. Recipient 1st prize sci. and tech. achievements, Yunnan Edn. Commn., 1995, 2d prize Nat. Sci. award Yunnan Province Govt., 1996-97, 3d prize Nat. Sci. award Yunnan Province Govt., 1999. Mem. IEEE, Chinese Math. Soc. Office: Yunnan Univ, Adult Edn Coll, 650091 Kunming China also: SE U, Dept Applied Math, 210096 Nanjing China

CAO, JINAN, polymer scientist; b. Changzhou, China, Oct. 18, 1955; s. Cangxian and Qiaozhen (Sun) C.; m. Feiyi Pang (div.); 1 child, George S. B of Engring., China Textile U., Shanghai, China, 1982; postgrad., Dailian Inst. Fgn. Langs., 1982; M of Engring., Tokyo Inst. Tech., 1985, PhD, 1988. Mechanic Changzhou (China) Factory of Packaging Materials, 1973-78; rsch. fellow Bio-Giken Inc., Tokyo, 1988-89, U. Queensland, Brisbane, Australia, 1989-90; rsch. scientist divsn. coal and energy tech. Com-

monwealth Sci. and Indsl. Rsch. Orgn., Sydney, Australia, 1990-92; sr. rsch. scientist Commonwealth Sci. and Indsl. Rsch. Orgn., Geelong, Australia, 1992—. Author, inventor in field. Recipient Platinum record for exceptional performance, 20th Century Achievement award and Man of Yr. medal Am. Biog. Inst., 1996; life fellow Internat. Biog. Assn., fellow Am. Biog. Assn. Mem. N.Y. Acad. Scis., Internat. Confedn. for Thermal Analysis and Calorimetry (Australian rep.), Australian X-Ray Analytical Assn. (sec. Victoria branch), Australasian Hair and Wool Rsch. Soc. Avocations: table tennis, swimming, go-chess, movie.

CAO, L. CHARLIE, structural engineer, consultant; b. Jiangsu, Peoples Republic of China, 1959. BS, S.E. U., Nanjing, China, 1982, MS, 1985; PhD, U. Colo., 1996. Registered profl. engr., Calif., Colo., Wash. Contbr. articles to profl. jours. including Jour. Structural Engring. Recipient Sci. and Tech. Hon. award China State Shipbuilding Co., 1990, medal of excellence, China State Commn. Engring. Software Appraisal, 1988. Mem. ASCE (Arthur M. Wellington prize 1997), S.E. of Structural Engrs. Assn. of Calif.

CAO, TONG, botanist, educator; b. Shanghai, China, Jan. 22, 1946; s. Youque Cao and Shizhao Lu; m. Chengying Yan, Apr. 1948; children: Hai, Yang. BS, Fudan U., 1968. Engr. Shenyang Biscuits Factory, China, 1968-78; rsch. assoc. Inst. Forestry & Soil Sci. Academia Sinica, Shenyang, China, 1978-84; vis. scholar dept. botany U. Alberta, Edmonton, Can., 1984-86; from assoc. prof. to prof. Inst. Applied Ecology Academia Sinica, Shenyang, 1986—. Editor: Bryoflora of China, vol. 1, 1994, vol. 2, 1996, Bryoflora of Xizang, 1985; contbr. articles to profl. jours. Mem. Chinese Acad. Scis. Office: Inst Applied Ecol Acad Sin, #72 Wunhua St, 110015 Shenyang China

CAO, WENJI, chemist; b. Dali, ShaanXi, China, Dec. 11, 1959. BS, Northwestern U., Xi'an, China, 1978; PhD, U. Utah, 1998. Chem. engr. Petrochemical Corp. China, Beijing, 1986-92; sr. analytical chemist Huntsman Polymers Corp., Odessa, Tex., 1998—. Author: Studies on Polymer Separation, Characterization and Universal Calibration by ThFFF, 1999; contbr. articles to profl. jours. Mem. Am. Chem. Soc., N.Y. Acad. Scis. Fax: 915-640-8440. Office: Huntsman Polymers Corp 2400 S Grandview Odessa TX 79766

CAO, XINMIN, molecular biologist; b. Lanzhou, Gansu Prov, China, Feb. 2, 1949; d. Zhi-Jie and Jing-Quan (Liang) Cao; m. Jianlin Fu, Dec. 24, 1975; 1 child, Huali. BS, Lanzhou U., 1982; MS, Tulane U., New Orleans, 1984; PhD, U. Chgo., 1989. Technician Jing Yuan Coal Miner's Hosp., Jing Yuan County, China, 1971-74; technician of chem. analysis Lanzhou Pharmacy, 1974-78; grad. rsch. asst. Tulane U., New Orleans, 1982-84, U. Chgo., 1984-89; postdoctoral fellow Howard Hughes Med. Inst., Chgo., 1989-90; rsch. fellow Nat. U. of Singapore, 1990-93, sr. scientist, prin. investigator, 1993-2000, assoc. prof., 2000—. Contbr. articles to profl. jours. Mem. Asia-Pacific Internat. Molecular Biology Network, Soc. of Chinese Bioscientists in Am. Home: Heritage View, Dover Rise 10 # 15-10, Singapore 138680, Singapore Office: Inst Molec and Cell Biology, 30 Medical Dr, Singapore 117609, Singapore

CAO, YE SHI, engineer, researcher; b. Shanghai, China, Aug. 20, 1949; arrived in Singapore, 1994; s. Xi Chong Cao and Shu Yi Yin; m. Xin Hong Liu, Jan. 17, 1980; 1 child, Xiao Yi. Degree, Ea. China U. Sci. & Tech., Shanghai, 1976; M in Engring., Nanjing (China) U. Chem. Tech., 1984; postgrad. diploma, Internat. Inst. Hydraulic and Environ. Engring., Delft, The Netherlands, 1986; PhD, Delft U. Tech., 1994. Process engr. Zhengjiang (China) Coke & Chem. Factory, 1977-80; asst. lectr. Suzhou (China) Inst. Silk and Textile Tech., 1980-82; lectr., dep. head dept. Suzhou Inst. Urban Constrn. and Environ. Protection, 1984-90; rsch. staff Internat. Inst. for Hydraulic and Environ. Engring., Delft, 1990-94; tech. studies mgr. Regional Inst. Environ. Tech., Singapore, 1994-98; sr. indsl. rsch. scientist Environ. Tech. Inst., Singapore, 1998—; cons. The European Commn., Brussels, 1995-97. Author: Aerobic Heterotrophic Biodegradation in Polluted Drain and Sewers, 1994; editor-in-chief: The China Environmental Market, 1996-2000, 1997, (procs.) 1st, 2nd and 3rd Sino-Europe Internat. Environ. Confs., 1995, 97, 99. Mem. Internat. Assn. on Water Quality (referee panel jour. water rsch. 1996—), Am. Soc. Microbiology. Avocations: table tennis, volleyball, reading. E-mail: yscao@eti.org.sg. Fax: 65 7921291. Office: Environ Tech Inst, 18 Nanyang Dr Blk 2 #237, Singapore 637723, Singapore

CAO, ZHENG YUAN, mechanics and optics educator and researcher; b. Taixin, Jaingsu, China, Aug. 8, 1938; s. Chengguan and Zan Zhu (Xu) C.; m. Yu Feng Zhang; children: Qinghong, Qingying. BS, Normal U. of East China, Shanghai, 1961. Educator dept. mechanics Tongji U., Peoples Republic of China. Editor: Photomechanic, 1982, Analysis of Experimental Stress, 1988, Course in Photomechanics, 1997. Recipient award Nat. Edn. Com., 1988, 93, Ni Tianzeng Edn. Found. award, 1995. Mem. Chinese Soc. Mechanics, Chinese Optical Soc. Home: 550/5 Tongji Xin Cun, 200092 Shanghai People's Republic of China Office: Tongji U, 1239 Shiping Rd, 200092 Shanghai People's Republic of China

CAO, ZHIGANG, electrical engineer, educator; b. Shanghai, July 31, 1939; s. Xianjun Cao and Weifang Zhang; m. Zhizhi Xu, Oct. 1, 1967; children: Yahui Cao, Yaxin Cao. BS in Radio Electronics, Tsinghua U., Beijing, 1962. Asst. prof. Tsinghua U., 1962-78, lectr., 1978-83, assoc. prof. electronic engring., 1987-92, prof. electronic engring., 1993—; vis. scholar Stanford (Calif.) U., 1984-86; exec. vice-chmn. tech. program com. Internat. Conf. Comm. Tech., Beijing, 1992—; vice-chmn. acad. com. China Inst. Comm., Beijing, 1995—; dep. dir. State Key Lab. on microwave and digital comm., 1990—, distance learning expert com. Ministry of Edn., 1999—. Author: Principles of Modern Communications, 1992 (1st prize Nat. Excellent engring. Textbook 1996); co-author: Modern Digital Communication Technology, 1987, Digital Processing of Speech Signals, 1995; interpreter: Computer Controlled Testing and Instrumentation, 1985; authored numerous technical papers. Fellow China Inst. Comm.; mem. IEEE (sr.), N.Y. Acad. Scis., China Satellite Comm. Broadcasting and TV User Assn. (bd. dirs. 1994—), Beijing Comm. and Info. Assn. (bd. dirs. 1996—). E-mail: czg-dee@tsinghua.edu.cn. Office: Dept Electronic Engring, Tsinghua U, Beijing 100084, China

CAPALBO, CARMEN, theater director and producer; b. Harrisburg, Pa., Nov. 1, 1925; s. Joseph and Concetta (Riggio) C.; m. Patricia McBride, July 9, 1950 (div. June 1961); children: Carla, Marco. Student, Yale Sch. Drama. prodns. include: dir., co-prodr. (plays) Juno and the Paycock, Shadow and Substance, Dear Brutus, Awake and Sing, The Threepenny Opera, The Potting Shed, A Moon for the Misbegotten, The Cave Dwellers, The Rise and Fall of the City of Mahagonny; dir. (opera) The Good Soldier Schweik, (plays) A Connecticut Yankee, Seidman and Son, The Strangers, The Sign in Sidney Brustein's Window, Enter Solly Gold, Slowly, By Thy Hand Unfurled, The Chosen; also TV prodn. The Power and the Glory; story cons.: Studio One, 1951-52; cons. The Bronx: After the Fires, Conversation with Eddie, 1983; prodn. mgr. Emlyn Williams as Charles Dickens, 1952-53, Jean-Louis Barrault-Madeleine Renaud Co., 1952; dir., prodr., writer 200 radio plays. Served with AUS, 1944-45. Decorated Bronze Star, Purple Heart. Recipient spl. Tony award 1956, Obie award 1956. Mem. League N.Y. Theatres, Dirs. Guild Am., Soc. Stage Dirs. and Choreographers, Dramatists Guild, League OffBroadway Theatres (co-founder 1958, exec. bd. 1958-60), Royal Philatelic Soc. (London). Address: 500 2nd Ave New York NY 10016-8606

CAPALDI, ELIZABETH ANN DEUTSCH, psychological sciences educator; b. N.Y.C., May 13, 1945; d. Frederick and Nettie (Tarasuck) Deutsch; m. Egidio J. Capaldi, Jan. 20, 1968 (div. May 1985). AB, U. Rochester, 1965; PhD, U. Tex., 1969. Asst. prof. dept. psychol. scis. Purdue U., West Lafayette, Ind., 1969-74, assoc. prof., 1974-78, prof., 1979-86, asst. dean Grad. Sch., 1982-86, head dept. psychol. scis., 1983-88, sec.-treas. council of grad. dept. psychology, 1986-88; prof. U. Fla., Gainesville, 1988-2000, provost, v.p. acad. affairs, 1996-99; provost SUNY, Buffalo, 2000—; spl. asst. to pres., U. Fla., 1991-96. Author: Psychology, 1989, 4th edit., 1996; cons. editor Jour. Exptl. Psychology, 1991-96; assoc. editor Psychonomic Bull. Rev., 1993-98; contbr. articles to profl. jours. NIMH grantee, 1984-94, NSF grantee, 1995-98. Fellow AAAS, APA, Am. Psychol. Soc. (mem. governing bd. 1991-96, pres. 1999); mem. Psychonomic Soc. (mem. governing bd. 1992-97), Midwestern Psychol. Assn. (sec.-treas. 1988-90, pres. 1991), Sigma Xi. Home: 6185 Heise Rd Clarence Center NY 14032-9311 Office: SUNY Office of Provost 562 Capen Hall Buffalo NY 14260-1600

CAPÃO-FILIPE, JOÃO ARTUR, ophthalmologist; b. Aveiro, Portugal, June 10, 1961; s. Artur Valente and Maria (Capão) F.; m. Claudia Capão Oliveira, Oct. 16, 1993. MD, Porto (Portugal) Med. Sch., 1985, MSc, 1994. Hosp. asst. S. João Hosp., Porto, 1993—. Contbr. articles to med. jours. Recipient Silva Pinto award, 1989, 94, Ophthalmology Portugal award, 1994. Mem. Am. Acad. Ophthalmology, Internat. Soc. Ocular Trauma, N.Y. Acad. Scis., Am. Coll. Sports Medicine, Am. Soc. Cataract and Refractive Surgery, Internat. Acad. Sports Vision, Assn. Rsch. in Vision and Opthalmology, Portuguese Soc. Opthalmology, Pan-Am. Soc. Opthalmology, Soc. Francaise d' Optalmologie. Mem. Portuguese Popular Party. Home: R Prof Luis de Pina 162, 4150-473 Porto Portugal Office: S João Hosp Porto Med Sc, Dept Ophthalmology, 4200 Porto Portugal

CAPASSO, GIOVANNI, orthopedic surgeon; b. Frattamaggiore, Italy, Jan. 6, 1950; s. Michele Capasso and Lidia Dattilo; m. Ida Vocaturo, July 2, 1981; children: Valerio, Daniele, Lydia. Degree in medicine, Facolta di Medicine, Neaples, Italy, 1974. Intern Clinica Ortopedica, Med. Sch. U. Neaples, 1975-82, rschr., 1982-87, attending orthopedic surgeon, 1987—, tchr. biomechanics/sports medicine, 1978-90, tchr. physiotherapy, 1990—. Author: La Spondilometria, 1992; co-author: Controversies in Orthopedic Sports Medicine, 1998. Mem. N.Y. Acad. Scis. Avocations: photography, history, bricolage, antiques.

CAPDEVILA, MARIANO LAZO, electro-mechanical company executive, industrial engineer; b. Santiago, Chile, Sept. 4, 1938; arrived in Spain, 1968; s. Ramon Ugarte Capdevila and Olga Zegers Lazo; m. Housnia el Idrissi; children: Lucia, Diana, Nancy, Francisco, Jaime, Heba, Mariano, Monserrat, Arturo, Olga. BBA, U. Chile, 1959; MS in Indsl. Engring., State Tech. U., Chile and Oxford U., Eng., 1962; D in Indsl. Engring., Ill. Inst. Tech., 1986; MBA in Mgmt., SUNY, 1986; D in Econs., Oxford U., Eng., 1987. Mgr. fgn. dept. Arica br. Banco Nacional del Trabajo, Chile, 1956-61; mgr. C.M. Dawson, Vanvarte, Chile, 1963-68; dir. Iwer Div. Engring., Barcelona, Spain, 1968-71; del. for Middle East Camer Internat. S.A., Madrid, 1971-73; mgr. for Middle East Echevarria Hnos. Internat., Madrid, 1973-78; vice chmn., comml. mgr. Energy S.A., Madrid, 1978-80; prin. elec. products export co., Madrid, 1981-82; comml. mgr. Middle East area Cobra, S.A., Madrid, 1983-88; chmn. Dr. Mariano Indsl. Consultant Bur., U.A.E., Oman and Egypt, 1988—; cons. in field. Fellow Inst. Profl. Mgrs. U.K. Roman Catholic.

ČÁPEK, VLADISLAV, physicist, educator; b. Prague, Czech Republic, Jan. 7, 1943; s. Karel and Milada (Čerychová) Č.; m. Jana Kyslingerová, Nov. 25, 1972; 1 child, Silvie. MSc, Charles U., Prague, 1965, DSc, 1989; PhD, Acad. Scis., Prague, 1971. Asst. Charles U., 1965-68, sr. asst., 1968-87, sci. coworker, 1987-91, assoc. prof. physics, 1991-94, prof. physics, 1994—. Contbr. over 160 articles to profl. jours. Avocations: music, sport. Home: Lužická 22, CZ 12000 Prague 2, Czech Republic Office: Inst Physics, Charles U Ke Karlovu 5, CZ-12116 Prague 2, Czech Republic

CAPELLA, ALPHONSE, physics researcher; b. Palafrugell, Girona, Spain, May 10, 1936; s. Pelayo and Montserrat (Noguer) C.; m. Maria Rosa Cristia, Dec. 26, 1959; children: Mercedes, Montserrat, Sylvie. Grad. in Physics, U. Barcelona (Spain), 1959; PhD, U. Paris, 1964, DSc, 1963. Stagiaire de recherche Nat. Ctr. Scientific Rsch., France, 1960-61; attaché recherche Nat. Ctr. Scientific Rsch., 1961-69, master rsch., 1969-92; mem. nat. com. Nat. Ctr. Sci. Rsch., France, 1975-80, dir. rsch., 1992; sci. visitor European Ctr. Nuclear Rsch., Switzerland, 1965-67, 75-76; mem. com. sci. Lab. Ecole Normale, France, 1977-78; mem. sci. com. Rencontres de Moriond, France, 1980-85, Quark Matter Conf., France, 1990. Author: Physics Reports, 1994; contbr. 170 articles to profl. jours. Avocations: skiing, sailing, opera. Office: U Paris XI Lab Phys Theorique & Hautes Energies, Batiment 211, 91405 Orsay Cedex, France

CAPELLA, GIOVANNI LUIGI, dermatologist; b. Milan, Italy, Dec. 18, 1963; s. Vittoriano and Wanda Bruna (Fagnani) C. MD, U. Milan, 1988. Vol. asst., resident Inst. of Dermatology, Milan, 1988-97, grantee, 1997-98; pvt. practice Milan, 1998—. Co-author: Orticaria-Angioedema, 1991; translator into Italian: Dermatologie et Vénéréologie, 1990, Dermatologie et Maladies sexuellement transmissibles, 1998; contbr. articles and abstracts to profl. jours. 2d lt. M.C., Italian Army, 1989-90. Mem. AAAS, N.Y. Acad. Sci., European Soc. Dermatol. Rsch., Soc. Italiana di Dermatologia e Venereologia. Avocations: electronic engineering, chess, piano, classical antiquities. Office: Via Sauli 7, 20127 Milan Italy

CAPELLAN, ANGEL, small business executive; b. Zorraquin, Spain, Apr. 10, 1942; s. Sotero Capellan and Damasa Gnozalo; m. Sonia C. Guadalupe, Aug. 27, 1971; children: Carlos Manuel, Amaya Isabel. Licentiate degree, U. Madrid, 1968; MA, NYU, 1969, NYU, 1970; PhD, NYU, 1977. Tchr. Colegio Santa Maria, Spain, 1962-66; instr. Spanish Hunter Coll., N.Y.C., 1969-78; dir. lang. arts South Bronx campus Sch. New Resources, Coll. New Rochelle, N.Y.C., 1978-83; assoc. dean Eugenio Maria de Hostos Community Coll., N.Y.C., 1983-84; pres. LEA, Book Distbrs., N.Y.C., 1984—; judge CEPI Literary Prizes, N.Y.C., 1972-89; founder, pub. Españoles en USA, Inc. Contbr. articles to profl. jours.; author of book revs., poems, and stories; author: Hemingway and the Hispanic World, 1985, Paisajes renacidos, 1982; contbg. author: Gran enciclopedia Rialp, Tomo 20, 1974, Tomo 23, 1974; founder, publisher Espanoles en USA; pres. Espanoles en USA, Inc., 1998—. Pres. Coun. Spanish Residents N.Y. Consular Area, 1997—; U.S. rep. Gen. Coun. for Emigration, Madrid, 1998—. Juan March fellow Juan March Found., Madrid, 1969-70, Fulbright scholar Fulbright Found., 1968-69; Elias Ahuja fellow Fulbright Found., Madrid, 1968-69. Mem. MLA, Am. Assn. Tchrs. Spanish and Portuguese, Am. Booksellers Assn., Assn. Empresarios Y Profesionales (U.S., Spain). Roman Catholic. Avocations: reading, stamp collecting, writing. Home and Office: 17023 83rd Ave Jamaica NY 11432-2101

CAPELLAS, MICHAEL D., computer company executive. Chief info. officer Compaq Computer Corp., Houston, 1998-99, pres., CEO, 1999—. Office: Compaq Computer Corp PO Box 692000 Houston TX 77269-2000 also: 20555 SH 249 Houston TX 77070-2698

CAPELLE-FRANK, JACQUELINE AIMEE, writer; b. Fond du Lac, Wis., Dec. 23, 1935; d. Ira Richard and Aimee Cecilia (Dignin) Capelle; divorced; children: P. Malachi, Tamara, Daria Frank-Weber. AA, Edison C.C., Naples, Fla., 1986; cert., U. Cambridge, Eng., 1991, U. Oxford, Eng., 1992, Paris Am. Acad., 1992; BA, Fla. Internat. U., 1994. part-time instr. Internat. Coll., 1999. Author: (children's book) What's a Library, 1974, (anthologies) Poetic Voices of America, 1996, 97. Mem. adv. bd. Greater Naples Leadership, Inc., 1999—. Mem. AAUW, Nat. Mus. Women, Collier County Hist. Soc. (bd. dirs. 1994—, pres. 1997-00), Nat. Trust for Hist. Preservation, Mus. Trustee Assn., Cooperstown Art Assn. Republican. Presbyterian. Avocations: reading, travel, country walks, gardening, swimming. Home: 143 4th Ave N Naples FL 34102-8421

CAPIE, FORREST HUNTER, economics educator; b. Glasgow, Scotland, Dec. 1, 1940; s. Daniel Forrest and Isabella Ferguson (Doughty) C.; m. Dianna Dix Harvey, Feb. 11, 1967;. BA, U. Auckland, 1967; MS, London Sch. Econs., 1969, PhD, 1973. Lectr. U. Warwick, Coventry, England, 1972-74, U. Leeds, England, 1974-79; prof. City U., London, 1979—. Editor: Econ. History Rev., 1991-99; author: Depression and Protectionism, 1983, Monetary History of the U.K., 1989, Tariffs and Growth, 1994, The Future of Central Banking, 1995, Monetary Economics in the 1990s, 1996, Asset Prices and the Real Economy, 1997, Capital Flows and Capital Controls, 2000. Office: City U Dept Banking Frobisher Cres, Barbican Ctr, London EC2Y 8HB, England

CAPLAN, ANN PATRICIA BAILEY, education educator; b. Neston, Cheshire, England, Mar. 13, 1942; d. Sylvester Launcelot and Marjorie (Parr) Bailey; m. Lionel Caplan, Mar. 31, 1967; children: Emma, Mark. BA in African Studies with honors, U. London, 1963, MA in Social Anthropology, 1965, PhD, 1968. Fellow Sch. Oriental & African Studies, London, 1968-70, 74-76; lectr. Goldsmiths Coll., London, 1976-88, prof., 1988—; head anthropology dept. Goldsmiths Coll., 1980-81, 83-84, 90-93; dir. Inst. Commonwealth Studies, Sch. Advanced Study, U. London, 1998-2000. Author: Priests & Cobblers, 1972, Choice & Constraint in a Swahili Community, 1975, Class & Gender in India: Women and Their Organizations in a South Indian City, 1985; editor: The Cultural Construction of Sexuality, 1987; (with J. Bujra) Women United, Women Divided: Cross-Cultural Perspectives, 1978; (with F. le Guennec-Coppens) Les Swahili entre Afrique et Arabie; (with D. Bell, W.J. Karim) Gendered Fields: Women, Men and Ethnography, 1993, Understanding Disputes: The Politics of Argument, 1995; African Voices, African Lives: Personal Narratives from a Swahili Village, 1997; Food, Health and Fertility, 1997; Risk Revisited, 2000; contbr. articles to profl. jours. Chair Forum Against Ethnic Violence, London, 1993-95. Nuffield Rsch. fellow 1994, Leverhulme Rsch. fellow. Mem. Assn. Social Anthropologists the U.K. and Commonwealth (chair 1997—), European Assn. Social Anthropologists, Acad. Learned Socs. in Social Scis. (coun.), Ctr. for South Asian Studies, Ctr. for African Studies, Internat. Union on Anthropol. and Ethnol. Sci., Forum Against Ethnic Violence (founder), Anthropology in Action, Assn. Univ. Tchrs., Britain-Tanzania Soc., Amnesty Internat., Nat. Coun. for Civil Liberties, Econ. and Social Rsch. Coun. Avocations: swimming, jogging, gardening, classical music. Office: Goldsmiths Coll, Dept Anthropology, London SE14 6NW, England

CAPLAN, BASIL, publisher; b. Liverpool, Lancashire, Eng., Jan. 8, 1927; s. David and Caroline (Cohen) C.; m. Marion Gedney, Feb. 16, 1962 (div. 1976); children: Jennifer, Jason. BA with honors, London U., 1951. Editor: The Complete Manual of Organic Gardening, 1992; founder, editor, author Organic Gardening, 1988-98. Avocations: gardening, writing, music, cooking. Home: Larcombes, Chipstable, Taunton, Somerset TA4 2PZ, England

CAPLAN, GIDEON A., physician, researcher; b. Sydney, Australia, Oct. 1, 1960; s. Leslie and Sophie Shoshana (Kemp) C.; m. Kim Suzanne Taylor, Jan. 12, 1986; children: Judah, Aaron. MBBS, U. Sydney, Australia, 1985. Cert. FRACP, Royal Australasian Coll. Physicians. Staff specialist geriatrician Prince of Wales Hosp., Sydney, 1993—, dir. post acute care svcs., 1993—; dir. Sir Moses Montefiore Home for Aged, Sydney, 1994—. Contbr. articles to profl. jours. Mem. steering com. of Commonwealth Dept. of Health and Family Svc. Cons. to advance Hosp. in the Home, Canberra, 1998-99, steering com. NSW Dept. Aging and Disability Action Plan on Dementia, Sydney, 1996—, steering com. Australian Resource Ctr. for Health Innovation Newcastle, 1997—, steering com. Commonwealth Dept. Health and Family Svc. Nat. Demonstration Hosps. Program II, Canberra, 1998—. Mem. Australian Soc. for Geriatric Medicine (NSW exec. treas. 1996—, Career Investigator award in Geriatric Medicine 1997), Brit. Geriatrics Soc., Australian Med. Assn., Australian Home and Outpatient Intravenous Therapy Assn. Avocations: jogging, gardening. Office: Prince of Wales Hosp, Barker St, Randwick 2031, Australia

CAPLES, RICHARD JAMES, dance company executive, lawyer; b. Balt., June 7, 1949; s. Delphin Delmas and Louise Skinner (Leigh) C. BA, Yale U., 1971; MA, Johns Hopkins U., 1974; JD, Cornell U., 1977. Bar: N.Y. 1978, U.S. Dist. Ct. (so. and ea. dists.) N.Y. 1978. Assoc. Donovan Leisure Newton & Irvine, N.Y.C., 1977-81, Shearman & Sterling, N.Y.C., 1981-83; exec. dir. Santa Fe Festival Theater, 1983-84, Lar Lubovitch Dance Co., N.Y.C., 1984—; dir. Doug Varone and Dancers, N.Y.C., 1995—; dir. Dance/USA, Washington, 1995—, also sec. bd., 1998-2000, treas., 2000—; bd. dirs. Park 58 Corp., , N.Y.C., 1989—, pres. 1994—; dir. Dean Dance and Music Found., N.Y.C., 1981-84. Mem. Am. Soc. Internat. Law, N.Y. State Bar Assn., Am. Coun. on Germany, Johns Hopkins Alumni Assn. (bd. dirs. N.Y.C. chpt. 1988-92), Univ. Club, Yale Club, Johns Hopkins Club (Balt.). Episcopalian. Home: 470 Park Ave New York NY 10022-1903 Office: Lar Lubovitch Dance Co 8th Fl 229 W 42d St New York NY 10036

CAPOLINO, GERARD-ANDRE, electrical engineering educator, dean; b. Marseille, France, Jan. 20, 1953; s. Jules-Andre and Raymonde-Marie (Manzon) C.; m. Danielle Orusa, July 12, 1975; children: Perrine, Tommy. BSc, U. Marseille, 1974, MSc, 1975, PhD, 1978; DSc, INP Grenoble, 1987. Researcher CNRS, Marseille, 1975-78; assoc. prof. U. Yaounde, Cameroon, 1978-81, U. Marseille, 1981-93; prof. U. Picardie, Amiens, France, 1993—; cons. Technicatome, Aix, France, 1987-89. Editor: Simulation of CAD for Electrical Machines, Power Electronics and Drives, 1991. Mem. IEEE (sr.), Soc. Elec. Engrs. (sr.). Avocations: soccer, skiing, badminton. Home: Vallon de Passe Temps, 13190 Allauch France Office: U Picardie, 33 rue St Leu, 80039 Amiens France

CAPOLONGO, DOMENICO, telecommunications executive; b. Roccarainola, Naples, Italy, Oct. 4, 1938; s. Vito Antonio and Emma (De Rinaldi) C.; m. Amparo Real, Sept. 5, 1965; children: Emma, Antonio Manuel, Emiliano. Laurea, U. Naples, 1962. Cert. engr. Head tech. projects SIP, Naples, 1963-79; exchanges responsible SIP, Bari, Italy, 1979-81; network planner SIP, Naples, 1981-85, transmissions responsible, 1985-88; Italian network planning responsible SIP, Rome, 1989-91; Italian network planning and programming responsible Telecom Italia, Rome, 1992-94, asst. of v.p., 1995-97; primer v.p. Empresa de Telecomunicaciones de Cuba (ETECSA), La Habana, Cuba, 1997-2000; prof. U. Naples, 1974-79. Author: Del Passato di Roccarainola e di Antichi Itinerari del Territorio Nolano, 1976-77, La Commenda Gerosolimitana di Cicciano Nel 1515, 1991; dir. cultural mag. periodical Atti Del Circolo Culturale B.G. Duns Scoto, 1975—; contbr. articles to profl. jours. Councillor Municipality, Roccarainola, 1972-87; assessor United Municipalities, Baiano, 1975-89. Recipient Accademico Associato, Accademia Tiberina, Rome, 1976. Mem. Italian Soc. Natural Sci., Circolo Culturale B.G. Duns Scoto (pres. 1971), N.Y. Acad. Scis., several biol. and hist. socs. Avocations: archaeology, history, biology. Home: Via Roma 8, 80030 Roccarainola Naples, Italy

CAPOMASI, LUIS ANTONIO, plastic industry executive; b. Buenos Aires, Nov. 26, 1950; s. Antonio Capomasi and Lydia Nelly (Camambrion) Chimenti. Student, U. Ciencias Empresariales y Sociales, Argentina, 1992. Sales tng. mgr. Gillette Co., Buenos Aires, 1974-86, sales mgr., 1992-94; mktg. mgr. Bic Co., Buenos Aires, 1987-92; sales dir. EMI Argentina, Buenos Aires, 1994-97; sales nat. mgr. Argentina, Uruguay and Chile Stafford Miller, Buenos Aires, 1997-99; ptnr. comml. dept., mktg. and sales dir. MERAK S.A., Buenos Aires, 1999—. Presenter Cath. Radio Program, Buenos Aires. With Argentine Navy, 1967-71. Mem. Argentine Mktg. Assn., Argentine Chamber Music Pubs., Radio Club Argentino. Avocation: amateur radio. Fax: 54-237-463-2592. Home: Palpa 3183, C1426DPG Buenos Aires Argentina Office: MERAK SA, Merlo 2460, B1744OEL Moreno Buenos Aires, Argentina

CAPONE, LUCIEN, JR., management consultant, former naval officer; b. Bristol, R.I.; s. Lucien and Louise Dolores (Malafronte) C.; m. Charlotte Loretta Lammers, July 22, 1950; children: Lucien, Judith Ann. B.S., U.S. Naval Acad., 1949; grad., Naval Postgrad. Sch., 1955, Indsl. Coll. Armed Forces, 1967; M.S. in Bus. Adminstrn, George Washington U., 1967, postgrad., 1970-71. Commd. ensign USN, 1949, advanced through grades to rear adm., served on destroyers Atlantic Fleet, 1949-54, mem. staff Office Chief Naval Ops. Dept. of Navy, 1955-57, exec. officer U.S.S. Huse, 1957-59; staff, comdr. Middle East Force USN, Persian Gulf, 1959-61; head plans, programs, and requirements br. Naval Communications System Hdqrs. USN, Washington, 1961-63; comdg. officer U.S.S. Hammerberg, 1963-64; dep. chief of staff Def. Comm. Agy., Washington, 1964-66; comdg. officer U.S.S. Dahlgren, 1967-69; asst. comdr. plans, programs, requirements Naval Telecommunications Command USN, Washington, 1969-72; comdg. officer U.S.S. Richmond K. Turner, 1972-74; dep. dir. nat. mil. command system tech. support Def. Comm. Agy., Washington, 1974-76; dir. command and control tech. ctr. Def. Comm. Agy., 1976-78; dep. dir. command and control Def. Communications Agy. USN, 1976-78; dir. Inter-Am. Def. Coll., Washington, 1978-79; exec. Booz, Allen & Hamilton, Inc., McLean, Va., 1979-97, v.p., 1983-88, sr. v.p., 1988-97; bd. dirs., operating coun. Booz, Allen & Hamilton, Inc., McLean, 1988-97. Decorated Legion of Merit, Def. Superior Service medal with oak leaf cluster. Mem. IEEE, AIAA, Armed Forces Communications and Electronics Assn. (past pres. D.C. chpt.). Office: Booz Allen & Hamilton Inc 8283 Greensboro Dr Ste 700 Mc Lean VA 22102-3838

CAPPA, STEFANO FRANCESCO, neurologist, researcher; b. Milan, July 1, 1953; s. Luigi and Adelia (Ripamonti) C.; m. Daniela Perani, Mar. 10,

1987; 1 child, Tommaso. MD, U. Milan, 1978. Intern, resident U. Milan, 1979-82; staff neurologist Niguarda Hosp., Milan, 1982-88; asst. prof. neurology U. Brescia (Italy), 1988-92, assoc. prof. neurology, 1992-99; prof. neuropsychology UHSR, Milan, 1999—; cons. Alzheimer's disease unit S. Cuore Sci. Inst., Brescia, 1995—. Editor: Neuropsychological Disorders After Subcortical Lesions, 1992; contbr. articles to profl. jours. Lt. Italian Med. Corps, 1980-81. Fellow NATO, 1980, European Sci. Found., 1987. Mem. Soc. Neurosci., Acad. of Aphasia, British Neuropsychol. Soc. Avocations: English Literature, cinema, skiing. Office: UHSR Dept Psychology, Via Olgettina 58, 20132 Milan Italy

CAPPATO, MARCO, member European parliament; b. Milano, Italy, May 25, 1971. Mem. European parliament, Italy, 1999—; mem. tech. group of ind. members, mixed group, European parliament; mem. com. on citizens' freedoms and rights, justice and home affairs; substitute mem. com. on employment and social affairs; mem. delegation for rels. with the member states of ASEAN, Southeast Asia and the Republic of Korea. Office: Via Torre Argentina 76, Terzo piano, I-00186 Roma Italy*

CAPPATO, RICCARDO PAOLO, physician; b. Ferrara, Italy, May 2, 1958; arrived in Germany, 1993; s. Igino and Norma (Boaretto) C. MD, U. Ferrara, 1983. Specialist in Cardiology, 1987. Asst. Arcisp. Santa Anna, Ferrara, 1984-93; sr. physician Univ. Hosp. Eppendorf, Hamburg, Germany, 1993-95; sr. physician AK, St. Georg, Hamburg, 1995—, co-dir. electrophysiology lab., 1995-97; cons. U. Hosp. Eppendorf, 1995-97, Osp. Civile Cento, Cento, Italy, 1997, Spitali Riuniti, Brescia, Italy, 1997, Osp. S. Raffaele, Milan, Italy, 1998; dir. electrophysiology 6 Arrythmia Ctr., Policlinico San Donato, San Donato Milanese, Milan, Italy, 2000. Contbr. articles to profl. jours. Recipient G. Binda award in rsch. Rsch. Foun., Milan, Italy, 1986. Home: u Testi 22, 44100 Ferrara Italy Office: AK St Georg II Medizin, Lohmuhlenstrasse 5, 20099 Hamburg Germany

CAPPEL, CONSTANCE, academic administrator, author; b. Dayton, Ohio, June 22, 1936; d. Adam Denison and Mary Louise (Henry) C.; m. R.A. Montgomery Jr., June 16, 1962 (div. Apr. 1980); children: Raymond A. Montgomery III, Anson Cappel Montgomery. BA, Sarah Lawrence Coll., 1959; MA, Columbia U., N.Y.C., 1961; PhD, The Union Inst., Cin., 1991. Editor Newsweek, N.Y.C., 1961-63, Vogue, N.Y.C., 1964-66; grad. prof. Goddard Coll., Plainfield, Vt., 1975-79; founder, chief exec. officer, pub. Vt. Crossroad Press, Waitsfield, 1972-82; comml. realtor Investmark, Dayton, 1985-87; prin., founder, CEO Cappel Cons., San Francisco, 1986-94; bus. advisor U.S. Peace Corps, Lodz, Poland, 1994-96; mgr. Price Waterhouse Nieruchomości, Warsaw, Poland, 1996-97; dir. devel. Conflict Resolution Catalysts, Montpelier, Vt., 1997; tchr. trainer U.S. Peace Corps., Kazakhstan, 1998; pres. Newport (N.H.) Earth Inst., 1999. Author: Hemingway in Michigan, 1966 (paperback 1977, 99), Vermont School Bus Ride, 1977, Utopian Colleges, 1999. Founder Women's Rights Project/ACLU, Vt., 1973-74; mem. grad. alumni/ae bd. The Union Inst., 1992-94, 99, 2000, sec., 1993. McDowell Colony fellow, Peterborough, N.H., 1972, 74. Mem. PEN Am. Ctr. Episcopalian. Office: Newport Earth Inst RR 1 Box 413A Claremont NH 03743-9406

CAPPELLO-ANGELLOTTI, RITA, artist; b. Naples, Italy, July 18, 1931; d. Alfredo and Agnese (Caprani) Angellotti; m. Vittorio Cappello, Dec. 4, 1955; children: Corrado, Francesco. One-woman shows include Isle of Capri, Italy, 1971, numerous others in Belgium, Germany, The Netherlands, Luxembourg, Phila., Paris, Monte Carlo, Miami, Fla., Nice, France, Padova, Italy, Switzerland, Japan. Mem. Acad. Tiberina Rome, Acad. Lutece Paris, Acad. Greci Marino. Avocations: classical music, opera, nature spotting.

CAPPER, WAYNE LOGAN, biomedical engineer, educator; b. Johannesburg, South Africa, 1959; s. Douglas Logan and Doreen Ivy (Fraser) C.; m. Jill Finlayson, Feb. 22, 1994. BS, Natal U., Durban, South Africa, 1981; MS, U. Cape Town, South Africa, 1984, PhD, 1988. Registered profl. engr., South Africa, profl. med. engr., South African Med. and Dental Coun. Prin. biomed. engr. Provincial Adminstrn. Western Cape, Cape Town, 1991—. Contbr. articles to profl. jours. Lt. South African Def. Force, 1989-90. Avocations: hiking, jogging, tennis.

CAPPIELLO, ACHILLE, chemist, educator; b. Rome, Feb. 19, 1957; s. Francesco and Tina (Ciasullo) C.; m. Pierangela Palma, Feb. 8, 1986; 1 child, Elena. Diploma, Tech. Inst. for Nuclear Energy, Rome, 1975; Diploma in Biology, La Sapienza U., 1981. Doctoral fellowship U. Urbino, Italy, 1984-87, rschr., 1987—; prof. U. Urbino, 1992—; postdoctoral assoc. MIT, Cambridge, 1987-89; cons. Waters Corp., U.S., 1998—. Author: (instrument design) Analytical Chemistry, 1993. Cpl. Italian Army, 1982-83. Mem. Italian Chem. Soc., Am. Soc. for Mass Spectrometry. Avocations: Alpine skiing, mountain biking. Office: U Urbino Inst Chem Sci, Piazza Rinascimento 6, 61029 Urbino Italy

CAPPO, JOSEPH C., publisher; b. Chgo., Feb. 24, 1936; s. Joseph V. and Frances (Maggio) Cacioppo; m. Mary Anne Cappo, May 7, 1967; children: Elizabeth, John. BA, DePaul U., 1957. Reporter Hollister Publs., Wilmette, Ill., 1961-62; reporter Chgo. Daily News, 1962-68, bus. columnist, 1968-78; columnist Crain's Chgo. Bus., 1978—, pub., 1979-89; v.p. Crain Comm., Inc., 1981-89, sr. v.p. group pub., 1989-95, sr. v.p. internat., 1996—; pub. Advt. Age, 1989-92, publishing dir, 1992—; dir. Assn. Area Bus. Publs., 1982-88, pres., 1985-86. Author: Future Scope: Succes Strategies for the 1990's and Beyond, 1990. Bd. dirs. Off the Street Club, Chgo., 1981—, Chgo. Advt. Fedn., 1987-93, Mus. Broadcast Comm., 1984-90, Ill. Coun. on Econ. Edn., 1990-95. With U.S. Army, 1959-61. Recipient award Ill. Press Assn., 1962, (with other Daily News staffers) Nat. Headliner award, 1966, Disting. Alumni award DePaul U., 1975, Page One award Chgo. Newspaper Guild, 1978, Peter Lisagor award Sigma Delta Chi, 1978, Outstanding Achievement award in comm., Justinian Soc. Lawyers, 1979, Champion award YWCA of Met. Chgo., 1984, Media Svc. award Chgo. Lung Assn., 1990. Mem. Internat. Advt. Assn. (world bd. 1994—, sr. v.p. 1996-98, world pres. 1998-2000), Econ. Club (Chgo.), Bus. and Econ. Writers (bd. govs. 1984-89), Ill. Small Bus. Adv. Commn., Delta Mu Delta (hon.). Roman Catholic. Office: Crain Communications Inc 740 N Rush St Chicago IL 60611-2546

CAPPONI, GIANFRANCO, company manager; b. Treviso, Veneto, Italy, May 18, 1941; s. Nicolo and Valeria (Petti) C.; m. Teresa Nava, May 31, 1976; children: Valeria, Stefano. D of Engring., Politecnico, Milan, 1967. Programmer Montechison, Milan, 1967-69; head of office Sprague Creas, Milan, 1969-72; head of dept. ATM, Milan, 1973—; nat. expert EEC, Brussels, 1991-93; cons. Law Ct., Milan, 1980-97; asst. Politecnico, Milan, 1975-85; chmn. VMI-CEI, Milan, 1985-97. Contbr. articles to profl. jours. Del. Dept. Coun., Milan, 1990-91. Mem. Inst. of Noise Control Engring., Order of Engrs., Commerce Chamber (expert mem.). Avocations: swimming, biking. Fax: 026-70-5532. E-mail: gfc@engineer.com. Home: Via Settembrini 27, 20124 Milan Italy

CAPPS, RICHARD HENRY, minister; b. Columbia, S.C., June 22, 1944; s. Henry Eddie and Maude Cecile (Simpson) Crapps; m. Joyce Dianne Wood, Aug. 2, 1968; children: Richard Henry (Hank) Jr., Elizabeth Cecille. AA, North Greenville Coll., 1965; BA, Furman U., 1967; ThM with honors, New Orleans Bapt. Theol. Sem., 1970, DMin, 1978. Ordained minister So. Bapt., 1965. Pastor Fairfield Bapt. Ch., Winnsboro, S.C., 1964-68, Society Hill Bapt. Ch., Oakvale, Miss., 1969-71, First Bapt. Ch., Gaston, S.C., 1971-79; interim pastor First Bapt. Ch., Cheraw, S.C., 1968; sr. pastor Laurel Bapt. Ch., Greenville, S.C., 1979-82; dir. missions South Roanoke Bapt. Assn., Greenville, 1982-93, Liberty Bapt. Assn., Thomasville, N.C., 1993-98; area dir. Piedmont/Western NC Prison Fellowship, Winston-Salem, N.C., 1999; min. missions & outreach Forsyth Park Bapt. Ch., Winston-Salem, N.C., 2000—; S.S. enlargement campaign cons. S.C. Bapt. State Conv., 1981-82; PACT cons. N.Am. Mission Bd., Atlanta, 1988-95; state disaster relief coord. N.C. Bapt. Men., Cary, 1989-93; ch. growth cons. Bapt. State Conv. of N.C., Cary, 1996-98. Contbr. articles to profl. publs. Bd. dirs. Greenville Boys Choir, 1986-90, Transplant Recipient Suport Sys., Pitt County Meml. Hosp., Greenville, 1991-93; mem. Greenville Choral Soc., 1990-93; mem. religion in schs. task force Pitt County Schs., Greenville, 1993; vice chmn. chaplains bd. Davidson Correction Ctr., Lexington, N.C., 1996-98; vol. greeter ARC, 2000—. Recipient Am. Legion award, 1965, Vol. of the Year, Davidson Correctional Ctr., 1997. Mem. Dir. of Missions Conf. (pres. 1986-87, treas. 1987-98), Thomasville C. of C., Lexington Ministerial Assn., Gaston Ruritan Club (chaplain 1973-77), Sierra Club. Democrat. Avocations: roses, antiques/collectibles, walking, collecting stamps and coins. Home: 198 Creekside Dr High Point NC 27265-9209 Office: Forsyth Park Bapt Ch 1600 S Hawthorne Rd Winston Salem NC 27103-4188

CAPPUCCIO, FRANCESCO PAOLO, internist; b. Naples, Italy, Aug. 29, 1956; arrived in U.K., 1983; s. Mario and Maria (Rispoli) C.; m. Alessandra De Martino, July 28, 1984; children: Amedeo Francesco, Eugenio Athos. MB BS, U. Naples Med. Sch., 1981, MD, 1984; MSc, London Sch. Hygiene & Tropical Medicine, 1993, diploma, 1997. Bd. cert., Naples, 1981, London, 1996. Lectr. U. Naples Med. Sch., 1982-83, 86-89; rsch. fellow Charing Cross & Westminster Med. Sch., London, 1983-86; lectr. London Sch. Hygiene & Tropical Medicine, 1994-96, St. George's Hosp. Med. Sch., London, 1989-94, 96—. Fellow Royal Coll. Physicians (London, mem. faculty pub. health medicine); mem. Brit. Hypertension Soc., European Soc. Hypertension, Am. Soc. Hypertension, Am. Heart Assn., Internat. Epidemiol. Assn., London Hypertension Soc. (steering com.). Office: St George's Hosp Med Sch, Cranmer Terr, London SW17 0RE, England

CAPRIO, ANTHONY S., university president; b. Providence, Apr. 12, 1945; s. Salvatore and Esther (Iafrati) C. BA, Wesleyan U., 1967; MA, Columbia U., 1969, PhD, 1973; BA (hon.), Western New Eng. Coll., 2000. Asst. prof. langs. and fgn. studies Lehman Coll., CUNY, Bronx, 1971-76; assoc. prof. Cedar Crest Coll., Allentown, Pa., 1976-80; prof., adminstr. Am. U., Washington, 1980-89; provost Oglethorpe U., Atlanta, 1989-96; pres. Western New Eng. Coll., Springfield, Mass., 1996—; mem. Nat. Humanities Faculty, 1977—; bd. dirs. Tuition Exch. Inc. Author: Reflets de la femme, 1973, En Français, 1976, 3d edit., 1985; also over 100 articles, book chpts. and revs. on pedagogy, lit. and transl. to profl. jours. including Columbia Dictionary of Modern European Lit., A Critical Bibliography of French Lit., others. Trustee Willie Ross Sch. for the Deaf, 1992—, Springfield Symphony Orch., 1998—; bd. dirs. Springfield Adult Edn. Coun., 1999—, Greater Springfield Convention and Visitors Bureau, 1999—, Pioneer Valley Econ. Devel. Coun., 2000—, Springfield Sch. Vols., 2000—; mem. exec. com. Assn. Ind. Colls. and Univs. in Mass., 1999—; mem. cabinet Cmty. United Way of Pioneer Valley, 1998—; co-chair Leadership Coun. of Springfield Mentoring Partnership, 1998—; corporator Springfield Libr. and Mus. Assn., 1998—; mem. task force on workforce devel. Pioneer Valley Planning Commn., 1998—; pres. Cooperating Colls. of Greater Springfield, 2000—. Recipient Adminstr.-Faculty award for outstanding performance Am. U., 1984, Disting. Adminstr. and Educator award Greater Washington Assn. Fgn. Lang. Educators, 1986. Mem. Am. Translators Assn., Am. Assn. Higher Edn., Am. Assn. Univ. Adminstrs., Soc. Coll. and Univ. Planning, Phi Beta Kappa, Omicron Delta Kappa, Phi Beta Delta, Phi Beta Kappa (fellow), others. Office: Western New Eng Coll Office of President 1215 Wilbraham Rd Springfield MA 01119-2612

CAPRIO, NICHOLAS FRANK, pension fund administrator, accountant, educator; b. Trenton, N.J., Oct. 15, 1939; s. Earl and Josephine Mapps; m. Julia R. Caprio, Nov. 7, 1959; 1 child, Julie Caprio Thompson. AA, Mercer County Community Coll., Trenton, 1972; BA, Trenton State U., 1974; MA, Rider Coll., 1977. Chief fiscal officer State of N.J., Trenton, 1972-83, dep. dir. div. pensions, 1983—; prin. Nicholas F. Caprio CPA, Trenton, 1980—; prof. Rider Coll., Lawrenceville, N.J., 1980—, Mercer County Community Coll., Trenton. Trustee Hamilton Ballet Theatre, Trenton; ptnr. Ballet Technique, Trenton. With USAF, 1961-65. Fellow N.J. Soc. CPAs; mem. AICPA. Avocations: bass, trombone. Home: 315 Sylvan Ave Trenton NJ 08610-5124 Office: State of NJ Div Pensions 50 W State St Trenton NJ 08608-1220

CĂPROIU, MIRON TEODOR, chemical engineer, educator; b. Ploiesti, Prahova, Romania, Aug. 8, 1946; s. Toma and Stela Ana (Minculescu) C.; m. Yvona Otilia-Eugenia Păuna, June 30, 1973; 1 child, Irina Mădălina. Chem. Engr., Poly. Inst., Bucharest, Romania, 1969, PhD in Chem. Engring., 1984. Researcher Inst. Chem. Rsch., Bucharest, 1969-79; sr. researcher Inst. Mil. Rsch., Bucharest, 1979-81, Ctr. Organic Chemistry, Bucharest, 1981—; asst. prof. dept. organic chemistry Faculty Chem. Engring., Bucharest, 1992—. Contbr. over 50 articles to profl. jours. including Tetrahedron, Tetrahedron Letters, Jour. Chem. Soc., Jour. Organic Chemistry, Bull. Soc. Chimique de France, others; patentee in field. Lt. in field artillery Mil. Sch., 1971. Recipient N. Teclu award Romanian Acad., 1988. Mem. Romanian Chem. Soc., Internat. E.P.R. Soc. Mem. Nat. Liberal Party. Christian Orthodox. Avocations: classical music, history, astronomy, geography. Home: Apt 12, 13 Aleea Baiut Bl A-34, 774381 Bucharest Romania Office: PO Box 15-258, Spl Independen ei 202B, 71141 Bucharest Romania

CAPRON, ANDRÉ, immunologist, researcher; b. Lens, Nord, France, Dec. 30, 1930; m. Monique Capron-Dupont; children: Stephanie, Alexis. MSC, U. Lille, 1954, LSc, 1959, MD, 1958. Rsch. asst. parasitology Faculty of Medicine U. Lille, 1955-58, asst. prof. parasitology, 1961-67, prof. immunology and parasite biology, 1970—, head dept. immunology U. Hosp., 1970-94; dir. Ctr. for Immunology of Parasites INSERM 167 Inst. Pasteur, Lille, 1975—, dir., 1994; expert de l'Orgn. Mondiale de la Santé; pres. du programme TDR OMS Immunology of Schistosomiasis, 1977-80; pres. steering com. Groupe Scientifique de Travail, 1980-83; vis. prof. London Sch. Tropical Medicine and Hygiene, 1982. Mem. edit. bd. Annals d'Immunolgie, Annales de Parasitologie Humaine et Comparee, Exptl. Parasitology, Parasite Immunology, Zeitschrift fur Parasitenkunde, European Jour. Immunology, IRCS Med. Jour., Jour. AMA, EOS. Recipient Prix Leveau Acad. de Medecine, 1959, Prix Recherche et Medecine de l'Inst. des Scis. de la Sante, 1984, Prix Richard Lounsbery Nat. Acad. Scis., 1986, Prix. Internat. de Medecine de la Found. FAICAL, 1990; named Officier Nat. Order of Merit, 1981, Comdr., 1990, Ordre du Lion, 1990, Ordre des Palme Academiques, 1991, Chevalier de la Legion d'Honneur, 1992. Mem. Soc. Francaise de Parasitologie, Soc. Francaise d'Immunologie (pres. 1981-85), Soc. Zoologique de France, Soc. de Pathologie Exotique, Am. Soc. Tropical Medicine and Hygiene (hon.), Am. Soc. Parasitology, Am. Soc. Immunology, Royal Soc. Tropical Medicine (London), AAAS, N.Y. Acad. Scis., Soc. Belge de Medecine Tropicale, Soc. Belge de Protozoologie, Soc. Internat. de Mycologie, Soc. Belge d'Immunologie, Soc. Portugaise de Parasitologie, Brit. Soc. for Parasitology (hon.), Soc. Suisse d'Immunologie (hon.), World Fedn. Parasitology (exec. bd. dirs. 1978-82), Am. Acad. Allergy and Immunology (internat. coun. 1987), Fedn. European des Soc. d'Immunologie (pres. 1989). Office: Inst Pasteur Unite INSERM, 1 rue du Pr A Calmette, 59019 Lille Cedex, France

CAPSHAW, TOMMIE DEAN, judge; b. Oklahoma City, Sept. 20, 1936; m. Dian Shipp; 1 child, Charles W. BS in Bus., Oklahoma City U., 1958; postrad., U. Ark., 1958-59; JD, U. Okla., 1961. Bar: Okla. 1961, Wyo. 1971, Ind. 1975. Assoc. Looney, Watts, Looney, Nichols and Johnson, Oklahoma City, 1961-63, Pierce, Duncan, Couch and Hendrickson, Oklahoma City, 1963-70; trial atty., v.p. Capshaw Well Service Co., Liberty Pipe and Supply Co., Casper, Wyo.; adminstrv. law judge Evansville, Ind., 1973-75, 96-99; hearing office chief adminstrv. law judge Chgo., 1975-96, acting regional chief adminstrv. law judge, 1977-78; sr. adminstrv. law judge, 1999—; acting appeals coun. mem., Arlington, Va., 1980, acting chief adminstrv. law judge, 1984; mem. faculty U. Evansville, 1977, Sch. Law Ill. U., 1988—, So. Ind. U., 1990; lectr. in field. Author: A Manual for Continuing Judicial Education, 1981, Practical Aspects of Handling Social Security Disability Claims, 1982, Judicial Practice Handbook, 1990, A Quest for Quality, Speedy Justice, 1991; contbr. numerous articles to profl. jours., chpt. to textbook. Mem. adv. coun. Boy Scouts Am., scoutmaster, den leader, 1969—, Nat. Jud. Coll. U. Nev.; bd. dirs. Casper Symphony, 1972-73, Casper United Fund, 1972-73, Midget Football Assn., Casper, 1972-73, German Twp. Water Dist., 1984-85; pres. Evansville Unitarian Universalist Ch., 1984-86; performer Evansville Philharmonic Orch., 1986-98; bd. dirs. German Twp. Vol. Fire Dept., 1998—. Recipient Kappa Alpha Order Ct. of Honor award, 1962, Silver Beaver award Boy Scouts Am., 1980, presentation for vol. svc. contbg. betterment of cmty. Office Hearings and Appeals, 1992, presentation outstanding jud. mentor tng. Supreme Ct. Iowa, 1992, presentation disting. mentor tng. Fla. Jud. Coll., 1992. Mem. Okla. Bar Assn., Okla. County Bar Assn. (v.p. 1967), Wyo. Bar Assn., Evansville Bar Assn. (jud. rep. 1986-87, James Bethel Gresham Freedom award 1988), Young Lawyers Assn., Assn. Adminstrv. Law Judges HHS (bd. dirs. 1979-82, Tic Vickery award 1998), Oklahoma City U. Alumni Assn. (bd. dirs. 1965). Home: 6105 School Rd # 6 Evansville IN 47720

CAPUANO, MAURICIO JACQUES, insurance company executive; b. Athens, Greece, Dec. 1, 1947; s. Jacques Moise and Mathilde (Maissa) C.; m. Christina Maria Carella, Aug. 29, 1977 (div. 1995); 1 child, Jacques; m. Golfo Papadimitriou, Dec. 3, 1995; children: Philippe, Polyxena-Alicia. Diplom in chem. engring., Nat. Poly. Sch., Athens, 1971. Stagiaire La Concorde, Paris, 1971-72; stagiaire Generali Ins. Co., Trieste, Italy, 1972, London, 1972-73; marine cargo and hull underwriter Generali Ins. Co., Athens, 1973-80, dep. gen. mgr. rep. office, 1980-81; mng. dir. Hellenic br. office Capuano Ins. Brokers, Athens, 1981—; prof. Hellenic Inst. Ins. Studies, Athens, 1996—. Mem. Chartered Inst. Inst. Avocations: sailing, tennis, Alpine skiing. Home: Meletopoulou # 6, 15452 Pal Psychico Greece Office: Capuano Ins Brokers, Aghias Varvaras 37, 15231 Alandri Greece

CAPUTO, DANIEL VINCENT, psychologist; b. N.Y.C.; s. Pasquale and Hortense C.; A.B., Bklyn. Coll., 1954; Ph.D., U. Ill., 1961. Prof. med. psychology Washington U., St. Louis, 1959-64; prof. psychology Queens Coll., CUNY, Flushing, 1964—, prof. emeritus, 1998—, chair dept. psychology, 1974-77; research assoc. St. Vincent's Med. Center, S.I., N.Y.; pvt. practice clin. psychology, 1973—. Registered psychologist, Nat. Register of Health Providers in Psychology; lic. psychologist, N.Y.; research grantee NIMH, 1963. Fellow N.Y. Acad. of Sci.; mem. N.Y. Acad. Scis., Am. Psychol. Assn., Eastern Psychol. Assn., N.Y. State Psychol. Assn. (rep. exec. com. 1981-83), Biofeedback Soc. Am. (cert.). Roman Catholic. Contbr. to Infants Born at Risk, 1979, Pre-term Birth: Relevance to Optimal Psychological Development, 1981, Multivariate Analysis of the Type A Personality, 1981. Office: 16-07 150th St Whitestone NY 11357-2545 Office: Queens Coll Dept of Psychology Kissena Blvd Flushing NY 11367

CAPUZZIELLO, PAUL THOMAS, senior financial advisor; b. Framingham, Mass., Oct. 8, 1969; s. Thomas James Capuzziello and Jeanne Marie (Boiteau) Mourey; m. Tracey Masse, Apr. 23, 1997. BSBA, Bryant Coll., Smithfield, R.I., 1991. CFP; master advisor. Sr. fin. advisor Am. Express Fin. Advisors, Lincoln, R.I., 1991—. Weekly columnist Woonsocket Call, 1993—. Treas. Bryant Coll. Alumni Bd., Smithfield, 1993-97; mem. fundraising com. Women's Ctr. of R.I., Providence, 1994-96; nominator Outstanding Young Men of Am., Montgomery, Ala., 1996-98; mem. planned giving com. Am. Cancer Soc., Providence, R.I., 1999—. Mem. Fin Planning Assn., R.I. Soc. Cert. Fin. Planners. Avocations: mountain biking, hiking, gardening, golfing. Office: Am Express Fin Advisors 6 Blackstone Valley Pl Ste 706 Lincoln RI 02865-1102

CÁRABE, JULIO, applied physicist, researcher; b. Tangier, Morocco, Oct. 14, 1959; (parents Spanish citizens); s. Julio Cárabe and Ana López; m. Delia Muñoz, July 28, 1989. BSc, U. Complutense, Madrid, 1981, MSc, 1983, PhD in Physics, 1990. Postgrad. Inst. Solar Energy, Poly. U., Madrid, 1981-83; mem. European State Agy. Space Rsch. & Technology Ctr., Noordwyk, The Netherlands, 1986-87; rschr. Ctr. Energy, Environ. and Technol. Rsch., Madrid, 1987—. Contbr. articles to sci. jours., including Materials Letters, Applied Surface Sci., Solar-Energy Materials and Solar Cells, Applied Physics Letters. 2d lt. Spanish Arty., 1984. Avocations: playing music, singing, cycling. E-mail: julio.carabe@ciemat.es. Office: CIEMAT, Avda Complutense 22, E-28040 Madrid Spain

CARABIAS LILLO, JULIA, government official; b. Mexico City, Mex., 1954. BA, MA, Nat. Autonomous, 1981. Sec. Environ., Natural Resources & Fisheries, 1998—; prof. sic. Nat. Autonomous U., 1981, U. Coun. UNAM, 1989-93; pres. Nat. Ecol. Inst.; mem. Coun. Nat. Solidarity Program; mem. adv. coun. Nat. Conservation Fund. Office: Sec Environ Natural Resourc, 4209 Freaccionamiento, Del Mexico*

CARABIN, HÉLÈNE, epidemiologist, veterinarian; b. Montreal, Que., Can., Apr. 21, 1970; d. Rene Carabin and Simonne Saint-Cyr. DVM, U. Montreal, 1992, MSc, 1994, PhD, 1998; postdoctorate, U. Oxford, Eng., 1998—. Vet. cons. Faculty of Med. Vet., Can., 1992-94; rsch. assoc. Faculty of Med. Vet., 1994; vis. scientist Food and Agrl. Orgn. of Unite Nations, Rome, summer 1999; tchr. U. Oxford, U.K., 1999—; tchr. faculty med. vet. U. Montreal, 1993-98; project dir., co-prin. investigator McGill U., Montreal, 1994-98, tchg. asst., cons., 1996-98; co-principal investigator, U. Oxford, 1998—. Contbr. articles to profl. jours. MS fellow Fonds pour la Formation de Chercheurs et l'Aide a la Recherche, Can., 1992-95, PhD fellow Nat. Health and Rsch. Devel. Program, Can., 1995-98, post-doctoral fellow Wellcome Trust Can. Med. Rsch. Coun., 1998—, Epidemiology prize, 2000. Mem. Assn. pour l'Etude de l'Epidemiologie des Maladies Animales, Royal Soc. for Tropical Medicine and Hygiene, Ordre des Medecins Vet., Internat. Soc. Environ. Epidemiology. Avocations: cycling, swimming, hiking, reading. Office: WTCEID Univ Oxford, South Parks Rd, Oxford OX1 3FY, England

CARACASIAN, LUSINE EHIA, thermal power engineer, educator; b. Bucharest, Romania, June 6, 1963; d. Ehia Artin and Maria Gheorghe (Radulescu) C. Degree in engring., U. Poly., Bucharest, Romania, 1986, PhD, 1999. Engr. Giurgiu (Romania) Power Plant, 1986-89; main engr. Inst. Power Studies and Design, Bucharest, 1998-99, Nat. Electricity & Heat Authority, Bucharest, 1999—; tchr. U. Poly., Bucharest, 1995-97. Avocations: astronomy, history, movies. Office: Nat Electricity & Heat Authority, 3 Constantine Naen, 70219 Bucharest Romania

CARAM, EVE LA SALLE, English educator, writer; b. Hot Springs, Ark., May 11, 1934; d. Raymond Briggs and Lois Elizabeth (Merritt) La Salle; m. Richard George Caram, Apr. 19, 1965 (div. Apr. 1978); 1 child, Bethel Eve. BA, Bard Coll., 1956; MA, U. Mo., 1977. English instr. Stephens Coll., Columbia, Mo., 1974,79-82; fiction writing grad. instr. Sch. Profl. Writing U. So. Calif., L.A., 1982-87; English lit. and writing instr. Calif. State U., Northridge, 1983—; sr. fiction writing instr. The Writers' Program UCLA, 1983—; fiction contest judge Calif. State U., Long Beach, 1992, 94, writer's conf. spkr., 1985-87, 94; spkr., mem. panel Tex. Am. Studies Assn., Wichita Falls, 1998. Author: (novel) Dear Corpus Christi, 1991, Wintershine, 1994, Rena, A Late Journey, 1999; editor: Palm Readings, Stories from Southern California, 1998; fiction editor West/Word, 1991. Mem. AAUP, Assn. Calif. State Profs., Nat. Assn. Tchrs. English, Poets and Writers, PEN Ctr. U.S.A. West. Democrat. Avocations: swimming, beach walks, outdoors. Home: 3400 Ben Lomond Pl Apt 121 Los Angeles CA 90027-2952 Office: UCLA Ext The Writers Program 10995 Le Conte Ave Los Angeles CA 90095-3001 also: Calif State U English Dept 1811 Nordoff Northridge CA 91330-0001

CARAMIHAI, MIHAI, engineer, educator; b. Bucharest, Romania, June 8, 1959; s. Gheorghe and Georgeta Caramihai; m. Simona Caramihai; 1 child, Giorgiana. MSc, U. Politehnica, Bucharest, 1984, PhD in Informatic Sys., 1987. Cert. trainer IBM-AS400, 1998. Engr. Midia Petrochem. Co., 1984-88; software devel. engr. Electrotehnica Enterprise, 1988-89; project mgr., adminstr. Datema Sys. SRL, 1992-95; software devel. engr. Kepler SRL, 1995-96; sr. rschr. dept. biotech. Rsch. Inst. of Chemistry, Politehnica Tech. U., Bucharest, 1989—; assoc. prof., project coord. Control & Info. Tech. Politehnica U., Bucharest, 1989-2000, prof. dept. Info. & Tech., 1999—; expert in automatic control & info. tech. Ministry Justice, 1993—, European Commn. Edn. & Culture Leonardo da Vinci Programme Nat. Coordination Unit, 1993—, European Commn. Rsch. & Devel., 1999—; vis. prof. Lab. d'Automatique de Grenoble, INat. Poly. Inst. Grenoble, 1997; cons. AMCSIT Politehnica U., Relansin Programme-IT, 1999—, Corint Programme-IT, 2000—, PLURI Cons SRL-IT, 2000—, Quantum Sys. Spa.-IT, Padova, 2000—. Author monographs; reviewer Computer Mag. USA, 1999-2000, Computing Reviews USA, 2000; contbr. articles to profl. jours.; patentee in field. Mem. IEEE, NaSPA, IEEE Computer Soc., N.Y. Acad. Sci., Internat. Fedn. Automatic Control, European Fedn. Biotech., Romanian Soc. for Bioengring. and Biotech., Romanian Info. Tech. & Comm. Assn., UNESCO Club for Bioinformatics and Knowledge Engring., World Wide Club for Biol. and Med. Cmty., Internat. Assn. Continuing Engring. Edn., Assn. Computing Machinery, Internat. Neural Network Soc., European Network Uncertainty Techniques Devels. Use Info. Tech., Internat. Assn. Computer Professionals, EUROFUSE, Tech. Coun. Software Engring. (com. software engring. edn., software process, requirement engring.), Soc. Bioinformatics Nordic Countries, Assn. Project Mgr., Forum

Europeen de l'Orientation Academique, Brit. Computer Soc., Royal Soc. New Zealand, Royal Soc. Victoria, Australia, Sigma Xi. Fax: 1-435-304-4726. E-mail: m.caramihai@ieee.org. Office: Rsch Inst Chem/Biotech Dept, Str Batistei 5 Sector II, 70131 Bucharest Romania

CARANGELO, LORI, writer, publisher, social activist, not-for-profit executive; b. New Haven, Apr. 3, 1945; 2 children. Student, Santa Barbara City Coll., Coll. of the Desert. Adminstrv. asst. Pvt. Industry Coun., Santa Barbara, Calif.; founder, pres. Americans for Open Records (AmFOR), Palm Desert, Calif.; pub. Access Press, Palm Desert, Calif. Author: Better than Sex Italian Cookbook, 2000, The Ultimate Search Book, 1998, 3rd edit. 2000, Born Losers: Billion Dollar Babies in America's Foster Care, Adoption and Penal Systems, 1999, Chose Children, 8 Ball Cafe, No Remorse; contbr. articles to profl. publs. Data reporting source Rights of the Child project UN, Hague Intercountry Adoption/Abduction Treaty Confs.; leader internat. adoption open records movement. Mem. Lit. Guild of Palm Springs, Open Records Movement. E-mail: accesspress@earthlink.net. Office: Access Press/AmFOR PO Box 401 Palm Desert CA 92261-0401

CARAPANCEA, MIHAI TITUS, ophthalmologist; b. Bucharest, Romania, Apr. 20, 1920; s. Titus Gh. and Eleonora (Zissu) C.; m. Elena Negru, Apr. 25, 1980. Dr. Medicine and Surgery, Faculty Medicine, Bucharest, 1944; DMS, U. Bucharest, 1967, Docent in Med. Scis., 1975; D of Therapeutic Philosophy (hon.), World U., 1983; D in Psychology (hon.), Parthasarathy Internat. Cultural Acad., 1993; Med. Sc. Dr. h.c. Complementary Medicines and Med. Alternativa, Open Internat. Univ., 1994. Asst. lectr. U. Bucharest, 1944-52; cons. eye specialist cons. ophthal. clinics, 1946-52; sci. rsch. worker D. Danielopolu Inst. Normal and Path. Physiology, Acad. Romania, Bucharest, 1951-53, interdisciplinary scientist, 1953-82, founder, head lab. clin. and exptl. physiology and physiopathology of eye, 1953-82, mgr. topics opthalmological rsch., 1956-82, sr. chief ophthalmologist, 1969-82, prin. sr. rsch. scientist, 1970-82, cons. adviser clin. and exptl. ophthalmology, 1983-90; mem. Aerospace Biol. sect. Astronautic Commn. Acad. Romania, Space Medicine and Cosmic. Biol. group Radiobiology Commn., Acad. Romania. Author: Amauroses, Amblyopiae and Ocular Disorders Caused by Quininic Intoxication, 1944, Physiopathology of Hypertensive, Clinical and Experimental, Manifestations of Retinal Vessels, 1970; research, over 390 publs. on corneal bio-architectonic structure; visual accommodation by topographic determinism of anatomo-functional mechanism of zonules; neurosis of hypermetropia; exophthalmia through hypertonia of striated periocular musculature; non-specific action of drugs on eye; pathognomonic ERG indications in gen. fatigue phenomenon; syndrome of ciliary plexus of orbit; clinical and experimental surgery of the orbital ciliary plexus; retinal vessels theshold excitability in experimental hypertension; alternating recidivation of rickettsial and/or pararickettsial uveitis; rickettsial and/or pararickettsial retinal arterites, cataract and glaucoma; corneo-conjunctival tactile sensibility, cilio-accommodation and retinal vessels modifications at high altitude; altitude hyperophthalmotony by transfer of hydrophilic ions from blood into aqueous humour and ophthalmotonico-homeostatic reactions of calcium and of Vitamin C; hypermetropic cilio-accommodation in altitude hyperophthalmotony and augmentation of hypermetropic amplitude by Vitamin C. Count Palatine, lt. Patriarchal Venerable Noble Guard Universal Orthodox Slav-Holy Ch., Italy, 2000. Decorated Centenary Medal of King Carol I with Pro Patria bar on Ribbon, 1940, Sanitary Merit Cross 2d class, 1942, Medal of Crusade against Bolshevism, 1942, Commemorative medal, 1944, Med. Order of the Queen Mary Cross 2d class, 1945, Disting. Mark Cross of the Red Cross, 1945, Medal of Antifascist Liberation, 1954, Mil. Order of the Star 5th class, 1955, Commemorative Cross WWII, 1994; named Knight Hon. Comdr. Cross of the Chivalrous Order St. Andrew (Austria), 1992, Knight Hon. Comdr. Cross of the Internat. Order for Peoples' Concordance (Switzerland) 1992, Knight Grand Cross of the Tambauense Merit of Brazil, 1992, Knight Grand Cross of the Sovereign and Royal Order of the Crown of Susiana, Italy, 1995, Knight Grand Cross of the Sovereign and Venerable Religious Order of Ambrosini's, Italy, 1995, Ancient Royal Order of Physicians, Sri Lanka, 1995, Knight Grand Cross of the Sovereign and Religious Chivalrous Order of St. Elisabeth's, Italy, 1997, Knight Royal civalrous Order of St. Lukas, Germany, 1999; recipient Honor medals Internat. Inst. Human Labor Problems-World Ctr. for Labor Promotion Belgium, bronze medal, 1971, silver medal, 1974, Commemorative Pennon, 1977, plaquette Labor U., Luxembourg, 1973, silver medal Soc. Encouragement Rsch. and Invention, France, 1974, Pro Mundi Beneficio medal Acad. Humanities, Brazil, 1975, gold plaquette of homage for self-devotion in social work activities and to the rich activity in behalf of labor promotion, Belgium, 1978, Silver and Gold medals Universal Acad., Switzerland, 1983, cert. of merit Universal Inst. Peace, Switzerland, 1984, Bronze medal with collar ribbon Albert Einstein Internat. Acad. Found., 1986; also numerous certs. and diplomas for disting. svcs. and outstanding achievements, 1976-99, Cert. Excellence, Sri Lanka U., 1997, Princely Gold medal and Knight Grand Officer, Chivalrous Order of St. Gereon, Germany, 1999; citation meritorious achievement Internat. Writers and Artists Assn., 2000; nobility title reconfirmed as Count of Kraina and Vraina, belonging to Ancestral House of Carapancea, Italy, 1998; nobility title conferred as Marquis of Derneck-Memmelsdorf, Germany, 1999; nobility title conferred as Count Palatine and Lt. in Patriarchal Venerable Noble Guard Universal Orthodox Slav Holy Ch., Italy, 2000. Mem. Acad. Romanian Scientists (titular mem. sci. coun.), Romanian Soc. Ophthalmology, Romanian Soc. Normal and Path. Physiology, Internat. Soc. Clin. Electrophysiology of Vision, Internat. Soc. Metabolic Eye Disease, Assn. Internat. Glaucoma Congress, French, Belgian, Italian socs. ophthalmology, Am. Soc. Ophthalmology and Optometry, Am. Soc. Contemporary Ophthalmology, Japanese Ophthal. Soc., Am. Soc. Photobiology, World U. (mem. roundtable, chmn. nat. chief del. for Rumania, internat. faculty mem.), Marquis Giuseppe Scicluna Internat. U. Found. (hon. v.p.), Diandra U. (hon. pres.), Internat. Inst. Human Labor Problems-World Ctr. for Labor Promotion (internat. v.p., mem. coun. bd., pres. Rumania sect., nat. chief del. for Rumania), Albert Einstein Internat. Acad. Found. (hon. v.p.), N.Y. Acad. Scis. (live), Universal Acad. (hon. life), Prof. Ambrosini Acad. Natural Scis. and Psychobiophysics (Academician in Med. Scis., mem. academicians' honor corps), Royal St. Lukas Gilde Antwerpen Internat. Acad. (prof. honoris causa, chief exec. counselor), Chrysalis Universal Heraldic Acad. (Academician of honor) , Mediterranean's Acad. (titular academician), Sicilian Acad. Scis. (effective mem.), Costantiniana Acad. (academician honoris causa), Acad. Internat. House of Intellectuals, F.R.G., Internat. Acad. Scis., F.R.G. and San Marino (free mem. Internat. Sci. Coll.), Cultural Ctr. Portugal (Academician ad honorem), Tambauense Acad., Brazil (Well-Deserved mem.), World Safety Orgn. (hon. internat. cons., cert. safety exec., v.p. for Ea. Europe, exec. v.p. dir. at large, bd. dirs.), Internat. Union Physiol. Scis., European Soc. Philosophy Med. and Healthcare, Albert Schweitzer Soc. (hon. mem., sci. coun., Albert Schweitzer medal 1992), Physicians in Help of Life Orgn. (internat. v.p.), Human Factors Soc., Ergonomic Soc. French Lang., Internat. Soc. Biometeorology, Aerospace Med. Assn., French Soc. Angiology, Internat. Soc. Cybernetic Medicine, Internat. Assn. Applied Psychology, Assn. Med. Renewal, Soc. Encouragement to Progress (life, Honour Gold medal 1997), Mgmt. Profls. Assn. (program com.), Rev. Scienza 2001 (internat. acad. com. mem. hon. sci.), Rev. Internat. Surgery (editl. bd.), Internat. Parliament for Safety and Peace (chargé d'affaires at large in Rumania), Universal Alliance for Peace by Knowledge, High Sch. Rsch. (prof., attache of rsch.), World Constitution and Parliament Assn. (hon. sponsor), European Chamber of Extra-Judiciary Arbitrators and Experts Tech. Counsellors (hon., expert of Europe for clin. and exptl. physiol. and physiopathology of the eye 1991—, dep. chargé with mission), Internat. Assn. Educators for World Peace (hon. diploma), Assn. Chivalrous Order of St. Andrews (assoc.), Phoenix Inst. (hon., life), Inst. Internat. Affairs (supreme coun.), Inst. Planetary Synthesis World Tchr. Trust, World Goodwill, Internat. Assn. Eco-spiritual Movement BEAULIEU, World Fedn. Europeans, Internat. Coll. Surgeons (Fellow in Opthalmology, founder, 1st pres. Rumanian nat. sect.), Psycho-Soc. Prophilactic Nat. Ctr. Nat. Ctr. (Italy), World Ctr. Scis. (sci. counsellor-expert in psychiatry), Sovereign and Royal Order of the Crown of Susiana (bailiff, lt. gen. Romania, Grand Master hon., Knight Grand Cross, 1995), Sovereign and Venerable Religious Order of Ambrosini's (Grand Master hon., Knight Grand Cross, 1995), Sovereign and Religious Chivalrous Order of St. Elisabeth's (Grand Prior for Rumania, Knight Grand Cross 1997), Royal Order of Benedictions and Holy Crusades (Grand Master hon. for Rumania 2000). Home: 21 Prof Ion Bogdan St, R-71149 Bucharest Romania

CARBALLO, JOSE MARIA, banker; b. La Laguna, Tenerife, Spain, Apr. 25, 1944; s. Antonio Carballo and Mercedes Cotanda; m. Gabriela M. Beautell, July 24, 196 9; children: Laura, Olivia. Grad. in econs., U. Bilbao, Spain, 11967; grad. in bus. mgmt., Cath. Inst. Bus. Adminstrn., Madrid, 1969; student, City U., London, 1970. Asst. mgr. Rodriguez Lopez, S.A., Tenerife, 1967-69, Hill Samuel & Co. Ltd., London, 1970-73; mgr. syndications Banco de Bilbao, 1973-75; U.S. joint gen. mgr. Banco de Bilbao, N.Y., Grand Cayman, Miami, 1975-79; head internat. dept., chief mgr. Banco de Bilbao, Madrid, 1979-82; U.S. gen. mgr. Banco de Bilbao, N.Y., Grand Cayman, Miami, 1982-83; U.K. gen. mgr. Banco de Bilbao, London, 1983-88; gen. mgr. Banco de Bilbao Vizcaya, Europe, 1988-89; CEO, Banco Santander de Negocios, Madrid, 1989-93; gen. mgr. Banco Santander, Madrid, 1993—; chmn. La Unión Resinera, Vista Capital de Expansión, BSCH Activos Inmobiliarios; bd. dirs. Servi-Pack, Teleférico Pico de Teide. Hon. treas., v.p. Iberoam. Benevolent Soc., London, 1983. Mem. Overseas Bankers Club, Royal Automobile Club, Met. Club (N.Y.C.). Avocations: astronomy, ham radio, classical music, jet skiing.

CARBAUGH, JOHN EDWARD, JR., lawyer; b. Greenville, S.C., Sept. 4, 1945; s. John Edward and Mary Lou (McCarley) C.; m. Mary Middleton Calhoun: children: John, Martha, Leacy, Miller. BA, U. of South, 1967; JD, U. S.C., 1973, postgrad., 1967-69; postgrad., Georgetown U., 1977-79. Bar: S.C. 1973, U.S. Ct. Appeals (4th cir.) 1982, U.S. Supreme Ct. 1982. With White House Staff, Washington, 1969-70; campaign dir. re-elect Thurmond campaign Washington, 1970-73; legis. asst. U.S. Senate, Washington, 1974-82; pvt. practice Washington, 1982—; bd. dirs. Westech. Internat., Inc., Washington Watch, Inc., Splty. Materials and Mfg., Inc., Tech. Holdings, Inc., The Stealth Corp., Inc.; mem. Pres. Commn. on Econ. Justice, Washington, 1985-87. Author: The Revisionists, 1991, We Need Each Other: U.S.-Japan Relations Approach the 21st Century, 1992; co-author: A Program for Military Independence, 1980; contbr. articles to profl. jours. Rep. Nat. Platform Staff, 1976, 80, 84, 88, 92, 96; Presdl. Transition Team, 1980-81. Sgt. USAR, 1969-77. Mem. Met. Club. Republican. Presbyterian. Avocations: tennis, travel, horticulture. Office: 1300 N 17th St Ste 1100 Rosslyn VA 22209

CARBIS, COLIN RICHARD, toxicologist, immunologist; b. Melbourne, Australia, Dec. 13, 1956; s. Allan Richard and Shirley Ainsley (McDonald) C. BS in Biol. Sci., LaTrobe U., Melbourne, 1980; cert. in journalism, 1992, cert. in TV presenting, 1993; PhD in Environ. Toxicology, LaTrobe U., Melbourne, 1996; diploma in hypnotic sci., 1997, diploma in psychotherapy, 1998. Rsch. scientist Victorian Inst. of Animal Sci., Melbourne, 1980-91; microbiology tchr. Kangan Inst., Melbourne, 1994—; sr. scientist, project mgr. CSL Ltd., Broadmeadows, Australia, 1997—. Contbr. articles to profl. jours. LaTrobe U. scholar, 1991-95. Office: Victorian Inst Animal Sci CSI Ltd, 189-209 Camp Rd, Broadmeadows VIC 3047, Australia

CARBÓ-DORCA, RAMON, chemistry educator, researcher; b. Girona, Catalonia, Spain, Oct. 19, 1940; s. Marcos and Clara (Carre) C.; m. Caterina Arnau, June 24, 1964 (div. 1986); 1 child, Joan-Marc; m. Loreto Giralt, Oct. 21, 1995; children: Ariadna, Alexis. PhDChemE, Inst. Químic de Sarrià, Barcelona, Spain, 1968; PhD in Chemistry, U. Autònoma de Barcelona, 1974. Prof. numerari Inst. Químic de Sarrià, Barcelona, 1964-86; prof. titular U. Autònoma de Barcelona, 1970-87; catedràtic Universitat de Girona, 1988—; dir. Inst. Computational Chemistry, 1993. Author of 15 books; contbr. more than 215 papers to sci. jours. Recipient Narcis Monturiol medal Generalitat de Catalunya, 1994. Mem. Am. Phys. Soc. (life), Am. Chem. Soc., N.Y. Acad. Scis., Real Soc. Española de Química, Soc. Catalana de Química, Grup de Química Teõrica de Catalunya, Internat. Soc. Quantum Biology (life). Avocations: gardening, Oriental languages, Oriental religions, science fiction, poetry. Home: Plaça d'Europa 4, 17005 Girona Spain Office: Universitat de Girona, Campus de Montilivi, 17071 Girona Spain

CARBOGNANI, LANTE ANTONIO, research chemist; b. Caracas, DF, Venezuela, May 16, 1951; s. Lante Giuseppe and Maria Josefa (Ortega) C.; m. Miren Josune Arambarri, Dec. 27, 1980; children: Natasha, Josune, Michelle, Lante. Licenciado Chemistry, Simon Bolivar U., Caracas, Venezuela, 1977. Tchr. Simon Bolivar U., Caracas, 1977-78; R&D flavor chemist Nectaroma, SCS, Los Teques, Venezuela, 1978-80; R&D chemist PDVSA-Intevep, S.A., Los Teques, 1980-84, unit head, 1984-87, project mgr., 1984-87, R&D chemist, 1987-91, sr. chemist, 1991—; presenter in field. Contbr. chpt. to book and articles to profl. jours. Recipient Meritory Achievement award HDH Tech., UNESCO, Intevep, 1991. Mem. AAAS, USB Grads. Assn., Venezuelan Scientist Assn. Roman Catholic. Avocations: reading, diving, listening to music, hiking, home mechanics. Office: PDVSA-INTEVEP, PO Box 76343, 1070A Caracas DF, Venezuela

CARBONEL, JEAN, retired benefits and pensions consultant; b. Le Val D'Ajol, Vosges, France, Nov. 22, 1929; s. Cyprien Antoine and Gabrielle (Brulez) C.; m. Josette Vignes, May 25, 1974. Student, Coll. J. Méline, Remiremont, France, 1945, Ctr. for Tech. Studies Banking, Paris, 1954; univ. doctorate in regional econs., Strasbourg (France) U., 1969. Br. mgr. Vittel BNP Bank, 1946-57; regional sales mgr. La Vie Nouvelle Life Ins. Co., Paris, 1958-64; nat. sales mgr. La Fédération Continentale Life Ins. Co., Paris, 1964-65; founder, prin. Carbonel Conseils d'Enterprises, Paris, 1965-94; co-owner Assurances St. Honoré, Edmond de Rothschild Group, Paris, 1991-94; pres. Previnter Assn. for Expatriates, Paris, 1974-94, Previnform SA, Paris, 1977-94, Carbonel & Assocs. Inc., N.Y.C., 1977-90; mem. Name at Lloyd's, London, 1986-95. Contbr. numerous articles and papers on employee benefits to profl. publs.; co-inventor (game) Jouarep, 1958. With N.C.O. Infantry, 1949-50. Mem. Club Avenir (BNP Bank subs., co-founder, v.p. 1985-92), Montreux Internat. Bus. Club. Avocations: walking, wild mushrooms, traveling, cooking, crosswords.

CARBONELL, EUDALD, anthropologist, archaeologist, paleoanthropologist; b. Ribes de Freser, Spain, Feb. 17, 1953; s. Francesc and Dolors (Roura) C. M, U. Autónoma Barcelona, Spain, 1976; PhD, U. Paris, 1986. Lectr. U. Rovira Virgili, Tarragonia, Spain, 1987-99; prof. U. Robira, Tarragonia, Spain, 1999—; leader Atapuerca Rsch. project. Contbr. articles to profl. jours. Mem. AAAS, French Soc. Prehistory, Soc. Catalana d'Arqueologia. Avocations: skiing, trekking, travel. Office: U Rovira Virgili, Plaza Imperial Tarraco 1, 43005 Taeragona Spain

CARBONELL, JOSEP ILUIS, medical administrator; b. Valencia, Pais, Spain, Feb. 5, 1955; s. Vicente Carbonell and Maria Esteve. PhD, U. Valencia, Valencia, 1980; diploma in social medicine, U. Mex., 1983; specialist in pub. health, U. Paris, 1985; M in Parasitary Illness, WHO, Valencia, 1989. Civil servant Ministry Pub. Health, 1981—; med. dir. Meditarrania Medica Clinic, Valencia, 1986—; chief rschr. program rsch. in med. abortion Eusebio Hernandez Hosp., Havana, Cuba; rschr. in oncology Nat. Initiative of Oncology, Havana, 1995-99. Contbr. articles to profl. jours. Cpl. Arty., 1984-85. Mem. European Soc. Contraception, Spanish Soc. Contraception, Nat. Abortion Fedn. Avocations: tennis, sailing. Home: C/Pintor Luis Arcas 9 6o, 46013 Valencia Spain Office: Mediterrania Medica Clinic, C/Maestro Sosa 2, 46007 Valencia Spain

CARBONINI, LORENZO, engineer; b. Vercelli, Italy, June 17, 1965; s. Dario and Graziella (De Filippi) C.; m. Adriana Alimonda, June 28, 1989. Physics degree, U. Degli Studi, Torino, Italy, 1989, math. degree, 1992. R & D electromagnetic engr. Alenia DAAS, Caselle, Italy, 1989-96; R & D sys. mgr. Comtest Italia, Torino, 1996-98; project mgr. Marconi Comms., SpA, Genoa, Italy, 1998—. Contbr. articles to profl. jours.; inventor and patentee in field. Sgt. Italian Army, 1988-89. Mem. IEEE. Home: Via Castagneto 21/25, 16032 Camogli Italy Office: Marconi Comms SpA Radio Lab, Via A Negrone 1/A, 16153 Genoa Cornigliano, Italy

CARBY-HALL, JOSEPH ROGER, lawyer, researcher, consultant, educator, diplomat; b. Lydda, Palestine, Dec. 1, 1933; s. Daniel and Nina (Caruana) C-H.; m. Hilary Virginia Rudd, Mar. 3, 1962; children: Felicity, Marie-Louise. MA, U. Aberdeen, Scotland, 1959, LLB, 1961; PhD, U. Hull, Eng., 1986; DLitt, Northland Open U., Can., 1986. Asst. legal advisor David Brown Industries, Huddersfield, Eng., 1962-65; lectr. in law, then reader Bristol (Eng.) Polytechnic, 1965-69; rschr. U. Bristol, 1969-70; sr. lectr. in law U. Hull, Eng., 1970—, dir. internat. legal rsch.; legal advisor, cons. Road Haulage Assn., East Yorkshire, Eng., 1974—; vis. prof. law U. Lodz, Poland, 1990—, Jean Monnet Partner prof. Nicolas Copernicus U., Torun, Poland, 1991—, invited prof. René Descartes (Paris V) U., 1995, Nantes U., 1997, U. Barcelona, Spain, 1997—, U. Geneva, Switzerland, 1998—, U. Thrace, Greece, 1999—, hon. prof. Bordeaux U., 2000—, U. Sofia, Bulgaria, 2000—; rsch. dir. Internat. U., Hull, 1991—. Author: Rethinking Labour-Management Relations-A Case for Arbitration, 1991; editor Managerial Law, 1970—; dep. editor Jour. Legis. Studies, 1995—; contbr. articles to profl. and acad. jours. Pilot officer RAF; capt. Royal Artillery; comdr. Royal Naval Reserve. Decorated Reserve Decoration, Ministry of Def. (Eng.), Knight of the Cross of the Order of Merit (Poland); hon. consul for Hull, Govt. of Poland, 1994—. Mem. Soc. Pub. Tchrs. of Law, Authors' Club. Roman Catholic. Avocations: karate, skiing, classic cars, sailing, cycling. Home: 41 North Bar Without, Beverley HU17 7AG, England Office: U Hull Ctr Legis Studies, Cottingham Rd, Hull HU6 7RX, England

CARCASCI, GIOVANNI MARIA, network engineer; b. Florence, Italy, Aug. 27, 1962; s. Paolo and Franca (Cambiati) C. Cert., IBM, Florence, 1992; graphic editl. diploma, ITI Leonardo da Vinci, Florence, 1995. Sys. adminstr. Casalini Libra Spa, Florence, 1992—. Co-editor (periodical) I Libri, 1997. Fellow IEEE; mem. ACM. Avocation: disc jockey. Home: Via del Gelsomino 40-42, 50125 Florence Italy Office: Casalini Libri Spa, Via Benedetto de Maiano 3, 50014 Fiesole Firenze, Italy

CARD, RICHARD IAN EDWARD, law educator; b. Guildford, Surrey, United Kingdom, Aug. 23, 1944; s. Wilfrid and Barbara (Hill) C.; m. Rachel Kathleen McElhinney, Aug. 4, 1967. LLB, Nottingham U., 1966; LLM, Birmingham U., 1973. Lectr. Birmingham U., 1966-73, Univ. Coll. of Wales, 1973-75; reader Reading U., 1975-80; head of law sch. Trent Polytechnic, Nottingham, 1981-88, De Montfort U., Leicester, 1989—. Author: Public Order, 1987, Police Law, 1994, Criminal Justice and Public Order Act, 1994, Criminal Procedure and Investigations Act, 1996, Crime and Disorder Act, 1998, Public Order Law, 2000; editor: Criminal Law, 1995. Mem. Lord Chancellor's Adv. Com. on Legal Edn. and Conduct, London, 1991-97. Fellow Royal Soc. Arts; mem. Naval Club. Avocations: sailing, boating. Office: DeMontfort Univ Law Sch, The Gateway, Leicester LE1 9BH, England

CARDEN, JOY CABBAGE, educational consultant; b. Livermore, Ky., Dec. 15, 1932; d. Henry L. and Lillie (Richardson) Cabbage; m. Donald G. Carden, Dec. 19, 1954; children: Lynn Kehlenbeck, Tom Carden, Bob Carden, Jan Blount, Jim Carden. BA, Ky. Wesleyan, 1955; MA, U. Ky., 1975. Instr. music Owensboro (Ky.) City Schs., 1955-57; founder, dir. Musical Arts Ctr., Lexington, Ky., 1980-88; edn. specialist Roland Corp., L.A., 1989, dir. edn., 1990-94, edn. cons., 1994—; music edn. cons., writer, clinician Yamaha Corp., 1994—. Author: Music in Lexington Before 1840, 1980, Guide to Electronic Keyboards, 1988; editor, author: Carden Keyboard Ensemble Series; editor: Ensemble the Resource of Keyboard Instructors; composer ensembles for electronic keyboards. Mem. Music Tchrs. Nat. Assn. (commd. composer 1987), Nat. Guild Piano Tchrs. (state chmn. 1980-88), Nat. Conf. Piano Pedagogy (com. chmn. 1990-94), Ky. Music Tchrs. Assn. (state chmn. 1980-88). Avocations: running, art. Home and Office: 10501 McMeekin Ln Unit 103 Louisville KY 40223-6132

CARDENAS, JUAN CARLOS, plastic surgeon, educator; b. Medellin, Antioquia, Colombia, July 3, 1964; s. Carlos Fidel and Lillian (Restrepo) C. MD, Medellin Coll., 1987. Physician Svc. Seccional de Salud de Antioquia, San Roque, Colombia, 1988-89; gen. physician Med. Ctr. San Roque, Envigado, Colombia, 188-89; resident in plastic surgery Univ. Hosp. San Vincente de Paul, Medellin, 1991-95; plastic surgeon Medellin, 1996—, CMSR, Medellin, 1996—. Contbr. articles to profl. jours. Mem. Colombian Soc. Plastic Surgery, Colombian Med. Soc. Avocations: swimming, astrology. Home: Cr 42A # 40csur-29 AP 301, Envigado Autioqui, Colombia Office: San Roque Medical Ctr, CR 43A #32B/Sur 15, Envigado Autioqui, Colombia

CARDENAS, RAUL ALFREDO, business educator, management consultant; b. Santa Barbara, Chihuahua, Mex., Nov. 11, 1935; s. Raul Adolfo C. and Maria E. Herrera; m. Julieta H. Hernandez, Sept. 22, 1962 (dec. Jan. 2000); children: R. Adam, Sylvia, Nora, L. Bernardo. BSChE, Nat. Autonomous U. Mex., Mexico City, 1959; MSChE, U. Calif., 1965; postgrad., Yale U., 1969-70. Shift engr. Monsanto Mexicana, Lecheria, Mex., 1959-63; various positions Coca-Cola, Mexico City and Toronto, 1968-78; gen. mgr. Industria Envasadora Coca-Cola, Queretaro, Mex., 1980-81; constrn. mgr. Ingersoll Rand, Queretaro, Mex., 1982-83; prof. Inst. Tech. Estudios Superiores Monterrey, Queretaro, Mex., 1984—, dir. Escuela Graduados en Adminstrn. y Direcion Empresas, dean MBA studies, 1996—; cons. in field. Author: How to Achieve Quality, 1992, Leadership, 1997. Mem. Am. Soc. Quality (sr.), AIChE. Avocations: reading, writing, music, geography, art. Home: Ezequiel Montes Nte 86 C202, CP7600 Queretaro Qro, Mexico Office: ITESM Campus, E Gonzalez #500, CP 76130 Queretaro Qro, Mexico

CARDENAS, RAUL RODOLFO, JR., engineering executive, educator; b. Galveston, Tex., Feb. 5, 1929; s. Raul Rodolfo and Clementina (Munoz) C.; m. Mary R. Gaglio, Nov. 23, 1961; children: Dianne, Randolph, Patricia. BA, U. Tex.-Austin, 1951, postgrad., 1955-57; MS in Environ. Health Sci., NYU, 1963, PhD, 1970. Asst. rsch. scientist NYU, N.Y.C., 1961-63, asst. prof., 1966-72; rsch. assoc. Manhattan Coll., 1963-66; prof. dept. civil engring. Poly. Inst. N.Y., Bklyn., 1972-87; pres. Internat. Technol., Inc., Northvale, N.J., 1997—; also bd. dirs. Internat. Technol., Inc., Northvale, N.J., Tel Aviv, Israel; bd. dirs. Advanced Compost Technol (ACT), v.p., tech. dir.; lab. dir. sewage dist. Rockland County; adj. prof. Hunter Coll., Polytech U., Cooper Union Coll., CCNY; lectr., cons. in field. Contbr. articles to profl. jours. and books. First chmn. elect PCB Settlement Com., N.Y. State, 1974-76; chmn. bd. dirs., pres. Carpenter Environ. Assoc., Inc., 1980-91; gov.'s tech. adv. bd. State of N.J., 1985; mem. pres. adv coun. Dominican Coll. 1st lt. U.S. Army, 1952-54. Fellow Scientists Inst. for Pub. Info.; mem. Water Environ. Assn. (Outstanding Analyst Achievement award 1996), Am. Soc. Microbiology, AAAS, Interam. Assn. San. Engrs., N.Y. Explorers Club, Sigma Xi. Home and Office: 66 Pine Tree Ln Tappan NY 10983-2112

CARDENAS-ARROYO, SANTIAGO, painter; b. Santafe de Bogotá, Colombia, Dec. 4, 1937; came to U.S., 1947; s. Jorge and Margarita (Arroyo) Cardenas; m. Cecilia Fischer, July 29, 1967; children: Maria Cristina, Guillermo, Nicolas. BFA, R.I. Sch. of Design, 1960; MFA, Yale U., 1964. Dir. art dept. U. Nacional, Bogota, Colombia, 1972-74. One man show Museo Rufino Tamayo, 1996; exhibitions include Museo de Arte Contemporaneo Caracas Paintings and Drawings, 1959-95, 1995, Biblioteca Luis Angel Arango, Bogota Paintings and Drawings, 1959-95, 1996, The Museum of Modern Art, N.Y., 1992. With U.S. Army, 1960-62. Recipient first prize for painting II Bienal de Coltejer, 1972, first prize for painting Salon Nacional, 1976. Roman Catholic. Fax: 571-216-3841. Home: A Aéreo 102989, Santafe de Bogota Colombia

CARDENS, JEANICE WYNCLARE MAYLEN, geriatrics nurse; b. Long Beach, Calif., Dec. 26, 1932; d. Harold Lee Sr. and Vera Charolette (Crosby) Maylen; m. Alphonse Frank Cardens Jr., June 4, 1956; 1 child, Alphonse Frank III. Diploma in nursing, Hotel Dieu Cath. Hosp., El Paso, Tex., 1954. R.N., Tex. Nurse Dr. J. Gordon Bateman, Long Beach, 1957-69, Foremost Dairy Plant, Long Beach, 1962-72; owner, mgr. Nursing Home, Wickenburg, Ariz., 1972-76; pvt. duty home care Long Beach, Hanford, Calif., 1977—. Vol. Kings County Adult Day Care, Hanford, 1991—, Sr. Companion Program, Fresno, Calif., 1999—; childcare provider 1st Presbyn. Ch., Hanford, 1994—; sec., treas. Kings County Commn. Aging Coun., 1998—; bd. dirs. Kings County Grandparent Mentoring Program, 1999—. Mem. Am. Assn. Retired Persons (health chmn. 1993—, pres. Hanford chpt. 1995-98). Republican. Avocations: needle work, photography, music, family history. Home and Office: 1175 Fitzgerald Ln Hanford CA 93230-2435

CARDIA, GIUSEPPE, surgeon; b. Messina, Italy, May 1, 1951; s. Luigi and Rosaria (Mastroeni) C.; m. Evelina Nappi; children: Ivanoe Fernando, Stefano Luigi. MD, U. Messina, 1975. Intern Inst. of Surg. Semiology, U. Messina, 1975-76; intern Surg. Clinic, U. Bari, Italy, 1976-81, surg. asst. emergency dept., 1981, surg. asst., 1981-92; gen. surgery rschr. U. Bari, Italy, 1992-95, vascular surgery rschr., 1995—, med. pathology prof. nursing sch.,

1977-81, vascular surgery prof., 1992-93, emergency surgery prof., 1996—, vascular surgery prof., 1998—; sci. sec. New Trends in Vascular Surgery congress, 1986. Cerebral Ischemia and Carotid Disease congress, 1992, Italian Soc. Emergency Surgery congress, 1994. Editor: Bioeurama '95 Abstract Book, 1996. Sec. Amiuca, Assn. Med. Internat. U., Bari, 1978-87; reg. vice-sec. CISL-Medici, Bari, 1982-91; sec. Assn. Rsch. U. Bari, 1992-98. Lt. Italian Army, 1976-77. Mem. Italian Soc. Vascular Pathology (sect. vi.p. 1993-96), European Soc. Vascular Surgery, M. De Bakey Internat. Surg. Soc. Christian Ch. Avocations: tennis, rugby. Office: U of Bari Surgery III, Policlinico, Bari Italy

CARDILLO, JOHN POLLARA, lawyer; b. Ft. Lee, N.J., July 1, 1942; s. John E. and Margaret (Pollara) C.; m. Linda Bentey, Sept. 25, 1976; children: John Thomas, Joseph Pollara, Margaret Celia, Mark Luigi. BA, Furman U., 1964; postgrad., W.Va. U., 1965; JD, U. S.C., 1968. Bar: S.C. 1968, N.Y. 1970, Fla. 1972, U.S. Ct. Appeals (2d cir., 4th cir. 5th cir. 11th cir.) 1972, U.S. Dist. Ct. (ea. and so. dists.) N.Y. 1972, U.S. Dist. Ct. S.C. 1968, U.S. Dist. Ct. (so. and mid. dists.) Fla. 1974, U.S. Tax Ct. 1972, U.S. Supreme Ct. 1984. Assoc. Cardillo & Corbett, N.Y.C., 1968-71, Mays & McLellan, Columbia, S.C., 1971-72, Sorokoty, Monaco & Cervelli, Naples, Fla., 1972-75; ptnr. Monaco, Cardillo & Keith, P.A., Naples, 1975-96, Cardillo, Keith & Bonaquist, P.A., 1997—. Mem. Furman U. Alumni Bd. Dirs., 1984-89; active Environ. Adv. Coun., Collier County, Fla., 1983-87, past chmn.; past pres. Pine Ridge Civic Assn.; bd. dirs. YMCA Collier County, past pres., 1978-80, United Arts Coun. of Collier County, pres., 1991-92, bd. dirs. Big Bros., 1974-76; past pres. Naples Leadership Sch., 1987-88; mem. Leadership Collier, 1992; mem. Gov.'s Task Force on Drug Abuse, 1985; bd. advisors Gene and Mary Sarazen FDN, 1997—; bd. trustees Edison C.C., 1998-99; past chair 14th Congl. Dist., Fla. State Dem. Party, State Jud. Coun., Fla. Dem. Party; founding bd. dirs. Neighborhood Health Clinic, 1998—. Mem. ATLA, ABA, Am. Arbitration Assn. (arbitrator), Acad. Fla. Trial Lawyers, Fla. Bar (20th jud. cir., bd. govs. 1992—), Fla. Criminal Def. Attys., Collier County Bar Assn. (past pres.), S.C. Bar Assn., Assn. Bar City N.Y., Maritime Law Assn., Naples Area C. of C. (bd. dirs. 1990-95, pres. 1994-95). Home: 395 Ridge Dr Naples FL 34108-2933 Office: Cardillo Keith & Bonaquist PA 3550 Tamiami Trl E Naples FL 34112-4999

CARDIN, PIERRE, fashion designer; b. San Biagio di Callalta, Italy, July 2, 1922. Ed., St. Etienne, France. Tailor with Manby (men's tailor), Vichy, France, 1939-40; adminstr. with French Red Cross, 1940-45; ambassadeur honoraire UNESCO, 1991; etoile d'or d'argent del; Pordre du tresor Sacre, Japan, 1991. Designer with Paquin, Paris, 1945-47, House of Dior, Paris, 1947-50, propr. own design house, Paris, 1950—; owner Maxim's Restaurants; founder, dir. Théatre des Ambassadeurs-Pierre Cardin, 1970, renamed Espace Cardin, 1971; mgr. Société Pierre Cardin, 1973—; designer costumes for films including La Belle et la bête, 1946, A New Kind of Love, 1963, The V.I.P.s, 1963, Eva, 1964, The Yellow Rolls Royce, 1965, Mata Hari, Agent H-21, 1967, A Dandy in Aspic, 1968, The Immortal Story, 1969, You Only Love Once, 1969, Little Fauss and Big Halsy, 1970. Decorated Officier Legion d' Honneur, les insignes de Comdr. de l'Ordre du Mérite de la République Italienne, 1976, ; recipient Basilica Palladiana prize, 1973, le prix de l'EUR (Italian theatre Oscar), 1974, Gold Thimble awards for most creative high fashion collections, 1977, 79, 82, Career Achievement award, Cutty Sark Men's Fashion Awards, 1984. Office: 59 rue du Faugourg-St Honoré, 75008 Paris France also: 27 Ave Marigny, 75008 Paris France*

CARDINAL, ROGER, literature and visual arts educator; b. Bromley, Kent, Eng., Feb. 27, 1940; s. Thomas and Ada (Eliza) Melbourne; m. Agnès Meyer, Aug. 15, 1965; children: Daniel, Felix. BA, U. Cambridge, Eng., 1962, PhD, 1966. Lectr., asst. prof. U. Manitoba, Winnipeg, Can., 1965-67; lectr. U. Warwick, Coventry, Eng., 1967-68; lectr. U. Kent, Canterbury, Eng., 1968-76, sr. lectr., 1976-81, reader, 1981-87, prof., 1987—. Author: Outsider Art, 1972, Figures of Reality, 1981, Expressionism, 1984, the Landscape Vision of Paul Nash, 1989, The Cultures of Collecting, 1994, Private Worlds, 1998, Messages d'Outre-Monde, 1999, Henry Moore: In the Light of Greece, 2000. Avocations: travel, diary-writing, ephemera collecting, collage-making, botany. Office: Rutherford Coll, U Kent at Canterbury, Canterbury CT2 7NX, England

CARDINALE, SALVATOR, government official; b. Mussomeli, Italy, June 20, 1948. Min. Ministry Posts & Telecomm., Rome, 1998—. Office: Ministry Posts & Telecomm, Viale America, 00144 Rome Italy*

CARDÓ, ANDRÉS SORIA, publishing company executive; b. Iquitos, Peru, Jan. 4, 1961; s. Andrés and Delicia (Soria) C.; m. Inés Múgica Olaran, Nov. 12, 1994; children: Magdalena, Lucia, María Paz, Ines. Diploma, Cath. U., 1980, BS, 1984; diploma in finance, ESAN, Lima, 1986; MBA, IESE, Madrid, 1991. Prof. Academia Trener, Lima, 1980-88; controller Petroleos del Peru, Lima, 1984-87; controller Hilados Peinados, Lima, 1987-88, v.p., 1988-89; contr. offshore investments Santillana Pub. Group, Madrid, 1990-94; gen. mgr. Santillana, La Paz, Bolivia, 1994—, also bd. dirs.; cons. CRESE, Lima, 1984-89. Mem. coun. cultural affairs Embassy of Spain, 1998—. Grantee Inst. de Cooperacion Iberoamericana, 1988. Mem. Camara Boliviana del Libro (v.p. 1996-98), IESE, Colegio de Economistas de Lima, Council of Cultural Affairs Embassy of the Kingdom of Spain, Camara Camercio Boliviano-Espanola (bd. dirs.), Fundación Orquesta Sinfóuica Nacional (bd. dirs.). Avocations: music, dance, theater, books, sports. E-mail: santilla@ceibo.entelnet.bo. Office: Santillana de Ediciones SA, Ave Arce # 2333, La Paz Bolivia

CARDONA, JOSE N., financial company executive; b. San Juan, P.R., May 5, 1950; arrived in Dominican Republic, 1985; s. Jose N. and Francisca (Lozada) C.; m. Karen Rivera, June 29, 1972; children: Michelle, Geraldine, Francisco, Victor. BBA, U. P.R., San Juan, 1972. CPA. From auditor to audit mgr. KPMG Peat Marwick, San Juan, 1972-80; office mgr. in charge KPMG Peat Marwick, Ponce, P.R., 1980-82; quality control, tng. and assurance ptnr. KPMG Peat Marwick, Santiago, Chile, 1982-85; audit ptnr. in charge KPMG Peat Marwick, Santo Domingo, Dominican Republic, 1985-87, exec. ptnr., 1987—; quality performance reviewer KPMG Peat Marwick, Latin Am., Miami, 1984; co-editor Dominican Republic Means Business, 1988. Editor: Doing Business in Santo Domingo, 1992. Bd. dirs. Am. C. of C., Santo Domingo, 1992-94; fin. com. Carol Morgan Sch., Santo Domingo, 1995; den leader Boy Scouts Am., Santiago, 1984-85; bd. dirs., treas. Cord Morgan Sch. Santo Domingo, 1999—. Mem. AICPA, Coll. CPA de P.R. Roman Catholic. Avocations: tennis, golf, dominoes, music. Office: KPMG Peat Marwick, Edificio Hache Piso 1 JFK, Santo Domingo Dominican Republic

CARDONE, FABIO, physicist; b. Chieti, Italy, Oct. 14, 1960; s. Mario Cardone and Maria Pia Palesse; m. Silvia Aquilani; 1 child, Cristina. PhD in Physics, U. L'Aquila, Italy, 1984; EPP diploma, U. Rome, 1985. Rschr. U. Wis., Madison, 1985-86; assoc. rschr. INFN, Rome, 1984-92, CERN, Geneva, 1989-92; prof. Gregoriana U., Rome, 1992-96, Tuscia U., Viterbo, Italy, 1996-99, L'Aquila (Italy) U., 1999—; advisor Senate of Italian Republic, Rome, 1995—. Author: (with G. Cherubini) Radon, 1997, Radioattivita, 1998; contbr. articles to profl. jours. Recipient Galilei prize in physics Galilei Found., 1985, Honor prize in scis. Abruzzo Region, 1991; Nat. Group of Math. Physics of Nat. Coun. Rschs. and Nat. Inst. High Math. fellow. Mem. Italian Physics Soc., N.Y. Acad. Scis. Mem. Alleanza Nat. Party. Avocations: World War I aircraft history and modeling. Fax: 207082. Home: Via Villaggio Italia 5, I-67039 Sulmona Italy

CARDOSO, ELIE PATRICK, physician, researcher, toxicologist; b. Beja, France, Apr. 24, 1949; s. Isaac Andre and Frida (Gozlan) C.; m. Simone Marie-Jeanne Beller; children: Ruth, Thomas. BS, Lycee Condorcet, Paris, 1968; MD, U. Paris, 1976; postgrad., U. Strasbourg, France, 1991. Vol. practitioner Paris, 1976-79; occupl. health physician Somie, Paris, 1974-76, Interco. Occupation Health Assn., Strasbourg, France, 1979-81, 91—; vol. physician Paris and Strasbourg, 1982-91; presenter in field. Contbr. articles to profl. jours.; inventor in field. Grantee Sci. Action in Rsch. and Occupation Health, 1993, CISME-ASMT, 1999. Avocations: music, sports. Office: AIMT, 3 Rue de Sarrelouis, 67080 Strasbourg Cedex France

CARDOSO, FERNANDO HENRIQUE, president of Brazil; b. Rio de Janeiro, June 18, 1931; m. Ruth Corrêa Leite Cardoso; 3 children. Senator São Paulo, Brazil, 1983-92; min. of fgn. affairs Brasília, Brazil, 1992-93, min. of finance, 1993-94, pres., 1995—; Founder Cebrap. Author: 21 books; (with Enzo Faletto) Dependency and Development in Latin America. Founder, mem. Partido da Social Democracia Brasileira, 1988. Office: Office of Pres, Praca Tres Poderes 3 andar, 70150900 Brasilia Brazil*

CARDOSO, PEDRO SOUSA, bank executive; b. Porto, Portugal, Mar. 2, 1959; s. Alcino and Zilda (Sousa) C.; 1 child, Alice. Degree in law, Cath. U., Lisbon, 1983. V.p. Mfrs. Hanover, N.Y.C., 1984-89; dir. Chem. Bank, Lisbon, 1989-96, Chem. France, Lisbon, 1996-98; dir. Banco de Investimento Global, Lisbon, 1998-99, also bd. dirs. Mem. Oporto Cricket & Lawn Tennis Club, Club Portuense. Home: Rua do Molhe 604-5 o DTO, 4150 Porto Portugal Office: Prasa Duqoe de Saldanha 1 8, Lisbon Portugal

CARDU, MIRCEA, mechanical engineer; b. Gradinari, Romania, Oct. 31, 1934; s. Aurel and Ana (Cotarla) C.; m. Cornelia Chirila, July 20, 1965; 1 child, Sandu Dana. Engr., Tech. U. Timisoara, 1957. Engr. IRA 13, Timisoara, Romania, 1957-59; design engr. Resita (Romania) Works, 1959-67; head design dept., gen. mgr. Rsch. and Design Inst., Bucharest, Romania, 1967-94; sr. advisor SOCET S.A., Bucharest, 1994—. Author: (book) Paths to the Alls Horizons, 1998; co-author: Steam Turbines, 1976; inventor in field; contbr. articles to profl. jours. Recipient Works Order Romanian State, 1981, Order Sci. Merit, 1983, Tudor Vladimirescu, 1984. Mem. N.Y. Acad. Scis. Home: Sect 3, Str Daniel Barceanu 26, 74137 Bucharest Romania Office: SOCET SA, Calea 13 Septembrie 168-184, 76302 Bucharest Romania

CARDWELL, DAVID ANTHONY, physicist, educator; b. Matlock, Derbyshire, United Kingdom, Nov. 18, 1960; s. William and Margaret Annie (Smith) C.; m. Sharon Redfern, Sept. 25, 1982; children: Mark Ian, James Richard. BSc in Physics, U. Warwick, Coventry, United Kingdom, 1983, PhD in Physics, 1987; BA in Engring., U. Cambridge, United Kingdom, 1997. Chartered physicist. Prin. scientist GEC-Marconi, Towcester, United Kingdom, 1986-92; asst. dir. rsch. Cambridge U., 1992-97, lectr., 1997—; assoc. lectr. Open U., 1987-98; fellow Fitzwilliam Coll., Cambridge, 1993—; cons. GEC-Marconi, 1995—, BNFL, Capenhurst, United Kingdom, 1995-97, Linklaters, London, 1997-98, Urenco, Capenhurst, 1999—. Contbr. numerous articles to profl. jours. Gov. Manchester Grammar Sch., Manchester, 1999, Chelmsford County H.S., 1999. Mem. Inst. Physics, Material Rsch. Soc. Avocations: soccer. E-mail: dc135@hermes.cam.ac.uk. Office: U Cambridge, Madingley Rd, Cambridge CB3 0HE, United Kingdom

CARDWELL, HAROLD DOUGLAS, SR., retired rehabilitation specialist; b. Varnell, Ga., July 17, 1926; s. Arlie Amber and Hettie Ellen (Eledge) C.; m. Priscilla Dean Rumley, July 3, 1954; children: Harold Douglas, Jr., Ruth Ellen Cardwell-Landau. AA, Daytona Beach C.C., 1972; student, U. Fla., 1970; BA, Fla. Tech. U., 1974; postgrad., Clemson U., 1975. Registered landscape architect, Fla. Chem. operator Fercleve Chem. Corp., Oak Ridge, Tenn., 1945-46; draftsman C.M. Price Constrn. Co., Daytona Beach, Fla., 1947-48; bookkeeper, expediter W.A. Cardwell Constrn. Co., Gatlinburg, Tenn., 1948-49; office mgr., sales rep. J.H. Gordon Lumber Co., St. Augustine, Fla., 1949-51; asst. mgr. King Bros. Lumber Co., St. Augustine, 1951-56; pvt. practice landscape architect Port Orange, Fla., 1956-67; sr. rehab. specialist State of Fla. Divsn. of Blind Svcs., Daytona Beach, 1967-99, ret., 1999. Vice chmn. Daytona Beach Preservation Bd., 1987-98; adv. mem. task force Daytona Beach City Govt., 1987; vice chmn. Volusia County Hist. Commn., Deland, Fla., 1989-92; mem. adv. bd. Volusia County Hist. Preservation Bd., Deland, 1992-94; adv. mem. Flagler Centennial Com., Tallahassee, Fla., 1986; pres. Fla. Anthropol. Soc., Gainesville, 1988-89; chmn. Daytona Beach Preservation Bd., 1998—. Recipient Historian of Yr. award Volusia County Hist. Commn., 1988, Lazarus award for Preservation, Fla. Anthropol. Soc., 1988. Mem. Am. Hort. Therapy Assn. (registered hort. therapist, nat. treas. 1978-80), Fla. Nurserymen and Growers Assn. (bd. dirs. 1963-64, 68-69), Halifax Hist. Soc. (bd. dirs. 1974—), Fla. Hist. Soc., Lions (Pres.' award in leadership Port Orange/South Halifax club 1988). Democrat. Methodist. Avocations: history, anthropology, historical tools, pre-historic tools, writing, research. Home: 1343 Woodbine St Daytona Beach FL 32114-5740

CARDWELL, RICHARD ANDREW, Hispanic literature educator; b. Gillingham, England, July 16, 1938; s. Albert Andrew and Mary Margarethe (Knight) C. BA with honors, U. Southampton, England, 1960; PhD, U. Nottingham, England, 1972. Cert. in edn., 1961. Asst. lectr. U. Coll. Wales, 1964-65, lectr., 1966-67; lectr. U. Nottingham, 1967-74, sr. lectr., 1974-78, reader Hispanic lit., 1974-83, prof., 1983—; examiner in Spanish, London Bd., 1964-70, chief examiner, 1970-83; examiner Cambridge Bd., 1964-83. Author: Blasco Ibanez: LaBarraca, 1972, Juan R. Jimenez: The Modern Apprenticeship, 1977; editor: Ricardo Gil, 1972, Manuel Reina, 1978, Francisco A. de Icaza, 1983, Gabriel Garcia Marquez: New Readings, 1987, What is Modernism, 1993, Zorrilla Centenary Readings, 1993, New Readings on Byron, 1995, Juan Ramon Jimenez, 1995, Byron The European, 1998, Byron Volume in Reception of Brit. Author Series; contbr. numerous articles on 19th and 20th century Spanish writers; co-editor Renaissance and Modern Studies Jour.; mem. editl. panel of internat. jours. Recipient bronze medal Royal Humane Soc., 1958, Silver Cross for Gallantry Boy Scouts Assn. Mem. Assn. Hispanists Great Brit., Anglo-Catalan Soc., Soc. Latin Am. Studies, Real Academia Sevillana de Buenas Letras. Avocations: gardening, music, creating beautoful things. Home: The Yews, 6 Town St, Sandiacre Nottingham NG10 5DP, England Office: U Nottingham, Dept Hispanic Studies Univ Park, Nottingham NG7 2RD, England

CARDWELL, SANDRA GAYLE BAVIDO, hospital admissions professional; b. Vinita, Okla., July 14, 1943; d. Amos Calvin Wilkins and Gretta Odell (Pool) Wilkins Kudlemyer; m. Phillip Patrick Bavido, Nov. 26, 1964 (div. Dec. 1973); 1 child, Phillip Patrick Bavido Jr.; m. Max Loyd Cardwell, Jan. 18, 1979 (div. Apr. 1992). AA, Tulsa Jr. Coll., 1973; BS cum laude, U. Tulsa, 1975. Sec. with various cos., 1966-69; sec. U.S. Dept. Fgn. Langs., West Point, N.Y., 1969-70; dep. ct. clk. civil div. Tulsa County Dist. Ct., Tulsa, 1975-76, dep. ct. clk. U.S. Passport Office,, 1976-77; broker-assoc. Gordona Duca, Inc., Realtors, Tulsa, 1977-91; mem. admissions staff St. Francis Hosp., Tulsa, 1997—. Mem. Polit. Action Com., Tulsa, 1980—; vol. in children's rights and child abuse legis. and statutes. Mem. AAUW, Tulsa Met. Bd. Realtors, Okla. Bd. Realtors, Tulsa Christian Women's Club (contact advisor 1988-89), Stonecroft Ministries (life publs. 1987-88), United Meth. Women (bd. dirs. 1986-87), Phi Theta Kappa (pres.), Pi Sigma Alpha (treas. 1974). Republican. Methodist. Avocations: piano, boating, gardening, reading, walking. Home: 3908 S St Louis Tulsa OK 74105-3317 Office: St Francis Hosp 6161 S Yale Ave Tulsa OK 74136-1992

CARDY, PATRICK ROBERT THOMAS, composer, educator; b. Toronto, Ont., Can., Aug. 22, 1953; s. Robert Thomas and Mary Agnes (McGarry) C.; m. Janet Marie Ashley, Aug. 4, 1990; children: Jonathan Fitzpatrick Alexander, Michael Robert James. MusB with honors, U. Western Ont., 1975; MMA, McGill U., 1977, MusD, 1981. Asst. prof. music Carleton U., 1977-82, assoc. prof. music, 1982-92, prof. music Sch. for Studies in Art and Culture, 1992—; resident composer Sch. Music, Meml. U. Nfld., 1992; composer-in-residence Vancouver Chamber Music Festival, 1993; music cons. Nat. Arts Ctr. Orch., 1996. Compositions include Golden Days, Silver Nights, 1976-77, Apokalypsis, 1978, The Snow Queen, 1980, Jig, Mirages, 1984, Virelai, 1985, Tombeau, Tango!, 1989, The Little Mermaid, 1990, Avalon, 1991, Autumn, Chaconne, Serenade, 1992, Dulce et decorum est..., 1993, Et in Arcadia ego, 1994, Fhir a Bhata: The Boatman, 1994, Dreams of the Sidhe, 1995, La Folia, 1996, Bonavista, 1997, The Return of the Hero, 1997, ...and in the night the gentle earth is falling into morning..., 1998, Kalenda Maya, 1999, Zodiac Dances, 2000; contbr. articles to profl. publs. Recipient Can. Fedn. U. Women Creative Arts award, 1976. Mem. Soc. Composers, Authors and Pubs. of Can., Am. Fedn. Musicians, Can. Univ. Music Soc. (bd. dirs., treas. 1987-91), Espace Musique (various exec. positions including pres. 1987-88), Can. Music Ctr., Can. League Composers (various exec. positions including pres. 1987-93), Can. Musical Reproduction Rights Assn. Avocations: reading, tennis, baseball, curling. E-mail: pcardy@ccs.carleton.ca. Home: 29 Morgan's Grant Way, Kanata, ON Canada K2K 2G2 Office: 1125 Colonel By Dr, Ottawa, ON Canada K1S 5B6

CARDYN, GEORGE DEON, marketing educator; b. Patras, Achaia, Greece, Dec. 23, 1946; arrived in Eng., 1980; s. George S. and Zoe P. (Vetopoulos) Zafiropoulos; m. Victoria A.C. Deon, Jan. 6, 1978; children: Alexis, Nicolai. BSc in Economics, Grad. Sch. Industry, Piraeus, Greece, 1968; Diploma in Logistics Mgmt., USAF U., 1969, Diploma in Civil Law, 1970; MBA, No. Ill. U., Dekalb, 1973. Product mgr. Reckitt & Colman, Athens, Greece, 1974, Sterling-Drug, Athens, Greece, 1974-76; account exec. Minos S.A., Athens, Greece, 1976-78; head bus. lectr. mktg. mgmt. John Cabot Internat., Rome, 1978-80; mktg. cons. Saudi Indsl. Devel. Fund, Riyadh, Saudi Arabia, 1980-83; sr. cons., ptnr. designate MKT Consulenti Assoc., Rome, 1983-86; regional dep. cons. Worldtech Ventures, Ltd., Stevenage, Herts, 1986-88; mng. dir. Europrise Mgmt. Strategy Ltd., Brussels, 1988-90; bus. tutor The Open U., Milton Keynes, Eng., 1990-92; sr. lectr. internat. mktg. strategy U. Humberside, Hull, Eng., 1992—; bd. dirs. Infogroup Cons. Svcs. S.A., Athens; mem. exec. com. British Inst. Mgmt., Canterbury, Eng., 1988-90; speaker in field. Author: Management, 1985; contbr. articles to profl. jours. Sgt. Hellenic Air Force, 1969-71. Grantee EEC, 1985-88, BP, 1994. Fellow Royal Soc. for Arts, Mfr. and Commerce; mem. Inst. Mgmt., Chartered Inst. Mktg., Assn. MBAs. Avocations: travelling. Home: 3 Quantock Dr, Ashford Kent TN24 8HR, England Office: U Humberside Sch Internat Bus, Cottingham Rd, N Humber Hull HU6 7RT, England

CAREATTI, DANIEL M., information systems specialist; b. Charleori, Pa., Mar. 7, 1952; s. Milio and Margaret A. (Kamoda) C.; m. Janet M. Shaw, May 6, 1978; 1 child, Carmen G. A, ECPI, 1971. Dir. info. systems T.L.F., Danville, N.C., 1996-97, GenCorp, Greensboro, N.C., 1997-99, Crumley & Assocs., Greensboro, N.C., 1999—; cons. in field. Home: 805 E Sheraton Park Rd Pleasant Garden NC 27313-9248 Office: Crumley & Assocs 500 W Friendly Ave Greensboro NC 27401-2203

CARELESS, SIMONE, company executive; b. London, Sept. 9, 1961; arrived in South Africa, 1969; d. Edsin Charles Careless and Rose Marianne Powers; m. John Powers; 4 children. B Com., UNISA, Johannesburg, South Africa, 1987; chartered inst. co. sec., Tech. Inst., Johannesburg, 1989. Acct. Criteria, Yeoville, 1979-82; credit mgr. Deweys Reitz Attys., Johannesburg, 1983-91; acct. Paul Shapiro Attys., Johannesburg, 1991-93; chmn. Egrinscu Co., Johannesburg, 1993—; dir. Global Investment Co., South Africa. Avocations: economics, business, internet, reading. Address: PO Box 1343, Rosettenville, Johannesburg 2130, South Africa

CAREW, PETER EDWARD, lawyer; b. Melbourne, Victoria, Australia, Dec. 5, 1953; s. Eric Cuthbert and Agnes Mary (Doyle) C.; m. Lisa Mary McNamara, April 23, 1983; children: Rachel, Danielle, Alexander. BA in Econs., Monash U., Australia, 1976, LLB, 1978; graduate, Leo Cussen Inst., Australia, 1979. Admitted Supreme Ct. Victoria as Barrister and Solicitor; cert. specialist in family law. Ptnr. Carew Counsel, Melbourne, Australia, 1979-83, Carew Counsel Holmes, Melbourne, Australia, 1983-90; dir. Carew Counsel Pty. Ltd., Melbourne, Australia, 1990—. Named Queen's Scout, Boy Scouts Assn., 1970. Mem. Kooyong Lawn Tennis Club, Nat. Golf Club, Melbourne Cricket Club, Sorrento Sailing Club. Avocations: golf, tennis, snow skiing. Office: Carew Counsel Pty Ltd, Level 7 555 Lansdale Street, Melbourne 3000 Victoria, Australia

CAREW, SIR RIVERS VERAIN, writer; b. Guildford, England, Oct. 17, 1935; m. Susan Babington Hill, Dec. 7, 1968 (div. 1991); children: Marcella, Marina, Miranda, Gerald; m. Siobhán Nic Chárthaigh, Apr. 9, 1992. B of Agrl. Sci., Trinity Coll., 1956, MA, 1960. Prodn. asst. Irish Tourist Bd., Dublin, 1962-67; asst. editor Ireland of the Welcomes (ITB Mag.), Dublin, 1964-67; sub editor Irish Nat. Broadcasting Orgn., Dublin, 1967-77, deputy chief sub editor, 1977-82, chief sub editor, 1982-87; chief sub editor BBC World Svc., London, 1987-93; retired, 1993. Co-editor: The Dubliner/ Dublin Mag., 1964-69; author of poems. Mem. Ch. of England. Avocations: music, reading. Home: Cherry Bounds, Hicks Ln, Cambridge CB3 0JS, England

CAREW POLE, SIR JOHN RICHARD, county government representative, farmer; b. Antony, Cornwall, Eng., Dec. 2, 1938; s. John Gawen and Cynthia Mary (Burns) C.P.; m. Victoria Marion Anne Lever, Sept. 26, 1966 (div. 1973); m. Mary Dawnay, 1974; children: John Tremayne, John Alexander George. Grad., Eton Coll., 1956; chartered surveyor, Royal Agrl. Coll., 1967. Qualified assoc. Royal Inst. Chartered Surveyors. Chartered surveyor Laws & Fiennes, Oxford, Eng., 1967-73; county councillor Cornwall County Coun., 1973-93, chmn. planning com., 1979-83, chmn. fin. com., 1985-89, chmn. property com., 1989-93; high sheriff Cornwall County, 1979, dep. lt., 1988—. Trustee Nat. Heritage Meml. Fund, 1991-2000, Tate Gallery, London, 1993—, Pilgrim Trust, 2000, Trust House Found., 1998—; commr. Countryside Commn., Cheltenham, Eng., 1991-96. Lt. Coldstream Guards, 1958-63. Mem. Fishmongers Co. (ct.), Royal Hort. Soc. (coun. 1999—). Mem. Ch. of Eng. Avocations: theater, gardening, collecting contemporary art, walking. Home: Antony House, Torpoint Cornwall PL112QA, England

CAREY, ALIDA LIVINGSTON, political scientist, writer, reporter; b. Phila., June 29, 1928; d. Henry Reginald and Margaret Howell (Bacon) C.; m. Isaac Kleinerman, Febr. 29, 1964 (div. Aug. 1967). Attended, Chatham (Va.) Hall Sch., 1947, Grad. Inst. of Internat. Studies, Geneva, Switzerland, 1949-50; BA, Smith Coll., Northampton, Mass., 1951. Promotion mgr. The Reporter Mag., N.Y.C., 1951-52; rschr., writer Newsweek Mag., N.Y.C., 1952-54; rschr. Edward R. Murrow series "See It Now" CBS-TV, Paris, 1954; reporter, writer Agence France-Presse, Paris, 1955; nat. U.S. correspondent The Reporter Mag., N.Y.C., 1968; reporter, writer Forbes Mag., N.Y.C., 1969-70; freelance writer various publs., 1955—. Contbr. numerous articles to profl. jours. including N.Y. Times Sunday Mag., Guardian of London, Christian Sci. Monitor, The North Am. Rev. Mem. com. to Oppose Sale of Saint Bartholomew's Ch., Inc., N.Y., 1986-91; vol. Saint James Ch. Soup Kitchen, N.Y., 1986—. Mem. ACLU, French Inst./Alliance Francaise, Mcpl. Art Soc., Editl. Freelancers Assn. Avocations: music, theater, film, photography. Office: 200 E 74th St Apt 4H New York NY 10021-3606

CAREY, ARTHUR BERNARD, JR., editor, writer, columnist; b. Phila., May 16, 1950; s. Arthur Bernard and Mary Louise (Lynch) C.; m. Katherine Ann White, Apr. 14, 1973 (div. Feb. 1980); m. Tanya Marie Walters, July 17, 1982; 1 child, Edward Lynch. A.B., Princeton U, 1972; M.S., Columbia U., 1975. Editor Fedn. Telephone Workers of Pa., Phila., 1972-74; reporter Bucks County Courier Times, Levittown, Pa., 1975-77, Phila. Inquirer, 1977—. Author: In Defense of Marriage, 1984, The United States of Incompetence, 1991; editor: That's Livin', 1984. Term trustee The Episcopal Acad., Merion, Pa., 1982-88, alumni trustee, 1990-93; mem. com. to nominate alumni trustees Princeton U., 1989-92. Recipient Edward J. Meeman Conservation award Scripps-Howard Found., 1977, Best Story of the Yr. award Nat. Conf. Sunday Mags., 1983, George Washington Honor medal Freedoms Found., 1984, Disting. Journalism award Epilepsy Found. Am., 1997, Robert Joplin Sci. Writers award Am. Orthopedic Foot and Ankle Soc., 1998; Robert E. Sherwood Traveling fellow Columbia U., 1975; best feature story Pa. Soc. Newspaper Editors, 1986, 91. Mem. Soc. Profl. Journalists (best newsfeature N.J. chpt. 1979). Democrat. Episcopalian. Avocations: running; weight lifting; carpentry; antique jeeps. Home: 928 Clover Hill Rd Wynnewood PA 19096-1631 Office: Phila Inquirer 400 N Broad St Philadelphia PA 19130-4099

CAREY, DEAN LAVERE, fruit canning company executive; b. Biglerville, Pa., Nov. 29, 1925; s. Earl E. and Ann Olivia (Newman) C.; m. Doris M. Dugan, July 21, 1949; children—Philip D., Juanita Ann. B.S., U. Pitts., 1949. With Knouse Foods Corp., Inc., Peach Glen, Pa., 1949—; contr. Knouse Foods Corp., Inc., 1955-59, asst. gen. mgr., 1960-62, gen. mgr., 1963-65, pres., 1966—, also dir. Dir. Blue Cross, Harrisburg, Pa.; chmn. Capital Blue Cross, Harrisburg. Served with USNR, 1944-46. Mem. Pa. Chamber Bus. and Industry (bd. dirs.). Lutheran. Clubs: Am. Legion, Masons, Shriners. Office: Knouse Foods Coop Inc 800 Peach Glen Idarille Rd Peach Glen PA 17375-0001

CAREY, EDWARD JOHN, insurance company executive; b. Kansas City, Aug. 12, 1947; s. Joseph George and Nelda (Roy) C.; m. Dana Marie LeMay, Mar. 30, 1985; children: Bridget C., Edward J. Jr., William T. BS in Polit. Sci., Rockhurst Coll., 1973. Multi line claims adjuster Safeco Ins. Co., Kansas City, 1973-79; risk mgr. Dolphin Titan Internat., Houston, 1980-85, Pennzoil Co., Houston, 1985-89; ins. broker Arthur J. Gallagher Co., Houston, 1989-99; ptnr. John L. Wortham & Son LLP Ins., Houston, 1999—; instr., assoc. risk mgmt. designation Risk and Ins. Mgmt. Soc., Houston, 1985-95. Charter mem. Offshore Energy Ctr. Soc., Galveston, Tex., 1996; scout leader Boy Scouts Am., Houston, 1999-2000. With USMC, 1966-70. Mem. Houston Club, Univ. Club. Roman Catholic. Avocations: golf, private pilot, collecting books on Albrecht Durer.

CAREY, ERNESTINE GILBRETH (MRS. CHARLES E. CAREY), writer, lecturer; b. N.Y.C., Apr. 5, 1908; d. Frank Bunker and Lillian (Moller) Gilbreth; m. Charles Everett Carey, Sept. 13, 1930; children: Lillian Carey Barley, Charles Everett. BA, Smith Coll., 1929. Buyer R. H. Macy & Co., N.Y.C., 1930-44, James McCreery, N.Y.C., 1947-49; Carey writer and lectr. Book reviewer, 1949—, syndicated newspaper articles, 1951, (with Lillian Moller Gilbreth) (McElligott medallion Assn. Marquette U. Women 1966); author: Jumping Jupiter, 1952, Rings Around Us, 1956, Giddy Moment, 1958, (with Frank B. Gilbreth, Jr.) Cheaper by the Dozen, 1949 (Prix Scarron French Internat. Humor award 1951, over 50 translations), Belles on Their Toes, 1951; contbg. author: Smith Voices—Selected Works by Smith College Women, 1990, 99; lifetime papers represented in collections at Smith Coll.; also mag. articles and book revs. Bd. dirs. Right to Read, Inc., 1968—, co-chmn., 1967; lay adv. com. Manhasset (N.Y.) Bd. Edn.; trustee Manhasset Pub. Libr., 1953-59, v.p., 1956-59; trustee Smith Coll., 1967-72; active in care-preservation and current student use of Frank B. and Lillian M. Gilbreth lifetime papers at Purdue U., Smith Coll. and interat. Montgomery award Friends of Phoenix Pub. Libr., 1981, honored guest Ariz. Lib. Friends, 1994; recipient Internat. Mgmt. award: the Gilbreth Medal, Soc. for Advancement of Mgmt., 1996. Mem. Authors Guild Am. (life mem., mem. guild council 1955-60), PEN, North Shore Club, Smith Coll. Club (asst. chmn. scholarship com. L.I. chpt. 1950-59), Smith Coll. Club (vice chmn. scholarship com. Phoenix chpt.). Home: 701 W Herbert Ave Apt 64 Reedley CA 93654-3951

CAREY, GEORGE LEONARD, archbishop of Canterbury; b. Nov. 13, 1935; s. George and Ruby Carey; m. Eileen Harmsworth Hood, 1960; 4 children. BD with honors, London Coll. Div., ThM; PhD, King's Coll., London. Ordained priest Ch. of Eng. Curate St. Mary's, Islington, Eng., 1962-66; lectr. Oak Hill Coll., Southgate, Eng., 1966-70, St. John's Coll., Nottingham, Eng., 1970-75; vicar St. Nicholas' Ch., Durham, Eng., 1975-82; prin. Trinity Coll., Stoke Hill, Bristol, Eng., 1982-87; hon. canon Bristol Cathedral, 1984-87; bishop of Bath and Wells Eng., 1987-91, archbishop of Canterbury, 1991—. Author: I Believe in Man, 1975, God Incarnate, 1976; co-author: The Great Aquittal, 1980, The Church in the Marketplace, 1984, The Meeting of the Waters, 1985, The Gate of Glory, 1986, The Message of the Bible, 1986, The Great God Robbery, 1989, I Believe, 1991, Sharing a Vision, 1993, Spiritual Journey, 1994, My Journey, Your Journey, 1996, Canterbury Letters to the Future, 1998, Jesus 2000, 1999; contbr. numerous articles to profl. publs. With RAF, 1954-56. Avocations: reading, writing, walking. Address: Lambeth Palace, London SE1 7JU, England

CAREY, LINDSAY BRIAN, minister, researcher; b. Perth, Australia, 1961. BA, Victoria U., 1985; BTheol, Melbourne U., 1989, BEd St, 1991; M of Applied Sci., LaTrobe U., 1996, postgrad., 2000. Educationalist RAAF, Australia, 1979-81; parish min. Uniting Ch., Australia, 1992—; journalist Australian Journalists Assn., Australia, 1982-86; indsl. chaplain Interchurch Trade & indsl. Mission, Australia, 1989-92; lectr., tutor LaTrobe U., 1989-92; nat. rsch. officer Australian Health and Welfare Chaplains Assn., 1999—. Author: Health and Well Being Hospital Chaplaincy: Health Policy in Australia, 1997, Prayer in the Clinical Context, 1999; editor: Chaplaincy in the Clinical Context, 1999; contbr. articles to profl. jours. Recipient Wagstaff award Theol. Hall Victoria, 1997-2000; Love to the World scholarship Uniting Ch. NSW, 1998. Mem. Uniting Ch. in Australia. Office: Sch Pub Health, LaTrobe Univ, Bundoora VIC 3083, Australia

CAREY, MARIAH, vocalist, songwriter; b. N.Y.C., 1969; d. Alfred Roy and Patricia Carey; m. Thomas Mottola, June 5, 1993. Back up vocalist with Brenda K. Starr. Albums: Mariah Carey, 1990, Emotions, 1991, Mariah Carey MTV Unplugged, 1992, Music Box, 1993 (Grammy nomination, Best Pop Female Vocal for "Dreamlover"), Merry Christmas, 1994, Daydream, 1995, Butterfly, 1997, #1's, 1998, Rainbow, 1999; appeared in movies All That Glitters, 1998, The Bachelor, 1999, (mini series) Motown 40: The Music Is Forever. Recipient Grammy awards Best New Artist of 1990, Best Pop Vocal Performance by Female, 1990. Office: Columbia Records 550 Madison Ave New York NY 10022-3211

CAREY, PETER PHILIP, novelist; b. Bacchus Marsh, Australia, May 7, 1943; m. Alison Summers, Mar. 16, 1985; 2 children. LittD, U. Queensland, Australia, 1989; LHD, The New Sch. Tchr. creative writing NYU, Princeton (N.J.) U., Columbia U., N.Y.C. Author: The Fat Man in History, 1974, War Crimes, 1979, Bliss, 1981, Illywhacker, 1985, Oscar and Lucinda, 1989 (Booker prize), (with Wim Wenders) Until the End of the World, 1990, The Tax Inspector, 1991, The Unusual Life of Tristan Smith, 1994, The Big Bazoohley, 1995, Jack Maggs, 1997 (Commonwealth prize 1998). Recipient NSW Premier's Literary award, Miles Franklin award (3), Nat. Book Coun. award (2), Age Book of Yr. award (3), Victorian Premier's Literary award. Fellow Royal Soc. Lit. Office: c/o Binky Urban ICM 40 W 57th St New York NY 10019-4001

CAREY, RONALD, former labor union leader; b. N.Y.C., Mar. 22, 1936; m. Barbara Murphy; 5 children. Pres. local union Internat. Brotherhood of Teamsters, Long Island City, NY, 1967—; pres. Internat. Brotherhood of Teamsters, Washington, 1992-99. Avocations: swimming, diving, fishing.

CAREY, ROY, physicist; b. Coventry, U.K., June 12, 1936; s. Leo Patrick and Annis (Pinnington) C.; m. Suzanne Elizabeth Marshall, Oct. 7, 1941; children: Petra, Tanya, Maxwell. DSc, U. Nottingham, 1999, BSc, 1958, PhD, 1961. Chartered physicist. Lectr. Coll. of Tech., Coventry, 1961-64, sr. lectr., 1964-68; prin. lectr. Polytechnic, Coventry, 1968-78; reader in physics Coventry U., 1978-86, prof., 1986—; dir. Ctr. for Data Storage Materials, Coventry U., 1992—. Author: Magnetic Domains and Techniques for their Observation, 1966; contbr. articles to profl. jours. Fellow Inst. of Physics, Royal Microscopical Soc.; mem. Coventry Aeroplane Club (pres. 1990-95, chmn. 1995-97, v.p. 1997—). Office: Coventry Univ, Priory St, Coventry CV1 5FB, England

CAREY, WILLIAM POLK, investment banker; b. Balt., May 11, 1930; s. Francis J. and Marjorie A. (Armstrong) C. Grad., Pomfret Sch., 1948; student, Princeton, 1948-50; BS in Econs., U. Pa., 1953; ScD. (Hon.), Ariz. State U., 1998. V.p., gen. mgr. A. J. Orbach Co., Plainfield, N.J., 1955-58; prin. W. P. Carey & Co., Bloomfield, N.J., 1958-63; pres., dir. Internat. Leasing Corp., N.Y.C., 1959-89; chmn. exec. com., dir. Hubbard, Westervelt & Mottelay, Inc. (now Merrill Lynch Hubbard, Inc.), N.Y.C., 1964-67; dept. head Loeb, Rhoades & Co. (now Lehman Bros.), N.Y.C., 1967-71; vice chmn. investment banking bd., dir. corporate finance duPont Glore Forgan Inc., 1971-73; pres., dir. W.P. Carey & Co., Inc. and affiliates, N.Y.C., 1973-83, chmn., 1983—; gen. ptnr. Corp. Property Assocs. (CPA), N.Y.C., 1978-97, chmn. CPA series of pub. ltd. partnerships and real estate investment trusts, 1979—; chmn. Carey Instnl. Properties, N.Y.C., 1991—, W.P. Carey & Co. LLC, W.P. Carey Internat. LLC, 2000—; chmn. exec. com. Carey Diversified LLC, 1997-2000; adv. com. U.S. Treasury Dept., 1986-92; exec. in residence Harvard Bus. Sch., 1999. Trustee Johns Hopkins U., Md. Hist. Soc.; adv. bd. Johns Hopkins Sch. Advanced Internat. Studies; life trustee Gilman Sch. Balt.; trustee, mem. exec. com. Rensselaerville (N.Y.) Inst., 1979—; chmn. bd. trustees Oxford Mgmt. Ctr. Assocs. Coun., 1984-94, hon. trustee 1994—; mem. coun. mgmt. Templeton Coll., Oxford U., 1970-95; chm. St. Elmo Found., W.P. Carey Found.; vis. com. econs. U. Pa.; dir. (hon.) Edmund Niles Huyck Preserve, Inc.; mem. leadership com. James A. Baker III Inst. for Pub. Policy Rice U.; gov. Nat. Assn. Real Estate Investment Trusts, 1993-97. 1st lt. USAF, 1953-55. Estab. William Polk Carey prize in econs., Carey term chairs in econs. and fin. U. Pa., Carey chair in math. Pomfret Sch., Carey prize in math. Calif. Inst. Tech., Armstrong law prize Ariz. State U. Mem. Soc. Mayflower Descs. (gov. emeritus), The Pilgrims, The Brook, Racquet and Tennis Club, Univ. Club, Penn Club (N.Y.), St. Elmo Club (Phila. and N.Y.C.), Maryland Club (Balt.), Harvard U. Faculty Club (Cambridge), N.E. Harbor Fleet (N.E. Harbor, Maine), Delta Phi. Episcopalian. Home: 525 Park Ave New York NY 10021-8141 also: Fullerlea Rensselaerville NY 12147 Office: 50 Rockefeller Plz New York NY 10020-1605

CAREZ, CHRISTIAN CHARLES-MARIE, photographer; b. Brussels, Belgium, Mar. 13, 1938; s. Leon and Germaine (Bertrand) C. Diploma, Nat. Sch. Visual Arts, Brussels, 1960. Freelance fashion and advt. photographer Brussels, 1963-74, San Francisco, 1970; prof. photography, Ecole Nat. Superieure des Arts Visuels de La Cambre, Brussels, 1981; presenter workshops. photographer series on various topics; one-man shows include: Palais des Beaux Arts, Brussels, 1974, 78, Canon Gallery, Amsterdam, 1979, Galerie Synergon, Brussels, Atelier Sainte-Anne, Brussels, 1985, 86, Maison de la Culture d'Amiens, France, 1986, Theatre du Ront-Point, Paris, 1986, De Brakke Grond, Amsterdam, 1988, Cultureel Centrum, Hasselt, 1991, Galerie Willy D'Huysser, Brussels, 1994, Galerie Focale, Nyon, 1994, Maison Culture, Namur, 1995, Galeirei Jean-Luc Pons, Paris, 1995, Mus. Photographie, Mont-sur-Marchienne, 1997, Maison Architectes, Ajaccio, 1998, Maison Braun, Prague, Inst. Francais, Bratislava, 2000; group shows include: Galerie Totem, Brussels, Maison d'Images, Brussels, 1983, Galerie Accent, Paris, 1984, Galerie Paule Pia, Antwerp, Belgium, 1985, Palais Expositions, Brussels, 1987, Maison Mutualites, Reims, 1988, Vlaams Cultureel Centrum, Amsterdam, 1989, Mois Photo, Nice, 1989, Ctr. Culturel Beaunord, Paris, 1990, Ctr. Culturel Botanique, Brussels, 1991, Tamagawa Arena Hall, Tokyo, 1992, Mus. Photographie, Mont-sur-Marchienne, 1993, Galerie Pons, Paris, 1994, Hotel Sully, Paris, 1996, Sala Exposicionnes Toree Canal Isabel II, 1997, ISELP, Brussels, 1999; represented in numerous collections, U.S. and Europe. Home and Studio: 40 Laarheidestraat, 1650 Beersel Belgium

CARGILL, BARBARA JOAN, management educator; b. Melbourne, Victoria, Australia, Feb. 6, 1950; d. Arthur Reginald and Doris Evelyn (Chaffey) Whitford; m. Michael James Faris, Jan. 1976 (div. July 1985); children: Nicholas, Louisa; m. Miles Nicholls, 1998. BA, U. Melbourne, 1970, MEd, 1995. Psychologist Dept. Labor, Melbourne, 1971-74; sr. psychologist Dept. Employment, Melbourne, 1974-79; pvt. cons. Melbourne, 1979-85; lectr. in orgnl. behavior Swinburne U. Tech., Melbourne, 1985-89, sr. lectr. orgnl. behavior, 1990-94, head Sch. Mgmt., 1994-97, head Sch. Bus., 1997—; cons./mgmt. trainer, 1971—; sec. Australian Inst. Human Rels., Victoria, 1977-78; spkr. numerous confs. in field. Contbr. articles to profl. publs. Mem. Australian Human Resources Inst. Avocations: historic architecture, gardening, family. Office: Swinburne U Tech, PO Box 218, Hawthorn Victoria 3122, Australia

CARGILL, PAULA MARIE, social worker, gerontologist; b. Henrietta, N.C., Sept. 18, 1943; d. John Edwin and Mabel Anne (Bridges) C. BA in Sociology/French, Winthrop Coll., 1965; MSW, So. Bapt. Theo. Sem., 1973; MS in Social Work, U. Louisville, 1975; grad. in gerontology, U. Mich., 1983. Lic. ind. social worker, lic. nursing home adminstr. Social worker Connie Maxwell Children's Home, Greenwood, S.C., 1965, 70-71; tchr. French secondary pub. schs., N.C., S.C., 1965-70; instr. sociology and French North Greenville Coll., Tigerville, S.C., 1973-74; adj. assoc. instr. North Greenville Coll., Tigerville, 1973-85; clin. social worker S.C. Dept. Mental Health, Simpsonville, 1975-77; social work supr. J Health Care Ctr., Inc., Simpsonville, 1977-84, S.C. Dept. Corrections, Greenville, 1984-89, 90-91; exec. dir. Grady H. Hipp Nursing Ctr., Greenville, S.C., 1989-90; access and in-home program dir. Sr. Action, Greenville, 1991-92; social worker S.C. Dept. Health and Environ. Control, 1992; social work cons. Interim Healthcare, 1992-96; dir. social work Richard Michael Campbell Vets. Nursing Home, Anderson, S.C., 1993; social worker, nursing home and rehab. agy. cons. Aging Cons. Svcs., Greenville, 1982—; ctr. dir. Choice Cmty. Mental Health, Greenville, 1996-97; with Bon Secours St. Francis Homecare, Greenville, 1997-2000, Bon Secours St. Francis Hosp., 2000—. Contbr. articles to religious mag. Bd. dirs. Greenville County Alcohol/Drug Abuse Commn., 1981-84, Ch. Cmty. Ministries, Greenville Bapt. Assn., 1982—, Grady H. Hipp Nursing Ctr., 1985-89, Rolling Green Village Retirement Ctr., 1990-91, 97-2000—, Upstate Alzheimer's Assn., 1990-92, 94-2000, Greenville County Mental Health Assn., 1999-2000; mission action cons. So. Bapt. Conv., 1982-83; coun. mem. Bapt. Women, Greenville, 1979-81, 88-91. Mem. NASW (bd. dirs. S.C. chpt. 1976-77, 79-81, 83-85, 90-91), S.C. Health Care Assn., Alumni Leadership Greenville. Avocations: building dollhouses and antique doll furniture, foreign languages, travel, walking. Home and Office: 1 Kenilworth Dr Greenville SC 29615-2320

CARGNELUTTI PLANISICH, MARIO LUIS, engineer, consultant; b. Reconquista, Santa Fe, Argentina, Nov. 16, 1945; s. Manuel F. and Maria T. (Planisich) C. Student, U. Sante Fe, 1964-73; M of Polit. Econs., U. Belgrano, Buenos Aires, 1986. Jefe control calidad Bouril Argentina, Sta. Elena, 1975-76; assessor O.E.A., Posadas, Misiones, 1978-81; tech. assessor Sec. Planeamiento, Posadas, 1978-81; jefe catedra U. Misiones, 1978-81, U. San Luis, V. Mercedes, 1981-82; cons., titular head MCy Assocs., Reconquista, 1983—. Author, editor: Banco Exportación, 1987, Determinación de variables Para Toma de Decisión en Incertidumbre, 1989, Sistema Argenex, 1990, Inversion Bejo Riesgo Economic Politica, 1990. Mem. Engring. Coun. Santa Fe. Avocation: tennis. Fax: 54-3482-442448. E-mail: mariolutti@arnet.com.ar. Home: Olesio 915, 3560 Reconquista Santa Fe, Argentina Office: MCy Asociados, Olesio 915, 3560 Reconquista Santa Fe, Argentina

CARIDAD Y OCERIN, JOSE MARIA, statistician educator; b. Seville, Andalucia, Spain, Mar. 29, 1949; s. Jose Maria Caridad Igelmo and Maria Teresa Ocerin Garcia; m. Rosa Maria Lopez Del Rio, Oct. 26, 1972; children: Daniel, Lorena. MS in Math., U. Seville, 1971, PhD in Math., 1973; MS in Econs., U. Málaga, Spain, 1973; Academico Corr. (hon.), Academia de Cordoba, Spain, 1988. Cert. statistitian and economist. Statistitian Banco de Bilbao, Spain, 1973-77; prof. Operationl Rsch. Inst., Bilbao, 1974-77, Bilbao (Spain) U., 1974-77; prof. stats., dir. computing Cordoba (Spain) U., 1977-80, vice-rector, 1984-90, chmn. dept. stats., 1990—; cons. statistitian Arvay, Bilbao, 1975-77; bd. dirs. Inst. de Prospectiva, Seville. Author: Tsp y Estimacion de Modelos Econometricos, 1990, Estadistica Aplicada, 1992, Econometria y Series Temporales, 1994, Design of Experiments, 1996; contbr. articles to profl. jours. Mem. Partido Popular, 1994; pres. Spanish Soc. of Tech. Info. in Agr. Res. officer Spanish Army. Mem. Assn. Statis. Computing, Biometric Soc., Club Pineda de Seville, Aeroclub de Cordoba. Roman Catholic. Avocation: tennis. Home: Aptdo 961, 14008 Cordoba Spain Office: Univ de Cordoba, Etsiam Aptdo 3048, 14080 Cordoba Spain

CARIGNAN, CLAUDE, astronomer, educator; b. Montreal, Dec. 20, 1950; s. Philippe and Gilberte (Frenette) C.; m. Lucie Houde, Aug. 1972 (div. Oct. 1985); children: Stephane, Veronik, Marilis. MSc, U. Montreal, 1978; PhD, Australian Nat. U., Canberra, 1983. Fellow Kapteyn Lab., Groningen, Holland, 1983-85; rsch. fellow U. Montreal, 1985-90, asst. prof., 1990-91, assoc. prof., 1991-97, prof., 1997—; dir. Ctr. de L'Observatoire Du Mont Megantic; bd. dirs. CFHT. Contbr. articles to profl. jours. Mem. Can. Astron. Soc. (bd. dirs. 1992-96, future radio astronomy nat. facility com. 1995-97), Am. Astron. Soc. Achievements include research in neutral hydrogen in galaxies from radio synthesis observations, detailed kinematics, mass distribution and properties of dark matter in spiral and dwarf galaxies. Home: 300 Joliette #801, Longueuil, PQ Canada J4H 2G5 Office: U Montreal Dept Physics, CP 6128 Succ Centre Ville, Montreal, PQ Canada H3C 3J7

CARINE, JAMES, association administrator; b. Isle of Man, Eng., Sept. 14, 1934; s. Amos and Kathleen Prudence (Kelly) C.; m. Carolyn Sally Taylor, Aug. 26, 1961; children: Andrew James, Malcolm John, Catriona Helena, Gregory Paul. Student, King Williams Coll., Isle of Man, 1945-50, Royal Naval Coll., Dartmouth, 1951-52. With Royal Navy, 1951-92; advanced through ranks to rear admiral; registrar, gen. mgr. Arab Horse Soc., Marlborough, 1992—; master Worshipful Co. of Chartered Secs., 1997-98. Dir. United Svcs. Trustee, 1995—. Decorated Knight of St. Gregory the Great, The Pope (Italy). Fellow Chartered Inst. Secs.; mem. Ex-Svcs. Mental Health Soc. (com. 1997—), Copyright Tribunal. Roman Catholic. Avocations: sailing, horse racing. Office: Arab Horse Soc, Ramsbury, Marlborough SN8 2PE, England

CARINO, LEDIVINA VIDALLON, public administration educator; b. Cavite, Philippines, Apr. 22, 1942; d. Leon Anonuevo and Dionisia Cajapin V.; m. Benjamin Vergara Carino; children: Benjamin, Jr., Hiyasmin Ledi. BA in Pub. Adminstrn. cum laude, U. Philippines, 1961; MA in Polit. Sci., U. Hawaii, 1964; PhD in Sociology, Ind. U., 1970. Dir. of rsch. Coll. of Pub. Adminstn./U. of Philippines, 1972—, dir. local govt. ctr., 1980-82, dean, 1982-84, 98—, v.p. for pub. affairs, 1992-93, prof., 1993—; system dir. Oblation Corps U. Philippines, 1994—; vis. prof. U. Hawaii, 1984-85; lead scholar various rsch. projects Asian and Pacific Devel. Ctr., Kuala Lumpur, 1992-94; cons. UN Devel. Program, N.Y., 1996-97. Author: Bureaucracy for Democracy, 1992; contbg. author/editor: Globalization and the Asian Public Sector, 1995, Education for Public Adminstration in Asia and Pacific, 1991, The Indang Experience, 1980 (Golden Book award 1980); co-author: Principal Reasons for Migration, 1977 (UP Ann. Rsch. award). Vol. cons. to constitutional commn. and Philippine Senate, 1986-92; pres. Philippine Assn. for Vol. Effort, 1997-99; nat. rep. Internat. Assn. for Vol. Effort, U.S., 1996-99; chmn. bd. stewards Ch. of the Risen Lord, 1993-95. Recipient Lifetime Achievement award in social scis., Nat. Rsch. Coun., Philippines, 1993; named Outstanding Alumna Philippine Christian, U. Philippines, 1994. Mem. Nat. Acad. of Sci. and Tech. (elected academician 1995), Philippine Sociol. Soc. (pres. 1975-76, 91-92), Nat. Rsch. Coun. of the Philippines (chmn. sociology, social work and demography 1986-87, chmn. political sci. and gov. 1988-89). Office: Nat Coll Pub Adminstrn and Gov, U of Philippines/Diliman, Quezon City 1101, Philippines

CARINO, LINDA SUSAN, business consultant; b. San Diego, Nov. 4, 1954; d. DeVona (Clarke) Dungan. Student, San Diego Mesa Coll., 1972-74, 89-90. Various positions Calif. Can. Bank, San Diego, 1974-77, ops. supr., 1977-80, ops. mgr., 1980-82; asst. v.p. ops. mgr. First Comml. Bank (formerly Calif. Can. Bank), San Diego, 1982-84; v.p. data processing mgr. First Nat. Bank, San Diego, 1984-91; v.p. conversion adminstr. Item Processing Ctr. Svc. Corp., Denver, 1991-92; mgr. computer ops. FIserv, Inc., Van Nuys, Calif., 1992-93; v.p., data processing mgr. So. Calif. Bank, La Mirada, Calif., 1993-94, v.p. tech. support mgr., 1994-96; ind. cons. First Nat. Bank of Ctrl. Calif., Salinas, Calif., 1996-97; project mgr. EDS Corp., Burbank, Calif., 1997-98; customer group mgr. EDS Corp., Charlotte, N.C., 1998-99, bus. svcs. rep., 1999—. Democrat. Avocations: swimming, bicycling, camping, knitting, sewing. Home: 9133 Kestral Ridge Dr Charlotte NC 28269 Office: EDS Corp 9014 Research Dr Charlotte NC 28262-8507

CARISTO-VERRILL, JANET ROSE, international management consultant; b. Quincy, Mass., Jan. 30, 1945; d. John J. and Adelaide Caristo; m. Richard M. Verrill, Mar. 31, 1984 (dec. Feb. 1995). BS, Boston U., 1968; diploma in social anthropology, Lady Margaret Hall, Oxford, Eng., 1974; M in Internat. Mgmt., Am. Grad. Sch. Internat. Mgmt., 1982. Social studies tchr. Boston, Pembroke & Cohasset Schs., Mass., 1969-81; summer planner, reunions MIT Alumni Office, Cambridge, 1973-76; pres. Macro Projects Internat., Wayland, Mass., 1984—; advisor Govt. Can., 1985, Nepal, 1986, Nizhny Novgorod, 1994, Algeria, 1994, Bosnia, 1996, 97, Ctr. for Religious Dialogue, Sarajevo, 1999, 2000, Montenegro, 2000, Habitat for Humanity, Belfast Unltd., 1994-96, Montenegro, 2000; guest spkr. energy conf. Govt. Turkey, Ankara, 1997; NGO del. UN Sci. & Tech. Commn., N.Y.C., 1993. Author: Civilian Military Cons. Corps, 1992,96;contbr. Macro Problems and World Projects, 1998. Filmmaker, vol. Mother Theresa's Hosps., Calcutta, India, summer 1980; vol. U.S. Peace Corps, Nigeria, 1964-66, U.S./China People's Friendship, Cambridge, 1982-83; guest White House Conf. Trade & Devel. No. Ireland, 1995; participant Friends Raoul Wallenberg Conf., Stockholm, 1997; adv. com. MIT Dewey Libr., Cambridge, 1993—; treas. Internat. Sunsat Energy Coun., 1986—; mem. dispute resolution forum Harvard Law Sch., 2000—. Mem. Internat. Assn. Macro-Engring. Socs. (dir. 1996—), Macro Engring. (pres. Boston chpt. 1985—), United Oxford & Cambridge U. Club (London), English Spkg. Union, Boston Ctr. Internat. Visitors, Oxford & Cambridge Club New Eng., Brookline Bird Club. Roman Catholic. Avocations: poetry, birdwatching, gardener, music, art and literature. Office: Macro Projects Internat Inc 174 Pelham Island Rd Wayland MA 01778-2513

CARLBERG, ULF BERTIL, entomologist; b. Nacka, Sweden, June 1, 1958; s. Bertil and Birgitta (Daněk) C. BSc in Chemistry, U. Stockholm, 1985, BSc in Biology, 1986, PhD Zoophysiology, 1992. From rsch. asst. to asst. Wenner-Gren Inst. Exptl. Biology U. Stockholm, 1982-92; biologist Swedish Mus. Natural History, Stockholm, 1993-94, coord. dept. info. technology, 1994—. Contbr. articles and book revs. to profl. publs. Mem. Swedish Linnean Soc., Swedish History of Sci. Soc., Nippon Bonsai Assn., Entomol. Soc. Stockholm, Phasmid Study Group.

CARLE, HARRY LLOYD, social worker; b. Chgo., Oct. 26, 1927; s. Lloyd Benjamin and Clara Bell (Lee) C.; m. Elva Diana Ulrich, Dec. 29, 1951 (div. 1966); adopted children: Joseph Francis, Catherine Marie; m. Karlen Elizabeth Howe, Oct. 14, 1967 (dec. Feb. 1991); children: Kristen Elizabeth and Sylvia Ann (twins), Eric Lloyd; m. Diane Wyland Gambs, May 23, 1993. BSS, Seattle U., 1952; postgrad., U. Wash., 1952-54, MSW, 1966. Pacific N.W. regional dir. Collegiate Coun. UN, 1952-53; rep. indsl. placement and employer rels. State of Wash., Seattle, 1955-57; parole and probation officer Seattle and Tacoma, 1957-61; parole employment splst., 1961-63, vocat. rehab. officer, 1963-64; clin. social worker Western State Hosp., Ft. Steilacoom, Wash., 1964-66, U.S. Penitentiary, McNeil Is., Wash., 1964-66; exec. dir. Shohomish County Cmty. Action Coun./Social Planning Coun., Everett, Wash., 1966-77; employment and edn. counselor Pierce County Jail Social Svcs., Tacoma, 1979-81; dir. employment devel. clinic coord. vocat. program North Rehab. Facility King County Divsn. Alcoholism and Substance Abuse, Seattle, 1981-90; counselor Northgate Outpatient Ctr. Lakeside Recovery, Inc., Seattle, 1991; staff deve. cons. Counseling for Ind. Living, Newport, R.I., 1992; cmty. orgn. agy. mgmt. cons., 1968-92; cons. to pres. Geneal. Inst., Salt Lake City, 1974-78. Vol. Vis. Nurse Svc. Wash. Hospice and Home Care, Montlake Terrace, Wash., 1996-98; mem. social svc. project staff Pacific Luth. U., Tacoma, 1979-81. Served with USN, 1944-46. U.S. Office Vocat. Rehab scholar, 1965-66; named First Honoree Hall of Success Iowa Tng. Sch. for Boys, 1969. Mem. NASW, Seattle Geneal. Soc. (pres. 1974-76), Soc. advancement Mgmt. (chpt. exec. v.p. 1970-71), Acad. Cert. Social Workers (ret. 1998), Henckel Family Nat. Assn., Seattle Japanese Garden Soc. (v.p. 1993-96), various hist. and geneal socs. in Pa. and Ill. Roman Catholic. Home: Poem Rising Garden 258 Two Crane Ln NW Poulsbo WA 98370-9700

CARLEHED, MAGNUS, mathematician; b. Längjum, Sweden, Aug. 3, 1961; s. Ingemar and Maritha (Bengtsson) Jacobson. BSc, Stockholm U., 1985; PhD, Umeå, 1998. Lectr. Mid Sweden U., Östersund, 1991-99, Linkoping U., 1999-2000; risk analyst Swedbank, Stockholm, 2000—. Contbr. articles to profl. jours. Polit. sec. Swedish Liberal Party, 1989. Grantee Magnuson's Found. for Maths., Swedish Royal Acad. Scis., 1997, Swedish Inst., 1998. Mem. Swedish Math. Soc., Am. Math. Soc. Avocations: chess, music, cooking, traveling. Home: Renstiernas gata 14, 116 28 Stockholm Sweden Office: Swedbank, Group Fin Risk Control, 10534 Stockholm Sweden

CARLÉN, STAFFAN CARL, museum director; b. Jönköping, Sweden, Jan. 7, 1944; s. Åke and Vera C. BA, U. Uppsala, Sweden, 1969, MA, 1970, attended Tchrs. Coll., 1971-72; PhD, U. Umeå, 1990. Curator The Nordic Mus., Stockholm, 1973-75, The Swedish Travelling Exhbns., Stockholm, 1976-83; dir. Millesgården, Stockholm, 1984-90, The Nordic Arts Ctr., Helsinki, Finland, 1990-94, Millesgården, Lidingö, Sweden, 1994—. Author: Exhibiting Culture: Concerning Culture Exhibitions Over A Period of 100 Years, 1990, Olga and Carl Milles, the home, the art, the food. Rotary Found. grantee Yale U. Mem. ICOM, Mus. Pub. Rels. Avocation, music. Office: Millesgården, Carl Milles Väg 2, 18134 Lidingö Sweden

CARLEONE, JOSEPH, aerospace executive; b. Phila., Jan. 30, 1946; s. Frank Anthony and Amelia (Ciaccia) C.; m. Shirley Elizabeth Atwell, June 29, 1968; children: Gia Maria, Joan Maria. BS, Drexel U., 1968, MS, 1970, PhD, 1972. Civilian engring. trainee, mech. engr. Phila. Naval Shipyard, 1963-68; grad. asst. in applied mechanics Drexel U., Phila., 1968-72, postdoctoral rsch. assoc., 1972-73; NDEA fellow Drexel U., 1968-71, adj. prof. mechanics, 1974-75, 77-82; chief rsch. engr. Dyna East Corp., Phila., 1973-82; chief scientist warhead tech. Aeroject Ordnance Co., Tustin, Calif., 1982-88; v.p., gen. mgr. warhead sys. divsn. GenCorp. Aeroject Precision

Weapons, Tustin, Calif., 1988-89; v.p., dir. armament sys. Aeroject Electronics Sys. Divsn., Azuza, Calif., 1989-94; v.p. tactical def. and armament products Aeroject, Calif., 1994-97, v.p. ops., 1997-99, v.p., gen. mgr. remote sensing sys. and ops., 1999—. Editor: Tactical Missile Warheads, 1993; contbr. articles to profl. jours.; rschr. explosive and metal interaction, ballistics, projectile penetration, impact of plates. Mem. ASME, AIAA, NDIA, Sigma Xi, Tau Beta Pi, Pi Tau Sigma, Phi Kappa Phi. Home: 2112 Campton Cir Gold River CA 95670-8302 Office: Aerojet PO Box 13222 Sacramento CA 95813-6000

CARLÈS, PIERRE, fluid mechanics researcher, educator; b. Nice, Alpes-Mari, France, Nov. 3, 1970; s. Lucien and Viviane (Grussenmeyer) C. Cert. proficiency in English, Cambridge (Eng.) U., 1991; BSc in Aeronautics, Ecole Nat. Supérieure d'Ingénieurs Constructions Aéronautiques, Toulouse, France, 1992; diploma (summer session), Internat. Space U., Barcelona, Spain, 1994; PhD in Fluid Mechanics, Inst. Nat. Polytech., Toulouse, France, 1995. Rsch. engr. French Space Agy., Toulouse, 1992-95; sci. officer Délégation Géné pour L'Armement Ctr. d'Essais Aéronautiques Toulouse, 1995-96; lectr. U. Pierre and Marie Curie, Paris, 1996. Contbr. articles to profl. jours. including Phys. Rev., Jour. Fluid Mechanics, Physics of Fluids, Physica. Sci. Officer French Air Force, 1995-96. Recipient Leopold Escande Sci. prize Inst. Nat. Polytech., Toulouse, 1996, medal Assn. Aéronautique et Astronautique de France, 1997. Mem. Planetary Soc. Avocations: pvt. pilot, profl. musician (drums), art. Office: U Paris 6, LMM, Tour 66 162, 4 Pl Jussieu, 75252 Paris Cedex 05, France

CARLES GORDO, RICARDO MARIA CARDINAL, archbishop; b. Valencia, Sept. 24, 1926. Archbishop of Barcelona, created and proclaimed cardinal, 1994. Office: Arzobispado, Carrer del Bisbe 5, 08002 Barcelona Spain*

CARLESON, ROBERT BAZIL, public policy consultant, corporation executive; b. Long Beach, Calif., Feb. 21, 1931; s. Bazil Upton and Grace Reynolds (Wilhite) C.; m. Betty Jane Nichols, Jan. 31, 1954 (div.); children: Eric Robert, Mark Andrew, Susan Lynn; m. Susan A. Dower, Feb. 11, 1984. Student, U. Utah, 1949-51; B.S., U. So. Calif., 1953, postgrad., 1956-58. Adminstrv. asst. City of Beverly Hills, Calif., 1956-57; asst. to city mgr. City of Claremont, Calif., 1957-58; sr. adminstrv. asst. to city mgr. City of Torrance, Calif., 1958-60; city mgr. City of San Dimas, Calif., 1960-64, Pico Rivera, Calif., 1964-68; chief dep. dir. Calif. Dept. Public Works, 1968-71; dir. Calif. Dept. Social Welfare, 1971-73; U.S. commr. welfare Washington, 1973-75; pres. Robert B. Carleson & Assocs., Sacramento, Calif. and Washington, 1975-81; chmn. Robert B. Carleson & Assocs., Washington, 1987-93, San Diego, 1993—; pres. Innovative Environ. Svcs. Ltd., Vancouver, B.C., Can., 1992; spl. asst. to U.S. pres. for policy devel. Washington, 1981-84; prin., dir. govt. rels. KMG Main Hurdman, Washington, 1984-87; dir. transition team Dept. HHS, Office of Pres.-Elect, 1980-81; spl. adviser Office of Policy Coordination; sr. policy advisor, chmn. welfare task force Reagan Campaign, 1980; bd. dirs. Fed. Home Loan Bank of Atlanta, 1987-90, I.E.S., Ltd., Can., Transenviro Co., USA, Churchill Co., USA; adv. com. Fed. Home Loan Mortgage Corp., 1985-87; mem. strengthening family policy coun. Nat. Policy Forum, Washington, 1994. Eagle Scout qtr. master sea scout, 1948; lt. gov. Calif. Boys' State, 1948; adv. coun. gen. govt. Rep. Nat. Com., Washington, 1980-81; sr. fellow Free Congress Found., 1994—; chmn. Am. Civil Rights Union, 1998—. Officer USN, 1953-56, USNR, 1956-63. Clubs: Masons, Rotary (pres. 1964), Army & Navy (Washington), Capitol Hill, Fairfax Hunt. Home and Office: 1911 Willow St San Diego CA 92106-1823

CHARLIE, ALEXANDER CHARLES (LORD CARLILE OF BERRIEN) British government official; b. Ruabon, Clwyd, Wales, Feb. 12, 1948; s. Erwin and Sabina Falik; m. Frances Anne Soley, Oct. 19, 1968; children: Anna, Eve, Ruth. Degree of law, King's Coll., London, 1969. Barrister Gray's Inn, London, 1970—, bencher, 1992—, Queen's Counsel, 1984—; hon. recorder City of Hereford, 1994—; dep. high court judge Montgomeryshire, 1983-97; lay mem. GMC, London, 1989-99; coun. mem. Justice, London, 1993—; non-exec. dir. Wynnstay and Chuyd Farmers Plc, 1997—; dir. UNICEF, U.K.; dir. Nat. Assn. fro the Care and Resettlement of Offenders. Liberal candidate, Flintshire East, 1974-79; chmn. Welsh Liberal Party, 1980-82; Liberal M.P., Montgomeryshire, 1983, 87, Liberal Dem. M.P., Montgomeryshire, 1992-97. Avocation: music.

CARLILE, MICHAEL JOHN, microbiologist, researcher; b. London, Dec. 16, 1930; s. John Hildred and Alice Clara (Ford) C.; m. Elizabeth Smith, Aug. 19, 1961; children: Margot, Susan. BA, U. Cambridge, Eng., 1954, MA, 1958, PhD, 1958, ScD, 1982. Lectr. in botany U. Bristol, Eng., 1956-61; sr.lectr. in botany U. Ibadan, Nigeria, 1961-63; asst. rsch. botanist U. Calif., Berkeley, 1963-64; sr. lectr. in biochemistry Imperial Coll., London, 1964-79, sr. lectr. in microbiology, 1979-87, hon. sr. lectr. in microbiology, 1987-2000. Sr. author: The Fungi, 1994; co-author: Introduction to the Biology of Microorganisms, 1960; editor: Evolution in the Microbial World, 1974, Primitive Sensory and Communication Systems, 1975, Molecular and Cellular Aspects of Microbial Evolution, 1981; contbr. numerous articles to profl. jours. Aldis scholar Trinity Hall, Cambridge, 1953-54. Mem. Soc. for Gen. Microbiology (coun. 1972-76, meeting sec. 1977-80), Brit. Mycological Soc. (v.p. 1991, chmn. conservation working party 1994-98, coun. 1994-96). Avocations: walking, natural history. Home: 42 Durleigh Rd, Somerset Bridgwater TA6 7HU, England

CARLIN, CLAIR MYRON, lawyer; b. Sharon, Pa., Apr. 20, 1947; s. Charles William and Carolyn L. (Vukasich) C.; children: Eric Richard, Elizabeth Marie, Alexander Myron. BS in Econs., Ohio State U., 1969, JD, 1972. Bar: Ohio 1973, Pa. 1973, U.S. Dist. Ct. (so. dist.) Ohio 1973, U.S. Dist. Ct. (no. dist.) Ohio 1975, U.S. Supreme Ct. 1976, U.S. Ct. Claims, 1983, U.S. Tax Ct. 1985. Staff atty. Ohio Dept. Taxation, Columbus, 1972-73; asst. atty. City of Warren, Ohio, 1973-75; assoc. McLaughlin, DiBlasio & Harshman, Youngstown, Ohio, 1975-80; ptnr. McLaughlin, McNally & Carlin, Youngstown, 1980-98, Carlin & Vasvari, LLC, Poland, Ohio, 1998-2000, Clair M. Carlin, LLC, 2000—. Mem. editl. bd. Ohio Trial mag. Mem. Trumbull County Bicentennial Commn., Ohio, 1976; v.p. Svcs. for the Aging, Trumbull County, 1976-77; mem. Pres.' Club Ohio State U. Maj. Ohio NG, 1972-82. Fellow Ohio State Bar Found.; mem. ATLA (bd. govs. 1996—, trustee PAC 1996-98), ABA, Ohio State Bar Assn. (negligence law com. 1991—), Ohio State Bar Coll., Mahoning County Bar Assn. (chmn. legal edn. com. 1985-86, counsel 1986-87), Ohio Acad. Trial Lawyers (trustee 1988-92, polit. action com. chmn. 1991, exec. com. 1991-97, treas. 1992-93, sec. 1993-94, pres.-elect 1994-95, pres. 1995-96), Mahoning-Trumbull Acad. Trial Lawyers (pres. 1991), Ohio State U. Alumni Assn. (pres. Trumbull County chpt. 1985—), Cath. War Vets. (Ohio state commdr., Vet. of Yr. 1988), Rotary. Democrat. Roman Catholic. Home: 3524 Hunters Hl Poland OH 44514-5303 Office: Carlin & Vasvari LLC PO Box 5369 Youngstown OH 44514-0369

CARLISLE, JAMES B., Antiguan and Barbudan head of state; b. Aug. 5, 1937; married; 5 children. LLD, Andrews U., Mich., 1996; student, Singapore U., 1963-64, Northhampton Coll. Tech., 1966-67; BDS, U. Dundee, 1972. Gen. dentistry practice Scotland, Wales, Eng., Antigua, 1972-92; gov. gen. St. John's, Antigua and Barbuda, 1993—. Chmn. Nat. Pks. Authority, 1986-90, Tabitha Sr. Citizens' Home, 1987-90; vol. dentist Bapt. Dental Clinic, 1981-83; mgr. flouride program Cath. Dental Ctr., 1983-86; initiator Free Dental Care Program Children & Elderly, 1993; founder, patron Clarence House Restoration Trust, Govt. House Restoration Trust, Antigua and Barbda Beautification Commn., Habitat for Humanity Antigua and Barbada, Can.-Antigua and Barbda Heritage and Ednl. Found.; mem. Royal Air Force Assn.; patron Antigua and Barbda Cricket Assn., Antigua Red Cross, Internat. Assn. Lions Club, Soroptimist Internat., Kiwanis Club; chief scout Antigua and Barbda. With Royal Air Force, 1961-66. Decorated knight grand cross Most Disting. Order St. Michael and St. George, knight grand cross Orderof the Queen of Sheba. Fellow Royal Coll. Surgeons of Edinburgh (hon.); mem. Am. Acad. Laser Dentistry, Internat. Assn. Laser Dentistry, Brit. Dental Assn. Seventh-day Adventist. Office: Office of Gov Gen, Govt House, Saint John's Antigua and Barbuda*

CARLO, LESLIE ALAN, electric utility executive, electrical engineer; b. Sudbury, Suffolk, Eng., Mar. 5, 1950; arrived in South Africa, 1983; s. Kenneth Frank and Peggy Winnifred (Collins) C.; m. Sarah Janina Lindsey-Renton, July 1, 1983. Nat. diploma, Mid-Essex Tech. Coll., Eng., 1971; postgrad., Mid-Essex Tech. Coll., 1972. Registered profl. engr., South Africa; chartered engr. U.K. Third engr. Ea. Electricity, Buby St. Edmunds, Eng., 1974-79; 1st engr. Ea. Electricity, Wherstead, Ipswich, Eng., 1979-83; engr. transmission protection Eskom, Johanesburg, South Africa, 1983-85; sr. engr. transmission protection Eskom, Johannesburg, South Africa, 1985-86; regional engring. mgr. Eskom, South Africa, 1986-95, bus. ops. mgr., 1995-97; distrn. bus. strategy mgr. Eskom, Johannesburg, 1997-98; bus. ops. mgr. Eskom, 1995-97; engr. mgr. Eskom, Pietersburg, South Africa, 1998-2000; ops. and field svcs. mgr. ESI-TEL, Eskom Enterprises, 2000—. Contbr. articles to profl. publs. Fellow Inst. of Elec. Engring., South African Inst. of Elec. Engring.; mem. European Fedn. of Nat. Engring. Inst. Avocation: bird watching. Fax: 27-11-871-3674. E-mail: les.carlo@eskom.co.za. Office: Eskom Enterprises, PO Box 107, Dermiston 1400, South Africa

CARLOS, BAUTISTA OJEDA, member European Parliament; b. Linares, Spain, Jan. 8, 1959. mem. European Parliament, Group of the Greens/European Free Alliance; mem. com. on agr. and rural devel., employment and social affairs; mem. del. for rels. with the Maghreb countries and the Arab Maghreb Union. Mem. Andalusian Party. Office: Parlamento Europeo, Rue Wiertz ASP 8H161, B-1047 Bruxelles Belgium*

CARLOS, ROBERTO DE SILVA (ROBERTO CARLOS DA SILVA), professional soccer player; b. Garca, Brazil, Apr. 10, 1973. Defender Uniao Sao Joao Football Club, Brazil, 1991-92, Palmeiras Football Club, Brazil, 1993-94, Inter Milan Football Club, Italy, 1995-96; with Brazilian Nat. Team World Cup, France, 1998; defender Real Madrid Football Club, Spain, 1998—. Office: Real Madrid Club Fútbol, Santiago Bernabeu C1 Condra Espina 1, 28036 Madrid Spain*

CARLOTTI, MARIE-ARLETTE, foreign diplomat; b. Béziers, France, Jan. 21, 1952. Mem. European Parliament, 1999—, mem. com. on devel. and coop., mem. com. on fgn. affairs/human rights/common security; mem. Group of the Party of European Socialists; vice chmn. Mems. from the European Parliament to the Joint Assembly of the Agreement between the African, Caribbean and Pacific States and the European Union. Socialist Party. Office: Immeuble Central Park bat B, Impasse Fissiaux, F-13004 Marseille France*

CARLOW, JOHN SYDNEY, research physicist, consultant; b. Kingston-upon-Thames, Surrey, Eng., May 8, 1943; s. Sidney George and Gwendoline (Craymer) C.; m. Carole Evelyn Harbidge, May 9, 1973; children: Anne-Marie Evelyn, Helen-Louise Gwendoline. BSc in Physics, Exeter U., Eng., 1964; PhD in Physics, Exeter (Eng.) U., 1971. Scientist GE (G.B.), Wembley, Eng., 1968-71; rsch. fellow chemistry dept. Dalhousie U., Halifax, N.S., Can., 1972-74; rsch. fellow Southampton U., Eng., 1974-77; sr. fellow CERN, Geneva, 1977-80; cons. Southampton, 1981-87; project mgr. AEA Tech., Abingdon, Eng., 1988—. Contbr. articles to sci. jours. Killam postdoctoral scholar Dalhousie U., 1972. Mem. Coun. European Engring. Assns., Engring. Coun. (U.K.) (chartered), Inst. Physics (U.K.) (chartered), Am. Phys. Soc., Inst. Materials, Brit. Computer Soc., Royal Soc. Chemistry (U.K.) (assoc.). Avocations: family history, astronomy, pollution control, home computer electronics and programming, home design. Home: 19 Elmsleigh Gardens, Bassett Southampton SO16 3GE, England Office: AEA Tech, Culham Sci Ctr, Abingdon, Oxford OX14 3ED, England

CARLSEN, KAI HAKON, health facility administrator; b. Moss, Norway, Jan. 3, 1946; s. Haakon and Kaya (Iversen) C.; m. Karin Lodrun, May 2, 1992; childree: Oda Cecilie, Eira Catharine; children from previous marriage: Espen, Preben, Benedicte. MD, U. Oslo, Norway, 1970, PhD, 1988. From cons. to sr. cons. dept. pediatrics Ullevaal Hosp., Oslo, Norway, 1980-84, 87-90; cons. Vo Ksentoppen Ctr., Oslo, Norway, 1984-87; sr. cons. Voksentoppen Ctr. Asthma & Allergy, Oslo, Norway, 1990-97, med. dir., 1997—; prof. Norwegian U. Sports & Phys. Edn., Oslo, 1992—. Author: Asthma and Training, 1996, Acute Asthma, 1996. Lt. Norwegian Army, 1972. Mem. European Respiratory Soc. (head pediat. assembly), Am. Thoracic Soc., Pediatric Respiratory Soc., Norwegian Soc. Allergy & Immunology. Avocations: medical research, photography, wildlife. Office: Voksentoppen Ctr Asthma, Ullveien 14, N-0791 Oslo Norway

CARLSEN, KARIN CECILIE LØDRUP, pediatrician; b. Oslo, Apr. 11, 1959; d. Sven Hanssøn and Helen Daphne Rosemary (Taylor) Lødrup; m. Kai-Håkon Carlsen, May 2, 1992; children: Oda Cecilie, Eira Catharine. Examen Philosoficum, U. Oslo, postgrad., 1980; MD, Royal Coll. Surgeons Ireland, 1986; PhD, U. Oslo, 1995. Med. intern Norway, 1986-88; mem. staff pediatric dept. Nordland Ctrl. Hosp., Bodo, Norway, 1988-89; mem. staff pediatric dept. Ullevål Hosp., Oslo, 1989-91, rsch. fellow pediatric dept., 1991-97, rschr. pediat. dept., 1996-99; rsch. fellow Nat. Inst. Pub. Health, Oslo, 1991-97; cons. pediatrician and rsch. fellow, 1999—; cons. pediatrician sect. allergology/pulmonology Dept. Pediats., Ullevål Hosp., 2000—; cons. pediatrician Ullevål Hosp., 2000—. Contbr. articles to profl. jours. Recipient Best Presentation award Pediatric Week Holland, 1994; recipient ann. prize for pediatric pulmonary rsch. Voksentopper Ctr., 1994, Ann. award Pediatric Assembly of European Respiratory Soc., 1995. Mem. Nordic Allergology Soc. (bd. dirs.), Nordic Soc. of Allergyology (pres. 1996-99, bd. dirs. 1999—). Office: Ullevål Hosp, Dept Pediatrics, N-0407 Oslo Norway

CARLSMITH, ROGER SNEDDEN, chemistry and energy conservation researcher; b. N.Y.C., Oct. 2, 1925; s. Leonard Eldon and Hope (Snedden) C.; m. Thelma Kathleen Sutton, July 31, 1954; children: David, Nancy Lynn. AB in Chemistry cum laude, Harvard, 1948; MSCE, MIT, 1950. Rsch. engr. Oak Ridge (Tenn.) Nat. Lab., 1950-62, group leader, 1962-70, sect. mgr., 1970-78, prog. dir. conservation and renewable energy, 1978-94; ret., 1994; mem. Gov.'s Energy Task Force, Tenn., 1972-74, adv. com. Fed. Power Commn., Washington, 1973; bd. dirs. Am. Coun. Energy Efficient Economy., Washington, Tenn. Citizens Wilderness Planning. Author: (book with others) World Energy Conference Survey of Energy Resourses, 1974. Sgt. USAF, 1943-46. Recipient Sadi Carnot medal for achievements in energy conservation rsch. Dept. Energy, 1996. Mem. AAAS, Sierra Club, The Wilderness Soc. Achievements include research and development of advanced technology for improved energy efficiency, alternative energy sources, environmental impacts of energy, energy and the economy. Home: 1052 W Outer Dr Oak Ridge TN 37830-8641

CARLSON, AMY L., lawyer. BSEE, Carnegie Mellon, 1986; MSEE, Rensselaer Poly. Inst., 1987; JD, MBA, U. So. Calif., 1991. Design engr. III Interconnection Products Inc., Santa Ana, Calif., 1987-88; assoc. Dewey Ballantine, L.A., 1992, Washington, 1992-94; assoc. Preston, Gates, Ellis & Rouvelas Meeds, Washington, 1994-99, ptnr., 2000—. Mem. Eta Kappa Nu, Tau Beta Pi. E-mail: amyc@prestongates.com. Office: Preston Gates Ellis & Rouvelas Meeds 1735 New York Ave NW Ste 500 Washington DC 20006-5209

CARLSON, DALE BICK, writer; b. N.Y.C., May 24, 1935; d. Edgar M. and Estelle (Cohen) Bick; children: Daniel, Hannah. BA, Wellesley Coll., 1957. Lic. wildlife rehabilitator, 1991. Pres. Bick Pub. House, 1993—; founder, pres. Bick Pub. House, 1993—. Author children's books, adult books 1961—, including: Perkins the Brain, 1964, The House of Perkins, 1965, Miss Maloo, 1966, The Brainstormers, 1966, Frankenstein, 1968, Counting Is Easy, 1969, Your Country, 1969, Arithmetic 1, 2, 3, 1969, The Electronic Teabowl, 1969, Warlord of the Genji, 1970, The Beggar King of China, 1971, The Mountain of Truth (Spring Festival Honor book, named Am. Library Assn. Notable Book), 1972, Good Morning Danny, 1972, Good Morning, Hannah, 1972, The Human Apes, 1973 (named Am. Library Assn. Notable Book), Girls Are Equal Too, 1973, 2d edit., 2000 (named Am. Library Assn. Notable Book), Baby Needs Shoes, 1974, Triple Boy, 1976, Where's Your Head?, 1971, 2d edit., 2000 (Christopher award), The Plant People, 1977, The Wild Heart, 1977, The Shining Pool, 1979, Lovingsex for Both Sexes, 1979, Boys Have Feelings Too, 1980, Call Me Amanda, 1981, Manners That Matter, 1982, The Frog People, 1982, Charlie the Hero, 1983, 1984-85: The Jenny Dean Science Fiction Mysteries, The Mystery of the Shining Children, The Mystery of the Hidden Trap, The Secret of the Third Eye, The James Budd Mysteries, The Mystery of Galaxy Games, The Mystery of Operation Brain, 1985, Miss Mary's Husbands, 1988, Basic Manuals in Wildlife Rehabilitation Series (6 vols.), 1993-94, Basic Manuals for Friends of the Disabled Series, 1995-96, Living With Disabilities, 1997, Wildlife Care for Birds and Mammals, 1997, Stop the Pain: Meditations for Teenagers, 1998, Confessions of a Brain-Impaired Writer: A Memoir, 1998, Stop the Pain: Adult Meditations, 2000. Mem. Authors League Am., Authors Guild. Address: 307 Neck Rd Madison CT 06443-2755

CARLSON, GEORGE RADCLIFFE, philosophy educator; b. Irvington, N.J., Oct. 14, 1935; s. Gustaf Bertil and Isabel Marple (Long) C.; m. Ingrid Waltraud Holz, Apr. 2, 1960. BA, Rutgers U., 1960; MA, U. Toronto, Ont., Can., 1965, PhD, 1970. Asst. prof. Trinity Coll., Toronto, 1967-71; sr. lectr. Witwatersrand U., Republic of South Africa, 1973-95, hon. lectr., 1996—. Mem. editl. bd. Philos. Papers, 1978-85; contbr. articles to profl. jours. With U.S. Army, 1961-63. Grad. fellow Province of Ont., 1964-67, vis. fellow Australian Nat. U., Canberra, 1986-87; sr. rsch. grantee Human Scis. Rsch. Coun., Republic of South Africa, 1986-87. Mem. Am. Philos. Assn. (internat.). Avocations: classical music, aerobic exercise. Home: 55 5th Ave Parktown North, 2193 Johannesburg Gauteng, South Africa Office: Witwatersrand U, 1 Jan Smuts Ave, 2001 Johannesburg Gauteng, South Africa

CARLSON, KATHLEEN BUSSART, law librarian; b. Charlotte, N.C., June 25, 1956; d. Dean Allyn and Joan (Parlette) Bussart; m. Gerald Mark Carlson, Aug. 15, 1987. BA in Polit. Sci., Ohio State U., 1977; JD, Capital U., 1980; MA in Libr. and Info. Sci., U. Iowa, 1986. Bar: Ohio 1980 (inactive). Editor Lawyers Coop. Pub. Co., Rochester, N.Y., 1980-83; asst. state law libr. State of Wyo., Cheyenne, 1987-88, state law libr., 1988—. 2d v.p., bd. dirs. Wyo. coun. Girl Scouts U.S., Casper, 1990-92, 1st v.p., bd. dirs., 1993-96. Mem. Am. Assn. Law Librs. (sec.-treas., State Ct. and County Law Librs. spl. interest sect. 1992-95, SCCLL edn. com. 1991-92, chair SCCLL grants com. 1997-98, nominating com. 1998-99, indexing legal periodical lit. adv. com. 1993-96, chair 1994-96, scholarship com. 1996-98, citation format com. 1998-2000, co-chair SCCLL membership com. 2000—, chair SCCLL edn. com. 2000—), Western Pacific Assn. Law Librs. (pres. 1996-97), Wyo. Libr. Assn. (sec. acad. and spl. librs. sect. 1990-92, pres. 1994-95), Bibliog. Ctr. for Rsch. (trustee 1991-95), Kappa Delta, Beta Phi Mu, Zonta Internat. Avocations: arts and crafts, baking. Home: 911 E 18th St Cheyenne WY 82001-4722 Office: State Law Libr 2301 Capitol Ave Cheyenne WY 82002-0001

CARLSON, LARS ANDERS, physician, educator; b. Stockholm, Sweden, Nov. 14, 1928; s. Fritz David and Marie Louise (Ljungberger) C.; m. Kerstin Rudin, Mar. 18, 1953 (div. Nov. 1978); children: Björn, Mats, Pia; m. Lena Johansson, Oct. 10, 1979 (div. Aug. 1989); children: Lars-Anders, Lena-Maria; m. Anette Maria Asplund, Nov. 24, 1989; children: Carolina Larsdotter, David Lars. MD, Karolinska Inst., Stockholm, 1956, PhD, 1960. Intern, resident dept. medicine Karolinska Hosp., Stockholm, 1956-61, assoc. prof., 1961-68; prof., chmn. dept. geriatrics Uppsala (Sweden) U., 1968-73; prof. dept. medicine Karolinska Hosp., Stockholm, 1973-93; chmn. King Gustav V Rsch. Inst., Stockholm, 1973-93, emeritus rsch. prof., 1994—; bd. dirs. Nobel Assembly, Stockholm, 1973-93. Contbr. more than 450 articles to internat. sci. publs. Recipient Minkowski prize European Diabetes Assn., 1968, Florman award Royal Swedish Acad., 1975, Alvarenga prize Swedish Med. Soc., 1985, Thureus Rsch. prize, Uppsala, 1971, Stockholm, 1980; CIBA Found. grantee in ageing rsch., 1956. Fellow Royal Coll. Physicians (Edinburgh); mem. European Soc. Clin. Investigation (pres. 1972-73), European Atherosclerosis Group (pres. 1973-77). Office: King Gustaf V Rsch Inst, Karolinska Hosp, Stockholm 171 76, Sweden

CARLSON, LAURA ANNE, psychology educator; b. Winchester, Mass., July 21, 1965; d. Werner A. and Elna M. (Eliasson) C.; m. Gabriel Allen Radvansky, Mar. 21, 1992; children: Hazel Eileen Radvansky, Grayson Peter Radvansky. BA, Dartmouth Coll., 1987; MA, Mich. State U., 1991; PhD, U. Ill., 1994. Asst. prof. psychology U. Notre Dame, Ind., 1994-99, assoc. prof., 1999—; mem. adv. panel Social, Behavioral and Econ. Scis. Powre grants NSF. Contbr. articles to profl. jours., including Jour. Memory and Lang., Jour. Exptl. Psychology, Perception and Psychophysics, Psychol. Sci. Grantee, NSF, 1996, 1998—, NIMH, 1996; grantee, award recipient APA. Mem. Am. Psychol. Soc., Psychonomics Soc., Cognitive Sci. Soc., Midwestern Psychol. Assn. Fax: 219-631-8883. E-mail: laura.c.radvansky.2@nd.edu. Office: Univ Notre Dame Dept Psychology 118D Haggar Hall Notre Dame IN 46556-5636

CARLSON, LAWRENCE ARVID, English language educator, real estate agent; b. San Diego, Dec. 29, 1935; s. Arvid Fritiof and Ruth Mathilda (Hedman) C.; m. Patricia Catherine Barlow, Sept. 8, 1963; children: Lawrence Stephen, Janine Catherine. BA in History, Roanoke Coll., 1957; MS in Edn., S.D. State U., 1962; MA in English, Calif. State U., Fullerton, 1966. Tchr. Edison Jr. High Sch., L.A., 1962-63, Anaheim (Calif.) High Sch., 1963-66; prof. English Orange Coast Coll., Costa Mesa, Calif., 1966—; instr. karate Orange Coast Coll., Costa Mesa, 1984-95; sales assoc. Real Estate Offices, San Juan Capistrano, Calif., 1993—. Host, writer (ednl. TV show) Creative Writers Viewpoint, 1975. Horseback riding tour leader Rock Creek Pack Sta., Bishop, Calif., 1990-95; leader 4-H, Orange County, Calif., 1983-93; vol. Liberty Walk, Dana Point, Calif., 1997. Maj. USMCR, 1957-67. Recipient Excellence award Nat. Inst. Staff Orgnl. Devel., 1993. Mem. Nat. Assn. Realtors, Calif. Assn. Realtors, Orange County Assn. Realtors, Faculty Assn. Calif. C.C.'s. Democrat. Lutheran. Avocations: horseback riding, karate, surfing. Home: PO Box 1266 Rancho Carrillo 10871 Verdugo Rd San Juan Capistrano CA 92693 Office: Orange Coast Cmty Coll 2701 Fairview Rd Costa Mesa CA 92626-5563

CARLSON, NANCY LEE, English language educator; b. Spokane, Wash., June 1, 1950; d. Catherine Esther Paight. BS, Wash. State U., 1973; MEd, curriculum specialist, Ea. Wash. U., 1987. Tchr. Stevenson-Carson Sch. Dist., Wash., 1973-74, Spokane Sch. Dist., 1974—; vis. faculty Ea. Wash. U., 1989-91, 93-95; active steering com. Spokane County Children's Alliance, 1992—. Spokane County co-chmn. Sen. Slade Gorton campaign, 1988, mem. adv. bd., 1989—; Rep. precinct committeeperson, 1988-90, 92-94; bd. dirs. West Ctrl. Cmty. Ctr., Spokane Civic Theater, sec., 1992-94; mem. affordable housing com. Spokane County, 1990-91; treas. Inland Empire for Africa, Spokane, 1985-86; vice chmn. Ea. Wash. phone bank for Sen. Dan Evans, Spokane, 1984; mem. Mayor's Task Force on the Homeless, 1987-88; mem. Spokane County adv. bd. City of Spokane Cmty. Ctr., 1990-92; lay min. First Presbyn. Ch., deacon, 1994—, sec. bd. deacons, 1994-96, vice moderator bd. deacons, 1996-97, moderator, 1997—, chair bd. deacons, 1997—; mem. Rep. George Nethercutt's Ednl. Adv. Bd., 1997—; bldg. rep. United Way, 1994—. Mem. NEA, ASCD, Nat. Coun. Tchrs. English, Wash. Coun. Tchrs. English, Wash. Edn. Assn., Spokane Edn. Assn., Wash. State U. Alumni Assn. (area rep. 1987-90). Republican. Presbyterian. Avocations: golfing, reading, stamp collecting, politics. Office: Rogers High Sch Sch Dist # 81 1622 E Wellesley Ave Spokane WA 99207-4299

CARLSON, PAUL EDWIN, real estate developer, writer; b. San Francisco, June 29, 1944; s. Carl John and Margueritte Eutha (Kovatch) C.; m. Sharon Raye Hammond, Nov. 14, 1964; children: Kimberley, Davin, Christina. AA, Yosemite Coll., 1964; BA, Calif. State U., Long Beach, 1971; cert. shopping ctr. mgr., Internat. Council of Shopping Ctrs. Mgmt. Sch., 1981. Vice and narcotics officer Modesto and Los Angeles Police Depts., Calif., 1964-69; owner Universal Prodns., N.Y.C. and Modesto, 1963-73; gen. mgr. City Investing Co., N.C.Y. and Beverly Hills, Calif., 1973-75; sr. v.p. The Koll Co., Newport Beach, Calif., 1975-79; v.p. Irvine Co., Newport Beach, 1979-80; owner Willows Shopping Ctr., Concord, Calif., 1980-83; sr. v.p. Lee Sammis Co., Irvine, 1983-85; pres. Am. Devel. Co., Costa Mesa, Calif., 1985-86; chmn. bd. The Carlson Co., Newport Beach, 1986-98, Coreland Carlson, Newport Beach, 1998—; guest lectr. U. So. Cal., U. Calif., Los Angeles, Orange Coast Coll.; real estate cons. Bank of Am., Union Bank, Chevron U.S.A., Aetna Life Ins. Co., James Lang Wooten, Eng., Peoples Republic of China. Author three screenplays for Police Story; comedy writer The Tonight Show, Sat. Night Live, Late Night with David Letterman; pub. Property Mgrs. Handbook. mem. Calif. State Juvenile Justice Commn., Rep. Senatorial Inner circle, Washington; past chmn. City of Newport Beach Traffic Commn.; pres. bd. trustees Mt. Diablo Hosp.; v.p., bd. dirs. City of Concord Pavillion; bd. dirs. Concord Visitors and Conv. Bur. Mem. Am. Cancer Soc. (bd. dirs. Contra Costa County), Internat. Coun. Shopping Ctrs. (state ops. chmn.). Republican. Avocation: youth counseling. Home: 29732

Orange Oak Laguna Niguel CA 92677-1963 Office: Coreland Carlson 1752 E 17th St Ste 420 Tustin CA 92780

CARLSON, RICHARD GREGORY, accountant; b. Chgo., Aug. 24, 1949; s. Richard George and S. Diane (Russell) C.; m. Annette Claire Bonneville, Aug. 30, 1969 (div. May 1982); children: Scott Richard, Amy Kristin; m. Pamela Catherine Punzelt, Sept. 25, 1982. BBA, Western Mich. U., 1971. CPA, Ill. With Deloitte & Touche, Chgo., 1971—, ptnr., 1980—, dir. Chgo. real estate svc. ctr., 1980-91, mem. nat. real estate com., 1982-91, dirs. client svcs. and devel., 1985-88, mem. Chgo. exec. com., 1985-88, mng. ptnrs. adv. coun., 1986-88, mng. dir. nat. real estate svcs., 1991—, nat. dir. real estate cons. svcs., 1997—. Author: Real Estate Accounting and Reporting Handbook, 1995; editor Real Estate Accounting and Taxation Journal, 1991-93, Real Estate Strategies, 1991—; contbr. articles to profl. jours. Mem. MIT Real Estate Cir., 1995—; adv. bd. Ctr. Real Estate Studies Ind. U.; mem. bd. advisors Real Estate Fin. Jour., 1993—; bd. dirs. Western Mich. U. Found., 1986, mem. investment com., 1986-88, 91-97, mem. exec. com., 1988-97, vice-chmn., 1992-93, chmn. 1994-97; bd. dirs. Pin Oak Homeowners Assn., treas. 1982-86. With USAR, 1971-77. Recipient Disting. Acctg. Alumni award Western Mich. U., 1987, Disting. Alumni award 1993. Mem. AICPA, Am. Acctg. Assn. (Midwest regional steering com. 1983-87), Ill. Soc. CPAs, Internat. Coun. Shopping Ctrs., Western Mich. U. Alumni Assn. (bd. dirs. 1984-91, treas. 1984-86, pres. 1986-88), Nat. Assn. Real Estate Cos., Nat. Realty Com. (bd. dirs., exec. com. 1992—), Nat. Coun. Real Estate Investment Fiduciaries (acctg. com. 1985—, pres. elect 1997, membership com. 1992-98, bd. dirs. 1993-99, pres. 1998-99), Plaza Club (Chgo.), Westmoreland Country Club (Wilmette, Ill., bd. dirs. 1988-92, treas. 1988-92), Ironwood Country Club (Palm Desert, Calif.). Republican. Office: Deloitte & Touche 2 Prudential Plz Chicago IL 60601

CARLSON, ROBERT EDWIN, lawyer; b. Bklyn., Oct. 11, 1930; s. Harry Victor and Lenore Marie (Hanrahan) C.; m. Maureen Eleanor Donnelly, Aug. 24, 1963; children: John T., Katherine L., Elizabeth A., Robert E. Jr. BS, U. Oreg., 1953; JD, U. Calif., San Francisco, 1958; LLM, Harvard U., 1963. Bar: Calif. 1959, U.S. Dist. Ct. (ctrl. dist.) Calif. 1959, U.S. Ct. Appeals (9th cir.) 1959. Assoc. Kindel & Anderson, L.A., 1958-63, ptnr., 1963-67; ptnr. Agnew, Miller & Carlson, L.A., 1967-80, Hufstedler, Miller, Carlson & Beardsley, L.A., 1980-88, Paul, Hastings, Janofsky & Walker, L.A., 1988—; pres. Constl. Rights Found., L.A., 1978-80, L.A. County Bar Found., 1988-89; mem. exec. com. bus. sect. L.A. Bar Assn., 1982-89; bd. dirs. Legal Aid Found., L.A. Bd. dirs. Westridge Sch. for Girls, Pasadena, Calif., 1985-91, Trust for Pub. Land, San Francisco, 1987—; chair bd. Skid Row Housing Trust, L.A., 1989—, Pasadena Cmty. Found.; bd. visitors Santa Clara Law Sch., 1986-92. With U.S. Army, 1953-55. Recipient Griffin Bell award Dispute Resolution Svcs., Inc., 1992, Katherine Krause award Inner City Law Ctr., 1996. Mem. ABA (mem. securities com., co-chair com. devel. investment svcs., mem. task force to prepare guidebook for dirs. mut. funds 1995, chairperson youth edn. for citizenship, Chgo. 1982-85), Calif. State Bar (mem. corp. com. 1990—), Valley Hunt Club, Chancery Club, Calif. Club. Democrat. Avocations: hiking, tennis, reading, skiing. Office: Paul Hastings Janofsky & Walker 555 S Flower St Fl 23 Los Angeles CA 90071-2300

CARLSON, ROBERT MARSHALL, hospital professional services official; b. Jamestown, N.Y., Oct. 6, 1950; s. Marshall Lawrence and Alice (Christine) C.; m. Robin Shankey, May 29, 1987; children: Todd Marshall, Scott Thomas. BS, Bowling Green (Ohio) State U., 1972; postgrad. in pub. health, U. Utah, 1972; ME in Health Edn., U. Toledo, 1977. Planning analyst, then found. dir. Riverside Hosp., Toledo, 1975-78; hosp. planning coord. Med. Coll. Ohio, Toledo, 1978-80, asst. hosp. dir. for ambulatory programs,, 1980-81; cons. P.M.S. (Planning & Mgmt. Services) Inc., Bloomington, Minn., 1981-82; dir. health tech. mktg., sr. cons. Ellerbe Cons. Group, Bloomington, 1983-85; mktg. dir. Ellerbe Assocs. Inc., Mpls., 1986; v.p. Ellerbe Assocs., 1987-89, Export USA Publs., Mpls., 1989-91; dir. physician svcs. HealthEast, St. Paul, 1991-95; exec. adminstr. OSF Med. Group, OSF Healthcare Systems, Peoria, Ill., 1995-99; dir. clin. svcs. Phycor, Inc., Nashville, 1999—. Served to commdr., Med. Svc. Corps., USNR, 1972-98. Mem. Med. Group Mgmt. Assn., Am. Coll. Med. Practice Execs., Assn. Mil. Surgeons of U.S., Profl. Ski Instrs. Am., Res. Officers Assn., Phi Kappa Phi, Kappa Sigma. Lutheran. Office: Phycor Inc 30 Burton Hills Blvd Ste 400 Nashville TN 37215-6140

CARLSON, RONALD LEE, lawyer, educator; b. Davenport, Iowa, Dec. 10, 1934; s. Arthur A. and Louise (Sehmann) C.; m. Mary Murphy, Apr. 10, 1965; children: Michael, Andrew. B.A., Augustana Coll., 1956; J.D. (Clarion DeWitt Hardy law scholar), Northwestern U., 1959; LL.M. (E. Barrett Prettyman law scholar), Georgetown U., 1961. Bar: Ill., Iowa 1959, D.C. 1960, U.S. Supreme Ct. 1966. Mem. firm Betty, Neuman, McMahon, Hellstrom & Bittner, Davenport, Iowa, 1961-65; U.S. commr. So. Dist. Iowa, 1964-64; prof. law U. Iowa, Iowa City, 1965-73, Washington U., St. Louis, 1973-84; John Byrd Martin prof. law U. Ga., 1984-95, Fuller E. Callaway prof. law, 1995—; vis. prof. Wayne State U., Detroit, summers 1974, 76, 77, 79, U. Tex., 1978, St. Louis U., 1982-86, 88, U. Iowa, 1986-87, 96; cons. Legis. Com. Criminal Code Revision Iowa, 1969-73; lectr. Nat. Coll. State Judiciary, Reno, 1974, Nat. Coll. Dist. Attys., West Palm Beach, Fla., 1980, Chgo., 1983, Inst. Continuing Legal Edn., Atlanta, 1990, 2000, Nat. Pract. Inst., Kansas City, 1991, 93, 98, Omaha, 1991, 96, Albuquerque, 1991, Milw., 1991, 97, 2000, Davenport, 2000, Des Moines, 1991, Chgo., 1991, San Francisco, 1991, 96, St. Louis, 1992, 93, 97, 98, Honolulu, 1992, 94, 96, New Orleans, 1992, Seattle, 1992, Minn., 1992, 93, 94, 95, 96, 97, Boston, 1992, Houston, 1992, 97, Cleve., 1992, 93, 97, Tampa, 1992, Miami, 1992, San Diego, 1993, L.A., 1993, Phoenix, 1993, 96, Detroit, 1993, Portland, 1993, Denver, 1993, 95, Washington, 1993, 97, Little Rock, 1993, 97, 98, Newark, 1994, Richmond, 1994, Atlanta, 1994, 95, 97, N.Y.C., 1994, Birmingham, 1995, Oklahoma City, 1995, 2000, Nashville, 1995, Salt Lake City, 1995, Charlotte, 1998, Phila., 1998, Las Vegas, 1998, Hartford, 2000, Columbus, Ohio, 2000, various other cities; lectr. Fed. Jud. Ctr., Orlando, 1994; Adler-Rosecan Disting. Lectr. St. Louis U., 1987; Cohen lectr. Wayne State U., 1989; Mason Ladd lectr. Fla. State U., 1981; Strasburger lectr. U. Tex., 1978; lectr. Am. Acad. Jud. Edn., 1980; disting. lectr. Tenn. Coll. Advocacy, 1980-85, 88, 90, 92, 94; moderator Robert Vance Forum on The Bill of Rights, 1990-96. Author: Criminal Justice Procedure, 1999, (with M. Ladd) Cases on Evidence, 1972, (with J. Yeager) Criminal Law and Procedure, 1979, Criminal Law Advocacy, 1982, Successful Techniques for Civil Trials, 1983, rev. edit., 1992, Adjudication of Criminal Justice, 1986, (with E. Imwinkelried, E. Kionka and K. Strachan) Evidence Teaching Materials for an Age of Science and Statutes, 1997, (with E. Imwinkelried) Dynamics of Trial Practice: Problems and Materials, 1995, (with M. Bright and E. Imwinkelried) Objections at Trial: A Concise Guide, 1998, (with M. Bright) Maine Objections at Trial, 1991, (with R. Aronson and M. Bright) Washington Objections at Trial, 1992, (with M. Bright) New Hampshire Objections at Trial, 1992, (with A. Montgomery and M. Bright) Minnesota Objections at Trial, 1992, (with M. Bright) Oregon Objections at Trial, 1992, Pocket Proof of Facts, 1993, Trial Handbook for Georgia Lawyers, 1993, (with J. Young, K. Curtis, and M. Bright) Virginia Objections at Trial, 1998. Vice pres. alumni bd. Augustana Coll., Rock Island, Ill., 1968. Recipient Disting. Teaching award Washington U., 1979, Founder's Day Teaching award Washington U., 1976, law faculty tchg. award U. Ga., 1985, ATLA Roscoe Pound Found. Jacobson award for excellence in trial law teaching, 1987, Josiah Meigs award U. Ga., 1989, Ethics award U. Ga. Law Sch. 1990, John C. O'Byrne Meml. Student Faculty award U. Ga. Law Sch., 1994, 98, Harrison Tweed award ALI-ABA. Mem. ABA, Am. Assn. Law Schs., Fed. Bar Assn. (chmn. law sch. divsn. 1978-79, nat. coun. 1994-95, Earl W. Kintner award for disting. svc. 1992), Iowa Bar Assn., Fed. Practice Inst. (dir. 1980-83, dean 1985-89), Am. Inns of Ct. Republican. Home: 283 Skyline Pkwy Athens GA 30606-3842 Office: U Ga School of Law Sch of Law Athens GA 30602

CARLSON, WARREN ORE, civil engineer; b. Woodbine, Kans., Apr. 11, 1926; s. Percy Franklin and Olivia Luella (Gugler) C.; m. Lenna Nadine Norman, Nov. 27, 1948; children: Teri Ann, Donna Elaine, Diana Lynn, Tina Marie, Randall Warren. BS in Civil Engring., U. Colo., 1946. Registered profl. engr., Alta., Can. Project engr. Brown & Root Ltd., Calgary, Alta., 1960-62, Bechtel Inc., Paris and Holland, 1962-72; engring. cons. Booz-Allen-Hamilton, Algiers, Algeria, 1972-74; project mgr. Worley-Protech, London and Holland, 1974-80, PDO (Shell I.P.M.), Sultanate of Oman, 1980-82; cons. J.P. Kenny Ltd., London and Denmark, 1982-84; sr. tech. advisor Petroleum Ministry Govt. of Oman, 1984-86; cons. Randall Cons., Germany and Portugal, 1986-93; sr. project mgr. Oman-India gas pipelines Intec Engring. Inc., Houston, 1994-95; quality assurance coord. Kvaerner R.J. Brown, Houston, 1995—. Lt. (j.g.) USNR, 1943-46. Mem. ASME, Am. Soc. Civil Engrs. Republican. Avocations: photography, travel, geneology. Home: 960 Berry Ave Los Altos CA 94024-5531

CARLSSON, BJÖRN, mechanical engineer, researcher; b. Stockholm, Sweden, Nov. 26, 1965; s. Jan and Birgit (Sjöström) C. MSc, Royal Inst. Tech., Stockholm, 1992, lic. in engring., 1996, PhD, 1997; MSc, Ohio U., 1992. Rsch. asst. Royal Inst. Tech., 1992-96; rschr. SSAB, Borlange, Sweden, 1996—. Contbr. articles to profl. jours. Mem. ASME. Avocation: squash. Home: Scheelegatan 11, 11228 Stockholm Sweden Office: SSAB Tunnplat, avd 97 UH, 78184 Borlange Sweden

CARLSSON, INGVAR GÖSTA, Swedish government official; b. Boras, Sweden, Nov. 9, 1934; m. Ingrid Melander, Oct. 7, 1957; children: Ingela, Pia. Degree in Polit. Sci. and Econs., Lund U., 1958; postgrad., Northwestern U., 1961. Sec. Prime Minister's Office, 1958-60; pres. Social Dem. Youth League, 1961-67; M.P., 1964-96; undersec. of state Statsradsberedningen, 1967-69; min. edn. and cultural affairs Govt. of Sweden, Stockholm, 1969-73, min. housing and phys. planning, 1973-76, dep. prime min., 1982-86, min. environment, 1985-86, prime min., 1986-91, 94-96; co-chmn. Commn. on Global Governance, 1992—; chmn. Olof Palme Internat. Ctr., 1999—, Ind. UN Inquiry of 1994 Genocide in Rwanda, 1999. Pres. Strategic Rsch. Found., 1997—. Mem. Social Dem. Party (exec. com. 1972-96, chmn. exec. com. 1986-96). Address: Gudöterassen 931, 13553 Tyresö Sweden

CARLSSON, PEDER ULF, science educator; b. Gothenburg, Sweden, Oct. 26, 1954; s. Lennart Karl and Marianne Greta (Eriksson) C.; m. Pia Susanne Olsson, May 28, 1994; children: Patrik, Elin. MS, Chalmers U. of Tech., Gothenburg, 1982, PhD, 1990. Lectr. Chalmers U. of Tech., Gothenburg, 1994—; cons. Nobel Biocare Inc., Gothenburg, 1985-96. Author: On Direct Bone Conduction Hearing Devices, 1990; patentee in field. Recipient 1st prize in Innovation Cup, Skandia & Dagens Industri, 1988, Cert. of Commendation IEE Prize for Helping Disabled People, 1989. Mem. Acoustical Soc. Am., N.Y. Acad. Scis. Avocations: skiing, gymnastics, music. Office: Chalmers U of Tech, Hörsalsvägen 9, 41296 Göteborg Sweden

CARLSSON, PER ARVID EMIL, pharmacologist, educator; b. Uppsala, Sweden, Jan. 25, 1923; s. Gottfrid and Lizzie (Steffenburg) C.; m. Ulla-Lisa Christoffersson, Dec. 29, 1945; children: Bo, Lena, Hans, Maria, Magnus. MD, PhD, U. Lund, Sweden, 1951. Assoc. prof. dept. pharmacology U. Lund, 1956-59; prof. pharmacology U. Göteborg, Sweden, 1959-89, prof. emeritus, 1989—; vis. scientist Lab. of Chem. Pharmacology, Nat. Heart Inst., Bethesda, Md., 1955-56; bd. mem. sci. adv. bd. and clin. adv. bd. ACADIA Pharms. Recipient Anders Jahre's Med. prize U. Oslo, 1974, Wolf prize in medicine, Jerusalem, 1979, Gairdner Found. award, Toronto, Can., 1982, 2d Ann. Bristol-Myers award for disting. achievement in neurosci. rsch., 1989, Japan prize in psychology and psychiatry Sci. and Tech. Found. Japan, 1994, Lieber prize for rsch. in schizophrenia Sci. Coun. of Nat. Alliance for Rsch. in Schizophrenia and Depression, 1994, rsch. prize Lundbeck Found., Denmark, 1995, Golden Kraepelin medal Max Planck Inst. Psychiatry, Munich, 1997, numerous others. Fellow Med. Soc. Gothenburg (hon.), World Fedn. Socs. Biol. Psychiatry (hon.), Collegium Internat. Neuropsychopharmacologicum (hon.), Academia Medicinae and Psychiatriae (hon.); mem. NAS (fgn. assoc.), Royal Soc. Sci. and Arts (Gothenburg), Japanese Pharmacological Soc. (fgn.), Am. Coll. Neuropsycholpharmacology (fgn.), German Pharmacological Soc. (corr.), Royal Swedish Acad. Sci., Acad. Europaea. Home: Torild Wulffsgatan 50, S-41319 Göteborg Sweden Office: ACADIA Pharms A/S, Fabriksparken 58, DK-2600 Glostrup Medicinaregatan 7, Denmark*

CARLTON, JAMES JOSEPH, Australian Red Cross administrator; b. Sydney, N.S.W., Australia, May 13, 1935; s. John Lyons and Alma Eileen (Kyle) C.; m. Diana Mary Wilson, May 9, 1964; children: Alexandra Jane, Freia Jo, Robert James. BSc, U. Sydney, Australia, 1955; Sr. Mgrs. in Govt. program, Kennedy Sch., Harvard U., 1983. Mgr. Dexlon Ltd., London, 1957-66; cons. McKinsey & Co., Inc., Melbourne, Australia, 1966-71; gen. sec. Liberal Party of Australia, Sydney, 1971-77; mem. Ho. of Reps., Canberra, Australia, 1977-94; minister for health Govt of Australia, Canberra, 1982-83; sec. gen. Australian Red Cross, 1994—; exec, councillor Commonwealth of Australia, 1982—; shadow minister Fed. Parliament, Australia, 1983-93; official commonwealth observer Zambian Elections, 1991; chmn. Nat. Adv. Coun. on Australian Archives, 1998—. Pres. Students' Rep. Coun., U. Sydney, 1956-57; sec. Friends of Australian Opera, Sydney, 1974-78. Mem. Union Club Sydney. Avocations: opera, music, bushwalking, cooking. Office: Australian Red Cross, 155 Pelham St, Carlton VIC 3053, Australia

CARLUCCI, JOSEPH P., lawyer; b. Port Chester, N.Y., Aug. 21, 1942; m. Elizabeth Smith; children: Susan Elizabeth, Kathleen Ann. BA in Econs., Georgetown U., 1964; JD, Fordham U., 1967. Bar: N.Y. 1969. Ptnr. Pierro & Carlucci, Port Chester, N.Y., 1969-76; pvt. practice, Rye, N.Y., 1977-78; mng. ptnr. Cuddy & Feder & Worby LLP, White Plains, N.Y., 1979-99; chief legis. counsel to N.Y. senator from Westchester County, 1971-73; chief counsel N.Y. State Select Com. on State's Economy, 1973-74; part. Nat. Conf. CHristians and Jews, 1999—. Co-founder, v.p. Rye Town-Port Chester Rep. Club, 1972; trustee Village of Port Chester, 1974-77; chmn. Port Chester Indsl. Devel. Agy., 1974-76; mem. Westchester County Econ. Devel. Coun., 1976-80, Narcotics Guidance Coun. Port Chester, 1970-74; chmn. Met. N.Y. YMCA Key Leaders Conf., 1984; mem. Parent's Coun., Wheaton Coll., 1986-87; bd. dirs. Port Chester YMCA, 1970-79, sec., 1972-77, v.p., 1978; mem. Port Chester Govt. Study Commn., 1971-73; commr. appraisal White Plains and Greenburgh Urban Renewal; counsel to South Shore Hotline, 1973-74; mem. Port Chester Pub. Employees Rels. Bd., 1973-77; mem. adv. bd. bd. dirs. Salvation Army, 1973-77; mem. adv. bd. Security Title and Guaranty Co., 1986-90; bd. dirs. Rye YMCA, 1979-87, pres., 1982-85, trustee, 1989—; trustee Rye Hist. Soc., 1979-83, 90-96, sec., 1980-81, v.p., 1982-83, 92-94, pres., 1994-96; interviewer alumni admissions program Georgetown U., 1988-96; bd. visitors Pace U. Sch. Law, 1990—; bd. dirs. Vol. Ctr. United Way Westchester County, 1991-97; mem. Westchester divsn. Cardinal's Com. for Laity, 1991—, vice chmn., 1992, chmn., 1993-95; mem. paralegal curriculum adv. com. SUNY-Westchester C.C., 1994; bd. dirs. March of Dimes Birth Defects Found., 1994-96, Westchester Bus. Partnership, 1995-98, Westchester Partnership for Econ. Devel., 1996—. Recipient Golden R award Renaissance Project, Inc., Gold Man award YMCA, 1985, Cmty. Svc. award Rotary Internat. Club, 1995. Mem. ABA (vice chmn. econs. of law practice com. on lawyering skills 1984-85), NCCJ, N.Y. State Bar Assn., Westchester County Bar Assn. (real property com. 1978-82), Port Chester-Rye Bar Assn. (sec. 1970-75, pres. 1976-77, bd. dirs. student assistance svcs. alcohol and drug abuse prevention program 1989-95, adv. bd. 1995—), Westchester C.C. Found. (bd. dirs. 1997—), NCCJ, Real Estate Fin. Assn., Coveleigh Club (bd. govs. 1978-86, sec. 1979, v.p. 1980, pres. 1981-84), Georgetown U. Met. Club (bd. dirs. 1980-82), Hundred Club Westchester (bd. dirs.).

CARL XVI GUSTAF, HIS MAJESTY KING, King of Sweden; b. Apr. 30, 1946; s. Prince Gustaf Adolf and Princess Sibylla (Princess Sache-Coburg-Gotha); m. Silvia Renate Sommerlath, June 19, 1976; children: Victoria, Carl Philip, Madeleine. Ed., Royal Naval Acad., Royal Nat. Def. Coll., U. Uppsala, Stockholm U.; hon. degree, Swedish U. Agrl. Scis., Royal Inst. of Tech., Stockholm Sch. Econs., Åbo Acad., Finland. King of Sweden, 1973—. Chmn. Swedish br. World-Wide Fund for Nature; hon. pres. World Scout Found. Office: Royal Palace, 11130 Stockholm Sweden

CARLYLE, RICHARD STANLEY, water transportation executive; b. Aug. 16, 1940. Student, Western Mont. State U., 1958-59; BS with honors, U.S. Merchant Marine Acad., 1963; diploma, Army Mgmt. Staff Coll., Ft. Belvoir, Va., 1993. Deck officer U.S. Merchant Marine, Balt., New Orleans,, Seattle, 1963-65, 69-70; tchr. Nicholls H.S., New Orleans, 1965-66, Page Navigation Sch., New Orleans, 1966-68; marine transp. officer Mil. Traffic Mgmt. Command, Seattle, 1972—; bd. dirs. N.W. Grad. Sch. of the Ministry, Redmond, Wash., 1998—; pres., author Rocky Point Press, Redmond, 1997—;. Author: An Answer to Prayer, 1998. Home: 14817 NE 64th St Redmond WA 98052-4746

CARMAN, JANICE FALLER (KIT CARMAN), psychology educator, consultant; b. Rochester, N.Y., Sept. 17, 1958; d. Raymond Owen and Laura Thompson F.; m. John Elwin Carman, Sept. 21, 1985 (div. Dec. 1998). BS, Ga. State U., 1982; MA, The Wright Inst., 1989, PhD, 1992. Advt. dir. McKendrick Corp., Atlanta, 1983-85, WARM-FM, Atlanta, 1985-86; creativity cons. Creativity Coach, San Francisco, 1990—; assoc. prof. psychology and mktg. Golden Gate U., San Francisco, 1990—, chair dept. psychology, 1994—; consumer psychologist, San Francisco, 1990—. Contbr. articles to profl. jours. Bd. dirs. NOW, San Francisco, 1987-88. Mem. APA, Am. Mktg. Assn. (v.p. bd. 1994-96). Avocations: walking, reading, travel. E-mail: kcarman@ggu.edu. Office: Golden Gate U 536 Mission St San Francisco CA 94105-2967

CARMAN, SUSAN HUFERT, nurse coordinator; b. Detroit, Oct. 2, 1940; d. Theodore Louis and Margaret L. (O'Connor) Hufert; children: Amy E., Holly C., John T. BSN, Johns Hopkins U., 1964; MEd, Northeastern U., 1975; MS in Health Care Adminstrn., Simmons Coll., 1988. Instr. psychiat. nursing Salem (Mass.) Hosp. Sch. Nursing, 1975-78, Curry Coll., Milton, Mass., 1978-80; editor Beacon Comm. Corp., Acton, Mass., 1980-84; writer health promotion Honeywell Inc., Waltham, Mass., 1984-85; mgr. mental health unit Heritage Hosp., Somerville, Mass., 1986-87; specialist adult psychiatry Mass. Dept. Mental Health, Boston, 1987-93; clinician intensive clin. svcs. MHMA, Boston, 1994-96; dir. Arbour Counseling Svcs. Boston, 1996—; with SHC Assocs., Boston, 1993—; bd. dirs. Com. to End. Elder Homelessness, Boston, Mass., 1993-99, Dept. Social Svcs., Lowell, sec., 1982-92. Chair health com. Jamaica Plain (Mass.) Tree of Life/Arbol da Vida, 1994—; docent Arnold Arboretum, Boston, 1989—. Mem. ANA, Mass. Nurses Assn. Avocations: travel, reading, walking, classical music.

CARMELI, MOSHE, theoretical physicist; b. Baghdad, Iraq, June 15, 1933; arrived in Israel, 1951; naturalized U.S. citizen, 1973; s. Eliaho and Neomi Carmeli-Chitayat; m. Elisheva Cohen, Aug. 17, 1961; children: Eli, Dorith, Yair. MSc, Hebrew U., Jerusalem, 1960; DSc, Technion-Israel Inst. Tech., Haifa, 1964. Rsch. assoc. Lehigh U., Bethlehem, Pa., 1964-65, Temple U., Phila., 1964-65; rsch. assoc. U. Md., College Park, 1965-67, asst. prof., 1967-68; rsch. physicist USAF Lab., Dayton, Ohio, 1967-72; assoc. prof. Ben Gurion U., Beer Sheva, 1972-74, head physics dept., 1973-77, prof. physics, 1974—, Albert Einstein prof. physics, 1979—, head Theoretical Physics Ctr., 1980-89; vis. prof. Inst. for Theoretical Physics, SUNY, Stony Brook, 1977-78, 81, U. Md., College Park, 1985-86, Inst. Henri Poincaré, Paris, 1975, Internat. Ctr. for Theoretical Physics, Trieste, 1977, 78, 79, 80, 81, 82, 85, 87, 88, Max-Planck Inst., Munich, 1980, U. Mass., Amherst, 1985, Colgate U., Hamilton, N.Y., 1987, Queen Mary Coll., U. London, 1988, State U. Campinas, São Paulo, Brazil, 1998. Author: Group Theory and General Relativity, 1977, Classical Fields: General Relativity and Gauge Theory, 1982, Statistical Theory and Random Matrices, 1983, Cosmological Special Relativity: The Large-Scale Structure of Space, Time and Velocity, 1997; co-author: Representations of the Rotation and Lorentz Groups, 1976, Gauge Fields: Classification and Equations of Motion, 1989, Gravitation: SL (2,C) Gauge Theory and Conservation Laws, 1990, Theory of Spinors, 2000; co-editor: Relativity, 1970; contbr. more than 100 articles to profl. jours. Fellow AAAS, Am. Phys. Soc.; mem. Israel Phys. Soc. (pres. 1982-85), Internat. Soc. for Gen. Relativity and Gravitation, N.Y. Acad. Scis., Sigma Xi. Home: 19 Erez St, Omer Israel Office: Ben Gurion U, Dept Physics, Beer Sheva 84105, Israel

CARMESIN, HANS-OTTO, physicist, educator; b. Speyer, Germany, Dec. 22, 1959; s. Ulrich and Maria-Luise (Meyer) C.; m. Ingeborg Schmidt, July 30, 1987; children: Johannes, Christian, Ellen, Matthias Carmesin. Diploma in physics, U. Mainz, Germany, 1986, PhD in Physics, 1988; Habilitation in physics, U. Bremen, Germany, 1995. Scientist U. Mainz, 1986-88; postdoctoral fellow NYU, N.Y.C., 1988-89, SUNY, Albany, 1989-90, U. Ga., Athens, 1990; sci. asst. U. Bremen, 1990—. Author: Consistent Calculus, 1994, Theorie Neuronaler Adaption, 1994, Neuronal Adaptation Theory, 1996, Grundideen der Relativitätstheorie, 1996; patentee in field. Recipient 3rd prize Bundeswettbewerb Mathematik, 1974. Fellow Alexander von Humboldt Found.; mem. Deutsche Physikalische Gesellschaft, Deutsche Neurowissenschaftliche Gesellschaft. Avocations: trumpet, piano, swimming. Office: Univ Bremen, Univ Inst Theor Physics, 28334 Bremen Germany

CARMICHAEL, JOHN CRAIG, JR., career counselor; b. Ft. Knox, Ky., Apr. 13, 1953; s. John Craig and Sara Alice (Booher) C.; m. Barbara Louise Werth, Aug. 18, 1984; 1 child, Jonathan Christian. BA, Western Ky. U., 1980, MEd, 1981. Employment counselor Ky. Dept. Human Resources, Bowling Green, 1980-81; residence hall dir. East Tex. State U., Commerce, 1981-84; career specialist, human devel. instr. Richland Coll., Dallas, 1987—; lectr. Richland Coll. Spkrs. Bur., 1993—; cons. Pvt. Industry Coun., Dallas, 1994—. Recipient Nat. Inst. for Staff and Orgnl. Devel. award for Tchg. Excellence, C.C. Leadership Program, U. Tex., Austin, 1994, Richland Coll. Excellence in Tchg. award, 1999-2000. Mem. Tex. Jr. Coll. Tchrs. Assn. Democrat. Episcopalian. Avocations: reading, travel. Home: 10227 Sunridge Trl Dallas TX 75243-2546 Office: Richland College 12800 Abrams Rd Dallas TX 75243-2199

CARMICHAEL, JUDY LEA, record industry executive, concert jazz pianist; b. Lynwood, Calif., Nov. 27, 1952; d. John Alvin and Jeanne Pauline (Boock) Hohenstein. Student, Calif. State U., Long Beach, 1970-73, Calif. State U., Fullerton. Owner C&D Prodns., N.Y.C., 1989—; chmn. jazz fellowships com. NEA, Washington, 1990-91; featured on Nat. Pub. Radio, Marian McPartland's Piano Jazz, 1990, Morning Edition Nat. Pub. Radio, also TV programs Entertainment Tonight, CBS, Sunday Morning with Charles Kuralt, 1993. Performed as pianist at Breda Jazz Festival, The Netherlands, 1986, Carnegie Hall, N.Y.C., 1988, 89, Rio de Janeiro, 1989, Peggy Guggenheim Mus., Venice, Italy, 1990, Am. Acad., Rome, 1990, 91, USIA Tour, Portugal, 1991, Spain, 1991, India, 1988, China, 1992, Singapore, 1994, S. Am., 1996, major U.S. tours 1993-95, also L.A., Zurich, Switzerland, Paris, Cannes, France; performer Stanford Symphony Pops with Skitch Henderson, 1997; author (music) Judy Carmichael's Complete Book of Stride Piano, 1987, You Can Play Stride Piano, 1996; prodr., artist (LP's) Jazz Piano, 1983, Two Handed Stride, 1980, (CD's) Trio, 1989, Old Friends, 1991, Pearls, 1985, ...And Basie Called Her Stride, 1993, Judy, 1994, Chops, 1995, PianoDisc, 1995, QRS piano rolls, 1996, (CD and player piano formats) High on Fats and Other Stuff, 1997; featured on CBS Sunday Morning with Charles Osgood, Entertainment Tonight, Prairie Home Companion, Nat. Pub. Radio's Morning Edit.; jazz editor Sheet Music mag., 1989-90; host, creator, prodr. Judy Carmichael's Jazz Inspired, Nat. Pub. Radio, 2000; contbr. numerous articles to profl. jours. NEA fellow, grantee; Grammy award nominee, 1980; chosen to be Steinway artist, 1986; nominated for Mac award Manhattan Assn. Cabarets and Clubs for Stage Show with Steve Ross, 1996. Avocations: golf, softball, tennis, skiing.

CARMICHAEL, MARY ALICE, artist, genealogist; b. Colon, Panama, Nov. 28, 1936; came to U.S., 1937; d. Donald Croom and Mary Alice (Gatling) Beatty; m. James Donald Carmichael, Oct. 28, 1961; children: James Donald Jr., Beatty Payseur, Daniel Troy. BA, Howard Coll., 1960. Contbr. articles to profl. jours. Organizing mem. Ala. Men's Hall of Fame, 1988—; mem. Women's Com. of 100 of Birmingham, pres. 1989-91; steering com. Reynold's Hist. Soc., 1988—; led successful efforts to keep local sch. from being closed and demolished. Named one of Outstanding Young Women of Am., 1972-73. Mem. DAR (Outstanding Jr. Mem. award 1968, Most Outstanding Hist. Paper award 1988), Soc. Mayflower Descendants Ala. (gov. 1990-94, registrar 1985-94), Rotary (helped initiate 1st heart pacemaker bank for the indigent in Bolivia). Presbyterian. Avocations: art, genealogy, photography, travel. Home: 2857 Canterbury Rd Birmingham AL 35223-1201

CARMICHAEL, PAUL LOUIS, ophthalmic surgeon; b. July 8, 1927; s. Louis and Christina Ciamaichela; m. Pauline Cecilia Lipsmire, Oct. 28, 1950; children: Paul Louis, Mary Catherine, John Michael, Kevin Anthony, Joseph William, Patricia Ann, Robert, Christopher. BS in Biology, Villanova U., 1945; MD, St. Louis U., 1949; MS in Medicine, U. Pa., 1954. Diplomate Am. Bd. Ophthalmology; cert. isotope methodology Hahnemann Med. Coll. Rotating intern St. Joseph's Hosp., Phila., 1949-50; resident in ophthalmology Phila. Gen. Hosp., 1952-54; asst. prof. ophthalmology Hahnemann Med. Coll., Phila., 1960-66, clin. assoc. prof. nuclear medicine, 1974-90; with radioactive isotope dept. Wills Eye Hosp., Phila., 1956-61, sr.

asst. surgeon, 1961-65, assoc. surgeon, 1966-72, assoc. surgeon retinal svc., 1972-90; attending ophthalmologist Holy Redeemer Hosp., Meadowbrook, Pa., 1963-65; assoc. ophthalmologist Grand View Hosp., Sellersville, Pa., 1958-75; instr. opthalmology Grad. Sch. Medicine, U. Pa., Phila., 1956-63; clin. assoc. prof. ophthalmology Temple U., Phila., 1967-72; clin. assoc. prof. ophthalmology Thomas Jefferson U. Sch. Medicine, Phila., 1971-90; chief ophthalmology North Pa. Hosp., Lansdale, 1959-90, pres. staff, 1959; pres. Ophthalmic Assocs., Lansdale, 1969-90. Co-author: Nuclear Ophthalmology, 1976; contbr. chpts. to books, papers to profl. confs., articles to publs. in field. Pres. bd. dirs. North Pa. Symphony, 1976-78. Capt. M.C., U.S. Army, 1950-51. Named Outstanding Young Man of Yr., Lansdale Jaycees, 1959, Outstanding Young Man, State of Pa. Jaycees, 1960. Fellow ACS, Internat. Coll. Surgeons, Coll. Physicians Phila.; mem. AMA, Montgomery County Med. Soc., Pa. Med. Soc., Am. Acad. Ophthalmology, Pa. Acad. Ophthalmology, Assn. Rsch. in Ophthalmology, Inter-County Ophthalmol. Soc. (co-founder, pres. 1975-78), Ophthalmic Club Phila. (pres. 1964), Delaware Valley Ophthalmic Soc. (pres. 1985-89). Roman Catholic. Home: Box 680308 2567 Columbine Ct Park City UT 84068

CARMICHAEL, RICHARD ARDEAN, marketing professional; b. Sigourney, Iowa, Jan. 2, 1930; children: Joseph, Laura, James, Janet, Jeanne, Cathy. Student, Wash. Jr. Coll., Iowa, 1949; D in Vet. Medicine, Iowa State U., 1955; student, Cambridge U., Eng., 1972. Owner, ptnr Speaker and Carmichael Vet. Clinic, Keota, Iowa, 1955-72; pres., gen. mgr. Maplehurst Ova Transplants, Inc., 1972-90; gen. mgr. Maplehurst Genetics Internat. Inc., 1990-97, 1997—. Contbr. articles to profl. jours. Recipient Award for Excellence Embryo Transfer Industry, 1988, The Tough Egg award Am. Embryo Transfer Assn., 1989. Mem. Iowa Vet. Med. Assn., Am. Vet. Med. Assn., Am. Assn. Bovine Practitioners, Internat. Embryo Transfer Soc. (com. chmn. 1974, bd. govs. 1975, sec., treas. 1976, pres. 1977, chmn. of workshop 1979, bd. dirs. 1982, v.p. 1982, pres. 1983, 84, govt. liaison and animal health and regulations com. chmn. 1983—), Soc. for Cryobiology, U.S. Animal Health Assn., Embryo Movement Symposium, Boy Scouts Am., Keota Cmty. Club, Knights of Columbus. Home: 32263 190th St Keota IA 52248-8551

CARMICHAEL, VIRGIL WESLY, mining, civil and geological engineer, former coal company executive; b. Pickering, Mo., Apr. 26, 1919; s. Ava Abraham and Rosevelt (Murphy) C.; m. Emma Margaret Freeman, Apr. 1, 1939 (dec.); m. Colleen Fern Wadsworth, Oct. 29, 1951; children: Bonnie Rae, Peggy Ellen, Jacki Ann. BS, U. Idaho, 1951, MS, 1956; PhD, Columbia Pacific U., San Rafael, Calif., 1980. Registered profl. geol., mining and civil engr., geologist, land surveyor. Asst. geologist Day Mines, Wallace, Idaho, 1950; mining engr. De Anza Engring. Co., Troy, Idaho, Santa Fe, 1950-52; hwy. engring. asst. N.Mex. Hwy. Dept., Santa Fe, 1952-53; asst. engr. U. Idaho, 1953-56; minerals analyst Idaho Bur. Mines, 1953-56; mining engr. No. Pacific Ry. Co., St. Paul, 1956-67; geologist N.Am. Coal Corp., Cleve., 1967-69, asst. v.p. engring., 1969-74, v.p., head exploration dept., 1974-84; travel host Satrom Travel and Tour, Bismarck, N.D., 1988-92; advisor photogeology for People to People "Hard Rock" Minerals Del. to China, 1981; leader People to People Coal Mechanization Del. to China, 1982; advisor (photogeology) to Carbocol, Colombia, S.A., 1984-85; mem. Bismarck Scottish Rite Children's Hearing Impairment Bd., 1991-97, 2000—. Asst. chief distbr. Emergency Mgmt. Fuel Resources of N.D., 1968-92; bd. dirs., chmn. fund dr. Bismarck-Mandan Orch. Assn., 1979-83; 1st v.p., bd. dirs., chmn. fund dr. Bismarck Arts and Galleries Assn., 1982-86; mem. and spl. advisor (Minerals) Nat. Def. Exec. Res., 1983—; mem. Fed. Emergency Mgmt. Agy., 1983—; life mem. adv. bd. Bismarck Salvation Army, 1988—, chmn., 1993-95; sci. rsch. bd. N.D. Acad. Sci. Found., 1986-91. Recipient A award for sci. writing Sigma Gamma Epsilon; J.C. Penney Golden Rule award finalist, 1996. Mem. Am. Inst. Profl. Geologists (past pres. local chpt.), Breezy Shores Resort and Beach Club (bd. dirs. 1986—), Kiwanis (past pres., dist. lt. gov., dist. chmn. internat. found. 1991-2000, Tablet of Honor, Mindacks Dist. appreciation, other awards), Masons (past master, trustee 1987-92, N.D. Masonic Found. 1987-92, 94-99, chmn. 1990-92, 97-99, Mason of Yr. Bismarck lodge 1992, Gen. Grand Masters award Cryptic Mason Med. Rsch. Found., Scottish Rite (Knight Comdr. Cross of Honor, Royal Order of Scotland), York Rite (Knight Templar Cross of Honor, Knight of York Cross of Honor), Bismarck Lodge Found., Elks (life), Am. Legion (life). Republican. Home: 1013 N Anderson St Bismarck ND 58501-3446

CARMIGNATO, GUILIO, financial company executive; b. Milan, Italy, May 5, 1965; s. Alberto and Milena (Guattari) C. Degree in econs., Bocconi U., Milan, 1990. Analyst Akros, Milan, 1990-93; mgr. corp. fin. and I.P.O. Santander Investment, Milan, 1993-96; mng. ptnr. T&A Testa & Assocs. SRL, Milan, 1996-99; mng. dir. info. tech. divsn. Banca del Gottasdo Group, 2000—. Lt. Italian Army, 1988-89. Avocations: travel, reading, sailing, soaring, collecting books. Office: Gestidsa, via Adamini 10a, CH 6901 Lugano Italy

CARMODY, ARTHUR RODERICK, JR., lawyer; b. Shreveport, La., Feb. 19, 1928; s. Arthur R. and Caroline (Gaughan) C.; m. Renee Aubry, Jan. 26, 1952 (div. 1980); children: Helen Bragg, Renee, Arthur Roderick, Patrick, Timothy, Mary, Virginia, Joseph; m. Mary Wells, Sept. 1, 1990. Grad. with honors, N.Mex. Mil. Inst.; BS, Fordham U., 1949; LLB, La. State U., 1952. Bar: La. 1952, U.S. Supreme Ct. 1971. Mem. firm Wilkinson, Carmody & Gilliam and its predecessors, Shreveport, 1952—; bd. dirs. Kansas City So. Transport Co., Kansas City, Shreveport and Gulf Terminal Co., Shreveport Braves Baseball Club (Tex. League), Sta. KDAQ-FM Pub. Radio, pres., 1991, chmn., 1992, RED River Pub. Radio Network; mem. Shreveport Steamer (World Football League) Partnership; pres. Touchdown Club of Shreveport, 1960. Author: Legal Problems in the Development and Mining of Lignite, 1976; legal history columnist Shreveport Bar Review, 1995—; La. adv. editor The Insurance Bar, 1961—. Chmn. Met. Shreveport Zoning Bd. Appeals, 1959-72; pres. bd. trustees Jesuit H.S., 1976-82; chmn. bd. govs. Loyola Found. Shreveport, 1991-94; trustee Schumpert Med. Ctr., 1965-85; bd. dirs. La. State U. Found., Baton Rouge, Agnew Day Sch., Shreveport, 1970-82, Ridgewood Montessori Sch.; nat. bd. dirs. N.Mex. Mil. Inst., Roswell, 1967-68 (named to Alumni Hall of Fame 1994); adv. coun. La. State U., Shreveport, 1982-86; govs. ad hoc com. for preparation rules and regulations for mining and reclamation of lignite in the State of La., Dept. Conservation, 1978-79; select com. mem. for rev. stds. jud. conduct Supreme Ct. of La., 1994—. 1st lt. USAR, 1948-50. Recipient Alumni Achievement award Fordham U., 1995; named Hon. Alumnus, elected to Ring of Honor Loyola Coll. Prep., 1993. Master Am. Inns of Ct.; fellow Am. Coll. Trial Lawyers, La. Bar Assn. (mem. com. on lawyer and judicial conduct 1996—); mem. ABA, Fed. Bar Assn., Shreveport Bar Assn., U.S. Supreme Ct. Hist. Soc., Fifth Fed. Cir. Bar Assn., Federalist Soc., North La. Hist. Soc., La. Hist. Assn., Confederate Meml. Lit. Soc., Nat. Soc. SAR (pres. Galvez chpt. 1997), Scribes Soc., Supreme Ct. of La. Hist. Soc., Univ. Assocs. of La. State U., Am. Judicature Soc., La. Law Inst., Trial Attys. Am., Nat. Assn. R.R. Trial Counsel, Internat. Assn. Def. Counsel, La. Assn. Def. Counsel, Nat. Acad. Law and Medicine, Am. Arbitration Assn. (panel arbitrators), Mid-Continent Oil and Gas Assn. (exec. com. 1984—), La. R.R. Assn. (exec. com. 1992—), Tarshar Soc., La. Assn. Bus. and Industry, Nat. Legal Ctr. for the Pub. Interest, Pub. Affairs Rsch. Coun., Shreveport C. of C. (dir. 1968-70), Kansas City So. Hist. Soc., Railway and Locomoitve Hist. Soc., Soc. Hosp. Counsel, La. Civil Svc. League, Res. Officers Assn., North La. Civil War Round Table, U.S. Horse Cavalry Assn., Soc. for Mil. History, Soc. for Civil War History, Crossed Saber Soc., Federalist Soc., Sovereign Mil. Order of Malta, Phi Delta Phi, Kappa Alpha Order. Home: 255 Forest Ave Shreveport LA 71104-4506 Office: Wilkinson Carmody & Gilliam 1700 Beck Bldg 400 Travis St Shreveport LA 71101-3108

CARMOSINO, GIANCARLO, pharmaceuticals company executive; b. Naples, Italy, Jan. 22, 1957; s. Carlo Carmosino and Civita Valerio; separated; children: Ilaria, Alessia. MD, U. Naples, 1982. Hormones specialist Hoechst Italy, Milan, 1985-88, head clin. rsch., 1989-90; med. mktg. dir. Master Pharma, Parma, Italy, 1991-98; regional med. mgr. Glaxo Wellcome, Verona, Italy, 1999—. Office: Glaxo Wellcome, Via Fleming 2, 37100 Verona Italy

CARNAHAN, GEORGE RICHARD, business educator, consultant; b. Zanesville, Ohio, May 20, 1935; s. George Edwin and Anna Eloise (Beymer) C.; m. Mary Linn Burbage, June 14, 1958; children: Elizabeth, George, Glenn, John. BS, Juniata Coll., 1957; MBA, Miami U., Oxford, Ohio, 1962; PhD, Ohio State U., 1967. Prof. mgmt. No. Mich. U., Marquette, 1964—, dept. head, 1985-93; bd. dirs. Bay Mills Community Coll., Brimley, Mich., 1985—. Co-author: T.I.M.E. To Improve Management Effectiveness, 1986; also articles. Elder Presbyn. Ch., Marquette. Mem. Acad. Mgmt., Decision Sci. Inst., Alpha Kappa Psi (v.p. 1983-87, pres. 1987-89). Democrat. Office: No Mich U Marquette MI 49855

CARNEGIE, RODERICK H., technological company executive, mining executive. Chmn. Hudson Conway Ltd., Adacel Techs. Ltd.

CARNEIRO, ANTONIO VAZ, internist, medical educator; b. Vila Real, Feb. 28, 1951; s. Antonio Reis and Maria Luisa (Vaz) C.; m. Cristina Goncalves, Sept. 23, 1992. MD, U. Lisbon, Portugal, 1976; PhD, U. Lisbon, 1994. Resident in internal medicine Santa Maria U. Hosp., Lisbon, 1977-82, attending staff in internal medicine, 1983-93; asst. clin. prof. U. Lisbon Sch. Medicine, 1994—. Roman Catholic. Avocations: cinema, tennis, classical music. E-mail: avc@ip.pt. Fax: 351 217 976758. Office: U Lisbon Hosp Santa Maria, Av Prof Egas Moniz, 1649-028 Lisbon Portugal

CARNEIRO, CELSO DEL RÉ, geology educator; b. São Paulo, Brazil, June 3, 1951; s. Florisvaldo Madureira and Elza Joanna (Dal Ré) C.; m. Marli Fernandes (div. Apr. 1999); children: Glauce Fernandes, Ivan Fernandes. Prof. Geoscis. Inst. U. São Paulo, 1973-78; researcher Technol. Rsch. Inst., São Paulo, 1978-95; prof. Geoscis. Inst. UNICAMP, Campinas, Brazil, 1986—; coord. DGRM-IFT, São Paulo, 1989-92, earth sci. course, Campinas, Brazil, 1998—. Editor-in-chief: Revista Brasileira Geociencias, 1983-89; editor: Projeção esterografica para analise, 1996. Mem. Brazilian Geol. Soc. (Martelo de Prata 1982), Brazilian Soc. Engring. Geology, Brazilian Soc. Advancement of Sci., Brazilian Acad. Scis. (assoc.). Office: State U Campinas Geoscis In, PO Box 6152, 13083970 Campinas SP, Brazil

CARNER, CHARLES ROBERT, JR., screenwriter, director; b. Chgo., Apr. 30, 1957; s. Charles Robert Carner Sr. and Barbara (Shields) Traeger. BA, Columbia Coll., 1978. Asst. to dir. TV show Dummy, Chgo., 1978; casting asst. film My Bodyguard, Chgo., 1979; story editor Tony Bill Prodns., Venice, Calif., 1979-81; screenwriter Fred Weintraub Prodns., Beverly Hills, Calif., 1981-82, Catalina Prodn. Group, Sherman Oaks, Calif., 1983-84, Trian Prodns./CBS-TV, Los Angeles, 1984-85; screenwriter, dir. Tristar Prodns., Los Angeles, 1985-89. Author: (screenplays) Seduced, 1985, Gymkata, 1985, Let's Get Harry, 1986, Blind Fury, 1988, Eyes of a Witness, 1991; writer, dir. TV series Midnight Caller, 1990, Reasonable Doubts, 1992, The Untouchables, 1993, TV movie A Killer Among Friends, 1992, One Woman's Courage, 1994, Vanishing Point, 1997, The Fixer, 1997, Who Killed Atlanta's Children?, 1999, Crossfire Trail, 2000. Active East African Wildlife Soc., Kenya, Los Angeles, 1984—. Recipient Best Student Film award Chgo. Internat. Film Festival, 1978. Mem. NRA (life), Writers Guild Am., Sierra Club (life). Roman Catholic.

CARNERO GONZALEZ, CARLOS, foreign diplomat; b. Madrid, Nov. 24, 1961. Mem. European Parliament, 1999—, mem. com. on constnl. affairs, substitute com. fgn. affairs/human rights/common security; mem. Group of the Party of European Socialists; mem. delegation to the EU-Turkey Joint Parliamentary Com.; substitute delegation to the EU-Malta Joint Parliamentary Com. *

CARNES, JOSEPH SYDNEY, clergyman; b. Memphis, Dec. 2, 1929; s. Samuel Leslye and Marion Rachel (Weaver) C.; m. Annie Frank Rutledge, June 22, 1952; children: Jane Ann, Joseph Sydney Jr., James Rutledge, John David. BS, Memphis State U., 1956; MDiv, Tex. Christian U., 1962, D Ministry, 1979. Ordained to ministry Christian Ch. (Disciples of Christ), 1949; cert. pastoral counselor Parkland Hosp., Dallas. Min. of membership 1st Christian Ch, Eugene, Oreg., 1962-65; sr. min. 1st Christian Ch, Nampa, Idaho, 1965-72, Lakeview Christian Ch., Dallas, 1972-81, Oak Cliff Christian Ch., Dallas, 1981—; pres. Christian Chs. in Idaho, Boise, 1971. Co-author: Communion Meditations, 1966. Founding dir. Nampa Christian Housing, 1967; bd. dirs. Mercy Hosp., Nampa, 1968-72, Idaho Mental Health Dept., 1969-72. Col. Tex. State Guard, chief chaplains, 1972-94. Mem. Mil. Chaplains Assn. U.S.A. (local pres. 1972—), Masons (33d degree, chaplain 1988-95), Lions (local pres. 1981-82), Order Ea. Star. Republican. Avocations: fishing, hunting, world travel. Home: 3738 Cripple Creek Dr Dallas TX 75224-3701 Office: 1222 W Kiest Blvd Dallas TX 75224-3233

CARNESALE, ALBERT, university chancellor; b. Bronx, N.Y., July 2, 1936; two children: Keith, Kimberly. BME, Cooper Union, 1957; MS, Drexel U., 1961, LLD (hon.), 1993; PhD, N.C. State U., 1966, LLD (hon.), 1997; AM (hon.), Harvard U., 1979; ScD (hon.), N.J. Inst. Technology, 1984. Prof. N.C. State U., Raleigh, 1962-69, 72-74; chief Def. Weapons Systems U.S. Arms Control and Disarmament Agy., Washington, 1969-72; prof. acad. dean John F. Kennedy Sch. Govt. Harvard U., Cambridge, Mass., 1974-97; dean John F. Kennedy Sch. of Govt., 1991-95; provost, Lucius N. Littauer Prof. Pub. Policy and Adminstrn. Harvard U., Cambridge, 1994-97; chancellor UCLA, 1997—. Author: New Nuclear Nations: Consequences for US Policy, 1993, Fateful Visions: Avoiding Nuclear Catastrophe, 1988, Superpower Arms Control: Setting the Record Straight, 1987, Hawks, Doves, and Owls: An Agenda for Avoiding Nuclear War, 1985, Living with Nuclear Weapons, 1983, Nuclear Power Issues and Choices: Report of the Nuclear Energy Policy Study Group, 1977. Gano Dunn award for Outstanding Profl. Achievement, Cooper Union, N.Y.C. Fellow Am. Acad. Arts and Scis.; mem. Coun. on Fgn. Rels., Internat. Inst. for Strategic Studies, L.A. World Affairs Coun. Office: U of California Office of the Chancellor 405 Hilgard Ave Los Angeles CA 90095-9000

CARNEVALE, LOUIS, civil engineer, inventor; b. Rome, Sept. 16, 1954; s. Loreto and Josephine Carnevale; m. Elizabeth T. Wrobel, Sept. 27, 1991; children: Ingrid, Patrick, Joseph. BA in Liberal Arts magna cum laude, Coll. at Old Westbury, N.Y., 1984; BS in Civil Engring. cum laude, U. Buffalo, 1989. Profl. engr., N.Y. Project mgr. Ea. Concrete Corp., Westhampton Beach, N.Y., 1989-91; civil engr. Suffolk County Water Authority, Oakdale, N.Y., 1991—. Author: How to Set Your VCR Clock, 1991; inventor detachable all terrain trailer. Cpl. USMC, 1977-81. Mem. Chi Epsilon. Avocations: camping, fishing, canoeing, hiking, running. Office: Suffolk County Water Authority Engring Dept PO Box 37 Oakdale NY 11769-0037

CARNEY, ANDREW SIMON, surgeon; b. South Shields, U.K., Aug. 17, 1965; arrived in Australia, 1999.; s. Michael Carney and Margaret Storey. BSc with 1st class honors, U. Edinburgh, Scotland, 1983, MB BChir with distinction in surgery, 1988. Sr. house officer Edinburgh Royal Infirmary, 1990-93; specialist registrar Queen's Med. Ctr., Nottingham, Eng., 1994-99; traveling fellow Mt. Sinai & N.Y. Hosps., N.Y.C., 1998; vis. fellow in head and neck surgery Royal Adelaide Hosp., Australia, 1999—. Mem. editl. bd. Scalpel; contbr. articles to profl. jours. Trustee Brit. Med. Students Trust, London; chmn. Brit. Jr. Drs. Conf., 1996-97, Brit. Med. Assn. Student Com., London, 1987-88. Recipient Gold medal sect. laryngology Royal Soc. Medicine, 1998, Rhinology prize Midland Inst. Otology, 1998, 99; traveling scholar Jour. Laryngology and Otology, 1998. Fellow Royal Coll. Surgeons Edinburgh. Avocation: sailing.

CARNEY, KAREN ROSE, music educator, pianist; b. Canton, Ohio, Dec. 9, 1940; d. Alex and Rose (Burky) Winkelman; 1 child, Miles. BMus, Baldwin-Wallace Coll., 1961; postgrad., Case Western Res. U., 1961; MA in Music Edn., Ohio State U., 1980, PhD in Music Edn., 1983. Cert. music tchr., N.C., Ohio. Accompanist, staff musician dance dept. Ohio State U., Columbus, 1983-85; asst. prof. N.C. Wesleyan Coll., Rocky Mount, 1985-87, U. S.D., Vermillion, 1987-88; pianist, spl. events The Ohio State U., Columbus, 1988-90; lectr., choir accompanist Fayetteville (N.C.) State U., 1990-91; instr. performing arts Meth. Coll., Fayetteville, N.C., 1990-91; asst. prof. Lincoln U., Pa., 1991-93; assoc. prof. Paine Coll., Augusta, Ga., 1993-95, Winston-Salem (N.C.) State U., 1995-99; elem. music tchr. New Hanover County Schs., Wilmington, N.C., 1999-2000; lectr. U. Ctrl. Ark., Conway, 2000—; PRAXIS item writer Ednl. Testing Svc., Princeton, N.J., 1997; com. music edn. UNC/NCCC Articulation Agreement, Chapel Hill, N.C., 1997; clinician Nat. Group Piano Symposium, U. Okla., Norman, 1985; judge music contests, Ohio, N.C., S.D. Vol. tchr., performer Winston-Salem/Forsyth County Pub. Schs., 1997-99; vol. pianist Baltic (Ohio) Country Manor, 1992-2000, nursing and retirement homes, Winston-alem, 1995-98; guest organist, pianist various chs., N.C. and Ohio. Rsch. grantee Lilly-Lincoln Univ., 1992; recipient Cert. of Recognition Winston-Salem State U. Friends of O'Kelly Libr., 1997. Mem. Am. Fedn. Musicians, Coll. Music Soc., Internat. Assn. Jazz Educators, Kodály of N.C., The Nat. Assn. Music Edn., Music Tchrs. Nat. Assn. (coll. faculty cert. in piano), Am. Mensa, Mu Phi Epsilon, Pi Kappa Lambda. Home: 2025A Silver Springs Cir Conway AR 72032-6085 Office: U Ctrl Ark 201 Donaghey Ave Conway AR 72035-5001

CARNEY, ROBERT ARTHUR, restaurant executive; b. Haddonfield, N.J., Aug. 20, 1937; s. George Albert and Margeret (Hollworth) C.; m. Janellen Sockol, may 31, 1996; 1 child, Lynn Ann. BA, Ursinus Coll., 1963. Procurement agt. Campbell Soup Co., Paris, Tex., 1963-69; mgr. procurement Campbell Soup Co., Salisbury, Md., 1969-72; dir. procurement Campbell Soup Co., Camden, N.J., 1972-78; v.p. procurement Burger King Corp., Miami, 1978-82; v.p. purchasing Pizza Hut, Inc., Wichita, 1982-95; sr. v.p. procurement Long John Silver's, Inc., Lexington, Ky., 1995-99. Mem. editl. adv. bd. Supplier Selection and Mgmt. Report. Mem. dean's adv. bd. Ala. State U. Capt. U.S. Army, 1958-60. Mem. Nat. Restaurant Assn. Roman Catholic. Home: 3154 Maria Dr Lexington KY 40516-9616

CARNEY, ROGER FRANCIS XAVIER, retired army officer; b. Bklyn., Oct. 20, 1933; s. Frank Clement and Clara Helen (Muller) C.; m. Linda Ann Bowlus, Aug. 11, 1963 (div. Mar. 1993); children: Kevin James, Stephen Jason, Brian Andrew. BS, Purdue U., 1960, MS in Indsl. Adminstrn., 1963; grad., U.S. Army Command and Gen. Staff Coll., 1975, U.S. Army War Coll., 1979; MA, U. Conn., 1992. Commd. 2d lt. U.S. Army, 1960, advanced through grades to lt. col., 1976; comdr. 583d Ordnance Co., Muenster, West Germany, 1969-72; R&D coord. Army Material Comman Field Office, Kirtland AFB, N.mex., 1972-74; logistic staff officer CENTAG Signal Support GP (NATO), Seckenheim, West Germany, 1975-78; chief nuc. weapons logistic element G4 CENTAG (NATO), Seckenheim, 1978; comdr. 15th Ordnance Bn., Darmstadt, West Germany, 1978-80; prof. mil. sci. head dept. Worcester (Mass.) Poly. Inst., 1980-84; prof. mil. sci., head dept. Fitchburg (Mass.) State Coll., 1980-84, Nichols Coll., Dudley, Mass., 1982-84; dean student affairs Nichols Coll., Dudley, 1985-98; dir. Robert C. Fischer Inst. Nichols Coll. Mem. Worchester Com. Fgn. Rels., Worchester Econ. Club (exec. com.), Mil. Adv. Coun. Ctr. for Def. Info. Decorated Legion of Merit, Bronze Star, 2 Meritorius Svc. medals, Army Commendation medal. Mem. Assn. U.S. Army, Assn. Former Intelligence Officers, Am. Legion, Ret. Officers Assn., U. Conn. Alumni Assn., Purdue Alumni Assn., Alpha Sigma Phi (pres. Purdue U. chpt. 1959-60), Pi Lambda Theta. Democrat. Home: 7 Thayer Pond Dr Apt 11 North Oxford MA 01537-1134

CARNEY, T. J, lawyer; b. Denver, July 18, 1952; s. Thomas Joseph Carney and Patricia (Amack) Carney Calkins; m. Deborah Leah Turner, Mar. 20, 1976; children: Amber Blythe, Sonia Briana, Ross Dillon. BA in Econs., U. Notre Dame, Ind., 1974; JD, U. Denver, 1976. Bar: Colo. 1977, Kans. 1977, U.S. Dist. Ct. Colo. 1977, U.S. Dist. Ct. Kans. 1977, U.S. Dist. Ct. Ariz. 1995, U.S. Ct. Appeals (10th cir.) 1983. Legal asst. Turner & Hensley, Chartered, Great Bend, Kans., 1977; atty.-shareholder Turner and Boisseau, Chartered, Great Bend, 1977-84; atty., shareholder Bradley, Campbell, Carney & Madsen, Golden, Colo., 1984-92, 95-97; atty.-shareholder Deborah & T.J. Carney, P.C., Lakewood and Golden, 1992-95; atty. officer Carney Law Office, Golden, Colo., 1997-99; spl. counsel Oliver & Kirven, P.C., Arvada, Colo., 1999; shareholder Oliver and Carney, P.C., Arvada, 1999—; CLE instr. Nat. Inst. Trial Advocacy, 1st Jud. Bar Assn., Colo. Inc., Rocky Mountain Child Advocacy Tng. Inst.; cons. Vocat. Econs., Inc., 1998, others. Precinct com. Rep. Party, Jefferson County, Colo., 1988-94, 2000—, area capt., 1994-96; bd. dirs. Jefferson County Libr. Found., 1999—. Mem. Colo. Bar Assn., Colo. Trial Lawyers Assn. (CLE), Kansas Bar Assn., Kans. Trial Lawyers Assn., 1st Jud. Dist. Bar Assn. (trustee 1990-94), Phi Delta Phi (Province Grad. of Yr. 1977). Avocations: flying, martial arts, skiing, lacrosse, ballroom dancing. Fax: 303-424-3629. Fax: (978) 334-5992. E-mail: tjc@carneylaw.net. Office: Oliver and Carney PC 7903 Ralston Rd Arvada CO 80002-2435

CARNEY NELSON, ELLEN B., elementary school educator; b. Soda Springs, Idaho, June 11, 1936; d. Clarence Lyle and Benda Gladys (Petersen) Burton; m. Earl J. Carney Jr., Mar. 17, 1954 (div. 1981); children: Dennis (dec.), Phyllis, Maureen, Wade, Gary; m. Lewis G. Nelson, June 7, 1996. BA in Edn., U. Ariz., 1972; MEd, U. Utah, 1976; postgrad., Idaho State U., 1990; student, U. Alaska, 1965, Brigham Young U., 1975. Cert. elem. tchr., Ariz., Idaho, Utah. Tchr. Kiddie Club Kindergarten, Ft. Walton Beach, Fla., 1967; substitute tchr. Tucson (Ariz.) Dist. Schs., 1971-72; tchr. Jordan Sch. Dist., Sandy, Utah, 1973-79; tchr., adminstr. Promised Horizons Pvt. Sch., Sandy, 1981; owner, operator Smart Start Preschool, Draper, Utah, 1978-81; tchr. Soda Springs Sch. Dist., 1981-90; grad. asst. Idaho State U., Pocatello, 1990-91; substitute tchr. Tooele Sch. Dist., 1991-95; tchr. Tooele Jr. H.S., 1996-2000; sch. bicentennial chmn. South Jordan (Utah) Elem. Sch., 1976; mem. GEMS program devel. team Jordan Sch. Dist., 1976-79; owner Wayan (Idaho) Cash Store, 1985-90. Author: Dr. Ellis Kackley-Best Damn Doctor in the West, 1989, Flora Whittemore, 1990, The Mountain: Carriboo and Other Gold Camps in Idaho, 1990, Way Out in Grays Lake, 1992, The Oregon Trail: Ruts, Rogues and Reminiscences, 1993 (Idaho Press Bk. of Yr. award Wyo. Hist. Soc.), River of Beaver, Stream of Gold, 1994 (award Nat. Fedn. Press Women's Hist. Novel Contest), Historic Soda Springs: Oasis on the Oregon Trail, 1998, (play) 200 Years Too Late, 1976; corr. Soda Springs Sun, Idaho State Jour., 1983-99. Den mother, cub scout leader, fin. coun. Boy and Girl Scouts Am., Anchorage, 1965-66, Ft. Walton Beach, 1967-68, Sandy, 1973-75; neighborhood chmn. ARC, Sandy, 1979-80, hosp. vol., Tucson, 1970; bd. dirs. Caribou County Hist. Preservation Commn., Soda Springs, 1988-94. Winner Bicentennial Contest Utah Edn. Assn., 1976. Mormon. Avocations: reading, writing, fishing, quiltmaking, handicrafts. Home: 389 Overland Rd Tooele UT 84074-1936

CARNIANI, CARLO, chemist; b. Bibbiena, Tuscany, Italy, July 31, 1960; s. Onorio and Rita (Lazzeri) C.; m. Maria Vittoria Enimmi, Feb. 14, 1987; children: Fiammetta, Davide. PhD in Chemistry, U. Florence, Italy, 1986. Rsch. chemist Enricerche, Milan, 1986-88; sr. rsch. chemist Enricerche, Milan, 1989-90; rsch. assoc. Clarkson U., Potsdam, N.Y., 1988-89; tech. advisor AGIP, Milan, 1990-93, sr. prodn. engr., 1993—. Contbr. articles to profl. jours.; patentee in field. Mem. Soc. Petroleum Engrs. Roman Catholic. Avocations: history, personal computing. Office: AGIP, Via Maritano 26, 20097 San Donato MI, Italy

CARNIEL, ELISABETH, microbiologist; b. Paris, Mar. 31, 1956; d. René and Huguette (Floch) C.; m. Patrick Perrin; children: Carniel-Perrin Brunehilde, Carniel-Perrin Adhéaume. Degree in Epidemiology, Pasteur Inst., France, 1981; Degree in Tropical Medicine, Paris V, 1984, MD, 1985; PhD, Paris VII U., 1990. Intern ICDDRB, Dakha, Bangladesh, 1983-84; rsch. fellow Pasteur Inst., Paris, 1986-88, asst., 1988—, head Yersinia Lab., 1990—; rschr. Brigham and Women's Hosp., Boston, 1993-95; dir. Yersinia Nat. Reference Lab., Pasteur Inst., Paris, 1990—; dir. WHO Collaborating Ctr. of Reference and Rsch. for Yersinia. Contbr. articles to profl. jours. Grantee Comite Consultatif des Applications de la Recherche, Pasteur Inst., Paris, 1991, 92, Inserm, France, 1993-95, Actions Concertees des Inst. Pasteur, 1995-96, Cen. D'Etude Du Bouchet, 1997, Direction Gen. des Armess/Direction des Sys de Force et die la Prospective, 1999-2001, Copernicus Program, EEC, 1999—. Mem. French Soc. Microbiology, Am. Soc. Microbiology. Office: Inst Pasteur Lab des Yersinia, 28 Rue du Dr Roux, 75724 Paris Cedex 15, France

CARNIOL, PAUL J., plastic and reconstructive surgeon, otolaryngologist; b. N.Y.C., Sept. 26, 1951; s. David A. and Diane (Hadler) C.; m. Renie Rich, Jan. 3, 1976; children: Michael P., Alan R., Eric T. BA, NYU, 1972; MD, U. Pa., 1976. Diplomate Am. Bd. Otolaryngology, Am. Bd. Cosmetic Surgery, Am. Bd. Med. Examiners, Am. Bd. Facial Plastic and Reconstructive Surgery. Surg. residency U. Pa., Phila., 1976-77, plastic and reconstructive surg. residency, 1981-83; surg. residency North Shore U. Hosp., Manhasset, N.Y., 1977-78; head and surg. residency, otolaryngology, clin. tchg. fellow Harvard Med. Sch., Boston, 1978-81; attending plastic surgeon, head and neck surgery Overlook Hosp., Summit, N.J., 1983—; clin. asst. prof. U. Medicine and Dentistry of N.J., Newark; cons. aesthetic, recon-

structive and pediatric plastic surgery; mem. bd. examiners Am. Bd. Cosmetic Surgery; instr. courses on lasers in plastic surgery, also numerous lectrs., TV presentations in field; chief sect. otolaryngology Overlook Hosp., 1992-97, Summit, N.J., otolaryngology resident tng. rotation; clin. asst. prof. U. Medicine and Dentistry N.J.; police surgeon, New Providence, N.J. and Summit. Editor: Laser Skin Rejuvenation, 1998, Facial Rejuvenation, 2000; spl. editor Am. Jour. Cosmetic Surgery; mem. editl. bd. Jour. Cutaneous Laser Surgery, Plastic Surgery Products; contbr. articles to profl. jours. Interviewer for admissions com. U. Pa., Phila., 1987—. Recipient Community Svc. award Ciba-Geigy, Summit, 1978, Found. award NYU, 1972, Alumni Gold Medal award NYU, 1972. Fellow ACS, Am. Acad. Otolaryngoloyy, Nead and Neck Surgery, Am. Acad. Cosmetic Surgery, Am. Acad. Facial Plastic and Reconstructive Surgery (dir. courses lasers facial plastic surgery and cosmetic surgery cosmetic body conturing surgery, 1996-98, care com., chmn. new tech. and surg. devices com., v.p. for R&D), N.J. Acad. Medicine, Am. Rhinologic soc.; mem. AMA, Internat. Soc. Cosmetic Laser Surgery (bd. dirs.), N.J. Med. Soc. (coun. on comm.), N.J. Acad. Otolaryngology (pres. 1993-96, 97—), Union County Med. Soc. (planning com. 1986-89, chmn. program com., exec. com., bd. dirs., treas.), Phi Beta Kappa. Avocations: golf, fishing, horseback riding. Office: Summit Med Group 33 Overlook Rd Ste 202 Summit NJ 07901-3562

CARON, MURIELLE HELLSTEN, physician, researcher; b. Eaubonne, Val D'oise, France, May 25, 1967; d. Bernard and Nicole (Blondin) C.; m. Hans Hellsten, Nov. 14, 1998; 1 child, Maxance. MD, Lund (Sweden) U., 1993. Physician Doctors Without Borders, Sri Lanka, 1993, Med. Neurochem., Lund, Sweden, 1994-96, 1998—; physician Lund U. Hosp., 1996-98; cons., Sweden, 1999—. Contbr. articles to profl. jours. including Cytogenet. Cell Genetics, Jour. Pharmacol. Exptl. Therapeutics, Addiction Biology and Life Sciences. Mem. Swedish Med. Assn. Avocations: horse riding, literature, philosophy, astronomy. Office: Lund U Hosp, Dept Med Neurochemistry, 22185 Lund Sweden

CARON, THOMAS JAMES, financial planner, estate planner; b. Evanston, IL, Jan. 30, 1962; s. Marcel James and Patricia M. (Pallys) C.; m. Kimberly Ann LeFrancois, Aug. 4, 1996; 1 child, Abigail Ann. BA, U. N.H., 1984. Fin. and estate planner Northeast Planning Assocs., Bedford, NH. Bd. dirs alumni coun. The Derryfield Sch., Manchester, N.H., 1997—; treas. Bedford Cmty. Ch., 1997—. Recipient Nat. Sales Achievement award Million Dollar Roundtable, 1990—, Nat. Quality award, 1991—. Mem. Nat. Assn. Life Underwriters, Internat. Assn. Fin. Planners, N.H. Estate Planning Coun. Republican. Office: Northeast Planning Assocs 18 Constitution Dr Bedford NH 03110-6076

CARPENTER, BETTY O., writer; b. Montreal, June 1, 1926; d. Harry and Dorothy (Schacher) Shmerling; m. David G. Ostroff, Apr. 6, 1946 (div. 1972); children: Jack Ostroff, Lucy Ostroff Harrow; m. Russell William Carpenter, Jr., Oct. 2, 1976 (dec.); stepchildren: Annette Marie Carpenter Freedman, Cynthia Carpenter Jefferson, Lori Carpenter Bembry. BA in Edn., Bklyn. Coll., 1947, MA in Edn., 1953; PhD in Adminstrn., NYU, 1973. Cert. sch. supt., prin., N.J., guidance counselor, elem. tchr., N.Y. Tchr. elem. grades N.Y.C. Pub. Schs. 54 and 139, Bklyn., 1946-54, 62; asst. prin. Pub. Sch. 139, Bklyn., 1962-67; pres. asst. prin. assoc. Ctrl. Office Bd. of Edn., N.Y.C., 1967-68, v.p. coun. suprs. and adminstrs., 1968-69, adminstrv. asst. pers., 1968-70; asst. supt. Plainfield (N.J.) Pub. Schs., 1970-74; supt. schs. Glen Rock (N.J.) Pub. Schs., 1974-84; ret. Author: Curriculum Guide to Public Schools of America, 1991, Tutoring for Pay, 1991, (book of poetry) Musings, The Brosh (Bionic Replacement of Species Humanoid), 1998, Lady of the Lake, 1999, Inherit the Rainbow, 2000. Trustee Glen Rock Libr. Bd., 1974-80, United Fund Bd., Glen Rock, 1975-77; vice chmn. Iredell County Bd. of Adjustment N.C., 1990-95; fellow mem. Lake Owners Gathered in Concern, N.C., 1985-88. Recipient Founders Day award NYU, 1973, Adminstrv. Leadership award NACEL, 1984. Mem. Soc. Children's Book Writers and Illustrators, Romance Writers Am., Nat. Writers Assn., Bergen County Supts. Assn. (pres.-elect), Nat. Scrabble Assn., Am. Contract Bridge League. Avocations: sculpture, golf, water aerobics, computers, bridge. Home: 11730 N 91st Pl Scottsdale AZ 85260-6866

CARPENTER, CHARLES JOHN, electrical engineer, consultant; b. Ilford, Essex, Eng., Apr. 30, 1927; s. Charles and Ruth Elizabeth (Hillary) C.; m. Rita Nellie Porter; children: David, Anne, Mary, Peter. BSc in Engring., London U., 1948, MSc in Engring., 1951, DSc in Engring., 1978. Chartered engr., Eng. Rsch. engr. Crompton Parkinson Ltd., Chelmsford, Eng., 1942-46, 49-53; lectr. Imperial Coll., London, 1953-61, sr. lectr., 1964-79; prof., head dept. elec. engring. U. of W. Indies, Trinidad, 1961-64; sr. lectr. Gwent Coll. of Higher Edn., Newport, Gwent, Wales, 1980-87; electromagnetics rschr., 1987—; cons. C.A. Carsons Ltd., Newcastle, Eng., 1969-79, various cos. Contbr. articles to profl. jours. Coord. Neighborhood Watch, Bath, 1980—. Fellow Instn. of Elec. Engrs. (mem. various coms., Instn. premium 1978, Maxwell premium 1993, Achievement medal 1995). Avocations: cycling, walking, skiing, swimming, skating. Office: Bristol Univ Dept Elec Engr, Woodland Rd, Bristol BS8 1UB, England

CARPENTER, DAVID ALLAN, lawyer; b. Cambridge, Mass., May 16, 1951; s. David Lawrence and Jane (Boucher) C.; m. Nancy Joan Surdyka, Apr. 29, 1973. BS in Bus. Adminstrn., Bucknell U., Lewisburg, Pa., 1972; MBA in Fin., Temple U., Phila., 1975; JD, Rutgers U., 1981. Banking officer Girard Bank, Phila., 1972-77, mng. ptnr., 1983-85, mng. ptnr. Mid Atlantic region, 1985-89, mng. ptnr. Atlantic region, 1989-92; nat. dir. litigation and claims svcs. Coopers & Lybrand, Phila., 1987-92; nat. dir. fin. adv. svcs. Coopers & Lybrand, Boston, 1992-94; founding ptnr. Ptnrs. for Mkt. Leadership, Inc., Atlanta, 1995—. Co-editor: Proving and Pricing Construction Claims, 1990, Environmental Dispute Handbook, 1991; contbr. articles to profl. jours., chpts. to books. Mem. Inst. Mgmt. Consultants, Turnaround Mgmt. Assn., Beta Gamma Sigma. Address: PO Box 903 Great Barrington MA 01230-0903 Office: Ptnrs for Mkt Leadership Inc 100 Galleria Pkwy SE Ste 400 Atlanta GA 30339-3122

CARPENTER, EDMUND NELSON, II, retired lawyer; b. Phila., Jan. 27, 1921; s. Walter S. and Mary (Wootten) C.; m. Carroll Morgan, July 18, 1970; children: Mary W., Edmund Nelson III, Katherine R.R., Elizabeth Lea; stepchildren: John D. Gates, Ashley du Pont Gates. AB, Princeton U., 1943; LLB, Harvard U., 1948; LLD (hon.), Widener U., 1985, U. Del., 1999. Bar: Del. 1949, U.S. Supreme Ct. 1957. Assoc. Richards, Layton & Finger, Wilmington, Del., 1949-53, ptnr., 1953-78, dir., 1978-91, pres., 1982-85; retired, 1991; dep. atty. gen. State of Del., 1953-54, spl. dep. atty., 1960-62; chmn. Del. Superior Ct. Jury Study Com., 1963-66, Del. Supreme Ct. Cts. Consol. Com., 1985-87; mem. Del. Gov.'s Commn. Law Enforcement and Adminstrn. Justice, 1969; chmn. Del. Supreme Ct. Adv. Com. on Profl. Fin. Accountability, 1974-75, Del. Jud. Nominating Commn., 1977-83, Del. Superior Ct. Study Com., 1991-92; mem. Long Range Cts. Planning Com., 1976-89, Del. Ct. Common Pleas Study Com., 1992, Del. Supreme Ct. Com. on Judicial Code of Conduct, 1991-93; co-chmn. Del. Justice Ctr. Com., 1994-97; mem. lawyers adv. com. U.S. Ct. Appeals (3d cir.) 1975-80, chmn., 1975-77; chmn. local rules com. U.S. Dist. Ct. Del., 1978-83, Del. Ct. on the Judiciary Rules Com., 1996-98; bd. dirs. Bank of Del., Barclay's Bank. Trustee Wilmington Med. Ctr., 1965—, U. Del., 1971-77, Princeton U., 1974-85, 86-91, Winterthur Mus., 1991-99, World Affairs Coun. Wilmington, 1968-80, Woodrow Wilson Found., 1985—, Lawrenceville Sch., 1953-74, trustee emeritus, 1974—; trustee Nat. Humanities Ctr., 1995-98; bd. dirs. Good Samaritan Inc., 1973—, pres., 1998—; mem. Del. Health Care Injury Ins. Study Commn., 1976-80. With U.S. Army, 1942-46, 50-52. Decorated Bronze Star, Soldier's medal, Chinese Order of the Flying Cloud with four battle stars; recipient 1st State Disting. Svc. award, Del. State Bar Assn., 1984, Josiah Marvel Cup award Del. State C. of C., 1990, Benjamin Franklin Disting. Pub. Svc. award Am. Philos. Soc., 1996. Fellow Am. Coll. Trial Lawyers, Am. Bar Found.; mem. ABA (ho. of dels. 1979-86), Del. State Bar Assn. (pres. 1971-72, Presdl. citation 1987), ATLA, Am. Judicature Soc. (bd. dirs. 1974-83, exec. com. 1978-80, v.p. 1980-81, pres. 1981-83, Justice award 1991). Home and Office: 600 Center Mill Rd Wilmington DE 19807-1502

CARPENTER, GORDON RUSSELL, lawyer, banker; b. Denton, Tex., Feb. 6, 1920; s. Solomon Lafayette and Grace L. (Fowler) C.; m. Muriel E. James, Sept. 18, 1943 (dec.); m. Mary Alice Borah, Aug. 4, 1962. BS, North Tex. State U., 1940; postgrad., Georgetown U., 1941-42; LL.B., So. Meth. U., 1948. Bar: Tex. 1947, U.S. Supreme Ct. 1960. Announcer KDNT, Denton, Tex., 1940-41; spl. agent FBI, 1941-46; exec. sec. Southwestern Legal Found., Dallas, 1947-56; exec. dir., 1956-58; adminstrv. asst. to dean Law Sch. So. Meth. U., 1951-58, asst. prof. law, 1956-68; trust officer 1st Nat. Bank, Dallas, 1958-60, v.p., 1960-79; v.p., sr. fin. planning officer InterfFirst Bank, Dallas, 1979-84. Bd. regents Tex. Sch. Trust Banking, 1981-82; bd. trustees Hatton W. Sumners Found., 1959—, exec. dir., 1985-95; chmn. North Tex. State U. Ednl. Found.; chmn. Luth. Med. Sys. Tex. Found., 1980-83; vice chmn. Farmers Br. Hosp. Authority, 1976-77. Recipient Pres.'s award State Bar Tex., 1963, Bd. Dirs. award, 1971, Gene Cavin award for excellence in con. legal edn., 1998. Fellow Tex. Bar Found.; mem. ABA (chmn. publs. com. mineral andnatural resources law sect. 1958-64), State Bar Tex. (chmn. cont. legal edn. com. 1952-54, 58-66, chmn. real estate, probate and trust law sect. 1964-65), Dallas Bar Assn. (dir. 1960-61, 65-66, chmn. centennial com. 1972-73), Dallas Bar Found. (trustee, sec.-treas.), Tex. Bankers Assn. (chmn. trust divsn. 1980-81), Soc. Former Spl. Agts. FBI (pres. 1963), Brookhaven Country Club, Masons, Delta Theta Phi. Republican. Presbyterian. Office: 325 N Saint Paul St Ste 3920 Dallas TX 75201-3821

CARPENTER, MARK LEO, book publishing executive, consultant, writer; b. Mishawaka, Ind., Apr. 9, 1957; s. Charles William and Mary Alice (Clancy) C.; m. Laurie Anne Crawford, Dec. 18, 1982; children: Alexander Lynn, Andrea Mary, Nicholas John. AA, Bethel Coll., Mishawaka, 1981, BA, 1981; student, Wheaton (Ill.) Coll., 1981-82; MA, U. de Sao Paulo, Brazil, 1997. Mng. editor Today in Michiana mag., South Bend, Mich., 1979-81, Christian Svc. Brigade, Wheaton, 1981-83; book editor Tyndale House Pubs., Wheaton, 1983-85; missionary World Ptnrs., Ft. Wayne, Ind., 1985—; CEO Editora Mundo Cristao, Sao Paulo, 1985-97, pres., chmn., 1997—; writer/editor, trainer Media Assocs. Internat., Bloomingdale, Ill., 1993-98, others, 1986—; conductor various seminars in field. Author: Brazil: An Awakening Giant, 2d edit., 1998; contbr. articles to Trad/Term, Modern Poetry in Translaton, others. Bd. dirs. Pan Am. Christian Acad., Sao Paulo, 1994-99. Recipient Alumni award for profl. achievement Bethel Coll., 1994. Mem. Associacao Brasileira de Editores Cristaos (bd. dirs., edtl. v.p.), Missao Informadora do Brasil (bd. dirs.), Media Assocs. Internat. Mem. The Missionary Ch. Inc. Avocations: reading, soccer (spectator), art museums. Office: Editora Mundo Cristao, R Antonio Carlos Tacconi 79, Sao Paulo 04810020, Brazil

CARPENTER, MICHAEL, financial services executive; b. London, Mar. 24, 1947; came to U.S., 1971; s. Walter and Kathleen Mary C.; m. Mary Aughton, Mar. 1, 1975; children—Nicholas James, Abigail Lee. B.Sc. with joint honors, U. Nottingham, Eng., 1968; M.B.A., Harvard U., 1973. Bus. analyst Mond div. Imperial Chem. Industries, Runcorn, Eng., 1968-71; cons., mgr. Boston Cons. Group, 1973-78, v.p., 1978-83; v.p. Gen. Electric Co., Fairfield, Conn., 1983-86; exec. v.p. Gen. Electric Credit Corp., Stamford, Conn., from 1986; also exec. v.p. GE Financial Services Inc.; joined Kidder Peabody & Co. Inc., 1989, chmn., pres., CEO, 1990-94; head life and annuity bus. Travelers Ins. Co., Hartford, 1994—; also exec. v.p. Travelers Group, Hartford, 1994—, vice chmn., chmn., CEO, pres. life and annuity; chmn., CEO Salomon Smith Barney, N.Y.C.; formerly chmn. Gen. Electric Venture Capital Corp. Baker scholar Harvard Bus. Sch., 1973. Office: Salomon Smith Barney 388 Greenwich St New York NY 10013-2339

CARPENTER, PAUL LYNN, cardiologist; b. Fairmont, Minn., Jan. 14, 1946; s. Orlo Earnest and Mae Elizabeth (Poulson) C.; m. Rhoda Ann Jordeth, Mar. 15, 1969; children: Amy Elizabeth, Emily Anne, Abigail Lynn. BSChE, U. Minn., 1968, MD, 1974. Diplomate Am. Bd. Internal Medicine. Chem. engr. 3M Co., St. Paul, 1968-69, USPHS, Cin., 1970-71; extern So. Bapt. Hosp., Ailoun, Jordan, 1975; resident in internal medicine Northwestern Hosp. U. Minn., Mpls., 1975-78, fellow in cardiology, 1978-80; invasive cardiologist Ctrl. Plains Clinic, Sioux Falls, S.D., 1980-81, North Ctrl. Heart, Ltd., Sioux Falls, 1981—; asst. clin. prof. dept. medicine U. S.D. Sch. Medicine, Sioux Falls, 1982-90, assoc. clin. prof. dept. medicine, 1990-98; clin. prof. medicine U. S.D. Sch. Medicine, 1998—; chmn. cardiac care com. Mckennan Hosp., Sioux Falls, 1984-98, co-dir. cardiac catheterization lab., 1988—, dir. cardiac rehab., 1990—; pres. North Ctrl. Heart, Ltd., 1984-85. Girls basketball coach YMCA, Sioux Falls, 1987-96; girls coach Sioux Falls Soccer Assn., 1991-94; Sunday sch. tchr. Ctrl. Bapt. Ch., Sioux Falls, 1987-94. Fellow Am. Coll. Cardiology (gov. S.D. 1987-90), Am. Coll. Chest Physicians; mem. ACP, AMA, S.D. State Med. Assn., Christian Med. Soc. (life), Alpha Omega Alpha, Tau Beta Pi. Avocations: Civil war and native American history, travel, sports, fishing. Office: No Ctrl Heart Ltd 911 E 20th St Sioux Falls SD 57105-1042

CARPENTER, RANDLE BURT, lawyer; b. Raleigh, N.C., Oct. 19, 1939; s. Randle Burt and Adonis (Watson) C.; m. Suzanne Gronemeyer, Aug. 21, 1965; children: Randle III, Christine. BA in Internat. Rels., Duke U., 1962, LLB, 1965; LLM in Fgn. Law, NYU, 1969. Bar: N.Y. 1967, N.C. 1965, U.S. Supreme Ct., U.S. Ct. Appeals (2d cir.), U.S. Dist. Ct., U.S. Ct. International. Trade. Official asst. First Nat. City Bank, N.Y.C., 1965-67; with Exxon Internat. Inc., N.Y.C., 1967-68; gen. counsel Occidental Crude Sales Inc., N.Y.C., 1968-75; v.p. law Wesco Internat. Inc., N.Y.C., 1975-76; gen. counsel A. Johnson & Co., Inc., N.Y.C., 1976-81; ptnr. Davidson Dawson & Clark, N.Y.C., 1981-84, Schoeman, Marsh & Updike, N.Y.C., 1984-97, Jackson & Nash, N.Y.C., 1997—; adj. prof. law Pace U., White Plains, N.Y., 1984—. Contbr. articles to profl. jours. Angier B. Duke scholar Duke U., 1958. Mem. Am. Arbitration Assn., Assn. of Bar of City of N.Y. (inter-Am. affairs com.), Maritime Law Assn., Church Club N.Y., Colonial Order of the Acorn (companion). Home: 29 Hazel Ln Larchmont NY 10538-4007 Office: Jackson & Nash 330 Madison Ave Rm 1800 New York NY 10017-5001

CARPENTER, RICHARD NORRIS, lawyer; b. Cortland, N.Y., Feb. 14, 1937; s. Robert P. and Sylvia (Norris) C.; m. Elizabeth Bigbee, Aug. 1961 (div. June 1975); 1 child, Andrew Norris; m. Leslie Nordby, July, 1991. BA magna cum laude, Syracuse U., 1958; LLB, Yale U., 1962. Bar: N.Y. 1962, N.Mex. 1963, U.S. Dist. Ct. (no. dist.) N.Y., U.S. Dist. Ct. N.Mex., U.S. Ct. Appeals (D.C. and 10th cirs.), U.S. Supreme Ct. Assoc. Breed, Abbott & Morgan, N.Y.C., 1962-63, Bigbee Law Firm, Santa Fe, 1963-78; ptnr. Carpenter Law Firm, Santa Fe, 1978—; spl. asst. atty. gen., State of N.Mex., 1963-74, 90-96; sec. Bokum Corp., Miami, Fla., 1969-70. Mem. adv. bd. Interstate Mining Compact, N.Mex., 1981-88; elder 1st Presbyn. Ch., Santa Fe, 1978-80, 86-89, trustee, 1975-77, pres., 1977; bd. dirs. Santa Fe Community Coun., 1965-67, St. Vincent Hosp. Found., Santa Fe, 1980-84; trustee Santa Fe Prep. Sch., 1981-84, pres., 1982-84; trustee St. Vincent Hosp., 1980-86, 87—, chmn. 1985-86, 90-93, 98—; bd. dirs. Santa Fe YMCA, 1964-69, pres., 1969; trustee Santa Fe Prep. Permanent Endowment Fund., 1987-90. Rotary Found. fellow, Panjab U., Pakistan, 1959-60. Mem. ABA, N.Mex. Bar Assn., 1st Jud. Bar Assn., N.Y. State Bar Assn., The Best Lawyers of Am., Phi Beta Kappa, Pi Sigma Alpha, Phi Beta Phi. Home: 1048 Bishops Lodge Rd Santa Fe NM 87501-1009 Office: PO Box 1837 Santa Fe NM 87504-1837

CARPENTIER, R, physician, astronomer; b. Bordeaux, Aquitaine, France, Aug. 24, 1934; m. Iwasaki Carpentier; children: Thomas, Philippe. MD, Bordeaux U., 1963. Sch. physician St. Quentin, France, 1963-65; reanimator Clamecy, France, 1965-74; workers inspector Coutances, 1974-76; inspector Social Security, Paris, 1976-94, dir., 1977-94; med. expert justice, Coutances, 1974. Mem. Astronomy Club Paris (pres. 1994—), Astro Club Planete (pres. 1994—). Avocation: astronomy. Home: Rue Marie Charles, 78700 Conflans Ste Honorin France

CARPI, DANIEL, historian; b. Milan, Italy, Aug. 3, 1926; s. Leone and Luisa (Modena) C.; m. Judith Treitel, Aug. 19, 1930. BA, Hebrew U., 1954, MA, 1958, PhD, 1967; Diploma, Inst. Latin Paleography, Rome, 1959. Prof. Tel-Aviv U., 1971-94, prof. emeritus, 1994—; fellow Oxford Ctr. Hebrew Studies, U.K., 1977; head of rsch. group Hebrew U., Jerusalem, 1987; vis. prof. Jewish Theol. Seminary, N.Y., 1976, Pontificia U. Gregoriana, Vatican, 1986; vis. fellow St. Antony's Coll., Oxford, U.K., 1992; dir. d'Etudes Assoc., Sorbonne, Paris, 1989. Author/editor books and publs. in field; editor: Letters of Zeev Jabotinsky, Vols. I-V. Chmn. acad. com. Jabotinsky Inst., Tel-Aviv, 1982—; mem. Supreme Coun. for Archives of Israel, 1972-94; chmn. acad. coun. Inst. of Diaspora, Tel Aviv, 1988-90; mem. acad. coun. Hist. Soc. of Israel, 1978-92. Capt. Israeli Def. Forces, 1968. Recipient Warburg prize Hebrew U., Jerusalem, 1962, 65; Commendatore Della Repub. Italiana, 1982, Leib Jaffe prize Keren Hayessod, Jerusalem, 1975, 93. Mem. World Union of Jewish Studies (hon.), Inst. for Advanced Studies (mem. acad. com. Hebrew U.). Office: Tel Aviv Univ, Carter Bld, 69978 Tel Aviv Israel

CARR, BERNARD FRANCIS, hospital administrator; b. Wilkes-Barre, Pa., July 13, 1919; s. John Daniel and Marjorie Veronica (Gallagher) C.; m. Mary Ann Reiss, Dec. 30, 1945; children: Bernard, Cathy, Irene, Patricia, Mary Ann. Grad., Rockland State Hosp. Sch. Nursing, 1942; B.S., NYU, 1949; M.B.A. in Hosp. Adminstrn., U. Chgo., 1951; student, Western State U. Coll. Law, 1981-82. R.N., Calif., Pa., Va.; lic. nursing home adminstr., Va.; lic. real estate agt., Calif.; lic. comml. aviator. Commd. USMCR, 1945; adminstrv. resident Ind. U. Med. Ctr., Indpls., 1950-51, adminstrv. asst., 1951-52, asst. adminstr., 1952-53; supt. Altoona (Pa.) Hosp., 1953-72; adminstr. South Coast Community Hosp., South Laguna, Calif., 1972-78, Bedford (Va.) County Meml. Hosp., 1978-79; exec. dir. South Coast Community Hosp. Found., 1976-77; dir., sec.-treas. Bedford Meml. Hosp. Found., 1978-79; regional mgr. Calif., Charter Med. Corp., Macon, Ga., 1978-81; div. mgr. Calif., Charter Med. Corp., Calif., 1981-84; adminstr., chief exec. officer Kellogg Psychiat (Charter Hosp.), Corona, Calif., 1981-82; pres., chief exec. officer New Riyadh (Saudi Arabia) Internat. Airport Hosp., 1980-81; assoc. dir. corporate quality assurance, dir. physician relations Charter Med. Corp., 1981-84; committeman Hosp. Coun. So. Calif., 1981; coord. home nursing svc. Kimberly Quality Svc. , Costa Mesa, Calif., 1992-96. Mem. Altoona Redevel. Authority, 1964-70, vice chmn., 1966-70; exec. com. Coordinating Council on Continuing Edn. in Health Care Systems, Pa. State U., 1971-73; mem. Blair County Child Welfare, Blair County Soc. for Crippled Children adv. bds., 1965-72; Blair County Human Devel. Task Force; mem. tech. adv. com. Altoona Community Renewal Program, 1971-73; fund raising chmn. Bedford area Piedmont div. Am. Heart Assn., 1978, White House Council on the Aged. Served at naval aviation cadet, 1943-45; cadet regimental comdr. Rensselaer Polytech. Inst., Chapel Hill, Glenview NAS, Pensacola, Fla. and Corpus Christi, Tex. 1st lt. USMCR, 1945-52. Fellow Am. Coll. Nursing Home Adminstrs., Am. Coll. Health Care Execs. (life); mem. Am. Hosp. Assn. (life, del. 1970—, mem. regional adv. bd., mem. council hosp. schs. nursing 1968-72), Calif. Hosp. Assn., Va. Hosp. Assn. (coms.), Hosp. Assn. Pa. (v.p. 1969-70, pres.-elect 1970-71, pres. 1971-72), Nat. League for Nursing (agy. rep. 1959—), Am. Health Care Assn., Va. Health Care Assn., Assn. Mental Health Adminstrs., Am. Pub. Health Assn., Hosp. Financial Mgmt. Assn., Nat. Council Community Hosps., Roanoke Area Hosp. Council, Laguna Beach C. of C. (dir.). Club: Rotarian (pres. elect Bedford 1979-80, pres. South-Laguna-Niguel 1976-77). Home: 31291 E Nine Dr Laguna Niguel CA 92677-2907

CARR, BESSIE, retired middle school educator; b. Nathalie, Va., Oct. 10, 1920; d. Henry C. and Sirlena (Ewell) C. BS, Elizabeth City Coll., N.C., 1942; MA, Columbia U. Tchrs. Coll., 1948, PhD, 1950, EdD, 1952. Cert. adminstr., supr., tchr. Prin. pub. sch., Halifax, Va., 1942-47, Nathalie-Halifax County, Va., 1947-51; prof. edn. So. U., Baton Rouge, 1952-53; supr. schs. Lackland Schs., Cin., 1953-54; prof. edn. Wilberforce U., Ohio, 1954-55; tchr. Leland Sch., Pittsfield, Mass., 1956-60; chair math. dept., tchr. Lakeland Mid. Sch., N.Y., 1961-83. Founder, organizer, sponsor 1st Math Bowl and Math Forum in area, 1970-76; founder Dr. Bessie Carr award Halifax County Sr. High Sch., 1962. Mem. Nat. Women's Hall of Fame. Mem. AAUW (auditor 1970-85), Delta Kappa Gamma (auditor internat. 1970-76), Assn. Suprs. of Math. (chair coordinating council 1976-80), Ret. Tchrs. Assn., Black Women Bus. and Profl. Assn. (charter mem. Senegal, Africa chpt.). Democrat. Avocations: travel, photography, souvenirs.

CARR, C. LYNN, sociology educator, researcher; b. Kansas City, Kans., Mar. 6, 1968; d. Gerson C. and Arleen Mae Carr. BA, Antioch Coll., 1989; MA, Rutgers U., New Brunswick, 1995. With dept. sociology Rutgers U., Piscataway, N.J. Contbr. articles to profl. jours., including Gender and Soc. Bd. dirs. George Street Coop, New Brunswick, 1997-99. Grantee Soc. for Psychol. Study Social Issues, 1998. Mem. Am. Sociol. Assn. Mem. Green Party. Avocation: reiki. E-mail: clcarr@rci.rutgers.edu. Office: Rutgers U Dept Sociology 54 Joyce Kilmer Ave Piscataway NJ 08854-8045

CARR, CHARLES ANTHONY BOWRINC, aerospace company executive; b. Hamburg, Germany, Oct. 15, 1958; s. William Bowrinc and Denise Ormond Selby (Yeatman) C.; m. Haylie Brookes, Oct. 16, 1998. Grad., Royal Mil. Acad., 1977. Sales rep. Lloyds Bowmaker, Cambridge, England, 1980-83; cons. Clifton Donkin, London, 1983-85; mktg. exec. Royal Ordnance, London, 1985-89; head pub. affairs Matra BDE Dynamics, U.K., 1989-97; v.p. comms. Eurofighter, Munich, Germany, 1998—. lt. Royal Arty. German Mil., 1977-80. Avocations: skiing, sailing, tennis. Office: Eurofighter GMBH, 17 AM Soldnermoos, 85399 Hallbergmoor Germany Address: Denninger Str 108, 81925 Munich Germany

CARR, CYNTHIA, lawyer; b. San Antonio, Nov. 4, 1953; d. Robert Claude Carr and Alta Mae (Bletsch) Holmes; m. Marc Allan Wallman; children: Lydia Michael, Aidan Holmes. BA, Austin Coll., 1975; JD, Harvard U., 1984; LLM, NYU, 1990. Bar: N.Y. 1985, Conn. 1988. Coord. Cambodian sect. Internat. Rescue Com., Bangkok, Thailand, 1980-81; legal intern Mental Health Legal Advisers Com., Boston, 1982-83; assoc. White & Case, N.Y.C., 1984-87; assoc. gen. counsel, exec. dir. planned giving Yale U., New Haven, 1988-2000; gen. counsel Save the Children, Westport, Conn., 2000—; vis. lectr. Yale U. Law Sch., New Haven, 1988-90. Vol. Peace Corps, West Africa, 1975-77, 79-80; bd. dirs. Yale Law Sch. Early Learning Ctr., 1990-95; trustee Yale U. Hong Kong Charitable Trust, 1997-2000, Oak Leaf Endowment Trust for Yale, 1997-2000. Mem. ABA (vice chair lifetime and charitable gift planning com. 2000—), Conn. Bar Assn. (mem. charitable giving exempt orgns. subcom.), Trusts and Estates Mag. (charitable giving mini bd. mem. 1996-99), Jewish Found. New Haven (tax and legal com. 1999—), Conn. Planned Giving Group (bd. dirs. 2000—). Home: 30 Hawley Rd Hamden CT 06517-2128 Office: Save the Children 54 Wilton Rd Westport CT 06880-3131

CARR, DANIEL BARRY, anesthesiologist, endocrinologist, medical researcher; b. N.Y.C., Apr. 6, 1948; s. Andrew Joseph and Florence (Glassman) C.; m. Justine M. Meehan, Nov. 11, 1978; children: Nora, Rebecca, Andrew. BA, Columbia U., 1968, MA, 1970, MD, 1976. Diplomate Am. Bd. Internal Medicine (subsplty. bds. Endocrinology and Metabolism, Anesthesiology, Pain Mgmt.). Intern Columbia-Presbyn. Med. Ctr., N.Y.C., 1976-78; resident med. svc. Mass. Gen. Hosp., Boston, 1978-79, endocrine fellow, 1979-82, staff physician endocrine unit, 1982-94, clin. assoc. physician, clin. rsch. ctr., 1982-84, fellow in anesthesiology, 1984-86, dir. analgesic peptide rsch. unit, 1986-94, staff physician anesthesia svc., co-dir. anesthesia pain unit, 1986-91, dir. divsn. pain mgmt., 1991-94; anesthetist, 1992-94; instr. medicine Harvard U. Med. Sch., 1982-84, asst.prof., 1984-88, assoc. prof., 1988-94; rsch. staff Shriners Burn Inst., Boston, 1986-94; Saltonstall prof. Pain Rsch. in anesthesia and medicine Tufts-New England Med. Ctr., 1994—; co-chair acute and cancer pain mgmt. guideline panels Agy. for Health Care Policy and Rsch., U.S. Dept. HHS, 1990-94; med. dir. pain mgmt. program Tufts-New Eng. Med. Ctr., 1995—; vice-chair rsch. dept. anesthesia New Eng. Med. Ctr., 1994—; pain revs. editor Cochrane Collaboration, 1998—; mem. Gov. Mass. spl. commn. pain mgmt., 1993-98; tech. expert Agy. Healthcare Rsch. and Quality, 1999-2000. Editor-in-chief IASP Pain: Clinical Updates, 1993—; mem. editl. bd. Clin. Jour. Pain, 1988—, Jour. Clin. Anesthesia, 1995—, Anesthesia and Analgesia, 1996-99, Jour. Pain, 1999—, Pain Medicine, 1999—; contbr. articles, rsch. reports, essays, revs. to profl. lib. Daland fellow Am. Philos. Soc., 1980-83. Mem. Am. Pain Soc. (bd. dirs. 1994-97), Am. Acad. Pain medicine (bd. dirs. 1995-98), France-Am. Pain Soc. (pres. 1996-98), Am. Soc. Anesthesiologists, Internat. Assn. for Study Pain (coun. 1996-99), Endocrine Soc., Soc. for Neurosci., Internat. Anesthesia Rsch. Soc., Assn. Univ. Anesthetists, Alpha Omega Alpha. Achievements include research on pain, analgesic peptides and stress responses; relationship between analgesia and clinical outcome; systematic reviews and guidelines for improved pain treatment in hospital, hospice and home care settings. Office: New Eng Med Ctr-Dept Anesthesia 750 Washington St Boston MA 02111-1526

CARR, EDWARD A., lawyer; b. Borger, Tex., July 31, 1962. AB with honors and distinction, Stanford U., 1984; JD, UCLA, 1987. Bar: Tex. 1988, D.C. 1989, U.S. Dist. Ct. (so. dist.) Tex. 1989, U.S. Ct. Appeals (5th cir.) 1989, U.S. Ct. Appeals (fed. cir.) 1989. Assoc. Vinson & Elkins, Houston, 1988-97, ptnr., 1997—; lectr. in field. Contbr. articles to profl. jours.,

contbg. author: (6-vol. book set) Business and Commercial Litigation in Federal Courts, 1998, Texas Legal Ethics, in the American Legal Ethics Library, 1998; mem. editl. bd. UCLA Law Review, 1986-87. Fellow Tex. Bar Found. (life); Mem. ABA (sects. antitrust law, litigation), Am. Judicature Soc. (life), Coll. State Bar Tex., D.C. Bar, Fed. Bar Assn., State Bar Tex., Houston Bar Assn. Address: Vinson & Elkins LLP First City Tower 1001 Fannin St Ste 2300 Houston TX 77002-6710

CARR, ELIZABETH DAVIS-JACKSON, municipal manager; b. Plymouth, N.C., May 13, 1932; d. Raleigh Sherman and Lillian Blanche (Davis) Jackson; m. Joseph Hargrove Bryan, Dec. 24, 1953; children: Joanna Davis, Peter-Michael. BA, East Carolina U., 1953; MA, Atlantic Christian Coll., 1955. Dir. Clinton (N.C.) C. of C., 1972-82; investments, venture capital Carr & Assocs., Inc., Atlantic Beach, N.C., 1985—; town mgr. Pine Knoll Shores, N.C., 1995—; bd. dirs. First Citizens Bank & Trust, Clinton, 1982-84; mem. bd. realtors Carteret County, 1989-91. Democrat. Presbyn. Avocations: reading, tennis, traveling.

CARR, JAMES MCLEOD, naval officer; b. Bethesda, Md., Sept. 21, 1956; s. James McLeod and Janet (Abbott) C.; m. Dana McBride, May 5, 1984; children: Natalie, Cavan, Doran Abbott. BS, U.S. Naval Acad., 1978; MA, U. Grenoble, France, 1983; M.Internat. Law, U. Lyons, France, 1984. Commd. USN, advanced through grades to capt.; commanding officer USS John Rodgers, Mayport, Fla., 1997-98; reactor officer USS Enterprise, Norfolk, Va., 1999—. Recipient Stephen B. Luce award Navy League, 1999; Olmsted scholar Olmsted Found., 1982.

CARR, KENNETH MONROE, naval officer; b. Mayfield, Ky., Mar. 17, 1925; s. Samuel Norman and Nancy Elmore (Monroe) C.; m. Mary Elizabeth Pace, June 10, 1949. Student, U. Louisville, 1944-45; B.S., U.S. Naval Acad., 1949. Served as enlisted man U.S. Navy, 1943-45, commd. ensign, 1949; advanced through grades to vice adm., 1977; mem. commissioning crew U.S.S. Nautilus, 1954; comdg. officer U.S.S. Flasher, 1964-67, U.S.S. John Adams, 1967-68; mil. asst. to Dep. Sec. Def., 1973-77; comdr. submarine force Atlantic Fleet, Norfolk, Va., 1977-80; vice dir. Strategic Target Planning, Offutt AFB, Nebr., 1980-83; later dep. comdr. U.S. Atlantic Fleet, Norfolk, Va., 1983-85; chmn. US Nuclear Regulatory Commn., 1989-91; bd. dirs. MDM Svcs. Corp. Decorated D.S.M. (4), Legion of Merit (2). Mem. N.Y. Yacht Club, Army-Navy Country Club. Baptist. Home: 2322 Ft Scott Dr Arlington VA 22202-2207

CARR, LARRY DEAN, health care management company executive; b. Mt. Vernon, Ill., Apr. 22, 1947; s. Jewell Dean and Mary Janet (Lawrence) C.; m. Jean Ann Swanson, May 12, 1973; 1 child, Lisa Diane. BS in Fin., U. Ill., 1969. CPCU. Analyst Allstate Ins. Co., Northbrook, Ill., 1970-75; controller Svc. Rev. Allstate Ins. Co., Arlington Heights, Ill., 1975-76; regional controller Allstate Ins. Co., Rochester, N.Y. and Murray Hiil, N.J., 1976-80; exec. info. dir. Allstate Ins. Co., Northbrook, 1980-82, dir. mktg., 1982-83; v.p. Crum and Forster Personal Ins. Co./U.S. Fire Ins. Co., Basking Ridge, N.J., 1983-84, sr. v.p., 1984-85, exec. v.p., 1985-86, chmn. bd. dirs., pres., CEO, 1986-90, also bd. dirs.; CEO Viking Inc. Co., 1986-90, Nat. Gen. Ins.Co., 1986-91; exec. v.p. Motors Ins. Corp., 1991; pres., CEO Presbyn. Ch. Found., 1993-99; pres., founding dir., chmn. bd. dirs. New Covenant Trust Co., N.A., 1997-99; pres. case mgmt. divsn. Concentra Managed Care, Inc., Waltham, Mass., 2000—. Treas., bd. dirs. Somerset Hills YMCA, Basking Ridge, 1984-85; trustee Kent Place Sch., 1989-90; mem. adv. bd. Resource Ctr. for Women and Their Families, 1989-90; dir. Jarvie Commonweal Svc., 1994-99, Ky. Shakespeare Festival, 1997, Presbyn. Outlook Found., 2000— . Served with USAR, 1969-74. Mem. Pres.' Assn., Am. Mgmt. Assn., Delta Sigma Pi. Republican. Presbyterian. Avocations: swimming, skiing. Office: Concentra Managed Care Inc 130 2d Ave Waltham MA 02154

CARR, OSCAR CLARK, III, lawyer; b. Apr. 9, 1951; s. Oscar Clark Carr Jr. and Billie (Fisher) Carr Houghton; m. Mary Leatherman, Aug. 4, 1973; children: Camilla Fisher, Oscar Clark V. BA in English with distinction, U. Va., 1973; JD with distinction, Emory U., 1976. Bar: Tenn. 1976, U.S. Dist. Ct. (we. dist.) Tenn. 1977, (no. dist.) Miss. 1977, U.S. Ct. Appeals (6th cir.) 1985, (5th cir.) 1995; cert. mediator Tenn. Assoc. Glankler Brown, PLLC (formerly Glankler, Brown, et al, Memphis, 1976-82, ptnr., 1982—, chief mgr., 1998-00. Bd. dirs. Memphis Ballet Soc., 1980, Memphis-Shelby County Unit Am. Cancer Soc., Memphis Oral Sch. for Deaf, 1988-91; treas., vestryman St. John's Espiscopal Ch., Memphis, 1988-91, sr. warden, 1991; mem. Commn. on Ministry Diocese of West Tenn., 1987-90, King of Carnival memphis, 1994; pres., dir. Juvenile Diabetes Found. Memphis chpt., 1998; bd. dirs. Carnival Memphis. Mem. ABA, Tenn. Bar Assn. (we. dist. coun. environ. law 1992—), Memphis-Shelby County Bar Assn. (bd. dirs. 1985-87), Memphis Country Club (atty. 1997—), U. Va. Alumni Assn. Office: Glankler Brown PLLC 1700 One Commerce Sq Memphis TN 38103

CARR, SIR (ALBERT) RAYMOND, retired educator; b. Bath, U.K., Apr. 4, 1919; s. Reginald and Marion (Maillard) C.; m. Sara Ann Strickland, 1950; children: Adam, Matthew, Charles, Laura. Student, U. Christ Church, Oxford; DLitt (hon.), Oxon, U. Madrid. Lectr. U. Coll., London, 1945-48; fellow All Souls Coll. Oxford (Eng.) U., 1946-60, dir. L.Am. Ctr., 1964-68, prof. history L.Am., 1967-68, warden St. Antony's Coll., 1968-86; disting. prof. Boston U., 1980; King Juan Carlos prof. Spanish history NYU, 1992. Author: Spain 1808-1939, 1966, Latin America, 1969; editor: The Republic and the Civil War in Spain, 1971, English Fox Hunting, 1976, The Spanish Tragedy: The Civil War in Perspective, 1977, Spain: Dictatorship to Democracy, 1979, Modern Spain, 1980, Fox-Hunting, 1982, Puerto Rico: A Colonial Experiment, 1984, The Spanish Civil War, 1986; contbr. articles to profl. jours. Recipient award of merit Soc. Spanish History, Order of Alfonso el Sabio, Prime of Asturias prize for Social Scis., 1999; hon. fellow Exeter U., 1987, St. Anthony's Coll., Oxford, 1988. Fellow Royal Hist. Soc., Royal Soc. Lit., Brit. Acad.; mem. Spanish Royal Acad. History (corr.). Conservative. Church of England. Avocation; fox hunting. Home: Burch, North Molton, South Molton EX36 3JU, England

CARR, RICHARD RAYMOND, editor, public relations administrator; b. Des Moines, Jan. 26, 1934; s. Raymond William and Myra Reuss (Stevens) C.; m. Kathryn S. Chapman, Jan. 9, 1954; children: Rochelle Carr Needham, Stephen Todd Carr. BJ, Kans. State U., 1956. News editor Headlight & Sun, Pittsburg, Kans., 1956-60; pub. rels. adminstr. Pittsburg State U., 1960-85; pub. rels. advisor Tri-Lakes Cmty. Theatre, Branson, Mo., 1985-87; mng. editor Alumni Today quar. jour. Ctrl. Mo. State U., Warrensburg, 1988-99, ret., 1999. Mem. Soc. Profl. Journalists, Kansas City Press Club, Alpha Tau Omega (trustee chpt.), Lions Club (past pres.), Kiwanis Club (past pres.). Methodist. Avocations: reading, collecting, history. E-mail: rcarr@i-land.net. Home: 99 Hawthorne Hill Dr Warrensburg MO 64093-2904

CARRAHER, SHAWN MICHAEL, management educator; b. Kansas City, Kans., Nov. 9, 1966; s. Charles E. and Loyalea Velda (Zimmerman) C. BBA with honors, Fla. Atlantic U., 1987; MBA, U. Cin., 1988; PhD, U. Okla., 1992. Delivery specialist Dayton Daily News, Beavercreek, Ohio, 1980-85; pres., owner Carraher & Sons, Beavercreek, 1982-87; tchr. U. Kans., Lawrence, 1988; rschr. Fla. Atlantic U., Boca Raton, 1989-90, U. Okla., Norman, 1990-92; vis. asst. prof. U. Wis., Milw., 1992-94; assoc. prof. Calif. State U., Chico, 1994-95, Ind. State U., Terre Haute, 1995-98, Ind. U., Bloomington, 1998-2000; prof. mgmt. and global entrepreneurship Tex. A&M U., Commerce, 2000—; pres. Carraher & Carraher Cons. Group, 1997—; cons. City of Norman, 1990-91, USAF, 1990-92, Pratt & Whitney, West Palm Beach, Fla., 1990; spkr. at more than 400 profl. presentations on goal-setting and mgmt. devel., including U. Okla., Norman, 1992. Author: (12 video tapes) Industrial Psychology, 1992; contbr. 60 articles to profl. jours. Pres. Christians In Action, Beavercreek, 1984-85; treas. Campus Crusade for Christ, Norman, 1991-92. Shuman fellow U. Okla., 1991; recipient award Delta Sigma Pi, 1996; named Outstanding Young Men of Am., 1992. Mem. Acad. Mgmt., Am. Ednl. Rsch. Assn., Am. Psychol. Soc., So. Mgmt. Assn., S.W. Acad. Mgmt. Avocations: research, speaking on goal-setting, martial arts, weight-lifting, cooking. Office: Tex A&M U-Commerce Dept Mgmt and Mgmt PO Box 3011 Commerce TX 74529-3011

CARRARD, FRANCOIS DENIS, international organization administrator, lawyer; b. Lausanne, Switzerland, Jan. 19, 1938; s. Jean-Louis and Erica (Godall) C.; m. Alba Gropetti, Sept. 29, 1966; children: Maud, Anne. JD, U. Lausanne, Switzerland, 1964. Bar: Canton of Vaud. Sr. ptnr. Carrard, Paschoud, Heim and Ptnrs., Lausanne, Switzerland, 1967—; dir. gen. Internat. Olympics Com., Lausanne, 1989—; chmn. bd. dirs. Beau-Rivage Palace, Lausanne, Vaudoise Assurances Group, Lausanne, Holdiprint Group, Lausanne, Bank Bruxelles Lambert (Suisse), Found. Moutreux Jazz Festival, Montreux, many others. Author: Les experts comptables, sociétés fiduciaires et syndicats de révision, 1964. Former mem. City Coun., Cully, Switzerland, 1985. Maj. Swiss Mil., 1983-95. Decorated comdr. Order of Civil Merit (Spain), officer Order of St. Charles (Monaco). Mem. Vaud Bar Assn. (former coun. mem.), Automobile Club of Switzerland (hon., former pres. 1969-78). Avocations: jazz pianist, swimming, skiing. Home: Route de Vevey 4, CH-1096 Cully Switzerland Office: Internat Olympic Com, Château de Vidy, CH-1007 Lausanne Switzerland

CARRARO, MASSIMO, member of European parliament; b. Camposampiero, Hungary, Mar. 8, 1959. Mem. European parliament, Hungary, 1999—; mem. Group of the Party of European Socialists; mem. com. on industry, external trade, rsch. and energy; substitute mem. com. on the environment, pub. health and consumer policy; mem. delegation for rels. with Switzerland, Iceland and Norway; substitute mem. delegation to the EU-Hungary Joint Parliamentary Com. Mem. Democratic Left. Office: c/o Morellato, Via Commerciale 29, I-35010 Fratte Di S Giustina Hungary*

CARRASQUERO, ARMANDO, chemist, educator; b. Maracay, Venezuela, Mar. 5, 1967; s. Armando and Delfina (Duran) C.; m. Petra Beatriz Navas, Aug. 23, 1998. Grad. in chemistry, U. Pedagogica, 1990; MEd, U. Bicentenaria, 1993; MSc, Ctrl. U. Maracay, 1999. Tchr. chemistry Ctrl. U. Venezuela, Maracay, 1991-94, U. Pedagogica, Maracay, 1994—; rschr. Inst. Natural Resources, Salamanca, Spain, 1999. Mem. Venezuelan Assn. Sci. Home: Sucre Ave Edif Sucre No 32, 2101 Maracay Aragua, Venezuela Office: Pedagogical U Dept Chem, Ave las Delicias, 2101 Maracay Aragua, Venezuela

CARRASQUILLA, GABRIEL, epidemiology educator, provincial health official; b. Bogotá, Colombia, Mar. 22, 1951; s. Juan Antonio Carrasquilla and Josefina Gutierrez; m. Olga Lucia Henao, Apr. 3, 1976; children: Adriana, Mauricio, Marcela. MD, U. Valle, Cali, Columbia, 1980, MPH, 1980; MSc, Harvard U., Boston, 1984; DPH, Harvard Sch. Pub. Health, Boston, 1993. MD Servicio Salud Valle 6751. Dir. health svcs. Dept. Pub. Health, Cali, Colombia, 1980-89; project dir. Save the Children, Santo Domingo, Dominican Republic, 1989-90; dir. divsn. health Fundacion para la Edn. Superior, Cali, Colombia, 1990-99; sec. of health State Valle del Cauca, 2000—; assoc. prof. U. Valle, Calli, 1986-96, prof., 1996—. Mem. Soc. Epidemol. Rsch., Am. Soc. Tropical Medicine and Hygiene, Royal Soc. Tropical Medicine and Hygiene. Home: Calle 12 #112-120, Cali Colombia Office: Fundacion Edn Superior, Edificio Gobernacion P11, Cali Colombia

CARRASQUILLO, RAMON LUIS, civil engineering educator, consultant; b. San Juan, P.R., July 28, 1953; s. Ramon L. and Abigail Carrasquillo; m. Gladys Mateu (div. 1983); children: Ramon L. Jr., Jessica Marie; m. Peggy Musser, 1985 (div. 1999); children: Travis Andrew, Austin Matthew, Bryant Matthew; m. Liby Moreno, 2000; 1 child, Maria Alejandra. BSCE, U. P.R., 1975; MSCE, Cornell U., 1978, PhD, 1980. Registered profl. engr., Tex. Grad. rsch. asst. Cornell U., Ithaca, N.Y., 1976-79; asst. prof. civil engring. U. Tex., Austin, 1980-84, assoc. prof. civil engring., 1984-89, prof. civil engring., 1989-99, adj. prof. civil engring., 1999—, researcher, 1980—; pres. CFX, Inc., Excellence in Engring., 1996-2000, Ceniza Internat., Inc., 1996—; ptnr. Carrasquillo Assocs., Austin, Tex., 1980—, Carrasquillo Trucking Svcs., 2000—; assoc. dir. Internat. Ctr. for Aggregates Rsch., Austin, 1992-96; pres. Rainbow Materials, Inc., 1994—, bd. dirs. Children's Advocacy Found., 1999. Co-author: Production of High Strength Concrete, 1986, also papers in field. Recipient Lockheed Ft. Worth Tchg. Excellence award, 1995; Austin Industries fellow, 1991-99; Dec. 14, 1995 named Ramon Carrasquillo Day, Austin. Fellow Am. Concrete Inst. (T.Y. Lin award 1990); mem. ASTM, ASCE, Tex. Aggregates and Concrete Assn. (Outstanding Speaker award 1980). Office: Carrasquillo Assocs 4534 W Gate Blvd Ste 230 Austin TX 78745-1468

CARRATÚ, ROMANO, gastroenterologist; b. Rome, June 1, 1933; s. Pasquale Carratú and Zore Tajetti; m. Angela Olivieri, Sept. 19, 1982; children: Margareth, Alexandra, Mary Gabriela. MD, U. Rome, 1958. Resident Clinic Med. U. Rome, 1970-80; prof. gastroenterology Somali U., Mogadishu, 1974; prof. gastroenterology U. Naples, Italy, 1980—, dir. postgrad. sch. gastroenterology, 1982—; co-pres. Nat. GI and Coloproctology Congresses, Naples, 1987, 96, 98; head gastrointestinal svc. U. Hosp. Naples, 1990—. Co-author: Handbook of Experimental Pharmacology Vol. 34, 1973; chief editor Italian Jour. Gastroenterology, 1989-96; mem. internat. bd. editors Jour. Clin. Gastroenterology, 1992-92; contbr. articles to profl. jours. Roman Catholic. Avocations: reading, travel, soccer. E-mail: rcarratu@tin.it. Home: Via Mecenate 59, 00184 Rome Italy Office: U Hosp, Pza Miraglia 2, 80138 Naples Italy

CARR-CHELLMAN, ALISON ALENE, education educator; b. Columbus, Ohio, Aug. 8, 1964; d. Richard Dean Carr and Patricia Mildred Burns; m. Davin Jules Chellman, June 12, 1998. BS, Syracuse U., 1986, MS, 1988; PhD, Ind. U., 1993. Dir. instrn. Sylvan Learning Ctrs., Syracuse, N.Y., 1987-88; instrnl. designer McDonnel Douglas, Denver, 1988-90; tchg. asst. Ind. U., Bloomington, 1990-93; asst. prof. Western Mich. U., Kalamazoo, 1993-94, Pa. State U., University Park, 1994—; cons. Compu-Kids, Columbus; course specific expert U. Access, L.A. Contbr. chpt. to book and articles to profl. jours. Dorothea Weinman scholar Dorothea Weinman Found., 1991, 92. Mem. Assn. Ednl. Comm. and Tech. (change divsn. pres. 1995-97, Meml. scholar 1991, 92), Am. Ednl. Rsch. Assn. (spl. interest group for instrnl. tech. chair 1998-99). Democrat. Roman Catholic. Avocation: singing. E-mail: aac3@psu.edu. Fax: 814-865-0128. Office: Penn State Univ 307 Keller Bldg University Park PA 16802-1303

CARRELL, HAMMEL LEE, jewelry designer; b. Lovington, N.Mex., Dec. 3, 1941; s. Hammel and Sudie Lee (Foust) C.; m. Linda Lee Koch; 1 child, Sativa Sunny Day January. BA, Ea. N.Mex. U., 1965; BFA, N.Mex. State U., 1973, MA, 1974; MFA, U. Kans., 1977. Owner, mgr. Fuego Del Sol, Cloudcroft, N.Mex., 1971-74, Platoro Del Fuego, Las Cruces, N.Mex., 1972-74; instr. design U. Kans., Lawrence, 1974-77; co-owner, mgr. The Oxbow Gallery, Lawrence, 1976-77; asst. prof. art No. Ariz. U., Flagstaff, 1977-80; designer, planner Carrell Carpet and Interiors, Austin, 1980-82; owner Creative Solutions, Austin, 1982-84; dir., founder The Austin Sch. of Jewelry and Design, Austin, 1984-97; owner New Horizon Studio, Austin, 1988—, Reflections of the West Gallery, Spicewood, 1998—; juror N.Mex. Designer-Craftsmans show, 1978, Albuquerque Designer-Craftsman competition, 1981, N.Mex. State U. Art Undergrad. Shows, 1972-74, Grad. and Faculty Shows, 1973-74. Group shows include Contemporary Jewelry show N.Mex. State Fair, 1972, Tex. Christian U., 1973, N.Mex. Gallery, 1973, Gallery Plus, Los Alamos, N.Mex., 1974, Nat. Metal Invitational Traveling Exhibit, U.S., Australia and New Zealand, 1975, Grad. Thesis Exhibit, Lawrence, Kans., 1977, S.W. Metalsmithing Exhbn., 1979, The Westside Gallery, Phoenix, 1980-82, Columbine Gallery, Breckenridge, Colo., 1984, Magic Mountain Gallery, Taos, N.Mex., 1985, Applied Arts Gallery, Austin, Tex., 1986, Littlefield Gallery, Austin, 1987, Red Poppy Gallery, Georgetown, Tex., 1988-90, El Taller Gallery, Austin, 1994-95, Spirit Echos Gallery, Austin, 1995—, Western Design Conf., 1998 (selected 1 of 2000 Artists/Designers 20th Century). Elected v.p. Art Students League N.Mex. State U., elected student rep. to faculty meetings. With USAF, 1966-70. Assistantship N.Mex. State U., U. Kans.; grantee Matthey-Johnson Inc. Mem. Delta Sigma Pi, Alpha Rho Gamma. Avocations: writing, painting, jewelry, sculpture, ceramics. Office: PO Box 196 Spicewood TX 78669-0196

CARREQO, PATRICIA, pharmacy educator, researcher; b. Vina Del Mar, Valparaiso, Chile, Sept. 30, 1958; d. Guillermo Carreqo and Yolanda Gonzalez. Cert. pharmacist. Tech. dir. Farmacia Knop, Quilpue, Chile, 1983-84; prof. U. Valparaiso, 1983—, dept. dir. pharmacy sch., 1996-98; cons. 3rd Local Ct. Justice, Valparaiso. Contbr. articles to profl. jours. Scholar Inst. de Cooperation Iberoamericana, Espaqa, Valencia, 1986, Ministry Fgn. Office, Perugia, Italy, 1991-92. Mem. Assn. Brasilera de Tecnologia Farmaceutica. Roman Catholic. Avocations: Tibetan yoga, camping, reading, watching movies. E-mail: pcarreno@uv.ci. Fax: 56-32-280417. Office: Univ Valparaiso, Gran Bretaqa 1093, 5001 Casilla Chile

CARRERA, JOSE, psychiatrist, child psychiatrist, psychoanalyst; b. Mexico City, Mex., July 19, 1929; s. Jose C. and Eva (Tamborrel) C.; m. Theresa Massa, Sept. 20, 1983; children: Eva, Maritza, Jose. MD, U. Nacional Autonoma de Mex., 1953; MPH, Sch. Pub. Health of Mex., 1960. Diplomate Am. Bd. Psychiatry and Neurology. Resident in internal medicine Inst. Nacional de Nutricion, Mex., 1952-55; resident in psychiatry U. Ill., Chgo., 1955-57, State U. N.Y., Syracuse, 1957-59; psychoanalyist Assn. Psicoanalitica Mex., Mex., 1960-65; instr. U. Nacional Autonoma de Mex., 1959-64; asst. prof. U. Mich., 1975-85; assoc. prof. U. S.D., 1985-95. Mem. AMA, Am. Psychiat. Assn. (life mem.), Am. Acad. Child and Adolescent Psychiatry, Mich. Psychoanalytic Soc. Avocations: computer, photography, gardening, cooking. Home: 13401 Trist Rd Grass Lake MI 49240-9159

CARRERA, VICTOR MANUEL, lawyer; b. Rio Grande City, Tex., Nov. 20, 1954; s. Eladio and Ines Olivia (Guerra) C. BS, U. Tex., 1975, BA with honors, 1976, JD, 1979. Bar: Tex. 1979, U.S. Dist. Ct. (so. dist.) Tex. 1980, U.S. Dist. Ct. (we. dist.) Tex. 1996, U.S. Ct. Appeals (5th cir.) 1986; cert. civil trial law, personal injury trial law, civil appellate law, Tex. Assoc. Cardenas & Whitis, McAllen, Tex., 1979-80; briefing atty. U.S. Dist. Ct. (so. dist.) Tex., Brownsville, 1980-81; assoc. Keys, Russell & Seaman, Corpus Christi, Tex., 1981-84; assoc. Wood, Boykin, Wolter & Keys, Corpus Christi, 1984-86, ptnr., 1987-88; participating mem. Law Offices of Ramon Garcia, P.C., Edinburg, Tex., 1988-90; ptnr. Munoz, Hockema & Reed, McAllen, Tex., 1990-96, Reed & Carrera, Edinburg, Tex., 1997, Reed, Carrera & McLain, Edinburg, TX, 1997—; lectr. South Tex. Coll. Law, Houston, 1987, U. Houston, 1989-90, 96-99, State Bar Tex., 1992. Mng. editor Tex. International Law Jour., 1978-79. Recipient Outstanding Individual Contbn. Award Vol. Lawyers of Coastal Bend, 1985. Mem. Tex. Bar Assn., Tex. Trial Lawyers Assn. (dir. 1991-96, lectr. 1993-94), Hidalgo County Bar Assn. Democrat. Avocations: history, archaeology. Home: 1208 Xanthisma Ave McAllen TX 78504-3520 Office: Reed Carrera & McLain PO Box 9702 Mcallen TX 78502-9702 also: Reed Carrera & McLain Bldg 101 1 Paseo del Prado Edinburg TX 78539

CARRERAS, RODRIGO, diplomat, political science educator; b. Desamparados, Costa Rica, Aug. 10, 1947; s. Benjamin Nunez and Daisy Jimenez; m. Marta Eugenia Mora; children: Isadora, Gustavo. BA, U. Costa Rica, 1974; MA, U. Calif., Berkeley, 1976. Amb. Costa Rica, Brasilia, Brazil, 1982-84; dir. fgn. policy Ministry Fgn. Affairs, San Jose, 1986-90; vice min. fgn. affairs Costa Rica, San Jose, 1994-98; amb. Costa Rica, Jerusalem, 1998—; chief of staff Ministry Fgn. Affairs, San Jose, Costa Rica, 1976-78; dir. Ceproceca, San Jose, 1984-86; prof. internat. rels., Nat. U., San Jose, 1976—. Decorated Knight, Order of Malta, 1997. Avocation: scuba diving. Office: 13 Diskin, Jerusalem Israel

CARRERE, CHARLES SCOTT, law educator, judge; b. Dublin, Ga., Sept. 26, 1937; 1 son, Daniel Austin. BA, U. Ga., 1959; LLB, Stetson U., 1961. Bar: Ga. 1960, Fla. 1961. Law clk. U.S. Dist. Judge, Orlando, Fla., 1962-63; asst. U.S. Atty. Middle Dist. Fla., 1963-66, 68-69, chief trial atty., 1965-66, 68-69; ptnr. Harrison, Greene, Mann, Rowe & Stanton, 1970-80; judge Pinellas County, Fla., 1980-96; vis. prof. law Stetson Coll. Law, 1997-98, Cumberland Law Sch., 1998-99. Recipient Jud. Appreciation award St. Petersburg Bar Assn., 1996, Alumnus of Yr. award Stetson Student Bar Assn., 1998. Mem. State Bar Ga., Fla. Bar, Phi Beta Kappa. Presbyterian. Address: PO Box 22034 Gateway Mall Sta Saint Petersburg FL 33742

CARREY, JIM, actor; b. Toronto, Ont., Can., Jan. 17, 1962; s. Percy and Kathleen Carrey; m. Melissa Womer, 1986 (div.); 1 child, Jane. Performances include (TV series) The Duck Factory, 1984, In Living Color, 1990-94; (TV films) Mike Hammer: Murder Takes All, 1989, Doing Time on Maple Drive, 1992; (films) Finders Keepers, 1984, Once Bitten, 1985, Peggy Sue Got Married, 1986, The Dead Pool, 1988, Earth Girls Are Easy, 1989, Pink Cadillac, 1989, High Strung, 1991, Ace Ventura: Pet Detective, 1993 (also screenwriter), The Mask, 1994, Dumb and Dumber, 1994 (MTV Movie awards), Batman Forever, 1995, Ace Ventura: When Nature Calls, 1995, The Mask's Revenge, 1996, Liar, Liar, 1996 (Blockbuster Entertainment award), The Cable Guy, 1996 (MTV Movie award), The Truman Show, 1997 (Golden Globe Best Performance award, MTV Movie award), Simon Birch, 1998, In My Life, 1998 (TV), Man on the Moon, 1999 (Golden Globe, 2000), Me, Myself and Irene, 3000, How the Grinch Stole Christmas, 2000. Star on the Hollywood Walk of Fame, 2000. Office: UTA 9560 Wilshire Blvd Fl 5 Beverly Hills CA 90212-2401

CARR-HILL, ROY ALEXANDER, statistician; b. Widnes, Eng., Aug. 29, 1943; s. Eric Arthur and Gwendoline (Rae) Carr-H.; m. Sylvaine Madeleine Marthe Bertin-Hugault(sepd); m. Susan Jenkins-Clarke; children: Aileen, Eva, Sita, Maya. BA, Cambridge U., Eng., 1965; M Criminology, U. Calif., Berkeley, 1968; PhD, U. Oxford, Eng., 1980. Lectr. U. Sussex, Brighton, Eng., 1971-74; adminstr. OECD, Paris, 1974-77; prof. U. Eduardo Mondlane, Maputo, Mozambique, 1978-81; rsch. fellow Med. Rsch. Coun., Aberdeen, 1981-83; prof. Ctr. for Health Econs., York, Eng., 1984—, Inst. of Edn./U. London, 1992—; cons. SIDA, Guinea-Bissau, Mozambique, 1983-96, Eurostat, 1996-98, WHO, So. Africa, 1987-93, IIEP, Paris, 1983-96. Co-author: (books) Crime Police and Criminal Statistics, 1978, Empirical Birthweight Standards, 1984, others; author: Social Conditions in Sun-Saharan Africa, 1991. Avocation: dry stone wall building. E-mail: irss23@york.ac.uk. Office: Ctr for Health Econs, U York, York Y01 5DD, England

CARRILLO, BERNARDO JORGE, veterinarian, researcher; b. S.S. Jujuy, Argentina, Nov. 18, 1931; s. Bernardo and Berta (Gonzalez) C.; m. Ingrid L. Estrup, Oct. 1, 1958; children: Jorge Ernesto, Pablo Javier. Degree in veterinary medicine, Buenos Aires U., 1956, DVM, 1967; MS, Cornell U., 1961; PhD, U. Calif., Davis, 1971. Researcher Nat. Inst. Agrl. Rsch., Balcarce, Argentina, 1958, co-dir., 1961-67, dep. chmn. dept. animal prodn., 1972-75; dep. chmn. vet. rsch. ctr. Nat. Inst. Agrl. Rsch., Castelar, Argentina, 1977-82, dir., 1982-87, 87-92, 1992-96; prof., organizer postgrad. course in pathology U. Rio, Brazil, 1975-77; dir. Cast. Found., 1996-2000; prof. U. Mar del Plata, Balcarce, 1965-75; vis. prof. U. Munich, 1982, U. Fla., Gainesville, 1982; coord. Internat. Relationship Project, Buenos Aires, 1983-85; pres. III Congress Vet. Medicine, Buenos Aires, 1980, VII Symposium WAVLD, Buenos Aires, 1994. FAO fellow, 1959, Ford fellow, 1967. Mem. World Assn. Vet. Medicine, , Argentine Assn. Vet. Lab. Diagnosis (pres. 1985-87), Am. Assn. Vet. Lab. Diagnosis, World Assn. Vet. Lab. Diagnosis (v.p. 1992—, acad. mem. 1994-96), Nat. Acad. Vet. Scis. Roman Catholic. Avocations: bike riding, tennis, horse riding. Home: Sanchez de Bustamante 2360, 1425 Buenos Aires Argentina Office: Vet Rsch Ctr INTA, CC 77, 1708 Morón Argentina

CARRILLO, JOSE ANTONIO, mathematician, researcher; b. Granada, Spain, Dec. 29, 1969; s. Antonio and Encarnacion (De La Plata) C.; m. Maria Victoria Roas. Degree in math., U. Granada, 1992, degree in computer scis., 1992, PhD in Math., 1996. Asst. prof. Univ. Granada, 1992—. Contbr. articles to profl. jours. Recipient Premio Fin de Carrera, Acad. Scis. Granada, 1992. Mem. Am. Math. Soc., Sociedad Española de Matemática Aplicada. Avocation: computer science. Office: U Granada, Dept Math Aplicada, 18071 Granada Spain

CARRILLO, LEONOR, microbiology educator, researcher; b. R. Saene Pena, Argentina, June 22, 1940; d. Oscar Enrique and Ana Leonor (Alvarado) C.; m. Pablo Cesareo Sisti, Sept. 26, 1978; children: Pablo Alberto, Francisco Javier, Enrique Carlos. D in Biochemistry, U. Nacional De La Plata, Argentina, 1972. Asst. U. Nacional De La Plata, Argentina, 1965-76; prof. U. Nacional De Jujuy, Argentina, 1976—, U. Nacional De Salta, Argentina, 1993—. Author: (book) Micologia De Los Alimentos, 1995; contbr. articles to profl. jours. Office: Facultad Ciencias Agrarias, Alberdi 47, 4600 San Salvador de Jujuy Argentina

CARRILLO-DE-LA-PEÑA, MARIA TERESA, psychologist; b. San Sebastian, Spain, Oct. 1, 1965; d. Fidel and Victoria (de la Pena) C. Grad. in psychology, U. Deusto, Spain, 1988; PhD in Psychology, U. Santiago de Compostela, Spain, 1993, Diplomate in Criminology, 1992. Rsch. asst. U. Santiago de Compostela, Spain, 1989-93, lectr., 1994—. Contbr. articles to profl. jours. Mem. Amnesty Internat., Internat. Soc. for Study of Individual Differences, Soc. Spanish Soc. Psicofisiologia. Avocations: trekking, travel,

meeting friends. Office:-U Santiago de Compostela, Faculty Psych Campus SUR, 15705 Santiago de Composta Spain

CARRINGTON, LORD (PETER ALEXANDER), former secretary general NATO, company executive; b. London, June 6, 1919; s. 5th Baron Carrington and Sybil Marion Colville; m. Iona McClean; 3 children. Ed., Eton Coll.; Doctorate, U. Buckingham, Sandhurst, Eng., 1989; LL.D., Cambridge U., 1981, Leeds U., 1981, U. Philippines, 1982; hon. fellow, St. Antony's Oxford, 1982; Doctorate, U. Essex, 1983; LLD (hon.), U. S.C., 1983; DSc (hon.), Cranfield, 1983; LLD, Aberdeen U., 1989; LLD (hon.), Harvard U., 1986; LLD, Sussex U., Reading U., 1989; LLD (hon.), U. Birmingham, 1993, U. Nottingham, 1993. Joined Grenadier Guards, 1939, served in N.W. Europe; chmn. Christies Internat. plc, 1988-93; parliamentary sec. to Minister of Agr., 1951-54, Ministry of Def., 1954-56; high commr. in Australia, 1956-59; First Lord of the Admiralty, 1959-63; minister without portfolio, leader House of Lords, 1963-64, leader opposition, 1964-70, 74-79; sec. of state for def., 1970-74, also minister aviation supply, 1971-74, chmn. Conservative Party, 1972-74; sec. of state for energy, 1974, for fgn. and commonwealth affairs, 1979-82, minister overseas devel., 1979-82; chmn. Gen. Electric Co., London, 1983-84; sec.-gen. NATO, Brussels, 1984-88; chmn. Australia and N.Z. Bank Ltd., 1969-70. Author: (autobiography) Reflect on Things Past, 1988. Sec. for fgn. corr., hon. mem. Royal Acad. Arts, 1982—; chmn. bd. trustees Victoria and Albert Mus., London, 1983-88; pres. The Pilgrims, 1983—; chancellor U. Reading, 1992; mem. Kissinger Assocs., 1982-84, 88-97; bd. dirs. The Telegraph, plc, 1990. Decorated Companion of Honour, knight Order of Garter, knight grand cross Order of St. Michael and St. George (chancellor 1984-94); recipient Medal of Freedom, 1988, Four Freedoms award Franklin and Eleanor Roosevelt Inst., 1992. Mem. Pratt's Club, White's Club. Address: 32a Ovington Sq, London SW3 1LR, England*

CARRINGTON, ALAN, chemistry educator; b. London, Jan. 6, 1934; s. Albert and Constance (Nelson) C.; m. Noreen Hilary Taylor, Nov. 7, 1959; children: Sarah Elizabeth, Rebecca Anne, Simon Francis. BSc, U. Southampton, Eng., 1955, PhD, 1959, DSc (hon.), 1984; MA, U. Cambridge, Eng., 1960. Rsch. fellow U. Minn., Mpls., 1957-58; asst. in rsch. U. Cambridge, 1960-63, asst. dir. rsch., 1963-67; fellow Downing Coll., Cambridge, 1960-67; prof. chemistry U. Southampton, 1967-76, SERC sr. fellow, 1976-79, Royal Soc. rsch. prof., 1979-84, 87—; Royal Soc. rsch. prof. U. Oxford, 1984-87. Author: Microwave Spectroscopy of Free Radicals, 1974, (with A.D. McLachlan) Introduction to Magnetic Resonance, 1967. Recipient Harrison Meml. medal and prize Chem. Soc., 1962, Marlow medal Faraday Soc., 1966, medal and award for structural chemistry Chem. Soc., 1970, others. Fellow Royal Soc. (Davy medal 1992), Royal Soc. Chemistry (pres. Faraday divsn. 1997—, Faraday medal 1986), Inst. of Physics; mem. CBE, Nat. Acad. Scis. (U.S.), Am. Acad. Arts and Scis. (fgn. hon.). Avocation: music (piano, organ). Home: 46 Lakewood Rd, Chandlers Ford SO53 1EX, England Office: U Southampton, Dept Chemistry, Southampton SO17 1BJ, England

CARRINGTON, CEDRIC GERALD, engineering physics educator, researcher; b. Oamaru, Otago, New Zealand, Oct. 16, 1943; s. Cedric Percy and Edith Florence (Willet) C.; m. Janet Michal Melville, Aug. 7, 1967; children: Ann Michelle, Sonya Jane, Richard Melville. BSc with honors, Otago U., Dunedin, New Zealand, 1966, MSc, 1967; DPhil, Oxford (Eng.) U., 1971, MA, 1972. Jr. rsch. fellow Merton Coll., Oxford, 1970-72; rsch. assoc. JILA, U. Colo., Boulder, 1972-73; lectr., sr. lectr., assoc. prof. engring. physics U. Otago, 1973-99, now prof. physics, 1999—; cons. Carrier Air-conditioning Ltd., Auckland, New Zealand, 1984-88, 95—, Energy Group Ltd., Dunedin, 1989—; mem. adv. panel New Zealand Found. for Rsch., Sci. and Tech., Wellington, New Zealand, 1993-2000. Author: Basic Thermodynamics, 1994; mem. editorial bd. Internat. Jour. Energy Rsch., 1984—; contbr. some 80 articles to profl. jours. Rutherford Meml. scholar Royal Soc., London, 1967; vis. fellow Keble Coll., Oxford, 1987; vis. rsch. fellow Melbourne U., 1994. Mem. ASHRAE, Internat. Inst. Refrigeration (v.p. commn. E2 1995—), Instn. Profl. Engrs. New Zealand. Achievements include two patents for devel. of improved heat pump heating systems. Office: U Otago Dept Physics, PO Box 56, Dunedin New Zealand

CARRINGTON, EDWIN WILBERFORCE, international organization administrator. Sec.-gen. Caribbean Cmty. Secretariat, Georgetown, Guyana. Office: Caribbean Cmty Secretariat, Ave of Republic, POB 10827, Georgetown Guyana*

CARRINGTON, J(OE) P(ETER) (JOSSIF PETER BARTOLOTTI), nutritionist, psychoanalyst, research scientist, educator; b. N.Y.C., Mar. 13, 1948; s. Nicholas S. and Yolanda Virginia (Luisi) B.; 1 child, Joseph Nicholas. Cert. advanced study, N.Y. Inst. Advanced Study, 1974; EdM, Harvard U., 1985; postgrad. in nuclear engring., MIT, 1985. Cert. psychol. assessment/analysis provider; lic. nutritionist. Med. nutritionist N.Y., 1970—, psychoanalyst, psychotherapist, 1985—; sr. fellow, prof. med. nutrition and theoretical physics N.Y. Inst. Advanced Study, N.Y.C., 1980—; founder Eugenics Corp., Del., 1994—; TV and radio guest ABC Nat. Network, 1992; host of Carrington Nutrition radio programs, WNN Radio, WSHE Radio, Fla., 1989. Electorate sr. governing bd. Harvard U. Fellow N.Y. Inst. Advanced Study (sr., pub. info. dir. on NASA 1983—, Albert Einstein Gold medal of Sci. 1985); mem. N.Y. Acad. Sci., Harvard Alumni Assn., Harvard Club, Phi Delta Kappa. Avocations: theoretical physics, Chinese medicine, natural scis., relativity, nutritional eugenics. Office: Eugenics Corp PO Box 770514 Coral Springs FL 33077-0514

CARRIÓ, ALEJANDRO DANIEL, lawyer, educator; b. Buenos Aires, Oct. 15, 1953; s. Genaro Ruben Carrió and Margarita Martha Baistrocchi; m. Alicia Angelica Maqueda de Carrió; children: Juan Francisco, Tomas. LLB, Buenos Aires U., 1976; LLM, La. State U., 1982. Ptnr. Law Firm Landaburu & Carrió, Buenos Aires, 1977—; adj. prof. law Buenos Aires U., 1984-88, prof. law, 1989—; rsch. assoc. La. State U., 1985; vis. prof. law Syracuse U., 1990, 91, 92, 94; vis. scholar Columbia U. Law Sch., N.Y., 1989. Author: Garantías Constitucionales en el Proceso Penal, 1984, 4th edit., 2000, The Criminal Justice System of Argentina, 1986, El Enjuiciamiento Penal en Argentina y Estados Unidos, 1989, Presidential Systems in Stress: Emergency Powers in Argentina and The United States (together with William C. Banks), 1993, La Corte Suprema y Su Independencia, 1996, (together with Alejandro M. Garro) Criminal Procedure: A Worldwide Study, Chapter 1: Argentina, 2000. Mem. Internat. Acad. Trial Lawyers, Assn. por Los Derechos Civiles (pres. 1996—). Home: Av Libertador 4710, 1426 Buenos Aires Argentina Office: Landaburu & Carrió, 25 de Mayo 555 Piso 12, 1002 Buenos Aires Argentina

CARRIOL, MICHEL-HENRI, import company executive; b. Paris, Apr. 11, 1940; s. Rene Carriol and Lucette Marot; m. Julie-Ann Zerky, Dec. 16, 1967; children—Jean-Marc, Jean-Philippe. Degree in Polit. Sci., Inst. Polit. Sci., France; degree in econs. U. Brussels. Diplomat, comml. attaché French Embassy, Australia, 1966-72; mng. dir. Trimex Pty., Ltd., Sydney, New South Wales, Sydney, Australia, 1973—. Adviser to French govt. on fgn. trade. Mem. French C. of C. (pres. 1981—). Clubs: Maxims Bus. Cercle Interalliee (Paris); Royal Sydney (Sydney). Avocations: skiing; stamp collecting. Office: Trimex Pty Ltd, 5 Crewe Place, Rosebery Sydney NSW 2018, Australia

CARRIVE, PASCAL LUC, neuroscientist; b. Abidjan, Ivory Coast, July 21, 1960; arrived in Australia, 1985; s. Jean-Pierre and Anne (Peugeot) C.; m. Isabelle Meyer, Dec. 2, 1989; 1 child, Clovis. PhD, U. Sydney, 1989. Rsch. fellow Nat. Health Med. Rsch. Coun., Sydney, 1995—; sr. lectr. U. NSW, Sydney, 1999—; rschr. U. Sydney, 1989—. Contbr. rsch. papers to profl. jours. Rsch. grantee Nat. Health Med. Rsch. Coun., Australia, 1995. Mem. Australian Neurosci. Assn., Am. Neurosci. Assn., French Neurosci. Assn. Avocations: graphic arts, hiking, sailing, ethnic cultures. Office: U New South Wales, Sch Anatomy, Sydney 2052, Australia

CARRO, CARL RAFAEL, executive search consultant; b. N.Y.C., Mar. 16, 1961; s. John and Victoria (Eugenia) C.; m. Inna Liban, Nov. 17, 1984. BA in Polit. Sci., Econs., Columbia U., 1983. With fin. svcs. Union Bank of Switzerland, 1983-87; cons. Korn Ferry Internat., N.Y.C., 1987-89; sr. exec. recruiter The Gap, Inc., N.Y.C., 1989-90; v.p. Exec. Placement Consultants subs. R.H. Macy & Co., N.Y.C., 1991-94; mng. dir. Exec. Search Cons. Internat., Inc., N.Y.C., 1994—. Republican. Roman Catholic. Avocations: karate, hiking, bicycling, old houses, chess. Office: Exec Search Cons Internat 350 5th Ave Ste 5501 New York NY 10118-5599

CARRO, DOMINGO, economist, consultant; b. Barcelona, Spain, July 5, 1970; s. Fernando Carro and Maria Luisa De Prada. B Bus., U. Navarra, Pamplona, Spain, 1994, M Econs., 1995. Pres. orgn. com. Latin America Investments, Madrid, 1992; gen. mgr. Servicios Navarra, Pamplona, 1993-95; exec. dir. Ctr. for Internat. Devel., Barcelona, 1996-96; cons. Econ. Commn. for Latin Am., UN, Santiago, Chile, 1997, Spanish Orgn. for Stds. and Cert., Madrid, 1998; sr. exec. Bertelsmann, 1999—; adviser Conf. Mins. and Heads of State, Madrid, 1992, World Summit on Social Devel., Copenhagen, 1995, Ctr. for Internat. Devel., Barcelona, 1997-98. Author: Desarrollo Productivo, 1997. Founder Internat. Assn. Students of Econ. and Comml. Scis., Navarra, Pamplona, 1990. Mem. Club Tenis Barcino. Roman Catholic. Avocations: politics, tennis, soccer, travel, reading. Home: Calle Luca 3 2ndo 1ra, 08022 Barcelona Spain

CARROLL, BILLY PRICE, artist; b. Memphis, Nov. 27, 1920; d. Robert Ray and Olive (Thomas) Price; m. Robert Ray Hosmer, May 3, 1941 (div. Aug. 1948); 1 child, Nadia Jan Woodall; m. David Donald Carroll, Dec. 25, 1964. Student, Memphis Acad. Arts, 1939-40, Farnsworth Sch. Painting, 1949, 50-51, Accademia Delle Belle Arte, Florence, Italy, 1959; also pvt. study, various museums, Uffizi, Florence, Italy. Lectr., Chinese, Western painting; lectr. Fine Arts Mus., Little Rock, Ark., 1954, Brooks Art Gallery, 1957, 62, 63, 69, 77, National TV interview, tape, Taiwan 1969, interview, Taipei, 1969, Lynchburg Fine Arts Ctr., 1971, 83, Memphis State U. Gallery, 1987, Memphis U., Lecture Memphis Racquet Club, Gallery Eng. Speaking Union, 1990, Memphis Brooks Mus. Art, 1984, 91, Shainberg Gallery, Memphis, Tenn. state conv. Nat. League Am. Pen Women. Exhibited one man shows, Fine Arts Mus., Little Rock, 1953, McCaughen and Burr Gallery Fine Arts, St. Louis, 1954, 64, 88, Brooks Meml. Art Gallery, Memphis, 1956, Greenville (Miss.) Art Assn., 1963, Hong Kong, 1968, Taiwan Nat. Art Center, Teipei, 1969, Mpls. Aquatennial Festival, 1970, Lynchburg Fine Arts Ctr., Va., 1971, 83, Memphis Brooks Mus. Art, 1984, Christian Bros. Univ. Art Gallery, 1993, others; exhibited group shows, Fla. Artists Group, 1952-53, 57-58, Brooks Meml. Art Gallery, 1953, 61, 66, 67, Painting of Year Exhbn., Atlanta, 1955, Mo. Athletic Club, St. Louis Fine Arts Collection, 1954, 1st Hunter Ann., Chattanooga, 1960, Shainberg Gallery, 1987; represented in permanent collections Ga. Inst. Tech., Atlanta, 1974, Mo. Athletic Club, St. Louis, U. Tenn. at Memphis, Memphis State U., United Chinese Bank, Hong Kong, Dr. Sun Yat Sen, 1st Pres. of China, 1969, City Hall Gallery of Memphis Mayor Wyeth Chandler, Portrait of Morrie Moss, major donor to Memphis Brooks Mus. Art, Christian Bros. U. Art Gallery, Judge Hu Anderson, Ct. Appeals, Jackson, Supreme Ct. Justice John Swepston, Memphis, 1952, Dean of Shelby County Jurists Judge Robert Hoffman, Memphis, 1956, Amherst Coll. Prof. Henry Steele Commager (family collection), 1972, Senator Howard Baker (family collection), 1973, Sr. Circuit Ct. Judge Harry Adams, Memphis, 1982, Circuit Ct. Judge Robert Hoffman, Memphis, 1982, two bishops of Tenn. Episcopal Diocese, Edmund P. Dandridge, Memphis, 1953, William E. Sanders, Knoxville, 1987, Mayor Elliott Shearer, Lynchburg, Va. (family collection), 1987, Judge U.S. Bankruptcy Ct., 1987, Judge William Leffler U.S. Bankruptcy Ct., 1987, U.S. Circuit Judge Harry Wellford, Memphis, 1988, others, portrait donor Morrie Moss Memphis Brooks Mus. Art, portrait Blanche Spain Christian Bros. U., 1993; career history listed with Nat. Mus. Women in Art, Washington, 1989, Nat. League of Am. Pen Women Regional Exhbn. Recipient Oil-first and Hon. award Tenn. Nat. League Am. Pen. Women Exhbn., 1969, numerous others; Jay Hambridge Found. fellow, 1954, Huntington Hartford Found. fellow, 1958. Mem. Memphis Brooks Mus. Art League. Home: 1956 Central Ave Memphis TN 38104-5237

CARROLL, BONNIE, publisher, editor; b. Salt Lake City, Nov. 20, 1941. Grad. high sch., Ogden, Utah. Owner The Peer Group, San Francisco, 1976-78; pub., editor The Reel Directory, Cotati, Calif., 1978—. Pub., editor The Reel Thing newsletter, San Francisco, 1977-78. Mem. Assn. Visual Communicators (bd. dirs. 1987-90), No. Calif. Women in Film, San Francisco Film Tape Council (exec. dir. 1979-81). Office: The Reel Directory PO Box 866 Cotati CA 94931-0866

CARROLL, CHARLES MICHAEL, music educator; b. Otterbein, Ind., Mar. 5, 1921; s. James William and Catherine Doretta (Bohan) C.; m. Mary Lipford Rosenbush, Sept. 4, 1951; children: Charles Michael, Mary Catherine, Theresa Jane, William Rosenbush. BM, Ind. U., Bloomington, 1949; MM, Fla. State U., Tallahassee, 1951, PhD, 1960. Asst. coordinator music services Ind. U., 1949-50; instr. music Fla. State U., 1950-53; concert mgr. symphony orchs. Toledo, Washington, Savannah, Ga., 1953-58; prof. music Pensacola (Fla.) Jr. Coll., 1960-64; prof. St. Petersburg (Fla.) Jr. Coll., 1964-89, chmn. communications dept.; music critic Tallahassee Democrat, 1950-53, St. Petersburg Evening Independent, 1976-86. Author: The Great Chess Automaton, 1975; contbr. articles to profl. jours., and encyclopaedias. Served to capt., AUS, 1942-46, ETO. Mem. Am. Symphony Orch. League (v.p. 1955-56), Am. Musicol. Soc. (nat. council 1974-77, chmn. chpt. 1974-76), Am. Soc. Eighteenth-Century Studies (exec. bd. region 1974-82, regional pres. 1979-80), Coll. Music Soc. (editor 1979-83, nat. council 1978-81, chmn. chpt. 1979-80), Société d'Etudes Philidoriennes (conseiller bibliographique 1988—). Home: 1701 80th St N Saint Petersburg FL 33710-3703

CARROLL, DAVID JOSEPH, actor; b. Stratford, N.J., July 9; s. David Ronald and Mary Jane (Popko) C. Student, Ctr. Talented Youth, 1991-92, ROGATE, 1991-92, Sch. Visual Arts, 1997—. Actor: (TV commls.) Rock & Roll Easter Eggs, 1989, British Knights, 1989, America's Funniest Home Videos, 1990, French Toast Clothes, 1990, Pizza Hut, 1990, Burger King, 1990, (films) Cadillac Man, 1989, Thank You and Goodnight, 1990. Mem. Screen Actors Guild. Avocations: biking, golf, computer animation, swimming, roller blading. Home: 385 Harlingen Rd Belle Mead NJ 08502-5313

CARROLL, FRANK EDWARD, radiologist, researcher; b. Phila., Oct. 25, 1941; s. Frank Edward Sr. and Marie Elizabeth (Mullen) C.; m. Saramae Dorothy Dever, Sept. 4, 1965; children: Frank Leonard, Mark Edward. BS in Biology, St. Joseph's Coll., 1963; MD, Hahnemann Med. Coll., 1967. Diplomate Am. Bd. Radiology. Rsch. asst. Hahnemann Med. Coll. and Hosp., Phila., 1965-66; rotating intern U.S. Naval Regional Med. Ctr., Oakland, Calif., 1967-68; submarine med. officer U.S. Submarine Med. Sch., U.S. Naval Submarine Base, Gorton, Conn., 1968, SSBN 659 Will Rogers Polaris Nuclear Submarine, 1968-69; staff physician Armed Forces Staff Coll., Norfolk, Va., 1969-70; diagnostic radiology resident St. Mary's Hosp. and Med. Ctr., San Francisco, 1970-72; resident, fellow, rschr. U. Calif. San Francisco Sch. Medicine, 1972-73; asst. prof. diagnostic radiology Yale U. Sch. Medicine, New Haven, 1973-74; staff radiologist Broadway Hosp., Vallejo, Calif., 1974-75, Franklin (Pa.) Regional Med. Ctr., 1975-83; asst. prof. diagnostic radiology Vanderbilt U. Med. Ctr., Nashville, 1983-87, chief sect. pulmonary imaging, 1983—, assoc. dir. divsn. diagnostic radiology, 1984, dir. lab. radiologic rsch., 1984-85, assoc. prof. diagnostic radiology, 1987-94, dir. diagnostic radiology, 1985-89, assoc. prof. physics and astronomy, 1993-99, prof. diagnostic radiology, 1994—; prof. physics and astronomy Vanderbilt U. Med. Ctr., 1999—; adj. asst. prof. diagnostic radiology Duke U. Med. Ctr., Durham, N.C., 1981-83; cons. in field; referee jours. in field, including Investigative Radiology, Acad. Radiology, Radiology, Chest, Jour. Applied Physiology, Archives of Internal Medicine, Am. Jour. Neuroradiology, others; grant reviewer NIH, Washington. Contbr. articles to profl. jours., chpts. to books. Bd. dirs. Nashville Opera, 1988-94, Franklin Emergency Ambulance Svc., 1975-83, St. Patrick's Sch. Bd., 1975-83; asst. scoutmaster Boy Scouts Am., Franklin, 1975-83, physician and merit badge counselor, Nashville, 1983—; pres. Am. Cancer Soc., Franklin, 1975-83; design prodn. vol. Cheekwood Fine Arts Mus., Nashville, 1995—. Lt. comdr. USNR, 1963-73. Fellow Am. Coll. Radiology, Am. Coll. Chest Physicians; mem. Am. Soc. Laser Medicine and Surgery, Soc. Photo-Optical Instrumentation Engrs., Soc. for Magnetic Resonance Imaging, Assn. Univ. Radiologists, Radiol. Soc. N.Am., Soc. thoracic Radiology, Tenn. Radiologic Soc., Mid. Tenn. Radiologic Soc. Achievements include production of pulsed, tunable, monochromatic X-rays by the free electron laser; evaluation of lung water by magnetic resonance imaging. Home: 1216 Vintage Pl Nashville TN 37215-4707 Office: Vanderbilt U Med Ctr 1161 21st Ave S Nashville TN 37232-0002

CARROLL, IRWIN DIXON, engineer; b. Many, La., Nov. 6, 1934; s. Andrew Dixon and Elizabeth Margaret (Irwin) C.; m. Claudia Laverne Bratcher, June 27, 1958; children: Richard Irwin, Claudia Elizabeth. BS in Mech. Engring., So. Meth. U., 1957, MS in Elec. Engring., 1967. Registered profl. engr., Tex. Design engr. Tex. Instruments, Dallas, 1957-66, engring. supr., 1966-71, engring. mgr., 1971-75, ops. mgr., 1975-77, European div. mgr., 1977-79, mfg. ops. mgr., 1979-80, dept. mgr., 1980-85; dept. mgr. George A. Greene Co., Campbell, Calif., 1985-86; cons. engr. Irwin Carroll Assocs., Dallas, 1986-88; dir. joint devel. programs, site mgr. Applied Materials, Inc., Austin, Tex., 1988—; tech. program dir. Semiconductor Equip. and Materials Inst., Dallas, 1983-85, speaker Zurich, Switzerland, 1986; mem. info. sys. adv. com. U.S. Dept. Commerce, 1990-96. Chmn. Zion Luth. Sch. Bd., Dallas, 1985-89; bd. dirs. Jr. Achievement of Ctrl. Tex., 1991-93, Japan-Am. Soc. of Austin, 1990-95, Austin Symphony Orch., 1994-97; pres. Austin Children's Mus., 1991-97; active Austin Choral Union, 1994-96; pres. Austin Comty. Found., 1996—. Mem. ASME, Greater Austin C. of C. (bd. dirs. 1991-95), Rotary. Lutheran. Home: PO Box 923 Salado TX 76571-0923 Office: Design Tech Group Inc (Roti-Chef Grills) PO Box 1056 Salado TX 76571-1056

CARROLL, JAMES J., business educator, litigation support consultant; b. Paterson, N.J., July 6, 1947; s. William J. and Mary K. (Koziol) C.; m. Andrea P. Nolan, June 28, 1970; children: Kathleen, Meredith, Alison. BSIE, N.J. Inst. Tech., 1969; MBA in Fin., Rutgers U., Newark, 1972; DBA in Mgmt., Nova Southea. U., 1987. CPA, N.J.; cert. mgmt. acct. Asst. prof. William Paterson Coll., Wayne, N.J., 1982-88, Fairleigh Dickinson U., Rutherford, N.J., 1988-91; assoc. prof. Georgian Ct. Coll., Lakewood, N.J., 1991-95, prof. bus., 1995—; cons. Deloitte & Touche, Allied-Signal, Engelhard Corp., Worthington Pump; CFO various cos.; speaker World Trade Coun. Witchita, Am. Small Bus. Administrn., Am. Assembly Collegiate Schs. Bus., Internat. Small Bus. Congress; fin. advisor various corps.; lectr. various colls. and univs.; expert witness James J. Carroll Consulting, Bridgewater, N.J., 1988—. Editor: Proceedings of Cases in Progress, 1991, 5th edit., 1995; mem. editl. bd. Jour. Small Bus. Mgmt. (Outstanding Editl. Reviewer award 1996), Jour. Managerial Issues, 1988-95, Jour. Small Bus. Strategy, Case Rsch. Jour.; ad hoc reviewer Acad. Mgmt. Rev., Entrepreneurship: Theory and Practice; reviewer numerous rsch. articles, textbooks; contbr. articles to profl. jours. Bd. dirs., treas. ARC, Somerset County, N.J., 1982-86. Recipient Econ. Edn. honor Freedoms Found. at Valley Forge, 1986, Leavey award Edn. Excellence, 1987; grantee in field. Fellow N.J. Soc. CPAs; mem. AICPA, Internat. Coun. Small Bus. Mgmt. (sr. v.p. rsch., pub., fin. 1992-94), Ea. Case Writers (pres. 1991-95), Acad. Mgmt. (dir. divsn. mgmt. edn. 1994—, Outstanding Reviewer award 1996), Ea. Acad. Mgmt. (treas. 1996—). Office: James J Carroll Cons 1374 Roger Ave Bridgewater NJ 08807-1251

CARROLL, LEWIS ANDREW, legal and management consultant; b. Huntington, W.Va., Nov. 22, 1920; s. Stephen Matthew and Florence Elizabeth (Ackerman) C.; m. Maria Helena Alves de Lima, June 27, 1959 (dec. May 1992); children: Margaret, Lewis. Bar: W.Va. 1949. Assoc. Todd, Dillon and Curtiss, Washington, 1950-51; asst. U.S. atty. U.S. Attys. Office, Washington, 1951-60, chief appellate sect., 1953-58; supr. trial atty. FPC, Washington, 1960-62; assoc. Ross, Marsh and Foster, Washington, 1962-65; sr. counsel So. Natural Gas Co., Birmingham, Ala., 1965-69; gen. counsel Asian Devel. Bank, 1969-75; v.p., gen. counsel Washington Gas Co., 1975-85; pvt. practice legal & mgmt. cons. McLean, Va., 1985—; cons. Am. Corp. Counsel Assn., 1986-91, Inter-Am. Devel. Bank, 1991-94; adj. prof. Cumberland Law Sch., 1969; trustee, pres. Rsch. Found., 1980-84. Lt. (j.g.) USNR, 1943-46. Named Disting. Alumnus, Marshall U., 1993. Mem. ABA (vice chmn. internat. pub. contracts 1974-75), Inter-Am. Bar Assn. (pres. Com. Corp. and Inst. Counsel 1990-97), FBA (pres. Birmingham chpt. 1968-69), Washington Met. Area Corp. Counsel Assn. (bd. dirs. 1983-86), Internat. Bar Assn., Bar Assn. D.C. (dir. 1977-80), Am. Corp. Counsel Assn., The Barristers, The Lawyers Club, Mil. Order of Carabao, John Carroll Soc., Am. Gas Assn. (legal com., chmn. editl. bd. Regulation of Gas Industry publ. 1978-87), W. Va. Bar Assn. Roman Catholic.

CARROLL, LUCY ELLEN, choral director, music coordinator, educator; b. N.Y.C., Oct. 11; d. Edward Joseph and Lucy Sophie (Czapszys) C. B in Music Edn., Temple U., 1968; MA, Trenton State Coll., 1973; D in Musical Arts, Combs Coll. Music, Phila., 1982. Cert. tchr. music, N.J., Pa., Nat. Cert., 1991. Tchr. music Log Coll. Jr. High Sch., Pa., 1968-72, Ind. (Pa.) High Sch., 1972-73; tchr. music William Tennent High Sch., Warminster, Pa., 1973-98, dir. mus. theater, 1973-98; choir dir. St. John Bosco Parish Choir, 1999—; music coord. Centennial Schs., 1991-98; founder, dir. Madrigal Singers, Warminster, Pa., 1971-98; choral dir. Cabrini Coll., Radnor, Pa., 1974-77, First Day Singers, Phila., 1979-83, Combs Coll. of Music, Phila., 1981-84, 87-88; choral adjudicator various Music festivals, 1973—; organist, Carmel of Phila, 1997—; theatre dir., Villa Joseph Marie (Holland), 1998-99; guest lectr. mus. seminars, convs., and writers' confs.; del. Internat. Arts Conf., Cambridge, Eng., 1992; columnist Polyphony mag.; scholar in residence Pa. Hist. and Mus. Commn. for Ephrata Hist. Site, 1999; Commonwealth Spkr. 2000, Pa. Humanities Coun. Singer (operas Ambler Festival) Street Scene, 1970, Death of Bishop of Brindisi (premiere); (Robin Hood Dell) La Boheme; dir. (jazz theater piece N.Y.C.) Murder of Agamemnon, 1980, (musi. drama) Power of Love (1705), 1986, (outdoor music theater) Vorspiel (Pa. Historic Commn. 1989); contbr. articles to profl. jours., also sci. fiction to sci. fiction mags. and anthologies. Recipient awards Writers of Future, 1985, 87, Andrew Ferraro award Combs Coll. Music, 1989, plaque for svc. to music Bucks County Commr., 1991, Disting. Citizen prize Southampton Twp., 1994, Harmony award Country Gentlemen Nat. Soc. for Preservation and Encouragement Barbershop Quartet Singing in Am., 1994; Scholar-In-Residence, Pa. Hist. and Museum Commn.; named Humanities Spkr. for 2000, Pa. Humanities Coun. Mem. Am. Choral Dirs. Assn., Sci. Fiction Fantasy Writers of Am., Theatre Assn. Pa., Del. Valley Composers (choral cons. 1988-90), Hist. Soc. Pa., Smithsonian Assocs., Music Fund Soc. of Phila., The Soc. for Am. Music, Pa. Music Educators Assn. (adv. bd. 1986-87), Ephrata Cloister Assocs., Sigma Alpha Iota. Republican. Roman Catholic. Avocations: travel, writing fiction. E-mail: LucyCarroll@worldnet.att.net. Home: 712 High Ave Hatboro PA 19040-2418

CARROLL, PATRICK THOMAS, communications executive; b. Bury St. Edmonds, Suffolk, Eng., July 12, 1956; 1 child from a previous marriage, Christopher; m. Kazue Mori; children: Sean, Alex. HND in Applied Physics, Stafford Poly., Eng., 1977; BSc, Southbank Poly., Eng., 1981. Sys. engr. Eddystone (Marconi), Eng., 1977-78; sys. engr., mgr. Marconi Comms., Eng., 1978-83; exec. Japan European Union, Japan, 1983-85; country mgr. Japan Marconi Ltd., Eng. and Japan, 1985—; rep. dir. BAE Sys. (formerly Marconi (Japan) Ltd.), Japan, 1994—; dir. GEC-Plessey Semiconductors, Japan, 1992-97; telecoms spokesman European Bus. Cmty., Japan, 1989—; expert mem. Japanese Ministry Posts and Telecom, 1990—; interpreter Royal Navy, Japan, 1995—. Mem. Brit. C. of C. Japan. (pres.), IEE (chartered engr.), Order of Brit. Empire. Avocations: sailing, diving, biking. Office: BAE Sys 8F Shin Toyo Aoyama Bldg, 7-1-15 Akasaka Minato-ku, Tokyo 107-0052, Japan

CARROLL, RAY DEAN, SR., veterinarian; b. Barry, Tex., Oct. 19, 1927; s. James William and Blanche Estelle (Jordan) C.; m. Lula Pearl Mayfield, June 6, 1957; children: James William, Ray Dean Jr. Assoc., Hillsboro Jr. Coll., 1948; BS in Animal Sci., Tex. A&M U., 1950, DVM, 1957. Vet. Carroll & Harpe Animal Hosp., Corsicana, Tex., 1957—; instr. Navarro Coll., Corsicana, 1970-95. Author: Beef Cattle Science Handbook, vol. 16, 1979. Mem. found. bd. Navarro Coll., 1985—, vice-chmn., trustee, 1990. With USN, 1945-46, 51-52. Mem. AVMA, Tex. Polled Hereford Assn. (pres. 1992-96), Navarro County Ext. Beef Commn. (chmn. 1960—). Democrat. Methodist. Home: 2203 Highland Cir Corsicana TX 75110-1611 Office: Carroll & Harper Animal Hosp 2508 W 2nd Ave Corsicana TX 75110-2520

CARROLL, THOMAS COLAS, lawyer, educator; b. Phila., Jan. 5, 1943; s. George Colas and Mary F. (Dempsey) C.; m. Peg Kelly, June 19, 1966; children: Kevin, Beth Ann. BS, St. Joseph's U., 1964; JD, Villanova U., 1967. Bar: Pa. 1967, U.S. Ct. Appeals (3d cir.) 1967, U.S. Ct. Appeals (D.C. cir.) 1988, U.S. Ct. Appeals (11th cir.) 1990, U.S. Supreme Ct. 1975. Assoc. Wolf, Block, Schorr & Solis-Cohen, Phila., 1967-69; staff atty., chief of family div., asst. chief fed. div. Defender Assn. of Phila., 1969-75; ptnr. Carroll

Creamer Carroll & Duffy, Phila., 1975-80, Carroll & Carroll, Phila., 1980-89; sole practitioner Phila., 1989-93; ptnr. Carroll & Cedrone, Phila., 1993—; adj. prof. law Villanova (Pa.) U., 1972—; lectr. Pa. Trial Lawyers Assn., Pa. Criminal Def. Lawyers Assn.; chmn. criminal justice act selection com. for ea. dist. Pa., 1980-89. Assoc. editor Law Review. Mem. Am. Arbitration Assn. (arbitrator), U. Pa. Am. Inn of Ct., Order of the Coif. Avocation: sailing. Office: Pub Ledger Bldg Ste94 150 S Independence Mall W Philadelphia PA 19106-3413

CARROLL, WILLIAM MACEWAN, neurologist, researcher; b. Perth, Australia, Feb. 23, 1949; s. Ian McEwan and Edith Marion (Rymer) C.; m. Kathryn Suzanne Monger, Feb. 1, 1974; children: Gemma Kathryn, Bonita Louise, Laura Jane. MBBS, U. West Australia, 1973, MD, 1985. Rsch. registrar Nat. Hosp. Queen Sq., London, 1978-80; assoc. vis. prof. U. Pa., Phila., 1980, U. Calif., Irvine, 1980; cons. neurologist SCGH, Perth, 1981—. Fellow Royal Australasian Coll. Physicians; mem. Australian Assn. Neurologists (councillor 1991-97, pres. 1998—), Multiple Sclerosis Soc. West Australia (med. dir. 1996-99), Multiple Sclerosis Soc. Australia (chmn. med. rsch. adv. bd. 1999—). Avocation: golf. Office: Subiaco Clinic, 25 McCourt St, Subiaco, Perth 6008, Australia

CARROW, MILTON MICHAEL, lawyer, educator; b. N.Y.C., Sept. 13, 1912; s. Samuel and Ethel (Berlin) C.; m. Betsey Wood Hall, Nov. 2, 1940 (div. 1968); children: David M., Thomas E., Deborah, James H., Emily W.; m. Eve Wagner Cooper; Feb. 28, 1969 (div. 1986); m. Barbara M. Barski, Nov. 2, 1996. AB, Syracuse U., 1933, postgrad., 1933-34; JD, Harvard U., 1937. Bar: N.Y. 1938. Assoc. Legal Aid Soc., Rochester, N.Y., 1937-38, Lincoln Epworth & Nathan Sweedler, 1938-42, Emil Schlesinger, 1946-48; pvt. practice, 1948-53; ptnr. Lavine & Carrow, N.Y.C., 1953-59, Landis, Carrow, Benson & Tucker, N.Y.C., 1959-70, Carrow, Bernson, Hoeniger, Freitag & Abbey, 1970-73; dir. Ctr. for Adminstrv. Justice, ABA, 1973-77, Nat. Center for Adminstrv. Justice, Consortium of Univs. of Washington Met. Area, 1977-79; pres. Nat. Center for Adminstrv. Justice, 1979-82; adj. asst. prof. Law Sch. NYU, 1964-68; vis. prof. Nat. Law Ctr., George Washington U., 1973-80; adj. prof. Georgetown U. Law Ctr., 1980-81; rsch. prof. pub. policy George Washington U., 1983—; mem. faculty appellate judges seminar Inst. Jud. Adminstrn., 1969, 70; cons. Nat. Adv. Com. Civil Disorders, 1967; vice chmn. Weston (Conn.) Charter Commn., 1965-66; counsel UN We Believe, 1962-72; vis. intervenor XVIII Internat. Congress of Adminstrv. Scis., Madrid, 1980; U.S. rep. to standing com. on law and sci. of pub. adminstrn. Internat. Inst. Adminstrv. Scis., 1982; cons. Block Island Charter Commn., 1988-89. Author: Background of Administrative Law, 1948, The Licensing Power in New York City, 1968, (with J.D. Nyhart) Law and Science in Collaboration, 1983; editor: (with Robert Paul Churchill and Joseph J. Cordes) Democracy, Social Values and Public Policy, 1998; also articles; editor Working Paper series, Grad. Program in Public Policy, 1985—. Dir. Washington Cir., George Washington U., 1988—. With AUS, 1943-46. Mem. ABA (chmn. sect. adminstrv. law 1971-72), Assn. of Bar of City of N.Y. (chmn. com. adminstrv. law 1964-67). Home: 914 25th St NW Washington DC 20037-2101 Office: George Washington Univ 2201 G St NW Rm 507 Washington DC 20052-0001

CARRUBBA, SALVATORE, journalist, art consultant; b. Catania, Italy, May 19, 1951; s. Concetto and Carmela (Ragusa) C.;m. Luisa De Martin; children: Carlotta, Tecla. Degree in law, U. Milan, 1974. Dep. editor Mondo Economico, Milan, 1984-86, editor-in-chief, 1990-93; dep. editor Il Sole 24 Ore, Milan, 1987-90, editor-in-chief, 1993-96, group mng. editor, journalist editor, 1997—. Author: (with Piero Bairati) La Trasparenza Difficile, 1990; Una Bussola per Il Nord, 1993. Counsellor for arts Town of Milan, 1997. Recipient goldene Ehrenfeichen award Govt. of Austria, 1997. Mem. Rotary Internat. Home: Viale Majno, 20123 Milan Italy Office: Il Sole 24 Ore, Via Tiziano 32, 20154 Milan Italy

CARSELLO, CARMEN JOSEPH, psychologist, educator; b. Chgo., July 16, 1915; s. Joseph and Mary Domenica (Tomasone) C.; m. Nicoletta Dalesio, June 18, 1939; children: Camille (dec.), Frank, Robert. BPE, DePaul U., 1938, MA, 1953; PhD, U. Sarasota, 1971; degree in gerontology, U. Ill., 1983. Registered psychologist, Ill. Tchr. parochial schs., Chgo., 1939-42; tchr. pub. schs., Cicero, Ill., 1942-43, Chgo., 1950-57; reading specialist Bur. Child Study Pub. Schs., Chgo., 1957-63; counselor, reading specialist U. Ill., Chgo., 1963-85, prof. emeritus, 1985—; prof. emeritus Nat.-Louis U., Evanston, Ill., 1986—; prof. emeritus psychology Triton Coll., River Grove, Ill., 1986-88. Contbr. articles to profl. jours. Vol. Loyola U., Chgo., 1960—; northwest rep. Mont-Clare Leyden Srs., Chgo., St. Williams Srs., 1985—; mem. career com. Joint Civic Com. Italian Ams., Chgo., 1985; pres. Mont Clare Leyden Srs., Chgo., 1989-91, St. Williams Srs., Chgo., 1989-91. Served with USN, 1943-45, PTO. Recipient Service award Loyola U., Chgo., WWII Victory medal, Asian Pacific Campaign medal, Philippine Liberation ribbon, Cook County Sheriff's Sr. Medal of Honor award, 1999, Chgo. Sr. Citizens Hall of Fame Cert. of Honor, 2000. Mem. Internat. Reading Assn., Chgo. Psychol. Assn., Asian-Am. Literacy Assn. of Internat. Reading Assn., U. Ill. Retirement Assn., U. Ill. Scholarship Assn., Chgo. Area Reading Assn., Gregroians Tchrs. Assn. (various offices Chgo. chpt.). Roman Catholic. Avocations: reading, swimming, dancing, travel, photography. Home and Office: 2154 N Nordica Ave Chicago IL 60707-3231

CARSON, ELLEN GODBEY, lawyer; b. Kingsport, Tenn., Apr. 30, 1955; d. Lewis Anderson and Doris Louise (Dempsey) C.; m. Robert Carson Godbey, June 2, 1979. BA, U. Tenn., Knoxville, 1976; JD, Harvard U., 1980. Consumer complaint specialist FTC, Boston, 1980; atty. civil rights divsn. HHS, Washington, 1980-81; assoc. Landis, Cohen, Rauh & Zelenko, Washington, 1981-87, Paul Johnson Alston & Hunt, Honolulu, 1987-91, Alston Hunt Floyd & Ing, Honolulu, 1991—. Former pres., dir. D.C. Rape Crisis Ctr., Washington, Sex Abuse Treatment Ctr., Honolulu, Hale Kipa Youth Svcs., Honolulu; trustee Ctrl. Union Ch. Named Outstanding Woman Profl., YWCA, 1990. Mem. Am. Arbitration Assn. (arbitrator, mediator), Hawaii State Bar Assn. (pres., dir. 1988-90, Pro Bono award 1989), Hawaii Women Lawyers (pres., dir. 1989-90, Women Lawyer of Yr. 1992), Hawaii Justice Found. (v.p., dir. 1996-2000), Inst. Human Svcs. (pres., dir. 1996-2000). Avocations: scuba, quilting. Office: Alston Hunt Floyd & Ing 18th Fl Pacific Tower 1001 Bishop St Ste 1800 Honolulu HI 96813-3689

CARSON, GORDON BLOOM, engineering executive; b. High Bridge, N.J., Aug. 1, 1911; s. Whitfield R. and Emily (Bloom) C.; m. Beth Lacy, June 19, 1937 (dec. Mar. 1998); children—Richard Whitfield, Emily Elizabeth (Mrs. Lee A. Duffus), Alice Lacy (Mrs. William P. Allman), Jeanne Helen (Mrs. Michael J. Gable). BSMechE, Case Inst. Tech., 1931, D Engring., 1957; MS, Yale U., 1932, ME, 1938; LLD, Rio Grande Coll., 1973. With Western Electric Co., 1930; instr. mech. engring. Case Inst. Tech., 1932-37, asst. prof., 1937-40, asso. prof. indsl. engring. charge indsl. div., 1940-44; with Am. Shipbldg. Co., 1936; patent litigation, 1937; research engr., dir. research Cleve. Automatic Machine Co., 1939-44; asst. to gen. mgr. Selby Shoe Co., 1944, mgr. engring., 1945-49, sec. of corp., 1949-53; sec., dir. Pyrrole Products Co., 1948-53; dean engring. Ohio State U., Columbus, 1953-58; v.p. bus. and finance, treas. Ohio State U., 1958-71; dir. Engring. Exptl. Sta., 1953-58, Accuray Corp., 1960-82, Cardinal Funds, Inc., 1962-98; exec. v.p. Albion (Mich.) Coll., 1971-76, exec. cons., 1976-77; asst. to chancellor, dir. fin. Northwood Inst., 1977-82; v.p. Mich. Molecular Inst., 1982-88; prin. Whitfield Robert Assocs., 1988—. Editor: The Production Handbook, 1958; cons. editor, 1972—; Author of tech. papers engring. subjects. Trustee White Cross Hosp. Assn., 1960-71; bd. dirs. Cardinal Funds, 1966-98; bd. d irs. Goodwill Industries, 1959-67, 1st v.p., 1963-64; bd. dirs. Orton Found., 1953-58; v.p. Ohio State U. Rsch. Found., 1958-71; v.p., chmn. adv. com. Ctr. for Automation and Soc., U. Ga., 1969-71; Chmn. tool and die com. 5th Regional War Labor Bd., 1943-45; chmn. Ohio State adv. com. for sci., tech. and specialized personnel SSS, 1965-70; pres. Larkin Parking Condo Assn., Inc., 1992—. Fellow ASME, AAAS, Inst. Indsl. Engrs. (pres. 1957-58); mem. Columbus Soc. Fin. Analysts (pres. 1974-75), Fin. Analysts Fedn. (bd. dirs. 1964-65), C. of C. (bd. dirs., treas. 1952-53), Am. Soc. Engring. Edn., Assn. Univs. for Rsch. in Astronomy (bd. dirs. 1958-71), Midwestern Univs. Rsch. Assn. (bd. dirs. 1958-71), U.S. Naval Inst., Nat. Soc. Profl. Engrs. (life), Romophos, Sphinx, Sigma Xi (fin. com. 1975-89, nat. treas. 1979-89), Masons (32 deg.), Tau Beta Pi, Zeta Psi, Phi Eta Sigma, Alpha Pi Mu, Omicron Delta Epsilon. Office: Whitfield Robert Assocs 5413 Gardenbrook Dr Midland MI 48642-3402

CARSON, STEVEN LEE, newspaper publisher; b. N.Y.C., Mar. 23, 1943; s. Harold and Mathilde (Seidel) C.; m. Yvonne DeDrozizhki, Aug. 8, 1971 (dec. Feb. 1980). BA, NYU, 1964, MA, 1965. Archivist, conf. dir. Nat. Archives, Washington, 1967-73; chmn. White House Conf. Pres. & Children, Washington, 1974; editor, writer Manuscript Soc. News, Washington, 1987—; conf. dir. The Manuscript Soc., 1974-80; dir. history pavilion Hall of Fame Great Am., N.Y.C., 1964; editor Pres. Commn. Civil Disorders, Washington, 1968; TV commentator, lectr. in field. Author: Maximilien Robespierre, 1988, (plays) The Last Lincoln, Princess Alice; contbr. articles to profl. jours. Speechwriter The White House, U.S. Congress, Md. Ho. Dels., 1974—. Ford Found. fellow, 1964, Johns Hopkins U. Chas Carroll Fulton fellow, 1965; grantee Md. Commn. Humanities, 1986, 87, U.S. Dept. Interior, 1985; recipient NYU Heights Daily News Alumni award, 1964, Archival medal Republic of Korea, 1972, Internat. Psychohistory Assn. award, 1983, Lincoln Group of N.Y. award, 1988, 92, Man of the Mo. award Washington Bus. Jour., 1989, Surratt Soc. award, 1993; delivered ofcl. Lincoln Day Address, Ford's Theatre, Washington, 1996, Smithsonian lectr., 1999—; named Man of Month Washington Bus. Jour., 1989. Fellow The Manuscript Soc.; mem. Nat. Press Club, Nat. Writers Union, Lincoln Group D.C. (pres. 1985-88), Wash. Ind. Writers, Lincoln Forum (trustee 1997—), Abraham Lincoln Inst. of the Mid. Atlantic (trustee 1997—), Lincoln Group Ill. (trustee 1986-91), NYU Hon. Soc., NYU Perstare et Praestare, NYU Soc. of the Torch. Avocation: collecting historic manuscripts & letters. Office: The Manuscript News 8811 Colesville Rd Ste 506 Silver Spring MD 20910-4332

CARSTAIRS, KARI SIGRID, clinical psychologist; b. Princeton, N.J., June 27, 1961; came to England, 1970; d. John Griggs and Diane Ella (Oenning) Thompson; m. Philip Justin Carstairs, June 2, 1986; children: Benjamin Thomas, Daniel Philip. BA (hons.), Oxford UNiv., 1981; D in psy., Widener Univ., 1991. Psychologist Phila. Child Guidance Clinic, Phila., 1991, Maidstone Priority Care NHS Trust, Maidstone, Eng., 1991-96, Oxleas NHS Trust, Bexley, Eng., 1996-98; psychologist in pvt. practice, Maidstone, 1993-98, Bromley, 1998—. Contbr. articles to profl. jours. Office: 7 Mayfield Rd, Bromley BR1 2HB, England

CARSTENS, JOHANN CHRISTIAAN, minister; b. Pretoria, Gauteng, South Africa, Jan. 7, 1947; s. Hendrik Gideon and Aletta Lourenza H. (DuToit) C.; m. Elizabeth Maria Lombard, Dec. 8, 1978; children: Johann Christiaan, Stefan Alexander, Tertius Christo, Rudolf Paul. BA, U. Pretoria, 1967, BD, 1970. Min. Dutch Reformed Ch., Villieria, Pretoria, 1972-75; camp organizer Dutch Reformed Ch.-Synod No. Transvaal, 1976-79; youth min. Dutch Reformed Ch.-Pietersburg North, South Africa, 1979-87; min. Dutch Reformed Ch.-Wierdapark South, Centurion, 1988—; scribe DRC Synod No. Transvaal, 1991-97, vice chmn. 1997—; scribe Commn. New Hymn Book DRC Gen. Synod, 1996—. Editor: Jeugsangbundel 2, 1993; co-author: History Afikaans Protestant Hymns, 1983. Named Youth Leader of Yr. Philatelic Fedn. So. Africa, 1995. Mem. Dendrological Soc. (chmn. 1995-97), South African Choral Soc. (treas. 1994-97, pres. 1997-2000), Afrikaans Philat. Soc. (sec. 1988—), Centurion Stamp Mates (leader), Philat. Fedn. So. Africa (pres. 1999-2000). Avocations: choral singing, stamps, Dendrology. Office: PO Box 52011, Wierdapark, Centurion 0149, South Africa

CARTA, RENZO MARIO S., chemical engineer, educator, researcher; b. Bonorva, Sardinia, Italy, July 27, 1950; s. Francesco and Maria (Soddu) C.; m. Raffaela Anna Pitzalis, May 11, 1999; 1 child, Francesca. PhD, State U., Cagliari, 1975. Prof. U. Cagliari, 1982—. Contbr. more than 30 articles to profl. jours. Home: Via Col d'Echele, 09122 Cagliari Sardinia, Italy Office: Dept Di Ingegneria Chimica, Piazza d'Armi, 09123 Cagliari Sardinia, Italy

CARTAGENA, FRANCISCO J., engineering executive; b. Bucaramanga, Colombia, May 18, 1966; s. Francisco A. and Angela (Mutis) C.; m. Sandra Florez, Dec. 17, 1987 (div. Oct. 1995); m. Sandra Lucia Alvarado, June 29, 1996; 1 child, Alejandra Cartagen. Degree indsl. engring., UIS, Bucaramanga, 1988; MBA, U. Miami, 1990. Mktg. mgr. N. Cartagena G. E. Hisos, Bucaramanga, Colombia, 1987-88, systems mgr., 1990-91, dir. engring., 1991—; bd. dirs. Conrepsa, Bogota. Amb. Great Lodge of Los Andes, 1995. Avocations: golfing, fishing, camping. Office: Nepomuceno Cartagena, GE Hisos, CRA 30 #14-12, Bogota Colombia

CARTELLA, PAOLO, electronics company executive; b. Reggio Calabria, Italy, July 8, 1967; s. Francesco and Maria Lucia (Pratticó) C. Degree in Fgn. Lang., U. Messina, Italy, 1993; MBA, U Trieste, Italy, 1994. Comml. asst. Marzotio Spa, Valdagno, Italy, 1994-95; export exec. Agrumaria Reggina, Reggio Calabria, 1995-97; export dir. Visa Electronics, Rome, 1997—. Avocations: reading, teenis, gymnastics. Home: Via Dei Veralli 20, 00163 Rome Italy Office: Visa Electronics, Via di Santa Cornelia 11, 00060 Formello Rome, Italy

CARTER, ANTHONY MICHAEL, physiology educator; b. Cowes, Isle of Wight, Eng., Mar. 28, 1942; arrived in Denmark, 1976; s. Alfred Douglas and Betty Audrey (Goodship) C.; m. Cathrine Sjöberg, 1965 (div. 1974); 1 child, Susanna; m. Inger Birgitta Grund, Jan. 5, 1980; 1 child, Jessica. BA, Cambridge (Eng.) U., 1964, MA, 1968; Fil. Lic., U. (Sweden) Lund, 1969, PhD, 1970. Asst. prof. U. Lund, 1970-76; assoc. prof. U. So. Denmark, Odense, 1976-88, dean medicine, 1987-88, sr. assoc. prof., 1988—; adj. prof. U. Western Ont., Can., 1999—. Author: An Introduction to Animal Physiology, 1984; contbr. articles to profl. jours. Mem. Am. Physiol. Soc., Internat. Fedn. Placenta Assns. (mem. exec. com.), Soc. Gynecologic Investigation, Physiol. Soc. Office: U So Odense/Physiol & Pharm, Winsloewparken 21, DK-5000 Odense Denmark

CARTER, BARRY EDWARD, lawyer, educator, administrator; b. L.A., Oct. 14, 1942; s. Byron Edward and Ethel Catherine (Turner) C.; m. Kathleen Anne Ambrose, May 17, 1987; children: Gregory Ambrose, Meghan Elisabeth. A.B. with great distinction, Stanford U., 1964; M.P.A., Princeton U., 1966; J.D., Yale U., 1969. Bar: Calif. 1970, D.C. 1972. Program analyst Office of Sec. Def., Washington, 1969-70; mem. staff NSC, Washington, 1970-72; rsch. fellow Kennedy Sch., Harvard U., Cambridge, Mass., 1972; internat. affairs fellow Coun. on Fgn. Rels., 1972; assoc. Wilmer, Cutler & Pickering, Washington, 1973-75; sr. counsel Select Com. on Intelligence Activities, U.S. Senate, Washington, 1975; assoc. Morrison & Foerster, San Francisco, 1976-79; assoc. prof. law Georgetown U. Law Ctr., Washington, 1979-89, prof., 1989-93, 96—; exec. dir. Am. Soc. Internat. Law, Washington, 1992-93; acting undersec. for export adminstrn. U.S. Dept. Commerce, Washington, 1993-94, deputy undersec., 1994-96; vis. prof. law Stanford U. Law Sch., 1990; bd. dirs. Nukem, Inc., 1998—; chmn. adv. bd. Def. Budget Project, 1990-93; mem. UN Assn. Soviet-Am. Parallel Studies Project, 1976-87. Author: International Economic Sanctions: Improving the Haphazard U.S. Legal Regime, 1988 (Am. Soc. Internat. Law Cert. of Merit 1989); co-author: International Law, 3d edit., 1999; contbr. articles to profl. jours. With U.S. Army, 1969-71. Mem. ABA, Am. Bar Found., Calif. Bar Assn., D.C. Bar Assn., Coun. on Fgn. Rels., Am. Soc. Internat. Law (hon. v.p. 1993-99, counselor, 1999-2000), Phi Beta Kappa. Democrat. Roman Catholic. Home: 2922 45th St NW Washington DC 20016-3559 Office: Georgetown U Law Ctr 600 New Jersey Ave NW Washington DC 20001-2075

CARTER, DAVID EDWARD, communications executive; b. Ashland, Ky., Nov. 24, 1942; s. Victor Byron and Lillie Elzena (Clarke) C.; m. Linda Louise Gibson, May 31, 1969; children: Christa Ann, Lauren Louise. AB, U. Ky., 1965; MS, Ohio U., 1967; MBA, Syracuse U., 1995; SMM, Harvard Bus. Sch., 1995, OPM, Harvard Bus Sch., 1998. Dir. advt. Wheeler & Williams Co., Ashland, 1965-66; instr. U. Ky., 1967-70; dir. communications Ky. Electric Steel Co., Ashland, 1970-77; pres. David E. Carter Inc., Ashland, 1977—; pres. Hollywood Ky. Corp. div. David E. Carter Inc., Ashland, Bangkok, Jakarta, Caracas, Hong Kong, 1986—; bd. dirs. Home Fed. Savs. & Loan Assn., Ashland, Decathlon Corp., Hanover Pub. Co.; exec. adv. bd. Ohio U. Sch. Bus.; alumni bd. dirs. U. Ky. Sch. Journalism; adj. prof. Thammasat U., Bangkok, 1992—. Scoutmaster, Tri-State Area Council Boy Scouts Am., 1970-77, dist. commr., 1977-78, recipient dist. award of merit, 1975, Recipient Clio award, N.Y.C., 1980, Disting. Alumnus award Ashland Community Coll., 1990. Mem. Nat. Acad. TV Arts and Scis. (3 Emmys for writing TV programs 1987), N.Y. Art Dirs. Club (2 Emmys for producing pub. TV program 1990, Am. Inst. Graphic Arts. Republican. Methodist. Author: It's Not the Money—It's The Principle, 1975, Book of American Trade Marks, 11 vols., 1972-89, Designing Corporate Symbols, 1975, Corporate Identity Manuals, 1976, Letterheads 7 vols., 1977-89, Ideas for Editors, 1977, Letterheads 5 vols. 1979-89, American Corporate Identity 5 vols. 1985-89, Designing Corporate Identity for Small Companies, 1985, How to Improve Your Corporate Identity, 1986, Logos of Major American Companies, 1989, International Corporate Design Symbols, 1990, Logos of Major World Corporations, 1990, World Corporate Identity, 1990; writer, producer: (TV series) Sassafrass, 1987-88; producer more than 12 sketches for The Johnny Carson Show, 1989-91 (2 Emmys, 1991). Avocations: sports collectibles, golf, photography. Home: 4727 Southern Hills Dr Ashland KY 41102-8213 also: 3225 W Gulf Dr Unit B301 Sanibel FL 33957-7700 Office: PO Box 2500 Ashland KY 41105-2500

CARTER, EDWARD GRAYDON, editor; b. Canada, July 14, 1949; s. E.P. and Margaret Ellen C.; m. Cynthia Williamson, 1982; 4 children. Student, Carleton U., U. Ottawa. Editor The Can. Rev., 1973-77; writer Time, 1978-83, Life, N.Y.C., 1983-86; founder, editor Spy, 1986-91; editor N.Y. Observer, 1991-92; hon. editor Harvard Lampoon, 1989; editor in chief Vanity Fair, N.Y.C., 1992—. Mem. Washington (Conn.) Club. Avocation: fly fishing. Office: Vanity Fair 4 Times Sq Fl 7 New York NY 10036-6522

CARTER, GERALD EMMETT, retired archbishop; b. Montreal, Que., Can., Mar. 1, 1912; s. Thomas Joseph and Mary (Kelty) C. BTh, Grand Sem. Montreal, 1936; BA, U. Montreal, 1933, MA, 1940, PhD, 1947, LTh, 1950; DHL, Duquesne U., 1963; LLD (hon.), U. Western Ont., 1966, Concordia U., 1976, U. Windsor, 1977, McGill U., Montreal, 1980, Notre Dame (Ind.) U., 1981, St. Francis Xavier U., 1998; LittD, St. Mary's U., Halifax, 1980; lic. (hon.) Medieval Studies, LittD (hon.) Midieval Studies, Pontificial Inst. Medieval Studies, 1995; D of Sacred Letters (hon.), U. St. Michael's Coll., 1998; LLD (hon.), Assumption U., 1999. Ordained priest Roman Cath. Ch., 1937. Founder, prin., prof. St. Joseph Tchrs. Coll., Montreal, 1939-61; chaplain Newan Club McGill U., 1941-56; charter mem., 1st pres. Thomas More Inst. Adult Edn., Montreal, 1945-61; mem. Montreal Cath. Sch. Commn., 1948-61; hon. canon Cathedral Basilica Montreal, 1952-61; aux. bishop London and titular bishop Altiburo, 1961; bishop of London, Ont., 1964-78; archbishop of Toronto, 1978-90, ret., 1990; elevated to cardinal, 1979; Chmn. Episcopal Commn. Liturgy Can., 1966-73; mem. Consilium of Liturgy, Rome, 1965, Sacred Congregation for Divine Worship, 1970; chmn. Internat. Com. for English in the Liturgy, 1971; appointee Econ. Affairs Coun. of Holy See, 1981; vice pres. Can. Cath. Conf., 1973, Cath. Conf. of Ont., 1971-73; pres. Can. Conf. Cath. Bishops, 1975; mem. coun. Synod of Bishops, 1977. Author: The Catholic Public Schools of Quebec, 1957, Psychology and the Cross, 1959, The Modern Challenge to Religious Education, 1961, A Shepherd Speaks, 1981. Decorated companion Order of Can. Office: Chancery Office, 1155 Yonge St, Toronto, ON Canada M4T IW2

CARTER, H. JOHN, sales executive, consultant; b. Melvindale, Mich., July 24, 1932; s. John Wesley Carter and Senia Spears; m. Marie Yvonne Goltry, Apr. 4, 1959; children: Timothy John, Yvonne Marie. AA, Henry Ford C.C., Dearborn, Mich., 1956; BA in Psychology, Wayne State U., 1963; BA in Philosophy and Theology, Madonna U., Livonia, Mich., 1984. Boy's counselor Boy's Rep., Livonia, 1954-57; buyer mdse. Montgomery Ward, Allen Park, Mich., 1958-63; liaison engr. Chevrolet Engring., Warren, Mich., 1963-67; buyer products and parts Am. Motors Co., Detroit, 1967-69; dist. sales mgr. Bundy Corp. TI, Detroit, 1969-71, Higbie Mfg. Co./IIT, Rochester, Mich., 1971-94; v.p. sales, mfg. representative Tubular Products Co., Rochester Hills, Mich., 1994—. Tchr. Ch. of the Nazarene, Dearborn, 1954-89, min. music, 1982-89; bd. dirs. Ch. of the Nazarene Dist. adv. bd., Brighton, Mich., 1985-89. With USAR, 1948-52. Avocation: boating. E-mail: hictpc@aol.com. Home: 5823 N Charlesworth St Dearborn Heights MI 48127-3980

CARTER, HARRY ROBERT, fire protection consultant; b. Neptune, N.J., July 29, 1947; s. Harry Barringer and Stella (Napiorkowski) C.; m. Jacalyn Roberta Miller, Apr. 29, 1972; children: Ellen, Kathleen, Todd. AA, Brookdale Coll., 1971; BA, Thomas Edison State Coll., 1975; BS magna cum laude, Jersey City State Coll., 1976; MA, Rutgers U., 1979; PhD, Western States U., 1984. Fire fighter Rahway (N.J.) Fire Dept., 1972-73; fire fighter Newark (N.J.) Fire Dept., 1972-77, fire capt., 1977-90, battalion fire chief, 1990-97, deputy fire chief, 1997-99, ret., 1999; adj. prof. Ocean County Coll., Toms River, N.J., 1977-81; pres. Carter Fire Protection, Inc., Adelphia, N.J., 1980—; fire marshal N.J. Army Nat. Guard, 1981-91. Author: Management in the Fire Service, 1989, Managing Fire Service Finances, 1989, Understanding Fire Behavior, 1995, Strategic Planning and Fire Protection, 1996, Tactics in Fire Department Management, 1997, Firefighting Strategy and Tactics, 1998, Management in the Fire Service, 3d edit., 1998; contbr. articles to profl. jours. Vol. fire fighter, officer Howell Twp. Fire Co. # 1, Adelphia, N.J., 1971—, tng. officer, 1978-91, fire chief, 1991. Capt. USAR, 1966-96. Mem. ISFSI (bd. dirs. 1989—, 1st v.p. bd. dirs. 1999), N.J. Soc. Fire Instrs. (bd. dirs. 1978-80, pres. 1980-82), Nat. Fire Protection Assn. (adv. coun. 1975-90), Internat. Assn. Fire Chiefs (scholarship 1975-76), Internat. Assn. Fire Fighters, Wall-Spring Lake Lodge F & AM, VFW, Am. Legion, Optimist Internat. Republican. Lutheran. Avocations: military music, playing the tuba, poetry, collecting military medals. Home: PO Box 100 Adelphia NJ 07710-0100

CARTER, JAMES ALFRED, lawyer; b. Shelbyville, Tenn., June 29, 1941; s. Granville Thomas and Elaine (Thrasher) C.; m. Kathleen Shaughness, Oct. 6, 1967; children: James Byrne, Stephen Thomas. BBA, U. Tex., Arlington, 1962; JD, U. Tex., 1967. Bar: U.S. Dist. Ct. (no. dist.) Tex. 1969, U.S. Tax Ct. 1970, U.S. Ct. Claims 1977, U.S. Supreme Ct. 1980, U.S. Ct. Appeals (5th cir.) 1985; CPA, Tex. Acct. Price Waterhouse, Ft. Worth, 1967; assoc. Smith, Carter, Rose & Finley, San Angelo, Tex., 1969-71; ptnr. Smith, Carter, Rose, Finley & Griffis, San Angelo, Tex., 1971-97; pvt. practice James A. Carter & Assocs., San Angelo, 1997—; chmn. estate planning, probate and tax law Tex. Bd. Legal Specialization, Austin, Tex., 1980-84. Chmn. March of Dimes, San Angelo, 1971; pres. West Tex. Boys Ranch, San Angelo, 1980-84; mem. St. John's Hosp. Yr. 2000, San Angelo, 1980-84, Century Club YMCA, San Angelo; bd. dirs. Rio Concho Manor, San Angelo, 1980-90; trustee San Angelo Ind. Sch. Dist., 1992-98, pres., 1997-98. Capt. U.S. Army, 1968-69. Fellow Tex. Bar Found.; mem. ABA, AICPA (chmn. regional trial bd.), Tex. Bar Assn. (cert. in tax law, estate planning, probate bd. legal specialization, chmn. tax specialization, estate planning and probate specialization coms., revision bd. Tex. guardianship statute, com. inheritance and state tax), Tex. State Soc. CPA's (chmn. by-laws com.), Kiwanis (pres. 1978-79). Republican. Mem. Ch. Christ. Avocations: handball, farming. Home: 915 Montecito Dr San Angelo TX 76901-4555 Office: 515 W Harris Ave Ste 100 San Angelo TX 76903-6362

CARTER, JAMES THOMAS, contractor, pilot; b. N.Y.C., Dec. 27, 1952; s. Wendell Green and Carolyn Elizabeth (Smith) C.; m. Mary Jane Zellers, Oct. 8, 1985. Cert. airline transport pilot, flight instr., FAA, advanced open water diver, PADI. Charter pilot, flight instr. Pompano Air Ctr., Pompano Beach, Fla., 1976-78; profl. pilot Profl. Pilot Svcs., Ft. Lauderdale, Fla., 1978-79; aviation operative CIA, 1978-79; pres., pilot Carter Charter Co., Inc., Ft. Lauderdale, 1979-92; novelist Ft. Lauderdale, 1992-94; account exec. Power Line Components, Inc., Lighthouse Point, Fla., 1994-96; exec. dir. Advanced Tech., Inc., Ft. Lauderdale, 1996-99; v.p. Advanced Mgmt. Svcs. Inc., Ft. Lauderdale, 1999; mem. missile program Lockheed Missile and Space, Huntsville, Ala., 1995-99, HRC program Smithsonian Astrophys. Obs., Cambridge, Mass., 1995-96, MIL-STAR program Electromagnetic Scis., Norcross, Ga., 1995-99, J-STARS program, 1996-99, Raytheon Missile Sys., Tucson, 1997-99, GEC Marconi, Norcross, Ga., 1997, airline capt. Profl. Air Charter, Ft. Lauderdale, Fla., 2000—. Author: Operation: Deepcover, 1994, A Twist of Fate, 1995, Stiletto, 1996, (poetry) Twilight, 1995, Christmas in the Snow, 1996. Recipient Editor's Choice award Nat. Libr. Poetry, 1996, 97. Mem. Aircraft Owners and Pilots Assn., Internat. Soc. Poets (disting.). Democrat. Presbyterian. Avocations: scuba diving, sailing, motorcycling, sea planes, snow skiing. Office: Profl Air Charter 1885 W Commercial Blvd Ste 120 Fort Lauderdale FL 33309-3066

CARTER, JANE FOSTER, agriculture industry executive; b. Stockton, Calif., Jan. 14, 1927; d. Chester William and Bertha Emily Foster; m. Robert Buffington Carter, Feb. 25, 1952 (dec. Dec. 1994); children: Ann Claire

Carter Palmer, Benjamin Foster; m. Frank Anthony Bauman, Aug. 15, 1998. BA, Stanford U., 1948; MS, NYU, 1949. Pres. Colusa (Calif.) Properties, Inc., 1953—; owner Carter Land and Livestock, Colusa, 1965—; sec.-treas. Carter Farms, Inc., Colusa, 1975-94, pres., 1994—. Author: If the Walls Could Talk, Colusa's Architectural Heritage, 1988; author, editor: Colusa County Survey and Plan for the Arts, 1981, 82, 83, Implementing the Colusa County Arts Plan, 1984, 85, 86. Adv. mem. Calif. Gov.'s Commn. on Agr., Sacramento, 1979-82, Calif. Rep. Ctrl. Com., 1976-94; del. Rep. Nat. Conv., Kansas City, Mo., 1976, Detroit, 1980, Dallas, 1984; trustee Calif. Hist. Soc., 1979-89, regional v.p., 1984-89; mem. Calif. Reclamation Bd., 1982-96, sec., 1986-96; mem. Calif. Hist. Resources Commn., 1994—, vice chair, 1996-97, chair person, 1997-99; mem. Colusa Heritage Preservation Com., 1976—, chmn., 1977-83, vice chmn., 1983-91; bd. dirs. Colusa Cmty. Theatre Found., 1980-99; bd. dirs. English-Speaking Union, San Francisco, 1992—, pres. , 1993-95, v.p., 1995—; bd. dirs. The English-Speaking Union of the U.S., N.Y.C., 1995—, bd. dirs. Leland Stanford Mansion Found., Sacramento, 1992—; trustee Calif. Preservation Found., 1989-95. Recipient award of Merit for Historic Preservation Calif. Hist. Soc., 1989, Design award Calif. Preservation Found., 1990. Mem. Sacramento River Water Contractors Assn. (sec. 1992—, exec. com. 1974—), Francisca Club, Kappa Alpha Theta. Episcopalian. Avocations: travel, the arts, hist. preservation. Home and Office: 4746 River Rd Colusa CA 95932-4200

CARTER, JEANNE WILMOT, lawyer, publisher; b. Iowa City, Iowa, Oct. 25, 1950; d. John Robert and Adelaide Wilmot (Briggs) Carter; m. Daniel Halpern, Dec. 31, 1982; 1 child, Lily Wilmot. BA cum laude, Barnard Coll., N.Y.C., 1973; MFA, Columbia U., 1977; JD, Yeshiva U., N.Y.C., 1986. Bar: N.Y. 1987. Assoc. Raoul Lionel Felder, P.C., N.Y.C., 1986—; pres., co-owner, dir. Ecco Press, Hopewell, N.J., 1992—. Author: Dirt Angel, 1997, Tales from the Rain Forest, 1997; editor: On Music, 1994; contbr. articles to profl. jours. and books including Reading the Fights, N.Am. Rev., O'Henry Prize Stories 1986, Antaeus, Antioch Rev., Arts and Entertainment Law Jour., Ont. Rev., Denver Quar., Jour. Blacks in Higher Edn., others. Bd. dirs. Nat. Poetry Series, 1981—, AIDS Helping Hand, N.Y.C., 1987-95, Planned Parenthood of Mercer County, 1998—; vol. litigator Womanspace, Princeton, N.J., 1994; mem. Jr. League of N.Y.C., 1980-91. N.Y. Found. of the Arts fellow, 1989. Mem. ABA, N.Y. State Bar Assn. Home: 60 Pheasant Hill Rd Princeton NJ 08540-7502

CARTER, JIMMY (JAMES EARL CARTER, JR.), former President of the United States; b. Plains, Ga., Oct. 1, 1924; s. James Earl and Lillian (Gordy) C.; m. Rosalynn Smith, July 7, 1946; children: John William, James Earl III, Donnel Jeffrey, Amy Lynn. Student, Ga. Southwestern Coll., 1941-42, Ga. Inst. Tech., 1942-43; BS, U.S. Naval Acad., 1946 (class of 1947); postgrad., Union Coll., 1952-53; LLD (hon.), Morris Brown Coll., 1972, Morehouse Coll., 1972, U. Notre Dame, 1977, Emory U., 1979, Kwansei Gakuin U., Japan, 1981, Ga. Southwestern Coll., 1981, N.Y. Law Sch., 1985, Bates Coll., 1985, Centre Coll., 1987, Creighton U., 1987; DEng (hon.), Ga. Inst. Tech., 1979; PhD (hon.), Weizmann Inst. Sci., 1980, Tel Aviv U., 1983, Haifa U., 1987; DHL (hon.), Cen. Conn. State U., 1985. Farmer, warehouseman Plains, Ga., 1953-77; mem. Ga. Senate, 1963-67; gov. State of Ga., Atlanta, 1971-75; President of United States, 1977-81; disting. prof. Emory U., Atlanta, 1982—; leader internat. observer teams Panama, 1989, Nicaragua, 1990, Dominican Republic, 1990, Haiti, 1990; host peace negotiations Ethiopia, 1989. Author: Why Not the Best?, 1975, A Government as Good as Its People, 1977, Keeping Faith/Memoirs of a President, 1982, Negotiation: The Alternative to Hostility, 1984, The Blood of Abraham, 1985, (with Rosalynn Carter) Everything to Gain: Making the Most of the Rest of Your Life, 1987, An Outdoor Journal, 1988, Turning Point: A Candidate, A State, and a Nation Come of Age, 1992, Talking Peace: A Vision for the Next Generation, 1993, Always a Reckoning, 1995. Mem. Sumter County (Ga.) Sch. Bd., 1955-62, chmn., 1960-62; mem. Americus and Sumter County Hosp. Authority, 1956-70; mem. Sumter County (Ga.) Library Bd., 1961; chmn. congl. campaign com. Dem. Nat. Com., 1974; founder Carter Ctr. Emory U., 1982; bd. dirs. Habitat for Humanity, 1984-87; chmn. bd. trustees Carter Ctr., Inc., 1986—, Carter-Menil Human Rights Found., 1986—, Global 2000 Inc., 1986—; chmn. Coun. of Freely-Elected Heads of Govt., 1986—; chmn. Coun. Internat. Negotiation Network, 1991—. Served to lt. USN, 1946-53. Recipient Gold medal Internat. Inst. Human Rights, 1979, Internat. Mediation medal Am. Arbitration Assn., 1979, Martin Luther King Jr. Nonviolent Peace prize, 1979, Internat. Human Rights award Synagogue Coun. Am., 1979, Conservationist of Yr. award, 1979, Harry S. Truman Pub. Svc. award, 1981, Ansel Adams Conservation award Wilderness Soc., 1982, Disting. Svc. award So. Bapt. Conv., 1982, Human Rights award Internat. League for Human Rights, 1983, World Meth. Peace award, 1985, Albert Schweitzer prize for Humanitarianism, 1987, Edwin C. Whitehead award Nat. Ctr. for Health Edn., 1989, Jefferson award Am. Inst. Pub. Svc., 1990, Phila. Liberty medal, 1990, Spirit of Am. award Nat. Coun. for Social Studies, 1990, Physicians for Social Responsibility award, 1991, Aristotle prize Alexander S. Onassis Found., 1991, Félix Houphouët-Boigny Peace prize UNESCO, 1995. Office: Carter Ctr 1 Copenhill 453 Freedom Pkwy NE Atlanta GA 30307-1406

CARTER, JOHN DALE, organizational development executive; b. Tuskegee, Ala., Apr. 9, 1944; s. Arthur L. and Ann (Bargyh) C.; m. Veronica Louise Helen Hopper, Oct. 12, 1986; children: Annelise Grace, Hopper Carter. AB, Ind. U., 1965, MS, 1967; PhD (NDEA fellow), Case Western Res. U., 1974. Dir. student affairs Dental Sch. Case Western Res. U., Cleve., 1974-75, asst. prof. applied behavioral sci., 1974-90, asst. dean orgn. devel. and student affairs, 1975-78; pres. John D. Carter and Assocs., Inc., Cleve., 1969—; ptnr. Portsmouth Cons. Group, 1984—; chmn. bd. Gestalt Inst. Cleve., 1974-80, chmn. orgn. and systems devel. program, 1980—, program dir., fin. dir. 1981-86, dir. corp. svcs., 1989-95, dean of faculty, 1992-96; pres. Orgn. and Systems Devel. Ctr., 1996—; mem. exec. bd. Nat. Tng. Labs., 1975-78; faculty Am. U., 1980-90, 94-96; mem. Nat. Tng. Labs., 1976—; bd. dirs. Behavioral Sci. Found., Cleve., Orgn. Devel. Network, 1999—; exec. bd. Fielding Inst., 1987-89; preceptor Shri Ram Chandra Mission, Sahag Marg Meditation, 1993—; Gestalt Inst. Cleve., 1996—; bd. mem. ODN Orgn. Devel. Network, 1999—. Author: Counselling the Helping Relationship, 1975, Managing the Merger Integration Process, 1986, Institutionalizing Change, 1995. Hon. fellow Gestalt Inst. Cleve., 1999. Fellow Gestalt Inst. of Cleve. (hon.); mem. Internat. Assn. Applied Social Scientists (cert. cons. Internat.), Kappa Alpha Psi (pres. Alpha chpt. 1964-65), Alpha Phi Omega. Home and Office: 2232 Harcourt Dr Cleveland OH 44106-4622

CARTER, JOHN NORMAN, endocrinologist, educator; b. Melbourne, Australia, Dec. 28, 1944; s. Norman and Vida (Robertson) C.; m. Merren Joan Rawson, May 3, 1975; four children. BSc in Medicine, U. Sydney, Australia, 1967, MBBS, 1969; MD, U. NSW, Australia, 1976. Resident, sr. med. registrar RNS Hosp., Sydney, 1969-72; fellow St. Vincent's Hosp., Sydney, 1973-75; postgrad. fellow U. Man., Winnipeg, Can., 1975-77; dir. endocrine unit Concord Hosp., Sydney, 1977-83; cons. endocrinologist Concord and Hornsby Hosps., Sydney, 1983—; clin. assoc. prof. U. Sydney; chmn. Commonwealth Ministerial Adv. Com. on Diabetes, 1995-99. Decorated officer Order of Australia. Fellow Royal Australasian Coll. Physicians; mem. Endocrine Soc. Australia, Australian Diabetes Soc. (past pres.). Avocations: golf, tennis, reading. Office: 39 Palmerston Rd, Hornsby NSW 2077, Australia

CARTER, KATHLEEN JANET JAN (JAN CARTER), sociologist; b. Perth, Australia, Oct. 29, 1941; d. Alexander Nathan and Kathleen Maude (Power) C. BA, U. Melbourne, 1967; MSc, London U., 1983; MPhil, U. Wester Australia, 1990. Prin. investigator Nat. Inst. Social Work, London, 1976-83; dir. Brotherhood of St. Laurence, 1986-92; prof., head social work Melbourne U., Australia, 1992-94; prof., dir. Deakin U., Melbourne, 1994&. Mem. Australian Assn. Social Workers. Avocations: philanthropy, arts, travel, writing, food. Office: Deakin Human Svcs Australia, 336 Glenferrie Rd, Malvern 3144, Australia

CARTER, LOUVENIA MCGEE, nursing educator; b. Bradley, Oct. 12, 1934; d. Henry Battle and Emma (Cox) McGee; m. Harvey L. Carter Jr., Jan. 15, 1956; children: Harvey III, Christopher, Richard, Robert. Diploma, Northwestern State Coll., Natchitoches, La., 1955; BSN, Northwestern State Coll., 1961; MSN, Northwestern State U. La., 1979; PhD, Tex. Women's U., 1990. Svc. dir. Upjohn Health Care Svcs., Shreveport, La., 1979-81; staff nurse VA Med. Ctr., Shreveport, 1955-56, 60, 82; assoc. prof. Northwestern State U., Shreveport, 1982-97. Mem. ANA (cert. in nursing adminstrn.), Nat. Conf. Gerontol. Nurse Practitioners, Sigma Theta Tau. Home: 830 Erie St Shreveport LA 71106-1506

CARTER, MICHAEL ANDREW, missionary center administrator; b. Eureka, Calif., Dec. 29, 1960; s. Walter Charles and Julia May Carter; m. Karla Ann Hobson, Oct. 27, 1982; children: Steven Brandon, Natalie Rachel, Nathan Spencer. BA, Brigham Young U., 1986, MEd, 1997, PhD, 2000. Missionary LDS Ch., Chgo., 1980-82; sys. engr. IBM, San Jose, Calif., 1982-84; sr. cons. and mgr. Sequent Computer Sys., Beaverton, Oreg., 1987-89; tchr. Missionary Tng. Ctr., Provo, Utah, 1985-86, tchr. supr., 1986-87, asst. adminstrv. dir., 1990-92, assoc. adminstrv. dir., 1992—; prin. cons. Carter, Johnson and Assocs., Provo, 1989-99. Author: Introduction to Dynamic UNIX, 1988, Introduction to Parallel Systems, 1989, System Security, 1996; contbr. chpt. to book. Coun., dist. and local adult leader Boy Scouts Am. Named to Outstanding Young Men of Am., 1996; Nat. Merit scholar, 1984; Brigham Young U. fellow, 1985; Baker Rsch. scholar, 1987. Mem. Inst. Mgmt. Accts., Data Processing Mgmt. Assn., Assn. Higher Edn. Facilities Officers (instn. rep.). Mormon. Avocations: family, outdoors, computers, reading. Office: Missionary Tng Ctr 2005 N 900 E Provo UT 84604-1763

CARTER, MICHELE A., biomedical ethicist, ethics educator; b. Okinawa, Japan, Apr. 24, 1949; parents Am. citizens; d. James Elbert and Dorothy (Curry) C. BS, U. Hawaii, 1972; MS, Tex. Women's U., 1982; PhD in Philosophy, U. Tenn., Knoxville, 1989. RN. Postdoctoral fellow in rsch. ethics Clin. Ctr., NIH, Bethesda, Md., 1989-90, acting chiefbioethics program, 1990-92; asst. prof. Inst. Med. Humanities, U. Tex., Galveston, 1993—, dir. ethics consultation svcs., 1993—, clin. asst. prof. Coll. Nursing, 1998—; ethics cons. to pvt., govt. and bus. settings in health care, 1993—; tchr. ethics U. Tex. Me.d Br., Galveston, 1993—, tchr. in philos. ethics, 1993—. Contbr. articles to jours. and encys. Bd. dirs. AIDS Coalition of Coastal Tex., 1999—; vol. Am. Cancer Soc. Rolf-Dieter Hermann scholar U. Tenn., Knoxville, 1984, Bacon-Beard schoalr in philosophy, 1985. Fellow Soc. for Philosophers in Am.; mem. AAUP, Am. Philos. Assn., Soc. Bioethics and Humanities, Oncology Nurse Soc., Sigma Theta Tau. E-mail: mcarter@utmbacdo. Office: U Tex Inst for Med Humanities 301 University Blvd Galveston TX 77555-5302

CARTER, PAUL RICHARD, physician; b. St. Louis, Apr. 14, 1922; s. Paul William and Lily Edith (Kreutzer) C.; m. Lenora Martha Parker, Dec. 24, 1944; children: Richard Brian, Janet Carol Becker. BA in English and History, Union Coll., 1944; MD, Loma Linda U., 1947. Diplomate Am. Bd. Gen. Surgery & Thoracic Surgery. Intern L.A. County Gen. Hosp., 1947-49, surg. resident, 1949-52, 54-56, head physician surgery, 1957-67; resident in chest surgery Olive View Sanitarium, 1956-57; chief of surgery Rancho Los Amigo Hosp., Downey, Calif., 1967-69; prof. of surgery Loma Linda (Calif.) U., 1960-98; clin. prof. surgery U. Calif., Irvine, 1960-95; pvt. practice surgery Covina, Calif., 1960-94; chief thoracic surgery Pettis VA Hosp., Loma Linda, 1978-94. Author about 90 articles and book chpts. in field; co-author: (2 vol.) History of the Pacific Coast Surgical Association, 1982, 88. Capt. USAMC, 1952-54, Korea. Recipient Fulbright scholarship, Oxford, 1959; named to editorial bd., Annals of Thoracic Surgery for 11 yrs. Fellow. ACS (recorder, sec., treas., pres. So. Calif. chpt. 1989, gov. 1991, exec. com. bd. govs. 1993-97); mem. Pacific Coast Surgical Assn. (v.p. 1987—, historian 1989-98), Am. Assn. Thoracic Surgery, Soc. Thoracic Surgeons, Western Surgical Assn., Societe Internat. Chirurgie, Coll. Chest Physicians, Gen. Thoracic Surgical Club, Internat. Soc. Diseases of the Esophagus. Republican. Avocations: travel, med. history, writing. Home: 75-310 14th Green Dr Indian Wells CA 92210-7421

CARTER, PRESTON HENRY, aerospace engineer; b. Spokane, Wash., Mar. 19, 1957; s. Lawrence Porter and Bethal Ann Carter; m. Nancy Dee Hess, Apr. 19, 1986; children: Albert, Cathy. BSAA, U. Wash., 1980; MSAE, U. Tex., 1986. Engr. Naval Air Weapons Ctr., China Lake, Calif., 1980-82, McDonnell Tech. Svcs. Co., Houston, 1982-84, Lockheed Engring. and Scis. Co., Houston, 1986-89; project engr. Space Industries Inc., Webster, Tex., 1989-91; prin. investigator Lawrence Livermore (Calif.) Nat. Lab., 1991—; co-founder Lunar Exploration, Inc., Houston, 1989-91; team mem. Clementine, Lunar Space Exploration. Achievements include inventor of HyperSoar. Avocations: fly fishing, metal working, reading, aviation. E-mail: phcarter@home.com and phc@llnl.gov. Fax: 925-423-5998. Home: 4201 Wilson Blvd # 110-456 Arlington VA 22203-1859 Office: Lawrence Livermore Nat Lab L-043 7000 East Ave # L-043 Livermore CA 94550-9516

CARTER, RUTH B. (MRS. JOSEPH C. CARTER), foundation administrator; b. Charlotte, Vt.; d. Ira E. and Sadie M. (Congdon) Burroughs; m. Joseph C. Carter, June 28, 1935. PhB, U. Vt., 1931. Prin. Newton Acad., Shoreham, Vt., 1931-35; substitute tchr. Spaulding High Sch., Barre, Vt., 1931-35, Woodbury (Vt.) High Sch., 1935-36; tchr. Craftsbury Acad., Craftsbury Common, Vt., 1936-38; sales mgr., buyer Vt. Music Co., Barre, 1939-44; statistician Syracuse U., 1944-46; instr. English Temple U., Phila., 1946-47; records clk. sec. Phila., 1947-56; tchr. English Cen. High Sch., Phila., 1957, Springfield Twp. Sr. High Sch., Montgomery County, Pa., 1964-65; exec. dir. White-Williams Found., 1966-82, trustee, 1982-95. Author: (with Joseph C. Carter) Anchors Aweigh Around the World with Ernest Vail Burroughs, 1960, Pilgrimage to the Lovely Lands of our Ancestors, 1984. Recipient Humanitarian award Chapel of Four Chaplains, 1981, city coun. citation City of Phila., 1982, citation White-Williams Found., 1994. Mem. AAUW (admissions chmn. Phila. chpt. 1959-61, sec. 1961-64, treas. 1965-67), DAR (treas., historian, com. chmn., budget dir., regent Germantown chpt. 1983-86, 89-92, treas. 1992-95, registrar 1995— pub. rels. chmn. 1986—), Women for Greater Phila., New Eng. Hist. Geneal. Soc., Geneal. Soc. Vt., Soc. Mayflower Descs. (bd. dirs. 1983-84, sec. 1985-91), Temple U. Faculty Wives Club (rec. sec. 1983-86, sec. 1997-2000, pres. Old York group), Temple U. Women's Club, The English Speaking Union, Regent's Club (Phila. chaplain 1986-88). Republican. Methodist. Home: 40 Mount Carmel Ave Apt D2 Glenside PA 19038-3429

CARTER, SAMUEL EMMANUEL, archbishop; b. St. Andrew, Jamaica, W.I., July 31, 1919; s. Wilfred George and Eugenie Marie (Williams) C. BA, MA in Theology, Weston (Mass.) Coll., 1950, STL in Theology, 1951; postgrad. in Ascetical Theology, St. Beuno's Coll., North Wales, 1955-56; MSW, Boston Coll., 1958, STD, 1988; DD (hon.), 1966; LLD (hon.), Coll. of Holy Cross, Worcester, Mass., 1970, LeMoyne Coll., Syracuse, N.Y., 1976, Loyola U., Chgo., 1979, U. W.I., 1988; DD, Bethany Coll., 1996. Ordained as priest Roman Cath. Ch., 1954, as bishop, 1966, appointed archbishop, 1970. Instr. Latin S. Simon's Coll., 1939-41; ivil servant Treas. Dept., 1941-44; instr. sociology Holy Cross Coll., Worcester, 1950-51; asst. parish priest, master ceremonies Holy Trinity Cathdeal Partish, Jamaica, 1958-59; founder, headmaster Campion Coll., 1960-64; rector St. George's Coll., 1964—; aux. bishop Kingston, Jamaica, 1966; vicar gen. Archdiocese of Kingston, pastor Holy Cross Ch. Kingston, 1966-70; archbishop of Kingston, 1970-95, archbishop emeritus, 1995—; dir. Pre-Cana Conf., 1959-65; vice chmn. Ecumenical Com. on Religious Edn., 1966-68; chmn. Archdiocesan Edn. Bd., 1968—; marriage counsellor Boston Children's Svc. and Family Svc. Greater Boston; del. 4th and final session of 2d Vatican Coun., Rome, as adviser to Bishop McEleney, 1965; chmn. Archdiocesan Commn. on Ecumenism,1966-70; chmn. Liturgical Commn. Antilles Episcopal Conf., 1966, pres., 1968, 70, 72, 74, 77, 79, 83, 86, 88; rep. 2d Synod of Bishops, Rome, 1969, rep. 3d Synod of Bishops, Rome, 1970; chmn. Caribbean Conf. Chs., 1973; mem. Commn. of Enquiry into adminstrn. justice, police brutality in State of Grenada, W.I., 1973; moderator Internat. Co-operation for Socio-Econ. Devel., mem. Bur., European Ch. Devel. Agy., 1975; chmn. Antilles Episcopal Commn. on Missions, 1975; chmn. Commn. for Missionary Activities, Communications Commn., Antilles Episcopal Conf., 1982; del. World Synod of Bishops, Rome, 1983; leader Caribbean Conf. Chs. Fact Finding Mission to Haiti, 1987. Editor in chief Mental Health Conf. Report, 1962. Chaplain Cath. Women's League, 1958-66; hon. sec. Jamaica Save the Children Fund, 1958-66, Fort Augusta Prison vis. com., 1960-74; mem. exec. com. Jamaica Mental Health Assn., 1961-63; moderator St. George's Coll. Old Boys' Assn., 1964-66; chmn. Archdiocesan Edn. Bd., 1968—, Holy Childhood High Sch. Bd., 1968-70, Holy Trinity Jr. Secondary Sch. Bd., 1968—; hon. v.p. Girl Guides Assn., Jamaica Scout Coun.; chmn. Dupont Primary Sch., Cockburn Pen.; mem. Coun. U. W.I., 1976—. Decorated Comdr. Order of Distinction Govt. Jamaica, Order of Jamaica, 1992; recipient Rale medallion, Bicentennial award Boston Coll. Sch. Social Work, 1976. Mem. Jamaica Coun. Chs. (pres. 1979, 80), Edn. Adv. Coun., Ministry Edn. Com. on Orgn. and Structure of Ednl. System (chmn.), Schs. and Colls. Labour Rels. Coun. (chm. 1965-66). Office: PO Box 36, 77 Halfway Tree Rd, Kingston Jamaica*

CARTER, THOMAS SMITH, JR., retired railroad executive; b. Dallas, June 6, 1921; s. Thomas S. and Mattie (Dowell) C.; m. Janet R. Hostetter, July 3, 1946 (dec. 1981); children: Diane Carter Petersen, Susan Carter Estes, Charles T., Carol Carter Koehler. BS in Civil Engring., So. Meth. U., 1944; MS in Engring. Mgmt., Kans. U., 1991. Registered profl. engr., Mo., Kans., Okla., Tex., La., Ark. With Mo. Kans. Tex. R.R., 1946-54, chief engr., 1954-61, v.p. ops., 1961-66; v.p. Kansas City So. Rlwy. Co., La. and Ark. Rlwy. Co., 1966-74; pres. Kansas City So. Rlwy. Co., 1973-86, also bd. dirs., chmn. bd., 1981-91; pres. La. and Ark. Rlwy. Co., 1974-86, also bd. dirs., chmn. bd., 1981-91, CEO, 1981-91. With U.S. Corps of Engrs., 1944-46. Fellow ASCE; mem. NSPE, Am. Rlwy. Engring. and Maintenance Assn. (life), Sun City Palm Desert Club, Hide-A-Way Lake Club. Home: 131 Clubview Dr Lindale TX 75771-5054

CARTER, VINCE, professional basketball player; b. Jan. 26, 1977. Grad., N.C. U., 1998. Forward Toronto (Can.) Raptors, 1998—; named NCAA Tournament All-East Regional Team, 1997, 98; mem. 1995 USA Basketball Jr. Team, World Championships. Established Embassy of Hope Found.; named Goodwill Amb., Big Bros./Big Sisters of Am. Recipient Schick Rookie of Yr. award 1998-99, selected Schick All-Rookie 1st Team. Office: c/o Toronto Raptors, 20 Bay St Ste 300, Toronto, ON Canada M5J 2N8

CARTER, WILLIAM ALLEN, sales executive, insurance company executive; b. Princess Anne, Md., Jan. 23, 1919; s. Orman Dallas and Mary Letitia (Porter) C.; m. Ann Whitmore, Apr. 12, 1943; children: William W. (dec.), Melinda Carter Luedtke, Richard B. BA, St. John's Coll., 1940; AA (hon.), Del. Tech. and C.C., Dover, 1993; PhD, Berne U., 1998. Commd. ensign U.S. Navy Acad., 1941; released to reserve duty USN, 1946; sales mgr. Houston-White Co., Millsboro, Del., 1946-58; dist. agent Northwestern Mutual Life Ins. Co., Millsboro, Del., 1958-84, emeritus agent, 1984—; sec., treas. Hub of Sussex, Inc., Millsboro, Del., 1965-82. Commr. Town of Millsboro, Del., 1953-62, pres. of commn., 1957-62; mem. Del. Gov.'s State Goals Commn., 1961-65, chmn. com. pub. edn.; mem. Del. Indsl. Bldg. Commn., 1962-69, chmn. 1965-69; founding chmn. Del. Higher Edn. Scholarship Coun., 1963-68; rep. Del. State Na.t Com. Support Pub. Schs., Washington, 1964-69; founding mem. bd. dirs. Rsch. for Better Schs., Inc., Phila., 1965-75, state bd. trustees Del. Tech. and C.C., sec., 1966-69, chmn., 1973-83; chmn. feasibility study com. Del. State C.C., 1965-66; mem. state bd. trustees Del. Tech. and C.C. Ednl. Found., 1967—; mem. Del. Higher Edn. Commn., 1993—, Del. Com. Pub. Health, 1995—, bd. trustees Del. Inst. Med. Edn. and Rsch. Comdr. USNR, 1953. Decorated Silver Star; Order of Great Patriotic War 1st class (USSR). Mem. Sussex Pines Country Club, Masons, Shriners. Democrat. Episcopalian. Home and Office: 227 Morris St Millsboro DE 19966-0248

CARTER, WILLIAM HAROLD, SR., physicist, researcher, electrical engineer; b. Houston, Nov. 17, 1938; s. William Henry and Fannie (Augusta) C.; children: William Harold Jr., Elizabeth Lee. BSEE, U. Tex., 1962, MSEE, 1963, PhD, 1966. Rsch. asst. U. Tex., Austin, 1962-66; rsch. assoc. U. Rochester, N.Y., 1969-70; rsch. physicist Naval Rsch. Lab., Washington, 1971-93; prof. U. Nebr., Lincoln, 1981-82; instr. Johns Hopkin's U., Balt., 1989-93; program dir. NSF, Arlington, Va., 1993-95; vis. rsch. fellow U. Reading, Eng., 1976-77; vis. scientist applied physics lab. Johns Hopkin's U., Columbia, Md., 1991-92. Contbr. numerous articles to profl. jours. Cellist Alexandria (Va.) Symphony, 1979-88, Georgetown Symphony, 1981—. Capt. U.S. Army, 1967-69. Fellow Optical Soc. Am., Internat. Soc. for Optical Engring. (chmn. tech. coun. 1980-82, chmn. pub. com. 1981-83, chmn. fellows com. 1986); mem. IEEE (sr., conf. chmn. 1988), Am. Phys. Soc., Cosmos Club. Achievements include co-discovery of the quasi-homogeneous source model; research in optical coherence, in applications of speckle phenomena, and in processing images and data from optical sensors. Home: 8301 Cherry Valley Ln Alexandria VA 22309-2117 Office: NSF 4201 Wilson Blvd Arlington VA 22230-0001

CARTER, WILLIE LEE, quality management professional; b. Alexandria, La., Jan. 22, 1946; s. Leola Carter; m. Hilde W. Wheeler, Apr. 4, 1970; children: Devin, Melissa. BA in Chemistry, So. Ill. U., 1969; MBA with honors, Roosevelt U., 1975. Devel. chemist Reliance Universal, Zion, Ill., 1969-74, plant chemist, 1974-76, plant svcs. mgr., 1976-78, prodn. mgr., 1978-81; plant mgr. Swift Adhesives, Oak Creek, Wis., 1980-81; ops. mgr. Swift Adhesives, Chgo., 1981-83, product mgr., 1983-86; dir. ops. Swift Adhesives, Downers Grove, Ill., 1986-89, dir. quality, 1989-91; dir. quality Dexter Automotive Coatings Div., Waukegan, Ill., 1991-93; v.p. quality and ops. support svcs. Internat. Jensen, Inc., Lincolnshire, Ill., 1993-97; pres., prin. cons. Quantum Assocs., Inc., Chgo., 1998—. Mem. Lake County (Ill.) Urban League, 1976-82, Waukegan (Ill.) Park Dist. Citizens Coun., 1981-83. Mem. NAACP, Am. Soc. Quality Control, Black MBA Assn., Beta Gamma Sigma, Kappa Alpha Psi (pres. Waukegan alumni chpt., 1975-82, Maywood-Wheaton alumni chpt., 1987-89). Baptist. Avocations: golf, gardening, reading. E-mail: wcarqual@compuserve.com. Home: 459 Lambert Tree Rd Highland Park IL 60035-5255

CARTHEW, CHRISTOPHER DAVID, software development executive; b. Adelaide, Australia, Oct. 12, 1962; s. David Alexander and Marie Carthew; m. Irina Czyczelis, June 24, 1994; 1 child, Thomas. BSc in Computer Engring. with honors, Adelaide U., 1983. Software engr. Electricity Trust of South Australia, Adelaide, 1984, Quickdraw, Adelaide, 1984-87; software devel. mgr. Caddsman, Adelaide, 1987-93; dir. Australian Software Industries, Adelaide, 1993—; dir., exec. tech. devel. CCIC, Adelaide, 1993—. Violinist, Unley Chamber Orch., Marlborough Players. Recipient IBM award for Computing Sci., 1982; finalist Young Achievers award, South Australia, 1985. Mem. Assn. Computing Machinery, Computer Soc. IEEE. Avocations: violin, cricket. Office: Australian Software Industr, 7 Hutton St, Vale Pk, S Austrl Adelaide 5081, Australia

CARTIER-BRESSON, HENRI, photographer; b. Chanteloup, France, Aug. 22, 1908; m. Martine Franck, 1970. Ed., Ecole Fènelon, Lycée Condorcet Paris; student painting at André Lhote, 1927-28; Dr. honoris causa, Oxford U., 1975. Asst. dir. to Jean Renoir, 1936-39; co-founder, assoc. Magnum Photos, 1947—; hon. prof. Acad. Fine Art of China, 1996. Photographs exhibited at Mus. Modern Art, N.Y.C., 1947, 68, 87, Louvre, Paris, 1955, 67, Victoria and Albert Mus., London, 1969, 99, Grand-Palais, Paris, 1970, Manege, Moscow, 1972, Edinburgh Festival, Hayward Gallery, London, 1978, 98, Mus. Modern Art, Paris, 1982, DeMesnil Found., Houston, Bibliotheque Nationale, Paris, U. Fine Arts, Osaka, also in major museums Mexico, Japan, Des Européens Maison de la Photo, Paris, 1997, Nat. Portrait Gallery, London, 1998, Washington, 1999 and other locations; drawings and paintings exhibited Carlton Gallery, N.Y.C., 1975, Bischofberger Gallery, Zurich, 1976, P.A.C. of Milan (Italy), 1983, U. Rome, 1983, Mus. Modern Art, Oxford, 1984, Palais Liechtenstein, Vienna, 1985, Arnold Herstand Gallery, N.Y.C., 1987, Ecole des Beaux Arts, Paris, 1989, Printemps, Tokyo, 1989, Fondation Gianadda, Switzerland, 1990, Villa Medicis, Rome, 1990, Musée de Louvain, Belgium, 1991, Mus. Modern Art, Taipei, 1991, Noyers Sur Serein, Yonne, France, 1992, Parma, Italy, 1992, Saragosse, Barcelona, Vienna, France, 1995, Mpls. Art Inst., 1996, O. Berggruen Gallery, London, 1996, Montreal, 1997, Gallery Claude Bernard, Paris, 1997, Kyoto, 1998, Royal Coll. Art, Kunsthaus, Zurich, 1998, Gallery E. Beyeler, Basel, London, 1998, Palazzo Medici Riccardi, 1998, Casino Veniera Firenze & Venice, Italy, 1998; documentary films: Victoire de la Vie, on hosps., Spanish Republic, 1937; (with Jacques Lemare) Le Retour, 1945; (with Jean Boffety) Impressions of California (CBS) 1969; Southern Exposures (with W. Dombrow) (CBS), 1970; author: The Decisive Moment, 1952, Images a la Sauvette, 1952, The Europeans, 1955, Verve, 1952, (text by Antonin Artaud) Danses à Bali, 1954, From One China to the Other (text by Jean Paul Satre) 1954, Moscow, 1955, The Galveston That Was (text by James Johnson Sweeney MacMullan), 1965; Les Cahiers de la photographie, 1985, (with François Nourissier) Vive la France, 1970 (with Etiemble) L'Homme et la Machine (IBM), 1972; The Face of Asia, 1972; A Propos de l'U.R.S.S., 1973;

Henri Cartier-Bresson Photographer (text by Yves Bonnefoy), 1979, rev. ed., 1999; Photoportraits 1932-1982, (text by A. de Mandiargues) 1982; Coll. Livre de Poche, 1983; The Early Work (text by Peter Galassi), 1987, Henri Cartier-Bressor in India, 1988, The Drawings of HCB Line by Line (text by John Russell and Jean Clair), 1989, America in Passing, 1991, Paris á vue d'oeil (text by Vera Feyder), 1994, Carnets Mexicains 1934-1964 (text by Carlos Fuentes), 1995, (study by Jean Pierre Montier) L'art sans Art, 1995, (text and photos by Henri Cartier-Bresson) André Breton, roi Soleil, 1995, L'Imaginaire d'Après Nature (texts by Henri Cartier-Bresson, edited by Fata Morgana), 1997, Des Européens (text by Jean Clair), Téte á Téte (text by E. Gombrich). Mem. Am. Acad. Art and Sci. Office: care Magnum Photos, 19 rue Hegesippe Moreau, 75018 Paris France Other: care Helen Wright 135 E 74th St New York NY 10021-3272

CARTLEDGE, TONY WALTER, editor, minister; b. Lincolnton, Ga., Dec. 5, 1951; s. William Crawford Jr. and Hollie (Williamson) C.; m. Jan Rush, May 26, 1984; children: Russ, Bethany (dec.), Samuel. BS, U. Ga., 1973; MDiv, SE Bapt. Theol. Sem., 1982; PhD, Duke U., 1989. Pastor Loco Baptist Ch., Lincolnton, Ga., 1972-74, Highland Baptist Ch., Hogansville, Ga., 1974-79, Tabbs Creek Baptist Ch., Oxford, N.C., 1979-84, Oak Grove Baptist Ch., Boone, N.C., 1984-88; sr. pastor Woodhaven Baptist Ch., Apex, N.C., 1988-98; editor, pres. The Biblical Recorder, Raleigh, N.C., 1998—; bd. dirs. The Copernicas Group, Cary, N.C. Author: Vows in the Old Testament and the Ancient Near East, 1992; contbr. articles to profl. jours. and bibl. reference books. Mem. Mothers Against Drunk Driving, Raleigh, 1994-96. Recipient Presidential medallion Campbell U., Buies Creek, N.C., 1999. Mem. Assn. Baptist Profs. of Religion. Avocations: reading, golf, children. E-mail: cartledge@mindspring.com. Home: 3912 Inkberry Ct Apex NC 27502-8867 Office: Biblical Recorder Inc 232 W Millbrook Rd Raleigh NC 27609-4304

CARTLIDGE, EDWARD SUTTERLEY, mechanical engineer; b. Trenton, N.J., Feb. 5, 1945; s. Leon James and Agnes Jean (Cinday) C.; m. Marilyn Spinuzza, July 21, 1979. BS in Marine Engring., U.S. Mcht. Marine Acad., 1968; MSME, N.J. Inst. Tech., 1971; MBA, Temple U., 1982; MA, Biblical Theol. Sem., 2000. Registered profl. engr., Pa., Ill., Del., Md., N.J., Va., Wis., Calif., Fla. Marine engr. Seatrain Lines, 1968-69; performance engr. Foster Wheeler Corp., Livingston, N.J., 1969-71; cons. engr. Fluor, Sargent & Lundy, and Kuljian Corp., 1971-75; chief engr. Gimpel Corp., Langhorne, Pa., 1976-79; sr. rsch. and devel. engr. Yarway Corp., Blue Bell, Pa., 1979-82; sr. project process engr. and power utilities supr. Merck & Co., Inc., West Point, Pa., 1982-91; sr. project mgr. Conmec, Inc., Bethlehem, Pa., 1992-93, Edward S. Cartlidge, PE and Assocs., Brandon, Fla., 1993-2000; cons. Pharm., Polymer Utilities, Semiconductor, Steel Fab., Gideon; Christian fin. counselor, lectr., seminar leader. Bd. dirs. Grand Old Gospel Fellowship. Served to comdr. USNR, 1968-91. Mem. NSPE (chpt. pres.), ASME, Pa. Soc. Profl. Engrs. (Young Engr. of Yr. 1980), Instruments Soc. Am., Am. Soc. Heat, Refrigerator, Air Conditioning Engrs., Soc. Mfg. Engrs., Am. Soc. Metals, Soc. Naval Architects and Marine Engrs., Naval Reserve Assn., Nat. Fire Prevention Assn., Gideons Internat. Home: 901 Stratford Manor Dr Brandon FL 33510-2810

CARTWRIGHT, THEODOR T., medical association administrator; b. Ft. Lauderdale, Fla., Feb. 28, 1972; s. John Gilbert and Clairce Jane C. BS, Mich. State U., 1995. Intern Congressman Frank R. Wolf, Washington, 1994, field rep., 1995-97; mgr. Flexible Packaging Assn., Washington, 1997-99, Am. Soc. for Microbiology, Washington, 1999—; mem. commonwealth adv. com. to gov., Va. sect., 1998—. Mgr. gubernatorial campaign Jim Gilmore, Va., 1998; campaign asst. Congressman Frank Wolf, Va., 1996. Presbyn. Avocations: mountain biking, scuba diving, ice hockey, soccer, wildlife observation. E-mail: autrakis@hotmail.org. Office: Am Soc Microbiology 1752 N St NW Washington DC 20036-2904

CARTY, DONALD J., airline company executive. Grad., Queen's U., Kingston, Ont., Harvard U. With Air Canada, Canadian Pacific Rwy.; gen. mgr. Montcel Distbrs. unit Celanese Can. Ltd., Montreal; sr. v.p. fin. Americana Hotels; v.p. profit improvement, v.p. ops. rsch. American Airlines, sr. v.p., controller, sr. v.p. airline planning, 1987-89; exec. v.p. fin. and planning AMR and Am. Airlines, DFW Airport, Tex., 1989-95; pres. AMR Airline Group and Am. Airlines, Inc., DFW Airport, Tex., 1995-98; pres., CEO CP Air; chmn., pres., CEO AMR Corp., Ft. Worth, 1998—; bd. dirs. Dell computer Corp., Can. Airlines Internat. Ltd.; adv. bd. Allendale Mut. Ins. Co. Bd. trustees Queen's U. Office: AMR Corp 4333 Amon Carter Blvd Fort Worth TX 76155-2605

CARTY, HEIDI MARLENE, educator, researcher; b. Salt Lake City, July 19, 1967; d. Richard Eathel Coon and Sharon (Pitcher) Smith; m. Shawn Patrick Carty. BS in Psychology with honors cum laude, Loyola U., 1992, MA in Rsch. Methodology and Stats., 1994, PhD in Rsch. Methodology and Stats., 1998. Rsch. asst. Loyola U. Med. Ctr., Maywood, Ill., 1993; rsch. asst. Loyola U., Chgo., 1993-94, grad. asst. statis. computing, 1992-94; statis. cons. Iota, Inc., Chgo., 1993-95; grad. asst. rsch. methodology Loyola U., Chgo., 1994-96; statis. cons. U. San Diego, 1996-98; asst. prof. rsch. Hofstra U., Hempstead, N.Y., 1998-99; asst. dir. stud. rsch. and information Univ. Calif. San Diego, San Diego, 1999—; part-time lectr. Loyola U., Chgo., 1992-96; lectr. biology dept. U. San Diego, 1998—. Contbr. articles to profl. jours. Recipient grad. assistantship Loyola U., 1992-94, 94-96; scholar Nat. AMBUCS, 1991. Fellow Am. Ednl. Rsch. Assn.; mem. APA, AERA, Psi Chi (pres.), Alpha Epsilon Delta. Avocations: sailing, reading, jogging, movies, theater. Office: UCSD 9500 Gilman Dr La Jolla CA 92093-5004

CARTY, JOHN CHARLES ANTHONY, advertising executive; b. Dublin, Ireland, Apr. 16, 1961; s. Owen and Ann (Costello) C. BSc, Trinity Coll., Dublin, 1983. Show jumper internationally; jockey for trainer Christy Kinane Cashel Co., Tipperary, Ireland, 1979-80; asst. trainer Carl Nafzger, 1983-84, Claude (Shug) McGaughey, Louisville & N.Y.C., 1985, Pat Brennan, Belmont Park, N.Y., 1985, Pat Hughes, Carlow, Ireland, 1986-88; polo player Mark Harris Rangiora, Churchill, New Zealand, 1989-90, Kerry Packer, Ellerston Scone, NSW, Australia, 1990-92; mng. dir. Stylish Advt., Dublin, 1992—. Avocations: cosmology, chess.

CARTY, JOHN WESLEY, lawyer; b. Lansing, N.C., Oct. 29, 1923; s. John Arthur and Bertha (Eller) C.; m. Doris Frances Barnes, June 27, 1948; children: Dixie Lynne, John Jeffrey. BA, Buena Vista Coll., 1950; JD, Drake U., 1952. Bar: Iowa 1952, U.S. Dist. Ct. (so. dist.) Iowa 1952, U.S. Ct. Appeals (8th cir.) 1965. Assoc. Pryor, Hale, Plock, Riley & Jones, Burlington, Iowa, 1952-54; ptnr. Carty & Jones, Des Moines, 1960-75; pvt. practice Winfield, Iowa, 1955—; Bd. dirs. Farmers Nat. Bank, Winfield, Iowa, pres., chmn. 1985—; pres. Oxidex, Inc., Winfield, 1971—; broker, dir. Winfield Realty Co., 1956-98; pres., chmn. Winfield Health Care & Retirement Ctr., 1972-77; dir., sec., treas. Satellite Mill, Inc., 1961-63. Co-author: Business Law & The Cooperative, 1962; assoc. editor Drake U. Law Rev., 1951-52. City atty. City of Winfield, Iowa, 1954-89, City of Wayland, Iowa, 1962-70; mem. Henry County Conservation Bd., Mt. Pleasant, Iowa, 1972-74; chmn. Henry County Compensation Commn., 1987-92; sec. S.E. Iowa Planning Coun., 1973-74; dir. S.E. Iowa Health Care Coun., Ft. Madison, 1974-76; mem. Iowa Archaeol. Soc., 1991—; mem. commn. eminent domain Henry County, 1993-98. With combat infantry U.S. Army, 1944-46, ETO. Decorated Combat Infantryman's badge, Bronze star; recipient Spl. award Bur. Nat. Affairs, 1952, Annual award Greene County Conservation Bd., 1987. Mem. Henry County Bar Assn. (pres. 1961-62), S.E. Iowa Bar Assn. (pres. 1962), Iowa State Bar Assn., Iowa Archeol. Soc., Hawkeye Archeol. Soc., Am. Legion, VFW, Masons, Phi Alpha Delta. Presbyterian. Home: 1586 Oasis Ave Mount Union IA 52644-9506 Office: Carty Law Office Farmers Nat Bank Bldg Winfield IA 52659

CARTY, MARY ELLEN, psychologist; b. N.Y.C., Aug. 7, 1958; d. Walter Vincent and Sally Rita (Clarke) C. BA, Coll. of New Rochelle, 1980, MS, 1991; PsychD, Yeshiva U., 1997. Cert. sch. psychologist, N.Y.; lic. psychologist., N.Y. Grad. asst. Coll. of New Rochelle, N.Y., 1989-90, rsch. asst., 1990-91; sch. psychologist intern Pawling (N.Y.) Ctrl. Sch. Dist., 1990-91; sch. psychologist Pawling Jr./Sr. H.S., 1991-93, Clarkstown H.S. South, West Nyack, N.Y., 1993-94; behavior specialist, psychologist Esperanza Ctr., N.Y.C., 1993-96; clin. psychology intern, postdoctoral fellow Ctr. Preventive Psychiatry, 1996-98; program psychologist So. Westchester Bd. Coop. Ednl. Svcs., Harrison, N.Y., 1998—; cons. acad. counselor Iona Coll., New Rochelle, N.Y., 1990-94, 96-97. Vol. English tchr. Immaculate Conception H.S., Jamaica, W.I., 1983-85; trustee, mem. ch. coun. St. Pius X Ch., Jamaica, 1983-85, mem. grad school adv. bd. Col. of New Rochelle, 1999—. Recipient Ursula Laurus citation, 2000; Empire Challenger fellow N.Y. State Edn. Dept., 1988-89. Mem. APA, N.Y. Assn. Sch. Psychologists (Ted Bernstein award 1996), Psi Chi. Democrat. Roman Catholic. Avocations: jogging, meditation, travel. Home: 434 N High St Mount Vernon NY 10552-3103 Office: So Westchester Bd Coop Ednl Svcs St Vincent's Hosp 275 North St Harrison NY 10528-1524

CARUSO, ANTHONY RALPH, mortgage banker, real estate developer; b. Cleve., Feb. 13, 1942; s. Ralph S. and Mary Louise C.; m. Ottalee Page Caruso, May 13, 1967. BA in Acctg. and Fin., John Carroll U., 1963. V.p. TransOhio Fin. Corp., Cleve., 1963-72; prin. CleveTrust Realty Advisors, Cleve., 1972-76; v.p. Cardinal Fed. Savs., Cleve., 1976-80, BankOne Corp., Cleve., 1980-83; sr. v.p. Equitable Fed. Savs., Columbus, Ohio, 1983-85; v.p. Huntington Nat. Bank, Cleve., 1985-88; exec. v.p., CEO, Stratford Mortgage Co., Mentor, Ohio, 1988—. Bus. faculty advisor Lakeland C.C., Mentor, 1977-80. Mem. Grand River Yachting Club (bd. trustees, treas.), Mid. Bass Island Yachting Club (commodore 1994-96). Republican. Roman Catholic. Avocations: power boating, skeet and trap shooting, cross-country skiing. Home: 9361 Canterbury Ln Mentor OH 44060-6406 Office: Stratford Mortgage Co 7537 Mentor Ave Mentor OH 44060-5442

CARUSO, CALOGERO, immunopathologist; b. Palermo, Italy, Dec. 1, 1947; s. Filippo and Francesca (Catalano) C.; m. Francesca Bulgarella, Apr. 6, 1974; children: Marco, Chiara. Student, Liceo Gonzaga, 1965; degree, U. Palermo, 1971. Asst. prof. U. Palermo, 1974-85, assoc. prof., 1985-94, full prof., 1994—, immunopathology unit chief, 1995—, dir. immunology course, 1997—, dir. pathobiology PhD course, 1998—, dir. lab. medicine PG course, 1999—. Author: Fisiopatologia della Flogosi, 1997; contbr. articles to profl. and sci. jours. Mem. Soc. Italiana di Patologia, Soc. Italiana di Immunologia ed Immunologia Clinica, European Found. for Immunogenetics. Fax: 390-9-1-655-5933. E-mail: marcoc@mbox.unipa.it. Home: Via G Ventura 1, 90143 Palermo Italy Office: U Palermo Dept Biopath & Biomed Methodol, Corso Tukory 211, 90134 Palermo Italy

CARUSO, ROSARIO ALBERTO, pathologist, researcher; b. Valledolmo, Palermo, Italy, Nov. 25, 1952; s. Michele Caruso; m. Luciana Rigoli; 1 child, Valerio. MD summa cum laude, U. Messina, Italy, 1977. Intern Inst. Morbid Anatomy U. Messina, Italy, 1975-77; rschr. in pathology U. Messina, 1977-99, assoc. prof. morbid anatomy, 1999—. Contbr. articles to profl. jours. Home: N Panoramica 690, I-98168 Messina Italy Office: Policlinico Universitario Dept Patologia Umana, Via Consolare Valeria, I-98125 Messina Italy

CARVAJALINO, MARIO RAFAEL, agroecological company executive; b. Bogotá, Colombia, Dec. 16, 1942; s. Luis Jose and Mary (Arevalo) C.; m. Silvia Batres, May 11, 1968 (dec. Jan. 1980); m. Olga Galofre, Oct. 5, 1981 (dec. Jan. 1990); children: Claudia, Juana, Diego; m. Sonia Martinez, Sept. 14, 1991. BS in Agrl. Engring., Nat. U. Colombia, Medellin, 1964; MS in Agrl. Econs., Mich. State U., 1966; postgrad. Instituto Alta Direccim de Emp, U De la Sabana, Bogotá, 1989; postgrad., Harvard U., 1996. Gen. mgr. Progen, Bogotá, 1966-92, Colinagro, 1968-80, Stoller, Bogotá, 1983-92; pres. Progen-Stoller-Incogua, Bogotá, 1992—; owner, pres. mgmt. co. Chmn. C. of C. Bogotá, 1994-97, CORFERIAS, Bogotá, 1995-96, 2000—, CORPARQUES, Bogotá, 1996, FUNDAC, Bogotá, 1993-97. Presdl. scholar Nat. U., 1964. Mem. Pres. Forum (bd. dirs. 1995-97), Andean Agroecol. Action, Programa Alta Direccim. Avocations: breeding horses and dogs, horseback riding, computers, music, camping. Home: Carrera 59 # 127B-53, Bogotá Colombia Office: Incogua Ltd Oficina 302 Edificio NOVA, Calle 125 # 31-84, Bogotá Colombia

CARVALHAES, AFFONSO LUIZ DE BARROS, steel products company executive; b. Marquês de Valença, Brazil, Apr. 4, 1938; s. Affonso de Barros and Beatriz (Rocha) C.; m. Rosaly Ratton; children: Affonso Henriques de Barros, Gustavo Luiz dos Reis. Student, Naval Sch., Rio de Janeiro, 1959; law degree, Law Sch. Cândido Mendes, Rio de Janeiro, 1968. From adminstrv. mgr. to gen. mgr. Litográfica Voltą Redonda, Barra Mansa, 1967-87; supt. Emesa S/A Indústria e Comércio de Metais, Barra Mansa, 1988—; ptnr., dir. Metalconsult Cons. Ltd., 1999—; indsl. dir. Comml. and Indsl. Assn. Barra Mansa, 1970-72. With Brazilian Navy, 1960-67. Named Businessman of Yr., Comml. and Indsl. Assn. Barra Mansa, 1992. Avocations: traveling, judging, tennis, theater, movies. Home: R Prof Manoel Ferreira, 144-ap 406, 22451000 Rio de Janeiro Brazil Office: Emesa S/A Ind E Com Metais, Rod Pres Dutra Km 288, 27365000 Barra Mansa Brazil

CARVALHO, JOSÉ RUY PORTO DE, statistician; b. Sao Paulo, Brazil, Jan. 24, 1953; s. Romeu and Edith (Porto) de C.; m. Ariadne Maria Brito Rizzoni, Jan. 25, 1980. BS, Campina U., 1975; MSc, Sao Paulo U., 1978; PhD, Reading U., 1988. From head statis. dept. to rschr. Embrapa, Campinas, Brazil, 1978—. Author: Plant-Soil Interaction at Low PH, 1991, Administration in Science and Technology: Agricultural Research, 1994, Planning of R&T Information Systems, 1999; contbr. articles to profl. jours. Mem. Brazilian Agrl. Rsch. Soc. Office: Embrapa/CNPTIA, Campus da Unicamp, Sao Paulo 13083970, Brazil

CARVALHO, JULIE ANN, psychologist; b. Washington, Apr. 11, 1940; d. Daniel Henry and Elizabeth Cecilia (Gardiner) Schmidt; children: Alan R., Dennis M., Melanie D., Celeste A., Joshua E. BA with honors, U. Md., 1962, postgrad., 1962-63, 68-73; MA, George Washington U., 1966; postgrad., Va. Poly. Inst., 1979-88. Social sci. rsch. analyst Mental Health Study Ctr., NIMH, Adelphi, Md., 1963-67; edn. and tng. analyst Computer Applications, Inc., Silver Spring, Md., 1967-68; edn. program specialist, program analyst Nat. Ctr. for Ednl. R&D, U.S. Office of Edn., Washington, 1969-73; equal opportunity specialist Office of Sec., HEW, Washington, 1973-77; legis. program, civil rights analyst Office for Civil Rights Dept. Health and Human Svcs., Washington, 1977-85; ind. cons.; adj. lectr., No. Va. C.C., George Mason U., Montgomery Coll., Strayer Coll., Shepherd Coll., Germanna Coll., U. Md. U. Coll., Prince William Hosp., Fairfax County Pub. Schs., Fairfax County Dept. Social Svcs., all Washington area, 1986—. Contbr. articles to profl. jours. Bd. dirs. Child Care Ctrs., 1970-76, HEW Employees Assn., 1973-78; mem. steering com. Alliance for Child Care, 1975-80; tchr. seminars for single-parent and spiritual groups. Mem. APA (panel condr. 1969-75, editor Bull. of Peace Psychology 1991-97, divsn. 48), ASPA (condr. panels 1975, 91), Capitol Area Social Psychologists Assn. (conf. chmn. 1985, 93), Psychologists Soc. Responsibility, Federally Employed Women (nat. editor 1975-79), Fairfax County Assn. for the Gifted (pres. 1980), Psi Chi, Phi Alpha Theta, Alpha Sigma Lambda (hon.). Address: PO Box 11500 Alexandria VA 22312-0500 Home and Office: 5927 Quantrell Ave Apt T3 Alexandria VA 22312-2762

CARVALHO, LUIZ PINTO DE, engineering company executive, consultant; b. Salvador, Bahia, Brazil, Apr. 6, 1938; s. Luiz Pinto de and Marina Pinto de (Maia) C.; m. Vera Tourinho Pinto De C., May 4, 1968; children: Cristina, Marcio. BSc, Inst. Tech. Aero., SJ Campos, Brazil, 1963, MSc, 1972; PhD, Stanford U., 1980. Cert. electronics engr. Asst. to dir. Telephone Co., Salvador, Brazil, 1966-69; engr. Secret Ciência Tecnol, Salvador, Brazil, 1969-71; asst. prof. Inst. Tech. Aero., SJ Campos, 1971-81; engr. ESCA Engenharia, Rio de Janeiro, 1981-90; ptnr. LPC Engenharia, Rio de Janeiro, 1991—; pres. Itaconsult-RJ, Rio de Janeiro, 1996-98; cons. in field; head dept. telecomm. Inst. Tech. Aero., SJ Campos, 1981; assoc. prof. dept. telecomms. U. Fed. Fluminense, Niteroi, 1999—. Mem. IEEE, Clube de Engenharia, Assn. Engrs. Inst. Tech. Aero. (pres. 1994-96). Avocations: cinema, music, literature, science, philosphy. E-mail: luizp-carvalho@uol.com.br. Home: R Paissandu 51 Ap 501, 22210080 Rio de Janeiro RJ, Brazil Office: LPC Engenharia 39/601, Av Franklin Roosevelt, 20021120 Rio de Janeiro RJ, Brazil

CARVALHO-RODRIGUES, FERNANDO ANTÓNIO, electrical engineer; b. Lisbon, Portugal, Jan. 28, 1947; s. Agostinho Vasco and Leontina Oliveira Carvalho; m. Maria Da Purificação, Sept. 28, 1969. MSc, U. Lisbon (Portugal), 1969; PhD, U. Liverpool (Eng.), 1974. Rsch. asst. Junta de Energia Nuclear, Sacavém, Portugal, 1974-76; rsch. fellow Junta de Energia Nuclear, Sacavém, 1976-79; sr. researcher Lneti, Lisbon, 1979-84, prin. scientist, 1984-90; prin. scientist INETI, Lisbon, 1990—; dir. Info. Tech. Inst., Lisbon, 1985—; leader Po-SAT consortium, Lisbon, 1990-94; cons. Portuguese-Am. Found., Lisbon, 1994—; bd. dirs. EID, Caparica, Portugal. Author: Sistemas Entropia Coesão, The Military Landscape--Mathematical Models of Combat, 1993, As Novas Tecnologias, O Futuro Dos Impérios e Os Quatro Cavaleiros Do Apocalipse, 1994. Lt. Portuguese Army, 1975. Recipient Pfizer prize, 1977, Gulbenkian prize, 1978, 82. Mem. N.Y. Acad. Sci., Acad. Das Ciências de Lisboa. Roman Catholic. Office: NATO Scientific and Environ Divsn, Boulevard Leopold 2, 1110 Brussels Belgium

CARVELL, JOHN EDWARD, trauma and orthopaedic surgeon, consultant; b. Dundee, Scotland, May 30, 1946; s. Robert Charles and Ivy (Dutch) C.; m. Carol Ritchie, July 22, 1972; children: Claire, Robin. MB, ChB, St. Andrews U., Scotland, 1970; M in Med. Sci., Dundee U., Scotland, 1974. House officer dept. orthops. DRI, Scotland, 1971; demonstrator in anatomy Dundee U., Scotland, 1971-73; S.H.O. Radcliffe Infirmary, Oxford, Eng., 1973-74; rotating surg. registrar Southampton (Eng.) Tchg. Hosp., 1974-75; orthop. registrar Royal United Bath Hosp., Wilshire, Eng., 1976-77; sr. orthop. registrar Nuffield Orthop. Ctr., Oxford, 1977-83; cons. orthop. surgeon Salisbury Dist. Hosp., Wilshire, 1983—; Welcome European traveling fellow Inst. Calot Berck Plage France, Pas-De Calais, 1980-81; chmn. Medisecs Ltd., Salisbury, 1983-99. Author: Surgery of the Knee, 1984. West Hants, South Wilts and East Dorset, Regional Salisbury Dist. pres. Arthritis Rsch. Campaign, 1985-98; pres. Arthritis and Rheumatism Coun., 1985-98. Recipient Ethicon award Ethicon Found., 1980, French Govt. award for med. sci. French Govt., 1980; Welcome European traveling scholar Welcome Trust, 1980. Fellow Royal Coll. Surgeons (Edinburgh), Royal Coll. Surgeons (Eng.) (surg. tutor 1996—, Brit. Orthop. Assn., Brit. Scoliosis Soc.; mem. Internat. Soc. Arthroscopy Knee Surgery and Orthop. Sports Medicine, Brit. Med. Assn. (hon. sec. Wessex regional cons. and specialist com. 1994-97, chmn. 1997—). Home: Newstead 143 Bouverie Ave S, Salisbury SP2 8EB, England Office: Salisbury Dist Hosp, Odstock, Salisbury SP2 8BJ, England

CARVER, KENDALL LYNN, insurance company executive; b. Spencer, Iowa, Nov. 4, 1936; s. Marion and Letha G.; m. Carol Lee Spiers, July 1, 1961; children: Merrian, Kendra, Lee, Christine. BS, U. Iowa, 1958. Rep. field sales Washington Nat. Ins. Co., Evanston, Ill., 1958-73; regional dir. Washington Nat. Ins. Co., 1974-77; pres. Washington Nat. Ins. Co., N.Y.C., 1977—; CEO Washington Nat. Ins. Co., 1978-94; mng. dir. Kendall Carver and Assocs. LLC, 1996-98; chmn. fin. com. First Benefit Ins. Co. of Phoenix, 1996-98; also bd. dirs. First Benefit Inst. Co. of Phoenix, 1997; founder, pres., CEO Confirmation-Plus LLC, 1998—; bd. dirs. Life Ins. Coun. N.Y., chmn., 1991; chmn. bd. dirs. Security Adminstrs. Inc., Binghamton, N.Y.; cons. to ins. industry. bd. dirs., mem. exec. com. Great Am. Life Ins. Co. of N.Y., 1999. Fellow Life Mgmt. Inst.; mem. Am. Coll. Life Underwriters, Life Ins. Council N.Y. (dir. 1979-82, 86-88). Republican.

CARWARDINE, RICHARD JOHN, historian, educator; b. Cardiff, Eng., Jan. 12, 1947; s. John Francis and Beryl (Jones) C.; m. Linda Margaret Kirk, May 17, 1975. MA, PhD, Oxford U., Eng., 1975. Prof. in Am. History U. Sheffield, Yorks, Eng., 1971—. Author: Transatlantic Revivalism, 1978, Evangelicals and Politics in Antellum America, 1993. Fellow Royal Hist. Soc.; mem. Orgn. of Am. Historians, British Assn. Am. Studies, Soc. for the History of the Early Republic, British Am. 19th Century Historians. Mem. Social and Liberal Democratic Party. Mem. Ch. of Eng. Avocation: drama. Office: U Sheffield, Dept History, Sheffield S10 2TN, England

CARY, JOHN WILLIAM, resource management educator, consultant; b. Melbourne, Australia, Feb. 4, 1945; s. William Joseph Cary and Lucy Tuomy; m. Roseann Coogen, Dec. 28, 1968; children: Joanna, Belinda, Alice. BS in Agrl. Sci., Massey U., N.Z., 1969; MS in Agrl. Sci., Melbourne U., 1975, PhD in Psychology, 1994. Farm mgmt. adviser Dept. Agr., Victoria, Australia, 1969-72, dairy policy adviser, 1973-77; lectr. mgmt. extension U. Melbourne, 1977-83, sr. lectr. mgmt. extension, 1984-94, assoc. prof., 1995-99, head dept. agr. and resource mgmt., 1996-98, prin. fellow, 1999—; prin. rsch. scientist Bureau Rural Scis., Australia, 1999—; vis. rsch. fellow U. Wis., Madison, 1983-84; vis. adviser Internat. Devel. Program, Australian Univs., Indonesia, 1980, 82; specialist adviser Parliamentary Select Comm. on Salinity, Victoria, 1984; vis. fellow U. Western Australia, 1990; vis. scholar U. Mich., Ann Arbor, 1995; cons. Lancare Rsch., New Zealand, 1994; bd. mem. Joint Ctr. Animal Welfare, 1997-99. Author: (with others) Agricultural and Livestock Extension, 1982, Financial Management, 1972, Greening a Brown Land: The Australian Quest for Sustainable Land Use, 1992; book editor Australian Jour. Agrl. Econs., 1986-88; contbr. articles to profl. jours. Research grantee Dairying Research Com., Australia, 1978, Commonwealth Extension Services, Canberra, Australia, 1979, Res. Bank, Australia, 1983; Australian Meat Research Council scholar, 1973; Commonwealth spl. rsch. grantee, 1986, grantee Australian Meat and Livestock Rsch. and Devel. Corp., 1987, Nat. Soil Conservation Program, 1988-90, Land and Water Resources Rsch. and Devel. Corp., 1991-92, 96-98, Environment Australia, 1997-98. Mem. Australian Agrl. and Resource Econ. Soc., Internat. Assn. Agrl. Economists, Rural Sociology Assn., Soc. European Rsch. Econ. psychology, Hobson's Bay Yacht Club, Univ. Club Melbourne. Avocations: yachting, fishing, music, wine. Home: 479-481 The Boulevard, East Ivanhoe VIC 3079, Australia Office: U Melbourne Burnley Coll, Burnley Gardens Yarra Blvd, Richmond VIC 3121, Australia

CARY, TRISTRAM OGILVIE, composer, writer; b. Oxford, Eng., May 14, 1925; arrived in Australia, 1974, dual citizenship; s. Arthur Joyce and Gertrude Margaret (Ogilvie) C.; m. Doris Enid Jukes, July 7, 1951 (div. 1978); children: John T.L., Robert A.J., Charlotte A. MA, Oxford U., 1948; hon. degree, Royal Coll. Music, London, 1970. lic. music tchr. Trinity Coll. Music, 1952; cert. engr. Inst. Elec. Engring., 1946. Self-employed composer, writer, tchr., 1952-74; lectr. (part-time) Royal Coll. Music., London, 1967-74; sr. lectr. U. Adelaide, Australia, 1974-78; assoc. prof. U. Adelaide, 1978-86, dean music, 1982-83, hon. vis. rsch. fellow, 1986—; self-employed composer, writer, tchr., 1986—; founder, dir. Electronic Music Studios, London, 1969-74; head Tristram Cary Creative Music Svcs., Adelaide, 1986—. Author: Dictionary of Musical Technology, 1992; composer: (film sound track) The Little Island, 1958 (Venice/Brit. Film Acad. awards, 1958), (radio score) The Ballad of Peckham Rye, 1962 (PrixItalia, 1962), numerous scores for concert and all media, 1955—. Lt. (spl.) Royal Navy, 1943-46, North Sea/Atlantic. Recipient Medal of the Order of Australia, 1991. Mem. British Acad. Composers and Songwriters. Avocations: sailing, billiards, wine, food. Home and Office: 30 Fowlers Rd, Glen Osmond SA 5064, Australia

CARY, WALTER RAY, small business owner; b. Paris, Ill., Nov. 21, 1943; s. Walter and Mable (Vidito) C.; m. Judith Kay Shively, June 3, 1967; children: Thad, Alta. Store mgr. Irish Florist, Paris, 1958-67; cabinet maker Johnson's Planing Mill, Paris, 1967-86; owner, pres. Ray's Lock Shop, Paris, 1986—, RJC Enterprises, Terre Haute, Ind., 1990—; pres., CEO JRC, Inc., 1998—; owner, pres. Penske Truck Leasing, Terre Haute. Chmn. adminstrv. coun. 1st United Meth. Ch., Paris, 1991-94, 95—, chmn. bd. trustees, 1988-90; vol. instr. Sec. State Rules of Road. Office: RJC Enterprises 1296 Ft Harrison Rd Terre Haute IN 47804-1238

CARYL, WILLIAM R., JR., orthodontist; b. Syracuse, N.Y., Sept. 7, 1953; s. William R. and Joyce L. (Downs) C.; m. Deborah S. Auerbach, April 25, 1975; children: Mark R., David M. BA in Biology, SUNY, Buffalo, 1975, DDS, 1979; MS in Oral Biology, Loyola U. of Chgo., Maywood, Ill., 1981. Assoc. orthodontist William B. Drake, DDS, MS, Liverpool, N.Y., 1981-84; orthodontist pvt. practice, Camillus, N.Y., 1983—; mem. adv. bd. Fairmount Gardens, Syracuse, N.Y., 1994—; co-chair Ctrl. N.Y. Study Group for Dentofacial Abnormalities, 1993-95. Nat. ski patroler Nat. Ski Patrol System Camillus Ski Assn., 1969-71, 81-93. Mem. ADA, Am. Assn. Orthodontists, Am. Cleft Palate Craniofacial Assn., Syracuse Dental Seminar (program chair, sec. 1987-88, 88—, pres. 89, 89-90), Rotary Internat. (sec., pres. 1989-90). Avocations: sailing, skiing, bicycling, tennis, reading. Office: 5102 W Genesee St Camillus NY 13031-2327

CASAL, JORGE JOSÉ, plant physiologist; b. Buenos Aires, Apr. 30, 1959; s. Julio Amadeo and Mariana Nélida (Morelli) C.; m. Maria Virginia Perez, Mar. 17, 1963; children: Javier José, Joaquin Federico, Tomas Esteban. Diploma in agronomy, U. Buenos Aires, 1982, MS, 1987; PhD in Biol. Scis., U. Leicester (Eng.), 1989. Fellow Nat. Rsch Coun., Buenos

Aires, 1983-87; overseas fellow Nat. Rsch. Coun., Leicester, 1987-89; lectr. U. Buenos Aires, 1990, adj. prof., 1991, assoc. prof., 1997—; adj. rsch. scientist Nat. Rsch. Coun., Buenos Aires, 1991-98, sr. rsch. scientist, 1998—. Contbr., co-contbr. over 60 articles to profl. jours. Mem. Argentine Soc. of Plant Physiology, Am. Soc. Plant Physiology. Roman Catholic. Home: Castro Barros 699, 1217 Buenos Aires Argentina Office: U Buenos Aires Faculty Agronomy, Avenida San Martín 4453, 1417 Buenos Aires Argentina

CASALBUONI, ROBERTO, physics educator; b. Florence, Italy, Sept. 21, 1942; s. Gino and Iolanda (Casini) C.; m. Marta Ballini, Oct. 18, 1969; children: Sara, Chiara. Laurea infisica, Univ. Florence, 1969. Researcher INFN, Florence, 1971-87; prof. Univ. Lecce, 1987-90; prof. Univ. Florence, 1990—, dean faculty of scis., 1999—; bd. dirs. INFN, Florence, 1982-87, Dept. of Physics Florence, 1995. Contbr. articles to profl. jours. Inducted in the Soc. of Scholars of Johns Hopkins, 1996. Office: Dept of Physics, L GO E Fermi 2, 50125 Florence Italy

CASAL-TATLOCK, ALVARO, journalist, museum director; b. Montevideo, Uruguay, Jan. 30, 1940; s. Eusebio José and Martha Margarita (Tatlock) C.; m. Maria Elvira Ramirez, Dec. 28, 1968; 1 child, Alvaro Casal; m. Maria Estela Abal, Sept. 28, 1995. LLB, Pub. Sch. Uruguay, Montevideo, 1958. Reporter El Plata, Uruguay, 1962-67; corr. Veteran & Vintage, Uruguay, 1968-74; reporter El Pais, Montevideo, 1972-76, editor, 1976-86, features writer, 1986—; mus. dir. Automobile Club, Uruguay, 1982—; prof. journalism Tech. Inst. Edn., Uruguay, 1984—; dir. Tintex, Uruguay, 1988-92; cons. Uruguay's Nat. Heritage Commn., 1992—. Author: El Automovile en el Uruguay, 1981, Enterado, Archivese, 1987, Introducción al periodismo, 1990, Los Uruguayos y sus automóviles, 1993, The Automobile in South America, 1996, La Doctrina Larreta, 1997; editor Tourism Mag., 1993. Mem. Soc. Automotive Historians, Montevideo Classic Car Club, Internat. Assn. Transport Museums, Internat. Coun. Mus. Uruguay (mem. bd. 1993—). Avocations: antique car restoration, photography, antique gun collecting. Home: 26 de Marzo 1217 A502, Montevideo Uruguay Office: El Pais Z Michelini 1283, Montevideo Uruguay

CASANOVA, JEAN-CLAUDE, political science educator; b. Ajaccio, Corsica, June 11, 1934; s. Jean and Marie-Antoinette (Luciani) C.; m. Marié à Marie-Thérèse Demargne, 1962; children: Jean-Laurent, Pierre. Student, Inst. Hautes Etudes, Tunis, 1951-54, U. Paris, 1954-57; diploma, Inst. d'Etudes Politiques, Paris, 1955-57; postgrad., Harvard U., 1957-58; cert. dept. law and econ. scis., 1964, D of Econ. Scis., 1964. Asst. lectr. law and econs. U. Dijon, 1963-64; prof. law U. Nancy, 1964; titular prof. U. Paris-Nanterre, 1968, l'Ist. d'Etudes Politiques, Paris, 1969—; vis. prof. U. Dakar, U. Harvard, Acad. Diplomatique, Vienna, Inst. Diplomatique Peking; mem. cabinet Ministre de l'Industrie, 1959-61; dir. rsch. and studies Fondation Nationale des Sciences Politiques, 1965—, co-dir. econ. studies, 1968, mem. adv. bd., 1971-86, 86-91; tech. adviser for higher edn. to Cabinet of the Min. Edn., 1972-74; mem. Commn. Trilatérale, 1973—; adviser to Prime Min., R. Barre, 1976-81; co-dir. econ. Thémis collection, 1988—. Author: Principes d'analyse Économique, 11 vols., 1972-86; contbr. articles to profl. jours.; columnist l'Express, 1985-95. 2d Lt. French res., hon. lt., 1961-63. Decorated Officier de l'Ordre de la LÉgion d'Honneur, Chevalier de l'Ordre national du Mérite, Officier des Palmes acadÉmies. Mem. Soc. Commentaire (adminstr., co-founder 1977—, editor 1978—), Fondation Saint-Simon (founding mem.). Home: 87 Blvd Saint-Michel, 75005 Paris France Office: Svc d'étude de l'activite econ, 4 rue Michelet, 75006 Paris France also: Revue Commentaire, 116 rue du Bac, 75007 Paris France

CASANOVAS, FEDERICO VALDERRAMA, aviation executive; b. Cochabamba, Tiraque, Bolivia, Nov. 26, 1924; s. Donaciano Blanco and Ubaldina Grageda (Valderrama) C.; m. Bertha Trigo Sainz, Jan. 20, 1950; children: Juan Carlos, Roberto Federico, Mauricio Javier. MS, Advanced Nat. Studies, La Paz, Bolivia, 1962, Internat. Studies Inst., La Paz, Bolivia, 1981. Gen. mgr. Air Transport Airline, Cochabamba, Bolivia, 1975-79; air transport expert adviser Wilbur Smith L.A., La Paz, 1980; under-sec. of civil aviation Min. of Aeronautics, La Paz, 1980-82; civil aviation project mgr. Internat. Civil Aviation Orgn., Panama, 1982-84; air transport officer Sam Regional Office Internat. Civil Aviation Orgn., Lima, Peru, 1984-88; civil aviation gen. dir. DGAC, La Paz, 1990-94; chief of Bolivian mission Internat. Civil Aviation Orgn., La Paz, 1994—; mgr.'s adviser N.E. Bolivian Airways, Cochabamba; nat. dir. of civil aeronautics, Bolivian Govt., La Paz; Air Force chief of gen. staff, Air Force Command, La Paz. Contbr. articles to profl. publs. Mem. The Highlander Club, Blat., 1998-99. Air Brigade Gen., Air Force, 1966. Decorated Bolivian Armed Forces, Perus, Argentina, Brazil, Paraguay, others. Mem. Cochamba Social Club, Cochamba Tennis Club, Nat. Geographic Soc. Roman Catholic. Avocations: tennis, swimming, horseback riding. Home: Buenos Aires Ave No 0303, PO Box 1476, Cochabamba Bolivia

CASANOVAS, JOAN, history educator; b. Barcelona, Catalonia, Spain, Dec. 14, 1962; s. Josep and Helena (Codina) C.; m. Magdalena Chocano. Lic. History, U. Barcelona, 1987; MA, SUNY, Stony Brook, 1988, PhD, 1994. Rschr. U. Pompeu Fabra, Barcelona, 1995-96; asst. prof. Latin-Am. history U. Rovira i Virgili, Tarragona, Spain, 1996—. Author: Bread, or Bullets!: Urban Labor and Spanish Colonialism in Cuba, 1850-1898, 1998, Spanish edit., 2000; contbr. articles to profl. jours. With Spanish Army, 1983-84. Fulbright fellow Ministry of Edn., Spain, 1990-94. Mem. Am. Hist. Assn., Conf. Latin Am. History, Latin Am. Studies Assn. E-mail: jcasanov@urv.es. Home: Ptge Montornes 7, 08023 Barcelona Spain Office: Univ Rovira i Virgili, Pl Imperial Tarraco 1, 43005 Tarragona Spain

CASÃO, ROY, agricultural engineer, researcher; b. Londrina, Paraná, Brazil, July 21, 1952; s. Ruy and Therezinha Antunes C.; m. Maria Helend Dias Cunha, July 2, 1977; children: Carolina Dias, Filipe Dias. MSc, UNICAMP/FEAGRI, Campinas, Brazil, 1984; PhD, UNICAMP/FEM, Campinas, Brazil, 1996. Rschr. IAPAR, Lonorina, Brazil, 1976—; mgr. farm IAPAR, Londrina, Brazil, 1978-80, rsch. mgr., 1986-91, 96-98. Author: Circular Técnica, 1998; contbr. articles to profl. jours.; inventor in field. 2d lt. Brasilian Army, 1971-72. Mem. Agricultural Engring. Brasilian Soc. Mem. Democracy Social Party. Avocations: basketball, submarine driving, running, aquatic sports. Home: Clevelandia 119 Ap 101 St, 86060470 Londrina Parana, Brazil Office: Agrl Inst Parana, Celso Garcia Cid Km 375, 86001970 Londrina Parana, Brazil

CASAS, ALBERTO, physics educator; b. Zaragoza, Spain, Oct. 31, 1958; s. Justiniano Casas and Maria Gonzalez; m. Resurreccion del Pozo, Sept. 8, 1991; children: Alberto. Grad. in physics, U. Zaragoza, 1980; PhD in Physics, U. Autonoma Madrid, Spain, 1985. Teaching asst., temporal staff U. Autonoma, Madrid, 1981-86; Flemming fellow U. Oxford, England, 1986-88; staff prof. U. Santiago, Spain, 1988-90; permanent staff mem. Consejo Superior de Investigaciones Cientificas, Madrid, 1990—; fellow CERN, Geneva, Switzerland, 1991-93; temporal staff mem. U. Calif., Santa Cruz, 1995-96; coord. for Spain, European Network on Astro-particle Physics, 1996. Contbr. articles to profl. jours.; referee Zeitschrift Physics, Germany, 1986—, Physics Letters, Amsterdam, The Netherlands, 1991—, Phys. Rev. Letters, N.Y., 1995—. Named assoc. CERN, Geneva, 1994, scientific assoc., 1999-2000, Hon. Prof., U. Autonoma, 1996-97; grantee European Union, Oxford, 1995. Mem. Royal Spanish Soc. Physics, U. Autonoma Madrid Inst. Theoretical Physics. Avocations: literature, music. Home: Av Artesanos 165, 28760 Tres Cantos Madrid Spain Office: Inst Estructura Mat CSIC, Serrano 123, 28006 Madrid Spain

CASAS, WALTER MARIO DE LAS, writer; b. Feb. 3, 1947; s. Mario C. Everardo de las C. and Aracelia Vivó. BA cum laude, Iona Coll., 1970; MA, Hunter Coll., 1977. Writer, 1968—; tchr. secondary schs. N.Y.C. region, 1970-96. Author: La niñez que dilata, 1986, Libido, 1989, Tributes, 1993, Discourse, 1999. Recipient Americanism medal Am. Legion, N.Y.C., 1965. Mem. Am. Assn. Tchrs. Spanish & Portuguese. Home: 323 Dahill Rd Apt 1A Brooklyn NY 11218-3848

CASATI, ANDREA, anesthesiologist, researcher; b. Milan, Dec. 27, 1966; s. Ermeneitalo and Basilia (Belloni) C.; m. Lucia De Santis, Mar. 9, 1989; children: Marco, Sofia. MD, U. Milan, 1991, specialization in anesthesiology, 1995. Postdoctoral fellow anesthesiology dept. U. Milan, 1991-94; anesthesiology physician H.S. Raffaele, Milan, 1994—; clin. investigator on anesthesia. Mem. editl. bd. Jour. Clin. Anesthesia, Jour. ALR, Minerva Anestesiology; contbr. articles to profl. jours. Mem. Italian Soc. Anesthesia (Soc. Italiana di Anestesia, Analgesia, Rianimazione e Terapia Intensiva grantee 1992), European Soc. Anesthesiologist (subcom. regional anesthsia), Italian Alpine Club (Ski Alpinism instr. 1980-2000). Avocation: mountaineering. E-mail: casati.andrea@hsr.it. Fax: 39022 641 2823. Office: IRCCS H S Raffaele, V Olgettina 60, 20132 Milan Italy

CASATI, GIULIO, theoretical physics educator; b. Brenna, Italy, Dec. 9, 1942; m. Antonia, Sept. 1, 1968; children: Davide, Fabio. Laurea in Fisica, Milan (Italy) U., 1968. Asst. prof. physics dept. Milan U., 1971-74, assoc. prof. physics dept., 1974-87, prof. physics dept., 1987—; dep. rector U. Dell' Insubria, Como, 1999—; sci. sec. Centro di Cultura Scientifica A. Volta, Como, Italy, 1981—; mem. exec. coun. European Sci. Found., Strasbourg, France, 1987—. Editor several vols. on classical and quantum chaos; contbr. articles to profl. jours. Recipient Italian prize for physics Francesco Somaini Found., 1991. Mem. Acad. Europaea, Internat. Union Pure and Applied Physics (internat. commn. C3), Italian Phys. Soc., European Phys. Soc., Am. Phys. Soc., Rotary. Office: Centro A Volta, Villa Olmo, 22100 Como Italy

CASAUBON, JUAN IGNACIO, physicist; b. Buenos Aires, Aug. 2, 1954; s. Juan Alfredo and Hemilce Maria (Peltzer) C. Licentiate, Rosario (Argentina) U., 1977; PhD in Physics, Buenos Aires U., 1984. Fellow CONICET, Buenos Aires, 1979-81, 82-84, rschr., 1985—; asst. Buenos Aires U., 1979-81, chief of practicals works, 1986-99, assoc. prof., 1997—; asst. Rosario (Argentina) U., 1982-85; sec. Litoral Univ. Residence, Rosario, 1974-77. Contbr. articles to profl. jours. Mem. Argentine Assn. Physics, Asociacion Quimica Argentina, Club Universitario de Buenos Aires. Avocations: golf, football, science and society, music. Office: U Belgrano, Villanueva 1324, 1426 Buenos Aires Argentina

CASAVANTES, RITA, defense electronics and engineering professional; b. El Paso, Tex., Jan. 18, 1959; d. Luis and Nancy (Elliott) C. BSIE, U. Tex.-El Paso, 1981. Indsl. engr. Tex. Instruments, Sherman, Tex., 1982-84, indsl. engring. supr., 1985-86, asst. strategy mgr., 1987-93; also mem. libr. adv. coun. Tex. Instruments, Sherman, 1985—; facilitator, instr., 1993-97. Editor Texoma Indsl. Newsletter, 1982-84 (Gold award 1984). Mem. ASTD, Inst. Indsl. Engrs. (chpt. sec. 1982-84, chpt. v.p. 1984-85), Methods Time Measurement Assn., Am. Contract Bridge League. Republican. Roman Catholic. Avocations: bridge, needlework, boating. Home: 4401 Savannah Dr Sherman TX 75092-4029 Office: Raytheon 6620 Chase Oaks Blvd PO Box 660246 Plano TX 75023

CASE, CHARLES PATRICK, histopathologist, researcher, musician; b. Oxford, Oxon, Eng., June 6, 1950; s. Humphrey John and Jean Allison (Orr) C.; m. Ruth Diana Bolland, Aug. 29, 1981; children: David Hugh, Matthew Julian, Jennifer Claire. MSc, Oxford (Eng.) U., 1976, DPhil, 1982; MBChB, U. Bristol, 1989. Rsch. asst. Oxford U., 1978-81; sr. scientist Midland Ctr. for Neurosurgery, Birmingham, 1982-84; house officer Royal Infirmary, Bristol, 1984-90; house officer Southmead Hosp., Bristol, 1990-91, registrar, 1991-93; lectr. U./Royal Infirmary, Bristol, 1993—; lectr. U. Bristol, 1993-98; sci. dir. Bimplant Rsch. Ctr., Bristol, 1997—; sr. lectr. U. Southmead Hosp., Bristol, 1998—. Contbr. articles to profl. jours. including Brit. Jour. Bone & Joint Surgery, Clin. Orthopaedics, Neursci., and Jour. Neurocytology. Named Fees scholar Wolfson Coll., 1978-81, Royal Coll. Surgeons, 1992; recipient 1st prize Brit. Orthopaedic Assn., 1993. Mem. ACP, Royal Coll. Pathology. Avocation: playing and recording music for the rock bands Circus and Immense. Office: Southmead Hosp Cell Path, Westbury-on-Tryn, Bristol B510 5N8, England

CASE, CLYDE WILLARD, JR., sales and marketing executive; b. Trenton, N.J.; s. Clyde Willard and Elizabeth (Rusling) C.; m. Margaret Jane Meyer; children: Nancy Elyse, Laura Elizabeth, Margaret Anne. BSEE, Rutgers U., 1948. Sales engr. GE, Newark, 1948-53; v.p. Gen. Office Supply Co., Union, N.J., 1953-62; dir. sales and mktg. Corry (Pa.) Jamestown div. Hon Ind., 1963-76; v.p. Lehigh Leopold div. Litton Ind., Burlington, 1976-78; v.p. All Steel div. R.C.A., Aurora, Ill., 1978-82; pres. Bill Case Assocs. Inc., Aurora, 1982-99. Pres. Taxpayers Assn., Metuchen, N.J., 1970-71. Sgt. U.S. Army, 1943-46. Mem. AIA (bd. dirs. Chgo. unit), Mchts. and Mfrs. Club of Chgo., Met. Planning Coun., Chgo. Archtl. Found., Chgo. Assn. Commerce and Industry, Rotary (N.Y.C.). Republican. Presbyterian. Avocations: recreational basketball, football, ice skating, hockey, golf. Home: 2361 Sans Souci Dr Aurora IL 60506-5262

CASE, DAVID BARTLETT, internist, educator; b. Plainfield, N.J., Mar. 17, 1942; s. George and Caroline (Bartlett) C.; m. Jean Brookhart, Aug. 2, 1969; children: Thayer Stimson, Nelson Chipman. AB, Princeton U., 1964; MD, Columbia U., 1968. Intern, then asst. resident Johns Hopkins Hosp., Balt., 1968-70; fellow Columbia Presbyn. Hosp., N.Y.C., 1972-75; asst., then assoc. prof. Cornell U. Med. Coll., N.Y.C., 1975-84, clin. assoc. prof., 1984—; mem. Council on High Blood Pressure Research, 1979—; vis. lectr. Columbia U. Coll. of Physicians and Surgeons, 1997—. Contbr. chpts. to books in field of hypertension, also articles to profl. jours. Recipient Andrew Mellon Tchr. Scientist award Cornell U., 1978. Master ACP (gov. downstate I); fellow Am. Coll. Clin. Pharmacology. Office: 635 Madison Ave New York NY 10022-1009

CASE, DAVID LEON, lawyer; b. Lansing, Mich., Sept. 22, 1948; s. Harlow Hoyt and Barbara Jean (Denman) C.; m. Cynthia Lou Rhinehart, Jan. 28, 1968; children: Beau, Ryan, Kimberly, Darren, Stephanie. BS with distinction, Ariz. State U., 1970, JD cum laude, 1973. Bar: Calif. 1973, U.S. Dist. Ct. (cen. dist.) Calif. 1973, U.S. Tax Ct. 1974, Ariz. 1976, U.S. Supreme Ct. 1997. Assoc. Willis, Butler & Scheifly, Los Angeles, 1973-75; from assoc. to mem. Ryley, Carlock & Applewhite, Phoenix, 1975—. Fellow Ariz. Bar Found., Am. Coll. Trust and Estate Counsel; mem. ABA (tax sect., corp. sect., probate and trust sect.), Ariz. Bar Assn., Ctrl. Ariz. Estate Planning Coun. (bd. dirs., pres. 1988-89), Beta Gamma Sigma. Republican. Presbyterian. Avocations: running, guitar, sports. Office: Ryley Carlock & Applewhite PO Box 634 Phoenix AZ 85001-0634

CASE, ELDON DARREL, materials science educator; b. Logan, Kans., Aug. 23, 1949; s. Eldon George and Ila Marie (Lewis) C.; m. Linda Lee Lubken, Aug. 29, 1975 (div. Mar. 1993); 1 child, Carl Allen; m. Rebecca J. Ervin, 1996. BA in Physics and Math., U. Colo., 1971; PhD in Materials Sci., Iowa State U., 1980. Rsch. asst. dept. materials sci. Iowa State U., Ames, 1976-80; NRC postdoctoral assoc. Nat. Bur. Standards, Gaithersburg, Md., 1980-82; rsch. engr. in materials sci. and mining engring. U. Calif., Berkeley, 1982-85; asst. prof. metallurgy, mechanics and materials sci. Mich. State U., East Lansing, 1985-88, assoc. prof., 1988-99, prof., 1999—; cons. Indsl. Tech. Inst., Ann Arbor, Mich., 1990, Westinghouse, West Mifflin, Pa., 1991-92; judge Nat. Am. Indian Sci. and Engring. Fair, 1993-2000; grand awards judge Internat. Sci. and Engring. Fair, 2000. Contbr. more than 95 tech. articles to profl. jours. and conf. procs. including Jour. Materials Sci., Materials Sci. Engring., Applied Physics Letters. Speaker to sch. groups Okemos (Mich.) Pub. Schs., 1986-90; asst. with middle-sch. activities Episcopal Ch., East Lansing, 1988-92; judge Nat. Am. Indian Sci. and Engring. Fair, 1993-2000. Recipient Tchr.-Scholar award Mich. State U., 1989, Withrow Excellence in Tchg. award Engring. Coll. Mich. State U., 1993, 95, 98; Regents scholar U. Colo., 1967-71; NRC postdoctoral assoc., 1980-82; grantee NASA, 1987, NSF, 1987-90, Mich. State U., 1989. Mem. AAUP, ASM (chair advanced joining tech. com. 1999—, tech. programming bd. for joining critical tech. sector 1999—), Nat. Inst. Ceramic Engrs., The Metall. Soc. (sec. structural materials div. 1988-91, chair non-metall. com. 1988-91), Am. Ceramic Soc. (pres. Mich. sect. 1998—, officer nominating com. engring. ceramics divsn.), Sigma Xi. Democrat. Achievements include first neutron scattering study from microcracks in a polycrystalline ceramic; statistical analysis of water drop impact damage cracks in infrared windows; microwave sintering and joining of ceramics and ceramic composites; adhesion studies of diamond thin-films on brittle substrates; thermal-shock and thermal fatigue studies on ceramics and ceramic composites, microwave sintering and joining of ceramics. Home: 4469 Fairlane Dr Okemos MI 48864-2407 Office: Materials Sci and Mechanics Sci Dept East Lansing MI 48824

CASE, GERARD RAMON, drafting technologist, paleontologist; b. Bklyn., Dec. 22, 1931; s. James Sanford and Adele Elizabeth (Harris) C. Student BFA program, Pratt Inst., Bklyn., 1955-59. Cert. coml. artist and draftsman. Pvt. practice advt. and art N.Y.C., 1955-72, Ultra Cooling Corp., N.Y.C., 1972-85; drafting technician Engring. div. Dept. of Pub. Works, Hackensack, N.J., 1986—; rsch. assoc. The Carnegie Mus. of Natural History, Pitts., Mich. State U. Mus., East Lansing; field assoc. dept. entomology The Am. Mus. of Natural History, N.Y.C. Author: Fossil Shark-Fish Remains of North America, 1967, Fossils Illustrated, 1968, Handbook of Fossil Collecting, 1972, Fossil Sharks: A Pictorial Review, 1973, Pictorial Guide to Fossils, 1982; contbr. 90 articles to profl. jours. With USN, 1951-55. Recipient Harrell L. Strimple award Paleontol. Soc., 1992; Rsch. grantee Griffis Found./Am. Littoral Soc., 1976-86. Mem. AAAS, Internat. Platform Asssn., Am. Littoral Soc., Soc. Vertebrate Palaeontology, Paleontol. Soc., Am. Legion, Korean War Vets. Soc., Soc. Col. Wars, Hereditary Order 1st Families Mass. (life), Sons of the Revolution (life). Republican. Baptist. Achievements include research in genera and species of fossil remains; discovery of insects in amber, new genera and species of fossil fish, and a new order of fossil fishes, the Iniopterygians.

CASE, HADLEY, oil company executive; b. N.Y.C., Mar. 28, 1909; s. Walter Summerhayes and Mary Soule (Hadley) C.; m. Julie Marguerite Ill, June 8, 1935 (dec. Mar. 1975); children: Mary C. Durham, Julie Anne, Rosalie C. Clark, Deborah Joan; m. Elizabeth M. McCabe, Nov., 1975. Student, Kent (Conn.) Sch., 1924-29, Antioch Coll., 1929-33; DSc (hon.), Antioch U., 1991, DS (hon.), 1991. Geol. field work Australia, 1933-34, Tex., 1935-36; with geol. dept. Case, Pomeroy & Co., Inc., N.Y.C., 1936-39, v.p., 1939-41, pres., 1941-83, CEO, 1983-93, chmn. bd., 1983-99, chmn. emeritus, 1999—; also bd. dirs.; pres., CEO Felmont Oil Corp., 1952-84; chmn. of bd., CEO Felmont Oil Corp. (merger Felmont and Homestake Mining Co.), 1972-84; dir. Homestake Mining Co., 1984-95, Brown Bros. Harriman Trust Co. Fla., 1986-93. Trustee Antioch U., 1987-93, Kent Sch., 1959-75, Brewster Acad., 1956-63, Boys' and Girls' Camps, Inc., Boston, 1971-76; trustee Hosp. St. Barnabas, Newark, 1942-59, pres. bd. trustees, 1949-52; bd. dirs. Greenwich Boys Club Assn., 1957-73, hon. mem., 1974—; trustee Naples (Fla.) Community Hosp., 1985-91; bd. dirs. Naples Philharm. Ctr. for Arts, 1988—; dir. The Conservancy, Naples, 1985-91; chancellor Kent Sch., 1985—, trustee, 1986—. Mem. Am. Inst. Mining and Metall. Engrs., Am. Petroleum Inst., Ind. Petroleum Assn. Am. (past v.p., dir.). Office: Case Pomeroy & Co Inc 529 5th Ave Fl 16 New York NY 10017-4684

CASE, RIC, computer company executive, consultant; b. Pottstown, Pa., Oct. 22, 1946; s. Richard I. and Amelia Elizabeth Case; m. Patricia Ann Anderson, Jan. 3, 1981 (div. Feb. 1987); 1 child, Steven Richard; m. Jacqueline Marie Utes, Oct. 25, 1997. B in Bus. Adminstrn., Tempe U., 1979. Mgr. Cotter & Co., Chgo., 1986-89; pres. Case Computer Consulting Corp., Lake Zurich, Ill., 1989—. With U.S. Army, 1967-68, Korea. Mem. Top Cats of Ill. (pres. 1997-2000). Republican. Lutheran. Avocations: motorcycling, snowmobiling, bowling, team sports. E-mail: riccase@earthlink.net and riccase@yahoo.com. Fax: 847-550-6543. Office: Case Computer Consulting Corp 1028 Aspen Ct Lake Zurich IL 60047-2232

CASE, ROSALIND See AVRETT, ROZ

CASEBEER, DOUGLAS KELLEY, artist, ceramist, consultant; b. Joplin, Mo., Nov. 1, 1956; s. Charles William and Sue (Dalby) C.; nm. Susan Roscoe, Dec. 22, 1979; children: Emily Clara, Logan Oliver. Student, U. Okla., 1974-76, Mo. Western Stat Coll., 1977-78; BFA in Ceramics, Wichita State U., 1980; MFA in Ceramics, Alfred U., 1982. Dir. ceramics and sculpture program, instr., resident artist Anderson Ranch Arts Ctr., Snowmass Village, Colo., 1985—, program dir. artist-in-residency program, 1987—, dir. programs, 1995-97; tchg. asst. advanced pottery and kilns N.Y. State Coll. Ceramics, Alfred U., 1980-82; instr. ceramics Jamaica Sch. Art, Kingston, 1984; ceramic cons. UN Indsl. Devel. Orgn., Vienna, Austria, 1982-85, German Agy. for Tech. Cooperation, Eschborn, 1985, Govt. of Nepal, Kathmandu, 1985, USIS, Washington, 1993, Hui Noeau Visual Arts Ctr., Makawao, Maui, Hawaii, 1998; prof. ceramics U. Ga., Cortona, Italy, 1993; mem. nat. adv. bd. Aspen Ednl. Rsch. Found., Woody Creek, Colo., 1998—; co-leader, instr. Gobardia project Potters to Nepal, ceramics study tour, Deohkuri, Dang Dist., Nepal, 1993-00; condr. workshops, lectr., vis. artist, 1983—. Exhibited in numerous group shows, 1978—, latest being Foothills Art Ctr., Golden, Colo., 1995, 98, Auckland (New Zealand) Studio Potters, 1996, 2000, U. So. Colo., Pueblo, 1996, Taller Huara-Huara, Santiago, Chile, 1996, Daniel Arvizu Gallery, Santa Ana, Calif., 1996, Mus. Nebr., Kearney, 1996, S.E. Ind. U., New Albany, 1997, Grosvenor Gallery, Kingston, Jamaica, 1997, Coll. of Ozarks, Point Lookout, Mo., 1997, Roundtree Art Ctr., Denver, 1997, Contemporary Artifacts Gallery, Brea, Ky., 1997, Greenwich House Pottery, N.Y.C., 1997, 98, 99, Adelson Gallery, Aspen, Colo., 1998, Evelyn Siegel Gallery, Ft. Worth, 1998, Ching-Tao Fang Ceramics Gallery, Kaohsiung, Taiwan, 1998, Odyssey Gallery, Asheville, N.C., 1999, Islip Art Mus., New Islip, N.Y., 1999, Yoyokaku Gallery, Karatsu-Chi, Saga, Japan, 1999, Gallery Ichibankan, Fukuoka, Japan, 1999, Andrews U., Beriene Springs, Mich., 2000, Hibberd/McGrath Gallery, Breckenridge, Colo., 2000, Signature Gallery, Atlanta, 2000; represented in permanent collections Islip Art Mus., Contemporary Ceramics Arts Inst., Taipei, Taiwan, Auckland Art Mus., Jamaica Nat. Gallery, Stetson U., Bemidji (Minn.) State U., Eccelson Harrison Mus. Art, Utah State U., Logan, N.Y. State Coll. Ceramics, Alfred U., Topeka Pub. Libr., also pvt. and corp. collections; work reviewed in newspapers and mags. Mem. Am. Craft Coun., Coll. Art Assn., Nat. Coun. on Edn. Ceramic Arts, Colo. Artist Craftsmen Assn. (bd. dirs. 1990-91). Achievements include development variety of kilns in U.S. and Caribbean; research on glazes and clay bodies in relation to demands of final project; discovered and developed 5 clays and variety of basic minerals for manufacture of ceramic products, 3 stoneware and 2 earthenware clays, 3 varieties of silica, dolomite, limestones, gypsum, haematite, steatite, and prophyry granites for feldspars. Office: Anderson Ranch Arts Ctr PO Box 5598 5263 Owl Creek Rd Snowmass Village CO 81615

CASELLA, PETER F(IORE), patent and licensing executive; b. June 5, 1922; s. Fiore Peter and Lucy (Grimaldi) C.; m. Marjorie Eloise Enos, March 9, 1946 (dec. Aug. 1989); children: William Peter, Susan Elaine, Richard Mark. BChE, Poly. U., Bklyn., 1943; student in chemistry, St. John's U., N.Y.C., 1940. Registered to practice by the U.S. Patent and Trademark Office, Can. Patent and Trademark Offices. Head patent sect. Hooker Electrochem. Co., Niagara Falls, N.Y., 1943-54; mgr. patent dept. Occidental Chem. Corp. (formerly Hooker Chem. Corp.), Niagara Falls, N.Y., 1954-64, dir. patents and licensing, 1964-81, asst. sec., 1966-81, ret., 1981; pres. TFA Products, Inc., Houston, Intra Gene Internat., Inc., Lewiston, N.Y., 1981-92; chmn. bd. In Vitro Internat., Inc., Linthicum, Md., 1983-86; cons. patents and licensing, Lewiston, N.Y., 1981—; Dept. Commerce del. on patents and licensing exchange, USSR, 1973, 90, Poland and German Dem. Rep., 1976. Editor: Drafting the Patent Application, 1957. Mem. Lewiston Bd. Edn., 1968-70. With AUS, 1944-46, Mediterranean Theater of Operation. Recipient Centennial citation Poly. U., Bklyn., 1955, Golden Jubilee Soc., 1993. Mem. ACS, AIChE, Assn. Corp. Patent Counsel (emeritus, exec. com. 1974-77, charter mem.), N.Y. Intellectual Property Law Assn. (Niagara Frontier chpt. pres. 1973-74, founder award 1974), Licensing Execs. Soc. (v.p. 1976-77, Trustees award 1977), Chartered Inst. Patent Agts. Gt. Britain (emeritus), Patent and Trademark Inst. Can., Internat. Patent and Trademark Assn. (emeritus), U.S. Trademark Assn., Nat. Assn. Mfrs. (patent com.), Mfg. Chemists Assn., Pacific Indsl. Property Assn., U.S. Patent Office Soc. (assoc.), U.S. Trademark Office Soc. (assoc.), Chemists Club (emeritus N.Y.C. chpt.), Niagara Club (Niagara Falls pres. 1973-74).

CASELLA, RUSSELL CARL, physicist; b. Framingham, Mass., Nov. 6, 1929; s. Rosario and Lena Casella; m. Marilyn Smith, Jan. 27, 1952; children: Sheryl M., Cynthia L. Conturie. BS in Physics, MIT, 1951, MS in Physics, 1953; PhD in Physics, U. Ill., 1956. Physicist Cambridge (Mass.) AF Rsch. Ctr., 1951-52; teaching and rsch. asst. physics dept. U. Ill., Urbana, 1953-55, rsch. fellow physics dept., 1955-56, rsch. assoc. physics dept., 1956-58; theoretical physicist IBM T.J. Watson Rsch. Ctr., Yorktown Heights, N.Y., 1958-65, Nat. Inst. Standards and Tech., Gaithersburg, Md., 1965-95. Contbr. numerous articles to profl. jours. Recipient Silver medal U.S. Dept. Commerce, 1973. Mem. Am. Phys. Soc., Sigma Xi. Achievements include development of theory of condensed-matter and of elementary-particle physics; research in (broken) symmetries; neutron scattering; Bose condensation of excitons; tests of time reversal and CPT symmetries in Kaon

physics; neutrino scattering; topology in neutron interferometry; high-temperature superconductivity; hydrogen in metals; quark-parton-sea content of the nucleon in deep-inelastic electroweak scattering. Home: 1485 Dunster Ln Potomac MD 20854-6107

CASELLAS, JOACHIM, art gallery executive; b. Gerona, Spain, Aug. 1, 1927; came to U.S., 1954; s. Juan and Dolores Farre (Carrera) C.; m. Elizabeth Reed Brannon, Mar. 17, 1952 (dec. Dec. 1984); m. Janice Mary Bezverkov, May 29, 1990. BA, Gerona Coll., 1948; MA, Sacred Heart Coll., 1953. Curator Mus. Provincial, Gerona, Spain, 1952; art appraiser Feist Co., N.Y.C., 1952-68, Mahan Co., New Orleans, 1968-72; pres. Casell Gallery, New Orleans, 1972—. One-man shows include Ft. Walton (Fla.) Beach Mus. Art, 1987. Mem. Ocean Springs Yacht Club. Republican. Episcopalian. Avocations: photography, plants. travel, antiques, boating. Home: 107 Shearwater Dr Ocean Springs MS 39564-4828 Office: Casell Gallery 818 Royal St New Orleans LA 70116-3115

CASELLES, VICENTE, physics educator; b. Gata, Alicante, Spain, Mar. 6, 1957; s. Vicente Caselles and Luisa Miralles; m. Elena Marti, July 19, 1981; children: Eduardo, Diego. BSc, U. Valencia, Spain, 1979, MSc, 1980, PhD, 1983. Rschr. U. Valencia, 1978-81, asst. prof., 1982-86, assoc. prof., 1987—, head inst., 1992—; cons. in field; bd. dirs. TIRS Group, Valencia. Author: Remote Sensing, 1991, Desertification, 1996, Agronomy, 1993; patentee in field. Vice chmn. AET, Madrid, 1997—; mem. for Spain Earsel, Paris, 1991-95. Officer Spanish Army, 1979-80. Fellow RSS, RSEF; mem. AGU (life), ASPRS. Avocations: football, skiing, handball. Home: Plz de Honduras 29, 46022 Valencia Spain Office: U Valencia Faculty Physics Dept Thermodynamics, Doctor Moliner 50, 46100 Burjassot Valencia Spain

CASER, SERGE JOSEPH, physicist; b. Inkermann, Oran, Algeria, Apr. 4, 1943; arrived in France, 1947; s. Domenico and Delphina (Loss-Franzin) C.; m. Marie Anne Bire, May 10, 1977 (div. Jan. 1999); 1 child, Sylvain. MSc, Strasbourg, France, 1965; specialty doctorate, Orsay, France, 1967; PhD in physics, Orsay, 1973. Rschr. Nat. Ctr. Sci. Rsch., Paris, Orsay, France, 1967-74, 76—; researcher Calif. Inst. Tech., Pasadena, Calif., 1974-76; cons. CNRS/Industry, France, 1980-82. Contbr. articles to internat. jours. Recipient 2nd prize best short story Fête du Livre, Palaiseau, 1987. Mem. N.Y. Acad. Scis. Avocations: novelist, short story author. Home: 96 Bis Ave de Paris, Versailles 78000, France Office: CNRS-LPT Bat 211, Univ Paris Sud, Orsay 91405, France

CASEY, BARBARA JEANNE, marketing professional; b. Glen Cove, N.Y., Mar. 6, 1970; d. William Royal DeMeo and Barbara Louise (Anderson) Terry; m. John Edward Casey, Sept. 12, 1998. BA, U. So. Calif., 1992; MBA, Columbia U., 1998. Client svcs. rep. Christie's Inc., N.Y.C., 1992-93, adminstr., 1993-94, overseas liaison, 1994-96; assoc. mktg. mgr. Time Inc., N.Y.C., 1998-99; dir. mktg. Onview.com., N.Y.C., 1999—. Mem. jr. com. Search and Care, Inc., 1993—. Mem. Am. Mktg. Assn., Choate N.Y.C. Alumni Club (v.p. 1996-98, co-pres. 1998—), Doubles Club (assocs. com. 1993—), Delta Gamma (v.p. programming alumni club 1994-95). Avocations: dogs, tennis, golf, skiing, arts and entertainment. Home: 945 Fifth Ave Apt 5E New York NY 10021-2655 Office: Onview.com 20 W 20th St Ste 904 New York NY 10011-4213

CASEY, BERNARD J., lawyer; b. June 4, 1942; s. Andrew J. and Theresa (Lennon) C.; m. Kathleen A. Wall; children: Brendan, B. John. AB, Providence Coll., 1964; JD, Catholic U., 1967. Bar: R.I. 1967, D.C. 1971, U.S. Supreme Ct. 1972, U.S. Cir. Ct. (D.C. cir., 4th cir., 6th cir.). Assoc. Gall, Lane & Powell, Washington, 1971-76, ptnr., 1976; ptnr. Reed Smith Shaw & McClay, Washington, 1976—. Bd. dirs. Cath. Charities, 1994-99, chmn., 1997-98. Served to capt. AUS, 1967-71. Decorated Bronze Star medal. Mem. ABA (litigation com.), D.C. Bar Assn., Barristers, Lawyers Club, Univ. Club (bd. govs. 1989-97, pres. 1990-92), Chevy Chase Country Club. Roman Catholic. Home: 4700 Connecticut Ave NW Apt 607 Washington DC 20008-5613 Office: Reed Smith Shaw & McClay East Tower 1301 K St NW Ste 1100 Washington DC 20005-3317

CASEY, CAROL ANN, librarian; b. Columbus, Ohio, Feb. 22, 1955; d. John P. and Eileen (Schupbach) C. MusB in Music Composition, So. Ill. U., 1975; MusM in Music Composition, U. Ill., 1978; MLS, Ind. U., 1985. Music catalog libr. So. Meth. U., Dallas, 1985-88; music catalong libr. U. Cin., 1988-90; catalog libr. Tex. Tech. U., Lubbock, 1990-92, coord. cataloging, 1992-95; head catalog dept. U. La., Lafayette, 1995—. Author: (book) Analytical Indexes to the Internet, 2000; contbr. articles to profl. jours. Mem. ALA, Nat. Writers Union. E-mail: ccasey@wsu.edu. Office: Holland Libr Wash State Univ Pullman WA 99165

CASEY, EDWARD DENNIS, newspaper editor; b. Binghamton, N.Y., Apr. 16, 1931; s. Edwin John and Agnes Mary (Casey) C.; m. E. Jacqueline Wilson, July 13, 1957; children—Daniel, Jeanne, Edward, John. B.A., St. Bonaventure U., 1952; postgrad., Armed Forces Pub. Information Sch., 1953, Syracuse U. Grad. Sch. Journalism, 1954. News editor Sun-Bull., Binghamton, 1960-65; editor Daily Advance, Dover, N.J., 1965-71; exec. editor Capital-Gazette Newspapers, Annapolis, Md., 1971—. Vice pres. Community Chest of Anne Arundel County.; bd. dirs. Annapolis Symphony Orch.; pres. Annapolis/Bywater Boys and Girls Club. With U.S. Army, 1952-54. Recipient Pub. Service award A.P., 1964, Nat. Headliners award, 1965. Mem. AP Mng. Editors Assn., Am. Soc. Newspaper Editors, KC, Sigma Delta Chi. Roman Catholic. Home: 1517 Riverdale Dr Annapolis MD 21401-5839 Office: The Capital 2000 Capital Dr Annapolis MD 21401-3157

CASEY, GAVIN, stock exchange executive; b. 1947. Various positions to dep. chief exec. County Nat. West Bank, from 1972; fin. dir. Smith New Court, 1989-94, COO, 1994; chief adminstrv. officer for internat. equities Merrill Lynch, 1994-96; chief exec. The Stock Exch., London, 1996—. Office: The Stock Exch, London EC2N 1HP, England Address: Dexter House, Royal Mint Ct, London EC3N 4QN, United Kingdom*

CASEY, JAMES FRANCIS, management consultant; b. Boston, May 22, 1935; s. James Francis and Elizabeth Mary (MacNeil) C.; m. Margaret Ann Flaherty, Jan. 22, 1977. BA in Philosophy cum laude, Weston Coll., 1957, BS/MS in Physics cum laude, 1962. Sales mgr. Xerox Corp., Stamford, Conn., 1963-79; dir. mktg. Computervision Corp., Bedford, Mass., 1979-82; v.p. CTX Corp., Sunnyvale, Calif., 1982-83; sr. mktg. exec. Hewlett-Packard Corp., Palo Alto, Calif., 1983-86; group mgr. Digital Equipment Corp., Maynard, Mass., 1986-92; mng. ptnr. Synergy Cons., Los Altos, Calif., 1992—; mem., dir., mem. exec. com. Agincourt Capital Plc, Dublin, Ireland, 1997-2000; pres. Mcpl. Utility Dist., State of Tex., 1998—, also bd. dirs.; cons. numerous clients, including IBM, Hewlett-Packard Co., Ceridian, Lexis-Nexis, E-Commerce Group, Reed Elsevier Plc. Group, others. Patron San Francisco Opera Co., 1982-99, San Francisco Orch., 1982-91; Friend Boston Symphony Orch., 1976-81; contbr. Austin Symphony Orch. Mem. Am. Mgmt. Assn. (bd. dirs. 1962-65), Am. Electronic Assn. (mktg. com. chmn. 1989-91), Hill Country Intergroup Assn. (chmn. bd. overseers), Del. Valley Reprographic Soc. (v.p.1965-69), Jr. C. of C. (pres. Phila. chpt. 1965-69). Fax: 512-346-6024. E-mail: casey78730@aol.com. Home and Office: 10123 Treasure Island Dr Austin TX 78730-3559

CASEY, MICHEAL WILLIAM, portfolio manager; b. Indpls., Oct. 4, 1955; s. Robert Ellsworth and Mildred Jane (Holland) C.; m. Christine McCarthy, Apr. 11, 1991 (div. Sept. 1997); children: Kathleen Maura, Thomas Robert, James Patrick. AB, Ind. U., 1978; MS, London Sch. Econs., 1985; PhD, New Sch. Social Rsch., 1996. Translator U. Graz, Austria, 1978-80; tchr. math. Peace Corps, Sierra Leone, 1981-83; economist McCarthy, Crisanti & Maffei, N.Y.C., 1986-90; internat. economist Maria Ramierz, Inc., N.Y.C., 1990-96; portfolio mgr. Federated Investors, N.Y.C., 1996—. Mem. Am. Econ. Assn., Ea. Econ. Assn., Internat. Economists Club N.Y. Office: Federated Investors 125 Water St Fl 15 New York NY 10005-1624

CASEY, PATRICK ANTHONY, lawyer; b. Apr. 20, 1944; s. Ivanhoe and Eutimia (Casados) C.; m. Gail Marie Johns, Aug. 1, 1970; children: Christopher Gaelen, Matthew Colin. BA, N.Mex. State U., 1970; JD, U. Ariz., 1973. Bar: N.Mex. 1973, Ariz. 1973, U.S. Dist. Ct. N.Mex. 1973, U.S. Ct. Appeals (10th cir.) 1979, U.S. Supreme Ct. 1980, U.S. Dist. Ct. Ariz. 1999. Assoc. Bachicha & Casey, Santa Fe, 1973-76; pvt. practice Santa Fe, 1976—. Bd. dirs. Santa Fe Sch. Arts and Crafts, 1974, Santa Fe Animal Shelter, 1975-81, Cath. Charities of Santa Fe, 1979-82, Old Santa Fe Assn., 1979-88, Santa Fe Fiesta Coun., 1982—; bd. dirs. United Way, 1986-89, N.Mex. State U. Found., 1985-93. With USN, 1961-67. Mem. ATLA (state del. 1988-89, bd. govs. 1990-91, 93-95), ABA, Western Trial Lawyers Assn. (bd. dirs. 1988-91, parliamentarian 1990-91, gov. 1987-90, treas. 1991-95, sec. 1991-92, pres.-elect 1995-96, pres. 1996-97), N.Mex. Trial Lawyers Assn. (dir. 1977-79, 85—, treas. 1979-83, pres. 1983-84), Bar Assn. 1st Jud. Dist. (pres. 1980), Hispanic Bar Assn., Am. Legion, Vietnam Vets. of Am., VFW, Elks. Office: 1421 Luisa St Ste P Santa Fe NM 87505-4073

CASEY, THOMAS JEFFERSON, investment banker, venture capitalist. Student, U.S. Naval Acad., 1964-65; MBA, Harvard U., 1970; PhD, U. London/Am. U., 1997—. Pres./COO New Eng. Furniture Group, Boston, 1968-71; chmn./CEO Commonwealth Industries, Inc., N.Y.C., 1971-75; pres./gen. mgr. Damson Oil Corp. AMEX, N.Y.C. and Houston, 1975-80; founder/chmn./CEO The Sovereign Group, Ltd., N.Y.C., 1980-90; chmn., CEO EnTech, Inc., N.Y.C., 1991—; guest lectr. Wharton Grad. Sch. Bus. Adminstrn.; former mem. faculty internat. mgmt. Northeastern U. Sch. Mgmt. and Adminstrn., Boston; sr. fin./investment advisor to several Fortune 500 cos., sovereign fgn. govts. and internat. fin. instns. Avocations: golf, tennis, skiing, sailing, flying. Office: EnTech Inc 730 5th Ave Ste 900 New York NY 10019-4105

CASEY, THOMAS WARREN, graphic design company executive, architect; b. Columbus, Ohio, Dec. 9, 1942; s. Warren Vale and Martha Elizabeth (Greene) C.; m. Susan Henrietta Davis, Oct. 1, 1966. BArch, Ohio State U., 1966. Registered architect, N.Y. Draftsman Skidmore Owings & Merrill, Chgo., 1964-66; architect U.S. Peace Corps, Tanzania, 1966-69; designer Brooks Barr Graeber & White, Austin, Tex., 1969-71, Hardy Holzman Pfeiffer, N.Y.C., 1971-73; design dir. Paul Arthur & Assoc., N.Y.C., 1973-74; designer Page, Artibrio & Resen, N.Y.C., 1974-79; ptnr. Greenboam & Casey Assocs., Inc., N.Y.C., 1979-94, The Casey Group, New Canaan, Conn., 1994—; con. Conn. Trust for Hist. Preservation, 1995, U.S. Gen. Svc. Adminstrn., 1996, juror Print Casebook Awards, N.Y.C., 1988, Hotel Sales & Mktg. Assoc., N.Y.C., 1987-90, Soc. Environ. Graphic Design 1997 Design Awards; adj. prof. N.J. Sch. of Architecture, Newark, 1980-82; guest lectr. Harvard U., Boston, 1982, U. Cin., 1990. Pres. Friends of New Canaan Libr., 1998—. Recipient Print Casebook 7 award, 1987. Mem. AIA (hist. resources com. Acad. of Architecture for Health), Soc. Environ. Graphic Design (bd. dirs. 1985-90, 96-99, pres. 1988-89), S.W. Pks. and Monuments Assn. (life), Conn. Trust for Hist. Preservation, Dutch Treat Club, Xi Grad. chpt. Phi Gamma Delta, Gridiron Club of New Canaan. Democrat. Fax: (203) 966-0250.

CASH, CAROL VIVIAN, sociologist; b. Port Arthur, Tex., Jan. 22, 1929; d. Mano Nathan and Floris Duval (Akin) C.; m. Robert Morrow Welch, Dec. 21, 1951 (div. 1966); children: Catherine Carol, Robert M. III, Candice Claire. AA, Lamar Jr. Coll., 1951; BS in Sociology, U. Houston, 1971. Sec. Port Arthur SS Co., 1948-50; with Gov's Office State of Tex., Austin, 1951-52; legal sec. Wesley W. West, Houston, 1953-55. Author numerous children's books. Active Houston area Boy Scouts Am., Girl Scouts U.S., 1960-76, Port Arthur Hist. Soc.; mem. Tex. Sesquicentennial Com., 1986; active in restoration of Tex. historic homes. Mem. AAUW (chmn. Port Arthur fund raiser 1982), Tex. Artist Mus. Soc., Planetary Soc., Fed. Women's Clubs, Writer's Club (v.p. 1983-84, pres. 1984-85, treas. 1985-90), U. Houston Alumni Assn. Avocations: concerts, theater, gardening.

CASHION, JOHN DIXON, physicist, educator; b. Launceston, Tasmania, Australia, Aug. 27, 1942; s. Albert Dixon and Ada Evelyn (Maynard) C.; m. Joan Margaret Lang, Sept. 16, 1967; children: Ian Campbell, Kathleen Joanne, Gillian Vikki. BSc, U. Melbourne, Australia, 1964, MSc, 1966; PhD, Oxford (Eng.) U., 1969. Lectr. Monash U., Melbourne, 1969-75, sr. lectr., 1976-83, assoc. prof., 1984—, head dept. physics, 2000—; vis. scientist Tech. U. Munich, 1974-75, Los Alamos Nat. Lab., N.Mex., 1980, Argonne (Ill.) Nat. Lab., 1980; CSIRO Divsn. Mineral Engring., Melbourne, 1988; cons. numerous mining cos. Contbr. over 100 sci. articles to profl. jours. Fellow Australian Inst. Physics; mem. Inst. Materials Engring. Australasia. Office: Monash U, Physics Dept, VIC Clayton 3168, Australia

CASHMAN, GIDEON, lawyer; b. N.Y.C., Sept. 10, 1929; s. Abba Morris and Rachel (Cashman) C.; m. Ruth Lucinda Parker, 1956 (div.); m. Kathryn Batchelder, 1985; children: Adam Parker, Lindsey Avril, Emily Parker Hyle. AB, NYU, 1951; JD, Columbia U., 1954. Bar: D.C. 1954, N.Y. 1954. Asst. counsel Waterfront Commn. N.Y., 1954-55; asst. U.S. atty. criminal divsn. So. Dist. Ct. N.Y., 1958-61, chief criminal apls., 1959-61; assoc. Christy Perkins & Christy, N.Y.C., 1961-63; sr. ptnr. Pryor, Cashman, Sherman & Flynn LLP, N.Y.C., 1963—; lectr. trial tactics Practicing Law Inst.; bd. dirs. Irvington Inst. for Med. Rsch. Trustee Friars Found., Heart Rsch. Found., Eugene O'Neill Teatre Ctr. 1st lt. U.S. Army, 1955-58. Mem. ABA, N.Y. State Bar Assn., Assn. Bar City N.Y., N.Y. County Lawyers Assn., Friars Club (N.Y.C.). Jewish. Home: 812 Park Ave New York NY 10021-2759 Office: 410 Park Ave New York NY 10022-4407

CASHMAN, MICHAEL RICHARD, small business owner; b. Owatonna, Minn., Sept. 26, 1926; s. Michael Richard and Mary (Quinn) C.; m. Antje Katrin Paulus, Jan. 22, 1972 (div. 1983); children: Janice Katrin, Joshua Paulus, Nina Carolin. BS, U.S. Mcht. Marine Acad., 1947; BA, U. Minn., 1951; MBA, Harvard U., 1953. Regional mgr. Air Products & Chems., Inc., Allentown, Pa., 1959-64; then pres. so. div. Air Products & Chems., Inc., Washington, 1964-68; mng. dir. Air Products & Chems., Inc. Europe, Brussels, 1968-72; internat. v.p. Airco Indsl. Gasses, Brussels, 1972-79; pres. Continental Elevator Co., Denver, 1979-81; assoc. Moore & Co., Denver, 1981-84; prin. Cashman & Co., Denver, 1984—. Committeeman Denver Rep. Com., 1986—, congl. candidate, 1988; chmn. "Two Forks or Dust" Ad Hoc Citizens Com.. Lt. (j.g.) USN, 1953-55. Mem. Bldg. Owners and Mgrs. Assn., Colo. Harvard Bus. Sch. Club, Am. Rights Union, Royal Golf de Belgique, Belgian Shooting Club, Rotary, Soc. St. George, Phi Beta Kappa. Avocations: skiing, golf, sailing, guitar, opera. Home: 2512 S University Blvd Apt 802 Denver CO 80210-6152

CASIANO VARGAS, ULISES AURELIO, bishop; b. Lajas, P.R., Sept. 25, 1933. Ordained priest Roman Cath. Ch., 1967. Elected to bishop, 1976 bishop of Mayaguez, P.R., 1976—. Address: Diocese of Mayaguez PO Box 2272 Mayaguez PR 00681-2272*

CASINI, PIER FERDINANDO, member European parliament; b. Bologna, Italy, Dec. 3, 1955. Mem. European parliament, Italy, 19996; mem. Group of the European People's Party (Christian Democrats) and European Democrats; mem. com. on devel. and cooperation, delegation for rels. with the member states of ASEAN, Southeast Asia and the Republic of Korea; substitute mem. delegation to the EU-Bulgaria Joint Parliamentary Com. Office: Via Due Macelli 66, I-00187 Roma Italy*

CASIRAGHI, GIOVANNI, organic chemistry educator; b. Monza, Italy, Dec. 9, 1939; s. Carlo and Massimiliana (Villa) C.; m. Daniela Andreolli, Nov. 21, 1970; children: Federico, Francesco. Diploma in chemistry, U. Pavia (Italy), 1964. Postdoctoral fellow U. Pavia (Italy), 1965-68; asst. prof. U. Parma (Italy), 1969-79, assoc. prof., 1980-85; prof. U. Sassari (Italy), 1986-91, dir. spectroscopy dept., 1988-91; prof., dir. organic chem. lab. U. Parma, 1992—. Contbr. over 150 articles to profl. jours.; patentee in field. Mem. Italian Chem. Soc., Italian Alpine Club (instr. ski mountaineering 1975—), Rotary Internat. Parma. Avocations: rock climbing, skiing. Home: Viale Martiri Libertà 5, I-43100 Parma Italy Office: Pharm Dept U Parma, Viale delle Scienze, I-43100 Parma Italy

CASLER, FREDERICK CLAIR, academic administrator, law enforcement educator; b. Corry, Pa., Mar. 7, 1946; s. Clair O. and Helen M. (Church) C.; m. Janice L. Newrick, Nov. 26, 1983; 1 child, Frederick Clair Jr. AA, Miami-Dade Jr. Coll., 1970; BGS, Rollins Coll., 1975, MS in Criminal Justice, 1979; cert., Kissimmee Police Acad., 1974, 88; postgrad.in Philosophy, Fla. Tech. U., 1995—. Cert. tchr., Fla. Tchr. criminal justice Orange County Schs., Orlando, Fla.; tchr., work experience coord. Osceola County Schs., Kissimmee, Fla.; police-sch. liaison officer Kissimmee Police Dept./Osceola County Schs.; vocat. adult and community education tchr. Kissimmee Police Acad./Osceola Dist. Schs.; coord. Kissimmee Criminal Justice Acad. Adviser various youth orgns. including SADD, Just Say No Club; mem. Osceola County Rep. Exec. Com.; cubmaster Boy Scouts Am. Mem. NEA, Am. Fedn. of Police, Internat. Conf. of Police Officers, Am. Soc. Law Enforcement Trainers, Nat. Assn. Chiefs Police, Fla. Assn. Sch. Resource Officers, Fla. Tchrs. Assn., Osceola County Tchrs. Assn., Fla. Criminal Justice Tng. Officers Assn., Fla. Peace Officers Assn., Internat. Conf. Police Chaplains, Am. Legion (post comdr. 1973), Kiwanis Club (dir.), Masons, Shriners, Scottish Rite, York Rite, B.P.O. Elks lodge # 1873, Loyal Order Moose Lodge 2056, Police Acad. Alumni Assn., Am. Police Hall of Fame, Am. Criminal Justice Assn., NRA (life), Am. Assn. Christian Counselors, Lambda Alpha Epsilon , Alpha Omega Epsilon (chpt. pres. 1996), Phi Delta Kappa.

CASO, ADOLPH, publishing company executive; b. Mirabella, Avellino, Italy, Jan. 7, 1934; came to U.S., 1947; s. Raffaele and Prisca (DeLuca) C.; divorced; children: Richard Anthony, Robert Ralph, Liana Cristina. BA, Northeastern U., 1957; AM, Harvard U., 1965. Dir. bilingual edn. Waltham (Mass.) Pub. Schs., 1964-83; pres., editor Branden Pub. Co. Inc., Boston, 1983—; tchg. fellow Harvard U., Cambridge, Mass., 1964. Author: The Straw Obelisk, 1973, Lives of Italian Americans, 1976, Water and Life, 1979, America's Italian Founding Fathers, 1984, Bilingual Two Language Battery of Tests, 1985, Mass Media vs. The Italian Americans, 1986, Issues in Foreign Language and Bilingual Education, 1987, Pages and Windows, 1991; (with Joseph Kinney) Young Rocky--The Life of Rocky Castellani, 1983; co-author: Tuskegee Airmen; contbg. editor: Dante in the 20th Century, 1985; editor: On Crimes and Punishments (Cesare Beccaria), 1985, Romeo and Juliet—Original Text, 1992, Straw Obelisk, 2d edit., 1995, We, The People, 1995, others. Pres. PTA, Newton, Mass., 1965, Waltham Overseas Studies, 1966-69; founder, pres. Dante U. Found., Boston, 1976—. With Signal Corps, U.S. Army, 1957-62; col. U.S. Army Res., 1963-87. Decorated cavaliere Republic of Italy; Fulbright scholar, 1966. Mem. Sons of Italy (commr.). Roman Catholic. Avocations: music, art, swimming, walking, Italian cuisine. Office: Branden Pub Co Inc PO Box 812 094 Wellesley MA 02482

CASOLIN, ARMAND, health facility administrator; b. Canberra, Australia, Aug. 23, 1967; s. Lino and Rosanna (Tento) C.; m. Corinna DiCristo, Sept. 12, 1993. MBBS, U. Sydney, 1992; Grad. Cert. Safety Sci., U. New South Wales, Sydney, 1999, M in Sci. and Tech. (Occupl. Medicine), 2000. Diplomate New South Wales Med. Bd. Intern/resident med. officer Repatriation Gen. Hosp. Concord, Sydney, 1992-93; sr. resident med. officer Auburn Dist. Hosp., Sydney, 1994; med. adviser Health Svcs. Australia, Sydney, 1995-99; dep. dir. HealthQuest, Sydney, 1999—. Author: Q Fever in New South Wales Deptartment of Agriculture Workers, 1998; contbr. articles to profl. jours. Mem. Australasian Faculty Occpl. Medicine. Office: HealthQuest/Level 2/187, Thomas St Haymarket, 2000 Sydney/NSW Australia

CASONATO, MARCO MARIO ALBERTO, psychology educator, psychoanalyst; b. Massa, Tuscany, Italy, Sept. 30, 1955; s. Giovanni Maria and Paola (Bertolucci) C. Degree in psychology with honors, U. Padua, Italy, 1983; degree in sexology, U. Siena, Italy, 1994. Psychology intern Milan (Italy) U., 1983-89; prof. psychology Palermo (Italy) U., 1989-91, Urbino (Italy) U., 1996-2000; prof. psychopathology U. Turin, Italy, 1998—; prof. psychodynamics U. Milan Bicocca, 2000—; vis. lectr. Inst. Contemporary Psychoanalysis, L.A., 1995; vis. prof. U. Milan, 1994-95, 96-97, 98-99, U. Siena, 1993-98. Author 6 books on psychotherapy, co-author 5 books, editor 11 books; contbr. over 120 articles on psychotherapy, psychoanalysis and psychopathology to profl. jours.; editor-in-chief (jour.) Psicoterapia, 1995; editor (jour.) Psichiatria e Territorio, 1991; mem. sci. com. (jours.) Pluriverso, 1995, Oikos, 1990-92. Recipient Scientific Rsch. 1st prize U. Bologna, 1968. Mem. APA (internat. affiliate), San Francisco Therapy Rsch. Group (grantee 1995), Inst. Contemporary Psychoanalysis (corr.). Liberal. Avocations: gardening, chess, playing with children. Fax: (0) 585-810865. E-mail: psicoterapia@yahoo.com. Office: Terzocentro Psicoterapia, Via Ravenna 9/C, I-00161 Rome Italy

CASPARI, FRITZ, retired foreign service officer, educator; b. Baden, Switzerland, Mar. 21, 1914; s. Eduard and Elli (Klussmann) C.; m. Elita Galdós Walker, Feb. 3, 1944; children: Hans Michael (dec.), Conrad, Elisabeth, Andrea. Student, Heidelberg (Germany) U., 1932-33; Diploma in Econs. and Polit. Sci., Oxford U., 1934, MLitt, 1936; PhD, Hamburg U., 1939, Golden Doctorate, 1990. Instr., asst. prof. Southwestern U., Memphis, 1936-37, Scripps Coll., Claremont, Calif., 1939-42; reference libr. Newberry Libr., Chgo., 1943-46; asst. prof. History and German U. Chgo., 1946-54; hon. prof. English intellectual history U. Cologne, Germany, 1955; head British, Irish, Common Wealth sect. Fgn. Office, Bonn, 1955-58; with German Fgn. Svc., 1954-69, 74-79; counselor Emb., London, 1958-63; min. mission to UN, N.Y.C., 1963-68; amb. Lisbon, Portugal, 1974-79; dep. chief, dir. Fed. Pres.'s Office, Bonn, 1969-74. Author: Humanism and the Social Order in Tudor England, 1954, German translation, 1988; contbr. articles to profl. jours. Fellow (hon.) St. Johns Coll. Oxford U., 1972—; decorated Grand Cross Order of Merit Fed. Republic of Germany, knight grand cross Order of Christ, Portugal, knight grand cross Order of St. Sylvester (Holy See), knight comdr. Royal Victorial Order, U.K., grand officer Order of Orange-Nassau (Netherlands), Order of St. Olav (Norway), others; Rhodes scholar Oxford U. Home: Chilgrove Farmhouse, Chilgrove, Chichester, West Sussex P018 9HU, England

CASPERSEN, FINN MICHAEL WESTBY, diversified financial services company executive; b. N.Y.C., Oct. 27, 1941; s. Olaus Westby and Freda Caspersen; m. Barbara Caspersen, June 17, 1967. BA With honors in Econs., Brown U., 1963; LLB cum laude, Harvard U., 1966; DHL (hon.), Johns Hopkins U., 1999; various hon. degrees. Assoc. Dewey, Ballantine, Bushby, Palmer & Wood, N.Y.C., 1969-72; chmn. bd., chief exec. officer, mem. exec. com. Beneficial Corp., Wilmington, Del., 1976-98; chmn. bd. dirs., CEO Knickerbocker LLC; past bd. dirs., mem. exec. com. Beneficial Nat. Bank; chmn. bd. dirs. Beneficial Bank, Plc; bd. advisors Inst. Law and Econs., U. Pa.; chmn. Coalition for Better Transp.; past co-chair Prosperity N.J.; chmn. U.S. Equestrian Team. Emeritus trustee Brown U.; bd. dirs. Clay Math. Inst.; chmn. Ellis Island Commn.; moderator, bd. dirs. Shelter Harbor Fire Dist.; pres. O.W. Caspersen Found.; trustee BGCN Life Camp Inc.; chmn. bd. trustees Peddie Sch., Hightstown, N.J.; chmn. bd. trust Gladstone Equestrian Assn. Inc.; bd. dirs. Drumthwacket Found.; charter mem. Partnership for N.J., New Brunswick; bd. dirs. Coalition of Svc. Industries, Inc., Washington, 1982-95, vice chair, 1995—; chmn. World Pair Championship, 1993; mem. corp. Cardigan Mountain Sch., 1981-96; mem. exec. com. Harvard Resources Com.; trustee BGCN Life Camp Inc., John Carter Libr.; chmn. dean's adv. com. Harvard Law Sch.; dir. Clay Math. Inst. Lt. USCG, 1966-69. Recipient Pres.'s medal Johns Hopkins U., Ethics in Bus. award BBB, 1992, Gov.'s award Alexander Hamilton Econ. Devel., 1997, President's medal Brown U., 1997, Brightest Star award Boys and Girls Clubs Newark, Inc., 1997, Humanities Citizen of Yr. award N.J. Coun. for Humanities, 1999; named Civic Leader of Yr., YMCA, 1982, Citizen of Yr., Morristown Meml. Hosp., 1993. Mem. Am. Fin. Svcs. Assn. (bd. dirs., chmn. govt. affairs com., chmn. membership com., adminstrn. com., past chmn.), Fla. Bar Assn., N.Y. Bar Assn., Harvard Club, Knickerbocker Club, Univ. Club, Wilmington Club. Office: Knickerbocker LLC 268 Main St Gladstone NJ 07934-2057

CASPERSEN, SVEN LARS, academic administrator, statistician; b. Aabenraa, Denmark, June 30, 1935; s. Jes Peter and Carla (Dahl) C.; m. Eva Skotte Henriksen, Dec. 1, 1962; children: Jes, Lars, Henrik. M Econs., Copenhagen U., 1961; D Honoris Causa, U. Ctrl. Fla., 1988, Vilnius Tech. U., Lithuania, 1993, U. Autonoma de Guadalajara, 1999. Asst. sec. Danish Ins. Cos., Copenhagen, 1962-64, dep. chief, 1964-68; asst. prof. stats. Copenhagen Sch. Econs., 1968-73; prof. stats. Aalborg (Denmark) U., 1973-76, rector, 1976—; chmn. Liaison Com. of Rectors in EU, Brussels, 1992-94; v.p. Fedn. European Stock Exch., Brussels, 1993-95, pres., 1995-96; chmn. bd. Copenhagen Stock Exch., 1989-96; chmn. European Capital Markets Inst., Copenhagen, 1994-95; pres. Internat. Assn. Univ. Pres., 1999. Chmn. Danish Parliaments Adv. Bd. on European Matters, Copenhagen, 1993—; chmn. bd. Aalborg Theatre, 1986—. Recipient Tribute of Appreciation Dept

of State of U.S., 1981. Avocations: chess, bridge, tennis. Home: Duebrødrevej 6, DK-9000 Ålborg Denmark Office: Aalborg U, Fredrik Bajers Vej 5, DK-9100 Ålborg Denmark

CASSAL ABUJDER, YUSEF SLEIMAN, business executive; b. Tarija, Cercado, Bolivia, Feb. 10, 1965; s. Baracat Jorge Cassal and Sofia Abujder Espinoza; m. Ginelda Yolands Eid Torchio, Nov. 26, 1983; children: Ezzidin, Angelina, Yazmin. Grad. h.s., Tarija, Bolivia. Inspector gen. Embotelladora, La Cascada, Bolivia, 1982-84; jefe de planta Embotelladora, La Paz, Bolivia, 1984-87; gerente tecnico Productos La Cascada, Tarija, 1988-89; gerente gen. Productos del Sur, Tarija, 1990—. Mem. Club De Caza y Pesca, Logia Narciso Campero, Asocincion Boliviann de Automovilismo. Roman Catholic. Avocations: caza, pesca, corredor de autos, karting, billas. Office: Productos del Sur SRL, Morros Blancos Zona Indsl, 128 Tarija Bolivia

CASSANDRAS, CHRISTOS GEORGE, engineering educator, consultant; b. Athens, Greece, Sept. 19, 1955; came to U.S., 1974; s. George and Venetsiana (Zervopoulou) C.; m. Carol Ellen Kamm, May 30, 1991; 1 child, Monica Georgia. BS, Yale U., 1977; MSEE, Stanford U., 1978; SM, Harvard U., 1979, PhD, 1982. Sr. systems engr. ITP Boston, Inc., Cambridge, Mass., 1982-84; asst. prof. U. Mass., Amherst, 1984-89, assoc. prof., 1989-93, prof. elec. and computer engring., 1993-97; prof. mfg. engring. Boston U., 1997—; cons., faculty affiliate Network Dynamics, Inc., Burlington, Mass., 1988—; vis. scholar Harvard U., Cambridge, Mass., 1990; vis. prof. U. Cath. de Louvain, Belgium, 1993. Author: Discrete Event Systems: Modelling and Performance Analysis, 1993 (Harold Chestnut prize 1999), Introduction to Discrete Event Systems, 1999; contbr. articles to profl. jours.; editor spl. issues various jours., 1990—. Fellow Lilly Found., 1991; rsch. grantee various fed. agys. and indsl. orgns., 1985—. Fellow IEEE (editor IEEE Transactions on Automatic Control 1994-98, editor-in-chief 1998—); mem. Inst. for Ops. Rsch. and Mgmt. Sci. (sr.), Control Systems Soc. (bd. govs.). Achievements include pioneering contributions to field of discrete event system theory and its applications to manufacturing, computer networks and transportation. Avocation: travel. Office: Dept Mfg Engring Boston U 15 Saint Marys St Boston MA 02215

CASSAR, JOANN, stone conservation scientist, researcher; b. Floriana, Malta, July 1, 1958; d. John Baptist and Pauline (Grech) c.; m. Robert Michael Cachia, Sept. 28, 1995. BSc, U. Malta, 1979, PhD, 1999. Stone conservator Nat. Mus. Archaeology, Malta, 1986-94; stone conservation scientist U. Malta, Msida, 1994—; external supr. faculty arch. U. Florence, Italy, 1989-93; mem. tech. experts com. Conservation Prehistoric Temples Malta, 1994-96; founding mem. Cosmos Nat. Com., Malta. Contbr. articles to profl. publs. UNESCO fellow, 1981-83, Salzburg Seminar fellow, 1990; short-term vis. grantee Smithsonian Instn., 1987. Mem. Internat. Coun. Monuments and Sites, Internat. Inst. Conservation of Hist. and Artistic Works, N.Y. Acad. Scis., Assn. for Preservation Tech. Office: U Malta, Inst Masonry Constrn Rsch, MSD 06 Msida Malta

CASSAR, JOSEPH, diplomat; b. Qrendi, Malta, Jan. 22, 1918; s. Giuseppe and Giovanna (Magri) C.; m. Jane Pace, 1948 (dec. 1989). Grad., Bishop's Sem., Gozo, Malta, U. Malta. Barrister, 1943—; mem. Coun. of Govt., 1945-46; spkr. Legis. Assembly, 1947-48; min. of justice Govt. of Malta, 1949-50, 51-53, 55-58, min. of labor, employment and welfare, 1971-74, min. of edn. and culture, 1974-76, min. justice, lands and parliamentary affairs, 1976, dep. prime min., 1976, dep. leader for govt. affairs, 1976, 81, min. fin., customs and people's fin. investments, 1979-81, sr. dep. prime min., min. justice and parliamentary affairs, 1981-87; mem. Maltese Ho. of Reps., 1987-92. Named Companion of the Order of the Maltese Rep., 1999. Address: Dar is-Sliem, Swiezi, Saint Andrew's Malta

CASSAR, JOSEPH PAUL, art historian, educator, art critic, artist; b. Pietà, Malta, Feb. 26, 1958; s. Carmel and Helen (Zammit) C. S.Th. Dip., Inst. Religious Studies, Malta, 1980; BA in Religious Studies, Inst. Religious Studies, 1983; BA in Ednl. Studies, U. Malta, 1982; MA, Columbia Pacific U., 1995; MPhil, U. Malta, 1997. Tchr. Edn. Dept. Malta, 1982-85; head of project Christoffel Blinden Mission, Kenya and Somalia, 1985-92; asst. prin. St. Martin's Coll., Malta, 1997-99; lectr. art unit faculty arch. U. Malta, 1995—; bd. examiners Art Unit, Malta, 1996-99; cons. Edn. Office, Malta, 1996-97; internat. baccalaureate examiner, Cardiff, Wales, 1996-99. Author: (children's workbook) Art in Malta Today, 2000; contbr. articles and monographs on Maltese contemporary art. Exhbn. organizer Friends of the Mus., 1995-97. Scholar Govt. of Italy, 1978-80; recipient Targa d'Onore Assn. Internat. Artistica, 1982. Mem. Nat. Soc. Edn. in Art and Design (assoc.). Roman Catholic. Avocation: swimming. Home: 35 Parish Priest Muscat Sq, Hamrun Malta Office: U Malta Faculty Arch, Art Unit, Msida Malta

CASSCELLS, SAMUEL WARD, III, cardiologist, educator; b. Wilmington, Del., Mar. 18, 1952; s. Samuel Ward and Oleda (Dyson) C.; m. Roxanne Bell, Feb. 10, 1990; children: Sam, Henry, Lillian. BS cum laude, Yale U., 1974; MD magna cum laude, Harvard U., 1979. Intern then resident Beth Israel Hosp., Boston, 1979-82; cardiology fellow Mass. Gen. Hosp., Boston, 1982-85; Kaiser fellow clin. epidemiology Brigham and Women's Hosp. and Harvard Sch. Pub. Health, 1984-85; rsch. fellow Nat. Heart, Lung, and Blood Inst., Bethesda, Md., 1985-91; vis. scientist Scripps Inst. Medicine and Sci., LaJolla, Calif., 1991-92; chief cardiology, T.R. and M. O'Driscoll Levy prof. medicine U. Tex. Med. Sch., Houston, 1994—; chief cardiology Hermann Hosp., Houston, 1994—; assoc. dir. cardiol. rsch. Tex. Heart Inst. and St. Luke's Episc. Hosp., Houston, 1992—; med. dir. U. Tex. Telemedicine; founder Prizm Pharms., La Jolla, 1992—, Selective Genetics, La Jolla, Dr. Red Duke.com, Houston, Volcano Therpeutics, Houston; cons. FDA, Advanced Rsch. Project Agy., NASA, NIH, VA; founder Pres. Bush Ctr. Cardiovasc. Health, Houston, DrRedDuke.com., Volcano Therapeutics, Selective Genetics. Mem. editl. bd. Circulation, 1992—, Am. Jour. Cardiology, 1992—, Tex. Heart Inst. Jour., 1992—, Vascular Medicine, 1995—, U.T. Lifetime Newsletter, 1996—; contbr. numerous articles to profl. jours. Mem. Am. Heart Assn. (Houston bd. dirs. 1992-96), Am. Fedn. Clin. Rsch., Am. Soc. Cell Biology, Soc. Vascular Biol. Medicine (bd. dirs.), Houston Cardiology Soc. (pres. 1995-96), Am. Coll. Cardiology, Assn. Univ. Cardiologists, Assn. Profs. of Cardiology (bd. dirs.), Chevy Chase (Md.) Club, Union Boat Club (Boston), Vicmead Hunt Club (Wilmington, Del.), Farmington Country Club (Charlottesville, Va.), City Tavern Club (Washington), Houston Country Club. Office: U Tex Med Sch 6431 Fannin St Houston TX 77030-1501

CASSEL, JOHN MICHAEL, plastic surgeon; b. Miami, Mar. 25, 1948; m. Robyn Cassel, July 12, 1987; children: (twins) Adrienne and Brandon. BS, U. Miami, 1972, MD, 1978. Diplomate Am. Bd. Plastic Surgery. Gen. surg. intern U. Va., Charlottesville, 1978-79, gen. surg. resident, 1979-80; gen. surg. resident Cedars-Sinai Med. Ctr., L.A., 1980-81; jr. resident in plastic surgery U. Miami Sch. Medicine, 1981-82, sr. resident in plastic surgery, 1982-83; microsurgery and hand surgery fellow Ralph K. Davies Med. Ctr., San Francisco, 1984; pvt. practice plastic surgery Miami, 1985—; clin. assoc. prof. plastic surgery U. Miami Sch. Medicine, 1984—. Fellow Am. Coll. Surgeons; mem. Am. Soc. Plastic & Reconstructive Surgeons, Am. Soc. Aesthetic Plastic Surgeons. Avocations: sculpture, stained glass, gem cutting, jewely design & fabrication. Office: 8950 N Kendall Dr Ste 106 Miami FL 33176-2131

CASSELL, LUCILLE RICHARDSON, small business owner; b. Sikeston, Mo., Feb. 23, 1958; d. Glen and Cenia (McCaster) Richardson; m. Arthur Earl Cassell, Apr. 12, 1986; children: Christopher Glen, Bryan Mitchell, David Arthur, Aaron Lamar. A in Bus. Admintrn., S.E. Mo. State U., 1980; deaconess lic., Green Meml. Bible Inst.-Coll., Sikeston, 1982; B in Bus. Mgmt., Frederick Taylor U., 1997. Shoe packer Wohl Shoe Co., Sikeston, 1980-84; sales clk. J.C. Penney, Sikeston, 1984-85; bookeeper, teller Bank of Sikeston, 1985-86; computer operator Sta. KBSI-TV, Cape Girardeau, Mo., 1986-89; data clk. Falcon Cable TV, Sikeston, 1989-90; owner, mgr. Wee=Care Daycare Ctr., Charleston, 1990-99; pres. CBD Enterprises, Inc., Charleston, 1999—; pre-Kindergarten tchr. Sikeston (Mo.) Pub. Schs., 2000; owner Cassell Cmty. Devel. Corp., 1995—, Wee-Care Christian Acad. Pre-School, 1998. Author: The Best That I Can Be, 1995; patented disposable diapers, adult diapers; inventor in field. Vol. Mo. Delta Med. Ctr., Sikeston, 1990; participant walk-a-thons Cystic Fibrosis Found., Charleston, 1992; Sunday sch. tchr. Green Meml. Ch., Sikeston, 1985-86, Opportunity Ch., Charleston; leader Kid's Beat Program, Opportunity COGIC Drill Team, Fancy Bottoms Diapers (displayed in Black Inventors Mus., St. Louis), leader youth drill team. Mem. Ch. of God in Christ. Avocations: reading, volleyball, music, bowling. Fax: 573-683-2152. E-mail: cbdenterprises@ldd.net. Home: PO Box 284 PO Box 284 Charleston MO 63834-0284

CASSELLA, DENNIS GENE, county official; b. Pratt, Kans., Oct. 24, 1946; s. Barney Joseph and Norma Jeanne Cassella. AA, Sacramento C.C., 1970; BA in History/Polit. Sci., U. Calif., Davis, 1971; MPA, East Tex. State U., 1975. City pers. dir. City of Texarkana, Ark., 1971-75; dir. adminstrv. svcs. Ark. Dept. Local Svcs., Little Rock, 1975-76; dir. gen. svcs. County of Nevada, Calif., 1977—; dir. emergency svcs. County of Nevada, 1988—; sr. adj. prof. Golden Gate U., Sacramento, 1979—. Mem. Nevada City Police Cmty. Rels. Commn., Nevada City, 1991-93, Nevada City Bicentennial of the Constitution Commn., 1986—. Staff sgt. USAF, 1966-69. Mem. Nevada County Libr. Found. (pres. 1998-99), Gold Country Lions (pres. 1987), Am. Soc. for Pub. Adminstrn. E-mail: henryv@nccn.net. Office: County of Nev Gen Svcs 950 Maidu Ave Nevada City CA 95959-8600

CASSELMAN, JACQUES A. EDUARD, urologist; b. Eernegem, Belgium, Nov. 12, 1936; s. Julien and Angele (Vanmaele) C.; m. Lili Heene, May 5, 1962; children: Katrien, Filip, Michel. MD, Cath. U., Leuven, Belgium, 1960. Tng. in urology St. John's Hosp., Brugge, 1960-64, Univ. Hosp. Clinico, Barcelona, Spain, 1965-66, Hosp. for Sick Children, London, 1966; head dept. urology St. Joseph Clinic, Ostend, Belgium, 1966—, H. Serruyn Hosp., Ostend, 1972-77; active mem. European Orgn. for Rsch. and Treatment of Cancer. Contbr. articles to nat. and internat. jours. Maj. Belgium mil. Mem. Belgian Soc. Urology (pres.), European Urol. Assn., Internat. Soc. Urology, Internat. Soc. Andrology, Am. Urology Assn., Rotary. Avocation: ornithology. Home: Boogschuttersstraat 4, B-8400 Oostende Belgium Office: Damiaan Ziekenhuis, Gouwelozestraat 100, B-8400 Oostende Belgium

CASSENS, NICHOLAS, JR., ceramics engineer; b. Sigourney, Iowa, Sept. 8, 1948; s. Nicholas and Wanda Fern (Lancaster) C.; m. Linda Joyce Morrow, Aug. 30, 1969; 1 son, Randall Scott, Jr. BS in Ceramic Engring., Iowa State U., 1971, BSChemE, 1971; MS in Material Sci. and Engring., U. Calif., Berkeley, 1979. Jr. rsch. engr. Nat. Refractories and Minerals Corp., Livermore, Calif., 1971-72; rsch. engr. Nat. Refractories and Minerals Corp., Livermore, 1972-74, sr. rsch. engr., 1974-77, staff rsch. engr., 1977-84, sr. staff rsch. engr., 1984—. Mem. Am. Ceramic Soc. Democrat. Achievements include patentee in field U.S., Australia, S.Am., Japan, Europe. Home: 4082 Suffolk Way Pleasanton CA 94588-4117 Office: 1852 Rutan Dr Livermore CA 94550-7635

CASSERLY, ALVARO ALONSO, investment management executive; b. Ocho Rios, Jamaica, June 4, 1932; s. Patrick Owen and Rachael (Smith) C.; m. Jean Allison Mair, Jan. 28, 1961; children: Marie, Bruce, Patrick, Robert. Student in edn., Excelsior Coll., Kingston, 1947-51; student, U. Colo., 1969, U. Mich., 1975, IMI, Geneva, 1981, IMD, Lausanne, 1999. Exec. sec. Electricity Frequency Standardization Commn., Kingston, 1957-63; sec., mgr. Electricity Authority, Kingston, 1963-67; sec. Pub. Utility Commn., Kingston, 1967-70; asst. to pres. Jamaica Pub. Service Co. Ltd., Kingston, 1970-72, treas., 1972-78, dir. fin., 1979-89; chmn. Jamaica Unit Trust Svcs. Ltd, Kingston, 1977-96; chief exec. Jamaica Unit Trust Svcs. Ltd., Kingston, 1990—; bd. dirs. Jamaica Unit Trust, Dyoll Group Ltd., Braco Resorts Ltd., Ind. Radio Co. Ltd.; chmn. Bd. Electricians Examiners, 1963-69. Pres., UN Assn., Jamaica, 1963-69; chmn. Jamaica Coun. for Handicapped, 1973-76, Coun. Voluntary Social Svcs., 1971-73; chmn. bd. govs. Muttall Meml. Hosp., 1993-99; trustee Caribbean L.Am. Action, 1997—. Mem. World Fedn. U.N. Assns. (v.p. 1966-69), Jamaica Club, Constant Spring Golf Club, Collegium Fabrorum (past master), Rotary (dist. gov. 1989-90). Home: 5 Paddington Terr, Kingston 6, Jamaica Office: Jamaica Unit Trust Svcs Ltd, 50 Knutsford Blvd, Kingston 5, Jamaica

CÁSSIA-MOURA, RITA DE, biophysicist, educator, researcher; b. Recife, Brazil, Feb. 25, 1964; d. Manoel João and Lúcia (Souza) M.; m. Carlos Raphael Lange. BSc in Biomedicine, Fed. U. Pernambuco, Recife, 1985, Specialist in Biophysics, 1992. Diplomate in biomedicine. Attending staff emergency dept. N.C. Hosp., Recife, 1987; fellow Fed. U. Pernambuco, 1987-92; cons. to med. lab. J.P. Hosp., Fusam, Jaboatão, Brazil, 1990—; rschr. U. Pernambuco, Recife, 1991—, prof. biophysics, 1991—, head biophysics divsn., 1992—. Contbr. articles to sci. jours. Mem. AAAS, N.Y. Acad. Sci., Bioelectrochem. Soc. Achievements include contributions to deployment of a membrane model in which it is possible to induce memory control. E-mail: rita@npd.ufpe.br. Home: Av Boa Viagem 118, 51011-000 Recife Pernambuco, Brazil Office: Univ de Pernambuco, Caixa Postal 7817, 50732-970 Recife PE, Brazil

CASSIDAY, BENJAMIN BUCKLES, III, lawyer; b. Honolulu, Sept. 6, 1950; s. Benjamin B. Jr. and Barbara (Dennison) C.; m. Maile Burgundy, May 8, 1996. BS, Stanford U., 1973; JD, Boston Coll., 1977. Bar: Colo. 1977, Hawaii 1980, U.S. Ct. Appeals (9th cir.) 1982. State pub. defender Pub. Defender's Office, Littleton, Colo., 1977-80; pvt. practice Honolulu, 1981-82, 88—; 1st dep. Fed. Pub. Defender's Office, Honolulu, 1982-87; lawyer rep. 9th Cir., 1993-95. Mem. Am. Bd. Criminal Lawyers, Hawaii Assns. Criminal Def. Lawyers (bd. dirs.). Avocations: poker, pool. E-mail: bencassiday@hotmail.com. Home: 5699 Kalanianaole Hwy Honolulu HI 96821-2303 Office: Law Office of Ben Cassiday 841 Bishop St Ste 2201 Honolulu HI 96813-3921

CASSIDY, BARRY ALLEN, physician assistant, clinical medical ethicist; b. Chgo., Aug. 28, 1947; s. Frank Thomas and Ann Marie (Panek) C.; m. JoAnn DeRue (div.); m. Robyn G. Lacher (div.); children: Colleen Conerky, Jason Lacher, Nathaniel Austin; m. Barbie A. Cassidy. Cert. physician assoc., Duke U., 1971; BS, Univ. State N.Y., Albany, 1992; PhD, Union Inst., 1995. Cert. physician asst. Physician assoc. Med. Offices of T.C. Rozema, MD, Waukegan, Ill., 1971-73; instr. in healthcare sci. Sch. Medicine George Washington U., Washington, 1973-75; med. cons. Medicolegal Rsch., Washington, 1975-79; CEO, dir. health svcs. Occucare, Inc., Research Triangle Park, N.C., 1979-81; v.p. Coastal Group, Inc., Durham, N.C., 1981-82; exec. v.p. So. Emergency Med. Assocs., Research Triangle Park, 1982-83; physician asst. Ariz. Heart Inst., Phoenix, 1983-86; pres. West Health Corp., Phoenix, 1986-87; thoracic and cardiovascular surgery physician asst. Mayo Clinic, Scottsdale, Ariz., 1987-96; assoc. prof., assoc. dir. physician asst. program Coll. Allied Health Scis. Midwe. U., Glendale, Ariz., 1996-99, dir. physician asst. program, 1998—; prof. health sci. Midwe. U., Glendale, 1999—, assoc. dean Coll. Health Scis., 1999—; adj. faculty S.W. Ctr. for Osteo. Med. Edn. and Health Scis., 1995-96; mem. Joint Bd. Regulation Physician Assts., 1998, pres., 1998—. Mem. editl. bd. Physician Assts. in Primary Care, 1985-88; inventor break-away catheter sys. Advisor on allied health Ill. Med. Soc., Chgo., 1972; advisor Gov.'s Health Licensure Comm., State of Ill., Chgo., 1972. Sgt. USAF, 1965-69. Mem. Ariz. Med. Assn., Ariz. Acad. Physician Assts., Hastings Ctr. for Med. Ethics (assoc.), Am. Soc. Law, Medicine and Ethics, Am. Acad. Physician Assts. (chmn. jud. affairs com., v.p. 1974). Jewish. Home: 6630 E Lafayette Blvd Scottsdale AZ 85251-3134 Office: Midwestern U Coll Coll Health Scis 19555 N 59th Ave Glendale AZ 85308-6813

CASSIDY, DAVID C., science educator, historian; b. Richmond, Va., Aug. 10, 1945. BA, Rutgers U., New Brunswick, N.J., 1967, MS, 1970; PhD, Purdue U., West Lafayette, Ind., 1976, DSc (hon.), 1997. Rsch. fellow U. Calif., Berkeley, 1976-77; A.V. Humboldt fellow U. Stuttgart, Germany, 1977-80; asst. prof. U. Regensburg, Germany, 1980-83; assoc. editor Einstein Papers Princeton (N.J.) U. Press, Princeton and Boston, 1983-90; assoc. prof. Hofstra U., Hempstead, N.Y., 1990-96; prof. Hofstra U., Hempstead, 1996—. Author: Uncertainty: Life and Science of W. Heisenberg, 1992, Einstein and Our World, 1995; assoc. editor Papers of A. Einstein, 1983-90; mem. editl. bd. Physics in Perspective, 19975, Isis, 19985; contbr. articles to profl. jours. Recipient sci. writing award Am. Inst. Physics, 1993. Fellow Am. Phys. Soc. (sec.-treas. forum hist. physics 1994-98); mem. History of Sci. Soc. (chair Pfizer prize com. 1994-97, Pfizer award 1995, runner-up Watson-Davis prize 1996), N.Y. Acad. Scis. (chair sect. hist. philos. sci. 1994-97). Office: Hofstra U Natural Sci Program Hempstead NY 11549-0001

CASSIDY, DENIS ANDREW, artist, architect; b. Bklyn., Mar. 9, 1961; s. John Joseph Cassidy and Monica Mary Gallagher. BA, Cath. U., 1984; postgrad., Pratt Inst., 1987-88. Student intern The White House, Washington, 1982-84; account exec. Telephone Mktg. Programs, N.Y.C., 1985; illustrator Gen. Rsch., Teaneck, N.J., 1985-86; arch., planner Port Authority of N.Y. and N.J., N.Y.C., 1986-94; arch., ptnr. Paul S. Marchese and Assocs., Greenwich, Conn., 1996—. Author: My Life as a Cartoon, 1996. Mem. Snug Harbor Cultural Ctr., Upper Catskill Cultural Coun., The Whitney Mus. of Am. Art. Named Most Outstanding Energetic Artist, Washington Arts Coun., 1984; recipient Exceptional Svc. medal Port Authority of N.Y. and N.J., 1993. Mem. Am. Inst. Archs., Schoharie Artists Coun. Office: Paul S Marchese & Assocs 15 Greenbriar Ln Greenwich CT 06831-3319

CASSIDY, EDWARD IDRIS CARDINAL, cardinal deacon; b. Sydney, NSW, Australia, July 5, 1924; s. Harold George and Dorothy May (Philipps) C. Student, St. Columba Sem., Springwood, Australia, 1943; grad., St. Patrick's Coll., Manly, Australia, 1949; JCD, Lateran U., Rome, 1955; Doctorate in Law (hon.), U. Notre Dame, 1995. Ordained priest Roman Cath. Ch., 1949, archbishop, 1970, created cardinal, 1991. Asst. priest Parish Yenda, Wagga Wagga, NSW, 1950-52; with Vatican Diplomatic Svc., India, Ireland, El Salvador, Argentina, 1955-70; titular archbishop of Amantia, 1970; Pontifical rep. China, Bangladesh, Burma, South Africa and Lesotho, The Netherlands, 1970-88; substitute Vatican Secretariat of State, 1988-89; pres. Pontifical Coun. for Promoting Christian Unity, Commn. Religious Rels. with the Jews, Vatican City, 1989—; Cardinal deacon of Santa Maria in Via Lata, 1991—. Mem. Coun. of Ctrl. com. for Jubilee Yr. 2000. Decorated Comendador en la Orden Nacional José Matias Delgado (El Salvador); Officer Order of Brilliant Star with Grand Cordon (Republic of China); Grootkruis in de Orde van Oranje-Nassau (The Netherlands); Cavaliere di Gran Croce dell'Ordine Al Merito della Repubblica Italiana; Companion in Gen. Div. of Order of Australia; Commandeur de la Légion d'Honneur (France); Gt. Cross of the Polar-star (Sweden); Grand Cross Order of Merit (Germany). Mem. Coun. of Secretariat of State's Second Sect. Congregation of Doctrine of Faith, Congregation for the Bishops, Congregation for the Oriental Chs., Adminstrn. of Patrimony of Apostolic See, Congregation for Evangelization of the Peoples, Congregation for Divine Worship and the Discipline of Sacraments, Pontifical Coun. Inter-religious Dialogue, Pontifical Coun. Cor Unum, Pontifical Commn. for Latin Am.

CASSIDY, JACK, educator; b. Phila., Mar. 12, 1941; married; 2 children. BA in English, Gettysburg Coll., Phila., 1962; MEd in Secondary Edn., Temple U., Phila., 1965, PhD in Ednl. Psychology, 1975. Tchr. Hawaii Dept. Pub. Instrn., Island Kauai, Lihue, 1965-69; instr. Temple U., 1970-71; reading supr. Newark (Del.) Sch. Dist., 1972-78; prof. Millersville (Pa.) U., 1981-98, Tex. A&M Univ., Corpus Christi, 1998—; spl. cons. Ednl. Testing Svc., 1977-93. Sr. author: Basic Life Skills, Macmillan Lit. Series, Read-Reason-Write, Scribner Reading Series; contbr. articles to profl. jours. Coach Community Swim Teams, Kapaa, Hawaii, 1967-68. Mem. Internat. Reading Assn. (legis. com. 1975-76, dir. 1976-79, pres. 1982-83), Diamond State Reading Assn. (pres. 1974-75), Nat. Coun. Tchrs. English, Coun. Exceptional Children, Assn. Gifted, Nat. Assn. Gifted, Nat. Coun. Accreditation Tchr. Edn. (exec. bd. 1986-88, chmn. 1988-89, 1997-2000), Coll. Reading Assn. (dir. 1994-97, pres. 1999-2000), Phi Delta Kappa. E-mail: jcassidy@falcon.tamucc.edu. Home: 322 Santa Monica Pl Corpus Christi TX 78411-1612 Office: Early Childhood Devel Ctr Tex A&M Univ 6300 Ocean Dr Corpus Christi TX 78412-5503

CASSIDY, JAMES MARK, construction company executive; b. Evanston, Ill., June 22, 1942; s. James Michael and Mary Ellen (Munroe) C.; m. Bonnie Marie Bercker, Aug. 1, 1964 (dec. Dec. 1981); children: Micaela Marie, Elizabeth Ann, Daniel James; m. Patricia Margaret Mary Murphy, Sept. 15, 1984. BA, St. Mary's Coll., 1963. Estimator Cassidy Bros., Inc., Rosemont, Ill., 1963-65, project mgr., 1965-67, v.p., 1967-71, exec. v.p., 1971-77, pres., 1978—; trustee Plasterer's Health & Welfare Trust, 1971-92; chmn. labor liaison com. Laborers Internat. Union N.Am. and Assn. Wall and Ceiling Industries, 1982-85, chmn. labor-mgmt. group, 1985-88; chmn. Chicagoland Assn. Wall and Ceiling Contractors' Carpenters Union Negotiating Team, 1983—; trustee, vice chmn. laborers dist. coun. Chgo. and Vicinity Laborers-Employers Cooperation and Edn. Trust Fund, 1999—. Area fund leader Constrn. Industry Salute to Boy Scouts Am., 1975; mem. president's coun. St. Mary's Coll. With U.S. Army, 1963-64, N.G., 1964-69. Mem. Chgo. Plastering Inst., Builder Uppers Club (pres. 1973-74), Chicagoland Assn. Wall and Ceiling Contractors (pres. 1976-79), Great Lakes Coun., Internat. Assn. Wall and Ceiling Contractors (chmn. 1977), Constrn. Employers Assn. Chgo. (bd. dirs. 1976—, pres.-elect 1989-90, pres. 1991-93, chmn. com. labor-mgmt. rels. 1983-93), Chicagoland Safety Coun. (bd. dirs. 1988-92), Joint Conf. Bd. Cook County (chmn. 1996-97, 98-99), Assn. Wall and Ceiling Industries Internat. (bd. dirs. 1978-81, 88-89, fin. v.p. 1990, 2d v.p. 1991, pres.-elect 1992, pres. 1993), Park Ridge Country Club (Ill.) (bd. dirs. 1994-97), Eagle Creek Country Club (Naples, Fla.).

CASSIDY, MICHAEL, evangelist, missionary, author; b. Johannesburg, South Africa, Sept. 24, 1936; s. Charles Stewart and Mary (Reading) C.; m. Carol Bam, Dec. 16, 1969; children: Catherine, Deborah, Martin. MA, Cambridge U., Eng., 1958; BD, Fuller Theol. Sem., 1963; HLD, Azusa Pacific U., Calif., 1993. Founder, internat. team leader African Enterprise, Pietermaritzburg, Kwazulu-Natal, South Africa, 1961—; Mem. Lausanne com. World Evangelisation; continuation com. Internat. Congress on World Evangelism. Writings include: Decade of Decisions, 1970, Prisoners of Hope, 1974, Relationship Tangle, 1974, Together in One Place, 1978, Christianity for the Open-Minded, 1979, Bursting the Wineskins, 1983, Chasing the Wind, 1985, The Passing Summer, 1989, Politics of Love, 1991, A Witness For Ever, 1995; editor: I Will Heal Their Land, 1974, Facing the New Challenges, 1978; contbr. numerous articles to profl. jours. Recipient St. Michael's award Michaelhouse, Paul Harris Fellow award Rotary Internat. Mem. Order Simon of Cyrene, Michaelhouse Old Boys Club, St. Catherine's Soc. Anglican. Office: care African Enterprise, PO Box 13140, Cascades 3202, South Africa

CASSIM, SIRAJUDDIN AKBARALLY, management consultant, stock broker; b. Nagpur, India, Sept. 6, 1942; s. Akbarally and Khatija (Meherally) C.; m. Yasmeen Sirajuddin Merchant, July 6, 1968; children: Riaz S., Maheen S., Saira S. BCom, Govt. Commerce Coll., Karachi, 1961. Chartered Acct., Sec. Ptnr. Duadally Siraj & Co., Karachi, 1968-84; proprietor Sirajuddin Cassim, Karachi, 1984—; pres. Karachi Stock Exchange, 1995, chmn. Cen. Depository Co. Pakistan Ltd., 1995; exec. dir. Standard Chartered Mercantile Leasing Co. Ltd., Karachi, Pakistan, 1997. Fellow ICSM; mem. Rotary Internat. Avocations: tennis, golf, swimming, cricket. Office: Sirajuddin Cassim, 26-29 Karachi Stock Exchg., Sindh Pakistan

CASSING, WOLFGANG, physicist, researcher; b. Bünde, Westfalen, Germany, June 20, 1953. Diploma in Physics, U. Münster, Germany, 1977, PhD in Philosophy, 1978, PhD in Physics, 1980. Sci. employee Gesellschaft für Schwerionenforschung, Darmstadt, Germany, 1980-85; pvt. docent Technische Hochschule, Darmstadt, 1986; acad. rschr. U. Giessen, Germany, 1985-91, prof. physics, 1992—; dir. Inst. Theoretical Physics, Giessen, 1993-94. Contbr. articles to profl. jours. Mem. Old Table. Avocation: photography. Office: Inst Theoretische Physik, Heinrich-Buff-Ring 16, 35392 Giessen Hessen, Germany

CASSIRER, CHRISTOPHER, healthcare educator; b. Lakewood, N.J., Apr. 18, 1964; s. Frederick Vernon and Rosemary Margaret (Daly) C. BA, Rutgers Coll., 1989; M in Pub. Health, Yale U., 1991; ScD, Johns Hopkins U., 1997. Salesman Jersey Coast Tobacco, Belmar, N.J., 1980-82; mgr. Behind the Sun, Inc., E. Brunswick, N.J., 1983-89; mgmt. cons. GE Co., Fairfield, Conn., 1990-91; rschr., mgmt. cons. Johns Hopkins U., Balt., 1991-97, postdoctoral fellow, dir. rsch. Gemini Cons., 1997, instr., 1997-99; asst. v.p. MMI Cos., Inc., Deerfield, Ill., 1998—; assoc. prof., chair ISP/Exec. Study program/healthcare mgmt. Carlson Sch. Mgmt., U. Minn., Mpls., 1999—; prin. cons. Harvard U. Sch. of Pub. Health, Boston, 1995-97, Healthcare Mgmt. Resources, Annapolis, Md., 1995, Arthur Andersen, Balt., 1997-98; instr. strategic planning and ops., Taiwan Elite Sr. Health Officers, John Hopkins, U., 1997, instr. risk mgmt. and inst. integrity, The Park Rigde Ctr. for Health, Faith and Ethics, Chgo., 1998, Adminstrv. Staff

Coll. India, Hyderabad, 1998, U. Hawaii Bus. Sch., Exec. Inst. for Leadership and Mgmt., Honolulu, 1999; spkr. hosp. risk/quality mgmt Congress on Quality in Medicine, U. Linz, Austria, 1998, Gen. Session Nat. Inst. Case Mgmt. Conf., New Orleans, 1999, Nat. Chronic Care Consortium Ann. Conf., San Francisco, 1999; presentor in field. Author: (dissertation) Maryland Hospital Risk Management Survey, 1997, Colorado and Utah Hospital Risk Management Surveys, 1998; inventor: (cocktail mix) Pearl Necklace. Grantee NIMH Rsch. Tng. grant, 1991; recipient Elinor and David Bodian Rsch. award, Balt., 1993, Health Svc. rsch. award, Johns Hopkins U., Balt., 1995. Mem. Am. Coll. Healthcare Execs., Chgo. Healthcare Execs., Nat. Patient Safety Found. (rsch. com. 1998). Avocations: writing, painting, teaching. Home: 2915 Dean Pkwy Apt 303 Minneapolis MN 55416-4409

CASSISI, NICHOLAS JOHN, otolaryngologist, dean; b. Portage, Pa., Mar. 2, 1935; s. Nicolo and Mary (Bonarrigo) C.; m. Elayne Ersay, Dec. 7, 1957; children: Jeffrey E., Nicole M. Cassisi Pope, Christopher M. BA, Case Western Res. U., 1957, DDS, 1961; MD, U. Miami, 1965. Diplomate Am. Bd. Otolarngology (assoc. examiner, sr. examiner 1993-99). Asst. clin. prof. U. Louisville Sch. Medicine, 1971-72; chief otolaryngology Ireland Army Hosp., Ft. Knox, Ky., 1971-73; joint appointments oral surgery U. Fla., Gainesville, 1973-91, assoc prof. surgery divsn. otolaryngology Coll. Medicine, 1973-77, prof. surgery, chief divsn. otolaryngology Coll. Medicine, 1977-91, prof., chmn. otolaryngology Coll. Medicine, 1991-2000, sr. assoc. dean clin. affairs Coll. Medicine, 1997—, chief staff Shands, 1999—; chief staff Shands Alachua Gen. Hosp., Gainesville, 1999—. Coord. editor: Practical Reviews in Otolaryngology - Head and Neck Surgery, 1992-98; editor: Management of Head and Neck Cancer: A Multidisciplinary Approach, 1993; co-author: A Handbook of Physicians, 4th edit., 1995, Otolaryngology, 1996. Lt. col. U.S. Army, 1971-73. Mem. NCAA, Southeastern Conf. of NCAA, Accrediation Coun. Grad. Med. Edn. (chmn. residency rev. com. 1995—), Am. Soc. Head and Neck Surgery. Fax: 352-392-6781. Home: 3105 SW 5th Ct Gainesville FL 32601-9043 Office: U Fla Coll Medicine Dept Otolaryngology 1600 SW Archer Rd Rm M228 Gainesville FL 32610-0264

CASSORLA, FERNANDO GOLUBOFF, physician, pediatric endocrinologist, researcher; b. Santiago, Chile, Aug. 28, 1948; s. Eduardo Levy Cassorla and Esther Slufman Goluboff; m. Antonieta Worm Elbo, Apr. 26, 1974 (div. 1985); children: Cristobal, Pablo. MD, U. Chile, Santiago, 1973. Diplomate Am. Bd. Pediat., Am. Bd. Pediat. Endocrinology. Resident pediat. Albany (N.Y.) Med. Coll., 1974-76; fellow pediat. endocrinology U. Pa., 1976-79; vis. assoc., sr. investigator NICHD, NIH, Bethesda, Md., 1979-89; clin. dir. NICHD, NIH, Bethesda, 1989-93; dir. Inst. Maternal and Child Rsch. U. Chile, Santiago, 1993—; dean adv. com. U. Chile Sch. Medicine, 1995-98. Contbr. chpts. to books and articles to profl. jours. Mem. Am. Acad. Pediats., L.Am. Soc. for Pediat. Endocrinology (pres. 1994), Soc. for Pediat. Rsch., Endocrine Soc., Lawson Wilkins Pediat. Endocrine Soc. Jewish. Avocations: traveling, sailing, skiing, photography. E-mail: fcassorl@machi.med.uchile.cl. Fax: 56-2-554-6890. Office: Inst Maternal & Child Rsch, Casilla 226-3, Santiago Chile

CASTADEDA-SEPULVEDA, ROMAN EDUARDO, physicist; b. Carolina, Colombia, Dec. 15, 1956; s. Roman de Jesus Castaneda-Echeverry and Nora Ines Sepulveda-Valdes; m. Margarita Maria Diez-Velez, Dec. 19, 1985; 1 child, Mariana Castaneda-Diez. BS in Physics, U. Antioquia, Medellin, Colombia, 1982, MS, 1986; PhD, Tech. U. Berlin, 1993. Prof. physics U. Nacional Sede Medellin, 1982-93, assoc. prof., 1993—; guest prof. U. Antioquia, 1993-96; acad. vice dean scis. faculty U. Nacional Sede Medellin, 1995-96, dir. rsch. and postgrad. studies in physics, 1994-95. Contbr. articles to profl. jours. DAAD fellow, 1988-93. Mem. Colombian Soc. Physics, Nat. Network for Optics Colombia, Assn. Colombiana para el avance de la ciencia, N.Y. Acad. Scis., Internat. Soc. Optical Engring., Abdus Salam Internat. Ctr. Theoretical Physics (head physics engring. program 1999—). Achievements include development of computerized system for automatic control of image quality of microscope lenses; procedures for distinguishing and reconstructing pseudo-identical objects; contributions to th theory of spatially partial coherent optical field (schell-model beams) and their applications. Office: U Nacional Medellin, AA 3840, Medellin Colombia

CASTAGNARO, MASSIMO, science educator; b. Sona, Verona, Italy, Dec. 10, 1958; s. Novenio Castagnaro and Lelia Bergamasco; m. Paola Mascarotto, June 7, 1986; children: Mattia, Sofia. DVM, U. Turin, Italy, 1982. Cert. in vet. medicine; diplomate European Coll. Vet. Pathology. Asst. prof. U. Turin, 1990-98; assoc. prof. U. Padua, Italy, 1998-99, prof., 1999—; vis. asst. prof. Tufts U. Sch. Medicine and Vet. Medicine, Boston, 1992. Roman Catholic. Avocation: music. Fax: 39049 8272602. E-mail: maxcasta@penta.agrip.unipd.it. Home: Via Turaza 48/C, 35129 Padova Italy Office: Faculty Vet Medicine, Agripolis, 35020 Legnaro Italy

CASTAGNOLA, GEORGE JOSEPH, JR., lawyer, mediator, secondary education educator; b. Scotia, Calif., July 6, 1950; s. George Joseph and Olga Esther Castagnola; m. Sandra Annette Castagnola, June 7, 1975; children: George Joseph III, Laura, Joseph. Grad., U. San Francisco, 1974; JD, N.W. Calif. U., Sacramento, 1990, D Juridical Sci., 1992. BAr: Calif. 1990. Tchr. El Molino H.S., Forestville, Calif., 1977—; charter boat capt. Castagnola Fishing, Petaluma, Calif., 1971—; prof. law N.W. Calif. U., 1990—; atty., mediator Law and Mediation Office of George Castagnola, Petaluma, Calif., 1990—. Cpl. USMCR, 1968-74. Mem. Calif. Bar Assn., Sonoma County Bar Assn., Calif. Tchrs. Assn., Golden Gate Sport Fishing Assn. Roman Catholic. Avocations: weightlifting, fishing. Home and Office: 802 Wine Ct Petaluma CA 94954-7420

CASTAÑEDA, MARINA, psychologist, writer; b. Mexico City, Apr. 1, 1956; d. Jorge and Neoma (Gutman) C. BA, Harvard U., 1978; MA, Stanford U., 1981, U.S. Internat. U., Mexico City, 1989. 3rd sec. Mexican Embassy, Paris, 1981-82; columnist The Mexico City News, 1984-86, nat. editor, 1985-86; pvt. practice psychologist Mexico City, 1989—; columnist The Mexico City Times, 1995-97; freelance translator/interpreter, 1976-97; co-dir. Milton H. Erickson Inst. Cuernavaca, Mex., 1997—. Translator: The Pre-Columbian Child, 1992, The Mexican Shock, 1995, New Times in Mexico, 1996, Compañero: The Life and Death of the Guevara, 1997. Author: Comprendre l'homosexualité, 1999; La Experiencia Homosexual, 1999. Mem. Internat. Soc. Hypnosis, Mexican Soc. Hypnosis. E-mail: castari@yahoo.com. Avocation: music. Home: Xicotencatl 137-B502, Col Del Carmen Coyoacan, 04100 Mexico City Mexico

CASTANO, EMANUELE, psychology educator; b. Verbania, Italy, Dec. 5, 1971; p. Umberto and Fausta (Gheza) C. Laurea, U. Padova, Italy, 1995; PhD, Cath. U. Louvain, Belgium, 1999. Rsch. fellow Cath. U. Louvain, 1995-99; postdoctoral fellow Ohio State U., columbus, 1999—; mem. faculty U. St. Andrews, Scotland, 1999—. Mem. Soc. Polit. Psychology, European Assn. Exptl. Social Psychology, Soc. for Psychol. Studies of Social Issues, Soc. Personality and Social Psychology. E-mail: castano.2@osu.edu. Office: Mershon Ctr Ohio State U 1501 Neil Ave Columbus OH 43201-2602

CASTAÑO, FERNANDO DANIEL, agronomist, educator; b. Balcarce, Argentina, Oct. 31, 1958; s. Raul Abel and Rosa Concepción (Blanco) C.; m. Mabel Noemí Colabelli, Aug. 26, 1988; children: Francisco, Facundo, Franco. Agrl. engr., Mar del Plata U., 1984; postgrad. diploma, Rennes I U., 1989; PhD, Rennes Nat. Coll. Agrl. Engring., 1992. Asst. Mar del Plata U., Balcarce, 1984-94, asst. prof., 1994—; cons. Context Consulting, West Des Moines, Iowa, 1998. Contbr. articles to profl. jours. Mem. Internat. Sunflower Assn., Rotary Club Balcarce (Goodwill amb. 1988). Roman Catholic. Avocations: football, rugby, horror and adventure movies, walking. Fax: 54 22 66 42 17 56. Home: Calle 4 #533, 7620 Balcarce Argentina Office: Mar del Plata U Agronomy, PO Box 276, 7620 Balcarce Argentina

CASTANO, GREGORY JOSEPH, lawyer; b. Kearny, N.J., Feb. 17, 1929; s. Nicholas and Marianna (Prestinaci) C.; m. June Dwyer, Oct. 15, 1966; children: Gregory, Christopher, John, Timothy. BS, Seton Hall U., 1950; JD, Fordham U., 1953; LLM, NYU, 1956. Bar: N.J. 1956, U.S. Ct. Appeals (3d cir.) 1957, U.S. Supreme Ct. 1959, U.S. Tax Ct. 1974, N.Y. 1985. Sports writer Newark Star-Ledger, 1946-53; pvt. practice Harrison, N.J., 1959-78; atty. Bd. Adjustment, Harrison, 1978; judge Superior Ct. N.J., Jersey City, 1978-85; ptnr. Tompkins, McGuire & Wachenfeld, Newark, 1985-88, Waters, McPherson & McNeill, Secaucus, N.J., 1988—; asst. atty. Town of Harrison, 1959-64; asst. prosecutor County of Hudson, N.J., 1963-71; atty. Town of West New York, N.J., 1977-78, Town of Kearny, N.J., 1999; adj. prof. Seton Hall U. Sch. Law, Newark, 1988—; master com. to computerize criminal cts. Essex County; mediator U.S. Dist. Ct., Superior Ct. Mem. editorial bd., The Cath. Adv., 1976-78. Tax assessor Town of Harrison, 1964-78; del. N.J. Constl. Conv., 1964; mem. juvenile conf. com. Twp. West Caldwell, N.J., 1977-78; trustee Caldwell (N.J.) Coll., 1985-91, chmn. acad. affairs com. bd. trustees, 1987-91; chmn. County Govt. Transition Com., Hudson County, 1987-88; mem. Hudson County Community Coll. Blue Ribbon Task Force, 1992-93. With U.S. Army, 1953-55. Named Man of Yr., Kearny Jaycees, 1963, Alumnus of Yr., Dorf Feature Service, 1987. Fellow Am. Bar Found.; mem. ABA, N.J. Bar Assn., Hudson County Bar Assn. (Justice medallion 1985), Essex County Bar Assn., West Hudson Bar Assn. (pres. 1977-78), Assn. Fed. Bar N.J., Essex Fells Country Club. Home: 19 Sunset Rd West Caldwell NJ 07006-6540 Office: Waters McPherson & McNeill 300 Lighting Way PO Box 1560 Secaucus NJ 07096-1560

CASTANO PINEDA, JORGE IVAN, chemist; b. Libano, Tolima, Colombia, Dec. 22, 1947; s. Castaño Garcia Josê Maria and Pineda Rubio Blanca Lucila; m. Peinado Portillo Matilde, Oct. 15, 1971; children: Jorge Hernan, Blanca Liliana, Juan Felipe, Jose Alejandro. Chemist, Antioquia U., 1975; MS, Nacional U., Colombia, 1986. Chemist Polimeros Colombianos, Medellin, 1972-73; prof. Univ. Nacional, Medellin, 1980-81; pres. Novaquimica Ltd., Medellin, 1989-93; prof. Univ. Antioquia, Medellin, 1990-92; r&d chem. mgr. Coltabaco S.A., Medellin, 1975—; lectr. O.E.A., Panama, 1980. Creator Noticias Quimicas Jour., 1975, others. Mem. Chemist and Tech. Soc. (pres. 1974-80), Colombian Chem. Soc. (pres. 1986-90), ICONTEC (pres. pesticides com. 1988-90), Am. Chem. Soc., AOAC, ASQUIMCO. Roman Catholic. Home: Calle 7 NO 83A-24, Medellin/Antioquia Colombia Office: Compania Colombiana Tabaco, Carrera 50 No 5-115, AA 828 Medellin/Antioquia Colombia

CASTBERG, ANDERS STANG, banking executive; b. Oslo, Norway, July 29, 1953; s. Torgrim and Hedevig (Stang) C.; m. Ann Catherine Englund, Aug. 20, 1980; children: Carl Fredrik, Sophie Caroline. MBA, Karlstad U., Sweden, 1978. V.p. shipping Christiania Bank, Oslo, 1980-82; dir. shipping/offshore Christiania Bank, London, 1982-88; sr. v.p. corp. clients Christiania Bank, Oslo, 1989-92, chief credit officer internat., 1992-94, project mgr. Sweden, 1994-96; br. mgr. Christiania Bank, Stockholm, 1996—. Mem. Norwegian-Swedish C. of C. (chmn. bd. dirs. 2000—), Norwegian-Swedish Corp. Assn. (bd. dirs. 1998—). Avocations: golfing, hiking, skiing. Office: Christiania Bank, Birger Jarlsgt 20, SE-11434 Stockholm Sweden

CASTEEN, JOHN THOMAS, III, university president; b. Portsmouth, Va., Dec. 11, 1943; s. John Thomas and Naomi Irene (Anderson) C.; children: John Thomas IV, Elizabeth, Lars. BA with high honors, U. Va., 1965, MA, 1966, PhD, 1970; LLD, Shenandoah Coll. and Conservatory Music, 1984; DHL, Bentley Coll., 1992; hon. degree, Piedmont (Va.) C.C., 1992; DPA, Bridgewater Coll., 1993; D honoris causa, U. Athens, Greece, 1996; DHL (hon.), Transylvania U., 1999. Asst. prof. English U. Calif., Berkeley, 1970-75; assoc. prof., dean admissions U. Va., Charlottesville, 1975-82; adj. prof. Va. Commonwealth U., Richmond, 1982-85; prof. English, pres. U. Conn., Storrs, 1985-90; pres. U. Va., 1990—, George M. Kaufman presdl. prof. of English, 1990—; bd. dirs. NCAA, Wachovia, Inc., Nellie Mae, Inc., Nellie Mae Found., Sallie Mae; mem. Assn. Acad. Health Ctrs.' Coun. Health Scis. and Univ.; mem. com. Nat. Inst. on Alcohol Abuse and Alcoholism and Misuse on Coll. Campuses; chair Coun. for Higher Edn. Accreditation, 2000—. Author: 16 Stories, 1981; contbr. articles to various publs.; mem. editl. adv. bd. The Presidency. Sec. edn. Commonwealth of Va., Richmond, 1982-85; trustee Mariner's Mus., 1990—, Coll. Entrance Exam Bd., N.Y.C., 1980-90, chmn. 1986-88; mem. So. Regional Edn. Bd., 1982-85. New Eng. Bd. of Higher Edn., 1986-90; mem. nat. adv. com. Nat. Domestic Violence Media Campaign, 1992—; dir. Am. Coun. on Edn., 1993-96. Recipient Outstanding Virginian award, 1993, Gold medal award Nat. Inst. Social Scis., 1998. Mem. Assn. Am. Univs. (exec. com.), So. Assn. Colls. and Schs. (chair commn. on colls. 1995-97, pres.-elect 1997, pres. 1998), Assn. Governing Bds. Colls. and Schs. (coun. of pres. 1992—), Keswick Club, Farmington County Club, Commonwealth Club (Richmond), Phi Beta Kappa. Episcopalian. Office: U Va Office of Pres Madison Hall PO Box 400224 Charlottesville VA 22904-4224

CASTEL, PHILIPPE, executive; b. Paris, Jan. 14, 1956. Lic. in Math., U. Paris, France, 1975; Lic. in Physics, U. Grenoble, 1976; Engring. degree, INPG, Grenoble, 1978. Rsch. & devel. dngr. L.C.I.E. (Pub. Lab.), Fontenay aux Roses, France, 1981-84; applied rsch. engr. Sopelem, Paris, 1984-87; project mgr. Omphale, Paris, 1987-89, Bendix, Paris, 1989-96; sr. project mgr. Delphi, Paris, 1996—. Contbr. articles to profl. jours.; inventor brake system for cars. Home: 8 Rue Monge, 75005 Paris France

CASTEL, VICTOR MIGUEL, linguistics researcher, educator; b. General Alvear, Mendoza, Argentina, Oct. 12, 1950; s. Esteban and Norma (Brovedani) C.; m. Julia Rosa Elmelaj, Feb. 21, 1975; children: Virginia, Víctor Mariano, Bernardo Ramón. Degree in English lang. and lit. edn., U. Cuyo, Mendoza, 1974; MA in Linguistics, U. Chgo., 1982; PhD in Lang. Scis., U. Blaise-Pascal, Clermont Ferrand, France, 1994. Assoc. prof. U. San Juan, Argentina, 1977-85, prof., 1985-88; rschr. CONICET, Mendoza, 1985—; prof. U. Cuyo, Mendoza, 1988—; dir. studies Maestría en Lingüística Aplicada, U. Cuyo, 1996—. Editor Revista Argentina de Lingüística, 1985—. Mem. Argentine Soc. Linguistics, Argentine Assn. Formal Linguistics and Computational Linguistics (v.p. 1996—). Home: Ruta de Uspallata 2615, 5513 Luzuriaga Mendoza, Argentina Office: CRICYT-INCIHUSA-UL, Bajada del Cerro s/n, 5500 Mendoza Argentina

CASTELAIN, PIERRE-YVES, retired dermatologist; b. Raismes, France, Feb. 23, 1927; s. Michel Auguste and Laure (Freville) C.; m. Agnes Marie Gueit, July 17, 1951; children: Genevieve, Marie-Helene, Michel. MD, Med. U., Marseille, 1951, MS, 1952. Practice medicine specializing in dermatology Marseille, 1953-92; cons. dermatologist Hotel Dieu Hosp., Marseille, 1953-73, Michel Levy Hosp., Marseille, 1973-86, St. Marguerite Hosp., 1987-92; lectr. Med. U. Marseille, 1977-92. Contbr. articles to profl. jours. Served to capt. French Army, 1954-55. Mem. European Acad. Allergology and Clin. Immunology, European Contact Dermatitis Soc., Soc. Française d'Allergie, Soc. Française de Dermatologie et Syphiligraphie, Groupe d'Etudes et de Recherches en Dermato-Allergie (pres. 1983-86). Roman Catholic. Lodge: Rotary (pres. 1984-85). Avocations: bridge, swimming, chess, travel. Home: 13 Avenue de Montredon, 13008 Marseille France

CASTELL, WILLIAM MARTIN, company executive; b. London, Apr. 10, 1947; s. William Gummer and Gladys (Doe) C.; m. Renice Mendelson, 1971; children: Sarah, Claire, William. BA, London Coll. FCA. With Wellcome Found. Ltd., U.K., 1976-86; mng. dir. Wellcome Biotech., U.K., 1984-87, Wellcome Biotech, U.K., 1984-87; comml. dir. Wellcome plc, U.K., 1987-89; CEO Nycomed Amersham plc (formerly Amersham Internat.), U.K., 1990—; vis. fellow Green Coll., 1993—; companion Inst. Mgmt., 1995—; non-exec. dir. Marconi plc (formerly GEC); chmn. The Prince's Trust, 1998—. Office: Nycomed Amersham plc, Amersham Place, Little Chalfont Bucks HP7 9NA, England

CASTELLANI, ANTONIO, aerospace engineering educator; b. Imola, Bologna, Italy, Apr. 18, 1936; s. Mario Castellani and Rina Morara; m. Serena Salvetti, Aug. 31, 1967; children: Flavia, Beatrice. Sch. Leaving Cert., Liceo E.Q. Visconti, Rome, 1956; M in Engring., U. Rome, 1960. Cert. in engring. Rschr. Nat. Coun. Rschrs., Rome, 1962-99; prof. U. La Sapienza, Rome, 1974—; nat. del. Fedn. Aero. Internat., Lausanne, Switzerland, 1995; gen. sec. Italian Assn. Aeronautics and Astronautics, Rome, 1977; sec. safety flight com. Nat. Coun. Researchers, Rome. Author 3 books in field; contbr. articles and reports to profl. jours. Lt. Italian Air Force, 1962-67. Recipient Gold medal Internat. Inst. Comm., Genoa, Italy. Home: Via Val D'Ala 28, 00141 Rome Italy Office: AIDAA, Via Nazionale 200, 00186 Rome Italy

CASTELLANO, JOSEPH ANTHONY, chemist, management consulting firm executive; b. N.Y.C., Oct. 28, 1937; s. Joseph John and Marie Antoinette (Gallo) C.; m. Rosalie Ann Fantaci, Aug. 28, 1960; children: Joseph, Thomas, Laura. BS in Chemistry, CCNY, 1959; MS in Chemistry, Poly. Inst. N.Y., 1964, PhD in Chemistry, 1969. Cert. profl. chemist; cert. community coll. instr. Research chemist Witco Chem. Co., Paterson, N.J., 1959-62; sr. research chemist Thiokol Chem. Corp., Denville, N.J., 1962-65; mem. tech. staff, project mgr. RCA Labs., Princeton, N.J., 1965-73; chmn., CEO Princeton Materials Sci., 1973-75; ops. mgr. Fairchild Camera and Inst. Corp., Palo Alto, Calif., 1975-77; mgr. ops. Kylex, Mt. View, Calif., 1977-78; pres. Stanford Resources, San Jose, Calif., 1978—; cons. scientist Princeton U., 1970-72; lectr. Rutgers U., Kent State U., SUNY-Binghamton, NASA Research Ctr., USAF Materials Lab., Office Naval Research, IBM Research Ctrs., RCA Labs., Motorola and various profl. and trade assns. Author: Handbook of Display Technology, 1992; publisher: Electronic Display World, The Electronic Display Industry Svc.; contbr. articles to profl. jours.; patents in field. Recipient RCA Doctoral Study award, RCA Labs. Outstanding Achievement award Indsl. Rsch. mag.'s IR-100 award, David Sarnoff Team award in Sci., Spl. Recognition award Soc. Info. Display. Fellow Am. Inst. Chemists; mem. AAAS, Am. Chem. Soc., Am. Assn. Advancement Sci., N.Y. Acad. Sci., Royal Chem. Soc., Soc. Info. Display, Profl. and Tech. Cons. Assn., Soc. Tech. Comm., N.Y. Acad. Sci., Sigma Xi. Roman Catholic. Home: 7017 Elmsdale Dr San Jose CA 95120-3225 Office: Stanford Resources Inc PO Box 20324 San Jose CA 95160-0324

CASTENELL, LOUIS ANTHONY, college dean; b. N.Y.C., Oct. 2, 1947; s. Louis Anthony Sr. and Marguerite (Barzon) C.; m. Mae Beckett, May 3, 1975; children: Louis Calvin, Elizabeth M. BA, Xavier U., 1968; MS, U. Wis., Milw., 1973; PhD, U. Ill., 1980. Cert. counselor and tchr. Elem. tchr. Orleans Parish Schs., New Orleans, 1968; academic advisor U. Wis., Milw., 1970-74; alumni dir. Xavier U., New Orleans, 1974-77, dean Grad Sch., 1980-89; dean Coll. Edn. U. Cin., 1990-99, U. Ga., 1999—; cons. in field. Contbr. chpts. to books and articles to profl. jours. Mem. edn. commn. Nativity Sch., Cin., 1990, NAACP, 1990; mem. steering com. Cin. Youth Collabarative, 1990; bd. dirs. Tri-State Edn. and Tech. Found., Cin., 1990. Sgt. U.S. Army, 1968-69, Korea. Recipient Presdl. Citation, Assn. Multicultural Counseling, Washington, 1983. HEW fellow, 1978-80. Mem. AACD, Am. Edn. Rsch. Assn., Am. Assn. Colls. Tchrs. Edn. (chmn.-elect), Nat. Bd. Profl. Tchg. Stds., Assn. Tchr. Educators, State U. Deans Edn., Kappa Delta Pi, Phi Delta Kappa. Democrat. Roman Catholic. Avocations: reading, travel, photography. Home: 1320 Beverly Dr Athens GA 30606-7610 Office: U Ga Coll Edn Aderhold Hall G-3 Athens GA 30602

CASTENSCHIOLD, RENÉ, engineering company executive, author, consultant; b. Mt. Kisco, N.Y., Feb. 7, 1923; s. Tage and Juno (Hagemeister) C.; m. Martha Naomi Stinson, Dec. 14, 1947; children: Gail F., Frederick T., Lynn Castenschiold Jones. BEE, Pratt Inst., 1944. Registered profl. engr., N.Y., N.J., Pa.; registered profl. planner, N.J. Test engr. (Manhattan Project) GE, Pittsfield, Mass., 1944-45; design engr. GE, Schenectady, 1946-47; sr. product engr. Am. Transformer Co., Newark, 1947-50; design engr. Automatic Switch Co., Florham Park, N.J., 1951-57; chief customer engr. Automatic Switch Co., Florham Park, 1957-74, exec. engring. mgr., 1974-85; pres. LCR Cons. Engrs. P.A., Green Village, N.J., 1986—; lectr. N.J. Inst. Tech., Newark, 1967-79; adviser Underwriters Labs., Inc., Melville, N.Y., 1973-85; chmn. U.S. Tech. Adv. Group and U.S. del. Internat. Electotech. Commn., Geneva, 1981-90; consulting editor, consulting-specifying engr., Des Plaines, Ill., 2000—. Consulting editor Consulting Specifying Engr., Des Plaines, Ill., 2000—; contbr. numerous articles and papers to profl. jours., chpts. to books, promulgation of numerous nat. and internat. elec. standards; patentee in fields transformer design, relays, automatic transfer switches and engine generator controls. Chmn. Bd. of Adjustment, Harding Twp., 1975-77, chmn. Planning Bd., 1982-85; dir. Civil Def., 1966-70; trustee Wash. Assn. N.J., Morristown, 1984-93, sec., 1985-88, v.p., 1989-92, pres., 1992-93; trustee Morristown Meml. Health Found., Inc., 1995—; co-chmn. Jefferson Soc., Morristown Meml. Hosp., 1995-98; vestryman Episcopal Ch., 1991-94. Named to Disting. Alumni Bd. Visitors, Pratt Inst., 1979; recipient Disting. Svc. award Morristown Nat. Hist. Park, 1993, achievement award Washington Assn. N.J., 1995. Listed in Danmarks Adel Aarbog, 1923—. Fellow IEEE (stds. bd. 1983-85, Achievement award 1988, Richard Harold Kaufmann award 1990), NSPE, Instrument Soc. Am., Nat. Elec. Mfrs. Assn. (chmn. automatic transfer switch com. 1982-88, James H. McGraw award 1986), Internat. Assn. Elec. Insps., Nat. Acad. Forensic Engrs., Coun. Engring. Splty. Bds. (bd. cert. diplomate), Am. Cons. Engrs. Coun., Nat. Fire Protection Assn., Internat. Platform Assn., N.J. Christmas Tree Growers' Assn., Can. Stds. Assn., Nat. Elec. Safety Found. (workplace safety com.), Nat. Forensic Ctr., Danish Am. Soc., Skytop Club (Pa.), Morristown (N.J.) Club. Republican. Avocations: swimming, tree farming, photography, hiking. Home: PO Box 154 Lees Hill Rd New Vernon NJ 07976 Office: LCR Cons Engrs PA PO Box 2 Green Village NJ 07935-0002

CASTIER, MARCELO, chemical engineering educator; b. Rio de Janeiro, Nov. 21, 1957; s. Eduardo and Angela Maria (Silva) C.; m. Ivone Beatriz Otazu, Dec. 8, 1998. BSc, Fed. U. Rio de Janeiro, 1981, MSc, 1985; PhD, Tech. U. Denmark, Lyngby, 1988. Cert. chem. engring. Faculty mem. Escola de Química, Rio de Janeiro, 1988—, dir. rsch., 1993, head grad. course, 1999-2000; cons. Petrobras, Rio de Janeiro, 1995; vis. rschr. U. Del., Newark, 1996, U. Vigo, Spain, 1999. Assoc. editor Brazilian Jour. Chem. Engring., 1995-98; contbr. articles to profl. jours. Office: U Fed Rio de Janeiro, Escola Quim Cp 68542, 21949900 Rio de Janeiro Brazil

CASTIGLIONI, PAOLO, researcher; b. Varese, Italy, July 20, 1961; s. Giulio and Giovanna (Pontiggia) C. PhD, Politecnico, Milan, 1993. Rschr. Centro Di Bioingegneria, Milan, 1989—. Contbr. articles to profl. jours. 2d lt. Italian Mil., 1988-89. Office: Larc-Centro Bioingegneria, via Gozzadini 7, I-20148 Milan Italy

CASTILE, RAND (JESSE RANDOLPH, III), retired museum director; b. N.C., July 15, 1938; s. Jesse Randolph II and Pauline Virginia (Simmons) C.; m. Sondra Meadow Myers, 1960; children: Leath Willow, Heather Rain. BA, Drew U., Madison, N.J., 1960; diploma, Urasenke Tea Ceremony, Kyoto, Japan, 1967; LHD (hon.), Drew U., 1992. With ARTnews, N.Y.C., 1963-65; dir. edn. Japan Soc., N.Y.C., 1967-71, dir. performing arts, 1981-86, dir. Japan House Gallery, 1971-86; dir. Asian Art Mus., San Francisco, 1986-94; ret.; vis. com. Met. Mus. Art, 1974—; sec., mem. U.S.-Japan Cultural and Ednl. Conf., 1972-86; mem. Maine Art Commn., 1997—. Author: The Way of Tea, 1971, 79; (exhbn. catalogue) Japanese Art Now: Tadaaki Kuwayama & Rikuro Okamoto, 1980, other catalogues; editor: Japanese Art Exhibitions with Catalogue in U.S., 1980; contbr. articles to profl. jours. Panelist Calif. Arts Coun., 1986-91; bd. dirs. West-East Coun. Cathedral Ch. of St. John the Devine, 1977-86, AAM/ICOM, 1982-85, Japan Soc. No. Calif., 1986-95, San Francisco Bay Area Dance Coalition, 1986-88, Rock and Roll Mus., San Francisco, 1988-89, U. San Francisco Ctr. for Pacific Rim, 1989-95, Seoul-San Francisco Sister City Com., 1987-93, Nat. Maritime Mus., San Francisco, 1989-93; mem. internat. adv. com. Ctr. for Internat. Contemporary Arts, 1989-95; chair co-chair gov. State Calif. awards for Art and Philanthropy, 1990-94, others; chmn. Eastport Area Millenium Festival, 1997-2000. Fulbright-Hayes fellow, 1966-67; recipient Mayor's award of Honor for Arts and Culture, N.Y.C., 1982, Alumni Achievement award Drew U., Madison, N.J., 1987, Plowshares Humanitarian award, 1990, Harry Mattin award Eastport Area C. of C., 2000. Mem. Assn. Art Mus. Dirs. (1974-95), Am. Assn. Mus. (bd. dirs. Internat. coun. 1982-86), Maine Arts Commn., Mus. Trustee Assn. (adv. coun. of dirs. 1989-95), Am. Fedn. Arts (nat. exhbn. com. 1980-95), Acad. Lacquer Rsch. Tokyo (Am. sec. 1977-86), Japan Soc. No. Calif. (bd. dirs. 1986-95, mem. collections com. Farnsworth mus. 2000—), Century Assn., St. Croix Country Club, Herring Cove Golf Club.

CASTILLA, CARLOS EDUARDO, surgeon; b. Buenos Aires, May 10, 1938; s. Carlos Martin and Aurora (Quatrini) C.; m. Maria Susana Alderete; children: Cristian, Cecilia, Martin. B, U. La Plata, Argentina, 1955; MD, U. La Plata, 1964. Rschr. La Plata Biol. Inst., 1970, chief med. rsch. dept., 1970-75; chief hepato-pancreato biliary dept. San Martin Hosp., La Plata, 1976-95; chief surgery admission unity San Martin Hosp., 1986-89, chief surgery unity, 1989-92, chief dept. surgery, 1992—; dir. City Bell Med. Ctr., La Plata, 1982-91, cons. surgeon Buenos Aires Med. Coll., 1994; asst. prof. med. sch., La Plata, 1982. Co-autho: Quotidian Surgery, 1979, Handbook of Surgery, 1996; contbr. over 100 papers to profl. jours. Mem. Prof. Dr. Jose M. Mainetti Found. for med. progress. Recipient Sci. Prodn. award Buenos Aires Med. Coll., 1975, 83. Fellow ACS; mem. Internat. Hepato Pancreato Biliary Assn., Argentine Soc. Surgery (Best Ann. Free Work of Surgery 1995), Soc. Surgery of La Plata (pres. 1995-96, Best Ann. Sci. Work 1993),

Argentine Acad. Surgery. Roman Catholic. Avocation: amateur radio. Home: Diagonal 74 No 1373, 1900 La Plata Argentina Office: San Martin Gen Hosp, 1 y 70, 1900 La Plata Argentina

CASTILLE, JEAN-PAUL GILBERT, researcher, innovation and management consultant; b. Semur en Auxois, Cote D'or, France, May 24, 1953; s. Paul Lucien and Odette Renée Rousseaux; (div.) children: Julie, Sophie; m. Odile Marcelle Mougeot. Student Engring, Arts Et Metiers Coll., Paris, 1976. Constrn. engr. USSI, Pierrelatte, France, 1977-80; project mgr. SGN, Paris, 1980-88; pres. Genese, Robion, France, 1989-97, innovation and mgmt. cons., 1997—; mktg. cons. Genese, N.Y.C., 1993-94. Inventor generic patents for interactive television, video on demand and streaming media over the internet, 1989 (Worldwide Invention award winner 1994). Avocations: movies, music, windsurfing, fly fishing, golf. Home: Cante Ploure, 84440 Robion France

CASTILLO, DEMETRIO, management educator, researcher; b. Naopa/Molango, Hidalgo, Mex., Dec. 22, 1939; s. Evodio and Reyna (Montaño) C.; m. Edilfonsa Hernández, Dec. 26, 1978; children: Demetrio, Karen, Katische, Dalia, Michael. Degree in Chem. Engring., Superior Sch. Chem. Engring. Extractive Industries, Mexico City, 1967; MSc, Superior Sch. Commerce and Adminstrn., Mexico City, 1994; DSc, Superior Sch. Commerce, Mexico City, 1996, Superior Sch. Commerce, Mexico City, 1999. Asst. to Vice Pres. Euzkadi, Mexico City, 1963-75; gen. mgr. Casmond, Guadalajara, Mex., 1975-78; planning dir. Gates Rubber, Mexico City, 1982-85; asst. to gen. mgr. Bandas Transportadoreas, Mexico City, 1985-88; mgmt. mgr. Tecnibandas, Mexico City, 1990-91; prof. Nat. Polytech. Inst., Mexico City, 1969—; pres. CONASUPO, Naopa/Molango, 1978-80. Mem. Acad. of Mgmt., Casa Blanca. Roman Catholic. Avocations: mountaineering, reading, walking, movies. Home: Colina de Mocusari No 37, 53140 Boulevares Naucalpan Mexico Office: Inst Politech Nac, Unidad Profl ALM, Edificio No 7, 00738 Mexico City Mexico

CASTILLO, SUSAN, American literature educator, poet, translator, human rights advocate; b. Jackson, Miss., Mar. 15, 1948; arrived in Portugal, 1971, in Scotland, 1996; d. Paul E. and Joree (Pierce) Parsons; m. Federico Perez Castillo, May 28, 1969 (div. 1998); children: Paul, Cristina. BA, Millsaps Coll., 1969; MA, Oporto (Portugal) Univ., 1981, PhD, 1989. Lectr. Oporto U., 1978-94; vice chancellor Fernando Pessoa U., 1994-96; lectr. dept. English lit. U. Glasgow, Scotland, 1996-99, reader, head dept., 1999—; specialist Native Am. culture, Am. colonial lit.; mem. internat. faculty Salzburg Seminar in Am. Studies. Author: Notes from the Periphery: Marginality in North American Literature and Culture, 1995; editor: (anthology) Engendering Identity, 1996, Native American Women in Literature and Culture, 1997, Post-Colonialism and Identity, 1998, The Literatures of Colonial America, 2000; translator: The Pottery of Estremoz (J. Vermelhinho), 1990, Oporto: The Paths of Memory (A. Fernandes), 1991, East Timor: Land of Hope, 1992, Lisbon 20th Century Tiles, 1993; editor Am. Studies in Britain; contbr. articles, book revs. to profl. jours., poetry and fiction to profl. publs. (winner 3d prize Internat. Scottish Open Poetry Competition 1999). Mem. MLA, Internat. Comparative Lit. Assn., British Assn. Am. Studies, European Assn. Am. Studies, Am. Studies Assn., Am. Indian Workshop, Amnesty Internat., Scottish Assn. for Study of Am. Avocations: writing poetry and fiction, collecting antique books, engravings, traveling. Office: U Glasgow, Dept English Lit, Glasgow G12 8QQ, Scotland

CASTILLO LARA, ROSALIO JOSE CARDINAL, archbishop; b. Sept. 4, 1922, San Casimiro, Venezuela; s. Rosalio Castillo Hernandez and Guillermina Lara Pena. J.C.D., Ateneo Salesiano, Torino, Italy, 1953. Ordained priest Roman Catholic Ch., 1949. Asst. for studies Liceo San Jose, Los Teques, Venezuela, 1949-50; pres. Assn. Venezuelana degli Educatori Cattolici, 1953; prof. Ateneo Salesiano, Torino, 1954-57, Rome, 1957-65; provincial superior Venezuela, Salesians, 1966-67, regional superior Latin Am., 1967-71, gen. councillor for pastoral care to youth, 1971-73; consecrated bishop Titular Ch. of Precausa, 1973, archbishop, 1982; co-adjutor bishop, Trujillo, Venezuela, 1973-74; del. Episcopal Conf. Venezuela, Synod of Bishops, Rome, 1974-75; sec. Pontifical Commn. for Revision of Code of Canon Law, Rome, 1975, pro-pres., 1982-84; pres. Disciplinary Commn. of Roman Curia, 1981, Pontifical Commn. for Authentic Interpretation of Code of Canon Law, 1984-89; elevated to cardinal, 1985; pres. Pontifical Coun. Interpretation of Legis. Texts, 1989-90, Adminstrn. of Patrimony of Apostolic See, 1989—; pres. Pontifical Commn. Vatican City State, 1990—. Contbr. articles to scholarly jours. Mem. Academia Ciencias Sociales y Politicas del Venezuela, Academia Nacional de la Historia di Venezuela (corr.). Address: Edo Aragua, San Casimiro Venezuela*

CASTILLO LÓPEZ, VICTOR, librarian, educator; b. Guatemala, Guatemala, Aug. 28, 1941; s. Manuel and Isabel (Lopez) Castillo. Asst. libr. Instituto Nutrición Centro Am. y Panama, Guatemala, 1970-80; libr. César Brañas Libr., Guatemala, 1980-82, Univ. del Valle, Guatemala, 1982-84, Univ. de San Carlos, Guatemala, 1984-90, Biblioteca Nacional, Guatemala, 1991—; dir. Biblioteca Nacional, 1999—; dir. Libr. Sch., Guatemala, 1994—. Author: Bibliography of José Batres Montúfar, 1982, Bibliography of Enrique Gómez Carrillo, 1984. Mem. Guatemalan Libr. Assn. Roman Catholic. Avocations: football, baseball, table tennis, reading, walking. Home: 11 Ave, Guatemala City 01002, Guatemala Office: Ministerio Cultura-Biblioteca Nat, 5a Avda 7 326 Zona 1, Guatemala City 01001, Guatemala*

CASTLE, LOUISE MARGARET, anti-trust lawyer; b. Sydney, Australia, Apr. 11, 1963; d. Peter John and Jennifer Anne (Walker) Benjamin; m. Timothy David Castle, July 18, 1987. BA, U. Sydney, 1984, LLB, 1986, LLM, 1993. Solicitor Priddle Gosling, Sydney, 1986-87; legal officer NSW Premier's Dept., Sydney, 1987-88; policy advisor Cabinet Office, Sydney, 1988-89; solicitor Allen, Allen & Hemsley, Sydney, 1989-95, ptnr., 1995—; mem. trade practices com. Bus. Law Coun., 1996—, dep. chairperson trade practices com., 2000—. Cons. editor CCH-Trade Practices Reproter, 1996-98. Sec. No. Nursery Sch. Mgmt. Com., 1997; mem. steering com. Jeans for Genes Charity, 1997. Recipient Restrictive Trade practices prize Sydney U., 1992. Office: Allen Allen & Hemsley, Chifley Tower, 2000 Sydney NSW, Australia

CASTLE, MICHAEL N., congressman, former governor, lawyer; b. Wilmington, Del., July 2, 1939; s. J. Manderson and Louisa B. Castle. BA, Hamilton Coll., 1961; JD, Georgetown U., 1964. Bar: Del. 1964, D.C. 1964. Assoc. firm Connolly Bove and Lodge, Wilmington, 1964-73; ptnr. firm Connolly Bove and Lodge, 1973-75; dept. atty. gen. State of Del., 1965-66; ptnr. firm Schnee and Castle (P.A.), 1975-80; lt. gov. State of Del., Wilmington, 1981-85; prin. Michael N. Castle (P.A.), 1981—; gov. State of Del., 1985-93; mem. Congress from Del. (at large), 1993—; mem. banking & fin. svcs. subcom. on Domestic and Internat. Monetary Policy, mem. edn. and workforce com., intelligence com., chmn. subcom. Early Childhood Youth and Families; mem. Del. Ho. of Reps., 1966-67, Del. State Senate, 1968-76, minority leader, 1976. Bd. dirs. Boys Club of Wilmington. Mem. Del. State Bar Assn., ABA, Council State Govts., Nat. Gov.'s Assn., Rep. Gov.'s Assn., Southern Gov.'s Assn. Republican. Roman Catholic. Office: US Ho of Reps 1227 Longworth Bldg Washington DC 20515-0801

CASTLEMAN, BREAUX BALLARD, health management company executive; b. Louisville, Aug. 19, 1940; s. John Pryor and Mary Jane (Ballard) C.; m. Sue Ann Foreman (div. 1995); children: Matthew B., Shea B. BA in Econs., Yale U., 1962; postgrad., NYU, 1963. Mgmt. trainee Bankers Trust Co., N.Y.C., 1963-65; mng. dir. Castleman and Co., Houston, 1965-71; dir. program planning, econ. U.S. Dept. HUD, Ft. Worth, Dallas, 1971-73; v.p., office mgr. Booz Allen and Hamilton, Dallas, Houston, 1973-85; mng. dir. Castleman Group, Houston, 1985-87; CEO Kelsey-Seybold Clinic, P.A., Houston, 1987-95; pres. physician resources divsn. Caremark Internat., Inc., 1994-96; pres. Scripps Clinic, La Jolla, Calif., 1996-99; CEO, Physia Corp., Houston, 2000—. Contbr. articles to profl. jours. Candidate state legislature, Houston, 1968. Mem. Am. Med. Group Assn. (bd. dirs. 1996-99), Planning Forum (chmn. 1985-86), Yale Club N.Y., Presidio Golf Club.

CASTLEMAN, HARRY WEISSINGER, financial planner; b. Louisville, Dec. 21, 1911; s. Samuel Torbitt and Margaret (Weissinger) C.; m. Cynthia Sortwell, Aug. 27, 1943; children: Cynthia, Margaret, Harry Jr., Anna, Joan. BA, Yale U., 1934; grad. Command and Gen. Staff Sch., U.S. Army, 1943. CLU. Ins. agt. Louisville, 1937; ins. gen. agt. The New Eng., Louisville, 1955-77, assoc. gen agt., 1977—; mem. exec. com., pres. Leaders Assn., New England Life Ins., Co., Boston, 1947-55, pres. 1955-56; founder, pres. Estate Planning Coun. of Louiville, 1948. Co-chmn. Oxmoor Steeplechase, Louisville, 1972-74. Lt. col. U.S. Army, 1940-45, ETO. Decorated Bronze Star, 1945; hon. mem. Million Dollar Round Table, Park Ridge, Ill., 1947—. Mem. various life ins. assns., Soc. of Colonial Wars, Yale Club of N.Y., Wynn-Stay Club (bd. dirs.), River Valley Club (bd. dirs.), Chi Psi. Republican. Episcopalian. Avocations: fox-hunting, polo. Address: PO Box 86 Brunswick ME 04011-0086

CASTON, PHILIP STEWART CHARLES, architect, researcher, educator; b. Dartford, Kent, Eng., Oct. 19, 1960; arrived in Germany, 1987; s. Ronald Edwin and Patricia Elisabeth (Kappeler) C. BA with hons., Thames Poly., London, 1982; degree in arch., Canterbury (Eng.) Coll. Art, 1985; certificate in conservation, Bamberg (Germany) U., 1988, PhD, 1996. Reg. arch. Arch. Registration Coun. United Kingdom. Arch. Ratcliffe Stott Assoc., Kent, Eng., 1985-86; excavation asst. German Archael. Inst., 1988-89; freelance bldg. rschr. Bamberg U., 1992—, lectr., 1993-2000, scholar, 1996-99; lectr. Regensburg (Germany) U., 2000; prof. bldg. documentation Fachhochschule Neubrandenburg, Germany, 2000—. Author: (Book) Late Medieval Crossing-Towers In The German-Speaking Lands-Construction and Building History, 1987; contbr. articles to profl. jours. Mem. Koldewey Assn. Avocations: skiing, swimming, restoring automobiles, restoring buildings. Office: Fachhochschule Neubrandenbg, Brodaerstr 2, 17033 Neubrandenburg Germany

CASTOR, JON STUART, electronics company executive; b. Lynchburg, Va., Dec. 15, 1951; s. William Stuart and Marilyn (Hughes) C.; m. Stephanie Lum, Jan. 7, 1989; 1 child, David Jon. BA, Northwestern U., 1973; MBA, Stanford U., 1975. Mgmt. cons. Menlo Park, Calif., 1981-96; pres. TeraLogic, Inc., 1996—. Dir. Midwest Consumer Adv. Bd. to FTC, 1971-73; v.p., bd. dirs. San Mateo coun. Boy Scouts Am., 1991-93; bd. dirs. Pacific Skyline Coun. Boy Scouts Am., 1994—; trustee Coyote Point Mus. Environ. Edn., San Mateo, 1992-95. Office: TeraLogic Inc 1240 Villa St Mountain View CA 94041-1124

CASTRATARO, BARBARA ANN, lawyer; b. Bethpage, N.Y., Apr. 25, 1958; d. Vincent James and Theresa (Chiarini) C. BA in Music, L.I. U., 1984; JD, N.Y. Law Sch., 1989. Bar. N.Y. 1990, U.S. Dist. Ct. (so. dist.) N.Y. 1990. Music dir. CBS Network, N.Y.C., 1979-81, exec. ops., 1985-88; music dir. NBC Network/Score Prodns., N.Y.C. and L.A., 1983-84, Score Prodns./ABC Network, N.Y.C. and L.A., 1980-84; assoc. Donald Frank Esq., N.Y.C., 1989-93, Law Offices of Joel C. Bender, White Plains, N.Y., 1993-99, Bender, Jenson, Silverstein & Castrataro, LLP, White Plains, 1999—; lectr. on divorce and separation; founder Castrataro Artist Mgmt., 1997-99; adj. faculty mem. Berkeley Coll., White Plains, N.Y. Recipient 3 Emmy nominations N.Y. Acad. TV Arts and Sci., 1979, 82-83. Mem. N.Y. State Bar Assn., Womens Bar Assn. Avocations: sailing, gourmet cooking, gardening. Office: 140 Grand St White Plains NY 10601-4831

CASTRO, EDUARDO ALBERTO, theoretical chemist and educator; b. Buenos Aires, Avellaneda, Argentina, July 14, 1944; s. Eduardo and Rosalia (Di Diego) C.; m. Alicia Haydée Jubert, Dec. 17, 1970. BS in Chemistry, La Plata (Argentina) U., Argentina, 1967; PhD in Chemistry, La Plata (Argentina) U., 1970. Technician Bunge & Born, Buenos Aires, 1959-60; chemist Duperial, Buenos Aires, 1961-62, Cristalux, Buenos Aires, 1962-64; prof. chemistry ENET #1, Buenos Aires, 1964-65; chemistry asst. La Plata U., 1965-74, prof. chemistry, 1974—; rschr. in chemistry CONICET, Buenos Aires, 1974—; dir. Annals of Argentinian Sci. Soc., 1989—; dir. Theoretical Chemistry Group, Argentina, 1974—, Theoretical Chemistry L.Am. Schs., 1981—. Author: Springer-Verlag Editorial, 1987, 2d edit. 1990 (Nat. Award in Sci. 1992); contbr. numerous articles to profl. jours. Recipient B. Houssay Award in Physics, CONICET, 1987, R. Labriola award in Chemistry, AQA, 1988, F.P.P. Moreno award Geog. Argentinian Soc., 1993. Fellow Argentine Chem. Assn. (bd. dirs. 1980—); Argentine Sci. Soc. (bd. dirs. 1980—), Internat. Union of Pure and Applied Chem. Avocations: tennis, classical literature, epistemology, jazz. Home: 65 #519, 1900 La Plata Argentina Office: Cequinor, Calle 47 y 115 CC962, 1900 La Plata Argentina

CASTRO, ENRIQUE ALFONSO, chemist, educator, researcher; b. Santiago, Chile, Jan. 30, 1941; s. Enrique Castro and Rosario Rubio; m. Carmen Alonso, Dec. 13, 1975; children: Cristobal, Andrea. Lic. chemist, Cath. U. Chile, Santiago, 1968; PhD in Chemistry, Exeter (Eng.) U., 1974. Asst. prof. Cath. U. Chile, Santiago, 1969-91, prof., 1991—. Contbr. articles to profl. jours. including Chem. Reviews, Jour. Am. Chem. Soc., Jour. Organic Chemistry, Internat. Jour. Chem. Kinetics and others. Grantee Direccion Investigacion Universidad Catolica de Chile, 1987, Fondecyt, Chile, 1989, 91. Mem. Chilean Chem. Soc., Am. Chem. Soc. Avocation: tennis. Home: San Pio X 2595 Dpto 61, 9 Santiago Chile Office: Cath U Chile, Vicuna Mackenna 4860, 22 Santiago Chile

CASTRO, FIDEL (FIDEL CASTRO RUZ), Cuban government official; b. Mayari, Oriente Province, Cuba, May 13, 1927; s. Angel Castro and Lina Ruz; m. Mirta Diaz Balart, Oct. 12, 1948 (div. 1955); 1 son, Fidel. Grad. with degree of bachelor, Colegio Belen, Havana, Cuba, 1945; law degree and doctorate, U. Havana, 1950. Practiced law, 1950-52, took part in revolutionary movement expdn. against govt. Dominican Republic, 1947; leader of armed forces attacking Batista govt. in Cuba, 1953-58, unsuccessfully attacked Moncada Barracks, Santiago de Cuba, July 1953; captured, imprisoned, 1953-55; in exile, Mex. and N.Y., 1955-56; returned to Cuba, 1956, and led armed attacks against Batista govt., using Oriente Province as hdqrs. for armed forces; following successful campaign these forces entered Havana, Jan. 1, 1959; designated Manuel Urrutia provisional pres., and was named by Pres. Urrutia comdr.-in-chief of Cuban armed forces, Jan. 2, 1959; became prime min., Feb. 1959-76; head state, pres. Council of State, 1976—; pres. Council of Mins., 1976—; 1st sec. Partido Unido de la Revolución Socialista, 1963-65, Partido Comunista, 1965—, mem. polit. bur., 1976—; head Nat. Def. Coun., 1992—. Author: Ten Years of Revolution, 1964, History Will Absolve Me, 1968, (with Frei Betto) Fidel, 1987, (with Nelson Mandella) How Far We Slaves Have Come: South Africa and Cuba in Today's World, 1991. Chmn. Agrarian Reform Inst., 1965—. Decorated Gold Star (Vietnam), Order of Lenin, Order of October Revolution, 1st class Somali Order, Order of Jamaica; recipient Lenin Peace prize, 1961, Dimitrov prize, 1980; named Hero of Soviet Union, 1963. Office: Office of the President/Council of State, Palacio del Gobierno, Havana Cuba*

CASTRO, FRANCISCO FERREIRA DE, lawyer, educator; b. Floriano, Piaui, Brazil, June 28, 1923; s. Cristino Raymundo and Maria José (Ferreira) de C.; m. Iracema Da Costa e Silva, Mar. 30, 1952; children: Maria Auxiliadora, Rosa Luisa, Francisco Filho. BS in Econs., Acad. Commerce Pe. Champagnat, Fortaleza, Brazil, 1941; LLB, Minas Gerais Fed. U., Belo Horizonte, Brazil, 1948; LLD, Brasilia U., 1967. State rep. Legis. Assembly, Piaui, Brazil, 1950-54; vice-gov., substitute gov. State Govt. Piaui, 1954-58; state lawyer Teresina, 1960-62; fed. dep. Nat. Congress, Brasilia, Brazil, 1958-62; adviser juridical affairs of presidency Fed. Govt., Brasilia, 1962-64; prof. constitutional law U. Brasilia, 1962-70, prof. polit. sci., 1989-93; atty. NOVACAP Co., Brasilia, 1961-64; 1st class atty. Fed. Dist. Govt., Brasilia, 1964-86; lawyer Supreme Tribunal and Superior Fed. Appeals Tribunal, Brasilia, 1964—. Author: The State's Aim-Main Doctrines, 1956, Modernization and Democracy, 1967; contbr. articles to profl. jours. Active Historic and Geographic Inst. Fed. Dist., Brasilia, 1992; mem., former pres. Fed. Dist. sect. Labor Party, Brasilia, 1986; candidate to fed. senate Nat. Congress, Brasilia, 1986. Recipient Juridical Medal, Medal of Centenary Clovis Bevilaqua Brazilian Govt., 1959, Grand Cross medal Piaui State Renasçença Merit Order, 1997, Medal Dist. Fed. Govt. Brazil, 1984. Mem. Brazil Lawyers Order (past pres.), Congress Club, Brazilian Tennis Acad. (hon.). Roman Catholic. Avocations: walking, jogging, swimming, reading, writing. E-mail: ffcastro@nuctecnet.com.br. Home and Office: SML MI 09, Conj 05 Casa 16, 71540095 Brasilia Distrito Federal, Brazil

CASTRO, GUILLERMO RAUL, chemist and researcher; b. La Plata, Argentina, June 20, 1956; s. Angel Raul and Adelia Celina (Actis Caporale) C. Bachellor, Nat. U. La Plata, 1974; MS, U. Buenos Aires, 1987, PhD, 1992. Lab. asst. Nat. Meteorol. Svc., Buenos Aires, 1981-83; instr. U. Buenos Aires, 1981-89, co-supr., 1989-91; lab. asst. Exptl. Biology and Medicine, Inst. Buenos Aires, 1983-86; rschr., co-supr. PROIMI, Tucuman, Argentina, 1992-96; lectr. U. Tucuman, 1992—; postdoctoral rschr. MIT, 1996-98; vice dir. PROIMI-Biotech., 1998-2000; mem. bd. PROIMI, 2000—. Contbr. articles to profl. jours. Recipient Younger Scientist award Antorchas Found., PROIMI, 1993, 94, 95, Tucumán Coun. Sch. Tech. Rsch. awards, 1995; grantee 3d World Acad. Scis., 1993-95, Argentine Anthartic Inst., U. Buenos Aires, 1988-90, Internat. Found. Sci., 1996; Pew fellow, 1996-98; Pew Found. grantee, 1998; Nat. Sci. Agy. grantee, 1999. Mem. Am. Soc. Microbiology, Am. Chem. Soc., Latin Assn. Biotech. and Bioengring., N.Y. Acad. Scis. Roman Catholic. Avocations: photography, soccer, rugby. Office: PROIMI, Avenida Belgrano y Pasaje, 4000 Tucuman Argentina

CASTRO, JOSEPH ARMAND, music director, pianist, composer, orchestrator; b. Miami, Ariz., Aug. 15, 1927; s. John Loya and Lucy (Sanchez) C.; m. Loretta Faith Haddad, Oct. 21, 1966; children: John Joseph, James Ernest. Student, San Jose State Coll., 1944-47. Mus. dir. Herb Jeffries, Hollywood, Calif., 1952, June Christy, Hollywood, 1959-63, Anita O'Day, Hollywood, 1963-65, Tony Martin, Hollywood, 1962-64, Tropicana Hotel, Las Vegas, Nev., 1980-97, Desert Inn, Las Vegas, 1992-93; orch. leader Mocambo Night Club, Hollywood, 1952-54; soloist Joe Castro Trio, L.A., N.Y.C., Honolulu, 1952-65, Sands Hotel, Desert Inn, Las Vegas, 1975-80; mus. dir. Folies Bergere, 1980-89; with Joe Castro Trio with Loretta Castro, 1995—. Recs. include Cool School with June Christy, 1960, Anita O'Day Sings Rodgers and Hart, 1961, Lush Life, 1966, Groove-Funk-Soul, Mood Jazz, Atlantic Records, also albums with Teddy Edwards, Stan Kenton, Jimmy Borges with Joe Castro Trio, 1990, Loretta Castro with Joe Castro Trio, 1990, Honolulu Symphony concerts; command performance, Queen Elizabeth II, London Palladium, 1989, Concerts with Jimmy Borges and Honolulu Symphony Pops Concerts, 1991; jazz concert (with Nigel Kennedy) Honolulu Symphony, 1990; jazz-fest, Kailua-Kona, Hawaii, 1990; leader orch. Tropicana Hotel, 1989-97. With U.S. Army, 1946-47. Roman Catholic. Home: 2812 Colanthe Ave Las Vegas NV 89102-2026

CASTRO, LEONARD EDWARD, lawyer; b. L.A., Mar. 18, 1934; s. Emil Galvez and Lily (Meyers) C.; 1 son, Stephen Paul. A.B., UCLA, 1959, J.D., 1962. Bar: Calif. 1963, U.S. Supreme Ct. 1970. Assoc. Musick, Peeler & Garrett, Los Angeles, 1962-68, ptnr., 1968—. Mem. ABA, Internat. Bar Assn., Los Angeles County Bar Assn. Office: Musick Peeler & Garrett 1 Wilshire Blvd Ste 2000 Los Angeles CA 90017-3876

CASTRO, LUIZ GUILHERME MARTINS, dermatologist; b. São Paulo, Brazil, Sept. 20, 1960; s. Raymundo Martins and Athaly Martins (Campos) C.; m. Vera Cecilia Paes de Barros, Dec. 17, 1987; 1 child, Ana Luiza. MD, U. São Paulo, 1986; Masters degree, Escola Paulista Medicina, São Paulo, 1992; doctorate, U. São Paulo, 1999. Diplomate Brazilian Med. Assn. Resident U. São Paulo, 1987-89, rsch. fellow, 1990-92, supervising physician, 1994—; dermatological cons. Galderma Lab, São Paulo, 1996-97; dermatological cons. Johnson & Johnson, Sao Paulo, 1990-96; gen. sec. Brazilian Soc. for Dermatol. Surgery, Sao Paulo, 1992-94. Mem. editl. bd. Annals Brasilian Dermatology, 1994—; contbr. articles to profl. jours. Recipient Young Dermatologist award Brazilian Soc. Dermatology, 1987, 88, 93, Perry Robins award Internat. Soc. Dermatol. Surgery and Oncology, 1991. Mem. Am. Acad. Dermatology, Ibero Latin Am. Coll. Dermatologists (Young Dermatologist award 1989). Avocation: tennis. E-mail: guiga@dermamail.com.br. Home: Rua Wanderley, 1261 apt 41, 05011001 Sao Paulo SP Brazil Office: Hosp Clinicas Faculdade Medicina, care Dept Dermatology Box 8091, 01065-970 São Paulo Brazil

CASTRO, MANUEL ALONSO, electrical and computer engineering educator; b. Caracas, Venezuela, Mar. 27, 1958; arrived in Spain, 1966; s. Manuel and Pilar (Gil) C.; m. Carmen Rocabert, Dec. 3, 1983; children: Marta, Iria. Degree in indsl. engring., ETSII/UPM, Madrid, 1983, D in Engring., 1988. Basic rschr. ETSII/UPM, Madrid, 1982-88; lectr. ETSII/UNED, Madrid, 1983-89, assoc. prof., 1989-93, 1993—, dir. computing and comm. svc. dept., 1996—; sr. sys. engr. Digital Equipment Co., Madrid, 1989-92, sr. tech. coord., 1992-93; computer cons. Euro Four, Madrid, 1991-94, Micromouse, Madrid, 1994-96; participant sci. confs. and workshops. Author: US-Spain Evaluation of the Solar One and Cesa-I Receiver and Storage Systems, 1989; author, editor: (book and software) Micro: Aprendizaje de Microprocesadores, Vols. 1, 1994, Vol. 2, 1996, Biblioteca Multimedia de las Energias Renovables, 1999; also books on electronics tchg. and use of simulation in electronics; contbr. articles to profl. jours.; rschr. on digital electronic design, microprocessor and embedded sys., renewable sys. design and comm., distance learning and multimedia application. Active Lions Internat., Madrid, 1989. Mem. IEEE (sr. mem.), IFAC, ISES (Spanish bd. mem.), Assn. for Computing Machinery, N.Y. Acad. Sci. Avocations: squash, skiing, stamp collecting. Office: ETSII/UNED Dept Elec Engr, Ciudad Universitaria s/n, 28040 Madrid Spain

CASTRO, MARCIA SALUSTIANO DE, marine biologist; b. Rio de Janeiro, Brazil, Aug. 10, 1969; d. Jose Goncalves de Castro and Judith Salustiano de Souza. BS, Fed. U. Rio de Janeiro, Brazil, 1995; Specialist, Fluminense Fed. U., Niteroi, Brazil, 1996, postgrad. Probationer Fed. U. Rio de Janeiro, 1990-95, autonomous biologist, 1995—.

CASTRO, MARIA GRACIELA, medical educator, gene therapy researcher; b. Buenos Aires, Mar. 2, 1955; d. Nestor Antonio Castro and Maria Esther Rodriquez; m. Pedro Ricardo Lowenstein, Jan. 12, 1988; 1 child, Elijah David. BSc 1st class in Chemistry, Nat. U. La Plata, Argentina, 1979, MSc in Biochemistry, 1981, PhD in Biochemistry, 1986. Fogarty postdoctoral fellow Lab. Neurochem. & Neuroimmunol. Nat. Inst. Child Health and Human Devel. NIH, Bethesda, Md., 1986-88; sr. rsch. fellow Lab. Molecular Endocrinology Dept. Biochemistry and Physiology U. Reading, U.K., 1988-90; lectr. dept. molecular and life scis. U. Abertay, Dundee, Scotland, 1991-92; lectr. in neurosci., dept. physiology U. Wales Coll. Cardiff, 1991-95; sr. lectr. medicine molecular medicine unit U. Manchester, Eng., 1995-98, prof. molecular medicine, 1998—; dir. Molecular Medicine and Gene Therapy Unit, Manchester, 1996—; expert Women in Sci. Tech., Sheffield, Eng., 1996—; mem. neurosci. panel Wellcome Trust, 1999—. Contbr. articles to high profl. sci. and med. jours.; mem. editl. bd. Jour. Endocrinology, Jour. Molecular Endocrinology, Current Gene Therapy, 2000—; patentee in field. Recipient Rsch. grant Brit. Heart Found., 1997, Rsch. grant Med. Rsch. Coun., 1998, Rsch. grant Biotechnology and Biol. Rsch. Coun., 1999, Rsch. grant Wellcome Trust, 1999. Mem. Am. Gene Therapy Assn., Endocrine Soc., Soc. for Neuroscience, Internat. Soc. Neurovirology (founding mem.). Fax: 44 0 161 275 5669. E-mail: mcastro@fs1.scg.man.ac.uk. Home: Didsbury Manchester, Lancashire United Kingdom Office: U Manchester Sch Med, Oxford Rd Stopford Bldg1302, Manchester M13 9PT, England

CASTRO, RAFAEL, pediatrician, hospital administrator; b. Santafé de Bogota, Colombia, Apr. 12, 1944; s. Rafael and Olga (Martinez) C.; m. Maria Mercedes Esguerra, Aug. 8, 1969; children: Juan P., Felipe, Santiago. MD, U. del Valle, Cali, Colombia, 1970. Diplomate Am. Bd. Pediatrics. Resident in pediatrics U. Tenn., Memphis, 1972-75; instr. pediatrics U. Javeriana, Bogota, 1975-77; asst. prof. pediatrics U. Militar Nueva Granada, Bogota, 1977-82, assoc. prof., 1982-87, titular prof. pediatrics, 1988—; chief pediatric svcs. Hosp. Militar Central, Bogota, 1988-91, head divsn. postgrad. med. edn., 1991-98; editor-in-chief Hosmil Medica, 1990-99. Editor-in-chief Hosmil Medica, 1990—; contbr. articles to profl. jours., chpts. to books. Recipient Med. Merit award Hosp. Militar Central, 1993. Mem. Colombian Assn. Med. Schs. (coun. of pediatric edn. and curriculum 1980—), Colombian Pediatric Soc. (pres. 1995-99), L.Am. Infectious Disease Soc., Colombian Assn. Infectious Diseases (pres. 2000-02), Gun Club, Club Los Lagartos. Liberal Party. Roman Catholic. Avocation: golf. Home: Carrera 12 79-07 (P-7), Bogota Colombia Office: Carrera 13 78-98, Bogota Colombia

CASTRO, RAUL (RAUL CASTRO RUZ), Cuban government official; b. June 3, 1931. Ed. Jesuit schs. Chief of armed forces, 1960, 1st dep. prime min., 1972-76, 1st v.p. coun. of state, 1976—, 1st v.p. coun. of mins., 1976—; assisted Fidel Castro's movement Mex., Cuba; imprisoned for insurrection, 1953, received amnesty, 1954. Decorated medal for Strengthening of Brotherhood in Arms, 1977, Order of Lenin, 1979, Order of Oct. Revolution, 1981. Address: Office of the President/Council of State, Palacio del Gobierno, Havana Cuba*

CASTRONOVO, VALERIO, historian, editor; b. Vercelli, Italy, Feb. 15, 1935; s. Rosario and Raffaella Castellana; m. Mariangela Chiabrando, Sept. 8, 1962; 1 child, Simona. Degree in polit. sci., U. Turin, Italy, 1959. Asst. lectr. U. Turin, 1959-66; rschr. L. Einaudi Found., Turin, 1966-68; lectr. modern history U. Milan, 1968-71; prof. contemporary history U. Turin, 1972—. Editor Prometeo; contbr. articles to profl. jours. Mem. Acad. Scis., Italian Coun. for Social Scis. Office: U Turin Fac Ednl Sci, Via S Ottavio 20, I-10124 Turin Italy

CASTRO-RUBIO, H. HUGO, engineering executive; b. Santiago, Chile, Feb. 3, 1943; s. Enrique Castro and Rosario Rubio; m. M. Teresa Barrenengoa, June 5, 1966; children: Paulina, Teresa, Soledad, José-Ignacio. Degree in civil engring., Cath. U., Santiago, 1965. Chief of dept. Chile State Rlwys., Santiago, 1966-71; v.p. INECO, Madrid, 1972-78; head of planning Ministry of Transport, Santiago, 1978-82; pres. Sonacol SA, Santiago, 1982—; chmn. Empremar, Valparaiso, Chile, 1980-83, Chile State Rlwys., Santiago, 1978-84. Mem. Engrs. Inst. (Chile), Transport Engring. Soc. (vice chmn. 1980—). Roman Catholic. Avocations: horseback riding, tennis, bridge. Office: Sonacol SA, Isabel La Catolica 4472, Santiago Chile

CASTRO-VAZQUEZ, ALFREDO, physiology educator, researcher; b. Buenos Aires, Dec. 27, 1945; s. Redento and Otilia Beatriz (Vazquez) Castro; m. Teresa Josefina Fornieles, May 3, 1975; children: Ezequiel, Ignacio, Sofia, Magdalena. MD, U. Salvador, Buenos Aires, 1971; PhD, U. Cuyo, Mendoza, 1993. Rsch. assoc. Med. Sch. U. Tex., Dallas, 1974-76; assoc. rschr. Lab. for Reprodn. and Lactation, Mendoza, 1976-85, ind. rschr., 1985-94, prin. rschr., 1994—; assoc. prof. physiology U. Cuyo Sch. Medicine, Mendoza, 1986-94, prof. physiology, 1994—, chmn., chair physiology, 1995—, dir. grad. program in biology, 1996—. Contbr. articles to profl. jours. Recipient Bernardo A. Houssay's Centennary award Nat. Rsch. Coun. Argentina, 1986. Mem. Am. Soc. Mammalogists, N.Y. Acad. Scis., L.Am. Assn. Human Reprodn. Rsch. (sec. 1977-81), Animal Behavior Soc. Roman Catholic. Office: Univ of Cuyo Sch Med, Casilla Correo 33, 5500 Mendoza Argentina

CASU, BENITO, biochemist; b. Brescia, Italy, Mar. 27, 1927; s. Luigi and Angela (Porcu) C.; m. Marta Mancini, May 6, 1954; children: Marco, Simona. D in Chemistry, U. Pavia, Italy, 1950; MD (hon.), U. Uppsala, Sweden, 1998. From rsch. fellow to dir. G. Ronzoni Inst., Milan, 1951-92, sci. coord., 1992—; vis. scientist McGill U., Montreal, Can., 1968-69; sci. com. Carbohydrates in Europe, 1992—; cons. in field. Co-author: (with J. Harenberg) Non-Anticoagulant Actions of Glycosaminoglycans, 1985; mem. internat. adv. bd. Biochem. Jour., 1973—; contbr. articles to profl. jours. Recipient Outstanding Achievement plaque Loyola U., Chgo., 1990. Mem. Italian Chem. Soc. (coord. carbohydrate group), 1984-96, Golden medal 1998), Internat. Carbohydrate Orgn. (nat. rep. 1976—, pres. 1996-98). Avocation: wood and stone carving. Home: via Giuseppe Colombo 81/A, 20133 Milan Italy Office: G Ronzoni Inst Chem Rsch, via G Colombo 81, 20133 Milan Italy

CASWELL, DOROTHY ANN COTTRELL, arts administrator; b. N.Y.C., Dec. 18, 1938; d. Donald Peery and Eleanor Hildaborg (Westberg) Cottrell; m. Allen Edward Caswell, Oct. 24, 1959; children: David Alan, Bruce Leland. Student, Carleton Coll., Northfield, MN., 1956-59; AB in Psych., George Wash. U., 1960-61; postgrad., SUNY, Oneonta, 1971-76. Sec. U.S. Fgn. Service, Tunis, Tunisia, 1959-61; mng. dir. Glimmerglass Opera, Inc., Cooperstown, N.Y., 1975-78; exec. dir. Upper Catskill Community Council on the Arts, Oneonta, N.Y., 1978-80; devel. officer Catskill Arts Consortium, Oneonta, 1981-83; devel. cons. Otsego Urban Rural Self-Devel. Assocs., Inc., Oneonta, 1982-83; co-founder, pres. Catskill Choral Soc., 1970-76, 81-84; assoc. producer Orpheus Theatre, Inc., Oneonta, 1984-91; voice tchr. Oneonta, 1984—; ptnr., co-owner OnStage Prodn. Svcs., 1991—; cons., arts adminstrv. Dorothy Caswell Assocs., Oneonta, 1981—; past pres., mem. sub-area coun. Health Sys. Agy. N.E. N.Y., also mem. planning adv. group and rev. adv. Singer/actress with Orpheus Theatre, 1984—; actress WSKG-TV Pub. TV film series Susquehanna Stories, 1990. Vol., mem. chorus Glimmerglass Opera Cooperstown, 1974—; mem. mil. acad. selection com. for Congressman Sherwood Boehlert of N.Y.; mem. Otsego County Health Planning Adv. Coun., Otsego Pub. Health Partnership; bd. dirs. Otsego County Tourism Bur., 1987-90, Oneonta Downtown Coalition, 1982-84. Honored for outstanding performance and svcs. to the community, SUNY, 1975. Democrat. Protestant. Avocations: singing, acting, gardening, swimming, skiing.

CASWELL, ROBERT DOUGLAS, aerospace engineer; b. Markdale, Ont., Can., Nov. 8, 1946; s. Robert G. and Helen (Hawken) C.; children: Laura, Andrea. BASc, U. Toronto, 1969; MASc, Inst. for Aerospace Studies, Toronto, 1970. Thermal engr. SPAR Aerospace, Toronto, 1970-73; systems space engr. Govt. of Can., Ottawa, Ont., 1973-76, shuttle arm test mgr., 1976-80, MSAT platform mgr., 1981-83, RADARSAT spacecraft mgr., 1983-86; space sta. robotics mgr. Nat. Rsch. Coun., Ottawa, Ont., 1986-88; Olympus platform mgr. ESA/ESTEC, Noordwijk, The Netherlands, 1988—. Tech. dir. film: Arm in Space, 1981; contbr. articles to profl. jours. Recipient J.A.D. McCurdy award U. Toronto, 1969, NASA Group Achievement award, 1981, Estec Performance award, 1990, Estec medal for Olympus Spacecraft Recovery, 1991, Recovery Team medal Academie Nationale del'Air et l'Espace, 1992. Mem. AIAA, Assn. Profl. Engrs. Ont., Can. Aeronautics and Space Inst. Home: Seinpostduin 74, 2586 EC Den Haag The Netherlands Office: Estec/CS, PO Box 299, 2200 AG Noordwijk The Netherlands

CATABELLE, JEAN-MARIE HENRI, industrial company executive; b. Dec. 10, 1941; s. Christian Aristide and Annette Marie (Lemonnier) C.; children by previous marraige: Laurent, Christine, Diane; m. Michèle Archambaud, Sept. 1, 1987. Engr., Ecole Cen. des Arts et Mfrs., Paris, 1963-66; MS with honors, Yale U., 1967; MBA with distinction, Harvard U., 1974. Dept. mgr. IBM France, Paris, 1969-72; asst. to contr. IBM Am. Far East, White Plains, N.Y., 1973; ops. mgr. Raychem S.A., Pontoise, France, 1974-78; mktg. mgr. Europe Raychem, Pontoise, 1978-81; gen. mgr. Compagnie Française des Isolants, France, 1981-82; mng. dir., COO DAV, Annemasse, France, 1982-90; v.p. sales and internat. activities Magneti Marelli, Milan, Italy, 1990-91; pres., CEO Marwal Sys. (joint venture Magneti Marelli/Walbro), 1991-99, also bd. dirs.; pres., CEO Magneti Marelli, France, 1998—; dir. ETUDOC, Annecy, France; chmn. bd. examiners LEP Profl. Sch., Annemasse, 1983-90; dir. ASDTN, Annecy, 1983-90; bd. dirs. French Nat. Edn. Com. Grenoble Acad., 1986-89; pres. Employer's Union (Marne, Champagne-Ardennes), Fedn. Industries Equipment Vehicules, Regional State Coun. Econ. and Social Affairs. Patentee in field; contbr. articles to profl. jours. Trustee LEP Profl. Sch., 1982. Lt. French Army, 1967-69. Fulbright fellow, 1966, 72, French Govt. fellow, 1972, Alliance Française fellow, 1966. Mem. Ecole Centrale Alumni Assn., Coun. Banque de France Marne, Golf Club, Tennis Club. Roman Catholic. Avocation: Traveling. Home: 17 Rue Duroc, 75007 Paris France Office: Magneti-Marelli France, 19 Rue Lavoisier, 92000 Nanterre France

CATACH, NINA ABIGNOLY, research director, deceased; b. Le Caire, Egypt, July 25, 1923; d. David Abignoly and Marie Dayan; m. David Catach; children: Irène, François, Laurent (dec.). Licence es lettres classiques, U. Paris, 1945; Maitrise lettres classiques, U. Aix-en-Provence, 1946; Capes Lettres Classiques, U. Paris, 1955; CNRS, Paris, 1962, D in Letters, 1968. Tchr., prof. Edn. Nationale, Paris, 1945-62; rschr. CNRS, Paris, 1962-92; educator U. Paris III, 1970-97; pres. Airoe Assn., Paris, 1983-97, Prix Saintour de l'Académie française, 1969, Grand Prix de l'Académie française, 1995; expert Conseil Superieur Langue Française, 1989-91. Author: L'Orthographe Française, 1978, 7th edit., 1997, La Ponctuation, 1994, 2d edit., 1995, others; author, editor: Dictionnaire Historique de l'Orthographe Française, 1994; editor: Pour une Théorie de la Langue écrite, 1988. Decorated chevalier Order Arts and Letters, 1997. Avocations: archeology, writing history.

CATA-DANIL, GHEORGHE, physicist; b. Sebes-Alba, Romania, Sept. 22, 1957; came to U.S., 1997; s. Nicolae and Aurelia (Danil) C.; m. Irina Ivascu, Oct. 22, 1988 (div. Jan. 1992); 1 child, Dragos. MS, U. Bucharest, Romania, 1982; PhD, Inst. Atomic Physics, Bucharest, 1991. With Inst. Power Reactors, Pitesti, Romania, 1982-84; scientist IFA, Bucharest, Romania, 1984-90; sr. scientist IFIN, Bucharest, Romania, 1990; matre de conf. ISN, Grenoble, France, 1990; assoc. rsch. scientist Yale U., New Haven, Conn., 1997-98; assoc. prof. BB U., Cluj-Napoca, Romania, 1997—; vis. scientist LMU, Munchen, Germany, 1990-96, INFN, Milan, 1992-96. Lt. Romanian Mil., 1996-97. Office: Inst Atomic Physics, PO box MG-6, 776163 Bucharest Romania

CATAL, HIKMET HUSEYIN, engineering educator; b. Usak, Turkey, Jan. 1, 1960; s. Yusuf and Meliha Catal. Diploma in Civil Engring., Ege U., Izmir, Turkey, 1982; MS, Dokuz Eylul U., Izmir, Turkey, 1986; PhD, Eylul U., Izmir, Turkey, 1992. Rsch. asst. dept. civil engring., architecture Dokuz Eylul U., Izmir, 1985-93, lectr., 1993-95, asst. prof., 1995-97, assoc. prof., 1997—. Asst. editor: Natural Sci. and Engring. Jour., 1998. Lt. Turkish mil., 1983-84. Office: Dokuz Eylul U/Civil Engring, Tinaztepe Campus, Buca-Izmir 35160, Turkey

CATALAN, CESAR ATILIO, chemistry educator; b. Tucuman, Argentina, Aug. 9, 1945; s. Emilio Rinaldo and Nelida Edit (Fanciotti) C.; m. Elsa del Valle Harlouchet, Oct. 30, 1972; children: Julieta Veronica, Patricia Elina. Grad., U. Tucuman, Argentina, 1968, PhD in Chemistry, 1977. Instr. Nat. U. Tucuman, Argentina, 1971-78, asst. prof., 1979-83, prof. chemistry, 1983—; pres. Nat. U. Tucuman, 1994-98; head organic chemistry inst. Sch. Chem., Biochem. & Pharmacy, Tucuman, Argentina, 1986-95; cons. in field. Co-author: (with I.J.S. Fenik and F.G. Venditti) Infrared Spectroscopy, Applications to Structural Problems in Organic Chemistry, 1985, UV and Visible Spectroscopy, Applications to Structural Problems in Organic Chemistry; contbr. articles to profl. jours. Postdoctoral fellow Stanford U. Chem. Dept., Palo Alto, Calif., 1982-83. Mem. Am. Soc. Pharm., Phytochem. Soc. Europe, N.Y. Acad. Scis. Avocations: walking, climbing. Home: 9 De Julio 620, 4000 Tucuman Argentina Office: U Tucuman, Ayacucho 471, 4000 Tucuman Argentina

CATALANO, JAMES ANTHONY, social worker; b. Lackawanna, N.Y., Nov. 5, 1954; s. George and Frances (McGowan) C. BA, Canisius Coll., 1977, Canisius Coll., 1992; MS, Columbia U., 1985, MA in Ednl. Psychology, 1999; MDiv, Weston Jesuit Sch. Theology, Cambridge, Mass., 1994, ThM, 1995. Cert. social worker, N.Y.; diploma clin. social work NASW, 1991. Caseworker Neighborhood Info. Ctr., Buffalo, N.Y., 1975-79; dir. Youth Svcs. Program Lincoln Community Ctr., Buffalo, N.Y., 1979-80; psychiatric social worker, discharge planner Bry-Lin Hosp., Buffalo, N.Y., 1981; social worker Cath. Charities of Western N.Y., Buffalo, N.Y., 1987-89; asst. to the dir. Inst. of Faith and Justice Canisius Coll., Buffalo, N.Y., 1989-90; pvt. practice Buffalo, N.Y., 1989—; relief worker Jesuit Refugee Svcs., San Salvador, El Salvador, 1985; chmn. Site Selection Com. for Residential Care Facilities, Buffalo, 1979-81; adv. to chmn. Pub. Svc. Commn. of N.Y., 1979-81; speaker on San Salvador Diocese of Buffalo, 1990-91; workshop leader Buffalo Taditional High Sch., Buffalo City High Sch. East Campus, 1988-89; com. mem. Dem. Orgn. Erie County, Buffalo, 1978-81. Recipient Vol. Svc. award VA, Syracuse, N.Y., 1982. Mem. NASW. Home and Office: 50 Glenwood Ave Jersey City NJ 07306-4606

CATALANO, LOUIS WILLIAM, JR., neurologist; b. Bklyn., Apr. 20, 1942; s. Louis William and Aileen (Bobb) C.; m. Diana Catalano; children: Louis William III, Jamea Elizabeth, Adriana Louise. BS cum laude, U. Pitts., 1963, MD, 1967. Diplomate Am. Bd. Psychiatry and Neurology, Am. Bd. Electroencephalography, Am. Bd. Pain Medicine, Am. Bd. Med. Examiners. Intern Presbyn.-St. Luke's Hosp., Chgo., 1967-68; rsch. assoc. NIH, Bethesda, Md., 1968-70; fellow neurology The Neurol. Inst., N.Y.C., 1970-73; clin. asst., prof. neurology U. Pitts. Sch. Med., 1973—; pvt. practice Greensburg, Pa., 1973—; staff Latrobe (Pa.) Area Hosp., 1973—, Westmoreland Regional Hosp., Greensburg, 1973—, Indiana (Pa.) Hosp., 1983—; cons. Jeannette (Pa.) Dist. Meml. Hosp., 1984—, Frick Cmty. Health Ctr., Mt. Pleasant, Pa., 1991—, Torrance (Pa.) State Hosp., 2000—; lectr. in field. Contbr. articles to profl. jours. Pres. Neurol. Inst. We. Pa. Spl. fellow Columbia U., NIH, 1970-73, epilepsy minifellow, Bowman Gray Sch. Medicine, Winston-Salem, N.C., 1988. Fellow Royal Soc. Medicine, Am. Acad. Neurology; mem. AMA, Am. Acad. Pain Mgmt., Am. Med. Electroencephalographic Assn., Am. Soc. Neuroimaging, Am. Acad. Clin. Neurophysiology, Am. Sleep Disorders Assn., Pa. Med. Soc., Westmoreland County Med. Soc., Latrobe Acad. Medicine, Pittsburgh Neurosci. Soc., Sigma Xi, Alpha Omega Alpha. Avocations: sport fishing, scuba diving, skiing, travel. Office: Cen Med Arts RD 7 Old Rte 30 Frye Farm Rd Greensburg PA 15601

CATALDO, FRANCO, chemist, researcher, educator; b. Asmara, Eritrea, Aug. 18, 1964; arrived in Italy, 1975; s. Francesco and Clotilde (Pagliaro); m. Stefania Lupi, Nov. 9, 1996; children: Francesca-Elena, Silvia. PhD in Chemistry, U. Rome, 1988. Prof. chemistry Tech. Sch., Rome, 1988-89; rschr. in chemistry ENI, Milan, 1989; rschr. in chemistry Bridgestone-Firestone, Rome, 1990-95, sr. rschr., 1995-99; gen. mgr. Progega s.n.c., Rome, 1999—; prof. indsl. chemistry U. Rome, 1997; R&D cons. Trelleborg-Pirelli, Tivoli, Rome. Author: Introduction to Macromolecular Chemistry, 1994; contbr. 77 articles to profl. jours.; patentee (20) in field. Fellow N.Y. Acad. Sci., Italian Chem. Soc. Office: Progega snc, Via casilina 1626/A, 00133 Rome Italy

CATALFO, BETTY MARIE, health service executive, nutritionist; b. N.Y.C., Nov. 2, 1942; d. Lawrence Santo and Gemma (Patrone) Lorefice; children—Anthony, Lawrence, Donna Marie. Grad. Newtown High Sch., Elmhurst, N.Y., 1958. Sec., clk. ABC-TV, N.Y.C., 1957-60; founder, lectr., nutritionist Weight Watchers, Manhasset, N.Y., 1964-75; founder, pres. Every-Bodys Diet, Inc. dba Stay Slim, Queens, N.Y., 1976—; dir. in-home program N.Y. State Dept. Health, N.Y.C., 1985—; founder, pres. Delitegul Diet Foods, Inc., 1988—; lectr. in field. Author: 101 Stay-Slim Recipes, 1983, Get Slim and Stay Slim Diet Cook Book, rev. ed., 1987, Diet Revolution, 1991, Holiday Cookbook, 1992, Fat Counts in Fast Food Spots, 1992, Choose to Loose!, 1993, You Are Not Alone, 1993, Eating Out, 1994, Change or Select, 1994, Calories Do Count!, 1994, Fat Free Receipes, 1994; author, dir., producer: (video) Dancersize for Overweight, 1986, Get Slim and Stay Slim Diet Cook Book, Eating Right for Your Life, Hello It's Me and I'm Slim, (videos) Stay Slim Line Dancing, 1989, Stay Slim Food Facts, 1989, Help Me Before I Give In, 1990, A New Year A New You!, 1991, Relax and Meditate, 1991, Come Shop with Me, 1991, Change or Accept, 1993, The Bag Lady, 1993, Sneak Eater, 1993, Sins That Every Dieter Makes, 1994, Stay Slim from Start to Finish, 1994, Here's Some Helpful Diet Tips, 1994, What Every Smart Dieter Knows, 1994, Mirror Mirror on the Wall, 1994, Weight Management Techniques, 1995; author, editor: (video) Eating Right For Life, 1985, Isometric Techniques for Weight Reduction, Dance Your Calories A-Weigh; author, producer: (video) Eating Habits, 1986—; (video) Isometric Techniques for Weight Reduction, 1986, Patience Is a Virtue When Weight Loss is the Goal, 1986, Slow Down you Eat to Fast, 1994, Always Giving Never Receiving, 1994, Relax and Don't You Worry, 1994; producer, dir.: (video) Positive and Negative Diet Forces, 1987, (video) Hello It's Me and I'm Thin, 1987, (video) Dance Your Calories A-Weigh, 1987, (video) Positive and Negative Diet Forces, 1987. Sponsor, lectr. St. Pauls Ctr., Bklyn., 1981—, Throgs Neck Assn. Retarded Children, Bronx, 1985—; active ARC, LWV, Am. Italian Assn., United Way Greenwich, Council Chs. and Synagogues, Heart Assn., N.Y. Meals on Wheels, 1985—, Health Assn. Fairfield County, Food Svcs. for Homeless People, 1993, 94, 95; chairperson, sponsor Battered Women, 1994—. Named Woman of Yr., Bayside Womens Club, N.Y., 1983, O, PK Woman of Yr., 1986—, Woman of Yr. Richmond Boys Club, 1987, Woman of Yr. Bronx Press Club Assn., 1987; recipient Merit award for Svc. Cath. Archdiocese of Bklyn., 1985, Merit award Svcs. Cath. Archdioces of Bklyn. and Queens, 1992, 93, 94, Community Service award Sr. Citizens Sacred Heart League Bklyn./Queens Archdiocese. N.Y. State Nutritional Guidance for Children Nat. Assn. Scis. Mem. Nat. C. of C. for Women (Woman of Yr. 1987, 90), Pres.'s Coun. on Nutrition, Roundtable for Women in Food Service, Bus. and Profl. Women's Club, Pres. Council for Phys. Fitness, Nat. Assn. Female Execs., Assn. for Fitness in Bus. Inc., Nat. Assn. Female Bus. Owners. Democrat. Roman Catholic. Club: Mothers Sacred Heart Sch. (chairperson 1979-82). Avocations: reading, travel, golf, family. Home: 21422 27th Ave Flushing NY 11360-2608 also: 58 Riverview Ct Greenwich CT 06831-4127 Office: 10005 101st Ave Ozone Park NY 11416-2601

CATANO, LUCY BACA, gallery manager; b. Roswell, N.Mex., Aug. 1, 1946; d. Mike Y. and Sostena (Sambrano) Baca; children: Teresa, Cuki, John, Robert. Asst. libr. Artesia (N.Mex.) Pub. Libr., 1966-72; arts and crafts tchr. WASA, Willcox, Ariz., 1990—; demonstrator Demos, Ltd., Tucson, 1989—; part-time mgr. Wildwood Gallery & Book Bank, Willcox, 1990—; spl. edn. tchr.'s aide, 1999—. Author children's stories; poet. Voter registrar Youth-Willcox Schs., 1992-94. Recipient award for Outstanding Dedication to Youth, City of Willcox, 1992, 1st place poetry award Willcox C. of C., 1996, 98; named Citizen of Yr., 1998, Outstanding Poet, 1998. Mem. Willcox Against Substance Abuse, Writer's Bloc, Friends of the Libr., Poet's Soc. Democrat. Mormon. Home: 408 N Arizona Ave Willcox AZ 85643-1526

CATANZARITI, JOSEPH JOHN, solicitor; b. Sydney, June 4, 1959; s. Raffaele and Antonia (Abiuso) C.; m. Maria Anna Ramaci, May 28, 1988; children: Elisa Antonia, Christina Maria, Gabriella Alana. BA, U. New South Wales, 1980, LLB, 1982. Bar: Australia 1982. Solicitor Clayton Utz, Sydney, 1988-90, ptnr., 1990—. Mem. Australian Human Resources Inst. (chartered), Indsl. Rels. Soc. New South Wales (com. 1983-91, asst. sec. 1991-93, pres. 1993-95, asst. sec. 1995—), Indsl. Rels. Soc. Australia (sec./treas. 1998—), Law Soc. New South Wales (councillor 2000). Roman Catholic. Avocations: theater, reading, writing. Office: Clayton Utz, 1 OConnell St Level 23-35, Sydney NSW 2000, Australia

CATE, PETER CARL, zoologist, researcher; b. Linz, Austria, July 23, 1948; s. Peter Mellon and Elfriede (Höfler) C.; m. Sylvia Brodowicz, June 20, 1981; children: Thomas, Sabine. D in phil., Vienna U., Vienna, 1982. Rsch. scientist Office of Rsch. Ctr. Agr., Vienna, Austria, 1979-87, sr. scientist, 1988—; cons. Mus. Nat. History, Vienna, 1984—, Nat. Hist. Mus. Prague, 1988—, Dept. Forestry, Bolzano, Italy, 1991—. Contbr. numerous articles to profl. jours. Mem. N.Y. Acad. Scis., Austrian Entomological Soc., Slovenian Entomological Soc., Soc. Coleopterologica, Assn. Europe of Coleopterologica. Avocations: skiing, entomology, travel. Home: Hebrag 4-18, 1090 Vienna Austria Office: Fed Office and Rsch Ctr Agr, Spargelfeldstr 191, A-1226 Vienna Austria

CATEDRA, MANUEL FELIPE, engineering educator; b. Santisteban, Jaen, Spain, Apr. 28, 1955; s. Manuel and Maria (Perez) C.; m. Virginia Castillo, Oct. 30, 1979; children: Begona, Jose. MS in Engring., U. Poly., Madrid, 1977, PhD in Telecomm., 1982. Asst. prof. U. Poly. Madrid, 1982-89; prof. U. Cantabria, Santander, Spain, 1989-98, U. Alcala, Spain, 1998—. Author: C6-FFT Method Application, 1995, IEEE Trans EMC, 1998, Cell Planning for Wireless Communication, 1999. Recipient Best Paper award Applied Elec. Soc., Monterey, Calif., 1997. Mem. IEEE, Applied Computational Electromagnetics Soc. Office: U Alcala, Escuela Politecnica, E-28806 Alcala Madrid, Spain

CATES, NELIA BARLETTA DE, diplomat of Dominican Republic; b. Santo Domingo, Dominican Republic, Dec. 21, 1932; d. Amadeo and Nelia (Ricart) Barletta; m. Miguel Morales Abreu, Oct. 29, 1953 (div. 1961); m. John Martin Cates, Nov. 19, 1976. Ed. in Argentina, Cuba and U.S.A.; diploma, Duchesne Coll., 1950. Cultural attache Embassy of Dominican Republic, London, 1975-85, amb., permanent rep. to Internat. Maritime Orgn., 1985-94; pres. Compania Editorial El Mundo S.A., La Habana, Cuba, 1994—. Mem. Maritime Orgn., 1985-86. Address: Erik Leonard Ekman 67, Arroyo Hondo Zona 5, Santo Domingo Dominican Republic

CATHCART-ROCA, MERCEDES LINA, humanities educator; b. Santiago de Cuba, Cuba, Sept. 20, 1937; d. José Cathcart-Grenot and Balbina Roca-Meléndez; m. Migdonio Causse, June 22, 1956 (div. Mar. 1970); 1 child, Mercedes Causse Cathcart. BL, U. Oriente, Santiago de Cuba, 1967; MS, Carolina U., Praga, 1977, PhD, 1978. Head Spanish dept. U. Oriente, 1967-70, dir. Sch. Letters, 1970-76, dean faculty philology, 1980-86, dean faculty arts and letters, 1986-91, head dept. faculty of letters, 1993—, cons. prof., 1995—; mem. PhD evaluating bd. Ministry of Higher Edn., Cuba, 1987-91; exec. sec. Linguistic and Lit. Conf., Cuba, 1980-90, 98-2000; mem. editing staff Rev. Santiago, Cuba, 1984-94; vis. prof. Universidad de Burdeos 3, France, 1999. Author: Historia de la Lengua Española, 1990; contbr. articles to profl. publs. Gen. sec. Syndicate for Edn., U. Oriente, 1978, mem. Syndicate for Edn., 1979. Recipient medal for campaign for literacy State Coun., Havana, 1983, Honor award for Cuban Culture, Ministry of Culture, Havana, 1993, Frank Pais award Ministry of Higher Edn., Havana, 1994. Mem. Cuban Linguist Assn., Circulo de la Lengua Española (bd. dirs. 1991-95), Cultural Ctr. of Cuban Embassy (bd. dirs. 1991-95). Avocations: reading, dancing, camping, music, travel. Home: Reparto Amplicacion Terraza, Calle 7 # 52, 90400 Santiago de Cuba Cuba Office: U Oriente Ciencias Sociales, Aveinda Patricio Lumumba SN, 90500 Santiago de Cuba Cuba

CATHEY, CATHARINE MELLON, investment company executive; b. Pitts.; d. Seward Prosser and Karen (Boyd) Mellon; m. John Murray Cathey, June 27, 1998. BA, Cornell U., 1989. With consignment svcs. Christie, Manson & Woods Plc, N.Y.C., 1989-90; assoc. Frank Russell Co., Tacoma, Wash., 1991; asst. v.p. Richard K. Mellon & Sons, Ligonier, Pa., 1990-91; asst. mgr. Brown Bros. Harriman & Co., N.Y.C., 1991-96; country coord. Schroders Investment Mgmt. Internat., London, 1996—. Active N.Y. Jr. League, N.Y.C., 1991-96.

CATHIE, KYLE ANNE BEWLEY, publishing executive; b. Guildford, Surrey, England, Oct. 10, 1948; d. Ian Asygarth Bewley and Marian Josephine (Cunning) C.; m. David Charles ap Simon, Apr. 23, 1973; children: Thomas, Nicholas, Josephine. Non-fiction editor Pan Books, London, 1973-83; editl. dir. Elm Tree Books/Hamish Hamilton, London, 1983-86, Macmillan London, 1986-89; mng. dir. Kyle Cathie Ltd, London, 1990—. Office: Kyle Cathie Ltd, 122 Arlington Rd, London NW1 7HP, England

CATHOMAS, BERNARD, arts council administrator; b. Breil/Brigels, Switzerland, June 11, 1946. PhD, U. Zurich, Switzerland, 1976. Prof. Tchr.'s Tng. Coll., Chur, Switzerland, 1973-80; sec. gen. Lia Rumantscha, Chur, Switzerland, 1980-97; dir. Pro Helvetia, Zurich, 1997—. Contbr. articles to profl. jours. Mem. parliament Swiss Canton Grisons, Chur, 1989-97. Home: Brunngasse 4, CH-8001 Zurich Switzerland Office: Pro Helvetia Arts Coun, Hirschengraben 22, CH-8024 Zurich Switzerland

CATLING, DOUGLAS GEORGE, product development company executive; b. Agra, India, Oct. 26, 1928; arrived in Australia, 1945; s. George Alfred and Olive Myrtle (Carville) C.; m. Julia Ann Rainford; 1 child, Rowland Douglas. Student, Sydney (Australia) U., 1977. Filing clk. JOYNSON-HICKS, London; chief mailing clk. Famous Artists Sch., Munich; tchr. lang. Berlitz, Dusserldorf, Germany; bd. dirs. Topa Ltd., London. Inventor of The Batsljetsl. With So. Provinces Mounted Rifles, Tuticorin, India, 1944-45. Mem. AAAS. Mem. Conservative Party. Mem. Early Ch. of England. Avocations: music, astronomy, archaeology.

CATOE, BETTE LORRINA, physician, health educator; b. Apr. 7, 1926; d. John Booker and Laura Beola (Adams) C.; m. Warren J. Strudwick, Sept. 17, 1949; children: Laura Christina, Warren J., William J. BS cum laude, Howard U., 1948, MD, 1951. Intern Freedmen's Hosp., Washington, 1951-52; pediat. resident Howard U./Freedman's Hosp., 1952-55; practice medicine specializing in pediatrics Howard U./Freedmen's Hosp., Washington, 1956—; instr. bacteriology Howard U., 1955-57; mem. staff Providence Hosp., Columbia Hosp., Howard U. Hosp., Wash., Hosp. Ctr.; sch. health officer Dept. Health, Washington, 1960-64; clin. instr. Howard U., 1956-58; mem. D.C. Health Planning Adv. Coun., 1967-77, chmn. 1973-77; chmn. D.C. Devel. Disabilities Adv. Coun., 1970-74; mem. D.C. Mayor's Commn. on Food and Nutrition, 1971-72, Mayor's Commn. on Maternal and Child Health, 1978-84, appt. vice chmn. Pub. Benefit Corp., 1997; mem. D.C. Commn. Jud. Tenure and Disabilities, 1977—, chmn. Bd. Public Benefit Corp. of D.C., 1998—; bd. govs. St. Alban's Sch., 1978-84; bd. dirs. D.C. Health and Welfare Coun., 1968-73, pres., 1973-74; del. Democratic Nat. Conv., 1976; bd. dirs. Met. Washington Health and Welfare Coun., 1970-72, Parent Coun. of Washington, 1974-75, Met. Med. Founds., Inc., Silver Spring YMCA, 1977-80, Kingsburg Ctr., 1997-99; mem. Mayor's Health Policy Coun.; chair emergency medicine com. Mem. AMA, D.C. Chirurg. Soc., D.C. Med. Soc. (bd. trustees 1996-99, nominating com. 2000—), Nat. Med. Assn. (chmn. pediat. sect. 1981-83), Am. Med. Women's Assn., NAACP, Urban League, Assn. Comprehensive Health Planners (dir. 1975-77), Women's Aux. Medico-Chirurg. Soc., Jack and Jill Am., Century

Club of Nat. Assn. negro Bus. and Profl. Women's Clubs (pres. 1985-89), Alpha Kappa Alpha, Links Club, Carrousels Club (nat. v.p. 1986-88, nat. pres. 1988-90), Women's Nat. Dem. Home: 1748 Sycamore St NW Washington DC 20012-1031 Office: 5505 5th St NW Washington DC 20011-6513

CATOIRE, VALERY, chemist, educator; b. Luce, France, June 19, 1966; s. Jean-Pierre and Claudette (Charlot) C.; m. Pascale Boutot, Aug. 28, 1993; children: Solène, Tristan. PhD, U. Bordeaux, 1994. Rschr. chemistry York U., North York, Can., 1995; prof. chemistry U. Orleans, France, 1996—. Office: Univ Orleans Sci Dept, Rue de Chartres, 45067 Orleans France

CATOVIC, ADNAN, dentist, educator; b. Zagreb, Croatia, June 9, 1953; parents Mustafa and Hatidza C.; m. Amira Alibegovic, 1989; children: Dina, Dzana, Hana. DDS, Sch. Dental Medicine Zagreb, 1977, MSc, 1981, PhD, 1986. From asst. to full prof. Sch. Dental Medicine, Zagreb, 1977—. Mem. Croatian Med. Acad. Scis., N.Y. Acad. Scis., Internat. Coll. Prosthodontists.

CATROUX, FRANCOIS PHILIPPE, interior designer; b. Mascara, Algeria, Dec. 5, 1936; arrived in France, 1955; s. Andre and Marie (Male) C.; m. Elisabeth Lage, Dec. 26, 1967; children: Maxime, Daphné. Interior designer Paris, 1967—. Office: 20 rue du Faubourg Saint-, Honoré, 75008 Paris France

CATSKY, JIRI, plant physiologist, researcher; b. Prague, Czech Republic, Feb. 27, 1932; s. Josef and Marie (Faitova) C.; m. Vlasta Volejnikova, Oct. 22, 1955; 1 child, Jana Catska-Kratukova. MS, Charles U., Prague, 1956; PhD, Czechoslovak Acad. Scis., Prague, 1961. Scientist Czech Acad. Sci., Prague, 1956-65, sr. scientist, 1965-82; sr. scientist Inst. Nat. Agrl. Rsch., Paris, 1968-70; chief scientist Czech Acad. Sci., Prague, 1982—. Editor: Methods of Studying Photosynthesis, 1965, Plant Photosynthetic Production: Manual of Methods, 1971; exec. editor Internat. Jour. Biologia Plantarum, 1970-89, editor-in-chief, 1989—; mem. editl. bd. Agronomie, 1975-97, European Jour. Agronomy, 1990-96; inventor in field; contbr. more than 120 articles to profl. jours. Recipient prize German and Czechoslovak Acads. Sci., 1987. Mem. Fedn. European Socs. of Plant Physiology. Avocations: photography, music. Home: Thurnova 13, CZ-16900 Prague 6, Czech Republic Office: Inst Exptl Botany/Acad Sci, Na Karlovce 1, CZ-16000 Prague 6, Czech Republic

CATTANEO, ANNA GIULIA, university technician; b. Busto Arsizio, Italy, May 13, 1952; d. Giovanni Luigi and Francesca Emilia (Dell'Acqua) C. MD, U. Milan, 1977, cert. diabetology specialist, 1980. Rsch. fellow Nat. Coun. Rsch., Milan, 1983-90; technician U. Milan, 1991-98, U. Insubria, Varese, Italy, 1999—. Contbr. articles to profl. jours. Mem. N.Y. Acad. Scis. Avocations: history, literature, swimming. Office: DBSF U Insubria, Via J H Dunant 3, 21100 Varese Italy

CATTANEO, JACQUELYN ANNETTE KAMMERER, artist, educator; b. Gallup, N.Mex., June 1, 1944; d. Ralph John and Gladys Agnes (O'Sullivan) Kammer; m. John Leo Cattaneo, Apr. 25, 1964; children: John Auro, Paul Anthony. Student, Tex. Woman's U., 1962-64. Portrait artist, tchr. Gallup, N.Mex., 1972; coord. Works Progress Adminstrn. art project renovation McKinley County, Gallup, Octavia Fellin Performing Arts wing dedication, Gallup Pub. Libr.; formation com. mem. Multi-Modal/Multi-Cultural Ctr. for Gallup; exch. with Soviet Women's Com. USSR Women Artists del., Moscow, Kiev, Leningrad, 1990; Women Artists del. and exch., Jerusalem, Tel Aviv, Cairo, Israel; mem. Artists Del. to Prague, Vienna and Budapest; mem. Women Artists Del. to Egypt, Israel and Italy, 1992, artist del., Brazil, 1994, Greece, Crete, Turkey, Spain, 1996. One-woman shows include Gallup Pub. Libr., 1963, 66, 77, 78, 81, 87, Gallup Lovelace Med. Clinic, Santa Fe Sta. Open House, 1981, Gallery 20, Farmington, N.Mex., 1985—, Red Mesa Art Gallery, 1989, Soviet Retrospect Carol's Art & Antiques Gallery, Liverpool, N.Y., 1992, 97, N.Mex. State Capitol Bldg., Santa Fe, 1992, Lt. Govt. Casey Luna-Office Complex, Women Artists N.Mex. Mus. Fine Arts, Carlsbad, 1992, Rio Rancho Country Club, N.Mex., 1995; exhibited in group shows including Navajo Nation Libr. Invitational, 1978, Santa Fe Festival of the Arts Invitational, 1979, N.Mex. State Fair, 1978, 79, 80, Catharine Lorrilard Wolfe, N.Y.C., 1980, 81, 84, 85, 86, 87, 88, 89, 90, 91, 92, 4th ann. exhbn. Salmagundi Club, 1984, 90, 98, 3d ann. Palm Beach Internat., New Orleans, 1984, Fine Arts Ctr., Taos, 1984, The Best and the Brightest O'Brien's Art Emporium, Scottsdale, Ariz., 1986, Gov.'s Gallery, 1989, N.Mex. State Capitol, Santa Fe, 1987, Pastel Soc. West Coast Ann. Exhbn., Sacramento Ctr. for Arts, Calif., 1986-90, gov.'s invitational Magnifico Fest. of the Arts, Albuquerque, 1991, Assn. pour la Promotion du Patrimone Artistique Française, Paris Nat. Mus. of the Arts for Women, Washington, 1991, Artists of N.Mex., Internat. Nexus '92 Fine Art Exhbn., Trammell Corw Pavillion, Dallas, Carlsbad (N.Mex.) Mus. Fine Art; represented in permanent collections Zuni Arts and Crafts Ednl. Bldg., U. N.Mex., C.J. Wiemar Collection, McKinley Manor, Gov.'s Office, State Capitol Bldg., Santa Fe, Hist. El Rancho Hotel, Gallup, Sunwest Bank, Fine Arts Ctr., Taos, Armand Hammer Pvt. Collection, Wilcox Canyon Collections, Sadona, Ariz., Galaria Impi, Netherlands, Woods Art and Antiques, Liverpool, N.Y., Stewarts Fine Art, Taos, N.Mex., Rehoboth McKinley Christian Hosp. & Sacred Heart Cathedral, Gallup, NM. Mem. Dora Cox del. to Soviet Union-U.S. Exch., 1990. Recipient Cert. of Recognition for Contbn. and Participation Assn. pour la Patrinome du Artistique Français, 1991, N.Mex. State Senate 14th Legislature Session Meml. # 101 for Artistic Achievements award, 1992, Award of Merit, Pastel Soc. West Coast Ann. Membership Exhbn., 1998, Holbein award for excellence in painting Pastel Soc. West Coast Internat. Juried Exhbn. Mem. Internat. Fine Arts Guild, Am. Portrait Soc. (cert.), Oil Painters of Am., Pastel Soc. of West Coast (cert., Hobein award, award of excellence mem.'s show 1999), Mus. N.Mex. Found., N.Mex. Archtl. Found., Mus. Women in the Arts, Fechin Inst., Artists' Co-op (co-chair), Gallup C. of C., Gallup Area Arts and Crafts Coun. (nat. and internat. artist of distinction award 1997), Am. Portrait Soc. Am., Pastel Soc. N.Mex., Catharine Lorillard Wolfe Art Club of N.Y.C. (oil and pastel juried membership), Oil Painters of Am., Pastel Soc. N.Mex., Soroptomists (Internat. Woman of Distinction 1990), Salmagundi Art Club. Address: 210 E Green St Gallup NM 87301-6130

CATTANI, DANTE THOMAS, artist, art educator, writer; b. Perth Amboy, N.J., Nov. 14, 1922; s. Louis and Catherine (Paone) C.; m. Alice Barone, Jan. 11, 1947 (div. Dec. 1951); 1 child, Dorian Mark (dec. 1980); m. Elizabeth Ann Peirce, Sept. 2, 1957. Diploma in advt. design, Phila. Coll. Art, 1945; BFA, Temple U., 1970. Ptnr. Cattani-Strome Studio, Phila., 1944-53; artist Hoedt Studios, Phila., 1953-56; freelance artist Phila., 1956—; lectr. U. Pa., Phila., 1969, Beaver Coll., 1975; prof. drawing and anatomy Phila. Coll. Art, 1945-85, head anatomy dept., 1954-85; ret., 1985—. Author: The Human Form, 1960; asst. with mural (Allen Saalberg) Bloomingdale, N.Y.C., (Jean Francksen) Parkway House, Phila., Helen Caro Store, Phila.; exhibited in shows at Dubin, Owen Joseph, Phila., Butcher and More, Phila., Civic Ctr., Phila., Allentown Mus., Phila., Ocean County Artists Guild, N.J., Oceanside Belmar, N.J., and numerous others. Mem. Center City Residents, Phila., 1975-83. Recipient best of show award, Ocean County Cultural & Hist. Soc., Toms River, N.J., 1988, Grumbacher Medal, Ocean County Art Guild, Toms River, 1991. Mem. Ocean County Art Guild. Avocations: reading, crosswords, guitar, piano. Home: 52 Williamsburg Dr Toms River NJ 08755-6306

CATTERALL, PETER, historian, educator; b. Preston, Eng., Dec. 23, 1961; s. Alfred Webster and Joan (Darbyshire) C.; m. Christine Margaret Lee, May 28, 1988; 3 children. Grad. with 1st class honors, Robinson Coll., Cambridge, 1984; PhD, Queen Mary Coll., London, 1989. Vis. lectr. modern Brit. history Queen Mary and Westfield Coll., 1992—; rsch. fellow Inst. Contemporary Brit. History, London, 1988-89, exec. dir., 1989—; cons. London Sch. Econ. for Brit. Polit. Archives; Fulbright-Robertson vis. prof. Brit. History, Westminster Coll., Fulton, Mo., 1999—. Author: British History, 1945-89: An Annotated Bibliography, 1990, History of Electrex, 1950-93; editor: (with C.J. Morris) Britain and the Threat to Stability in Europe, 1993, (with James Obelkevich) Understanding the Post-War British Society, 1994, (with Sean McDougall) The Northern Ireland Question in British Politics, 1996, The Making of Channel 4, 1999; editor Modern History Rev.; co-editor Contemporary British History, Contemporary Britain: An Annual Review National Identities; contbr. to profl. jours. Mem. London SE Valuation Tribunal. F-llow Royal Hist. Soc., Royal Soc. Arts; mem. Inst. Commonwealth Studies, Wesley Hist. Soc., Sociology of Religion Group. Methodist. Office: Inst Contemporary Brit Hist, Malet St Senate House Rm 357 Mile End Rd, London E14NS, England*

CATTHOOR, FRANCKY VICTOR MARCELLINE, electrical engineer, researcher; b. Temse, Belgium, Oct. 12, 1959; s. Rene and Maria (Maes) C. Grad. in Elec. Engring. summa cum laude, Cath. U. Leuven, Belgium, 1982, PhD in Engring. summa cum laude, 1987. Head applications and archtl. strategies group Inter-Univ. Micro-Electronics Ctr., Leuven, 1987-89, head high-throughput archtl. strategies and synthesis domain, 1990-92, head sys. exploration for memory and power domain, 1993—; assoc. prof. dept. elec. engring. Cath. U. Leuven, 1990-2000, part-time prof., 2000——; lectr. in field. Co-author: (textbook) Accelerator Data-Paths Synthesis for High-Throughput Signal Processing Applications, 1996, (textbook) Custom memory mgmt. methodology, 1998, Modelling, Verification and Exploration of Task-Level Concurrent in Real-Time Embelled Systems, 1999; editor: Unified Low Power Designflow for Data-dominated Multi-media and Telecom Applications, 2000; co-editor: Application-video Architecture Synthesis, 1993, VLSI Video/Image Signal Processing, 1993, Algorithms and Parallel VLSI Architectures III, 1995; contbr. over 30260 articles to profl. pus.; patentee in field. Recipient Young Scientist award Marconi Internat. Fellowship, 1985. Mem. IEEE (sr. mem., assoc. editor Transactions on VLSI Sys. 1995-98, assoc. editor Transactions on Multi-media, 1999—). Office: IMEC, Kapeldreef 75, B-3001 Leuven Belgium

CATTIER, JEAN JACQUES, champagne and wine company executive; b. Chigny Les Roses, Champagne, France, June 10, 1944; s. Jean Jules and Nelly Marie (Adam) C.; m. Gisele Labruyere, Dec. 27, 1975; 1 child, Alexandre. MS, U. reims, France, 1968; Nat. Diploma of Oenology, U. reims, 1969. With Institut d'Astrophysique, Paris, 1969; mgr. lab. Terres Australes et Antarctiques Francaises, Kerguelen Island, 1969-71; pres. Champagne Cattier, Chigny les Roses, 1971—. Mem. city coun. Town Coun. of Chigny les Roses, 1995. Roman Catholic. Avocations: sports, aircraft piloting, travel, cultural activities. E-mail: jeancatt@cattier.com. Home: 23 rue de Rilly, 51500 Chigny les Roses France Office: Champagne Cattier, 11 Rue Dom Perignon, 51500 Chigny les Roses France

CATTO, HENRY EDWARD, former government official, former ambassador; b. Dallas, Dec. 6, 1930; s. Henry Edward and Maurine (Halsell) C.; m. Jessica Oveta Hobby, Feb. 15, 1958; children: Heather, John, William, Elizabeth. BA, Williams Coll., 1952; JD (hon.), U. Aberdeen, 1990. Ptnr. Catto & Catto, San Antonio, 1955—; dep. rep. Orgn. Am. States, Washington, 1969-71; ambassador to El Salvador, 1971-73; U.S. chief protocol White House, Washington, 1974-76; ambassador to UN, Geneva, 1976-77; asst. sec. def. Pentagon, Washington, 1981-83; vice chmn. H & C Communications, 1983-89; amb. to U.K., 1989-91; dir. U.S. Info. Agy., Washington, 1991-93; adj. prof. U. Tex., San Antonio, 1993—; mem. Coun. on Fgn. Rels., N.Y.C., 1973; bd. dirs. Cullen-Frost Bankers; bd. dirs. Nat. Pub. Radio; vice chmn. The Aspen Inst., 1993—; chmn. Atlantic Coun. U.S., 1999—. Mem. Metro Club (Washington). Republican. Office: 110 E Crockett St San Antonio TX 78205-2612

CATULLO, DORIS JANE, sculptor; b. Phila., Aug. 17, 1929; d. Charles J. and Jane M. (Karsner) Corrigan; m. Albert Catullo, May 18, 1949 (dec. Sept. 6, 1993); 1 child, Jayne-Leslie; m. Frank Riggenbach, May 20, 1995. Student, No. Va. C.C., Mary Washington Coll., Corcoran Sch. Art, Washington, Art League Sch., Alexandria, Va., 1986-87, Biani and Cacia Art Foundry, Pietrasanta, Italy, 1988, Bruno Cacciatori Marble Studio, Pietrasanta, Italy, 1988, Scottsdale (Ariz.) Artist Sch., 1989-90, Loveland Acad. Fine Arts, Loveland, Colo., 1996. Sculptor, 1986—. Sculptor: (bronze bas relief) Aaron Burr (at site of birth) Newark, N.J., 1997, (5 foot bronze ballerina) Attitude (lobby Concert Hall) George Mason U., 1993, (bust) Gen. Lewis B. Hershey (Selective Svc. hdqts.) Washington, William Ford Bldg., William Ford NPWA, Alexandria Park, Alexandria, Va., Norman Hamilton Bldg., Washington, Md.; exhbns. include Arts Club of Washington, 1988, Art League Gallery, Alexandria, Va., 1988, 89, Allied Artists of Am. 78th ann. exhibit, Nat. Arts Club, .Y.C., 1991, Nat. Acad. Design, N.Y., 1994, Nat. Sculpture Soc. "Making Faces", Americas Tower, N.Y.C., 1996; solo show Campbell House, Southern Pines, N.C., 2000. Recipient Elaine and Albert Ominsky award for Portraiture Knickerbocker Artists N.Y., 1992, Traditional Sculpture Catherine Lorrilard Wolfe award, 1993, Elected Signature Artist award Knickerbocker Artist Internat., 1993, Award of Excellence Art League, Alexandria, Va., 1988, 89. Mem. Nat. Sculpture Soc., Knickerbocker Artist Internat., Pen and Brush N.Y. Home and Studio: 7 Piney Pt Whispering Pines NC 28327-9475

CATZ, AMIRAM, physiatrist; b. Haifa, Israel, June 24, 1952; s. Iona and Klara (Graif) C.; m. Yehudit Rosenberg, June 19, 1975; children: Noa, Eyal, Neta. MD, Hebrew U., Jerusalem, 1981; diploma in rehab. medicine, Tel Aviv U., 1986, Master's, 1990. Lic. MD, Israel. Resident in neurosurgery Tel Aviv Med. Ctr., 1982-83; resident in phys. medicine and rehab. Loewenstein Rehab. Hosp., Raanana, Israel, 1983-90, specialist in phys. medicine and rehab., 1990-93, med. dir. spinal dept., 1994—; sr. house officer in spinal injuries Stoke (Eng.) Mandeveile Hosp., 1988; instr. faculty of medicine Tel Aviv U., 1989-94, lectr., 1994—. Author (chpts. in books) Introduction to Rehabilitation Medicine, 1990, Handbook of Neurology: Aging and the Autonomic Nervous System, 1999; author, rschr. numerous monographs; contbr. articles to profl. jours. in the fields of rehabilitation, spinal injuries, and neurophysiology. Maj. Israeli Def. Force, 1978-94. Mem. Israel Med. Assn. (exam. com. phys. med. rehab. 1992—, adv. com. degree in phys. med. rehab. 1995—), Israel Assn. of Phys. Medicine and Rehab., The Internat. Med. Soc. of Paraplegia. Achievements include development of a disability scale specific for spinal injuries and an aiding device for tetraplegia. Home: Rupin 23, 44209 Kfar Sava Israel Office: Loewenstein Rehab Hosp, 273 Ahuza St, 43100 Raanana Israel

CAUDILL, DELANA RENEE, civilian military employee; b. Jan. 18, 1950. AA in Mgmt., St. Leo Coll., Eglin AFB, Fla., 1987. Svcs. bus. mgr. Army & Air Force Exch., Eglin AFB, 1986-93, Keesler AFB, Miss., 1994-98, Tuzla, Bosnia, 1996-97, Fort Carson, Colo., 1998—; mediator Army & Air Force Exch., Fort Carson, 2000. Vol. ARC. Home: PO Box 12845 Fort Carson CO 80913-2845 Office: AAFES Colo Springs Exchs Bldg 2140 KHE SANH St Ft Carson CO 80913

CAUDILL, STEVEN BRENT, economics educator; b. Portsmouth, Ohio, Oct. 4, 1954; s. Donal Caudill and Nona Justine Hess; m. Janice Elaine Jackson, May 18, 1996. BA, Ohio Wesleyan U., 1976; MA, U. Fla., 1978, PhD, 1982. Asst. prof. econs. Auburn (Ala.) U., 1982-89, assoc. prof. econs., 1989-94, prof. econs., 1994—. Contbr. articles to profl. jours. Named Outstanding Rschr., Coll. Bus., Auburn U., 1991, Tchr. of Yr. Assn. Grad. Bus. Students, 1999. Mem. Am. Econ. Assn., So. Econ. Assn. Avocation: basketball. Home: 2349 Rockdell Ln Auburn AL 36830-7241 Office: Dept Econs Auburn U Auburn University AL 36849

CAUDRON, GÉRARD, foreign diplomat; b. Royaucourt et Chailvet, France, Feb. 27, 1945. Mem. European Parliament, 1999—, mem. com. on industry, external trade, rsch. and energy, substitute com. fgn. affairs/human rights/common security; mem. Group of the Party of European Socialists; mem. bur. of the European Parliament; mem. delegation to the EU-Poland Joint Parliamentary Com.; substitute delegation to the EU-Cyprus Joint Parliamentary Com. Socialist Party. Office: Maison du Citoyen d'Europe, 1 chaussee de l'Hotel Ville, F-59650 Villeneuve d'Ascq France*

CAUGHFIELD, LANCE ERIC, lawyer; b. Abilene, Tex., Jan. 14, 1970; s. Dwight A. and Alice M. Caughfield; m. Adrienne Helenne Rigsby, May 22, 1993. BA i n Comm., Abilene Christian U., 1993, BA in Polit. Sci., 1993; JD, U. Tex., 1996. Bar: Tex. 1996. Intern Supreme Ct. Tex., Austin, 1995; assoc. Fletcher & Springer, LLP, Dallas, 1996—, sect. head Yr. 2000 sect., 1999—. Articles editor Tex. Intellectual Property Law Jour., 1996. Mem. Abilene Christian U. Alumni Assn. (dir. 1993-2000, bd. dirs.). Republican. Mem. Church of Christ. Avocations: woodworking, militaria, scuba diving. E-mail: entropy1@airmail.net and lance@fletchspring.com. Fax: 214-987-9866. Office: Fletcher & Springer LLP 9400 N Central Expy Ste 1400 Dallas TX 75231-5043

CAULLERY, ISABELLE, foreign diplomat; b. Bordeaux, France, Aug. 17, 1955. Mem. European Parliament, 1999—, mem. com. on budgetary control, substitute com. on econ. and monetary affairs; treas. Union for Europe of the Nations Group; mem. delegations to the parliamentary coop. coms. and delegations for relations with Ukraine, Belarus and Moldova. *

CAUQUIL, CHANTAL, foreign diplomat; b. Montauban, France, July 3, 1949. Mem. European Parliament, 1999—, mem. com. on budgets; substitute com. on employment and social affairs; mem. Confederal Group of the European United Left/Nordic Green Left; mem. delegation for relations with Switzerland, Iceland and Norway. Office: Lutte Ouvrière, BP233, F-75865 Paris Cedex 18, France*

CAUSEY, G(EORGE) DONALD, medical educator; b. Balt., July 9, 1926; s. George Hopkins and Jessie Hitchens (Webster) C.; m. Alice Sherman Meredith, Mar., 1951 (div.); 1 child, Susan Victoria; m. Linda Marie McGranahan, Jan. 15, 1961; children: Christopher, Aimee, Julia. BA, U. Md., 1950, MA, 1951; PhD, Purdue U., 1954. Asst. clinic chief Dept. Pub. Health, Washington, 1954-55; audiology clinic chief VA Med. Ctr., Washington, 1955-68, dir. auditory rsch. lab., 1968-82; rsch. prof. U. Md., College Park, 1956-80; vis. prof. audiology Syracuse U., N.Y., summer 1968; affiliate prof. engring. Colo. State U., Fort Collins, 1975-78; clin. assoc. prof. surgery Georgetown U. Med. Ctr., Washington, 1976-82; rsch. prof. Cath. U. Am., Washington, 1980-91; pres. Causey Assocs., Chevy Chase, 1987-92. Author 65 jour. publs., 6 book chpts; co-inventor: 5 U.S. patents, 1977-80, 1 Brit. patent, 1980. Elder, auditor Presbyn. Ch. With USN, 1944-46, PTO. Recipient rsch. grants NIH, 1961-63, VA, 1967-79, Pub. Health Svc., 1971-72, EPA, 1979. Fellow Md. Speech and Hearing Assn. (pres. 1973-74), Am. Speech, Lang., Hearing Assn.; mem. IEEE (sr.), Acoustical Soc. Am., Am. Nat. Stds. Inst. (S-3-48 com.), Sigma Xi (hon.). Home: 3504 Dunlop St Chevy Chase MD 20815-5932

CAUSSE, JEAN-BERNARD R.M., otologist, surgeon; b. Beziers, Hérault, France, May 13, 1944; s. Jean René and Simone (Coulombie) C.; m. Isabelle Meslin, July 19, 1968; children: Jerome, Annabelle. MD, U. Strasbourg, France, 1975. Intern Strasbourg, 1972-75; mem. staff Caune Clinic, 1975-99, U. Hosp. Montpellier, 1999—; corr. mem. Nat. Coun. of Noise, French Ministry of Environmen; instr. Am. Acad. Author: (monograph) On Otosclerosis, 1991; Contbr. more than 130 articles to sci. mags. Recipient Rsch. and Tng. award Am. Acad., Pioneer award Consul Gen. Hérault, award French Legion of Honor, 1999. Mem. Am. Otol. Soc. (corr.), Am. Acad. (corr.), Soc. Hôpitaux Paris. Avocation: photography. Home and Office: 53 Allées Paul Riquet BP 4226, 34543 Beziers France

CAUTHEN, CHARLES EDWARD, JR., retail executive, business consultant; b. Columbia, S.C., Oct. 26, 1931; s. Charles Edward and Rachel (Macaulay) C.; m. Hazel Electa Peery, June 13, 1959; children: Portia Cauthen White, Rachel Cauthen Rohrer, Sara Cauthen Landfear, Sidney Cauthen Bullard. BA, Wofford Coll., 1952; cert. Charlotte Meml. Hosp., Sch. Hosp. Adminstrn., 1956; MS in Bus. Adminstrn. and Labor Mgmt., Kennedy-Western U., 1986, PhD in Bus. Adminstrn., 1986; LLD, Montreat-Anderson Coll., 1991. Asst. adminstr. Union Meml. Hosp., Monroe, N.C., 1956-58; adminstr. Lowrance Hosp., Inc., Mooresville, N.C., 1958-61; v.p., mgr. Va. Acme Market, Bluefield, W.Va., 1961-68; v.p. Acme Markets and A-Mart Stores (now Acme Markets of Tazewell, Va., Inc.), North Tazewell, Va., 1965-87; adminstr. Lowrance Hosp., Inc., Mooresville, N.C., 1958-61; v.p., mgr. Va. Acme Market, Bluefield, W.Va., 1961-68; v.p. Acme Markets and A-Mart Stores (now Acme Markets of tazewell, Va., Inc.), North Tazewell, Va., 1965-87, exec. v.p., 1968-71, pres., 1971-87; provost King Coll., Bristol, Tenn., 1987-89, pres., 1989-92; pres. Doran Devel. Corp., 1971-87, Big A Market, Inc., 1981-87; cons. in field. Author: Evaluation of the Small Company for Strategic Planning, Merger or Acquisition, 1987. Deacon, elder, trustee Westminster Presbyn. Ch., Bluefield, W.Va.; mem. Internat. Adv. Coun. Han Nam U., Korea, 1991; mem. exec. bd. Sequoyah Coun. Boy Scouts Am.; bd. dirs. Internat. Inst. Christian Studies, 1993-97, Tenn. Inst. for Pub. Policy, 1994—. Served to 1st lt. AUS, 1952-54. Mem. W.Va. Assn. Retail Grocers (v.p., dir. 1968-82), Va. Food Dealers Assn. (dir. 1978), Bluefield Sales Exec. Club (dir. 1965-67), Rotary (bd. dirs. 1966). Republican. Home and Office: PO Box 725 Bristol TN 37621-0725

CAVACO SILVA, ANIBAL, former Portuguese government official, economist, educator; b. Loule, Portugal, July 15, 1939; s. Teodoro Silva and Maria do Nascimento Cavaco; m. Maria Alves, 1963; children: Patricia, Bruno. Grad. in fin., Superior Inst. Econs. and Fin. Scis., Lisbon, Portugal, 1964; PhD, York U., U.K., 1973, D honoris causa, 1993; D honoris causa, U. Coruña, Spain, 1996. Tchr. pub. econs. and polit. economy Inst. Econ. and Fin. Studies, 1965-67, Cath. U., 1975—, New U. of Lisbon, 1977—; rsch. fellow Calouste Gulbenkian Found., 1967-77; dir. rsch. and statis. dept. Bank of Portugal, 1977-79, 81-85; min. fin. and planning, 1980-81; pres. Coun. for Nat. Planning, 1981-84; prime min. of Portugal, 1985-95; econ. adviser Ctrl. Bank; dir. Economia. Author: Budgetary Policy and Economic Stabilization, 1976, Economic Effects of Public Debt, 1977, Public Finance and Macroeconomic Policy, 1982, The Economic Policy of Sa Carneiro's Government, 1982, A Decade of Reforms, 1995, Main Speeches as Prime Minister, 5 vols., 1987, 89, 91, 93, 95; contbr. articles on fin. mkts., pub. economies and Portuguese econ. policy to profl. jours. Recipient Joseph Bech prize 1991, Academico Honorario of Real Academia de Ciencias Morales y Politicas, Spain, 1994, Freedom prize Max Schmidheiny Found., Switzerland, 1995. Social Democrat. Office: U Nova Econs Facilty, Tv Estevao Pinto, P1099032 Lisbon Portugal

CAVAILLON, JEAN-MARC, immunology researcher, educator; b. Paris, May 28, 1952; s. Jean-Pierre and Liliane (Zisman) C.; m. Nicole Haeffner, Nov. 27, 1976; children: Alexis, Sebastien, Yann. PhD, U. Paris VII, 1977; DSc, U. Paris VI, 1980. Rsch. fellow Med. Rsch. Coun., Toronto, Can., 1977-79; rsch. fellow Inst. Pasteur, Paris, 1979-80, asst., 1981-83, chief of rsch., 1984-90, chief of lab., 1991—; assoc. dir. gen. immunology course, Inst. Pasteur, 1994-97, dir., 1997—; mem. editl. bd. Jour. Endotoxin Rsch., 1994—, Jour. Shock, 1999—, Jour. Sepsis, 1999—. Author: Cytokines, 1993, 96. Recipient Allergy 2000 prize, Schering-Plough, Paris, 1990. Mem. Internat. Endotoxin Soc. (pres.-elect 1996-98, pres. 1998-2000). Avocations: fencing, skiing, stamps, travel. Office: Inst Pasteur, 28 rue Dr Roux, F-75015 Paris France

CAVALCANTI, SOLANGE BESSA, physicist, educator; b. Nitersi, Brazil, Aug. 12, 1952; d. Theophilo Araujo and Selda Bessa Cavalcanti; m. Raimundo Rocha Dos Santos, July 23, 1975 (div. July 1982); 1 child, Mariana; m. Walmar Amazonas Buarque, Dec. 7, 1992; children: Pedro, Olivia. BSc, Pontifmcia U. Catslica, Rio de Janeiro, 1975; PhD, U. London, 1984. Adj. prof. U. Fed. de Alagoas, Maceis, Brazil, 1984—; cons. Conselho de Cijncia e Tecnologia do Estado de Alagoas, Fundag'o de Apoio Pesquisa do Estado de Alagoas, Maceis. Avocations: playing piano, body boarding. E-mail: solange@lux.ufal.br. Fax: 082-214-1645. Home: Rua Bom Destino 82, 57045260 Maceis Alagoas, Brazil Office: Univ Fed de Alagoas, Cidade Univ CCEN/FISICA, 57045260 Maceis Alagoas, Brazil

CAVALERI, PIERO, librarian; b. Milan, Jan. 28, 1957; s. Elia Cavaleri and Giuliana Romerio; m. Mariangela Vago, Oct. 4, 1992. Grad. pub. sch., Monza, Italy. Libr. Comune di Renate, Italy, 1982-86, U. Bocconi, Milan, 1986-91, U. Cattaneo, Castellanza, 1991—. Mem. Assn. Italian Biblioteche. Home: Via Della Torre 8, 20045 Besana Brianza Milan, Italy Office: U Cattaneo, Corso Matteotti 22, 21053 Castellanza VA, Italy

CAVALIERE, FRANK JOSEPH, lawyer, educator; b. N.Y.C., Dec. 29, 1949; s. Alfred and Margaret Joan Cavaliere. BA in Econs., Bklyn. Coll., 1970; BBA in Acctg., Lamar U., 1976; JD, U. Tex., 1979. Bar: Tex. 1979. Atty. Coke & Coke, Dallas, 1979-81, Weller, Wheelus & Green, Beaumont, Tex., 1981-84; pvt. practice law Beaumont, 1985 ; from asst. to full prof. bus. law Lamar U., Beaumont, 1985—; mem. editl. adv. bd. CPA Internet Connection, Harcourt Brace Co., 1997-99; tech. advisor Am. Law Inst.-ABA, 1998—; continuing legal edn. spkr. Am. Law Inst.-ABA. Author (column) Web-Wise Lawyer, The Practical Lawyer, 1996 ; contbr. articles to profl. jours. Advisor Pi Kappa Alpha Fraternity, Beaumont, 1987-90, Delta Sigma Pi Fraternity, Beaumont, 1994-97. Lt. USNR, 1970-75. Mem. ABA, Tex. Bar Assn., Coll. of the State Bar Tex., Jefferson County Bar Assn., Phi Beta Kappa. Office: 148 S Dowlen Rd PMB 683 Beaumont TX 77707-1755

CAVALLARO, JOSEPH JOHN, microbiologist; b. Lawrence, Mass., Mar. 18, 1932; s. John and Salvatrice (Zappala) C.; m. Kathleen Frances Kraus, Dec. 2, 1972; children: Theresa Margaret, Sandra Marie, Elizabeth Camille, Danielle Kay, Gina Kathleen. BS, Tufts U., 1952; MS, U. Mass., 1954; PhD, U. Mich., 1966. Pub. health sanitarian Hartford (Conn.) Health Dept., 1954-55, 57-61; teaching assoc. dept. microbiology U. Mass., Amherst, 1961-62; rsch. virologist Med. Rsch. Labs., Charles Pfizer & Co., Groton, Conn., 1966-67; rsch. assoc. dept. epidemiology Sch. Pub. Health, U. Mich., Ann Arbor, 1967-70; microbiologist, diagnostic immunology tng. br. Ctrs. for Disease Control, Atlanta, 1971-86, research microbiologist anaerobic bacteria br., Ctrs. for Disease Control, 1986—; lectr. resident pathologists Grady Meml. Hosp., Atlanta, 1975; asst. prof. pathology Morehouse Sch. Medicine, 1982-85, clin. assoc. prof., 1986-97; adj. asst. prof. pathology and lab. medicine Emory U. Sch. of Medicine, 1985—; cons. Pan Am. Health Orgn., Colombia and Brazil, 1976, 77. Served with M.C., AUS, 1955-57. Registered specialist microbiologist Nat. Registry Microbiologist, Am. Acad. Microbiology. Fellow Am. Acad. Microbiology; mem. Am. Soc. Microbiology, Am. Assn. Immunologists, N.Y. Acad. Sci., KC, Sigma Xi. Democrat. Roman Catholic. Prin. author/co-author over 11 lab. manuals; contbr. articles to profl. jours., chpts. to books. Home: 1325 Balsam Dr Decatur GA 30033-2905 Office: 1600 Clifton Rd Atlanta GA 30333

CAVALLI, PIETRO, geneticist, consultant, researcher; b. Lecco, Lombardy, Italy, Apr. 18, 1951; s. Erminio Cavalli and Maddalena Sassi; m. Maria Rosa Gosi, May 2, 1988; 1 child, Giulio. Degree in Medicine and Surgery, Graduate U. Parma, Italy, 1976, degree in Hematology, 1979, degree in Preventive Medicine, Hygiene, 1983; degree in Cytogenetics, Graduate U. Pavia, Italy, 1986. Medical Doctor. Fellow in medical pathology U. Parma, Italy, 1976-77; asst. Cremona (Italy) Gen. Hosp., 1980-90, chief asst. immunohematology, 1990-95, chief dept. genetics, 1995—; cons. NIH, 1979-81; prof. Brescia U., 1995-99. Contbr. articles to profl. jours. Capt. Army Med. Svcs., 1989-90. Grantee Luppi-Quaranta, 1998, Lega Italiana Lotta contro i Tumori (LILT), 1999, A.O.C., 1999. Mem. AAAS, Italian Soc. Human Genetics, Italian Immunohematology Soc., European Soc. Human Genetics. Avocations: free climbing, running, cycling. Office: Dept Genetics, Cremona General Hospital, 26100 Cremona Italy

CAVALLO, DOMINGO, Argentinian politician; b. Cordoba, Argentina, July 21, 1946. PhD in Econs., Harvard U.; hon. diploma, U. Nat. de Córdoba, 1968. Former v.p. pub. bank Córdoba; pres. cen. bank Argentina, 1982; rep. to Nat. Congress Parliament Córdoba Province-PJ, 1987-89; min. of fgn. rels. Buenos Aires, Argentina, 1989-91, min. economy, pub. works & svcs., 1992-96; rep. from Córdoba Province to Nat. Congress Parliament, 1987-89; founder Mediterranean Found. Author: Volver a Crecer, 1986, El Desfio Federal, 1986, Economia en Tiempos de Crisis, 1989, La Argentina que pudo ser, 1989; mem. rsch. observa editl. bd. World Bank, 1987—; contbr. articles to newspapers. Recipient Gold medal and honor diploma Nat. U. Cordoba, 1968. Office: c/o Group of Thirty 1990 M St NW Ste 450 Washington DC 20036-3466*

CAVALLO, FRANCESCA ROMANA, physicist; b. Ascoli Piceno, Italy, Mar. 20, 1958; d. Silvio and Alberta (Bonelli) C.; m. Alberto Monti, May 13, 1978; 1 child, Matteo. Laurea in fisica, U. Bologna, 1984, PhD, 1989. Assoc. Istituto Nazionale di Fisica Nucleare, Italy, 1984-89; rschr. Istituto Nazionale di Fisica Nucleare, Italy, 1990—; physics tchr. Italian Govt., 1987-89; prof. Bologna U., Italy, 1994—. Mem. Delphi Collaboration, CMS Collaboration. Avocations: traveling, children, literature. Office: INFN, Viale Berti Pichat 6/2, 140127 Bologna Italy

CAVANAGH, JOHN BARR, neuropathologist; b. Sheerness, Kent, Eng., May 5, 1921; s. John Duncan Macaulay Cavanagh and Laura Elena Louise Gladys Barr; m. Sheila Ross Fisher, Mar. 31, 1951 (div. 1964); children: Charlotte Patricia, Eleanor Louise Hamilton, John Francis; m. Marion Elisabeth Dennison, Dec. 6, 1965; children: Elisabeth Clare, Amy Madeleine. MBBS, London Hosp. Med. Sch., 1945; MD, London U., 1966. FRCPath., FRCP(London). Lectr. in pathology London Hosp. Med. Coll., 1948-50; rsch. fellow in neuropathology Guy's Hosp. Med. Sch., 1951-62, reader in neuropathology, 1962-64; dir. rsch. group in applied neurobiology Inst. Neurology, London, 1964-75, prof. applied neurobiology, 1970-86, prof. emeritus, 1986—; vis. fellow St. Edmunds Coll., Cambridge, Eng., 1986-87; hon. rsch. fellow Inst. Psychiat., 1994—; cons. MRC toxicology unit U. Leicester, 1992—. Editor: Neuropathology and Applied Neurobiology jour., 1975-90, (ann. reviews) Recent Advances in Neuropathology, Vols. 1, 2, and 3, 1979-86; contbr. articles to profl. jours. Capt. RAMC, 1946-48. Avocation: ceramics. Home: 51 Chestnut Rd, West Norwood, London SE27 9EZ, England Office: Dept Neurology, Inst Psy/De Crespigny Park, London SE5 8AF, England

CAVANAGH, RICHARD EDWARD, business policy organization executive; b. Buffalo, June 15, 1946; s. Joseph John and Mary Celeste (Stack) C.; m. Patricia Sypher, 1995; 1 child. BA, Wesleyan U., Middletown, Conn., 1968; MBA, Harvard U., 1970. Assoc. McKinsey & Co. Inc., Washington, 1970-77, ptnr., 1980-88; exec. dir. fed. cash mgmt. U.S. Office Mgmt. and Budget, Washington, 1977-79; exec. dean Kennedy Sch. Govt. Harvard U., Cambridge, Mass., 1988-95; pres., CEO The Conference Board, Inc., N.Y.C., 1995—; cons. Carter-Mondale Presdl. Transition, 1976-77; domestic coord. Pres.' Reorgn. Project, The White House, Washington, 1978-79; mem. exec. com. Pres.' Pvt. Sector Survey on Cost Control, Grace Commn., 1982-83. Co-author: (with Donald K. Clifford Jr.) The Winning Performance: How America's High-Growth Midsize Companies Succeed, 1985, 2d edit., 1988 (pub. in 11 fgn. langs.). Mem. bd. judges Dively Award, Harvard U., 1984-94; trustee Ctr. for Excellence in Govt., 1985, 96—, Drucker Found., 1998—, Ednl. Testing Svc., 1997; trustee Wesleyan U., 1988-2000, vice chair, 1997-2000; trustee, dir. Black Rock Mut. Funds, 1994—; dir. Fremont Group, 1997—, The Guardian Ins., 1998—, Arch Chems., Inc., 1996—, Airplanes Group and Aircraft Fin. Trust, 1999—. With U.S. Army, 1968. Recipient Presdl. commendation, 1979, 80, 83; John Reilly Knox fellow, 1969, Clark fellow, 1969. Mem. Am. Soc. Pub. Adminstrn., Acad. Polit. Sci., Coun. on Fgn. Rels., Raimond Duy Baird Assn., Wesleyan U. Alumni Assn. (chmn. 1985-87), Met Club (D.C.), Harvard Club (N.Y.C.), Beta Theta Pi. Democrat. Roman Catholic. Home: 921 Palmer Rd Bronxville NY 10708-3304 Office: The Conference Board Inc 845 3rd Ave Fl 2 New York NY 10022-6600

CAVARNOS, CONSTANTINE PETER, writer, philosopher; b. Boston, Oct. 19, 1918; s. Peter (Panagiotes) John and Irene (Maistrou) C. AB magna cum laude, Harvard U., 1942, AM, 1947, PhD, 1948. Tchg. asst. in philosophy Harvard U., Radcliffe Coll., 1945-46; teaching fellow in philosophy Harvard U., Cambridge, Mass., 1946-47; teaching asst. in philosophy Tufts U., Wellesley (Mass.) Coll., 1948-49; asst. prof. philosophy U. N.C., Chapel Hill, 1949-54; assoc. prof., prof. philosophy and Byzantine art Greek Orthodox Sch. Theology, Brookline, Mass., 1954-56; vis. assoc. prof. philosophy Wheaton Coll., Norton, Mass., 1965-67, Clark U., Worcester, Mass., 1967-68; pres. Inst. for Byzantine and Modern Greek Studies, Belmont, Mass., 1969—; adj. prof. philosophy and Byzantine art Hellenic Coll., Brookline, 1978-82. Author: A Dialogue between Bergson, Aristotle and Philologos, 1949, Byzantine Sacred Art, 1957, Anchored in God, 1959, Man and the Universe in American Philosophy, 1959, Symbols and Proofs of Immortality, 1964, Modern Greek Philosophers on the Human Soul, 1967, Byzantine Thought and Art, 1968, Modern Greek Thought, 1969, The Holy Mountain, 1973, Plato's Theory of Fine Art, 1973, 2d edit., 1998, The Classical Theory of Relations, 1975, Plato's View of Man, 1975, Orthodox Iconography, 1977, Japanese edit., 1999, A Dialogue on G.E. Moore's Ethical Philosophy, 1979, Paths and Means to Holiness, 1980, Modern Orthodox Saints, Vols. I-XIII, 1971-99, St. Nectarios of Aegina, 1981, 2d edit., 1988, 95, The Future Life According to Orthodox Teaching, 1984, The Educational Theory of Benjamin Lesvos, 1984, Meetings with Kontoglou, 1985, Bysanttilainen Taide, 1987, The Goodness of God and the Self-Willed Wickedness of Man, 1987, St. Methodia of Kimolos, 1987, Smoking and the Orthodox Christian, 1988, Fasting and Science, 1988, The Hellenic-Christian Philosophical Tradition, 1989, New Library, Vol. 1, 1989, Vol. 2, 1992, Vol. 3, 1995, Immortality of the Soul, 1993, Guide to Byzantine Iconography, Vol. I, 1993, Vol. II, 2000, Pythagoras on the Fine Arts as Therapy, 1994, Biological Evolutionism, 1994, 2nd ed. 1997, Orthodox Christian Terminology, 1994, Cultural and Educational Continuity of Greece, 1995, To Haigion Oros (Greek version of The Holy Mountain-1973), 2000; editor: Greek Language and Culture: Their Vitality and Importance Today, 1995, Byzantine Churches of Thessaloniki, 1995, He Hiera Byzantine Techne, 1995, Spiritual Beauty, 1996, The Concept of Christian Love, 1996, The Seven Sages of Ancient Greece, 1996, Ecumenism Examined, 1996, Victories of Orthodoxy, 1997, St. Nectarios' Study on Holy Icons, 1997, Byzantine Chant, 1998, Fine Arts as Therapy, 1998, St. Photios The Great: Philosopher and Theologian, 1998, Dostoievsky's Philosophy of Man, 1998, Koncepti i Dashurise Kristiane, 1998, The Hellenic Heritage, 1999, St. Gregory of Nyssa on the Human Soul, 2000. Sheldon Travel fellow in philosophy, Harvard/Athens-Paris-Cambridge (Eng.)-Oxford, 1947-48, Fulbright Rsch. scholar U. Athens, 1957-59; recipient Archon of the Oecumenical Patriarchate, Constantinople, 1979, Ann. Faculty award Hellenic Coll., 1986, The Florovsky Theol. prize Ctr. for Traditionalist Orthodox Studies, 1992. Mem. Am. Philos. Assn., The Metaphysical Soc. of Am. (past treas. 1949), Internat. Inst. Arts & Letters, Revista de la Soc. Argentina of Philosophy, Plomaritan Soc. of Boston (past pres.), Ctr. de Estudios Bizantinos y Neohelénicos Fotios Malleros U. Chile (hon.). Greek Orthodox. Avocations: music, restoration of icons, walking. Office: Inst Byzantine & Greek Studies 115 Gilbert Rd Belmont MA 02478-2200

CAVATHAS, CONSTANTINE, journalist, publisher; b. Athens, Greece, Mar. 2, 1939; s. Dimitrios and Erasmia Cavathas; m. Sofia Cavatha. Cert. in civil engring., Regent St. Polytech., 1959; student, No. Polytech., 1960-61. Sci. editor Mesimvrini Newspaper, Athens, 1964-67; chief editor Auto Express mag., Athens, 1967-69; editor, pub. 4 Wheels Mag., Athens, 1970—, Sound & Hi-Fi Mag., Athens, 1974—, Ptisi (Flight) Mag., Athens, 1979—, 2 Wheels Mag., Athens, 1987-90; fgn. news editor sci. and tech. Kathimerini, Eleftherotypia, Athens, 1974-82; automotive editor Vima, Athens, 1987-98; publ. cons. daily newspaper Kathimerini, Athens, 1998—; editor, pub. Taste mag., Athens, 1996—, 2nd Hand mag., Athens, 1997—, Computer Arts mag., Athens, 1998—, Taste Kitchen mag., Athens, 1998, Gardening Anthology mag., Athens, 1999, Cyber Week newspaper, Athens, 2000, Odigontas mag., 2000; owner Techlink Internet Svc. Provider, Athens, 1993—; mem. Car of the Yr. Jury, Amsterdam, Holland, 1984—; owner Radio Sta. 94.4 FM En Lefko BBC World Svc., Athens, 1998. Author: Driving, 1982. 1st lt. Grecian Army, 1962-64. Mem. Guild Motoring Writers, Athens Union Journalists, Athens Gliding Club. Avocations: flying, gliding, car racing. Office: Tech Press SA, 2-4 Hellioupoleos St, GR 17237 Athens Greece

CAVAZZA, WILLIAM, geologist, educator; b. Bologna, Italy, June 11, 1957; s. Walter Cavazza and Graziella Madaschi. BS, U. Bologna, 1983; MS, U. Calif., L.A., 1985, PhD, 1989. Rschr. U. Bologna, 1987-98; assoc. prof. U. Basilicata, Potenza, Italy, 1998—; nat. corr. Internat. Assn. Sedimentologists, 1991-94; dir. UNESCO-Internat. Geol. Correlation Program Project 369, 1994-99; bd. dirs. Interdepartmental Ctr. for Marine Scis., U. Bologna. Mem. Italian Fedn. Earth Scis. (mem. exec. com. 1997). Office: U Basilicata Dept Geol Scis, Contrada Macchia Romana, 85100 Potenza Italy

CAVE, TERENCE CHRISTOPHER, literature educator; b. Bournemouth, U.K., Dec. 1, 1938; s. Alfred Cyril and Sylvia Norah (Norman) C.; m. Helen Elizabeth Robb, July 31, 1965 (div. 1990); children: Christopher James, Hilary Ann. BA, Cambridge (Eng.) U., 1960, PhD, 1966. Asst. U. St. Andrews, Scotland, 1962-63, lectr., 1963-65; lectr. U. Warwick, Coventry, Eng., 1965-70, sr. lectr., 1970-72; fellow, tutor St. John's Coll., Oxford, Eng., 1972—; prof. French lit. U. Oxford, 1989—; vis. prof., Oxford, U.S., Can., Norway, France. Author: Devotional Poetry in France, 1969, The Cornucopian Text, 1979, Recognitions: A Study in Poetics, 1988, Pré-Histoires: Textes Troublés Au Seuil De La Modernité, 1999; contbr. articles to profl. publs., chpts. to books; translations from French. Hon. fellow Gonville and Caius Coll., Cambridge. Fellow Brit. Acad., Inst. Romance Studies (hon. sr. rsch. fellow); mem. Academia Europaea, Royal Norwegian Soc. Scis. and Letters. Avocations: music, languages, travel. Office: St John's Coll, Oxford OX1 3JP, England

CAVENDISH, JONATHAN STEWART, film producer; b. Nairobi, Kenya, Apr. 2, 1959; arrived in Eng., 1959; s. Robin Francis and Diana Mary (Blacker) C.; m. Lesles Ann Rogers; children: Teddy, Polly, Willow. Degree in history, Oxford (Eng.) U., 1980. Account mgr. Boade Massing Ct., London, 1981-83; film prodr. Little Bird, London, 1983—. Prodr. December Bride, 1989 (European Film award 1990), Into the West, 1991 (Best Film Netherlands Film Festival 1992), Nothing Personal, 1995 (Best Actor Lenide Film Festival 1995), Ordinary Decent Criminal, 1999, among others. Office: Little Bird, 7 Lower James St, London W1, England

CAVENDISH, RUPERT EDWARD GREVILLE, antique dealer, furniture designer; b. Bath, Eng., Sept. 4, 1955; s. Greville Adrian and Hazel Colleen (May) C. BA in Politics, Newcastle-Upon-Tyne (Eng.) U., 1977. Owner Rupert Cavendish Antiques, London, 1981—; dir. A.J. Brett & Co., London, 1996—. Liberal Democrat. Avocations: history, travel, swimming, riding. Office: Rupert Cavendish Antiques, 610 King's Rd, London SW6 2DX, England

CAVENEY, ROBERT JOHN, quality assurance professional; b. Chester, Cheshire, Eng., Feb. 19, 1941; s. Alan Joseph and Catherine Mary (Reynolds) C.; m. Carol Blanche Lorn Miller, July 3, 1965; children: Deborah Ann, Michael John, Sean Mark. BSc, U. Witwatersrand, Johannesburg, South Africa, 1961, BSc with honors, 1962, MSc, 1964, PhD, 1970. Rsch. asst. U. Witwatersrand, Johannesburg, 1964-66; rschr. Adamant Rsch. Lab., Johannesburg, 1967-74; patent mgr. DeBeers Indsl. Diamonds divsn., Johannesburg, 1974-78; group quality mgr. DeBeers Indsl. Diamonds divsn., Johannesburg & Shannon, Ireland, 1994—; rsch. mgr. DeBeers Diamond Rsch. Lab., Johannesburg, 1978-83, dep. dir. rsch., 1983-89, dir. rsch., 1989-93; mem. South African liaison com. Internat. Union Pure and Applied Physics, 1988-96; mem. exec. com. Specialist Group of South African Inst. Physics, Solid State Physics/Materials Sci., 1992—; mem. rsch. com. U. Witwatersrand, Johannesburg, 1994—. Contbr. articles to profl. jours., chpt. to book; patentee in field. Chmn. PTA Sandringham H.S., Johannesburg, 1980-93, sec. governing body, 1980-93; chmn. governing body and PTA, Sandringham Primary Sch., Johannesburg, 1970's and 80's; chmn. Jabula Nursery Sch., 1970's and 80's. Mem. South African Inst. Physics, Country Club Johannesburg. Methodist. Avocations: running, reading, walking in mountains, watching sports (rugby, cricket). Home: PO Box 3106, Cramerview 2060, South Africa Office: De Beers Indsl Diamond Div, PO Box 1770, Southdale 2135, South Africa

CAVENY, LEONARD HUGH, mechanical engineer, aerospace scientist, consultant; b. Atlanta, Oct. 30, 1934; s. Elmer Leonard and Dorothy (Franklin) C.; m. Joyce Rodal, Apr. 10, 1957; children: Polly J., Rebecca R., Teresa L., Leslie Y., Susan C. BME, Ga. Inst. Tech., 1956, MSME, 1960; PhD in Mech. Engring., U. Ala., 1969. Registered profl. engr. Ala., 1965. Supr. aerothermodynamics Thiokol Chem. Corp., Huntsville, Ala., 1960-67; sr. tech. staff Princeton (N.J.) U., 1969-80; program mgr. Air Force Office Sci. Rsch., Washington, 1980-85; dep. dir. sci. and tech. Strategic Defense Initiative Orgn., Washington, 1985-93; dir. sci. & tech. Ballistic Missile Defense Orgn., Washington, 1993-97; cons. in field. Editor: Orbit-Raising and Maneuvering Propulsion, 1984; inventor in field. Lt. (j.g.) USN, 1956-59. Recipient Yuri Gagarin medal, Moscow, 1993. Fellow AIAA (chair elec. propulsion tech. com. 1984-86, chair Princeton sect. 1974-75, tech. chair internat. elec. propulsion conf. 1985, editorial adv. bd. 1988—, Wyld Propulsion medal 1997); mem. The Combustion Inst. Avocations: photography, construction, tennis. Home: 13715 Piscataway Dr Fort Washington MD 20744-6635

CAVIGLI, HENRY JAMES, petroleum engineer; b. Colfax, Calif., Mar. 14, 1914; s. Giovanni and Angelina (Giachi) C.; m. Ruth Loree Denton, June 11, 1942; children: Henry James Jr., Robert D., Paul R., Loree Ann McIntire. BS in Petroleum Engring., U. Calif., Berkeley, 1937, MS in Mech. Engring., 1947. Sr. engr. Chevron Corp., Rio Vista, Calif., 1954-57, supt. No. Calif., 1958-69; mgr. non operated joint ventures Chevron Corp., LaHabra, Calif., 1970-76; cons. Cavigli & Mee, petroleum cons., Sacramento, Calif., 1976—. Author: Escapades in the Blue, 1996. Mem. sch. bd. Rio Vista High Sch., 1962-67. Maj. USAF, 1942-47. Decorated Bronze Star with 4 oak leaf clusters. Mem. Soc. Petroleum Engrs., Petroleum Prodn. Pioneers, Calif. Conservation Comm. Oil Producers (chmn. 1971-72), Sutter Club, C. of C., Lion, Sigma Xi, Theta Tau Epsilon. Republican. Roman Catholic. Achievements include research in mech. sampling-field oil tanks, determination of minimum chem., productivity index of pumping wells, rotating piston pressure recorder. Home: 6271 Eichler St Sacramento CA 95831-1864 Office: Cavigli & Mee PO Box 22815 Sacramento CA 95822-0815

CAVINA, STEFANO, structural engineer; b. Ravenna, Italy, Jan. 6, 1955; s. Antonio and Giuseppina (Laghi) C.; m. Franca Samorini, Sept. 18, 1983; 1 child, Roberto. Degree in engring., welding inspection, Istituto Italiano Saldatura, 1994. Design specialist On-Offshore Mfr., Italy, 1975-79; project engr. M.I.R. SRL-Ravenna, Italy, 1980-85; supr. AGIPspa - oil co., Ravenna, 1986-90, project engr., 1991-92, constrn. engr., off-shore coord., 1993-95, constrn. mgr., 1995—; lectr. City Planetarium, 1992—; promoter astronautics show, 1978, astronomy-astronautics show, 1979, aeronautics-astronautics-astronomy show, 1992, 93, astronautics show Gianni Caproni Air Mus. of Trento, 1995, astronautics show San Pelagio Air Mus., 1996, Planet Mars show San Pelagio Air Mus., 1997, Red Star in the Space show Planetarium of Ravenna, 1997; founder Associazione Astrofili Rheyta Ravenna-Arar, 1974; freelance writer; webmaster Pianetta Marte (Planet Mars). Contbr. articles to profl. jours. Mem. Planetary Soc. Home: Viale del Gabbiano No 4, 48020 Punta Marina Terme Ravenna, Italy Office: AGIPspa, Via del Marchesato 13, 48023 Marina di Ravenna Italy

CAVOUNIDIS, SPYROS, civil engineer; b. Athens, Dec. 20, 1944; s. Constantine and Domnitsa (Lanitou) C.; children: Constantine, Athena. Diploma Civil Engring., Nat. Tech. U. Athens, 1968; MS Civil Engring., Stanford U., 1970, PhD Civil Engring., 1975. Tchg. asst. Stanford (Calif.) U., 1970-72; soils engr. Geomechaniki S.A., Athens, 1974-78; lectr. Imperial Coll., London, 1978-80; cons. Athens, 1982-89; sec. gen. Ministry of Interior/Greece, Athens, 1989; dir., ptnr. Geotechnical Design Co. Ltd., Athens, 1989-93, Edafos Ltd., Athens, 1993—; organizing com. First Geotech. Conf., Greece, 1985-88; mem. Soils Mechanics Com., Athens, 1975-78, 80-89, pres., 1998—; mem. Com. on Rsch., Tech. Chamber, Athens, 1975-78. Author: Leptomeries; contbr. articles to profl. jours. Pres. Fgn. Students Assn., Stanford, 1969-70; mem. cen. com. Party-Pasok, Athens, 1974-75, Party-Sosialistiki Poreia, Athens, 1975-78, Party-Synaspismos, Athens, 1989-2000. Mem. Am. Soc. Civil Engring., Tech. Chamber of Greece, Civil Engrs. Assn. Greece, Athens Coll. Alumni Assn., Brit. Geotech. Soc. Achievements include rsch. on coupled consolidation during constrn. of earth dams, engring. behaviour of Marls; rsch. on three-dimensional slope stability analysis. Home: 5 Pendelis St, Athens 10557, Greece Office: Edafos Ltd, 9 Yperidou St, Athens 10558, Greece

ÇAVUSOĞLU, IBRAHIM ERFÜS, lawyer, economist; b. Ankara, Turkey, Sept. 3, 1934; s. Ali Resat and Fatma Müeyyet (Tözün) C.; children: Ali Haluk, Asli Hande. Economy license, U. Istanbul, Turkey, 1957; law license, U. Ankara, 1982. Credential of law of the Ankara Bar. Receptionist Hotel Cihan Palace, Ankara, 1957-60, chief receptionist, 1960-61, dep. gen. mgr., 1961-62, gen. mgr., 1964-67; mem. bd. Çavusoğullari Turizm A.S., Ankara, 1967-78, chmn. bd., 1978—; mem. Touristic Hoteliers Assembly, Ankara, 1957-57, The Ankara Bar, 1983-93; lectr., instr. Hotel Tng. Sch., Ankara, 1971-73. Pres. Found. of Çavusoğullari Mosque, Ankara, 1978-95; dep. pres. Assn. Hist. Monuments of Turkey, Ankara, 1990-95; mem. Internat. Airline Passengers Assn., Eng., 1994-95. Lt. Turkish Mil., 1962-64. Mem. Internat. Hotel Assn., Ankara Tennis Club, Ankara Horse Riding Club, Ankara Contract Bridge. Office: Çavusoğullari TurizmA Ş, Tuna Caddesi 18/6 Yenisehi, 06420 Ankara Turkey

CAWALING, MANUEL ROBERTO, artist, cultural organization administrator; b. Seattle, Sept. 1969; s. Manuel and Isabel C. Student, Shoreline Cmty. Coll., 1987-89, Seattle Ctrl. Cmty. Coll., 1989-91. Theatre dir., artistic dir. Pilgrim Ctr. for the Arts, 1989-94; prodn. mgr. Northwest Asian Am. Theatre, 1992-95, assoc. artistic dir., 1995-97, acting artistic dir., 1997; rental mgr. Nippon Kan Theatre, 1994-95; co-mgr. Rainier Vista Arts Program Seattle Children's Mus., 1998—; tchr. in field; adv. com. Seattle Ctr. Pub. Programs, 1996—; bd. dirs. G.A.P. Theatre Co., Seattle's League of Fringe Theatres. dir. numerous prodns. Program coord. Youth Can Now Program, Wing Luke Asian Mus.; panelist King County Arts Commn. Special Projects Program, 1998, King County Arts Commn. Cultural Facilities Program, 1996, 98; curator Theatre Programming Bumbershoot, 1994, Seattle Poetry Festival, 11th Hour Prodns., 1998, 12 Minutes Max, On the Boards; program facilitator Seattle Center's 1997 artsEdge Festival. Recipient Outstanding Supr. award SYEP, 1995, 97, Appreciation award NWAAT. E-mail: cawala@aol.com.

CAWOOD, CHARLES DAVID, urologist; b. Lexington, Ky., May 22, 1937; s. Charles David and Helen Elizabeth (Rinke) C.; m. Susan Ruth O'Dell, June 10, 1962 (dec. July 1986); children: Todd Christopher, Amy Elizabeth; m. Charlotte Dee Barton, June 18, 1988; children: Elizabeth Ann Maddeaux, Scott Edward Maddeaux. BS cum laude, U. Ky., 1957; MD, U. Louisville, 1961. Diplomate Am. Bd. Urology. Intern St. Joseph's Infirmary, Louisville, 1961-62; urology resident Baylor Coll. of Medicine, 1964-68, instr. divsn. of urology, 1968-71, asst. clin. prof., 1971-83; assoc. chief of urology Ben Taub Gen. Hosp., 1968-72; ret., 1997; chief of urology St. Luke's Episcopal Hosp., Tex. Med. Ctr., 1991-94; clin. prof., dept. urology Baylor Coll. of Medicine, ret. 1997; presenter in field; cons. Am. Cystoscope Makers Inc./Baxter, 1981-84, Advanced Clin. Products, 1988-90, N.Am. Med., 1994-98. Contbr. articles to profl. jours.; patentee in field. Mem. Harris County Med. Soc., Houston Urologic Soc., Am. Urol. Assn. (south ctrl. sect.), Tex. Assn. of Genitourinary Surgeons, Phi Beta Kappa.

CAWS, MARY ANN, French language and comparative literature educator, critic; b. Wilmington, N.C., Sept. 10, 1933; d. Harmon Chadbourn and Margaret Devereux (Lippitt) Rorison; m. Peter Caws, June 2, 1956 (div. 1987); children: Matthew, Hilary. BA, Bryn Mawr Coll., 1954; MA, Yale U., 1956; PhD, U. Kans., 1962; D.Humane Letters, Union Coll., 1983. Asst. instr. Romance Langs. U. Kans., Lawrence, 1957-62, asst. editor univ. press, 1957-58, vis. asst. prof., spring 1963; lectr. Barnard Coll. Columbia U., N.Y.C., 1962-63; mem. faculty Sarah Lawrence Coll., Bronxville, N.Y., 1963-64, Hunter Coll. CCNY, N.Y.C., 1966-88; prof. Grad. Sch. CCNY, N.Y.C., 1969-88, exec. officer comparative lit. program Grad. Sch., 1977-79, exec. officer French program Grad. Sch., 1979-86, Disting. prof. French and comparative lit. Grad. Sch., 1983—; prof. English CUNY, 1985—; Disting. prof. French, comparative lit., English Grad. Sch. CUNY, N.Y.C., 1987—; Phi Beta Kappa vis. scholar, 1982-83; dir. NIH summer seminars for coll. tchrs., 1978, 85; mem. faculty Sch. of Criticism and Theory, Dartmouth U., 1988, Sch. Visual Arts, 1993; professeur associé Université de Paris VII, 1993-94; co-chair Henri Peyre Inst. for the Humanities, 1980—, French Inst., 1997—; lectr. N.Y. Coun. for Humanities, 1992-96. Author: Surrealism and the Literary Imagination, 1966, The Poetry of Dada and Surrealism, 1970, The Inner Theatre of Recent French Poetry, 1972, The Presence of René Char, 1976, René Char, 1977, The Surrealist Voice of Robert Desnos, 1977, La Main de Pierre Reverdy, 1979, The Eye in the Text, Essays on Perception, Mannerist to Modern, 1981, André Breton, 1982, 96, The Metapoetics of the Passage, Architextures in Surrealism and After, 1982, Yves Bonnefoy, 1984, Reading Frames in Modern Fiction, 1988, Edmond Jabès, 1988, The Art of Interference: Stressed Readings in Visual and Verbal Texts, 1989, Women of Bloomsbury, 1991, Robert Motherwell: What Art Holds, 1996, Carrington and Lytton: Alone Together, 1996, The Surrealist Look: An Erotics of Encounter, 1997; co-author: Bloomsbury and France: Art and Friends, 1999; contbr. articles to profl. jours.; editor: Dada-Surrealism, 1972, co-editor, 1980—, Le Siècle éclaté, 1974-78, About French Poetry from Dada to Tel Quel, 1974, Selected Poetry Prose of Stéphane Mallarmé, 1982, Selected Poems of St.-John Perse, 1983, Writing in a Modern Temper, 1984, Textual Analysis, 1986, Perspectives on Perception: Philosophy, Art, and Literature, 1989, City Images, 1992, Joseph Cornell's Theater of the Mind: Selected Diaries, Letters and Files, 1994; co-editor: Selected Poems of René Char, 1992, Contre-Courants: Les femmes s'écrivent à travers les siècles, 1994, Écritures de femmes: Nouvelles Cartographies, 1996; translator: Poems of René Char, 1976, Approximate Man and other Writings of Tristan Tzara, 1975, Mad Love, 1987, The Secret Art of Antonin Artaud, 1998; co-translator: Poems of André Breton, 1984, Communicating Vessels, 1990, Break of Day, 1999; chief editor Harper Collins World Reader, 1994. Decorated officier Palmes Académiques, France; fellow Guggenheim Found., 1972-73 NEH, 1979-80, Fulbright traveling fellow, 1972-73, Rockefeller Found. fellow, 1994; Getty scholar, 1990. Mem. MLA (exec. coun. 1973-77, v.p.

1982-83, pres. 1983-84), Am. Assn. Tchrs. French, Assn. for Study Dada and Surrealism (pres. 1982-86), Internat. Assn. Philosophy and Lit. (exec. bd. 1982—, chmn. 1984), Acad. Lit. Studies (pres. 1985), Am. Comparative Lit. Assn. (exec. com. 1981, v.p. 1986—, pres. 1989-91). Home: 140 E 81st St New York NY 10028-1805 Office: CUNY Grad Ctr 33 W 42d St New York NY 10036-8003

CAWTHON, FRANK H., retired construction company executive; b. Kissimmee, Fla., Apr. 3, 1930; s. Benjamin Hill and Eva Elizabeth (Mullins) C.; m. Mary Elizabeth Dickert, July 10, 1959; 1 child, Frank H. Grad. high sch. Asst. sec.-treas. Orange Belt Truck & Tractor, Orlando, Fla., 1948-52, Murdock Constrn. Co., Inc., Orlando, 1954-59; sec.-treas. Amick Constrn. Co., Inc., Orlando, 1959-90; ret., 1990; bd. dirs. Amick Constrn. Co., Inc. Bd. dirs. Conway Little League, Orlando, 1977. With U.S. Army, 1952-54. Mem. Cen. Fla. Rd. Bldrs. Assn. Democrat. Lutheran. Avocations: oil painting, gardening, fishing. Home: 391 Brushwood Ln Casselberry FL 32708-4955 Office: Amick Constrn Co 401 Ferguson Dr Orlando FL 32805-1009

CAWTHON, WILLIAM CONNELL, operations management consultant; b. Roxton, Tex., Sept. 1, 1922; s. William Arthur and Lura (Denton) C.; m. Flora Keith Campbell, May 31, 1947; children: William Connell, Clark Campbell, Flora Keith. B.M.E., Cornell U., 1944; M.S.M.E., U. Tex., 1947; M. Automotive Engring., Chrysler Inst., Detroit, 1949. Mfg. exec. Chrysler Corp., Detroit, 1955-59; dir. purchasing Chrysler Corp., 1959-62; v.p. mfg. Am. Standard Corp., N.Y.C., 1962-66; v.p., dir. indsl. engring. and mfg. worldwide ITT, N.Y.C., 1966-68; exec. v.p. Weatherhead Co., Cleve., 1968-70; prin. William C. Cawthon (cons.), Hudson, Ohio, 1970-72; v.p., gen. mgr. parts div., textile machinery div. Rockwell Internat., Hopedale, Mass., 1972-73; v.p. mfg. No Telecom Ltd. (former No. Electric Co., Ltd.), Montreal, Que., Can., 1973-77; v.p. mfg. No. Telecom Inc., Nashville, 1973-80, v.p. ops., 1980-85, v.p. corp. devel., 1985-87; prin. William C. Cawthon Cons., Nashville, 1987—; mem. chancellor's council U. Tex. Served to lt. comdr. USNR, 1945-46, 51-53, PTO, Korea. Named Distinguished Grad. U. Tex., 1961. Fellow Boston U. Mfg. Roundtable; mem. Newcomen Soc. Republican. Mem. Ch. of Christ. Home and Office: 1024 Lynwood Blvd Nashville TN 37215-4512

CAYEA, DONALD JOSEPH, lawyer; b. Bklyn., Mar. 3, 1948; s. Glendon Vernon and Marie Nicola (Gesualdo) C. BA, L.I. U., 1969; JD, Western New Eng. Coll., 1975. Bar: N.Y. 1976, U.S. Dist. Ct. (so. and ea. dists.) N.Y. 1978, D.C. 1979, U.S. Supreme Ct. 1979. Prin. Donald J. Cayea & Assoc., N.Y.C., 1976—; ptnr. Kroll & Tract, N.Y.C., 1988-90, Levitan, Frieland & Cayea, N.Y.C., 1990-94, Klepner & Cayea, N.Y.C., 1994-98, Brand, Cayea & Brand, LLC, N.Y.C., 1998—; gen. counsel Entertainment USA, 1990—; lectr. Paralegal Inst., NYU, 1984—, adult edn. program Nassau County Bar Assn., Mineola, N.Y., 1978-79; panelist trial advocacy program Cardozo Law Sch., Yeshiva U., N.Y.C., 1984—; spkr. Ft. Lauderdale (Fla.) Film Festival, 1989, 90, Coun. on Mgmt. Worker's Compensation Update, N.Y.C., 1995, 96; guest panelist Property Loss Rsch. Bur., Washington, 1989, Chgo., 1991. Prodr.: (video) Dahmer, the Secret Life, 1993, (off Broadway) West Side Stories, Theatre Airelle, N.Y.C., 1993, Conversations with My Daughter; exec. prodr. (film) The Hunt for CM24, 1997; prodr. (theatre) The Remarkable Thing About Star Dust, Mother Lode, 1999, (off-Broadway) Panache, 2000. Pres. Seascape Condominium, Westhampton Beach, N.Y., 1986-92; sponsor Richmond Roller Hocker Assn., Staten Island, N.Y., 1984-89; mem. Pres.'s Coun., L.I. Univ. Served in U.S. Army, 1970-71. Mem. ABA (editor TIPS publ. editorial bd. 1990-93), Assn. Trial Lawyers Am., N.Y. State Bar Assn., Internat. Bar Assn., Assn. of Bar of City of N.Y., New York County Lawyers Assn., Phi Epsilon Pi. Office: 720 5th Ave Fl 14 New York NY 10019-4107

CAYER, JOANNE M., sales executive; b. Lawrence, Mass., June 19, 1970; d. Roland W. and Cynthia M. Cayer. AS, Plymouth State Coll., 1991, BS, 1993. Maj. account exec. Applied Theory, Syracuse, N.Y.; sales dir. Omtool Ltd., Salem, N.H.; sales asst. Labtech, Wilmington, Mass. Mem. Eta Sigma Gamma. Republican. Roman Catholic. E-mail: jcayer@msn.com. Home: 61 Windsor Blvd Londonderry NH 03053-3619

CAYNE, JAMES E., investment banker; b. 1934. With Bonn Bush Mach, 1954-66, Lebenthal and Co., 1966-69; pres., past sr. mng. dir. Bear Stearns and Co. Inc., also bd. dirs.; CEO, pres. Bear Stearns and Co. Inc., N.Y.C., 1993—. Office: Bear Stearns & Co Inc 245 Park Ave Fl 9A New York NY 10167-0002

CAYOT, PHILIPPE, food scientist, reseacher; b. Auxerre, Yonne, France, May 9, 1965; s. Jean-Philippe and Denise (Deranty) P.; m. Nathalie Villermain-Lecolier, July 2, 1988; children: Sarah, Diane, Myrtille. Degree, Nat. Higher Sch. Biology, Dijon, France, 1985; D, Burgundy U., Dijon, France, 1993. Lectr., asst. Burgundy U., 1991-93, reader, 1997—; engr. Arilait-Recherche, Paris, 1993-94; lectr. Claude Bernard U., Lyon, France, 1994-97; advisor post graduate program, Burgundy U. Author: Structure and Technofunctions of Milk Proteins, 1998; contbr. author: Food Proteins and their Applications, 1997, Structure-Function Relationship of Whey Proteins, 1997. Recipient Xavier Bernard Price award French Agrl. Acad., Paris, 1990. Avocations: running, mountain biking, painting, tennis. Home: 53 Grande Rue, 21 310 Mirebeau Sur Beze France Office: Ensbana Univ de Bourgogne, 1 Esplanade Erasme, 21 000 Dijon France

CAZABAT, EDUARDO HORACIO, psychologist; b. Junin, B.A., Argentina, May 14, 1955; s. Castor Eduardo Cazabat and Judith Maricela Mendez; m. Nora Maria Carrara (div. Apr. 1989); 1 child, Melina Julia; m. Maria Leticia Lahitte; 1 child, Rocio Abril. Grad. in psychology, U. Complutense, Madrid, 1984. Cert. supr. Assn. Sistemica de Buenos Aires. Chief of residents Hosp. Paroissien, La Matanza, Argentina, 1988-91; psychotherapist C. Priv. Psicoterapias, Buenos Aires, 1986—; pvt. practice psychology, Buenos Aires, 1985—; coord. editl. bd. Sistemas Familiares, Buenos Aires, 1997—; mem. internat. bd. Cuadernos Teraria Familiar, Madrid, 1999. Founder Assn. Latin Am. Stress Traum., Mem. APA (internat.), Internat. Family Therpay Assn., Traumatology Inst. Achievements include pioneer in introducing power therapies in Argentina. E-mail: cazabat@yahoo.com. Home and Office: Angel J Carranza 2400 12o A, C1425FXF Buenos Aires Argentina

CAZALAS, MARY REBECCA WILLIAMS, lawyer, nurse; b. Atlanta, Nov. 11, 1927; d. George Edgar and Mary Annie (Slappey) Williams; m. Albert Joseph Cazalas (dec.). BS in Pre-medicine, Oglethorpe U., Atlanta, 1954; MS in Anatomy, Emory U., 1960; JD, Loyola U., 1967, Loyola U., New Orleans, 1967. RN, Ga.; Bar: La. 1967, U.S. Dist. Ct. (ea. dist.) La. 1967, U.S. Ct. Appeals (5th cir.) 1972, U.S. Supreme Ct. 1975, U.S. Ct. Appeals (fed. cir.) 1999. Gen. duty nurse, 1948-68; instr. maternity nursing St. Josephs Infirmary Sch. Nursing, Atlanta, 1954-59; med. rschr. in urology Tulane U. Sch. Medicine, New Orleans, 1961-65; legal rschr. for presiding judge La. Ct. Appeals (4th cir.), New Orleans, 1965-71; pvt. practice New Orleans, 1967-71, asst. U.S. atty., 1971-79; sr. trial atty. Equal Employment Opportunity Commn., New Orleans, 1979-84; owner Cazalas Apts., New Orleans, 1962—; lectr. in field. Contbr. articles to profl. jours. Bd. advisors Loyola U. Sch. Law, New Orleans, 1974, v.p. adv. bd., 1975; active New Orleans Drug Abuse Adv. Com., 1976-80; task force Area Agy. on Aging, 1976-80, pres. coun. Loyola U., 1978—; adv. bd. Odyssey House, Inc., New Orleans, 1973; chmn. womens com. Fed. Exec. Bd., 1974; bd. dirs. Bethlehem House of Bread, 1975-79. Named Hon. La. State Senator, 1974; recipient Superior Performance award U.S. Dept. Justice, 1974, Cert. Appreciation Fed. Exec. Bd., 1975-78, Rev. E.A. Doyle award, 1976, Commendation for tchg. Guam Legislature, 1977, Career Achievement award Mt. de Sales Acad., 1995. Mem. Am. Judicature Soc., La. Sate Bar Assn., Fed. Bus. Assn. (v.p. 1976—, pres. 1976-78, bd. dirs. 1972-75), Fed. Bar Assn. (1st v.p. 1973, pres. New Orleans chpt. 1974-75, nat. coun. 1974-79), Assn. Women Lawyers, Nat. Health Lawyers Assn., DAR, Bus. and Profl. Womens Club, Am. Heart Assn., Emory Alumni Assn., Oglethorpe U. Alumni Assn., Loyola U. Alumni Assn. (bd. dirs. 1974-75, 77, v.p. 1976), Jefferson Parish Hist. Soc., Sierra Club, Zonta, Leconte Hon. Sci. Soc., Phi Delta Delta (merged with Phi Alpha Delta pres. 1970-72, bd. dirs., vice justice 1974-75), Alpha Epsilon Delta, Phi Sigma. Democrat.

CAZALET, PETER GRENVILLE, business executive; b. Weymouth, Eng., Feb. 26, 1929; s. Peter Grenville Lyon and B. Elise (Winterbotham) C.; m. Jane Jennifer Rew, June 15, 1957; children: Peter, Andrew, William. Ed., Uppingham Sch., Magdalene Coll., Cambridge U. Gen. mgr. BP Tanker Co. (now BP Shipping), 1968-70; regional coordinator BP, Australasia, Far East, 1970-72; pres. BP N.Am., N.Y.C., 1972-75; dir. BP Trading, 1975-81; chmn. BP Oil Internat. Ltd., 1981-89; mng. dir. Brit. Petroleum Co., London, 1981-89; dep. chmn. Brit. Petroleum Co., 1986-89; chmn. APV PLC, 1989-96; dep. chmn. GKN, Plc., 1989-96; chmn. Hakluyt & Co., 1998-99; mem. Hakluyt Found., 1996—; mem. gen. com. Lloyd's Register, 1981-99, Energy Capital Investment Co., 1994-98, Seascope Shipping Holdings, 1997—. Trustee Uppingham Sch., 1976-94. Mem. Middle East Assn. (v.p. 1981—), China Britain Trade Group (v.p. 1993-96, pres. 1996-98), Brooks's Royal Wimbledon Golf Club, MCC. Address: 22 Hill St, London W1X 7FU, England

CAZAN, MATTHEW JOHN, political science educator; b. Beclean, Romania, Mar. 10, 1912; s. John and Marie (Sipos) C.; m. Sylvia Marie Buday, July 14, 1935; 1 child, Matthew John George. Student, U. Bucharest Law Sch., Youngstown Coll., Georgetown U. Sch. Fgn. Svc. Lectr. Georgetown U., Washington, 1942-44; spl. lectr. Indsl. Coll. Armed Forces, 1947; assoc. in Romanian, Georgetown U. Inst. Langs. and Linguistics, 1949—; lectr. polit. sci. and econs. Sch. Fgn. Svc., 1943-57; lectr. The Inst. Fgn. Service Officer Preparation, 1953—; lectr. polit. sci. George Washington U., 1963—; spl. employee U.S. Dept. Justice, 1947-60, FBI, 1963-94, ret., 1994; internat. claims analyst Fgn. Claims Settlement Commn., 1960-63. Chmn. Labarca youth guidance com. Va. Gov.'s Conf. on Youth. Mem. AAUP, Am. Polit. Sci. Assn., Am. Soc. Internat. Law, Conf. Dem. Theory, Pi Gamma Mu. Home: 6369 Lakeview Dr Lake Barcroft Estates Falls Church VA 22041

CAZAUBON, CHICHÉLE CAROLINE, physician, editor; b. Reuilly, France, Apr. 12, 1948; d. Rene Gerard and Madeleine Geanne (Cincet) C. Bachelor, U. Paris, 1967, MD, 1975. Pvt. practice, 1975—; physician Am. Hosp. of Paris, 1996—; organizer Internat. Congress, 1996—. Editor-in-chief Angeiologie, 1996—. Mem. French Soc. of Angology (gen. sec. 1996), French Soc. of Phlebologie (sec.). Roman Catholic. Avocation: horse racing. Home and Office: 145 Rue de la Pompe, 75116 Paris France

CAZAVAN, LARRY O., television executive; b. Cin., Aug. 21, 1945; s. Norman A. and Lily A. (Shafer) C.; m. Karen E. Cranor (div.); children: Kimberly, Kelly. BFA, U. Cin., 1967; MCP, Vanderbilt U., 1999. Dir. Sta. WCPO-TV, Cin., 1967; dir. Sta. KMBC-TV, Kansas City, Mo., 1967-70, program dir., 1970-71; asst. program dir. Sta. WLS-TV, Chgo., 1972; program dir. Sta. WXYZ-TV, Detroit, 1972-75, Sta. WISH-TV, Indpls., 1975-78; mgr. Sta. KITV-TV, Honolulu, 1978-85; program mgr. Sta. WTSP-TV, Tampa, Fla., 1985-91; sta. mgr. Sta. WATE-TV, Knoxville, Tenn., 1991-95; v.p. ops. Sta. WNAB-TV, Nashville, 1995-97; exec. v.p. Fla. Assn. Broadcasters, Tallahassee, 1997-99, Barcazmor Consulting, 1999—. Exec. producer: (syndicated TV show) Hot Fudge, 1973. Pres. Hawaii chpt. Muscular Dystrophy Assn., Honolulu, 1984; sec., treas. Christmas Toy Network, Tampa, 1986-87; bd. dirs. St. Petersburg Urban League, 1986-90, Operation PAR, St. Petersburg, 1986—. With USNR, 1963-67. Recipient Silver medal N.Y. Film Festival, 1982, 84, Bronze medal N.Y. Film Festival, 1984. Mem. Nat. Assn. TV Program Execs. (Iris award 1980, 83). Avocations: flying, golf. Home: 413 Brentwood Oaks Dr Nashville TN 37211-6526

CAZELLES, HENRI, humanities educator; b. Paris, June 8, 1912; s. Pierre and Clotilde (Duflot) C. B, St. Croix de Neuilly, 1926-29; diploma, Science Politique, Paris, 1932; D Droit, U. Paris; PhD, U. Rome; D honoris causa, Bonn U. Prof. Inst. Catholique, Paris; dir. d'etudes Ecole Pratique de Hautes Etudes, Sorbonne, France, 1972-80; prof. San Francisco Claremont, Washington, 1972-79, Rome, 1982-89, Louvan, Jerusalem, 1980-86; mem. edn. bd. dirs. Velus Testamentum, 1950-75. Contbr. articles to profl. jours. Recipient Chevelir de la legion d'Honneur. Mem. Royal Acad. Belgium, Soc. Old Testament Studies. Home: 277 B Raspail, 75012 Paris France Office: Bibliothèque Biblique, Occumenique 21 Rue d'Assas, Paris 75006, France

CAZES, BERNARD, long-term planner; b. Hanoi, North Vietnam, Feb. 14, 1927; s. Antoine and Yvonne (Charrier) C.; m. Georgette Beros, Feb. 2, 1952; children: Jerome, Vincent (dec.). BA in History, U.Bordeaux, France, 1948; Grad., Nat. Sch. Adminstrn, Paris, 1955. Jr. civil servant French Treasury, Paris, 1956-59; staff mem. Commissariat Gen. du Plan, Paris, 1960-78, head div. long-term studies, 1978-92. Author: La Vie Economique, 1966, L'Histoire des Futurs, 1986; editor Turgot's Economic Writings; book rev. editor (fgn.) Societal, 1992; book review editor Sociedad and Politique Etrangise!. Comdr. order Alfonso X the Wise, officer Legion D'Honneur. Mem. Agorametrie Survey Assn. (past pres.). Home: 60B rue Benoit Malon, 92130 Issy France Office: Commissariat du Plan, 18 rue de Martignac, 75007 Paris France

CAZES, JEAN-MICHEL, food products executive; b. Bordeaux, Girond, France, Mar. 25, 1935; s. André and Claudine (Lavinal) C.; m. Maria-Thereza Carregal Ferreira, Dec. 2, 1968; children: Anne Christine, Marina, Catherine, Jean Charles. Student, Paris Sch. Mines, 1959; degree in Engring., U. Tex., 1960. Sales mgr. IBM France, Paris, 1962-71; pres. STAD (Empain-Schneider Group), Paris, 1971-73; chmn. Chateau Lynch Bages S.A., Pauillac, France, 1973—; exec. v.p. Chateau Pichon-Longueville, Pavillac, France, 1987—; bd. dirs. Compagnie Medocaine, Bordeaux, France, ID Systemes, Bordeaux, Chateau de Cordeilan-Bages, Pauillac; gen. ptnr.Axamillesines, Pavillac, 1987—. Served to lt. Paris Air Force, 1960-62. Mem. Pavillac Wine Producers Assn. (pres. 1974-87), Bordeaux Wine Council (bd. dirs. 1976—), Commanderie Bontemps Medoc Graves Medoc Wine Council (grand-neûtre 1997—). Roman Catholic. Lodge: Rotary (Medoc). Home and Office: Chateau Lynch-Bages, 33250 Pauillac France

CAZZULLO, CARLO LORENZO, psychiatrist; b. Gallarate, Italy, Jan. 30, 1915; m. Adriana Guareschi; 1 child, Allessandra. MD summa cum laude, U. Milan, Italy, 1940. Cert. Bd. Speciality in Nervous and Mental Diseases, 1943. Vis. investigator Rockefeller Inst. Med. Rsch., N.Y.C., 1947; rsch. asst. N.Y. State Psychiatric Inst./Columbia U., 1948; vis. investigator Montreal Neurol. Inst., 1949; prof. nervous & mental diseases U. Milan, Italy, 1958; prof. psychiatry U. Milan, 1959, emeritus prof. psychiatry, 1991; cons. IRCCS, Milan, 1995; expert aids commn. Ministry Health, Milan, 1998; dir. course for doctors as sci. in psychosocial psychiatry, 1980; expert commn. on AIDS, Ministry of Health, 1998. Author: (book) Family Therapy and Psychoeducation, 1995; editor: (jour.) Italian Jour. Psychiatry and Behavioural Scis.; contbr. over 630 articles to profl. jours. Spkr. in field. Recipient Gold Medal, Italian Soc. Psychiatry, 1991, Polish Acad. Medicine, 1996, Italian Ministry Pub. Edn., 1976, Italian Ministry Health, 1970; Academic award, Sakel found., 1962, others. Founder Italian Soc. Psycheneuropharmacology, Multiple Sclerosis Cen., Gallarate; mem. Italian Psychiatric Assn. (pres.), World Health Orgn. (bd. dirs.), World Psychiatric Assn. (exec. com. mem. 1990-93, coun. mem. 1966-90, chmn. several coms.); hon. mem. Swiss Psychiatric Assn., World Biological Psychiatric Assn., Epyptian Psychiatric Soc., others. Home: Piazza Duse 1, 20122 Milano Italy

CÉ, MARCO CARDINAL, patriarch of Venice, former bishop of Bologna; b. Izano, Italy, July 8, 1925. Ordained priest Roman Catholic Ch., 1948; tchr. sacred scripture and dogmatic theology at sem. in Diocese of Crema (Italy); rector seminary, 1957; presided over diocesan liturgical commn., preached youth retreats; ordained titular bishop of Vulturia, 1970; aux. bishop of Bologna (Italy), 1970-76; gen. eccles. asst. of Italian Cath. Action, 1976-78; patriarch of Venice, 1978—, elevated to Sacred Coll. of Cardinals, 1979; titular ch., St. Mark. Mem. congregations Clergy, Cath. Edn. Office: Curia Patriarcale, S Marco 318, 30124 Venice Italy*

CEBRIÁN ECHARRI, JUAN LUIS, publisher, journalist, editor, author; b. Madrid, Spain, Oct. 30, 1944; s. Vicente Cebrián Carabias and Carmen Echarri; divorced; children: Daniel, Eva, Juan, Rebecca; m. Teresa Aranda, 1988; children: Rafael, Teresa. Grad. in Journalism, EOP, Madrid, 1963; Hon. Prof., Iberoamericana U., Santo Domingo, Dominican Republic. Founding mem. Cuadernos para el Dialogo, Madrid, 1962-67; sr. editor Informaciones, Madrid, 1963, dep. editor in chief, 1969-75; dir. news programming Spanish TV, Madrid, 1974; editor-in-chief El Pais newspaper, Madrid, 1976-88, pub., CEO, 1988—; dep. chmn. Cinco Dias newspaper, Madrid, 1988—; CEO Grupo Prisa, Madrid, 1988—; dep. chmn. Canal Plus (now Sogecable), Madrid, 1988—; mem. bd. Cadena Ser, Madrid; mem. Spanish Royal Acad. Author: La Prensa y la Calle, La España que Bosteza, Què pasa en el mundo, Crónicas de mi pais, La Rusa, El tamaño del Elefante, Retreto ole Gabriel Gurcie Marquez, La Isla del Viento, El Siglo de las Sombras, Cartas a un joven Periodiste, La Red, La afsuia del diajon; contbr. articles to profl. jours. Recipient 1st prize Control to dir. of an info. medium, 1976-77, 77-78, 78-79, 79-80, 80-81, best journalist award, 1979, Editor-of-Yr. awawrd World Press Rev., 1980, Spanish Nat. Journalism prize, 1983, Honour medal U. Miss., 1986, Freedom of Expression medal F.D. Roosevelt Four Freedoms Found., 1986, Trento Internat. prize, 1987. Mem. Internat. Press Inst. (exec. bd. 1978—, working com. 1980, v.p. 1982-86, chmn. 1986-88), Sociedad Económica Madritense, Asociación de la Prensa, Chevalier des Arts et Lettres France. Office: Gran Vía 32, 28013 Madrid Spain

CEBULA, RICHARD JOHN, economist, educator; b. Bklyn., Mar. 24, 1944; s. Jerome Matthew and Miriam (Lyons) C.; m. Louise E. Bedrossian, June 2, 1965 (div. Dec. 1981); children: David, Christina. BA, Fordham Coll., 1966; MA, U. Ga., 1968; PhD, Ga. State U., 1971. Asst. prof. Ohio U., Athens, 1971-73; from assoc. to full prof. Emory U., Atlanta, 1973-92; prof. econs. Ga. Inst. Tech., Atlanta, 1992-99; Shirley and Philip Solomons Eminent Scholar Chair in Econs. Armstrong Atlantic State U., 1999—. Author: Determinants of Human Migration, 1979, The Deficit Problem in Perspective, 1987, Crisis in Commercial Banking, 1993, Geographic Living Cost Differentials, 1983, Economics of the Sports Industry, 1995, Savings and Loan Crisis, 1992, Microeconomics Alive!, 1997, Macroeconomics Alive!, 1997; editor Jour. Econs. and Fin., 1996-98; assoc. editor Annals of Regional Sci., 1998—; regional editor Internat. Advances in Econ. Rsch., 1996—; mem. editl. bd. Am. Jour. Econs.; mem. editl. bd., adv. editor Pub. Fin. Rev., East Econ. Jour., Rev. Fin. Econ.; contbr. more than 100 articles to profl. jours. Econ. advisor U.S. Congressman Levitas, Washington, 1974-84, Fed. Res. Bank Atlanta, 1984, U.S. Senator Sam Nunn, Washington, 1995. Recipient citation of excellence Anbar Electronic Intelligence, U.K., 1996. Mem. Am. Econs. and Fin., Am. Econ. Assn., Acad. of Econs. and Fin. (v.p. 1999—). Achievements include research on effects of welfare on migration, determinants of geographic living-cost differentials, effects of budget deficits on interest rates, economic growth, causes of bank and thrift failures. Avocations: jogging, tennis.

CECCHI, MARIO, vascular surgeon, consultant; b. Marina di Carrara, Italy, Mar. 27, 1942; s. Luigi and Emilia (Cucurnia) C.; m. Annalisa Coppi, Feb. 27, 1964; children: Chiara, Giulia, Elisa, Lucia, Anna. Assoc. vascular surgery Nuovo Ospedale San Giovanni di Dio, Florence, 1974-91, head vascular surgery, 1997—, head dept. surgery, 1997—; head sect. vascular surgery Civil Hosp., Arezzo, 1991-96; head gen. surgery Civil Hosp., Pistoia, 1996-97. Councillor Montecantini Terme, 1990-98. E-mail: cecchie@tin.it. Office: Nuovo Ospedale San Giovanni, via Torregalli 3, 50143 Tuscany Italy

CECCHINI, LEO, entrepreneur; b. Washington, June 13, 1940; s. Leo Francis and Ruth Elizabeth Cecchini; m. Sandra Jean Cecchini, Feb. 4, 1978; children: Chiara, Sabrina. BS in Econs., U. Md., 1962; MA in Bus., Schiller Internat., 1985. Vol. Peace Corps, Asmara, Eritrea, 1962-64; diplomat U.S. Dept. State, Washington, 1965-90; mng. dir. Hill & Knowlton, Ankara, Turkey, 1990-91; owner NK Internat., Windhoek, Namibia, 1991-94; gen. mgr. South African Trade Ctr., Orlando, Fla., 1994-95; dir. Gemmex Intertrade Am., McLean, Va., 1996—; assoc. Global Bus. Access, Washington, 1995—; bd. dirs. N'FETN Co., Asmara. Bd. dirs. E&E Returned Peace Corps Vols., Pittsford, N.Y., 1994—, Balkan Forum, Washington, 1999—, Nat. Peace Corps Assn., Washington, 1999—. Recipient Outstanding Svc. award City of Saigon, Vietnam, 1969, Spl. Achievement award Union C. of C., Ankara, 1980, Outstanding Am. award Am. Club, Madrid, 1984. Mem. Mensa Internat., Order of St. George. Republican. Roman Catholic. Avocations: travel, writing, motorcycles. E-mail: leo@cecchini.org. Home: PM1-D4 Paseo Arta, E07579 Betlem Mallorea, Spain Office: Gia Inc PO Box 3274 Mc Lean VA 22103-3274

CECH, PETR, communication executive; b. Prague, Czech Republic, Oct. 10, 1967; s. Zdenek and Eva (Flanderkova) C. MS, Czech Tech. U., Prague, 1993; postgrad., Coll. des Ingeniers, Paris, 1994. Rsch. asst. Czech Tech. U., Prague, 1987-93; bus. mgmt. asst. Sofreavia, Paris, 1994-95, comm. mgr., 1996—. Mem. Assn. Aeronentique Astronomique de France, Czech Mgmt. Assn., Czech Aeronautical Soc. Office: Sofreavia, 3 Carrefour de Weiden, 92441 Issy-les-Moulineaux Cedex, France

ČECH, SVATOPLUK, embryologist, educator, researcher; b. Josefov, S. Moravia, Czech Republic, Jan. 14, 1940; s. Antonin and Frantiska (Lysonkova) C.; m. Jana Kleinwächterova, Mar. 17, 1962; children: Lenka, Barbora. MD, Masaryk U., Brno, Czech Republic, 1963, PhD, 1975; DSc, Charles U., Prague, Czech Republic, 1985. Fellow Masaryk U., 1963-77, sr. lectr., 1978-85, prof., 1986—; rsch. fellow U. Copenhagen, 1975, Med. H.S., Hannover, Germany, 1978, Univ. Clinic, Essen, Germany, 1981; vis. prof. Med. U. Luebeck, Germany, 1987; guest investigator U. Bonn, Germany, 1995; vice-dean Med. Faculty Masaryk U., 2000—. Author: (with M. Dvorak, J. Stastna, P. Travnik, and D. Horky) The Differentiation of Rat Ova during Cleavage, 1978 (Czech Med. Soc. prize 1979), Stored Materials in the Course of Development of the Mammalian Ovum, 1983, (with M. Dvorak, J. Stastna, P. Travnik and J. Tesarik) The Differentiation of Preimplantation Mouse Embryos, 1985 (Czech Med.Soc. prize, 1987); contbr. over 140 articles to profl. publs. and more than 20 learning texts (including textbook) for undergraduates in field of histology and embryology. Recipient J.E. Purkyne medal Czechoslovak Biol. Soc., 1990, 2000, silver medal Med. Faculty J.E. Purkyne U., 1990, bronze medal Masaryk U., 1994, hon. medal Palacky U., 2000, hon. medal Med. Faculty Masaryk U., 2000. Mem. Czechoslovak Biol. Soc. (sci. sec., chmn. 1976-89, 90—), Anatomische Gesellschaft Germany, Czech Anat. Soc., European Cell Biology Orgn., Czech Soc. Histochem. and Cytochem., Czechoslovak Soc. Electron Microscopy, N.Y. Acad. Scis. Roman Catholic. Avocations: music, history of medicine. Office: Masaryk U Dept Histology, Jostova St 10, 66243 Brno Czech Republic

CECH, THOMAS ROBERT, chemistry and biochemistry educator; b. Chgo., Dec. 8, 1947; m. Carol Lynn Martinson; children: Allison E., Jennifer N. BA in Chemistry, Grinnell Coll., 1970; PhD in Chem., U. Calif., Berkeley, 1975; DSc (hon.), Grinnell Coll., 1987, U. Chgo., 1991, Drury Coll., 1994, Colo. Coll., 1999, U. Md., 2000. Postdoctoral fellow dept. biology MIT, Cambridge, Mass., 1975-77; from asst. prof. to assoc. prof. chemistry U. Colo., Boulder, 1978-83, prof. chemistry and biochemistry also molecular cellular and devel. biology, 1983—, disting. prof., 1990—; rsch. prof. Am. Cancer Soc., 1987—; investigator Howard Hughes Med. Inst., 1988-99, pres., 2000—; co-chmn. Nucleic Acids Gordon Conf., 1984; Phillips disting. visitor Haverford Coll., 1984; Vivian Ernst meml. lectr. Brandeis U., 1984, Cynthia Chan meml. lectr. U. Calif., Berkeley; mem. Welch Found. Symposium, 1985; Danforth lectr. Grinnell Coll. 1986; Pfizer lectr. Harvard U., 1986, Hastings lectr., 1992; Verna and Marrs McLean lectr. Baylor Coll. Medicine, 1987; Harvey lectr., 1987; Mayer lectr. MIT, 1987, HHMI lectr., 1989, T.Y. Shen lectr., 1994; Martin D. Kamen disting. lectureship, U. Calif., San Diego, 1988; Alfred Burger lectr. U. Va., 1988; Berzelius lectr. Karolinska Inst., 1988; Osamu Hayaishi lectr. Internat. Union Biochemistry, Prague, 1988; Beckman lectr. U. Utah, 1989; Max Tishler lectr. Merck, 1989; Abbott vis. scholar U. Chgo., 1989; Herriott lectr. Johns Hopkins U., 1990; J.T. Baker lectr., 1990; G.N. Lewis lectr. U. Calif., Berkeley, 1990; Sonneborn lectr. Ind. U., 1991; Sternbach lectr. Yale U., 1991; W. Pauli lectr., Zürich, 1992; Carter-Wallace lectr. Princeton U., 1992; Stetten lectr. NIH, 1992; Dauben lectr. U. Wash., 1992; Marker lectr. U. Md., 1993; Hirschmann lectr. Oberlin Coll., 1993; Beach lectr. Purdue U., 1993; Abe White lectr. Syntex, 1993; Robbins lectr. Pomona Coll., 1994; Bren lectr. U. Calif., Irvine, 1994; Wawzonek lectr. U. Iowa, 1994; Sumner lectr. Cornell U., 1994; Steenbock lectr. U. Wis., 1995; Murachi lectr. FAOB Congress, Sydney, 1995; Streck award lectr. U. Nebr., 1996; Gardner-Davern lectr. U. Utah, 1996, Priestley lectr. Pa. State U., 1996; Beckman lectr. Calif. Inst. Tech., 1996, Lemieux lectr. U. Alta., Can., 1997, Hogg Award lectr. MD Anderson Cancer Ctr., 1997, DeCoursey Nobel Lectr. Trinity U., 1998, Tschirgi lectr. U. Calif. San Diego, 1998. Assoc. editor Cell, 1986-87, RNA Jour.; mem. editl. bd. Genes and Devel.tep. editor Sci. mag., to 1999. Nonresident fellow Salk Inst., to 1999; trustee Grinnell Coll. NSF fellow, 1970-

75, Pub. Health Svc. rsch. fellow Nat. Cancer Inst. 1975-77, Guggenheim fellow, 1985-86; recipient medal Am. Inst. Chemists, 1970, Rsch. Career Devel. award Nat. Cancer Inst., 1980-85, Young Sci. award Passano Found., 1984, Harrison Howe award, 1984, Pfizer award, 1985, U.S. Steel award NAS, 1987, V.D. Mattia award, 1987, Louisa Gross Horowitz prize Columbia U., 1988, Newcombe-Cleveland award AAAS, 1988, Heineken prize Royal Netherlands Acad. Arts and Scis., 1988, Gairdner Found. Internat. award, 1988, Lasker Basic Med. Rsch. award, 1988, Rosenstiel award Brandeis U., 1989, Warren Triennial prize, 1989, Nobel prize in Chemistry, 1989, Hopkins medal Brit. Biochem. Soc., 1992, Feodor Lynen medal, 1995, Nat. Sci. medal, 1995, Mike Hogg award M.D. Anderson, 1997, Wright prize Harvey Mudd Coll., 1998; named to Esquire Mag. Register, 1985, Westerner of Yr. Denver Post, 1986. Mem. AAAS, Am. Soc. Biochem. Molecular Biology, NAS, Am. Acad. Arts and Scis., European Molecular Biology Orgn., RNA Soc. (v.p. 1993-96). E-mail: cecht@hhmi.org. Fax: 301-215-8558. Office: Howard Hughes Med Inst 4000 Jones Bridge Rd Chevy Chase MD 20815-6789

CECI, RUGGERO LENNART, psychology researcher; b. Stockholm, Aug. 25, 1956; s. Arturo and Elin Marta (Eriksson) C.; m. Katarina Hedvig Berglund, Aug. 24, 1996; children: Ceci, Antonella, Ida, Adrian, Johannes. BS, Stockholm U., 1982, Lic. Philosophy, 1987, PhD, 1990. Rsch. asst. prof. Stockholm U., 1980, asst. prof., course adminstr., 1990; asst. prof., course adminstr. U. Coll. of Falun, 1991; rschr. Karolinska Hosp., Stockholm, 1992; project mgr. Swedish Nat. Rd. Adminstrn., Stockholm, 1995-2000, nat. coord. human factors in traffic, 1999—; vis. scholar U. Pitts., 1987-88; rsch. cons. Nat. Sports Confedn., Sweden, 1993-95; program adminstr., U. Coll. Falun, Sweden, 1994; cons. prof. Stockholm U., 1994-95. Contbr. articles to profl. jours. Rep. for doctoral students, dept. psychology, 1988-90. Telegraphist Swedish Army, 1976-77. Recipient scholarships Swedish Inst., Pitts., 1987-88, Wallenberg Found., N.Y., 1994, Wenner-Gren Found., Dallas, 1992. Mem. Am. Coll. Sports Medicine, Internat. Soc. Psychophysics, Swedish Soc. Behavior Sci. in Sports, Internat. Coun. on Alcohol and Addictions, Human Factors and Ergonomics Soc. Avocations: sports, family, reading, social life. Office: Swedish Nat Rd Adminstrn, PO Box 4202, S-17104 Solna Stockholm Sweden

CECIL, DORCAS ANN, property management executive; b. Greensboro, N.C., Mar. 31, 1945; d. George Joseph and Marianne Elizabeth (Zimmerman) Ernst; m. Richard Lee Cecil, June 8, 1968; children: Sarah, Matthew. BA, U. Ark., 1967. Pres. B & C Enterprises Property Mgmt., Ltd., O'Fallon, Ill., 1977-93, Cecil Mgmt. Group, Inc., O'Fallon and St. Louis, 1993—; bd. dirs. Mid-Am. Behavioral Healthcare. Bd. dirs. O'Fallon Pub. Libr., 1983—, v.p., 1986-87, pres., 1987-99; sec. St. Vincent de Paul Soc., 1987—; bd. dirs. Leadership Coun. Southwestern Ill., 1994—. Named Realtor of Yr., Belleville Area Assn. Realtors, 1994. Mem. Inst. Real Estate Mgmt. (cert., v.p. 1987, pres. St. Louis chpt. 1990, vice chmn. Nat. IREM std. coms. 1991—, regional v.p. 1992-93, governing councillor 1994-96, nat. ethics and discipline hearing bd. 1994-96), St. Louis Multi-Housing Coun., Profl. Housing Mgmt. Assn., Cmty. Assns. Inst., Nat. Assn. Realtors, Ill. Assn. Realtors (housing com. 1994—), Belleville Assn. Realtors (bd. dirs. 1991-94, Realtor of Yr. 1994), Mo. Assn. Realtors, Belleville Bd. Realtors C. of C. (bd. dirs. 1987-96, v.p. 1988, pres. 1992-93), O'Fallon C. of C. Office: Cecil Mgmt Group Inc PO Box 459 O'Fallon IL 62269-0459

CECIL, LINDA MARIE, obstetrician/gynecologist; b. Huntsville, Tex., Apr. 10, 1944. MD, U. Tex., 1971. Diplomate Am. Bd. Ob-Gyn. Intern U. Tex., 1971-72, resident in ob-gyn, 1972-75; fellow in fetal maternal medicine Baylor U., 1979-80; staff Med. Ctr. Hosp., Conroe, Tex.; courtesy staff Meml. Hosp., Woodlands, Tex.; asst. clin. prof. Baylor Coll. Med. Mem. ACOG, AMA, Tex. Med. Assn., Tex. Assn. Ob-Gyn., So. Med. Assn. Fax: 409-539-3349. Office: 500 Med Ctr Blvd # 240 Conroe TX 77304

CEDAR, PAUL ARNOLD, church executive, minister; b. Mpls., Nov. 4, 1938; s. Carl Benjamin and Bernice M. (Peterson) C.; m. Jean Helen Lier, Aug. 25, 1959; children: Daniel Paul, Mark John, Deborah Jean. BS, No. State Coll., Aberdeen, S.D., 1960; MDiv, No. Bap. Theol. Sem., 1968; Calif. State U., Fullerton, 1971; DMin, Am. Baptist Sem. of the West, 1973. Ordained to ministry Evang. Free Ch. of Am., 1966. Youth for Christ, crusade dir. Billy Graham Evang. Assn., Leighton Ford Team, 1960-65; pastor Evang. Free Ch., Naperville, Ill., 1965-67, Yorba Linda, Calif., 1969-73; exec. pastor 1st Presbyn. Ch. Hollywood, Calif., 1975-81; sr. pastor Lake Ave. Congl. Ch., Pasadena, Calif., 1981-90; pres. Evang. Free Ch. Am., Mpls., 1990-96; chmn., CEO Mission Am., 1995—; guest dean Billy Graham Sch. Evangelism, Mpls., 1983—; vis. prof. Fuller Theol. Sem., Pasadena, Talbot Theol. Sem., La Habra, Calif., Trinity Div. Sch., Deerfield, Ill. Author: How to Make Love Your Motive, 1977, Becoming a Lover, 1978, Seven Keys to Maximum Communication, 1980, Sharing the Good Life, 1980, Communicators Commentary, 1983, Strength in Servant Leadership, 1987, Mastering the Pastoral Role, 1991, Where Is Hope?, 1992, A Life of Prayer, 1998. Chmn. U.S. Lausanne Com. for World Evangelization, 1992—, AD 2000 and Beyond Movement; mem. adv. bd. African Enterprise; mem. exec. com. Nat. Prayer Com. Mem. Christian TV and Film Commn., Internat. Students, Worldwide Leadership Coun., Caleb Ministries, Leadership Renewal Ctr., John M. Perkins Found., Revival Prayer Fellowship, Barnabas Internat., Pioneer Clubs. Avocations: athletics, music, writing, carpentry. Office: Mission Am 5666 Lincoln Dr Ste 100 Edina MN 55436-1673

CEDERHOLM, MARITA BRITA VIKTORIA, lawyer; b. Sweden, Mar. 27, 1959. LLM, U. Stockholm, 1992. Assoc. Advokatfirman Delphi & Co., Stockholm, 1992—. Office: Delphi Lawyers, Box 1432, Stockholm 111 84, Sweden

CEDERVALL, GOESTA HUGO, metallurgical company executive, management consultant; b. Vaestanfors, Sweden, Feb. 7, 1925; arrived in W. Germany, 1968; s. Carl Gustaf and Aina Maria (Goerling) C.; m. Viveka Margareta Huitfeldt, Jan. 4, 1963; children: Camilla, Christina, Patrik. Degree in Mining and Metall. Engring., Royal Inst. Tech., Stockholm, 1949. Asst. to mgr. R-N process Agy., Brussels, Belgium, 1958-61; tech. adviser Ferrox SA, Geneva, 1961-65; metall. engr. Stora Kopparberg, Falun, Sweden, 1965-68; mgr. tech. svcs. QIT-Fer et Titane GmbH, Frankfurt, Germany, 1968-69, mng. dir., 1969-90; chmn. ductile iron com. Internat. Pig Iron Secretariat, Duesseldorf, W.Ger., 1970-72, chmn. tech. devel. com., 1987-89. Patentee in stell casting; contbr. articles to profl. jours. Chmn. Alliance Francaise, Falun, Sweden, 1965-68; bd. dirs. Swedish Ch., Frankfurt, 1972-88, 89-91, chmn. 91-99. Recipient Dropsy medal, 1968. Mem. Iron and Steel Inst., Metals Soc., Verein Deutscher Eisenhuettenleute, Svenska Bergsmannafoereningen, Svenska Metallograffoerbundet, Sancte oerjens Gille (Stockholm).

CEHRELI, ZAFER CAVIT, dental educator, researcher; b. Ankara, Turkey, Feb. 7, 1969; s. Cavit Cehreli and Sevim Gultepe. DDS, Hacettepe U., Ankara, 1997. Asst. prof. Sch. Dentistry Hacettepe U., Ankara, 1997—. Mem. editl. bd. Jour. Hacettepe Faculty of Dentistry, 1992—; contbr. articles to profl. jours. Mem. Internat. Assn. Pediat. Dentistry (Jury Spl. award 1996), Turkish Dental Assn. (bd. dirs. 1998—). Avocations: scuba diving, Zen meditation, astrology, philosophy, Shakespearean age literature. Office: Hacettepe U Sch Dentistry, Dept Pedodontics Sihhiye, 06100 Ankara Turkey

ČEJKA, JIŘÍ, chemist, researcher, museum director; b. Roudnice, N.L., Czech Republic, Sept. 2, 1929; s. Josef and Božena (Roudnická) C.; m. Marie Sedláčková, July 26, 1958; children: Jiří, Jan. MSc, Inst. Chem. Tech., Prague, Czechoslovakia, 1961, PhD, 1970; DSc, Acad. of Scis. of Czech Republic, 1994. Rsch. chemist Reagencia, Kralupy, Czechoslovakia, 1954-59, Glazura, Roudnice, 1959-72; head. rsch. chem. divsn. Nat. Mus.-Natural History Mus., Prague, 1972-93, scientist, 1972-88, sr. rsch. scientist, 1988—, dir., 1991—. Author: Secondary Uranium Minerals, 1990; editor Acta Mus. Nat. Pragae, Hist. Natur., 1974-93; regional editor Czech Republic Art and Archaeology Tech. Abstracts, The Getty Conservation Inst., Marina del Rey, Calif., 1988-94; holder patents. Mem. Confederation Polit. Prisoners Czech Republic (award 1998), Czech Chem. Soc., Slovak Chem. Soc., Crystallographic Soc., Junák Boy Scout and Girl Guide Orgn. (award 1947, 87, 90, 92, 99). Avocations: classical music, jazz, fine arts, philosophy of the world scout movement. Fax: 420-2-24226488. E-mail: jiri.cejka@nm.cz. Home: Michálkova 1672, 413 01 Roudnice Czech Republic Office: Nat Scis Mus of Nat Mus, Václavské náměstí 68, 115 79 Prague 1, Czech Republic

CEJPEK, JIŘÍ, art educator; b. Jevíčko, Czech Republic, Feb. 20, 1928; s. Jan and Marie (Lerlová) C.; m. Iluše Jindrová, Apr. 8, 1950; children: Jana, Aleš, Martina. Grad., Charles U., Prague, Czechoslovakia, 1957, PhD, 1966. Head of libr. Masaryk's Pub. Edn. Inst., Prague, 1950-51; asst. dept. libr. sci. and sci. info. Charles U., Prague, 1953-68, asst. prof., 1968-73, prof., dir. Inst. of Info. Studies and Librarianship, 1990-94, prof. emeritus, 1997—; head Inst. Bohemistic and Librarianship Silasian U., Opava, Czech Republic, 1994-98; mem. nat. com. Federation Internat. of Documentation, 1992—. Author 11 textbooks; contbr. over 270 articles to profl. jours. Mem. Assn. Czech Librs. and Info. Workers/Profls. (pres. 1968-70, v.p. 1989-95, bd. dirs.). Avocations: music, literature, traveling, hiking. Home: Fantova 10/1793, 155 00 Prague 5, Czech Republic Office: Faculty of Arts Inst Info, Faculty of Arts Inst Info, U Krize 10 Charles U, 15500 Prague 5, Czech Republic

CEKIC, OSMAN, ophthalmology educator; b. Bursa, Turkey, Aug. 19, 1966; s. Muhsin and Gönül (Kuzucoglu) Č. MD, Hacettepe U., Ankara, Turkey, 1990; postgrad., Osaka (Japan) U., 1999—. Tng. in ophthalmology Ankara U. Med. Faculty, 1991-96; cons. ophthalmic surgeon SSK Eye Hosp., Ankara, 1996-97; asst. prof. ophthalmology Inönü U. Med. Faculty, Malatya, Turkey, 1997—; rschr. Osaka U. Med. Faculty, 1998-99, vitreoretinal surgery fellow, 1999—. Grantee Monbusho, Japan, 1998. Avocation: painting. Office: Osaka U Med Fac Dept Oph, 2-2 Yamadaoka, Suita-shi, Osaka 565-0871, Japan

CELA, CAMILO JOSÉ, author; b. Iria Flavia, Corunna, Spain, May 11, 1916; m. María del Rosario Conde Picavea, 1944 (div. 1989); 1 son; m. Marina Castaño, 1991. D (hon.), U. Madrid, 1933-36, 39-43, Syracuse U., 1933-36, 39-43. Dir., pub. Papeles de Son Armadans, 1956-79. Writings include: (fiction) La Familia de Pascual Duarte, 1942, Pabellón de reposo, 1943, Nuevas andanzas y desventuras de Lazarillo de Tormes, 1944, Esas nubes que pasas, 1945, El bonito crimen del carabinero, y otras invenciones, 1947, El gallego y su cuadrilla, y otros apuntes carpetovetónicos, 1949, La colmena, 1951, Santa Balbina 37, gas en cada piso, 1952, Timoteo el incomprendido, 1952, Café de artistas, 1952, Baraja de invenciones, 1953, Mrs. Caldwell habla con su hijo, 1953, La Catira, 1955, El molino de viento, 1956, Nuevo retablo de don Cristobita, 1957, Cajón de Sastre, 1957, Las viejas amigos, 2 vols., 1960-61, Gavilla de Fábulas sin amor, 1962, Tobogán de hambrientos, 1962, Once cuentos de Fútbol, 1963, Las compañías convenientes, y otros fingimientos y cegueras, 1963, El solitario, Los sueños de Quesada, 1963, Garito de hospicianos y bambollas, 1963, Toreo de salón, 1963, Izas rabizas y colipoterras, 1964, Cuentas 1941-1953, Apuntes carpetovetónicos, 1965, Historias de España, 4 vols., 1965-67, Nuevas escenas matritenses, 7 vols., 1965-66, San Camilo 1936, 1969, Obras selectas, 1971, Oficio de tinieblas 5, 1973, Cuentos para leer despues del baño, 1974, Prosa, 1974, Café de artistas y otras papeles volanderos, 1978, El espejo y otras cuentos, 1981, Mazurca para dos muertos, 1983 (Spanish Nat. prize for lit. 1984), Cristo versus Arizona, 1988, Desde el palomar de Hita, 1991, Cachondeos, escareos y otros meneos, 1991, O Camaleón solteiro, 1991, La Sima de las penúltimas inocencias, 1993; (plays) Homenaje al Bosco I, 1969; (poetry) Poemas de una adolescencial cruel, 1945, Maria Sabina, 1967, Cancionero de la Alcarria, 1987, Reloj de Sangre, 1989 (other writings) Mesa revuelta, 1945, San Juan de la Cruz, 1948, Viaje a la Alcarria, 1964, Ávila, 1952, Del Miño al Bidasoa, 1952, Ensueños y figuraciones, 1954, Vagabundo por Castilla, 1955, Mis páginas preferidas, 1956, Judíos, moros y cristianos, 1956, La rueda de los ocios, 1957, La obra literaria del pintor Solana, 1957, Recuerdo de don Pío Baroja, 1958, La cucaña: memorias, 1959, Primer viaje andaluz, 1959, Cuaderno del Guadarrama, 1959, Curatro figuras del '98, 1961, Obra Completa, 14 vols., 1962-83, Páginas de geografía errabunda, 1965, Viaje al Pirineo de Lérida, 1965, Viajes por España, 3 vols., 1965-68, Madrid, 1966, Calidoscopio callejero, marítimo y campestre de Camilo José Cela para el reino y ultramar, 1966, Xam, 1966, Diccionario secreto, 2 vols., 1968-72, Al servicio de algo, 1969, La bandada de palomas, 1969, Barcelona, 1970, La Mancha en el corazón y en los ojos, 1971, La bola del mundo, 1972, A vueltas con España, 1973, Cristina Mallo, 1973, Balada del vagabundo sin suerte y otros papeles volanderos, 1973, Diccionari manual castellá-catalá, catalá, castellá, 1974, Danza de las gigantes amorosas, 1975, Rol de cornudos, 1976, Crónica del cipote de Archidona, 1977, La rosa, 1979, Los sueños vanos, los ángeles curiosos, 1980, Vuelta de hoja, 1981, Los vasos comunicantes, 1981, Album de taller, 1981, Enciclopedia de erotismo, 3 vols., 1982-86, El jugo de los tres madroños, 1983, Madrid, color y siluta, 1985, Nuevo viaje a la Alcarria, 1986, El asno de Buridán, 1986, Of Genes, Gods and Tyrants, 1987, Conversaciones españoles, 1987, Los caprichos de Francisco de Goya y Lucientes, Las Orejas del niño Raul, 1989, Vocación de repartidor, 1989, Obras y completas, 25 vols., 1989-90, Galicia, 1990, Blanquito, peón de Brega, 1991, Páginas escogidas, 1991, Torerías, 1991, El huero del juicio, 1993, Memorias, entendimientos y voluntades, 1993; editor: Homenaje y recuerdo a Gregorio Marañón, 1961. Recipient Premio de la critica, 1955, Premio Nacional de Literatura, 1984, Premio Principe de Asturias, 1987, Nobel prize in Literature, 1989. Mem. Real Acad. Espanola, Royal Galician Lang. Acad., Royal Acad. Lit. Barcelona, Hispanic Soc. Am., Am. Assn. Tchrs. of Spanish and Portuguese, Soc. Spanish and Spanish-Am. Studies, Acad. du Monde Latin, Acad. Porteña del Lunfardo, Inst. Cultural Relations between Israel, Latin Am., Spain and Portugal. Office: c/o Carmen Balcella, Diagonal 580, Barcelona 08021, Spain*

CELEBI, GURBUZ, biophysics educator; b. Atca, Turkey, May 18, 1943; s. Muammer and Vecihe (Sari) C.; m. Sol Kohen, Apr. 11, 1975; 1 child, Nil. BSEE, Robert Coll. Istanbul, 1965, MSEE, 1967; PhD, Clark U., 1971. Rsch. asst. Robert Coll., Istanbul, 1965-67, Clark U., Worcester, Mass., 1967-70, Monell Chem. Senses Ctr., Phila., 1970-71; project mgr. Miralin Co., Wayland, Mass., 1971-74; from asst. prof. to prof. Ege U. Med. Sch., Izmir, Turkey, 1974—. Author: Biophysics, 1989, Biomedical Physics, 1994; translator: Nerve, Muscle & Synapse, 1984. Mem. Nat. Geographic Soc., Turkish Biophysics Soc., EEG, EMG and Clin. Neurophysiology Soc., Sports Traumatology, Arthroscopy and Knee Surgery Soc. Avocations: swimming, skiing, ice skating, carpentry, classical music. Home: Universiteliler Sitesi, 321 Sok #18, Bornova Guzelbahce 35310, Turkey Office: Ege U Med Sch, Ege U Med Sch, Biophysics Dept, 35040 Bornova Turkey

CELEBIC, ASJA, dentist; b. Zagreb, Croatia, Nov. 5, 1956; s. Fuad and Tatjana (Gazzari) C.; m. Ivica Prga (div. 1983); 1 child, Vedran. DDS, Sch. Dental Medicine, Zagreb, 1980, MS, 1984, specialist in dental prosthodontics, 1987, PhD, 1993. Teaching asst. Sch. Dental Medicine, 1982-95, assoc. prof., 1995—; rschr. Ministry of Sci., Croatia, 1990; cons. postgrad. study Sch. Dental Medicine, 1995. Contbr. articles to profl. jours. Mem. Croatian Med. Union, Croatian Prosthodontic Assn., European Prosthodontic Assn. (Dentsply Shield award 1995), Croatian and World Anthropologic Soc. Mem. Croatian Med. Union, Croatian Prosthodontic Assn., European Prosthodontic Assn. (Dentsply Shield award 1995), Croatian Anthropol. Soc., World Anthropol. Soc., Internat. Assn. Dental Rsch. Avocations: recreational activities, travel, swimming, sports. Home: Primorska 7, 10000 Zagreb Croatia Office: Sch Dental Medicine, Gunduliceva 5, 10000 Zagreb Croatia

CELENTANO, LINDA, industrial designer; b. N.J., May 11, 1958; d. Edward and Ruth Celentano. Student design, U. Copenhagen, 1978; B Indsl. Design, Pratt Inst., 1980. Indsl. designer Lebowitz/Gould Design, N.Y.C. 1979-81, Smart Design, N.Y.C., 1981-85; product design dir. Medin Corp., Wallington, N.J., 1985-95; indsl. designer Pfizer Howmedica, 1995-97; prof. indsl. design Pratt Inst., N.Y.C., 1998—; lectr. Pratt Inst. Alumni Series, Bklyn., 1986-87. Published in Indsl. Design Mag., 1986, 90, Product Design II, 1987, Product Design VI, 1994, Internat. Design Yearbook, 1988, 89, N.Y. Times, 1990, ID Mag., 1990, New and Notable Product Design, 1991, Crain's N.Y. Bus., 1998, Design Exch., Toronto, 1998, also salad servers; represented in permanent collections Cooper-Hewitt Collection, N.Y.C., Nambe Picture Frames and Desk Top Accessories Chgo. Athenaeum Design Mus. Vol. Libr. for Recording for Blind, N.Y.C., 1990; co-founder Rowena Reed Kostellow Fund, 1990—, active exec. com.. Recipient Design Excellence award Indsl. Design Mag., 1986. Mem. Indusl. Designer Soc. Am. Lutheran. Avocations: cooking, travel, photography. E-mail: celentano@aol.com. Home and Office: 8 Whites Ln Waldwick NJ 07463-1716

CELESTE, RICHARD F., ambassador, former governor; b. Cleve., Nov. 11, 1937; s. Frank C.; m. Dagmar Braun, 1962; children: Eric, Christopher, Gabriella, Noelle, Natalie, Stephen. B.A. in History magna cum laude, Yale U., 1959; Ph.B. in Politics, Oxford U., 1962. Staff liaison officer Peace Corps, 1963; dir. Peace Corps, Washington, 1979-81; spl. asst. to U.S. amb. to India, 1963-67; mem. Ohio Ho. of Reps., Columbus, 1970-74, majority whip, 1972-74; lt. gov. State of Ohio, Columbus, 1974-79, gov., 1983-91; mng. ptnr. Celeste & Sabety, Ltd., Columbus, Ohio; amb. to India New Delhi, 1997—. Mem. Ohio Dem. Exec. Com. Rhodes scholar Oxford U., Eng. Mem. Am. Soc. Pub. Adminstrn., Italian Sons and Daus. Am. Methodist. Office: Am Embassy New Delhi India Dept State Washington DC 20521-0001

CELI, ANA, humanities educator; b. Rio Cuarto, Cordoba, Argentina, Feb. 3, 1947; d. Jose and Italia (Coatti) C.; m. Juan Torti; 1 child, Santiago. MA, Calif. State U., 1972. Tutor Calif. State U., 1970-72; asst. prof. U. Nacional de Rio Cuarto, 1973-76, adj. prof., 1977-82, assoc. prof., 1982-87, prof., 1987—; charter mem., coord. scholarships Fulbright-Laspau-U. Nacional de Rio Cuarto, 1990-93; charter mem., coord. Ctr. for Am. Studies in Rio Cuarto, 1992—; vis. scholar Iowa U., 2000. Editor Las XXVIII de Estudios Americanos, 1997; editor, author: Saul Bellow: The Critical Essays, 1998; contbr. articles to profl. jours. including Am. Studies Jour. Internat. Fulbright scholar, 1970; grantee Am. Studies Assn., 1994, European Assn. Am. U., 1998. Mem. Argentina Assn. Am. Studies, Argentine Comparative Lit. Assn., Argentine Assn. Writers, Assn. Argentine Univ. Women, Rotary (Rio Cuarto). Roman Catholic. Avocations: biking, tennis, music. Office: U Nacional de Rio Cuarto, Ruta 6 y 36, Rio Cuarto Cordoba, Argentina

CELICHOWSKI, JAN STEFAN, science educator; b. Poznań, Poland, Aug. 3, 1960; s. Bogdan and Krystyna (Rostafińska) C.; m. Hanna Maria Olejniczak, Feb. 20, 1982; children: Jan Paweł, Maria, Stanisław. MS, U. Sch. Agr., Poznań, 1982; PhD, Nencki Inst. Exptl. Biology, Warsaw, 1989. Asst. U. Sch. Phys. Edn., Poznań, 1981-89, adj., 1989-97, prof., 1997—; dir. Fondation Poznań Ille et Vilaine, Poznań, 1993—. Author: (handbook) Muscle Organization and Movement Control, 1992; co-author: (handbook) Applied Physiology, 1997. Recipient award Ministry Sport and Phys. Edn., 1992, 98. Mem. Internat. Brain Rsch. Orgn., Polish Neuroscience Assn., Polish Physiol. Soc. Roman Catholic. Avocations: tourism, sports. Home: 9/9 Chełmońskiego St, 60 754 Poznań Poland Office: Dept Neurobiology, 55 Grunwaldzka St, 60-352 Poznań Poland

CELIER, ODILE MARIE, religious organization administrator; b. Orléans, France, Apr. 18, 1945; d. Bernard and Geneviéve (O'Mahony) Mace de Gastines; children: Alexandre, Clément, Félicité, Espérance. M in Modern Lit., U. Paris, 1967; Lic. Theology, U. Strasbourg, 1978; Canonical degree, Inst. cath. Paris, 1989. Head Inst. Theology Lais Inst. Cath. Paris, 1990—. Author: (book) The Sign of the Shroud, 1992. Home: 37 Rue de L'Université, 75007 Paris France Office: Inst Cath Paris, Rue d'Assas, 75006 Paris France

CELIK, GULFEM ELIF, allergist, researcher; b. Samsun, Turkey, Mar. 12, 1966; d. Zeki and Ayla (Pervane) Ozdemir; m. Ismail Celik, Nov. 4, 1990. MD, Hacettepe U., Ankara, Turkey, 1990. Resident dept. chest diseases and TB Ankara U., 1991-96, resident dept. allergic diseases, 1996—, chief resident, 1995-96, specialist dept. allergic diseases, 1999—. Author: Respiratory Diseases, 1997; asst. editor Turkish jour. Asthma and Allergy, 1999—; contbr. articles to profl. jours. Recipient sci. award Nat. Allergy Congress, 1998, Poster Presentation award Congress Nat. Turkish Respiratory Rsch. Soc., 1999, Nat. Asthma and Allergic Diseases Congress, 1999. Mem. Turkish Thorax Assn., European Respiratory Soc., Turkish Nat. Allergy Assn. Avocations: interior design, guitar, reading. Home: Esat Caddesi 37/20, 06660 Ankara Turkey Office: Ankara U Sch Medicine, Divsn Allergic Diseases, 06300 Ankara Turkey

CELIKEL, AYLA, physicist, researcher, educator; b. Ankara, Turkey, Nov. 6, 1943; d. Adem and Vehibe (Arayan) C. BSc, Ankara U., 1966, MSc, 1970; PhD, U. Sussex, Brighton, Eng., 1976. Engr. Elec. Rsch. Coun., Ankara, 1966-67; asst. prof. Ankara U., 1967-71, 1976-87, assoc. prof., 1987-96, prof. high energy physics, 1996—. Contbr. articles to profl. jours. Scholar UNESCO, 1971-73, 75-76, Fulbright Found., 1980-81. Mem. Turkish Phys. Soc., N.Y. Acad. Scis. Avocations: philosophy of science, music, literature, painting, swimming. Office: Ankara U Faculty Scis, Dept Physics, 06100 Tandogan Ankara Turkey

CELIS, JEAN-PIERRE P.J.C., educator; b. Leuven, Belgium, Oct. 13, 1947; m. Denise Delepine. PhD, Cath. U. Leuven, 1976. Cert. in metall. engring. Rschr. Cath. U. Leuven, 1971-88, prof., 1989—. Fellow Inst. Metal Finishings. Office: Cath U Leuven, De Croylaan, 3001 Leuven Belgium

CELIS, JULIO ENRIQUE, biochemist and educator; b. Santiago, Chile, May 21, 1941; s. Julio E. and Aura (Allende) C.; m. Ariana Pfeifer, Dec. 24, 1964 (dec.); children: Cynthia, Pamela, Juan Pablo. B. Biochemistry, U. Chile, Santiago, 1964; PhD in Biochemistry, U. Iowa, 1968. Asst. prof. U. Chile, Santiago, 1970-73; mem. sci. staff MRC Lab. of Molecular Biology, Cambridge, U.K., 1973-75; assoc. prof. U. Aarhus, Denmark, 1975-86, prof. biochemistry, 1986—, prof. and chmn. dept. biochemistry, 1987—; chmn. Danish Human Genome Ctr., Aarhus, 1991—; vice chmn. sci. com. Danish Cancer Soc., 1991-97, chmn. symposium and prize com., 1992—; Bio-Rad, San Francisco, Unilever, UK; Danish del. to EMBL Coun. and European Molecular Biology Conf., 1994—; chmn of EMBL coun., 1997, 98; European Union observer to Internat. Adv. Com. for the Nucleotide Sequence Databases, 1996; leader Danish delegation to OECD Megasci. Forum on Bioinfortics, 1996-99; sec. gen. Fedn. European Biochem. Socs., 1998; v.p. European Molecular Biology Conf., 1997, 98, founding mem. European Life Sci. Forum. Editor: Nonsense Mutations and tRNA Supressors, 1979, Two-Dimensional Gel Electrophoresis of Proteins, 1984, Microinjection and Organelle Transplantation techniques, 1986, Cell Biology: A Laboratory Handbook, 1994, 97; Danish del. European Molecular Biology Lab. Coun., Heidelberg, Germany, 1994—, European Molecular Biology Conf., Heidelberg, 1994—; editor (Internet site) Human 2-D Gel database. Recipient medal Coll. de France, 1987, Wonderful Copenhagen Congress Amb. of the Yr. prize, 1998, Hirai Meml. award, Japan, 1999. Mem. Chilean Acad. Sci., Nordic Molecular Biology Orgn. (chmn. 1990-94), European Molecular Biology Orgn., Academia Europaea, Danish Royal Soc. Sci. and Letters, Danish Acad. Natural Scis., Human Genome Orgn. Home: Toftebakken 10, 8250 Egaa Denmark Office: Aarhus U Dept Med Biochem, Ole Worms Allé Bldg 170, DK-8000 Århus C, Denmark

CELLARY, WOJCIECH STEFAN, computer science educator; b. Poznań, Poland, Sept. 2, 1951; s. Jerzy and Halina Cellary; m. Daromira Mende, 1952; children: Katarzyna, Marcin, Przemysław. MSc in Automatics, Tech. U. Poznan, 1974, PhD in Computer Engring., 1977. Dir. sci. of computer sci. inst. Tech. U. Poznan, 1987-92; sci. dir. Franco-Polish Sch. New Info. and Comm. Tech., Poznan, 1992-96; head of dept. info. tech. U. Econs. Poznan, 1996—. Author: Examples of Microcomputer Applications to Process Control, 1980, Algorithms of Task and Resource Allocation in a Complex of Operations, 1981, Resource Allocation in Computer Systems: an Attempt to a Global Approach, 1981, Operation Research for Computer Scientists, 1983, Scheduling under Resource Constraints-Deterministic Models, 1986, Real-Time Operating System iRMX-88, 1988, Operating System CP/J for Elwro-800 Junior Microcomputers, 1988, Concurrency Control in Distributed Database Systems, 1988, Relational Databases for Microcomputers, 1989, Lexicon of LOGO, 1989; contbr. numerous articles to profl. jours. Mem. IEEE, Polish Info. Processing Soc., Armed Forces Comm. and Electronics Assn. Home: Braniborska 17, 60-179 Poznań Poland Office: U Econs Poznań, Mansfelda 4, 60-854 Poznań Poland

CELLI, GIORGIO, member European parliament; b. Verona, Italy, July 16, 1935. Mem. European Parliament, Italy, 1999—; mem. Group of the Greens/European Free Alliance; mem. com. on agr. and rural devel.; substitute mem. com. on culture, youth, edn., the media and sport; mem. delegation to the EU-Bulgaria Joint Parliamentary Com. Office: Via Filippo Re 6, I-40126 Bologna Italy*

CEM, ISMAIL, Turkish government official. Min. fgn. affairs Govt. of Turkey, Ankara, 1997—. Office: Disisleri Bakanliği, Yeni Hizmet Binasi Balgat, 06100 Balgat Turkey*

CÉNAC, ARNAUD GUY, internist, educator; b. Chartres, France, Nov. 24, 1943; s. Louis and Françoise (Liébaut) C.; m. Michèle Klotz, Jan. 11, 1967; 1 child, Juliette. MD, Broussais Hotel Dieu, Paris, 1974, cardiology, 1974; internal medicine, Créteil, France, 1976; tropical medicine, Brest, France, 1989. Intern des Hôpitaux de Paris Assistance Publique, Paris, 1970-74; chief de clinique Univ. Créteil, Créteil, 1974-81; prof. Faculté des Scis. de La Santé, Niamey, Niger, 1981-88, U. de Bretagne Occidentale, Brest, 1988—; bd. dirs. Network, West Africa, Network, Vietnam. Author: Cahiers de Pathologie Medicale, 1972-77, Dictionnaire Pratique de Medecine Clinique, 1977; contbr. articles to profl. jours. Recipient Prince Albert 1er de Monaco prize Acad. Nat. de Medicine, 1995. Mem. Soc. Nat. Française de Medicine Interne, Soc. de Pathologie Exotique, Soc. Medicale des Hosp. de Brest (pres. 1993-96). Avocations: photography, history, birdwatching in Africa. Office: Ctr Hosp Reg & U Cavale, Svc de Medicine Interne, 29609 Brest Bretagne, France

CENGIZKAN, ALI, architectural design educator; b. Ankara, Turkey, Oct. 29, 1954; s. Recep Cengizkan and Lütfiye Suna (Ergün) C. BArch, Mid. East Tech. U., Ankara, 1978, MArch, 1981, PhD in Arch., 2000. Rsch. asst. Mid. East Tech. U., 1981-84, instr., 1984—, chmn. dept. architecture, 1994-98; cons. UM:AG Found., Ankara, 1995—; mem. editl. bd. Chamber of Architects, 1985-86, METUPRESS, Ankara, 1996—, 2nd Maastrichts Internat. Poetry Nights, 2000. Author: (poetry) Senlere, 1981 (Acad. Poetry prize 1981), Cocuk Ömrümüz, 1982 (Toprak Poetry prize 1983), Yunan Dosyasi, 1983 (Peace and Friendship prize Abdi Ipekçi 1983), Sürek Avinda Dünya, 1994 (Ceyhun Atuf Kansu Poetry prize 1995). Recipient Rome Reading award Artists Assn. Italy, 1992, Cambridge Seminar award Brit. Coun., 1995. Mem. Sanart, Chamber Architects, Turkish PEN, Writers' Assn. Turkey (founder, vice chmn. 1993-97, chmn. 1997-98). Avocations: book cover design, editing, collecting butterflies, translating, photography. Office: Mid East Tech U, 06531 Ankara Turkey

CENTO, WILLIAM FRANCIS, retired newspaper editor; b. St. Louis, Mar. 20, 1932; s. Frank and Augusta (Albietz) C.; m. Vera Ann Shaide, May 16, 1964. BS, St. Louis U., 1954. Gen. assignment reporter East St. Louis (Ill.) Jour., 1954-56; suburban editor Globe-Democrat, St. Louis, 1956-61; copy-editor Post-Dispatch, St. Louis, 1961-62; make-up editor Pioneer Press, St. Paul, 1962-65, wire editor, 1965-67, Sunday editor, 1967-73; graphics editor Pioneer Press & Dispatch, St. Paul, 1974-77; mng. editor St. Paul Dispatch, 1977-84; assoc. editor Pioneer Press, St. Paul, 1984-90; owner Give Me Rewrite, West St. Paul, 1990—; editor, pub. Letter from Minn., West St. Paul, 1995—. Editor: Fifty and Feisty APME: 1933 to 1983, 1983. Recipient numerous awards including Twin Cities Newspaper Guild Page 1 award Makeup 1st pl. award, 1969, 71, 74, 2d pl., 1971, 72, Award of Appreciation, AP Mng. Editors Assn., 1983. Mem. Soc. Profl. Journalists, AP Mng. Editors Assn. (bd. dirs. 1982-88). Roman Catholic. Avocations: painting, graphic design. Home: 111 Imperial Dr W Apt 103 West Saint Paul MN 55118-2249

CERAJ-CERIĆ, MIHAJLO, chemical engineer; b. Zagreb, Croatia, Apr. 15, 1944; s. Josip and Jelena (Erlich) C.; m. Ljerka Klier, April 4, 1970; children: Sanja, Zlatko. BS, Zagreb (Croatia) U., 1967, MS in Chemical Tech., 1976. Rschr. PLIVA Rsch. Inst., Zagreb, 1968-77, head quality assurance lab., 1978-88, mgr., 1988-89, dir. rsch., 1990-95, regulatory affairs tech. exec., 1995—. Contbr. articles to profl jours. Mem. Croatian Chem. Soc., Croatian Engrs. Soc., Regulatory Affairs Profls. Soc. Avocations: sailing, skiing, travel. Office: PLIVA Regulatory Affairs, Prilaz baruna Filipovica 25, 10000 Zagreb Croatia

CERBONE, ROBERT, sales and marketing exeuctive; b. Bklyn., Jan. 29, 1960; s. Frank James Sr. and Margaret (Castore) C. BA in Physics, Adelphi U., 1982; MBA in Mktg., L.I. U., 1985. Sales engr. Logitek, Farmingdale, N.Y., 1981-82; systems support specialist Porta Systems Corp., Syosset, N.Y., 1982-83; sales engr. Rhode & Schwarz, New Hyde Park, N.Y., 1983-84; regional sales rep. Chyron Corp., Melville, N.Y., 1984-86; sales engr. Ampex Systems Corp., Redwood City, Calif., 1986-87, dist. mgr., 1987-89, dir. southcentral region, 1989-91, mgr. hdqs. sales programs, 1991, dir. eastern region, 1991-93; mgr. group sales Dynatech Video Group, Salt Lake City, 1993-94; regional sales mgr. Leitch Inc., Chesapeake, Va., 1994-95; dir. of mktg. Tektronix, Inc., Beaverton, Oreg., 1995-99; market devel. mgr. Intel Corp., Hillsbror, Oreg., 1999—. Mem. Soc. Broadcast Engrs. Roman Catholic.

CERCAS, ALEJANDRO, foreign diplomat; b. Bahernando (Caceres), Spain, May 25, 1949. Mem. European Parliament, 1999—, mem. com. on employment and social affairs, substitute com. on agr. and rural devel.; mem. Group of the Party of European Socialists; mem. delegation for relations with Israel. Mem. Spanish Socialist Workers' Party. *

CERCHEZ, LIDIA CECILIA, science researcher; b. Bucuresti, Romania, Feb. 2, 1939; d. Constantin and Maria M.; m. Mihai Vasile C., July 14, 1967; 1 child, Mihnea Alexandru. Diploma, U. Bucuresti, Romani, 1965. Chem. engrng. diplomate. Chem. engr. Geol. Prospecting Enterprise, Bucuresti, 1965-67; rschr., chief of lab. Forestry Rsch. Inst., Bucuresti, 1967-74; mani rschr. III, chief of refractory Bldg. Materials Rsch. Inst., Bucuresti, 1974-87, mani rschr. II, chief of refractory, 1987-90, mani rsch. I, chief of refractory, 1996-97, chief engr., 1996-97, rsch., devel. dir., 1997—. Contbg. author: (books) The Extension of the Spruce Fir Tree Culture in Romania, 1974, Engineering Ceramics, Vol. III, 1993; patentee in field. 1st lt. Romania Army, 1972. Mem. Romanian Assn. Materials (v.p. 1997-99, 1st prize award 1995), Romanian Ceramic Soc., European Ceramic Soc., Gen. Engrs. Assn. Democratic. Avocations: music, lit., history. Office: Rsch Inst Bldg Materials, Calea Grivitei 132/Sector 1, 78122 Bucuresti Romania

CERDÀ, A., geologist, researcher; b. Xàtiva Valencia, Spain, June 22, 1966; p. Jose Maria and Raquel (Bolinches) C.; m. Rosina Navarro, Feb. 8, 1992; children: Naia, Lluna. Degree in geography and History, U. Valencia, 1989, D in Geography, 1993, cert. in geography, 1999. Sr. rschr. U. Valencia, 1989-93, sr. tchr., 1996-97, rsch. asst., 1998—; rschr. Bar-Ilan U., Ramat-Gan, Israel, 1993; rsch. asst. Crandfield (U.K.) Ecotechnology Inst., 1994, U. Amsterdam, The Netherlands, 1994-96; meteorologist Valencis TV, 1997-98; with Spanish Coun. for Sci. Rsch., 1999—; cons. Swedish Devel. Rsch., 1997—, EPYPSA, Madrid, 1997—. Med. asst. Red Cross, Valencia, 1990-96. Grantee Valencia Govt, 1989-93, Spanish Govt., 1994—. Mem. European Soc. Soil Sci. Avocations: volleyball, music, gardening, trekking. Office: U Valencia Dept Geography, Blasco Ibañez 28, 46010 Valencia Spain

CERDEIRA MORTERERO, CARMEN, foreign diplomat; b. Ceuta, Spain, Sept. 27, 1958. Mem. European Parliament, 1999—, mem. com. on regional policy, transport and tourism, substitute com. on citizens freedoms, rights, justice; mem. Group of the Party of European Socialists; mem. delegation for relations with the countries of S.Am. and Mercosur. Mem. Spanish Socialist Workers' Party. *

CERESKO, ANTHONY RAYMOND, Old Testament educator; b. Detroit, Aug. 20, 1942; s. Anthony Raymond and Mary Elizabeth (Tyrie) C. BA, Niagara U., Niagara Falls, N.Y., 1967; STB, Cath. U. Am., Washington, 1970, Lic. Sacred Theology, 1971; D Sacred Scripture, Pontifical Bibl. Inst., Rome, 1981. Lectr. SS Cyril and Methodius Sem., Orchard Lake, Mich., 1975-78; assoc. prof. U. St. Michael's Coll., Toronto, Ont., Can., 1978-91; prof. O.T. St. Peter's Pontifical Inst., Bangalore, India, 1991—. Author: Job 29-31 in the Light of Northwest Semitic: A Translation and Philological Commentary, 1980, Introduction to the Old Testament: A Liberation Perspective, 1992, Psalmists and Sages: Essays on Old Testament Poetry and Religion, 1993. Mem. Cath. Bibl. Assn. Am. (assoc. editor Cath. Bibl. Quar. 1984-91), Soc. Bibl. Lit., Soc. Bibl. Studies (India) (mem. exec. com. 1994-96), Indian Theol. Assn. Home and Office: Divine Word Sem, Tagaytay City, Cavite 4120, The Philippines

CERIĆ, EMIR JOSIP, oil company executive; b. Bosanska Dubica, Bosnia and Herzegovina, Apr. 19, 1944; s. Adem and Vera (Devčić) C.; m. Nada Meić, Nov. 18, 1972; 1 child, Igor. BSc, U. Tech., Zagreb, 1968, MSc, 1976, DSc, 1979. Registered engr. Engr. Ina Refinery, Rijeka, Croatia, 1968-71, asst. product mgr., 1971-74, product mgr., 1974-79, chief engr. R&D, 1979-84, mgr. R&D, 1984-94, project mgr., 1994—; cons. Engrng. Co. BJ, Zagreb, 1992-96; sci. asst. U. Tech., Zagreb, 1978—, lectr., 1981-82; lectr. Bus. Sch., Zagreb, 1992-93; mem. Croatian Nat. Copm. of World Petroleum Congress, Zagreb, 1991—. Author: Petroleum Technology, 1984, Technology of Base Oils, 1994; contbr. articles to profl. jours. Mem. Croatian Com. for Fuel and Lubricants, Com. for Petroleum Croatian Acad. Sci., Croatian Soc. Chemists. Roman Catholic. Avocations: sports (tennis, chess), stamp collecting. Home: F-Candeka 23A, 51000 Rijeka Croatia Office: Ina Rafinerija Nafte, Industriyska 26, 51000 Rijeka Croatia

CERING, DOJE, government official; b. Ziahe County, China, 1939. Magistrate Nagarze County and Gyaza County, China, 1962-66; sec. Communist Youth League, Tibet Cmty. Com., China, 1970's; standing com. CPC Tibet Regional Com., China, 1977; mem. CPC CC Commn. Discipline Inspection, China, 1978-82; vice chmn. Tibet Regional People's Congress, China, 1982-83; vice chmn. Tibet Regional People's Govt., China, 1983-86, chmn., 1986-90; vice min. Ministry Civil Affairs, China, 1990-93, min., 1993—. Office: Min Civil Affairs, 9 Xihuang Cheng Gennan, Jie 11 Beijing 100032, China*

ČERMÁK, FRANTIŠEK, science educator; b. Prague, Czech Republic, Jan. 30, 1940; s. František and Ružena (Pešková) Č.; m. Hilkka Annikki Lindroos, Dec. 11, 1940; children: Anna, Marie. CSc, Charles Univ., Prague, 1990, DSc, 1990, dozent, 1991. Lectr. Charles Univ., Prague, 1962-94, prof. Czech, 1994—; head lexicographic dept. Acad. Scis., Prague, 1991-93; dir. Czech Nat. Corpus Inst. Charles Univ., 1994—. Author: Foundations of Linguistic Methodology, 1993, Language and Linguistics, 1994; co-author, co-editor: Dictionary of Czech Idioms, 1983, 88, 94, The Dutch-Czech Dictionary, 1989; co-editor: Manual of Lexicography, 1995; translator: F. de Saussure: Course in General Linguistics, 1989, 96. Mem. Soc. Linguistica Europea, Euralex. Avocations: languages, science, travel, philosophy, art. Office: Charles Univ Faculty Phil, J Palacha 2, 110 00 Prague Czech Republic

CERMAK, JAN JIRI KAREL, mechanical engineering educator; b. Prague, Czechoslovakia, Feb. 24, 1939; s. Karel and Ludmila (Bohuslavova) C.; m. Eva Klimesova, Aug. 21, 1997; children: Edith, Ludmila. MA, Czech Tech. U., Prague, 1961, PhD, 1975, Doctorate, 1992. Asst. Czech Tech. U., Prague, 1961-64, lectr., 1964-81, sr. lectr., 1983-91, dept. head, 1991-94, asst. prof., 1994—; maitre asst. Centre U., Tizi-Ouzou, Algeria, 1981-83; vice dean internat. rels. Centre U. Tizi-Ouzou, Prague, 2000—; cons. Praga n.p., Prague, 1982-91. Author: (student handbook) Selected Methods of Forming 1981 (univ. rector's prize 1982); co-author: Handbook of Metal Forming Tools, 1993, Analysis of Techniques for Selecting Manufacturing Technology, 1995. Assoc. judge local ct. Prague 2, 1986-91. Fellow Internat. Inst. of Forging Technology; mem. Czech Forging Industry Assn., Tech. Com. of EuroForge. Avocations: tourism, sports, literature. Office: Czech Tech U Fac Mech Engr, Technicka 4, 16607 Prague Czech Republic

CERMAK, JOSEF RUDOLF CENEK, lawyer; b. Skury, Czech Republic, Nov. 15, 1924; s. Rudolf and Rosalie (Zahalkova) C. JUC, Charles U., Prague, 1945; LLB, U. Toronto, Ont., Can., 1958. Called to Ont. bar, 1960, created Queen's counsel, 1975. Mem. firm Borden, Elliot, Kelley & Palmer, Toronto, 1960-61, Wahn, Mayer, Smith, Creber, Lyons, Torrance & Stevenson, Toronto, 1962-92; ptnr. Smith, Lyons, Torrance, Stevenson & Mayer (and predecessors), Toronto, 1967-92; bd. dirs. pvt. Can. corps. Author: Pokorne Navraty, 1955, Going Home, 1963, My Toronto, 1984, Fragmenty ze zivota Cechu a Slovaku v Kanade, 2000, Winston Churchill, Nástin zivota, 2000; editor: Zpravy News, 1965-67; chmn. editl. bd. Nase Hlasy, Toronto Czech Weekly, 1960-68; host (Czechoslovak TV show) The Window, Can.; contbr. articles to various Czechlovakian newspapers in Can. and U.S. Actor, New Theatre, Toronto, Snizek Theatre, N.Y.C., CBC Radio and more; mem. Exec. Pro Arte Orch. Assn., 1963-66; bd. dirs. Can. Ethnic Heritage Found., Pro Arte Orch. Soc. Recipient Panhellenic prize, Epstein award Univ. Coll., U. Toronto, Masarykova cena CSSK Arbor award U. Toronto, Commemorative Medal of Pres. of Czech Republic. Mem. Can. Bar Assn., Ont. Bar Assn., Czechoslovak Soc. Arts and Scis. Am. (pres. Toronto chpt. 1970-79), Czechoslovak Nat. Assn. Can. (mem. exec. com. 1958-70, pres. 1999—), Pres.'s Cir. U. Toronto, Group of 175 U. Toronto. Clubs: Sokol Gymnastic Assn., Lawyers.

CERNA, MARIE, physician, immunogeneticist; b. Jihlava, Czech Republic, Sept. 7, 1964; d. Bohuslav and Zdeňka (Bohackova) Stepanova; m. Robert Černy, May 27, 1989; children: Marie, Robert. MD, Charles U., Prague, Czech Republic, 1989, PhD, 1994. Rsch. fellow Inst. for Clin. and Exptl. Medicine, Prague, 1989-90, U. Tex., Dallas, 1990-93; rschr. Inst. for Clin. and Exptl. Medicine, 1993-99; asst. prof. Charles U. Med. Sch., Prague, 1999—. Author: Systemic Lupus Erythematosus, 1997; contbr. articles to profl. jours. Mem. European Fedn. for Immunogenetics, Czech Immunology Soc., Czech Biochem. Soc. Home: Hrudickova 2097, CZ14800 Prague 4 Czech Republic Office: CBO Cell/Molecular Biology, LF3 UK Ruska 87, CZ 10000 Prague 10 Czech Republic

CERNAJSEK, TILLFRIED, librarian, geologist; b. Vienna, Austria, Nov. 24, 1943; s. Friedrich Rudolf and Sophie (Steger) C.; m. Helfriede Daubek, July 21, 1971; children: Uwe, Werner, Gernot. Matura, Gymnasium, Vienna, 1963; PhD, Vienna, 1971. Cert. geologist, paleontologist, libr. Asst. U. Salzburg, Austria, 1969-71; geologist geol. survey Austria, 1977-74; libr. geol. survey, 1975—. Author and editor, books, procs. Mem. mcpl. coun., Perchtoldsdorf, 1990-92. Recipient silver badge Perchtoldsdorf Mcpl. coun., 1987, Sci. Coun. Pribram medal, 1990. Mem. Österreiche Gesellschaft Wissenscheftpeschichte, Österreichische Geologische Gesellschaft, Vereinipung Österreichischer Bibliothekare. Protestant. Avocations: book-plates, collecting, publishing. Home: Walzengasse 35A, A-2380 Perchtoldsdorf Niederösterreich, Austria Office: Geol Survey Austria, Libr Tongasse 12 PO Box 127, A-1031 Wien Austria

CERNEA, MINERVA, executive search company executive; b. Bucharest, Romania, Dec. 22, 1962; d. Remus and Maria (Doncu) Bunea; m. Dominic Paul Laurent Cernea, Oct. 11, 1985; children: Ana-Maria Romana, Patrick Paul. MSc, Poly. U., Bucharest, 1986; MBA, IEDC, Brdo, Slovenia, 1996. Engr. IEMI, Bucharest, 1986-89, Inst. Sci. Rsch. and Technol. Engrng. for Automation, Bucharest, 1989-90; sci. rschr. IPA, Bucharest, 1990-94; mktg. mgr. Integrated Romanian Info. Sys., Bucharest, 1994-96; dir. purchasing and sales Cardinal 2000, Bucharest, 1997; cons. Amrop Internat., Stein Ptnrs. Mgmt. Cons., Bucharest, 1997-99; mng. dir. PMC Internat. Romania, Bucharest, 1999—; owner, Pyramid srl, Bucharest, 1993—; cons. Soros Found., Bucharest, 1997. Roman Catholic. Avocations: profl. literature, music. Home: Calea Floreasca 104 Et 1, 71402 Bucharest Romania Office: PMC Internat Romania, Str Caragea Voda 14 Sector1, 71262 Bucharest Romania

CERNOSEK, KITTY, interior decorator; b. Dallas, Aug. 9, 1938; d. G.V. and Martha M. (Watkins) Whitefield; m. Larry A. Cernosek, June 17, 1979; children: Melinda A. Morris, Curt Robbins, Katrina Burgess. Student, Abilene Christian U., 1954-57; cert. in floral design, Lamar U., 1982. Floral designer, area floral trainer Safeway Stores, Inc., Port Arthur, Tex., 1982-86; display designer, saleswoman Teters Floral Co., Irving, Tex., 1986-88; owner, designer, bd. dirs., cons. Decorating Den, Austin, Tex., 1988-95; owner Accessories by Kitty, Taylor, Tex., 1995—; freelance interior decorator, 1985-88; seminar dir. Balcones Woods Women's Assn., Austin, 1989; chmn. Tex. Home Owners Show Sale, Austin, 1988, 89. Vol. Blue Santa, Austin, 1988-89, ARC, Austin, 1988; founding mem. Austin Lyric Opera Chorus, Austin Choral Union; vol. receptionist Taylor C. of C., 1996—. Mem. Nat. Home Furnishing Assn., Austin C. of C. Avocations: singing, reading, travel. Home and Office: Accessories by Kitty 912 James St Taylor TX 76574-2654

CERNUSHI-FRIAS, BRUNO, electrical engineer; b. Montevideo, Uruguay, Apr. 7, 1952; became citizen of Argentina, 1978; s. Felix and Zulema (Frias) Cernuschi. BEE, U. Buenos Aires, 1976; MEE, Brown U., Providence, R.I., 1983, PhD in Elec. Engring., 1984. Asst. faculty engring. U. Buenos Aires, 1976-78, chief asst., 1979-83, asst. prof., 1984-87, sec. for rsch. and PhD studies, 1987-89, prof. dept. elec. engring., 1990-94, prof., 1995—; rschr. Consejo Nacional de Investigaciones Cientificas y Tecnicas, 1984—, prin. rschr., 1995—. Contbr. articles to profl. jours. Recipient 1st prize for ship engine control design, Secretaria de Estado de Intereses Maritimos, Buenos Aires, 1978, Bernardo Houssay prize Consejo Nacional de Investigaciones Cientificas y Tecnicas, 1987, Konex-Canon prize, 1993, Elec. Engring. prize Acad. Nacional de Ciencias Exactas, Fisicas y Naturles, 1995. Mem. IEEE, AAAS, Assn. Computing Machinery, Am. Math. Soc., Sigma Xi. Roman Catholic. Home: Las Heras 2269 (4A), 1127 Buenos Aires Argentina Office: Cassilla 8, Sucursal 12 B, 1412 Buenos Aires Argentina

CERNY, FRANTISEK, science educator, researcher; b. Trebic, Czech Republic, Jan. 19, 1944; s. Frantisek and Ruzena (Palikova) C.; m. Jana Timrova, June 1, 1968; 1 child: Eva. MSc, Czech Tech. U., Prague, 1966; PhD, Czech Tech. U., 1995. Rschr. Semiconductor Rsch. Inst., Prague, 1967-78; dept. head Material Rsch. Inst., Prague, 1979-91; asst. prof. Czech Tech. U., 1992-99, assoc. prof., 1999—. Contbr. articles to profl. jours. Grantee Grant Agy. of Czech Republic, Prague, 1997. Avocation: hiking. Office: Czech Tech U, Technicka 4, 16607 Prague Czech Republic

CERNY, HARALD, soccer player. Forward, now midfielder 1860 Munich, Germany. Address: Deutscher Fussball-Bund, PO Box 71 02 65, D-60492 Frankfurt am Main Germany Also: Grünwalder Str 114, 81547 München Germany*

CERNY, JAROSLAV, mathematics educator; b. Prague, Czech Republic, Jan. 13, 1950; s. Jaroslav and Vera (Krckova) C.; m. Nadezda Kubisova, Mar. 13, 1956; children: Vit, Jiri. Grad., Charles U., Prague, 1973, Dr, 1982, PhD, 1982. Asst. lectr. dept. math. Faculty Civil Engring., Czech Tech. U., Prague, 1973-76, sr. lectr., 1976-86, from asst. prof. to prof., head dept., 1986—; sr. lectr. Pub. Acad. Prague, 1985-88. Author: Descriptive Geometry, 1988 (Univ. award 1988), Geometry in Practice, 1992 (medal of J.A. Comenius) 1993, Constructive Geometry, 1998. Mem. Soc. Europeenne pour la Formation des Ingenieurs, Internat. Gesellschaft fur Ingenierupadogogic, Assn. Czech Mathematicians and Physicists (chmn. com. math. of tech. univs.). Avocations: travel, fruit growing. Home: Pirinska 3242, 14300 Prague Czech Republic Office: Faculty Civil Engring, Tha'kurova 7, 16629 Prague Czech Republic

CERNY, JOSEPH CHARLES, urologist, educator; b. Apr. 20, 1930; s. Joseph James and Mary (Turek) C.; m. Patti Bobette Pickens, Nov. 10, 1962; children: Joseph Charles, Rebecca Anne. BA, Knox Coll., 1952; MD, Yale U., 1956. Diplomate Am. Bd. Urology. Intern U. Mich. Hosp., Ann Arbor, 1956-57, resident, 1957-62; practice medicine specializing in urology Ann Arbor and Detroit, 1962—; instr. surgery (urology) U. Mich., Ann Arbor, 1962-64, asst. prof., 1964-66, assoc. prof., 1961-77, clin. prof., 1971—; chmn. dept. urology Henry Ford Hosp., Detroit, 1971—, chmn. emeritus urology Henry Ford Hosp., 1998; pres. Resistors, Inc., Chgo., 1960—; cons. St. Joseph Hosp., Ann Arbor, 1973—; chief urology sect., dept. surgery Ann Arbor VA Hosp., 1999—. Mem. editl. bd. Am. Jour. Kidney Diseases, 1988—; contbr. articles to profl. jours., chpts. to books. Bd. dirs., trustee Nat. Kidney Found. Mich., Ann Arbor, 1988—, chmn. urology coun., 1987—, exec. com., 1987—, pres., 1988—, emeritus trustee, 1997; bd. dirs. Ann Arbor Amateur Hockey Assn., 1980-83; pres. PTO, Ann Arbor Pub. Schs., 1980. Lt. USNR, 1956-76. Recipient Disting. Svc. award Transplantation Soc. Mich., 1982, Disting. Svc. award Nat. Kidney Found. Mich., 1993, Champion of Hope award Nat. Kidney Found., 1997. Fellow ACS (pres.-elect Mich. br. 1984-85, pres. 1985—); mem. Am. Acad. Med. Dirs., Am. Coll. Physician Execs., Internat. Soc. Urology, Am. Urol. Assn. (pres. Mich. br. 1980-81, pres. North Cen. sect. 1985-86, manpower com. 1987-88, 90-92, jud. rev. com. 1987-91, tech. exhibits 1987-88, fiscal affairs rev. commn. 1985-89, audit commn. 1992-96, chmn. 1995, exec. commn. 1993—, bd. dirs. 1994—, work force com., publs. com. 1995—, chmn. publs. com. 1999, Best Sci. Exhibit award 1978, Best Sci. Films award 1980, 82, audio-visual com. 1994—, program rev. com. 1994—, urology work force com. 1995—, jud. and ethics com. 1997—), Transplantation Soc. Mich. (pres. Mich. 1983-85), Am. Assn. Transplant Surgeons, Endocrine Surgeons, Soc. Univ. Urologists, Am. Assn. Urologic Oncology, Am. Fertilitiy Soc., Am. Coll. Physician Execs., Am. Acad. Med. Dirs., S.W. Oncology Group, Barton Hills Country Club, Ann Arbor Racquet Club. Avocations: tennis, fishing, Civil War. Home: 2800 Fairlane St Ann Arbor MI 48104-4110 Office: U Mich Health Sys Sect Urology Dept Surgery 1500 E Medical Center Dr Ann Arbor MI 48109-0005

CERNY, PHILIP GEORGE, political scientist, educator; b. N.Y.C., Mar. 13, 1946; arrived in Eng., 1967; s. Paul Joseph Cerny and Nona Kathleen (Reed) Bell; div., 1977; children: Alexander, Marcus. BA, Kenyon Coll., Gambier, Ohio, 1967; PhD, U. Manchester, Eng., 1976. Rsch. asst. in govt. U. Manchester, 1967-70; lectr., sr. lectr. politics U. York, Eng., 1970-95; prof. internat. polit. economy U. Leeds, Eng., 1996-2000; prof. govt. U. Manchester (Eng.), 2000—; vis. scholar Harvard U., Cambridge, Mass., 1982; vis. assoc. prof. Dartmouth Coll., Hanover, N.H., 1983-84; vis. prof. NYU, N.Y.C., 1988-89. Author: The Politics of Grandeur: Ideological Aspects of De Gaulle's Foreign Policy, 1980, The Changing Architecture of Politics, 1990; contbr. articles to profl. jours. Recipient Harold D. Lasswell prize, 1995. Mem. Internat. Studies Assn. (mem. gov.'s coun. 1995), Am. Polit. Sci. Assn. Avocations: folk and roots music. Home: 7 Warburton St, Didsbury, Manchester M20 6WA, England Office: U Manchester, Dept Govt, Manchester M13 9PL, England

CERNY, RADOVAN, physicist, researcher; b. Vsetin, Czechoslovakia, Jan. 25, 1957; s. Miroslav and Zofie (Langerova) C.; m. Ilja Stupkova, Aug. 25, 1986 (div. 1993); 1 child, Jakub. MSc, Charles U., Prague, Czechoslovakia, 1981, PhD in Solid State Physics, 1990. Sci. worker Charles U., Prague, Czechoslovakia, 1987-91; asst. post doctoral U. Geneva, Switzerland, 1991-93, master asst., 1993-95, master of rsch., 1995—. Contbr. articles to profl. jours. Recipient Achievemnt award Czechoslovak Acad. Scis., 1985. Mem. Czechoslovak Soc. Crystallography (sec. 1990-93), Swiss Users Group SNBL, (sec. 1996—), Swiss Soc. Crystallography (com. mem. 1996—), Internat. Ctr. for Diffraction Data. Avocations: mountaineering, skiing, music, history. Office: U Geneva, 24 Quai Ernest-Ansermet, Ch-1211 Geneva Geneva, Switzerland

CERNY, ROBERT, physicist educator; b. Rakovnik, Czech Republic, Oct. 12, 1958; s. Miloslav and Vlasta (Leitnerova) C.; m. Marie Stepanova, May 27, 1989; children: Marie, Robert. MS, Czech Tech. U., Prague, Czechoslovakia, 1983, PhD, 1988, DSc, 1995. Profl. civil engr. Asst. prof. Czech Tech. U., Prague, 1988-91, 92-94; rsch. fellow Rice U., Houston, 1991-92; assoc. prof. Czech Tech. U., Prague, 1994-98; prof. Czech Tech. U., 1998—. Author: (book) Physics-Transport Phenomena, 1993; contbr. articles to profl. jours. Mem. N.Y. Acad. Scis., European Materials Rsch. Soc., Materials Rsch. Soc. Avocations: tennis, table tennis. Home: Hrudickova 2097, CZ-14800 Prague 4, Czech Republic Office: Czech Tech U, Thakurova 7, CZ-16629 Prague 6, Czech Republic

ČERNY, SLAVOJ, physical chemist, researcher; b. Prague, Czechoslovakia, Dec. 19, 1932; s. Slavoj and Anna (Lorenzová) Č; m. Tatana Jirkovská, June 1, 1963; children; Ivan, Martin. D of Natural Scis., Charles U., Prague, 1963; CSc in Phys. Chemistry, Czechoslovak Acad. Scis., Prague, 1963. Rsch. scientist J. Heyrovsky Inst. Phys. Chemistry, Czechoslovak Acad. Sci., 1964-70, sr. rsch. scientist, 1970—, vice dir., 1991-96, sci. sec., 1996—. Co-author: Active Carbon, 1970, Adsorption on Solids, 1974; contbr. over 60 articles to chem. jours. Avocations: classical music, history. Office: Heyrovsky Inst Phys Chemist, Acad Sci Czech Rep Dolejškova 3, 182 23 Prague 8, Czech Republic

CERON, HECTOR, civil engineer; b. Santiago, Chile, Aug. 12, 1941; s. Hector Ceron and Leonor Polanco; m. Hueche Alejandra, May 30, 1981; children: Alejandra, Hector. Degree in civil engring., Cath. U. Engr. Dictuc, Santiago, Chile, 1975-76, Min. de Vivienda y Urb, Concepcion, Chile, 1977—. Avocation: antique car restoration. Office: Min Vivienda y Urbanismo, Rengo 476, Concepcion Chile

CEROVSKY, NEVENKA, pharmaceuticals company executive; b. Zagreb, Croatia, Nov. 16, 1958; d. Zvonko and Slavica (Pusec) Kozina; m. Davor

Cerovsky, July 13, 1985; 1 child, Iva. B in Econs., Zagreb U., 1982. Exec. Zagreb Baking Industry, 1982-84; from fgn. fin. coord. to dir. cosmetics & hygiene divsn. Neva d.o.o. Pliva Group, Zagreb, Croatia, 1984—; bd. dirs., CFO, Podravka d.d. Food Industry, 2000—; cons. in field. Decorated by Pres. of Croatia. Avocations: music, travel, sports, art collecting. Office: Podravka Group, A Starcevica 32, 48000 Koprivnica Croatia

CERRI, ALBERTO, management consultant executive; b. Mar del Pata, Buenos Aires, Argentina, Oct. 13, 1948; came to U.S., 1964; s. Alberto Roman and Milagro (Climent) C.; m. Christina M. Gastaldi, Jan. 17, 1978; children: Alberto A., Patrick L. AA in Bus. Adminstrn., Santa Ana Coll., 1970; Contracts in Architecture/Engring., U. Buenos Aires, 1978; postgrad. studies in small bus. mgmt., Cath. U. La Plata, Argentina, 1985; BS in bus. mgmt., U. La Salle, 1994. Lic. income tax preparer. Acctg. dept. supr. Security Indsl. Supply, South Gate, Calif., 1970-71; fin. mgr. Ullom, Kahn & Assoc., Santa Ana, Calif., 1971-74; mng. ptnr. Estudio Enterprise, La Plata, 1974-86; exec. dir. Cerrico Enterprises, Santa Ana, 1986—. Contbr. articles to profl. jours. Pres. Buenos Aires regional chpt. Argentine Coun. Small Bus., 1983-86; treas. C. of C., Argentina, 1985-86; mem. Entrepreneurs' Guild, 1989; com. chair Orange County coun. Boy Scouts Am., 1990-91. Mem. Nat. Soc. Pub. Accts., Calif. Assn. Ind. Accts. Roman Catholic. Avocations: researching small business, coin and stamp collecting, walking, biking.

CERRI, GIOVANNI GUIDO, radiologist, educator; b. Milan, Oct. 9, 1953; arrived in Brazil, 1955; s. Vittorio and Elma (Facchin) C.; m. Luciana Mendes de Oliveira, May 28, 1994; children: Eduardo, Luiza, Júlia. MD, U. São Paulo, 1976, degree in radiology, 1979, PhD, 1984. Bd. cert. Brazilian Coll. Radiology. Asst. prof. U. São Paulo, 1980-86, assoc. prof., 1986-96, chmn. dept. radiology, 1996—; chief dept. radiology Hosp. Das Clínicas, São Paulo, 1990-94, dir. radiology divsn., 1996—; dir. imaging divsn. Heart Inst., São Paulo, 1990—; pres. postgrad. commn. Sch. Medicine U. São Paulo, 1991—; cons. WHO, Geneva, 1988—. Author: Contribution of Ultrasound in Schistosomiasis, 1984 (Lafi's prize 1985), Abdominal Ultrasound, 1993, Doppler, 1996, Ultrasound Gynecology-Obstetrics, 1997. Bd. dirs. Internat. Soc. Radiology, Zürich, Switzerland, 1994-97. Mem. L.Am. Fedn. Ultrasound (hon., pres. São Paulo chpt. 1991-93, honor Mex. chpt. 1995), Brazilian Med. Assn., São Paulo Med. Assn., World Fedn. Ultasound in Medicine and Biology. Home: R Henrique Martins 377, 04504-000 São Paulo Brazil Office: Hosp Das Clínicas, Av Dr Eneas Carvalho Aguiar 255 3o, 05403-001 São Paulo Brazil

CERRI, ROBERT NOEL, photographer; b. Boston, Dec. 25, 1947; s. Lawrence Alfred and Angelina (Arena) C. BA, Georgetown Coll., 1972. Dir., head counselor The Open Door, Boca Raton, Fla., 1972-77; actor, model Miami, 1977-79; photojournalist Newsweek/Nat. Geographic, Miami, 1979-85; comml. advt. photographer Miami, 1985-98; pres. Robert Cerri Photography (now RC Photo & Design), Miami, NY, LA, Orlando, The Caribbean, 1985—, Dream Light Prodns., 1994—, RC Photo & Design, 1999—. Mem. USGA, Acad. Model Aeronautics, Tasters Guild, U.S. Golf Assn.,* Meeting Profl. Internat., Nat. Trust for Historic Preservation, Williamsburg Preservation Soc., PGA Ptnrs. Club. Republican. Avocations: golf, inline skating, horseback riding, travel, model planes & rockets. Fax: (561) 447-8684. E-mail: rcp-d@worldnet.att.net. Office: RC Photo & Design PO Box 618121 Orlando FL 32861-8121

CERRUTI, ROBERTO, executive; b. Turin, Italy, Dec. 19, 1968. B of Aerospace Engring., Turin Poly Tech., 1993. Rsch. & devel. engr. Varian VVT, Turin, Italy, 1994-98, prodn. mgr., 1998—. Mem. AVS, ASTM. Avocations: soccer, volleyball, skiing, music. Office: Varian VVT, Via Fratelli Varian 54, 10040 Turin Italy

CERTIK, MILAN, scientist in biotechnology, educator; b. Bojnice, Slovak Republic, July 28, 1962; s. Milan and Maria (Cicmancova) C.; m. Daniela Babinska, Aug. 18, 1990; 1 child, Ema. MSc, Slovak Tech. U., Bratislava, Slovak Republic, 1985, PhD, 1992. Rschr. Biotika, Slovenska Lupca, Slovak Republic, 1985-86; head of fermentation divsn. Rsch. Inst. Gerontology, Malacky, 1986-96; scientist, tchr. Slovak Tech. U., Bratislava, 1996—; advisor Rsch. Inst. Liko, Bratislava, 1987-94. Galena Co., Opava, Czech Republic, 1991-94; cons. ZTS Industry, Martin, Slovak Republic, 1991-92, Palma-Tumis Oil Co., Bratislava, 1996; invited prof. Kyoto (Japan) U., 1997-98. Author: Recent Research Developments in Oil Industry, 1998, Research Advances in Biosciences and Bioengineering, 2000; contbr. articles to profl. jours.; patentee in field. 1st lt. Czechoslovak Army, 1985-86. Sci. and Tech. Agy. fellow, Tsukuba, Japan, 1994-95; Japan Soc. for Promotion of Scis. fellow, 1998-2000. Mem. Am. Oil Chem. Soc., Japanese Soc. Biosci., Biotech. and Agr. Roman Catholic. Avocations: sports, travel, photography, cooking. E-mail: mcertik@yahoo.com. Office: Slovak Tech U/Fac Chem Tech, Radlinskeho 9, 812 37 Bratislava Slovak Republic

CERVANTES, EMILIO, biologist, scientist; b. Pamplona, Navarra, Spain, Nov. 15, 1958; s. Emilio Cervantes and Carmen Ruiz de la Torre; m. Juana Gutierrez, Aug. 8, 1983; children: Julia, Emilio, Ana. Scientist IRNA-CSIC, Salamanca, Spain. Home: c/ Ancha, 37002 Salamanca Salamanca, Spain Office: IRNA-CSIC, c/Cordel de Merinas 40-52, 37072 Salamanca Salamanca, Spain

CERVANTES AGUIRRE, ENRIQUE, Mexican government official; b. Puebla, Mex., Jan. 20, 1935; married; 4 children. Grad., Heroico Mil. Coll., Mex., 1954. Enlisted Mex. Army, 1952; dep. of chief staff 35th Mil. Zone Mex. Army, Chilpancingo, Guerrero, 1972-74; chief of staff 27th Mil. Zone Mex. Army, Alcapulco, Guerrero, 1974-76; advanced through grades to two star brigade gen. Mex. Army, 1980, divsn. three star gen., 1982, comdr. several Mil. Regions; dir. gen. def. prodn. Govt. of Mex., Mexico City, 1988, sec. nat. def., 1994—. Office: Blvd Manuel Avila Camacho, Esquina con Av Batalia Celaya 1, Colonia Lomas de Sotelo Mexico City Codigo Posta 11200, Mexico Address: Avila Camacho e Ind, Lomas de Sotelo, 11640 Mexico City Mexico*

ČERVENKA, MIROSLAV, humanities educator, researcher; b. Praha, Czech Republic, Nov. 5, 1932; s. František and Věra (Chocová) Č.; divorced, 1967; children: Jindřich, Jan; m. Marcela Pittermannová, Aug. 24, 1967. Degree in philology, Charles U., Praha, Czech Republic, 1956; DS, Acad. Scis., Praha, Czech Republic, 1969. Asst. Acad. Scis., Praha, 1956-61, rschr., 1961-71, 90—; prof. Charles U., Praha, 1994—, head dept. Czech lit., 1997-2000. Author: Der Bedeutungsaufbau des Literarischen Werks, 1978, A Siege from Within (in Czech), 1996, including 10 more books on theory and history of literature; editor-in-chief Česká Lit., 1990—. Recipient Joseph Dobrovsky medal for the merits in humanities Acad. Scis., 1997. Mem. Prague Linguistic Cir. (v.p. 1991), Czech PEN Club. Home: Schnirchova 4, 17000 Praha Czech Republic Office: Filozofická Fakulta UK, nám V Jana Palacha 2, 11638 Praha Czech Republic

ČERVENY, LIBOR, chemistry educator; b. Prague, Czech Republic, July 2, 1942; s. Josef and Ludmila (Kubešová) Č.; m. Milada Smitková, Dec. 2, 1971. Ing., Inst. Chem. Tech., 1964, Dr., 1969. Rschr. Rsch. Inst. of Organ. Syntheses, Pardubice, Czech Republic, 1969-70; scientific worker Inst. Chem. Tech., Prague, 1970-90, prof., 1990—, head dept. organic tech., 1994; cons. Aroma, Prague, 1975. Editor: Catalytic Hydrogenation, 1986; contbr. over 200 articles to profl. jours. Recipient Nat. Prize Czech Parliament, 1987. Mem. Am. Chem. Soc. Achievements include more than 50 patents in field; research in catalysis, technology, syntheses and technologies of chemical specialties such as flavors and fragrances. Home: U smaltovny 32, 170 00 Prague 7 Czech Republic Office: Inst Chem Tech, Technická 5, 166 28 Prague Czech Republic

ČERVINKA, OTAKAR, chemistry educator; b. Lázně Toušeň, Czech Rep., May 20, 1925; s. Otakar and Eliška (Melicharová) C.; m. Alexandra Králíková, June 24, 1970; children: Filip, Jakub, Otakar. Chem. engr., Inst. Chem. Tech., Prague, Czech Rep., 1949, DTech, 1950, DSc, 1968. Asst. prof. Inst. Chem. Tech., 1950-61, lectr., 1961-68, prof., 1968-95, prof. emeritus, 1995—. Author: Organic Chemistry, Enantioselective Reactions in Organic Chemistry, Mechanism of Organic Reactions. Recipient medal Coll. France, 1978, F. Stolby, 1990, E. Voteuk, 1995. Mem. Czech Chem. Soc. (hon., Hanuš medal 1976), Swiss Chem. Soc. Office: Inst Chem Tech Organic Chem, Technicka 5, 166 28 Prague 6, Czech Republic

CERVINKOVA, ZUZANA, physiology educator; b. Pardubice, Czech Republic, Apr. 11, 1951; d. Bedrich Jansa and Olga (Vinarova) Jansova; m. Miroslav Cervinka, Nov. 10, 1973; children: Petra, Katerina. MD, Charles U., Prague, 1975, PhD, 1985. Lectr. Charles U. Faculty of Medicine, Hradec Kralove, Czech Republic, 1975-78, sr. lectr., 1979-91, assoc. prof., 1991—, head dept. physiology, 1990—. Contbr. articles to profl. jours. Agy. of the Czech Republic grantee, 1994-96; Ministry of Edn. grantee, 1993. Mem. Assn. Univs. in Czech Republic, European Assn. for Study of the Liver, Czech Soc. Hepatology (bd. dirs.) Czech Soc. Physiology (bd. dirs., treas.). Avocations: travel, sports, music. Home: Kubelikova 481, 500 03 Hradec Králové Czech Republic Office: Charles U Fac of Medicine, Simkova 870, 500 01 Hradec Králové Czech Republic

CESA, MICHAEL PETER, cardiologist, consultant; b. N.Y.C., Sept. 4, 1946; s. John J. and Catherine R. (Brunialti) C.; m. Barbara A. Perrelli, June 21, 1969; children: Christopher, Thomas, Gregory, Meredith. BS, Manhattan Coll., 1968; MD, SUNY, Bklyn., 1972. Diplomate Am. Bd. Internal Medicine, Am. Bd. Cardiovasc. Disease. Intern dept. medicine Kings County Hosp., Bklyn., 1972-72, med. resident dept. medicine, 1973-75, cardiology fellow dept. medicine, 1975-77; clin. asst. prof. medicine SUNY, Stony Brook, 1994—; pres. med. staff St. Johns Episcopal Hosp., Smithtown, N.Y., 1984, chief cardiology, 1997—; pres., COO North Suffolk Cardiology Assocs., Stony Brook, 1984—. Fellow Am. Heart Assn. (coun. on clin. cardiology), Am. Coll. Cardiology, Am. Coll. Chest Physicians; mem. Am. Soc. Nuc. Cardiology (cert.). Roman Catholic. Avocations: collecting toy trains, baseball cards, hi fi stereos, sports. Office: North Suffolk Cardiology 2500 Nesconset Hwy Ste 1 Stony Brook NY 11790-2561

CESARI, EDUARD, physics educator, materials science researcher; b. Barcelona, June 6, 1951; s. Joan and Mercè (Aliberch) C.; m. Mercè Bohigas, Jan. 4, 1975; children: Albert, Joan. Grad. in physics, U. Barcelona, 1974, PhD in Physics, 1979. Lectr. U. Politècnica Catalunya, Barcelona, 1979-82; assoc. prof. U. Barcelona, 1983-86; prof. U. Illes Balears, Palma de Mallorca, 1986—, head dept. physics, 1990-94, vice chancellor for rsch., 1995-99. Contbr. numerous articles to profl. jours.; patentee in field. Mem. Materials Rsch. Soc., European Materials Rsch. Soc., Soc. Catalana de Fisica, Real Soc. Española de Fisica. E-mail: eduard.cesari@vib.es. Office: U Illes Balears, Crtra Valldemossa KM 7.5, 07071 Palma de Mallorca Spain

CESARIO, ROBERT CHARLES, franchise executive, consultant; b. Chgo., Apr. 6, 1941; s. Valentino A. and Mary Ethel (Kenny) C.; m. Susan Kay DePoutee; children: Jeffrey, Bradley. B.S. in Gen. Edn., Northwestern U., 1975; postgrad. in bus. adminstrn. DePaul U., 1975. Mgr. fin. ops. Midas Internat. Corp., Chgo., 1968-73; dir. staff ops. Am. Hosp. Supply Corp., McGaw Park, Ill., 1973-76; v.p. Car X Svc. Systems Inc., Chgo., 1976-78, v.p. oil svcs., 1983-84; v.p. Chicken Unltd. Enterprises Inc., Chgo., 1978-83; pres. Growth Strategies, Inc., 1984-87; pres. CEO Lube Pro's Internat., Inc., 1987—. Served with USMC, 1960-62. Office: Lube Pros Internat Inc 1630 W Colonial Pkwy Palatine IL 60067-1209

CESARO, LUIGI, member European parliament. Mem. European Parliament, Italy, 1999—; mem. Group of the European People's Party (Christian Democrats) and European Democrats; mem. com. on regional policy, transport and tourism; substitute mem. com. on agrl. and rural devel.; vice-chmn. delegation for rels. with Australia and new Zealand. Office: Palazzo Comit, Via Roma 157, I-80029 S Antimo Italy*

CESAROTTI, VITTORIO, industrial engineer; b. Rome, Apr. 8, 1968; s. Enrico and Evelina (Fortini) C. Grad. Mech. Engring., U. Rome; PhD in Indsl. Mgmt., U. Naples, Federico II. Cons. Olivetti, Rome, 1990-92, Fiat, Naples, Italy, 1992, Technova, Naples, 1993-94, European Found. for Quality Mgmt., Brussels, 1994-95; rschr. U. Rome Tor Vergata, 1996-99, prof. indsl. engring., 1999—; ptnr. Gens Cons., Rome, 1996—. Author: (books) La Produzione Snella, 1992, The European Way for Excellence. E-mail: cesarotti@uniroma2.it. Office: U Rome/Dept Mech Engring, Via di tor Vergata 110, 00133 Roma Italy

CESPEDES, J. MARTIN, chemical engineer; b. Medellin, Antioquia, Colombia, Oct. 2, 1948; s. Jenaro Cespedes and Elvira Galeano; m. Esther Herrera, June 14, 1978; children: Andres, Manuel. Chem. engr. degree, Univ. de Antioquia, Medellin, 1974; postgrad., Sch. Tech. Chemistry, Prague, Czechoslovakia, 1982. Quality control head Andercol, S.A., Medellin, 1974-77, R&D head, 1977-84, tech. dir., 1984-94; chemistry and phys. chemistry prof. U. de Medellin Politécnico Jaime Isaza, 1994—. Mem. Am. Soc. for Quality Control, Am. Chem. Soc., Colombian Chem. Engrs. Soc. Avocations: music, cyclism. E-mail: cesher@epm.net.co. Home: Carrera 43C No 4 Sur-143, Casa 132, Medellin Colombia

CESZKOWSKI, DANIEL DAVID, financial analyst; b. Geneva, Dec. 9, 1954; s. Ignaz Ceszkowski and Veronika Noemi (Goldstein) Blanc; children: Axel, Jeremy, Leah. Lic. Sci. Commerce & Industry, U. Geneva, 1977; MBA, Internat. Mgmt. Devel. Inst., Lausanne, Switzerland, 1985. Systems engr. Honeywell Bull, Geneva, 1977-80; dir. Corinfo S.A., Geneva, 1980-81; systems analyst Hewlett Packard, Meyrin, Switzerland, 1981-84; fin. cons. Merrill Lynch Internat., Inc., Geneva, 1986-89; pvt. practice fin., investment advisor Geneva, 1988—; portfolio mgr. Great Pacific Capital S.A., Geneva, 1989-90; fin. mgr. Fed. Express Switzerland, Geneva, 1990-94; bd. dirs. Telos Holding AG, Inc., Mievda S.A., Geneva.

CETE, MÜKERREM, surgeon, health facility administrator; b. Ankara, Turkey, Oct. 19, 1955; s. Celâl and Nevin (Gürsoy) C.; m. Nesrin Evirgen, May 14, 1985; children: Onur, Mine. MD, Med. Faculty Ankara (Turkey), 1985. Resident gen. surgery Ankara (Turkey) Numune Hosp., 1981-85, registrar, 1985-88, sr. registrar, 1988-92, dep. chief clinic, 1992—; head rsch. team clin. rsch. oral presentation Nat. Surg. Congress, 1996. Contbr. 54 articles to med. jours. Recipient Disting. Physician award Ministry Health, 1986, 1991, Very Satisfactory Cert. Coun. Europe, 1997. Mem. Turkish Surg. Assn., Assn. Gastroenterology, Assn. Turkish Colon and Rectal Surgery, Assn. Turkish Endoscopic and Laparoscopic Surgery, Turkish-Am. Assn. Avocations: philately, swimming. Fax: 90-312 3103460. E-mail: mcete@yahoo.com. Home: 60 Sokak No 4/2-A Emek, 06510 Ankara Turkey Office: Ankara Numune Tng & Rsch Hosp, Talatpasa St, 06100 Ankara Turkey

CETÍN, ANTON, artist; b. Bojana, Croatia, Sept. 18, 1936; arrived in Can., 1968, naturalized, 1973; s. Tomo and Terezija (Grcic) C.; m. Milka Katalenic, Dec. 16, 1962; 1 child, Dawn Antonia. Diploma, Sch. Applied Arts, Zagreb, 1959; masters diploma, Acad. Fine Arts, Zagreb, 1964. One-man shows include Art Gallery Hamilton, 1978, Mus. Arts and Crafts, Zagreb, 1986, Beverly Gordon Gallery, Dallas, 1987, Nat. and Univ. Libr., Zagreb, 1988, Oberhausmuseum, Passau, Germany, 1990, Sony Plaza Art Gallery, Tokyo, 1991, Gallery 7, Hong Kong, 1993, Museo del Chopo, Mexico City, 1993, Salas Nactionales de Cultura-Palais de Glace, Buenos Aires, Argentina, 1994, Museo Mcpl. de Arte J.C. Castagnino, Mar del Plata, Argentina, 1995, Mus. and Gallery Ctr., Zagreb, 1996, Art Gallery, Split, Croatia, 1998; group exhbns. include Mus. Modern Art, Crakow, Poland, 1972, Brockton Art Ctr., 1974, Nat. Libr. France, 1978, 2d Cabo Frio Internat. Print Biennial, Brazil, 1985, Del Bello Gallery, Toronto, 1986, 87, 89, 90, Crespano del Grappa, Italy, 1988, Nat. Libr. Can., 1990, Art Asia, 1993, Olympic Games, Atlanta, 1996, Shenzhen Fine Art Inst., Shenzhen Mus. Modern Art, Shanghai, 2000, others; represented in permanent collections at nat. librs. France, Croatia, Can., U.N., Japan and Salas Nacionales-Palais de Glace, Buenos Aires, Museo del Chopo, Mexico City, Vatican, Italy, Mus. Arts and Crafts, Mus. and Gallery Ctr., Zagreb, Can. Cultural Ctr., France, others; author: Eve and the Moon, 1975; co-author: Amerika Croatan America, 1988. Named Artist of Yr., Can. Croatian Artists Soc., 1986. Home: PH3, 5 Greystone Walk Dr, Scarborough, ON Canada M1K 5J5 Studio: 37 Hanna Ave 13A, Toronto, ON Canada M6K 1W9

CETRULO, JERRY, artist, sculptor; b. Jersey City, N.J., Sept. 10, 1941; s. Gerardo Cetrulo and Eva Augustine; m. Renate Cetrulo, 1961 (div.); children: Michael, Mark, Heidi; m. Barbara Cetrulo, Aug. 2, 1998. Customer engr. IBM, Cranford, N.J., 1967-99; ret., 1999; instr. Am. Woodcarving Sch., Wayne, N.J., 1992—. With U.S. Army, 1959-62. Avocations: woodcarving, painting. E-mail: njcarver@worldnet.att.net. Home: 18 Cayuga Ave Rockaway NJ 07866-1012 Office: Am Woodcarving Sch 21 Pompton Plains Xrd Wayne NJ 07470-6326

CETTO, ANA MARIA, physicist, researcher; b. Mexico City, Mexico, Feb. 18, 1946; d. Max L. and Catarina (Kramis) C.; m. Luis Fernando de la Peña, Dec. 13, 1968; 1 child, Carolina. Physics Diplomate, U. Nac. Autonoma de Mexico, Mexico City, 1967, MS in Physics, 1970, PhD in Physics, 1971; MA in Biophysics, Harvard U., 1969. Cert. physics. Assoc. lectr. UNAM, Mexico City, 1966-69, assoc. rschr. Inst. Fisica, 1970-84, lectr., 1969—, rsch. prof., 1984—, dean faculty scis., 1978-82, head theoretical physics dept., 1991-93; chair project Mus. on Light Sci. Ctr., 1994-96; vis. prof. London U., 1971-72, 93-94, U. Paris VI, 1977-78, U. Rome, 1984-85; sci. advisor UNESCO, Paris, 1996—, cons. world conf. on sci., 1998—. Co-author: The World of Physics (in Spanish), 3 vols., 1977, 90, The Quantum Dice, 1996; editor: Scientific Publications in Latin America, 1995, Scientific Journals in Latin America, 1999; editor Revista Mexicana de Fisica, 1990-92; contbr. articles to profl. jours. Mem. exec. coun. Internat. Network Engrs. and Scientists, Germany, 1992-98; mem. press com. Internat. Coun. Sci. Unions, Paris, 1993-99; v.p. Third World Orgn. Women in Sci., Trieste, Italy, 1993-99; vice-chair Com. on Sci. and Tech. in Developing Countries, 1995-97; v.p. Interciencia Assn., 1997-2000; mem. UN Univ. Coun., 1998-99. Nat. rsch. fellow Ministry Edn., Mexico, 1984—. Fellow Third World Acad. Scis.; mem. Pugwash Confs. (mem. coun. 1992—, chair exec. com. 1997—, Nobel Peace prize 1995), Mexican Physics Soc. (adv. coun. 1992—), Mexican Acad. Scis., Am. Phys. Soc., Coun. on Ideas. Home: Retorno Cerro Del Agua 98, 04360 Mexico City Mexico Office: Inst de Fisica UNAM, Apartado Postal 20-364, 01000 Mexico City Mexico

CEVETILLO, GERRI MARIE, manufacturing company executive; b. Bronx, N.Y., May 27, 1946; d. Gennaro Dominick and Jean Marie (Cucchiello) Luizzi; m. Louis Anthony Cevetillo, Aug. 6, 1967 (div. May 1978); children: Christopher Dante, Michael Gennaro. Mgr. mktg. J.F. Jeleko & Co., Armonk, N.Y., 1978-85; mgr. sales and mktg. Coltene Whaledent Dental Lab. Tech., Mahwah, N.J., 1985-90; gen. mgr. UL-TRONICS, Mahwah, 1990—, Dentronix, Ivyland, Pa., 2000—; cons. infection control Assn. Barber Bds. Am., 1996—; spkr. in field. Cons. Milady Publs., 1998-99, Hair Internat., 1998-99, Pivot Pt. Internat., 1999; contbr. articles to profl. jours. Mem. Am. Beauty Assn. (chair mktg./pub. rels. com. 1997-99, bd. dirs. 2000—), Nat. Interstate Coun. State Cosmetology Bds. (mem. infection control com. 1994—), Nail Mfrs. Coun. (v.p. 1996-98, pres. 1999-2000). Avocations: travel, sailing, public speaking. Office: UL-TRONICS Mahwah NJ 07430-0526 also: Dentronix Ivyland PA

CEYHUN, OZAN, member of the European Parliament; b. Adana, Turkey, Oct. 10, 1960. Mem. European Parliament, Russelsheim, Germany, 1999—; mem. Group of the Greens/European Free Alliance, European Parliament; mem. com. on citizen's freedoms and rights, justice and home affairs; substitute mem. com. on petitions; mem. delegation to the EU-Turkey Joint Parliamentary Com. Office: Ferdinand-Stuttmann, StraBe 13, D-65428 Russelsheim Germany

CÉZARD, FRANCOIS, financial executive; b. Paris, Mar. 26, 1962; m. Florence David. Maitrise Bus. Adminstrn., U. de la Sorbonne, Paris, 1983; diploma, Inst. D'Etudes Politiques, Paris, 1985; Dess Controle de Gestion, U. Dauphine, Paris, 1985. Fin. analyst Barclays Bank, Paris, 1987-88; bond trader Meeschaert Rousselle, Paris, 1989; primary dealer Banque Indosuez, Paris, 1990-92, structured fin., 1993-96; CFO La Henin Vie Life Ins., 1996—. Lt. jr. grade French Navy, 1985-86. Avocations: organ, opera, golf. Home: 13 rue Monsieur, 75007 Paris France Office: Banque Indosuez, Banque Indosuez LaHenin Vie, 14 rue Roquepine, 75008 Paris Cedex 08, France

CHA, JAE-HO, psychology educator; b. Yuchoo, Republic of Korea, Mar. 1, 1934; s. Suk-Hwan Cha and Hyang-Ja Yi; m. Choon-Ja Ryu, Oct. 24, 1969; children: Guang-Ho Cha, Oona Cha. BA, Seoul Nat. U., Republic of Korea, 1956, MA, 1962; MA, U. Ariz., 1967; PhD, UCLA, 1971. Lectr., rschr. Seoul Nat. U., 1962-64; lectr. Calif. State U., L.A., Dominguez Hills, 1971; asst. prof. psychology Seoul Nat. U., 1974-79, assoc. prof. psychology, 1979-84, prof. psychology, 1984—; dir., mem. com. Korean Social Sci. Rsch. Coun., Seoul, 1977—; chmn. com. promotion acad. rsch., Ministry Edn., Seoul, 1998—, mem. ctrl. edn. adv. bd., 1994-98, grant proposal evaluation com., 1995-96. Author: Psychology of Culture Design, Theoretical Contributions: Collected Work, 1999; translator: Culture and Organizations, 1995 (Free Econ. Culture award 1996). V.p. Ctr. Healthy Family Action, Seoul, 1996—; pres. Nat. Conf. Univ. Student Guidance Ctrs., Seoul, 1987-88. With Army of Republic of Korea (attached to U.S. 7th Inf. Divsn.), Dongduch'on. Fulbright scholar, 1964-66. Fellow Korean Psychol. Assn. (pres. divsn. social psychology 1977-78, 80-82; pres. 1982-83); mem. Sigma Xi. Avocations: tennis, fishing. Home: Arum'maul 515-1001, Yimae-Dong Pundang-Ku, Sung'nam, Kyunggi-Do 463-060, Republic of Korea Office: Seoul Nat U Dept Psych, San 56-1 Shinrim-Dong, Kwanak Seoul 151-742, Republic of Korea

CHA, JIN SOON, linguistics educator; b. Seoul, Dec. 26, 1945; s. Kyun Sang and Kyung Do Cha. BA, H.U.F.S., 1968; MA, Korea U., 1970, York U., 1977; postgrad., York U., 1978; PhD, McGill U., 1983. R.A. York U., 1975-78; teaching asst. McGill U., 1978-81; prof. Sookmyung Women's U., Seoul, 1983-98; Korean coord. U. So. Colo., Pueblo, 1994—; rschr. Washington Coll., Chestertown, 1996—; mentor McGill U., Montreal, 1997—; interviewer Korea Travel Bur., 1987; chmn. English com. Nat. Bur. Ednl. Evaluation, Korea, 1990; examiner Korean Govt., 1992; dep. gov. ABIRA; dep. dir. gen. (Asia) IBC; sec. RSCG, 1968; rschr. Pres.'s Coun. Econ. and Sci. Advisors, Korea, 1975; dir. Korean Lang. Rsch. Inst., 1998—; pres. Songsan Pub. Co., 2000—. Author: Linguistic Cohesion in Texts: Theory and Description, 1993; editor: Current Papers of Noam Chomsky, 1997, Current Papers of M.A.K. Halliday, 1994, Before and Towards Communication Linguistics: Essays by Michael Gregory and Associates, 1995, TOEFL, 1987-91, Essays, 1994, rev. edit., 1999. With Korean Army, 1974. Fulbright scholar; recipient Brit. Ambs. award, H.U.F.S. Fellow IBA (life, life patron, Order of Internat. Ambs.), ABI (life, rsch. fellow); mem. MLA, IWWP (hon.), IBC (hon. adv. coun.), Linguistic Assn. Can. and U.S., Linguistics Assn. Gt. Britain, Linguistic Soc. Am. (life), World Comm. Assn. (life), N.Y. Acad. Scis., Nat. Geographic Soc., United Bible Socs., Internat. Living (life), Philological Soc., Internat. Sash Academia, Poetry Soc., Planetary Soc., Exec. Club Internat., Oxford Club (life CLA, ALS). Presbyterian. Avocations: fishing, calligraphy, sports, photography, mountaineering. Office: Korean Lang Rsch Inst, 89-45 Sinjeong-dong, Yangcheon-gu Seoul 158-849, Republic of Korea

CHA, SE DO, internist; b. Seoul, Korea, Dec. 17, 1942; came to U.S., 1966, naturalized, 1977; s. Young Sun and Hee Joo (Chang) C.; m. Elsa Jane Greene, Dec. 21, 1974; 1 child, Elizabeth. M.D., Yon Sei U., 1966. Diplomate Am. Bd. Internal Medicine. Intern Presbyn.-U. Pa. Med. Ctr., Phila., 1966-67; resident in medicine Harrisburg (Pa.) Hosp., 1967-70; chief resident in medicine Roger Williams Gen. Hosp., Providence, 1970-71, cardiologist, 1973-75; fellow in cardiology Deborah Heart and Lung Center, Browns Mills, N.J., 1971-73, cardiologist, 1975—, asst. dir. adult cardiac catheterization lab., 1975-86, dir., 1987—; clin. asst. prof. U. Medicine and Dentistry N.J., 1987; instr. Brown U., Providence, 1973-75. Contbr. articles to profl. jours. Fellow ACP, Soc. for Cardiac Angiography; mem. AMA, Fedn. Clin. Rsch., Am. Heart Assn. Office: Deborah Heart and Lung Ctr Trenton Rd Browns Mills NJ 08015

CHA, SOYOUNG STEPHEN, mechanical engineer, educator; b. Inchon, Korea, June 25, 1944; came to U.S., 1974; s. Sang O. and Sook S. (Lee) C.; m. Young W. Park, Sept. 4, 1974. BS, Seoul (Korea) Nat. U., 1969; MS, Mich. State U., 1976; PhD, U. Mich., 1980. Project rsch. engr. Northrop corp., Rsch. Triangle Park, N.C., 1979-84; prof., dir. opto-mech. lab. U. Ill., Chgo., 1984—; spkr. in field. Guest editor Optics Lasers Engring., 5 vol., 1992; contbr. over 100 articles to profl. and tech. jours. Dept. of Energy fellow, 1987, NASA fellow, 1994, USAF fellow, 1996. Fellow Internat. Soc. Optical Engring. (conf. chair, co-chair 1991—), ASME (tech. com. 1983-87), Am. Soc. Aeronautics and Astronautics (tech. com. 1994-97, 1998—), Visu-

alization Soc. Japan (conf. co-chair 1998). Methodist. Achievements include patent for holographic velocimetry. Office: U Ill Chgo 2039 ERF 842 W Taylor St Chicago IL 60607

CHABANE, MOHAMMED HABIB, allergist, immunologist; b. Oran, Algeria, June 22, 1956; s. Mohamed and Khedidja (Elagoune) C.; m. Micheline Musitelli, Apr. 16, 1986; children: Soumeya, Mohamed Nasr-Eddine. Diploma in Immunology and allergy, U. Paris VI, 1982, PhD in Immunology, 1991. Tng. in immunology, hematology and genetics U. Paris VI, 1982-85, asst. prof., 1999—; rsch. mgr. Rothschild Hosp., Paris, 1982-98; advisor med. affairs Allerbio Labs., 2000—. Contbr. articles to med. jours., including Allergy, Jour. Allergy and Clin. Immunology, Clin. exptl. Immunology, Am. Jour. Contact Dermatis. Mem. French Soc. Allergy, French Med. Doctors from Maghreb. Avocations: chess, hiking, bowling, table tennis. Email: habib.chabane@rth.ap-hop-paris.fr. Home: 11 Ave Gallieni, 98300 Epinay Sur Seine France Office: Rothschild Hosp, 33 Blvd de Picpus, 75012 Paris France

CHABARD, JEAN-PAUL, engineer, researcher; b. Clermont-Fed, Auvergne, France, Nov. 18, 1959; s. J. Louis and Marie P. (Doly) C.; m. Nicole F. Bevillard, Dec. 22, 1984; children: Guillaume, Anne F., Lucie. Engr., Ecole Cen des Arts et Mfg, Paris, 1983. Rschr. EDF, Chatou, France, 1986-90; prof. Ecole Cen. des Arts et Mfg., Chatenay, France, 1987, Ecole Nat. des Ponts et Chausses, Paris, 1988; mgr. EDF, Chatou, 1990-97, 1997—. Contbr. articles to profl. jours. Recipient Cray France prize Computational Mechanics, 1988. Fellow Soc. de Math. Appliquees a L'Industrie; mem. Internat. Assn. for Hydraulic Rsch. (chmn. divsn. II). Home: 7 route de Croissy, 78110 Le Vesinet France Office: EDF-Lab Nat D'Hydraulique, EDF, 6 Quai Watier, 78400 Chatou France

CHABOCHE, JEAN-LOUIS, mechanical engineer; b. Blanquefort, France, Feb. 3, 1945; s. André and Thérese (Dugravier) C.; m. Solange Pestel, July 4, 1969; children: Laetitia, Patricia, Sebastien, Marika, Benjamin. MS, U. Orsay, France, 1967; PhD, Paris VI U., 1978. Rsch. engr. Nat. Office of Aerospace Studies and Rsch., Chatillon, France, 1972-80, group chief, 1980-86, divsn. head, 1986, rsch. dir., 1992—; assoc. prof. Ecole Ctrl., Paris, 1983-96, U. Tech., Compiegne, France, 1986-95, Troyes, France, 1996. Author: Mechanics of Solid Materials, 1990; mem. editl. bd. Internat. Jour. Plasticity, 1986-96, Internat. Jour. Damage Mechanics, 1992. Pres. Cath. Family Assn., Chevreuse, France, 1989-96. Recipient Caméré prize French Acad. Sci., 1980, Silver medal Ctr. Nat. Rsch. Sci., 1999. Roman Catholic. Office: ONERA, 29 Ave Division Leclerc, 92 320 Chatillon France

CHABOT, DIANE, telecommunications executive; b. Montreal, Que., Can.; d. Andre and Henriette (Beauchemin) C. Student, Univ. Montreal-Coll. Sophie, Barat, Montreal, Univ. Montreal, Hautes Etudes Commerciales. Apptd. v.p. regional performance Bell Can., Toronto, 1983-84; pres. Info Pro, Toronto, 1984-87, v.p. pub. affairs, 1987-88; v.p. pub. rels. Nortel, 1988-90; v.p. logistics Bell Can., 1990; group v.p. logistics Bell Can., Toronto, 1993-95; pres. DCM Enterprises, 1996—; chmn. Mt. Pleasant Group; chmn. bd. Ont. Film Devel. Corp., 1992-98; pres. Ont./Rhone-Alpes Com., 1990-97. Gala com. mem. 1994 Can. Olympic Assn.; chmn. The Bishop Strachan Sch., 1993-97; dir. conf. of Ind. Schs., 1993-95; vice-chmn. Premier's Coun. on Health, Well-being and Social Justice, 1991-94; mem. Adv. Com. on Cultural Industries Sectoral Strategy, 1993-94; dir. Arts Found. Greater Toronto, 1988-96; bd. dirs. Toronto 2008 Olympic Bid, War Child Can., Invest in Kids Found., Can. Stage. Office: 268 Spadina Rd, Toronto, ON Canada M5R 2VI

CHABOT, JEAN-LUC, political science educator; b. Noyal sur Vilaine, France, July 2, 1944; s. Jean and Jeanine (Fremont) C. Student, U. Paris, 1965-67; LLM, U. Grenoble, France, 1969, Superior Degree in Pub. Law, 1970, D in Polit. Sci., 1978. Lectr. U. Pierre Mendes France, Grenoble, 1970-81, sr. lectr., 1981—, dir. Human Rights Ctr. Faculty of Law. Author: Nationalism, 1986, 4th edit., 1996, History of Political Thought XIX-XX, 1988, Social Doctrine of the Catholic Church, 1989, 2d edit., 1992, Introduction to Politics, 1991, Social Science Methods, 1995. Roman Catholic. Avocations: philosophy, tennis, nordic skiing. Office: U Pierre Mendes France, Faculty of Law, Grenoble France

CHABRA, OM PARKASH, heavy electrical equipment company executive; b. Village Kumhariwala, Punjab, Pakistan, Oct. 8, 1936; arrived in India, 1947; s. Ram Lal and Kaushalya Chabra; m. Sudesh Bhatla, Oct. 11, 1968; children: Sonali, Anuj. Ed., Ropar, India, 1954; B of Elec. Engring., Delhi (India) U., 1958; diploma in Russian, Kiev U., 1962; PhD in Tech., Moscow Power Inst., 1965. Chartered engr., India. Mgr. BHEL, Hardwar, India, 1975-77, sr.mgr., 1977-82, dep. gen. mgr., 1982-88; gen. mgr. BHEL, Hardwar, 1988-94; advisor, cons. Bharat Heavy Electric Ltd., Hardwar, 1994-97, R&D mgr./in charge Generator Rsch. Inst., 1987-94; advisor Lakshmanan Isola Pvt. Ltd., Bangalore, 1998—; chmn. insulation com. Bur. Indian Standards, New Delhi, 1980—; mem. nat. subcom. for com. 15, CIGRE, New Delhi, 1988—. Contbr. articles to profl. jours. Chmn. Soc. Soviet Ed. Profls., Hardwar, 1989-90. Fellow Inst. of Engrs., Inst. Standards Engrs.; mem. IEEE (sr.), N.Y. Acad. Scis. (exec. com. 1989—). Avocations: gardening, listening to music, science fiction, outings, mountaineering. Fax: 91-8113-71166. Home: BHEL, 1 Type VI Sector 5-A, 249 403 Hardwar 249 403, India Office: Lakshmanan Isola Pvt Ltd, 5 Primrose Rd, Bangalore 560 025, India

CHABRILLAT, SABINE, geophysicist, researcher; b. Toulouse, France, Dec. 16, 1968; came to U.S., 1996; d. Jean-Claude and Anne-Marie (Lacheze) C. BS in Physics, U. Toulouse, 1990, MS, 1991, PhD in Spectral Geology, 1995. Post doctoral fellow U. Colo., Boulder, 1996-97; rsch. assoc. U. Colo., 1997-2000. Developer procedures identification and mapping of expansive clay soils in Colo. using field spectrometry and hyperspectral data.

CHACHOLIADES, MILTIADES, economics educator; b. Omodos, Limassol, Cyprus, June 22, 1937; came to U.S. 1962; s. Panagis Themistokli and Hariclea (Miltiadou) C.; m. Mary Modenos, Dec. 30, 1962; children: Lea, Marina, Linda. BA, Sch. Bus. & Econs., Athens, 1961; PhD, MIT, 1965. Asst. prof. NYU, 1965-68; vis. assoc. prof. UCLA, 1970; assoc. prof. econs. Ga. State U., Atlanta, 1968-71; prof. econs. Ga. State U., 1971-73, rsch. prof. econs., 1973-87, chmn. dept. econs., 1986-89, prof. econs., 1989-93; prof. emeritus Ga. State U., Atlanta, 1995—; prof. econs. U. Cyprus, Nicosia, 1993—, rector, 1995-99. Author: The Pure Theory of International Trade, 1973, Brit. edit. 1974, Internat. Monetary Theory and Policy, 1978, internat. student edit., 1978, International Trade Theory and Policy, 1978, internat. student edit., 1978, Principles of International Economics, 1981, Spanish edit., 1982, Malaysian edit. 1988, Microeconomics, 1986, Greek edit., 1989, Microeconomics: Instructors Manual, 1986, internat. econs. edit., 1990, International Economics: Instructors Manual, 1990; contbr. articles to profl. jours.; editorial advisor Greek Econ. Rev. Athens Sch. fellow, Am. Hellenic Ednl. and Welfare Fund fellow, 1962-64, MIT Sloan rsch. assistantship, 1962-63, econs. fellow, 1963-64, others. Mem. Royal Econ. Soc., Ea. Econ. Assn., Greek Econ. Assn., So. Econ. Assn., Am. Econ. Assn. Office: U Cyprus Dept Econs, PO Box 20537, Nicosia TT1678, Cyprus

CHACKO, SAMUEL, association official; b. Mezhuveli, Kerala, India, Aug. 1, 1942; came to U.S., 1970; s. Chanda Pillai and Sosamma (Cheriyan) C.; m. Omana Chellimalayil George, May 21, 1979; children: Roshen Samuel, Renee Susan. BA in Econs., U. Kerala, 1963, MA in History, 1966, MA in Polit. Sci., 1968; BA in Social Sci., Olivet Nazarene U., Kankakee, Ill., 1971; MA in Comm., Govs. State U., 1974; postgrad., U. Ill., Chgo., 1981-86. Cert. in gerontology, cmty. nutrition. Dir. dept. aging Kankakee Land Community Action Agy., 1972-76; head sr. citizens dept. Oakland-Livingston Human Svcs. Agy., Pontiac, Mich., 1976-78; dir. Benton Harbor (Mich.) Area Parks and Recreation Bd., 1978-79; program analyst Ill. Migrant Coun., Chgo., 1980-84; dir. energy svcs. Community and Econ. Devel. Assn. Cook County, Inc., Chgo., 1985—; mem. Ill. State Commerce Comm. Task Force on Rewriting Utility Svc. Rules, 1995—, Ill. State Energy Assistance Program Working Group, 1991-93. Vice chmn. State Assn. Dirs. Foster Grandparent Program, 1974-76; chmn. com. on bylaws Nat. Dirs. Assn. Foster Grandparent Programs; bd. dirs. Kankakee-Will County Citizens Coun., 1975-76, NAACP, 1973-76. Office: Cmty and Econ Devel Assn Cook Cty Inc 208 S Lasalle St Ste 850 Chicago IL 60604-1000

CHACON, GRACIELA GOMEZ, chemistry educator, consultant; b. Quezaltepeque, El Salvador, Apr. 20, 1925; d. Santos Chacon and Ana Josefa Gomez Araujo. Chemist pharmacist, U. El Salvador, 1952; degree in nutrition-dietetics, Nutrition Inst. C.Am. & Panama, Guatemala, 1961; degree in food scis., nutrition, U. Louvain, Belgium, 1972; degree in food contaminants, Ctrl. Food Technol. Rsch Inst., Mysore, India, 1979; meritorious hon. diploma, U. El Salvador, 1986. Cert. nutritionist-dietist. Nutritionist INCAP, 1965-67; nutritionist Nutrition Inst. C.Am. and Panama, Social Welfare and Pub. Health Ministry, San Salvador, El Salvador, 1962-64, 68-71; head biochemistry dept. Sch. Pharmacy U. El Salvador, San Salvador, 1973-85, prof. biochemistry Sch. Pharmacy, 1974-89, dean Sch. Pharmacy, 1986-87; coord. biochemistry Sch. Medicine U. Evangélica, San Salvador, 1990—; dir. food chemistry Sch. Medicine, U. Evangélica, San Salvador, 1990—; thesis cons. Sch. Pharmacy, U. El Salvador, San Salvador, 1982—, Sch. Pharmacy, U. Alberto Masferrer, San Salvador, 1996. Bd. dirs. Universitarian Women Assn., San Salvador, 1964, Pharm. Women Assn., San Salvador, 1974; v.p. Cen. Am. Nutritionist Assn., San Salvador, 1972-74; rep. Univ. Superior Coun., U. El Salvador, 1974; currency collaborator Piety Ministry, San Salvador, 1993—. Fellow State Dept. U.S., Kans. U., 1957-58, Internat. Orgn. for Atomic Energy, Sao Paulo, Brazil, 1974, FAO, Mysore, 1987-88, Honoring Women Pharmacist of World, FIP, 1998. Fellow López Labs. Pharm. (diploma 1995); mem. Nutrition-Dietetics Assn. El Salvador (founder, diploma 1976), Pharm. Assn. (honor diploma 1985); mem. Am. Chem. Soc. Avocations: classical music, reading, writing, playing with children, aerobics. Home: 2a Calle Poniente # 7-9, Santa Tecla El Salvadore Office: U Evangélica, 49a Av Sur y Av Olimpica, San Salvador El Salvador

CHACON ARIAS, VIRGINIA, national archives director; b. Alajuela, Costa Rica, July 16, 1956; d. Roberto and Virginia (Arias) Chacón Murillo; m. Mario Blanco; 1 child, Alejandro; m. Alvaro Morales, Nov. 1991; 1 child, Ana María. Licentiate in Laws, U. Costa Rica, 1979, Diploma in Archival Studies, 1982. Head notarial archives Nat. Archives of Costa Rica, San José, 1978-80, subdir., 1980-91, gen. dir., 1991—; prof. archival legislation U. Costa Rica, San José, 1987—, Nat. Archives of Costa Rica, 1990—. Editor Revista del ARchivo Nacional, 1991—; contbr. articles to profl. jours. Collaborator Sch. for the Rehab. of Children with Cerebral Palsy, San José. Recipient scholarship O.A.S., 1989. Mem. Asociaciú332n Latinoamericana de Archivos (sec. 1992-95, v.p. 1995-97, pres. 1999—), Colegio de Abogados de Costa Rica (sec. of bd. 1992-93), Inst. Costarricense de Derecho Notarial (v.p. 1992—). Roman Catholic. Office: Archivo Nacional de Costa Rica, PO Box 41-2020, Zapote Costa Rica

CHADBOURNE, JOHN FREDERICK, JR., engineering executive; b. Detroit, Oct. 10, 1948; s. John Frederick and Wilhelmina (Williams) C.; m. Deborah Ann Bennett, Aug. 13, 1968. BSChemE, U. Fla., 1970, MS in Engring., 1971, PhD in Environ. Engring., 1977. Staff cons. environ. sci. and engring. U. Fla., Gainesville, 1971-74; proprietor Environ. Cons. Svcs., Orlando, Fla., 1974-77; corp. environ. mgr. Lafarge Corp., Dallas, 1977-87, dir. environment and indsl. hygiene, 1992-94; v.p. tech. and regulatory affairs Systech Environ. Corp., Dallas, 1987-92; pres. Chadbourne Environment and Safety Programs Inc., Dallas, 1994—; vis. prof. environ. engring. so. Meth. U., 1997—. Author (book chpt.) Burning Hazardous Waste in Cement Kilns, 1989, 97. Mem. AAAS, AIChE, Air and Waste Mgmt. Assn. (com. chair 1977-97), N.Y. Acad. Scis. Achievements include having secured permits to replace fosssil fuel with hazardous waste on many cement kilns. Avocations: scuba diving, trekking, Wu Chi Chuan. Office: CESP Inc 13106 Roaring Springs Ln Dallas TX 75240-5643

CHADDERTON, LEWIS TAYLOR, physicist, educator, researcher; b. May 22, 1938; s. A. Chadderton; m. June Carding, Aug. 15, 1959; 3 children. BSc, U. Durham, Eng., PhD; DSc, Gonville and Caius Coll., Cambridge, MA. Rsch. fellow in physics Cavendish Lab. Cambridge U., 1963-64, demonstrator in physics, 1964-66, asst. dir. rsch. physics and chemistry of solids, 1964-66; mem. tech. staff N.Am. Corp., 1966-70; prof. physics H.C. Orsted Inst., U. Copenhagen, Denmark, 1970-79, head dept. physics, 1972-79, Regius prof. physics, 1980—; chief div. chem. physics CSIRO, 1980-87, chief rsch. scientist, 1987-98; adj. prof. physics Rsch. Sch. Phys. Scis., Australian Nat. U., Canberra, 1987—. Author: Radiation Damage in Crystals, 1965, Fission Damage in Crystals, 1968, Radiation Effects, 1969, also articles. Mem. Monash Club, Nat. Press Club, Cambridge Union, Oxford and Cambridge Club (London). Avocations: writing, communication of science, viticulture. Office: Wolverley, RMB 296, Gundaroo Rd, Bungendore NSW 2621, Australia

CHADEAU, EMMANUEL VINCENT, historian; b. Paris, Jan. 13, 1956; s. André Louis and Yvonne (Humbert) C.; m. Madeleine Mazars, May 29, 1981 (div. 1994); children: Mathilde, Cécile. Agregé d'histoire, Ecole Normale Superieure, 1979; doctor, U. Paris, 1986. Rsch. fellow CNRS, Paris, 1981-85, CNRS/IHTP, Paris, 1985-88; prof. Charles de Gaulle U., Lille, France, 1988—; jr. mem. Inst. Univ. France, Paris, 1993-98; dir. Inst. d'Histoire de l'Industrie, Paris, 1993-97, Ministry of Def., 1994—; editl. fellow Smithsonian Instn. Press, Washington, 1992-96; rsch. exec. IFRESI/CNRS, 1991-95. Editor Entreprises et Histoire, 1992; co-editor Les Cahiers de Science, 1992-96; editor: Ambition Technologique: Naissance d'Ariane, 1995; author: Saint-Exupery, 1994, Thermoz 2000, Dream and Power, A Century of Aviation, 1996. Mem. Aero-Club de France. Avocations: detective stories, swimming, oenology, aviation. Home: 44 Rue de la Sabliere, 92600 Asnieres France Office: Charles de Gaulle Univ, BP149, 59653 Villeneuve D'ascq France

CHADEGANIPOUR, MOSTAFA, science educator, microbiologist, mycologist; b. Isfahan, Iran, June 15, 1956; s. Abolfath Chadeganipour and Sedigheh Moosavi; m. Shahy Nilipour. BS, Isfahan U., 1979; MA, Clark U., 1986, PhD, 1990; MSPH, Tehran (Iran) U., 1981. Instr. Med. Tech. Inst., Isfahan, 1981-84, Worcester State Coll., 1987; microbiology technologist St. Vincent Hosp., Worcester, 1990-91; asst. prof. dept. mycology Isfahan U. Med. Scis., 1991-96, assoc. prof., 1996-2000; dir. Kashani Hosp. Lab., Isfahan, 1992-94. Author: Scientific Writing, 1994; contbr. over 50 articles to profl. jours., including Mycoses, Mycologia; editor-in-chief Jour. Med. Rsch., 1991—. Mem. Am. Soc. Clin. Pathologists, Med. Mycol. Soc. Ams. Avocation: fishing, mountaineering. Office: Mycology Dept, Isfahan U Med Scis, Isfahan Iran

CHADWICK, ALAN FRANK, adult educator; b. London, Jan. 13, 1935; s. Frank and Nora May (Widdowson) C.; m. Angela Elizabeth Scott, July 30, 1963; children: Anna, Alison, Mark. MEd, U. Manchester, 1971, PhD, 1976. Diploma in Adult Edn. Tchr. East Suffolk/Local Edn. Authority, Eye, Eng., 1960-61; head of sch. dept. Warwickshire/Local Edn. Authority, Sutton Coldfield, Eng., 1961-70; further edn. coll. lectr. Countyborough Edn. Authority, Derby, Eng., 1970-74; lectr. U. Nottingham, Eng., 1974-78; sr. lectr., dir. Ctr. for Commonwealth European Edn. Devel. U. Surrey, Guildford, Eng., 1978-99; cons. Swedish Internat. Devel. Agy., Stockholm, 1993-96; chmn. nat. adv. edn. com. for edn., tng. and devel. City and Guilds, London, 1986-98, vice chmn. policy com. for edn. and tng., 1996-99; mem. edn. adv. com. Victoria and Albert Mus., London, 1994—; mem. internat. edn. adv. com. Victoria and Albert Mus., London, 1994—; mem. internat. grad. faculty, CBL, Brisbane, Australia, 1997—. Author: The Role of the Museum and Art Gallery in Community Education, 1980; co-author: The Training of Adult Educators/Internat. Ency. of Edn., 2d edit., 1994; coeditor: The Training of Adult Educators in Western Europe, 1991, Museums and the Education of Adults, 1996, Museums and Adults Learning: Perspectives From Europe, 2000. Fellow Royal Soc. Arts (hon), City and Guilds London Inst. (vice-chmn. policy com., edn. and training 1996-99, councillor 1996—); mem. Edn. for Devel. (trustee 1990-2000). Avocations: horse, equestrian pursuits, music, museum and gallery vis., films. Home: Martlets Kings Ln, Mare Hill, Pulborough West Sussex RH20 2EB, England Office: U Surrey Stag Hill, Sch Edn, Guildford Surrey GU2 5XH, England

CHADWICK, DEREK JAMES, foundation administrator; b. Carshalton, Surrey, Eng., Feb. 9, 1948; s. Dennis Edmund and Ida (Kay) C.; m. Susan Reid, Dec. 20, 1980; children: Andrew John, Frederick Mark. BA in Chemistry, Oxford U., 1969, BSc, 1970, MA, 1972, D Philosophy, 1972. ICI fellow Cambridge U., 1972-73; Prize fellow Magdalen Coll., Oxford U., 1973-77; Royal Soc. European exch. fellow Eidgenössische Technische Hochschule, Zurich, Switzerland, 1975-77; lectr., sr. lectr., reader Liverpool U., 1977-88; vis. prof. U. Alsace, Mulhouse, France, 1988; dir. The Ciba Found. (now named The Novartis Found.), London, 1988—; coun. mem. Louis Jeantet Found., Geneva, 1988-98, Assn. Med. Rsch. Charities, London, 1991—; vice-chmn., 1994— mem. steering com. Scientists Inst. for Pub. Info., N.Y.C., 1989-96; vis. prof. U. Trondheim, Norway, 1996—. Editor 37 books; author 100 papers and chpts. in sci. jours. and books. Fellow Royal Soc. Chemistry; mem. Am. Chem. Soc., Worshipful Soc. Apothecaries London, Hague Club Dirs. European Founds. (sec. 1993-97). Avocations: music, gardening, skiing. Office: The Novartis Found, 41 Portland Pl, London W1N 4BN, England

CHADWICK, OWEN, historian, educator; b. Bromley, Kent, Eng., May 20, 1916; s. John and Edith (Horrocks) C.; m. Ruth Hallward, Dec. 28, 1949; children: Charles, Stephen, Helen, Andre. BA, Cambridge U., Eng., 1939, LittD (hon.); LittD (hon.), Bristol U., 1939, London U., Columbia U., East Anglia U., Eng., U. Kent, Eng., Leeds U., Eng.; DD (hon.), Oxford U., St. Andrews U., Wales U.; LLD (hon.), Aberdeen U. Ordained priest to Ch. of Eng. Prof. ecclesiastical history Cambridge U., 1958-68, Regius prof. modern history, 1968-83, master of Selwyn Coll., 1956-83, vice chancellor, 1969-71; pres. Brit. Acad., London, 1981-85. Author: The Victorian Church (2 vols.), 1966-70; The Popes and European Revolution, 1981, History of the Popes 1830-1914, 1998, Acton on History, 1998, Created Knight; author 19 books on church history. Decorated Order of Merit (England); recipient Wolfson prize for historical writing, 1981. Office: Cambridge U, Dept History, Cambridge CB3, England

CHADWICK, RUTH FELICITY, bioethics educator; b. Birmingham, Eng., Oct. 16, 1951; d. Edwin and Beatrice Maud (Checkley) C. BA with hons. class I, St. Hugh's Coll., Oxford, Eng., 1974, BPhil, 1976, DPhil, 1980; LLB, U. London, 1986. Lectr. in philosophy Trinity Coll., Oxford, Eng., 1976-77; lectr. in ancient philosophy St. Hugh's Coll., Oxford, 1979; lectr. in philosophy Liverpool U., 1979-80; sr. lectr. in law, moral philosophy St. Martin's Coll., Lancaster, 1981-86; lectr. in philosophy U. Wales, Cardiff, 1987-93, dir. Ctr. Applied Ethics, 1989-93; prof. moral philosophy U. Ctrl. Lancashire, Eng., 1993-2000, head Ctr. Profl. Ethics, 1995-2000; prof. U. Lancaster, 2000—; mem. ethics com. Genome Orgn., 1995—, vice-chair, 1999—; mem. Nat. Com. Philosophy, Eng., 1995—, stds. and ethics com. U.K. Ctrl. Coun. for Nursing, Midwifery and Health Vis., 1989-96, Food Ethics Coun., 1998—; vis. prof. U. Tsukuba, 1998; hon. prof. U. Lancaster, 1998-99. Co-author: Ethics and Nursing Practice, 1992; co-author, editor: Ethics, Reproduction and Genetic Control, 1987, rev. ed., 1992; editor: (4 vol. collection) Kant: Critical Assessments, 1992; co-editor: The Right to Know and the Right Not to Know, 1997; editor-in-chief: Encyclopedia of Applied Ethics, 4 vols., 1998; contbr. articles to profl. jours. Mem. dept. health working party on priority setting, London, 1996; evidence House of Commons select com. sci. and tech., London, 1995. Recipient grants to coordinate Euroscreen European Commn., 1994, Project on Biotechnology, 94, Euroscreen II, 1996, Projects for European Parliament, Scientific and Technol. Options Assessment Unit, 1997, 98. Fellow Royal Soc. Arts; mem. Soc. Applied Philosophy, Assn. Legal and Social Philosophy, Internat. Assn. Bioethics, European Soc. for Philosophy of Medicine and Health Care. E-mail: r.chadwick@lancaster.ac.uk.

CHADZELEK, THOMAS, software engineer; b. Völklingen, Saarland, Germany, Mar. 29, 1969; s. Manfred and Ursula (Dilling) C. M in Computer Sci., U. Saarland, Saarbrücken, Germany, 1995, PhD in Computer Sci., 1998. Sci. asst. U. Saarlande, Saarbrücken, 1995-99; software engr. SAP Retail Solutions, St. Ingbert, Germany, 1999—. Avocation: cycling. E-mail: thomas.chadzelek@sap.com.

CHAFFEE, STEVEN, communications educator; b. South Gate, Calif., Aug. 21, 1935; s. Edwin W. and Nancy M. Chaffee; m. Sheila McGoldrick, 1966 (div. 1987); children: Laura, Adam, Amy; m. Debra Lieberman, 1989; 1 child, Eliot.; BA in History, U. of Redlands, 1957; MS in Journalism, UCLA, 1962; PhD in Comm., Stanford U., 1965. News editor Angeles Mesa News-Advertiser, L.A., 1957; reporter Santa Monica (Calif.) Evening Outlook, 1962; from asst. prof. to full prof. U. Wis., Madison, 1965-81; prof. comm. Stanford (Calif.) U., 1981-2000, U. Calif., Santa Barbara, 2000—. Author: Communication Concepts 1: Explication, 1991; co-editor: handbook of Communication Science, 1987; co-author: Television and Human Behavior, 1978; editor: Political Communication, 1975. Lt. (j.g.) USN, 1957-61. Fellow Internat. Comm. Assn. (pres. 1981); mem. Assn. for Edn. in Journalism and Mass Comm. Democrat. Avocation: hiking. Office: U Calif Dept Comm Santa Barbara CA 93106

CHAFFIN, WILLIAM MICHAEL, lawyer; b. Memphis, Jan. 27, 1947; s. William Emmett and Mary (DeWeese) C.; m. Paula Gayle Young, Apr. 5, 1969; children: Katherine Young, Courtney DeWeese. BBA, U. Miss., 1969, JD, 1972. Bar: Miss. 1972, U.S. Dist. Ct. (no. and so. dists.) Miss. 1972, U.S. Dist. Ct. Ark. 1992. Assoc. Maynard, Fitzgerald & Bradley, Clarksdale, Miss., 1972-73; ptnr. Maynard, Fitzgerald, Bradley & Chaffin, Clarksdale, 1973-74; assoc. Holcomb, Dunbar, Connell, Merkel & Tollison, Clarksdale, 1975-78; ptnr. Holcomb, Dunbar, Connell, Chaffin & Willard, Clarksdale, 1978—; counsel to bd. dirs. United So. Bank, Clarksdale, 1982-90, N.W. Miss. Regional Med. Ctr., Clarksdale, 1988—; former chmn. Commn. Continuing Legal Edn. for State of Miss. Mem. Dem. exec. com. Coahoma County, Miss., 1976-84; counsel to Coahoma County Bd. Suprs., 1984-94. Fellow Miss. Bar Found.; mem. ABA, Miss. Bar Found., Miss. Defense Lawyers Assn., Assn. County Bd. Attys., Miss. State Bar. Episcopalian. Avocations: hunting, scuba diving, golf. Home: 111 Cypress Ave Clarksdale MS 38614-2603 Office: Holcomb Dunbar Connell Chaffin & Willard 152 Delta Ave Clarksdale MS 38614-4212*

CHAHAL, SUKH MOHINDER SINGH, human genetics researcher, educator; b. Khokhar, India, July 24, 1955; s. Ghuman Singh and Bhagwant Kaur (Bhattal) C.; m. Ramanjit Kaur Brar, July 4, 1993; 1 child, Sarah. BSc, Delhi U., 1974, MSc in Anthropology, 1976; PhD in Human Genetics, U. Newcastle, Eng., 1981. Pool officer Coun. Scientific Indsl. Rsch., Delhi U., 1982-83; lectr. Punjabi U., Patiala, India, 1983-88; rsch. scientist Punjabi U., Patiala, 1988-93, lectr., 1993-95, reader, 1995—. Field and rsch. worker in populations of N.W. India, especially in the Himalayas. Jr. rsch. fellow D.S.T./Govt. of India, Delhi, 1976; Commonwealth scholar U.K. Govt., 1978. Home: Q-6 Campus, 147 002 Patiala Punjab, India Office: Punjabi U, 147 002 Patiala Punjab, India

CHAHINE, YOUSSEF, film director. Dir. (films): Daddy Honest, 1950, Nile boy, 1951, Dark Waters, 1956, Cairo Station, 1958, The Ring Seller (Order of Lebanon-Beyrouth), 1965, The Choice, 1970 (Grand Prize Carthage-Tunisia), Alexandria Why (Silver Bear-Berlin Festival), Cairo...as told by Chahine, 1991, Destiny, 1997 (Cannes Film Festival award), numerous others. Office: Misr Internat Films, 35 Champollion St, Cairo Egypt

CHAHINIAN, A(RAM) PHILIPPE, oncologist; b. Paris, June 21, 1942; came to U.S., 1974; m. Marjorie Ellen; 1 child, Michael J. B., Buffon Coll., Paris, 1960; MD, Paris U., 1969. Diplomate Am. Bd. Internal Medicine, Am. Bd. Med. Oncology. Intern, resident Paris Univ. Hosps., France, 1968-74; fellow noeplastic diseases Mt. Sinai Sch. Medicine, N.Y.C., 1974-76, asst. prof., 1976-79, assoc. prof., 1980-88; prof. clin. medicine Coll. Physicians and Surgeons Columbia U., N.Y.C., 1990-92; prof. dept. medicine Mt. Sinai Sch. Medicine, N.Y.C., 1995—, prof., 1995—; adj. prof. dept. neoplastic diseases Mt. Sinai Sch. Medicine, N.Y.C., 1992-95. Author: Lung Cancer, 1976; author (with others) of books; contbr. articles to profl. jours. Lt. Med. Corps, French Army, 1970. Rsch. grantee Nat. Cancer Inst., 1984. Fellow Am. Coll. Physicians; mem. Am. Soc. Clin. Oncology, Am. Assn. Cancer Rsch., Am. Fedn. Clin. Rsch., N.Y. Acad. Scis. Achievements include research in treatment of various cancers including lung cancer, asbestos related cancers, and mesothelioma by transplantation of human cancers into mice. Office: Mt Sinai Sch of Medicine Dept NeoPlastic 1 Gustave L Levy Pl New York NY 10029-6500

CHAHL, LORIS AVRIL, pharmacologist, educator; b. Goondiwindi, Australia, Aug. 16, 1940; d. Ralph Murray and Beatrice May (Mathers) Sherrington; m. Jaswant Singh Chahl, Jan. 7, 1966; children: Javaan Singh, Thari Janet. BSc, U. Queensland, 1960, MSc, 1966, PhD, 1970, DSc, 1990. Tutor in physiology U. Queensland, Brisbane, Australia, 1960-70, tutor in pharmacology, 1974-79; postdoctoral fellow U. Edinburgh, Scotland, 1971-72; lectr. in pharmacology U. Papua New Guinea, Port Moresby, 1972-73;

from lectr. to sr. lectr. U. Newcastle, Australia, 1979-90, assoc. prof., 1990—. Contbr. articles to profl. jours. Mem. Internat. Assn. for Study of Pain, Internat. Neuropeptide Soc., Australian Neurosci. Soc., Australasian Soc. for Clin. and Exptl. Pharmacologists and Toxicologists, Australian Physiol. and Pharmacol. Soc. Office: U Newcastle, Faculty Medicine, Newcastle 2308, Australia

CHAI, CHENG SHENG, mechanical and electrical research and development engineer, educator; b. Singapore, Jan. 13, 1965; s. Kim Hooi and Fook Yew (Chan) C.; m. Moy Choon Ng, Mar. 28, 1992. Diploma in mech. engring., Ngee Ann Poly., Singapore, 1985; AD in Electronics, ICS, Singapore, 1991; BSc in Engring. Tech., Pacific Western U., U.S., 1993; PhD in Computer Sci., Pacific Western U., 1997; MSEE, LaSalle U., 1996; MSc in Precision Engring., Nanyang Tech. U., Singapore. Technician Matsushita Tech., Singapore, 1988-90, asst. engr., 1990-91, engr., 1991-93, sr. engr., 1993-97, prin. engr., engring. mgr., 1997-98, mgr., 1997—. Sgt. specialist Singapore Armed Forces, 1986-87. ICS scholar, 1990. Mem. ASME, IEEE, Nat. Soc. Profl. Engrs., Singapore Armed Forces Reservist Assn., Soc. of Tribologists and Lubrication Engrs., Inst. of Engrs. (Singapore), Singapore Inst. Mgmt., The Microelectronics Soc., Internat. Biog. Assn. (dep.-dir.-gen.). Avocations: reading, sky-watching, experimenting, jogging, interior designing. Home: Block 869 # 06-349, Street 83, 730869 Singapore Singapore Office: Matsushita Tech (S) Pte Ltd, 285 Jalan Ahmad Ibrahim, 639931 Singapore Singapore

CHAI, JOHN CHEE-KIONG, mechanical engineering educator; b. Kota-Kinabalu, Sabah, Malaysia, July 16, 1962; s. Kong Lim and Alice C.; m. Stacy Chai, Aug. 31, 1991. BSME, U. Windsor, 1986; MSME, U. Wis., 1989; PhD, U. Minn., 1994. Rsch. asst. U. Wis., Milw., 1986-89, tchg. asst., 1987-89; rsch. asst. U. Minn., Mpls., 1989-94, tchg. asst., 1989-91; rsch. engr. Innovative Rsch. Inc., Mpls., 1994-95; asst. prof. Tenn. Tech. U., Cookeville, 1995-2000, assoc. prof., 2000—; cons. Ford Motor Co., Detroit, 1994, Sandia Nat. Lab., Alberqueque, 1994, Synergetic Tech. Inc., Delmar, N.Y., 1996—. Contbr. articles to profl. jours. Fellow to the Czech Republic Nat. Rsch. Ctr., 1996; Rsch. grant NASA Hdqtrs., Washington, 1996; named Mech. Engring. Faculty of the Yr., Tenn. Tech. U., 1996; recipient Grad. of Last Decade award U. Wis., Milw., 1999. Mem. ASME, AIAA, Phi Kappa Phi, Sigma Xi, Pi Tau Sigma (hon.). Office: Tenn Technol U Dept Mech Engring 115 W 10th St Cookeville TN 38505-0001

CHAI, ZHEN-MING, electrical engineering educator, researcher; b. Ninghai, China, Aug. 17, 1933; s. Yi-Zhong Chai and Su-Juan Teng; m. Hua-Xian Zhou, May 15, 1963; children: Zhi-Hong, Li-Hong, Ning. BSc, Shanghai Chiao-Tung U., Shanghai, 1955; PhD, Academia Sinica, Beijing, 1962. Designer Tianjin Radio Factory, China, 1955-57; rsch. assoc. Inst. Electronics Academia Sinica, Beijing, 1963-77, assoc. prof. dept. head, 1978-79; rsch. fellow Tech. U. Aachen, Germany, 1979-81; rsch. prof., dep. dir. Academia Sinica, 1982-83, prof., inst. dir., 1984-91, prof., chmn. sci. coun., 1992-98. Editor: Advances in Circuits and Systems, 1985; contbr. over 100 articles to tech. publs. Fellow IEEE (sr., chmn. Beijing chpt. 1988—), China Assn. Med. Imaging Tech. (v.p. 1984—), China Inst. Electronics (dir. 1993—); mem. N.Y. Acad. Scis. Home: Zhong-Guan-Cun, Bldg 811 Apt 604, Beijing 100080, China Office: Inst Electronics Academia Sinica, PO Box 2702, Beijing 100080, China

CHAIBI, MOHAMED BEN M'BAREK, military officer, researcher; b. Tazouguert, Errachidia, Morocco, Apr. 28, 1956; s. M'Barek Chaibi and Sfia Azzedine; m. Malika Assif, Feb. 9, 1985; children: Leila, Loubna. B of mathematics, Mil. Royal Acad., Meknes, Morocco, 1976; deck officer, Naval Royal Acad., Casablanca, Morocco, 1979; telecommunication engr., Telecom. Inst., Rabat, Morocco, 1988; profound studies diploma, Hassan II U., Casablanca, 1990, D of electronics, 1993. Cert. telecom. engr. Deck officer Moroccan Royal Navy, Casablanca, 1979-88; chief telecom. officer Moroccan Royal Navy, Rabat, 1988-89, 92-93; chief electronic dept. Moroccan Royal Navy, Casablanca, 1989-92, dir. Telecom. Sch., 1993-94; chief studies and planning officer Moroccan Royal Navy, Rabat, 1994—. Contbr. articles to profl. jours. Moslem. Avocations: painting, sports. Home: BP 6321 Rabat Instituts, Rabat Morocco

CHAIDRON, ANDRE, Belgium government official; b. Brussels, Oct. 4, 1935; s. Louis and Ida (Ister) C.; m. Dewolf, July 12, 1985; 1 child, Caroline. Student pub. schs., Belgium. Asst. to stockbroker Brussels, 1954-55; with Soc. Nat. Distbn. Eau, Brussels, 1955-56; exec. agt. Ministry Fin. - Tax Svc., Brussels, 1957-60; gen. auditor Ministry Fin. 6th Treasury, Brussels, 1960-2000. Decorated chevalier Order of Leopold, officier Order of Leopold II, Medal 1st Class, Civic Cross 1st Class, comdr. of Crown Order (Belgium). Mem. Acacias Tennis Club (pres.), Internos (pres.), T. Invest (pres.). Home: Ave du Pois de Senteur 60, Brabant 1020 Brussels Belgium Office: Ministry Fin, Ave des Arts 30 Brabant, 1040 Brussels Belgium

CHAIKA, YURI, federal official; b. 1951. Prosecutor gen.; 1st dep. sec. Security Coun., 1999; min. of justice Moscow, 1999—. Office: Ministry of Justice, 4 Vorontsovo Pole, Moscow Russia*

CHAIKEN, JAN MICHAEL, government agency official; b. Phila., Oct. 19, 1939; s. Joseph and Evelyn Fox C.; m. Marcia R. Rosenblum, June 16, 1963; children: David, Shama. BS in Physics, Carnegie-Mellong U., 1960; PhD in Math., MIT, 1996. Asst. prof. Cornell U., Ithaca, N.Y., 1964-67; rsch. assoc. MIT, Cambridge, 1967-68; sr. math. Rand, Santa Monica, Calif., 1968-84; sr. scientist Abt Assocs., Inc., Cambridge, Mass., 1984-94; dir. Bur. of Justice Stats. U.S. Dept. of Justice, Washington, 1994—. Recipient Pres.'s award Inst. for Opers. Rsch. and the Mgmt. Scis., Balt., 1999, O.J. Hawkins award for Innovative Leadership and Outstanding Contbns. in Criminal Justice Info. Systems, SEARCH, Sacramento, Calif., 1999. Mem. Am. Soc. Criminology, INFORMS, Sigma Xi. E-mail: chaikenj@usdoj.gov. Office: Bur Justice Stats 810 Seventh St NW Washington DC 20531-0001

CHAIKEN, SHELLY L., psychologist, educator; b. Washington, June 7, 1949; d. Bernard and Harriet H. C. BS, U. Md., 1971; MS, U. Mass., 1975, PhD, 1978. Asst. prof. U. Toronto, 1977-82; from asst. to assoc. prof. psychology Vanderbilt U., Nashville, 1982-85; from assoc. prof. to prof. NYU, N.Y.C., 1985-89, prof., 1989—. Co-author: (with A. Eagly) The Psychology of Amituler, 1993; co-editor: (with Y. Trope) Dual Process Theory in Social Psychology, 1999; contbr. 45 articles to profl. jours. Grantee NSF, 1983-86, Nat. Inst. Mental Health, 1988-92, 1993-95; fellow Ctr. for Advanced Study in Behavioral Scis., Palo Alto, Calif., 1997-98. Fellow Am. Psychology Assn., Am. Psychological Soc., Soc. Personality Soc. Psychology, Soc. Experimental Social Psychology (pres. 1983). Democrat. Avocations: gardening, tennis, reading fiction, dog walking. E-mail: chaiken@nyu.edu. Office: Dept Psychology NYU 6 Washington Pl New York NY 10003-6603

CHAILLY, RICCARDO, conductor; b. Milan, Feb. 20, 1953; s. Luciano and Anna Maria (Motta) C.; ed. conservatories Giuseppe Verdi, Milan, Perugia. Asst. to condr. La Scala, Milan, 1972-74; debut as condr. with Chgo. Opera, 1974, at La Scala, 1978; Brit. operatic debut at Covent Garden, 1979; Brit. concert debut London Symphony Orch., Edinburgh Festival, 1979; Met. Opera debut, 1982; engagements with major orchs. including Vienna and Berlin philharm. orchs., Concertgebouw, Orch. de Paris, London Symphony Philharm., Royal Philharm., Cleve. Orch., Chgo. Symphony Orch., Phila. Orch., N.Y. Philharm. Orch.; condr. Salzburg Festival, 1984-86; prin. guest condr. London Philharm., 1982-85; chief condr. Teatro Comunale, Bologna, Italy, 1986-93; chief condr. Berlin Radio Symphony Orch., 1982-89; chief condr. Royal Concertgebouw Orch., Amsterdam, 1988—, Orch. Sinfonica di Milano Guiseppe Verdi, 1998—; recs. for Decca records. Decorated grand ufficiale della Repubblica Italiana, knight of the Order of the Netherlands Lion, Cavaliere Di Gran Croce (Italia), Abrogino d'Oro, Comune Milano. Mem. Royal Acad. Music London (hon.). Office: care Jacob Obrechtstraat 51, 1071 KJ Amsterdam The Netherlands

CHAIN, BOBBY LEE, electrical contractor, former mayor; b. Hattiesburg, Miss., Sept. 19, 1929; s. Zollie Lee and Grace (Sellers) C.; m. Betty Sue Green, June 30, 1967; children: Robin Ann, Laura Grace, Bobby Lee, John Webster. BS, U. So. Miss., Hattiesburg, 1974; DBA (hon.), William Carey Coll., Hattiesburg, 1983. Chief electrician Miss. Power & Light Co., Natchez, 1950-53; asst. to gen. supt. atomic energy plant Allegany Electric Co., Oak Ridge, 1954-55; owner, chmn. bd. Chain Electric Co., Hattiesburg, 1955, Chain Lighting & Appliance Co., Hattiesburg, 1960; owner, pres. Chainco, Inc., oil properties, Hattiesburg, 1974—; bd. dirs. Deposit Guaranty Nat. Bank, Jackson; adv. dir. Deposit Guaranty Nat. Bank, Hattiesburg, 1965-00; mem. Interstate Oil Compact Commn., 1972—; mem. nat. adv. coun. SBA, 1966-67; bd. dirs. Miss. Econ. Coun., 1991-93; mayor city of Hattiesburg, 1980-85; adv. dir. Am. South Bank, 2000. Past mem., past pres. Miss. Trustees Instns. Higher Learning; past mem. So. Regional Edn. Bd., Mississippians for Quality Edn.; past chmn. Commn. on Efficiency in Govt., Miss. Econ. Coun.; mem. Miss. State Workforce Devel. Coun.; chmn. Pearl River County Dist. Workforce Coun.; past bd. dirs. Pub. Edn. Forum of Miss.; mem. commissioning com. USS John C. Stennis CVN-74 Aircraft Carrier, 1995. With U.S. Army, 1950-51, Korea. Recipient Disting. Svc. award U. So. Miss., 1976, Hub award, 1979, Continuous Outstanding Svc. award, 1980, Liberty Bell award Forrest County Bar Assn., 1980, Svc. to Edn. award Phi Delta Kappa, 1980, Disting. Citizen award Pine Burr Area Coun. Boy Scouts Am., 1995; named to Hall U. So. Miss., Miss. Bus. Hall of Fame, 1994; Bobby L. Chain Tech. Ctr. named in his honor; Bobby L. Chain Hattiesburg Mcpl. Airport named in his honor; Paul Harris fellow Rotary Internat., 1990. Mem. Newcomen Soc. N.Am., U. So. Miss. Alumni Assn. (Outstanding Svc. award 1972, Sales and Mktg. Man of Yr. award 1981), Hattiesburg C. of C. (past dir.), Miss. Bus. Roundtable, Kiwanis, Hattiesburg Country Club (past pres.), U. So. Miss. Century Club, Shriners, Omicron Delta Kappa, Beta Gamma Sigma. Baptist. Home: 312 6th Ave Hattiesburg MS 39401-4294 Office: PO Box 2058 Hattiesburg MS 39403-2058

CHAIT-MAGEN, SUZANNE, psychotherapist; b. Albany, N.Y.; d. Samuel and Ida (Rosenthal) C.; m. C. Magen. BA, Skidmore Coll., Saratoga, N.Y.; MSW, Adelphi U., 1978; grad., Psychoanalytic Tng. Inst., N.Y.C., 1982. Cert. social worker, N.Y.; cert. fellow inmanaged care, N.Y., Fla.; cert. psychoanalytic psychotherapy; cert. managed care in mental health care; cert. public procurement buyer. Med. social work supr. Div. Med. Rev.-Med. Assistance Program, N.Y.C., 1987-88; asst. dir. pub. affairs N.Y.C. Med. Assistance Program, 1988-89; contract specialist N.Y.C., 1990-94; dir. staff devel. and tng. bur. Sch. Health Program N.Y.C. Dept. Health, 1994—; pvt. practice psychotherapy N.Y.C., 1982—. V.p., chmn. beautification com. 82nd St. Assn., N.Y.C., 1983-84. Fellow N.Y. State Soc. Clin. Social Workers; mem. NASW. Avocations: travel, cross-country skiing, dancing, sailing, photography.

CHAJDA, IVAN, mathematics educator, researcher; b. Přerov, Czechoslovakia, Dec. 13, 1946; s. Jan Hampl and Božena C.; m. Věra Studeníková, Sept. 24, 1971; children: Martin, Radek. MSc, Palacky U., Olomouc, Czechoslovakia, 1970; PhD, Masaryk U., Brno, Czechoslovakia, 1974, DrSc, 1985. Scientific worker Meopta Přerov, 1970-85, chief tech. devel., 1985-86; prof. math. Palacky U., Olomouc, Czech Republic, 1987—, dir. PhD studies, 1991—. Author: Algebraic Theory of Tolerance Relations, 1991; contbr. articles to Algebra Universalis, 1984, 85, 87, 94, 96; referee: Mathematica Revs., 1975—, Zentralblatt Math., 1975—. Grant linkage NATO, Brussels, 1993, grantee Grant Agy. Czech Republic, Prague, 1994. Mem. Am. Math. Soc., Union Czech Mathematicians. Avocations: cycling, hiking, cross-country skiing. Home: Třída 17 Listopad 22, 750 00 Přerov Czech Republic Office: Palacky U Dept Algebra, Tomkova 40, 779 00 Olomouc Czech Republic

CHAKAROV, ANTON GOTCHEV, barrister; b. Simeonovgrad, Haskovo, Bulgaria, June 14, 1930; s. Gotcho Siderov and Tianka Zhekova (Popova) C.; m. Irina Dimitrova Siarov, Jan. 29, 1961; children: Temenuga, Antonova, Guergana Antonova. MS in Law, U. Sofia, 1952. Journalist Septemvri Newspaper, St. Zagora, 1952-59; barrister St. Zagora, 1959-75, 92—; lawyer Building Co., Dimitrovgrad, 1975-92; lawyer, cons. OverGaz, St. Zagora, 1997—; internat. chess referee Internat. Chess Fedn., 1965. Author: 1600 Selected Aphorisms and Jokes, 1999. Recipient Barrister award Ministry of Legis., 1976. Mem. Nat. Chess Fedn., Info. Globe Assn. (founder 1997). Avocations: chess, bridge, checkers, collecting autographs of chess masters and world champions, world travel. Home: 51 Gen Gurko St, 6000 Stara Zagora Bulgaria Office: 9B Metody Kusev St, 6000 Stara Zagora Bulgaria

CHAKRABARTI, BIKAS KANTA, nuclear physicist; b. Calcutta, India, Dec. 14, 1952; s. Bimal Kanja and Pratima (Roychowdhury) C.; m. Kaberi Banerjee, May 9, 1978; children: Kalyan-Sundar, Anindya-Sundar. BSc, Calcutta U., 1971, MSc, 1973, PhD, 1979. From lectr. to prof. Saha Inst. Nuclear Physics, Calcutta, 1983—. Fellow Indian Acad. Scis. Office: Saha Inst Nuclear Physics, 1/AF Bidhannagar, 700064 Calcutta India

CHAKRABARTI, PARTHASARATHI, electronics engineer, researcher; b. Dakshin Barasat, India, Jan. 18, 1958; s. Prafulla Kumar and Deepti (Bhattacharyya) C.; m. Runa Chakrabarti, Jan. 22, 1987; 1 child, Ishita. BS in Physics with honors, U. Calcutta, India, 1978, B of Tech. in Radiophysics & Electronics, 1981, M of Tech. in Radiophysics & Electronics, 1983; PhD in Electronics Engring., Banaras Hindu U., Varanasi, India, 1988. Asst. lectr. Birla Inst. Tech. and Sci., Pilani, India, 1984; rsch. assoc. Banaras Hindu U., 1984-86; asst. prof. Birla Inst. Tech., Ranchi, India, 1986-88, assoc. prof., 1988-93; reader Banaras Hindu U., 1993-97, prof., 1998—; prin. investigator rsch. project Min. Sci. and Tech., Govt. India. Author: Analog Communication Systems, 1998, Principles of Digital Communication, 1999; contbr. articles to profl. jours. Recipient Nat. scholarship Govt. of India, 1974, Gold medal Vidyasagar Coll., Calcutta, 1978, Vis. fellowship Indian Nat. Sci. Acad., New Delhi, 1993, Vis. fellowship Sci. and Engring. Rsch. Coun., Govt. of India, 1994. Fellow Optical Soc. India; mem. IEEE, Instn. Engrs. India (life), Indian Soc. Tech. Edn. (life). Hindu. Achievements include research in photodetectors for application in integrated optoelectronic circuits; development of computer aided models of optoelectronic devices; fabrication and development of metal-insulator semiconductor capacitor for optically controlled applications for the study of radiation tolerance of semiconductor denus and circuits. Office: Banaras Hindu U Inst Tech, Dept Electronic Engring, 221 005 Varanasi India

CHAKRABARTI, SUBHASH RANJAN, dairy technology educator, researcher, consultant; b. Jagannathpur, Bangladesh, Jan. 1, 1945; arrived in India, 1947; s. Sukhesh Ranjan and Binodini (Bhattacharjee) C.; m. Anita Bhattacharjee, Feb. 12, 1977; 1 child, Saurabh. BSc, Calcutta U., 1965; BSc in Dairy Tech., Punjab U., 1969, MSc in Dairying, 1971, PhD in Dairying, 1976. Rsch. tech. asst. Nat. Dairy Rsch. Inst., Karna, 1971-76; asst. mgr., chief quality control Dudhsagar Dairy, Mehsana, 1976-78, Mother Dairy, Calcutta, 1978-82; reader, head dept. dairy tech. Bidhan Chandra Krishi Viswavidyalaya, Mohanpur, 1982-96, West Bengal U. of Animal and Fishery Scis., Mohanpur, 1995-98. Fellow Indian Coun. of Agrl. Rsch., 1969, 71. Mem. Assn. of Food Scientists and Technologists (India). Home: B-7/277, Kalyani Nadia 741235, India Office: W Bengal U Animal/Fish Scis, 68 Kshudiram Bose Sarani, Calcutta 700037, India

CHAKRABARTI, SUBIR KUMAR, economics educator; b. Shillong, India, Jan. 21, 1958; s. Sunil and Maya C.; m. Tuhina Chakrabarti, Feb. 14, 1989; children: Anisha, Devika, Sharmistha. BSc (hon.), Northeastern Hill U., Shillong, Meghalya, 1976; MA in Econ., Jawaharlal Nehru U., New Delhi, India, 1978; PhD in Econ., U. Iowa, 1985, MS in Math., 1985. Jr. rsch. fellow Presidency Coll. Calcutta, India, 1979-81; grad. asst. U. Iowa, Iowa City, 1981-85; asst. prof. Ind. U., Purdue U., Indpls., 1985-91, assoc. prof., 1991-98, prof., 1998—. Author: Games and Decision Making, 1999; contbr. articles to profl. jours. Mem. Econometric Soc., Phi Beta Kappa. Hindu. Avocations: tennis, jogging, culture. E-mail address: imxl100@iupui.edu. Home: 700 Warren Rd Apt 20-1F Ithaca NY 14850-1230 Office: Indiana U Purdue U Indpls 425 University Blvd Indianapolis IN 46202-5148

CHAKRABARTI, SUBRATA KUMAR, marine research engineer; b. Calcutta, India, Feb. 3, 1941; came to U.S., 1964, naturalized, 1981; s. Asutosh and Shefali C.; m. Prakriti Bhaduri, July 23, 1967; children: Sumita, Prabal. BSME, Jadavpur U., Calcutta, India, 1963; MSME, U. Colo., 1965, PhD, 1968. Registered profl. engr., Ill. Asst. engr. Kuljian Corp., Calcutta, 1963-64, Simon Carves Ltd., Calcutta, 1964; instr. engring. U. Colo., Boulder, 1965-66; hydrodynamicist CB&I Tech. Svcs. Co. (formerly Chgo. Bridge and Iron Co.), Plainfield, Ill., 1968-70, head analytical group, 1970-79, dir. marine rsch., 1979-95, dir. structural devel., 1995-96; pres. Offshore Structure Analysis, Inc., Plainfield, 1996—; vis. prof. U.S. Naval Acad., Annapolis, Md., 1986, 88, Indian Inst. Tech., Madras, 1996; presenter in field. Author: Hydrodynamics of Offshore Structures, 1987, Nonlinear Methods in Offshore Engineering, 1990, Offshore Structure Modeling, 1994; editor: Fluid Structure Interaction in Offshore Engineering, 1994; tech. editor Applied Ocean Rsch., 1998—; mem. editl. bd. Applied Ocean Rsch., Marine Structures, Topics in Engring., Advances in Fluid Mechanics series; assoc. editor Energy Resources Tech.; contbr. articles to profl. jours. and chpts. to books; patentee in field. Recipient Jadavpur U. Gold medal, 1963; U. Colo. fellow, 1968; named Outstanding New Citizen, 1981-82. Fellow AAAS, ASCE (publ. com. waterway divsn., James R. Cross Gold medal 1974, Freeman scholar 1979), ASME (exec. com., editor jour. offshore mechanics and arctic engring. divsn. 1986-96, chmn. divsn., 1987-88; awards com. 1983-96, tech. session devloper, chmn. 1983—, chmn. tech. program com. 1988-89, Ralph James award 1984, co-editor proc. internat. symposium, Offshore Mechanics and Arctic Engring. achievement award 1990, Ten Paper award 1991, Disting. Svcs. award 1998), NAS (design group, marine structures group 1989-91, chmn. 1992-95), Sigma Xi. Office: Offshore Structure Analysis Inc 13613 Capista Dr Plainfield IL 60544-7966

CHAKRABARTY, ANANDA MOHAN, microbiologist; b. Sainthia, India, Apr. 4, 1938; s. Satya Dos and Sasthi Bala (Mukherjee) C.; m. Krishna Chakraverty, May 26, 1965; children: Kaberi, Asit. BSc, St. Xavier's Coll., 1958; MSc, U. Calcutta, 1960, PhD, 1965. Sr. research officer U. Calcutta, 1964-65; research asso. in biochemistry U. Ill., Urbana, 1965-71; mem. staff Gen. Electric Research and Devel. Center, Schenectady, 1971-79; prof. dept. microbiology U. Ill. Med. Center, 1979-89; disting. prof., 1989—. Editor: Genetic Engineering, 1977, Biodegradation and Detoxification of Environmental Pollutants, 1982. Named Scientist of Yr. Indsl. Rsch. Mag., 1975, Univ. scholar U. Ill., 1989; recipient Inventor of Yr. award Patent Lawyers' Assn., 1982, Pub. Affairs award Am. Chem. Soc., 1984, Disting. Scientist award EPA, 1985, Merit award NIH, 1986, Pasteur award, 1991, Disting. Svc. award U.S. Army, 1993, Proctor & Gamble award, 1995. Mem. Am. Soc. Microbiology, Am. Soc. Biol. Chemists. Home: 206 E Julia Dr Villa Park IL 60181-3340 Office: U Ill Med Ctr Dept Microbiology M/C 790 835 S Wolcott Ave Chicago IL 60612-7340

CHAKRABORTI, NIRUPAM, engineering educator; b. Coochbehar, W.Bengal, India, Apr. 30, 1955; s. Nalini Kanta and Reba (Biswas) C.; m. Chhanda Roy, July 30, 1979; 1 child, Sankhamala. B.Met.E., Jadavpur U., Calcutta, India, 1977; MS, N.Mex. Tech., 1979; PhC, U. Wash., 1982, PhD, 1983. Rsch. asst. N.Mex. Tech., Socorro, 1977-79; rsch./tchg. asst. U. Wash., Seattle, 1979-83; from vis. faculty to assoc. prof. Indian Inst. Tech., Kanpur, 1984-95, prof. engring., 1995-2000; prof. engring. Indian Inst. Tech., Kharagpur, 2000—; vis. scientist Max Planck Inst., Stuttgart, Germany, 1988-89; vis. asst. prof. U. Utah, Salt Lake City, 1990-92; internat. expert/vis. prof. Nat. Steel Co./Fluminense Fed. U., Brazil, 1994, 95, 96; vis. prof. Fed. U. Ouro Preto, Brazil, 1997. Contbr. articles to profl. jours. Avocation: literature. Office: Indian Inst Tech, Dept Matls/Metall Engring, Kharagpur 721302, India

CHAKRABORTY, ASIT KUMAR, biotechnology products executive, scientist; b. Midnapore, West Bengal, India, June 19, 1958; temporary resident U.S., 1990-95, 98-99; s. Kalipada and Binapani (Babarta) C.; m. Anjana Chatterjee, Oct. 20, 1989; children: Anindita, Anupama. PU in Sci., Calcutta U., 1975, BSc in Chemistry with honors, 1979, MSc in Biochemistry, 1981, PhD in Biochemistry, 1990. Rsch. fellow Ind. Inst. Chem. Biology, Calcutta, 1983-89; postdoctoral rsch. virologist U. Calif., Berkeley, 1990-91; sr. postdoctoral fellow Creighton U. Sch. Medicine, Omaha, 1992-94; postdoctoral scientist Med. U. S.C., Charleston, 1994-95; scientist Ind. Inst. Chem. Biology, Calcutta, 1995-98; vis. scientist Sch. Medicine Creighton U., Omaha, 1998-99, The Johns Hopkins Sch. Medicine, Balt., 1999; pres. Kali-sita Bio Tech Rsch. Pvt. Ltd., India, 2000—; sci. evaluator Current Drugs, Ltd., London, 1994—; reviewer sci. paper B.B. Acta, U.S., 1999—. Rsch. fellow, Indian Coun. Med. Rsch., 1984, Coun. Sci. & Indsl. Rsch., 1985-89; rsch. scholar Indian Inst. Chem. Biology, 1983. Mem. AAAS, N.Y. Acad. Sci., Soc. Biol. Chemists (life). Republican. Hindu. Avocations: music, thriller movies, soccer, writing poetry and fiction. Home: 466 Garfa Main Rd Aditi # 6, 700075 Calcutta Jadavpur, India

CHAKRABORTY, SUPRIYA, chemistry researcher; b. Cacutta, India, June 16, 1962; s. Dharani Dhar and Mira (Chatterjee) C.; m. Prakriti Mukherjee, Jan. 15, 1999. BSc, Indina Inst. Tech., Kharagpur, 1984, MSc, 1986; PhD, M.S. U. of Baroda, Vadodara, India, 1995. Postgrad. tchr. Ctrl. Sch., Kalaikunda, India, 1986-87; rsch. fellow Indian Sch. Mines, Dhanbad, India, 1987; rsch. scholar Phys. Rsch. Lab., Ahmedabad, India, 1987-93, postdoctoral fellow, 1994-95; postgrad. rschr. U. Calif., Santa Barbara, 1995-96; rsch. chemist U. Calif., San Diego, 1996-98; project scientist Phys. Rsch. Lab., Ahmedabad, 1999—. Mem. Kharagpur Vivekan and Yuva Mahamondal, Kharagpur, 1975—. Mem. Am. Geophys. Union, Am. Inst. Physics, Indian Soc. for Mass Spectrometry. Avocations: photography, drawing, sketching, calligraphy, writing poetry. Home: PDF Quarter A2, PRL Campus, 380 009 Ahmedabad, Gujarat India Office: Phys Rsch Lab, Navrangpura, 380 009 Ahmedabad, Gujarat India

CHAKRAVARTY, NIRMAL KUMAR, pharmacologist, educator; b. Calcutta, India, June 1, 1919; arrived in Denmark, 1969; s. Jitendranath and Usha (Ukil) C.; m. Kerstin B.M. Stenson, Mar. 21, 1964; children: Anna Mira, Arjun Anders. MB, Calcutta U., 1943, MD, 1952, DPhil, 1956; MD, Karolinska Inst., Stockholm, 1959. House physician Calcutta Med. Coll. Hosp., 1944-45; rschr. Calcutta Sch. Tropical Medicine Indian Coun. Med. Rsch., 1945-54; Rockefeller Found. rsch. fellow U. Utah, 1954-55; rschr. Venezuelan Inst. Sci. Rsch., Caracas, 1960-62; rsch. fellow Carlsberg Found. Biol. Inst., Copenhagen, 1962-64; docent, prof. pharmacology Umeå (Sweden) U., 1964-68; vis. prof. pharmacology Southwestern Med. Sch. U. Tex., Dallas, 1966; prof. pharmacology Odense (Denmark) U., 1969-89, prof. emeritus, 1989—; censor in pharmacology Århus (Denmark) U., 1969-89. Contbr. chpts. to books, numerous articles to profl. jours. Named Knight of Order of Dannebrog Queen of Denmark, 1976, Knight of First Grade Order, 1988; recipient Svend Petersen's Meml. Fund prize, 1988. Mem. European Histamine Rsch. Soc., Danish Pharmacol. Soc. Home: Bødtchersvej 20, 5230 Odense M, Denmark Office: Dept Pharmacology Inst Med Biology, Winslowparken 19, 5000 Odense Denmark

CHALABY, JEAN KARIM, sociologist; b. Geneva, Switzerland; s. Reda and Raphaelle (Giordani) C. BS in Sociology, U. Lausanne, Switzerland, 1989; MS in Sociology, London Sch. Econs., 1991, PhD in Sociology, 1994. Rsch. assoc. London Sch. Econs., 1995—; lectr. sociology City U., London, 2000; cons. in field. Contbr. articles to profl. jours. Grantee SNSF, Bern, Switzerland, 1995, 97—. Roman Catholic. Avocations: cello, chamber music. Office: City Univ, Northampton Sq, London EC1V 0HB, England

CHALAM, KAKARLA VENKATA, physician, educator; b. Pedamuttevi, India, Aug. 1, 1959; s. Kasturi C.; m. Aruna Potla, June 3, 1982; 1 child, Sandeep. BS, Loyola Coll., 1972; MD, Guntur (India) Med. Sch., 1978; MS, Postgrad. Inst., Chandigarh, India, 1983. Diplomate Am. Bd. Ophthalmology. Asst. instr. U. Tex. Southwestern Med. Sch., Dallas, 1992-94; asst. prof. U. S.C. Sch. Medicine, Columbia, 1994-97, assoc. prof., 1997-2000, program dir., 1994-2000; assoc. chmn. U. Fla. Sch. Medicine, Jacksonville, 2000—. Sect. editor Ocular Pharmacology, 1997-98. Fellow Royal Coll. Surgeons Edinburgh. Republican. Avocations: photography, classical music, technical writing, table tennis. E-mail: kvchalam@aol.com. Fax: 904-549-3883. Address: 653 W 8th St Jacksonville FL 32209-6511

CHALKER, ROBERT PHELPS, retired association executive; b. Linden, Ala., Mar. 16, 1914; s. Isaac Watts and Harriet Marshall (Phelps) C.; m. Edna Violet Wood, Nov. 8, 1946 (dec. 1985); children: Janet, Jeffrey; m. Louise Studley, 1990. Student, Birmingham (Ala.) So. Coll., 1929-31; AB, Duke U., 1933, MA, 1935; postgrad., Heidelberg (Germany) U., 1936, U. Chgo., 1937, U. Paris, 1938, Fgn. Service Inst., Columbia U., 1950-51. Instr. pub. schs. Marianna and Panama City, Fla., 1934-35; Pensacola, Fla., 1935-38; instr. extension service U. Ala., 1939; vice consul Berlin, 1939-42, sec. embassy, 1941-42; interned Bad Neuheim, Germany, 1941-42; vice counsul Lisbon, Portugal, 1942, Birmingham, Eng., 1942-44; consul, sec. embassy London, 1944-48; consul Madras, India, 1948-49, Bremen, Fed. Republic

Germany, 1949-50, Duesseldorf, Fed. Republic Germany, 1951-54; personnel ops officer Office of Personnel, Dept. State, Washington, 1954-56; consul gen. Amsterdam, The Netherlands, 1956-59; with U.S. Naval War Coll., 1959-60; Am. consul gen. Kobe-Osaka, Japan, 1960-64; counsellor Am. Embassy Dublin, Ireland, 1964-68; exec. dir. U.S. C. of C., Dublin, Ireland, until 1995, ret., 1995. Mem. Alpha Tau Omega. Clubs: Stephen's Green, Milltown Golf. Lodge: Rotary (past pres.).

CHALKLEY, JACQUELINE ANN, retail company executive; b. Benson, Minn., Jan. 3, 1946; d. Vincent Otto and Dorothy Mildred (Alsaker) Kaehler; m. C. Wayne Callaway. BA in Art History cum laude, Brown U., 1967; MA, Columbia U., 1968; postgrad. in Contemporary Art, New Sch. for Social Rsch., N.Y.C., 1968-70; postgrad. in Ceramics, U. Md., 1970-72. Art tchr. Summit (N.J.) High Sch., 1968-70, Rockville (Md.) High Sch., 1970-74; adj. prof. ceramics Montgomery Coll., Rockville, 1974-78; owner Jackie Chalkley at Foxhall Square, Washington, 1978-99, Jackie Chalkley at Willard Collection, Washington, 1986-99, Jackie Chalkley at Chevy Chase Plz., Washington, 1989-99; juror Rhinebeck Craft Fair, 1981, New Eng. Buyers Market, Boston, 1982, Craft Art '82, Richmond, Va. Craft Show, 1983, Smithsonian Crafts Exhbn. '83, Smithsonian Instn. Women's Com. Craft Show, 1984, Annie Albers fashion show at Renwick Gallery, 1984, Morristown Craft Fair, 1984, Washington Craft Show, 1986, Potomac Craftsmen's Guild Show, 1987, Harrisburg Arts Festival, 1987, Ceramic Guild Washington, 1987, Washington Guild Goldsmiths, 1987, 18th Bienniel Exhbn. Creative Crafts Coun., 1988, others; appointee screening com. Piedmont Craftsman's Guild, Winston-Salem, N.C., 1983-86, D.C. Commn. Arts, 1983-85; mem. hon. com. Brandeis Art Exhbn., 1984; mem. hon. com. various exhbns. and fundraisers Textile Mus., 1984-86. Featured in Ceramics Monthly, 1994, Women's Wear Daily, 1995. Mem. hon. com. 2d Ann. 34th St. Art Fair, John Eaton Sch., 1985; mem. benefit com. Washington Charitable Fund, 1989; hon. bd. trustees D.C. chpt. Design Industries Found. for AIDS, 1989, 90; mem. auction ann. benefit com. Washington Project for Arts, 1989, 90, benefit com. Source Theater, 1993, benefit com. Corcoran Mus. Jazz Evening, 1993, honorary com. Lab Sch. Wash., 1992, honorary benefit com. Arena Stage Living Theater, 1997, 98; sponsor Wearable Art Fashion Show, Renwick Mus., 1993; juried Smithsonian Craft Show, 1994; hon. chmn. Friends of the Corcoran Mus. Benefit, 1999-00; mem. benefit com. Living Stage & Arena Theatre, 1997, 98, 99; chmn. Craft Leaders Caucus Day 2000; mem. nat. resource bd. James Renwick Alliance of Renwick Mus., 2000—. Appeared on cover of Forecast Mag., 1978; recipient Best Taste in Washington award Washingtonian Mag., 1982, 1st Ann. Outstanding Accessories Merchandising award Accessories Mag., 1985; named one of 23 People to Watch in 1983, Washingtonian Mag., 1982; her apt. chosen as Residential Interior of Yr., Am. Soc. Interior Designers, 1985, 92; her store named 1986 Comml. Interior of Yr., Am. Soc. Interior Designers; nat. award for logo design Am. Corp. Identity, 1988, 91. Mem. Am. Craft Coun., Washington Fashion Group, James Renwick Craft Leaders Caucus, Friends of the Corcoran Gallery of Art, Friends of the Phillips Collection, Friends of the Textile Mus. Avocations: travel, food, modern dance, visual arts, swimming. Office: Jackie Chalkley 2130 Cathedral Ave NW Washington DC 20008-1502

CHALLA, SUBHASH, researcher in electrical engineering; b. Hyderabad, A.P., India, Aug. 10, 1970; s. Raji Reddy and Laxmi Reddy (Katta) C.; m. Lalitha Vadlapalli, June 29, 1997. B.Tech., Jawaharlal Nehru Technol. U., Hyderabad, India, 1993; PhD, Queensland U. Tech., Brisbane, Australia, 1998. Lectr. Queensland U. Tech., Brisbane, 1994-98, rsch. asst., 1994-95; rsch. fellow dept. elec. and electronics engring. U. Melbourne, 1998-2000, sr. rsch. fellow, 2000—; vis. scholar Harvard U., Boston, 1997; cons. Sci. Systems, Boston, 1997; co-founder ASHA-Australia. Contbr. articles to profl. jours. Child sponsor World Vision, Australia, 1995-97; pres. Indian Students Orgn., Australia, 1996-97. Overseas Postgrad. Rsch. scholar Commonwealth Govt. Australia, 1995; Harvard U. scholar, 1997. Avocations: reading, music, playing violin, philosophy. Office: Dept Elec & Electronic Engr, Univ Melbourne, Parkville VIC 3052, Australia

CHALMERS, JOHN MURDO, vibrational spectroscopist, researcher; b. London, Nov. 13, 1946; s. Frank Ernest and Margaret Mary (Maciver) C.; m. Shelley Cliff, Apr. 26, 1975; 1 child, Elizabeth Margaret. Lab. asst. plastics div. ICI, Welwyn Garden City, Eng., 1965-68, exptl. scientist petrochems. and plastics div., 1968-82; rsch. scientist advanced materials ICI, Wilton, Cleveland, Eng., 1982-88, sr. rsch. scientist materials rsch. ctr., 1988-91; bus. rsch. assoc. Wilton Rsch. Ctr. ICI, 1991-99; cons. VSConsulting, Stokesley, Eng., 2000—; vis. lectr. Sch. of Chem. Scis., U. East Anglia, Norwich, Eng., 1992—; part-time sr. rsch. fellow U. Nottingham Sch. Chemistry, 2000—. Co-author: Industrial Analysis with Vibrational Spectroscopy, 1997; editor: Spectroscopy in Process Analysis, 2000—; mem. editl. adv. bd. Spectroscopy, 1989—, Spectroscopy Internat., 1989-92, Spectroscopy Europe, 1992—, Vibrational Spectroscopy, 1990-95; contbr. chpts. to books, articles to profl. jours. Recipient Williams-Wright award Coblentz Soc., 1994. Fellow Royal Soc. Chemistry (com. analytical div. molecular spectroscopy group, hon. treas. 1991-95, vice chmn. 1995-98, chmn. 1996-98, 1998), Infrared and Raman Discussion Group (meetings sec. 1993-95, chmn. 1995—), Soc. for Applied Spectroscopy, Coblentz Soc. (Williams-Wright award 1994), U.K. Microspectrometry Applications Group, Microbeam Analysis Soc., Assn. Brit. Spectroscopists (chmn. 1998—). Mem. Ch. of Eng. Avocations: sailing, gardening, walking, do-it-yourself. Office: VSConsulting, 14 Croft Hills Tame Bridge, Stokesley TS9 5NW, England

CHALUPSKY, JOSEF (JIRI), parasitologist, educator; b. Prague, Czech Republic, Mar. 12, 1931; s. Josef and Anna (Rydlová) C.; m. Dagmar Haderová, May 22, 1954; children: Josef, Dagmar. PhD, Charles U., Prague, 1953, Rerum naturalium doctor, 1973; MS, Charles U. Asst. prof. dept. parasitology Charles U., 1957-91, assoc. prof. dept. parasitology, 1991—. Co-author: Keys of Czechoslovac Dipterans, 1977, Blood-Sucking Dipterans and Maggots, 1980, Basic Parasitology, 1988, Special Medical Microbiology and Parasitology, 1994, 2d edit., 1998; co-author (film) Mosquitoes, 1994 (Main prize Academia Film Olomouc), Flagellates, 1995 (J.A. Comenius prize Academia Film Olomouc); contbr. articles to profl. jours. Mem. Czech Zool. Soc., Assn. Collectors and Friends of Bookplates, Czech Parasitological Soc. Avocations: bibliophilie, bookplates, small scale graphic art, poetry. E-mail: chalupsk@natur.cuni.cz. Home: Druzstevni ochoz 52, 140 00 Prague 4 Czech Republic Office: Charles U Dept Parasitology, Fac Natural Scis, 12844 Prague 2 Czech Republic

CHALY, ALEXEY MICHAILOVICH, electrical engineer, business executive; b. Moscow, June 13, 1961; s. Michael Vasil'evich and Alevtina Tikhonovna (Yarovaya) C.; m. Elena Vasil'evna Mamotchenko, Aug. 29, 1986; 1 child, Michail Alexeevich. BS, Sevastopol Inst. Indsl. Design, USSR, 1983; DSE, Russian Electrotech. Acad., Moscow, 1997. Rsch. engr. Sevastopol Inst. of Indsl. Design, 1983-88, mgr. rsch. lab., 1988-90; dir. R&D venture Tavrida-Electric, Sevastopol, 1990-92; gen. mgr. indsl. group Tavrida-Electric, Sevastopol, Ukraine, 1992—; mem. permanent internat. scientific com. Internat. Symposium on Discharge and Elec. Insulation in Vacuum, Edinburgh, U.K., 1996—. Patentee in field. Mem. N.Y. Acad. Sci., Russian Electrotech. Acad. Avocations: soccer, world history. Home: Kazach'ya Buh 9-27, Sevastopol 99011, Ukraine Office: Vakulenchuck Str 22, Sevastopol 99053, Ukraine also: Marshal Biriuzov Str 1, 123298 Moscow Russia

CHAM, JESUS C., food distribution company executive; b. Dagupan City, Philippines, Dec. 25, 1954; s. Chua Cham and Bee Ching Co; m. Flora Chua Hao, Aug. 5, 1979; children: Colleen, Candice, Charisse, Jezreel Chester. BS in Chem. Engring., U. Philippines, 1976. From asst. sales mgr. to mng. dir. Mayon Consolidated, Inc., Philippines, 1976—; bd. dirs. Sub-0 Foods Corp., Manila, Philippines, Malabon Candy Co., Manila, Unique Lumber, Inc., Dagupan City, Philippines, Mayden Cleaning Solutions, Inc., Manila, Aztec Constrn. Co., Dagupan City, Penguin Agro Marine Corp., Dagupan City, Baguio Devel. Corp., Hong Kong. Mem. Mensa. Avocations: reading, gym, swimming, singing, piano.

CHAM, WAI KUEN, engineering educator; b. Hong Kong, July 20, 1957. BS, Chinese U. Hong Kong, 1979; MS, Loughborough U. Tech., U.K., 1980, PhD, 1983. Sr. engr. Datacraft H.K. Ltd., Hong Kong, 1984; lectr. Hong Kong Poly., 1984-85; lectr. Chinese U. Hong Kong, 1985-91, sr. lectr., 1992-96, assoc. prof., 1996-97, prof., 1997—; cons. JPL, NASA, 1993; chmn. engring. panel Chinese U. Hong Kong, 1995-96; fellow coll. assembly United Coll., Chinese U. Hong Kong, 1991—; mem. engring. panel Rsch. Grant Coun., Hong Kong Govt., 1993-98. Author: (book chpt.) Advances in Electronics and Electron Physics, 1994; contbr. articles to profl. jours. Mem. IEEE (sr.), Inst. Elec. Engrs., Chinese Inst. Engring. (exec. com. Circuits and Sys. Soc. 1997—). Avocations: badminton, music, reading. Office: Chinese U of Hong Kong, Dept Electronic Engring, Shatin Hong Kong

CHAMA, CHRISTOPHER CHAMBULA, physical metallurgy educator, consultant; b. Mansa, Luapula, Zambia, Dec. 10, 1956; s. Crispin Myala C. and Abiya Kunda Sota. BS, U. Zambia, 1980; MS, Pa. State U., 1983, PhD, 1986. Asst. dean U. Zambia, Lusaka, 1987-88, lectr., 1987-95, acting head of dept., 1988-89, 91-92, head of dept., 1992-94, sr. lectr., 1995-99, assoc. prof., 2000—; cons. Lusaka Engring. Co., 1988-93, Chinese Team of Engring., Lusaka, 1988, Engring. Svcs. Corp., Lusaka, 1992, Zambia Electricity Supply Corp., Lusaka, 1998. Judge Nat. Essay Competition UN Fund for Population Activities, Zambia, 1987; assesor applications Fulbright Scholarships, Lusaka, 1996—. Staff Devel. fellow U. Zambia, 1983, rsch. fellow Japanese Agy. Indsl. Sci. and Tech., 1999; Fulbright scholar U.S. Govt., 1981; recipient Labour Day award U. Zambia, 1995. Mem. ASM, South African Inst. Steel Constrn., Internat. Metallographic Soc. Roman Catholic. Avocations: music, watching sports, current world affairs, gardening. Home: U Zambia, F13 Handsworth Ct, Lusaka Lusaka, Zambia Office: U Zambia Sch Mines, PO Box 32379, Lusaka Lusaka, Zambia

CHAMBEL, MANUEL MATOS, airline official, consultant; b. Margem, Portugal, Dec. 17, 1951; s. José Elias and Maria (Florinda) Gravicha; m. Isabel Santos Ferreira, Oct. 16, 1976; children: Hugo, Ricardo. Grad. in aero. engring., Mil. Acad., Lisbon, Portugal, 1977; postgrad., ITA-CTA, San José dos Campos, Brazil, 1982, LEQUAL, Lisbon, 1989. Commd. officer Portuguese Air Force, 1977, advanced through grades to col.; ACFT program mgr. Portuguese Air Force, Lisbon, 1977-81, chief ACFT divsn., 1987-97; tchr. Air Force Acad., Sintra, Portugal, 1982-87; resigned, 1997; dep. dir. quality assurance OGMA-S.A., Alverca, Portugal, 1997—. Home: Praceta do Comércio No 7, 60 Esq-Alfragide, 2720111A Amadora Portugal Office: OGMA SA, Industria Aero do Portugal, 2615 Alverca Portugal

CHAMBERLAIN, BRUCE ANTHONY, Parliamentarian; b. Brighton, Victoria, Australia, Aug. 9, 1939; s. Peter Henry and Eileen Veronica (Haddad) C.; m. Paula Swan, Feb. 6, 1965; 4 children. BA, Melbourne (Australia) U., 1963, LLB, 1963. Mem. Parliament of Victoria, 1973—, shadow minister, 1982-91, pres. legis. coun., 1992—, leader opposition legis. coun., 1986-88. Bd. dirs. Greening Australia, Victoria, 1994—. Mem. Australasian Study of Parliament Group (v.p. Victorian chpt.), Commonwealth Parliamentary Assn. (joint pres. Victorian br.), Lions Internat. (past pres. Hamilton Victoria br.). Liberal. Roman Catholic. Avocations: golf, internet. E-mail: president@parliament.vic.gov.au. Office: Parliament of Victoria, Spring St, Melbourne Victoria 3002, Australia

CHAMBERLAIN, JEAN NASH, county government department director; b. Chgo., Oct. 14, 1934; d. William Edmund and Virginia Jean (La Fon) Nash; m. James Staffeld Chamberlain, Dec. 29, 1953; children: James W., William S., Caren T., Martha J. Student, U. S.C., 1951-53. Polit. dir. Tribune/United Cablevision, Huntington Woods, Mich., 1982; orgn. dir. polit. campaign, Oakland, Mich., 1983-84; dir. fin. Dan Murphy for Gov., Mich., 1985-86; exec. mgr. Greater Royal Oak (Mich.)/Oak Park C. of C., 1986-93. Vice chair Rep. com., Oakland County, Mich., 1971-73; chair Rep. 18th congl. dist., 1973-77; del. Rep. Nat. Conv., Kansas City, Mo., 1976; bd. dirs. Oakland County Mental Health Bd., 1976-93, chair 1984-86. Named among top thirty Outstanding Women State Mich., Mich's. Womens Commn., 1998. Mem. U.S. C. of C., Mich. State C. of C., South Oakland Boys and Girls Club (bd. dirs.), South Oakland Salvation Army (bd. dirs.), Harnack Firefighters Scholarship Fund (bd. dirs.), Woodward Dream Cruise (bd. chair). Roman Catholic. Avocations: tennis, biking, sports, cooking. Office: Oakland County Exec Office Bldg 1200 N Telegraph Rd Pontiac MI 48341-1032

CHAMBERLAIN, JOHN LOOMIS, III, retired pediatrician, educator; b. Balt., July 18, 1930; s. John Loomis Jr. and Marie (Brosius) C.; m. Eleanor Fulton, 1956 (div. Apr. 1976); m. Amelie Marie Chamberlain, Apr. 29, 1977; children: Carolyn, Allison, John Loomis IV. BA, Amherst Coll., 1953; MD, U. Va., 1957. Pediatrician Lexington (Ky.) Clinic, 1962-66; asst. prof. pediat. U. Ky. Sch. Medicine, Lexington, 1962-66; clin. prof. child health and devel. George Washington Sch. Medicine, Washington, 1966—; pediatrician Office of Drs. Howard, Daisley and Ong, Washington, 1966-70; ret., 1992; chmn. med. staff Children's Hosp., 1976-79. Editor-in-chief Clin. Proceedings, 1979-84; mem. editl. rev. bd. Contemporary Pediat., 1984-87, Pediat. in Review, 1985-88. Col. U.S. Army, 1991-93. Fellow Am. Acad. Pediat. (v.p. Washington chpt. 1985-88); mem. Vis. Nurse Assn. (med. adv. bd. 1972-89), Rotary, Cosmos Club. Republican. Episcopalian. Avocations: tennis, flying, SCUBA diving. Home: 4321 Westover Pl NW Washington DC 20016-5553

CHAMBERLAIN, NEVILLE, nuclear energy industry executive; b. Oct. 3, 1939; s. Leslie and Doris Ann (Thompson) C.; m. Joy Rachel Wellings, 1971; four children. BSc, U. Durham, 1961, MSc, 1962. With UKAEA, 1962-71, Urenco Ltd., 1971-77; from fuel prodn. to dep. chmn. Brit. Nuclear Fuels, 1977-99; chmn. TEC Nat. Coun., 1999—; dir. Energy Strategists Cons. Ltd. Office: BNFL Oaklands/2 The Paddock, Hinderton Rd, Neston Cheshire CH64 9PH, England

CHAMBERLAIN, OWEN, nuclear physicist; b. San Francisco, July 10, 1920; m. Babette Copper, 1943 (div. 1978; 4 children; m. June Steingart, 1980 (dec.); m. Senta Pugh, 1998. AB (Cramer fellow), Dartmouth Coll., 1941; PhD, U. Chgo., 1949. Instr. physics U. Calif., Berkeley, 1948-50, asst. prof., 1950-54, assoc. prof., 1954-58, prof., 1958-89, prof. emeritus, 1989—; civilian physicist Manhattan Dist., Berkeley, Los Alamos, 1942-46. Recipient Nobel prize (with Emilio Segré) for physics, for discovery antiproton, 1959, The Berkeley citation U. Calif., 1989; Guggenheim fellow, 1957-58; Loeb lectr. at Harvard U., 1959. Fellow Am. Phys. Soc., Am. Acad. Arts and Scis.; mem. Nat. Acad. Scis., Berkeley Fellows. Office: U Calif Phys Dept Berkeley CA 94720-0001

CHAMBERLIN, EUGENE KEITH, retired historian, educator; b. Gustine, Calif., Feb. 15, 1916; s. Charles Eugene and Anina Marguerite (Williams) C.; m. Margaret Rae Jackson, Sept. 1, 1940; children: Linda, Thomas, Rebecca, Adrienne (dec.), Eric. BA in History, U. Calif., Berkeley, 1939, MA, 1940, PhD, 1949. Tchr. Spanish, Latin Lassen Union H.S. and Jr. Coll., Susanville, Calif., 1941-43; tchr. history Elk Grove (Calif.) Joint Union H.S., 1943-45; tchg. asst. history U. Calif., Berkeley, 1946-48; instr. history Mont. State U., Missoula, 1948-51, asst. prof., 1951-54; asst. prof. to prof. San Diego City Coll., 1954-78; prof. history San Diego Miramar Coll., 1978-83, San Diego Mesa Coll., 1983-86; ret., 1986; cab driver San Diego Yellow Cab Co., 1955-74, 79, 86; vis. prof. history Mont. State Coll., Bozeman, summer 1953, U. Calif. Ext., 1964-68, San Diego State Coll., 1965-68, others; instr., coord. history lectr. San Diego C.C.-TV, 1969-77; prof. history MiraCosta Coll., 1998; mem. adv. com. Quechan Crossing Master Plan Project, 1989-90; historian San Diego First Ch. of the Brethren, 1954-98. Author booklets on S.W. Am. history; contbr. articles on Mexican N.W. to profl. jours. Recipient Merit award Congress of History San Diego County, 1978, award for dedicated svc. to local history San Diego Hist. Soc., 1991, Ben Dixon award Congress History, San Diego and Imperial Counties, 1997; grantee Huntington Libr.-Rockefeller Found., 1952, Fulbright-Hays, Peru, 1982. Mem. AAUP (com. mem., nat. coun. 1967-70, pres. Calif. conf. 1968-70, acting exec. sec. 1970-72, 50 Yr. Mem. 1999), San Diego County Congress of History (pres. 1976-77, newsletter editor 1977-78), Am. Hist. Assn. (life, Beveridge-Dunning com. 1982-84, chmn. 1984), Pacific Coast Coun. on Latin Am. Studies, Cultural Assn. of the Californias, The Westerners (Calafia, S.D. chpt.), E Clampus Vitus Squibob Chpt. (historian 1970-96, emeritus historian and archivist 1996—, chpt. pres. 1972-73, dir. proctor 1983-89, grand coun. mem. 1972-93, dir. T.R.A.S.H. 1979-93, pres. 1983-84), San Diego Hist. Soc. (hon. life), Assn. Calif. Cmty. Colls. (founding, life), Phi Alpha Theta (sec. 1948-54), U. Calif. Berkeley chpt. 1947-48, organizer and faculty adv. Mont. State U. chpt. 1948-54). Democrat. Mem. Church of the Brethren. Home: 3033 Dale St San Diego CA 92104-4929

CHAMBERS, ALLAN ANTHONY, investment banker; b. Liverpool, Eng., July 14, 1948; s. James and Catherine Elizabeth (Lewis) C.; m. Monica Jean Pope, Oct. 23, 1971; children: Ashley, Justin. MSc, Cranfield (Eng.) Inst. Tech., 1971; SM, MBA, MIT and Harvard U., 1975. V.p. Bankers Trust Co., London, 1979-82; mgr. Hambros Merchant Bank, London, 1982-84; sr. mgr. Commerzbank AG, London, 1984-87; dir. Comml. Union Assurance Co plc, London, 1987-92; v.p., sr. banker Merrill Lynch, London, 1992-96; sr. dir. Daiwa Securities, London, 1996—. Cons. various charities, 1990-97. Travelling fellow Worshipful Co. Sci. Instrument Makers-Livery, London, 1973, MIT & Harvard Bus. Sch., 1973-75. Mem. Harvard Bus. Sch. Club of London, Cranfield Inst. Tech. Alumni Assn., MIT Alumni Assn. Avocations: chess, golf, antique collecting, travel, internet development. E-mail: allan.chambers@lineone.net. Home: Mt Shell Farm, Langford Rd, Wickham Bishops CM8 3JG, England

CHAMBERS, CLYTIA MONTLLOR, public relations consultant; b. Rochester, N.Y., Oct. 23, 1922; d. Anthony and Marie (Bambace) Capraro; m. Joseph John Montllor, July 2, 1941 (div. 1958); children: Michele, Thomas, Clytia; m. Robert Chambers, May 28, 1965. BA, Barnard Coll., N.Y.C., 1942; Licence en droit, Faculte de Droit, U. Lyon, France, 1948; MA, Howard U., Washington, 1958. Assoc. dir. dept. rsch. Coun. for Fin. Aid to Edn., N.Y.C., 1958-60; asst. to v.p. indsl. rels. Sinclair Oil Corp., N.Y.C., 1961-65; writer pub. rels. dept. Am. Oil Co., Chgo., 1965-67; dir. editorial svcs., v.p. Hill & Knowlton Inc., N.Y.C., 1967-77; sr. v.p., dir. spl. svcs. Hill & Knowlton Inc., L.A., 1977-90, sr. cons., 1990—; cons. and trustee Childen's Inst. Internat., L.A., 1988-93. Co-author: The News Twisters, 1971; editor: Critical Issues in Public Relations, 1975. Mem. Calif. Rare Fruit Growers (editor Fruit Gardener 1979-2000, editor emeritus 2000—). E-mail: clytia@112358.com. Home: 11439 Laurelcrest Dr Studio City CA 91604-3872

CHAMBERS, DAVID WADE, science educator; b. Elk City, Okla., June 21, 1938; came to Australia, 1977; s. Elmer Wade and Anita Marie (Sims) C.; m. Rachel Ann Faggetter, Feb. 18, 1968; 1 child, Susannah Rachel. B.A., U. Okla., 1960; M.A., Harvard U., 1966, Ph.D., 1969. Tutor, Harvard U., Cambridge, Mass., 1962-66; asst. prof. So. Meth. U., Dallas, 1966-69; assoc. prof. McGill U., Montreal, Que., Can., 1969-76; sr. lectr. Deakin U., Melbourne, Victoria, Australia, 1977—. Author: Liberation and Control, 1979 (ABA award 1979); Worm in the Bud, 1984; Red and Expert, 1984; Imagining Nature, 1985 (Fabinyi award 1985); several textbooks. Home: PO Box 73, Airley's Inlet Victoria 3221, Australia Office: Deakin U, Melbourne Victoria 3217, Australia

CHAMBERS, DONALD ARTHUR, biochemistry and molecular medicine educator; b. N.Y.C., Sept. 24, 1936. AB, Columbia U., 1959, PhD, 1972. Rsch. biochemist dept. surgery Harvard Med. Sch./Mass. Gen. Hosp., Boston, 1961-66; rsch. fellow in hematology dept. surgery Harvard Med. Sch./Beth Israel Hosp., Boston, 1967-68; faculty fellow in chem. biology Columbia U., N.Y.C., 1969-71; asst. rsch. biochemist Ctr. for Med. Genetics dept. medicine U. Calif. Med. Ctr., San Francisco, 1972-74, lectr. in biochemistry and biophysics, 1972-74, asst. prof. molecular biology and biochemistry, 1974-75; asst. prof. biol. chemistry and dermatology U. Mich., Ann Arbor, 1975-79, assoc. prof. biol. chemistry, 1979; prof. molecular biology U. Ill., Chgo., 1979—, prof. biol. chemistry, 1980—, rsch. prof. dermatology, 1981—, prof. biol. psychiatry, 1996; assoc. mem. Dental Rsch. Inst. U. Mich., 1978-79, adj. rsch. investigator Dept. Biol. Chemistry, 1979—; dir. Ctr. for Molecular Biology of Oral Disease, U. Ill., Chgo., 1979—, interim head dept. biochemistry, 1985, head dept. biochemistry, 1986—; vis. scholar Green Coll., Oxford U., 1989-93, hon. vis. fellow, 1993—; fellow Honors Coll., 1985—, Phi Kappa Phi lectr., 1991; nat. action com. Am. Assn. Dental Rsch., 1981—; study sect. rev. NIH, 1983-86, 92, 98—. Mem. editl. bd. Perspectives in Biology and Medicine. Recipient James Howard McGregor prize Columbia U., 1971; named Inventor of Yr., U. Ill., 1990; fellow in hematology NIH, 1967-68, fellow in chem. biology, 1969-71; Rsch. grantee NIH, Am. Cancer Soc., Office of Naval Rsch., 1986—, Helene Curtis, Inc., 1988—, Tng. grantee NIH-NIGMS, 1975-79, NIH-NIAMDD, 1976-79, 77-80, NIH-NIDR-NIAMDD, 1980—, NIH-NCI, 1982-88. Mem. AAAS, Am. Assn. Med. Colls., Am. Chem. Soc., Am. Fedn. Clin. Rsch., Am. Soc. Biol. Chemistry, Am. Soc. Cell Biology, Am. Soc. Microbiology, Internat. Assn. Dental Rsch. (com. on rsch. progress 1982-85, chmn. 1984-85, chmn. grad. tng. forum com. exptl. pathology sect. 1983), Assn. Dept. Chmn. Biol. Chemistry, Chgo. Assn. Immunologists, Chgo. Cancer Assn., N.Y. Acad. Scis. (organizer meeting The Double Helix, 40 Yrs. 1993), Royal Soc. Medicine, Soc. Investigative Dermatology, Phi Kappa Phi, Sigma Xi (special englbrice panel, NIDER-NIH 1998—). Achievements include patents (U.S., Can.) for method of determining periodontal disease, (with other) method of quantifying aspartate amino transferase in periodontal disease; research in role of cyclic nucleotides, prostaglandins, hormones and other regulatory factors in the regulation of cell function, proliferation and differentiation, in molecular medicine in neural-immune interactions, the regulatory mechanisms of host-microbial interactions, in the history and devel. of concepts in the bio-med. scis. Office: U Ill Coll Med Dept Biochemistry 1819 W Polk St # C 536 Chicago IL 60612-7331 Office: Ctr Molecular Biol Oral Diseases 801 S Paulina St # C 860 Chicago IL 60612-7210

CHAMBERS, GLENN DARRELL, wildlife photographer, artist; b. Butler, Mo., June 14, 1936; s. E. Glenn and Fern M. (Woods) C.; m. Marilyn Janell Henry, Aug. 29, 1959 (div. Jan. 1980); children: James D. (dec.), Russell G., Lindell C.; m. Jeannie Bay Erwin, Feb. 27, 1980; stepchildren: Robert Roemer, Matthew Roemer. BS, Central Mo. State U., 1958; MA, U. Mo.-Columbia, 1961. Area mgr. Mo. Dept. Conservation, Jefferson City, 1961-62, research biologist, 1962-69, biologist, photographer, 1969-79; regional dir. Ducks Unltd., Columbia, Mo., 1979-83, wildlife photographer, 1984-88; pres. Niska Art, Inc., Columbia, Mo., 1984—, Paddlefoot Prodns., Inc., 1994—; motion picture specialist Mo. Dept. Conservation, 1988-95; exec. v.p. Mo. Bird Obs., 1988; freelance cinematographer, 1995—. Films include: (with Charles and Elizabeth Schwartz) Return of the Wild Turkey (2d place award Outdoor Writers Assn. Am.), 1971, The Show-Me Hunter (2d place award Outdoor Writers Assn. Am.), 1972, Wild Chorus: The Story of the Canada Goose (1st place award Outdoor Writers Assn. Am.), 1974, (Best Motion Picture award Wildlife Soc.), 1974; More Than Trees: Ecology of the Forest (2d place award Forestry Film Festival, 1st place award Outdoor Writers Assn. Am.), 1977, It's Your Choice, 1990 (Teddy Roosevelt award Mich. Outdoor Writers Assn.), Forests for the Future, 1991 (Teddy Roosevelt award Mich. Outdoor Writers Assn.), Back to the Wild, 1998 (3 Emmy awards); prodr. Otter Chaos, Nat. Geog. TV, 2000; tech. articles to Jour. Wildlife Mgmt., 1961-77; winner 1984-85 Mo. Waterfowl Stamp Design Contest; recipient TV Emmy award for Best Non-News Feature Glenn and the Geese, 1990, Where Eagles Soar, 1995 (2d Place award Assn. for Conservation Info.), Furbearers of Mo., 1997. Bd. dirs. Conservation Fedn. Mo., 1998—, Mo. Conservation Heritage Found., 1990—. Mem. Wildlife Soc. (E. Sidney Stephens award 1990). Democrat. Baptist. Home: 807 Cornell Columbia MO 65203-1828

CHAMBERS, JOHN WHITECLAY, II, history educator; b. West Chester, Pa., Aug. 6, 1936; s. John McCausland and Le-Arie P. Chambers; m. Dorothy Roman, 1958; children: John Bret, Jeffrey Mark, Michael Adam; m. Amy Russo Piro, 1982; 1 child, Tacy Elizabeth. Reporter Pasadena (Calif.) Ind. Star-News, 1958-60, San Rafael (Calif.) Ind.-Jour., 1960-61; news and documentary writer/prodr. KRON-TV, San Francisco, 1961-65; asst. prof. history Barnard Coll., Columbia U., N.Y.C., 1972-82; asst. prof. history Rutgers U., New Brunswick, N.J., 1982-87, assoc. prof., 1987-93, prof., 1993—, dept. chair, 1997-98; Fulbright lectr. U. Rome, spring 1982; project dir. Rutgers Ctr. Hist. Analysis, 1993-95; vis. lectr. U. Tokyo, 1997. Author: Three Generals on War, 1973; Draftees or Volunteers, 1975; The Eagle and the Dove: The Peace Movement and U.S. Foreign Policy, 1900-1922, 1976, 2d edit., 1991; The Tyranny of Change: America in the Progressive Era, 1890-1920, 1980, 2d edit., 1992, 3rd edit., 2000; (with Warren Susman) American History Reading Lists, 3 vols., 1983; To Raise an Army: The Draft Comes to Modern America, 1987 (Best Book award Soc. Mil. History 1988, Best Book on Mil. History 1987); (with Charles C. Moskos) The New Conscientious Objection: From Sacred To Secular Resistance, 1993; (with David Culbert) World War II Film and History, 1996; (with G. Kurt Piehler) Major Problems in American Military History, 1998; editor-in-chief Oxford Co. to Am. Military History, 1999. NEH grantee, 1974; humanities fellow Rockefeller Found., 1981-82, vis. fellow Inst. Advanced

Study, Princeton, 1995-96. Mem. Peace History Soc. (pres. 1975-77), Am. Hist. Assn., Orgn. Am. Historians, Soc. Historians of Am. Fgn. Rels., Soc. Mil. History. Office: Rutgers U 16 Seminary Pl New Brunswick NJ 08901-1108

CHAMBERS, JOHNNIE LOIS (TUCKER CHAMBERS), retired elementary school educator, rancher; b. Crocket County, Tex., Sept. 28, 1929; d. Robert Leo and Lois K. (Slaughter) Tucker; m. R. Boyd Chambers; children: Theresa A., Glyn Robert, Boyd James, John Trox. BEd, Sul Ross State U., Alpine, Tex., 1971. Tchr. 1st and 2d grades Candelaria (Tex.) Elem. Sch., 1971-73; head tchr. K-8 Ruidosa (Tex.) Elem. Sch., 1973-77; head tchr. K-8 Presidio Ind. Sch. Dist. at Candelaria Elem. Sch., 1977-91, tchr. 2d and 3d grades, 1991-93, tchr. pre-kindergarten, kindergarten and 1st grade, 1993-98; acting prin. Candelaria Elem. and Jr. High, 1995-98, head tchr. pre-K to 8th grades, 1996-98, tchr. pre-K, kindergarten, 1st and 2d grades, 1996-99, ret., 1999; mem. sight-base decision making, Presidio, 1991-94; mem. Chihuahuan Desert Rsch. Inst., Alpine, 1982-94. Leader Boy Scouts Am., Ruidosa and Candelaria, 1973-91, Cub Scout leader, 1973-91; chpt. mem. Sheriffs Assn. Tex., Austin, 1980. Recipient awards Boy Scouts Am., 1969, 83, winner Litter Gitter award, 1994-95. Mem. Tex. State Tchrs. Assn., Phi Alpha Theta. Avocations: hiking, camping, anthropologic digs, cave exploring, cooking. Home: 99 Retirement Cir Candelaria TX 79843

CHAMBERS, MARJORIE BELL, historian; b. N.Y.C., Mar. 11, 1923; d. Kenneth Carter and Katherine (Totman) Bell; m. William Hyland Chambers, Aug. 8, 1945; children: Lee Chambers-Schiller, William Bell, Leslie Chambers Trujillo, Kenneth Carter. AB cum laude, Mt. Holyoke Coll., South Hadley, Mass., 1943; MA, Cornell U., 1948; PhD, U. N.Mex., 1974; LLD honoris causa, Ctrl. Mich. U., 1977; LHD (hon.), Wilson Coll., 1980, Northern Michigan U., 1982. Staff asst. Am. Assn. UN, League of Nations Assn., N.Y.C., 1944-45; program specialist dept. rural sociology Cornell U., Ithaca, N.Y., 1945-46, rsch. asst. dept. speech and drama, 1946-48; substitute tchr. Los Alamos (N.Mex.) Pub. Schs., 1962-65; project historian U.S. AEC, Los Alamos, 1965-69; adj. prof. U. N.Mex., Los Alamos, 1970-76, 84-85; pres. Colo. Women's Coll., Denver, 1976-78; dean Grad. Sch. Union Inst., Cin., 1979-82, mem. core faculty Grad. Sch., 1979—; interim pres. Colby-Sawyer Coll., New London, N.H., 1985-86; vis. prof. Cameron U., Lawton, Okla., 1974; commr., vice-chair N.Mex. Commn. on Higher Edn., Santa Fe, 1987-91; chair citizen adv. bd. U.S. Army Command and Gen. Staff Coll., Ft. Leavenworth, Kans., 1990—; mem. bd. dirs. Coun. Ind. Colls. and Univs., Santa Fe, 1991—; rep. Los Alamos County Labor Mgmt. Bd. Contbr. articles to profl. jours. Chair Los Alamos County Coun., 1976, councilor, 1975-76, 79; candidate N.Mex. 3d Congl. Dist., 1982, lt. gov. N.Mex., 1986; chair Sec. of Navy's Advisor Bd. on Edn. and Tng., Washington and Pensacola, Fla., 1987-89; chair Citizen Bd. of U.S. Army Command and Gen. Staff Coll., Fort Leavenworth, Kans.; acting chair, vice-chair adminstrn. Pres. Carter's Com. for Women, Washington, 1977-80; chair Pres. Ford's Nat. Adv. Bd. on Women's Ednl. Programs, Washington, Los Alamos County Pers. Bd., 1983-90; mem. nat. adv. coun . U.S. SBA, 1990—; mem. Los Alamos and N.Mex. Rep. Ctrl. com., 1982—; trustee Colby-Sawyer Coll., New London, N.H., 1980-89; pub. mem. U.S. Dept. State Fgn. Svc. selection bd., 1978; mem. U.S. del. UN Conf. Women, Copenhagen, 1980; bd. dirs. N.Mex. Endowment for the Humanities, 1997—. Recipient Teresa d'Avila award Coll. St. Teresa, Winona, Minn., 1978, Disting. Woman award U. N.Mex. Alumni Assn., Albuquerque, 1990, N.Mex. Disting. Pub. Svc. award Gov. and Awards Coun., Albuquerque, 1991; named Outstanding N.Mex. Woman Gov. and Com. on Status of Women, Albuquerque, 1988, 89. Mem. AAUW (life), U.S. rep. coun. 1973-75, nat. pres. 1975-79, pres. Edn. Found.), DAR, Bus. and Profl. Women (Los Alamos parliamentarian and dist. parliamentarian 1991-93), Women's Polit. Caucus (gov. bd. conv., keynoter, vice-chair Rep. caucus 1971—), Internat. Women's Forum, N.Mex. Hist. Soc., Los Alamos Hist. Soc. (pres., Sangre de Cristo Girl Scouts "Woman of Distinction" 1996). Presbyterian. Avocations: figure skating, skiing, swimming, painting, public speaking.

CHAMBERS, ROBERT WILLIAM, marketing professional, consultant; b. Atlanta, Apr. 4, 1943; s. Robert William Chambers and Mary Emily (Martin) Nalley; m. Wendy Ann Treneer, Dec. 28, 1967 (div. 1979); 1 child, Robert William III. AB, Princeton U., 1965; MA, Indiana U., 1970, PhD, 1974. Assoc. instr. Ind. U., Bloomington, 1970-73; instr. Kans. State U., Manhattan, 1973-74; gen. mgr. Standard Cellulose Products Inc., Atlanta, 1974-75; mgr. sales, ops. Disposable Plastic Systems Inc., Marietta, Ga., 1975-77; asst. v.p., account exec. instl. sales Robinson-Humphrey Co. Inc., Atlanta, 1977-80; columnist, fin. reporter Atlanta Journal, 1980-81; account exec. Hill and Knowlton (J. Walter Thompson Group), Atlanta, 1981-83; sr. v.p., sales mgr. eastern div. Colonial Investment Svcs. Inc., Atlanta, 1983-90; sr. fin. cons. The Gwent Group, Atlanta, 1990-92; v.p., treas. Rabun Gap Film Corp., Atlanta, 1993—; dir. Bus. Svcs. Div. Porraro and Assocs., Atlanta, 1993-95; mgr. accts. divsn. Atlanta Rsch. and Trading, 1994-95; regional mktg. dir. Stephens, Inc., Atlanta, 1996-97; fin. reporter Atlanta-Jour.-Constn., 1997-99; mktg. dir. Macey-Holland & Co., Atlanta, 1999; COO The Resource Ctr., Atlanta, 2000—; Ga. correspondent The Economist, London, 1978-83, 995; Am. Bankers Assn. fellowship, 1998. Mem. bd. Oglethorpe U. Art Mus., 1998—. Mem. Soc. Colonial Wars, The Author's Guild. Episcopal. Clubs: Piedmont Driving, Nine O'Clocks (Atlanta). Home: 335 Franklin Rd NE Atlanta GA 30342-2711 Office: RWC Ltd PO Box 421612 Atlanta GA 30342-8612

CHAMBERS-MANGUM, FRANSENNA ETHEL, special education educator; b. Meridian, Miss., June 27, 1957; d. Forrest S. and Betty (Wade) Chambers; 1 child, Richard Jomar Sullivan. BS, Jackson State U., 1979, MA, 1980, EdS, 1986. Cert. tchr., Miss., secondary adminstr., Miss. Chpt. tchr. Meridian Pub. Schs., 1979; tchr. spl. edn. Magee (Miss.) Pub. Sch., 1980-84; speech pathologist Heritage Sch. Learning Disability, Jackson, Miss., 1984-85; speech pathologist Canton (Miss.) Pub. Schs., 1985-86, spl. edn. tchr., 1986-88, pre-sch. coord., 1988-89; tchr. spl. edn. lang. delayed Jackson (Miss.) Pub. Schs., 1989-90, tchr. spl. edn., 1990—, mid. sch. reading tchr., 1993—; Miss. Writing Project cons. tchr., 1989—, Adult Edn. tchr. (ages 16-65). Writer and editor poems. Mem. Miss. Registrar Voters Com., Jackson, 1975—, Vista/Peace Corps, Jackson, 1980, NAACP, Jackson, 1982-85; bd. dirs., sec. and coord. Roshea Recovery Ctr., 1993—; tchr. Sunday sch., Jackson, 1992. Named Miss Miss. Elks, 1972-74, Miss Miss. Congeniality, Jaycees, 1972; Black Women's Assn. partial scholar, 1975. Mem. Miss. Writers of Am., Miss. Assn. Colls. and Evaluator Univs., Miss. Assn. Tchrs. (evaluator 1986—, Educator of Yr.), Learning Disabled Assn. Miss., Miss. Assn. Edn., Eastern Star, Daus. of Isis. Democrat. Avocations: writing poetry, public relations. Home: 1772 Casteel Dr Jackson MS 39204-3508

CHAMBOLLE, THIERRY JEAN-FRANCOIS, environmental scientist; b. Beychac et Cailleau, Gironde, France, June 12, 1939; s. Jean Michel and Renée Marie (Minchini) C.; m. Claude Elisabeth Delord, Aug. 29, 1963; children: Damien, David, Antonin, Étienne, Thomas. Baccalauréat in Math and Philosophy, Lycée Montesquieu, Bordeaux, France; diploma of engineering, Ecole Polytechnique, Paris, 1959-61, Ecole Nationale des Ponts et Chaussées, Paris, 1962-64. Dir. de l Eau et la Prévention des Pollutions, 1978-88; délégué aux risques majeurs Ministère de l Environment France; directeur de la recherche Lyonnaise Des Eaux, Dumez, France, 1989-91, dir. gen., 1991-95, dir. gén. dél., 1995—; pres. CEMAGREF, France, 1989-99. Decorated Officier, Legion of Honor, Mérite Nat. (France). Mem. Acad. Scis. (com. applications). Office: Suez Lyonnaise des Eaux, 1 rue d'Astorg, 75008 Paris France

CHAMBONET, JEAN-YVES, physician; b. Paris, Jan. 2, 1944. MD, U. Paris, 1974. Extern Hosp. Paris, 1967-72; family physician Liberal, Nantes, France, 1975—. UFR Medicine, Nantes, France, 1993—. Co-author: Guide Aides Sociales, 1996. Mem. Coll. Nat. Géneralistes Enseignants. Office: Faculty Medicine, 1 Rue Veil, 44035 Nantes France

CHAMI, ROGER LOUIS, heavy construction company executive; b. Cairo, Egypt, July 28, 1940; s. Louis Fathallah and Alice Rebecca (Seidah) C.; m. Judith de Bocay, June 4, 1965; children—David, Sarah. Grad. Am. U., Beirut, Lebanon; Doctorate, Sorbonne U., Paris. Engr. Internat. Engring. Corp., Cairo, 1965-70; chief engr. Societe Internat. de Constructions, Beirut, 1970-75; pres. Les Constructeurs Reunis, Cairo, 1970-80, chmn., Paris., Cairo, 1980—; sec. Bridge Com., Cairo, 1965-70, Golf com., Cairo, 1970-75; v.p. Swedish Com., Stockholm, 1975-80; pres. Christian Assn., Cairo, 1980—. Contbr. articles to profl. jours. Sec. Guisa Constrn. Coop., 1967. Mem. National Party. Maronite. Clubs: Automobile (Cairo), Gezira. Lodge: Grand. Avocations: bridge; golf; music; literature. Office: Les Constructeurs Reunis,, 10 Elwi St., 11000 Cairo Egypt

CHAMIS, CHRISTOS CONSTANTINOS, aerospace scientist, educator; b. Sotira, Greece, May 16, 1930; came to U.S., 1948; s. Constantinos and Anastasia (Kyriakos) C.; m. Alice Yanosko, Aug. 20, 1966; children: Chrysanthe, Anna-Lisa, Constantinos. BS in Civil Engring., Cleve. State U., 1960; MS, Case Western Res. U., 1962, PhD, 1967. Draftsman, designer Cons. Engring., Cleve., 1955-60; rsch. asst. Case Western Res. U., Cleve., 1960-62, rsch. assoc., 1964-68; rsch. mathematician B.F. Goodrich, Brecksville, Ohio, 1962-64; aerospace engr. Glenn Rsch. Ctr. NASA, Cleve., 1968-78, sr. rsch. engr., 1978-86, sr. aerospace scientist, 1986—; cons. Lawrence Livermore Labs., Calif., 1974-79; adj. prof. Cleve. State U., 1968—, Akron U., 1980—, Case Western Res. U., 1984—. Editor: Composites Analysis/Design, 1975, Test Methods and Design Allowables for Composites, 1979, 89; mem. editl. bd. Jour. Composites Rsch. and Tech., Reinforced Plastics and Composites, Internat. Jour. Damage Mechanics, Theoretical and Applied Fracture Mechanics; contbr. numerous articles to sci. jours.; patentee in field for Intraply Hybrid Composites; rschr. in hygrothermal composite micromechanics, computational composite mechanics-computer codes, high-temperature composite structures, structural tailoring of engine structures, computational simulation of progressive fracture, engine structures computational simulations, computational simulation/tailoring of coupled multi-discipline problems, and probabilistic structural analysis. Served with USMC, 1952-53. Fellow ASME, AIAA (assoc. editor 1986-88), ASCE, ASTM, Soc. Advancement Materials and Process Engring.; mem. Soc. Exptl. Mechanics, Soc. Automotive Engrs., Am. Soc. Metals, Am. Soc. Composites, Soc. Engring. Sci., Am. Ceramic Soc., Sigma Xi, Dodoni Club, Hellenic U. Club. Home: 24534 Framingham Dr Cleveland OH 44145-4902

CHAMPA, JOHN JOSEPH, telecommunications engineer, consultant; b. Columbus, Ohio, Oct. 16, 1944; s. Antonio John and Helen Catherine (Izzie) C.; ; children: Lea Christine Kuhn, Susan Catherine Muscat, Rebecca Lynn McLaughlin, Patrick John C. BA, Ohio State U., Columbus, 1974; MA, Cen. Mich U., Mt. Pleasant, 1975; MS, Columbia Pacific U., San Rafael, Calif., 1985, PhD, 1986. Cert. telecom. engr. Mem. U.S. police Fed. Protective Svc., Nashville & Columbus, 1972-74; safety engr. Borden Corp., Columbus, 1974-76; plant safety engr. Buckeye Steel Castings, Columbus, 1976-80; divsn. safety engr. Cooper Energy Svcs., Mount Vernon, Ohio, 1980-82; sr. safety engr. Goodyear Atomic Corp., Piketon, Ohio, 1982-83; corp. safety engr. Unisys Corp., Detroit, 1984-88; mgr., chief engr. Unisys Worldwide Videoconferencing, Detroit, 1988-94; dir. Multimedia Comms. Svcs., Plymouth, Mich., 1994—; exec. v.p. Radio Amateur Satellite Corp., Washington, 1988-91; adj. prof. Franklin U., Columbus, 1979-81. Inventor: Digital Video Switch for Videoconferencing, 1992; author: CD-ROM Unisys Multimedia and Video Conferencing Solutions; co-author: Am. Nat. Stds. Inst. (ANSI) Z241 Std.; contbr. articles to profl. jours. Capt. U.S. Army, 1967-71. Mem. Internat. Teleconferencing Assoc. (bd. dirs. 1993-99, exec. com. 1996-97), Nat. Assn. Radio and Telecom. Engrs., Nat. Rifle Assn., Nat. Arbor Day Found., Nature Conservancy Mich. Chpt.-Great Lakes Soc., Nat. Geog. Soc., Mich. Bear Hunters Assn., Upper Peninsula Bear Houndsman Assn., Mich. United Conservation Clubs, Desktop Users Group, PictureTel Users Group, VFW (past post comdr. and trustee), Safari Club Internat., Am. Radio Relay League, Am. Canoe Assn., Livingston County Amateur Radio Club. Avocations: hunting, cartography, camping, amateur radio. Office: Unisys Corp Bldg 1 41100 Plymouth Rd Ste 350 Plymouth MI 48170-1892

CHAMPAGNE, JOSEPH ERNEST, corporate consultant, industrial psychologist; b. Norwich, Conn., May 19, 1938; s. Fred Joseph and Loretta Eva (Lucier) C.; m. Emilie Lind, Dec. 27, 1969; children: Jennifer, Juliana, Johanna. A.B., St. Mary's U., 1960; M.A., Fordham U., 1962; Ph.D., Purdue U., 1966. Lic. cert. psychologist, Tex. Psychology instr., research asst., cons. various orgns., 1962-71; pres. Houston Community Coll. System, 1971-73, pres. emeritus; assoc. dir. Ctr. Human Resources U. Houston, 1969-71, 73-76; coordinator extended acad. and pub. service programs U. Houston System Office, 1977-78, assoc. v.p. office of exec. v.p., 1977-78; prof. dept. organizational behavior and mgmt. U. Houston, 1967-81, v.p. acad. affairs, 1978-81; pres. Oakland U., Rochester, Mich., 1981-91; pres., chief exec. officer Crittenton Corp., Rochester, Mich., 1991-93; chancellor Lamar U. System, Beaumont, Tex., 1994-95; chmn. bd. dirs. Ross Controls Corp., Munder Funds. Contbr. articles to numerous publs. Pres. Houston Area Rehab. Assn., 1971; bd. dirs. Tex. Rehab. Assn, 1971-72; mem. adv. com. Community Colls., Houston, 1970-71; bd. dirs. Ctr. Multiple Handicapped Children, 1973-81, Assn. Univ. Related Rsch., pres. 1990-91; chmn. bd. dirs. Houston Lighthouse for Blind, 1976-81; bd. dirs. Detroit Symphony Orch., Detroit Econ. Club, Oakland U. Found.; mem. nat. adv. council Ctr. for Study of Presidency; pres., bd. dirs. Nat. Accreditation Coun., 1976-85, 88-91. Named Citizen of Yr. Houston Area Rehab. Assn. Mem. Am. Psychol. Assn., Am. Assn. Higher Edn., Am. Mgmt. Assn. Roman Catholic.

CHAMPION, ANTHONY GERARD, population geography educator; b. Canterbury, Kent, Eng., Apr. 19, 1946; s. Thomas Alan and Winifred Margaret (Balmer) C.; m. Marilyn Evans, Apr. 14, 1980; children: Katherine, Victoria. BA in Geography with honors, Oxford (Eng.) U., 1967; MPhil in Geography, U. London, 1969; PhD in Geography, Oxford U., 1972. Temp. lectr. U. Newcastle Upon Tyne, Eng., 1972-74, lectr., 1974-89, sr. lectr., 1989-93, reader in population geography, 1993-96, prof. population geography, 1996—, hon. dir. Housing and Soc. Rsch. Group, 1990—. Author, editor: Counterurbanization, 1989, Population Matters, 1993; author: Contemporary Britain, 1990, The Population of Britain in the 1990's, 1996. Vol. com. mem. Nomad Housing Assn., Newcastle Upon Tyne, 1978—. Recipient Rsch. grants Econ. and Social Rsch. Coun., 1986, 92, 94, 97, Brit. Acad., 1997, Wellcome Trust, 1992, Joseph Rowntree Found., 1991, Royal Soc. Mem. Coun. Brit. Geography (hon. treas. 1994-97). Office: Univ Newcastle, Dept Geography, Newcastle upon Tyne NE1 7RU, England

CHAMPION, KENNETH STANLEY WARNER, physicist; b. Sydney, NSW, Australia, Dec. 7, 1923; s. Cecil Alexander Buckingham and Ellen Catherine (Moxham) C.; m. Mavis Audrey Hinckley, Nov. 27, 1948; children: Annette, Gwendalyn, Geoffrey, Sandra. BS, U. Sydney, 1945; PhD, U. Birmingham, Eng., 1951. Asst. lectr. physics U. Queensland, Australia, 1946-49; rsch. fellow Australian Nat. U., 1949-52; rsch. assoc. MIT, Cambridge, Mass., 1952-54; asst. prof. physics Tufts U., Medford, Mass., 1954-59; rsch. scientist, sr. scientist Atmospheric Physics/Br. Chief, 1959-64; sr. exec. AF Cambridge Rsch. Labs./Phillips Lab., 1964-94; Brit. Coun. Rsch. scholar, 1947-49; vis. prof. U. Adelaide, Australia, 1964; presenter in field in 21 countries. Contbr. articles to 6 internat. profl. jours. Co-pres. PTA, Lexington, Mass., 1965-75. Fellow Phys. Soc. of London; mem. AIAA (assoc. fellow), N.Y. Acad. Scis., Am. Phys. Soc., Am. Geophys. Union, Am. Meteorol. Soc., Sigma Xi. Episcopalian. Achievements include being a pioneer in early plasma fusion oriented rsch.; pioneer in space rsch. with rocket and satellite measurements and development of internationally accepted atmospheric models. Home: 6 Rolfe Rd Lexington MA 02420-2308

CHAMPION, PIERRE DHEILLY, surgeon, researcher; b. Chatou, Ile de France, France, Nov. 26, 1936; s. Julien Joseph and Raymonde (Dheilly) C.; m. Genevieve Massonnet, June 25, 1964; children: Marie-Blandine, Herve, Christian. MD, U. Paris, 1964. Asst. surgeon Argenteuil Hosp., France, 1969-73; oral surgeon Beaumont, France, 1973-75; mgr. Centre Med., Bourg-la-Reine, France, 1975-99. Mem. Soc. Stomatologie Chirurgie Maxillo Faciale (sec. 1966). Roman Catholic. Avocation: equestrian. Office: 5 La Calcine, 66300 Llauro France

CHAMPION, TERENCE JOHN, marketing professional; b. London, Dec. 8, 1941; came to U.S., 1982; s. Anthony William and Emily Agnes (Taylor) C.; m. Madeleine Lee Geddes, Oct. 7, 1967; 1 child, Vanessa Sian. BA, Durham (Eng.) U., 1964. Various, 1964-82; gen. mgr. Moss Dynamics, Easton, Pa., 1982-89; pres. McQuay-Norris World Trade Corp., Easton, 1989-92, Champion Techs., Phila., 1993—; cons. in internat. mktg. various Fortune 500 corps. Mem. Lloyds of London (Bolivian rep. 1976-81). Office: Champion Technologies 2020 Walnut St Apt 8E Philadelphia PA 19103-5660

CHAMPION DE CRESPIGNY, RICHARD RAFE, academic administrator, educator; b. Adelaide, Australia, Mar. 16, 1936; s. Richard Geoffrey and Kathleen Cavanagh (Cudmore) Champion de C.; m. Christa Charlotte Boltz, May 17, 1959; children: Christine Anne Young, Richard Mark. MA, Cambridge U., Eng., 1961; BA in Oriental Studies, Australian Nat. U., Canberra, 1962, MA, 1964, PhD, 1968. With faculty Asian studies Australian Nat. U., 1965—, reader in Chinese, 1973-98, dean Asian studies, 1979-82, master univ. house, 1991—, adj. prof. Asian studies, 1999—; sec.-gen. 28 Internat. Cong. Orientalists, Canberra, 1971. Author: Last of the Han, 1969, China This Century, 1975, 2d edit., 1992, Northern Frontier, 1984, Emperor Huan and Emperor Ling, 1989, Generals of the South, 1990, To Establish Peace, 1996. Fellow Australian Acad. Humanities; mem. Chinese Studies Assn. Australia (pres. 1999—). Anglican. Avocations: walking, gardening, heraldry. Office: Univ House, Australian Nat U, Canberra 0200, Australia

CHAMPY, WILLIAM, JR., mathematician, educator, researcher, scientist, writer; b. Orangeburg, S.C., July 23, 1949; s. Buster and Mamie (Brown) C.. BS in Profl. Chemistry, S.C. State Coll., 1977, MEd, 1985, postgrad.; cert. prodn. operator, Orangeburg-Calhoun Tech. Coll., Orangeburg, S.C., 1990; cert. computer operator, Orangeburg-Calhoun Tech. Coll., 1997. Cert. critical needs tchr. in sci.; lic. bus driver, S.C., armed security guard, small bus. owner, operator. Mgr., owner Champy's Night Club, Orangeburg, S.C., 1968-84; tchr. chemistry, physics, sci. Quinas H.S., Augusta, Ga., 1980; instr. math. Orangeburg-Calhoun Tech. Coll., Orangeburg, S.C., 1985-87; tchr. math Branchville (S.C.) H.S., 1987; coord. devel. lab., math instr. Denmark (S.C.) Tech. Coll., 1989-90; lab. mgr., adminstr. Voorhees Coll., Denmark, S.C., 1991-92; math instr. Midlands Tech. Coll., Columbia, S.C., 1994; security officer Security Force, Inc., 1992-94, Spartan Security, 1995-96, Pinkerton, Inc., 1988—, Sizemore Security, Columbia, 1996—; rsch. asst. dept. energy, divsn. ecology S.C. State U., Orangeburg, unit mgr. dormatory, student svc. program coord. I, 1999—; with U.S. Census, 2000—; truck driver, laborer City of Columbia, 1980; edgefiler, tool sharpener Utica Tool Co., Inc., Orangeburg, 1982; security officer Wells Fargo, Orangeburg, 1990-92, Security Force, Inc., 1992-94, others; substitute tchr., bus driver Orangeburg Sch. Dist. # 5, 1988—; freelance personal income tax preparer, 1998—; coord. Swapop Tutoring Program S.C. State U./NASA, Orangeburg, 1998—; press operator, blademaker Frigidaire Corp., Orangeburg, 1998—; saw operator, laborer, inspector N.Am. Container, Orangeburg, 1996. Census enumerator, summer 1990; custodian, maint., set-up helper Episcopal Ch. of the Redeemer, 1997; field rep. U.S. Census Bur., 1997; security officer Am. Security, Inc. Mem. AAAS, ACS, NAACP, Nat. Inst. Sci., Am. Mgmt. Assn., S.C. State U. Nat. Alumni Assn., S.C. Tech. Edn. Assn., Nat. Inst. Sci., Nat. Soc. Black Engrs., Nat. Assn. Black Engrs., Ernest E. Just Sci. Club, Masons (sec.), Phi Delta Kappa, Omega Psi Phi. Avocations: pocket billiards, reading, fishing, hunting, checkers. E-mail: wchampy@scsu.edn. Home: 327 Champy Rd Orangeburg SC 29115-8923 Office: SC State U Dormitory/Unit Dept Orangeburg SC 29117-0001

CHAMULEAU, ROBERT ANTOINE FRANÇOIS MARIE, internist, educator; b. Maastricht, The Netherlands, Nov. 11, 1941; s. F.J. Chamalaun and Elisabeth Van Der Voort; m. Wilhelmina L.J.M. Loonen, Oct. 25, 1965; children: Martine E.D., Steven A.J., Boudewyn F. MD, U. Amsterdam, The Netherlands, 1968, PhD, 1971. Assoc. prof. dept. gastroenterology-hepatology Acad. Med. Ctr., U. Amsterdam, 1975—. E-mail: R.A.Chamuleau@amc.uva.nl. Office: Acad Med Ctr U Amsterdam, PO Box 22660, 1100 DD Amsterdam The Netherlands

CHAMZAS, CHRISTODOULOS C., electrical engineer, educator; b. Komotini, Thrace, Greece, Sept. 6, 1951; s. Constantinos C. and Evanthia A. (Lyrantzopoulos) C.; m. Elpida D. Antonopoulou, May 29, 1993; children: Constantinos, Dimitrios, Athanasios. Diploma in Elec. Engring., Nat. Tech. U., Athens, Greece, 1974; M. in Sys. Engring., Poly. Inst. Bklyn., 1975; PhD in Elec. Engring., Poly. Inst. N.Y., 1979. Registered engr., Greece. Acad. assoc. Poly. Inst. N.Y., Bklyn., 1976-79, asst. prof., 1979-82; mem. tech. staff AT&T Bell Labs., Holmdel, N.J., 1982-87, disting. mem. tech. staff, 1988-90; asst. prof. computer sci. U. Crete, Heraklion, 1987-88; assoc. prof. elec. engring. Democritus U. of Trace, Xanthi, 1990-97, prof., 1997—, dir. electric circuits analysis lab., 1990—, dir. image processing and multimedia unit, 1996—, dir. Cultural and Edn. Techs. Inst., 1998—; Editor IEEE Comms. Transactions, 1988. Mem. IEEE (sr.), Tech. Chamber of Greece, Sigma Xi. Greek Orthodox. Achievements include 6 international patents on image compression. Avocation: sailing. Office: Democritus Univ of Thrace, Dept of Elec Engring, 67100 Xanthi Greece

CHAN, ANDREW YIU CHUNG, environmental scientist; b. Hong Kong, Nov. 8, 1959; arrived in Australia, 1992; s. Yuen Hoi and Sze Nui (Wong) C.; m. Louisa Mun Yi Kwok. BSc, Chinese U. Hong Kong, 1981, dip. ed., 1984; MSc, Leeds (Eng.) U., 1991; PhD, Griffith U., Australia, 1998. Tchr. Kwun Tong Maryknoll Coll., Hong Kong, 1981-85, Hong Kong Buddhist Secondary Sch., 1985-87, Kwok Tak Seng Cath. Secondary Sch., Hong Kong, 1987-90, 91-92; lectr. Sch. Biochem. and Biol. Scis., Ctrl. Queensland U., Australia, 1998; lectr. Australian Sch. Environ. Scis., Griffith U., Nathan, Australia, 1998—. Contbr. articles to profl. jours., including Atmospheric Environment, Chemosphere, Internat. Jour. Environ. and Analytical Chemistry. Mem. Royal Australian Chem. Inst. Avocations: badminton, bridge, chess, reading, travel. Office: Australian Sch Environ Sci, Griffith U, Nathan QLD 4111, Australia

CHAN, BERNARD WAN BUN, transplant physician, biomedical consultant; b. Hong Kong, Oct. 31, 1935; s. Shing Chue and So Chun (Chung) C.; m. Dieneke Kroeze, Mar. 9, 1968; children: Robert, George, Marius. MB, BS, U. London, 1960, MD, 1970. Mem. sci. staff Med. Rsch. Coun., Eng., 1964-66; Elmore rsch. scholar Cambridge (Eng.) U., 1966-70; chief resident in hematology McMaster U., Can., 1970-72; chief hematologist Kitchener Waterloo Hosp., Ont., Can., 1972-89; bone marrow transplant dir. Hong Kong Sanatorium Hosp., 1998—; hon. assoc. prof. dept. pathology Chinese U. Hong Kong, 1993—; pres. Phoenix BioSci. Ltd., Hong Kong, 1993—. Contbr. articles to profl. jours. including Nature, Blood, Brit. Jour. Hematology. Chmn. med. affairs. Can. Cancer Soc., Ont., 1987. Fellow Royal Coll. Physicians (Can.), Royal Coll. Physicians (U.K.), Hong Kong Acad. Medicine; mem. Rotary (Hong Kong). Avocations: music, gardening. Office: Rm 602 Manning House 48 Queens Rd, Central Hong Kong

CHAN, BUDDY TAK-BIU, investment company executive; b. Hong Kong, Oct. 1, 1961; s. Peter P.F. and Vivian P.K. (Chan) Chan; m. Yuko Takeshita, Apr. 27, 1988; children: Christina Akie, Catherine Yoshie, Cary Toshiki. Diploma, Oxford Coll. Applied Sci., Eng., 1984; BSc, DSc, Pacific Western U., 1986. Founder, dir. Buddy Electronics & Systems Ltd., Hong Kong, 1979—; exec. dir. Peter Chan (Secs.) Ltd., Hong Kong, 1983—; gen. mgr. Pacific Essential Ltd., Hong Kong, 1987-92, dir., 1987—; editor Hong Kong Economist Newspaper Ltd., 1987-92; mng. dir. Concord Securities Ltd., Hong Kong, 1987—; mgr. Essential Projects Corp., U.S., 1988-92, Essential Tech. Ltd., Can., 1988—; bd. dirs. Pacific Essential Ltd., Buddy Electronics & Sys. Ltd., Concord Securities Ltd., Essential Tech. Ltd., Hong Kong Economist Newspaper Ltd. Author: Application of Robotic Technology in Rehabilitation Medicine, A Restaurant Served by Robots--A Feasibility Study, The Illustrated Encyclopedia of Robotic Technology, The Share Registration Program--An Advance Approach. Recipient cert. Dir. of the Assn. for Mgmt. Excellence, U.S., 1989, Internat. Bus. Inst., U.S., 1989, Hong Kong Productivity Coun., 1988, Japan Found. and Japan Assn. Internat. Edn., 1987, Stock Exch. of Hong Kong Ltd., 1987, Hallmark Medallion, World Decoration of Excellence, 1989, Leader in Sci. award Am. Biog. Inst., 1989, Award of Honor, Internat. Civil Aviation Orgn., 1979; fellow Oxford Coll. Applied Sci., 1984. Fellow Internat. Biog. Assn. UK; mem. Robotic Internat. (sr.), Soc. Mfg. Engrs. USA (sr.), Nat. Svc. Robot Assn. USA (charter), Hong Kong Inst. Fishery (exec. com.), N.Y. Acad. Scis. (sustaining), Am. Biog. Inst. Rsch. Assn. (dep. gov. 1989-90), ASME, German Assn. Engrs., French Soc. Mech. Engrs., Robotic Soc. Am., Japan Indsl. Robot Assn., Robotics Soc. Japan, Engring. Mgmt. Soc., IEEE, Inst. Sci. Tech. UK, Laser Soc. Japan, ABI Rsch. Bd. Advisers. Avocations: aeronautical science, criminology, horseback riding, tennis. Office: 2620 Sandstone Crescent, Coquitlam, BC Canada V3E 2T9

CHAN, CARLYLE HUNG-LUN, psychiatrist, educator; b. Clarksdale, Miss., July 4, 1949; s. Henry Howe and Jennie (Wong) C.; m. Patricia

Meyer, June 18, 1977; children: Christopher, Diana. BS, U. Wis., 1971; MD, Med. Coll. Wis., 1975. Diplomate Am. Bd. Psychiatry and Neurology. Resident in psychiatry U. Chgo., 1975-78; postdoctoral fellow R.W. Johnson clin. scholar Yale U. Sch. Medicine, 1978-80; asst. prof. Med. Coll. Wis., Milw., 1980-86, assoc. prof., 1986-98; prof. Med. Coll. of Wis., Milw., 1998—; dir. residency edn. Med. Coll. Wis., Milw., 1987—, prof., 1998—, vice chair edn. and informatics, 1997—, dir. continuing med. edn., 1990—; dir. catchment area Milw. County Mental Health Complex, 1981-82; chief psychiatrist Psychiatrist Ctr., Columbia Hosp., Milw., 1982-87; dir. continuing med. edn. Soc. Tchg. Scholars, 1994; dir. course annual psychiat. conf., 1982—; dir. Door County (Wis.) Summer Inst., 1987—. Asst. editor Asian-Am. Psychiatry Newsletter, Washington, 1983-84; assoc. editor Acad. Psychiatry Newsletter, 1991-94; contbr. articles to profl. jours. Bd. dirs. Planning Council for Mental Health and Social Service, 1983—. Jr. Faculty Devel. award NIMH, 1983-85; Community Devel. award Apple Computer Co., Milw., 1984. Fellow Am. Psychiat. Assn.; mem. Am. Coll. Psychiatrists, Wis. Psychiat. Assn. (pres. Milw. chpt. 1990-91, chair edn. com. 1995—), Assn. Acad. Psychiatry (regional coord. 1987—, regional coord. dir. 1993-96, treas. 1996—), Am. Assn. Dirs. Psychiat. Residency Tng. (sec. 1994-95, pres.-elect 1995, pres. 1996, treas. 1990-92, program com. chair 1993-94), Wis. State Med. Soc., Milw. County Med. Soc. Med. Coll. of Wis., Soc. Teaching Scholars. Avocations: tennis, golf, running. Office: Med Coll Wis Dept Psychiatry 8701 W Watertown Plank Rd Milwaukee WI 53226-3548

CHAN, CHAK-FU, hotel executive, real estate investment company executive; b. Hong Kong, Apr. 18, 1918; s. Kwan-Tung and Kwei-Heung (Cheng) C.; m. Esther Chi-Lan Wong, Oct. 22, 1953; children: Lawrence M. Y., Charles M. W., Joseph M. C. Civil engring. degree, Lingnam U., 1937. Mng. dir. Fu Investment Co. Ltd., Hong Kong, 1961—, Internat. Hoteliers Ltd., Hong Kong, 1972—; chmn., pres. Fu Investment Co., Ltd., Los Angeles, 1973—, Pearl City Investment Corp., Los Angeles, 1974—; chmn. Pacific Renaissance Assocs., San Francisco, 1986—, Park Lane Hotels Internat., Hong Kong and N.Y.C., 1986—; mng. gen. ptnr. U.S. Hotelier Assn., San Francisco, 1981—; dir. Real Estate Developers Assn., Hong Kong, 1974—, Newco Holding Corp., Nauru, 1987, Panilla Holdings BVI, Ltd., Brit. Virgin Island, 1988. Mem. Am. Soc. Travel Agts., Pacific Area Travel Assn., Country Club, Jockey Club (Hong Kong). Office: Park Lane Hotel, 310 Gloucester Rd 7th Fl, Causeway Bay Hong Kong

CHAN, DAVID MOON CHEUNG, physician, educator; b. Hong Kong, July 19, 1946; s. Tak Sang and Shau Wah (Lee) C.; m. Livia Suk Lun Lai; children: Leslie, Mercedes, Cordia, Nathan, Joshua. MB, BChir, Hong Kong U., 1970. Diplomate Am. Bd. Pediat. Fellow in hematology and oncology Harvard U., 1973-74; clin. instr. U. B.C., 1976-80, clin. asst. prof., 1980-87, clin. assoc. prof., 1987-91, clin. prof., 1991—; head dept. pediats. Mount St. Joseph Hosp., Vancouver, 1987-93; dir. World Vision (Hong Kong); hon. clin. prof. Suzhou Med. Coll., China; dean's rep. U. B.C. Faculty Medicine, 1995; chmn. Quality Camp Internat., Hong Kong Br., 1995, Cmty. Care Found, Vancouver, 1995; spl. China rep. Evang. Med. Aid Soc., 1995. Author: Young Courage. Chmn. Save Elizabeth Liu Bone Marrow Registration Campaign, Vancouver, 1990, Miracle Network Telephone, China Sect., 1991. Nuffield scholar Nuffield Fdt., London, 1969; fellow Hong Kong Acad. of Sci., 1998. Fellow Royal Coll. Physicians Can. (cert.), Am. Acad. Medicine; mem. N.Y. Acad. Sci. Baptist. Office: # 1102 528 Nathan Rd, Kowloon Hong Kong China also: 3983 Dumfries St, Vancouver, BC Canada

CHAN, DONALD PIN-KWAN, orthopaedic surgeon, educator; b. Rangoon, Burma, Jan. 21, 1937; s. Charles Y.C. and Josephine (Golamco) C.; m. Dorothy Chan, July 31, 1966; children: Joanne, Elaine. BS, U. Rangoon, Burma, 1955, MD, 1960. Intern medicine U. Hong Kong, 1960-61, resident surgery and orthopaedics, 1961-68; resident orthopaedic surgery U. Vt., 1968-71; assoc. orthopaedist Strong Meml. Hosp., Rochester, N.Y., 1972-80, sr. assoc. orthopaedist, 1980-86, attending orthopaedist, 1986—; asst. prof. U. Rochester, 1972-80, assoc. prof., 1980-87, prof., 1987-93; prof., head of divsn. spine surgery U. Va., Charlottesville, 1994—; dir. Goldstein Fellowship, Rochester, Orthopaedic Clin. Svcs., Rochester; chief sect. spine surgery dept. orthopaedics, Rochester, 1993. Contbr. articles on clin. rsch. related to the spine. Bd. dirs. Rochester Chinese Assn., 1991. Traveling fellow Scoliosis Rsch. Soc. Fellow ACS, Am. Acad. Orthopaedic Surgeons, Am. Orthopaedic Assn., Scoliosis Rsch. Soc. (1st v.p. 1995, pres. 1997-98); mem. AMA, N.Am. Spine Soc., Am. Spinal Injury Assn., Ea. Orthopaedic Assn. Avocations: tennis, fishing. Office: Univ Va Health Scis Ctr PO Box 159 Charlottesville VA 22902-0159

CHAN, DWIGHT KUNG-SANG, automobile accessories company executive, musician; b. Sept. 24, 1934; s. Yin Cheung and Phoebe (Nee) C; m. Victoria Chan, Apr. 2, 1966; 1 child, Nathanael. BS, Chung Chi Coll., Hon Kong, 1958. Salesman Dow Chem. Internat. S.A., 1960-66; pres. Le Mans (Taisi) Ltd., Hong Kong, 1966—; propr. Francolux Société, 1975—; pres. Carrie Children's Fashion; founder, chmn. bd. Hosanna Chanters, Hong Kong, 1991—, Hosaana Chanters, Sydney, 1995—. Bass-baritone soloist Hong Kong Oratorio Soc., 1958—; operatic debut in Marriage of Figaro, 1967, Hong Kong City Hall L'Elixier d'Amor, 1968, The Bartered Bride, 1976, The Sweet Maiden (Chinese), 1978, Messiah Cultural Centre, Manila, 1972, Der Freischütz, 1989, Taipei Bastien Und Bastienna New HK Cultural Centre, 1989; oratorio solos include Samson, Judas Maccabaeus, Israel in Egypt, Creations, Seasons, Mount of Olive, Mass in C, Missa Solemnis, St. Paul Requiems, (Brahms, Mozart, Verdi), Twelfth Mass, St. John's Passion, St. Matthew's Passion. Mem. Hong Kong Oratorio Soc. (chmn.), Y's Men of Hong Kong, Chung Chi Execs. (charter mem., 1st exec. bd., hon. treas.). Office: A2-19 Kin Lee Bldg 138, Jaffe Rd, Hong Kong Hong Kong

CHAN, HARVEY THOMAS, JR., food technology researcher; b. Astoria, Oreg., Mar. 5, 1940; m. Doreen Eiko Yoshizumi, Dec. 26, 1964; children: Baron D., Dwight D., Teruko M. BS, Oreg. State U., 1963, PhD, 1968; MS, U. Hawaii, 1965. Food technologist Agrl. Rsch. Svc. USDA, Honolulu, 1968-79, Hilo, Hawaii, 1979-98; cons. Internat. Exec. Svc. Corp., Guatamala, 1986—, Dominican Republic, 1987—, USAID, Winrock, India, 1988. Author: Tropical Fruit Processing, 1988; editor: Handbook of Tropical Foods, 1983; contbr. articles to profl. jours.; inventor device for removal of Papaya seeds. Cubmaster Boy Scouts Am., Hilo, 1980-83, asst. scoutmaster, 1986-99. Mem. Inst. Food Technologists (chmn. Hawaii sect. 1977-78, chmn.-elect, 1976-77, sec.-treas. 1973-75), Am. Chem. Soc., Am. Hort. Soc., Sigma Xi. E-mail: hchan@aloha.net. Home: 932 Komomala Dr Hilo HI 96720-2728

CHAN, HSIAO CHANG, physiology educator; b. Canton, China, June 12, 1957; s. Chuang Yi Chen and Zi Yu Huo; m. York Ming Hwe, Apr. 12, 1989; 1 child, Alan. ND, U. Ill., 1983, PhD, 1988. Postdoctoral assoc. U. Ill., Champaign-Urbana, 1988-89, U. Chgo., 1989-92; asst. prof. physiology Chinese U. Hong Kong, 1993-95, assoc. prof., 1996—; dir. Epithelial Cell Biology Rsch. Ctr., 1999—. Contbr. articles to sci. jours., including Sci., Am. Jour. Physiology, Jour. Physiology, chpt. to book; mem. editl. bd. Devel. and Reproductive Biology. Grantee Assisted Reprodn. Tech. and Andrology Internat., 1994, travel grantee DuPont Merck, 1996; recipient Nat. Natural Sci. award, China, 1997. Mem. Physiol. Soc., Am. Physiol. Soc., Soc. for Study Reprodn., Biophys. Soc. Achievements include discovery of cell shrinkage-induced cation conductance, discovery of a functional role of annexin IV; investigation of Cl-channel regulation in normal and cystic fibrosis epithelial cells; elucidation of bioelectric properties of the male and female reproductive tracts. Office: Chinese U Hong Kong, Dept Physiology, Shatin Hong Kong China

CHAN, JULIUS, Papua New Guinean government official; b. Tanga, New Ireland, Papua New Guinea, Aug. 29, 1939; m. Stella Ahmat, 1966; 4 children. Student, Marist Bros. Coll., Ashgrove, Queensland; grad., U. Queensland, Australia; D. of Econ. (hon.), Dankook U., Seoul, 1978; D. of Tech. (hon.), U. Tech., Papua New Guinea, 1983. Cooperative officer Papua New Guinea Adminstrn., 1960-62; mng. dir. Coastal Shipping Co. Ltd., 1963-70; elected M.P., 1968, 72, 77, 82, 87, 92; dep. speaker, vice chmn. pub. accounts com. House of Assembly, Papua New Guinea, 1968-72; min. finance Govt. of Papua New Guinea, 1975, dep. prime min., min. primary industry, 1977, prime min., 1980-82, dep. prime min., min. trade and industry, 1986, dep. prime min., min. finance and planning, 1992-94, prime min., min. fgn. affairs and trade, 1994-96; parliamentary leader People's Progress Party, Papua New Guinea, 1970-97; gov. IBRD/IMI, 1992—; Gov. Papua New Guinea, vice chair Asian Devt. Bank 1975-77. Address: PO Box 6030, Boroto Papua New Guinea

CHAN, KA CHING, manufacturing engineer, researcher, consultant; b. Kowloon, Hong Kong, Jan. 27, 1965; arrived in Australia, 1989; s. Kau Chan and Lau Sum (Ha) C.; m. Miranda Wong, June 12, 1990; children: David Bertrand, James Michael. BASc, U. Toronto, 1987, MASc, 1989; PhD, U. New South Wales, Sydney, Australia, 1995. Cert. and chartered profl. engr. Rsch. ast., tchr. asst. in mech. engring. U. Toronto, 1987-89; devel. engr. Inst. for Mfg. Mgmt. and Tech., Sydney, 1989-90, sr. engr., 1990-91; lectr. mech. engring. U. New South Wales, 1991-97, sr. lectr. mech. engring., 1997—; vis. asst. prof. indsl. engring. Hong Kong U. Sci. and Tech., 1996-97; cons. CSIRO, Sydney, 1993-94, Formica, Sydney, 1991-92. Contbr. articles to profl. jours. U. Toronto Open Master's fellow, 1988-89, McAllister Summer Rsch. fellow, 1986; grantee U. New South Wales, ARC, CSIRO, others. Mem. ASME, Instn. of Engrs. Australia, Inst. Indsl. Engrs., Soc. Mfg. Engrs (assoc.). Achievements include design and development of a number of computer controlled flexible fixturing systems; development of a new concept called virtual fuzzy set to improve fuzzy system accuracy. Office: U NSW, Sch Mech and Mfg Engring, Sydney 2052, Australia

CHAN, KAR MING HENRY, administrator; b. Hong Kong, July 15, 1958; s. Peter and Pick Lin (Wan) C. BSc, Chinese U. Hong Kong, 1981. Mgr. Hong Kong Royal Pub., Hong Kong, 1981-82; analyst programmer Hong Kong Govt., 1982-94; mgr., dir. Intellegent Office Co., Hong Kong, 1994—; Intelligent Recruitment Svcs., Hong Kong, 1994-98. Mem. China Software Industry Assn. (AI subcom., coun. mem.), HKITF (exec. coun.), STFC (adv. panel), HKSPIN, HKCS, IMIS, Intellegent I.T. Personnel, Hong Kong, 1998-99. Avocations: volleyball, badminton, squash, reading. Office: Intelligent Office Co, Flat 4B 41 Chi Kiang St, Kowloon Hong Kong

CHAN, KEN, ecology and physiology educator, researcher; b. Guangchou, Guangdong, China, Feb. 17, 1956; s. King-ah Chan and Kit-wan Lau; m. Anne Stacey Bermingham, Apr. 16, 1992; children: Zuleka Sachelle, Kolya Lucas. BSc, U. New Eng., Armidale, Australia, 1987, BSc with 1st class honors, 1988; PhD, U. Queensland, Brisbane, Australia, 1993. Tutorial asst. U. Queensland, 1989-92; rsch. asst. Australian Nat. U., Canberra, 1993-94; lectr. in physiology Ctrl. Queensland U., Rockhampton, Australia, 1994-97; lectr. U. Sunshine Coast, Sippy Downs, Queensland, 1997—; hon. fellow Ctrl. Queensland U., 1998—; project dir. Habitat Fragmentation of Migratory Birds Project, Rockhampton, Australia, 1996—. Contbr. articles to profl. jours. Recipient High Priority Australian Postgrad. award Australian Govt., 1989-92, numerous rsch. grants, 1991—. Mem. Sunshine Coast Ornithol. Soc. Inc. (founding pres. 1997—). Office: U Sunshine Coast, Sippy Downs Dr, Sippy Downs QLD 4556, Australia

CHAN, KIONG KONG, gynecological oncologist, consultant; b. Singapore, June 22, 1945; arrived in Eng., 1960; s. Kee Shoon and Mee Heung (Tung) C.; m. Patricia Anne Phillips, July 17, 1981; children: Alexander, Olivia, Barnaby. MBBS, London U., 1970. Sr. lectr. U. Birmingham, Eng., 1980-86; cons. gynecol. oncologist, surgeon Birmingham Women's Hosp., 1986—; coord. Brit. Surg. Gynecol. Oncology Group, 1996—. Editor, author: Management of Ovarian Cancer, 1996. Grantee Cancer Rsch. Campaign. Fellow Royal Coll. Surgeons, Royal Coll. Obs. and Gynecology; mem. Internat. Gynecol. Cancer Soc., Brit. Gynecol. Cancer Soc. Avocations: skiing, golf, bridge. Home: 126 Metchley Ln, Birmingham B17 0JA, England Office: Birmingham Women's Hosp, Metchley Park Rd, Birmingham B15 2TG, England

CHAN, KOWK-TAI, engineering educator; b. Canton, China, Nov. 7, 1954; s. Chi-Sang and Kam-Kiu (Wong) C.; m. Lai-Oh Chow, Sept. 6, 1984; children: Chun-On, Chun-Hang. BS, U. Hong Kong, 1978; MBA, Chinese U. Hong Kong, 1987; PhD, Hong Kong Polytech U., 1996. Engr. Ryoden Elec. Engring. Co., Hong Kong, 1978-84, JRP Cons. Engrs., Hong Kong, 1984-85; lectr. Vocat. Tng. Coun., Hong Kong, 1985-88; lectr., asst. prof. Hong Kong Polytech U., 1989-94, assoc. prof., 1995—. Mem. Chartered Instn. Bldg. Svcs. Engrs., Hong Kong Instn. Engrs., Am. Soc. Heating, Refrigerating and Air Conditioning Engrs. Office: Hong Kong Polytech U, Dept BSE, Hung Hom Hong Kong China

CHAN, KWOK LEUNG, mechanical engineer; b. Hong Kong, Mar. 11, 1970; s. Kang Por Chan and So Han Yim; m. Kong Yuen Yee, Dec. 23, 1998. BS with honors, Hong Kong Polytechnic, 1992. Grad. trainee Hong Kong Electric Co., 1992-94; engr. Parsons Brinckerhoff Asia Ltd., Hong Kong, 1995-96; with water supplies dept. Hong Kong Govt., 1996—. Mem. Inst. Mech. Engrs., Inst. Engrs. Australia, U.S. Naval Inst. Avocations: cycling, photography, shooting sports, flying, model making.

CHAN, KWONG YIN, soil scientist; b. Hong Kong, Sept. 7, 1950; s. Tsan and Sau-Fong (Yiu) C.; m. Sau-Wan Wu, Jan. 3, 1977; children: Wei-Ling, Jee-Lin. BSc with honors, U. of Hong Kong, 1973; dip. nat. res., U. New England, 1975; PhD, U. Sydney, 1979. Scientific officer NSW Agrl., Narrabri, Australia, 1979-80; scientific officer NSW Agrl., Rydalmere, Australia, 1983-88, rsch. scientist soils, 1988-91, sr. rsch. scientist, 1991-96; prin. rsch. scientist soils NSW Agrl., Wagga Wagga, Australia, 1996—; scientific officer Pollution Control Commn., Sydney, 1980-83. Editl. bd. Soil and Tillage Rsch., 1992—. U. rsch. scholar U. Sydney, 1975-79; fellow U. We. Sydney. Fellow U. New England Postgrad. Suprs. (hon.), Internat. Soil and Tillage Rsch. Orgn., Internat. Soil Sci. soc. Avocations: swimming, bush walking, table tennis. Office: Wagga Agrl Inst, Private Mail Bag, Wagga Wagga NSW 2650, Australia

CHAN, NOR NORMAN, physician; b. Wu Han, China, May 27, 1967; s. Yeh Chan and Or Lai Wong; m. Karolina Aleksandra Bogotko, July 7, 1996; children: Jennifer Megan, Timothy Dylan. MB, BChir, U. Liverpool, Eng., 1991; DCh, Royal Coll. Physicians, 1995. Sr. ho. officer in oncology Royal Marsden Hosp., London, 1994-95; specialist registrar in diabetes and endocrinology Hemel Hempstead Gen. Hosp., Herts, Eng., 1995-96, Watford Gen. Hosp., Herts, Eng., 1996-97, Chelsea & Westminster, London, 1997-98, Charing Cross Hosp., London, 1998; rsch. fellow U. Coll., London, 1998—. Reviewer Diabetologia, Diab Med. Jour.; contbr. articles to profl. jours. Rsch. grantee Astra Pharm., 1998, Brit. Heart Found., 1998; Brit. Heart Found. Rsch. fellow U. Coll., London, 1998—. Master Royal Coll. Physicians; mem. Brit. Diabetic Assn., Soc. Endocrinology. Avocations: economy, finance. Office: Eurodiab U Coll London, 1-19 Torrington Pl, London WC1E 6BT, England

CHAN, PAUL KAY-SHEUNG, clinical virologist, educator; b. Hong Kong, July 1, 1964; s. Shu and Shui King (Luk) C. MBBS, U. Hong Kong, 1988; MSc, U. London, 1995; diploma in virology, London Sch. Hygiene Trop. Med., 1996. Med. and health officer Govt. of Honk Kong, Dept. Health, Virus Unit, 1991-96; assoc. prof. microbiology Chinese U. of Hong Kong, 1996—. Contbr. articles to profl. jours. Fellow Hong Kong Coll. Pathology, Hong Kong Acad. Medicine; mem. Royal Coll. Pathology. Avocation: photography. Office: Chinese U of Hong Kong, Dept Microbiology, Shatin Hong Kong China

CHAN, PAUL S.L., scientist, researcher; b. Amoy, Fujian, China, Mar. 18, 1937; s. King Hsin and Ming Kam (Yuen) C.; m. Alice C.S. Li, Aug. 29, 1965; 1 child, John Y.Y. NBSc, Wuhan (China) U., 1961; MSc, Chinese U. Hong Kong, 1980. Rsch. chemist Shanghai Inst. Organic Chemistry, Chinese Acad., 1961-78; grad. asst. Chinese U. Hong Kong, 1978-80; mgr. chem. dept. Sunda Enterprises, Hong Kong, 1980-82; mgr. polymers R&D, Guertin Bros. Coating and Sealants Ltd., Winnipeg, Man., Can., 1982-90, 94-97; sr. polymer chemist Ashland Chems., Mississauga, Ont., Can., 1990-94; R&D fellow, dept. mgr. materials design and synthesis Polymer Coating Techs. of Singapore, 1997—. Patentee in field. Deacon, Winnipeg Chinese Alliance Ch., 1988; vice chmn. ch. coun. Logos Bapt. Ch., Mississauga, 1992; mem. mission com. Grace (Singapore Chinese Christian) Ch., 1999; del. Citizen Amb. Program, Seattle, 1995. Recipient Can. award for bus. excellence Min. Regional Indsl. Expansion, 1988. Mem. AAAS, TAPPI, Am. Chem. Soc. Christian. Avocations: reading, travel, classical music. Home: 19A Hillview Ave # 05-03, 669554 Singapore Singapore Office: Polymer Techs Singapore Pte, 16 Joo Koon Crescent, 629018 Singapore Singapore

CHAN, PETER WING KWONG, pharmacist; b. L.A., Feb. 3, 1949; s. Sherwin T.S. and Shirley W. (Lee) C.; children: Kristina Dionne, Kelly Alison, David Shoichi. BS, U. So. Calif., 1970, D in Pharmacy, 1974. Lic. pharmacist, Calif. Clin. instr. U. So. Calif., 1974-76; staff clin. pharmacist Cedars-Sinai Med. Ctr., L.A., 1974-76; 1st clin. pharmacist in ophthalmology Alcon Labs., Inc., Ft. Worth, 1977—; formerly in Phila. monitoring patient drug therapy, teaching residents, nurses, pharmacy students, then assigned to Tumu Tumu hosp., Karatina, Kenya, also lectr. clin. ocular pharmacology tng. course, Nairobi, Cairo, Athens, formerly dist. sales mgr. Alcon/BP, ophthal. products div. Alcon Labs., Inc., Denver, v.p., gen. mgr. Optikem Internat., Sereine Products, Dvi., Optacryl, Inc., Denver, 1980-81, product mgr. hosp. pharmacy prodcuts Am. McGaw div. Am. Hosp. Supply Corp., 1981-83; internat. market mgr. IOLAB subs. Johnson & Johnson, 1983-86, dir. new bus. devel. Iolab Pharms., 1986-87. dir. Internat. Mktg., 1987-89, dir. new products mktg., 1989; bus. and mktg. strategies cons. to pharm. and med. device cos. Chan & Assocs., Northridge, Calif., 1989-98; regional mng. dir. Pacific Rim, Leiner Health Products, Inc., Carson, Calif., 1998-2000; pres. Universal Alliance, Oceanside, Calif., 2000—; ptnr., chmn., CEO PreFree Techs. Inc., 1992-96; med. dir., Clin. Profl. Affairs, Nexstar Pharms., Inc., Boulder, 1996-97; ptnr. Vitamin Specialties Corp., 1993-95, JSP Ptnrs., Ltd., 1992—; med. dir., clin. and profl. affairs, Nexstar Pharm., Inc., Boulder, Colo.; regional mng. dir. Pacific Rim Leiner Health Products, 1998—; bd. dirs. SUDCO Internat., L.A. Del. Am. Pharm. Assn. Ho. Dels., 1976-78, Calif. Youth Theatre at Paramount Studios, Hollyood, 1986-2000; bd. councillors U. So. Calif. Sch. Pharmacy, 1995—. Recipient Hollywood-Wilshire Pharm. assn. spl. award for outstanding svc., 1974. Mem. Chinese Am. Pharm. Assn., Am. Pharm. Assn., Calif. Pharm. Assn., Hollywood-Wilshire Pharm. Assn. (bd. dirs. 1972-76), Am. Soc. Hosp. Pharmacists, Am. Pharm. Assn. Acad. Pharmacy Practice, U. So. Calif. Assocs. (life), U. So. Calif. Gen. Alumni Assn., U. So. Calif. (steering com. lifescies info. networking coun.), Granada Hills H.S. Highlanders Booster Club (bd. dirs. 1991, 92, 93, chmn.-Project 2000), QSAD Centurions, U. So. Calif. Lifetime Assocs., Gamma Epsilon Omega Alumni Assn. (bd. dirs.), Phi Delta Chi, NRA (life), Golden Eagle, Calif. Rifle & Pistol Assn. (life). Republican. Fax: 760-639-4493. E-mail: vitadoc007@cs.com. Home: 49 Bridgeport St Dana Point CA 92629-3242 Office: Chan and Assocs 32545B Golden Lantern #257 Dana Point CA 92629

CHAN, RAYMOND TAK MING, computer scientist; b. Hong Kong, Dec. 15, 1964; s. So and Yue Chu (Yan) C. BS, Chinese U. Hong Kong, 1989; MS, City Polytechnic of Hong Kong, 1993. Systems engr. NCR Hong Kong Ltd., 1989; analyst programmer City Polytechnic of Hong Kong, 1989-93; applications developer IKEA Trading Hong Kong Ltd., 1993-94; cons. D&M (Asia) Ltd., Hong Kong, 1994-95; sr. analyst Kingston-SCL Ltd., Wanchai, Hong Kong; cons. D&M (Asia) Ltd., Hong Kong, 1996; technology cons. Platinum Technol. (HK), Ltd., Hong Kong, 1996-98; sr. mgr. SUNDAY O/B Mandarin Comms. Ltd., 1998—. Mem. IEEE. Democrat. Avocations: chess, football. Office: Taikoo Pl 979 Kings Rd, 16/F Warwick House Quarry Bay Hong Kong

CHAN, THOMAS TAK-WAH, lawyer; b. Kowloon, Hong Kong, 1950. BA magna cum laude, U. Wis., Whitewater, 1973; JD, U. Wis., 1979. Bar: Wis. 1979, U.S. Dist. Ct. (ea. dist.) Wis. 1979, Minn. 1983, Calif. 1987. Judicial intern Wis. Supreme Ct., 1978; atty. Wausau (Wis.) Ins., 1979-82; staff atty. CPT Corp., Eden Prairie, Minn., 1982-84; gen. counsel Lee Data Corp., Eden Prairie, 1984-85; dep. gen. counsel Ashton-Tate Corp., Torrance, Calif., 1985-87; pres. Chan Law Group LC, L.A., 1987—; mem. adv. bd. SBA Export Devel. Ctr., 1992—; founder Bus. Software Alliance, Washington, 1987; mem. industry sector adv. com. and U.S. trade rep., U.S. Dept. Commerce, 1988-91; founder Asian Pacific Am. Coord. Com., 1996. Mem. Asian Pacific Am. Bar Assn. (founder, dir. 1998—), Wis. Bar Assn., Calif. Bar Assn. (lectr. 1988) Computer Law Assn., So. Calif. Chinese Lawyers Assn. (gov. 1990-92) Export Mgrs. Assn. So. Calif. (dir. 1990-92), S.Bay Chinese Am. C. of C. (founder, dir. 1997—), S.Bay Chinese Culture Ctr. (dir. 1998—), Cause (dir. 1994-97, chmn. 1995-96), Phi Kappa Phi. Avocations: skiing, hiking. Office: Chan Law Group 911 Wilshire Blvd Ste 2288 Los Angeles CA 90017-3451

CHAN, WENG-KONG, engineering educator, researcher; b. Singapore, Apr. 7, 1957; s. Kai-Soon Tan and Luan Leong; m. Julie Bee-Gek Lee, May 15, 1980; children: Elaine Yilin, Lorraine Yalin. B in Engring., U. Singapore, 1980; D in Engring., Ecole Nat. D'Arts et Metiers, Paris, 1984. Project engr. Def. Sci. Orgn. Nanyang Tech. U., Singapore, 1984-86, from lectr. to sr. lectr., 1986-97, assoc. prof., 1998—. Contbr. articles to profl. jours. Mem. Singapore Spastic Assn., 1992—. Pub. Svc. Commn. scholar U. Singapore, 1976-80, French postgrad. scholar, Paris, 1980-84. Mem. AIAA, ASME (pres. Singapore chpt. 1995-96), Singapore Spastic Assn. Buddhist. Avocations: bridge, swimming, reading. Office: Nanyang Tech U Sch Mech & Prodn Engring, Nanyang Ave, Singapore 2263, Singapore

CHAN, WING-CHUNG, pathologist, educator; b. Hong Kong, Oct. 11, 1947; came to U.S., 1975; s. Kwok-Ping and Yuet-Wah (Ching) C.; m. Angelina H. Li, May 16, 1981; children: Eric J., Jason E. MBBS, U. Hong Kong, 1973, MD, 1988. Diplomate in anat. pathology, clin. pathology and hematology Am. Bd. Pathology. Resident in pathology U. Chgo., 1975-79, rsch. assoc. in immunology, 1979-80; asst. prof. pathology Emory U. Sch. Medicine, Atlanta, 1980-86, assoc. prof., 1986-91; prof. pathology U. Nebr. Med. Ctr., Omaha, 1991—. Mem. editorial bd. Am. Jour. Clin. Pathology, 1990—; assoc. editor Am. Jour. Pathology, 2000—; contbr. chpts. to books, numerous articles to profl. jours. Mem. U.S. and Can. Acad. Pathology, Hematopathology Soc. (charter), Am. Soc. Hematology, Am. Assn. Immunologists. Achievements include research in the lymphoproliferative disorder involving large granular lymphocytes; study of myeloperoxidase gene expression in health and in leukemic conditions; study of retroviral gene sequences in lymphomas and leukemias; study of lineage and clonality of Hodgkin's disease and gene expression pattern of non-Hodgekin's lymphoma. Home: 10617 Castelar St Omaha NE 68124-1841 Office: 983135 Nebr Med Ctr Omaha NE 68198-0001

CHAN, XIANGLIN, automotive executive. Pres. Shanghai Automotive Indsutry Corp. Group; chmn. Shanghai Auto Sci. and Tech. Devel. Fund. Fax: 86-21-6433-0518. Office: 309 Wukang Rd, Shanghai 200031, China*

CHAN, YOKE KAI, finance educator; b. Singapore, Singapore, Dec. 17, 1948; m. Irene Li-Eng Seah, May 28, 1977; children: Joy Boon-Min, Justin Boon-Pin, Joel Boon-Jin. B in Accountg. with honors, U. Singapore, 1971; M in Commerce with honors, U. N.S.W., Sydney, Australia, 1986. CPA. Internal auditor Keppel Corp. Ltd., Singapore, 1971-75; acctg. mgr. Hewlett Packard Co., Singapore, 1975-79; prin. acct. Housing and Devel. Bd., Singapore, 1980-81; lectr. Nat. U. Singapore, Singapore, 1981-87; sr. lectr. Nanyang Tech. U., Singapore, 1987-98, assoc. prof., 1999—; vis. scholar U. Sydney, N.S.W., 1997-98; cons. Jurong Town Corp., Singapore, 1988-90, external examiner Ngee Ann Poly., Singapore, 1993-97. Contbr. articles to profl. and rsch. jours. Pres. Coral Park Residents Assn., Singapore, 1988-90; counsellor Nanyang Tech. U. Residence Hall, Singapore, 1988-98; mem. com. Bukit Batok Town Coun., Singapore, 1991-96; mem. panel of inquiry Pub. Accts. Bd., Singapore, 1992—. Recipient award Australian Govt., 1983. Fellow Chartered Inst. Mgmt. Accts. U.K. (cert., pres. 1989-94), Inst. CPAs Singapore (cert., chmn., dep. chmn., com. mem., 1986—). Avocations: reading, golf, swimming. Office: Nanyang Tech U, S3 #01B-63 Nanyang Ave, 639798 Singapore Singapore

CHAN, YUK-SHEE, finance educator; b. Haikou, Hainan, China, Aug. 18, 1953; s. Kwan-Ng and Wai-Ching (Wong) C.; m. Chiu-Ha Teresa Lai, 1977; children: Owen Man-On, Joanna Man-Jung. BBA, Chinese U. Hong Kong, 1975; MBA, U. Calif. Berkeley, 1976, MA in Econs., 1981, PhD, 1982. Asst. prof., assoc. prof. fin. Northwestern U., Evanston, Ill., 1982-86; assoc. prof., prof. fin. U. So. Calif., 1986-93; prof. fin. Hong Kong U. Sci. and Tech., 1992—, founding dean Bus. Sch., 1993—; dep. chmn. bd. Hong Kong Securities Clearing Co., 1994-98; pres. Asia Pacific Fin. Assoc., 1997-99; Mem. adv. com. HSI Svcs. Co. Ltd., 1994—. Assoc. editor Jour. Banking and Fin., 1994—; contbr. articles to profl. jours. Mem. Asia Pacific Fin. Assn. (bd. dirs.), Am. Fin. Assn., Internat. Assn. for Mgmt. Edn. (dir.

AACSB 1999—), Beta Gamma Sigma. Office: Hong Kong U Sci & Tech, Sch Bus & Mgmt, Clearwater Bay Hong Kong Hong Kong

CHANCE, GRAHAM WILFRID, pediatrician, emeritus educator; b. Birmingham, Eng., May 9, 1933; arrived in Can., 1970; s. Wilfrid Joseph and Edith (Rumsey) C.; m. Mary Eugenia Lewis, Mar. 25, 1961; children: Valerie Mary, Andrea Jane, Christine Anne. MB ChB, U. Birmingham, Eng., 1956. Diplomate in child health. Tng. positions several hosps., various cities, Eng., 1956-64; lectr. U. Birmingham, 1965-67, sr. lectr., 1967-70; assoc. prof. U. Toronto, 1970-78, prof., 1978-79; prof. U. Western Ont., London, Can., 1979-96; cons. pediatrician United Birmingham Hosps., 1967-70; dir. neonatal intensive care unit Hosp. for Sick Children, Toronto, 1970-78; chair divsn. neonatal/perinatal medicine U. Western Ont. and St. Joseph's Health Ctr., London, Ont., 1979-96. Editr: Textbook of Perinatal Medicine, 1975; contbr. numerous articles to profl. jours.; author govt. publs. Vol. chair Can. Inst. Child Health, 1994-99; served on numerous nat., provincial, local bds. and coms. for profl. socs., govts. and ednl. instns. Capt.Royal Army, 1957-59, Malaya and Singapore. Recipient Sisters of St. Joseph award for excellence, London, Can., 1995, Dean's award for excellence U. Western Ont., 1996; Mary Crosse meml. lectr. U. Birmingham, 1981; Martha May Elliott Forum lectr. APHA, 1982, others. Fellow Royal Coll. Physicians (London), Royal Coll. Physicians (Can.), Can. Pediatric Soc., Am. Acad. Pediatrics, Westminster Inst. Ethics and Human Values; mem. Sirmoor Club. Anglican. Avocations: child health advocacy, classical music, gardening. Office: Can Inst Child Health, 885 Meadowlands Dr E, Ottawa, ON Canada K2C 3N2

CHANCE, KENNETH BERNARD, endodontist, educator, university official; b. N.Y.C., Dec. 8, 1953; s. George E. and Janie L. (Bolles).; m. Sharon Lee Lewis, July 11, 1981; children: Kenneth Bernard, Dana Marie, Christopher, Jacquelyn. BS, Fordham U., 1975; DDS, Case Western Res. U., 1979; Cert. in Endodontics, U. Medicine and Dentistry N.J., 1982. Asst. attending Jamaica Hosp., Queens, N.Y., 1981-87; chief endodontics Kings County Med. Ctr., Bklyn., 1982-91; assoc. prof. endodontics U. Medicine and Dentistry N.J., 1987; also dir. external affairs N.J. Dental Sch.; asst. attending North Ctrl. Bronx (N.Y.) Hosp., 1983-91, Kingsbrook Jewish Med. Ctr., 1986-92; asst. dean external affairs and urban resource devel. N.J. Dental Sch., 1989; cons. Harlem Hosp., N.Y.C., 1982-90; health policy advisor to U.S. Senator Frank Lautenberg of N.J., 1991—; dir. health policy program The Joint Ctr. Polit. and Econ. Studies, 1993-94; acting chmn. dept. endodontics N.J. Dental Sch., 1994-97; fed. rels. adv. com. U. Medicine and Dentistry N.J., 1994-97; dean, prof. endodontics Meharry Med. Coll. Sch. Dentistry, 1997—. Min. of music, sr. organist Sharon Bapt. Ch., Bronx, 1983; mem. healthcare task force Congl. Black Caucus, 1994—. Recipient Dr. Paul F. Sherwood award for excellence in endodontics Case Western Res. U. Dental Sch., 1979, Cmty. Svc. award U. Medicine and Dentistry N.J., 1997, Tenn. Outstanding Achievement award, 1998, Outstanding Academician award U. Medicine and Dentistry N.J., 1999; Found. grant award U. Medicine and Dentistry N.J., 1984, Exceptional Merit award, 1985, Excellence award, 1990; fellow Nat. Dental Leadership Devel. PEW, 1991, Robert Wood Johnson Health Policy, 1991, Pierre Fauchard Acad., 1996. Fellow Am. Coll. Dentists, Internat. Coll. Dentists; mem. ADA, Internat. Assn. Dental Rsch., Am. Assn. Dental Schs., Nat. Dental Assn., Am. Assn. Endodontists, Greater Met. Dental Soc. N.Y. (pres.-elect 1986-87, v.p. 1984-86), Omicron Kappa Upsilon. Home: 1500 Braebury Cir Nashville TN 37211-8501

CHAND, PREM, career officer; s. Lal Chand and Durga Devi C.; m. Kirti Pawar; children: Niti, Anirudh, Srishti. BSEE, GNEC, Ludhiana, India, 1971; MTech in Guidance and Ctonrol, IIT, Madras, 1978; PhD, BITS, Pilani, India, 1997. Dep. elec. officer Vizag, India, 1974-75; instr. Vizag, 1975-76; asst. dir. Naval Hdqtrs., New Delhi, 1978-83; dep. elec. officer Bombay, 1983-84; dep. dir. NHQ, New Delhi, 1987-89; sr. systems mgr. WESEE, New Delhi, 1989-91, joint dir., 1991-97, additional dir. gen., 1997—; mem. Prime Minister's Nat. IT task force, Working Group Nat. Rsch./Task Force, New Delhi, 1998—; chmn. com. for evaluation of IT Enterpeneurship Devel. Programme, New Delhi, 1999—; mem. Defence-IT industry task force, 1998. Author: (book series) Programme Complexities of India Information Infrastructure Security and Information Warfare Initiatives, 10 vols., 1999, Concept Architecture and Configuration of National C41 Systems. Commodore IN, 1997-2000. Mem. IEEE. Avocations: Indian classical music, studying effects of magnetic therapy. Office: Mahindra Brit Telecom (MBT), 8 Parliament St, New Delhi 110001, India

CHAND, SURESH, life science educator; b. Meerut, India, July 15, 1954; s. Ramchandra and Chandrakanta; m. Lata Kamal, Sept. 4, 1957; children: Anuvrat, Apurv. BSc, Meerut Coll., India, 1974, MS, 1976; PhD in Tissue Culture, U. Calcutta, India, 1981. Rsch. fellow U. Calcutta, India, 1976-80; fellow Jawaharlal Nehru U., New Delhi, 1980-81; lectr. Meerut Coll., India, 1981-89; reader Devi Ahilya U., Indore, India, 1990-98, prof., 1998—; vis. Commonwealth fellow U. Nottingham, Eng., 1985-86; vis. scientist Inst. Plant Physiology, B.R.C., Szeged, Hungary, 1982; vis. fellow U. Jerusalem, 1998. Contbr. over 50 articles to profl. jours. Mem. Internat. Assn. Plant Tissue Culture, Soc. Plant Biochemistry and Biotechnology, Assn. Cell & Chromosome Rsch., Soc. Adv. Botany, Brit. Soc. Cell Biology. Hindu. Avocations: reading, music, cultural programme. Fax: 0091-731-470372. Home: F2 Univ Flats Khandwa Rd, Indore 452 017, India Office: Devi Ahilya U Sch Life Scis, Khandwa Rd, Indore 452 017, India

CHANDAKAS, STEFANOS, medical researcher, military officer; b. Athens, Greece, Mar. 27, 1972; s. Athanassios and Panayiota (Christopoulou) C. Degree, U. Paris, 1988; MD, U. Athens, 1996, PhD, 1999. Med. diplomate. Breast cancer rschr. U. Athens, 1996—; gen. practitioner Ipokration Hosp., Athens, 1997-98; sr. ho. officer Athens Policlinic, 1998-99; naval officer-physician Greek Navy, 1999—. Named Best Young Athlete, Greek Navy, 1988. Greek Orthodox. Avocations: sailing (Greek Olympic team 1992, 96), water skiing, snow skiing, diving. Office: Bas Sofias 121, Athens Greece

CHANDEZON, JEAN GABRIEL, electromagnetism educator; b. Martres de Veyre, France, Dec. 10, 1941; s. Eugène and Germaine (Espinasset) C.; m. Christiane Roux, Mar. 2, 1963; children: Christophe, Frédéric. Lic. Scis., Blaise Pascal U., Clermont-Ferrand, France, 1962, D 3d Cycle, 1966, DSc, 1979. Asst. Clermont-Ferrand U., Aubiere Cedex, 1964-67, maitre de confs., 1967-88, prof. 2d class, 1988-95, prof. 1st class, 1995, dir. Electromagnetism Lab., 1983—. Mem. Optical Soc. Am., European Optical Soc., Soc. Francaise d'Optique, Soc. Electriciens Electroniciens. Roman Catholic. Achievements include research on theoretical and numerical studies on Maxwell's equations in covariant form in electromagnetic optics, propagation in waveguides and scattering by gratings and surfaces. Home: 31 Ave Presle, 63960 Veyre-Monton France Office: 24 Ave Des Landais, 63177 Aubiere Cedex, France

CHANDLER, CLIFFORD, photographer, airline company executive; b. N.Y.C., Mar. 6, 1931; s. Clifford and Margaret Aurelia (Greene) C.; m. Johnnie M. Brooks (div. 1981); 1 child, Keith; m. Velma Olive Jackson, Nov. 7, 1981; 1 child, Cassandra. Student Germain Sch. Photography, N.Y.C., N.Y. Sch. Radio Announcing, Pratt Inst., Bklyn. Publicity photographer Latin Quarter, N.Y.C., 1955-63; photographer, writer Etcetera mag., Bklyn., 1963-69; asst. to pres. J.C. Mandel Security, N.Y.C., 1969-73, security exec., acctg. dir., 1987—; dir. security Pratt Inst., Bklyn., 1973-79; darkroom attendant NYU Med. Ctr., N.Y.C., 1983-87; gen. mgr. internat. total services Am. Airlines, N.Y.C., 1986-87, accounts dir. John C. Mandel Security Bur., Bklyn., 1988—. Exhibited in group shows: Fulton Art Fair, Bklyn., Carver Fed. Savs., Bklyn., Bethany Bapt. Ch., Bklyn., Black Arts Repertories Theatre, N.Y.C., Hariett Tubman Hist. and Cultural Mus., Macon, Ga., One man shows: Pratt Inst., Bklyn., St. Peters Luth. Ch., N.Y.C., Ledel Gallery, N.Y.C. Cover photographer Duke Ellington in Person, Houghton, Mifflin, Boston, 1978; contbg. writer Big Red News, Bklyn. Recipient awards Germain Sch. Photography, Pratt Inst., N.Y.C. Police Dept. Home: 480 2nd Ave New York NY 10016-9151 Office: John C Mandel Security Bur 100 Water St Brooklyn NY 11201-1045

CHANDLER, EDWARD WILLIAM, communications systems engineer; b. Milw., Oct. 10, 1953; s. Donald Harold and Helen Aliedia (Wonders) C.; m. Christine Anne Wohl, June 13, 1987; children: Rebecca Marie, Marcella Anne, Mary Elizabeth, Andrew Donald. BS, U. Wis., Milw., 1975; MSEE, Ill. Inst. Tech., 1978; PhD, Purdue U., 1985. Registered profl. engr., Wis. Electronics engr. Communications and Electronics div. Motorola Inc., Schaumburg, Ill., 1976-77; instr. elec. engring. Milw. Sch. Engring., 1977-79, asst. prof., 1979-80, assoc. prof., 1982-84, prof., 1992—, acting head electronic communications engring. tech. program, 1978-79, head, 1979-80, dir. elec. engring. program, 1982-84, dir. MS in Engring. program, 1992—; asst. prof. elec. engring. Marquette U., Milw., 1984-86; sr. engr. Titan Corp. (formerly Govt Sys. divsn. M/A-COM, Inc.), San Diego, 1986-88, mem. tech. staff, 1988-92; engring. cons. Linkabit Wireless, 1992—; lectr. U. Wis., Milw., part-time 1979-83; invited lectr. Czech Tech. U., 1997, 98, Tech. U. Budapest, 1998, Fachhoschchule, Lübeck, Germany, 2000; grad. instr. rsch. Purdue U., West Lafayette, Ind., 1980-82; rsch. cons. Naval Ocean Systems Ctr., San Diego, 1986. Contbr. articles to profl. jours. David Ross summer grantee, 1981; faculty rsch. grantee Milw. Sch. Engring., 1983; recipient Outstanding Tchr. award Marquette U. Coll. Engring., 1986, Titan Most Valuable Performer award, 1990, Noel Amherd Tech. Performer award, 1991. Mem. IEEE (sr., newsletter editor Milw. sect. 1985-86), Am. Soc. Engring. Edn., Armed Forces Communications Electronics Assn., Air Force Assn., Triangle, Sigma Xi, Tau Beta Pi, Eta Kappa Nu. Home: 7030 N Range Line Rd Glendale WI 53209-2621 Office: Milw Sch Engring 1025 N Broadway Milwaukee WI 53202-3109

CHANDLER, ELISABETH GORDON (MRS. LACI DE GERENDAY), sculptor, harpist; b. St. Louis, June 10, 1913; d. Henry Brace and Sara Ellen (Sallee) Gordon; m. Robert Kirkland Chandler, May 27, 1946 (dec.); m. Laci de Gerenday, May 12, 1979. Grad., Lenox Sch., 1931; pvt. study sculpture and harp. Mem. Mildred Dilling Harp Ensemble, 1934-45; prof. sculpture Lyme Acad. Fine Arts, 1976—, chair sculpture dept. Exhibited sculpture NAD, Nat. Sculpture Soc., Allied Artists Am., Nat. Arts Club, Pen and Brush, Lyme Art Assn., Mattatuck Mus., Catherine Lorillard Wolfe Art Club, Am. Artists Profl. League, Hudson Valley Art Assn., USIA, 1976-78, Lyme Art Ctr., 1979, retrospective exhbn. Lyme Acad. Fine Arts, 1987, Madison Gallery, 1987, Old State House, Hartford, Conn., 1989, Mellon Art Ctr., Wallingford, Conn., 1989, Fairfield U. Walsh Gallery, 1991, Brit. Mus., London, Am. Medallic Sculptors Assn. Traveling Exhbn., 1994, Slater Mus. Cropsey Found., 1995, Nat. Sculpture Exhbn. Lyme Acad. Fine Arts, 1995-96, Lever House, N.Y.C., 1996, America's Tower, 1996-98, Hillsdale (Mich.) Coll., 1997, Nat. Acad. Mus., N.Y.C., 1998; represented in permanent collections Aircraft Carrier USS Forrestal, Gov. Dummer Acad., James Forrestal Research Ctr. of Princeton U., Lenox Sch., James L. Collins Parochial Sch., Tex., Storm King Art Ctr., Columbia U., Pace U., White Plains, N.Y., St. Patrick's Cathedral, N.Y.C., McAuley Ctr., St. Joseph's Coll., West Hartford, Conn., Nat. Acad. Mus.; designed and executed Brookgreen Gardens medal, Forrestal Meml. Medal, Timoschenko Medal for Applied Mechanics, Benjamin Franklin Medal, Albert A. Michelson Medal, Jonathan Edwards Medal, Shafto Broadcasting Award Medal, Enrichment of Life medal Soc. Medallists, Brookgreen Gardens Medal, Adlai Stevenson bronze bust for Woodrow Wilson Sch. of Princeton U., 250 Ann. George Washington medal,Owen R. Cheatham bronze bust for Ga. Pacific Bldg., Atlanta, Messiah Coll., Grantham, Pa., Adlai E. Stevenson High Sch., Ill., Queen Anne's County Courthouse Square, Md., Our Lady Mercy Hosp., N.Y.C., Albert A. Michelson bust in Hall of Fame for Great Americans, pvt. collections. With mus. therapy div. Am. Theatre Wing, 1942-45; trustee The Lenox Sch., 1953-55; chmn. Associated Taxpayers Old Lyme, 1969-72; mem., trustee Brookgreen Gardens, S.C., 1989-97; founder, life trustee Lyme Acad. Fine Arts, 1976, prof. sculpture, 1976—. Recipient 1st prize Bklyn. War Meml. competition, 1945, 1st prize sculpture Catherine Lorillard Wolfe Art Club, 1951, 58, 63, Gold medal, 1969, Founders prize Pen & Brush, 1954, 76, 78, Gold medal, 1957, 61, 63, 69, 74, 76, Am. Heritage award, 1968, Solo Show award, 1961, 69, 75, Thomas R. Proctor prize NAD, 1956, Dessie Greer prize, 1960, 79, 85, Sculpture prize Nat. Arts Club, 1959, 60, 62, Gold medal, 1971, Gold medal Am. Artists Profl. League, 1960, 69, 73, 75, prize, 1981, Anna Hyatt Huntington prize, 1970, 76, Harriet Mayer Meml. prize, 1961, Gold medal Hudson Valley Art Assn., 1956, 69, 74, Mrs. John Newington award, 1976, 78, Lindsey Morris Meml. prize Allied Artists Am., 1973, Gold medal, 1982, Sculpture prize Acad. Artists, 1974, Sydney Taylor Meml. prize Knickerbocker Artists, 1975, New Netherlands DAR Bicentennial medal, 1976, Pietro Montana Meml. prize Hudson Valley Art Assn., 1995, Citation, State of Conn., 1995; named Citizen of Yr., Town of Old Lyme, Conn., 1985. Fellow NAD (academician), Nat. Sculpture Soc. (coun. 1976-85, Tallix Foundry award 1979, John Spring Founder's award 1986, John Cavanaugh Meml. prize 1991, Silver medal, citation 1992, Herbert Adams Meml. medal for svc. to Am. Sculpture), Am. Artists Profl. League, Internat. Inst. Arts and Letters; mem. Federation International de la Medaille, Nat. Arts Club, Allied Artists Am., Am. Medallic Art Soc., Pen and Brush, Catherine Lorillard Wolf Art Club, Lyme Art Assn. (pres. 1973-75), Coun. Am. Artists Socs. (dir. 1970-73), Am. Artists Profl. League (dir. 1970-73). Home and Studio: 2 Mill Pond Ln Old Lyme CT 06371-1118

CHANDLER, GRIFFON PORTER, civil engineer; b. Prattville, Ala., Apr. 2, 1928; s. Charles Jackson and Fannie H. (Hall) C.; m. Elizabeth Strawbridge (dec.); children: Michael Griffon, Mary Ann, Joseph Porter. BS in Civil Engring., Auburn U., 1953. Engr.'s asst. to divsn. engr. St. Louis, San Francisco Railway Co.; gen. mgr. Holiday Inn Indsl. Properties Holiday Inns, Inc.; self-employed home builder, developer Miss. Bd. dirs. C. of C. Olive Br., Miss., 1987, Miss. Indsl. Devel. Assn., 1988, DeSoto County (Miss.) Economic Devel. Coun., 1989. Mem. Rotary. Home: 2860 Castleman St Memphis TN 38118-2625

CHANDLER, JAMES BARTON, international education consultant; b. Conway Springs, Kans., May 27, 1922; s. James Perry and Bessie May (Stone) C.; m. Madeleine Racoux, July 27, 1946; children: Paul A., Peter R., Michele A. Chandler Dore. AB, U. Kans., 1947, MA, 1949; postgrad., U. Mich., 1950-54. Asst. prof., fgn. student advisor Ea. Mich. U., 1953-55, 57-58; lang. edn. advisor Okla. A&M/Ethiopia, 1955-57, U. Mich./Laos, 1958-60; tchr. edn., advisor U.S. AID-Laos, Vientiane, Laos. 1960-61, edn. div. chief, 1961-63, asst. dir. manpower, industry, pub. adminstrn., 1965-69, deputy mission dir., 1969-73; higher edn. advisor U.S. AID-Tunisia, Tunis, Tunisia, 1963-65; dir. Office of Edn. AID, Washington, 1973-76, assoc. asst. adminstr., 1976-77; dir. Internat. Bur. Edn. UNESCO, Geneva, 1977-83; cons. Ann Arbor, 1983-88; St. Louis, 1989—; sec. Rotary, Vientiane, Laos, 1968-69. Capt. U.S. Army, 1943-47, ETO. Decorated Bronze Star, 1945; recipient Meritorious Honor award AID, 1973, Disting. Career Svc. award, 1977, Cert. Appreciation Pres. Gerald Ford, 1975, Letter Appreciation Dir. Gen. UNESCO, Geneva, 1983; S.L. Whitcomb fellow U. Kansas, 1948-49; fellow Ford Found., 1951-52. Mem. Am. Acad. Social and Polit. Sci., Am. Fgn. Svc. Assn., NRA, Nat. Icarian Soc., Nat. Assn. Scholars, Nat. Parks and Conservation Assn., Am. Assn. Retired Persons, Nat. Wildlife Fedn., Archaeol. Inst. Am., Ind. Rights Found., Comparative and Internat. Edn. Soc., Diplomatic and Consular Officers Ret. (regional corr.), Nat. Assn. Ret. Fed. Employees (pres. Ann Arbor chpt. 1986-89, v.p. St Louis chpt. 1989-90, pres. 1991-93, bd. dirs. 1992-93), Mo. Hist. Soc., Richmond Heights Srs. (v.p., pres.), Smithsonian Assocs., World Affairs Coun., Wilson Ctr. Assn., Nature Conservancy, Assn. Former Internat. Civil Servants, VFW, Am. Legion, 4th Cavalry Assn., Austrian Soc. of St. Louis, Soc. Francaise St. Louis (bd. dirs., v.p., pres., sec., sgt.-at.-arms), Ctr. for Internat. Understanding, Alliance Francaise, St. Louis-Lyon Sister Cities Com., Rotary (bd. dirs., officer), St. Louis Discussion Club, Great Decisions Discussion Group, UN Assn. U.S.A., Phi Beta Kappa, Pi Delta Phi. Roman Catholic. Avocations: bowling, bridge, billiards, oil painting, writing memoirs, stamps and coins. Home and Office: 7449 Rupert Ave Richmond Hts MO 63117-2426

CHANDLER, JOHN ANDREW, financial investor; b. Chgo., Dec. 4, 1961; s. Franklin Irwin and Linda Diane C. BS, Kans. State U., Manhattan, 1984. Mktg. mgr. The Mktg. Co., St. Louis, Mo., 1984-89; sales mgr. N. River Homes, Hamilton, Ala., 1989-92; sr. v.p. Midland Credit Mgmt., Hutchinson, Kans., 1992—. Mem. Praire Dunes C. of C., 1992—. Mem. Debt Buyers Assn. Avocation: golf. Home: 3103 Mission Dr Hutchinson KS 67502-9109 Office: Midland Credit Mgmt 5775 Roscoe Ct San Diego CA 92123-1399

CHANDLER, JULIETTE ANNE, writer, communications executive; b. Denver, Jan. 10, 1959; d. Peter James Bissell and Ruby Louise (Chandler) Racine; m. Gregory Lanigan, May 9, 1992 (div. July 1996); 1 child, Brendan; m. Roy Boggie, Oct. 18, 1997. BA in Journalism, U. Md., 1981; cert. in writing, U. Calif., San Diego, 1990, cert. in hatha yoga, 1994. Tech. writer, trainer Computer Scis. Corp., San Diego, 1982-85; documentation mgr. Mantech Math. Corp., San Diego, 1985-88; bus. owner, writer, CFO, sec. Chandler Comms., Inc., Ventura, Calif., 1988—; pub. rels. writer Westroots Bus. Writing, La Jolla, Calif., 1990; journalist; spkr. in field. Contbr. articles, columns to newspapers. Vol. 12-step recovery programs, Calif., 1987-97. Mem. Ventura County Writer's Club. Home: 654 Bellefontaine St Pasadena CA 91105-2441 Office: Chandler Comms Inc 1349 E Santa Clara St Apt 207 Ventura CA 93001-3248

CHANDLER, KIMBERLEY LYNN, gifted education resource specialist; b. Waynesboro, Va., Sept. 28, 1961; d. Alden Hugh and Cecille Frances (Brooks) C. BA in Elem. Edn., Coll. William and Mary, 1984, MA in Edn./Gifted Edn., 1992, postgrad. Lic. educator, Va. Tchr. Fredericksburg (Va.) Pub. Schs., 1984-87, Henrico County Pub. Schs., Richmond, Va., 1987-98; gifted edn. resource specialist Hanover County Pub. Schs., Richmond, Va., 1998—; summer sch. coord. Henrico County Pub. Schs., 1996, 97, staff devel. presenter, 1996, 97; curriculum cons. Coll. of William and Mary, Williamsburg, Va., 1996; presenter in field.; mem. gifted edn. staff devel. talent bank, mem. tchr. stds. com. Va. Dept. Edn.; mem. peer coaching program, Prin.'s Acad.; sch. renewal planning team facilitator Hanover County Pub. Schs. Author: (curriculum unit) Literary Reflections, 1992; author: (with others) NAGC PreK-12 Gifted Program Standards Document; editor (newsletter): Va. Assn. for the Gifted, 1999—. Vol. Hanover Humane Soc., 1994—, Habitat for Humanity Global Village Program, Nicaragua Disaster Relief Mission Team, 1999, Brazil VBS Mission Team, 2000. Grantee Henrico Edn. Found., 1997, Henrico Gifted Adv. Coun., 1997, Pntrs. in Arts grantee Richmond Arts Coun., 1996, Hanover Edn. Found., 1999. Mem. Nat. Assn. for Gifted Children (Harry Passow Classroom Tchr. scholarship 1997, sec./treas. technol. divsn. 1997-99, sec./treas. profl. devel. divsn. 1997-99), Hanover County Prins. Acad., Va. Soc. for Tech. in Edn., Va. Assn. for the Gifted (ex officio bd. dirs.), Kappa Delta Pi (chpt. sec.). Home: 11444 New Farrington Ct Glen Allen VA 23059-1629 Office: Hanover County Pub Sch 200 Berkley St Ashland VA 23005-1302

CHANDLER, ROBERT LESLIE, public relations executive; b. Phila., Mar. 3, 1948; s. Joel leslie and Evelyn Laney (DeLaney) C.; m. Maureen O'Keefe, Mar. 21, 1970. AS, Atlantic C.C., 1969; BS, Bowling Green State U., 1971; MS, Ohio U., 1972; MBA in Hosp. Adminstrn., Wagner Coll., 1980. Dir. pub. rels. Athens Mental Health Ctr., Ohio, 1972; internal comms. editor, pub. affairs dept. Owens-Corning Fiberglas Corp., Toledo, 1972-74; dir. cmty. rels. Wyandotte Gen. Hosp., Mich., 1974-76; v.p. asst. adminstr. mktg./pub. affairs Meth. Hosp., Bklyn., 1976-82; exec. v.p. Burson-Marsteller Pub. Rels., N.Y.C., 1982-95; pres. Chandler-Chicco Agy., 1995. Mem. budget com. United Way Mich., 1975-76; bd. dirs. N.Y. chpt. Am. Heart Assn. Am. Heart Assn. N.J./N.Y. State scholar, 1969. Mem. Pub. Rels. soc. Am., Am. soc. Health Care Mktg. and Planning, Am. Coll. Healthcare Execs. (assoc. mem.), Sigma Delta Chi, Kappa Tau Alpha. Home: 525 W 22nd St Apt 6D New York NY 10011-1100 Office: Chandler Chicco Agy 450 W 15th St Ste 700 New York NY 10011-7014

CHANDLER, STEPHEN ANTHONY, electrical engineer; b. Farnborough, England, Aug. 31, 1948; s. Gerard and Rosina (Patton) C.; m. Anne Elizabeth Osborn; children: James, Clare, Mary. BA, Cambridge U., 1969, MA, 1973; PhD, Southampton U., 1973. Rsch. fellow U. Southampton, England, 1972-76; lectr. U. Sierra Leone, Freetown, 1976-80, U. London, 1980-81, U. Warwick, Coventry, England, 1981-98; tech. dir. Rural Radio Systems, Ltd, Coventry, 1998—. Mem. IEEE, Inst. Elec. Engrs. Roman Catholic. Avocations: mountaineering, music, art, organic gardening, running. Office: Rural Radio Sys Ltd, 94 Cannon Park Rd, Coventry CV4 7AY, England

CHANDRA, ARUN, computer engineer, educator; b. Patiala, Punjab, India, Oct. 2, 1963; came to U.S., 1985; s. Ramesh and Veena Chandra; m. Renee Parks, June 11, 1994. BE in Elec. Engring., U. Delhi, 1985; MS in Computer Engring., U. Tex., Austin, 1988, PhD in Computer Engring., 1993. Mem. devel. staff IBM, Austin, Tex., 1993-98; adj. lectr. U. Tex., Austin, 1995-98; tech. staff engirng. Motorola, Austin, 1998; mem. tech. staff Sun Micro Sys., Sunnyvale, Calif., 1999-2000, Nexsi, San Jose, Calif., 2000—. Contbr. numerous articles to profl. jours.; patentee in field. Mem. AAAS, IEEE (vice-chair POSIX-SRASS 1993-96), N.Y. Acad. Scis., Internat. Assn. Sci. and Tech. for Devel., Tau Beta Pi, Beta Alpha Pi. Avocations: sports, art, toy trains. E-mail: arun.chandra@nexsi.com.

CHANDRA, BRIJESH, engineering educator; b. Akbarpur, India, Feb. 12, 1937; s. Darshanimal and Shanti Agrawal; m. Sneh Bala, June 22, 1966; children: Divya, Gopika. BSc, Agra (India) U., 1956; BE, U. Roorkee, India, 1959, ME in Applied Electronics & Servomech., 1968; PhD, MJP Rohalkhand U., Bareilly, India, 1999. Asst. prof. elect. engring. HBT Inst., Kanpur, India, 1960-62; lect. in elect. engring. U. Roorkee, 1962-70; reader in elect. engring. WRDTG, Roorkee, 1970-84; scientist E AHEC, WRDT, Roorkee, 1984-85; prof. U. Roorkee Water Resources Devel. Tng. Ctr., 1985-96, BPT Inst., Bahardar, Ethiopia, 1996—; dean students U. Roorkee, 1975-77. Chief editor Indian Water Resources Jour., 1989-91, editor, 1995-96; chief editor, editor Lions Mag.; chief editor (newsletter) Univ. News Bulletin. Served with India mil., 1956-59. Fellow IE (life, hon. sec., Merit cert. 1971, 93), IWRS (life, exec. v.p. 1992-95); mem. Grand Lodge India (Worshipful Master 1990-91), Lions Club (pres. 1977-78), IETE (life). Hindu. Avocations: social work, sports, gardening, travel, reading. Office: Univ Roorkee, Water Res Devel Tng Ctr, 247667 Roorkee India

CHANDRA, KIRTUNIA JURAN, fish biology educator; b. Tangail, Bangladesh, Feb. 1, 1953; s. Radha Nath and Surabala (Sarkar) Kirtunia; m. Krishna Raychoudhury, Jan. 30, 1986; two children. BSc in Fisheries with honors, Bangladesh Agrl. U., Mymensingh, 1973, MSc in Fisheries, 1974; PhD, Andhra U., Waltair, India, 1982. Cert. aquaculturist. Tchg. fellow Bangladesh Agrl. U., Mymensingh, 1975-77, lectr., 1977-82, asst. prof., 1982-87, assoc. prof., 1987-92, prof., 1992—, head dept. fisheries biology and limnology, 1989-91, dean fisheries faculty, 1995—; acad. staff fellow Liverpool (Eng.) U., 1988-89; project dir. Bangladesh Agrl. U. Overseas Devel. Adminstrn. Link, Bangladesh Agrl. U., 1995-96, convener dean coun., 1995-97. Joint editor Bangladesh Jour. Fisheries, 1982-84, Bangladesh Jour. Aquaculture, 1982-84; contbr. articles to profl. jours. Recipient Rsch. awards Assn. Commonwealth Univs., 1988-89, Internat. Found. for Sci., 1992, Aquatic Animal Health Rsch. Inst., 1997. Mem. Asiatic Soc. Bangladesh, Asian Fisheries Sci. Avocations: sight seeing, traveling, cricket, football. Office: Bangladesh Agrl Univ, Mymensingh 2202, Bangladesh

CHANDRA, NARESH, diplomat. PhD (Mathematics), Allahabad University, India. With Indian Adminstrv. Svc., India, 1956—; advisor on export industrialization & policy commonwealth secretariat, Colombo, India, 1981-1984; advisor to the gov. of Jammu & Kashmir India, 19896; sec. of water resources Fed. Indian Govt., 1987—, sec. of defense, sec. of interior & justice, cabinet sec., 1990-92, sr. advisor to the Prime Minister, 1992—; gov. State of Gujarat, India; amb. to U.S. Fed. Indian Govt., Washington, 1996—; mem. Indian Space Commn., 1990-92, mem. Indian Atomic Energy Commn., 1990-92. Office: Embassy of India 2107 Massachusetts Ave NW Washington DC 20008-2878*

CHANDRA, PRAKASH, molecular biologist, educator; b. Calcutta, India, Oct. 16, 1936; arrived in Germany, 1960; s. Niranjan Lal and Tara Devi (Gupta) Jain; m. Angelika Chandra; children: Ramon, Robin, Tamir. BSc, U. Delhi, 1956; MSc, U. Nagpur, 1958; Dr. phil. nat., U. Frankfurt, 1965, Dr. med. habil, 1971. Rsch. asst. U. Calif., Berkeley, 1958-60; rsch. assoc. U. Hamburg, Germany, 1960-63; rsch. assoc., lectr., prof. U. Frankfurt, Germany, 1971-73; prof., head dept. U. Frankfurt, 1973—; dir. NATO-ASI, Corfu, Greece, 1978, 81, Maratea, Italy, 1985. Author: Methods of Molecular Biology, 1973; contbr. more than 200 articles to profl. jours. Recipient Leukemia prize German Soc. Pediatrics Oncology, 1978, Semmelweis medal U. Budapest, 1980, Univ. medal Tel-Aviv U., 1986. Fellow Royal Soc. Chemistry London, N.Y. Acad. Sci.; mem. Rotary Club Frankfurt (bd. dirs.). Avocation: tennis. Office: Univ Med Sch, Theodor Stern Kai 7, D-60590 Frankfurt Germany

CHANDRA, SHEEL, textiles executive; b. Shimla, India, Sept. 1, 1941; s. Nandau Chand and Indumati Devi Carol; m. Nanda Sheel Pardesi, Jan. 30, 1973; children: Nishant, Nandita, Pranan, Saudamani. BA, Punjab (India)

U., 1965. Trainee State Govt., Himachal Pradesh, 1966-69; mgr. Hoechst Dyes, Delhi, India, 1969-75; divsn. mgr. Thakersay's, Delhi, 1975-77; resident mgr. Assoc. Capsules, Delhi, 1977-78; chief exec. Kismet Carpets Inc., New Delhi, 1978—. Office: Kismet Carpets Inc, C-12 Gulmohar Park, New Delhi 110 049, India

CHANDRA, SULEKH, chemist, educator; b. Khurja, India, Nov. 7, 1953; s. Deep Chand and Ramwati Devi; m. Shashi Bala; children: Swati, Amit. BSc, Meerut (India) U., 1974, MSc, 1976; PhD, Delhi U., 1979. Lectr. Zakir Husain Coll., Delhi, 1980-86, sr. lectr., 1986-93, reader, 1993—; supr. PhD program Zakir Husain Coll., Delhi, 1988, 93, 96, 98; vis. fellow Dept. Sci. Tech. Major Rsch. Project, Delhi, 1993, 98. Pres. Nature & Environment, Delhi, 1987-88. Life mem. Indian Chem. Soc., Indian Sci. Congress, Analytical Sci. Soc., Chem. & Rsch. Soc., Instn. of Chemists. Hindu. Avocation: reading research books. Home: C-1/340 Yamuna Vihar, Delhi 110053, India Office: Zakir Husain Coll, JLN Marg, Delhi 110002, India

CHANDRAN, CHITRA, consultant pediatrician; b. Delhi, India, Oct. 21, 1947; arrived in Australia, 1974; d. Kitianda C. and Kodandera T. Ganapathy.; m. Natteri V. Chandran, Nov. 12, 1973; children: Aditi, Shiv. MBBS, Madras U., India. Diplomate Am. Bd. Pediatrics. Resident Govt. Gen. Hosp., Madras, 1970-71; sr. resident in pediatrics Inst. Child Health/Hosp. of Sick Children, Madras, 1971; pediatric intern Jewish Hosp. and Med. Ctr./Greenpoint Hosp., Bklyn., 1971-72, sr resident in pediatrics, 1972-73; fellow in pediatric genetics, asst. instr. pediatrics SUNY Downstate Med. Ctr., Bklyn., 1972-74; med. officer St. Nicholas Hosp. and Tng. Ctr., Australia, 1974-76, pediatrician, 1976-79, acting. med. supt., coord. diagnostic svcs., 1979-84; hon. vis. assoc. pediatrician Children's Hosp., Melbourne, Australia, 1980-82; cons. pediatrician cmty. svcs. Early Childhood Svcs., Victoria, Australia, 1984-92; hon. clin. asst. Devel. Disabilities Clinic, Monash (Australia) Med. Ctr., 1989—; cons. pediatrician in pvt. practice, 1992—. Contbr. articles to profl. jours. Trustee The East West Ctr., Melbourne, 1992—, The East West Found. of Australia, 1992—, The East West Found. of India, 1995—. Recipient Pres. of India Silver medal, 1962, Gold medal U. Madras, 1966. Fellow Am. Acad. Pediatrics, Royal Australian Coll. Physicians; mem. Pediatric Soc. Victoria, Australian Med. Assn. Victorian Med. Women's Soc. Home: Apt 703, Treasury Gardens, 30 St Andrews Pl, Melbourne, Victoria 3000, Australia Office: Druid's House, 6th Fl, 407-409 Swanston St, Melbourne, Victoria 3000, Australia

CHANDRASEKARAN, MARGAM, mechanical engineer, researcher; b. Thanjavur, India, July 29, 1966; s. C. Neelakantan and Rajeswari Margam. BMechE, Regional Engring. Coll., Silchar, India, 1988; MS, Indian Inst. Tech., Madras, 1994; PhD, Nanyang Technol. U., Singapore, 1998. Rsch. assoc. Indian Inst. Tech., Madras, 1989-90, 93-94, rsch. engr. Sch. Mech. and Prodn. Engring., 1998-99; rsch. fellow Sch. Mech. and Prodn. Engring. Namyang Technol. U., Singapore, 1999—. Author: Materials Degradation and Its Control by Surface Engineering, 1999; patentee in field; contbr. articles to profl. jours. Indian Inst. Tech. scholar, 1990-93, 94-95. Mem. ASME (assoc.), Powder Metallurgy Assn. India (life), Am. Powder Metallurgy Inst., N.Y. Acad. Scis. Avocations: reading, music, sports, traveling. Home: Bukit Batok W Ave 6, Bl 132 # 04-318, Singapore 650132, Singapore Office: Sch Mech Prodn Engring, Nanyang Technol U, Singapore 639798, Singapore

CHANDRASEKHAR, KULANGAREZHATHU P., physician, consultant, cardiologist, educator; b. Thaikattucherry, Kerala, India, Aug. 29, 1934; s. K. Parameswaran Pillai and P. Lakshmikutty Amma; m. Gita Pillai, Apr. 27, 1964; children: Ajit, Anand. MB BS, U. Travancore, 1956; MD, U. Kerala, 1964. MRCP (Glasgow, Edinburgh), FRCP (Edinburgh). Tutor in anatomy, physiology, and medicine U. Travancore, 1957-63, asst. prof. medicine, 1963-68, assoc. prof. medicine, 1968-72, assoc. prof. cardiology, 1972-74, prof. cardiology, 1974-81; prof., head dept. medcine Calabar (Nigeria) U., 1981-83; dir., prof. medicine Calicut U., 1983-87, vice-prin. Med. Coll., 1986-87; dir., prof. medicine Med. Coll. Trivandrum, Kerala, 1987-89, vice-prin., 1987-89, prin., dir. med. edn., 1989-90; ret., 1990; cons. physician pvt. practice Kerala Govt. Svc., 1990—; cons. physician, cardiologist PMR Hosp., Kollam, 1990—, G.G. Hosp., Trivandrum, 1990-91; cons. physician, cardiologist Gopala Pillai Hosps., Nagercoil, Kanyakumari Dist., Tamil Nadu, 1992-99; commonwealth med. fellow Regional Cardiothoracic Centre, Sheffield, 1969-70, sr. registrar in cardiology, 1970-71; MB BS examiner U. Kerala, U. Calicut and U. Madurai, U. Mangalore, U. Coimbatore, U. Tirupati, 1972-89; examiner Nat. Bd. Exams. in Medicine, 1980s; referee JAPI, Bombay, 1980s; postgrad. examiner in MD gen. medicine various univs.; expert/adviser to Union Pub. Svc. Commn., India, Kerala Pub. Svc. Commn.; bd. studies in medicine U. Calicut, U. Kerala; adviser/tech. expert Union Pub. Svc. Commn. India, Kerala Pub. Svc. Commn., 1972—; joint dir. med. edn., Kerala, 1989-90. Contbr. more than 100 articles to profl. jours. including JAPI, Indian Ht. Jour., BMJ, Cardiology, Indian Practitioner, Antiseptic, Kerala Med. Jour., among others. Fellow Royal Coll. Physicians (Edinburgh); mem. Royal Coll. Physicians and Surgeons (Glasgow), Assn. Physicians of India, Cardiol. Soc. India. Avocation: reading medical books and periodicals. Home: Sangeet, Bapuji Nagar Rd, Trivandrum Kerala 695011, India

CHANDRASEKHARAM, DORNADULA, earth sciences educator; b. Madras, India, Mar. 14, 1948; s. Devar and Bharati Baliah; m. Rama Koteswaram, Aug. 31, 1977; children: Varun, Rohini. BSc in Geology, Madras U., 1969; MSc in Applied Geology, Indian Inst. Tech., Bombay, 1972, PhD, 1978. Rsch. assoc. Indian Inst. Tech., Bombay, 1978-80; sr. scientist Centre for Water Resources Mgmt., Calicut, Kerala, India, 1980-85, Ctr. for Earth Sci. Studies, Trivandrum, India, 1985-87; prof. dept. earth scis. Indian Inst. Tech., Bombay, 1987—, head dept. earth scis.; Third World Acad. Scis. vis. prof. Sana' U., Republic Yemen, 1997—; Internat. Ctr. Theoretical Physics fellow, Trieste, Italy, 1997—. Contbr. articles to nat. and internat. jours., chpts. to books. Mem. Internat. Geothermal Assn., Gerthermal Resources Coun., Current Sci. Assn. India, Internat. Assn. Volcanology and Chemistry Earth's Interior. Avocations: origami, carroms champion in the campus. Office: Indian Inst Tech, Dept Earth Scis, Bombay 400076, India

CHANDRASHEKARAN, MAROLI KRISHNAYYA, biologist; b. Salem, Tamil Nadu, India, Jan. 4, 1937; s. Maroli and Rukmini (Bantwal) Krishnayya; m. Shashikala Shamanna, June 17, 1968; children: Sujata, Sonali. BS, Madras U., 1958, MS, 1960, PhD, 1964, DSc, 1985. Alexander v. Humoldt fellow Tuebingen, Germany, 1964-68; Miller fellow Berkeley U., Calif., 1968-70; rsch. assoc. DFG, Germany, 1970-75; reader Kamaraj U., India, 1975-80; prof. MKU, India, 1980-96; sr. prof. MKU, 1994-96, syndicate mem., 1994-96, chmn. syndicate, 1995; prof. JNCASR, Bangalore, 1996—. Author: Biological Rhythms, 1985, Basic Experiments in Neurophysiology, 1987. Recipient S.S. Bhatnagar prize CSIR, New Delhi, 1979, Sir J.C. Bose prize, 1989. Fellow Indian Acad. Sci. (editor 1991-96), Indian Nat. Sci. Acad. (editor 1997-99, vice-pres. 1999-2000), Third World Acad. Sci. Hindu. Avocations: reading, writing, travel. Home: 411 103 15th Cross, Jayanagar II Block, 560011 Bangalore India Office: JNCASR, Jakkur PO, 560064 Bangalore India

CHANDROMONI, veterinarian, educator; b. Munger, Bihar, India, June 2, 1957; s. Jugal Kishore Prasad and Nirmala Sinha; m. Kanak Lata, Mar. 11, 1986; children: Bhaskar Moni, Pushkar Moni. BSc, Ranchi (India) Vet. Coll., 1980; MSc, Bihar Vet. Coll., Patna, India, 1985; PhD, Indian Vet. Resch. Inst., Izatnagar, 1997. Vet. officer Bihar Govt., Patna, 1981-85; assoc. prof. Rajindra Agrl. U., Patna, 1985—. Scholar, Ranchi Vet. Coll.; Univ. fellow Ranchi Vet. Coll. Mem. Coll. Tchrs. Assn. (gen. sec. 1997-98)., Animal Nutrition Soc. India. Avocation: table tennis. Home: H No. 27, Patna 800023, India Office: S G Inst Dairy Tech, Dehlwan-Lohia Nagar, Patna 800020, India

CHAN DUKI See SU CHEE CHEN

CHANDY, RAJESH K., business educator; b. Ernakulam, India, Oct. 2, 1969; came to U.S., 1990; s. Koshy and Rachel Chandy; m. Pattana Thaivanich, Mar. 2, 1996. B in Engring., Madurai Kamaraj U., Madurai, India, 1990; MBA, U. Okla., 1992; PhD, U. So. Calif., 1996. Vis. asst. prof. UCLA, 1996-97; asst. prof. bus., Melcher Faculty fellow U. Houston, 1997—; asst. prof. U. Minn., 2000—. Contbr. articles to profl. jours. Grantee Inst. Study Bus. Mkts., 1995, Alden Clayton award Mktg. Sci. Inst., 1995. Mem. Am. Mktg. Assn., Acad. Mktg. Sci. (Mary Kay award 1998), Inst. Mgmt. Scis., Acad. Mgmt. Avocations: travel, reading. E-mail: rchandy@csom.umn.edu. Office: U Minn U Minn Carlson Sch of Mgmt Minneapolis MN 55455

CHANEY, FREDERICK MICHAEL, senator, lawyer; b. Perth, Asutralia, Oct. 28, 1941; s. Frederick Charles and Mavis Mary (Bond) C.; m. Angela Margaret Clifton, Apr. 18, 1964; children: Frederick, Gervase, Patrick. LLB, U. Western Australia, Perth, 1962. Pvt. practice, 1966-74; senator Australian Parliament, Western Australia, 1974-90, opposition whip, 1975, govt. whip, 1975-78, min. adminstrv. svcs., 1978, min. Aboriginal affairs, 1978-80, min. social security, 1980-83, leader opposition in the Senate, 1983-90, deputy leader of opposition and parliamentary Liberal Party, 1989-90, shadow min. for resources and energy, 1983-84, shadow min. for industry, tech. & commerce, 1984-87, 88-89, shadow min. for indsl. rels., 1987-88, 89-90, shadow min. environ. & sustainable devel., 1990—; mem. several senate and joint selection coms., 1976-77, mem. Commonwealth parliamentary del. to Can., 1976, to U.S., 1976, joint leader parliamentary del. to Bangladesh, India and Sri Lanka, 1978. Sr. v.p. Liberal Party of Western Australia, 1970-74, mem. fed. exec. com., 1973-74, fed. platform com., 1973-74; mem. Nat. Native Title Tribunal, 1994-2000, dep. pres., 2000—; chancellor Murdoch U., 1995—; apptd. officer Order of Australia, 1997. Rsch. fellow Grad. Sch. Mgmt., U. Western Australia, 1993-95. Roman Catholic. Home: 23 B Brown St, Claremont 6010, Australia

CHANG, ANNE BERNADETTE, pediatrician; b. Johor, Malaysia, Aug. 24, 1963; d. Anthony Chang and Kim Hua Kam. MBBS, U. Melbourne, 1988, PhD, 1997. FRACP/Australia. Intern St. Vincent's Hosp., Melbourne, 1989; registrar Mater Misericordiae Children's Hosp., Brisbane, Australia, 1991-94; fellow Royal Children's Hosp., Melbourne, 1995-97; pediat. respiratory cons. Mater Hosp., Brisbane, 1997-2000; assoc. prof. pediats. Flinders U. No. Territory Clin. Sch., 2000—. Contbr. articles to profl. jours. Grad. scholar Nat. Health and Med. Rsch. Coun., 1995-97; St. Vincent's Hosp. Grad. award, Melbourne, 1987; exhibitionist Queen's Coll., Melbourne, 1987. Fellow Royal Coll. Physicians; mem. The Royal Soc. of Australia and New Zealand, Am. Thoracic Soc., European Respiratory Soc. Roman Catholic. Avocations: bush walking, guitar, environ. issues., indigenous health issues. Office: Alice Springs Hosp, Dept Paediatrics, 3052 Melbourne NT 0871, Australia

CHANG, BAOCHONG BOLIN, oncologist; b. Dongtai, China, Sept. 17, 1967; came to U.S., 1990; s. Tao and Youzhu (Lü) C.; m. Tian Gu, July 31, 1990; children: Andrew, Bruce. BS, MD, Suzhou U. Med. Coll., 1989; MS, U. Mass., 1993; PhD, Clark U., 1998. Lic. physician, Mich.; diplomate U.S. Edn. Commn. for Fgn. Med. Grads. Oncologist Suzhou (China) Med. Coll. Hosps., 1989-90; rsch. asst. U. Mass. Med. Ctr., Worcester, 1990-92; rsch. assoc. Worcester Found. Biomed. Rsch., Shrewsbury, Mass., 1993-97; postdoctoral fellow U. Mass., Worcester, 1997-98; med. resident, instr., prin. investigator McLaren-Mich. State U., Flint, Mich., 1998—; oncology fellow M.D. Anderson Cancer Ctr., Houston, 2001—; founder Frontier Med., Inc. Contbr. articles to profl. jours. Fellow U. Mass., 1990-92, The Fairlawn Found. Biomed. Rsch., 1994-96. Mem. AAAS, ACP, AMA, Am. Assn. Cancer Rsch., N.Y. Acad. Scis., Am. Soc. Internal Medicine, Am. Chinese Med. Assn. (founder Mich. chpt.). Achievements include being the first in world to characterize human TrkA gene promoter which may lead to treatment of neuroblastoma. E-mail: b chang@dr.com. Office: Int Med Residency McLaren Med Ctr 401 S Ballenger Hwy Flint MI 48532-3638

CHANG, BYEONG-MO, computer scientist, educator, researcher; b. Mokpo, Chonnam, South Korea; s. Jaenam and Samrae (Kim) C. BS in Computer Engring., Seoul (Korea) Nat. U., 1988; MS in Computer Sci., Korea Adv. Inst. Sci. & Tech., 1990, PhD in Computer Sci., 1994. Rsch. asst. Korea Advanced Inst. Sci. and Tech., Taejon, 1990-94; postdoctoral rschr. Electronics and Telecom. Rsch. Inst., Taejon, 1994-95; assoc. prof. dept. computer sci. Sookmyung Women's U., Seoul, 1995—, chmn. dept. computer sci., 1996—; vis. rschr. Korea Sci. and Engring. Found., 1996. Contbr. articles to profl. jours. Rsch. grantee Korea Sci. and Engring. Found., 1995, Electronics and Telecom. Rsch. Inst., 1996. Mem. Korea Info. Sci. Soc., Assn. Computing Machinery. Avocations: swimming, tennis, climbing. Office: Sookmyung Womens Univ, Chongpadong Yongsanku, Seoul 140-742, Republic of Korea

CHANG, BYUNG-CHUL, surgeon, educator; b. Daegu, Korea, Apr. 7, 1953; s. Soo-Ik Chang and Tae-Suk Kim; m. In Kyung Kim, June 14, 1981; children: Joon Young, Joon Ha. MD, Yonsei U., Seoul, Korea, 1977; MS, Yonsei U., Seoul, 1981, PhD, 1991. Cert. in thoracic and cardiovascular surgery Ministry of Health and Social Affairs, Republic of Korea. Rsch. instr. dept. thoracic and cardiovascular surgery Yonsei U., 1985-87, asst. prof., 1987-92; Evarts A. Graham fellow Am. Assn. Thoracic Surgery, Boston, 1987-88; rsch. assoc. Washington U. Sch. Medicine, St. Louis, 1988-89; assoc. prof. divsn. cardiovascular surgery Yonsei Cardiovascular Ctr., Seoul, 1992-99, prof., 1999—, chief divsn. cardiovascular surgery, 1997—. Contbr. chpts. to med. books. Capt. Republic of Korea Army, 1982-95. Recipient Acad. award Korean Soc. Biomed. Engring., Dongshin SmithKline Beecham prize for rsch. achievement, 1996. Mem. Korean Soc. Thoracic and Cardiovascular Surgery, Korean Soc. Circulation, Korean Soc. Heart Transplantation, Internat. Soc. Cardiovascular Surgery. Avocations: golf, mountain climbing. Fax: 82-2-313-2992. E-mail: bcchang@yumc.yonsei.ac.kr. Home: # 202 Sae-Seoul Apg 46, Banpo-dong Seocho-ku, Seoul 137-044, Korea Office: Yonsei U Divsn Cardiovasc, 134 Shinchon-dong Seodaemun, Seoul 120-752, Korea

CHANG, CHAO-FU, microbiologist, educator; b. Taichung, Taiwan, Nov. 10, 1940; s. Fu-Chen and Kuan (Jang) C.; m. Chu Lin; children: Hong-E, E-Ching, E-Ting. Diploma, Nat. Pingtung Inst. Agr., Taiwan, 1965; MS, N.C. State U., 1976, PhD, 1978. Jr. specialist Taichung Agrl. Sta., 1966-67; asst. Nat. Pingtung Inst. Agr., 1967-73, instr., 1973-79, assoc. prof., 1979-82, prof., 1982-91, head dept., 1982-86, dir. vet. hosp., 1983-86; prof. Nat. Taiwan U., Taipei, 1991—. Editor-in-chief Jour. Chinese Soc. vet. Sci., 1992-95; contbr. articles to profl. jours. 2d lt. Taiwanese army, 1965-66. Mem. Am. Soc. Microbiology, Taiwan Assn. Vet. Medicine and Animal Husbandry (dir.), Chinese Soc. Vet. Sci. (dir.), Chinese Soc. Microbiology, Chinese Soc. Lab. Animals (dir.), Chinese Soc. Traditional Vet. Sci. (dir.). Avocations: horticulture, mountain climbing, music, jogging. Fax: 886-2-2363-2436. E-mail: cfchang@ccms.ntu.edu.tw. Home: 5th Fl 2-6 Lane 3, Chaozhou St, Taipei 100, Taiwan Office: National Taiwan Univ, 142 Zhoushan rd, Taipei 106, Taiwan

CHANG, CHENG-JEN, surgeon, researcher; b. Taipei, Taiwan, Aug. 24, 1958; s. Yang-Lieh and Shiow-Shya (Lay) C.; m. Ingrid Yin-Yin Han, Apr. 19, 1986; 1 child, Hsi-Wen. MD, China Med. Coll., Taichung, Taiwan, 1982; MS, Newport (Calif.) U., 1998. Intern Chang Gung Meml. Hosp, Taipei, 1981-82, resident in gen. surgery, 1987-89, resident in plastic surgery, 1989-90, chief resident in plastic surgery, 1990—, attending physician in plastic surgery, 1991—, clin. lectr., 1998—, asst. prof., 1995; asst. prof. Chang Gung U., Tao-Yuan, 1991-97; presenter in field. Author: Year Book of Dermatology, 1997; chief in editor Chang Gung Surg. News, 1998—; contbr. articles to profl. jours. including Plastic and Reconstructive Surgery, Jour. Clin. Laser Medicine, Chang Gung Med. Jour., Laser and Light in Ophthalmology. 2d lt. Taiwanese Air Force, 1982-84. Recipient Johnsen Johnsen Med. scholarship, 1981, Best Article award Nat. Sci. Coun., 1996, 9th Congress Internat. Nd. Yag Laser Symposium, 1997; internat. clin. fellow U. Calif., Irvine, 1994-95. Mem. AAAS, Congress Internat. Soc. for Laser Surgery and Medicine, Internat. Soc. for Photodynamic Therapy, Soc. Photo-Optical Instrumentation Engrs., Internat. Soc. Optical Engring., Oriental Soc. Aesthetic Plastic Surgery, Am. Soc. Plastic and Reconstructive Surgery, Am. Soc. for Laser Surgery and Medicine (publs. com. 1998-99), Formosan Med. assn., Laser Medicine Soc., Surg. Assn., Hand Surgery Soc., Radiology Soc., Plastic and Reconstructive Assn., Internat. Soc. for Burn Injuries, Lions (award 1985). Buddhist. Avocations: golf, swimming, painting, classical music, dance. Home: Tung Hwa North Rd, 10105 Taipei Taiwan Office: Chang Gung Meml Hosp, 199 Tung Hwa North Rd, 10105 Taipei Taiwan

CHANG, CHEW KIENT, management company executive; b. Sandakan, Sabah, Malaysia, Oct. 10, 1962; arrived in Singapore, 1988; s. Kwong Yui and Nyuk Ha (Chan) Chang; m. Lisa Ngo, July 25, 1992; children: Chang Hin Yun, Chang Hin Keat. BA, U. Toronto, Can., 1985; MBA, Saint Mary's U., Halifax, Can., 1987; diploma, Inst. Basic Life Principles. Indsl. engr. Tilley of Can., Toronto, 1984-86; user svc. cons. Saint Mary's U., Halifax, Can., 1987, lectr., 1987-88; sr. cons. MBA Svcs., Halifax, 1988; ops. mgr. McAlister Servicemaster, Singapore, 1989; gen. mgr. MHL ServiceMaster, 1990; gen. mgr. Asia Servicemaster, Singapore, 1992—; dir. ServiceMaster, Hong Kong, 1995, Taiwan, 1994—, Singapore, 1993—; dir. MHL ServiceMaster Sdn Bhd, Malaysia, 1995—; United MHL (Malaysia) Sdn Bhd, 1995—. Vol. Salvation Army, Singapore, 1990-94; asst. camp dir. Christian Horizon, Can., Beacon Bible Camp. Engrs., Can.; chmn. host and hostess Inst. of Basic Life Principles, Singapore chpt. Govt. of Ont. merit scholar, 1980; Can Tire Corp. scholar, 1988; Sant Mary's ggrad. fellowship. Mem. Am. Bus. Coun., AnCham (internat. regional policy com., IT policy com., govt. liaison com. com.). Office: Pico Creative Ctr, Level 2 20 Kallang Ave, Singapore 339411, Singapore

CHANG, CHIA-CHENG, educator; b. Tamsui, Taipei, Taiwan, May 28, 1939; came to the U.S., 1966; s. Chi Chang and Kwei Wang; m. Li-Hwa Wu, Sept. 19, 1964; children: Li-Chee, Helen, Catherine. BS, Chung-Hsing U., Taichung, Taiwan, 1962; PhD, U. Mo., 1971. Postdoctoral investigator Oak Ridge (Tenn.) Nat. Lab., 1971-72; postdoctoral rsch. fellow U. Mich., Ann Arbor, 1972-74; rsch. assoc. Mich. State U., East Lansing, 1974-75, asst. prof., 1975-79, assoc. prof., 1979-89, prof., 1989—; mem. site visiting teams NIH, 1977, 79, 80, 87; mem. grant rev. panels U.S. Army Med. Rsch. and Materiel Command, 1995, 96, 2000. Contbr. articles to profl. jours. V.p. Taiwanese Am. Assn., 1975. 2nd lt. Taiwanese Mil., 1962-63. Recipient Young Environ. Scientist award Nat. Inst. Environ. Health Scis., NIH, 1978-81; grantee NCI, NIH, 1989-94, Nat. Inst. Environ. Health Scis., NIH, 1994-98, U.S. Army Med. Rsch. and Materiel Command, 1996-2000. Mem. AAAS, N.Am. Taiwanese Profs. Assn. (pres. Mich. chpt. 1989, 99), Am. Assn. for Cancer Rsch., Genetic Soc. Am., Tissue Culture Assn. Achievements include patents for human breast epithelial cell type with stem cell and luminal cell characteristics. Avocations: tennis, Tai-chi. E-mail: cc.chang@ht.msu.edu. Fax: 517-432-6340. Home: 4096 Wabaningo Rd Okemos MI 48864-3437 Office: Mich State Univ 252 Food Safety/Toxicology East Lansing MI 48824

CHANG, CHIH JEN, family physician, educator; b. Taipei, Taiwan, China, Dec. 31, 1954; s. Tong Yang and Yueh Nu (Chen) Chang; m. Tzu Chen Chang, Dec. 21, 1980; children: Chieh Chun, Chieh Yu. MD, China Med. Coll., Taichung, Taiwan, 1981. Cert. family physician, endocrinologist, diabetes specialist. Intern Nat. Taiwan U. Hosp., Taipei, 1980-81, resident, 1981-83; resident Tao-Yuan (Taiwan) Hosp., 1983-85; prof. Med. Coll. Nat. Cheng-Kung Univ., Tainan, 1998—; head dept. family medicine Nat. Cheng-Kung Univ. Hosp., Tainan, 1987—; dir. Diabetes Rsch. Ctr., Tainan, 1995-99. Contbr. articles to profl. jours.; editl. bd. Chin Jour. Family Medicine, 1995-99. Mem. Am. Diabetes Assn. (mem. profl. sect.), World Orgn. Nat. Colls., Acads. and Academic Assn. of Gen. Practice/Family Physicians, , Family Medicine Soc. (cert. bd. 1987-99), Geriatric Soc. (ednl. com. 1995-99), N.Y. Acad. Scis. Buddhist. Avocations: tea drinking, swimming, singing, reading, diving. Office: Nat Cheng-Kung Univ Hosp, #138 Sheng-Li Rd, Tainan 70428, Taiwan

CHANG, CHIN-CHEN, computer science educator, academic administrator; b. Taichung, Republic of China, Nov. 12, 1954; s. Ching-shui Chang and Shiow-Yueh Lin; m. Ling-Hui Huang; children: Ching-Chieh, Ching-Yun, Ching-Chun. BS, Nat. Tsing-Hua U., 1977, MS, 1979; PhD, Nat. Chiao-Tung U., 1982. Chmn. computer sci. and info. engring. Nat. Chung Cheng U., Taiwan, 1989-92, dean of engring., 1992-95, chmn. automation rsch. ctr., 1993-95, dean acad. affairs, 1995-97, acting pres., 1996-97; dir. adv. office Ministry of Edn., Taiwan, 1998—; cons. computer ctr., Nat. Chung Hsing U., Taiwan, 1985-89, Chin-Yi- Inst. of Tech., Taiwan, 1986-87, Chia-Yi County Govt., Taiwan, 1994—. Author: Database Management Systems, 1991 (Outstanding Teaching Material award 1992). Recipient Disting. Rsch. awards, Nat. Sci. Coun., Republic of China, Outstanding Scholarly Contbrn. award, Internat. Inst. Advanced Systems, Can., 1999. Fellow IEEE. Buddhist. Avocations: golf, swimming, basketball. Office: Chiayi County, 160 San-Hsing Village, Ming-Shung Taiwan

CHANG, CHING-I EUGENE, retired insurance executive; b. Taichung, Republic of China, June 16, 1938; came to U.S., 1965; s. Chang T. and Tsai Chang; m. Lucia S. Chen, Sept. 9, 1967; 1 child, Michael K. BBA, Chang Kung U., 1962; MS in Stats., Mich. State U., 1967. Chief actuary Chrysler Ins. Group, Troy, Mich., 1970-80; v.p. ITT Lyndon Ins. Group, St. Louis, 1980; asst. v.p. actuary Citizens Ins. Co. Am., Howell, Mich., 1980-85; pres., COO Lake States Ins. Co., Traverse City, Mich., 1985-97; ret., 1997; mem. Mich. Bilateral Trade Team to Taiwan, 1993-98. Trustee Lake Superior State U., 1996—; mem. adv. bd. Boys and Girls Club of Grand Traverse, Mich., 1991—. Inductee Mich. Ins. Hall of Fame, 1997. Mem. Am. Acad. Actuaries, Soc. Actuaries (assoc.), Mich. Actuarial Soc. (pres. 1981-82), Internat. Actuarial Assn., Econ. Club Traverse City (pres. 1993-94). Avocation: tennis. Home: 6176 Singletree Williamsburg MI 49690-9570

CHANG, CHING-JER, medicinal chemistry educator; b. Hsinchu, Taiwan, China, Oct. 17, 1942; came to the U.S., 1968; s. Tin-lian and Awei (Lai) C.; m. Shu-fang Kuo, Dec. 25, 1978; children: Philip, Sylvia. BS, Nat. Taiwan Cheng Kung U., 1965; PhD, Ind. U., 1972. Asst. prof. Purdue U., West Lafayette, Ind., 1973-78; assoc. prof. Purdue U., West Lafayette, 1978-84, prof., 1984—; mem. bioorganic and natural products chemistry study sect., NIH, Bethesda, Md., 1986-90, spl. study sect., 1991—; editl. adv. bd. Jour. Natural Products, 1989—; assoc. editor: Jour. Asian Nat. Products; reviewer Human Frontier Sci. Program, Strassbourg, France, 1992—. Contbr. articles to profl. jours. Mem. Am. Soc. Pharmacognosy (exec. com. 1993—), Am. Chem. Soc., Am. Assn. for Cancer Rsch., Phytochem. Soc. N.Am., Argentinian Soc. Organic Chemistry (hon. mem.). Achievements include 3 patents. Office: Dept Medicinal Chemistry Purdue Univ West Lafayette IN 47907

CHANG, CHI-SEN, gastroenterologist; b. Taichung, Taiwan, Aug. 30, 1957; s. Te-Jung and Su-Ping (Tsai) C.; m. Chuan-Huei Hsiung, Sept. 3, 1984; children: Yun-Hsuan, Yun-Tsui, Yun-Fang. MB, Kaoshiung (Taiwan) Med. Coll., 1982. Intern Chang-Gung Meml. Hosp., Taipei, 1981-82; med. officer Chinese Army Field Hosp., 1982-84; resident Taichung (Taiwan) Vets. Gen. Hosp., 1984-87, fellow gastroenterology, 1987-89, attending physician, 1989—; cons. Nutrition Support Team Taichung, Vets. Gen. Hosp., 1994—, cons. Hospice Care Taichung, 1995—. Recipient Award of Outstanding Dr., Bur. Health, Taichung City, 1994, 96., Outstanding Gastroenterology Article award J-L Sung's Rsch. Found., 1997, Outstanding Rsch. Article award Taichung Veterans Gen. Hosp., 1998. Mem. Med. Dr. Soc. Republic of China, Gastroenterology Soc. Republic of China, Chinese Soc. Parenteral and Enteral Nutrition. Avocations: tennis, golf, bowling. Home: 66-20 Sec 1 Nan-Tun Rd, 403 Taichung Taiwan Office: Taichung Vets Gen Hosp, 160 Sec 3 Chung-Kang Rd, 407 Taichung Taiwan

CHANG, CHONG EUN, chemical engineer; b. Seoul, Korea, Dec. 4, 1938; came to U.S., 1968; BS in Chem. Engring., Seoul Nat. U., 1964; PhD in Chem. Engring., U. So. Calif., 1973, MS in Mech. Engring., 1977. Asst. chief of lab. Hyundai Co., Seoul, 1964-68; postdoctoral rsch. assoc. U. So. Calif., L.A., 1973-75; sr. process engr. Allis-Chalmers Corp., Stansteel Products, L.A., 1976-78; mgr. process devel. Alpha Therapeurics Corp., L.A., 1979-81, sr. prin. scientist, 1981-92; v.p. RAAS, Inc., Agoura Hills, Calif., 1992-94; exec. advisor Korea Green Cross Corp., Seoul, Korea, 1996—. Contbr. articles to Jour. Crystal Growth, Internat. Jour. Heat and Mass Trans. With Korean Army, 1959-60. Archimedes Cir. scholar. 1971. Mem. AICHE. Achievements include patents for fractionation of blood plasma, albumin purification. Home: 5833 Briartree Dr La Canada Flintridge CA 91011-1826 Office: Korea Green Cross Corp, 227 Kugal-ri, Yongin Kyunggi-do Korea

CHANG, CHUEI-TIN, chemical engineering educator; b. Taipei, Taiwan, Jan. 29, 1954; s. Perng-Sen and Harn-Jui (Tung) C.; m. Yu-Wen Wang, Jan. 7, 1982; children: Fenway, Chihway. BS, Nat. Taiwan U., 1976; MS, Columbia U., 1979, Phd, 1982. Process engr. FMC Corp., Princeton, N.J., 1982-85; asst. prof. U. Nebr., Lincoln, 1985-89; assoc. prof. Nat. Cheng

Kung U., Tainan, Taiwan, 1989-93, prof., 1993—; adj. lectr. N.J. Inst. Tech., Newark, 1984. Contbr. articles to profl. jours. 2d lt. Army of Taiwan, 1976-78. Recipient citation for Outstanding Achievement, Columbia U., 1981, Lai Zai Teh award ChiChE, 1999; Nat. Sci. Coun. grantee, 1990—. Fellow Chinese Chem. Engring. Soc.; mem. AIChE, Sigma Xi. Avocations: jogging, fishing. Home: Apt 3F No 36 Lane 52, Sheng Li Rd, Tainan 70101, Taiwan Office: Nat Cheng King U, Dept Chem Engring, Tainan 70101, Taiwan

CHANG, CHUN-YEN, engineering educator; b. Kaoshiung, Taiwan, Oct. 12, 1937; s. Moo-huo and Shu-Yu Chang; m. Cheng-Hwei; children: Wei-Heng, Wei-Jen, Wei-Lun. PhD, Nat. Chiao Tung U., Hsinchu, Taiwan, 1970. Mem. tech. staff Bell Labs., 1981-90; prof., dir., dean engring. dept. Nat. Nano Device Lab. Nat. Chiao Tung U., Hsinchu, 1990—; president Nat. Chiao Tung U., Hsinchu, Taiwan; vis. prof. U. Fla., 1987, Stuttgart U., 1989; cons. Nippon Seiki, 1985, Electronics Rsch. and Svc. Orgn. of Indsl. Tech. Rsch. Inst., 1985—. Recipient Engr. Acad. award Ministry of Edn., Republic of China, 1988, Outstanding Rsch. awawrd Nat. Sci. Coun., Republic of China, 1983—. Fellow IEEE; mem. Am. Physics Soc. (life). Avocation: golf. Office: Nat Chiao Tung U, 1001 Univ Rd, Hsinchu Taiwan*

CHANG, DAH-CHUNG, design engineer, educator; b. Chia-yi, Taiwan, June 13, 1969; parents Chuan-Chian Chang and Hsian-Chu Luo. BSEE, Fu-Jen Cath. U., Taipei, Taiwan, 1991; MSEE, Nat. Chiao Tung U., Hsinchu, Taiwan, 1993, PhD in Elec. Engring., 1998. Tchg. asst. Nat. Chiao Tung U., 1991-92, rsch. asst., 1992-98; design engr. ITRI, Hsinchu, 1998—; asst. prof. Fu-Jen Cath. U., Taipei, 1998—; part-time design engr. Indsl. Tech. Rsch. Inst., Hsinchu, 1998. Author: (textbook) Data and Digital Communication Systems and Principles, 1996; contbr. articles to profl. jours. Named Excellent Younger of 1994, Chinese Ret. Soldier Assn., 1994. Mem. IEEE. Avocations: medicine, music, movies, traveling. Fax: 886-3-5820081. E-mail: dcchang@itri.org.tw. Home: 3F-1 73 Fu-Ruei St, Taichung 407, Taiwan Office: Indsl Tech Rsch Inst, N100 Bldg 14 Chung Hsing Rd, Chutung 310, Taiwan

CHANG, DEH-MING, rheumatologist, immunologist, medical educator; b. Taipei, Taiwan, May 3, 1955; s. Tao Chang and Yi-Chang Lin; m. Chi Lei, Nov. 20, 1983; children: Da-Wei, Da-Jung, Da-Fang. MD, Nat. Def. Med. Ctr., Taipei, 1981; MS, Harvard U., 1990. Med. diplomate in rheumatology and immunology, 1987. Resident Tri-Svc. Gen. Hosp., Taipei, 1981-86; instr. Nat. Def. Med. Ctr., 1986-90; attending physician Tri-Svc. Gen. Hosp., 1987-92; assoc. prof. medicine Nat. Def. Med. Ctr., 1991-95; chief, dept. rheumatology/immunology Tri-Svc. Med. Hosp., 1993—; prof. medicine Nat. Def. Med. Ctr., 1995—. Inventor in fields of clinical immunology and immunopathology, 1994, 95. Capt., Navy Gen. Hosp., 1983-84, Kao-H. Fellow Am. Coll. Rheumatology; mem. N.Y. Acad. Scis., Mass. Med. Soc., Rheumatology Assn. (sec. gen. 1993—), Immunology Assn. (bd. dirs. 1994—), Lupus Found. (bd. dirs. 1993—), Asthma Ctr. (bd. dirs. 1993—). Avocations: tennis, chess. Office: Tri-Svc Gen Hosp Rheumatol/, Ting-Chow Rd, Taipei Taiwan

CHANG, DING-KWO, biophysicist; b. Keelung, Taiwan; s. Shiou-Chin Chang and Yue-Er Tu; m. Man-Li Chuang, Sept. 1984; children: Kevin Yi, Greta Shin-Yi. BS, Nat. Taiwan U., 1973; MS, U. Akron, 1978; PhD, U. Wis., 1984. Rsch. instr. U. Ala., Birmingham, 1987-90; lab. mgr. U. Mo., Columbia, 1990-91; rsch. fellow Rice U., Houston, 1991; assoc. rsch. prof. biophysics Academia Sinica, Taipei, Taiwan, 1991-97, rsch. prof., 1997—. Author:J. Virology, 1997; contbr. articles to profl. jours. Nat. Sci. Coun. grantee, 1996. Mem. AAAS, Chinese Chem. Soc. (sect. coord. 1993—). Avocations: basketball, swimming. Office: Inst Chemistry, Academia Sinica, Taipei 11529, Taiwan

CHANG, EDWARD H., computer company executive; b. Taipei, Taiwan, Jan. 10, 1958; came to U.S., 1975; s. James T. and Yu-Chin Chang. BA, U. Hawaii, 1981. Cert. Inst. for Cert. Bus. Counselor. Mktg. dir. Prometheus World Enterprise, Santa Ana, Calif., 1983-88; gen. mgr. Trans PC, Inc., Norwalk, Calif., 1989-91; v.p. consumer products Microtome, Inc., St. Louis, 1992-95; exec. dir. Lotus Profl., L.A., Calif., 1996—; exec. dir. EKM Computer, Inc., Buena Park, Calif., 1997-99, LPS Telemgmt., L.A., 1995—. Bd. dirs. Vairotsana Found., pres., 1996-98. Buddhist. Achievements include co-patent for system and apparatus for electronic communication. E-mail: edward8888@aol.com. Office: Lotus Profl Media Tower II Rm 411 1600 Taft Ave Los Angeles CA 90028-3707

CHANG, EUGENE YU-SHENG, political science educator; b. Chungking, Shih-chuan, China, Oct. 3, 1940; s. Ke-chang and Yun-chi (Tang) C.; m. Shirley Shih-Lan Tsai, Oct. 3, 1970; children: Nancy Shih-chi, George Shih-chieh. BA in Polit. Sci., Tunghai U., Taichung, Taiwan, 1963; MA in Polit. Sci., Syracuse U., 1969; postgrad. studies, U. Pitts., 1973-75. English tchr. Kaohsiung (Taiwan) Third Middle Sch., 1964-65; tech. libr. clk. Air Asia Co., Tianan, Taiwan, 1965; grad. asst. Tunghai U., Taichung, Taiwan, 1965-68, lectr. in polit. sci., 1969-72, assoc. prof. polit sci., 1972-81, prof., 1981-95, assoc. prof., 1995—; rsch. fellow Princeton U. Ctr. Internat. Studies, Princeton, N.J., 1987-88. Author: (books) American Ocean Policy Since 1945, 1992, Chinese (R.O.C.) Participation in the Creation of the United Nations, 1994, Essays on American Politics and the United Nations, 1994; also articles in political sci. jours. 2d lt. Republic of China Air Force, 1963-64. Recipient Syracuse in Asia fellowship Syracuse U., N.Y., 1968-69; Fulbright Jr. Scholar fellowship, Inst. Internat. Edn., N.Y.C., 1973-75, Nat. Sci. Coun. fellowship, Taipei, Taiwan, 1987-88. Mem. Am. Polit. Sci. Assn., Chinese Polit. Sci. Assn., Internat. Studies Assn., Internat. Polit. Sci. Assn., Am. Studies Assn. Mem. KMT.. Avocations: travel, classical music, photography, stamp collection. E-mail: yschang@mail.thu.edu.tw. Home: No 1 Tunghai Rd, 407 Taichung Taiwan Office: Tunghai U Dept Polit Sci, PO Box 870, T'aichung 407, Taiwan

CHANG, FLORA CHIA-I, university administrator; b. Taipei, Taiwan, China, June 19, 1957; d. Clement C.P. and Carrie W.T. (Chiang) C. BA, Chengchi U., Taipei, 1979; MA, San Francisco State U., 1982, Stanford U., 1983; EdD, Stanford U., 1995. Lectr. Tamkang U., Tamsui, China, 1984-89, assoc. prof., 1989-90, 93—, v.p., 1986—. Author: Gender Differences in Faculty Hiring in Taiwan, 1996. Mem. AAUW, AERA, IAFFE. Buddhist. Avocations: reading, golf, tennis, travel, Internet. Office: Tamkang U, 151 Ying-Chuan Rd, Taiwan Tamsui 25137, China

CHANG, GENE HSIN, economics educator, humanities educator; b. Shanghai, China, Feb. 22, 1952; came to U.S., 1982.; s. Huaisheng Chang and Jiahui Huang; m. Jinmei Chang, Aug. 12, 1985; children: Elaine, Emily. BA, Fudan U., Shanghai, 1982; MA, U. Calif., Berkeley, 1984; PhD, U. Mich., 1989. Asst. prof. U. Toledo, 1989-92, assoc. prof., 1995—, dir. Asian Studies Inst., 1997—; prof. Zhejiang Asia-Pacific Rsch. Inst., Hangzhou, China, 1992-95. Editor: China Economic Reform, 1991; co-editor China Econ. Rev., 1997—; contbr. articles to profl. jours., chpts. to books. Wheeler fellow U. Calif., Berkeley, 1983-84, Rackham fellow U. Mich., Ann Arbor, 1988-89;. Mem. Am. Econ. Assn., Assn. Asian Studies, Assn. for Comparative Econ. Studies, Royal Econ. Assn. Britain, Chinese Economist Soc. (bd. dirs. 1985-88, pres. 1990-91). Avocations: ping-pong, reading. Office: U Ohio Dept Econs Toledo OH 43606

CHANG, H. K., biomedical engineer, educator; b. Shenyang, Liaoning, China, July 9, 1940; came to U.S., 1963; s. En Shu and Li (Kwan) C.; m. Min-min Chou, Sept. 5, 1965; children: Y. Katharine, W. Michael. BCE, Nat. Taiwan U., Taipei, 1962; MCE, Stanford U., 1964; PhD in Biomed. Engring., Northwestern U., 1969. Asst. prof. SUNY, Buffalo, 1969-75, assoc. prof., 1975-76; assoc. prof. McGill U., Montreal, Que., Can., 1976-80, prof. biomed. engring., physiology and medicine, 1980-84; prof. biomed. engring. and physiology U. So. Calif., L.A., 1984-90, chmn. dept. biomed. engring., 1985-90; founding dean sch. engring., prof. chem. engring. Hong Kong U. Sci. and Tech., 1990-94; dean sch. engring., prof. chem. engring., prof. medicine U. Pitts., 1994-96; pres., Univ. prof. City U. Hong Kong, 1996—; mem. study sect. NIH, Bethesda, Md., 1987-90; hon. prof. Chinese Acad. Med. Scis., Beijing, 1987—, Peking Union Med. Coll., 1987—. Author: Respiratory Physiology: An Analytical Approach, 1989, Fluid and Solute Transport in the Airspaces of the Lungs, 1993; mem. editorial bd. Jour. Applied Physiology, 1979-85; contbr. over 100 articles to profl. jours.; patentee in field. Grantee Nat. Heart Lung Blood Inst., 1974-89. Fellow Hong Kong Instn. Engrs., Hong Kong Acad. Engring. Scis.; mem. ASCE (sr.) AIChE, Am. Inst. Med. and Biol. Engring. (founding fellow), Am. Physiol. Soc., Biomed. Engring. Soc. (sr.; bd. dirs. 1985—, pres. 1989-90), Am. Thoracic Soc. Office: City U Hong Kong, Office of Pres 83 Tat Chee Ave, Kowloon Hong Kong China*

CHANG, HANG, emergency physician; b. Taipei, Taiwan, Nov. 20, 1955; s. Yuen-Hwa C. and Hwei-Ping Hwu. MD, Nat. Taiwan U., Taipei, 1982, PhD, 1992. Resident Nat. Taiwan U. Hosp., Taipei, 1984-88, attending surgeon, 1988-89, vice-chief emergency dept., 1989-92; assoc. prof. Nat. Taiwan U. Hosp., 1995-99; chmn. emergency dept. Shin Kong Hosp., Taipei, 1992-99, vice supt., 1999—; dir. emergency med. svcs. coun. Dept. Health, China, 1991—, exec. hosp. accreditation program, 1990—; chmn. Nat. Resuscitation Coun. Taiwan, 1999—; adv. Taipei City Govt., 1999—. Lt. Taiwan Army, 1982-84. Recipient Nat. award Health Care, Dept. Health, Taipei, China, 1998. Mem. Am. Coll. Emergency Physicians, World Assn. Disaster and Emergency Medicine, Formosan Med. Assn., Soc. Emergency Medicine (hon. pres. 1996—), Taipei Med. Assn. (acting dir. 1999—), Assn. Injury Prevention (acting dir. 1998—), Taiwan Surg. Assn. (dir. trauma com. 1996—), Assn. Quality Health Care (dir. 1996—). Avocations: tennis, squash, swimming, skiing. Office: Shin-Kong Hosp, 95# Wen-Chang Rd, Taipei 111, Taiwan

CHANG, HELEN CHUNG-HUNG HSIANG, piano pedagogy specialist; b. Shanghai, July 20, 1937; d. Shou-Tsu Edward and Chen-Tze Kiang Hsiang; m. Nai Lin Chang; children: Tai Deborah, Huan Justina, Lan Samantha, Ling Patricia. BA cum laude, Mt. Mercy Coll., Cedar Rapids, Iowa, 1960; BMus cum laude, Lawrence U., 1980; postgrad. in pedagogical study, Am. Suzuki Inst., Stevens Point, Wis., 1972, 83, 88-89. Cert. tchr. Music Tchrs. Nat. Assn., Wis. Music Tchr. Assn., Suzuki Assn. of the Ams. Co-chair Fox Valley Keyboard Tchrs., Appleton, Wis., 1981-82, chair, 1982-83, treas., 1996-97; recital chair Suzuki Edn. Assn. of the Fox Valley, Appleton, 1984-96; judge regional competitions Wis. Music Tchrs. Assn., 1988-97, state competition, 1994, 95, others, coach numerous students. Mem. Northeast Wis. Chinese Assn. (Chinese lang. instr. 1972-76), Wis. Music Tchrs. Assn. (award of excellence 1981, 94, 99), Music Tchr. Nat. Assn., Suzuki Assn. of the Ams., Suzuki Assn. of Wis.

CHANG, HIANG-CHU AUSILIA, education educator, researcher; b. Yong-Goang, South Korea, Dec. 10, 1945; arrived in Italy, 1964; d. Yoon-Hwan and Ok-Nim (Kim) C. BA, U. Auxilium, Turin, Italy, 1969, MA, 1972; PhD, U. Auxilium, Rome, 1980. Prof. didactics Pontifical Faculty Scis. of Edn., Turin, Rome, 1975—, prof. comparative edn., 1980—, vice dir., 1989-95, 98—, dir. Inst. of Edn., 1987-93; cons. exptl. lycées, Turin, Rome, Montecatini, Italy, 1982-92; cons. Nat. Com. of Salesian Schs., Rome, 1990-95, Com. for Salesian Schs. of Europe, 1992—, Internt. Found. Nova Spes, Rome, 1998—. Author: Comparative Education as Educational Discipline, 1982, Interdisciplinarity and Discovery Method in School, 1985, (with M. Checchin) Intercultural Education, 1996; co-editor: Women and Humanization of Culture at the Threshold of the Third Millenium. The Way of Education, 1998. Mem. Cath. Ctr. Univ. Profs. Edn., Comparative Edn. Socs. in Europe, Internat. Office of Cath. Edn. Office: Pontifical Fac Scis of Edn, Auxilium, Rome 00166, Italy

CHANG, HONG-CHAN, electrical engineer educator, consultant; b. Taipei, Taiwan, Republic of China, Mar. 5, 1959; s. Wen-Chiang and Shiu-Chu (Hsu) C.; m. Wen-Ching Chang Lin, Dec. 24, 1983; children: Yu Shan, Wei Shan, Yu Cheng. BS, Cheng-Kung U., 1981, MS, 1983, PhD, 1987. Assoc. prof. Nat. Taiwan U. of Sci. and Tech., Taipei, 1987-95, prof., 1995—, chmn. dept. elec. engring., 1997—; mem. task force Ministry of Econ. Affairs, Taipei, 1999—; rev. com. mem. Taipei City Govt., 1999—; reviewer rsch. project Nat. Sci. Coun., Republic of China, 1990—. Contbr. articles to profl. publs. Mem. IEEE, The Instn. of Elec. Engrs. (reviewer papers 1997), Chinese Inst. of Engrs. Avocations: playing badminton, reading, music, hiking, swimming. Office: Nat Taiwan U Sci and Tech, 43 Keelung Rd Sec 4, Taipei 106, Republic of China

CHANG, HSUEH-WEN, educator; b. Taichung, China, Mar. 3, 1956; s. Tso-Peng and Chiao-Shin (Wong) C.; m. Fieng-Lan Sun, Dec. 25, 1984; children: Che, Chin. BS, Tunghai U., Taichung, China, 1978; MS, Ind. State U., 1981; PhD, Ind. U., 1988; MS, Harvard U., 1988. Assoc. prof. Nat. Sun Yat-Sen U., Kaohsiung, China, 1988—; statis. analyst Brigham and Women's Hosp., Boston, 1988; dir. grad. affairs Nat. Sun Yat-Sen U., 1993-95. Mem. environ. impact assessment com. Kaohsiung City Govt., 1994—. 2d lt. Chinese Army, 1978-80. Mem. Chinese Biol. Soc., Ecol. Soc. Am. Avocation: choir conducting. Home: 5 Alley 32 Ln, 458 Chung-Ho St, Taipei Taiwan Office: Nat Sun Yat-Sen U, Nat Sun Yat-Sen U, Dept Biol Scis, Kaohsiung/Taiwan Republic of China

CHANG, HYOUN KAB, psychology educator; b. Chilkokgun, South Korea, Apr. 14, 1942; parents Tae Hee Chang and Kwang Hwang Choi; m. Bang Ja Chung, May 10, 1968 (dec. June 1997); m. Mee Hyang Cho, Oct. 16, 1999. BA in Psychology, Seoul Nat. U., 1965; MA in Psychology, Korea U., 1967; PhD in Psychology, Seoul Nat. U., 1984. Rsch. fellow Cath. Med. Coll., Seoul, 1965-70; asst. prof. Seoul Nat. U., 1970-79; assoc. prof. Yeungnam U., Kyungsan, Korea, 1979-84, prof., 1984—; vis. prof. N.Y. State Inst. Basic Rsch., N.Y.C., 1986, U. Ariz., Tucson, 1997; dir. Inst. Humanities, Yeungnam U., Kyungsan, 1999—. Author: (books) Social Isolation and Behavioral Disorder, 1984, Biological Psychology, 1995, Stress and Mental Health, 1996. Mem. APA, Korean Neurobiol. Soc. (v.p. 1991-95), Korean Psychol. Assn., Soc. for Neurosci. Avocation: meditation. Office: Yeungnam U, Daedong, Kyungsang BukDo, Korea

CHANG, I-SHIH, aerospace engineer; b. Taipei, Taiwan, Dec. 2, 1945; came to U.S., 1968; s. I.H. and T.C. Chang; m. O.J. Chang, May 25, 1974; children: Anna, Brandon. Degree in mech. engring., Taipei Inst. of Tech., 1965; MS, U. Kans., 1969; PhD, U. Ill., 1973. Scientist assoc.-rsch. Lockheed Missiles & Space, Huntsville, Ala., 1973-76; mem. tech. staff Rockwell Internat., Anaheim, Calif., 1976-77; mem. tech. staff The Aerospace Corp., El Segundo, Calif., 1977-80, engring. specialist, 1980-90, sr. engring. specialist, 1990-91, disting. engr., 1991—. Contbr. articles to profl. jours. Fellow AIAA (assoc.); mem. Phi Kappa phi. Democrat. Home: 890 S Calle Venado Anaheim CA 92807-5004 Office: The Aerospace Corp M4/967 2350 E El Segundo Blvd El Segundo CA 90245-4691

CHANG, JANICE MAY, lawyer, administrator, notary public; b. Loma Linda, Calif., May 24, 1970; d. Belden Shiu-Wah (dec.) and Sylvia (Tan) C. BA, Calif. State U., San Bernardino, 1990, cert. paralegal studies, 1990, cert. creative writing, 1991; JD, LaSalle U., 1993; D in Naturopathy, Clayton Sch. Natural Healing, 1993; MS in Psychology, Calif. Coast U., 1997; PhD in Bus. Adminstrn., Columbia State U., 1997; DFA in Creative Writing: Poetry, Am. Internat. U., 1999. Notary pub., Calif. Victim/witness contact clk.-paralegal Dist. Atty.'s Office Victim/Witness Assistance Program, San Bernardino, Calif., 1990; gen. counsel JMC Enterprises, Inc., Loma Linda, Calif., 1993-98; law prof. LaSalle U., Mandeville, La., 1994-97; corp. counsel, CFO, JDS Assocs., Inc., Loma Linda, 1998-99; corp. counsel, CFO DJS, L.P., Loma Linda, 1998-99; with trust mgmt.-legal dept./trust svcs. Southeastern Calif. Assn. Seventh-Day Adventists, Riverside, 1998—; spkr. Internat. U. Graduation Ceremony/Conv., Las Vegas, 1998; sponsor La Sierra U. Student Employment Recognition Banquet, Riverside, Calif., 1999, 2000, La Sierra U. Path of the Just Tree Project, 1998, vol. La Sierra U., Riverside, Ca. Health Fair Expo, 1988, 89, Am. Red Cross First Aid & CPR classes, 1994—. Contbr. poetry to anthologies, including Am. Poetry Anthology, 1987-90, The Pacific Rev., 1991, The Piquant, 1991, River of Dreams, 1994, Reflections of Light, 1994, Musings, 1994 (Honorable Mention award 1994), Best Poems of 1995 (Celebrating Excellence award 1995, Inspirations award 1995), Am. Poetry Annual, 1996, 99, Best New Poems of 1996, Interludes, 1996, Meditations, 1996, Perspectives, 1996 (Honorable Mention award 1996), Keepsakes, 1997 (Honorable Mention award 1997), Best Poems of 1997, Poetic Voices of America, 1997, The Isle of View, 1997, The Other Side of Midnight, 1997, Treasures, 1998, Best Poems of 1998, Writingscapes: Insights & Approaches to Creative Writing, 1998, Am. Poetry Ann., 1999, Mirrors, 1999, America at the Millennium, 2000; contbr. to photog. anthologies Tapestry of Dreams to Internat. Libr. Photography, 1999, Mystical Seasons to Internat. Libr. Photography, 1999. Donor Loma Linda Indonesian SDA Ch. Belden S. Chang Meml. Fund-Bldg. Annex, 1998—. Recipient Poet of Merit award Am. Poetry Assn., San Francisco, 1989, Golden Poet award World of Poetry, Washington, 1989, Publisher's Choice award Watermark Press, 1990, Editor's Choice award The Nat. Libr. of Poetry, 1990-97, Pres.'s award for lit. excellence Iliad Press, 1995-97. Mem. APA, ATLA, Nat. Notary Assn. Republican. Seventh-Day Adventist. Avocations: poetry writing, music, drama, lit., numismatics. Home: 1025 Crestbrook Dr Riverside CA 92506-5662 Office: Southeastern Calif Assn 7th-Day Adventists PO Box 8050 11330 Pierce St Riverside CA 92515-8050

CHANG, JAU-WOIE, mechanical engineer, researcher; b. Tainan Hsien, Taiwan, Dec. 25, 1966; parents Chung Lee Chang and King Zue Don ChangDon; m. Hu Lin Lin, Feb. 13, 1993. ME, Nat. Cheng Kung U., Tainan, 1991; PhD, Nat. Taiwan U., 1997. Registered mech. engr. Rschr. Indsl. Tech. Rsch. Inst., HsinChu, Taiwan, 1997—. Contbr. articles to profl. jours. Home: 47 Kueigun Village, Tainan Hsien 73406, Taiwan Office: Indsl Tech Rsch Inst, Chung Hsing Rd Sect 4, Chutung Hsinchu 310, Taiwan

CHANG, JEFFREY CHAI, dentist, educator, researcher; b. Canton, China, Dec. 19, 1946; came to U.S., 1967; s. Po Wing and Wai Ming (Chan) C.; m. Frances Fuhnan Liang; children: Sheila Sai, Kenneth Kiu. BA with honors, Northeastern U., 1971; DDS, Georgetown U., 1976; MS in Dentistry, U. Tex. Dental Br., Houston, 1996. Commd. 2d lt. U.S. Army, 1976, advanced through grades to maj.; gen. dental officer Dental Corps U.S. Army, Ft. Bliss, Tex., 1976-79; officer-in-charge Dental Clinic U.S. Army, Pusan, Korea, 1979-80; asst. chief clinician dental activity U.S. Army, Ft. Momouth, N.J., 1980-83; chief dental emergency svc. dental activity U.S. Army, Ft. Hood, Tex., 1984-85; resigned U.S. Army, 1985; clin. asst. prof. Dental Sch. U. Calif., San Francisco, 1985-88; clin. asst. prof. NYU Coll. Dentistry, N.Y.C., 1988-90; asst. prof. U. Tex. Dental Br., 1990-92, assoc. prof., 1992—; cons. VA Med. Ctr., San Francisco, 1987-88, St. Barnabas Hosp., Bronx, N.Y., 1988-90, VA Med. Ctr., Houston, 1993—, ADA Coun. on Sci. Affairs, 1996—; scientist Houston Biomaterials Rsch. Ctr., 1996—. Contbr. 40 articles, 20 abstracts to profl. jours. Col. USAR, 1996—. Fellow Acad. Gen. Dentistry, Am. Coll. Dentists, Acad. Dentistry Internat.; mem. ADA, Am. Coll. Prosthodontists, Am. Assn. Dental Rsch., Internat. Assn. Dental Rsch., Chinese Am. Drs. Assn. (bd. dirs. 1994—), Am. Legion, Omicron Kappa Upsilon, Delta Sigma Delta. Avocations: soccer, stamps, contemporary music, photography, hi-fi systems. Home: 4123 Custer Creek Dr Missouri City TX 77459-1545

CHANG, JENGHWA, biomedical and electrical engineer, medical physicist; b. Taipei, June 18, 1962; came to U.S., 1989; s. Tsen-Ming Chang and Yu-Jeng Huang; m. Shiaoching Gong. BS in Control Engring., Nat. Chiao-Tung U., Hsinchu, Taiwan, 1984, MS in Comm. Engring., 1986; MS in Elec. Engring., Poly. U. N.Y., 1991, PhD in Elec. Engring., 1995. Cert. med. dosimetrist, med. physicist. Rsch. and tchg. asst. Nat. Chiao-Tung U., Hsinchu, Taiwan, 1984-86; rsch. asst. Academia Sinica, Taipei, 1988-89, N.Y. Hosp.-Cornell Med. Ctr., N.Y.C., 1991-93; rsch. asst. prof. SUNY Health Sci. Ctr., Bklyn., 1993-98; clin. med. physicist Rahway (N.J.) Hosp., 1994-97, Peninsula Hosp. Ctr., Far Rockaway, N.Y., 1996-97; asst. attending physicist and asst. lab. mem. Meml. Sloan-Kettering Cancer Ctr., N.Y.C., 1997—. Contbr. chpt. to book, over 20 articles to profl. jours. Scholar for Spl. Tech. Chinese Min. Edn. Affairs, 1985, 86; named Excellent Officer award Chinese Marine Corps, 1988. Mem. IEEE, Am. Assn. Physicists in Medicine, AAAS, Radiol. and Med. Physics Soc. N.Y., Am. Soc. for Therapeutic Radiology Oncology. Achievements include pioneering in reconstructing tomographic images of biological tissues from scattered light source and verification of intensity modulated beam for radiation treatment of cancers using electronic portal imaging devices. Avocations: music, philosophy, art, exercise. Office: Meml Sloan-Kettering Cancer Ctr Dept Med Physics 1275 York Ave New York NY 10021-6094

CHANG, JIH-MING, retired Islamic studies educator; b. Chunli, Taiwan, Sept. 4, 1932; s. Yue-Chien and Tsuen-Mei (Jan) C.; m. Michèle Marthe Mélessy, Nov. 3, 1944 (div.); children: Xavier, Emmanuel; m. Yu-Lin Wu, Dec. 26, 1947; 1 child, Monica Man-Hsien. BA, Nat. Chenchi U., Taipei, Taiwan, 1961; MA, Ind. U., 1970; PhD, U. Paris, 1976. Assoc. prof. dept. Arabic lang. Nat. Chenchi U., 1976-83, prof., 1983-98; dir. dept. Arabic lang. Nat. Chenchi U., 1981-84. Author: (in French) Les Musulmans Sous la Chine des Tang, 1976, (in Chinese) The World of Islam, 1987, (Arabic and Chinese edits.) A Study on Legends and Poetry of Pre-Islam, 1981. Served with Taiwanese mil., 1961-62. Avocations: travel, fast walking. Home: 78 109 Ln Mu Cha Rd, 2d Sect Mucha, Taipei Taiwan

CHANG, JOSEPH SYLVESTER, electronics executive, engineering educator; b. Johor Bahru, Malaysia, Dec. 28, 1960; arrived in Singapore, 1992; s. Yuan Wan Chang and Kim Kwa Kam; m. Chai Lung Lee, Jan. 23, 1988; 1 child, Sebastian Ming Jie. B in Engring., Monash U., Australia, 1983; PhD, U. Melbourne, Australia, 1990. Devel. engr. Commonwealth Sci. and Indsl. Rsch., Melbourne, 1983; test engr. Tex. Instruments, Singapore, 1984-85; sr. rsch. scientist Human Comm. Rsch. Ctr., Melbourne, 1986-92; assoc. prof. Nanyang Tech. U., Singapore, 1992—; dir. R&D, co-founder Multitech Products Pte Ltd, Singapore, 1995—; cons. to several hearing aid cos., Australia, 1988—. Contbr. articles to profl. jours.; patentee in field. Tech. mem. Australian Deafness Coun., Melbourne, 1988-92; tech. advisor H.E.A.R., Australia, 1990-92; mem. com. Welfare 2000, Singapore, 1995—. Recipient Best Paper prize Microelectronics Conf., Australia, 1989, Best Math. prize Nat. Edn. Ministry, Malaysia, 1977; grantee NSTB, EDB, AcRF. Avocations: running, swimming. Office: 223A-225 Innovation Ctr, Nanyang Ave, Singapore 637720, Singapore

CHANG, KUANG-YEH, microelectronics technologist; b. Nanjing, China, Sept. 1, 1948; came to U.S., 1971; s. Yi and Wen-Teh (Tang) C.; m. Huey-Lian Ding, June 30, 1975; children: Fen, Wendy, Sherry, Sean. BSEE, Nat. Taiwan U., 1970; MSEE, U. Tenn., 1973; PhD, U. Pitts., 1978. Mem. tech. staff Hughes Aircraft Co., Newport Beach, Calif., 1978-83; mem. tech. staff Advanced Micro Devices, Sunnyvale, Calif., 1983-85, tech. integration mgr., 1994-96; device mgr. Motorola, Austin, Tex., 1985-89; engring. mgr. VLSI Tech., San Jose, Calif., 1989-91; fellow Compass Design Automation, San Jose, 1991-94; dir. ops. United Microelectronics Corp. Science Park, Hsinchu, Taiwan, 1996—; com. mem. ASIC Conf., Rochester, 1993-94. Patentee in field. 2d lt. Chinese Army, 1970-71. Mem. IEEE, Phi Kappa Phi. Avocations: swimming, skiing, classical guitar, saxaphone, camping. Home: PO Box 2922 Saratoga CA 95070-0922 Office: UMC Science Park, 10 Innovation Rd 1, Hsinchu Taiwan

CHANG, LAWRENCE HOOI-TUANG, mathematics educator; b. Teluk Anson, Malaysia, Jan. 26, 1963; s. Anthony Swee-Chong and Jacintha Ah-Soi (Tan) C. BS with honors, U. Pertanian, Malaysia, 1987; MS, U. Sains, Malaysia, 1991, PhD, 1997. Rsch. asst. Univ., Malaya, 1988; rsch. officer U. Sains, Malaysia, 1991-92, 97, lectr., 1997—. Contbr. articles to profl. jours. Roman Catholic. Avocations: reading, swimming, scuba diving. E-mail: upalhtc@kcp.usm.my. Office: UPA U Sains, Perak Br Campus, Tronoh 31750, Malaysia

CHANG, LEROY L., physicist; b. Kaifung, China, Jan. 20, 1936; came to U.S., 1959; s. Hsin-Fu and Hsien-Hen (Lee) C.; m. Helen H. Chang, 1962; children: Justin, Leslie. BS, Taiwan U., 1957; MS, U. S.C., 1961; PhD, Stanford U., 1963. Mem. rsch. staff IBM T.J. Watson Rsch. Ctr., Yorktown Heights, N.Y., 1963-68, 69-75, mgr. molecular beam epitaxy, 1975-84, tech. planning staff, 1984-85, mgr. quantum structures, 1985-92; dean of sci. Hong Kong U. of Sci. Tech., 1993-98, v.p. acad. affairs, 1998—. Fellow IEEE (David Sarnoff award 1990), Am. Phys. Soc. (Internat. prize New Materials 1985); mem. NAS, NAE, Chinese Acad. Scis., Franklin Inst. (Stuart Ballantine award 1993), Academia Sinica. Office: Office of VP Acad Affairs, Hong Kong U of Sci & Tech, Kowloon Hong Kong China

CHANG, MARIAN S., filmmaker, composer; b. Atlanta, Aug. 19, 1958; d. C.H. Joseph and C.S. (Chun) C. BA in Music, Harvard U., 1981; MFA in Filmmaking, Columbia U., 1994. Composer, dir., choreographer Exptl. Theatre, Dance, Boston, 1981-88; composer for modern dance co. Performing Arts Ensemble, Boston, 1986-88; co-dir., choreographer, performer Theatre S., Boston, 1987-88; prodr., dir., writer, sound designer, composer N.Y.C., 1991—; founder, prodr. Shy Artists Prodns., Boston, N.Y.C., 1988-94.

Recipient Mass. Artists Fellowship Program award in choreography, 1987, in music composition, 1988; recipient First Prize Kans. City Music Scholarship Competition, 1976, Nino Cerruti Film award, 1995; grantee N.Y. Coun. for the Humanities, 1998. Home: 220 E 27th St Apt 7 New York NY 10016-9234

CHANG, MICHAEL, tennis player; b. Hoboken, N.J., Feb. 22, 1972; s. Joe and Betty Chang. Round of 16 U.S. Open, N.Y.C., 1988, 89, 91, 94; round of 16 Wimbledon, London, 1989, 90, quarterfinalist, 1994; champion French Open, Paris, 1989, quarterfinalist, 1990, 91, finalist, 1995; semifinalist Australian Open, Melbourne, 1995, finalist, 1996; finalist U.S. Open, N.Y.C., 1996; champion Infiniti Open, L.A., 1996, Legg Mason Tennis Classic, Washington, 1996, Newsweek Champions Cup, Indian Wells, Calif., 1996; other tournaments include: semifinalist WCT Scottsdale (Ariz.) Open, 1987; champion Transamerica Open, San Francisco, 1988; semifinalist Volvo Tennis Indoor, Memphis, 1989, semifinalist, 1991; finalist Volvo Tennis L.A., 1989, 90, 93; champion Silk Cuts Championships, Wembley, Eng., 1989; semifinalist Sovran Bank Classic, Washington, 1990; champion Player's Ltd. Internat. Can. Open, Toronto, 1990; semifinalist Suntory Japan Open, Tokyo, 1991, 92; semifinalist Open de la Ville de Paris, 1991, 94; finalist Compaq Grand Slam Cup, Munich, 1991, 92; champion Diet Pepsi Indoor Challenge, Birmingham, Eng., 1991; semifinalist Thriftway ATP Championships, Cin., 1992, champion, 1993, 94, finalist, 1995; semifinalist Waldbaum's Hamlet Cup, L.I., N.Y., 1992; semifinalist Seiko Super Tennis, Tokyo, 1992, finalist, 1994, champion, 1995; semifinalist European Cmty. Championships, Antwerp, Belgium, 1992; finalist Salem Open, Hong Kong, 1992, champion, 1994, 95, champion, Osaka, 1993, champion, Kuala Lumpur, 1993, champion, Beijing, 1993, 94, 95; champion Volvo Tennis/San Francisco, 1992; champion Newsweek Champions Cup, Indian Wells, Calif., 1992, semifinalist, 1993; champion Lipton Internat. Players Championships, Key Biscayne, Fla., 1992; semifinalist Kroger St. Jude Internat., Memphis, 1993, finalist, 1998; Ford Australian Open, Melbourne, 1997, U.S. Open, N.Y.C., 1997; champion Indonesian Open, Jakarta, 1993; finalist Japan Open, Tokyo, 1994, semifinalist, 1995; champion Indonesian Men's Open, Jakarta, 1994; champion Comcast U.S. Indoor, Phila., 1994, finalist, 1995; champion AT&T Challenge, Atlanta, 1994, 95, Infiniti Open, L.A., 1996, U.S. Men's Clay Ct. Championships, 1997, Salem Open, Hong Kong, 1997, Legg Mason Tennis Classic, Washington, 1996, 97, Kroger St. Jude, 1997, Newsweek Champions Cup, Indian Wells, Calif., 1996, 97; finalist Sybase Open, San Jose, Calif., 1995, semifinalist, 1996, 1998; finalist ATP World Tour Championships, Frankfurt, Germany, 1995; mem. U.S. Davis Cup Squad, 1989-91; semifinalist du Maurier Open, Montreal, Canada, 1997; semifinalist Great Amer. Insurance ATP Championship, Cincinnati, Oh., 1997; semifinalist Heineken Open, Rosmalen, The Netherlands, 1997. Achievements include being the youngest player to win USTA Boys' Nat. Championships, 1987; youngest male to advance to semifinals of Super Series tournament, 1987; youngest male to win match at U.S. Open, 1987; youngest male to win match at Wimbledon, 1988; youngest player to win Super Series tournament, 1988; youngest player to be named to U.S. Davis Cup Squad, 1989; youngest male Grand Slam Champion in Open Era, 1989; youngest ever French Open Champion, 1989; first Am. since Tony Trabert to win French Open, 1989. Address: Advantage Internat 1751 Pinnacle Dr Ste 1500 Mc Lean VA 22102-3833

CHANG, NI-BIN, environmental pollution control educator; b. Taipei, Taiwan, China, Apr. 21, 1960; s. T.Y. and Y.C. (Roam) C. BS, Chung-Tung U., Taiwan, 1983; MS, Cornell U., 1989, PhD, 1991. Engr. Koohsiung City Govt., Tainan, Taiwan, 1985-86, Taiwan, Provincial Govt., 1986-87; deputy mgr. Ecology & Environ. Inc., Taipei, Taiwan, 1991-92, Fichtner Pacific Engring. Inc., Taipei, Taiwan, 1992; assoc. prof. Nat. Cheng-Kung U., Tainan, Taiwan, 1992-97, prof., 1997—. Mem. ASCE, ASME, Air and Waste Mgmt. Assn., Internat. Solid Waste Mgmt. Assn., Internat. Assn. Water Quality. Office: Nat Cheng-Kung U, Dept Environ Engring, T'ainan Taiwan

CHANG, PAUL CHEE MY, neurologist; b. Hong Kong, Sept. 16, 1954; s. Tsing Hsiang and Ling Sung (Poon) C.; m. Anita Liang, Aug. 5, 1979; children: Heidi, Ray, Ruth. M.B.B.S., U. Hong Kong, 1978. Med. officer Tung Wah Hosp., Hong Kong, 1979-85; sr. med. officer Kwong Wah Hosp., Hong Kong, 1985-89; lectr. dept. medicine U. Hong Kong, 1989-92; cons. and head dept. medicine Ruttonjee Hosp., Hong Kong, 1992—. Fellow Royal Coll. Physicians (Glasgow), Royal Coll. Physicians (Edinburgh), Royal Coll. Physicians (London), Hong Kong Acad. Medicine, Hong Kong Coll. Physicians, Hong Kong Neurol. Soc. (v.p. 1997-99, pres. 1999—). Office: Ruttonjee Hosp Dept Medicine, 266 Queens Rd E, Hong Kong Hong Kong

CHANG, PAUL P.C., inventor, researcher; b. Taiping, Malaysia, Oct. 20, 1944; s. Fook and Tai (Lee) C.; m. Eveline Rosemarie Symons, Feb. 24, 1973; children: Paulina, Edwin, Felicia Ann. Diploma in Tchg., Tech. Tchrs. Coll., Kuala Lumpur, Malaysia, 1966; Diploma, Inst. Motor Industry, U.K., 1970. Tech. tchr. Ministry of Edn., Malaysia, 1966-73; mfg. supt. SGS Electronics, Malaysia, 1974-79, prodn. control mgr., 1980-82; R&D mgr. Caltona Lab., Malaysia, 1982-89, CEO, 1990—. Mem. Soc. Mfg. Engrs. (sr.), Malaysian Invention and Design Soc. (Malaysia). Achievements include invention of a method and apparatus that enabled the first lightning surge protection system in the world good enough to dare provide performance guarantee from lightning surge of any magnitude. Home: 90 Taman Mutiara, 84000 Muar Johor Malaysia Office: Caltona Lab, 30 Lrg Kurau 9 Taman Sg Ab, 84000 Muar Johor Malaysia

CHANG, PING-TUNG, mathematics educator; b. Nan-King, China, Oct. 16, 1935; came to U.S., 1963; s. Sun and Y.K. (Wang) C.; 1 child, Susanna San-San. BE, Nat. Taiwan Normal U., Taipei, 1960; MS in Math., Ind. State U., 1966; PhD, Ga. State U., 1977. Asst. prof., chair div. natural sci. Mt. St. Paul Coll., Waukesha, Wis., 1966-68; tchr. math. Brooker T. Washington High Sch., Atlanta, 1970-73; asst. prof. math. Gordon Jr. Coll., Barnesville, Ga., 1973-78; assoc. prof. math. Augusta (Ga.) Coll., 1978-83; assoc. prof. Laredo (Tex.) State U., 1983-88; coord. math., prof. math. U. Alaska, Anchorage, 1988—; vis. prof. math. Taiwan Normal U. Grad Sch. Math., Taipei, summer 1979. Author: A Comparative Study of Math Education Between ROC & USA, 1985, Teach Mathematics in Junior High School, 1985, Remedial Math Education for Disadvantaged, 1985; (coll. textbook) Teaching Mathematics in the Elementary School, 1989; contbr. several articles to profl. jours. Recipient awards; grantee Pacific Cultural Found., 1982-83, Laredo State U., 1984, U. Alaska Dept. Edn., Dwight D. Eisenhower Math. and Sci. grant Mat-Su Math Coop. Project, 1990-92. Mem. Am. Math. Soc., Math. Assn. Am., Nat. Coun. Tchrs. Math., N.Y. Acad. Scis., Math. Assn. Two-Yr. Colls. (nat. devel. program in math. com. 1974-80), Assn. for Supervision and Curriculum Devel., Pi Mu Epsilon, Matanuska-Susitna Lion Club. Achievements include development of curriculum, teacher training, and remedial activities for slower learners, of mathematics education seminars. Office: U Alaska Anchorage Matanuska-Susitna Coll PO Box 2889 Palmer AK 99645-2889

CHANG, REI-YEUH, cardiologist, hospital administrator; b. Shih-Kang, Taichung, Taiwan, June 4, 1963; s. Tsai-Miao and Chen (Lin) C. Student, China Med. Coll., Taichung, 1989. Intern Mackay Meml. Hosp., Taipei, Taiwan, 1988-89; resident in internal medicine Feng-Chia Hosp., Tainan, Taiwan, 1989-90; resident in internal medicine Mackay Meml. Hosp., Taipei, Taiwan, 1990-93, chief resident, resident cardiology, 1993-95; chief coronary care unit Chia-Yi (Taiwan) Christian Hosp., 1995—. Contbr. articles to med. jours. Mem. Soc. of Internal Medicine of Republic of China (specialist), Soc. of Emergency and Critical Care Medicine (specialist, advanced cardiac life support instr.), Soc. of Cardiology of Republic of China (specialist), Taiwan Soc. of Critical Care Med. (specialist), Soc. Ultrasound in Medicine of Republic of China. Avocations: jogging, swimming, hiking. Office: Chia-Yi Christian Hosp, 539 Chung Shiao Rd, Chia-Yi Taiwan

CHANG, ROCSON CHI MENG, government agency administrator; b. Singapore, Nov. 21, 1961; s. Richard Wing Chee and Katherine (Ho) C. BS, So. Ill. U., 1987, MBA, 1988. Asst. pub. rels. and mktg. mgr., gen. mgr. Ise Mgmt. Pte., Ltd., Singapore, 1982-84; student campus mgr. AT&T, Ill., 1987-88; merchandiser Archer Daniels Midland, Ill., 1989-90; trader, asst. trading mgr. Toepfer Internat.-Asia Pte. Ltd., Singapore, 1990-94; asst. dir. exhbns. and convs. Singapore Tourist Promotion Bd., N.Y.C., 1995-98; v.p. Ea. U.S.A., Singapore Tourism Bd., N.Y.C., 1998—; mem. working com. Global Indian Entrepreneurs Conf., Singapore, 1995-96; advisor steering com. Global Franchising Conf., Singapore, 1996—; mem. steering com. Asia-Pacific Petroleum Conf., Singapore, 1997—; organizing com. Asean-Eu Partenariat, Singapore, 1997—; chmn. Asean Tourism Ea. USA, N.Y., 1998—. Mem. Golden Key Nat. Honor Soc. Avocations: tennis, badminton, scuba diving, chess, reading. Address: 100 UN Plz Condos 327 E 48th St Apt 16D New York NY 10017-1713 Office: Singapore Tourism Bd 590 5th Ave Fl 12 New York NY 10036-4702

CHANG, RODNEY EIU JOON, artist, dentist; b. Honolulu, Nov. 26, 1945; s. Alfred Koon Bo and Mary Yet Moi (Char) C.; m. Erlinda C. Feliciano, Dec. 4, 1987; children: Bronson York, Houston Travis, Rochelle Jessica. BA in Zoology, U. Hawaii, 1968; AA in Art, Triton Coll., 1972; DDS, Loyola U., 1972; MS in Edn., U. So. Calif., 1974; MA in Painting and Drawing, U. No. Ill., 1975; MA in Community Leadership, Cen. Mich. U., 1976; BA in Psychology, Hawaii Pacific U., 1977; MA in Psychology of Counseling, U. No. Colo., 1980; PhD in Art Psychology, The Union Inst., 1980; MA in Computer Art, Columbia Pacific U., 1989. Pvt. practice dentist Honolulu, 1975—; dir. SOHO too Gallery and Loft, Honolulu, 1985-89; freelance artist Honolulu, 1982—; curator Webfelt Mus. of Early Cyberart, Honolulu, 1996—; founder Pygoya Internat. Art Group, 1990—, Art Cap Group, Slap Caps Co., Honolulu, 1993, Ctr. Cyberspace.com; columnist Milk Cap News; dir. ann. Honolulu City Hall Hawaiian Computer Art Exhbn., 1990-92; speaker on art psychology and computer art, also numerous TV and radio interviews; dir. centerofcyberspace.com, 2000. Author: Mental Evolution and Art, 1980, Rodney Chang: Computer Artist, 1988, Commentaries on the Psychology of Art, 1980; host (radio show) Disco Doc Hour, Sta. KISA; one-man shows include Honolulu Acad. Arts, 1986, Shanghai State Art Mus., People's Republic of China, 1988, Retrospective Exhbn. 1967-87, Ramsay Gallery, Honolulu, 1987, Visual Encounters Gallery, Denver, 1987, The Bronx Mus. of the Arts, N.Y.C., 1987, Nishi Noho Gallery, N.Y.C., 1987, Eastern Wash. U. Gallery of Art, 1988, Salon de la Jeune Peinture, Paris, 1989, Holter Art Mus., Mont., 1989, Las Vegas Art Mus., 1990, Forum Art Sch. Gütershoh, Fed. Republic of Germany, 1990, Siggraph-Dallas, 1990, Tartu State Art Mus., Estonia/USSR, 1990, U. Oregon Continuation Ctr., Portland, 1991—, Kauai Art Mus., Hawaii, 1993, RC Gallery of Computer Art, Honolulu, 1994, Archtl. Design of the Pygoya Home Mus., 1994; conceived, produced 1st milk cap art exhbn., Arts of Paradise Gallery, Waikiki Beach, 1993; organizer, artist 1st internat. digital art exhbn., Bombay, India; founder New York Net Gallery.com; featured artist Indian 1st Internat. Digital Art Exhbn., Calcutta, 1999. Judge Jr. Miss Contest, Honolulu, 1981. Served to capt., U.S. Army, 1973-74. Mem. ADA, Hawaii Dental Assn., Assn. of Honolulu Artists (pres. 1989, v.p. 1999), Nat. Computer Graphics, Acad. Gen. Dentistry, Hawaii Space Soc., Bernice Bishop Mus. Honolulu. Roman Catholic. Achievements include publication and issue of world's first pre-paid long distance telephone cards as signed and numbered, limited edition fine art prints, Pygoya Webmuseum of Cyberart on Internet, 1997; dir. Internet Programs, Las Vegas Art Mus., eobituary.com. and centerofcyberspace.com., 2000, lifeportraits.org, centerofcyberculture.com. Office: 2119 N King St Ste 206 Honolulu HI 96819-4550

CHANG, SAM SHIFENG, meteorologist; b. Shanghai, China, Jan. 15, 1938; s. Yu Qing Zhang and Xing Lin Zhou; m. Rui Lian Chang, July 15, 1964; children: Hong Gao, Heather. BS, Nanjing U., 1959, MS, 1962; PhD, U. Wash., 1988. Asst. prof. Nanjing U., China, 1976-79; vis. scholar U. Wis., Madison, 1979-81; vis. scientist NCAR, Boulder, Colo., 1981-82, Oreg. State U., Corvallis, 1982; rsch. asst. U. Wash., Seattle, 1983-88; rsch. assoc. U. Chgo., 1988-89; meteorologist Air Force Rsch. Lab., Lexington, Mass., 1989-99, Army Rsch. Lab., Adelphi, Md., 1999—; invited lectr. Nagoya U., Japan, 1996. Author: Cumulus Dynamics, 1965; contbr. articles to profl. jours. Mem. Am. Geophys. Union, Am. Meteorol. Soc., European Geophys. Soc., Sci. Rsch. Soc., Sigma Xi. Avocations: ping pong, basketball. Home: 1836 Metzerott Rd Apt 1404 Adelphi MD 20783-3449 Office: Army Rsch Lab 2800 Powder Mill Rd Adelphi MD 20783-1138

CHANG, SHAN-CHWEN, medical educator, researcher, physician; b. Shin-Chu, Taiwan, June 11, 1956; s. Jin-Chaw and Yu-Ing (Sheu) C.; m. Fung-Rong Hu, July 31, 1983; children: Hao-Chun, Hao-Yun. MD, Nat. Taiwan U., 1981, PhD, 1992. Intern Nat. Taiwan U. Hosp., Taipei, 1980-81, resident, 1983-86, fellow in infectious diseases, 1986-88, attending staff, 1988—; lectr. in internal medicine Nat. Taiwan U., 1990-92, assoc. prof., 1992—, chief sect. infectious diseases, dept. internal medicine Nat. Taiwan U. Hosp., 1996—; cons. Sun Yat-Sen Cancer Ctr., Taipei, 1990-95, Lo-Ton (Taiwan) Po-Ai Hosp., 1991—, Dept. Health, Taiwan, 1992—; councilor nosocomial infection control com. Nat. Taiwan U. Hosp., 1987—, mem. antibiotics com., 1996—; mem. infection control adv. com. Dept. Health, Taiwan, 1992—, mem. drug rev. com., 1997—, adv. com. control of AIDS, 1999—, adv. com. immunization practice, 2000—. Contbr. articles to profl. jours.; editor: Nosocomial Infection Control Newsletter, 1991-95; dep. editor-in-chief Jour. Infectious Diseases Soc., 1990-97; dep. editor-in-chief Nosocomial Infection Control Jour., 1996—; editor: Jour. Microbiology, Immunology and Infection, 1998—. Ensign Taiwanese Navy, 1981-83. Grantee Nat. Taiwan U., 1990—, Nat. Sci. Coun., 1989—, Dept. Health, 1991—. Mem. Formosan Med. Assn., Chinese Soc. Microbiology (bd. dirs. 1998—), Infectious Diseases Soc. Republic of China (sec. in gen. 1993-96, bd. dirs. 1996—), Nosocomial Infection Control Soc. (bd. dirs. 1993-2000, pres. 2000—), Am. Soc. for Microbiology, European Soc. Clin. Microbiology and Infectious Diseases, Taita Jing-Fu Alumni Assn. (dep. sec.-in-gen. 1991-99, sec.-in-gen. 2000—). Avocations: sports, classical music, tennis, table tennis, badminton. Office: Nat Taiwan Univ Hosp, No 7 Chung-Shan S Rd, Taipei 100, Taiwan

CHANG, SHI-CHUAN, chest physician, researcher; b. Ping-Tung, Taiwan, Republic of China, Oct. 16, 1954; s. Hsi-Mu and Yu-Mei (Kuo) C.; m. Jung-Shu Lin, Dec. 25, 1980; children: Shu-Luen, Shu-Wei. MD, China Med. Coll., Tai-Chung, Taiwan, 1980; PhD, Nat. Yang-Ming U., Taipei, Taiwan, 1990. Resident Vets. Gen. Hosp., Taipei, 1980-85, chief resident, 1985-86, attending physician, 1986—; lectr. Nat. Yang-Ming U., Taipei, 1987-90, assoc. prof., 1990-96, prof., 1996—. Author: Year Book of Pulmonary Disease, 1994, Year Book of Medicine, 1994, Archives of Internal Medicine, 1994; exec. editor Jour. Internal Medicine, 1990-94; editor Chinese Med. Jour., 1994—; dep. editor Thoracic Medicine, 1997—. Mem. Tzu-Chi Buddhist Found., Huea-Lian, Taiwan, 1986, Lit. Taiwan Found., Kao-Hsiung, 1997, Horng-I Reverent Meml. Assn., Taipei, 1987. Recipient Rsch. award Nat. Sci. Coun., 1989-95. Fellow Am. Coll. Chest Physicians; mem. Am. Thoracic Soc., N.Y. Acad. Scis. Buddhist. Avocations: writing, pencil drawing, juvenile literature, swimming, baseball. Office: Vets Gen Hosp Chest Dept, No 201 Sect 2 Shih-Pai Rd, Taipei 11217, Taiwan

CHANG, SHIRLEY LIN (HSIU-CHU CHANG), librarian; b. Chia-yi, Taiwan, June 22, 1937; came to U.S., 1962; naturalized, 1977.; d. Tzu-kun and Ying (Chang) Lin; m. Parris H. Chang, Aug. 3, 1963; children: Yvette Y., Elaine Y., Bohdan P. BA, Nat. Taiwan U., Taipei, 1960; postgrad., U. Wasn., 1962-63; MLS, Columbia U., 1967; MA, Pa. State U., 1988. Libr. asst. Yale U., New Haven, 1964-67; asst. ref. libr. Pa. State U., University Park, 1971-75; cataloguer Australian Nat. U., Canberra, 1978; catalog/ref. libr. Lock Haven U., 1979—, asst. prof., 1982-88, assoc. prof., 1988—, chairperson libr. dept., 2000—; chmn. dept. libr. Lock Haven U., Pa. Author: Taiwan's Brain Drain and Its Reversal, 1999. Mem. ALA, Chinese-Am. Librs. Assn. (chmn. awards com. 1982-83), Asian/Pacific Am. Librs. Assn., Assn. for Asian Studies, Pa. Libr. Assn., Phi Beta Delta Honor Soc. Home: 1221 Edwards St State College PA 16801-6930 Office: Lock Haven U Stevenson Libr Lock Haven PA 17745

CHANG, SHU TING, fungal geneticist, mushroom biologist; b. Yuanping, Shanxi, China, Sept. 30, 1930; arrived in Australia, 1972; s. Huang-Kuan and Tsan-Li (Kuo) C.; m. Judy Li-Ju Lee; children: David Ming-Tsan, Barbara Ming-Wai, Judy Ming-Sze, Ernest Ming-Cheng, Jennifer Ming-Jing. BSc, Nat. Taiwan U., 1953; MSc, U. Wis., 1958, PhD, 1960; Diploma, Nat. Tsing Hua U., Taiwan, 1963; postgrad., Harvard U., 1966-67. Asst. lectr. in biology Chinese U. Hong Kong, 1960-61, lectr. in biology, 1961-70, sr. lectr. in biology, 1970-74, reader in biology, 1974-78, prof. biology, 1978-95, emeritus prof. biology, 1995—; dir. Hong Kong Microbial Resources Centres, 1990—; dir. Center for Internat. Svcs. to Mushroom Biotech., 1993-96; dir. Inst. Sci. and Tech., Chinese U. Hong Kong, 1985-92, dean Faculty of Sci., 1975-77, chmn. dept of biology, 1983-94, dir. of the office of student affairs, 1979-81. Author: The Chinese Mushroom, 1972, Edible Mushrooms and Their Cultivation, 1989Technical Guidelines for Mushroom Growing in Tropics, 1990, Hong Kong Mushrooms, 1995, Mushroom Biology: Concise Basics and Current Developments, 1997; editor: The Cultivation of Edible Mushrooms, 1978, Tropical Mushrooms, Biological Nature and Cultivation Methods, 1982, Genetics and Breeding of Edible Mushrooms, 1993, Mushroom Biology and Mushroom Products, 1993. Decorated officer Order Brit. Empire, 1994. Fellow World Acad. Art and Sci. (Stockholm), Internat. Inst. Biotech. (London), World Acad. Productivity Sci. (Stockholm); mem. Internat. Mushroom Soc. for the Tropics (pres.), Brit. Mycological Soc. (hon., life), Internat. Soc. for Mushroom Sci. (hon., life, Internat. Cooperation award for light industry 1990). Christian. Avocations: travel, reading, swimming. Home: 3 Britton Pl, McKellar, Canberra ACT 2617, Australia Office: Chinese U Hong Kong, Univ Sci Ctr Dept Biology, Shatin Hong Kong China

CHANG, SU HUI, executive; b. Taiwan, Feb. 7, 1949; d. Pi Po and Jui Chu (Hwang) C. Grad., Nat. Chung Hsing U., China, 1969. Reporter China Television, Taiwan, 1970-76; rep. CTS, Hong Kong, 1980-91; bur. chief China Times, Hong Kong, 1980-91; dir. Free China Rev., Hong Kong, 1991-93, Kwang Hwa Info. & Culture Ctr., Hong Kong, 1993—; rsch. councilor Nat. Unification Coun., 1997—. Contbr. articles to profl. jours. Mem. Hong Kong Chinese Pen (dir.). Home: Kwang Hwa Info & Culture, 40/F One Pacific Pl 88 Queensway, Hong Kong Hong Kong

CHANG, SUNG-GOO, urological oncologist; b. Yeo-chu, Kyungkido, Korea, Nov. 23, 1952; s. Woo-Myun Chang and Jung-Young Shin; m. Soon-Hee Choi, Mar. 22, 1980; children: Ki-Baik, Ki-Sul. MD, Kyung Hee U., Seoul, 1977, MS, 1981; PhD, Inje U., Pusan, Korea, 1991; M in Adminstrn., Han Yang U., Seoul, 1994. Prof. Kyung Hee U. Med. Ctr., 1986—, chief dept. edn., 1995-97, dept. chief spl. diagnostic lab., 2000—; clin. and rsch. fellow Roswell Park Cancer Inst., Buffalo, N.Y., 1989-90; mem. ctrl. pharm. affairs coun. Ministry of Health and Social Affairs Korea, 1998—. Editor-in-chief Korean Jour. of Urology, 1999—; mem. editl. bd. Korean Jour. of Urology, 1992-96. Capt. Med., 1982-85, Korea. Recipient Yrs. Excellent Sci. Article award Korean Fedn. Sci. and Tech., 1994, Minister's award Dept. Ednl. Ministry Republic of Korea, 2000. Mem. Am. Urol. Assn., Am. Assn. Cancer Rsch., Korean Urol. Assn. (treas. 1996-99), Internat. Soc. Urol., Korean Cancer Assn. (sec. 2000—), Kyung-Hee Internat. Med. Coop. Soc. (exec. com. 1993—). Confucianism. Home: 9-605 Woo Sung Apt, 503 Tae-Chi-Tong Kang Nam Ku, Seoul 135-281, Korea Office: Kyung Hee U Med Ctr Dept Urology, # 1 Hoeki-Dong Dongdaemunku, Seoul 130-702, Republic of Korea

CHANG, TAI-PING, educator; b. Chia-Yi, China, Dec. 15, 1954; s. Tao-chen and Shu (Hsu) C.; m. Quey-Jen Yeh. B, Nat. Taiwan U., 1977; M of Civil Engring., Pa. State U., 1981, M of Math., 1982; PhD, Columbia U., 1985. Civil engr. Taiwan Power Co., Taipei, 1977-79; structural engr. Sargent & Lundy, Chgo., 1985-86; computer systems analyst Louis Berger, Inc., East Orange, N.J., 1986-88; project engr. Malcolm Pirnie, Inc., White Plains, N.Y., 1988-89; assoc. prof. Nat. Chung-Hsing U., Taichung, Taiwan, 1989-94, prof., 1994—, chmn., 1997-99. Contbr. articles to profl. jours. Recipient Acad. Rsch. award Nat. Sci. Coun., Taiwan, 1991-99. Avocations: bridge, tennis. Office: Nat Chung-Hsing U, Dept Applied Math, Taichung Taiwan China

CHANG, TE LIN, architect; b. Canton, China, Oct. 8, 1919; s. Pei Ye and Yu Cheun (Chen) C.; m. Shih Wei Yen, Jan. 15, 1950. B, Hangchow Christian U., 1943. Reg. architect. Col. Army, China, 1944-66; chief Lab. Med. Equipage, Taipei, 1953-58; chief engr. Vets. Gen. Hosp., Taipei, 1958-62; dept. head Med. Engring. NDMC, Taipei, 1962-66; architect-prin. T.L. Chang and Assocs., Architects-Engrs., Taipei, 1966—. Architect of numerous medical buildings and residences, 1963-98. Recipient Precious Star medal, Royalty & Diligence medal, Peih Liang medal Chinese Army. Mem. ASHRAE, AIA (hon. fellow), Internat. Fedn. Hosp. Engring., Inst. Architects (pres. 1969-70). Office: TL Chang & Assocs Architects & Engrs, 5-2 Ln 27 Linyi St, Taipei 100, Taiwan

CHANG, THEODORE CHIEN-HSIN, psychologist; b. Shanghai, Kiangsu, Peoples Republic of China, June 21, 1926; came to U.S., 1949; s. Yu-Tung and Yin-Fen (Wen) C. MD, St. John's U., Shanghai, 1947; PhD, NYU, 1957. Cert. tchr., Iowa; cert. psychologist. Psychologist NYU/Bellevue Med. Ctr., N.Y.C., 1954-56, Springfield (Md.) State Hosp., 1957-58, Kans. Neurol. Inst., Topeka, Kans., 1958-61, Larned (Kans.) State Hosp., 1961-62, Camarillo (Calif.) State Hosp., 1962-63, Musctatuck State Hosp., Ind., 1963-65; chief psychologist Cumberland Comprehensive Care Ctr., Somerset, Ky., 1965-69; psychologist VA Med. Ctr., Knoxville, Iowa, 1969-71; sales Lincoln Benefit Life Ins., 1975-93, Life USA, 1993-95, World Ins., 1995—; assst. prof. Fu-tung U., Shanghai, 1995—. Recipient fellowship Econ. Corp. Adminstrn., 1950-56. Mem. Am. Psychol. Assn., Iowa Psychol. Assn. Home: 13 Cobblefield Dr Mendham NJ 07945

CHANG, WALTER HONG-SHONG, biomedical engineering educator; b. Lotung, Taiwan, Republic of China, Nov. 2, 1943; s. Hung-Ying and Hsi (Lin) C.; m. Jan Jyu Song, Jan. 29, 1969; children: An-Pei, Su-Pei, Kae-Lin. BS, Chung Yuan Chrisitan U., 1966; MS, Yonsei U., 1974; postgrad., Tokyo Denki U. Lectr. electronic engring. dept. Chung Yuan Christian U., Taiwan, 1971-75, assoc. prof., chmn. dept. biomed. engring., 1975-81, prof., chmn. dept. biomed. engring., 1981-83, prof., dean biomed. engring./gen. affairs, 1983-89, prof., dir. biomed. engring., libr., 1989-95; gen. sec. Nat. Youth Commn. Executive Yuan of the Republic of China, Taiwan, 1995-96; prof., dir. biomed. engring., alumni & placement office Chung Yuan Christian U., 1997-99, prof. dean biomed. engring./rsch. & development, 1999—; vis. prof. Human Performance Lab., U. Calgary, 1999; patent examiner, drafting com. Nat. Bur. of Stds., Taipei, 1975—; standing dir. biomed. engring. Soc. of Republic of China, 1980—, pres. Biomed. Engring. Soc. of Republic of China, 1999—; mem. World Coun. for Biomechanics, 1984—; chmn. working group on Asian-Pacific activities, mem. adminstrv. coun. Internat. Fedn. for Med. and Biol. Engring., 1997—. Contbr. articles to profl. jours. Chmn. Chinese Oversea Student Assn., Seoul, 1977-78. Lt. Chinese Air Force, 1966-67. Fellowship The Advancement of Christian Higher Edn. in Asia, 1972-74, Nat. Sic. Coun. of the Republic of China, 1977-78. Mem. IEEE/EMBS, Assn. for the Advancement of Med. Instrumentation,, Internat. Fedn. Med. and Biol. Engring. (coun. 1997—), World Acad. Biomed. Tech. Avocations: tennis, baseball, sports. Home: No 1 Jen Al Lo, Chung Yuan Shin Chun, Chung-Li Taiwan Office: Chung Yuan Christian U, Dept Biomed, Chung-Li Taiwan

CHANG, WALTER TUCK, SR., drafting and autoCAD educator, real estate agent, national defense instructor; b. Honolulu, Feb. 16, 1920; s. Awai Abner and Clara Pau'au'au (Fairman) C.; m. Rita AnaMarie Yee Chang, Aug. 16, 1950 (div. June 1959); children: Walter Tuck Jr., Nani; m. Mercedes Arroyo Chang, June 15, 1961 (div. June 1973); m. Evelyn Show Chiao Huang, Aug. 25, 1973. BA in Indsl. Arts with honors, San Jose State U., 1945; postgrad., U. Calif., Berkeley, 1949-55; MA in Edn. and Adminstrn., San Francisco State U., 1959; postgrad., U. Hawaii, 1959-64, U. Md., 1967-68. Gen. secondary credential, Calif., spl. subject supervision vocat. class A, spl. subject supervision vocat. class C1, spl. secondary life diploma in indsl. arts, secondary sch. adminstrn., suprvision secondary sch. tchrs, Calif.; profl. secondary cert. in indsl. arts, Hawaii. Drafting apprenticeship engring. and estimation dept. Hawaiian Elec. Co., Honolulu, 1937-39; journeyman machinist, leadman, nat. war manpower job instr. Joshua Henry Iron Works, Sunnyvale, Calif., 1942-45; vocat. instr. San Jose State U., 1942-45; automotive machinist Garden City Sales and Svc. Co., San Jose, Calif., 1945-46; journeyman machinist Oliver M. Johnson Machine Shop, San Jose, Calif., 1946; machinist Food Machine Corp., San Jose, Calif., 1946; machinist, tool maker Ames Aeronautical Lab., Moffett Field, Calif., 1946-51; adult evening vocat. instr. Leland Evening H.S., San Jose, 1951; vocat. inst., supr., driver edn., tng. John Swett Union H.S., Crockett, Calif., 1951-59; journeyman machinist Oliver United Filters Inc., Oakland, Calif., 1952-53; vocat. dir., night prin. John Swett Union H.S., Crockett, Calif., 1952-59; indsl. arts, English, World Hist. instr. McKinley H.S., Honolulu, 1959-62; indsl. arts metal works instr. Kailua H.S., Oahu, 1962; indsl. arts tchr. edn. instr., supr. indsl. arts student tchrs. U. Hawaii Coll. Edn. Manoa Campus,

Honolulu, 1962-64; drafting instr. archtl. engring., auto-cad, supr. driver edn. tng. Kamehameha Schs., Honolulu, 1964-90; built over 1,000 engines for liberty, cargo steam ships, minesweepers during WWII, 1942-45. Author: Getting Started With the Calipro, 1965, The Kidjel Ratio Concept in Designing and Drafting. Hawaiian musician entertainer ARC, San Francisco Bay Area, 1942-49; Sunday Sch. tchr. Hayward (Calif.) Missionary Bapt. Ch., 1958-59, Missionary Bapt. Chs. on Oahu, Hawaii, 1960—; pres. PTA of New Keolu Elem. Sch., 1961, v.p. monthly meetings; designed and built 4 chs., Calif. and Hawaii; support Missionary Bapt. Chs. and Missions, U.S., Can., South Am., The Philippines, Japan, China, India, Africa, Russia, Jerusalem, 1958—. Recipient Nat. Merit Honor Soc. award, 1938, Best Auto-CAD Architecture in Hawaii award Sausilito Software, 1985, Nat. Hon. Edn. Fraternity award Phi Delta Kappa, 1962, award Solid Koa Poi Pounder, Best Designed 4 Million Dollar Indsl. Arts Complex in Hawaii award Kamehameha Schs.; named Most Outstanding Educator, Kamahameha Alumni Assn., Honolulu, 1984. Mem. Oahu Indsl. Arts Tchrs. Assn. (exec. bd. 1959, v.p. in charge of monthly workshops 1960, pres. 1961), Epsilon Pi Tau, Kappa Delta Pi. Avocations: photography, raising gold fish, travel, reading books, sports. Home: 98-410 Koauka Loop Apt 11D Aiea HI 96701-4520

CHANG, WINSHIH, orthopedic surgeon; b. Taiwan, Aug. 25, 1957; came to U.S., 1967; s. Tehmeng and Kungmin (Liu) C.; m. Risa Cohen, July 4, 1991; 1 child, Paula. BS magna cum laude, CUNY, 1979; MD with distinction, U. Rochester, 1982. Diplomate Nat. Bd. Med. Examiners, Am. Bd. Orthopedic Surgery. Intern in gen. surgery UCLA Hosp., 1982-83; med. officer USPHS, Billings, Mont., 1983-85; bioengring. fellow Hosp. for Joint Diseases Orthopedic Inst., N.Y.C., 1985-86, resident in orthopedic surgery, 1986-90, chief resident in orthopedic surgery, 1990; spl. fellow adult reconstructive surgery Mayo Clinic, Rochester, Minn., 1990-91, instr. orthopedic surgery, 1990-91; pvt. practice orthopedic surgery Somers (N.Y.) Orthopedic Surgery and Sports Medicine Group, 1991—. Winner Alfred A. Richman Rsch. contest Am. Coll. Chest Physicians, 1981, Otto Aufranc award Hip Soc., 1987; resident scholar Ea. Orthopedic Assn., 1986, Frauenthal scholar, 1990. Fellow Am. Acad. Orthopaedic Surgeons, Internat. Coll. Surgeons; mem. AMA, N.Y. State Med. Soc., N.Y. State Orthopedic Soc. Avocations: tennis, photography, philosophy.

CHANG, WOONG-SEONG, metallurgist, researcher; b. Pusan, Korea, Oct. 13, 1959; s. Soo-Seong Chang and In-Soon Kim; m. Hee-Jeong Lee, Jan. 30, 1988; children Hye-Min, Hyun-Jin. B in Engring., Pusan (Korea) Nat. U., 1982, M in Engring., 1984; PhD, Monash U., Melbourne, Australia, 1995. Rsch. asst. Pusan Nat U., 1982-84; rsch. engr. Pohang (Korea) Iron & Steel Co., 1984-88; sr. rsch. engr. Rsch. Inst. Indsl. Sci. & Tech., Pohang, 1988-91; rsch. assoc. Monash U., Melbourne, Australia, 1993-95; prin. rsch. scientist Rsch. Inst. Indsl. Sci. and Tech., Pohang, 1995—; reviewer Korean Welding Soc., Taejon, Korea. Inventor: holds 25 patents in metallic alloys and mfg. methods: co-author: (book) Welding Handbook (Korean), 1996, 98; (thesis) Multiphase AL-Ti-V Intermetallic Alloys, 1995 (K.H. Hunt award for best PhD thesis 1996); contbr. over 30 articles to profl. refereed jours. Recipient Monograph of Yr. award Australian Soc. Electron Microscopy, 1994. Mem. Minerals, Metals and Materials Soc., Am. Welding Soc., Korean Inst. Metals and Materials (Best Micrograph 1995, Best Poster Presentation 1997), Korean Welding Soc. (life). Office: Rsch Inst Indsl Sci & Tech, PO Box 135, 790-600 Pohang Kyungbok, Korea

CHANG, WUNG, business advisor, researcher, lecturer; b. Kangke Pyongbuk, Republic of Korea, Apr. 24, 1942; came to U.S., 1973; s. Jae Sun and Key Bok (Yoo) C.; m. Han Jin Yang, Nov. 14, 1970; children: Min, Won. MPA, Yon-Sei U., 1971; PhD in Bus. Mgmt., Union U., 1983. Editor-in-chief Korea Photo Times, Seoul, 1970-73; sec.-gen. Wum Found., L.A., 1986-87; sr. analyst Pacific Rsch. Inst., L.A., 1988-92; advisor Korea Travel News, Seoul, 1988-93; controller U.S. Top Capital Corp., L.A., 1991—; vice chmn. Mid-Wilshire Vocat. Tng. Ctr. divsn. Adult and Career Edn., L.A. Unified Sch. Dist. Adv. Coun., 1994-96; vol. lectr. The Korean Sr. Citizens Assn. of San Fernando Valley Coll, 1995-96; co-chmn. Internat. Rsch. Inst. Govt. and Pub. Adminstrn., L.A., 1995—; commentator Radio Korea, USA, 1997-99. Mem. Rep. Presdl. Adv. Commn., Washington, 1991; active Rep. Senatorial Com., Washington, 1991; nat. campaign advisor Rep. Senatorial Inner Circle, Washington, 1995—. Capt. Korean Army, 1966-70. Recipient Presdl. Order of Merit, 1991, Rep. Presdl. Task Force Wall of Honor, 1992. Avocations: fishing, swimming, music, baseball. Home: 7625 Radford Ave North Hollywood CA 91605-2858

CHANG, YIH, materials science educator, researcher; b. Tainan, Taiwan, July 12, 1958; s. Han-Sun and Chuan-Jiang (Yang) C.; m. Shine Lu, Dec. 16, 1984; children: Wendy, Sam. BSME, Chung Cheng Inst. Tech., Taoyuan, Taiwan, 1980; MSME, Nat. Chiao-Tung U., Hsinchu, Taiwan, 1984; PhD in Materials Sci. Engring., Stanford U., 1991. Teaching asst. Chung Cheng Inst Tech., Taoyuan, 1980-82, lectr., 1984-87; assoc.prof. Nat. Chiao-Tung U., Hsinchu, 1991-92; assoc. prof. Chung Cheng Inst. Tech., 1992-96, prof., 1996-98; dir. flat panel display divsn. Ritek Co., 1999—; cons. Vehicle Testing Ctr., Hsinghu, 1983-84; mem. project evaluation com. Dept. Health, Exec. Yuan, Taipei, Taiwan, 1983-84, Dept. Labor Affairs, Exec. Yuan, 1995-97. Contbr. articles to profl. jours.; patentee in field. Recipient Rsch. award Nat. Sci. Coun., Taipei, 1994. Mem. ASME, IEEE, TMS, ASM, AAAS, Nat. Geographic Soc., Chinese Soc. Def. Sci. & Tech. Chinese Crystal Growth Soc., Chinese Soc. Mech. Engrs., Am. Phys. Soc., Abrasive Machining Soc., Materials Rsch. Soc. Office: RiTek Co, No 10 Kuangfu N Rd, Taipei 30316, Taiwan

CHANG, YING KUANG, banker; b. Shanghai, Jan. 19, 1927; m. Ya Ching Woo, 1952; children: Maidie Yee, Otto Yen Ching. Grad., Nat. Shanghai Inst. of Comm., 1948. From traineee to dept. head China State Bank Ltd., Shanghai,, Hong Kong, 1970-86; dep. mgr. Liu Chong Hing Bank Ltd., Hong Kong, 1970-86, dir., mgr., 1986-94, exec. dir., 1994-97, non-exec. dir., 1997—; bd. dirs. Liu Chong Hing Fin. Ltd., Hong Kong, Liu Chong Hing (Nominees) Ltd., Hong Kong, Galbraith Ltd., Hong Kong, Man Hing Express & Godown Co. Ltd., Hong Kong. Office: Liu Chong Hing Bank Ltd, 24 Des Voeux Rd, Central, Hong Kong Hong Kong

CHANG, YONGSUNG, economist; b. Seoul, Korea, Jan. 19, 1966; came to U.S., 1992; s. Byeongsoo Chang and Myoungsook Hahm; m. Yoonji Lee, Sept. 2, 1994. BA, Seoul Nat. U., 1989, MA, 1991; PhD, U. Rochester, 1997. Asst. prof. U. Pa., Phila., 1997—; assoc. mem. Ctr. East Asian Studies, Phila., 1998—. Mem. Am. Econ. Assn., Korean-Am. Econ. Assn. Avocation: tennis. Home: 527 Williamson Cir Media PA 19063-5132

CHANG, YOON-YOUNG, geoenvironmentalist; b. Seoul, Korea, Jan. 25, 1965; parents Won-Sik Chang and Ki-Won Min; m. Yoon-Sun Oh, May 21, 1994; 1 child, Susanna. BS, Yonsei U., 1987; MS, Oreg. State U., 1989; PhD, Tex. A&M U., 1996. Rsch. scientist, sr. rsch. scientist Korea Inst. Sci. & Technology, Seoul, 1991—. Mem. Internat. Assn. Water Quality, Am. Geophys. Union. Office: Kwangwoon U Dept Envir Eng, 447-1 Wolgye-Dong Nowon-Ku, Seoul Korea 139-701

CHANG, YUN CHUAN, civil engineer; b. Medan, Sumatra, Indonesia, July 19, 1932; arrived in Hong Kong, 1976; s. Nieng Tung and Sui Lien (Chi) C.; m. Jung Lan Chang, Aug. 8, 1963; 1 child, Kit. BSCE, Dairen Inst. of Tech., 1957. Asst. engr. Wuhan Design Inst., Ministry of Electric Power, Peoples Republic of China, 1957-58; hydraulic design rschr., resident engr. Hydroelectric Power of The People's Republic of China; head dam structure dept. Mid-South Design Inst. Hydroelec. Min. of Water Resources & Electric Power, People's Republic of China, 1959-76; chief materials engr. Nishimatus Contrn. Co. Ltd., Hong Kong, 1979-82; materials technologist Mass Transit Railway Corp., 1982-85; cons. engr. French CFEM Facades Co. Ltd., Suresnes, France, 1986-88; dep. gen. mgr. Hasket Ltd., Hong Kong, 1988-90; chief engr., dir. Bill Kwong Universal Internat. Engring. Co. Ltd., Hong Kong, 1990—. Contbr. articles to profl. jours. Mem. ASCE, Am. Concrete Inst. Achievements include rsch. on the problem of concrete blockage in pipeline while pumping in tunnel under compressed air by designing a special pumped mix incorporated with superplasticizer and water reducing agent. Office: Unit 1116 11th Fl Star House, 3 Salisbury Rd, Tsimshatsui Kowloon Hong Kong China

CHANG, YUN SIL, pediatrician, researcher; b. Pusan, South Korea, Dec. 6, 1964; d. Jung Bu Chang and Keum Sook Lee; m. Kyung Min Noh; children: Jong Hyun, Eu Na. MD, Seoul (South Korea) Nat. U., 1989, MS in Medicine, 1994, PhD in Medicine, 1999. Intern Seoul Nat. U. Hosp., 1989-90, resident, 1990-94; fellow in neonatology Seoul Nat. U. Children's Hosp., Seoul, 1994; fellow in neonatology Samsung Med. Ctr., Seoul, 1995-96, staff pediat., 1996—; asst. prof. Sung Kyun Kwan U. Sch. Medicine, South Korea, 1999—. Contbr. articles to profl. jours. Mem. Korean Med. Assn., Korean Pediat. Assn., Korean Soc. Neonatology, Korean Soc. Perinatology. Avocations: piano, music. Office: Samsung Med Ctr, 50 Ilwon-dong Kangnam-ku, Seoul 135 710, South Korea

CHANG, ZONG-LIANG, biochemist; b. Shanghai, China, Nov. 29, 1937. BS, Fudan U., 1962; equivalent PhD, Shanghai Inst. Cell Biology, 1981. Rsch. assoc. Shanghai Inst. Cell Biology Chinese Acad. Scis., 1977-81, assoc. prof. Shanghai Inst. Cell Biology, 1983-87; vis. assoc. NIH, Bethesda, Md., 1981-83; vis. faculty U. Pitts., 1987-88, U. Kans., Kansas City, 1988-90; vis. scientist Guthrie Rsch. Inst., Sayre, Pa., 1990-94; prof., chief of section signal transduction Shanghai Inst. Cell Biology, 1995—; vis. scientist Case Western Res. U., Cleve., 1992. Co-author: Differentiation and Tissue Maintenance, 1990, Experimental Tumor Biology, 1992; mem. editl. bd. Jour. Cell Biology (China), Shanghai Jour. Immunology; contbr. articles to profl. jours. Mem. China Assn. Cell Biology, Chinese Assn. Cancer Rsch., Chinese Assn. Immunology. Office: Grad Sch Med Divsn Hematology-Oncology Dept Med Rsch Bldg Rm 414 1924 Alcoa Hwy Knoxville TN 37920

CHANG-MOTA, ROBERTO, electrical engineer; b. Caracas, Venezuela, Dec. 28, 1935; came to US, 1948; s. Roberto W. and Mary C. (Mota) Chang; m. Alicia Santamaria-Gonzales, May 4, 1968; children: Roberto Ignacio, Roxana Ivette, Ricardo Ignacio. DEE, U. Cen. Venezuela, 1960; MS, U. Ill., 1962; AR, Harvard U., 1970; PhD, UCLA, 1983. Dir. sch. engring., prof. Ctrl. U., Caracas, 1964-69; pro., dean Simon Bolivar U., Caracas, 1971-77; pres. Colegio de Ingenieros de Venezuela, Caracas, 1974-79; dir. Venezuelan Power Co., Caracas, 1974-79; pres. Latin Am. Orgn. Engring., Quito, Ecuador, 1977-79, Corporoil, Caracas, 1981-85, Audio Interface Corp., Caracas, 1983-96; v.p. ESCA Corp., Caracas, 1991-95; pres. 3R Corp., Caracas, 1995—; spl. cons. Venezuelan Navy and Army, 1971-75, Venezuelan Congress, 1989-96; mem. tech. com. Venezuelan Supreme Election Coun., 1971-81, exec. dir., 1981-82, gen. dir., 1982-97; gen. dir. Consejo Nacional Electoral, 1991-98; cons. Ministry of Interior, 1990; v.p. Electronic Cir. Corp., 1991-2000; trustee Simon Bolivar U., 1985-98; bd. dirs. Sistemas y Procesos Automatizados, SEPAI Corp. Gen. dir. Nat. Election Coun., 1985-99, Sistemas Electorales y Procesos Automatizados, 1999. Mem. IEEE, Am. Soc. Engring. Edn., Venezuelan Soc. Elec. and Mech. Engring. (pres. 1972-73), Instn. Elec. Engrs., Puerto Azul Club, Playa Pintada Club, Caracas Racquet Club. Roman Catholic. Home: 7861 SW 180th St Miami FL 33157-6216 also: Prados del Este, Calle Colon Quinta Cumana, Caracas 1080, Venezuela

CHANIN, MICHAEL HENRY, lawyer; b. Atlanta, Nov. 11, 1943; s. Henry and Herma Irene (Blumenthal) C.; m. Margaret L. Jennings, June 15, 1968; children: Herma Louise, Richard Henry, Patrick Jennings. A.B., U. N.C., 1965; J.D., Emory U., 1968. Bar: Ga. 1968, D.C. 1981. Dir. So. Ctr. for Studies in Pub. Policy, Atlanta, 1968-69; asst. and acting legal officer 1st Coast Guard Dist., Boston, 1969-72; atty. Powell, Goldstein Frazer & Murphy, Atlanta, 1972-77; spl. asst. to sec. U.S. Dept. Commerce, Washington, 1977-78; dep. asst. to pres. The White House, Washington, 1978-81; ptnr. Powell, Goldstein, Frazer & Murphy, Washington, 1981—. Served to lt. USCGR, 1969-72. Mem. ABA, D.C. Bar Assn., State Bar Ga. Democrat. Office: Powell Goldstein Frazer & Murphy 1001 Pennsylvania Ave NW Fl 6 Washington DC 20004-2505

CHANLEY, VIRGINIA ANN, political science educator; b. Clark AFB, The Philippines, Sept. 2, 1961; came to U.S., 1963; d. Jesse Jerome and Carol Lavonne Chanley; m. Lewis Clyde Clemmens, Jr., June 12, 1992. BA, Ariz. State U., 1989, MA, 1991; PhD, U. Minn., 1997. Tchg. and rsch. asst. polit. sci. dept. Ariz. State U., Tempe, 1989-91; tchg. asst. polit. sci. dept. U. Minn., Mpls., 1991-92, rsch. asst. Arlene Carlson Data Analysis Lab., 1992-94, rsch. and tchg. asst. polit. sci. dept., 1995-96; dissertation fellow Mershon Ctr., Ohio State U., Columbus, 1994-95; instr. polit. sci. dept. Fla. Internat. U., Miami, 1996-97, asst. prof. polit. sci. dept., 1997—; cons., rschr. Inst. for Pub. Opinion Rsch., Miami, 1997-2000. Contbr. articles to profl. jours. Hubert H. Humphrey fellow U. Minn., Mpls., 1992; Summer Inst. Polit. Psychology gratnee U. Minn., Mpls., 1992. Mem. Internat. Soc. Polit. Psychology, Am. Polit. Sci. Assn., Western Polit. Sci. Assn., Midwest Polit. Sci. Assn. Avocation: gardening. E-mail: chanleyv@fiu.edu. Office: Fla Internat Univ Dept Polit Sci University Park Miami FL 33199-0001

CHAN-LING, TAILOI, optometrist, neurobiologist, educator; b. Hong Kong, Aug. 30, 1958; d. Oi Kwan Chan and Siu Ying Chang; m. Daniel Sydney Ling, Apr. 28, 1984; children: Matthew Daniel, Katherine Elizabeth. B of Optometry with honours, U. NSW, Sydney, Australia, 1981, M of Optometry, 1982, PhD, 1986. Cons. optometrist Telecom Australia, Sydney, NSW, 1981-82, Met. Water Sewerage and Drainage Bd., Sydney, NSW, 1983-88; clin. supr. Sch. Optometry, U. NSW, Sydney, 1982-86; vis. lectr. Sch. Optometry U. NSW, Sydney, 1988-93; vis. lectr. dept. anatomy U. Sydney, 1988-93, postdoctoral fellow dept. anatomy, 1987-90; Wellcome-Ramaciotti vis. rsch. fellow dept. biology Univ. Coll. London, 1989; R. Douglas Wright rsch. fellow dept. anatomy U. Sydney, 1991-93, Nat. Health-Med. Rsch. Coun. sr. rsch. fellow dept. anatomy, 1994—, prof., 1994—; reviewer Investigative Ophthalmology Visual Sci., Jour. of Comparative Neurology, Glia, Developmental Brain Rsch., Neurochemistry Internat., Neurosci. Letters. Contbr. chpts. to books; contbr. articles to profl. jours. Sec. Chinese Cath. Cmty., Sydney, 1991-94. Recipient Optometric Vision Rsch. Found. prize, 1980, Hydron Contact Lens prize, 1981, Wellcome-Ramaciotti Travelling fellowship, 1989, Australian Perinatal Soc. Best Presentation award, 1994, Today's Life Sci. Rsch. award, 1994; grantee in field. Fellow Am. Acad. Optometry; mem. N.Y. Acad. Scis., Assn. for Rsch. in Vision and Ophthalmology, Australian Neurosci. Soc. (A.W. Campbell award, 1993), Nat. Assn. Rsch. Fellows of Nat. Health and Med. Rsch. Coun. (R. Douglas Wright award, 1991-94), Australian and New Zealand Microcirculation Soc. (v.p., Frank C. Courtice-Young Investigator award 1991, sec. 1997—), Australian Soc. for Med. Rsch., Contact Lens Soc. of Australia (Rsch. award, 1983-85). Avocations: gardening, bush walking, sailing. Home: 62 Janet St Russell Lea, Sydney 2046, Australia Office: U Sydney, Dept Anatomy and Histology, Sydney 2006, Australia

CHANSAY WILMOTTE, PHILIPPE, lawyer; b. Liège, Belgium, Aug. 12, 1957; s. Robert Chansay Wilmotte and Frédérique De Bruyn; m. Soraya Benmestoura, May 14, 1994; 1 child, Elisabeth. LLB, Cath. U. Louvain, 1984. Bar: Brussels. Pvt. practice Brussels, 1985—. Author: (study) The Lockerbie Case, 1995. Former chmn. internat. com. Social Christian Party's Youth, 1989; rep. in Vienna UN Econ. and Social Com. North South XXI, Geneva, 1995. Mem. Kiwanis Internat. (club officer 1989). Avocation: horseback riding. Home: 37 Chée de Liège, B 4500 Huy Belgium Office: 25 ave de la Porte de Hal, B-1060 Brussels Belgium

CHANT, SYLVIA HAMILTON, geography educator; b. Dundee, Scotland, Dec. 24, 1958; arrived in Eng., 1960; d. Stuart Ralston and June Dollis (McCartney) C.; m. Andrew Laurence McInally, May 14, 1992 (div. Dec. 1994). BA in Geography, Cambridge (Eng.) U., 1981; PhD, U. London, 1984. Rsch. asst. devel. planning union U. Coll. London, 1985, 1985; rsch. assoc. Inst. Geografia U. Autonoma Mexico, Mexico City, 1985-86; lectr. geography and L.Am. studies Liverpool (Eng.) U., 1987-88; lectr. geography London Sch. Econs., 1988-95, reader geography, 1995—; mem. internat. adv. bd. Third World Planning Rev., U.K., 1991—, Singapore Jour. Tropical Geography, 1999—; mem. rd. adv. bd. Bull. Latin Am. Rsch., 1993—, Jour. Migration Studies, 1996—; cons. UN Univ., Helsinki, Finland, 1995, Commonwealth Sec., London, 1995—, Rockefeller Found., N.Y., 1996, UN Devel. Program, N.Y., 1996, World Bank, 1999, ILO, 2000. Author: Women and Survival in Mexican Cities, 1991, Women-headed Households: Diversity and Dynamics in the Developing World, 1997; co-author: (with L. Brydon) Women in the Third World, 1989, (with C. McIlwaine) Women of a Lesser Cost: Female Labour Foreign Exchange and Philippine Development, 1995, (with C. McIlwaine) Three Generations, Two Genders, One World: Woman and Men in a Changing Century, 1998; editor: Gender and Migration in Developing Countries, 1992. Rsch. grantee Econ. and Social Rsch. Coun., U.K., 1989, 93-94; Social Sci. Rsch. fellow Nuffield Found., London, 1994-95. Fellow Inst. L.Am. Studies U. London (assoc. 1994-99); mem. Soc. L.Am. Studies (v.p. 1993-97, pres. 1997-99). Avocations: fitness training, playing piano, traveling, attending films. Office: London Sch Econs Geography, and Environment Houghton St, London WC2A 2AE, England

CHAO, JAMES MIN-TZU, architect; b. Dairen, China, Feb. 27, 1940; came to U.S., 1949; naturalized, 1962; m. Kirsti Helena Lehtonen, May 15, 1968. BArch, U. Calif., Berkeley, 1965. Registered arch., Calif., Ariz., Colo., Ill., N.Mex.; cert. instr. real estate, Calif. Intermediate draftsman Spencer, Lee & Busse, Archs., San Francisco, 1966-67; asst. to pres. Import Plus Inc., Santa Clara, Calif., 1967-69; job capt. Hammaberg and Herman, Archs., Oakland, Calif., 1969-71; project mgr. B A Premises Corp., San Francisco, 1971-79; constrn. mgr. The Straw Hat Restaurant Corp., San Francisco, 1979-81, mem. sr. mgmt., dir. real estate and constrn., 1981-87; mem. mktg. com. Straw Hat Coop. Corp., San Francisco, 1988-91; pvt. practice Berkeley, 1987—; dir. real estate Papillon Devel. Inc., 1998—; pres. Food Svc. Cons. Inc., 1987-89; pres., CEO Stratsac, Inc., 1987-92; prin. arch. Alpha Cons. Group Inc., 1991-98; v.p. Intersyn Industries Calif., 1993-99; nat. tng. dir. Excel Telecom., Inc., 1995-99; CEO Nuts and Bolts Books, 1997—; lectr. comml. real estate site analysis and selection for profl. real estate seminars; coord. minority vending program, solar application program Bank of Am.; guest faculty mem. N.W. Ctr. for Profl. Edn.; mem. Nat. Coun. Archtl. Registration Bds., 1998—. Author: The Street-Smart Restaurant Development Handbook, 1996; patentee tidal electric generating system; author 1st comprehensive consumer orientated performance specification for remote banking transaction. Mem. AIA, Encinal Yacht Club (bd. dirs. 1977-78). Republican.

CHAO, TSAI CHUNG, physician, residency program director; b. Hangzhou, Zhejiang, China, Oct. 13, 1944; came to U.S., 1981; s. Chi Chang and Chi Hsiao (Sun) C.; m. Hsian Fang Hsiang; children: Charlene, James. Diploma, Zhejiang Med. U., 1969; MD, SUNY, N.Y.C., 1993. Diplomate Am. Bd. Phys. Medicine and Rehab. Ind. Med. Examiners, Am. Acad. Pain Mgmt. Surg. intern Xiaoshan County Hosp., Xiaoshan City, China, 1969-70; gen. practitioner Xiaoshan Coal & Iron Mining, 1970-72; surg. ho. physician Linpu People's Hosp., Xiaoshan City, 1972-74; surg. resident Zhejiang Med. U., Hangzhou City, 1974-80; surg. oncology fellow Hangzhou Cancer Inst., 1980; asst. prof., staff surgeon Zhejiang Med. U., Hangzhou City, 1980-81; instr. S. Baylo U., Garden Grove, Calif., 1984-86, SAMRA U. Oriental Medicine, L.A., 1985-86; surg. resident Interfaith Med. Ctr., Bklyn., 1986-88; rehab. medicine resident SUNY Health Sci. Ctr., Bklyn., 1988-91, clinic asst. prof., attending physician, 1991-97, dir. rehab. med. residency program, 1997—. Contbr. articles to profl. jours. Fellow Am. Acad. Phys. Med. and Rehab.; mem. AMA, Am. Congress Rehab. Medicine, Am. Acad. Med. Acupunture, Am. Coll. Occupl. and Environ. Medicine, N.Y. Acad. Scis. Home: 330 E 38th St Apt 37N New York NY 10016-2782 Office: SUNY Health Sci Ctr PO Box 30 Brooklyn NY 11203-0030

CHAO, TZU-CHIEH, surgeon, researcher; b. Taichung, Taiwan, Sept. 3, 1953; s. Ling-Cheng and Su-Chen (Chang) C.; m. I-Shiu Chen, May 6, 1984; children: Allen, Albert. MB, China Med. Coll., Taichung, 1979; MS, U. Ill., Chgo., 1989, PhD, 1993. Cert. surgeon, gastrointestinal surgeon, endoscopic surgeon, Taiwan Surg. Bds. Surg. resident Chang Gung Meml. Hosp., Taipei, Taiwan, 1981-85, gen. surg. fellow, 1985-86, attending gen. surgeon, 1986—; rsch. assoc. U. Ill. Coll. Medicine, Dept. Surgery, Chgo., 1989-92; lectr. Chang Gung U. Coll. Med., Taoyuan, Taiwan, 1993, assoc. prof. surgery, 1993—; mem. com. med. ins. payment, Bur. Labor Ins., Taipei, 1994-95, Bur. Nat. Health Ins., Taipei, 1995—; dir. surg. intensive care unit Chang Gung Meml. Hosp., Taipei, 1996-98. Contbr. articles to scientific jours. Biomed. rsch. scholar Chang Gung Meml. Hosp., 1987-92, Eleanor B. Pillsbury scholar U. Ill. Hosp., 1990-92. Mem. Internat. Coll. Digestive Surgeons, Soc. Leukocyte Biology, Soc. Exptl. Biology and Medicine. Avocations: swimming, golf, music. Home: 12th fl, 406 Chang Gung Med Village, Taoyuan 33333, Taiwan Office: Chang Gung Meml Hosp Surg, 199 Tung Hwa North Rd, Taipei 10591, Taiwan

CHAOUAT, ARI, physician; b. Paris, Dec. 24, 1960. MD, 1992. Asst. U. Hosp., Strasbourg, France, 1992-97, cons. physician, 1997—. Contbr. articles to profl. jours. Office: Svc De Pneumologie, Hopital De Hautepierre, 67000 Strasbourg France

CHAOUAT, DIDIER, physician, rheumatologist; b. Paris, Oct. 10, 1968; s. Yves and Jacqueline (Balensi) C.; m. Brigitte Alon, Feb. 28, 1980; children: Mathieu, Benjamin. MD, U. Paris, 1970. Intern Hosps. of Paris, 1978; chief of svc. Fondation Rochschild, Paris, 1982—; prof. Med. Coll. Paris Hosp. Editor Rheumatology Revs. Pres. med. commn., mem. directorial bd. French Golf Fedn. Mem. Racing Club of France. Avocation: golf. Home: 5 rue Lyautey, Paris 75016, France Office: Fondation Rothschild, 25-29 rue Manin, 75019 Paris France

CHAOUAT, GERARD CHARLES PAUL, researcher; b. Alger, France, May 6, 1944; s. Yves David and Jacqueline (Balewski) Balensi. Bachelor's degree, U. Paris, 1962; MD, Faculty Lariboisière, Paris, 1968; PhD, U. Paris 6, 1979; cert. in immunology, Inst. Pasteur, 1969; Dr. Honoris Causa, Pecs U., Hungary, 1998. Intern Hosp. Region de Paris, 1968-72; chercheur benevole Inst. Nat. Santé et Recherche Med., 1973-76; grants for tng. Med. Rsch. Coun., Brit. Coun., Wellcome Rsch. Lab., 1974; attache de recherche Ctr. Nat. Recherche Scientifique, 1974; vis. scientist NIH, Bethesda, Md., 1981-82; from charge de recherches to checteur de recherches, 1982-99; dir. rsch. Ctr. Nat. Recherche Scientifique. Treas., mem. Nat. Bur. Syndicat Nat. des Cherchers Sci. Recipient award Am. Soc. Immunology. Mem. Internat. Soc. Immunology of Reprodn. (sec.-gen., pres. elect). Office: Hopital A Béclève, U131 IWSERM, 92141 Clamart Cedex, France

CHAPA, ELIA KAY, health administration educator; b. Apr. 9, 1960; d. Domingo Prado and Elida (Vaca) C. BA, Baylor U., 1982; postgrad., Southwestern Bapt. Theol. Sem., 1983-85; MPA, Tex. Tech U., 1993; postgrad., U. North Tex. Health Sci. Ctr., 1995—. Adj. instr. health svcs. adminstr. Dallas Bapt. U., 1998—; adj. instr. health svcs. adminstrn. Dallas Bapt. U., 1998.

CHAPDELAINE, PERRY ANTHONY, JR., public health physician, educator; b. Mason City, Iowa, Feb. 23, 1950; s. Perry Anthony Sr. and Ruby Elizabeth (McCurley) C.; m. Catherine Joan Tidwell, May 22, 1981; 1 child, Rachel Maria. BA in Sociology, St. Ambrose U., 1972; MD, Meharry Med. Coll., 1989, MSPH, 1992. Diplomate Am. Bd. Preventive Medicine. CEO, pres. AC Projects Inc., Franklin, Tenn., 1974-86; epidemiologist Meharry Med. Coll., Nashville, 1992-95, asst. prof., 1993-95, dir. preventive medicine residency program, 1995; chief med. physician City of Nashville, Metro Health Dept., 1995-2000; pvt. cons. practice, 2000—; assoc. Meharry Med. Coll., 2000—; cons. St. Thomas Hosp. Clin. Ethics Ctr., Nashville, 1993-98, Nashville Prevention Mktg. Initiative, 1994-96; med. dir. Samaritan Recovery Cmty., Nashville, 1993-95; mem. Access Med Plus Peer Rev. Com., Nashville, 1996-2000. Co-editor: The John W. Campbell Letters, 1985 (Hugo award nominee 1986). Mem. Tenn. Pub. Health Assn., Alpha Chi, Alpha Omega Alpha. Avocations: writing, photography, dulcimer, hiking. E-mail: chapdelaine@1nol.com. Home: 7376 Walker Rd Fairview TN 37062-8141

CHAPIN, MARY Q., arbitrator, mediator, writer, performing artist; b. Shepherdstown, W.VA., May 5, 1933; d. Guy Estil and Anne Mildred (Jones) Quisenberry; m. Edward John Chapin Jr.; children: John Edward, Susan Q. (dec.). SUNY Regent's Degree, 1985; AAS, SUNY, Binghamton, BS, 1991. Pers. adminstr. Mohawk Valley Psychiatric Ctr., Utica, N.Y., 1976-89; arbitrator Am. Arbitration Assn., N.Y.C., 1989-99; pres. Dispute Resolution Internat., New Hartford, N.Y., 1993—; neutral chair NYSDOL Office of Labor Mgmt., Albany, N.Y., 1993—; mem. adv. coun. on safety and security in N.Y. State schs. N.Y. State Dept. Edn., Albany, 1995-97; founder, mem., bd. dirs. Forum on Conflict and Concensus, 1993-941 chiar Mohawk Valley Women's History Project, 1998—. Author: Woman's Suffrage: A Dream of Full Citizenship; author, performer An Afternoon with Susan B. Anthony; contbr. articles to profl. jours. Pres. Utica/Rome Metro

League of Women Voters, 1992-97; coord. Com. on Met. Orgn., 1995-97; coord. of multicultural commn. League of Women Voters Edn. Fund, 1997; trustee Mohawk Valley Cmty. Coll., 1996—; mem. edn. com. Assn. Bd. of Trustees of C.C., 1997—; Utica C. of C., 1995-98. Recipient Found. award The Found. of SUNY at Binghamton, 1992, Recognition award NYS League of Women Voters, 1995, 97, Recognition award U.S. LWV Edn. Fund, 1998, Labor Mgmt. award Office of Mental Health, 1988. Mem. AAUW (v.p.), Central N.Y. Futurist, Bd. Neighborhood Ctr. Avocations: medical herbalist, human rights and women's rights. Home and Office: 56 Woodbrooke Rd New Hartford NY 13413-4805

CHAPIN, MARYAN FOX, civic worker; b. Easton, Pa., Apr. 26, 1933; d. Louis Rodman and Mary Catherine (Cannon) Fox; m. Richard Chapin, Nov. 3, 1956; children: Aldus Higgins II, Margery Rodman, Marya Marsh, Richard Dickinson. AB, Vassar Coll., 1954. Sec. editl. office New Yorker Mag., Inc., 1954-55; mem. staff admissions office Harvard Coll., Cambridge, Mass., 1956; contr. Chapin's Market, Cambridge, 1986-88; trustee Longy Sch. Music, 1974-75; pres. founding bd. trustees New Sch. Music, 1976-77; bd. dirs. Young Audiences of Mass., 1976-83, chairman, 1980-82; adv. bd. Wheelock Coll. Family Theatre, 1985-92; treas. Richards Libr., Georgetown, Maine; chmn., bd. trustees Bowdoin Summer Music Festival, 1997-99, treas. 1999—. Bd. dirs. Lark Soc. for Chamber Music, 1997—. Mem. New Eng. Conservatory (bd. overseers 1987-92), Vincent Club (bd. mgrs. 1961-67). Home: Knubble Rd Georgetown ME 04548

CHAPIREAU, FRANÇOIS PIERRE, psychiatrist; b. Sainte-Adresse, France, Sept. 2, 1947; s. Pierre Nicolas and Marie-Louise (Fegrai) C.; m. Genevieve Henriette Hertzog; 1 child, Boris. MD, U. Paris, 1973, psychiatrist, 1975. Head of dept. Hosp., France, 1978—; assoc. rschr. WHO Collaborating Ctr., Paris, 1994—; cons. expert Coun. of Europe, Strasburg, France, 1990; med. editl. bd. French Fedn. of Psychiatry, 1997—. Author: Le Handicap Mental Chez L'Enfant, 1997. Mem. Evolution Psychiatrique (Prize 1975), Societe Medico Psychologique. Office: Hosp Erasme, 143 ave Armand Guillebaud BP 85, 92160 Antony France

CHAPIRO, ADOLPHE, education educator, consultant; b. Moscow, USSR, Feb. 13, 1924; arrived in France, 1933; s. Georges and Bronislawa (Shulman) C.; m. Josette Schubert, Aug. 25, 1950; children: Marianne, Marc. Chemist, U. Paris, 1947, PhD, 1950. Rsch. prof. Centre Nat. de La recherche Scientifique, Paris, 1947—. Author: Radiation Chemistry of Polymeric Systems, 1982, Jean-Antoine Lepine, Horloger, 1988, La Montre Francaise du XVIe siècle à 1900, 1990; contbr. articles to profl. jours. Avocations: antique watches and clocks. Office: Centre National de La, Recherche Scientifique, 2 Rue Henry Dunant, 94320 Thiais France

CHAPLIN, GEORGE, newspaper editor; b. Columbia, S.C., Apr. 28, 1914; s. Morris and Netty (Brown) C.; m. Esta Lillian Solomon, Jan. 26, 1937; children: Stephen Michael, Jerry Gay. BS, Clemson Coll., 1935; Nieman fellow, Harvard U., 1940-41; HHD (hon.), Clemson U., 1989; LHD (hon.), Hawaii Loa Coll., 1990. Reporter, later city editor Greenville (S.C.) Piedmont, 1935-42; mng. editor Camden (N.J.) Courier-Post, 1946-47, San Diego Jour., 1948-49; mng. editor, then editor New Orleans Item, 1949-58; asso. editor Honolulu Advertiser, 1958-59, editor in chief, 1959-86, editor at large, 1986—; mem. selection com. Jefferson fellowships East-West Ctr.; chmn. Gov.'s Conf. on Year 2000, 1970; chmn. Hawaii Commn. on Year 2000, 1971-74; co-chmn. Conf. on Alt. Econ. Futures for Hawaii, 1973-75; charter mem. Goals for Hawaii, 1979-81; alt. U.S. rep. South Pacific Commn., 1978-81; chmn. search com. for pres. U. Hawaii, 1983; chmn. Hawaii Gov.'s Adv. Coun. on Fgn. Lang. and Internat. Studies, 1983-94; rep. of World Press Freedom Com. on missions to Sri Lanka, Hong Kong, Singapore, 1987. Editor, officer-in-charge: Mid-Pacific edit. Stars and Stripes World War II; editor: (with Glenn Paige) Hawaii 2000, 1973, Presstime in Paradise: The Life and Times of the Honolulu Advertiser 1856-1995, 1998. Bd. dirs. U. Hawaii Rsch. Corp., 1970-72, Inst. for Religion and Social Change, Hawaii Jewish Welfare Fund, Charleston Christian-Jewish Coun.; mem. bd. govs. East-West Ctr., Honolulu, 1980-89, chmn., 1983-89; mem. bd. govs. Pacific Health Rsch. Inst., 1984-90, 93-97, pres., 1995-96; bd. govs. Straub Med. Found., 1989-98, Hawaii Pub. Schs. Found., 1986-87; trustee Clarence T. C. Ching Found., 1986-95; mem. Temple K.K. Beth Elohim; Am. media chmn. U.S.-Japan Conf. on Cultural and Ednl. Interchange, 1978-86; co-founder, v.p. Coalition for Drug-Free Hawaii, 1987-90; panelist ABA Conf., 1989; mem. Civilian Adv. Group, U.S. Army, Hawaii, 1985-95; co-chair Hawaii State Commn. on Judicial Salaries, 1995-98. Capt. AUS, 1942-46. Decorated Star Solidarity (Italy), Order Rising Sun (Japan), Prime Minister's medal (Israel); recipient citations Overseas Press Club, 1961, 72, Headliners award, 1962, John Hancock award, 1972, 74, Distinguished Alumni award Clemson U., 1974, E.W. Scripps award Scripps-Howard Found., 1976, Champion Media award for Econ. Understanding, 1981, Judah Magnes Gold medal Hebrew U. Jerusalem, 1987, Herbert Harley award Am. Judicature Soc., 1991, Regents medal of distinction U. Hawaii, 1998; inductee Honolulu Press Club Hall of Fame, 1987. Mem. Honolulu Symphony Soc., Pacific and Asian Affairs Council (dir.), Internat. Press Inst., Am. Soc. Newspaper Editors (dir., treas. 1973, sec. 1974, v.p. 1975, pres. 1976), Friends of East-West Ctr., Country Club of Charleston, Harbour Club.

CHAPMAN, ANTHONY BRADLEY, psychiatrist; b. Salem, Mass., June 22, 1938; s. Anthony Bredick and Gladys Gwendolyn (Poole) C.; m. Ella Mueller, Aug. 30, 1963; children: Bradley, Jeffrey. BS with honors, Northeastern U., 1961; MD, Stanford U., 1966. Diplomate Am. Bd. Psychiatry and Neurology. Rsch. asst. Harvard Med. Sch., Boston, 1957-61; intern Case-Western Res. U., Cleve., 1966-67; resident Johns Hopkins Hosp., Balt., 1967-69, fellow in behavioral medicine, 1967-69; fellow in child psychiatry U. Pa., Phila., 1969-71; pvt. practice Alexandria, Va., 1973—; dir. Attention Disorder Ctr. No. Va., Alexandria, 1991—; guest lectr. Children and Adults with Attention Deficit Disorder, Arlington, Va., 1990-96. Editor Hyperactive Child Newsletter, 1974-78. Maj. U.S. Army, 1971-73. Recipient Outstanding Tchr. award Am. Acad. Family Practice, 1976-81. Mem. Am. Med. Soc., Am. Psychiat. Electrophysiology Assn., Va. Med. Soc., Alexandria Med. Soc., Attention Deficit Disorders Profls. No. Va. (pres. 1990-92). Avocations: jazz, Brazilian music, tennis, skiing. Office: 2059 Huntington Ave Ste 108 Alexandria VA 22303-1602

CHAPMAN, AUDREY, science association executive, clergywoman. AB summa cum laude, Wellesley Coll., 1963; MA in Polit. Sci., Columbia, 1965, PhD in Pub. Law, Govt.-African Studies, 1967; MDiv, N.Y. Theol. Sem., 1986; STM, Union Theol. Sem., 1991. Ordained to ministry United Ch. of Christ, 1986. Instr. dept. polit. sci. Barnard Coll., Columbia U., N.Y.C., 1966-67, asst. prof. dept. polit. sci., 1967-69; lectr. dept. polit. sci. and sociology U. Ghana, 1970-72; cons. Middle East Office, Ford Found., Lebanon, 1972-73; cons. task force on women Ford Found., N.Y.C., 1974-75, cons. Office V.P. Internat. divsn., 1975; cons. Office V.P. Internat. divsn. Ford Found., Kenya, 1976-77; advisor social stats. divsn. Crl. Bur. Stats., Kenya, 1977-79; dir. Kenya edn. setor analysis program U.S. AID, 1979-81; dir. World Issues Office, sec. United Ch. Bd. for World Ministries, N.Y.C. and Washington, 1981-90; dir. sci. and human rights program AAAS, Washington, 1991—, dir. dialogue on sci., ethics and religion, 1995—; vis. scholar Mid. East Inst., Columbia U., 1973-74; vis. sr. rsch. fellow Inst. for Devel. Studies, U. Nairobi, 1977-78; adj. prof. N.Y. Theol. Sem., 1986, Wesley Theol. Sem., 1992, 93, Andover Newton Theol. Sem., 1996; adj. prof. dept. theology Georgetown U., Washington, 1996. Author: Ibo Politics: The Role of Ethnic Unions in Eastern Nigeria, 1972, Women's Education in Five Developing Countries: Opportunities and Outcomes, 1981, Faith, Power, and Politics: Political Ministry in Mainline Churches, 1991, Exploring a Human Rights Approach to Health Care Reform, 1993, Unprecedented Choices: Religious Ethics at the Frontiers of Genetic Science, 1999, (with David R. Smock) The Cultural and Political Aspects of Rural Development: The Case of Eastern Nigeria, 1973, The Politics of Pluralism: A Comparison of Lebanon and Ghana, 1975; editor: Comparative Politics: A Reader in Institutionalization and Mobilization, 1973, (with Rodney Petersen) Consumption, Population and the Environment: Perspectives from Science and Religion, 1999; prin. author, editor (with Janet Z. Giele) Women: Roles and Status in Eight Countries, 1977; co-author, editor (with Leonard Rubenstein) Human Rights and Health: The Legacy of Apartheid, 1998; editor, co-author: Health Care Reform: A Human Rights Approach, 1994, Health Care and Informatoin Ethics: Protecting Fundamental Human Rights, 1997, Perspectives on Genetic Patenting: Science, Religion, Industry and Government in Dialogue, 1999; contbr. articles and monographs to profl. jours. and conf. procs., chpts. to books. Bd. dirs. Am. Near East Refugee Aid. Mem. Am. Theol. Soc., Am. Acad. Religion, Soc. for Christian Ethics (com. for 21st century), Hastings Ctr. on Bioethics (assoc.), Am. Assn. Bioethics, Inst. for Religion in Age of Sci., Assn. for Politics and Life Scis. Fax: 202-289-4950. E-mail: achapman@aaas.org. Home: 20142 Darlington Dr Montgomry Vlg MD 20886-1008 Office: AAAS 1200 New York Ave NW Ste 100 Washington DC 20005-3941

CHAPMAN, BRUCE JAMES, academic economist; b. Canberra, A.C.T., Australia, Sept. 16, 1951; s. James and Hazel (Harman) C.; m. Pamela Ann Lyndon; children: Chapman, James Oscar, Lyndon, Jack. B of Econs., Australian Nat. U., 1973; PhD, Yale U., U.S.A., 1981. Lectr. U. Adelaide, Australia, 1980-83; rsch. fellow Australian Nat. U., Canberra, 1983-85, sr. rsch. fellow, 1986-94, dir. Ctr. for Econ. Policy Rsch., 1994—; cons. Govt. of Ausralia, 1987-89, World Bank, Washington, 1990-99; sr. econ. cons. Australian Prime Min., 1994-96. Contbr. articles to profl. jours. Interviews for radio and TV. Fellow Australian Acad. Social Scis.; mem. Econ. Soc. Australia (pres. ACT br. 1991-94). Achievements include first income contingent charge for higher education, the Australian Higher Education Contribution Scheme. Avocations: cricket, conversation, cooking, children. Home: Yarralumla, 6 Denman St, Canberra ACT 2600, Australia Office: Australian Nat U, PO Box 4 GPO, Canberra ACT 0900, Australia

CHAPMAN, DAVID, intensive care physician; b. Dunstable, U.K., Jan. 14, 1948; s. Harold and Gladys (Holt) C.; m. Roberta Chapman McAvoy, Mar. 8, 1968 (div. 1986); children: James, Ruth; m. Bridget Langham, Oct. 15, 1988. B Medicine B Surgery, Liverpool (Eng.) U., 1971. Cons. Derbyshire Royal Infirmary, U.K., 1979—; tutor Royal Coll. Anaesthesiologists, 1984-90; paramedic trainer East Midlands Ambulance Svc., U.K., 1988. Fellow Royal Coll. Anesthaesiologists; mem. Intensive Care Soc., N.Y. Acad. Scis., Planetary Soc. Home: Tithebarn Ln, Ashbourne DE6 5JH, England

CHAPMAN, GILBERT BRYANT, physicist; b. Uniontown, Ala., July 8, 1935; s. Gilbert Bryant and Annie Lillie (Stallworth) C.; m. Loretta Woodward, June 5, 1960 (dec. Sept. 1994); children: Annie L., Bernice M., Cedric N., David O., Ernest P., Frances Q.H., Gilbert Bryant III; m. Betty J. Chapman, June 27, 1999. BS in Math. and Chemistry, Baldwin Wallace Coll., Berea, Ohio, 1968; MS in Physics, Cleve. State U., 1973; MBA, Mich. State U., 1990; postgrad, Kent State U., Ohio, 1974-76. Phys. sci. technician NASA-Lewis Rsch. Ctr., Cleve., 1953-68, emission spectroscopist, 1968-75, materials engr., 1975-77; sr. rsch. engr. Ford Motor Co., Redford Twp., Mich., 1977-83, project engr., 1983-86; adv. materials testing specialist Chrysler Corp., Highland Park, Mich., 1986-89; adv. materials specialist Chrysler Corp., Madison Heights, Mich., 1989-91, advanced materials and product exec., 1991-95, advanced materials cons., 1995-98; sr. mgr. advanced materials and product devel. DaimlerChrylser Corp., Rochester Hills, Mich., 1998—; chmn. auto. com. '87 Soc. Mfg. Engrs. Composites Group, Dearborn, 1987, chair bd., 1996; chmn. ind. adv. bd. NDE/Ctr., Iowa State U., Ames, 1989, 90; mem. indsl. adv. bd. Inst. for Mfg. Rsch., Wayne State U., Ctrl. State U., U. Tex.-Pan Am., U. Mich.-Dearborn; chair Internat. Symposium on Automotive Tech. and Automation Materials Conf., 1996, 98, Automotive Composites Consortium, 1996. Contbr. articles to profl. jours., chpts. to books. Lay leader, elder SDA Ch. of Southfield, Mich., 1983-95, elder, 2000—; bd. trustees Mt. Vernon Acad., Ohio, 1972-76; lay adv. coun. Ohio Conf. SDA, 1974-77. With USAF, 1959-61. Recipient Group Achievement award, NASA Lewis Rsch. Ctr., 1970, Apollo Achievement award, 1968, Mayor Archer's Proclamation, Motor City Youth Fedn., 1994, Spirit of Detroit award Detroit City Coun., 1994; named one of Best and Brightest Profls., Dollars and Sense Mag., 1993, Black Engr. of Yr. and Career Achievement award U.S. Black Engr. and Info. Tech. mag., 1999. Fellow Am. Soc. Nondestructive Testing (cert. level III 6 NDT methods); mem. AAAS, ASM (polymer composites program com. paper 1986), ASTM, IEEE, SAE (award for excellence in oral presentation), Am. Chem. Soc., Am. Phys. Soc., Am. Soc. for Composites, Engring. Soc. Detroit (sci. com., ASM/ESD Best Paper award 1993), Fedn. of Analytical Chemists, Nat. Tech. Assn. (Cleve. program com.), Soc. for Applied Spectroscopy (Cleve. vice chair, sec.), Soc. Mfg. Engrs. (chaired CMA adv. bd.), Soc. Physics Students (pres.), Internat. Symposium on Automotive Tech. and Automation (chair materials conf. 1996). Achievements include patent for infrared inspection method for friction welds in thermoplastics and advanced vehicle concepts; development of low-frequency ultrasonic inspection methods for polymer composites and adhesive bond joints; co-development of D.C. arc method of determining work functions of refractory alloys, spectrochemical analysis of microgram-size samples. Home: 38671 Greenbrook Ct Farmingtn Hls MI 48331-2979 Office: DaimlerChrysler Corp Liberty and Tech Affairs 2730 Research Dr Rochester Hls MI 48309-3574

CHAPMAN, HILTON EVELEIGH, legal counsel; b. Sydney, NSW, Australia, July 28, 1955; s. Graham Eveleigh and Virginia Alison Chapman; m. Penelope Jane Booth, Dec. 13, 1980; children: Andrew James, Claire Louise. B in Comm., U. NSW, 1978, LLB, 1978; FCIS, Inst. Corp. Mgrs., Sydney, Australia, 1992. Dep. group sec. TNT Ltd., Redfern, NSW, Australia, 1978-92; group sec. TNT Ltd., Redfern, 1992-97; co. sec., gen. counsel Burns Philp & Co. Ltd., Sydney, Australia, 1997-98; gen. counsel TNT Australia Pty Ltd., 1998—. Avocations: cricket, wine and food appreciation, golf. Office: TNT Plaza Tower 1, Lowsen Square, Redfern NSW 2016, Australia

CHAPMAN, HOPE HORAN, psychologist; b. Chgo., Feb. 13, 1954; d. Theodore George and Idelle (Poll) H.; m. Stuart G. Chapman, Dec. 4, 1983. BS, U. Ill., 1976; MA, No. Ill. U., 1979; cert. lawyer's asst. program, Roosevelt U., Chgo., 1996, 97; student, Ballet Russe Sch., 1999-2000. Lic. pharmacy technician, Ill. Psychologist Glenwood (Iowa) State Hosp. Sch., 1979-83, Gov. Samuel H. Shapiro Devel. Ctr., Kankakee, Ill., 1985-86; dir. staff tng. and devel. Gov. Samuel H. Shapiro Devel. Ctr., Glenkirk, 1988-90; clin. assoc. Bennett & Assocs., 1990-91; psychologist Singer Mental Health & Devel. Ctr., Rockford, Ill., 1992-93; forensic psychologist Elgin (Ill.) Mental Health Ctr., 1993-94. Contbr. papers to profl. confs., articles to jours. Active Omaha Symphonic Chorus, 1981-83; mem. Omaha Pub. Schs. Citizens Adv. Com., 1980-81; mem. edn. com. Anti-Defamation League, 1980-85, chmn. com. anti-Semitism and Jewish youth, 1981-84; commr. youth commn. Village of Hoffman Estates, Ill., 1988-94; vice chmn. oversight com. Vogelei Teen Ctr., 1988-94; commr. Environ. Commn., Village of Hoffman Estates, 1994-2000, chmn. Schaumburg Twp. Mental Health Bd., 1993-94; election judge Cook County, 1992—; judge's asst. Cook County Cir. Ct., 1996-2000. Scholar State of Ill. Mem. APA, Midwest Psychol. Assn., Am. Coll. Forensic Examiners, Am. Bd. Disability Analysts, Ill. Paralegal Assn., Phi Kappa Phi, Psi Chi. Jewish.

CHAPMAN, JEREMY ROBERT, renal physician; b. London, Sept. 20, 1953; arrived in Australia, 1987; s. John Brian and Barbara Elsie (Champion) C.; m. Clare M.C. Harris; children: Robert, Matthew, Elizabeth. MA, Cambridge (Eng.) U., 1972, MB BChir, 1978, MD, 1987. MRC rsch. fellow Oxford (Eng.) U., 1983-87; cons. dir. tissue typing NSW Red Cross, Sydney, Australia, 1987—; renal physician Westmead Hosp., Sydney, 1987-93, dir. renal medicine, 1993—; mem. chmn. Australian Bone Marrow Donor Registry, 1990—, E. Treasurer Transplantation Soc. Author: Manual of Renal Transplantation, 1993. Project grantee Nat. Health and Med. Rsch. Coun. Australia, 1987-2002. Fellow Royal Australian Coll. Physicians; mem. Royal Coll. Physicians, Transplantation Soc. of Australia and New Zealand. Office: Westmead Hosp, Renal Medicine, Westmead 2145, Australia

CHAPMAN, KENNETH MAYNARD, retired workforce development specialist; b. Corinth, Ky., Sept. 30, 1938; s. Leonard N. and Rachel (Howard) C.; m. Patricia L. Gross Barnhill, July 15, 1960 (div. May 1976); children: Kenneth L., Karen L.; m. Virginia L. Robinson, June 6, 1976; stepchildren: Stephen E. Howell, Michael A. Howell. AAS in Chem. Tech., Ohio Coll. Applied Sci., Cin., 1958; BS in Chem. Engring., MIT, 1961; MA in Adult Edn., George Washington U., Washington, 1969. Acting head chem. tech. Ohio Coll. Applied Sci., Cin., 1961-63; head chem. engring. tech. Temple U., Phila., 1963-67; asst. edn. sec. for 2-yr. colls. Am. Chem. Soc., Washington, 1967-69; assoc. dir. chem. tech. project Am. Chem. Soc., Berkeley, Calif., 1969-72; mgr. spl. programs Am. Chem. Soc., Washington, 1973-82, head R&D in edn., 1982-90, spl. asst. to dir., 1990-99, head tech. resources/edn., 1993-99; v.p. Computer-Based Instrnl. Sys., San Antonio, 1972-73; ret., 1999. Co-author: The Chemical Technicians Handbook, 1973; co-author/editor: (book series) Modern Chemical Technology, 1973; co-author: Foundations for Excellence in the C.P.I., 1997; co-author/editor: (booklet) Gaining the Competitive Edge, 1993. Mem. Triangle Coalition for Sci. and Tech. Edn. (bd. dirs., sec.-treas. 1990-97), Nat. Vo-Tech Honor Soc. (bd. dirs.).

CHAPOUTHIER, GEORGES, biologist, writer; b. Libourne, Gironde, France, Mar. 27, 1965; s. Fernand and Odette (Mazaubert) C.; m. Wan Hua Chapouthier, Dec. 1, 1972; children: Catherine, Amandine, Henri, Emeline. PhD in Sci., U. Strasbourg, France, 1973; PhD in Arts, U. Lyon, France, 1986. Rsch. scientist Centre Nat. de la Recherche Scientifique, France, 1968-84, rsch. dir., 1984—; rsch. assoc. Baylor Coll., Houston, 1969-71; lectr. U. Strasbourg, 1968-72, U. Paris, 1974—; expert Centre Nat. de la Recherche Scientifique, 1985; mem. jury Prix Kastler, France, 1993-96; expert Conseil de Recherches Scis. Humaines, Can., 1996. Author: Psychophysiologie, 980, Au Bon Vouloir de C'Homme L'Animal, 1990, The Universal Declaration of Animal Rights, 1998, others; mem. editl. team several sci and philos. jours.; contbr. articles to profl. jours. Recipient silver medal Soc. D'Encouragement au Progres, France, 1991. Avocations: journalism, writing. Home: 11 Bis Rue Du Val de Grace, 75005 Paris France

CHAPOVAL, ANDREI, immunologist; b. Barnaul, Russia, June 1, 1967; arrived in U.S., 1994; s. Ivan A. and Antonina I. C.; m. Svetlana P. Chapoval, June 30, 1995; 1 child: Dennis A. MS in biology, Altai State Univ., Barnaul, Russia, 1989; PhD in immunology, Russian Cancer Ctr., Moscow, 1994. Rsch. fellow Mayo Clinic, Rochester, Minn., 1994-96; postdoctoral assoc. The Jackson Lab., Bar Harbor, Maine, 1996-98; rsch. fellow Mayo Clinic, 1998—. Author (chpt. in book) Molecular Medicine, 2000; contbr. articles to profl. jours. Recipient rsch. grant The Jackson Lab., 1996. Mem. Am. Assn. Cancer Rsch., Am. Assn. Advancement of Sci. Avocations: downhill skiing, beer brewering. E-mail: chapoval.andrei@mayo.edu. Office: Mayo Clinic 200 1st St SW Rochester MN 55905-0002

CHAPPELL, MILTON LEROY, lawyer; b. Accra, Ghana, Mar. 25, 1951; (parents Am. citizens); s. Derwood Lee and Helen Jean (Freeman) C.; m. Margot Cecelia Shields, Dec. 18, 1972; children: Marton Gerald, Monet Louise. BA summa cum laude, Columbia Union Coll., 1973; JD, Cath. U., 1976; diploma, Nat. Inst. Trial Advocacy, Boulder, Colo., 1978; cert., U. Miami, 1982. Bar: Md. 1976, D.C. 1977, U.S. Ct. Appeals (4th, 5th, 9th and D.C. cirs.) 1977, U.S. Dist. Ct. D.C. 1978, U.S. Ct. Appeals (6th cir.) 1979, U.S. Supreme Ct. 1980, U.S. Ct. Appeals (11th cir.) 1981, U.S. Dist. Ct. Md. 1982, U.S. Ct. Appeals (7th cir.) 1988, U.S. Dist. Ct. (no. dist.) Calif., 1990. Sole practice Silver Spring, Md., 1976—; staff atty. Nat. Right to Work Legal Def. Found., Springfield, Va., 1976—; lectr. Columbia Union Coll., Takoma Park, Md., 1976-77; legal cons. JNA Elem. Sch., Takoma Park, 1980-83; gen. counsel Playgrounds Unltd., Inc., 1988-2000, Internat. Play Equipment Mfrs. Assn., Inc., 1995—; participant play settings subcom. recreation access adv. com. U.S. Archtl. and Transp. Barriers Compliance Bd., 1993-94. Contbr. to Ohio No. U. Law Rev., Govt. Union Rev. Mem. Hillandale Civic Assn., Silver Spring, 1980—; legal cons., bd. dirs. Silver Spring Seventh-day Adventist Ch., 1976-84, Takoma Park.; participant U.S. Arch. and Trans. Barriers Compliance Bd., Recreation Access Adv. Com., Play Settings subcom., 1993-94. Mem. ABA, Md. Bar Assn. D.C. Bar assn. (assoc.). Home: 10321 Royal Rd Silver Spring MD 20903-1616 Office: Nat Right to Work Legal Def Found 8001 Braddock Rd # 600 Springfield VA 22151-2110

CHAPUT, EUGENE MICHAEL, advertising executive; b. San Francisco, July 5, 1941; s. Eugene Rene and Lucille Marie (Longuy) C.; m. Susan Mary Oliphant, Dec. 18, 1965; children: J. Michael, E. John, Thomas Patrick. BS, U. So. Calif., 1963, MBA, 1965. Sr. media planner Young & Rubicam, San Francisco, 1965-69; v.p., dir. mktg. svcs. Grey Advertising, San Francisco, 1969-78; v.p., mgmt. supr. Hoefer, Dieterich & Brown, San Francisco, 1978-79; v.p. Young & Rubicam, San Francisco, 1979—. Patentee; inflatable portable sofa, 1996, electronic self defense weapon disguised as personal accessory, 1999; copyright holder parent-child bonding exercise program; contbr. to numerous creative advertising concepts. Coach Little League Baseball, Youth Soccer, Portola Valley, Calif., 1973-86; chmn. Portola Valley Parks and Recreation, 1978-83. Recipient numerous advt. awards, 1985—; named first honoree Top of the Dial award, No. Calif. Broadcasters Assn., 1995. Mem. San Francisco Olympic Club (physical fitness commr. 1982-87, Weight Lifting record 1998, 2000). Avocations: physical fitness, skiing, tennis, motorcycling. Office: Young & Rubicam Inc 100 1st St Ste 1800 San Francisco CA 94105-2600

CHAPUT, MICHEL ALBERT, science educator, researcher; b. Lyon, Rhone, France, Dec. 1, 1948; s. Albert Chaput and Clemence Varigny; m. Josiane Branche, Oct. 21, 1972; children: Sebastien, Audrey. Diploma, Inst. U. Tech., Lyon-Villeurbanne, France, 1970. Tchr. U. Inst. Tech., Lyon-Villeurbanne, 1972-75; rschr. Nat. Ctr. Sci. Rsch. U. Claude Bernard Lyon 1, Lyon-Villeurbanne, 1976—. Author, co-editor: Glossaire de Sciences Cognitives (Glossary of Cognitive Sciences), 1997. Fellow European Chemoreception Orgn., Assn. Physiologists. Fax: 04 78 94 95 85. Office: Univ Claude Bernard Lyon 1, 43 Blvd du 11 NOvembre 1918, 69622 Rhone France

CHARABI, SAMIH AHMED, otolaryngologist; b. Cairo, Egypt, Jan. 25, 1949; s. Ahmed Mohamed and Awatef Mohamed (El Shazly) C.; m. Birgitte Wittenborg Paulsen, Dec. 17, 1990; children: Salem, Salma. MD, Copenhagen U., 1983, DMSc, 1997. Physician Nat. Hosp./Rigshospitalet, Copenhagen, 1983-85, 90, Bispebjerg Hosp., Copenhagen, 1986-88, Glostrup (Denmark) U. Hosp., 1987-88, Aalborg (Denmark) U. Hosp., 1989; physician, specialist in ENT/head and neck surgery Gentofte U. Hosp., Hellerup, Denmark, 1991—; assoc. prof. Copenhagen U., 2000—. Contbr. articles to profl. jours. Named Best Rschr., Scandinavian Soc. Otolaryngology, 1996. Mem. Barany Soc., European Acad. Otology/Neurotology, Coll. Oto-Rhino-Laryngologicum Amicitiae Sacrum. Avocations: squash, tennis, swimming, chess. Home: Ahlmanns Alle 12, 2900 Hellerup Denmark Office: Gentofte U Hosp, Dept Otol/Head & Neck Surg, 2900 Hellerup Denmark

CHARACHON, ROBERT LOUIS, medical educator; b. Lyon, France, Sept. 14, 1932; s. Jean and Marguerite (Roche) C.; m. Claude Magdelaine, Sept. 7, 1957; children: Delphine, Rémi, Guillaume, Jérôme. MD, U. Lyon, 1961. Asst. prof. Univ. Hosp., Grenoble, 1965-71, prof., 1971—, head of dept. ENT dept., 1971-99. Recipient Croix de la Valeur Militaire, 1955, Chevalier de L'Ordre du Mérite, 1990. Office: CHU de Grenoble, 38043 Grenoble Cedex France

CHARALABOUS, EPAMINONDAS, bank executive, stock derivatives consultant; b. Thessaloniki, Greece, July 7, 1962; s. Spiridon and Veatriki (Komi) C. Degree in Econs., U. Thessaloniki, 1988, Degree in Balkan Langs., 1989; Degree in Mktg., U. Macedonia, Degree in Human Resources. Jr. mgr. adminstrn. Bank S.A.R., Thessaloniki, 1981—. Author: Annual Report, 1996, Bank Capital Increase Procedures, 1996. Sgt. Engrs., 1990-91. Mem. Mktg. Inst., Soc. Bus. Adminstrn., Club of Dx'ers (pres. 1997—), Club Maths. (pres. 1997—), Club PC Users (pres. 1997—). Greek Orthodox. Avocations: personal computers, geography, Internet, mathematics.

CHARALAMBIDES, CHARALAMBOS A., shipping executive; b. Athens, Greece, Oct. 26, 1961; s. Athanassios and Olga (Roubi) C. Diploma, U. Wales, 1990. In ops. dept. Seven Seas Maritime Ltd., London, 1991-92, Square Ltd., Piraeus, Greece, 1993-95, Pronoia Ship Agts., Piraeus, 1995-98; port capt. Atlantic Corp., Piraeus, 1998—. Mem. Nautical Inst., Chartered Inst. Transport, Baltic Exch. Home: 119 Tritonos St, GR 17562 Athens Greece

CHARALAMBOUS, STEFANOS, nuclear physics educator, laboratory director; b. Pireus, Greece, May 20, 1927; m. Elefteria Ntemi, June 7, 1960; children: Avgui, Hara, Melissa. B, U. Athens, 1954, PhD, 1960. Asst. U. Athens, 1954-59; fellow CERN, Geneva, 1959-62, rschr., 1962-71; asst. prof.

U. Thessaloniki, Greece, 1967-74, prof., 1974—, dir. nuclear physics lab., 1974—. Author 7 books on physics; contbr. more than 160 rsch. articles to physics jours. Home: Roussidou 12, GR 55131 Thessaloniki Greece Office: Aristotle U of Thessaloniki, Univ Campus, GR 54006 Thessaloniki GR 54006, Greece

CHARAMIS, SPILIOS JOHN, broadcast executive; b. Athens, Greece, Jan. 6, 1937; s. John and Angela (Politis) C.; m. Lilia Pesnikides, July 8, 1958 (div. Jan. 1981); children: John, Spyros, Alexis; m. Barbara Van Der Zee, Nov. 21, 1982. Degree in law studies, Athens U., 1957. Mng. dir. Vioplastic S.A., Athens, 1962-64, Pagosmios Asphalistiki S.A., Athens, 1975-77; gen. mgr. Mole-Richardson (Hellas) Ltd., Athens, 1964-74; dir. of TV ERT nat. TV and radio network, Athens, 1978-81; vice chmn. Hellas - Radio Ltd., London, 1982-89; dep. dir. gen. Antenna TV S.A., Athens, 1989-94, dir. gen., 1994—; dir. gen. Antenna TV Cyprus Ltd., Nicosia, 1992—; dep. dir. gen. ERT, 1980-81; fgn. corr. Politika Themata, London, 1982-89. Producer video Keep Athens Clean, 1979. Mem. State Orgn. for Audiovisual Matters, Athens, 1974-78. Lt. Greek Navy, 1958-61. Recipient Medal of the Flag, State of Yugoslavia, 1961, Medal of Liechtenstein, 1964. Mem. Royal TV Soc., Soc. Friends of P. Kanellopoulos, Fgn. Press Assn., Liberal Club, Yachting Club of Greece, Naval Mus. of Greece. Greek Orthodox. Avocations: sailing, hunting, fishing. Home: Dikearhou 68 Mets, 116 36 Athens Greece Office: Antenna TV SA, 10-12 Kifissias Ave, 151 25 Maroussi Athens Greece

CHARI, SREEMATHI, endocrinologist, researcher; b. Mysore, Karnataka, India, Sept. 25, 1945; arrived in Germany, 1976; parents: H. K. Gopalakishnan and Jayalakshmi (Sosale) C. BSc, U. Mysore, India, 1963; MSc, U. Bangalore, India, 1965; PhD, U. Delhi, India, 1972. Rsch. asst. U. Delhi dept zoology, 1967-73; postdoctoral fellow Radioimmunoassay Lab. Univ. Liége, Belgium, 1973-75; rsch. officer Univ. Marburg (Germany) Women's Hosp., 1976—; vis. scientist U. So. Calif. Women's Hosp., L.A., 1987-88. Contbr. articles to profl. jours. Recipient Schöller-Junkmann prize, Germany, 1977. Mem. Soc. for Study of Fertility, German Endocrine Soc. Office: Univ Frauenklinik, Pilgrimstein 3, 35037 Marburg Hessen, Germany

CHARITY, JULIA ANNE, research scientist; b. Christchurch, N.Z., Aug. 17, 1970; d. Laurence Michael and Lois Ivy (Walker) Connelly; m. Iain Charity, Dec. 31, 1994. BSc with honors, U. Canterbury, Christchurch, N.Z., 1992; PhD, Australian Nat. U., Canberra, 1996. Vacation scholar Australian Nat. U., Canberra, 1991-92; tech. asst. Crop and Food Rsch., Christchurch, 1992-93; rsch. scientist Forest Rsch., Rotorua, 1997-99, project leader, 1999—; Editl. reviewer Forest Rsch., 1997—. Announcer 2XX Cmty. Radio, Canberra, 1995; student rep. mgmt. com. Coop. Rsch. Ctr. for Plant Sci., Canberra, 1994-96; v.p. Canberra Ginninderra Rotoract Club, 1993-94. Recipient Sadie Balkind Travel award N.Z. fedn. of Univ. Women, 1992, Plant Sci. Ctr. grad. award, 1995, Young Investigator award Amrad Bhaimacia Biotech, 1995. Mem. Internat. Assn. for Plant Tissue (conf. organizer 1999), N.Z. Soc. Biochemistry and Molecular Biology. Avocations: running, mountain biking, crafts, travel, socializing. Office: Forest Research, Pvt Bag 3020, Rotorua New Zealand

CHARLES (PHILIP ARTHUR GEORGE CHARLES), Prince of Wales, Earl of Chester, Duke of Cornwall and Rothesay, Baron of Renfrew, Earl of Carrick, Lord of the Isles, Great Steward of Scotland; b. Nov. 14, 1948; s. Prince Philip, Duke of Edinburgh and Queen Elizabeth II; m. Lady Diana Spencer, July 29, 1981 (div. 1996); children: William Arthur Philip Louis (Prince William of Wales), Henry Charles Albert David (Prince Henry of Wales). B.A., Trinity Coll., Cambridge U., 1970, M.A., 1975; barrister, Gray's Inn, 1974; hon. bencher, 1975; student, U. Wales, 1975. Became Duke of Cornwall and Rothesay, Earl of Carrick, Baron of Renfrew, Lord of the Isles and Gt. Steward of Scotland, 1952, created Prince of Wales and Earl of Chester, 1958, invested, 1969, created knight Order of Garter, 1958, invested, 1968; col.-in-chief Royal Regiment Wales, 1969—, Cheshire Regiment, 1977—, Air Res. Group of Air Command in Can., 1977—, Lord Strathcona's Horse Regiment, 1977—, Parachute Regiment, 1977—, Royal Australian Armoured Corps, 1977—, Royal Regiment Canada, 1977—, Royal Gurkha Rifles, 1994, Royal Winnepeg Rifles, 1977—, The Royal Pacific Islands Regiment, 1984—, Royal Can. Dragoons, 1985—, Army Air Corps, 1992—, Royal Dragoon Guards, 1992—, The Highlanders, Deputy Col. in chief, 1994; col. Welsh Guards, 1974—; rear admiral Royal Navy, 1998; maj. gen. Royal Army, 1998; air vice marshall Royal Air Force, 1998; pres. The Prince's Trust-Bro., 1996—; high steward Royal Borough Windsor and Maidenhead, 1974—; pres. Prince's Trust, 1977—, The Prince of Wale's Found. for Architecture and The Urban Environment,1992—, Prince of Wales Bus. Leaders Forum, 1990—, Royal Coll. Music, 1993; chancellor U. Wales, 1976—; pres. United World Colls., 1978-92; v.p. Nat. Trust, 1996. Author: The Old Man of Lochnagar, 1980, A Vision of Britain: A Personal View of Architecture, 1989, H.R.H. The Prince of Wales Watercolors, 1990, Highgrove: Portrait of an Estate, 1993. Patron The Queen's Trust, 1977—, Nat. Gallery, 1993—, Oxford Ctr. for Islanic Studies, 1993—, Nat. Trust Centenary Appeal, 1995—. Group capt. RAF, 1971, capt. Royal Navy, 1988. Decorated grand cross So. Cross (Brazil), The White Rose (Finland), House of Orange (The Netherlands), Order of Oak Crown (Luxembourg), Order of Ojasvi Rajanya (Nepal), Legion of Honor (France); knight Order of Elephant (Denmark); grand cordon Supreme of the Chrysanthemum (Japan); Order of Republic of Egypt; great master Order of Bath (U.K.); recipient Coronation medal, 1953, The Queen's Silver Jubilee medal, 1977, Spoleto prize, 1989, Premio Fregene, 1990, Freedom of City of Cardiff, 1969, Royal Borough of New Windsor, 1970, of City of London, 1971, of Chester, 1973, of City of Canterbury, 1978, of City of Portsmouth, 1979, of City of Lancaster, 1993, of City of Swansea, 1994; named Author of Yr., 1989, Hon. fellow Trinity Coll., Cambridge, 1988, Liveryman, Fishmongers Co., 1971, Freeman, Drapers' Co., 1971, Freeman, Shipwrights' Co., 1978, Hon. Freeman, Goldsmith's Co., Liveryman, Farmers' Co., 1980, Liveryman, Pewterers' Co., 1982, Liveryman, Fruiterers' Co., 1989, Master Mariners of Mchts., City of Edinburgh, 1979. Fellow Royal Coll. Surgeons (hon.), Royal Aero. Soc. (hon.), Inst. Mech. Engrs. (hon.); Royal fellow Australian Acad. Sci.; mem. Soc. St. George's and Descendents of Knights of the Garters (pres. 1975—), Royal Thames Yacht Club (adm. 1974—), Royal Forestry Soc., Incorporation of Gardeners of Glasgow (hon. life). Home: HRH The Prince of Wales, St James's Palace, London SW1A 1BS, England also: Highgrove House Doughton, Tetbury, Gloucestershire GL8 8TG, England*

CHARLES, BLANCHE, retired elementary education educator; b. Spartanburg, S.C., Aug. 7, 1912; d. Franklin Grady and Alice Florida (Hatchette) C. BA, Humboldt State U., 1934; adminstrv. cert., U. So. Calif., 1940. Tchr. Calexico (Calif) Unified Sch. Dist., 1958-94; libr. Calexico Pub. Libr., El Centro Pub. Libr. Elem. sch. named in her honor, 1987. Mem. NEA, ACT, Calif. Tchrs. Assn., Nat. Soc. DAR, Nat. Soc. Daus. of Confederacy, Delta Kappa Gamma. Avocations: gardening, reading. Home: 37133 Highway 94 Sp # 3 Boulevard CA 91905-9524

CHARLES, BRUCE GORDON, pharmaceutical educator; b. Nambour, Queensland, Australia, May 17, 1949; s. Gordon Robert David and Clarice May Barnet (Bieber) C.; m. Kathryn Lynne Wight, Jan. 12, 1979; children: Robert, David. B of Pharmacy, U. Queensland, Brisbane, 1970, B of Pharmacy with honors, 1971, PhD, 1976; grad. diploma in bus. adminstrn., Queensland Inst. Tech., Brisbane, 1985. Harkness fellow U. Iowa Coll. Pharmacy, Iowa City, Iowa, Australia, 1975-77; sr. scientist dept. clin. pharmacology Princess Alexandra Hosp., Brisbane, 1979-88; tutor dept. pharmacy U. Queensland, Australia, 1972-75; Nat. Health & Med. Rsch. Coun. rsch. officer Dept. of Medicine U. Queensland, 1978-79, sr. lectr. dept. pharmacy, 1988-99; assoc. prof. U. Queensland Sch. Pharmacy, 2000—; cons. to pharm. industry, including Therapeutic Goods Adminstrn., Drug Evaluation Br., Canberra, Australia, 1987—; dir. Aust Ctr. for Pediat. Pharmacokinetics, 1999—. Mem. editl. bd. Jour. Chromatography, 1999—; contbr. over 85 articles to profl. jours. Recipient Postgrad. Rsch. award Commonwealth of Australia, 1972-75; Harkness fellow Commonwealth Fund of N.Y., 1975-77. Mem. Australasian Soc. Clin. Exptl. Pharmacologists and Toxicologists, Australian Pharm. Scis. Assn., Australian Perinatal Soc., Internat. Assn. Therapeutic Drug Monitoring & Clin. Toxicology. Anglican. Avocations: reading, fishing, cricket. Home: 32 Parklane Tce, Brookfield QLD 4069, Australia Office: U Queensland, Sch Pharmacy, Brisbane 4072, Australia

CHARLES, CHERYL, non-profit and business executive; b. Seattle, Nov. 4, 1947; d. Tom E. Charles and Irene D. (Brown) Shelver; m. Robert E. Samples, Sept. 15, 1973; 1 child, Stician M. BA, U. Ariz., 1969; MA, Ariz. State U., 1971; PhD, U. Wash., 1982. Lic. secondary edn. Tchr. Phoenix Union H.S., 1969-71; staff assoc. Social Sci. Edn. Consortium, Boulder, Colo., 1971-72; social studies dept. chmn. Trevor Browne H.S., Phoenix, 1972-73; asst. dir. Essentia: Environ. Studies for Urban Youth, Olympia, Wash., 1973-75; nat. dir. Project Learning Tree, Tiburon, Calif. & Boulder, Colo., 1976-84; exec. dir. Project Wild, Boulder, 1981-93; pres. Sol y Sombra Found., Santa Fe, N.Mex., 1991—; exec. dir. Ctr. for Study of Cmty., Santa Fe, 1993—; COO The Santa Fe Group, 1996—; owner Hawksong Assocs.; prin. investigator MacArthur Found., Chgo., 1993-94, Bradley Found., Milw., 1995-99, Ednl. Found. Am., Westport, Conn., 1995-2000; project dir. McCune Found., Santa Fe, N.Mex., 1995-97; sr. dir. Banking Industry Tech. Secretariat, 1997—. Co-author: The Whole School Book, 1977; editor: Project Wild Elementary and Secondary Guide, 1983-92, Project Wild Aquatic Guide, 1987-92; co-editor, designer Windstar Jour., 1987-90. Mem. nat. adv. com. U. Mich. Coll. Engring., East Lansing, Mich., 1990-93; nat. judge Seiko Youth Challenge, 1994; bd. advisors Aspen (Colo.) Global Change Inst., 1990—; bd. trustees Hispanic Culture Found., Albuquerque, 1995-98; pres. bd. trustees Windstar Land Conservancy, 1996—; chair bd. trustees Windstar Found., 1995—. Recipient Leadership award U.S. Forest Svc., internat. region, 1985, L.B. Sharp award excellence in outdoor/environ. edn., 1993, Gold medal Pres. Environ. and Conservation Challenge award, Washington, 1991; named Profl. of Yr. Western Assn. Fish/Wildlife Agys., 1991. Mem. N.Am. Assn. Environ. Edn., Nat. Coun. Social Studies, N.Mex. First Town Hall, No. N.Mex. Grant Makers. Avocations: writing, horseback riding, dancing, cooking, reading. Office: The Santa Fe Group 3 N Chamisa Dr Ste 2 Santa Fe NM 87505-9463

CHARLES, CHRISTIAN, software professional; b. Paris, June 26, 1952; s. René and Claire C.; m. Christine Dosson, Dec. 6, 1986. M Maths., U. Paris Dauphine, 1974, M Econs., 1976, PhD Math., 1977. Math. asst. U. Paris Dauphine, 1975-78; computer engr. Tymshare, Paris, 1978-80; computer engr. STSC France, Paris, 1981, mgr., 1982-84; creator, organizer Uniware, Paris, 1984—; Author: (statis. software) Unistat, 1985. With French mil., 1978. Avocation: stamp collections. Home: 140 Bd Bineau, Neuilly 92200, France Office: Uniwin Tour Neptune, Sigma-Plus, 29 Rue Lauriston, 92086 Paris 75116, France

CHARLES, JEAN-FRANÇOIS MIGUEL, entomologist; b. Paris, France, Mar. 6, 1955; s. Jean and Micheline (Candoret) C.; m. Michele F. Jacquet, Sept. 10, 1988; children: Elaine, Marie-Lou. MSc in Animal Biology, U. Paris 6, 1978, PhD of Entomology, 1981, DSc of Entomology, 1987. Rsch. asst. Inst. Pasteur, Paris, 1979-85, rsch. scientist, 1985—; vis. scientist U. Calif., Riverside, 1988-89. Mem. AAAS, Am. Soc. Microbiology, Soc. Invertebrate Pathology. Avocations: music, bird watching, photography. Home: 6 Rue Jolly, 94160 Saint-Mande France Office: Inst Pasteur Bacteries Entomopathogenes, 25 Rue du Docteur Roux, 75724 Paris France

CHARLES, JOEL, forensic audio and video tape analyst, voice identification consultant; b. Phila., Jan. 12, 1914; s. Samuel William and Minnie (Fink) Blumenstein; m. Lillian DuBowe, May 31, 1938 (div. 1964); children: Mark Blumenstein, Richard Blumenstein; m. Nancy Sher, Oct. 24, 1988. BSChemE, Drexel U., 1938. Pres. The Charles Agy., Phila., 1938-42, 45-64; physicist Naval Air Exptl. Station, Phila., 1942-45; pres. The Dento-Med. Tapes, Upper Darby, Pa., 1957-73, Associated TV Prodns., Inc., Phila., 1948-52, Computerized Electronic Edn., Upper Darby, Pa., 1969-73; dir. continuing edn., media instructional methodology Pa. Coll. of Podiatric Medicine, Phila., 1973-77; pvt. practice Plantation, Fla., 1977-96, Coral Springs, Fla., 1996—; expert witness on tape recordings; lectr. Tex. Criminal Def. Lawyers Inst., La. Pub. Def. Criminal Lit. Seminar, Broward Criminal Def. Lawyers Assn., Dade Criminal Def. Lawyers Assn., Phoenix Pub. Defenders, Dade Fed. Pub. Defenders, Fla. Investigators Assn. Contbr. articles to profl. jours. Mem. NACDL (assoc.), Nat. Forensic Ctr., Internat. Assn. for Forensic Phonetics, Am. Fedn. Musicians, Am. Dialect Soc., Audio Engring. Soc. (chmn. forensic tape com.). Achievements include development of early rapid form of computerized voice identification, designed first high-speed portable audio cassette duplicator. Home and Office: St Johns Woods 1109 NW 97th Dr Coral Springs FL 33071-5961

CHARLES, KWAME RICHARD, management consultant, educator; b. Port of Spain, Trinidad and Tobago, Nov. 7, 1952; s. John Alston and Sylvia Elizabeth (Wallace) C.; m. Marcelline Genevieve Mendez, Nov. 19, 1981; 1 child, Machel. BA, U. Toronto, Can., 1976; MS, Howard U., 1978, PhD, 1980. Job analyst Govt. Trinidad & Tobago, 1980-81; mgmt. cons. Trinidad & Tobago Mgmt. Devel. Ctr., 1981-81; human resource mgr. Nat. Gas Co. Trinidad & Tobago, Ltd., 1982-88; lectr. U. West Indies, Bahamas, 1988-92, Trinidad & Tobago, 1992-96; cons. Quality Cons., Trinidad & Tobago, 1996—; gov. Nat. Inst. Higher Edn., Trinidad & Tobago, 1994-96. Co-editor: Tourism Education and Human Resource Development for the Decade of the '90s, 1991, Competing in the Markets of the Americas, 1995. Founding mem. Caribbean Ctr. for Quality and People Devel., Bahamas 1992—; mem. Caribbean Hospitality Tng. Adv. Coun., Puerto Rico, 1994—, Nat. Quality Coun. of Trinidad & Tobago, 1997-98; bd. dirs. Caribbean Ctr. for Excellence, Puerto Rico, 1997—. Avocations: music, weight tng. Fax: (868) 628-2752; e-mail: kcharles@wow.net. Home: 6A Fondes Amandes Rd, Saint Anns Trinidad & Tobago Office: Quality Cons, 66A Picton St, Newtown Port of Spain Trinidad & Tobago

CHARLES, LYN ELLEN, marketing executive, commercial artist, photograph; b. Little Falls, N.Y., Sept. 1, 1951; d. Searle and Barbara Charles. BA, U. Conn., 1973; grad., Art Instrn. Schs. Inc., 1976. Rsch. asst. Conn. State U., New Britain, 1974; comml. artist Conn. C.C., Hartford, 1978; market rschr. Karen Assocs., Simsbury, Conn., 1981; market rsch. operator Consumer Surveys Telemarketing, Inc., Dedham, Mass., 1981-87; receptionist, file clk. Jobpro Temp. Svcs., 1987-88; field rep. Actnow, Westhampton Beach, N.Y., 1987-88; with Inventory Control Co., South Hackensack, N.J., 1988-98, Fred Meyer Vanguard Mktg. Svcs., Portland, Oreg., 1997, Regional Inventory Specialists, 1997; artist, vol. Farmington Valley Arts, Avon, Conn., 1982-84; freelance artist West Hartford Art League, 1978-81, Northwestern Conn. Art Assn., 1979-81, Wadsworth Atheneum, 1980-82. Vol. med. receptionist Hosp. and Clin. Info. Desk, U. Conn. Health Ctr., 1975, 76-78, Office Cultural Affairs, Pub. Survey to Select Artist for Art Work at Coliseum, Hartford Civic Ctr., 1979; mem. Childreach Sponsorship of PLAN Internat. USA, 1992—, Corvallis Arts Ctr., 1995—; vol. Cmty. Outreach, Inc., 1999. Recipient Alice Collins Dunham prize, 69th Ann. Exhbn. of Conn. Acad. Fine Arts, 1980; named Duchess of Bedfordshire, Eng., Cromwell Estate and Covent Garden, 1990. Mem. Christian Ch. Avocations: hiking, swimming, ballet, bicycling, horseback riding.

CHARLES, MBALA LHEMBA, pediatrician, researcher; b. Luzumu, The Congo, June 3, 1960; arrived in South Africa, 1997; s. Lhemba Mazona Pierre and Nsona Nsamu Pauline; m. Dimasi Kussa Clarisse, Dec. 3, 1988; children: Dave Lhemba, Blonde Mbala, Nsona Mbala. Diploma in biomed. sci., U. Kinshasa, Congo, 1983, MD, 1986, spl. cert. pediat., 1990, specialist pediatrician, 1993. Gen. med. practitioner Hosp. Ime Kimpese, Congo, 1986-88, dir. pediats., 1993—; pediat. resident Univ. Hosp. Kinshasa, 1988-93; pediatrician specialist cons. Projet Nkebolo Edinburgh U. & Ime Kimpese Hosp., 1993-96; tchr. pediats. Med. Sch. Kimpese, 1993—; coord. clin. practice med. students & young doctors U. Kinshasa, U. Bas Congo, Ime Kimpese Hosp., 1993—; dir. planning com. Inst. Ime Kimpese, 1994-97, dir. sci/ med. meetings, 1994—; sci. dir. "medicine a" rev. Med. Svc. Bas-Congo, 1996—. Author: Medicine and Therapeutics in Tropical Countries, 1998; editor Medecine A, 1996, 97, 98; contbr. articles to profl. jours. Pres. Choral Chothec Christian Ch. Kimpese, 1996—, support com., 1996—; with Christian People Protection Ecology Christian Ch. Bas-Congo, 1997. Mem. U. Pediatricians Republic Dem. Congo, Union Pediatricians African Countries, Order Physicians. Avocations: music, football, theatre, reading. Office: Ime Kimpese Hosp, Maison 0032 PO Box 68, Kimpese Republic of Congo

CHARLES, ROBERT BRUCE, lawyer; b. Portsmouth, Va., Aug. 23, 1960; s. Roland Wilbur Charles Jr. and Doris Anne (Hassell) Barbineau; m. Marina Timasheff, Oct. 16, 1988; 1 child, Nicholas Westcote. AB, Dartmouth Coll., 1982; MA, Oxford U., 1984; JD, Columbia U., 1987. Bar: N.Y. 1989, Conn. 1989, Maine 1990. Law clk. to judge U.S. Ct. Appeals (9th cir.), Seattle, 1987-88; assoc. Kramer, Levin, Nessen, Kamin & Frankel, N.Y.C., 1988-91; assoc. Weil, Gotshal & Manges, N.Y.C., 1991-92, Washington, 1993-95; dep. assoc. dir. office of policy devel The White House, Washington, 1992-93; chief staff, chief counsel nat. security, internat. affairs and criminal justice subcommittee U.S. Ho. of Reps., Washington, 1995-99; prof. govt. and cyberlaw Harvard U. Extension Sch., 1998-99; pres. Direct Impact, L.L.C., 1999—; summer assoc. The White House, Washington, 1982-84, Supreme Ct. India, 1985. Contbr. articles to profl. jours., chpts. to books. Active Coun. on Fgn. Rels. Theodore Roosevelt Assn. Officer USNR, 1998—. Keasbey scholar, Phila. 1982, Tony Patino fellow Columbia U., 1984. Republican. Avocations: distance running, cycling, hiking, writing.

CHARLES, RON, archaeologist, researcher; b. Kilgore, Tex., Aug. 9, 1949; s. Kenneth F. and Lorene M. (Graham) C.; m. Paula J. Crandall, Sept. 25, 1971; children: Ronnie, Bradley. BS, U. Southwest La., Lafayette, 1970; BA, Berea Coll., Springfield, Mo., 1976; MA, Fla. Internat., Miami, 1978; PhD, Fla. Internat., 1980, ThD, 1982. Cert. secondary tchr. La., Tex. Self-employed contract rsch. and archaeology, 1971-78; project dir. Owens-Corning-Fiberglass, Toledo, 1979-85; sr. pastor North Ga. Assembly, Gainesville, 1985-93; pres./archeol. chief officer Found. for Internat. Exploration, Gainesville, 1990-97; rschr. Christian Fin. Concepts, Gainesville, 1996—; mem. adv. bd. Pacific U., Sydney, Australia, 1990-97; conductor contract archeol. tours. Piedmont Coll., Demorst, Ga., 1996—; co-founder Albanian/Am. Archeol. Soc., Tirana, Albania, 1991—. Author: (books) Milk to Meat, 1982, Street Walkin, 1985, Worlds of Noah, 1991, Search, 1996. Active internat. humanitarian relief Found. for Internat. Exploration & Rsch.. Recipient Nat. Merit scholarship 1967, archeol. rsch. grants, 1987-97. Rhodes scholar designate 1968. Mem. Am. Tchrs. Assn., Archeol. Inst. Am., Phi Beta Kappa. Republican. Assembly of God. Avocations: archeol. rsch., writing, internat. archeol. tours, mountain climbing, hist. tours. E-mail: rpalban@msn.com. Home: 4344 Price Rd Gainesville GA 30506-5370

CHARLES, RUTH PATRICIA, nutritionist; b. Dublin, Ireland, Apr. 17, 1970; d. Patrick and Bernadette (Quigley) McMahon; m. Ronald Jude Charles, July 15, 1995; children: Jonathan, Martha. BSc hons, U. Dublin, 1992; diploma in human nutrition hons, City of Dublin Inst. Tech., 1992. Basic grade dietitian Beaumont Hosp., Dublin, 1993-94; dep. prin. dietitian Federated Dublin Hosps., 1994-98; paediatric dietitian Our Ladys Hosp. for Sick Children, Dublin, 1998—; rsch. dietitian Dept. Surgery Beaumont Hosp., Dublin, 1994, Age Related Healthcare Meath Hosp., Dublin, 1995-96. Contbr. articles to profl. jours. Mem. Irish Nutrician and Dietetic Inst. Avocations: horseriding, swimming, keeping fit, reading, travel. Office: Our Ladys Hosp Sick Chldrn, Dept Nutrition & Dietetics, Crumlin Dublin 12, Ireland

CHARLES, WALTER, actor; b. East Stroudsburg, Pa., Apr. 4, 1945; s. Theodore Edmund and Catherine Alexandra (Carstensen) Jacobsen. MusB, Boston U., 1968. Appeared in Broadway shows La Cage Aux Folles, Aspects of Love, Me & My Girl, Cats, Sweeney Todd, Grease, Knickerbocker Holiday, Call Me Madam, A Christmas Carol, Sunset Boulevard (Can. co.), others; off Broadway, Wit; films: A Fine Mess, Weeds, Fletch Lives, Prancer, TV programs Cagney & Lacey, Kate & Allie, Law & Order, 1981 Tony Awards, PBS Great Performances, 1983 Grammy awards, All My Children, others, also various nat. tours, regional and stock theatrical prodns., commls. and voice-overs. Recipient Best Actor in Musical award Bay Area Drama Critics, 1984. Fax: (914) 482-3204.

CHARLEY, ROBERT CLIVE, agricultural products company executive; b. Coventry, Eng., Feb. 27, 1955; s. Cyril and Violet (Richardson) C.; m. Linda Dorothy Briggs, July 22, 1978; children: Suzanne Elizabeth, Lauren Amelia. BScTech. with honours, U. Wales, Cardiff, 1978; PhD, U. Strathclyde, Glasgow, Scotland, 1981. Chartered biologist. Rsch. scientist Weston Rsch. Ctr., Toronto, Ont., Can., 1981-82, mgr. pilot plant, 1982-84; rsch. scientist Allelix, Mississauga, Ont., Can., 1984-86; prodn. mgr. Agrl. Genetics Co., Cambridge, Eng., 1986-89; various positions Biotal Ltd., Cardiff, 1986-96, mng. dir., 1996-98; pres. Biotal Can. Ltd., 1999—. Mem. Inst. Biology, Soc. for Gen. Microbiology, Farmer's Club. Avocations: his family, travel. Home: 50 Harmony Dr, Niagara on the Lake, ON Canada LO5 1JO Office: PO Box 8000-272, Niagara on the Lake, ON Canada L0S 1J0

CHARLIER, ETIENNE BERNARD, telecommunication equipment executive; b. Koln, Germany, July 2, 1964; s. Jose and Jacqueline (Bastogne) C. Ingenieur civil electricien, UCL, Louvain, Belgium, 1988, B in phil., 1988; MS in mgmt., MIT Sloan, 1993. Devel. engr. Alcatel, Antwerp, Belgium, 1988-91; strategic project leader Alcatel, Antwerp, 1993-95; dep. regional dir. access systems divsn. Alcatel, Shanghai, Peoples Republic China, 1995-99, regional dir. carrier data divsn., 1999—. V.p. Conf. Olivaint De Belgique, Brussels, 1987-88. With Belgium Artillery, 1990. Recipient Belgian Am. Ednl. Foun. fellow, 1992-93. Avocations: music, history, jogging, literature, finance. Home: 5 Ave General Cambronne, B1380 Lasne Belgium Office: Alcatel China Ltd, 500 Zhang Yang Rd, Shanghai Pudong 200122, Peoples Republic of China

CHARLIER, JEAN PIERRE, management consultant; b. Warmeriville, Marne, France, Apr. 27, 1937; s. Roger Jean and Marcelle (Camus) C.; m. Heide Marie Meyer, June 4, 1966; children: Nina, Bruno. Engr. Bull, Paris, 1960-63, London, 1963-65; tech. mgr. Bull, Cologne, Fed. Republic Germany, 1965-67; gen. mgr. ops. Europe: Wang Labs., Brussels, 1967-73; mng. dir. C&M Trading, Brussels, 1973-77, Outirop Fasteners, Kembs, France, 1977-79; pres. Inter Mutuelles Assistance, Niort, France, 1980-82; mng. ptnr. Internat. Bus. Cons., Niort, 1983—, Internat. Mgmt. and Bus., Niort, 1986—. Home: 1 Rue Andre Gide, 79000 Niort France Office: Internat Mgmt and Bus, 1 Rue Andre Gide, 79000 Niort France

CHARLSON, DAVID HARVEY, executive search company professional; b. Pitts., May 26, 1947; s. Raymond Milton and Helen Joan (Wesley) C.; m. Michal Brooke Riley, Aug. 22, 1969; 1 child, Adam David. BS, U. Ariz., 1969. Personnel dir. internat. div. Bank of Am., San Francisco, 1969-73; mgr. employment Gen. Foods Corp., White Plains, N.Y., 1973-74; staff v.p. Staub-Warmbold Assocs., San Francisco, 1974-76; mng. dir., sr. ptnr. Korn-Ferry Internat., Chgo., 1976-84; exec. v.p., mng. dir. Richards Cons., Chgo., 1984-89; pres., CEO Chestnut Hill Internat., Chgo., 1989-98; mng. dir. Midwest Ops. Foster Ptnrs., Chgo., 1998—; bd. dirs. Highland Pk. Hosp., Dental Network Am., I.V.T. Corp., Biogen, WEA. Contbr. articles to profl. publs. Mem. Oak Park (Ill.) Sch. Dist. Bd. Edn., 1978-80; bd. dirs. U. Chgo. Grad. Sch. Bus., 1982-84, mem. bd. advisors; bd. dirs. Better Boys Found., Chgo., 1982-84; treas. Chgo. Dist. Tennis Assn., 1984-86; chmn. Ill. Citizens for Perot, 1992; sr. advisor Clinton-Gore Presdl. Campaign, 1992, Ill. Dem. Com., 1992—; mem. adv. bd. Little City Found.; mem., advisor to White House pers. Dem. Nat. Com. Recipient NFL Players Assn. award Better Boys Found., 1984; named One of Am.'s Top 100 Exec. Recruiters, Harper & Row Publs., One of 150 Top Exec. Recruiters in Am., 1992, One of 200 Top Exec. Recruiters in N.Am., 1994. Mem. Internat. Motor Sports Assn., Pharm. Mfrs. Assn., Assn. Exec. Recruitment Cos., Univ. Club Chgo., Pres.' Club U. Ariz., Sports Car Club Am., Execs. Club Chgo. Avocations: automobile racing, golf, tennis, Tae Kwon Do. Home: 3210 N Seminary Ave # 2 Chicago IL 60657-3311 Office: Foster Ptnrs 363 E Wacker Dr Chicago IL 60601-5278

CHARLTON, BRUCE GRAHAM, psychology educator, physician; b. Torquay, Devon, England, Feb. 13, 1959; s. Graham Charlton and Stella Dobson; m. Gillian Patricia Rye. MA, U. Durham, 1989; MB BS with honors, U. Newcastle upon Tyne, 1982, MD, 1988. Rsch. fellow MRC Neuroendocrinology Unit, 1984-87; resident don U. Coll., Durham, 1987-88; sr. demonstrator physiology Newcastle U., 1988-89, lectr. epidemiology, 1993-96, lectr psychology, 1996—; lectr. anatomy Glasgow U., 1989-93; vis. prof. UEL Ctr. at St. Bartholomew's Hosp., London, 1999—; vis. disting. millenial fellow Kings. Coll. London, 2000—. Co-author: The Making of a Doctor, 1992; author: Psychiatry and the Human Condition, 2000; author (radio drama) Solitude, Exile and Ecstasy, 1991. Mem. Literary and Philos. Soc. of Newcastle upon Tyne. Office: Dept Psychology Ridley Bldg, U Newcastle upon Tyne, Newcastle upon Tyne NE1 7RU, England

CHARLTON, SHIRLEY MARIE, educational consultant; b. Nashville, Nov. 20, 1934; d. Ottis Ruby and Irene Lenoir (Cabler) C.; children: David Matthew Christian Sironen, Charlton Gwynn Cabler Sironen. BS, George Peabody Coll. Tchrs., 1954; MA in Ednl. Adminstrn. and Supervision, U. Tenn., Chattanooga, 1970. Cert. supr., Tenn. Classroom tchr. Albany (Ga.) Pub. Schs., 1954-55, 56-57, Orlando (Fla.) Pub. Schs., 1960-61, Grand Forks (N.D.) Pub. Schs., 1962-65; TV and resource tchr. Chattanooga Publ Schs., 1965-67, supr., 1967-97; cons., 1997-99. Mem. NEA, Tenn. Edn. Assn., Chattanooga Edn. Assn. (charter mem. negotiating team 1979-81), Alpha Delta Kappa (v.p. 1981-83). Episcopalian. Avocations: history, genealogy, acting, art, music.

CHARMANDARIS, VASSILIS, astronomer; b. Serres, Greece, Aug. 14, 1967. BSc in Physics, U. Thessaloniki, Greece, 1989; PhD in Astrophysics, Iowa State U., 1995. Postdoctoral rschr. Centre d'Etudes de Saclay, Paris, 1996-97; postdoctoral fellow Observatoire de Paris, 1997-99; staff astronomer Cornell U., Ithaca, N.Y., 1999—. Contbr. articles to profl. jours. Marie Curie fellow European Union, 1996. Mem. Am. Astron. Soc., European Astron. Soc., Hellenic Astron. Soc. E-mail: vassilis@astro.cornell.edu. Fax: 607-255-5875. Office: Cornell Univ 106 Space Scis Bldg Ithaca NY 14853

CHARMES, JEAN-PIERRE, physician, researcher; b. Rodez, Aveyron, France, Apr. 11, 1944; s. Roger and Louise (Berliat) C.; m. Marie-Germaine Lecussan, Aug. 23, 1969; children: Ludovic, Benedicte, Emmanuel, Guillaume. MD, Med. Sch., Limoges, France, 1971, gerontologist, 1990; nephrologist, Med. Sch., Paris, 1975. Asst. U. Hosp., Limoges, 1974, médecins des hôpitaux, 1981, chief geriatric divsn., 1990, chief geriatric dept., 1999; chargé de cours Med. Sch., Limoges, 1974—; mem. Med. Commn. Univ. Hosp., Limoges, 1982-99, v.p., 1990-99; mem. Adminstrn. Coun. Univ. Hosp., Limoges, 1987-99. Co-author: (with others) L'insuffisance rénale chronique: du diagnostic à la dialyse, 1988; contbr. articles to profl. jours. Pres. Assn. Soins Palliatifs Haute-Vienne, Limoges, 1990. Mem. European Dialysis and Transplant Assn., European Renal Assn., French Soc. Gerontology, Soc. Nephrology, Home Dialysis Assn. (gen. sec. 1977—). Avocation: horse riding. Office: Ctr Hospitalier Univ, 2 ave Martin Luther King, 87042 Limoges France

CHARMLEY, JOHN DENIS, historian; b. Birkenhead, England, Nov. 9, 1955; s. John and Doris (Halliwell) C.; m. Dorothea Bartlett, July 23, 1979 (div. 1992); children: Gervase, Gerard (twins), Kit; m. Lorraine Fegan, July 4, 1992. BA, Pembroke Coll., Oxford U., 1977; DPhil, Oxford U., 1982. From lectr. to prof. modern history U. East Anglia, Norwich, England, 1979—; Fulbright prof. Westminster Coll., Fulton, Mo., 1992-93. Author: Duff Cooper, 1986, Lord Lloyd, 1987, Chamberlain and the Lost Peace, 1989, Churchill: The End of Glory, 1993, Churchill's Grand Alliance, 1995, A History of Conservative Politics, 1996, Splendid Isloation: Britain and the Balance of Power, 1874-1914, 1999. Fellow Royal Hist. Soc.; mem. Savile Club, Norfolk Club. Avocations: history, politics, dining out. Office: U East Anglia, Norwich NR4 7TJ, England

CHARMOT, GUY DENIS, epidemiologist, retired health officer; b. Toulon, France, Sept. 10, 1914; s. Ulysse Joseph and Claire (Esmieu) C.; m. Edith Marie DuBuisson, Nov. 30, 1948; 1 child, Dominique. MD, Lyon (France) U., 1938. Col., Troupes de Marine French Army Health Svcs., 1938-66; physician Inst. Pasteur Hosp., Paris, 1966-79, Claude Bernard Hosp., Paris, 1979-94; adminstrv. cons. Inst. African Medicine and Epidemiology, Paris, 1994—; physician, French African and sub-Saharan colonies, 1945-66; former chief tropical disease medicine, Inst. Pasteur Hosp. and Claude Bernard Hosp. Contbr. chpts. to books, over 300 articles to med. jours. Decorated Croix de Guerre, 1940-45, Compagnon de la Libération, 1944, Commandeur de la Legion d'Honneur, 1965. Mem. Soc. Exotic Pathology (pres. 1982-86), Acad. Scis. d'Entre-Mer, Soc. Infectious Pathology. Avocation: alpinism. Home: 72 blvd de Reuilly, F-75012 Paris France Office: Inst Med et d'Epidemiol Afr, 46 rue Henri-Huchard, F-75018 Paris France

CHARNAYA, ELENA VLADIMIROVNA, physics educator, researcher; b. Leningrad, Russia, Oct. 24, 1947; d. Vladimir Il'ich and Marina Germanovna (Paschenko) C.; m. Sergei Petrovich Brel, Apr. 6, 1970; 1 child, Brel Vladimir. Master, St. Petersburg (Russia) State U., 1972, PhD, 1975, DSc, 1988. Asst. prof. Leningrad Electrotech. Inst., 1976-80; asst. prof. physics St. Petersburg (Russia) State U., 1980-83, sr. rschr., 1983-88, prof., head rsch. group, 1988-99, head lab., 1999—; vis. prof. Cheng Kung Nat. U., Tainan, Taiwan, 1993-94, 97, 98, U. Leipzig, Germany, 1995, 97, 98, 99, U. Copenhagen, 1995. Author: (with V.M. Mikushev) Fundamentals of Nuclear Magnetic Resonance in Solids (in Russian), 1995; contbg. author: Fundamental Physics of Ultrasound, 1988; contbr. over 110 articles to profl. jours. Avocations: travels, gardening. Home: R Zorge St 12 apt 278, 198328 St Petersburg Russia Office: Inst Physics, Petrodvorets, 198904 St Petersburg Russia

CHARNE, MICHAEL MORDECHI, entrepreneur; b. Johannesburg, Gauteng, South Africa, Sept. 2, 1947; s. Louis and Raina (Cohen) C.; m. Suzette Cheryl Flax, Mar. 15, 1987; children: Rijon, Laurelle. BCom in Acctg., Witwatersrand U., Johannesburg, 1969. Mng. dir. British Glass Co. Ltd., 1968-69, Float Glass Co. Ltd., Johannesburg, 1969-78, Grants Furniture Group, Johannesburg, 1979-96; mng. dir., chmn. Charne Group of Cos., Johannesburg, 1990—; CEO, Mathomo Group Ltd., Johannesburg, 1995—. Chmn. bd. dirs. Assocs. of Ben-Gurion U., South Africa, 1990—. Mem. Houghton Golf Club (league capt., mem. com.). Jewish. Avocations: piano, golf, music. Home: Sunray PO Box 518, 287 Marion Rd Sundown 24, Strathavon 2031, South Africa Office: Mathomo Group Ltd, PO Box 688, Johannesburg South Africa

CHARNIN, MARTIN, theatrical director, lyricist, producer; b. N.Y.C., Nov. 24, 1934; s. William and Birdie (Blakeman) C.; m. Lynn Ross, Mar. 2, 1958 (div.); 1 son, Randy; m. Genii Prior, Jan. 8, 1962 (div.); 1 dau., Sasha; m. Jade Hobson, Dec. 1985. BA, Cooper Union, 1955. Acting stage debut West Side Story, 1957; also appeared in The Girls Against the Boys, 1959; writer: lyrics and sketches Fallout Revue, 1959; lyricist: revue Pieces of Eight, 1959, Little Revue, 1960, Hot Spot (Broadway), 1963, Zenda, 1963, Mata Hari, 1967; lyricist, dir. Ballad for a Firing Squad, 1968; lyricist: Two by Two, 1970; conceived and directed: revue Nash at Nine (Broadway), 1973; dir.: revue Music! Music!, 1974; lyricist, dir., creator: Annie (Tony award for lyrics), 1977 (2 Drama Desk awards for lyrics and direction); dir. 4 nat. cos., 1978, also London prodn., 1978; dir. Bar Mitzvah Boy, London, 1978; lyricist: I Remember Mama, 1979; lyricist, dir., co-book writer The First (2 Tony nominations), 1981; lyricist: TV spl. Feathertop, 1961, Jackie Gleason Show, 1961; conceived and produced: TV spl. the Women in the Life of a Man, 1970 (2 Emmy awards); conceived, produced, directed and wrote TV spls. George M, 1970, Jack Lemmon in 'S Wonderful, 'S Marvelous, 'S Gershwin (2 Emmy awards), 1972 (Peabody award for Broadcasting), Jack Lemmon in Get Happy—The Music of Harold Arlen, 1973, Dames at Sea, 1972, Cole Porter in Paris, 1973, Annie and the Hoods, 1974, The Annie Xmas Show, 1977, C'mon Saturday, 1977; author: TV spls. The Giraffe Who Sounded Like Ol' Blue Eyes, 1976, Annie: A Theatre Memoir, 1977; dir. On the Swing Shift, A Backer's Audition, 1983; creator, writer, dir. Upstairs at the O'Neals, 1983; dir. Jokers at Goodspeed, 1986, An Evening of Neil Simon at the Public Theater, 1986; creator, writer, dir. The No-Frills Revue, 1987; dir. Cafe Crown at the Public Theater, 1988, Cafe Crown on Broadway, 1989, Laughing Matters, Off Broadway Sid Caeser and Co., Annie 2, 1990, N.Y. premiere Jules 'Feiffers Carnal Knowledge, 1991; lyrics and dir. Annie Warbucks at Goodspeed, Mata Hari, N.Y., 1996; producer N.Y. Shakespeare Festival Evenings for Joseph Papp, 1990, 91; one show Rainbow and Stars, N.Y.C.; lyrics, co-writer, dir. Winchell, 1991; lyrics, dir. Galileo, 1992, Annie Warbucks, 1993; dir. Loose Lips Revue, 1995, Can Can, rev. 1995; dir. Jeanne, Montreal, 1996. Office: care Richard Ticktin 1345 Avenue Of The Americas New York NY 10105-0302

CHARNOCK, JOHN STEWART, biologist; b. Adelaide, Australia, Dec. 29, 1930; s. Albert Edward and Winifred Marjorie (Scott) C.; m. Barbara Joan Schubert, Nov. 1, 1957; children: Cathryn, Elizabeth, Christopher Stewart. BSc, U. Adelaide, 1956, PhD, 1961, DSc, 1979. Asst. prof. Vanderbilt U., Nashville, 1962-63; sr. lect. dept. med. sci. U. Adelaide, Australia, 1964-68; prof. pharmacology U. Alberta, Can., 1968-70; prof., chmn. dept. pharmacology U. Alberta, 1970-80; chief rsch. scientist CSIRO, Australia, 1980-93; cons. in field Australia, 1993—; cons. Palm Oil Rsch. Inst. Malaysia, Kuala Lumpur, 1986-88, Nestlé Foods, Vevey, Switzerland, 1990-92; prin. cons. John Charnock & Assocs., Normanville, 1998—. Fellow Nuffield Found., 1974-75, Nat. Health & Med. Rsch. Coun. Australia, 1961-63. Mem. N.Y. acad. Sci., Am. Oil Chem. Soc. Avocations: reading, walking, swimming. Office: John Charnock & Assocs, PO Box 2060, Normanville SA 5204, Australia

CHARNY, ISRAEL WOLF, psychologist, educator; b. N.Y.C., July 18, 1931; arrived in Israel, 1973; s. Bernard and Anna (Aichenbaum) C.; m. Phyllis Ellen, Apr. 14, 1957 (div. 1981); children: Adam, Anna, Rena; m. Judy Schott, Oct. 13, 1982; children: Michelle, David, Aviv. AB, Temple U., 1952; PhD, U. Rochester, 1957. Pvt. practice psychology, Paoli, Pa., 1958-73, Jerusalem, 1973—; assoc. prof. psychology Tel Aviv U., 1973-93; exec. dir. Inst. Holocaust & Genocide, Jerusalem, 1979—; prof. psychology Hebrew U., Jerusalem, 1993—. Author: Marital Love and Hate, 1972, How Can We Commit the Unthinkable?: Genocide, the Human Cancer, 1982, Existential/Dialectical Marital Therapy: Breaking the Secret Code of Marriage, 1992; editor: Strategies Against Violence: Design for Nonviolent Change, 1978, The Book of the International Conference on the Holocaust and Genocide, 1983, Toward the Understanding and Prevention of Genocide, 1984; founder series, editor: Genocide: A Critical Bibliographical Review, 1988, Vol. 1, 1988, Vol. 2, 1991, Vol. 3, 1994, The Widening Circle of Genocide, Vol. 4, 1997; series editor: Medical and Psychological Effects of Concentration Camps on Holocaust Victims, 1997; Holding on to Humanity - The Message of Holocaust Survivors: The Shamai Davidson Papers, 1992, co-editor (with Samuel Totten and William Parsons): Genocide in the Twentieth Century: Critical Essays and Eyewitness Accounts, 1995; revised and expanded paperback: Century of Genocide: Eyewitness Accounts and Critical Views, 1997; editor-in-chief: Encylopedia of Genocide, 1999. Mem. Israel Family Therapy Assn. (pres. 1977-79), Internat. Family Therapy Assn. (pres. 1995-97), Assn. Genocide Scholars. Home: Ben Azzay 4, 93507 Jerusalem Israel Office: Inst Holocaust and Genocide, PO Box 10311, 91102 Jerusalem Israel

CHAROCOPOS, ANTHONY NICHOLAOS, philosopher, educator; b. Vrontados, Chios, Greece, Dec. 23, 1926; s. Nicholaos George and Maria Anthony (Tellis) C.; m. Katerina Constantinos Kokkinos, Aug. 27, 1961; 1 child, Nicholaos. Diploma in Ancient Greek Lit., U. Athens, Greece, 1953; MA, Columbia U., 1960; PhD, U. Athens, 1965. Prof. secondary schs. Greek Min. Edn., Chios, 1954-71; supt. high schs. Greek Min. Edn., Athens, 1971-83, prof. philosophy Arsakio Acad., 1983-89; retired, 1989. Author: Vrontados and its History, 1955, Administration of Chios Island during the Turkish Occupation (First award 1960), Linguistic studies on Erithe - Erithiani, 1960, About the Existance of Ancient Church to Kybele at Vruntados Chios, 1963, Homer and Chios Island, 1963, The Liberation struggles of Chians against Genoans and Turks, 1964, The structure of Homeric Poems, 1967, The Ideal of Education according to Hesiodos, 1980, The contribution of the Greek Philosophy during the 18th century (First award 1982), Olympic Principles and Greek Education, 1982, The Longevity According to Psuedo-Lukiano, 1984, Introduction to Philosophy—Part I: Ethics and Aesthetics, 1986, The Ancient Jonia and the Chios Spirityal Tradition, The Chois High School and the Revival of Greece, 1994, The Saint Anthinos of Chois, 1996, Adam Corvais, 250 Years After His Birth, 1998, p.A. Margaronis, A Greek Shipowner, 1998, Saint Anthimos Speeches Vol. 1, 2000; contbr. numerous articles to jours. and newspapers. With inf. Greek Army, 1949-51. Mem. Greek Philologist Assn., Greek Humanities Assn., Vroutaldus Prog. Assn. (gen. sec. 1953-55, pres. 1963-71), Vroutados Citizens Union Attica, Chian Philologist Assn., Chian Assn. Attica (bd. dirs. 1995—), Philol. Assn. Athens, Byzantine Studies Assn., Popular U. Athens. Greek Orthodox. Avocation: Byzantine music. Home: Laskaridou 105, Kallithea, 17676 Athens Greece

CHAROENRATANAKUL, SUCHAI, chest physician; b. Bangkok, Thailand, Feb. 1, 1955; s. Virat and Nongnut Charoenratanakul. BSc, Mahidol U., Bangkok, 1976, MD, 1979. Sr. house officer Freeman Hosp., Newcastle, Eng., 1980-83, Weston Gen. Hosp., Bristol, Eng., 1983-84; registrar Falkirk (Eng.) Royal Infirmary, 1984-85; cons. chest physician Siriraj Hosp., Bangkok, 1985-86; asst. prof. Mahidol U., Bangkok, 1986-87, assoc. prof., 1987-96, prof. medicine, 1987—; dir. divsn. pulmonary disease Siriraj Hosp., 1997—. Editor-in-chief thai Jour. Tuberculosis and Chest Diseases, 1992—; editl. bd. The Respirology, 1996—; editor: Textbook of Respiratory Diseases, 1995. Knight Grand Cross (1st class) of the Most Noble Order of the Crown of thailand, 1992, Knight Grand Cross of the Most Order of the Crown of Thailand, 1997. Fellow Royal Coll. Physicians of Edinburgh, Royal Coll. Physicians of London, Am. Coll. Chest Physicians; mem. Thoracic Soc. Thailand (chmn. 1993—), Anti-tuberculosis Assn. Thailand (exec. com. 1992—). Avocations: tennis, golf. Home: Mungtongthani Jangnattara, 52/499 Soi 15, Nonthaburi 11120, Thailand Office: Siriraj Hosp Dept Medicine, Divsn Respiratory Disease, Bangkok 10700, Thailand

CHARP, SYLVIA, educator, consultant; b. Phila.. PhD, U. Pa., 1978. Dir. instnl. sys. Sci. Dist. Phila., 1989—; sr. fellow U. Pa., Phila., 1997—; tchr. math. and sci. Sci. Dist. Phila.; founder Charp Assocs, Upper Darby, 1999—; cons. Bell Atlantic, IBM, N.Y. Inst. Tech., also others, 1979—; bd. dirs. Liberty Net, Phila., Tchg., Learning with Tech., Washington; cons. Charp Assocs., Upper Darby, Pa. Author: (booklets) Be a Computer Literate, 1985, Telecommunications Fundamentals, 1988; editor-in-chief Tech. Horizons in Edn. Jour., 1976—. Recipient Silver Core award Internat. Fedn. Info. Processing Socs., 1984, Pioneer award Nat. Computing Conf., 1999. Mem. Am. Soc. for Tchrs. Math., Am. Fedn. for Info. Processing Socs., Internat. Soc. for Computers in Edn. (pres.). Avocations: reading, theater, walking. E-mail: charp@seas.upenn.edu. Office: Charp Assocs 39 Maple Ave Upper Darby PA 19082-1902

CHARPAK, GEORGES, physicist, nuclear scientist; b. Dabrovica, Poland, Aug. 1, 1924; naturalized in France, 1946; s. Maurice and Anna (Szapiro) C.; m. Dominique Vidal, 1953; children: Yves, Nathalie, Serge. Student, Ecole des Mines de Paris, 1945-47, BSc in Engring., 1948; D of Physics, Coll. of France, 1954; PhD in Physics, Collège de France, 1954; hon. doctorate, U. Geneva, 1977, U. Thessalonica, Greece, 1993, Vrije Univ. Brussels, 1994, U. Coimbra, Portugal, 1994, U. Ottawa, Canada, 1995. Lic. civil mining engr. Prof. Centre Nation de la Recherche Scientifique, 1948-59, Centre Européen pour la Recherche Nucléaire, Geneva, 1959—; rschr. Cern Lab. for Particle Physics, Geneva; Joliot-Curie prof. Ecole Supérieure de Physique et Chimie de la Ville de Paris, 1984—. Contbr. articles to profl. jours. With French Army, prisoner of war, Dachau. Decorated chevalier Legion of Honor, Mil. Cross 39-45, Croix de Guerre (France); recipient Ricard prize European Physics Soc., 1980, High Energy and Particle Physics prize, 1989, Nobel prize for physics, 1992. Mem. NAS (fgn. assoc.), French Acad. Scis. (Commissariat prize of Atomic Energy 1984), Austrian Acad. Scis. (hon.), Russian Acad. Scis. (fgn.), Lisboa Acad. Scis. (corr.). Achievements include invention of multiwire proportional chambers, drift chambers, diverse types of flash chambers without photography; development of particle detectors in high energy physics, installations for biological research using Beta-ray imagery; research in nuclear structure by reactions. Home: 2 rue de Poissy, 75005 Paris France Office: CERN Lab for Particle Physics, CH 1211 Geneva Switzerland

CHARPENTIER, JEAN-CLAUDE, engineering educator; b. Paris, Jan. 11, 1939; s. Gaston Emile and Genevieve (Deville) C.; m. Claude Mengin, Nov. 18, 1972; children: Caroline, Stephanie, Charlotte, Emilie. Engr., IDN, Lille, France, 1964; D in Chem. Engring., ENSIC, Nancy, France, 1968. Stagiaire de recherche Ctr. Nat. de la Recherche Scientifique, Nancy, 1964-65; attache de recherche CNRS, Nancy, 1965-70, charge de recherche, 1970-74, maitre de recherche, 1974-81, dir. de recherche, 1981-85; dir. scientifique dept. engring. scis. CNRS, Paris, 1985-91; cons. Elf Atochem, Lacq, France, 1975-85, Exxon, Florham Park, N.J., 1980-85; dir. Ctr. de Perfectionnement des Industries Chimiques, Nancy, 1985-94; del. sci. region Lorraine, CNRS, Nancy, 1979-85. Editor: Entropie Jour., 1979—, Recents Progres en Genie des Procedes, 1995; assoc. editor: Techniques de L'Ingenieur, 1982—, Chemical Engineering Science, 1992—; contbr. articles to profl. jours. Dep. dir. Lab. des Scis. de Genie Crmique, CNRS, Nancy, 1980-85; dir. Ecole Nat. Superieure des Industries Chimiques, Nancy, 1983-85; scientific dir. Engring. Sci. Dept. Ctr. Nat. de la Recherche Scientifique, CNRS, Paris, 1985-91; dir. Ecole Superieure de Chimie Industrielle de Lyon, 1992—, Ecole Superieure de Chimie Physique Electronique de Lyon, 1994—. Decorated Chevalier Dans Ordre Nat. du Merite, Rep. France, Paris, 1989, Chevalier Dans, Paris, 1992, Order Nat. Legion of Honor., Paris, 1992, Chevalier Dans Ordre du Merite Agricole, Paris, 2000. Fellow Am. Inst. Chem. Engrs.; mem. Acad. Europeenne, N.Y. Acad. Sci., sci. pres. Soc. Francaise de Genie des Procéoles. Avocations: angling, music/piano. Office: Ecole Superieure Chimie Physique Electronique Lyon, bd 11 Novembre 1918, Villeurbanne Cedex, France

CHARRIER, JACQUES ROBERT, materials educator; b. Niort, France, May 2, 1939; s. Jean Leon and Jeanne (Derre) C.; m. Claudine Marie Squires, Jan. 21, 1961; children: Sylvie, Christine, Philippe. Licence scis., U. Poitiers, 1962, doctorat 3 cycle, 1964, doctorat d'etat, 1978. Adviser U. Poitiers, France, 1961-64; rschr., prof. U. Poitiers, 1970—; rschr. CNRS, Poitiers, 1964-70; study-directorship IUT/GMP, Poitiers, 1971-73; survey lab. dir. GMP/U. Poitiers, 1975; rsch. dir. LMPM/ENSMA, Chasseneuil, France, 1980. Contbr. articles to profl. jours. including Nondest. Test Eval., Sci. Rev. Metal. Mem. FCPE-CES Jardin des Plantes, 1968, SILC, 1970; v.p. SCAS-IUT, 1994. Recipient Medal of Jeunesse et Sport, Sport Ministery, 1970. Mem. N.V. Sci. Acad., COFREND, GT60fSF2M. Office: ENSMA-LMPM, 1 rue Clement Ader, BP40109 Futuroscope Cedex, France

CHARRIER, MICHAEL EDWARD, investment banker; b. Columbia, S.C., July 6, 1945; s. Raymond Joseph and Anne Mary (Toth) C.; m. Elizabeth Andrea Alexandra Thyssen, June 17, 1967. Grad., Anson Acad., 1963; BA, Columbia U., 1967, MA, 1968; postgrad., Harvard U., 1977, Yale U., 1988. Cert. national croquet referee; cert. croquet instr. II. With strategic planning and devel. TWA, N.Y.C., 1970-73; dir. devel. City Fed. Savs. Bank, Elizabeth, N.J., 1974-76; fin. cons. Pan Am., N.Y.C., 1976; CFO Jet Aviation Internat., N.Y.C., 1976, pres., 1977—; also bd. dirs.; pres. Charrier, Girrard and Townsand, 1977; CEO Hardwick, Wells & Winthrop, N.Y.C., 1978-84; also bd. dirs.; sr. ptnr. Ardsley, Milbank & Co., Inc., N.Y.C., 1985—; also bd. dirs.; pres. Hamilton Sci. Corp., Greenwich, Conn., N.Y.C., 1986-95; also bd. dirs.; pres. Hamilton Chem. Corp., N.Y.C., 1988-95, also bd. dirs.; mem. exec. com. Hamilton Chem. Internat., 1990—; bd. dirs. Hamilton Chem. Ltd., London, 1990-95; sci. instr. Manhattan Country Day Sch.; cons. Columbia U., N.Y.C., 1985; bd. dirs. CIL, Palm Beach, Fla.; pres. Soundcrest Vinyards, N.Y.; CEO, bd. dirs. B&M Book corp., N.Y.C.; mem. Archtl. Rev. Bd., Southampton, N.Y. Pub. Yale Croquet Manual, USCA Collegiate Manual, 1991, Collegiate Croquet Coaching Manual, 1992; contbr. articles to mags. Dir. Rep. Speakers Bur., N.Y.C., 1986; strategist Reagan-Bush campaign, N.Y.C., 1984; mem. adv. bd. Def. Fire Protection Assn., 1987—; advisor Urban Design and City Planning, City of N.Y., 1973—; head coach Yale Croquet Team, 1988—, U.S. Naval Acad. Croquet Team, 1990, Nat. Collegiate Croquet Championship Team, Yale U., 1990, 91, World Collegiate Croquet Championship Team, Yale U., 1991; sports commr. for croquet U.S. Spl. Olympics, 1993—. With U.S. Army, 1968-70, ETO. Recipient Proclamation City of N.Y., 1978, Citation for Bus. Devel. City of N.Y., 1978, Medal of Merit Presdl. Task Force, Washington, 1983; named Collegiate Croquet Coach of Yr., USCA ,1991, Croquet Comm. Spl. Olympics, 1993. Mem. AIAA, AAAS, ASTM, Naval Inst., Navy League, N.Y. Acad. Scis., Am. Acad. Sci. and Tech. (sci. judge 1987—), Soc. for Advancement of Material and Process Engring., Global Econ. Action Com., Am. Chem. Soc., Def. Mfrs. and Suppliers Assn. Am., Nat. Fire Protection Assn., U.S. Croquet Assn. (Palm Beach, Fla., chmn. collegiate divsn., mgmt. com. 1993), Def. Fire Protection Assn., N.Y. Archtl. League, N.Y. Croquet Club (bd. dirs. 1989, chmn. lawn com. 1990—, 1st v.p. 1993-95, pres. 1998), Yale Club of N.Y.C., N.Y. Stock Exch. Club, New Eng. Soc., Columbia U. Faculty Club, LeClub, Ivy League Soc. Club, West Side Tennis Club, Forrest Hills, N.Y., Greenwich Polo Club, Grad. Club. Home: PO Box 746 New York NY 10163-0746 also: 122 Lynn Ave Southampton NY 11969

CHARRON, JOSEPH L., bishop; b. Redfield, SD, Dec. 30, 1939. ordained priest June 3, 1967. Asst. Theology prof. St. John's U., Collegeville, MN, 1970-76; asst. gen. sec. U.S. Catholic Conf., 1976-79; assoc. gen. sec. Nat. Conf. of Catholic Bishops, 1976-79; Kansas City Provincial dir. CPPS, 1979-87; aux. bishop Diocese of St. Paul/Minneapolis, 1990-93; bishop Diocese of Des Moines, 1994—; mem. Soc. of Precious Blood, Kansas City Province, 1961—; mem. Catholic Theological Soc. of Amer.; mem. Nat. Conf. of Catholic Bishops/U.S. Catholic Conference admin. comm. Office: Chancery PO Box 1816 Des Moines IA 50306-1816

CHARTERS, ALEXANDER NATHANIEL, retired adult education educator; b. Verdant Valley, Alta., Can., Aug. 22, 1916; came to U.S., 1948, naturalized, 1957.; s. Alexander Allen and Louisa Magdalena (Kern) C.; m. Margaret Anne MacNaughton, Mar. 29, 1952; children: A. William, David W., John C., Louisa A. Vike. BA, U. B.C., 1938; PhD, U. Chgo., 1948. Tchr. pub. schs., Fernie, B.C., 1939-41, Vancouver, 1941-42; asst. to dean Univ. Coll., Syracuse U., 1948-50, asst. dean, 1950-52, dean, 1952-64, asst. prof. Sch. Edn., 1950-54, assoc. prof., 1954-59, prof., 1959-83, prof. emeritus, 1983—, area chmn. for adult edn., 1950-80, univ. v.p. for continuing edn., 1964-73; vis. mem. faculty U. Chgo., 1958; UNESCO del. Internat. Conf. on Adult Edn., UNESCO, 1972; observer, del., Tokyo, 1972, Paris, 1985; coord. US participation pvt. sector CONFINTEA V, Hamburg, also observer and U.S. del., 1997, mem. U.S. del. team, 1997; cons. UNESCO Inst. for Edn., 1998; mem. standing com. 5th World Conf. on History of Adult Edn., 1991; mem. steering com. Internat. Assocs., 1991—; chmn. program com. Internat. Conf. Rethinking Adult Edn. for Devel., Ljubljana, Slovenia, 1993; adv. S. Rodriguez U., Caracas, Venezuela, 1994; external examiner adult edn. U. Madras, 1996; presenter edn. conf., Jena, Germany, 1996; cons. in adult edn. Inst. Pedagogida Rural, Venezuela, 1998; founding cons. Academic Inst. Educators of Adults, 1998; cons. to numerous acad. instns. Author numerous books and publs. multi-media formats. Mem. bd. Ctr. Study Liberal Edn. Adults, 1957-67, chmn., 1964-65; mem. Internat. Coun. for Adult Edn. (hon. 1998); founding mem., treas. Internat. Congress U. Adult Edn., 1962-67; mem. N.Y. State Adv. Bd. on Continuing Higher Edn.; chmn. Galaxy Conf. Adult Edn. Orgns., 1969; chmn. priorities com. Cmty. Chest and Coun.; trustee Chautauqua Inst., 1960-69; bd. mem. Laubach Literacy Internat., 1965-70, sec., 1967-70; trustee Ctrl. N.Y. UN Assn., Syracuse World Affairs Edn. Orgns.; mem. U.S. Nat. Com. UNESCO, presenter 5th world assembly, Cairo, 1994; bd. visitors U. Pitts., Washington U., St. Louis; founding mem., bd. dirs. Coalition Adult Edn. Orgn., 1964-82; exec. bd. dirs. Westminster Manor Ctr.; bd. dirs., treas. Vandercamp Conf. and Recreation Ctr., 1991-95, Ctrl. N.Y. Presbytery Conf. Ctr., 1991; clk. of session, elder Park Ctrl. Presbyn. Ch. With Royal Can. Naval Vol. Res., 1942-45. Recipient William Pearson Tolley medal for disting. leadership in adult edn. Syracuse U., 1986, Lifetime Achievement award Ctrl. N.Y. Coalition on Adult and Cont. Edn.; Alexander Charters Libr. Resources for Educators of Adults named for him Syracuse U., 1998. Mem. Assn. Continuing Higher Edn. (pres. 1947-48, Leadership citation 1973), Am. Assn. Adult Continuing Edn. (Pioneer award 1980), Nat. U. Continuing Edn. Assn. (pres. 1965-66, Bitner award 1973, Alexander N. Charters award 1999), Internat. Coun. Adult Edn. (founder 1972, chair documentation 1974, coord. confs., mem. Internat. Adult and Continuing Edn. Hall of Fame 1996), Internat. Soc. Comparative Adult Edn. (founding pres. 1992), Acad. Inst. Educators of Adults (founding cons. 1998), Ctrl. N.Y. Coalition on Adult and Continuing Edn. (lifetime achievement award 1998), Rotary (internat. Paul Harris fellow 1992), Beta Theta Pi. Home: 216 Lockwood Rd Syracuse NY 13214-2035

CHARTERS D'AZEVEDO, RICARDO, management executive; b. Lisbon, Portugal, July 29, 1942. Degree in elec. engring., Tech. U. Lisbon, 1970. Secondary tech. sch. tchr. Lisbon, 1969-71; prof. telecom., electronics, dir. elec. and electronic lab. Portuguese Mil. Acad., Lisbon, 1973-78; asst. prof. Inst. Superior Técnico Tech. U. Lisbon, 1970-78; rschr. Portuguese Nat. Inst. Sci. Rsch., Lisbon, 1970-78; dir. short cycle higher edn. coord. office Portuguese Ministry of Edn., Lisbon, 1978-83; dep. dir. gen. higher edn. Portuguese Ministry of Edn., 1978-83, dir. gen. studies and planning office, 1983-88; head divsn. edn. and tng. for new techs. EC, Brussels, 1988-93, head divsn. evolution of jobs, open and distance learning, 1993-97; mem. thessalonique mgmt. bd. CEDEFOP, 1991-97; dir. European Commn. Representation, Portugal, 1997—; Portuguese rep. OECD Com. of Edn., 1983-88, Internat. Assn. for Evaluation of Edn. Achievement, 1983-88; mem. Portuguese Statis. Nat. Body, 1983-88; mem. comissao Nat. Emprego of Portuguese Ministry of Labor; mem. Portuguese Nat. Commn. for Planning, 1983-88; pres. Schs. Network Planning Body, 1983-88; mem. Comissao de Reforma do Sistema Educativo, 1983-88. Contbr. articles to profl. publs.

Mem. Ordem dos Engenheiros, Clube Portugues do Benelux. Home: Rua Sacadura Cabral 304, P-2765 S Pedro Estoril Portugal Office: European Commn Rep, Largo Jean Monnet n:1-10, 1269 068 Lisbon Portugal

CHARTIER, GERMAIN HENRI, science educator; b. Fontainebleau, France, Nov. 4, 1936; s. Robert and Marie Céline (Desenfant) C.; m. Anne Marie Marcelle Danjean, Apr. 29, 1940; children: Alain, Isabelle, Philippe. Grad., Ecole Normale, Paris, 1960; agregation physique, Paris, 1960; D Physics, U. Paris-Orsay, 1970. Secondary sch. tchr. Paris, 1960-63; asst. prof. U. Paris-Orsay, 1963-72; sci. attache French Embassy, London, 1972-73; prof. Inst. Nat. Poly., Grenoble, France, 1973-98, prof. emeritus, 1998—; dir. Univ. Internat. Dept., Grenoble, 1990-94; mem. editl. bd. Jour. Applied Physics, London, 1985-91; sci. dir., cons. Schneider Elec., Grenoble, 1987-97; dir. Lab. CNRS, Grenoble, 1983-91; sci. dir. creation of a cooperating lab. industry, 1983. Author: Les Lasers, 1990, Manuel D'Optique, 1997. Lt. French Navy, 1961-63. E-mail: g.chartier@teemphotonics.com. Home: 8 Blvd Agutte Sembat, 38000 Grenoble France Office: Teem Photonics, 13 Chemin de Vieux Chere, 38246 Meylan cedex France

CHARTIER, JANELLEN OLSEN, airline service coordinator; b. Chgo., Sept. 12, 1951; d. Roger Carl and Genevieve Ann (McCormick) Olsen; m. Lionel Pierre-Paul Chartier, Nov. 6, 1982; 1 child, Régine Anne. BA in French and Home Econs., U. Ill., 1973, MA in Tchg. French, 1974; student, U. Rouen (France), 1971-72. Cert. tchr., Ill. Flight attendant Delta Airlines, Atlanta, 1974—; Spanish qualified Delta Airlines, 1977-82, German qualified, 1980—, in-flight svc. coord., 1980—, European in-flight svc. coord., 1983—; French examiner In-Flight Svc., 1984-95; interpreter Formax, Inc., Mokena, Ill., 1976-82; staff interpreter Acad. Legal and Tech. Translation, Ltd., 1991—, part time instr. French Northea. Ill. U., 1995—. Bd. dirs. One Plus One Dance Co., Champaign, Ill., 1977-78. Mem. Am. Assn. Tchrs. French, NAFE, Alliance Maison Francaise de Chgo., Phi Delta Kappa, Alpha Lambda Delta. Roman Catholic. Home: 1406 S State St # A Chicago IL 60605-2803

CHARTIER, PIERRE, educator; b. Neuilly sur Seine, France, Dec. 3, 1937; s. René and Renée (Charret) C.; m. Monique Rougier, Oct. 20, 1934. D, Strasbourg U., France, 1968. Asst. U. Strasbourg, 1960-73; sr. asst. prof. U. Dakar, Senegal, 1974-77; rsch. assoc. NYU, 1968-69; prof. of electrochemistry U. Louis Pasteur, Strasbourg, 1979—; dir. Unite Form et Recherche, 1987-90; vis. prof. UCLA, L.A., 1990. Co-author: Application de la Thermodynanique du Non Equilibre, 1975; contbr. articles to profl. jours. Mem. Internat. Soc. Electrochemistry, Soc. Francaise de Chimie. Avocations: tennis, bridge. Home: 9 rue de Londres, 67000 Strasbourg France Office: U Louis Pasteur, 1-4 rue Blaise Pascal, 67000 Strasbourg France

CHARTIN, JACKIE GERMAIN, physician; b. Romorantin, Loir et Cher, France, Dec. 4, 1933; s. Germain and Paulette (Millot) C.; m. Nicole Jeanine le Dour, Aug. 7, 1961; children: Bruno, Marie-Laure, Patrice, Hubert, Nicolas. MD, U. Paris, 1968. Cert. pneumologist. Extern Hosp. of Paris, 1959-65; physician Centre Medico-Chirurgical de Normandie, Evreux, France, 1965-70; pvt. practice medicine specializing in pneumology Lorient, France, 1970-96; asst. pneumologist Lorient Hosp., 1974-96. Contbr. articles to polit. jour. Pres. Assn. France-Etats-Unis, 1983-90, Comité-de Lorient, France, 1986-87; involved in devel. rels. with Romaina. Served with French mil., 1960-62. Mem. Societe de Pneumologie de L'Ouvest. Roman Catholic. Avocations: French and English lit., archeology, photography. Home: 41 rue de la Villeneuve, 56100 Lorient, Britanny France

CHARTRES, COLIN JOHN, soil scientist; b. Hertford, United Kingdom, Dec. 10, 1951; arrived in Australia, 1978; s. Ronald Arthur and Jean Cicely (Barton) C.; m. Margaret Vivienne Preece, Sept. 20, 1975; children: Andrew Paul, Christopher Allen. BS, U. Bristol, 1972; PhD, U. Reading, 1975. Soil scientist Booker Agr. Internat., London, 1976-78; lectr. dept. geography U. New South Wales, Sydney, Australia, 1978-83; sr. prin. rsch. scientist Divsn. of Soils Commonwealth Sci. Rsch. Orgn., Canberra, Australia, 1984-97; chief divsn. geohazards land and water resources Australian Geol. Survey Orgn., Canberra, 1997-98; chief divsn. land and water scis. Bur. Rural Scis., Kingston, Australia, 1998—; chmn. Subcommn. B Internat. Soc. Soil Sci., 1992-96. Contbr. articles to profl. jours. and books. Recipient Rsch. award Landcare Australia, 1991. Mem. Soil Sci. Soc. of Am., Soil Sci. Soc. of Australia (pres. Australian Capital Territory br. 1986-88, 96-98, Publ. medal 1983). Avocations: gardening, bush walking, travel. Office: Bur Rural Scis, PO Box E11, Kingston ACT 2604, Australia

CHARVATOVA, IVANKA, geophysicist, astronomer; b. Jilemnice, Czech Republic, Dec. 3, 1941; d. Karel and Bozena (Hanusova) K.; m. Vitezslav Jakubec, Apr. 16, 1965 (div. 1982); children: Veronika, Stepan; m. Ivan Charvat, Nov. 25, 1986. Engr., Czech Tech. U., Prague, 1963; postgrad., Charles U., Prague, 1976; PhD, Czechoslovak Acad. Sci., 1990. Scientist Acad. of Scis. of Czech Republic, 1968-89, sr. scientist, 1990—. Author: Encyclopedia of Planetary Sciences, 1997; contbr. articles to profl. jours. Grantee Agy. of the Czech Republic, 1993-96, 97-99. Avocations: poetry translation, art. Office: Geophys Inst AS CR, Bochni II, 141 31 Prague 4, Czech Republic

CHASE, ERIC LEWIS, lawyer; b. Princeton, N.J., Sept. 21, 1946; s. Harold William and Bernice Mae (Fadden) C.; m. Jamie Campbell, Dec. 29, 1979; children: Eric Campbell, Kathryn Dianne, John Harold. BA, Princeton U., 1968; JD cum laude, U. Minn., 1974. Bar: N.J. 1974, D.C. 1975, U.S. Ct. Appeals (3d cir.) 1979, U.S. Supreme Ct. 1981, U.S. Claims Ct. 1982, U.S. Tax Ct. 1982, N.Y. 1983. Trial atty. FCC, 1974-78; asst. U.S. atty. Dist. N.J., Newark, 1978-80; ptnr. Margolis Chase, Verona, N.J., 1980-90, Hannoch Weisman, Roseland, N.J., 1990-93, Bressler, Amery & Ross, Florham Park, N.J., 1993—; prof. law of war Marine Corps Command and Staff Coll., Quantico, Va., 1990-99. Author: Automobile Dealers and the Law, 1994, 7th edit., 2000; contbr. articles on law and mil. to profl. publs., including N.Y. Times, Washington Post, Newsweek mag. With USMC, 1968-71; col. Res., ret. Mem. ABA (mem. task force on internat. criminal ct.), N.J. State Bar Assn. (franchise com 1997 , co-chair franchise com. 1999-00). Office: Bressler Amery & Ross 325 Columbia Tpke Ste 8 Florham Park NJ 07932-1212

CHASE, PEARLINE, adult education educator; b. Lake Providence, La., Jan. 25, 1949; d. Willie and Rebecca (Thompson) C. BS in Liberal Studies and Math., So. U., 1970; MS in Math. Edn., La. Tech. U., 1977; EdM in Adminstrn. Planning Social Policy, Harvard U., 1984, EdD, 1987. Tchr. Caddo Parish Schs., Shreveport, La., 1970-78, East Carroll Parish Schs., Lake Providence, La., 1980-81; program coord., staff asst. Harvard U., Cambridge, Mass., 1983-84; exec. asst. to pres. Ky. State U., 1985-86, assoc. v.p. acad. affairs, 1986-87, v.p. student affairs, 1987-88; dir. bd. programs and policy analysis City Colls. Chgo., 1988-89; v.p. acad. affairs Paul Quinn Coll., Dallas, 1990-92; cons. Wilmington Inst., Dallas, 1992-96; assoc. prof. math. DeVry inst. Tech., Irving, Tex., 1996—. Teaching fellow U. Okla., Norman, 1981-83; fellow Congl. Black Caucus, Washington, 98th Congress, U.S. Ho. of Reps., Woodrow Wilson fellow; T.H. Harris scholar. Mem. Nat. Coun. Tchrs. Math., Nat. Assn. Devel. Educators, Alpha Kappa Alpha. Office: DeVry Inst 4800 Regent Blvd Irving TX 75063-2439

CHASE, SANDRA LEE, clinical pharmacist, consultant; b. Oak Park, Ill., July 31, 1959; d. William Warren and Charlene Lois (Johnson) C.; m. Christopher Paul Bloch, Sept. 8, 1984; children: Kyle Thaddeus, Matthew William. Student, Mich. State U., 1977-80; BS in Pharmacy, U. Mich., 1983, PharmD, 1984. Lic. pharmacist, Del., Mich., Pa.; cert. leader aquatic fitness YMCA aquatic program. Rsch. asst. U. Mich., Ann Arbor, 1980-81; pharmacy intern Three Rivers (Mich.) Hosp., 1981, Cmty. Pharmacy, Ann Arbor, 1980-83; pharmacy intern, grad. intern St. Francis Hosp., Wilmington, Del., 1982-83; resident in hosp. pharmacy Thomas Jefferson U. Hosp., Phila., 1984-85, clin. pharmacist in cardiopulmonary medicine, 1985-89; sr. med. info. coord. ICI Pharms. Group, Wilmington, Del., 1989-92; clin. pharmacist Thomas Jefferson U. Hosp., Phila., 1989-93, clin. pharmacist drug use policy and clin. svcs., 1993-98; clin. pharmacy specialist Spectrum Health, Grand Rapids, Mich., 1999—; adj. asst. prof. clin. pharmacy Temple U. Coll. Pharmacy, 1997-98, Ferris State U. Coll. Pharmacy, 1999—; clin. instr. in pharmacy practice Phila. Coll. Pharmacy and Sci., Phila., 1985-87, clin. asst. prof., 1987-88, clin. assoc. prof., 1988-98; instr. critical care cardiopulmonary medicine in nursing Episcopal Hosp., Phila., 1986-88, Thomas Jefferson U. Hosp., Phila., 1985-91, Our Lady of Lourdes Med. Ctr., Camden, N.J., 1988-91; coord., prof. pharmacology and drug therapeutic for advanced nursing practice course Sch. Nursing, Ctr. for Profl. Devel., U. Pa., Phila., 1994—; adj. prof. pharmacy Coll. Pharmacy Ferris State U., 1999—; mem. Pa. Osteoporosis Soc. Bd., 1996-98; presenter in field. Mem. editl. bd. RN, Med. Econs.; referee AHFS Drug Info., Am. Druggist, Am. Jour. Hosp. Pharmacy, Nursing 96 Drug Handbook, Nursing 97 Drug Handbook, Pharmacotherapy, RN Mag., Annals of Pharmacotherapy, U. Hosp. Consortium Monographs; contbg. editor RN Mag., mem. editl. bd.; contbr. numerous articles to profl. jours. Mem. adv. bd. Nursing Mothers Network; bd. dirs. Coll. Pharmacy Alumni Soc., 1991-97, 99-01; cert. leader aquatic program Arthritis Found. YMCA, 2000—. Mem. Am. Coll. Clin. Pharmacy, Am. Soc. Health Sys. Pharmacists, Am. Pharm. Assn., Del. Pharm. Soc. (conv. com. 1990-94, ACPE com. 1990-94), Western Mich. Soc. Health-Sys. Pharmacists (bd. dirs. 1998—), Mich. Pharmacists Assn., Rho Chi Pharm. Soc., Aerobics and Fitness Assn. Am. Republican. Lutheran. Avocations: aerobics, waterskiing, cross-country skiing, gardening. Office: Spectrum Health Downtown Campus Dept Pharmacy 100 Michigan St NE Grand Rapids MI 49503-2560

CHASTAIN, JAMES WILLIAM, construction professional; b. El Centro, Calif., Aug. 25, 1957; s. James William Chastain and Mary Evelyn Cable; m. Eileen Marie Webb, June 5, 1995; children: Angela Marie Britt, Kari Collins Davis. Grad. H.S., Huntington, W.Va. Pulpwood laborer Internat. Paper Co., Columbia, La.; dry wall taper Greene Enterprises, Tucson, Western Am. Drywall, Tucson; law svc. staff Chastain Lawn Svc., Redding, Calif., Coo's Bay, Oreg. Author: Best Poetic Classics of 97. Life mem., tv prodr. Tucson Cmty. Cable Cooperation-Oasis TV, Tucson, 1987-2000; civil rights activist Huguenot Party, Tucson, Huntington, 1991. Recipient award Pima County Libr., Tucson, 1994. Avocations: camping, fishing, reading, inventing, song writing. Address: Delta Publications 1901 Breckenridge Pl Toms River NJ 08755-0900

CHATEAU, GEORGES MICHEL, petroleum engineer, consultant; b. St. Leonard de Noblat, France, May 13, 1934; came to U.S., 1981; s. Jean Roger and Marcelle M. (Lachaise) C.; m. Ruth M. Loeffler, June 12, 1964. Engr., Ecole Nationale Superieure de Mecanique de Nantes, France, 1957, Ecole Nationale Superieure des Petroles, Rueil-Malmaison, France, 1959. Drilling engr. S.N. Repal, Algiers, Algeria, 1962-65; offshore engr. Elf Aquitaine, Pau-Paris-Bordeaux, France, 1965-81, Port-Gentil, Gabon, 1968; frontiers arctic and offshore studies and ops. staff Elf Aquitaine Petroleum, Houston, 1981-90, Paris, 1990-95; cons., France, 1995—. Contbr. articles to profl. publs. Patentee in field. Served with French Armed Forces, 1959-62. Mem. Soc. Petroleum Engrs., ASME, Assn. Francaise des Techniciens du Petrole. Current work: Deep sea and Arctic engineering for oil and gas production facilities. Subspecialties: Petroleum engineering; Mechanical engineering consultant. Address: BP23, 87400 Saint Leonard-de-Noblat France

CHATELAIN, PETER JOHN, research scientist; b. Rabat, Morocco, Jan. 12, 1962; arrived in australia, 1982, naturalized, 1965; s. Jean-Claude Louis Castellano and Annetta Josephine Kay. B Applied Sci. in Geophysics, U. Queensland, Brisbane, Australia, 1986; diploma in computer sci., U. Melbourne, Australia, 1990; PhD in Elec. and Electronics, Queensland U. Tech., Brisbane, 1997. Rsch. scientist Aero. and Maritime Rsch. Lab., Melbourne, 1987-93, Electronics and Surveillance Rsch. Lab., Adelaide, Australia, 1998—; scientist Queensland U. Tech., Brisbane, 1993-97; cons. in forensic sci. Queensland U. Tech., 1995-96; mem. Nat. Accredited Authority Translators and Interpreters, Australia, 1991—. Contbr. articles to profl. jours. With French Armed Forces, 1980-82. Mem. Def. Sci. and Tech. Orgn. Avocation: military history. Office: ESRL-ITD 205 Labs, PO Box 1500, Salisbury SA 5108, Australia

CHATER, KEITH FREDERICK, microbiologist; b. Croydon, Eng., Apr. 23, 1944; s. Frederick Ernest and Marjorie Inez (Palmer) C.; m. Jean Wallbridge, Sept. 3, 1966; children: Alison Clare, Simon Frederick, Julian David, Timothy Felix. BS with honors, U. Birmingham, Eng., 1966, PhD, 1969. Rsch. sci. dept. genetics John Innes Centre, Norwich, Eng., 1969—, head dept. genetics, 1998—; hon. prof. U. East Anglia, Norwich, 1988—, Chinese Acad. Scis. Inst. Microbiology, Beijing, 1999—, Huazhong Agrl. U., Wuhan, 2000—. Co-author: Genetic Manipulation of Streptomyces, 1985, Practical Streptomyces Genetics, 2000; co-editor: Genetics of Bacterial Diversity, 1989; mem. editl. bd. Jour. Bacteriology, 1983-97, Gene, 1983-97. Active Campaign for Nuc. Disarmament. Fulbright scholar Harvard U., 1983. Fellow Royal Soc.; mem. Am. Soc. Microbiology, Nat. Conf. Univ. Profs., Soc. Gen. Microbiology, Genetical Soc. (Gt. Britain). Mem. Labor Party. Avocations: painting, gardening, birdwatching. Home: 6 Coach House Ct, Norwich NR4 7QR, England Office: John Innes Centre, Norwich Rsch Park, Colney, Norwich NR4 7UH. England

CHATT, ALLEN BARRETT, psychologist, neuroscientist; b. Phoenix, July 17, 1949; s. Arthur Beecher Ellis and Helen Scheidt Chatt; m. Gail Nancy Anguish, Aug. 21, 1971. BS in Psychology with honors, SUNY, Buffalo, 1971; MS in Psychology, Fla. State U., 1974, PhD in Psychology and Neuroscience, 1978. Rsch. asst. Fla. State U., Tallahassee, 1971-76; predoctoral fellow U. Tex. Med. Br., Galveston, 1977; postdoctoral fellow sch. medicine Yale U., New Haven, Conn., 1978-80; rsch. psychologist VA Med. Ctr., West Haven, Conn., 1978-84, sr. rsch. psychologist, 1985-90; rsch. asst. prof. sch. medicine Yale U., New Haven, Conn., 1981-87; rsch. assoc. prof. Yale U., New Haven, 1988-90; founder, exec. dir., consulting psychologist Phoenix Fund for Neurologically Challenged, Madison and Tallahassee, 1991—; vis. prof. neurosci. Beijing Normal U., 1987, U. Glasgow, 1994-95; grant reviewer NSF, NIH, VA, 1982—; neurosci. reviewer Am. Psychol. Soc. Convs., 1991—; sci.-by-mail scientist Mus. Sci., Boston, 1991—; psychol. cons., case mgr. for neurologically impaired; pvt. funding of neurol. rsch.; prof. movement scis. Fla. State U., 1999—. Contbr. chpts. and forewards to books, articles to profl. jours.; mem. editorial bd. Brain Rsch., 1983-86, Exptl. Neurology, 1982-86, Quar. Jour. Exptl. Physiology, 1986, Exptl. Brain Rsch., 1984-88. Mem. Rep. Senatorial Inner Circle, Washington, 1985, Rep. Town Com., Guilford, 1992; life mem. Rep. Nat. Com., 1993—, Eisenhower Commn., 1995, Pres. Club, 1991, Chmn.'s Adv. Bd., 1994; sponsor The Phoenix Fund Grad. Rsch. fellowship Dept. of Movement Sci. Fla. State U., 1999—, Jennifer Harrison Meml. Golf Tournament, 1991—, Freedom Scholarship Batavia H.S. Class 1965, 1992—, Bobby Bowden Classic Fellowship Christian Athletes, 1992—, Goodspeed Opera House, 1995—, Bill Campbell Challenge Children's Miracle Network, 1996—, Fla. State U. Seminole Classic, 1998—, Phoenix Fund Collegiate Scholarship for Applied Biomed. Undergrad. Study for Leon County, Fla., 1999—, Boy's Town Invitational of North Fla., 1998—, Camp Sunshine, 1992—; mem. devel. bd. Coll. Human Scis. Fla. State U., 1998—; bd. dirs. Wal-Mart/Children's Miracle Network, No. Fla., 1998—, Jennifer Harrison Fund, 1995—; judge Sam Walton Cmty. Leader Scholarship Program, The Phoenix Fund Collegiate Scholarship in Human Scis., 1999—; adv. bd. The Ellingsworth Press, 1998—. Merit Review Rsch grantee VA Med. Ctr., 1982-90; RO-1 Rsch. grantee NIH, 1982-87; recipient Most Sr. Benefactor award Children's Miracle Network, 1997—. Mem. Am. Psychol. Soc., AAAS, Epilepsy Found. Am., Soc. for Neurosci., Am. Epilepsy Soc., Yale Neurology Alumni Adv. Assn. (charter). Republican. Methodist. Achievements include the development of a neurosurgical procedure increasing the effectiveness of stellate ganglion blocks for the treatment of reflex sympathetic dystrophy in humans, discovery of differential neuronal circuits involved in focal and secondarily generalized seizure activity in neocortical model of epilepsy, brain cells that become abnormal initially in focal and secondarily generalized seizure activity, mid brain neuronal circuits modulating pain, thermal evoked potential in humans and the localization of cortical cells responsive to pain. Home: PO Box 1449 Guilford CT 06437-0549 also: 2949 Golden Eagle Dr E Tallahassee FL 32312-4008

CHATTERJEE, AMAR, physiologist, educator; b. Howrah, India, Sept. 1, 1938; s. Jitendranath and Bina (Mukherjee) C.; m. Rita Basu, June 9, 1970; children: Kanak, Kanistha. MSc, U. Calcutta, 1960, PhD, 1966, DSc, 1976; postgrad., U. Kans., 1970. Lectr. RPM Coll., Calcutta, 1962-69, assoc. prof., 1969-76; prof. U. Lusaka, Zambia, 1976-79, U. Khartoom, Sudan, 1979-90; prof., chmn. Al.A. Med. Coll., Bijapur, India, 1990-91; prof. U. Sains Malaysia, P. Pinang, 1991—; mem. editl. bd. Biomed. Rsch., 1982. Contbr. articles to profl. publs. Ford Found. scholar, 1968-70; rsch. grantee WHO, Ford Found., Population Coun., 1970-80; recipient Rsch. Carrier Devel. award Family Planning Found., 1976. Mem. Soc. Study Reproduction, Soc. Study Fertility. Office: U Sains Malaysia, Sch Med Scis, Kubang Kerian 16150, Malaysia

CHATTERJEE, AMITAVA, finance educator, consultant; b. Calcutta, India, Jan. 10, 1961; came to U.S., 1986; s. Nepal and Shila Chatterjee; m. Rupa Bhattacharjya, Dec. 15, 1993; 1 child, Anirudha. BS, U. Calcutta, 1983, MS, 1985; Postgrad. Diploma in Operational Rsch., Ops. Rsch. Soc. India, Calcutta, 1985; PhD, U. Miss., 1992. Jr. rsch. fellow U. Calcutta, 1985-86; tchg. and rsch. asst. U. Miss., University, 1987-90, statis. cons., 1990-92; coord. area econs. and fin., asst. prof. fin. Lemoyne Owen Coll., Memphis, 1992-96; asst. prof. fin. Fayetteville (N.C.) State U., 1996-99, assoc. prof. fin., 1999—; advisor Econs. and Fin. Club, Fayetteville, 1996—; bd. dirs. Acad. Econs. and Fin., Hattisburg, Miss., 1999—. Co-author: Principles of Finance, 2d edit., 1998—; mem. editl. bd. Jour. Fin. Case Rsch., 1999—; contbr. articles to profl. jours. Grad. fellow Internat. Fedn. Operational Rsch., 1985—; Classroom Tchg./Learning grantee Carolina Colloquy for Univ. Tchg., Cullowhee, N.C., 1999. Mem. Acad. Fin. Case Rsch. (founder, mem. editl. bd. 1999—), Acad. Econs. and Fin. (track chair 1999), Am. Fin. Assn., Fin. Mgmt. Assn. Hindu. Avocations: reading, cooking. E-mail: chatteramit@hotmail.com and achatterjee@uncfsu.edu. Fax: 910-823-2427. Home: 213 Tallstone Dr Fayetteville NC 28311-1461 Office: Fayetteville State Univ 1200 Murchison Rd Fayetteville NC 28301-4298

CHATTERJEE, ANIRUDDHA, pediatrition; b. New Delhi, May 7, 1968; s. Siba Prasad and Dolly Chatterjee. MBBS, All India Inst. Med. Scis., New Delhi, MD in Pediat.; MD in Pediat., Children's Hosp. Mich. Resident in pediat. All India Inst. Med. Scis., New Delhi, 1992-95, chief resident, 1995-97; resident pediat. Detroit Med. Ctr., 1997-99; assoc. prof. dept. pediat. Sitaram Bhartia Inst., New Delhi, 1999—; attending cons. Sitaram Bhartia Inst., New Delhi. Fellow Am. Acad. Pediat., 1997. Mem. Med. Coun. India. Hindu. Achievements: computers, home improvement, electronics, stamp collecting. E-mail: ac@pediatrician.com. Home: d-113 Lajpat Nagar-I, New Delhi India Office: B-16, Mehrauli Instnl Area, New Delhi 110016, India

CHATTERJEE, ASHOK KUMAR, naval architect; b. Krishnagar, India, Feb. 28, 1953; s. Siva Das and Lila (Banerjee) C.; m. Mridula Roy, June 21, 1991; children: Prerana, Aparna. BTech with honors, Indian Inst. Tech., Kharagpur, 1975; MSc, U. Strathclyde, Glasgow, Scotland, 1979; PhD, U. Glasgow, 1982. Asst. naval architect Garden Reach Shipbuilders Ltd., Calcutta, 1975-76; naval architect Bombay Marine Engring. Works Pvt. Ltd., 1976-77; pool officer Indian Inst. Tech., Kharagpur, 1982-83; reader U. Cochin, Kerala, India, 1983-84; dep. dir. Directorate of Naval R&D, New Delhi, 1984-85; asst. dir. Directorate of Naval Design, New Delhi, 1986-94; sr. engr. Def. Materiel Orgn., Singapore, 1994-2000; cons. SeaQuest, Singapore, 2000—. Contbr. articles to profl. jours. India MInistry of Edn. scholar, 1977. Avocations: painting, photography, Hindi classical music and movies. Home: Jurong East Ave 1, Block 339 # 02-1530, Singapore 600339, Republic of Singapore Office: SeaQuest Tech Pvt Ltd, No 1 6th Lok Yang Rd, Singapore 628099, Republic of Singapore

CHATTERJEE, DEBABRATA, surgeon; b. Chandernagore, India, Dec. 1, 1937; s. Debendranath and Nandarani (Mukherjee) C.; m. Adele Patricia Powell, Sept. 17, 1971 (dec. Mar. 1999); children: Crispin Dara, Justin Sanjay. MB BS, Calcutta (India) U., 1960; ChM, Liverpool (Eng.) U., 1973. House surgeon medicine, surgery, gynae, ortho, urology N.R.S. Med. Coll. Hosp., Calcutta and Kent, Eng., 1960-64; univ. rsch. fellow U. Liverpool, Eng., 1965-67; surg. registrar London, Liverpool & Leeds, Eng., 1965-70; sr. surg. registrar, tutor, asst. gen. surgery Univ. Coll. Cork, Ireland, 1970-71; asst. gen. surgeon Ireland, 1971-74; lectr., cons. gen. surgeon Univ. Hosp. W.I., Jamaica, 1974-77; cons. surgeon N.W. Thames Regional Authority London & Plymouth Gen. & Royal Infirmary, Edingubrh, Scotland, 1977-81; cons. gen. surgery BUPA Hosp., Harpenden, Eng., 1978-95; cons. gen. surgeon Daliburgh Hosp., South Uist, Scotland, 1982-95; med. practitioner South Uist, Scotland, 1982—; tching, rsch. and svc. adminstr. London, Leeds, Liverpool, Cork, Jamaica and Edinburgh, 1965—, univ. undergrad. and postgrad. tchr., 1965-81; rschr. in field; examiner U. W.I., 1974-77. Contbr. articles to profl. jours. Rsch. fellow/grantee Medica Rsch. Com., Liverpool U., 1966, 67, rsch. and publs. grantee U. W.I., Jamaica, 1974, 75, 76, grantee Med. Rsch. Coun. Eire, 1971, Med. Edn. & Rsch. Coun., Belfast, 1972, 73. Fellow Royal Coll. Surgeons England and Edinburgh, Royal Soc. Medicine, Internat. Coll. Surgeons (sr. fellow), Assn. Surgeons Gt. Britain; mem. AAMS, Brit. Assn. Advacement of Sci., Brit. Assn. Surg. Oncologists (founding mem.), Assn. Endoscopic Surgeons (founding mem.), Soc. Laparoscopic Surgeons U.S.A., N.Y. Acad. Scis. (Charles Darwin Assoc. 1999), Brit. Med. Assn., Hosp. Cons. Specialists Assn., European Assn. Endoscopic Surgery. Avocations: history of philosophy, playing Indian classical musical instruments. Office: Doctors House, Lochboisdale, South Uist HS8 5TH, Scotland

CHATTERJEE, MALAYA, immunologist; b. Cooch-Behar, W. Bengal, India, Jan. 16, 1946; came to US, 1969; d. Nalini Nath and Kanak Prova (Chakraborty) Bhattacharya; m. Sunil K. Chatterjee, Oct. 25, 1972; children: Indranil, Sumana. BS, Presidency Coll., Calcutta, India, 1963; MS, U. Calcutta, 1965, PhD, 1969. Cancer rsch. scientist III Roswell Park Cancer Inst., Buffalo, N.Y., 1972-78; cancer rsch. scientist IV Roswell Park Cancer Inst., Buffalo, 1979-92; assoc. prof. U. Ky., Lexington, 1993-97, prof. dept. medicine, 1997-99; prof. dept. medicine U. Cin., 1999—; mem. The Barrett Cancer Ctr., Cin., 1999—; cons. study sect. Nat. Cancer Inst.-NIH, Bethesda, Md., 1992-96, 97—. Contbr. numerous articles to profl. jours., 12 chpts. to books; patentee in field (3). Mem. Hindu Cultural Soc. We N.Y., Buffalo, 1972-92. Grantee Nat. Cancer Inst. NIH, 1976-79, 89—, Am. Cancer Soc., 1979-82, Pharm. Corp., 1996-99, Dept. Def., 1995-98. Mem. Am. Assn. Immunologists, Am. Assn. Cancer Rsch., N.Y. Acad. Scis., Blue Grass Indo-Am. Assn. Democrat. Hindu. Avocations: travel, music, camping, gardening, international cooking. Office: U Cin Med Ctr 3125 Eden Ave Cincinnati OH 45267-0001

CHATTERJEE, SMRITI NARAYAN, biophysicist, researcher, educator; b. Chandernagar, India, May 1, 1932; s. Abinash Chandra and Bibha Bati (Banerjee) C.; m. Amala Dhar, May 12, 1961; 1 child, Saugata. BSc with honours in Physics, Calcutta (India) U., 1953, MSc in Physics, 1955, PhD in Sci., 1958. Head biophysics div. Sch. Tropical Medicine, Calcutta, 1961-73; asst. dir. Indian Inst. Chem. Biology, Calcutta, 1973-77; sr. prof. biophysics, chmn. biophysics divsn. Saha Inst. Nuclear Physics, Calcutta, 1977-92, dir., 1990-91, Indian Nat. Sci. Acad. sr. scientist emeritus, 1992-97; Platinum Jubilee lectr. India Sci. Congress Assn., 1993; mem. governing coun. Bose Inst., 1993—; Prof. A.K. Chandra meml. lectr. Calcutta U., 1996.; Prof. Sambhu Nath De meml. lectr. Indian Nat. Sci. Acad., 1996. Contbg. author: Advances in Virus Research, 1984, Free Radicals in Biology and Medicine, 1988; editor: Physical Techniques in Biology, 1986; contbr. over 150 articles to sci. jours. Inaugurator Dist. Sci. Fair, Burdwan, West Bengal, India, 1993. Recipient award Rockefeller Found., 1962, Shakuntala Amirchand prize Indian Coun. Med. Rsch., 1966, Basanti Devi Amirchand prize Indian Coun. Med. Rsch., 1983, Foundation Day Oration medal Sch. Tropical Medicine, 1992. Fellow Indian Nat. Sci. Acad. (sect. com. 1989-91, sr. scientist emeritus award 1992), Nat. Acad. Scis. (India), West Bengal Acad. Sci. and Tech. (coun. mem., convenor sect. commn. IX); mem. Indian Biophys. Soc. (life, v.p. 1986-88), Indian Phys. Soc. (life, v.p. 1986-88), Environ. Mutagen Soc. India (life), Electron Microscope Soc. India, Indian Sci. Congress Assn., Indian Sci. News Assn. (life), N.Y. Acad. Scis., Rotary. Hindu. Avocations: writing popular science, watching football and cricket games. Home: Bidhannagar, Block CF-69, West Bengal Calcutta 700 064, India

CHATTERJEE, UDIT, physics educator, researcher; b. Calcutta, India, Aug. 23, 1962; s. Biswanath and Bandana (Banerjee) C.; m. Debjani Chakraborty, Apr. 28, 1998; 1 child, Reelee. BSc in Physics with honors, Burdwan (India) U., 1983, MSc in Physics, 1985, PhD in Physics, 1992. Project prin. investigator dept. sci. tech. Burdwan U., 1993-95, pool officer Coun. Sci. and Indsl. Rsch., 1995-96, lectr., 1996—; vis. scientist Electrotech. Lab., Tsukuba, Japan, 1996, 97, 98, 99. Contbr. articles to profl. jours. including Applied Physics Letters, Optics Letters, among others. Recipient

Young Scientist Project award DST, Govt. of India, 1993, Jr. Associateship Internat. Ctr. Theoretical Physics, Trieste (Italy), 1995. Mem. Indian Laser Assn. (life), Indian Physics Assn. (life). Hinduism. Avocations: photography, detective stories, music. Home: Fatakgora, Chandannagar 712136, India Office: Burdwan U, Golapbag, Burdwan 713104, India

CHATTERTON, ROBERT TREAT, JR., reproductive endocrinology educator; b. Catskill, N.Y., Aug. 9, 1935; s. Robert Treat and Irene (Spoor) C.; m. Patricia A. Holland, June 24, 1956 (div. 1965); children: Ruth Ellen, William Matthew, James Daniel; m. Astrida J. Vanags, June 4, 1966 (div. 1977); 1 child, Derek Scott; m. Carol J. Lewis, May 24, 1985. BS, Cornell U., 1958, PhD, 1963; MS, U. Conn., 1959. Postdoctoral fellow Med. Sch. Harvard U., 1963-65; rsch. assoc. div. oncology Inst. Steroid Rsch. Montefiore Hosp. and Med. Ctr., N.Y.C., 1965-70; asst. prof. Coll. Medicine U. Ill., 1970-72, assoc. prof. Coll. Medicine, 1972-79; prof. Med. Sch. Northwestern U., Chgo., 1979—; mem. sci. adv. com. AID; chairperson Instl. Review Bd. Northwestern U., 1982-83, Intellectual Properties Com., Northwestern U., 1987-95; dir. Immunoassay Facility, R.H. Lurie Cancer Ctr., Northwestern U. Med. Sch., 1997—; dir. Clin. Labs., dept. ob-gyn., Northwestern Med. Faculty Found., 1996-99, dir. shared clin. labs., 1999—. Contbr. numerous articles to sci. jours.; patents: method of totally suppressing ovarian follicular devel. and method of ovulation detection. Grantee NIH, 1972-90, 95—, NSF, 1975, 95-98, AID, 1971-86, Army Office Rsch., 1987-94. Mem. AAAS, N.Y. Acad. Scis., Am. Chem. Soc., Endocrine Soc., Soc. Gynecologic Investigation, Soc. Study Reprodn., Chgo. Assn. Reproductive Endocrinologists (pres. 1987-88), Sigma Xi, Phi Kappa Phi. Presbyterian (deacon). Home: 6001 N Knox Ave Chicago IL 60646-5821 Office: Northwestern U Prentice 1516 333 E Superior St Chicago IL 60611-3015

CHATTIN-MCNICHOLS, JOHN PATRICK, education educator; b. N.Y.C., July 12, 1950; s. Robert and Frances (Graff) McNichols; m. Barbara J. Chattin, June 11, 1977; children: Gregory B., David S. AB, UCLA, 1973; PhD, Stanford U., 1979. Vis. prof. in devel. psychology Purdue U., West Lafayette, Ind., 1978-79; asst. prof. in edn. Seattle U., 1979-85, assoc. prof., 1985—. Author texts: Understanding the Computer Age, 1983, Microworks, 1986, Montessori Controversy, 1991. Bd. dirs. Seattle Children's Mus., Am. Montessori Soc. Recipient numerous grants in field. Roman Catholic. Office: Seattle U Sch Edn Seattle WA 98122

CHATTOPADHYAY, AJIT KUMAR, electrical engineering educator; b. Nachankonda, India, Feb. 29, 1936; s. Dibakar and Karunamayee (Chattopadhyay) C.; m. Sumitra Gangoly, May 10, 1966; children: Mitrajit, Suryamita. BEE, Calcutta U., 1958; MTech, Indian Inst. Tech., Kharagpur, 1963; PhD, Manchester (Eng.) U., 1971. Lectr. elec. engring. Indian Inst. Tech., Kharagpur, 1962-68, asst. prof. elec. engring., 1968-76, prof. elec. engring., 1976-96, head dept. elec. engring., 1992-95; AICTE emeritus fellow BE Coll., Calcutta, 1996-99, CSIR emeritus scienti, 1999—; vis. prof. U. Tech., Baghdad, Iraq, 1980-81; cons. Tata Iron and Steel Co., Jamshedpur, Bharat Heavy Electricals Ltd., Bangalore, India, Electronic R&D Ctr., Bangalore; mem. governing body R.E. Coll., Rourkela, India, 1990-93. Mem. editl. bd. Electrosoft, 1990-93; author 2 video courses on machine drives; contbr. over 100 articles to profl. jours. Governing body KG Engring. Inst., Bishnupur, India, 1981-87, 91—. Colombo Plan fellow, 1968. Fellow IEEE, Indian Nat. Acad. Engrs., Inst. of Engrs. India (Tata Rao prize 1993-94), Inst. Electronic and Telecom. Engrs. (Bimal Bose award 1986); mem. Indian Soc. Tech. Edn. Hindu. Avocations: reading literature, writing, travel, dramatics, TV. Home: Flat 3B, 48/1 Laxmi Narayan Tala Rd, 711-103 Howrah, West Bengal India Office: Bengal Engring Coll, PO Botanic Garden, 711 103 Howrah, West Bengal India

CHATTOPADHYAY, NITIN, chemistry educator, researcher; b. Midnapore, India, Feb. 12, 1960; s. Abinash Chandra and Kanak Prabha (Goswami) C.; m. Kalpana Maity, Feb. 8, 1988; 1 child, Nilabja. BSc with honors, Calcutta (India) U., 1981, MSc, 1983; PhD, Jadavpur U., India, 1990. Rsch. fellow Indian Assn. for Cultivation of Sci., 1984-89; lectr. Kanyapur Poly., India, 1989-91; lectr. Jadavpur U., 1990-91, sr. lectr., 1991—; guest lectr. Vidyasagar U., India, 1988-90; lectr. R.K. Misison, Vidyamandira, India, 1991. Contbr. articles to profl. jours. Nat. Merit scholar Govt. of West Bengal, 1976, 78; Ranit Protibha Puraskar fellow, Calcutta, 1986; Boyscast fellow, 1996; Katholieke U. Leuven rsch. fellow, 1996. Mem. IUPAC (affil.), Indian Photobiology Soc. (life), Indian Soc. for Radiatio and Photochem. Scis. (life), Indian Soc. for Surface Sci. and Tech. (life). Avocation: listening to music. Office: Jadavpur U Dept Chemistry, PO Jadavpur, 700 032 Calcutta India

CHATTOPADHYAY, PRITHVIRAJ, management educator; b. Calcutta, India, Oct. 26, 1961; s. Gouranga and Arati C.; m. Elizabeth George, July 4, 1991. Diploma in mgmt., XLRI, Jamshedpur, India, 1988; PhD, U. Tex., 1996. Sales exec. Eureka Forbes Ltd., Calcutta, 1984-85; faculty mem. Tata Mgmt. Tng. Ctr., Pune, India, 1988-90; asst. prof. Western Mich. U., Kalamazoo, 1996-98; lectr. U. Queensland, Brisbane, Australia, 1998—. Contbr. articles to profl. jours. Rsch. grantee U. Tex., 1995, U. Queensland, 1999, Soc. for Human Resource Mgmt., 1997, Australian Rsch. Coun., 1999. Mem. Acad. Mgmt., Inst. for Ops. Rsch. and Mgmt. Sci. E-mail: r.chattopadhyay@gsm.uq.edu.au. Office: Grad Sch Mgmt U Queensland, Blair Dr, Brisbane 4072, Australia

CHATTOPADHYAY, SUBRATA, medical physiologist, researcher; b. Malda, India, Feb. 8, 1961; p. Nemai and Jayashri Chattopadhyay. MB, BChir, Calcutta (India) Med. Coll., 1984; MD, J.N. Med. Coll., Aligarh, India, 1989; PhD, U. Conn., 1998. E-mail: suc94001@usa.net. Fax: 212-860-9279. Office: Mount Sinai Sch Medicine Bopx 1126 One Gustave L Levy Pl New York NY 10029

CHATURANI, PURSHOTAM, applied mathematics educator, researcher; b. Mirpurkhas, India, Apr. 15, 1940; s. Tanumal and Parvati (Jethani) C.; m. Prabha Tandon, July 7, 1971; children: Manish, Kishor. BSc, Agra (India) U., 1961, MSc, 1963; PhD in Math., Indian Inst. Tech., Bombay, 1969. Assoc. lectr. applied math. Indian Inst. Tech., Bombay, 1966-67, lectr., 1968-76, asst. prof. applied math., 1976-83, assoc. prof. applied math., 1983-84, prof. applied math., 1984—; postdoctoral fellow U. Windsor, Ont., Can., 1974-75; chmn. Bombay adv. com. C.L. Chandna Math. Award, Nat. Level, Windsor, 1997—; participant numerous confs. and symposia; chmn. tech. sessions numerous confs., including 7th Congress Vijnan Parashad of India, 1997, others; mem. adv. bd. nat. confs.; referee and reviewer Indian Nat. Sci. Acad., Coun. Scientific & Indsl. Rsch. India, others; referee numerous Indian and internat. jours. and procs., including Biorheology, Internat. Jour. Engring. Sci., Indian Jour. Pure and Applied Math., Jour. Math. and Phys. Scis., others. Contbr. over 100 articles to nat. and internat. profl. jours.; mem. editl. bd. Indian Jour. Pure & Applied Math., 1982-85. V.p. Faculty Forum, Indian Inst. Tech., 1989-90, chmn. standing adv. com. for security arrangemetns, 1997—, gen. sec. staff club, 1977, warden hostel no. 8, Bombay, 1983. Recipient rsch. associateship Rsch. Coun. Can., U. Windsor, 1983-84, vis. fellowship Can. Commonwealth, Regina, 1992; rsch. grantee Coun. Scientific and Indsl. Rsch. India, New Delhi, 1995-2000. Mem. Internat. Soc. Biorheology, Vijnan Parishad of India (life; exec. com. 1997—, chmn. best paper award com. 1997), Indian Soc. Theoretical and Applied Math. (life; exec. com. 1995—, joint sec. 1983-86, v.p. 1987-88), Nat. Soc. Fluid Mechanics and Power (sec. 1988). Hindu. Avocations: tennis, swimming, cricket, music, travel. Home: A-17 Hill Side, Indian Inst Tech Powai, Bombay 400 076, India Office: Indian Inst Tech Bombay, Math Dept Powai, Bombay 400 076, India

CHATURVEDI, PUSHPA, paediatrician, educator, consultant; b. Naushera, Sind, India, Dec. 4, 1942; d. Chandiram Teumal and Sati Chandiram (Kishnani) Abichandani; m. Vishwanath Chaturvedi, June 2, 1971; children: Amit, Rajiv, Sona. MB BS, Sri-Ram-Chandra Bhanj Med. Coll., Cuttack, 1965; MD, All India Inst. Med. Scis., Delhi. Clin. resident All India Inst. Med. Scis., Delhi, 1967-70; registrar Kalavati Saran Children's Hosp. and Safdurjung Hosp., Delhi, 1970-72; lectr. Mahatma Gandhi Inst. Med. Scis., Sevagram, 1972-73; reader Mahatma Gandhi Inst. Med. Scis., Sewagram, 1975-77, assoc. prof., head, 1977-81, 84—; reader, head Indira Gandhi Med. Coll., Nagpur, 1974-75; assoc. prof. Garyounis U., Benghazi, Libya, 1981-83; head infectious diseases Disease Unit Alfateh Children's Hosp., Benghazi, Libya, 1981-83; prof., head pediatrics MGIMS Sevagram, Wardha, India. Contbr. over 100 articles to profl. jours. Health educator Local Women's Orgn., Wardha, 1984—. Mem. FIAP, Indian Acad. Paediatrics (life, exec. mem. 1989-90), Indian Med. Assn., Breast Feeding Task Force, Thallessimia and Sickle Cell Disease Soc. (pres.). Avocations: health education talks, reading, gardening, stitching.

CHATWIN, CHRISTOPHER REGINALD, engineering educator, researcher; b. Birmingham, U.K., Dec. 9, 1950; s. Gordon Roy and Grace Thelma (Hughes) C.; m. Catherine MacGregor, Feb. 15, 1984; children: Lesley, Craig, Andrew. BSc, Aston U., Birmingham, 1973; MSc, Birmingham U., 1977, PhD, 1979. Mgmt. trainee Austin/Rover, Birmingham, 1973-75, mfg. mgr., 1975-76; rsch. fellow Birmingham U., 1979-80; reader Glasgow (Scotland) U., 1980-95; prof. Sussex U., Brighton, Eng., 1995—; dir. S.E. advanced tech. hub Inc. Tech. Ltd., Glasgow, 1992-95. Author: Computational Moving Boundary Problems, 1994, Frequency Domain Filtering Strategies for Hybrid Optical Information Processing, 1996; mem. editl. bd. Lasers Engring.; contbr. articles to profl. jours. including Optical Computing, Signal Processing, Holography, Lasers, Computer Integrated Manufacture, Robotics, Instrumentation, Digital Image Processing, Control Systems, Digital Electronics, Laser Materials Processing. Fellow Inst. Mech. Engrs., Inst. Elec. Engrs., Inst. Physics; mem. IEEE, Internat. Soc. Optical Engring, European Optical Soc., Laser Inst. Am., Assn. Indsl. Laser Users, Optical Soc. Am. Avocations: skiing, oil painting, music, bird watching, gardening. Office: Sch Engring, U Sussex Falmer, Brighton BN1 9QT, England

CHAU, AMY SUK KWAI, computer consultant; b. Kowloon, Hong Kong, May 26, 1961; arrived in Eng., 1979; d. Wing-Kit and Wai-Hing (Chan) Lau; m. Tony Kai-Wai Chau, Oct. 2, 1987; 1 child. BEE, U. Coll. London, 1983, PhD, 1988. Rsch. assoc. Univ. Coll. London, 1986-89; engr. software M&R Computer Consultancy, London, 1989-90; analyst Abbey Nat. Bank, London, 1990-94; tech. architect assoc. J.P. Morgan, London, 1994-97; asst. v.p. Merrill Lynch, London, 1997—; bd. dirs. T.K.C. Rsch., London. Mem. IEEE, IEE London (assoc.), BCS (assoc.), Brit. Machine Vision Assn. Avocations: badminton, squash, tennis, swimming, gardening. Home: Traps Lodge 23 11 Acre Rise, Essex Loughton IG10 1AN, England Office: Merrill Lynch, 25 Ropemaker St, London EC2Y 9LY, England

CHAU, FOO-TIM, chemistry educator; b. Namghai, Guangdong, China, Mar. 7, 1948; s. Pun and Siu-Mui (Ho) C.; m. Pui-Ki Pauline Liu, Sept. 22, 1975. BSc with honors, Chinese U. Hong Kong, 1970, MSc, 1972; PhD, U. B.C., 1975. Overseas postdoctoral fellow Nat. Rsch. Coun. Can., 1975-77; grad. master tchr. Kowloon Pentecostal Sch., Hong Kong, 1978-82; lectr. Hong Kong Poly., 1983-88, sr. lectr., 1988-90, reader, 1990-94, prof., 1994—; referee Computer in Physics, 1988-92. Editl. bd. Lab. Microcomputer U.K., 1991-96; contbr. articles to profl. jours. Deacon Christian Fellowship Ctr., Hong Kong, 1982—. Fellow Royal Soc. Chemistry U.K. (chartered chemist); mem. Am. Chem. Soc., Hong Kong Instn. Sci. (founding mem.), Rsch. Grant Coun. Avocations: sports, music, gardening. Office: Dept Applied Biology, and Chemical Technology, The Hong Kong Poly U, Hung Hom Kowloon, Hong Kong

CHAU, HOI FUNG, physicist, astrophysicist; b. Kowloon, Hong Kong, Feb. 28, 1968; came to U.S., 1992; s. Kui Wah and Wai Fong (Kam) C. BS, U. Hong Kong, 1989, PhD, 1992. Postdoctoral rsch. assoc. U. Ill., Urbana-Champaign, 1992-94; mem. Inst. for Advanced Study, Princeton, N.J., 1994-96; asst. prof. U. Hong Kong, 1996—. Contbr. articles to profl. jours.; patent on certain quantum cryptographic systems. Recipient Outstanding Young Rsch. award, 2000. Mem. IEEE, AAAS, Am. Astron. Soc., Am. Phys. Soc., Am. Math. Soc., Hong Kong Phys. Soc. (coun. 1990-91, 97-99, hon. sec. 99—). Achievements include a consistent description of post-glitch response of various pulsars (neutron stars), the proof of security of quantum cryptography against evasdropper's attack. Office: U Hong Kong Dept Physics, Pokfulam Rd, Pokfulam Hong Kong

CHAU, KAI BONG, lawyer, consultant; b. Hong Kong, Sept. 25, 1934; s. Sik Nin and Ida Hing Kwai (Lau) C.; m. Brenda Yuet Ching Tam, July 4, 1956; 1 child, Brandon Kwok Fung. MA in Law with honors, Cambridge (Eng.) U., 1957. Bar: England 1962, Hong Kong 1963; notary pub. Prin. K.B. Chau & Co., Solicitors, Hong Kong, 1963—; hon. consul Cook Islands, South Pacific, 1982; chmn. Oriental Express Travel Agts. IATA, Hong Kong Internat. Import and Export Co. Ltd.; dir. Pearl City Restaurants, 1990, Ying Bong Co. Ltd., Hong Kong, 1963-79. Subject of numerous TV, mag. and newspaper interviews. Named one of 12 Most Interesting Personalities in World, Marie France mag., 1986, one of 6 personalities in The Best of Hong Kong, Womens' Wear Daily, 1988; appearances in Robin Leach's "Lifestyle of the Rich and Famous" (U.S. TV), Alan Whicker show "Barry Norman's Quest in Hong Kong" (BBC), "60 Minutes" (Australian TV) and others. Mem. Royal Hong Kong Jockey Club.

CHAU, KAM-TIM, engineering educator, researcher; b. Hong Kong, Oct. 29, 1960; s. Yat-wing Chow and Sou-chun Chan; m. Wai-lim Ho, Aug. 9, 1993; children: Magnum Mak-Lam, Jaquelee Chit Yu. M in Engring., Asian Inst. Tech., 1987; PhD, Northwestern U., 1991. Site engr. asst. Mei Cheong Contrn. Co., Hong Kong, 1983; tutor, demonstrator Hong Kong Baptist Coll., Hong Kong, 1984-85; rsch. assoc. Asian Inst. Tech., Bangkok, 1987; from rsch. asst. to post-doctoral fellow Northwestern U., Evanston, Ill., 1991-92; lectr. Hong Kong Poly., 1992-94; asst. prof. Hong Kong Poly. U., 1995-96, assoc. prof., 1996—; Reviewer Internat. Jour. Solids and Structures, 1993—, Jour. Engring. Math., Jour. Engring. Mechanics, Jour. Infrastructure Systems, Internat. Jour. Fracture, Rock Mechanics and Rock Engring, Jour. Sound and Vibration, Mechanics Rsch. Comms., Jour. Applied Mechanics, Internat. Jour. Rock Mechanics and Mining Scis.; mem. editl. team Advances in Structural Engring. Mem. ASME (geomechanics com. applied mechanics div. 1993—, elasticity com. 1993—), Japan Soc. Soil Mechanics and Found. Engring. (Asian tech. com. 1994—), Am. Soc. Engring. Edn. Avocations: swimming, running marathons, travel, hiking, photography. Office: Hong Kong Poly U, Dept Civil/Structural Engr, Hung Hom Kowloon Hong Kong China

CHAU, LAP PUI, engineering researcher; b. Hong Kong, June 19, 1967; s. Pak Ling and Siu Han (Yip) C.; m. Loo Sim Yap. BEE (hon.), Oxford Brookes U., 1992; PhD in Elec. Engring., Hong Kong Polytech. U., 1996. Engr. Dataworld Internat. Ltd., Hong Kong, 1989-91, sr. engr., 1992-93; sr. engr. Tritech Microelectronic Internat. ltd., Singapore, 1996-97; rsch. fellow Ctr. for Signal Processing Nanyang Tech. U., Singapore, 1997—; asst. prof. Sch. Elec. and Electronic Engring. Nanyang Technol. U., Singapore, 2000—. Inventor: IEEE transactions on circuits and systems for video technology, 1994, IEEE transactions on circuits and systems, 1995, Internat. jour. of electronics, 1996. IEEE. Fax: 65-7910128. E-mail: elphchau@ntu.edu.sg.

CHAUDHARI, GHANASHYAM NARAYAN, pharmaceutical professional; b. Jalgaon, India, Apr. 19, 1953; s. Narayan R. and Dwarka N. C.; m. Pratibha Ghanashyam Mahajan, Dec. 8, 1984. BPharm, K.M.K. Coll. Pharmacy, Mumbai, India, 1976; MPharm, Bombay Coll. Pharmacy, Mumbai, India, 1979; PhD in Technology, U. Mumbai, 1983. Lectr. Mumbai Coll. Pharmacy, 1977-83; asst. prof. K.M.K. Coll. Pharmacy, Mumbai, 1983-95; tech. svc. mgr. J.B. Chems., Mumbai, 1985-87; R&D mgr. Glenmark Pharms., Nasik, 1987-99, R&D v.p. formulation, 1999—. Contbr. articles to profl. jours. Mem. Indian Pharm. Assn. (life), Rotary. Avocations: reading, photography, movies, travel, friendship.

CHAUDHARI, PRADIP RAMDAS, veterinarian, scientist; b. Jalgaon, India, Dec. 17, 1968; s. Ramdas Vithoba and Prabha Ramdas (Patil) C.; m. Vatsal Pradip Ahirrao, Dec. 1990. B Vet. Sci. and Animal Husbandry, Punjabrao Agr. U., Nagpur, India, 1991; M Vet. Sci., Konkan Agr. U., Bombay, India, 1994; DMRIT, Mumbai (India) U., 1998. Sci. officer Bhabha Atomic Rsch. Ctr., Mumbai, 1994—; hon. animal welfare officer Animal Welfare Bd. India, Chennai, 1997. Author: About Veterinary Nuclear Medicine, 1999; contbr. articles to profl. jours.)Best Article award 1995, Best Surgeon award 1998, Young Scientist award 1999). Office: Radiation Med Ctr BARC, Tata Meml Ctr Parel, Mumbai India

CHAUDHARY, NAEEM SARWAR, helicopter pilot; b. Kasur, Punjab, Pakistan, June 12, 1968; s. Mohammed Sarwar and Khursheed (Sarwar) C.; m. Lubna Naeem, Feb. 16, 1997; children: Mahnoor Naeem, Abdullah Naeem. BSc in Naval Scis., Naval Acad., Karachi, Pakistan, 1990; diploma in Air Safety. Cert. pilot, Pakistan; nav., gunnery, torpedo anti submarine, comms., Naval Warfare, ops. Lt. comdr. Naval Aviation Pakistan Navy, Karachi, 1995-96, staff officer tng., 1999—, exec. officer, sr. pilot 333 ASW Squadron, 1987—; commd. lt. comdr. Pakistan Navy, 1999, advanced through grades to lt. comdr., 1999, helicopter pilot; bridge watch PNS BABUR; flyer 333 ASW Sqn. Islam. Avocations: tennis, squash, golf, billiards. Office: 333 ASW Squadron, PNS Mehran Sharah-e-Faisal, 75350 Karachi Sindh, Pakistan

CHAUDHARY, NEENA, otolaryngologist, surgeon; b. Chandigarh, Punjab, India, May 28, 1962; d. Jugal Kishore and Prem Lata (Anand) Sondhi; m. Deepak Chaudhary, Nov. 25, 1988; children: Kshitij, Akshit. MB, BChir, Bhopal U., 1985, MS in ENT, 1991. Sr. rsch. fellow Lady Hardinge Med. Coll., New Delhi, 1991-92; sr. resident Safdarjang Hosp., New Delhi, 1992-95, sr. rsch. assoc., 1995-99, ENT specialist, 1999—. Contbr. articles to profl. jours. Mem. Assn. Otolaryngologists India, Ctrl. Svcs. Officers Inst. Avocations: music, watching movies, cooking. Home: 241 Laxmi Bai Nagar, New Delhi 110023, India Office: Safdarjang Hosp, New Delhi 110021, India

CHAUDHARY, SUJEET, physicist, research scientist; b. Pilkhuwa, Ghaziabad, India, Sept. 1, 1968; s. Chander Pal and Summitra Kumari (Devi) C.; m. Geeta Rani, June 23, 1999; 1 child, Sanskar. BS of Physics with honors, Meerut U., Ghaziabad, India, 1987; MS of Physics, Indian Inst. Tech., New Delhi, 1990, M of Tech., 1992, PhD, 1997. Sr. rsch. fellow Indian Inst. Tech., New Delhi, 1992-96; sci. officer Centre for Advanced Tech., Indore, 1997—; sci. officer Dept. Atomic Energy, Govt. India. Contbr. more than 20 articles to profl. jours. including Phys. Rev. B, Physica C., Solid State Comms., among others. Rsch. fellow Grad. Aptitude Test Engring., 1990; scholar Nat. Scholarship Scheme, 1987. Avocations: reading, music. Home: 74-B Umesh Nagar, Indore 452009, India Office: Centre for Advanced Tech, PO-CAT, Indore 452013, India

CHAUDHARY, ZAFAR IQBAL, pathologist, consultant; b. Lahore, Punjab, Pakistan, May 3, 1949; arrived in United Arab Emirates, 1993; s. Noor Elahi and Noor (Begum) C.; m. Perveen Zafar, Dec. 2, 1966; children: Naheed, Asif, Mazhar, Saima. BVSc, BSc, U. Punjab, Lahore, Pakistan, 1970; MSc with honors, U. Agr., Faisalabad, Pakistan, 1978; MSc in Animal Growth, U. Alta., Edmonton, Can., 1985; PhD, U. Punjab, 1998. Lectr. Coll. Vet. Scis. U. Punjab, 1971-85, asst. prof., 1985-91, assoc. prof., 1991-93; pathologist vet. sect. Abu Dhabi Municipality, United Arab Emirates, 1993-96, dir., 1996—. Contbr. more than 50 articles to profl. jours. Recipient numerous scholarships. Mem. Soc. for the Advancement of Sci. (exec. coun.). Office: Abu Dhabi Municipality, Dirs Vet Sect/PO Box 10829, Abu Dhabi United Arab Emirates

CHAUDHRY, HUMAYUN JAVAID, physician, medical educator, writer; b. Karachi, Pakistan, Nov. 17, 1965; came to U.S., 1971, naturalized, 1978; s. Hukam Dad and Riffat Sultana (Bhatti) C.; m. Nazli Tabasum Iqbal, June 7, 1992; children: Shaun Hatim, Haris Iqbal. BA, NYU, 1986, MS, 1989; DO, N.Y. Coll. Osteo. Medicine, 1991; postgrad., Harvard U. Diplomate Nat. Bd. Osteo. Med. Examiners, Am. Bd. Internal Medicine; lic. physician, surgeon, N.Y. Intern St. Barnabas Hosp., Bronx, N.Y., 1991-92; resident in internal medicine Winthrop-U. Hosp., Mineola, N.Y., 1992-95, chief med. resident, 1995-96; clin. asst. prof. medicine N.Y. Coll. Osteo. Medicine, Old Westbury, 1997—; attending physician, dir. med. edn. Long Beach (N.Y.) Med. Ctr., 1996—; attending physician Island Park Med. Care, 1996-98, Family Care Ctr., Long Beach, N.Y., 1996-99, Westbury Total Health Care, 2000—; adj. instr. anatomy N.Y. Coll. Osteo. medicine, Old Westbury, 1996—; reporter, news editor, TV anchorman Third World Broadcasting Network, N.Y.C., 1986-95, 99—; asst. clin. instr. medicine SUNY Stony Brook Sch. Medicine, 1995-96. Mem. editl. bd. New Physician, Reston, Va., 1991-99; founding editor The NYSSIM Resident newsletter, 1996-97; contbr. articles to profl. jours. Press sec. Pakistan Independence Day Parade N.Y., 1987-88; inaugural spkr. 1st ann. Pakistan Day Festival Bklyn., 1991; founding mem. Pakistan Press Club Am., N.Y.C., 1990-93, v.p., 1992-93. Capt. USAFR, 1999—. Regents Coll. scholar State of N.Y., Albany, 1982; recipient Essay Competition award N.Y.C. Fire Dept., 1979. Fellow ACP, Royal Soc. Medicine U.K., Nassau Acad. of Medicine; mem. AMA, Am. Osteo. Assn., N.Y. State Soc. Internal Medicine (pres. resident physicians sect. 1995-96, bd. dirs. 1996-2000), Am. Coll. Osteo. Internists (founding pres. N.Y. chpt. 1998—, bd. dirs. 1999—), Islamic Med. Assn. N.Am., Assn. Pakistani Physicians N.Am., Amnesty Internat., Am. Muslim Coun., Kashmiri-Am. Coun., N.Y. Coll. Osteo. Medicine Alumni Assn. (sec. bd. dirs. 1995-98, pres. 1998-2000, bd. dirs. 2000—), Assn. Osteo. Dirs. Med. Educators, N.Y. State Osteo. Med. Soc., Nassau Soc. Internal Medicine (bd. dirs. 1996-98, v.p. 1998-99, pres. 1999-2000), Islamic Ctr. of L.I., Islamic Soc. N.Am., World Wildlife Fund, Med. Soc. State of N.Y., Am. Acad. Osteopathy. Republican. Muslim. Avocations: tennis, reading, rare books, travel. Home: 1022 Commack Rd Dix Hills NY 11746-8209 Office: Long Beach Med Ctr 455 E Bay Dr Long Beach NY 11561-2301

CHAUDHRY, PRAVEEN K., adult education educator, researcher; b. Patna, Bihar, India, Oct. 24, 1961; came to U.S., 1990; s. Shree Krishna and Sudha Chaudhry; 1 child, Omar Kabeer. MA, Hindu Coll., Delhi, India, 1984; MPhil, U. Delhi, 1985; PhD, U. Pa., 2000. Asst. prof. U. Delhi, 1987-94; rsch. assoc. Ctr. Advanced Study India U. Pa., Phila., 1994; asst. prof. Swarthmore (Pa.) Coll., 1999—. Mem. Internat. Studies Assn., Am. Polit. Sci. Assn., Assn. Asian Studies. Office: Swarthmore Coll 500 College Ave Swarthmore PA 19081-1306

CHAUDHRY, RIAZ AHMAD, librarian; b. Lahore, Punjab, Pakistan, Dec. 25, 1952. BA, U. Punjab, 1975; B Arts in Libr. and Info. Scis., Allama Iqbal Open U., 1986. Libr. Crescent Model Sch., Lahore, 1975-78; libr. asst. Pakistan Atomic Energy, Lahore, 1978-79; tech. libr. Packages, Ltd., Lahore, 1979—. Office: ShahrahERoome PO Amer Sidhu, 54760 Lahore Punjab, Pakistan

CHAUDHURI, BIDYUT BARAN, computer scientist, educator; b. Bangladesh, Dec. 7, 1950; s. Jagadananda and Renuka Saha C.; m. Subhra Poddar, May 6, 1985; children: Amanda, Anwesha. BS with honors, Calcutta U., 1969, B Technology, 1972, M Technology, 1974; PhD, IIT, Kanpur, 1980. Computer engr. Indian Statis. Inst., Calcutta, 1978-81, assoc. prof., 1982-86, prof., 1987—, dpet. head, CVPRU, 1993—; Leverhulme vis. fellow, Queen's U., U.K., 1981-82; vis. prof. GSF, Munich and Tech. U., Hannover, Germany, 1986-88; adminstrv. head P&ES Divsn., Indian Statis. Inst., 1990-92, prin. coord. NCKBC, CVPRU, 1992—; expert rev. com. Dept. Sci. and Technology, India, 1993—; sec. Internat. Acad. of Sci., Germany, 1992—. Inventor in field. Recipient J.C. Bose Meml. award, 1986, Achuta Menon prize, 1996; Nodal Centre grantee UN Devel. Programme, 1988, Indo-German Collaboration grantee Internat. Buro, Munich, 1989, Homi Bhabha fellow, 1992, Vikram Sarbhai rsch. awardee, 1995. Fellow Indian Nat. Acad. of Engring., Indian Nat. Acad. Scis., Internat. Assn. Pattern Recognition, Inst. Electronics Telecomm. Engring. Avocations: volleyball, music, lit. Home: 87/29 AK Mukherjee Rd, West Bengal 700 090 Calcutta India Office: Indian Statis Inst, 203 B T Rd, West Bengal 700035 Calcutta India

CHAUDHURI, SUBHASIS, engineering educator, consultant; b. Bahutali, W. Bengal, India, Mar. 1, 1963; s. Nihar Kumar and Santa C.; m. Sucharita Chatterjee, June 8, 1991; children: Ushasi, Syomantak. BTech, Indian Inst. Tech., Kharagapur, 1985; MS, U. Calgary, Alta., Can., 1987; PhD, U. Calif., San Diego, 1990. Asst. prof. Indian Inst. Tech., Bombay, 1990-94, assoc. prof., 1994-98, prof., 1998—; vis. prof. U. Erlangen, Germany, 1996. Co-author: Depth from De Focus, 1999. Alexander von Humboldt fellow, 1997, fellow Inst. Electronics and Telecomm. Engrs., India, 1999. Mem. IEEE. Hindu. Avocations: reading, philosophizing, music, cooking. Home: Quarter No C-68, IIT Powai, Bombay 400076, India Office: Indian Inst Tech, Dept Elec Engring, Powai Bombay 400076, India

CHAUDOIR, JACQUES, company executive; b. Liege, Belgium, June 1, 1929; s. Camille and Gabrielle (Vivario) C.; m. Gilberte Juzen, May 27, 1977. Degree in indsl. engring., Inst. Gramme, Angleur, Belgium. Comml. mgr. Maison Noirfalise & Cie, S.A., Angleur, 1954-74; asst. mgr. Intranet, S.A., Clermont, Belgium, 1974-78; dir. Maison Noirfalise & Cie, S.A., 1974-

85; mgr. Groupe Chaudoir SPRL, Liege, 1980—. Mem. Cercle Liegeois Des Assureurs (past pres.), Cercle Royal Des Assureurs De Belgique. Home: Rue Des Pins 1, 4130 Tilff Belgium

CHAUHAN, RAMSWAROOP SINGH, physician, veterinarian; b. Aligarh, India, Sept. 10, 1958; s. Rajpal Singh and Prakash Vati (Raghaw) C.; m. Vandana Singh, Nov. 16, 1984; children: Mahima Singh, Yatishwar. B in Vet. Sci. and Animal Husbandry, G.B. Pant U., India, 1981, M in Vet. Sci. in Pathology, 1982, PhD in Pathology, 1991. Tchg. assoc. G.B. Pant U., India, 1983; assoc. prof. G.B. Pant U., 1996-99, nat. fellow, 1999—; asst. disease investigation officer CCSHAU Hisar, India, 1983-88, sr. ADIO, 1988-96. Author: Veterinary Clinical and Laboratory Diagnosis, 1995, Aflatoxicosis in Animals and Man, 1997, An Introduction to Immunopathology, 1998; mng. editor Jour. Immunology and Immunopathology, 1999—. Gen. sec. Rastriya Shekshic Mahasaryh, Pantnagar, 1997—. Recipient award Indian Assn. for the Advancement of Vet. Rsch., 1996, Nat. Fellow award Indian Coun. Agrl. Rsch., 1999. Mem. R.S.M., Indian Assn. Vet. Pathologists (zonal sec. 1999—, Best Young Scientist award 1992), Soc. for Immunology and Immunopathology (sec. gen. 1998—). Achievements include inventor of dot immunobinding assay for rapid diagnosis of diseases. Avocations: reading, writing, research on herbal medicines, research on environmental pollutions. Home: V 1346 Ta Colony, Pantnagar 263145, India Office: GB Pant Univ, Coll Vet Scis, Pantnagar 263145, India

CHAULET, PIERRE, chest disease physician, consultant; b. Algiers, Algeria, Mar. 27, 1930; s. Alexandre Edme and Suzanne Claire (Tamiatto) C.; m. Claudine Simone Guillot; children: Luc, Anne, Eve-Marie. MD, U. Paris, 1957; specialist in TB and chest diseases, U. Tunis, Tunisia, 1960; assoc. prof. medicine, U. Algiers, 1967. Med. specialist Ministry of Pub. Health, Tunis, 1957-62; asst. clinician Univ. Hosp. Ctr., Algiers, 1962-67, lectr., 1967-71; prof. Univ. Hosp. Ctr. West, Algiers, 1971-94; med. officer WHO/GTB, Geneva, 1994-98; chief physician Med. Svcs. Tunis, 1957-62, Algiers, 1962-94; rsch. program mgr. Nat. Orgn. Scientific Rsch., Algiers, 1971-2000; nat. expert Ministry of Health, Algiers, 1967-99; internat. cons. Internat. Union Against Tuberculosis and Lung Disease and WHO, 1981-2000; sr. cons. WHO, 2000. Co-author (WHO tech. documents): TB/HIV Clinical Manual, 1996, Guidelines for the Management of Drug Resistant Tuberculosis, 1996, Treatment of TB, Guidelines for National Programmes, 1997, Tuberculosis Handbook, 1998; contbr. more than 500 articles and reports to profl. jours. and conf. procs. Del. to Popular Communal Assembly of Algiers City, Algeria, 1967-71; mem. exec. bur. Algerian Med. Union, 1977-82; v.p. Nat. Human Rights Observatory, Algeria, 1992-96; health advisor to head of govt., Algeria, 1992-94. Capt.-physician, Nat. Liberation Army, Algeria, 1957-62. recipient Ricaux Tuberculosis prize, Nat. Acad. Medicine, Paris, 1967, Algerian Resistance medal, Pres. Algerian Republic, 1984, Social Merit medal, Republic of Senegal, 1989, Internat. award Princess Chichibu Meml. Found., 1999. Mem. Am. Coll. Chest Physicians, Fedn. Maghrebine of Respiratory Diseases, Algerian Soc. Pneumophtisiology (exec. com. 1964-94), N.Y. Acad. Scis. Avocations: literature, history, economy, politics. Home: Rue du Hoggar 8, Hydra, 16035 Algiers Algeria

CHAUMBA, JEFFERSON BRIGHTON, geologist; b. Dorowa, Zimbabwe, Mar. 18, 1969; s. Augustine Kapuno and Scholarstica (Mavura) C. BS, U. Zimbabwe, 1992; MS, U. Natal, S. Africa, 1995; PhD, U. Cape Town, S. Africa, 1999. Process geologist Independence Mining, Zimbabwe, 1999—. Roman Catholic. Home: PO Box 3328 Paulington, Mutare Zimbabwe Office: Independence Mining, Box 56, Shamua Zimbabwe

CHAUNU, PIERRE RENE, history educator; b. Aug. 17, 1923; s. Jean and Heloise (Charles) C.; m. Huguette Catella, Sept. 13, 1947; 6 children (1 dec.). Mem. faculty Sch. Advanced Hispanic Studies, Madrid, 1948-51; with CNRS, 1956-59, now mem. directorate, mem. sci. com., history sec., 1980—; with U. Caen, France, 1959-70; prof. history Sorbonne, U. Paris, 1970—; assoc. prof. Faculte de Theologie Reformee, Aix-en-Provence, France, 1974; mem. sect. Conseil Econ. et Social, 1976-77; pres. Conseil Superieur des Corps Universitaires, 1977. Author: Seville et l'Atlantique (1504-1650) (12 vols.), Histoire et Foi, 1980, Histoire et imagination, 1980, Rèforme et contre-rèforme, 1981, Histoire et Dècadence, 1981, La France, 1982, Ce que je crois, 1982, Le chemin des mages, 1983, Combats pour l'histoire, 1983, L'historien dans tous ses ètats, 1984, L'Historien en Cet Instant, 1985, Rèhistoire, 1986, Au coeur religieux de l'histoire, 1986, L'aventure de la rèforme, 1986, Une autre voie, 1986, Du Big Bang è l'enfant, 1987, L'Obscure Mémoire de la France, 1988, Apologie pour l'histoire, 1988, Le Grand Dèclassement, 1989, Journal de Jeau Hèroard, 1989, Trois Millions d'Années, 1990, Colère Contre Colère Seghers, 1991, Miroirs et Reflets de L'Histoire, Economica, 1991, Dieu, Apologie, 1991, L'Aventure de la Reforme, le monde de Jean Calvin, 1992, Brève Histoire de Dieu, Lalfont, 1992, Danse avec l'Histoire de Fallois, 1992, Colomb ou la Loyique de l'imprivisible, 1993, Les fon dements de la pèaix, 1993, L'axe du temps, 1993, L'instant eclate, 1994, Lesenjeux de la faix, 1995, L'Hèritage, 1995, Baptime de Clovis, Baptime de la France, 1996, Balland, 1996, Danse avec l'histoire de Paris, 1998, Le basculement religieux, 1998, Charles Quint Feyard, 1999; contbr. numerous articles to profl. jours. Decorated Commandeur d'la Legion d'honneur. Mem. Acad. Scis. morales et politiques,. Office: U Paris-Sorbonne, 1 Rue Victor-Cousin, 75005 Paris France also: 12 rue des Cordeliers, 14300 Caen France

CHAURET, CHRISTIAN PIERRE, microbiologist, educator; b. Buckingham, Que., Can., Dec. 19, 1965; came to U.S., 1996; s. Raymond C. and Marie-Paule M. (Renaud) C.; m. Denise C. Schwerdtfeger, July 6, 1991; children: Renaud C., Eric C. BS in Agr., McGill U., 1988, MS, 1990; PhD, U. Waterloo, Ont., Can., 1994. Post-doctoral rschr. U. Ottawa, Ottawa, Can., 1994-96; asst. prof. Ind. U., Kokomo, 1996—; mem. project advisory com. Am. Water Works Assn. Rsch. Found., Denver, 1997-99. Contbr. articles to profl. jours. Recipient rsch. grant Chlorine Chemistry Coun., Kokomo, 1998—, rsch. grants Am. Water Works Assn. Rsch. Found., 1997-99, 1997, 1995-96. Mem. Am. Soc. for Microbiology, Am. Water Works Assn., Ind. Br. Am. Soc. for Microbiology (edn. rep. 1997—). E-mail: cchauret@iuk.edu. Office: Ind U Kokomo 2300 S Washinton St Kokomo IN 46904-9003

CHAUVEL, CHRISTOPHE JACQUES, physician; b. Paris, July 13, 1963; s. Philippe Francis and Francine Marie (Dubois) C.; m. Annick Marie Jacquemin, Nov. 15, 1986; children: Remi, Caroline, Hélène, Chloé, Noémie. MD, 1990. Resident Hosp., Paris, 1986-90, asst., 1991-95; physician Clinique St.-Augustin, Bordeaux, France, 1996—; cons. med. labs., 1995—. Contbr. articles to profl. jours. Home: 2 Rue Kleber, 33200 Bordeaux France Office: Clinique Saint-Augustin, 114 Ave D'Ares, 33000 Bordeaux France

CHAUVET, GILBERT ANDRÉ, mathematics educator; b. Nueil, France, Oct. 2, 1942; s. Eugene Chauvet and Antonia Mainchain; m. Marie Elizabeth Cottet, June 27, 1940; children: Pierre, Anne, Line. M Maths., Poitiers U., France, 1965; PhD in Molecular Physics, Nantes U., France, 1974; MD, Angers U., France, 1976. Researcher Angers U., 1964-72, assoc. prof., 1972-76; prof. biomath. Angers U., 1976-80; prof. theoretical biology Angers U., 1980—; dir. Med. Computing Dept. Angers Hosp., 1984—; dir., founder Inst. Theoretical Biology/Angers U., 1988—; rsch. prof. U. So. Calif., L.A., 1994—, Pitts. U., 1988-92; dir. Theoretical Biology Svcs., Masson, Paris, 1987—. Author: Theoretical Physiology, 3 vols., 1987-90, La Vie Dans La Matiere, Flammarion, Paris, 1995, Theoretical Systems in Biology: Hierarchical and Functional Integration, 3 vols., 1996; contbr. articles to profl. jours. Avocation: hist. monuments. Office: IBT Physiol Systems Sim Lab, 10 rue A Boquel, Angers 49100, France

CHAVAN, BIR SINGH, psychiatrist, consultant; b. Ambala, Haryana, India, Mar. 25, 1961; s. Tulsi Ram and Kartari Devi (Kataria) C.; m. Kavita Banswal, Apr. 30, 1988; 2 children. M.B.B.S., Rohtak Med. Coll., Haryana, 1983; MD, Postgrad. Inst., Chandigarh, India, 1987. Jr. resident Postgrad. Inst., Chandigarh, 1985-87, sr. resident, 1988; asst. prof. All India Inst. Med. Scis., New Delhi, 1988-92, assoc. prof., 1992-96, cons., 1990-96, cmty. cons., 1993-96; prof. Govt. Med. Coll., Chandigarh, 1996—, head dept., 1996—; cons. in-chg. All India Inst. Med. Scis., New Delhi, 1990-96, cons. in-chg. cmty., 1993-96. Contbr. articles to profl. jours. Coord. Free Health Camp Socially Cultured and Sci. Trained Med. Assn., Haryana, 1990—. WHO fellow, 1996. Fellow Indian Psychiat. Assn.; mem. Delhi Psychiatry Assn., Indian Assn. Social Psychiatry. Home: 513 Arya Nagar, Ambala Cantt Haryana, India Office: Government Medical Coll, Sector 32, Chandigarh 160047, India

CHAVANCY, GÉRARD JEAN, research scientist; b. Lyon, France, Mar. 22, 1946; s. Paul Joseph and Louise Elidie (Varagnat) C.; m. Marianne Peres, Sept. 9, 1967; 1 child, Philippe. Degree in sci., U. Claude Bernard, Lyon, 1967, PhD in Speciality Biology, 1970, State Doctorate in Sci., 1980. Lectr. U. Claude Bernard, Lyon, 1967-71; asst. prof. U. Laval, Quebec, Can., 1971-73; from rsch. asst. to sci. officer Ctr. Nat. Rsch. Sci., Lyon, 1973—; dir. Unité Nat. Séricicole Inst. Nat. de la Recherche Agronomique, Lyon, 1986—; sec.-gen. Internat. Sericultural Commn., Lyon, 1990—; cons. FAO World Bank, 1986—. Editor: Sericologia, 1986—. Recipient Chevalier Merit Agricole Min. Agriculture, France, 1986. Mem. AAAS, Soc. France Biochemistry Biol. Molecular, Soc. Biology Cellular, N.Y. Acad. Scis., Acad. Sci. Ardè (corr.), Acad. Sci. Lyon. Avocations: reading, theatre. Home: 2 Ave Roberto Rossellini, 69100 Villeurbanne France Office: Unité Nat Séricicole, 25 Quai Jean-Jacques Rousseau, 69350 La Mulati 69350, France

CHAVARRIA, FEBRONIO EDUARDO, engineering company executive, consultant; b. Monterrey, Nuevo Leon, Mex., May 4, 1952; s. Febronio Eduardo and Soledad (Fernandez) C.; m. Elia Teresa Aldrete, Oct. 27, 1977; children: Bertrand, Sebastian. Civil engr., U Autonoma Nuevo Leon, Monterrey, 1974, M of Engring., 1976; D of Engring., Ecole Nat. Traveaux Pubs. Etat, Lyon, France, 1980; postgrad., U. Tex., 1981. Cert. engr. CEO Kappak Consultores, Monterrey, 1981-86; pres., CEO Grupo FCH, Monterrey, 1986—; cons. Pemex, Monterrey, 1981-83, Protexa, Monterrey, 1992-96, Enermex, Monterrey, 1992—. Contbr. articles to profl. jours. Sec. of ecology Municipality of Apodaca, Nuevo Leon, 1994. Recipient Olin-Tonatiuh award Coparmex, 1992. Mem. Internat. Assn. Water Quality, Am. Water Works Assn., Water Environment Fedn. Avocations: classical guitar, chess, karate. Home: Cumbres 4o Sector ACP, Paseo Navegants 121 Norte, 64619 Monterrey Mexico Office: Grupo FCH, Blvd Puerta Del Sol 934, 64630 Monterrey Mexico

CHAVES, CARLOS MAURICIO G.F., physicist, educator, researcher; b. Rio de Janeiro, Aug. 12, 1940; s. Bento Ferreira and Yvette Ferreira (Giesbrecht) C.; m. Therezinha Ferreira Souza da Costa, Jan. 29, 1965 (div. July 1973); 1 child, Adriana; m. Renate Eva Katharina Weiss, Sept. 13, 1978; children: Fabio, Leonardo. B degree, Fed. U., Rio de Janeiro, 1964; PhD, Cath. U., Rio de Janeiro, 1973. Postdoctoral fellow U. de Paris, Orsay, 1976, U. Pa., Phila., 1977; assoc. prof. Cath. U., Rio de Janeiro, 1974—, dir. dept. physics, 1978-80; vis. scientist Max Planck Inst., Stuttgart, Germany, 1984-86. Author: (ednl. software) A Multimedia Tutorial for University Physics, 1994, A Multimedia Course in Mechanics for High School, 1994; contbr. articles to profl. jours. Mem. Brazilian Phys. Soc., N.Y. Acad. Scis. Avocations: horse riding, diving. E-mail: cmch@fis.puc-rio.br. Office: Cath U Dept Physics, Rua Marques S Vicente 225, 22453900 Rio de Janeiro Brazil

CHAVES, FRANCISCO DE PAULA, JR., criminalist; b. Aragargas, Brazil, Aug. 22, 1954; s. Francisco de Paula Chaves and Schelle Chaves de Ziree; m. Maria Socorro Gomes; children: Francisco Guanna Damasceno, Eudesio Guanna Gomes, Desirée Gomex, Gustavo Guanna Junquire. Degree in adminstrn., U. Católica de Goiás, Brazil, 1979. Document examiner IPEC, Goiania, Brazil, 1997—. Author: Abordagem Geral sobre os Pitules de Divida Pública, 1988, Cobetanea de Documentis sobre a Economic Virtual de Republica, 1998, Iconografia das Apólices de di Vida Pública, 1999; (CD rom) Papeis de Valor Circulautes—Dinheiro e Apólices, 1999. Mem. Assn. Brasileira Criminalística, Internat. Assn. for Identification. Roman Catholic. Avocations: ancient documents, martial arts. Home: r J-54 Ad 91 Lt 13, St Jao, 74574200 Goiania Brazil Office: IPEC Inst Fran de Paula, Rua J54 QD 91 LT13 St J, 74574200 Goinia Go Brazil

CHAVES, JOSE MARIA, diplomat, foundation administrator, lawyer, educator; b. Bogotá, Colombia, Aug. 19, 1922; s. Carlos Chaves and María García de C.; m. Elena Gómez y Samperio; children: Cristina María, Tómás José. Bachiller, Bogotá, 1939, cert. in anthropology, 1942, JD, 1945; DSc (hon.), U. Antióquia, 1948; MA, Columbia U., 1951, PhD, 1953; LLD, U. Popayán, Colombia, 1957, Mercy Coll., 1991. Bar: Columbia 1944, Inter-American 1953. Editor in chief Revista Colegio del Rosario (arts and letters mag.), Colombia, 1944; gen. legal duties specializing in public adminstrn. Bogotá, 1942-45; instr. Romance langs. Columbia U., N.Y.C., 1945-48, 50-51; founder, 1st dean faculty U. Andes, Bogotá, 1948-49; head area studies Queens Coll. NYU, 1951-53; counselor Colombian Embassy, Washington, 1953-55; prof. internat. law U. Colombia, 1955-58, U. Paris, 1957; guest prof. internat. law and relations Brit. Council, various univs. Eng., Scotland, 1957; dir., chief exec. Am. Found. for Cultural Popular Action, Inc. (pvt. internat. orgn. for mass edn. by radio), N.Y.C., 1958—; amb. of Kyrgyzstan to UN, 1992—; dir. Center Latin Am. Studies, CUNY; chmn. Hispanic Am. editorial bd. Grolier, Inc., 1971—; ambassador extraordinary, permanent del. Iberoam. Bur. Edn. to UN; A.E. and P., permanent rep. Grenada to OAS; permanent rep. orgn. Iberoam. Countries to UN and OAS, 1986—; alt. gov. World Bank and Internat. Monetary Fund, 1974-77, 94; chmn. C.I.P., 1972—; organizer, dir. tech. assistance mission Unitarian Service Com. in Latin Am.; dir. gen. Nat. Univ. Fund, Colombia, 1955-58; amb. extraordinary Spl. Mission to Brazil, 1995. Editor-in-chief: Grolier Spanish Universal Ency; author: Chaves Plan for settlement religious conflict between Caths. and Protestants in Latin Am; Author: Francisco de Vitoria. Founder International Law, 1945, Intergroup relations in the Spain of Cervantes, 1953, University Reform in Colombia, 1957. Pres. Assn. Latin Am. Unity, 1984; chmn. Summit Coun. World Peace, 1985-92; ambassador extraordinary and plenipotentiary of Kyrgyztan to the UN, 1992-93. Decorated Legion of Honor (France); gran cruz Order of St. Constantine the Great; comdr., knight comdr. Grand Order Isabel La Católica (Spain); knight comdr. Alfonso El Sabio; grand cross Vasco N'nez de Balboa Panama, 1970; grand cross Juan P. Duarte Sanchez y Mella Dominican Republic, 1970, Medal of Jerusalem Israel, 1972; grand cross Order of Malta, 1976; grand cross Order Justice Law and Peace of Mex., 1977, grand cross Order Latin Am. Unity 1986, grand cross Order of St. Michael (Portugal), 1990; grand cross Order of Holy Cross of Jerusalem, 1991, grand cross of Saint Dennis of Zanthe, 1991; recipient medaglia universitaria U. Po Deo, Rome, 1957, medalla de los Andes U., 1958, medaille de Versailles, France, 1990, medalla Universidad, Lima, 1990, Lord Perry World prize for Edn., 1993, Order of Manas of Kyrgyzstan 1995. Mem. Internat. Law Assn., Inter-Am. Bar. Assn., Acad. Polit. Sci., MLA, Academia Hispano Americana, Assn. for Latin Am. Unity (founder, pres. 1984), Summit Coun. for World Peace (dir. 1987), Met. Club, Columbia U. Club (N.Y.C.), Quill Club USA (pres.), Brook Club, Phi Delta Kappa (v.p. Univ. World). Clubs: Metropolitan, Brook, Columbia U. (N.Y.C.), Quill of U.S.A. (pres.). Home: 118 E 60th St New York NY 10022-1103 Office: 401 5th Ave New York NY 10016-3317

CHAVES, WILSON LUIZ CAETANO, metallurgist; b. Raul Soares, Brazil, May 11, 1946; s. Wilson Cory and Nazira Caetano (Alves) C.; m. Maria Nazareth Avelar, Mar. 4, 1972; children: Daniela, Renata, Carolina. Grad., Coll. Arquidiocesano, Ouro Preto, Brazil, 1965. Metallurgist Morro Velho Mining, Nova Lima, Brazil, 1974-76, supr., 1976-80, head divsn., 1980-81, head dept., 1981-86, prodn. supt., 1986-91, metallurgical mgr., 1991-97; metallurgical mgr. Minorco Brazil, Nova Lima, 1997-98, Minorco Gold, Nova Lima, 1998—. Mem. Brazilian Metals Assn., Minas Gerais State Engrs. Assn. Roman Catholic. Avocations: soccer, music, movies, internet. Home: Rua Dos Andes 60, 34000000 Nova Lima Brazil Office: Anglo Gold, Praca Do Mineiro 83, 34000000 Nova Lima MG, Brazil

CHAVEZ, GERTRUDE MACASAET, editor, correspondent; b. Manila, Philippines, Nov. 16, 1963; d. Mariano and Valeria Macasaet (Napolis) Chavez. AB in Econs., Ateneo de Manila, 1983. Fin. analyst AFP Pension Fund, Manila, 1985-87; fin. editor Businessworld, Manila, 1987-95; editor-analyst Peregrine Securities, Manila, 1996; bur. chief Asia Times, Manila, 1997; editor AFX-Asia News, Manila, 1998—. Contbr. articles to profl. jours. Reuters fellow Oxford U., 1993-94; Gannett/Freedom Forum fellow U. Tex., 1995. Mem. Econ. Journalists Assn. Manila, Fgn. Corrs. Assn. Philippines. Avocations: swimming, reading, mountain trekking. Home: 2429 Amatista St, San Andres, Manila Philippines Office: AFX-Asia, King's Ct II Bldg 5th Fl, Pasong Tamo, Makati Philippines

CHÁVEZ, IGNACIO SANCHEZ, cardiologist; b. Mexico City, Nov. 14, 1928; s. Ignacio Sánchez and Celia (Rivera) Chávez; m. Ofelia Areyzaga, Nov. 24, 1956; children: Ofelia, Ignacio, Georgina, Fernando. MD, Nat. Autonomous U. of Mexico, 1952. Resident in internal medicine Nutrition's Hosp., Mexico City, 1952-54; resident in cardiology Nat. Inst. Cardiology, Mexico City, 1954-56; head in clin. svcs. and tchg. divsn. Nat. Inst. Cardiology, 1959-89, gen. dir., 1989-99; rsch. fellow Mass. Gen. Hosp., Boston, 1957, Peter Bent Brigham Hosp., Harvard U., Boston, 1958-59; prof. in cardiology Nat. Autonomous U. of Mexico, Mexico City, 1961-99. Contbr. to 6 cardiol. books, articles to profl. jours. Bd. Govs. Nat. Autonomous U. of Mexico, 1985-97. Mem. Nat. Acad. Medicine (pres. 1985), Mex. Soc. Cardiology (pres. 1976-78), Interamerican Soc. Cardiology (gen. sec. 1972-76), Internat. Soc. & Fedn. of Cardiology (nominating com. 1983-86, exec. bd. 1987-90), Mexican Bd. Cardiology (founding 1979-80, 2d pres. 1980-81). Home: Arenal 28 Chimalistac, Deleg A Obregon, 01070 Mexico City Mexico Office: Inst Nacional Cardiologia, Juan Badiano No 1 Tlalpan, 14080 Mexico City Mexico

CHAVEZ, MARY ANN, osteopathic family physician; b. York, Pa., Dec. 6, 1942; d. Henry David Gross and Mary Ellen (Ness) Rhoads; m. Richard L. Ziegler, Dec. 24, 1965 (div. Jan. 1983); children: Richard L. Ziegler Jr., Mara L. Tammaro, Brian L. Ziegler. BS, Alvernia Coll., 1983; DO, Coll. Osteo. Medicine, Phila., 1992. Legal sec. Louis Sager, Esquire, Pottstown, Pa., 1962-67; homemaker, tailor in pvt. practice Pottstown, 1967-85; intern Riverside Hosp., Wilmington, Del., 1992-93, resident in family practice, 1993-95; pvt. practice Spring Grove, Pa., 1995-97, Lancaster, Pa., 1997-999, Chillicothe, Ohio, 1999—. Pell grantee, Beog grantee Alvernia Coll., 1979-83. Mem. AMA, Am. Osteo. Assn., Am. Coll. Osteo. Family Physicians, Am. Acad. Osteopathy, Pa. Osteo. Med. Assn., York County Osteo. Med. Assn, Nat. Osteo. Women's Physicians Assn., Ohio Osteo. Medicine, Ohio State Med. Soc., Ross County Med. Soc., First Capitol Rotary Club. United Methodist. Avocations: oil painting, piano, tailoring. Home: 76 Fruithill Dr Chillicothe OH 45601-1135 Office: Mead Family Health Ctr PO Box 2500 311 Caldwell St Chillicothe OH 45601-3332

CHAVEZ, MARY LYNN, pharmacy educator; b. Detroit, May 8, 1950; d. Gilbert E. and Dorothea J. (Munro) Van Sickle; m. Pedro I. Chavez, May 12, 1973; children: Pedro C., Stephen J. BS in Pharmacy, U. Tex., 1973; PharmD, Purdue U., 1985. Instr. Coll. Pharmacy U. P.R., San Juan, 1983-84, 87-88, asst. prof. pharmacy practice, 1988-92, clin. pharmacy specialist Med. Sch.-Pediat. Oncology Group, 1990-93, assoc. prof. pharmacy, 1990-93; assoc. prof. dept. pharmacy practice Chgo. Coll. Pharmacy, Midwestern U., Downers Grove, Ill., 1993-98, acting asst. chmn. clin. edn., 1997-98; dir. didactic edn. Midwestern U. Coll. Pharmacy, Glendale, Ariz., 1998—; dir. complementary therapies Rsch. Ctr. Advancement Pharmacy Practice, Glendale, 1998—; writer pharmacy exam. CAT-NAPLEX/NABPLEX Licensure, Park Ridge, Ill., 1996; reviewer posters and presentations Am. Assn. Health Sys. Pharmacies, Bethesda, Md., 1996—; reviewer manuscripts Annals of Pharmacotherapy, Cin. Therapeutics, Am. Jour. Pharm. Edn., Jour. Pharmacy Tech., Am. Jour. Health Sys. Pharmacy, 1995—. Mem. editl. bd. Jour. Am. Pharmacy Assn., Prima Pub.; contbg. editor Hosp. Pharmacy. Asst. to cub pack leader area coun. Boy Scouts Am., Naperville, Ill., 1995, 96. Mem. Am. Pharm. Assn., Am. Assn. Colls. of Pharmacy, Am. Soc. Hosp. Pharmacists, Am. Coll. Clin. Pharmacists, Sigma Xi, Rho Chi. Office: Midwestern U Coll Pharmacy Glendale AZ 85308

CHAVEZ, VICTOR MANUEL, process engineer; b. Trujillo, Peru, Mar. 10, 1946; came to U.S., 1976; s. Alfonso Manuel Chavez and Paulina Leon Flores; m. Carmen Rosa Herrera, July 19, 1974; children: Leslie, Natalie, Valerie. BSChemE, UNMSM, Lima, Peru, 1970; engring. degree in petrochimie, U. Libre, Brussels, 1976. Registered profl. engr., Tex. Process engr. Nueces Petrochem., Corpus Christi, Tex., 1977-80; sr. process engr. HDR, Houston, 1980-82, Litwin Engrs. & Constrn., Houston, 1982-84; lead process engr. M.W. Kellogg, Houston, 1984-91; process engr. specialist Va. Indonesia Co., Houston and Bontang, Indonesia, 1991-96; prin. process engr. Fluor Daniel, Houston, 1996-97, The Bechtel Corp., Houston, 1997—. Mem. AIChE, NSPE. Avocations: golf, jogging. Home: 1415 Kelliwood Oaks Dr Katy TX 77450-4349

CHAVIS, ERIC NOEL, religious organization executive, minister. BS in Acctg. and Bus. Mgmt., Hampton (Va.) U., 1971; postgrad., L.I. U., 1973; MDiv, Duke U., 1977; D of Ministry, McCormick Theol. Sem., Chgo., 1996. Ordained minister Presbyn. Ch., 1983. Bank examiner Irving Trust Co., N.Y.C., 1971-74; supply pastor John Hall Presbyn. Ch., Carthage, N.C., 1974-78, 7th Presbyn. Ch., Chgo., 1978-80; asst. v.p. ops. Independence Bank of Chgo., 1978-80; auditor Main Bank of Chgo., 1980-83; assoc. exec. presbyter Presbytery of Giddings-Lovejoy, St. Louis, 1983-88; exec. dir. Gateway East Met. Ministry, East St. Louis, Ill., 1983-88; assoc. exec./treas. Synod of South Atlantic, Jacksonville, Fla., 1988-96; parish assoc. Woodlawn Presbyn. Ch., Jacksonville, 1988—; devel. officer Presbyn. Ch. (U.S.A.) Found., Jacksonville, Fla., Alaska, Wash., Idaho, 1996—; process cons. Jamaica Ecumenical Ministry, United Theol. Coll. of W.I., Kingston, Jamaica, Synod of the Nile, Egypt. Bd. dirs. South Austin Cmty. Devel. Project; foster care parent State of Fla., 1993—; mem. Homeless Feeding Program, 1991—; chmn. task force Ch. and Soc., Presbytery of Chgo., 1980-83; bd. dirs. Nat. Presbyn. Men, Louisville, 1984-88, Presbyn. Health, Edn. and Welfare Assn., Louisville, 1986-93, Boggs Rural Life Ctr., Keysville, Ga., 1994-96; mem. jud. bus. com. Presbytery of St. Augustine, Jacksonville, 1990-96; bd. visitors Johnson C. Smith Sem., Atlanta, 1993-97. Mem. Jacksonville Golfers Guild, Hampton U. Alumni Assn. Home: P401 1901 Merrill Creek Pkwy Everett WA 98203-5891 Address: 217 7th Ave North Seattle WA 98109-5005

CHAWLA, HARPINDER SINGH, pediatric dentist, consultant, researcher; b. Amritsar, India, Mar. 15, 1945; s. Sukhdev Singh and Iqbal Kaur (Bagga) C.; m. Kiran Chaudhary, May 28, 1972; children: Amit, Amrita. BDS, Govt. Dental Coll. & Hosp., Amritsar, 1967, MDS, 1970; MNAMS, Nat. Acad. Med. Scis., India, 1986. Registrar Postgrad. Inst. Med. Edn. & Rsch., Chandigarh, India, 1970-72, lectr., 1972-78, asst. prof., 1978-85, assoc. prof., 1985-86, prof., 1986—, head oral health scis. ctr., 1998—. Editor Jour. Indian Soc. Pedodontics & Preventive Dentistry, 1980-95. Fellow Internat. Coll. Dentistry. Sikh. Avocations: oil painting, badminton, meditation. Home: House No 67 Sector 24A, Chandigarh 160012, India Office: Postgrad Inst Med Edn, Sector 12 Dept Oral Health, Chandigarh 160012, India

CHAWLA, HARVINDER SINGH, science educator; b. Delhi, India, Mar. 15, 1955; s. Gian Singh and Parkash Kaur (Dhingra) C.; m. Paramjit Kaur Panesar, Nov. 20, 1983; children: Komaljit Kaur, Jasmit Singh. BSc, Delhi U., 1973; MSc, Govind Ballabh Pant U., Pantnagar, India, 1975; PhD, Punjab Agrl. U., Ludhiana, India, 1978. Cert. geneticist. Scientist CSIR, Ludhiana, 1979; asst. prof. Govind Ballabh U., Pantnagar, 1979-92, assoc. prof., 1992—; chief editor CD-ROM prep. on agrl. biotech. Monsanto and Govind Ballabh Pant U., 1998-99. Author: (books) Lab Exercises in Genetics and Cytogenetics, 1995, Principles and Techniques in Plant Tissue Culture, 1997, Biotechnology in Crop Improvement, 1998, Introduction to Plant Biotechnology, 2000. DAAD fellow, Germany, 1985, 97, Dept. Biotech. Overseas associateship, 1993. Fellow Indian Soc. Genetics and Plant Breeding; mem. N.Y. Acad. Scis. Sikh. Office: Govind Ballabh Pant U, Dept Genetics/Plant Breed, 263 145 Pantnagar India

CHAWLA, SANTA, research scientist; b. Raiganj, India, Jan. 4, 1955; d. Sita Kanta and Suniti Rani (Chaudhury) Acharya; m. Anil Kumar Chawla, Dec. 10, 1982; children: Nandini, Bhaskar. BSc with honors, U. North Bengal, India, 1974; MSc, Banaras Hindu U., India, 1977, diploma French lang., 1981, PhD, 1984; diploma in German lang., Banaras Hindu U., 1992. Jr. rsch. fellow Banaras Hindu U., Varanasi, India, 1978-80; sr. rsch. fellow Banaras Hindu U., Varanasi, 1980-83; pool officer Phys. Rsch. Lab., Ahmedabad, India, 1986-89; postdoctoral fellow Phys. Rsch. Lab., Ahmedabad, 1989-90, scientist, 1992—; rsch. assoc. Gujarat U., Ahmedabad, 1991-92. Contbr. articles to profl. jours. Nat. Merit scholar Govt. India, 1972-77; rsch. grantee Nat. Phys. Lab., India, 1997, Dept. Atomic Energy, India, 1998. Mem. Indian Laser Assn. (life), Indian Women Scientists Assn. (life), Swadeshi Sci. Movement (life). Hindu. Avocations:

reading, music, watching television, gardening. Office: Nat Phys Lab, Dr KS Krishnan Rd, New Delhi 110012, India

CHAWLA, SUSHMA, obstetrician/gynecologist; b. Lahore, India, Aug. 26, 1944; d. Prem and Sushila (Vaid) Sudan; m. Ghansham Dass Chawla, May 11, 1971 (dec. 1986); children: Luthra, Deepak. MBBS, Med. Coll. Amritsar, India, 1968; MD, Postgrad. Inst. Med. Sci., Chandigarh, India, 1973. Med. officer Civil Hosp., Pathankot, India, 1977; gynecologist Civil Hosp., Jalandhar, India, 1977-80, Jalandhar Nursing Home, 1980-85; obstetrician gynecologist Chawla Nursing Home & Maternity Hosp., India, 1985-99. Fellow Indian Coll. Maternal-Child Health, Indian Coll. Gynecology. Home: Chawla Nursing Home and, Maternity Hosp, 144001 Jalandhar India

CHAWNER, LUCIA MARTHA, English educator; b. Ithaca, N.Y., Dec. 2, 1933; d. Lowell Jenkins and Lucia Mary (Soule) C.; m. Movses Guichen Andreassian, Mar. 18, 1967 (div. June 1971). Student, Earlham Coll., 1951-53; BA, U. Colo., 1956; MA, So. Meth. U., 1975. Provisional cert. elem., secondary and talented and gifted, Tex.; profl. cert. reading specialist, Tex. Tchr. grade 7 lang. arts and social studies Stonewall Jackson, Dallas Ind. Sch. Dist., 1959-63; reading clinician Reinhardt, Dallas Ind. Sch. Dist., 1963-66; Reading Resource Pilot Project Lakewood, Dallas Ind. Sch. Dist., 1972-74; devel. curriculum specialist El Centro Coll., Dallas County C.C. Dist., Dallas, 1977-78; English tchr. Health Magnet, Dallas Ind. Sch. Dist., 1979-95; univ. supervising tchr. U. Tex. Dallas, Richardson, 1996—; part-time instr. El Centro & Richland Colls., Dallas, 1978-88, Brookhaven Coll., Farmers Branch, Tex., 1996-98; mem. English lit. textbook adoption com. Dallas Ind. Sch. Dist., 1988-89; chmn. English dept. Health Magnet, Dallas Ind. Sch. Dist., 1989-94, mgr. innovative grant, 1994-95. Co-leader child and youth study U. Md., Dallas, 1967-69; pres. English-Speaking Union-Dallas Br., 1992-96; Leadership Arts, Dallas Bus. Com. Arts, 1994-95; region 7 chmn., nat. bd. mem. English-Speaking Union of USA, 1996—. Recipient Instrnl. grant Richland Coll., 1980; Advanced Study grantee Dallas Ind. Sch. Dist., 1973; Named Tchr. of the Yr., Health Magnet, 1991, Rotary Tchr. of the Yr., Health Magnet, 1993. Mem. Dallas Mus. Art League (bd. mem. 1997—), New Conservatory of Dallas (bd. mem. 1999—), Friends SMU Librs. (bd. mem. 1995-98), Assemblage (pres. 1987-88), Brit. Am. Commerce Assn., Dau. British Empire, Delta Delta Delta, Phi Delta Kappa, Pi Lambda Theta. Avocations: sculpture, needlepoint, fitness exercise, travel. Office: PO Box 141179 Dallas TX 75214-1179

CHAYKIN, ROBERT LEROY, manufacturing and marketing executive; b. Miami, Fla., May 2, 1944; s. Allan Leroy and Ruth (Levine) C.; m. Patty Jean Patton, Feb. 1971 (div. May 1975); m. Evalyn Marcy Slodzina, Sept. 3, 1989; children: Stephanie Lee, Michelle Alee, Catrina Celia, Ally Sue. BA in Polit. Sci., U. Miami, Fla., 1965, LLB, 1969. Owner, operator Serrating Svcs. Miami, 1969-71, Serrating Svcs. Las Vegas, Nev., 1971-84; pres. Ser-Sharp Mfg., Inc., Las Vegas, 1984—; nat. mktg. dir. Coserco Corp., Las Vegas, 1987—. Patentee in mfg. field. With U.S. Army, 1962. Recipient 2d degree black belt Tae Kwon Do, Profl. Karate Assn., 1954-61. Avocations: travel, camping.

CHAZINE, JEAN MICHEL, ethno-archaeologist; b. Apt, France, Dec. 22, 1941; s. Robert and Simone (Vincent) C. Bachellor, Honfleur's Coll., 1960; physico-metallography engr., E.S.L., 1969; MA in Ethnology, Sorbonne U., 1978; DEA, Art and Archaeology Inst., 1982. Head of workshop projects Degremont, France, 1969-73; head of archaeol. projects CNRS, Tahiti, 1974-79, head dept. archaeology, 1979-82; head ethno-archaeological programs CNRS, East Pacific area, 1983-91, W. Pacific, S.E. Asia, Solomon Islands, Palawan (Philippines), Borneo, 1992—. Co-author: (TV documentary) le Sable, l'eau et l'humus, 1987, A la decouverte des grottes ornees de Borneo, 1997; contbr. articles to profl. jours. Mem. Assn. for Archaeology Polynesienne (v.p. 1975), Soc. Océanistes (bd. dirs.), IPPA, WAC. Avocations: garbage social archaeology, photo/video. E-mail: jmchazine@lycos.com. Home: La Brémonde, 84480 Buoux France Office: U St Charles, Maison Asie-Pacifique, 13331 Marseille France

CHEA, CHANTO, banker; b. Kampong, Thom Prov., Cambodia, Oct. 9, 1951; married. Grad. in commerce sci., U. Phnom Penh, Cambodia, 1975; PhD in Econ. Sci., U. Hanoi, Vietnam, 1990; PhD in Bus. Adminstrn. (hon.), U. So. Calif., 1995. Dir. Municipality Bank Phnom Penh, 1979-81; min. planning Govt. of Cambodia, Phnom Penh, 1986-98; M.P. for Kompong Thom Area, Cambodian Parliament, Phnom Penh, 1993-98; dep. gov. Nat. Bank of Cambodia, Phnom Penh, 1981-86; gov. Nat. Bank Cambodia, Phnom Penh, 1998—. Author: Reform of the State-owned Enterprises, 1989, Problems of Socio-Economic Development in Cambodia, 1990, Option of Socio-Economic Development in Cambodia from 1990 up to 2000, 1991. Office: Nat Bank Cambodia, POB 25, 22-24 Preah Norodom Blvd, Phnom Penh Cambodia

CHEAH, CHIEN CHERN, engineering educator, researcher; b. Singapore, Singapore, July 26, 1965; s. Sim Bee Cheah and Siew Tan Goh; m. Bee Lan Ng; children: Dawn, Shen. B in Engring., Nat. U. Singapore, 1990; M in Engring., Nanyang Tech. U., Singapore, 1993, PhD, 1996. Design engr. Chartered Electronics Industries, Singapore, 1990-91; rsch. asst. Nanyang Tech. U., Singapore, 1991-93, tchg. asst., 1993-96, lectr., 1998-99, asst. prof., 1999—; rsch. fellow Ritsumeikan U., Japan, 1996-98. Contbr. articles to profl. jours. Recipient Rsch. fellowship Toyota Motor, 1996; scholarship Nan Ann, 1988-90. Mem. IEEE (developing country fellowship 1995, session co-chair conf. on robotics and automation 1999), IFAC (affialiate mem.). Avocations: swimming, jogging, photography. Office: Nanyang Tech U, Blck S1 Nanyang Ave, Singapore 639798, Singapore

CHEAH, JONATHON KIAN THONG, engineering executive; b. Ipoh, Perak, Malaysia, Oct. 21, 1962; arrived in Singapore, 1982; s. Alan Chet Peng Cheah and Hung Kuen Ho. B in Engring, Nanyang Technol. U., Singapore, 1986; M in Entrepreneurship, Swinburne, Melbourne, Australia, 1995. Product engr. Hanna Instruments, Singapore, 1986-88; sales/mktg. mgr. Mentor Graphics, Singapore, 1989-94; gen. mgr. Altium AP, Singapore, 1994-95, Atlas Telecom, Singapore, 1995-97; dir. Asian ops. Xynetix, San Jose, Calif., 1997—. Mem. IEEE. Office: Avant! Corp 46871 Bayside Pkwy Fremont CA 94538-6572

CHEAH, KEONG-CHYE, psychiatrist, educator; b. Georgetown, Penang, West Malaysia, Mar. 15, 1939; came to U.S., 1959; s. Thean Hoe and Hun Kin (Keong) C.; m. Sandra Massey, June 10, 1968; children: Chylynn, Maylynn. BA in Psychology, U. Ark., 1962; MD, U. Ark., Little Rock, 1967, MS in Microbiology, 1968. Diplomate Am. Bd. Psychiatry and Neurology (examiner 1982, 85); cert. Ark. State Sci. Bd., Ark. State Med. Bd. Intern U. Ark. Med. Ctr., 1967-68; resident VA Med. Ctr. and U. Ark. Med. Ctr., Little Rock, 1968-72; chief addiction sect. Little Rock VA Med. Ctr., 1972-73, staff psychiatrist, 1975-80; chief psychiatry American Lake VA Med. Ctr., Tacoma, 1981-86; chief consultation, liason Am. Lake divsn. Puget Sound Health Care Sys., Tacoma, 1986-94; asst. prof. medicine, psychiatry U. Ark., Little Rock, 1975-81; asst. prof. psychiatry and behavioral scis. U. Wash., Seattle, 1981-86, clin. assoc. prof., 1987—; mem. dist. br. com. The CHAMPUS, 1977-91; surveyor JCAHO, 1990-93; site visitor AMA Continuing Med. Edn., 1979-83; book reviewer Jour. Am. Geriatrics Soc., 1984-85; mem. task force alcohol abuse VA Med. Dist. 27, 1984, survey mem. Sytematic External Rev. Process, 1985; mem. mental health plan adv. com. State of Ark., 1976-81, chmn. 1979-81, chmn. steering com., 1979; mem. Vietnamese Resettlement Program, 1979; many coms. Am. Lake VA Med. Ctr. including chmn. mental health coun. 1981-84, utilization rev. com., 1981-86. Contbr. articles and abstracts to profl. jours.; presenter to confs. and meetings of profl. socs. Mem. Parents Adv. Com., Lakes H.S., Wash., 1987-91; mem. Mayor's Budget and Fin. Foresight Com., 1992—, chmn. 1990-92; sch. cons. Child Study Ctr. U. Ark., 1972-74; bd. dirs. Crisis Ctr. Ark., 1974-79, chmn. pub. rels. com., 1975-79, mem. pers. com. 1974, vice chmn. bd. 1977; pres. Chinese Assn. Ctrl. Ark., 1977; mem. gifted edn. adv. coun. Clover Park Sch. Dist. 400, Wash., 1983-85, Parent Tchr. Student Orgn. Recipient U.S. Govt. scholarship 1959, cert. merit State of Ark., 1973, Leadership award, Mental Health Svcs. Divsn., State of Ark., 1980. Fellow Am. Psychiat. Assn. (sec. treas. Asian Am. caucus 1985-87, pres. 1987-94); mem. Assn. Mil. Surgeons U.S., Wash. State Psychiat. Assn. (mem. peer rev. com. 1982-92, chmn. pub. psychiatry com. 1985-93, exec. coun. 1985-93), N. Pacific Soc. Neurology and Psychiatry Assn. (sec.-treas. 1986-99, pres. 1993), S. Puget Sound Psychiat. Assn., Assn. Chinese-Am. Psychiatrists, Chapel of Four Chaplains, Ark. Caduceus Club, Alpha Epsilon Delta, Psi Chi, Phi Beta Kappa, Alpha Omega Alpha. Avocations: reading, target shooting. Office: American Lake Divsn Puget Sound Health Care Sys Tacoma WA 98493-0001

CHEAH, PEH YEAN, research scientist; b. Teluk Intan, Perak, Malaysia, June 15, 1958; d. Yuk Ling Cheah and Chai Mooi Tan; m. Soo Chin Liew; children: Kaiyang, Kaiyi. BSc in Edn. with 1st class honors, Sci. U. Malaysia, 1982; MEd, U. Malaya, Malaysia, 1985; PhD, U. Ariz., 1989. Vis. fellow U. Malaya, 1983-85; grad. tchg. asst. U. Ariz., 1986, grad. rsch. asst., 1986-89; postdoctoral fellow Children's Hosp. L.A., 1989-90; rsch. fellow Inst. Molecular and Cell Biology, Singapore, 1990-96; sr. scientist Singapore Gen. Hosp., 1996—. Contbr. articles to profl. jours. Grantee Nat. Med. Rsch. Coun., 1997, 99, Singapore Cancer Soc., 1997-99. Mem. Am. Assn. Cancer Rsch. Avocations: reading, classical music, gardening, interior decoration. Office: Singapore Gen Hosp, Dept Colorectal Surgery, Singapore 169608, Republic of Singapore

CHEBEZ, JUAN CARLOS, foundation administrator; b. Buenos Aires, Oct. 31, 1962; s. Juan Carlos and Ana Anunciacion (Torregiani) C.; m. Sofia Helena Heinonen Fortabat, Apr. 16, 1994; children: Lautaro Inacayal, Camila. BS, Inst. Ednl. Fátima, Martínez, Argentina, 1980. Pres. Assn. Conservation Naturaleza, Argentina, 1976-82; coord. tech. Fundacion Vida Silvestre Argentina, Buenos Aires, 1982-90; assessor Ministerio de Ecologia de Misiones, Posadas, Argentina, 1987-89; dir. manejo Adminstrn. Parques Nacionales, Buenos Aires, 1990-93; dir. Delegacion Nordeste Adminstrn. de Parques Nacionales, 1994—; pres. Aves Argentinas-Assn. Ornitológica del Plata, Buenos Aires, 1996—; hon. assessor Ministerio de Ecología de Misiones, 1995. Co-author: Mamiferos Fueguinos, 1993, Reservas Naturales Misioneras, 1998; author: Los Que Se Van-Especies Argentinas en Peligro, 1994, Fauna Misionera, 1996 (Mención Especial Feria del Libro award 1997). Roman Catholic. Avocations: writing poems and songs. Office: Delegacion Regional NEA-APN, Av Victoria Aguirre 66, 3370 Puerto Iguazu Argentina

CHEBLAKOVA, ELENA ANATOL'EVNA, mathematician, researcher; b. Barnaul, Russia, Sept. 12, 1972; d. Anatolii Vasilievich Dvurechenskii and Serafima Yakovlevna Dvurechenskaya; m. Georgii Borisovich Cheblakov, Dec. 9, 1994; 1 child, Irina Georgievna. Bachelor's degree, Novosibirsk State U., 1993, Master's degree, 1995. Aspirant Inst. Computational Techs., Novosibirsk, 1995—. Soros student Internat. Soros Program of Edn. in Exact Scis., 1995, Soros aspirant, 1996. Avocations: dancing, embroidery, films, picnics, traveling. Fax: 3832 341342. E-mail: lena@net.ict.nsc.ru. Office: Inst Computational Techs, Lavrentyev ave 6, 630090 Novosibirsk Russia

CHECCHI, ALFRED A., airline company executive; b. 1948; m. BA, Amherst Coll., 1970; MBA, Harvard Univ., 1974. V.p. Marriott Corp., 1975-82; with Bass Bros., 1982-86; pres. Alfred Checchi Assocs., Inc., 1986—; co-chmn., bd. dirs. NWA Inc., 1997—, Northwest Airlines Inc., 1997—, Wings Holdings Inc., 1997—; bd. dirs. Northwest Airlines, Inc., St. Paul, 1997—. Office: NW Airlines Inc 5101 Northwest Dr Saint Paul MN 55111-3034

CHECHENYA, KOSTYANTYN ANATOLIJOVYCH, musician, conductor; b. Kyiv, Ukraine, June 1, 1959; s. Anatoliy Evgenovych and Nadia Elisevna (Truschenko) C.; m. Jryna Mykolaiyvna Levchenko; children: Maria, Kostya. Musician, State High Msic Coll., Kyiv, Ukraine, 1985; Condr., Kyiv State Pedagogical U., 1990. Soloist Musica Aeterna Ensemble, Kyiv, 1981-90; tchr. Music Sch., Kyiv, 1981-96, dir. folk instruments dept., 1997—; head early music ensemble House of Tchrs., Kyiv, 1990—; sci. cons. People's Medicine Assn., Kyiv, 1996; dir. music cycle Early Ukrainian Music in European Contest, Kyiv, 1997-99, Ancient Mus. Instruments, Kyiv, 194-98, Masterpieces of Early Music, Kyiv, 1992-96. Author: Only Blues, 1999, Ragtime, 2000, Country Music, 2000; condr., actor: The Poem About Igor, 1987. Recipianet Plaque, Kyiv State City Adminstrn., 1999, Lawreat 1st pl. All-Ukrainian Contest, Ministry of Culture, 1996, 2nd pl., 1999. Orthodox Christian. Avocations: music therapy, archeology, excavations, jogging. Home: 12 Pryvokzalna Str Apt 139, 02096 Kyiv Ukraine Office: House of Tchrs., 57 Volodymyrska St, 04030 Kyiv Ukraine

CHECHIN, VALERY ANDREEVICH, physicist; b. Moscow, Apr. 22, 1941; s. Andrei Chechin and Antonina Nedotko; m. Olga Odintsova, Dec. 8, 1964 (div. 1975); 1 child, Sergei; m. Helen Bodenkova, Mar. 7, 1987. Grad., Moscow State U., 1964, PhD, 1972. Jr. rschr. Lebedev Phys. Inst., Moscow, 1964-71, sr. rschr., 1971-85, leading rschr., 1986—. Author: Neutrinos for Geophysics, 1985, Ionization Measurements in High Energy Physics, 1993. Mem. N.Y. Acad. Scis., House of Scientists. Avocations: speleology, arctic ski tours. Home: ul Miklukhi-Maklaya 29, Korp 1 Kv 29, 117485 Moscow Russia Office: PN Lebedev Phys Inst, Leninsky Prospect 53, 117924 Moscow Russia

CHEDORE, ADRIAN GENGE, marketing professional; b. Cardiff, Wales, Oct. 28, 1951; arrived in Hong Kong, 1979; s. Philip Lester and Wendy Patricia (Genge-Andrews) C.; m. Salome Bermudez, Mar. 4, 1989 (div. Sept. 1996). BA, U. Sussex, 1973. Rsch. exec. Taylor Nelson, London, 1973-75; brand mgr. Harp Lager, London, 1975-77; planner Allen Brady & Marsh, London, 1977-79; mng. dir. Allen Brady & Marsh, Hong Kong, 1979-85; regional dir. Frank Small & Assocs., Hong Kong, 1985-91; CEO Asia Market Intelligence Ltd., Hong Kong, 1991—. Invented analysis procedure (AMI PinPoint), 1994, ad pre-testing sys. (AMI AdCheck), 1995. Mem. European Soc. for Opinion and Market Rsch., U.K. Market Rsch. Soc., European Soc. Opinion & Mktg. Rsch., Am. Mktg. Assn. Office: Asia Market Intelligence Ltd 9/F Leighton Ctr, 77 Leighton Rd, Causeway Bay Hong Kong China

CHEE, PERCIVAL HON YIN, ophthalmologist; b. Honolulu, Aug. 29, 1936; s. Young Sing and Den Kyau (Ching) C.; m. Carolyn Tong, Jan. 27, 1966; children: Lara Wai Lung, Shera Wai Sum. BA, U. Hawaii, 1958; MD, U. Rochester, 1962. Intern Travis AFB Hosp., Fairfield, Calif., 1962-63; resident Bascom Palmer Eye Inst., Miami, Fla., 1965-68, Jackson Meml. Hosp., Miami, 1965-68; partner Straub Clinic, Inc., Honolulu, 1968-71; practice medicine specializing in ophthalmology, Honolulu, 1972—; mem. staffs Queen's Med. Center, St. Francis Hosp., Kapiolani Children's Med. Center, Honolulu; clin. assoc. prof. surgery U. Hawaii Sch. Medicine, 1971—; cons. Tripler Army Med. Center. Mem. adv. bd. Services to Blind; bd. dirs. Lions Eye Bank and Makana Found. (organ bank), Multiple Sclerosis Soc. Served to capt. USAF, 1962-65. Fellow Am. Acad. Ophthalmology, ACS; mem. AMA, Pan Am. Med. Assn., Pan Pacific Surg. Assn., Am. Assn. Ophthalmology, Soc. Eye Surgeons, Hawaii Ophthal. Soc. Pacific Coast Ophthal. Soc., Am. Assn. for Study Headache, Pan Am. Ophthal. Found. Contbr. articles to profl. pubs. Home: 3755 Poka Pl Honolulu HI 96816-4409 Office: Kukui Pla 50 S Beretania St Ste C116 Honolulu HI 96813-2225

CHEE-HWA, TUNG, government official; b. Shanghai, May 29, 1937; married; three children. BS in Marine Engring., U. Liverpool, U.K., 1960. Mgr. family shipping bus.; mem. consultative com. for basic law, mem. exec. com. Hong Kong Govt., 1992-96, adviser to People's Rep. of China, first chief exec. Spl. Adminstrv. Region, 1996—. Office: Office of Chief Exec/Govt, Upper Albert Rd, Hong Kong Hong Kong*

CHEEK, HOWARD LEE, JR., political science and philosophy educator; b. Winston-Salem, N.C., Oct. 27, 1960; s. Howard Lee and Ann Marie Clinch Cheek; m. Kathy Braun, Dec. 18, 1994. BA in Polit. Sci. and History, Western Carolina U., 1983; MDiv, Duke U., 1986; PhD, Cath. U. Am., 1998. Ordained minister United Meth. Ch., 1993. Legis. asst. U.S. Ho. of Reps., Washington, 1982; min. United Meth. Ch., N.C., 1983—; prof. polit. sci. and philosophy Brewton-Parker Coll., Mt. Vernon, Ga., 1997-2000; exec. dir. Wesley Studies Soc., Greensboro, N.C., 1994-2000; prof. polit. sci. and philosophy Lee Univ., Cleveland, Tenn., 2000—. Author: Calhoun and Popular Rule, 2000; editor: Political Philosophy and Cultural Renewal, 2000. Capt. Chaplaincy Corps, U.S. Army, 1994-99. Recipient Antinian award So. Polit. Sci. Assn., 1999; rsch. grantee various founds., 1983—. Avocations: fishing, hiking, collecting fine writing instruments. E-mail: lcheek@leeuniversity.edu. Home: 172 Georgia Bell Cir SE Cleveland TN 37323-7728 Office: Brewton-Parker Coll Dept Polit Sci Lee University Cleveland TN 37323

CHEEK, JAMES RICHARD, ambassador; b. Decatur, Ga., Apr. 27, 1936; s. Woodrow Wilson and Dorothy (Webb) C.; m. Carol Ruth Rozzell, Sept. 1, 1957; children—Leesa Lynn, Forrest Craig, Surya Tamang. B.A., Ark. State Tchrs. Coll., 1959; M. Internat. Service, Am. U., 1961. Dep. chief mission Am. Embassy, Montevideo, Uruguay, 1977-79; dep. asst. sec. state U.S. Dept. State, D.C., 1979-81; dep. chief mission Am. Embassy, Kathmandu, Nepal, 1982-85; charge d'affaires, chief mission Am. Embassy, Addis Ababa, Ethiopia, 1985-88; diplomat-in-residence Howard U., Washington, 1988-89; U.S. amb. to Sudan Am. Embassy, Khartoum, 1989-92; U.S. amb. to Argentina Am. Embassy, Buenos Aires, 1993-96; global cons., ambassador in residence U. Ark., Little Rock, 1997—. Served to capt. U.S. Army, 1954-56. Recipient spl. commendation Women's Orgn., Dept. State, 1979, Disting. Alumnus award U. Ark., 1992, U. Ctrl. Ark., 1997. Mem. Am. Fgn. Service Assn. (William R. Rivkin award 1974). Avocations: antique clocks, fishing, trekking, playing squash. Home: 31 Saint Andrews Dr Little Rock AR 72212-2908 Office: U Ark 2801 S University Ave Little Rock AR 72204-1099

CHEEK, MICHAEL CARROLL, lawyer; b. Fostoria, Ohio, Aug. 28, 1948; s. Carroll Wright and Mabel A. (Smith) C. BA, Hanover Coll., 1970; JD, U. Cin., 1974. Bar: Ohio 1974, Fla. 1974, U.S. Dist. Ct. (mid. dist.) Fla. 1975. Pub. defender Clearwater, Fla., 1974-77, lawyer sole practice, 1977—; vice chmn. bar grievance Clearwater, 1990-94; trustee Pinellas County Law Libr., Clearwater, 1977-92; chmn. Ct. Law Libr., 1982-89. Pres. 1st Step Corp., Clearwater, 1986-93; vice chmn. Long Ctr. Found., Clearwater, 1994-95; founder Head Start Learn-to-Swim Program, 1994. Mem. Nat. Assn. Criminal Def. Lawyers, Pinellas Criminal Def. Assn. (v.p. 1987), Am. Inn of Ct. Office: 480 Poinsettia Rd Belleair FL 33756-1081

CHEEVER, EDDIE, formula I driver; b. Phoenix, Jan. 10, 1958; children: Estelle, Eddie. Test diver Ferrari Formula One team, 1977; race car driver Team Hesketh Formula One, 1978-89, Indy Cir., 1990. Recipient Winner 1998 Indpls. 500, Indy 200 Walt Disney World, 1997, Rookie of Yr. Indy 500, 1992. Office: Team Cheever LLC Ste 600 8435 George Town Rd Indianapolis IN 46268*

CHEIDO, MARGARITA ALEKSANDROVNA, physiologist, researcher; b. Voronezh, Russia, Feb. 2, 1939; d. Aleksandr Makarovich Okorokov and Polina Aleksandrovna Okorokova; m. Gennadiyi Petrovich Cheido (div. 1981); 1 child, Iya. Grad., Acad. Selskogo Hosyaistva, Voronezh, 1961; PhD, Inst. Physiology, Sbramn Novosibirsk, 1983. Biologist Acad. Selskogo Hosyaistva, Voronezh, 1956-61; rschr. Inst. Physiology Sbrams, Novosibirsk, 1962-84, sr. rschr., 1984-96, leading rschr., 1996—. Contbr. articles to profl. jours. Recipient individual grant Internat. Sci. Found., 1992, grant Russian Found. Fundamental Investigations, 1992-95, 99—. Mem. Russian Soc. Physiologists, Russian Soc. Immunologists. Avocations: travel, swimming, reading literature, classic music. Home: Geroev Truda 20-47, 630055 Novosibirsk Russia Office: Inst Physiology Sbrams, Timakova Str 4, 630117 Novosibirsk Russia

CHEIRIF, JORGE BERKSTEIN, cardiologist, consultant; b. Mexico City, June 21, 1956; came to U.S., 1981; s. Benito C. and Raquel Berkstein; m. Heidy Derzrvitch, June 14, 1981; children: Benjamin, Michelle, Mark. MD, Nat. U. Mexico, 1981; degree in internal medicine, Baylor U., 1984, degree in cardiology, 1987. Dir. echocardiography VA Med. Ctr., Houston, 1987-92, Oschler Clin., New Orleans, 1992-97, Ppresbyn. Hosp. of Dallas, 1998—; bd. dirs. Cardiopulmonary Rsch. Sci. and Tech. Inst., Dallas. Contbr. over 50 articles to med. jours. Fellow Am. Coll. Cardiology; mem. Am. Soc. Echocardiography, Am. Heart Assn. (clinician-scientist award 1992-97). Office: N Tex Heart Ctr 8440 Walnut Hill Ln Ste 700 Dallas TX 75231-3824

CHEITEN, MARVIN HAROLD, writer, hardware manufacturing company executive; b. New Brunswick, N.J., Apr. 24, 1943; s. Samuel and Sarah (Peretzman) C. BA summa cum laude, Rutgers U., 1965; MA, Princeton U., 1967, PhD, 1971, AB (hon.), 1985. Ptnr. The Water Master Co., Highland Park, N.J., 1971-76, v.p., 1976-86, pres., 1986—. Author: (plays) Trial by Fire, 1972, Queen Jane, 1976, The Vault, 1978, The Golden Spy, 1996, Chowder, She Wrote, 1996, Le Coq d'Or, 2000; (novella) The Long Hello, 1995, (essays) The Fate of Princeton Graduate School, 1991, Touching A Goddess, 1996, Two Voices In The Darkness, 1997, To The Millstone, 1997, Escape from Raritan Prep, 1998, Songs for My Love, 2000, (lyrics) The Inn Cabaret, 1978-80, Deborah, 1996, A Princess In Death, 1998, Dorothea, 2000; also short stories; mem. editl. bd. Princeton Alumni Weekly, 1983-87. Bd. dirs. Princeton Rep. Assn., 1972-74; bd. trustees Princeton Chamber Symphony, 1993—; bd. trustees Friends of Theatre Intime, 1996—. Mem. Assn. Princeton Grad. Alumni (gov. bd. 1973-88), Nassau Club, Campus Club, Dramatists Guild, Alliance L.A. Playwrights. Jewish. Office: The Water Master Co PO Box 1186 New Brunswick NJ 08903-1186

CHEKANOV (CHAKANAU), SERGEI VLADIMIROVICH, physicist; b. Minsk, Belarus, June 9, 1969; s. Vladimir Sergeevich and Nina Konstantinovna (Zuk) C. Master's degree, hon. degree in physics, Belorussian State U., Minsk, 1993; D of Physics, U. Nijmegen, The Netherlands, 1997. Cert. in high-energy physics. Postdoctorate High Energy Physics Inst. Nijmegen U. Nijmegen, 1997-98; postdoctorate Argonne Nat. Lab., 1998—; coord. Zeus QED Group, Hamburg, Germany, 2000—. Contbr. articles to profl. jours. Sr. sgt. Soviet Army, 1987-89. Recipient Soros award, 1995. Avocation: music. Home: Slavinskogo 37-175, 220086 Minsk Belarus Office: Zeus Argonne Nat Lab, Notkestrasse 85, 22607 Hamburg Germany

CHEKHUN, VASYL FEDOROVYCH, oncologist, researcher; b. Trostynka, Ukraine, Nov. 15, 1956; s. Fedor Mykitovych and Olga Safronivna (Semenets) C.; m. Nataliya Vasylivna Kutsenok. July 30, 1987; children: Svyatoslav, Olga. MD, Med. Inst. Kyiv, Ukraine, 1980; PhD, Kavetsky Inst. Exptl. Pathology, Oncology, Radiobiology, Kyiv, 1986; DSc, R. Kavetsky Inst., Kyiv, 1994. Lab. asst. R. Kavetsky Inst. Exptl. Pathology, Oncology, Radiobiology, Kyiv, 1980-83, jr. rsch. worker, 1983-86, rsch. worker, 1986-88, scientific sec., 1988-96, dir., 1996—; prof. Sci. and Technologies Ministery of Ukraine, Kyiv, 1997; lectr. Nat. U. Kyiv, 1996. Editor (jour.) Exptl. Oncology, 1996. Pres. Unity Against Cancer Fund, Ukraine, 1997. Avocations: modern and classical music, poetry, tennis, cycling, swimming. Home: ap 99, 94 Chervonoarmijska Str, 03150 Kyiv Ukraine Office: R Kavetsky Inst Exptl Path, 45 Vasylkivska Str, 03022 Kyiv Ukraine

CHELES, LUCIANO, art history educator; b. Cairo, Sept. 7, 1948; arrived in Eng., 1965; s. Alberto and Agata (Di Stefano) C. BA, Reading (Eng.) U., 1973; Postgrad. Cert. in Edn., U. Wales, Cardiff, 1974; MPhil, Essex U., Colchester, Eng., 1980; PhD, Lancaster (Eng.) U., 1992. Lectr. Italian dept. Lancaster U., 1978-94, sr. lectr. Italian dept., 1994—; vis. prof. dept. art history U. Lyons, France, 1994-95, 96, 97; reader Princeton U. Press, 1994, Longman, London, 1994; cons. BBC, London, 1994-95. Author: The Studiolo of Urbino, 1986 (Frontino-Montefeltro prize 1992); co-editor: The Far Right in Western & Eastern Europe, 1995, Grafica Utile. L'Affiche d'Utilé Publique en Italie, 2000. Grantee Italian Min. Fgn. Affairs, 1989, British Acad., 1990, 93, 97, Scouloudi Found., 1995. Mem. Assn. Study Modern Italy (bd. dirs. 1992—), Soc. Italian Studies, Soc. Renaissance Studies, Com. French History Art. Mem. Labour Party. Avocations: cinema, painting, swimming. Office: Dept D'Etudes Italiennes, Universite de Poitiers, Poitiers 86022, England Office: D'Etudes Italiennes, Universite de Poitiers, 86022 Poitiers France

CHELIDZE, TAMAZ LUCKA, science administrator; b. Kutaisi, Georgia, Dec. 24, 1934; s. Lucka Alexander and Liuba Peter (Darchia) C.; m. Venera Besarion Tevdoradze, Mar. 4, 1957; children: Lia, Zurab. Geophysicist, Moscow State U., 1957; Candidate Physics and Mth., Tbilisi (Russia) State U., 1964; D Chemistry, Inst. Chemistry Colloids, Kiev, Russia, 1975; D Physics and Math., Inst. Physics of Earth, Moscow, 1986. Rsch. worker Inst. Geophysics, Tbilisi, Georgia, 1957-76, head dept., 1976-85, asst. dir., 1985-92, dir., 1992—; chair geophysical prospecting Tbilisi State U.; dir. European Ctr. Geodynamical Hazards of High Dams Coun. of Europe; cons. Ctr. Natural Disasters, Tbilisi, 1992-94; mem. coun. experts Coun.

Earthquake Prediction, Moscow, 1988-94; invited prof. U. Strasbourg, 1987, 92; Rennes (France) U., 1995-97; Ecole Normale Superieure (Paris), 1999. Co-author: Electric Spectroscopy of Heterogeneous System, 1977, Percolation Theory in Mechanics of Geomaterials, 1987. Grantee Ministry Rsch. and Higher Edn., Paris, 1994. Mem. Am. Geophys. Union (assoc.), Georgian Geophys. Soc. (pres. 1992-2000), Georgian Acad. Scis. (corr.), Acad. Ecol. Scis. (corr.). Avocation: farming. Home: N5 Mitskevich, 380094 Tbilisi Georgia Office: Inst Geophysics, 1 Alexidze St, 380093 Tbilisi Georgia

CHELLAPPA, NAITHIRITHI TIRUVENKATACHARY, environmental science educator, consultant; b. Madras, Tamil Nadu, India, Mar. 24, 1943; arrived in Brazil; s. Naithirithi Tiruvenratachary and Ranganayaki Durai Kutty Srinivasaraghavan; m. Sathyabama Ramanathan Chellappa, Oct. 8, 1979; children: Sarah L., Thingo. BSc, U. Madras, India, 1965; MSc, U. Madras, 1968, PhD, 1973; PhD, U. Glasgow, Scotland, 1985; FLS (hon.), Linnean Soc., London, 1978; MI in Biology (hon.), Inst. of Biology, London, 1980. Sr. rsch. fellow U. Madras, India, 1972-74; rsch. assoc. U. Madras, 1974-76; lectr. botany NEHU, Shulong, India, 1976-77; vis. prof. Univ. Fed. Rio Grande do Norte, Natal, Brazil, 1977-81, assoc. prof., 1981—; post doctoral rsch. assoc. U. Glasgow, Scotland, 1986-88; post-grad. coord. Univ. Fed. Rio Grande do Norte, Natal, 1999—, vice dir., 1995-99, senate mem. univ. coun., 1992-95; cons. CNPQ, Brasilia, Brazil, 1989—. Co-author textbook on basic biology, 1974. Vol. Social Svcs., Natal, 1994—. Fellow Am. Phycological Soc.; mem. Brit. Inst. Biology. Avocations: novel writing, chess, internet, service to poor people. Home: Rva Joaquim Fabricio 299, 59012340 Natal RN Petropol, Brazil

CHELSTROM, MARILYN ANN, political education consultant; b. Mpls., Dec. 5; d. Arthur Rudolph and Signe (Johnson) C. BA, U. Minn., 1950; LHD, Oklahoma City U., 1981. Staff asst. Mpls. Citizens Com. Public Edn., 1950-57; coord. policies and procedures Lithium Corp. Am., Inc., Mpls., N.Y.C., 1957-62; exec. dir. The Robert A. Taft Inst. Govt., N.Y.C., 1962-77, exec. v.p., 1977-78, pres., 1978-89, pres. emeritus, 1990—; polit. edn. cons., 1990—; pres. Chelstrom Connection, 1992—. Home: 9600 Portland Ave Minneapolis MN 55420-4564 Office: 155 E 38th St New York NY 10016-2660

CHELTSOV, VLADISLAV FEODOROVITS, physicist, theorist; b. Moscow, June 24, 1934; s. Feodor Andreievitch Tahrahsov and Julia Sergeevna Cheltsova; m. Lubuv Dimitirievna Kahshkova, Aug. 22, 1970 (div. Oct. 1983); children: Andrei, Anton. Diploma in Theoretical Nuclear Physics, Moscow Phys. Engring. Inst., 1958; PhD in Theoretical Physics, Kahzahn (Russia) U., 1969. Instr. Moscow Phys. Engring. Inst., 1958-61; rschr. Rschr. Inst., Moscow, 1961-69; assoc. prof. Textile Acad., Moscow, 1969-78; journalist Priroda Mag., Moscow, 1978-81; assoc. prof. Acad. of Mgmt., Moscow, 1981-88; assoc. prof. physics Moscow Mining U., 1988—. Contbr. numerous articles to profl. jours. including Quantum Optics and Quantum Electronics. Peter Kapitza grantee Royal Soc. London-Imperial Coll., 1991. Mem. Laser and Electrooptical Soc. of IEEE (sr.), European Phys. Soc., Inst. of Physics. Achievements include development of new theory of radiation from atoms trapped in damped microcavity. Avocations: swimming, diving, mountain skiing, hiking, music. E-mail: vcheltsov@mtu-net.ru. Home: Novatorov Str 18-7-2, 117421 Moscow V421, Russia Office: Moscow Mining U Dept Physic, Lenin Ave 6, 117935 Moscow GSP 1, Russia also: PO Box 31, 117313 Moscow V313, Russia

CHE MAN, YAAKOB BIN, food technology educator, researcher; b. Kuala Terengganu, Malaysia, May 2, 1954; s. Che Man Bin Yusof and Kah Binti Embong; m. Wan Jamilah Binti Wan Abdullah, Aug. 5, 1982; children: Nadiah, Yazid, Hanisah, Nafisah, Muhammad Ariff, Najihah, Hasanah. Diploma in food tech., Inst. Tech. Mara, Shah Alam, Malaysia, 1976; BS with high hons., U. Tenn., 1977, MS, 1979; postgrad. diploma in food sci. nutrition, U. Agr., Wageningen, The Netherlands, 1982; cert. in sci. & tech. mgmt., Nat. Inst. Pub. Adminstrn. Malaysia and Internat. Devel. Program of Australian Univs. and Colls. Ltd., 1992; PhD in Food Sci., U. Ill., 1988. Head food tech. dept. U. Putra Serdang, Malaysia, 1992-93; dep. dean faculty food sci. & biotech. U. Putra, Serdang, Malaysia, 1993-95, acting dean, 1993-95; rsch. fellow Palm Oil Rsch. Inst. Malaysia, Bangi, 1996-97; prof. food tech. U. Putra, 1997—; vis. prof. McGill U., Montreal, Que., Can., 1997; cons. FITRIA ASEAN Food, Sungai, Besi, Malaysia, 1996—, Ilham Daya Bd., Puchong, Malaysia, 1998—, State of Penang, Malaysia, 1998—, Ajinomoto Co., Inc., Tokyo, 1998—. Mem. editl. bd. Jour. Food Lipids, 1996—, ASEAN Food Jour., 1996—; mem. adv./editl. bd. Jour. Hospitality, Leisure and Tourism Mgmt., 1996—. Fellow Internat. Inst. Islamic Thought; mem. Inst. Food Tech., Am. Oil Chemists Soc., N.Y. Acad. Scis., Malaysian Inst. Food Tech. (exec. coun. 1996—), Malaysian Oil Sci. & Tech. Assn. (exec. coun. 1996—). Avocations: fishing, badminton, soccer. Home: No 40, Taman Universiti Indah, Seri Kembangan 43300, Malaysia Office: U Putra, Dept Food Tech, UPM Serdang 43400, Malaysia

CHEMLA, KARINE CAROLE-CAMILLE, mathematical researcher; b. Tunis, Tunisia, Feb. 8, 1957; arrived in France, 1964; d. Maurice and Andree Francine (Cohen) C. Masters, U. Paris VII, 1977, Agregation de Math., 1978; PhD in Math., U. Paris XIII, 1982. Researcher French Nat. Ctr. Sci. Research, Paris, 1982—. Editor sect. in Ency. Maths., 1987; contbr. articles to profl. jours.; chief editor: Extrême-Orient Extrême-Occident; mem. editl. bd. Revue d'histoire des mathématiques. Recipient Prix du meilleur rapport Found. Finger Polignac, 1982. Mem. AAS, Soc. Math. de France, Brit. Soc. Inst. Math., European Assn. Chinese Studies. Home: 3 Square Bolivar, 75019 Paris France

CHEN, ALBERT HUNG-YEE, academic dean. Lectr. law Univ. of Hong Kong, 1984-88, sr. lectr., 1988-93, head, dept. of law, 1993—. Author: (books) An Introduction to the Legal System of the People's Republic of China, 1992, Law and Politics in Hong Kong, 1990; contbg. author books in field, including Developing Theories of Rights and Human Rights in China, 1993; contbr. articles to profl. jours. Fax: 852-2559-3543. Office: Faculty of Law/U Hong Kong, 4/F KK Leung Bldg/Pokfulam, Hong Kong Hong Kong*

CHEN, ANDREA YA-HUEI, lawyer, arbitrator; b. Tainan City, Taiwan, Oct. 25, 1957. LLB, Taiwan U., 1979; LLM, U. Pa., 1983, Harvard U., 1984. Inhouse counselor Acer Inc., Taipei, Taiwan, 1986-87; lectr. Chinese Culture U. Law Sch., Taipei, 1987-91; assoc. prof. Soochow U. Law Sch., Taipei, 1987-97; arbitrator Comml. Arbitration Assn., Taipei, 1987—; lawyer China-Pacific Law Offices, Taipei, 1993-96, World Law Office, Taipei, 1996—. Author: Legal Forms of Computer Contract, 1996. Commr. Environ. Protection Assn. of Republic of China Enterprises, Taipei, 1991-93, Nat. Fedn. of Industries, Taipei, 1991-96, bd. appeals Environ. Protection Adminstrn., Taipei, 1993-99, bd. of petition Directorate Gen. of Telecomm., Ministry of Transp., Taipei, 1995-97, rules and regulations com. Taipei Mcpl. Govt., 1995-98; commr. of law biotech. and pharm. industries program office Ministry of Econ. Affairs, Taipei, 1998-2000; mediator com. on environ. dispute mediation Taipei Mcpl. Govt., 1994-99, mediation office for dispute on shipment inspection and supervision, Ministry of Econ. Affairs, Taipei, 1999-2000; chair assessors com. on edn!. disputes resolution Bur. of Edn., Taipei Mcpl. Govt., 1995-97; sec. gen. New Environment Found., Taipei, 1989-91; exec. dir. EPA Found. for Waste Disposal and Resource Recovery, Taipei, 1993-96. Scholar Ministry of Edn., Taipei. Mem. Inter-Pacific Bar Assn. (vice chair environ. protection com. 1996-99), Taiwan Bar Assn. (chair environ. protection com. 1993-96, bd. dirs. 1996-99), Taipei Bar Assn. (chair environ. protection com. 1990-96, bd. dirs. 1993-96), Taoyuan Bar Assn. Avocations: travel, swimming. Office: World Law Office, 12 F-1 No 311 Sec 4 Chung Hsiao E Rd, Taipei 10515, Taiwan

CHEN, BOR SEN, electrical engineer, educator; b. Hsin-Ying, Tainan, Taiwan, Apr. 17, 1947; s. Teng Hui and Su Tou Chen; m. Show Fen Tsay, July 20, 1975; 2 children. BS, Tatung Inst. Tech., Taipei, Taiwan, 1970; MS, Nat. Ctrl. U., Chungli, Taiwan, 1973; PhD, U. So. Calif., 1982. Lectr. elec. engring. Tatung Inst. Tech., 1973-76, assoc. prof., 1976-83, prof., 1983-87; prof. Nat. Tsing Hua U., Hsinchu, Taiwan, 1987—; cons. Tatung Corp., Taipei, 1982-87, Yuan Ze Inst. Tech., Chungli, 1993—. Assoc. editor Jour. Control Sys. and Tech., 1992—; contbr. articles to sci. jours. Lt. Taiwan Army, 1970-71. Fellow Nat. Sci. Coun. Taiwan (Disting. Rsch. award 1991, 93, 95); mem. IEEE (sr.). Avocations: hiking, folk music. Home: Nat Hsing Hua Univ, 19-6F Western Yard, Hsinchu 30043, Taiwan Office: Nat Hsing Hua U, Kuang Fu Rd, Dept Elec Engr, Hsinchu 30043, Taiwan

CHEN, CARLSON S., mechanical engineer; b. Orange, N.J., Mar. 17, 1960; s. Kao and May Chen; m. Lynn Duong, Dec. 5, 1992; 1 child, Christopher D. BSME, Brown U., 1982; MBA, U. Pitts., 1987. Engr. Westinghouse Corp., Pitts., 1982-89; sr. engr. Gen. Dynamics, San Diego, 1989-91, GPS Techs., San Diego, 1991-93; sr. mech. engr. Nat. Steel & Shipbuilding (Gen. Dymnanics divsn. since 1998), San Diego, 1993—. Contbg. author Standard Handbook of Powerplant Engineering, 1997. Active Brown Cmty. Outreach, 1979-80. Mem. ASME, Soc. Naval Architects & Marine Engrs. (publicity, meetings, membership chmn. San Diego chpt. 1998-99, chmn. membership 2000, sec. 2000—), Brown Club of San Diego. Office: Nat Steel & Shipbuilding Co Harbor Dr & 28th St San Diego CA 92186

CHEN, CHANGKANG, physico-chemist, researcher; b. Fuzhou, Fujing, China, June 20, 1943; arrived in Eng., 1989; s. H. Chen and M. Lai; m. Yongle Hu, May 28, 1969; 1 child, Xin. B. U. Sci. and Tech. of China, 1965; D. Chinese Acad. Scis., 1978. Rsch. asst. Chinese Acad. Scis., Fuzhou, 1965-78, assoc. rsch. fellow, 1978-89; rsch. fellow Oxford (Eng.) U., 1989—; sr. rsch. assoc. Balliol Coll., Oxford, Eng., 1994-97. Author: Studies of High Temperature Superconductors, 1995, Phase Design and its Application to High Temperature Superconductors, 98. Named Advanced Investigator, Academica Sinica, Beijing, 1984, 85; The Royal Soc. fellowship, London, 1987-88. Mem. Chinese Chem. Soc., Brit. Assn. for Crystal Growth. Avocations: table tennis, Chinese chess, fishing, novels, movies. Office: Clarendon Labs U Oxford, Parks Rd, Oxford OX1 3PU, England

CHEN, CHANG-NEW, engineering educator; b. Fang Yang, Taiwan, China, Jan. 20, 1953; s. Yu-Chi Chen and Chiean Hsieh. BS, Nat. Cheng Kung U., Tainan, Taiwan, 1975; MS, Tokyo U., 1978; PhD, U. So. Calif., 1986. Lectr. Nat. Cheng Kung U., Tainan, 1978-81, assoc. prof., 1989-99, prof., 1999—. Contbr. articles to profl. jours. Recipient Disting. Paper award Soc. Naval Architecture and Marine Engrs., 1989, Disting. Paper award Soc. Chinese Engrs., 1990. Mem. ASME (OOMAE Divsn. Appreciation award 1999). Avocation: swimming, music. Fax: 886-06-2747019. Office: Nat Cheng Kung U, No. 1, Ta-Hsueh Rd, Tainan 70101, China

CHEN, CHAO, finance educator; b. Chia-Yi, Taiwan, Jan. 22, 1953; s. Chen-Po and Yen Ping Chen; m. Ping Peng, Mar. 29, 1979; children: Jerry, Andrea. BA, Nat. Chengchi U., Taipei, Taiwan, 1976, MA, 1980; PhD, U. Md., 1988. Fgn. exch. specialist Internat. Cmml. Bank China, Taipei, 1981-82; asst. rsch. fellow Chung Hua Inst. Econ. Rsch., Taipei, 1982-83; instr. U. Md., College Park, 1987-88; assoc. prof. fin. Calif. State U., Northridge, 1988-93, prof., 1994—, dir. Ctr. for China Fin. and Bus. Rsch., 1998—; advisor Seven Arrows Mgmt., Albuquerque. Contbr. articles to profl. jours. Faculty devel. grantee China Inst., Northridge, 1998, rsch. grantee Calif. State U., 1999, Calif. State U. Coll. Bus. Adminstrn., 1999. Mem. Fin. Mgmt. Assn., Am. Fin. Assn., Global Fin. Assn. (best paper award 1994), Acad. Fin. Svc. Assns. Avocations: movies, music, tennis. Fax: 818-677-6079. E-mail: chao.chen@csun.edu. Home: 17510 Tuba St Northridge CA 91325-1435 Office: Calif State U 18111 Nordhoff St Northridge CA 91330-0001

CHEN, CHAOMEI, computer scientist; b. Beijing, China, Sept. 26, 1960; s. Xiqian and Jinli (Du) C.; m. Baohuan Zhang, Jan. 25, 1988; 2 children: Calvin and Steven. BSc in Math., Nankai U., Tianjin, China, 1983; MSc in Computation, U. Oxford, Eng., 1991; PhD in Computer Sci., U. Liverpool, Eng., 1995. Asst. libr. Libr. of Chinese Acad. Scis., Beijing, 1983-85, libr., 1985-89; software engr. Rsch. Machines Plc, Oxford, 1990; rsch. asst. U. Liverpool, 1991-92, 95; lectr. in computer studies Glasgow Caledonian U., Scotland, 1995-97; lectr. in info. sys. Brunel U., Uxbridge, Eng., 1997-2000, reader in info. sci., 2000—. Author: Information Visualisation and Virtual Environments, 1999; contbr. articles to profl. jours. Recipient award for excellence of instnl. project, 1986; named Disting. Young Scientist, Chinese Acad. Scis., 1987; vis. scholar U. Oxford, 1989-90; rsch. fellow Brit. Telecomms. Plc, 1997; grantee Engring. and Phys. Scis. Rsch. Coun., 1997, Libr. and Info. Commn., 1999, European Commn. 5th Framework Program, 2000. Mem. Assn. for Computing Machinery, Brit. Computer Soc. (human computer interaction specialist group), Soc. of Info. Visualisation (exec. com.), Am. Soc. Info. Sci. Office: Brunel U, Dept Info Sys & Computing, Uxbridge Middlesex UB8 3PH, England

CHEN, CHEN, medical research scientist; b. Xian, Shaanxi, China, Apr. 21, 1957; s. Jin Dian and Zhen (Guo) C.; m. Jin Zhang, July 18, 1985; children: Clifford, Jenny. MD, Shanghai Med. U., 1982; PhD, U. Bordeaux, 1989. Intern Peking Union Hosp., Beijing, 1981-82; postgrad. fellow Peking Union Med. Coll., 1982-86; postdoctoral fellow Inserm-U 176, Bordeaux, France, 1986-89, Glaxo Rsch. Inst., Research Triangle Park, N.C., 1989-91; sr. rsch. scientist Prince Henry's Inst., Melbourne, Australia, 1991—; sr. rsch. officer Australian NH and MRC, Melbourne, 1994-95, sr. rsch. fellow, 1996—; hon. sr. lectr. physiology Monash U., 1996—; hon. rsch. fellow, prof. physiology Peking U. Med. Coll., Chinese Acad. Med. Scis., 1998—; hon. prof. pharmacology U. Alta., Can., 1998—; hon. prof. physiology Mil. Med. U., China, 1999—. Contbr. articles to profl. jours. Recipient growth rsch. award Eli Lilly, Melbourne, 1992, Servier award, Brisbane, 1994. Mem. Soc. Neurosci., Endocrine Soc. Australia (Servier award), Australia Neurosci. Soc., Internat. Soc. Neurochemistry. Avocations: soccer, travel, reading, movies, gardening. Office: Prince Henrys Inst, PO Box 5152, Clayton 3168, Australia

CHEN, CHENGGANG, research scientist; b. Wenling, Zhejiang, China, Mar. 16, 1967; p. Rongquan Chen and Xiaohua Cao; m. Hong Zeng, Nov. 1, 1995. BS, Hangzhou (Zhejiang) U., 1987; MS, Zhejiang U., Hangzhou, 1989; PhD, Case Western Res. U., 1999. Rsch. asst. Zhejiang U., Hangzhou, 1987-89; asst. engr., lectr. Hangzhou U., 1990-93; rsch. asst. Case Western Res. U., Cleve., 1993-98; postdoctoral rsch. fellow Northwestern U., Evanston, Ill., 1998-99; postdoctoral rsch. assoc. Case Western Res. U., Cleve., 1999, The BFGoodrich Co., Cleve., 1999; assoc. rsch. scientist U. Dayton (Ohio) Rsch. Inst./Air Force Rsch. Lab., 2000—; cons. The BFGoodrich Co., Cleve., 1999. Author: Polymer Preprints, 1998, Organic/Inorganic Hybrid Materials, 1998. Alumni Grad. fellow Case Western Res. U., Cleve., 1995. Mem. Am. Chem. Soc., Materials Rsch. Soc. Achievements include 4 U.S. patents and 3 European patents. Avocation: stamp collecting. E-mail: cxc88@po.cwru.edu. Fax: 937-258-8075. Office: U Dayton Rsch Inst Air Force Rsch Lab 300 College Park Dayton OH 45469-0001

CHEN, CHERN-LIN, electrical engineer, educator; b. Taipei, Taiwan, China, Oct. 15, 1962; s. Chin-Yuan Chen and Yon-Tze Liang; m. Ching-Yi Lee, Jan. 7, 1993; children: Sun-Yung, Ru-Hsin. B, Nat. Taiwan U., Taipei, 1984, PhD, 1987. Assoc. prof. dept. elec. engring. Nat. Taiwan U., Taipei, 1987-95, prof., 1995-2000; cons. Great New Devel. & Care, Taipei, 1990—, Acer Peripheral, Inc., Taoyuan, Taiwan, 1996-97, Acer Display Tech., Hsinchu, Taiwan, 1997—. Contbr. articles to profl. jours. Recipient Outstanding Rsch. award Nat. Sci. Coun., 1998, Disting. Young Elec. Engr. award Chinese Elec. Engr. Assn., 1999. Mem. IEEE (sr.). Achievements include 12 inventions; 10 patents, China. Avocations: swimming, basketball, table tennis, kong-fu, jogging. Office: Nat Taiwan U, Dept EE, Roosevelt Rd, Sec 4, No. 1, Taipei 10617, China

CHEN, CHIAO-CHICY, psychiatrist; b. Tainan, Taiwan, Nov. 1, 1951; s. Chin-Shan and Tsun-Tien (Tsai) C.; m. Sou-Chen Wang, Dec. 23, 1978; children: Anne Chia-Yin, Luke Lian-Kwea. MD, Chung-Shan Med. Coll., 1970; PhD, Okayama (Japan) U., 1981. Med. diplomate; specialist in psychiatry. Psychiatric resident Taipei City Psychiat. Ctr., 1980-81, staff psychiatrist, 1982-86, chief-in-psychiatrist, 1986-89, 1989—; cons. psychiatrist Taiwan Nat. U., Taipei, 1986-90, assoc. prof., 1993—. Contbr. articles to profl. jours. Mem. Found. of Med. Profls. Alliance in Taiwan, 1993. 2d lt. Navy, 1975-77, Taiwan. Recipient Rsch. award Nat. Sci. Coun., 1988, 91. Fellow Soc. of Psychiatry (contr. 1989-93, sec. gen. 1993-95, dir. 1995—, Youth Rsch. award 1981); mem. Rotary Club. Presbyterian. Office: Taipei City Psychiat Ctr, 309 Sung-Te Rd, Taipei 110, Taiwan

CHEN, CHIEN-JEN, epidemiologist; b. Kaohsiung, Taiwan, June 6, 1951; s. Hsin-An Chen and Lien-Tze Wei; m. Fong-Ping Lo, Aug. 14, 1977; children: Yi-Ju, Yi-Wen. BS, Nat. Taiwan U., Taipei, 1973, MPH, 1977; DSc, Johns Hopkins U., 1982. Prof. Grad. Inst. Pub. Health Nat. Taiwan U., 1986-93, dir., 1992-93, prof. Grad. Inst. Epidemiology, 1994—, dir., 1994-97; dean Coll. Pub. Health, 1999—; sr. assoc. dept. epidemiology Johns Hopkins U., 1995—; adj. prof. dept. epidemiology and biostats. Tulane U., 1995—; dir. gen. divsn. life scis. Nat. Sci. Coun., Taipei, 1997-99. Contbr. 280 articles to sci. jours. Rsch. fellow Columbia U., 1989-90, Inst. Biomed. Scis.-Acad. Sinica, 1988-93. Fellow Am. Coll. Epidemiology; mem. Acad. Sinica (academician). Home: 76-3F King-Hwa St, Taipei 10606, Taiwan Office: Grad Inst Epidemiology, 1 Jen-Ai Rd Sect 1, Taipei 10018, Taiwan

CHEN, CHIEN-TZUNG, surgeon; b. Taipei, Republic of China, Jan. 2, 1961; m. Meng-Chen Ho, Sept. 10, 1994; children: Yi-Hseuh, Yi-Haur. MD, Kaoshiung (Taiwan) Med. Coll., 1987. Resident in gen. surgery Chang Gung Meml. Hosp., Taipei, 1987-90, from resident to chief resident in plastic surgery, 1990-93, attending staff trauma and emergency surgery, 1993-96, asst. prof. trauma and emergency surgery, 1996—; rsch. fellow U. Tex. S.W. Med. Sch., Dallas, 1997-98. Contbr. articles to profl. jours. Mem. Surg. Assn. Rep. of China, Plastic & Reconstruction Surg. Assn. (Best Paper of Yrs. award 1993), Oriental Soc. Aesthetic Plastic Surgery. Avocations: travel, swimming, photography, golf. Office: Chang Gung Meml Hosp, 5 Fu-Hsing St Trauma Dept, 333 Kweishan Taiwan

CHEN, CHIH-FAN, electrical engineer; b. Pa, Hopei, China, June 19, 1924; s. Shu-Chuang and Tung C. PhD, Cambridge U., 1971; LLD (hon.), Lewis Coll., 1963. Rsch. prof. Boston U., 1985—. Fellow Inst. Elec. Engrs. Office: Boston U Met Coll 808 Commonwealth Ave Boston MA 02215-1206

CHEN, CHIH-YING, mathematics and computer science educator, researcher; b. Taichung, Taiwan, June 26, 1951; s. Tain-Sheng and Yueh-Er (Wang) C.; m. Shwu-Jyy Lee, Mar. 29, 1981; children: Yi-Jen, yi-Hwan. B, Tamkang U., Taipei, Taiwan, 1974; M, Cen. U., Chungli, Taiwan, 1976; PhD, TsingHua U., Hsinchu, Taiwan, 1995. Instr. Feng Chia U., Taichung, Taiwan, 1976-82; assoc. prof. math. Feng Chia U., Taichung, 1982-93, prof., 1993—; cons. Consulting Ctr. of Statistics, Feng Chia U., 1979-82. Contbr. numerous articles to profl. jours. Recipient Rsch. award Nat. Sci. Coun., Taiwan, 1987-89. Mem. IEEE Computer Soc., Math. Soc. Republic of China, Chinese Statistics Assn., Computer Soc. Republic of China, Yang Ann Tennis Club (capt. 1980—), Phi Tau Phi. Home: 7F 537-1 Wen Shin Nan 3d Rd, Taichung 40408, Taiwan Office: Feng Chia U, 100 Wenhwa Rd Seatwen, Taichung 40724, Taiwan

CHEN, CHIN-CHIN, music educator; b. Taipei, Taiwan, Jan. 29, 1964; came to the U.S., 1991.; MMus in Piano Performance, U. Ill., 1993, MMus, 1995, DMA in Composition/Theory, 2000. Tchg. asst. U. Ill., Urbana, 1995-99; asst. prof. Grand Valley State U., Allendale, Mich., 1999—; adj. asst. prof. Millikin U., Decatur, Ill., 1998-99. Author (music for vibraphone and tape) Points of Departure, 1996, (music for 2-channel tape) Points of No Return, 1997 (first prize 1997), (music for violin and tape) Points of Arrival, 1998, (music for orch.) The Marks of Life, 1999. Recipient electroacoustic music commn. U. Ill., Urbana-Champaign, 1995, 98. Mem. Internat. Computer Music Assn., Soc. Composers, Inc., Soc. for the Electro-Acoustic Music in the U.S., Broadcast Music, Inc. E-mail: chenc@gvsu.edu. Fax: 616-895-3100. Office: Grand Valley State Univ One Campus Dr Allendale MI 49401

CHEN, CHI-YAO, insurance underwriter, educator; b. I-Lan, Taiwan, Nov. 19, 1930; s. Yen-Kun and A-Shang (Huang) C.; m. Shou-Huei Chen, Nov. 14, 1959; children: Chern-Chyi, I-Yung, In-Han. B of Liberal Arts, Nat. Taiwan U., Taipei, 1953. Cert. non-life underwriter, non-life mgmt. Mgr. underwriting dept. Taiwan Fire & Marine Ins. Co., Ltd., Taipei, 1980; exec. v.p. Fubon Ins. Co., Ltd., Taipei, 1980-91; assoc. prof. Nat. Chengchi U., Taipei, 1991-2000; chmn. ins. com. Consumers Assn., 1996-97, 98-99, chmn. bd. dirs.; bd. dirs. Guarantee Fund, Compuls ory Auto Ins.; advisor compulsory automobile ins. prep. com. Ministry of Transp. and Comm., 1997; mem. coun. ins. Min. of Fin., 1998—; exam. bd. Spl. Exam., Min. Exam.; chmn./mem. various target working coms. of various govt. and pvt. orgns. Author: Studies on Reinsurance, 1976, Reinsurance Principles and Practice, 1987, Reinsurance, 1992, Risk Management, 1993, Automobile Insurance Claims, 1995, Reins in Theory and Practice, revised, enlarged, 1993, 96, 2000, Automobile Insurance, Principles and Practice, 1999. Recipient Outstanding award Ministry of Fin., 1978, Acad. prize Japan Risk Mgmt. Soc., 1994; named Outstanding Author of Yr., Nat. Coun. Sci., 1994. Mem. Rotary Club of Taipei S.E. (pres. 1993-94), Taipei Fire Prevention Assn. (dir.), Non-Life Underwriters Soc. (chmn. 1990-96, hon. chmn. 1997—), Soc. Risk Mgmt. (chmn. 1998—), Chi-yung Ins. Edn. Found. (chmn. 1998—), Internat. Fedn. of Risk and Ins. Mgmt. Assn. (bd. dirs. 1998—), Fedn. of Asian, Pacific and African Mgmt. Orgns. (bd. dirs. 1998—). Avocations: hiking, travel. Home: 2d Fl #5 Ally 5 Ln 5 Sec 3, Ren-Ai Rd, Taipei Taiwan Office: Nat Chenchi U Risk Mgmt Ins Dept, No 64 Sec 2 Chu-Nan Rd, Taipei Taiwan

CHEN, CHUNGTE WILLIAM, optical engineer; b. Taipei, Taiwan, June 24, 1950; came to U.S., 1974; s. Dwan-In and Atz Chen; m. Jenna Angela Chen, Jan. 18, 1975; children: Julia Shouann, Stacy Shouru. BS, Tunghai U., Taichung, Taiwan, 1972; MS, Creighton U., 1976; PhD, U. Ariz., 1980. Sr. engr. Perkin-Elmer Co., Norwalk, Conn., 1980-82; chief optical designer Hughes Optical Products Inc., Des Plaines, Ill., 1982-84; sr. optical designer Perkin-Elmer Co., Danbury, Conn., 1984-88; R&D mgr. Perkin-Elmer Co., Garden Grove, Calif., 1988-89; sr. scientist Hughes Aircraft Co., El Segunda, Calif., 1989-97; engring. fellow Raytheon Systems, El Segunda, Calif., 1997—. Over 30 patents in field. Mem. Zool. Soc. San Diego, 1989—. Recipient Optical Tech. award Electro-Optics Network, 1994, Electro-Optic Sensor and Tech. award Hughes Aircraft Co., 1996. Mem. Internat. Soc. Optical Engrs. (guest editor 1980), Optical Soc. Am., Soc. Info. Display. Avocations: tennis, tai-chi, camping, spending time with family. E-mail: cbchen@west.raytheon.com. Home: 33 Allegheny Irvine CA 92620-2604

CHEN, CHUN-JEN, engineer; b. Kaohsiung, Taiwan, July 17, 1971; s. Deng-Kai and Hsiu-Hsia (Lin) C.; m. Yi-Lin Wei, Jan. 8, 1999; 1 child, Rui-Ting. B, Nat. Cheng Kung U., Taiwan, 1994, M, 1996. Tchg. asst. Nat. Cheng Kung U., Dept. Materials Sci. and Engring., 1995-97, rsch. asst., 1995—. Contbr. articles to profl. jours. Mem. Chinese Soc. Materials Sci., Chinese Inst. Engrs. Avocations: reading, baseball, bowling, computer. Home: No 15 Fu Shing 3rd Rd, Kaohsiung 806, Taiwan Office: Nat Cheng Kung U, Materials Sci & Engring, Tainan 701, Taiwan

CHEN, CHWEN CHENG, psychiatrist; b. Kaohsiung, Taiwan, Jan. 2, 1958; s. A-Kong and Chuan-Chen (Huang) C.; m. Wan-Ya Chang, Mar. 29, 1986. MB, China Med. Coll., 1984; PhD, Kings Coll. U. London, 1994. Med. diplomate, Taiwan. Resident in psychiatry Nat. Taiwan U. Hosp., Taipei, 1984-87, chief resident, 1987-88; lectr. in psychiatry Nat. Cheng Kung U., Tainan, Taiwan, 1988-95, dir. student counseling ctr., 1988-90, 95—, assoc. prof., dir., 1995—; cons. Tainan Counseling Guidance Ctr., 1995-97, Tainan Women Orgn., 1995-97. Contbr. articles to profl. jours. Scholar Ministry of Edn., 1990-94. Mem. Royal Coll. Psychiatrists (U.K.), Taiwan Soc. Psychiatrists (exec. bd. 1995-97, 99-2001), N.Y. Acad. Sci., Nat. Geographic Soc., Eastern Asia Acad. Sociocultural Psychiatry. Lutheran. Achievements include research in previous adverse life event effects on risk of breast cancer. Office: Nat Cheng Kung U Dept Psych, 139 Sheng-Li Rd, Tainan 70428, Taiwan

CHEN, CHYI CHANG (JIMMY), engineering company executive; b. Taiwan, July 15, 1939; s. Meng Hui Chen and Sun Ruo Ho; m. Yeh Er Liao, June 19, 1963; children: David, Peter. BSc in Mech. Engring., Nat. Taiwan U., Taipei, 1961. Workshop supr. Taiwan Aluminum Co., 1962-65; design engr. Taiwan Cement Co., 1965-66; project engr. Philco Ford Microelectronic, Taiwan, 1966-70; supt. SGS-Thomson, Singapore, 1970-73; engring. mgr. Wah Chang Internat., Singapore, 1973-89; engring. mgr. San Teh Ltd., Singapore, 1990-94, asst. chmn., 1994—. Recipient Best Engring. Support award Motorola, Singapore, 1991, Best Enterprise of Singapore award Govt. Singapore, 1992. Avocations: golf, swimming. Home: 22 Yio Chu Kang Rd # 03-01, Singapore 545535, Singapore Office: San Teh Ltd, 100 Eunos Ave 7, Singapore 405972, Singapore

CHEN, C.L. PHILIP, engineering educator; b. Pu-Li, Taiwan, July 4, 1959; s. Cheng-Kwan Chen and Yu Liu; m. Chien-Chiu Chien, July 2, 1984; children: Oriana, Melinda, Nelson. BS, Nat. Tapei U. Tech., Taiwan, 1979; MS, U. Mich., 1985; PhD, Purdue U., 1988. Vis. asst. prof. Ind. U.-Purdue U., Indpls., 1988-89; assoc. prof. Wright State U., Dayton, Ohio, 1995-2000, prof., 2000—, asst. prof., 1989-95; cons. Wright-Patterson AFB, Dayton, 1990-99. Author: Fuzzy Neural Systems, 2000, editor Smart Engineering System Design, 1996, Intelligent Engineering Systems Through Artificial Neural Networks, 1995; contbr. articles to profl. jours. V.P. bd. trustees Dayton Am. Chinese Assn., 1995. Fellow NRC, 1995; recipient Rsch. Initiation award NSF, 1989. Mem. IEEE (sr.), Taiwanese Assn. Dayton (trustee, v.p.). Avocations: golf, tennis, astronomy.

CHEN, CONCORDIA CHAO, mathematician; b. Peiping, China; came to U.S., 1955, naturalized, 1969; d. Chun-fu and Kwie Hwa (Wong) Chao; BA in Bus. Adminstrn., Nat. Taiwan U., 1954; MS in Math., Marquette U., 1958; postgrad. Purdue U., 1958-60, M.I.T., 1961-62; m. Chin Chen, July 2, 1960; children: Marie Hui-mei, Albert Chao. Teaching asst. Purdue U., Lafayette, Ind., 1958-60; system analysis engr. electronic data processing div. Mpls.-Honeywell, Newton Highlands, Mass., 1960-63; mgmt. planning asst. Lederle Labs., Am. Cyanamid Co., Pearl River, N.Y., 1964, computer applications specialist, 1967, ops. analyst, 1967; staff programmer IBM, Sterling Forest, N.Y., 1968-73, adv. programmer Data Processing Mktg. Group, Poughkeepsie, 1973-80, mgr. systems programming and systems architecture, Princeton, N.J., 1980-82, sr. systems analyst, 1982-83, data processing mktg. cons., Beijing, 1983-88; sr. planner IBM DSD, Poughkeepsie, 1988-92; program mgr. Chiang Indsl. Charity Found Ltd., 1993-94; mgr. software engring. China Weal Bus. Machinery Co., Ltd., Hong Kong, 1995-99, exec. gen. mgr., 1999—. Chmn. ednl. council Hudson region MIT. Mem. Am. Math. Soc., Soc. Indsl. and Applied Maths., MIT Club Hudson Valley (pres.). Home: 12 Mountain Pass Rd Hopewell Junction NY 12533-5331 Office: Guangzhou World Trade Ctr, Huan Shi East Rd 52709-13, Guangzhou 510095, China

CHEN, DAVID YUXIAO, electrical engineer, researcher; b. Sichuan, China, Mar. 19, 1970; came to U.S., 1991; parents Shunling and Yuli Tu. BA in Chemistry/Physics, Lawrence U., Appleton, Wis., 1993; MS in Elec. Engring., U. Wis., 1997, PhD in Materials Sci., 1997. Cert. exec. edn. Wharton Sch. U. Pa., 1999. Tchg. asst. U. Wis., Madison, 1993-94, rsch. asst., 1994-97; mem. tech. staff microelectronics group Lucent Techs. Inc., Reading, Pa., 1997-2000; product specialist, prog. mgr. Avanti Corp., Allentown, Pa., 2000—. Contbr. articles to profl. jours. Mem. IEEE (mem. exec. com. 1997—, chair Grads. of Last Decade 1997—), Soc. Mfg. Engrs. (sr.), Am. Soc. Engring. Edn., Reading Area Chinese Assn. (pres. 1998), N.Y. Acad. Sci., Phi Beta Kappa, Sigma Xi. Achievements include resarch in the thermodynamic exchange mechanism in forming ohmic contacts to compound semiconductor; Indium-based ohmic contacts to n-GaAs; low pressure chemical vapor deposition in fabricating integrate circuits for telecommunications. Avocations: travel, tennis, windsurfing. Office: Avanti Corp 5366 Andrea Dr Allentown PA 18106-9458

CHEN, DONG, hematologist; b. Beijing, Mar. 5, 1968; s. Chen Mingsen and Wenrong Liu; m. Ping He, May, 12, 1994. MD, Beijing Med. U., 1992; MS, Peking Union Med. Coll., Beijing, 1994; PhD, U. Ky., 1999. Rsch. assoc. Peking Union Med. Coll., 1992-94; rsch. asst. U. Ky., Lexington, 1994-99, rsch. scientist, 1999—. Mem. Am. Assn. Hematology (cert.), Am. Assn. Cell Biology. Avocations: travel, computers, hiking, swimming. Fax: (606) 323-1037. E-mail: chendon@pop.uky.edu. Office: U Ky 800 Rose St Lexington KY 40506-0001

CHEN, DU-XING, physicist; b. Shanghai, China, May 8, 1941; arrived in Sweden, 1985; arrived in Spain, 1989; s. Shi-Zhong and Zuo-Min (Wang) C.; m. Jia-Ying Wu, Sept. 17, 1969; 1 child, Chen-Si Wu. Student, Peking (China) U., 1958-64; M in Physics, Chinese Acad. Scis., Beijing, China, 1981; PhD in Materials Sci. and Engring., Ctrl. Iron & Steel Rsch. Inst., Beijing, China, 1985. Technician, engr. Beijing (China) Metallurgical Rsch. Inst., 1964-82; engr. Ctrl Iron and Steel Rsch. Inst., Beijing, China, 1982—; postdoc. rschr. Royal Inst. Tech., Stockholm, Sweden, 1985-89; guest rschr. NIST, Boulder, Colo., 1988,90,92; vis. prof. U. Autonoman Barcelona, Spain, 1989-91; prof. Inst. Magnetismo Aplicado RENFE-UCM, Madrid, Spain, 1992—; supv. doctoral students Barcelona, Madrid, Spain, 1989—; referee apptd. by Phys. Review, Phys. Review Letters, IEEE, 1993—. Author: Physical Bases of Magnetic Measurements, China Mechanical Industry, 1985, Ballistic and Bridge Methods of Magnetic Measurements of Materials, China Metrology, 1990; contbr. articlest to profl. jours. Recipient Significant Achievements The First China Sci. Conf., Beijing, 1978, Highest Rank for Indiv. Beijing Mcpl., 1981, Successful Completion of Assignment, NIST, U.S. Dept. Commerce, 1988, 90. Office: Inst Mag Apds, PO Box 155, 28230 Las Rozas Spain

CHEN, EDEN HSIEN-CHANG, engineering consultant; b. Koachsiung, China, Mar. 1, 1954; came to U.S., 1976; s. Wen-Wu and Wen-Chian (Tien) C.; m. Marilyn L. Haugan, Jan. 18, 1982; children: Jessica, Joshua, Justin, Jerilyn. BS in Indsl. Engring., Chung Yuan U., 1976; MS in Indsl. Engring., N.D. State U., 1980. Sr. engr. Gen. Instruments, Kaohsiung, Taiwan, 1976-78, Litton Industries, Sioux Falls, S.D., 1980-86; engring. mgr. DICKEY-John Corp., Auburn, Ill., 1986-88, TRW, Marshall, Ill., 1988-90; prin. cons. CTI, Springfield, Ill., 1990—; adj. instr. George Washington U., Washington, 1989—, U. Wis., Madison, 1989, U. Dayton, 1996—; instr. Soc. Automotive Engrs., Warrendale, Pa., 1986—, Soc. Mfg. Engrs., Dearborn, Mich., 1989—. Chmn. Springfield Commn. Internat. Visitors, 1995-96, commr., 1992-97; advisor Ill. Staet Treas. Pat Quinn, Chgo., 1992-94, Overseas Chinese Affairs Commn., Taipei, Taiwan, 1995—. Office: CTI PO Box 9302 Springfield IL 62791-9302

CHEN, ERIC YEN-PO, accountant, consultant; b. Kaohsiung City, Taiwan, Nov. 7, 1971; came to the U.S., 1994; s. Jeng-Quey and Hsiu-Chuan (Sun) C.; m. Irene Hsiao-pu Jao, May 22, 1997. BS in Atmospheric Sci., Nat. Taiwan U., 1994; MBA in Accountancy, CUNY, 1996. CPA, N.Y., N.J. Account analyst Dean Witter Trust Co., Jersey City, 1994-95; contr. APWM, Inc. (Roven Dino), Pine Brook, N.J., 1995-96; assoc., tax specialist Kuan C. Tsai & Assocs., P.C., CPA's, Metuchen, N.J., 1996-98; assoc. Rothstein, Kass & Co., P.C., CPA's, Roseland, N.J., 1998-99; bus. analyst mgr. Formosa Plastics Corp., Livingston, N.J., 1999—; cons. Keydata Internat., Inc., South Plainfield, N.J., 1996-98, Aaeon Electronics, Inc., Hazlet, N.J., 1997-98, New Bay Corp., N.Y.C., 1997-98, Pine Tech. USA, Edison, N.J., 1997-98. Supporter Nutley (N.J.) Fire Dept., 1994-98, Nutley Police Dept., 1994-98. Mem. AICPA, N.J. Soc. CPAs (mem. polit. action com. 1998 , internat. taxation, young CPAs com.), Beta Gamma Sigma.

CHEN, ER-PING, engineering executive; b. Ping-Liang, Kansu, China, May 19, 1944; came to U.S., 1967; s. Sheng-Huang and Tze-Yu (Chou) C.; m. Regina C. Chen, Mar. 31, 1973; children: Candice S., Benjamin B. BS, Nat. Chung-Hsing U., Taiwan, 1966; MS, Lehigh U., 1969, PhD, 1972. Asst., assoc. prof. Lehigh U., Bethlehem, Pa., 1972-78; mem. tech. staff Sandia Nat. Labs., Albuquerque, 1978-93; disting. mem. tech. staff Sandia Nat. Labs., 1993-97; mgr. Sandia Nat. Labs., Livermore, Calif., 1997—. Co-author: Cracks in Composite Materials, 1981; contbr. more than 100 articles to profl. jours. V.p. Albuquerque Sister Cities Found., 1986; pres. N.Mex. Chinese Assn., 1985, Assn. Chinese Engrs. and Scientists of N.Mex., 1990. Fellow ASME (chair tech. com. 1984-86). Avocation: tennis. Home: 303 Bonaire Ct Danville CA 94506-1414 Office: Sandia Nat Labs PO Box 969 Livermore CA 94551-0969

CHEN, ESTHER EVA, psychologist, educator; b. Budapest, Hungary, Mar. 17, 1938; arrived in Israel, 1947; d. Gyula Zvi and Magda (Benedict) Fried; m. Jacob Chen, Mar. 25, 1958; children: Michal, Tamar, Arnon, Orit. Tchg. diploma, Bar-Ilan U., Tel-Aviv, 1963, BA in Psychology, 1976; MA in Psychology, Edmonton, Can., 1983. Cert. hypnotherapist, family and child therapist. Tchr. H.S., Hod-Hasaron, Israel, 1971-76; sch. counselor Dormitary, 1976-83; psychologist spl. edn. Pardes-Cana, 1983—; pvt. practice psychology Hod-Hasaron, 1987—; cons. in field. Active Civil Movement, Tel-Aviv, 1972-79. Sgt. Israeli Def. Force, 1956-58. Avocations: yoga, swimming, traveling, gardening, painting. Home: Aliyat-Hanoar 7, 45101 Hod-Hasaron Israel Office: Dormitory Spl Edn, Pardes-Cana, 67089 Tokayer Israel

CHEN, FENG, mechanics educator; b. Shanghai, Oct. 22, 1947; s. Shau Long and Xin Yun Chen; m. Xun Hu, Oct. 1, 1984; 1 child, Shu La. Degree, Ctrl. South U. Tech., Changsha, China, 1982, MS, 1985, PhD, 1998; diploma (hon.), Beijing Fgn. Lang. U., 1998. Asst. prof. Ctrl. South U. Tech., 1982-85, lectr., 1985-89, prof., 1995—; sr. vis. scholar Royal Inst. Tech., Stockholm, 1989-92; guest rschr. Voice Inst., Göteborg, Sweden. Author: Theorem of Movement, 1982 (1st prize 1983). Grantee Gen. Co. Nonferrous Metals China, 1995, China Nat. Nature Sci. Found., 1995. Mem. Assn. Mechanics China, Assn. Mech. Engring China, Assn. Failure Analysis China, Inst. Material Fracture and Strength (vice dean 1995—). Avocations: classical music, table tennis. Home: Pu Dong Da Dau 2641 Long, No 15 Rm 201, Shanghai 200129, China Office: Ctrl S U Tech, Opening Lab Mechs, Changsha Hunan 410083, China

CHEN, FU-MIN, gynecologist; b. Hong-chow, China, Apr. 21, 1936; s. Hong-Tno and Wen-Jen (Song) C.; m. Chou-Mai Chang, Mar. 15, 1964. MB, Nat. Defence Med. Coll., 1962. Resident ob/gyn. Trisvc. Gen. Hosp., Taipei, Republic of China, 1964-68, Beth Israel Med. Cen., N.Y., 1968-71; chief ob/gyn. Trisvc. Gen. Hosp., Taipei, 1972-79; assoc. prof. ob/gyn. Nat. Defence Med. Coll., Taipei, 1978-91; supt. and dir. dept. ob/gyn. Chung-Shan Hosp., Taipei, 1981-82, pres./dir. dept. ob/gyn., 1982—. Author: (books) Book for Pregnent Women, 1994, Health for Women, 1996, Clinical Stories of An Old Doctor, 1999. Pres. Med. Adv. and Svc. Assn., China, 1989-91. Major, Navy/Army, China, 1962-63. Fellow Am. Coll. Obsterics and Gynecology, Am. Coll Surgeons, Internat. Coll. Surgeons, Taipei Med. Soc. Avocations: swimming, bridge. Office: Chung-Shan Hosp, No 11 Ln 112 Sect 4 Jen-Ai, 106 Taipei Republic China

CHEN, GANG See SHENG, GANG

CHEN, GEN-HUEY, computer science educator; b. Taipei, China, Oct. 10, 1959; s. Pi-chin and Su-hsin (Ho) C.; m. Yin-Ling Liao; children: Yen-Jean, Yen-Tim. B, Nat. Taiwan Univ., Taipei, 1981; M, Nat. Tsing-Hua Univ., Hsinchu, Taiwan, 1983, PhD, 1987. Assoc. prof. Nat. Taiwan Univ., Taipei, 1987-92, prof., 1992—; cons. Nat. Sci. Coun., Taiwan, 1994—. Contbr. articles to profl. jours. Recipient Disting. Rsch. award Nat. Sci. Coun., 1993, 95, 97, 99. Fax: 886 2 223628167. Home and Office: Nat Taiwan Univ, Dept Computer Sci, Taipei Taiwan

CHEN, GEORGE CHI-MING, energy company executive; b. Shanghai, China, Sept. 21, 1923; s. Harvey Kun-Fan and Margaret Wen-Yao (Sang) C.; m. Nora Tzu-Ling Pan, Oct. 15, 1953; children: Priscilla Hsu-Lu, Peter Hsu-Ling. BS, Harvard U., 1946. Mgr. Kian Gwan Co., Shanghai, 1947-49, Hong Kong, 1949-50; mng. dir. Kian Gwan Co., Taipei, 1950-51; chmn. George Chen & Co., Taipei, 1951-87, Lien Chen Ltd., Taipei, 1951-87; mng. dir. Shing Nung Group, Tai Chung, 1961-87; chmn. Shell Pacific Devel., Singapore, 1970-87. Trustee Northfield Mt. Hermon Sch., Mass., 1988-98, Libr. Found. of San Francisco, 1996—; mem. bd. overseers Harvard U., 1998—. Lt. Col. Chinese Army. Mem. China Petroleum Soc. (life). Republican. Roman Catholic.

CHEN, GEORGE MIN-YEN, minister; b. Shanghai, China, Feb. 2, 1934; s. Xin-Chang and Shu-Fen (Dong) C.; m. Wen-Yu Shum, June 10, 1975; children: Hui-fu, Mary. Ordained minister. Exec. dir. Bonisa Found., Lisse, Holland, 1985—; sr. advisor Internat. Aid Inc., Spring Lake, Mich., 1986—; missionary Asian Outreach Internat., Hong Kong, 1987—; cons. Action Love, Hong Kong, 1995—; min. at large, 1952—; hon. chmn. Huancheng Social Welfare Found., Zhongshan, China; hon. pres. Huancheng Hosp., Zhongshan, AnQing Mcpl. Hosp., Anhui, China, QianWu Hosp., Zhuhai, China, DaYe Christianity Hosp., Hupei, China. Avocation: travel. Home: Flat B 5/F Block 6, Villa Esplanada/Tsing Yi, Hong Kong China

CHEN, GUANG-WEI, surgeon, educator; b. Taichung, Taiwan, May 3, 1957; s. Hung-Gun Chen and Su-Chin Lai; m. Hui-Na Yeh, June 27, 1987; children: Edward, Eddie. M, China Med. Coll., Taichung, Taiwan, 1993, PhD, 1998. Resident surgery dept. CMCH, Taichung, Taiwan, 1984-88, chief resident surgery dept., 1988-89, attending physician colon rectal surgery dept., 1990-93, chief physician colon rectal surgery dept., 1993—, assoc. prof. surgery dept., 1998—; chief Inst. Assoc. Chinese and Western Medicine, 2000—. Mem. N.Y. Acad. Scis., Surgery Soc. China, Colon Rectal Surgery Soc. China, Biomolecular Soc. China. Avocations: art, photo. Home: No 330 Sect 3 San Ming Rd, Taichung 400, Taiwan Office: China Med Coll Hosp, No 2 Yuh-Der Rd, Taichung 400, Taiwan

CHEN, GUI-QIANG, mathematician, educator, researcher; b. Ningbao, Zhejiang, People's Republic of China, May 25, 1963; came to U.S., 1987; parents Zhi-Biao and Jin-Er (Hu) C. BS, Fudan U., Shanghai, People's Republic China, 1982; PhD, Acad. Sinica, Beijing, 1987. Asst. prof. Inst. Systems Sci., Acad. Sinica, 1987; vis. scientist Courant Inst. Math. Scis., N.Y.C., 1987-89; asst. prof. math. U. Chgo., 1989-94; assoc. prof. math. Northwestern U., 1994-96, prof., 1996—; cons. Argonne Nat. Lab., Chgo., 1989-95. Recipient Young Investigator award NSF, Beijing, China, 1987, Nat. Medal of Sci., People's Republic of China, 1989; Alfred P. Sloan Rsch. fellow, 1991; named Excellent Young Scientist, Beijing Soc. for Sci. and Tech., 1988. Mem. Am. Math. Soc., Soc. for Indsl. and Applied Math. Office: Northwestern Univ Dept Math Evanston IL 60208-0001

CHEN, GUODONG, scientist, chemical engineer; b. Huaian, Jiangsu, China, July 23, 1963; s. Tingzhu Chen and Xiuying Shi; m. Dan Tao, Jan. 3, 1996; 1 child, Lydia Sijia. B in Engring., Nanjing Inst. Chem. Tech., Nanjing, China, 1985, M in Engring., 1988; MSChemE, Tenn. Technol. U., 1992; PhD in Bioengring., U. Toledo, 1996. Engr. Rsch. Inst. Petroleum Processing, Beijing, 1988-90; postdoctoral scientist Ohio U., Athens, 1997-99; sr. mfg. scientist Wyeth-Lederle Vaccines and Pediatrics, Pearl River, N.Y., 1999—; presenter in field. Contbr. articles to Enzyme and Microbial Tech., Biotechnology and Bioengring., Biochemistry, Biofunctional Membranes, Biophysical Jour. Mem. AIChE, Am. Soc. for Engring. Edn., Parenteral Drug Assn., Sigma Xi. Achievements include development of the optimal pH control technique; rsch. in Helicobacter pylori survival in the gastric acidity of the human stomach, enzymology of vitamin B12; development of the dual automatic pH control and dextrose feeding technique for vaccine production. Office: Wyeth-Lederle Vaccines/Pediatrics 401 N Middletown Rd Pearl River NY 10965-1215

CHEN, HAN-FU, control scientist; b. Hangzhou, China, Feb. 10, 1937; s. Kien Kwong Chen and Liang-Bi Zhu; m. Shu-Jun Wang, Dec. 23, 1963; 1 child, He-Yi Chen. Diploma, Leningrad (USSR) U., 1961. Rsch. asst. Inst. Math. Chinese Acad. Scis., Beijing, 1961-78, rsch. assoc., 1979, assoc. prof. math., 1979-80; assoc. prof. math. Inst. Systems Scis., Chinese Acad. Scis., Beijing, 1980-86, prof. math., 1986—, dep. dir., 1987-91, dir., 1995-98; mem. tech bd. Internat. Fedn. Automatic Control, 1993—. Author: Recursive Estimation and Control for Stochastic Systems, 1985; co-author: Identification and Stochastic Adaptive Control, 1991, Stochastic Approximation, 1996. Recipient Nat. Natural Sci. awards State Commn. Sci. and Tech. for China, 1987, 97. Fellow IEEE; mem. Chinese Acad. Scis., Chinese Assn. Automation (pres. 1993—). Office: Inst Systems Science CAS, Zhongguancun, Beijing 100080, China

CHEN, HO-HONG H., industrial engineering executive, educator; b. Taiwan, Apr. 11, 1933; s. Shui-Cheng and Mei (Lin) C.; m. Yuki-Lihua Jenny, Mar. 10, 1959; children: Benjamin Kuen-Tsai, Carl Joseph Chao-Kuang, Charles Chao-Yu, Eric Chao-Ying, Charmine Tsuey-Ling, Dolly Hsiao-Ying, Edith Yi-Wen, Yvonne Yi-Fang, Grace Yi-Sing, Julia Yi-Jiun. Owner Tai Chang Indsl. Supplies Co., Ltd., 1967—; pres. Pan Pacific Indsl. Supplies, Inc., Ont., Can., 1975—, Maker Group Inc., Md., 1986—, Wako Internat. Co., Ltd., Md., 1986—; prof. First Econ. U., Japan. Author: 500 Creative Designs for Future Business, 1961; A Summary of Suggestions for the Economic Development in Central America Countries, 1979; Access and Utilize the Potential Fund in Asia, 1980. Mem. Univ. Club (Washington), Kenwood Golf & Country Club (Bethesda, Md.). Office: PO Box 5674 Washington DC 20016-1274

CHEN, HONG-I, hospital administrator, educator; b. Tainan City, Taiwan, Feb. 18, 1949; s. Su-Shiun and Su-Tsueylien (Su) C.; m. Wang-Hsunyu Wang, Dec. 24, 1978; children: Yu-Nein, Chiang-Nein. BM, Nat. Def. Med. Ctr., Taipei, Taiwan, 1973; PhD, U. Oxford, Eng., 1990. Diplomate in surgery and urology. Chief surgery The 804 Mil. Gen. Hosp., Taiwan, 1984-87, vice dir., 1990-93, dir., 1993—; cons. Min-Teh Mcpl. Mid. Sch., Tainan, Taiwan, 1991-94, The Tainan 1st Provincial H.S., 1994—. Col. Taiwan Mil., 1993-96. Recipient medal of study merit Ministry Nat. Def., 1991. Mem. Urol. Assn. Republic of China (Dr. Y.F. Shieh's prize 1992), Brit. Assn. Urol. Surgeons, European Assn. Urology, N.Y. Acad. Scis., Royal Soc. Medicine. Buddhist. Avocations: tennis, golf. Home: 17F-4 # 50, Lane 355 Chong-Hwa Rd, Yung-Kang City Tainan Hsiang Taiwan Office: Tri-Svc Gen Hosp, PO Box 90055, Taipei Taiwan

CHEN, HSING-YI, electrical engineering educator; b. Tainan, China, Oct. 20, 1954; s. Wen-Chang and Hsiu-Luan (Shih) C.; m. Phone-Mei Chou, Jan. 14, 1984; children: Goan-Yi, Gawn-Chi. BSEE, Chung Yuan Christian Univ., Chung-Li, Taiwan, 1978; MS elec. engr., Nat. Tsing Hua Univ., Hsin-Chu, Taiwan, 1981; PhD in elec. engr., Univ. Utah, 1989. Engr. Chinese Petroleum Corp., Taipei, Taiwan, 1978-79, Gibson Engnrs. Ltd., Taipei, 1981-82; pres. Hsing-Yi Profl. Elec. Engrs. Office, Taipei, 1982-85, Sine-Valve Profl. Elec. Engrs. Office, Taipei, 1994—; dir. R & D, Ctr. for Far East, Yuan Ze U., Chung-Li, Taiwan, 1995-99; prof., chmn. dept. elec. engring. Yuan Ze U., Taiwan, 1995—; cons. Joyful Mech. & Elec. Corp. Ltd., Taipei, 1994—, Chung Shan Inst. of Sci. & Tech., Taiwan, 1993, SINE & Assocs. M/Elec COns. & Engrs. 1989—. Assoc. editor: Jour. of Occupational Safety & Health, 1996; contbr. numerous articles to profl. jours. Rsch. project reviewer Inst. of Occupational Safety and Health, Coun. of Labor Affairs, Yuan, 1995-96. With Army, 1974. Recipient Class A Rsch. award Nat. Sci. Coun., 1990, 91, 94-99, Outstanding award Yuan Ze U., 1990, Outstanding Alumnus of Tainan 2d H.S., 1995. Mem. Taipei Assn. of Profl. Elec. Engrs., The Inst. of Elec. and Electronics Engrs., The Chinese Automatic Control Soc., Phi Tau Phi. Avocations: swimming, table tennis, chinese chess, music.

CHEN, HSUAN-CHIH, psychologist; s. C.X. Chen and Fang Chu; m. Nancy Chen, 1978; children: Sen-Lay Robert, Liang-Jun Timothy. PhD, U. Kans., 1982; postdoctoral fellow, U. Colo., 1982-83. Lectr. to sr. lectr. Chinese U. of Hong Kong, 1983-95; rsch. fellow Inst. for Perception Rsch., The Netherlands, 1989-90; summer rsch. fellow Max Planck Inst. for Psycholinguistics, The Netherlands, 1992-96; prof. Chinese U. of Hong Kong, 1995—. Assoc. editor: Acta Psychologica Sinica, China, 1995—; co-editor: Cognitive Aspects of the Chinese Language, 1988, Language and Cognitive Processes, U.K., 1997—; editor: Language Processing in Chinese, 1992, The Cognitive Processing of Chinese and Related Asian Languages, 1997. Recipient fellowship Internat. Reading Assn., U.S.A., 1987. Mem. Internat. Assn. for Study of Attention and Performance/The Netherlands, Psychonomic Soc., Cognitive Sci. Soc. Avocations: reading, travel. Home: Dept Psychology, The Chinese U of Hong Kong, Shatin New Territories China

CHEN, HUAITAO, veterinary pathologist, consultant; b. Huayin, Shaanxi, China, Aug. 10, 1938; p. Zixiu Chen and Dengcao Wang; m. Qiuchang Wang, Dec. 25, 1968; children: Wenjie, Wenhong. Grad., Gansu Agrl. U., Lanzhou, China, 1961; diploma in Vet. Scis., N.Bălcescu Agrl. Inst., Bucharest, Romania, 1981. Asst. Gansu Agrl. U., 1961-78, lectr., 1978-79; lectr. N.Bălcescu Agrl. Inst., 1979-81; asst. prof. Gansu Agrl. U., 1987-91, prof., 1992—; discipline specialist Nat. Natural Sci. Found. China, Beijing, 1996—; cons. editl. office Inner Mongolian Animal Scis. and Prodn., Huhhot, China, 1993—. Author: (textbook) Veterinary Pathology, 2000, Clinical Zoopathology, 1995; contbr. articles to profl. jours. Recipient award Govt. Gansu Province, 1989, grant State Coun. China, 1992, award Ministry Agr., China, 1996. Mem. AAAS, N.Y. Acad. Sics., Chinese Assn. Animal Sci. and Vet. Medicine, Chinese Assn. Vet. Pathology, Internat. Vet. Acad. on Disaster Medicine. Avocations: sports, touring, reading, music. Office: Gansu Agrl Univ, 1 Yingmencun Anning Dist, 730070 Lanzhou China

CHEN, HUITANG, educator; b. Chao Yan City, China, July 1, 1933; s. Huanwen C. and Qinyin Zhou; m. Yuejuan Wang, Aug. 17, 1935; 1 child, Yinong. B, Jiaotong U., Shanghai, China, 1953, M, 1956. Asst. Jiaoting U., Shanghai, China, 1956-58, lectr., assoc. prof., 1958-86, prof., 1986—; scientific rschr. Dybna Nuclear Rsch. Inst., Russia, 1962-65; vis. prof. Keio U., Yokohama, Japan, 1981-82. Inventor in field. Mem. IEEE (sr.). Avocations: music, reading. Home: Tongji New Village 636/303, Shanghai 200092, China Office: Tongji U Dept Elec Engring, 1239 Siping Rd, Shanghai 200092, China

CHEN, I-SHIN, physicist; b. Tainan, Taiwan, China, Sept. 1, 1949; s. Gin-Jung and Wu-Gung C.; m. Mei-Jiang Lin, Jan. 30, 1980; children: Li-Ru, Ching-Yuang. BS, Taiwan Normal U., 1974, M, 1978; PhD, Ohio State U., 1991. Instr. Taipei (China) Mcpl. Tchrs. Coll., 1978-84, assoc. prof., 1984-94, prof., 1994—; chmn. dept. sci. & math. Taipei Mcpl. Tchrs. Coll., 1987-88, chief fin. dept., 1986-87. Author of software. 2d lt. Chinese Army, 1973-74. Execute Yuan scholar, Taipei, 1975, Nat. Sco. Coun. scholar, Taipei, 1988-91. Mem. Nat. Assn. Sci. Rsch. in Teaching, Nat. Sci. Tchrs. Assn. Avocations: table tennis, baseball, Chinese chess. Home: 11F-6 162 Sec 4 Roosevelt, Taipei Taiwan Office: 1 I-Kou W Rd, Taipei Taiwan

CHEN, JAMES TSING-FANG, artist, educator, cultural center administrator; b. Tainan, Taiwan, June 2, 1936; came to U.S., 1975; m. Lucia Hou, Dec. 20, 1975; children: Ted, Julie. BA, Nat. Taiwan U., Taipei, 1959; cert., Beaux Arts, Paris, 1972; MA in Contemporary French Lit., U. Paris, 1965; PhD in History of Modern Art, La Sorbonne, Paris, 1970. Editor-in-chief Formosan Report, Paris, 1973-80; founder T.F. Chen Cultural Ctr., N.Y.C., 1996—, New World Art Ctr., N.Y.C., 1996—; chmn. fine arts sect. Internat. Conf. Arts, Paris, 1987, N.Y.C., 1988. Author of 12 books: Ten Year's of My Pictorial Voyages, 1974, The Spirit of Liberty, 1986, The Art of Dr. T.F. Chen: Neo-Iconography, 1990, Dreaming Towards A New Renaissance, 1990, My Days in Paris, 1996, Towards the 21st Century, 1999, others; over 100 one-man shows in Europe, N.Am. and Asia, including Phila. Art Alliance 1978, State World Forum, 1998; lectr. and tour show throughout Taiwan, 1987; retroactive show New World Art Ctr., 1996; exhibited in numerous group shows in Europe, N.Am., Asia; prodr. series The Statue of Liberty, Post-Van Gogh, East-West, Space Age, Humanity, Princess Diana, others; represented in permanent collections Mus. Modern Art, Paris, Smithsonian Instn., Washington, Pacific Asia Mus., Taipei Fine Arts Mus., also pvt. collections. Organizer, sec.-gen. Fedn. World Formosan Assns., Paris and N.Y.C., 1974-80. Recipient Achievement award in arts and humanities Taiwanese-Am. Found., L.A., 1983, Disting. Alumnus award Tainan 1st H.S., 1995; scholar Govt. of France, 1963. Avocations: music, cooking, chess, hiking. Fax: 212-966-5285. Home and Office: TF Chen Museum Bldg 250 Lafayette St New York NY 10012-4040

CHEN, JAW-WEN, cardiologist, researcher; b. Taipei, Taiwan, Apr. 10, 1959; s. Jong-Peng Chen and Ju-Ying Neu. MD, Kaohsiung Med. U., Taiwan, 1984. Resident Vet. Gen. Hosp., Taipei, 1986-90, chief resident, 1990-91, fellow, 1991-93, vis. staff, 1993—; postdoctoral rschr. Stanford (Calif.) U., 1997-98, asst. prof., 1997—; asst. prof. Nat. Yang-Ming U. Sch. Medicine, Taipei, 1997—, Nat. Def. Med. Coll., Taipei, 1991—. Author: When You Can Not Hide, 1984; contbr. articles to profl. jours. Mem. Am. Heart Assn., Internat. Soc. Lipids Arthersclerosis, N.Y. Acad. Sci. Avocations: reading, writing, chess. Office: Vet Gen Hosp, 201 Shih-Pai Rd Sect 2, Taipei Taiwan

CHEN, JEFF WILLIAM, neurosurgeon; b. Pasadena, Dec. 30, 1959; s. William S. and Susan (Wong) C.; m. Jeanne Chu, May 30, 1987; children: Patrick, Therese. BS/MS, Calif. Inst. Tech., 1981; MD, PhD, Johns Hopkins U., Balt., 1987. Diplomate Am. Bd. Neurol. Surgeons. Surg. intern U. Calif., San Diego, 1987-88, neurosurgery resident, 1988-93; fellow in neurovascular surgery Barrow Neurol. Inst., Phoenix, 1993-94; asst. prof. neurosurgery U. Tex. Med. Br., Galveston, 1994-99; dir. neurotrauma Legacy Hosp. Sys., Portland, Oreg., 1999—; vis. scientist LaJolla Cancer Rsch. Found., 1988-93. Contbr. articles to profl. jours. NIH traineeship, 1981-87, N.Y. Acad. Sci. traineeship, 1986. Fellow ACS; mem. Am. Assn. Neurol. Surgeons, N.Y. Acad. Sci., Congress of Neurol. Surgeons, Tau Beta Pi. Roman Catholic. Achievements include discovery of lysosomal membrane proteins, p53 and pituitary tumors. Office: Legacy Emanuel Hosp 501 N Graham St Ste 580 Portland OR 97227-2003

CHEN, JEN-PING, atmospheric sciences educator; b. Taipei, Taiwan, Aug. 11, 1959; s. Nai-Hung and Hwa-Chueh (Chen) C. BS, Nat. Taiwan U., 1982; MS, S.D. Sch. Mines and Tech., 1986; PhD, Pa. State U., 1992. Tchg. asst. Nat. Taiwan U., Taipei, 1984-85; rsch. asst. S.D. Sch. Mines and Tech., Rapid City, 1985-86, Pa. State U., University Park, 1987-92; postgrad. rsch. Scripps Instn. Oceanography, La Jolla, Calif., 1992-94; assoc. prof. dept. atmospheric scis. Nat. Taiwan U., 1994-98, prof. dept. atmospheric scis., 1999—. Translator: Atmosphere, Climate and Change, 1997; editor Jour. Terrestrial, Atmospheric and Oceanic Scis., 1997. Chmn. Alumni Assn. of Dept. Atmospheric Scis., Nat. Taiwan U., 1997-99. Mem. Am. Meteorol. Soc., Am. Geophys. Union, Meteorol. Soc. Republic of China. Avocations: bridge, GO, basketball, table tennis, tennis. Office: Nat Taiwan U Dept Atmos Sci, 61 Ln 144 Sect 4 Keelung Rd, 107 Taipei Taiwan

CHEN, JIABI, educator; b. Nanjing, Jiangsu, China, Sept. 8, 1946; s. Qingyi Chen and Meihong Guo; m. Yannan Zhang, July 30, 1979 (dec. Aug. 1988); 1 child, Xi; m. Lingman Zhai, Mar. 31, 1992. BS, Tsinghua (China) U., 1968. Engr. Changchun 4th Optical Factory, China, 1968-75; asst. prof. Huazhong U. Sci. and Tech., China, 1975-80, lectr., 1980-86, assoc. prof., 1986-91; prof. Nanjing Normal U., China, 1992-97, Shanghai (China) U. Sci. and Tech., 1997—. Author: Principle and Problems of Fourier Optics, 1985, Principle and Problems of Statistical Optics, 1992, Holographic and Special Metrology, 1995, Lesar Metrology, 1998. Mem. SPIE, Chinese Optical Assn., Shanghai Laser Assn. (v.p. 1997-99). Avocation: reading. Office: Shanghai U Sci & Tech, 516 Jungong Rd, Shanghai 200093, China

CHEN, JIANDE, biomedical engineer, researcher; b. Ningbo, Zhejiang, China, Dec. 4, 1956; came to U.S., 1989; s. Shitang and Liyue (Zhao) C.; m. Xiuxia Du, Feb. 6, 1983; children: Dennis, Sidney, Juliana. BS, East China Normal U., Shanghai, 1982; PhD in Applied Sci., Katholieke U. Leuven, Belgium, 1989. Asst. prof. internal medicine U. Va., 1990-94; dir. electrophysiology lab. Baptist Med. Ctr., Oklahoma City, 1995-96; scientific dir. Lynn Health Sci. Inst., Oklahoma City, 1996—; v.p. Lynn Health Sci. Inst., 1997—; adj. assoc. prof. U. Okla., 1997—; cons. Synectics Med., Inc., Sweden, 1993-96. Editor: Electrogastrography: Principles & Applications, 1995; author 7 book chpts.; contbr. more than 100 articles to profl. jours.; patentee in field. V.p. Okla. Chinese Profl. Assn., Oklahoma City, 1997. Recipient Young Investigator award Whitaker Found., Washington, 1994, 21 rsch. grants, 1992—. Fellow Am. Coll. Gastroenterology; mem. IEEE (sr.), Internat. Electrogastrography Soc. (pres. 1996-98, Alvarez award 1995). Avocations: music, playing cards. Home: 15511 Turtle Oak Ct Houston TX 77059-3133 Office: U Tex Med Br Div Gastroenterology 4.106 Mccullough Bldg Galveston TX 77555-0001

CHEN, JIM NAN, physician; b. Taichung, Taiwan, Aug. 6, 1940; s. Abe Pin Ho and Wen Chi (Huang) C.; m. Lind Rwei-Yin Chiu, Nov. 30, 1969; children: Steven, Jasmin. MD, Kaoshiung Med. Coll., Taiwan, 1968. Med. diplomate. Intern St. Francis Hosp., Trenton, N.J., 1971-72; resident in surgery Mac Kay Meml. Hosp., Taipei, Republic of China, 1969-71, Rochester (N.Y.) U., 1972-73, Beckely (W.Va.) VA Hosp., 1977-78; resident in urology N.Y. Mt. Sinai Hosp., N.Y.C., 1974-75, Tulane U., New Orleans, 1972-78, U. Western Ont., Can., 1973-74; chmn. Chen Clinic, Taichung, 1983—. Lt. Taiwan Navy, 1967-68. Avocations: tennis, golf. Office: Chen Clinic, 3-5 Sec 1 Chung Hua Rd, 403 Taichung Taiwan

CHEN, JOHN CALVIN, child and adolescent psychiatrist; b. Augusta, Ga., Apr. 30, 1949; s. Calvin H. Chen and Lora L. Liu. BA in History, Pacific Union Coll., 1971; MD, Loma Linda U., 1974; PhD in Philosophy, Claremont Grad. U., 1984; JD, UCLA, 1987. Bar: Calif. 1987, U.S. Dist. Ct. (ctrl. dist.) Calif. 1988; diplomate Am. Bd. Psychiatry and Neurology, Child and Adolescent Psychiatry. Resident in psychiatry Loma Linda U. Med. Ctr., 1975-77; fellow in child and family psychiatry Cedars-Sinai Med. Ctr., L.A., 1977-78; psychiat. cons. San Bernardino (Calif.) County Mental Health Dept., 1979-83; pvt. practice Claremont, Calif., 1980-84; fellow in child and adolescent psychiatry U. So. Calif., L.A., 1983-84; law clk. to Hon. William P. Gray U.S. Dist. Ct., L.A., 1987-88; mental health psychiatrist Los Angeles County Dept. Mental Health, L.A., 1988-94, Alameda County Health Care Svcs. Agy., Fremont, Calif., 1994-97; physician specialist L.A. County Health Care Svcs. Agy., L.A., 1997—; sr. physician, 1999—; attending physician Martin Luther King Jr. Hosp., L.A., 1997—; child and adolescent psychiatrist Augustus F. Hawkins Mental Health Ctr., L.A., 1997—, chief child/adolescent svc., 1998—; adj. instr. philosophy Fullerton (Calif.) Coll., 1989-90; adj. asst. prof. psychiatry Charles Drew U., 1998—; asst. clin. prof. psychiatry UCLA Sch. of Medicine, 1998—. Mem. Calif. Hist. Soc. Recipient Cert. Recognition L.A. County Mental Health Dept., 1993; univ. fellow Claremont Grad. Sch., 1980-81. Mem. ABA, Am. Philos. Assn., Chinese for Affirmative Action, Soc. for Exploration of Psychotherapy Integration, Chinese Hist. Soc. Am. Office: 745 E Valley Blvd PMB 120 San Gabriel CA 91776-3549

CHEN, JOHN J. J., chemical and materials engineering educator; b. Jesselton, British North Borneo, Dec. 26, 1950; arrived in New Zealand, 1970.; PhD, U. Auckland, New Zealand, 1980. Prof. chem. and materials engrng. dept. U. Auckland. Fellow Royal Soc. New Zealand, Instn. Chem. Engrs. (London), Instn. Profl. Engrs. (New Zealand). Office: U Auckland Chem-Materials, Engrng Dept, Pvt Bag 92019, Auckland New Zealand

CHEN, JU-CHIN, oceanography educator; b. Yenling, Honan, China, Mar. 3, 1940; s. Chao-Yuen and Kwei-Wen (Cheng) C.; m. Pi-hsiu Huang, Sept. 25, 1965; children: Chih-kuang, Ping-kuang. BS, Nat. Taiwan U., Taipei, 1962; MA, Rice U., 1965, PhD, 1967. Rsch. scientist S.W. Ctr. of Advanced Studies, Dallas, 1967-70; assoc. porf. Inst. Oceanography Nat. Taiwan U., Tapei, 1970-74, dir., 1974-80, prof., 1974—; Mem. Republic of China Nat. Com. IGBP, Taipei, 1988-96, Nat. Com. SCOPE, 1991—; pres. Nat. Com. on Ocean Rsch., 1992-97, chmn. Chinese Taipei ODP Consortium, Taipei, 1996-98. Contbr. more than 100 sci. articles to nat. and internat. jours including Acta Geochimica and Cosmochimica, Am. Mineralogist. 2d lt. Rep. of China Army, 1962-63, Taiwan. Recipient Dr. Sun Yat Sen rsch. publ. award Dr. Sun Yat Sen Found., 1973, Outstanding Rsch. award Nat. Sci. Coun., Taipei, 1985-87, Excellence in Tchg. award Ministry of Edn., Taipei, 1989. Mem. Geolog. Soc. China in Taipei (pres. 1983), Am. Geophys. Union, Geolog. Soc. Am., Geochem. Soc. Avocation: stamp collecting. Home: Chou Shan Rd, No 11 Alley 5 Lane 30, Taipei Taiwan Office: Nat Taiwan U, Inst Oceanography, Taipei Taiwan

CHEN, KAO, consulting electrical engineer; b. Shanghai, China, Mar. 21, 1919; came to U.S., 1947; s. Chi-son and Wei C. (Hsu) C.; m. May Yee Yoh, Nov. 14, 1948; children: Jennifer H., Arthur B., Carlson s. BSEE, Jiao Tong U., Shanghai, 1942; postgrad., Brit. Industries scholar, Rugby, Eng., 1945-47; MSEE, Harvard U., 1948; postgrad. degree in Elec. Engring., NYU, 1953. Registered profl. engr., N.J., N.Y. Relay specialist Am. Gas & Electric Co., N.Y.C., 1950-52; project supr. Ebasco Internat., N.Y.C., 1953-55; sr. project engr. Westinghouse Electric Corp., Bloomfield, N.J., 1956-67, fellow engr., 1968-83; fellow engr., cons. N.Am. Philips Lighting Corp., Bloomfield, N.J., 1983-86; pres. Carlsons Cons. Engrs., San Diego, Calif., 1987—; vis. prof. Fudan U., 1982; cons. in field. Author: Industrial Power Distribution and Illuminating Systems, 1990, Energy Effective Industrial Illuminating Systems, 1994; editor-in-chief Std. Handbook Powerplant Engring., 1997, Energy Management in Illuminating Systems, 1999; contbr. chpts. to 3 engring. handbooks, 6 IEEE stds., over 100 articles and papers to profl. jours.; patentee in field. Exec. PTA, Cedar Grove, N.J., 1960-62; exec. Essex coun. Boy Scouts Am., West Orange, 1966-70; mem. Repub. Presdl. Task Force, 1989—. Recipient Rep. Presdl. award, 1994. Fellow IEEE (life fellow, del. to visit China 1982, vice chmn. indsl. utilization sys. dept. 1981-84, chmn. 1985-87, chmn. prodn. and application of light com. 1983-84, mem. new stds. com. 1985-86, IEEE rep. to IEC TC34 lamps and related equipment 1997—, Soc. best paper awards 1981, 83, IEEE Centennial medal 1984, IEEE-IAS award of merit 1985, Richard Harold Kaufmann award 1992, IEEE-IAS Disting. Lectr. 1996-97, IAS Recognition award to disting. lect. 1997, RAB Larry K. Wilson transnational award 1998), Power Engring. Soc. (energy engring. seminar leader 1991), Industry Applications Soc. (mem. transactions adv. bd. 1981-84); mem. NSPE (life), Assn. Energy Engrs., Illuminating Engring. Soc. (emeritus, mem. Centennial Club), U.S. Nat. Com. of the Internat. Commn. on Illumination, Am. Biog. Inst. (rsch. bd. advisors, Commemorative Medal of Honor 1987), Energy Svcs. Mktg. Soc. (charter), Jiao Tong Alumni Assn. (v.p. 1962-63), Harvard Club (N.J., sch. com. 1975-83), Harvard Club (San Diego). Achievements include research and development in energy management of industrial power and illuminating systems. Home: 11816 Caminito Corriente San Diego CA 92128-4550

CHEN, KENNETH TING, information systems specialist; b. Tainan, Taiwan; came to U.S., 1978; s. Shih Tsung and Hsing-Chu C.; m. Chien-Yi. BS in Computer Sci., Trinity U., 1988; MBA, U. Houston, 1994. Microsoft Cert. Profl. Internet, 1997, Microsoft Cert. Sys. Engr., 1998. Advanced sys. engr. Texaco Inc., Houston, 1988-95; info. sys. team leader Star Enterprise, Houston, 1995-98, Equiva Svcs. LLC, Houston, 1998—. Recipient Cio Web award Cio Magazine, 1998. Office: Equiva Svcs LLC 12700 Northborough Dr Houston TX 77067-2502

CHEN, KOK-CHOO, lawyer, educator; b. Hong Kong, Oct. 24, 1947; d. Chin Poo and Kim Suan (Lin) Tan; m. Heung-tat Ng; children: Shahn Y., Mei-Mei. Barrister-at-law, Inns of Ct., Eng., 1968. Bar: Calif., 1974. Assoc. Law Offices of Tan, Rajah and Cheah, Singapore, 1969-70; lectr. Nanyang U., Singapore, 1970-71; law clk. Sullivan and Cromwell, N.Y.C., 1971-74; assoc. Heller, Ehrman, White and McAuliffe, Calif., 1974-75; founding ptnr. Ding and Ding, Taipei, Taiwan, 1975-88, Ding, Ding and Chan, Calif., 1983-88; sr. ptnr. Chen & Assocs., Taipei, 1988, Republic of China, 1988—; v.p. Echo Pub., 1992; atty. Jones Day Reavis & Pogue, 1992—; pres. Nat. Culture and Arts Found., Taiwan, 1995-97; sr. v.p. Taiwan Semiconductor Mftg. Co., Ltd., 1997—. Author: Licensing Technology to Chinese Enterprise (Chia Hsin Found. award), 1986. Named One of Ten Most Outstanding Women of Yr., Taiwan, 1982. Mem. Honorable Soc. of Inner Temple, Calif. Bar Assn., Zonta Internat.

CHEN, KO-RON, dermatologist, medical educator; b. Taipei, Taiwan, Feb. 9, 1954; s. Kung-pei Chen and Shiu-Chin Chen-Ko; m. Miki Kitayama, Sept. 24, 1989; children: Akinori, Akiyoshi, Akiteru. BS in Agr., Nat. Taiwan U., Taipei, 1976; MD, Keio U., Tokyo, 1985, PhD in Med. Sci., 1989. Sr. resident in dermatology Saiseikai Ctrl. Hosp., Tokyo, 1989-91; vis. clinician Mayo Clin., Rochester, Minn., 1991-92, rsch. fellow, 1992-93; vice head dept. dermatology Kawasaki (Japan) City Hosp., 1993-96; chief divsn. dermatology Ogikubo Hosp., Tokyo, 1996—; instr. dermatology Keio U., Tokyo, 1996—. Contbr. articles to med. jours. Lt. Armored Corps. Taiwan Army, 1976-78. Rsch. grantee Roche Dermatologics Found., Washington, 1993. Mem. Japanese Derm. Assn., Asian Derm. Assn., Internat. Soc. Dermatopathology. Avocations: classical music, travel, playing guitar. Office: Ogikubo Hosp Dept Dermatol, 3-1-24 Imagawa, Suginami Tokyo 167-0035, Japan

CHEN, KUEN HAI, physician; b. Tachia, Taiwan, May 23, 1937; came to U.S., 1966, naturalized, 1976; s. John Bei and Yeh (Liang) C.; m. Fu Mei Lai, Jan. 1, 1966; children: Richard, Humphrey, Christopher. BS, Nat. Taiwan U., Taipei, 1959, MD, 1964. Diplomate Am. Bd. Family Practice. Intern Ill. Central Hosp., Chgo., 1966-67; resident in gen. surgery Sisters Hosp., Buffalo, 1967-69, C & O Hosp., Huntington, W.Va., 1970-71; fellow spinal cord injury service VA Hosp., East Orange, N.J., 1971-72, chief, 1972-76; mem. staff First Ave. Med. Center, N.Y.C.; mem. adv. bds. Dupont, McNeil Health Network, 1999—; Shering/Key cons. Glaxo Wellcome Inc. Nat. Irritable Bowel Syndrome Awareness Registry, 2000—; mem. med. adv. bd. Agouron, Bristol Myers Roche, 2000—; physicians coun. Heritage Found., 1994—; dir. K.F.C. Corp; analyst Am. Bd. of Disability, 1999. Author: American Spoken English; founding prodr. GOP-TV, 1994—. Active Taiwan Union Presbyn. Ch. in N.Y., chmn. exec. com., 1983, pres. Parents' Assn., 1980-84; mem. Presdl. Adv. Commn., 1992, Presdl. Commn. Am. Agenda, 1992; del. Presdl. Trust, 1992; adv. mem. Rep. Nat. Commn. Am. Agenda, 1992—; hon. co-chmn. bus. adv. coun. Rep. Nat. Com., 1998; del. N.J. Rep. Presdl. Task Force, 1994-98; mem., chmn. adv. bd. Rep. Nat. Com., 1994—, hon. co-chmn. bus. adv. com., 1998, hon. chmn. bus. adv. coun. 1999—; founding mem. Rep. Campaign Coun., 1994—, nat. campaign advisor, 1995—, Eisenhower Commn., 1995-96; mem. Rep. Senator Adv. Coun., 1997—, Rep. Senator Inner Circle, 1998—; hon. co-chmn., 1999—, adv. coun. Rep. Nat. Com., 1998, chmn. adv. coun. 1999. Served with Taiwan Air Force, 1965. Recipient Physician Recognition award AMA, 1969, 72, 75, 78, 81, 84, 87, 90, 93; Disting. Service and Leadership award Nat. Taiwan U.; Patriotic award medal Pres. of U.S.; named Mem. of Yr. Rep. Presdl. Task Force, 1996. Fellow Am. Acad. Family Physicians, Am. Geriatric Soc.; mem. Am. Bd. Disability Analysts, N.Y. Acad. Sci., Am. Coll. Emergency Physicians, AMA, N.Y. County Med. Soc. (com. health care agy.), Internat. Soc. Paraplegia, Heritage Found., Taita Jing-Fu Med. Found. (hon. dir.), Nat. Taiwan U. Med. Coll. Alumni Assn. (exec. dir. 1979-81, pres. 1981-83, permanent bd. dirs. 1984, chmn. edn. com. 1987-95, chmn. fund campaign com. 1988-94, N.Y. chpt. bd. dirs. 1994, bd. trustees 1985-88, chmn. by-law com. 1994—), Am. Spinal Injury Assn., Nat. Bd. Addiction Examiners (dr. addiction counselor), W.Va. Med. Inst., N. Am. Taiwanese Med. Assn. (bd. dirs. greater N.Y. chpt. 1985—, pres. 1987-89, chmn. edn. com. 1989-95), Nat. Taiwan U. Alumni Assn. (bd. dirs. 1981—, chmn. edn. com. 1984-94, chmn. by-law com. 1994-96, treas. 1991-94, pres. 1999-2001). Presbyterian.

CHEN, LAN ZHUANG, agricultural studies educator; b. Zaoqiang, Hebei, China, Dec. 16, 1956; s. Gui Hang Chen and Su Lan Liu; m. Li Ming Guan; 1 child, Xi Chen. B, Hebei Agrl. U., Baoding, China, 1982; M, Yamagata U., Tsuruoka, Japan, 1989; D, Kagoshima (Japan) U., 1992. Rsch. asst. Hebei Acad. Agr., Shijiazhuang, China, 1982-86; vis. scientist Yamagata U./China Edn. Com., Tsuruoka, Japan, 1986-87; postdoct. fellow Agy. Sci. and Tech. Japan, Tsukuba, 1992-95; asst. prof. Miyazaki (Japan) U., 1995—; judge Miyazaki Prefecture Japanese Contest for Returnees, 1989—. Contbr. articles to profl. jours. Rsch. grantee Ministry Edn. Japan, 1997-99, 98—, Iijima Found., 1998; reipient prize Japanese Soc. Breeding for Young Scientist, 1997. Office: Miyazaki U Gene Rsch Ctr, 1-1 Gakuen Kibanadai Nishi, Miyazaki 889-2192, Japan

CHEN, LI, computer scientist, software engineer; b. Lishui, Jian Su, China, Apr. 23, 1961; came to U.S., 1991; s. Zhengxi and Suqin (Wang) C.; m. Lan Zhang, Apr. 18, 1987; 1 child, Boxi. BS, Wahan (China) U., 1982; MS, Utah State U., 1995; postgrad., U. Luton, U.K., 1999—. Asst. engr. Rsch. Inst. of Geophys. Prospecting, Nanjing, China, 1982-85; lectr. Nanjing Inst. Tech., 1985-89, Wuhan U., 1989-91; sr. software engr. Spiricon, Inc., Logan, Utah, 1994-2000, Sorenson Media, Salt Lake City, 2000—; prin. rsch. scientist Sci. and Practical Computing Lab., North Logan, 1997-2000; adj. assoc. prof. Wuhan U., China, 1997—. Contbr. articles to profl. jours. Recipient Award Rsch. Fund of Chinese Acad. Sci. for Young Scientists, 1987, 2d Class award Chinese Min. Geology, 1991; named Outstanding Scientist of Wuhan U., 1991. Achievements include definition of gradually varied surfaces and interpolation algorithms; the definition of general discrete manifolds and the classification of digital surface points; optimal algorithm for optimal minimum odd-weigh-column SEC-DED code's check matrix; inventor fuzzy sub-fiber, possibility-based neural networks. Avocation: Chinese flute. Office: Sorenson Media Inc 4393 Riverboat Rd Ste 300 Salt Lake City UT 84123-2524

CHEN, LIN XIANG-QUN, chemist; b. Beijing; came to U.S., 1981; d. R.Y. Chen and Y.X. Sha; m. Di Jia Liu, 1983; 1 child, Vicky Liu. BS, Peking U., Beijing, 1982; PhD, U. Chgo., 1987. Rsch. assoc. U. Calif., Berkeley, 1988-89; asst. chemist Argonne (Ill.) Nat. Lab., 1989-94, chemist, 1994—. Patentee in field. Travelling fellow NATO, 1986; grantee Dept. of Energy, Washington, 1996-98. Mem. AAAS, Am. Chem. Soc., Optical Soc. Am., Sigma Xi. E-mail: lchen@anl.gov. Office: Argonne Nat Lab 9700 S Cass Ave Bldg 200 Argonne IL 60439-4831

CHEN, LINFENG, electrical engineer; b. Tiantai, Zhejiang, China, Nov. 2, 1968; s. Kegui Chen and Yuequi Xu. BS, B in Engring., Tsinghua U., Beijing, 1991. Asst. lectr. Tsinghua U., Beijing, 1991-94; rsch. scholar Nat. U. Singapore, 1994-97; project engr. Def. Sci. Orgn. Nat. Labs., Singapore, 1997-99; mem. tech. staff DSO Nat. Labs., Singapore, 1999—. Contbr. articles to profl. jours. Mem. AIAA, Materias Rsch. Soc. Avocations: music, reading, swimming. Home: #07-04, Block 601, Clementi St 1, Singapore 120601, Singapore Office: Def Sci Orgn Nat Labs, 20 Science Park Dr, Singapore 118230, Singapore

CHEN, LU, figure skater; b. Changchun, Jilin, China, Nov. 24, 1976. Figure skater China, 1981—; mem. Chinese Nat. Figure Skating Team, 1988—. Recipient Bronze medal Olympic Games, Nagano, 1998, 7 time Chinese Nat. Champion and 2 time Olympic Bronze medalist. Avocations: reading, music, dancing. Address: c/o Yuki Saegusa 22 E 71st New York NY 10021*

CHEN, MEI-LIEN, environmental studies educator; b. Chuang-Hwai, Taiwan, Nov. 15, 1958; s. Ting-Fu Chen and Ging-Yung Chuang; m. Pei-Jung Kuo, Jan. 25, 1986; 1 child, Hsiang. B of Pub. Health, Nat. Taiwan U., Taipei, 1981, MPH, 1983, PhD, 1992. Cert. sr. and jr. civil svc. exam., Taiwan. Tchg. asst. Nat. Taiwan U., 1982-85; lectr. Nat. Yang-Ming U., Taipei, 1985-92, assoc. prof., 1992—; vis. scholar UCLA, 1995-96. Contbr. articles to profl. jours. including Am. Indsl. Hygien Assn. Jour., Sci. of Total Environment, Toxicol. and Environ. Chemistry, Internat. Jour. Environ. Analytical Chemistry. Recipient Acad. award Nat. Sci. Coun. of Republic of China, 1992, 93, 94, 96, 97, 98, 99. Mem. Nat. Pub. Health Assn. of Republic of China, Chinese Occupl. Health Assn. Taiwan. Avocations: traveling, swimming. Fax: (886-2-28221942). E-mail: mlchen@ym.edu.tw. Office: Nat Yang-Ming U, 155 Li-Long St Shih-Pai, Taipei Taiwan

CHEN, MICHAEL SHIH-TA, banker; b. India, Sept. 30, 1945; s. Chih-Ping and Lilleo Yung-Chieh (Wong) C.; children: Te-kuang, Te-Ming. AB with honors, U. Calif., 1966; MA, Cornell U., 1969; PhD, 1973; MBA, Harvard U., 1972. Staff officer Citybank N.A., N.Y.C., 1973-76; mgr. Hong Kong, 1976-78, asst. v.p., 1979-80, v.p., 1980-86; chmn. Chen Group Internat. Ltd., Hong Kong, 1986-89; regional dir. Asia Internat. Pvt. Banking Nat. Westminster Bank PLC, Hong Kong, 1982-92; head wealth mgmt. group Std. Chartered BAnk Internat. Pvt. Banking, 1994-95; cons. Chen Group Intenat., Hong Kong, 1992-94; mem. coordinating com. of mgmt. for exec. devel. program, Chinese U. Hong Kong; mem. adv. com. Hong Kong Poly. U.; vis. lectr. MBA programs; chmn. adv. com. for mgmt. edn., mgmt. devel., mem. exec. com. for fin. and adminstrn. Hong Kong Coun. Social Svc.; mem. social work com. Caritas, Hong Kong; mem. adv. com. City Polytechnic U. Hong Kong. Contbr. articles to profl. publs. Mem. Harvard Bus. Sch. Assn. Hong Kong (pres., dir., chmn. 1980-86), Asia Soc., Harvard (pres. 1979-80), Royal Hong Kong Jockey, Fgn. Corrs., Am., Taipei Bankers, Hong Kong Country. Home: 9B Skyline Mansions, 51 Conduit Rd, Hong Kong Hong Kong also: 4244 Ridgemont Ct Oakland CA 94619-3727 Office: Std Chartered Bank, Hong Kong Hong Kong

CHEN, MING-DER, biochemist, researcher; b. Taipei, Taiwan, Republic of China, Nov. 4, 1961; s. Shui-Kui and Hsiao Yu-Mei; m. Hui-Ling Yu, Feb. 13, 1992; children: Chen, Chi-Chung. MSc, Tunghai U., Taichung, Taiwan, 1986, PhD, 1994. Asst. Tunghai U., Taichung, Taiwan, 1984-85; rsch. asst. Vets. Gen. Hosp., Taichung, 1985-86, asst. rschr., 1988-89, assoc. rsch. specialist, 1989—; lectr. Tunghai U., Taichung, 1996—. Contbr. articles to profl. jours. Mem. Internat. Assn. Bioinorganic Sci., Am. Diabetes Assn., N.Y. Acad. Scis. Avocations: badminton, bowling, billiards, pencil drawing, Chinese chess. Office: Vets Gen Hosp Div Endo/Meta, #160 Sec 3 Taichung-Kang Rd, 40705 Taichang Taiwan R.O.C.

CHEN, MINGYI, pharmacologist; b. Tnag Shan, China, Aug. 13, 1968. MD, Beijing Med. U., China, 1992; postgrad., Kyoto (Japan) U., 1996. Cardiologist Beijing Med. U., 1992-96; rsch. fellow Rsch. Inst. Nat. Cardiovasc. Ctr., Osaka, Japan, 1998—. Co-author: Nursing Pharmacology Protocols, 1996, Lipoprotein Metabolism and Atherogenesis, 1998, Method in Molecular Medicine: Vascular Disease, 1999. Fax: 81-66-872-7485. Office: Nat Cardiovasc Ctr Rsch Ins, Fujishirodai 5-7-1, Osaka 565-8565, Japan

CHEN, NIAN, toxicologist, government official; b. Shanghai, Oct. 31, 1948; arrived in Australia, 1984; s. Mou Yong Chen and Ye Qing Wang; m. Nai Li Wang, Dec. 6, 1976; children: Yi, James Ian. MB, Shanghai Med. U., 1982, M in Medicine, 1984; PharmM, Queensland (Australia) U., 1984, PhD in Medicine, 1992. Mech. engr. Shangahi Numbering Machine Co., 1968-73, elec. engr., 1973-78; rsch. officer Queensland U., 1989-92; pharmacologist Princess Alexandra Hosp., Brisbane, Australia, 1993-94; sr. toxicologist Nat. Occupl. Health Safety Commn., Australia, 1994—; tchr. Sydney (Australia) Inst. Tech., 1995—, U. Western Sydney, 1997-98; dir. Nellian Australia, 1996-2000, mem. Nat. Gene Tech. Regulation Task Force, 1998-2000. Contbr. articles to Acta Pharmacologica Sinica, Clin. Exp. Pharmacological Physiology, Biochem. Pharmacology, Human and Exptl. Toxicology. San Hao scholar Shanghai Med. U., 1978-83, Ernest Singer scholar Queensland U., 1985-89, Rsch. scholar, 1989. Mem. Australian Soc. Biochemist Molecular Biologist, Australian Soc. Clin. Exptl. Pharmacologists Toxicologists. Achievements include antibody studies, polyamine receptor studies, reversion of toxic effects by their specific antibodies in animals and humans, clinical pharmacology of organ transplantation, clinical monitoring in drug overdose and drug interaction, risk assessment on agricultural and veterinary chemicals and new industrial chemicals in Australia. Home: 2 A Elsinore St, Merrylands 2160, Australia Office: Nat Occupl Health Safety Cm, GPO Box 58, Sydney 2001, Australia

CHEN, OSCAL TZYH-CHIANG, electrical engineering educator, researcher; b. Chia-Yi, Taiwan, Jan. 1, 1965; s. Szu-Shen Chen and Pei-Pei Chang; m. Hui-Yi Wei, May 27, 1995. BS, Nat. Taiwan U., 1987; MS, U. So. Calif., 1990, PhD in Elec. Engring., 1994. Engr. Computer and Comms. Rsch. Lab., ITRI, Taiwan, 1994-95, project leader, 1995; assoc. prof. dept. elec. engring. Nat. Chung Cheng U., Chia-Yi, 1995—. Contbr. chpt. to book, articles to profl. jours.; author procs.; assoc. editor IEEE Circuits and Devices Mag., 1995-99. Exec. sec. VLSI/CAD program, divsn. engring. and applied sci. Nat. Sci. Coun., Taiwan, 1994-96, co-chair devel. program So. Telecomms. Rsch. Ctr., 1996-99. Mem. IEEE (co-chair tech. program com. 1996, others; Best Paper award 1995), Chinese Fuzzy Systems Assn. Achievements include VLSI design of vector quantization, biomedical hippocampus chip, image compression, learning schemes of artificial neural networks. Office: Nat Chung Cheng U Dept EE, 160 San-Hsing Ming Hsiung, 621 Chia-Yi Taiwan

CHEN, PANG-CHI, gastroenterologist, educator; b. Taichung, Taiwan, China Rep., Sept. 8, 1947; m. Ying-Erl Lin, Dec. 24, 1976; children: Chang-Ming, Jeffrey P. MD, Kaohsiung Med. Coll., Taiwan, 1973. Attending physician Chang Gung Meml. Hosp., Taipei, Taiwan, 1979—, dir. digestive endoscopy, 1990—; assoc. prof. China Med. Coll., Taichung, 1979-94, Chang Gung Med. Coll., Taipei, 1988—. Editor-in-chief Gastroenterological Jour. Taiwan; editorial adv. Chang Gung Med. Jour.; author: Gastrointestinal Endoscopy. Recipient Dr. Takemitaro award Taiwan Med. Assn., 1979, Cheng-Hsing Found. award, 1984, The 20th Century Achievement award IBC and ABI, 1995, World Lifetime Achievement award ABI, 1996; named Honorable Citizen City of Taipei, 1996. Mem. Digestive Endoscopy Soc. Taiwan (exec. bd.), Gastroenterol. Soc. Taiwan (exec. bd., pres. 28th annual congress), European Assn. Gastroenterology & Endoscopy, Formosan Med. Assn., Am. Soc. for Gastrointestinal Endoscopy (corres. mem.), Internat. Gastro-Surg. Club (permanent mem.). Office: Chang Gung Meml Hosp, 199 Tung Hwa N Rd, Taipei Taiwan 105

CHEN, PATSY FANG, music educator; b. Taipei, Taiwan, May 31, 1948; came to U.S., 1968; d. Kuo Chiao and Shui Lien (Liao) Fang; m. Wen Jer Chen, June 15, 1968; children: Wendy Fang, Justine Fang. Diploma in piano performance, Nat. Taiwan Coll. Arts, Taipei, 1968; M in Music Edn., NYU, 1980, postgrad., 1980-84. Sec. med. edn. Norwegian-Am. Hosp., Chgo., 1968-70; instr. piano Taipei and N.Y., 1967—; concert mgr. KYVAS Arts Mgmt., N.Y.C., 1987—; cmty. liaison Queens Symphony Orch., N.Y.C., 1993—. V.p. N.Am. Elite Youth Orch., Dallas, 1996-97; artistic dir. Youth Orch., CYCNY, 1998—; bd. dirs. Si-Yo Music Soc., 1994—, Ling Nan Art Assn., 1995—; mem. adv. com. N.J. Performing Arts Ctr. World Festival, 2000—. Named Outstanding Alumnus, Nat. Taiwan Coll. Arts, 1997. Mem. Internat. Chinese Soc. Photography and Arts, N.Y. State Music Tchr. Assn., Taiwanese Am. Assn. in Greater N.Y./N.Y.C. (v.p. 1997-98), Union Taiwan Univs. and Colls. Alumni Assn. Greater N.Y./N.Y.C. (pres. 1997-98, contbg. editor jour. 1998). Avocations: cooking, gardening, photography, travel. E-mail: patsychen@aol.com. Home: 175 Willoughby St Apt 2A Brooklyn NY 11201-5447

CHEN, PEIDE, mathematics educator; b. Mienhu, Kwang Tung, China, Jan. 3, 1940; s. Minfu and Pixia (Liu) C.; m. Lejun Lin, Nov. 9, 1969 (div. Dec. 1987); 1 child, Weixin. Grad., Peking U., 1964, Chinese Acad. of Scis.,

Peking, 1968; PhD, Colo. State U., 1997. Asst. researcher Inst. of Maths., Peking, 1968-77, asst. prof., 1977-79; vis. scholar U. of Paris, 1980-81; asst. prof. Inst. of Applied Maths., Peking, 1982, assoc. prof., 1983-89, prof., 1989—; postdoctoral fellow U. Windsor, Ont., Can., 1997; dep. dir. Lab. of Probability and Stats., Peking, 1990, dir., 1991-92; vis. scholar Colo. State U., Ft. Collins, 1993. Contbr. numerous articles to profl. jours. Recipient J.L. Madison award Colo. State U., 1995, 97, Bose-Srivastava Exptl. Design award, 1997; fellow Univ. Windsor, Ont. Can., 1996, 98. Mem. Am. Math. Soc., Math. Assn. Am., Inst. Math. Stats., Am. Statis. Assn. Office: Inst Applied Maths, 100080 Beijing China

CHEN, PETER WEI-TEH, mental health services administrator; b. Fuchow, Fukien, China, July 20, 1942; came to U.S., 1966; s. Mao-Chuang and Sheu-Lin (Wang) C.; m. Lai-Wah Mui, Nov. 8, 1969; children: Ophelia Mei-Chuang, Audrey Mei-Hui. BA, Nat. Chung Hsing U., Taipei, Taiwan, Republic of China, 1964; MSW, Calif. State U., Fresno, 1968; D of Social Work, U. So. Calif., 1976. Case worker Cath. Welfare Bur., L.A., 1968-69; psychiat. social worker L.A. County Mental Health Svcs., 1969-78, mental health svcs. coordinator, 1978; sr. rsch. analyst Jud. and Legis. Bur. L.A. County Dept. Mental Health, 1978-79; Forensic In-Patient Program dir. L.A. County Dept. Mental Health, 1979-86, chief Jail Mental Health Svcs., 1986-89, asst. dep. dir. Adult Svc. Bur., 1989, dir. cmty. care programs, 1989—; clin. prof. dept. psychiatry Harbor/UCLA Med. Ctr., 1997—; pres. Orient Social and Health Soc., Los Angeles, 1973-75; bd. dirs. Am. Correctional Health Assn., 1986-87. Author: Chinese-Americans View Their Mental Health, 1976. Bd. dirs. San Marino (Calif.) Cmty. Chest, 1986-87; trustee San Marino Schs. Found., 1987-90; advisor San Marino United Way, 1989-92, AIDS Commn. L.A. County, 1993; founder, past chmn., bd. dirs. Chinese Sch. of San Marino, 1981—. 2d lt. Chinese Marine Corps, Taiwan, Republic of China, 1964-65. Recipient several cmty. svc. awards, 3 spl. awards Nat. Assn. County Orgn. Mem. Nat. Assn. Social Workers (bd. dirs. Calif. chpt. 1979-80), Nat. Correctional Health Assn., Forensic Mental Health Assn. Calif., L.A. World Affairs Coun., Chinese Am. Profl. Soc. (pres. 1997-98, chmn. bd. dirs. 1998—). Clubs: Chinese of San Marino (pres. 1987-88), San Marino City. Avocations: sports, fishing, bridge. Home: 2161 E California Blvd San Marino CA 91108-1348 Office: LA County Dept Mental Health 1925 Daly St Los Angeles CA 90031-3309

CHEN, ROBERT KUO-CHENG, environmental science educator, consultant; b. Beijing, China, June 27, 1930; s. Yuan and Lin Ching-Ying Chen; m. Judy Ju-Hu Chen, Oct. 18, 1953; children: David, Abraham, Eunice. M of Food Sci. and Tech., U. Calif., Davis; postgrad., Taiwan U. Dir. Sci. Edn. Ctr., Taichung, Taiwan, 1972-80; chief editor Youth Sci. Dictionary Youth Cultural Enterprise Co., Ltd., Taipei, Taiwan, 1974-81; prof., chmn. dept. environ. engring. Nat. Chung Hsing U., Taichung, 1958—; Chinese editorial cons. Time Life, 1976; chief cons. World Green Biotech, Taiwan, 1998—. Recipient Nat. Gold Ting award, 1977, 81, Nat. award for editing nature mag., 1983, others. Mem. Assn. Food Sci. and Tech., German Carl Duisberg Gesellschaft e.V., Deutsche Stiftung fuer Internationale Entwicklung, N.Y. Acad. Sci. Office: Nat Chung-Hsing U Dept Environ, Engring 250 Kuo-kuang Rd, Taichung Taiwan

CHEN, ROGER LEI, fashion designer; b. Shanghai; s. Zhi-xue Chen and Yulin Hang. MA, Oreg. State U., 1994; AAS, Fashion Inst. Tech., N.Y.C., 1995. Asst. fashion designer Nike, Inc., Beaverton, Oreg., 1993-94; assoc. designer Blassport by Bill Blass, N.Y.C., 1995-98; head designer Millershor/Shomi, N.Y.C., 1996—. Mem. Fashion Group Internat. (exec. mem.), Assn. for Chinese Fashion DEsigners (bd. dirs.). Avocations: painting, photography.

CHEN, RONG-CHI, neurologist, educator; b. Hsinchu, Taiwan, Nov. 10, 1938; s. Jing-shing Chen and Ju-huan Chen-Jeng; m. Chaw-fang Chou, Dec. 4, 1964; children: Linda Tzu-ling, Wendy Wen-yu, George Chia-ji. MD, Nat. Taiwan U., Taipei, 1964; PhD, Medicina Alternativa Internat. Colombo, Sri Lanka, 1987. Resident in neuropsychiatry Nat. Taiwan U. Hosp., 1965-69, staff physician, 1969-97; resident in neurology U. Wis., Madison, 1971-73; lectr. Nat. Taiwan U. Med. Coll., Taipei, 1973-76, assoc. prof., 1976-82, prof., 1982—; chmn. neurology Nat. Taiwan U. Med. Coll., Nat. Taiwan U. Hosp., 1986-92; vice-supr. Nat. Taiwan U. Hosp., 1992-96; supr. En Chu Kong Hosp., 1997—. Editor: Clinical Neurology, 1990; editor-in-chief Acta Neurologica Taiwanica, 1992-97. Chmn. bd. suprs. Consumer Found. Taiwan, 1991-93; pres. Buddhist Lotus Hospice Found, Taiwan, 1994—, Buddhist Med. Assn., Taiwan, 1995—, Taiwan Hospice Orgn., 1999—; nat. del. World Fedn. Neurology, 1989-91. 2nd lt. Taiwanese Army, 1964-65. Recipient Paper Excellence award Wis. Neurol. Soc., 1973, Rsch. Article Excellence award Chinese Med. Assn., 1986, Excellent Textbook award Ministry Edn., 1990. Mem. Am. Neurol. Assn. (corr.), Am. Acad. Neurology (assoc.), Taiwan Neurol. Soc. (pres. 1989-91), Taiwan Epilepsy Soc., Taiwan Stroke Soc., Formosan Med. Assn. Buddhist. Avocations: reading, ping-pong, hiking, camping. Fax: 886-2-2673-0920. E-mail. rcchen@mail.eck.org.tw. Office: En Chu Kong Hosp, 399 Fuhsing Rd Sanhsia Town, Taipei Hsien 237, Taiwan

CHEN, RUEY-HWA, biochemistry educator; b. Taipei, Taiwan, May 8, 1961; d. Hsin-You and Elaine (Sha) C.; m. Yuh-Shan Jou, May 30, 1987; children: Nancy Jou, Grace Yuh-Hsin Jou. BS, Nat. Taiwan U., 1983, MS, 1985; PhD, Mich. State U., 1991. Postdoctoral fellow dept. growth and devel. U. Calif., San Francisco, 1992-95, asst. biochemist, 1995-96; assoc. prof. Inst. Molecular Medicine Nat. Taiwan U., Taipei, 1996—; mem. grant rev. panel Nat. Sci. Coun., Republic of China, Taipei, 1998, 99. Contbr. articles to profl. jours. Leukemia Soc. Am. fellow, 1995; Nast. Sci. Coun./Republic of China grantee, 1998—, 99. Mem. Am. Soc. for Cell Biology, Genetic Soc. Taiwan. Avocations: music, reading. E-mail: rhchen@ha.mc.ntu.edu.tw. Office: Inst Molec Med/Nat Taiwan U, 7 Chung Shan S Rd, Taipei Taiwan

CHEN, SHAN-TARNG, physics educator; b. Madow, Taiwan, May 24, 1957; s. Ming-Shyan Chen and Gann Lin; m. Shu-Chin Wang, May 22, 1985; 1 child, Mei-Guang. BS, Nat. Changhua U. Edn., Taiwan, 1981, MS, 1991. Asst. in physics Nat. Chunghsing U., Taichung, Taiwan, 1986-93, lectr., 1993—. Author: University Physics, 1996; contbr. articles to profl. jours. Avocations: tennis, table tennis, fishing. Fax: 011-886-4-2862534. Office: Nat Chunghsing U Dept Phys, Kuo Kuang Rd, T'aichung 40227, Taiwan

CHEN, SHI KUN, electrical engineering educator; b. Shanghai, Dec. 29, 1927; s. Wen Qi Chen and Mu Ying Zhang; m. Ming Rui Gu, Sept. 9, 1951; children: Sui, Yi, Gang, Pei. B, Jiaotong U., Shanghai, 1949. Engring. diplomate. Asst. Jiaotong U., 1949-54, lectr., 1954-57; lectr. Xi'an (China) Jiaotong U., 1957-62, assoc. prof., 1962-82, prof., 1982—; dean elec. machinery divsn. Xi'an Jiaotong U., 1984-90, dir. postdoctoral fellow program, 1990-98. Editor: Testing of Electrical Machines, 1954; chief editor: Design of Electrical Machines, 1982; inventor in field. Recipient Nat. Inventor award Nat. Commn. Sci. and Tech., Beijing, 1981, cert. of honor Nat. Edn. Commn., Beijing, 1990; grantee State Coun., Beijing, 1992. Mem. Chinese Engring. Soc. (sr., bd. dirs. 1990-94, cert. honor 1995, chmn. linear elec. machines com. 1988-96, vice chmn. elec. machine com. Shaanxi chpt. 1982—, elec. machine com. for editing textbooks 1982-96). Avocations: table tennis, Chinese classical music. Home: 1-45-303 Xian Jiaotong U, Xian 710048, China Office: Xian Jiaotong U, 28 Xian-ning Rd, Xian 710049, China

CHEN, SHUANG, computer science professional; b. China, Jan. 29, 1958; m. Hongwen Yan, Aug. 3, 1987; children: Jessica Y., Julia Y. BSEE, Nanjing Aeronautical U., 1982; MSEE, South China U. Sci. and Tech., Guangzhou, China, 1985; MPH in Computer Engring., Rutgers U., 1990, PhD in Computer Engring., 1991. Mem. faculty South China U. Sci. and Tech., Guangzhou, 1985-86; rsch. asst. Rutgers U., New Brunswick, 1986-91; sr. rsch. engr. Comm. Intelligence Corp., Redwood Shores, Calif., 1991-95; rsch. staff mem. IBM Thomas J. Watson Rsch. Ctr., Yorktown Heights, N.Y., 1995-98; pres., CEO Internat. Interactive Commerce, Ltd., Armonk, N.Y., 1999—; reviewer profl. jours.. Author: (with others) Studies in Pattern Recognition, 1997. Grad. Rsch. Assistantship, Rutgers U., 1987-91. Mem. IEEE, Sigma Xi. Office: Internat Interactive Commerce Ltd 84 Bus Park Dr Armonk NY 10504

CHEN, SHU-YING, bank executive; b. Taipei, Taiwan; d. Ping-Chung and Chin-Mei C.; m. Chang-Pyng Lu; children: Po-Kuan Lu, Po-Hsuan Lu. LLB, Nat. Taiwan U., 1965; LLM, Nat. Kyoto U., 1970. Asst. dir. Dept. Monetary Affairs Min. of Fin., 1982-87, deputy dir., 1987-89, counsellor and deputy dir., 1989-91; exec. v.p. The Export-Import Bank of ROC, 1991—; com. mem. The Supervisory Com. on Res. Against New Taiwan Currency Issue, 1980-87; dir. of bd. The Farmers Bank of China, 1987-91; mng. dir. of bd. Small and Medium Bus. Credit Guarantee Fund, 1987-91. Author: A Research of the Foreign Exchange Control System in Taiwan, 1986; contbr. articles to profl. jours. Home: 52 Chung-She Rd, Shilin Taipei 11104, Taiwan Office: The Export-Import Bank ROC, 8th Fl 3 Nan-Hai Rd, Taipei 100, Taiwan

CHEN, SHYI-MING, computer science educator; b. Taipei, Taiwan, Republic of China, Jan. 16, 1960; s. Ching-Tien and Pi-Hong (Huang) C. BSEE in Electronic Engring., Nat. Taiwan U. Sci. and Tech., Taipei, 1982, MSEE, 1986; PhDEE elec. engrg., Nat. Taiwan U., Taipei, 1991. Instr. electronic engring. Fu-Jen U., Taipei, 1987-89, 90-91; assoc. prof. dept. computer info. sci. Nat. Chiao Tung U., Hsinchu, Taiwan, 1991-96, prof., 1996-98; prof. dept. electronic engring. Nat. Taiwan U. Sci. and Tech., Taipei, 1998—. Contbr. chpts. to books: Fuzzy Reasoning in Information, Decision, and Control Systems, 1994, Fuzziness in Petri Nets, 1999, Fuzzy Theory Systems: Techniques and Applications, 1999; contbr. over 110 articles to profl. jours. and conf. proceedings. Recipient Nat. Sci. Coun. rsch. awards, 1992-2000, Outstanding paper award Jour. of Info. and Edn., 1994, Outstanding Paper award Computer Soc. of Republic of China, 1995, Outstanding Youth Elec. Engr. award Chinese Inst. of Elec. Engring., Republic of China, 1997, Best Paper award Nat. Computer Symposium, Republic of China, 1999, Outstanding Paper award Computer Soc. Republic of China, 1999. Mem. IFSA, IEEE (sr.), ACM, Phi Tau Phi. Avocations: volleyball, movies, music, TV, travel. Office: Nat Taiwan U Sci/Tech Elec, Engr 43 Sect 4 Keelung Rd, 106 Taipei Taiwan

CHEN, STEPHEN S. F., retired diplomat; b. Nanking, China, Feb. 11, 1934; m. Rosa Te Chen; three children. BA, U. Santo Tomas, Philippines, 1957, MA, 1959; postgrad., U. Santo Tomas, 1959-60; DBA (hon.), Kensington U. Various positions in field to dir. gen. Coord. Coun. for N.Am. Affairs, L.A., 1988-89; dep. rep. Coord. Coun. for N.Am. Affairs, Washington, 1989-93; vice-min. fgn. affairs Ministry Fgn. Affairs, China, 1993-96; dep. sec.-gen. Office of Pres., China, 1996-97; rep. TECRO, Washington, 1997-2000; ret., 2000. Avocations: fgn. langs. including Chinese, English, Spanish, Portuguese and six Chinese dialects.

CHEN, TAK-MING, civil engineer; b. Changning, Hunan, China, July 29, 1936; came to U.S., 1970; s. Jenn-Chiu and Yin (Peng) C.; m. Taining Chou, July 1, 1973; children: Merry, Terry. BS in River/Harbor Engring., Taiwan Provincial Coll. of Marine Sci. and Tech., 1966; MSCE, U. Mo., 1971. Registered profl. engr., N.Y., Md., D.C. Project engr. Chinese Petroleum Corp., Taipei, Taiwan, 1973; structural designer Bellante, Clauss, Miller & Nolan, inc., Scranton, Pa., 1974-76; structural engr. Wayman C. Wings, Cons. Engrs., N.Y.C., 1978-80, Gibbs & Hills, Inc., N.Y.C., 1980-81; civil/structural engr. Bechtel Power Corp., Gaithersburg, Md., 1981-84; structural engr. Hazen & Sawyer, P.C., N.Y.C., 1984-85; civil/structural engr. N.Y.C. Dept. Sanitation, 1985-87; civil engr. N.Y.C. Dept. Bldgs., 1987-94, N.Y.C. Comptroller's Office, 1994—; pres. Chen's Cons. Engrs., Queens, N.Y., 1985-87. Bd. dirs. RFK Dem. Assn., Inc., Forest Hills, N.Y., 1994—. Recipient Cert. of Honor for leadership Dem. Nat. Com. Mem. NSPE, N.Y. State Soc. Profl. Engrs., Chinese Am. Assn. City of N.Y., MSM-UMR Alumni Assn., Comptr. Engrs. Assn. Home: 82-28 255th St Floral Park NY 11004 Office: New York City Comptrollers Office Bur of Engring 2 Lafayette St Rm 204 New York NY 10007-1307

CHEN, TE TSAW, healthcare executive; b. Hou-Long, Taiwan, Jan. 16, 1934; s. Kai Ju Chen and Duann Ong; m. Shaw Jane Lai; children: Steve Wei, Lily Wei. Postgrad., U. Pa., 1972. Diplomate Am. Bd. Ophthalmology, Japanese Bd. Ophthalmology, Taiwan Bd. Ophthalmology. Resident Nat. Taiwan U. Coll. Medicine, 1960-64, chief resident, 1965; staff ophthalmologist Mackay Meml. Hosp., Taiwan, 1967-72; rotating intern Mt. Sinai Hosp., N.Y.C., 1972; fellow N.Y. Med. Coll., 1975; clin. fellow Albany (N.Y.) Med. Coll., 1976; pvt. practice N.Y.C, 1976-78; chmn., prof. ophthalmology dept. Chang Gung Meml. Hosp., Taiwan, 1978-87; prof. ophthalmology Taipei (Taiwan) Med. Coll., 1980—; dir. Te Tsaw Eye Ctr., Taiwan, 1987—; ednl. mem., med. supr. Customer Found. Republic of China, 1984-85; chmn. credential com. Chang Gund Meml. Hosp., Taiwan, 1981-83, supervising mem. hosp. affairs, 1985-86, dir. edn. and tng., 1986-87. Fellow Am. Acad. Ophthalmology and Otolaryngology; mem. Am. Intra-Ocular Implant Soc., Kerto-Refractive Soc., Internat. Coll. Surgeons, Societas Ophthalmologica Japonica, Japan Ophthalmologists Assn., Ophthalmol. Soc. Japan, Am. Soc. Cataract and Refractive Surgery, Assn. for Rsch. in Vision and Ophthalmology, Asia-Pacific Intraocular Implant Assn. (founder), Internat. Soc. Refractive Keratoplasty, Ophthal. Soc. Republic of China (bd. dirs. 1965-69, 86—, pres. 1996-2000). Avocations: swimming, tennis, table tennis, billiards, jogging. E-mail: sjanec@ms35.hinet.net. Fax: 886-2-27176613. Office: Te Tsaw Eye Ctr MinSheng E, No 2-1 Ln 130 Sect 3, Taipei Taiwan

CHEN, TEH-HSUN BEAN, government safety official; b. Ho-Long, Miau-Li, Taiwan, Mar. 15, 1951; s. Kai-Ee Chen and Yue-Mei Cheng; m. Wey-Tsyr Shaw, Mar. 26, 1983; 1 child: Stephanie. BS in Physics, Tunghai U., Taichung, Taiwan, 1974; MS in Biophysics, U. Rochester, 1979, PhD in Biophysics, 1982. Post doctoral fellow Inhalation Toxicology Rsch. Inst., Albuquerque, 1983-85, staff scientist, 1985-95; sr. risk assessment specialist GRAM Inc., Albuquerque, 1995-96; team leader Nat. Inst. for Occupl. Safeth and Health, Morgantown, W.Va., 1996—; adj. prof. U. N.Mex., Albuquerque, 1990-95; cons. site-wide environ. impact statement GRAM Inc., Dept. Energy, Los Alamos Nat. Lab., N.Mex., 1995-96. Author: (book chpts.) Encyclopedia of Environmental Control Technology, 1989, Aerosol Measurement: Principles, Techniques and Applications, 1993, 2000, Air Sampling Instruments, 1995, 2000; contbr. over 50 articles to profl. jours.; patentee virtual impactor. Mem. cmty. adv. bd. KNME TV5, Albuquerque. Grantee HUD, 2000—, Dept. Energy, 1984-95, NIH, 1993-95. Mem. Am. Indsl. Hygiene Assn. (mem. aerosol tech. com. 1988—, best poster award 1999), Am. Assn. Aerosol Rsch., European Aerosol Assn., Chinese Assn. Aerosol Rsch. (life, mem. editl. adv. bd. 1993—). Avocations: reading, singing, playing tennis and volleyball. Office: NIOSH/HELD/EAB MS3030 1095 Willowdale Rd Morgantown WV 26505

CHEN, TIAN HONG, computer systems/software engineer; b. Guangzhou, Guangdong, China, July 25, 1958; arrived in Australia, 1987; d. Shixun Chen and Yanlan Zhang; m. Yaping Shao, Feb. 18, 1990; children: Scross Dounan, Emily Ximin. BS, Zhongshan U., Guangzhou, 1983, MS, 1986; PhD, Flinders U. South Australia, Adelaide, Australia, 1993. Rsch. assoc. South China Sea Inst. Oceanography Academia Sinica, Guangzhou, 1986-91; rsch. asst. Australian Nat. U., Canberra, 1991-94; rsch. fellow MacQuarie U., Sydney, Australia, 1994-96; info. tech. officer Australian Oceanographic Data Ctr, Sydney, 1996-98; sr. programmer/analyst Dept. Atty. Gen., Sydney, 1998—. Avocations: bushwalking, dancing. Home: 3 Asquith Ave Rosebery, Sydney NSW 2018, Australia Office: 201 Elizabeth St, Sydney NSW 2000, Australia

CHEN, TSAI-HSIANG, engineering educator; b. Hsinchu, Taiwan, Mar. 15, 1953; s. Chao Chuan and Hsiu Ying (Liu) C.; m. Feng-I Lin, Sept. 23, 1984; children: Wei-Chu Patrick, Fang-Jer. BS, Nat. Taiwan U. Sci. and Tech., Taipei, 1980, MSc, 1982; PhD, U. Tex., Arlington, 1990. Technician Taiwan Water Co., Hsinchu, China, 1976-78, Taiwan Telecomm. Administrn., Taipei, 1979; jr. engr. Indsl. Tech. Rsch. Inst., Hsinchu, 1980; lectr. Nat. Taiwan U. Sci. and Tech., Taipei, 1982-89; assoc. prof. Nat. Taiwan Inst. Tech., Taipei, 1989-96, prof., 1996—; cons. Power Rsch. Inst. Taiwan Power Co., Taipei, 1991-92, Provisional Engring. Office High-Speed Rail Ministry Comm., Taipei, 1992-94, Coun. Labor Affairs, Taipei, 1993-94; reviewer Nat. Compilation Com., Taipei, 1990—. Author: (with others) Advanced in Control and Dynamic System, vol. 43; contbr. articles to profl. jours. 2d lt. Chinese Air Force, 1974-76. Recipient Rsch. award Nat. Sci. Coun. China, 1985, 86, 90, 91, 92, 93, 94, 95, 96, 98. Mem. IEEE Power Engring. Soc., Chinese Inst. Engring. (Outstanding Young Rschr. award 1982, life), Chinese Inst. Elec. Engring. (sr.), Phi Beta Delta, Tau Beta Pi. Home: 1F # 10 Alley 68 Ln 41, Taipei 106, Taiwan Office: Nat Taiwan U Sci and Tech, 43 Keelung Rd Sect 4, Taipei 106, Taiwan

CHEN, WEI, epidemiologist; b. People's Republic of China, Dec. 28, 1968. BS in Biology, Nanjing U., People's Republic of China, 1990; MS in Molecular Biology, U. Houston, 1995. Pharmacist in Chinese herbal medicine Inst. Medicinal Ctl., Jiangyin, Jiangsu, People's Republic of China, 1990-92; asst. rsch. and tchg. in molecular genetics U. Houston, 1993-95; molecular biologist U. Tex., 1995-99; genetic epidemiologist U.Tex./M.D. Anderson Cancer Ctr., 1999—; designer of maps, posters. Contbr. articles to profl. jours., chpts. to books. Recipient scholarships acad. excellence Nanjing U., 1987-89. Mem. Am. Soc. Human Genetics, Internat. Genetic Epidemiology Soc., Sigma Xi. Fax: 713-792-8261. E-mail: weichen@notes.mdacc.tmc.edu.

CHEN, WEI-JAO, surgeon, educator; b. Taichung, Taiwan, Nov. 15, 1939; s. Wen-Chiang and Pin (Wu) C.; m. Shiang-Yang Tang, Jan. 1, 1970; children: Yo-Shen, Yo-Yi. BM, Nat. Taiwan U., Taipei, 1965; D in Med. Scis., Tohoku U., Sendai, Japan, 1973; MPH, Johns Hopkins U., 1989. Resident dept. surgery Nat. Taiwan Univ. Hosp., Taipei, 1966-70, dep. dir., 1987-91; faculty mem. Nat. Taiwan U. Coll. Medicine, Taipei, 1975—, dean, 1991-93; pres. Nat. Taiwan U., Taipei, 1993—. Author: Story of Separation of Conjoined Twins, 1980; editor: Asia Pacific Jour. Clin. Nutrition, 1993—, Nutrition, 1994—. Active Press Coun., Taiwan, 1994—. With Taiwanese Air Force, 1965-66. Recipient Ten Outstanding Young Person award JCA Club, 1979, Outstanding Sci. Achievement award Exec. Yuen, 1980. Mem. Am. Soc. Parenteral and Enteral Nutrition, European Soc. Parenteral and Enteral Nutrition, Surg. Soc. Taiwan, Taiwanese Assn. Pediatric Surgery (pres. 1990-92), Chinese Assn. Parenteral and Enteral Nutrition (pres. 1992-96), Formusa Med. Assn. (pres. 1995-98). Avocations: hiking, jog, golf. Home: 20 Fu Chow St, Taipei 106, Taiwan Office: Nat Taiwan U Hosp Dept Surg, 7 Chung-Shan S Rd, Taipei 100, Taiwan

CHEN, WENDE, systems engineering educator, scientist; b. Shanghai, China, Oct. 16, 1941; s. Xin Zhen and Yi Xian (Zhou) C.; m. Qin Ning Cao, May 1, 1968; children: Hui, Xin Mei. BA, Chinese U. Sci. and Tech., Beijing, 1964, D degree, 1968. Registered rsch. profl. engr., People's Republic of China. Engr. Lab. Digital Systems Tianshui (People's Republic of China) Electric Drive Inst., 1969-78; rsch. assoc. Inst. of Math., Academia Sinica, Beijing, 1979-80; assoc. prof. Inst. Systems Sci. Academia Sinica, Beijing, 1982-89, prof., 1989—; vis. prof. Math. Ctr., Amsterdam, Netherlands, 1985, U. Linkoping, Sweden, 1988, U. Linz, Austria, 1988, U. Bergen, Norway, 1988, 92, 95-98, 2000; vis. prof. dept. math. U. Turku, Finland, 1987-88, 91, Basic Rsch. Inst. Math. Scis., Hewlett-Packard Co., Bristol, Eng., 1995; reviewer Math. Rev. U.S., 1989—; participant internat. symposiums, Germany, 1985, Italy, 1989, Austria, 1991, Japan, 1994, U.S.A., 1999. Author: Walsh Function and Transformation, 1985, Applied Discrete Mathematics, 1991, Discrete Event Dynamic Systems, 1994. Recipient Ho Pan Ching Yi award Prof. Y.C. Ho, Harvard U., 1994. Mem. China Math. Soc., Am. Math. Soc., China Info. Theory Soc. (commissary com. 1997—). Office: Academia Sinica Inst Sys Sci, Zhongguancun, Beijing 100080, China

CHEN, WEN-PING, astronomy educator; b. Ping-Tung, Taiwan, Nov. 22, 1958; s. Ren-Yinn and Hsueh (Fan) C.; m. Rwei-Ju Stella Chuang, June 30, 1984; children: Kenneth, Kevin. BS, Nat. Ctrl. U., Taiwan, 1980; PhD, SUNY, Stony Brook, 1990. Rsch. fellow Carnegie Instn. Wash., 1990-92; assoc. prof. Nat. Ctrl. U., Taiwan, 1992—. Mem. editl. bd. Sci. Monthly (Taiwan). Mem. Chinese Astron. Soc., Internat. Astron. Union, Am. Astron. Soc. Avocation: bridge. Office: Nat Ctrl U, Inst Astronomy, Chung-Li 32054, Taiwan

CHEN, WENTING, chemist; b. Beijing; came to U.S., 1991; s. Shenyi Chen and Xingfeng Bu; m. Mu Zhang. BEng, Tsinghua U., Beijing, 1990; MS, N.Mex. State U., 1994. Engr. Beijing Xing Da Sci. Co., Beijing, 1990-91; rsch. asst. N.Mex. State U., Las Cruces, 1991-93; scientist SmithKline Beecham Pharm., King of Prussia, Pa., 1993-97; staff scientist DuPont Pharm. Co., Wilmington, Del., 1997-99, sr. staff scientist, 1999—. Contbr. articles to sci. publs., including Jour. Medicinal Chemistry, Jour. Organometalic Chemistry, Jour. Organic Chemistry, others. Mem. AAAS, Am. Chem. Soc., N.Y. Acad. Scis. E-mail: wenting.chen@dupontpharma.com. Office: DuPont Pharm Co E500/4206A Rt 141 & Henry Clay Rd Wilmington DE 19880

CHEN, WESLEY, lawyer; b. N.Y.C., Nov. 29, 1954; s. Tom Y.M. and Mary (Don) C.; m. Vivien Wong, Dec. 10, 1983; 2 children: Marissa, Jocelyn. BA, N.Y. U., 1976, JD, 1980. Bar: N.Y. 1981, U.S. Dist. Ct. (so. and ea. dists.) N.Y. 1981. Lawyer Meissner, Tisch & Kleinberg, N.Y.C., 1980-81; pvt. practice N.Y.C., 1982-85, 89, 91—; of counsel Serchuk, Wolfe & Zelermyer, White Plains, N.Y., 1985-88; ptnr. Cantwell & Chen, N.Y.C., 1988, Kimmelman, Sexter, Warmflash & Leitner, N.Y.C., 1990-91, Krasner & Chen, N.Y.C., 1992-94, Serchuk & Zelermyer, N.Y.C., 1995—; bd. dirs. United Orient Bank, N.Y.C., 1982-92, MFY Legal Svcs., Inc., 1993-96; mem. N.Y. State Banking Bd., 1992—. Trustee Union Ch. of Pocantico Hills, 2000—. Mem. ABA, N.Y. State Bar Assn. (mem. banking law com.), N.Y.County Lawyers Assn. (mem. banking law com.), Asian-Am. Bar Assn. of N.Y., Chinese C. of C. (legal adviser 1982—). Office: 641 Lexington Ave Fl 20 New York NY 10022-4503

CHEN, XI, engineering educator; b. Taizhou, Jiangsu, China, June 3, 1936; s. Xiushan and Su (Huang) C.; m. Pingyang Sun, July 20, 1963; 1 child, Ji. Diploma, Tsinghua U., Beijing, 1961. Asst. Tsinghua U., Beijing, 1961-79, lectr., 1979-85, assoc. prof., 1985-91, prof. dept. engring. mechanics, 1991—; hon. fellow U. Minn., Mpls., 1981-83, vis. assoc. prof., 1989. Author: Heat Transfer and Fluid Flow Under Thermal Plasma Conditions, 1993, Kinetic Theory and its Application in the Study of Heat Transfer and Fluid Flow, 1996; contbr. articles to profl. jours. Recipient Nat. Natural Sci. Prize of China, Chinese Govt., 1991, Sci. and Tech. Achievement prize Nat. Edn. Commn. of China, 1988, 93. Mem. Chinese Soc. for Engring. thermophysics, Chinese Soc. for Aeronautics, Internat. Union of Pure and Applied Chemistry (subcom. on plasma chemistry 1996—). Avocations: reading, Chinese chess. Office: Tsinghua U Dept Engr Mech, 1 Qinghua Yuan, Beijing 100084, China

CHEN, XI-QING, mechanical engineer; b. Quan-Jiao, Anhui, China, Sept. 10, 1964; s. Jin-Luo Chen and You-Zhen Huang; m. Ping Cui, Jan. 23, 1990. BSc, Hohai U., China, 1985; PhD, Inst. Superior Tecnico, Lisbon, Portugal, 1994. Rsch. engr. Inst. Superior Tecnico, Lisbon, 1990-91, postdoctoral rschr., 1995-97; rsch. assoc. U. Waterloo, 1998-2000; safety analyst Atomic Energy Can. Ltd., Mississauga, Ont., Can., 2000—. Contbr. articles to profl. jours. Mem. AIAA, N.Y. Acad. Scis. E-Mail: chenxq@scientist.com. Home: 5962 Greensboro Dr, Mississauga, ON Canada L5M 5S5 Office: Atomic Energy Can Ltd, 2251 Speakman Dr, Mississauga, ON Canada L5K 1B2

CHEN, YEONG SHENG, computer educator, researcher; b. Tainan, Taiwan, Sept. 21, 1965; s. A-Chung Chen and A-Chiao Wu. B Engring., Nat. Chiao-Tung U., Hsinchu, Taiwan, 1988, M Engring., 1990; PhD, Nat. Taiwan U., Taipei, 1996. Lectr. computer ctr. elec. engring. dept. Nat. Taiwan U., 1992-93; instr. Hwa-Hsia Coll. Tech., Chung-Ho, Taipei, 1993-95, assoc. prof., 1996—, chmn. dept. info. mgmt., 2000—. Avocation: table tennis. Office: Hwa-Hsia Coll Tech Elec Eng, No 111 Hwa-Hsin Rd, Chung-Ho Taipei 235, Taiwan

CHEN, YIH MING, botany educator; b. Tainan, Taiwan, Aug. 23, 1940; m. Ling Huang; children: Choo-Huang, Terry, Nicholas. BS, Nat. Taiwan U., Taipei, 1964, MS, 1968. Tchg. asst. dept. botany Nat. Taiwan U., 1967-68, instr. dept. botany, 1968-74, assoc. prof. botany, 1975-79, prof. botany, 1979—, chmn. dept. boatny, 1988-94, chmn. Grad. Inst. Botany, 1988-94; asst. rsch. fellow dept. botany U. Ga., Athens, 1972-74; dean Office of Gen. Affairs Nat. Taiwan U., 1994-98, pres. special asst., 1998—, head biotech. rsch. ctr., 1999—; rsch. fellow dept. botany U. Ga., Athens, 1981; rsch. prof. botany U. S.C., Columbia, 1982. Editor-in-chief Taiwania, 1988-94. Mem. acad. and cultural exch. with Mainland China, Straits Acad. and Cultural Exch. Assn., Taipei, 1992. 1d lt. ROTC, Taiwan, 1963-64. Recipient Outstanding Acad. Achievement award Ministry of Edn., Taiwan, 1982,

Outstanding Rsch. Achievement award Nat. Sci. Coun. Taiwan, 1990, 91, 92, 93, Sci. Achievment award for Outstanding Contbn. in Field of Agrl. Chem. Sci. in Taiwan, 1995. Mem. Internat. Assn. for Plant Tissue Culture, Bot. Soc. Republic of China (pres. 1992-93), Biol. Soc. China (pres. 1994-95, Outstanding Rsch. Achievement award 1987), Chinese Biochem. Soc., Internat. Union Biol. Scis. (Republic of China nat. com. 1994-96), Am. Soc. Plant Physiologists, Japanese Soc. Plant Physiologists, The Weed Sci. Soc., Biol. Soc. China, Internat. Assn. Plant Tissue Culture and Biotech., Phi Tau Phi. E-mail: yihmingc@ccms.ntu.edu.tw. Home: 346-1 5F Fu-chin St, 105 Taipei Taiwan Office: Nat Taiwan U Dept Botany No 1, Roosevelt Rd Sec 4, 106 Taipei Taiwan

CHEN, YI-MING ARTHUR, preventive medicine researcher and educator; b. Taipei, Taiwan, Dec. 28, 1956; s. Pao-Huei and Yin-O Chen. MD, Nat. Yang-Ming U., Taipei, 1982, MS, 1984; DSc, Harvard U., 1990. Rsch. fellow Harvard AIDS Inst., Boston, 1989-90; vis. scientist Nat. Cancer Inst., Frederick, Md., 1990-92; assoc. prof. Nat. Yang-Ming U., Taipei, 1992-98, prof. Inst. Pub. Health, Inst. Microbiology, Immunology, 1998—, chmn. Inst. Pub. Health, 1994-97, 2000—, dir. AIDS Prevention and Rsch. Ctr., 1998—. Translator: AIDS in the World, 2d edit., 1999, Promotion of AIDS Awareness, 1993; contbr. articles to profl. jours.; patentee in field. Founder Living with Hope Orgn., Taipei, 1994—; cons. Consumer Found. of Republic of China, 1994—; mem. coun. of reps. Asia Pacific AIDS Svc. Orgn., 1998—. Rsch. grantee Nat. Sci. Coun.-Taiwan, 1992-99, Dept. Health/Taiwan, 1992-99. Mem. Chinese Soc. of Preventive Medicine (pres. 1999—), Am. Soc. Microbiology, Internat. AIDS Soc., Soc. Chinese Biomed. Scientists in Am. KMT Party. Buddhist. Avocations: antiquarian, interior design, painting, opera, classical music. Office: Nat Yang-Min U Inst Pub Hlt, 155 Li Noun St Spc 2, Taipei 112, Taiwan

CHEN, YU, acupuncturist, Chinese herbologist; b. Beijing, China, Sept. 10, 1942; came to U.S., 1985; d. Hai Chen and Xiu (Wang) C.; m. Paul L. Munson, Feb. 27, 1987; 1 child by previous marriage: Ming An. MD, Capital Med. Coll., Beijing, 1965; D Traditional Chinese Medicine, Chinese Traditional Med. Sch., Beijing, 1977; MS, Chinese Acad. Med. Sci., Beijing, 1981. Diplomate in acupuncture Nat. Commn. Cert. Acupuncture; cert. Chinese herbologist; lic. acupuncturist, Md. Physician Govt. China, Ching Yang, Gan Su, 1968-73; resident physician dept. ob-gyn. Worker's Hosp., Yen Shan Oil Factory, Beijing, 1974-78; attending physician dept. genetics Nat. Rsch. Inst. Family Planning, Beijing, 1982-83; WHO postdoctoral fellow Karolinska Inst., Stockholm, 1983-85; postdoctoral fellow dept. physiology U. Tex., Houston, 1985-87; postdoctoral fellow dept. pharmacology U. N.C., Chapel Hill, 1987-90; pvt. practice acupuncture and herbology Cmty. Wholistic Health Ctr., Carrboro, N.C., 1989-93; pvt. practice acupuncture, Chinese herbology, magnet therapy Pikesville and Parkville, Md., 1993—. Contbr. articles to profl. jours.; patentee in field; inventor of simple and effective way to treat panic attack by acupuncture and magnet hammer, ear magnet therapy to treat diabetes mellitus, scalp magnet therapy to treat attention deficit disorder, herbal suppository for treatment of vaginal yeast infection, herbal treatment of AIDS meningitis. Recipient Best Essay award 1st Internat. Conf. Micro-Acupuncture Therapy, San Francisco, 1995. Democrat. Lutheran. Avocations: painting, photography, travel, classical music, gardening. Office: Beijing Acupuncture Chinese Herb & Magnetic Ctr 1401 Reisterstown Rd Baltimore MD 21208-6502

CHEN, YUH-MIN, engineering educator, consultant; b. Taichung, Taiwan, Republic of China, Apr. 16, 1958; s. Chi-Cheng Chen and Sheo Liou. BS, Nat. Tsing-Hua U., 1981, MS, 1983; PhD, Ohio State U., 1991. Lectr. Chinese Air Force, Gan-San, Republic of China, 1983-85; asst. rsch. fellow Academia Sinica, Taipei, 1985-87; rsch. assoc. NSF/ERC/OSU, Columbus, Ohio, 1987-91, engr., 1991-92; engr. S.D.R.C., Cin., 1992-94; assoc. prof. Nat. Cheng-Kung U., Tainan, Taiwan, 1994-99, prof., 1999—; cons. MIRL/ITRI, Hsin-chu, 1995-96, YJS Food Co., Tai-Chun, 1994—, Xerox, Rochester, 1994. Contbr. articles to profl. jours. Chmn. Buddhist Assn. of Columbus, 1991-92. Recipient Rsch. award Nat. Sci. Coun., 1996, 97, 98, 99. Mem. ASME, IEE, Assn. of Automation, Buddhist Assn. of Compassion (chmn. 1994—). Avocation: mediation practice. Office: Nat Cheng-Kung U, No 1 University Rd, Tainan 70101, Republic of China

CHEN, YULIU, engineering educator; b. Shanghai, July 13, 1937; s. Yafu and Shanwei (He) C.; m. Yizhuang Huang; children: Bin, Rui. Grad., Tsinghua U., Beijing, 1959. Tchr. Tsinghua U., 1959-78, lectr., 1978-85, assoc. prof., 1985-89, prof., 1989—; vis. scholar U. Manchester Inst. of Sci. and Tech., 1979-81, U. Strathclyde, Glasgow, 1981-82, Hong Kong U. of Sci. and Tech., 1994-96. Author: Large-scale Systems Theory and its Applications, 1992 (Excellent Book of Tsinghua express 1992), Computer Integrated Manufacturing Systems Implementation Methodology, 1996, Advanced Operation Patters of Manufacturing Enterprises, 1998, Design Methods for Complex Systems, 1991, IDEF Modeling Methods (in Chinese), 1998; editl. bd. Internat. Jour. of Prodn. Planning and Control. Fellow Hong Kong Inst. Engrs.; mem. IEEE (sr.), IFAC/MIA. Avocation: choral conducting. Office: Tsinghua U, Dept Automation, Beijing 100084, China

CHEN, YUNG SHENG, electrical engineer, educator; b. Miao-Li, Taiwan, June 30, 1961; s. Chin and Mei (Chiu) C.; m. Tsuey Ping Chung, Sept. 28, 1991; children: Ya-Han, Wei-En. B in Engring., Chung Yuan Christian U., 1983; M in Engring., Nat. Tsing Hua U., 1985, PhD, 1989. From assoc. prof. to prof. Yuan-Ze Inst. Tech., Taoyuan, Taiwan, 1991—. Avocations: photography, music, sports. Office: Yuan Ze U Dept Elec Engring, 135 Yuan-Tung Rd Nei-Li, 320 Taoyuan Taiwan

CHEN, ZENGQIAN, neurosurgeon; b. Zhaoyuan, China, Oct. 25, 1945; m. Yibin Zhao; children: Hong, Liang, Rong. MB, Qingdao Med. Coll., China, 1970. Surgeon Weishan County Hosp., Shandong, China, 1970-80, ShanDong Tumor Hosp. & Inst., Jinan, China, 1980—; edn. dir. Weishan Med. Sch., China, 1970-80. Contbr. articles to profl. jours.; inventor in field. Mem. China Laser Soc., Shongdong Med. Laser Soc. (chief sec. 1980-96). Home: 440 Ji Yan Rd, Jinan 250117, CHina Office: ShanDong Tumor Hosp & Inst, 440 JiYan Rd, Jinan 250 117, China

CHEN, ZHANGXIN JOHN, mathematics educator; b. Boying, Jiangxi, China, Oct. 15, 1962; came to the U.S., 1986; s. Furong Chen and Hao-e Fang; m. Aijie Li, Jan. 5, 1986; children: Christina C., Paul Z. BS, U. Jiangxi, Nanchang, 1983; MS, Xi'an (Shaanxi) Jiaotong U., 1985; PhD in Math., Purdue U., 1991. Asst. prof. Xi'an Jiaotong U., 1985-86; rsch. assoc. U. Minn., Mpls., 1991-93; vis. asst. prof. Tex. A&M U., College Station, 1993-95; asst. prof. So. Meth. U., Dallas, 1995-98, assoc. prof., 1999—; cons. Rush Presbyn. St. Luke's Med. Ctr., Chgo., 1994-95; reviewer Math. Revs., Providence, 1994—. Contbr. articles to profl. jours. Recipient Sigma Xi Outstanding Rsch. award, 1999; grantee NSF, 1996—; univ. fellow Jiangxi U., 1981, 82; David Ross fellow Purdue U., West Lafayette, Ind., 1989, 90. Mem. Am. Math. Soc., Soc. for Indsl. and Applied Math., N.Y. Acad. Scis. Avocation: playing sports. Office: So Meth Univ Dept Math PO Box 750156 Dallas TX 75275-0156

CHEN, ZHAOQING, electronics engineer; b. Nanchang, China, Jan. 18, 1956; s. Yuxiao and Yunkun (Ao) C.; m. Ying Hua; children: Xu, Wynter. BS, Jiangxi U., Nanchang, 1982; M in engring., Tsinghua U., Beijing, China, 1985; PhD, Tsinghua U., Beijing, 1989. Instr. Tsinghua Univ., 1989-91; vis. scholar Univ. Calif., Berkeley, 1991-92; assoc. prof. Tsinghua Univ., 1992-94; vis. scholar SUNY, Binghamton, 1994-97; sr. staff engr. Motorola, Austin, Tex., 1997-98; adv. engr. IBM, Poughkeepsie, N.Y., 1999—. Co-author: Cad of Microwave Circuits, 1988, Application Tech. for Microwave CAD, 1996; inventor in field. Recipient Outstanding Paper award, Chinese Inst. Electronics, 1986, Advanced Sci. and Tech. award Chinese State Coun., 1988. Mem. IEEE, Internat. Microelectronics and Packaging Soc. Office: IBM P310 2455 South Rd # P310 Poughkeepsie NY 12601-5463

CHEN, ZHIPING, engineer; b. Nankang, Jiangxi, China, Apr. 24, 1960; s. Shaolin and Juyin (Zeng) C.; m. Wei Dai, July 6, 1987; children: Nan, Ray. BSc, South China U. of Tech., 1982, MSc, 1985; PhD, Monash U., 1998. Lectr. Guangdong Inst. of Tech., Guangzhou, China, 1985-91; rsch. scientist Comalco Rsch. Ctr., Melbourne, 1993; mfg. engr. Hawker de Havilland Victoria Ltd., Australia, 1994—. Author: International Conference on Residual Stresses, 1988, Intelligent Processing and Manufacturing of Material, 1997; contbr. articles to profl. publs. Com. mem. Chinese Student and Scholar Club of Monash U., 1992-94. Strategic Partnership with Industry Rsch. and Tng. Support grant Australian Rsch. Coun., 1998; rsch. fellowship Victorian Edn. Found., 1994; Australia Devel. and Cooperation scholarship Australian Internat. Devel. Asst. Bur., 1992. Mem. Chinese Profls. Club of Australia. Avocations: computer programming, badminton, music, electronics. Office: Hawker Havilland Vic Ltd, 31 Wharf Rd, Port Melbourne 3207, Australia

CHEN, ZUENG-SANG, soil science educator, researcher; b. Taipei, Taiwan, Nov. 6, 1952; s. Tzen-Tein and Wu-Shuang (Wu) C.; m. Hsien-Tzu Lee, Aug. 11, 1977; children: Yee-Tzu, Yee-Chung. Bachelor, Nat. Taiwan U., 1975, Master, 1978, PhD, 1984. Lectr. Nat. Taiwan U., 1984-85, assoc. prof., 1985-89, prof., 1989—; mem. steering com. Internat. Series of Biogeochemistry of Trace Elements, Aiken, Ga., 1992—, Internat. Series of Soil Contamination Rsch. in Asia and Pacific, Adelida, Australia, 1996—; dir. com. soil pollution EPA of Taiwan, 1997—. Author: (chpt.) Biogeochemistry of Trace Elements, 1992, (chpt.) Sampling of Environmental Materials for Trace Analysis, 1994; editor: Biogeochemistry of Trace Elements (II), 1997, Soil Sci Soc. Am. Jour., 1996, 98, 99, 2000, Jour. Vegetation Sci., 1998, Soil Sci., 1999, 2000, numerous others. Lt. Taiwan Mil., 1978-80. Mem. Internat. Union Soil Sci., Chinese Agrl. Chemistry Soc. (Sci. Achievement award 1997), Soil Sci. Soc. Am., Agrl. Assn. China (Sci. Achievement award 1998). Avocations: climbing mountains, music, photography, reading, movies. Office: Dept Agr Chem Nat Taiwan U, No 1 4th Sect Roosevelt Rd, 10617 Taipei Taiwan

CHENAULT, KENNETH IRVINE, financial services company executive; b. N.Y.C., June 2, 1951; s. Hortenius and Anne N. (Quick) Ch.; m. Kathryn Cassell, Aug. 20, 1977; children: Kenneth I. Jr., Kevin A. BA, Bowdoin Coll., 1973; JD, Harvard U., 1976; PhD (hon.), Morgan State U., 1990, Stony Brook U., 1996, Adelphi U., 1995, Bowdoin Coll., 1996, U. Notre Dame, 1998, Xavier U., 1997, S.C. State U., 1997, Howard U., 1998, U. Notre Dame, 1998. Bar: Mass. 1981. Assoc. Rogers & Wells, N.Y.C., 1977-79; cons. Bain & Co., Boston, 1979-81; dir. strategic planning Am. Express Co., N.Y.C., 1981-83; from v.p. to sr. v.p. Am. Express Travel Related Svcs. Co., Inc., N.Y.C., 1983-96, exec. v.p. platinum card/gold, 1986-88, exec. v.p. personal card divsn., 1988-89, pres. consumer card and fin. svcs. group, 1990-93, pres. U.S.A., 1993-95; vice-chmn. Am. Express Co., N.Y.C., 1995-97, pres., COO, 1997—; bd. dirs. IBM, Am. Express Co., Mt. Sinai-NYU Med. Ctr. & Health Sys., NCAA, CASA, The Ron Brown Award for Corp. Leadership, Arthur Ashe Inst. for Urban Health. Dean's adv. bd. Harvard Law Sch.; mem. Coun. Fgn. Rels., N.Y.C., 1988. Mem. ABA. Congregationalist. Office: Am Express Co Am Express Tower World Fin Ctr 200 Vesey St New York NY 10285-1000

CHÊNEAU, JACQUES PIERRE JOSEPH, orthopedist; b. Tunis, Tunisia, May 14, 1927; s. Maurice Charles and Appoline Marie (Isanove) C.; m. Giraud Gisèle, Sept. 6, 1952 (dec. Jan. 1986); 1 child, Françoise; m. Gire Marie Paule, July 6, 1992. MD, Faculty of Medicine, Toulouse, France, 1953. Pvt. practice medicine Toulouse, France, 1955-63, pvt. practice medicine specializing in rehab., 1965-85; pvt. practice medicine specializing in rehab. Werner Wicker Clinic, Bad Wildungen, Fed. Republic Germany, 1986; pvt. practice specializing in orthoses Midi Oxygene Orthoses, Marseille, France, 1987-89, Centre Hospitalier Universitaire, Toulouse, France, 1989—. Author: C.T.M. Korzet, 1953, Handbuch zur Herstellung des C.T.M. Korsetts, 1986, also publs. on treatment of scoliosis. Lt. with French army, 1954, Vietnam. Fellow Soc. Phys. Medicine, Soc. Osteopathy (adminstr.), Skoliose Selbsthilfe Verband, Deutsche Gesellschaft fur arthrologie und Chirotheraphie, Internat. Soc. for Prosthetics and Orthotics. Home: 39 rue des Chanterelles, 31650 Saint Orens France

CHENEY, DAVID WARREN, science and technology policy analyst, executive; b. La Jolla, Calif., Jan. 27, 1958; s. Elliott Ward C. and Elizabeth Jean (Helsley) Root; m. Alexandra S. Fairfield, Dec. 27, 1990; children: Alexander Ward, Austin Elizabeth. BS in Geology-Biology, Brown U., 1979; MS in Tech. and Policy, MIT, 1983. Engr. Core Lbs. Internat., Inc., Dallas, 1979-81; analyst sci. and tech. Congl. Rsch. Svc. Libr. of Congress, Washington, 1983-89; sr. assoc. Coun. on Competitiveness, Washington, 1989-94; staff dir. tech. subcoun. Competitiveness Policy Coun., Washington, 1992-94; assoc. dep. undersec. U.S. DOE, Washington, 1994-97; sr. tech. policy analyst SRI Internat., Arlington, Va., 1998—; v.p. Internet Policy Inst., Washington, 1999-2000; adj. lectr. George Mason U., Fairfax, Va., 1991; vis. rschr. Saitama U., Urawa, Japan, 1987, 88; exec. dir. Optoelectronics Industry Devel. Assn., 1993-94; cons. U.S. Dept. Commerce, other orgns., 1998, 99. Witness hearing Com. on Sci. U.S. Congress, Washington, 1989, 91. Mem. AAAS, Sigma Xi. Achievements include contributions to the Clinton administration's technology policy. Avocations: masters swimming, running, hiking. Office: Internet Policy Inst North Bldg Ste 250 601 Pennsylvania Ave NW Washington DC 20004-2601

CHENG, CHEANYEH, chemistry educator, researcher; b. Taipei, Taiwan, Dec. 22, 1951; s. Yet-Sen and Yen-In (Chen) C.; m. Mei-Lung Fei, Aug 25, 1985; children: Shihshin, Shihjung, Shihtung. BS, Chung Yuan Christian U., Chungli, Taiwan, 1974; MS in Chemistry, U. Ky., 1978, MSChemE, 1981; PhD, Rutgers U., 1987. Asst. rsch. scientist N.Y. Inst. Basic Rsch. in Mental Retardation, N.Y.C., 1982; assoc. prof. Chung Yuan Christian U., Chung-Li, Taiwan, 1987-99, prof., 1999—; mem. editorial adv. bd. Chemistry, The Chinese Chem. Soc., Taiwan, 1989-91. Contbr. articles to profl. jours. 2nd lt. Chinese Army ROTC, 1974-76. Nat. Sci. Coun. grant, Taiwan, 1989—. Mem. AAAS, N.Y. Acad. Scis., Chinese Chem. Soc. (editl. bd. 1989-91). Christian. Avocations: singing, bridge, stamp and coin collecting, travel. Office: Chung Yuan Christian U, Dept Chemistry, 320 Chung-Li Taiwan

CHENG, CHU YUAN, economics educator; b. Kwangtung Province, China, Apr. 8, 1927; came to U.S., 1959, naturalized, 1964; s. Hung Shan and Shu Sheng (Yang) C.; m. Alice Hua Liang, Aug. 15, 1964; children: Anita tung I, Andrew Y.S. BA in Econs., Nat. Chengchi U., Nanking, China, 1947; MA, Georgetown U., 1962, PhD, 1964. Rsch. prof. Seton Hall U., 1960-64; vis. prof. George Washington U., Washington, 1963; sr. rsch. economist U. Mich., Ann Arbor, 1964-69; assoc. prof. Lawrence U., Appleton, Wis., 1970-71; assoc. prof. econs., chmn. Asian studies com. Ball State U., Muncie, Ind., 1971-73, prof. econs., 1974—; cons. NSF, Washington, 1964—; rsch. mem. presdl. Coun. for Nat. Unification, Republic of China, 1992—. Author: Scientific and Engineering Manpower in Communist China, 1966, The Machine-Building Industry in Communist China, 1971, China's Petroleum Industry: Output Growth and Export Potential, 1976, China's Economic Development: Growth and Structural Change, 1981, The Demand and Supply of Primary Energy in Mainland China, 1984, Taiwan as a Model for China's Modernization, 1986, Sun Yat-sen's Doctrine in Modern World, 1988, Taiwan Experience and China's Reconstruction, 1989, Behind the Tiananmen Massacre, Social, Political and Economic Ferment in China, 1990, Economic Development and Interaction between Two Sides of the Taiwan Straits, 1993, The Transformation of Social, Political and Economic Structure in China, 1994, China's Transition From A Planned to A Market Economy, 1994, Township-Village Enterprises: China's New Route to Industrialization, 1995, China's Economic Reform: Programs, Effects and Prospects, 1997, China's Economic Reform and Cross-Strait Economic Relations, 2000. Bd. dirs., pres. Dr. Sun Yat-sen Inst., Chgo., 1978—. Grantee NSF, 1960-64, Social Sci. Rsch. Coun., 1965-67, 74, Chiang ching-Kuo Found., 1996; recipient Outstanding Rsch. award Ball State U., 1976, Outstanding Educator in Econs., Ball State U., 1981-82. Mem. Am. Econ. Assn., Assn. Asian Studies, Assn. Comparative Econ. Studies, Am. Acad. Polit. and Social Sci., Assn. Chinese Social Scientists in N.Am. (bd. dirs., pres. 1994-96), Am. Assn. Chinese Studies (bd. dirs., pres. 1996-98), Chinese-Am. Soc. (pres. Washington 1989-92), Chinese Acad. and Profl. Assn. Mid-am. (pres. 1983-84), Ind. Acad. Social Sci., Omicron Delta Epsilon. Home: 1211 N Greenbriar Rd Muncie IN 47304-2934 Office: Ball State U Coll Bus Rm 123 Muncie IN 47306-0001

CHENG, CHUEN YAN, biochemist, educator; b. Hong Kong, June 18, 1954; came to the U.S., 1981, naturalized, 1993; s. C. Yin and Tak Ying (Ho) C.; m. Po Lee, Mar. 17, 1978; children; Yan Ho, Chin Ho. BS with honors, Chinese U., Hong Kong, 1978; PhD, U. Newcastle, Australia, 1982. Fellow Population Coun., N.Y.C., 1981-82, rsch. investigator, 1983-84, staff scientist, 1985-87, scientist, 1988-90, sr. scientist, 1991—; assoc. dir. Internat. Consortium on Male Contraception, N.Y.C., 1994-95, dir., 1996—; asst. prof. Rockefeller U., N.Y.C., 1986-90; prof. U. Rome, 1990—; cons. Angelini Pharms., Inc., River Edge, N.J., 1985-91, Angelini Rsch. Inst., Rome, 1992-93, Fidia Pharms., Inc., Italy, 1997. Contbr. numerous articles to profl. jours. Recipient Sea Horse award, Newcastle U., Australia, 1982. Mem. Am. Soc. Andrology (Best Sci. Paper award 1996), Endocrine Soc. (Richard E. Weitzman Meml. award 1988). Achievements include patents for abnormally glycosylated variants of alpha-2-macroglobulin and serum proteins used to detect autoimmune disease, monoclonal antibody specifically detects abnormal glycosylation site on α-antitrypsin used to detect autoimmune conditions, testicular protein that regulates androgen production for male fertility control; 3-substituted 1-benzyl-1H indazole derivatives as antifertility agents. Office: Population Coun 1230 York Ave New York NY 10021-6307

CHENG, CHUNWEI, physicist; b. Beijing, Jan. 12, 1957; arrived in Eng., 1985; s. Dianyang and Shumin (Zhang) C.; m. Sophia Lihong Wang, Sept. 14, 1985; 1 child, Ken. BSc, Beijing U., 1982, MSc, 1985; PhD, Heriot-Watt U., Edinburgh, Eng., 1987. Asst. lectr. Beijing U., 1985; rsch. assoc. U. Manchester Inst. Sci. and Technology, Eng., 1987-89, Queen Mary Coll., London, 1989-90; rsch. fellow Leed (Eng.) U., 1990-96; tech. designer, cons. Renishaw Plc., Gloucestershire, Eng., 1996—. Inventor in field. Mem. AAAS, Inst. Physics. Avocations: reading, countryside, walking, swimming. Office: Renishaw Plc, Old Town, GL12 7OH Gloucester England

CHENG, FAI CHUT, electrical engineering researcher; b. Shanghai, Jiangsu, China, July 15, 1933; s. Sui Hoi and Yuk Chi (Chow) C. BSc in Engring., Tsing Hua U., Beijing, 1957; MPhil, U. Hong Kong, 1990. Engr. N.E. Power Adminstrn. Ctrl. Lab., Harbin, 1957-73; technician Tomoe Electronics Co., Hong Kong, 1973-76; lectr. Sch. of Sci. and Tech., Hong Kong, 1976-80; rsch. asst. Hong Kong Polytech. U., 1989-92, tchg. asst., 1992-93, evening vis. lectr., 1988-89, 90-93, hon. rsch. assoc., 1993-94, part-time rsch. asst., 1994-97, hon. rsch. fellow, 1998-99, hon. fellow, 2000—; part-time demonstrator U. Hong Kong, 1980-88; temp. tchr. Haking Wong Tech. Inst., Hong Kong, 1987-88. Contbr. articles to profl. jours. including IEEE Transactions. Mem. IEEE (sr.), Instn. Elec. Engrs. (assoc., U.K.), Hong Kong Instn. Engrs. (assoc.), N.Y. Acad. Scis. Avocations: philosophy, traditional Chinese medicine, literature, Qigong, walking. Office: Hong Kong Polytech U, Dept Elec Engring, Hung Hom Kowloon Hong Kong China

CHENG, FAN-TIEN, manufacturing engineering educator; b. Tainan, Taiwan, Sept. 12, 1953; s. Shien-Shi Cheng and Yen-King Chen; m. Mei-Mei Chen, July 30, 1978; children: Hui-Wen, Kai-Wen. BS, Nat. Cheng Kung U., Tainan, 1976; MS, Ohio State U., 1982, PhD, 1989. Rsch. asst. to asst. scientist Chung Shan Inst. of Sci. and Tech., Taiwan, 1976-86, assoc. scientist, 1986-94, sr. scientist, 1994-95; assoc. prof. engring. Nat. Cheng Kung U., 1995-97, prof. engring., 1997—, dir., 1998—; sect. head Chung Shan Inst. of Sci. and Tech., 1990-95,. Assoc. editor IEEE Trans. on Robotics and Automation, 2000; contbr. articles to profl. jours. Mem. IEEE (Sr. mem. award 1998, Kayamori Best Paper award ICRA '99), IEEE Internat. Conf. on Robotics and Automation. Avocations: bowling, sightseeing, music. Office: Inst Mfg Engring, Nat Cheng Kung U, Tainan 701, Taiwan

CHENG, HSING-HSIEN, biochemist, educator; b. Cho-chi, China, Feb. 11, 1945; s. Ting-Chia Yuan Ping Cheng and Pei Rou Hsu. BS, Chung Hsing U., Taichung, China, 1968; Master's, Nat. Taiwan U., Taipei, China, 1983, PhD, 1987. Rschr. Taiwan Provincial Agrl. Rsch. Ctr., Taichung, Taiwan, 1973-82; assoc. prof. Taipei (Taiwan) Med. Coll., 1988-95, prof., 1995—. Contbr. articles to sci. and profl. jours. Recipient rsch. award Nat. Sci. Coun. of Republic of China, 1992-96. Mem. AAAS, Nutrition Soc. (editor 1999—, rsch. award 1992, 93, 94, 95, 96), Asian-Pacific Soc. Atherosclerosis and Vascular Diseases. Avocations: travel, cooking. Office: Taipei Med Coll Sch Nutriti, Health Sci 250 Wu-Hsing St, Taipei 110, Taiwan

CHENG, HU, software engineering educator; b. Shanghai, China, July 22, 1938; p. Yizhong Cheng and Huan Zhuang; m. Qi Liu, Jan. 5, 1968; 1 child, Guangyao. BSc, Peking U., Beijing, 1960. With Inst. Computing Tech., Chinese Acad. Scis., Beijing, 1960-80, assoc. prof., 1980-85; assoc. prof. Inst. Software, Chinese Acad. Scis., Beijing, 1985-90, prof., 1990—. Contbr. articles to profl. jours. Mem. IEEE (software engring. std. com.), Internat. Neural Network Soc., N.Y. Acad. Scis. Fax: 86-10-62562533. E-mail: chenghu@126.com. Home: Room 502, Zhong Guancun Bldg 952, Beijing 100080, China Office: Inst Software CAS, PO Box 8718, Beijing 100080, China

CHENG, I-JIUNN, marine biology educator; b. Hsinchu, Taiwan, July 29, 1953; s. Tao-Yu and Bin-Zin (Chen) C.; m. Chich-ping Kuo, Sept. 18, 1983; children: Wan-Hwa Cheng, Yue-Hwa Cheng. BS, Nat. Taiwan Ocean U., Keelung, 1976; MS, SUNY, Stony Brook, 1984, PhD, 1989. Postdoctoral rschr. SUNY, Stony Brook, 1989-91; assoc. prof. marine biology Nat. Taiwan Ocean U., 1991-97, full prof. marine biology, 1997—; vis. scholar Argos Marine Lab., Banyulus, France, 1993; mem. editl. bd. Sci. Monthly Jour., Taipei, 1997—, Chinese Amphibian and Reptilian Jour., 1998-99; lectr. Nat. Sci. Edn. Hall, Taipei, 1995—; mem. dissertation com. Andhra (India) U., 1995-97; mem. com. APEC Marine Resource Conservation Working Group, biol. sect., Taipei, 1998—. Contbr. articles to profl. jours. (Li-Kuo-Din Gen. Scientific Writing 1st award 1998). Mem. Keelung City com. for pub. hazard dispute negotiation, 1998—; cons. com. Nat. Mus. Marine Biology, Kentung, Taiwan, 1998—. 2d lt., Air Force Def. Arty., 1976-78, Kimmen, Taiwan. Rsch. grantee Nat. Sci. Coun., Taipei, Taiwan, 1993, 96. Mem. Internat. Union Conservation for Nature (Marine Turtle and Chinese Amphibian & Reptilian Specialist Groups), Fishery Soc. Taiwan, Sigma Xi. Home: 3d fl # 5 55 Alley, Fu-Yang Rd, Taipei 110, Taiwan Office: Inst Marine Biol Nat Taiwan, # 2 Pei-ning Rd, Keelung 202-24, Taiwan

CHENG, JAMES KUO-CHIANG, Chinese culture educator; b. Nanking, People's Republic of China, Aug. 20, 1936; naturalized, 1977.; s. Lieh and Chih-Chen (Chu) C.; m. Lolan Lo, July 25, 1959; children: Wen-Chun, Phillip Josephine, Irene, Lorraine, Katherine, Shan-Yun (Alice). BA, George Fox Coll., 1960; MA, Seton Hall U., 1963; MLS, Vanderbilt U., 1965; PhD, Pacific U., 1993. Reporter Cen. News Agy., Vancouver, B.C., Can., 1965-70; asst. prof. U. Alberta, Edmonton, Can., 1966-68; chief libr. Okanagan Coll., Kelowna, B.C., 1968-70; sec. gen. Chinese Nationalist League, Vancouver, 1970-75; pres. The New Republic Daily, Vancouver, 1970-75, Hua-Kang Pub. Co., Chinese Culture U., Taipei, Taiwan, 1975-79; chief libr. Chinese Culture U., Taipei, Taiwan, 1975-79; prof. Chinese Culture U., Taipei, People's Rep. China, 1975—, dean, 1977-79, pres. Hua Hsir Cultural Ctr., 1980-95; adv. Commn. Overseas Chinese Affairs, 1980—; vice chmn. bd. Hua-Hsin Cultural Ctr., 1995—; vis. scholar Harvard U., 1965, Hamline U., 1966; pres. Vets. Weekly, 1980—; adv. ctrl. com. KMT, 1993—. Author: The Stranger, 1963, Man Without A Country, 1964, Cry, Beloved Country, 1968, The Collected Short Stories, 1970, American History, 1985, My Homeland, 1993. Mem. Chinese Nationalist League, Taipei, 1955—. Recipient Lit. award Fedn. Overseas Chinese, 1970, Lit. award Chinese Lit. and Arts Fedn., 1993, Lit. award Asian Writers Fedn. Korea, 1993, outstanding svc. award Kuo-Ming-Tang, 1999, 2d class grand award, 2000; named Outstanding Young Man of Am., 1967, Outstanding Young Man of China, 1972, Pres. Chiang Kai-shek's aard KMT, 1973, Pres. Lee Teng Hui's Citation, 1993, Pres. Bill Clinton's White House citation, 1994. Mem. Pubs. Assn. China (bd. dirs. 1982—), Latin Am. Assn. (bd. dirs. 1991—), Vets. Writers Soc. (pres. 1991—), Chinese Writers Assn. (pres. 1992—, del. 5th conv. 1996), Chinese Culture Exch. Assn. (pres. 1993—), Chinese Mags. Assn. (bd. dirs. 1993—), Chinese Lit. and Arts Fedn. (bd. dirs. 1994—), Chinese Mags. Assn. (hon. pres. 1999—). Roman Catholic. Home: 38 Ally 27, Ln 133 Chung-Yang Rd, Hsin-Dien Taipei, Taiwan Office: Hua Hsin Culture Ctr, 133 Kuang Fu North Rd, Taipei Taiwan

CHENG, JIAYANG, agricultural engineering educator; b. Duchang, Jiangxi, China, Aug. 12, 1962; came to U.S., 1991; s. Chuanyu Cheng and Xinge Cao; m. Yan Long, June 26, 1991; 1 child, Kerry. BS, Nanchang (China) U., 1982; MS, St. Cyril and Methodius U., Skopje, Macedonia, 1987; PhD, U. Cin., 1996. Engr.-in-tng., Ohio. Tchg. asst. Jiangxi Poly. U., Nanchang, 1982-85, lectr., divsn. dir., 1987-91; rsch. asst. St. Cyril and Methodius U.,

1985-87; rsch. asst. U. Cin., 1991-96, rsch. assoc., 1996-97; asst. prof. dept. biol. and agrl. engring. N.C. State U., Raleigh, 1997—. Contbr. articles to sci. jours., including Water Rsch., Water Sci. and Tech., Bioresource Tech. Gen. sec. Chinese Am. Friendship Assn., Raleigh, 1999. Mem. Am. Soc. Agrl. Engrs., Water Environ. Fedn. (founding mem. U. Cin. chpt., pres. 1995), Internat. Water Assn. Avocations: swimming, ping pong, racquetball. E-mail: jay cheng@ncsu.edu. Office: NC State U PO Box 7625 Raleigh NC 27695-0001

CHENG, JIN-PEI, chemistry educator, academic administrator; b. Tianjin, China, June 1, 1948; s. Binghu Cheng and Yongqing Yang; m. Yunru Huang, Oct. 31, 1976. MSc, Nankai U., Tianjin, China, 1981; PhD, Northwestern U., 1987. Postdoctoral rsch. assoc. Duke U., Durham, N.C., 1987-88; assoc. prof. Nankai U., Tianjin, China, 1988-90, prof. chemistry, 1990—; vis. prof. Utah State U., Logan, 1992, Duke U., Durham, N.C., 1995, U. Hong Kong, China, 1997; mem. editorial bd. Chem. Jour. Chinese Univs., 1993—; v.p. Nankai U., Tianjin, 1995—; mem. instr. com. of higher edn. State Ednl. Commn. China, 1995—; cons. acad. degree com. The State Coun., China, 1997—. Contbr. numerous articles to nat. and internat. profl. jours. including Science, Jour. Am. Chem. Soc., Jour. Organic Chemistry. Mem. nat. commn. The Chinese Peoples' Political Consultant Commn., 1993—, mem. standing com., 1998—. Grantee: Nat. Sci. Found. China, State Edn. Commn., Others, 1993—. Mem. Am. Chem. Soc. Avocations: music, musical instruments. Office: Nankai U Dept Chemistry, 94 Weijin Rd, Tianjin 300071, China

CHENG, JOSEPH YU-SHEK, political scientist, educator; b. Hong Kong, Nov. 11, 1949; s. Kan Yau and Suk Chun (Pang) C.; m. Grace Wong, Feb. 18, 1973; children: Felicia, Laurence. B in Social Sci., U. Hong Kong, 1972; BA, Victoria U., Wellington, New Zealand, 1973; PhD, Flinders U., South Australia, 1979. E-mail: rcccrc@cityu.edu.hk. Fax: 852-2788-7328. Office: City U Hong Kong, Tat Chee Ave Kowloon Tong, Kowloon Hong Kong

CHENG, KEVIN HON-KIT, marketing professional; b. Hong Kong, Aug. 29, 1955; s. Nam Ngok and Kwai Fai (Lam) C.; m. Shirley Chui-Wan Yeung, Aug. 4, 1988; children: Eric, Florence. BA in Econs with honors, Wilfrid Laurier U., 1979; MA in Econs., York U., Toronto, Ont., Can., 1980. Mgr. rsch. Hong Kong Bank, 1980-87; treasury economist, advisor Westpac Banking Corp., Sydney, Australia, 1987-93; head econ. rsch. and product devel. Hong Kong Futures Exch., 1993—; econ. lectr. Hong Kong Polytech. U., 1981-87. Author: Asia by the Year 2000 Europe, 1992. Avocations: swimming, reading, music, strategic thinking and driving. Office: Hong Kong Future Exch, Rm 407 Shui On Centre, Wanchai Hong Kong

CHENG, MEI-FANG, psychobiology educator, neuroethology researcher; b. Kee Lung, Taiwan, Republic of China, Nov. 24, 1938; came to U.S., 1959; d. Chao-Chin Hsieh and Ai Tsu; m. Wen-Kwei Cheng; m. June 7, 1963; children: Suzanne, Po-Yuan, Julie. BS summa cum laude, Nat. Taiwan U., Taipei, 1958; PhD, Brywn Mawr Coll., 1965. Postdoctoral fellow U. Pa., Phila., 1965-68; asst. rsch. prof. Inst. Animal Behavior Rutgers U., Newark, 1969-73, assoc. prof., 1973-79, prof., 1979—, acting dir. Inst. Animal Behavior, 1989-91, dir., 1991-95; cons. NIMH, mem. neurosci. study sect., 1991-95; cons., mem. behavioral neurobiology br. NSF; mem. NIH Reviewers Res., 1995—; cons. numerous granting agys. Author: Advance in the Study of Behavior, 1979; co-editor: Reproduction: A Behavorial and Neuroscientific Perspective, 1986; assoc. editor Hormones and Behavior, 1986-96; cons. Brain Rsch., Sci., others; contbr. articles to profl. jours. Fulbright scholar, 1959; recipient Rsch. Scientist Devel. award NIMH, 1974-79, 79-84, Johnson & Johnson Discovery award, 1989, Hoechst-Celanese Innovative award, 1993, award of excellence in rsch. Rutgers Bd. Trustees, 1998. Mem. Internat. Conf. Neuroethology, Neurosci. Achievements include discovery that a bird's own songs stimulate the endocrine changes; identification and demonstration of the auditory-endocrine pathways involved in voice and sound mediated endocrine change, the emotional state; discovery that brain cell loss in the adult brain is not imminent, proper social stimuli facilitate cell repair following injury induced cell loss. Office: Rutgers U Inst Animal Behavior 101 Warren St Newark NJ 07102-1811

CHENG, MICHAEL C.H., integrated circuit design engineer; b. Singapore, Oct. 31, 1961. BS summa cum laude, U. Mass., 1985; PhD, U. London, 1993; diploma, Imperial Coll., 1993. IC devel. engr. Matsushita Denshi, Japan and Singapore, 1985-88; IC design engr. Silicon Compilation Tech., Singapore, 1988-90; rsch. engr. Imperial Coll., U. London, 1990-93; sr. engr. Tritech Microelectronics Internat., Singapore, 1993-95; engring. mgr. Chartered Semiconductor Mfg. Ltd., Singapore, 1996—. Contbr. papers to profl. publs. Rsch. scholar Singapore Techs., 1990-93, Commonwealth scholar U. Mass., 1985; recipient ORS award Com. of Vice-Chancellors and Prins. of Univs. of U.K., 1991-93. Mem. IEEE, N.Y. Acad. Scis., Tau Beta Pi, Phi Kappa Phi, Eta Kappa Nu, Alpha Lambda Delta. Avocations: antique pens, reading, running, swimming, diving. Office: Chartered Semiconductor Mfg Ltd, 60 Woodlands Indsl Park D, St 2, Singapore 738406, Singapore

CHENG, PHILIP SHU-YING, insurance company executive,; b. Kwang Tung, China, July 24, 1943. BS in Mech. Engring., U. Minn., 1965; MBA, St. Louis U., 1969. Internat. planning officer Chase Manhattan Bank, N.Y.C., 1974-77; corp. banking mgr. Chase Manhattan Bank, Hong Kong, 1977-81; v.p. instnl. banking Chase Manhattan Bank, Taipei, Taiwan, 1981-85; v.p. consumer banking Chase Manhattan Bank, N.Y.C., 1986-96; v.p. investments Met. Ins., Taipei, 1996—. Contbr. article to profl. jour. Assoc. instr. U.S. Profl. Tennis Registry, Hilton Head, S.C., 1989. Mem. Am. C. of C. Hong Kong (chmn. membership com. 1981), Am. C. of C. Taiwan (mem. ins. com. 1996-99). Avocations: tennis, sailing, golf. Office: Met Ins and Annutiy co, 11 Fl 85 Jen Ai Sect Rd, Taipei 106, Taiwan

CHENG, PING, engineering educator; b. Canton, China; m. Sabrina H.T. Yuen; children: Albert H., Bonnie J. BS in Mech. Engring., Okla. State U., 1958; MS in Mech. Engring., MIT, 1960; PhD in Aeronautics & Astronautics, Stanford U., 1965. Vis. prof. Nat. Taiwan U., Taipei, 1968-70; assoc. prof. U. Hawaii, Honolulu, 1970-74; vis. prof. Stanford U., Palo Alto, Calif., 1976-77; guest prof. Tech. U. Munich, Germany, 1984; prof. mech. engring. U. Hawaii, 1974-94, chmn. dept. mech. engring., 1989-94; head dept. mech. engring. Hong Kong U. Sci. and Tech., 1995—. Editor: (jour.) AAIA Jour. of Thermophysics & Heat Transfer, 1988—; mem. editl. bd. Jour. Numerical Heat Transfer, 1996—, Jour. Exptl. Heat Transfer; contbr. articles to scientific jours. including Internat. Jour. Heat Mass Transfer, Jour. Heat Transfer. Recipient Fujio Matsuda scholar award U. Hawaii Found., 1989; recipient Dist. Scientific Achievement award Chung Shan Found., 1969. Fellow ASME (Heat Transfer Meml. award in sci. 1996). Office: Hong Kong U Sci & Tech, Dept Mech Engring Clearwater Bay, Kowloon Hong Kong

CHENG, STEPHEN KIN KWOK, psychologist, consultant, business consultant; b. Hong Kong, May 21, 1947; arrived in Australia, 1973; s. Tung Fai and Shui Mui (Young) C.; m. Wilai Surapathana; children: Adrian, Rowena, Caleb. BA with honors, U. Hong Kong, 1971; BD, Melbourne Coll. Divinity, Australia, 1979; BSW, U. We. Australia, Perth, 1979; PhD, Murdoch U., Perth, 1998. High sch. tchr. Dept. Edn., Hong Kong, 1971-73; curate Diocese of Perth, 1976; social worker Graylands Hosp., Perth, 1979-84; sr. social worker Multicultural Psychiatric Ctr., Perth, 1984-93; multicultural cons. Curtin U., Perth, 1994-95; dir. East Asia Access Consulting, Perth, 1995—; Sapphire dir. GNLD Internat., Perth, 1995—; mem. multicultural rsch. group O.M.I., Perth, 1992-93. Author: Multicultural Social Work, 1995; cons. editor: Jour. World Psychology, 1997—; contbr. articles to profl. jours. chair accreditation panel Edith Cowan U., Perth, 1986-87; dep. chair Cath. Migrant Ctr., Perth, 1987-95; mem. bd. mgmt. Fremantle Migrant Ctr., Perth, 1985-88. Mem. Am. Psychol. Assn., Internat. Coun. Psychologists, Chung Wah Assn. (dep. chair 1985-88). Avocations: reading, swimming, travel, rowing, Internet.

CHENG, TING-WONG, academic administrator. BA, Nat. Chengchi U., Taipei, Taiwan, 1964, ML, 1968; MA, U. Mo., Columbia, 1970, PhD, 1974. Prof., chmn. dept. acctg. Nat. Chengchi U., Taipei, Taiwan, 1975-85, dean coll. of commerce, 1986-92, provost, 1993-94; chmn. Chinese Acctg. Edn. Assn., Taiwan, 1995-99; pres. Nat. Chengchi U., Taipei, Taiwan; supr. Chang Hwa Comml. Bank, Taiwan, 1980-92, Ctrl. Bank China, Taiwan, 1985-93, Chinese Petroleum Corp., Taiwan, 1985-93. Fax: 886-2-29398043. Office: Nat Chengchi U, 64 Chih-nan Rd Sec 2, Taipei Taiwan

CHENG, TSUNG O., cardiologist, educator; b. Shanghai, Mar. 30, 1925; came to U.S., 1950, naturalized, 1960; s. Keith S. and Fanny (Wang) C.; m. Marie Ellen Roe, June 18, 1955; children: Mark Dudley, Yvonne Joyce. BS, St. John's U., China, 1945; MD, U. Pa., 1950, MS in Medicine, 1956. Diplomate Am. Bd. Internal Medicine (subsplty. cardiovasc. disease), Nat. Bd. Med. Examiners. Intern St. Barnabas Hosp., Newark, 1950-51; resident Cook County Hosp., Chgo., 1952-55; fellow in cardiovasc. disease George Washington U., D.C. Gen. Hosp., Washington, 1955-56; instr. cardiology Harvard Med. Sch. Mass. Gen. Hosp., Boston, 1956-57; fellow in cardiorespiratory physiology Johns Hopkins U. Sch. Medicine and Hosp., 1957-59; practice medicine specializing in cardiology Washington, 1970—; asst. prof. medicine SUNY Downstate, 1959-70; assoc. prof. medicine George Washington U., 1970-72; chief cardiology D.C. Gen. Hosp., 1971-72; prof. George Washington U., 1972—; dir. cardiac catheterization lab. George Washington U. Med. Center, 1972-78, assoc. dir. cardiology, 1972-75; asst. physician Cardiac Clinic, Johns Hopkins Hosp., 1957-59, mem. staff cardiac catheterization lab., 1957-59; dir. cardiopulmonary lab. Bklyn. Hosp., 1959-66; co-chief Pediatric Cardiac Clinic, 1959-66; chief Adolescent Cardiac Clinic, 1961-66; attending physician Adult Cardiac Clinic, 1959-66; chief Pediatric Cardiac Clinic Cumberland Hosp., Bkly., 1963-66; asst. chief cardiology VA Hosp., Bklyn., 1966-69; chief Cardiovascular Lab., 1966-70, chief cardiology, 1969-70; asst. vis. physician Kings County Hosp. Med. Center, Bklyn., 1964-70; attending physician Univ. Hosp., SUNY, Bklyn., 1967-70; cons. Beth Israel Med. Ctr., N.Y.C., 1970-82; guest lectr. Chinese Med. Assn., 1972, 73, 75, 77, 79, 83, 86, 89, 92, Chinese Ministry Health, 1990; hon. prof. Shanghai 2d Med. Univ. 1986—, Qingdao Med. Coll., 1989—, Binzhou Med. Coll., 1992—, Taishan Med. Coll., 1992—, Tongji Med. U., Wuhan, China, 1993—, Jiujiang Med. Coll., Jiangxi, China 1994—, U. Cape Town, South Africa, 1995—; hon. dir. Qingdao Cardiovascular Rsch. Inst., 1989—, Guangdong Provincial Cardiovascular Inst., 1990—; hon. pres. Dandong 1st Hosp., Dandong, Liaoning Province, People's Republic of China 1988—, Shanghai St. Luke's Hosp., 1990—, Binzhou Med. Coll. Affiliated Hosp., 1992—, Taishan Med. Coll. Affiliated Hosp., 1992—, Jiujiang Med. Coll. Affiliated Hosp., Jiujiang, Jiangxi, China, 1994—, Second People's Hosp., Jin De Zhen, Jiangxi, 1994—; vis. prof., Peking Union Med. Coll., 1986—; hon. cons. Beijing Hosp., 1989—; vis. prof. Sun Yatsen Med. U., Canton, 1992—, Cairo U., Egypt, 1994—, U. Oxford, Eng., 1995—, U. Witwatersrand Med. Sch., Johannesburg, South Africa, 1995—, U. Paris Hosp., Tenon, France, 1995—, U. Natal, Durban, South Africa, 1995—, Cath. U. Inst. Cardiology, Rome, 1996—, Inst. Clin. Physiology, Nat. Rsch. Coun., U. Pisa, Italy, 1996—, Inst. Clin. Physiology of the Nat. Rsch. Coun., Milan, Inst. of Pathol. Anatomy Med. Sch. U. Milan, 1996—, U. Dusseldorf (Germany), 1997—, U. Hamburg (Germany), 1997—, U. Hannover (Germany), 1997—, U. Melbourne (Australia), 1997—, U. NSW, Sydney, Australia, 1997—, U. Instanbul (Turkey), 1999—, U. Athens (Greece), 1999—, U. Cordoba (Spain), 2000—, U. Las Palmas (Spain), 2000—, U. Complutense, Madrid, 2000—; v.p. Am. Ctr. for Chinese Med. Sci., 1982-91; pres. Friends St. Luke's Hosp. Shanghai, 1991—, chmn. bd., 1992—; hon. dir. Inst. Invasive Therapy PLA 150th Ctrl. Hosp., Luoyang, China 1994—; disting. sr. visitor Royal Brompton Hosp./Nat. Heart and Lung Inst., London, 1995—; hon. advisor Guangdong Soc. Interventional Cardiology, Guangzhou, China, 1996—. Sr. editor Vascular Medicine, 1983-88, Angiology, 1986-97; editor: The International Textbook of Cardiology, 1986, 87, Percutaneous Balloon Valvuloplasty, 1992; mem. editl. bd. Catheterization and Cardiovasc. Diagnosis, 1991—, Catheterization and Cardiovasc. Interventions, 1999—, Jour. Noninvasive Cardiology, 1997iagnostics, 1999—; co-editor: Congestive Heart Failure, 1991, Modern Cardiology, 1994, Genetics of Cardiovasc. Diseases, 1995, Congestive Heart Failure, 2nd edit., 1997; contbg. med. editor: Cortlandt Forum, 1997-98; contbr. numerous articles to sci. and med. jours. Fellow ACP, Am. Coll. Chest Physicians, Am. Coll. Cardiology (ofcl. rep. to stds. com. on catheters Assn. Advancement Med. Instrumentation 1971—), Am. Heart Assn., Coun. Clin. Cardiology, Soc. Cardiac Angiography and Interventions, Internat. Coll. Angiology, Am. Coll. Angiology, Soc. Geriat. Cardiology (founding), Royal Soc. Medicine; mem. AAAS, Am. Fedn. Clin. Rsch., Am. Heart Assn., Washington Heart Assn. Home: 7508 Cayuga Ave Bethesda MD 20817-4822 Office: George Washington U Med Ctr 2150 Pennsylvania Ave NW Washington DC 20037-3201

CHENG, VOON YEEN, semiconductor researcher; b. Ipoh, Perak, Malaysia, Nov. 10, 1971; d. Foo Lai and Mooi (Loo) Cheng; m. Chen Hung Tan, Apr. 30, 1997. BSc in Sci., Malaya U., Malaysia, 1995. Engr. UNISEM Berhad, Perak, Malaysia, 1995-98, semicondr. rschr., 1998—. Office: UNISEM (M) Berhad, no 1 Persiaran Pulai Jaya 9, 31300 Ipoh, Perak Malaysia

CHENG, WEIMING, optical engineering educator; b. Ningbo, China, July 11, 1955; s. Mingde and Aiju (Cai) C.; m. Yi Wu, Jan. 10, 1987; 1 child, Xin Cheng. BS, Shanghai Inst. Mech. Engring., 1982, MS, 1986; PhD, Shanghai Inst. Optics and Fine Mech., Academia Sinica. Asst. prof. Shanghai Inst. Mech. Engring., 1986-89; lectr. Shanghai U. Sci. Tech., 1989-93, assoc. prof., 1993-94; assoc. prof. Shanghai Univ., 1994-98, prof., 1998—, vice chmn. dept., 1995—. Contbr. articles to profl. jours.; inventor in field. Named Outstanding Young Tchr., Shanghai Mcpl. Govt., 1993, Outstanding Tchr., 1995. Mem. China Optical Soc. Avocations: photography, swimming. Office: Shanghai Univ Dept Precision Mech Engring, 20 Chengzhong Rd, 201800 Jiading Shanghai, China

CHENG, WU C., patent examiner; b. Shanghai, China, Aug. 11, 1922; came to U.S., 1948; s. Ting-yih and Wei-chi (Kiang) C.; m. Wenying Liu, 1963; 1 child, Robert C. BS, St. John's U., Shanghai, 1944; MS, Kans. State Coll., 1949; PhD, Ga. Inst. Tech., Atlanta, 1954. Asst. prof. to prof., head chemistry dept. Union U., Jackson, Tenn., 1955-66; assoc. prof. chemistry George Peabody Coll., Nashville, 1966-72; tchr. with rank I Lyman H.S., Longwood, Fla., 1972-75; asst. prof. chemistry to assoc. prof. physics Paine Coll., Augusta, Ga., 1975-89; patent examiner U.S. Dept. Commerce, Washington, 1990-99; vis. instr. chemistry Ga. Inst. Tech., Atlanta, summer 1956; chemist No. Regional Rsch. Ctr., Peoria, Ill., summer 1976, 88; faculty rsch. participant Savannah River Lab., Aiken, S.C., summer 1977, Argonne Nat. Lab., Chgo., summer 1982, Oak Ridge (Tenn.) Nat. Lab., summer 1984; mem. faculty Rockwell Hanford (Wash.) Ops., summer 1979; faculty rsch. fellow USAF Acad., Colorado Springs, Colo., summer 1986. Contbr. articles to profl. jours. Mem. Am. Chem. Soc., Armed Forces Comms. and Electronics Assn., Ga. Acad. Sci., N.Y. Acad. Scis., Sigma Xi. Achievements include patents in field. Address: PO Box 211336 Augusta GA 30917-1336

CHENG, YEN CHUAN, physician; b. Singapore, Sept. 28, 1971; s. Chia Pan Cheng and Geok Eng Tar; m. Poh Yee Whey, Nov. 7, 1998. MB, BChir, Nat. U. Singapore, 1995. Physician dept. orthopaedic surgery Alexandra Hosp., Singapore, 1995-96; physician dept. respiratory medicine Tar Tock Seng Hosp., Singapore, 1996; physician dept. otolaryngology surgery Singapore Gen. Hosp., 1996-97; physician dept. anaethesia Urargi Gen. Hosp., Singapore, 1997-98; physician accident and emergency dept. Singapore Gen. Hosp., 1999—. Coun. mem. students union Nat. U. Singapore, 1991-92, pres. med. faculty, 1991-92; active Wesley Meth. Ch. Capt. Singapore Armed Forces, 1998-99. Mem. Singapore Swimming Club. Avocations: tennis, swimming, running. Home: Blk 27, Oxley Rd #12-08, Singapore 238621, Singapore

CHENG, YIU-CHUNG, academic administrator. Vice chancellor U. Hong Kong. Office: U Hong Kong, Pokfulan Rd, Hong Kong Hong Kong*

CHENG, YUE, molecular geneticist, pathologist; b. Wenzhou, Zhijiang, China, Aug. 23, 1958; s. Renbin Cheng and Benzhao Zhou; m. Yuxing Xiong, Mar. 16, 1988. MBBS, Anhui Med. Coll., Hefei, China, 1982; MS, Sun Yatsen U. Med. Sci., Guangzhou, China, 1987. Asst. prof. Sun Yatsen U. Med. Sci., Guangzhou, 1989-93; vis. asst. rschr. U. Calif., Irvine, 1993-95; vis. scholar Hong Kong U. Sci. and Tech., 1995—; dir. grad. course Sun Yatsen U. Med. Sci., Guangzhou, 1991-93. Contbr. articles to profl. jours. Grantee Sun Yatsen U. Med. Sci., 1991. Mem. Chinese Med. Assn., Chinese Med. Assn. Hong Kong. E-mail: yuecheny@hotmail.com. Office: Hong Kong U Sci and Tech, Dept Biol Clear Water Bay, Kowloon Hong Kong

CHENVIDHYA, DHIRAPHOL ZALVINO, hospital executive, surgeon; b. Bangkok, Jan. 18, 1952; s. Philip Bhatsorn and Suthee Josephine (Wiratkul) C.; m. Urai Vilamas, Jan. 20, 1981; children: Kroekphorn, Kuepong. BS, Mahidol U., Thailand, 1973, MD, 1975. Diplomate Thai Bd. Surgery. Surgeon Sappasitthiprasong Hosp., Ubon, Thailand, 1980-98, chief tech. sect., 1991-98, chmn. dept. surgery, 1993-97, chmn. dept. cmty. medicine, 1997-98, med. dep. dir., 1998, v.p. Savs. Coop. Ltd. of the hosp., 1998-2000; examiner surgery Royal Coll. Surgeons, Thailand, 1991-2000; chmn. Clin. Epidemiology Group, Ubon, 1994-2000; vis. cons. Regional Cancer Ctr., Ubon, 1997-2000; chief surveyor Regional Com. Hosp. Accreditation, Thailand, 1998; spkr. Regional Health Svc. Devel. Commn., Ubon, 1994. Contbr. articles to profl. jours. Vol. The Princess Mother's Med. Vol. Found., 1983-2000; guest lectr. Cath. Family Promotion Ctr. Ubon, 1984-98; discussant Social Security Office, Thailand, 1994-99. Recipient Outstanding Civil Svc. award Govt., 1986; named to Order Crown Thailand 1st class, 1996, Order Royal White Elephants 1st class, 1999. Fellow Royal Coll. Surgeons Thailand, Pub. Health Exec. Assn. Thailand; mem. Internat. Coll. Surgeons (envoy fellow, regent Thailand sect. 1994—), Pub. Health Exec. Assn. Roman Catholic. Avocations: aerobic walking, reading, Internet exploration, traveling. Office: Sappasitthiprasong Hosp, Sappasit Rd, Ubon Mueng 34000, Thailand

CHEON, IL-TONG, physicist, educator; b. Seoul, Korea, Feb. 9, 1936; s. Kap Kum and Maen Soo (Park) C.; m. Yang Ja Lee, Nov. 18, 1970; 2 children. BS, Osaka (Japan) U., 1961; MS, Kyoto (Japan) U., 1963, ScD, 1966. Prof. Kobe-Gakuin U., Kobe, Japan, 1967-72; vis. prof. Liege (Belgium) U., 1972-74, Munich Tech. U., Garching, Germany, 1974, McMaster U., Hamilton, Ont., Can., 1974-76; prof. physics Yonsei U., Seoul, 1976—, head dept. physics, 1989-91, dir. Natural Sci. Rsch. Inst., 1991-93; vis. prof. Rensselaer Poly. Inst., Troy, N.Y., 1980-81; guest prof. U. Tokyo, 1994-95. Editor: Recent development of Nuclear Study using Electron and Photon Beams, 1995, Procs. of 4th Asia-Pacific Physics Conf., 1991; author: Quantum Mechanics, 1985, A Short Table of Constants, Coefficients and Mathematical Formulae in Physics. Mem. Sci. and Tech. Cons. Corps., Seoul, 1996-99. Fellow Korean Acad. Sci. and Tech.; mem. Korean Phys. Soc. (chmn. nuclear physics divsn. 1984-86, Phys. Soc. award 1983), Phys. Soc. Japan, Internat. Union Pure and Applied Physics (C12 commr. 1999—). Avocations: swimming, reading. Office: Yonsei Univ Dept Physics, Shinchon-dong 134 Seodae Moon Ku, 120-749 Seoul Republic of Korea

CHEONG, ELLA SHUK KI, lawyer; b. Hong Kong, Dec. 14; d. Wai Fund and Yin Ching (Cheuk) C.; m. Sil Chiu Yu (dec. 1985); children: Wai Yan, Wai Yee, Wai Ching, Wai Hong. Bar: Hong Kong 1963, U.K. 1967. Asst. Wilkinson & Grist, Hong Kong, 1963-72, ptnr., 1972-88, sr. ptnr., 1988—. Contbr. articles to profl. jours. Justice of Peace, Hong Kong, 1995. Recipient Merit award AIPPI, Vienna, Austria, 1997. Mem. Hong Kong Women Profls. & Entrepreneurs Assn., Law Soc. Hong Kong, Hong Kong Soc. Notaries. Avocations: travel, home entertaining, lecturing. Office: Wilkinson & Grist, 10 Chater Rd 6th Fl, Hong Kong Hong Kong

CHEONG, KENNETH KENG-LIANG, academic administrator; b. Singapore, Apr. 22, 1958; s. Kok-Kee and Hun-Khoon (Chew) C. BS with honors, Teesside Poly. U., 1983; MSc, U. Manchester, 1985; LTCL, Trinity Coll. of Music, London, 1987; diploma in bus. adminstrn., Nat. U. Singapore, 1993. Chartered engr.; cert. data processor. Asst. registrar Nat. U., Singapore, 1985-94; info. systems officer Nat. Computer Bd., 1985-94; sr. cons. Internat. Corp. Mgmt. Pte Ltd., 1987-94. Recipient Good Svc. medal Singapore Armed Forces. Mem. IEEE, Br. Computer Soc., Singapore Computer Soc., Mensa Singapore.

CHEOUR, MARIE KATARIINA, research scientist; b. Helsinki, Oct. 16, 1965; d. Moshe Ben C. and Tuula Soile (Samulin) Tamminen; m. Kari Juhani Luhtanen, July 4, 1987 (div. 1992); children: Daniel, Julian. MA, U. Helsinki, 1994, PhD, 1998; postgrad., Northwestern U., 1998-99. Rschr. U. Helsinki, 1993-98, supr. developmental brain rsch. lab., 1996-98; sr. scientist, head lang. and the developin brain group U. Turku, Finland, 2000—. Contbr. articles to profl. jours. Mem. Nordic Psychophysiology Soc. Avocations: modern art, literature, cooking. Home: Rikunkuja 4, 01420 Vantaa Finland Office: U Turku Ctr Cogn Neurosci, Lemminkaisenk 14A, 200014 Turku Finland

CHEP, ALAIN, science educator, researcher; b. Kremlin-Bicêtre, France, Jan. 27, 1962; s. Louis and Françoise (Gauthier) C.; m. Farida Laroui, Jan. 27, 1990; 1 child, Tommy. BA, H.S. Raspail, Paris, 1984; MA, Ecole Normale Superieure, Cachan, France, 1985, Agrégation exam., 1986, searching study degree, 1987; PhD, Ecole Centrale Paris, 1992. Cert. in mech. engring. Schoolmaster Tech. Sch., Vitry-Sur-Seine, France, 1992-93; lectr. Inst. U. Info. des Maitres, Creteil, France, 1993—; rschr. U. Lab. in Automated Prodn. Rsch./Ecole Normale Superieure, Cachan, 1986—; specialist com. Ecole Normale Superieure, Cachan, 1995-98; v.p. specialist com. Inst. U. Info. des Maitres, Creteil, 1996-98, specialist com., 1998-99; cons. Alphatom, Marcoussis, France, 1999—. Author: Technologies and Trainings, 1998; contbr. articles to profl. jours. Dir. Holiday Ctr., Town Hall Drancy, France, 1989-90. Scientist of contingent Land Forces, 1987-88. Recipient Dir.'s Cert., Ministry of Youth and Sports, 1989. Mem. Ecole Normale Superieure Cachan (entry competition exam. 1991-93), Nat. Exhbn./City of Scis. and Industry (organizer), Gama Group/Assn. Francaise Scis. Tech. Info. des Sys. Avocations: jogging, tennis, swimming, travel, sport fishing. E-mail: chep@lurpa.ens-cachan.fr. Home: 37 Ave de l'étang neuf, 91460 Marcoussis Essonne, France Office: U Lab Automated Prodn Rsch, 61 Ave Président Wilson, 94235 Cachan Cedex, France

CHEPEL, VITALY YURIEVICH, physicist, researcher; b. Lvov, Ukraine, USSR, Jan. 17, 1957; s. Yuri Prokofievitch and Margarita Sergeevna (Ilyina) Ch.; m. Oxana Anatolievna Rainesh, Jan. 30, 1988; 1 child, Dmitry. MSc, Moscow Engring. Physics Inst., 1980, PhD, 1988. Engr. Moscow Engring. and Physics Inst., 1980-82, rschr., 1986-92; invited scientist Lab. for Instrumentation and Particle Physics, Coimbra, Portugal, 1992-93; sr. rschr. Lab. for Instrumentation and Particle Physics, Coimbra, 1993—; vis. prof. U. Coimbra, 1993, invited assoc. prof., 1996—. Contbr. articles to profl. jours. Mem. N.Y. Acad. Sci., Portuguese Soc. Radiation Protection. Office: LIP Coimbra Physics Dept, Univ Coimbra, 3000 Coimbra Portugal

CHEPESIUK, RON JOSEPH, librarian, educator; b. Thunderbay, Canada, June 14, 1944; s. Joseph Peter and Anne Kating C.; m. Karen Rene Harmon, Aug. 14, 1968 (div. 1975); m. Magdalena Aranda, Aug. 7, 1988. BA, Moorhead State U., 1968; MLS, Clack Atlanta U., 1972, Diploma in Archival Studies, 1986. With Nat. U. Ireland, Dublin, 1979-90; prof. Winthrop U., Rock Hill, S.C., 2000—. Author 14 Books; contbr. over 2000 articles for profl. jours.; columnist S.C. newspapers and mags. Mem. Moose, Omicron Delta Kappa. Avocations: weight training, karate. Home: 781 Wofford St # It Rock Hill SC 29730-3380 Office: Winthrop U 701 Oakland Ave Rock Hill SC 29730-3525

CHEPURNENKO, VICTOR PAVEL, refrigeration engineer, educator; b. Odessa, Ukraine, Feb. 9, 1930; s. Pavel Ivan and Maria Vasil (Glavatskaya) C.; m. Eleonora Peter Platonova, Oct. 6, 1956; 1 child, Tanya. DSc, Odessa Tech. Inst. Food, 1954; postgrad., Odessa Tech. Inst. Food, Odessa, 1957. Engring. diplomate. Lectr. Odessa Tech. Inst. Food and Refrigeration Industry, 1957-65, assoc. prof., 1965-86, prof., 1986-88; dep. rector Odessa State Acad. Refrigeration, 1988—. Author books, 1991, 93, 95; patentee in field. Recipient Charter of Honour for Pedagogical Activity, 1977, Order of Honour, 1981, Silver medal for achievements in USSR Nat. Economy, 1984; named Honoured Sci. and Engring. Worker of Ukrainian SSR, 1991. Mem. Odessa State Acad. Refrigeration (spl. sci. counsel for awarding sci. degrees), Odessa State of Food Techs. (spl. sci. counsel for awarding sci. degrees), European Assn. Internat. Edn., Internat. Acad. Refrigeration (v.p. Ukrainian br. 1995). Avocations: gardening, yachting, fishing, skiing. Office: Odessa State Acad Refriger, 1/3 Dvoryanskaya, 270026 Odessa Ukraine

CHEPURNOV, ALEXANDR ALEXEI, virology and biotechnology researcher; b. Chita, Russia, Aug. 24, 1951; s. Alexei Pavel and Zoretta Boris Chepurnov; m. Tat'yana Savost'yn Obushenko, July 8, 1978; 1 child, Arseniya. Grad., Irkutsk (Russia) State U., 1973; PhD, Siberian Inst. Physiology, Irkutsk, 1978; DSc, State Rsch. Ctr. Virology & Biotech., Novosibirsk, Russia, 1999. Postgrad. fellow Siberian Inst. Physiology and

Biochemistry, Irkutsk, 1973-76; scientist Ctrl. Siberian Bot. Garden, Novosibirsk, 1977-81; asst. prof. Agrl. U., Novosibirsk, 1981-83; staff scientist State Rsch. Ctr. Virology & Biotech. Vector, Novosibirsk, 1983-85, head lab., 1986—; cons. in field. Contbr. articles to profl. jours. Mem. Russian Soc. Biotech. Russian Orthodox. Avocation: travel. Home: Home 23 app 25, Koltsovo 630559, Russia Office: SRCVB Vector, Koltsovo 633159, Russia

CHÉREAU, PATRICE, theater, opera and film director; b. Lèzigne, France, Nov. 2, 1944; s. Jean-Baptiste and Marguerite (Pélicier) C. Ed., Lycèe Louis-le-Grand and Faculté de Lettres, Paris, 1958-62. Co-dir. Théatre National Populaire, 1972-81; dir. Théatre des Amandiers, Nanterre, 1982-90. Theatre prodns. include: L'Intervention, 1964, L'Affaire de la rue de Lourcine, 1966, Les Soldats, 1967, La Révolte au Marchè noir, 1968, Don Juan, L'Italienne a Alger, 1969, Richard II, Splendeur et Mort de Joaquin Murieta, 1970, La Finta Serva, 1971, Massacre à Paris, 1972, Toller, 1973, La Dispute, 1973, Lear, 1975, Peer Gynt, 1981, Les Paravents, 1983, Combat de Nègre et de Chiens, 1983, La Fausse Suivante, 1985, Quartett, 1985, Quai Ouest, 1986, Dans la solitude des Champs de Coton, 1987, Hamlet, 1987, 95, Le Retour au désert, 1988, Le Temps et la Chambre, 1991; operas include: L'Italiana in Algeri, 1969, The Tale of Hoffman, 1974, Der Ring des Nibelungen, Bayreuth, 1976-80, Lulu, 1979, Lucio Silla, 1985, Wozzeck, 1992-98, Don Giovanni, 1994-96; films include: La Chair de l'Orchidée, 1974, Judith Therpauve, 1978, L'Homme blessé, 1982, Hôtel de France, 1987, Le Temps et la Chambre, 1993, La Reine Margot, 1994 (Cannes Internat. Film Festival Jury Prize), Those Who Love Me Can Take the Train, 1998 (Cannes Film Festival 1998), Intimacy, 2000. Office: Artmedia, 10 ave Georges V, 75008 Paris France also: French Film 745 5th Ave New York NY 10151-0099

CHEREM, LAZARO, physician; b. Mexico City, Sept. 21, 1951; s. Elias and Victoria (Behar) C.; m. Monica A. Cherem, June 30, 1978; children: Deborah Joanna, Elias Daniel, Jessica Diane, Alex David. MD with honors, U. Guadalajara, Mex., 1973. Intern Dalhousie U., Halifax, N.S., Can., 1973-74; fellow Nat. Heart Inst., Mexico City, 1974-76; resident Mt. Sinai Sch. Medicine, N.Y.c., 1976-78; fellow Washington U. Med. Sch., St. Louis, 1978-80; asst. prof. medicine Nat. Heart Inst., Mexico City, 1980-82; ptnr., owner AKDHC, Ltd., Phoenix, 1982-95; ptnr., owner, v.p. Grupo Medico Lomas, Mexico City, 1995—; v.p. AKDHC, Ltd., Phoenix, 1988-93, pres., 1993-95. Mem. editl. bd. Anales Medicos, 1996—; contbr. articles to profl. jours. Mem. ACP. Republican. Jewish. Avocations: reading, music, internet. Home: Prolongacion Bosque Reforma, 1440 Torre II-601, 11700 Mexico City Mexico Office: Grupo Medico Lomas, TEAPA # 4 Lomas Virreyes, 11000 Mexico City Mexico

CHEREMISIN, ALEKSANDER ALEKSEEVICH, physicist, educator; b. Tobolsk, Russia, Nov. 6, 1951; s. Aleksey Prokopievich and Evdokia Jacoblevna (Bateegina) C.; m. Maria Davidovna Sopova, Jan. 17, 1974; children: Anna, Ksenya. PhD in Physics and Math., USSR Acad. Scis., 1980; D in Physics and Math., Krasnoyarsk State Tech. U., 1999. Engr. Novosibirsk Inst. Organic Chemistry, USSR Acad. Sci., 1979-81; assoc. prof. dept. physics Krasnoyarsk (Russia) State U., 1981-99, prof., 1999—, head atmospheric optics lab. Rsch. Phys. Engring. Inst., 1992—; sr. executor USSR Govt. Program Krasnoyarsk State U., 1986-91, head theoretical and exptl. space physics lab., 1986-91, head of structural methods lab., 1983-86, dep. dean dept. physics, 1981-85, co-organizer schs. for talented children, 1985-87. Contbr. articles to sci. and profl. jours. Grantee Scie. and Edn. State Com., Russia, 1996-2000. Mem. Dr.'s Club. Avocations: literature, classical music, recreational activities. Office: Krasnoyarsk State U Rsch Phys Engring Inst, PO Box 8678 Akademgorodok, 660036 Krasnoyarsk Russia

CHÉRET, ROGER, atomic engineering executive; b. St.-Brice-Sous-Foret, France, Nov. 25, 1939; m. Jacqueline Daniele Altschuller, July 6, 1973; 1 child, Emmanuel. Degree in engring., Ecole Poly., Paris, 1960; DSc, U. Poitiers, France, 1971. Dir. leader Commissariat a l'Energie Atomique, France, 1976-86, sci. dir. dep., 1986-89, dir. rsch., 1986, tech. inspector, 1989—, bd. dirs., 1986; tchr., Ecole Poly., 1973-85. Author: La Détonation des Explosifs Condensés, 1989; co-author: Classic Papers in Shock Compression Science Stringer, 1999; contbr. articles to profl. publs. Recipient Gen. Muteau prize Acad. Scis. Paris, 1979, Chevalier de l'Ordre Nat. Merit, 1976, Chevalier des Palmes Acad., 1982, Chevalier de l'Ordre Nat. Legion Honor, 1990. Office: Commn l'Energie Atomique, 33 Rue de la Federation, 75015 Paris France

CHERGINETS, VICTOR LEONIDOVITCH, chemist, researcher; b. Kiev, Ukraine, Sept. 30, 1962; s. Leonid Andreevitch and Anna Filippovna (Khod'kova) C.; m. Nadezhda Mikhailovna Lazareva, Dec. 3, 1988; 1 child, Anton. Degree, Kharkov State U., USSR, 1984; D, Kharkov State U., 1991. Jr. rschr. Inst. for Single Crystals, Kharkov, 1986-91, rschr., 1991-93, sr. rschr., 1993—. Contbr. articles to profl. jours. Sr. lt. Forces of Spl. Appointment, 1984-86. Recipient grant Internat. Sci. Found., 1993, Pres. of Ukraine, 1994, 96, ISSEP, 1998. Avocations: fishing, soccer, chess. Email addresses: cherginets@isc.kharkov.com, cherginets@isc.kharkov.ua. Home: Gagarin ave 2a ft60, Kharkov 61125, Ukraine Office: Inst for Single Crystals, Lenin ave 60, Kharkov 61001, Ukraine

CHERIAN, DHIRAJ CHANDAPILLA, strategic management executive, information technologist; b. Cochin, India, Dec. 7, 1968. B of Commerce, Bangalore (India) U., 1990; Hons. Diploma in Sys. Mgmt., Nat. Inst. Info. Tech., India, 1992; MBA in Euro-Mgmt., U. Libre de Bruxelles, Brussels, 1996. Sales mgr. Shell Products, Bangalore, 1990-93; country mgr. Transcend Group, Bangalore and Chgo., 1993-95; fin. initiatives mgr. Mitsubishi Corp., Tokyo, 1997—; bus. cons. Erin Group, Bangalore. Com. leader Table Tennis Assn. India, Bangalore, 1993; internat. projects mgr. Inst. Cultural Affairs, Tokyo and Phoenix, 1997. Mem. Knight Templars Japan (Chevalier 1997—). Fax: 407-852-1123. Home: 12504 Bohannon Blvd Orlando FL 32824-6062

CHERIAN, MATHEW PUNNACHALIL, pediatrician, consultant; b. Thiruvamkulam, Ernakulam, India, Sept. 5, 1949; s. Ipe and Kunjamma (Varkey) C.; m. Aleena Varkey, Dec. 31, 1978; children: Amit George, Arun Abraham, Anjali Maria. MB, BS, Calicut (India) Med. Coll., 1972; diploma in child health, Christian Med. Coll., Ludhiana, Punjab, India, 1976, MD in Pediatrics, 1977. Med. diplomate pediat. Royal Coll. Physicians Ireland. Jr. resident Sofdarjing Hosp., New Delhi, 1974, C.M.C. Hosp., Ludhiana, Punjab, India, 1975-76; registrar pediatrics C.M.C. Hosp., LLudhiana, Punjab, India, 1977-78; cons. pediatrician Med. Trust Hosp., Cochin, India, 1978-80; cons. pediatrician Aramco Med. Orgn., Rastanura, Saudi Arabia, 1980—, dir. clin. lab., 1994—. Contbr. articles to profl. jours. Chief donation campaign to India and Africa, 1997. Recipient scholarship Kerala U., 1966-67. Fellow Royal Coll. Physicians Ireland, Am. Coll. Tropical Medicine, Internat. Coll. Tropical Medicine; mem. Indian Acad. Pediatrics, Royal Coll. Physicians Ireland, N.Y. Acad. Sci. Avocations: stamp collecting, coin collecting, tennis, badminton, weight training. Home: Saudi Aramco, PO Box 1356, 31311 Ras Tanura Saudi Arabia

CHERIAN, VARGHESE IEPEN, psychologist, educator; b. Mepral, India, Feb. 24, 1941; arrived in South Africa,1992; s. Eapen and Sossammma Varghese; m. Lily Ninan, May 31, 1971; children: Bindu, Bilu. BSc, Kerala U., 1961, DSS, 1963; BEd, Mysore U., 1964; MA, Tribhuavan U., 1965, Kerala U., 1971; PhD, U. Wales, 1987. Asst. Nair Meml. Secondary Sch., India, 1965-66; gen. asst., warden Alwaye Settlement H.S., India, 1966-67; lectr. Govt. Victoria Coll., India, 1967-68, Peet Meml. Tng. Coll., India, 1969-71; lectr., dept. head Min. Edn., Zambia, 1972-82; head dept. ednl. rsch., dir. ednl. rsch. bur. U. Transkei, South Africa, 1982-91; prof., head dept. psychology edn. U. of the North, South Africa, 1992—. Co-author: An Educational Psychology for Schools in Africa, 1986; contbr. articles to profl. jours. Fellow Royal Coll. Preceptors (London, assoc.), Brit. Psychol. Soc.; mem. AAAS, South African Psychol. Soc., N.Y. Acad. Scis., Internat. Assn. Cognitive Edn. Avocations: swimming, reading, TV and radio programs, music, pets. Office: U of the North, Turfloop PBX 1106, 0727 Sovenga South Africa

CHERIS, ELAINE GAYLE INGRAM, business owner; b. Ashford, Ala., Jan. 8, 1946; m. Samuel David Cheris, June 8, 1980; 1 child, Zachariah Adam Abraham. BS, Troy State U., 1971. Aquatics dir. Yale U., New Haven, 1976-79; owner, CEO Cheyenne Fencing Soc., Denver, 1980—; chmn. organizing com. World Fencing Championships, 1989, World Jr./ Cadet Fencing Championships, 1993; nat. devel. coord. Modern Pentathlon, 1998. Author: Handbook for Parents - Fencing, 1988, 2d edit., 1992; editor Yofen Mag., 1988-90, 1992—. Mem. Gov.'s Coun. on Sports and Fitness, Colo., 1990-2000; commr. Colo. State Games-Fencing, 1989-95; nat. chair jr. cadet, youth. Modern Penthathlon, 1997—; sec. U.S. Olypmians, Colo. chpt., 1999—. Mem. U.S. Olympic Foil Team, 1980, 88 (6th place fencing), U.S. Olympic Epee Team, 96 (8th place, oldest athlete on U.S. team), ranked #1 U.S. Fencing Women's Epee, 1999-2000, mem. U.S. Pan-Am. Games Team, 1987 (Gold medal women's foil team), 1991 (Gold medal women's epee team, 1999, Pan Am. Games Epee Team; named Sportswoman of Yr. Fencing, YWCA, 1980, 81, 82, to Sportswoman Hall of Fame, 1982; mem. U.S. World Championship Fencing Team, 1982, 83, 85, 87, 90, 91, 92, 93, 98, 99, U.S. Maccabiah Fencing Team, 1981 (1 gold, 1 silver medal); U.S. world team coach U.S. Modern Penthathlon; recipient Gold Medal of Honor from Fedn. Internat. d'Escrime, 1993. Mem. AAPHERD, U.S. Fencing Assn. (youth chmn. 1988-90, editor Youth mag., 1988-90, 92—, chmn. Colo. divsn., 1992-94), Fedn. Internat. d'Escrime (chmn. Atlanta fencing project '96, chmn. World Fencing Day 1994). Jewish. E-mail: elainecheris@aol.com. Office: Cheyenne Fencing Soc 5818 E Colfax Ave Denver CO 80220-1507

CHERKAOUI, MOHAMED, sociologist; b. Boujad, Morocco, Apr. 22, 1945; s. Abdelaziz and Saadia (Moutawakil) C.; m. Khadija Sadif, Feb. 17, 1985; children: Youssef, Selma, Anas. MA in Philosophy, Sorbonne, Paris, 1967, MA in Sociology, 1972, BSc in Stats., 1972, PhD in Sociology, 1975, PhD in Scis. Humaines, 1981. Asst. prof. Sorbonne, Paris, 1972-73; cons. Private Co., Paris, 1974-75; rsch. officer Nat. Ctr. for Sci. Rsch., Paris, 1976-85, rsch. dir., 1986—; prof. U. Lausanne, 1989-94, Sorbonne, 1995—; prof. U. Geneva, 1995—; cons. French Min. of Planning, Paris, 1976-85, UNESCO, Paris, 1975; expert and cons. Nat. Com., CNRS, 1995—. Author: Les Paradoxes de la Réussite Scolaire, 1979, Les Changements du Système Éducatif en France, 1982, Sociologie de l'education, 1986, Naissance d'une Science Sociale, 1998; co-author: The Classical Tradition in Sociology, 1997, Ctrl. Currents in Social Theory, 1999, Dictionnaire de Sociologie, 1999, Le Suicide. Un Sèecle apreès Durkéum, 2000. Mem. French Sociol. Soc., Internat. Sociol. Assn. Avocation: collecting 19th century English and French silver. Office: 54 Blvd Raspail, Maison des Scis de l'Homme, 75006 Paris France

CHERKIN, ADINA, interpreter, translator; b. Geneva, Nov. 22, 1921; came to U.S., 1940; d. Herz N. and Genia (Kodriansky) Mantchik; m. Arthur Cherkin, Mar. 14, 1943 (div. Sept. 1980); children: Della Peretti, Daniel Craig. BA in Premed. Studies, UCLA, 1942, MA in Russian Linguistics, 1977. Pvt. practice med. interpreter in 5 langs. L.A., 1942-80; translator UCLA Med. Sch., 1970-79; pres. acad. forum Jewish studies Herz Mantchik Amity Cir., L.A., 1973-99. Author: Terse Verse and Oodles of Doodles, 1999; author numerous poems. Active L.A. Internat. Vis. Coun., 1991—; pub. rels. Judge Stanley Mosk's Campaign, L.A., 1960; vol. Senator Cranston's Campaign, 1960. Recipient Community Svc. award L.A. City Coun., 1992. Mem. Am. Soc. for Technion Israel Inst. Tech. (bd. regents). Avocations: dance improvisation, figure skating. Home and Office: 2369 N Vermont Ave Los Angeles CA 90027-1253

CHERMANN, JEAN CLAUDE, virologist; b. Paris, Mar. 23, 1939; s. Camille Andre and Benbeneda (Montoya) C.; m. Pearron Daniele, Dec. 22, 1962; children: Jean Francois, Olivier. Bachelor, Michelet, 1959; Maitrise Biochemistry, Paris U., 1963, PhD, 1967. Rsch. asst. Pasteur Inst., Paris, 1963-77, head lab., 1977-87; chief viral oncology lab., Pasteur Inst., Paris; rsch. dir. Insti. Nat. de le Recherche Medicale, Marseille, France, 1988—; vis. scientist Nat. Cancer Inst., Bethesda, Md., 1971. Decorated Ordre Nat. du Merite Pres. de la Republique (France), Ordre Nat. Legion d'Honneur(France); co-recipient King Faisal Internat. prize Medicine, 1993. Developer with Francoise Barre-Sinoussi and Luc Montagnier isolation of HIV-the causative agt. of AIDS. Office: Campus Univ Luminy Bt INSERM, Laboratoire de Recherches, F-13273 Marseille 9, France Address: care Inst Pasteur, 25-28 rue du Dr Roux, 75015 Paris France

CHERMASHENTSEV, VALERIJ MICHAILOVICH, chemist; b. Novosibirsk, Russia, June 18, 1946; s. Michail Petrovich and Alexandra Federovna (Varenicheva) C.; m. Galina Konstantinovna Rubina, Aug. 23, 1969; 1 child, Andrej. BS in Chemistry, Novosibirsk State U., 1969; MS in Chem. Scis., Inst. of Neorganic Chemistry, 1980; PhD of Chem. Scis., State Sci. Ctr., Koltsovo, Russia, 1990. Rschr. Inst. Catalysis, Novosibirsk, Russia, 1969-72, Inst. Neorganic Chemistry, Novosibirsk, 1972-82; head of lab. State Sci. Ctr. Vector, Novosibirsk, 1982-93; head of dept. Inst. Bioorganic Chemistry, Novosibirsk, 1993-96; head of lab. State of Architecture Civil Engring. U., Novosibirsk, 1996—. Mem. N.Y. Acad. Scis. Avocations: chess, Go. Home: Morskoj 20-3, 630090 Novosibirsk Russia Office: State Arch Civil Engring U, 113 Leningradskaj Ave, 630090 Novosibirsk Russia

CHERMITI, AMOR, agronomist, researcher; b. Kabbara, Tunisia, 1956; s. Ali and Fadha Chermiti; m. Dalila Rejaibi, July 28, 1984; children: Ines, Foued. MS in Agronomic Engring., U. Tunis, Tunisia, 1982; PhD, Cath. U. Louvain, Belgium, 1994. Author: The Role of Cereal Straws in Animal Feeding, 1999; patentee in field; contbr. articles to profl. publs. Mem. Agronomic Rschrs. Tunisian Assn. (pres.). Address: chermiti.amor@iresa.agrinet.tn. Office: Tunisian Agrl Rsch Nat Inst, Rue Hedi Karray, 2049 Ariana Tunisia

CHERN, JIAMING, chemical engineering educator, researcher; b. Chia-Yi, Taiwan, June 12, 1960; s. Far-Shong and Ling-Tsi (Wu) C.; m Shu-Min Hou, Aug. 1, 1987; children: Frederick, Franklin. BS, Nat. Taiwan U., 1982; MS, U. Del., 1987; PhD, Pa. State U., 1990. Rsch. engr. USI Far East Corp., Taipei, 1986-87; sr. project engr. GTE Products Corp., Towanda, Pa., 1990-92; assoc. prof. Tatung Inst. Tech., Taipei, 1993-99; prof. chem. engring. Tatung U., Taipei, 2000—. Patentee in field. Founder Taipei Human Svc. Soc., 1994, chmn., 1994-96. Mem. AIChE, Am. Chem. Soc., Chinese Inst. Chem. Engrs. Avocations: reading, music, drama, opera. Office: Tatung U, 40 Chungshan N Rd 3d Sec, Taipei 104, Taiwan

CHERNENKO, VLADIMIR ANDREYEVICH, physicist, researcher, educator; b. Lokhviza, Poltava, Ukraine, May 14, 1953; s. Andrey Illich and Maria Grigorevna (Chernenko) Shish; m. Larisa Zakharivna Stonoga, May 16, 1979; children: Vladislav, Eugen. MS, Moscow State U., 1975, Candidate of Scis., 1980. Asst. Moscow State U., 1975-78; jr. rsch. scientist Inst. Metal Physics, Nat. Acad. Scis. Ukraine, Kiev, 1978-85, sr. rsch. scientist, 1985-95; sr. rsch. scientist Inst. Magnetism Nat. Acad. Scis. Ukraine, Kiev, 1996—; invited prof. U. Balearic Islands, Palma, Spain, 1993, 95, 96, 98, 99, 2000, Univ. VI, Paris, 1997; cons. Inst. Electrotechnico Nat., Galileo Ferraris, Torino, Italy. Contbr. articles to profl. jours.; inventor in field. Gledden Sr. Vis. fellow U. Western Australia, Nedlands, 1997—. Mem. Ukrainian Phys. Soc. Avocations: winter swimming, cultivation of vegetables, repairing old cars. Home: Priozyornaya St 8 Apt 12, 03211 Kiev Ukraine Office: Inst Magnetism, Vernadsky St 36-B, 03142 Kiev Ukraine

CHERNETSOF, NIKITA, zoologist, researcher; b. St. Petersburg, Russia, Sept. 28, 1972; s. Sevir and Milena (Rozhdestvenskaya) C. MSc, St. Petersburg State U., 1994, postgrad., 1996-99. Rsch. asst. Biol. Sta. Rybachy, Russia, 1994-96, rschr., 1999—. Contbr. articles to profl. jours.; translator. Adminstrn. of St. Petersburg grantee, 1997. E-mail: nchernetsov!bioryb.koenig.su. Office: Biol Sta Rybachy, 32 Pobedy, Rybachy, Kaliningrad Russia 238535

CHERNEY, JAMES ALAN, lawyer; b. Boston, Mar. 19, 1948; s. Alvin George and Janice (Elaine) Cherney; m. Linda Bienenfeld. BA, Tufts U., 1969; JD, Columbia U., 1973. Bar: Ill. 1973, U.S. Supreme Ct. 1977, U.S. Ct. Appeals (7th cir.) 1979, U.S. Ct. Appeals (3d cir.) 1982, U.S. Ct. Appeals (10th cir.) 1984, U.S. Ct. Appeals (8th and 9th cirs.) 1987. Assoc. Kirkland & Ellis, Chgo., 1973-76; assoc. Hedlund, Hunter & Lynch, Chgo., 1976-79, ptnr., 1979-82; ptnr. Latham & Watkins, Chgo., 1982—. Mem. ABA, Chgo. Bar Assn., Saddle and Cycle Club (sec. 1989, v.p. 1991-92, pres. 1992-94). Office: Latham & Watkins Sears Tower Ste 5800 Chicago IL 60606-6306

CHERNIAK, SAUL SAMUILOVICH, materials science educator; b. Kursk, Russia, Mar. 24, 1926; s. Samuil V. and Hana A. (Butinskaya) C.; m. Idea G. Kudasheva, Nov. 4, 1948; 1 child, Anna S. Lontsikh. Degree, Mining and Metall. Inst., Irkutsk, Russia, 1953, PhD, 1965, D of Tech. Scis., 1973. Mem. Acad. of Transport of Russian Fedn., N.Y. Acad. Scis. Grinder Def. Works, Penza, Russia, 1941-43; foreman technologist Irkutsk Heavy Engring. Plant, 1946-57, chief metallographic lab., chief ctrl. lab. of plant, 1957-82; chief dept. metal engring. and materials sci. Irkutsk Inst. Rlwy. Transport Engrs., 1982—; cons. Irkutsk Heavy Engring. Plant, 1982—. Author: High Manganese Steel in Dredge Construction, 1996, Steels of Scooping Mechanisms of Mining Machines for Siberia and Extreme North, 1997; contbr. articles to profl. jours. Home: ul Krasnokazachya 2-10, 664007 Irkutsk Russia Office: Inst Rlwy Transport Engrs, ul Chernyshevskogo 15, 664074 Irkutsk Russia

CHERNIAKOV, MIKHAIL, engineering educator, researcher; b. Nikolaev, Russia, June 8, 1950; arrived in Australia, 1995; s. Solomon Cherniakov and Raisa (Egudic) Cherniakova; m. Irina Levit, Oct. 24, 1976; children: Pavel, Alexei, Andrei. B, MIEE, Moscow, 1974, PhD, 1981, DSc, 1992. Engr. MIEE, Moscow, 1974-81, sr. rschr., 1981-85, head R&D lab., 1985-93, prof., 1993-95; sr. lectr. U. Queensland, Brisbane, Australia, 1995-2000, U. Birmingham, Edgbaston, Australia, 2000—. Contbr. articles to profl. jours. Office: U Birmingham Sch Electronic, and Elec Engring, Edgbaston B15 2TT, England

CHERNIN, RALPH, construction executive; b. Wilkes-Barre, Pa., Apr. 3, 1937; s. Alex and Yetta Chernin; m. Adeline Marilyn Chernin, Feb. 13, 1960; children: Alan, Susan, David. Grad. h.s., Wilkes-Barre. Estimator David M. Abel, Miami, Fla., 1954-58; owner MRC Constrn., Miami, 1958-64; dir. constrn. melvin Simon & Assocs., Indpls., 1964-72; owner Ralph Chernin & Assocs., Miami, 1972-94; v.p., chmn. Konover Constrn. Corp., Miami, 1994—. Bd. dirs. Am. H.S., Miami, 1989-94, Miami Jewish Fedn., 1982-92, Miami Jewish Home, 1992—. With USMC, 1991-93. Avocation: golf. Office: Konover Constrn Corp S 700 W Hillsboro Blvd Deerfield Beach FL 33441-1612

CHERNISH, STANLEY MICHAEL, physician; b. N.Y.C., Jan. 27, 1924; s. Michael B. and Veronica (Hodon) C.; m. Lelia M. Higgins, June 19, 1949; 1 child, Dwight. BA, U. N.C., 1945; MD, Georgetown U., 1949. Diplomate Nat. Bd. Med. Examiners, Am. Bd. Internal Medicine. Intern Washington Gen. Hosp., 1949-51; resident Marion County Gen. Hosp., Indpls., 1953-55; with clin. rsch. div. Eli Lilly & Co., Indpls., 1954-85; from asst. to assoc. in medicine Sch. Medicine, Ind. U., 1957-66, asst. prof., 1967-76, clin. assoc. prof., 1977-80, assoc. prof., 1981-94; rsch. cons. Meth. Hosp., Indpls., 1986—; mem. vis. staff Marion County Gen. Hosp., 1965-94. Contbr. more than 115 articles to profl. jours., chpts. to books. Served with USNR, 1943-45, 50-53, ret. comdr. 1984. Fellow ACP, Am. Coll. Gastroenterology; mem. Am. Coll. Clin. Pharmacology and Therapeutics, AMA (Physicians Recognition award in continuing med. edn. 1972—), Ind. State Med. Soc. (mem. subcommn. on accreditation), Marion County Med. Soc., Assn. Am. Physicians and Surgeons, Am. Fedn. Clin. Rsch., Am. Gastroent. Assn., Sci. Rsch. Soc., Sigma Xi.

CHERNITSKII, ALEXANDER ALEKSANDROVICH, physicist; b. Leningrad, Russia, Mar. 16, 1955; s. Alexander Nikolaevich and Zoya Stanislavovna (Dobrzhanskaya) C.; m. Lubov Ilinichna Generalskaya, Nov. 19, 1976 (div. June 1984); children: Sergei, Konstantin; m. Irina Anatolievna Korochkina, Apr. 6, 1994; children: Ekaterina, Mihail. Grad., Inst. Fine Mechs. and Optics, Leningrad, Russia, 1982, PhD, 2000. Rschr. Leningrad Inst. Fine Mechs. and Optics, 1982-85, All Union Elec. Machine-Bldg. Inst., Leningrad, 1985-88, St. Petersburg Electro-Tech. U., Russia, 1988—. Contbr. articles to Theoretical and Mathematical Physics, Helvetica Physica Acta, Jour. High Energy Physics. With Russian Mil., 1973-75. Home: Krasnogo Kursanta 7-14, 197110 Saint Petersburg Russia Office: St Petersburg Electrotech U, 5 Prof Popov St, 197376 Saint Petersburg Russia

CHERNOGUBOVSKY, MICHAEL ALEXANDROVICH, physicist, researcher; b. Leningrad, USSR, June 22, 1957; s. Alexander Victorovich and Nina Mikhaylovna (Bordukova) C.; m. Nadejda Victornovna Mitina, Sept. 8, 1984; 1 child, Ilia Mikhaylovich. Engr., Leningrad Electroengrin. Inst., 1980; PhD, Leningrad, 1988; MS in Radioengring cum laude, D in Physics and Maths. Asst. Leningrad Electroengring. Inst., 1975-80; engr., 1980-85, researcher, 1981-85; sr. rsch. scientist D.V. Efremov Inst., St. Petersburg, 1985-95; leading researcher D.V. Efremov Inst., 1999—; rsch. fellow Japan Atomic Energy Rsch. Inst., Tokai-mura, 1995-98. Contbr. article to profl. jour.; patentee in field. Avocations: classical music, fishing. Home: Apt 27, Makarova Emb 18, 199053 Saint Petersburg Russia

CHERNOMYRDIN, VIKTOR STEPANOVICH, Russian government official; b. Apr. 9, 1938. Operator Oil Refinery, 1960-67; mem. CPSU, 1961-91; with Orsk City Com., 1967-73; dep. chief engr., dir. Orenburg Gas Plant, 1973-78; with CPSU Ctrl. Com., 1978-82, 86-90; dep. min., chief of all union production, gas exploitation USSR Gas Industry, 1982-85, min., 1985-89; dep. USSR Supreme Soviet, 1987-89; chmn. bd. dirs. Gasprom, 1989-92; dep. prime min. Ministry of Fuel and Energy, 1992; chair. Coun. of Ministers, 1992—; chairman Russian Federation, Russia, 1993-98; chmn. bd. All-Russian Movement-Our Home, 1995—; chmn. Our Home is Russia Party; bd. dirs. Gazprom Oil Co. Office: Gazprom, 16 Nametkina, 117884 Moscow B-420, Russia*

CHERNOV, STANISLAV, physicist; b. Leninskoie, USSR, Mar. 27, 1938; s. Alexander and Roza (Kantor) C.; m. Maya Pleple, Feb. 26, 1966; children: Lev, Elena. MS in Physics, U. Latvia, Riga, 1962. Engr. semiconductor plant, Riga, 1962-64, technol. dept. head, 1964; postgrad. student Inst. Physics, USSR Acad. Sci., Riga, 1964-67, rsch. officer, 1967-85, head of lab., 1985-90; head of lab. Inst. Solid State Physics, U. Latvia, Riga, 1991—. Office: Inst Solid State Physics, U Latvia, 8 Kengaraga St, LV-1063 Riga Latvia

CHERNOV, VLADIMIR IVANOVICH, cardiologist; b. Tomsk, Russia, Apr. 21, 1962; s. Ivan Petrovich and Nadejda Anisimovna (Bezzubceva) C.; m. Nina Nikolaevna Bezmaternyh, May 20, 1988; children: Ekaterina, Dmitriy. MD, Tomsk (Russia) Med. Inst., 1985; PhD, Inst. Cardiology, Tomsk, 1990. Cardiologist Inst. Cardiology, Tomsk, 1985-90, sr. rschr., 1990—. Author: Myocardial Scintigraphy in Nuclear Cardiology, 1997; contbr. articles o profl. jours. Recipient awards 2d Congress of Cardiologists Ctrl. Asia, 1996, European Academia Young Scientists, 1996, Tomsk Region Young Scientists, 1996. Mem. European Soc. Nuclear Medicine, Russian Soc. Nuclear Medicine. Office: Inst Cardiology, Kievskaya St 111/2, 634012 Tomsk Russia

CHERNOW, BART, critical care physician; b. N.Y.C., June 26, 1947. BA, Queens Coll., 1968; MD, SUNY, N.Y.C., 1976. Internal medicine intern Nat. Naval Med. Ctr., Bethesda, Md., 1976-77, internal medicine resident, 1977-79, endocrine fellow, 1979-81; dir. rsch. dept. critical care medicine Bethesda Naval Hosp., 1981-85, head acad. affairs, 1985-86; assoc. prof. anesthesia Harvard Med. Sch., Boston, 1986-90; assoc. dir. surg. ICU Mass. Gen. Hosp., Boston, 1986-90; prof. medicine, anesthesia and critical care Johns Hopkins U. Sch. Medicine, Balt., 1990-99; physician-in-chief Sinai Hosp., Balt., 1990-97; program dir. John Hopkins U./Sinai Hosp. Program in Internal Medicine, Balt., 1990-97; vice dean for rsch. and tech. Sch. Medicine Johns Hopkins U. Sch. Medicine, Balt., 1997-99; pres. GMP Cos. Inc., Ft. Lauderdale, Fla., 1999—; adj. prof. medicine, anesthesia and critical care Johns Hopkins U. Sch. Medicine, 1999—. Editor: Pharmacologic Approach to the Critically Ill Patient, 1983, 88, 94; editor-in-chief: Critical Care Medicine, 1990-97. Comdr. med. corps USNR, 1969-86. Recipient Achievement award Am. Coll. Nutrition, 1995. Fellow ACP (master), Am. Coll. Critical Care Medicine; mem. Soc. Critical Care Medicine (Presdl. citation 1997), Am. Coll. Chest Physicians (regent 1990-98, pres. 1996-97, master fellow CHEST found. pres. 1996-99). Fax: 954-745-3511. Home: 2100 N Ocean Blvd Ph 30 Fort Lauderdale FL 33305-1940 Office: GMP Cos Inc Ste 1701 One E Broward Blvd Fort Lauderdale FL 33301

CHERNS, DAVID, physicist, educator; b. Lemsford, Eng., May 31, 1948; s. Aubrey and Joan (Relleen) C.; m. Gillian Grace Jeffrey, Aug. 19, 1972;

children: Helen, Peter. BA in Nat. Scis. with hons., Cambridge (Eng.) U., 1970, PhD, 1973, MA, 1974. Rsch. fellow Atomic Energy Rsch. Establishment, Harwell, Eng., 1974-77; rsch. asst. dept. materials Oxford U., 1977-83; lectr. dept. physics Bristol (Eng.) U., 1983-91, reader dept. physics, 1991—; vis. scientist IBM, Yorktown Heights, N.Y., 1980; dir. advanced rsch. workshop NATO, 1987; chmn. organizing com. Electron Microscopy and Analysis Group Conf., 1993; sec. electron microscopy analysis group Inst. Physics, 1990-92, chmn., 1992-94; mem. com. Condensed Matter and Materials Physics, Inst. Physics, 1989-92. Author chpts. in books, editor books, contbr. over 140 articles to profl. publs. Grantee in field. Mem. Royal Mircoscopical Soc. Avocations: squash, cycling, gardening, reading. Office: HH Wills Physics Lab, U Bristol Tyndall Ave, Bristol BS8 1TL, England

CHERNY, DAVID EDWARD, lawyer; b. Brookline, Mass., Jan. 21, 1957; s. Jacob and Anne (Gray) C.; m. Elise Joan Sallen, June 4, 1978; children: Michael Aaron, Allyson Jill. BSBA cum laude, Boston U., 1978; JD cum laude, Suffolk U., 1981. Bar: Mass. 1981, U.S. Dist. Ct. Mass. 1982, U.S. Tax Ct. 1982, U.S. Ct. Appeals (1st cir.) 1982, U.S. Supreme Ct. 1985, Tex. 1990. Assoc. Atwood & Wright, Boston, 1981-84, Jacob M. Atwood P.C., Boston, 1984-86; ptnr. Atwood & Cherny, Boston, 1986—; prin. Algonquin Assocs., Boston, 1986—; pres. Geneva/Roth Holdings Ltd., 1989—. Fellow Am. Acad. Matrimonial Lawyers, Internat. Acad. Matrimonial Lawyers; mem. ABA, Mass. Bar Assn., Boston Bar Assn., Assn. Trial Lawyers Am., Mass. Acad. Trial Attys. (lectr. family law), Blue Hill Country Club, Algonquin Club, Phi Delta Phi. Office: Atwood & Cherny 393 Commonwealth Ave Boston MA 02115-1802

CHERNYAK (CHARNIAK), ARKADIY ALEXANDROVICH, mathematician, researcher, educator; b. Kremenchug, Poltavskaya, USSR, July 12, 1955; s. Alexandr and Asja (Amrom) C.; m. Zhanna Albertovna, Apr. 4, 1976; 1 child, Dasha. MS of Math. with honors, Byelorussian State U., Minsk, USSR, 1977; PhD of Math., Math. Inst. Acad. Sci., Minsk, USSR, 1986, DS, 2000. Engr., mathematician, programmer Inst. Problems of Reliability Machine, Minsk, 1977-82, from jr. rsch. scientist to rsch. scientist, 1982-87, sr. rsch. scientist, 1987-91, leading rsch. scientist, 1992-97; sr. lectr. Byelurus State Econ. U., Minsk, 1997-2000; prof. Belarus State U., Minsk, 2000; prof. math. Internat. Inst. Social and Econ. Rels., 2000—. Author 3 textbooks on math.; contbr. articles to profl. jours.; inventor in field. Named Sr. Rsch. Sci., State Sci. Com., Moscow, 1990, Laureat Premium Acad. Sci., Soros Internat. Found., Minsk, 1990. Mem. Am. Math. Soc. (reviewer 1983—). Avocations: poetry, swimming. Home: Russiyanova 10 299, Minsk 220141, Belarus Office: Kazinca Str 21, Minsk 220099, Belarus

CHERNYAKOV, SERGEI MIKHAILOVICH, physicist, researcher; b. Port Vladimir, Murmansk, Russia, Jan. 29, 1950; s. Mikhail Vasilevich and Stepanida Maksimovna (Egolaeva) C.; children: Ilya, Julia. Diploma, U. Petrozavodsk, Russia, 1972. Comdr. platoon Soviet Army, Pechenga, Russia, 1972-74; engr. Polar Geophys. Inst., Murmansk, 1974-85, scientist, 1985-96; head of obs. Polar Geophys. Unit, Murmansk, 1996—; pres. SM LLC, 1992—; lectr. Murmansk State Tchg. Inst., 1998—. Contbr. articles to jours. in field. Leader Komsomol Orgn., Polar Geophys. Inst., Murmansk, 1976-80, dep. sec. Communist Party, 1980-81. Grantee Internat. Sci. Found., 1993. Mem. European-Asian Geophys. Soc., Nat. Philosophy Alliance, Interstellar Propulsion Soc., Nat. Geog. Soc. Avocations: music, skiing, travel. Home: 45 Kirova St Apt 3, 183032 Murmansk Russia Office: Polar Geophys Inst, 15 Khalturina St, 183010 Murmansk Russia

CHERNYKH, VALENTIN PETROVICH, chemist, educator; b. Rechitsa, Russia, Jan. 5, 1940; s. Piotr Kouszmich Chernykh and Ekaterina Petrovna Starostina; m. Valentina Frankovna Bednarchuk, Apr. 30, 1987; children: Yulia Valentinovna, Vladislava Valentinovna. Pharmacist, Pharm. Inst., Kharkov, Ukraine, 1959, M in Pharmacy, 1964, D in Pharmacy, 1976, D in Chemistry, 1991. Lectr. Pharm. Inst., Kharkov, 1967-71, asst. prof., 1971-78, vice dean, 1971; dean pharmacy faculty Pharm. Inst., 1971-74; vice rector Pharm. Inst., Kharkov, 1976-80, prof. organic chemistry, 1978—, head, organic chemistry dept., 1979—; rector Ukrainian Acad. Pharmacy, Kharkov, 1980—. Author: Handbook for Laboratory Work and Seminars in Organic Chemistry, 1980, 2d edit., 1991, Pharmacology of Sulphanilamide and Sulphamide Drugs: Pharmacokinetics, Pharmadynamics, Pharmacotherapy, 1982, 2d edit., 1991, Organic Chemistry: Textbook for Pharmacy Students, 3 vols., 1993, 95, 97, Hepatic Diseases and Diseases of Biliferous Tract: Cholelithic Diseases, Hepatitis, Cirrhosis, Cancer, 1994, Diabetes Mellitus, 1994, Gastric and Duodenal Diseases: Gastritis, Ulcer, Cancer, 1995, Hypertension, 1995, Large Intestine Diseases, 1996; patentee in field.; contbr. articles to profl. jours.; editor-in-chief Visnic Pharmatsiyi Jour., 1992—. Dept. Dist. Coun. People's Deps., Kharkov, 1982; dep. City Coun. People's Deps., Kharkov, 1985, 87; chmn. Rep. Com. Pharmacy, 1980—; mem. state awards com. in sci. and engring., Kiev, 1996—; mem. pharmacol. com., Pharmacopeia Com. of Ukraine, Kiev, 1992—. Recipient order for svcs. III grade, Govt. Ukraine, 1996, order of Red Banner of Labor, 1986, badge of honor, 1971. Mem. Ukrainian Scientific Soc. Pharmacists (vice chmn. 1980—, assoc. mem.), Nat. Acad. Scis. Ukraine. Avocations: photography, music, singing. Office: Nat Ukrainian Acad Pharmacy, Pushkinskaya Str 53, 310002 Kharkov Ukraine

CHERNYSHEV, EVGENII ANDREEVICH, chemistry researcher, chemistry educator; b. Moscow, Feb. 16, 1928; s. Andrew Borisovich and Leokadiya Romanovna (Vol'skaya) C.; m. Tat'yana Ivanovna Grigos, Nov. 10, 1950 (Oct. 1971); 1 child, Andrei; m. Galina L'vovna Shiplevskaya, Feb. 23, 1974; 1 child, Anna. Chem. Engr., Coll., Moscow, 1949; PhD, Postgrad., Moscow, 1952; D in Chemistry, U. Moscow, 1963. Rschr. Inst. Organic Chemistry, Acad. Sci. USSR, Moscow, 1952-55, prof., 1969, sr. rschr., 1955-65; head dept. Sci. Rsch. Inst. Chemistry and Tech. Organoelement Compounds, Moscow, 1965-70, head lab., 1970-73, dept. dir., 1973-75; dir., chmn. coun. State Rsch. Ctr., Moscow, 1975-94; mem. couns. Moscow Acad. Fine Chem. Tech., 1985—, chair dept. chemistry and tech. organoelement compounds, 1988—; gen. dir. State Rsch. Ctr., Moscow, 1994—; mem. couns. Inst. Organoelement Compounds, Acad. Sci. RF, Moscow, 1975—. Author: Synthesis of the Organosilicon Monomers, 1961; mem. editl. bd. Khimicheskaya Promyshlennost. Recipient Order of Red Banner of Labour, Govt. USSR, 1980, Nat. Prize of USSR for Novel Chems., Govt. USSR, 1984, S. Korolev Medal for Space Rsch., Ctr. for Space Rsch., 1988, Badge of Honour, RF Pres., 1998; named Honoured Scientist of RF, Pres. of RF, 1994, academical of Internat. Acad. for Integration Sci. Bus, 2000. Avocations: gardening, floriculture, plant-growing. Office: SRC RF GNIIChTEOS, 38 shosse Entuziastov, 111123 Moscow Russia

CHÉRON, BRUNO JEAN MICHEL, manufacturing executive; b. Mulhouse, France, June 25, 1976; s. Etienne and Annie Chéron. Degree in engring., Ecole Poly., Palaiseau, France, 1997; MS, MIT, 1998. Rsch. asst. Russian Acad. Sci., Novosibirsk, 1997, MIT, Cambridge, Mass., 1998; tech. engr. Procter & Gamble, Euskirchen, Germany, 1998-99, Mequinenza, Spain, 1999—. 2d lt. French Air Force, 1994-95. Mem. Sigma Xi. Avocation: basketball. Home: 33 Rue de Hirsingue, 68200 Mulhouse France

CHERPITEL, DIDIER J., international organization executive; b. France, 1944; married; 3 children. M in Polits. and Econs., MBA in Econs. From trainee banker to mng. dir. French oper. J.P. Morgan, 1971; mng. dir. Security Capital Group, London; sec. gen. Internat. Fedn. Red Cross and Red Crescent Soc., Geneva. Vol. tchr. adult evening classes, Abidjan, Ivory Coast. Office: Internat Fedn Red Cross &, PO Box 372, CH-1211 Geneva Switzerland*

CHERRY, BARBARA WATERMAN, speech and language pathologist, physical therapist; b. Norfolk, Va., June 25, 1949; d. Robert Bullock and Dorothy Estelle (Walsh) Waterman; m. Albert Glen Cherry, Sept. 17, 1977; 1 child, Dorothy Louise. BS in Phys. Therapy, U. Fla., 1972, MA in Speech-Lang. Pathology, 1982. Lic. phys. therapist, speech and lang. pathologist, Fla.; cert. tchr., Fla. Staff phys. therapist Retreat for the Sick Hosp., Richmond, Va., 1973-75; clin. instr. in phys. therapy Sch. of Rehab. Scis., Tehran, Iran, 1975-76; staff phys. therapist Sulmaniya Hosp., Manama, Bahrain, 1976-77, Cathedral Rehab. Ctr., Jacksonville, Fla., 1978-80; staff speech-lang. pathologist S. Allen Smith Clinic, Jacksonville, Fla., 1982-87, Mt. Herman Exceptional Child Ctr., Jacksonville, Fla., 1987-91, Duval County Sch. System, Jacksonville, Fla., 1991—. Mem. Am. Speech, Lang., and Hearing Assn., Am. Phys. Therapy Assn., Phi Kappa Phi. Episcopalian. Home: 8821 Ivey Rd Jacksonville FL 32216-3369 Office: Mt Herman Exceptional Student Ctr 1741 Francis St Jacksonville FL 32209

CHERRY, BRAD CHARLES, real estate sales professional; b. L.A., July 23, 1962; s. Robert Thomas and Tay Ann Cherry; m. Amanda Palmer, Oct. 5, 1984; children: Jessica, Kelly, Brett. BSBA, U. So. Calif., 1984. Sales agt. Coldwell Banker, Charlotte, N.C., 1985-92, Trammell Crow Co., Charlotte, 1992—. Avocation: tennis. E-mail: bcherry@trammellcrow.com. Home: 2612 Whitney Hill Rd Charlotte NC 28226-4342 Office: Trammell Crow Co 121 W Trade St Ste 1900 Charlotte NC 28202-1161

CHERRY, KENNETH JEROME, JR., surgeon, educator; b. Richmond, Va., Oct. 22, 1947. MD, U. Va., 1974. Diplomate Am. Bd. Surgery, Gen. Vascular Surgery. Intern, resident surgery U. Va., Charlottesville, 1974-80; resident vascular surgery U. Calif. San Francisco, 1980-81; prof. surgery Mayo Sch. Medicine, Rochester, Minn., 1981—; surgeon Rochester Meth. Hosp., St. Mary's Hosps., Rochester. Mem. ACS, Internat. Soc. Cardiovascular Surgeons, Midwestern Vascular Surg. Soc., Peripheral Vascular Soc., Soc. for Vascular Surgeons. Home: 3581 Wright Rd SW Rochester MN 55902-1416 Office: Mayo Clin West6 B Rochester MN 55905-0001

CHERRY, RICHARD JOHN, biophysicist; b. Hitchin, Herts, Eng., Jan. 3, 1939; s. Leslie George and Dorothy Emily (Tasker) C.; m. Georgine Mary Ansell, June 23, 1962; children: Simon Richard, Matthew James. BA, St. John's Coll., Oxford, Eng., 1960; PhD, U. Sheffield (Eng.), 1972. Scientific officer Svcs. Electronics Rsch. Lab., Baldock, Eng., 1960-64; scientist Unilever Rsch., Welwyn, Eng., 1964-70; rsch. fellow U. Sheffield (Eng.), 1970-73; privat dozent Eidgenössische Tech. Hochschule, Zürich, Switzerland, 1973-82; prof. biol. chemistry U. Essex (Eng.), 1982—; Coord. membrane initiative Sci. and Engring. Rsch. Coun., Swindon, 1989-93; mem. biochemistry, cell biology com. Biotech. and Biol. Scis. Rsch. Coun., Swindon, 1994-96. Editor: New Techniques of Optical Microscopy and Microspectroscopy, 1991; co-editor: Techniques for the Analysis of Membrane Proteins, 1986, Structural and Dynamic Properties of Lipids and Membranes, 1992; contbr. over 100 articles to profl. jours. Mem. molecular, cell panel Wellcome Trust, London, 1988-91. Recipient open scholarship St. John's Coll., Oxford, Eng., 1957, Ruzicka prize for chemistry, Switzerland, 1981. Mem. Brit. Biophys. Soc., Biochem. Soc. Avocations: photography, gardening, music. Office: U Essex, Dept Biol Scis, C04 3SQ Colchester England

CHERTKOV, VICTOR YAKOV, research scientist; b. Tashkent, Russia, Feb. 5, 1942; arrived in Israel, 1992; s. Yakov Boris and Bella Pavel; (Kreingaus) C.; m. Ludmila Vasili Obuhov, Nov. 29, 1966 (div. Nov. 1976); 1 child, Michael. MS, Moscow State U., 1965; PhD, Geol. Prospecting Inst., Moscow, 1972; DS, Mining Inst., St. Petersburg, Russia, 1991. Jr. rschr. Inst. Nuclear Geophys. & Geochem., Moscow, 1965-69, Geophys. Faculty, Geol. Prospecting Inst., Moscow, 1969-73; sr. rschr. All-Union Rsch. & Design Inst. Bldg. Materials Sources, Moscow, 1974-87; leading rschr. All-Union Rsch. & Design Inst. Bldg. Materials Sci., Moscow, 1987-92; rsch. scientist Faculty Agrl. Engring., Technion, Haifa, Israel, 1994—; translator All Union Translation Ctr., Moscow, 1976-89. Contbr. articles to profl. jours. Rsch. grantee Min. Sci. & Arts, Israel, 1996-98. Mem. European Geophys. Soc., Am. Geophys. Union, N.Y. Acad. Scis. Jewish. Avocations: reading, jogging, skiing. Office: Faculty Agrl Engring, Technion, 32000 Haifa Israel

CHERUBIM, VICTOR EMMANUEL, business executive, shipbroker; b. Colombo, Ceylon, Sri Lanka, Oct. 29, 1934; s. Victor Ernest and Constance Vanderkoen Vanderkoen; m. Vasanthi Josephine Sandrasagra; 1 child, Romer. BA with honors, St. Patrick's Coll., Jaffna, Ceylon, 1953, Aquinas U. Coll., Colombo, 1957, Albion Coll., Mich., 1958, City London Coll., 1968. Coll. visitor staff World U. Svc., N.Y., 1958-62; founder, sec. Jaffna Dist. Coop. Harbour Svcs. Union Ltd., Jaffna, Ceylon, 1962-64; shipping asst. Campbell, Booker Carter Ltd., London, 1966-73; freight bookings officer Booker Export Svcs. Ltd., London, 1966-73; mgr. shipping Permutit Ltd., Isleworth, 1973-74; ship ops. exec. Polish Ocean Lines, London, 1974-85; mgmt. ext. programme Manpower Svcs. Commn., London, 1985-86, Royal Mail, London, 1987-99; cons. shipping, chartering and realty, sr. ptnr. Cargo & Ship Agy., Essex, 1995—; mgmt. cons. to English Folk Song & Dance Soc., London, 1985-86; chmn. Tamil Refugee Action Group, London, dir. 1988-2000; co-sec. Tamil Refugee Housing Assn. Ltd., London, 1989-98; dir. Tamil Cmty. Housing Assn. Ltd., London, 1989-2000; gen. sec. Com. Cultural Affairs of Tamils, U.K., 1993—; spkr. in field. Contbr. articles to newspapers in Sri Lanka and U.K. Travel grantee Asia Found., 1957; U.S. State Dept. scholar Inst. Internat. Ednl. Exchange, 1957-58; named Hon. Citizen of Albion, Mich., 1958. Fellow Inst. Chartered Shipbrokers. Avocations: world travel, collecting medals (British), collecting stamps. E-mail: victorcherubim@aol.com. Address: 35 Crystal Way, Dagenham Essex RM8 1UE, United Kingdom

CHERUBINI, GIOVANNI, electrical engineer; b. Padua, Italy, Aug. 31, 1957; s. Bruno and Clotilde (Lazzaro) C.; m. Mariuccia Bazzolo, May 7, 1988; children: Antonio, Claudia. DEE, U. Padua, 1981; MS, U. Calif., San Diego, 1984, PhD, 1986. Profl. elec. engr. Rsch. staff IBM Zurich Rsch Lab., 1987—; cons. M/A-COM Linkabit, San Diego, 1984-86; vis. prof. U. Padua, 1995-96. Patentee self-training adaptive equalization, adaptive equalization for token-ring transmission system, trellis augmented precoding; coeditor IEEE Standard 802.3 for Fast Ethernet Physical Layer Specification, 1998; guest editor: IEEE Jour. on Selected Areas in Communications, 1995; contbr. chpts. to books. Lt. Italian Air Force, 1982-83. Scholar Italian Soc. Electrotechnology, 1983. Mem. IEEE (sr., editor Transactions on Comm. 1999—). Avocation: tennis. Office: IBM Zurich Rsch Lab, Saumerstrasse 4, CH-8803 Rueschlikon Zurich, Switzerland

CHERUKU, SRINIVASA RAO, research scientist; b. Karimnagar, India, Aug. 9, 1961; came to U.S., 1998; s. Trilochan Rao and Prasuna Cheruku; m. Sudha Madhavi, Apr. 22, 1992; 1 child, Prasuna. BSc, Osmania U., Hyderabad, India, 1981, MSc, 1984; PhD, N. Ea. Hill U., Shillong, India, 1994. Rsch. fellow Regional Rsch. Lab., Hyderabad, 1984-88; jr. rsch. fellow N. Ea. Hill U., Shillong, 1988-90, sr. rsch. fellow, 1990-94; postdoctoral rsch. fellow U. Rene Descartes, Paris, 1994-95; quick-hire scientist Indian Inst. Chem. Tech., Hyderabad, 1995-96; postdoctoral rsch. assoc. Nat. Tsing Hua U., Hsinchu, China, 1997-98, U. Nebr. Med. Ctr., Omaha, 1998—. Contbr. articles to profl. jours. Mem. AAAS, Am. Chem. Soc., Indian Network Found. Avocations: science reading, industrial news and trends, cricket, travel. Office: U Nebr Med Ctr 986025 Nebr Med Ctr Omaha NE 68198-0001

CHESER, RAYMOND NORRIS, III, medical devices company executive; b. Louisville, Oct. 17, 1947; s. Raymond N. II and Martha June C.; 1 child, Stephanie Cheser. BS, Tex. A&M U., 1970, MS, 1976; MBA, U. Conn., 1983; DBA, Nova Southeastern U., 1996. Rsch. chemist The Dow Chem. Co., Freeport, Tex., 1970-76; engring., mfg. mgr. Johnson and Johnson, Skillman, N.J., 1977-80; engring., mfg. mgr. Johnson and Johnson, Southington, Conn., 1980-92, dir. quality assurance, 1995-96; engring. mgr. C.R. Bard, Billerica, Mass., 1992-95; dir. continous improvement U.S. Surg. Corp., North Haven, Conn., 1997—; adj. faculty Boston U., 1994-95; adj. assoc. prof. Albertus Magnus Coll., New Haven, 1996—, U. New Haven, 2000—; spkr. in field. Contbr. articles to profl. jours. Bd. dirs. New Britain Symphony, 1989-90. Recipient Shingo prize for mfg. rsch., 1999. Mem. Acad. of Mgmt., Assn. for Mfg. Excellence, Internat. Assn. of Facilitators. Avocations: music composition, clay sculpture, art collector. E-mail: rayc@ziplink.net.

CHESEREM, MICAH, bank executive. Gov. Ctrl. Bank of Kenya, Nairobi. Office: Ctrl Bank of Kenya, Haile Selassie Ave P O Box 60000, Nairobi Kenya

CHESHANKOV, BOZHIDAR IVANOV, mathematics educator; b. Sofia, Bulgaria, Dec. 17, 1935; s. Ivan Sotirov and Christina (Dimcheva) C.; m. Militza Grigorova Batchvarova, July 30, 1961 (dec. Mar. 1986); children: Vessela, Ivan. MS, Tech. U. Sofia, Bulgaria, 1959; MS in Math., U. Sofia, Bulgaria, 1966; PhD, Tech. U. Sofia, Bulgaria, 1965; DS, U. Sofia, Bulgaria, 1974. Asst. prof. Tech. U. Sofia, 1960-68, assoc. prof., 1968-79, prof., 1979—; head dept. Tech. U. Sofia, 1980-95, dir. inst., 1995—. Author: Optimal Control, 1980, Theory of Oscillations, 1982. Mem. AMS. Home: ul GS Rakovsky No 166 A, 1000 Sofia Bulgaria Office: Tech U Sofia, Inst Applied Math & Info, 1156 Sofia Bulgaria

CHESHIRE, CAROLYN IRENE, personal trainer, fitness and health consultant; b. Castle Donnington, Eng., July 23, 1948; d. William Henry and Constance May Cheshire; m. James Lewis, May 3, 1986. Diploma in bus. studies, Loughborough Coll., 1965; diploma in fitness tchrs. cert., 1991. Sec. dept. agrl. econs. U. Nottingham; pvt. sec. Fgn. Office, London; asst. to dir. fin. London Broadcasting Co.; Mem. internat. women's com. Internat. Fedn. Body Bldg., Gt. Britain, 1981, internat. women's judge, Malmö, Sweden, 1985, Brit. rep., Czechoslovakia, 1985; commentator World Games, Channel 4 TV, 1985. Author: Body Chic, 1985, Body Dynamics, 1996; appeared in TV documentary Muscle Madness, 1981, feature film Pumping Iron II—The Women, 1983. Named 1st Ms. Olympia (first Brit. competitor) Internat. Fedn. Body Bldg., 1980, 1st World Couples Champion, Internat. Fedn. Body Bldg., 1982, 7th Ms. Olympia, 1983, 1st Brit. Champion, English Fedn. Body Bldg., 1981; named Britain's Best Personal Trainer, 1993. Mem. Fitness Profls., Soc. Authors. Avocations: travel, cooking, listening to music. E-mail: carolyn-cheshire@hotmail. com. Home: 109 Howard House Dolphin Sq, SW1V 3PE London England

CHESLER, DORIS ADELLE, real estate professional; b. Lincoln, Ill., Sept. 23, 1924; d. Harry and Esther Pearl (Campbell) Schoth; m. Eugene Albert Aughenbaugh, May 23, 1943 (div. Sept. 1970); children: Judith C., Rodney E., Paula Sue; m. Arthur Bernard Chesler, Oct. 16, 1972. Lic. real estate broker, Fla. Realtor, assoc. Kilgore Real Estate, Brandon, Fla., 1969-76; broker Doris A. Chesler, Brandon, 1976—. Den mother Cub Scouts Am., Tampa, 1961-62; leader 4-H Club, Decatur, Ill., 1956. Republican. Presbyterian. Avocations: interior decorating, sewing, gardening, music, square dancing.

CHESLEY, STANLEY MORRIS, lawyer; b. Cin., Mar. 26, 1936; s. Frank and Rachel (Kinsburg) C.; children: Richard A., Lauren B. BA, U. Cin., 1958, LLB, 1960. Bar: Ohio 1960, Ky. 1978, W.Va., Tex., Nev. 1981. Ptnr. Waite, Schneider, Bayless & Chesley Co., Cin., 1960; Contbr. articles to profl. jours. Past chmn. bd. commrs. on grievances and discipline Supreme Ct. Ohio; past pres. Jewish Fedn. Cin.; nat. vice chair, bd. govs., trustee, joint distbn. com. United Jewish Coms; exec. bd., nat. bd. govs. Am. Jewish Com.; nat. bd. govs. Hebrew Union Coll.; exec. com. U.S. Holocaust Meml. Mus. Mem. ABA, ATLA, Am. Judicature Soc., Fed. Bar Assn., Melvin M. Belli Soc., Ohio Bar Assn., Ky. Bar Assn., W.Va. Bar Assn., Tex. Bar Assn., Nev. Bar Assn., Cin. Bar Assn. Office: Waite Schneider Bayless & Chesley 1513 Central Trust Towers Cincinnati OH 45202

CHESNEY, ANTONY, chemist, research scientist; b. Manchester, Eng., Feb. 14, 1968; s. Graham and June (Jackson) C. BSc in Chemistry with honors, U. Sheffield, Eng., 1989, MPhil in Chemistry, 1990, PhD in Chemistry, 1993. Sr. rsch. asst. U. Durham, 1993-98; sr. scientist Millipore-Bioprocessing, Newcastle, 1998-2000, ICI (Synetix), Cleveland, England, 2000—. Contbr. articles to profl. jours. including Chemistry: A European Jour., Chem. Comms., Jour. Materials Chemistry. Grantee EPSRC, 1996. Mem. Am. Chem. Soc., Royal Soc. Chemistry. Avocations: rugby union, golf, mountaineering, association football. Office: Synetix Ltd, Belasis Ave PO Box 1, Consett Billingham Cleveland TS23, England

CHESNEY, ROBERT HENRY, communications executive, consultant; b. Rockville Centre, N.Y., Aug. 12, 1950; s. Robert Lewis and Maureen C. (Oates) C.; m. Donna Marie Mazian, May 1, 1976; 1 child, Alexis Mary. BA in Indsl. Psychology, Hofstra U., 1972, MBA in Qualitative & Quantitative Analysis, 1979. Internal auditor Grumman Aerospace, Bethpage, N.Y., 1974-77, sr. ops. specialist, 1978; sr. systems analyst Sta. WNET, N.Y.C., 1978-79, mgr. mgmt. info. systems and procedures, 1979-81, asst. dir. mgmt. info. systems and procedures, 1981-82; sr. tech. cons. N.Y. Telephone, Melville, 1982-83, AT&T Info. Systems, Melville, 1983-89; from sr. exec. data sales to mgr. territory AT&T Computer Systems, Melville, 1990-94; from sr. client cons. to mng. client cons. AT&T Ops. Cons. Group, Manhasset, N.Y., 1994-95; ptnr. AT&T Bus. Consulting, Manhasset, N.Y., 1995; dist. mgr. AT&T Bus. Cons., Atlanta, Ga., 1996-97; dist. mgr. CFO SAP Lucent Technologies Inc., Warren, N.J., 1997-99, dist. mgr. GSP IPS, 1999-2000; sr. mgr. SPN NNS CFO sys. and procurement Lucent Technologies Inc., Warren, 2000—. Mem. IEEE, IEEE Computer Soc., IEEE Comms. Soc., Assn. Computing Machinery, N.Y. Acad. Scis., Hofstra U. Alumni Assn. Republican. Roman Catholic. Office: Lucent Technologies Inc 283 King George Rd Warren NJ 07059-5134

CHESNOKOVA, NATALJA BORISOVNA, biochemist; b. Moscow, Dec. 5, 1946; d. Boris Michailovich Chystiakov and Luba Michailovna Spivakova; m. Alexei Grigorievich, July 26, 1969; 1 child, Helene. Degree in biochemistry, Med. Inst. Moscow, 1970; degree in biology, Helmholtz Inst., Moscow, 1973, D of Biology, 1992. Rschr. Helmholtz Inst., Moscow, 1973-89, sr. rschr., 1989-90, head of rsch. group, 1989-98, chief of divsn. of pathophysiology and biochemistry, 1998—. Contbr. articles to profl. jours. Mem. Biochem. Soc., Ophthalmol. Soc. Russia. Home: 2 Peschanaja St 2/1-111, 125252 Moscow Russia Office: Helmholtz Eye Disease Rsch, Sadovaja-Chernogriazskaya, 14/19 Moscow 103064, Russia

CHESNUT, CAROL FITTING, lawyer; b. Pecos, Tex., June 17, 1937; d. Ralph Ulf and Carol (Lowe) Fitting; m. Dwayne A. Chesnut, Dec. 27, 1955; children: Carol Marie, Stephanie Michelle, Mark Steven. BA magna cum laude, U. Colo., 1971; JD, U. Calif., San Francisco, 1994. Rsch. asst. U. Colo., 1972; head quality controller Mathematics, Inc., Denver, 1973-74; cons. Mincome Man., Winnipeg, Can., 1974; cons. economist Energy Cons. Assocs. Inc., Denver, 1974-79; exec. v.p. tng. ECA Intercomp, 1980-81; gen. ptnr. Chestnut Consortium, S.F., 1981—; sec. Critical Resources, Inc., 1981-83. Rep. Lakehurst Civic Assn., 1968; staff aide Senator Gary Hart, 1978; Dem. precinct capt., 1982-88. Mem. ABA, ACLU, AAUW (1st v.p. 1989-90), LWV, Soc. Petroleum Engrs., Am. Nuc. Soc. (chair conv. space activities 1989, chair of spouse activities 1989), Am. Geophys. Union, Assn. Women Geoscientists (treas. Denver 1983-85), Associated Students of Hastings (rep. 1994), Calif. State Bar, Nev. State Bar, Nat. Acad. Elder Law Attys., Clark County Bar Assn. (coun. com. 1999), Canyon Ranch Homeowners Assn. (sec. bd. dirs. 1994-97), Phi Beta Kappa, Phi Chi Theta, Phi Delta Phi. Unitarian. Office: Ste 319 2921 N Tenaya Way Las Vegas NV 89128-0454

CHESNUTT, WILLIAM JAMES, barrister; b. Wanganui, New Zealand, Nov. 29, 1955; m. Shu-Hui Kuo, Aug. 14, 1994. BCom, U. Western Australia, 1986, B Juris, 1988, LLB, 1989, LLM, 1998. Solicitor Robinson Cox, Perth, Australia, 1989-91; barrister Bar Chambers, Perth, 1991-99, London Ct. Chambers, 1999—. Mem. Law Soc. of Western Australia, Bar Assn. of Western Australia. Office: London Ct Chambers 2nd Fl, 56 St George's Ter, Perth Australia

CHESSON, MICHAEL BEDOUT, history educator; b. Richmond, Va., Sept. 5, 1947; s. Wesley Earle and Virginia Winborne (Ramsey) Chesson. AB with high honors in History, Coll. William and Mary, 1969; postgrad. (Gilman fellow), Johns Hopkins U., 1972-73; PhD in History (Grad. fellow), Harvard U., 1978. Clk. R.F. & P. R.R., Richmond, 1966-69; park ranger-historian Colonial Nat. Hist. Park, Nat. Park Svc., Yorktown and Jamestown, Va., 1969-70, 72, 73; tchg. fellow Harvard U., 1975-78; asst. prof. history U. Mass., Boston, 1978-82, assoc. prof. history, 1982-96, prof. history, 1996—. Author: Richmond After the War, 1865-1890, 1981. Served to capt. USNR, 1969—. Fellow Mass. Hist. Soc.; mem. Am. Hist. Assn., So. Hist. Assn., Va. Hist. Assn., Orgn. Am. Historians, Peabody Essex Mus., Cape Ann Hist. Assn., Mil. Hist. Soc. Mass., Naval Res. Assn., Res. Officer Assn., Fleet Res. Assn., Navy League. Democrat. Club: Wardroom Club (Boston).

CHESTER, MICHAEL ALAN, biochemist; b. Doncaster, Yorkshire, Eng., Apr. 14, 1943; arrived in Sweden, 1973; m. Christina Wiman, June

1978. BTech, Loughborough U., Eng., 1966; MSc, Warwick U., Eng., 1967; PhD, London U., 1971. Beit meml. fellow Lister Inst. London U., 1970-73; Wellcome European fellow Uppsala (Sweden) U., 1973-75; clin. chemist Lund (Sweden) U., 1975-78, 79-83; assoc. prof. med. faculty Kuwait U., 1978-79; proj. dir., dir. scientific affairs, project coord. BioCarb AB, Lund, Sweden, 1983-91; lab. head blood ctr. U. Hosp., Lund, 1992-98; head quality and devel. Blood Ctr. Skåne, 1998-99, head rsch. and devel., 1999—; sec. Internat. Glycoconjugate Orgn., 1989—; mem. Internat. Union Biochemistry and Molecular Biology-Internat. Union Pure and Applied Chemistry joint commn. on biochem. nomenclature (JCBN), 1989-97, assoc. mem., 1998—; head dept. transfusion medicine Lund U., 1998—. Founding editor: Glycoconjugate Jour., 1984-93. Fellow Royal Soc. Chemistry, Biochem. Soc. Avocations: squash, sailing, gardening, tennis. Office: Blood Ctr, U Hosp, 221 85 Lund Sweden

CHESTER, NORMAN CHARLES, bank executive; b. Glen Ridge, N.J., Dec. 7, 1953; s. Norman Harding Chester and Barbara Wanda (Barber) Tessier; m. Vivian Leslie Tarallo, Aug. 15, 1987; children: Alfred Eduardo, Caroline Carmen. BBA, Bucknell U., 1976; MBA, Rutgers U., 1981. Cert. mgmt. acct. Adj. instr. Bergen C.C., Paramus, N.J., 1983-85; rep. Equitable Life, E. Orange, N.J., 1976-77; mgmt. trainee U.S. Life Ins. Co., N.Y.C., 1977-79; from acct. to v.p. Chase Manhattan Bank, N.Y.C., 1979-97; v.p., contr. ABN-AMRO Bank, N.Am. Spcl. Credits, N.Y.C., 1997—; guest speaker Exec. Enterprises, 1993-94. Trustee Westwood (N.J.) United Meth. Ch., 1988-92, fin. chair, 1989-94, sec. adminstrv. coun., 1986-89; publicity chair Hillsdale Vol. Ambulance Svc., 1986-99, fin. chair, 1993—, treas., 1994—; dir. Oradell Kids Found., 1996-97. Mem. Inst. of Mgmt. Accts. Methodist. Avocations: running, photography. Home: 782 Martin Ave Oradell NJ 07649-2338 Office: ABN-AMRO Bank 10 E 53rd St New York NY 10022-5244

CHESTER, THOMAS WAYNE, state agency administrator; b. Clarksville, Tenn., July 19, 1950; s. Douglas Bell and Ida Mae Chester; m. Betty Ruth Davis, Feb. 14, 1990; 1 child, Andrew Douglas. BSBA, Austin Peay State U., 1973; MPA, Tenn. State U., 1999. Cert. govt. fin. mgr. Acct. I dept. fin. and adminstrn. State of Tenn., Nashville, 1973-76, acct. II dept. fin. and adminstrn., 1976-79, asst. dir. fiscal affairs dept. gen. svcs., 1979-81, asst. chief fiscal svcs. dept. gen. svcs., 1981-84, dir. of fin. I dept. gen. svcs., 1984-93, dir. fin. III dept. gen. svcs., 1993—; notary pub. at large, Tenn., 1996—. Treas. Cub Scout Pack #753, Mt. Juliet, Tenn., 1999—; coach Mt. Juliet (Tenn.) Little League Baseball, 1999-2000, 2000—. Mem. Am. Soc. Pub. Adminstrn. (bd. dirs., treas. 1995-97, pres.-elect 1998-2000, pres. 1999-2000), Assn. Records Mgrs. and Adminstrs. (audit com. 1995-96). Presbyterian. Avocation: team sports. Home: 803 Ridgetop Dr Mount Juliet TN 37122-4136

CHETA, DAN MIRCEA, diabetologist, medical educator; b. Satulung, Brasov, Romania, Nov. 29, 1943; s. Gheorghe and Margareta (Marinescu) C.; m. Nina Silvia Giurescu, June 16, 1973; children: Dana Viorica, Alexandru Costin. MD, Bucharest U. Medicine, Romania, 1967; PhD, Bucharest Acad. Medicine, 1977. Intern various hosps., Bucharest, 1966-69; gen. practitioner various med. ctrs., Bucharest, 1969-76; asst. prof. Bucharest U. Medicine, 1976-91, sr. lectr., 1991-94, assoc. prof., 1994-99, prof., 1999—; prin. physician Diabetes Clinic, Bucharest, 1976-90, cons. physician 1990—; chief dept. N. Paulescu Inst., Bucharest, 1995—. Author: Immuno-Metabolic Interrelations, 1987 (Romanian Acad. award 1987); author/coauthor 11 other books; contbr. numerous articles to sci. jours. Recipient I. Pavel prize, Bucharest Acad. Medicine, 1993. Mem. N.Y. Acad. Scis., European Assn. Study of Diabetes. Orthodox Church. Avocation: travel. Home: 28 Alexandru Donici, 70238 Bucharest II, Romania Office: N Paulescu Institute, 5 Ion Movila, 79811 Bucharest II, Romania

CHETTIAR, ANGIDI VERRIAH, federal official; b. Apr. 28, 1929; m. Milliaga Malliah; 6 children. Grad., Royal Coll. Sch., Port Louis. Mem. Labour Party Govt. of Mauritius, 1952—, mem. legis. assembly, 1967-82, chmn. ex-servicemen welfare fund, 1969-82, chmn. MBC gen. adv. coun., 1970-82, treas. Labour Party, 1976-97; adminstr. S.S.R. House Govt. of Mauritius, Port Louis; mem. exec. com. Labour Party Govt. of Mauritius, until 1997, chief whip, 1976-80, minister of state to prime minister's office, 1981, v.p., 1997—. 1st Labour mayor, Vacoas-Phoenix, 1970; gen. sec. Tamil Temple Fedn. Mauritius, 1971-73, chmn., 1973-76. Office: Govt Ctr Office of VP, 30 Faraqauhar Ave, Quarte Bornes Port Louis Mauritius*

CHETTLE, A(LVIN) B(ASIL), JR., lawyer, educator; b. Hollywood, Calif., Apr. 13, 1937; s. Alvin Basil Sr. and Evelyn Teresa (Olsen) C. BS, Georgetown U., 1959, JD, 1962, LLM, 1964. Bar: Va. 1962, D.C. 1962, U.S. Ct. Mil. Appeals 1962, U.S. Ct. Appeals (D.C. cir.) 1962, U.S. Ct. Claims 1963, U.S. Tax Ct. 1963, U.S. Ct. Appeals (9th cir.) 1964, Calif. 1965, U.S. Dist. Ct. (cen. dist.) Calif. 1965, U.S. Supreme Ct. 1975, U.S. Dist. Ct. (so. dist.) Calif. 1977. Adminstrv. asst. to dir. claims div. Nat. Canners Assn. (now Nat. Food Processors Assn.), Washington, 1962-64; assoc. Keel & Pressman, Hawthorne, Calif., 1964; ptnr. Keel & Chettle, Hawthorne, Calif., 1965, Keel, Chettle & Valentine, Hawthorne, Calif., 1966-71; city prosecutor City of Hawthorne, 1965-69; sr. ptnr. Chettle & Valentine, Manhattan Beach, Calif., 1971-92; pvt. practice Manhattan Beach, 1971—; lectr. Food Processors Inst., Washington, Massey U., New Zealand, 1983; spl. counsel City of Inglewood, Calif., 1971, City of Hawthorne, Calif., 1977-84, City of Torrance, Calif., 1979—; arbitrator South Bay Mcpl. Ct., Torrance and L.A. Superior Ct.; judge pro tem L.A. Jud. Dist., 1982-00, South Bay Jud. Dist., Torrance, 1985-00, L.A. County Superior Ct., 1990—; hearing officer City of Garden Grove, 1989-92, City of Hawthorne, 1992-94; guest lectr. UCLA, 2000. Active L.A. chpt. ARC, 1966-96, ARC Blood and Tissue Svcs., 1966-96; 1st chair emeritus bd. dirs. ARC Blood Svcs.-So. Calif. Region, 1997—; bd. dirs. Coalition of Food Industry Counsel; mem. bd. advisors Cath. Distance U., 1983-98. Recipient Life Time Achievements award Nat. Food Processors Assn. Mem. D.C. Bar Assn., Calif. Bar Assn. (del. conf. of dels. 1969), Va. Bar Assn., Assn. So. Calif. Def. Counsel, Inglewood Dist. Bar Assn. (trustee 1967, 70, treas. 1967, nominating com. 1966, 75, 76, 77, v.p. 1968, pres. 1969). Office: PO Box 7 Manhattan Beach CA 90267-0007

CHETTY, GIRIJA M., economics and computers educator, researcher; b. Hyderabad, A.P., India, Feb. 3, 1962; arrived in Australia, 1993; d. Raghaviah Veera Raghaviah and Sita (Mahalakshmi) Ghantala; m. Madhusudan Rajgopal Chetty, Nov. 4, 1985; 1 child, Kritika. B Engring. (Electronics), RCE, Nagpur, India, 1983, M Engring. (Electronics), 1988. Chartered profl. engr., India. Lectr. electronics VRCE, Nagpur U., 1983-86, sr. lectr., 1986-93, coord. women in engring. program, 1989; rsch. scholar U. South Australia, Australia, 1993; assoc. lectr. electronics Deakin U., Australia, 1994-95; lectr. electronics and computing Monash U., Churchill, Australia, 1995—; cons. on electronic and computer engring., Australia, 1994—; presenter in field; participant internat. confs. on electronics and computing. Contbr. articles to profl. publs. Rsch. scholar Delft (The Netherlands) U. Tech., 1988. Mem. IEEE, Instn. Engrs., IICA. Avocations: reading, computing, sports, community service, working towards equal opportunity for women in professional and business areas. Office: Monash U, Switchback Rd, Churchill Vic 3842, Australia

CHETTY, MANORANJENNI, pharmacology educator, researcher; b. Pietermaritzburg, South Africa, Feb. 5, 1958; d. Visvanathan Subbiah and Lutchmee (Naidoo) Pillay; m. Vasudevan Viswanatha, Sept. 12, 1982; 1 child, Vahini. BPharm, U. Durban-Westville, South Africa, 1980; MS in Pharmacology, Rhodes U., South Africa, 1983; PhD, U. Durban-Westville, 1992. Pharmacist State Hosp., South Africa, 1982-88; lectr. U. Durban-Westville, 1988-94; pharm. documentation mgr. Hoechst Marion Roussel Pharms., South Africa, 1995-97; sr. lectr. U. Witwatersrand, South Africa, 1997-99; head Sch. Pharmacy Technikon, Pretoria, South Africa, 1999—; acting dir. Drug Studies Unit, South Africa, 1994; mem. coun. South African Pharmacy Coun., 1994. Contbr. articles to profl. jours. Mem. health policy com. African Nat. Congress, 1992-93; drug policy com. Dept. Health, South Africa, 1994. Recipient Silver medal Lennon Pharms., South Africa, 1987, Gold medal Lennon Pharms., 1988, scholarship Med. Rsch. Coun., South Africa, 1990-92. Mem. South African Pharmacy Coun., Neuroscis. Group South Africa, South African Pharmcol. Soc. Hindu. Avocations: walking, birdwatching, travel. Home: 11 Ferero St, 1609 Edenglen South Africa Office: Technikon Pretoria Sch Phar, Pvt Bag X68, 0001 Pretoria South Africa

CHETTY, RAVINDRA, barrister; b. Dar es Salaam, Tanzania, Oct. 18, 1962; came to Mauritius, 1966; s. Valaydon and Ethrajam (Naiken) C.; m. Shalmila Moodely, Nov. 7, 1990; children: Khavi Shankara, Manushyam, Kathirasam. BA in Law, Balliol Coll., Oxford U., 1986. Called to bar Middle Temple, London, 1987; qualified as barrister, London, 1987. Pvt. practice Port Louis, Mauritius, 1987—; lectr. Mauritius Coun. Legal Edn., 1991—. Vice chmn. Mauritius Child Care Soc., 1994—; pres. Mauritius Football Assn., 1996—. Mem. Rotary (pres. 1995-96). Avocations: football, cycling, reading, films, swimming. E-mail: rchetty@chambers.sirhamid.intnet.mu. Home: GIDC, Floreal Mauritius Office: 6th Fl PCL Bldg, 43 Sir William Newton St, Port Louis Mauritius

CHETVERIN, ALEXANDER BORISOVICH, molecular biologist; b. Salsk, Rostov, Russia, May 20, 1953; s. Boris Vladimirovich and Claudia Fedorovna (Luk'yanenkova) C.; m. Helena Vladimirovna Khlyustova, May 17, 1980; children: Olga, Dahrya. BS in Biology, Moscow State U., 1973, MS in Molecular Biology, 1975, PhD in Molecular Biology, 1985, DSc in Molecular Biology, 1995. Rsch. fellow Inst. Protein Rsch. Russian Acad. Scis., Pushchino, 1977-80, jr. scientist Inst. Protein Rsch., 1980-85, sr. scientist Inst. Protein Rsch., 1985-89, lead scientist Inst. Protein Rsch., 1989-96, prin. scientist Inst. Protein Rsch., 1996—; advisor Molecular Biology jour., Moscow, 1995—. Contbr. articles to profl. jours. Mem. Russian Acad. Scis. Achievements include patent in method for amplification of nucleic acids in solid media. Avocation: gardening. Fax: 7-095-924-04-93. E-mail: alexch@vega.protres.ru. Home: 24 Mikroraion AB Apt 238, 142290 Pushchino Russia Office: Russian Acad Science, Inst Protein Research, 142290 Pushchino Russia

CHEUNG, FANNY MUI-CHING, educator, foundation administrator; b. Hong Kong, Oct. 3, 1950; d. Yuk-kai Cheung and You-fong Chan; m. Japhet Sebastian Law. BA, U. Calif., Berkeley, 1970; PhD, U. Minn., 1975. Clin. psychologist United Christian Hosp., Hong Kong, 1975-77; prof. psychology Chinese U. Hong Kong, 1977—; chairperson Equal Opportunities Commn., Hong Kong, 1996-99; dept. chmn., 2000—; dean faculty social sci. Chinese U. Hong Kong, 1995-96; prin. author, rschr. Chinese Personality Assessment Inventory, 1991—; transl., prin. rschr. Chinese Minn. Multiphasic Personality Inventory, 1979—; founding dir. Gender Rsch. Program, Hong Kong, 1985-96; dir. Gender Rsch. Ctr., Chinese U., Hong Kong, 2000-01. Contbr. numerous book chpts. and articles to profl. jours. Advisor on Hong Kong affairs Hong Kong and Macau Office of State Dept., China, 1995-97; founding chairperson The Women's Ctr., Hong Kong, 1981-93; founding pres. Hong Kong Fedn. Women's Ctrs., 1993-96; vice-chmn. New Life Psychiat. Rehab. Assn., Hong Kong, 1976-96; justice of peace Hong Kong Govt., 1988. Decorated Officer of Most Excellent Order of Brit. Empire, Queen Elizabeth II, 1997; recipient Badge of Honor, Queen Elizabeth II, 1986. Fellow Hong Kong Psychol. Soc. (pres. 1984-85); mem. Internat. Assn. Applied Psychology (pres. divsn. clin. and comty. psychology 1990-94).

CHEUNG, GORDON CHI KAI, education educator; b. Hong Kong, Oct. 16, 1966; s. Yip Nan Cheung and Siu-iong Chan; m. So Fan Lee, Mar. 17, 1996; 1 child, Edmund. Honors Diploma, Lingnan Coll. (now Lingnan U.), Hong Kong, 1990; MSc, U. Bristol, 1992; PhD, Chinese U. of Hong Kong, 1997. Tutor The Chinese U. of Hong Kong, 1997-98; rsch. assoc. Lingnan U., 1998—; sec. Overseas Chinese Studies Found., 1998—. Author: Market Liberalism: American Foreign Policy Toward China, 1998, The Political Economy of Japan, 2000; contbr. articles to profl. jours. Recipient Eu Tong Sen scholarship U. Hawaii, Manoa, 1995, Lee Found. award, Singapore, 1995. Mem. Acad. Polit. Sci., Assn. Asian Studies. Avocations: reading, fishing, badminton. Office: Lingnan U/Chinese Bus, Tuen Mun NT, Hong Kong China

CHEUNG, HEE TAI ANDREW, pharmaceutical chemistry educator, researcher; b. Hong Kong, Mar. 4, 1936; came to Australia, 1970; s. Shiu Fan and Wai Iu (Tsao) C.; m. Agnes J. Shen, Aug. 17, 1966, 1 child, Stephen L. MSc, U. Hong Kong, 1959; PhD, diploma, Imperial Coll. U. London, 1962; DSc, U. London, 1989. Rsch. fellow Harvard U. Med. Sch., Boston, 1962-63, rsch. assoc., 1963-64; rsch. assoc. Columbia U., N.Y.C., 1964-65; lectr. pharm. chemistry U. Sydney, Australia, 1970-73, sr. lectr., 1974-80, reader, 1981—; vis. scientist Nat. Inst. for Med. Rsch., London, 1976, 84, 91, 92, 94. Rsch. grantee Australian Rsch. Coun., Nat. Health and Med. Rsch. Coun., Australia, various dates. Fellow Royal Soc. Chemistry (London), Royal Australian Chem. Inst.; mem. Australian Pharm. Sci. Assn. Avocations: music, art. Office: Faculty Pharmacy, U Sydney, Sydney NSW 2006, Australia

CHEUNG, LINUS W. L., telecommunications executive. BS in Social Sci., U. Hong Kong, 1971, postgrad., 1978; postgrad., Harvard U., Oxford (Eng.) U., INSEAD, France. To dep. mng. dir. Cathay Pacific Airways Ltd., 1980-94; chief exec. Hong Kong Telecom. Ltd., Wanchai, 1994—; now dep. chmn. Pacific Century Cyberworsk Ltd., Hong Kong; bd. dirs. Cable & Wireless PLC, Hong Kong; mem. Pacific Bus. Forum APEC. Former mem. Hong Kong govt. Ctrl. Policy Unit; mem. numerous civic, bus. and polit. orgns. Avocations: reading, contemporary Chinese art, music, swimming, golf. Fax: 852-2962-2888. Office: Pacific Century Cyberworks, 3 Garden Rd, Ctrl 38th Fl, Hong Hong 070, Hong Kong*

CHEUNG, MAN KEN, chemist, chemical engineer, educator; b. Hong Kong; s. Pak Nam Cheung and Oi In Pang; m. Janet Hui-Chen, July 11, 1992; 1 child, Lemuel. BS, U. Wis., 1987; PhD, Northwestern U., 1992. Postdoctoral fellow U. Calif., Davis, 1992-94; vis. scholar Hong Kong U. Sci. & Technology, 1994-95; from asst. prof. to sr. lectr. Hong Kong Poly. U., 1995—. Mem. AIChE, Am. Chem. Soc., N.Y. Acad. Scis., Hong Kong Chem. Soc., Golden Key Honor Soc., Phi Eta Sigma, Tau Beta Pi, Alpha Chi Sigma. Office: Hong Kong Poly U ABCT, Hung Hom, Kowloon Hong Kong China

CHEUNG, PAUL V.S., dean, engineering educator. Dean engring. U. Hong Kong. Office: U Hong Kong, Porkfulam Rd, Hong Kong Hong Kong*

CHEUNG, TO-YAT, computer science educator, consultant; b. Hong Kong, July 31, 1937; arrived in Can., 1972; s. Kwun-Hin and Sau-Fong (Yeung) C.; m. Molly Mo-Jing Ko, June 5, 1970; children: Yolanda Wing-See, Calista Wing-Kum. BA with honours, U. Hong Kong, 1961, BSc with spl. honors, 1962; MSc, U. Wis., 1967, PhD, 1970. Systems analyst Nat. Cash Register Co., L.A., 1970-72; network analyst Computel Ltd., Ottawa, Ont., Can., 1972-73; vis. prof. computer sci. U. Alberta, 1973-74; prof. U. Ottawa, 1974-94; computer cons. Can. Dept. Supply and Svcs., Ottawa, 1982; network cons. UN, 1983; computer auditor Revenue Can., Ottawa, 1986-89; database cons. Stats. Can., Ottawa, 1989-90; chair, prof. City U. of Hong Kong, 1992—. Contbr. numerous articles on networks, databases, ops. rsch., numerical analysis, and distributed computing to sci. jours. and proc. Rsch. fellow Telecommunications Rsch. Inst. Ont., 1989—, Can. Inst. Telecommunications Rsch., 1990—. Mem. IEEE Computer Soc. Avocations: badminton, chess. Home: B5, 81 Tat Chee Ave, Hong Kong Hong Kong Office: Dept Computer Sci, City U Hong Kong, Hong Kong Hong Kong

CHEVALIER, BARBARA LANSBURGH, interior designer; b. San Francisco, Aug. 19, 1907; d. S. Laz and Ethel (Newman) Lansburgh; children: Suzanne Chevalier-Skolnikoff, Haakon L. Chevalier. Student, Mills Coll., 1926, Stanford U., 1927; BA, U. Calif., Berkeley, 1931. Social worker U.S. Govt. (Alameda County), Calif., 1936-37; apprentice interior designer San Francisco, 1938-43; personal sec. to Elizabeth Arden, 1944; owner, mgr. Barbara Chevalier Interiors, San Francisco, 1947—; pres. Chevalier-Rogers, Inc., San Francisco, 1962-70. Designer Stinson Beach Wedding Gardens and many residencies. Bd. dirs. San Francisco Boys Chorus. Mem. Am. Soc. Interior Designers, Phi Beta Kappa. Fax: 415-346-5434. Home and Office: Barbara Chevalier Interiors 2298 Pacific Ave # 3 San Francisco CA 94115-1435

CHEVALIER, FRANÇOIS, historian, educator; b. Montluçon, Allier, France, May 27, 1914; s. Jacques and Marie (Mercier) C.; m. Josèphe Charvet, June 1, 1949; children: Manuel, Miguel, Vincent. Lic. in history in geography, U. Grenoble, France, 1936; archiviste paleographe degree, Ecole Nat. Chartes, Paris, 1940; Doctorate, The Sorbonne, Paris, 1949. Rschr., prof. French Inst. Mex., 1946-49; dir. French Inst. L.Am., Mex., 1949-62; prof. U. Bordeaux, 1962-66; dir. Casa Velazquez, Madrid, 1967-79; prof. U. Sorbonne, Paris, 1970-84, prof. emeritus, 1984—. Author books about Mex. translated to English and Spanish; contbr. numerous articles to profl. jours. 2d lt. French Army, 1939-40. Named Chevalier Legion d'honneur, 1959. Roman Catholic. Avocations: skiing, hiking. Home: 76 Ave Ledru Rollin, 75012 Paris France Office: L Am Ctr U Paris I, 17 rue de la Sorbonne, 75005 Paris France

CHEVENEMENT, JEAN-PIERRE, French government official; b. Belfort, France, Mar. 9, 1939; s. Pierre Chevènement and Juliette Garessus; m. Nisa Grünberg, June 29, 1970; children: Raphaël, Jean-Christophe. Ed., U. Paris, Ecole Nat. Adminstrn. Dep. to Nat. Assembly, Paris, 1973-81, 86-88; dep. to Nat. Assembly Paris, 1991—; pres. Deptl. Assembly Franche-Comté, 1981-82; mayor Town of Belfort, 1983-89, 89—; minister state, minister research and tech. France, Paris, 1981-82, minister industry, 1982-83, minister nat. edn., 1984-86, minister def., 1988-91, min. of interior. Mem. Socialist Party. Avocations: chess. Home: 22 rue Descartes, 75005 Paris France Office: Ministry of Interior, Place Beauvau, 75800 Paris France*

CHEVRIER, CHRISTINE DENISE, research engineer; b. Nancy, Lorraine, France, Mar. 3, 1969; d. Daniel and Françoise (Denys) C. Engring. Degree, DEA Info., Nat. Inst. Applied Scis., Lyon, France, 1992; PhD, U. Henri Poincaré, Nancy, France, 1996. Rsch. engr. Ctr. for Rsch. in Architecture and Engring., Nancy, 1995—. Avocation: painting. Office: CRAI, 2 rue Bastien Lepage, 54001 Nancy France

CHEVRILLON, CYRILLE LOUIS, investment banking executive; b. Paris, May 29, 1953; s. Remi Louis and Louise Marie (de Boysson) C.; m. Princess Aleth de Broglie, June 9, 1979; children: Paul, Remi, Laure, Victor. Diploma of fine arts, Santander, Spain, 1973; MBA, Hautes Etudes Commerciales, Paris, 1976. Cert. comml. banking mgmt. program. Investment banker JP Morgan, N.Y.C., Paris, 1976-84; fin. dir. Gaumont, Paris, 1984-86; dir. Salomon Bros. Internat. Ltd., London, 1986-91; mng. dir. Salomon Bros. S.A., Paris, 1991-92; sr. ptnr. Chevrillon-Philippe S.C.A., 1992-99, Chevrillon & Associés, 2000—; chmn. Imprimerie Bussiere-BCP, Financière Herissey, Hexaflux-Technol, Chevrillon-Candover, CPI Printing Industries; dir. CCR-CP Commerty Bank Group, Dupont -Med. Avocation: sailing. Home: 3 rue du Canivet, 75006 Paris France Office: Chevrillon & Associés SCA, 6 Rond Point Des Champs, 75008 Paris France

CHEVRILLON, OLIVIER, research company executive; b. Paris, Jan. 28, 1929; s. Louis and Hedwige C.; m. Marie France Renaud; 1 child, Melisande. Student, Inst. Nat. d'Etude Polit., Paris, 1946-49, Nat. d'Adminstrn., 1949-52. With French Coun. State, Paris, 1953-68; v.p. L'Express, Paris, 1968-70, chmn. bd., editor, 1970-71; chmn., columnist Le Point, Paris, 1972-86; dir. French museums Ministry Culture, Paris, 1987-90; chmn. Lab. Delagrange, 1990-91; vice-chmn. Groupe Cofremca, Paris, 1991-96; chmn. Cofremca-Sociovision, Bussiere, Brodard et Taupin, Paris, 1996—. Vice-chmn. French-Am. Found., Paris, 1978-88. Lt. French Air Force, 1952-53. Mem. Le Siecle Club. Home: 15 rue Maitre Albert, 75005 Paris France Office: Cofremca-Sociovsion, 16 rue d'Athènes, 75009 Paris France

CHEVROLLE, FRANÇOISE, chemist; b. Paris, Mar. 12, 1948; d. Jean and Madeleine Lambert Baroux; m. Jean-François Chevrolle , Dec. 15, 1978. PhD in Chemistry, U. Paris, 1975; PhD, Nat. Pub. Health, Rennes, 1985; postgrad., Scis. Politiques, Paris. Chemist Hosp., Montpellier, 1979-81, French Health Ministry, Paris, 1985-89, Sanofi, Paris, 1989-93, French Blood Agy., Paris, 1993-2000, French Nat. Blood Svc., Paris, 2000—. Author: Transfusion Clinique et Biologique, 1998; contbr. articles to profl. jours. Mem. Gercle Rep., Paris, 1998. Mem. Quality Health Soc., CoFRAC (lab. accreditation com. 1997). Avocations: hike in mountains, French history. Home: 218 Boulevard Raspail, 75014 Paris France Office: Etabussement Français, 100 ave de Suffren, 75015 Paris France

CHEW, DAVID K. M., company executive; b. Singapore, May 2, 1958; s. Shin Khiong and Lucy (Ng) C.; m. Sook Ching Leong, Apr. 29, 1995; 1 child, Phoebe Rong-Qi. PhD, U. So. Calif., 1986. Exec. chmn. Stratech Ltd., Singapore, 1989—. Capt. Singapore Armed Forces, 1976-79. Recipient employers award SAF, 1992, Enterpreneur of Yr. award ASME/Rotary, 1999, Enterprise 50 award EDB, AC, BT, 1999. Achievements include patent for portable weapons scoring system, intelligent car park system. Home: 52 Bayshore Pk Apt 09-02, Singapore 469978, Singapore Office: Stratech Ltd, 1 Internat Bus Pk 05-13/14, Singapore 609917, Singapore

CHEW, FOOK TIM, research scientist; b. Kuala Lumpur, Malaysia, Sept. 25, 1969; s. Pang Yin and Geat Choo (Yap) C.; m. Chye Fong Liew, July 8, 1995; 1 child, Joshua Chew Jian Xiang. BS in Biotech. with honors, Argl. U., Malaysia, 1993; PhD, Nat. U., Singapore, 1998. Lab. tech. Nat. U., Singapore, 1993, rsch. asst., 1994-98, rsch. fellow, 1998—; vis. rsch. assoc. Inst. Med. Rsch., Kuala Lumpur, Malaysia, 1994, U. Md., Balt., 1998. Inventor in field. Mem. Am. Acad. Allergy, Asthma & Immunology. Avocations: coin collecting, soccer. Office: Nat U Singapore, Lower Kent Ridge Rd, Singapore 119 074, Singapore

CHEW, JESSICA ALLEN, genetics researcher; b. Huntsville, Ala., Sept. 3, 1976; d. William Mahlon and Amy Allen Chew. BA in Molecular Biology with honors, Kenyon Coll., 1998. Rsch. apprentice U.S. Army Missile Command, Redstone Arsenal, Ala., summer 1994-96; tchg. asst. Kenyon Coll., Gambier, Ohio, 1996-97, sci. scholar, summer 1997; rsch. asst. Case Western Res. U., Cleve., 1998—. Tutor for study buddy program Big Bros./Big Sisters, Topeka, 1999—; vol. Shawnee County Health Dept., Topeka, 2000. Mem. Sigma Xi. Avocations: flute, handbells. Home: 1401 Old Carriage Ln SE Huntsville AL 35802-2762

CHEY, WILLIAM YOON, physician; b. Ki Jang, Korea, Jan. 21, 1930; s. Kee Bok and Myungkwon (Lee) C.; m. Fan K. Tang, May 21, 1959; children: William D., Donna C., Richard D., Laura C. MD, Seoul (Korea) Nat. U., 1953; MSc, U. Pa., 1962, DSc, 1966. Intern N.Y.C. Hosp., 1954-55, resident, 1955-56; resident in pathology Mount Sinai Hosp., N.Y.C., 1956-57; fellow in hepatology Seton Hall Med Coll., Jersey City, 1957-58; practice medicine specializing in gastroenterology Phila., 1967-71; attending physician Temple U. Med Center, Phila., 1963—; rsch. fellow in gastroenterology Samuel S. Fels Rsch. Inst., 1959-60; rsch. assoc. Samuel S. Fells Rsch. Inst., 1961, instr. medicine, 1961, assoc., 1963, asst. prof., 1965-68, assoc. prof., 1968-71; prof. medicine U. Rochester, N.Y., 1971-77, clin. prof., 1977-88, prof. medicine, 1988—; sr. attending physician, founding dir. Isaac Gordon Ctr. for Digestive Diseases and Nutrition, The Genesee Hosp., 1971-91; dir. divsn. gastroenterology and hepatology U. Rochester Sch. Medicine and Dentistry, 1992-2000, physician Strong Meml. Hosp., Rochester, 1992-2000; founding dir. William B. and Sheila Konar Ctr. for Digestive Liver Disease, Rochester, 1995—; dir. Rochester Inst. for Digestive Diseases and Scis., Rochester, N.Y., 2000—; cons. gastroenterologist Canandaigua (N.Y.) VA Hosp., 1977—; hon. prof. Catholic U. Med. Coll., Seoul, Korea, 1983; clin. prof. medicine Yunsei U. Sch. Medicine, Seoul, Korea, 1984; vis. prof. Peking Union Med. Coll., Beijing, Chinese Acad. Med. Scis., Beijing, 1985, Hallym U. Coll. of Medicine, Choonchun, Korea, 1986, Shanghai (People's Rep. China) Med. U., 1987, Korea U. Coll. Medicine, Seoul, 1991; mem. surgery and bioengring. study sect. Nat. Inst. of Diabetes, Digestive and Kidney Diseases, NIH, Bethesda, Md., 1982-86. Contbr. articles to profl. and sci. jours and textbooks; mem. editorial bd. The Pancreas, Am. Jour. Physiology. Fellow Am. Coll. Gastroent.; mem. AAAS, Am. Fedn. Clin. Rsch., Am. Gastroent. Assn., Am. Physiol. Soc., Am. Assn. Study Liver Disease, Am. Pancreatic Assn. (pres. 1999-2000), Internat. Assn. Pancreatology, Am. Motility Soc., Am. Soc. Gastrointestinal Endoscopy, Am. Soc. Acupuncture, Am. Coll. Acupuncture, Sigma Xi. Home: 133 Crescent Hill Rd Pittsford NY 14534-2406 Office: U Rochester Med Ctr 601 Elmwood Ave Rochester NY 14642-0001

CHEYNET DE BEAUPRE, BERTRAND CONSTANTIN, thermochemist, researcher; b. Lyon, France, Nov. 7, 1948; s. Maurice Charles and Jeanne Marie (Pellissier) C. de B.; m. Marie Claude Chambrion, July 31, 1976; children: Julien, Antoine. Diploma, U. Tech., Grenoble, France, 1973; MSc,

U. Grenoble, 1975, diploma profound studies, 1976; D, Nat. Poly. Inst., Grenoble, 1978. Engr. Thermodata, Grenoble, 1978-94, gen. mgr., 1994—; adminstr. sci. group Thermodata Europe. Author: Thermodynamic Properties of Inorganic Substances, 1989; author computer software COACH (Computer Assisted CHemistry), GEMINI (Gibbs Energy MINImizer). With inf. French Army, 1968-69. Mem. Soc. of Cincinnati. Avocations: snowboarding, skiing, biking, sailing. Home: 131 rue des Maquis du Gresivaudan, 38920 Crolles Cidex 250B, France Office: Thermodata, Grenoble Campus BP 66, 38402 Saint-Martin d'Heres Cedex, France

CHEZEM, DAVID EMIL, multimedia specialist; b. Denville, N.J., Mar. 11, 1974; s. Robert Emil and Helen Elizabeth Chezem; m. Amy Lee Siegrist, May 24, 1998. BS, Rowan U., 1996. Lab. technician Rowan U., Glassboro, N.J., 1996-97, computer technician, 1997, multimedia specialist, 1997—; cons. CRS, Wenonah, N.J.; Synchronized Multimedia Integration Lang. developer Real Networks Developer; mem. mobile adv. coun. Internat. Data Corp.; streaming audio and video developer, Flash developer, mem. Rsch. and Tech. Com. Avocations: construction, history, volleyball. Fax: (856) 256-4915. E-mail: chezem@rowan.edu. Home: 578 Princeton Blvd Wenonah NJ 08090-1401 Office: Rowan U 201 Mullica Hill Rd Glassboro NJ 08028-1702

CHHABRA, TARLOK SINGH, advertising company executive; b. Ludhiana, Punjab, India, Feb. 7, 1942; s. Arjun Singh Chhabra; m. Santosh K. Kaur Arora, 1965; 2 children. BA, Punjab U., Patiala, India, 1961; MA, Utkal U., Bhubaneswar, India, 1963; LLB, Kurukshtra (India) U. Advt. cons. Universal Internat. Advt. Inc., Chandigarh, India, 1965—; mgmt. cons., 1994—. Avocations: traveling, correspondence. Office: Univ Intl Inc, 889 Sector 60, 160059 Chandigarh Mohali, India

CHHATWAL, AMAR SINGH, editor; b. Bhalwal, Punjab, Pakistan, Oct. 1, 1912; arrived in Eng., 1962; s. Sundar Singh and Sat Bharai (Bindra) C.; m. Satwant Sita Kaur Kapany, Oct. 14, 1937 (dec. Mar. 1991); children: Hardaman Kaur Chopra, Mohin Preet Kaur Magon, Harjas Kaur Bharara. Student, Khalsa Coll., Gujranwala, Pakistan, 1930; grad., Forman Christian Coll., Lahore, Pakistan, 1932; 1st Examination in Law, Law Coll., Lahore, 1935. Salesman Goodyear Tire Co., Lahore, 1935-37; mng. dir. exec. Chhatwal & Co. Ltd., Lahore, 1935-47; proprietor Chhatwal & Co., Delhi, India, 1947-53; ptnr. Chhatwal Mfg. Corp., Amritsar, India, 1953-61; exec. officer Dept. Trade and Industry, London, 1962-77; mng. editor Sikh Courier Internat., London, 1962—. Pres. Punjabee Soc. Brit. Isles, London, 1966-68, Edgware Gurdwara, Middlesex, London, 1970-90; trustee World Congress Faiths, London, 1975-90; exec. mem. World Conf. Religions for Peace, London, 1980-90; gen. sec. World Sikh Found., London. Mem. Cen. Sikh Temple. Avocations: reading, writing, traveling. Home: Russells 43 Stradbroke Dr, IG7 5RA Chigwell Essex, England Office: 33 Wargrave Rd South Harrow, Middlesex HA2 8LL, England

CHHATWAL, VIKRAM JIT SINGH, surgeon, consultant, researcher; b. Silchar, Assam, India, Nov. 6, 1969; s. Mohinder Jit Singh and Sushma (Renjen) C. MBBS, Jawaharlal Nehru Med. Coll., Belgaum, India, 1991; diploma in Journalism, Bharitiya Vidya Bhavan, Delhi, India, 1996; PhD, Nat. U. Singapore, 1996; diploma in healthcare adminstrn., Inst. Health Care Adminstrn., Chennai, India, 1998; MBA, Ecole Nat des Ponts et, Chausseurs, Paris, 1998; Grad. Fletcher Sch. of Law/Diplomacy, Tufts U., 1999. Intern Safdargum Hosp., Delhi, 1992-93; vis. fellow NUH, Singapore, 1993; post graduate NUS, Singapore, 1993-96; dy. gen. mgr. Strategic Planning FDS Gainwell, Bangalore, India, 1996-97, gen. mgr. Strategic Planning, 1997-98; assoc. UTI Securities Exch., Mumbai, India, 1998-99; CEO Apollo Health St, Hyderabad, India, 2000—; cons. Med. TV, Jain TV, New Delhi, India, 1992-93, Jour. Am. Med. Assn., New Delhi, 1992-93, Ronak Engring., Bangalore, 1996-98, Venu Eye Ctr., New Delhi, 1997; cons. palliative medicine Indraprastha Apollo Hosp., New Delhi, 1997—. Contbr. articles to profl. jours. Vol. Nat. Cadet Corps., Delhi, 1986, Hospice Care Assn., Singapore, 1993. Recipient Best Free Paper award Acad. Med., Singapore, 1994. Mem. Sikh Ch. Avocations: golf, rifle shooting, reading, travelling. Fax: 9140-3608050. E-mail: vchhatwal@system3.net. Home: 352 Sector 29, Noida UP 201303, India Office: Apollo Health St, Jubilee Hills, Hyderabad 500 033, India

CHI, BENJAMIN E., computer network executive; b. Tianjian, China, June 18, 1933; came to U.S., 1940; s. Hilary Shou-Yu and Emily Exner Chi; m. Virginia, Feb. 17, 1967. BS, Antioch Coll., 1955; PhD, Rensselaer Poly. Inst., Troy, N.Y., 1962. Postdoctoral fellow, instr. Case Western Res. U., Cleve., 1962-65; summer rsch. fellow U. Minn., Mpls., 1963; from asst. prof. to assoc. prof. physics, dir. computer ctr. SUNY, Albany, 1965-99; dir. advanced technologies NYSERNet, Troy, 1999—; cons. in field. Mem. Assn. Computing Machinery, Sigma Xi. E-mail: bec@nysernet.org. Home: 1424 River Rd Selkirk NY 12158-1603 Office: NYSERNet 385 Jordan Rd Troy NY 12180-7620

CHI, HAOTIAN, federal official. Min. of nat. def. China. Office: 25 Huang Si Da Jie, De Sheng Men Wai East Dist, Beijing 100011, China*

CHI, TONG CHINI, materials scientist; b. Johok Bahru City, Malaysia, Aug. 6, 1955; s. Tong Chua Chor and Ng Ou Tiow. Grad. h.s., Malaysia, 1973. Supr. Bird Park, Singapore, 1971-77; material advisor Sentosa, Singapore, 1978-87; material specialist Singapore Zoo, 1989-90, Motorola, 1990—. Mem. Nature Soc. Singapore. Avocations: swimming, reading, running, camping, soccer.

CHIA, PEI-YUAN, banking executive; b. Hong Kong, Jan. 27, 1939; came to U.S., 1962, naturalized, 1970; s. Dewey T.H. and Kitty C.; m. Frances T.C. Yen, Feb. 20, 1965; children: Katherine, Douglas, Candice. BA, Tunghai U., Taiwan, 1961; MBA, U. Pa., 1965. Products group mgr. Gen. Foods Corp., White Plains, N.Y., 1965-73; mktg. dir. Citibank (N.A.), N.Y.C., 1974-77; mng. dir. Famibank, Belgium, 1978-80; pres., chief exec. officer Diner Club/Carte Blanche Corp., L.A., 1980, divsn. exec., 1982-84; group exec., mem. policy com. Diner Club/Carte Blanche Corp., 1985-90; sector exec. global consumer banking Citibank, N.Y.C., 1991-92; sr. exec. v.p., mem. mgmt. com. Citicorp, 1992, vice chmn., 1994-96; bd. dirs. Am. Internat. Group, Inc., Baxter Internat., CNH Global, N.V. Trustee Mt. Sinai-NYU Med. Ctr. Health Sys., Asia Soc.; mem. grad. exec. bd., sr. fellow SEI Ctr. for Advanced Studies in Mgmt., U. Pa. Wharton Sch.; adv. coun. Rockefeller U. Office: 298 Bedford-banksville Rd Bedford NY 10506-1925

CHIA, TIMOTHY CHEE MING, investment banker; b. Singapore, Jan. 5, 1950; s. Cheng Guan and Janet Yoke Leng (Leong) C. BS in Mgmt. cum laude, Fairleigh Dickinson U., 1972. Exec. trainee Am. Express, Singapore, 1972-74; investment asst. AIA Co. Ltd., Singapore, 1974, investment adminstr., 1976; asst. v.p. investments AIA Co. Ltd., Hong Kong, 1978, 81-82, v.p. investments, 1983-86; pres. Unithai Oxide Co Ltd. and Thai Lysaght Co. Ltd., Thailand, 1981-82, Prudential Asset Mgmt. Asia Ltd., Hong Kong, 1986—; mng. dir. PAMA (Singapore) Pte. Ltd., 1986—. Office: PAMA (Singapore) Pvt Ltd, 20 Collyer Quay 21-02 Tung, Singapore 049319, Singapore

CHIACCHIERE, MARK DOMINIC, lawyer; b. Phila., Dec. 10, 1966; s. Dominic Joseph and Diana (Alosi) C. BSBA, Georgetown U., 1989; JD, Villanova U., 1992. Bar: Pa. 1992, N.J. 1992, U.S. Dist. Ct. (ea. dist.) Pa. 1993, U.S. Ct. Appeals (3d cir.) 1993, U.S. Dist. Ct. N.J. 1992. Assoc. O'Brien & Ryan, Plymouth Meeting, Pa., 1992-94, White & Williams, Phila., 1994-97; bd. dirs. The Savoy Co. Phila., treas., 1999—. Facilitator Parish Coun., Phila., 1996-97. Mem. ABA, Phila. Bar Assn., Savoy Co. (bd. dirs., treas.), Alpha Phi Omega (Mu Alpha alumni sec. 1991-97, bd. dirs. 1995—). Office: 1500 Locust St Apt 3507 Philadelphia PA 19102-4324

CHIAIA, BERNARDINO MARIA, engineering educator, consultant; b. Bari, Italy, May 7, 1966; s. Carlo Chiaia and Adriana Concetta Della Ratta; m. Silvia Bettocchi, Oct. 18, 1997; 1 child, Irene. M in Civil Engring., U. Bari, 1991; PhD in Structural Engring., Politechnic Turin, Italy, 1995. Cert. profl. civil engr. Civil engr. A. Chiaia & Assocs., Bari, 1991-93; asst. rschr. Politechnic Turin, 1992-95, asst. prof., 1995-98, prof. structural mechanics, 1998—; cons. A. Chiaia & Assocs., Bari, 1991-93, Ct. Justice, Bari, 1991—. Contbr. articles to profl. jours. Rsch. grantee Delft U. Tech., 1995. Mem. Italian Soc. Fracture (mem. directive coun. 1997—), Com. Scaling Quasi-Brittle Fracture. Roman Catholic. Office: Polytechnic Turin, Corso Duca degli Abruzzi 24, 10129 Turin Italy

CHIANG, ALBERT CHINFA, polymer chemist; b. Pai-ho, Tainan, Taiwan, Jan. 3, 1946; came to U.S., 1973; s. Long and Ping (Su) C.; m. Geraldine Chin, June 4, 1978; 1 child, Scott Jinlong. BS, Nat. Chung-Hsing U., Taichung, Taiwan, 1970; MS, Georgetown U., 1977; PhD, Am. U., 1980. Teaching asst. Georgetown U., Washington, 1974-77, Am. U., Washington, 1977-80; assoc. chemist Pitney Bowes, Stamford, Conn., 1980-81, chemist, 1982-83, staff chemist, 1984-86, sr. chemist, 1987-89, tech. advisor, 1989-92; v.p. R&D Mearthane Products, Cranston, R.I., 1992-97, v.p., 1998—; mem. Chinese Oversea Scholar, Taipei, Taiwan, 1980—. Mem. adv. bd. Am. Security Coun., Washington, 1984. Dissertation fellow Am. U., 1979. Mem. Am. Chem. Soc. (rubber div. 1987—), Soc. Plastics Engring. (sr. mem.), Photography of Sci. and Engring. Achievements include 11 patents and 4 patents pending; development of processes for preparation of polypheynlacetylene and desulfurization of coal; invention of materials for electrophotographic toners, high solid content emulsion formation, flourescent thermal transfer ribbon formation, new dual-step thermal transfer printing; research in rubber, photopolymers, thermal printing, polyurethane manufacturing, conducting polymers including conductive urethane, acrylate, highly conjugated rubber and plastics, and high temperature superconducting material formation, non-impact printing technology and printing materials for postage meter and other mailing system machines; development and production of laser printer rollers including charge roller, developer roller, toner pick-up roller, paper transport roller, in-line skate wheel and live action skate wheel having a breaking mechanism; developed toner for office machine application and medical grade urethane for medical applications. Home: 112 Deerfield Ridge Dr Mystic CT 06355-1150

CHIANG, BENJAMIN BI-NIN, research foundation administrator; b. Republic of China, July 8, 1929; m. Annie Ying-Wha Shai, Aug. 23, 1958; children: Jane, Lily. MD, Nat. Def. Med. Ctr., Taipei, Taiwan, 1954. Chief cardiology div. Vets. Gen. Hosp., Taipei, 1966-80, chmn. dept. of medicine, 1980-85, dir. clin. research ctr., 1982-96, dep. dir., 1985-96; ret., 1996; prof., chmn. dept. of medicine Nat. Yang Ming Med. Coll., Taipei, 1980-85, dir. inst. clin. medicine, 1986—, dean sch. of medicine, 1985—; pres. Rsch. Found. Cardiovasc. Medicine; physician to late Pres. of China, Chiang Chin Kuo, 1978-88. Author: Clinical Echocardiography, 1979, Clinical Electrocardiography, 1983; editor Jour. Echocardiography, 1984, Jour. AMA (Southeast Asia div.), 1984, Jour. Medicine Digest, 1984. Named one of 10 Most Outstanding Young Men Jr. Chamber of Commerce, Taipei, 1966, one of 10 Most Outstanding Vets. Vocat. Aaasistance Commn. of Retired Servicemen, Taipei, 1979; research fellow U. London, 1962-64, U. Mich, 1967-69. Fellow Royal Coll. Physicians, Am. Coll. Cardiology, Am. Coll. Chest Physicians; mem. Republic of China Soc. Cardiology (pres. 1987-90), Chinese Med. Assn. (exec. bd. 1969—). Home: 128-9B Sect 4, Chung Hsiao E Rd, Taipei 10646, Taiwan

CHIANG, KAO FEI, electronics engineering educator; b. Kiangsi, China, Mar. 23, 1947; arrived in New Zealand, 1996; s. Shih Sheng Chiang and Feng Fung Shev; m. Han Shiow Liu, July 22, 1973; children: Ming-Ling, Ming-Shan. BSEE, Chung Cheng Inst Tech, Taiwan, 1968, MSEE, 1972; degree in engring., U. So. Calif., 1977; PhD, Nat. Chen-Kung U., Taiwan, 1988. Sr. engr., dir. Chung Shan Inst. Sci. Tech., 1972-93; assoc. prof. electronic engring. Nan-Tai Inst. Tech., Tai-Nan City, Taiwan, 1993—. Contbr. articles to engring. jours. Col. Army Signal Corps, 1983-93, Taiwan. Stanford U. vis. scholar, 1986. Mem. IEEE, Armored Forces Comm. Electronics Assn. Avocations: music, travel. Home: 5F #28 Alley 14 Lane 283, Sect 3 Roosevelt Rd, Taipei Taiwan Office: So Taiwan U Electronic Dept Nai-Tan Inst Tech EE Dept, Nai-Tan St #1, Tainan 710, Taiwan

CHIANG, KIN SENG, optical physicist, engineering educator; b. Zhongshan, Guangdong, People's Republic China, Aug. 18, 1957; d. Arthur and Lai Kam (Lei) Jan; m. Yuan Li Chiang, July 3, 1984; children: Cordelia, Shannon. BEE, U. NSW, Sydney, Australia, 1982, PhD, 1986. Rsch. officer Australian Def. Force Acad., Canberra, Australia, 1986; from rsch. scientist to sr. rsch. scientist div. applied physics Commonwealth Sci. and Indsl. Rsch. Orgn., Sydney, 1986-93; from sr. lectr. to prof. City U. Hong Kong, 1993—; vis. scientist Electrotech. Lab., Tsukuba City, Japan, 1987-88; vis. fellow City Polytechnic Hong Kong, 1992. Contbr. articles to profl. jours., chpt. to book; inventor, patentee optical fiber ultrasonic sensors. Recipient rsch. award for fgn. specialists Govt. of Japan, 1987; rsch. scholar Govt. of Australia, 1982; Croucher Sr. fellow Croucher Found., 2000. Mem. IEEE, Optical Soc. Am., Internat. Soc. for Optical Engring., Australian Optical Soc. Avocations: travel, reading, badminton, table tennis, Chinese literature, translation. Office: City Univ Hong Kong, 83 Tat Chee Ave, Hong Kong Kowloon, China

CHIANG, WEN-YEN, engineering educator, consultant; b. Taichung, Taiwan, Aug. 9, 1938; s. Wei-Kung and Chin-Yun (Chien) C.; m. Mei-Jung Chang, Mar. 25, 1966; 2 children. BS, Nat. Taiwan U., 1961; MS in Engring., Tokyo U., 1965, D in Engring., 1969. Researcher Ctrl. Rsch. Labs. Kuraray Co., Kurashiki, Japan, 1969-73; researcher Inst. of Resource Utilization, Tokyo Inst. Tech., Tokyo, 1973-74; prof. Inst. Chem. Engring., Nat. Taiwan U., Taipei, 1979-80; plant gen. mgr. Tatung Co., Taoyuan, Taiwan, 1979-81; dir. preparatory divsn. Tatung Co., Taoyuan, 1985-89; dean Tatung Inst. Tech., Taipei, 1981-89; cons. Tatung Co., 1979-97; mem. com. Nat. Sci. Coun., Taipei, 1994—. Author: An Essay of Science and Technology, 1981. Patentee in field. Lt. in Res. Officers Tng. Corps, 1961-62. Recipient Rotary Yoneyama Meml. Found. award, Tokyo, 1966-69, 1990, Hsie-Chih Assn. Found. award, Taipei, 1975, 76, 78, 84-99, Excellent Rsch. award Nat. Sci. Coun., Taipei, 1975—. Mem. Soc. Plastic Engrs. Avocations: collecting stamps, jogging, travel, reading and writing. Home: 7F 11-4 Ln 69 Tien Mu E Rd, Taipei 11131, Taiwan Office: Tatung Inst Tech, 40 Chungshan N Rd 3d Sec, Taipei 10451, Taiwan

CHIANG, YUNG FRANK, law educator; b. Taichung, Taiwan, Jan. 2, 1936; came to U.S., 1961; s. Ruey-ting and Yueh-yin (Ho) C.; m. Quay-yin Lin, Nov. 1, 1969; children: Amy P., David H. LLB, Nat. Taiwan U., 1958; LLM, Northwestern U., 1962; JD, U. Chgo., 1965. Bar: Taiwan 1960, N.Y. 1974. Assoc. Yen & Lai Law Office, Taipei, Taiwan, 1960-61; editor The Lawyers Co-op Pub. Co., Rochester, N.Y., 1965; rsch. assoc. in law Harvard Law Sch., Cambridge, Mass., 1965-67; asst. prof. law U. Ga. Sch. Law, Athens, 1967-72; assoc. prof. law Fordham U. Sch. Law, N.Y.C., 1972-76, prof. law, 1976—; legal cons., vice chmn. Asia Bank, N.A., Flushing, N.Y., 1983-88; leader N.Y. judge and lawyers del. to China and Hong Kong, People to People Internat., 1994; organizer, moderator 5 Russian delegations to U.S., People to People Amb. Program, 1994-95; pres. Fordham U. Law Faculty Union, 2000—. Contbr. articles to law jours. Organizer, bd. dirs. The Taiwan Mcht. Assn. N.Y., Flushing, 1976-96, pres., 1980-84; pres. N.Y. chpt. Formosan Assn. for Pub. Affairs, Washington, 1991, 92. Mem. N.Y. State Bar Assn., N.Am. Taiwanese Profs. Assn. (bd. dirs. 1994-96, 1997—, v.p. 1997-98, pres. 1998-99), Nat. Assn. of Securities Dealers (arbitrator 1976-98), Order of Coif. Avocations: reading, skiing, archery, swimming. Office: Fordham U Sch Law 140 W 62nd St New York NY 10023-7407

CHIAPELLA, ANNE PAGE, epidemiologist; b. Oakland, Calif., Oct. 12, 1942; d. Karl Josef and Anne Elizabeth (Gorrill) C. BA in Polit. Sci., Stanford U., 1964, PhD in Neurosci., 1982, MS in Stats., 1985; MPH in Epidemiology, Johns Hopkins U., 1986. Med. rschr. Stanford (Calif.) U., 1966-75, postdoctoral fellow, 1983-85; postdoctoral fellow Johns Hopkins U., Balt., 1986-88; program officer Inst. Medicine NAS, Washington, 1989-91; sr. analyst Nat. Inst. on Alcohol and Alcohol Abuse, Rockville, Md., 1991—; statis. and intellectual property cons. various orgns., Washington, 1983—; internat. rsch. on alcohol-related problems, 1993—. Writer humorous, tech. and travel speeches, 1985—; reviewer grants and sci. jours., 1992—; contbr. articles to sci. jours. Pres. Nebr. Ave. Neighborhood Assn., Washington, 1987-91, 2000—; assoc. Smithsonian Instn., Washington, 1987—; active in Friends of Kennedy Ctr., Washington, 1987—, Friends of Nat. Zoo, Washington, 1987—, Textile Mus., Washington, 1986—, WETA, Pub. Broadcasting Svc., 1997—. Grantee and fellow NIH, 1975, 77, 83, 86; grantee Environ. Health Sci. Ctr., 1986. Mem. AAAS, APHA, Soc. Epidemiologic Rsch., Toastmasters Internat. (officer 1987-89), Am. Statis. Assn. Avocations: travel, writing, photography. Home: 5126 Nebraska Ave NW Washington DC 20008-2047

CHIAPPARELLI, MARCO, pharmaceutical company executive; b. Rome, Feb. 18, 1955; s. Italo and Rosa Maria (Miceli) C.; m. Emi Morroni, Feb. 20, 1980 (div. 1987). MD, U. La Sapienza, Rome, 1979, Specialist in Obstetrics and Gynecology, 1983. Med. diplomate. Clin. rsch. assoc. Abbott, Campoverde, Italy, 1983-86; asst. to med. dir. Biomedica Foscama, Rome, 1986-93; dir. med. affairs Sankyo Pharma Italia (formerly Luitpold), Rome, 1993—. Contbr. articles to profl. jours.; patentee in field. 1st lt. Health Svc., Italian Army, 1980-82. Mem. Faculty of Pharm. Med., Societa di Scienze Farmacologiche Applicate. Home: Via Arta Terme 50, 00188 Rome Italy Office: Sankyo Pharma Italia, Via Montecassiano 157, 00156 Rome Italy

CHIARELLI, ROBERT CHARLES, audio engineer; b. Mass., Jan. 13, 1963; s. Carmello Charles C.; m. Theresa Pauline; 1 child, Robert Michael. Student, U. Miami. CEO 3.6 Music, L.A. Mixer albums for Will Smith, Christina Aguilera, Madonna, Ricky Martin, Temptations, Michael Bolton, Janet Jackson. Bd. dirs. Great Leap, Santa Monica, Calif. Mem. Am. Fedn. Musicians, Nat. Acad. Arts & Scis. Office: Final Mix Inc 2219 W Olive Ave Ste 102 Burbank CA 91506-2625

CHIARI, ADRIANA, dentist, artist; b. Milan, Milano, Italy, Sept. 5, 1957; d. Adriano and Gioconda (Arimini) C.; m. Marco Bruno Gusmeroli, Aug. 15, 1995; 1 child, Rodolfo. Grad., U. Milan, Italy, 1982, specialty Odontoiatric and Prosthetics, 1985, specialty Orthodontics, 1987. cons. U. Milan, 1985-90, 1998—. Artist, sculptor: 2d prize Pop Art Sculpture, 1994, Critic's prize, 1995, Monbadori Art prize, 1996 (2d); Featured in Article "Fish Out of Water" ARCA Jour., 1992. Mem. Am. Assn. Orthodontics, Assn. Me4d. Dentists Italian, Societe Italians di Ortodoncia. Home: Corso Repubblica 54, 28041 Arona Italy Office: Corso Liberazione 39, 28041 Arona Italy

CHIAROTTI, GIANFRANCO, physics educator; b. Como, Italy, July 6, 1928; s. Luigi and Maria (Paltrinieri) C.; m. Aida Repanai, Oct. 26, 1959; children: Guido, Laura, Ugo. PhD in Physics, U. Pavia, Italy, 1951. Asst. U. Pavia, 1951-55; asst. prof. U. Ill., Urbana, 1955-57; prof. U. Messina, Italy, 1962-65, U. Rome, 1965—; Francqui prof. U. Liege, Belgium, 1975; chmn. nat. com. for physics Nat. Rsch. Coun., Rome, 1988-94. Editor: Current Trends in the Physics of Materials, 1990, Physics of Solid Surfaces (4 vols.), 1993. Fellow Am. Phys. Soc.; mem. Nat. Acad. Italy (Feltrinelli Prize for Physics 1991). Office: Dept Physics U of Rome, Via Ricerca Scientifica 1, 00133 Rome Italy

CHIBBER, PANNA, bioenvrionmental engineer; b. Chandigarh, India, Oct. 14, 1974; came to U.S., 1975; d. Pradeep and Kamlesh (Dutta) C. BS in Polit. Sci., Pa. State U., 1996; M of Aeronautic Sci., Embry Riddle U. Commd. airman 1st class USAF, 1997; bioenvironmental engr. technician USAF, Lakenheath, Eng., 1997—. Author: Anonymous, 1997; editor Hubris, 1995. Jr. asst. Congressman Paul McHale, 1995. Democrat. Hindu. Avocations: piano, running, writing, painting, weight training. Home: 1980 Linden Ln Whitehall PA 18052-3740

CHIBUZO, GREGORY ANENONU, veterinary educator; b. Abor, Enugu, Nigeria, July 25, 1943; s. Onyemahalu Paul and Nwakaku Jannet (Offiah) C.; m. Elizabeth Chinyere Onwu, Aug. 8, 1972; children: Chinyere, Uzoego, Chukwuemeka, Ijeoma. BSc, Tuskegee U., 1968, DVM, 1970, MSc, 1975; PhD, Cornell U., 1979. Asst. prof. anatomy Tuskegee U., 1973-76, assoc. prof. anatomy, 1976-79, prof. anatomy, 1979-82; prof. vet. anatomy U. Maiduguri, Nigeria, 1982—; founding dean faculty vet. medicine U. Maiduguri, 1983-93, chmn. dept. vet. anatomy, 1984-88; biomed. cons. So. Vocat. Coll., Tuskegee, 1980-82; external examiner U. Ibadan, Nigeria, 1984-86, U. Nigeria, Nsukka, 1995-97. Author: Our Reactions and The Nervous System, 1986, Ruminant Dissection Guide, 1994; contbr. articles to profl. jours.; cons. editor Tropical Veterinarian, 1989-93. Mem. governing coun. Abubakar T.B. U., Nigeria, 1989-93, U. Maiduguri, 1993-96; chmn. electoral com. Igbo Welfare Assn., Maiduguri, 1993; assessor Nigeria Nat. Merit Award, 1997-2000. Recipient Traveling award to Can. univs. Assn. Commonwealth Univs., London, 1988; health faculty rsch. fellow NIH, Bethesda, Md., 1977. Mem. Internat. Goat Assn., Nigerian Vet. Med. Assn., Borno State Vet. Med. Assn. (pres.). Avocations: tennis, jugging, traveling, reading. Home: H-12 Quarters, Univ Maiduguri, Maiduguri Borno, Nigeria Office: U Maiduguri Fac Vet Med, PMB 1069, Maiduguri Borno, Nigeria

CHICCO, BRUNO, research scientist; b. Isola, Italy, Jan. 27, 1939; arrived in Australia, 1954; s. Giusto and Gisella Chicco; m. Nina Christina Petersen, May 11, 1968; children: Christina, David. BTech, U. Adelaide, Australia, 1963. Cadet chemist DHA Pty. Ltd., Adelaide, 1957-61; chemist F.H. Faulding & Co., Adelaide, 1961-64, prodn. supr., 1964-67; exptl. officer Dept. Def., Adelaide, 1967-77; exptl. scientist Commonwealth Scientific & Indsl. Rsch. Orgn., Adelaide, 1977-93, sr. scientist, 1993—. Contbr. articles to profl. jours. Roman Catholic. Avocations: reading, tennis, roses, soccer, travel. Office: CSIRO-MST, 32 Audley St, Woodville North SA 5012, Australia

CHICHE, BERNARD, surgeon, researcher; b. Alger, Algeria, Nov. 16, 1942; s. Martin and Mireille Amsellem C.; m. Claudine Fau, Dec. 15, 1976; children Frederic, Caroline. MD, Med. Sch. Paris, 1973. Cert. in laparoscopy. Specialized tchr. anatomy Med. U. Paris, 1968-73, asst. head dept. anatomy, 1973-80; chief staff surgery St. Anne Hosp., Paris, 1980—, René Descartes U., 1980—; gen. surgeon Blomet Hosp., 1980—; prof. Coll. Medicine Hosp., Paris, 1980—; tchr. surgical procedure, medical law U. Paris, 1980—; pvt. practice Paris, 1980—; pvt. hosp. practice Clinic Blomet, Paris, 1980—. Author: (with D. Buthiau) Imagerie Clinique in Gynecology, 1993, Emergencies in Surgery, 1976; contbr. over 80 articles in profl. jours.; developed laparoscopic surgery in both digestive (gallblader, colonic surgery, hernia) and gynecologic tracts; developed open surgery: esophagus, pancreas, colon and rectum. Elected medical expert Paris Court, 1986. Fellow ACS, French Acad. Surgery, French Soc. Gynecology, French Soc. Phlebology, French Coll. Vascular Pathology. Home: 48 Ave de Saxe, 75007 Paris France Office: Hosp Sainte Anne, 1 Rue Cabanis, 75014 Paris France

CHICHETTO, JAMES WILLIAM, editor, educator; b. Boston, June 5, 1941; s. Francis Anthony and Christina McInnis C. B of Philosophy, Stonehill Coll., 1964; M of Theology, Holy Cross Coll., 1968; MA, Wesleyan U., 1978. Ordained to ministry, Cath. Ch. the Congregation of Holy Cross, 1968. Assoc. editor Gargoyle Mag., Cambridge, Mass., 1975-81, Conn. Poetry Rev., Stonington, 1981-84, 1984-88, asoc. editor, art editor, 1988-89, editor, 1989-91; prof. writing Stonehill Coll., North Easton, Mass., 1991—; art editor East & West Lit. Quar., San Francisco, 1995—. Author of poems, essays, revs. and plays. Mem. Easton Arts Coun., 1994-98. Recipient Sri Chinmoy award, 1986; NEA grantee, 1980, 83. Fellow World Lit. Assn.; mem. Assn. Lit. Scholars. Democrat. Avocations: painting, sketching. Home: 474 Washington St North Easton MA 02357-0001 Office: Stonehill Coll 430 Washington St Easton MA 02357

CHICHILNISKY, GRACIELA, mathematician, economist, educator, consultant; b. Buenos Aires, Mar. 27, 1946; came to U.S., 1968, naturalized citizen, 1992; d. Salomon Chichilnisky and Raquel Gavensky; children: Eduardo Jose, Natasha Sable. Student, MIT, 1967-68; MA, U. Calif., Berkeley, 1970, PhD in Math., 1971, PhD in Econs., 1976. Postdoctoral fellow Harvard U., 1974, lectr. dept. econs., 1975-77, fellow Harvard inst. internat. devel., 1978; assoc. prof. Columbia U., N.Y.C., 1977-80, prof., 1981—, dir. program on info. and resources, 1994—, prof. stats, 1996—, dir. Ctr. for Risk Mgmt., 1998—; UNESCO chair math. and econs., 1995—; chmn., CEO Cross Border Exch. Corp., 1999—; mem. presdl. cabinet Banco Ctrl. Repubica Argentina, 1971-74; co-prin. investigator Urban Inst., Washington, 1975-77; vis. scholar Internat. Inst. Applied Sys, Analysis Laxenburg, Austria, 1975-77; prin. investigator U.S. Dept. Labor, 1977-78, Rockefeller Found. Project Internat. Rels., 1981-83; project dir. UN Inst. Tng. and Rsch., N.Y., 1979-83; chaired prof. econs. U. Essex, 1980-81; vis. prof. inst. math and its applications U. Minn., 1983-84, U. Siena, Italy, summers, 1991-93; vis. prof. Stanford Inst. Theoretical Econs., Stanford U., summers, 1991-

93, dept. econs., Inst. Internat. Studies, 1993—, vis. prof. depts., econ. and ops. rsch. Stanford U., 1993-94; prof. missionaire U. des Antilles et de la Guyane, spring 1984-85; NSF prof. dept. math. U. Calif., Berkeley, 1985-86; CEO, chmn. FITEL Ltd., 1985-89; exec. dir. Sci. Internat. Ltd., 1989-90; vis. prof. U. Cath. Buenos Aires, Aug. 1993; cons. in field; UNESCO chair in math. and econs., Columbia U., 1995—; Salinbemi chair U. Siena, Italy, 1994-95. Co-author: Catastrophe or New Society? A Latin American World Model, 1976; author: (with G. Heal) The Evolving International Economy, 1986, Oil in the International Economy, 1991, Sustainability: Dynamics and Uncertainty, 1998, Mathematical Economics, 1998, Topology and Markets, 1998, Markets, Information and Uncertainty, 1998, Environmental Markets: Equity and Efficiency, 1999; assoc. editor Jour. Devel. Econs., 1976-86, Advances in Mathematics, 1985, Risk Decision and Policy; mem. various editorial bds.; contbr. articles to profl. jours. Bd. trustees Nat. Resources Def. Coun., N.Y., 1994—. Recipient Internat. Rels. award Rockefeller Found., 1983-84; named Most Disting. Woman Economist, Newcombe Found. and Omega Delta Epsilon, 1991, Leif Johansen award U. Oslo, Norway, 1995; grantee NSF, 1974—; fellow Ford Found., 1967-69, Banco Ctrl. Republica Argentina, 1972-74, spl. fellow UN Inst. Tng. and Rsch., 1977-76. Mem. Coun. Social Choice and Welfare Soc. Office: Columbia U Program Info and Resources 405 Low Libr 116th & Broadway New York NY 10027

CHICHINADZE, VAKCHTANG KONSTANTINE, mathematician; b. Tbilisi, Georgia, Sept. 23, 1918; s. Konstantine and Alexandra (Gotsiridze) C.; m. Ketevan Gachechiladze, Jan. 9, 1951; children: Eliso, Revaz. Engr., Poly. Inst. Tbilisi, 1947; MS, Control Problem Inst. Moscow, 1952, DSc, 1968. Dep. dir. Inst. Electronics and Automatics, Tbilisi, 1956-71; dir. Inst. Microelectronics, Tbilisi, 1971-74; dep. minster High edn. Ministry, Tbilisi, 1974-78; adviser of dir. Inst. Computing Maths., Tbilisi, 1978—; prof. Poly. Inst., Tbilisi, 1949. Author: Numerical Optimizaiton of Dynamic Problems, 1980, The Solution of Unconvex Non-Linear Optimal Problems, 1983. With Georgian Mil., 1941-45, WWII. Decorated Order of the Red Star, Order of the Patriotic War. Mem., IEEE (sr.), Nat. Geographic Soc., Planetary Soc., Acad. Scis. Home: 16 Chavchavadze Ave, 380079 Tbilisi Georgia Office: Inst Computing Maths, 8 Akurskaya, 380093 Tbilisi Georgia

CHI-CHU, LO, pesticide educator; b. Hwa-lien, Taiwan, China, Nov. 12, 1952; s. Dei-Hsing and Yu-In (Wu) Lo; m. Chang Chai-Ju, Jan. 8, 1982; children: Ta-tung, Shou-Ju, Hsiao-Shan. BS, Nat. Chung-Hsing U., Taichung, China, 1976; MS, Nat. Taiwan U., Taipei, China, 1980; PhD, Tex. A&M U., 1983. Instr. Nat. Taiwan U., Taipei, China, 1983-84; assoc. prof. Tunghai U., China, 1984-85; dept. head, sr. scientist Taiwan Agrl. Chems. & Toxic Substance Rsch. Inst., 1986-96; advisor pesticide and toxic chem. ctrl. Chinese Agrl. Tech. Team, Ministry of Agr. and Water, Riyadh, Saudi Arabia, 1997-98; prof. Nat. Chung Hsing U., 1995-96. Author: Pesticide Formulation and Application Systems, 1989; contbr. articles to profl. jours. Mem. Am. Chem. Soc., Chinese Chem. Soc. Office: Taiwan Agrl Chem Rsch Inst, 11 Kuang Ming Rd Wu-Feng, Taichung Hsien China

CHIDNESE, PATRICK N., lawyer; b. Neptune, N.J., May 26, 1940; s. Louis and Helen C.; 1 child, Krista; m. Kathy J. Chidnese, Feb. 16, 1985; children: Patrick, Nicole. B.A., U. Miami, 1964, J.D., 1968. Assoc. Sinclair, Louis & Huttoe, Miami, 1968-69; assoc. Stephens, Demos, Magil & Thornton, Miami, 1969-70; assoc. Howell, Kirby, Montgomery, D'Aiuto, Dean & Hallowes, Fort Lauderdale, Fla., 1970-71; sole practice, Fort Lauderdale, 1971—; county atty. Broward County Juvenile Ct., 1971-72. Mem. Fla. Bar Assn. (chmn. auto ins. com. 1977-78, chmn. 17th jud. circuit legis. com. 1977-80), Broward County Bar Assn., Acad. Fla. Trial Lawyers, Broward County Trial Lawyers Assn. (bd. dirs. 1974-80). Home: PO Box 18419 Asheville NC 28814-0419

CHIEFFI, GIOVANNI, biology educator; b. Naples, Italy, July 19, 1927; s. Lorenzo and Matilde (Notarloberti) C.; m. Anna Maria Valentino; children: Matilde, Lorenzo, Gabriella, Sergio, Silvia, Paolo. MD, Faculty Medicine & Surgery, Italy, 1950. Asst. to prof. Univ. Naples, 1950-62; rsch. assoc. Wayne State Univ., 1954-55, State Univ. Iowa, 1955-56; prof. Univ. Messina, Italy, 1962-63, Univ. Camerino, Italy, 1963-68, Univ. Naples, 1968—; bd. dirs. Genetica. Co-author: Biologia, 1995, Nature, London, 1958, 61, Internat. Review of Citology, 1996. Mem. Acad. Nazionale Dei Lincei, Acad. Pontaniana, Soc. Nazionale Sci. Home: Via Ligorio Pirro 20, 80129 Naples Italy Office: Univ Naples, VIa Costantinopoli 16, 80138 Naples Italy

CHIEGBOKA, PATRICIA CHINYERE, psychology administrator, consultant; b. Onitsha, Nigeria, Aug. 19, 1967; d. Godwin Igwekwube Ezenwobodo and Veronica Obiageli Obienyenwa; m. Leo Ifeanachor Chiegboka, Oct. 15, 1988; children: Chisom, Afoma, Ugochukwu, Onyekachi, Chidubem. Diploma in Hotel and Catering Mgmt., Inst. Mgmt. and Tech. Enugu, Nigeria, 1986; BSc in Gen. and Applied Psychology, U. Jos, Nigeria, 1995; diploma in computer programming, U. Lagos, Nigeria, 1996, MSc in Clin. Psychology, 1998. Tchr. home econs. and English lit. Social Centre Secondary Sch., Nigeria, 1987-88; lectr. hotel and catering mgmt. courses Social Centre Vocat. Sch., 1987-88; dir. Leonidas Assocs. Ltd., Lagos, 1990—; intern Jos U. Tchg. Hosp., 1994-95, Nigerian Army Base Hosp., Lagos, 1997-98; dir. Chiegboka Ventures Ltd., Lagos, 1997—; cons. marriage and family, 1995—; advisor Isuofia Women's Wing, Lagos, 1995—. Mem. APA, Internat. Coun. Psychologists, Nigeria Psychol. Assn. Roman Catholic. Avocations: helping people in difficulties, counselling, addressing the public, sports, music. E-mail: leonidas@micro.com.ng. Home: PO Box 4963, No 32 Bishop St, Surulere Lagos Nigeria Office: Chiegboka Ventures Ltd, No 32 Bishop St PO Box 4963, Surulere Lagos Nigeria

CHIEN, FRANCOISE FANG-LIN, immigration and education consultant; b. Taipei County, China, Oct. 23, 1965; d. Ching-tu and Wen Chen C.; m. Robert Fang, Sept. 10, 1992; children: Kenny Fang, Tina Fang, Trina Fang. BA, Soochow U., 1992. Sec. Advance Taiwan Co., Taipei, 1987-89; exec. sec. No. Maple Co., Ltd., Taipei, 1989-91; from mgr. to gen. mgr. E&C Overseas Enterprise Co., Ltd., Taipei, 1991—. Author, editor: Guide to American Private Secondary Schools, 1997, Stop, Look & Listen to American Immigration, 1999. Pres. Taipei Internat. Lion's Club, 1997-98, bd. dirs. 1998-99. Mem. Taipei Immigration Cons. Assn., Taiwan Overseas Study Assn. Fax: 886-2-27294940. E-mail: encmall@mszb.hinet.net. Home: 10-3F 6 Lane 79 Antei St, Nei-hu Dist Taipei, China

CHIEN, FREDRICK FU, Taiwan government official; b. Peiping, China, Feb. 17, 1935; s. Shih-liang and Wan-tu Chien; m. Julie Tien, Sept. 22, 1963; children: Carl, Carol. BA, Nat. Taiwan U., Taipei, 1956; MA, Yale U., 1959, PhD, 1962; LLD (hon.), Sung Kyun Kwan U., Republic of Korea, 1972, Caribbean Am. U., 1988, Boston U., 1997, Idaho State U., 1997; D in Literature (hon.), Wilson Coll., 1993; D in Pub. Svc. (hon.), Fla. Internat. U., 1994. Sec. to the premier Exec. Yuan, 1962-63; specialist, section chief Dept. North American affairs Min. Fgn Affairs., 1964-67, dep. dir. Dept. North American affairs, 1967-69, dir. Dept. North American affairs, 1969-72, dir.-gen. Govt. Info. Office, 1972-75, adminstrv. vice min., 1975-79, polit. vice min., 1979-82; U.S.A. rep. Coordination Coun. for North Am. Affairs, 1983-88; min. state, chmn. Coun. for Econ. Planning and Devel. Exec. Yuan, 1988-90; min. Ministry Fgn. Affairs, Republic of China, 1990-96; speaker Nat. Assembly, Taipei, 1996-98; pres. Control Yuan, Republic of China, 1999—; vis. assoc. prof. Nat. Chengchi U., 1962-64; vis. prof. Nat. Taiwan U., 1970-72, 97099, Soochow U., 1997-98. Author: The Opening of Korea, 1967, Speaking as a Friend, 1975, More Views of a Friend, 1976, Faith and Resilience, 1988, The Republic of China under the New International Order in the Post-Cold War Era, 1991, The Emerging Economic and Security Situation in Asia and Taiwan's Role in It, 1993, Prospects for Economic Growth in the Asia-Pacific Region: The Role of the Republic of China on Taiwan, 1994, Opportunity and Challenge, 1995. Active ctrl. standing com. Kuomintang, Taipei, 1988-99. 2d lt. Army, 1956-58. Decorated Order of Brilliant Star with Grand Cordon of Republic of China; Order of Diplomatic Svc. Merit (Republic of Korea); Kim Khanh Medal (Republic of Vietnam); Orden Nat. Del Merito en el Grado Del Gran Cruz, (Paraguay); El Grado de Gran Cruz Placa de Plata (Dominican Republic); Gran Cruz de Plata de la Orden De Jose Cecilio (Honduras); Orden Nat. "Jose Matias Delgado" en el Grado de Gran Cruz Placa de Plata (Salvador); grand officier L'Ordre Nat. Ordre Honneur et Merite (Haiti); Order of Good Hope in the Grand Cross Class (South Africa); Orden Merito en el Grado de Gran Cruz Extraordinario (Paraguay); Royal Order of Sobhuza II (Swaziland); Orden de Morazan Gran Cruz Placa de Plata (Honduras); grand officier Ordre Du Merite Centrafricain; Order of the Propitious Clouds with Grand Cordon (Republic of China). Avocations: reading, golf. Home: 25 Sung-chih Rd 4th Fl, Taipei Taiwan Office: Control Yuan, 2 Chung Hsiao E Rd Sec 1, Taipei Taiwan 10048, Republic of China

CHIEN, I JY (STEVEN CHIEN), engineering educator; b. Taipei, Taiwan, Oct. 15, 1960; came to U.S., 1989; s. Chung-Yueh Chien and Zuei-Chi Chang; m. Chin-Mann W. Chien, Feb. 25, 1989; children: Jeffrey, Angela. BS, Tamkang U., Taipei, 1983; MS, U. Md., 1991, PhD, 1995. Sys. engr. China Engr. Cons. Inc., Taipei, 1985-89; rsch. asst. U. Md., College Park, 1989-93; sr. transp. engr. Info. Dynamic Inc., Washington, 1993-96; asst. prof. N.J. Inst. Tech., Newark, 1996—. Contbr. articles to profl. jours. Mem. ASCE, Transp. Rsch. Bd., Inst. Transp. Engrng., Sigma Xi. Avocation: calligraphy. Office: Inst for Transp 161 Warren St Newark NJ 07103-3537

CH'IEN, RAYMOND KUO-FUNG, industrialist; b. Tokyo, Jan. 26, 1952; arrived in Hong Kong, 1957; s. James M.N. and Ellen A.L. (Ma) C.; m. Hwee Leng Whang, 1978; children: Kay Z.J., Karla Z.T., Karsten Z.T. BA in Econs., Rockford Coll., 1973; MA, U. Pa., 1976, PhD in Econs., 1978. Group mng. dir. Lam Soon H.K. Group, Hong Kong, 1984-97; chmn. Inchcape Pacific Ltd., Hong Kong, 1997—; chmn. HSBC Pvt. Equity Mgmt. Ltd. Mem. exec. coun. Hong Kong Govt., 1992-97, Hong Kong Spl. Adminstrv. Region of People's Republic of China, 1997—; chmn. Hong Kong/Japan Bus. Coop. Com., Hong Kong, 1995—, Hong Kong Indsl. Tech. Ctr. Corp., 1993—, Industry and Tech. Devel. Coun., Hong Kong, 1993—. Recipient Young Industrialist award Fedn. of Hong Kong Industries, 1988, Non-Offcl. Justice of the Peace for Hong Kong Gov. of Hong Kong, 1993, Comdr. of the Most Excellent Order of the British Empire Her Majesty the Queen, 1994. Mem. Global Leaders of Tomorrow of World Econ. Forum, Young Pres. Orgn. *

CHIEN, RONG-NAN, hepatologist; b. Changhwa, Taiwan, Oct. 22, 1958; s. Te-Yuan and Yang Nu (Yang) C.; m. Pao-Chin Tseng, Apr. 3, 1987; children: Chien Yu-Nien, Chien Yu-Hsuan. MD, China Med. Coll., Taichung, 1984. Diplomate Bd. Internal Medicine, Bd. Gastroenterology; cert. educator. Resident in internal medicine Chang Gung Meml. Hosp., Taipei, Taiwan, 1986-89, fellow hepato-gastroenterology, 1989-91, attending physician, 1991—; clin. instr. Chang Gung Med. Coll., Tao-Yuan, 1991—, instr. 1994—; assoc. prof. Chang Gung Nursing Inst., Tao-Yuan, 1997—. Inventor in field. Mem. European Assn. Study Liver, Taiwan Assn. Study Liver, Gastroenterolog. Soc. Taiwan. Avocations: jogging, movies, tennis, table tennis, basketball. Office: Liver Rsch Unit, 199 Tung Hwa N Rd, Taipei 10591, Taiwan

CHIEN, SUFAN, surgeon, educator; b. Zhejiang Province, China, July 20, 1938; came to U.S., 1982; s. Jiaxing and Julian (You) C.; m. Lorrain Wilson; children: Samson, Lynn. MD, Shanghai 1st Med. Coll., 1962. Resident dept. gen. surgery Zhongshan Hosp. Shanghai 1st Med. Coll., 1962-66, attending gen. surgeon, 1975-79; supr. cardiopulmonary bypass Shanghai Inst. Cardiovasc. Diseases, 1975-82, attending surgeon cardiovascular surgery, 1979-82; vis. scientist cardiovascular divsn. Mayo Clinic, Rochester, Minn., 1982-84; vis. scientist physiology and biophysics La. State U. Med. Ctr., Shreveport, 1984-85; vis. scientist surgery, physiology and biophysics U. Ky. Med. Ctr., Lexington, 1985-87, asst. prof. divsn. cardio-thoracic surgery, 1987-93, assoc. prof., 1993-96; assoc. prof. surgery U. Louisville, 1996—; invited lectr., presenter in field; mem. sci. rev. com. study sect. NIH. Author: Hibernation Induction Trigger for Organ Preservation, 1993; mem. editl. bd. Internat. Medicine Rev., 1979-84; contbr. articles and abstracts to med. jours., chpts. to books. Grantee NIH, VA, U.S. Army, AHA, Univ. Fellow Am. Coll. Angiology; mem. AHA, N.Y. Acad. Scis., Chinese Med. Assn., Chinese Surg. Assn., Chinese Soc. Thoracic Surgeons, Shanghai Med. Soc., Internat. Soc. Heart and Lung Transplantation. Office: U Louisville Sch Medicine Rudd Heart-Lung Ctr 1200 201 Abraham Flexner Way Louisville KY 40202-3841

CHIERICI, GIAN LUIGI, petroleum engineer, educator; b. Parma, Italy, Dec. 1, 1926; s. Giuseppe and Anna (Ferrari) C.; m. Graziella Antonioli, Jan. 7, 1956; 1 child, Marcello. ChD, U. Parma, 1949; D Chem. Engring, U. Padua, 1955; D Physics, U. Parma, 1965; PhD in Petroleum Engring., U. Bologna, 1963. Rsch. chemist Carlo Erba, 1949-51; head thermodynamics lab. AGIP SpA, 1951-55, head reservoir physics dept., 1955-70, head dept. phys. chemistry, 1970-78, v.p. fields devel. and prodn., 1978-82, v.p. petroleum engring., 1982-87, chmn. R&D com., 1984-91; chmn. working group on exploration and exploitation ENI Coll. for Rsch., 1991-93; assoc. prof. petroleum engring. U. Bologna, 1961-85, prof. petroleum reservoir engring., 1987-99; hon. prof. U. Patagonia, Argentina, 1962—, State Gubkin Acad. Oil and Gas, Moscow, 1996—; lectr. petroleum engring. for mgrs. in energy industry ENI Postgrad. Sch., Milan, 1993—; mem. adv. com. mgmt. projects on geothermal energy EEC, Brussels, 1976-83, cons. to dirs. gen., 1987-95; mem. Italian nat. com. for World Petroleum Congresses, 1980-91, mem. permanent coun., 1982-91, mem. sci. program com., 1983-91; chmn. com. for tech. and sci. cooperation Ministry of Oil Industry of USSR and Agip SpA, 1980-91; chmn. steering com. for rsch. on petroleum recovery Norsk Agip/Statoil/IKU, 1980-85; mem. sci. program com. European Symposium on Enhanced Oil Recovery, 1982-96; mem. sci. com. Rogalandsforskning U., Stavanger, Norway, 1987-91; mem. sci. com. Osservatorio Geofisico Sperimentale, Trieste, Italy, 1993-97; mem. Italian State tech. com. oil, gas and geothermal energy Min. Industry, Rome, 1997—. Author: Volumetric and Phase Behaviour of Hydrocarbon Reservoir Fluids, 1962, Enhanced Oil Recovery - A State-of-the-Art Review, 1980, Principles of Petroleum Reservoir Engineering, 1994; assoc. editor Jour. Petroleum Sci. and Engring.; mem. editl. bd. Petroleum Geosci.; contbr. articles to internat. tech. mags. Mem. AIME, Soc. Petroleum Engrs. (Internat. Reservoir Engring. award 1996). Home: Via Triulziana 36/A, San Donato Milanese, I-20097 Milan Italy

CHIERIGHINO, BRIANNE SIDDALL, voice-over, actress, assistant location manager; b. Encino, Calif., Aug. 25, 1963; d. Earl Richard and Loretta Jeanette Siddall; m. D. Deven Chierighino, Apr. 4, 1987. AA in Art cum laude, L.A. Valley Coll., Van Nuys, Calif., 1985; student, Glendale (Calif.) C.C., 1990-94; BA in Art magna cum laude, Calif. State U., Northridge, 1995; postgrad., Loyola Marymount U., L.A., 1995—. Freelance asst. sound editor L.A., 1985-89, illustrator, 1985—; voice over artist, actor Tisherman Agy., L.A., 1990—; location asst., 1996—. Art exhibited at San Bernardino (Calif.) County Mus., 1995. Civic vol. fundraiser AIDS Meml. Quilt, Northridge, 1995. Recipient Outstanding Citizen award Coun. City L.A., 1987, L.A. Police Dept., 1987. Mem. SAG, AFTRA, Golden Kay Nat. Honor Soc., Phi Kappa Phi, Psi Chi. Avocations: ice skating, in-line skating, bicycling, softball, tennis.

CHIESA, MARIA DONATELLA, economics educator; b. Torino, Italy, Jan. 4, 1946; m. Riccardo Bonetti; 1 child, Stefano. Degree in bus. adminstrn., 1971, grad. in comml. law, 1977. Rschr., 1971, tchr., 1974; internat. tchr. program London Bus. Sch., 1976; auditor accounts, 1986. Author: (books) Pirelli Case, 1973, The Management of Travel Agency, 1994. Home: Strada Dei Tadini 17, 10131 Torino Italy Office: Facolta di Economia, Corso Unione Sovietica 218, 10134 Torino Italy

CHIEW, FRANCIS HOCK SOON, hydrologist, researcher; b. Kuala Lumpur, Malaysia, Nov. 29, 1964; arrived in Australia, 1983; s. Daniel and Julie (Toh) C.; m. Mei San Lee, May 17, 1992; 1 child, Meghan. B in Civil Engring., U. Melbourne, Australia, 1986, PhD, 1990. Registered profl. engr., Australia. Rsch. fellow Ctr. for Environ. Applied Hydrology, Melbourne, Australia, 1991-93; project leader Cooperative Rsch. Ctr. for Catchment Hydrology, Melbourne, Australia, 1994—. Co-author: The Myth Report - Some Ideas on the Future of Hydrology, 1993, Urban Stormwater Pollution, 1997, Stormwater Gross Pollutants, 1998; assoc. editor Hydrological Scis. jour.; contbr. chpts. to books, articles, reviews. Mem. Internat. Water Assn., Am. Geophysical Union, Instn. of Engrs. (Australia). Avocations: tennis, soccer, traveling, golf. Office: Univ Melbourne, Dept Civil & Environ Eng, Parkville VIC 3052, Australia

CHIH, CHUNG-YING, physicist, consultant; b. Yuki, Fukien, China, Dec. 11, 1916; s. Lai Sui and Sung-Yee (Lin) C.; BSc, Nat. Tsing Hua U., Peking, China, 1937; PhD, U. Calif., Berkeley, 1954; m. Alice Yuen, Aug. 15, 1955; came to U.S., 1948, naturalized, 1962. Instr. physics Fukien Med. Coll., 1937-40; instr., then asso. prof. Fukien Tchrs. Coll., 1940-44; assoc. prof., then prof. physics Nat. Chi-Nan U., 1944-45; prof. physics Kiang-su Coll., 1945-48; physicist Radiation Lab., U. Calif., Berkeley, 1948-54, summer 1956; mem. faculty Middlebury (Vt.) Coll., 1954-68, prof. physics, 1966-68; sci. cons., Bridgeport, Conn., 1968—. NSF grantee, 1957-60. Mem. Am. Phys. Soc. Address: PO Box 2556 Noble Sta Bridgeport CT 06608

CHI HAOTIAN, Chinese government official; b. Zhaoyuan County, Shandong, China, 1929; married; two children. Grad., People's Liberation Army Acad., 1960. Battalion instr. Chinese People's Vols., Korea, 1950-52; dir., polit. dept. Chinese Army Regiment, 1952-58; mayor Army Unit in Nanjing Mil. Region, 1958-60; polit. commissar Chinese Army Regiment, 1960-70, Chinese Army Divsn., 1970-73; dep. polit. commissar Beijing Mil. Region, 1973-75, dep. chief of staff, 1975-77; dep. chief People's Liberation Army Gen. Staff, 1977-85; polit. commissar Jinan Mil. Region, 1985-87; chief People's Liberation Army Gen. Staff, 1987-92; mem. 14th Communist Party of China Ctrl. Com., 1993—; state councillor, min. nat. def. Beijing People's Govt., 1993—. Mem. Communist Party of China, 1950—. Office: De Sheng Men Wai, 25 Huang Si Da Jie, East Dist Beijing 100011, China also: Ministry Nat Defense, Beijing China Address: 11 Qing Men Dong Da Jie, Beijing 100006, China*

CHIHARA, GORO, biologist; b. Tokyo, July 20, 1927; s. Tsuneto and Tsuguko (Sezaki) C.; m. Suzuko Yasuda, May 27, 1960; children: Chie, Tomihiko. B of Pharm. Sci., Tokyo U., 1952, PhD, 1957, D in Pharm. Sci., 1962. Head biochemistry Tokyo U. Hosp., 1956-62; head chemotherapy Nat. Cancer Ctr. Rsch. Inst., Tokyo, 1962-88; prof. cancer rsch. Inst. Chemistry, Kyoto (Japan) U., 1985-91; prof. pharm. chemistry Pharm. U. Kyoto, 1991-93; prof. biotech. Biotech. Rsch. Ctr., Teikyo U., Kawasaki, Japan, 1988-93; vis. prof. pharm. chemistry Keio U., Tokyo, 1982-93; vis. prof. immunology Yamagata (Japan) U., 1984-95; cons. sci. Ajinomoto Co., Tokyo, 1993—. Author: Immunopotentiation, Ciba Found. Symp., 1973, Cancer and Immunopotentiation, 1980, Immune Modulation Agents and Their Mechanisms, 1984, Immunotherapy of Infections, 1994, Immunoduratory Agents from Plants, 1999. Tokyo U. fellow, 1952-56; Recipient Asahi Sci. award Asahi Shinbun, 1958, Princess Takamatsu Found. award, 1973, Future Trends in Chemotherapy Internat. award Intersci. World Conf. on Inflamation, 1988. Mem. European Assn. Cancer Rsch., Hungarian Assn. Oncology (hon.), Internat. Soc. Preventive Oncology. Avocations: exploring hot springs, mountain climbing. Home: Tanacho 49-15 Aoba-ku, Yokohama 227-0064, Japan

CHIHMAN, ANDREW VALERIEVICH, engineer; b. Leningrad, Russia, Mar. 4, 1973; s. Valery Nikolaevich and Nina Ivanovna (Volskaya) C.; m. Dina Igorevna Nikitina, Apr. 24, 1999; 1 child, Artem. Student, Tech. U., St. Petersburg, 1996. Cert. in engring. Engr. Pavlov's Inst. Physiology, St. Petersburg, 1995-97, Alcatel Telecom, St. Petersburg, 1997—; tchr. computer sci. St. Petersburg sch., 1995-97. Contbr. articles and abstracts to profl. jours. Officer Naval Res. Orthodox. Avocations: football, volleyball, traveling. Home: Bykov St 39 Flat 94, 188680 Saint Petersburg Pavlovo, Russia

CHIHOREK, JOHN PAUL, electronics company executive; b. Wilkes-Barre, Pa., June 22, 1943; s. Stanley Joseph and Caroline Mary C.; m. Cristina Maria Marroquin, Dec. 28, 1968; children: Jonathan, David, Crista, Daniel. BSEE, Pa. State U., 1965; postgrad., Calif. State U., San Diego, 1970-71; MBA, Calif. State U., Sacramento, 1972. Program officer Hdqrs. Air Force Logistic Command, Dayton, Ohio, 1972-75; sr. engr. Hdqrs. Air Force Space Div., L.A., 1975-78; mgr. software systems dept. Logicon Inc., San Pedro, Calif., 1978; mgr. software product assurance dept. Loral Aeronutronics, Rancho Santa Margarita, Calif., 1978-85, mgr. software engring., 1985—; pres. CMC Sys. Inc. Mem. Congl. Adv. Bd., 1980; active PTA, mem. Republican Nat. com. Served with USN, 1965-70, Vietnam. Decorated Bronze Star. Mem. IEEE (mgmt. bd. Computer Soc., exec. com. on standard), AAAS, Engring. Mgmt. Soc. (v.p. publs.), Air Force Assn., Internat. Platform Assn. Roman Catholic. Clubs: Lions, Odd Fellows. Office: Loral Aeronutronics Ford Rd Newport Beach CA 92633

CHIKAONDA, MATHEW, bank executive. Gov. Res. Bank of Malawi, Lilongwe; min. fin. and econ. planning Malawi. Office: Res Bank of Malawi, PO Box 30049, Capital City Lilongwe Malawi*

CHILAVERT, JOSE LUIS, professional soccer player; b. Luque, Paraguay, July 27, 1965. Goalkeeper Cucuta Deportivo Football Club, Colombia, Atletico Nacional Football Club, Colombia, Real Zaragoza Football Club, Spain, Velez Sarsfield Football Club, Argentina; goalkeeper, capt. Paraguay Nat. Team. Recipient 1997 Copa America, 1998 World Cup, Mercosur Cup 2000, Clausura 2000, Apertura 2000. Office: Assn Futbol Argentina, Viamonte 1366/76, 1053 Buenos Aires Argentina also: Club Atletico Velez Sarsfield, Av Juan B Justo 9200, Capital Federal Argentina*

CHILCOTE, SAMUEL DAY, JR., trade association administrator; b. Casper, Wyo., Aug. 24, 1937; s. Sam D. and Juanita C. (Cornelison) C.; m. Ellen Sheridan Spear, Nov. 11, 1966. BS, Idaho State U., 1959. Adminstrv. asst. Continental Oil Co., Glenrock, Wyo., 1960-63; asst. supt. public instrn., dir. Wyo. Surplus Property Agy., Wyo. Sch. Lunch Program, Cheyenne Wyo. Dept. Edn., 1963-67; supr. N. Central region Distilled Spirits Inst., Denver, 1967-71; exec. dir., chief operating officer N. Central region Distilled Spirits Inst., Washington, 1971-73; exec. v.p., chief operating officer Distilled Spirits Council, Inc., Washington, 1973-77, pres., chief exec. officer, 1978-81; pres. Tobacco Inst., Washington, 1981-99; chmn. Chilcote Enterprises, 1999—; mem. industry sect. adv. council consumer goods, Dept. Commerce. Pres. Sky Ranch Found. for Boys, 1975-81, pres. emeritus, 1981—; treas. Ford's Theatre, 1984-88, vice chmn., trustee, 1988—, chmn., 1997—; bd. dirs., exec. com. Art Barn; chmn. Awards Dinner Com., 1989—, USO Met. Washington, past pres. Capt. U.S. Army, 1959-60. Recipient Profl. Achievement award Idaho State U. Coll. Bus., 1986, Man of Yr. award Anti-Defamation league, 1986, Humanitarian of the Yr. award Tobacco and Confectionery Div. Dinner for the UJA-Fedn. 1991 campaign, Good Scout award Greater N.Y. Coun. Boy Scouts Am., 1996. Mem. Georgetown Club, Congl. Country Club (past pres., exec. com., bd. govs.), Burning Tree Club, Nat. Press Club, Capitol Hill Club, City Club, F St. Club, TPC Avenel (Washington), Jefferson Islands Club (bd. govs.), Masons, Elks, Shriners. Office: Chilcoe Enterprises Chilcote Enterprises 9116 Falls Bridge Ln Potomac MD 20854-3946

CHILDERS, CHARLES EUGENE, mining company executive; b. West Frankfort, Ill., Oct. 29, 1932; s. Joel Marion and Cora E. (Choate) C.; m. Norma A. Casper, June 8, 1952; children: Joel M., Katrina K. BS, U. Ill., 1955; LLD (hon.), U. Saskatchewan, 1994. With Duval Corp., Carlsbad, N.Mex., 1955-62, Internat. Minerals Corp. (IMC), 1963-77; v.p. Esterhazy oper. IMC, 1977-79; pres. IMC Coal, Lexington, 1979-81; v.p. potash oper. IMC, 1981-82, v.p. expansion and devel., 1982-87; pres., chief exec. officer Potash Corp. of Sask., Inc., Saskatoon, Can., 1987-90, chmn., pres., chief exec. officer, 1990-98, chmn., chief exec. officer, 1998-99, chmn., 1999—; bd. dirs., past chmn. bd. Canpotex Ltd., Sask., Found. for Agronomic Rsch.; past chmn. bd. The Fertilizer Inst.; bd. dirs. Conf. Bd. Can., Battle Mountain Gold Corp.; past chmn. Potash and Phosphate Inst.; mem. fertilizer industry adv. com. to FAO. Dir. at large Jr. Achievement of Can. 1st lt. U.S. Army, 1955-57. Mem. AIME, Can. Inst. Mining and Metallurgy, Sask. Potash Producers Assn. (past. chmn.), Internat. Fertilizer Industry Assn. (past pres.). Republican Baptist. Home: 3835 E Placita De Piacho Tucson AZ 85718-7414 Office: Potash Corp of Sask, 122 1st Ave S, Saskatoon, SK Canada S7K 7G3

CHILDERS, SUSAN LYNN BOHN, special education educator, administrator, human resources and transition specialist, consultant; b. Zanesville, Ohio, Mar. 1, 1948; m. Lawrence J. Childers; 1 child, Jeffrey Scott. AA, Ohio U., 1978, BS in Edn. cum laude, 1982; MEd in Supervision, Ashland U., 1991. Profl. cert. 1-8 elem. tchr., K-12 edn. handicapped and supervision; spl. edn. tchr., Ohio; permanent cert., supervision. Educator learning disabilities, developmentally handicapped Maysville Local Sch. Dist., South Zanesville, Ohio, 1982-89; work-study coord. Holmes County Office Edn., Millersburg, Ohio, 1990, editor spl. edn. newsletter, 1990-93, cons.,

supervisor work-study programming, 1991-93; spl. edn. supr. Wayne County Bd. Edn., Wooster, Ohio, 1993-94; adminstr. severe behavior handicapped program, supr. special edn. Ashland-Wayne County Bd. Edn., Wooster, 1994-95; cons. Tri-County Ednl. Svc. Ctr., Wooster, 1996-99; supr. spl. edn., supr. instrn. support Zanesville (Ohio) City Schs., 1999; dir. spl. edn. Licking County Ednl. Svc. Ctr., Newark, Ohio, 2000—; mem. Holmes County Spl. Edn. Adv. Coun., 1990-93, E. Holmes Local Sch. Dist. Strategic Planning Action Team Job/Life Skills, 1993; spkr. in field; rep. Ohio Devel. Handicapped Issues Forum; mem. steering com. Ohio Speaks, 1991-94; mem. strategic planning com. Ashland-Wayne County Bd. Edn., 1994-95; mem. Chippewa Local Sch. Dist. Child Care Bd., 1995-96; chmn. Direct Student Svcs. Strategic Planning Com., 1995-96; mem. safety com. Ashland-Wayne Ednl. Svc. Ctr., 1994-96; mem. svc. coordination com. Wayne County Children and Family First Initiative, 1995, 96; Edn. Rep. Safety Com., Tri-County Ednl. Svc. Ctr., Wooster, 1997-99. Editor Spl. Edn. Newsletter Holmes County Office Edn., 1990-93. Mem. adv. bd. Holmes County Job Placement, Holmes County Litter Prevention Cmty. Action Plan com., 1993; vol. Ohio Buckeye Book Fair, 1991-93, 99, Holmes County Spl. Olympics, 1990-93, chairperson vols., 1993; mem. jr. assembly Bethesda Hosp., 1970-78; mem. Beaux Arts Zanesville Art Ctr., 1972-78; mem. spl. needs adv. bd. Ashland-West Holmes Career Ctr., 1990-93; mem. Transition and Comm. Consortium on Learning Disabilities, Ohio U. Alumni Career Resource Network, Holmes County Abuse Prevention Cmty. Action Plan com., 1993, Ohio Staff Devel. Coun., Wayne County Family and Children First Coun. (Clin. Cluster), 1994-96; co-chairperson fundraising com. Creating Connections Symposium, Akron, Ohio, 1994; mem. Ashland-Wayne-Holmes Counties Adv. Com. for Tech. and Tng. subcom., Ohio, 1996-97; adv. com. for tech. 3-county rep., Ashland, Wayne, Holmes, Ohio, 1996-98, mem. A-site tech. tng. com., 1996-97, regional rep. for School/Net Communities of Practice, 1996. Recipient award Muskingum County Office Litter Prevention, 1988, Kids Care Project, 1989, Maysville Bd. Edn. commendation, 1989, Merit award Keep Ohio Beautiful program, 1991, Ohio Future Forum's Exemplary Transition from Sch.-to-Work Model award, 1993, Model Program designation Ohio's Employability Skills Project, 1987, Franklin B. Walter Outstanding Educator award, 1996, 98. Mem. ASCD, Career Edn. Assn., Coun. Exceptional Children, Ohio Rural Edn. Assn., Ohio Sch. Suprs. Assn., Ohio Assn. Vocat. Edn. Spl. Needs Pers., Ohio Assn. Suprs. and Work-Study coords. (award of Excellence 1992, reg. pres. 1993-94), Am. Assn. Univ. Women, Wayne-Holmes Elem. Adminstrs. Assn., Ohio Pupil Pers. Assn., Phi Delta Kappa. Office: Licking County Ednl Svc Ctr 675 Price Rd NE Newark OH 43055-9454

CHILDS, DONALD SAMUEL, truck driver; b. Wichita, Kans., Apr. 22, 1941; s. Donald and Dora Viola (Miner) C.; m. Jeannette Louise MacMillan, Apr. 11, 1969; 1 child, Jennifer Louise. BBA, Wichita State U., 1967. Petroleum landman Denver, 1968-89; truck driver various, Denver, 1989—. With USN, 1961-63. Methodist. Home: PO Box 1665 Arvada CO 80001-1665

CHILDS, MARILYN CARLSON, journalist, educator; b. Springfield, Mass., Aug. 26, 1923; d. Carl Oscar and Dorothy M. (Davis) Carlson; m. Harold Lofton Childs, Febr. 2, 1952; children: David Loring, Robert Stuart, Carl Albert. AA, Vermont Jr. Coll., 1942; BA, Am. Internat., Springfield, 1945. Cert. tchr., Vt. Reporter Montpelier (Vt.) Argus, 1942, Springfield Union, 1943-45; assoc. editor Am. Horseman, Lexington, Ky., 1945-47; mng. editor Popular Horsemen, Harrisburg, Pa., 1948-52; freelance writer various publs., 1953-90; tchr. Chelsea (Vt.) H.S., 1966-88, debate coach, 1970-99, asst. prin., 1975-85. Author: Riding Show Horses, 1963, Mandate For A Morgan Horse, 1967, Training Your Colt to Ride and Drive, 1969, Men Behind the Morgan Horse, 1979; co-author: Training Your Colt to Ride and Drive, revised edit., 1994. Del. Vt. State Rep. Party, Montpelier, 1982-99; chmn. Rep. Fun Days, Chelsea, 1986-92; justice of the peace, Chelsea, 1986-94; mem. Orange County Reparative Bd., 1997—. Named Outstanding Speech Educator Nat. Fedn. State H.S. Assns., 1989, Debate Coach of the Yr. Vt. Debate/Forensics League, Burlington, 1995, VFW's Vt. Citizenship Tchr., 2000. Mem. Am. Horse Shows Assn., Am. Morgan Horse Assn. (life), Am. Saddlebred Horse Assn., Nat. Fedn. Interscholastic Speech/Debate (zone rep. 1986-89), New England Horseman's Coun. (past pres. 1990-95, judge), Delta Kappa Gamma Internat. (pres. 1994-96). Republican. Christian Scientist. Avocations: horses, travel. Home: 48 Harolyn Hill Rd Tunbridge VT 05077-9660

CHILDS, RAND HAMPTON, data processing executive; b. Charlotte, N.C., Oct. 20, 1949; s. Wade Hampton and Francis Marion (Rand) C.; m. Anne Elizabeth Turner, Jan. 4, 1986; children: Ian Peter, Ryan Patrick. BS in Chemistry, Ga. Inst. Tech., 1971, MS in Chemistry, 1977; postgrad., Eidgenossische Technische Hochschule, Zurich, Switzerland, 1971-72. Sys. analyst computing svcs. dept. Ga. Inst. Tech., Atlanta, 1974-80, mgr. data processing computing svcs. dept., 1980-83, assoc. dir. office of computing svcs., 1983-87; v.p. software devel. Sirsi Corp., 1987-94, acting mgr. data conversion dept., 1995-97, v.p. R&D, 1994—; cons. in field. Contbr. articles to profl. jours.; compiler: (with Naugle and Sherry) A Concordance to the Poems of Samuel Johnson. World Student Fund scholar Ga. Inst. Tech. and Swiss Govt., 1971-72. Mem. AAAS, Am. Chem. Soc., Assn. Computing Machinery, Info. Industry Assn., VIM (6000) (Control Data Corp. User Group), Sigma Xi, Alpha Iota Delta of Chi Psi (Atlanta). Home: 12451 N Shawdee Rd SE Huntsville AL 35803-3717 Office: SIRSI Corp 101 Washington St SE Huntsville AL 35801-4827

CHILLEMI, JOHN VINCENT, electrical utility executive; b. Albany, Georgia, Apr. 29, 1967; s. Tom Nicholas and Jana (Lewis) C.; m. Daniela Lee Zimmermann, Nov. 6, 1993; children: Jack, Olivia. B Mech Engring., Ga. Inst. Tech., 1991; MBA, Ga. State U., 1998. Engr.-in-tng., Ga.; cert. energy mgr. Key account mgr. Ga. Power, Atlanta, 1991-95; mem. pipeline exec. tng. program So. Co., Atlanta, 1996-97; asst. to exec. v.p. internat. rels. So. Energy, Inc., Atlanta, 1998; dir. asset optimization So. Energy, Amsterdam, The Netherlands, 1999; dir. Italian ops. So. Energy-Italia S.R.L., Milan, 1999—, also bd. dirs. Republican. Roman Catholic. Avocations: golf, running, backpacking.

CHILLIARD, YVES, research scientist; b. Vinay, France, July 5, 1951; s. Rene and Colette (Chevallier) C.; m. Sylvette Oullier, Mar. 29, 1975 (dec. 1995); 1 child, Nicolas. Degree in engring., Agronomy Nat. Inst., Paris, 1973; DS, U. Paris 6, 1985. Rschr. Inst. Nat. Rsch. Agronomy, Paris, 1975-81; rschr. Inst. Nat. Rsch. Agronomy, Theix, France, 1981-91, head rsch. unit, 1992-98, assoc. head rsch. dept., 1999—. Hon. fellow Hannah Rsch. Inst., Scotland, 1995—. Mem. Am. Dairy Sci. Assn., Am. Soc. Animal Sci., French Nutrition Soc. (v.p. 1996-99). Avocations: skiing, hiking, climbing, music. Office: INRA, Theix, 63122 St Genes Champanelle France

CHILTON, BRADLEY STEWART, law educator; b. Rockford, Ill., Oct. 28, 1955; s. Ermal Rural and Maybelle Rose (McNair) C.; m. Lisa Marie Hartmann, May 21, 1977. BA, Milton Coll., 1977; JD, U. Toledo, Ohio, 1980, MA, 1981; MA, U. Wis., 1982; PhD, U. Ga., 1988; MLS, U. So. Miss., 1989. Instr. S.E. Mo. State U., Cape Girardeau, 1985-86; asst. prof. U. So. Miss., Hattiesburg, 1986-89, Wash. State U., Pullman, 1989-93; assoc. prof. U. Toledo, 1993-2000, U. North Tex., 2000—. Author: Prisons Under the Gavel, 1991. Mem. Acad. Criminal Justice Scis., Am. Polit. Sci. Assn., Am. Soc. Criminology, Am. Soc. Pub. Adminstrn. Congregationalist. Avocations: music, home design and building, religion. Office: Criminal Justice Univ North Texas PO Box 305130 Denton TX 76203-5130

CHILTON, MEREDITH, curator, museum administrator; b. Woking, Surrey, Eng., Apr. 23, 1953; d. Boone Grubbs and Joan Deborah (Clarkson) Miller; m. David Chilton, July 12, 1981; 1 child, Thomas Clarkson. BA in with honors, U. E. Anglia, 1979; grad. diploma, Manchester U., 1980. Curator Mildenhall Mus., Suffolk, Eng., 1977-78; curatorial asst. Gibson House Mus., Suffolk, 1981-83; sr. asst. curator George R. Gardiner Mus. Ceramic Art, Toronto, 1984-96, dir.-curator, 1997-99; chief curator George R. Gardiner Mus. Ceramic Art, 2000—; faculty mem. Grad. Ctr. for Studies in Decorative Arts, Bard Coll., 1994—; joint course dir. Cooper Hewitt Mus., N.Y., Parsons Sch. Design; curator 15 exhbns. Gardiner Mus. Contbr. articles to profl. jours. Mem. Keramic Freunde deer Schweiz, Conn. Ceramic Circle (hon.), Am. Ceramic Cir. (bd. mem. 1985-93, jour. editor 1987-93), English Ceramic Cir., Gesellschaft der Keramikfreunde, French Porcelain Soc. Office: 111 Queens Park, Toronto, ON Canada M5S 2C7

CHILTON, ST. JOHN POINDEXTER, retired plant pathology educator, farm owner; b. Phila., Feb. 3, 1909; s. St. John P. and Helen Frances (McGloin) C.; m. Alice Pleasance Hunter, Mar. 2, 1935. BS, La. State U., 1935, MS, 1936; PhD, U. Minn., 1938. Agt. plant pathology U.S. Dept. Agr., 1938-40; faculty La. State U., 1940—, prof., 1948—, chmn. dept. botany and plant pathology, 1950-70; plant pathologist, head dept. plant pathology La. Agr. Expt. Sta., 1950-76; rep. div. biology and agr. NRC, 1952-57; pres., dir. LaPlace Enterprises, Inc., 1961-89; pres., mgr. Esperanza Farms, 1974-83; cons. Nicaragua Sugar Estates, Ingenio San Antonio, 1964-86. Fellow AAAS; mem. Am. Phytopath. Soc. (ex-counselor), Internat. Soc. Sugarcane Technologists (vice-chmn. 10th congress), Am. Soc. Sugarcane Technologists (past pres.), SAR (past pres. Phil Thomas chpt.), La. Acad. Sci. (past pres.), La. Geneal. and Hist. Soc. (pres. 1972-76), Hist. Assn. Central La. (pres. 1980-82), Am. Sugarcane League U.S. (life), Rotary. Club: Rotarian. Home: 431 Belgard Bnd Boyce LA 71409-9276

CHILUBA, FREDERICK JACOB TITUS, Zambian government official; b. Kitwe, Zambia, Apr. 30, 1943; s. Jacob Tiutus Chiluba Nkonde and Diana Kaimba; m. Vera Tembo; 9 children. Pers. clk. Tanzania; accounts asst. Atlas Copco, Ndolo, Zambia, 1966-67; mem. Nat. Union Bldg., Engring. and Gen. Workers, Zambia, 1967-87; pres. Govt. of Zambia, Lusaka, 1991—; mem. Zambian delegation Gen. Assembly UN, 1973; chmn. Zambia Congress Trade Unions; pres. Movement for Multiparty Democracy. Office: State House, PO Box 30208, Lusaka Zambia*

CHILUKURI, NAGESWARARAO, biochemist; b. Pangulur, India, July 1, 1952; came to U.S., 1981; s. Venkatasubbaiah and Kamalamma C.; m. Satyavani, Aug. 7, 1974; children: Krishna, Rupa, Bhavana. BS, Andhra U., 1972, MSc, 1974; PhD, Madras U., 1981. Vis. fellow, then vis. assoc. Nat. Cancer Inst., Bethesda, Md., 1981-88; sr. scientist Connective Tissue Rsch. Inst., Phila., 1988-91; sr. staff fellow Nat. Cancer Inst., 1991-93; rsch. assoc. prof. Northwestern U., Chgo., 1993-98; asst. prof. M.D. Anderson Cancer Ctr./U. Tex., Houston, 1998—. Mem. Am. Assn. Cancer Rsch., Soc. Investigative Dermatology. E-mail: crao@notes.mdacc.tmc.edu.

CHILUMPHA, CASSIM, Malawi government official, law educator; b. Nkhota Kota, Nov. 20, 1958; married; 3 children. LLB, U. Malawi, 1982; PhD, U. Hull, 1987. State advocate Ministry of Justice, 1982-83; lectr. comml. law U. Malawi, 1988-92, sr. law lectr., head bus. adminstrn. dept., 1992-94, assoc. prof., 1994—; min. Malawi Ministry of Def., 1994-96; min. justice and constl. affairs Govt. of Malawi, from 1996, atty. gen., 1996—, now min. edn., sports and culture; mem. Nat. Exec. Coun., 1993-94, Nat. Consultative Coun., 1993-94; vice chmn. Constl. Drafting Com., 1994; mem. Nat. Adv. Coun. on Edn., 1989—. Office: Ministry of Education, Pvt Bag 328 Capital City, Lilongwe 3, Malawi*

CHIMISSO, CRISTINA, historian, educator, philosopher; b. Perugia, Italy, July 28, 1964; d. Alfredo Chimisso and Giuseppina Bucci. Degree in philosophy, U. Perugia, 1990; PhD, U. Cambridge, Eng., 1996. rsch. Rsch. fellow Max Planck Inst. for History of Sci., Berlin, 1997-98; Sarton fellow Am. Acad. Arts and Scis., Cambridge, Mass., 1999; lectr. cultural history U. Aberdeen, Scotland, 2000; lectr. European studies Open U., Milton Keynes, Eng., 2000—. Mem. History of Sci. Soc. E-mail: c.chimisso@open.ac.uk. Office: Open U, Walton Hall, Milton Keynes MK7 6AA, England

CHIMURA, AKIRA, economist; b. Shizuoka City, Japan, June 6, 1936; s. Koji and Mitsu (Ikeyama) C.; m. Misao Fujishita, May 30, 1947; children: Kaoru, Atsushi. BA, Tokyo U., 1959, LLB, 1961. Mktg. dept. Sumitomo Metal Inds., Ltd., Tokyo, 1961-63; rsch. dept. Sumitomo Metal Inds., Ltd., 1963-96; visiting rsch. fellow Inst. Energy Economics, Tokyo, 1979-83, 88-96; adv. rsch. fellow Japan Coal Energy Ctr., Hibiya, Tokyo, 1998—. Contbr. articles to profl. jours. Dir. Local Town Assn., Kujike/Abiko, 1980, 96. Avocations: gardening, hiking. Fax: 81-3-3214-3724.

CHIN, CHI CHUNG, physicist, electrical engineer, researcher; s. Wah Kin Chin and Luen Tam; m. Winnie Wong, Jan. 27, 1990. BSc, U. Hong Kong, 1983; MSc, Iowa State U., 1985; PhD, MIT, 1991. Rsch. scientist Mtrial Lab. ITRI, Hsinchu, Taiwan, 1993-95; assoc. rsch. fellow Inst. Astronomy and Astrophysics, Academia Sinica, Nankang, Taipei, Taiwan, 1995—. Contbr. articles to sci. jours., including Phys. Rev. B., Jour. Materials Rsch., Advances in Superconductivity, Physica C, Jour. Crystal Growth, IEEE Trans. on Applied Superconductivity, Applied Physics Letter, Rev. Sci. Instruments. Recipient dir.'s award ISTEC, Tokyo, 1993; grantee Nat. Sci. Coun., Taiwan, 1997-99. Mem. European Applied Superconductivity Soc. Avocation: classical music. Office: Acad Sinica Inst Astronomy, 128 Yen Chju Yuan Rd Sec 2, Taipei Nankang 115, Taiwan

CHIN, DAVIS, lawyer; b. Evansville, Ind., Dec. 13, 1947; s. Frank S. M. and Mamie (Shu) C.; m. Pauline C., Aug. 3, 1974; 1 child, Davis M. BS, Rose-Hulman Inst. Tech., Terre Haute, Ind., 1969; JD, U. Balt., 1974; LLM in Taxation, John Marshall Law Sch., 1981. Bar: Ill. 1974, U.S. Dist. Ct. (no. dist.) 1974, U.S. Ct. Appeals (7th cir.) 1974, U.S. Patent and Trademark Office 1974, U.S. Claims Ct. 1977, U. S. Tax Ct. 1977, U.S. Supreme Ct. 1977, U.S. Ct. Appeals (fed. cir.) 1982. Staff atty. CTS Corp., Elkhart, Ind., 1974; assoc. Petherbridge, Lindgren & Gilhooly, Chtd., Chgo., 1974-78; staff atty. Borg-Warner Corp., Chgo., 1978-80, Container Corp. Am., Chgo., 1980-84; pvt. practice Chgo., 1984—; instr. Prairie State Coll., Chgo. Heights, 1987-90, 94, South Suburban Coll., South Holland, Ill., 1989-91, Roosevelt U., Olympia Fields, Ill., 1990-93. Elder United Presbyn. Ch., South Holland, 1986—; panel program atty. Chgo. Vol. Legal Svcs., 1988—. Mem. Am. Intellectual Property Law Assn., Chgo. Bar Assn., Intellectual Property Law Assn. Chgo., Patent Law Assn. Chgo. (bd. mgrs. 1985-87, 94-96). Avocations: tennis, golf, travel. Home: 11428 Plattner Dr Mokena IL 60448-9228 Office: 111 W Washington St Ste 1025 Chicago IL 60602-2745

CHIN, DER-TAU, chemical engineer, educator; b. Zhejiang, China, Sept. 14, 1939; came to U.S., 1963, naturalized, 1977; s. Tsu-Kang and Shou-Chen (Chen) C.; m. Lorna Fe Gencianeo, July 17, 1971; children: Janet G., Lynn G. BSChemE, Chungyuan Coll. Sci. & Engring, 1962; MSChemE, Tufts U., 1965; PhD in Chem. Engring., U. Pa., 1969. Plant engr. Lungyen Sugar Factory, 1962-63; sci. programmer USAF Cambridge (Mass.) Rsch. Lab., Lexington, Mass., 1965; sr. rsch. engr. rsch. labs. GM Corp., Warren, Mich., 1969-75; prof. Clarkson U., Potsdam, N.Y., 1975—; vis. scientist Brookhaven Nat. Lab., Upton, N.Y., summers 1977, 80, U.S. Army Belvoir Research Devel. Ctr., Ft. Belvoir, Va., summer 1985, U.S. Army Electronics Tech. and Devices Lab., Ft. Mammouth, N.J., summer, 1986, Armstrong Lab. Tyndall Air Force Base, Fla., summer 1995; vis. prof. U. Calif., Berkeley, 1981, Swiss Fed. Inst. Tech., Zurich, 1981, Nat. U. Singapore, 1982, 87, Nat. Tsing Hua UNI, 1989; cons. Centro de Pesquisas do Energia Electrica, Rio de Janeiro, Brazil, summer 1979. Fellow Electrochem. Soc. (Young Authors award 1971); mem. AIChE, Am. Electroplaters Soc., Am. Chem. Soc. Office: Clarkson U PO Box 5705 Potsdam NY 13699-0001

CHIN, FRANCIS YUK LUN, computer science educator; b. Hong Kong, Apr. 8, 1948; arrived in Hong Kong, 1983; s. Chuen and Suk Ching (Cheng) C.; m. Bethany Mee Yee Chan, Oct. 27, 1989; children: Grace Ho Yun, Justin Ho Jing, Jerome Balmen, Vivian Waimen. BASc, U. Toronto, Ont., Can., 1972; MA, MSc, Princeton (N.J.) U., 1974, PhD, 1976. Asst. prof. dept. math. U. Md., Balt., 1975-76; asst. to assoc. prof. dept. computer sci. U. Alberta, Edmonton, 1976-83; sr. lectr. dept. computer sci. Chinese U. of Hong Kong, 1983-85; head dept. computer sci. U. Hong Kong, 1985-99, chair computer sci., 1988—; asst. dept. EECS U. Calif. San Diego, La Jolla, 1980-81; gov. bd. mem. Chinese Lang. Computer Edn., 1986—. Editorial bd.: Journal of Information Processing Letters, International Journal of Foundations of Computer Science, Computer Processing of Chinese and Oriental Languages; contbr. articles to profl. jours. Named one of Ten Outstanding Young Persons award, Hong Kong, 1987. Fellow Hong Kong Assn. for Computer Edn. (hon.), IEEE. Roman Catholic. Office: Univ Hong Kong, Dept Computer Sci, Hong Kong Hong Kong

CHIN, JANET SAU-YING, data processing executive, consultant; b. Hong Kong, July 27, 1949; came to U.S., 1959; d. Arthur Quock-Ming and Jenny (Loo) C. BS in Math, U. Ill., Chgo., 1970; MS in Computer Sci., U. Ill., Urbana, 1973. Sys. programmer Lawrence Livermore (Calif.) Lab., 1972-79; sect. mgr. Tymshare Inc., Cupertino, Calif., 1979-83, Fortune Systems, Redwood City, Calif., 1983-85; div. mgr. Impell Corp, Berkeley, Calif., 1985; pres. Chin Assocs., Oakland, Calif., 1985-88; bus. devel. mgr. Sun Microsystems, Mountain View, Calif., 1988-92; engring. dir. Cadence Design Systems, San Jose, Calif., 1992-94; quality dir. Cadence Design Sys., San Jose, Calif., 1994-95; asst. to CEO, Avant! Corp., Fremont, Calif., 1995-99; provost World Inst. Tech., Fremont, Calif., 1996-98; cons. Second Resource, Oakland, 2000—; vice-chmn. Am. Nat. Standards Inst. X3H3, N.Y.C., 1979-82, internat. rep. X3H3, 1982-88. Co-author: The Computer Graphics Interface, 1991; contbr. tech. papers to profl. publs. Mem. Assn. Computing Machinery, Sigma Xi. Avocations: karate, iaido, taiko, science fiction/fantasy.

CH'IN, MICHAEL KUO-HSING, international conference and travel management executive; b. Singapore, Sept. 19, 1921; s. Chin-cho and Wen-chih (Chang) C.; m. Edith Tzu-lin Fang; children: Lucy Wei-Tzu, May An-Tzu, Peggy Hsien-Tzu, Judy Pei-Tzu. BS, Yen Ching U., Cheng-tu, Republic of China, 1945. Asst. proctor's office Yenching U., Cheng-tu, Republic of China, 1945-46; asst. bur. of relief Chinese Nat. Rural Rehab. Adminstrn., Nanking, Republic of China, 1946-48; statistician-in-charge, personnel-in-charge Nanking Phys. Rehab. Ctr., Republic of China, 1948-50; technician soil analysis Pub. Health Research Inst., Taipei, Taiwan, Republic of China, 1950-51; asst., jr. adminstrv. asst., adminstrv. asst., sr. adminstrv. asst. Sino-Am. Joint Commn. on Rural Reconstrn., Taipei, Taiwan, Republic of China, 1951-72; exec. officer Asian Vegetable R&D Ctr., Shanhua, Taiwan, Republic of China, 1972-83, dir. adminstrn., 1983-91; exec. v.p. Taiwan Conf. Mgmt. Co., Ltd., Taipei, Republic of China, 1991-93, gen. mgr., exec. v.p., 1993-94, sr. advisor, 1996—; dep. gov. Am. Biog. Inst. Rsch. Assn., Raleigh, N.C., 1990—; dep. dir. gen. Internat. Biog. Ctr., Cambridge, Eng., 1990—; advisor Zion Tours Internat. Co. Ltd., Taipei, 1991-95, sr. advisor, 1996—; adv., editorial bd., Yenching U History, Beijing, 1998, advisor Taiwan Rail Tours Ctr., 1995—; dir. Internat. Conv. Devel. Assn., Taipei, 1991—; coord. Taipei host com., mem. working com. 31st Internat. Congress and Conv. Assn. Gen. Assembly, 1991-92; TCM rep. agt. Excerpta Medica, 1992-94; mktg. contact Taiwan Conf. Mgmt. Co. Ltd./CONGREX, Internat. Congress and Conv. Assn., 1992-94. Mem. Meeting Planners Internat. (Asia Pacific adv. group 1993-94). Baptist. Home: 2 Fl 5 Ln 16 PuCheng St, Taipei 106, Taiwan Office: Taiwan Conf Mgmt Co Ltd, PO Box 68-439, Taipei Taiwan

CHIN, SUE SOONE MARIAN (SUCHIN CHIN), conceptual artist, portraitist, photographer, community affairs activist; b. San Francisco; d. William W. and Soo-Up (Swebe) C. Grad., Calif. Coll. Art, Mpls. Arts Inst.; scholar, Schaeffer Design Ctr.; student, Yasuo Kuniyoshi, Louis Hamon, Rico LeBrun. Photojournalist All Together Now Show, 1973, East-West News, Third World Newscasting, 1975-78, Sta. KNBC Sunday Show, L.A., 1975, 76, Live on 4, 1981, Bay Area Scene, 1981; chmn. Full Moon Products; pres., bd. dirs. Alumni Oracle Inc. Graphics printer, exhbns. include: Kaiser Ctr., Zellerbach Pla., Chinese Culture Ctr. Galleries, Capricorn Asunder Art Commn. Gallery (all San Francisco), Newspace Galleries, New Coll. of Calif., L.A. County Mus. Art, Peace Pla. Japan Ctr., Congress Arts Comm., Washington, 1989; SFWA Galleries, Inner Focus Show, 1989—, Calif. Mus. Sci. and Industry, Lucien Labaudt Gallery, Salon de Medici, Madrid, Salon Renacimento, Madrid, 1995, Life is a Circus, SFWA Gallery, 1991, 94, UN/50 Exhibit, Bayfront Galleries, 1995, Somar Galleries, 1997, Sacramento State Fair, 2000, Star Child, Women thru the Ages - Somarts Gallery, 2000, AFL-CIO Labor Studies Ctr., Washington, Asian Women Artists (1st prize for conceptual painting, 1st prize photography), 1978, Yerba Buena Arts Ctr. for the Arts Festival, 1994; represented in permanent collections L.A. County Fedn. Labor, Calif. Mus. Sci. and Industry, AFL-CIO Labor Studies Ctr., Australian Trades Coun., Hazeland and Co., also pvt. collections; author: (poetry) Yuri and Malcolm, The Desert Sun, 1994 (Editors Choice award 1993-94). Del. nat., state convs. Nat. Women's Polit. Caucus, 1977-83, San Francisco chpt. affirmative action chairperson, 1978-82, nat. conv. del., 1978-81, Calif. del., 1976-81. Recipient Honorarium AFL-CIO Labor Studies Ctr., Washington, 1975-76; award Centro Studi Ricerche delle Nazioni, Italy, 1985; bd. advisors Psycho Neurology Found. Bicentennial award L.A. County Mus. Art, 1976, 77, 78. Mem. Asian Women Artists (founding v.p., award 1978-79, 1st award in photography of Orient 1978-79), Calif. Chinese Artists (sec.-treas. 1978-81), Japanese Am. Art Coun. (chairperson 1978-84, dir.), San Francisco Women Artists, San Francisco Graphics Guild, Pacific/Asian Women Coalition Bay Area, Chinatown Coun. Performing and Visual Arts. Address: PO Box 421415 San Francisco CA 94142-1415

CHIN, TAKAAKI, orthopedic surgeon; b. Kobe, Hyogo, Japan, Oct. 4, 1960; s. Gokyu and Shouei C.; m. Kazuko Hayashi, Oct. 16, 1989; 1 child. B in Medicine, Tokushima (Japan) U., 1986; PhD, Kobe U., 1992. Med. diplomate. Resident Kobe U. Hosp., 1986-87; rsch. fellow McGill U., Montreal, Can., 1990-92; head physician Hyogo Rehab. Ctr., Kobe, 1992—; cons. Japanese Soc. Prosthetics and Orthotics, 1998—. Contbr. articles to profl. jours. Mem. Japanese Orthopaedic Assn., Internat. Soc. Prosthetics and Orthotics, Internat. Soc. Orthopaedic Surgery and Traumatology (amputation and prosthesis). Avocations: body-building, travel. Office: Hyogo Rehab Ctr, 1070 Akebono-Cho Nishi-ku, 651-2181 Kobe Japan

CHINABUT, SUPRANEE, fisheries scientist; b. Phichit, Thailand, Feb. 25, 1947; d. Leang and Komkum Bumrongsuk; m. Narong Chinabut, Aug. 10, 1972; 1 child, Patsuda. BSc, Kasetsart U., 1969; MSc, Auburn U., 1979; PhD, Stirling U., 1989. Fish biologist Dept. Fisheries, Bangkok, Thailand, 1969-79, head fish pathology unit, 1979-95, dir. aquatic animal health rsch. inst., 1995—. Mem. Asian Fisheries Soc., Am. Fisheries Soc. Avocation: needlework.

CHINDAH, ALEX CHUKS, biologist; b. Rumuokwurusi, Nigeria, July 2, 1956; s. George Adiele and Dorathy Ufe (Murphy) C.; m. Templar Ese Shdigben, Apr. 14, 1989; children: Ruhuoma, Chitugah, Jakirichi, Souis, Bisinuchi. BS with hon., U. Calabar, Nigeria, 1980; MS, U. Portharcourt, Nigeria, 1985; PhD, U. Sci. & Tech., Nigeria, 1998. Rsch. asst. Inst. Pollution Studies, Portharcourt, Nigeria, 1983-87; rsch. fellow Inst. Pollution Studies, Portharcourt, 1987-91, sr. rsch. fellow, 1993—; coord. biological soc., Portharcourt, 1990-97. Contbr. articles to profl. jours. Vice-chmn., sec. Rumuokwurusi Town Coun., 1985-93; vice-chmn. Esara Co. Coun., 1996—. Mem. Fishories Soc. Nigeria, Ecological Soc. Nigeria, N.Y. Acad. Sci. Avocations: golf, hockey, fishing. Home: No 33 Igwuruta Rd, Rumuokwurusi Box 5400, Portharcourt Nigeria Office: Inst Pollution Studies, U Sci & Tech, PMB 5080 Portharcourt Nigeria

CHIN-DUSTING, JAYE PUI FONG, research scientist; b. Johor Baru, Johor, Malaysia, Oct. 17, 1963; arrived in Australia, 1982; d. Robert Joon Keng and Alee (Liang) Chin; m. Gregory James Dusting, Jan. 8, 1995; children: Cameron James Sze Ming, Julian Robert Sze Chin. BSc with honors, Monash U., Melbourne, Australia, 1986, PhD, 1990. Tutor Monash U., 1989, sr. tutor, 1990; postdoctoral rsch. scientist Alfred and Baker med. unit Baker Med. Rsch. Inst., Melbourne, 1990-95, sr. postdoctoral rsch. scientist, 1995—, R.D. Wright Rsch. fellow, 1997—, head Vascular Pharmacology Lab., 1997—; presenter in field. Reviewer Brit. Jour. Pharmacology, Clin. and Exptl. Physiology and Pharmacology, Hypertension, Endothelium: Jour. Endothelial Cell Rsch.; contbr. articles to profl. jours. Recipient Internat. Travel award Nat. Heart Found. Australia, 1993, 94, Young Investigator award ASTRA, 1993, Am. Heart Assn., 1995; postgrad. scholar Monash U., 1986-89. Fellow Wellcome Trust Travel, 2000; mem. Australian Soc. Clin. and Exptl. Pharm acologists and Toxicologists (Young Investigators Award grantee 1989, Internat. Travel award 1993), Australian Vascular Biology Soc., Internat. Soc. Heart Rsch. (Internat. Travel award 1992). Office: Alfred & Baker Med Unit, Commercial Rd, Prahran 3181 VIC, Australia

CHINEME, CHIJIOKE NWANKWO, veterinary pathologist, educator; b. Awka, Anambra, Nigeria, Dec. 4, 1935; s. Nweke and Nwabalum Mary (Anakweze) C.; m. Philippa Obiageli Nwobu, July 21, 1971; children: Nkechi, Chukwuemeka, Ikechukwu, Nneka. DVM, Tuskegee U., 1967; PhD, Cornell U., 1975. Vet. rsch. officer Vet. Divsn., Enugu, Nigeria, 1967-70; asst. prof. Tuskegee U., 1970-73; resident pathologist Cornell U., Ithaca, N.Y., 1975-76; reader Ahmadu Bello U., Zaria, Nigeria, 1978-80; prof. Ahmadu Bello U., Zaria, 1980-83; prof. U. Nigeria, Nsukka, 1983—, dean faculty vet. medicine, 1984-86, dep. vice-chancellor, 1987-91, co-dir. Svc.

Tng. Ctr., 1989-97, 1997—. Contbr. articles to profl. jours. Pres. Village Health Found., Awka, 1990—. Assn. Commonwealth U. sr. traveling fellow, 1988. Fellow Coll. Vet. Surgeons Nigeria; mem. Vet. Coun. Nigeria, Phi Kappa Phi. Roman Catholic. Avocations: table tennis, walking, music appreciation. Home: U Nigeria, 629 Odim St, Nsukka Enugu, Nigeria Office: Dept Vet Pathology, Univ Nigeria, Nsukka Enugu, Nigeria

CHING, CHIAO-LIANG JULIANA, development company executive, physician; b. Kowloon, Hong Kong, Feb. 23, 1955; d. Tan and Vivien (Kiang) Ching. BS in Biology with honors, Yale U., 1977; MD summa cum laude, U. Calif., Davis, 1981. Resident UCLA Hosps. and Clinics, 1981-83, Harvard U. Hosps., Boston, 1983-85; dir. Ideal Choice Devel. Ltd., Hong Kong, 1987—. Mem. Hong Kong Assn. Univ. Women. Avocations: music, reading. Office: Internat Fin Ctr, 1 Harbour View Street, Central Hong Kong China

CHING, SHUK CHI EMILY, physicist; b. Hong Kong, June 23, 1964; d. Lam-Siu Ching and So-Chun Lam; m. Ip-Wing Yu; 1 child, Ying-Ngai. BSc with 1st class honors, U. Hong Kong, 1986; MPhil in Physics, Chinese U. of Hong Kong, 1988; PhD in Physics, U. Chgo., 1992. Postdoctoral fellow Inst. Theoretical Physics, U. Calif., Santa Barbara, 1992-93; C.N. Yang rsch. fellow dept. physics Chinese U. Hong Kong, 1994, hon. and vis. lectr. dept. physics, 1994, asst. prof. dept. physics, 1995-97, assoc. prof. dept. physics, 1997—. Contbr. articles to profl. jours.; referee jours.; spkr. in field. Recipient Achievement in Asia award Overseas Chinese Physics Assn., 1999. Avocations: reading, hiking, listening to music. Office: Chinese U Hong Kong, Dept Physics, Shatin New Territories, Hong Kong

CHING, WAI KI, mathematics educator; b. Hong Kong, Feb. 22, 1969; s. Shun Tai and Kam Koo (Wong) C.; m. Shuet Yee Lee. BS in Math., U. Hong Kong, 1991, MPhil in Applied Math., 1994; PhD in Systems Engring., Chinese U. Hong Kong, 1998. Teaching asst. Hong Kong Polytech U., 1995-97, Hong Kong U. Sci. & Tech., 1997-98; statistician Hong Kong Spl. Adminstrn. Region Govt., Wanchai, China, 1998—. Co-author: (chpts.) :ecture Notes in Control and Information, 1996, Lectures in Applied Mathematics, 1997. Mem. IEEE, Soc. Indsl. and Applied Math. Avocations: reading, football, music. Home: Rm 2 6/F 526 Queens Rd West, Hong Kong China Office: Hong Kong SAR Govt, 22/F Wanchai Tower, Wanchai China

CHINN, MARK ALLAN, lawyer; b. Jackson, Miss., June 9, 1953; s. Rollin J. and Ann M. (Heiberg) C.; m. Cathy Hawkinson, Aug. 6, 1978; children: Courtney, Casey, Carly, Conley. BA in Polit. Sci., Iowa State U., 1975; JD, U. Miss., 1978. Bar: U.S. Dist. Ct. (no. dist.) Miss. 1978, U.S. Dist. Ct. (so. dist.) Miss. 1980; U.S. Ct. Appeals (5th and 11th cirs.) 1981; U.S. Supreme Ct. 1980; cert. civil trial expert Nat. Bd. Trial Advocacy. Staff atty. Miss. Senate, Jackson, 1978-79; spl. asst. Atty. Gen. Office, Jackson, 1979-80; assoc. Louis Baine, Jackson, 1980-82, Law Office William Latham, Jackson, 1982-88; atty. pvt. practice, Jackson, 1988—; adj. prof. law Miss. Coll. Sch. Law. Bd. dirs. Arts Alliance, Jackson, 1990-97, Miss. Children's Home, Jackson, 1990-95; pres. Jackson Urban League Bd., 1995-2000; bd. dirs. Jubilee Jam Found., 1995-97, chmn. Jubilee! Jam '96. Recipient Award of Merit, Miss. Bar Assn., 1996, Lamar Order U. Miss. Law Alumni, Miss. Bar Found. Mem. ABA, Lamar Order, Miss. Bar Assn. (chmn. family law sect. 1995-96, chmn. small firm practice com. 1995-96, Award of Merit 1996), Miss. Trial Lawyers Assn., Hinds County Bar Assn. (dir. 1994-95, pres. 1998—), Am. Inn of Ct. (master Charles Clark), Rotary, Jackson C. of C., Miss. Bar Found. (supreme ct. gender fairness task force). Avocations: golf, physical fitness, Karate, Tae Kwan Do (Black Belt), flying. E-mail: divorce@meta3.net. Office: Chinn & Assocs 4316 Old Canton Rd Ste 200 Jackson MS 39211-5920

CHINN, MENZIE DAVID, economics educator; b. Richland, Wash., June 4, 1961; s. Gene S. and Susan F. (Louie) C. BA, Harvard U., 1984; MA in Econs., U. Calif., Berkeley, 1988, PhD in Econs., 1991. Rsch. asst. Kennedy Sch. Govt., Harvard U., Cambridge, Mass., 1982-84, Brookings Inst., Washington, 1984-85; rsch. asst. Inst. for Internat. Studies U. Calif., Berkeley, 1985-86, lectr. econs. dept., 1988-90, researcher Inst. for Bus. & Econ. Rsch., 1990-91; asst. prof. econs. U. Calif., Santa Cruz, 1991—, assoc. prof., 1997—; sr. economist Pres. Coun. Economic Advisors, 2000—; faculty rsch. fellow Nat. Bur. Econ. Rsch., Inc., 1996—. Co-editor-in-chief Harvard Internat. Rev., 1982-83; assoc. editor Jour. Internat. Econs., 1996—; contbr. articles to profl. jours. Recipient Young Economist prize Am. Express Bank Rev. Awards, London, 1988. Mem. Am. Econs. Assn., Econometric Soc., Internat. Econs. and Fin. Soc. Office: U Calif Dept of Econs Santa Cruz CA 95064

CHINN, SIR TREVOR (EDWIN), business executive; b. July 24, 1935; s. Rosser and Susie Chinn; m. Susan Speelman, 1965; 2 children. Ed., Clifton Coll., King's Coll. Chmn. Lex Svc. PLC, London, 1959—; bd. dirs. Hampstead Theatre. Pres. Joint Israel Appeal; chmn. Brit./Israel Pub. Affairs Ctr.; vice chmn. Wishing Well Appeal, Gt. Ormond St. Hosp. for Sick Children, 1985-89; trustee Royal Acad. Trust, 1989—; freeman City of London. Mem. Variety Club Gt. Britain (chief barker 1977, 78). Office: Lex Svc PLC, Lex Ho Boston Dr Bourne End, Buckinghamshire SL8 5YS, England*

CHINNALA, AYODHYA RAMULU, biotechnologist, researcher; b. Ghattikal, India, Nov. 15, 1960; s. Venkatakishtaiah and Radhamma Chinnala; m. Indira Chinnala, Sept. 1994. BSc, Chanda Kantaiah Meml. Coll., Warangal, India, 1980; MSc in Plant Sci., Kakatiya U., Warangal, India, 1984, PhD, 1989; postgrad. diploma in higher edn., Indira Gandhi Nat. Open U., 1999; postgrad. diploma in portfolio mgmt., Pondicherry U., 2000. Cert. tchr. plant biotech. Lectr.prof. Kakatiya U., 1989-94; postdoctoral scientist U. Ill., Urbana-Champaign, 1994-96; scientist CSIR, New Delhi, 1996-97; asst. prof. Nat Coun. Edn. Rsch. and Tng. (NCERT), Ajmeer, India, 1997—; cons. Social Forestry Plantations, Warangal, 1981-86. Unv. Grants Commn. grantee, New Delhi, 1993. Fellow Indian Bot. Soc., Am. Soc. Plant Physiology, N.Y. Acad. Scis.; mem. In Vitro Biology Md., Plant Tissue Culture Assn. India, Indian Inst. Pub. Adminstrn. (life). Avocation: creative scientific awareness in rural people, extension education amd and teacher education programs. Home: Vill Ghattikal, Mandal, Rayaparthy, 506314 Warangal India Office: Regional Coll NCERT, Puskar Rd, 305 004 Ajmer India

CHINNIAN, RAJARATNAM RAWLIN, psychologist; b. Nagercoil, Tamilnadu, India, Nov. 29, 1940; s. Rajaratnam John and Lily Chinnian; m. Sylvia Olive, Sept. 16, 1970; children: Rawlin R., Joshua V. MA in Psychology, Annamala U., India, 1964; MPhil in Clin. Psychology, Nat. Inst. Health, Bangalore, India, 1969; PhD, Maduaikamaraj U., Madurai, India, 1979. Tutor, asst. prof. psychology Presidency Coll., Madras, India, 1964-66; asst. prof. clin. psychology Madurai Med. Coll., 1971-91; cons. psychologist, head dept. psychology Alamal Hosp., Riyadh, Saudi Arabia, 1991-97; vis. prof. psychology Fisk U., Nashville, 1986-87; hon. asst. prof. psychology King Saud U., Riyadh, 1992-97. Mem. editl. bd. Indian Jour. Clin. Psychology, 1977-80, Indian Jour. Psychiatry, 1977-78. Mem. APA (internat. affiliate). Mem. Christian Protestant Ch. of South India. Avocation: Indian and western music. Fax: 0091-452-521566. Home and Office: 83-A Singarayar Colony, North Ext, Madurai Tamilnadu 625002, India

CHINO, YOSHITOKI, securities company executive; b. Mar. 18, 1923; s. Hisakichi and Tokiyo Chino; m. Sachiko Kawabata, 1950; 2 children. BA, Keio U., Japan, 1946. Adviser Daiwa Securities Co. Ltd., 1991-97; vice chmn. Daiwa Anglo-Japanese Found., Tokyo. Named Hon. Knight Comdr. of the Most Excellent Order of the Brit. Empire, 1992, Grande Ufficiale dell Ordine al Merito della Repubblica Italiana, 1995. Avocation: reading, personal computer, fishing. Office: The Daiwa Anglo-Japanese, 1-1-9 Nihonbashi Kayabacho, Chuo-ku Tokyo 103-0025, Japan*

CHINOT, OLIVIER LOUIS, medical oncologist; b. Abidjan, Ivory Coast, Sept. 24, 1959; s. René and Brigitte (Butot) C.; m. Emmanuele Ribereau-Gayon, Aug. 31, 1991. Degree in med., 1985; Ed Lycee Janson de Sailly Faculty Paris Quest, U. R Descartes, France, 1991; MD, U. Aix Marseille II, France, 1992; M in biol., U. Paris, 1992; spec. degree in med. onc., 1992, degree in biol., 1994. Interne des hopitaux Marseille, 1985-92, hosp. asst., 1992-96, hosp. practitioner, 1997—; asst. lectr. U. Medicine, Marseille, 1992-96, lectr., 1997—; mem. faculty Paris-Ouest, U.R. Descartes, France; tchr. European Sch. Oncology, 1997—, Faculty Medicine, Marseille, 1992—; mem. tchg. cmty. Faculty Medicine, Marseille, 1997—. Author: Biologie des Gliomes Malins, 1996, Imagerie des Gliomes, 1999. Served with French Military in Cameroun, 1985-86. Mem. European Orgn. for Rsch. on Treatment in Cancer Brain Tumors Study Group, European Assn. Neuro-Oncology, European Soc. Therapeutic Radiotherapy and Oncology. Roman Catholic. E-mail: ochinot@mail.ap hm.fr. Office: Dept Neurosurgery, Chu Timone rue St Pierre, 13385 Marseille Cedex 5, France

CHINTALAPATI, SASIKALA, microbiology researcher, educator; b. Kadiri, India, Mar. 9, 1963; d. Lakshminarayanarao and Sundari (Jois) Kogileru; m. Venkata Ramana Chintalapati, May 5, 1992; children: Sarath, Ashrith. BS, Osmania U., Hyderabad, India, 1983, BEdn, 1984, PhD in Microbiology, 1990; MS, Bharatiyar (India) U., 1986. Lectr. V.V. Coll. Sci. and Arts, Hospet, India, 1986-87; jr. rsch. fellow Osmania U., Hyderabad, 1987-89, sr. rsch. fellow, 1989-92, rsch. assoc., 1992-94, rsch. scientist, 1994-96; rsch. scientist Jawaharal Nehru Tech. U., Hyderabad, 1996-99, asst. prof., 1999—. Office: Jawaharal Nehru Tech U, IPGS&R Ctr Environ, Hyderabad 500 028, India

CHIOGIOJI, MELVIN HIROAKI, former government official, entrepreneur; b. Hiroshima, Japan, Aug. 21, 1939; came to U.S., 1939; s. Yutaka and Harumi (Yamasaki) C.; m. Eleanor Nobuko Oura, June 4, 1960; children: Wendy A., Alan K. B.S. in Elec. Engring., Purdue U., 1961; M.B.A., U. Hawaii, 1968; D.Bus. Adminstrn., George Washington U., 1972. Registered profl. engr., Hawaii. Head weapons gen. component div. Quality Evaluation Lab., Oahu, Hawaii, 1965-69; dir. weapons evaluation and engring. div. Naval Ordinance Systems Command, Washington, 1969-73; dir. Office Indsl. Analysis Fed. Energy Adminstrn., Washington, 1973-75; asst. dir., div. bldg. and community systems Dept. Energy, Washington, 1975-79, dir. fed. program div., 1980—, dep. asst. sec. state and local assistance program, 1980-85, dir. office of transp. systems, 1985-90; constrn. mgr. Office of New Prodn. Reactors, Washington, 1990-92; pres. EFC, Inc., 1980-99, Precision Auto Care, Inc., 1989-97, Intemco, 1993-96, Mele Assocs., Inc., 1999—; prof. mgmt. sci. George Washington U., 1972—. Author: Industrial Energy Conservation, 1979, Energy Conservation in Commercial and Residential Buildings, 1982; contbr. articles to profl. jours. Mem. Md. State Adv. Com. on Civil Rights, 1976—; mem. Nat. Naval Res. Policy Bd., 1977—; vestryman Grace Episcopal Ch., Silver Spring, Md., 1982—; bd. dirs. Japanese Am. Nat. Mus., 1996—; chmn. Nat. Japanese Am. Meml. Found., 1995—. With USN, 1961-65; rear adm. USNR. Decorated Navy Commendation medal, Meritorious Svc. medal, Legion Merit medal. Mem. IEEE (sr.), NSPE, Acad. Mgmt., Naval Res. Assn., Assn. for Sci., Tech. and Innovation (pres. 1979-81), Soc. Am. Mil. Engrs., Armed Forces Mgmt. Assn., Seabee Meml. Scholarship Assn. (bd. dirs. 1973—), Triangle Fraternity Edn. Found. (bd. dirs. 1995—), Purdue U. Alumni Assn., Nat. Japanese Am. Meml. Found. (chmn.), Japanese Am. Nat. Mus. (bd. dirs.). Address: 15702 Thistlebridge Dr Rockville MD 20853-3226 Office: 14660 Rothgeb Dr Rockville MD 20850-5309

CHIOLIS, MARK JOSEPH, television executive; b. Walnut Creek, Calif., Dec. 29, 1959; s. Richard Spiro and Muriel Marie (Kottinger) C. Student aeronautics, Sacramento C.C., 1980-82; student, American River Coll., 1982. With on-air ops. Sta. KRBK-TV, Sacramento, 1979-81; on-air ops. trainer, crew chief Sta. KVIE-TV, Sacramento, 1981-85; trainer on air ops., ops. crew chief Sta. KRBK-TV, Sacramento, 1981-84; producer, dir., ops. crew chief Sta. KVIE-TV, Sacramento, 1985-87, Sta. KRBK-TV, Sacramento, 1984-87; prodn. mgr., producer, dir. Sta. KVIE-TV, Sacramento, 1987—; production mgr., producer, dir. spl. programs, comml. productions Sta. KRBK-TV, Sacramento, 1987—; with on-air ops. Sta. KVIE-TV, Sacramento, 1980-82; regional sales mgr. BTS-Broadcast T.V. Systems, Inc., 1992—; promotion chmn. Capital Concour d'Elegance, Sacramento, 1984—, gen. chmn., 1987-89. Producer (music videos) Running Wild, Running Fee, 1984, Rocket Hot-/The Image, 1984 (Joey award 1985); producer, dir. (music video) Haunting Melodies, 1991; dir. (documentary) Behind Closed Doors, 1984; producer, dir. FLIGHTLOG, The Jerry Reynolds Show, CountryMile country music show, 1991; dir. (video camera) Reno Nat. Championship Air Races, 1992, 93, 94, 95, 96, 97, dir. photography, 1998; Money Insights, 1993; tech. video dir. for state franchise bd. Tax Talk, 1992, 93, 94, 96, Teleconf. uplinks; segment prodr. Daylight Run 97 Camrac Studios. Video producer Calif. N.G., 1980-82; video trainer Am. Cancer Soc., Sacramento, 1983-85; cons. Sacramento Sheriff's Dept., Sacramento, 1984—, United Way-WEAVE, Sacramento, 1984-85; bd. dirs. Woodside Homeowners Assn., 1989—. Recipient Gold Addy award, 1986, 87, Addy award, 1989. Mem. Calif. Broadcasters Assn. (bd. dirs. 1996—), Am. Advt. Fedn., Sacramento Advt. Club (awards video producer 1984—, chmn. judging 1988-89, bd. dirs. 1989—, co-chair awards banquet 1989-90), Aircraft Owners and Pilots Assn., Computer Users Group. Republican. Avocations: flying, helicopters, writing, tennis, racquetball. Office: Philips Broadcast TV Sys 111 N 1st St Ste 100 Burbank CA 91502-1851

CHIOREAN, MIRCEA IOAN, physician; b. Ceanul, Romania, May 6, 1933; s. Ioan and Valeria C.; m. Sabina Usurel, Oct. 28, 1957; children: Barbu August, Luminita Antonela. Grad., The Babes-Bolyai U., 1957, U. Medicine and Pharmacy, Cluj-Napoca, 1964; PhD in Medicine, U. Bucharest, 1982. Family doctor Romania, 1964-69, resident doctor in anesthesiology and intensive care, 1969-73; specialist doctor in intensive care, rschr. The Med. Sci. Acad., Targu-Mures, 1973-75, specialist doctor in intensive care and anesthesiology, 1975-92; univ. lectr. The Targu-Mures U. of Medicine and Pharmacy, 1992-94, univ. prof., 1994—; dir. prof. dept. Mures County Coll. of Physicians; pres./coord. The Pilot Ctr. of Emergency Medicine and Catastrophic Medicine, 1991-98; pres. Coun. of Adminstrn./pvt. med. practice, 1993-99, Dir. Coun. of Hipocrate 2000, 1997-99, others. Mem. editl. bd. The Romanian Jour. of Intensive Care Medicine, 1993—, The Romanian Mag. of Intensive Care Medicine, 1993—; author: (book) Immunobiology for Surgeons and Anesthesiology, 1983; editor: Practical Guide of Prehospital Emergency Medicine, 1995, Intensive Medicine, Vols. 1-3, 1997-99; editor: Romanian Jour. of Emergency and Disaster Medicine, 1993-97; others. Capt. doctor The Min. of Nat. Def. Mil., 1967—. Mem. World Fedn. Soc. of Anesthesiologists. Avocations: hitchhiking, classical music. Office: Intensive Care Dept, Gheorghe Marinescu nr 50, 4300 Targu-Mures Romania

CHIOTELLIS, PHILIP NICOS, cardiologist; b. Kyrenia, Cyprus, May 31, 1942; s. Nicos Philip and Maria (Constantinides) C.; m. Lavinia Conroy; children: Nicos, Peter, Fiona. MD, Athens U., 1966. Resident in medicine N.J. Med. Sch., Newark, 1968-71; fellow in cardiology Mass. Gen. Hosp./Harvard Med. Sch., Boston, 1972-74; instr medicine Harvard Med. Sch., Boston, 1974-75; practice cardiology Boston/Cape Cod Area, 1974—; pres. Heart Ctr., Hyannis, Mass. Fellow Am. Coll. Cardiology, Paul Dudley Med. Soc., Algonquin Club (Boston), Everglades Club (Palm Beach, Fla.). Office: Heart Ctr 52 Park St Hyannis MA 02601-5206

CHIOU, YAHN-KUN, gynecologic oncologist; b. Miaoli, Taiwan, Feb. 17, 1960; s. Chien-Shao and Poon Ran-Woo (Poon) C.; m. Chun-Ying Lin, Oct. 5, 1985; children: Andrew, Edward, Michelle. MD, Taiwan U., Taipei, 1985. Pediat. resident Hsin-chu (Taiwan) Air Force Hosp., 1985-87; ob-gyn resident Taiwan Univ. Hosp., Taipei, 1987-90, ob-gyn chief resident, 1990-91; gynecologic oncology rsch. fellow U. Va., Charlottesville, 1992-93, gynecologic oncology clin. fellow, 1993-95; divsn. head gynecologic oncology dept. Sun Yat-Sen Cancer Ctr., Taiwan U., Taipei, 1995—, attending in gynecologic oncology, 1996—; cons. gynecologic oncology fellow program Taiwan Coop. Oncology Group, Taipei, 1995—; clin. tchr. Nat. Taiwan U. Med. Sch., Taipei, 1996—. Contbr. articles to med. jours. Recipient Taiwan U. rsch. fund Taiwan Rsch. Inst., 1991, Koo Found. tng. fund, 1992. Mem. AMA, Internat. Gynecologic Cancer Soc., Soc. Ob-Gyn. Avocations: tennis, swimming, golf. Office: 125 Lih-Der Rd Pei-Tou Dist, Taipei Taiwan Address: No 9 Alley 24 Ln 358, Tah-hsing East Rd, Tah-hsing Taipei 111, Taiwan

CHIPARA, MIRCEA, physicist; b. Constanta, Romania, Apr. 16, 1953; s. Ioan and Elena Chipara; m. Dorina Magdalena Marica, June 29, 1978; children: Octav, Alin Cristian. BS in Physics, U. Bucharest, Romania, 1975, MS in Ploymer Physics, 1977; PhD in Physics, Inst. for Atomic Physics, Bucharest, 1997. Rschr. Inst. for Atomic Physics, 1979-90; sr. rschr. Nat. Inst. for Materials Physics, Bucharest, 1990-98; postdoctral rsch. assoc. U. Nebr., Lincoln, 1999—; vis. prof. physics U. Bucharest; sci. editor, computer processor Romanian Reports, Romanian Acad. Scis., Bucharest. Contbr. or co-contbr. articles to sci. publs. NATO grantee for East European Scientists, Italy, 1998; award recipient French Vacuum Soc., 1992, Internat. Conf. for Radiation Rsch., Edinburgh, Scotland, 1985; recipient Constantin Budeanu award Romanian Acad. Scis., Bucharest, 1991. Mem. European Phys. Soc., Romanian Phys. Soc. Fax: 402-472-5385. E-mail: chipara@mciworld.com. Home: 2259 Y St Apt 29 Lincoln NE 68503-1669 Office: Univ Nebr Behlen Lab Physics Lincoln NE 65855-0111

CHIRAC, JACQUES RENÉ, president of France; b. Paris, Nov. 29, 1932; s. François and Marie-Louise (Valette) C.; m. Bernadette Chodron de Courcel, 1956; children: Laurence, Claude. Ed., Lycee Carnot, Lycee Louisle-Grand, Ecole Nationale d'Administration. Auditor Cour de Comptes, 1959-62; pres. Govt. of France, Paris, 1995—; head dept. sec. gen. govt., 1962; head dept. Pvt. Office of M. Pompidou, 1962-65; counselor Cour des Comptes, 1965-67; sec. state for employment problems, 1967-68; sec. state of economy and fin., 1968-71; minister for parliamentary relations, 1971-72, minister for agr. and rural devel., 1972-74; minister of the interior, 1974; prime minister, 1974-76, 86-88; sec. gen. Union des Democrates pour la Republique (UDR), 1975, hon. sec.-gen., 1975-76; pres. Rassemblement pour la République (formerly UDR), 1976, 80-81, 82-94, hon. sec. gen., 1977-80; mem. Nat. Assembly, 1967, 68, 73, 76, 78; mem. European Parliament, 1979, 80; pres. gen. council La Correze, 1970-79; mayor, Paris, 1977-95; pres. French Republic, 1995—. Treas. Fondation Claude Pompidou, from 1969. Decorated Gt. Cross, Order of Merit, knight Order of Agrl. Merit, Order of Arts and Letters, Croix de la Valeur Militaire, Chevalier de l'Etoile Noire, du Mérite Sjortit, du Mérite Touristique, Médaille de l'Aéronautique. Office: Palais de l'Elysee, 55-57 rue du Fauborg Saint-Honore, 75008 Paris France

CHIRAN, AUREL, agronomics educator; b. Tandarei, Ialomita, Romania, Jan. 17, 1942; s. Cristea and Maria (Serban) C.; m. Zenovia Craciun, Feb. 22, 1965; children: Cornelia, Mihai. Engr., Agronomical U., Bucarest, Romania, 1965. Cert. engr. Preparator Agronomical U. Iasi, Romania, 1965-68, asst., 1968-77, lectr., 1977-90, assoc. prof., 1990-92, prof., 1992—, sci. sec. agrl. faculty, 1992-96, dean agrl. faculty, 1996-2000. Author: Marketing Agrar, 1997, Marketing Agrar-Practical Guide, 1997, Piata Produselor Agricole si Agroalimentare, 1999, Zooeconomie, 1999, Agromarketing, 1999. Mem. Agronomics Engrs. Orgn. Mem. Orthodox Ch. Avocations: soccer, travel, performances. Home: ScB et III ap lo, Aleea M Sadoveanu 4 Bl A1, 6600 Iasi Romania Office: Agronomical U, Aleea M Sadoveanu 3, 6600 Iasi Romania

CHIRAS, JACQUES STEPHANE, neuroradiology educator; b. Paris, Oct. 7, 1949; s. Etienne and Jacqueline (Bonnemort) C.; m. Brigitte Marie Antoinette Blondé, June 23, 1973; children: Laure, Guillaume, Anne Gabrielle. Degree in medicine, St. Antoine, Paris, 1977; MD, U. Paris VI, 1979; specialist degree in radiology and imaging, Paris, 1983. Asst. in radiology Hosp. Salpetriere, Paris, 1979-89; prof.neuroradiology Faculty Medicine Pitie Salpetriere U. Paris VI, 1989—; chief dept. neuroradiology Hosp. Salpetriere, 1995—; dir. postgrad. edn. neuroradiology, U. Paris VI, 1990—. Author: Arderiography of the Pelvis, 1981, Art Chemotherapy in Interventional Neuroradiology, 1993, Vertebroplasty in Spine Metastases, 1997, 99, Maxillofacial Imaging, 1997; contbr. numerous articles to profl. jours. Served with French mil., 1974-75. Mem. AAAS, French Soc. Neuroradiology (exec. bd.), European Soc. Neuroradiology (prize 1983, 86), World Fedn. Interventional Neuroradiology, French Soc. Radiology, World Fedn. Neurol. Soc. Roman Catholic. Avocation: sailing. Fax: 93 142161906. Office: Hopital Salpetriere, 47 Blvd de l'Hopital, 75013 Paris France

CHIRGADZE, YURI NICKOLAIEVICH, biologist; b. Tashkent, Russia, Sept. 18, 1935; s. Nickolay Mikhailovich and Antonina Konstantinovna (Voronina) C.; m. Lubov Ivanovna Kleshevskaya, Dec. 18, 1963; children: Nickolay, Dmitri. BS, Moscow State U., 1959; PhD, Russian Acad. Scis., 1963, DSc, 1977. Rschr. Inst. Biophysics Russian Acad. Scis., Moscow, 1962-67; head lab. protein spectroscopy Inst. Protein Rsch. Russian Acad. Scis., Pushchino, 1967-74, head lab. protein structure analysis Inst. Protein Rsch., 1974—; prof. molecular biology Russian Acad. Scis., Pushchino, 1986; vis. rschr. U. Oreg., Eugene, 1975; vis. prof. Birkbeck Coll. U. London, 1993. Contbr. articles to profl. jours. Recipient State Order Sign of Honor Supreme Soviet of USSR, 1976; grantee Am. Crystallographic Assn., 1993, Brit. Royal Soc., 1993, Russian Acad. Sci., 1998—. Office: Inst Protein Rsch, Russian Acad Scis, Moscow Pushchino 142290, Russia

CHIRIBOGA KLEIN, SYLVIA INES, developmental pediatrician, educator; b. Lima, Peru, June 22, 1957; came to U.S., 1959; d. Jorge Chiriboga and Olga Ines Klein; m. Alfredo Gustavo Caviglia, Apr. 30, 1982; children: Selene Ines, Andrés Julian, Arian Ignacio. MD, U. Buenos Aires, 1981. Diplomate Am. Bd. Pediat. Pediatrician Mt. Sinai Sch. Medicine and Hosp./Beth Isreal Med. Ctr., N.Y.C., 1985; postdoctoral fellow, jr. attending in pediat. St. Luke's Roosevelt Hosp., Columbia U., N.Y.C., 1986-88; devel. pediatrician Booth Meml. Med. Ctr., N.Y.C., 1987-88; attending physician in pediat. Sanatoria Junin, Argentina, 1988—; physician spl. edn., moderate and severe mental retardation Bd. Edn., Junin, Argentina, 1990—; chief pediat. Ferroviario Hosp., Junin, Argentina, 1991-94; prof. neurophysiology and neuropsychopathology Inst. No. 20 for Spl. Educators, Junin, Argentina, 1992—; attending physician pediat. Clin. Pequena Familia, Junin, Argentina, 1998—; cons. physician Minors at Risk Minors State Ct., Junin, Argentina, 1997—, Bd. for Spl. Edn., Province of BsAs, 1994—; vis. physician Hosp. Garrahan Interdisciplinary Clins., Buenos Aires, 1997—; cmty. tchr. prevention in devel. pediat., Bd. Edn. Dist. VII Province of Buenos Aires, 1990—. Contbr. articles to profl. jours. Coord. Parents Assn. for Children with Autism Argentina. Fellow Soc. Argentina de Pediatria (cert. specialist), Am. Acad. Pediat. (corr. mem). Avocations: reading, teaching, painting, gardening, writing. Home: Ataliva Roca 26 Junin, 6000 Buenos Aires Argentina Office: Centro Medico Famyl, Lebenson 29 Junin, 6000 Buenos Aires Argentina

CHIRKIN, ANATOLY STEPANOVICH, physicist, educator; b. Moscow, May 4, 1939; s. Stepan Andreevich and Evdokiya Egorovna Chirkin; m. Tat'yana Alekseevna Sarychikhina, Feb. 22, 1969; children: Ludmila, Ol'ga. Diploma of physics, Lomonosov Moscow State U., 1963, Candidate of Sci. in Physics and Math., 1968, DSc in Physics and Math., 1980. Cert. prof.'s title in field of laser physics. Jr. sci. rschr. dept. sci. info. M.V. Lomonosov Moscow State U., 1966-68, sr. sci. rschr. dept. sci. info., 1969-87, chief sci. rschr. faculty of physics, 1987-97, prof. faculty of physics, 1997—; vis. prof. Kamensky U., Bratislava, Slovakia, 1991, Palacky U. Olomouc, Czech Republic, 1997. Author 6 books, 6 inventions, numerous articles. Recipient State prize, 1997, Lomonosov prize, 1997. Mem. Internat. Soc. for Optical Engring. (editor 3 vols. of procs.), Internat. Info. Acad. Avocations: history, football. E-mail: chirkin@foton.ilc.msu.su. Office: MV Lomonosov Moscow State U, Faculty of Physics, 119899 Moscow Russia

CHIRON, JEAN-PAUL MICHEL ANDRÉ, microbiology educator; b. Bressuire, Poitou, France, Sept. 3, 1947; s. André and Madeleine (Sourisseau) C.; children: Sophie-Anne, Aude-Emmanuelle; m. Janine Lamandé. Degree in pharmacy, U. Tours, 1970, PharmD, 1977. Asst. prof. pharmacy U. Tours, 1971-76, prof., 1979-90, 92—, dean, 1981-88; chef de travaux U. Dakar, Senegal, 1975-79; dir. Rsch. Inst., Bobo Dioulasso, 1990-92; cons. Inst. Medicament, Tours, 1981-90, Assn. Devel.Res. Expertise Microb. Imm. Tours, 1994—, Tours, 1992—; expert Pharmacopee Francaise, Paris, 1986-93, Assn. Frans Normalisation, Paris, 1988—. Mem. editl. bd. Bull. Acad. Nat. de Pharmacie. Lt. French Air Force, 1974-75. Decorated officer Order of Merit (Senegal), officier Ordre des Palmes Académiques (France); laureat Nat. Acad. Medicine; recipient prix Leon Baratz. Mem. Academie Nat. Pharmacie, Am. Soc. for Microbiology, N.Y. Acad. Scis., Internat. Soc. for Infectious Diseases. Avocations: sports, travel. Home: 9 rue Robert Marchand, 94250 Gentilly France Office: U Tours Lab Micro and Immun Fac Sc Pharm, Philippe Maupas, 37200 Tours France

CHIRVA, VASSILY YAKOVLEVICH, dean, researcher; b. Kirovograd, Ukraine, July 19, 1939; s. Yakov Sergeevich Chirva and Marfa Zakharovna Krjachko; m. Alla Konstantinovna Zymbaljuk, Apr. 10, 1965; 1 child, Natalja. Candidate Chem. Scis., Kishinev (Moldova) State U., 1965; post-grad., Inst. Natural Chemistry Prods., Russia, 1962-65; D of Chem. Scis., Tashkent (Uzbekistan) State U., 1973. Rsch. worker Moldova Acad. Scis., Inst. Chemistry, Kishinev, 1965-74; head of organic chemistry dept., dean natural scis. faculty Simferopol (Ukraine) State U., 1974—; participant in-ternat. confs. and symposia on chemistry of natural products and bioorganic chemistry; mem. Ukrainian Certifying Commn. Expert Coun. Author monographs; contbr. numerous articles and papers to sci. jours.; patentee in field. Recipient Soros Prof. award Soros Found., 1996. Mem. Ukrainian Chem. Soc. Avocations: numismatics, philately, collecting books. Home: Pervomajskaya St 3a, 95007 Simferopol Ukraine Office: Simferopol State U, Simferopol State U, Yaltinskaya 4, 950366 Simferopol Ukraine

CHIRVASE, ANA AURELIA, research scientist; b. Dumbraveni, Vrancea, Romania, Apr. 13, 1948; d. Ion and Elena Valeria (Georgescu) Martinciuc; m. Nicolae Beganu, Feb. 20, 1973 (div. Dec. 1973); m. Ion Marcel Chirvase, Jan. 30, 1974; 1 child, Ion Gabriel. BS, Unirea H.S., Focsani, Romania, 1966; MSChemE, Ecole Nat. Sup. Ind. Chem., Nancy, France, 1972; PhD in Biotech., Poly. U., Bucharest, Romania, 1998. Chem. engr. Inst. Chem. Pharm. Rsch., Bucharest, 1972-77, Danubiana fgn. trade co., Bucharest, 1977-78; rschr. Inst. Chem. Pharm. Rsch., Bucharest, 1978-84; sr. rschr. Inst. Chem. Rsch., Bucharest, 1984—; cons., rsch. projects evaluator Rsch. and Tech. Ministry, Bucharest, 1992-95; program monitor European Commn. Dir.-Gen. XII, Brussels, 1999; tchr. Poly. U., Bucharest, 1992-94. Contbr. articles to profl. jours.; patentee in field. Mem. European Fedn. Biotech., Romanian Soc. Biotech. (v.p. 1992—). Mem. Romanian Christian Democrat Party. Orthodox. Avocations: reading, travel, study of Far East culture. Home: Bl 117C Sc A App 6, 14 Str Sachelarie Visarion, 73331 Bucharest Romania Office: Inst Chem Rsch, 202 Splaiul Independentei, 77208 Bucharest Sect 6, Romania

CHISHOLM, COLIN ALEXANDER JOSEPH, III, media professional; b. Salem, Mass., Nov. 23, 1951; s. Colin Alexander William XI and Mary Elizabeth (Brennan) C.; m. Virginia Louise Nance, June 24, 1973; 1 child, Mary Kathryn. MS, New England Inst., 1976. Dir. sales United Artists TV, 1979-80; v.p. Turner Program Svcs., 1981-85; pres. CST Entertainment, 1986-88; vice chmn., CEO Comship Corp., 1989; chmn., CEO Chisholm Bros. Inc.; founder, chmn. bd. The Caribbean Network, 1994, CaribTel Telephone Co., 1994. Contbr. articles to profl. jours. Bd. dirs. St. Andrew's Soc. of the State of N.Y., Maine Golf Hall of Fame; dinner com. The Bal Polonaise, 1988, 89; mem. English Speaking Union; patron Debutante Assembly; mem. Nat. Found. of Scottish Medieval and Mus. With USMC, 1969-74, Res., 1974-76. Mem. NATAS, N.Y. State Broadcasters Assn. (bd. dirs.), Internat. Radio and TV Soc. (com.), Nat. Assn. of TV Program Execs. (com.), Am. Film Inst. (com.), Am. Legion, Scottish-Am. Found., Clan Chisholm Soc., Scottish Heritage U.S.A., Nat. Trust for Scotland, Rotary (N.Y.), Squadron A Assn., OverSeas Press Club Am., Coffee House N.Y. Office: 280 Railroad Ave Greenwich CT 06830-6338

CHISHOLM, DONALD JOHN, endocrinologist, educator; b. Sydney, NSW, Australia, Feb. 14, 1941; s. Henry John and Joan Maud (Meagher) C.; m. Judith Connor, Aug. 16, 1968; children: David Alexander, James Lachlan, Sarah Caroline. MB BS, Sydney U., 1963. Rsch. fellow Garvan Inst. of Med. Rsch., Sydney, 1968-69; clin. rsch. fellow McGill U., Montreal, 1969-71; asst. dept. medicine St. Vincents Hosp.-Melbourne U., 1971-78; resident, registrar St. Vincent's Hosp., Sydney, 1964-67; sr. staff endocrinologist St. Vincents Hosp., 1978—; from asst. prof. to prof. medicine U. New South Wales, Sydney, 1980—; from asst. dir. to head metabolic divsn. Garvan Inst. Med. Rsch., Sydney, 1978—; bd. dirs. Sisters of Charity Health Care Svc., Australia, 1996—; chmn. program CTEE, XIII Congress, Internat. Diabetes Fedn., 1985-88. Contbr. chpts. to books; contbr. over 170 articles to internat. med. jours. Mem. coun. Diabetes Australia, 1984-86, 94, bd. dirs., NSW br., 1987—. Decorated officer Order of Australia; Multiple rsch. grantee Nat. Health and Med. Rsch. Coun., Australia, 1972—. Fellow Royal Australasian Coll. Physicians (councilor 1986-96); mem. Australian Diabetes Soc. (pres. 1984-86), Am. Diabetes Assn., Endocrine Soc. Australia (councilor 1978-80), Australia Soc. Med. Rsch., Roseville Golf Club. Roman Catholic. Avocations: golf, squash, music. Home: 7 Belgium Ave, NSW Sydney 2069, Australia Office: Garvan Inst Med Rsch, St Vincents Hosp, NSW Sydney 2010, Australia

CHISHOLM, TOMMY, lawyer, utility company executive; b. Baldwyn, Miss., Apr. 14, 1941; s. Thomas Vaniver and Rubel (Duncan) C.; m. Janice McClanahan, June 20, 1964; children: Mark Alan (dec.), Andrea, Stephen Thomas, Patrick Ervin. BSCE, Tenn. Tech. U., 1963; JD, Samford U., 1969; MBA, Ga. State U., 1984. Registered profl. engr., Ala., Ark., Del., Ga., Fla., Ky., La., N.H., Miss., N.C., Pa., Tenn., S.C., Va., W.Va. Civil engr. TVA, Knoxville, Tenn., 1963-64; design engr. So. Co. Svcs., Birmingham, Ala., 1964-69; coord. spl. projects So. Co. Svcs., Atlanta, 1969-73, sec., house counsel, 1977-82, v.p., sec., house counsel, 1982-98; v.p., assoc. gen. counsel, sec. So. Co., Atlanta, 1998—, asst. to pres., 1973-75, sec., asst. treas., 1977—; mgr. adminstrv. svcs. Gulf Power Co., Pensacola, Fla., 1975-77; sec. So. Energy, Inc., Atlanta, 1981-82; v.p., sec. So. Energy Resources Inc., Atlanta, 1982—. Mem. ABA, State Bar Ala., Am. Soc. Corp. Secs., Am. Corp. Counsel Assn., Nat. Assn. Corp. Dirs., Phi Alpha Delta, Beta Gamma Sigma. Office: The Southern Co 270 Peachtree St NW Ste 2200 Atlanta GA 30303-1247*

CHISSANO, JOAQUIM ALBERTO, president of Mozambique; b. Chibuto, Gaza Province, Mozambique, Oct. 22, 1939. Ed., Lourenco Marques. Sec. svc. ministry Frente de Libertacao de Mozambique, 1964-74, mem. cen. com., also charge conduct and coordination of war against Portuguese Army; prime min. Transitional Govt. of Mozambique, Maputo, 1974-75; min. fgn. affairs Govt. of Mozambique, Maputo, 1975-86, pres., comdr.-in chief armed forces, 1986—. Address: Office of Pres, Avenida Julius Nyerere 2000, CP 285 Maputo Mozambique*

CHISUM, GENE H., II, municipal official; b. Uvalde, Tex., July 31, 1954; s. Gene H. Chisum and Elizabeth R. Martin; m. Nancy E. C., Feb. 18, 1978; children: Gene H. III, Jade Elizabeth Reynolds. Student, Southwest Tex. Jr. Coll., Uvalde, 1972-78. Owner, operator Chisum Constrn. Co., Uvalde, 1990-93; gen. supt. Waggoner Constrn. Co., San Antonio, 1993-94; dir. pub. works City of Ingleside, Tex., 1994-97; gen. mgr. Kingsland (Tex.) Mcplty. Utility Dist., 1997—; sec., treas. Highland Lakes Corp., Marble Falls, Tex., 1999-00. Chair law enforcement adv. panel Llano County Crime Stoppers, 1997—; sec., treas. Highland Lakes Coop., 1999-00. Mem. Tex. Water Utility Assn. (sec./treas. Highland Lakes Dist. 1997-99, v.p. 1999-00, Outstanding Mem. 1999), Kingsland C. of C. (bd. dirs. 1999-01), Kingsland Lions Club, Ingleside Lions Club (v.p. 1996-97), Double A Club, Masons. Episcopalian. E-mail: genechisum@281.com. Office: Kingsland Mcpl Utility Dist 100 Ingram St Kingsland TX 78639-5244

CHITRE, SHARADCHANDRA RAGHUNANDAN, physician; b. Apr. 11, 1936; came to U.S., 1968; s. Raghunandan Ballal and Sarojini Chitre; m. Rekha Balkrishna Chitnis, May 6, 1961; children: Nanda, Priya, Yash. MB, BChir, M.S. U., Baroda, India, 1961, MS, 1966. Resident in orthopaedic surgery Royal Sea Bathing Hosp., Margate, Eng., 1967-68; resident in surgery Beverly (Mass.) Hosp., 1968-70, emergency physician, 1971—, chief emergency and outpatient dept., 1975-85; fellow in plastic surgery Meth. Hosp., Bklyn., 1970-71; instr. North Shore Community Coll., Beverly; former mem. state adv. bd. on emergency med. Services. Fellow Royal Soc. Health (London); mem. Mass. Med. Soc., Essex South Dist. Med. Soc., Indian Med. Assn. New Eng. (trustee), Am. Coll. Emergency Physicians, Baroda Med. Coll. Alumni Assn. (pres. 1987-90, trustee 1997-00). Home: 901 Bay Rd Hamilton MA 01936-0327 Office: 75 Herrick St Beverly MA 01915-5900

CHITSOMBOON, BENJAMART, science educator; b. Bangkok, May 25, 1954; d. Prayuth Kotarapinit and Supasri Srisuchart; m. Tawit Chitsomboon, Sept. 15, 1986; 1 child, Bhodhipal. BSc, Chulalongkorn U., Bangkok, 1977; MPH, U. Mich., 1980; PhD, Utah State U., 1986. Rsch. assoc. Mahidol U., Bangkok, 1977-78; rschr. Chulalongkorn U., Bangkok, 1980-82; grad. rsch. asst. Utah State U., 1982-86; postdoctoral fellow Med. Coll. Va., 1986-89; spl. fellow Cleve. Clinic Found., 1990-91; rsch. assoc. Case Western U., Cleve., 1991-95; asst. prof. Suranaree U. Tech., Nakhon Ratchasima, Thailand, 1995—. Author: Biochemical Pharmacology, 1986; contbr. articles to profl. publs. Disting. Student scholar Chulalongkorn U., 1975, 76, 77, Royal Thai Govt. scholar, 1978-80. Mem. Biotech. of Thailand, Toxicol. Soc. Thailand, Environ. Mutagen Soc. Buddhist. Avocations: swimming, tennis. Office: Suranee U Tech Inst Sci, 111/144 Univ Ave, 30000 Nakhon Ratchasima Thailand

CHITTY, NAREN JAYANTHA, international communication educator, consultant; b. Colombo, Ceylon, Apr. 27, 1949; s. Samuel Alexis and Doris Saraswathy (Aserappa) C.; m. Gina Ismene Shenaz De Souza, Dec. 17, 1959; children: Sabina Alexa Theodora, Grischa George Armand. MA, Am. U., Washington, 1984, PhD, 1992. Cons. Ministry of State, Colombo, Sri Lanka, 1979-82; counselor Embassy of Sri Lanka, Washington, 1982-87; resident rep. Worldview Internat. Found., Washington, 1988; lectr. Macquarie U., Sydney, Australia, 1989-92, sr. lectr., 1992-99; assoc. prof., head of media and comm. dept. Macquarie U., Sydney, 2000—; dir. Ctr. Internat. Comm., 2000—. Author: Framing South Asian Transformation, 1994; editor Jour. Internat. Comm. Mem. Internat. Assn. Media and Comm. Rsch. (sec.-gen. 1996—), Worldview Internat. Found., AsiaPacific Media Info. Ctr. Avocation: oil painting. Office: Macquarie Univ Dept Media, North Ryde, 2109 Sydney NSW, Australia

CHIU, ALLEN WEN-HSIANG, surgeon, educator; b. Taipei, Taiwan, Dec. 16, 1958; s. Shang-Ming and A-Ju (Hsieh) C.; m. Catherine Jui-Ling Liu, Sept. 20, 1986; children: Albert, Amory. MD, Nat. Yang-Ming U., Taipei, 1984, PhD, 1995. Resident Vet. Gen. Hosp., Taipei, 1986-90; instr. Nat. Yang-Ming U., Taipei, 1990-95, assoc. prof., 1995—; cons. Indsl. Tech. Rsch. Inst., Hsin Chu, Taiwan, 1996; chief urology Chi-Mei Found. Hosp., Tainan, 1997—. Editor (video) Video Urology Times, 1996; contbr. articles to profl. jours. Boston U. Med. Ctr. fellow, 1992-93. Mem. Urol. Soc. China, Am. Urol. Assn., Endourological Soc. Avocations: golfing, swimming, tennis, basketball. Home: No 46-4 Tien-Mou West Rd, Taipei 11132, Taiwan Office: Urology Chi Mi Found Hosp, No 901 Chung-Hwa Rd, Yung-Kang Tainan Taiwan

CHIU, CHENG-HSUN, pediatrician, researcher; b. Miaoli, Taiwan, July 14, 1963; s. Hsi-Hu and Hsieh Ching-Mei Chiu; m. Tzu-Ying Lee, Oct. 29, 1995; children: Huei-Chen, Catherine, David, Ethan. MD, Chung-Shan Med. Coll., Taichung, Taiwan, 1989; PhD in Clin. medicine, Chang Gung U., Taoyuan, Taiwan, 1997; postgrad., U. B.C., Vancouver, Can., 1997-99. Med. diplomate. Resident dept. pediatrics Chang Gung Children's Hosp., Taoyuan, 1989-92, chief resident, 1992-93, attending physician, 1993—; clin. cons. Microbiology Lab., dept. clin. pathology Chang Gung Meml. Hosp., Taoyuan, 1994—; asst. prof. dept. pediatrics Chang Gung U., Taoyuan, 1996—. Contbr. articles to profl. jours. Recipient Louis Pasteur award First World Congress Pediatric Infectious Diseases, World Soc. Pediatric Infectious Diseases, 1996, Merck Found. rsch. award Chinese Taipei Pediatric Assn., 1997. Mem. Pediatric Infectious Disease Soc. Am., Am. Soc. Microbiology, Infectious Disease Soc. Republic of China, Chinese Taipei Pediatric Assn. Avocations: sports, movies, classical music, travel. Home: 3F No 17 Aly 18 Lane 130, Sec 3 Ming-Sheng E Rd, Taipei Taiwan Office: Chang Gung Childrens Hosp, Dept Peds 5 Fu-shin St, Kwei-San Tao Yuan 333, Taiwan

CHIU, DAVID TAK WAI, surgeon; b. Kwangtung, China, Oct. 23, 1945; s. Bud Yick and Lai Kwai (Lum) C.; m. Lilian Wah-Ying Shen, June 19, 1973; children: Vincent, Edmund, Jerome, Miranda. BA, U. Mo., St. Louis, 1969; MD, Columbia U., 1973. Diplomate Am. Bd. Plastic Surgery. Intern Barnes Hosp., St. Louis, 1973-74, resident in gen. surgery, 1974-77, resident in plastic surgery, 1977-79; fellow NYU Med. Ctr., N.Y.C., 1980, instr. surgery, 1981, asst. prof., 1981-89; supervisory attending Bellevue Hosp. Hand Clinic, N.Y.C., 1981-89; assoc. dir. plastic surgery, chief hand/microsurgery and replantation surgery divsn. plastic surgery Columbia Presbyn. Med. Ctr., N.Y.C., 1989-94, dir. microsurgery ctr., 1993, chief plastic surgery divsn. dept. surgery, 1994-97, prof. clin. surgery, 1990—, Thomas S. Zimmer prof., 1994-2000, Calvin F. Berber prof., 2000—. Author: Introduction to Microsurgery: A Lab Manual, 1985; mem. editorial bd. Jour. Reconstructive Microsurgery, 1990—. Recipient Alumni Fedn. Columbia U. medal, 1995. Fellow ACS; mem. AMA, Fedn. Chinese Am. and Chinese Can. Med. Socs. (founding pres. 1994-96, chmn. bd. dirs. 1996-98), Chinese Am. Med. Soc. (dir. 1983—, pres. 1985-87), Am. Assn. Plastic Surgeons, Am. Soc. Reconstructive Microsurgery, N.Y. County Med. Soc., N.Y. State Med. Soc., N.Y. Soc. Surgery of Hand (pres. 1996-97), Plastic Surgery Rsch. Council, Coll. Physicians and Surgeons Alumni Assn. (dir. 1984, Bronze medal 1973, Gold medal 1997), N.Y. Regional Soc. Plastic and Reconstructive Plastic Surgery (pres. 1996-97), Am. Soc. Reconstructive Microsurgery (pres. 1998-99), Am. Soc. Surgery of Hand, Am. Soc. Plastic and Reconstructive Surgeons, Am. Assn. Hand Surgery, Am. Soc. Peripheral Nerve Surgery (founding, pres. 1999—), Royal Soc. Medicine, Northeast Soc. Plastic Surgery, Chinese Am. Med. Soc. (Presdl. medal 1987, Disting. Service award 1988), Internat. Soc. of Reconstructive Microsurgery, Am. Acad. Pediatrics (splty. fellow 1992), Fedn. Chinese Am. and Chinese Can. Med. Socs. (founding pres. 1994-96, outstanding achievement award 1994, chmn. bd. dirs. 1996-98), Sunderland Soc., Tissue Engring. Soc. Office: 900 Park Ave New York NY 10021-0231

CHIU, DIRK MOON, engineering educator; b. Kuala Lumpur, Selangor, Malaysia, May 26, 1948; arrived in Australia, 1983; s. Kon Fah and Chui (Lee) C.; m. Lee Huang Lim, Nov. 8, 1969; children: Jhin Hann, Shen Yih. BS in Engring., U. London, 1969; MSc, U. Edinburgh, Scotland, 1976; PhD, U. Manchester, Eng., 1978. Telecomms. engr. STC, U.K., 1969-70; electronics design engr. Control Sys., U.K., 1970-72; sr. electronic engr. London U., 1973-75; lectr. in electronics Singapore Poly., 1978-81, Paisley (Scotland) U., U.K., 1981-83; course coord. Victoria U., Melbourne, Australia, 1983-98; assoc. prof. Agrl. U. Malaysia, Selangor, 1998—; vis. prof. Nankai U., China, 1994—. Author: Electronic Science and Education, 1995; contbr. over 100 articles to profl. jours. and confs. procs. Edn. grant Lee Found., 1969, Rsch. grant SRC, 1976, advanced studentship, 1975. Mem. Inst. Elec. Engrs., Engring. Bd. (Malaysia). Avocations: Chinese history and literature, classical music, fiction. Home: 71 Long Valley Way, Doncaster VIC 3109, Australia Office: Agrl Univ Malaysia, Serdang, Selangor Malaysia

CHIU, STEPHEN KA WAI, chemicals company executive; b. Macau, Portugal, Nov. 20, 1951; arrived in China, 1995; s. Kok Yuen Chiu and Shau Man Cheung; m. Jessica Rong Hui Fan, Mar. 21, 1997. BSChemE, U. Nebr., 1974, MBA, 1976. Supply analyst, sr. bus. analyst, staff investment analyst Exxon Chem. Asia Pacific Ltd., Hong Kong, 1977-82; mgr. paramins and performance chems. Exxon Chem. China Ltd., Hong Kong, 1982-84; bus. devel. mgr. Monsanto Far East Ltd., Hong Kong, 1984-86, mgr. sales and mktg. devel., 1986-89; mng. dir. Biesterfeld Far East Ltd., Hong Kong, 1989-93; dir. China agr. product group FMC Corp., Shanghai, China, 1993—; bd. dirs. Suzhou (China) Fumeishi Crop Protection Co. Ltd. Mem. Crop Protection Assn. China (sec. 1997—). Avocations: music, reading, traveling. Home: 39 Rose Garden, 165 Guiping Rd, Shanghai China Office: FMC Asia-Pacific Inc, 13A Zao Fong Univ Bldg, Shanghai China

CHIU, WEIHSUEH ALBERT, researcher; b. Taipei, Taiwan, Dec. 12, 1971; came to U.S., 1972.; s. Hungdah and Yuan-Yuan C.; m. Jill Kirsten Cetina, Aug. 3, 1997. AB, Harvard U., 1993; MA, Princeton U., 1995, PhD, 1998. Evaluator U.S. Gen. Acctg. Office, Washington, 1998—. Contbr. articles to profl. jours. Williams fellow Princeton U., 1994; recipient Barry M. Goldwater scholarship, 1991-93. Mem. AAAS, Am. Phys. Soc., Am. Astron. Soc., Phi Beta Kappa. Avocation: violin. E-mail: chiuw.nsiad@gao.gov. Office: U S Gen Acctg Office 441 G St NW Washington DC 20548-0001

CHIU, YISHU (ISU KYU), environmental educator, researcher; b. Hsinchu, Taiwan, Jan. 28, 1933; s. Holiang and Yeichiau (Peng) C.; m. Mizuko Taniguchi Oka, Oct. 10, 1969; children: Mari, Kenya, Ami, Shinya. BS, Taiwan U., 1956; MS, Kyoto (Japan) U., 1966; PhD, U. Western Ont., Can., 1973. Engr. New Japan Engring. Cons., Osaka, 1966-67; rsch. assoc. Inst. for Virus Rsch. Kyoto U., 1967-68; rsch. assoc. biochem. and environ. engring. group U. Western Ont., 1968-73; asst. prof. George Washington U., Washington, 1973-77; tech. advisor Nihon Suido Cons., Tokyo, 1977-81; expert Jomo Kenyatta Coll. A&T, Nairobi, Kenya, 1983-86; prof. Tunghai U., Taichung, Taiwan, 1986-96; vis. prof. Beijing Normal U., 1994—; instr. Japan Internat. Coop. Agy., Tokyo, 1977-81; editor, coord. Ea. Asian Rsch. Group, Tokyo, 1980—; advisor Natural Mind-up Coll., Tokyo, 2000—. Author: A Dictionary for Unit Conversion, 1975. Recipient Rsch. on Environ. Pollution Control System award NSF, 1975. Mem. ASCE. Avocation: touring. Fax: (03) 3207-1335. Office: 3-12-5-406 Nishi-Waseda, Shinjuku-ku Tokyo 169-0051, Japan

CHIVAS, ALLAN ROSS, geosciences, educator, research scientist; b. Sydney, Australia, May 14, 1950; s. Charles William and Muriel Ruth (Brown) C. BS with honors, U. Sydney, 1972, PhD, 1977. Geologist AMAX Exploration, Perth, Australia, 1972-73; rsch. fellow CRPG, Nancy, France, 1978-79; sr. fellow, leader environ. geochemistry group The Australian Nat. U., 1979-95; head Sch. of Geosci. U. Wollongong, 1995-99, found. prof. of geosciences, 1995—; vis. scientist U.S. Geol. Survey, Menlo Park, Calif., 1977-78; chair steering com. Climates of the Past/project of UNESCO/Internat. Union of Geol. Scis., 1995-99; leader working group on dating, IGCP Project on Continental Shelves in the Quaternary, 1996-2000; treas. Internat. Union Quartenary Rsch., 1999—, sec. com on Quaternary Econ. Deposits, 1999—. Contbr. more than 120 articles to profl. jours. and publs.; mem. editl. bd. of various jours. Recipient Edgeworth David Travel scholarship, U. Sydney, 1976. Mem. Australian Inst. Nuclear Sci. and Engring. (mem. accelerator mass spectrometry specialist com. 1995—, chmn. 1998—). Avocations: travel, fieldwork, photography. Home: 15 Toorak Ave, Mangerton NSW 2500, Australia Office: Sch Geoscis, U Wollongong, Wollongong NSW 2522, Australia

CHIVERTON, PATRICIA ANN, nursing educator, dean; b. Rochester, N.Y., Nov. 21, 1947; d. Paul and Eleanor (Buyck) Gilmore; 1 child, Laura. BS, Ctrl. Mo. State U., 1970; MS, U. Rochester, 1980, EdD, 1990. Exec. dir. Alzheimer's Assn., Rochester, N.Y., 1987-89; clin. assoc. U. Rochester, 1987-89, clin. chief psychiat. mental health nursing, 1990-97, asst. prof. clin. nursing, 1994-95, interim chair health care sys. divsn., 1994-95, assoc. prof. clin. clin. nursing, 1996—, CEO cmty. nursing ctr., 1996—, assoc. dean clin. affairs Sch. Nursing and Med. Ctr., 1996—, interim dean Sch. Nursing and Med. Ctr., 1999—; judge Book of the Yr., Am. Jour. Nursing, 1999, reviewer, 1998-99; cons. F.F. Thompson Continuing Care Facility, Canadaigua, N.Y., 1997-99. Contbr. chpts. to books in field. Rep. N.Y. State Alzheimer's Assn., 1985-88; bd. dirs. Health and Wellness Ctr., Livingston County, N.Y., Monroe County Long Term Care Agy., Rochester, 1997—. Mem. Am. Psychiat. Nurses Assn. (pres. Northwestern chpt. 1995-97, Excellence in Leadership award 1994), Soc. Edn. and Rsch. in Psychiat. Mental Health Nursing, Ea. Nursing Rsch. Soc., Nat. Acads. Practice (Disting. Practitioner), Sigma Theta Tau. E-mail: patricia chiverton@urmc.rochester.edu. Office: U Rochester Sch Nursing 601 Elmwood Ave Rochester NY 14642-0001

CHIZHENKOVA, ROGNEDA ALEXANDROVNA, neurophysiologist, researcher; b. Alma-Ata, USSR, Dec. 23, 1938; d. Alexandr Semenovich and Galina Petrovna (Brazhnikova) C.; m. Yuriy Mikhaylovich Cherhukhin, Oct. 10, 1970 (div. Apr. 1972); 1 child, Vladislav Yuryevich. MD, Med. Inst. Tashkent, USSR, 1962; postgrad. med. scis., Acad. Scis. of Russia, Moscow, 1966, MD, 1992. Postgrad. rschr. Inst. Higher Nervous Activity and Neurophysiol., Acad. Scis., Moscow, 1962-65; jr. rsch. worker Inst. Higher Nervous Activity and Neurophysiol., Acad. Scis., 1965-68; jr. rsch. worker Inst. Biophysics Acad. Scis. USSR, Pushchino, 1968-76, sr. rsch. worker, 1976-91, 1991-93, leading rsch. worker, 1993—; organizer seminars, 1973-83; head of seminar Philos. Problems of Neurophysiology, 1973-83. Author: Structural-functional Organization of Sensorimotor Cortex, 1986; contbr. articles to profl. jours. Grantee Russian Found. Fundamental Investigations for Support of Prominent Scientists, 1996; recipient medal Govt. of USSR, 1970. Mem. European Bioelectromagnetics Assn., Internat. Brain Rsch. Orgn., Acad. Problems of Life Protection. Avocations: music, singing, painting. Home: Distric V 22 Apt 56, 142292 Pushchino Russia Office: Acad Scis Russia Inst Cell, Biophysics, 142292 Pushchino Russia

CHIZZOLA, REMIGIUS KARL, biologist, plant physiologist; b. Vienna, Austria, June 12, 1958; s. Karl and Sirylle (Froeschl) C. MS, U. Vienna, Austria, 1981; PhD, U. Vienna, 1986. Asst. U. Veterinary Medicine, Vienna, 1986-97, asst. prof., 1998—. Mem. Soc. Medicinal Plant Rsch., N.Y. Acad. Scis. Roman Catholic. E-mail: Remigius.chizzola@vu.wien.ac.at. Home: Sternwartes Strasse G7, A-1180 Vienna Austria Office: Veterinaer Med U Vienna, Veterinaer Platz 1, A-1210 Vienna Austria

CHKHEIDZE, PETER, diplomat; b. Georgia, Oct. 22, 1941; m. Manana Chkheidze; 2 children. Grad. in Law, Tbilisi State U.; postgrad., Soviet Ministry Fgn. Affairs Diplomatic Acad. With dept. internat. orgns. Soviet Ministry Fgn. Affairs, 1977-78; from 1st sec. to counselor Soviet Mission to UN, N.Y.C., 1978-84; head fgn. rels. Communist Ctrl. Com. Govt. USSR, 1984-89; chmn. Ga. Trade Union Fedn., 1989-91; permanent rep. to Russia Govt. Georgia, 1991-93; amb. to U.S. Govt. Georgia, Washington, 1993-95; perm. rep. to UN Govt. Georgia, 1993—; elected vice chmn. 53rd Session UN Gen. Assembly, 1998. Office: Permanent Mission of Georgia to UN Perm Mission Georgia to UN One UN Plaza 26th Fl New York NY 10017

CHLAMTAC, IMRICH, computer company executive, educator; b. Zlate Moravce, Czechoslovakia, Mar. 21, 1949; came to U.S., 1977; s. Zoltan and Klara (Csato) C.; children: Eddie, Noga. BS, Tel Aviv U., 1975, MS, 1977; PhD in Computer Sci., U. Minn., 1979. Prin. engr. Digital Equipment Co., Tewksbury, Mass., 1980-82; sr. lectr. Technion, Haifa, Israel, 1987-93; Fulbright prof. U. Mass., Amherst, 1993-94; founder, CEO BCN, Inc., Boston, 1990—, pres.; prof. Boston U., 1995—; disting. chair in telecom. prof. U. Tex., Dallas; cons. Motorola, Austin, Tex., 1983-86, Intel, Haifa, 1982-84, Fibronics, Hyannis, Md., 1984-86, Codex, Mansfield, Mass., 1985-89, GTE, Waltham, Mass., 1991-92, Digital Equipment Co., Littleton, Mass., 1992-93; U.S. del. Internat. Union Radio Sci., 1987, 90; lectr. and presenter in field. Co-author: Local Networks, 1980; editor-in-chief Wireless Networks Jour., 1995—, Jour. Spl. Topics on Mobile Networking and Applications, 1996—, Optical Networks Mag.; contbr. articles to profl. jours. Recipient New Talents in Simulation award Soc. for Computer Simulation, 1982. Fellow IEEE (IEEE TOC jour. editor 1989-93, founder, chair MobiComm Conf. 1995—), Assn. for Computing Machinery (gen. chmn. Sigcomm conf. 1993—). Office: Univ Texas Dallas Engring EC-38 PO Box 830688 Richardson TX 75083-0688

CHLUPÁČ, IVO, geologist, paleontologist, educator; b. Benešov, Czech Republic, Dec. 6, 1931; s. Karel and Marie (Kodetová) C.; m. Marta Světlíková, 1955 (div. 1967); children: Jan, Tomáš; m. Olga Hofmanová, Aug. 12, 1967; 1 child, Martin. Diploma, Charles U., Prague, Czech Republic, 1955. Geologist Geol. Survey, Prague, 1955-91; prof. faculty of scis. Charles U., Prague, 1991—; sci. worker Geol. Survey, Prague, 1962-91; head dept. geology Charles U., 1991-96. Contbr. over 270 articles on paleontology and geology to profl. jours. Recipient award Czech Literary Found., Prague, 1988. Mem. Czech Geol. Soc., Acad. Leopoldina. Roman Catholic. Avocations: fossil collecting, archaeology. Home: Daškova 3077, 143 00 Prague Czech Republic Office: Charles U Faculty of Scis, Albertov 6, 128 43 Prague Czech Republic

CHMELA, PAVEL, physics educator, researcher; b. Pozděchov, Moravia, Czechoslovakia, July 2, 1936; s. Josef and Milada Bozena (Rolčíková) C.; m. Marie Františka. BS, Polacky U., Olomouc, Czechoslovakia, 1959, MS, 1967, PhD, 1968; D. habil., A. Mickiewicz U., Poznań, Poland, 1986. Diplomate in physics and math. Asst., head sect. Polacky U., Olomouc, Czechoslovakia, 1960-66, rsch. fellow, 1966-74, 76-88; assoc. prof. Mil. Tech. Coll., Cairo, 1974-76; head physics dept., 1975-76; prin. rsch. fellow Tech. U., Brno, Czechoslovakia, 1988-95, prof. physics, 1995—; coord. Optical Quantum and Statis. Properties of Sys. state rsch. program, Czechoslovakia, 1985-89; sec. Czechoslovak Com. for Fundamental Rsch. in Optics, Czechoslovakia, 1984-85; mem. Czech Com. for Optics of Internat. Commn. for Optics, 1990—; lectr. in field. Author: Introduction to Nonlinear Optics, 1982; co-author: Modern Nonlinear Optics, 1993; mem. editl. bd. Czechoslovak Jour. Physics, 1973-90; contbr. over 70 articles to profl. jours. Mem. Union Czech Mathematicians and Physicists (v.p. phys. sect. 1981—, chmn. optical divsn. phys. sect. 1985—, hon. 1981, hon. phys. sect. 1987). Avocations: history, tourism, folklore music. Home: Úvoz 6, 602 00 Brno Moravia,

Czech Republic Office: Tech U Brno Technická 2, Inst Phys Engring, 616 69 Brno Moravia, Czech Republic

CHMIELARZ, PAWEL, scientist; b. Mosina, Poland, June 14, 1963; s. Romuald and Bozena (Walorczyk) C.; m. Jolanta Kubica, Jan. 9, 1989; children: Katarzyna, Jakub. BA, U. Poznan, Poland, 1982; MS, Agrl. U., Poznan, 1987, PhD, 1997. Asst. Inst. Dendrology Polish Acad. Scis., Kornik, 1989-90, sr. asst., 1991-98, head cryogenic lab., 1999. Contbr. articles to profl. jours. Grantee Com. Scientific Rsch., Warsaw, Poland, 1992-95, 95-98, 2000—, Polonium France-Poland, 1999-2000. Avocations: gardening, classical music. Home: Krosno Tylna 25, 62-050 Mosina Poland Office: Polish Acad Scis, Parkowa 5, 62-035 Kornik Poland

CHMIELEWSKI, HENRYK MIKOLAY, neurologist, educator; b. Myszyniec, Warszawa, Poland, Sept. 10, 1934; s. Yózef and Mieczyslawa (Yakalska) C.; widowed; m. Wanda Serafin, May 2, 1935; children: Elzbieta, Yanusz. MD, Med. U., Łódź, Poland, 1958; PhD, Mil. Med. U., Łódź, Poland, 1966, assoc. prof., 1974, extraordinary prof., 1982, ordinary prof., 1990. Cert. neurologist. Head dept. neurology Mil. Med. U., Łódź, 1974—, dep. dean, 1977-85, dep. rector clin. and didactic affairs, 1985-87; comdr. postgrad. med. ctr. Mil. Med. U., Warszava, 1987-91; rector Mil. Med. U., Łódź, 1991-98; cons. Neurologist Sanatorium Hosp., Busko-Zdr., Poland, 1975—. Contbr. articles to profl. jours. Mem. Parliament, Poland, 1989-91. Brig. gen. Polish Army, 1991-98. Recipient Pro Ecclesia et Pontifice Cross of Vatican, Pope John Paul II, 1996, Polonia Restituta Commodore Cross, Pres. of Polish Republic, 1997. Mem. Polish Acad. Scis. (mem. neurochemistry commn. neurol. scis. com. 1984—, mem. commn. pain, clin. pathophysiology com. 1986—), Polish Soc. Neurology (sec. 1982-87, v.p. 1987-90). Roman Catholic. Home: ul Kochanowskiego 10m8, 91-469 Łódź Poland

CHMIELEWSKI, TADEUSZ, engineer; b. Siestrzanki, Poland, Feb. 1, 1941; s. Waclaw and Waleria (Dobrzycka) C.; m. Wieslawa Maria Weselinska, Dec. 26, 1964; children: Marcin, Pawel. M in eng., Tech. Univ. Gdansk, Poland, 1964, PhD, 1972, DSc, 1978. Asst. Tech. Univ. Gdansk, 1964-72, asst. prof., 1972; asst. prof. Tech. Univ. Opole, Opole, Poland, 1973-78, assoc. prof., 1978-89, prof., 1989—; rsch. scholar Tech. Univ., Aachen, Germany, 1991; cons. Milihouse, Damaskus, Syria, 1985-86. Co-author: Dynamics of Civil Engineers Structures, 1996, Structural Mechanics, 1996; author: Structural Static Analysis, 1987, Probability Methods in Dynamics of Structure, 1982. Prorector for scientific affairs Tech. Univ Opole, 1981-84, dean dept. civil engring., 1987-93, 99—. Recipient Rsch. award for Fgn. Specialists Japanese Gov., 1997, Mutual Edn. Exchange grant U.S. Dept. of State, 1976-77, rsch. fellowship Commn. of European Communities, 1993. Mem. Polish Assn of Theoretical and Applied Mechanics (chmn. 1986-90), Polish Assn. Civil Engrs. Roman Catholic. Avocations: tennis, volleyball, ski. E-mail address: tch@po.opole.pl. Fax number: 48 77 456 50 84. Home: Zamiejska 19, Opole 45 851, Poland Office: Tech Univ Opole, Katowicka 48, Opole 45 061, Poland

CHMIL, VITALY DANILOVICH, chemist, researcher; b. Kharkov, Ukraine, Apr. 14, 1937; s. Daniil Ivanovich and Anna Fedorovna (Kravcova) C.; m. Lydmila Nikolaevna Ropackaya, Apr. 26, 1959; 1 child, Golochova Elena. Chemist, U. Kharkov, Ukraine, 1959, cand. in sci. in Chemistry, 1966; PhD in Biology, Rsch. Inst. Common Hygiene, Moscow, 1989. Rschr. Rsch. Inst. of Chem.-Pharms., Kharkov, Ukraine, 1959-69, All-Union Sci. Rsch. Inst. of Pesticides, Polymers, Plastics, Kiev, Ukraine, 1969-86; lab. chief All-Union Sci. Rsch. Inst. of Pesticides, Polymers, Plastics, Kiev, 1986-89; dept. head Inst. Echohygiene and Toxicology by L.I. Medyed, Kiev, Ukraine, 1989—; expert Comecon, Moscow, 1975-91; mem. legis. metrology commn. of sci. coun. by Chromatography Acad. Scis., Moscow, 1980-91, commn. for standards, Govt. of USSR, Moscow, 1981-91, nat. work group ZD-4 Internat. Orgn., 1984-91; expert mem. Govt. Chem. Commn. Ukraine, reporting to Cabinet Ministers of Ukraine, 1992—, regulation com. of th Commn. of Ukranian Hygienic Ministry of Health, 1995—; observer Internat. Collaborative Analytical Coun. on Pesticides, Eng., 1993—, corr., 1998—. Author: (book) Methods of Determination of Microquantities of Pesticides, 1984; inventor: method for extracting substances from water solutions, 1961, method for extracting pesticides from water solutions, 1981, method for extracting pesticides from plants, 1989, method of determination of kaunter in air, 1989; contbr. approximately 300 articles, abstracts etc. to profl. jours. Recipient Cert. of Achievement, U.S. Agy. for Internat. Devel. in field of pesticide mgmt., 1994; grantee Internat. Sci. Found., Wash., 1993. Mem. N.Y. Acad. Scis., Assn. Chromatographists of Ukraine, (head in Kiev 1994-97), Ukranian Chem. Soc., Ukranian Hygienic Soc. Avocations: skiing, mushroom hunting, fishing. Home: 18 Tarasovskaya Str, 01033 Kiev Ukraine Office: Inst Echohygiene & Toxicol, 6 Geroev Oborony Str, 03022 Kiev Ukraine

CHMURZYŃSKI, JERZY ANDRZEJ, ethologist; b. Warsaw, Poland, Mar. 11, 1929; s. Czeslaw and Jozefa Eugenia (Zak) C.; m. Wanda Czeslawa Rudzka, Dec. 15, 1956; children: Ryszard Jerzy, Anna Elzbieta. MPhil, Warsaw U., 1952; PhD, Nencki Inst. Exptl. Biology, Warsaw, 1961, Dr habil/DSc, 1973. Jr. asst. Warsaw U., 1950-52; asst. Nencki Inst. Exptl. Biology, Warsaw, 1952-53, sr. asst., 1953-57, adj./asst. prof., 1957-75, docent/assoc. prof., 1975-92, prof., 1993—, acting head of lab., 1964-69, 80-81, head lab., 1990-99; ret., 2000. Co-author: (textbook) Biological Mechanisms of Behavior, 1989 (Polish Acad. Sci. award 1990); sci. editor: An Introduction to Animal Behaviour, 1976; author over 120 articles to sci. jours. Mem. Polish Tchrs. Assn., 1950-80, Solidarnosc Trade Union, 1980-92. Decorated Golden Cross of Merit; recipient Medal of 25 Yrs., Polish Acad. Sci., 1978, Medal of XL Anniversary of People's Poland, 1984. Mem. Polish Ethol. Soc. (pres.), Com. for Evolutionary and Theoretical Biology. Roman Catholic. Avocations: oil painting, playing piano, cycling, astronomy, reading science fiction. E-mail: jch@nencki.gov.pl. Home: ul Smolna 14 m 10a, PL00-375 Warsaw Poland Office: Nencki Inst Exptl Biology, PO Box 38-ul Pasteura 3, PL02-093 Warsaw Poland

CHO, ALFRED YI, electrical engineer; b. Beijing, China, July 10, 1937; came to U.S., 1955, naturalized, 1962; s. Edward I-Lai and Mildred (Chen) C.; m. Mona Lee Willoughby, June 16, 1968; children: Derek Ming, Deidre Lin, Brynna Ying, Wendy Li. BSEE, U. Ill., 1960, MS, 1961, PhD, 1968, D Engring. (hon.), 1999. Rsch. physicist Ion Physics Corp., Burlington, Mass., 1961-62; mem. tech. staff TRW-Space Tech. Labs., Redondo Beach, Calif., 1962-65; mem. tech. staff Bell Labs., Murray Hill, N.J., 1968-84, dept. head, 1984-87; dir. Materials Processing Rsch. Lab. AT&T Bell Labs., Murray Hill, 1987-90; semicondr. rsch. lab. v.p. Bell Labs. Lucent Techs. (formerly AT&T Bell Labs.), Murray Hill, 1990—; fellow Bell Labs., Lucent Techs. (formerly AT&T Bell Labs.), 1992—; rsch. asst. U. Ill., Urbana, 1965-68; vis. prof. dept. elec. engring., vis. rsch. prof. coordinated sci. lab. U. Ill., Urbana, 1977-78, adj. prof. dept. elec. engring., adj. rsch. prof. coordinated sci. lab., 1978—; bd. dirs. Riber, Edison, N.J.; trustee Coll. of N.J., 1996—. Contbr. over 480 articles to profl. jours.; 51 patents in field; developer molecular beam epitaxy. Recipient Disting. Tech. Staff award AT&T Bell Labs., 1982, Elec. and Computer Engring. Disting. Alumnus award U. Ill., 1985, Disting. Achievement award Chinese Inst. Engrs., U.S.A., 1985, Internat. Gallium Arsenide Symposium award, 1986, Heinrich Welker Gold medal, 1986, The Coll. Engring. Alumni Honor award U. Ill., 1988, World Materials Congress award ASM Internat., 1988, Achievement award Indsl. Rsch. Inst., Inc., 1988, Thomas Alva Edison Sci. award N.J. Gov., 1990, Internat. Crystal Growth award Am. Assn. for Crystal Growth, 1990, Asian Am. Corp. Achievement award, 1992, Chinese Am. Engrs. and Scientists Assn. So. Achievement award, 1993, Nat. Medal of Sci. NSF, 1993, Elliott Cresson medal The Franklin Inst., 1995, Computer and Comm. prize, Japan, 1995, W.E. Lamb medal for laser sci. and quantum optics, 2000; inductee N.J. Inventors Hall of Fame, 1997. Fellow IEEE (Morris N. Liebman award 1982, IEEE Medal of Honor 1994), Am. Phys. Soc. (Internat. prize for new materials 1982); mem. Am. Vacuum Soc. (Gaede-Langmuir award 1988), Electrochem. Soc. (electronic divsn. award 1977, Solid State Sci. and Tech. medal 1987), Materials Rsch. Soc. (Von Hippel award 1994), Academia Sinica (Taiwan), Chinese Acad. Scis., Am. Philos. Soc., Nat. Acad. Engring., Nat. Acad. Scis., Am. Acad. Art & Scis., Sigma Xi, Tau Beta Pi, Eta Kappa Nu, Sigma Tau. Fax: 908-582-2043. E-mail: ayc@lucent.com. Office: Bell Labs Lucent Tech PO Box 636 New Providence NJ 07974-0636

CHO, BYUNG JIN, engineering educator; b. Pusan, South Korea, July 5, 1964; arrived in Singapore, 1997; s. Rai Hwa and Kyung Suk (Lee) Cho; m. Eun Bae Park; children: Jae Sung, Jae Won. B.Engring., Korea U., Seoul, 1985; M.Engring., Korea Adv. Inst. Sci. & Tech., Taejon, 1987, PhD, 1991. Rsch. fellow IMEC, Leuven, Belgium, 1991-93; sect. mgr. Hyundai Electronics Co. Ltd., Korea, 1993-97; asst. prof. engring. Nat. U. Singapore, 1997-99; assoc. prof. Nat. U., Singapore, 2000—. Patentee (over 50) in field; contbr. numerous articles to profl. jours. Mem. IEEE, Electrochem. Soc. Presbyterian. Avocations: musical instruments, worshop song leader. Office: National Univ of Singapore, 10 Kent Ridge Crescent, Singapore 119260, Republic of Singapore

CHO, BYUNG-SUN, law educator; b. Seoul, Apr. 28, 1959; parents Bo-Won Cho and Myung-Hi Huh; m. Hye-Ryung Um, Feb. 6, 1990; children: Min-Ha, Min-Hyung. BA, Sung-Kyun-Kwan U., Seoul, 1982, ML, 1985; JD, Albert-Ludwigs-U. Freiburg, Germany, 1989. Prof. Chongju (Korea) U. Coll. Law, 1990—; cons. Korea Inst. Nuclear Safety, Taejon, 1990—; exch. prof. Max-Planck-Inst. for Fgn. and Internat. Criminal Law, Freiburg, 1995-97. Author: Law on Regulatory Offenses, 1991, International Environmental Criminal Law, 1995, Environmental Criminal Law, 1998. Cons., rschr. Civic Orgn. for Environ. Protection, Seoul, 1995—. 2d lt. Land Forces Army, 1985-86. Humboldt Rsch. fellow Alexander von Humboldt Found., 1996. Mem. Internat. Assn. Criminal Law (France), Korea Assn. Criminal Law, Korea Assn. Environ. Law. Avocation: skiing. Fax: 82 (043) 233 0227. E-mail: chobs@chongju.ac.kr. Home: Heungdok-ku Kagyung-dong, Byuksan Apt 104-701, Chungbuk Chongju-shi 361-260, South Korea Office: Chongju U Coll Law, Sangdang-ku Naedok-dong 36, Chungbuk Chongju-shi 360-764, South Korea

CHO, DONG-YOON, surgeon; b. Nampyong, Korea, June 27, 1956; s. Byong Suk and Jeong Soon (Tark) C.; m. Jeong Ran Suh, Dec. 5, 1981; children: Yu Ri, Yu Jin, Yu Na. B, Chonnam U., Kwangju, Korea, 1981, M, 1983, D, 1990. Dir. Cho's Surg. Clinic, Naju, Korea, 1989-93, Hakmoon Surg. Clinic, Kwangju, Korea, 1993-2000. Capt. Korean Army, 1986-89. Chonnam Med. Sch. grantee, Kwangju, 1978. Mem. Internat. Soc. Univ. Colon and Rectal Surgeons, Korean Surg. Soc., Korean Soc. Gastrointestinal Endoscopy, Korean Soc. Coloproctology (dir. 1997-2000), Am. Soc. Colon and Rectal Surgeons. Avocations: golf, horseback riding, classical guitar. Home: 103-902 Samick, Apt Jinwoldong, Kwangju 503-330, Korea Office: Hakmoon Surg Clinic, 26-12 Hakdong Dongku, Kwangju 501-190, Korea

CHO, FUJIO, automobile company executive; b. Tokyo, 1937. Grad. law dept., Tokyo U., 1960. With Toyota Motors, 1960—; pres. Toyota Motor Mfg. USA, 1988, mng. dir., 1994, exec. dir., 1996, v.p., 1998, pres., 1999. Office: Toyota Motor Corp, 1 Toyota-cho, Toyota City 471-8571, Japan*

CHO, GYUSEONG, nuclear engineering educator; b. Kwangju, Korea, July 23, 1960; s. Yongsub and Yongsoon (Han) C.; m. Sunja Kim, May 18, 1986; children: Ina, Yuna. BA, Seoul Nat. U., Korea, 1983, MS, 1985; PhD, U. Calif., Berkeley, 1992. Ast. prof. Korea Advanced Inst. Sci. & Tech., Taejon, 1994-97, assoc. prof., 1998—. Mem. IEEE. Avocations: tennis, golf. Office: Korea Advanced Inst Sci, 373-1 Kusongdong, Taejon 305-701, Korea

CHO, HYO-NAM, civil engineering educator; s. Sung-Ku Cho and Sung-Ok Kang; m. Geum-Choon Park; children: Junsuk, Haelin, Soojung, Jungyun. BS, Korea Mil. Acad., Seoul, 1967; MS, Mich. State U., 1970, PhD in Civil Engring., 1972. Prof. civil engring. Korea Mil. Acad., 1973-87, dir. dept. R & D, 1980-82; dir. Hwarangdae Rsch. Inst., Seoul, 1983-84; prof. civil engring. Hanyang U., Ansan, Republic of Korea, 1988—; com. mem. Ctrl. Constrn. Tech. Rev., Ministry of Constrn., Republic of Korea, 1981-97; mem. constrn. tech. adv. com., Seoul, 1986—, design rev. com., Ministry of Def., 1982—, Korea Hwy. Co., 1993—. Author: Structural Analysis, 1997, Structural Steel Engineering, 1995, Bridge Engineering, 1999; contbr. articles to profl. jours. Full col., Korean Mil. Acad., 1967-87. Recipient Presdl. award Pres. Republic of Korea, 1980, Samil honor award, 1980, excellent paper awards Korean Soc. Civil Engring., 1984, Korean Sci & Engring. Assn., 1991, 99. Fellow Nat. Acad. Engring. Korea; mem. Korean Soc. Civil Engring. (dir. 1986-88), Korean Soc. Steel Constrn. (v.p. 1997—), Computational Structural Engirng. Inst. Korea (pres. 1998—). Buddhist. Avocations: Ki-gong (yoga), Zen meditation. Office: Hanyang U, Dept Civil, Environ Engring Sadong, Ansan 425-791, Republic of Korea

CHO, IN-KOO, economist, educator; b. Seoul, Korea, Sept. 26, 1958; s. Dong-Sun Cho and Chan-Mo Chung; m. Jeong Eun Lee, Mar. 22, 1989; 1 child, Nicholas. BA, Seoul Nat. U., 1981; PhD, Princeton U., 1986. Asst. prof. U. Chgo., 1986-91, assoc. prof., 1991-95; assoc. prof., prof. Brown U., Providence, R.I., 1995-98; William Kinkead Prof. U. Ill., Champaign, 1998—. Alfred P. Sloan Found. fellow, 1991-93; NSF grantee, 1987—. Mem. Econometric Soc. Office: U Ill Dept Econs 1206 S 6th St Champaign IL 61820-6978

CHO, JUNDONG, computer scientist, educator, electronic engineer; b. Seoul, Republic of Korea, July 21, 1957; s. Taehyuk Cho and Heungbok Lee; m. Keumju Choi, Aug. 6, 1988; children: Youngho, Yongjae. BS in Electronic Engring., Sun Kyun Kwan U., Suwon, Republic of Korea, 1980; MS, Bklyn. Polytech. U., 1989; PhD, Northwestern U., 1993. Comm. officer Republic of Korea Marine Corps, Kimpo, 1980-83; computer-aided design engr. Samsung Electronics, Suwon, 1983-87; sr. engr. Samsung Electronics, Buchun, Republic of Korea, 1993-95; asst. prof. electronic engring. Sung Kyun Kwan U., Suwon, 1995—; assoc. editor Korea Info. Sci. Soc., 1997—. Editor: High Performance Design Automation for MCM and Packages, 1996; guest editor Internat. Jour. Custom Chip Design, Simulation and Testing, 1995, Internat. Jour. High Speed Electronics, 1994, 95. Mem. IEEE (sr., session chair, program com. Internat. Conf. on VLSI Design, 1996-97, program com. Multi-Chip Module Conf., 1996-97, Best Paper award IEEE/Assn. Computing Machinery, Design Automation Conf. 1993), Inst. Electronic Engrs. of Korea (editl. mem.), Korea Info. and Sci. Soc. (editl. mem.). Avocations: tennis, climbing. E-mail: jdcho@yurim.skku.ac.kr. Home: Apt 128, 202 Kwacheon, Kyunggi-Do 427-040, Republic of Korea Office: Sung Kyun Kwan U Elec Engrg, 300 Chunchun-Dong, Suwon Kyung-Gi Do 440-746, Republic of Korea

CHO, KEUMNAM, mechanical engineering educator, researcher; b. Seoul, Republic of Korea, Sept. 2, 1956; s. Kibum and Imsun (Ahn) C.; m. Hannah Hanghee Chun, June 8, 1985; children: Edward H., Constance H. BS Seoul Nat. U., 1980; MS, SUNY, Stony Brook, 1986, PhD in Mech. Engring., dd1989. Rschr. Korean Advanced Inst. Sci. and Tech., Seoul, 1982-83; tchg. asst. SUNY, Stony Brook, 1984-89; instr. Drexel U., Phila., 1990-91; rsch. scientist Korean Advanced Energy Rsch. Inst., Taejon, Republic of Korea, 1992-93; asst. prof. mech. engring. Sung Kyun Kwan U., Suwon, Republic of Korea, 1993-97, head dept. mech. engring., 1995-97, assoc. prof. mech. engring., 1997—. Editor Korean Soc. Energy Engring., 1998—; contbr. articles to profl. jours. Sgt., Republic of Korea Marine Corps, 1980-82, Pohang. Recipient grants Korean Sci. and Engring. Found., Taejon, 1994, 99, Korean Ministry Edn., Seoul, 1994, 95, 96, 97., Korean Rsch. Found., 1998, 99. Mem. ASME, ASHRAE, IIR (Korean com. 1998—), Korean Soc. Mech. Engrs. Roman Catholic. Avocation: skiing. Home: Choongang-Dong 65, Chukkong Apt 1009-403, Kyungido Kwachun 427-010, Republic of Korea Office: Sung Kyun Kwan U, Chunchon-Dong 300 Changanku, Suwon 440-746, Republic of Korea

CHO, KUN-WOO, nuclear engineer; b. Soon-Cheon, Chon-Nam, Rep. of Korea, Oct. 9, 1959; s. Kye-Sun Cho and Bok-Nam Lee; m. Soon-Hee Bank, Apr. 21, 1984; children: Min-Hyung, Min-Ki. BS, Seoul Nat. U., Rep. of Korea, 1981; MS, Seoul Nat. U., 1983; PhD, U. Cin., 1989. Researcher Korean Inst. Nuclear Safety, 1982-86, sr. researcher, 1989-92, RPM radiation safety group, 1994-99, head radiation protection dept., 1999—; rsch. asst. U. Cin., 1986-89; sci. attache Emb. of Korea, Vienna, Austria, 1992-94. Mem. Korean Nuclear Safety, Korean Radiation Protecion Soc. Presbyterian. Avocations: sports, reading books, swimming, bicycling, tennis. Home: 135-1401 Hanbit Apt, Eudong-Dong Yusong-ku, 305-333 Taejon Republic of Korea Office: Korea Inst Nuclear Safety, PO Box 114, Yusong Taejon 305-600, Republic of Korea

CHO, KYU-KAB, engineering educator; b. Osaka, Japan, Nov. 27, 1942; s. In-Hwan and Soon-Jeon (Bae) C.; m. Soo-Seon Kim, Aug. 25, 1974; children: Jeong-Won, Jeong-Ah, Jeong-Yeon. BSME, Pusan (Korea) Nat. U., 1966, MSME, 1969; MSIE, U. Ala., Tuscaloosa, 1973; PhD, Pa. State U., 1982. Prof. dept. mech. engring. Pusan Nat. U., 1970-85, dir. Univ. Computer Ctr., 1991-92, dean Coll. Engring., 1992-94, dir. Rsch. Inst. Mech. Tech., 1994-98, prof. dept. indsl. engring., 1985—; vis. scholar U. Ill., Urbana, 1989-90. Author: Introduction to Industrial Engineering, 1988; assoc. editor Jour. Mfg. Sys., 1999; contbr. articles to profl. jours. Dir. Kochon Scholarship Found., Pusan, 1994, Yeonchul Scholarship Found., Pusan, 1995. 1st lt. Korean Army, 1966-68. Mem. Korean Inst. Indsl. Engrs. (pres. 1995-96, Outstanding Acad. award 1993), Korea Sci. and Engring. Found. (R&D com. 1997-98), Info. Promotion Assn. (chair 1995), Inst. Indsl. Engrs. (sr.), Nat. Acad. Engring. Korea, Soc. Mfg. Engrs. (sr.). Avocation: mountain climbing. Home: Kyungdong Apt 102-1503, Cheongryong-Dong, 609-350 Pusan Korea Office: Pusan Nat U, 30 Jangjeon Kumjeong-Ku, 609-735 Pusan Korea

CHO, KYUNAM, marine architect and engineer, educator; b. Kunsan, Korea, July 6, 1953; s. Kwangjin and Jungsook (Park) C.; m. Haekyung Kang, July 6, 1980; children: Jahyun, Eunhae. BS, Seoul Nat. U., 1976; M in Naval Architecture, U. Mich., 1981, M in Applied Mechs., 1982, PhD, 1985. Engr. Korea Shipping Co., Seoul, 1979-80; lectr. U. Ulsan, Korea, 1986-93, Pusan (Korea) Nat. U., 1987-88; head dept. ocean engring. rsch. Hyundai Maritime Rsch. Inst., Ulsan, 1986-93; prof. dept. naval architecture and ocean engring. Hongik U., Chungnam, Korea, 1993—; dir. Korea Com. for Ocean Engring., Pusan, 1989—; mem. tech. com. Internat. Ship Structure Congress, 1984—; mem. internat. tech. com. Tech. Exch. and Adv. Meeting, Asia Zone, 1994—. Author: Finite Element Methods for Engineers, 1987, Design of Offshore Structures, 1994; editor Jour. Soc. Naval Architecture, 1993—, Jour. Ocean Engring., 1989—. Prin., Sunday Sch. of Hoam Ch., Seoul, 1973-75; mem. com. Korean Govt. Ocean Devel. Com., Seoul, 1989-94; advisor Korean Register of Shipping, Daejeon, 1994—, Korea Ocean Rsch. Devel. Inst., Asnan, 1994—. Officer Korean Navy, 1976-79. U.S. Ship Structure Com. grantee; recipient scholarships. Mem. ASME, Soc. Naval Architects of U.S.A., Internat. Soc. Offshore and Polar Engrs., Korean Soc. Naval Architects, Korean Soc. Civil Engrs., Computational Engring. Inst. Korea (bd. dirs. 1994—). Roman Catholic. Avocations: tennis, golf, music appreciation. Office: Hongik U, 310 Shinan, Chochiwon Chungnam 339-701, Republic of Korea

CHO, MYONG WON, retired English language, linguistics researcher; b. Kwangju, Chonnam, Republic of Korea, Sept. 2, 1932; s. Chongju C. and Pan Chun; m. Yong Jwa Suh, Dec. 25, 1969; children: Cho Jake Jaiho, Cho Yunki. MA, Chonnam Nat. U., Kwangju, Republic of Korea, 1959; PhD in Lit., 1974; MA, U. Hawaii, 1967. Instr. Chonnam Nat. U., Kwangju, Republic of Korea, 1959-68; asst. prof. Chonnam Nat. U., Kwangju, 1968-73, assoc. prof., 1974-79, prof., 1979-98, prof. emeritus, 1998—, dir. Lang. Edn. Ctr., 1969-80, academic dean Grad. Sch., 1982-84, dean Coll. Edn., 1984-86; postdoct. fellow U. Edinburgh (Scotland), 1980; profl. The East-West Cultural Learning Inst., Honolulu, 1973-74;. Author: Modern Foreign Language Education, 1981, Travels: Landscape, Peoplescape and Self-Escape, 1993, Out There, 1998, Language Learnability, vol. I & II, 1998; author, editor: Dictionary of English Teaching, 1991. Postdoct. fellow Hornby Found. and Brit. Coun., 1979-80; scholar The East West Ctr., 1965-67; recipient Profl. Rsch. award The East West Ctr., 1973-74. Mem. Korea Assn. Tchrs. of English (pres. 1986-90, Best Thesis of Yr. 1998), Internat. Assn. Tchrs. of English as a Fgn. Lang., TESOL. Home: Yang 2 Dong Suhku, Keumho Apt 3-201, 502-222 Kwangju Chonnam, Republic of Korea Office: Chonnam U Coll Edn, Yongbongdong Buk-ku, 500-757 Kwangju Chonnam, Republic of Korea

CHO, NAM ZIN, nuclear engineering educator; b. Choongnam, Korea, Mar. 6, 1949; m. Young Ock C. BS Nuclear Engring., Seoul Nat. U., 1971; MS Nuclear Engring., U. Calif., Berkeley, 1976, PhD Nuclear Engring., 1980. Tchr., rsch. assoc. U. Calif., Berkeley, 1975-80; staff scientist Sci. Applications, Inc., Palo Alto, Calif., 1980-82; nuclear engr. Brookhaven Nat. Lab., Upton, N.Y., 1983-87; asst. prof. Korea Advanced Inst. Sci. and Tech., Taejon, 1987-89, assoc. prof., 1989-93, prof., 1993—; chmn. dept. nuclear engring. Korea Advanced Inst. Sci. and Tech., 1994-96; dir. Nat. R&D Program STEPI for Ministry of Sci. and Tech., Seoul, 1996-99; spkr. in field. Author: Neutron Transport Theory-Computational Algorithms and Applications, 2000; editor: (book) Special Lectures on Reactor Physics, 1993; assoc. editor Nuclear Sci. and Engring., 1996—; contbr. articles to profl. jours. Mem. Korean Nuclear Soc. (publs. sec. 1991-96, Acad. Excellence award 1993, Best Paper award 1999), Am. Nuclear Soc. (exec. com. reactor physics divsn. 1997—, Best Paper award 2000), N.Y. Acad. Scis., Soc. Indsl. and Applied Math., others. Presbyterian. Office: KAIST, 373-1 Kusongdong Yusong-gu, Taejon 305-701, Korea

CHO, SIU-YEUNG DAVID, electrical engineer; b. Hong Kong, Oct. 1, 1970; s. Hoi-Kit Cho and Shek-Ha Yip. B in Engring., U. Brighton, 1994; PhD, City U. Hong Kong, 1999. Asst. engr. Wharf Cable TV Ltd., Hong Kong, 1994-95; contract programmer Mitsubishi Heavy Indsl. Ltd., Japan, 1997; rsch. asst. City U. Hong Kong, 1998-99, sr. rsch. asst., 1999—. Rsch. fellow City U. Hong Kong, 2000—. Mem. IEEE, Inst. Elec. Engrs. U.K., N.Y. Acad. Scis. Office: City U Hong Kong, Tat Chee Ave, Kowloon Hong Kong

CHO, SONG-TAE, federal official; b. Nov. 3, 1942. Grad., Korea Mil. Acad., 1964; student, ROK Army Coll., 1974; MBA, Kyoung-Book U., 1987; M in Adminstrn., Dong-Kook U., 1991. Chief mgmt. divsn. Hdqrs. SROKA, 1986-88; dir. Mil. Rsch. Inst. ROK Army Hdqrs., 1988-89, commdg. gen. 56th Inf. Divsn., 1989-91; dir. policy and planning MND ROK, 1991-92; commdg. gen. 1st Corps, 1992-93; chief policy and planning divsn. MND ROK, 1993-95; commdg. gen. SROKA, 1995-96; ret., min. nat. def., 1999—. Office: 3-1 Yong San-dong, Yongsan-gu, Seoul Korea*

CHO, SOOHYUN, research communications engineer; b. Kimhae, Republic of Korea, Apr. 13, 1967; s. Hungsik Cho and Hyunnam Son. BS, Korea U., Seoul, Republic of Korea, 1990, MS, 1997. Rsch. engr. Samsung Electronics, Seoul, 1990-95, TNRL, Korea Telecom, Seoul, 1997—. Mem. IEEE, Korean Inst. Comm. Scis., Inst. Electronics Korea. Office: TNRL Korea Telecom, 17 Woomyun-dong Sucho-gu, Seoul 137-792, Republic of Korea

CHO, SUK JOON, public administration educator, consultant; b. Bukchong, Hannam, Korea, Mar. 25, 1929; s. Jae Il and Duk Soon (Chon) C.; m. Sung Ja Song, Dec. 23, 1961. LLB, Chung-Ang U., Seoul, Korea, 1955; LLM, Seoul Nat. U., Seoul, Korea, 1957; MA in Pub. Adminstrn., U. Minn., 1961, PhD, 1965. Asst. prof. pub. adminstrn. Seoul Nat. U., 1961-69, assoc. prof. pub. adminstrn., 1969-73, prof. pub. adminstrn., 1973-94, dean Grad. Sch. Pub. Adminstrn., 1984-88, prof. emeritus, 1994—; sr. fellow East-West Ctr., Hawaii, 1973-74; recognized student Oxford (Eng.) U., 1978-79; vice chmn. Pres.'s Commn. for Adminstrv. Reform, Korean Govt., 1987-88. Author: Organization Theories, 1975, Modern Office Management, 1982, Public Administration in Korea, 1980, Korean Organization for Public Administration, 1993. Pres. Citizen's Coalition for Better Govt., Seoul, 1997—. Recipient Disting. Svc. medal Pres. of Korea, 1994. Mem. Korean Inst. Orgnl. Studies (dir. 1994—), Korean Assn. Pub. Adminstrn. (pres. 1979-80), Am. Sociol. Assn. Presbyterian. Avocations: fishing, photography, archery. Home: Olympic Sonsuchon, Apt 307-301, Songpa-ku, Seoul 138-788, South Korea Office: Korean Inst Orgnl Studies, Kongduk-Dong 404, Mapo-ku, Seoul 121-020, South Korea

CHO, SUNG YOON, law librarian; b. Shinuiju, Pyongan Pukto, Republic of Korea, Sept. 10, 1928; came to U.S., 1955; s. Bong Soon Cho and Yong Soon Kim; m. Won Kyung Bae, Oct. 20, 1962 (dec. Nov. 1982); children: David, Margaret; m. Kyung Soo Kim, Aug. 31, 1985. LLB, Seoul (Republic of Korea) Nat. U., 1953; MA, Tulane U., 1957, PhD, 1963; M in Comparative Law, George Washington U., 1966. Korean atty. Civil Assistance Command UN, Seoul, 1953-55; legal specialist Korean and Japanese law Far Ea. Law div. Libr. of Congress, Washington, 1959-68, sr. legal specialist, 1968-77, asst. to chief, 1977-83, asst. chief, 1983-95, spl. law group leader eastern law divsn., 1995—; cons. Rsch. Analysis Corp., McLean, Va., 1968-71. Author: Asian Survey, 1971, Japanese Writings on Communist Chinese Law, 1977, Law and Legal Literature of North Korea: A Guide, 1988;

contbr. articles to profl. jours. Chmn. bd. trustees Korean Ch. Greater Washington, McLean, 1980-82, chmn. adminstrv. bd., 1988-90. Mem. Internat. Assn. Law Librs., Am. Soc. Internat. Law, Am. Assn. Law Librs. (com. fgn. law indexing 1973-79), Assn. Asian Studies (com. Asian law 1982-86), Japanese-Am. Soc. Legal Studies. Methodist. Avocations; music, fishing, reading, golf. Fax no.: (202)707-1820. E-mail: scho@loc.gov. Office: Libr Congress Ea Law Div 101 Independence Ave SE Washington DC 20540-0002

CHO, SUNG-BAE, computer scientist; b. Seoul, July 17, 1965; s. Sang-Yeon Cho and Jong-Im Lee; m. Jung Kim, Oct. 5, 1993; children: Yoon-Bin, Joon-Hee. BS, Yonsei U., 1988; MS, Korea Advanced Inst. Sci. Tech, Taejeon, 1990, PhD, 1993. Tech. staff computer ctr. Korea Advanced Inst. Sci. & Technology, 1991-92; rsch. staff Ctr. Artificial Intelligence Rsch., Taejeon, 1992-95; rschr. ATR Human Info. Processing Rsch. Labs., Kyoto, Japan, 1993-95; sr. rschr. Rsch. Inst. Software Application, Seoul, 1995—; vis. rschr. U. New South Wales, Canberra, 1998; assoc. prof. Yonsei U., Seoul, 1995—. Mem. IEEE (fellow), Internat. Neural Networks Soc. Avocations: basketball, reading, travel. Home: 463-48 Myunmok, 3 dong Jungrang-ku, Seoul 131-203, Republic of Korea Office: Yonsei U Dept Computer Sci, 134 Shinchon-dong Sudaemoon-ku, Seoul 120-749, Republic of Korea

CHO, TAE-GEUN, mathematics educator; b. Seoul, Korea, Sept. 28, 1935; s. Rae-Sun and Won-Ye (Lee) C.; m. Chung-Hee Lee, Feb. 25, 1961; children: Yeh-Dong, Catherine Mee-Hie. BA, Seoul Nat. U., 1959; MS, Koryo U., Seoul, 1963; PhD, UCLA, 1969. Tchg. asst. UCLA, 1964-69; asst. prof. SUNY, Albany, 1969-72; prof. Sogang U., Seoul, 1972—; dean acad. affairs Sogang U., 1991-93, dean grad. sch., 1994-97. Author: Real Analysis, 1979; contbr. articles to profl. jours. Recipient Seokryu Medal of Honor, Pres. Office Republic Korea, 1989. Mem. Korean Math. Soc., Am. Math. Soc. (pres. 1984-86, Merit Medal of Honor 1992). Office: Sogang Univ, Shinsoodong Mapo-koo, Seoul 121-742, Republic of Korea

CHO, YANGLAI, physicist; b. Sachun, Kyung Nam, Korea, Nov. 11, 1932; came to U.S., 1957; parents Sung Je and Du Lee (Lee) C.; m. Marion White; children: H. Eugene, H. Adrian, H. Elliot. BS in Physics, Seoul Nat. U., Korea, 1956; PhD in Physics, Carnegie Inst. Tech., 1966. Instr. Vassar Coll., Poughkeepsie, N.Y., 1960-62; post-doctoral assoc. Argonne (Ill.) Nat. Lab., 1967-68, asst. physicist, 1969-72, physicist, 1972-84, sr. physicist, 1984—, project dir. advanced photon source, 1984-91; dep. assoc. lab. dir., 1991—; mem. adv. bd. European Synchotron Radiation Facility, Grenoble, France, 1986—, Spring-8 Synchrotron Facility, Harima, Japan, 1990—. Recipient Disting. Performance award, U. Chgo., 1986. Mem. Am. Physical Soc., Sigma Xi. Office: Argonne Nat Lab D-401 9700 Cass Ave Lemont IL 60439-4803

CHO, YOUNG JUNE, mechanical engineer; b. Seoul, Korea, Oct. 22, 1955; s. Soo Hyun Cho and Chun Hee Lee; m. Sae-Sil Kwon; children: Baum Suk, Han-Suk. BS, Hanyang U., 1979; M in Engring., Korea Advanced Inst. Sci., 1981, PhD, 1986. Mgr. rsch. & devel. Daewoo Shipbuilding, Okpo, Korea, 1986-89; sr. rsch. engr. Korea Inst. Sci. & Tech., Seoul, 1989; prin. rsch. engr. KITECH, Seoul, 1989-98. Mem. IEEE, Internat. Fedn. Automatic Control (nat. orgn. com. 1997), Soc. Automation and Sys. Engring. (editl. bd. 1996), Korean Soc. Mech. Engrs. Avocation: golf. E-mail: choyj@kitech.re.kr. Office: KITECH Indsl Automation Ctr, 35-3 Hongchon-R1 Ibjangmyun, Chonansi 330-820, Republic of Korea

CHOA, WALTER KONG, technical service professional; b. Rangoon, Burma, Aug. 10, 1948; came to U.S., 1974; s. Keng Hong and Kim (Tan) C.; m. Teresa Yeap Myint, Sept. 29, 1979; 1 child, Patricia. BS in Chemistry, Rangoon U., 1967. R & D chemist Diversey Chems., Des Plaines, Ill., 1975-80; mgr. tech. svc. Diversey Wyandotte, Mich., 1980-85, Diversey Wyandotte Metals, 1985-88; western mgr. tech. svc. Henkel Surface Technologies, Madison Heights, Mich., 1988—. Mem. Am. Electgroplaters and Surface Finishers Assn. (appreciation award L.A. br. 1983), Chem. Coaters Assn. Internat. Home: 3561 Cotter Rim Ln Diamond Bar CA 91765-3763 Office: Henkel Surface Techs 1615 Johnson Rd NW Atlanta GA 30318-8937

CHOATE, EDWARD LEE, lawyer, educator; b. Carbondale, Ill., Jan. 8, 1951; s. Loree and Geraldine Louise (Minton) C.; m. Lenetta Kay Blackburn, Sept. 10, 1983. BA with honors in History, So. Ill. U., 1972; JD, U. Notre Dame, 1975. Bar: Ill. 1975, U.S. Dist. Ct. (so. dist.) Ill. 1981, U.S. Ct. Appeals (7th cir.) 1981, Conn. 1996, U.S. Supreme Ct. 2000. Sole practice Carterville, Ill., 1975-92; assoc. to v.p. student and univ. affairs So. Conn. State U., New Haven, 1992—; asst. state's atty. Williamson County, Ill., 1982-84; asst. vis. prof. aviation law Sch. Tech. Careers, So. Ill. U., Carbondale, 1981, 82. Precinct committeeman Carterville Rep. Com., 1982-92. Named one of Outstanding Young Men in Am., 1985; So. Ill. U. Pres.'s scholar. Mem. ABA, Phi Alpha Theta. Baptist. Clubs: Masons (32 degree, numerous offices in various local and state divsns.), Shriners, KT (past comdr.), Order Eastern Star (past pastron). Home: 68 Nutmeg Hill Rd Hamden CT 06514-1163 Office: 501 Crescent St 144 Engleman Hall New Haven CT 06515

CHOAY, PATRICK HENRI, pharmaceutical executive. Nat. pharmacist diploma, U. Paris, 1969, DSc, 1973, PharmD, 1977. Rsch. asst. Centre Nat. de la Recherche Scientifique, Paris, 1969-75; gen. mgr. Laboratoire Choay, Paris, 1982-83; dir. rsch. Inst. Choay, Paris, 1975-84; pres. Lab. CCD, Paris, 1986—, Lab. Bailly, 1995—; lectr. biochemist and biophysics U. San Francisco, 1977; lectr. organic chemistry Worcester Found., Shrewsbury, Mass., 1975. Col. French Army Med. Corps. Mem. French Nat. Pharm. Acad. Office: Patrick Choay SA, 60 rue Pierre Charron, 75008 Paris France

CHOBANOVA, ROSSITSA DOBREVA, economist, researcher; b. Harmanli, Haskovo, Bulgaria, Dec. 2, 1956; d. Dobri Yankov and Tzanka Dobreva (Ivanova) C.; m. Atanas Dimitrov Kovatchev; children: Dobromira, Dessisslava. BA, MA in Econs., U. for Nat. and World Economy, Sofia, Bulgaria, 1978; PhD in Econs., Moscow State U., 1983. Asst. prof. U. for Nat. and World Economy, Sofia, 1983; sr. rschr. Inst. Econs., Bulgarian Acad. Scis., Sofia, 1984-93, project leader, 1994-98, sr. rsch. fellow, 1998—; lectr. U. for Nat. and World Economy, Sofia, 1984, Veliko Turnovo (Bulgaria) U. St. Cyril and St. Methodi, 1992; individual rschr. Ctrl. European U., Prague, Czech Republic, 1992-94; team leader Rotterdam (The Netherlands) U., 1994-96; cons. EU Phare Programme for Bulgaria, 1997. Author: Investing in Transitional Economy, 1995, Foreign Direct Investment to Central and Eastern Europe, 1996, Barriers to Innovation, 1998, Economy and Technology: Contradictions, 1999, Innovation Systems in Central and Eastern Europe, 1999; editor in chief Economy and Ecology in Transition, 1994—. Pres. Assn. Economy and Democracy, Sofia, 1990—; convenor econony and ecology commn. Helsinki Citizens Assembly, Prague and The Hague, 1992—. Mem. Internat. Inst. for Self Mgmt. (dir. 1991), Union Bulgarian Scientists (gen. sec. of the union 1999—). Home: Apt 22, Mladost 2 Bl 219-V, 1799 Sofia Bulgaria Office: Assn Economy & Democracy, Mladost 2 Bl 219V Kab 14, 1790 Sofia Bulgaria Office: Bulgarian Acad Scis, Int Econs, 3 Aksakov St, 1040 Sofia Bulgaria

CHOBAUT, JEAN-CLAUDE, physician, educator; b. Diarville, Lorraine, France, June 6, 1946; s. Andre Leon and Josiane (Chenevard) C.; m. Marie-Claire Humbert, May 15, 1970; children: Guillaume, Mathieu, Elise. MD, U. Nancy, France, 1971. Resident Hopital Ctrl., Nancy, 1970-71, Hopital Saint-Jacques, Besancon, 1972-76; ENT specialist Centre Hospitalier U., Nancy, 1976-79; ENT specialist Centre Hospitalier U., Besancon, 1979-88, prof., 1988—, chief dept., 1989—. Contbr. articles to profl. jours. including European Respiratory Jour., Am. Jour. Otolaryngology. Capt. French Army Res., 1972-98. Mem. Rotary. Avocations: skiing, sailing, hunting, fishing. Home: 9 Rue du Tremblois, 25910 Saint-Vit France Office: Chu Jean-Minjoz, 3 Bd Fleming, 25000 Besancon France

CHOCK, ALVIN KEALI'I, retired botanist; b. Honolulu, June 18, 1931; s. Hon and Eleanor Kam Hoon (Au) C.; m. Yona Nahenahe Bielefeldt, June 18, 1962; children: T. Makana, D. 'Alana, D. Malama. BA, U. Hawaii, Manoa, 1951, MS in Botany, 1953; postgrad., U. Mich., 1953-55, U.S. Dept. Agr. Grad. Sch., 1959, Pacific Asian Mgmt. Inst., 1988, 90, U. Hawaii, 1988, 90. Tech. adminstrv. asst. European Exchange Svc., Katterbach bei Ansbach/Mfr., Germany, 1958-59; plant quarantine insp. Agrl. Rsch. Svc., U.S. Dept. Agr., N.Y.C., 1959-60, Honolulu, 1961-67; supervisory insp. Agrl. Rsch. Svc., U.S. Dept. Agr., Balt., 1967-70; program specialist Office of Pesticide Programs, EPA, Washington, 1970-71, supervisory program specialist, 1971-74, supervisory biologist, 1975; agrl. officer (plant quarantine) FAO, Rome, 1975-78; also tech. sec. Near East Plant and Caribbean Plant Protection Commn., 1976; supervisory biologist, registration div. Office of Pesticide Programs, EPA, Washington, 1978-81; acting coord. internat. programs Dept. Agr., Hyattsville, Md., 1981-82; dir. (Europe, Near East and Africa) Region II, 1981-82; dir. (European, Near East and Africe) Region II, The Hague, The Netherlands, 1982-88; dir. (Asia and Pacific) Region III, Hyattsville, 1988-92; lectr. botany U. Hawaii, 1961-67, 69, 72, 79, 84, 86, 88, 90, 93, 95—, adj. instr. botany, 1993-95, adj. colleague, 1995—; asst. botanist B.P. Bishop Mus., Honolulu, 1961-65; botanist Kokee Natural History Mus., Hawaii, 1953-55; bot. cons. Nat. Park Svc., 1962-63; mem. work panels European and Mediterranean Plant Protection Orgn., Paris, 1976-78; plant quarantine cons. Coun. Agr. Rep. China, Taiwan, 1993; artist-in-residence Am. Folk Dance, Hawaii Dept. Edn. Founding editor Hawaii Bot. Soc. Newsletter, 1962-63, 66; editor Fed. Plant Quarantine Insps. Nat. Assn. newsletter, 1963-65, Ka Nupepa, 1968-71; chmn. editl. com. FAO Plant Protection Bull., 1976-78; contbg. author books; editor (with G.L. Addicott) Pavorite Songs of the Hawaii State Society, 1973; contbr. articles to profl. jours.; mem. Nā Kúpuna o Ko'olau Hawaiian Entertainment Group. Mem. governing bd. Nat. Conf. State Socs., Washington, 1972-75, dep. dir. gen., 1973-74, 2d v.p., 1974-75; governing bd. Asian Pacific Am. Heritage Coun., Inc., 1979-81, 88-92; sec. PTA, Overseas Sch. Rome, 1976-77l USDA rep., 1988, observer, 1990-91, governing bd. Am. Fgn. Svc. Assn., 1989-91; co-spokesperson Mayor's Ewa-Kapolei Vision Team, Honolulu, 1998-99. Served with inf. U.S. Army, 1955-57. Plant species Cyanea chockii named in his honor; recipient other awards in field. Mem. Hawaiian Acad. Sci. (dir. jr. acad. 1963-64), Lloyd Shaw Found., Assn. Tropical Biology (charter), Hawaiian Bot. Soc. (sec. 1962, dir. 1963, 65, 94-95, pres. 1964), Internat. Assn. Plant Taxonomists, Pacific Sci. Assn., Soc. Econ. Botany, FAO Assn. Profl. Staff (appeals and procedures com. 1976-77, standing com. career devel. 1976-78), Nat. Capital Area Square Dance Leaders Assn. (editor newsletter 1980-81), Mediterranean Area Callers and Tchrs. Assn. (founder, publicity dir. 1977-78), European Callers and Tchrs. Assn., Contralab, Hawaii State Soc. D.C. (dir. 1968-69, 89-91, 1st v.p. 1969-71, pres. 1971-72, adv. 1978-79, 2d. v.p. 1979-80, Hawaii rep. 1995—), Hawaii Fedn. Square & Round Dance Clubs (treas. 1996-98), Hawaii State Dance Coun. (bd. dirs. 1996—, sec. 1997-99), Consumers Union, Bishop Mus. Assn., Ramblin' Romans Sq. Dance Club (founder), Ewa Gentry Cmty. Assn. (v.p. 1993-95, pres. 1995-96, newsletter editor 1993-94), Arbors Assn. Apt. Owners (bd. dirs. 1994—, v.p. 1997—, newsletter editor 1994—), Roosevelt H.S. Alumni Assn. (bd. dirs. 1993—), Roosevelt Alumni Found. (v.p. 1994-96, pres. 1996-99, bd. dirs. 1994—), Pacific Sci. Assn., Benevolent and Protective Order of Elk (inner guard 2000—), Internat. Order Odd Fellows, Sigma Xi. Home: 91-1064 Laaulu St Apt E Ewa HI 96706-3866

CHOCKALINGAM, MARY JULIANA, research and development executive; b. Valayapatty, Chennai, India, July 14, 1940; d. Tanjore Athisayanathan Mangalam Pillai and Rosary Ammal (Thiruchelvam) Mangalampilli; m. Sillanatham Chockalingam, May 26, 1969; children: C.A.J. Amudha, Francis Mohan, C. Mary Jaya Priya. BS, Am. Coll., Madurai, India, 1959; MS, Madras U., India, 1962, PhD, 1987; post-grad. diploma Computer Applications, Alagappa U., Karaikudi, India, 1994. Sr. sci. asst. Ctrl. Electrochem. Rsch. Inst., Karaikudi, 1964-69, scientist "A", 1969-74, scientist "B", 1974-79, scientist "C", 1979-84, scientist E I, 1984-89, scientist E II, 1989-96, dep. dir., 1996—. 12 patents in field. Recipient Invention Promotion Bd. award Nat. Rsch. Devel. Bd., New Delhi, 1973. Fellow Soc. Advancement of Electrochem. Sci. and Tech., Inst. Chemists India, Solar Energy Soc. India; mem. Photoptical Instrumentation Engrs., Materials Rsch. Soc. Avocations: photography, drawing, language learning (French, German, Russian, Tamil, English, Hindi, Telugu). Home: 120 Ezhilaham V St, TT Nagar Karaikudi, 630 002 Chenaai State India Office: Ctrl Electrochem Rsch Inst, Karaikudi, 630 006 Tamilnadu India

CHODES, JOHN JAY, photographer, writer; b. N.Y.C., Feb. 23, 1939; s. Ralph and Henrietta (Jonas) C. Comml. cert., Germain Sch. Photography, N.Y.C., 1963. Asst. editor Kauri, N.Y.C., 1966-67; sales promotion writer Business Week, N.Y.C., 1967-69, Fortune, N.Y.C., 1970, Forbes, N.Y.C., 1971, The N.Y. Times, N.Y.C., 1972-74; comms. dir. Libertarian Party of N.Y., 1980-93; photographer Long Distance Log, Phila., 1961-63; photographer publicity Newsweek, N.Y.C., 1960-61, Athletics Weekly, London, 1963-64, Track & Field News, Los Altos, Calif., 1961-63, Brooklyn Eagle, 1997-99, Brooklyn Heights Press, 1998-00. Author Corbitt, 1973, Bruce Jenner, 1976; numerous plays; contbr numerous articles to profl. jours. Recipient Journalistic Excellence award Road Runners Club of Am., 1974, Outstanding Svc. award Libertarian Party of N.Y., 1988. Mem. League of the South, Road Runners Club, Libertarian Party of N.Y. Jewish. Avocation: road racing. Home: 411 E 10th St Apt 22G New York NY 10009-4213

CHODOROW, NANCY JULIA, sociology educator; b. N.Y.C., Jan. 20, 1944; d. Marvin and Leah (Turitz) C.; children: Rachel Esther Chodorow-Reich, Gabriel Issac Chodorow-Reich. BA, Radcliffe Coll., 1966; PhD, Brandeis U., 1975; grad., San Francisco Psychoanalytic, 1993, cert. in adult psychoanalysis, 2000. From lectr. to assoc. prof. U. Calif., Santa Cruz, 1974-86; from asst prof. sociology to prof. U. Calif., Berkeley, 1986—, clin. prof. dept. psychology, 1999—; faculty San Francisco Psychoanalytic Inst., 1994—. Author: The Reproduction of Mothering, 1978 (Jessie Bernard award 1979, named one of Ten Most Influential Books of Past 25 Years, Contemporary Sociology 1996), 2nd edit., 1999, Feminism and Psychoanalytic Theory, 1989, Femininities, Masculinities, Sexualities, 1994, The Power of Feelings: Personal Meaning in Psychoanalysis, Gender, and Culture, 1999; contbr. articles to profl. jours. Fellow Russell Sage Found., NEH, Ctr. Advanced Study Behavioral Scis., ACLS, Guggenheim fellow; recipient Contbn. to Women and Psychoanalysis award APA. Mem. Internat. Psychoanalytic Assn., Am. Psychoanalytic Assn., San Francisco Psychoanalytic Soc. Office: U Calif Dept Sociology 410 Barrows Hall Berkeley CA 94720-1980

CHODOSH, SANFORD, pulmonologist; b. Carteret, N.J., Jan. 14, 1928; s. m. Harriet Reznick; 3 children. BA in Biology and Chemistry, U. VA., 1948; MD, Johns Hopkins U., 1952. Intern Boston City Hosp., 1952-53, resident, 1956-58, fellow Lung Sta., 1958-59, physician-in-charge Sputum Lab., 1959-85, dir. dept. inhalation therapy, 1971-79, 80-81, dir. pulmonary outpatient dept., 1973-76; instr. in medicine Tufts U., Boston, 1960-61, asst. prof. medicine, 1962-70, assoc.. prof. medicine, 1970-74; assoc. prof. medicine Sch. Medicine Boston U., 1974—; chief pulmonary clinic VA Outpatient Clinic, Boston, 1979-2000, chief medicine, 1984-88, acting chief staff, 1986-87, chief staff, 1987-2000, assoc. chief medicine, 1988-91; rsch. asst. dept. psychobiology Johns Hopkins U., 1949-51; asst. vis. physician I & III Tufts Med. Svc., Boston City Hosp., 1964-67, assoc. vis. physician, 1968-73; vis. physician Univ. Hosp., 1977-88; vis. physician VA Hosp., Boston, 1975-77; mem. utilization evaluation com. Dept. Health and Hosps., 1966-71, chmn. accreditation subcom., 1966-68, chmn. human studies com., 1972-84; mem. tuberculosis adv. com. Deans Com. Boston, 1967-68, tuberculosis implementation com., 1969-71; mem. pulmonary com. Tufts U. Sch. Medicine, 1969-71, sci. affairs com., 1972-74; chmn. pharmacy and therapeutics com. Dept. Health and Hosps., 1972-75, patient care com., 1972-74, human studies com., 1973-84; cons. in field. Contbr. numerous articles to profl. publs., chpts. to books. Active Am. Lung Assn. of Mass.; mem. Applied Rsch. Ethics Nat. Assn. Coun., 1986. With U.S. Army and USAF Med. Corps, 1953-56. Fellow Nat. Tuberculosis Assn., 1958-60, 60-61, Edward Livingstone Trudeau fellow Nat. Tuberculosis Assn., 1961-62; recipient Rsch. Career Devel. award USPHS, 1963-67. Fellow Am. Coll. Chest Physicians; mem. Am. Thoracic Soc., Mass. Thoracic Soc. (v.p. 1968-70, pres. 1970-72, mem. coun. 1967-77, 79-82, mem. rsch. allocations com. 1982-84), Am. Coll. Chest Physicians, Mass. Med. Soc., Johns Hopkins Med. and Surg. Assn., Suffolk Dist. Med. Soc., Pub. Responsibility in Medicine and Rsch., Inc. (founding mem., bd. dirs. 1974—, pres. 1979—), Assn. Accreditation Human Rsch. Protections, Inc. (founding mem., pres. 1999—), Sigma Xi, Phi Beta Kappa. Home: 35 Oak Hill Rd Wayland MA 01778-2917

CHOE, SEUNGHO, physicist, researcher; b. Kwang-Joo, Republic of Korea, July 1, 1967; s. Kyu-Jin Choi and Jung-Soon Kim. BS, Yonsei U., Republic of Korea, 1989, MS, 1992, PhD, 1997. Tchg. asst. Yonsei U., Seoul, Republic of Korea, 1990-94, rschr., 1992-97, 98—; lectr. Bucheon Tech. Coll., Republic of Korea, 1995-97; vis. post-doc Adelaide U., Australia, 1997-98. Contbr. articles to profl. jours. Scholar Korean Air Lines, 1987-88; rsch. fellow Ctr. Theoretical Physics, 1997; fellow Korea Rsch. Found., 1997. Mem. Korean Phys. Soc. Avocations: collecting stamps, playing soccer. Home: Jinju Apt 502-707, Gajoa 2 Dong, Seogu, Incheon 404-252, Republic of Korea Office: Yonsei U, Dept Physics, Seoul 120-749, Republic of Korea

CHOE WON IK, judge. Pres. Ctrl. Ct., Pyongyang, Dem. People's Republic of Korea. Office: Mansudong Central District, Pyongyang Peoples Republic of Korea*

CHOH, SUNG HO, physics educator; b. Chungjin, Hamkyung, Korea, Nov. 7, 1935; s. Dae Haeng and Kum Ok (Koh) C.; m. Sul Ja Kim, Sept. 3, 1966; children: Suk-Joo, Yun-Joo. BS, Seoul (Korea) Nat. U., 1958, MS, 1960; PhD, Brown U., Providence, 1968. Instr. Yon Sei U., Seoul, 1961-63; postdoctoral fellow McMaster U., Hamilton, Ont., Can., 1968-71; assoc. prof. Korea U., Seoul, 1971-74, prof. physics, 1974—, dean Coll. Sci., 1992-94; vis. scientist Oxford (U.K.) U., 1979-80; vis. prof. Brown U., Providence, 1987-88, Monash U., Melbourne, Australia, 1996-97; com. mem. Korea Sci. and Engring. Found., Seoul, 1981-82; dir. Seoul br. Korea Basic Sci. Inst., 1994-96; mem. Presdl. Coun. on Sci. and Tech., Seoul, 1995-96. Author: Magnetic Resonance Methods, 1985, 2nd printing, 1991; editor-in-chief Jour. Korean Phys. Soc., 1989-93; patentee in magnetic field measuring technique. Recipient Nat. Order Mokreon Korean Govt., 1987, Acad. award Samil Moonwha Found., Seoul, 1990. Fellow Korean Phys. Soc. (v.p. 1989-93, trustee 1993-97, pub. papers award 1983, 8th Sung Bong Physics award 2000), Korean Acad. Sci. and Tech., Inst. Physics (U.K.). Presbyterian. Avocations: Korean chess, golf. Home: Joogong Apt 1001-402, Choongang-dong 67, Gwacheon Kyunggi-do 427-010, Republic of Korea Office: Korea U Dept Physics, Sungbuk-ku Ahnam-dong, Seoul 136-701, Republic of Korea

CHOI, AN-SEOP, civil engineer; b. Seoul, Korea, Oct. 4, 1967; s. Byung-Eun and Hae-Eun; m. Gab-Joo Chae; 1 child, Kyu-Won. BS, Hanyang U., Seoul, 1991; MS, Pa. State U., University Park, 1993, PhD, 1997. Rsch. asst. Pa. State U., University Park, 1993-96; sr. rschr. Samsung Co., Yongin, Korea, 1997-2000; asst. prof. Sejong U., Seoul, Korea, 2000—. Contbr. articles to profl. jours. Recipient scholarship, Dongboo found., Seoul, 1989-90. Avocations: baseball, basketball. Office: Sejong U Dept Archtl, 98 kunja-Dong, 143-747 Seoul Korea

CHOI, BYUNG HAN, plant breeder, researcher; b. Inpyung, Chonnam, Korea, June 20, 1942; s. Jung Hew Choi and Gae Nyou Park; m. Young Ae Kim, Nov. 28, 1968; children: Jung In, Dong Suk. BS, Seoul Nat. U., Suwon, Korea, 1964; MS, Oreg. State U., 1982, PhD, 1984. Jr. rschr. Nat. Crop Experiment Sta., Suwon, 1964-75; sr. rschr. Crop Experiment sta., Suwon, 1975-99; crop specialist Korea Agr. Mission to Vietnam, 1971-75. Author or co-author: (books) Sesame, 1986, Rapeseed, 1988, Peanuts, 1992, Buckwheat, 1993, Introduction to Agricultural Science, 1994, Pearl Millet, 1995, What Crop Is Maize?, 1998, Tea Culture, 1998, Organic Agriculture, 1998, Crop Breeding for Quality Improvement, 1994, Crop Breeding Guide Book, 1996, In Vitro Haploid Production in Higher Plants, Vol. 4: Cereals, 1997. Crop sci. rsch. grantee Korean Soc. Crop Sci., 1991. Mem. Buckwheat Rsch. Assn. (v.p. 1997—), Crop Sci. Soc. Am. Avocations: climbing, swimming, reading, TV. Home: Daerim Apt 12-201, 156-093 Sadang Seoul, Korea Office: Nat Crop Experiment Sta, Seodundong, 441-100 Suwon Korea

CHOI, BYUNG IHN, radiology educator; b. Seoul, Jan. 2, 1950; parents Sun Geun Choi and Byung Jin Lee; m. Eun Kyung Lee, Sept. 18, 1977; children. Yoon Young, Yoon Suk. MD cum laude, Seoul Nat. U., 1974, PhD, 1983. Cert. med. dr. Ministry Health and Welfare; cert. diagnostic radiologist. Radiologist-in-chief dept. radiology Capital Armed Forces Hosp., Korean Army, Seoul, 1979-82; prof. dept. radiology Coll. Medicine Seoul Nat. U., 1982—; vis. rsch. fellow U. Calif., San Francisco, 1985-86; vis. radiologist faculty medicine U. Tokyo, 1988, Mass. Gen. Hosp., Boston, 1990; vis. prof. dept. radiology Pitts. U. Med. Ctr., 1994, U. Tex., M.D. Anderson Cancer Ctr., Houston, 1990, dept. radiology U. Wash. Med. Ctr., Seattle, 1994; cons. Korean Army, Seoul, 1989—; dir. Office Edn. and Rsch., Seoul Nat. U. Hosp., 1998—. Contbr. articles and papers to sci. jours. Recipient award for outstanding sci. paper in sci. and tech. Korean Fedn. Socs. for Sci. and Tech., 1992, Gold Medal award for outstanding sci. exhbn. Korean Soc. Med. Ultrasound, 1995. Mem. World Fedn. Ultrasound in Medicine and Biology (co-opted councilor 1997—), Asian Fedn. Socs. of Ultrasound in Medicine and Biology (treas. 1992-98, sec. 1998—), Am. Inst. Ultrasound Medicine (sr.). Avocations: tennis, golf, swimming. Fax: 82 2 7436385. E-mail: choibi@radcom.snu.ar.kr. Office: Seoul Nat U Hosp, 28 Yongon-dong Chongno-gu, Seoul 110-744, Korea

CHOI, CHANG-HOON, electrical engineer; b. Pusan, Korea, Jan. 7, 1964; came to U.S., 1997; m. Sung-Dal Choi and Boon-Yee Lee; m. Ju-Hee Kim, Apr. 15, 1990; children: Seung-Yeon, Seung-Woo. BS, Sogang U., 1988, MS, 1990. Sr. engr. Samsung Electronics Co. Ltd., Kyungki-do, Korea, 1990-97; summer intern Advanced Micro Devices, Inc., Sunnyvale, Calif., 1999. Mem. IEEE. Avocation: cinema. E-mail: chchoi@stanford.edu.

CHOI, CHINTAE, research mechanical engineer; b. Pusan, Republic of Korea, May 30, 1959; s. Hakrak Choi and Youngkum Chang; m. Soonyoung Hong; children: Eurah, Sahnkyu. BSME, Pusan Nat. U., 1982, MSME, 1984, PhD in Mech. Engring., 1997. Rsch. engr. Rsch. Inst. Indsl. Sci. and Tech., Pohang, Republic of Korea, 1986-98, sr. rsch. engr., 1995—, team leader, 1998—; postdoctoral rsch. assoc. U. Ill., Urbana-Champaign, 1997-98; adj. prof. Uiduk U., Kyungjoo, Republic of Korea, 1999—. Contbr. articles to sci. jours., including IEEE Trans. Sys., Man and Cybernetics, Procs. Instn. Mech. Engrs., Mechatronics, also Am. Control Conf. 2d lt. Korean Army, 1984-85. Recipient award for best project on Autonomous Reclaimer Sys., 1997, award for best project on steel-making process Pohang Iron and Steel Making Co., Ltd., 1999. Mem. IEEE. Avocations: fishing, listening to music. Office: Rsch Inst Indsl Sci-Tech, San 32, Kyungbok Pohang 790-330, Republic of Korea

CHOI, CHONG WHAN, construction company executive; b. Seoul, May 10, 1925; s. Sang Lim and Lim Ja (Kim) C.; m. Kwang Young Chai, Feb. 7, 1949 (dec. 1999); children: Yong Kwon, Yong Ju. BA in Econs., Kun Kuk U., 1958; D of Engring. (hon.), St. Petersburg Mining Inst., 1993. Founder, hon. chmn. Samwhan Corp., 1946—; chmn. Woosung Devel. Co., Ltd., 1967—, Woosung Food Stuff Industry Co., Ltd., 1969—, Samwhan Engring. Co., Ltd., 1976—, Sun Travel Co., Ltd., 1977—; chmn. Samwhan Corp., 1978-96, hon. chmn., 1996—; chmn. Shinmin Mut. Savs. & Fin. Co., Ltd., 1978—, Hoehyon Co., Ltd., 1978—; Hoehyon Co., Ltd., Samwhan Camus Co., Ltd., 1978—, Samwhan Platt Co., Ltd., 1979—, Samsam Investment & Fin. Corp., 1982-97; hon. consul-gen. in Korea for Kingdom of Swaziland, 1971—. Author: Autobiography of Choi, 1996. Chmn., Korea-Saudi Arabia Econ. Cooperation Coun., 1979—; vice-chmn. Korea-U.S. Econ. Coun., 1980-95; mem. Adv. Coun. Peaceful Unification Policy, Rep. of Korea, 1981—; dean Corps Hon. Consuls in Korea, 1982—; v.p. Korea-Arab Friendship soc., 1976-82. Decorated Order of Indsl. Svc. Merit, 1967, 70, 72, 74, 75, 76, Silver Tower, 79, Gold Tower, 84, others; Royal Order of Sobhuza II (Swaziland), 1981; Order Indsl. Svc. Merit; Silver Tower, 1979, Gold Tower, 1984; others. Mem. Korea Mil. Constrn. Contractors Assn. (chmn. 1966), Internat. Fedn. Asian and Western Pacific Contractors Assns. (pres. 1974-75, hon. mem. award, 1989), Internat. Pvt. Econ. Coun. of Korea (vice-chmn. 1988-91), Korea-USSR Econ. Assn. (vice-chmn. 1989-92), Korea-Commonwealth Ind. States Econ. Assn. (chmn. 1992-97), Constrn. Assn. Korea (pres. 1975-81, hon. pres. 1981—), Korea C. of C. and Industry (v.p. 1976-82), Fedn. Korean Industries (dep. chmn. 1983-92, advisor 1993), Confedn. of Internat. Contractors Assn. (pres. 1983-85), Korea-Japan Econ. Assn. (vice-chmn. 1987-95). Home: 1-216 Gahoe-Dong, Chongro-ku, Seoul 110-260, Republic of Korea Office: Samwhan Corp, 98-20 Unni-Dong Chongro-ku, Seoul Republic of Korea also: Samwhan Corp 2701 Saint Cloud Dr San Bruno CA 94066-1743

CHOI, HOON, technical educator; b. Seoul, South Korea, May 19, 1960; parents Seung-Hyun and Min-Young Do Choi; m. Hyweon Suk, Sept. 2,

1986; children: YoungWu, HeeJu. BS, Seoul Nat. U., 1983; MS, Duke U., 1990, PhD, 1993. Sr. mem. tech. staff Electronics and Telecomms. Rsch. Inst., Taejon, Korea, 1983-96; mem. steering com. SIGIN of Korea Info. Sci. Soc., Seoul, 1994-98; chmn. Student Assn., dept. computer engring. Seoul Nat. U., 1980. Contbr. rsch. papers to profl. jours.; patentee in field. Recipient 1st prize Korea Info. Sci. Soc. and IBM Korea, 1982, Grad. Fellowship award IBM, 1992. Mem. IEEE, Korea Info. Sci. Soc., Korean Inst. Comm. Scis. Roman Catholic. Avocations: sightseeing, mountain climbing, listening to music. Fax: 82 42 822 4997. E-mail: hchoi@comeng.chungnam.ac.kr. Office: Chungnam Nat U, Dept Comp Eng 220 Kung-Dong, 305-764 Taejon Korea

CHOI, HOON, electrical engineer; b. Seoul, Aug. 14, 1970; parents Young Choi and Young-ae Yim; m. Jeong-won Hwang, June 19, 1996. BSEE, Yonsei U., Seoul, 1993; MSEE, Korea Advanced Inst. Sci. and Tech., Taejon, Korea, 1995; PhD in Elec. Engring., Korea Advanced Inst. Sci. and. Taejon, Korea, 1999. Cert. in Very Large Scale Integration/Computer Aided Design/design engring. Engr. Samsung Electronics, Kyungki-do, Korea, 1993-95, jr. engr., 1995-99; sr. engr. Samsung Electronics, Kyungki-do, 2000—. Contbr. papers to profl. jours. and confs. Avocations: swimming, body building. Fax: 82 2 6413 0106. E-mail: hchoi@ieee.org. Home: 5-1001 Meesung Apt, Songpa-dong Songpa-gu, Seoul 138-172, South Korea Office: Samsung Electronics, San #24 Nongseo-Ri, Yongin Kyungki-Do 449-711, South Korea

CHOI, IK-SOO, engineering educator; b. Kimje, Republic of Korea, Aug. 25, 1945; child of Gui Dong and Tae Soon Bae; m. Boo Yul Kim, Nov. 24, 1973; children: O-Hyun, Jin Woong, Dong Woong. BS, Korea U., Seoul, 1972, MS, 1975, PhD, 1978; postgrad., Chgo. U., 1981. Advisor KORSTIC, Seoul, 1975-77; dir. Korea Inst. Energy Rsch., Taejeon, 1982-87, v.p., 1987-88, acting pres., 1987, pub., editor, 1987-88; dir. Korea Inst. Energy Rsch., Nice, France, 1989-90; prof. Korea Advanced Inst. Sci. & Tech., 1984-90, Kongju (Republic of Korea) Nat. U., 1999—. Chmn. Korea Taekyun Assn., 1998, Korea-China Civilization Assn., 1999. Sgt. Repubic of Korea Army, 1967-70. Recipient Technonet Asia prize, 1976, Superior Rschr. award Ministry Sci. & Tech., 1985, Nat. prize, 1987. Fellow Korea Inst. Chem. Engrs. (permanent); mem. Assn. Energy Engrs. Achievements include invention of re-refinery process of waste lube-oil; manufacturing and composition of combust tube for Yoon-Tan; pellet type activated carbon manufacturing with non-cocking coal; manufacturing of fuel from waste lube-oil. Avocation: golf. Home: 397-31 Yousung, Taejeon 305-343, Korea Office: Korea Inst Energy Rsch, 71-2 Yousung, Taejeon 305-343, Korea

CHOI, IN-HO, life science educator; b. Daegu, Korea, Dec. 30, 1957; s. Jong-Rok Choi and Malcho Yoon; m. Kyoungsook Park; 1 child. BS, Yonsei U., Seoul, Korea, 1981; MA, Ind. State U., 1985, PhD, 1989. Postdoctoral rschr. U. Pa., Phila., 1989-91; asst. prof. Yonsei U., Wonju, Korea, 1991-94, assoc. prof., 1994-99, prof., 1999—; vis. scientist Smithsonian Tropical Rsch. Inst., Panama City, Panama, 1997-98; cons. Daewoo Found., Seoul, 1992. Contbr. articles to profl. jours. Rsch. grantee Ind. Acad. Sci., Indpls., 1988, Korea Sci. and Engring. Found., Seoul, 1994-96, Internat. Rsch. Exch. Program, Korea Rsch. Found., 1996-98. Mem. Korean Assn. Biol. Sci., Soc. Comparative and Integrative Biology, Japanese Soc. Biol. Sci. in Space. Avocations: collecting shells, photography, writing poetry, movies, travel. Office: Yonsei U Dept Life Sci, 234 Maeji-Ri Heungup-Myon, Wonju, Kangwon-Do 222-710, Republic of Korea

CHOI, JAE HOON, retired university administrator, legal educator; b. San Cheong, Korea, Apr. 8, 1929; s. Ki Seop and Bok Cho (Jeong) C.; m. So Hee Kim, Apr. 15, 1952; children: Shi Hyun, Jang Hyun, Jee Hee. LLB, Seoul Nat. U., 1953, LLM, 1955; PhD, Pusan Nat. U., 1971; researcher The Hague (Netherlands) Acad. Internat. Law, 1971; LL.D. (hon.), Nat. Chengchi U., Republic of China, 1984; LL.D. (hon.), U. S.C., 1987. Prof. law Pusan Nat. U., 1956-83, dean Coll. Law and Polit. Sci., 1971-73, dir. Inst. Problem of Korean Unification, 1974-77, dean Grad. Sch. Public Adminstrn., 1981-83, pres., 1983-87, prof. emeritus, 1990—; prof. law Kyushu Nat. U., Japan, 1988-89; chmn., pres. Hyunbum Rsch. Inst. for Internat. Affairs, 1990—; prof. law Seinangakuin U., Fukuoka, Japan, 1992-2000. Mem. Korean Assn. Internat. Law (v.p. 1974-77, pres. 1983-84), Am. Soc. Internat. Law, Japanese Assn. Internat. Law. Author: International Law, 1984; contbr. articles to profl. jours. Office: # 1407 Samhwan B/D, 830-295 Bumil-Dong, Tong-ku Pusan 601-062, Republic of Korea

CHOI, JAI WON, mathematical statistician, researcher; b. Kum-Ho-Up, Korea, Jan. 1, 1937; came to U.S., 1963; s. Byung Zoo Choi and Ky Cho Kim; m. Grace Gemma Park, Mar. 27, 1971; 1 child, Eleanor Park Choi. BA, Yonsei U., Seoul, Korea, 1959; BS magna cum laude, Calif. Bapt. Coll., 1966; postgrad., Harvard U., 1966-67; MA, U. Minn., 1970, PhD, 1980. Tchr. high sch. Seoul, 1960-63; statistician Ohio Dept. Health, Columbus, 1973-74; mathematical statistician U.S. Dept. Health & Human Svcs., Hyattsville, Md., 1976—; vis. rsch. assoc. Johns Hopkins U., Balt., 1985; program chair Washington Statis. Soc., 1984-90; cons. Univ. Student Health Svc., Mpls., 1975; invited spkr. Internat. Statis. Inst., 1995, Korean Sch. Health Assn., 1989; invited prof. Korea U., Seoul, 1996. Recipient Dir.'s award Nat. Ctr. for Health Statistics, 1980, Best Statistical Paper award CDC, 1990; USPHS trainee U. Minn., Mpls., 1974-76. Mem. Am. Statis. Assn., Korean Pub. Health Assn. (invited spkr. 1989), Korean Scientist and Engr. Assn. (invited spkr. 1988), Toastmasters (pres. Club 1260 1989), Internat. Statis. Inst. Home: 9504 Mary Knoll Rd Rockville MD 20850-3469 Office: Nat Ctr Health Statistics 6525 Belcrest Rd Ste 915 Hyattsville MD 20782-2003

CHOI, JEONG-WOO, chemical engineering educator; b. Seoul, Korea, Nov. 12, 1959; s. Jeong-Chan and Keum-Ok (Chun) C.; m. Hee-Myong Kim, May 24, 1986; children: Keun-Young, Hye-Gyu. BS cum laude, Sogang U., Seoul, 1982, MS, 1984; PhD, Rutgers U., 1990. Prof. chem. engring. Sogang U., 1990—, chmn. dept. chem. engring., 1995-96; vis. scientist IBM Almaden Rsch. Ctr., San Jose, Calif., 1993-94, Mitsubishi Electronics Advanced Tech. R&D Ctr., Osaka, Japan, 1996; vis. prof. Tokyo Inst. Tech., Nagatsuta, Japan, 1997, U. Tokyo, 1999; mem. editl. bd. Biotech. and Bioprocess Engring., Seoul, 1999—; mem. adv. bd. tech. Korean Ministry Commerce, Industry and Engring., Seoul, 1998-99; cons. Korean Inst. Energy Rsch., Taejeon, 1997; rschr. in field. Author: Bioengineering, 1995; contbr. articles to profl. jours. 2d lt. Korean Army, 1984-85. Recipient Young Scientist prize Korean Soc. Biotech. and Bioengring., 1998, Bumsuk Best Paper prize Korean Inst. Chem. Engring., 1998. Mem. AAAS, N.Y. Acad. Scis., Internat. Soc. Molecular Electronics and Biocomputing. Home: 403-1502 Daemyong Apt, Daehwa-Dong Ilsan-Ku, Koyang-Si Kyungkido 411-410, Korea Office: Sogang U Dept Chem Engring, CPO Box 1142, Seoul 100-611, Korea

CHOI, JUN-SEOP, engineer, educator, researcher; b. Korea, May 20, 1952; s. Sang-Kon and Nam-Soon (Rhyu) C.; m. Jin-Soo Kim, Apr. 23, 1988; children: Su-A, Su-Min, Si-Yeon. B in Engring., Hanyang U., Seoul, Korea, 1976; M in Engring., Tohoku U., Sendai, Japan, 1984, D in Engring., 1987. Sr. rschr. Korea Inst. Machinery and Metals, Taejeon, 1987-93; assoc. prof. Korea Nat. U. Edn., Chungwon, 1993—; cons. Taeyang Engring., Ansan, Korea, 1993—; chief editor Korean Tech. Edn. Assn., 2000—. Editor Jour. Korea Inst. Indsl. Educators, 1993—, Korea Soc. Mech. Engrs., 1987—. With Korean Army, 1973-74. Recipient Cert. award Internat. Heat Transfer Conf., 1986. Mem. Korea Soc. Mech. Engrs. Roman Catholic. Avocations: mountain climbing, hiking. Office: Korea Nat U Edn, Kangne-Myon, Chungwon-Gun, Chungbuk 363-791, Korea

CHOI, SANG DON, physics educator, researcher; b. Taegu, Republic of Korea, Jan. 20, 1939; s. Jung K. and Num I. (Lee) C.; m. Soo Gyeon Lee, Jan. 6, 1969; children: Joon Hyuck, Jung An. BS, Kyungpook Nat. U., Taegu, Korea, 1962, MS, 1964; PhD, SUNY, Buffalo, 1980. Prof. Kyung-Il U., Taegu, 1966-81; rsch. fellow SUNY, Buffalo, 1980-81; prof. Kyungpook Nat. U., Taegu, 1981—, chmn. pre-dental dept., 1983-84, chmn. physics dept., 1991-93, grad. chmn. physics dept., 1993-94, dir. Basic Sci. Rsch. Inst., 1993-96; lectr. Yeung-nam U., Taegu, 1965-75, Ulsan U., 1975, Korean Nursing Mil. Acad., Taegu, 1995-96. Author: Thermodynamics and Statistical Mechanics, 1986, Modern Physics for Life Sciences, 1991; co-author: Natural Science, 1992, University Physics, 1993. Mem. Korean Phys. Soc. (trustee 1981—, Outstanding Paper award 1989, Outstanding Rsch. award 1997). Avocations: classical literature, walking, meditation. Office: Kyungpook Nat U, Dept Physics Sankyuck-dong, 702-701 Taegu Republic of Korea

CHOI, SING-KI XAVIER, research scientist; b. Hong Kong, Dec. 13, 1953; s. Kee and Soon-Eu (Ton) C.; m. Anne Mui-Chin Ng, Oct. 13, 1984; children: Sarah-Jane Sau-Wei. B of Engring., Monash U., 1980, PhD, 1984, grad. diploma, 1989. Rsch. scientist CSIRO, Australia, 1984-90, sr. rsch. scientist, 1990-94, prin. rsch. scientist, 1994—; external rsch. cons. Comalco, Australia, 1987-95; hon. rsch. cons. U. Queensland, Australia, 1994-97; overseas specialist referee Rsch. Grants Coun., Hong Kong, 1995—; panel of assessors Australian Rsch. Coun., 1995—. Author: (with others) Huber's Yield Criterion in Plasticity, 1994; contbr. articles to profl. jours. Bishop Bianco scholarship St. Charles Sch., 1964-66, Monash grad. scholarship Monash U., 1980-83. Mem. N.Y. Acad. Scis., Soc. of Petroleum Engrs., Internat. Soc. for Rock Mechanics. Avocations: table-tennis, music, swimming, reading. Home: 1 Genoa St, Dandenong North 3175, Melbourne Australia

CHOI, STEPHEN U.S., mechanical engineer; b. Sunsan, Korea, Feb. 15, 1942; s. Yong Soo and Boon Soon (Cho) C.; m. Sunja Kang, Oct. 20, 1969; children: Samuel, David, John, Paul. BS, Seoul Nat. U., 1964; MS, U. Tex., 1974; PhD, U. Calif., Berkeley, 1978; MDiv, No. Bapt. Theol. Sem., 1997. Asst. prodn. mgr. Monier Papr Mfg. Co., Ltd., Taegu, Korea, 1964-69; assoc. investigator Korea Inst. Sci. and Tech., Seoul, 1969-73; nuclear staff Bechtel Power Corp., San Francisco, 1978-79; staff scientist Lawrence Berkeley Nat. Lab., Berkeley, Calif., 1980-83; mech. engr. Argonne (Ill.) Nat. Lab., 1983—; vis. prof. Purdue U. Calumet, Hammond, Ind., 1990-93; chmn. Internat. Energy Agy. Advanced Fluids Expert Group, 1990-93. Contbr. articles to profl. jours. Mem. ASME, Korean-Am. Scientists and Engrs. Assn., Phi Kappa Phi. Mem. Bible Ch. Achievements include invention of nanofluids, an innovative new class of heat transfer fluids which can be engineered by suspending nanoparticles in conventional heat transfer fluids. Avocations: walking, hiking, reading, meditation, biking. Home: 6413 Pruthmore Ct Lisle IL 60532-3255 Office: Argonne Nat Lab 9700 S Cass Ave Argonne IL 60439-4803

CHOI, YAT MAN, engineering company executive, educator; b. Hong Kong, June 1, 1950; arrived in Australia, 1989; s. Shek Yu and Chun Fong (Pang) C.; m. Suet Kam Leung, Dec. 23, 1983; children: Tin Lun, Tin Kin. BEng with 1st class honours, U. Wales, 1978, PhD, 1982. Lab. technician Sing Yin Secondary Sch., Hong Kong, 1972-75; lectr. Hong Kong Poly. U., 1982-87, sr. lectr., 1987-89; rsch. scientist Def. Sci. and Tech. Orgn., Adelaide, Australia, 1989-90, sr. rsch. scientist, head of sect., 1990-92; prin. lectr., assoc. prof. City U. Hong Kong, 1992-95; dir. ISO-Ing Centre, Hong Kong, 1995—; mem. acad. bd. Hong Kong Poly. U., 1987-89. Contbr. more than 60 articles to profl. jours. Pres. Overseas Chinese Student Assn., U. Wales, 1978-79. Sr. mem. IEEE, Instn. Elec. Engrs. Hong Kong Centre (com. mem. 1995-98), Hong Kong Instn. Engrs. (divsn. rep. electronic divsn. 1994-97, com. mem. 98—, program mgr. and newsletter editor info. tech. divsn. 1995-98). Avocations: literary thinking, swimming, outings, sports. Home: Flat 5 Block R 26/F, Sunshine City Ma On Shan, Shatin Hong Kong China Office: Hong Kong Indsl Tech Ctr, 72 Tat Chee Ave, Kowloon Hong Kong China

CHOI, YEARN-IK, educator; b. Daejun-City, Korea, Nov. 23, 1953; s. Yoon-Sik and Wol-Hang (Yoo) C.; m. Hye-Rhee Chee, Aug. 9, 1982; children: Yoon-Chul, Moon-Chul. BS, Seoul Nat. U., 1976; MS, Korea Advanced Inst. of Sci., Seoul, 1978, PhD, 1981. Postdoctoral rsch. fellow Korea Advanced Inst. of Sci. and Tech., Seoul, 1981-84; rsch. assoc. U. Calif., Berkeley, 1982-84; prof. Ajou Univ., Suwon-City, 1984—. Contbr. more than 100 articles to profl. jours. Mem. IEEE, Soc. for Info. Display, Korea Inst. Elec. Engrs. (editor, awards 1991), Korea Inst. Telematics and Electronics, Korea Acad. Indsl. Tech. (com. 1989—), Internat. Symposium Power Semiconductor Devices (tech. mem. 1994—). Office: Ajou Univ, 5 Wonchun-Dong Paldal-Ku, Suwon 442-749, Republic of Korea

CHOI, YONG-EUI, plant biologist, researcher; b. Kimje-Kun, South Korea, June 29, 1960; s. Kong-In and Rack-Do (Choi) C.; m. Joung-Yeon Han, Apr. 23, 1994; children: Han-Bin, Han-Seok. BSc, Chonbuk Nat. U., Chonju, South Korea, 1994, MSc, 1994, PhD, 1994. Rsch. assoc. Agrl. Biotech. Inst., Suwon, South Korea, 1985-86; tchg. asst. Chonbuk Nat. U., Chonju, 1994-96; postdoctoral rschr. Korea Ginseng Tobacco Rsch. Inst., Taejon, South Korea, 1996-98, rschr., 1998—. Contbr. articles to Plant Cell Reports, Plant Cell Tissue and Organ Culture, Plant Sci., Jour. Plant Biology, Phytomorphology, others. Sgt. South Korean Army, 1986-88. Mem. Korean Soc. Plant Tissue Culture (dir. 1996-98), Agrl. Biotech. Inst., Bot. Soc. Korea, Plant Resources Soc. Korea, Internat. Soc. Plant Morphologists. Christian. Avocations: tennis, playing violin, listening to music. Home: 1314-94 Douckjin-Dong, 561-190 Chonju Republic of Korea

CHOI, YOUNG DEUK, medical educator; b. Seoul, Republic of Korea, May 12, 1961; s. Man Jin Choi and Bok Soon Park; m. Kwang Hee Baek, Oct. 9, 1986; children: Hye Seung, Hye Cho. MD, Yonsei U., Seoul, 1986, MS, 1993, PhD, 1998. Med. diplomate. Intern Coll. Medicine Yonsei U., Seoul, 1986-87, resident Coll. Medicine, 1987-91, instr. Coll. Medicine, 1995-98, asst. prof. Coll. Medicine, 1998—; chief Masan (Rep. of Korea) Hosp., 1991-94; fellow Ewha Woman's U. Mokdong Hosp., Seoul, 1994-95; with Yongdong Severance Hosp., Seoul, 1998. Cons. Chungang mag. health care, 1999, Chosun mag. cancer cons., 1999; contbr. articles to profl. jours. Cons. Befrienders, Seoul, 1998. Grantee Coll. Medicine Yonsei U., 1997, 98, Ginseng grantee Korean Soc. Ginseng, 1999. Mem. Korean Andrology Assn. (dir. 1998), Korean Soc. Urology, Korean Med. Assn., Am. Urol. Assn., Soc. Basic Urol. Rsch. Avocations: golf, driving, antique collection. Office: Dept Urology Kangnam-ku, Dogok-dong Yongdong Severance Hosp, Seoul 135-270, Republic of Korea

CHOI, YOUNG SOO, pharmacologist, toxicologist; b. Chonju, Rep. of Korea, Dec. 20, 1936; came to U.S., 1961; d. Sung Wook and Woo Bok Choi. BS, Chosun U., Kwangju, Rep. of Korea, 1959; MS in Pharmacology, U. R.I., 1963; PhD in Pharmacology, Hahnemann Med. Coll., Phila., 1968. Rsch. asst. U. R.I., 1961-63; rsch. fellow Hahnemann Med. Coll., 1963-65, grad. student instr., 1965-67; postdoctoral fellow Downstate Med. Ctr. SUNY, Bklyn., 1967-68; assoc. rsch. scientist NYU Med. Ctr., N.Y.C., 1969-74; asst. prof. Howard U. Med. Sch., Washington, 1974-76; cons. FDA, Rockville, Md., 1975-76, pharmacologist, 1976-90, expert pharmacologist, 1990-97; guest worker NIH, Bethesda, Md., 1977-80. Mem. Soc. of Toxicology, Korean-Am. Scientists and Engrs. Assn. (mem. editl. bd. 1979), Phi Sigma, Rho Chi. Roman Catholic. Achievements include development of 3 sets of guidelines for toxicity studies required for FDA approval for new drug applications; research in pulmonary surfactants, intralipids, leukotriene antagonists, and immunotoxic and pulmonary drugs. Avocations: gardening, sewing, singing, brush writing, painting. Home: 4200 Warner St Kensington MD 20895-4058

CHOI, YOUNGBOK, engineering educator; b. Pohang, Republic of Korea, May 17, 1959; s. Moonsu and Jungja (Lee) C.; m. Won Kyung Lee, Aug. 17; children: Hyungyoon, Junghyun, Youngeun. B, Kyungbook Nat. U., Republic of Korea, 1984, M, 1988; PhD, Osaka U., Japan, 1996. Engr. LG Electronics Co., Kumi, Republic of Korea, 1984-85; sr. mem. tech. staff ETRI, Taejun, Republic of Korea, 1985-92; asst. prof. Tongmyong U. Info. Tech., Pusan, 1996—. Contbr. articles to profl. jours. Sgt. Army, Pohang, Republic of Korea, 1980-82. Mem. IEEE, Inst. Electronics, Info. and Commn. Engrs., Inst. Electronics Engrs. Korea. Office: Tongmyong U Info Tech, 535 Yongdang-Dong, Nam-Gu Pusan 608-711, Republic of Korea

CHOI, YU-LEUK, civil engineer, retired; b. Guang Dong, China, June 26, 1939; s. Tit-Long and Man-Ching (Ng) Tsoi; m. So-Lang Shiu, Nov. 14, 1975; children: King-Chow, King-Lun. BS in Engring., Hong Kong U., 1960; BS in Math., London U., 1963; ME, NSW U., Australia, 1966; PhD, Cornell U., 1971; postgrad., Henley Mgmt. Coll., Eng., 1991, Tsinghua U., China, 1993. Apprentice engr., asst. engr. Pub. Works Dept., Hong Kong, 1960-64, engr., 1965-71, sr. engr., 1972-77, chief engr., 1978-81; govt. engr. Transport Dept. and Govt. Secretariat, Hong Kong, 1982-87; from deputy project mgr. to dep. dir. Ter. Devel. Dept., Hong Kong, 1987-94; prin. govt. civil engr. Civil Engring. Dept., Hong Kong, 1994-96; dir. bldgs. Bldgs. Dept., Hong Kong, 1996-99, ret., 2000; hon. sr lectr., adj. prof. Hong Kong U., 1983—; external examiner for BEng. honors course Hong Kong Poly. U., 1984-90; examiner profl. exam. Instn. of Civil Engring., U.K., 1984-96, Hong Kong Instn. of Engrs., 1990-96; bd. dirs. Beijing-Hong Kong Acad. Exchange Ctr.; organizer of several internat. confs. and seminars on engring. and urban devel., Hong Kong. Editor: Coastal Infrastructure Development in Hong Kong, 1996, Building Construction in Hong Kong, 1998; contbr. articles to profl. jours. Recipient Postgrad. scholarship Australian Govt., 1965, Overseas Study scholarship Hong Kong Govt., 1968-70. Fellow Inst. Civil Engrs. U.K., Hong Kong Instn. Engrs.; mem. ASCE, Hong Kong Jockey Club. Achievements include creation of LUTO model which is the first operational computer-based planning model for joint optimisation of land use and transport; derivation of Hong Kong's Territorial Development Strategy; planning and management of New Town Development; design and implementation of Hong Kong's new legal requirement of site safety management system on building sites; design and implementation of horizontal drains for slope stabilization; research in thermal stratification, investigation of failure of reinforced concrete balconies and canopies. Home: 3A 205-207 Prince Edward Rd, Kowloon Hong Kong China Office: Nathan Ctr Rm 402 4/F, 580 Nathan Rd, Kowloon Hong Kong

CHOI-CHEUNG, VIVIEN L.F., university administrator; b. Hong Kong, Aug. 25, 1957; d. Kam-man Choi and Man-hing Chan; m. Patrick T.L. Cheung; 1 child, Alvin. BS with honors, Loma Linda U., 1982; MS, Kans. State U., 1984. Food prodn. mgr. Porter Meml. Hosp., 1984-85; dietitian Our Lady of Maryknoll Hosp., Hong Kong, 1985-86; lectr. Hong Kong Polytech U., 1986-88; catering mgr. City U. Hong Kong, 1988-93; dir. campus svcs. Hong Kong U. Sci. & Tech., 1993—; lectr. Hong Kong U., 1997-98; cons. Hong Kong Sports Inst., 1989-90; spkr. in field. Bd. dirs. FS CSI World-wide; contbr. articles to profl. jours. Fellow ADA; mem. FCSI, IACP. Avocations: ethnic cooking, reading, music, travel. Office: CSO HKUST, Clear Water Bay, Kowloon Hong Kong

CHOJNACKI, JULIUSZ C., hydrobiologist, oceanographer, educator; b. Kamionka, Lublin, Poland, Nov. 20, 1943; s. Kazimierz and Janina (Kubacka) C.; m. Elżbieta Żókiewicz, Dec. 25, 1949; children: Anna, Barbara; stepdaughter, Hanna. BS in Marine Fisheries, Agrl. U. Szczecin, 1968, dr. nat. sci., 1976, PhD of Oceanography, 1984. Asst. faculty marine fisheries Agrl. U., Szczecin, Poland, 1968-75, 77-85; asst. Inst. Ecology Antarctic expeditions Polish Acad. Sci., 1975-76, 77-78; assoc. prof. Agrl. U., Szczecin, 1985-91, prof., 1991—; prof. Maritime U. of Szczecin, 1999—; assoc. prof. Internat. Ctr. Ecology, Szczecin, 1996—; pres. Szczecin br. Polish Ecol. Club, 1990-96; head investigations in artificial reefs Polish Found. Scis., Baltic Sea, 1990-96; mem. regl. commn. Nature Protection, 1994—, mem. sci. bd. Wolin Nat. Park, 1997—. Author: Outline of Water Ecology, 1996, Basic in Water Ecology, 1998, Lexicon of Water Ecology, 1999; co-author: What Happened with the Baltic Sea, 1992; contbr. articles to profl. jours. Fellow World Assn. Copepodologists; mem. Polish Acad. Sci. (bd. dirs. com. Marine Investigation, head br. ICE 1996-98, bd. dirs. com. Polar Rsch. 1990—), European Union Coastal Conservation Polish br., European Artificial Reefs Rsch. Network, Biopolitics Internat. Orgn., Polish Hydrobiol. Assn., Polish Union Nature Photographers, Szczecin Assn. Scis., Baltic Marine Biology (chmn. WG 1974-98). Avocations: art, photography, literature, computers, cars. E-mail: marecol@fish.ar.szczecin.pl. Home: Budzysza Wosia 14/1, 71-273 Szczecin Poland Office: Agrl U Dept Marine Ecology, Str Kazimierza Krolewicza 4/H-19, Szczecin Poland also: Maritime U Szczecin Dept Ec, Str Waly Chrobrego 1-2, 70-500 Szczecin Poland

CHOJNOWSKI, JULIAN JOZEF, chemist, educator; b. Warsaw, Poland, June 17, 1935; s. Joseph Richard and Aldona (Wisniewski) C.; m. Alexandra Bebłowski, June 20, 1959; children: Gregory, Justyna. MSc, Łódź (Poland) Tech. U., 1957, PhD, 1963, Habilitation, 1971. Asst. Tech. U., Łódź, 1958-63, adj., 1963-71; postdoctoral rsch. assoc. U. Wis., Milw., 1966-67; assoc. prof., head lab. Polish Acad. Scis., Łódź, 1972-83, prof., head lab., 1983—; vis. prof. U.Sci. and Tech., Montpellier, France, 1982, Ind. U., Indpls., 1989, U. Paris XIII, 1994, 98; cons. Dow Corning Europe, Barry, 1994-99; mem. adv. bd. Main Group Chemistry News, Jour. Inorganic and Organometallic Polymer, 1993-98. Editor: Progress in Organosilicon Chemistry, 1995; contbr. chpts. to books. Grantee Polish Acad. Scis., Warsaw, 1978, 81, 90. Mem. Polish Chem. Soc. (head Lodz divsn. 1998—), Prof. Club. Roman Catholic. Avocations: hiking, boating, skiing. Home: ul Wileńska 36, 94-011 Lodz Poland Office: Polish Acad Scis, ul Sienkiewicza 112, 90-363 Lodz Poland

CHOK, TIMOTHY KON FUI, microbiologist, researcher; b. Tawan, Saban, Malaysia, Apr. 11, 1952; s. Dean Fook Chok and Khiun Kiaw Wong; m. Gek Eng Gon; children: Jun Mei, Jun Lei. B in Applied Sci., U. Malborough, 1998. Mng. ptnr. Kwong Fui, Tawau, Malaysia, 1975-87, Syt Mahkota, Tawau, 1988—. Home: No 3687 Taman Setia, Chong Thien Vun Rd, Tawan 91000, Malaysia Office: PO Box 60240, Tawan 91012, Malaysia

CHOKSY, JAMSHEED KAIRSHASP, historian, religious scholar, language professional, humanities educator; b. Bombay, India, Jan. 8, 1962; arrived in Sri Lanka, 1962; permanent resident, U.S. 1995, naturalized, 1999.; s. Kairshasp Nariman and Freny Kairshasp (Cooper) C.; m. Carol Emma Burnside, Sept. 12, 1993; 1 child, Darius Jamsheed. AB in Mid.-Ea. Langs. and Culture, Columbia U., 1985; PhD in History and Religions, Harvard U., 1991. Tchg. fellow dept. anthropology and archaeology Harvard U., 1988, jr. fellow, 1988-91; vis. asst. prof. depts. history and internat. rels. Stanford U., 1991-93; asst. prof. dept. ctrl. Eurasian studies, India studies, medieval studies, near eastern lang. and cultures, religious studies Ind. U., Bloomington, 1993-97, assoc. prof., 1997-2000; dir. undergrad. studies dept. near Ea. langs. and cultures Ind. U., 1995-99, chmn. dept. near Ea. langs. and cultures, 1999-2000, dir. middle ea. studies program, 1999-2000, prof., 2000—; mem. Sch. Hist. Studies, Inst. for Advanced Study-Princeton, 1993-94; cons. PBS-TV, 1990, L.A. Times, 1998, Am. Mus. Natural History, 1998, Am. Hist. Rev., 1999—; active Ctr. for Advanced Study in the Behavioral Scis., 1999; presenter in field. Author: Purity and Pollution in Zoroastrianism, 1989, Conflict and Cooperation, 1997, Earliest Zoroastrianism, 2000, Archeological Surveys in Pakistan, 1988-90, 1999; contbr. numerous articles to profl. publs. Rsch. fellow Govt. India, Bombay, 1998; John Simon Guggenheim Meml. Found. fellow, 1996-97; resident scholar Ind. U., 1996-97, grantee 1994—, grantee Am. Acad. Religion, 1995-96, Andrew W. Mellon fellow, 1991-93. NEH fellow, Inst. for Advanced Study, Princeton, 1993-94, fellow Royal Asiatic Soc. Great Britain, Ireland. Office: Ind U Dept Near Ea Langs Goodbody Hall 102 1011 E 3rd St Bloomington IN 47405-7005

CHÖLER, ULLA GERTRUD SOPHIA, retired physician, physiotherapist; b. Länghem, Sweden, Aug. 31, 1924; d. Carl Gustaf Ernst Anders Chöler and Kerstin Maria Sophie Sparre of Söfdeborg. MD, Karolinska Inst., U. Stockholm, 1954, MB, 1959. Lic. physiotherapist; cert. specialist in med. and neurol. rehab., cert. specialist in orthopedic surgery. Physiotherapist Stockholm, London, Amsterdam, 1947-52; asst. physician in depts. surgery and neurosurgery Stockholm, 1959-61, asst. physician in depts. orthopedics and rehab., 1961-67; asst. prof. Sch. Physiotherapy, U. Gothenburg, 1967-70; asst. head physician depts. rehab. Gothenburg and Stockholm, 1967-76; head physician dept. orthopedics Hosp. of Skövde, 1976-89; asst. dept. anatomy Royal Caroline Inst., 1953-56; orthopedic cons. of occupational disorders and disability pensions Ins. Med. Offices, County of Stockholm, 1989-94; lectr. in Sweden, U.S. and Tailand, 1964-94. Translator: Fearless Childbirth; contbr. numerous articles to profl. jours. Recipient Athletic Shield/1st prize for sports Örebro, 1943; AAUW scholar, 1970. Mem. Swedish Assn. Physicians, Swedish Orthopedic Soc., Swedish Soc. Head Physicians, Nordic Orthopedic Fedn., Ruth Jackson Orthopedic Soc. Mem. Swedish State Ch. Avocations: skiing, skating, mountaineering, bicycling, swimming.

CHOMSKY, NOAM (AVRAM CHOMSKY), linguistics and philosophy educator; b. Phila., Dec. 7, 1928; s. William and Elsie (Simonofsky) C.; m. Carol Doris Schatz, Dec. 24, 1949; children: Aviva, Diane, Harry Alan. BA, U. Pa., 1949, MA, 1951, PhD, 1955, DHL (hon.), 1984; DHL (hon.), U. Chgo., 1967, Loyola U., Chgo., 1970, Swarthmore Coll., 1970, Bard Coll., 1971, U. Mass., 1973, U. Maine, 1992, Gettysburg Coll., 1992, Amherst Coll., Buenos Aires, 1996, U. Rovira i Virgili, Catalonia, 1998, U. Guelph, Can., 1999, Columbia U., 1999, U. Conn., 1999, U. Toronto, 2000, U. Western Ont., 2000; LittD (hon.), U. London, 1967, Delhi (India) U., 1972,

Visva-Bharati U., Santiniketan, West Bengal, 1980, Cambridge (Eng.) U., 1995; Doctorate (hon.), Scuola Normale Superiore, Pisa, Italy, 1999; LLD, Harvard U., 2000. Mem. faculty MIT, 1955—, prof. modern langs., 1961—, Ferrari P. Ward prof. modern lang. and linguistics, 1966—, Inst. prof., 1976—; vis. prof. Columbia U., N.Y.C., 1957-58; mem. Inst. Advanced Study Princeton U., 1958-59, Am. U. of Cairo, 1993; Linguistic Soc. Am. prof. UCLA, summer 1966; Beckman prof. U. Calif.-Berkeley, 1966-67; John Locke lectr. Oxford U., 1969; Bertrand Russell Meml. lectr., Cambridge, 1971; Nehru Meml. lectr., New Delhi, 1972; Huizinga lectr. U. Leiden, 1977; Woodbridge lectr. Columbia U., 1978; Kant lectr. Stanford U., 1979; Jeanette K. Watson disting. vis. prof. Syracuse U., 1982; Pauling Meml. lectr. Oreg. State U., 1995. Author: Syntactic Structures, 1957, Current Issues in Linguistic Theory, 1964, Aspects of the Theory of Syntax, 1965, Cartesian Linguistics, 1966, Topics in the Theory of Generative Grammar, 1966, (with Morris Halle) Sound Pattern of English, 1968, Language and Mind, 1968, American Power and the New Mandarins, 1969, At War with Asia, 1970, Problems of Knowledge and Freedom, 1971, Studies on Semantics in Generative Grammar, 1972, For Reasons of State, 1973, (with Edward Herman) Counterrevolutionary Violence, 1973, Peace in The Middle East, 1974, Logical Structure of Linguistic Theory, 1975, Reflections on Language, 1975, Essays on Form and Interpretation, 1977, Human Rights and American Foreign Policy, 1978, (with Edward Herman) The Political Economy of Human Rights, 2 vols., 1979, Language and Responsibility, 1979, Rules and Representations, 1980, Lectures on Government and Binding, 1981, Concepts and Consequences of the Theory of Government and Binding, 1982, Towards a New Cold War, 1982, Radical Priorities, 1982, Fateful Triangle, 1983, Turning the Tide, 1985, Barriers, 1986, Knowledge of Language, 1986, Pirates and Emperors, 1986, On Power and Ideology, 1987, Language and Problems of Knowledge, 1987, Language in a Psychological Setting, 1987, Generative Grammar, 1987, Culture of Terrorism, 1988, (with Edward Herman) Manufacturing Consent, 1988, Language and Politics, 1988, Necessary Illusions, 1989, Deterring Democracy, 1991, Chronicles of Dissent, 1992, What Uncle Sam Really Wants, 1992, Year 501, 1993, Rethinking Camelot, 1993, Letters from Lexington, 1993, The Prosperous Few and the Restless Many, 1993, Language and Thought, 1994, World Orders, Old and New, 1994, The Minimalist Program, 1995, Powers and Prospects, 1996, The Common Good, 1998, Profits Over People, 1998, The New Military Humanism, 1999, New Horizons in the Study of Language and Mind, 2000. Recipient Disting. Sci. Contbn. award APA, 1984, Kyoto prize, 1988, George Orwell award Nat. Coun. Tchrs. English, 1987, 89, James Killian faculty award MIT, 1992, Lannan Lit. award for nonfiction, 1992, Joel Seldin Peace award Psychologists for Social Responsibility, 1993, Homer Smith award NYU Sch. Medicine, 1994, Loyola Mellon Humanities award Loyola U., Chgo., 1994, Helmholtz medal Berlin-Brandenburgische Akademie Wissenschaften, 1996, Benjamin Franklin Inst, award, 1999; jr. fellow Soc. Fellows, Harvard U., 1951-55, rsch. fellow Harvard Cognitive Studies Ctr., 1964-67. Fellow AAAS, Brit. Acad. (corr.), Brit. Psychol. Soc. (hon.), Royal Anthrop. Inst. Gt. Britain, Royal Anthrop. Inst. of Ireland, Utrecht Soc. Arts and Scis. (hon.), Gesellschaft für Sprachwissenschaft (hon.), Am. Acad. Philosophy; mem. APA (William James fellow 1990), NAS, Am. Acad. Arts and Scis., Linguistic Soc. Am., Deutsche Akademie der Naturforscher Leopoldina, Assn. for Edn. in Journalism and Mass Comm. (Profl. Excellence award 1991). Home: 15 Suzanne Rd Lexington MA 02420-1831 Office: MIT 77 Massachusetts Ave Cambridge MA 02139-4307

CHON, KYE-SUNG (KAYE CHON), educator; b. Chonju, South Korea, May 25, 1954; came to U.S., 1980; s. Eul-Soo Chon and Chom-Soon Choe; m. Mee-Sook Chon, Apr. 29, 1979; children: June, Harah. BS, Ga. State U., 1984; MS, U. Nev., 1985; PhD, Va. Tech., 1990. CHE, Am. Hotel and Motel Assn. Instr. Va. Tech., Blacksburg, Va., 1986-90; assoc. prof. U. Nev., Las Vegas, 1991-94; prof. U. Houston, 1995—. Editor Jour. Travel and Tourism Mktg., 1991—, Jour. Hosp. and Tourism Rsch., 1995—. Sgt. U.S. Army, 1974-77. Recipient John Wiley and Sons award CHRIE, 1993. Mem. Internat. Soc. Travel and Tourism Educators (Martin Opperman award 1999), Asia Pacific Tourism Assn. (nat. rpe. 1995-99). Avocations: photography, travel. E-mail: kchon@uh.edu. Office: Univ Houston 4800 Calhoun St Houston TX 77204-0001

CHONDROS, THOMAS G., mechanical engineering educator, consultant; b. Lamia, Greece, Oct. 17, 1953; s. George T. and Anastasia (Karapli) C.; m. Sofia Panteliou, Dec. 23, 1982; chi ldren: Irini, Dafni. MS in Mech. Engring., U. Patras, Greece, 1977, PhD in Mech. Engring., 1982. Engring. rschr. Brit. Petroleum of Greece Ltd., Athens, 1978-79; engr. Piraiki-Patraiki SA Cotton Mfg., Patras, 1979-82; plant mgr. Frigorex Abee, Patras, 1983-84; tech. dir. Ministry Transp., Patras, 1984-88; mng. dir. EGL Western Greece Papers Mills SA, Patras, 1989-90; asst. prof. mech. engring. U. Patras, 1990—; cons. Indsl. Reconstrn. Orgn., Athens, 1991-92; vis. prof. Washington U., St. Louis, 1994-95. Lt., Greek Air Force, 1982-83, Araxos Base. Mem. ASME, Soc. Aero. Engrs., Tech. Chamber Greece, Assn. Motor Vehicles Importers Reps. (gen. dir. 1999—). Achievements include design and construction of E-240, the electric mini-car of the University of Patras. Home: Elafonisou 6, 26 442 Patras Greece Office: Univ Patras, Mech and Aero Engring Dept, 261 10 Patras Greece

CHONG, BENG HOCK, hematologist, educator; b. Ipoh, Perak, Malaysia, Oct. 29, 1945; arrived in Australia, 1977; s. Yew Aik and Poh Tin (Quah) C.; m. Saw Gaik Lim; children: James, Phillip. MB BS, U. Malaya, Kuala Lumpur, Malaysia, 1972. Asst. hematologist Royal Melbourne (Australia) Hosp., 1983-86; staff hematologist St. George Hosp., Sydney, 1986-90; sr. staff hematologist Prince of Wales Hosp., Sydney, 1990—; acad. assoc. U. Melbourne, 1984-86; sr. lectr. U. N.S.W., Sydney, 1987-90, assoc. prof., 1990-96, prof., 1997—. Contbr. articles to profl. jours.; editl. bd. Thrombosis and Haemostasis, 1997—. Nat. Health and Med. Rsch. Coun. Australia Program grantee, 1994—, Commonwealth AIDS Rsch. grantee, 1995-97, Australian Agy. for Internat. Devel. Rsch. grantee, 1996—. Fellow Royal Coll. Pathologists of Australasia, Royal Australasian Coll. Physicians, Royal Coll. Physicians (Glasgow); mem. Royal Coll. Physicians (U.K.), Australasian Soc. Thrombosis and Haemostasis (founding mem.), Am. Soc. Hematology, Haematology Soc. Australia. Avocations: tennis, swimming, jogging. Office: Prince of Wales Hosp, High St, Randwick NSW 2031, Australia

CHONG, PAUL JOE, chemist; b. Che-Ju City, Korea, Jan. 7, 1938; s. Tu Jung Chong and Yim Saeng Oh; m. Kyung Rang Hong. BSc in Pharmacy, Seoul (Korea) Nat. U., 1962, MSc in Pharmacy, 1969; MSc in Chemistry, U. Newcastle, Australia, 1978, PhD in Chemistry, 1982. Chemist U.S. Armed Forces Far East Engring. Corps, Seoul, 1965-68; rsch. chemist ACI Tech. Ctr., Sydney, Australia, 1969-72; chief chemist Rutile & Zircon Mines Ltd., Newcastle, Australia, 1973-78; prin. chemist Korean Rsch. Inst. Chem. Tech., Taejon City, 1982—; vis. rschr. Osaka (Japan) U., 1988-89; lectr. Grad. Sch. Chung-Nam Nat. U., Tae-Jon City, 1983-90; vis. prof. Korea U., Sung-Kyun Kwan U., Seoul, 1992-96; external patent examiner Govt. Patent Office, Seoul, 1982-91; vis. rschr. La Trobe (Australia) U., 1996-97. Contbr. articles to profl. jours.; patentee in field. Recipient Commercialization of Zeolite Synthetic Tech. award Korean Ministry of Sci. and Tech., 1992. Fellow Royal Chem. Soc.; mem. Korean Chem. Soc., Am. Chem. Soc. Avocations: horseback riding, tennis, classical music. Office: Korean Rsch Inst Chem Tech, PO Box 107 You-Sung Dauck, Daduck Science Town 305-606, Republic of Korea

CHONG, STEPHEN CHU LING, lawyer; b. Lakewood, Ohio, Aug. 1, 1957; s. Richard Seng Hoon C. and Betty J. (Chong) Wamego; m. Sheryl Kay Horton, Nov. 23, 1984; children: Evan M. G., Erin M.L., Elena M.L., Eric M.K., Ethan M.L. BA, Calvin Coll., 1979; JD, Ohio State U., 1982. Bar: Fla. 1982, U.S. Dist. Ct. (mid. dist.) Fla. 1983, U.S. Ct. Appeals (11th cir.) 1982, U.S. Tax Ct. 1985; bd. cert. real estate lawyer Fla. Bar Bd. Legal Specialization and Edn. Assoc. Caudill, Drage, de Beaubien, Orlando, Fla., 1982-83; shareholder Caudill, Chong & Migliaccio, Winter Garden, Fla., 1983-84; assoc. Thomas R. Rogers & Assocs., Longwood, Fla., 1984-90; of counsel Litchford, Christopher, Orlando, 1990-92; pres., shareholder Marks & Chong, Orlando, 1992—; mem. nominating bd. City of Orlando, 1993-98, chmn. 1996-97; mem. area bus. com. Naval Tng. Ctr. Reuse Com., Orlando, 1994-95; bd. trustees Minority/Women Bus. Enterprise Alliance, Orlando, 1994—; chair Realtor Rels. Com., Orlando, 1992-93; presenter in field. Contbr. articles to profl. jours. Mem. cultural diversity com. Orlando Sci. Ctr., 1993—; mem. cmty. adv. bd. WMFE-TV/FM, Orlando, 1994-95; mem. adv. bd. Ctrl. Fla. Family, Orlando, 1994—; pres. Asian Am. C. of C., Orlando, 1993-94, 1999—; trustee Calvin Coll., Grand Rapids, Mich. Recipient Vision award-Small Bus. Downtown Orlando Partnership, 1994. Mem. ABA, Fla. Bar Assn., Orange County Bar Assn., Christian Legal Soc. Ctr. Fla. (pres. 1999-2000). Presbyterian. Office: Marks & Chong 605 E Robinson St Ste 510 Orlando FL 32801-2045

CHONG, TAI-LEUNG TERENCE, economist, educator; b. Hui An, Fujian, China, July 19, 1968; parents Ngan-Wah and Yuk-Wah Chong. BSSC, Chinese U. Hong Kong, 1991; MA, U. Rochester, 1993, PhD, 1995. Asst. prof. Chinese U. Hong Kong, 1995—; invited seminar spkr. Citibank, Hong Kong, 1999; invited discussant Fin. Sec. Hong Kong, 1998, 99. Contbr. articles to profl. jours. RGC rsch. grantee Hong Kong Govt., 1997, 98; univ. fellow U. Rochester, 1992-95; Sun Han Chang Meml. scholar Chinese U. Hong Kong, 1991. Fax: 852 26035805. E-mail: b792703@mailserv.cuhk.edu.hk. Home: Parc Versailles, Tai Po NT, Hong Kong China Office: Chinese U Hong Kong, Shatin Hong Kong China

CHONG SONG-TAEK, banker. Pres. Ctrl. Bank Dem. People's Republic Korea. Office: Ctrl Bank Dem People's Rep Korea, Munsudong, Ctrl Dist Pyongyang Dem Peoples Republic of Korea*

CHONMAITREE, TASNEE, pediatrician, educator, infectious disease specialist; b. Bangkok, Thailand, Dec. 9, 1949; came to U.S., 1975; d. Surajit and Arporn (Maitong) C.; m. Somkiat Laungthaleong Pong, June 27, 1981; children: Ann L. Pong, Dan L. Pong. BS, Mahidol U., Bangkok, 1971; MD, Siriraj Med. Sch., Bangkok, 1973. Diplomate Am. Bd. Pediatrics, Am. Bd. Pediatric Infectious Diseases. Rotating intern Siriraj Hosp., Bangkok, 1973-74, resident in pediatrics, 1974-75; resident in pediatrics Lloyd Noland Hosp., U. Ala., Birmingham, 1975-78; fellow infectious disease U. Rochester (N.Y.), 1978-81; asst. prof. pediatrics U. Tex. Med. Br., Galveston, 1981-87, asst. prof. pathology, 1985-87, assoc. prof. pediatrics and pathology, 1987-94; prof. pediatrics and pathology, 1994—; assoc. dir. clin. virology lab. U. Tex. Med. Br., Galveston, 1985-92, dir. divsn. pediatric infectious disease, 1985-92. Contbr. 65 articles to profl. jours. Grantee NIH, 1993—. Fellow Am. Acad. Pediatrics, Pediatric Infectious Diseases Soc., Infectious Diseases Soc. Am.; mem. Soc. Pediatric Rsch., European Soc. for Pediatric Rsch., Tex. Infectious Disease Soc. Buddhist. Avocation: classical music. Home: 1906 Cherrytree Park Cir Houston TX 77062-2327 Office: U Tex Dept Pediatrics Med Br Ninth Street & Market Galveston TX 77555-0001

CHOO, DANIEL CHUNG ANN, cardiologist; b. Singapore, Jan. 20, 1965; s. Yoon Kian and Esther Choo; m. Selina Chan. BS, Pacific Union Coll., 1985; MD, Loma Linda U., 1990. Diplomate Am. Bd. Internal Medicine, Nat. Bd. Med. Examiners. Intern in internal medicine Loma Linda U., 1990-91, resident in internal medicine, 1993-95, fellow in cardiovascular disease, 1999—; acting chief of medicine Sir Run Run Shau Hosp., Haunzhon, China, 1995-99. Home: 11824 Saint Andrews Pl Loma Linda CA 92354-4165

CHOO, SHIN JANN, retail business development manager; b. Alor Setar, Kedah, Malaysia, May 24, 1967; parents Saik Eng Choo and Aoi Seok Tan. B of Surveying, U. Tech. Malaysia, 1996. Valuation exec. Henry Bucher, Lim, Long & Teoh (S) Sdn Bhd, Johor Bahru, Malaysia, 1991-92; project exec. The Lion Group, Kuala Lumpur, Malaysia, 1992-94; project mgr. The Lion Group, Beijing, 1994-98; real estate devel. mgr. BP Guangdong Ltd., Guangzhou, China, 1998-2000; retail bus. devel. mgr. BP Guangdong Ltd., Guangzhou, 2000—. Mem. ISM, MIM. Avocations: music, computer, taking photographs. Fax: 8620 87520595. E-mail: ChooShj@bp.com and choosj@sina.com. Home: # 404 Block G8 sec 2, Bdr Baru Wangsa Maju, Kuala Lumpur 53300, Malaysia Office: BP Guangdong Ltd Level 18, Citic Plz 233 Tianhe Bei Lu, Guangdong 510613, China

CHOO, YEN, molecular biologist, researcher; b. Athens, Greece, Aug. 24, 1970; s. Hoey and Alexandra (Avgeropoulou) C. BSc, U. Bristol, Eng., 1991; PhD, U. Cambridge, Eng., 1995. Scientist Med. Rsch. Coun., Cambridge, 1995—; founding scientist, dir. rsch. Gendaq, Ltd. Contbr. articles in profl. jours.; patentee design of DNA binding proteins. Office: Med Rsch Coun, Lab Molecular Bio Hills Rd, Cambridge CB2 2QH, England

CHOOB, VLADIMIR VICTOROVICH, biologist, educator; b. Alma-Ata, USSR, Dec. 3, 1966; s. Victor Ivanovich and Ludmila Deomidovna (Porotnikova) C.; m. Larisa Alexandrovna Axyonova, Dec. 22, 1987; 1 child, Maria Vladimirovna. MS, Lomonosov Moscow State U., 1988, PhD, 1995. Rschr. Lomonosov Moscow State U., 1988-91, asst. prof., 1991-98, assoc. prof., 1998—; lectr. Gymnasium 1543, Moscow, 1991-93. Author: (book) Tractaus de Divisionibus Cellularum, 1995; co-author: (with M. B. Berkenblit) Biology—6, 1991, (with Yu. V. Maleeva) Biology—7, 1993, (with K. D . Lezinak) Pot Plants, 1999. Avocations: gardening, swimming, music. Office: Lomonosov Moscow State U, Dept Plant Physiology, 119899 Moscow Russia

CHOOI, SIMON, R&D engineer, chemistry educator; b. Singapore, May 28, 1965; s. Steven and Sophia (Wong) C.; m. Stacia Tan Chooi, July 1, 1995; children: Chooi, Sarah. BS (hon.), Nat. U. Singapore, 1990, PhD, 1995. Engr. Chartered Semicondr. Mfg., Singapore, 1994-95, sr. engr., 1995-97, group leader, 1997-99, prin. engr., 1999-2000, sr. prin. engr., 2000—. Contbr. articles to profl. jours.; patentee in field. Mem. Singapore Nat. Inst. Chemistry, Electrochem. Soc. Avocations: reading, photography, soccer, travel, jogging. Office: Chartered Semiconductor Mfg, 60 Woodlands Indsl Pk D St2, Singapore 738406, Singapore

CHOOK, EDWARD KONGYEN, university administrator, disaster medicine educator; b. Shanghai, Apr. 15, 1937; s. Shiu-heng and Shuiking (Shek) C.; m. Ping Ping Chew, Oct. 30, 1973; children by previous marriage: Miranda, Bradman. MD, Nat. Def. Med. Ctr., Taiwan, 1959; MPH, U. Calif., Berkeley, 1964, PhD, 1969; ScD, Phila. Coll. Pharmacy & Sci., 1971; JD, La Salle U., 1994. Assoc. prof. U. Calif., Berkeley, 1966-68; dir. higher edn. Bay Area Bilingual Edn. League, Berkeley, 1970-75; prof., chancellor United U. Am., Oakland and Berkeley, Calif., 1975-84; regional adminstr. U. So. Calif., L.A., 1984-90; pres. Pacific Internat. U., Berkeley and Pomona, Calif., and Guam, 1996—, Shanghai Internat. Coll., 1997—; chancellor Bi-Lingual Coll. Zhuhai (China)-Pacific Internat. Joint U., Hong Kong, 1998—; pres. Main Coin Investment Mgmt., LTD., Oakland, Calif., 1999—; mem. staff Pacific Internat. U., Guangdong, 2000—; internat. dir. Silver State Air Corp., Las Vegas, Nev.; vis. prof. Nat. Def. Med. Ctr., Taiwan Armed Forces U., 1982—, Tongji U., Shanghai, 1992, Foshan U., China, 1992—; cons. specialist Beijing Hosp., 1988—; founder, pres. United Svc. Coun., Inc., 1971—; pres. Pan Internat. Acad., Changchun, China and San Francisco, 1979—, China Gen. Devel. Corp., U.S., 1992—; pub. Unity Jour./Power News, San Francisco, 1979—; Goodwill Amb. of Asia, Federated States of Micronesia, 1997—, mem. NAS-NRC, Washington, 1968-71; spl. cons. cultural sensitivity seminars; spl. lectr. KPMG/Peat Warwick Accts., 1996; advisor Ka Wa Bank, Hong Kong, 1986-96. Assoc. editor U.S.-Chinese Times, 1996-98; pub. US-China Times, 1996—, Unity Jour. N.Am. edit., 1996—; contbr. articles to profl. jours. Trustee Rep. Presdl. Task Force, Washington, 1978—; advisor on mainland China affairs Ctrl. Com. Chinese Nationalist party, Taiwan, 1994-97; pres. Oakland Chinese Nationalist Party, 1998—; deacon Am. Bapt. Ch.; sr. advisor U.S. Congl. Adv. Bd.; mem. Presdl. Adv. Commn., 1991—; hon. dep. sec. of state State of Calif., 1990-93; spl. advisor to sec. of state, 1991—; pres. Yuen Kong Found. for Internat. Understanding (aka March Fong EU Found.), 1994-96, 96—; mem. Nat. Heart Coun., 1994—, Capital Hill Club, Washington, 1992—; senatorial commn. Rep. Senatorial Inner Cir., 1996. August 9, 1997 proclaimed Ed Chook Day by City of Oakland. Mem. World Affairs Coun. San Francisco, Rotary (com. chmn. 1971—). Achievements include rsch. on hearing conservation program in U.S. Army, criteria for return to work, principles and practices of nuclear, biol. and chem. weapons. Address: PIU Adminstrn Office 1212 Broadway Ste 808 Oakland CA 94612-1810

CHOONG, PETER FOOK MENG, orthopedic surgeon, educator; b. Kuala Lumpur, Malaysia, Nov. 8, 1961; s. Lee Son and Siew Chin (Quan) C.; m. Kerry Maree Hames, Mar. 21, 1993; children: Emma Lai Peng, Annabelle Lai Cheng, Erika Li Kai. B Medicine B Surgery, U. Melbourne, Australia, 1984, MD, 1994. Vis. surgeon U. Hosp., Lund, Sweden, 1993-94, 95-96; spl. fellow in orthopedic oncology Mayo Clinic, 1994-95; mem. hosp. exec. com. St. Vincent's Hosp., Melbourne, 1997, dir. orthopedics, prof. orthopedics, 1996—, clin. dir. spl. surgery, 1997—; chief clin. advisor in orthopedics, Melbourne, 1997-98. Contbr. articles to profl. jours. John Loewenthal fellow RACS, 1991, rsch. found. fellow, 1992; Gordan Gordan Taylor scholar U. Melbourne, 1993. Fellow Royal Coll. Surgeons; mem. Orthopedic Oncology Soc. Australia (sec.-treas. 1996—), Anz Orthopedic Rsch. Soc. (pres. 1998—), Internat. Soc. Limb Salvage Surgery. Avocations: golf, fly fishing, tennis, wine. Office: 55 Victoria Parade, Fitzroy Victoria 3065, Australia

CHOONG, POH LIAN, electrical engineer, educator; b. Ipoh, Perak, Malaysia, Aug. 17, 1966; d. Soon Kim Choong and Guat Ngoh Yeoh; m. Tendy The, Jan. 27, 1996. BEng with honors, U. Auckland, New Zealand, 1991; PhD, U. We. Australia, Perth, 1996. Software engr. Dominion Svcs. Ltd., Auckland, 1990-91; lectr. engring. U. We. Australia, 1995-98; rsch. scientist DSTO, Adelaide, Australia, 1998—; master and profl. course coord. Ctr. Intelligent Info. Processing Sys., Perth, 1995-98. Contbr. articles to profl. jours. including, Breast Cancer Research & Treatment, Australia Computer Journal, IEEE Transaction of Neural Networks. Recipient Med. Oncology Studentship award Cancer Found. We. Australia, 1992; Stanford Women's fellow Univ. We. Australia, 1996. Mem. IEEE, Inst. Engrs. Australia. Avocations: gardening, camping.

CHOPADE, BALU ANANDA, microbiologist, researcher, educator; b. Salshirambe, India, July 1, 1956; s. Ananda Balu and Yashodha Ananda (Kamble) C.; m. Nalini Ganpatrao Shirolkar, July 10, 1988; children: Snehal, Niraja. BSc, Shivaji U., Kolhapur, India, 1978; MSc, U. Pune, India, 1980; PhD, U. Nottingham, Eng., 1986. Lectr. Shivaji U., Kolhapur, 1980-81; lectr. U. Pune, 1982-83, sr. lectr., 1986-91, reader, 1992-2000, head dept., 1994, 96-2000; rsch. scholar U. Nottingham, 1983-86; prin. investigator Coun. of Sci. and Indsl. Rsch., New Delhi, Pune, 1989-91; coord. Alis Program Brit. Coun. London, Pune, 1994; prin. investigator rsch. projects Univ. Grants Commn., New Delhi and Indian Space Rsch. Orgn., Bangalore, 1999-2001. Contbr. articles to profl. jours. Mem. exhbn. com. Indian Sci. Congress, Pune, 1988. Recipient Best Tchr. award Pune Corp., 1993; Nat. Overseas scholar Govt. India, 1983-86; Fogarty Internat. fellow Fogarty NIH, 1994-96. Mem. Am. Soc. Microbiology, Assn. Microbiologists India (life, sec. Pune AMI unit 1988-91), Soc. Biol. Chem. India (life). Buddhist. Avocations: photography, writing, reading, music, travel. Home: Yashodhan Coop Hsg Soc, Flat 3 Bldg 18C Baner Rd, Pune 411007, India Office: U Pune, Dept Microbiology, Ganeshkhind, Pune 411007, India

CHOPELAS, ANASTASIA, geophysicist; b. Springfield, Mass., Nov. 13, 1952; came to Germany, 1986.; d. Alec Peter and Zafiria C.; m. Reinhard Boehler, July 22, 1984 (div. Dec., 1997); children: Marika Boehler, Alexander Boehler. BS in Chem., UCLA, 1974; MS in Geochem., Cal. Inst. Tech., 1976; PhD in Chem., UCLA, 1981. Rsch. chemist Chevron Oil Field Rsch., La Habra, Calif., 1982-85, TRW, Redondo Beach, Calif., 1985-86; rsch. scientist Max Planck Inst., Mainz, Germany, 1986-99; sr. scientist physics dept. U. Nev., Las Vegas, 1999—; women's advocate Max Plank Inst., Mainz, Germany, 1997-99. Assoc. editor Am. Mineralogist, 1997—; contbr. chpts. to books, articles to profl. jours. Mem. Am. Geophysical Union, Am. Mineral Soc. Greek Orthodox. Avocations: running, guitar, singing. Office: U Nev Physics Dept Las Vegas NV 89154

CHOPIN, SUSAN GARDINER, lawyer; b. Miami, Fla., Feb. 23, 1947; d. Maurice and Judith (Warden) Gardiner; m. M.S. Rukeyser, Jr. Mar. 10, 1997; children: Philip, Alexandra, Christopher. BBA, Loyola U., New Orleans, 1966; JD cum laude, U. Miami, 1972; MLitt (Law), Oxford U., Eng., 1983. Bar: Fla. 1972, Iowa 1979. Sr. law clk. to judge U.S. Dist. Ct. (so. dist.) Fla., Miami, 1972-73; ptnr. Chopin & Chopin, Miami, 1973-77; assoc. prof. law sch. Drake U., Des Moines, 1979-80; pvt. practice law Palm Beach, Fla., 1981—; ptnr. Chopin & Chopin, 1999—. Mem. editorial bd. Fla. Bar Jour., 1975—; contbr. articles to profl. jours., legal revs. Trustee Preservation Found. of Palm Beach, 1986-89. Mem. ABA, Fla. Bar Assn., Iowa Bar Assn., Fed. Bar Assn., Internat. Bar Assn., Fla. Assn. Women Lawyers, Soc. Wig and Robe, Palm Beach County Bar Assn., English Speaking Union, Phi Kappa Phi, Phi Alpha Delta. Office: Esperante Bldg 222 Lakeview Ave Ste 1150 West Palm Beach FL 33401-6149

CHOPPIN, PURNELL WHITTINGTON, research administrator, virology researcher, educator; b. Baton Rouge, July 4, 1929; s. Arthur Richard and Eunice Dolores (Bolin) C.; m. Joan Harriet Macdonald, Oct. 17, 1959; 1 dau., Kathleen Marie. MD, La. State U., 1953; DSc (hon.), Emory U., 1988, La. State U., 1988, Tulane U., 1989, Washington U., 1991, Med. U. S.C., 1995, U. Md., Baltimore County, 1995, U. Mass., 1999, U. Mass., 1999; MD (hon.), U. Cologne, 1988; DSc (hon.), Northwestern U., 1999; MD (hon.), U. Cologne, 1988, D Medicine (hon.), 1988; DHL (hon.), Mt. Sinai Sch. Medicine, 1996; LLD (hon.), St. Francis Xavier U., 2000; DSc (hon.), Rockefeller U., 2000. Diplomate Am. Bd. Internal Medicine. Intern Barnes Hosp., St. Louis, 1953-54, asst. resident, 1956-57; fellow, rsch. assoc. Rockefeller U., N.Y.C., 1957-60, asst. prof., 1960-64, assoc. prof., 1957-60, prof., sr. physician, 1970-85, Leon Hess prof. virology, 1980-85, v.p. acad. programs, 1983-85, dean grad. studies, 1985; v.p., chief sci. officer Howard Hughes Med. Inst., Chevy Chase, Md., 1985-87, pres., 1987-99, pres. emeritus, 2000—; chmn. sect. 43 microbiology and immunology NAS, 1989-92, chmn. class IV med. scis., 1983-86, mem. com. on reorganization structure, 1985-86; coun. Inst. Medicine, 1987-92, exec. com., 1988-91; mem. virology study sect. NIH, 1968-72, chmn. virology study sect., 1975-78; bd. dirs. Royal Soc. Medicine Found. Inc., N.Y.C., 1978-93; mem. adv. com. fundamental rsch. Nat. Multiple Sclerosis Soc., 1979-84; chmn. adv. com. fundamental rsch., 1983-84; mem. adv. coun. Nat. Inst. Allergy and Infectious Diseases, 1980-83; mem. bd. scis., cons. Meml. Sloan-Kettering Cancer Ctr., N.Y.C., 1981-86; chmn. bd. scis., 1983-84; mem. commn. on life scis. NRC, Washington, 1982-87; mem. sci. rev. com. Scripps Clinic and Rsch. Found., La Jolla, Calif., 1983-85, chmn. sci. rev. com., La Jolla, Calif., 1984; mem. coun. for rsch. and clin. investigation Am. Cancer Soc., N.Y.C., 1983-85; mem. com. priorities for vaccine devel. Inst. Medicine, Washington; mem. governing bd. NRC, 1990-92. Contbr. numerous articles to profl. pubs., chpts. on virology, cell biology, infectious diseases to profl. publs., 1958—; editor: Procs. Soc. Exptl. Biology and Medicine, 1966-69; assoc. editor Virology, 1969-72, editor, 1973-86; assoc. editor: Jour. Immunology, 1968-72, Jour. Supramolecular Structure, 1972-75; mem. editorial bd. Jour. Virology, 1972-85, Comprehensive Virology, 1972; mem. overseas adv. panel Biochem. Jour., 1973-77. Capt. USAF, 1954-56, Japan. Recipient Howard Taylor Ricketts award U. Chgo., 1978; Waksman award for excellence in microbiology Nat. Acad. Scis., 1984, Alumni Achievement award Washington U. Sch. Medicine, 1990, Meml. Sloan-Kettering medal for outstanding contbns. to biomed. rsch., 1998, Spl. Recognition award Assn. Am. Med. Colls., 1999; named to alumni Hall of Distinction La. State U., Baton Rouge, 1983, Dean's medal Harvard Med. Sch., 1992. Fellow AAAS; mem. NAS, Am. Acad. Arts and Scis., Am. Philos. Soc. (coun. 1998—), Assn. Am. Physicians, Am. Soc. Clin. Investigation, Am. Soc. Microbiology (chmn. virology div. 1977-79, div. group councilor 1983-85), Harvey Soc., Am. Assn. Immunologists, Soc. Cell Biology, Infectious Diseases Soc. Am., Practitioners Soc. N.Y., Am. Clin. and Climatological Assn., Am. Soc. Virology (pres. 1985-86), Sigma Xi (chpt. pres. 1980-81), Alpha Omega Alpha. Office: Howard Hughes Med Inst 4000 Jones Bridge Rd Chevy Chase MD 20815-6789

CHOPRA, DEEPAK, writer. Author: Return of the Rishi, 1989, Quantum Healing, 1990, Perfect Health, 1990, Unconditional Life, 1991, Creating Health, 1991, Creating Affluence, 1993, Ageless Body, Timeless Mind, 1993, Restful Sleep, 1994, Perfect Weight, 1994, Journey Into Healing, 1994, The Seven Spiritual Laws of Success, 1995, Return of Merlin, 1995, Como Crear Abundancia/How to Create Wealth, 1999, How to Know God: The Soul's Journey into the Mystery of Mysteries, 2000, Everyday Immorality: A Concise Course in Spiritual Transformation, 1999. Office: Chopra Ctr for Well Being 7630 Fay Ave La Jolla CA 92037-4841

CHOPRA, KAMAL NAIN, engineering executive; b. Lahore, Punjab, India, June 6, 1945; s. Tara Chand and Pushpa Wati (Bajaj) C.; m. Sushil Bala Malik, Dec. 10, 1974; children: Rishika, Sonalee, Rakshit. BSc, Delhi U., 1965; MSc, Indian Inst. Tech., Delhi, 1967, MTech, 1969, PhD, 1974. Lectr. Delhi U., 1972; sr. sci. officer Instruments R&D Orgn., Dehradun, India,

1972-79; scientist C, Thin Films Group Def. Sci. Ctr., Delhi, 1980-86, scientist D, 1986-91, scientist E, 1991-96, scientist F, 1996—; vis. scientist Thin Films Lab., U. St. Jerome, Marseille, France, 1984-85; thin films engr. M/S Balzers, Liechtenstein, Switzerland, 1995; thin films coatings technologist Thin Films sect. U. Innsbruck, Austria, 1995. Contbr. more than 85 articles to profl. jours. Indian Inst. Tech. Sr. Rsch. fellow, 1969-72. Mem. Def. Rsch. and Devel. Orgn. Officers Club. Hindu. Avocations: singing, music, sports, fabrication of decorative coatings.

CHOPRA, SAWARAN JIT, engineering company executive; b. Delhi, India, Apr. 29, 1941; s. Sardari Lal and Bimla Wati (Sabharwal) C.; m. Neelam Mehta; two children. B in Chem. Engring., Delhi U., 1962; D in Chem. Engring., IIT, Delhi, 1971. Shift chemist Gwalior Rayons, Nagda, India, 1962-65; prodn. supt. Amsar Pvt. Ltd., Indore, India, 1965-66; sr. rsch. scholar IIT, Delhi, 1966-70; process engr. Engrs. India Ltd., Delhi, 1970-73, sr. engr., 1973-76, supervising engr., 1976-80, sr. mgr., 1980-86, dep. gen. mgr., 1986-92, gen. mgr., 1992-95, exec. dir., 1995-97, dir. (tech.), 1997—. Recipient Independence Day award Nat. Rsch. Devel. Corp., New Delhi, 1987. Mem. Indian Inst. Chem. Engrs. (exec. com. North Indian regional ctr.). Home: 96 Munirka Enclave, New Delhi 110067, India Office: Engrs India Ltd, 1 Bhikaiji Cama Place, New Delhi 110066, India

CHOPRA, VIRENDER LAL, government official, agricultural studies educator; b. Adhwal, Pakistan, Aug. 9, 1936; s. Harbans Lal and Sukwanti C. BSc with honors, Delhi Univ., 1955; PhD, U. Edinburgh, 1967; DSc (hon.), CSA Univ. Agriculture and TEch., India, 1989, Banaras Hindu U., India, 1992. Prof. genetics Indian Agrl. Rsch. Inst., New Delhi, 1970-84, head divsn. genetics, 1974-75, 77-80, dir., prof. eminence biotech. ctr., 1985-90; dir. gen. Indian Coun. Agrl. Rsch. and Sec. Gov. of India, New Delhi, 1992-94; nat. prof. Indian Agrl. Rsch. Inst., New Delhi, 1994—; cons. FAO, chief tech. advisor Govt. Vietnam, Hanoi, 1990-91; sec. Indian Dept. Agrl. Rsch. and Edn., New Delhi, 1992-94; Vice chmn. IBPGR, Rome, 1989, ICRISAT, Hyderabad, 1992; trustee CYMMIT, Mex., 1993, IRRI, Manila, 1994. Contbr. chpts. to books, articles to profl. jours. Recipient Padma Bhushan award Govt. India, 1985; fellow 3d World Acad. Arts and Scis., European Acad. Arts and Scis., 1994. Avocations: reading, cooking. Office: NRC on Plant Biotech, Indian Agrl Rsch Inst, New Delhi 110 012, India

CHOPRA, YASH RAJ, film director; b. Jullundur City, Punjab, India, Sept. 27, 1932; s. Walaiti Ram and Draupadi Chopra; m. Pamela Chopra; children: Aditya, Uday. BA. Founder Yash Raj Films, 1971, Yash Raj Films Pvt. Ltd., 1973; Dir. (films) Dhool Ka Phool, 1958, Dharamputra, 1962, Waqt, 1965, Ittefaq, 1969, Admi Aur Insan, 1970, Joshila, 1973, Deewar, 1975, Trishul, 1978, Parampara, 1992; prodr., dir. (films) Daag, 1973, Kabhi Kabhi, 1976, Kala Patthar, 1979, Silsila, 1981, Mashaal, 1984, Faasle, 1985, Vijay, 1988, Chandni, 1989, Lamhe, 1991, Darr, 1993, Dil to Pagal Hai, 1997. Prodr. (films) Doosra Aadmi, 1977, Noorie, 1979, Sawaal, 1981, Nakhuda, 1981, Aaina, 1993, Yeh Kilagi, 1994, Dilwale Dulhania Le Jayenge, 1995. Recipient 5 Nat. awards, 7 Filmfare awards. Mem. Film Prodrs. Guild India. Fax: 91-22-6113460/6116714. E-mail: distribution@yashrajfilms.com. and YRFilmsUK@aol.com. Home: 21 Adityodaya 12th Rd, JVPD Scheme, Juhu Mumbai 400049, India Office: Yash Raj Films Pvt Ltd, 17 Vikas Park, Juhu Mumbai 400049, India*

CHOQUETTE, WILLIAM H., construction company executive; b. Webster, Mass., Jan. 9, 1941; s. Paul J. and Virginia (Gilbane) C.; m. Lynn Devaney, Aug. 12, 1967; children: William, Madeleine. B.A., U. Notre Dame, 1962; M.B.A., Columbia U., 1966. Field supt. Gilbane Bldg. Co., Providence, R.I., 1966-68, asst. adminstrv. mgr., 1968-71, mgr. sales engring., 1971-75, v.p. bus. devel., 1975-79; v.p., regional mgr. Gilbane Bldg. Co., Landover, Md., 1980-82, sr. v.p., regional mgr., 1982—, sr. v.p., dir. federal mktg., 1991—; sr. v.p., Gilbane Properties, Bethesda, Md., 1993—. Co-chmn. United Way Prince George's County, Md., 1983, 84, Corp. heroes' chmn., 1985; mem. steering com. Greater Washington Bd. Trade, 1983, 84, co-chmn. planning and devel. com., 1986-87; bd. dirs. Wash. area chpt. Boy Scouts Am. Explorers div.; chmn. Nat. Capitol Area; mem. enterprise task force Greater Balt. Com., 1983. Served to 1st lt. Signal Corps, U.S. Army, 1962-64. Mem. Washington Bldg. Congress (bd. govs. 1982-88). Home: 7704 Glendale Rd Bethesda MD 20815-4908 Office: Gilbane Bldg Co 4330 East West Hwy Ste 314 Bethesda MD 20814-4408 also: Gilbane Bldg Co 7 Jackson Walkway Providence RI 02903-3623

CHORBA, TIMOTHY A., former ambassador to Singapore; b. Yonkers, N.Y., Sept. 23, 1946. BA magna cum laude, Georgetown U., 1968; JD, Harvard U., 1972. Bar: N.Y. 1973, D.C. 1977. Legis. counsel to Hon. Jonathan B. Bingham U.S. Ho. of Reps., 1972-73; ptnr. Patton, Boggs & Blow, Washington, 1977-94, 98—; amb. to Singapore, 1994-97. Fulbright scholar in Internat. Law and Internat. Rels., U. Heidelberg, West Germany, 1968-69. Mem. D.C. Bar, Phi Beta Kappa, Coun. Am. Ambs. Office: Patton Boggs 2550 M St NW Washington DC 20037-1301

CHOROT, PALOMA, clinical psychologist, lecturer; b. Madrid, June 4, 1959; s. Jose Luis Chorot and Carmen Raso. PhD in Psychology, U. Nacional Edn. Distancia, Madrid, 1986. Researcher U. Nacional Edn. Distancia, Madrid, 1981—, prof. psychodiagnostics, 1983-89, prof. psychopathology, 1986—. Author: Researches on Skin and Salivary pH and its Relationship with Anxiety and Phobic Fear, 1982, Experimental Studies About the Incubation Model of Fear, 1983—, Theorists Work at Psychological Assessment, 1983; advisor Internat. Jour. Psychosomatics, Phila, 1984, Revista de Psicopa tologia y Psicologia Clinica, 1996; contbr. articles to profl. jours. Mem. Internat. Psychosomatics Inst., Soc. Espanola de Psicopatologia y Psicologia Clin., Assn. Espanola de Estres y Ansiedad. Achievements include research on stress, emotional, psychosocial variables on cancer and screening, anxiety sensitivity and panic disorders, and psychosomatics disorders. E-mail: pchorot@psi.uned.es. Home: C/Serbal # 3, 28023 Madrid Spain Office: U Nacional Edn Distancia, PO Box 60148, 28040 Madrid Spain

CHORUS, ROGIER, federal official; b. Nijmegen, Gelderland, The Netherlands, Aug. 7, 1943; s. Alfons Chorus and Herma Borgers; m. Mirjam Meijer, May 30, 1973; children: Felix, Caspar, Sarah. LLM, Leiden U., 1967. Trainee, account mgr. ABN Bank, Rotterdam, The Netherlands, 1970-74; adminstr. Ministry of Finance, The Hague, The Netherlands, 1975-80; dir. internat. rels. Netherlands Christian Employers' Assn., The Hague, 1980-90; sec. gen. Cerame-Unie, Brussels, Belgium, 1990—. Contbr. articles to profl. jours. Chmn. Soc. European Affairs Practitioners, Brussels, 1997—; treas. Union European Federalists, Brussels, 1997—; bd. dirs. Verbond Kristelyke Werkgevers Mechelen. Capt. The Netherlands Infantry, 1976-90. Roman Catholic. Office: Cerame-Unie, Rue Les Colonies 18-24, 1000 Brussels Belgium

CHOTARD, THIERRY JEAN, mechanical engineer, educator; b. La Rochelle, France, Mar. 27, 1964; s. Rodolphe and Jeanine (Lemmo) C.; m. Roxana Ghodsnia, July 20, 1996. BS, Inst. U. de Tech., Limoges, France, 1984; DEST, Conservatoire Nat. Des Arts et Metiers, Paris, 1991; diploma in engring., U. Tech. Compiegne, France, 1994, MS, 1994; PhD in Mech. Engring. with honors, UTC, Compiegne, France, 1997. Technician GEC-Alsthom, France, 1987-89; engr. Jaeger, France, 1989-92; asst. prof. U. Limoges, 1998—. Contbr. articles to profl. publs. 1st lt. French Air Force, 1986-87.

CHOU, C. PERRY, chemical engineering educator; b. Taipei, Taiwan, July 26, 1962; m. H. Jennifer Wu, July 2, 1988; 1 child, Stephen. BS, Nat. Taiwan U., 1984, MS, 1988; PhD, Rice U., 1995. Assoc. rschr. Union Chem. Lab., Hsinchu, Taiwan, 1987-90; assoc. prof. Feng Chia U., Taichung, Taiwan, 1995—; cons. Yung Shin Pharm. Co., Taichung, 1996-97, Plant Evaluation Project, Taichung, 1996—, EPA, Taiwan, 1997—, Miaoli. Editor Bioindustry, 1998—; contbr. articles to profl. jours. 2d lt. Chinese Air Force, 1984-86. Office: Feng Chia U Chem Engring, 100 Wenhwa Rd, Taichung 407, Taiwan

CHOU, CHEN-CHIA, mechanical engineering educator, researcher; b. Hualien, Taiwan, Aug. 16, 1959; s. Chin-Tsai and Tsau-May (Hwang) C.; m. Fan-yi Li, Aug. 11, 1988; children: Liyoung, Liling. Bachelor, Chiao Tung U., Hsinchu, Taiwan, 1981; master, Sun-Yat-Sen U., Kaohsiung, Taiwan, 1983; PhD, U. Ill., 1990. Postdoctoral rsch. assoc. U. Ill., Champaign, 1990-92, vis. asst. prof., 1992; assoc. prof. Nat. Taiwan U. of Sci. and Tech., Taipei, 1992-99, prof., 1999—; cons. Tex. Instrument, Taipei, Taiwan, 1994. Contbr. articles to profl. publs. Recipient First Prize Polaroid Corp., 1992. Mem. Chinese Ceramic Soc. (Young Scholar medal 1998), Am. Ceramic Soc., Chinese Soc. for Materials Sci. Avocations: photography, swimming, camping. Office: Nat Taiwan U Sci/Tech, 43 Keelung Rd Sec 4, 106 Taipei Taiwan

CHOU, CHUNG KUAO, radiologist; b. Taichung, Taiwan, May 25, 1957; s. Zen Tee and Su Fan (Chu) C.; m. Mei Lian Wu; children: Y. Scarlet, Y. Robert, Y. Elizabeth. B in Medicine, Kaohsiung (Taiwan) Med. Sch., 1982; MPH, Johns Hopkins U., 1987. From resident to attending staff Dept. Radiology Kaohsiung Med. Coll., 1987-93; attending staff Radiology Dept. Chi Mei Found. Hosp., Tainan, Taiwan, 1993—. Contbr. articles to profl. jours. Buddhist. Office: Chi Mei Found Hosp Radiol, 901 Chung Hwa Rd, Tainan 710, Taiwan

CHOU, DAVID CHENDER, computer science, educator; b. Taichung, Taiwan, Apr. 30, 1953; s. Yun-chang and Yu-ing (Liu) C.; m. Amy Y. Chou, June 7, 1981; children: Ann, Beverly. BA, Feng-chia U., 1978; MS, Nat. Taiwan U., 1980, Ga. State U., 1987; PhD, Ga. State U., 1987. Cert. computer profl. Instr. Overseas Chinese Bus. Coll., Taichung, Taiwan, 1978-80; grad. rsch. asst., instr. Ga. State U., Atlanta, 1982-87; asst. prof. No. State U., Aberdeen, S.D., 1987-88; asst. prof., assoc. prof., prof. West Tex. A&M U., Canyon, 1988—; prof. St. Cloud (Minn.) U., 1998—; cons. Corp. Sys., Amarillo, Tex., 1993—. Contbr. articles to profl. jours. Recipient Recognition award Tex. Instruments, Inc., 1993. Mem. IEEE Computer Soc., Internat. Chinese Info. Sys. Assn. (pres. 1997), Assn. Chinese Mgmt. Edn. (v.p. 1997-98, pres. elect 1999, pres. 2000), Decision Scis. Inst. (Southwest coun. 1992-96, sec. 1996-99). Avocations: sports, music. Office: Dept BCIS St Cloud State U Saint Cloud MN 56301

CHOU, JASON LUCAS, chemist, technology company executive; b. Yanji, Xinjiang, China, June 30, 1957; came to the U.S., 1982; s. Zuo Qing and Mei Fang (Luo) Zhou; m. Wenting Yu Chou, June 14, 1986; children: Eric Lawrence, Kevin Richard. BS in Chemistry, U. Sci. and Tech. China, 1981; PhD in Polymer Chemistry, U. Md., 1987; MBA in Internat. Bus., Washington Internat. U., Wayne, Pa., 2000. Tchg. asst. U. Md., College Park, 1982-83, rsch. asst., 1982-87; sr. rsch. chemist PPG Industries, Allison Park, Pa., 1987-92; scientist, project leader Henkel Corp., Ambler, Pa., 1992-96; internat. tech. mgr. Henkel Corp., Ambler, 1997-99; asst. gen. mgr. Shanghai (China) Henkel Oleochemicals, 1996-97; gen. mgr. Material Innovation, Lenonia, N.J., 1999—; founder, pres. East West Tech., Dresher, Pa., 1994—. Contbr. articles to profl. jours. Mem. Am. Chem. Soc. Achievements include patents for Fluorine Containing Polymer Having A Terminal Ester Group, Fluorine Containing Polymers and Coatings Compositions, Curing Agents for Aqueous Epoxy Resins (2); research interest include synthesized monomers for ring opening polymerization with low shrinkage or expansion; designed, developed and commercialized products for coatings, adhesives, additives, textiles, cables and hydraulic fluids applications. Avocations: reading, sightseeing, golf, fishing, carpentry. Office: East West Tech 712 Castlewood Dr Dresher PA 19025-2014

CHOU, KUO-CHEN, biophysical chemist; b. Guangdong, China, Aug. 14, 1938; came to U.S., 1980; s. Hsiu-Chi Chou and Bi-Kun Luo; m. Wei-Zhu Zhong, Apr. 12, 1968; 1 child, James Jeiwen Chou. BS, Nanking (Peoples Republic China) U., 1960, MS, 1962; PhD equivalent, Shanghai (Peoples Republic China) Inst. Biochemistry, 1976; DSc, Kyoto (Japan) U., 1983. Jr. scientist Shanghai Inst. Biochemistry, Chinese Acad. Sci., 1976-78, assoc. prof., 1978-79; vis. assoc., prof. Chem. Ctr. Lund (Sweden) U., 1979-80; vis. assoc. prof. Max-Planck Inst. Biophys. Chemistry, Göttingen, Fed. Republic Germany, 1979-80; vis. assoc. prof. chemistry Cornell U., Ithaca, N.Y., 1980-83, sr. scientist Baker Lab., 1984-85; vis. prof. biophysics U. Rochester, N.Y., 1985-86; sr. scientist Eastman Kodak Co., Rochester, 1986-87, Upjohn Labs., Kalamazoo, Mich., 1987-94, Pharmacia & Upjohn, Kalamazoo, 1995—. Editor Jour. Molecular Sci., 1983-86, Progress in Physics, 1981-85; mem. editl. bd. Current Peptide and Protein Sci., 2000—; contbr. more than 200 rsch. articles and rev. papers to profl. jours. Recipient Sci. and Tech. award Shanghai Com. of Sci. and Tech., 1977, Nat. medal of Sci., Nat. Acad. of Sci., China, 1978, Disting. Leadership award Am. Biog. Inst., N.C., 1989, Commemorative medal of Honor, Am. Biog. Inst., 1991; named for Leadership and Achievement, Internat. Biog. Ctr., Cambridge, U.K., 1990. Fellow Am. Inst. Chemistry; mem. AAAS, N.Y. Acad. Scis., Biophysical Soc., Am. Chem. Soc., Sigma Xi. Achievements include rsch. in protein conformation and folding; graph theory in chem. reaction systems; enzyme kinetics; DNA codon usage analysis; prediction of protein cellular location and structural class; structure and function of antifreeze protein; prediction of HIV protease cleavage site; low-frequency collective motions of biomacromolecules and their biol. functions; structures of growth hormone and membrane proteins, proton-pumping mechanism of membrane proteins, inhibition kinetics of HIV reverse transcriptase, structure and binding site of adhesion proteins, apoptosis, cyclin-dependent kinases, molecular mechanism of Alzheimer's Disease, prediction signal peptides and their cleavage sites. Home: 7088 Arbor Valley Ave Kalamazoo MI 49009-8540 Office: Pharmacia & Upjohn Labs Computer-Aided Drug Discov 301 Henrietta St Kalamazoo MI 49007-4940

CHOU, LOUIS SHENG-TSI, science administrator, educator; b. Taipei, Taiwan, Mar. 18, 1944; s. Chin-Bao and Gea Chen C.; m. Maria Ih-Shin Chang, Sept. 21, 1968; children: Andy Shao-Bin, Paula An-Ting. BS, Nat. Taiwan U., Taipei, 1967; MS, U. Mass., 1971; PhD, U. Maine, 1973. Prof., chmn., dir. Nat. Chiao-Tung U., Hsinchu, Taiwan, 1974-81; dir. gen. Nat. Youth Commn., Taipei, Taiwan, 1981-83; dir. Coord. Coun. North Am. Affairs, L.A., 1984-87; dir. gen. Ministry Transp. and Comms., Taipei, 1987-94, 95—; chmn. TAISEL, Taipei, 1994-95; researcher Taiwan Rsch. Inst., Taipei, 1993—. Contbr. articles to profl. jours. 2d lt. Republic of China Army, 1967-68. Mem. China Liquid Crystal Soc. (pres. 1995-99), Chinese Cath. Culture Assn. (sec. gen. 1975—), Chinese Sci. and Tech. Mgmt. Assn. (bd. dirs. 1995—). Avocations: kung-fu, soccer, basketball. Office: Ministry Transp and Comms, 2 Chang Sha St Sec 1, 1001 Taipei Taiwan

CHOU, RICHARD CHUNWAH, neuroscientist; b. Tsuen Wan, Hong Kong, Apr. 27, 1964; came to U.S., 1989; s. Sun Po and Hoy Tei (Chiu) C. BS (hon.), Chinese U. Hong Kong, 1987; PhD in Pathology, SUNY, Buffalo, 1995. Instr. dept. pathology SUNY, Buffalo, 1994-95, postdoctoral fellow dept. neurology, 1995-97, rsch. scientist neurology, 1997—, instr. dept. neurology, 1995—. Contbr. articles to profl. jours. Lam Oi Tong fellow, 1987-88; Mark Diamond Rsch. grantee, 1993-94, Sigma Xi grantee, 1994-95. Mem. N.Y. Acad. Scis., Soc. for Neurosci., Sigma Xi. Achievements include research on relationship between neural function and the inflammatory response during experimental arthritis; cell cycle regulation in astrocytes and its implications in neurological disorders. Avocation: jogging. Office: SUNY-Buffalo Dept Neurology 646 Biomed Rsch Bldg Buffalo NY 14214

CHOU, WUSHOW, computer scientist, educator; b. Shanghai, Kiangsu, China, Feb. 12, 1939; m. Lena Sun, Apr. 17, 1965; children: Warren, Wesley. BEE, Cheng Kung U., Tainan, Taiwan, 1961; MEE, U. N.Mex., 1965; PhD in Elec. Engring. and Computer Sci., U. Calif., Berkeley, 1968. Acting asst. prof. U. Calif., Berkeley, 1968-69; v.p. Network Analysis Corp., Glen Cove, N.Y., 1969-76; vis. prof. SUNY, Stony Brook, 1976; rsch. prof. George Washington U., Washington, 1975-76; prof. computer sci. dept. and elec. and computer engring. dept. N.C. State U., Raleigh, 1976—, dir. computer studies, 1976-88; dep. asst. sec. for info. systems U.S. Dept. Treasury, Washington, 1994-97, chief info. officer, 1996-97; vis. prof. Poly. U., Bklyn., 1988-89; pres. ACK Computer Applications, Cary, N.C., 1978-93; cons. AT&T, IBM, U.S. Govt., Singapore Govt., French Govt, over 40 corp. and other internat. corps. and orgns. Author, editor: Computer Communication, Vol. 1, 1984, Vol. 2, 1985, Advances in Telecommunication, 1985-88; editor in chief Jour. of Telecom., 1982-85, IT Profl., 1998—; contbr. over 70 articles to profl. jours. and confs. Recipient award GSA, Washington, 1988, Treasury Dept., 1997; rsch. grantee NSF, 1978, rsch. grantee Army Rsch. Office, Research Triangle Park, N.C., 1982, rsch grantee AT&T, 1987. Fellow IEEE, Assn. Computing Machines. Office: NC State U Dept Computer Sci PO Box 8206 Raleigh NC 27695-0001

CHOU, YUNG-MING, lawyer; b. Tainan, Taiwan, Jan. 29, 1959; came to U.S., 1985; s. Ming-Chien and Hong-Hsi Chou; m. Chueh Wang; 1 child, Hsueh-Ting. LLB, Fu Jen Cath. U., Taipei, Taiwan, 1981; M of Criminal Justice Adminstrn., Oklahoma City U., 1986, JD, 1993. Bar: Calif. 1994, N.Y. 1994, U.S. Dist. (no. dist.) Calif. 1995, U.S. Dist. Ct. (ctrl. dist.) Calif. 1996, U.S. Tax Ct. 1998. In-house legal counsel, claim adjuster The First Ins. Co., Ltd., Taipei, 1983-85; lectr. Taiwan Police Coll., Taipei, 1988-89; claims mgr. Ins. Co. N.Am., Taipei, 1987-91; copr. counsel Aces Rsch., Inc., Fremont, Calif., 1994-96; pvt. practice Yung-Ming Chou, Atty. at Law, Fremont, Calif., 1995—. Recipient Dr. Sun Yat Sen scholarship Kuomintang, Taipei, 1991-93; named Amb. at Large, Oklahoma City Mayor, 1986, Hon. Citizen, Oklahoma City Mayor, 1986. Mem. Alameda County Bar Assn. Office: 39111 Paseo Padre Pkwy Ste 207 Fremont CA 94538-1695

CHOUARD, CLAUDE HENRI, surgeon; b. Paris, July 3, 1931; s. Pierre and Denise (Petit-Dutaillis) C.; m. Isabelle Sainflou, July 7, 1959; children: Christophe, Mathieu, Julien, Clement. Prof. ear, nose & throat U. Paris, 1962—. Mem. French Med. Acad. Home: 10 Bd Flandrin, F-75116 Paris France Office: Hosp St Antoine, 187 rue du FBG, F-75012 Paris France

CHOUBEY, VEERENDRA KUMAR, research scientist; b. Jabalpur, Madhya, India, Apr. 30, 1952; s. Ishwari Prasad and Ramwati Mishra Choubey; m. Rani Veerendra Choubey, Mar. 10, 1984; children: Varun, Vani. BS, Jabalpur U., 1973, MS, 1976; P.G. Diploma, Indian Inst. Tech., 1978; Doctorate, Jawaharlal Nehru U., India, 1990. Air photo interpreter Min. of Home Affairs, New Delhi, 1980-87; scientist Nat. Inst. of Hydrology, Roorkee, India, 1987—. Author numerous articles on remote sensing applications in hydrology. Recipient Nat. Hydrology award Nat. Inst. Hydrology, 1995, Cert. Appreciation, Rotary, 1979. Mem. Internat. Assn. Hydrol. Scis., Indian Soc. Remote Sensing (life), Indian Assn. Hydrologists (life). Office: Nat Inst Hydrology, 247 667 Roorkee UP, India

CHOUDHURI, P.C., veterinarian educator; b. Nov. 5, 1941; s. Sri Kaibalya Choudhuri; m. Sandhya, 1974; children: Snigdharani, Siddhartha. BVSc&AH with honors, Orissa Vet. Coll., Bhubaneswar, 1963; MVSc, U.P. Coll. Vet. Sci., Mathura, 1968; PhD, Ctrl. Drug Rsch. Inst., Lucknow, 1973; ISc, Khalikote Coll., Berhampur. Veterinary asst. surgeon Orissa, 1963-66; jr. rsch. fellow U.P. Coll. Veterinary Sci., Mathura, 1966-68; rsch. asst. Orissa Biological Products Inst., Bhubaneswar, 1968-70; sr. rsch. fellow Cen. Drug Rsch. Inst., Lucknow, 1970-73; asst. prof. G.B. Pant Agricultural U., Pantnagar, 1973-78; assoc. prof. internal medicine Coll. Veterinary Sci., Punjab Agrl. U., Ludhiana; prof. head dept. medicine Coll. Veterinary Sci., Acharya N.G. Ranga Agrl.U, India, 1982—; prin. Coll. Vet. Sci., Tirupati, 1995-97. Author: (books) Veterinary Clinician's Guide, Management and Care of Dogs; mem. editl. bd. Indian Jour. Veterinary Medicine, The Orissa Veterinary Jour., The Indian Jour. Idigenous Medicine, Advances in Agrl. Rsch. in India, others. Recipient Narayana Rao Gold medal, Indian Soc. Veterinary Medicine, 1992, State Best Tcrh. award, Govt. Andhra Pradesh, Dr. K.S. Nair Meml. prize, Indian Veterinary Assn., certificate of merit, Indian Soc. Veterinary Medicine. Fellow Indian Soc. Veterinary Medicine (life mem., gen. sec./treas.), Nat. Acad. Veterinary Sci.; mem. APAU Tchrs. Assn. (pres., bd. mgmt.). Home: 5-1-75 (G) SD Rd, Tirupati 517 507, India

CHOUDHURY, ANWARUDDIN, civil servant; b. Shillong, Meghalaya, India, Oct. 25, 1958; s. Alauddin and Shaukatunnessa (Mazumder) C.; m. Bilkis Begum, Apr. 1994; 1 child, Jevian Farhin. BA in Geography with honors, B. Borooah Coll., Guwahati, India, 1981; MA in Geography, Gauhati U., 1985, PhD in Primatology, 1989. Exec. magistrate Govt. Assam, Guwahati, 1983-88, rsch. officer, 1988; dep. dir. Welfare of Plains Tribes & Backward Classes, Guwahati, 1988-89; sub-divisional officer Govt. Assam, Dhakuakhana, 1989-91; addl. dist. magistrate Diphu, 1991-92; project dir. Dist. Rural Devel. Agy., Tinsukia & Lakhimpur, 1992-95; dep. sec. Cooperation Dept., Guwahati, 1996—; CEO The Rhino Found., Guwahati, 1995—; adviser WWF-India N.E. Regional Office, Guwahati, 1996—; mem. waterbird spl. group World Conservation Union, Switzerland, 1996—, mem. Asian Rhino spl. group, 1997—. Author of 8 books and monographs; contbr. articles to profl. jours. Mem. Bombay Natural History Soc., Oriental Bird Club, N.Y. Acad. Scis. Home: Islampur Rd, Guwahati 781 007, India Office: The Rhino Found, G Bordoloi Path Bamunimaidn, Assam 781 021, India

CHOUDHURY, DILIP KUMAR, physicist, educator; b. Pakowa, Assam, India, Sept. 1, 1946; s. Dandi Ram and Hemlata (Datta) C.; m. Nilima Niogi, Aug. 7, 1974; children: Sanghamitra, Subhamitra. BSc with hons., Cotton Coll., Guwahati, India, 1965; MSc, Delhi U., 1967, PhD, 1970. Postdoc. Delhi U., 1970-71; overseas fellow Oxford (Eng.) U., 1971-74; sr. rsch. assoc. Daresbury (Eng.) Lab., 1974-76; vis. fellow Tata Inst. of Fundamental Rsch., Bombay, 1976-78; from lectr. to reader Gauhati U., Guwahati, India, 1978-88; prof. Gauhati U., Guwahati, 1988—, head dept. physics, 1993-95, head computer ctr., 1994-95; consulting panel sci. tech. All India Radio, Guwahati, 1995-96; assoc. Internat. Ctr. for Theoretical Physics, Triste, Italy, 1992-98. Author: Elementary Particle, 1985, Lives and Works of Five Nobel Prize Winning Physicists, 1988, Science Series for Children, 1990, Science and Scientists in India and Abroad, 1995. V.D. Thawani fellow Assam Sci. Soc., 1988; recipient Kamal Kumari Nat. award Kamal Kumari Found., 1994. Mem. Indian Physics Assn. (life), N.Y. Acad. Sci., Physics Acad. N.E. (v.p. 1998—). Hindu. Avocations: cycling, reading, music. Home: 51 Univ Campus, Guwahati 781014, India Office: Dept Physics, Gauhati Univ, Guwahati 781014, India

CHOUDHURY, NABAJYOTI, osteopath, medical educator; b. Tezpur, Assam, India, Dec. 1, 1959; s. Narendra Chandra and Lily (Das) C.; m. Nandita Das, Apr. 24, 1989; children: Khushboo Nabajyoti Choudhury, Pradumnya Nabajyoti Choudhury. MBBS, Gauhati Med. Coll., India, 1982; PhD, Inst. Med. Edn. and Rsch., Chandigarh, India, 1991. Lic. med. doctor, osteopath. Intern, jr. resident Gauhati Med. Coll., Assam, India, 1983-85; osteopathic tutor, 1986; rsch. scholar Postgrad. Inst. Med. Edn. and Rsch., Chandigarh, India, 1986-90; sr. resident Sanjay Gandhi Postgrad. Inst. Med. Scis., Lucknow, India, 1991-92, asst. prof., 1992-96, assoc. prof., 1996—. Author: (book chpt.) Transfusion Safety in Components; contbr. articles to profl. jours. Marie Curie fellow Commn. of European Cmty., Brussels, 1995-96. Mem. Internat. Soc. Blood Transfusion, Am. Assn. Blood Banks, Indian Soc. Blood Transfusion & Immunohematology (life), Indian Soc. Hematology & Blood Transfusion (life). Home: Rupnagar Kumarpara, Gauhati Assam 781009, India Office: Sanjay Gandhi Postgrad Inst, Rae Barely Rd, Lucknow 226014, India

CHOUDHURY, NAMITA ROY, polymer scientist, educator; b. Calcutta, India, July 14, 1960; arrived in Australia, 1994; d. Samarendra Nath Roy and Jyotirmoyee Roy Choudhury; m. Naba Kumar Dutta; Nov. 20, 1990; 1 child, Ankit K. Dutta. BSc in Chemistry with honors, Lady Brabourne Coll., Calcutta, 1980; B in Tech., U. Calcutta, 1983, M in Tech., 1985; PhD, Indian Inst. Tech., Kharagpur, 1991. Tech. officer Himalay Rubber Products Ltd., India, 1984-86; rsch. assoc. Indian Inst. Tech., Kharagpur, 1989-91; vis. rsch. scientist Nat. Ctr. for Sci. Rsch., Mulhouse, France, 1991-93; sr. rsch. scientist Royal Mica Insulating Co., India, 1993-94; rsch. engr. Royal Melbourne (Australia) Inst. Tech., 1994-96; sect. leader Ian Wark Rsch. Inst., Australia, 1996—. Contbr. chpt. to book, articles to profl. jours. Mem. Royal Australian Chem. Inst., N.Am. Thermal Analysis Soc., Polymer Processing Soc., Am. Chem. Soc. Fax: 61-8-8302-3683. Office: U S Australia, Ian Wark Rsch Inst, Adelaide 5095, Australia

CHOUDUM, SHESHAYYA ANJINAYYA, mathematics educator, researcher; b. Manvi, Karnataka, India, Feb. 12, 1947; s. Anjinayya and Lakshmi C.; m. Uma Peddakotla, Dec. 1, 1976; children: Meenakshi, Vidya. Secondary sch. leaving cert., Govt. Sch., Manvi, India, 1963; BSc, P.C. Jabin Coll., Hubli, India, 1967; MSc, Karnataka U., Dharwar, India, 1969; PhD, Indian Inst. Tech., Madras, 1975. Lectr. Madurai (India) U., 1978-85, reader, 1985-93; asst. prof. Indian Inst. Tech., Madras, 1993-95, assoc. prof., 1995—. Author: A First Course in Graph Theory, 1986. Commonwealth Acad. Staff fellowship Assn. Commonwealth Univs., London, 1996. Mem. Ramanujan Math. Soc. Avocations: reading, watching sports, carpentry, gardening. E-mail: sac@acer.iitm.ernet.in. Home: C4-5 3rd Cross Rd, 600 036 ITT Madras Tamil Nadu, India Office: IIT, IIT Dept Math, 600 036 Madras Tamil Nadu, India

CHOUE, YOUNG SEEK, university administrator, association executive; b. Unsan, Korea, Nov. 22, 1921; s. Man Duk and Kook Soo (Kang) C.; m. Chung-Myung Oh, Oct. 26, 1942; children—Chung Won, Ryo Won, Mi Yun, In Won. LL.B., Seoul Nat. U., 1950; LL.D., U. Miami, 1959; Dr. Pub. Service (hon.), Ohio No. U., 1977; D.H.L. (hon.), N.C. Central U., 1983. Pres., founder Kyung Hee U., Seoul, 1955, Su Won Campus Kyung Hee U., 1979, Inst. Internat. Peace Studies, Seoul, 1979; chmn. Korean Assembly Reunion 10 Million Separated Families; pres. Global Coop. Soc. Club Internat.; pres. Inst. Brighter Soc.; perpetual pres. emeritus Internat. Assn. Univ. Pres.; chmn. bd. trustees Ko Whang Found. Kyung Hee U. Author: The Creation of a New Civilized World, 1951; Reconstruction of the Human Society, 1975; Oughtopia, 1979; World Peace: The Great Imperative, 1981. Gov. Korean Dist. Civitan Internat., 1975; internat. advisor Internat. Peace Acad., 1983. Recipient Highest award of Humanities World Congress Humanities, 1974; Moran Decoration of Highest Nat. Order, Pres. Korea, 1975; Gt. World Peace award Internat. Assn. Univ. Pres., 1981; Priz Internat. Dag Hammarskjold in Cultural Merit Pax Mundi Found., Belgium, 1983. Mem. Chinese Writers' Assn. (medal of culture 1962), Am. Assn. State Colls. and Univs. (Internat. Ednl. Leadership award 1975). Club: GCS Internat. Home: 7-36, 1-ka Myungryun-dong, Chongro-ku, Seoul 110, Republic of Korea Office: Office of Chancellor Kyung Hee Univ, 1 Hoiki-dong dongdaemunku, Seoul 130-701, Republic of Korea*

CHOUEKA, YAACOV, computer science educator, consultant; b. Cairo, Egypt, June 16, 1936; arrived in Israel, 1957; s. Aharon and Sarina (Dishi) C.; m. Sara Choueka; children: Aharon, Avi, Yinon, Renanit, Yehonatan, Roey, Elyasaf, Shirat. MSc with distinction, Hebrew U., 1962, PhD, 1971. Faculty dept. math. and computer sci. Bar Ilan U., Ramat Gan, Israel, 1964—, prof. computer sci., 1990—; head Inst. for Info. Retrieval and Computational Linguistics Faculty of Natural Scis., 1975—; head, prin. investigator Response Project, 1975-86; invited rschr. Bellcore, N.J., 1979-80; head, prin. investigator Rav-Milim Project, Hebrew Computational Linguistics, 1988-97; invited prof. dept. computer sci. Inst. for Medieval Studies U. Montreal, Can., 1979-80; spkr. in field. Editor-in-chief: Rav-Milim Complete Dictionary of Modern Hebrew, 6 vols., 1997; contbr. numerous articles to profl. publs. Capt Tsahal-Israeli Army, 1962-65. Recipient 15 grants; recipient Annual prize Israel Info. Processing Assn., 1981, 92; (with others) Israel Prime Minister prize, 1997. Office: Bar Ilan U, Ramat-Gan, 52900 Ramat-Gan Israel

CHOUKAS-BRADLEY, JAMES RICHARD, lawyer; b. Hartford, Conn., Sept. 11, 1950; s. William Lee and Paula Ann (Elliott) Bradley; m. Melanie Rose Choukas, June 21, 1975; children: Sophia Crane, Jesse Elliott. BA cum laude, U. Vt., 1974; JD cum laude, Georgetown U., 1980. Bar: D.C. 1980, U.S. Ct. Appeals (D.C. cir.) 1981, U.S. Ct. Appeals (11th cir.) 1984, U.S. Ct. Appeals (10th cir.) 1985, U.S. Ct. Appeals (4th cir.) 1990. Reporter, editor The Berlin (N.H.) Reporter, 1974; editor, pub., creative dir. Ad Lib, Gorham, N.H., 1974-75; asst. to city mgr. City of Berlin, 1975-77; legal intern Congl. Budget Office, Washington, 1978; rsch. assoc. Schlossberg-Cassidy & Assocs., Washington, 1978-80; assoc. Miller, Balis & O'Neil, P.C., Washington, 1980-84, mem., v.p., 1985—, mem. exec. com., 1993-97; legal advisor, first v.p. Sugarloaf Citizens Assn., Barnesville, Md., 1987-2000; counsel Mcpl. Gas Authority of Ga., Natural Gas Acquisition Corp. of City of Clarksville, Tenn., S.E. Ala. Gas Dist., Mcpl. Gas Authority of Miss.; gen. counsel Tenn. Energy Acquisition Corp., Lower Ala. Gas Dist.; spkr. in field; pioneer in joint action and pub. financing in deregulated natural gas industry. Author: The Early Days, 1975. Pres. D.C. Dukes Athletic Club, Washington, 1978-81, Montgomery Dukes, 1987-92; com. chmn. Berlin Bicentennial Commn., Berlin, 1975-76; youth soccer coach Seneca Sports Assn. Regents scholar State of N.Y., 1968. 278-553d. Energy Bar Assn., Nat. Youth Sports Coaches Assn., Sugarloaf Citizen Assn., Randolph Mountain Club, Sugarloaf Citizens Assn., For a Rural Montgomery, Phi Beta Kappa. Avocations: softball, guitar, songwriting, hiking, travel.

CHOUKROUN, JACQUES ANDRE, ambulance and fire service physician, commander; b. Oujda, Morocco; s. Lucien and Daniele (Chekroun) C.; m. Françoise Breitenstein; children: Mathieu, Pierre, Rose, Jean. MD, Lariboisiere St. Louis, Paris, 1984; specialist in Emergency Medicine, Pr Saint Marc, Rennes, France, 1986; specialist in Disaster Medicine, Pr Larcan, Nancy, France, 1988; Medicine for Underwater Diving, Frejus St Raphel, France, 1991; Method and Reasoning Tactics, Nat. Sch. Officers sapeurs-po, Nainville Les Roches, France, 1993; Hyperbaric Medicine, Pr Achard, Angiers, France, 1995. Pvt. practice gen. medicine Mamers, France, 1985—; MD emergency dept. Ctr. Hosp., Mamers, 1997—; med. captain Fire and Ambulance Svcs., Le Mans, France, 1986; med. commander Fire and Ambulance Svcs., Le Mans, 1995. Mem. Am. Coll. Emergency Physicians, Soc. Francophone d'Urgence Medicale. Avocations: riding (mil. and jumping), motor biking. Office: Emergency Dept, Ctr Hosp de Mamers, 72600 Mamers France

CHOULIS, NICOLAS H., pharmacy educator; b. Athens, Greece, Nov. 17, 1930; Divorced 1986. BPharm, U. Athens, Athens, 1958; PhD, U. London, London, 1964. Vis. tchr. U. London, 1964; rsch. assoc. U. Kansas, 1964-65; assoc. prof. U. Houston, 1965-70; prof. U. W.Va., 1970-79, U. Athens, 1979—; cons. WHO, 1973—; dean Sch. Pharm., U. Athens, 1982-96; pres. European Union Com. on Pharmacy Edn., 1988-92. Author: (book) Pharmaceutical Technology, 1982, Laboratories in Pharmaceutical Technology, 1984, Identification of Drugs of Abuse, 1978; contbr. 145 articles to profl. jours. Recipient Mead Johnson Rsch. award, 1966, Lederle Pharmacy Faculty award, 1967, Danford Found. fellow, 1978. Mem. Greek Pharm. Soc. (pres. 1980—), Greek Antismoking Soc. (sec. gen. 1986—). Greek Orthodox. Home: P.O. Box 51173, 14510 Kifissia Greece Office: Sch Pharmacy, U Athens, 15771 Athens Greece

CHOUNG, JUNG TAE, investment banker; b. Kwangju City, Rep. of Korea, May 10, 1959; s. Soo Sun Choung and Young Im Lee; m. Ji In Chang, Apr. 21, 1990; children: Jiae, Jisoo. Diploma, St. Aldates Coll., Oxford, Eng., 1985; DMS, U. Hertfordshire, Hertford, Eng., 1986; MBA, Brunel U., London, 1989. Qualified mgmt. cons., Korea Productivity Ctr. Head of mergers and acquisitions Tong Yang Securities, Seoul, Korea, 1989-94; head of investment banking and fin. instns. ING Bank, Seoul, 1994-97; asst. dir. Asian Securitization Group, ING Barings, Hong Kong, 1997-98; head Deutsche Bank, Seoul, Korea, 1998-2000; pres. TG Corp., Korea, 2000—; CFO KVC Net Group, Korea, 2000—; Lectr. Korea Productivity Ctr., 1990—, Fedn. Korean Industries, 1996—. Author: Strategic Management of Mergers and Acquisitions, 1989, International Mergers and Acquisitions, 1989. Sgt. Korean Marine Corps., 1980-82. Mem. Mergers and Acquisitions Experts Assn. Avocations: golf, travel, climbing, swimming. Home: 133-103 Olympic Athlete Apt, 89 Bangie-dong Songpa-ku, Seoul Korea Office: Haesung 1 Bldg Fl 3, 942 Daech 3-dong, 135-725 Kangnam-ku Seoul, Korea

CHOURAKI, LUCIEN, rheumatologist; b. Tunis, Tunisia, Mar. 2, 1931; s. Joseph and Rachel (Aidan) C.; m. Monique Bessudo, Mar. 19, 1966; children: Olivier, Laurent, Heloise. MD, Faculte de Medicine, Paris, 1962. Extern Paris hosps., 1950-55, intern, 1956-62; practice medicine specializing in rheumatology Paris, 1964—; cons. Hopital Cochin, Paris, 1964—, Hopital Rothschild, Paris, 1964-94. Served as lt. French Air Force Med. Service, 1957-59. Jewish. Home and Office: 37 Ave de Lowendal, 75015 Paris France

CHOUSSAT, MARC HENRI, power company executive; b. Suresnes, France, Sept. 8, 1962; s. Jean and Claire (Zizine) C.; m. Nathalie Ours, July 17, 1999; 1 child, Penelope. MBA, Columbia U., 1990; M, Ecole Nat. des Ponts/Chaussees, Paris, 1986. Prin. Booz Allen & Hamilton, Paris, 1990-98; v.p. M&A, Alstom, Paris, 1999; dir. Abb-Alstom Power, Brussels, 1999—. Office: AAP, 489 Ave Louise, B1050 Brussels Belgium

CHOUTEAU, CHRISTIAN, physician; b. Paris, France, Jan. 24, 1929; s. Ernest and Alice (Durinck) C.; m. Nichole Richard, July 28, 1954; children: Dominique, Philippe, Didier, Anne, Cecile. MD, U. Paris, 1956. Interne Hosp. de St. Briex, France, 1954-57; practice medicine Penvenan, France, 1958—; medecin attache Hosp. de St. Brieuc anexe de Trestel, Trevou, France, 1965—; pres. various med. assns. Served to capt. French mil., 1957-58. Mem. Assn. Formation Médicale Continue de Lannion (founder, pres. 1967), Fedn. Régionale Assns. Enseignement Médicale Continue de Bretagne (founder, sec. gen. 1979, pres. 1982—), Cunseil Régional de Formation Médicale Coninue de Bretagne (founder, pres. 1982—, pres. fundraising com.), Bd. Observatoire Régional de Santé de Bretagne (past v.p.), Commn. Études Médicales de Bretagne, Conseil Adminstrn. Union Nat. Formation Médicale Continue (del. de la Bretagne á Paris), Syndicat Mèdecins (v.p.), Conf. Syndicats Médicaux Français (regional del.).

CHOW, AMY, gymnast, Olympic athlete; b. San Jose, Calif., May 15, 1978. Mem. USA Team, Hamamatsu, Japan, 1993, World Championships Team, Dortmund, Germany, 1994, Pan Am. Games Team, Mar del Plata, Argentina, 1995, U.S. Olympic Team, Atlanta, 1996. Placed 1st vault U.S. Gymnastics Championships, Ohio, 1992, 1st all around, vault, uneven bars, balance beam, 2d floor exercise, Mex. Olympic Festival, 1992, 3rd all around, vault, 1st floor exercise, USA/Japan Competition, Hamamatsu, Japan, 1993, 3rd vault Coca-Cola Nat. Championships, Nashville, Tenn., 1994, 1st vault, 2d uneven bars, 3rd all around Pan Am. Games, Mar del Plata, Argentina, 1995; recipient Gold medal Women's Gymnastics Team competition and Silver medal uneven bars, Olympic Games, Atlanta, 1996. Office: care USA Gymnastics Pan American Plaza 201 S Capitol Ave Ste 300 Indianapolis IN 46225-1058

CHOW, AMY HAU KUEN, lawyer, contract negotiator, consultant; b. Hong Kong, Hong Kong, May 31, 1963; d. Yun-Yin and Lin-Wan (Wong) C. B in Social Scis., U. Hong Kong, 1985; M in Japanese Bus. Studies, Chaminade U., Honolulu, Hawaii, 1987; B in Law, Beijing (China) U., 1996. Bar: solicitor Hong Kong, solicitor Eng. and Wales. Tchg. asst. Chinese U. of Hong Kong, 1985-86; officer Fuji Bank Ltd., Hong Kong, 1987-88; asst. to gen. mgr. Devel. Co., Ltd., Hong Kong, 1988-90; trainee solicitor Peter C. Hong, Chow & Chow Solicitors, Hong Kong, 1992-94; solictor and China gen. counsel Counselors at Large Ltd., Hong Kong, 1994-95; sr. contract consultant Hewlett Packard Asia Pacific Ltd., Hong Kong, 1995-98; asst. solicitor Johnston Stokes & Master, Hong Kong, 1998, Jenken Chan & Ptnrs., Hong Kong, 1999; legal mgr. Beijing Oriental Plaza Co., 1999—; bd. dirs. Chediston Co., Ltd., Hong Kong, 1993—; cons. Cal Internat. Ltd., Hong Kong, 1996—. Sec. The Incorporated Owners of Happy Ct., Hong Kong, 1995-97; chairlady Owners of Happy Ct., Hong Kong, 1997-98; mem. St. Andrew's Ch. Choir. Named Model Teenager of Hong Kong, Island Jaycees, Hong Kong, 1978; recipient Fujitsu scholarship, Fujitsu Ltd., Honolulu, Tokyo, 1986-87. Mem. The Law Soc. Hong Kong, Hong Kong Lawyers Tng. Course Alumni Ltd. (bd. dirs. 1995-98, v.p. Happy Valley Hong Kong 1998-99), Rotary Club (dir. comty. svcs. Happy Valley, Hong Kong 1996—). Mem. Anglican Ch. Avocations: squash, badminton, swimming, scuba diving. Home: Flat A 6th Fl Happy Ct, 39E Sing Woo Rd, H Valley Hong Kong China Office: 6F Beijing Tower, 10 East Chang An St, Beijing 100006, China

CHOW, CELIA CHUNG, physics educator; b. Jinghua, Zhejiang, China, May 25, 1940; d. Tin Wen and Shang Chew Chung; m. David Chow, Nov. 28, 1968. BS, Taiwan Cheng-Kung U., Tainan, Taiwan, 1962; MS, U. Detroit, 1965; PhD, U. Ill., 1970. Asst. prof. Conn. State U., New Britain, 1968-73, assoc. prof., 1973-92, prof. physics, 1992—; cons. NSF, Washington, 1986, 99; test writer Grad. Record Exam, Princeton. Contbr. articles to profl. jours. Rsch. grantee AAUP, 1985, 92, 93, 95. Mem. AAUW (chair ednl. found. 1993—), Am. Assn. Physics Tchrs. E-mail: chow@ccsu.edu. Office: Conn State U Stanley St New Britain CT 06050

CHOW, CHARN KI KENNETH, lawyer; b. Hong Kong, Oct. 3, 1953; s. Edmund Wai-Hung and Tak-Ching (Poon) C.; m. Priscilla Wai-Man Li, Dec. 19, 1987. LLb, London U., 1976, LLM, 1976. Admitted to English Supreme Ct., 1979, Hong Kong Supreme Ct., 1980. Articled clk. Messrs. Slaughter & May, Eng., 1977; solicitor Edmund W. H. Chow & Co., Hong Kong, 1980; ptnr. Edmund W. H. Chow & Co., 1982-88; pvt. practice law Hong Kong, 1988—; barrister Middle Temple, U.K.; part-time lectr. U. Hong Kong Sch. Law, 1980-83, hon. lectr., 1983-85; lectr. and cons. in field; cons. All China Law Assn. (Inst. for Rsch. on Hong Kong Law); hon. pres., legal advisor Chinese Reform Assn., convenor Rsch. Group on Trans 1997 Hong Kong Laws; mem. Prep. Com. for Hong Kong Spl. Adminstrv. Region (sub-group on law, sub-group on fin. and economy); spl. dir., legal advisor China Coun. for Promotion of Area Devel.; mem. Inland Revenue Bd. Rev.; cons. China Assn. Oriental Culture Studies. Cons. editor The Company Lawyer jour., Asian Pacific Comml. Lawyers; English cons. editor China Law Quar.; freelance contbr. to profl. jours., newspapers and mags. Mem. Basic Law Cons. Com., Hong Kong, nat. com. Chinese People's Polit. Cons. Conf. China; exec. legal cons. Wushu Union Ltd.; hon. pres. Hong Kong Badminton Assn.; legal advisor Hong Kong United Youth Assn. Ltd. Mem. Chinese Brit.-Returned Students Assn., Queen Mary Coll. Grads. Assn. (past pres.), U London Grad. Assn. (past pres.), Chinese Gen. c. of C. (bd. dirs.). Avocations: badminton, Chinese martial arts (Wushu), computers, music, operatic vocal arts.

CHOW, FRANKLIN SZU-CHIEN, obstetrician, gynecologist; b. Hong Kong, Apr. 15, 1956; came to U.S., 1967; s. Walter Wen-Tsao and Jane Ju-Hsien (Tang) C. BS, CCNY, 1977; MD, U. Rochester, 1979. Diplomate Am. Bd. Ob-Gyn. Intern Wilmington (Del.) Med. Ctr., 1979-80, resident in ob-gyn, 1980-83; practice medicine specializing in ob-gyn Vail (Colo.) Valley Med. Ctr., 1983—, chmn. obstetrics com., 1984-85, 86-87, chmn. surg. com., 1987-88, vice chief of staff, 1989-91, chief of staff, 1991-92. Named to Athletic Hall of Fame, CCNY, 1983. Fellow Am. Coll. Ob-Gyn's; mem. AMA, Colo. Med. Soc., Intermountain Med. Soc. (pres. 1985-86), Internat. Fedn. Gynecol. Endoscopists, Am. Assn. Gynecol. Laparoscopists, Gynecologic Laser Soc., Am. Soc. Colposcopy and Cervical Pathology. Avocations: skiing, swimming, photography. Home: P O Box 5657 274 Beard Creek Rd C3 Vail CO 81658-5657

CHOW, HUMPHREY WAI, mechanical engineer; b. Hoi Ping, Canton, China, Feb. 7, 1954; came to U.S., 1972; s. Lai and Ming-Kuen (Wong) C.; m. Joanna Qi Deng, Nov. 17, 1988; children: Genevieve Daisy, Daphne Jolie. BSME, U. Mass., Lowell, 1978; MS, Ga. Inst. Tech., 1984; PhD, Rensselaer Poly. Inst., 1993. Product design engr. GE Co., Rome, Ga., 1979-82; mech. design engr. GE Co., Pittsfield, Mass., 1984-85; rsch. asst. Rensselaer Poly. Inst., Troy, N.Y., 1985-87; sr. mech. design engr. GE Co., Schenectady, N.Y., 1987-90; teaching asst. Rensselaer Poly. Inst., Troy, 1990-93; dynamic analysis engr. GE Co., Fitchburg, Mass., 1993-94; method devel. engr. Knolls Atomic Power Lab., Schenectady, 1994-96; staff engr. GE Aircraft Engines, Lynn, Mass., 1996-98, 99—; lead engr. GE Deutschland, Frankfurt, Germany, 1998-99. Contbr. articles to profl. jours. including European Jour. Mechanics. Mem. ASME, AIAA. Achievements include patents for rotor coil connectors of turbine generators; design of propulsion turbine generator for the Navy's integrated electric drive program; method development for nuclear fuel and core design analysis in the naval reactors program; metal forming process; modeling of fan and compressor airfoils manufacturing for aircraft engines. Office: GE Aircraft Engines 1000 Western Ave Lynn MA 01910-0001

CHOW, LUNG-HEN HENRY, laboratory project manager; b. Keelung, Taiwan, Feb. 24, 1958; s. Jui-Chien and Yu-Hwa C. (Chang) C.; m. Chin-Yun Sun, Mar. 14, 1993; children: Johann, Jo Ann. BSME, Chung Yuan Christian U., Chungli, Taiwan, 1980; MS in Applied Mechanics, Lehigh U., 1982, PhD in Mech. Engring., 1988. Assoc. prof. cert., Min. Edn., Republic of China. Rsch. asst. Computer Aided Design Lab./Lehigh U., Bethlehem, Pa., 1984-88; specialist Hung Hui Tech., L.A., 1988-89; rschr. Flow Measurement Lab./Ctr. for Measurement Stds., Hsinchu, Taiwan, 1989-90; sect. mgr. liquid flow sect. Ctr. for Measurement Stds., Hsinchu, 1990-92; project mgr. Flow Measurement Lab./Ctr. for Measurement Stds., Hsinchu, 1992—; assoc. prof. dept. Chung Yuan U., Chungli, Taiwan, 1991-92; com. mem. Exam. Com. for Type Approval of Watermeter, Nat. Bur. Stds. Ministry Econ. Affairs, Taipei, 1992—; presenter in field. Contbr. articles to profl. jours. Mem. ASME, The Chinese Metrology Soc. Presbyterian. Avocations: tennis, jogging, golfing, pottery arts. Home: 3rd Fl 20 Lane 181, An Ho Rd Sect 2, Taipei 10663, Taiwan Office: Ctr for Measurement Stds, 321 Kuang Fu Rd Sect 2, Hsinchu 30042, Taiwan

CHOW, NAN-HAW, pathologist; b. Taipei, Taiwan, Oct. 9, 1958; s. Jin-Chi and Ging-Ing (Hwang) C.; m. Ying-Chen Wang, Jan. 7, 1989. MD, China Med. Coll., Taichung, 1983; MS, Nat. Taiwan U., Taipei, 1986. Intern Vets. Gen. Hosp., Taipei, 1981-83; resident Nat. Taiwan U. Hosp., Taipei, 1983-86; teaching asst. Nat. Taiwan U., Taipei, 1983-86; resident Nat. Cheng Kung U. Hosp., Tainan, 1988-89; asst. prof. Nat. Cheng Kung U., Tainan, 1989-96, assoc. prof., 1996—; staff pathologist Nat. Cheng Kung U. Hosp., Tainan, 1989—. Contbr. articles to profl. jours. Mem. Am. Assn. Clin. Chemistry, U.S. and Can. Acad. Pathology, Am. Assn. Cancer Rsch. Avocations: music, tea-pot collecting, making tea. Office: Nat Cheng Kung Univ Hosp, Dept Pathology, 704 Tainan Taiwan

CHOW, RAYMOND, entertainment company executive; b. Hong Kong. BS in Journalism, St. Johns' U., 1949. Reporter Hong Kong Standard, Voice of Am., Hong Kong, 1951-59; publicity mgr., head prodn. Shaw Bros. Film Studio, Hong Kong, 1959-69; chmn. Golden Harvest Entertainment (Holdings) Ltd., Kowloon, Hong Kong, 1970—. Prodr. films The Big Boss, Enter the Dragon, Amsterdam Kill, The Boys in Company C., Cannonball Run, 1980 (Showman of Yr. award, Golden Horse award), Teenage Mutant Ninja Turtles. Fax: 852-2351-1683. Office: 8 King Tung St, Hammerhill Rd, Fu Shan Kowloon Hong Kong*

CHOW, TOMMY WAI-SHING, electronic engineering educator; b. Hong Kong, Apr. 27, 1959; naturalized U.K. citizen; s. Tim Kai and Poon Mei (Chan) C.; m. Shui Kit Law, Dec. 24, 1984; children: Adrian H.Y., Ian H.H. BSc with 1st class honours, U. Sunderland, Eng., 1984, PhD, 1988. Chartered engr., U.K. Undergrad. trainee NEI Reyrolle Tech. Orgn., Hebburn, Eng., 1983; rsch. asst. U. Sunderland, 1985-88; lectr. electronic engring. City U. Hong Kong, 1988-92, sr. lectr., 1992-95, assoc. prof., 1995—; invited lectr. Hong Kong Sci. Mus., 1998, also others; host radio series Info. Comm. and Computer Tech., Radio TV Hong Kong, 1998; reviewer internat. jours.; cons. Foilbourn Enterprise Ltd., Hong Kong, 1990, Kowloon-Canton Rlwy. Corp., Hong Kong, 1992-93, Pulse Ltd., Dung Goon, China, 1995, Mass. Transit Rlwy. Corp., Hong Kong, 1997, Fed-Supremetech Co. Ltd., Hong Kong, 1997; collaborative rschr. Royal Obs. Hong Kong, 1994-96, Internat. R & D Co. Ltd., Newcastle-upon-Tyne, Eng., 1985-88; collaborative R & D cons. Hong Kong Electric Co. Lt.d, 1993-95; expert W.K. To&Co Solicitors, Hong Kong, 1998; tech. referee Hong Kong Govt. Industry Dept., 1998; tech. reviewer Univ. Grant Com. (H.K.) on Rsch. Grant Allocation, 1998; mem. Occupl. Safety and Health Coun. on Electronics and Comm., Hong Kong, 1998—. Contbr. articles to intrnat. jours., including IEEE Trans. on Neural Networks, IEEE Trans. on Circuits and Sys., IEEE Trans. on Indsl. Electronics, IEEE Trans. on Sys., Man and Cybernetics, Computer Jour., Neural Processing Letters, Engring. Application Artificial Intelligence, Internat. Jour. Knowledge Based INtelligent Engring. Sys., Signal Processing, Neural Computing, Artificial Intelligence, Internat. Jour. Electronics, Jour. South China U. Tech. Natural Sci., Wear, also numerous conf. procs. Strategic rsch. grantee, 1989, 91, 94, 96, 98. Mem. IEEE, Instn. Elec. Engrs. U.K. (undergrad. scholar 1983), Hong Kong Instn. Engrs. (vice chmn. control automation and instrumentation divsn. 1996-97, chmn. 1997-98). Baptist. Avocations: tennis, football, reading. Office: City U Hong Kong Dept Elec, Engring, Tat Chee Ave, Kowloon Hong Kong China

CHOW, VINCENT TAK-KWONG, biomedical scientist, educator; b. Georgetown, Penang, Malaysia, Sept. 3, 1958; arrived in Singapore, 1978; s. Michael and Maureen (Li) C.; m. Mei-Choo Loke, Dec. 16, 1984; children: Joel, Jerome, Clara-Anne. MB BS, Nat. U. Singapore, 1983, PhD, 1991, MD, 1996; MSc, U. London, 1986; diploma in microbiology, U. Coll. London, 1987. Registered Singapore Med. Coun., Gen. Med. Coun. U.K. House officer Ministry of Health, Singapore, 1983-84, med. officer, 1984; sr. tutor Nat. U. Singapore, 1984-91, lectr., 1991-93, sr. lectr., 1994-98, assoc. prof., 1998—; mem. adv. com. biotech. exhbn. Singapore Sci. Ctr., 1991-95; vis. scientist Japan Soc. for Promotion of Sci., 1991, 97. Contbr. over 60 articles to sci. publs. Vol. lectr. Singapore Cancer Soc., 1992—. Overseas grad. scholar, 1985-87; acad. rsch. grantee Nat. U. Singapore, 1985—; Asian Molecular Biology Orgn. fellow, 1991; recipient Murex Virologist award Asia Pacific Soc., 1995. Mem. Internat. Soc. for Infectious Diseases, N.Y. Acad. Scis. Roman Catholic. Achievements include British patent for detection of dengue and other flaviviruses using NS3 gene primers and probes; isolation of novel human genes HEP-COP, DENN, Huel. Avocations: reading, motoring. Office: Nat U Singapore, Kent Ridge 117597, Singapore

CHOW, WINSTON, engineering research executive; b. San Francisco, Dec. 21, 1946; s. Raymond and Pearl C.; m. Lilly Fah, Aug. 15, 1971; children: Stephen, Kathryn. BSChemE, U. Calif. Berkeley, 1968; MSChemE, Calif. State U., San Jose, 1972; MBA cum laude, Calif. State U., San Francisco, 1985. Registered profl. chem. and mech. engr.; instr.'s credential Calif. Community Coll. Chem. engr. Sondell Sci. Instruments, Inc., Mountain View, Calif., 1971; mem. R & D staff Raychem Corp., Menlo Park, Calif., 1971-72; supervising engr. Bechtel Power Corp., San Francisco, 1972-79; sr. project mgr. water quality and toxic substances control program Electric Power Rsch. Inst., Palo Alto, Calif., 1979-89, program mgr., 1990-97, product line mgr. environ. market sector, 1997-99, indsl. and agrl. energy techs. and svcs. bus. area mgr., 1999—, exec. dir. ctrs. network, 1999—; mem. steering com. Industrial Energy Tech. Conf. Editor: Hazardous Air Pollutants: State-of-the-Art, 1993; co-editor: Clean Water: Factors that Influence Its Availability, Quality and Its Use, 1996; co-author: Water Chlorination, vols. 4, 6; co-editor 1997 Internat. Clean Water Conf.-Today's Sci. for Tomorrows Policies, The Environ. Profl., 1997; contbr. articles to profl. jours. Pres., CEO Directions, Inc., San Francisco, 1985-86, bd. dirs., 1984-87, chmn. strategic planning com., 1984-85; industry com. Am. Power Conf., 1988—; with strategic long-range planning and restructuring com. Sequoia Union H.S. Dist., 1990-93, chmn. dist. ctrl. com., 1992-94. Recipient Grad. Disting. Achievement award, 1985; Calif. Gov.'s Exec. fellow, 1982-83. Mem. ASME, AIChE (profl. devel. recognition award), NSPE, Calif. Soc. Profl. Engrs. (pres. Golden Gate chpt. 1983-84, v.p. 1982-83, state dir.), Water Environ. Fedn., Air and Waste Mgmt. Assn. (mem. electric utility com. 1990—), Calif. State U. Alumni Assn. (bd. dirs., treas. 1989-91), U. Calif. Alumni Assn., Beta Gamma Sigma. Democrat. Presbyterian. Office: Electric Power Rsch Inst 3412 Hillview Ave Palo Alto CA 94304-1344

CHOW, YUK-TAK, physicist, educator; b. Hong Kong; s. Wah and King (Hon) C.; m. Linda Hon, Nov. 12, 1993. BSc, Heriot-Watt U., Edinburgh, Scotland, 1982; MSc, U. St. Andrews, St. Andrews, Scotland, 1983; PhD, Heriot-Watt U., Edinburgh, 1988. Rsch. assoc. Heriot-Watt U., Edinburgh, Scotland, 1986-88; rsch. fellow U. Southampton, U.K., 1989-91; assoc. prof. City U. of Hong Kong, 1992—. Contbr. articles to physics jours. Recipient Croucher scholarship, 1982, 83, J.H. Murray prize for Optics, 1982. Mem. IEEE, Instn. Elec. Engrs., Optical Soc. of Am., Inst. Physics. Avocations: laboratory research, flying model helicopter, reading, golfing. Office: City U Hong Kong Dept EE, 83 Tat Chee Ave, Kowloon Hong Kong China

CHOW, YUN-FAT, actor; b. Nam Nga Island, Hong Kong, May 18, 1955; p. Jasmine Chow. Appeared in Two Times: Hong Kong 1941, 1985 (Best Actor award Won Taiwan Golden Horse, Best Actor award Won Asian Pacific Festival 1985), An Autumn's Tale, 1987 (Best Actor award Won Taiwan Golden Horse), Three Times: A Better Tomorrow, 1987 (Best Actor award Won Hong Kong Acad.), City On Fire, 1988 (Best Actor award Won Hong Kong Acad.), The Eighth Happiness, 1988, All About Ah Long, 1989 (Best Actor award Won Hong Kong Acad.), A Better Tomorrow III, 1989, Triad Savages, 1989, Triads: The Inside Story, 1989, The Fun, the Luck and the Tycoon, 1989, God of Gamblers, 1989, The Killer, 1989, Wild Search, 1989, Once a Thief, 1990, Black Vengeance, 1990, Prison on Fire II, 1991, Full Contact, 1992, Now You See Love, Now You Don't, 1992, Ruthless Super-Cop, 1992, Hot-Handed God of Cops, 1992, All for the Winner, 1992, Treasure Hunt, 1994, God of Gamblers' Return, 1994, The Peace Hotel, 1995, The Replacement Killers, 1998, King's Ransom, 1998, The Corruptor, 1999, Anna and the King, 1999, and others. Named Star of the Decade, CineAsia-The Asian Theatre Owners Conv.

CHOWDHARY, BRAHMA RAM, veterinarian; b. Surpaliya, Nagaur, India, Dec. 12, 1941; s. Ganga Ramji and Hira (Devi) C.; m. Bhanwari Devi, May 12, 1945; children: Arachana, Kalpana, Anjana, Arati, Alok. B.Vet. Sci. and Animal Husbandry, Coll. Vet. and Animal Sci., Bikaner, India, 1963, PhD, 1980; MSc, Lincoln Coll., Christchurch, N.Z., 1967. Demonstrator Coll. Vet. and Animal Sci., Bikaner, 1963-65, asst. prof., 1967-75, assoc. prof., 1975-90, prof., 1991—; officer in charge Camel Rsch. Ctr., Bikander, 1980-84. Author: Sheep and Wool Production, 1975, Wool

Science, 1976, Desert Diet and Man, 1984, Camel Behaviour Production and Management, 1994, Eco-culture Nutrition and Livestock Production, 1998. World U. fellow, 1965-67. Mem. Soc. Animal Prodn., Soc. Desert Tech. Avocations: gardening, chess, fossil collection, travel, yoga. Home: Hirakunj-Alok Sadan, Sharma Colony Rani Bazar, Bikaner 334001, India Office: Coll Vet and Animal Sci, Livestock Prodn Dept, Bikaner 334002, India

CHOWDHURI, PRITINDRA, electrical engineer, educator; b. Calcutta, July 12, 1927; came to U.S., 1949, naturalized, 1962; s. Ahindra and Sudhira (Mitra) C.; m. Sharon Elsie Hackebeil, Dec. 28, 1962; children: Naomi, Leslie, Robindro, Rajendro. B.Sc. in Physics with honors, Calcutta U., 1945, M.Sc., 1948; M.S., Ill. Inst. Tech., 1951; D.Eng., Rensselaer Poly. Inst., 1966. Jr. engr. lightning arresters sect. Westinghouse Electric Corp., East Pittsburgh, Pa., 1951-52; elec. engr. high voltage lab. Maschinenfabrik Oerlikon, Zurich, 1952-53; research engr. High Voltage Rsch. Commn., Daeniken, Switzerland, 1953-56; devel. engr. high voltage lab. GE, Pittsfield, Mass., 1956-59; elec. engr. research and devel. ctr. GE, Schenectady, N.Y., 1959-62; engr. elec. investigations transp. systems div. GE, Erie, Pa., 1962-75; staff mem. Los Alamos (N.Mex.) Nat. Lab., 1975-86; prof. elec. engring. Ctr. Elec. Power Tenn. Technol. U., Cookeville, 1986—; lectr. Pa. State U. Behrend Grad. Ctr., Erie, 1969-75. Author: Electromagnetic Transients in Power Systems, 1996. Patentee in field. Fellow AAAS, IEEE, Instn. Elec. Engrs. (U.K.), N.Y. Acad. Scis. Democrat. Unitarian. Home: 690 Valley Forge Rd Cookeville TN 38501-1574 Office: Tenn Technol U Ctr Elec Power PO Box 5032 Cookeville TN 38505-0001

CHOWDHURY, GOBINDA GOPAL, library and information science educator; b. West Bengal, India, Nov. 5, 1959; s. Ananda G. and Uma (Goswami) C.; m. Sudatta Chowdhury, Jan. 23, 1991; children: Avirup, Anubhav. BSc with honors, U. Burdnan, India, 1979, BLISc, 1982, MLISc, 1984; PhD, Jadavpur U., India, 1991, U. Sheffield, U.K., 1992. Asst. libr. DCIL, India, 1985-87; lectr. Vidyasagar U., India, 1987-89; commonwealth scholar U. Sheffield, U.K., 1989-92; scientist fellow INSDOC, India, 1992-93; assoc. prof. Sch. of Info. Studies of Africa, Ethiopia, 1993-97; sr. lectr. Nanyang Technol. U., Sinapore, 1998—, assoc. prof., 2000—. Author: Introduction to Modern Information Retrieval, 1999, Text Retrieval Systems in Information Management, 1996, PRECIS: A Workbook, 1995, Information Retrieval System, 1994, (with others) Trends in Information Retrieval Resarch, 1997, Knowing the Social Science User: Some Preliminaries for the Investigator, 1990; contbr. articles to profl. jours. Recipient Ranganathan medal, 1992, U. and Bani Bose Gold medal U. Burdnan, 1982, 84. Fellow Libr. Assn.; mem. Bengal Libr. Assn. Avocations: Indian music, surfing the net. Home: 35F Nan Yang Ave, 03-11 Nanyang Heights, Singapore 639808, Singapore Office: Sch Computer Engring NTU, N4 #2a-32 Nanyang Ave, Singapore 639798, Singapore

CHOWDHURY, HUMAYUN QUADER, executive scientific instrument company; b. Barisal, Bangladesh, Feb. 19, 1953; s. Abdul Quader Chowdhury and Amina Begum; m. Sharmeen Soneya Murshid, Dec. 12, 1984; 1 child, Saiqu'a Shabnam. BS with honors, Dhaka (Bangladesh) U., 1974. Mktg. exec. A. Q. Chowdhury & Co, Dhaka, Bangladesh, 1974-75; mktg. mgr. A. Q. Chowdhury & Co, Dhaka, 1975-80, team leader electron optics divsn., 1982-84, CEO, 1985—; chief cons. Spatial Edn. & Rsch., Houston, 1988—; CEO, founder Plasma Plus, Dhaka, 1992—; founder Continuing Edn. in Sci. and Medicine, Bangladesh. Columnist (free lance) for Hindustani Film Music. With Guerilla forces Liberation War, Bangladesh, 1971. Named Freedom Fighter Bangladesh Govt., 1971. Mem. Assn. for Advancement of Med. Instrumentation, Am. Assn. Physicists in Medicine (assoc.), Extraordinary Svc. award Dhaka W. chpt. 1989-90, named Paul Harris fellow Rotary Internat. 1992), Am. Water Works Assn. Avocations: music, sports, reading, travel, meeting people. Home: Baridhara Apt E-1, 20 Dootabash Rd, Dhaka 1212, Bangladesh Office: Plasma Plus KJH Mansion, 83 Laboratory Rd Spectrachrome Fl, Dhaka 1205, Bangladesh

CHOWDHURY, MAHIUDDIN, engineering educator, researcher; b. Dhaka, Bangladesh, Oct. 31, 1945; s. Amir Hossain and Peara (Begum) C.; m. Laila Anwara, May 10, 1978; 1 child, Yasar Athar. BSc in Engring., Bangladesh U. Engring. & Tech., Dhaka, 1968; PhD, U Newcastle-on-tyne, Eng., 1978. Rsch. assoc. U. Newcastle-upon-tyne, Eng., 1975-77; lectr. Bangladesh Univ. Engring. and Tech., Dhaka, 1969-72, asst. prof., 1978-81, assoc. prof., 1981-85, prof., 1985-89; sr. lectr. U. New South Wales, Sydney, Australia, 1989—; head of dept. Naval Arch. and Marine Engring., Bangladesh U. Engring and Tech., Dhaka, 1978-89; chmn. Nat. Com. on Safety of Passenger Vessels, Shipping Ministry, Govt. Bangladesh; cons. Govt. Bangladesh ministries shipping, forest, inland water transport. Contbr. articles to profl. jours., presented papers to many internat. sci. confs. and symposiums, 1979—. Recipient scholarship Commonwealth U.K., 1972-74. Fellow Royal Instn. Naval Architects, Instn. Engineers Bangladesh; mem. Inst. Engrs. Australia. Avocations: travel, fishing, bushwalking. Office: U New South Wales, Sch Mech and Mfg Engring, Sydney Australia

CHOWDHURY, NIRMALENDU, veterinary, educator; b. Karimganj, Assam, India, Feb. 1, 1942; s. Raimohan and Prafulla Bala (Das) C.; m. Amita Dutta, Nov. 17, 1973; 1 child, Rooh. BVSc, Assam Agrl. U., 1964; MVSc, U.P. Coll. Vet. Sci., 1968; DSc, State U. Gent, 1975; postgrad., Kumamoto U. Med. Sch., 1980-81. Rsch. scholar Indian Vet. Rsch. Inst., 1969-70, State U. Gent, Belgium, 1971-75; assoc. prof. Assam Agrl. U., 1975-80; assoc. prof. Punjab (India) Agrl. U., 1982-87, prof., 1988—. Editor: Helminthology, 1994, Helminths of Wildlife, 2000. Rsch. fellow Coun. Sci. and Indsl. Rsch., Indian Coun. Agrl. Rsch., 1969, Belgian Ministry Edn., 1970, Japan Soc. Promotion Sci., 1980. Fellow Belgian Soc. Parasitology (corr.); mem. Indian Soc. Parasitology, World Assn. Advancement Vet. Parasitology. Avocations: photography, stamp collecting, story writing, reading, research. Home: Nilmani Rd, Assam Karimganj 788 710, India

CHOWDHURY, ZAFRULLAH A.T.M., healthcare activist, surgeon, consultant; b. Chittagong, Bangladesh, Dec. 27, 1941; s. Humayun Murshed and Hasina (Begum) C.; m. Susanne Ehrhardt, Dec. 17, 1972 (div. Sept. 1991); m. Shireen Parveen Huq, Jan. 1992; children: Brishti Anna, Bareesh Hasan. Degree, Dhaka (Bangladesh) Coll., 1958, BS, 1964; Primary F.R.C.S., Royal Coll. of Surgeons, Glasgow, Scotland, 1969; F.C.G.P. (hon.), Coll. Gen. Practitioners, Dhaka, 1990. Sr. house surgeon Brit. Nat. Health Svc., Eng., 1965-69, registrar, 1969-71; cons. surgeon Bangladesh Freedom Fighters (govt. in exile), Dhaka, 1972; cons. surgeon (hon.) Bangladesh Army, Dhaka, 1972; cons. surgeon Gonoshasthaya Kendra, Dhaka, 1972—; projects dir. Gonoshasthaya Kendra (G.K.), Savar, Bangladesh, 1972-82, coord., Dhaka, 1982—; chmn. (hon.) Gonoshasthaya Pharms. Ltd., Bangladesh, 1981—; chmn. various G.K. enterprises, 1988—. Author: The Politics of Essential Drugs, 1995; chief editor Monthly Gonoshasthaya (People's Health), Bengali, 1974—; contbr. articles to profl. jours. Mem. Socialist by Conviction, Bangladesh, 1956—; health activist G.K., 1972—. Recipient Independence Day award Govt. of Bangladesh, 1977, Magsaysay award R. Magsaysay Found., The Philippines, 1985, Right Livelihood award R.L. Found., Sweden, 1992, Swedish Youth Peace prize Swedish Youth Peace Found., 1974. Mem. Brit. Med. Assn., Bangladesh Pvt. Med. Practitioners Assn., Health for All. Avocations: reading, travelling, women's devel., disaster mgmt. Home: Bakshibazar, 8 Umesh Datta Rd, Dhaka 1211, Bangladesh Office: Gonoshasthaya Kendra, Mirzanagar via Savar Cantt, Dhaka 1350, Bangladesh

CHOWDRI, NISAR AHMAD, general and plastic surgeon, consultant; b. Srinagar, India, Apr. 15, 1959; s. Ghulam Nabi and Rajia Begum (Kaling) C.; m. Neelofer Nisar Rigoo, Nov. 7, 1989; children: Iqra Nisar, Obaid Ahmad. MB BS, Govt. Med. Coll., Srinagar, 1984; MS, S.K. Inst. Med. Scis., Srinigar, 1988. House surgeon SMHS Hosp., Srinagar, 1984-85; asst. surgeon J&K Health Svcs., India, 1985-86; jr. resident S.K. Inst. Med. Scis., 1986, postgrad. resident, 1986-88, sr. resident in surgery, 1988-91, cons. surgeon in plastic surgery, 1991-96; cons. surgeon, 1997—. Contbr. articles to profl. jours. Recipient Bronze medal U. Kashmir, India, 1980. Fellow Assn. Indian Surgeons; mem. Assn. Surgeons of India (life), Assn. Plastic Surgeons (life), Nat. Acad. Burns India (life). Avocations: gardening, photography, reading medical literature. Home: Hassi Bhat Rainawari, 190003 Srinagar India Office: Dept Surgery, SK Inst Med Scis Soura, 190011 Srinagar India

CHOWE, FLORY FA-LONG, sculptor, art educator, consultant; b. Hong Chow, China, Apr. 27, 1936; came to U.S., 1954; d. Lung-Wan and Jean-Yin Chao; m. John Sie, Feb. 15, 1958 (div. Dec. 17, 1966); children: Susan Sie, Deborah Sie, James Sie; m. Arthur G. Hedley, July 11, 1972. BA, Barry U., 1957; postgrad. in sculpture, Art Students' League N.Y., 1966-70. Acting dean, assoc. prof. fine arts Dharma Realm Buddhist U., Talmage, Calif., 1979-81; art cons., designer, executor for specific sites The Orient Golf Clubs, Pen Holdings Inc., Internat., Taipei, Xiamen, Taiwan, China and Nashville, 1993-96; chief organizer, propr. Studio Gallery, Ukiah, Calif., 1996—; artist-in-residence Art Acad. Rome, 1970. Represented in permanent sculpture collections in Italy, Switzerland, America, Japan, Taiwan, and China; featured interview in Sojourn, 1999. Recipient 1st award in sculpture 23d Taiwan Arts Exhbn., 1968, Emily Lowe scholarship Art Students' League N.Y., 1968, Edward G. McDowell Traveling scholarship, 1970. E-mail: falong@pacific.net. Home and Office: Studio Gallery 3299 Bus Mcgall Rd Ukiah CA 95482-9339

CHOWNING, ORR-LYDA BROWN, dietitian; b. Cottage Grove, Oreg., Nov. 30, 1920; d. Fred Harrison and Mary Ann (Bartels) Brown; m. Kenneth Bassett Williams, Oct. 23, 1944 (dec. Mar. 1945); m. Eldon Wayne Chowning, Dec. 31, 1959. BS, Oreg. State Coll., 1943; MA, Columbia U., 1950. Dietetic intern Scripps Metabolic Clinic, LaJolla, Calif., 1944; sr. asst. dietitian Providence Hosp., Portland, Oreg., 1945-49; contact dietitian St. Lukes Hosp., N.Y.C., summer 1949; cafeteria food svc. supr. Met. Life Ins. Co., N.Y.C., 1950-52; set up food svc. and head dietitian McKenzie-Willamette Meml. Hosp., Springfield, Oreg., 1955-59; foods dir. Erb Meml. Student Union, Eugene, Oreg., 1960-63; set up food svc. and head dietitian Cascade Manor Retirement Home, Eugene, 1967-68; owner, operator Veranda Kafe, Inc., Albany, Oreg., 1971-80; owner, operator, sec.-treas. Chownings Adult Foster Home, Albany, 1984-98. Contbr. articles to profl. jours. Lin County Women's chair Hatfield for Senator Spaghetti Rally, Albany H.S., 1966; food preparation chair Yi for You, Mae Yih for State Senate, Albany Lebanon, Sweet Home, 1982; Silver Clover Club sponsor Oreg. 4-H Found., Oreg. State U., Corvallis, 1994-96. Recipient coll. scholarship Nat. 4-H Food Preparation Contest, Chgo., 1939. Mem. Am. Dietetic Assn. (registered dietitian, gerontol. nutritionist dietetic practice group 1988—), Oreg. Dietetic Assn. (diet therapy chair, newsletter editor 1963-64), Willamette Dietetic Assn., Kappa Delta Pi (Kappa chpt.), Mu Beta Beta. Republican. Mem. Disciples of Christ. Avocations: gardening, genealogy, swimming, travel, pet therapy. Home and Office: 4440 Woods Rd NE Albany OR 97321-7353

CHOY, KIM FUN, human resource consultant; b. Hong Kong, Dec. 20, 1931; children: Orpheus, Hercules, Hermes. BA with honors, U. Hong Kong, 1958; diploma in applied social studies, Nottingham (Eng.) U., 1964. Fellow Birmingham (Eng.) U.; probation officer Hong Kong Govt., 1958-72, prin. social welfare officer, 1972-74, sr. tng. officer, 1974-91; indsl. resource cons. Gladiolus Co. Ltd., Hong Kong, 1991—; dir. Floral Land Co. Ltd., Hong Kong, 2000—; hon. cons. to Cultural Gallery Mgmt. and Reform Group of 30 Provincial Cities, China; MBO program del. Asian Productivity Orgn., Tokyo; profl. asst. to Dir. Social Welfare, Hong Kong, 1970-71; tng. advisor Overseas Trust Bank, Hong Kong; extramural lectr. Chinese U. of Hong Kong, 1970-73; hon. adviser Hong Kong Nursing Assn.; spkr., presenter in field; seminar leader Chinese South West Mil. Region Corps; invited guest China QCC Nat. Conv., 1991-92; organizer ISO 9000 Quality Assurance Certification Agys. Conf., Guangzhou, China; mgmt. trainer Bank of China Group, Hong Kong; appraiser for vis. trainers Sr. Pers. Officer Tng. Inst., Beijing. Translator: Tao Te Qing; editor Hong Kong Social Workers' Assn. Jour.; author, composer, editor (poetic work) The Missing Link, 1963; contbr. poems to profl. publs. Founding chmn. The Masquers Dramatic Group. Mem. ASTD, Assn. Mgmt. Edn. and Devel., Hong Kong Inst. Pers. Mgmt. (assoc.), Hong Kong Quality Mgmt. Assn. (consultancy chmn. 1993—), Asia Soc. (Hong Kong). Avocations: writing poetry, para-normal healing translation, cultural exchange. E-mail: glado@pacific.net.hk. Home: 2 King Tak St B/10, Homatin Hong Kong Office: Gladiolus Co Ltd, PO Box 71718, Hong Kong China

CHOYCE, DAVID PETER, ophthalmologist; b. London, Mar. 1, 1919; s. Charles Coley and Gwendolen Alice (Dobbing) C.; m. Diana Graham, Sept. 3, 1949; children: Jonathan, David Gregory, Matthew Quentin. BSc, U. London, 1939, MB, BS, 1943, MS, 1962. Cons. Southend Hosp., Essex, Eng., 1954-84; ophthalmologist Hosp. for Tropical Diseases, London, 1953-88; overseas cons., ophthalmologist Henry Ford Hosp., Detroit, 1980—; pvt. practice London, 1955—; cons. London Centre for Refractive Surgery, 1987—; mem. Brit. Acad. Experts, 1991—. Author: Intraocular Lenses and Implants, 1964; contbr. numerous articles to profl. jours. Med. Officer, Brit. Navy, 1943-46. Recipient Disting. Achievement award Am. Soc. Contemporary Ophthalmology, 1986, Mericos award Mericos Eye Inst., La Jolla, Calif., 1986, Binkhorst medal Am. Implant Soc., 1981, Internat. award of excellence in ophthalmology Hawaiian Eye Found., 1991, Innovators Lecture, ASCRS, 1993. Fellow Royal Coll. Surgeons (Eng.; Hunterian prof.), Japanese Implant Soc.; mem. Yugoslav Implant Soc. (hon.), Kerato-Refractive Soc. (pres. 1986-89, Palaeologus medal 1984), Am. Soc. Cataract and Refractive Soc. (40th Anniversary Pioneer award 1989, nominated for induction in the Ophthalmology Hall of Fame 2000), Internat. Intraocular Implant Club (pres. 1977-80), U.K. Intraocular Implant Soc. (pres. 1980-82), So. African Implant Soc., Brit. Acad. of Experts, Expert Witness Inst., Moor Park Golf Club. Mem. Conservative Party. Achievements include research in the correction of high myopia with minus optic anterior chamber implants; medico-legal work including allegations of negligence. Avocation: golf. Fax: 44 (0) 1702 342611. E-mail: professorchoyce@aol.com. Home: 9 Drake Rd, Westcliff-on-Sea SS0 8LR, England Office: 45 Wimpole St, London W1M 7DG, England

CHRAI, SUGGY SINGH, pharmacist; b. Amristsar, India, Oct. 13, 1947; csme to U.S., 1969; s. Sohan and Beant (Kaur) C.; m. Jane M. Limpert; children: Brian, Emily. BS in Pharmacy, Jadavpur U., Calcutta, India, 1969; MS, U. Wis., 1971, PhD, 1973; MBA, Fairleigh Dickinson U., 1977. Dir. pharm. tech. Bristol-Myers Squibb, New Brunswick, N.J., 1977-95; v.p. tech. affairs Mova Pharm. Corp., Cagaus, P.R., 1995; v.p. devel. Liposome Co., Plainsboro, N.J., 1995-97; v.p. tech. ops. Delsy's Pharm. Corp., Princeton, N.J., 1997—. Contbr. articles to profl. jours. Active Boy Scouts Am., N.J., 1996—. Fellow Am. Pharm. Assn., Am. Assn. Indian Pharm. Scientists. Home: 16 Bodine Dr Cranbury NJ 08512-3159 Office: Delsys Pharm Corp 201 Washington Rd Princeton NJ 08540-6449

CHRÉTIEN, (JOSEPH JACQUES) JEAN (JOSEPH JACQUES JEAN CHRÉTIEN), prime minister of Canada, lawyer; b. Shawinigan, Que., Can., Jan. 11, 1934; s. Wellie and Marie (Boisvert) C.; m. Aline Chaîné, Sept. 10, 1957; children: France, Hubert, Michel. Law degree, Laval (Que.) U., 1958; LLD (hon.), Wilfred Laurier U., 1981, Laurentian U., 1982, U. Western Ont., 1982, York U., 1986, U. Alta., 1987, Lakehead U., 1988, U. Ottawa, 1994, Meiji U., 1996; D (hon.), Warsaw Sch. Econs., Poland, 1999, Mich. State U., 1999, Hebrew U., Israel, 2000, Memorial U., 2000. Bar: Que. 1958. Former mem. firm Chrétien, Landry, Deschênes, Trudel & Normand; M.P. from St. Maurice Ho. of Commons, 1963-86; Parliamentary sec. to prime min., 1965, Parliamentary sec. to min. of fin., 1966, min. without portfolio, 1967, min. of nat. revenue, 1968, min. of Indian Affairs and No. devel., 1968-74; pres. Treasury Bd. Can., 1974-76; min. of industry, trade and commerce, 1976-77, min. of fin., 1977-79, min. of justice, atty. gen. of Can., min. of state for social devel., min. responsible for Constln. negotiations, 1980-82, min. of energy, mines and resources, 1982-84, deputy prime min., sec. state for external affairs, 1984, external affairs critic for the official opposition, 1984-86; counsel Lang, Michener, Lawrence & Shaw, Toronto, Ottawa and Vancouver, 1986-90; leader Liberal Party of Can., 1990; M.P. from Riding of Beauséjour, 1990-93; M.P. from Riding of St. Maurice Que.; prime min., 1993—. Mem. Can. Bar Assn., Shawinigan Sr. C. of C. (dir. 1962). Office: Parliament Bldgs, Langevin Block 80 Willington St, Ottawa, ON Canada K1A 0A2

CHRÉTIEN, RAYMOND A. J., ambassador; b. Shawinigan, Que., Can., May 20, 1942; s. Maurice and Cécile (Marcotte) C.; m. Kay Rousseau; children: Caroline, Louis-François. BA, Sém. de Joliette, 1962; LLL, U. Laval, 1965. Bar: Que. 1966. Mem. legal affairs div. Div. External Affairs Govt. of Can., 1966-67, policy dir. industry, investments and competition, asst. undersec. mfg., tech. and transp., insp. gen., assoc. undersec. state for external affairs, 1988-91; 3rd sec. permanent mission to UN Govt. of Can., N.Y.C., 1967-68; asst. sec. fed. and provincial rels. com. Privy Coun. Office Govt. of Can., 1968-70, exec. asst. to sec., mem. treasury bd. Privy Coun. Office, 1970-71; exec. asst. to pres. Can. Internat. Devel. Agy., 1971-72; 1st sec. Can. Embassy, Beirut, 1972-75; 1st sec., counsellor Can. Embassy, Paris, 1975-78; Can. amb. to Zaïre, 1978-81, Can. amb. to Mexico, 1985-88; Can. amb. to Belgium and Luxembourg Brussels, 1991-94; Can. amb. to U.S. Washington, 1994—. Awarded Order of Aztec Eagle, Mex. Office: Canadian Embassy 501 Pennsylvania Ave NW Washington DC 20001-2111*

CHRISANT, ROSEMARIE KATHRYN, law library administrator; b. Chgo., Oct. 9, 1946; d. Theodore and Angeline Frances (Pawlik) Layne; 1 child, Paula Ellen Marie. BS in Edn., No. Ill. U., 1967; MLS, Rosary Coll., 1971. High sch. English tchr. Chgo. Sch. System, 1967-70; asst. libr. Akron (Ohio) Law Libr. Assn., 1971-76, libr. dir., 1976—; cons. law firms, Akron. Contbr. articles to profl. jours. Mem. ABA, Am. Assn. Law Librs., Ohio Regional Assn. Law Librs. (Outstanding Svc. award 1986), Spl. Libr. Assn., Ohio Libr. Assn. E-mail: allarkc@en.com. Office: Akron Law Libr Assn Summit County Courthouse 209 S High St Rm 4 Akron OH 44308-1625

CHRIST, DUANE MARLAND, computer systems engineer; b. Lakota, Iowa, Jan. 5, 1932; s. George Andrew and Esther Gertrude (Franke) C.; m. Lily Esther Shih, Sept. 14, 1963; 1 child, Wesley Anzo. BS, Iowa State U., 1953; MA, U. Minn., 1960; PhD, Rutgers U., 1998. Sci. programmer United Aircraft Corp., Hartford, Conn., 1960-63; computer sys. analyst IBM, N.Y.C., 1963-68, staff instr., 1968-76, adv. sys. engr., 1976-82, sr. sys. engr., 1982-87, prin., 1987—. 1st lt. USAF, 1953-56. Recipient Ea. Regional Dir. award, 1983; named Area Specialist of Yr., 1986; IBM Resident Study fellow, 1966-68. Mem. Assn. Computing Machinery, Soc. Indsl. and Applied Math., Math. Assn. Am., Inst. Ops. Rsch. and Mgmt. Scis., Am. Math. Soc. Home and Office: 15 Tilton Dr Freehold NJ 07728-3359

CHRIST, JACOB, psychiatrist; b. Langenbruck, Baselland, Switzerland, Feb. 10, 1926; s. Anton Leonard and Anna Alice (Kambli) C.; m. Cornelia A. van der Horst, Sept. 30, 1950 (dec. May 1952); 1 child, Frans; m. Barbara R. Fierke, Sept. 15, 1956 (dec. Nov. 1968); children: Charlotte, Martin, Catherine; m. Jane Lippincott Smith, Jan. 6, 1979; children: Heidi, Jonathan. MD, U. Lausanne (Switzerland), 1951, U. Amsterdam (the Netherlands), 1952; MD (Thesis), U. Zürich (Switzerland), 1952. Diplomate Am. Bd. Psychiatry and Neurology; cert. Specialty Bd. Psychiatry, Switzerland. Intern U. Amsterdam Hosps., 1949-52; resident Med. Coll. Va., Richmond, 1952-53, N.Y. Hosp., Cornell Med. Ctr., 1953-54, Yale Psychiatric Inst., New Haven, Conn., 1954-55; asst. instr., clin. assoc. psychiatrist Harvard U. Med. Sch., McLean Hosp., Boston, 1956-70; assoc. prof. Emory U. Med. Sch., Atlanta, 1970-79; cons. staff Northside Community Mental Health Ctr., Atlanta, 1973-79; psychiatrist in chief External Psychiat. Svcs. of Canton Baselland, Liestal, Switzerland, 1979-91; pvt. practice psychiatry Basel, Switzerland, 1991—; vis. instr. Med. U. of S.C., Charleston, 1970-77; instr. Sch. for Social Work, Basel, 1979—. Co-editor: Contemporary Marriage, 1976. Lt. USN, 1955-57. Rsch. grantee NIMH, 1967-69. Fellow Am. Psychiat. Assn., Am. Group Psychotherapy Assn. E-mail: jjchr@attglobal.net. Home and Office: Sevogelplatz 2, 4052 Basel Switzerland

CHRIST, KARYN LYNN, clothing and swimwear designer, poet; b. Balt., Aug. 16, 1956; d. Robert John and Lois Mae Requard; m. Dale Robert Christ, Nov. 1, 1996. Diploma, Belair (Md.) H.S. Clothing designer Dress-Ups, Balt., 1974-86; master cutting contract designer Costume World, Pompano, Fla., 1994—; master designer, owner Jita Original Bodywear, 1987—. Contract for swimwear designs and Spandex specialist; designer for theatrical prodns.; poet: A Journey Thru a Love, 1996. Fundraiser swim and fashion shows Cancer & Leukaemia in Childhood Trust, Bristol, Eng., 1993. E-mail: vita@ibm.net. Home and Office: 59 Acacia St Clearwater FL 33767

CHRIST, LILY ESTHER SHIH, mathematics educator; b. Korea, Sept. 19, 1936; came to U.S., 1955; d. Whan-Chang and Shin-Tze (Lin) Shih; m. Duane M. Christ, Sept. 14, 1963; 1 child, Wesley Anzo. BS, U. Minn., 1960; MA, Western Res. U., 1962; EdD, Columbia U., 1967. Tchr. Cleve. Pub. Schs., 1960-62; stats. lab. asst. Tchrs. Coll., Columbia U., N.Y.C., 1964-71; asst. prof. Coll. of Mt. St. Vincent, N.Y.C., 1966-68; asst. prof. John Jay Coll. Criminal Justice, CUNY, N.Y.C., 1969-73, assoc. prof., 1974—; HI-TECH PREP dir., 1993—. Fulbright-Hays Sr. scholar, 1972. Mem. Math. Assn. Am. (gov. 1990-93, Cert. of Merit Svc. 1987), Am. Statis. Assn. (dist. 2 gov. 1990-91), Nat. Coun. Tchrs. Mathematics. E-mail: christle@j-jay.cuny.edu. Office: CUNY John Jay Coll Criminal Justice 445 W 59th St New York NY 10019-1104

CHRIST, MICHAEL, physician; b. Rosenheim, Bavaria, Germany, Mar. 19, 1964; s. Hermann and Erika (Padeller) C.; m. Sabine Bentlage, July 1, 1993; children: Marius, Lea. MD, U. Munich, Germany, 1990. Intern U. Munich, 1991-92, approbation as physician, 1992; resident U. Munich, U. Heidelberg, 1992-99; prin. investigator U. Heidelberg, Germany, 1996, clin. pharmacologist, 1999—; prin. investigator Clin. Pharmacology, Mannheim, Germany, 1996—; cons., lectr. Klinikum Mannheim, 1998. Author: From Hypertension to Heart Failure, 1998, Vitamins and Hormones, 1999; contbr. articles to profl. jours. Chmn. Local Standby Duty of Pub. Health, Schwetzingen, 1997—. Recipient Searle Young Investigators award, 1995, Hans Dengler stipendium, 1999. Mem. German Soc. Clin. Pharmacology, German Soc. Internal Medicine, German Soc. Cardiology. Avocations: tennis, jogging, joinery, reading, mountaineering. Office: Inst Clin Pharmacology, Theodor Kutzer Ufer 1-3, 68167 Mannheim Germany

CHRISTE, KARL OTTO, research chemist; b. Ulm, Fed. Republic Germany, July 24, 1936; s. Eugen A. and Elsa M. (Heller) C.; m. Brigitte F. Fischer, Jan. 27, 1962; children: Ralf, Mark, Tina. BS, Tech. U., Stuttgart, Fed. Republic Germany, 1957, MS, 1960, PhD, 1961; postgrad., U. Vienna, Austria, 1957-58. Sr. rsch. chemist Stauffer Chem. Co., Richmond, Calif., 1962-67; tech. staff Rocketdyne Divsn. Rockwell Internat., Canoga Park, Calif., 1967-78, mgr. rsch., 1978-94; sr. staff advisor Air Force Rsch. Lab., Edwards AFB, Calif., 1994—; prof. chemistry U. So. Calif., L.A., 1994—. Contbr. articles to profl. jours.; patentee in field. Recipient Apollo award NASA, 1969, Star Team award USAF, 1999, Prix Moissan award, 2000. Mem. AAAS, Am. Chem. Soc. (Creative Work in Fluorine Chemistry award 1986), N.Y. Acad. Scis. Avocations: tennis, fencing (2 times U.S. champion). Home: 5645 Parkmor Rd Calabasas CA 91302-1036 Office: ERC Air Force Rsch Lab Edwards AFB CA 93524-0001

CHRISTEN, EVAN WILFRED, drainage engineer, researcher; b. Kericho, Kenya, May 6, 1967. MSc in Soil and Water Engring., Cranfield U., Eng., 1991, PhD in Agrl. and Environ. Engring., 1994. Postdoctoral fellow divsn. water resources Commonwealth Scientific and Industrial Rsch. Org., Griffith, NSW, Australia, 1991-94, project leader land and water, 1996—; sec. tile drainage com. Murrumbidgee Irrigation Area, Griffith, 1994-98. Mem. Murrumbidgee Field Naturalists, Griffith, 1998—. Grantee Natural Resources Mgmt. Strategy, 1994, Murray Darling Basin Commn., 1996, Nat. Program Irrigation R&D, 1999. Mem. Australian Soil Sci. Soc. (v.p. Riverina br. 1998—). Fax: 61-269630439. Office: CSIRO Land and Water, Research Station Rd, Griffith 2680, Australia

CHRISTEN, JOSÉ ANDRÉS, statistician, researcher; b. Mexico City, June 17, 1966; s. J. Joaquin and Lucila (Gracia) C.; m. Tzarara López, May 2, 1997. BS, U. Nat. Autonoma Mex., Mexico City, 1989; PhD, U. Nottingham (Eng.), 1994. Researcher Inst. Maths. U. Nat. Autonoma Mex., Morelia, Michoacan, 1994—; const. archeologists, Hawaii, 1995-96. Contbr. articles to profl. jours. Grantee Sistema Nacional Investigadores. Mem. SSM, AME. Avocations: soccer, high cuisine, travel. Office: UNAM Inst Matemáticas, Nicolás Romer 150 Centro, 58000 Morelia Mich, Mexico

CHRISTENSEN, ALLEN CLARE, agriculturist, educator; b. Lehi, Utah, Apr. 14, 1935; s. Clare Bernard and Relia Sarah (Allen) C.; m. Kathleen Ruth Atwater, Dec. 19, 1958; children: Ann Marie, Allen Clare Jr., james Lynn, Niel Daniel, Eric Wayne. BS with honors, Brigham Young U., 1957; MS, U. Calif., Davis, 1960; PhD, Utah State U., 1979. Cert. Am. Registry Profl. Animal Scientists. Vocat. agr. tchr. White Pine County Schs., Lund, Nev., 1961-64; from asst. to assoc. prof. agr. Calif. State Poly. U., Pomona, 1964-73; prof., 1973-94, dean coll. agr., 1980-85, 87-94, acting provost and

acad. v.p., 1985-87; pres. Philippines San Fernando Mission The Ch. Jesus Christ of Latter Day Saints, 1994-97, dir. pub. affairs Pacific Islands area, 1998-00; pvt. cons., 1997-98; cons. Agrl. Edn. Found., Templeton, Calif., 1971-85, AID, Washington, 1983-87, 89, W.K. Lesotho Agrl. Coll., Maseru, 1989; trustee Consortium for Internat. Devel., Tucson, Ariz., 1980-94, vice chair bd., 1988-89, chmn., 1992-94; mem. deans's coun. Calif. Agr. Leadership Program, Templeton, 1980-85, 87-94, chair, 1989-91; mem. joint com. on agr. rsch. and devel. AID, 1982-87, chmn. strengthening grant panel bd. internat. food and agrl. devel., 1983-87; chair BIFAD panel Human Capital Devel., 1985-87; apptd. by Gov. Wilson to Calif. State Bd. for Food and Agr., 1991-94, NASULGC Bd. on Agr., 1992-94. Author: (with others) Working in Animal Science, 1978; contbr. articles to profl. jours. Pres. Chino (Calif.) Latter-Day Saint Stake, 1979-88; mem. exec. bd. Old Baldy coun. Boy Scouts Am., 1988-89; bd. dirs. so. Calif. Agrl. Land Found., 1988-94. Recipient Hon. State Farmer Degree Calif. Assn. Future Farmers Am., 1983, Disting. Svc. award Calif. Assn. Future Farmers Am., 1992, hon. Am. FFA degree Nat. future Farmers Am. Orgn., 1993. Mem. Am. Soc. Animal Scis., Poultry Sci. Assn., Golden Key Nat. Honor Soc. (hon.), Phi Beta Delta, Phi Kappa Phi, Gamma Sigma Delta (Outstanding Faculty award of Merit 1976, Spl. award of Merit in Adminstrn. 1994, pres. 1969-70), Alpha Zeta. Republican. Mem. LDS Ch.

CHRISTENSEN, BIRGITTE VIEBAEK, anesthesiologist, physician; b. Karise, Denmark, May 20, 1956; d. Knud and Herdis (Christensen) C.; m. Geert Petersen (div.); children: Nicky, Christina. MD, Copenhagen U., 1983. Cert. specialist in anaesthetics, Denmark, Norway. Physician Denmark, 1983-96; sr. house med. officer hosp. in Denmark, 1997; anaesthetist Denmark, 1997—. Contbr. articles to profl. jours. Mem. Danish Med. Assn., Danish Assn. Anaesthetists, Danish Assn. Acupuncture. Office: Dept Anes/Amtssygehuset, i Glostrup, Ndr Ringvej, 2600 Glostrup Denmark

CHRISTENSEN, C(HARLES) LEWIS, real estate developer; b. Laramie, Wyo., June 3, 1936; s. Raymond H. and Elizabeth C. (Cady) C.; m. Sandra Stadheim, June 11, 1960; children: Kim, Brett. BS in Indsl. Engring., U. Wyo., 1959. Mgmt. trainee Gen. Mills, Chgo., 1959, Mountain Bell, Helena, Mont., 1962-63; data comms. mgr. Mountain Bell, Phoenix, 1964-66, dist. mktg. mgr., so. Colo., 1970-73; seminar leader AT&T Co., Chgo., 1966-68; mktg. supr. AT&T Co., N.Y.C., 1968-70; land planner and developer Village Assocs., Colorado Springs, Colo., 1973, exec. v.p., 1975-77; v.p. Cimarron Corp., Colorado Springs, 1974-75; pres. Lew Christensen & Assocs., Inc.; ptnr., gen. mgr. Briargate Joint Venture, 1977-82; pres. Vintage Comtys., Inc., 1982-95. Bd. dirs. Pikes Peak coun. Boy Scouts Am., Citizens Goals, Colo. Coun. on Econ. Edn., Cheyenne Mountain Zoo, U. Wyo. Found., engring. adv. bd.; chmn. Colorado Springs Econ. Devel. Coun., 1978, 89; bd. dirs., chmn. bd. Penrose St. Francis Hosp., chmn. 1999—. Served with USAF, 1959-62. Mem. Colorado Springs Home Builders Assn. (bd. dirs.), Urban Land Inst., Colorado Springs C. of C. (bd. dirs., chmn. bd.), Colorado Springs Country Club (bd. dirs.), Garden of Gods Club. Republican. Presbyterian. Achievements include development of 1,000-acre Peregrine planned community, south of USAF Academy; the 7,000 acre planned community of Briargate, just east of the USAF Academy. Office: Lew Christensen & Assocs Inc 2520 Stagsleap Pt Colorado Springs CO 80904-1192

CHRISTENSEN, DAN CHARLY, historian; b. Copenhagen, Dec. 24, 1941; s. Asger Charly and Margrethe Emma Eleonora (Møller) C.; m. Anne Møllegaard, Sept. 29, 1985 (div. 1990); children: Peter Andreas, Nils Olav; m. Hanne Lopdrup; 1 child, Signe Malene. Candidate in philosophy, Copenhagen U., 1970, PhD in History, 1996. H.s. tchr. Frederiksborg, Denmark, 1968-70; lectr. Tchrs.' Tng. Coll., Silkeborg, Denmark, 1970-72, Roskilde (Denmark) U. Ctr., 1972—; advisor Rsch. Inst. Devel. Studies, Copenhagen; cons. Jordens Verden, Viborg, Denmark; rschr. Rsch. Coun., 1990-95. Author: History of Danish Constitution 1830-48, 1970 (Gold medal 1970), Grundtvig and Industrialization, 1983, Det Moderne Project, 1996; contbr. articles to profl. jours. Fellow Agrl. History Soc. Avocations: farming, mountaineering. Home: Kvanløse Havremark, 4300 Holbaek Sjaelland, Denmark Office: Roskilde U, Marbjergvej, 4000 Roskilde Sjaelland, Denmark

CHRISTENSEN, DONNA RAY, educator; b. Chgo., Oct. 26, 1940; d. Raymond and Eleanor Grace (Kuempel) C. BA, Rosary Coll., 1986; MA, Concordia U., 1993. Instr. adult edn. Ctrl. YMCA Coll., Chgo., 1965-68; adminstr. St. James-Christie Acad., Oak Park, Ill., 1969-86; educator Sch. Dist. #89, Maywood, Ill., 1986-91; reading specialist Sch. Dist. #92, Broadview, Ill., 1991—; adj. faculty Concordia U., River Forest, Ill., 1995, Aurora (Ill.) U., 1996; featured spkr. Ill. Reading Conf., 1993-97, Concordia U. Reading Conf., 1994-2000. Bd. dirs. Oak Park-River Forest Symphony, 1992-94; mem. festival chorus Concordia U., 1988—. Grantee Ill. Math. & Sci. Acad., Olympic Com., 1997-2000. Mem. West Suburban Reading Coun. (bd. dirs. 1994-96), Internat. Reading Assn., Ill. Reading Coun. Avocations: Egyptology, writing children's books, collecting royal memorabilia, collecting historic dolls.

CHRISTENSEN, ERIK M(ARTIN), Scandinavian literature educator; b. Sønderborg, Denmark, Apr. 5, 1931; arrived in Germany, 1973; s. Aage Marius and Eva Margrethe (Kruuse) C.; m. Birgit Bøgeskov Hansen, Nov. 9, 1970 (div. 1986); 1 child, Sophus; m. Sabine Renner, Dec. 21, 1990; children: Jens, Søren, Marius. Mag.art., Aarhus Univ., Denmark, 1962; PhD, Odense Univ., Denmark, 1972. Apprentice The East Asiatic Co., Copenhagen, Denmark, 1949-51; conscript Danish Mil. Svc., Denmark, 1951-52; trainee The East Asiatic Co., N.Y.C., 1952-53; employee The East Asiatic Co., Cali, Colombia, 1953-54; bus. organizer Importadores Aliados, Cali, 1954-55; amanuensis Aarhus Univ., 1962-68; lectr. Odense U., 1968-73; prof. Freie Univ. Berlin, 1973-94; prof. Humboldt-Univ. Berlin, 1994-96, prof. emeritus, 1996—. Author: Ex auditorio Martin A. Hansen, 1965, Verifikationsproblemet, 1971, Henrik Ibsens realisme, 1985, Henrik Ibsens anarkisme, 1989, Complete Bibliography in Uriasposten, 1990; editor: Johannes V. Jensen for Det Danske Sprog-og Litteraturselskab, Copenhagen. Recipient Golden medal Aarhus U., 1961. Home: Flade klit 16, DK-7900 Nyk Mors Denmark

CHRISTENSEN, JAMES EDWARD, editor, publisher, author; b. Stella, Mo., July 18, 1941; arrived in Australia, 1974; s. Alvin Fey and Ollie Maxine (Sherwood) C.; m. Joan Frances Smith, June 30, 1962; m. Margaret Douglas McClintock Marks, Apr. 26, 1985; children: Jolene Michelle, Kim Ann, Todd Alan. BA, U. Calif., Berkeley, 1963; MA, Calif. State U., 1970; PhD, UCLA, 1972. Tchr. Kabaa (Kenya) Boys High Sch., 1964, Machakos (Kenya) Boys High Sch., 1965-66, Fountain Valley (Calif.) High Sch., 1966-69; grad. asst. UCLA, 1970-72; asst. prof. So. Ill. U., Carbondale, 1972-74; lectr. Charles Sturt U., Wagga Wagga, NSW, Australia, 1974-89; editor Educology Rsch. Assocs., Sydney, NSW, Australia, 1989—. Co-author: (with J.E. Fisher) Analytic Philosophy of Education as a Subdiscipline of Educology, 1979, Organization and Colleges of Education-An Educological Perspective, 1983, (with D. Lane), The School Librarian's Guide to Curriculum Development, 1985; editor: Perspectives on Education as Educology, 1981; author: Curriculum, Education and Educology, 1981, Education and Human Development, 1981; editorial cons.: Jour. Abstracts in Internat. Edn.; co-editor: Internat. Jour. of Educology. Recipient Wood Meml. Fund scholarship, 1959-63, Calif. State scholarship, 1959-63, U. Calif. Alumni scholarship, 1959-60, Fulbright-Hays Rsch. Abroad fellowship, 1972 (declined); grantee NDEA Title IV fellowship in Edn., 1969-72. Mem. ASCD, African Studies Assn. Australia, Am. Assn. Higher Edn., Am. Ednl. Rsch. Assn., Am. Ednl. Studies Assn., Assn. Tchr. Edn., Australian and New Zealand Comparative and Internat. Edn. Assn., Australian Assn. Rsch. in Edn., Australian Curriculum Studies Assn., Comparative and Internat. Edn. Soc. N.Am., Internat. Coun. Computers in Edn., Nat. Soc. for Study of Edn., Soc. Profs. in Edn., Phi Delta Kappa. Avocations: photography, dog breeding. Office: Educology Resch Asso, PO Box 216, Terrigal NSW 2260, Australia

CHRISTENSEN, JENS JØRGEN ELMER, clinical microbiologist; b. Nestved, Sealand, Denmark, Oct. 20, 1952; s. Aage Elmer and Inger (Madsen) C.; m. Birgitte Steen Hansen, Aug. 22, 1992; children: Martin, David. MD, U. Copenhagen, 1980; DSc, U. Aarhus, 1999. Med. diplomate. Physician dept. clin. microbiology Bispeboerg Hosp., Copenhagen, 1982-85; physician dept. medicine Kalundborg (Denmark) Hosp., 1985-88; physician dept. clin. microbiology Hillerød (Denmark) Hosp., 1990-92, Herlev (Denmark) Hosp., 1992-95; physician, co-head dept. clin. microbiology Århus (Denmark) U. Hosp., 1995-96; physician Statens Seruminst., Copenhagen, 1988-90, staff specialist dept. clin. microbiology, 1996-2000, head dept. clin. microbiology, 2000—; mem. bd., chmn. Young Microbiologists, Copenhagen, 1987-90; guest rschr. Ctrs. for Disease Control and Prevention, Atlanta, 1995. Contbr. articles to profl. jours. Mem. Danish Soc. Clin. Microbiology (bd. sec. 1990-96), Danish Soc. Immunology, Orgn. Clin. Microbiologists (bd. dirs. 1996—), N.Y. Acad. Scis. Avocations: tennis, badminton, wind-surfing. Office: Statens Seruminst Dept Clin, Microbiol Artilleri vej 5, 2300 Copenhagen S, Denmark

CHRISTENSEN, KAARE, geneticist, epidemiologist; b. Holstebro, Denmark, June 20, 1959; s. Kaj and Marie C.; m. Anne Maria Herskind, June 4, 1988; children: Sofie, Therese, Mads. MD, Odense U., 1987, PhD, 1994, DrMedSci, 1999. Resident Svendborg Hosp., Denmark, 1987-90; from rsch. fellow to prof. Odense U., Denmark, 1990—. Home: 117 Paeregrenen, 5220-SO Odense Denmark Office: Danish Twin Registry, Danish Twin Registry, Sdr Boulevard 23A, 5000-C Odense Denmark

CHRISTENSEN, KARIN, librarian; b. Tversted, Denmark, Dec. 17, 1955; d. Osvald Hartman and Gerda Signe (Poulsen) C. Libr., Royal Sch. Librarianship, Aalborg, Denmark, 1983. Libr. Pub. Libr., Bov, Denmark, 1985-86; head libr. Luth. Sch. Theology, Aarhus, Denmark, 1986—. Coeditor Teologi for Kirken, 1993; editor Teologi for Tanken og Troen, 1997. Avocations: languages, music. Office: Luth Sch Theology, Katrinebjergvej 75, DK-8200 Århus N, Denmark

CHRISTENSEN, KARL-CHRISTIAN HULDGAARD, finance manager; b. Assens, Funen, Denmark, June 16, 1961; s. Mogens Kjeld and Grethe (Huldgaard) C.; m. Jette Madsen, May 7, 1994; children: Jesper, Lene, Lars. MBA in Econs., HHA, Aarhus, Denmark, 1988. Mktg. cons. Jydsk Telefon, Aarhus, Denmark, 1984-87, Danfoss, Nordborg, Denmark, 1987-93; sr. cons. Danfoss, Nordborg, 1993-95; mktg. mgr. s.p. 2.00 Danfoss, Warsaw, 1995-97; mktg. support mgr. MD divsn. Danfoss, Nordborg, 1997-99, fin., human resources mgr., 1999—; tchr. Syddansk U., Sonderborg, Denmark, 1999—.

CHRISTENSEN, PAMELA KAREN, pediatric nurse; b. Mason City, Iowa, Aug. 5, 1957; d. Buford LeRoy and Violet Mae (Shepherd) C. AS, North Iowa Area Community Coll, Mason City, 1982. Cert. med. asst. Lakeland Med. Acad., Mpls., 1977. Staff nurse pediat. and med.-surg. unit Boone County Hosp., Boone, Iowa, 1982-84; traveling nurse, pediat. and adult Yuma (Ariz.) Med. Ctr., 1985-86, 89, 90-92, White Meml. Hosp., L.A., 1985, City of Faith Hosp., Tulsa, Okla., 1985; charge nurse pediat., staff nurse pediat. ICU City of Faith Hosp., Tulsa, 1986-89; traveling nurse charge pediat. Chinle (Ariz.) Navajo Hosp., 1985; traveling charge nurse pediat. and adult Dallas Children's Med. Ctr., 1989; traveling nurse in pediat. Havasu Samaritan Hosp., Lake Havasu City, Ariz., 1990, 93; traveling pediatric nurse Univ. Med. Ctr., Lubbock, Tex., 1990; traveling pediatric and adult nurse Vanderbilt U. Med. Ctr., Nashville, Tenn., 1991-92; adult charge nurse and NICU Audubon Humana Hosp., Louisville, 1991-92; traveling pediatric nurse City of Hope Med. Ctr., Duarte, Calif., 1993; traveling pediatric charge nurse St. Vincent Meml. Hosp., Taylorville, Ill., 1993-94; traveling pediatric nurse Jersey Shore Med. Ctr., Neptune, N.J., 1994, Ark. Children's Hosp., Little Rock, 1994; traveling nurse in pediat. Phoenix Children's Hosp., 1995; staff nurse in pediats. ICU Mayo Eugenio Litta Children's Hosp., Rochester, Minn., 1995-98; triage nurse Mayo Med. Ctr., 1998—; spkr. pediat. ICU conf. Mem. Am. Assn. Med. Assts. (past local pres. and state sec.). Home: 329 Chestnut St Osage IA 50461-1920

CHRISTENSEN, PER REX, astrophysicist; b. Kolding, Denmark, May 3, 1936; s. Svend Aage and Ragnhild Christensen; m. Hanne Rossen Hansen, June 8, 1957; children: Lars, Helle, Anders. MSc in Exptl. Physics, U. Copenhagen, 1960, PhD in Exptl. Physics, 1970. Amanuensis Niels Bohr Inst., Copenhagen, 1960-69, assoc. prof., 1969—, dir., 1989-93; adminstrv. dir. Theoretical Astrophysics Ctr., Copenhagen, 1994—; postdoctoral fellow Calif. Tech. Inst., Pasadena, 1965-66, rsch. assoc., 1974-75; vis. assoc. European So. Obs., La Silla, Chile, 1983; chmn. DK-Planck Consortium, Copenhagen, 1998—. Mem. Internat. Astronimal Union, Danish Nat. Com. for Astronomy. Fax: 45 35 32 59 01. E-mail: perrex@tac.dk. Office: Theoretical Astrophysics Ctr, Juliane Maries Vej 30, 2100 Copenhagen Denmark

CHRISTENSEN, PETER BRØGGER, neurologist, consultant; b. Odense, Denmark, Nov. 27, 1954; s. Ib and Birthe (Rohde-Jensen) C.; m. Grethe Villumsen, Jan. 19, 1984; children: Louise, Henrik. Grad., Aarhus (Denmark) U., 1983. Cons. neurologist, dept. neurology Aarhus (Denmark) U. Hosp., 1998—; mem. European ALS Rsch. Group. Author articles on amyotrophic lateral sclerosis and myasthenia gravis. Recipient Mogens Fog prize, 1992, also grants in field. Mem. Danish Soc. for Rsch. in Amyotrophic Lateral Sclerosis, Danish Neurol. Soc., European Neurol. Soc. Home: Jacob Adelborgs Alle 15, 8240 Risskov Denmark Office: Aarhus Univ Hosp, Dept Neurology, 8000 Århus Denmark

CHRISTENSEN, ROBERT WAYNE, oral maxillofacial surgeon, minister; b. N.Y.C., Apr. 6, 1925; s. Charles Joseph Brophy and Eva Sutherland (Hart) Christensen; m. Ann Forsyth (div.); children: Robert, Joan, Elizabeth, Peter, Mary, Colleen, Patricia, Michelle; m. Lynne Blindbury; children: Andrew, Matthew. DDS, NYU, 1948. Oral surgery tng. L.A. County Gen. Hosp., 1950; oral maxillofacial surgeon, 1950-88; pres. TMJ Implants, Inc., Golden, Colo., 1988—; minister, founder Covenant Marriages Ministry, Golden, 1988—; pres. Design Dynamics Internat., Golden, 1994—; R&D med. adv. bd. mem. Sch. Medicine LLU, Loma Linda, Calif.; pres.'s cabinet mem. Jerry Savelle Ministry, Ft. Worth, 1994—; adj. prof. bioengring. Sch. Engring., Clemson U., 1997; pres. Med. Modeling Corp., 1997; biomed. engring. program adv. bd. Colo. State U., 1999. Inventor of 5 U.S. patents. Lt. USNR. Robert W. Christensen fellow TM Joint Surgery, U. Tenn. Sch. Med., 1997. Republican. Avocations: skiing, gardening, photography. Office: TMJ Implants Inc 17301 W Colfax Ave Ste 135 Golden CO 80401-4880

CHRISTENSON, EILEEN ESTHER, geriatrics nurse; b. Fosston, Minn., July 26, 1950; d. Arthur L. and Gertrude E. (Jaworsky) Maruska; m. Leonard Dale Christenson, Mar. 16, 1968; children: Kristy, Dale, Melissa, Alicia. Grad., Thief River Fall Tech. Inst., Minn., 1967. LPN, Ill., N.Mex., Minn. Staff nurse Beltram (Minn.) Nursing Home, 1990—, Clearwater County Meml. Hosp., Bagley, Minn. Troop leader Land O'Lakes coun. Girl Scouts U.S., 1974-89. 1st lt. USAF, 1968-76, Vietnam. Decorated Purple Heart, Silver Cross, Bronze Star with bronze oak leaf cluster. Mem. VFW, Am. Legion, Eagles 351. Home: RR 5 Box 330A Bemidji MN 56601-8531

CHRISTENSSON, LEO STAUN, mechanical engineer, consultant; b. Odense, Fuenen, Denmark, Nov. 26, 1941; s. Paul Gustaf Johannes and Grethe (Staun) C.; m. Elisabeth Schramm, Oct. 14, 1965 (div. Nov. 1972); children: Paul, Annette, Birgitte; m. Annette Ellekilde Smidt, Oct. 15, 1972. BSc, Odense Inst. Mech. Engring., 1965. Gen. mgr., dir. Superfos Feeds Ltd., London, 1973-77; sr. engr. Cimbria Unigrain A/S, Thisted, Denmark, 1977-80; tech. mgr., regional mgr. Grundfos A/S, Singapore, 1980-83; gen. mgr. I. Kruger A/S-Scanwater, Singapore, 1983-85; regional v.p. Damrow Co., Inc., Kolding, Denmark, 1985-92; mgr. pilot plant NIRO A/S, Soeborg, Denmark, 1992-97; tech. mgr. Biofiber A/S, Thisted, 1997-98; cons. engr. LSC-Consulting Engr., Badajoz, Spain, 1998—; mem. Coun. for Tech. Coop. with Developing Countries, Copenhagen, 1971-73. Mem. Am. Soc. Agrl. Engring., Danish Soc. Engrs., N.Y. Acad. Sci., European Register Engring. Professions. Avocations: music, photography, sailing. E-mail: isc@post4.netmaster.dk. Office: AGRAZ SA, Ctra Madrid-Lisboa km 309, E-06195 Badajoz Spain

CHRISTENSEN, JOHN DENIS, business educator; b. N.Y.C., July 16, 1936; s. Charles Nicholas and Mary Antoinette (Koza) C.; AB, Lehman Coll. CUNY, 1970; MBA with distinction, Pace U., 1975; postgrad. Columbia U., 1976—; Doctor of Industrial Mgmnt. (hon.), U. Industrial Mgmt.; Credit mgr. Butler Lumber Co., 1961-62; fiscal, comptroller, sales staff Lever Bros., 1962-67; contr., sales v.p. Cycle Circus, Inc., 1967-70; v.p. Putnam Bicycle Importers Co., 1970-73; curriculum chmn. bus. adminstrn., prof. mgmt., dept. chmn. bus. adminstrn. & pub. svc. SUNY Westchester C.C., Valhalla, N.Y., 1975—, dir. Mgmt. Inst., chmn. faculty devel. conf., v.p. Faculty-Student Assn., Joseph and Sophia Abeles Disting. chair of bus., 1994—; vis. prof. econs. Mercy Coll., Dobbs Ferry, N.Y.; adj. assoc. prof. mgmt. Iona Coll., New Rochelle, N.Y. bd. dirs. Investment Properties Corp., Computweather Corp., Bio Med. Concepts, Inc.; adv. bd. U. Indsl. Mgmt.; cons. N.Y. State Bd. Regents, N.Y. State Edn. Dept.; chmn. Urba Devel. Corp. of Lewisboro N.Y., Town of Lewisboro Housing Com.; bd. mem. Westchester Minority Devel. Corp., 1983-84. Recipient Medallion Edn. award WCCF. Mem. Am. Acad. Mgmt., Nat. Econs. Club, Am. Inst. Higher Edn., Am. Acad. Polit. and Social Scis., Assn. MBA Execs., N.Y. State Assn. Two-Year Colls. (exec. bd. 1980-84), Nat. Bus. Honor Soc., Alpha Beta Gamma (nat. chmn. 1978-79, nat. devel. chmn. 1980-81, chief exec. officer 1983—), Sigma Lambda, Delta Mu Delta, others. Republican. Roman Catholic. Author: (with R. Wunsch) The Complete Resume Handbook, 1967; Management Miscellany, 1978, 4th edit., 1990; Introduction to Business (film series), 1980; Introduction to Finance (film series), 1982; (with Heinz Weirich) Instructor's Manual for Management, 1984; dir. editor: The Honors Jour., 1995—. Home: 1160 Midland Ave Apt 4C Bronxville NY 10708-6430 Office: Westchester Community Coll 75 Grasslands Rd Valhalla NY 10595-1636

CHRISTIAANS, PETER ALBERT, financial consultant; b. Antilles, The Netherlands, Sept. 25, 1968; Came to U.S., 1980; s. Piet Henderik and Anne Cornelia (Leising) C. BS, U. Miami, Fla., 1991, MBA, 1993, MS, 1994, postgrad., 1995—. Mgr. Abvu Inc., Miami, 1993-95; cons. Andersen Worldwide, Miami, 1995-97, sr. cons., 1997—; cons. Abvu Inc., 1995—. Active Netherlands Assn. South Fla., Miami Coun. Internat. Visitors; mem. adv. bd. Iron Arrow Honor Soc., U. Miami. Mem. Am. Sociol. Assn., Acad. Mgmt., Phi Alpha Theta, Alpha Epsilon Lambda (pres. 1993-95), Omicron Delta Kappa, mem. adv. brd. Iron Arrow Hon. Soc., U. Miami. Avocations: fly fishing, racquetball. Home: 11824 SW 99th Ave Miami FL 33176-4112 Office: Arthur Andersen 1 Biscayne Tower #2100 Miami FL 33131

CHRISTIAEN, HUBERT GEORGES T., physics educator; b. Bruges, Belgium, Sept. 26, 1936; s. Frans and Lucie (Plovie) C.; m. Simone St. Meykens, Oct. 25, 1975; children: Bruno, Mark, Liesbet. Lic. Physics, K.U. Leuven, Belgium, 1969, DSc, 1978. With Nuclear Rsch. Ctr., Mol, Belgium, 1969-70; asst. K.U. Leuven, 1970-80, werkleider, 1980-91, lector, 1991-92, asst. prof. analytical mechanics, 1992-99, assoc. prof., 1999—; consul; nat. coord. for European Schs. Project, 1991—. Editor mag. School and Computer, 1981-93. Mem. Internat. Fedn. for Info. Processing (working group 3.1 1988—), Fedn. Belgian Assns. for Informatics (treas. 1992-95, pres. 1997-99), Assn. for Computing Machinery, Internat. Soc. for Tech. in Edn. Avocation: sailing. Home: Bloesemlaan 17, B-3360 Korbeek-Lo Belgium Office: K U Leuven, Celestijnenlaan 200A, Heverlee B-3001, Belgium

CHRISTIAN, CURT, mathematician; b. Linz, Austria, May 30, 1920; s. Camillo and Christine (Vicek) C.; m. Ekaterina Trendafilowa, 1946; 1 dau., Claudia. MD, U. Vienna, 1947, PhD, 1953. Practice gen. and psychiat. medicine, 1947-66; mem. faculty U. Vienna, 1966—, prof. math., 1969-98; dir. Inst. Logistic, 1967-90; hon. prof. Tech. U., Vienna, 1972—. Author papers in field. Fellow Internat. Biog. Assn. (life); mem. Austrian Acad. Scis., Acad. Scis. Bologna (Italy), Am. Math. Soc., Assn. Symbolic Logic, Oesterreichische Mathematische Gesellschaft, Oesterreichische Computer Gesellschaft, Gesellschaft Sprachwissenschaften, Philosophische Gesellschaft, Oesterreichische Ä rztekammer. Roman Catholic. Home: 45 Strassergasse, Vienna A-1190, Austria Office: 25 Wachringer Strasse, A-1090 Vienna Austria

CHRISTIAN, DAVID GILBERT, historian; b. N.Y.C., Dec. 8, 1946; arrived in Australia, 1975; s. John and Carol Cathay (Tuttle) C.; m. Richarda Haidin Randall, Oct. 17, 1969; children: Joshua Richard, Emily Carol Sophia. BA, Oxford U., 1968; MA, U. West Ontario, 1970; DPhil, Oxford U., 1974. Lectr. Macquarie U., Sydney, Australia, 1975-82; sr. lectr. Macquarie U., Sydney, Australia, 1982-91; assoc. prof. Malquarie U., Sydney, Australia, 1991—. Author: Living Water: Vodka and Russian Society on the Eve of Emancipation, 1990, Power & Privilege: The Russian Empire and the Soviet Union in the 19th and 20th Centuries, 1994; co-author: Bread and Salt: A Social and Economic History of Food & Drink in Russia, 1984. Mem. Australian Acad. Humanities. Avocations: singing, walking. Office: Macquarie U, Dept History, Sydney 2109, Australia

CHRISTIAN, GARY IRVIN, lawyer; b. Albany, Ga., July 7, 1951; s. Rupert Irvin and Alice Amelia (Smith) C.; 1 child, Amy Margaret. BA in History, Polit. Sci., David Lipscomb Coll., 1973; MPA, U. Tenn., 1974; JD, Vanderbilt U., 1979. Bar: Fla. 1979, U.S. Dist. Ct. (no. and mid. dists.) Fla 1979. Rsch. dir. Ala. League of Mcpls., Montgomery, 1974-76; instr. in pub. adminstrn. David Lipscomb Coll., Nashville, 1977-79; assoc. Rogers, Towers, Bailey, Jones & Gay, Jacksonville, Fla., 1979-83, Foley & Lardner, Jacksonville, 1983-86; ptnr. Christian, Prom, Korn & Zehmer, Jacksonville, 1986-92, Rumph, Stoddard & Christian, Jacksonville, 1992—. Editor-in-chief Vanderbilt Jour. of Transnational Law, 1978-79. Bd. dirs. PACE Ctr. for Girls, Inc., Jacksonville, 1984—, pres., 1984-86; mem. leadership Jacksonville, 1986-87; chmn. site selection com. St. Johns County Sch. Bd., 1993-95; mem. site selection com., St. Johns County Sch. Bd., 1989-91. Mem. ABA (condominiums and planned devels. com.), Jacksonville Bar Assn. (coord. continuing edn. 1984-85, vice chmn. real property sect. 1986-87, chmn. 1987-88, chmn. corps., banking & bus. sect. 1991-92), Wavemasters Soc. (pres. 1986-87), Jacksonville C. of C. (com. 100 1986-94), Southpoint Bus. Assn. (bd. dirs. 1990-98, pres. 1991-93), Oak Bridge Country Club, Seminole Club, Salt Creek Homeowners Assn. (bd. dirs. 1993-97, pres. 1994-96), Univ. Club, Deer Creek Country Club. Republican. Mem. Ch. of Christ. Avocations: golf, fishing, racquetball, hunting, stamp collecting. Home: 1719 Girvin Rd Jacksonville FL 32225-2620 Office: Rumph Stoddard & Christian 3100 University Blvd S Ste 101 Jacksonville FL 32216-2777

CHRISTIAN, JACKIE DON, JR., television production executive; b. Stockton, Calif., Dec. 14, 1970; s. Jackie Don and Paula Marie Christian; m. Tres Mali Scott-Christian, July 27, 1996. BA in Broadcast Journalism, Langston (Okla.) U., 1999. Cert. audio engr. Sound Masters Rec. & Engring. Sch., North Hollywood, Calif., 1991. Audio engr. Blast Creco & Virgin Rock Radio, L.A., 1988--98; dir. music, mktg., promotions, pers., and audio engring. Dion Promotions, L.A., 1989-98; staff writer Langston U. Gazette, 1993-97; radio prodn. mgr., TV 2-3 prodn. mgr. KALU, Langston, 1993-99; promoter LBM Promotions, Groove Daddy Promotions, Oklahoma City, 1997-98; CEO BU! Prodns., Guthrie, Okla., 1997—; videotape operator TV-9 (CBS affiliate), Oklahoma City, 1999—. Exec. prodr. (album) Langston Centennial Compilation Album, 1997; prodr. numerous commls., radio and TV. Mem. Nat. Assn. Black Journalists, Okla. Small Bus. Devel. Ctr., Pride of Stillwater (lodge 238), Omega Psi Phi.

CHRISTIAN, JOHN WYRILL, metallurgy educator; b. Scarborough, England, Apr. 9, 1926; s. John William and Louisa Christian; m. Maureen Smith; children: Louise Hilda, John William, Timothy James (dec.). BA, Oxford U., 1945, PhD, 1949. Lectr. in metallurgy Oxford U., 1955-62, reader, 1958-67, prof., 1967-89, emeritus prof., 1989—. Contbr. books and articles to profl. jours. Fax: 01815-511419. Home: 11 Charlbury Rd, Oxford OX2 6UT, England Office: Dept of Materials, Oxford Univ, Oxford OX1 3PH, England

CHRISTIAN, RICHARD CARLTON, university dean, former advertising agency executive; b. Dayton, Ohio, Nov. 29, 1924; s. Raymond A. and Louise (Gamber) C.; m. Audrey Bongartz, Sept. 10, 1949; children: Ann Christian Carra, Richard Carlton Jr. B.S. in Bus. Adminstrn, Miami U., Oxford, Ohio, 1948; MBA, Northwestern U., 1949; LLD (hon.), Nat.-Louis U., 1986; postgrad., Denison U., The Citadel, Biarritz Am. U. Mktg. analyst Rockwell Mfg. Co., Pitts., 1949-50; exec. v.p. Marsteller Inc., Chgo., 1951-60; pres. Marsteller Inc., 1960-75; bd. dirs., exec. com. Young and Rubicam, Inc., 1979-84; chmn. bd. Marsteller Inc., 1975-84, chmn. emeritus, 1984—; assoc. dean Kellogg Grad. Sch. Mgmt. Northwestern U., 1984-91, assoc. dean Medill Sch. Journalism, 1991-99; dir., chmn. Bus. Publs. Audit Circulation, Inc., 1969-75; Speaker, author marketing, sales mgmt., marketing research and advt. Trustee Northwestern U., 1970-74, Nat.-Louis U., Evanston, Ill., 1970-92, James Webb Young Fund for Edn., U. Ill., 1962-95; pres.

Nat. Advt. Rev. Coun., 1976-77; bd. adv. coun. mem. Miami U.; mem. adv. coun. J.L. Kellogg Grad. Sch. Mgmt., Northwestern U.; v.p., dir. Mus. Broadcast Comm.; dir. Can. U.S. Ednl. Exch. (Fulbright Found.). With inf. AUS, 1942-46, ETO. Recipient Ohio Gov.'s award 1977, Alumni medal, Alumni, Merit and Svc. awards Northwestern U.; named to the Advt. Hall of Fame, 1991. Mem. Am. Mktg. assn., Indsl. Mktg. Assn. (founder, chmn. 1951), Bus. Profl. Advt. Assn. (life mem. Chgo., pres. Chgo. 1954-55, nat. v.p. 1955-58, G. D. Crain award 1977), U. Ill. Found., Northwestern U. Bus. Sch. Alumni Assn. (founder, pres.), Am. Assn. Advt. Agys. (dir., chmn. 1976-77), Am. Acad. Advt. (1st disting. svc. award 1978), Northwestern U. Alumni Assn. (nat. pres. 1968-70), Mid-Am. Club, Comml. Club, Econ. Club Chgo., Kenilworth Club, Westmoreland Country Club, Alpha Delta Sigma, Beta Gamma Sigma, Delta Sigma Pi, Phi Gamma Delta. Baptist.

CHRISTIAN, SUZANNE HALL, financial planner; b. Hollywood, Calif., Apr. 28, 1935; d. Peirson M. and Gertrude (Engel) Hall; children: Colleen, Carolyn, Claudia, Cynthia. BA, UCLA, 1956; MA, Redlands U., 1979; cert. in fin. planning, U. So. Calif., 1986. CFP. Instr. L.A. City Schs., 1958-59; instr. Claremont (Calif.) Unified Schs., 1972-84, dept. chair, 1981-84; fin. planner Waddell & Reed, Upland, Calif., 1982-96, sr. account exec., 1986; br. mgr. Hornor, Townsend & Kent, Claremont, 1996—; corp. mem. Pilgrim Place Found., Claremont; lectr. on fin., estate and tax planning for civic and profl. groups. Author: Strands in Composition, 1979; host Money Talks with Suzanne Christian on local TV cable, 1993—. Mem. legal and estate planning com. Am. Cancer Soc., 1988—; profl. adv. com. YWCA-Inland Empire, 1987; treas. Fine Arts Scripps Coll., 1993-94; bd. dirs. Casa Colina Hosp., Galelio Soc. Harvey Mudd Coll. Recipient Athena Internat. Businesswoman of Yr. award, 1997. Mem. Inst. CFPs, Fin. Planning Assn., Planned Giving Roundtable, Estate Planning Coun. Pomona Valley (pres.-elect, bd. dirs.), Claremont C. of C. (pres., bd. dirs. 1994-95), Curtain Raisers Club Garrison (pres. 1972-75), Circle of Champions (pres.'s coun. 1994-95, Silver Crest award 1985-87, 94, 95, HTK top ten leader 1996, 97, 98, 99), Harvey Mudd Coll. Galelio Soc. (bd. dirs. 1997-98), Kappa Kappa Gamma (pres. 1970-74). Avocations: tennis, gardening, archaeology. Fax: 909-625-3661. Home: PO Box 1237 Claremont CA 91711-1237 Office: Hornor Townsend & Kent 419 Yale Ave Claremont CA 91711-4340

CHRISTIANSEN, ERLING N., biochemist, educator; b. Bergen, Norway, Dec. 15, 1931; s. Erling Bruun and Esther (Neumann) C. MS, U. Oslo, 1959, PhD, 1975. Asst. prof. nutritional biochemistry U. Oslo, 1969-92, prof., 1993-98, sr. scientist, 1998—; prof. II, U. Bergen, 1992-95; gen. sec. Scandanavian Forum for Lipid Rsch. and Tech. (Lipidforum), 1997—. Contbr. articles to profl. publs. Mem. Am. Oil Chemistry Soc., European Acad. Nutrition Soc., Norwegian Biochem. Soc. Fax: 47-2285-1341. Home: Pres Harbitz Gt 22 B, N 0259 Oslo Norway Office: Inst Nutrition Rsch, U Oslo Box 1046, N 0316 Oslo Norway

CHRISTIANSEN, ROY HVIDKAER, lawyer; b. Detroit, Dec. 24, 1932; s. Rasmus H. and Gudrun (Lohmann-Sorensen) C.; m. Barbara L. Stauffer, June 9, 1956; children: Kathryn G. Hardy, Patricia L. Kalbfleich, Kai H., Karl H. BA, U. Mich., 1954, JD, 1957. Bar: Mich. 1957, U.S. Dist. Ct. (ea. dist.) Mich. 1957, U.S. Supreme Ct. 1962, U.S. Ct. Appeals (6th cir.) 1966, U.S. Dist. Ct. (we. dist.) Mich. 1989. Assoc. Erickson, Dyll, Marentary & Van Alsburg, Detroit, 1958-59; gen. counsel Transam. Freight Lines, Inc., Detroit, 1959-71; of counsel Kerr, Russell and Weber, Detroit, 1972-98; vis. cir. judge 6th Cir. of Mich., 1999-2000. Judge City of Huntington Mcpl. Ct., Huntington Woods, Mich., 1969-76, City of Detroit Recorders Ct., 1971-73; past mayor, councilman City of Huntington Woods. Fielding H. Yost scholar. Fellow Am. Coll. Trial Lawyers, Mich. State Bar Found.; mem. ABA, Mich. Bar Assn., Detroit Bar Assn., Oakland County Bar Assn. Republican. Presbyterian. Avocations: travel, fishing, music, gardening, sports observing. Office: Kerr Russell and Weber 500 Woodward Ave Ste 2500 Detroit MI 48226-3427

CHRISTIE, AMIEL COLIN, pathologist; b. Sydney, NSW, Australia, Mar. 26, 1920; s. Colin and Helen Mary (Seton) C.; m. Betty Margaret Stewart, Oct. 5, 1955; children: Andrew, Jonathan, Rosemary, David. MBBS, Sydney U., 1942, MD, 1955; Diploma Clin. Pathology, London U., 1948. Med. diplomate. Pathology registrar Royal Prince Alfred Hosp., Sydney, 1942-44; dir. pathology Repatriation Hosp., Perth, 1946-47; asst. pathologist Royal Marsden Hosp., London, 1949-54; dir. pathology Royal Hosp. for Women, Sydney, 1955-61; cons. pathologist The Wollongong Hosp., Australia, 1962-84, emeritus cons., 1984—. Contbr. articles to profl. jours. Capt. Australian Army Med. Corps, 1944-46. Fellow Royal Coll. Pathologists of Australasia, Royal Coll. Pathologists (Eng.); mem. AAAS, Am. Soc. Clin. Pathologists, Assn. Clin. Pathologists (Gt. Britain), Internat. Soc. Dermatopathology, Internat. Soc. Haematology. Mem. Ch. of England. Avocations: tennis, reading. Home: 170 Edinburgh Rd Castlecrag, Sydney NSW 2068, Australia Office: 39 Market St, NSW 2500 Wollongong Australia

CHRISTIE, DAVID JOHN, energy conservation administrator; b. Olympia, Wash., June 15, 1947; s. Edwin John and Joanne Lenore Christie; m. Patricia Lynne Christie, Jan. 20, 1989; children: Todd Martin, Cody Martin, Carole Gibbs, Bonnie Gibbs. BS in Physics, So. Oreg. U., 1969; postgrad., Wash. State U., 1969-75. Cert. energy mgr. Ptnr. Seahorse Bay Restaurant, Beaverton, Oreg., 1978-81; restaurant energy cons. Portland, 1981-82; energy analyst, insp. Farwest Energy Mgmt., Kelso, Wash., 1982-87; conservation program auditor Braco Energy Svcs., Seattle, 1986-90; comml./ind. energy auditor Braco Energy Svcs., Portland, Oreg., 1990-95; conservation program mgr. McMinnville (Oreg.) Water and Light, 1995—. Author: BPA Residential Auditor/Inspector Training Manual, 1984, (tng. manual) Lighting Analysis Guide, 1992. With USNG, 1970-76. Recipient Green Lights Surveyor Ally award EPA, 1993-98, Achievement and Leadership award Oreg. Mcpl. Electric Conservation Agy., 1997. Mem. Assn. Profl. Energy Mgrs. Avocations: chess, tennis. E-mail: davidj@mc-power.com. Home: 1224 NE Kirby St Mcminnville OR 97128-3706 Office: McMinnville Water and Light 855 NE Marsh Ln Mcminnville OR 97128-9309

CHRISTIE, DAVID THOMAS, information systems specialist, conductor; b. Beckenham, Kent, Eng., Nov. 11, 1957; arrived in Switzerland, 1987.; s. Leslie Arthur and Vera Lilian (Lipscombe) C.; m. Jacqueline Imhof, June 23, 1995; children: Séan Alexander, Aedán Tavish. MA, Balliol Coll., Oxford, Eng., 1980. Software engr. Logica Ltd., London, 1980-83; software project mgr. Logica SA/NV, Brussels, 1983-87; software projects cons. Digital Equipment, Zürich, 1987-90; software cons., project mgr. Logica Informatik, Zürich, 1990-96; account mgr. Union Bank Switzerland, Zürich, 1996-98; v.p. strategic projects markets divsn. Swiss Exch., Zürich, 1998—. Orchestral mgr. Cantiere Internat. d'Arte, Montepulciano, Italy, 1980-82; condr., founder Orch. Con Brio, Brussels, 1986-87; condr. Orchestergesellschaft Winterthur, Switzerland, 1991-99; mus. dir. MusicMakers, 2000—. Sec. Jr. Common Room, Balliol Coll., Oxford, 1978-79; treas. Gyrenbad Water Co., 1999—. Mem. IEEE, British Computer Soc., Condrs. Guild. Avocations: music, skiing, walking, cooking. Office: Swiss Exch, Selnaustr 30 Postfach, CH-8021 Zürich Switzerland

CHRISTIE, JULIE, actress; b. Chukua, India, Apr. 14, 1940; d. Frank St. John and Rosemary Ramsden C. Student, Central Sch. Dramatic Art, London, Brighton Coll. Tech. Profl. Debut in Brit. TV series A is for Andromeda, 1962; (TV movies) Dadah is Death, 1988, The Railway Station Man, 1992; (TV miniseries) Karaoke, 1996; (films) Crooks Anonymous, 1962, The Fast Lady, 1963, Billy Liar, 1963, Young Cassidy, 1964, Darling, 1965, Dr. Zhivago, 1965, Fahrenheit 451, 1966, Far From the Madding Crowd, 1967, Petulia, 1968, In Search of Gregory, 1969, The Go-Between, 1971, McCabe and Mrs. Miller, 1971, Don't Look Now, 1974, Shampoo, 1975, Demon Seed, 1977, Heaven Can Wait, 1978, The Return of the Soldier, 1981, Heat and Dust, 1983, The Gold Diggers, 1984, The Tattoed Memory, 1986, Fathers and Sons, 1988, The Railway Station, 1991, Power, 1986, Miss Mary, 1987, La Memoire tatouél, Fools of Fortune, 1990, Hamlet, 1996, Dragonheart, 1996, Afterglow, 1997; appeared with Birmingham Repertory Co., 1963, Royal Shakespeare Co., 1964; appeared in plays Old Times, Wyndham's, 1995; other TV appearances include: Sins of the Fathers, 1988, The Miracle Maker, 1999. Recipient Academy award for best actress in Darling, 1965; N.Y. Film Critics Circle award, 1965; Best Dramatic Actress Laurel award and Herald award, 1967. Office: 23 Linden Gardens, London W2 4HD, England also: c/o Agents Associes, 201 rue Fauburg St Honore, 75008 Paris France

CHRISTIE, RENFREW LESLIE, dean; b. Johannesburg, South Africa, Sept. 11, 1949; s. Frederick John and Lindsay Chapman (Taylor) C.; m. Menan du Plessis, June 14, 1990; children: Camilla Rose, Aurora Lindsay. BA with honors, U Cape Town, South Africa, 1974, MA, 1975; DPhil, Oxford U., England, 1979; B of Comm., U. South Africa, 1985. Deputy pres. Nat. Unin South African Students, 1971-72; jr. lectr. U. Cape Town, South Africa, 1975, acad. planner, 1987-90; dean rsch. U. Western Cape, South Africa, 1990—. Author: Electricity, Industry and Class in South Africa, 1984; co-author: (chpt.) Strikes, Machinery, Productivity and Colour in the South African Mines, 1995. Polit. prisoner African Nat. Congress, Pretoria, 1979-86. With South African Mil., 1967. Field Marshal Smuts scholar Oxford U., 1975-79, guest scholar Woodrow Wilson Ctr., Washington, 1994; sr. rsch. fellow Stiftung Fir Wissenschaft, Germany, 1994. Avocations: parenting, reading, music, swimming, scepticism. Home: 2 Glade Rd Rondebosch, Cape Town 7700, South Africa Office: U West Cape, Pvt Bag X17, Bellville 7535, South Africa

CHRISTIE, RICHARD WALLACE, retired structural engineer; b. Ridgewood, N.J., Jan. 21, 1928; s. William Donald and Dorothy Seberne (Bensen) C.; m. Jean Anne Grebenstein, Feb. 6, 1954; children: Susan, Douglas, Martha. BS in Engring., U. Mich., 1950; MEngring., Yale U., 1951. Registered profl. engr., N.Y., N.J., Conn., Calif. Engr. Hardesty & Hanover, N.Y.C., 1951-56; assoc. Hardesty & Hanover, 1956-71, ptnr., 1972-94, ptnr. emeritus, 1995—; Mem. steel structures com., 1974—, chmn. movable bridge subcom., 1993— Am. Railway Engring. Assn.; mem. structural welding com., 1971-96 Am. Welding Soc.; mem. Can./CSA movable bridge design code com., 1992—. Co-author: 50-Yr. History of Movable Bridge Constrn., 1975. Mem. Ridgewood Planning Bd., 1976-81. Fellow ASCE (Roebling award 1989). Mem. Reformed Ch. of Am. (elder). Avocations: woodworking. Home: 87 Green Knolls Dr Wayne NJ 07470-6123 Office: Hardesty & Hanover 1501 Broadway Ste 310 New York NY 10036-5587

CHRISTING, ADAM, performing company executive; b. Inglewood, Calif., Feb. 28, 1964; s. Paul Duane and Marianne (Stoddard) Brown. BA, Biola U., 1986. Pres. CLEAN COMEDIANS, La Mirada, Calif., 1990—. Editor: Comedy Comes Clean I, 1996, II, 1997. Mem. The Magic Castle. Office: CLEAN COMEDIANS 14752 Beach Blvd Ste 207 La Mirada CA 90638-4256

CHRISTMAN, IRENE RANCK, retired music education association administrator; b. Lancaster, Pa., Nov. 27, 1918; d. David Garfield and Kathryn Elizabeth (Mentzer) Ranck; m. Russell Berlin Christman, Dec. 12, 1949 (dec.); children: Robert Randolph Miller, John David. BS in Music Edn. and Music Supervision, Lebanon Valley Coll., 1939; cert., U. Pa., 1940; postgrad., U. R.I., 1951, Pa. State U., 1953. Cert. educator, Pa. Music supr., band dir. Warwick Twp. (Pa.) Schs., 1939-49; music supr. Middletown (Pa.) Schs., 1949-53; chmn. music edn. Cen. Dauphin Schs., Harrisburg, Pa., 1953-84; bd. dirs., edn. com. Symphony Orch., Hershey, Pa., 1991-94, bd. sec. 1994-96; organist, band/choral dir., vocal soloist. Contr. articles to profl. jours. Fund-raiser cancer and heart assns.; ch. choir mem. Recipient Nat. award Music Industry Conf., 1991, Silver Burdett Ginn Publ. Citation, 1993. Mem. Pa. Music Educators Assn. (life, exec. dir. 1953-96, emeritus 1996—), Music Educators Nat. Conf. (chmn. nat. coun. state sects. 1981-83, state sec. div. 1953—, Nat. Svc. award 1990), Pa. Soc. Assn. Execs. (sec., pres. 1991-97), Dauphin County Music Educators Assn. (pres. 1953-55), Pilot Club of Harrisburg, Pi Gamma Mu. Republican. Presbyterian. Avocations: travel, art, reading, voice and piano, antiques. Home and Office: Real Estate 3512 Cloverfield Rd Harrisburg PA 17109-2029

CHRISTODOULIDES, ANDREAS DEMOSTHENES, educational administrator, researcher, editor; b. Oekos, Nicosia, Cyprus, Oct. 24, 1918; s. Demosthenes and Eleni Christodoulides; m. Loulla Theocharides; children: Stella, Costas. BA, U. London, 1953, diploma in edn., 1955; diploma ednl. adminstrn. and supervision, Northwestern U., 1961. Tchr. Govt. Cyprus, Nicosia, 1939-46; lectr. Tchrs. Coll. Morphou, Cyprus, 1946-49; sch. prin. Dept. Edn., Morphou, 1949-51; sch. inspector Dept. Edn., Nicosia, 1951-60, chief inspector schs., 1960-70; dir. primary edn. Ministry Edn., Nicosia, 1970-77; dir. overseas svcs. Ministry for Affairs, Nicosia, 1977-82; dean of adminstrn. Internat. Coll., Nicosia, 1983—; pres. Nat. Com. for Internat. Yr. of Child, Cyprus, 1978-81; del. Coun. Europe Out-of-Sch. Edn., Strasbourg, 1963-77; papers presented to numerous orgns. Author: Reading Primer, 1959, The Story of Communications, 1950, Talks to Parents, 1967, We and Our Children, 1981; editor, contbr. Cyprus Edn. Rsch. Bull. (hon. pres. 1995), Family and Sch. (hon. pres. 1996), (children's periodical) Avgerinos, 1983-96. Pres. Pancyprian Sch. for Parents, founder, 1963-96; pres. Expatriates Assn., Nicosia, 1979-83, Kalopanayiotis, 1981—; pres. New Generation Assn., Nicosia, 1983—, Kalopanayiotis Cultural Centre, 1990—; mem. Anti-Cancer Soc., 1976—, Cyprus Internat. Bd. Books for Young People, 1980—. Recipient hon. plaque Parents Found., 1971. Mem. Cyprus Edn. Rsch. Assn. (pres. 1961-84, hon. plaque 1995), Cyprus Assn. for Books for Children and Young People, Cyprus Assn. for Family Planning, Pancyprian Assn. for Mental Hygiene, Am. Ednl. Rsch. Assn. Mem. Progressive Dem. Party. Greek Orthodox. Avocations: reading, writing, gardening, stamp collecting, violin. Home: Flat 53, 24 Michalakopoulos Str, 1075 Nicosia Cyprus Office: Avgerinos Periodical, PO Box 5105, 1307 Nicosia Cyprus

CHRISTODOULOS, ARCHBISHOP, archbishop; b. Xanthi, 1939. PhD in Theology, law degree. Ordained as deacon, 1964, priest, 1965. Pastor of ch. Dormition of the Virgin in the Phaleron, Volos, 1966; chief sec. Holy Synod; elected Metropolitan of Dimitriados, Volos, 1974; archbishop Greek Orthodox Ch. Office: Church of Greece, Ag Philotheis 21, 10556 Athens Greece*

CHRISTODOULOU, CHRIS, management professional, educator; b. Melbourne, Australia, Apr. 25, 1944; s. Sofocles and Maria (Giasoumi) C.; m. Despina Petrou, Nov. 4, 1967; children: David, Danielle, John. B in Agrl. Sci., U. Melbourne, 1965; MSc, Monash U., 1967, MBA, 1974, PhD, 1984. Dept. head rsch. svc., process devel. H.J. Heinz Co. Australia Ltd., Melbourne, 1968-75; asst. to mng. dir. Brown & Dureau Ltd., Melbourne, 1975; from lectr. to assoc. prof. mgmt. Swinburne U. Tech., Melbourne, 1976-99, adj. assoc. prof., 1999—; adj. prof. Royal Melbourne Inst. Tech., 1999—; vis. prof. UNITEC, Auckland, New Zealand, 1999. Mem. Australia-New Zealand Acad. Mgmt., Strategic Mgmt. Soc. Office: Swinburne U Tech Grad Sch, John St Hawthorn, 3122 Melbourne Victoria, Australia

CHRISTODOULOU, CHRISTODOULOS, government official; b. Avgorou, Famagusta, Cyprus, Apr. 13, 1939; married; 1 child. Grad., Pantios Univ. Polit. Sci., Athens, 1968; degree in law, Aristotelian U., Salonica, Greece, 1972; PhD in Law, U. Wales, 1992. Tchr. primary edn., 1962; with publs. sect. Pub. Info. Office Govt. of Cyprus, Nicosia, 1962-66, dir. Govt. Printing Office, 1972-85, permanent sec. Ministry of Labor and Social Ins., 1985-89, permanent sec. Ministry Agr. and Natural Resources, 1989-94, min. finance, 1994-99, min. interior, 1999—. Contbr. articles to profl. jours. Office: Minister of Interior, Dem Severis Av-Ex-Sec Compd, Nicosia Cyprus

CHRISTODOULOU, EFTHYMIOS NICOLAS, government official, banker; b. Larissa, Greece, Dec. 2, 1932; s. Nicolaos and Electra Christodoulou; m. Eftychia Boboli; children: Nicolaos, Natalia, Alexander. Diploma, Athens Coll., 1951; BA in Econs., Hamilton Coll., 1953; MA in Econs., Columbia U., 1955. Econ. adviser, dir. Nat. Bank of Greece, Athens, 1959-74; dir. Nat. Investment Bank for Indsl. Devel. (ETEBA), Athens, 1959-74, dir. gen., 1974-79; chmn., CEO Olympic Airways, Athens, 1977-79; gov., CEO Nat. Bank of Greece, Athens, 1979-81; pres. Union of Greek Banks, Athens, 1979-81; mem. european parliament People's Party, 1984-90, 94-99; alt. min. Ministry of Fgn. Affairs, Athens, 1990; from alt. min. to min. Ministry of Nat. Economy, Athens, 1990-92; gov. Bank of Greece, Athens, 1992-93; mem. budget com. Rapporteur for '86 budget of EEC, Brussels, 1986. Office: Bank of Greece, 18 Alex.Soutsou St, 10250 Athens 10671, Greece

CHRISTODOULOU, MANOLIS A., electronics educator, consultant, engineer, researcher; b. Athens, Greece, Oct. 9, 1955; s. Adonis M. and Mary E. (Grimani) C.; m. Kallia P. Papadoyiannis, Aug. 20, 1980; children: Adonis, Panos. Diploma in electricity, Nat. Tech. U. Athens, 1978; MSEE, U. Md., 1979; diploma in engring., U. So. Calif., L.A., 1982; PhD in Elec. Engring., Democritus U., Thrace, Greece, 1984. Registered profl. engr., Greece. Teaching asst. U. Md., College Park, 1978-79, U. So. Calif., L.A., 1979-82; rsch., teaching asst. Democritus U., Xanthi, Greece, 1982-84; asst. prof. U. Patras, Greece, 1984-87; assoc. prof. Syracuse (N.Y.) U., 1987-89; prof. U. Crete, Chania, Greece, 1989—; cons. Alpha, SAI, Athens, 1984—. Contbr. numerous articles to profl. jours. St. Fellow Found. of Athens fellow, 1973-78. Mem. IEEE (sr.), Tech. Chamber Greece. Avocations: swimming, skiing. Home: 53 Moreos St, 16561 Glyfada Athens, Greece Office: Tech U Crete, Univ Campus, 73100 Chania Crete, Greece

CHRISTOFF, CHRISTIAN SERGE, foreign trade consultant; b. Ixelles, Brabant, Belgium, Jan. 2, 1936; s. Stoyan and Persa (Shopoff) C.; m. Martine Claire Vanderlinden, Dec. 21, 1963; children: Ivan, Olivier. Degree in Indsl. Chemistry Engring., C.E.R.I.A., Brussels, 1962. Quality control officer paint and varnish industry, Vilvoorde, Belgium, 1962-65; master of rsch. plastics industry, Brussels, 1966-74; tech., comml. rep. Argus Chem., Drogenbos, Belgium, 1975-79; area sales mgr. Ea. Europe-Mid. East Diamond Shamrock Europe, Drogenbos, 1980-85; area sales exec. Ea. Europe-Mid. East Harcros Chems., Brussels, 1986-89; area sales mgr. Ea. Europe Pitts. Corning Europe, Brussels, 1990; cons.-owner agreed by the Commn. of European Union Fgn. Trade Advisory Svcs., Braine-L'Alleud, Belgium, 1991—. Avocations: historical research, woodworking, music (piano), walking. Home: Rue du Faisan 6, 1420 Braine-l'Alleud Belgium Office: Fgn Trade Advisory Svcs, Rue du Faisan 6, 1420 Braine-l'Alleud Belgium

CHRISTOFFEL, DAVID ALEC, geophysicist, educator; b. New Plymouth, New Zealand, June 7, 1929; s. Wieland and Mary Eliza (Berntsen) C.; m. Marie Geraldine Valentine, Dec. 14, 1957; children: Paul, Penelope, Michael. BSc, Canterbury U., Christchurch, New Zealand, 1949, MSc with honors in Physics, 1952; PhD in Physics, Nottingham U., 1957. Rsch. fellow in geophysics U. B.C., Vancouver, Can., 1959-62; sr. lectr. in physics Victoria U., Wellington, New Zealand, 1962-66, assoc. prof. physics and earth scis., 1966-93; semi-ret., cons. in Earth scis., 1993. Contbr. articles to profl. jours. Lt. New Zealand Sci. Def. Corps, 1952-54. Mem. Citizen's Advice Bur., Otaki, New Zealand, 1998—. Fellow Royal Soc. New Zealand; mem. Am. Geophys. Union, Rotary Internat. (pres.-elect Otaki br. 2000—). Anglican. Avocations: choral singing, lawn bowls, hiking, skiing, small farming. Home: 62 Old Coach Rd N, Otaki New Zealand Office: Inst Geophysics, Victoria U PO Box 600, Wellington New Zealand

CHRISTOFFERSEN, MARTIN LINDSEY, evolutionary theory educator, researcher; b. São Paulo, Brazil, Apr. 10, 1953; s. Finn Elwarth and Joan Audrey (Lindsey) C.; m. Maria de Fatima Gomes de Lima; children: Hana Gomes de Lima Lindsey, Mauri Kanagawa. BS in Zoology, U. São Paulo, 1975, MS in Zoology, 1977; specialization in marine ecology, Duke U., 1978; PhD in Scis., U. São Paulo, 1980. Coord. Marine Sci. Rsch. Ctr. and grad. course in zoology Fed. U. Paraiba, João Pessoa, Brazil, 1980-84, prof. ecology, 1980, prof. invertebrate zoology, 1981-93, prof. carcinology, 1980-90, prof. comparative biology, 1991—, prof. evolution, 1994—; collector and curator Brazilian coastal marine invertebrates, establishing rep. collection in João Pessoa, 1977-90; vis. rschr., Smithsonian Instn., Washington, Am. Mus., Harvard U., Cambridge, Mass., 1978; scientific ad hoc cons. several nat. instns. and jours., 1980—; pres. Scientific Commn., Brazilian Congress Zoology, João Pessoa, 1988. Contbr. articles to profl. jours.; editor (jour.) Revista Nordestina de Biologia, 1986-94; mem. editl. com. Jour. Comparative Biology, 1995—. UNESCO/Rockefeller Found. fellow, 1978; rsch. scholar São Paulo State Found., 1975-79, Fed. Dist. Nat. Coun., 1981—; recipient A.R. Ferreira award for best paper, Brazilian Soc. Zoology, 1989. Mem. AAAS, Willy Hennig Soc. Avocations: tennis, classical guitar, cave exploration, languages, real estate. E-mail: mlchrist@dse.ufpb.br. Home: Ave Sapé 1800 Apt 102, 58038382 João Pessoa Brazil Office: Fed U Paraiba, Dept Sistematica & Ecologia, 58059900 João Pessoa Paraiba, Brazil

CHRISTOL, CARL Q(UIMBY), lawyer, political science educator; b. Gallup, S.D., June 28, 1913; s. Carl and Winifred (Quimby) C.; m. Jeannette Stearns, Dec. 18, 1949; children: Susan Quimby Christol-Deacon, Richard Stearns (dec.). AB, U. SD., 1934, LLD (hon.), 1977; AM, Fletcher Sch. Law and Diplomacy, 1936; postgrad., Institut Universitaire des Hautes Etudes Internationales, Geneva, 1937-38, U. Geneva, 1937-38; PhD, U. Chgo., 1941; LLB, Yale U., 1947; postgrad., Acad. Internat. Law, The Hague, 1950. Bar: Calif. 1949, S.D. 1948. Assoc. firm Guthrie, Darling and Shattuck, Los Angeles, 1948-49; of counsel Fizzolio, Fizzolio & McLeod, Sherman Oaks, Calif., 1949-94; assoc. prof. polit. sci. U. So. Calif., 1949-59, prof., 1959-87, prof. emeritus, 1987—, chmn. dept. polit. sci., 1960-64, 75-77; Stockton chair internat. law U.S. Naval War Coll., 1962-63, cons., 1963-70; cons. World Law Fund; mem. L.A. Mayor's Adv. Com. Human Rels., Commn. to Study Orgn. of Peace; mem. adv. panel on internat. law Dept. State, 1970-76; v.p. Ct. of Man Found., 1971-77; scholar-in-residence Rockefeller Found. Bellagio Conf. and Study Ctr., Italy, 1980. Author: Transit by Air in International Law, 1941, Introduction to Political Science, 1957, 4th edit., 1982, Readings in International Law, 1959, The International Law of Outer Space, 1966, The International Legal and Institutional Aspects of the Stratosphere Ozone Problem, 1975, The Modern International Law of Outer Space, 1982, Space Law: Past, Present and Future, 1991; bd. editors: Western Polit. Quar, 1970-75, Internat. Lawyer, 1975-84, Space Policy, 1985—, Internat. Legal Materials, 1985—, Australian Internat. Law Jour., 1998—; contbr. articles on legal, polit. and mil. subjects to profl. jours. Bd. dirs. Los Angeles County Heart Assn., 1956-61. Served to lt. col. AUS, 1941-46; col. Res. ret. Decorated Bronze Star medal; recipient Dart award U. So. Calif., 1970, Assos. award for excellence in teaching, 1977, Raubenheimer award, 1982, Disting. Emeritus award, 1990, Rockefeller Found. fellow, 1958-59. Mem. Am., Los Angeles bar assns., Am. Soc. Internat. Law (exec. council 1973-76), Internat. Studies Assn. (chmn. internat. law sect. 1977-78), Internat. Acad. Astronautics, State Bar Calif., UN Assn. Los Angeles (pres. 1961-63), Am. Polit. Sci. Assn., Internat. Inst. Space Law (pres. Am. br. 1973-75, Lifetime Achievement award 1998), Town Hall, AIAA, Internat. Law Assn., UN Assn. U.S. (dir. 1967-69), Masons, Blue Key, Skull and Dagger, Rotary, Phi Beta Kappa, Phi Kappa Phi (award 1987), Alpha Tau Omega. Republican. Presbyterian. Home: 1041 Anoka Pl Pacific Palisades CA 90272-2414 Office: U So Calif Polit Sci Dept Los Angeles CA 90089-0001

CHRISTOPHE, ARMAND BRUNO, nutrition educator, consultant; b. Berchem, Flanders, Belgium, Apr. 21, 1941; s. Raymond and Emmerencia (Van Camp) C.; m. Maria Dekoninck, Sept. 15, 1966; children: Guy, Nadine, Filip, Veronique. Licentiate Chemistry, U. Ghent, Belgium, 1962, PhD in Sci., 1966, Doctorate in Biochemistry, 1978. Rsch. asst. U. Ghent, 1963-66, 1st asst., 1966-72, rsch. leader, 1972-78, mem. faculty aggregate, 1978-85, 88-91, prof., 1991—; sr. rsch. assoc. Rice U., Houston, 1985-88; cons. in field, 1991—. Author: Introduction to Biochemistry, 1966, Introduction to Nutrition, 1994, Structural Modified Food Fats: Synthesis, Biochemistry and Use, 1998, Fat Digestion and Absorption, 2000, also over 200 rsch. papers in field; assoc. editor INFORM. Recipient Prize Stas. Belgian prize Belgian Royal Acad. Medicine, 1971-73, Prize MSW DeVooght, Cystic Fibrosis Assn., 1983; Hormel fellow U. Minn., 1984. Mem. Belgian Soc. Biochemistry, Am. Oil Chemist Soc., Royal Flemish Soc. Chemistry, Internat. Soc. Study Fats and Fatty Acids, European Acad. Nutritional Scis. E-mail: Armand.Christophe@rug.ac.be. Office: Univ Hosp, De Pintelaan 185, B 9000 Ghent Belgium

CHRISTOPHER, IRENE, librarian, consultant; b. Greece, Nov. 17, 1922; came to U.S., 1923; d. George and Helen (Stephens) C. AB, Boston U., 1944; BLS, Simmons Coll., 1945. Gen. asst. Robbins Pub. Libr., Arlington, Mass., 1945-46; gen. asst. Boston U. Chenery Libr., 1946-47, head circulation dept., 1947-48, head reference dept., 1948-62; dir. libr. Emerson Coll., Boston, 1962-68; dir. Gordon McKay libr. Harvard U., Cambridge, Mass., 1968-70; chief libr. Boston U. Med. Ctr., 1970-92. Mem. AAUW, ALA (various coms. 1962-82, coun. 1970-74), Spl. Librs. Assn. (various coms. Boston chpt. 1952-75), Am. Soc. Info. Sci., Women's Nat. Book Assn., North Atlantic Health Scis. Librs., Med. Libr. Assn., New Eng. Online Users Group, Inc., Mass. Libr. Assn., Boston U. Women's Coun. Home: 790 Boylston St Apt 11C Boston MA 02199-7911

CHRISTOPHER, JAMES CHARLES, theater and film critic; b. Dublin, Ireland, Mar. 25, 1966; s. Lloyd Jerome and Mairin Margaret (Hargaden) C.; m. Dina Mary Southwell, Nov. 2, 1996; 1 child, Samson. MA with honors, Edinburgh (Scotland) U., 1986. Dep. theater editor Time Out, London, 1987-96; theater critic Sunday Express, London, 1996; theater critic The Times, London, 1997-99, film critic, 1999—; lectr. Brit. Am. Dramatic Arts, London, 1997-98; judge Perrier Comedy Awards, Edinburgh, 1997. Author: (biography) Elizabeth Taylor, 1999; editor jours. Fringe Frisk, 1996, Fringe in Focus, 1997 (Nat. West Livewire award); dir. stage play The Shoeshop of Desire, 1997. Mem. Critics Cir. Avocations: motorbikes, golf, fantasizing, skiing. Home: 84 A Savernake Rd, London NW3 2JR, England

CHRISTOPHER, JAMES ROY, executive director; b. Fort Worth, Aug. 4, 1942; s. Roy Leslie and Mary Ruth (Hudson) C. Student, U. Tex., 1962-64, UCLA, 1978-79. Program dir. Priority One Outpatient Treatment Ctr., Beverly Hills, Calif., 1987-89; founder, exec. dir. SOS/Secular Orgns. for Sobriety, L.A., 1986—; lectr. in field; originator events Funeral for the Unknown Smoker (annual), Unknown Smoker's Day, 2000, Memorial to the Unknown Smoker. Author: How to Stay Sober: Recovery Without Religion, 1988, Unhooked: Staying Sober and Drug Free, 1989, SOS Sobriety: The Proven Alternative to 12 Step Programs, 1992, Escape from Nicotine Country; How to Stop Smoking Painlessly, 1999; contbr. articles to profl. jours.; over 300 appearances in radio and TV. Mem. ACA, Am. Coun. on Alcoholism. Unitarian. Avocations: hiking, running, theatre, film. Office: Secular Orgns for Sobriety SOS Internat Clearinghouse 5521 Grosvenor Blvd Los Angeles CA 90066-6915

CHRISTOPHER, RUPERT LAWRENCE, diplomat; b. Berbice, Guyana, Feb. 2, 1956; s. Robert Louis Christopher and Linda Harriéte Simons; m. Nadia Georgine Klaverweide, June 4, 1977; children: Tamara, Roel, Robert, John. Degree in mil. scis., Army Staff Coll., Brazil, 1993, D Mil. Applications, Planning, Studies, 1997. Mil. police officer Ministry of Def., Suriname, 1982-84, head info. svc., 1984-89; def. negotiator Ministry of Def., 1984-89, 94-96; min. def. Ministry of Def., Suriname, 1991, head def. strategic planning, 1994-96; ambassador fgn. affairs Embassy of Suriname, Brasilia, Brazil, 1996—; def. negotiator M.O.D., 1984-89, 94-96; chief negotiator Free Trade Area of the Ams., 1997—; non-resident ambassador to Mercosur, Mercosul, 2000. Author: The F.T.A.A., 1998 (award L.Am. Noticias and Amazone Post 1999), (monograph) War and Irregular War, 1993. Hon. pres. Assn. L.Am. and Caribbean Freight Forwarders, Suriname, 1998; pres. Zwaluw Soccer Team, 1986-89; co-founder, hon. pres. C. of C. Suriname-Brasil. Recipient Medal of the Pacifist Brazilian Armed Forces. Mem. Assn. War Coll., Mem. Nat. Geographic Soc. Avocations: reading, jogging, writing. Office: Embassy of Suriname, Q1-9 Conj-8 Casa 24, 70454900 Brasilia Brazil

CHRISTOPHER, WARREN, lawyer, former government official; b. Scranton, N.D., Oct. 27, 1925; s. Ernest W. and Catharine Anna (Lemen) C.; m. Marie Josephine Wyllis, Dec. 21, 1956; children—Lynn, Scott, Thomas, Kristen. Student, U. Redlands, 1942-43; B.S. magna cum laude, U. So. Calif., 1945; LL.B., Stanford, 1949; LL.D. (hon.), Occidental U., 1977, Bates Coll., 1981, Brown U., 1981, Claremont Coll., 1981. Bar: Calif. 1949, N.Y., U.S. Supreme Ct. 1949. Law clk. U.S. Supreme Ct. Justice William O. Douglas, Washington, 1949-50; practice in Los Angeles, 1950-67, 69-76, 81-93, 97—; mem. firm O'Melveny & Myers, 1950-67, 69, ptnr., 1958-67, 69-76, 81-93, sr. ptnr., 1997—; dep. atty. gen. U.S., Washington, 1967-69; dep. sec. of state Dept. State, Washington, 1977-81; sec. U.S. Dept. of State, Washington, 1993-97; spl. counsel to Gov. Calif., 1959; cons. Office Under Sec. State, 1961-65; mem. bd. bar examiners State Bar Calif., 1966-67; dir. So. Calif. Edison Co., First Interstate Bancorp, Lockheed Corp.; chmn., trustee Carnegie Corp. N.Y.; mem. Calif. Coordinating Coun. for Higher Edn., 1960-67, pres., 1963-65; vice chmn. Gov.'s Commn. on L.A. Riots, 1965-66; chmn. U.S. delegations to U.S.-Japan Cotton Textile Negotiations, 1961, Geneva Conf. on Cotton Textiles, 1961; spl. rep. sec. state for Wool Textile Meetings, London, Rome, Tokyo, 1964-65; mem. Trilateral Commn., 1975-77, 81-88; mem. internat. adv. coun. Inst. Internat. Studies; chmn. Ind. Commn. on L.A. Police Dept., 1991. Author: In the Stream of History, 1998; co-author: American Hostages in Iran: The Conduct of a Crisis, 1985. Trustee Stanford U., 1971-77, 81-93, pres. bd. trustees, 1985-88; bd. dirs., vice chmn. Coun. on Fgn. Rels., 1982-91; bd. dirs. L.A. World Affairs Coun.; mem. exec. com. Am. Agenda, 1988; mem. U.S.-Korea Wisemen Coun., 1991-93. Lt. (j.g.) USNR, 1943-46. Decorated Medal of Freedom 1981; recipient Harold Weill award NYU, 1981, Louis Stein award Fordham U., 1981, Jefferson award Am. Inst. for Pub. Svc., UCLA medal, Thomas Jefferson award in law U. Va. Fellow Am. Bar Found., Am. Coll. Trial Lawyers, AAAS; mem. ABA (ho. dels. 1975-77, chmn. standing com. fed. judiciary 1975-77), Calif. Bar Assn. (gov. 1975-77), L.A. County Bar Assn. (pres. 1974-75), Am. Law Inst., Order of Coif, Calif. Club, Chancery Club, Phi Kappa Phi. Office: O'Melveny & Meyers 1999 Ave Of Stars Fl 7 Los Angeles CA 90067-6022

CHRISTOPHERSON, ELIZABETH GOOD, broadcast executive; b. Cin.; d. Walter R. and Jean S. Good; m. Paul C. Christopherson, July 3, 1971; 1 child, Katharine. BA, Wellesley Coll., 1971. Bd. dirs. N.J. State Coun. Arts, 1982—, chmn., CEO, 1989-91; exec. dir., CEO N.J. Network, Trenton, 1994—; pres., CEO NJN Found., 1994—; bd. dirs., mem. adv. coun. PNC Bank N.J.; bd. dirs. PBS, McCarter Theater; bd. dirs., mem. bus. leadership coun. Wellesly Coll. Pres., bd. dirs. Leadership Am. Assn., Alexandria, Va., 1991-92. Mem. N.J. C. of C. (bd. dirs.), Internat. Women's Forum (pres. N.J. chpt.). Office: NJ Network PO Box 777 Trenton NJ 08625-0777

CHRISTOPHERSON, MYRVIN FREDERICK, college president; b. Milltown, Wis., July 21, 1939; s. Fred J. and Inger J. (Haug) C.; m. Anne Christine Marking, June 10, 1967; children: Kirsten, Berit, Bjorn, Nisse. BA, Dana Coll., 1961; MS, Purdue U., 1963, PhD, 1965; DD (hon.), Wartburg Theol. Sem., 1998. Teaching asst., instr. Purdue U., West Lafayette, Ind., 1961-65; asst. prof. speech U. Wis., Madison, 1965-69; assoc. prof. communication U. Wis., Stevens Point, 1969-76, prof. communication, 1976-86, assoc. dean. fine arts and communication, 1970-86; pres. Dana Coll., Blair, Nebr., 1986—; cons. Wis. Telephone, Milw., 1968-78, AT&T, N.Y.C., 1969-71, 1st Fin. Corp., Stevens Point, 1980-86; commr. Nebr. Coordinating Commn. for Post Sec. Edn., 1989-91. Author: Speaker's Trainer's Guide, 1970, The Company Speaker, 1979; editor Jour. of the Wis. Communication Assn., 1978-80. Mem. Nebr. Ednl. Fin. Authority, 1991—, chmn., 1992-99; mem. adv. bd. The Lutheran, 1987-94, chmn., 1992-94; bd. dirs. Blair Cmty. Found., 1999—; bd. dirs. Planned Giving Svcs., Nebr., chmn., 1992-94; ann. fund appeal chmn. Meml. Cmty. Hosp., 1994; mem. pastoral call com. First Luth. Ch., 1995, mem. ch. coun., 1999; trustee Palmer Chiropractic U., 1998—; mem. coun. of presidents Evangel. Luth. Ch. in Am., 1999—, vice chmn., 1999-2000, chmn., 2000—. Inducted into Wall of Honor, Unity High Sch., Polk County, Wis.; fellow Palmer Coll. Chiropractic, Palmer Coll. Chiropractic-West; named Knight of The Order of the Dannebrog, Queen Margrethe II of Denmark, 1997. Mem. Nat. Assn. Ind. Colls. and Univs. (bd. dirs. 1997-99), Assn. Ind. Colls. Nebr. (chmn. 1992-93), Nebr. Ind. Coll. Found. (exec. com. 1990-92, vice chmn. 1992-93, chmn. 1994-95), Luth. Edn. Conf. N.Am., (vice chmn. 1994-95, chmn. 1995-96), Nebr. Ednl. TV Coun. for Higher Edn. (chmn. 1990-91), North Ctrl. Assn. Colls. and Schs. (cons.-evaluator 1997—), Nat. Assn. Intercoll. Athletics (coun. of presidents 1999—). Avocations: international travel, reading, writing, antique collecting, study of theology. Office: Dana Coll Office of Pres Blair NE 68008

CHRISTOPHORY, JUL ALFRED, government official, former library administrator; b. Luxembourg, Luxembourg, Apr. 22, 1939; s. Edouard and Marguerite (Jeitz) C.; m. Marielle Ruppert, July 19, 1966; children: Tom, Nadia. Cert. in modern letters, U. Sorbonne, Paris, 1962; student, King's Coll., London, 1963-64; PhD, U. Luxembourg, 1966. Prof. Lycée de Garçons, Luxembourg, 1966-72, Miami U. European Ctr., Luxembourg, 1970-77, Lycée Michel-Rodange, Luxembourg, 1972-83; dir. Nat. Library, Luxembourg, 1984-96; dir. European Commn. Represenation Office European Commn., Luxembourg, 1996—. Author: Who's Afraid of Luxembourgish?, 1973, The Luxembourgers in Their Own Words, 1978, Luxembourgeois, Qui Êtes-vous?, 1984, A Short History of Literature in Luxembourgish, 1994; co-author: Luxembourg, Vol. 23, 1981, rev. edit., 1997. Roman Catholic. Avocations: swimming, music, travel. Home: Ferme de Grevels, 8059 Bertrange, Luxembourg Luxembourg Office: Bâtiment Jean Monnet, L 2920 Luxembourg Luxembourg

CHRISTY, ALFRED ANTONY, research scientist; b. Jaffna, Sri Lanka, Dec. 21, 1952; came to Norway, 1983; s. Joseph and Maryppillai (Saverimutthu) Alfred; m. Marie Lilani Frederick, Jan. 31, 1977; children: Gehan, Salrina S., Kevin. BS in Chemistry, U. Ceylon, Sri Lanka, 1976; MS, U. Bergen, Norway, 1987; PhD, U. Bergen, 1990. Asst. lectr. U. Jaffna, 1976-77; sr. sci. master Nigerian Schs. Bd., 1977-83; asst. lectr. U. Bergen, 1983-87, rsch. officer, 1987-90, rsch. scientist, 1990-98; prof.-elect in analytical chemistry Agder Coll., Kristiansand, Norway, 1998—; chmn. Scandinavian Symposium on Infrared and Raman Spectroscopy dept. chemistry U. Bergen, 1994. Contbr. articles to profl. jours. Recipient Best Poster award European Assn. Organic Chemists, 1987, Rsch. scholarship U. Bergen, 1987. Roman Catholic. Avocations: reading, motor sport, micro mechanics. Home: Rodhettesvei - 18, Kristiansand 4638, Norway Office: Univ Bergen, Dept Chemistry, Bergen N-5007, Norway

CHRISTY, ARTHUR HILL, lawyer; b. Bklyn., July 25, 1923; s. Francis Taggart and Catherine Virginia (Damon) C.; m. Gloria Garvin Osborne, Feb. 14, 1980; children by previous marriage: Duncan Hill, Alexandra. A.B., Yale U., 1945; LL.B., Columbia U., 1949. Bar: N.Y. 1950. Assoc. firm Baldwin, Todd & Lefferts, N.Y.C., 1950-52; spl. asst. atty. gen. Saratoga Investigation, N.Y., 1952-53; asst. U.S. atty. So. Dist. N.Y., 1953-54; chief prosecutor spl. asst. atty. gen. Saratoga and Columbia County Investigations, 1954-55; asst. atty. gen. N.Y., 1955; chief criminal div. U.S. atty.'s Office, So. Dist. N.Y., 1955-57; chief asst. U.S. atty., 1957-58, U.S. atty., 1958-59; partner firm Christy & Viener (and predecessors), N.Y.C., 1959—; spl. asst. to Gov. Rockefeller, 1959-61; apptd. 1st spl. prosecutor Under Ethics in Govt. Act of 1978 to investigate charges against White House Chief of Staff, 1979-80. Artist in scrimshaw. Trustee, vice chmn. Bklyn. Hosp., Cmty. Svc. Soc.; v.p., gen. counsel, mem. coun. N.Y. Heart Assn. Lt. USNR, 1944-46. Mem. ABA, N.Y. State Bar Assn., Fed. Bar Assn., Assn. Bar City N.Y. (chmn. exec. com. 1966-67, v.p. 1968-69), Am. Coll. Trial Lawyers, Century Assn., Rockefeller Luncheon Club, Univ. Club (N.Y.C.), Mastigouche Fish and Game Club (Que., Can.). Republican. Episcopalian. Home: 430 E 57th St New York NY 10022-3061 Office: 620 5th Ave New York NY 10020-2402

CHRISTY, CHARLES WESLEY, III, industrial engineering educator; b. Chester County, Pa., Apr. 29, 1942; s. Charles Wesley Jr. and Violet R. (Pierpont) C.; m. D. Jean Cullmann, Jan. 25, 1972; children: Richard Townsend, Charles Wesley IV, Michael Pierpont. BS, Widener U., 1973; MBA, Temple U., 1980. Chmn. indsl. engring. tech. Del. Tech. and C.C., Newark, 1970—; pres. Pierpont Industries, Inc., Wilmington, Del., 1985—; adj. assoc. prof. U. Del., Newark, 1994; examiner Del. Quality Award, Wilmington, 1994. Bd. dirs., past pres. Opportunity Ctr., Inc., Wilmington, 1972—. Mem. Am. Inst. Indsl. Engrs. (bd. dirs. Del. chpt. 1970—, past pres.), Am. Soc. Quality Control. Home: 11 Harlech Dr Wilmington DE 19807-2507 Office: Del Tech & CC 400 Stanton Christiana Rd Newark DE 19713-2111

CHRISTY, ROBERT ALLEN, investment broker, investment advisor; b. Butler, Pa., Feb. 22, 1956; s. Allen B. and Jane (McMinn) C.; m. Diana Lynn Hinson, June 2, 1984; children: Kenneth Robert, Ashley Lynn. BA in Econs., Grove City (Pa.) Coll., 1978. Investment broker Bache, Halsey, Stuart & Shields, Charlotte, N.C., 1982-87; v.p. investments Prudential-Bache Securities, Atlanta, 1987-90; v.p. Paine Webber, Inc., Atlanta, 1990-95, Oppenheimer & Co., Inc., 1995-96; chief fin. officer Profl. Karate Assocs.; pres., CEO Christy Investment Group, Roswell, Ga., 1996—; pres. North-South Ventures, Atlanta. Pres. Roswell Jaycees, 1990-91; chmn. North Fulton Jr. C. of C., 1991-92; Served to capt. USMC, 1978-82. Mem. Am. Mgmt. Assn., Ga. Securities Dealers Assn., N.C. Securities Dealers Assn., Internat. Assn. Fin. Planning, Ofcls. Unltd. (assoc.), Atlanta Sports Coun., Yes! Atlanta Coun., North Fulton Jr. C. of C. (chmn. 1991-92), North Fulton Found. chmn. 1992), Rotary (editor Charlotte chpt. 1984-85, Paul Harris fellow 1986). Republican. Presbyterian. Avocations: golf, baseball, umpiring, kickboxing. Office: Christy Investment Group 10800 Alpharetta Hwy Ste 555 Roswell GA 30076-1423

CHRISTY, STÉPHANE, computer science engineer, researcher, educator; b. Neuilly-sur-Seine, France, Sept. 18, 1971. Degree in engring., Grande Ecole Engring. in Computer Sci and Applied Math., Grenoble, France, 1994; postgrad. cert., Nat. Poly. Inst. of Grenoble, 1994, PhD, 1998. Mil. engr. Aérospatiale Co., Paris, 1995-96; rschr. Graphics Vision Robotics Lab., Inst. Computer Sci. and Applied Math. and Nat. Rsch. Inst. Computer Sci. and Automation, Grenoble, 1994-95, 96-98; head oral tests prep. classes for entrance to Grandes Ecoles, Neuilly-sur-Seine, 1995-96, Grenoble, 1996-98; tchr. Joseph Fourier U., Grenoble, 1996-98; software engr. Thomson-CSF Detexis Co., Saint Cloud 1998-99, engr. Computer Sci., CNES French Space Agy., Toulouse, 1999—. Contbr. articles to profl. jours., conf. procs. Avocations: skiing, travel, hiking. Home: 74 rue Pauline Borghèse, 92200 Neuilly-sur-Seine France Office: CNES, 18 Ave Edouard Belin, 31401 Toulouse cedex 4 France

CHRITTON, GEORGE A., theater producer; b. Chgo.; s. George A. and Dorothea G. Chritton; m. Martha Gilman, Aug. 26, 1956; children: Stewart, Andrew, Douglas, Laura, Neil, Lyle. BA, Occidental Coll., 1955; postgrad., Princeton U., 1955-57. With CIA & various U.S. govt. agys., 1960-89; gen. ptnr. Margeo Investment Co., L.A., 1963-76; pres. Wildacre Prodns., Inc., L.A., 1990—; pres., CEO Fin. Svcs. Bancorp, Reno, 1990—; pres. Sycamore Prodns. Ltd., Nev. and Calif., 1994—. Prodr. theater prodns. Thornton Wilder's Youth, In Shakespeare and The Bible, A Ringing of Doorbells, The Rivers under the Earth, 1999. Mem. Am. Fgn. Svc. Assn., Washington, 1960—; chmn. bd. Neighborhood Learning Ctr., Capitol Hill, Washington, 1985-87; vol. Options House, Hollywood, Calif.; vol. coord. Rebuild L.A.; spl. advocate L.A. County Juvenile Ct., 2000—. Maj. USAF, 1957-60. Named Princeton Nat. Fellow, 1955-56, Vis. Fellow & Lectr. U. Calif., 1987-88. Mem. AFTRA, Am. Film Inst., Nat. Assn. Ind. Film & T.V. Prodrs., L.A. World Affairs Coun., Phi Beta Kappa, Phi Gamma Delta, Alpha Mu Gamma, Alpha Phi Gamma, Princeton Club (So. Calif.). Office: Wildacre Prodns Inc PO Box 719 Beverly Hills CA 90213-0719

CHROBAK, LADISLAV, hematologist; b. Hrabyne, Czech Republic, Apr. 11, 1927; s. Ludvik and Bozena (Polaskova) C.; m. Hana Dulickova, July 28, 1951; children: Jiri, Ludmila, Pavel. MD, Charles U., 1951, PhD, 1962. From resident to prof. medicine U. Hradec Kralove, Czech Republic, 1952-98, prof. emeritus, 1998—; prof. hematology, Kuwait U., 1982-84; cons. Min. Health, Kuwait, 1968-71. Author: Paroxysmal Nocturnal Hemoglobinuria, 1967, (with T. Gral and J. Kvasnička) Physical Examination in Internal Medicine, 1997, Hairy Cell Leukemia, 1999. Recipient Silver medal, Charles U., Prague, 1995, Golden medal, Hradec Faculty of Medicine, 1997. Mem. Internat. Soc. Hematology (coun. 1981-86, 90-98), Internat. Soc. Hemostasis and Thrombosis, Czech Soc. Hematology (v.p. 1986-92, pres. 1992-94, Hematology award 1963, 96), Soc. Hematology Hungary (hon.), Soc. Hematology Poland (hon.), Soc. Hematology Slovakia (hon.), Soc. Hematology Czech Republic (hon.), Czech Med. Soc. (hon.), Slovak Med. Soc. (Golden medal 1987). Avocation: history. Home: Urxova 296, 500 06 Hradec Kralové Czech Republic Office: Faculty Hosp, Dept Hematology, 500 05 Hradec Kralové Czech Republic

CHROBOG, JUERGEN, ambassador; b. Berlin, Feb. 28, 1940; m. Magda Gohar; 3 children. Degree in law, U. Goettingen, Germany. Atty.; joined German Fgn. Svc., 1972; mem. German rep. UN, N.Y.C., 1972-73; responsible for European, Third World affairs and econs. Office of Fgn. Min., Bonn, 1973-77; dep. amb. Embassy of Germany, Singapore, 1977-80; spokesman German del. European Cmty., Brussels, 1980-83; dep. spokesman Fgn. Office, Bonn, 1983-84, spokesman, head press office, 1984, spokesman, head mgmt. staff, 1984-91, dir. polit. dept., 1991-94; amb. to U.S. Embassy of Germany, Washington, 1995—. Office: Embassy of Germany 4645 Reservoir Rd NW Washington DC 20007-1998

CHRUŚCICKI, TADEUSZ JERZY, museum director, museology researcher; b. Cracow, Poland, Sept. 11, 1934; s. Tadeusz Karol and Antonina (Sitarz) C.; divorced; children: Eve, Peter. MA, Jagiellonian U., Cracow, Poland, 1959. Cert. art hist. Dir. Regional Mus., Nysa, Poland, 1960-64, Provincial Mus., Opole, Poland, 1964-70; dep. dir. Nat. Mus., Cracow, Poland, 1970-74, dir., 1974-85, 1989-2000; ret., 2000; dep. dir. Jagiellonian U. Mus., Cracow, Poland, 1986-89; lectr. in museology Jagiellonian U., Cracow, Poland, 1973-90. Author: Museums of Cracow, 1981, National Museum in Cracow, 1987. Mem. Polish United Workers Party, 1963-90; pres. Cracow-Kyoto Found., 1989—, Princes Czartoryski Found., 1991—; v.p. Polish Nat. Com. ICOM, 1982—. Recipient Polonia Restituta Cross State Coun., 1979, medal of Nat. Edn. Ministry of Edn., 1977, Silver and Gold Cross of Merit State Coun., 1970, 76. Fellow Polish Art Historian Soc.; mem. Internat. Print Art Triennale (hon.), Cracow Polish-Japanese Soc. (pres. 1979—). E-mail: dyrekaja@muz-nar.krakow.pl. Home: 23/75 Krowoderskich Zuchow, 31-271 Cracow Poland

CHRUŚCIEL, TADEUSZ LESŁAW, pharmacologist; b. Lwów, Poland, Jan. 30, 1926; s. Stanisław and Bronisława (Markowska) C.; m. Maria Józefa Sliz; children: Magdalena, Piotr, Wojciech. MD, Jagiell U., Cracow, 1951; Dr. hon. causa, Siles Acad. Medicine, Katowice, Poland, 1996. Staff Jagiell U., Cracow, 1950-58; chmn. dept. pharmacology Siles Acad., Zabrze, Poland, 1955-68; prof. Siles Acad., Zabrze, 1955-68; sr. med. officer Mental Health Office, WHO, Geneva, 1968-75; dep. dir. Inst. Drug Rsch., Warsaw, Poland, 1975-83; prof., chmn. dept. clin. pharmacology Postgrad. Med. Sch., Warsaw, 1983-96; mem. Internat. Narcotics Control Bd., 1978-82; chmn. Ntl Physicians Chamber, 1989-93; cons. in clin. pharmacology. Co-author: Lexicon of Medicaments, 1971, Commentary to Drug Law, 2000; contbr. chpts. to books and over 300 articles to profl. jours. Recipient medal Med. Trade Union, 1953, Silesian County, 1965, Warsaw County Coun., 1972, Order Polonia Restituta, Coun. of State, 1982. Mem. Polish Pharmacol. Soc., Polish Acad. Sci. (com. mem.), Physicians Chamber, Polish Med. Soc., Roman Cath. Physicians Assn. Roman Catholic. Avocations: philately, swimming, literature. Home: Dzika 6/284, 00-172 Warsaw Poland

CHRYSANTHOPOULOS, THEMISTOCLES LEONIDAS, retired ambassador; b. Canea, Crete, Greece, Aug. 9, 1915; s. Leonidas Themistocles and Jeanne (Gallenca) C.; m. Maria Botsaris, Dec. 3, 1944 (div. 1981); children: Leonidas, Daphne; m. Marie-Hermine de Magnin, Mar. 1, 1984. Degree in law, Athens (Greece) U., 1938. Attache Greek Ministry Fgn. Affairs, Athens, 1945-46; mem. Paris Peace Conf., 1946; polit. advisor Greek Mil. Govt., Rhodes Dodecanese, Greece, 1947-49; vice-consul Greek Consulate Gen., Cairo, 1949-51; 2d sec. Greek Embassy, Beirut, 1951-52; press officer Greek Embassy, Washington, 1952-53, 1st sec., 1953-58, counsellor, 1958-59, charge d'affaires, 1958; del. for Greece Founding Conf., IAEA, N.Y., 1956, UN Gen. Assembly, N.Y., 1956; consul gen. Istanbul, Turkey, 1961-65; amb. Sofia, Bulgaria, 1966-67, Tokyo, 1971-75, Ottawa, Ont., Can., 1975-78, Beijing, 1978-80. Contbr. articles to profl. jours. 2d lt. Greek mil. 1938-45. Decorated knight comdr. (Greece), Grand Cross St. Andrew (Constantinople), Grand Cross Madara (Bulgaria), Grand Cross Rising Sun (Japan), Silver Cross (Sweden). Mem. Internat. Inst. for Strategic Studies. Greek Orthodox. Avocation: citrus fruit grower in Aeghion, Greece. Home: 20 Omirou St, 10672 Athens Attica, Greece Country Home: 45 Odos Aghion Apostolon, 251-00 Aeghion Achaia, Greece

CHRYSIKOPOULOS, CHARALABOS S. (HARRIS CHRYSIKOPOULOS), physician; b. Corfu, Greece, Aug. 15, 1961; s. Spyridon and Dolly (Maneta) C. MD, Washington U., St. Louis, 1986. Diplomate Am. Bd. Radiology. Resident in radiology U. Calif., San Diego, 1986-91; staff radiologist Hygeia Hosp., Athens, 1992-97, Hyanous Stavros Hosp., Athens, 1997—. Contbr. articles to profl. jours. Office: Kyanous Stavros Hosp Radiol, 102 Vass Sofias Ave, 15123 Marousi Athens 11528, Greece

CHRYSOS, MICHAEL GEORGE, physics educator, researcher; b. Heraklion, Crete, Greece, June 4, 1961; arrived in France, 1992; s. George Michael and Maria Xenophon (Spithacki) C.; 1 child, Elena. Diploma in elec. engring., Nat. Tech. U. Athens, 1985; PhD in Atomic and Molecular Physics, U. Athens, 1990; Habilitation, U. Angers, France, 1997. Postdoctoral fellow CNRS Lab. de Photophysique-Moleculaire, Orsay, France, 1992-93; rsch. assoc. CNRS Lab. de Photophysique-Moleculaire, Orsay, 1993, postdoctoral fellow EEC fellow, 1993-95; rschr., tchr. Faculty Scis. Angers U., 1994—, full prof., 1997—, group leader, 1999—; vis. prof. Technion Polytechnic Inst. Tech., Haifa, Israel, 1993; part-time rschr. groupe de Spectrometrie Moleculaire et Atmospherique, Reims, France, 1992-94. Author 2 text books, including Introduction à la Mécanique Quantique, Introduction à la Relativité Restreinte; contbr. numerous articles to profl. jours. including Phys. Rev. Letter, Phys. Rev., Jour. Physics B: Atomic, Molecular, and Optical Physics, Chem. Physics Letters, Jour. Chem. Physics, Internat. Jour. Quantum Chemistry. Served Greek Army (Corps Engrs.), 1990-91. Mem. Christian-Orthodox Ch. Avocations: drawing, painting. Home: 88 rue Larévellière, 49100 Angers France Office: U Angers Lab Optiques Propr, UMR CNRS 130 2 bd Lavoisier, 49045 Angers France

CHRYSOSTOMOS (CHRISTOFOROS ARISTODIMOU), archbishop of Cyprus; b. Statos, Cyprus, Sept. 27, 1927. Ordained deacon Greek Orthodox Ch., 1951, priest, 1961. Suffragan bishop, 1968-73, met. of Paphos, 1973-77; archbishop of Nova Justiniana and all Cyprus, Nicosia, 1977—. Office: Archbishop Nova Justiniana, PO Box 1130 Arch Kyprianos St, Nicosia Cyprus*

CHRYSSANTHOU, CHRYSSANTHOS, pathologist, educator; b. Thessaloniki, Greece, Oct. 15, 1925; came to U.S., 1954; s. Prodromos and Despina Chryssanthou; m. Iphigenie Fotiadis, Oct. 14, 1958 (div. 1969); children: Despina, Helen Chryssanthou-Huska; m. Gariele Franke, Dec. 11, 1970. MD, Aristotelean U., Thessaloniki, 1953; postgrad., Hahnemann Med. Coll., 1963; diploma (hon.), Luis A. Schreiber Ctrl. Hosp., Lima, Peru, 1978. Cert. clin. lab. dir., N.Y. Instr. in pathology NYU Med. Sch., N.Y.C., 1957; assoc. dir. pathology Beth Israel Med. Ctr., N.Y.C., 1976-82, dir. office of rsch., 1983-96, hon. attending physician, 1997—; assoc. prof. pathology Mt. Sinai Sch. Medicine, N.Y.C., 1967-80, prof. pathology, 1980-96, professorial lectr., 1997—; prof. extraordinario pathology U. Guadalajara (Mex.) Med. Sch., 1986; vis. prof. C. Bernard Inst., U. Montreal, Can., 1966, C. Heredia Med. Sch., Lima, 1978. Contbr. over 100 articles to profl. jours., poetry to book (Gold medal 1989); exhibitor laser photocoagulation in sci. exhibit, 1976 (1st pl. award). Rsch. grantee USPHS, 1967-72, Office Naval Rsch., 1968-82, NASA, 1983-88. Mem. Am. Soc. for Investigative Pathology, Sigma Xi. Achievements include patents for microscope attachment to obtain successive intermediate magnifications, process and apparatus for detection of specific biological factors. Avocations: painting, poetry, tennis. Home: 100 Winston Dr Apt 15K Cliffside Park NJ 07010-3240 Office: Beth Israel Med Ctr 1st Ave at 16th St New York NY 10003

CHRZANOWSKI, LIONEL MICHEL, financial executive; b. Creteil, France, Aug. 1, 1958; s. Stefan and Paulette (Van De Ponseele) C. Brevet de Technicien Superieur, Paul Doumer, 1978, CNTE, Vanves, France, 1980. Student, free-lance advt. Société des Centres Commerciaux, Boissy and Ulis, France, 1977-79; mgr. Pharmacy, Ulis, 1980-81; probationer Soc. Gen. Paris Stock Exchange, 1976-78; fin. counselor Savs. Bank, Evry, France, 1981—; speculator, mgr. Chrzanowski FC, Santeny, France, 1980—. Author: Le Petit Dictionnaire A Mourir de Rire Tomes 1 and 2, 1983, The D.S.E. Management Method, 1980, Small Laughing Death Dictionary, 1985, The Small Pocket Macho, 1986. Founder Santeny Oposition, 1983, Santeny Avenir, 1989. Mem. French Assn. Mktg., Rasenblement Pour la Republique. Avocations: humor, politics, history, genealogy, creativity. Office: Chrzanowski Lionel FC, 9 rue de Lesigny, Val de Marne, 94440 Santeny France

CHU, ALLEN YUM-CHING, automation company executive, systems consultant; b. Hong Kong, June 19, 1951; arrived in Can., 1972; s. Luke King-Sang and Kim Kam (Lee) C.; m. Connie Ge Chen, June 29, 1999. BSc in Computer Sci., U. B.C., Vancover, Can., 1977; BA in Econs., U. Alta., Edmonton, Can., 1986. Rsch. asst. dept. neuropsychology and rsch. Alta. Hosp., Edmonton, 1977-78; systems analyst dept. agr. Govt. of Alta., Edmonton, 1978-81; systems analyst for computing resources City of Edmonton, 1981-86; pres. ANO Automation Inc., Vancouver, 1986-92; v.p., bd. dirs. ANNOVA Bus. Group, Inc., Can., 1993-98; dir. Capital Alliance Group, 1998—; mem. Vancouver Bd. Trade. Mem. IEEE Computer Soc., N.Y. Acad. Sci. Office: Capital Alliance Group, # 1108 777 W Broadway, Vancouver, BC Canada V5Z 4J7

CHU, CHAO-HSIEN, information science and technology educator; b. Kaohsiung, Taiwan, June 22, 1951; s. Tsong-Jui and Chin-Lien (Wang) C.; m. Fang-Mei Kuo, July 1, 1982; children: Karen L., Emily J. BE, Chung Yuan U., Taiwan, 1974; MBA, Tatung Inst. of Tech., Taipei, Taiwan, 1978;

PhD, Pa. State U., 1984. Sect. chief Tatung Co., Taipei, 1978-80; grad. asst., instr. Pa. State U., University Park, 1980-84; asst. prof. Baruch Coll. CUNY, N.Y.C., 1984-86; asst. prof. Iowa State U., Ames, 1986-90, assoc. prof., 1990-99; assoc. prof. Pa. State U., University Park, 1999—; mem. edit. rev. bd. Info. Resource Mgmt. Assn., 1989-97, Prodn. Ops. Mgmt. Soc., 1990-99. Contbr. over 20 articles to profl. jours. Mem. Am. Prodn. & Inventory Control, Decision Sci. Inst., Inst. Mgmt. Sci., Japanese Soc. Fuzzy Theory and Systems. Office: Sch of Info Sci & Tech 515 Rider Bldg University Park PA 16801-3857

CHU, CHUNG KWANG, medicinal chemistry educator; b. Seoul, Republic of Korea, May 18, 1941; s. Jee Young Huh; children: Susan, Jackie. BS, Seoul Nat. U., 1964; MS, Idaho State U., 1970; PhD, SUNY, Buffalo, 1974. Rsch. assoc. Sloan-Kettering Cancer Inst., N.Y.C., 1974-80; asst. prof. Idaho State U., Pocatello, 1990-82; asst. prof. medicinal chemistry U. Ga., Athens, 1982-87, assoc. prof., 1997-90, prof., 1990-98, rsch. prof., 1998—; mem. adv. bd. NIH, Pharmasset, Atlanta. Lt. (j.g.). Mem. Am. Chem. Soc. (rsch. grantee 1988), Am. Assn. for Cancer Rsch., Am. Assn. Colls. Pharmacy, Internat. Soc. Antiviral Rsch. Achievements include numerous patents in drug discovery field. Fax: 706-542-5381. E-mail: dchu@rx.uga.edu. Office: U Ga Coll Pharmacy Brooks Dr Athens GA 30602

CHU, DAVID S. C., economist; b. N.Y.C., May 28, 1944; s. H.T. and Esther (Briney) C.; m. Laura L. Tosi, Apr. 1, 1978. BA, Yale U., 1964, PhD, 1972. Asst. dir. nat. security and internat. affairs Congl. Budget Office, Washington, 1978-81; dir. then asst. sec. def. for program analysis and evaluation Dept. Def., Washington, 1981-93; economist RAND, Santa Monica, Calif., 1970-78; sr. fellow RAND, Washington, 1993-94, dir. Washington rsch. dept., 1994-96, dir. Washington office, assoc. chmn. of rsch. staff, 1996-98; v.p. army rsch. divsn., dir. Arroyo Ctr., 1998—. Capt. U.S. Army, 1968-70, Vietnam. Decorated Bronze Star, Army Commendation medal. Fellow Nat. Acad. Pub. Adminstrn. (chmn., bd. trustees 1999—); mem. Phi Beta Kappa. Office: Rand 1200 S Hayes St Arlington VA 22202-5050

CHU, EDWARD KAWAH, bank administrator; b. Hong Kong, May 21, 1955; s. Peter and Helen (Chang) C.; m. Mee-Ling Lai, Nov. 14, 1987; children: Tin-Lok, Yan-Lok, Chun-Lok. B of Social Scis., U. Hong Kong, 1978. Asst. analyst Nomura Rsch. Internat. Co. Ltd., Hong Kong, 1978-79; exec. trainee Shanghai Comml. Bank Ltd., Hong Kong, 1979-81, jr. economist, 1981-82, economist, 1982-83, asst. mgr., 1984-88, asst. corp. sec., 1989, corp. sec., 1989—. Mem. Inst. of Chartered Secs. and Adminstrs. (assoc.), Hong Kong Inst. of Company Secs. (assoc.). Avocations: tennis, swimming. Office: Shanghai Comml Bank Ltd, 12 Queen's Rd Ctrl, Hong Kong Hong Kong

CHU, ELIZABETH Y.F., diplomat; b. Pengfu, Taiwan, July 30, 1955; d. Tze-ming Chu and Chiu Hua Yang; m. Chao-wen Yu; children: Judy, Howard. B, Tunghai U., Taiwan, 1977; M in Social Sci., San Francisco State U., 1991, M in Econs., 1992; D (hon.), Baker U., 1999. Desk officer Ministry of Fgn. Affairs of Republic of China, Taipei, 1978-86, asst. on home assignment, 1992, sect. chief, 1992-95, asst. counselor, sect. chief, 1995-96, dep. dir. gen., 1996-98; asst. Taipei Econ. and Cultural Office, San Francisco, 1986-92; dir. gen. Taipei Econ. and Cultural Office, Kansas City, Mo., 1998—; bd. dirs. Trade Promoting Fund, Bur. Trade Affairs, Ministry Econ. Affairs, Taipei, 1996-98. Artist: Nature and Art, 1998; exhibited in group shows. Named Model Civil Servant, Cabinet of the Republic of China, Taipei, 1994, 20 Yr. Civil Svc. award, 1998; named Hon. Nebr. Citizen, 1998. Mem. Greater Kansas City C. of C. (appreciation award 1998), Internat. Trade Club, World Trade Coun. of Wichita (appreciation award 1999), Phi Beta Delta. Avocations: art, golf. Office: Taipei Econ and Cultural Office 3100 Broadway Kansas City KS 64111

CHU, GE-LIN See ZHU, GE-LIN

CHU, HORN DEAN, chemical engineer; b. China, Sept. 9, 1933; s. Johnson S.T. and Daisy (Hsia) C.; m. Pik Yu Cheung, June 23, 1962. BS, Waseda U., Tokyo, 1959, MS, 1961; MS, U. Pa., 1963; PhD, U. Ala., 1965. Project engr. Selas Corp., Dresher, Pa., 1965-71; asst. and adj. prof. Rutgers U., New Brunswick, N.J., 1971-79; sr. process engr. MacAndrews & Forbes Co., Camden, N.J., 1979-81; pres. Berkorp, Inc., Haddonfield, N.J., 1981—. Contbr. articles to profl. jours. Fellow Am. Inst. Chemists; mem. AIChE, Am. Chem. Soc., Inst. Food Technologists, AAAS, Sigma Xi. Office: Berkorp Inc 6-10S Haddon Ave Haddonfield NJ 08033-1860

CHU, HSIEN MING, investment company executive; b. Tai-an, Shandon, China, Sept. 17, 1936; came to the U.S., 1965; s. Yung-Bao and I-Ing Chu; m. Anita (Yung) Chu, Sept. 6, 1970; children: Antony, Lawrence, Frederick. BA, Nat. Taiwan U., Taipei, 1964; MA, U. Wis., 1968, PhD, 1978. Acad. staff U. Wis., Madison, 1968-78, rsch. assoc., 1978-84, assoc. rschr., 1984-86; pres. Lanteen Internat. Investment Co., Madison, 1986—; also bd. dirs. Lanteen Internat., Madison. Contbr. articles to profl. jours. Mem. Am. Culinary Fedn., Sigma Xi. Home: 7310 New Washburn Way Madison WI 53719-3010

CHU, HSIEN-KUN, chemist, researcher; b. Shanghai, People's Republic of China, Oct. 14, 1947; came to U.S., 1971; s. Hwei-Teh and Yun-Hsiang (Chang) C.; m. Winnie K.S. Wong, Dec. 23, 1976; children: James C., Jason C. BS, Nat. Taiwan U., Taipei, Republic of China, 1970; PhD, Vanderbilt U., 1976. Vis. instr. U. Tex., Arlington, 1976-77; rsch. assoc. Tex. Christian U., Ft. Worth, 1977-80; rsch. specialist Dow Corning Corp., Midland, Mich., 1980-88; sr. scientist Loctite Corp., Rocky Hill, Conn., 1988—. Contbr. rsch. articles to sci. jours. Mem. Am. Chem. Soc., Sigma Xi. Achievements include patents on silicone sealants; research into mechanistic studies of organic reactions, silicone research. Home: 6 Harvest Hl Wethersfield CT 06109-2422 Office: Loctite Corp 1001 Trout Brook Xing Rocky Hill CT 06067-3910

CHU, JOHNSON CHIN SHENG, retired physician; b. Peiping, China, Sept. 25, 1918; came to U.S., 1948, naturalized, 1957; s. Harry S.P. and Florence (Young) C.; m. Sylvia Cheng, June 11, 1949; children—Stephen, Timothy. M.D., St. John's U., 1945. Intern Univ. Hosp., Shanghai, 1944-45; resident, research fellow NYU Hosp., 1948-50; resident physician in charge State Hosp. and Med. Ctr., Weston, W.Va., 1951-56; chief services, clin. dir. State Hosp., Logansport, Ind., 1957-84, ret., 1998; active mem. Meml. Hosp., Logansport, Ind., 1968—. Research in cardiology and pharmacology; contbr. articles to profl. jours. Fellow Am. Psychiat. Assn., Am. Coll. Chest Physicians; mem. AMA, Ind. Med. Assn., Cass County Med. Soc., AAAS. Home: 36 E Lake Shafer Monticello IN 47960 Office: Southeastern Med Ctr Walton IN 46994

CHU, KWANGIL, ombudsman, lawyer; b. Inchon, Korea, Aug. 12, 1943; s. Muyong Chu and Gumre Chung; m. Eunkyung Suh, Nov. 23, 1969; children: Heesun, Heekyung, Heeyong, Heewon, Sungkyu. BA, Seoul (Korea) Nat. U., 1965, MA, 1967, LLD, 1979. Judge adv. Ministry Def., Korea, 1967-70; pub. prosecutor Ministry Justice, Seoul, Korea, 1971-81; sr. prosecutor Ministry Justice, Pusan, Korea, 1981-92; chief prosecutor Ministry Justice, Inchon, 1992-95; sr. chief prosecutor Ministry Justice, Seoul, 1995-98, chief ombudsman, 1998—; prof. Jud. Inst. for Rsch. and Tng., Seoul, 1985-87. Author: A Study of the Hearsay Rule, 1979, Collection of Poems, Bell Sound under Evening Dusk, 1992; co-author: The Legal Analysis of UR Agreements, 1994, The Study of UR Dispute Settlement, 1994. Capt. Korean Army, 1967-70. Recipient Medal Hongjo Svc., Pres. Korea, 1989, medal Hwangjo Svc., Pres. Korea, 1996; named Proud Alumnus, George Washington U., 1995. Mem. Korean Criminal Law Soc., Korean Bar Assn. Roman Catholic. Avocations: oil painting, golfing, mountain climbing. Home: 25-205 Sampung Apt, Sochodong Sochogu, Seoul 137-074, Korea Office: Ombudsman of Korea, 267 Migeundong Seodaemungu, 120-020 Seoul Korea

CHU, PATRICK TAK-LONG, marketing professional; b. Hong Kong, Feb. 22, 1950; s. Hang and Yuk Kuen (Kit) C.; m. Betty Po Kuen Chan, July 14, 1985. BSBA, Northeastern U., 1976; MBA, U. Wis., 1977. Asst. mgr. Fuji Marden & Co. Ltd., 1978-79; mktg. and ops. mgr. Paterson Simons (HK) Ltd., 1979-81; product mgr. The Friestland Trading Co. (HK) Ltd., 1981-82; mktg. mgr. Am. Express Internat. Inc. (HK), 1982—; mgr. Samsonite United Agencies Ltd., 1983-86; mng. dir. Inexo Ltd., Hong Kong, 1986-99, Champion San Ltd., Kwai Chung, Hong Kong, 1999—; bd. dirs. Macsee Ltd., Hong Kong, Grand Sight Indsl. Ltd., Hong Kong, Multi Top Ltd., Hong Kong, Seatac Holdings Ltd.; mem. Mktg. Mgmt. Com., Hong Kong, 1989-91. Com. mem. Yuen Long (Hong Kong) Dist. Bd., 1991-94; bd. dirs. Yuen Long Town Hall Mgmt. Bd., 1983—. Named Senator, Jaycees Internat., 1984. Mem. Hong Kong Mgmt. Assn., Hong Kong Tourist Assn., Hong Kong Tourism Assn. (com. rels.), Hong Kong Advertisers Assn., Assn. of Retailers and Tourism Svcs. (mem. gov. coun. 1993, chmn. 1995-97), Chinese Exec. Club (mem. exec. com. 1991-95, 99—), Sales and Mktg. Exec. Club (pres. 1989-91), Retailers Mgmt. Assn., Hong Kong Gen. C. of C., Hong Kong Jr. C. of C., Yuen Long Jaycees (pres. 1982). Avocations: golf, tennis, squash, reading. Office: Inexo Ltd, Champion San Ltd 1208 Vanta, Ind Ctr 33 Tai Lin Pai Rd, Kwai Chung Hong Kong

CHU, STEVEN, physics educator; b. St. Louis, Feb. 28, 1948; s. Ju Chin and Ching Chen (Li) C.; children: Geoffrey, Michael. BS in Physics, AB in Math., U. Rochester, 1970; PhD in Physics, U. Calif., Berkeley, 1976. Post doctoral fellow U. Calif., Berkeley, 1976-78; mem. tech. staff Bell Labs., Murray Hill, N.J., 1978-83; head quantum electronics rsch. dept. AT&T Bell Labs., Holmdel, N.J., 1983-87; prof. physics and applied physics Stanford (Calif.) U., 1987—, Frances and Theodore Geballe prof. physics and applied physics, 1990—, chmn. physics dept., 1990-93; Morris Loeb lectr. Harvard U., Cambridge, Mass., 1987-88; vis. prof. Coll. de France, fall 1990; Richtmeyer Meml. lectr., 1990. Contbr. papers in laser spectroscopy and atomic physics, especially laser cooling and trapping, and precision spectroscopy of leptonic atoms, polymer and biophysics. Recipient Humboldt sr. scientist award, Sci. for Art prize, 1995; co-recipient King Faisal prize for sci., 1993, Nobel prize for physics, 1997; Woodrow Wilson fellow 1970, doctoral fellow NSF, 1970-74, postdoctoral fellow 1977-78, Guggenheim fellow, 1996. Fellow Am. Phys. Soc. (Herbert P. Broida prize for laser spectroscopy 1987, chair laser sci. topical group 1989, A.L. Schawlow prize 1994), Optical Soc. Am. (William F. Meggars award 1994), Am. Acad. Arts and Scis.; mem. NAS, Academica Sinica, Am. Philos. Soc., Chinese Acad. Sci. (fgn.), Korean Acad. Sci. and Tech. (fgn.). Office: Stanford Univ Varian Bldg Rm 230 Stanford CA 94305-4060

CHU, SZU-TE, economics educator; b. Lien-Shui, Chiangsu, China, June 2, 1928; s. Tzong-Hwa and Shyh (Chen) C.; m. Pey-Hsien Chen, 1962; children: Churngwei, Churngwen. B in Law, U. Taiwan, 1958; M in Letters, Oxford (Eng.) U., 1980. Asst. land econs. and adminstrn. Nat. Chung-Hsing U., Taipei, 1958-65, instr., 1965-70, assoc. prof., 1970-79, prof., 1979-80, 86—, head prof., 1980-86. Commr. Spl. Group for Equalization of Land Ownership, Taiwan, 1987—; standing supr. Land Reform Assn., Taiwan, 1988—. Author: Land Utilization in U.S.A., 1970, Land System in Selected Countries, 1979, rev. edit., 1999, Rural Economic Problems in China, 1930-50, 1980, Location Theory, 1986, Land Policy, 1989, rev. edit., 1993. Mem. Sino-Brit. Cultural and Econ. Assn., Oxford Soc. Avocation: mountaineering. Office: Nat Chung Hsing U, Dept Land Econs & Admin Chan Kao N Rd, Taipei Taiwan

CHU, WANG BO, university administrator, educator, researcher; b. Yixing, Jiangsu, Peoples Republic of China, Oct. 2, 1962; s. Wang Shun and Zhong Feng (Di) Xiang; m. Cheng Yan Song, Aug. 12, 1986. Bachelor's, Chonghing U., People's Republic of China, 1986, master, 1988, PhD, 1996. Lectr. Bioengring. Ctr. Chongqing U., People's Republic of China, 1988-92, assoc. prof., 1992-97, prof. Bioengring. Ctr., 1997—; vis. prof. Gunma U., Japan, 1997-98, 99; mem. corp. rsch. Cardiovascular Rsch. Ctr., Japan, 1991-92. Editor-in-chief Clinical Cell Rheology, 1998, Plant Biomechanics, 1999; author: Foundation of Continuum Mechanics, 1998. Mem. Chongqing Soc. for BME (mng. dir. 1998—), Chongqing Soc. for Food Engring. (mng. dir. 1997—). Avocations: sports, singing songs. Home: Donglin Cun 5, Chongqing Univ, Chongqing 400044, People's Republic of China Office: Bioengring Ctr Chongqing U, Shapinba, Chongqing 400044, People's Republic of China

CHUA, HWEE HONG GARY, import and export company executive; b. Singapore, Nov. 27, 1971; s. Chua Ban Seng and Tan Kek Huay. Cert., Beijing U., 1994; BSc in Econs., Nat. U. of Singapore, 1995. Med. rep. Pfizer Pte Ltd., Singapore, 1995, profl. svc. rep., 1996-97; mng. dir. T.G. Kiatz co. Pte Ltd., Singapore, 1997—; bd. dirs. Rose Syrup Mfg. Co., Gallop Hardware Trading Pte. Ltd. Sgt. Singapor Air Force, 1990-92. Avocations: soccer, basketball, community work, skiing. Office: TG Kiat & Co (Pte) Ltd, Blk 15 Woodlands Loop 01-23, SC738322 Woodlands East Republic of Singapore

CHUA, JAMES HAI-JOO, nuclear scientist; b. N.Y., June 19, 1951. BS in Nuclear Engring., Manchester U., U.K., 1975; M.Nuclear Sci., Columbia U., 1977, PhD in Nuclear Sci., 1977. Pres. The Big Apple Internat. Group of Cos., Aerospace & Sci. Rsch., Inc., Advance Tech. (China) Ltd., The Big Apple Design team, Missile Fabrication Composites, Inc., Space Sci. Inc., Wailic Investments (HK) Ltd., Mamina (Tokyo) Group of Cos.; v.p. Am. Aerospace corp., China (PRC) Procurement Group, JC Star Consortium (Europe); dir. Starlight Mfg. Group of Cos., Biotech Rsch. Capital Funds, The Big Apple (Internat.) Trusts. Baron's Who's Who fellow, 1997—. Mem. aIAA, AAAS. Office: The Big Apple Internat Grp, Macpherson Rd PO Box 103, Singapore 913404, Singapore

CHUA, MARIA CORA Y., legislative counsel; b. Koronadal, The Philippines, July 7, 1971; d. Dionisio B. and Maxima Y. Chua. BA, U. Md., 1993; JD, Am. U., 1996. Rsch. lab. asst. Am. U. Social Sci. Lab., Washington, 1993-94; law clk. APA, Washington, 1994, D.C. Office of the Corp. Counsel, Family Svcs., Washington, 1995; pub. interest law clinic dean's fellow Am. U. Pub. Interest Law Clinic, Washington, 1995-96; legis. aide State Md. Ho. Dels., Annapolis, 1996; disability adv., adminstrv. hearing specialist Health Mgmt. Assocs., Inc., Balt., 1996; legal counsel Conn. Gen. Assembly's Ho. Rep. Office, Hartford, 1996-97; legis. counsel Conn. Commn. on Children, Hartford, 1997—; advisor The Aetna Found. Children's Ctr., St. Francis Hosp., Hartford, 1997—; dir. Nat. Conf. State Legislatures' Rsch. and Com. Staff, Denver, 1998—. Facilitator Parent Leadership Tng. Inst., Hartford, 1997—; vol. neonatal ICU, John Dempsey Hosp., U. Farmington, Conn., 1997—; chairwoman Conn. Jr. Leagues' State Pub. Affairs Com., Hartford, 1998—; advisor Truglia Thumbelina Fund, Stamford, Conn., 1998—. Roman Catholic. Avocations: singing, hiking, jogging, running, athletics. Office: Conn Commn on Children 18-20 Trinity St Hartford CT 06032

CHUA, SOO-JIN, electronics engineering educator; b. Muar, Johor, Malaysia, Apr. 7, 1951; s. Joo-Lai and Yang-Liew (Goh) C.; m. Foong-Chin Liow; children: Clara, Adeline, Hong-Shing. BEE, U. Singapore, 1974; PhD, U. Wales, 1977. Rsch. engr. Std. Telecom. Labs., Harlow, U.K., 1977-79; lectr., sr. lectr. electronic engring. Nat. U. Singapore, 1979-89, assoc. prof., 1990-96, prof., 1997—, dir. Ctr. for OptoElectronics, 1990—, asst. dir. Inst. Microelectronics, 1991-95, program dir. Inst. Materials Rsch. and Engring., 1996—; dep. dir. Singapore-MIT Alliance, 1998—. Contbr. articles to profl. jours. Mem. IEEE (sr. mem., chmn. Singapore sect. 1984-86, chmn. 1987), Soc. Photo-Optical Instrumentation Engrs. (vice chmn. 1994-97). Avocations: badminton, swimming, tennis. Office: Nat U Singapore Dept Elec Engring, 10 Kent Ridge Crescent, 119260 Singapore Singapore

CHUA, TUAN MENG HOCKCHUA, real estate developer, community leader; b. Muar, Johor, Malaysia, Jan. 20, 1944; s. Song Lim and Sai Eng (Koh) C.; m. Siow Gek Seah, Sept. 16, 1970; children: Chong Jan, Chongee, Chongson. BA, Comml. Mgmt. Inst., Jersey, Eng., 1980; BA in Mgmt., Ctrl. Pacific Sch., Magville, Australia, 1984; D in Cmty. Leadership, U. St. Clements U., Eng., 1999. Chief exec. Song Lim Group Estates, Johor, 1970-93; CEO Hockchua Group of Cos., Muar, 1992—; exec. chmn. Syt. Sri Meriah Sdn. Bhd., Muar, 1978—; bd. dirs. Ban Heng Hong Sdn. Bhd., Muar, Direct Devel. Sd. Bhd., Jojoya Devel. Sdn. Bhd., Muar; mem. bus. del. ofcl. visit ot Hon. Dr. Mahathir Mohamad, Prime Min. of Malaysia, to Kyrgyz, Kazakhstan, 1996; bus. del. Beijing Dialogue, 1996, M'sia P.M., Cuba, Chile, Uruguay, Argentina, 1997; bus. del. ofcl. visit led by trade min. Rafidah Aziz to Sydney, Melbourne and Parth, Australia, 1999. Chmn. Chung Hwa Primary Schs., Muar, 1992—, Moral Uplifting Soc., Muar, 1992—, WTF T'k'do Assn., Muar, 1990, C. of C. Johor State (v.p., apptd. asst. marriage-registrar, 1997—), Muar. Recipient D of Univ., St. Clements U., Eng., 1999. Fellow Internat. Comml. Mgmt. (U.K.), Inst. Comml. Mgmt. (U.K.); mem. Am. Inst. Mgmt. (fellow pres. coun. 1980—), Lions Internat. (Disting. Mem. award 1991). Kuan-Yin. Avocations: travel, golf, reading, landscaping. Home: PO Box 45, 5-1 Jalan Mohamadiah, Johor Muar 84000, Malaysia Office: 111 Jalan Abdullah, Johor Muar 84000, Malaysia

CHUAH, MENG INN, anatomist, educator; b. Ayer Itam, Penang, Malaysia, Mar. 24, 1956; arrived in Hong Kong, 1983, arrived in Australia, 1994; d. Kim Hye and Soon May (Tan) C.; m. David Wai Lun Yick, May 28, 1983 (dec.); 1 child, Jonah Lee. BA in Biology cum laude, U. Rochester, 1979; PhD in Cell Biology and Anatomy, Northwestern U., 1984. Lectr. Dept. Anatomy Chinese U. Hongkong, Shatin, 1983-94; sr. lectr. dept. anatomy and physiology U. Tasmania, 1994—; vis. scientist Neurosci. Unit Montreal Gen. Hosp., Crouche Found., 1988. Co-author: A Lab Manual of Neuroanatomy, 1986; contbr. articles in neurosci. jours. Genesee scholar U. Rochester, 1975-79, Schunselaar Rsch. scholar, 1997; fellow Northwestern U., 1979-83, Croucher Found., 1988-89. Mem. Soc. for Neurosci., Internat. Brain Research Orgn., Assn. for Chemoreception Scis., Australian Neurosci. Soc. Avocation: reading. Office: Dept Anatomy & Physiology, GPO Box 252-24, 7001 Hobart Tasmania, Australia

CHUAN, LEEKPAI, Prime Minister of Thailand; b. Muang Dist., Trang, Thailand, July 28, 1938. Cert. in painting and sculpture, Silpakorn Pre-U.; LLB, Thammasat U., 1962; PhD in Polit. Sci. (hon.), Srinakharinwirot U., 1985, Ramkhamhaeng U., 1987; PhD in Laws (hon.), U. of the Philippines, 1993. Barrister-at-law, Thai Bar Assn., 1964. Mem. parliament Govt. of Thailand, Bangkok, 1969, 75-76, 79, 1983, 86, 88, 1992, 95, 96; spkr. ho. of reps. Govt. of Thailand, 1986-88, dep. min. justice, 1975; min. to prime min.'s office Govt. of Thailand, Bangkok, 1976, min. of justice, 1980, min. of commerce, 1981; min. agr. and coops. Govt. of Thailand, 1981-83, min. edn., 1983-86; min. pub. health Govt. of Thailand, Bangkok, 1988-89, dep. prime min., 1990, min. agr. and cooperatives, 1990, prime min., 1992-95, 97—; leader of the opposition Govt. of Thailand, 1995-96; vis. lectr. forensic medicine dept. faculty medicine Chulalongkorn U. Mem. Silpakorn U. Coun., Srinakharinwirot U. Coun. Named Knight Grand Commdr., Most Illustrious Order of Chula Chom Klao, 1996, Knight Grand Cordon spl. class of Most Exalted Order of the White Elephant, 1982. Office: Office of Prime Min, Thanon Nakhon Pathom, Bangkok 10300, Thailand*

CHUANG, FRANK SHIUNN-JEA, engineering executive, consultant; b. Taiwan, China, Sept. 5, 1942; came to U.S., 1966, naturalized, 1974; s. Swiss S. and Chin-May C.; m. Lily L. Chuang, Aug. 14, 1971; 1 child, Eugene. BS, Nat. Taiwan U., 1964; MS, U. Mass., 1968, PhD, 1971. Instr. engring. U. Conn., 1971-72; dept. mgr. C.E. Maguire; cons. engrs. New Britain, Conn., 1972-78; v.p., cons. engrs. Hayden, Harding & Buchanan, Inc., East Hartford, Conn., 1978-82; pres., cons. engrs. L-C Assocs., Inc., Rocky Hills, Conn., 1982—; bd. dirs. Equity Bank, Wethersfield Conn.; mem. Conn. State Bd. Examiners for Profl. Engrs. and Land Surveyors. Chmn. Wethersfield Flood Encroachment Control Bd. U. Mass. Water Resource Rsch. Ctr. grantee, 1966-71. Mem. ASCE, Nat. Soc. Profl. Engrs., Water Pollution Control Fedn., Wethersfield Country Club. Home: 38 Stonegate Dr Wethersfield CT 06109-3652 Office: L-C Assocs Inc 1960 Silas Deane Hwy Rocky Hill CT 06067-1310

CHUANG, SHOU-HWA, zoologist; b. Siantan, Indonesia, June 10, 1919; s. Cho-Yun and Hong-Neo (Oei) C.; m. Elsie Lee-Chuen Loo, Sept. 13, 1951; children: Catherine Hsueh-Jau, Helen Hsueh-Ruey. BS, Nat. Amoy U., Xiamen, China, 1941; MS, Bristol U., England, 1948; PhD, U. Malaya, Singapore, 1957. Teaching asst. Amoy U., Changting, China, 1941-43, Nat. Shanghai Med. Coll., Chungking, China, 1943-44; asst. prof. Nat. Taiwan U., Taipei, 1948-49; lectr. U. Malaya, Singapore, 1950-60, sr. lectr., 1960-70; assoc. prof. U. Singapore, 1970-71, prof., 1971-77, chmn. zoology dept., 1971-77; dir. Regional Marine Biol. Ctr., Singapore, 1973-77; retired, 1977; cons. in field. Author: On Malayan Shores, 1961; co-author, editor: Animal and Nature in Singapore, 1973; contbr. articles to profl. jours. Mem. Sentosa Coral Com., Singapore, 1970-76, Nat. Mus. Bd., Singapore, 1970-72, Great Barrier Reef Com., Brisbane, Australia, 1973. Mem. Zool. Soc. London, Paleontological Soc. Am. Avocations: scuba diving, music. Home: 144 Pasir Ris Rd, Singapore 519131, Singapore

CHUANG, TSU-YI, dermatologist, epidemiologist, educator; b. Amoy, China, May 21, 1946; s. Hsi and Kia-Ling (Hwang) C.; m. Lydia Ling-Chuan Lee, Dec. 22, 1973; children: Chester, Nancy. B of Medicine, Nat. Taiwan U., Taipei, 1971; MPH, U. Wash., 1978. Diplomate Am. Bd. Dermatology, Am. Bd. Preventive Medicine. From asst. prof. to assoc. prof. dermatology U. Wis., Madison, 1984-92; chief dermatology svc. Middleton VA Med. Ctr., Madison, 1984-90; assoc. prof. dermatology Wright State U., Dayton, Ohio, 1990-95, dir. immunopathology lab., 1994-95; dir. dermatology clinic Frederick A. White Health Ctr., Dayton, 1995; prof. dermatology Ind. U., Indpls., 1995—, med. dir. melanoma program, 1996—, Arthur L. Norins prof., dir. dermatology clinic, 1999—; vis. prof. Nat. Taiwan U., Taipei, 1991-97. Co-author: Conn's Current Therapy, 1992, The Challenge of Dermato-Epidemiology, 1997; editl. cons. Arch Dermatol., Chg., 1990-97; editor Dermatologica Sinica, Taipei, 1994-96; contbr. over 100 articles to profl. jours. Pres. Rochester (Minn.) Chinese Culture Assn., 1980-82; v.p. Orgn. of Chinese Ams., Madison, 1986-90; pres. Midwest Chinese Christian Assn., Dayton, 1993-94, Indpls., 1996-97. Rsch. grantee U. Wis., 1985-89, VA merit rev. bd. grantee Dept. Vets. Affairs, 1986-88, 90-94; recipient Burdette-Kunkel award Mary Margaret Walther Program for Cancer Care Rsch., 1996-97. Fellow Am. Acad. Dermatology (editl. cons. Am. Acad. Dermatology jour. 1986-2000), Am. Soc. for Dermatol. Surgery; mem. Soc. for Investigative Dermatology, Ind. Chinese Profls. Assn. (pres. 1998). Achievements include first historical cohort study of human papilloma virus infection in U.S. in a defined population, first historical cohort study of genital herpes virus infection in U.S. in a defined population, first incidence study of polymyalgia rheumatica in the U.S. in a defined population, first population-based incidence study of skin cancer in U.S. in two well-defined populations. Home: 7314 Chestnut Hills Blvd Indianapolis IN 46278-1793 Office: Ind U 550 University Blvd Indianapolis IN 46202-5149

CHUANG, YII-DER, diplomat; b. Chekiang, China, July 1, 1934; came to U.S., 1964; s. W.C. Chuang and Y.F. Chang; m. Chung-hwa Lee, Jan. 6, 1968; children: David, Michael, Nancy. BS in Automotive Engring., Chung-Cheng Inst., 1957; MS in Metall. Engring., Mich. State U., 1966; PhD in Materials Sci., NYU, 1971. Dir. hot lab. Inst. Nuclear Energy Rsch. Atomic Energy Coun., Exec. Yuan, Taoyuan, Taiwan, 1972-82; sr. scientist sci and tech. adv. group Exec. Yuan, Taipei, Taiwan, 1980-84; dep. dir. prep. office materials rsch. lab. Indsl. Tech. Rsch. Inst., Hsinchu, Taiwan, 1981-82; dep. dir. materials rsch. and devel. ctr. Chung Shan Inst. Sci. and Tech., Taoyuan, Taiwan, 1982-84; dir. sci. divsn. Coord. Coun. N.Am. Affairs, Houston, 1984-86, San Francisco, 1986-92; dir. sci. divsn. Taipei Econ. and Cultural Rep. Office, Washington, 1992—; exec. sec. materials steering com. Exec. Yuan, 1981-84; dir. Rep. Office Hsin-Chu Sci.-based Indsl. Park Adminstrn., Taiwan, 1986-92; patent reviewer Nat. Bur. Standards, Taiwan, 1973-83; exec. sec. Commn. Third Asian-Pacific Corrosion Control Conf., 1981-83. Editor Nuclear Sci. Jour., 1978-79; contbr. over 35 articles to profl. jours. Scholar NYU, 1972. Mem. Nuclear Energy Soc. of Rep. of China, Chinese Soc. Materials Sci. (editor Materials Sci. Quarterly 1972-78), Chinese Inst. Mining and Metall. Engrs., Chinese Soc. Mech. Engrs., Monte Jade Sci. and Tech. Assn., Alpha Sigma Mu. E-mail: yiider chuang@hotmail.com. Office: TECRO Sci Divsn 4201 Wis Ave NW MB-09 Washington DC 20016

CHUBAIS, ANATOLY BORISOVICH, utilities energy executive; b. Borisov, Belarussia, June 16, 1955; married; 2 children. Grad., Leningrad Engr. & Econ. Inst. Engr., asst. of chair Leningrad Inst. Econ. and Engring., 1977-82, docent, 1982-90; dep., 1st dep.-chair Leningrad Mcpl. Coun., 1991; min. Russia, chair State Com. for Mgmt. State Property, 1991—; dep. prime min., chair Co-ordination Coun. for Privatization, 1992—; mem. State Duma, 1993—; 1st Dep. Prime Min. Economy and Fin. Russian Govt., 1994-96, head residential adminstrn., 1996, 1st dep. prime min., min. finance, 1997; CEO RAO United Energy Sys. Russia, Moscow, 1998—. Office: 7 Kitaigorodsky proezd, 103074 Moscow Russia

CHUBAROV, LEONID BORISOVICH, mathematician, educator; b. Beltsy, Moldova, Sept. 11, 1948; s. Shpitalnic Boris Zakharovich and Sofia

Abramovna Chubarova; m. Emilia Smirnova, Oct. 25, 1973; 1 child, Dmitri. BSc, Tomsk (Russia) U., 1969; MSc, Novosibirsk (Russia) U., 1971, PhD, 1981. Jr. rschr. Computing Ctr. SB Russian Acad. Scis., Novosibirsk, 1971-76; jr. rschr. Inst. Pure and Applied Mechanics SB Russian Acad. Scis., Novosibirsk, 1976-81, head rsch. group, 1981-83; head lab. Computing Ctr. SB Russian Acad. Scis., Krasnoyarsk, Russia, 1983-91, Inst. Computation Technologies SB Russian Acad. Scis., Novosibirsk, 1991—; assoc. prof. Novosibirsk U., 1991-99; vis. prof. Linkoping (Sweden) U., 1996-99. Author: Numerical Simulation of Tsunami Waves Propagation, 1983, Computer Experiment in the Problem of Tsunami Waves, 1989, Software Environment for Mathematicians, 1999. Recipient All-Union award for young scientist Fed. Govt. USSR, 1981; named G. Soros Disting. Assoc. Prof., ISSEP, 1997, 98. Mem. Russian Nat. Tsunami Commn. Avocations: theatre, soccer, cinema, literature. E-mail: chubarov@adm.ict.nsc.ru. Fax: 7 3832 341342. Office: SB RAS Inst Comp Tech, Ac Lavrentjev Ave 6, 630090 Novosibirsk Russia

CHUBYKALO, ANDREW EVGENIEVICH, physics researcher, educator; b. Polotsk, Vitebsk, Bielorussia, Apr. 30, 1959; s. Evgenii Andreevich and Mayia Petrovna Chubykalo; m. Blanca Isela Ibarra-Murillo; 1 child, Evgenii Andreevich. MSc, U. Kharkov, Ukraine, 1986; PhD in Theoretical Physics, Acad. Sci., Ukraine, 1992. Rsch. assoc. U. Kharkov, 1986-92; rsch. scientist Inst. Materials Science, Madrid, 1993-95; prof. Sch. of Physics U. Autonoma de Zacatecas, Mex., 1995—; rschr. 1 level Nat. Sys. Rschr., Mex., 1998—. Contbr. articles to sci. jours. Soldier 1st class Spetznaz, 1979-81. Mem. Mex. Soc. Physics, N.Y. Acad. Scis. Communist. Avocations: athletics, science fiction, Chinese language. Home: Av de la Vid 145, 98068 Zacatecas Mexico Office: U Autonomas Zacatecas, Sch Physics A P 580, 98068 Zacatecas Mexico

CHUDINOVICH, IGOR YURIEVICH, mathematics educator; b. Makeevka, Donetsk, Ukraine, Dec. 15, 1949; s. Yuri and Evgenia Chudinovich; m. Olga Mikhailovna Dolberg, Jan. 16, 1971; 1 child, Evgenia. MSc in Math. and Tchg. of Math., Kharkov (Ukraine) State U., 1971; Candidate Sci. in Math., Inst. for Theoretical Physics, Kiev, Ukraine, 1975; DSc in Math., Kharkov Inst. Low Temperature Physics & Engring., 1993. Asst. prof. math. Kharkov State U., 1974-79, sr. lectr., 1979-82, assoc. prof., 1982-95, prof., 1995—. Author: Boundary Equation Method in Dynamic Problems for Elastic Media, 1991; contbr. articles to sci. jours., including Math. Methods in Applied Scis., IMA Jour. Applied Math. Grantee Internat. Sci. Found., Ukraine and U.S., 1995, Engring. and Physics Sci. Rsch. Coun., U.K., 1996, 97. Mem. Am. Math. Soc., Kharkov Math. Soc. Avocation: classical music. Office: Kharkov State U Dept Math, 4 Svobody Sq, 61074 Kharkov Ukraine

CHUDZIKIEWICZ, RYSZARD JERZY, foundry educator; b. Tarnopol, Ukraine, June 20, 1923; s. Antoni and Janina (Czekańska) C.; m. Bożena Maria Sauter, Dec. 9, 1948; two children. Engr., Tech. U., Gliwice, Poland, 1946; D in Tech. Sci., Tech. U.-Akademia Górniczo-Hutnicza, Cracow, Poland, 1962. Chief engr. of foundry Gliwice, 1946-56; asst. Tech. U., Gliwice, 1946-56; prof. Tech. U., Szczecin, Poland, 1956—; rector Tech. U., Szczecin, 1975-78; adviser Foundry Dozament, Nowa Sól, Poland, 1956-77. Author: Hot Blast Cupolas, 1962 (State's award for tech. progress Poland 1964), Mouldig in Selfhardening Sands, 1971, Founry Mechanization and Automatization, 3rd edit., 1980. Mem. Polish Acad. Sci. (sect. of foundry process theory). Avocation: hunting. E-mail: lukas@shiptech.tuniv.szczecin.pl. Home: Potulicka 57/15, 70-230 Szczecin Poland Office: Technical Univ, Piastów 41, 71-065 Szczecin Poland

CHUDZINSKI, MARK ADAM, lawyer; b. Chgo., Oct. 13, 1956; s. Brunon and Maria (Chmielinski) C.; m. Barbara Podkul, July 31, 1993; 1 child, Anna. BA, Northwestern U., 1977, MBA, 1981, JD, 1981; Diplome d'Etudes Approfondies, U. Paris, 1982. Bar: N.Y. 1982, Ill. 1990, U.S. Supreme Ct. 1994. Assoc. Coudert Bros., N.Y.C., 1982-85, London, 1985-88, Sydney, Australia, 1988-89; sr. assoc. Winston & Strawn, Chgo., 1990-95, ptnr., 1995-96; gen. counsel Ameritech Internat., 1996-99. Articles editor Northwestern Jour. Internat. Law and Bus., 1981. Trustee Window To The World Comm., Inc. (Stas. WTTW-TV and WFMT-FM), Chgo., Kosciuszko Found., N.Y.C.; mem. adv. bd. Sta. WBEZ-FM, Chgo.; bd. dirs. Chgo. Legal Clinic, Inc., Polish Mus. Am., 1991-98, Polish Am. Congress, 1992-96. Austin scholar 1978; fellow Leadership Greater Chgo., 1990; U.S. Champ Jessup Moot Ct., 1979. Mem. ABA, N.Y. State Bar Assn., Am. Soc. Internat. Law, French-Am. C. of C., German-Am. C. of C., U.S.-Poland C. of C. (founder, chmn. 1991-95). Roman Catholic.

CHUEIRI, RENAN RACHID, mechanical engineer; b. Ibaiti, Parana, Brazil, Feb. 12, 1958; s. Alexandre Rachid and Olga Melo Chueiri; m. Maria Regina Rebello; children: Felipe, Caio. Degree in Mech. Engring., U. Mogi Das Cruzes, Sao Paulo, Brazil, 1980; M in Material Application Engring., Hannover U., Germany, 1987. Engring. mgr. Pety Bom, Sao Jose Dos Campus, Brazil, 1981-84; gen. mgr. Haas Do Brazil, Sao Paulo, 1987-90; mgr. tech. Santista Alimentus, Sao Paulo, 1990-93; CEO Petybonm, Goiania, 1993-95, Plus Vita, Rio de Janeiro, 1995-98, Cafe Tres Corações, Belo Horizonte, 1998—. Named Hon. Citizen, Govt. Parana State.

CHUGHTAI, SELINA, psychologist; b. London, June 26, 1970; d. Mohammed Tufail and Iqbal Chughtai. BS in Psychology with honors, London Guildhall U., 1994, MS in Applied Psychology, 1996. Lectr. study skills London Guildhall U., 1996-97; occupl. psychologist Career Analysts, London, 1997-98; clin. audit project officer South London and Maudsley Hosp. (NHS Trust), London, 1998—. Mem. APA (affiliate). Avocations: fitness, charity, running. Fax: 0207-411-6587. E-mail: laviza.chughtai@virgin.net; selina.chughtai@slam-tr.nhs.uk. Home: 113 The Roundway, London N17 7HD, England

CHUKHLOMIN, VALERIY DMITRIEVICH, economics educator, academic administrator; b. Petrovsk, Chita Oblast, USSR, Oct. 24, 1959; s. Chukhlomin Ipatovich Dmitriy and Kazanova Feodosyevna Tatyana; m. Irina Victorovna Ivanishko, July 19, 1979; children: Marina, Anna. Specialist Degree in Math. Econs., Novosibirsk State U., USSR, 1982; Degree in Polit. Econs., Inst. Economics, Novosibirsk, 1986, PhD, 1986. Assoc. prof. econs. Omsk (Russia) Rlwys. Inst., 1986-91; vice rector Omsk (Russia) State U., 1991-98, chair dept. bus. studies, 1993-99; dean sch. internat. bus. Omsk State U., 1999—; sr. rschr. Inst. Econs., Omsk, Russia, 1992—. Co-author: The New Economic Thinking, 1990, Road to Market Economy, 1991. Recipient best student's diploma of the year award Ministry Edn., Moscow, 1983. Mem. European Assn. for Evolutionary Polit. Economy, Internat. Acad. Bus. Avocation: chess. Home: PO Box 3077, 644070 Omsk Russia Office: Omsk State U, 55A Prospekt Mira, 644077 Omsk Russia

CHUKHRAI, PAVEL GRIGORYEVICH, film director; b. Moscow, Oct. 14, 1946; s. Grigori Chukhrai. Grad., All-Union State Inst. Cinema, 1971. Dir., writer: (films) Lyudi v okeane, 1980, Vor, 1997; dir.: (films) Kletka dlya kanareyek, 1983, Zina-Zinuyla, 1986; script writer Who Will Pay For the Fortune, The Thief, 1997. Office: NUT-Profit Office 430, 12-A Chistoprudny Blvd, 101000 Moscow Russia also: Confedn Filmmakers Unions, Vasilyevskaya St 13, 123825 Moscow Russia*

CHUKOVA, YULIA PETROVNA, physicist; b. Velikodvorie, Vladimir, Russia, May 5, 1935; d. Peter Nicholaevich and Lubov Georgievna (Kireeva) C. BSc with honors, Sch. 79, Moscow, 1953; MSc with honors, Lomonosov State U. Moscow, 1959; PhD in physics and math, Lebedev Phys. Inst. Russian Acad. Scis., Moscow, 1968; sr. rsch. scientist diploma, Nat. Illuminating Engring. Inst., Moscow, 1968. Cert. scientist wide field natural Scis. Engr., sr. rsch. scientist Nat. Illuminating Engring. Inst., 1959-75; sr. rsch. scientistnatural diamond rsch. lab. USSR Ministry Fin., Moscow, 1975-85; sr. rsch. scientist Acad. Med. Scis. USSR, Moscow, 1985-86, Temp. Sci. Group Otlik, Kiev, USSR, 1987; dir. Krasnopresnenskiy Ecol. Fund, Moscow, 1991—; lectr. Moscow Inst. Radio Art Electronics and Automatics, 1966-70; head Electromagnetics Lab. Inst. Human Ecology Rassian Acad. Tech. Scis., Moscow, 1998—; lectr. Moscow Inst. Raising the Level of Tchr. Skill, 1998—. Author: Anti-Stokes Luminescense and New Possibilities For Its Apllications, 1980, Will We Die From Cancer?, 1995, others; contr. to profl. jours. Patenteein field. Recipient Golden medal R.S.F.S.R., Soviet Govt., Moscow, 1953, Silver medal Prin. Com. USSR Exhbn. Nat. Economy Achievement, 1975, Moscow 850 medal Russian Govt, 1997. Mem. Presidium Russian People Acad. Scis. (corr. mem., academician, 1998, 1999), Russian Geog. Soc., European Bioelectromagnetics Assn. Avocations: poetry, arctic travels, skiing, painting. Home: Malaya Gruzinskaya St. 6-42, 123242 Moscow Russia

CHUKWU, UMUNNEOCHI, pharmacist, educator, researcher, consultant; b. Amuda-Umunneochi, Abia, Nigeria, May 25, 1955; s. Akabueze Ikere and Ekwuforo Priscilla (Iwe-Ezeala) C.; m. Chinomnso Amarauche Chukwumerije, Dec. 1, 1984; children: Chizaram, Oluebube, Otutodirichukwu, Chizuroke, Udochiamaka. B Pharmacy, U. Nigeria, Nsukka, 1981, MPharm, 1983, PhD, 1986; postgrad., Victoria U., Manchester, Eng., 1985. Registered pharmacist, Nigeria; lic. fed. govt. drug analyst, Nigeria. Asst. lectr. pharmaceutical tech. and indsl. pharmacy U. Nigeria, 1983-84, lectr. II, 1984-86, lectr. I, 1986-88, sr. lectr., acting head pharm. tech., 1988-95, 98-00, acting dean Faculty Pharm. Scis., 1995, prodn. mgr. pilot drug prodn. unit, 1986—; cons. Drug Info. Health Clinics, Nigeria, 1988—; drug analyst Fed. Ministry Health, Nigeria, 1990—; resource person Raw Materials R & D Coun., Nigeria, 1991—; reviewer Colour Atlas of Pharmacology, 1997. Mem. editl. adv. bd. Nigeria Jour. Pharmacy, 2000—; contbr. articles to sci. jours., including Drug Devel. and Indsl. Pharmacy, Bull. Chimico Farmaceutico, STP Pharma Sci., Analytical Letters, Acta Pharm. Staff adviser Christian Union, U. Nigeria, 1994—, joint Christian body, 1994—; mem. area com. Scripture Union, Nigeria, 1996—. Recipient Chemist prize Kingsway Ltd., Nigeria, 1978; rsch. grantee U. Nigeria Senate, 1982, Brit. Coun. grantee U. Manchester, 1985. Mem. Nat. Assn. Acad. Pharmacists (coord. U. Nigeria 1986—), Pharm. Soc. Nigeria (zonal coord. 1986—), Internat. Bioencapsulation Rsch. Orgn., Third World Acad. Scis. (assoc., vis. rschr. 1998—). Methodist. Avocations: Bible reading, football, lawn tennis. Office: U Nigeria, Dept Pharm Tech, Nsukka Enugu, Nigeria

CHULAVACHANA, TAVISAK, ophthalmologist, resort owner; b. Bangkok, Apr. 27, 1931; s. Sanoh amd Soi (Sukandhavanich) C.; m. Lola Jeanette Mangus, Dec. 6, 1959. MD, Chulalongkorn U., Bangkok, 1954; MPH, Harvard U., 1955. Diplomate Am. Bd. Ophthalmology. Instr. Tulane U., La., 1960-61, Chulalongkorn U., Bangkok, 1961-62; pvt. practice Pirompesuj Hosp., Bangkok, 1962—. Author: Eye Disease, 1989. Fellow Am. Coll. Surgeons, Am. Acad. Ophthalmology. Home and Office: Pirompesuj Hosp, 117/1 Phyathai Rd, 10400 Bangkok Thailand

CHUMACHENKO, EVGENIY, mathematician; b. Melitopol, USSR, Dec. 28, 1951; s. Nikolay and Antonina (Flerova) C.; m. Tatiana Bardakova, Oct. 27, 1973; children: Sergey, Lana. MS, Moscow State U., 1979; PhD, Moscow Steel & Alloys Inst., 1981, DSc, 1995. Engr., programmer Computer Ctr. Min. Energy, Moscow, 1974-79; asst. prof. Moscow Steel & Alloys Inst., 1981-82; rschr. All-Union Rsch. Inst. Metallurgic Machine Bldg., Moscow, 1982-89; prof. Moscow State Inst. Electronics & Maths., 1989—. Author: Application of the Finite Element Method to Calculation of Part of Metallurgic Machine for Problem of Forging of Metal, 1989, Mathematical Simulation of Shape-Changing for Forging, 1998. Home: Kashirskoye Shosse h87 f 22, 142040 Domodedovo Moscow, Russia

CHUN, BYUNG SUK, publishing executive; b. Hongsung, Republic of Korea, Sept. 1, 1937; s. Kwang Soo Chun and Sa In Kim; m. Myung Hee Kim, Mar. 24, 1963; children: Joon Bae, Hyun Bae, Jin Bae. B in Econs., Korea U., Seoul, 1960. Mng. editor Jin-Myung Pub. Co., 1960-66; exec. Moonye Pub. Co., Seoul, 1966—. Chief editor The Korean Pub. Jour., Seoul, 1994-99. Recipient Official commendation Minister of Culture and Pub. Info., 1982, citation Prime Minister of Korea, 1988, Publ. Ethics award Korean Publ. Ethics Commn., 1994, Korean Pub. Culture award HanKook Ilbo, 1996, prize Korean Pub. Sci. Soc., 1996, award Korean Soc. of Translation, 1997, Journalism Culture award Chung-Ang U., 1997, Seoul City Culture award Seoul Met. Govt., 1999; named to Order for Cultural Merit, Pres. of Korea, 1993. Mem. Korean Pub. Assn. (bd. dirs. 1975—), Korean Pubs. Coop. (bd. dirs. 1982-99), Korean Pubs. Assn. (v.p. 1985-87), Korean Pub. Rsch. Inst. (bd. dirs. 1991-92, 98—), Korean Pub. Fund (bd. dirs. 1994—). Avocation: appreciation of old Korean painting and writings. Home: Dohwa-Dong Mapo-Gu, Mapo Samsung Apt 112-1404, Seoul 121-040, Republic of Korea Office: Moonye Pub Co Kyunggi Bd 3F, 184-4 Chungjeong-no 2 ga, Seodaemun-gu Seoul 120-012, Republic of Korea

CHUN, SAE-IL, physician, educator, hospital administrator; b. Seohung, Korea, Sept. 25, 1936; s. Jin Kun and Yong Wha (Yoon) C.; m. Soon Ok Choi, Sept. 18, 1965; children: Joseph, Scott, Sam. MD, Yonsei U., Seoul, Korea, 1961. Resident in family medicine St. Agnes Med. Ctr., Phila., 1967-70; resident in rehab. medicine Hosp. U. Pa., 1970-72; dir. Del. Curative Workshop, Wilmington, 1973-79; prof. U. Pa. Med. Sch., 1979-88, Yonsei U. Med. Sch., 1988—; dir. Yonsei U. Rehab. Hosp., Seoul, 1992—; chmn. World Congress Acupuncture, 1974, Korean Acad. Rehab. Medicine, 1992-94; dir. Rsch. Inst. Traditional Medicine, 1995-98. Author: Rehabilitative Treatment of Stroke, 1992; editor Yonsei Med. Jour., 1992-96; editor-in-chief Internat. Acupuncture Jour., 1979-87; med. editor Acupuncture Rsch. jour., 1974-78. Pres. Korean-Am. Assn. N.J., 1983-85, Korea-Am. Music Found., 1986-88, East-West Med. Assn., 1991—; chmn. Veneratio Vitae Club, Korea, 1990—. Capt. Korean Army, 1961-67. Recipient Recognition award Philippine Acupuncture Assn., 1977. Fellow Am. Acad. Phys. Medicine and Rehab., Korean Acad. Rehab. Medicine (chmn. 1992-94); mem. Internat. Acupuncture Assn. (pres. 1979-87), Internat. Rehab. Medicine Assn. (bd. govs. 1997—). Presbyterian. Avocations: travel, music, drawing, caligraphy, golf. Home: 536-1105 Samsung Apt, 870 Whatjungdong, Koyang City Republic of Korea Office: Yonsei Univ, Rehab Hosp, 120-752 Seoul Republic of Korea

CHUNG, BUHM JIN, university educator; b. Seoul, Korea, Feb. 7, 1935; m. Kang Yoon-Se, Sept. 9, 1960; children: Chung Hea-Yang, Chung Sona. BA, Sung Kyun Kwan U., 1959, PhD, 1978; MA, Nat. Taiwan Normal U., 1961. Lectr. Sung Kyun Kwan U., Seoul, Korea, 1961-70, asst. prof., 1970-75, vice prof., 1975-80, prof., 1980—, dean coll. of humanities, 1986-88, pres., admin. dir., 1995—. Author: The History of Chinese Literature, 1988, A Study on Novel of Tang Dynasty, 1982; editor: Standard Chinese Language, 1969, Chinese Pronunciation, 1982. Mem. Soc. for Chinese Studies (pres. 1984-86, 88—), Soc. for Chinese Lang. and Lit. (pres. 1979-80). Avocations: go, tenis. Office: Sungkyunkwan U, 53 3-Ga Myongnyundong, Chongo-gu Seoul 110-745, Republic of Korea*

CHUNG, CAROLINE, airline professional; b. Washington, Apr. 27, 1970; d. Jae Wan and Soojun Chung. BS, U. Wis., 1992; MBA, Vanderbilt U., 1997. Cert. Mad Dogg Spinning, Aerobics and Fitness Assn. Am. Mgr. product devel. U.S. Airways, Washington, 1999—. Roman Catholic. Avocations: professional aerobics instructor, travel, reading, world maps, music. E-mail: cchung@usairways.com. Office: US Airways 2345 Crystal Dr Arlington VA 22227-0001

CHUNG, CHE-SHUM, banker; b. Macao, Feb. 2, 1947. BA, U. Hong Kong, 1971. Mgr. and sec. Wing Lung Bank Ltd., Hong Kong, 1985-87, asst. gen. mgr., sec., 1987-90, gen. mgr., sec., 1990-91, exec. dir. and gen. mgr., 1991—; CEO Wing Lung Fin. Ltd., Hong Kong, 1985—; bd. dirs. Wing Lung Fin. Ltd., Hong Kong, Wing Lung Bank (Trustee) Ltd., Hong Kong, Wing Lung Bank (Nominees) Ltd., Hong Kong, Wing Lung Credit Ltd., Hong Kong, Wing Lung Agy. Ltd., Hong Kong, Wing Lung Ins. Co. Ltd., Hong Kong, Wing Lung Ins. Brokers Ltd., Hong Kong, Hongnet Ltd., Hong Kong, Wing Lung Securities Ltd., Hong Kong, Sea Wing Investments Ltd., Hong Kong, Wing Lung Futures Ltd., Hong Kong. Office: Wing Lung Bank Ltd, Wing Lung Bank Ltd, 45 Des Voeux Rd Ctrl, Hong Kong Hong Kong

CHUNG, CHI YUNG, college administrator; b. Hunan, China, July 29, 1920; d. Ling and Chan (Shi) C.; m. Henry H. L. Hu, Nov. 12, 1945; children: Y.S. Hu, F.C. Hu. LLB, Wuhan U., (China), 1944; PhD, U. Paris, 1953. Judge Dist. Ct., Chung King, China, 1943-45; lectr. Bapt. Coll., 1955-66, Chung Chi Coll., 1960-67; sr. lectr., head sociology, social work dept., dean arts faculty Bapt. Coll., 1967-71; founder, v.p. Hong Kong Shue Yan Coll., 1971—; prin. Shue Yan Secondary Coll., Hong Kong, 1972-93; hon. prof. Wuhan U., People's U. China, hon. adv. prof. Beijing Inst.of Tech.; mem. consultative com. for basic law Hong Kong Spl. Adminstrv. Region, People's Republic of China, mem. exec. com., 1996—, Release Under Supervision Bd. Hong Kong; apptd. adv. of Hong Kong affairs by PRC; mem. eletion com., chief exec. Provisional Legis. Coun., 1996. Author: Ta Tsing Lu Li in Hong Kong, 1957, Human Rights and Questions of Nationality, 1957, A Study of Social Legislation, 1963, Chinese Law and Custom, 1963, Problem of Juvenile Delinquency in Hong Kong, 1965, Youth Problem and Education in Hong Kong, 1966. Democrated Badge of Honor by H.E. the Gov. Mem. Hong Kong Tchr.'s Assn. (hon. pres., advisor). Home: 114 Macdonnell Rd Flat 404, Hong Kong China Office: Shue Yan Coll, 10 Wai Tsui Cresc Braemar Hill Rd, North Point Hong Kong

CHUNG, CHI-KIT RONALD, computer engineering educator, researcher; b. Hong Kong, Hong Kong, Aug. 3, 1963; s. Ping Kwai and Hoi Kuen (Lo) C. BS in Elec. Engring. with honors, U. Hong Kong, 1986; MS in Elec. Engring., U. So. Calif., 1988, PhD in Computer Engring., 1992. Chartered engr. Engring. Coun. U.K. IC design engr. RCL Semiconductors, Ltd., Hong Kong, 1986-87; application electronics engr. Outboard Marine, Asia, Ltd., Hong Kong, 1987; rsch. asst. Inst. for Robotics and Intelligent Systems U. So. Calif., L.A., 1988-92; assoc. prof. automation and computer aided engring. The Chinese U. of Hong Kong, Shatin, 1992—. Contbr. articles to profl. jours. Grantee: Hong Kong RGC. Mem. IEEE (sr.), Brit. Computer Soc., Mensa. Office: Chinese U Hong Kong, Dept Automation, Shatin NT Hong Kong

CHUNG, GYUHWA, plant geneticist, educator; b. Chinju, Korea, Apr. 24, 1954; s. Ilyeong Chung and Daesoo Yun; m. Jiyeon Ha, Apr. 12, 1989; children: Yeongyeong, Yeonji. BA, Gyeongsang Nat. U., Chinju, 1976, MS, 1985, PhD, 1988. Rschr. Seoul Nat. U., 1988; lectr. Gyeongsang Nat. U., 1989-91; prof. Yosu (Korea) Nat. U., 1992—; advisor Jinyang Seed Devel. Co., Chinju, Nat. Fisheries Rsch. and Devel. Inst. Avocations: habkido, music composition. E-mail: ghchung@yosu.yous.ac.kr. Fax: 061-659-3302. Office: Yosu Nat U, Doonduk-Dong San 96-1, Chonnam Yosu 550 749, Korea

CHUNG, HAI WON, geneticist, educator; b. Seoul, Korea, July 8, 1950; s. Seung Whang and Taek Ja (Shon) C.; m. Young Sook Bae, Dec. 5, 1979. BS, Seoul Nat. U., 1973, MPH, 1978, PhD, 1983. Lectr. 3d Mil. Acad., Young cheon, Korea, 1973-75; from rschr. to sr. rschr. Korea Atomic Energy Rsch. Inst., Seoul, 1975-85; from asst. prof. to prof. Sch. Pub. Health Seoul Nat. U., 1985—, dir. Inst. Health and Environ. Scis., 1992-94; vis. scientist U. Calif., San Francisco, 1988-89; cons. Ministry of Labor, Seoul, 1992-94, Korea Atomic Energy Rsch. Inst., Daejeon, 1996-97. Author: Introduction to Public Health, 1996, Radiation Biology, 1997, Industrial Toxicology, 2000. 1st lt. Korean Mil., 1973-75. Mem. Korean Environ. Mutagen Soc. (editor-in-chief 1999—), Genetics Soc. Korea (bd. dirs. 1986—), Environ. Mutagen Soc. Avocation: table tennis. Home: 106-1506 Dae-A Apt, Gayang 1 dong Kangsu-gu, 157-200 Seoul Korea Office: Seoul Nat U Sch Pub Health, 28 Yun Keun-dong Chongro-ku, 110-460 Seoul Korea

CHUNG, HAN-GIL, dermatologist; b. Seoul, Korea, Feb. 10, 1969; s. No-Pal Chung and Jung-Ja Park; So-Young Jang, Oct. 15, 1994; 1 child, Sung-Youn. MD, Yonsei U., Seoul, 1993; MSc, Yonsei U., 1999. Dermatologist Yonsei U. Coll. Medicine, Seoul, 1997—, chief resident, 1999. Lt. Korean Navy, 1994-97. E-mail: onewayc@hotmail.com. Fax: 82-2-393-9157. Office: Yonsei U Coll Medicine, Shinchondong 134, Seoul Korea

CHUNG, HENRY SHU-HUNG, electrical and electronic engineering educator; b. Hong Kong, Jan. 25, 1966; s. Yuen-Yun and Yuk-Hing (Lam) C.; m. Vonney Pui-Man Cheng, Nov. 17, 1997. Higher Diploma in E.E. with distinction, Hong Kong Poly. U., 1988, BEng with 1st class honors, 1991, PhD, 1994. Electronic engr. BERT Corp. Ltd., Hong Kong, 1994-95; asst. prof. City U. Hong Kong, 1995-98, assoc. prof., 1998—; vis. lectr. Hong Kong Poly. U., 1995; cons. ECO-GEA Ltd., 1997, Popular Signs Ltd., Hong Kong, 1998, Universe Dragon Ltd., 1998; chmn. subject com. Hong Kong Exams. Authority, 1996—; mem. com. of disciplinary tribunal panel, elec. and mech. svcs. dept. Hong Kong Govt., 1996—. Contbr. articles to profl. jours. Recipient China Light and Power prize, 1991; Li Po Chun scholar, 1986, silver medal Internat. Chinese Invention Exposition, 1998; NanShing/Nanco scholar, 1989, 90; Sir. Edward Youde Meml. Fund scholar and fellow, 1991, 92; Croucher Found. scholar, 1993; Taipei Trade Ctr. scholar, 1994. Mem. IEEE, IEEE Circuits and Sys. Soc. (tech. com. 1997-98), Sir Edward Scholars Assn. (chmn. exec. com. 1992-94), Sir Edward Youde Scholars Assn. (coun. chair 1997—). Avocations: hiking, reading, swimming. Office: City U Hong Kong, Tat Chee Ave, Kowloon Tong, Hong Kong China

CHUNG, HUI-SUK, company executive, educator; b. Kyunggi Province, Korea, Apr. 25, 1939; s. Kyung-Sik and Soon-Nyu (Kim) C.; m. Lynna G. Goyma, Mar. 1, 1978; 1 child, Jae-Woo. BA, Keun Kook U., Seoul, Korea, 1965; MBE, U. Asia and Pacific, Manila, 1993; PhD, Philippine Christian U., Manila, 1998. Asst. mgr. YuHan Pharm. Co. Ltd., Seoul, 1957-59; Korea rep. Nestles Products (HK) Ltd., Hong Kong, 1959-61; pres. Daerim Fancy Yarn Mfg. Co., Korea, 1980-90, Kisco Inc., Philippines, 1991—; prof. postgrad. studies Philippine Christian U., Manila, 1998—. Mem. Rotary Club of Pasig (chmn. internat. svc.). E-mail: kisco@pacific.net.ph. Office: Kisco Inc Unit 408, 37 Annapolis St, San Juan Manila, Philippines

CHUNG, HUNG-YUAN, electrical engineering educator; b. Taiwan, Aug. 10, 1952; s. Kun-Chu and Yu-Luan (Su) C.; m. Mei-Ying Liu, Feb. 28, 1982; children: Yao-Liang, Wan-Rung, Yao-Ching.ng. PhD in Elec. Engring., Nat. Cheng-Kung U., Taiwan, 1987. Assoc. scientist Chung Shang Inst. Sci. and Tech., Taiwan, 1982-84; lectr. Nat. Cheng-Kung U., Taiwan, 1984-87, assoc. prof., 1987-92; prof. Nat. Ctrl. U., Taiwan, 1992—. Contbr. articles to profl. jours. Mem. IEEE. Office: Nat Ctrl U, Dept Elec Engring, Chung-Li 32054, Taiwan

CHUNG, JAE HO, electronics engineering educator, researcher; b. Incheon, Korea, Aug. 26, 1957; s. Ku Chang and Bok Nam (Kim) C.; m. Sunnie Kim, Dec. 15, 1984; children: Jonathan, Michael, Steven. BS, U. Md., 1982, MS, 1984; PhD, Ga. Inst. Tech., 1990. Electronic engr. Naval Surface Warfare Ctr., White Oak, 1984-85; mem. tech. staff AT&T Bell Labs., Naperville, Ill., 1991-92; prof. electornic engring. Inha U., Incheon, 1992—; invited rschr. Electronics and Telecomms. Rsch. Inst., Taejon, Korea, 1995-97. Author: Advances in Speech Coding, 1991, A New Homomorphic Vocoder Framework Using Analysis-by-Synthesis Excitation, 1991; contbr. articles to profl. jours. Mem. Sci. Rsch. Soc., Tau Beta Pi, Eta Kappa Nu. Office: Inha U, Dept Electronic Engring, 402-751 Incheon Korea

CHUNG, JAY YOUNG, business educator, researcher; b. Taejon, Republic of Korea, Oct. 15, 1944; s. Ku Geun Chung and Soon Yea Rhee; m. Sook Hee Lee, Jan. 28, 1974; children: In Suk, Jin Hyuk, Seruk. BA in Bus. Mgmt., Sung Kyun Kwan U., Seoul, 1968; MA in Commerce, Waseda U., Tokyo, 1972, D Commerce, 1980. Prof. bus. Sung Kyun Kwan U., 1984—, dean Sch. Econs. and Bus., 1994-96, dean Grad. Sch. Bus. Adminstrn., 1995-96; pres. Info. Telecom. Inst. Ctr., Seoul, 1996—; bd. dirs. Korea Telecom., Seoul, 1994-97, Phhang Steel Corp., Seoul; mem. Presdl. Commn. on Edn. Reform, Seoul, 1996-98. Author: The Lobbying Economics, 1987; contbr. articles to profl. jours. Dir. gen. Neo Libertarian Soc., Seoul, 1997—. Avocations: tracking, gardening. Fax: 812-762-7835. E-mail: jyjung@yurim.skku.ac.kr. Home: Han Yang Apt 22 Dong 1201, 493 Upkujong Dong Kang Nam, Seoul Republic of Korea Office: Sung Kyun Kwan U, 3ka Myung Yun-Dong Jong Ro, Seoul 110-745, Republic of Korea

CHUNG, JEN-KING, communications executive; b. Ping-Tong, Taiwan, China, Dec. 2, 1960; s. Ren-Syh Chung and Shiow-Jwu Lee; m. Wen-Huey Chang, May 9, 1987; children: Hsing-Yuan, Hsing-Chen. B in Engring., Nat. Cheng-Kung U., Tainan, China, 1983, MS, 1985; PhD, Nat. Ctrl. U., Chung-Li, China, 1997. Asst. rschr. Telecom. Lab. Chunghwa Telecom. Co., Ltd., Chung-Li, 1985-90, assoc. rschr., 1990-96, sr. rschr., 1996-99; dir. info. sys. dept. So. Bus. Group, Koashown, China, 1999—. Mem. IEEE. Achievements include Chinese patent, 1995. Avocation: tennis, music. Office: Chunghwa Telecom Co Ltd, 20, Chi-Hsen 1st Rd, 800 Kaoshown China

CHUNG, JING-GUNG, physician, educator; b. Kaohsiung-Hsien, Taiwan, Republic of China, Apr. 7, 1950; s. Feng-Ding and Jinn-Maan (Ven) C.; m. Ming-Ming Yin, Sept. 13, 1980; 1 child, Tzu-Wei. MS, N.Mex. Highland U., 1983, La. Tech. U., 1986, U. Miss., 1989; PhD, U. Miss., 1992. Tchg. asst. Tchg. Coll. Tainan Journzor, 1980-82; tchg. asst. N.Mex. Highland U., Las Vegas, 1982-83, La. Tech. U., Ruston, 1984-86, U. Miss. Med. Ctr., Jackson, 1986-92; postdoctoral fellow U. Mich., Ann Arbor, 1992-93; assoc. prof. China Med. Coll., Taichung, 1993—. Mem. editl. bd. Chinese Jour. Immunology, 1993-99; contbr. articles to profl. jours. Kao-Jih mem. Gwo-Min Danng, Taichun, Taiwan, 1996-99. Comd. officer Mil. Police Taiwan mil., 1970-72. Named Outstanding Tutor China Med. Coll., 1994. Mem. N.Y. Acad. Scis. Buddhist. Avocations: movies, music, basketball, tennis, swimming. Home: No 46 8F, Second St of Bor Goan 400, Taiwan Republic of China Office: China Med Coll, No 91 Hsueh-Shih 400, Taichung Taiwan Republic of China

CHUNG, JUNG GIT, aerospace engineer; b. Sun Wai, Moy Kok, Canton, Republic of China, Apr. 12, 1922; s. Pak Wing and Yow Fun (Dong) C.; m. Fay Yung Ma, May 3, 1951; 1 child, John Gingkeong. BAE, NYU, 1949, MAE, 1951. With Fairchild Republic, Farmingdale, N.Y., 1951-86, airloads and performance engr., 1962-64; head transonic, supersonic and hypersonic wind tunnels Republic Aviation, 1963-65; airloads and performance engr. M-30 Aerospace Plane Fairchild Republic, Farmingdale, 1964-66; design air loads engr. Boeing 757, Boeing Aircraft, Seattle, 1979; NATO fighter design specification team Fokker, Amsterdam, 1969-70; preliminary design and performance FRC/SAAB Transport, Swearingen Aviation, San Antonio, 1980; loads and dynamics engr. Grumman E-2C, Grumman Aircraft, Bethpage, 1981, preliminary design of aerial refueling tank, 1982; AMRAM missile ejection and separation dynamics Grumman F-14, Bethpage, 1983, with ASW-340 store carriage and separation, F-15 dispenser tech., 1984, with A-10 performance maintenance, capacity acctg., interface mgmt., aircraft accident analysis, 1985, T-46 aeroperformance, quality control flying surfaces, 1986; mem. faculty N.Y. Inst. Tech., 1969; instr. H&R Block, 1986; instr., tax preparer Vol. Income Tax Assistance, 1986-92; instr. SeniorNet Dorest Hills Learning Ctr., 1993-95; sr. connections adv. bd. Adelphi U. Sch. Social Work, 1991-95, Nassau Libr. Sys., 1995—. Coord. and instr. Tax Counseling for the Elderly, AARP ADC/Tax Assistance, 1985—, tech. specialist, 1996-98, instr. AARP 55-Alive Mature Driving, 1998—; vol. Am. Fedn. Arts; program and membership chair Fairchild Republic Retirees, 1986-91; mem. adv. coun. planning and priorities com. Nassau County Dept. Sr. Citizen Affairs, 1996—; tutor English for spkrs. of other langs. Lit. Vols. Am., Nassau County chpt., 1993— (Tutor of Yr. 1998). Mem. CAP, AAAS, AAIA, AARP (1st v.p. Farmingdale chpt. 1988-89, pres. 1992-93, alt. del. biennial conv. 1994, legis. com. 1990-94, L.I. sect. coun. 1996—), Met. Mus. Art, Mus. Natural History, Am. Fedn. Arts, U.S. Coast Guard Aux., Data Processing Mgmt. Assn., Air Force Assn., Am. Def. Preparedness Assn., N.Y. Acad. Sci., Nat. Assn. Tax Practitioners, Nat. Mgmt. Assn., Portrait Inst., Internat. Platform Assn. Republican. Presbyterian. Home: 32 Mulberry St Apt 5 New York NY 10013-4339 Office: Sr Connections South Farmingdale Libr Farmingdale NY 11735

CHUNG, KYU-SUN, nuclear engineering educator; b. Chun-Chon, Korea, June 11, 1957. BS cum laude, Seoul (Korea) Nat. U., 1980, MS, 1982; PhD, MIT, 1989. Sr. rsch. assoc. Northeastern U., Boston, 1989; asst. prof. Hanyang U., Seoul, 1989-95, assoc. prof., 1995—; vis. scientist Jet Joint Undertaking, Culham, U.K., 1993, U. Tex., Austin, 1995. Contbr. articles to profl. jours. 2d lt. Korean Army, 1982. Korea Sci. and Engring. fellow Korea Sci. Engring. Found., 1983-85. Mem. IEEE, Am. Phys. Soc., Korean Nuclear Soc., Korean Phys. Soc. (editor 1997—), Korean Inst. Christian Studies (gen. sec. 1996-98). Office: Hanyang U Dept Nucl Engring, 17 Haeng-Dang Dong, 133-791 Seoul Korea

CHUNG, MAN CHIN, medicinal chemistry educator, researcher; b. Farien, China, May 24, 1961; d. Chung Dar Wen and Lih-Jen (Lee) C.; m. Francisco de Paula Garcia Caravante Jr., Mar. 19, 1994; children: Ana Lucia Chung Caravante, Luis Henrique Chung Caravante. Degree in Pharmacy-Biochemistry, U. S.P. State, Brazil, 1983; MS, U. Sao Paulo, 1988, PhD, 1997. Aux. lectr. Faculty of Pharm. Sci. Estadual U. Sao Paulo, 1985-88, asst. prof., 1988-97, 1997—; cons. Revista de Ciencias Farmaceuticas da UNESP, Araraquara, Sao Paulo, Farma & Cia, Santo Andre. contbr. articles to profl. jours. Mem. Am. Chem. Assn., Brazilian Chem. Soc. Roman Catholic. Avocation: swimming. Home: 533 Joaquim Alves, São Paulo Brazil Office: UNESP Faculty Pharm Sci, Rodovia Araraquara-Jau Km 1, São Paulo Brazil

CHUNG, SANG-KOO, engineering educator, electrical engineer; b. Kimhae, Korea, Jan. 6, 1938; s. In-Chul Chung and Wea-Sun Kim; m. Kyung-In Lee, June 10, 1971; children: Jae Wook, Jin Hee. BSEE, Seoul Nat. U., 1962; student, Tech. U., Berlin, 1964-66; MSEE, Washington U., St. Louis, 1972, DSc, 1974. Postdoctoral fellow Washington U., 1974-75; rsch. fellow Regensburg (Germany) U., 1975-78; prof. Ajou U., Suwon, Korea, 1978—, dean Sch. Engring., 1981-83, dean Grad. Sch., 1990-94; vis. scholar UCLA, 1983-84; guest rschr. ABB Semiconductor AG, Switzerland, 1996. Contbr. tech. articles to profl. jours. including Jour. Electronic Materials, Solid-State Electronics, IEEE Transactions on Electron Devices, others. Fellow Korea Inst. Telematics and Electronics (mem. com. semiconductor devices and electronic materials 1986); mem. IEEE, Korean Inst. Elec. Engrs., N.Y. Acad. Scis. Presbyterian. Office: Ajou U, 5 Wonchun-Dong Paldal-ku, Kyung-gi Suwon 442-749, Republic of Korea

CHUNG, STEPHEN YUE PING, academic dean. BA, Oreg. State U.; MA, Mich. State U.; MA, PhD, Stanford U. Former sch. tchr., class master primary and secondary schs.; dean faculty of edn. Chinese U. of Hong Kong, Shatin, Hong Kong; vis. scholar Stanford U.; rsch. fellow U. Calif., Berkeley; guest prof. Peking U., Nanjing U.; cons. for ILO on legislation of labour tng. law in China; cons. World Bank. Office: Chinese Univ Hong Kong, Faculty of Edn, Shatin NT Hong Kong*

CHUNG, STEVE SHAO-SHIUN, electrical engineer, educator; b. Hsinchu, Taiwan, Apr. 23, 1950; m. Jane Y. Tsai, Jan. 11, 1980; children: David W., Cindy Y. BEE, Nat. Cheng-Kung U., Taiwan, 1973; MEE, Nat. Taiwan U., 1975; PhD, U. Ill., 1985. Mgr. rsch. and devel. San San Electronics Co., Taipei, Taiwan, 1976-78; instr. Nat. Taiwan Inst. Tech., Taipei, 1978-83, assoc. prof., 1985-87; rsch. asst. U. Ill., Urbana, 1983-85; assoc. prof. Nat. Chiao Tung U., Taiwan, 1987-89, prof., 1989—; dep. dir. Instruments Calibration Svc. Ctr., Taipei, 1978-82; cons. in field. Author: Network Analysis, 1986; contbr. articles to profl. jours.; patentee in field. Recipient Excellent Rsch. award Nat. Sci. Coun., 1989-95, Outstanding Rsch. award, 1996-98, Outstanding Paper award Electron Devices and Materials Assn., 1996. Mem. IEEE (sr., chair Taipei chpt. EDS, mem. tech. com. Symposium VLSI Tech. 2000—), Chinese Inst. Engrs. Avocations: painting. Home: 30 Alley 14 Lane 393, Ming-Hu Rd/Hsinchu 300, Taiwan Office: Nat Chiao Tung U, 1001 Ta-Hsueh Rd, Hsinchu 300, Taiwan

CHUNG, SUK HO, mechanical engineering educator; b. Yechon, Kyungbuk, Republic of Korea, Feb. 20, 1954; s. Yonghan and Ilhyun (Rho) C.; m. Seonil Yoo, May 4, 1978; 1 child, Mijung. BS, Seoul Nat. U., Republic of Korea, 1976; MS, Northwestern U., 1980, PhD, 1983. Cert. mech. engr. Rsch. engr. Korea Inst. Sci. and Tech., Seoul, 1977-78; post-doctoral fellow Northwestern U., Evanston, Ill., 1983; vis. scholar Princeton U., N.J., 1988, U. Calif. San Diego, La Jolla, 1988-89; prof. Seoul Nat. U., 1984—; chmn. dept. Seoul Nat. U., 1990-94; div. chief Turbo and Power Machinery Rsch. Ctr., Seoul, 1994—; dir. Automotive Rsch. Ctr./Inst. Advanced Machinery and Design, Seoul, 1997—; adv. mem. Min. Constrn., Seoul, 1996-98, Min. Industry, Seoul, 1998—. Co-author: Handbook of Heat and Mass Transfer, Vol. 4, 1990; mem. editl. bd. Jour. Combustion and Flame, 1997—; contbr. articles to profl. jours. Adv. mem. Seoul City, 1998—. With Air Force, 1976-77. Recipient R.B. Cabell fellow Northwestern U., Evanston, 1982-83. Mem. Korea Soc. Mech. Engrs. (Acad. Achievement award 1996, dir. 1996-97), Korea Soc. Automotive Engrs. (bd. dirs.), The Combustion Inst., Tau Beta Pi. Home: Rex Apt 15-309, Ichon Yongsan, Seoul Republic of Korea Office: Dept Mech Engring, Seoul Nat U, 151-742 Seoul Republic of Korea

CHUNG, SUNG-CHONG, mechanical engineering educator; b. Seoul, Korea, Dec. 12, 1956; s. Chai-Choon Chung and Ran-In Han; m. Wha-Jin Lee, Feb. 15, 1986; children: Si-Yon, Youn-Jei, Youn-Seo. BS, Hanyang U., Seoul, 1979; MS, Korea Advanced Inst. Sci/Tech, Seoul, 1981, PhD, 1987. Rsch. asst. Korea Advanced Inst. Sci/Tech, Seoul, 1981-83; instr. Hanyang U., Seoul, 1983-86, asst. prof., 1986-92, assoc. prof., 1992-97, prof., 1997—; vis. prof. Purdue U., West Lafayette, Ind., 1988-89; vis. rschr. Korea Inst. Machinery and Metals, Changwon, 1989-90; dir. Mech. Engring. and Tech. Rsch. Inst., Hanyang U., Seoul, 1994—, chmn. mech. design and prodn. engring. dept., 1995-97; mem. engring. tech. coun. Ministry of Trade, Industry and Energy, Korea, 1992—; tech. advisor Hwacheon Machinery Works Co. Ltd., Seoul, 1997—, ACE Indst. Co. Ltd., Incheon, 1996—, Mfg. Engrs. Network (MENET) Co., Ltd., Seoul, 1998—; coun. Inst. Industry Standards of Korea, 1995—, Nat. Inst. Quality and Technology, Korea, 1996—; engring. coun. Small & Medium Bus. Adminstrn., Korea, 1997—; mem. tech. com. ISO/TC39, Machine Tool Divsn., 1998—. Contbr. papers to profl. jours.; inventor in field. Recipient Disting. Rsch. award Hanyang U., 1998, 99, 2000, Paper award 28th N.Am. Mfg. Rsch. Conf. hosted by U. Ky., 2000. Mem. ASME, Korean Soc. Mech. Engrs. (exec. sec. 1994-95), Korean Soc. Machine Tool Engrs. (chmn. structural design divsn. 1996-98, editl. dir. 1998—), Korean Soc. Precision Engring. (mem. editl. bd. 1996—), N.Am. Mfg. Rsch. Instn., Soc. of Mfg. Engrs., Am. Soc. for Precision Engring., Internat. Conf. on Precision Engring. Singapore Expo 2000 (internat. adv. com.). Roman Catholic. Avocations: climbing, swimming. Office: Hanyang U Sch Mech Engring, 133-791 Seongdong-Gu Seoul, Republic of Korea

CHUNG, TAI HO, medical educator; b. Taegu, Korea; s. Yong Sam Chung and Kee Bun Lee; m. Hyuk Ja Kwon; 1 child, Chong Chan. MD, Kyungpook U., Taegu, Korea, 1958, MS, 1962, D Medicine, 1968. Med. officer, intern Korean Army, 1st Army Hosp., Taegu, 1958-59; chief clin. chemistry Capital Army Hosp., Seoul, 1961-62; fellow Kyungpook U., 1963-64, instr., 1964-67, asst. prof., 1967-71, assoc. prof., 1972-77, prof. biochemistry and immunology, 1964-98, dean Med. Sch., 1988-90, dir. WHO Hepatitis Ctr., 1990—, head dept. immunology, 1996-98; dir. Liber Rsch. Instn., 1996-98; attending prof. dept. pharamcology Yonsei U., Seoul, 1979-97; rsch. fellow dept. biochemistry George Washington U. Sch. Medicine, Washington, 1966-67; resdient, rsch. fellow VA Hosp., Richmond, Va., Med. Coll. Va., 1971-73; vis. rschr. dept. cellular immuno-hematology U. Burssels Hosp., 1975; vis. prof. dept. biochemistry SUNY, Buffalo, 1975-76; vis. prof. Rigshospitalet, Bispebjerg Hosp. and State Serum Inst., Denmark, 1979, Walter Reed Army Inst. Rsch., 1982, UCLA Tissue Typing Lab., 1987. Author: Stomach Cancer, 1980, Text Book of Immunology, 1996; contbr. numerous articles to profl. jours. Recipient Decoration of Moran Jang, Korean Govt., 1989. Mem. Korean Assn. Biochemistry and Molecular Genetics (trustee), Korean Cancer Soc. (trustee), Korean Immunology Soc. (trustee), n.Y. Acad. Scis. Home: No 111-1, Dae Bong-Dong, Taegu Korea Office: Kyungpook Nat U Sch Med, Liver Rsch Instn, Taegu Korea

CHUNG, YOUNG RYUN, educator, research scientist; b. Pusan, Korea, Feb. 16, 1954; s. Tae Gyu and Sung Jin (Lee) C.; m. Eun Kyoung Kim, Feb. 26, 1983; children: Jayeon, Hayeon. BS, Seoul (Korea) Nat. U., 1976, MS, 1981; PhD, Ohio State U., 1988. Cert. environ. mgmt. engr. Korea Manpower Agy. Jr. rsch. scientist Korea Ginseng and Tobacco Rsch. Inst., Seoul, 1979-84; rsch. assoc. Ohio State U., Columbus, 1985-87; sr. rsch. scientist Korea Rsch. Inst. Chem. Tech., Taejeon, 1988-92; prof. Gyeongsang Nat. U., Chinju, Korea, 1992—, dean assoc., 1996-97, dep. dir. Office of Planning and Rsch., 1999-2000; mem. environ. forum Nat. Parliament, Seoul, 1996; advisor Kyeongnam Province, Rural Devel. Assn., Changwon, Korea, 1995. Contbr. articles to profl. jours.; patentee in field. Lance cpl. Korean Army, 1976-79. Mem. Am. Phytopathological Soc., Korea Phytopathological Soc., Korea Organic Waste Recycling Coun. (acad. advisor 1993-98), Microbiol. Soc. Korea, N.Y. Acad. Scis. E-mail: yrchung@nongae.gsnu.ac.kr. Fax: 82-591-759-0187. Home: Sangdae-dong, Hyundai apt 108-303, Chinju 660-421, Republic of Korea Office: Gyeongsang Nat Univ, Dept Microbiology, Chinju 660-701, Republic of Korea

CHUNG-KWONG, POON, academic administrator; b. Hong Kong, Feb. 28, 1940; married; three children. BS with 1st class hons., U. Hong Kong, 1963, 64; PhD, Univ. of London, 1967, DSc, 1979. Fellow Royal Soc. of Chemistry/London; chartered chemist. Lectr. to read in chemistry U. Hong Kong, 1968-82, prof. in chemistry, 1982-90, dean of faculty of sci., 1983-90; dir. Hong Kong Polytechnic, 1991-94; pres. Hong Kong Polytechnic U., 1994—; postdoctoral rsch. fellow U. Coll., London, 1967, Calif. Inst. of Tech., 1967-68, vis. rsch. assoc., 1976, 79; vis. rsch. assoc. U. So. Calif., 1972; vis. prof. U. Toronto, 1984; hon. prof. East China U. of Sci. and Technology, Nanjing U. of Aeronautics and Astronautics, China, South China U. of Technology, U. Warwick, U.K.; numerous govtl. appointments including chmn. Radiol. Protection Adv. Group, 1989-2001; numerous bus. appointments including dir., chmn. bd. dirs. PolyU Technology and Consultancy Co., Ltd.; dir., vice-chmn. bd. dirs. Hong Kong Plastics Technology Ctr., Ltd.; adviser China Assn. for Sci. and Soc., 1996—, The Chinese History and Culture Ednl. Found., 1999—; chmn. Consumer Liaison Group, Hong Kong Electric Co., Ltd., 1992—; others. Contbr. articles to profl. jours. Mem. Nat. Com. of the Chinese People's Polit. Consultative Conf., 1998-2002; sci. and technology adviser Govt. of Hainan Province; adviser Guangzhou Assn. of Sci. and Technology, Sci. and Technology Devel. Found. of Hainan Province, 1995—, Guangzhou Found. Sci. and Tech. Progression; mem. Huaqiao Univ. Coun., 1992-2001; mem. Nuclear Safety Consultative Com. for Guangdong Daya Bay Nuclear Power Sta., 1999-2001; others. Recipient U.K. Commonwealth scholarship, 1964-67, U.S. Fulbright scholarship, 1967-68, named one of Ten Outstanding Young Persons in Hong Kong, 1979; recipient visitorship U.K. Coun. for Internat. Cooperation in Higher Edn., 1984, invitation to nominate candidates for award of Nobel Prize for Chemistry, Swedish Royal Acad. of Scis., 1985, 91, others; fellow Univ. Coll./Univ. London, 1996. Mem. Internat. Fedn. Assns. for the Advancement Sci. and Tech. (founding mem. exec. com.), World Assn. for Co-operative Edn. Coun. (v.p. 1998-2000), The Hong Kong Post-Secondary Colls. Athletic Assn. (pres. 1999-2000, hon. chmn.), Fedn. of Hong Kong Machinery and Metal Industries, Hong Kong Tourist Assn. (Hong Kong Conv. Amb.), Hong Kong Assn. for the Advancement of Real Estate and Constrn. Technology, Ltd. (hon. advisor), Hong Kong Assn. for Advancement of Sci. and Technology (past pres. 1986-87), others. E-mail: pckpoon@polyu.edu.hk. Office: The Hong Kong Polytechnic U, Hunghom, Kowloon Hong Kong

CHUNG TEH, LEE, lawyer; b. Taipei, Taiwan, China, Aug. 11; s. Chou Zan Lee and Ru Sin Yao; m. Jaclyn Tsai, July 18, 1982; children: James, Joseph. LLB, Nat. Taiwan U., Taipei, 1977; LLM, U. Calif., Berkeley, 1981, JSD, 1986. Judge Dist. Ct., Yunlin and Changhwa, Taiwan, 1982-85; ptnr. Tsar and Tsai Law Firm, Taipei, 1986-98; mng. ptnr. Lee, Tsai Ptnrs. Attys. at Law, Taipei, 1998—. Office: Lee Tsai & Ptnrs, 5A 218 Tun Hwa S Rd Sec 2, Taipei 106, China

CHUNZE, JIANG, economist, educator; b. Jinde County, Anhui, China, Mar. 30, 1935; d. Jiang QiangShi and Liu lianZhen H.; m. Xie Minggan, Oct. 30, 1933; 1 child, Jiang Xie. Crwin Econs., Shanghai Fudan U., 1956; MA in Econs., Chinese People's U., 1965; postgrad., Ga. U. Tech. Prof. comparative econ. studies grad. sch. Chinese Acad. Social Scis., 1978-88, sr. rsch. fellow Inst. World Economy and Politics, 1978-88; dep. dir. dept. fgn. econ. sys. State Commn. for Restructuring Econ. Sys., 1988-93; dir. coordinate dept. Acad. Macro-Econ. Studies State Planning Commn., 1994—; prof. Tsinghua U., Beijing, 1994—, dir. Asian Inst., 1999—; rschr. in comparative econs. and transition econs.; vis. prof. U. Calif., Berkeley, U. Ill., Smithsonian Instn., 1984-86; vis. rschr. OECD, Paris, EEC, Belgium, Bank of Tokyo, others; project guest fellow Ctr. for Econ. Rsch., Peking U., 1998-99. Author: Comparative Economic Systems-The Theory and Method for Choosing Optimal Economic System, 1992, International Economic Comparative Studies: Reform and Development and Tendency, 1992, On the Target Model of Chinese Reform: Market Economy with Government Coordination, 1992, Inevitability of Transition to Market Economy with Necessary Government Functions, 1992, China is Going to Socialist Market Economy, 1992, On Target Model of China's Economic Reform and Comparative Economic Systems, 1992, Research on Factors of Inflation and Policies for Anti-inflation During 1996-2000 in China, 1996, On Setting Up the Group of Industries Connected with Development of Agriculture in China, 1996, The Russian Economy During Transition, 1996, A Comparison of Tranformation of Russian & Chinese Economic Systems, 1996, Comparative Transition Economy, 1997, Striding Toward 2020, 2 vols., 1997, 98, Analysis and Research on Current Pension System in China; contbr. 400 articles to profl. publs., including Jour. East Asian Studies, Reform; also over 20 chpts. to books. Mem. Mainland Assn. for Rels. Across Taiwan Straits (exec. bd. 1994), Chinese Soc. World Econ. Studies, Chinese Soc. Internat. Econ. Rels., Chinese Soc. Asia and Europe Studies (vice chair econ. subcom.), Chinese Soc. for Modern Market Economy (acad. subcom.), Chinese Social Univ., All China Assn. Macro Economy, Western Returned Scholars Assn. Home: Apt 5-3-426, 2 Shou Du Ti Yu Guan S Rd, Beijing 100044, China

CHUPRINA, VALENTYNA GRYGORIYIVNA, physicist, researcher; b. Makoshino, Chernigiv, Ukraine, Sept. 20, 1930; d. Grygoriy Ivanovich and Fedora Grygoriyivna (Chyberun) Chuprina; 1 child, Olena Yuriyivna Chebanyuk. MSc, Shevchenko State U., Kiev, 1954; PhD, Inst. Metalo-Ceramics, Kiev, 1966. Asst. Pedagogical U., Stanislav, 1954-56; engr. IMSS, Kiev, 1956-59; sr. engr. Inst. Materials Sci. Problems, Kiev, 1962-67, rsch. asst., 1967-70, sr. scientist, 1970—. Inventor refractory coatings; contbr. articles to profl. jours. Mem. Assn. zeleny Svit, Kiev, 1988, Assn. Meml., Kiev, 1989, Human Right Def. Com., Ukraine, 1993. Recipient Inventor in the USSR medal, 1980. Mem. N.Y. Acad. Scis., Ukrainian Physics Soc. Orthodox Ch. Avocations: painting, swimming. Office: Inst Materials Sci Problems, 3 Krzhizhanowsky St, 252 142 Kiev Ukraine

CHURCH, CLIVE HILBORNE, humanities educator; b. London, June 12, 1939; s. John Hilborne and Florence Mabel (Rolt) C.; m. Margaret Ann Blasby, Sept. 2, 1965; children: Hilary Jane, Joanna Clare. BA in History with honors, U. Exeter, U.K., 1960; PhD in History, U. London, 1963. Jr. lectr. modern history Trinity Coll., Dublin, Ireland, 1963-65; lectr. French history U. Lancaster, U.K., 1965-75; sr. lectr. in European studies U. Lancaster, 1975-81, U. Kent, U.K., 1982-88; reader European studies U. Kent, 1988-92, prof. European studies, 1992—, Jean Monnet prof., 1995. Author: Europe in 1830, 1983, Practice and Perspective in Validation, 1984, Switzerland and Europe, 1993, The Not So Model Republic, 1994, Where is Switzerland, 1995, European Union and European Community, 1995, Continuity and Change, 1995, European Integration Theory in the 1990s, 1996, European Union Economic & Political Aspects, 2000; rev. editor Jour. Common Market Studies, 1993-96. Chmn. Thanington Without Civil Parish Coun., U.K., 1987-91. Mem. Univ. Assn. for Euro Studies (treas. 1989-93), Kent County Cricket Club. Avocation: watching cricket.

CHURCH, FRANK FORRESTER, minister, author, columnist; b. Boise, Idaho, Sept. 23, 1948; s. Frank Forrester and Bethine (Clark) C.; m. Amy Furth, May 30, 1970 (div. 1991); children: Frank Forrester, Nina Wynne; m. Carolyn Buck Luce, July 25, 1992. AB, Stanford U., 1970; MDiv, Harvard U., 1974, PhD, 1978. Sr. min. All Souls Unitarian Ch., N.Y.C., 1978—; columnist The Chicago Tribune, 1987-88, The New York Post, 1989; vis. prof. Dartmouth Coll., Hanover, N.H., 1989. Author: Father and Son: A Personal Biography of Senator Frank Church of Idaho, 1985, The Devil and Dr. Church, 1985, Entertaining Angels, 1987, The Seven Deadly Virtues, 1988, Everyday Miracles, 1988, Our Chosen Faith: An Introduction to Unitarian Universalism, 1989, God and Other Famous Liberals, 1991, Life Lines, 1996, A Chosen Faith, 1998, Lifecraft, 2000; translator: Greek Word-Building (Matthias Stehle), 1976; editor: Continuity and Discontinuity in Church History, 1978, The Essential Tillich, 1987, 2d edit., 1999, The Macmillan Book of Earliest Christian Prayers, 1988, The Macmillan Book of Earliest Christian Hymns, 1988, The MacMillan Book of Earliest Christian Meditations, 1989, One Prayer at a Time: A 12 Step Anthology, 1989, The Jefferson Bible, 1989, Without Apology: The Liberal Faith of A. Powell Davies, 1998; contbr. articles to Harvard Theol. Rev., Church and State Quar., Vigiliae Christianae, Bill Moyer's World of Ideas, Philip Berman's The Search for Meaning, others; contbr. speeches to Rep. Am. Speeches, 1983-84, 86-87, 87-88, 89-90, 92-93, 95-96, 97-98. Bd. dirs. Union Theol. Sem., N.Y.C., Coun. on Econ. Priorities, N.Y.C., 1984-91, Religion in Am. Life, Christianity in Christ, 1991, Franklin and Eleanor Roosevelt Found., N.Y.C., 1990—, N.Y. Correctional Assn., Osborne Inst., 1991-94, Enterprise Found., N.Y.C. HIV Planning Coun.; chmn. Coun. on Environment N.Y.C., 1995—; mem. svc. com. Unitarian Universalist Ch., 1978—; founder Lifelines Ctr., 1999. Montgomery fellow Dartmouth Coll., 1989. Mem. Am. Acad. Religion, Unitarian Universalist Mins. Assn., Soc. Bibl. Lit., Citizens United for Separation of Church and State. Democrat. Home: 201 E 80th St New York NY 10021-0511 Office: All Souls Unitarian Church 1157 Lexington Ave New York NY 10021-0440

CHURCH, GRAHAM JASPER, communications educator; b. July 7, 1972. BS, Ctrl. Mich. U., MA. Instr. Mid-Mich. C.C., Harrison, 1997—, Saginaw (Mich.) Valley State U., 1998—. Home: 701 Center Ave Apt 1 Bay City MI 48708-5979 Office: Mid Mich CC 7904 N Saint Helen Rd Saint Helen MI 48656-9771

CHURCH, JANE EVELYN, executive director, counselor; b. Phila., May 5, 1930; d. Carl Roger Dillman and Elizabeth Jane Powell; m. Allen Clarke Church, June 28, 1952; children: Allen, Thomas, Kenneth, Steven. BA, U. Pa., 1952; M in Ednl. Guidance and Counseling, Xavier U., 1977. Intermediate head counselor, tennis instr. Crystal Lake Camp, N.Y., 1948-51; social worker Hamilton County Sch. for Under Privileged Children, Scranton, Pa., 1953; cert. coord. Carlson Learning Inst., various cities, 1978-98; founder, exec. dir. One Earth One People, Cin., 1990—; lectr. in field. Contbr. articles to profl. jours. Founder Christmas Gift project for under-privileged children, 1968; mem. devel. com. Cin./Kharkov Sister City project, 1989-91; pres. internat. study group Am. Women's Club, Brussels; drug chair Hamilton County PTA, Cin., 1974-76. Recipient Cert. of Appreciation, Cin. Pub. Schs., 1994, Excellence in Ecology award Movimento Ecologista Mexicano, Mexico City, 1995, recognition Pres. Clinton for outstanding achievement in environment protection svcs., 1997, 98, J.C. Penney Golden Rule award, 1999, 2000. Mem. Delta Delta Delta. E-mail: jchurch@goodnews.org. Office: One Earth One People PO Box 43144 Cincinnati OH 45243-0144

CHURCH, RICHARD DWIGHT, electrical engineer, scientist; b. Ogdensburg, N.Y., June 27, 1936; s. Dwight Perry and Carmeta Elizabeth (Walters) C.; m. Vernice Naomi Ives, Aug. 26, 1961; children: Joel, Benjamin. B of Elec. Engring., Clarkson Coll. Tech., 1963. Elec. design engr. IBM, Owego, N.Y., 1963-69; prin. engr., pres. ASL Systems, Inc., Afton, N.Y., 1969-94, chmn. bd. dirs.; sr. elec. design engr. Magnetic Labs., Inc., Apalachin, N.Y., 1980-82, power supply engring. cons., 1982—; sci. Two Forty-Eight Co., Afton, 1994—; guest lectr. Afton Sch., Clarkson U. Co-author: Career Oriented Problems for Secondary Mathematics, 1974; contbr. articles to profl. jours.; patentee in field. Treas., trustee Candor Congregational Ch., 1972-84; vice chmn. Town Planning Bd. Candor, 1975-82; rep., mem. Candor Fire Co., 1972-87; bd. dirs., treas. Candor Cmty. Club, 1970-72. With USAF, 1955-59. Recipient Dr. Carl Michel award Clarkson Coll. Tech., 1960. Mem. IEEE (sr. mem.), Am. Water Works Assn., Assn. Energy Engrs. (sr.), Afton Bd. Fire Commrs., Candor Coin Club (pres. 1978-81), Union of Concerned Scientists, The Cousteau Soc., N.Y. Forest Owners Assn. (dir. 2000—), Am. Soc. Dowsers, Nat. Warplane Mus. Avocations: maple syrup production, maple tree farm development, pyramid geometry, bicycling. Home: 1249 County Road 30 Afton NY 13730-2181 Office: PO Box 235 Afton NY 13730-0235

CHURCHILL, JAMES GARTON, retired international finance consultant; b. Bklyn., July 16, 1930; s. S. Garton and Mary Ellen (Peck) C.; m. Nancy Barrett Wickers, July 31, 1954 (dec. Jan. 1997); children: Glenn Garton, Bruce Barrett, Ellen Wickers. BA, Dartmouth Coll., 1952; MBA, Harvard U., 1954. Fin. analyst Mobil Oil Corp., N.Y.C., 1958-62; treas. Mobil Inner Europe, Geneva, 1962-65, Mobil Europe, London, 1965-68; fin. dir. Mobil Sekiyu, Tokyo, 1968-70; treas. internat. ops. Kaiser Aluminum & Chem. Corp., Oakland, Calif., 1970-81, treas., 1981-87; pvt. practice fin. cons. San Francisco, 1987-90. Served to lt. USNR, 1954-57. Avocations: history and French language study, reading. Home and Office: 2001 Grassy Ln Woodstock VT 05091-8053

CHURCHILL, STUART WINSTON, chemical engineering educator; b. Imlay City, Mich., June 13, 1920; s. Howard Heenan and Faye Erma (Shurte) C.; m. Donna Belle Lewis, Feb. 22, 1946 (div.); children: Stuart Lewis, Diana Gail, Cathy Marie, Emily Elizabeth; m. Renate Ursula Treibmann, Aug. 3, 1974. BS in Math, U. Mich., 1942, BSChemE, 1942, MS, 1948, PhD, 1952; MA (hon.), U. Pa., 1972. Technologist Shell Oil Co.,

1942-46; tech. supr. Frontier Chem. Co., 1946-47; mem. faculty U. Mich., 1949-67, prof. chem. engring., 1957-67, chmn. dept. chem. and metall. engring., 1962-67; mem. faculty U. Pa., 1967—, Carl V.S. Patterson prof. chem. engring., 1967-90, Carl V.S. Patterson prof. emeritus, 1990—; chmn. region 2 edn. and accreditation com. Engrs. Council Profl. Devel., 1961-65, mem. nat. council, 1965-71, exec. com., 1968-71; mem. bd. trustees Chemical Heritage Found., 1983-99; mem. bd. dirs., 1999—, mem. fin. com., 1987—; cons. heat transfer and combustion. Recipient S. Reid Warren, Jr. award for disting. teaching U. Pa., 1976, Max Jakob Meml. award for heat transfer ASME/ Am. Inst. Chem. Engrs., 1979, medal for disting. achievement U. Pa., 1993; Japan Soc. for Promotion of Sci. grantee, 1977. Fellow AIChe (nat. coun. 1962-64, pres. 1966, Profl. Progress award 1964, William H. Walker award 1969, Warren K. Lewis award 1978, Founders award 1980, eminent chmn. engr. Diamond Jubilee 1983, heat transfer and energy conversion divsn. award 1997, inst. lectr. 1998); mem. Nat. Acad. Engring., Combustion Inst., Am. Chem. Soc., Am. Soc. for Engring. Edn. (Corcoran award for best paper 1993), Verein Deutscher Ingenieure (corr. mem.), Sigma Xi, Phi Kappa Phi, Phi Lambda Upsilon (award U. Mich. chpt. 1961), Tau Beta Pi. Unitarian. Home: 137 Pole Cat Rd Glen Mills PA 19342-1301

CHURCHILL, THOMAS JOHN, broadcast meteorologist; b. Dubuque, Iowa, Mar. 4, 1961; s. John Victor and Thoma Margaret (Grutz) C.; m. Rita Lucia Daniels, Apr. 25, 1987; 1 child, Georan Thomas Churchill. Meteorologist Sta. WDBQ, Dubuque, 1974-76, Teleprompter, Dubuque, 1976-79, Sta. KLXL-FM, Dubuque, 1979-81, Stas. WDBQ/KIWI-FM, Dubuque, 1981-82; meteorologist, pres. No. Data Group, Inc., Dubuque, 1982-87; chief meteorologist Athena Svcs. Group, Inc., Dubuque, 1987-91; pres. Weatheradio, Dubuque, 1992-2000; ret., 2000; tech. cons. AccuWeather, State College, Pa., 1998-2000; guest meteorologist Sta. KRON-TV, San Francisco, July 1975, Tomorrow Show on NBC-TV, N.Y.C., Aug. 1976, Good Morning Am. on ABC-TV, N.Y.C., Sept. 1978; cons. in field. inventor digital weatherman, weather automation system. Commr. Dubuque Cable Regulatory Commn., 1983; co-founder, spokesperson Citizens United for Respect Equality, Dubuque; voting mem. Dubuque County Rep. Ctrl. Com. Mem. Am. Meteorol. Soc. Republican. Roman Catholic. Avocations: electronics, politics. Office: Weatheradio Box 1400 Dubuque IA 52004-1400

CHURESIGAEW, SUNCHAI, physician, consultant, researcher, educator; b. Ubolrathani, Thailand; s. Chote and Tepin (Watanasingha) C.; m. Amittada Yuvanatemiya, Nov. 11, 1969; children: Sarocha, Manisa. MD, Chulalongkorn U., Thailand, 1966. Diplomate Am. Bd. Pediatrics. Pediatrician Children's Hosp., Thailand, 1975—; dep. dir. Queen Sirikit Nat. Inst. of Child Health, Bangkok, 1996—. Author: Manual of Pediatric and Endocrinology, 1995; contbr. articles to profl. publs. Mem. Pediatric Endocrinology Assn. (vice chmn. 1990—), Pediatric Assn. of Thailand, Thai Acad. of Pediatrics, Endocrinology Soc. of Thailand, Pediatric Endorcine Soc. of Thailand. Home: 22/5 Soi Charoenmitr, Ekamai, Bangkok 10110, Thailand Office: Queen Sirikit Nat Inst, Rajvithi Rd, Bangkok Thailand

CHURILLA, BARBARA ANN KURYAN, secondary education educator; b. Feb. 5, 1941. BA, Rutgers U., 1979, MFA, 1983. Tchr. E. Windsor Regional Sch. Dist., Hightstown H.S., Hightstown, N.J., 1980—; instr. Triangle Art, Lawrenceville, N.J., 1996—. Mem. NEA, Nat. Art Edn. Assn., Coll. Art Assn., Art Educators N.J., E. Windsor Edn. Assn. Home: 414 Trumbull Ct Newtown PA 18940-1771 Office: Hightstown High Sch 25 Leshin Ln Hightstown NJ 08520-4001

CHUTE, HAROLD LEROY, veterinary pathologist, former chemical company executive; b. Winnipeg, Man., Can., Sept. 4, 1921; came to U.S., 1949; naturalized, 1955; s. Kenneth Karl and Hilda Mae (Stoddart) C.; m. Marion B. Baker, Aug. 9, 1947; children: Pamela D., Hazel Lee., Cameron C. Student, N.S. Agrl. Coll., 1942-44, hon. assoc., 1976; DVM, Ont. Vet. Coll., U. Guelph, 1949; MS, Ohio State U., 1953; DVSc, U. Toronto, 1955; LLD (hon.), Dalhousie U., 1998. Poultry pathologist U. Maine, Orono, 1950-80, prof., 1949-76; treas., dir. MeBio Labs Inc., 1958-66; dir. pullorum typhoid testing U. Maine, Orono, 1958-68, dir. devel., 1967-76; pres. Chute Chem. Co., Bangor, Maine, 1977-95; bd. dirs. Blue Cross Blue Shield, Maine, 1988-99, dir. Key Bank of Eastern Maine. Contbr. over 200 articles to profl. jours. Mem. cmty. rels. Coun. of Job Corps; mem. EMTEC, 1990—; dir. Machigonne Agy.,; pres., CEO Margaret Villa Inc.; bd. dirs. U. Maine Found.; trustee Grand Lodge Charity Fund, 1969—; mem. Orono Town Coun., 1963-72; pres. Pine Tree 4-H Found., 1986-93; mem., trustee, deacon Ch. Univ. Fellowship, U. Maine. Mem. Am. Assn. Avian Pathologists (past pres.), Am. Assn. Vet. Lab. Diagnosticians (past pres., Pope award 1990), AVMA (del. 1978-2000), Maine Vet. Med. Assn. (past pres.), Shriners (potentate Anah Shrine Temple, Bangor 1981), Order of DeMolay (exec. officer Maine 1971-80, grand master grand lodge of Maine 1968-70), Mason (33 degree). Republican. Home: 432 Main St Orono ME 04473-3435

CHVÁLA, MILAN, entomologist, educator; b. Prague, Apr. 18, 1936; s. Ladislav and Marie (Šverepová)C.; m. Milena Havírová,Aug. 6, 1964; 1 child, Martina. MS in Biology, Charles U., Prague, 1960, PhD, 1966; DSc, Acad. of Scis., Prague, 1989. Dir. Dist. Museum, Slany, Czech Republic, 1960-62; postgrad. rschr. Univ. Museum, Copenhagen, 1968-69; asst. prof. Charles U., Prague, 1966-94, prof., 1995—, head dept. zoology, 1994-95, vice dean, 1991-94; vice chmn. Coun. for Internat. Congresses of Dipterology, 1986-94, chmn., 1994—. Co-author: The Horse Flies of Europe, 1972, Bloodsucking Flies and Gad-Flies, 1980, Insects: A Comprehensive Illustrated Guide to Insects of Britain and Europe, 1989; author: Fauna Entomologica Scandinavica, vols. 3, 12 and 29, 1975-94; contbr. articles to profl. jours.; head editl. bd. Acta Univ. Carolinae-Biologica, Prague, 1991—. Fellow Royal Entomol. Soc. London; mem. Czech Zool. Soc., Czechoslovak Entomol. Soc. (sci. sec. 1979-88), Finnish Entomol. Soc. (corr.). Avocations: travel, cottage in village. Home: Milevská 1111, CZ-14000 Prague 4 Czech Republic Office: Charles U Dept Zoology, Viničná 7, CZ-12844 Prague 2 Czech Republic

CHVIRUK, VLADIMIR PETROVICH, electrochemical engineering educator; b. Lisovcy, Kiev, Ukraine, Sept. 10, 1935; s. Peter Jakovlevich and Ellen Nicholayevna (Khmaruk) C.; m. Olga Vasilyevna Bogmat, Oct. 23, 1934; 1 child, Alexander. PhD, Kiev Poly. Inst., Ukraine, 1965; D Tech. Scis., U. Moscow, 1984. Sci. worker Kiev Chlorine Sci. Rsch. Inst., 1958-61, head sci. rsch. lab., 1965-82, chief sci rsch. dept., 1982-86; head dept. electrochem. engring. Nat. Tech. U. Ukraine, Kiev, 1986—, chmn. doctor sci. advice, 1993—, head sci. rsch. lab. electrochem. kinetics, 1994—. Patentee in field. Recipient medal Chem. Industry USSR, Moscow, 1978. Mem. N.Y. Acad. Scis., Internat. Soc. Electrochemistry. Home: Apt 125, Street L Gavro h, 9e, 254211 Kiev Ukraine Office: Nat Tech U Ukraine, Pobeda Ave 37, 252056 Kiev Ukraine

CHYLARECKI, CHRISTOPH, trauma surgeon; b. Srem, Potnan, Poland, Oct. 22, 1956; arrived in Germany, 1981; s. Henryk and Wanda (Ptakik) C.; m. Irene Szepska, Jan. 7, 1978 (div. Nov. 1997); 1 child, Frederic. MD, Med. Acad., Poznan, 1981. Resident St. Elisabeth Hosp., Wadern, Germany, 1982-86, St. Vinzenz Hosp., Duisburg, Germany, 1986-88; resident Berufsgenossensch Trauma Ctr., Duisburg, 1989-91, sr. officer, 1991—. Contbg. author: Gutachten Kolloquium, 1993, 95, 96, 97, Elbow Surgery, 1998; contbr. articles to med. jours., including Jour. Joint and Bone Surgery, Langenbeck's Arch. Chir. Mem. Am. Acad. Orthopaedic Surgeons, German Assn. for Orthopaedics and Trauma, German Soc. for Traumatology. Avocations: underwater diving, gliding. Home: Grossenbaumer Allee, D-47249 Duisburg Germany Office: BG-Unfallklinik, Grossenbaumer Allee 250, D-47249 Duisburg Germany

CHYNOWETH, W. EDWARD, retired lawyer, farmer; b. Washington, Sept. 1, 1923; s. Bradford Grethen and Grace (Woodruff) C. BS in Mil. Sci. and Engring., U.S. Mil. Acad., 1946; MS in Mech. Engring., U. Calif., Berkeley, 1959; LLB, Stanford U., 1963. Bar: Calif. Pvt. practice law Fresno, Calif., 1963-69; dep. dist. atty. Tulane County, Visalia, Calif., 1969-78; farmer Sanger, Calif., 1968—. Contbr. articles to profl. jours. Maj. U.S. Army, 1946-57. Home: 403 S Indianola Ave Sanger CA 93657-9436

CHYTIL, METHOD K., mathematician; b. Prague, Czech Republic, Nov. 22, 1926; s. Method S. and Milada (Tuma) C.; m. Marie Petruj, Sept. 14, 1957; children: Vladimir, Paula, Miriam. Diploma in engring., Tech. U., Prague, 1950; PhD in Logic, Charles U., Prague, 1970. Rsch. asst. Inst. Engring. Rsch., Prague, 1951-55; with State Census Inst., Prague, 1955-63; dir. Ctr. for Biomath. Czechoslovak Acad. Scis., Prague, 1963-87; owner Omnipress Prague Ltd., 1989—. Contbr. numerous articles to profl. jours. Mem. Christian Dem. Party. Roman Catholic. Home: Na Sypcine 9, CZ-14700 Prague Czech Republic

CHYUN, SANG JIN, retired diplomat; b. Chol-won, Kangwon-Do, Korea, Mar. 15, 1929; s. Dong Chan and Soon Duk (Ahn) C.; m. In Won Kim, Apr. 17, 1954; children: Sun Jae, Seung Jae, Jin Jae, Kwang Jae. BA, Yon Sei U., Seoul, Korea, 1951; postgrad., NYU, N.Y.C., 1954-55. Cert. High Civil Svc. Exam., diplomatic br. Entered Ministry Fgn. Affairs, 1950; vice consul Korean Consulate Gen., N.Y.C., 1952-56; 1st sec. Korean Embassy, Washington, 1959-61; dir. Polit. Affairs Bur. Ministry Fgn. Affairs, 1961-62; counselor Korean Embassy, Taipei, 1962-64; dir Econ. Affairs Bur. Ministry Fgn. Affairs, 1964-66, asst. min. fgn. affairs, 1966-67; min. Korean Embassy, Washington, 1967-69; amb. to Cameroon, 1969-72, amb. to Peru, 1972-75, amb. to Malaysia, 1975-79; amb. Korean Mission to UN, 1979-80; rsch. commr. Inst. Fgn. Affairs and Nat. Security, 1980; fellow Ctr. Internat. Affairs, Harvard U., 1979-80; pres. Korean Coun. Fgn. Rels., Seoul, 1992-96, advisor, 1996—; mem. Korean Olympic Com. Seoul, 1993—; bd. mem. Korean Com. for UNICEF, 1993—, Seoul Peace Prize Cultural Found., 1995—; advisor internat. affairs Fedn. Korean Industries, 1989-93; pres. Korea Diplomatic Cons., 1993-98; vis. prof. Kangneung Nat. U., 1997-99. Author: The World to Seoul, 1990. V.p. Korea Amateur Sports Assn. and Korean Olympic Com., 1981; dep. sec. gen. for internat. rels. Seoul Olympic Organizing Com., 1981-89, sec. gen. settlement bd., 1989. Decorated Korean Order of Service Merit, Green Stripes, 1960, Yellow Stripes, 1984, Heung-In medal Order of Diplomatic Svc. Merit, 1961, Moran medal Order of Civil Merit, 1987, fgn. decorations, Argentina, Italy, Vietnam, Cameroon, Peru. Mem. Rotary of Seoul Olympic Town (pres. 1993-94). Avocation: photography. Home: Kangnam-ku, 593-22 Shinsa-Dong, Seoul 135-120, Republic of Korea

CHYUNG, CHI HAN, management consultant; b. Seoul, Korea, Jan. 27, 1933; s. Do Soon and Boksoon (Kim) C.; came to U.S., 1954, naturalized, 1963, BS, Kans. Wesleyan U., 1958; M.BA, Mich. State U., 1960; postgrad. Mass. Inst. Tech.; m. Alice Yvonne Whorley, Dec. 23, 1961; children: Eric, Diana. Ops. analyst Chevrolet div. Gen. Motors Corp., Detroit and Flint, Mich., 1959-61; economist Internat. Harvester Co., Chgo., 1961-63; sr. analyst market div. Internat. Minerals & Chem. Corp., Skokie, Ill., 1963-66; mgr. market info. and planning Gulf & Western Industries, N.Y.C., 1966-68; dir. market planning and devel. Am. Standard, Inc., N.Y.C., 1968-71; pres. Oxytech Corp., Medcraft Industries, Inc.; mgmt. cons., internat. market devel., Darien, Conn., 1971—; dir. Korea Hapsum Co.; cons. Govt. of Korea, Taisei Constrn. Co., Tokyo. Served with Korean Army, 1951-53. Mem. Inst. Mgmt. Scis., Am. Mktg. Assn., Ops. Research Soc., Am. Chem., N.Am. Corp. Planning Soc., Beta Gamma Sigma. Contbr. papers to profl. lit. Office: Oxytech Corp 433 Post Rd Darien CT 06820-3606

CIA, MANUEL LOPEZ, artist; b. Las Cruces, N.Mex., Jan. 4, 1937; s. Anastacio Cea Lopez and Mercedes Rivera. Student, Am. Acad. Art, Chgo., 1958-61, Art Inst. San Francisco, 1962, L.A. Trade Tech., 1963-64, U. N.Mex., 1990. Author: Color Quest, 1991, Theory of Sophisticism, 1993; Exhibited in group shows at The Fundacion Teleton de Honduras, Teguicigalpa, 1989, France-USA, Paris, 1991, Arts and the Quincentennial, Albuquerque, 1992, U.S. Artists, Phila., 1993, State of the Art, Boston, 1993, Miniatures 1993, Albuquerque, 1993, Montserrat Gallery, N.Y.C., 1995; one man shows include El Prado Galleries, Sedonia, Ariz. and Santa Fe, N.Mex., 1989, 90, 95. With USAF, 1954-57. Recipient Outstanding Individual award Youth Devel., Albuquerque, 1991. Mem. Internat. Assn. Contemporary Art, Soc. Am. Impressionists. Avocations: study and writing of aesthetics. Home: PO Box 7332 Albuquerque NM 87194-7332

CIAMPI, CARLO AZEGLIO, President of Italy; b. Livorno, Italy, Dec. 9, 1920; m. Franca Pilla; children: Gabriella, Claudio. Diploma, Scuola Normale Superiore, Pisa, Italy, 1941; BA, U. Pisa, LLB, 1946. Various positions Bank of Italy, Rome, 1946-60, economist rsch. dept., 1960-70, head rsch. dept., 1970-73, sec. gen., 1973-76, dep. dir. gen., 1976-78, dir. gen., 1978-79; gov. Bank of Italy, Rome, 1979-93; pres. Italian Coun. Ministers, Rome, 1993-94; v.p. Bank Internat. Settlements, Basle, Italy, 1994-96; min. treasury, budget and econ. programming govts. Prime Mins. Prodi and D'Alema Govt. Italy, 1996-99, pres., 1999—; dep. chmn. Ufficio Italiano Cambi, Rome, 1978-79, chmn., 1979-93; gov. for Italy IBRD-IDA-IFC, Washington, 1979-93, ADB, Manila, 1982-93; bd. dirs. Bank Internat. Settlements, Basle, 1979-83, Consiglio Nazionale delle Ricerche, Rome, 1979-93, Instuto l'Enciclopedia Treccani, Rome, 1996-99; pres. coun. ministers, 1993-94; hon. gov. Bank Italy, 1993—; vice chmn. BIS, 1994-96; chmn. competitiveness adv. group (European Commn.), 1995-96; 1996-99; pres. Ente "Luigi Einaudi", Rome, 1995-96; pres. Venice Internat. U., 1996-99; chmn. Interim Com. IMF, Washington, 1998-99, Ente Einaudi for Monetary, Banking and Fin. Studies, 1995—. Author of numerous articles, speeches, reports and addresses. With Italian Army, 1941-44. Decorated Mil. Cross Italian Army, Grand Cross Order of Merit Fed. Republic Germany, Grand Cordon Order of Rising Sun Govt. Japan; named Commandeur Legion Honor, Order Merit, Govt. France. Mem. SocietÀ degli Economisti. Office: Office of Pres, Palazzo del Quirinale, 00187 Rome Italy

CIANCAGLINI, HUMBERTO RAFAEL, electronics educator; b. Salta, Argentina, Sept. 6, 1918; s. Alfonso Atilio and Maria Teresa (Ilvento) C.; m. Cora Matilde Gutierrez, June 20, 1920; children: Rolando M., Alejandro M. Civil Engr., U. Buenos Aires, 1943, Comm. Engr., 1945. Cert. engr. Electronic engr. Philips Argentina, Buenos Aires, 1943-46; prof. Tech. Sch., Buenos Aires, 1946-52; design and rsch. engr. Philips Argentina, Buenos Aires, 1953-59, tech. adviser, 1970-78; head prof. U. Buenos Aires, 1947-66, emeritus prof., 1984—; nuclear electronics expert Internat. Atomic Energy Agy.-UN, 1966-85; comm. state sec. Argentina, 1983-85; tech. adviser Instituto Nacional de Tecnologia Indsl., Buenos Aires, 1996-99; dir. Conae Argentina, Buenos Aires, 1991-97. Inventor automatic telephone recorder, 1945, electronic heating sys. control, 1963, electronic simulator of real golf playing, 1983, automatic TV rating rec. Bd. dirs. Argentine Coun. Sci. and Tech., Buenos, 1958-66, Argentine Atomio Energy Commn., Buenos Aires, 1959-61, Argentine Space Rsch., Buenos Aires, 1959-66, Argentine Space Activities Commn., Buenos Aires, 1991-97. Recipient diploma de merito Funhdacion Konex, Buenos Aires, 1983. Mem. IEEE (life, chmn. Buenos Aires sect. 1965, Eminent Engr. Latin Am. region 1985), N.Y. Acad. Scis., Academia Argentina de Ciencias Espaciales, Argentine Acad. Nacional de Ingenieria. Avocations: golf, mechanical hobbies, woodworking. Home: Lafinur 3383 Dto 12A, 1425 Buenos Aires Argentina Office: Facultad de Ingenieria, Paseo Colon 850, Buenos Aires Argentina

CIANCI, GIOVANNI, humanities educator; b. Milan, Apr. 1, 1940; s. Nicola and Giuseppina (Navoni) C. BA, U. Milan, 1967. Assoc. prof. U. Palermo, Italy, 1970-82; prof. U. Genoa, Italy, 1982-94, U. Milan, 1994—. Avocations: art, music. Home: Via de Sanctis 29, Milan Italy 20141 Office: Istituto di Aglistica, Piazza S Alessandro 1, Milan 20123, Italy

CIANFRIGLIA, FRANCESO, physician; b. Rome, Jan. 8, 1948; s. Francesco Cianfriglia and Annamaria Lopez; m. Givlia Calabresi, May 10, 1972; children: Cristina, Carlotta. MD, 1972. Asst. Nat. Cancer Inst., Rome, 1973-88; vice chief Regional Ctr. for Mouth Neoplasms and Prevention of Oral, 1988-90; chief Regional Ctr. for Mouth Neoplasms and Prevention of Oral Precancerous Lesions, 1990—. Author: Malignant Tumors of Upper Maxilla, 1994, Oral Carcinoma, 1995; author Nat. Campaign Against Oral Tumors, 1993-97. Roman Catholic. Avocations: music, skiing, diving. Home: Via Lombardia 30, 00187 Rome Italy Office: Studio Cianfrigua, via Lombardia 30, 00187 Rome Italy

CIANNELLA, JOEEN MOORE, legislative staff member, small business owner; b. Warren, Ohio, Mar. 20, 1948; d. Joseph Alvie and Elizabeth Dorthea Moore; m. Christopher M. Ciannella, July 31, 1976 (div. Jan. 1987); children: Bryce C., Tara E. BA in French, Denison U., 1970. Profl. staff U.S. Senate Rep. Policy Com., Washington, 1971-75; owner Jo Moore-Sophisticated Country, Park Ridge, N.J., 1984—; dir. cmty. affairs Congresswoman Marge Roukema U.S. Ho. Reps., Ridgewood, N.J., 1985—. Elected mem. Park Ridge County Com., 1983—, mcpl. chairperson, 1986-96; active Bergen County (N.J.) Rep. County Com., 1983—, Park Ridge Rep. Orgn., 1983—, v.p., 1988-89; active N.E. Rep. Orgn. Dist. 39, State N.J., 1984—, sec., 1990-91, treas., 1991-92, chairperson, 1992-93; active Bush for Pres. Campaign, 1988, 92, Dole for Pres. Campaign, 1996; ofcl. com. mem. N.J. GOP Conv., 1991; charter mem. Women Leadership Summit, Rep. Network to Elect Women, 1996-97; trustee Greater Roles and Opportunities for Women, N.J. GOP, 1997—; mem. Park Ridge Bd. Health, 1984-86; founding mem. Pioneer Women Bergen County, 1992—; mem. exec. bd. Bergen Coun.-Boy Scouts Am., 1991-98, co-chairperson Pascack Valley Dist. Luncheree, 1991-92, chairperson spl. events fin., 1993-94, mem. exec. com., 1993-98, vice chmn. fin., 1995-98; mem. Nat. Coun.-Boy Scouts Am., 1995-98; mem. exec. bd. No. N.J. Coun.-Boy Scouts Am., 1999— (Silver Beaver award), Northern N.J. Coun. Boy Scouts Am., 1999, vice chair fin., 2000; mem. exec. bd. Ramapo Coll. Found., 1991—, theme chairperson fundraiser, 1991-94, disting. citizen dinner com., 1991—, bus. network com., 1994-97, chmn. pub. rels. and mktg. com., 1996-2000, mem. exec. com., 1996—, chmn. mktg./instnl. rels., 2000—. Recipient Mission award Ramapo Coll. Found., 1999. Mem. N.J. Fedn. Rep. Women, Rep. Women of the 90's State N.J., Bergen County Women's Rep. Club, Ridgewood Unit Rep. Women, Jr. League Bergen County (com. mem. Festival of Trees 1988), Park Ridge Rotary Club (com. mem. annual auction 1990—, chairperson holiday party 1991—). Republican. Avocations: gardening, antiquing, sports, travel. E-mail: joeen.ciannella@mail.house.gov. Home: 34 Spring Valley Rd Park Ridge NJ 07656-1860 Office: Congresswoman Marge Roukema US Ho of Reps 1200 E Ridgewood Ave Ridgewood NJ 07450-3937

CICCI, RAFAEL ALEJANDRO, government agency financial executive; b. May 7, 1968. MBA in Internat. Mgmt., South Bank U., London, 1993; M in Pub. Sector Econs., Ctr. for Macroecon. Studies, Buenos Aires, Argentina, 1997. CPA, Argentina, Spain. Prof. econs., acctg. and fin. H.S. Manuel Belgrano, Cordoba, 1992; from asst. prof. to assoc. prof. acctg. Nat. U. Cordoba, 1990-92; analyst South Bank U., 1993; chief dept. planning and control Nat. Bank of Argentina, 1993-94, advisor to pres., 1994-95; project analyst Nat. Office for Projects with Intl. Orgns. Ministry of Econs., Argentina, 1996, advisor to sec. legal and tech. coord., 1997, adminstrn. and fin. mgr. Aiport Regulation Agy./Sec. Transp., 1998—. Avocations: soccer, drama studies. E-mail: rafael cicci@yahoo.com. Office: Hidalgo 561 Piso, 13 Depto I Torre B, 1405 Capital Federal Argentina

CICCIARELLI, JAMES CARL, immunology educator; b. Toluca, Ill., May 26, 1947; s. Maurice Cicciarelli and Helen Ippolito; 1 child, Nicola; m. Mavy Jane Manning, June 2000. BS, Tulane U., 1969; PhD, So. Ill. U., 1977. Lic. clin. lab. dir., Calif. Fellow dept. surgery UCLA, 1977-79, asst. prof. immunology, 1980-87, assoc. prof., 1987-91; prof. urology and microbiology U. So. Calif., L.A., 1992—; lab. dir. Metic Transplant Lab., Inc., L.A., 1984—; bd. dirs. So. Calif. Organ Procurement Agy.; clin. lab. dir. Am. Bd. Bioanalysis, 1991—; mem. histocompatibility com. United Network Organ Sharing, 1991-94; mem. scientific adv. com. United Network for Organ Sharing, 1997—; lab. dir. Sharp Hosp. and Clinic, San Diego. Contbr. articles to profl. jours., chpts. to books. Rsch. grant NIH, 1985-88. Mem. Am. Soc. Histocompatibility and Immunogenetics, Internat. Transplant Soc., Am. Soc. Transplant Physicians, Internat. Soc. Heart Lung Transplantation. Libertarian. Roman Catholic. Avocations: boating, biking, skiing, tennis, running. Home: 5 Ringbit Rd W Rolling Hills CA 90274-5241 Office: USC Dept Urology Metic Transplant Lab 2100 W 3rd St Ste 280 Los Angeles CA 90057-1922

CICCONE, J. RICHARD, psychiatrist; b. N.Y.C., Mar. 21, 1943; s. Louis and Vilma Olga (Musacchio) C.; m. Natalie A. Caputo, Dec. 9, 1967; children: Regina, Louis, Robert. AB, Columbia U., 1963; MD, U. Pitts., 1968. Diplomate Am. Bd. Psychiatry and Neurology (additional qualifications in forensic psychiatry). Intern Montefiore Hosp., Pitts., 1968-69; USPHS fellow in psychiatry Strong Meml. Hosp., Rochester, N.Y., 1969-72, asst. resident in psychiatry, 1969-70, assoc. resident in psychiatry, 1970-71, chief resident in psychiatry, 1971-72; instr. U. Rochester, 1971-72, asst. prof. Sch. Medicine, 1974-79, assoc. prof. Sch. Medicine, 1979-89, prof., 1989—, dir. residency edn., 1979-85, dir. psychiatry and law program, 1985—, dir. psychiatry and law fellowship, 1987—, prof. Sch. of Medicine, 1989—; mem. Gov.'s Task Force to Study Reporting of Crimes at Psychiat. Ctrs., 1985, N.Y. State Commn. Quality Care, 1985-93; chair N.Y. State Med. Records Access Rev. Com., 1987—; vis. prof. U. Siena, Italy, 1994, 95, 97, 98, 2000. Assoc. editor: Bull. Am. Acad. Psychiatry and the Law; contbr. articles to profl. jours.; co-author: The Mental Health Professional and the Legal System, 1991. Served to lt. cmmdr. USN, 1972-74. Fellow Am. Psychiat. Assn. (vice chair coun. on psychiatry and law 1988-93, chair, commn. on jud. action 1993-2000, chair com. pub. policy, litigation & advocacy 2000—); mem. Genesee Valley Psychiat. Assn. (pres. 1983-85), Am. Acad. Psychiatry and Law (pres. 1986-87), Assn. of Dirs. of Forensic Fellowship Programs (pres. 1992-96). Home: 70 Edgemoor Rd Rochester NY 14618-1206 Office: Strong Meml Hosp 300 Crittenden Blvd Rochester NY 14642-0001

CICCONE, MADONNA LOUISE VERONICA See MADONNA

CICCONI, CHRISTOPHER M., lawyer; b. Anaheim, Calif., Aug. 19, 1949; s. Samuel A. and Ercilia (Silva) C.; m. Cynthia Anne June 20, 1981; children: Christina Michelle, Kelly Melissa. BA in Comm. Arts, U. Notre Dame, 1971; JD, Villanova U., 1974; LLM in Taxation, Temple U., 1978. Bar: Pa., U.S. Dist. Ct. (ea. and mid. dists.) Pa., U.S. Ct. Appeals (3d dist.), U.S. Tax Ct., U.S. Supreme Ct. Assoc. Rocap, Rocap & Guinta, Media, Pa., 1974-77; 1st asst. pub. defender Pub. Defender's Office of Delaware County, Media, 1977-78; ptnr. Hepford Zimmerman & Swartz, Harrisburg, Pa., 1978-90, mng. ptnr., 1985-90; atty., mem. Eckert Seamans Cherin & Mellott, Harrisburg, 1990—, chairperson corp. dept., 1999—; bd. dirs. York Saw & Knife Co., Inc., dBi Labs., Inc., Harrisburg, Ollie's Bargain Outlets, Inc., Harrisburg, sellstufflocal.com., Inc.; instr. Coll. Med., Pa. State U., 1992-98. Author, editor: Buying and Selling a Business, 1998. Mem., chair Zoning Hearing Bd., Derry Twp., Pa., 1984-89; mem. Preservation of Hershey Com., Derry Twp., 1987-88. Recipient Cmty. Achievement award Derry Twp., 1989, award of yr. Notre Dame Alumni Assn., 1995. Mem. Pa. Bar Assn. (chair legal affairs of older persons com. 1986-88, arbitrator dispute resolution com. 1988—), Dauphin County Bar Assn., Estate Planning Coun. Ctrl. Pa., Sorin Soc. of U. Notre Dame. Avocations: playing piano, wine collecting, travel, golf. Home: 1045 Fairdell Dr Hummelstown PA 17036-8710 Office: Eckert Seamans et al 213 Market St Harrisburg PA 17101-2132

ÇIÇEKOGLU, MEHMET OGUZHAN, electronics educator, researcher; b. Istanbul, Turkey, Jan. 1, 1963; s. Mehmet Burhanettin and Emine Nebahat Çi'3oekoglu. BS, Boğaziçi U., Istanbul, 1985, MS, 1988; PHD, Istanbul Tech. U., 1996. Rsch. asst. computer engring. dept. Boğaziçi U., 1988-91, instr., 1991-97, asst. prof., 1997-99, assoc. prof. Biomed. Engring. Inst., 1999—, head electronics program, 1993-94, 97-98, vice dir. Sch. for Advanced Vocat. Studies, 1993-96, vice head tech. programs Sch. for Advanced Vocat. Studies, 1998-99. Contbr. over 60 articles to profl. jours. and conf. procs. Mem. IEEE. Office: Boğaziçi U MYO Electron, 80815 Bebek Istanbul, Turkey

CICELLIS, KAY, novelist, translator, short story writer; b. Marseilles, France, Sept. 24, 1926; d. Gerasimos and Vasso (Saliaris) C.; m. Nicholas Michael Paleologos, Apr. 7, 1957; children: Michael (dec.), Anna Francesca. Grad., Greek State Gymnasium, Athens, Greece, 1946. Author: The Easy Way, 1950, No Name in the Street, 1952, Death of a Town, 1956, Ten Seconds from Now, 1954, The Way to Colonos, 1960, The Missing Floor, 1984, The Dance of the Hours, 1998. Recipient Greek State prize for short stories, 1999. Mem. Greek Soc. Authors. Avocations: cinema, cooking, Scrabble. Home: 13 Hadzicostas St, 11521 Athens Greece

CICERCHI, ELEANOR ANN TOMB, fundraising executive; b. Sayre, Pa., Dec. 11, 1944; d. William Horton and Brinton Elizabeth (Cauffiel) Tomb; m. Robert A. Weskerna, Nov. 19, 1966 (div. Feb. 1981); children: Amy Marie, Robert Campbell; m. Philip J. Cicerchi, July 1982. AB with great distinction, Mt. Holyoke Coll., 1966; MS, New Sch. Social Rsch., 1992. Cert. fundraising exec. Sr. mktg. rep. Group Health Plan, Guttenberg, N.J., 1976-79; dir. comty. rels. Burke Rehab. Ctr., White Plains, N.Y., 1979-84; exec. dir. Bergen comty. Coll. Fedn., Paramus, N.J., 1984-86; campaign counsel Brakeley John Price Jones, Inc., Stanford, Conn., 1986-88; v.p. instnl. advancement Marymount Coll., Tarrytown, N.Y., 1988-93; dir. maj. gifts Am. Found. for AIDS Rsch., N.Y.C., 1993-95, chief devel. officer, 1995-96;

v.p. devel. and external affairs ORBIS Internat., Inc., N.Y.C., 1996-2000; assoc. v.p. devel. Save the Children, Westport, Conn., 2000—; faculty mem. Fundraising Sch., Ctr. Philanthropy, Ind. U., Indpls., 1989—; adj. grad. faculty mem. NYU, N.Y.C., 1990-97, New Sch. for Social Rsch., N.Y.C., 1995—, chmn. PR Group for Vision 2000: The Right to Sight, Geneva, 1998-99; bd. dirs. AMD Alliance, 1999—. Author: Raid!, 1978, Anonymous Giving, 1991; co-author: The Earth Shook and the Sky Was Red, 1976, The Flower of the Virginian, 1980. Pres. Dem. Club, River Vale, N.J., 1978-81; bd. dirs., immediate past chmn. Philharmonia Virtuosi, Dobbs Ferry, N.Y., 1985—; bd. dirs., sec. Am. Anorexia-Bulimia Assn., N.Y.C., 1984-1999. Woodrow Wilson fellow, 1966; Sarah Williston scholar, 1964, Mt. Holyoke scholar, 1963. Mem. Nat. Soc. Fundraising Execs. (Greater N.Y. chpt. v.p. 1993-95), Women in Fin. Devel., Phi Beta Kappa. Home: 14 Calhoun Ave Trumbull CT 06611-2424 Office: Save the Children 54 Wilton Rd Westport CT 06880-3131

CICERO, SILVIO MOURE, educator, researcher; b. São Paulo, Brazil, Aug. 4, 1948; s. Joséand Ester Moure Cicero; m. Maria Fernanda de Moraes, Feb. 9, 1978; children: Maria Thereza De Moraes, Pedro Henrique De. Agronomist, U. São Paulo, 1973, MSc, 1976, PhD, 1979. Cert. agronomist. Rschr. Empesa Brasileira de Pesquisa Agropecuaria, São Paulo, 1974-76; asst. prof. U. São Paulo, 1976-79, assoc. prof., 1979-96, prof., 1996, head Escola Superior de Agricultura Dept. Agrl., 1991-97, pres., 1999—. Author: (with others) Actualization in Seed Production, 1986, Seed Quality Evaluation, 1987, Cold Test, 1994, 99. Mem. Brazilian Seed Tech. Assn. E-mail: smicero@carpa.ciagri.usp.br. Fax: 10 429-4269. Office: Avenida Padua Dias 9, Piracicaba, 13418000 São Paulo Brazil

CICERONE, RALPH JOHN, academic administrator, geophysicist; b. New Castle, Pa., May 2, 1943; married; 1 child. SB, MIT, 1965; MS, U. Ill., 1967, PhD in Elec. Enging. and Physics, 1970. Physicist U.S. Dept. Commerce, 1967; rsch. asst. aeronomy U. Ill., 1967-70; assoc. rsch. scientist aeronomy space physics rsch. lab. U. Mich., Ann Arbor, 1970-78; assoc. rsch. chemist ocean rsch. divsn. U. Calif., San Diego, 1978-80, rsch. chemist Scripps inst. oceanography, 1980-81; Daniel G. Aldrich prof., chair geosci. dept. U. Calif., Irvine, 1989-94, dean Sch. Phys. Scis., 1994-98, chancellor, 1998—; sr. scientist, dir. atmospheric chemistry divsn. Nat. Ctr. Atmospheric Rsch., Boulder, Colo., 1980-89; lectr., asst. prof. elec. engring. U. Mich., Ann Arbor, 1973-75; mem. Bd. Sustainable Devel., 1995-99, Coun. of NAS, 1996-99. Assoc. editor Jour. Geophysics Rsch., 1977-79, editor, 1979-83. Recipient Bower award for Achievement in Sci., Franklin Inst., 1999. Fellow AAAS, Am. Chem. Soc., Am. Meteorol. Soc., Am. Geophysical Union (Macelwane award 1979); mem. NAS (elected 1990, mem. com. atmospheric sci. 1980-82, mem. bd. atmospheric sci. and climate 1987-89, mem. commn. geosci., environment and resources), Am. Acad. Arts and Scis., Am. Philos. Soc. Office: U Calif Irvine Chancellors Office 501 Administration Bldg Ofc Irvine CA 92697-1900

ČIČIN-ŠAIN, VJERA, editor; b. Split, Dalmatia, Croatia, Apr. 1, 1937; d. Jerko and Anka (Jerkovic) Č-Š; m. Željko Senečić, June 1, 1967 (div. 1976). Diploma in Philology, Germanistics, and Anglistics, U. Zagreb, Croatia, 1960. Translator Maierform S.A., Geneva, 1961; asst. in press and cultural svc. U.S. Am. Consulate Gen., Zagreb, Croatia, 1962-67; prodn. sec. Mozaik-Film, Zagreb, 1968-70; editor Univ. Press Liber, Zagreb, 1970-89, Nakladni Zavod Matice Hrvatske, Zagreb, 1989-91; counsellor Ministry of Culture, Zagreb, 1991-92; editor Matica Hrvatska, Zagreb, 1992-97; founder The Mediterranean Inst. G. Novak For Internat. Studies, Hvar, Croatia, 1998. Editor: (books) History of World Literature, 1975; translator: Nietzsche: The Birth of Tragedy, 1983 (award for Best Translation 1983). Counsellor for multilateral cooperatin in the field of culture, Croatian Ministry of Culture and Edn., Zagreb, 1991-92; gen. sec. Croatian PEN Ctr., Zagreb, 1992—. Recipient award Goethe Inst., Gottingen, 1986, Inst. Italiano di Cultura, Zagreb, 1995. Mem. Croatian PEN Ctr./Zagreb (gen. sec. 1992, 96-2000). Mem. Liberal Party of Croatia. Roman Catholic. Avocations: swimming, skiing, mountain climbing. FAX: 385-1-4810191. Home: Amruseva 11, 10 00 Zagreb Croatia Office: Croatian PEN Ctr, TRG B Jelacica 7, 10 000 Zagreb Croatia

CICOLANI, ANGELO GEORGE, research company executive, operating engineer; b. Norwood, Mass., Mar. 4, 1933; s. Luigi and Maria (Fossa) C.; m. Marilyn Adell Griffith, June 4, 1955 (div. 1968); children: George, Susanne, Diana; m. Patricia Anne Kirsch, Nov. 1, 1979 (dec. July 1995). Student, Northeastern U., 1950; BS, U.S. Naval Acad., Annapolis, Md., 1955, Naval Postgrad. Sch., 1969. Commd. ensign U.S. Navy, 1955, advanced through grades to lt. comdr., 1975, chief reactor operator, 1958-62, exec. officer, 1963-67; systems analyst for Strategic Sys. Project Office U.S. Navy, Arlington, Va., 1969-75; cons. Arlington, 1975-77; sr. rschr. R&D Assocs., Arlington, 1977-82, program mgr., sr. scientist, 1982-87, chief of staff, tech. dir. Springfield Rsch. Facility, 1988—. Author: The Role of Systems Analysis, 1974; author, editor Mineral Minutes Jour., 1972-74; author numerous reports on command and control survivability rsch., 1978-86, numerous reports on underground mil. facilities rsch., 1987—; developer installation vulnerability assessment techniques and courses of instrn., 1987—; designer Low Speed Ram-Jet, 1954 (Inst. Aero. Scis. 1st Pl. award). Pres. emeritus bd. dirs. Dumbarton Concert Series, Washington, 1982—. Mem. Ops. Rsch. Soc. Am., Naval Inst., Mineral Soc. D.C. (pres. 1972-77), Naval Submarine League, Ret. Officers Assn., Nature Conservancy. Office: Springfield Rsch Facility 6801 Telegraph Rd Alexandria VA 22310-3398

CICUREL, DAVID ELIE, investment consultant; b. Boulogne, France, May 23, 1949; arrived in U.K., 1985; s. Raymond Cicurel and Rosemary (Naggar) de Cazaux; m. Alejandra Dolfino, Dec. 11, 1988; children: Deborah, Sam. Engr., Polytechnique Paris, 1971; MBA, INSEAD, 1973. Exec. Keyser Ullmann, London, 1973-75; rep. Keyser Ullmann, Paris, 1975-76; dir. Co. de Navigation Mixte, Paris, 1976-78; chmn. Duc Lamothe Ledru, Paris, 1978-83, Continental Foods, London, 1990-98; dir. David Cicurel (Investments) Ltd., London, 1998—; chmn. Internat. Comm. and Data, London, 1992-95; cons. Paris, London, 1983-90. Lt. French Artillery, 1970-71. Mem. Eagle Ski Club, Cercle Interallie, Lansdowne Club. Jewish. Office: David Cicurel Investment, 14 New Burlington St, London W1S 3BQ, England

CID, CONSUELO, physicist, educator; b. Guadalajara, Spain, Sept. 29, 1967; d. Vincente Cid Bayo and Conseulo Tortuero Cobeqa; m. Felix Diaz Martinez, Dec. 8, 1990; children: Felix, Maria. BS in Physics, U. Complutense, Madrid, 1990. Rschr. Ciemat, Madrid, 1990-91; prof. U. Alcala, Madrid, 1998-99. Co-author: Rayos Cosmicos 98, 1998. Mem. Am. Geophys. Union. Office: U Alcala Apartado 20, 28871 Alcala de Henares, 99999 Madrid Spain

CIERESZKO, ANDRZEJ, science educator; b. Torun, Poland, Dec. 27, 1956. MSc, U. Agr. and Tech., Olsztyn, Poland, 1980, PhD, 1988; DSc, Inland Fisheries Inst., Olsztyn, 1998. Vis. prof. Ohio State U., Columbus, 1991-96; assoc. prof. Inst. Animal Reproduction and Food Rsch. Polish Acad. Sci., Olsztyn, 1996-99, asst. prof., 1999—. Office: Polish Acad Sci, Tuwima 10, 10-747 Olsztyn Poland

CIERNIEWSKI, JERZY LESZEK, soil science and remote sensing educator; b. Poznań, Poland, July 12, 1948; s. Stanisław and Teodora (Skrzypczak) C.; m. Anna Maria Skuratowicz, Oct. 25, 1975; children: Maciej, Katarzyna. MSc, Agrl. U., Poznan, 1971; PhD, Agrl. U., 1979, Habilitation, 1989, Prof., 2000. Asst. Agrl. U., 1971-79, tutor, 1979-87; tutor Adam Mickiewicz U., Poznan, 1987-89, asst. prof. soil sci., 1989-91, prof., 1991—, vice dean Geography and Geology Faculty, 1996-99. Contbr. over 60 articles on soil sci. and remote sensing to sci. jours., including Remote Sensing of Environment, Internat. Jour. Remote Sensing, Remote Sensing Revs., Internat. Agrophysics, Photogrammetry & Remote Sensing of Environ., Polish jours. Mem. Solidarity Trade Union, Poznan, 1980—. Mem. Polish Soil Sci. Soc. Avocations: angling, gardening. Home: Lisowskiego 6/2, 61-606 Poznań Poland Office: Adam Mickiewicz U, Fredry 10, 61-701 Poznań Poland

CIERPKA, MANFRED, physician, psychoanalyst, researcher; b. Nuertingen, Germany, Apr. 13, 1950; s. Erich and Maria (Gehring) C.; m. Astrid Bruess, Feb. 14, 1952; children: Lukas, Arne. MD, U. Ulm, Germany, 1977; degree in psychiatry and psychotherapeutic medicine, U. Goettingen, Germany, 1991. Resident in psychosomatics U. Ulm, 1978; resident BKH Guenzburg, 1979-83, resident Outpatient Clinic of Psychotherapy, 1984-87, dir. Outpatient Clinic of Psychotherapy, 1987-91; prof. Ctr. Family Therapy, Goettingen, 1991-98, Heidelberg, 1998—; dir. Lindau Psychotherapy Weeks, 1989—; cons. German Med. Assn., 1995—. Author: Assessment of Families with a Schizophrenic Offspring, 1990; editor: Family Diagnostics, 1988, Textbook of Family Diagnostics, 1996, Psychotherapy of Eating Disorders, 1997; jour. editor Psychotherapeut, 1994—, Praxis der Kinderpsychologie und Kinderpsychiatrie, 1994—. Fellow Studienstiftung des Deutschen Volkes, 1973-77. Mem. Internat. Psychoanalytic Assn., Soc. for Psychotherapeutic Rsch. Office: U Heidelberg Ctr Fam Therap, Bergheimerstr 54, 69115 Heidelberg Germany

CIESIELSKA, JOANNA KRYSTYNA, science educator; b. Wodzisław OElski, Poland, Jan. 30, 1969; d. Wiesław and Barbara Krystyna Dedko; m. Krzysztof Ciesielski, Dec. 16, 1995; 1 child, Krzysztof. MSc, Marie Curie Skłodowska U., Lublin, 1994. Cert. in biophysics. Tchr. Zespół Szkół Rolniczych, Ludwin, 1997-99, Zespół Szkół Ogólnokształcych nr 1, OEwidnik k. Lublina, 1999—. Avocations: science fiction, computers. E-mail: jkciesielska@poczta.onet.pl. Office: Zespó Szkó Ogólnoksztaccych nr 1, Wojska Polskiego 24, OEwidnik Poland

CIESIELSKI, JACEK, toy manufacturing company executive; b. Warsaw, Poland, Jan. 15, 1956; s. Adam and Sydonia (Gromek) C.; m. Maria Zywicka, Nov. 11, 1978; children: Piotr, Jan, Zuzanna. LLM, U. Warsaw, 1980; MBA, U. Minn., 1998. Editor Karjowa Agencja Wydaunicza, Warsaw, 1984-85; journalist Mlodziezowa Agencja Wydawnicza, Warsaw, 1985-89; gen. mgr. Ultima Ltd., Warsaw, 1989-92, Joker Ltd., Warsaw, 1992-94, Hasbro Poland, Warsaw, 1995—. Mem. Fgn. Investors Chamber Industry & Commerce, Confedn. Polish Pvt. Employers. Office: Hasbro Poland, Solec 22, 11-410 Warsaw Poland

CIESLAK-GOLONKA, MARIA TERESA, chemist, educator; b. Chelm, Lublin, Poland, Jan. 4, 1944; d. Leon and Stanislawa (Sadurska) Cieslak; m. Leszek Jan Golonka, Dec. 29, 1973; children: Jan, Hanna, Maria, Aleksandra. MS, U. Lublin, Poland, 1966; PhD, Tech. U. Wrocław, Poland, 1974, DSc, 1993. Chem. diplomate. Asst. Tech. U., Szczecin, Poland, 1967-70; asst. prof. U. Tech. Wrocław, 1974-93, assoc. prof. chemistry, 1993—; lectr. Pedagogical U., Kielce, Poland, 1993-94. Contbr. articles to profl. jours. Organizer Free Flying U., Wrocław, 1985-90. Grantee Ministry Edn., Warsaw, 1990. Mem. Polish Chem. Soc. Roman Catholic. Avocations: history of science, women in science. E-mail: golonka@fichn.ch.pwr.wroc.pl. Home: 9 Stefki St, 52-428 Wroclaw Poland Office: Univ Tech, WYB Wyspianskiego 27, 50-370 Wroclaw Poland

CIESZEWSKI, SANDRA JOSEPHINE, manufacturing company manager; b. Cleve., June 7, 1941; d. Chester L. and Cecilia (Laska) C. BA in Chemistry, Ursuline Coll., 1962; BA in Art History, Cleve. State U., 1981; Exec. MBA, Baldwin Wallace Coll., 1989. Chemist Harshaw Chem. Co., Cleve., 1962-65, Union Carbide Corp., Parma, Ohio, 1965-79; project mgr. Gould, Inc., Eastlake, Ohio, 1979-91; product engring. mgr.- lithium Duracell Global Bus. Mgmt. Group, Lexington, N.C., 1992—. Mem. Soc. of Women Engrs. (N.E. Ohio sect.) Cleve. Garden Ctr., Cleve. Mus. Art. Mem. Am. Chem. Soc., Soc. Applied Spectroscopy, Electrochem. Soc. (treas 1980), Women's Club (sec. Walton Hills chpt. 1985, treas. 1991), Assoc. Artists of Winston-Salem (bd. dirs. 1998—), Southeastern Ctr. Contemporary Art, Winston-Salem Cinema Soc. (programming chmn. 1997-98, treas. 1998—). Avocations: painting, gardening, skiing, cycling.

CIESZYŃSKI, TOMASZ MARIA, surgeon, researcher; b. Poznań, Poland, Nov. 6, 1920; s. Antoni and Róza)Troczyńska) C.; m. Maria Elzbieta Garbacz, Oct. 7, 1961; children: Jakub, Jagoda Derkowska. Diploma, Jagiellonian U., Cracov, Poland, 1945; MPhil in Chemistry, U. Wrocław, Poland, 1952; MD, U. and Tech. U. Wrocław, 1947; Docent in Surgery, Med. Acad., Wrocław, 1968. Lab asst. Inst. Exanthem Fever Res ., Weigl Lvov, Poland, 1941-44; jr. sci. worker Inst. Mother/Child Welfare, Lvov, 1945-46; jr. asst. Stomalogical Clinic, U. Wrocław, 1946-47; asst. Soc. Care Stomalogical Inst., Zabrze, Poland, 1947-48; sr. asst. Physiol. Chemistry Inst. Med. Acad., Wrocław, 1949-50; sr. asst. adj. Univ. Chair Crystallography, Wrocław, 1950-52; sr. asst. Orthop. Clinic Med. Acad., Warsaw, 1953; sr. asst., adj., docent, extraordin prof. 2nd Surg. Clinic Med. Acad., Wrocław, 1953-91; prof. med. sci. Pres. of Poland, 1992; lectr. Codivilla-Putti Inst., Cortina d Ampezzo, Italy, 1981, Tokyo U. Orthop., 1982; mem. faculty Stockholm Internat. Symposium, 1986. Contbr. articles to profl. jours. Recipient Golden Cross of Merit, Polish State, 1975, Cross de Chevalier Order of Polonia Restituta, Polish State, 1990, medals U. Tokyo, 1982, Med. Acad Wrocław, Poland, 1990. Avocations: poetry, painting, sculpture. Home: Modrzewiowa 20, 55-120 Oborniki Ślaskie Poland

CIFERRI, ALBERTO, chemist, educator; b. Rome, Italy, Feb. 16, 1930; s. Pietro and Elsa (Canestri) C.; m. Erminia Chiuminatto, April 20, 1953 (dec. 1991); 1 child, Paolo. DSc, U. Rome, 1953, libero docente, 1964. Asst. prof. U. Rome, 1953-57; fellow Mellon Inst., Pitts., 1957-59; scientist Monsanto Co., Durham, N.C., 1959-68; dir. rsch. CNR, Rome, 1968-82; scholar Duke U., Durham, N.C., 1975—; prof. U. Genoa, Italy, 1982—; vis. prof. Weizmann Inst., Rehovot, Israel, 1964, Washington U., St. Louis, Mo., 1971, Calif. Inst. Tech., Pasadena, 1973, U. Witwatersrand, Johannesburg, South Africa, 1984, Kyoto (Japan) U., 1985, N.C. State U., Raleigh, 1990; cons. Ministry of Planning, Mogadishu, Somalia, 1980, Acad. Sci. of P.R. of Mongolia, Ulan Bator, 1988-92, FAO, Santiago, Chile, 1991, others; lectr. in field. Author, editor: Ultra-High Modulus Polymers, 1979, Polymer Liquid Crystals, 1982, Liquid Crystallinity in Polymers, 1991, Supramolecular Polymers, 2000; contbr. over 170 articles to profl. jours. Mem. E-mail: cifjepa@chimica.unige.it. Office: Univ Genoa Dept Chemistry, Via Dodecaneso 31, 16146 Genoa Italy

CIFOLETTI, GIOVANNA CLEONICE, education educator; b. Milan, Italy, Apr. 28, 1952; d. Carlo and Maria (Tanner) C.; 1 child, Adina. Grad., U. Milan, 1977; PhD in Philosophy, U. Montreal, Que., Can., 1987; PhD in History, Princeton U., 1992. Fellow math. dept. U. Aarhus, Denmark, 1977-78; fellow, lectr. U. Montreal, 1978-82, Princeton (N.J.) U., 1983-88; fellow European Union, Florence, Italy, 1988-89, Italian Ministry Edn., Paris, 1989-91, Ctr. Nat. Libre, Paris, 1992-93; vis. prof. U. Siene, Italy, 1992-93; prof. lyceum Italian Ministry Edn., Milan, 1993-94; assoc. prof. Ecole Hautes Études en Sci. Sociales, Paris, 1996—. Author: La Methode de Fermat son Statut et Sa Diffusion, 1990, (exhibit and catalog of 16th century books) Subtillor: Arithmetica ou Une Science Brieve et Claire, 1991; contbr. articles to profl. jours. Fulbright Found. fellow, 1989-93, Jean Mornet fellow European Union, 1988-89, Wolfenbittel fellow, 1991, Max Planck Inst. Wissenschaftesgeschichte, 1998. Mem. History of Sci. Soc., Internat. Soc. for History of Rhetoric. Avocations: classical music, jazz, folk dance. Office: Ctr Koyre Ehess, 57 Rue Cuvier, 75005 Paris France

CIFTCIOGLU, NEVA, microbiologist; b. Erzurum, Turkey, July 1, 1963; s. Ayhan and Songul (Akdag) G. BS, Hacettepe U., Ankara, Turkey, 1985; MS, U. Ankara, 1988, PhD, 1991. Cert. med. microbiologist. Rsch. scientist U. Ankara, Turkey, 1985-91, U. Kuopio, Finland, 1991-93; clin. microbiologist Baskent U. Hosp., Ankara, Turkey, 1993-95; sr. scientist U. Kuopio, Finland, 1995—. Contbr. articles to profl. jours. Recipient FIM 100.000 award Finnish Min. Edn., Kuopio, Finland, 1991, Acad. Finland, 1995, FIM 15000 award Savon Tech., Finland, 1996, FIM 20000 award Jenny and Antii Wihuri Found., Finland, 1997, 98, FIM 10000 award Savon Tech., 1998, FIM 20000 award Minerva Medix, Finland, 1999. Mem. Am. Soc. Microbiology, N.Y. Acad. Sci., Am. Soc. for Cell Biology, Finland Soc. Biochemistry and Microbiology, Finland Soc. Physiology. Muslim. Avocations: singing, swimming, painting. E-mail: neva.ciftcioglu@uku.fi. Fax: 358 17 2811510. Office: U Kuopio, Salvilahdentie POB 1627, FIN70211 Kuopio Finland

CIGNA, ARRIGO ANGELO, physicist, consultant; b. Milano, Italy, Dec. 18, 1932; s. Giuseppe and Camilla (Castelli) C.; m. Luciana Rossi, Mar. 12, 1961; children: Alessandra, Margherita. D Physics, Univ., Milano, 1958. Scientist CNRN, Ispra, Italy, 1958-59; lab. dir. CNEN, Casaccia, Italy, 1961-74; div. dir. CNEN, Casaccia, 1974-81; ctr. dir. CNEN, La Spezia, Italy, 1981-85; project dir. ENEA, Saluggia, Italy, 1984-90; sci. adv. ENEA, Saluggia, 1990-94; ret., 1994; Italian del. Radiation Protection Com. European Cmty., 1971-95; chmn., 1980, 87-89; chmn., coord. rsch. environ. surveillance program OECD-NEA, Paris, 1986-95. Contbr. articles to sci. jours. mem. Italian Speleological Soc. (pres. 1970-74), Union Int. Radioecologie (pres. 1992-98), Union Int. Speleologie (pres. 1973-81). Roman Catholic. Avocations: antiques, painting restoration, history. E-mail: cigna@biemmenet.it. Home: Fraz. Tuffo, I-14023 Cocconato Italy

CIGOLINI, ROBERTO DAVIDE, engineering educator; b. Milan, Jan. 6, 1969; s. Erminio and Carla (Gorla) G.; m. Cristina Sabrina Pasqualato, Apr. 10, 1999. M in Engring., Poli. Milan, 1994; Witness Instr. Diploma, AT&T Istel, Milan, 1994. Engr. 1996. Jr. cons. Busacca & Assoc., Milan, 1994; lectr. Poli. Milan, 1994-96, prof., 1996—; dir. MIP-Poli. Milan, 1998—; cons. Efeso Cons., Milan, 1995-97, Asset Cons., Milan, 1997—, See Carrier History 1,3,5, Milan, 1994—; mem. auditors bd. co. in milling bus., Lodi, Italy, 1989-92. Author: Case Studies of Industrial Plants, 1995, Industrial Plants Management, 1997; contbr. articles to profl. jours. Recipient G. Gandini prize Town Coun., Lodi, 1988, Milano Richerche prize Milan Rsch. Consortium, 1994. Fellow Soc. for Computer Simulation (Belgium), Nat. Assn. Plant Design and Mgmt., Nat. Assn. Bus. Mgmt. Engring., European Ops. Mgmt. Assn., Intellectual Property Ctr. Roman Catholic. Avocations: chess, ancient Latin literature, skiing, tennis. Office: Poli Milan, Piazza L da Vinci 32, 20133 Milan Italy

CIJAN, RAFAEL VICTOR, judge; b. Celje, Slovenia, Sept. 25, 1935; s. Viktor Alojz and Blanka Margarita (Kramer) C.; m. Desanka Vlastimir Rogić, Mar. 8, 1963; children: Vladimir Rafael, Boris Rafael. Graduated jurist, Law Sch., Belgrade, Yugoslavia, 1961; M of Law Scis., Law Sch., Begrade, 1964, D of Law Scis., 1966. Teaching fellow of adminstrv. law Law Sch., Belgrade, 1962-64, asst. prof. of adminstrv. law, 1964-67; dept. head The Republic Inst. for Pub. Adminstrn., Belgrade, 1967-70; dir. Fed. Adminstrn. Advancement Cen., Belgrade, 1973-75; undersecretary Fed. Secretariate of Justice and Adminstrv. Orgn., Belgrade, 1975-80, Fed. Secretariate for Info., Belgrade, 1980-82; dep. of sec. gen. Presidency of Yugoslavia, Belgrade, 1982-86; judge Fed. Ct., Belgrade, 1986-90, pres., 1990—; councillor State Adminstrn. Revision Bd., Belgrade, 1969-71; prof. Welfare Officers' Coll., Belgrade, 1976-80; prof. Law Sch., Maribor, Slovenia, 1989. Author: Supplement to the Bibliography of the Constitution and Administrative Law 1918-62, 1962, Practical Course Book of Administrative Law, 1964; co-author (with others) textbook on administrative law, 1965, public law, 1966. Active Internat. Congress of Adminstrv. Law, Copenhagen, 1967, Inter Action Coun., Brioni, Yugoslavia, 1984, 8th UN Congress on Prevention of Crime, Havana, Cuba, 1990. Mem. Lawyers Assn. Yugoslavia, Assn. Adminstrv. Scis. and Practices, Adminstrv. Law Theory and Practice Assn. of Yugoslavia (sec. 1965-75). Roman Catholic. Home: Vladetina 3, 11000 Belgrade Slovenia*

CIKRLE, VOJTĚCH, bishop; b. Brno-Bosonohy, Czech Republic, Aug. 20, 1946; s. Růžena (Svobodová) Cikrlova. Diploma of theology, Cyril/Method Faculty Theology, Litoměřice, Czech Republic, 1976, ThLic. Ordained priest, Roman Cath. Ch., 1976, ordained bishop, 1990. Diocesan priest Diocese of Brno, Czech Republic, 1976-82, bishop, 1990—; prefect Cyril & Method Faculty of Theology, Litoměřice, 1982-87, rector, dir., 1987-90; Bishop of Brno, 1990—. Avocations: music, literature, astronomy, sports, hiking. Office: Bishopric of Brno, Petrov 8, 601 43 Brno Czech Republic

CILARDO, AGOSTINO, political scientist, educator; b. San Prisco, Italy, Aug. 19, 1947; s. Alessandro and Pasqua (Merola) G.; m. Anna Teresa del Vecchio, Apr. 11, 1977; children: Alessandro, Antonio Augusto Marcello, Chiara. Degree in polit. scis., Oriental Inst., 1974, degree in Islamic studies, 1981; degree in theology, Istituto Superiore di Scienze Religiose, Capua, Italy, 1993. Asst. Oriental Inst., Naples, Italy, 1974-80, rschr., 1980-90, prof., 1990—; prof. Inst. Superiore Sci. Religiose, Capua, Italy, 1994—. Author: The Evolution of Muslim Family Law in Egypt, 1985, Studies on the Islamic Law of Inheritance, 1990, Teorie sulle origini del diritto islamico, 1990, Diritto ereditario islamico I, 1993, II, 1994, The Qur'anic Term Kalala, 1997; editor: Presenza araba e islamica in Campania, 1992, L'Islam Oggi, 1993, Lezioni sull'Islam, 2000. Chmn. Associazione Culturale Kampanom, 1994—. Mem. Inst. per l'Oriente, Union Europeenne des Arabisants et Islamisants. E-mail: acilardo@iuo.it. Home: Viale Trieste 150, 81054 San Prisco CE, Italy

ÇILLI, AYKUT, physician, educator; b. Erzincan, Turkey, Jan. 2, 1968; s. Halil and Hafize Çilli. MD, Gazi U., Ankara, Turkey. Rsch. asst. respiratory medicine Gazi U. Med. Sch., Ankara, 1991-97; rsch. fellow U. Edinburgh, Scotland, 1998; assoc. prof. Akdeniz U. Med. Sch., Antalya, Turkey, 1998—. Mem. Turkish Med. Assn., Assn. Thorax. Avocations: tennis, football, music. Fax: 90 242 2274490. Home: 17.sokak, 48/3, Bahçelievler, 06490 Ankara Turkey Office: Akdeniz U Med Sch, Dumlupinar Caddesi, Antalya Turkey

CIMINO, CARLO, equity analyst; b. Milan, Italy, Mar. 14, 1961; s. Bruno and Paola (Isacco) C.; m. Claudia Vignati, May 27, 1995. Degree in Law, U. Milan. Equity analyst Analitica SpA, Milan, 1992-93; equity analyst AFB SIM, Milan, 1993-96, head of rsch., 1996-97; head equity rsch. CENTROSIM SpA, Milan, 1998-99; head of rsch. Metzler Capital Markets Italy SpA, Milan, 1999—. Sgt. Italian Air Force, 1984-85. Avocations: diving, theatre, fishing. E-mail: ccmino@metzler.com. Office: Metzler Capital Mkts Italy, Corso Europa 12, Milan Italy 20122

CINFICI, WILLIAM FRANK, historian; b. Little Rock AFB, Dec. 6, 1969; s. William and Rose Concetta (Floriani) C. BA in History cum laude, Gettysburg (Pa.) Coll., 1991; student, Widener U. Sch. of Law, 1991-92. Rsch. specialist Berks County Register of Wills Office, Reading, Pa., 1992-94; office support Berks County Employment and Tng. Office, Reading, 1994-95; supr. victim/witness assistance unit Berks Country Dist. Atty.'s Office, Reading, 1995; temp. adminstrv. asst. Chris Talarico Assocs., Inc., West Reading, Pa., 1995-97; mem. election staff Pennsylvanians for Effective Govt., Muhlenberg, 1996; exec. dir. Berks County Rep. Com., Reading, 1997; local registrar divsn. vital records Pa. Dept. Health, Reading, 1997—. Contbr. articles to Italian-Am. Perspective. Recording sec. Berks County Young Reps., 1998—; elected mem. Berks County Rep. Com., 1992—, Rep. State Com. Pa., 1998—. Mem. Italian-Am. Cultural Ctr. (bd. dirs.), Order Sons of Italy, Phi Beta Kappa. Home and Office: 1238 Linden St Reading PA 19604-2017

CINGOSKI, VLATKO TOMISLAV, electrical engineering educator, researcher; b. Ohrid, Macedonia, June 11, 1962; s. Tomislav and Vasilka (Kurtelova) C.; m. Vesna Snegar, Jan. 27, 1991; 1 child, Marija. BSEE, U. Sts. Cyril and Methodius, Skopje, Macedonia, 1986, MSEE, 1990; PhD in Electrical Engring., Hiroshima U., Japan, 1996. Asst. prof. U. Sts. Cyril and Methodius, Skopje, Macedonia, 1986-91; rschr. Hiroshima U., Japan, 1991-93, asst. prof., 1996-99; mgr. for devel. and investments Electric Power Co. Macedonia, Skopje, 1999—. Author: Studies in Applied Electromagnetics and Mechanics, 1995, 96, Elsevier Studies in Applied Electromagnetics in Matherials, 1995; editor Jour. Japanese Soc. for Applied Electromagnetics and Mechanics; contbr. articles to profl. jours. Mem. IEEE, Internat. Compumag Soc., Nat. Geog. Soc., Japanese IEE, Japan Soc. for Applied Electromagnetics and Mechanics. Office: Elec Power Co Macedonia, 11 October 9, Dept Devel/Invest, 91000 Skopje Macedonia

CINI, MARCELLO, physicist, educator; b. Firenze, Italy, July 29, 1923; s. Giulio and Margheria (Del Valle de Paz) C. D of Engring., Poly. Turin, Italy, 1946; D of Physics, U. Turin, 1947. Cert. theoretical physicist. Prof. U. La Sapienza, Rome, 1957—; dir. CIRMS, U. La Sapienza, Rome, 1993-98. Author: (books) L'Ape e L'Architetto, 1976, Quantum Theory Without Reduction, 1990, Un Paradiso Perduto, 1994; contbr. papers to profl. jours. Mem. Italian Phys. Soc. (dir. 1971-78, v.p. 1968-71). Office: U La Sapienza, Piazza a Moro 2, 00185 Rome Italy

CINI, MICHELE, physicist, educator; b. Pisa, Tuscany, Italy, Nov. 29, 1946; s. Francesco and Fernanda (Cappelli) C.; m. Anna Ursino, Apr. 17, 1971; 1 child, Massimo. Degree in Physics cum laude, U. Pisa, Italy, 1969. Rsch. worker Istituto Donegani, Novara, Italy, 1970, Agip Nucleare, Pisa, 1970-73, Snam Progetti, Monterotondo, Rome, Italy, 1973-78, Assoreni, Monterotondo, 1978-82, Nat. Rsch. Coun., Rome, 1982-88; prof. U. Rome, Tor Vergata, Italy, 1988—; group leader Esprit Project-Auger Spectroscopy,

1985-88, Esprit Project-Nonlinear Optics, 1989-92; rsch. cons. CNR, Rome, 1988-90. Author: Corso di Fisica Atomica e Molecolare, 1992; contbr.: Dictionary of Physical Science; contbr. articles to profl. jours. Mem. Italian Phys. Soc., Internat. Workshop on Auger Spectroscopy and Electronic Structure (mem. sci. com.). Avocations: classical music, chess, astronomy, history. Home: via Peccioli 44, 00139 Rome Italy Office: Dept di Fisica, via della Ricerca Scientifica, 00133 Rome Italy

CINQUE, DEAN ANTHONY, lawyer; b. L'Aquila, Paganica, Italy, Sept. 24, 1947; arrived in Australia, 1956; s. Mario and Flavia Cinque; m. Janet Hall, Dec. 12, 1973; children: Katherine, Michelle, Elizabeth. Assoc. Ins. Inst. degree, Australian Ins. Inst., Melbourne, 1973; LLB, U. Melbourne, 1987. Cert. lawyer. Claims officer Royal Ins. Co., Melbourne, 1966-71, Royal Automobile Club Victoria Ins. Co., 1971-73, Westminster Ins. Co., London, 1973; legal exec. Cleary Ross & Doherty, Melbourne, 1974-76, Morrow & Morrow, Ballarat, Victoria, 1976-84; prin. Doyle Cinque & Co., Ballarat, Victoria, 1984—; mng. dir. Pro Share Investments Pty Ltd., Ballarat, 1993—. Mem. Law Coun. Australia, High Ct. Australia, Supreme Ct. Victoria (barrister, solicitor), Law Inst. Victoria, Alumni Assn. U. Melbourne, Buninyong Golf Club, Pambula-Merimbula Golf Club, Ballarat Tennis Club (pres. 1989-91, mng. dir. 1992-93), Australian Royal Tennis Assn. (chmn. 1994-98), Internat. Com. Royal Tennis, Royal Melbourne Tennis Club, Hatfield House Tennis Club U.K., Old Ballarat Royal Tennis Club (pres. 1989-91), Romsey Royal Tennis Club (dir.), Lions Internat. (pres. Buninyong Mt. Helen club 1993-94, 15 Yr. Monarch award 1993), Ballarat Sportsmen Club, Old Colonist Club Ballarat. Roman Catholic. Avocations: golf, royal tennis, theatre. Office: Doyle Cinque & Co, 17 Dawson St, Ballarat Vic 3350, Australia

CIOCLOV, DRAGOS DUMITRU, education educator, researcher; b. Turnu-Severin, Oltenia, Romania, Oct. 26, 1937; s. Gheorghe and Maria (Stoenescu) C.; m. Ana Dragomir; children: Buruiana Elena-Maria, Cioclov-Olaru Gabriela Ana. BA, Coll. C.D. Loga, Timisoara, Romania, 1954; Diploma in Mech. Engring., Polytech. U., Timisoara, 1959, D Tech. Scis., 1971. Devel. engr. Heay Mech. Plants and Inst. Architecture, Timisoara, 1960-65; sr. rschr. Romanian Acad. of Sci., Timisoara, 1965-70; head lab., scientific dir. and gen. dir. Inst. of Welding and Material Testing, Timisoara, 1970-95; prof. of strength of materials Polytech. U., Timisoara, 1981—; prof. of mech. engring. Univ. Inst. of Tech. and Cath. U., Lille, 1994—; prof. fracture mechanics Fraunhofer Inst. of Non-Destructive Testing/U. Saarbrucken, Germany, 1995—; cons. Assn. Tech. Supervision, Sulzbach, Germany, 1996—, ind. agys., 1995—. Author: (book) Strength and Reliability Under Variable Loading, 1975, Fracture Mechanics, 1977, Pressure Vessels: Stress, Strain and Fracture Analysis, 1981, 2d. edit. 1998; contbg. author: Probabilistic Modeling of Structural Fatigue in Uncertainty Modeling and Analysis in Civil Engineering, 1998. Recipient Nat. prize in tech. scis., Romanian Acad., Bucharest, 1975. Mem. ASME, Am. Soc. Welding, Romanian Soc. of Welding (founding pres. 1992-97). Avocations: lit., arts, tennis, winter sports. Office: Fraunhofer Inst Non-Destrct, Test/Saarbruecken Univ/# 37, D-66123 Saarbrüken Germany

CIOFFI, MICHAEL LAWRENCE, lawyer; b. Cin., Feb. 2, 1953; s. Patrick Anthony and Patricia (Schroeder) C.; children: Michael A., David P., Gina M. BA magna cum laude, U. Notre Dame, 1975; JD, U. Cin., 1979. Bar: Ohio 1979, U.S. Dist. Ct. (so. dist.) Ohio 1980, U.S. Dist. Ct. (no. dist.) Ohio 1983, U.S. Ct. Appeals (6th cir.) 1985. Asst. atty. gen. Ohio Atty. Gen., Columbus, 1979-81; from assoc. to ptnr. Frost & Jacobs, Cin., 1981-87; staff v.p., asst. gen. counsel Penn Cen. Corp., Cin., 1988-93; v.p., asst. gen. counsel Am. Fin. Group, Cin., 1993—; adj. prof. law U. Cin. Coll. Law, 1983—. Author: Ohio Pretrial Litigation, 1991; co-author: Sixth Circuit Federal Practice Manual, 1993. Bd. dirs. Charter Com. of Greater Cin., 1985-88. Recipient Goldman Prize for Tchg. Excellence U. Cin. Coll. Law, 1995, Nicholas Longworth Disting. Alumni award, 1996. Mem. ABA, Fed. Bar Assn. (mem. exec. com., pres.1994), Ohio Bar Assn., Cin. Bar Assn. Avocations: tennis, travel. Office: Am Fin Group 1 E 4th St Cincinnati OH 45202-3717

CIOLA, EGIDIO, psychologist, consultant; b. Bolzano, BZ, Italy, Aug. 26, 1942; s. Aldo and Mitzi (Seeber) C.; m. Carla Arnulfo, July 6, 1941; children: Maria, Enrico. Grad. Edn., U. Turin, Italy, 1979; M Psychotherapy, Italian Family Therapy Assn., Milan, 1990. Diplomate psychology, psychotherapeutics. Personnel selector and trainer Fossano, Italy, 1969-86; pvt. practice psychologist, psychotherapist Cuneo, Italy, 1986—; psychologist cons. primary indsl. groups, Italy, 1986—; dir. Family Adv. Bur., Cuneo, 1980—, Alcoholist Therapy Ctr., Cuneo, 1988-96; supr. Cmty. Care Ctrs., Municipality of Turin, 1996-98; rschr. Union Premarital and Marital Cons., Cuneo, 1994—. Author: Alcohol: The Uncertain Enjoyment, 1997, Try to Understand, 1998. Mem. APA, Italian Psychol. Assn., European Family Therapy Assn. Roman Catholic. Fax: 0171-602749. E-mail: ciola@multiwire.net. Office: Via Bersezio Nr 57, 12100 Cuneo Italy

CIONGOLI, ALFRED KENNETH, neurologist; b. Phila., Jan. 11, 1943; s. Alfred Anthony and Antoinette Marie (Ragano) C.; m. Barbara, Nov. 22, 1966; children: Adam, Happy, Gregory, Alessandra, Antonio. AB, U. Pa., 1964; DO, Phila. Coll. Osteopathic Med., 1968. Diplomate Am. Bd. Psychiatry & Neurology. Resident in neurology, chief resident neurology unit U. Vt. Coll. Medicine, 1968-73; attending neurologist U. Pa. Med. Sch., Phila., 1974-75; rsch. fellow in neuroimmunology Danish Muscular Sclerosis Soc., Copenhagen, 1973-74, Hosp. U. Pa., Phila., 1975-77; pres. Neurol. Assocs. Vt., Burlington, 1977—; attending neurologist Hosp. U. Pa. Med. Sch., 1975-77; clin. asst. prof. neurology U. Vt. Coll. Medicine, Burlington, 1977-87, clin. assoc. prof., 1987—, dir. Multiple Sclerosis clinic, 1975; pres. Bd. Alumni Dirs. Phila. Coll. Osteopathic Med., 1994—, chmn. internat. fellowship com., 1990—; chmn. com. NIH, 1990—. Apptd. boxing commr. State of Vt., 1982; sr. med. officer U.S. Olympics team, 1986. Recipient Ellis Island Medal of Honor, 1997, Grand Officiale Order Merit Republic Italy, Italian Pres. Scalfero, 1998. Mem. AMA, Am. Assn. Neurology, Phila. Neurol. Soc., Ethan Allan Club (bd. gov.), Nat. Italian-Am. Found. (sr. v.p. 1992-95, pres. 1996—, vice chmn. 1999—). Office: Neurol Assn Vt 89 S Williams St Burlington VT 05401-3405

CIORNEI, IOAN, mechanical engineering educator; b. Arborea, Romania, Aug. 25, 1950; s. Mihai and Elena (Calancea) C.; m. Modesta Sericiuc, Feb. 4, 1956; 1 child, Catinca. Degree in engring., Gh. Asachi U., Iasi, Romania, 1974; PhD, Politehnica U., Bucharest, Romania, 1986; grad. (hon.), Grigore Ghica Coll., Dorohoi, Romania, 1999. Mech. engr. Mobstrat, Suceava, Romania, 1974-78; asst. U Stefan Cel Mare, Suceava, 1978-82, lectr., 1982-90, asst. prof., reader, 1990-92, prof., 1992—, head dept. engring., 1990-92, dean mech. engring. faculty, 1992—; state rep. bearing firm URB Rulmenti, Suceava, 1999—, Mobstrat, Suceava, 1990-92; hon. lectr. Nat. Edn. Ministry, 1986. Mem. editl. bd. Acta Tribologica, 1994—; contbr. over 100 articles to profl. jours.; patentee (16) in field. Lt. Romanian armed forces res., 1975—. Mem. Romanian Tribology Assn., Scientists' Assn. Romania. Greek Orthodox. Avocations: mountaineering, music, fiction, conversation. Home: Oituz St # 11 Bl A7 Sc C 10, 5800 Suceava Romania Office: U Stefan Cel Mare, University St # 1, 5800 Suceava Romania

CIOSEK, JERZY FELIKS, physicist; b. Warsaw, Poland, May 17, 1954; s. Feliks Bonifacy and Danuta Genowefa (Marcinkowska) C.; m. Magdalena Klecz, Aug. 5, 1977; 2 children. MS, Mil. U. Tech., Warsaw, Poland, 1979, DS, 1985. Asst. Inst. Optical Elecs., Warsaw, Poland, 1979-81, asst. lectr., 1981-85, lectr., 1986-95, head film lab., 1995—. Inventor in field. Mem. SPIE, OSA, Polish Vacuum Soc. Avocations: skiing, sailing, photography, travel. Office: IOEMVT, 2 Kaliski Str, 00-908 Warsaw Poland

CIPOLLA, ROBERTO, information scientist; b. Solihull, England, May 3, 1963; s. Salvatore and Concetta (Criminisi) C. MS in Engring., U. Pa., 1985; M in Engring., U. Electro Comms., Tokyo, 1988; DPhil, U. Oxford, 1991; BA with hons., U. Cambridge, 1984. Lectr. U. Cambridge, Eng., 1991-97; reader U. Cambridge, 1997—; cons. Toshiba Corp., Tokyo, 1997—. Author: Active Visual Inference of Surface Shape, 1995, Visual Motion of Curves and Surfaces, 2000; contbr. articles to profl. jours. U. Oxford fellow, 1990-91, Toshiba Corp. fellow, 1991-92; recipient Best Paper prize European Conf. Computer Vision, 1992, 96, British Machine Vision Conf., 1994, 97, 99, British Robot Assn., 1993. Roman Catholic. Avocations: photography, japanese culture and language. Home: 7 New Sq, Cambridge CB1 1EY, England Office: Dept Engring, Univ Cambridge, Cambridge CB2 1PZ, England

CIPUTRA, real estate developer; b. Sulawesi, 1931. Grad. in arch., Bandung Inst. Tech. Founder, pres., commr. Pembangunan Jaya Group, Jakarta, Indonesia, 1960—; commr. PT Pembangunan, Jakarta; chmn. Ciputra Devel., Jakarta; founder, pres., bd. dirs. Ciputra Group. Avocation: golf. Fax: 62321-324-017. Office: Jaya Bldg, Jalan MH Thamrin No 12, Jakarta 10340, Indonesia*

CIRELLO, JOHN, utility and engineering company executive; b. Bound Brook, N.J., Apr. 17, 1943; s. Fiore Avanti and Assunta C.; m. Sherron Anne Thomas, July 31, 1965; children: Assunta Anne, Elizabeth Rose, Sherron Marie. BS, Rutgers U., 1965, MS, 1971, PhD, 1975. Registered profl. engr., N.J., Pa. Engr. Calif. Dept. Water, L.A., 1965-66, U.S. Army Corps of Engrs., Ft. Belvoir, Va., 1966-68, Balt. Gas and Elec., 1968-69; rschr. Rutgers Water Resources Inst., New Brunswick, N.J., 1969-71; asst. prof. Rutgers U., New Brunswick, 1971-80; pres. Princeton Aqua Sci., Edison, N.J., 1980-85; v.p. IT Corp., Edison, N.J., 1985-88; v.p. ea. region Chem. Waste Mgmt., Inc., Princeton, N.J., 1988-92; pres. Metcalf & Eddy Svcs., Inc., Branchburg, N.J., 1992-95; Environ. Engring. Svcs. Inc., 1995-96; pres., CEO Fla. Water Svcs. Corp., 1995—; exec. v.p. Minn. P&L, Duluth, Minn., 1995—; pres.'s coun. U. Fla.; mem. dean's exec. coun. U. Ctrl. Fla. Editor (tng. manuals) Land Application of Effluents & Sludges, 1976, Ultimate Disposal of Organic and Inorganic Sludges, 1976, Water and Wastewater Polishing and Rennovation Techniques, 1976; co-editor (tng. manual) Construction and Environmental Inspectors Training Manual, 1977; contbr. articles to profl. jours. Mem. Bd. Adjustment, Bound Brook, N.J., 1976-81; councilman, pres., Bound Brook Town Coun., 1981-87; chmn. Dem. com. Bound Brook, 1982-86; Grad. Leadership Fla. Class XVI. Capt. U.S. Army Engr. Corps, 1966-68. Recipient award N.J. Water Pollution Control Assn., 1990. Mem. ASCE, Water Environ. Fedn., Am. Chem. Soc., Fla. Water Works Assn., Nat. Assn. Water Cos., Water Utilities Exec. Coun., Fla. State C. of C. (bd. dirs. 1997—). Roman Catholic. Avocations: antique and classic cars, golf. Home: 540 Winding Creek Pl Longwood FL 32779-6119 Office: Fla Water Svcs Corp PO Box 609520 Orlando FL 32860-9520

CIRIACO, SERGIO, financial consultant; b. Macerata, Italy, July 10, 1960; s. Nazareno and Rosa (Brunori) C.; m. Maria Adelaide Talevi, Sept. 19, 1987; 1 child, Francesca. Degree in economy and commerce, U. Ancona, Italy, 1984; M in Fin. Mgmt., U. Bocconi, Milan, 1987. Cons. C.B.F. spa, Milan, 1984-85; v.p. Gestione Fondi Fininvest, Milan, 1985-93, Murchio Sim spa, Milan, 1993-98; cons. Arpa SPA, Loreto, Italy, Casa Rurale Ed Artigiana Cantu, Italy. Roman Catholic. Avocations: sailing, skiing. E-mail: ciriacose@hotmail.com. Fax: 0039-2-67148473. Office: Cassa Rurale ed Artigiana, Cso Unita D'Italia 11, 20100 Cantu Co Italy

CIRILO, AMELIA MEDINA, educational consultant, supervisor; b. Parks, Tex., May 23, 1925; d. Constancio and Guadalupe (Guerra) C.; m. Arturo Medina, May 31, 1953 (div. June 1979); children: Dennis Glenn, Keith Allen, Sheryl Amelia, Jacqueline Kim. B.S. in Chemistry, U. North Tex., 1950; M.Ed., U. Houston, 1954; Ph.D. in Edn. and Nuclear Engring., Tex. A&M U., 1975; cert. in radioisotope tech. Tex. Woman's U., Denton, 1962; cert. in Pub. Speaking Dale Carnegie, 1993. Cert. in supervision, bilingual Spanish, Tex.; cert. permament profl. tchr., Tex. Tchr. sci., dept. Starr County Schs., Rio Grande City, Tex., 1950-53; elem. tchr. San Benito-Brownsville, Tex., 1953-54, Kingsville (Tex.) Schs., 1954-56; tchr. sci. dept. head chem. physics LaJoya (Tex.) Pub. Schs., 1956-70; teaching asst. Tex. A&M U., College Station, 1970-74; instr. fire chemistry Del Mar Jr. Coll., Corpus Christi, Tex., 1974-75; exec. dir Hispanic Ednl. Research Mgmt. Analysis Nat. Assn., Inc., Corpus Christi, 1975-79; head dept. chem. physics San Isidro (Tex.) High Sch., 1979-82; tchr. chemistry W.H. Adamson High Sch., Dallas, 1982-84, Skyline High Sch. 1984-92; ednl. cons., 1992—; chmn. faculty adv. com., 1983-84; tchr. high intensity lang. sci. Skyline High Sch., Dallas, 1984-86, chem. tchr. 1986-92; mem. core faculty Union Grad. Coll., Cin., P.R., Ft. Lauderdale, and San Diego, 1975-79; mathematician Well Instrument Devel. Co., Houston, summers 1950-54; panelist, program evaluator Dept. of Edn., Washington, 1977-79; program evaluator, Robstown, Tex., 1975-79; tchr. trainer Edn. 20 and 2 Region Ctrs., Corpus Christi and San Antonio, 1975-79; researcher, writer Coll. Edn. and Urban Studies, Harvard U., Cambridge, Mass., 1978-80; vis. prof. bilingual dept. East Tex. State Coll., Commerce, 1978; ednl. cons. and supv. Adult Basic Edn., Dallas Pub. Schs., 1994-99, kindergarten tchr., 1999-00; conf. presenter program evaluation, 1977-79. Author, rschr.: contr. chapt. to book, Harvard U., 1983, Comparative Evaluation of Bilingual Programs (named one of best U.S. books), 1978; Reflections (poetry), 1983. NSF grantee The Women's U., 1963-65; Recipient Educator of Yr., Literary Couns. of Greater Dallas, 1997-98; bd. dirs. Meth. Home for Elderly, Weslaco, Tex., 1968, Am. Cancer Soc. fund drive, College Station, 1971-74; Brazos County advisor Tex. Constl. Revision Commn., 1973-74; sec. Goals for Corpus Christi Com. of 100; Corpus Christi rep. Southwestern Ednl. Authority, Edinburg, Tex., 1977-79; co-founder, bd. dirs. Women's Shelter, Corpus Christi, 1977-78; exec. bd. Nat. Com. Domestic Violence, 1978-80; pres. Elem. PTA, 1972-75; mem. Women's Polit. Caucus, Mex. Am. Democrats. Recipient Sr. Salute award for achievements in edn. City of Dallas and NYL Care 65, 1996. Mem. Tex. Tchrs. Assn., NEA, Tex. Assn. Bilingual Educators, AAUW, Chem. Soc., Pan Am. Round Table, So. Sociol. Assn., Rocky Mountain Sociol. Assn., Metroplex Educators Sci. Assn., League United Latin Am. Citizens (pres. College Station 1973-74, past dist. dir. Corpus Christi), Fiesta Bilingual Toastmasters; bd. trustees Sci Cluster Skyline H.S., 1994—; Srs. Active in Life Adv. Com. Dallas City Parks & Recreation. Avocations: ballroom dancing, comedy. Home and Office: 5005 Oak Trl Dallas TX 75232-1643

CÎRLAN, MARIUS-PAUL VASILE, veterinarian, educator; b. Aiud, Romania, Mar. 29, 1938; s. Vasile Mihai and Paulina Petre (Păunescu) C.; m. Maria Dumitru Olaru, Feb. 7, 1981; 1 child, Andrea. Vet. Doctor, U. Iasi, Romania, 1968, DVM, 1976. Farm chief collective farm, Mogosesti-Siret, Romania, 1969-75; veterinarian Ctr. Artificial Inseminations, Iasi, 1976-80; prin. veterinarian Vet. Inspectorate, Iasi, 1981-91; prof. genetics faculty vet. medicine U. Iasi, 1992—. Author: Elements of Normal Animal Genetics, 1996 (medal 1997), Elements of Pathologic Animal Genetics, 1998; contbr. articles to profl. jours. Grantee Inst. Agronomical Rsch., France, 1999. Mem. Romanian Assn. Veterinarians, European Cytogeneticists Assn., 1997—, N.Y. Acad. Scis. Orthodox. Home: Vasile Alecsandri 7 Apt 1, 6600 Iasi Moldavia, Romania Office: Faculty Vet. Medicine, Aleea M Sadoveanu 6-8, 6600 Iasi Moldavia, Romania

CIRLINCI, MASSIMO, consulting company executive; b. Orvieto, Umbria, Italy, July 12, 1949; s. Salvatore and Filomena (Tilli) C.; m. Maria Giulia Brunetta, Apr. 26, 1983. Laurea in Mech. Engring., U. Rome, 1978. Cert. in engring. Indsl. engr. Playtex, Pomezia, Italy, 1979-80; sales engr. Asco Malugani, Milan, 1980-81; product mgr. Delchi-Carrier, 1981-86; mktg. mgr. Landis & Gyr, Milan, 1986-87; founder, owner Cirlinci Consulting Group, Milan, 1987—; strategic cons. Cirlinci Consulting Group, 1992—; strategic decision making ENAGP, Florence, Italy, 1999; mem. com. for seasonal adjustment Nat. Coun. Rsch., Rome; bd. dirs. ENAIP. Author: The Exercise Book, 1994, The Charge, 1997, Why Does He/She Do It?, 1998. 1st lt. Italian Air Force, 1975-76. Mem. Am. Mktg. Assn. Avocations: biking, skiing, diving, mountain trekking. E-mail: cirlinci@tin.it. Office: Cirlinci Consulting Group, Via Fiordalisi 6/3, 20146 Milan Italy

CIRONE, WILLIAM JOSEPH, educational administrator; b. Bklyn., Dec. 27, 1937; s. Joseph Nicholas and Marie Ann (Basile) C.; m. Barbara Jane Skirkie, Dec. 22, 1962; 1 child, Peter Craig. BA, Providence Coll., 1959; MA, NYU, 1960; adminstrv. cert., U. Calif., Santa Barbara, 1977. Tchr. N.Y.C. Pub. Schs., 1960-68; dir. product devel. ednl. divsn. Mead Corp., Atlanta, 1968-70, dir. mktg., 1970-73; founder, dir. Ctr. Cmty. Edn. and Citizen Participation, Santa Barbara, Calif., 1973-82; supt. schs. Santa Barbara County, 1983—; vis. fellow Chisholm Inst. Tech., Melbourne, Australia, 1986; vis. scholar Ctr. for excellence Tenn. State U., 1986. Host (cable talk shows) Education On-Line-A Line to Learning, Cirone on Schools. Bd. dirs., v.p., chair student aide com., S.B. Cmty. Found.; bd. dirs. Cmty. Action Commn., 1973-81, Cmty. Resource Info. Svc., 1978-82, Fin. Crisis Mgmt. Assistance Team, 1993—, Nat. Partnership in Edn., 1998—, Calif. Alliance for Arts Edn., 1999—; bd. dirs., sec. Pvt. Industry Coun., Santa Barbara, 1983-89; bd. dirs. Industry Edn. Coun. Santa Barbara, 1983—, pres., 1990, 99; bd. dirs. Coun. of Alcoholism and Drug Abuse, 1998—, Santa Barbara Lung Assn., 1983-87, Philip Francis Siff Ednl. Found., 1986—; bd. dirs. Impact II, 1989—, pres., 1993-99; bd. dirs. Nat. Comm. Edn. Assn., 1989-92, pres., 1990; regional chair Calif. County Supt. Assn., 1990—, bd. dirs. media and values, 1989-92; hon. bd. dirs. So. Coast Spl. Olympics; mem. Gov.'s Commn. on Earthquake Hazards, 1981; mem. state bd. Common Cause, 1974-77, organizer and 1st state chmn., Ga., 1970-73; mem. voter accessibility adv. bd. Santa Barbara County, 1986—; mem. adv. bd. CALM, Peace Resource Ctr., Marymount Sch., Women's Cmty. Bldg., Jodi House, Boy Scouts Am., Girl Scouts U.S.; comdrs. cmty. liaison com. Vandenberg AFB; mem. Access Theatre; mem. Hon. Commn. for Goleta Hosp.; mem. campaign cabinet Santa Barbara United Way, 1991, 98; adv. bd. Santa Barbara Brand Opera Assn., 1996—; co-chair State Supts. Statewide Arts Task Force, 1997. Recipient Smallheiser award United Fedn. Tchrs., 1968, Hon. Svc. award 15th Dist. PTA, 1979, 81, Intercongregation Orgn. Project Action award, 1995, Anti-Defamation League Santa Barbara Disting. Svc. award, 1996, Meritorious Svc. award Cmty. Action Com., Santa Barbara, 1981, Ind. Living Resource Ctr., 1985, Hon. Svc. award Calif. State PTA, 1995, 99 for '99 award, Santa Barbara C. of C., 1993-99, Profl. Publ. award Calif. County Supts. Assn., Comm. Achievement award Toastmasters Internat., 1999, Santa Barbara Wildlife Care Network award, 2000, Excellence in Svc. award South Coast Bus. and Tech., 2000; named Calif. Cmty. Educator of Yr., Calif. Cmty. Edn. Assn., 1984, Pub. Servant of Yr., Santa Barbara County, 1987. Mem. World Future Soc. (life), Am. Assn. Sch. Adminstrs., Assn. Calif. Sch. Adminstrs., So. Coast Coord. Coun. (past chmn., past exec. com.), Nat. Soc. Fundraising Execs., Automobile Assn. Am. (So. Calif. adv. bd.), Phi Delta Kappa. Democrat. Unitarian. Home: 953 Elk Grove Ln Solvang CA 93463-9608 Office: PO Box 6307 Santa Barbara CA 93160-6307

CIRRITO, JOSEPH JAMES, geographer; b. Caltavuturo, Italy, June 21, 1926; s. Bartolo and Mary (Cuccia) C.; m. Daphne Faith Lemmer, July 2, 1965. BA, U. of the Ams., 1954; cert., Aeronautical Chart/Info. Ctr., 1958, Air U., 1959, Indsl. Coll. Armed Forces, 1963, Alexander Hamilton Inst., 1967, Newspaper Inst. Am., 1968, Am. Mgmt. Assn., 1974. Designer Buffalo, N.Y., 1954-57; rsch. analyst Aeronautical Chart and Info. Ctr., St. Louis, 1957-59; assoc. The Editl. Group Ltd., Buffalo and Johannesburg, South Africa, 1960—; cons. J J Cirrito Assocs., Johannesburg, 1978—; cons. Small Bus. Devel. Corp., Johannesburg, 1991-96, South African Unemployed Workers Orgn., Johannesburg, 1995-96. Contbr. articles to profl. jours. With USN, 1943-46. Recipient Klein Meml. Writing award Newspaper Inst. of Am., 1967. Mem. South African Vol. Euthanasia Soc., Nat. Def. Indsl. Assn. (life), Loyal Order of Moose, Transvaal Aviation Club. Avocations: bridge, chess, photography, jogging. Office: JJ Cirrito Assocs, Box 4171, Witbeeck 1729, South Africa

CISNEROS, HENRY G., former federal official, broadcast executive; b. San Antonio, June 11, 1947; s. J. George and Elvira (Munguia) C.; m. Mary Alice Perez; children: Teresa Angelica, Mercedes Christina, John Paul. BA, Tex. A&M U., 1969, M. Urban and Regional Planning, 1970; MPA, Harvard U., 1973; D.Public Adminstrn., George Washington U., 1975. Adminstrv. asst. to city mgr. San Antonio, 1968, Bryan, Tex., 1969-70; asst. dir. dept. model cities San Antonio, 1969-70; asst. to exec. v.p. Nat. League Cities, Washington, 1970-71; White House fellow asst. Sec. of HEW, Washington, 1971-72; teaching asst. dept. urban studies and planning M.I.T., 1972; mem. City Coun., San Antonio, 1975-81; mayor City of San Antonio, 1981-89; sec. U.S. Dept. HUD, Washington, 1993-97; pres., COO, Univision Comm., Inc., L.A., 1997-2000; chmn. Am. Cityvista, San Antonio, 2000—. Trustee City Pub. Service Bd., City Water Bd., San Antonio; chmn. Fire and Police Pension Fund; mem. strategy council Nat. Democratic Party; mem. Twentieth Century Fund Ednl. Task Force, Eisenhower Found., com. on visual arts Tex. A & M U., bus. adv. com. Trinity U.; tri-chmn. United San Antonio; bd. dirs. San Antonio Symphony Soc., 1974-75. Recipient Thomas Jefferson award for pub. architecture AIA, 1995. Office: Am Cityvista 454 Soledad St Ste 300 San Antonio TX 78205-1555

CISSE, SOUMAILA, Malian government official. Min. fin. and trade Govt. of Mali, Bamako, min. fin., now min. environ. Office: Min of Finance and Trade, BP 234 Koulouba, Bamako Mali Mailing Address: Quartier du Fleuve, BP 790, Bamako Mali*

CISTERNAS, LUIS ALBERTO, engineering educator, consultant; b. Oficina Victoria, Tarapaca, Chile, Jan. 7, 1961; s. Carlos Alberto C. and Bernardina del Carmen Arapio; m. Edelmira Delfina Galvez, Aug. 9, 1986. BS in Chem. Engring., U. del Norte, Chile, 1986; PhD in Chem. Engring., U. Wis., 1993. Prof. part-time U. Catolica del Norte, Antofagasta, Chile, 1986-88; asst. prof. U. Antofagasta, 1988-93, assoc. prof., 1993—, chief grad. studies, 1995—, rsch. dean of engring., 1996—. Author: (with H. R. Gallejuillos, T. A. Graber, and M. E. Taboada) Fundamentos de Procejamiento de No Metálicos, 1998, (with M. Montenegro and C. Urqueta) Tecnologia de Los Procesos Químicos, 1999; editor: Innovacion, 1996—; contbr. articles to profl. jours. Mem. AIChE. Roman Catholic. E-mail: lcisternas@vantof.cl. Office: U Antofagasta, Casilla 170, Antofagasta Chile

ČÍTEK, JINDŘICH, agriculture sciences educator, geneticist; b. České Budejovice, Czech Republic, May 25, 1959; s. Jindřich and Anna (Frühbauerová) Č.; m. Vladimíra Křížová, Sept. 27, 1986; 1 child, Jindřich. Diploma in agrl. engring., U. South Bohemia, Č. Budějovice, 1983; CSc om Agr., U. Prague, Czech Republic, 1991. Cattle breeder agrl. coop., Vodňany, Czech Republic, 1983-86; instr. agr., geneticist U. South Bohemia, 1986—. Author: Beef Cattle Raising, 1992, Pastoral Technology, 1993, Rearing of Young Cattle, 1994. Fellow Czech Sci. and Tech. Soc. Avocations: travel, skiing. Fax: 00420 777 2593. E-mail: citek@zf.jcu.cz. Office: U South Bohemia, Studentská 13, 370 05 Ceske Budejovice Czech Republic

CITERNE, PHILIPPE, bank executive. CEO Soc. Generale, Paris. Office: Soc Gen, 17 Cours Valmy, 92972 Paris - La Defense France

CITRIN, YALE, light industry executive. BA, NYU, 1950; JD, Bklyn. Law Sch., 1954. Bar: N.Y. 1954. CEO Millar Elevator, Inc., N.Y.C., 1959-83; bus. cons. N.Y.C., 1983—; head rschr. neuropsychobiology pvt. found., N.Y.C., 1975—. Home: 54 Bradford Rd Scarsdale NY 10583-7650

CITRON, KLAUS-JÜRGEN, diplomat; b. Berlin, May 16, 1929; s. Fritz and Charlotte (Furbach) C.; m. Karin Bille Hansen, June 17, 1961; children: Reinhard, Bettina. Dr. Philosophy, U. Kiel, Germany, 1954. Asst. lectr. in German Ecole Centrale des Arts et Manufactures, Paris, 1955-56; asst. prof. German lit. U. Bologna, Italy, 1956-59; consul of Fed. Republic of Germany San Francisco, 1963-66; cultural counsellor Embassy of Germany, New Delhi, 1966-68; dep. chief of mission Embassy of Germany, Kuala Lumpur, 1968-72; dep. head of U.S. desk Ministry Fgn. Affairs, Bonn, Germany, 1972-74; head polit. desk German Del. to NATO, Brussels, 1974-78; head of desk nuclear and worlwide arms control Bonn, 1978-82, dep. commr. for arms control, 1982-84; head of German del. Conf. on CSBM, Stockholm, 1984-86; head of del. Vienna for Mandate Negotiations for Conventional Disarmament, 1987; head policy planning Ministry Fgn. Affairs, Bonn, 1988-90; amb. of Germany Hague, The Netherlands, 1990-94; spl. amb. European Stability Pact, 1994. Mem. German Atlantic Soc. (bd. dirs. 1994—). Office: Auf der Mertenbitze 17, 53639 Königswinter Germany

CITRON, RICHARD IRA, management consultant; b. Chgo., Apr. 1, 1944; s. Irving I. and Ruth (Katz) C.; m. Phyllis Sarah Kalifey, Dec. 26, 1971; children: Brian Todd, Dana Ann. BS, Roosevelt U., Chgo., 1966; MS, Ill. Inst. Tech., 1968, PhD, 1972. Enrolled Actuary. Consulting prin. A.S. Hansen, Inc., Chgo., 1972-79; mng. prin. A.S. Hansen, Inc., N.Y.C., 1979-82; exec. v.p. Frank B. Hall Consulting Co., N.Y.C., 1982-86; pres., CEO W F Corroon, Inc., Stamford, Conn., 1986-92; pres. Benefit Svcs. div., exec. v.p., dir. Hogg Robinson, Inc., N.Y.C., 1992-95; CEO Penn Gen. Svcs. Corp., Inc., N.Y.C., 1992-95; chmn. Hogg Robinson Consulting Group, Inc., N.Y.C., 1992-95, Group Plan Cons., Inc., N.Y.C., 1992-95; chmn., CEO Citron & Assocs., Inc.; corp. dir. Worlwide Benefits Cambell Soup Co., Inc., 1996; bd. dirs. Employee Benefit Rsch. Inst., Washington, HRI, Inc., N.A. Author articles in profl. jours. Trustee Optometric Ctr. of N.Y., mem. Coll. Council of SUNY; cons. State of Ill. Pension Laws Commn. 1974-78. Recipient: Blum-Kolver Found. grant 1963-66, Nat. Sci. Found. grant 1968-

70. Mem. Am. Acad. of Actuaries, Internat. Found. Employee Benefits (chmn actuaries com. 1981-82), Assn. of Private Pension and Welfare Plans, Am. Soc. for Advancement of Sci., Boardroom, Landmark, Elmwood Country Club. Office: Campbell Pl Camden NJ 08106

CIUBOTARU, ALEXANDRU AURELIAN, electronics engineer; b. Galati, Romania, Apr. 12, 1965; s. Constantin and Aurelia C.; m. Dana Mihaela Bedivan, Sept. 8, 1993. Diploma de inginer, Inst. Politehnic Iasi, Romania, 1989; PhD, Univ. Tex., 1996. Design engr. Tehnoton, Iasi, 1989-91; asst. instr. Inst. Politehnic, Iasi, Tex., 1991-92; grad. rsch., tchg. asst. Univ. Tex., Arlington, 1992-96; intermediate product/device engr. Nat. Semiconductor Corp., Arlington, Tex., 1996-98; lead design engr. Intersil Corp., Palm Bay, Fla., 1998—. Contbr. articles to profl. jours. E-mail: alex ciubotaru@yahoo.com. Fax: 321 729-4885. Home: 6900 Woodlake Dr NE Apt 101 Palm Bay FL 32905-6122 Office: Intersil Corp 2401 Palm Bay Rd NE Palm Bay FL 32905-3378

CIUFOLINI, IGNAZIO, physicist; b. Rome, Dec. 27, 1951; s. Giuseppe and Loreta (Fabi) C. M in Math. with hons., U. Rome, 1980; PhD in Physics, U. Tex., 1984. From tchg. asst. to lectr. U. Tex., Austin, 1982-86, rsch. assoc., 1986-88; vis. prof. U. Trento, Italy, 1989; rsch. assoc. CNR of Italy, Rome, 1989-99; prof. U. Lecce, Italy, 1999—; vis. prof. U. Rome, 1995-96; mem. fundamental phys. in space com. European Space Agy., 1993-94. Author: Gravitation and Inertia, 1995 (Best Book in Phys. Astronomy award Am. Assn. Pub. 1995), (with S.T. Hawking and J.A. Wheeler, audiobook) Theories of the Universe, 1996; editor: Gravitational Waves: Sources and Detectors, 1997, Gravitational Waves: Theory and Experiment, 2000. Prin. investigator Italian Space Agy., Rome, 1990-98; fellow U.S. Nat. Rsch. Coun., 1988. Mem. AAAS, Italian Soc. Gravitation (bd. dirs. 1996—), Internat. Sci. Found. Avocations: music, travel, arts, nature. Office: Ingegneria Innovacione, U Lecce Via Monteroni, 73100 Lecce Italy

CIUGUREANU, CONSTANTIN TEODOR, chemistry educator, researcher; b. Iasi, Moldova, Romania, Oct. 30, 1940; s. Petru Teodor and Magdalena (Bodogan) C.; m. Maria Mantea, Dec. 25, 1968; 1 child, Elena Doina. Diploma, U. Al. I. Cuza, Iasi, 1965, D in Chemistry, 1973. Instr. Al. I. Cuza U., Iasi, 1965-68, asst., 1969-75, lectr., 1976-90, sr. lectr., 1990-95, prof., 1996—. Author: General Chemistry, 1993, Matter in the Making, 1997, Chemistry, 1998; contbr. articles to jours. in field; inventor in field. Mem. Romanian Assn. Zeolites and Molecular Sieves, N.Y. Acad. Scis. Eastern Orthodox. Avocations: literature, philosophy, tourism. Home: C Negri, 6600 Iasi Romania Office: Al I Cuza U, Copou St 11, 6600 Iasi Romania

CIULLI, SORIN, theoretical physicist, educator; b. Bucharest, July 16, 1933; s. Tascu and Maria (Hogas) C.; m. Ioana Vladescu, Jan. 23, 1957 (div. 1962); m. Michaela Sorescu, May 25, 1968; 1 child, Alexandre-Cedric. MS, U. Bucharest, 1955; PhD, Joint Inst. Nuclear Rsch., 1968. Asst. prof. U. Bucharest, 1955-56; rsch. scientist Joint Inst. for Nuclear Rsch., Dubna, Russia, 1957-62; rsch. scientist Inst. for Atomic Physics, Bucharest, 1962-66, sr. rsch. sci., 1970-75; vis. scientist C.E.R.N., NORDITA, Geneva, Copenhagen, 1967-69, 75-76; ord. prof. U. Montpelier, France, 1983—; vis. prof. U. Groningen, Birmingham, Bern Karlsruhe, Trinity Coll., Inst. Hautes Etud. Sci., 1976-82, Oxford Brookes, 1995-96. Contbr. articles on analytic methods in element particles, regularization of unstable problems and electric impedance tomography to sci. jours. Mem. N.Y. Acad. Scis., Am. Phys. Soc., European Phys. Soc. Avocation: Himalayan mountaineering. Office: U Montpellier II, Dept Math Phys, F-34095 Montpellier France

CIVASAQUI, JOSE (SOSUKE SHIBASAKI), poet; b. Saitama Prefecture, Japan, Jan. 2, 1916; s. Namitaro and Sato (Izawa) Shibasaki; m. Setsuko Hirose, Sept. 18, 1940; children: Takashi, Seishi, Sonoe. Grad., Saitama County Sch., 1935, studied writing with Edmund Blunden, 1947-50; LHD (hon.), L'Univ. Libre D'Asie, Karachi, Pakistan, 1977; HHD, World U., Tucson, 1977; PhD (hon.), Nat. Acad. Mgmt., Tapiei, 1987; DLitt (hon.), Albert Einstein Internat. Acad. Found., 1991. Adviser liaison dept. Hakodate Dock Co. Ltd., Tokyo, 1948-51; mgr. liaison sect. Watanabe Confectionary Co., Ltd., Tokyo, 1951-54; mem. lit. staff Toshiba EMI Co., Ltd., Tokyo, 1955-76; lectr. Japan Transl. Acad., Tokyo, 1978-84, Sunshine Coll., Tokyo, 1985-94. Author: In His Bosom, 1950, In Thy Grace, 1971, Beyond Seeing, 1977, Living Water, 1984, Invitation to the World of Haiku, 1985; translator: Doshin Shien (R.L. Stevenson's A Child's Garden of Verse), 1973, Kusa no Tsuyu (Novin Afrouz's Dew of Grass), 1987, Chosuichi Doro no Boken (Erna M. Holyer's Reservoir Road Adventure, 1990; author: (poetry) Green Pastures, 1993; also numerous songs. Recipient World Poetry award 3rd World Congress Poets, 1976, 4th World Congress Poets, 1979, 8th World Congress Poets, 1985, Gerald L.K. Smith award, 1985, Platformers USA, 1985, Italia '85 indetto del Centro Nazionale Culturale, 1985, Amando M. Yuzon Meml. award 10th World Congress Poets, 1987, runner-up prize writing competition IBC, 1987, Medal for Peace, Albert Einstein Internat. Acad. Found., 1990, medallion Poetry Day Australia and Melbourne Poetry Soc. Competition, 1991-92, Michael Madhusudan Acad. award, 1992, 4th Order of Merit, Japan, 1993, Congress medallion for Disting. Participation, Internat. Biographical Ctr., Am. Biog. Ctr., 1993, Silver medallion Dove in Peace, Poetry Day Australia, 1995. Fellow Internat. Soc. Lit. (Eng.), Internat. Acad. Poets (Eng.); mem. United Poets Laureate Internat. (hon. pres., decretum hon. 1988), Japan Guild Authors and Composers (mng. dir.), Japan League Poets (mng. dir.), Japan Song Translators Soc. (pres.), Internat. Shakespeare Assn., World Jnana Sadahk Soc. (India), Poetry Soc. Japan (pres.), Acad. Mentis, Italia Tagore Inst. Creative Writing Internat. (India), Poetry Soc. (London), PEN. Address: 2-12-11 Honcho Ikebukuro, Toshima-ku, Tokyo 170, Japan

CIVIDJIAN, GRIGORE ALEXANDRU, electrical engineering educator; b. Kishinev, Moldavia, Jan. 12, 1936; s. Alexandru Gregory and Iuliana Aleksei (Solearsky) C.; m. Xenia Andrei Kishinsky, June 6, 1964; children: Natalia, Andrei. Diploma in engring., Poly. Inst., Bucharest, Romania, 1958; PhD, Poly. Inst., Iassy, Romania, 1970; degree in Math., U. Craiova, 1971. Worker local industry Craiova, Romania, 1958-60; designer Project Instn., Craiova, 1960-67; asst. prof. U. Craiova, 1967-69, lectr., 1969-77, assoc. prof. engring., 1977-89, prof., head dept. elec. apparatus, 1989—; cons. Electroputer Rsch. Inst., Craiova, 1970-95, Elec. Engring. Rsch. Inst., Bucharest, 1981-95. Author (textbook) Electrical Apparatus, 1972, 96; contbr. articles to profl. jours. St. Petersburg Tech. U. grantee Ministry of Edn., 1973, U. Ctrl. Lancashire (Eng.) grantee, 1994, U. Paul Sabatier grantee, 1995. Mem. Elec. Fuses Club, Electrostatica Soc., Internat. Electrotechnical Commn. Nat. Com. Avocations: music, swimming. Home: Dezrobirii F 1-1-1, RO-1100 Craiova Romania Office: Univ Lapus 5, RO-1100 Craiova Romania

CIXOUS, HÉLÈNE, comparative literature educator, author; b. Oran, Algeria, June 5, 1937; arrived in France, 1955.; d. Georges and Eve (Klein) C.; 2 children. Agrégation in Eng. Lit., Paris, 1959, D ès Lettres, 1968; D (hon.), Queen's U, Canada, 1991, Edmonton U., Canada, 1992, York U., England, 1993, Georgetown U., 1995, Northwestern U., 1996, U. Wis., Madison, 1999, Saint Andrews U., Fife, Scotland, 1999. Co-founder U. Paris 8, 1968, chair prof. English lit., 1968—, head Ctr. Women's Studies, 1974—; vis. prof., lectr. numerous confs. and symposia in Europe and N.Am., Japan, India; disting. vis. prof. Northwestern U., 1995—. Author: Le prénom de Dieu, 1967, Dedans, 1969, English translation), 1986, Le troisième corps, 1970, (English translation), 1999, Les Commencements, 1970, Un Vrai Jardin, 1971, Neutre, 1972, Tombe, 1973, Portrait du soleil, 1973, Revolution pour plus d'un Faust, 1975, Souffles, 1975, La, 1976, Partie, 1976, Angst, 1977, Préparatifs de Noces au-delà de l'abîme, 1978, Vivre L'Orange (bilingual), 1979, Anankè, 1979, Illa, 1980, With ou l'art de l'innocence, 1981, Limonade Tout Était si Infini, 1982, Le Livre de Promethea, 1983 (English translation 1991), La bataille d'Arcachon, 1986, Manne, 1988 (English translation 1994), Jours of L'an, 1990 (English translation 1998), L'Ange au Secret, 1991, Déluge, 1992, Beethoven à jamais, 1993, La Fiancée Juive, 1995, Messie, 1996, OR, Les Lettres de Mon Père, 1997, Osnabrück, 1999, Les Rêveries de la Femme Savage 2000, Le Jour o388 je N'étais pa Lá, 2000; (essays) L'Exile of James Joyce, 1969 (English translation 1976), Prénoms de Personne, 1974, La Jeune Née, 1975 (English translation 1986), La Venue à L'Ecriture, 1977, (English translation), 1991, Entre l'Écriture, 1986, L'Heure de Clarice Lispector, 1989, Reading with Clarice Lispector, 1990, Readings, the Poetics of Blanchot, Joyce, Kafka, Lispector, Tsvetaeva, 1992, Three Steps on the Ladder of Writing, 1993, Photos de Racines, 1994 (English trans. 1997), Stigmata, 1998; theater: La Pupille, 1971, Portrait de Dora, 1976 (English trans. 1983), Le Nom d'Oedipe, 1978 (English trans. 1991), La Prise de L'école de Madhubaï, 1984 (English trans. 1986), L'Histoire terrible inachevée de Norodom Sihanouk, Roi du Cambodge, 1985 (English trans. 1994), L'Indiade ou l'Inde de leurs rêves, 1987, On ne part pas on ne revient pas, 1991, La Ville Parjure, 1994 (best play of yr. Critic's award), Voile Noire Voile Blanche (bilingual), 1994, L'Histoire, 1994, Tambours Sur La Digue, 1999. Recipient Prix Médicis, 1969, Croix du Sud, Brazil, 1989, Chevalier de la légion d'honneur, 1994, Officier de L'Ordre Nat du Mérite, 1998. Mem. Conseil Sci. Fond. de France. Office: Centre d'Etudes Féminines, U Paris VIII 2 rue de la Liberte, 93526 Saint-Denis Cedex 02, France

CIZEK, DAVID JOHN, sales engineer, small business owner; b. Chgo., Sept. 29, 1959; s. John Jacob and Cecelia Ursula (Shway) C.; m. Kimberly Ann Kral, May 12, 1984. BSEE, U. Ill., 1981. Asst. sales engr. control divsn. Westinghouse Electric Co., Chgo., 1981-83; product line engr. control divsn. Westinghouse Electric Co., Fayetteville, N.C., 1983-85; sales engr. field sales divsn. Westinghouse Electric Co., Chgo., 1985-86, aerospace and def. automation specialist, 1987-88, engr. distbn. support sales, 1988-94; field sales divsn. sales engr. Cutler-Hammer, 1994-95; pres., owner Lakeridge Electric Supply Co., Inc., Romeoville, Ill., 1995—. Mem. U. Ill. Alumni Assn., Girl Scouts of Am., Kappa Sigma Alumni Assn. Republican. Presbyterian. Avocations: real estate investing, fishing, hunting, tennis. Home: 8409 Willow West Dr Willow Springs IL 60480-1139 Office: Lakeridge Electric Supply 734 Oakridge Dr Romeoville IL 60446-1395

CIZEK, GREGORY J., educator; b. Cin., Apr. 26, 1958; s. Donald F. and Helen L. Cizek; m. Rita L. Olson, June 25, 1977; children: Caroline R., David I., Stephen F.G. BA in Elem. Edn., Mich. State U., 1979, MA in Curriculum and Instrn., 1984, PhD in Measurement, Evaluation and Rsch. Design, 1991. Cert. elem. tchr., Ohio, Mich., Iowa; cert. elem. prin., Iowa. Elem. sch. tchr. Living God Christian Sch., Traverse City, Mich., 1979-84; test devel. specialist Mich. Dept. Edn., Lansing, 1985-86; program mgr. Am. Coll. Testing, Iowa City, 1987-91; asst. prof. ednl. rsch. and measurement U. Toledo, 1991-95, 1995-99; assoc. prof. ednl. measurement and evaluation U. N.C., Chapel Hill, 1999—; cons. Nat. Assessment Governing Bd., Washington, 1993-99, N.J. Dept. Edn., Trenton, 1995—. Author: Cheating on Tests: How To Do It, Detect It, and Prevent It, 1999, (monograph) Filling in the Blanks: Putting Standardized Tests to the Test; editor, author: Handbook of Educational Policy, 1999, Setting Performance Standards, 2000. V.p. Sylvania (Ohio) Pub. Schs. Bd. Edn., 1998, mem., 1999. Mem. Am. Ednl. Rsch. Assn. (com.), Nat. Coun. on Measurement in Edn. (com.). Home: 111 Middlebrook Ct Chapel Hill NC 27514-5228 Office: U NC Sch Edn Cb3500 Chapel Hill NC 27599-0001

CIZIK, ROBERT, manufacturing company executive; b. Scranton, Pa., Apr. 4, 1931; s. John and Anna (Paraska) C.; m. Jane Morin, Oct. 3, 1953; children: Robert Morin, Jan Catherine, Paula Jane, Gregory Alan, Peter Nicholas. BS, U. Conn., 1953; MBA, Harvard U., 1958; LLD (hon.), Kenyon Coll., 1983. Acct. Price Waterhouse & Co. (CPAs), N.Y.C., 1953-54, 56; fin. analyst Exxon U.S.A., N.J., 1958-61; exec. asst. Cooper Industries, Inc., Houston, 1961-63, treas., 1963-64, contr., 1964-67, v.p. planning, 1967-69, exec. v.p., 1969-73, pres., 1973-92, COO, 1973-75, CEO, 1975-95, chmn., 1983-96; propr. Cizik Interests, Houston, 1996—; dir. Am. Indsl. Ptnrs., 1996-98; adv. dir. Wingate Ptnrs., 1994—; chmn. bd. dirs. Easco, Inc., 1997-98; chmn. bd. dirs. Stanadyne Automotive, Koppers Industries; bd. dirs. Temple Inland, Air Products and Chems., Inc.; mem. Bus. Roundtable, 1978-95; mem. host com. Houston Econ. Summit Meeting, 1990. Bd. dirs. Assocs. Harvard Bus. Sch., Boston, 1984-96; mem. Tex. Bus. and Edn. Coalition, 1991-94; chmn. Heartstrings Benefit, Design Industries Found. for AIDS, 1991-92; mem. nat. adv. coun., trustee Tex. Heart Inst.; mem. devel. bd. U. Tex. Houston Health Sci. Ctr.; campaign co-chair Wortham Theater Ctr., 1981-83, United Way of Tex., Gulf Coast, 1994-95. 1st lt. USAF, 1954-56. Recipient Gen. Maurice Hirsch award Bus. Com. for Arts, 1984, CEO of Yr. bronze award Fin. World Mag., 1987, CEO of Decade bronze award in Indsl. Equipment Cos., 1988, Masterson award Houston Grand Opera, 1998, Maurice Hirsch award for philanthropy, 1999; named Best CEO in Machinery Industry, Wall St. Transcript, 1980, 81, 83, 86, 87, 88, 89, 90-91, Internat. Exec. of Yr., Greater Houston Partnership and Houston World Trade Assn., 1990. Mem. NAM (chmn. 1992-93), Elec. Mfrs. Club (bd. govs. 1984—, pres. 1990-92), River Oaks Country Club, Forum Club Houston (founding), Houston Ctr. Office: Cizik Interests Chase Tower 600 Travis St Ste 3628 Houston TX 77002-2910

CLAASSEN, WYNAND, architect, editor; b. Schweizer-Reneke, South Africa, Jan. 16, 1951; s. George Nicolaas and Petronella (Theunissen) C.; m. Jeanette Delport, Dec. 10, 1982; children: Antonie, Jeanelle, Jeanrá, Jeanandi. BArch, U. Pretoria, South Africa, 1978. Architect Dept. Plural Rels., Pretoria, 1979, Stauch Vorster & Ptnrs., Durban, South Africa, 1979-81; ptnr. Partnership Wynand Claassen, Durban, 1981-82, Wynand Claassen, Smuts-Erasmus & Ptnrs., Durban, 1982-87, Wynand Claassen Architects, Durban, 1987-91, Bau Architects Inc., Durban, 1991—; capt. Springbok Nat. Rugby, 1981-82, rugby selector, 1985, selector, mng. Seven-A-Side, 1995—. Author: (with Dan Retief) More Than Just Rugby, 1985 (Best Sellers List), The Final Chapter, 1996; pub., co-author (with Chris Schoeman) Who's Who of South African Rugby, 1996; editor, columnist monthly mag. Rugby 15 International, 1992-98; contbr. weekly column on rugby A Touch of Claassen to Sunday Tribune, 1989-97; one-man shows at Sanlam Ctr., Cape Town, South Africa, 1982, Sasolburg, 1983, Standerton, 1985; artist of Springbok rugby capts. for South African Rugby Football Union Centennary, 1989; cartoonist Springbok team mems., 1981, monthly rugby cartoon for Rugby 15 mag., 1994-98. Trustee Chris Burger Rugby Players Meml. Fund, Cape Town, 1984-98. Recipient Civic award for environ. excellence City of Pietermaritzburg, 1999, Regional award for design and quality Brick Devel. Assn. (2), 1989. Mem. Inst. South African Architects, South African Rugby Supporters Club (chmn. bd. dirs. 1996—). Mem. Dutch Reformed Ch. Avocations: painting cartons, music, road running, social golf. Office: BAU Architects, PO Box 4003, Durban Kwazulu-Natal 4000, South Africa

CLACK, JERRY, classics educator; b. N.Y.C., July 22, 1926; s. Christopher Thrower and Mildred Taylor (VanDyke) C. AB, Princeton U., 1946, MA, 1958; PhD, U. Pitts 1962; MA, Duquesne U., Pitts., 1977. Documents officer U.S. Nat. Commn. for UNESCO, 1946-52; exec. dir. Allegheny County chpt. Nat. Found., Pitts., 1953-68; asst. prof. dept. classics Duquesne U., Pitts., 1968-71, assoc. prof., 1971-75, prof., 1975—, chmn. dept., 1973-75, 80-83, n.em. preprofl. health com., 1970-76, mem. univ. library com., 1979-93, mem. univ. due process, core curriculum, arts and scis. curriculum coms., 1986-94, mem. univ. promotion and tenure com., 1988-90. Editor: The Classical World, 1977-93, Anthology of Hellenistic Poetry, 1982, Meleager: The Poems, 1992, Asclepiades of Samos and Leonidas of Tarentum: The Poems, 1999; mem. editl. bd. Duquesne Univ. Press, 1991-94; author books, articles, revs. in field. Pres. Western Pa. Pub. Health Conf., 1967; v.p. Western Pa. Council World Federalists, 1965-88, treas., 1987—; mem. U.S. del. to 3d UNESCO Gen. Conf., Florence, Italy, 4th UNESCO Gen. Conf., Paris. Mem. Classical Assn. Pitts. and Vicinity (treas. 1970-78, 85—, sec. 1988—), Pa. Classical Assn. (treas. 1977-99), Classical Assn. Atlantic States (pres. 1987, exec. com. 1974—, 2d v.p. 1975, 1st v.p. 1976, exec. dir. 1993—), Am. Philol. Assn. (chmn. working group editors classical jours. 1982-93, chmn. com. regional classical orgns. 1986-95), Vergilian Soc. Am. (trustee 1985-87), Phi Sigma Iota, Delta Phi Alpha, Alpha Epsilon Delta, Phi Alpha Theta. E-mail: clack@duq.edu. Home: 5920 Kentucky Ave Pittsburgh PA 15232-2824 Office: Duquesne U Department Of Classics Pittsburgh PA 15282-0001

CLACKSON, STEPHEN GREGORY, communications executive; b. Taunton, Somerset, Eng., Apr. 23, 1961; arrived in Germany, 1995; s. Kenneth Alan and Joyce Ruth (Ginger) C.; m. Ute Kriesten, Apr. 28, 1995; children: Aelfleda Iona Christiane, Wulfric Kenneth Rainer. BSc, U. London, 1984, PhD, 1989; MSc, U. Wales, 1995. European physicist. Fellow in edn. Brunel U., Eng., 1988-89; fellow and tutor in natural philosophy U. Aberdeen, Scotland, 1990-92; info. technologist & mediator Informationsverarbeitung-Leverkusen GmbH, Germany, 1995-98; established tech. lang. bur., 1998—. Author: Die Traurigen Löwen von Göttingen, 1995; contbr. articles to profl. jours.; author, narrator, performer (sound recording) Mortier Magic, 1993. Chmn. Friends of Albania, Somerset, Eng., 1991-92. Fellow Royal Soc. Arts. Avocations: genealogy, numismatics, heraldry, angling. Home and Office: Robert-Stolz-Strasse 18c, 42929 Wermelskirchen Germany

CLAES, DANIEL JOHN, physician; b. Glendale, Calif., Dec. 3, 1931; s. John Vernon and Claribel (Fleming) C.; AB magna cum laude, Harvard U., 1953, MD cum laude, 1957; m. Gayla Christine Blasdel, Jan. 19, 1974. Intern, UCLA, 1957-58; Bowyer Found. fellow for rsch. in medicine, L.A., 1958-61; pvt. practice specializing in diabetes, L.A., 1962—; biotech. cons. SIRA Techs., 1995—; v.p. Am. Eye Bank Found., 1978-83, pres., 1983—, dir. rsch., 1980—, chmn., CEO 1995—; pres. Heuristic Corp., 1981—. Mem. L.A. Mus. Art, 1960—. Mem. AMA, AAAS, Calif. Med. Assn., L.A. County Med. Assn., Am. Diabetes Assn. (profl. coun. on immunology, immunogenetics and transplantation), Internat. Diabetes Fedn., Internat. Pancreas & Islet Transplant Assn. Clubs: Harvard and Harvard Med. Sch. of So. Calif.; Royal Commonwealth (London). Contbr. papers on diabetes mellitus, computers in medicine to profl. lit. Office: Am Eyebank Found 15237 W Sunset Blvd Ste 108 Pacific Palisades CA 90272-3690

CLAESEN, LUC JOSEPH MARIE, electrical engineer and educator; b. Hasselt, Belgium, May 23, 1956; s. Emiel and Paula (Lambrichts) C.; m. Leona Vanschoenwinkel, July 19, 1980; children: Jan, Karel. Burg.Ir., Kath. U. Leuven, Belgium, 1979, PhD, 1984. Rschr. Cath. U. Leuven, 1979-84, prof. elec. engring., 1989—; group leader IMEC, Leuven, 1984—; CAD-track chmn. IEEE ICCD Conf., Cambridge, Mass., 1993-94; chmn. Higher Order Logic-92 Workshop, Leuven, 1992, Applied Formal Methods W.S., Houthalen, Belgium, 1989; program chmn. Internat. Fedn. Info. Processing Computer Hardware Description Langs.'93 Conf., Ottawa, Ont., Can., 1993. Editor: Formal VLSI Correctness Verification, 1989, Formal VLSI Specifications and Synthesis, 1989, Higher Order Logic Theorem Proving, 1992, Computer Hardware Description Languages, 1993; editorial bd. Formal Methods in System design jour. Mem. IEEE (sr., Best paper award ICCD-86 conf. 1986), Internat. FEdn. Info. Processing Working Group 10.2 (sec. 1991—), IFIP WG 10.5. Home: Klameerstraat 21, Alken Limburg 3570, Belgium Office: IMEC, Kapeldreef 75, Leuven 3001, Belgium

CLAGETT, ARTHUR F(RANK), psychologist, sociologist, qualitative research writer, retired sociology educator; b. Little Rock, Dec. 3, 1916; s. A.F. and Mary Gertrude (Bell) C.; m. Dorothy Ruth Pinckard, Dec. 23, 1954. BA in Chemistry, Baylor U., 1943; MA in Psychology, U. Ark., 1957; PhD in Sociology, La. State U., 1968. Shift chemist Celanese Corp., Cumberland, Md., 1942-44; shift supr. penicillin prodn. Comml. Solvents Corp., Terre Haute, Ind., 1944-45; rsch. supr. streptomycin pilot plant Schenley Labs., Lawrenceburg, Ind., 1945-48; asst. mgr. Clagett's Feed and Seed Store, Donna, Tex., 1948-50; med. svc. rep. Blue Line Chem. Co., St. Louis, 1952-56; prison classification officer La. State Penitentiary, 1956-59, classification supr. new admissions, 1959-60; instl. sponsor inmate Sober Alcohol Anonymous Group; organizer Hew Hope Alcohol Anonymous Group; condr. group counseling studies; counseling psychologist Baker, La., 1960-64; asst. prof. sociology Lamar State Coll. Tech., Beaumont, Tex., 1964-66; assoc. prof. sociology Stephen F. Austin State U., 1968-83, prof., 1983-85, prof. emeritus, 1986—; consulting sociologist, social psychologist, criminologist, Nacogdoches, Tex., 1986-91; qualitative rsch. writer, 1992—. Mem. editl. bd. Quar. Jour. Ideology, 1982-93; contbr. numerous articles to profl. jours. including Jour. Offender Counseling, Internat. Rev. Mod. Sociol., Jour. Offender Rehab., Criminal Justice Policy Rev. Mem. univ. rsch. coun., 1973-75, Sch. Liberal Arts coun., 1970-71. Mem. Am. Assn. Individual Investors, Internat. Platform Assn., So. Sociol. Soc., Am. Soc. Criminology, Am. Acad. Criminal Justice Scis., Am. Sociol. Assn. (chaired annual meetings, presented 33 papers). Methodist. Avocations: reading, internet, classical music. Home and Office: 619 E Oak Ln Nacogdoches TX 75961-4771

CLAGUE, JOHN ROGERS, sculptor; b. Cleve., Mar. 14, 1928; s. John Rogers and Ernestine Marie (Honsberg) C.; m. Sarah Eddy Reynolds, Aug. 2, 1958; children: Jeannette R., Elizabeth H. BFA, Cleve. Inst. of Art, 1956. Instr. Western Res. U., Cleve., 1956; sculpture instr. Oberlin (Ohio) Coll., 1957-61; prof. sculpture Cleve. Inst. of Art, 1957-71. One man show at Waddell Gallery, N.Y.C., 1966; group exhbn. at Whitney Mus. Art, N.Y.C., 1965, sculpture in permanent collections: Flower of Erebus, Cleve. Mus. of Art, Syllogistic Construction, Art Gallery of Ont., Auriculum I, Ashland U., Astra, Trumbull Meml. Hosp. Cpl. U.S. Army, 1950-52. Recipient Cleve. Arts prize Women's City Club of Cleve., 1967; Ohio Arts Coun. Individual Artist grantee, 1977.

CLAIRE, DENNIS DANIEL, JR., secondary education educator; b. Port Jefferson, N.Y., Aug. 14, 1949; s. Dennis Daniel and Genevieve C.; m. Janice Marie Claire, July 17, 1976; children: Dennis Patrick, Ryan J., Patrick J. BA, Marist Coll., Poughkeepsie, N.Y., 1974; MS, L.I. U., 1991; ArtsD, St. John's U., 1999. Cert. secondary tchr., N.Y. Tchr. Rhinecliff (N.Y.) Union Free Sch. Dist., 1974-77; prin., master electrician Dennis Clair Electric Co., Mattituck, N.Y., 1977-79; tchr. Greenport (N.Y.) Union Free Sch. Dist., 1979—; adj. prof. Suffolk County C.C., Riverhead, N.Y., 1998—. Pres. Greenport Tchrs. Assn., 1987-89 (v.p., 1986-87). Mem. World Jewish Congress, N.Y.C., 1995—. Educator of Yr. Suffolk Times, 1990. Mem. MLA, N.Y. State English Coun. (Tchr. of Excellence 1991), L.I. Lang. Arts Coun. Avocations: reading, sailing. E-mail: d4eire@hamptons.com. Home: 845 Rosewood Dr PO Box 1138 Mattituck NY 11952-0920 Office: Greenport Union Free Sch Dist 720 Front St Greenport NY 11944-1500

CLAIRIS, CHRISTOS, linguistics educator; b. Istanbul, Turkey, Nov. 27, 1941; s. Ilias and Meropi (Vassiliadis) C.; m. Lydia Peridis, Apr. 27, 1990; 1 child, Nicolas. Diploma, Megalé tou Genous Scholè À Istanbul; PhD in Gen. Linguistics, Sorbonne U., Paris, 1982. Prof. Cath. U. Valparaiso, Chile, 1970-76, U. René Descartes Sorbonne, Paris, 1978—. Author: Fuegian Linguistics, 1987, Grammar of Modern Greek, 1996. E-mail: clairis@paris5.sorbonne.fr. Home: 5 rue Vercingétorix, 75014 Paris France Office: Univ René Descartes, 12 rue Cujas, 75005 Paris France

CLAMANN, YORK H., biologist, educator; b. Berlin, Germany, Sept. 24, 1942; came to U.S., 1947; naturalized, 1960; s. Hans Georg and Maria C. C.; m. Andrea Mary Ryza, June 10, 1967; children: Christina Marie, Andrew York. BA, St. Mary's U., 1964; MA, Incarnate Word Coll., 1966; PhD, Tex. A&M U., 1976. Biology tchr. Northeast Ind. Sch. Dist., San Antonio, 1964-67; clin. chemist U.S. Army, Houston, 1968-71; student tchr. supervisor Tex. A&M U., College Station, 1974-76; sci. supervisor Abiline (Tex.) Ind. Sch. Dist., 1976-94; curriculum dir. St. John's Sch., Abilene, 1995-96; adj. prof. Abilene Christian U., 1996-97, Our Lady of the Lake U., San Antonio, 1997—; cons. Pearson Edn. Corp., 1997—; dir. Morgan Jones Planetarium, Abilene, 1980-95; dir. sci. fair Abilene Ind. Sch. Dist., 1978-91. Citizens adv. bd. Abilene Jr. League, 1979; regional dir. CPR, Am. Heart. Assn., 1990-96; dir. Holy Family Sabbath Choir, 1994—; precinct election judge Taylor County, Abilene, 1988—. Served in U.S. Army, 1968-71. Fellow Internat. Planetarium Soc.; mem. AAAS, Sci. Tchrs. Assn. Tex., PTA. Avocations: amateur radio, swimming, international travel, motorcycle riding, directing choir. Home: 4000 Witte Cove Round Rock TX 78681-1046 Office: Our Lady of Lake U San Antonio TX 78207

CLAMPITT, OTIS CLINTON, JR., health agency executive; b. Burlington, N.C., Nov. 17, 1947; s. Otis Clinton and Audrey Mae (Brafford) C.; m. Martha Jane Redding, Apr. 3, 1971. BA in English, Guilford Coll., 1971. Unit exec. dir. N.C. div. Am. Cancer Soc., Winston-Salem, 1972-73, area rep., 1973-74, met. area dir., 1974-75; dir. pub. edn./info. S.C. div. Am. Cancer Soc., Columbia, 1976-78, dir. devel., 1978-79, dep. exec. v.p., 1979-81; exec. v.p. Miss. div. Am. Cancer Soc., Jackson, 1981-89; nat. v.p. Am. Cancer Soc., Washington, 1989—; faculty, cons. Am. Cancer Soc. Acad., Atlanta, 1989—. Co-founder, pres. Forsyth County Interagy. Health Coun., Winston-Salem, 1975; chmn. Miss. Combined Fed. Campaign, Jackson, 1987-89, Miss. Com. on Indigent Patient Care, Jackson, 1989; appointed Govs. Task Force on Agy. Registration, Jackson, 1989; bd. dirs. Miss. Seatbelt Coalition, Jackson, 1986-90, Nat. Vol. Health Agency Capital Area, 1994—. Mem. Miss. Soc. Assn. Execs., Nat. Soc. of Fund Raising Execs. Avocations: sailing, snow skiing, water skiing, traveling. Home: 1712 Woodlore Rd Annapolis MD 21401-6568 Office: Am Cancer Soc PO Box 6640 Annapolis MD 21401-0640

CLANCY, EDWARD BEDE CARDINAL, archbishop; b. Lithgow, NSW, Australia, Dec. 13, 1923; s. John Bede and Ellen Lucy (Edwards) C. Grad., St. Columba's Coll., Springwood, NSW, St. Patrick's Coll., Manly, NSW; LSS, Pontifical Bibl. Inst., Rome; DD, Propaganda Fide U., Rome. Ordained priest Roman Cath. Ch., 1949, ordained bishop, 1974. Parish min. Belmore, NSW, 1950-51, Liverpool, NSW, 1955; sem. staff Springwood, NSW, 1958, Manly, 1966-73; aux. bishop Archdiocese of Sydney, Australia, 1974-78; apptd. and installed archbishop of Canberra and Goulburn Australia, 1979; archbishop of Sydney, 1983—, created cardinal,, 1988; chancellor Australian Cath. U., 1992—; installed as chancellor Australian Cath. U., 1992. Author: The Bible-The Church's Book, 1974; contbr. to Australian Cath. Record. Decorated Order of Austrlia, 1984, Companion of Australia, 1992. Avocations: reading, golf. Office: St Mary's Cathedral 13th Fl, Polding House 276 Pitt St, Sydney NSW 2000, Australia

CLANET, FRANK EMILE, physicist, educator; b. Fontenay-le-Comte, France, July 1, 1929; s. Emile and Denise (Aulagnier) C.; m. Marie Christiane Dellerm, Dec. 21, 1953; children: Marie-Carole, Marie-Luce, Fabienne. BS, U. Bordeaux, France, 1952, PhD in Pharm. Scis., 1953; PhD in Phys. Scis., U. Paris, 1968. Cert. univ. prof. Head chemist Nat. Marine, Paris, 1955-68; dir. svc. Commissariat de l'Energie Atomique, Paris, 1958-69; prof. edn. and rsch. U. François Rabelais, Tours, France, 1969—; acad. dean pharmaceutic scis. Faculty Tours, 1971-74; rschr. Inst. Radium, Paris, 1964-66. Translator: Electrochemistry (Milazzo) 1969; patentee in field. Mem. AAAS, Royal Soc. Chemistry Gt. Britain, Ste Francaise de Chimie, Assn. Sci. Europeene Pour Eau et Santé. Achievements include U.S. and European patents for Method for Filling an Aerosol Can with 2 Compartments, Collapsible and Inflatable Piston for Multi-Compartmental Containers, French patent for Procedure to Eliminate Impurities from a Liquid, U.S. and European patent for dispenser device with sealed closure for the contents of a receptacle that is pressurized or that has a pump. Office: 4 bis Sentier des Voisinoux, 92190 Meudon France

CLARAMMA, NARIVELIL MATHEW, chemist; b. Kottayam, India, Sept. 15, 1950; d. Mathew and Mariam Narivelil; m. Palackal Augustine Stanes, Aug. 20, 1978; children: Deepa Rani, Binu Roy. MS, St. Thomas Coll., Kottayam, India, 1972; PhD, Cochin U. Sci. & Tech., Kochi, India, 1998. Lab. asst. Rubber Bd., Kottayam, India, 1973-77, rsch. asst., 1977-84, asst. rubber chemist, 1984-88, rubber chemist, 1988—; rschr. in field. Avocation: reading. Home: Palackal House, Kottayam 686 018, India Office: Rubber Rsch Inst India, Rubber Bd PO, Kottayam 686 009, India

CLARAMUNT-VALLESPI, ROSA MARÍA, chemistry educator; b. Barcelona, Spain, Apr. 29, 1948; d. Francisco Claramunt and Primitiva Vallespí; children: David, Isabel. MS in Chemistry, U. Barcelona, 1969, PhD in Chemistry, 1973; DEA in Organic Chemistry, U. Montpellier, France, 1971; Thèse D'état in Organic Chemistry, U. Montpellier, 1976. Asst. prof. U. Barcelona, 1969-71; asst. étrangère U. Montpellier, 1971; rsch. worker U. East Anglia, Eng., 1973-74, U. Aix-Marseille III, France, 1974-79; tituar prof. U. Nacional Educación a Distancia, Madrid, 1981-86; prof. U. Nacional Educación a Distancia, 1986—; head dept. organic chemistry, 1986—; rsch. fellow U. Mons (Belgium), 1974-75, U. Lund (Sweden), 1974-75. Author 5 books on organic chemistry; contbr. 250 articles to profl. jours., 10 chpts. to books. Office: UNED Dept Quim Organ & Biol, Senda del Rey 9, 28040 Madrid Spain

CLARE, ANTHONY WARD, psychiatry educator, hospital administrator; b. Dublin, Ireland, Dec. 24, 1942; s. Bernard Joseph Clare and Mary Agnes Dunne; m. Jane Carmel Hogan, Oct. 4, 1966; children: Rachel, Simon, Eleanor, Peter, Sophie, Justine, Sebastian. MB BChir, Univ. Coll., Dublin, 1966; MPhil, London U., 1972; MD, Nat. U. Ireland, 1983; DSc (hon.), U. East Anglia, 1996; DPhil (hon.), Open U., Eng., 1994. Registrar St. Patrick's Hosp., Dublin, 1967-69; registrar, sr. registrar Maudsley Hosp., London, 1970-75; lectr., sr. lectr. Inst. Psychiatry, London, 1976-82; prof. psychol. medicine St. Bartholomew's Hosp., London, 1983-89; med. dir. St. Patrick's Hosp., Dublin, 1989—; clin. prof. psychiatry Trinity Coll., Dublin, 1989—; chmn. cen. com. King's Fund, London, 1984-89, Prince of Wales Adv. Group on Disability, London, 1989-97, Agy. for Personal Svc. Overseas, Dublin, 1994-99. Author: (books) Psychiatry in Dissent, 1976, Let's Talk About Me, 1981, In the Psychiatrist's Chair, 1984, vol. II, 1995, vol. III, 1998, On Men: Crisis in Masculinity, 2000. Recipient Sony award for Best Radio Interview of Yr., Sony Corp., 1996. Fellow Royal Coll. Physicians of Ireland, Royal Coll. Psychiatrists (London; v.p. 1994-96), Royal Coll. Physicians (London); mem. Garrick Club. Avocations: broadcasting, theater, writing, family life. Office: St Patrick's Hosp, James St, Dublin 8, Ireland

CLARE, BRIAN WILLIAM, computational and medicinal chemist, researcher; b. Wagerup, Australia, Dec. 13, 1940; s. Mario Dalla and Dorothy C. BS with honours, U. Western Australia, Nedlands, Australia, 1965, PhD, 1973. Chartered chemist. Rsch. asst. U. WA, Nedlands, Australia, 1973-75; rsch. technician Murdoch (Australia) U., 1975-80; profl. officer, 1981-99; rsch. officer U. Western Australia, 1981—; cons. Heartlink Pty. Ltd., 1999—. Contbr. numerous papers and articles to profl. jours. Mem. Royal Australian Chem. Inst., Royal Soc. Chemistry, N.Y. Acad. Scis. Home: 6 Antigonus St, Coolbellup 6163, Australia Office: Murdoch U, Dept Chemistry, Murdoch 6150, Australia

CLARE, GEORGE, safety engineer, systems safety consultant; b. Apr. 8, 1930; s. George Washington and Hildegard Marie (Sommer) C.; m. Catherine Saidee Hamel, Jan. 12, 1956; children: George Christopher, Kristine Ren.è. Student, U. So. Calif., 1961, U. Tex., Arlington, 1963-71, U. Wash., 1980. Cert. product safety mgr. Enlisted USN, 1948, advanced through grades to comdr., 1968, naval aviator, 1951-70; served in Korea; comdr. Res., 1963-70, ret., 1970; mgr. sys. safety missiles divsn. LTV Missiles and Electronics Group, Dallas, 1963-90. Mem. Nat. Rep. Com., Rep. Senatorial Com., Rep. Congl. Com., Rep. Senatorial Com., Rep. Congl. Com., Tex. Rep. Com., Citizens for Republic. Decorated Air medal with gold star, others. Mem. AIAA, Am. Security Coun., Internat. Soc. Air Safety Investigators, Sys. Safety Soc., Am. Def. Preparedness Assn., Naval Aviation, Ret. Officers Assn., Air Group 7 Assn. (pres.). Roman Catholic. Home and Office: 825 Bayshore Dr Apt 500 Pensacola FL 32507-3463

CLARIÁ, JUAN JOSÉ, astrophysics researcher, educator; b. Córdoba, Argentina, June 13, 1945; s. Roger Arturo and Delia Agueda (Rabellini) C.; m. Graciela Beatriz Somaré, Feb. 23, 1973; children: Juan J., Alejandro J., Santiago A., María Agustina, María Belén. BS, Nat. Coll. Montserrat, Córdoba, 1962; lic. in astronomy, Nat. U. Córdoba, 1969, PhD in Astronomy, 1973. Rsch. astronomer Córdoba Observatory, 1970-72; asst. prof. astrophysics Nat. U. Córdoba, 1973-74; assoc. prof. astrophysics U. Los Andes, Mérida, Venezuela, 1974-76, Fed. U. Rio Grande do Sul, Porto Alegre, Brazil, 1977-79; assoc. prof. astrophysics Nat. U. Córdoba, 1979-82, full prof. astrophysics, 1983—; dir. Astron. Observatory Córdoba, 1995—; pres. Scientific Com. CASLEO, San Juan, Argentina, 1994-95; Coun. Scientific and Technol. Rsch., Córdoba, 1993—. Author 2 books; contbr. over 160 articles to profl. jours. in field of astrophysics. Recipient award Scientific Soc. Argentina, Buenos Aires, 1995. Mem. Astron. Soc. Argentina (pres. 1987-90), Internat. Astron. Union, Royal Astron. Soc. Eng. Roman Catholic. Avocations: tennis, music, football, socializing. Home: Alonso de Alfaro 1761, Cordoba 5014, Argentina Office: Astronomical Observatory, Laprida 854, Cordoba 5000, Argentina

CLARIDGE, ELMOND LOWELL, retired engineering educator, consultant; b. Delaplaine, Ark., June 5, 1917; s. Elmond Lee and Irene Cynthia Gates (Compton) C.; m. Zola Ruth McDowell, Jan. 1, 1939 (dec. Oct. 9, 1990); children: David Elmond, Jonathan McDowell; m. Mary Lasley Moore, Feb. 11, 1995 (dec. Feb. 16, 1999). BS in Chem. Engring., U. Mo., Rolla, 1939, MS in Chem. Engring., 1941; PhD in Chem. Engring., U. Houston, 1979. Registered profl. engr., Tex. Rsch. chemist Shell Oil Co., Wood River, Ill., 1941-43, technologist, 1943-48; asst. chief rsch. Shell Oil Co., Houston, 1948-55, 57-60; sr. technologist head office Shell Oil Co., N.Y.C., 1960-64; group leader Royal Dutch Shell, Amsterdam, 1955-57; sr. rsch. assoc. Shell Devel. Co., Houston, 1964-79; assoc. prof. chem. engring. dept. U. Houston, 1979-91, dir. petroleum engring. grad. program, 1979-87; cons. Gulf Univs. Rsch. Consortium, Houston, 1979-85, TCA Reservoir Engring. Svcs., Houston, 1979—. Author: PE 506, Miscible Processes, 1992; contbr. articles to profl. jours. Recipient Disting. Life award St. Luke's United Meth. Ch., 1990. Mem. AIChE, AAAS, Am. Chem. Soc. (chmn. sub com. petroleum res. fund adv. com. 1985-88), Am. Petroleum Inst. (rsch. adv. bd. prodn. divsn. 1978-81), Petroleum Soc./Can. Inst. Mining, Metallurgy and Petroleum, Soc. Petroleum Engrs. (editor reprint book Surfactant/Polymer Chemical Flooding vols. I, II, 1982, Enhanced Oil Recovery Pioneer 1980), Sigma Xi, Alpha Chi Sigma. Achievements include ten patents. Home and Office: 5439 Paisley St Houston TX 77096-4025

CLARK, ALASTAIR TREVOR, barrister, museum administrator; b. Glasgow, U.K., June 10, 1923; s. William George and Gladys Catherine (Harrison) C.; m. Hilary Agnes Mackenzie Anderson, May 1, 1965. BA, Magdalen Coll., 1947, MA, 1948; postgrad., Ashridge Mgmt. Coll., 1963; called to bar, Inns of Ct., 1963. Sec. to cabinet, sr. dist. officer H.M. Overseas Civil Svc., Northern Nigeria, 1948-59; clk. of couns., dir. social welfare, prin. asst. Urban Coun., Hong Kong, 1960-72, colonial sec., acting chmn., 1960-72; chief sec. Western pacific high commn., acting gov. Solomon Islands, 1972-77; councillor City of Edinburgh Coun., Scotland, 1980-88; chmn. Scottish Mus. Coun., Scotland, 1981-84, 87-90; trustee Nat. Mus. of Scotland and Charitable Trust, 1985-87, 87—; dir. Royal Lyceum Theatre, Edinburgh, 1982-84, Edinburgh Acad., 1979-84; gov. Edinburgh Filmhouse, 1980-81, 87—; vice chmn. Almond Valley Heritage Trust, Livingston, Scotland, 1990—. Author: A Right Honorable Gentleman: Abubakar From the Black Rock, 1991; contbr. articles to profl. jours. Trustee Smith Art Gallery and Mus., Stirling, Scotland, 1993—; councillor Edinburgh Internat. Festival, 1980-86, 90-94; sec. St. John's Cathedral Coun., Hong Kong, 1963-72; assessor Scottish Sheriff Cts. Race Rels. Adv. Panel, Scotland, 1983—. Maj. Cameron Highlanders and Royal West African Frontier Force, 1942-46. Country leader fellowship U.S. State Dept., 1972; grantee Leverhulme Trust, 1979-81. Fellow Soc. of Antiquaries of Scotland, Royal Scotish Soc. of Arts; mem. The Athenaeum, The New Club. Avocations: music, theatre, collecting netsuke, reading, museums and galleries. E-mail: at-clark@globenet.co.uk. Home: 11 Ramsay Garden 2d Fl, Edinburgh EH1 2NA, Scotland

CLARK, ALFRED WILLIAM, retired sociology educator; b. Ouyen, Victoria, Australia, Aug. 31, 1925; s. Alfred Hoswell and Ida (Foulsham) C.; m. Lorel Mary Curry, May 15, 1994; children: Alice, Simon. BA with honors, U. Melbourne, Australia, 1956, MA, 1958; PhD, U. New South Wales, Sydney, Australia, 1966. Lic. Psychologist. Ednl. psychologist Victoria Edn. Dept., Australia, 1954-57; clin. psychologist Royal Children's Hosp., Melbourne, Australia, 1958-59; sr. lectr. U. New South Wales, Sydney, Australia, 1959-69; sr. social scientist Tavistock Inst., London, 1970-75; prof. La Trobe U., Melbourne, Australia, 1975-90, prof. emeritus, 1990—. Author: Social Science: Introduction to Theory and Method, 1983, Understanding and Managing Social Conflict: The Social Role Approach, 1992; co-author: Fraser House: Theory Practice and Evaluation of a Therapeutic Community, 1969; editor: Experimenting with Organizational Life, 1976; contbr. numerous articles to profl. jours. With Royal Australian Air Force, 1944-46, Darwin, Australia. Avocations: painting, golf. Home: 49 Warburton Rd, Canterbury VIC 3126, Australia

CLARK, ALICIA GARCIA, political party official; b. Vera Cruz, Mex.; came to U.S., 1970; d. Rafael Garcia Aully and Maria Luisa (Cobos) Garcia; m. Edward E. Clark, Oct. 20, 1970; 1 child, Edward E. MS in Chem. Engring., Nat. U. Mex., Mexico City, 1951. Chemist Celanese Mexicana, Mexico City, 1951-53, lab. mgr., 1951-53, sales promotion mgr., 1958-65, sales promotion and advt. mgr., 1965-70; nat. chmn. Libertarian Party, Houston, 1981-83, coord. coun. state chairs, 1987-95; pres. San Marino (Calif.) Guild of Huntington Hosps., 1981-82, chmn. Celebrity Series, 1989-90, 90-91. Pres. Multiple Sclerosis Soc., San Gabriel Valley, Calif., 1977-78, San Marino Woman's Club, 1989-90; bd. dirs. L.A. Opera League, 1990-96; founder, co-chair Hispanics for L.A. Opera, 1991-98; bd. dirs. L.A. Opera Assn., 1994—, Guild Opera Co., 1994-96, L.A. Music and Art Sch., 1995—; exec. brd. Club 100, 1996-99; v.p. bd. dirs. L.A. Opera, 1995—; mem. opera panel Nat. Endowment for Arts, 1997. Recipient award La Mujer de Hoy mag., 1969, Heroes of L.A. award Hispanic Traditions and Heritage Coun., 1995, Star of Our Culture award Mex. Cultural Inst. L.A., 1998. Mem. Fashion Group (treas. 1969-70, award 1970), San Marino Woman's Club (ways and means chmn. 1987-88).

CLARK, ANDREW ERIC, educator of economics; b. Newbury Park, Essex, Eng., Feb. 21, 1963; came to U.S., 1989; s. Frederick Lawrence and Joyce Aileen Gorton (Davies) C. BA, U. Warwick, Eng., 1985; MSc with distinction, London Sch. Econs., 1986, PhD, 1989. Vis. asst. prof. Dartmouth Coll., Hanover, N.H., 1989—; sr. rsch. officer U. Orléans, France, 1997—, U. Essex, 1991—; rsch. fellow CEPREMAP and Delta, 1993—; cons. OECD, 1995—; sr. rsch. prof. U. d'Orléans, 2000—. Author: U.K. Unemployment, 1989, 3rd edit., 1997. Mem. Am. Econ. Assn., Royal Econ. Soc. Office: Univ Orléans, LEO, 45067 Orléans France

CLARK, DAVID MCKENZIE, lawyer; b. Greenville, N.C., Sept. 1, 1929; s. David McKenzie and Myrtle Estelle (Brogdon) C.; m. Martha McKellar Early; children: David, Martha Dockery, Marietta Brogdon, Carolyn Elizabeth; m. Susan Summers Mullally; 1 child, McKenzie Lawrence. BA, Wake Forest Coll., 1951; LLD, NYU, 1957. Law clerk Chambers of Justice Black U.S. Supreme Court, Washington, D.C., 1957-59; assoc. Smith, Moore, Smith, Schell & Hunter, Greensboro, N.C., 1959-63; ptnr. Stern Rendleman & Clark, Greensboro, N.C., 1964-68, Clark & Wharton, Greensboro, N.C., 1968-98, Clark Bloss & McIver, Greensboro, 1999—. Mem. bd. dirs. Legal Svcs. of N.C., Raleigh, 1976-82; pres. Summit Rotary Club, Greensboro, 1967; mem. bd. trustees W. Market Street Methodist Ch., Greensboro; chmn., co-founder Greensboro Legal Aid Found., 1965-68. Mem. ABA, Am. Trial Lawyers Assn., Am. Bd. Trial Advocates, N.C. Bar Assn. (bd. govs. 1982-85), N.C. Acad. Trial Lawyers, Greensboro Bar Assn. (bd. dirs.). Avocations: golf, tennis. Home: 328 E Greenway Dr N Greensboro NC 27403-1560 Office: Clark & Wharton 125 S Elm St Ste 600 Greensboro NC 27401-2644

CLARK, FAYE LOUISE, drama and speech educator; b. La., Oct. 9, 1936; m. Warren James Clark, Aug. 8, 1969; children: Roy, Kay Natalie. Student, Centenary Coll., 1954-55; BA with honors, U. Southwestern La., 1962; MA, U. Ga., 1966; PhD, Ga. State U., 1992. Tchr. Nova Exptl. Schs., Ft. Lauderdale, Fla., 1963-65; faculty dept. drama and speech Ga. Perimeter Coll. (formerly DeKalb Coll.), Atlanta, 1967—; chmn. dept., 1977-81. Pres. Hawthorne Sch. PTA, 1983-84. Mem. Nat. Comm. Assn., Ga. Theatre Conf. (sec. 1968-69, rep. to Southeastern Theatre Conf. 1969), Ga. Psychol. Assn., Ga. Comm. Assn., Atlanta Press Club, , Friends of Atlanta Opera, Oglethorpe Mus., Southeastern Theatre Conf., Atlanta Hist. Soc., Atlanta Artists Club (sec. 1981-83, dir. 1983-89), Thalian-Blackfriars, Lake Lanier Sailing Club, Phi Kappa Phi, Pi Kappa Delta, Sigma Delta Pi, Kappa Delta Pi. Home: 2521 Melinda Dr NE Atlanta GA 30345-1918 Office: Ga Perimeter Coll Humanities Dept Dunwoody Campus Dunwoody GA 30338

CLARK, FRED, legal writer, editor; b. Limón, Costa Rica, Dec. 12, 1930; came to U.S., 1968; s. Thomas and Irene (Penney) C.; m. Dorothy Hyacinth James, Aug. 4, 1956; children: Paul, Fred Jr., Lydia Ramona. Student, Ctrl. Am. Acad., 1944-49; BLitt, U. Costa Rica, 1951; postgrad., Stafford Coll., 1956-57; barrister-at-law, Inner Temple, London, 1960. Bar: Eng. 1960, Jamaica 1960; cert. in law Coun. Legal Edn. Master of langs. Merl Grove Sch., 1951-55; trust officer Govt. of Jamaica, 1960-61; pvt. law practice Kingston, Jamaica, 1961-67; legal editor Corp. Trust Co., N.Y.C., 1968-69; sr. legal editor Prentice-Hall, Inc., Englewood Cliffs, N.J., 1969-91; cons. commonwealth law. Editor The Corp. Jour., 1968-69. Trustee United Ch. of Christ, 1970-78; spl. advisor U.S. Congl. Adv. Bd.; nat. adv. bd. Am. Security Coun. Recipient Disting. Leadership award, 1984, Presdl. medal of merit, 1986. Mem. Am. Mgmt. Assn., Internat. Platform Assn., Internat. Commn. Jurists, Am. Mus. Natural History, Nat. Geog. Soc., N.Y. Acad. Scis., Am. Ballet Theater, Met. Opera Guild, U.S. Naval Inst., Freeport Bus. Promotion (bd. dirs.), U.S. Power Squadron (asst. sec.), Inter-Am. Soc., Rosicrucians. Home: PO Box 291 Bergenfield NJ 07621-0291

CLARK, GORDON LESLIE, educator; b. Yallourn, Victoria, Australia, Sept. 10, 1950; s. Bryan and Leslie (Cowley) C.; m. Shirley Anne Clark, Dec. 19, 1972; 1 child, Peter. BA in Econs., Monash U., Melbourne, Australia, 1973, MA, 1975; PhD, McMasters U., Hmailton, Ontario, Canada, 1978. Asst. prof. Harvard U., Cambridge, Mass., 1978-83; assoc. prof. U. Chgo., 1983-85; prof. Carnegie Mellon U., Pitts., 1985—. Author: Unions and Communities Under Siege, 1989, Judges and the Cities, 1985, Interregional Migration, 1983. Co-author: Regional Dynamics, 1986, State Apparatus, 1984. Recipient Conf. Medal Royal Australian Planning Inst., 1988, Andrew Mellon Fellowship Nat. Research Coucil, 1981, Cert. of Appreciation Am. Inst. Architects, 1979. Mem. Am. Econ. Assn., Assn. Am. Geographers. Home: 5000 Forbes Ave Pittsburgh PA 15213-3815 Office: Ctr for Labor Studies Carnegie Mellon U Pittsburgh PA 15213

CLARK, GRANT LAWRENCE, corporate lawyer; b. Syracuse, N.Y., Apr. 15, 1954; s. Robert William and Linda (Grant) C.; m. Diana Christine Baker, Aug. 5, 1983. BA, Framingham State Coll., 1979; JD, Suffolk U., 1983. Bar: Mass. 1983, Calif. 1992, U.S. Dist. Ct. Mass. 1983, U.S. Dist. Ct. (so. dist.) Calif. 1992, U.S. Ct. Appeals (D.C. cir.) 1995, U.S. Ct. Claims 1995, U.S. Ct. Mil. Appeals 1984. Staff judge advocate USAF, Washington, 1983-87; asst. gen. counsel GSA, Washington, 1987-88; assoc. Rivkin, Radler, Dunne & Bayh, Washington, 1988-91; assoc./ptnr. McKenna & Cuneo, Washington, 1991-94; asst. gen. counsel Sci. Applications Internat. Corp., San Diego, 1994-99; v.p.-gen. counsel Telcordia Tech., Inc., Morristown, N.J., 1999—; instr. Fed. Publs., Inc., Washington, 1991—. Mem. pres.'s coun. Scripps Rsch. Found., LaJolla, Calif., 1998-99; mem. Founder's Soc., Morris Animal Found., Englewood, Colo., 1998-99. Capt., USAF, 1983-87. Mem. ABA, Fed. Bar Assn., Nat. Contracts Mgmt. Assn. Avocations: mountain biking, Latin dance, medieval history. Home: 229 Mount Kemble Ave Morristown NJ 07960-6209 Office: Telcordia Tech Inc 445 South St Morristown NJ 07960-6454

CLARK, IRA GRANVILLE, historian, educator; b. Amarillo, Tex., Jan. 23, 1909; s. Ira Granville and Centennial Germany (Seeger) C.; m. Jennalee McFall, Aug. 8, 1937 (dec. 1994); children: Ira Granville, David McFall. BA, West Tex. State Tchrs. Coll., 1931; MA, U. Okla., 1937; PhD, U. Calif., 1947. Tchr. pub. schs., Hollister, Okla., 1931-35; instr. Cen. High Sch. and Jr. Coll., Muskogee, Okla., 1937-42; from instr. to assoc. prof. N.Mex. State U., Las Cruces, 1942-51, prof., 1951-75, prof. emeritus, 1975—; state supr. Emergency Farm Labor program Agrl. Extension Svc., Las Cruces, 1943-45; cons. N.Mex. State Engr. Office, Santa Fe, 1981-82, Rio Grande Hist. Collections, N.Mex. State U. Libr., 1984, N.Mex. State Land Office, Santa Fe, 1988-89. Author: Then Came the Railroads, 1958, Water in New Mexico, 1987 (Border Regional Libr. Assn. award 1988); author (with others): Aridity and Man, 1963. Recipient Cert. of Recognition Gov. N.Mex., Santa Fe, 1976, Paso por Aqui award Rio Grande Hist. Collections, Las Cruces, N.Mex. 1987, Hon. Mention Abel Wolman award Am. Pub. Works Assn., 1988, Heritage Preservation award State N.Mex. 1988. Fellow AAAS; mem. Am. Hist. Assn., Orgn. Am. Historians, Western Hist. Assn. (coun. 1971-73, award of honor 1976), Agrl. Hist. Soc., Hist. Soc. N.Mex. (patron, bd. dirs. award 1988), Dona Ana County Hist. Soc. (patron, Pasajero del Camino Real award 1989). Democrat. United Methodist. Avocations: walking, bridge. Home: PO Box 253 Mesilla Park NM 88047-0253

CLARK, JAMES S., marketing executive; b. Stockholm, Sept. 19, 1942; s. Melvin James and Gun Elisabeth (Cederberg) C.; m. Inger Margareta Hansson, May 23, 1970; children: Tony, Robert. Degree in mktg. cons., Berghs/RMI, Stockholm, 1969, degree in advt. cons., 1970; degree in br. mgmt., Internat. Tng. Ctr., Rive-Reine, Switzerland, 1975. Brand mgr. John Norelid AB, Stockholm, 1969-73, Nestle, Bjuv, Sweden, 1973-77, GB-Glace subs. Unilever, Stockholm, 1977-82; mktg. mgr. Friggs Naturprodukter, Ekerö, Sweden, 1982-84; CEO A-Byrån advt. agy., Örebro, Sweden, 1984-85, Clark Mktg. AB, Örebro, 1986—. Author: Masterclass Sponsorship, 1996, Sponsorship in Summary, 1997, Finding and Keeping Sponsors, 1999; editor, author newsletter Aktuellt om Sponsring, 1988-99; contbr. articles to profl. jours. Leader Boy Scouts, Lidingö, Sweden; youth leader IK Frej, Taby, Sweden, 1978-84; bd. dirs. Örebro Chamber Choir, 1986-93. Mem. European Sponsorship Cons. Assn. (bd. dirs. 1997-99), Mktg. Assn. Stockholm (chmn. sponsorship group 1978-84), Örebro Västra Rotary Club (various offices), Stockholm Mktg. Assn., Swedish Pub. Rels. Assn., Swedish Acad. Bd. Dirs. Office: Clark Mktg AB, PO Box 1336, SE-70113 Örebro Sweden

CLARK, JANET, retired health services executive; b. Detroit, Oct. 3, 1941; d. John Francis Bullock and Martha Barbara (Bauer) Clark; m. Donald Bruce Tyson, Feb. 29, 1964; children: William John, Barbara June; m. Herman John Husmann, Nov. 11, 1988. AAS in Dental Hygiene, Broome C.C., 1961; BS in Health Edn., SUNY, Cortland, 1963; MPA in Mgmt., SUNY, Albany, 1993. Dental hygiene tchr. West Genessee Ctrl. Schs., Camillus, N.Y., 1964-65; health educator N.Y. State Dept. of Health, Syracuse, 1965-70; sr. sanitarian N.Y. State Dept. of Health, Monticello, 1977-80; prin. sanitarian N.Y. State Dept. of Health, N.Y.C., 1980-86; field ops. rep. N.Y. State Dept. of Health, Albany, 1986-89, mgr. Indian health, 1990-95, ret., 1995; sanitarian, health educator Onondaga County Health Dept., Syracuse, 1970-77; chmn., CEO Ha'awi Found. for Econ. Deve. in Indigenous Nations, 1994-2000; CEO J. Clark Enterprises LLC, 1999—; office mgr. Latham Area C. of C., 1995-97; CEO, CFO Workplace Safety Svcs. LLC, 1998-99, Alpha Strike Computers, 1998—. Mem. AAUW, NAFE, Am. Legion Aux., Nat. Environ. Health Assn., N.Y. Soc. Profl. Sanitarians (sec. 1970-84), N.Y. State Registry of Sanitarians (treas. 1987-90, pres. 1990-95, Meritorious Svc. award 1986), Hawaii C. of C., Elks. Avocations: reading, real estate, music, snorkeling, cards. Office: PO Box 6190 Hilo HI 96720-8924

CLARK, JESSIE DONA, social worker; b. Rochester, N.Y., Feb. 28, 1922; d. Robert Edward and Florence Virginia (Nelson) Bray; m. James Governeau Banks, Jan. 23, 1943 (div. Nov. 1972); children: James Governeau, Franklin Frazier, David Robert; m. Paul Andrews Clark, Jan. 21, 1973. BA, Howard U., 1947, MSW, 1960. Psychiat. social worker St. Elizabeths Hosp., Washington, 1960-65; family relocation officer D.C. Redey, Land Agy., 1965-73; supr. social worker Dept. Community Mental Health, St. Thomas, V.I., 1975; spl. asst. to comptroller V.I. Housing Auth., St. Thomas, 1975-85; evaluator, vice chmn. Operation Sisters United, St. Thomas, 1975-83; cons. V.I. Labor Mgmt. Com., St. Thomas, 1984—; cons. human resources dept. U. V.I., 1992—. Bd. dirs. YWCA (Phyllis Wheatley Br.), Washington; commr. Youth Coun., Washington, Vis. Nurses Assn., Washington, Ptnrs. for Health, St. Thomas (editor mo. newsletter 1988-89). Recipient Disting. Lady award Plymouth Congl. Ch., 1967, Outstanding Performance award D.C. Redevelopment Agy., 1971; NIMH fellow 1957-60. Mem. Internat. Assn. Pers. Mgrs. (v.p.), Nat. Assn. Housing & Renewal Officials, Nat. Assn. Social Workers (V.I. chpt., pres. 1985-87, Social Worker of Yr. 1983), Eta Phi Beta (v.p. 1988-89). Home: PO Box 8485 Saint Thomas VI 00801-1485

CLARK, JOAN HARDY, retired journalist; b. Toronto, Ont., Can., Apr. 17, 1934; came to the U.S., 1960; d. Henry Hardy and Irene Elsie Stevens; children: Lisa Anne Hanson, Anthony David Stuart Hanson. BA, Carleton U., Ottawa, Can., 1954; postgrad., Sarah Lawrence Coll., 1973-75. Bd. mem. Whitney Mus., N.Y.C., 1983—; chmn. coun. conservators N.Y. Pub. Libr., N.Y.C., 1986—, bd. mem., 1996—. Mem. Cosmopolitan Club. Home: 1 Gracie Sq New York NY 10028-8001

CLARK, JONATHAN MALCOLM, publishing director; b. Birmingham, U.K., Aug. 9, 1962; s. Malcolm Brian and Jennifer Anne (Thonger) C.; m. Elly Nijhoff, June 1, 1996; children: Alexander, Emma. BSc (hons.), U. Newscastle-upon-Tyne, U.K., 1983, PhD, 1987. Rsch. scientist Shell Rsch., Amstedam, The Netherlands, 1987-90; publ. editor Elsevier Sci., Amstedam, The Netherlands, 1990-93, mktg. mgr., 1993-95, assoc. publ., 1995-99, publ. dir., 1999—; guest lectr. Amsterdam Coll., Internat. Bus. Sch. Utrecht, The Netherlands. Contbr. articles to profl. jours.; patentee in field. Recipient Indsl. Chemistry Grad. award Salter's Inst. Indsl. Chem., 1983. Mem. KNRB (amateur rowing coach 1995—), Cornelis Tromp Rowing Club (regatta sec. 1998—). Avocations: rowing, mountaineering, cooking. Home: Rembrandtlaan 12, Loosdrecht 1231 AC, The Netherlands Office: Elsevier Science, Sara Burgherhartsfraat 25, Amsterdam 1055 KV, The Netherlands

CLARK, JOSEPH FLOYD, research scientist; b. White Plains, N.Y., Aug. 27, 1961; s. James Patrick and Beatrice Dill (Scova) C. BA, Susquehanna U., Selingsgrove, Pa., 1984; MS, Mich. State U., 1986; PhD, 1990. Rsch.

asst. Dept. Health and Exercise Mich. State U., E. Lansing, 1984-86; postdoctoral fellow Dept. Biophysics Centre U., Paris-Sud, France, 1990-91; lectr. and rschr. in biochemistry Oxford U., Eng., 1991-97; lectr. biochemistry Oxford U., 1997—; group leader Vasospasm Rsch. Group, Mill Hill, London, 1997—; cert. mem. Nat. Athletic Trainers Assn., 1984-94; guest spkr., adviser John Jay Sch. Sys., Cross River, N.Y., 1990-94; lectr. biochemistry Worcester Coll. Oxford; mem. Franco-Soviet Rsch. Exch., Paris, Moscow, 1990-91; lic. emergency med. tech. Dept. Health, N.Y., 1979-90; cons. in field. Author, editor: Creatine and Creatine Phosphate, 1996; contbr. articles to profl. jours.; patentee in field of vascular spasm diagnosis, 1996. Emergency room vol. Northern Westchester Hosp., Ctr. Mt. Kisto, 1979-84; ambulance vol. Katonah (N.Y.) Ambulance, 1979-89; mem. Rsch. Def. Soc., London, 1993-94. Recipient Jr. Rsch. fellow Linacre Coll., Oxford, Eng., 1992, Fogarty Internat. Rsch. award NIH, Bethesda, Md., 1990, travelling fellow Sasakawa Found., Nagoya, Japan, 1993, Rsch. grantee Knoll Pharm., Germany, 1993. Mem. Physiology Soc., Metabolic and Energetic Rsch. Group in Europe, Biochemical Soc., Biophysical Soc., Interna. Soc. Heart Rsch. Avocations: travel, photography, karate, skate boarding, water skiing. Office: U Oxford Biochemistry Dept, South Parks Rd, Oxford OX1 3QU, England

CLARK, JOSEPH FRANCIS, JR., lawyer; b. Tulsa, Okla., Jan. 20, 1949; s. Joseph F. and Betty Sue C.; m. Carol J. Coleman, Nov. 2, 1974 (div. 1981); m. Cathy A. Baker, Jan. 6, 1989; children: Joseph F. Clark III, Thomas S. Clark, Joshua B. Baker. BA, Villanova U., 1971; JD, Tulsa U., 1973. Bar: Okla. 1974. Atty. Gibbon, Gladd, Clark et al, Tulsa, 1974-78; pvt. practice Tulsa, 1979-80; atty. Williams, Clark et al, Tulsa, 1980-90; ptnr. Clark & Stainer, Tulsa, 1990-94, Layon, Cronin, Clark & Kaiser, P.L.L.C., Tulsa, 1994-99; pvt. practice Tulsa, 1999—. Mem. Am. Inns of Ct. (Council Oak chpt., term master 1996-98, master 1999—), Tulsa County Bar Assn. (fee dispute com. 1998-99). Democrat. Roman Catholic. E-mail: jclarkatt@aol.com. Home: 2922 E 39th St Tulsa OK 74105-3704 Office: 1605 S Denver Ave Tulsa OK 74119-4232

CLARK, KAREN SUE, editor, communications educator; b. Spokane, Wash., Aug. 15, 1952; d. Clifford French and Patty Ann (Ellis) C. BS in Wildlife Biology, Wash. State U., Pullman, 1974; MS in Comm., Ea. Wash. U., Cheney, 1993. Lab. technician molecular genetics dept., plant pathology dept. Wash. State U., Pullman, 1972-75; accounts payable supr. Gen. Store, Spokane, 1975-77; purchasing bookkeeper B.J. Carney & Co., 1977-81; supr. accounts payable Romac Corp., Spokane, 1981-82; bookkeeper lodge #228 Elks, Spokane, 1982-84; copy editor Internat. Amb. Programs, Spokane, 1984-86, sr. sci. editor, 1986-88, dir. publs. dept., 1988-89; grad. asst. comm. program Ea. Wash. U., Cheney, 1991-92; instr. intercultural and interperson comm., pub. speaking Spokane C.C., 1994—, Gonzaga U., Spokane, 1996—. Editor: Aerospace Education, 1988, Wildlife Management, 1988, Automatic Control Technology, 1988, Shellfish Production, 1987. Sch. bd. dir. Dist. 325/179, 9 Mile Falls, Wash., 1988-95, chair; acad. coach, Wash. State Nat. 4-H Horse Bowl Team, Washington, Denver, 1981, 83, 85; Spokane County alt. del. Rep. Convention, 1986, 88, 90; monitor water quality Assn. for Protection of Lake Spokane; founding sponsor Challenger Ctr. for Space Sci. Edn.; mem. comm. subject adv. com. Wash. State Commn. on Student Learning. Mem. Wash. State Sch. Dirs. Assn. (rep. 5th legis. dist. network 1989, 90, 91), Spokane Astron. Soc. Avocation: saddlemaking.

CLARK, KATHLEEN MARGARET CLAIRE, political scientist; b. Townsville, Australia, June 18, 1939; d. Russell and Leila (Harris) Skerman; m. Nicholas Forgan Clark, Apr. 1, 1961; children: Tanya, Douglas, Russell, Nicola. BA, U. Queensland, 1962, MA, 1964; PhD, U. Melbourne, 1969. Tutor U. Queensland, Brisbane, Australia, 1962-63; lectr. U. Melbourne and Royal Melbourne Inst. Tech., Australia, 1965-67, 69-73; pub. servant. Australian Pub. Svc., Canberra, 1973-89, asst. sec., 1983-89; asst. sec. Australian Capital Ter. Pub. Svc., Canberra, 1989-96; vis. fellow Australian Nat. U., Canberra, 1991-98. Editor: Australian Foreign Policy: Towards a Reassessment, 1973, Creating a Culture to Encourage Students with Disabilities, 1995; contbr. articles to profl. jours. Fellow Inst. Pub. Adminstrn. Australia (pres. Australian Capital Ter. divsn. 1987-89); mem. Internat. Inst. Strategic Studies, Australasian Polit. Studies Assn.

CLARK, KEITH COLLAR, musician, educator; b. Grand Rapids, Mich., Nov. 21, 1927; s. Harry Holt and Bethyl June (Collar) C.; m. Marjorie Ruth Park, Dec. 8, 1951; children: Nancy Joy McColley, Sandra Lynn Masse, Karen Jean Moore, Beth Anne Barnard. Student of trumpet, Nat. Music Camp, Interlochen, Mich., 1943, 44, 45; studied under Lloyd Geisler, 1947-48, studied under Armando Ghitalla, 1974. Trumpet player Grand Rapids Symphony Orch., 1943-46; with U.S. Army, 1946, advanced through grades to master sgt., 1966; trumpet player U.S. Army Band, Washington, 1946-66; ret., 1966; assoc. prof. brass Houghton (N.Y.) Coll., 1966-80; cons., asst. project dir. Dictionary Am. Hymnology, Bethesda, Md., 1980-81; prin. trumpet S.W. Fla. Symphony Orch., Ft. Myers, 1982-86, Treasure Coast Symphony Orch., Ft. Pierce, Fla., 1989-94, Atlantic Classical Orch., Vero Beach, Fla., 1991—; adj. prof. Edison C.C., Ft. Myers, 1984-89, Indian River C.C., Ft. Pierce, 1989-94; instr. Montgomery Coll., Bethesda, 1964-66, Roberts Wesleyan Coll., Rochester, N.Y., 1969-70; condr. Houghton Coll. Symphony Orch., 1966-78, Concert Band, 1975-80; lectr. Inst. Musica Suera Mexicana, Pueblo, 1973; guest condr. Buffalo Philharm. Orch., 1969, Treasure Coast Symphony Orch., 1990. Author: A Selective Bibliography for the Study of Hymns, 1980; assoc. editor The Instrumentalist mag., 1974-76; contbr. articles to profl. publs. Music dir. Maryland Avenue Bapt. Ch., Washington, 1947-51, Cherrydale Bapt. Ch., Arlington, Va., 1953-60, Christ Meth. Ch., Arlington, 1961-65, Vero Beach Alliance Ch., 1990-93. Recipient honor awards Nat. Sch. Orch. Assn., 1976, 80. Mem. Internat. Trumpet Guild (charter, project dir. 1978-80), Hymn Soc. of U.S. and Can. (life, grantee 1980-81), Ch. Music Soc. (Eng.) (life), Hymn Soc. Gt. Britain and Ireland (life), Nat. Ch. Music Fellowship (pres. 1967-69), Soc. of Am. Music. Avocations: collecting books and early records, jogging. Home: 801 Linnaen Ter NW Port Charlotte FL 33948-3616

CLARK, KENNETH JAMES, astronomer, educator; b. Wallasey, Merseyside, Eng., Dec. 22, 1950; s. James William and Elsie Victorine (Wilson) C.; children: Susan, Deborah, Neil. Nurseryman Wallasey Coun., 1967-70; engr. Brit. Telecom, 1970—. Mem. Brit. Astron. Assn., Liverpool Astron. Soc. (sec. 1990—). Avocations: photography, art, classical music, model-making, horticulture. Home and Office: 31 Sandymount Dr, Wallasey L45 0LJ, England

CLARK, MARK JEFFREY, paralegal, researcher; b. Alton, Ill., Nov. 2, 1953; s. William Alfred and Winifred May (Young) C.; m. Patricia Ann Newell, July 29, 1989; children: Jason William, Brandi Leigh. AS in Bus. Adminstrn., Lewis & Clark Coll., 1978; cert. paralegal, Paralegal Inst., Atlanta, 1994, diploma in civil lit. and bus. law, 1994. Commd. spl. officer Lake Ozark (Mo.) Police Dept., 1975-78; ind. paralegal J & B Enterprises, Woodriver, Ill., 1994—; criminal rschr. Pinkerton Svcs. Group, Charlotte, N.C., 1998—, MPC Legal Rsch. Consulting Svcs., Battle Creek, Mich., 1999—; cons., rschr. Nationwide Corps., 1994—. With USN, 1972-75, Vietnam. Mem. Nat. Paralegal Assn., KC (4th degree), Am. Legion. Democrat. Roman Catholic. Avocations: scuba diving, golf, bowling. Home: Rt # 71 Box 272 Camdenton MO 65020

CLARK, MARTIN PHILIP, telecommunications executive; b. Reading, Berkshire, Eng., Dec. 20, 1959; arrived in Germany, 1991; s. Colin Douglas and Sonia Gillian (Osborne) C.; m. Marabel Helen Goatly, July 8, 1989; children: Eliot, Joseph, Patrick. BA, Oxford (Eng.) U., 1981, MA, 1986; diploma in Econs., London Sch. Econs., 1992. Chartered engr.; registered European engr. Network planning mgr. Brit. Telecom Internat., London, 1981-89; group telecom mgr. Grandmet, London, 1989-91; network devel. mgr. Cable & Wireless Europe, Frankfurt, Germany, 1991-92; sr. mgr. Comm. Network Internat. GmbH, Frankfurt, 1993-95; telecomm. cons. Eppstein, Germany, 1995—; tech. dir., Europe Netro GmbH, Frankfurt, 1996-2000. Author: Networks and Telecommunications, 1991, 2d edit., 1997, Managing to Communicate, 1994, ATM Networks, 1996, Wireless Access Networks, 2000. Recipient Maurice Lubbock prize Oxford U., 1981, CEGB scholar, 1978-81. Mem. Instn. Elec. Engrs. (prizes 1979, 81). Avocations: rowing, piano playing.

CLARK, MARY JO, community health nurse; b. Omaha, Oct. 21, 1945; d. Jerome Martin and Mary Caroline (Seeger) Dummer; m. Philip Earl Clark, Mar. 10, 1979; 1 child, Philip Earl II. BSN, U. San Francisco, 1967; Pediatric Nurse Practitioner, UCLA, 1973; MSN, Tex. Women's U., 1979; PhD in Nursing, U. Tex., 1988. RN, Calif. Community health nurse U.S. Peace Corp, Vita, India, 1967-69; instr., asst. prof. East Tenn. State U. Sch. of Nursing, Johnson City, 1976-82; asst. prof. Med. Coll. of Ga. Sch. of Nursing, Augusta, 1982-86; prof. U. San Diego, Hahn Sch. of Nursing and Health Sci., Alcala Park, San Diego, 1986—; Univ. prof. U. San Diego, Philip Y. Hahn Sch. of Nursing, Alcala Park, San Diego, 1997; cons. Westinghouse Health Systems Agy., 1977-82; pediatric nurse practitioner L.A. County Dept. of Health Svcs., Whittier, Calif., 1973-76, pub. health nurse, 1970-73. Producer: (videotape) Intradermal Tuberculin Skin Testing, 1986; author: The Mentoring Game, 1984, Nursing in the Community, 1999, Community Health Nursing Handbook, 1999; contbr. numerous articles to profl. jours. Scout facilitator Boy Scout Troop 980, 1992, 91, health and safety coord., 1991—, pub. health merit badge counselor, 1991—; instr. positive parenting St. Therese Acad., 1987-90; mem. Red Cross Health and Safety Adv. Com., San Diego, 1986—; cons. San Diego County Health Dept., 1986-87; dir. Cmty. Outreach Partnership Ctr. Info. and Referral Svcs., 1996—. Nominated as Outstanding Faculty Mem. of Sch. of Nursing, Med. Coll. of Ga., 1984, 85, Outstanding Faculty Mem., East Tenn. State U., 1982; recipient Mother Mary Russell award U. San Francisco Sch. of Nursing, 1967. Mem. APHA, Nat. League for Nursing, Epsilon Sigma Chpt. Sigma Theta Tau, Zeta Mu Chpt., Sigma Theta Tau. Democrat. Roman Catholic. Avocations: reading, needlework, crafts. Home: 8359 Carlton Oaks Dr Santee CA 92071-2207 Office: U of San Diego Hahn Sch Nursing & Health Sci 5998 Alcala Park San Diego CA 92110-2476

CLARK, MAYREE CARROLL, investment banking executive; b. Norman, Okla., Mar. 9, 1957; d. Benton C. Clark and Joan M. (Harris) Richards; m. Jeffrey P. Williams, Apr. 28, 1984. BS, U. So. Calif., 1976; MBA, Stanford U., 1981. Econ. analyst Nat. Econ. Rsch., L.A., 1976-79; assoc. Morgan Stanley, N.Y.C., 1981-84, v.p., 1985-87, prin., 1987-89, mng. dir., 1990—, global rsch. dir., 1994—; adj. prof. Columbia U., N.Y.C., 1988-89. Chmn. Student Sponsor Partnership, N.Y.C., 1996-99. Republican. Office: Morgan Stanley and Co 1585 Broadway Fl 14 New York NY 10036-8200

CLARK, MERRELL MAYS, management consultant; b. Clifton Springs, N.Y., Feb. 8, 1935; s. Arthur Tillotson and Ruthanna Frame (Anderson) C.; m. Lynne Ruth Butcher, June 14, 1957; children: Elisabeth Lynne Clark Jenks, Aimee Ruthanna Clark Peterson, Catherine Merrell Clark Seda. BA, Yale U., 1957, MA in Religion, 1970. Asst. to advt. mgr. Armstrong Rubber Co., West Haven, Conn., 1959-60; mktg. analyst SSC & B, N.Y.C., 1960-62, account exec., 1962-64, v.p., account supr., 1964-68, v.p. mgmt. supr., 1968-70; prin. Knight, Gladieux & Smith, N.Y.C., 1970-72; v.p. Edna McConnell Clark Found., N.Y.C., 1972-77; exec. v.p. Acad. for Ednl. Devel., N.Y.C., 1977-81; prin. Clark Co., Scarsdale, N.Y., 1981—. Contbr. articles to profl. jours. Bd. dirs. Westchester Cmty. Svcs. Coun., White Plains, 1965-72, Elderhostel, Boston, 1977—, pres. Elderworks, Scarsdale, 1978—, Nat. Sch. Vol. Program, Alexandria, Va., 1977-89, chmn. nat. adv. bd., Coun. for the Arts in Westchester, White Plains, 1978-83, Scarsdale Found., 1981-90; advisor Nat. Exec. Svc. Corps, N.Y.C., 1977-87, United Way Scarsdale-Edgemont, 1989-97; treas. Greenacres Assn. Scarsdale, Inc. 1993-97; treas. Yale Westchester Alumni Assn., 1995-97, pres., 1997—. Mem. Fox Meadow Tennis Club, Yale Club. Republican. Presbyterian. Avocations: piano, organ, painting, platform tennis. Office: PO Box 1385 Scarsdale NY 10583-9385

CLARK, NOEL BRYAN, chemist, forester; b. Yallourn, Victoria, Australia, Dec. 16, 1953; s. Bryan Victor and Florence Lesley Clark; m. Merran Louise Coster, Feb. 3, 1990; 1 child, Lauren. Diploma in applied sci., Gippsland Inst. Advanced Edn., Churchill, Australia, 1976; PhD, U. Melbourne, Australia, 1998. Lab. supr. Unichema Australia, Melbourne, 1976-81; lab. and quality control supr. Sts. Ice Cream, Melbourne, 1981-84; exptl. scientist Commonwealth Sci. & Indsl Rsch. Orgn. Forestry and Forest Products, Melbourne, 1984-99; cons. Dept. Primary Industries, Brisbane, Australia. Co-author: The Young Eucalypt Report, 1991. Mem. Tech. Assn. Australian and New Zealand Pulp and Paper (mem. exec. com. 1985-99). Avocations: sailboarding, yachting. Office: CSIRO Forestry & Forest Products, Bayview Ave, Clayton 3169, Australia

CLARK, OLIVER NICHOLAS HUNTINGDON, management consultant; b. N.Y.C., Sept. 9, 1960; s. Richard Howland and Nancy (Schlumberger) C. BL, U. Sorbonne, Paris, 1982, lic., 1984; MSc, ESC, Rouen, France, 1996; MBA, Purdue U., 1996. Registered with World Bank, European Union, U.S. AID for overseas missions in devel. econs. Tng. mgr. Alexander Proudfoot, Brussels, 1984-85; asst. adminstrv. mgr. Cogefar, Tanzania, 1986-87; mktg. mgr. Enjeux de l'Europe, France, 1992-93; mng. ptnr. Sobic Internat., Belgium, 1993-95; ind. mgmt. cons., 1987-92, 95—. Author client tng. manuals, 1984—; contbr. articles to profl. publs. Aide de camp Marine Nat., 1980-81. Mem. Soc. of the Cincinnati (jr., life). Avocations: orchids, opera, antiques, horsemanship, gemology. Home: 39 Rue Fg St Denis, 75010 Paris France

CLARK, PAUL, airline analyst; b. London, Mar. 16, 1954; arrived in France, 1984; m. Judith Ann Holt, July 15, 1978. MSc, Poly. Inst. Cen. London, 1983. Various positions Brit. Railways Bd., London, 1972-84; gen. mgr. mktg. dept. Airbus Industrie, Toulouse, France, 1984—. Author: Railways of Devil's Dyke, 1976, Chichester and Midhurst Railway, 1980, Buying the Big Jets, 2000; producer film Devil's Dyke-A Victorian Pastime, 1980. Mem. Chartered Inst. Transport. Avocations: photography, chess. Home: 16 rue des Demoiselles, 31330 Ondes France Office: Airbus Industrie, 31700 Blagnac France

CLARK, PAUL ERNEST, university administrator; b. Radlett, Eng., Mar. 5, 1945; arrived in Australia, 1970; s. Ernest Leslie and Dorothy May (Holden) C.; m. Jean Siddall, Sept. 20, 1969; children: Jennifer Ann, Andrew Robert James. BSc with honors, Exeter U., Eng., 1966, PhD, 1970; Diploma Edn., Monash U., Australia, 1973. Lectr., sr. lectr. Monash U., Melbourne, Australia, 1970-81; head dept. physics Capricornia Inst., Rockhampton, Australia, 1981-88, dean sci., 1985-88; dep. dir. Footscray Inst. Tech., Melbourne, 1988-91; pro vice-chancellor rsch., prof. Victoria U. Tech., Melbourne, 1991-94, dep. vice-chancellor, prof., 1994-2000; dep. vice chancellor, prof. U. Sunshine Coast, Queensland, 2000—; bd. chmn. Victoria Univ. Enterprises, 1991-2000, Victoria U. Found., Melbourne, 1993-98; trustee Com. for Econ. Devel. Australia, 1994-2000; bd. dirs. Aust Food Industry Sci. Ctr., 1994-96. Contbr. 60 articles to profl. jours. Bd. mem. Regional Econ. Devel. Orgn. for Western Melbourne, 1994—. Fellow Australian Inst. Physics, Inst. Instrumentation and Control. Avocations: reading, gardening, bushwalking. Office: U Sunshine Coast, Maroochydore DC, Queensland 4558, Australia

CLARK, PHILIP HART, retired urban and regional planner; b. Hartford, Conn., May 23, 1938; s. Raymond Gilbert and Phyllis Angeline (Hart) C. BArch, Cornell U., 1961, M in Regional Planning, 1968. Asst. project mgr. W.R. Grimshaw Co., Denver, 1964-65; project coord. U. Pa., 1968-69; sr. planner County of Fairfax, Va., 1969-72; urban planner Hellmuth, Obata & Kassabaum, Washington, 1972-73; chief air transp. planning Met. Washington Coun. Govts., 1973-77; urban planning cons. Reston, Va., 1977-78; with Gordian Assocs., Washington, 1978-79; program mgr. base comprehensive planning USAF Engring. and Svcs. Ctr., Tyndall AFB, Fla., 1979-81; program mgr. base comprehensive planning hdqrs. USAF Pentagon, Washington, 1981-92; environ. restoration program mgr. Sta. Hdqrs. USAF Pentagon, Washington, 1992-98; ret., 1998; vis. lectr. George Washington U., 1975, Am. U. 1976-77, Air Force Inst. Tech., 1979-91, USAF Acad., 1989; speaker Soc. Am. Mil. Engrs. Mtgs., aviation assn. meetings. Mem. Paul Hill Chorale, 1970-76, Choral Arts Soc., 1977-79, 81-83, Reston Chorale, 1983-95, 99—, Kaleidoscope Theatre, Panama City, Fla., 1980-81, Washington Men's Camerata, 1995-97. Capt. USAF, 1961-64. Fellow Am. Inst. Cert. Planners; mem. Am. Planning Assn., Theta Chi. Democrat. Avocations: music, reading, swimming, travel, photography.

CLARK, REESE HUNTER, pediatric research executive, educator; b. Charlotte, N.C., Mar. 7, 1956; s. Eric III and Bettie C.; m. Carol B. Bedsole, Aug. 15, 1981; children: Reese Hunter Jr., Sheldon Dunham. MD, U. N.C., 1982. Residency in pediatrics Wilford Hall USAF Med. Ctr., San Antonio, 1982-85, fellow in neonatology, 1985-87; adj. scientist S.W. Found. for Biomed. Rsch., San Antonio, 1987-90; asst. prof. pediatrics Emory U. Sch. Medicine, Atlanta, 1990-93, assoc. prof., 1993-97; assoc. prof. Duke U. Sch. Medicine, Durham, N.C., 1997-99; consulting assoc. prof. pediatrics Duke U. Sch. Medicine, 1999—; dir. rsch. Pediatrix Med. Group Inc., Ft. Lauderdale, Fla., 1998—. Contbr. rsch. articles to profl. jours. Advisor FDA, Washington, 1995—. Major USAF, 1982-90, Tex. Recipient Andrew M. Margileth award for Clin. Rsch. in Pediat., 1990. Fellow Am. Acad. Pediat.; mem. So. Soc. Pediatric Rsch., Am. Thoracic Soc., Soc. Pediatric Rsch., Extracorporeal Life Support Orgn. (head protocols com. 1997—). Methodist. Avocations: running, biking. E-mail: reese clark@pediatrix.com. Office: Pediatrix Med Group Inc PO Box 559001 Fort Lauderdale FL 33355-9001

CLARK, ROBERT HENRY, JR., holding company executive; b. Manchester, N.H., Mar. 4, 1941; s. Robert Henry and Elva C. (Stearns) C.; m. Rosalie Foster Case, Dec. 21, 1963; children: Robert Henry III, Hilary Eagan, Hadley Case. BSBA, Boston U., 1964. Mcpl. bond underwriter Merrill Lynch, Pierce, Fenner & Smith, N.Y.C., 1964-70; v.p. Case, Pomeroy & Co., Inc., N.Y.C., 1971-75, exec. v.p., 1975-83; pres. Case, Pomeroy & Co., Inc., 1983—, CEO, 1993—, chmn., 1999—; v.p. fin. Felmont Oil Corp., 1972-79, exec. v.p., 1979-84; bd. dirs. Homestake Mining Co., FINOVA Group, Inc. Trustee Boston U., 1984-87. Mem. Sigma Alpha Epsilon. Office: Case Pomeroy & Co Inc 529 5th Ave Fl 16 New York NY 10017-4684

CLARK, ROBERT PHILLIPS, newspaper editor, consultant; b. Randolph, Vt., Dec. 3, 1921; s. James S. and Gladys M. (Phillips) C.; m. Jeanne Orr Rice, Dec. 14, 1949; children: Patricia Orr Clark Blackstone, Elizabeth Phillips Clark Christiansen. AB, Tufts U., 1942; MA, U. Mo., 1948. Reporter Owensboro (Ky.) Messenger & Inquirer, 1948-49; reporter, sci. writer Courier-Jour., Louisville, 1949-62; Washington corr. Courier-Jour., 1958; mng. editor Louisville Times, 1962-71; exec. editor Courier-Jour. and Louisville Times, 1971-79; exec. editor Fla. Times-Union and Jacksonville Jour., 1979-82; v.p news Harte-Hanks Newspapers, 1983-86; co-chmn. rsch. com. Newspaper Readership Project, 1982-83; news, editorial cons., 1987—; disting. vis. prof. Baylor U., 1990-92, Slippery Rock U., 1990; mem. accrediting com. Accrediting Coun. on Edn. in Journalism and Mass Comm., 1986-89. Author: Success Stories: What 28 Newspapers Are Doing to Gain and Retain Readers, 1988, Keys to Success: Strategies for Newspaper Marketing in the '90s, 1989; also numerous articles. Bd. dirs. Louisville Presbyn. Theol. Sem., 1968-73, past sec.; trustee S.W. Sch. of Art and Craft, 1993-96; bd. dirs. San Antonio Bot. Soc., 1996—; Pulitzer Prize juror, 1968, 69, 88, 89. Served to capt. U.S. Army, WWII, PTO. Decorated Bronze Star, Purple Heart; Nieman fellow Harvard U., 1960-61; named Editor of Yr., Nat. Press Photographers Assn., 1967. Mem. Am. Soc. Newspaper Editors (pres. 1985-86, v.p. Found. 1980-81, 85-86, contbr. Bull.), Soc. Profl. Journalists (contbr. Quill Jour.), AP Mng. Editors Assn. (pres. 1974-75, chmn. regents 1979-80), Internat. Press Inst. (bd. dirs. Am. com. 1981-87), Soc. Mayflower Descendants (capt. San Antonio colony 1999—), Club Giraud, Torch Club (San Antonio, pres. 1997-98), Harvard Club, Delta Tau Delta. Democrat. Presbyterian. Home: 3506 Elm Knoll St San Antonio TX 78230-2706

CLARK, ROSS BERT, II, lawyer; b. Lafayette, Ind., Dec. 23, 1932; s. Ross Bert and Pauline Frances (Wilkinson) C.; m. Madge Logan, Dec. 27, 1959; 1 stepchild, George W. Johnson III. BA in History, U. of the South, 1954; JD, U. Tenn., 1960. Bar: Tenn. 1961, U.S. Dist. Ct. (we. dist.) Tenn. 1961, U.S. Dist. Ct. (no. dist.) Miss. 1981, U.S. Dist. Ct. (ea. dist.) Ark. 1996, U.S. Ct. Appeals (6th cir.) 1962. Law clk. to presiding judge U.S. Dist. Ct. (we. dist.) Tenn., Memphis, 1961-62; assoc. Rupert & Ewing, Memphis, 1962-64, Laughlin, Watson, Garthright & Halle, Memphis, 1964-68; ptnr. Laughlin, Halle, Clark, Gibson, McBride, Memphis, 1968-84, McKnight, Hudson, Lewis, Henderson & Clark, Memphis, 1985-91, Apperson, Crump, Duzane & Maxwell, Memphis, 1991-96, Armstrong, Allen, Prewitt, Gentry, Johnston & Holmes, Memphis, 1996—; instr. med. and dental jurisprudence U. Tenn., Memphis, 1963-72; asst. city atty. City of Memphis, 1972-78. Chmn. bd. dirs. Memphis Heart Assn., 1971-72; mem. U. Tenn. Law Sch. Adv. Coun., 1983-90, chmn., 1986-88; trustee U. of The South, 1992-95, 98-2000. Fellow Am. Bar Found., Tenn. Bar Found. (trustee 1989-98, chmn. 1996-97); mem. ABA, Nat. Conf. Commrs. on Uniform State Laws (Tenn. commr. 1998—), Tenn. Bar Assn. (ho. of dels. 1986-88, bd. govs. 1988-94), Memphis Bar Assn. (treas. 1981, sec. 1982, v.p. 1983, pres. 1984), Rotary (sec. 1988, bd. dirs. 1988-90). Republican. Episcopalian. Office: Armstrong Allen Prewitt Gentry Johnston & Holmes LLP Brinkley Plz Ste 700 80 Monroe Ave Memphis TN 38103-2481

CLARK, R(UFUS) BRADBURY, lawyer; b. Des Moines, May 11, 1924; s. Rufus Bradbury and Gertrude Martha (Burns) C.; m. Polly Ann King, Sept. 6, 1949; children: Cynthia Clark Maxwell, Rufus Bradbury, John Atherton. BA, Harvard U., 1948, JD, 1951; diploma in law, Oxford U., Eng., 1952; D.H.L., Ch. Div. Sch. Pacific, San Francisco, 1983. Bar: Calif. 1952. Assoc. O'Melveny & Myers, L.A., 1952-62, sr. ptnr., 1961-93; mem. mgmt. com., 1983-90; of counsel O'Melveny & Myers LLP, L.A., 1993—; bd. dirs. Econ. Resources Corp., Brown Internat. Corp., Brown Citrus Sys., Inc., Avoco Internat. Corp., John Tracy Clinic, also pres. 1982-88, Tracy Family Hearing Ctrs. Editor: California Corporation Laws, 7 vols, 1976—. Chancellor Prot. Episcopal Ch. in the Diocese of L.A., 1967—, hon. canon, 1983—. Capt. U.S. Army, 1943-46. Decorated Bronze Star with oak leaf cluster, Purple Heart with oak leaf cluster; Fulbright grantee, 1952. Mem. ABA (com. law and acctg., task force on audit letters 1976-93, com. on opinions 1988-92), State Bar Calif. (chmn. drafting com. on gen. corp. law 1973-81, drafting com. on nonprofit corp. law 1980-84, mem. exec. com. bus. law sect. 1977-78, 84-87, sec. 1986-87, mem. com. nonprofit orgns. 1991—, mem. task force on opinions 1999—), L.A. County Bar Assn., Harvard Club, Chancery Club, Alamitos Bay Yacht Club (Long Beach, Calif.). Republican. Office: O'Melveny & Myers LLP 400 S Hope St Los Angeles CA 90071-2899

CLARK, SHELIA ROXANNE, sports association executive, legislative analyst; b. June 28, 1959; d. Milton Cornell and Mable Juanita (Grubb) C. BS in Polit. Sci., Radford U., 1983; MPA, James Madison U., Harrisonburg, Va., 1987. Dir. Black Teenage World Scholarship Program, Va., 1977-88; intern Field Found., New River Valley, Va., 1984-85, Rep. Rick Boucher, Washington, 1987; adminstrv. asst. OMB Watch, Washington, 1988; legis. asst. Nat. Community Action Found., Washington, 1988-93; exec. dir. Gary Clark's Sports Camp, 1990—; interim dir. talent search program Va. Tech. U., Blacksburg, 1997-98, athletic acad. advisor/lectr., 1998—, asst. coord.-student athletic Office of Acad. Enrichment, 1998—; project coord. Student Coalition Against Tobacco, 1994-95; cons., asst. Nat. Children's Day Found., Washington, 1991-93; advisor Soc. of African Am. Scholars, Alpha Kappa Mu, Va. Tech. U., Blacksburg. program dir. Project Unity, Va., 1984; bd. mem. VA Action, 1985, Grassroots Leadership Project, N.C., 1987; campaign worker Clinton Presdl. Campaign/Transition, Washington, 1992. Internship The Field Found., 1984-85, Congressman Rick Boucher, Washington, 1987. Mem. Nat. Council Negro Women. Office: Gary Clarks Sports Camp PO Box 202 Dublin VA 24084-0202

CLARK, STEPHEN RICHARD LYSTER, philosophy educator; b. Luton, Bedfordshr, U.K., Oct. 30, 1945; s. David Allen Richard and Mary Kathleen (Finney) C.; m. Edith Gillian Metford, July 1, 1972; children: Samuel, Alexandra, Verity. BA, Oxford U., 1968, MA, 1973, DPhil, 1973. Fellow All Souls Coll., Oxford, 1968-75; lectr. Glasgow U., 1974-83; prof. Liverpool U., 1984—, dean of arts faculty, 1995-98; Stanton lectr. Cambridge U., 1988-90, Wilde lectr. Oxford U., 1991. Author: The Moral Status of Animals, 1977, From Athens to Jerusalem, 1984, Limits and Renewals, Vols. 1-3, 1989-91, How to Think About the Earth, 1993, How To Live Forever, 1995, Animals and their Moral Standing, 1997, God, Religion and Reality, 1998, The Political Animal, 1999, Biology and Christian Ethics, 2000; editor: Jour. of Applied Philosophy, 1990-2000; list owner/internet bull. bd. Philos-L, 1989—. Scott Holland Lectureship, SH Trustees, 1992, Read Tuckwell Lectureship, Bristol U., 1994. Fellow Royal Soc. Arts; mem. Greenpeace (U.K.), Farm Animal Welfare Coun. (animal procedures com.). Anglican. Avocations: sci. fiction, computers. Office: U Liverpool, Dept Philosophy, Merseyside Liverpool L69 3BX, England

CLARK, SUSAN JEANNE, economics educator; b. Flint, Mich., Mar. 11, 1948; d. Daniel Robert and Joyce Ann (Ambrose) Glasson; m. John David Clark, Jan. 26, 1968; children: J. Daniel, Crystal A. BS, U. Mich., 1974; MA, U. Okla., 1982. Cert. tchr., Mich. Tchr. programming Genesee County Skills Ctr., 1973-74; tchg. asst. U. Okla., Norman, 1980-82; comml. realtor Barbara Lee & Assocs., Ft. Smith, Ark., 1982-84; instr. part-time Westark Coll., Ft. Smith, 1986-89, instr. econs., 1989—. Trustee, chmn. Ft. Smith Libr. Bd., 1982-92; sec. treas. Ft. Smith Symphony Guild, 1982-84; bd. trustees Immaculate Conception Sch., Ft. Smith, 1985-88. Office: Westark Coll PO Box 3649 Fort Smith AR 72913-3649

CLARK, TERESA WATKINS, psychotherapist, clinical counselor; b. Hobart, Okla., Dec. 18, 1953; d. Aaron Jack Watkins and Patricia Ann (Flurry) Greer and Ralph Gordon Greer; m. Philip Winston Clark, Dec. 29, 1979; children: Philip Aaron, Alisa Lauren. BA in Psychology, U. N.Mex., 1979, MA in Counseling and Family Studies, 1989. Lic. profl. clin. counselor, N.Mex.; nat. cert. counselor. Child care worker social svcs. divsn. Family Resource Ctr., Albuquerque, 1978-79; head tchr., asst. dir. Kinder Care Learning Ctr., Albuquerque, 1979-80; psychiat. asst. Vista Sandia Psychiat. Hosp., Albuquerque, 1980-87; psychotherapist outpatient clinic Bernalillo County Mental Health Ctr.-Heights, 1989-91; therapist adult program Charter/Heights Behavioral Health Sys., Albuquerque, 1991-2000. Vol. mental health svcs. disasters ARC. Mem. ACA, Am. Assn. Multicultural Counseling and Devel., Nat. Bd. Cert. Counselors, N.Mex. Health Counselors Assn. (former cen. regional rep., ethics chair, bd. dirs.), Mental Health Counselor's Assn., Billy The Kid Outlaw Gang Hist. Soc. Democrat. Avocations: music, camping, horseback riding, reading. Office: Charter Health Behav Hlth Sys 103 Hospital Loop NE Albuquerque NM 87109-2115

CLARK, THOMAS FETZER, sculptor, religious art educator; b. Elizabethtown, N.C., Oct. 19, 1928; s. James Hector and Angelyn (Fetzer) C. AB, Davidson Coll., 1949; BD, Union Theol. Sem., 1953; PhD, U. Aberdeen, Scotland, 1957. Youth dir. First Presbyn. Ch., Burlington, N.C., 1949-50; asst. pastor Westminster Presbyn. Ch., Bluefield, W.Va., 1953-55; assoc. prof. Davidson (N.C.) Coll., 1958-85; lead artist Cairn Studio, Davidson, N.C., 1978—. Office: Cairn Studio PO Box 400 Davidson NC 28036-0400

CLARK, THOMAS RYAN, retired federal agency executive, business and technical consultant; b. Aberdeen, Wash., Sept. 16, 1925; s. George O. and Gladys (Ryan) C.; m. Barbara Ann Thiele, June 14, 1948; children: Thomas R. III, Kathleen Clark Sandberg, Christopher J.T. Student, U. Kans., 1943-44; BS, U.S. Mil. Acad., 1948; MSEE, Purdue U., 1955; cert., U.S. Army Command and Gen. Staff Coll., 1960, Harvard U., 1979. Commd. C.E., U.S. Army, 1948, advanced through grades to col., 1968; ret. U.S. Army, 1968; program mgr. U.S. AEC, Washington, 1968-75; dep. mgr. Dept. of Energy, Albuquerque, 1976-83; sr. exec. svc., 1977; mgr. Nev. ops. Dept. of Energy, Las Vegas, 1983-87, ret., 1987; cons. in field Las Vegas and Albuquerque, 1987—; mem. adv. bd. Dept. Chem. and Nuclear Engring., U. N.Mex., 1984-91; mem. statewide adv. bd. Desert Research Inst., U. Nev., 1985-88. Editor, co-author: Nuclear Fuel Cycle, 1975. Trustee Nev. Devel. Authority, Las Vegas, 1984-88, Nat. Atomic Mus. Found., 1993—, pres., 1997-99. Decorated Legion of Merit, Bronze Star; named Disting. Exec., Pres. of U.S., 1982. Mem. Las Vegas C. of C. (bd. dirs. 1983-87), Sigma Xi, Tau Beta Pi, Eta Kappa Nu, Rotary Club of Albuquerque (pres. 1993-94). Episcopalian. Lodge: Rotary.

CLARK, WILLIAM, JR., political advisor; b. Oakland, Calif., Oct. 12, 1930; s. William and Mary Edith (Coady) C.; m. Judith Lee Riley, Sept. 11, 1954; 1 child, Jared Riley. BA, San Jose State U., 1955; postgrad., Columbia U., 1967-68; diploma with distinction, Nat. War Coll., 1977; LittD (hon.), Calif. State U., 1992. Dir. liaison dept. U.S. Civil Adminstrn., Naha, Japan, 1970-72; U.S.-Japan Trade Officer Am. Embassy, Tokyo, 1972-74, minister, 1981-85; polit. counselor Am. Embassy, Seoul, Republic of Korea, 1977-80; minister Am. Embassy, Cairo, 1985-86, charge d'affaires, 1986; dir. spl. trade activities Dept. of State, Washington, 1974-76, dir. Japanese Affairs, 1980-81, dep. asst. sec. state, 1986-89; ambassador to India, 1989-92; asst. sec. of state East Asian and Pacific affairs Dept. of State, Washington, 1992-93; Japan chair, sr. advisor Ctr. for Strategic and Internat. Studies, Washington, 1993-95; pres. Japan Soc., N.Y.C., 1996—; sr. advisor Ctr. for Strategic and Internat. Studies, Washington, 1996—. Lt. (j.g.) USN, 1950-53. Recipient Superior Svc. award Dept. Army, 1971, Outstanding Svc. award Dept. Army, 1972, Disting. Svc. award Pres. U.S., 1985, Meritorious Svc. award Pres. U.S., 1987, 89, Disting. Honor award Dept. State, 1989, Charles E. Cobb award Dept. State, 1991, Disting. lectr. Fgn. Svc. Inst., 1995. Mem. Am. Fgn. Svc. Assn., Asia Soc., Japan Am. Soc. (bd. dirs. 1994—), Am. Japan Soc. (bd. dirs. 1981-85, coun. fgn. rels. 1995—), Am. C. of C. (hon. mem. Tokyo 1981-85, Cairo 1985-86), Gizira Club (Cairo), Tokyo Am. Club, Pres.'s Estate Polo Club (New Delhi), Chevy Chase Club (Washington). Episcopalian. Avocations: tennis, riding, skiing, golf. Home: 420 E 54th St Apt 5J New York NY 10022-5150

CLARK, WILLIAM ARTHUR V., geographer, demographer; b. Christchurch, N.Z., Mar. 21, 1938; came to U.S., 1961; s. Edward Arthur and Gertrude Rita (MacDonald) C.; m. Valmai Ruth Kirklam, July 1, 1961 (div. Oct. 1971); m. Irene Stephanee Borah, Mar. 25, 1978; children: Elisa, Louisa, Clifton, Justin. BA, U. N.Z., 1960; MA, U. Canterbury, N.Z., 1961; PhD, U. Ill., 1964; Doctorem Honoris Causa, U. Utrecht, The Netherlands, 1992; DSc, U. Auckland, N.Z., 1994. Lectr. U. Canterbury, 1964-66; asst./assoc. prof. U. Wis., Madison, 1966-70; prof. geography UCLA, 1970—, chmn. dept. geography, 1987-92, 95-97, assoc. dir. Inst. Social Sci. Rsch., 1984-87; vis. prof. U. Amsterdam, 1981; Belle Van Zuylen prof. U. Utrecht, 1989; cons. state atty. gens. Mo., Calif., Wis., Minn. Author: Human Migration, 1986, Households and Housing, 1996, The California Cauldron: Immigration and the Fortunes of Local Communities, 1998; author/editor: Residential Mobility and Public Policy, 1980, Rediscovering Geography: New Relevance for Science and Society, 1997. Fellow-in-residence Netherlands Inst. Advanced Studies, The Hague, 1993, Guggenheim fellow, 1994-95. Fellow Royal Soc. New Zealand (elected hon. 1997); mem. Assn. Am. Geographers (Honors award 1986), Population Assn. Am. Anglican Ch. Achievements include research in district and appellate court rulings on demographic change and school desegregation. Avocations: skiing, scuba diving, sailing, music. Office: UCLA Dept Geography 405 Hilgard Ave Los Angeles CA 90095-9000

CLARK, WILMA JEAN MARSHALL, English language educator; b. Akron, Ohio, Apr. 18, 1928; d. Paul Marshall and Laura Mae Haught; m. Gerald F. Clark, Apr. 11, 1947; children: Thomas M., G. Michael, Kathleen S., Deborah J. BA, Akron U., 1961; MA, Morgan State U., 1970; PhD, U. Md., 1980. Tchr. English, Journalism, French Overlea Sr. H.S., 1961-67; tchr. English and Journalism Perry Hall Sr. H.S., 1967-68; chair English dept. Towsontown Jr. H.S., 1968-70; asst. prof. English Dundalk (Md.) C.C., 1970-72; assoc. prof. English Morgan State U., Balt., 1970-94; prof. English Ea. Christian Coll., Belair, Md., 1989-95; adj. prof. English Lincoln (Ill.) Christian Coll.-East Coast, 1995—; mem. Mountain Christian Sch. Bd., Harford County, Md., 1992—; founding mem. Mountain Christian High Sch., Harford County, 1996—. Contbr. articles to profl. jours. Mem. AAUP, Balt. Alliance of H.S./Coll. Educators, Coll. English Assn. (panel mem. nat. conf., treas./exec. bd. mid-Atlantic group). Home: 11518 Chapman Rd Kingsville MD 21087-1526

CLARKE, ADRIENNE ELIZABETH, biochemist; b. Melbourne, Victoria, Australia, Jan. 6, 1938; d. Valentine Clifford and Alice Louise (Patterson) Petty; m. Charles Peter Clarke, Aug. 14, 1959; children: Stephen Peter, Penelope Anne (dec.), Catherine Marjorie. BSc in Biochemistry with hons., U. Melbourne, Melbourne, 1958, PhD in Biochemistry, 1963. Sr. lectr. sch. botany to prof. U. Melbourne, 1979-85, prof., 1985—, laureate prof., 1999—; lt. gov. State of Victoria, 1997—; dir. Plant Cell Biology Rsch. Ctr., Melbourne, 1982—, Alcoa of Australia Ltd., 1993-96, Woolworths Ltd., Australia, 1994—, Western Mining Corp. Ltd., Australia, 1996—; mem. Prime Min.'s Supermarket to Asia Coun., Canberra, 1996—; mem. Prime Min.'s Sci. Coun., Canberra, 1990-96; head sch. botany U. Melbourne, 1991-93; chmn. CSIRO, Canberra, Australia, 1992-96. Author: Chemistry and Biology of (1-3)-B-glucans, 1992; co-editor: Carbohydrate-Protein Recognition, 1988, Genetic Control of Self-incompatibility and Reproductive Development in Flowering Plants, 1994; mem. editl. bd. Sci., Plant Ce Plant Jour., others. Mem. adv. coun. Aid Policy, Canberra, 1992-96. Fellow Australian Acad. Sci., Australian Acad. Technol. Sci. Engring., Janet Clarke Hall; mem. Nat. Acad. Sci., Order Australia, Internat. Soc. Plant Molecular Biology (pres. 1996—), Australian Mutual Provident Soc. (dir. 1994—), Victorian Bus. Round Table. Achievements include discovery that the gene controlling self-incompatibility in plants encodes a series of alletic ribonucleasus. Office: Sch Botany, U Melbourne, Parkville 3052, Australia

CLARKE, SIR ARTHUR CHARLES, author; b. Minehead, Somerset, Eng., Dec. 16, 1917; s. Charles Wright and Norah (Willis) C.; m. Marilyn Mayfield, June 15, 1953 (div. 1964). B.Sc. in Physics and Math. with 1st class honors, King's Coll., London, 1948; D.Sc. (hon.), Beaver Coll., 1971, U. Moratuwa, 1979; D.Litt. (hon.), U. Bath, Eng., 1988, U. Liverpool, Eng., 1995, U. Hong Kong, Beijing, 1996. Auditor British Civil Service, His Majesty's Exchequer and Audit Dept., London, 1936-41; asst. editor Science Abstracts Inst. of Elec. Engineers, London, 1949-50; lectr., author, 1951—; chancellor U. Moratuwa, Sri Lanka, 1979—; Vikram Sarabhai prof. Phys. Research Lab., Ahmedabad, India, 1980; underwater explorer, photographer Great Barrier Reef of Australia and coast of Ceylon, 1954-64; commentator with Walter Cronkite Apollo missions, 1968-70; dir. Rocket Pub. Co., Underwater Safaris, Sri Lanka; founder Arthur C. Clarke Centre for Modern Technologies, Sri Lanka, 1984—; trustee Inst. Integral Edn.; fellow Franklin Inst., 1971, King's Coll., 1977, Inst. of Robotics, Carnegie-Mellon U., 1981; lectr. U.S. and Britain, 1957-74; bd. dirs. Nat. Space Soc., Space Generation Found., Internat. Astronomical Union, Planetary Soc., Rocket Pub. Co., Eng., Underwater Safaris, Sri Lanka; chmn. Second Internat. Astronautics Congress, London, 1951; moderator "Space Flight Report to the Nation", N.Y., 1961; fgn. assoc. Nat. Acad. Engring. (U.S.); mem. adv. coun. Internat. Sci. Policy Found., Fauna Internat., Sri Lanka, Earth Trust. Author: (non-fiction) Interplanetary Flight, 1950, The Exploration of Space, 1951 (Internat. Fantasy award 1952), The Young Traveller in Space, 1953 (pub. as Going Into Space, 1954), (with R.A. Smith) The Exploration of the Moon, 1955, The Coast of Coral, 1956, The Making of a Moon, 1957, The Reefs of Taprobane, 1957, The Scottie Book of Space Travel, 1957, (with Mike Wilson) Boy Beneath the Sea, 1958, Voice Across the Sea, 1958, The Challenge of the Spaceship, 1959, The Challenge of the Sea, 1960, (with Wilson) The First Five Fathoms, 1960, (with Wilson) Indian Ocean Adventure, 1961, Profiles of the Future, 1962, The Treasure of the Great Reef, 1964, (with Wilson) Indian Ocean Treasure, 1964, (with editors of Life mag.) Man and Space, 1964, Voices from the Sky, 1965, The Promise of Space, 1968, (with astronauts) First on the Moon, 1970, Report on Planet Three, 1972, (with Chesley Bonestell) Beyond Jupiter, 1972, The View from Serendip, 1977, (with Simon Welfare and John Fairley) Arthur C. Clarke's Mysterious World, 1980, Ascent to Orbit, 1984, 1984: Spring-A Choice of Futures, 1984, (with Welfare and Fairley) Arthur C. Clarke's World of Strange Powers, 1984, (with Peter Hyams) The Odyssey File, 1985, Arthur C. Clarke's July 20, 2019: Life in the 21st Century, 1986, Arthur C. Clarke's Chronicles of the Strange and Mysterious, 1987, Astounding Days, 1989, Opus 700, 1990, How the World Was One, 1992, (with Welfare and Fairley) Arthur C. Clarke's A-Z of Mysteries, 1993, By Space Possessed, 1993, The Snows of Olympus, 1994, Front Line of Discovery: Science on the Brink of Tomorrow, 1994, Greetings, Carbon-based Bipeds, 1999; (fiction) The Sands of Mars, 1951, Prelude to Space, 1951, Islands in the Sky, 1952, Against the Fall of Night, 1953, Childhood's End, 1953, Expedition to Earth, 1953, Earthlight, 1955, Reach For Tomorrow, 1956, The City and the Stars, 1956, Tales from the White Hart, 1957, The Deep Range, 1957, The Other Side of the Sky, 1958, Across the Sea of Stars, 1959, A Fall of Moondust, 1961, From the Oceans, from the Stars, 1962, Tales of Ten Worlds, 1962, Dolphin Island, 1963, Glide Path, 1963, Prelude to Mars, 1965, The Nine Billion Names of God, 1967, (with Stanley Kubrick) 2001: A Space Odyssey, 1968, The Final Odyssey, 1997, The Lion of Comarre and Against the Fall of Night, 1968, The Wind from the Sun, 1972, Of Time and Stars, 1972, The Lost Worlds of 2001, 1972, Rendezvous with Rama, 1973 (Nebula award Sci. Fiction Writers Am. 1973, Hugo award World Sci. Fiction Conv. 1974, John W. Campbell Meml. award Sci. Fiction Rsch. Assn. 1974, Jupiter award Instructors of Sci. Fiction in Higher Edn. 1974), The Best of Arthur C. Clarke, 1973, Imperial Earth, 1975, The Fountains of Paradise, 1979 (Nebula award Sci. Fiction Writers Am. 1980, Hugo award World Sci. Fiction Conv. 1980), 2010: Odyssey Two, 1982, The Sentinel, 1983, Selected Works, 1985, The Songs of Distant Earth, 1986, 2061: Odyssey Three, 1988, (with Gentry Lee) Cradle, 1988, A Meeting with Medusa, 1988, (with Lee) Rama II, 1989, Tales from Planet Earth, 1989, (with Gregory Benford) Beyond the Fall of Night, 1990, Ghost from the Grand Banks, 1990, (with Lee) Garden of Rama, 1991, More Than One Universe, 1991, The Hammer of God, 1993, (with Lee) Rama Revealed: The Ultimate Encounter, 1994, (with Mike McQuay) Richter 10, 1996, 3001: The Final Odyssey, 1997, (with Mike-Kube-McDowell) Trigger, 1999, (with Stephen Baxter) The Light of Other Days, 2000; screenwriter: (films) (with Stanley Kubrick) 2001: A Space Odyssey, 1968 (Academy award nomination best original screenplay 1968, Second Internat. Film Festival Spl. award 1969); writer, host: (TV series) Arthur C. Clarke's Mysterious World, 1980, Arthur C. Clarke's World of Strange Powers, 1984, Mysterious Universe, 1994; actor: (films) Beddagama, 1979; editor: Time Probe: The Science in Science Fiction, 1966, The Coming of the Space Age, 1967, Three for Tomorrow, 1972, The Science Fiction Hall of Fame Vol. III, 1982. With Lindbergh Award Noms. Com. Served to flight lt. RAF, 1941-46. Recipient Presdl. award U. Ill., 1997. Fellow Royal Astron. Soc., Royal Soc. Arts; mem. Brit. Interplanetary Soc. (chmn. 1947-50, 53), Internat. Council Integrative Studies, AIAA, Inst. Engrs. Sri Lanka (named hon. fellow 1983), Sri Lanka Astron. Soc., Royal Astron. Soc., Assn. Brit. Sci. Writers (life), Internat. Acad. Astronautics, World Acad. Art and Sci., Nat. Space Inst. (dir.), Brit. Sci. Fiction Assn. (pres.), Royal Soc. Arts, Brit. Sub-Aqua Club, Brit. Astron. Assn., H.G. Wells Soc. (hon. v.p.), Sci. Fiction Writers Am., Internat. Sci. Writers Assn., Sci. Fiction Found., Soc. Authors (mem. coun.), Am. Astronautical Assn., Am. Assn. for Advancement of Sci., Nat. Acad. Engring., Third World Acad. of Scis. (assoc. fellow), Sri Lanka Animal Welfare Assn., Sri Lanka Assn. Advancement Sci., Sri Lanka Nat. Inst. Paraplegics, Astron. Soc. Haringey, Soc. Satellite Profls. (hon. chmn., Hall of Fame 1987), Nat. Space Soc. (bd. dirs., R.A. Heinlein Meml. award 1990), Royal Asiatic Soc., Astron. Soc. Pacific, Nat. Acad. Engring. (fgn. assoc.), U.N. Assn. Sri Lanka (hon. life pres.). Office: David Higham Assocs, 5 Lower John St Golden Sq, London W1R 4HA, England*

CLARKE, CATHRINE SYLVIA, jewelry designer; b. Santos, Brazil, Mar. 23, 1950; d. Robert and Lucy Sylvia (White) C.; m. Carlos Alberto de Ulhoa Canto, June 29, 1970 (div. Aug. 1988); children: Christian, Patrick, Sabrina. Student, Atelier Caio Mourão, Rio de Janeiro, 1990-91, Atelier Andrea Nicácio, Rio de Janeiro, 1997-98; studied gemology with, Walter Leite, Rio de Janeiro, 1999. Tchr. IBEU, Rio de Janeiro, 1982-87; owner Kate's Jewelry, Rio de Janeiro, 1988—. Exhibited jewelry at Brazil Pavillion Art Expo, 1998, Brazil Creative Zone Hong Kong Jewelry Fair, 1999; contbr. article to Ventura Cultural Bilingual Mag., 1999, and to book Design in the 21st Century, 1999. Recipient award for collection DeBeers, 1997, awards for handmade jewelry Brazilian Inst. Gems and Minerals, 1997, 98, Brazil's 500 Yrs. Commemorative award BSB Design, 1999. Mem. Ajorio Jewely Assn. Mem. Ch. of Eng. Avocations: travel, movies. E-mail: kates@domain.com.br. Office: Kate's Jewelry, Rua Visconde Piraja 547, LJ110 Rio de Janeiro 22410003, Brazil

CLARKE, DARREN, golfer; b. No. Ireland, Aug. 14, 1968; m. Heather; 1 chile, Tyrone. Turned profl., 1990; winner Ulster PGA, 1992, Alfred Dunhill Belgian Open, 1993, Irish PGA, 1994, Linde German Masters, 1996; 2d pl. finish Open Championship, 1997, Volvo PGA Championship, 1997; mem. winning team Ryder Cup, 1997. Placed 1st The Compass Group English Open, 1999-2000. Avocations: cars. Office: PGA 100 Avenue Of Champions Palm Bch Gdns FL 33418-3665 Office: Internat Sports Mgmt Ltd, Stocks Ln Over Peover, Knutsford Cheshire WA16 8TW, England*

CLARKE, DAVID MURRAY, psychiatrist; b. Melbourne, Victoria, Australia, Sept. 1, 1952; s. James Eric and Elizabeth Josephine (Kinross) C.; m. Denise Anne Cooper, Oct. 19, 1974; children: Nathanael, Hannah, Naomi. MBBS, Melbourne U., 1977; M in Psychol. Medicine, Monash U., 1989, PhD, 1996. Clin. asst. Royal Children's Hosp., Melbourne, 1981-83; registrar, psychiatrist St. Vincent's Hosp., Melbourne, 1984-87; registrar Prince Henry's Hosp., Melbourne, 1988; lectr. Monash U., Melbourne, 1989-98, assoc. prof., 1999—; dep. head cons. liaison psychiat unit Monash U. Med. Ctr., Melbourne, 1992—, head, 1994; chmn. bd. Keriva, Melbourne, 1988—. Contbr. chpt. in book and articles to profl. jours. Grantee Nat. Health and Med. Rsch., 1992-94, Doctoral Trustees, 1994. Fellow Royal Australian Coll. Gen. Practitioners, Royal Australian and New Zealand Coll. Psychiatrists (grant 1988); mem. Australasian Soc. Psychiat. Rsch., Internat. Coll. Psychosomatic Medicine, Acad. Psychosomatic Medicine. Office: Monash Med Ctr Dept Psychol Med, 246 Clayton Rd, Clayton Victoria 3168, Australia

CLARKE, EVELYN WOODMAN, volunteer; b. National City, Calif., May 24, 1917; d. William Irving and Lena Edah (Crouse) Woodman; m. George Samuel Clarke, May 25, 1935 (dec. Nov. 1974); children: Peter Brian, August William, George Woodman. Grad., Herbert Hoover H.S., San Diego, 1935; student, San Diego State Coll., 1935. Clk. U.S. Post Office, Grossmont, Calif., 1943-70. Del. 49th Congl. Dist. Calif. White House Conf. on Aging, 1995-96; mem. San Diego County Dem. Cen. Com., 1978-83; chair 78th Assembly Dist., 1985-86; alt. del. Dem. Nat. Conv., N.Y., 1980; commr. San Diego City Pub. Utilities Adv. Commn., 1992—, San Diego County Commn. on Status of Women, 1980-83; mem. program/budget rev. panel United Way, 1980-83; observer U.S. Nat. Conf. for Women, Houston, 1977, UN Internat. Women's Yr. Tribunal, Mexico City, 1975; mem. U.S. Dem. Congl. Campaign Com., U.S. Dem. Senatorial Campaign Com., Clinton/Gore '96 Campaign. Recipient Vol.'s commendation United Way, San Diego, 1983, Susan B. Anthony cert. NOW, San Diego, 1982; named Hon. Life Mem. Calif. Congress Parents and Tchrs., 1948. Mem. YWCA, Uptown Dem. Club, Emily's List, Nat. Women's Polit. Caucus (Spl. Recognition award 1993, Alice Paul award 1985), Older Women's League (Wonderful Older Woman's award 1985), San Diego Hist. Soc., San Diego Opera, San Diego Zool. Soc., UN Assn. Avocations: current events, photography. Home: 605 W Walnut Ave Apt A San Diego CA 92103-3987

CLARKE, FRANCIS GORDON, history educator, researcher; b. Melbourne, Australia, July 6, 1943; s. Walter Sinclair Nelson and Norma Mary (McDermott) Clarke; m. Janice Kerry Braysher, Dec. 28, 1963; children: Leon, Paul, Chifley. BA, U. Western Australia, Perth, 1965, MA, 1970; PhD, Dalhousie U., Halifax, N.S., Can., 1973. Sr. tutor in history Macquarie U., North Ryde, Australia, 1973-76, lectr. in history, 1976-79, sr. lectr. in history, 1980-91, assoc. prof. history, 1992—. Author: The Land of Contrarieties, 1979, Will-O'-The-Whisp, 1983, Australia: A Concise History, 1st edit., 1989, 2d edit., 1992, Korean lang. translation, 1995, The Big History Question: Snapshots of Australian History, 1998, Japanese translation, 2000, vol. 2, 2000. Avocations: walking, reading, yoga. Office: Macquarie U, School of History, North Ryde NSW 2109, Australia

CLARKE, GARY NORMAN, reproductive biologist; b. Ouyen, Victoria, Australia, Sept. 10, 1951; s. Mervyn and Norma Clarke; m. Susan Biggs; children: Emily, Oliver. BSc, Monash U., Melbourne, Australia, 1971, BSc with honors, 1972, MSc, 1976; postgrad., Melbourne U. Accredited Nat. Assn. Testing Authorities. Scientist Royal Women's Hosp., Melbourne, 1976-84, sr. scientist, 1985-95, unit mgr., 1995—; vis. scientist U. Hawaii, 1977-78; cons. Hamad Hosp., Qatar, 1988; plenary lectr. 4th World In Vitro Fertilization Congress, 1985. Contbr. book chpt.: CRC Handbook of the Laboratory Diagnosis and Treatment of Infertility, 1990; contbr. sci. papers and rsch. articles to profl. jours. Rsch. grantee Royal Women's Hosp., 1988, traveling scholar, 1992; rsch. grantee Nat. Health and Med. Rsch. Coun., 1989. Mem. Birds Australia, Med. Scientists Assn. Victoria, Fertility Soc. Australia (founding mem., bd. dirs. 1991-96), Scientists in Reproductive Tech. (founding mem., nat. coun. 1994-96). Avocations: bird watching, art appreciation, traveling, reading. E-mail: clarkga@cryptic.rch.unimelb.edu.au. Office: The Royal Women's Hosp, Andrology Unit, 132 Grattan St, 3053 Carlton Victoria, Australia

CLARKE, GEORGE ELLIOTT, writer; b. Windsor, N.S., Can., Feb. 12, 1960; s. William Lloyd and Geraldine Elizabeth (Johnson) C. Cert., Banff Ctr. Sch. Fine Arts, 1983; BA with honors, U. Waterloo, 1984; MA, Dalhousie U., 1989, LLD, 1999; PhD in English, Queen's U., 1993. Legis. intern Ont. Legis. Assembly, 1982-83; editor-in-chief, treas. Imprint Pubs., U. Waterloo, 1984-85; cmty. devel. worker Black U. Front of N.S., 1985-86; legis. asst. to Howard D. McCurdy MP, 1987-91; tchg. asst. English dept. Queen's U., 1991-93, asst. adj. prof., 1994; asst. prof. English and Can. studies Duke U., 1994-99; asst. prof. English U. Toronto, 1999—; writer-in-residence St. Mary's U., 1990, Selkirk Coll., 1991. Author: Saltwater Spirituals and Deeper Blues, 1983, Whylah Falls, 1990, Lush Dreams, Blue Exile, 1994, Beatrice Chancy, 1999, Whylah Falls: The Play, 1999; editor: Fire on the Water: An Anthology of Black Nova Scotian Literature 2 vols., 1991, 92, Eyeing the North Star: Directions in African-Canadian Literature, 1997; co-editor: Border Lines: Contemporary Poems in English, 1995; contbr. poetry to anthologies; columnist Halifax Herald Ltd., 1992—; weekly columnist The Daily News, Halifax, 1988-89. Recipient 1st prize adult poetry Writers' Fed. N.S., 1981, Archibald Lampman award for poetry Ottawa Ind. Writers, 1991, Portia White prize N.S. Arts Coun., 1998, Arts Alumni award U. Waterloo, 1999; Ont. Arts Coun. grantee, 1989, Can. Coun. grantee, 1990; Bellagio Ctr. resident Rockefeller Found., 1998. Mem. MLA, Writers' Fedn. N.S., Writers' Union Can., League Can. Poets, Can. Artists Network, Black Artists in Action, Black Cultural Soc. N.S. Baptist. Avocations: cinema, music. Office: U Toronto, 7 Kings Coll Cir, Toronto, ON Canada M5S 3K1

CLARKE, GRAEME WILBER, humanities educator, researcher; b. Nelson, New Zealand, Oct. 31, 1934; arrived in Australia, 1957; s. Wilber Patrick and Marjorie Edna (Le May) C.; m. Nancy Jean Jordan, Jan. 20, 1963; children: Brigid, Thomas, Edward, William. MA, U. New Zealand, 1956; BA, Oxford U., England, 1959; LittD, U. Melbourne, Australia, 1976. Lectr. Australian Nat. U., Canberra, 1957, 61-63; sr. lectr. U. Western Australia, Perth, 1964-66; assoc. prof. Monash U., Melbourne, 1967-68; prof. U. Melbourne, 1969-81; dir. humanities rsch. ctr. Australian Nat. U., Canberra, 1982-99. Author: The Octavius of Marcus Minocius Feliz, 1974, The Letters of St. Cyprian of Carthage, 4 vols., 1984, 86, 89; editor: Rediscovering Hellenism: The Hellenic Inheritance and The English Imagination, 1989, Reading the Past in Late Antiquity, 1989, Identities in the Eastern Mediterranean in Antiquity, 1998, Jebel Khalid on the Euphrates: Report on Excavations 1986-1996, vol. 1, 2000. Recipient fellowship Nat. Humanities Ctr., 1991-92, Trendall fellowship Brit. Sch. Rome, 1998-99. Fellow Soc. Antiquaries of London, Australian Acad. Humanities; mem. Inst. for Advanced Study. Roman Catholic. Avocations: gardening, home maintenance, archaeology. Home: 62 Wybalena Grove, Canberra 2614, Australia Office: Australian Nat U, History Dept, Canberra 0200, Australia

CLARKE, H(AROLD) DIGBY, clinical thanatologist, consultant; b. Montreal, Que., Can., July 4, 1931; s. Harold George and Florence Mae (Turner) C.; m. Jean McGowan, Sept. 6, 1963 (dec. May 1990); children: Christopher Digby, Sean Christian, Tamara A. Siobhan. BA, Concordia U., Montreal, 1955, B in Commerce, 1956; B in Civil Law, McGill U., Montreal, 1959; MA in Counseling Psychology, Adler Sch. Profl. Psychology, Chgo., 1994; cert. in thanatology, Mt. Ida Coll., Newton, Mass., 1995; postgrad., Pacific Western U., Hawaii, 1997. Bar: Que. 1960. Corp. solicitor Canadair Ltd., Montreal, 1960-63; assoc. advocate Laidley, Walsh, Campbell, Montreal, 1963-66; ptnr. Lesyk & Clarke, Montreal, 1966-72; sr. ptnr. Clarke, Kooiman & Wiley, Montreal, 1972-79; sr. counsel Adessky, Kingstone, Montreal, 1979-82; sr. ptnr. Heller, Clarke, Blond, Montreal, 1982-91; counselor, cons. Montreal, 1991-94; dir. Clarke, Wise & Villeneuve, 1960-75; profl. spkr. and writer. Contbr. articles to profl. jours.; web editor RecipesforLife (monthly newsletter). Bd. dirs. Victorian Order of Nurses, 1980-90, Hospice of So. Maine, Saco, 1993-96; mem. Old Orchard Beach Zoning Bd. Appeals, 1995-97. Fellow Am. Assn. Grief Counselors; mem. ABA, ACA, Assn. Death Edn. and Counseling, N.Am. Soc. Adlerian Psychology, New Eng. League Mid. Schs., Can. Guidance and Counselling Assn., Ont. Assn. Cons., Counsellors, Psychometrists, and Psychotherapists, Que. Bar Assn., Toastmasters (pres. Portland, Maine 1997). Anglican. Avocations: biking, skiing, sailing, study. E-mail: digcave@recipesforlife.com.

CLARKE, HENRY LEE, foreign service officer, former ambassador; b. Ft. Benning, Ga., Nov. 15, 1941; s. Edwin Lee and Jane Iredell (Jones) C.; m. Kathleen Ann Smith, May 19, 1973 (div. 1996); children: Ann Marie, Edwin Lee; m. Elena Anatolyevna Fedyai, Jan. 8, 1997; children: Julia Chikerenda, Christopher Lee. AB, Dartmouth Coll., 1962; MPA, Harvard U., 1967. U.S. fgn. svc. officer Dept. State, 1967-99; econ. counselor Am. Embassy, Moscow, 1982-85; dep. chief Am. Embassy, Bucharest, Romania, 1985-89;

econ. counselor Am. Embassy, Tel Aviv, 1989-92; amb. to Uzbekistan, Am. Embassy, Tashkent, 1992-95; internat. affairs advisor Nat. War Coll., Washington, 1995-98; sr. advisor for property restitution in Europe, Dept. State, Washington, 1998-2000; bd. dirs. Addex Inc., Boston. Chmn. bd. Am. Sch., Bucharest, 1985-89, Tashkent Internat. Sch., 1994-95.

CLARKE, J(OHN) NEIL, accountant; b. Aug. 7, 1934; s. George Philip and Norah Marie (Bailey) C.; m. Sonia Heather Beckett, 1958; 3 sons. LLB, U. London. Chartered acct. Ptnr. Rowley, Pemberton, Roberts and Co., Eng., 1960-69; with Charter Consolidated, 1969-88, dep. chmn., chief exec., 1982-88; chmn. Brit. Coal Corp., London, 1991-97; chmn. Johnson Matthey, 1984-89, Anderson Strathclyde, 1987-88, Molins, 1989-91, Genchem Holdings, 1989—; bd. dirs. Travis Perkins. Mem. MCC, Royal West Norfolk Golf Club, Addington Golf Club. Avocations: music, tennis, golf. Office: High Willows, 18 Park Ave Farnborough Pk, Orpington Kent BR6 8LL, England

CLARKE, LAMBUTH MCGEEHEE, retired college president; b. Salisbury, Md., Oct. 4, 1923; s. Hawes Palmore and Jessie Lee (Ham) C.; m. Alice Royall Acree, July 16, 1955; children: Leighton Krips, Palmore, Jessica, Virginia Hitch. BA, Randolph-Macon Coll., 1944, LLD (hon.), 1969; MA, Johns Hopkins U., 1948; postgrad., U. Birmingham, 1948, Harvard U., 1982. English instr. Randolph-Macon Coll., Ashland, Va., 1948-51, asst. to pres., 1951-58, v.p. devel., 1958-66; pres. Va. Wesleyan Coll., Norfolk, 1966-92, pres. emeritus, 1992—, also trustee; acting pres. Randolph-Macon Womans' Coll., 1993-94. Bd. dirs. Va. Symphony, Norfolk, 1970-88, trustee, 1990—; bd. dirs. Leigh Meml. Hosp., later Med. Ctr. Hosps., 1970-82, Norfolk Forum, 1970-80, World Affairs Coun., 1972-76, YMCA, Norfolk, 1972-78, Sta. WHRO-TV, 1972-76, Greater Norfolk Corp., 1978-92, Com. of 101-Future of Hampton Rds., Norfolk, 1983-92, Order of Cape Henry 1607, Norfolk, Va. Eye Found., Norfolk, 1973-92, Va. Coun. Chs., 1978-82; trustee Va. Found. Ind. Colls., Richmond, 1982-92, vice-chmn., 1990-92, assoc., 1992-97; trustee Randolph-Macon Womans Coll., 1992-97, hon. trustee, 1998—; mem. univ. senate United Meth. Ch., Nashville, 1988-92, bd. dirs., gen. bd. higher edn., 1980-88, del. jurisdictional conf., 1976-96, gen. conf., 1980-92; adv. bd. DePaul Med. Ctr., Norfolk, 1988-96; bd. dirs. Lee's Friends, 1993-99, adv. bd., 1999—; bd. dirs. Tidewater Scholarship Found., Westminster-Canterbury of Hampton Rds., Portsmouth Mus. Found., Inc., 1997-2000, Norfolk Bot. Gardens Found.; chmn. adminstrv. bd. Larchmont United Meth. Ch., 1993. Lt. (j.g.) USNR, 1943-46. Recipient Brotherhood citation NCCJ, 1991, John Wesley Disting. Educator award, 1991, Francis Asbury Educator award, 1995, Jerry G. Bray Dist. Svc. medal Va. Wesleyan Coll., 1997, Lambuth M. Clarke Acad. Ctr. of Va. Wesleyan Coll., 1999. Mem. Soc. Alumni Randolph-Macon Coll. (bd. dirs. 1993-99), Soc. of the Cin., Rotary Club Norfolk, Phi Beta Kappa, Omicron Delta Kappa, Phi Kappa Phi, Lambda Chi Alpha. Methodist. Avocations: volunteerism, reading, music, art and church architecture, philately.

CLARKE, MICHAEL PATRICK, ophthalmologist; b. Manchester, Eng., Mar. 30, 1959; s. William Joseph and Rose Veronica (O'Brien) C.; m. Hilary Geraldine Clarke, July 20, 1984; children: Thomas, Nicola, Laura, Felicity. MA, Cambridge U., 1982, MB B in Surgery, 1982. Registrar Leeds, U.K., 1986-88; sr. registrar Nottingham, U.K., 1988-90; fellow Hosp. for Sick Children, Toronto, Can., 1990-91; cons. ophthalmology Newcastle, U.K., 1991-99; sr. lectr. U. Newcastle, 1998—; head univ. dept. ophthalmology, Newcastle, 1995—; assoc. clin. sub dean Faculty of Medicine, U. Newcastle, 1999—. Editl. bd. Jour. of Pediatric Ophthalmology and Strabismus; contbr. articles to profl. jours. Sch. gov. Ponteland County Mid. Sch., 1997—. Fellow Royal Coll. Surgeons, Royal Coll. Ophthamologists; mem. Children's Eye Group (co-chmn.). Mem. Labour Party. Roman Catholic. Avocations: fishing, tennis. Office: Eye Dept, RVI, Newcastle upon Tyne NE1 4LP, United Kingdom

CLARKE, NICHOLAS CHARLES, metallurgical executive, mineral technologist; b. Ipswich, Suffolk, Eng., Feb. 2, 1948; s. Stanley Charles and Edna May (Howes) C.; m. Juliana S.C. Yap, June, 1998; 1 child, Frances May Lin. BS in Mineral Tech. with honors, Imperial Coll., London, 1969; Assoc., Royal Sch. of Mines, London, 1969; PhD, Leeds (Eng.) U., 1975. Registered profl. engr. Operator Falconbridge Nickel Mine, Sudbury, Ont., Can., 1968; mineral dressing engr. Sierra Leone Devel. Co. Ltd., Marampa, 1969-71; lectr. U. Tech., Lae, Papua New Guinea, 1975-77; sr. metallurgist Bougainville Copper Ltd., Panguna, Papua New Guinea, 1977-86; mgr. metallurgy Agnew (West Australia) Mining Co. Proprietary Ltd., 1986; resident mgr. Golden Spec Mine, Nullagine, West Australia, 1986-87; prin. cons. Normet Proprietary Ltd., Perth, West Australia, 1987-89; mng. dir., prin. cons. Normet (Malaysia) Sdn Bhd, Kuala Lumpur, 1989-92; prin. Imtech P/L, Applecross, W.A., Australia, 1992—. Fellow Instn. Mining and Metallurgy; mem. Australasian Instn. Mining and Metallurgy. Avocations: sailing, stage lighting, carpentry, theatre and cinema.

CLARKE, (MARY) PATRICIA, writer, editor, journalist; b. Melbourne, Victoria, Australia, July 30, 1926; d. John Laurence Riyan and Annie Teresa (McSweeney); m. Hugh Vincent Clarke, 1961; children: John, Justin, Brigid. Journalist News and Info. Bur., Australia, 1951-61, ABC, 1963-68; journalist, editor M. Newton Publications, 1968-73; editor Nat. Capital Devel. Commn., 1973-79. Author: The Governesses, 1985, A Colonial Woman, 1986, Pen Portraits, 1988, Pioneer Writer, 1990, Life Lines, 1992, Tasma, 1994 (Non-Fiction award Soc. Women Writers 1995), Tasma's Diaries, 1995, Rosa! Rosa!, 1999; editor: Canberra Hist. Jour., 1987—. Mem. classifications com. Nat. Trust, 1994-97; mem. programs com. Ctr. for Australian Cultural Studies, 1993—. Harold D. White fellow Nat. Libr. Australia, 1993, Literary fellow Literature Bd. Australia Coun., 1995; grantee several literary projects Literature Bd. Australia Coun., 1988-90. Mem. Canberra Dist. Hist. Soc. (councillor 1987—, v.p. 1995-97, pres. 1997-99), Ind. Scholars Assn. Australia (sec. 1995—), Nat. Press Club, Australian Soc. Authors, Australian Soc. Editors, Australian Soc. Indexers. Avocations: study of history. Home and Office: 14 Chermside St, Deakin Canberra ACT 2600, Australia

CLARKE, PETER GEOFFREY HATHERLEY, neurobiologist, educator; b. London, Dec. 29, 1946; arrived in Switzerland, 1977; s. John G.H. and Dorothy Joan (Rackham) C.; m. Stephanie Hosek, Oct. 6, 1979; children: Lydia, Christine. BA, U. Oxford, Eng., 1968, MA, 1972; PhD, U. Keele, Eng., 1972; MA, U. Oxford, Eng., 1972. Rsch. asst. U. Oxford, 1971-74; Wellcome rsch. fellow Washington U., St. Louis, 1974-75; rsch. officer U. Oxford, 1975-77; premier asst. U. Lausanne (Switzerland), 1977-80, maitre asst., 1980-85, asst prof., 1985—. Contbr. articles to profl. jours. Jr. Rsch. fellow U. Oxford, 1976-77; recipient Demuth award for Med. Rsch. Demuth Found., 1983. Mem. Physiol. Soc. U.K., European Neurosci. Assn., European Cell Death Orgn.

CLARKE, PHILIP H., law educator, university administrator; b. Newcastle, N. Umbrld, Eng., June 25, 1949; arrived in Australia, 1962; LLB, U. Western Australia, Perth, 1971; LLM, U. Auckland, New Zealand, 1974. Barrister and Solicitor. Lectr. in law Australian Nat. U., Canberra, 1974-79; dir. Law Reform Commn., Perth, Australia, 1980-82; sr. lectr. in law Monash U., Melbourne, 1983-88; assoc. prof. law Deakin U., Geelong, Australia, 1989-92; prof. of law Deakin U., Geelong, 1992—; dean faculty bus. and law Deakin U., 1999—; warden Garan Hall, Australian Nat. U., Canberra, 1976; mem. Consultative Com., TPC, Canberra, 1989-91, Coun. of Legal Edn., Melbourne, 1992—; head Sch. of Law, Deakin, Geelong, 1993—. Author: (books) Vertical Price Fixing, 1991, Contract Law, 1993; (encyclopedia sect.) Misleading Conduct, 1993, (with Corones) Consumer Protection and Product Liability, 1997, (with Corones) Competition Law & Policy, 1999, (with Gamble and Brebner) Contract Companion, 2000. Grantee: Com. for Advancement of Univ. Teaching, 1993, Nat. Priority Reserve Fund, 1994. Mem. ABA (assoc.) Law Inst. Office: Deakin U, Faculty Bus and Law, Geelong Vic 3217, Australia

CLARKE, RICHARD ALAN, electric and gas utility company executive, lawyer; b. San Francisco, May 18, 1930; s. Chauncey Frederick and Carolyn (Shannon) C.; m. Mary Dell Fisher, Feb. 5, 1955; children: Suzanne, Nancy C. Stephen, Douglas Alan. AB Polit. Sci. cum laude, U. Calif., Berkeley, 1952, JD, 1955. Bar: Calif. 1955. Pres. Pacific Gas and Electric Co., San Francisco, 1985-86, chmn. bd., CEO, 1986-94, chmn. bd., 1994-95; ptnr. Rockwell, Fulkerson and Clarke, San Rafael, Calif., 1960-69; bd. dirs. Pacific Gas & Electric Co., Potlatch Corp., CNF TransInc.; mem. Bus. Coun. Pres.' Coun. on Sustainable Devel. Bd. dirs., past chmn. Bay Area Coun.; trustee Boalt Hall Trust, Sch. Law U. Calif., Berkeley, U. Calif. Berkeley Found.; mem. adv. bd. Walter A. Haas Sch. Bus., U. Calif., Berkeley; chmn. adv. bd. Ctr. for Orgnl. and Human Resource Effectiveness, U. Calif., Berkeley; bd. dirs. Nature Conservancy of Calif.; co-chair U. Calif. Regents Outreach Adv. Bd.; mem. Pres.'s Coun. on Environ. Quality; chair Bay Area Econ. Coun. Mem. Calif. C. of C. (past dir.), San Francisco C. of C. (past dir., v.p. econ. devel.), Edison Elect. Inst. Office: Pacific Gas & Electric Co 123 Mission St # H17F San Francisco CA 94105-1551

CLARKE, ROBERT R., biochemist, researcher; b. Londonderry, Northern Ireland, Mar. 3, 1956; s. Thomas and Eileen (Mateer) C.; m. Leena Anikki Hilakivi, Sept. 24, 1989; children: Tomas, Johan, Robin. BSc, U. Ulster, Northern Ireland, 1980; MSc, Queen's U., Belfast, Northern Ireland, 1982, PhD, 1986, DSc, 1999. Fellow Royal Soc. Chemistry; Fellow Inst. Biology. Guest rschr. NIH, Bethesda, Md., 1987-88; asst. prof. physiology and biophysics Georgetown U., Washington, 1989-95, assoc. prof. physiology and biophysics, 1995-99, prof. oncology, physiology and biophysics, 1999—; cons. Am. Inst. for Cancer Rsch., 1990—, Cancer Rsch. Found. of Am., 1995—, NIH, 1996—, U.S. Dept. Def., Frederick, Md., 1995—, State of Nebr., 1999—, State of Calif., 1999. Mem. editl. bds.: Breast Cancer Rsch. and Treatment, 1992—, Oncology Reports, 1997—, Brit. Jour. of Cancer, 1997—, Jour. of Mammary Gland Biology and Neoplasia, 1999—; guest editor (monographs): Breast Cancer Research and Treatment, 1996, 97; patentee in field of breast cancer treatment; contbr. over 100 articles to profl. jours. and chpts. to books. Grantee NIH 1992—, 95—, 89—, Dept. Def. 1996—, 98—, 99—. E-mail: clarker@gunet.georgetown.edu Fax: 202-687-7505. Office: Georgetown Sch Medicine VT Lombardi Cancer Ctr 3970 Reservoir Rd NW Washington DC 20007-2126

CLARKE, RONALD JAMES, chemist, chemical engineer, consultant; b. Huddersfield, Yorkshire, Eng., Jan. 1, 1919; s. Walter James and Clarissa Mary (Burton) C. BA (hons.) in Chemistry, Oxford U., 1941, MA, 1946. Rsch. chemist Unilever Ctrl. Rsch., 1941-46; devel. mgr. Pears Ltd., Unilever, London, 1946-52; rsch. scientist Gen. Foods Ltd. (UK), London, 1957-84; ret.; coffee cons. Chichester, 1984—; tech. sec. Tech. Commn. of Assn. Fabricants de Cafe Soluble Europeen, Paris, 1980-84; vis. lectr. Queen Elizabeth Coll., U. London, 1972-74. Author: Process Engineering in the Food Industries, 1957, Memoirs, Down the Supermarket Aisles, 1999; author/co-editor: Coffee, vols. I-VI, 1985-88; contbr. articles to profl. jours.; patentee in field. Recipient Disting. Svc. cert. brit. Stds. Instn., 1993. Mem. Soc. of Chem. Industry (food engring. group com. mem. 1963—), Internat. Stds. Orgn. (coffee com. chmn. 1990-98), Assn. Scientifique Internat. Cafe (mem. coun. 1982—, medal 1982), Birdham Yacht Club (commodore 1987-88). Conservative Party. Ch. of Eng. Avocations: gardening, historical studies, yachting. Home: Ashby Cottage, Donnington, Chichester P020 7PW, England

CLARKE, THEO, management consultant; b. Southampton, Eng., June 11, 1958; s. Geoffrey Denzil and Hilda Margery (Thompson) C.; m. Cathy Simpson, Nov. 15, 1980 (div. Feb. 1986); m. Sonia Jane Duncan, Dec. 30, 1987. MBA, Open U., U.K., 1997. Project mgmt. profl., 1997; chartered info. sys. practitioner; cert. mgmt. cons.; chartered marketer. Archaeologist Eng. and Norway, 1976-80; computer operator Esso Petroleum Co. Ltd., London, 1981-83, tech. planner, 1983-86; cons. BSL Internat., Bromley, Kent, Eng., 1986-88, systems mgr., 1988-90; devel. environ. mgr. Woolwich Bldg. Soc., Bexleyheath, Kent, 1990-94, prin. mgmt. cons., 1994-95; sec. Hogshead Pub. Ltd., London, 1995-98; dir. Tignosis Ltd., London, 1993—, Modelmaking Supplies Ltd., London, Scensetters Ltd., London, SFC Press Ltd., London; CEO Chart Internat. Ltd., East Preston, West Sussex, 1997-99; chmn. Chart Internat. Group plc, 1999-2000; mng. dir. Playing Games, Ltd., London, 1999—, Not Just Games, Ltd., London, 1999—. Contbg. editor SFC Press, 1986-94, Games, Games, Games, 1994-98, Number, 1977-97; chair editl. bd. Project, 1995-98; contbr. articles to profl. jours. Freeman City of London, Worshipful Co. of Info. Technologists. Fellow Royal Soc. Arts; mem. IEEE (sr., cons. 1993—), Inst. Mgmt. Cons., Freeman Co. Mgmt. Cons. (ct. assts. 1996-99), Assn. Project Mgmt. (mem. exec. bd. 1996-98), Brit. Computer Soc. (cons. 1995-97), Inst. Mgmt. Info. Sys., Assn. Computing Machinery, Inst. Mgmt., Inst. Dirs., Royal Inst. Navigation, Project Mgmt. Inst., Assn. MBAs, Assn. Archaeol. Illustrators and Surveyors (licentiate), Inst. Field Archaeology (practitioner), Soc. Authors, Chartered Inst. Mktg. Avocations: board games, underwater archaeology, scuba diving, books and theatre. Office: Tignosis Ltd, 98 Choumert Rd, London SE15 4AX, England

CLARKSON, ADRIENNE, federal government official; b. Hong Kong, 1939; m. John Ralston Saul. BA with honours, U. Toronto, MA in English Lit.; postgrad., Sorbonne, Paris. Host, writer, prodr. CBC TV, 1965-82; first agt.-gen. for Ont. Paris, 1982-87; pres, pub. McClelland & Stewart, 1987-88; exec. prodr., host, writer Adrienne Clarkson's Summer Festival, Adrienne Clarkson Presents, 1988-98; gov. gen. Govt. of Can., 1999—; Chair, bd. trustees Can. Museum of Civilization, Hull, Que.; pres. exec. bd. IMZ, Vienna; active numerous arts and charitable orgns. exec. prodr., host CBC TV program Something Special, others; writer, dir. several films, Can. Named to Order of Can., 1992; recipient numerous awards. Office: Rideau Hall, 1 Sussex Dr, Ottawa, ON Canada K1A 0A1

CLARKSON, ELISABETH ANN HUDNUT, civic worker; b. Youngstown, Ohio, Apr. 20, 1925; d. Herbert Beecher and Edith (Schaaf) Hudnut;. AB, Wilson Coll., 1947; MA, State U. N.Y., 1973, also postgrad; LHD, Wilson Coll., 1985. m. William M.E. Clarkson, Sept. 23, 1950; children: Alison H., David B., Andrew E. With J.L. Hudson Co., Detroit, 1947-50; writer The Minute Parade daily Sta. WGR, Detroit, 1948-50. Author: You Can Always Tell a Freshman, 1949, An Adirondack Archive: The Trail to Windover, 1993; author articles, dramatic presentations, archival materials Adirondack Mus., 1950-77. Trustee Wilson Coll., Chambersburg, Pa., 1970-83, chmn. bd. trustees, 1979-82; bd. dirs. Buffalo Mus. Sci., 1972-87, 90-96; mem. Trinity Episcopal Ch., 1950—, Trinity Vestry, 1996-99, mem. cultural leadership group, 1994-96, 98—; mem. racism commn. Episcopal Diocese of Western N.Y., 1989-92; bd. dirs., companion-in-charge soc. Companion of the Holy Cross, 1986-90, N.Y. State Mus., 1985-90; pst chmn. jr. group Albright Knox Art Gallery; collector, curator Graphic Controls Corp. art collection, 1976-83; bd. dirs. Bischoff Clarkson Hudnut corp., North Creek, N.Y., 1973-83; bd. dirs. windover corp., 1997—, pres., 1998—; trustee Clarkson Ctr. for Human Svcs., 1995-2000, Irish Classical Theatre, 1998—; mem. Buffalo Art Commn., 1983—, chmn., 1990-96; mem. cmty. adv. panel Niagara Frontier Transp. Authority, 1991-94; mem. exec. bd. arts adv. coun. SUNY at Buffalo, 1985-95; bd. dirs. N.Y. State Mus. Assn., Albany, 1985-90; sustainer Jr. League, 1983—. Recipient Trustee award for disting. svc. Wilson Coll., 1983, award in the Arts, NCCJ, 1998. Mem. Garret Club, Buffalo Tennis and Squash Club, Sloane Club (London). Episcopalian. Home: 156 Bryant St Buffalo NY 14222-2003

CLARKSON, LAWRENCE WILLIAM, airplane company executive; b. Grove City, Pa., Apr. 29, 1938; s. Harold William and Jean Henrietta (Jaxtheimer) C.; m. Barbara Louise Stevenson, Aug. 20, 1960; children: Michael, Elizabeth, Jennifer. BA, DePauw U., 1960; JD, U. Fla., 1962. Counsel Pratt & Whitney, West Palm Beach, Fla., 1967-72, program dep. dir., 1972-75, program mgr., 1974-75; v.p., mng. dir. Pratt & Whitney, Brussels, Belgium, 1975-78; v.p. mktg. Pratt & Whitney, West Palm Beach, 1978-80; v.p. contracts Pratt & Whitney, Hartford, Conn., 1980-82, pres. comml. products div., 1982-87; sr. v.p. Boeing Comml. Airplanes Group, Seattle, 1988-91; corp. v.p. planning and internat. devel. Boeing Co., Seattle, 1992-93, sr. v.p., 1994-99; pres. Boeing Enterprises, Seattle, 1997-99; sr. v.p. Project Internat., Seattle, 2000—; bd. dirs. Partnership for Improved Air Travel, Washington, 1988-91; bd. dirs. Atlas Air, Avnet Inc., Interturbine NV, chmn., 2000—. Trustee DePauw U., Greencastle, Ind., 1987—; overseer Tuck Sch. Dartmouth, Hanover, N.H., 1993-99; corp. coun. Interlochen (Mich.) Ctr. for Arts, 1987, trustee, 1988—, chmn., 1996—; trustee Seattle Opera, 1990—, chmn., 1991—; pres. Japan-Am. Soc., Wash., 1993, pres. Wash. State China Rels. com., 1992-93; chmn. Nat. Bur. of Asia Rsch., Coun. Fgn. Rels.; chmn. U.S. Pacific Econ. Corp. Coun., 1993—. Mem. Nat. Assn. Mfrs. (bd. dirs. 1993-99), N.Y. Yacht Club, Seattle Yacht Club, Met. Opera Club, Wings Club (bd. govs. 1987-91, Order of St. John (comdr. 1994-99), Met. Club D.C., Am. Inst. Contemporary German Studies (bd. dirs.). Episcopalian. Home: 10127 NE 66th Ln Kirkland WA 98033-6870

CLARKSON, RICHARD CLAIR, publisher, editor, photographer; b. Aug. 11, 1932; s. Maurice Wolford and Mary Meta (Murphy) C. BS in Journalism, U. Kansas, 1956. Dir. photography Topeka (Kans.) Capital-Jour., 1958-79; asst. mng. editor/graphics The Denver Post, 1980-84; dir. photography, sr. asst. editor Nat. Geographic Soc., Washington, 1985-87; prin. Rich Clarkson and Assocs., LLC, Denver, 1987—; organizer, producer ann. workshops in sports photography with U.S. Olympic Com., and editorial and wildlife photography in Jackson Hole, Wyo; past lectr. adj. faculty U. Kansas Sch. of Journalism; lectr. at Mo. and Maine photographic workshops and at the Internat. Ctr. of Photography, N.Y.C.; juror Pulitzer prize in photography, 1986-87; judge and advisor Sasakawa Sports Found. and Competition, Tokyo. Co-author: (books) (with Cordner Nelson) The Jim Ryun Story, 1967, (with Bill Bruns), Sooner, 1972, Montreal 76, 1976, (with Bob Hammel) Knight with the Hoosiers, 1975, Silver Knight, 1996, (with Billy Reed) The Final Four, 1988; compiling editor The Kansas Century: 100 Years of Jayhawk Basketball, 1997; dir. of photography (book) A Day in the Life of America, 1986; producer-coord. (Brian Lanker project) I Dream a World: Portraits of Black Women Who Changed America, 1989; compiling editor World Champion Broncos, 1998. Trustee William Allen White Found., U. Kans; mem. hon. adv. coun. Nat. Mus. Wildlife Art, Jackson, Wyo., exec. com. W. Eugene Smith Meml. Fund, chmn. grant jury, 1995; founding officer Nat. Press Photographers Found. Named 1 of 50 most influential individuals in Am. photography, Am. Photo Mag., 1988. Mem. Nat. Press Photographers' Assn. (pres. 1975-76, past chmn. edn. com., twice chmn. Picture of Yr. jury). Office: Rich Clarkson & Assocs Denver Place Plaza Tower 1099 18th St Ste 1840 Denver CO 80202-1918

CLAROTTI, PAOLO CASIMIR, diplomat; b. Rome, Feb. 12, 1933; s. Giorgio Luciano and Janina (Rutkowska) C.; m. Laura S. Pane, Oct. 26, 1961; children: Giorgio, Silvia. Grad. law and econ. sci., Paris U., 1956. Prin. Ctr. for Productivity in Commerce, Rome, 1952-53; head sect. Fedn. Tradesmen, Milan, Italy, 1956-58; head rsch. dept. Fedn. Pub. Houses (Horeca), Rome, 1958-59; prin. adminstr. Commn. Eur. Communities, Brussels, 1959-71, adviser, 1971-72, head banking and fin. establishments div., 1972-86; adviser Commn. Eur. Communities, 1986-98, ret. hon. dir.; rep. officer Banca Popolare di Novara, Brussels, 1998—. Contbr. numerous articles to profl. jours. Sec. Brussels fedn. Italian Christian Dem. Party, 1975-79; chmn. Brussels sect. People's Eur. Party, 1979-84, Coun. Fgn. Residents, Auderghem, Belgium, 1976-88. Mem. Eur. Civil Servant Fedn. (founding, chmn. 1972-76). Roman Catholic. Office: Banca Popolare di Novara, Rue de l Industrie 40, 1040 Brussels Belgium

CLARY, BRADLEY G., lawyer, educator; b. Richmond, Va., Sept. 7, 1950; s. Sidney G. and Jean B. Clary; m. Mary-Louise Hunt, July 31, 1982; children: Benjamin, Samuel. BA magna cum laude, Carleton Coll., 1972; JD cum laude, U. Minn., 1975. Bar: Minn. 1975, U.S. Dist. Ct. Minn. 1975, U.S. Ct. Appeals (10th cir.) 1977, U.S. Ct. Appeals (8th cir.) 1979, U.S. Ct. Appeals (6th cir.) 1980, U.S. Ct. Appeals (7th cir.) 1981, U.S. Supreme Ct. 1986, U.S. Ct. Appeals (4th cir.) 1989, U.S. Ct. Appeals (9th cir.) 1991. Assoc. Oppenheimer Wolff & Donnelly, St. Paul, 1975-81, ptnr., 1982-2000; legal writing dir. Law Sch. U. Minn., 1999—; adj. prof. Law Sch. U. Minn., Mpls., 1985-99; adj. instr. William Mitchell Coll. Law, St. Paul, 1995-96, 98, adj. prof., 1997, 99. Author: Primer on the Analysis and Presentation of Legal Argument, 1992. Vestryman St. John Evangelist Ch., St. Paul, 1978-81, 98-00, pledge drive co-chmn., 1989-90, sr. warden, 2000—; mem. alumni bd. Breck Sch., Mpls., 1981-85, 89-96, exec. com., 1991-96, dir. emeritus, 1996—; mem. adv. bd. Glass Theatre Co., West St. Paul, Minn., 1982-87; mem. antitrust adv. panel dept. health State of Minn., 1992-93. Mem. ABA (adv. group antitrust sect. 1987-89, corp. counseling com.), Minn. Bar Assn. (program chmn. antitrust sect. 1986-87, treas. 1987-88, vice-chmn. 1989-90, co-chmn. 1990-92), Phi Beta Kappa. Avocations: tennis, sailing. Office: U Minn Law Sch 229 19th Ave S Rm 444 Minneapolis MN 55455-0400

CLARY, RICHARD WAYLAND, lawyer; b. Tarboro, N.C., Oct. 10, 1953; s. S. Grayson and Jean (Beazley) C.; m. Suzanne Clerkin, July 21, 1991; children: Grayson Edward, Taryn Fenner. BA magna cum laude, Amherst Coll., 1975; JD magna cum laude, Harvard U., 1978. Bar: N.Y. 1981, U.S. Dist. Ct. (so. and ea. dists.) N.Y. 1981, U.S. Dist. Ct. (no. dist.) Calif., 1982, U.S. Ct. Appeals (9th cir.) 1983, U.S. Supreme Ct. 1989, U.S. Ct. Appeals (3d cir.) 1990, U.S. Ct. Appeals (2d cir.) 1994, U.S. Ct. Appeals (fed. cir.) 1995, U.S. Ct. Appeals (11th cir.) 1999, U.S. Ct. Appeals (6th cir.) 2000. Law clk. to judge U.S. Ct. Appeals (2d cir.), N.Y.C., 1978-79; law clk. to Justice Thurgood Marshall U.S. Supreme Ct., Washington, 1979-80; assoc. Cravath, Swaine & Moore, N.Y.C., 1980-85, ptnr., 1985—, mng. ptnr. litigation, 1997—. Bd. dirs. Legal Aid Soc., 1998—. John Woodruff Simpson fellow Amherst Coll., 1975-76. Mem. ABA, Fed. Bar Found. (bd. dirs. 1998—), N.Y. State Bar Assn., Assn. Bar City N.Y., Fed. Bar Coun., Phi Beta Kappa. Episcopalian. Office: Cravath Swaine & Moore Worldwide Pla 825 8th Ave New York NY 10019-7475

CLARY, RONALD GORDON, insurance agency executive; b. Moultrie, Ga., May 2, 1940; s. Ronald Ward and Hazel (Collins) C.; m. Adrian Irene Baker; children: Lynn, Beth, Lindsay, Baker. Student, Young Harris Coll., 1958-60; BBA in Ins., U. Ga., 1963; LLB, Woodrow Wilson Coll. Law, 1966. Registered rep. fin. planner. Field rep. Comml. Union Ins. Cos., 1962-67; ind. ins. agt., 1967—; ins. agt., sec. of agy. Day, Reynolds & Parks, Gainesville, Ga., 1970-93, pres., 1993—; fin. planner, registered rep. Am. Express Fin. Advisors, Inc. Mem. Profl. Ins. Agts. Am., Ga. Assn. Ind. Ins. Agts., Gainesville Assn. Ind. Ins. Agts. (past pres.), Young Agts. Com. Ga. (past chmn.), Am. Legion, Elks, Rotary. Republican. Baptist. Avocations: tennis, sailing. Fax: 770-754-9690. Home: PO Box 211 Gainesville GA 30503-0211 Office: 2475 Northwinds Pky Ste 100 Alpharetta GA 30004-4800

CLARY, ROY, hospital administration executive; b. Winnipeg, Man., Can., Aug. 20, 1939; s. Omar LeRoy and Lois Ruth (Corey) C.; m. Marlene Alice Kogan; children: Megan Jennifer, Ethan Samuel. BA, Ohio State U., 1961; BFA/MFA, Art Inst. Chgo., 1964. Actor Seattle Repertory Theatre, 1964-66, Barter Theatre, Abingdon, Va., 1969-70, Great Lakes Shakespeare Festival, Lakewood, Ohio, 1970-71; campaign dir. USO of Metro. N.Y.C., 1973-78; assoc. dir. devel. NYU, 1978-87; exec. v.p. Calvary Hosp. Fund, Bronx, 1987—. Mem. Rotary (pres. Bronx club 1996-97). Avocations: chess, golf, theatre. Office: Calvary Hosp Fund 1740 Eastchester Rd Bronx NY 10461-2322

CLAUBERG, ROLF, physicist; b. Solingen, Germany, May 31, 1956; arrived in Switzerland, 1985; s. Werner and Luise A. (Pickelein) C. Diploma in Physics, U. Cologne, Germany, 1980, D Natural Sci., 1984. Sci. asst. Forschungszentrum Zülich, Germany, 1979-84, rsch. staff mem., 1984-85; rsch. staff mem. IBM Rsch., Rüschlikon, Switzerland, 1985-91, mgr. laser characterization and modeling, 1991-92, mgr. VLSI design, 1992-97, mgr. high-speed adapters, 1997—; mem. contractless testing com. Informationstechn. Ges./Verein Deutscher Elektro-techniker, 1988-92, Cost 216 Project of European Union, 1990-91; working group vice-chmn. Cost 240 Project of European Union, 1991-93. Contbr. articles to profl. jours., chpts. to books; patentee in field. Recipient Max Auwärter award Auwärter Found. and Austrian Vacuum Soc., Balzers, 1981. Mem. Am. Phys. Soc., German Phys. Soc., Informationstechn. Ges./Verein Deutscher Elektro-techniker. Office: IBM Rsch Divsn, Säumerstr 4, 8803 Rueschlikon Switzerland

CLAUDEL, NICOLAS, hepatogastroenterologist; b. Saigon, South Vietnam, Mar. 22, 1960; s. Roger and Yolande (Huard) C.; m. Pascale Koch, July 19, 1980; children: Anne, Edouard. MD, Faculty of Medicine, 1984, specialist gastroenterology, 1989; cert. pharmacology, U. Lyon I, 1992; diploma of med. statistics, U. Paris VI, 1993. Intern Hosp. Complex, Lyon, 1984-89; asst. H.I.A. Desgenettes, Lyon, 1990-93, sr. registrar, 1993-94, hosp. svc. head, 1995—; cons. Hosp. Complex, Lyon, 1990—; tchr. U. Lyon I, France, 1990—. Commdr. Health Svc. of French Army, 1994—. Fellow Soc. Francaise D'Endoscopie Digestive, Soc. Francaise de Medecine des Armées. Avocations: motorbiking, stunt-riding, theatre, traveling. Office: HIA Desgenettes, 108 Boulevard Pinel, 69275 Lyon France

CLAUS, JÜRGEN, visual artist, writer; b. Berlin, Germany, May 28, 1935; s. Hermann and Helene (Kochs) C.; m. Nora Toni Koch Claus, August 11,

1987. U. Marburg, 1954-60, U. Munich, 1954-60. Fellow rsch. affiliate MIT Media Arts, Cambridge, Mass., 1983-88; lectr. Acad. Fine Arts, Munich, 1986—; prof. Acad. Media Arts, Cologne, 1991-2000. Author: Expansion of Art, Rowohlt Verlag Hamburg, 1970, The Electronic Bauhaus, Zurich, 1987, Sonnenmeer, 1995, Kulturelement Sonne, 1997; one-man shows include exhibitions from 1958— at Berlin, Lisbon, Cologne, Milan, Rome, Osaka, Munich and other cities; solar sculptures in pub. spaces, 1995, 98. Recipient Prix Lago Maggiore, Video Art Festival, Locarno, 1988, European Solar prize Eurosolar, Bonn, Germany, 1995. Home and Office: Overoth 5, B-4837 Baelen Belgium

CLAUSEN, AMIE JO, adult day center administrator; b. Blair, Nebr., Aug. 6, 1970; d. Richard Lee and Lorraine Leah (Lorsch) Hansen; m. Clint Ray Clausen, Sept. 15, 1990; children: Jolee Kay, Jordan James. A Human Svcs., S.E. C.C., Lincoln, Nebr., 1990; cert. nursing asst., Good Shepherd Luth. Home, Blair, 1993. Cert. nursing asst., activity dir., Nebr. Activity dir. Crowell Meml. Home, Blair, 1990-92; asst. dir. Shepherd's Watch Adult Day Ctr., Blair, 1993-97, dir., 1997—; mem. Ea. Nebr. Office on Aging, Blair, 1998—; presenter in field, 1997—. Mem. social concerns com. Arlington (Nebr.) Cmty. Ch., 1994-96; mem. Washington County Ext. Bd., Blair, 1997—; mem. Christian edn. com. 1st Luth. Ch., Blair, 1999—; mem. bd. Good Tidings Presch., Blair, 1999—. Mem. Nat. Coun. on Aging, Nat. Adult Day Svcs. Assn., Nebr. Adult Day Car Assn. (sec. 1997-98, pres. 1999-01), Nebr. Rural Health Assn., Nebr. Homes and Svcs. for Aging Assn. Republican. Avocations: crafts, gardening, rubber stamping, family time.ž. Home: 2607 College Dr Blair NE 68008-1036 Office: Good Shepherd Luth Home 2242 Wright St Blair NE 68008-1148

CLAUSEN, CLAUS ANDREAS, marine biologist; b. Fredrikstad, Norway, Aug. 1, 1922; s. Olaf Georg and Marie Elise (Johansen) C.; m. Astrid Bolette Bech, July 17, 1955; children: Inger Anne, Berit Elisabeth. PhD in Sci., U. Oslo, 1955. Lectr. H.S., Elverum, Norway, 1955-57; lectr. U. Bergen, Norway, 1957-65, assoc. prof., 1965-92. Contbr. articles to profl. jours. Mem. Internat. Assn. Meiobenthologists. Avocations: astronomy, local history. Home: Ekornvegen 19, N-5236 Bergen Norway Office: Inst Zoology, Univ Bergen/Allegt 41, N-5007 Bergen Norway

CLAUSEN, THOMAS HANS WILHELM, chemist; b. Luebeck, Fed. Republic Germany, Apr. 20, 1950; s. Hans August and Lotte Henny Adele (Stubbendorf) C.; m. Monika Maria Epe, June 21, 1980; children: Lars Christopher, Lisa Katharina Joseline. Diploma in Chemistry, U. Kiel, Fed. Republic Germany, 1974, PhD in Chemistry, 1977. Asst. Christian Albrechts U., Kiel, 1974-78; hair dye rschr. Wella Ag, Darmstadt, Fed. Republic Germany, 1978-83, head dept. rsch. hair dyes, organic chemistry, 1983-87, head dept. chem. rsch., 1987-89, R&D hair care, 1989-97, v.p. R&D personal care, 1997-99; sr. v.p. R&D Wella Ag, Darmstadt, 1999—. Co-author: Ullmann Encyclopedia, 1989, 97; spkr. various congresses, 1988; contbr. articles to profl. jours.; patentee in field of hair dyes, hair care and organic chemistry. Mem. Gesellschaft Deutscher Chemiker, Am. Chem. Soc. Avocations: house and garden activities, photography, video, electronics. Home: Auf dem Kreuzberg 8, D 64342 Seeheim Germany

CLAUSS, FREDERIC, sales executive; b. Stratbourg, France, July 3, 1967; s. Charles and Narlene (Nunch) C.; m. Valerie Dereonaucourt; 1 child, Jeremy. Sales Alcatel Cable Switzerland, 1991-94, sales mgr., 1994-96, sales mgr. North and South Am., 1996-97, head comml. svcs., 1997—. Avocations: mountain biking, skiing. Office: Alcatel Cable Switzerland, Rue Francois Borel, 2016 Cortaillod Switzerland

CLAUSSEN, BJÖRGULF, medical researcher; b. Oslo, Aug. 16, 1944; s. Odvar and Marit (Norderhaug) C.; m. Liv Knutsson, Jan. 3, 1966; children: Harald, Laila, Unni. MD, Oslo U., 1969, PhD, 1994. Asst. psychiatry Ullevaal (Norway) Hosp., 1971, gen. practitioner, 1972-87; rsch. fellow Oslo U., 1988-91, asst. prof., 1992—. Author: Without Work and Health, 1994; contbr. articles to profl. jours. Rsch. fellow Oslo U., 1988-91. Home and Office: Social Security Medicine, PO Box 1130, N-0317 Oslo Norway

CLAUSSEN, LISA RENEE, engineering executive; b. Cedar Grove, Wis., Mar. 28, 1964; d. Erwin John and Shirley Ann (Winkelhorst) C. BS in Indsl. Engring., U. Wis., Platteville, 1987; MS in Ops. Mgmt., U. Ark., Fayetteville, 1990. Registered profl. engr., Wis. Quality engring. process coord. Speed Queen Co., Ripon, Wis., 1987-88; plant quality control engr. Speed Queen Co., Searcy, Ark., 1988-90; quality engring. rep. Snap-on Inc., Kenosha, Wis., 1990-92, quality engr. med. products divsn., 1992-94; quality assurance supr. Snap-on Inc., Elizabethton, Tenn., 1994—. Active Nat. Kidney Found. Wis., Milw., 1994—. Recipient Outstanding Recent Alumnus award U. Wis.-Platteville, 1999. Mem. NAFE, Am. Soc. for Quality (sr., cert. quality engr., cert. quality auditor, SMP coord. Racine-Kenosha sect. 1992-94, membership chair N.E. Tenn. 1995-96, chair elect 1996-97, chair 1997-98, past chmn. 1998-99, dir. 1999—), Inst. Indsl. Engrs. (sr., bd. dirs. Ctrl. Ark. 1989-90, dir. support Tri-Cities Tenn. 1995-97, pres.-elect 1998-99, pres. 1999-2000, past pres. 2000—, asst. regional v.p. region 3 2000—). Avocations: music, literature, travel, science/science fiction. Office: Snap On Inc 2195 State Line Rd Elizabethton TN 37643-4683

CLAVEL, BERNARD CHARLES HENRI, writer; b. Lons-le-Saunier, France, May 29, 1923; s. Henri and Heloise (Dubois) C.; m. Andrée David, 1945 (div. 1982); children: Roland, Gérard, Yves; m. 2d Josette Pratte, 1982. Author: L'ouvrier de la nuit, 1956, Pirates du Rhône, 1957, Qui m'emporte, 1958, Paul Gauguin, 1958, L'Espagnol, 1959, Malataverne, 1960, La célébration du bois, 1962, Le voyage du père, 1965, L'Hercule sur la place, 1966, Leonard de Vinci, 1967, L'Arbre qui chante, 1967, La maison des autres, 1962, Celui qui voulait voir la mer, 1963, Le coeur des vivants, 1964, Les fruits de l'hiver, 1968, Victoire au Mans, 1968, L'espion aux yeux verts, 1969, Le tambour du bief, 1970, Le massacre des innocents, 1970, Le seigneur du fleuve, 1972, Le silence des armes, 1974, Lettre à un képi blanc, 1975, La voyage de la boule de neige, 1975, La saison des loups, 1976, La lumière du lac, 1977, Ecrit sur la neige, 1977, Fleur de sel, 1977, La femme de guerre, 1978, le Rhône ou les métamorphoses d'un dieu, 1979, Le chien des Laurentides, 1979, L'Iroquoise, 1979, Marie Bon Pain, 1980, La bourrelle, 1980; (with Josette Pratte) Felicien le fantôme, 1980; Compagnons du Nouveau-Monde, 1981; Terres de mémoire, 1981; Arbres, 1981; Poèmes et Comptines, 1981; Le hibou qui avait avalé la lune, 1981: Odile et le vent du large, 1981; Rouge Pomme, 1982; l'Homme du Labrador, 1982; Harricana, 1983; l'Or de la terre, 1984; Le roi des poissons, 1984; Le mouton noir et le loup blanc, 1984; Miserere, 1985; L'oie qui avait perdu le nord, 1985; Au cochon qui danse, 1986, Amarok, 1987; l'Angélus du soir, 1988, le Grand voyage de Quick Beaver, 1988; Maudits sauvages, 1989, Quand j 'etais capitaine, 1990; Meurtre sur la Grandvaux, 1991; La révolte à deux sous, 1992; Cargo pour l'enfer, 1993; Les Roses de Verdun, 1994; Le Carcajou, 1996; Jésus, le fils du charpentier, 1996; La Guinguette, 1997; Contes et Légendes du Bordelais, 1997; Le Soleil de Morts, 1998; Achille, le singe, 1999; Les petots bonheurs, 1999; le commencement du monde, 1999; author numerous plays for radio and TV; contbr. revs. for jours. Recipient Prix Eugene Leroy, 1956, Prix Populiste, 1962, Prix Jean Mace, 1968, Prix Goncourt, 1968, Grand Prix litteraire de la Ville de Paris, 1968, Prix Albert Olivier, 1968, Prix de la Paulee de Meursault, 1992, Grand Prix litteraire de la Ville de Bordeaux, 1994, Prix Ardua de l'Université de Bourdeaux, 1996, Prix des Maisons de la Presse, 1998. Office: l'Ecritoire, 1134 Vufflens-le-Chateau Switzerland

CLAVERIE, CHRISTINE, marketing specialist; b. Bois Colombes, France, Apr. 17, 1960; d. Marcel and Noelle (Thoreau) Chastagner; married, Feb. 25, 1989; children: Thomas, Laura. Grad. bus. sch., ESCP, France, 1983. Mktg./sales mgr. Philips France, 1986-90; mktg. dir. France Philips Interactive, 1990-93; sales mgr. Europe Thomson Multimedia, France, 1992-95, mktg. mgr. Europe, 1995-97; mktg. dir. Europe Essilor, Charenton, France, 1997—. Home: 16 Rue Des Bouleaux Blancs, 92390 Villeneuve France Office: Essilor Internat, 147 Rue De Paris, 94227 Charenton France

CLAVERO, ANTONIO, economist, educator; b. Malaga, Spain, Dec. 14, 1953; s. Antonio and Ana (Barranquero) C.; m. Isabel, May 12, 1979; 1 child, Antonio. Grad., U. Malaga, 1977, PhD, 1982. From tchg. asst. to prof. U. Malaga, Spain, 1979—; vice-chancellor U. Malaga, 1984-87; prin. Malaga Sch. Social Work, 1988-96, Dept. Econometrics, 1998—. Co-author: Need of Public Investment in Andalusia, 1984; contbr. articles to profl. jours. Grantee Min. Edn., Madrid, 1990, regional govt. Sevilla, Spain, 1993-97. Mem. Economist's Coll. Roman Catholic. Avocations: reading, music, swimming, trekking. Home: Luis de Milan, 29018 Malaga Spain Office: Dept Econometrics, PO Box Divsn #4, 29071 Malaga Spain

CLAY, CLIFTON FORD, motion picture producer, writer; b. Galveston, Tex., Nov. 2, 1939; s. James Henry and Catherine (Royal) C.; m. Ann Chandler, Oct. 4, 1964; children: Mary Kim, Jason Anthony, Tara Ann. BS, U. Calif., Berkeley, 1962; MA, Am. Film Inst., Beverly Hills, Calif., 1977; postgrad., Citrus Coll., Azusa, Calif., 1978. Actor Screen Actor's Guild, Hollywood, Calif., 1968-75; freelance writer L.A., 1972—; film producer Turner-Clay Prodn., L.A., 1972-74; v.p. Motion Picture Group, Beverly Hills, 1982-83; chief ops. officer Oak Tree Films, Ltd., London, 1984—; mem. exec. bd. Park Ave. Entertainment, L.A., 1986, Am. Film Inst. Alumni Writers Workshop, 1984—; v.p. Am. Film Inst. Alumni, 1985-87, pres., 1987-88; lectr. high schs., 1987—; v.p. Courtroom Gunfighters, Inc., 1991—; pres. NKOSI Internat. House, 1992—. Producer: Maxi, 1972; screenwriter: Sunflower, 1973, Sweetwine & Tyree, 1975, This Land Yesterday, 1976, Delaney Street Feud, 1978, Grannie's Rebels, 1978, Destiny's Journey, 1982, Autumn Rain, 1984, Jammer, 1984, Bramber House, 1985, Augusta Rose, 1986, The Concrete Garden, 1990, Courtroom Gunfighters, 1991, Freeborn-The Roundtable, 1992, The Ebony Rope, 1992, The Dragon's Mouth, 1993, Justice For No One, 1994, Uncle Bubba, 1995, The Cedar Street Boys, 1995, My Lover, My Friend, 1995, Till Tomorrow Comes, 1996, Clear Lake Meadow, 1996, Grandma's Hat, 1997, A Whisper of Truth, 1997, Mama's Song, 1997, Strawberry Kisses, 1998, Bakala, 1998, Moonlight and Soft Waves, 1999, Naked Sisters, 1999. Den leader Cub Scouts Am., Covina, Calif., 1978; coach Little League Football, Covina, 1979. Mem. Assn. Ind. Video & Filmmakers, Inc., Producers Assn. LA., Britain Film & TV Producers, Vintage Sports Car Club, Ltd. (Eng.). Episcopalian. Avocations: shooting, sky diving, lecturing, racing cars, collecting model trains. Home: 679 Antiquity Dr Green Valley CA 94585-4073 Office: Oak Tree Films Ltd, 42a Devonshire Close, CM23 5ED London WI, England

CLAYBURGH, JILL, actress; b. N.Y.C., Apr. 30, 1944; d. Albert Henry and Julia (Door) C.; m. David Rabe, Mar., 1979. BA, Sarah Lawrence Coll., 1966. Former mem., Charles Playhouse, Boston; Off-Broadway plays include The Nest; Broadway debut in The Rothschilds, 1970; stage appearances include In the Boom Boom Room (David Rabe), Design for Living (Noel Coward); film appearances include The Wedding Party, 1969, The Telephone Book, 1971, Portnoy's Complaint, 1972, The Thief Who Came to Dinner, 1973, The Terminal Man, 1974, Gable and Lombard, 1976, Silver Streak, 1976, Gable and Lombard, 1976, Semi-Tough, 1977, An Unmarried Woman, 1978, Luna, 1979, Starting Over, 1979, It's My Turn, 1980, First Monday in October, 1981, I'm Dancing as Fast as I Can, 1982, Hannah K, 1983, In Our Hands, 1984, Where Are The Children, 1986, Shy People, 1987, Beyond the Ocean, 1990, Whispers in the Dark, 1992, Le Grand Pardon II, 1992, Rich in Love, 1993, Naked in New York, 1994, Fools Rush In, 1997, Going All the Way, 1997; appeared in TV films Snoop Sisters, 1972, The Art of Crime, 1975, Hustling, 1975, Griffin and Phoenix, 1976, Miles to Go..., 1986, Who Gets the Friends?, 1988, Fear Stalk, 1989, Unspeakable Acts, 1990, Reason for Living: the Jill Ireland Story, 1991, Trial: The Price of Passion, 1993, Firestorm: A Catastrophe in Oakland, 1993, For the Love of Nancy, 1994, Honor Thy Father and Mother: The True Story of the Menendez Brothers, 1994, The Face on the Milk Carton, 1995, When Innocence is Lost, 1997, Sins of the Mind, 1997, Crowned and Dangerous, 1998, My Little Assassin, 1999; TV documentary: Ask Me Anything: How to Talk to Kids About Sex, 1989; TV series Trinity, 1998, Everything's Relative, 1999. Recipient Best Actress award for An Unmarried Woman, Cannes Film Festival; Golden Apple award for best film actress in An Unmarried Woman. Office: 12424 Wilshire Blvd Ste 1000 Los Angeles CA 90025-1071

CLAYTON, EVA M., congresswoman, former county commissioner; b. Savannah, Ga., Sept. 16, 1934; m. Theaoseus T. Clayton; children: Theaoseus Jr., Martin, Reuben, Joanne. BS, Johnson C. Smith U.; MS, North Carolina Central U. Former commr. Warren County, N.C.; mem. 103rd Congress from 1st N.C. dist., Washington, D.C., 1993—; mem. agriculture com. resource conservation, rsch. and forestry 103rd Congress from 1st N.C. dist., mem. house democratic policy com., mem. com. on budget. Democrat. Office: US Ho of Reps 2440 Rayburn Bldg Washington DC 20515-3301

CLAYTON, MARVIN COURTLAND, engineering, manufacturing sourcing and health wellness consultant; b. Norwich, Conn., Feb. 19, 1938; s. Marvin C. and Peggy (Farmer) C.; children: Cheryll, Michelle, Deborah. BS in Indsl. Engring., Purdue U., 1963; MBA, U. Louisville, 1971; MPA, Penn. State U., 1986; grad., U.S. Army War Coll., 1986. Registered profl. engr., Calif., Ky., Mo., Pa.; cert. purchasing mgr., mfg. engr., mfg. mgr., profl. mgmt. cons., logistician, exec. in logistics. Mgr. shop ops. GE Appliances, Louisville, 1968-69, prog. mgr. mfg. engring., 1969-71, contracting agt. material handling and computer systems, 1973-76, program mgr., material resource systems, 1976-80, mgr., advance and indirect material purchasing, 1980-82, program mgr., purchasing programs, 1982-87, program mgr., sourcing integration, 1987-89, mgr. supplier productivity engring., 1989-93, puchasing mgr. range products bus., 1993; prin. The Clayton Group, Louisville, 1993-94; mgr. range bus. purchasing GE Appliances, Louisville, 1992-94; mgr. Strategic Sourcing, Louisville, 1994; mgr. mfg. engring. Emerson Electric Co., St. Louis, 1971-72; corp. engring. and mfg. cons. AMEDCO, Springfield, Mo., 1972-73; pres. Clayton Cons., Louisville, Ky., 1994—; prin. The Clayton Group, Global Cons., Exec. Distbrs., NuSkin, Pharmanex, Big Planet, 1992—; pres. CC Global, Louisville, Queretaro, Mex., 1996—. Patentee in field. Chmn. bd. deacons Bapt. Ch., Louisville, 1975; dir. ch. choir Bapt. Ch., Arkansas City, Kans., 1963. Col. USAR, 1963-93. Named to Honorable Order of Ky. Cols. Mem. Res. Officers Assn. (exec. bd., pres. 1984, nat. councilman 1990-94), Ky. Res. Officers Assn., Inst. Indsl. Engrs., Assn. Internal Mgmt. Cons., Assn. of U.S. Army, Purdue Alumni Assn., U. Louisville Alumni Assn., Pa. State Alumni Assn., Army War Coll. Alumni Assn. Republican. Avocations: piano, gardening, sports. E-mail: clayton-group@bigplanet.com. Home and Office: 8215 Camberley Dr Louisville KY 40222-5534

CLAYTON, ORVILLE WOOLFORD, surgeon; b. Ft. Payne, Ala., May 30, 1921; s. Olney Walker Clayton and Flora Pauline Wheeler; m. Dorothy Nell Meadows, June 20, 1944; children: Stephen W., Kathy L. Stockham, Shelley E. BA, U. Ala., Tuscaloosa, 1943; B in Medicine, Northwestern U., 1945, MD, 1946. Post surgeon U.S. Army, Huntsville, Ala., 1946-48; chief resident surgery Univ. Hosp., Birmingham, Ala., 1948; chief surgery Bapt. Med. Montclair, Birmingham, 1969-74, pres. staff, 1982; clin. assoc. prof. surgery U. Ala., Birmingham, 1973-91; bd. dirs. Am. Pulmonary Inst., Birmingham, 1996-99. Capt. U.S. Army, 1946-48. Fellow ACS, So. Thoracic Soc. Avocations: gardening, genealogy. Home: 3133 Ryecroft Rd Birmingham AL 35223-2715

CLAYTON, PETER ROBERT, library educator; b. Maclean, Australia, Nov. 24, 1947; s. Frederick George and Edna Gwen (Richards) C.; m. Rosanne Helen Walker (div.); children: Cathie Koina, Philip, Robert; m. Adela L. Love. BA, U. Sydney, Australia, 1968; diploma in librarianship, U. NSW, Australia, 1969, PhD, 1993; MA, U. Canberra, Australia, 1990. Libr. Australian Nat. U., 1970-74; documentation officer Royal Commn. on Australian Govt. Adminstrn., 1974-75; from reader svcs. libr. to assoc. libr. Canberra Coll. Advanced Edn., 1975-89; sr. lectr. U. Canberra, 1989-98, assoc. prof., 1999—, dir., libr. and info. studies, 1991-95, dir. ctr. for comm. policy rsch., 1996-99; cons. in field. Editor Australian Acad. and Rsch. Libr., 1997—; contbr. articles to profl. jours. Gen. sec. Libr. Assn. Australia, 1976. Ctr. for Info. Studies fellow Charles Stunt U., 1995. Fellow Australian Inst. Mgmt. (assoc.); mem. Australian Libr. and Info. Assn. (assoc., pres. univ., coll. and rsch. libr. sect. 1991-92), Australian Coll. Edn. Avocations: music, opera, photography, film, walking. Office: U Canberra Faculty Comm, PO Box 1, Canberra ACT 2616, Australia

CLAYTON, RAYMOND ARTHUR, purchasing executive; b. Newark, May 22, 1930; s. John Raymond and Marion Caroline (Haster) C.; m. Barbara Russell Langdon, Feb. 11, 1956; children: Matthew Arthur, Mark Thomas. BSBA, NYU, 1951, MBA in Indsl. Rels., 1962. Lifetime cert. purchasing mgr. Minor league baseball player Cin. Reds, Inc., Columbia, S.C., 1951, Detroit Tigers, Jamestown, N.Y., 1954; adminstrv. staff Western Elec. Co., Inc., N.Y.C., 1954-55, sect. chief, contract buyer, 1956-59; dept. chief, contract buyer Bell Telephone Labs., Inc., Whippany, N.J., 1960-63, exec. asst., 1964-67; head svc. ops. Bell Telephone Labs., Inc., North Andover, Mass., 1968-74; head purchasing Bell Telephone Labs., Inc., Whippany, N.J., 1975-76, Murray Hill, N.J., 1977-78, 81-83; head personnel systems Bell Telephone Labs., Inc., Short Hills, N.J., 1979-80; mgr. purchasing, resident AT&T Bell Labs. North N.J. AT&T Techs. Inc., 1984-87; assoc. dir. materials mgmt. inst. Bloomfield (N.J.) Coll., 1989-95, dir., 1996-98; pvt. practice as cons. purchasing and materials mgmt. Stanton, N.J., 1989—. Contbr. articles to profl. jours. Dir. Prep Club Greater Lawrence (Mass.) C. of C., 1969-74, v.p. socio-econ. divsn., 1972; organizer, advisor Jr. Achievement, Lawrence, 1970-74; pres. Boxford (Mass.) Athletic Assn., 1973-74; treas., mem. exec. com. Union (N.J.) County Econ. Devel. Corp., 1979-83. Mil. svc., 1952-53, Korea. Mem. Nat. Assn. Purchasing Mgmt. (orgn. and planning com. 1994-97, J. Shipman award com. 1996, 98, nat. bd. dirs. 1992-94, 2000—, asst. dir. 1990-91, N.J. chpt. program chair 1979-83, exec. v.p. 1983-84, pres. 1984-85, 89-90, dir. nat. affairs 1985-86, 90-91, 93-94, 96-97, trustee 1984-2000, dir. ednl. liaison 1999—, mktg. mgr. 2000, fin. com., 2000—, policy com., 2000—, C.P.M. instr. 1989—, W.M. Moon award 1991, H.L. Erlicher award 1996), Luth. Ch. Mo. Synod (N.J. dist. fin. com. 1992-95, bd. dirs. 1995—, chair 2000—, chair ops. coun. 1995—). Republican. Lutheran. Avocations: hiking, tennis, coaching little league baseball. Home: PO Box 145 Stanton NJ 08885-0145

CLAYTON, SIMON ANTHONY, financial executive; b. Birmingham, U.K., Oct. 25, 1956; s. Norman and Margaret (Tooth) C.; m. Judy Mary McLennan, June 6, 1981; children: Emma, Ben. BA in Econs. with Honors, U. Manchester, 1979. Chartered acct. Acct. Arthur Andersen & Co., Manchester, 1979-82; mng. dir. corp. fin. HSBC Investment Bank, 1982-98; group fin. dir. DHL Worldwide Network, Brussels, 1998—. Mem. Royal Automobile Club (London), Walton Heath Golf Club, Pinheiros Altos Golf Club. Avocations: golf, tennis, flying, music. Office: DHL Worldwide Express Bv, De Kleetlaan 1, 1831 Diegem Belgium

CLEARY, DAVID MICHAEL, composer, critic, library assistant; b. Chelsea, Mass., Nov. 11, 1954; s. Robert Joseph and Sally Ann (Deuker) C. MusB, New Eng. Conservatory Music, 1976; MusM, U. Hartford, 1978; MusD, U. Cin., 1982. Asst. to composition dept. New Eng. Conservatory Music, Boston, 1974-76; teaching asst. in music theory U. Hartford (Conn.), 1976-78; teaching asst. in music theory U. Cin., 1978-80, rotating instr. in music theory, 1980-81; libr. asst. Harvard U., Cambridge, Mass., 1984—; assoc. prodr. The Composers Show, Sta. WGBH-FM, Boston, 1974-75; co-dir. Composers in Red Sneakers, 1994—, pres., 1997—. Compositions include Five Character Studies, 1979, A Gathering of Quokkas, 1985 (commd. Dinosaur Annex Ensemble), Lake George Overture, 1988, String Quartet no. 1, 1988, Gryllus, 1988-89, Cruikshank Fantasy, 1989 (commd. Alea III), Woodwind Quintet no. 2, 1990 (commd. Arcadian Winds), String Quartet no. 2, 1991 (commd. Artaria Quartet Boston), Linsner Sextet, 1992 (commd. Northwestern U. Trombone Ensemble), Western Wind Fragments, 1993-94 (commd. Eos Ensemble), Fanfares for Teddy Roosevelt, 1994-95, The Deeper Magic, 1995-96 (commd. Duo Renard), Fourteen Movie Characters, 1996-97 (commd. Am. Composers Forum Boston Area chpt.), Postcards from Annaghmakerrig, 1998; contbg. music writer (website) All-Music Guide, 1997—, (book) All Music Guide to Rock, 2d edit., 1997—; contbg. music critic New Music Connoisseur, 1999—, The Enterprise, 1999—; contbr. articles, revs., chpts. to profl. publs., books and websites; recordings on Centaur, Vienna Modern Masters CD labels. Mem. fellows coun. Va. Ctr. for the Creative Arts, 1999—; mem. bd. advisors Kalvos and Damian's New Music Bazaar, 1999—. Recipient 1st pl. Rosenberger Meml. Comm. Competition, Cin., 1989, Harvey Gaul Composition Competition, 1990; ASCAP grantee U. Hartford, 1978, grantee Somerville Arts Coun., 1987, 90, Meet the Composer, 1990, ASTRAL grantee Nat. Found. for Advancement in Arts, 1994; rsch. fellow U. Cin., 1980, Douglas W. Bryant fellow, 1988, fellow Va. Ctr. for Creative Arts, 1988, 89, Yaddo fellow, 1988, Cummington fellow, 1989, Millay fellow, 1990, fellow Ella Lyman Cabot Trust, 1990, Ragdale fellow, 1992, MacDowell fellow, 1995, Tyrone Guthrie Ctr. fellow, 1998. Mem. BMI, Am. Music Ctr., Am. Composers Forum, Soc. Composers. Email: dcleary@fas.harvard.edu. Home: 7 Arlington St Apt 34 Cambridge MA 02140-2736 Office: Harvard U Biolabs Libr 16 Divinity Ave Cambridge MA 02138-2020

CLEARY, JAMES C., audio-visual producer; b. N.Y.C., Mar. 15, 1921; s. James Charles and Elizabeth Adelaide (Anglin) C.; m. Adele Lillian Coe, Nov. 28, 1954. Grad., Scarsdale (N.Y.) H.S., 1940. Lithographer, camerman Advt. Lit. Inc., N.Y.C., 1940-41; advt. copy writer Grosset & Dunlap, book pubs., N.Y.C., 1942-44; advt. copy writer, editor Baker & Taylor, book wholesalers, N.Y.C., 1945-46; asst. mgr. sales Camera Craft Inc., retail photog. sales, White Plains, N.Y., 1946-50, Colortone Camera Inc., White Plains, 1950-57; prodr., lectr. Ansco divsn. Gen. Aniline & Film Corp., Binghamton, N.Y., 1959-61; lab. photographer Nevis Lab. Nuc. Rsch., Columbia U., 1959-75; audio-visual specialist Edgemont Sch. Dist., Scarsdale, 1975-83; owner-prodr. Cleary Sound-Slides, New Rochelle, N.Y., 1950—. Mem. Scarsdale Camera Club (pres. 1948-49), Color Camera Club Westchester N.Y. (dir. 1958-59), Am. Security Coun. (advisory bd. 1970—), USAF Assn., Am. Def. Preparedness Assn., Westchester County Grand Jurors Assn., The Baker Street Irregulars, Three Garridebs, Sherlock Holmes Socs., Thomas Wolfe Soc. Achievements include patentee of complete sound-synchronized, dissolving slide project control system, 1966; pioneer in use of dissolve projection and synchronized sound in presentation of color slide continuities. Address: Cleary Sound-Slides 28 Pengilly Dr New Rochelle NY 10804-3016

CLEARY, SEAN MICHAEL, executive; b. Somerset West, South Africa, Oct. 26, 1948; s. Thomas Stanislaus and Isobel Forsyth Cranston (Bell) C.; m. Sophia Natalie Smit, June 5, 1971; children: Sean Michael, Mary Siobhan. BA, U. South Africa, 1969; MBA, Brunel U., England, 1999. Vice consul, consul SA Consulate Gen., Tehran, Iran, 1971-75; deputy head econ. & fin. rels. divsn. Min. Fgn. Affairs, Pretoria, South Africa, 1976-77, head tng. divsn., 1978; polit. counsellor South African Embassy, Washington, 1978-82; consul gen. SA Consulate Gen., Beverly Hills, Calif., 1982-83; chief dir. Office of Adminstr. Gen., Windhoek, Nambia, 1983-85; mng. dir. Strategic Concepts Ltd., Johannesburg, South Africa, 1985—; guest lectr. Sch. Bus. Leadership, U. South Africa, 1986—; faculty mem. Grad. Inst. Mgmt. & Tech., Johannesburg, 1995—, Internat. Ctr. Mgmt. Devel., Johannesburg, 1996—; vice chmn. Meridian Worldwide LLC, 1998—; mng. dir. Ctr. for Advanced Governance Think Tools AG, 1999— (mgmt. bd.); mem. facilitating and prep. coms. Nat. Peace Accord, 1992, EXCO; chair Working Group on Code of Conduct for Polit. Parties/Orgns. Contbr. articles to profl. jours. Mem. South African Inst. Internat. Affairs, Africa Inst. South Africa, Soc. Advancement Socio-Econs. Avocations: fishing, riding, writing, music. Home: The Lodge Silverhurst, Silverhurst Est, Constantia, Cape Town South Africa Office: Strategic Concepts, Stratcon Ho Waterfall Park, Halfway House 1685, South Africa

CLEATON-JONES, PETER EIDDON, physician, dentist; b. Johannesburg, Mar. 5, 1941; s. Ioan Prichard and Zélie Janet Mary (Swanson) C.; m. Marguerite Ginette France Thorpe, Mar. 11, 1967; 1 child, Ioan Philippe. B of Dental Surgery, U. Witwatersrand, 1963, B of Medicine/B of Surgery, 1967, PhD, 1975, D of Sci. in Dentistry, 1991. Surg. intern Baragwanath Hosp., Johannesburg, 1968, med. intern, 1968; sr. then chief rsch. officer Med. Rsch. Coun., U. Witwatersrand, Johannesburg, 1969-76; prof. exptl. odontology U. Witwatersrand, 1977—; dir. dental rsch. inst., med. rsch. coun. U. Witwatersrand, Capetown, Johannesburg, 1977—; emergency medicine med. officer Hillbrow Hosp., Johannesburg, 1969-84; anaesthetist Baragwanath Hosp., 1969-75, Johannesburg Hosp., 1975—. Author: Essential Medicine for Dental Research, 1971, 2d edit., 1996; contbr. articles to profl. jours.; presenter in field. Group chmn. Boy Scout Troop, Johannesburg, 1985-87; trustee Fund for Foster Parenting, Johannesburg, 1994—; weekly med. nat. radio broadcaster S.A. Broadcasting Corp., Johannesburg, 1984-92. Recipient Silver medal Med. Rsch. Coun., 1990, 1999. Mem. South African Sugar Assn. (rsch. panel mem.), Internat. Assn. for Dental Rsch. (pres., Colgate Palmolive prize South African divsn. 1969, H. Trendley Dean Meml. award 1998, disting. svc. award 2000), So. African Assn. for Advancement of Sci. (S. Africa medal). Avocations: model engineering, genealogy. Office: MRC U Witwatersrand, Dental Rsch Inst Pvt Bag 3, Wits 2050, South Africa

CLEESE, JOHN MARWOOD, writer, businessman, comedian; b. Weston-super-Mare, Eng., Oct. 27, 1939; s. Reginald and Muriel C.; m. Connie Booth, 1968 (div. 1978); 1 child, Cynthia; m. Barbara Trentham, 1981 (div. 1990); 1 child, Camilla; m. Alyce Faye Eichelberger, 1992. Student, Clifton Coll., Bristol, Eng.; MA, Downing Coll., Cambridge U., Eng.; LLD (hon.), St. Andrews U. Andrew D. White prof.-at-large Cornell U., 1999—. First appearance on Brit. TV as writer, performer on The Frost Report, 1966; other TV series include At Last the 48 Show; actor Monty Python's Flying Circus, Fawlty Towers; guest TV appearance Cheers (Emmy award); appeared in BBC prodn. The Taming of the Shrew, 1981; guest TV appearance Third Rock from the Sun, 1998 (Emmy nom.); film appearances include Interlude, 1968, The Magic Christian, 1970, The Rise and Rise of Michael Rimmer, 1970, And Now for Something Completely Different, 1972, Monty Python and the Holy Grail, 1975, Romance with a Double Bass, 1975, Life of Brian, 1979, The Secret Policeman's Ball, 1979, Time Bandits, 1981, Monty Python Live at the Hollywood Bowl, 1982, The Secret Policeman's Other Ball, 1982, Privates on Parade, Yellowbeard, 1983, The Meaning of Life, 1983, Silverado, 1984, Clockwise, 1986, A Fish Called Wanda (author screenplay, Best Actor Brit. Acad. Film and TV Arts), 1988, Erik the Viking, 1988, Splitting Heirs, 1992, Mary Shelley's Frankenstein, 1994, Jungle Book, 1994, (voice) Fierce Creatures, 1997, The Out of Towners, Isn't She Great, 1998, The World is Not Enough, 1999, Rat Race, 2000; co-author: The Strange Case of the End of Civilization as We Know It, 1977; founder, former dir. Video Arts Ltd., London, 1979-91, also created series of TV & radio commls. for products advertised internationally; co-author: Monty Python's Big Red Book, 1975, Families and How to Survive Them, 1983, Life and How to Survive It, 1993. Recipient Queen's award for Exports (awarded to Video Arts Ltd.), 1982. Office: care David Wilkinson, 115 Hazlebury Rd, London SW6 2LX, England

CLEETON, DAVID LAWRENCE, economist, educational administrator; b. Chillicothe, Mo., Aug. 10, 1952; s. Sam Jr. and Doris Maxine (Clark) C.; m. Betty Howell, July 19, 1986; children: Sarah Howell, Rebecca Lebo. AB, U. Mo., 1973, AM, 1975; PhD, Washington U., St. Louis, 1980. Asst. prof. econs. Oberlin (Ohio) Coll., 1980-85, chmn. dept. econs., 1986-92, 97—, chmn. social sci. div., 1988-92, prof., 1991—, chmn. Ctr. European studies, 1996—; vis. prof. Washington U., 1984, U. Wis., Madison, 1986-88, Econs. Inst., Boulder, Colo., 1990, 2000, U. Strasbourg, 1994-95; treas. bd. Allen Meml. Hosp., Oberlin, 1992-99. European Union corr. Tax Notes Internat., 1998—; contbr. articles to profl. jours. NIMH fellow, 1987-88, Sloan fellow, 1984-85, Earhart fellow, 1979-80. Mem. Am. Econ. Assn., Am. Fin. Assn., Am. Statis. Assn., Fin. Mgmt. Assn., Internat. Pub. Fin. Inst., Nat. Tax. Assn., European Econ. Assn., European Fin. Mgmt. Assn. Office: Oberlin Coll Rice Hall Oberlin OH 44074

CLEGHORN, JOHN EDWARD, bank executive; b. Montreal, July 7, 1941; m. Pattie E. Hart; children: Charles, Ian, Andrea. B in Commerce, McGill U., Montreal, 1962; DCL (hon.), Bishop's U., 1989; LLD (hon.), Wilfrid Laurier U., 1991; DCL (hon.), Acadia U., 1996. Chartered acct. Articled with Clarkson Gordon, chartered Accts., Montreal, 1962-64; sugar and futures trader St. Lawrence Sugar Ltd., Montreal, 1964-66; with assignments Citibank, NY, Montreal, Winnipeg & Vancouver, 1966-74; various posts Royal Bank of Canada, Montreal, Toronto & Vancouver, 1974-86; pres. Royal Bank of Canada, 1986-90; pres. and COO RBC, 1990-94; CEO Royal Bankof Can., Montreal, 1994-95; chmn., CEO, 1995—; bd. dirs. Royal Bank of Canada; bd. dirs. RBC Dominion Securities, Ltd., Inc., Finning Internat. Inc.; chmn. Conf. Bd. of Can.; vice chmn. Bus. Coun. on Nat. Issues, Gov. McGill U.; chmn. McGill Fund Coun., Nat. Gallery of Can. Found.; dir. Can. Spl. Olympics Found.; chancellor Wilfrid Laurier Univ.; dir. Internat. Monetary Conf. Fellow Order of Chartered Accts. Quebec, Inst. Chartered Accts. Ont.; mem. Can. Inst. Chartered Accts., Inst. Chartered Accts. Brit. Columbia. Office: Royal Bank Can, 200 Bay St Royal Bank Plz, Toronto, ON Canada M5J 2J5

CLEMA, JOE KOTOUC, computer scientist; b. Omaha, Sept. 23, 1938; s. Joseph Arthur and Sylva Marie (Kotouc) C.; m. Maria Estela Cobos, Apr. 1, 1960; children: Jennifer, Arta. Student, U.S. Mil. Acad., 1957-60; BS, U. Nebr., 1963; MS, U. Miami, 1969; PhD, Colo. State U., 1973. Systems analyst Gen. Electric, Louisville, 1969-70; head sci. applications Colo. State U., Ft. Collins, 1970-73; project engr. Gen. Dynamics, Ft. Worth, 1973-77; sr. mgr. Simulation Tech., Inc., Dayton, Ohio, 1977-79; program mgr. Pratt and Whitney, West Palm Beach, Fla., 1979-82; dept. mgr. CACI, Dayton, 1982-83; dir. spl. projects Systems and Applied Scis., Vienna, Va., 1983-85; chief software engr. IIT Rsch. Inst., Annapolis, Md., 1985-90; cons. to IBM with, pres. Neurosystems, Inc., Bethesda, Md., 1991-98; cons. on IRS tax system modernization TRW, Merrifield, Va., 1993-95, cons. simplified tax & wage sys., 1995-96; mgr. Sys. Resources Corp., 1997-98, Houston Assocs., Inc., 1998—. Contbr. articles to profl. jours. Sustaining mem. Rep. Nat. Com., Washington, 1983—. Served to capt. U.S. Army, 1963-67. First Ann. Simulation Symposium Rsch. grantee, 1972; recipient Outstanding Svc. award Ann. Simulation Symposium Bd. Dirs., 1980. Mem. IEEE (sr.), ACM (nat. lectr. 1978-83), Soc. Computer Simulation (bd. dirs. , program chmn. 1988-96), Mid Atlantic Electronic Commerce Network (bd. dirs. 1995-98), Spl. Interest Group on Simulation (chmn. 1979-81), Ann. Simulation Symposium (chmn. bd. dirs. 1979), Internat. Platform Assn., Armed Forces Comms. and Elec. Assn., Toastmasters, Herndon C. of C., Hidden Creek Country Club, Worldgate Athletic Club. Republican. Avocations: bridge, tennis. Home: 301 Missouri Ave Herndon VA 20170-5426 Office: Houston Assocs Inc 4601 Fairfax Dr Arlington VA 22203-1500

CLEMEDSON, ULRIKA CECILIA, toxicologist, researcher, consultant; b. Danderyd, Sweden, Nov. 30, 1960; d. Carl-Johan and Margit Ulla (Malmquist) C.; m. Per Torbjörn Larsson, June 2, 1990; children: Per Johan, Carl Emil. BS, Uppsala (Sweden) U., 1986; licentiate philosophy, Stockholm U., 1989, PhD, 1992. Rsch. scientist dept. pharm. biosci. div. toxicology Uppsala U., 1992-96; cons., mng. dir. CCTox Cons. and Nordic Info. Ctr. for Alt. Methods (NICA), Stocksund, Sweden, 1997—. Co-author: The Brain in Bits and Pieces, 1992; contbr. articles to Pharmacology and Toxicology, Toxicology in Vitro, Neurotoxicology and Teratology. Recipient rsch. prize Juliana von Wendt Animal Protection Fund, 1995. Mem. Scandinavian Soc. for Cell Toxicology (treas. 1992-98), Swedish Soc. Toxicology, Soc. for In Vitro Biology, European Soc. Toxicology in Vitro (mem. exec. com. 1998—), Swedish Fund Rsch. Without Animal Expts. (mem. exec. com. 1998—). Avocations: skiing, restoring antiques, outdoor life, decorating. Home: Mittspåret 36, SE-18754 Täby Sweden Office: CCTox Cons, Vintervägen 17, SE-18274 Stocksund Sweden

CLEMENS, ALVIN HONEY, insurance company executive; b. Pa., July 10, 1937; m. Valerie Crooker, Aug. 26, 1989; children: Kelli, Julie, Tracy, Wendy, Amy, Alvin H. Jr., Conner. BA, Pa. State U., 1959; postgrad. in ins., San Diego State U. Supr. sales assn. group dept. Ins. Co. Am., 1959-63; founder, ptnr. Butera, Clemens & Beyer Ins. Cons., Norristown, Pa., 1963-67; founder, dir., pres., chmn. Ex. Commn. Acad. Ins. Group, Valley Forge, Pa., 1967-85; dir., chmn., CEO Acad. Ins. Group (formerly Unicom Ins. Group), 1984-85; founder, dir., chmn. CEO Exec. Internat. Life, Bermuda, 1981-89; chmn., CEO Maine Nat. Life Ins. Co., Portland, 1985-96; chmn., CEO, pres. Provident Am. Corp., Norristown, 1989—, Provident Indemnity Life Ins. Co., Norristown, 1989-99; chmn. Health Axis Inc., 1999—; mem. exec. com. bd. dirs. Ins. Fedn. Pa. trustee Pa. State U., mem. bd. visitors bus. sch.; apptd. to Banking and Ins. Transition Team, Pa., 1995—; co-chmn. Ins. Task Force of Pa. IMPACCT Commn. on Banking and Ins. trustee Pa. State U., mem. bd. visitors bus. sch. Mem. Young Pres. Orgn., Phila. Pres. Orgn., World Pres. Orgn., Aronimink Golf Club, Pyramid Club. Office: Health Axis Inc PO Box 511 Norristown PA 19404-0511

CLEMENS, DANIEL, physicist; b. Berlin, Feb. 3, 1961; s. Axel and Barbara (Schubert) C. Diploma in physics, Tech. U., Berlin, 1989, D of Natural Scis., 1993. Sci. collaborator, fellow Hahn-Meitner-Inst., Berlin, 1989-93, Paul Scherrer Inst., Villigen, Switzerland, 1994—. Mem. Swiss Soc. for Neutron Scattering. Avocation: sports. Office: Paul Scherrer Inst, CH-5232 Villigen Switzerland

CLEMENS, PETER CLAUS, physicist; b. Garmisch-Partenkirchen, Bavaria, Germany, Mar. 11, 1945; s. Johann and Aloisia (Gotz) C.; m. Hella Maria Kirschsieper, Apr. 9, 1976; 1 child, Patrick. Diploma in Physics, Tech. U., Munich, 1973. Project scientist Siemens AG, Munich, 1973—. Contbr. articles to profl. jours.; inventor in field-assisted ion exchange. Gefreiter Gebirgsjager, 1964-66, Straubing, Germany. Avocations: squash, biking, windsurfing, homeworking. Office: Siemens AG, Otto-Hahn-Ring 6, Bayern Munich D-81739, Germany

CLEMENS, T. PAT, manufacturing company executive; b. Hibbing, Minn., July 26, 1944; s. Jack LeRoy and Mildred (Coss) C.; m. 1966 (div. 1992); children: Patrick Michael, Heather Kristen. BS in Econs. and Mgmt., St. Cloud State U., 1968; student of theology, Coll. St. Thomas, 1985-87. Sales adminstr. Transistor Electronics Co., Eden Prarie, Minn., 1969; head instnl. sales Chiquita Brands, Edina, Minn., 1970; dist. sales mgr. Menley & James Labs., Phila., 1971-75; owner, pres. T.P. Clemens Labs., Eagan, Minn., 1975—; instr community edn. Rosemount, Minn., 1977-78; bd. dirs. Rosemount Hockey, 1977-78, Relocation Assistance Assn. Am., 1984-85; v.p. Sch. Dist. #196 Booster Club, 1984-85; lectr. econs. to corps., high schs. and colls. in U.S., Scotland, Ireland, and Jamaica, 1979—. Author, editor: How Prejudice and Narcissism Control Economics of the United States and the World, 1979. Mem. Rosemont Cmty. Edn. Bd., 1985, chmn., 1986-87; chmn. speakers bur. Citizens Steering Com., 1984-85; coach Little League, 1970-82, 88-91; coach high sch. weight lifting team, 1975-95; vol. worker with comatose children, 1975-96, 97—. Recipient letter of recognition for stopping armed robbery Dakota County Atty.'s Dept., 1979, 93. Mem. Internat. Platform Assn., Kids-N-Kinship Program 1988-92. Home and Office: 1276 Vildmark Dr Eagan MN 55123-2801

CLEMENT, CHRISTOPHE, plant biologist, researcher; b. Saint-Dizier, France, Mar. 20, 1964; s. Jean and Roseline (Thieblemont) C.; m. Yannick Louchie; children: Denis, Mathilde, Antoine. MSc, U. Reims, France, 1987; agregation, U. Lille, France, 1988; DEA, U. Paris VI, 1990; PhD, U. Reims, 1994. Biology tchr. Nat. Edn. Min., France, 1989-94; asst. prof. biology U. Reims, 1988-93, assoc. prof. biology of plants, 1994—; orgnanizer Congress on Anther and Pollen, 1998. Reviewer jours. Protoplasma, 1996—, Internat. Jour. Plant Scis., 1998—; contbr. articles to profl. jours. Sgt. French Air Army, 1988-89. Recipient spl. prize Assn. des Palynologues de Langue Française, 1995. Mem. Internat. Assn. Plant Tissue Culture, Bot. Soc. Am. Avocation: subaquatic diving. Office: URCA-UFR Sci, Biol Phys Vegetales BP 1039, F-51687 Reims 2, France

CLEMENT, CLAUDE JEAN, retired gas company director, consultant, educator; b. Paris, France, Feb. 25, 1931; s. Roger and Genevieve Marie (Charron) C.; m. Francoise Marie Laffineur (dec. 1998); children: Sylvie, Pierre. BS in Math., Physics, Univ. Paris, 1956; degree in Engring., Nat. Sch. Chem. Engring., Lille, France, 1956; PhD in Physical Sci., Univ. Paris, 1965. Registered Chem. Engr. Probationer Nat. Nuclear Ctr., Bruyere-Le-Chatel, France, 1956; rsch. engr., group leader French Petroleum Inst., Rueil, France, 1959-66; from head process rsch. dept. to dir. Shell Oil, various, France, U.S.A., 1966-86; dir. scientific rels. Shell Oil, Paris, 1986-91, retired, 1991; assoc. prof. Paris VI Univ., 1989-94; cons. Directorate of French Civil Aviation, Paris, 1992-93, Framatome, Paris, 1994. Contbr. articles to profl. jours.; 20 patents in field. Adminstr. U. Pamoth Curie, Paris, 1990—. Lt. Engr. Corps., 1956-59. Mem. ACS, French Nat. Coun. Civil Engrs. Commn. of Profls., Assn. Francasse Des Techniciens du Petrole, The Higher Edn. Commn. of French Patronate, N.Y. Acad. Scis. Avocations: painting, research in numbers theory. Home: 35 Rue Malherbe, 76100 Rouen France

CLEMENT, DANIEL ROY, III, accountant, assistant nurse, small business owner; b. Kirtland, Ohio, Apr. 2, 1943; s. Roy A. Jr. and Evelyn Violet (Hale Chase) C.; m. Jennifer Ilean Handley, July 10, 1965 (div. 1975); children: Elizabeth Ann Clement Baitt, Catherine Lynn Clement Holder; m. Barbara Jane Griffiths, Dec. 10, 1985. Student, Fenn Coll., 1961-63, Alexander Hamilton Inst., 1963-67, Am. Inst. of Banking, 1963-65, Lakeland Coll., 1965-70, Case Western Res. U., 1970-73, Lake Erie Coll., 1973-85. Shipping and cost acctg. Mentor (Ohio) Products, 1961; acctg. asst. N.Y. Cen. Transport, Cleve., 1963-65; acct. mgr. Am. Soc. of Metals, Novelty, Ohio, 1965-67; corp. fleet mgr. Addressograph Multigraph, Euclid, Ohio, 1967-72; treas. Debevec Salo & Assocs., Painesville, Ohio, 1972-74; with sales Pontiac Cadillac-Record Shack, Mentor, 1974-78; shipping coord. Ajax Mfg., Euclid, 1978-82; notary pub. Active Jr. C. of C., Mentor, Willoughby, Brunswick, Novelty, Lake County, 1962-78; mem. Congl. Task Force Pres. Bush, 1981-94. Republican. Methodist. Avocations: gardening, dogs, cats, tropical fish. Home and Office: 344 N Saint Clair St Painesville OH 44077-4039

CLEMENT, PAUL PLATTS, JR., performance technologist, educator; b. Geneva, Ill., Aug. 30, 1935; s. Paul P. and Vera Elizabeth (Dahlquist) C.; m. Susan Alice Aikins, June 7, 1958; children: Paul P. IV, Kathleen Elizabeth. BA in Math., Coe Coll., 1957. Sales tech. rep. Burroughs Corp., Chgo., 1960-63; mgr. EDP, Harding-Williams Corp., Chgo., 1963-65; edn. coord. Standard Oil Co., Chgo., 1965-69; mgr. product planning Edutronics Systems Internat., Chgo., 1969-71; interactive video instrn. specialist Advanced Systems Inc., Chgo., 1971-88; ind. cons. in tng., media use, computers Downers Grove, Ill., 1988; prin. instr., developer UNISYS Corp., Lisle, Ill., 1988-89; mgr. employee devel. CNA Ins. Cos., Chgo., 1990-91; cons. media tng. Internet Systems Corp., Chgo., 1990-93; prin. Clement Consulting Group, Downers Grove, 1993—; part-time data processing faculty Coll. of DuPage and Coll. extension, Harper Coll., Ill., DeVry Inst.; invited spkr. numerous computer and tng. confs., nat. and internat. assns.; developer, presenter workshops in field; mem. adv. bd. Northeastern Ill. U., Chgo. Developer and pub. 12 animated films with supplementary texts, 84 videotapes, 17 interactive videodiscs and over 7000 pages of expository texts; collaborator 100 other videotapes with supplementary texts; prin. developer micro-computer based People Compatability System, 1983; developer Decision Table Algorithms, 1986, 94th Inf. Div. Assn. Info. System, 1977, Basic Computer Programmer Tng. Curriculum for Eng. Govt., 1979, computerized Data Processing Curricula Devel. System, 1973, Early COBOL Lang. precompiler, 1967, AutoMagic Glossary, 1992; contbr. articles to Datamation Mag., Data Tng. Mag. Capt. USAF, 1958-60. Recipient Silver award WPC, 1996, Gold award, 1998. Mem. Nat. Soc. Performance and Instrn. (contbr. to jour.). E-mail: PaulClementJr@IBM.net. Home and Office: 4942 Linscott Ave Downers Grove IL 60515-3537

CLEMENT, PETER ADELIN RICHARD, otorhinolaryngologist, educator; b. Izegem, Belgium, Nov. 11, 1941; s. Max and Yvonne (van Camfort) C.; m. Thongsoy Chalor, 1996. Student, U. Ghent, Belgium, 1960-62; MD, U. Brussels, 1967. Registered ear, nose and throat specialist, The Netherlands, Belgium. Training in ear, nose and throat U. Amsterdam, The Netherlands, 1967-70, 71-74; rsch. assoc. Cedars of Lebanon Med. Ctr., L.A., 1970-71; postdoctoral scholar UCLA, 1970-71; ear, nose and throat specialist St. Pieters Hosp., Brussels, 1974, Brugmann Hosp., Brussels, 1974-78; head ear, nose and throat dept. Free U. Brussels, 1979—, prof. otorhinolaryngology, head dept. spltys., 1980—, coord. med. students prespecialization, 1985—; chmn. Internat. Standardization Com. on Rhinomanometry; mem. internat. adv. coun. Internat. Symposium on Infection and Allergy of Nose. Mem. editorial bd. Jour. Heat and Neck Pathology, Med. Trends; contbr. over 210 articles to med. jours. Mem. Am. Coll. Allergy, Am. Acad. Facial, Plastic and Reconstructive Surgery, Am. Acad. Allergy and Immunology, Am. Acad. Otolaryngic Allergy, Am. Acad. Otolaryngology-Head and Neck Surgery Found., European Rhinologic Soc., Internat. Rhinologic Soc. (sec. gen., treas. 1990—), Royal Soc. Medicine, Nederlandse Vereniging voor Allergologie, Nederlandse Vereniging voor Schisis en Craniofaciale Afwijkingen, Barany Soc., Joseph Soc., Internat. Orgns. Med. Scis. (coun.), numerous others. Home: Klaproosstraat 12, B-1731 Zellik Belgium Office: Free U Brussels, ENT Dept, Laarbeeklaan 101, 1090 Brussels Belgium

CLEMENT, RICHARD WOLCOTT, librarian, educator; b. Phila., Aug. 28, 1951; s. Danforth and Patricia (Harshman) C.; m. Susanne Kofod, Aug. 24, 1974; children: Kristina Alexandra, Elizabeth Wolcott. BA, U. Nev., 1975, MA, 1977; AM, U. Chgo., 1984. Asst. prof. English Ill. State U., Normal, 1981-84; rare book cataloger U. Chgo. Libr., 1985-86; assoc. spl. collections libr. Spencer Libr., U. Kans., Lawrence, 1996-2000, spl. collections libr., head, 2000—. Author: The Book in America, 1996; editor: Iberia and the Mediterranean, 1989, Greece and the Mediterranean, 1990, Spain and the Mediterranean, 1992. Summer fellowship NEH, 1983, fellowship Newberry Libr., Chgo., 1982, Andrew W. Mellon Found., St. Louis U., 1982. Mem. ALA, Mediterranean Studies Assn. (bd. dirs. 1994-2000, pres. 1994-98), Medieval Acad. of Am., Soc. for the History of Authorship, Reading and Publishing. Avocations: travel, reading, music, building houses. Fax: 785-864-5803. E-mail: rclement@ukans.edu. Home: 2205 Riviera Dr Lawrence KS 66047-1990 Office: Spencer Rsch Libr U Kans Lawrence KS 66045-0001

CLEMENTE, JAVIER, soccer coach; b. Barakaldo, Spain, Mar. 12, 1950. Profl. soccer player Athletic Bilbao, 1974; head coach nat. soccer team Athletic Bilbao, Spain, 1981—, World Cup Championships, 1994; nat. mgr., coach Spanish Nat. Team, 1992-2000; coach Real Sociedad, 1999—. *

CLEMENTE, PAOLO, research engineer; b. Benevento, Italy, May 5, 1959; s. Saverio and Bianca (Liguori) C.; m. Giuliana Zullo, Dec. 10, 1986; children: Sara, Francesco. Degree in civil engring., U. Federico II, Naples, Italy, 1983, PhD in Structural Engring., 1992. Registered profl. engr., Italy. Freelance structural engr. Benevento, Italy, 1983-85; rsch. structural engr. ENEA, Rome, 1985-87, sr. rsch. structural engr., 1988—, head exptl. dynamic analysis structure/system identification, 1992—; referee internat. jours. in field; contract prof. U. Trento, Italy, 1999, 2000. Contbr. articles to profl. publs. Grantee Min. Sci. Rsch., Italy, 1989-91, U. Federico II, 1993-95, NATO, 1996-97. Mem. EERI, N.Y. Acad. Scis. Office: ENEA CR Casaccia, Via Anguillarese 301, 00060 Rome San Maria Di Galeria, Italy

CLEMENTE, PATROCINIO ABLOLA, secondary education educator; b. Manila, Philippines, Apr. 23, 1941; s. Elpidio San Jose and Amparo (Ablola) C.; came to U.S., 1965; BSE, U. Philippines, 1960; postgrad. Nat. U., Manila, 1961-64; MA, Ball State U., 1966, EdD, 1969; postgrad. U. Calif., Riverside, 1970, Calif. State Coll., Fullerton, 1971-72. High sch. tchr. gen. sci. and biology, div. city schs., Quezon City, Philippines, 1960-65; doctoral fellow dept. psychology Ball State U., Muncie, Ind., 1966-67, dept. spl. edn., 1967-68, grad. asst. dept. gen. and exptl. psychology, 1968-69; tchr. educable mentally retarded high sch. level Fontana (Calif.) Unified Sch. Dist., 1969-70, intermediate level, 1970-73, dist. sch. psychologist, 1973-79, bilingual edn. counselor, 1979-81; resource specialist Morongo (Calif.) Unified Sch. Dist., 1981-83, spl. day class tchr., 1983-90, tchr. math, sci., Spanish, English, 1990—; adj. assoc. prof. Chapman Coll., Orange, Calif., 1982-91. Adult leader Girl Scouts of Philippines, 1963-65; mem. sch. bd. Blessed Sacrament Sch., Twentynine Palms, Calif. State bd. scholar Ball State U., 1965-66. Fellow Am. Biographical Inst. (hon. mem. research bd. advisors, life); mem. ASCD, NEA, Coun. for Exceptional Children, Am. Assn. on Mental Deficiency, Nat. Assn. of Sch. Psychologists, Found. Exceptional Children, Assn. for Children with Learning Disabilities, Nat. Geographic Soc., Calif. Tchrs. Assn., Morongo Tchrs. Assn., Smithsonian Inst. Roman Catholic. Home: PO Box 637 Twentynine Palms CA 92277-0637

CLEMENTE, ROBERT JOHN, education executive; b. Brisbane, Queensland, Australia, Feb. 21, 1951; m. Caroline A. Coffey, Sept. 1981; children: Camilla, Julia. LLB with honors, U. Melbourne, Australia, 1972. Bar: Supreme Ct. Victoria 1973. Mng. dir. Bus. Law Edn. Ctr., Australia, 1975-91; chmn. TV Edn. Network Inc., N.Y., 1987-92; mng. dir. TV Edn. Network Inc., London, 1992-96, dir., 1996—; dep. chmn. com. of mgmt. Trinity Edn. Ctr., Australia, 1989-99; chmn. TV Edn. Network, Ltd., Australia, 1991—. Editor Melbourne U. Law Rev., 1971. Mem. Trinity Coll. Coun., Melbourne, 1989—; chmn. Trinity Coll. Strategy Com., 1994-95. Fellow Trinity Coll., 1997. Mem. Internat. Industry Assn. (dir. 1998—), East India Club (London), Australian Interactive Multimedia Assn. (treas. 1996-97, v.p. 1997-98, pres. 1998-99), Australian Club. Avocations: skiing, bushwalking, opera. Office: 7th Fl, 395 Collins St, Melbourne Victoria 3000, Australia

CLEMENTI, EMILIO, pharmacology educator; b. Milan, Apr. 1, 1964; s. Francesco Clementi and Tullia Scamazzo. B in Classical Sci., Licaeum G. Carducci, Milan, 1982; M in Piano, Conservatory Music G. Verdi, Milan, 1983; MD, U. Milan, 1988; PhD in Pharmacology, U. Brescia, Italy, 1994. Asst. prof. U. Reggio Calabria, Catanzaro, Italy, 1992-98; assoc. prof. U. Calabria, Cosenza, Italy, 1998—; vis. scientist U. Coll. London, 1997-99; cons. Schering Plough, Milan. Mem. editl. adv. bd. Current Topics Pharmacology, 1994—; composer music Orthodox Divine Svcs. Recipient A. Benedicenti prize Italian Soc. Pharmacology. Christian Orthodox. Avocations: music, reading, swimming. Office: Dibit H San Raffaele Inst, Via Olgettina 58, 20132 Milan Italy

CLEMENTS, CHRISTOPHER JOHN, epidemiologist, public health physician; b. Ledsham, Cheshire, Eng., Jan. 21, 1946; arrived in New Zealand, 1980; s. Henry Walter and Mary (Jordan) C.; m. Vivienne Mary Driscoll, Dec. 11, 1976; children: Tristan, Ashley. MBBS, London Hosp. Med. Sch., London, 1969; diploma Obstetrics and Neonatal Medicine, U. Auckland, 1972; diploma in Child Health, Royal Coll. Physicians, London, 1973; MSc, U. Manchester, 1980. House surgeon London Hosp., Whitechapel, 1969; house physician St. Richard's Hosp., Chichester, Eng., 1969; resident pediatrics U. Western Ont., London, Can., 1970; registrar obstetrics Waikato Hosp., Hamilton, New Zealand, 1971; sr. house officer Alder Hey Childrens Hosp., Liverpool, Eng., 1972; med. dir. Hosp. del Valle Apurimac, Peru, 1973; registrar pediatrics Lancaster Royal Infirmary, 1974-76; registrar cmty. medicine N.W. Regional Health Authority, 1978-80; dep. med. officer health Wellington, New Zealand, 1980-83; asst. dir., head disease control Dept. Health, Wellington, 1983-85; med. officer Expanded Programme on Immunization WHO, Geneva, 1985—; tchr. dept. pediatrics U. Western Ont., dept. child health U. Liverpool, dept. health policy U. Lancaster, dept. cmty. medicine U. Otago, New Zealand; chief med. officer Save the Children Fund, Bangladesh, 1977, Afghanistan, 1977. Cons. editor Annals of Tropical Pediatrics, 1980-85; reviewer Biologicals, Bull. of WHO, Bull. Pan Am. Health Orgn., Weekly Epid. Record, Vaccine; contbr. over 100 articles to profl. jours. Elder local evangelical ch. Fellow Australasian Faculty Pub. Health Medicine of Royal Australian Coll. Physicians; mem. Faculty Pub. Health Medicine of Royal Coll. Physicians. Avocations: windsurfing, guitar, photography, jogging, gardening. E-mail: clem@who.ch. Office: WHO Expanded Programme Immunization, 1121 Geneva 27, Switzerland

CLEMENTS, GEORGE NICKERSON, linguist, educator, researcher; b. Cin., Oct. 5, 1940; s. George Love and Rosalie Frances (Bangs) C.; companion Annie Louise Emilie Rialland; children: William Riwal, Celia Anabel. BA, Yale U., 1962; PhD, U. London, 1973. Asst. prof. Harvard U., Cambridge, Mass., 1975-79, assoc. prof., 1979-82; assoc. prof. Cornell U., Ithaca, N.Y., 1982-86, prof., 1986-93; rsch. dir. C.N.R.S. UPRESA 7018, Paris, 1992—; vis. faculty Vrije U., Amsterdam, CIEFL, Hyderabad, U. Paris VII, U. Groningen, U. Salzburg, U. Amsterdam, U. Wash., U. Nairobi, U. Legon, Ghana; cons. Am. Heritage Dictionary, Boston, 1982—; invited faculty Linguistic Soc. Am., Stanford, Calif., 1987, Columbus, Ohio, 1993, Ithaca, N.Y., 1997, Australian Linguistic Soc., Sydney, 1992. Co-author: (with S.J. Keyser) CV Phonology, 1983, (with M. Halle) Problem Book in Phonology, 1983; co-editor: (with J. Goldsmith) Autosegmental Studies in Bantu Tone, 1984; contbr. articles to profl. jours. With U.S. Army, 1963-65. Fulbright grantee, 1984, NSF grantee, 1988-90; Whiting Found. fellow, Kenya, 1978. Mem. Linguistic Soc. Am., Acoustical Soc. Am., European Speech Community Assn. Office: ILPGA, 19 Rue des Bernardins, Paris France 75005

CLEMENTS, JAMES DAVID, retired psychiatry educator, physician; b. Pineview, Ga., May 7, 1931; s. Marcus Monroe and Dewey Thelma (Gammage) C.; m. Janet Collier Swan, Aug. 25, 1952; children—Leiliar Ann, David Marcus. B.A., Emory U., 1952; M.D., Med. Coll. Ga., 1956. Intern Temple U., Phila., 1956-57; resident in pediatrics Temple U., 1957-59; fellow mental retardation Sch. Medicine, Yale U., 1959-60; med. dir. Gracewood (Ga.) State Sch. Hosp., 1960-62, asst. supt., 1963-64; dir. planning mental retardation Ga. Dept. Pub. Health, Atlanta, 1964-65; dir. Ga. Retardation Center, Atlanta, 1964-79; med. cons. mental retardation Ga. Dept. Human Resources, 1979-81; resident in psychiatry Emory U., Sch. Medicine, Atlanta, 1983-86; clin. asst. prof. pediatrics and psychiatry Emory U. Sch. Medicine, Atlanta, from 1964, asst. prof. psychiatry, 1985-95; ret., 1995; assoc. clin. prof. neurology, asst. clin. prof pediatrics Med. Coll. Ga., Augusta, 1970—; spl. cons. neurology mental retardation dept. pediatrics Ga. Bapt. Hosp., 1965—; mem. adv. com. program exceptional children Ga. Dept. Edn., 1968-70; mem. adv. bd. Sch. Allied Health Sci., Ga. State U., 1971-76; mem. accreditation council mental retardation council Joint Commn. on Accreditation Hosps., Chgo., 1975-79; del. White House conf.

Ga. com. children youth, 1970; mem. Pres.'s Com. on Mental Retardation, 1975-78; chmn. Willowbrook rev. panel Fed. Ct. Eastern Dist. N.Y.; reviewer NSF; cons. Inst. Society, Ethics and Life Scis., Hastings Center; commr. Am. Bar Assn., 1976-80. Contbr. articles to profl. jours., anthologies, seminars. Mem. adv. bd. Arbor Acad., DeKalb County (Ga.) Dept. Edn., 1973-75; mem. bd. founders, adv. com. Ashdun Hall, 1965-70; trustee Gatchell Sch., Mental Health Law Project (now Bazelon Ctr. for Mental Health Law); adv. com. Kennedy Center, Johns Hopkins U. Recipient Leadership award Am. Assn. Mental Deficiency, 1980. Fellow Am. Acad. Pediatrics (cons. head start med. cons. service), Am. Assn. Mental Deficiency (pres. 1974-75), Pan Am. Med. Assn., Am. Geriatrics Soc.; mem. Ga. Pediatric Soc., Nat. Assn. Supts. Pub. Residential Facilities Mentally Retarded, Nat. Assn. Retarded Citizens (legal advocacy adv. com. 1975), Internat. Assn. Sci. Study Mental Deficiency (chmn. local organizing com. 4th internat. congress, mem. council 1976-78), Am. Psychiatric Assocs. Home: 475 Grant St SE Atlanta GA 30312-3154

CLEMENTS, JOHN ROBERT, real estate professional; b. Richmond, Ind., Nov. 2, 1950; s. George Howard and Mary Amanda (McKown) C. Grad. high sch., Phoenix. Sales assoc. Clements Realty, Inc., Phoenix, 1973-75; office mgr. Clements Realty, Inc., Mesa, Ariz., 1975-78; v.p., co-owner Clements Realty, Inc., Phoenix, 1978-80; broker, assoc. Ben Brooks & Assocs., Phoenix, 1980-88; pres. John R. Clements, P.C., 1984—; broker Keller Williams Realty, Phoenix and Mesa, Ariz., 1994-96; facilities dir., gen. mgr. mall divsn. Infinity Outdoor, Phoenix, 1996—. Real estate dir. Circle K Corp., Western Region, 1989-92; bd. dirs., v.p. Big Sisters Ariz., Phoenix, 1974-80; trustee Ariz. Realtors Polit. Action Com., 1975-85, Realtors Polit. Action Com., Ill., 1985-88; appointee Govtl. Mall Co., Ariz., 19865, commr. chair, 1991-95. Mem. Ariz. Assn. Realtors (bd. dirs., pres. 1981), Mesa-Chandler-Tempe Bd. Realtors (past bd. dirs., pres., 1978), Nat. Assn. Realtors (past bd. dirs., exec. com.), Coun. Residential Specialists (bd. govs. 19865, v.p. 1990, pres. 1991), Ariz. Country Club. Republican. Presbyterian. Home: 3618 N 60th St Phoenix AZ 85018-6708 Office: Outdoor Sys 2502 N Black Canyon Hwy Phoenix AZ 85009-1800

CLEMENTS, LYNNE FLEMING, family therapist, programmer; b. Bklyn., Aug. 8, 1945; d. Daniel Gillies and Dorothy Frances (Zitzmann) Fleming; m. Louis Myrick Clements, Feb. 19, 1972; children: Ryan Louis, Glenn Fleming. BA in Sociology, Bradley U., 1967; MSW, Fordham U., 1973; postgrad. studies, Columbia U., 1970-71; cert. family therapy, Inst. for Mental Health Edn., 1990. Lic. clin. social worker, N.J.; cert. social wrk mgr. Computer programmer Employer's Comml. Union Group Ins. Cos., Boston, 1967-69, Harvard Bus. Sch., Cambridge, Mass., 1969-70, Volkswagon of Am., Englewood Cliffs, N.J., 1971; psychiat. social worker Associated Cath. Charities Family and Children's Svcs., Paramus, N.J., 1973-74, Christian Health Ctr., Wyckoff, N.J., 1976; owner, mgr. Wicker Wagon, Bergenfield, N.J., 1977-85; psychotherapist The Psychotherapy Counseling Ctr., Bergenfield, N.J., 1982-89; programmer analyst Atlas Computing Svcs., Secaucus, N.J., 1984-86; program coord., family therapist Divsn. Family Guidance, Hackensack, N.J., 1986-91; pres. Corp. Family Resources, Ridgewood, N.J., 1989—; family therapist cons. Family Recovery of Valley View, White Plains, N.Y., 1992-94, Furman Clinic, Fair Lawn, N.J., 1995-96, Van Ost Inst. for Family Living, Englewood, N.J., 1996; cert. social work mgr., 1997—; part-time family therapist N.J. Ctr. for Psychotherapy Inc., Ridgefield Park, 1990. Sunday sch. tchr. All Saints Ch., 1982-89, 94—, chmn. bd. cmty. play ctr., 1977-78; mem. Twin-Boro Youth Ministry Coun., 1989—, Bergen County Family Day Care Coalition, 1989—; apptd. sec. Mayor's Beautify Bergenfield Com., 1991-95; chmn. entertainment Bergen County Children's Festival, 1993; apptd. chmn., designer Bergenfield's Coun. for Arts, 1993-99, chmn. author/poet program, 1996—; chmn. curriculum enhancement com. Bergen County Acad. for Advancement of Sci. and Tech., 1992-96. Recipient 1st and 2nd pl. awards Bergenfield 1980 Art Contest; NIMH grantee, 1973. Mem. AAUW, Gifted Child Soc. (parent workshop coord. 1989—, bd. dirs. 1991—), NASW, Acad. Cert. Social Workers, Am. Orthopsychiat. Assn., Fordham U. Alumni Assn., N.J. Commerce and Industry Assn. (child care com. 1990—, mem. human resources com. 1990—), N.J. Soc. Clin. Social Workers (chmn. mktg. and vendor com. 1999—), Zonta (Amelia Earhart chmn. 1987-88, literacy com. 1995—, chmn. status of women com. 1993-94), Women of Accomplishment (founder, pres. 1990—, chmn. women's coalition conf. 1993—). Episcopalian. Avocations: walking, art, music, crafts, boating. Home: 148 Harcourt Ave Bergenfield NJ 07621-1917 Office: Corp Family Resources 15 Godwin Ave Ste 1 Ridgewood NJ 07450-3739

CLEMENTS, ROBIN EDWARD, lawyer, company director; b. Melbourne, Australia, June 29, 1941; s. Kenneth John and Margaret Mawbey (Harty) C.; m. Deirdre Griffiths, Mar. 28, 1969; children: Jonathan William, David Anthony. LLB, U. Melbourne, 1964. Bar: Victoria Supreme Ct., 1966, NSW Supreme Ct., 1990. Sr. ptnr. Gadens Ridgeway, Lawyers, Melbourne, 1970-93, nat. chmn., 1989-92; sr. cons. Deacons Lawyers, Melbourne, 1994—; chmn. Austin Group Ltd., 1993-97, Victorian Plantations Corp., 1993-99; mem. adv. bd. Buchan Comm. Group, 1995-98; bd. dirs. Adorina Group Pty. Ltd., Thomas Warburton Group Pty. Ltd., Johnson Taylor Porter Group Ltd., RMG Limited; chmn. V/Line Freight Corp., 1997-99, Hillside Trains Corp., 1998-99, Genomic Disorders Rsch. Ctr. Limited. Chmn. urban land authority rev. com. Victoria State Govt., 1996; bd. dirs. Victoria divsn. Nat. Heart Found., 1996-98. Mem. Law Coun. Australia, Australian Inst. Co. Dirs., Australian Club (pres. 1994-95), Moonee Valley Racing Club (com. 1989-2000). Avocations: sports, gardening, reading. Office: Deacons, 385 Bourke St, Melbourne Vic 3000, Australia

CLEMONS, BILL, lawyer; b. Hardshell, Ky., Oct. 16, 1944; s. Urban and Irene N. Clemons; m. Joan Williams (div.); children: Wanda Faye, Randal Scot. AA, Hazard (Ky.) C.C., 1992; BA, Berea (Ky.) Coll., 1994; JD, U. Ky., 1997. Miner Falcon Coal Co., Jackson, Ky., 1978-91; dep. cir. clk. Adminstrv. Office of Cts., Lexington, Ky., 1995-96; pre-trial officer Adminstrv. Office of Cts., Lexington, 1996-97; staff atty. Henderson (Ky.) Cir. Ct., 1997, Legal Aid Svcs., Lexington, 1997-98; assoc. pub. advocate Dept. Pub. Advocacy Commonwealth of Ky., 1998—. With U.S. Army, 1965-67, Vietnam. Mem. ABA, Ky. Bar Assn. Avocations: reading, computers, travel. Home: 1350 Bethel Church Rd Hardshell KY 41348-9038 Office: Dept Pub Advocacy 205 Lovern St Hazard KY 41701-1727

CLEMONS, LYNN ALLAN, land use planner; b. New Orleans, Oct. 23, 1946; s. Gaylord Wilson and Jessica Monica (McDonald) C. BS, Colo. State U., 1973. Planner outdoor recreation Bur. Outdoor Recreation, Denver, 1974-75; planner outdoor recreation Bur. Land Mgmt., Golden, Co., 1975-77, Winnemucca, Nev., 1977—; pub. affairs officer Bur. Land Mgmt., Winnemucca, 1989-93. Co-author environ. impact statements. With USN, 1968-69, Vietnam. Recipient Spl. Achievement award Dept. of Interior, 1988, 91. Mem. Am. Radio Relay League, U.S. Chess Fedn., No. Nev. Amateur Radio Club (sec.-treas. 1992), Winnemucca Amateur Trap Assn. (sec.-treas. 1981), Assn. for Preservation Tech., Wilderness Soc., One Moccasin Toastmasters Club (officer, Competent Toastmaster award 1988). Roman Catholic. Avocations: woodworking, backpacking, gourmet cooking, reading for the blind, guitar. Office: Bur Land Mgmt 5100 E Winnemucca Blvd Winnemucca NV 89445-2921

CLEMONS, ROBERT EARL, non-profit organization administrator; b. Wagoner, Okla., Aug. 25, 1932; s. Ernest and Exzee (Smith) C. BFA, Calif. Coll. Arts and Crafts, 1971. Pres., dir. Ctrl. East Oakland (Calif.) Neighborhood Housing, 1979—, Ctrl. East Oakland (Calif.) Local Devel. Corp., 1979—. With USAF, 1951-55, Korea. Democrat. Baptist. Avocations: pen and ink drawing, watercolor painting, wood sculpture. Home and Office: Ctrl East Oakland Local Devel Corp PO Box 896 Oakland CA 94604-0896

CLERGERIE, JEAN-LOUIS, law educator, researcher; b. Tours, France, Apr. 13, 1949; s. Yves and Jacqueline (Petibon) C.; m. Bénédicte Dubois, Jan. 29, 1977; children: Caroline, Marine, Alix. M in Law, U. Tours, 1979; DES in Polit. Sci., U. Poitiers, France, 1975, DEA in Pub. Law, 1977, D of State, 1984; lic. rsch. direction, U. Besançon, France, 1987. Prof. U. Angers, France, 1975-76, U. Tours, 1976-85, U. Besançon, 1985-90; prof. U. Limoges, France, 1990—, Jean Monnet chair, 1992—; dir. Ctr. U. Regional Studies Territorials Limousin, France, 1993—; dir. degree European law, U. Limoges, 1994—, bd. dirs. faculty law; vis. prof. Inst. d'Etudes Europeennes, Brussels. Mem. editl. bd. Cahiers Paneuropéens, 1995—; contbr. articles to profl. joursincluding R.D.P., AJDA, Recueil Dalloz, Gazette du Palais, Semaine Junidigue, Petites Affiches, Knisis, Cahiens Paneunofeens, Europe; author: The Crisis of Biafna, 1994, The principle of subsidiariry, 1997, The judiciary power of U.E., 1999, The European Union, 2000, The prejudicial adjournment, 2000. Mem. Commn. Study Communautés European, Sci. Coun. Europa. Avocations: cycling, music, drawing, country, literature. Office: Univ Limoges Faculty Law, 4 Place du Présidial, 87031 Limoges France

CLERGUE, LUCIEN GEORGES, photographer; b. Arles, France, Aug. 14, 1934; s. Etienne and Jeanne (Grangeon) C.; m. Yolande Wartel, Jan. 10, 1963; children: Anne, Olivia. Dr. es Letters in Photography, U. Provence, 1979. tchr. workshops New Sch., N.Y.C., Art Ctr., Pasadena, Osaka U., Japan, other U.S. univs. and colls. Freelance photographer, 1959—; artistic dir. Arles Festival, 1971-75, 86-88; founder, Rencontres Internationales de la Photographie, Arles, 1969, art dir. XXVth anniversary, 1994; one-man exhbns. include Kunstgewerbe Mus., Zurich, 1958, 63, Mus. Modern Art, N.Y.C., 1961—, Musée d'Arts Decoratifs, Paris, 1962—, Moderna Museet, Stockholm, 1969—, Art Inst. Chgo., 1970—, Kunsthalle, Düsseldorf, Fed. Republic Germany, 1970—, Gallery Witkin, N.Y.C., 1972-79, Bruxelles Musee d'Ixelles, 1974—, Israel Mus., Jerusalem, 1974—, Ctr. Pompidou, Paris, 1980—, Musée d'Art Moderne Paris, 1984, George Eastman House, Rochester, 1985, ICP, N.Y.,1986, Amos Anderson Mus., Helsinki, 1987, Real Maestranza Sevilla, 1991, Houston Photo Fest, 1992, Milw. Art Mus., 1993, Calif. Mus. Photography, Riverside, 1997, Centro de la Imagen, Mexico, 1997, Kunstmuseum Dortmund, 1999, John Stevenson Gallery, N.Y., 2000; works rep. books, movies; represented in permanent collection Fogg Mus., Harvard U., Cambridge, Mass.; films include Picasso War Love and Peace; books include Footprints of the Gods, 1988, Picasso my Friend, 1993, Grands Nus, 1999; author of 50 publs. Decorated chevalier Nat. Order Merit, 1980; recipient Louis Lumière prize, 1966, Grand Prix of Higashikawa Photo Fest, 1986, 3rd prize World Press Photo Internat., Amsterdam, 1997, Prix Polyedre, Aix, France, 1998. Mem. Assn. Nat. Photographers Createurs, Parc Regional Camargue, Ste. des Amis Jean Cocteau, Ste des Amis de La Fond, St. J. Perse, Aix en Pr., Rencontres Internat. de la Photographie Arles, Memoire 2000. Roman Catholic. Home: 17 Rue Aristide Briand, BP 84, 13632 Arles Cedex, France

CLERGUE, YOLANDE, executive; b. Paris, Feb. 16, 1929; d. Pierre Wartel and Geneviève Masson; m. Lucien Clergue, Jan. 1, 1963; children: Anne, Olivia. Flight hostess Air France, 1954-59; founder Found. Van Gogh Arles, 1985—. Avocations: painting, music, planes. Email: fondwga@wanadoo.fr. Fax: 04 90 496132. Home: 17 rue Aristide Briand, 13200 Arles France Office: Vincent Van Gogh Found, 24 bis Rond Point Arenes, 13200 Arles France

CLERICI, ALFONSO, import/export company executive; b. Genoa, Italy, Mar. 9, 1953; married; 4 children. With Group CoeClerici, Italy; CEO CoeClerici, N.Y.C.; CEO logistic sub-holding CoeClerici, Italy; founder, owner Clerici Spa Logistic Group, Italy, 1995—; v.p. Assologistica. Hon. consul of India in Genoa. Mem. Italian Yacht Club, Golf Club, Colline del Gavi, Tunnel Club. Avocations: painting, skiing, fishing, golfing. E-mail: aclerici@clerici.com. Home: Salita Santa Caterina 4/5, Genoa Italy

CLERIDES, GLAFCOS JOHN, president of Cyprus, lawyer; b. Nicosia, Cyprus, Apr. 24, 1919; s. John and Elli C. Grad., Pancyprian Gymnasium, Nicosia, London U. Bar: Gray's Inn 1951. Practiced law Cyprus, 1951-60; min. justice, 1959-60; mem. Ho. Reps., 1960-76, 81-93, pres., 1960-76; acting pres. Cyprus, 1974, pres. Cyprus, 1993—; head Greek Cypriot Del. Joint Constnl. Com., 1959-60; Greek Cypriot del. London Conf., 1964; rep. negotiator Greek Cypriot Cmty. Intercommunal Talks, 1968. Author: My Deposition, vol. 1, 1988, vol. 2, 1989, vol. 3, 1990, vol. 4, 1991. Pres. Red Cross, 1961-63, hon. cert., hon. life mem., Recognition Disting. Svc.; founder Unified Party, 1969, Dem. Nat. Front; leading mem. Unified Party, Progressive Front, Dem. Nat. Front, 1976. Decorated Gold Medal-Order Holy Sepulchre, Recognized Svcs. and Understanding Roman Cath. Religious Group by approval of His Holiness Pope John XXIII, Grand Cross of Saviour, Greece. Office: Presidential Palace, Nicosia Cyprus

CLERMONT, CHARLES M., entrepreneur, consultant; b. Port-Au-Prince, Haiti, Jan. 16, 1950; s. Marcel and Louisette (Gaillard) C.; m. Frederique Nicolas; children: Carl Frederic, Louis-Olivier. MS in Engring., Inst. Nat. Sci Appliquees, Toulouse, France, 1973; MA, Tufts U., 1982. Sales mgr. Haytian Tractor and Equipment Co., S.A., Port-Au-Prince, 1976-81, fin. mgr., 1982-83; credit mgr. Sofihdes, Port-Au-Prince, 1983-85, Banque de Credit Immobilier, Port-Au-Prince, 1985-88; gen. mgr. Sogebel, 1988-93, Sogebank, 1993-2000; ret., 2000; cons. Capital Consult/Multiplan, Port-Au-Prince, 1978-83. Coordinator Movement Action Dem., Port-Au-Prince, 1986—. Office: 14 Rue Panamericaine, Petion-Ville Haiti

CLEVE, GUNNEL INGA-LILL, English language educator; b. Helsinki, Finland, May 13, 1930; d. Georg Osvald and Aili Adeline (Hellbom) Lehtinen; m. Johan Fredric Cleve, June 15, 1952; 1 child, Johan Georg Ola. Diploma in philosophy, Helsinki U., 1960, Licentiate in Philosophy, 1978; PhD, Turku (Finland) U., 1987. Translator ins. dept. Ministry Social Affairs, Helsinki, 1951-58; secondary sch. tchr. English Svenska Flicklycéet, Helsinki, 1960-61, Brändö Svenska Samskola, Helsinki, 1961-67; asst. Helsinki U., 1967-71, Tampere (Finland) U., 1972-73; lectr. The Swedish Sch. Bus., Helsinki, 1973-77, The Turku (Finland) Sch. Bus., 1977-79; lectr. Turku U., 1979-80, asst., 1981-83; lectr. Åbo Akad. U., Turku, 1983-89, assoc. prof., 1989-93; ret. Åbo Acad. U., Turku, 1993; corr. editor Mystics Quarterly, 1986—; docent Turku U., 1987-95; mem. direction Inst. Women's Studies Åbo Akad. U., 1992-93. Contbr. numerous articles to profl. jours. and newspapers. Mem. cultural bd. City of Kaarina, Finland, 1989-92, 97—, 1st dep. mem. town coun., 1990-92, mem. health ctr. coun., 1993-96. Avocations: traveling, literature, language studies.

CLEVELAND, JULIA LYNN, elementary school educator; b. Ft. Dodge, Iowa, May 1, 1952; d. Euzema Hendrix and Mildred Helen (Harris) C. BS, Berry Coll., Mt. Berry, Ga., 1973, MEd, 1978. Cert. tchr. in early childhood and middle grades. Tchr. Cloverleaf Elem. Sch., Cartersville, Ga., 1873-85, Cass Middle Sch., Cartersville, 1985—; team leader Cass Middle Sch., Cartersville, Ga., 1989-95; mem. site based mgmt. com. Cass Mid. Sch., 1993-98, mem. tech. com., 1993-96, mem. sch. improvement com., 1998—. Editor Casszine jour., 1989—. Mem. People for the Ethical Treatment of Animals, Nat. Mus. of Women in the Arts, Greenpeace, Humane Soc. U.S., ASPCA, Physicians Com. for Responsible Medicine, Amnesty Internat. Named Tchr. of the Yr., Cass Middle Sch., 1992. Mem. NEA, Ga. Assn. Educators, Profl. Assn. Ga. Educators. Methodist. Avocations: writing poetry and short stories, drawing. Home: PO Box 313 Armuchee GA 30105-0313 Office: Cass Middle School 195 Firetower Rd NW Cartersville GA 30120-4648

CLEVELAND, RAY LEROY, history educator; b. Scottsbluff, Nebr., Apr. 29, 1929; s. Harold and Florence Cleveland. BA, Westmont Coll., 1951; MA, Johns Hopkins U., 1956, PhD, 1958; SCd (hon.), U. of the Pacific, 1970. Rsch. assoc. Johns Hopkins U., Balt., 1959-64; rsch. fellow Am. Found. for Study of Man, 1964-66; assoc. prof. U. Sask., Regina, Can., 1966-72, prof. history, 1972-74; prof. history U. Regina, 1974-94, prof. emeritus, 1994—; assoc. editor Bull. of Am. Schs. of Oriental Rsch., 1960-64; editor publs. Am. Found. for Study of Man, 1959-75. Author: An Ancient South Arabian Necropolis, 1965, Middle East and South Asia, 20 edits., 1967-88; co-editor: Alexander The Great, 1992; contbr. numerous articles to profl. jours. Fellow Am. Sch. Oriental Rsch. in Jerusalem, 1955-56. Office: U Regina, History Dept, Regina, SK Canada S4S 0A2

CLEWLOW, WARREN A. M., manufacturing company executive, sugar cane farmer; b. Durban, Natal, South Africa, July 13, 1936; s. Percy Edward and Eunice Rose (Penrose) C.; m. Margaret Brokensha; 5 children. CA, U. Natal, D in Econ. (hon.), 1988. Acct. Halsey Button & Perry, South Africa and Zimbabwe, 1958-62; acct., sec. tractor divsn. Barlow, Bloemfontein, then Durban, South Africa, 1963-67; fin. dir. Thos Barlow & Sons (SWA) Ltd. (now Sonnex Pty Ltd.), Namibia, 1968, mng. dir., 1969-71; mng. dir. Barlows Mfg. Co. Ltd., South Africa, 1972-74; chief ops. dir. Barlow Rand Ltd., South Africa, 1983-85, dep. chmn., chief exec., 1985-90; vice chmn., chief exec. Barlow Rand Ltd., 1988; chmn. Barlow Ltd. (formerly Barlow Rand Ltd.), 1991—; also bd. dirs.; chmn. Pretoria Portland Cement Co. Ltd., 1993—; dep. chmn. Old Mutual, SA; dir. SA Mutual Life Assurance Soc., South Africa, Iscor Ltd., South Africa, Sasol Ltd., South Africa, Comparex Holdings Ltd., South Africa, J. Bibby & Sons, Ltd., U.K., Old Mutual plc. Past chmn. State Pres. Econ. Adv. Coun., 1990-93, mem. 1985-93; hon. pres. South Africa Found., trustee, 1983—, coun. mem., 1985—, pres. 1989-93; dir. SAFTO, 1979, chmn., 1985-88; hon. treas. African Children's Feeding Scheme, 1981—; bd. govs. Urban Found. (now Nat. Bus. Initiative), 1985-95; bd. Assn. Marketers, 1988—; v.p. Inst. Dirs. So. Africa, 1993—; chmn. U. Natal Devel. Found., 1994—. Decorated Order of Meritorious Svc. Class 1-Gold, 1988; recipient Dr. E.G. Malherbe award for outstanding contbns. to edn., sci., industry U. Natal, 1986; named Marketing Man of Yr. by Inst. Mktg. Mgmt., 1984; awarded hon. professorship in bus. mgmt. and adminstrn. Stellenbosch, 1986; Inst. Mktg. Mgmt. fellow, 1984. Mem. Whites (London), Rand Club (Johannesburg), Durban Club. Avocations: tennis, horticulture, hist. reading, fishing. Office: Barlow Ltd, PO Box 782248, Sandton 2146, South Africa*

CLIET, ISABELLE MARIE, biologist; b. St. Jean de Maurienne, Savoie, France, Apr. 3, 1961; d. Jean Alexandre and Ginette (Taravel) Clement; m. Christian Felix Cliet, Sept. 6, 1986; children: Mathilde, Vincent, Charles. M in Cellular Biology, U. Sci., Grenoble, France, 1986; postgrad., U. Paris VII, 1987. Toxicologist Rhone-Poulenc Rorer, Paris, 1986-94, sr. labelling specialist, 1994-96, regulatory affairs sr. mgr., 1996—; study dir. Rhone-Poulenc Rorer, Paris, 1987-88, mgr., 1988-93. Contbr. articles to profl. jours. Mem. Soc. Française de Toxicologie Génétique, Assn. pour la Recherche en Toxicologie, Soc. de Biologie Cellulaire Francaise. Avocations: reading, golf, sailing. Office: Aventis, 20 Ave Raymond Aron, 92160 Antony France

CLIFF, JOHNNIE MARIE, mathematics and chemistry educator; b. Lamkin, Miss., May 10, 1935; d. John and Modest Alma (Lewis) Walton; m. William Henry Cliff, Apr. 1, 1961 (dec. 1983); 1 child, Karen Marie. BA in Chemistry, Math., U. Indpls., 1956; postgrad., NSF Inst., Butler U., 1960; MA in Chemistry, Ind. U., 1964; MS in Math., U. Notre Dame, 1980. Cert. tchr., Ind. Rsch. chemist Ind. U. Med. Ctr., Indpls., 1956-59; tchr. sci. and math. Indpls. Pub. Schs., 1960-88; tchr. chemistry, math. Martin U., Indpls., 1989—, chmn. math. dept., 1990—, divsn. chmn. depts. sci. and math., 1993—; adj. instr. math. U. Indpls., 1991. Contbr. rsch. papers to sci. jours. Grantee NSF, 1961-64, 73-76, 78-79, Woodrow Wilson Found., 1987-88; scholarship U. Indpls., 1952-56, NSF Inst. Reed Coll., 1961, C. of C., 1963. Mem. AAUW, NAACP, NEA, Assn. Women in Sci., Urban League, N.Y. Acad. Scis., Am. Chem. Soc., Nat. Coun. Math. Tchrs., Am. Assn. Physics Tchrs., Nat. Sci. Tchrs. Assn., Am. Statis. Assn., Am. Assn. Ret. Persons, Neal-Marshall-Ind. U. Alumni Assn., U. Indpls. Alumni Assn., U. Notre Dame Alumni Assn., Ind. U. Chemist Assn., Notre Dame Club Indpls., Kappa Delta Pi, Delta Sigma Theta. Democrat. Baptist. Avocations: gardening, sewing. Home: 405 Golf Ln Indianapolis IN 46260-4108 Office: Martin U 2171 Avondale Pl Indianapolis IN 46218-3878

CLIFF, STEVEN BURRIS, engineering executive; b. Knoxville, Tenn., Mar. 30, 1952; s. Edgar Burris and Otella (Patterson) C.; m. Sharon Grace Davis, Sept. 11, 1971 ; children: Sarah Elizabeth, Susan Rebecca, Steven John. BS in Engring. Sci., U. Tenn., 1974, MS in Engring. Sci., 1976; postgrad., So. Sem., 1974-75. Rsch. asst. U. Tenn., Knoxville, 1972-75, asst. rsch. prof., 1975-76; program analyst Oak Ridge (Tenn.) Nat. Lab., 1976-77, rsch. engr., 1977-79; chief tech. officer Computer Concepts Corp., Knoxville, 1979-81; pres. Productive Programming Inc., Knoxville, 1981-82; v.p. R&D Control Tech. Inc., Knoxville, 1982-98, sr. v.p. R&D, 1998—, corp. sec., 1991—; ptnr. Middlebrook Indsl. Properties, 1985—, Cliff Bros. Investments, 1988—. Contbr. articles to profl. jours. Exec. bd. Rocky Hill Parent-Tchr. Orgn., Knoxville, 1987, 91-97, pres. 1994-95; deacon West Knoxville Bapt. Ch., 1984-87, Loveland Bapt. Ch., Knoxville, 1976-82; tech. com. Bearden (Tenn.) Mid. Sch., 1996-97; bd. dirs. Rocky Hill Baseball League, 1995-2000. U. Tenn. scholar, 1970. Mem. Soc. Mfgs. Engrs. (sr.), Nat. Electronic Mfg. Assn. (chmn. com. 1987-94, seminar spkr. 1988-94), Am. Assn. for Artificial Intelligence, Instrument Soc. Am., Open DeviceNet Vendors Assn. (com. chair 1998—), Contro Net Internat. (com. chair 2000—). Avocations: photography, home improvement projects, fishing, bluegrass guitar. Home: 8210 Northshore Dr SW Knoxville TN 37919-8711

CLIFFE, MARK ALAN, economist; b. Sheffield, Yorkshire, England, Feb. 4, 1959; s. Bernard William and Florence (Timmins) C.; m. Carol Johnstone, Apr. 11, 1987; children: Matthew, Helen, Frances. MA in Econs., Christ's Coll., Cambridge, Eng., 1980. Cert. diploma in acctg. and fin., Assn. Cert. Accts. Economist Overseas Containers Ltd., London, 1980-82; chief economist Anz Merchant Bank, London, 1983-87, Nomura Rsch. Inst. Europe, London, 1987-94; chief internat. economist HSBC Markets, London, 1994-98; chief economist ING Barings, London, 1998—; chmn. Item Club, London, 1986-93. Columnist The Times, London, 1984-97, Evening Standard, London, 1993-96, Independent (Sunday), London, 1999—. Mem. Soc. Bus. Economists. Home: 9 Woodville Gardens, W5 2LG Ealing London, England Office: ING Barings, 60 London Wall, London EC2M 5TQ, England

CLIFFORD, STEVEN FRANCIS, science research director; b. Boston, Jan. 4, 1943; s. Joseph Nelson and Margaret Dorothy (Savage) C.; children from previous marriage: Cheryl Ann, Michelle Lynn, David Arthur; m. Theresa Kavanagh, Aug. 1996. BSEE, Northeastern U., Boston, 1965; PhD, Dartmouth Coll., 1969. Postdoctoral fellow NRC, Boulder, Colo., 1969-70; physicist Wave Propagation Lab., NOAA, Boulder, 1970-82, program chief, 1982-87, dir. environ. tech. lab., 1987—; mem. electromagnetic propagation panel, NATO, 1989-93; vis. sci. closed acad. city Tomsk, Siberia, USSR; apptd. mem. NAS Bd. on Atmospheric Sci. and Climate, 1999—. Author: (with others) Remote Sensing of the Troposhpere, 1978; contbr. 125 articles to profl. jours.; patentee in acoustic scintillation liquid flow measurement, single-ended optical spatial filter, acoustic sensor of surface ocean current and waves, high resolution GPS scatterometer. Recipient 5 Outstanding publs. awards Dept. Commerce, 1972, 75, 89, 96, Outstanding Career Performance, U.S. Presidental award, 1998; inducted NAE, 1997. Fellow Optical Soc. Am. (editor atmospheric optics 1978-84, advisor atmospheric optics 1982-84), Acoustical Soc. Am.; mem. IEEE (sr.), Nat. Acad. Engring., Internat. Radio Sci. Union, Am. Geophys. Union, Nat. Acad. Scis. Avocations: running, cross country skiing. Office: NOAA Environ Tech Lab 325 Broadway St Boulder CO 80305-3337

CLIFFORD, STEWART BURNETT, banker; b. Boston, Feb. 17, 1929; s. Stewart Hilton and Ellinor (Burnett) C.; m. Cornelia Park Woolley, Apr. 26, 1952; children: Cornelia Lee Wareham, Rebecca Lyn Mailer-Howat, Jennifer Leggett Danner, Stewart Burnett. AB, Harvard U., 1951, MBA, 1956. Asst. cashier Citibank, N.A., N.Y.C., 1958-60, asst. v.p., 1960-63; exec. v.p., gen. mgr. Merc Bank, Montreal, Que., Can., 1963-67, v.p. planning Overseas div., 1967-68; v.p., adminstr. comml. banking group Citibank, N.Y.C., 1969-72; v.p. head world corp. dept. Citibank, London, 1973-75; sr. v.p. domestic energy Citibank, N.Y.C., 1975-80, sr. v.p., head pvt. banking and investment div., 1981-87, div. exec., head investment div., 1987-93; sr. banker Pvt. Bank U.S., 1993-94; cons. Munn Bernhard & Assocs., N.Y.C., 1995—; dir. Monumental Corp., Balt., 1974-89. Pres. 120 East End Ave. Corp., Woolley-Clifford Found.; life trustee Spence Sch.; vice chmn. Asphalt Green; elder and trustee Brick Ch.; trustee Princeton Theol. Sem., Presbyn. Ch. (USA) Found.; mem. com. univ. resources Harvard Coll. 1st lt. U.S. Army, 1951-54. Republican. Clubs: Pilgrims, Union, University (N.Y.C.); Duxbury Yacht (Mass.), Bath & Tennis (Palm Beach). Avocations: squash, tennis. Home: 120 E End Ave New York NY 10028-7552 Office: Munn Bernhard & Assocs 6 E 43rd St New York NY 10017-4609

CLIFTON, BOBBIE JEAN, elementary education educator; b. Shaw, Miss., Apr. 29, 1952; d. Tilmon and Inez (Hacklen) C.; m. Willie Norris, July 19, 1970 (div. Oct. 10, 1977); children: Gerald, Rodney, Willie Jr. BS in Edn., Delta State U., 1991. tchr. cons. Delta State U., Cleveland, Miss., Writing/Thinking Inst., Starkville, Miss.; state textbook rating com. mem. Miss. State Dept. Edn., Jackson, Miss. Tchr. fifth grade Mound Bayou (Miss.) Pub. Schs., 1991—; Treas. Bolivar County Dem. Exec. Com., Cleveland, 1996—, Silhouette Club, Mound Bayou, Miss., 1994—; Miss. Language Arts Framework writing team mem. 1996; Miss. State Dept. Edn. Primary Guide

writing team mem., 1998; facilitator Success For All Programs, 1999—. Mem. Miss. Assn. Educators (pres. 1983—), Miss. Reading Assn. (bd. dirs. 1996-97), Miss. Assn. Educators (bd. dirs. 1986-91), Delta Reading Coun. (pres. 1996-97), Miss. Coun. Tchrs. English. Democrat. Baptist. Avocations: sewing, teaching, reading, fishing, meeting people. Home: 504 W South St Mound Bayou MS 38762-9789 Office: Mound Bayou Pub Schs PO Box 901 Mound Bayou MS 38762-0901

CLIMENT, MIGUEL LLORET, mathematics educator; b. Villajoyosa, Alicante, Spain, May 1, 1959; s. Tomas Lloret Ruiz and Magdalena Climent Lloret; m. Pilar Ramon Sanchez; children: Marina, Carles. Licentiate in math., U. Valencia, Spain, 1983, postgrad., 1986; postgrad., U. Alicante, Spain, 1996. Assoc. prof. U. Politechnical, Valencia, 1984-89, full prof., 1989-92; full prof. U. Alicante, 1992—. Contbr. articles to profl. jours. Avocation: chess. Office: Dept Analisis Matematico, Univ de Alicante, 03071 Alicante Spain

CLINCH, NICHOLAS BAYARD, III, business executive; b. Evanston, Ill., Nov. 9, 1930; s. Nicholas Bayard Jr. and Virginia Lee (Campbell) C.; m. Elizabeth Wallace Campbell, July 11, 1964; children: Virginia Lee, Alison Campbell. Student, N.Mex. Mil. Inst., Roswell, 1948-49; AB, Stanford U., 1952, LLB, 1955. Bar: Calif. 1959. Expedition leader First Ascent, Gasherbrum I (26,470 ft.), Pakistan, 1958, First Ascent, Masherbrum (25, 660 ft.), Pakistan, 1959-60; assoc. Voegelin, Barton, Harris & Callister, L.A., 1961-68; pvt. practice Washington, 1968-70; v.p., counsel Lincoln Savs. & Loan Assn., L.A., 1970-74; exec. dir. Sierra Club Found., San Francisco, 1975-81; environ. cons. Fluor Corp., Grass Valley, Calif., 1981-84; v.p., sec. CCA, Inc., Denver, 1984—; bd. dirs. Growth Stock Outlook Inc., Potomac, Md., Recreational Equipment Inc., Seattle. Author: A Walk in the Sky, 1982. Leader Am. Antarctic Mountaineering Expdn., Sentinel Range, 1966-67; co-leader Chinese Am. Ulugh Muztagh Expdn., Kun Lun Range, Xinjiang, 1985, Am. Expdns. to Kang Karpo Range, Yunnan-Tibet border, 1988, 89, 92, 93; co-founder, trustee Calif. League Conservation Voters, San Francisco, 1972-97. 1st lt. USAF, 1956-57. Recipient John Oliver La Gorce medal Nat. Geog. Soc., Washington, 1967. Fellow Royal Geog. Soc., Explorers Club; mem. ABA, Am. Alpine Club (hon., pres. 1967-70), Appalachian Mountain Club (hon.), State Bar Calif., Alpine Club (hon. London), Chinese Assn. Sci. Expdns. (hon.). Republican. Episcopalian. Avocations: mountaineering, skiing, book collecting. Home: 2001 Bryant St Palo Alto CA 94301-3714 Office: CCA Inc 4100 E Mississippi Ave Ste 1750 Denver CO 80246-3067

CLINE, CAROLYN JOAN, plastic and reconstructive surgeon; b. Boston; d. Paul S. and Elizabeth (Flom) Cline. BA, Wellesley Coll., 1962; MA, U. Cin., 1966; PhD, Washington U., 1970; diploma Washington Sch. Psychiatry, 1972; MD, U. Miami (Fla.) 1975. Diplomate Am. Bd. Plastic and Reconstructive Surgery. Rsch. asst. Harvard Dental Sch., Boston, 1962-64; rsch. asst. physiology Laser Lab., Children's Hosp. Research Found., Cin., 1964, psychology dept. U. Cin., 1964-65; intern in clin. psychology St. Elizabeth's Hosp., Washington, 1966-67; psychologist Alexandria (Va.) Community Mental Health Ctr., 1967-68; research fellow NIH, Washington, 1968-69; chief psychologist Kingsbury Ctr. for Children, Washington, 1969-73; sole practice clin. psychology, Washington, 1970-73; intern internal medicine U. Wis. Hosps., Ctr. for Health Sci., Madison, 1975-76; resident in surgery Stanford U. Med. Ctr., 1976-78; fellow microvascular surgery dept. surgery U. Calif.-San Francisco, 1978-79; resident in plastic surgery St. Francis Hosp., San Francisco, 1979-82; practice medicine, specializing in plastic and reconstructive surgery, San Francisco, 1982—. Contbr. chpt. to plastic surgery textbook, articles to profl. jours. Mem. Am. Soc. Plastic and Reconstructive Surgeons, Royal Soc. Medicine, Calif. Medicine Assn., Calif. Soc. Plastic and Reconstructive Surgeons, San Francisco Med. Soc.

CLINE, CHARLES WILLIAM, poet, pianist, rhetoric and literature educator; b. Waleska, Ga., Mar. 1, 1937; s. Paul Ardell and Mary Montarie (Pittman) C.; m. Sandra Lee Williamson, June 11, 1966 (div. 1996); 1 son, Jeffrey Charles. Student, U. Cin. Conservatory of Music, 1957-58; AA, Reinhardt Coll., 1957; BA, George Peabody Coll. for Tchrs., 1960; MA, Vanderbilt U., 1963; LittD, World U., 1981 DFA (hon.), Australian Inst. Coordinated Rsch., 1996. Asst. prof. English Shorter Coll., Rome, Ga., 1963-64; instr. English West Ga. Coll., Carrollton, 1964-68; manuscript procurement editor Fideler Co., Grand Rapids, Mich, 1968; assoc. prof. English Kellogg Community Coll., Battle Creek, Mich., 1969-75, prof. English and resident poet, 1975—; chmn. creative writing sect. Midwest Conf. on English, 1976; condr. poetry readings and workshops. Piano recitals at Internat. Congress on Arts and Comm., 1992, 93, 94, 95, 96, 99; author: Crossing the Ohio, 1976, Questions for the Snow, 1979, Ultima Thule, 1984, (with Amal Ghose and others) Wholeness of Dream, 1989; editor: Forty Salutes to Mich. Poets, 1975; contbr. Gifts of Music, 1994; contbr. poems to jours. and anthologies. Decorated knight comdr. Lofsensischen Ursinusordens, 1991, knight Order of Knights Templars of Jerusalem, 1991, knight Order of Circulo Nobilario de los Caballeros Universales, 1993, knight Order of Holy Grail, 1996, baron Royal Order of the Bohemian Crown, 1996, count Order of San Ciriaco, 1996; recipient Poetry awards Modus Operandi, 1975, Internat. Belles-Lettres Soc., 1975, Poetry Soc. Mich., 1975, N. Am. Mentor, 1977, 78, Lit. Prize World Inst. Achievement, 1986, 88, Star of Distinction, 19th Internat. Congress on Art and Comm., St. John's Coll., U. Cambridge, 1992, Disting. Participation medallion 20th Congress, Cambridge, Mass., 1993, 26th Congress, Lisbon, 1999, Diplôme d'Honneur en Littérature et Musique, Inst. des Affaires Internats., 1996; resolutions recognition Kalamazoo City Commn., Mich. Ho. of Reps. and Senate, 1981, others. Fellow World Literary Acad. (founding, prize 1983), Internat. Soc. Lit. (life), Am. Biog. Inst. (life, World Fellowship award 1987, Internat. Hall of Leaders 1988, hon. advisor rsch. bd. advisors nat. divsn. 1994); mem. Tagore Inst. Creative Writing Internat. (life), World Poetry Soc. Intercontinental, Centro Studi e Scambi Internazionali (Poet Laureate award, Diploma di Benemerenza, Diploma d'Onore), Accademia Leonardo da Vinci, Poetry Soc. Am., Poets and Writers Inc., Acad. Am. Poets, Am. Biog. Inst. Rsch. Assn. (dep. gov.), Internat. Biog. Assn. (life patron), World U. Roundtable, Internat. Biog. Ctr. (dep. dir. gen. 1991, 20th Century award for achievement 1992, World Intellectual 1993, cert. of mutual loyalty between dir. gen. and deps. 1999, pictorial testimonial for outstanding scholars of the 20th century 1999), Accademia Internationale di Pontzen (distintivo palmato 1991, lauro d'oro for literary merit 1991, grande medaglia Aurata della fondazione 1997, scettro d'argento 1998), Maison Internat. des Intellectuels, Acad. M.I.D.I., Wordsworth-Coleridge Assn., Assn. Lit. Scholars and Critics. Presbyterian. Office: Kellogg Community Coll 450 North Ave Battle Creek MI 49017-3306

CLINE, FRED ALBERT, JR., retired librarian, conservationist; b. Santa Barbara, Calif., Oct. 23, 1929; s. Fred Albert and Anna Cecelia (Haberl) C. AB in Asian Studies, U. Calif., Berkeley, 1952, MLS, 1962. Resident Internat. House, Berkeley, 1950-51; trainee, officer Bank of Am., San Francisco, Düsseldorf, Fed. Republic Germany, Kuala Lumpur, 1954-60; adminstrv. reference libr. Calif. State Libr., Sacramento, 1962-67; head libr. Asian Art Mus. San Francisco, 1967-93; ret., 1993. Contbg. author: Chinese, Korean and Japanese Sculpture in the Avery Brundage Collection, 1974; author, editor: Ruth Hill Cooke, 1985; contbr. articles and book revs. on AIDS to various publs. Bd. dirs. Tamalpais Conservation Club, 1990-94, 98-99; AIDS activist. Sgt. M.C., U.S. Army, 1952-54. Mem. Metaphys. Alliance (sec., bd. dirs. San Francisco chpt. 1988-91), Sierra Club. Democrat. Avocations: hiking, music, reading. Home: 825 Lincoln Way San Francisco CA 94122-2369

CLINE, JANET E. SAFFORD, school district administrator, desktop publisher; b. London, Aug. 28, 1945; came to U.S., 1946; d. Don F. and Elizabeth G. (Taylor) Safford; m. Raymond D. Cline, Aug. 23, 1966; children: Roger D., Martin A. BA, West Tex. State U., Canyon, 1967. Admissions clk. North Tex. State U., Denton, 1971-72; comms. dir. United Meth. Temple, Port Arthur, Tex., 1973-75; edn. and health reporter Port Arthur News, 1977-82; coord. sch./cmty. rels. Port Arthur Ind. Sch. Dist., 1982-97, dir. comms., 1997—; owner Janet Cline Pub. Author, editor numerous PAISD Publs.; contbr. articles to profl. jours. Mem. Mayor's Com. on Edn., Port Arthur, 1994-96chmn. Port Arthur Centennial Activities Commn., 1996—; pres. Mid/South Jefferson County chpt. Am. Heart Assn., 1997—, Samaritan Counseling Ctr., Jefferson County, 1997—. Recipient Anson Jones award Tex. Med. Assn., 1983, Silver Star of Tex. award Tex. Hosp. Assn., 1983. Mem. Tex. Sch. Pub. Rels. Assn. (regional v.p. 1988-89, chair com. 1983-97, Bright Idea award 1997), North Port Arthur Rotary Club (v.p. 1997—). Methodist. Avocations: reading, bridge, cross stitch, travel.

CLINE, JOHN CARROLL, clinical psychologist; b. Staunton, Va., Sept. 6, 1955; s. Carroll Hubert and Naomi Edith (Hevener) C.; m. Diane Jeannette Goudreau, May 21, 1983; 1 child, Virginia Goudreau Cline. BA, U. Va., 1977; PhD, U. Toledo, 1984. Lic. psychologist, Conn.; cert. biofeedback; clin. assoc. Am. Bd. Med. Psychotherapists; diplomate Am. Acad. Pain Mgmt. Psychology intern U. Toledo, 1980-81; predoctoral intern VA Med. Ctr., West Haven, Conn., 1981-82, attending psychologist, 1984-85; clinician Alcohol Svcs. Orgn., New Haven, 1982-85; team leader, staff psychologist Elmcrest Hosp., Portland, Conn., 1985-86, asst. unit chief, 1986, dir. behavioral medicine svc., 1986-90; pvt. practice psychologist Hamden, Conn., 1986-94; dir. adult outpatient svcs. Inst. of Living, Hartford, Conn., 1990-93; psychol. svcs. cons. Hamden, Conn., 1994—; clin. dir. dept. counseling and psychiat. svcs. Grove Hill Med. Ctr., New Britain, Conn., 1994—, chair quality assurance & outcomes mgmt. dept. psychiat. svcs., 1995—; clin. affiliate Yale Psychol. Svcs. Clinic, Yale U., New Haven, 1985—; cons. psychologist VA Med. Ctr., West Haven, 1985-91; asst. prof. clin. psychiatry U. Conn. Med. Sch., Farmington, Conn., 1991-94; instr. orthopaedic phys. therapy program Sch. Grad. and Continuing Edn. Quinnipiac Coll., Hamden, Conn., 1992—; sr. cons. network devel. Inst. of Living, Hartford, 1993-94. Mem. mission study com. 1st Presbyn. Ch., New Haven, 1990-91; mem. Conn. Coun. Mental Health Providers, 1993-96, chair, 1993-94. Mem. AAAS, APA (coun. rep. 1997—), Conn. Psychol. Assn. (chair hosp. practice com. 1990-92, practice directorate coord. 1993, pres.-elect 1994, pres. 1995-96, past pres. 1997), Conn. Behavior Therapy Assn. (mem. exec. com. 1992—), N.Y. Acad. Scis., Soc. for Psychotherapy Rsch., Assn. Psychiat. Clinics of Conn. (mem. polit. com. 1993-94, mem. edn. com. 1993-94), Assn. for Applied Psychophysiology and Biofeedback, Soc. Behavioral Medicine. Avocations: microcomputers, fitness walking, fatherhood. Home: 4 Lamkin St Hamden CT 06517-3309 Office: Grove Hill Med Ctr 300 Kensington Ave New Britain CT 06051-3916

CLINE, MICHAEL PATRICK, association executive; b. Washington, Oct. 31, 1945; s. William E. and Anna (Kraynik) C.; m. Diana Cline, Dec. 31, 1989; children: Tammy, Mike, Bill, John, Terri, Nikki. AA in Bus., Cuyahoga C.C., Cleve., 1988; BA in Bus. Mgmt., Malone Coll., North Canton, Ohio, 1989. Cert. tchr., Ohio; lic. real estate, Ohio. With Phoebus Trucking, Cleve., 1967-68, Allied Delivery Sys., Cleve., 1968-86; owner M&N Auto Truck Body, Cleve., 1968-90; exec. dir. Enlisted Assn. of the N.G., Alexandria, Va., 1990—; notary pub., Va. Author: How to Improve Office Efficiency, 1989, How to Work with Congress, 1991. Pres. Homeowners Assn. Woodbridge, Va., 1993-98; trustee Nat. Guard Ins. Trust, Washington, 1993—; co-chmn. Mil. Coalition; mem. Sec. of Vets. Adv. Panel on Edn; mem. com. on edn. Vet. Affairs Com.; co-chmn. Mil. Coalition; hon. chief master sgt. Air N.G. With U.S. Army, 1963-67, Ohio N.G., 1967-92. Recipient Cert. of Merit, Mil. Coalition, Washington, 1995, Dedication/Appreciation award Medal of Honor Soc., 1992, U.S. Army Disting. Svc. ribbon with cluster. Mem. Enlisted Assn. of N.G. (life, exec. coun.), Md. Enlisted Assn. N.G., NRA, ASAE. Methodist. Avocations: computers, camping, antiques, travel. Office: Enlisted Assn NG of US 1219 Prince St Alexandria VA 22314-2916

CLINGAN, CHARLES EDMUND, historian; b. N.Y.C., Oct. 12, 1962; s. Eldon Ray and JoAnn Kay (McNamara) C. BA, CUNY, Queens, 1985; MA, U. Wis., 1987, PhD, 1991. Vis. asst. prof. Montclair State Coll., Upper Montclair, N.J., 1991-92, CUNY, 1992-95, NYU, 1994-95; asst. prof. history U. N.D., Grand Forks, 1995-2000, assoc. prof., 2000—. Author: From the General Manager's Files, 1993, Finance from Kaiser to Führer: German Budget Politics, 1912-34, 2000. Vice pres. Broadway Dem. Club, N.Y.C., 1994-95. Fulbright scholar, 1988-89. Mem. Am. Hist. Assn., German Studies Assn., Austrian Studies Ctr., Conf. Group on Ctrl. European History, Soc. for French Hist. Studies, Fulbright Assn. (pres. No. Prairie chpt. 1995—), Phi Beta Kappa. Office: Univ ND PO Box 8096 Grand Forks ND 58202-8096

CLINKENBEARD, JAMES HOWARD, principal; b. Alexandria, Va., Apr. 1, 1950; s. Howard Samuel and Ethel Jane (Schwager) C.; m. Janelle Darlene Turner, May 27, 1972; children: Adam James, Nathan Linton, Evan Joel. BS, Murray State U., 1977; MEd, Xavier U., 1985, postgrad., 1986-87, 89-92. Cert. tchr. and adminstr., Ky. Tchr. art Newport (Ky.) Ind. Schs., 1978-88, chief negotiator, 1985-88, asst. prin., 1988-91, 92-96, dir. Title V, 1991-92, acting prin., 1992, 94-95, prin., 1996—; freelance artist, designer Bellevue, Ky., 1977—; juror various sch. and profl. art shows; speaker pub. sch. in-service programs. Featured in Kentucky Artist and Craftsman mag., 1977; author various documents, ednl. reports. State advisor Ky. Imagination Celebration, 1984-85; bd. dirs. Ky. Citizens for the Arts in Edn., 1983-85; advisor Ky. Task Force for Comprehensive Arts, 1984, Ky. Task Force on Acad. Competition, 1985; active Ft. Thomas and Newport PTAs, Bellevue Civic Assn.; chmn. Citizens for Bellevue Schs., 1980-81, Arts Subcom., Coun. on Higher Edn., 1985-86, Ky. Foster Care Rev. Bd., 1991-97; deacon First Christian Ch., Ft. Thomas, 1976—, chmn. bd., 1982-83, Sunday Sch. tchr., 1976-97, 99-2000; mem. select panel Ky. Disting. Educators Program; chmn. Sch. Based Decision Making Coun., 1996—; chair com. Troop 70, Boy Scouts Am., 1997—. Recipient commendation Ky. Supt. Pub. Instrn., 1984. Mem. NEA, ASCD, Nat. Art Edn. Assn. (Ky. del. 1976-77, 81), Ky. Art Edn. Assn. (various offices including pres. 1983-84, Project Art Tchr. award 1980), Ky. Edn. Assn. (svcs. com. 1985-87, del. 1986-88, mem. task force 1987-88), Newport Tchrs. Assn. (sec. 1982-83, treas. 1985-88, pres. 1988, vice chmn. polit. action com. 1984), Newport Adminstrs. Assn. (pres. 1994-97), Washington Evening Star Cartoonists Guild, Ft. Thomas Swim Club (bd. dirs. 1994—, pres. 1995—), Alpha Tau Omega (chpt. advisor 1987-91, chpt. housing corp. pres. 1993—, chpt. bd. trustees 1995—). Republican. Mem. Christian Ch. (Disciples of Christ). Avocations: reading, sports, working with children. E-mail: jclink.nky@fuse.net. Home: 30 Kathy Ln Fort Thomas KY 41075-1914 Office: Newport Ind Schs 101 E 4th St Newport KY 41071-1615

CLINTON, HILLARY RODHAM, First Lady of United States, lawyer; b. Chgo., Oct. 26, 1947; d. Hugh Ellsworth and Dorothy (Howell) Rodham; m. William J. Clinton, Oct. 11, 1975; 1 child, Chelsea Victoria. BA with high honors, Wellesley Coll., 1969; JD, Yale U., 1973; LLD (hon.), U. Ark., Little Rock, 1985, Ark. Coll., 1988, Hendrix Coll., 1992, U. Sunderland, 1993, U. Pa., 1993, U. Mich., 1993, U. Ill., 1994, U. Minn., 1995, San Francisco State U., 1995; D Pub. Svc. (hon.), George Washington U., 1994, U. Md., College Park, 1996; DHL (hon.), Drew U., 1996, Ohio U., 1997. Bar: Ark. 1973, U.S. Dist. Ct. (ea. and we. dists.) Ark. 1973, U.S. Ct. Appeals (8th cir.) 1973, U.S. Supreme Ct. 1975. Atty. Children's Def. Fund, Cambridge, Mass. and Washington, 1973-74; legal cons. Carnegie Coun. on Children, New Haven, 1973-74; counsel, impeachment inquiry staff Judiciary Com. U.S. Ho. of Reps., Washington, 1974; asst. prof. law, dir. Legal Aid Clinic U. Ark. Sch. Law, Fayetteville, 1974-77; asst. prof. law U. Ark. Sch. Law, Little Rock, 1979-80; ptnr. Rose Law Firm, Little Rock, 1977-92; chair Presdl. Task Force on Nat. Health Care Reform, 1993. Author: Handbook on Legal Rights for Arkansas Women, 1977, 87, It Takes a Village: And Other Lessons Children Teach Us, 1996; syndicated columnist Talking It Over, 1995—; contbr. articles to profl. jours. Bd. dirs. Childrens Def. Fund, Washington, 1976-92, chair, 1986-92, Legal Svcs. Corp., Washington, 1977-81, chair, 1978-80; founder, pres., bd. dirs. Ark. Advs. for Children and Families, 1977-84; bd. dirs. Child Care Action Campaign, 1986-92, Nat. Ctr. on Edn. and the Economy, 1987-92, Ark. Children's Hosp., 1988-92, Franklin and Eleanor Roosevelt Inst., 1988-92, Children's TV Workshop, 1989-92, Pub./Pvt. Ventures, 1990-92; chmn. Ark. Edn. Stds. Com., 1983-84; mem. commn. on quality edn. So. Regional Edn. Bd., 1984-92; chair ABA Commn. on Women in the Profession, 1987-91; hon. pres. Girl Scouts of Am., 1993—; mem. adv. bd. HIPPY, 1988-92, bd. dirs.; hon. chair Pres.' Com. on the Arts and Humanities, 1993—, U.S. Del., UN Fourth World Conf. on Women, 1995; hon. mem. The Pen and Brush, 1996—. Named Outstanding Layman of Yr. Phi Delta Kappa, 1984, Health Educator of Yr., Ryan White Found., 1995; recipient Lewis Hine award Nat. Child Labor Law Com., 1993, Albert Schweitzer Leadership award Hugh O'Brian Youth Found., 1993, Iris Cantor Humanitarian award UCLA Med. Ctr., 1993, Friend of Family award Am. Home Econs. Assn., 1993, Charles Wilson Lee Citizen Svc. award Com. for Edn. Funding, 1993, Claude D. Pepper award Nat. Assn. for Home Care, 1993, Commitment to Life award AIDS Project L.A., 1994, Disting. Svc., Health Edn. and Prevention award Nat. Ctr. for Health Edn., 1994, First Ann. Eleanor Roosevelt Freedom Fighter award, 1994, Brandeis award U. Louisville Sch. of Law, 1994, Social Justice award United Auto Workers, 1994, Ernie Banks Positivism trophy Emil Verban Meml. Soc., 1994, Humanitarian award Alzheimer's Assn., 1994, Elie Wiesel Found., 1994, Internat. Broadcasting award Hollywood Radio and TV Soc., 1994, Ellen Browning Scripps medal Scripps Coll., 1994, Disting. Pro Bono Svc. award San Diego Vol. Lawyer Program, 1994, HIPPY U.S.A. award, 1994, C. Everett Koop medal Am. Diabetes Assn., 1994, Women's Legal Def. Fund award, 1994, Martin Luther King, Jr. award Progressive Nat. Bapt. Conv., 1994, 30th Anniversary Women at Work award in Pub. Policy, Nat. Commn. on Working Women, 1994, Greater Washington Urban League award, 1995, Servant of Justice award N.Y. Legal Aid Soc., 1995, Presdl. award Bklyn. Coll., 1995, Outstanding Mother award Nat. Mother's Day Com., 1995, Dedication, Annual Survey Am. Law, NYU, 1995, Nat. Breast Cancer Coalition Leadership award, 1995, Faith in Humanity award Nat. Coun. Jewish Women, 1996, NICHE Humanitarian award, 1996, Nat. Assn. Elem. Sch. Prins. Dist. Svc. award, 1996, Grammy award, 1997, Bully Pulpit award Nat. Coun. for Adoption, 1997, Nat. Family Advocate award Parents' Plus Newspaper, 1997, Disting. Svc. to Edn. award Coll. Bd., 1997, Disting. Svc. award Columbia U. Ctr. of Addiction and Substance Abuse, 1997, Commitment to Children award The Elizabeth Glaser Pediat. AIDS Found., 1997, Eleanor Roosevelt Living World award Peace Links, 1997; Paul Harris fellow Rotary Found., 1996. Fellow Am. Bar Found.; mem. Ark. Bar Assn., Ark. Trial Lawyers Assn., Ark. Women Lawyers Assn., Am. Trial Lawyers Assn., Pulaski County Bar Assn. Home and Office: The White House 1600 Pennsylvania Ave NW Washington DC 20500-0003

CLINTON, LAWRENCE PAUL, psychiatrist; b. Lubbock, Tex., Apr. 27, 1945; s. Lewis Paul Clinton and Dorothy E. (Higgins) Clinton-Billingslea; m. Bonnie Gail Orenstein, June 22, 1969; children: Kerry Elizabeth, Andrew James, Alexander Geoffrey, Kaylin Lee. BA with honors, So. Conn. State Coll., 1966; postgrad., Ohio State U., 1966-68; MD, Hahnemann U., 1972. Diplomate Am. Bd. Psychiatry and Neurology, Am. Bd. Forensic Examiners, Am. Acad. Experts in Traumatic Stress. Teaching asst. Ohio State U., Columbus, 1966-68, research fellow, 1966-68; clin. instr. psychiatry Hahnemann U., Phila., 1975-82, asst. clin. prof., 1982—; chief exec. officer Bldg. Mgmt. Group, Vineland, N.J., 1986—; psychiat. dir. James Guiffre Med. Ctr., Phila., 1976-79; med. dir. PSI Group, 1990—; cons. Superior Ct. N.J., 1975—, Ranch Hope, Alloway, N.J., 1989-92. Contbr. articles to profl. jours. Mem. Am. Security Coun., 1975—, Rep. Senatorial Com., 1978—, Rep. Nat. Com., 1978, The Pres.'s Club, 1990—. Recipient awards Am. Security Coun., 1982, Buena Regional Sch. Dist., N.J., 1983, Vineland Parent Support and Adv. Group, 1990, Rep. Presdl. Legion of Merit medal, 1992; decorated Chevalier Comdr. Ordre Souverain et Militaire de la Milice du Saint Sepulcre, 1990—. Fellow Am. Bd. Forensic Examiners, Phila. Coll. Physicians and Surgeons; mem. AMA, Am. Psychiat. Assn., Internat. Assn. Group Psychotherapy, N.J. Psychiat. Soc., Internat. Platform Soc., Med. Club Phila., World Fedn. Mental Health, InterAm. Coll. Physicians and Surgeons, Hahnemann Undergrad. Rsch. Soc. (treas. 1971-72), Confedn. of Chivalry, Am. Chem. Soc., Phi Lambda Kappa (v.p. 1972), Societe d'Chemie (pres. 1965-66), South Jersey Psychiat. Soc. (sec.-treas. 1994—), SPQR Club (pres. 1961-62, pres.2001) (Milford, Conn.), Union League Phila., Union League Phila. Yatch Club. Avocations: gardening, art collecting, book collecting, historical biography, golf, sailing. Office: 1138 E Chestnut Ave Bldg 6 Vineland NJ 08360-5053

CLINTON, RICHARD LEE, international relations educator; b. Cookeville, Tenn., Sept. 20, 1938; s. Howard Cecil Clinton and Nelva Dee Webb; m. Susan Jeffries Clinton, Sept. 17, 1964 (div. Dec. 1985); children: Lara Franklin, Lisa Laurens; m. Rosalie Norwood, Nov. 1, 1986. BA, Vanderbilt U., 1960, MA, 1964; PhD, U. N.C., 1971. Asst. prof. U. N.C., Chapel Hill, 1971-76; asst. prof. Oreg. State U., Corvallis, 1976-78, assoc. dean Coll. Liberal Arts, 1978-82, assoc. prof. Coll. Liberal Arts, 1982-85, prof. Coll. Liberal Arts, 1985—; cons. UN Fund for Population Activities, Bolivia and Guatemala, 1988, Internat. Planned Parenthood Fedn., Costa Rica and Honduras, 1984, Ford Found., Peru, 1977, U.S. Dept. State, Peru, 1974; Hanna Disting. Prof., Rollins Coll., Winter Park, Fla., 1990, 93, 94, 95; Fulbright sr. lectr. U.S. Govt., Peru, 1982, 97. Author: (book) Problems of Population Policy Formation in Peru, 1971, Poblacion y desarrollo en el Peru, 1985; editor: (books) Political Science in Population Studies, 1972, Research in the Politics of Population, 1973, Population and Politics, 1973. Lance cpl., USMCR, 1958-64. Mem. Latin Am. Studies Assn. E-mail: richard.clinton@orst.edu. Office: Oreg State U Dept Polit Sci Corvallis OR 97331

CLINTON, WILLIAM JEFFERSON, President of the United States; b. Hope, Ark., Aug. 19, 1946; m. Hillary Rodham, Oct. 11, 1975; 1 child, Chelsea Victoria. BS in Internat. Affairs, Georgetown U., 1968; postgrad., Oxford U., 1968-70; JD, Yale U., 1973. Prof. U. Ark. Sch. Law, Fayetteville, 1973-76; pvt. practice law, 1973-76; atty. gen. State of Ark., Little Rock, 1977-79; gov. State of Ark., 1979-81, 83-92; of counsel Wright, Lindsey & Jennings, Little Rock, 1981-82; President of the United States, 1993—; chmn. So. Growth Policies Bd., 1985-86. Chmn. Edn. Commn. of the States, 1986-87, mem. steering com.; mem. Task Force on Adolescent Edn., Carnegie Found.; chmn. Dem. Leadership Coun., 1990-91. Rhodes scholar Univ. Coll., Oxford U., 1968-70. Mem. ABA, Ark. Bar Assn., Nat. Govs. Assn. (vice chmn. 1986, chmn. 1986-87, exec. com., fin. com., com. on human resources, com. on internat. trade and fgn. rels., task force on rural devel., co-chmn. task force for edn. 1990-92). Home and Office: The White House 1600 Pennsylvania Ave NW Washington DC 20500-0003*

CLOD, BENTE, scriptwriter, screenwriter, educator, consultant; b. Copenhagen, Mar. 7, 1946; d. Eigil Bredo Frederik Poulsen and Elsebet Clod-Svensson. Degree, Gladsaxe Sem., 1969, Danish Film Sch., Copenhagen, 1980, Gøsselskolen, Copenhagen, 1983. 'uthor: Wait Until You Hear Me Laugh, 1983, (tv play) Red Threads, 1983, Write! , 1987, Write a Film, 1997, Angel Power 2000, poems, short stories, articles. Founder Kvindetryk women's press. Address: Faelledvej 14 2 TV, 2200 Copenhagen Denmark

CLODE, WILLIAM HENRY, microbiologist; b. Funchal, Madeira, Portugal, July 20, 1927; s. William Edward Clode and Maria Carolina Monteiro C.; m. Maria Helena Migueis, May 22, 1957; children: Paulo, Nuno, Pilar, Joao, Helena. MD, Faculdade Medicina Lisboa, Portugal, 1952. Med. diplomate. Internist Hosp. Santa Maria, Lisboa, 1961-65; med. rsch. assoc. Brookhaven Nat. Lab., N.Y.C., 1961-62; asst. Inst. Portugues Oncologia, Lisboa, 1963-72; chief of svc. Inst. Oncologia, Lisboa, 1972—; mem. responsible nuclear medicine Inst. Oncologia, Lisboa, 1954-87, Biotery Inst., 1987-97. Col. Angolan med. svc., 1973-75. Roman Catholic. Avocations: poetry, plastic arts. Home: Av Roma 85-5 Dt, 1700 Lisboa Portugal

CLOETE, CHRISTIAAN JOHANNES, energy executive; b. Ermelo, South Africa, Aug. 12, 1947; s. Christiaan Johannes and Maria Elizabeth (DeJager) C.; m. Marie Janse van Rensburg, Jan. 6, 1973; children: Yvonne, Christiaan, Lise-Marie. BSc, Wits U., 1971; MBL, Unisa, 1981. Sr. project engr. Gencor, Johannesburg, Gauteng, South Africa, 1976-78; mgr. mine Sigma Mine, Sasol, Free State, South Africa, 1978-80; from asst. gen. mgr. to gen. mgr. Sasol Coal, Sigma, Secunda, South Africa, 1980-93; mng. dir. Sasol Coal, Johannesburg, Gauteng, 1993-98; owner Powerhouse Consultation, Estates Ins. Risks and Forestry, Pretoria, South Africa, 1996—; dir. U. Pretoria, 1998—; dir. Richards Bay Coal Terminal, Natal, 1996, SDB, Maumalanga, 1990, Pretoria U. Bus. Sch.; adv. bd. Dept. Mining. Engrs., 1994. Contbr. articles to profl. jours. Mem. Highveld Reformation and Devel. Forum, 1996; chmn. Johannes Stegmann Theatre, 1991. Mem. SAIMM, SACPE, Nat. Productivity Inst. Avocations: golf, fitness, reading, nature. Address: Powerhouse Cons, 103 Shongweni 232 Schroder, Groenkloof 0181, South Africa

CLONEY, GORDON JEREMIAH, II, insurance executive; b. Binghamton, N.Y., Dec. 29, 1939; s. Gordon J. and Kaisa M. Karikka Cloney; m. Mary Kay Shepston; children: Maureen Jannette, Michelle Margaret. BA, Colgate U., 1961. Program officer U.S. Peace Corps, Washington, 1963-65; pres. Andean Found., Washington, 1965-69; loan officer Inter Am. Devel. Bank, Washington, 1970-73; dir. western hemisphere affairs U.S. C. of C., Washington, 1973-79, dir. svc. trade policy, 1980-87; pres., CEO Internat. Ins.

Coun., Washington, 1988-98; chmn., CEO Inst. Internat. Ins. Devel., Washington, 1999—; sec.-gen. Assn. Am. C. of C. in L.Am., Washington, 1973-78; U.S. dir. InterAm. Fedn. Ins. Cos., Bogota, Colombia, 1990-99; founding mem. U.S. Govt. Industry; sect. advisor Com. for Svc. Industry Trade, 1985—. Prin. architect gen. agreement on trade in svcs. World Trade Orgn. Avocations: carpentry, woodworking. Home: 10902 Wilder Point Ln Reston VA 20191-5008

CLOONAN, PATRICK MICHAEL, radio news producer, writer; b. Pitts., Oct. 13, 1954; s. Joseph Patrick and Margaret (Leister) C. BA in Journalism, Pa. State U., 1976. Freelance journalist AP, 1975-82, 89—; news dir. WNCC-AM, Barnesboro, Pa., 1976-82; assignment editor WTAJ-TV, Altoona, Pa., 1982-83; editor, reporter News Publishing Co., Homestead, Pa., 1984-85; cashier's clk. Legg Mason Masten Inc., Pitts., 1986-87; columnist Expression, Pitts., 1986-97; freelance corr. Post-Gazette, Pitts., 1989-92; freelance journalist CBS Radio Network, N.Y.C., 1989-2000; prodr. KQV-AM, Pitts., 1989-2000; commentator WPLW-AM, Pitts., 1996-97; news writer WPXI-TV, Pitts., 1997-98; staff writer Daily News, McKeesport, Pa., 2000—. Editor The Keystone State Times Newsletter, Munhall, Pa., 1997—; contbr. articles to newspapers. Vol. Bush-Quayle '88, Pitts., 1988, Robertson for Pres., Pitts., 1987; Munhall, Pa., Mayor's adv. bd. rep. Salvation Army, Homestead, Pa., 1985-87. Mem. Soc. Profl. Journalists, Am. Fedn. TV and Radio Artists, Pa. State Alumni Assn., South Hills Coin Club (newsletter writer 1988), KC. Roman Catholic. Avocations: reading, travel, shortwave radio, dogs, lay ministry.

CLOQUETTE, ERIC, cable television company exective, consultant; b. Brussels, Apr. 18, 1957; s. Gaston J.J. Cloquette and Nelly Andry; m. Anne Lambrechts, Aug. 27, 1988; 1 child, Pierre-Olivier. Comml. engr. grad., Warocque U., Mons, Belgium, 1982. Cert. engr., Belgium. Semi-sr. auditor Arthur Andersen, Brussels, 1982-84, Abidjan, Ivory Coast, 1984, Dakar, Senegal, 1984; mgr. fin. and adminstrn. Banner Industries Inc., Brussels, 1985-88; mgr. fin. and adminstrn., mgr. human resources Canal Belgium, Brussels, 1988—; CEO, Ryand Belgium, Mons, 1984—, Canal Belgium, LBO Prodn., Quevy, Belgium, 1995—; cons. in fin. Canal Polska, Warsaw, Poland, 1994-95, Tevece, Montevideo, Uruguay, 1994-95. CEO, Atelier des Ressources Assn. sans But Lucratif, Lillois, Belgium, 1994—. Mem. Fin. Execs. Inst. Belgium, Assn. des Ingenieurs Commerciaux de Mons. Avocations: golf, tennis. Home: Ave des Alouettes 72, 1428 Lillois Belgium Office: Canal & Belgium, Chaussée de Louvain 656, 1030 Brussels Belgium

CLOSE, GLENN, actress; b. Greenwich, Conn., Mar. 19, 1947; d. William and Bettine Close; m. Cabot Wade (div.); m. James Marlas, 1984 (div.); 1 child, Annie Maude Starke. B.A., Coll. William and Mary, 1974. Profl. actress, also accomplished mus. performer (lyric soprano); co-owner The Leaf and Bean Coffee House, Bozeman, Montana, 1991—. Joined New Phoenix Repertory Co., 1974; made Broadway debut in Love for Love; other Broadway appearences include The Rules of the Game, The Member of the Wedding, 1974-75, Rex, Barnum, 1980-81 (Tony award nominee), The Real Thing, 1984-85 (Tony award for Best Actress in Drama), Benefactors, 1986, Wine Untouched, Death and the Maiden, 1992 (Drama League N.Y. Distinguished Performance award, 1992, Tony award for Best Actress in Drama, 1992), Sunset Boulevard, 1994-95 (Tony award Lead Actress in a Musical, 1995); other theatre appearences include Uncommon Women and Others, The Singular Life of Albert Nobbs, 1982 (Obie award), Childhood, 1985, one performance oratorio Joan of Arc at the Stake, 1985, Sunset Boulevard (L.A.), 1993-94, and other repertory and regional theatres; films include The World According to Garp, 1982 (Acad. award nominee), The Big Chill, 1983 (Acad. award nominee), The Natural, 1984 (Acad. award nominee), Greystoke: The Legend of Tarzan, Lord of the Apes (voice), 1984, The Stone Boy, 1984, Maxie, 1985, Jagged Edge, 1985, Fatal Attraction, 1987, Light Years (voice), 1988, Dangerous Liaisons, 1988, Immediate Family, 1989, Reversal of Fortune, 1990, Hamlet, 1990, Hook (cameo), 1991, Meeting Venus, 1991, The House of the Spirits, 1994, The Paper, 1994, 101 Dalmations, Mars Attacks!, 1996, Air Force One, 1997, Paradise Road, 1997; TV films include Too Far To Go, 1979, Orphan Train, 1979, The Elephant Man, 1982, Something about Amelia, 1984 (Emmy award nominee), The Elephant's Child (host), 1987, The Emperor's New Clothes (host), 1987, The Legend of Sleepy Hollow (narrator), 1988, Stones for Ibarra, 1988, (also exec. prodr.) Sarah, Plain and Tall, 1991, Skylark, 1993 (Emmy award nomine for Lead Actress in a Miniseries, 1993), Serving in Silence: The Margarethe Cammermeyer Story, 1995 (Emmy award), In the Gloaming, 1997, The Vagina Monologues, 1998. Recipient Woman of Yr. award Hasty Pudding Theatricals, 1990, Dartmouth Film Soc. award, 1990. Mem. Phi Beta Kappa. Office: CAA 9830 Wilshire Blvd Beverly Hills CA 90212-1804

CLOSE, MELANIE JANE, disability information and advice service coordinator; b. Preston, Lancashire, Eng., Dec. 18, 1963; d. Derek and Barbara (Noon) Sergeant; m. Neil Anthony Close, July 16, 1988; 1 child, Natalie Frances. BSc in Psychology with honors, U. Cen. Lancashire, Preston, 1997; cert. in vol. skills, U. Wales, Lampeter, 1997. Clerical asst. Race Rels. Bd., Preston, 1980-82; coord. Preston Info. Project, 1997—. Vol. counselor Preston Victim Support, 1994—; dir. Preston Womens Refuge, 1996—. Mem. Brit. Psychology Soc., Brit. Assn. Counseling. Anglican. Avocations: socializing, walking, spending time with family. Home: 55 Elmsley St, Preston PR1 7XE, England

CLOSON, JACQUES HENRI LUCIEN, physician; b. Liège, Belgium, July 14, 1921; s. Camille and Jeanne Catherine Charlotte (Becasseau) C.; m. Marie Henreitte Graulich, Oct. 19, 1966; children: Thierry, Vincent, Patrice, Beatrice. D.Sc., Univ. Paris, 1959; PhD, Univ. Liège, Belgium, 1964. Asst. in radiotherapy and oncology Baviere Hosp. Univ. Liège, 1949-66, med. prof., dir., 1966-86, hon. prof., 1986—. Decorated comdr. Order de la Couronne, grand officer Order Leopold II (Belgium). Mem. Lions. Roman Catholic.

CLOSSET, GERARD PAUL, forest products company executive; b. Longwy, France, Nov. 17, 1943; came to U.S., 1965, naturalized, 1976; s. Robert Joseph and Renee (Jacquemet) C.; m. Nicki Lynn Okin, June 29, 1968; children: Juliette, Jennifer. BS, U. Pitts., 1966, MS, 1968, PhD, 1973. Engr. Allied Chem. Corp., Morristown, N.J., 1968-69; rsch. engr. Westvaco Corp., Laurel, Md., 1973-77; mgr. coating St. Regis Paper Co., West Nyack, N.Y., 1977-83, dir. materials, 1983-85; dir. papermaking Champion Internat., 1985-87, v.p. tech., 1987-96; v.p. applied techs. Champion Internat., Stamford, Conn., 1996—. Contbr. articles to profl. jours. Pres. Rockland Suburban Symphony, 1984-89; bd. dirs. Rockland County Assn., 1987-92. Fellow TAPPI (past chmn., rsch. mgmt. com., trustee TAPPI found.); mem. AIChE, Am. Forest Products Assn. (chmn. agenda 2020 com.). Avocations: photography, skiing, scuba diving.

CLOSSON, WALTER FRANKLIN, prosecutor; b. Phila., Dec. 24, 1944; s. David Mayard Jr. and Florence Louise (Anderson) C.; m. Irene Veronica Jones, Aug. 10, 1968; children: Forrest Troy, Carey-Walter Franklin. BS in Music Edn., West Chester U., 1967; JD, Potomac Sch. Law, Washington, 1981. Bar: Ga. 1983, Md. 1985. Tchr. music D.C. Pub. Schs., Washington, 1967-77; tchr. woodwinds D.C. Youth Orch. Program, Washington, 1969-71; dist. ct. commr. Dist. Ct. of Md., Ellicott City, 1978-89; supervising dist. ct. commr. Dist. Ct. of Howard County, Ellicott City, 1984-89; asst. state's atty. State's Atty.'s Office, Ellicott City, 1989-99; chief child support divn. State's Atty.'s Office, 1999—. Mem.. Howard County Bar Assn., Waring-Mitchell Law Soc. (pres. 1992-94, Man of Yr. 1990), Masons (sr. deacon 1996-97, sr. warden 1997-98, worshipful master, 1998-99), Delta Theta Phi (v.p. 1979-80). Office: Howard County States Atty 7121 Columbia Gateway Dr Columbia MD 21046

CLOTTES, JEAN JOSE, archaeologist, researcher; b. Espéraza, Aude, France, July 8, 1933; s. Bernard and Marie (Huedo) C.; m. Renée Paule Caussanel, Apr. 13, 1957; children: Jean-François, Isabelle, Christine. BA, Carcassonne U., France, 1950; Licentiate of Letters, U. Toulouse, France, 1954, D of Letters, 1975. Tchr. Lycée, Foix, France, 1959-74; dir. prehistoric antiquities Ministry of Culture, Toulouse, France, 1971-90; gen. insp. of archaeology Paris, 1991-92; sci. advisor Ministry of Culture, France, 1992-99; pres. Internat. Com. for Rock Art, 1991-99; collection dir. Editions de Seuil, 1996—, Editions La Maison des Roches, 1997—. Author: (with Jean Courtin) The Cave Beneath the Sea, 1995 (Harry Abrams, pub.), Les Cavernes de Niaux, 1995, Voyage en Préhistoire, 1998, (with David Lewis-Williams) The Shamans of Prehistory in Le Musée des Roches, 2000, Grandes Girafes et Fourmis Vertes, 2000. With French Nat. Svc., 1959-62, Rochefort, Toulouse. Decorated chevalier Order Arts and Letters, officer Order Acad. Palms, officer Order of Merit, Chevalier Legion of Honor (France). Fellow Soc. of Antiquaries of London (hon.). Avocations: hiking, skiing. Home and Office: 11 Rue du Fourcat, 09000 Foix Ariege France

CLOUDSLEY-THOMPSON, JOHN LEONARD, retired zoology educator, author; b. Murree, India, May 23, 1921; s. Ashley George Gyton and Muriel Elaine (Griffiths) Thompson; m. Jessie Anne Cloudsley, 1944; children: John Hugh, Timothy, Peter Leslie. BA, Cambridge (Eng.) U., 1946, MA, 1949, PhD in Zoology, 1950; DSc, U. London, 1960; DSc (hon.), U. Khartoum, Sudan, 1981. Lectr. zoology King's Coll., U. London, 1950-60; prof., keeper of Sudan Nat. History Mus. U. Khartoum, 1960-71; prof. zoology Birkbeck Coll., U. London, 1970-86, prof. emeritus, 1986—; vis. prof. U. Kuwait, 1978, 83, U. Nigeria, Nsukka, 1981, U. Qatar, 1986, Sultan Qaboos U., Muscat, 1988; vis. rsch. fellow Australian Nat. U., 1987; hon. cons. U. Malaya, 1969, Arabian Gulf U., Bahrain, 1986, U. Kuwait, 1990; participant numerous expdns. to Iceland, 1947, So. Tunisia, 1954, Africa, 1960-73. Author: Spiders, Scorpions, Centipedes and Mites, 1958, 2d edit., 1968, Animal Behaviour, 1960, Rhythmic Activity in Animal Physiology and Behaviour, 1951, (with John Sankey) Land Invertebrates, 1961, (with M.J. Chadwick) Life in Deserts, 1964, Desert Life, 1963, Animal Conflict and Adaption, 1963, Animal Twilight: man and game in eastern Africa, 1967, Microecology, 1967, Zoology of Tropical Africa, 1969, The Temperature and Water Relations of Reptiles, 1971, Desert Life, 1974, Terrestrial Environments, 1975, Insects and History, 1976, Evolutionary Trends in the Mating of Arthropoda, 1976, Man and the Biology of Arid Zones, 1977, The Water and Temperature Relations of Woodlice, 1977, The Desert, 1977, Animal Migration, 1978, Why the Dinosaurs Became Extinct, 1978, Wildlife of the Desert, 1979, Biological Clocks: their functions in nature, 1980, Tooth and Claw: defensive strategies in the animal world, 1980, Guide to Woodlands, 1985, Evolution and Adaption of Terrestrial Arthropods, 1988, Ecophysiology of Desert Arthropods and Reptiles, 1991, The Diversity of Desert Life, 1993, (novel) The Nile Quest, 1994, Predation and Defence Amongst Reptiles, 1994, Biotic Interactions in Arid Lands, 1996, Teach Yourself Ecology, 1998, The Diversity of Amphibians and Reptiles: an introduction, 1999; editor: Sahara Desert, 1984; editor-in-chief Jour. Arid Environs., Vol. 1, 1978-Vol. 37, 1997, now editor emeritus; editor book series (with wife) Natural History of the Arabian Gulf, 1981-82, Adaptations of Desert Organisms, 1989-2000, also numerous articles in sci. jours. and encys. Freeman City of London, 1945; Liveryman Worshipful Co. Skinners, 1952. Capt. 7th Armoured Divsn. 4th County London Yeomanry, 1940-44; hon. capt. Brit. Army, 1944; ETO. Recipient medal Royal African Soc., 1969, J.H. Grundy Meml. medal Royal Army Med. Coll., 1987, Found. for Environ. Conservation prize, Geneva, 1989, Peter Scott Meml. award Brit. Naturalists Assn., 1993; NSF sr. rsch. fellow U. N.Mex., Albuquerque, 1969. Fellow Linnean Soc. London (hon. FLS 1997, v.p. 1975-76, 77-78), Royal Entomol. Soc. London, Zool. Soc., Inst. Biol. (K.S.S. Charter award 1981), World Acad. of Art and Sci. Avocations: music (especially opera), photography, traveling. Home: 10 Battishill St, Islington, London N1 1TE, England

CLOUGHLEY, T(ERENCE) MICHAEL GROGAN, retired oil company executive; b. Blackpool, Eng., Mar. 23, 1941; s. H. Thomas G. and Dorothea (Harrison) C.; m. Elisabeth Faure Didelle, Sept. 3, 1966; children: Patrick J., P. Andrew, C. Marc. BA in Mech. Scis. with honors, Trinity Coll., Cambridge, Eng., MA, 1963, PhD, 1968. Engring. mgr. Brunei Shell, 1982-85, tech. dir., 1986-90; head prodn. liason Europe Shell Internat., Hague, The Netherlands, 1985-86; project mgr. Shell Internat., London, 1992-94; gen. mgr. ops., dir. Shell Nigeria, 1991-92; exec. sec. Internat. Oil Industry Exploration Prodn. Forum, London, 1994-98; indsl. adv. Eng. Sci. Rsch. Coun., London, 1978; dir. Billiton Exploration, The Netherlands, 1985-86. Contbr. articles to profl. publs. Chartered engr. Mem. Inst. Civil Engrs. (scholar 1960). Avocations: sports, reading, music, art.

CLOULAS, IVAN, archivist; b. St. Junien, France, Dec. 26, 1932; s. Adrien and Lucie (Boutet) C.; m. Annie Brousseau, July 16, 1962; children: Catherine, Sophie, Silvain, Cecile. Diploma archivist paleograph, Ecole des Chartes, Paris, 1957; D in History, U. Paris Sorbonne, 1968. Conservator Archives Nationales, Paris, 1957, conservator of modern series, 1965, chief automated data processing, 1972-85, chief history dept., 1985-98; rschr. Ecole Francaise de Rome, 1957-59, Casa de Velazquez, Madrid, 1965-68; chief departmental archives Evreux, France, 1968-72; gen. sec. Reg. Com. for Automation, UNESCO, 1972-84. Author: Catherine de Medecis, 1979, Laurent le Magnifique, 1982, Vie Quotidienne in Renaissance Castels, 1983, Henri II, 1985, Charles VIII, 1986, Les Borgia, 1987, Chambord, 1989, Jules II, 1989, Philippe II, 1992, Savanarole, 1994, Diane de Poitiers, 1996, Catherine de Medicis: la passion du pouvoir, 1999, Bérengère et Richard Coeur de Lion, 1999. Arts and letters officer, Paris, Merite officer, Paris. Decorated Legion of Honor (France); recipient grand prize Ville de Paris, 1982, Histoire de L'Academie Francaise, 1986. Fellow Soc. de l'Ecole des Chartes, Soc. de L'Histoire de France, Soc. Libre de l"Eure (gen. sec.), Acad. de Rouen, Soc. Archeologique et Historique du Limousin, Soc. Hist. Plantagenêts. Office: Archives Nationale, 44 rue du Bois de Boulogne, 92200 Neuilly-Sur-Seine France

CLOUSE, JOHN DANIEL, lawyer; b. Evansville, Ind., Sept. 4, 1925; s. Frank Paul and Anna Lucille (Frank) C.; m. Georgia L. Ross, Dec. 7, 1978; 1 child, George Chauncey. AB, U. Evansville, 1950; JD, Ind. U., 1952. Bar: Ind. 1952, U.S. Supreme Ct. 1962, U.S. Ct. Appeals (7th cir.) 1965. Assoc. Firm of James D. Lopp, Evansville, 1952-56; pvt. practice law James D. Lopp, Evansville, 1956—; guest editorialist Viewpoint, Evansville Courier, 1978-86, Evansville Press, 1986-98, Focus, Radio Sta. WGBF, 1978-84; 2d asst. city atty. Evansville, 1954-55; mem. appellate rules sub-com. Ind. Supreme Ct. Com. on Rules of Practice and Procedure, 1980.. Pres. Civil Svc. Commn. Evansville Police Dept., 1961-62, v.p., 1988; pres. Ind. War Memls. Com., 1963-69; mem. jud. nominating com. Vanderburgh County, Ind., 1976-80; dir. Ind. Fed. Cmty. Defender Project, Inc., 1993-98. With inf. U.S. Army, 1943-46. Decorated Bronze Star; named one of World's Most travelled Man Guinness Book of Records, 1993, Most Travelled Man, 1995-2000. Fellow Ind. Bar Found.; mem. Evansville Bar Assn. (v.p. 1972, James Bethel Gresham Freedom award 1997), Ind. Bar Assn. (chmn. com. on civil rights 1991-92), Travelers Century Club (L.A.), Pi Gamma Mu. Republican. Methodist. Office: 123 NW 4th St Ste 317 Evansville IN 47708-1712

CLOWES, GARTH ANTHONY, electronics executive, consultant; b. Didsbury, Eng., Aug. 30, 1926; came to U.S., 1957; s. Eric and Doris Gladys (Worthington) C.; m. Katharine Allman Crewdson, July 29, 1950 (dec. Jan. 1998); children: John Howard Brett, Peter Miles, Vicki Anne. BSc, Stockport Coll., Cheshire, Eng., 1953; postgrad., UCLA, 1965-66; higher nat. cert., Birmingham (Eng.) Coll. Tech., 1955-56. Gen. mgr., v.p., dir. Eldon Industries, Inc., El Segundo, Calif., 1962-69; CEO, founder Entex Industries, Inc., Compton, Calif., 1969-83; pres., founder Entex Electronics, Inc., Valley Ford, Calif., 1983—; pres., founder TTC, Inc., Carson, Calif., 1984-86; pres. Universal Telesis Electronics, Inc., Carson, 1986-87; gen. mgr. Matchbox Toys (U.S.A.) Ltd., Moonachie, N.J., 1987-88; dir. gen. Matchbox Spain, S.A., Valencia, 1988-89; cons. Matchbox Internat. Ltd., worldwide, 1986-89; spkr. in bus. field. Inventor electronic voice recognition devices, numerous others. Mem. pres.'s com. UNICEF, N.Y., 1972-74, Senate Adv. Bd., Washington, 1982-83; cons. Interracial Coun., L.A., 1967-69; mem. adv. bd. Santa Rosa Coll., 1993-99. Decorated Knight of Malta. Avocations: antiques, gardening, art, breeding Scotch Highland cattle. Home: 68 W Cross Island Rd Camano Island WA 98282-6667

CLOYD, JOHN ASBILL, county assessor; b. Columbia, S.C., Nov. 25, 1937; s. William Joseph and Doris Neeley (Asbill) C.; m. Mary Lou Crum, June 19, 1963; children: Jane Elizabeth, Edward Asbill. BS, U. S.C., 1959. With Calhoun Life Ins. Co., Columbia, S.C., 1960-66; asst. sec. supr. claims Palmetto State Life Ins. Co., Columbia, 1966-71; staff appraiser S.C. Fed. Savs. and Loan Assn., Columbia, 1971-78; assessor Richland County, S.C., 1978—. Pres. Family Service Ctr., 1987, 90, 93, bd. dirs. 1982-95. Served to lt. col. S.C. Army Nat. Guard, 1954-93. Mem. Soc. Real Estate Appraisers (pres. Columbia chpt. 1986-88, lt. gov.), Am. Inst. Real Estate Appraisers, Assessors of S.C. (pres. 1976, 87, 88), S.C. Assn. Assessing Officials (chmn. 1997, 98). Clubs: Columbia Ball, Tarantella, Forest Lake. Lodge: Kiwanis (pres. Columbia club 1985-86, lt. gov. 1988). Avocations: golf, South Carolina history.

CLOYD, THOMAS EARL, broadcast designer, consultant; b. Washington, Sept. 1, 1944; s. Buford Thomas Cloyd and Florence Elizabeth (Green) Paterson; m. Linda Oblak, Apr. 17, 1968 (div. Mar. 1989); 1 child from previous marriage, Lisa; 1 child, Tobey. Broadcast designer Sta KYW-TV/CBS, Phila., 1965-90; owner Barboza Assocs., Blackwood, N.J., 1970—; cons. emerging techs. Broadcast Designers Assn., San Francisco, 1981-89. Designer: (TV show) Mike Douglas Show, 1965-76, Sta. WWL-TV News Set, 1974, Shattered Dreams, 1985 (Emmy nomination 1985), (TV show logo) Steve Allen Show, 1971, and corp. trade exhibits. With U.S. Army, 1962-65, ETO. Home: 590 Lower Landing Rd Apt 183 Blackwood NJ 08012-4125

CLOZEL, MARTINE, research scientist; b. Nancy, France, Dec. 27, 1955; d. Etienne and Gilberte Caen; m. Jean-Paul Clozel, June 24, 1978; children: Sophie, Thomas, Sarah. MD, U. Nancy, 1980, M Pharmacology, 1980, postgrad. in pediatrics, 1983. Rsch. fellow McGill U., Montreal, Que., Can., 1980-82; fellow U. Calif., San Francisco, 1984-85; rschr. Hoffmann-LaRoche, Basel, Switzerland, 1987-92, sci. specialist, 1992-94, sci. expert, 1994-97; v.p., head preclin. drug devel. Actelion Ltd., Allschwil, Switzerland, 1999—. Contbr. over 90 articles to profl. publs.; 11 patents in field; discovered first orally active endothelin receptor antagonist. Eli-Lilly rsch. fellow, 1984; recipient spl. prize Fondation de France, 1983-84, Roche Prize, 1997. Avocations: skiing, tennis, classical music, travel, reading. Home: 11 rue Oberlin, 68300 Saint-Louis France Office: Actelion Ltd, Gewerbestrasse 16, 4123 Allschwil Switzerland

CLUA, OSVALDO, computer educator; b. Buenos Aires, June 4, 1953; s. Antonio and Julia Rosa (Pillez) C.; m. Maria Feldgen, Feb. 1, 1987. Engr., Facultad of Engring., Buenos Aires, 1978; Licenciado in Analysis of Sys., U. Buenos Aires, 1981. System programmer Faculty of Engring., U. Buenos Aires, 1980-81; sr. system programmer Agua Y Energia Electrica, Buenos Aires, 1982-83, project leader, 1983-89, mgr. R&D., 1989—; prof. computers Faculty of Engring., Buenos Aires, 1993—; prof. La Plata U., Buenos Aires, 1995—; part-time prof. Univ. Ausfral, 1995—; cons. mem. Depto Computacion, Facultad Ingenieria, Buenos Aires, 1990—, ext. chmn., 1994—; part-time prof. Cath. U. Argentina, Buenos Aires, 1993—, U. Ausfral, 1995-97. Mem. ACM, IEEE Computer Soc. Avocation: treking. Home: Caseros 3580, 1263 Buenos Aires Argentina Office: Univ of Buenos Aires, Faculty of Engring, Paseo Colon 850, 1063 Buenos Aires Argentina

CLUBB, BRUCE EDWIN, retired lawyer; b. Blackduck, Minn., Feb. 6, 1931; s. Ernest and Abigail (Gordy) C.; m. Martha Lucia Trapp, Dec. 19, 1954; children: Bruce Allen, Christopher Wade. B.B.A., U. Minn., 1955, LL.B. cum laude, 1958. Bar: D.C. 1959. Atty. Covington & Burling, 1958-61, Devel. Loan Fund, 1961-62, Chapman, DiSalle and Friedman, 1962-67; commr. U.S. Tariff Commn., 1967-71; ptnr. firm Baker & McKenzie, Washington, 1971-96; disting. lawyer in residence U. Minn. Law Sch., 1981-82; chmn. bd. dirs. Sunrise Properties, Inc., 1989-99. Author: (treatise) United States Foreign Trade Law (2 vols.), 1991; contbr. law revs. Served with AUS, 1952-54. Mem. D.C. Bar Assn., Am. Arbitration Assn. (arbitrator 1994-2000), Order of Coif. Republican. Clubs: Cosmos (pres. 1986), Metropolitan, Army Navy. Home: 630 Tennis Club Dr Fort Lauderdale FL 33311-4055

CLUDTS, STEPHAN, economist; b. Brussels, Nov. 10, 1974; m. Marie Mertens de Wilmars, June 26, 1998. Lic. Bus. Adminstrn., Cath. U. Leuven, Belgium, 1996; Lic. Philosophy, Free U. Brussels, 1999. Rsch. asst. Cath. U. Leuven, 1996—; advisor Ethibel, Brussels, 1999—; audit verificator Hefboom, Brussels, 1999. Contbr. articles to profl. jours. Home: 244 Ave Rogier, B-1030 Brussels Belgium Office: Cath Univ of Leuven, 69 Naamsestraat, B-3000 Leuven Belgium

CLUGSTON, GRAEME ALISTAIR, nutritionist, pediatrician, health organization administrator; b. Melbourne, Victoria, Australia, May 10, 1946; s. Colin William and Norma Mavis (McLeod) C.; m. Meena Pakhrin, Aug. 30, 1974; children: Andrew, Stephen. MBBS, U. New South Wales, Sydney, Australia, 1972; DCH, Royal Coll. Physicians, London, 1974; MSc, London Sch. Hygiene & Medicine, 1976, PhD, 1982, DLSHTM, 1996. Resident in pediat. Prince Wales Children's Hosp., Sydney; pediatrician Shanta Bhawan Hosp., Kathmandu, Nepal, 1973-74; hon. clin. asst. to Prof. J.C. Waterlow, London Sch. Hygiene and Tropical Medicine, 1975-80; pub. health nutritionist for Nepal, WHO, Kathmandu, 1981-82; regional nutrition advisor S.E. Asia, WHO, New Delhi, 1982-89; dir. nutrition program WHO, Geneva, 1992—. Contbr. over 40 articles to profl. pubs. Recipient prize of Australian Coll. Ophthalmologists, 1971, Hecht prize in Human Nutrition, U. London, 1975. Office: World Health Orgn Nutrition, Ave Appia, 1211 Geneva Switzerland

CLUNIE, GORDON JAMES AITKEN, surgeon, researcher; b. Suva, Fiji, Mar. 29, 1932; s. Thomas Anderson Clunie and Agnes Smith Aitken; m. Jess Anne Crozier, Dec. 29, 1957; children: David Alexander, Christine Louise, Pamela Elizabeth. MB ChB, U. Edinburgh, Scotland, 1956, ChM, 1968, DSc, 1993. Fellow Royal Coll. Surgeons, Edinburgh, 1961, Eng., 1962, Royal Australian Coll. Surgeons, Melbourne, 1969. Lectr. surg. sci. U. Edinburgh, 1964-67; reader in surgery U. Queensland, Brisbane, Australia, 1968-73, prof. surgery, 1973-78; prof. surgery U. Melbourne, 1978-95; deputy dean Faculty of Medicine, U. Melbourne, 1986-95; dean Faculty of Medicine, Dentistry & Health Scis. U. Melbourne, 1995-97; sr. med. cons. Anti-Cancer Coun. Victoria, Carlton, Australia, 1998—; sr. examiner gen. surgery Royal Australian Coll. Surgeons, Melbourne, 1988-92, chmn. bd. basic surg. a tng., 1995-99, chmn. ct. or examiners, 1999-2000; chmn. med. and sci. com. Anti-Cancer Coun. of Victoria, Australia, 1984-88. Editor-in-chief Australian & New Zealand Jour. of Surgery, 1990-95; editor Integrated Therapy of Cancer, 1984, Textbook of Surgery, 1997. Capt. Royal Army Med. Corps, 1957-59. Mem. Surg. Rsch. Soc. Australia and New Zealand (pres. 1975-77), Clin. Oncological Soc. Australia (pres. 1983-85), Internat. Surg. Soc., Transplantation Soc., Australian Soc. Immunology, Internat. Assn. Endocrine Surgeons, Transplantation Soc. Australia and New Zealand. Avocations: reading, music, swimming. Office: Anti-Cancer Coun Victoria, 1 Rathdowne St, Carlton 3053, Australia

CLUNIES-ROSS, CHRISTOPHER MYLES, environmental company executive; b. Adelaide, Australia, Oct. 7, 1963; s. Graham George and Rosemary Gweneth (Keen) C-R.; m. Katrina Judith Sporton, Nov. 27, 1993; children: Caitlin Louise, Kyle Aiden. BSc, Latrobe U., Melbourne, Australia, 1986; diploma in edn., U. Melbourne, 1987; M in Engring. Sci., U. Queensland, Brisbane, Australia, 1994, PhD in Chem. Engring., 2000. Rsch. officer Commonwealth Sci. and Indsl. Rsch. Orgn., Melbourne, 1986; sci. officer Environment Protection Agy., Melbourne, 1987-89; prin. scientist Nat. Analytical Labs., Melbourne, 1989-92; prin. sci., mng. dir. Unilabs Environ., Brisbane, 1992—; cons. U. Queensland, 1993—. Contbr. articles to profl. jours. Grantee Commonwealth Govt., Australia, 1994-97, 95. Mem. Royal Australian Chem. Inst., Clean Air Soc. of Australia and New Zealand. Avocations: skiing, photography, reading. Fax: (61-7) 3801 4645. E-mail: unilabs@geocities.com. Office: Unilabs Environ, 149 Bryants Rd, Loganholme 4129, Australia

CLYBURN, LUTHER LINN, real estate broker, appraiser, ship captain; b. Evansville, Ind., May 17, 1942; s. Luther and Robbie (Cobb) C.; children: Lisa Michelle, Luther Brent. Grad., Am. Savs. and Loan Inst., 1970; ABA, Pontiac (Mich.) Bus. Inst., 1972; BS, Detroit Coll. Bus., 1972; M of Bus. Mgmt., Ctrl. Mich. U., 1983. Lic. merchant marine; cert. scuba instr. Chief loan officer First Fed. Savs. and Loan Assn. Oakland, Pontiac, 1964-74; assoc. broker Bateman Real Estate Corp., Pontiac, 1975-77; regional rep. United Guaranty Residential Ins., Troy, Mich., 1977-83; sr. account mgr. Investors Mortgage Ins. Co., Boston, 1983-87; real estate broker, appraiser White Lake, Mich., 1977—, Clyburn Appraisal Svcs., White Lake, 1987—. Project dir., capt.: (documentary film) Angels of the Sea, 1982 (N.Y. Film Festival award 1983); photographer for Tundra Tours 25th anniversary of Alaska's Iditarod dog sled race, 1997, 2000. Capt., comdr. "Noble Odyssey" Tng. Ship, Mt. Clemens, Mich., 1977-89; dir., comdr. U.S. Naval Sea Cadet Corps Great Lakes div., Mt. Clemens, Mich., 1973—; nat. bd. dirs. U.S. Naval Sea Cadet Corps, 1988; project dir. Interseas Inc., Pontiac, 1982; ship capt. Great Lakes Botanical Island research project for Cranbrook Inst. Sci.

(Thunder Bay Islands, Lake Huron, 1987, Islands of Green Bay, 1989, 90); dir. of Underwater Cinitofu; capt. Pride of Mich., 1989—; capt. Great Lakes Island Rsch. Project for Oakland U., Fox Islands, 1996; project dir. In Search of the Griffin, Great Lakes Rsch. Bd., Pride of Mich., 1998—; founder/pres. Inter-Seas Exploration Ltd., 1999—. Recipient Cert. Appreciation award Southfield Bicentennial Commn., 1976, Letter of Commendation award Sec. of Navy, 1983, Quality People award Meritorious Cmty. Svc., 1993, Oakland County Q2 award, 1993, Unsung Hero award Mich. Ho. of Reps., 1994. Mem. Internat. Ship Masters Assn., Navy League of U.S., Am. Soc. Appraisers, Mich. Assn. Real Estate Appraisers. Home and Office: 9000 Gale Rd White Lake MI 48386-1411

CLYNE, MICHAEL GEORGE, linguistics educator; b. Melbourne, Victoria, Australia; s. John and Edith (Timar) C.; m. Irene Donohoue, Dec. 28, 1977; 1 child, Joanna. BA, U. Melbourne (Australia), 1960, MA, 1962; PhD, Monash U., Melbourne, Australia, 1965; DPhil (hon.), U. Munich, 1997. Tchg. fellow in German Monash U., Melbourne, Australia, 1962-64, lectr. in German, 1964-68, sr. lectr. in German, 1969-72, assoc. prof. German, 1972-88, prof. linguistics, 1988—; vis. prof. linguistics U. Stuttgart, Germany, 1972-73, Heidelberg, Germany, 1997; dir. rsch. Lang. and Soc. Ctr. Nat. Inst. Langs. and Literacy Australia, 1990—. Author: Community Languages-The Australian Experience, 1991, Inter-Cultural Communication at Work, 1994, The German Language in a Changing Europe, 1995, Undoing and Redoing Corpus Planning, 1997, Pluricentric Languages in an Immigrant Context, 1999, others; editor: Jour. Intercultural Studies, 1977-86, 93-96; contbr. over 250 articles to profl. jours.; mem. editl. bd. jours., book series. Mem. Ministerial Adv. Com. Multi-Cultural and Migrant Edn., Victoria, Australia, 1983-87. Mem. Order of Australia, 1993; decorated Cross of Hon. Sci. and The Arts 1st Class (Austria), 1996; recipient Jakob and Wilhelm Grimm prize, 1999. Fellow Acad. Social Scis. Australia, Australian Acad. Humanities; mem. Applied Linguistics Assn. Australia (hon. life), Inst. Deutsche Sprache (corr.), Australian Linguistic Soc. Office: Monash U, Dept Linguistics, 3168 Clayton Victoria, Australia

CLYNE, PATRICK FRANCIS, solicitor; b. Drogheda, Ireland, Jan. 23, 1946; s. Thomas Anthony and Philomena Ita (Begley) C. BA, Trinity Coll., Dublin, 1972, LLB, 1972, MA, 1976. Solicitor, Ireland, 1973, England and Wales, 1994. Solicitor, atty. Martin E. Marren and Co., Dublin, 1973—; commr. for oaths Supreme Ct., Ireland, 1984—; lectr., examiner Inc. Law Soc. of Ireland, Dublin, 1974-84. Freeman City of London, 1997; liveryman Worshipful Loriners' Co., London, 1998. Named Knight of Magistral Grace Sovereign Mil. Order of Malta, 1973; recipient Silver medal U. Philos. Soc., 1972, Cross of Officer of Merit, Sovereign Mil. Order of Malta, 2000. Mem. Royal Dublin Soc. (mem. gen. purposes com. 1999), Kildare St. and Univ. Club (hon. sec. 1996—), Friendly Bros. of St. Patrick (pres. 1996-98), Royal Irish Yacht Club. Roman Catholic. Avocations: travelling, antique collecting, practicing social virtues. Home: 59 Trees Rd, Mount Merrion Dublin, Ireland Office: Martin E Marren & Co, 10 Northumberland Rd, Dublin 4, Ireland

CLYNE, PETER ROBERT, medical practitioner, educator; b. Sydney, Australia, Jan. 7, 1952. MB, BChir with honors, Sydney U., Australia, 1976; Grad. Diploma in Epidemiology, U. Newcastle, 1996; Master of Med. Sci. in Clin. Epedemiology, Univ. Newcastle, 1999. Intern The Sydney Hosp., NSW, Australia, 1976-77; resident med. officer Prince of Wales Hosp., NSW, Australia, 1977-78; med. resident, registrar Royal Hobart Hosp., Australia, 1978-79; pvt. practice London, 1980-81, Roselands, Sydney, Australia, 1981-96; hon. clin. lectr. Univ. NSW, 1995—, hon. vis. fell., 1995—; med. educator, tng. prog. NSW, Royal Australian Coll. of Gen. Practitioners, 1995-98; pvt. practice Burwood, Sydney, Australia, 1996-99; pvt. prac. South Strathfield, Sydney, 1999—; chief exec. ofcr. Western Sydney Divsn. of Gen. Prac., 1996—; vice chmn., mem. exec. com. Canterbury Divsn. Gen. Practice, 1992-96, vice chmn., NSW Fac., Royal Australian Coll. of Gen. Practitioners, 1991-94, mem. mgmt. com., 1992—; mem. aged care liason com. S.W. Area Health Bd., 1993; hon. vis. fellow, hon. clin. lectr. U. NSW, 1995—; cons. Abbott Diagnostics, Sydney, 1986, Kodak Australia, Sydney, 1987; mem. mgmt. com. Doctors' Health Adv. Svcs., Sydney, 1993; mem. com., working party com. Chmn. NSW State Com. Med Colls., 1994-97; mem. ministerial gen. practitioner taskforce NSW Health Dept., 1994-95, gen. practice adv. com., 1996—, mem. adv. group forum legal implications clin. practice guidelines, mem. clin. ref. group, 1997—; dir. Western Sydney Divsn. Gen. Practice, 1996—; mem. adv. com. NSW Breast Cancer, 1996—; mem. profl. svcs. rev., mem. com. post operative care in med. benefits schedule, Medicare schedule rev. task force Dept. Health and Family Svcs., 1997—, mem. gen. practice adv. group, 1998—, mem. specialist recognition adv. com., 1998—; mem. clin. streaming com. Western Sydney Area Health Svc., 1997—, chmn. of counc., Royal Australian Coll. of Gen. Practitioners, 1999—, chmn. edn. and tng. adv. bd., Royal Australian Coll. of Gen. Practitioners, 1999—, NSW Fac. Rep. on Counc., Royal Australian Coll. of Gen. Practitioners, 1998-99, examiner, Royal Australian Coll. of Gen. Practitioners, 1995—, ex-officio mem. of bd., NSW Fac., Royal Australian Coll. of Gen Practitioners, 1988—, founding chmn., expert panel, NSW Fac., Royal Australian Coll. of Gen. Practitioners, 1995-99, RACGP Rep. on Gen. Prac. Subcom. of Med. Svcs. Com. NSW, 1989-99. Co-author: (video) An Introduction to Office Pathology, 1993; author: Manual of Office Bacteriology, 1988, (monograph) Standards for Office Procedures in General Practice, 1992; contbr. articles to profl. jours., chpts. to books. Mem. gen. practice liason com. Nat. Heart Found. Australia, 1993-94. Recipient James McRae Yeats prize for surgery Sydney Hosp., 1973. Fellow Royal Australian Coll. Gen. Practitioners (mem. faculty bd. 1988—, founding chmn., vice chmn. office pathology subcom. 1989-95, chmn. practice mgmt. com. 1988-94, chmn. planning com. 1993-94, chmn. expert panel NSW faculty 1994-97, founding chmn. expert panel NSW faculty, 1995—, med. educator tng. program, 1995—, examiner 1995—, chmn. medico-pharmacy liaison com., 1996-97, vice chmn. NSW faculty 1991-94, chmn. 1994-97, vice chmn. Canterbury divsn. gen. practice 1994-96, profl. rev. panel 1996—, rep., mem. editl. panel Australian Family Physician 1996—), Australian Med. Soc. (mem. advt. monitoring subcom. NSW br. 1994—), Nat. Assn. Testing Authorities (category 5 lab. inspector 1987-95, mem. med. testing registration adv. com. 1995-99). Avocations: computer programming, piano, photography, public speaking, time management. Office: PO Box 291, Strathfield 2135, Australia

ČMAKAL, TOMÁŠ RUDOLF, information and communication system manager; b. Prague, Czech Republic, May 9, 1948; s. Rudolf and Marie Marieanna (Reinischová) Č; m. Martina Krotká, Mar. 24, 1952; children: Hana, Zuzana. Ing., ČVUT, Prague, Czech Republic, 1972; CSc, ČSAV-UTIA, Prague, Czech Republic, 1982. Asst. Transgas, Prague, Czech Republic, 1972-73, specialist of control, 1973-82, mgr. control dept., 1982-89, mgr. info. divns., 1989—. Contbr. numerous articles to profl. jours. Avocations: jogging, swimming, raiting. Home: Křenická 68, 100 00 Prague Czech Republic Office: Transgas, Limuzská 12, 100 98 Prague Czech Republic

COAD, NOEL KENNETH, private country club administrator; b. Pembroke, Bermuda, Dec. 24, 1948; came to U.S., 1981; m. Kenneth Henry and Winifred Treco C.; m. Judith T. MacGillis, Sept. 7, 1974; children: Therese Ann, Daniel Roy. BA, Bournemouth Mcpl. Coll., 1971. Asst. mgr. The Princess Hotel, Hamilton, Bermuda, 1971-73; resident mgr. Southampton Princess Hotel, Bermuda, 1973-78; gen.mgr. Mid-Ocean Club, Tucker's Town, Bermuda, 1978-81, Stanwich Club, Greenwich, Conn., 1981-85, Rumson (N.J.) Country Club, 1985-88, Rockaway River Country Club, Denville, N.J., 1988—. Mem. Club Mgrs. Assn., N.J. Club Mgrs. Assn. (treas. 1997-99, v.p. 1999—), N.J. Club Found. (sec. 1997—). Avocations: music, photography, gardening. Home: 2 Decamp Dr Boonton Twp NJ 07005 Office: Rockaway River Country Club 39 Pocono Rd Denville NJ 07834-2960

COAKER, A. WILLIAM, chemical engineer, consultant; b. Johannesburg, South Africa, Oct. 8, 1927; came to U.S., 1953; s. Norwood Edward and Vera Louise (Gilfillan) C.; m. Mary Leonard West, Oct. 16, 1954 (dec. Feb. 25, 1980); children: Hillary, Evan, Timothy; m. Barbara Isabelle Wikander, June 14, 1980. BS in Engring., U. Witwatersrand, 1949, PhD, 1953. R&D engr., group leader Monsanto Chem. Co., Springfield, Mass., 1953-64; sr. R&D group leader Monsanto Co., St. Louis, 1964-69, market mgr., 1970-75; v.p. tech. Triple R Industries, Basking Ridge, N.J., 1976-77; dir. mfg. svcs. Tenn. Chem. Co., Piscataway, N.J., 1978-81; prin. Coaker Consulting, Morristown, N.J., 1981-83; sr. R&D assoc. BF Goodrich Co., Avon Lake, Ohio, 1983-93; sec./treas. A.W. Coaker & Assocs., Inc., North Olmsted, Ohio, 1993—. Author chpt. in 2 books; patentee in field. Stephen min. Trinity Cathedral, Cleve., 1995—. Fellow Soc. Plastics Engrs. (editor vinyl divsn. newsletter 1981-95, bd. dirs. vinyl divsn. 1982—); mem. AIChE, Am. Chem. Soc. Episcopalian. Avocations: tennis, hiking, gardening. Home and Office: A W Coaker & Assocs Inc 6726 Chadbourne Dr North Olmsted OH 44070-5039

COASE, RONALD HARRY, economics educator; b. Willesden, Eng., Dec. 29, 1910; came to U.S., 1951; s. Henry Joseph and Rosalie (Giles) C.; m. Marian Ruth Hartung, Aug. 7, 1937. B of Commerce, London Sch. Econs., 1932, DSc, 1951; Dr. Rer. Pol. honoris causa, Cologne U., Fed. Republic Germany, 1988; D of Social Sci. (hon.), Yale U., 1989; LLD (hon.), Washington U., St. Louis, 1991, U. Dundee, Scotland, 1992; DSc (hon.), U. Buckingham, Eng., 1995; DHL (hon.), Beloit Coll., 1996; docteur honoris causa, U. Paris, 1996. Sir Ernest Cassel Travelling scholar, 1931-32; asst. lectr. Dundee Sch. Econs., 1932-34, U. Liverpool, Eng., 1934-35; from asst. lectr. to lectr. to reader London Sch. Econs., 1935-51; prof. U. Buffalo, 1951-58, U. Va., Charlottesville, 1958-64; prof. U. Chgo., 1964—, now Clifton R. Musser prof. emeritus, sr. fellow in law and econs. Law Sch.; statistician, then chief statistician Central Statis. Office, Offices War Cabinet, Eng., 1941-46. Author: British Broadcasting, A Study in Monopoly, 1950, The Firm, the Market and the Law, 1988, Essays on Economics and Economists, 1994; editor Jour. Law and Econs., 1964-92. Mem. hon. com. Eurosci. Recipient Nobel prize in Econs., 1991; Rockefeller fellow, 1948; fellow Center for Advanced Study Behavioral Scis., 1958-59; sr. rsch. fellow Hoover Instn., Stanford U., 1977; hon. fellow London Sch. Econs. Fellow Am. Acad. Arts and Scis., Am. Econ. Assn. (disting.), Brit. Acad. (corr.), European Acad.; mem. Royal Econ. Soc., Mont Pelerin Soc., Internat. Soc. for New Instnl. Econs. (founding pres. 1997). Home: 1515 N Astor St Chicago IL 60610-1627 Office: U Chgo Laird Bell Law Quadrangle 1111 E 60th St Chicago IL 60637-2776

COATES, ALAN STUART, physician, clinical researcher; b. Kew, Australia, June 27, 1943; s. Thomas Hampton and Joan Glazebrook (Courtney-Pratt) C.; m. Marylon Slade Bodkin, Jan. 2, 1967; children: Andrew, Catherine, Elizabeth, James. MB BS, U. Melbourne, 1966, MD, 1973. Resident med. officer Royal Melbourne Hosp., 1967-68; registrar U. Melbourne, 1969-70; rsch. fellow Walter and Eliza Hall Inst., Melbourne, 1971-76; vis. fellow Wis. Cancer Ctr., Madison, 1976-78; med. oncologist N.S.W. Cancer Coun., Sydney, Australia, 1978-80, Ludwig Inst. Cancer Rsch., Sydney, 1980-88; sr. specialist Royal Prince Alfred Hosp., Sydney, 1984-98; rsch. dir. Sydney Melanoma Unit, 1985-98; assoc. prof. U. Sydney, 1985-98, prof., 1998—; CEO Australian Cancer Soc., 1998—; dir. Australia New Zealand Breast Cancer Trials Group, Sydney, 1990—; mem. sci. com. Internat. Breast Cancer Study Group, St. Gallen, Switzerland, 1990—; vis. prof. U. Ulm, Germany, 1993, Harvard U., 1994. Author articles and editorials. Recipient prize in clin. surgery U. Melbourne, 1966; Nat. Health and Med. Rsch. Coun. Australia grantee, 1973-99. Mem. Clin. Oncol. Soc. Australia (pres. 1994-95), Am. Soc. for Clin. Oncology (bd. dirs.), Am. Assn. for Cancer Rsch., European Soc. for Med. Oncology. Anglican. Avocations: computing, sailing, golf, music. E-mail: alancoates@cancer.org.au. Home: 40 Cook Rd, Centennial Park NSW 2021, Australia Office: Australian Cancer Soc, GPO Box 4708, Sydney NSW 2001, Australia

COATES, GLENN RICHARD, lawyer; b. Thorp, Wis., June 8, 1923; s. Richard and Alma (Borck) C.; m. Dolores Milburn, June 24, 1944; children—Richard Ward, Cristie Joan. Student, Milw. State Tchrs. Coll., 1940-42, NMA and MA, 1943-44; LLB, U. Wis., 1949, SJD, 1953. Bar: Wis. 1949. Atty. Mil. Sea Transp. Service, Dept. Navy, 1951-52; pvt. practice law Racine, Wis., 1952—; of counsel Dye, Foley, Krohn, Shannon, S.E.; sec., gen. counsel Racine Federated Inc.; lectr. U. Wis. Law Sch., 1955-56. Author: Chattel Secured Farm Credit, 1953; contbr. articles to profl. publs. Chmn. bd. St. Luke's Meml. Hosp., 1973-76, bd. dirs., 1990-91; pres. Racine Area United Way, 1979-81; bd. curators State Hist. Soc. Wis., 1986—, pres., 1995-97; bd. dirs. Racine County Area Found., 1983-89; bd. dirs. Wis. History Found., Inc., 1983-99, Hist. Sites Found., Inc., 1987-89, St. Luke's Hosp./St. Mary's Med. Ctr. Healthcare Found., 1992-96. With U.S. Army, 1943-46. Fellow Am. Bar Found. (life); mem. ABA, State Bar Wis. (bd. govs. 1969-74, chmn. bd. 1973-74), Wis. Jud. Coun. (chmn. 1969-72), Am. Law Inst. (life), Order of Coif. Methodist (chmn. fin. com. 1961-67). Club: Racine Country. Lodge: Masons. Home: 2830 Michigan Blvd Racine WI 53402-4254 Office: 1300 S Green Bay Rd Racine WI 53406-4469

COATES, JOHN PETER, technical executive; b. Coventry, Eng., Apr. 4, 1946; came to U.S., 1978; s. Harry and Barbara Joan (Snape) C.; m. Laura Frances Curran, July 28, 1979; children: Jonathan Edmund, Kristen Elizabeth, Ross James. BS/MS in Chemistry, Slough Coll. of Tech. now Thames Valley Univ., Eng., 1972; PhD in Chemistry, Brunel U., London, 1987. Analytical chemist Castrol Oil Co., Bracknell, Eng., 1964-73; sr. chromatographer Burmah Oil, Bromboro, Eng., 1973-74; sr., chief chemist Perkin-Elmer Ltd., Beaconsfield, Eng., 1974-78; sr. staff scientist Perkin-Elmer Corp., Norwalk, Conn., 1978-85; dir. mktg. Spectra-Tech Inc., Stamford, Conn., 1985-88; dir. analyzer div. Nicolet Instrument Corp., Madison, Wis., 1988-92; dir. mktg. real time systems divsn. (PAI) Perkin-Elmer, Norwalk, Conn., 1992-96; prin. cons. Coates Cons., Newtown, Conn., 1996—; dir. techs. Global Tecnhovations, Inc., Atlanta, Ga., 1998—; interim dir. MCEC, U. Tenn., Knoxville, 1999—. Co-author: (with L.C. Setti) Oils, Lubricants and Petroleum Products--Characterization by Infrared Spectra, 1985; patentee in field; contbr. chpts. to books and articles to profl. jours. Fellow Royal Soc. Chemistry; mem. Am. Chem. Soc., Instrument Soc. Am., Soc. Automotive Engrs., Soc. Applied Spectroscopy. Avocations: writing, photography, music, computers. Office: Coates Cons PO Box 3176 Newtown CT 06470-3176

COATES, WAYNE EVAN, agricultural engineer; b. Edmonton, Alta., Can., Nov. 28, 1947; came to U.S., 1981; s. Orval Bruce Wright and Leora (Raesler) C.; m. Patricia Louise Williams, Aug. 28, 1970. BS in Agr., U. Alta., 1969, MS in Agrl. Engring., 1970; PhD in Agrl. Engring., Okla. State U., 1973. Registered profl. engr., Ariz., Sask. Forage systems engr. Agr. Can., Melfort, Sask., 1973-75; project engr., tech. advisor, asst. sta. mgr. Prairie Agrl. Machinery Inst., Humboldt, Sask., 1975-81; cattle, grain farmer pvt. practice, Humboldt, 1975-81; assoc. prof. U. Ariz., Tucson, 1981-91, prof., 1991—; prof. titular ad honorem U. Nat. de Catamarca, Argentina, 1993—; cons. Vols. in Coop. Assts. and Ptnrs. of Ams., 1991-98, Paraguayan Govt. UN Devel. Program, 1987-90, Argentine Govt., univs. and pvt. industry, 1991—, govt., univ. and agrl. orgns., Mid East agrl. projects, 1986-89, 98-99; spkr. at internat. confs., Australia, Paraguay, Argentina, Peru, Chile, U.S.; expert witness in field. Designer farm equipment primarily for alternative crops and tillage; patentee in field; contbr. articles to profl. jours. Pres. Sunrise Ter. Village Townhomes Homeowners Assn., Tucson, 1990-92, 98-2000. Grantee USDA, Washington, 1981—, Ariz. Dept. Environ. Quality, Phoenix, 1989-98, U.S. Dept. of Energy, Washington, 1991-98, agrl. industries western U.S., 1982—. Mem. AAAS, NSPE, Am. Soc. Agrl. Engrs. (chmn. Ariz. sect. 1984-85, vice-chmn. Pacific region 1988-89, dir. dist. 4 1991-93, rep. to AAAS Consortium of Affiliates for Internat. Programs 1992-97, internat. dir. 1994-96), Assn. for Advancement of Indsl. Crops (pres. 1994-95, Outstanding Rschr. award 1997), Soc. Automotive Engrs., Air and Waste Mgmt. Assn., Coun. for Agrl. Sci. and Tech., Can. Soc. Agrl. Engring., Australian Soc. for Agrl. Engring., Asian Assn. for Agrl. Engring., Asociacion Latinoamericana de Ingenieria Agricola, Sigma Xi. Avocations: jogging, hiking. Office: U Ariz Office Arid Lands Studies 250 E Valencia Rd Tucson AZ 85706-6800

COATS, WARREN L., JR., economist; b. Bakersfield, Calif., May 19, 1942; s. Warren L. and Sara Jane C.; m. Louise Wilkinson, Feb. 15, 1968 (div. June 1980); children: Brandon, Daylin. BA in Econs., U. Calif., Berkeley, 1965; MA in Econs., U. Chgo., 1967, PhD in Econs., 1972. Instr. econs. Ill. Inst. Tech., Chgo., 1966-67, 68-70; asst. prof. econs. U. Hawaii, Honolulu, 1968; asst. prof. econs. U. Va., Charlottesville, 1970-76, asst. dep. chmn., 1972-74, dir. honors program, 1974-76; economist, sr. economist ctrl. banking dept. Internat. Monetary Fund, Washington, 1976-81, chief opers. divsn. SDRs, administered accts. treas.'s dept., 1982-88, advisor treas.'s dept., 1989-91, advisor monetary and exch. affairs dept., 1992-99, asst. dir. monetary and exch. affairs dept., 1999—; technical asst., advisor ctrl. banks Bulgaria, Croatia, Czech Republic, Hungary, Kazakhstan, Kyrgyz Republic, Malta, Moldova, Bosnia, Kosovo, Turkey, other countries; presenter in field. Co-author: The World Development Report, 1989, The Simple Analytics of Digital Money: Finance in Cyberspace, 1996; co-editor: Money and Monteary Policy in Less Developed Countries: Survey of Issues and Evidence, 1980; contbr. numerous articles to profl. jours. Mem. Am. Econ. Assn., We. Econ. Assn. Internat. (past mem. exec. com.), Order of the Golden Bear, Phil. Soc. (past bd. dirs.), Mt. Peleron Soc., Alpha Tau Omega (past pres.). Home: 1300 Crystal Dr # 1707 Arlington VA 22202-3234 Office: Internat Monetary Fund 700 19th St NW Washington DC 20431-0001

COBB, BRIAN ERIC, broadcasting executive; b. Berlin, N.H., Jan. 3, 1945; s. Everett Bryan and Eleanore (Bouchard) C.; m. Denise Leclair, Sept. 20, 1986; children: Jennifer, Heather. BS, U. Nev., 1967. Gen. sales mgr. Sta. WNGE-TV, Nashville, 1972; mktg. mgr. Sta. WNGE-TV, 1973-76, v.p., gen. mgr., 1977; v.p., gen. mgr. Sta. WSIX AM/FM, Nashville, 1977, Gen. Electric Broadcasting of Colo., stas. KOA-AM, KOAQ, KOA-TV, Denver, 1978-81; v.p. TV Chapman Assocs., Washington, 1982-87; ptnr. Media Venture Ptnrs., Naples, Fla., 1987—; cons. Denver Broncos, 1982—; pres. Media Venture Mgmt., Biltmore Broadcasting. Comml. chmn. Mile-Hi United Way, 1980; bd. dirs. Vanderbilt Children's Hosp., 1973-76; founder Naples Children and Edn. Found. Named an Outstanding Young Man of Yr., Nashville Jaycees, 1978. Mem. Nat. Assn. Broadcasters, Nat. Assn. TV Program Execs., Tenn. Assn. Broadcasters (bd. dirs. 1975-77), Nat. Assn. Media Brokers (pres. 1993-95), Rotary. Republican. Roman Catholic. Avocations: golfing, reading. Office: Media Venture Ptnrs 8889 Pelican Bay Blvd Ste 500 Naples FL 34108-7512

COBB, JOHN CECIL, JR. (JACK COBB), Latin America area specialist, communications specialist and executive; b. Walton, Ky., Apr. 10, 1927; s. John Cecil and Lucy (Dean) C. B.A. in Sociology, Antioch Coll., 1950; postgrad., U. Ams., Mex., 1950; M.A. in Communication, Mich. State U., 1964. Fgn. corr., pub. exec. Vision, Inc., Rio de Janeiro, N.Y.C., 1950-55; writer Mexico City, 1956-57; dir. Antioch Coll. Program, Guanajuato, Mex., 1958-62; communication research asst. Mich. State U., East Lansing, 1962-64, mem. research staff Computer Inst. Social Sci. Research, 1964-67; Fulbright prof. U. El Salvador, San Salvador, 1967-68; cons. Peace Corps, Lima, Peru, 1968-69, San Jose, Costa Rica, 1968-69; exec. dir. Latin Am. Studies Assn., Washington, 1969-71; cons. Washington, 1972-78; pres. Human Comm. Sys., Reston, Va., 1978-93, prin., 1994—; cons. on new internat. curriculum Antioch Coll., 1990; prodn. mgr. Peace in Action mag., 1994-97; cons. World Wide Web, 1996. Author: (with Howard I. Blutstein) Area Handbook of El Salvador, 1971; also monographs on land reform in El Salvador, 1980-86, study of urban family income in Bolivia, 1986, 3 software manuals on linking of electronic mail networks, 1991-92. Mem. Common Cause No. Va., 1975-77, publicity chmn., 1975-77; mem. exec. com. Washington area UN Assn., 1977-79; mem. Fairfax County Democratic Com., 1975-78; mem. Cherrydale Tap Dancers, 1997-98, Gotta Dance troupe, 1998—. Served with USN, 1945-46. Mem. Social Sci. Computing Assn. (chair), Latin Am. Studies Assn., Inter-Am. Coun. (v.p. 1994-95, pres. 1995-96), Soc. Internat. Devel., Mid-Atlantic Conf. Latin Am. Studies (panelist 1997), Fulbright Assn., The Internet Soc. Office: Reston Internat Ctr 11800 Sunrise Valley Dr Ste 32 Reston VA 20191-5302

COBB, ROWENA NOELANI BLAKE, real estate broker; b. Kauai, Hawaii, May 1, 1939; d. Bernard K. Blake and Hattie Kanui Yuen; m. James Jackson Cobb, Dec. 22, 1962; children: Shelly Ranelle Noelani, Bret Kimo Jackson. BS in Edn., Bob Jones U., 1961; broker's lic., Vitousek Sch. Real Estate, Honolulu, 1981. Lic. real estate broker, Honolulu; cert. residential broker. Med. supr. Hawaii Med. Svc. Assn., 1964-65, 66-68; bus. mgr. Micronesian Occupl. Ctr., Koror Palau, 1968-70; prin. broker Cobb Realty, Lihue, Hawaii, 1983—; sec. Neighbor Island MLS Svc., Honolulu, 1985-87, vice chmn., 1987-88; chmn. MLS Hawaii, Inc., Honolulu, 1988-90. Assoc. editor Jour Entymology, 1965-66. Sec. Koloa Cmty. Assn., 1981-98, pres., 1989; mem. Kauai Humane Soc., YWCA, Kauai Mus., Kauai Visitors Bur.; bd. dirs. Wong Care Home, Hoi'Ke Pub. TV, 1998—, v.p., treas., 1999, pres. 2000; vice chairperson Kauai Schs. Adv. Coun., 1995-98, pres., 2000; mem. adv. bd. KKCR Radio, 2000, dir. Kekohu Found, 1999-2000. Mem. Nat. Assn. Realtors (grad. Realtors Inst., cert. residential specialist), Hawaii Assn. Realtors (cert. tchr., state bd. dirs. 1984, v.p. 1985, dir. 1995-96), Kauai Bd. Realtors (v.p. 1984, pres. 1985, bd. dirs. 1995-97, treas. 1999, Realtor Assoc. of Yr. award 1983, Realtor of Yr. award 1986), Kauai C. of C., Soroptomists (bd. dirs. Lihue chpt. 1986-89, treas. 1989). Avocations: reading, music, travel. E-mail: rcobb@hawaiian.net. Office: PO Box 157 Koloa HI 96756-0157

COBB, STUART ROBERT, medical educator; b. Durham, Eng., Jan. 19, 1970; arrived in in Scotland, 1973; s. Andrew Robertson and Dorothy Robina (Williamson) C.; m. Cheryl Alexandra Rachel McMaster, Apr. 7, 1998; 1 child, Stella Dorothy Cobb. BSc, Glasgow (Scotland) U., 1993; DPhil, Oxford (Eng.) U., 1996. Rschr. Inveresk Rsch. Internat., Edinburgh, Scotland, 1987-89; rschr., neuropharmacology educator Edinburgh U., 1996-99. Contbr. articles to profl. jours. Fellow Caledonian Rsch. Found., Glasgow, 1999—. Mem. Physiol. Soc. Gt. Britain, Brit. Neurosci. Assn. Avocation: skiing. Home: 11 Church Hill Pl, Edinburgh EH10 4BE, Scotland Office: Univ Glasgow, University Ave, Glasgow G12 8QQ, Scotland

COBB, TY, lawyer; b. Great Bend, Kans., Aug. 25, 1950; s. Grover Cowling and Elizabeth Anne (McCleary) C.; m. Leigh Elliott Stevenson, Aug. 21, 1976; children: Chance Wyatt, Chelsea Leigh, Brady Elliott, Chloe Elizabeth. AB, Harvard U., 1972; JD, Georgetown U., 1978. Bar: D.C. 1979, U.S. Dist. Ct. D.C. 1979, U.S. Dist. Ct. Md. 1979, U.S. Ct. Appeals (4th and D.C. cirs.) 1979, U.S. Ct. Internat. Trade 1980, U.S. Ct. Appeals (3d cir.) 1987, U.S. Supreme Ct. 1986, Md. 1987, Colo. 1998, U.S. Ct. Appeals (10th cir.) 1999. Legis. adminstrv. asst. U.S. Ho. of Reps., Washington, 1974-75; law clk. to fed. judge U.S. Dist. Ct., Balt., 1978-79; assoc. Collier, Shannon, Rill & Scott, Washington, 1979-81; asst. U.S. atty. Office of U.S. Atty., Balt., 1981-86; chief criminal cases Office U.S. Attorney, Balt., 1984-86; ptnr. Hogan & Hartson LLP, Washington and Balt., 1988-98; mng. ptnr. Hogan & Hartson LLP, Denver, 1998—; mid-atlantic regional coord. Organized Crime Drug Enforcement Task Force, U.S. Dept. Justice, Balt., 1985-86, spl. trial counsel Office of Ind. Counsel HUD, 1994-95; instr. U.S. Atty. Gen.'s Adv. Inst., U.S. Dept. Justice, 1983-86; mem. Jud. Conf. of U.S. Ct. Appeals (4th cir.). Contbr. articles to ABA Complex Crimes Jour. Chmn. Md. lawyers Dole for Pres., 1986-87; counsel Forest Glen Park Civic Assn., Montgomery County, Md., 1981-84. Fellow Am. Coll. Trial Lawyers; mem. ABA, Harvard Alumni Assn. (bd. dirs. 1990-92). Republican. Office: Hogan & Hartson LLP 555 13th St NW Ste 800 E Washington DC 20004-1161 also: Hogan & Hartson 1200 17th St Ste 1500 Denver CO 80202-5835

COBBETT, STUART HANSON, lawyer; b. Montreal, June 3, 1948; s. Stuart Ashton and Adrienne Edythe (Hanson) C.; m. Jill Rankin, Sept. 7, 1973; children: Alexander, William, Anne. BA, McGill U., 1969, BCL, 1972. Bar: Que. Ptnr. Heenan Blaikie, Montreal, 1974-85; sr. v.p., dir. Astral Comms., Montreal, 1985-92; sr. ptnr. Stikeman Elliott, Montreal, 1992; mng. prin. Stikeman Elliott, London, 1996-99; mng. ptnr. Stikeman Elliott, Montreal, 2000—; bd. dirs. ABL Can. Inc., Montreal, Formula Growth Ltd., Montreal, McCord St. Sites, Montreal. Bd. dirs. Bishop's Coll. Sch., Lennoxville, Que., Can., 1982-95; chmn., bd. dirs. McGill News, Montreal, 1991-96; chmn. bd. visitors in arts McGill U., 1991-96. Mem. Can. Bar Assn., Internat. Bar Assn., N.Y. State Bar Assn., McGill Alumni U.K. (pres. 1996). Anglican. Avocations: skiing, tennis, golf, walking. Office: Stikeman Elliott, 1155 Rene Levesque Blvd, Montreal, PQ Canada H3B 3V2

COBBS, PRICE MASHAW, social psychiatrist; b. L.A., Nov. 2, 1928; s. Peter Price and Rosa (Mashaw) C.; m. Evadne Priester, May 30, 1957 (dec. Oct. 1973); children—Price Priester, Marion Renata; m. Frederica Maxwell, May 26, 1985. A.B., U. Calif.-Berkeley, 1953; M.D., Meharry Med. Coll., 1958. Intern San Francisco Gen. Hosp., 1958-59; psychiat. resident Mendocino State Hosp., Talmage, Calif., 1959-61, Langley Porter Neuro-Psychiat. Inst., San Francisco, 1961-62; pres. Pacific Mgmt. Systems, San Francisco, 1967—; CEO Cobbs, Inc.; mgmt. cons. in workforce diversity numerous cos., govt. agys. and community projects; conducted seminars UN,

Dept. State; guest lectr. leading colls. and univs.; chair 1st Ann. Nat. Diversity Conf., San Francisco, 1991; speaker 1st Internat. Diversity Conf., Johannesburg, South Africa, 1991; vis. cons., lectr. workforce diversity, South Africa, 1993; co-founder, pres. Renaissance Books, Inc.; adv. bd. Black Scholar. Author: (with William H. Grier) Black Rage, 1968, The Jesus Bag, 1971, (with Judith L. Turnock) Cracking the Corporate Code: From Survival to Mastery, 2000; contbr. State of Black America 1988, 89; pub. Mother Jones Mag. Bd. dirs. Found. for Nat. Progress, Lucille Packard Found. for Children's Health. Served to cpl. U.S. Army, 1951-53. Recipient Pathfinder award Assn. Humanistic Psychology, 1993. Fellow Am. Psychiat. Assn.; mem. Nat. Med. Assn., NAACP (life), Nat. Acad. Scis.; charter mem. Nat. Urban League. Achievements include pioneering in discipline of ethnotherapy to understand differences in race, culture and ethnicity. Avocations: bicycling, walking, reading, blues singing. Office: Pacific Mgmt System 3528 Sacramento St San Francisco CA 94118-1850

COBERLY, PATRICIA GAIL, elementary education educator, adult education educator; b. Fort Smith, Ark., Jan. 7, 1962; d. Charles Joe and Marie Opal Stracener; m. Mark Windfield Coberly, Nov. 6, 1990; children: Laura Kendrick, Christy Gail. BS with honors, Ark. Tech. U., 1987; MEd, U. Ark., 1993, EdD, 1995. Cert. tchr., Ark. Tchr. Ozark (Ark.) Sch. Dist., 1988-96; asst. prof. Armstrong Atlantic State U., Savannah, Ga., 1996—, adminstrv. dept. head middle and secondary edn., 1997—; cons. in field. Contbr. chpts. to books, articles to profl. jours. Mem. Am. Assn. Colls. Tchr. Edn., Ga. Assn. Tchr. Educators, Ga. Assn. Colls. Tchr. Edn., Ga. Profl. Mid. Edn., Nat. Middle Grades Assn., Ga. Middle Grades Assn., Nat. Sci. Tchrs. Assn., So. Futurists, World Futures Soc., Nat. Sci. Tchrs. Assn., Profs. Mid. Level Edn., Phi Delta Kappa, Phi Kappa Phi, Alphi Chi. Home: 718 Plantation Dr Rincon GA 31326-9708 Office: Armstong Atlantic State U 11935 Abercorn St Savannah GA 31419-1909

COBEY, CHRISTOPHER EARLE, lawyer; b. Merced, Calif., Mar. 18, 1949; s. James and Virginia Cobey; m. Elizabeth Jordan Rantz, Aug. 26, 1972; children: Sarah Elizabeth, Carolyn Branum. Student, Pomona Coll., 1967-69; BA with distinction and honors, Stanford U., 1971; JD, U. Calif., Davis, 1974. Bar: Calif. 1974, U.S. Dist. Ct. (no. dist.) Calif. 1981, U.S. Supreme Ct. 1983, U.S. Ct. Appeals (9th cir.) 1984, U.S. Dist. Ct. (ea. dist.) Calif. 1985. Dep. dist. atty. Los Angeles County, 1974-75, San Mateo County, Redwood City, Calif., 1975-77; assoc. ptnr. Hession & Creedon, San Mateo, Calif., 1979-85; of counsel Jackson, Lewis, Schnitzler & Krupman, San Francisco, 1985-88; ptnr. Seyfarth, Shaw, Fairweather & Geraldson, 1988-93, Ferrari, Alvarez, Olsen & Ottoboni, San Jose, 1993-96, Schachter, Kristoff, Orenstein & Berkowitz, Menlo Park, 1996-99; sr. counsel Littler Mendelson, San Jose, 1999—. Mem. San Mateo County Dem. Cen. Com., 1975-84, Calif. Dem. State Cen. Com., 1978-80; chmn. Town of Atherton Planning Commn., 1985-86; mem. Atherton Town Council, 1986-94, mayor, 1990-92; bd. dirs. Calif. Common Cause, 1980-81. Mem. ABA, San Mateo County Bar Assn. (bd. dirs. 1982-86, chmn. conf. on dels. delegation 1987), State Bar Calif. (resolutions com., conf. of dels. 1980-85, chmn. 1985), Stanford Alumni Assn. Presbyterian. Office: Littler Mendelson 50 W San Fernando St Ste 1400 San Jose CA 95113-2431*

COBEY, JOHN GEOFFREY, lawyer; b. Cleve., Aug. 16, 1943; s. Herbert Todd and Phyllis Jean (Weston) C.; m. Jan M. Frankel, 1983; children: Max Todd, David William. BS, Cornell U., 1966; postgrad., U. de Deusto, Balboa, Spain, 1968, Exeter (Eng.) U., 1969; JD, U. Cin., 1969. Bar: Ohio 1969, U.S. Dist. Ct. (so. dist.) Ohio 1969, U.S. Ct. Appeals (6th cir.) 1970, Ky. 1978, U.S. Dist. Ct. (no. dist.) Ky. 1978. Mem. Cohen, Todd, Kite and Stanford LLC, 1969—; bd. dirs. 1st Nat. Bank No. Ky., C&W Equipment Repair, Armstrong Coffee Co.; sec. bd. dirs. Elegant Fare; bd. dirs., sec. Apt. Assn. Title Co.; bd. dirs. Real Time Syss., Inc.; counsel coop. housing City of Cin. Founder, pres. Young Men's Wing, Mercantile Libr., 1971, regional amb. Cornell U., 1998, 99, 2000; trustee Ohio chpt. Nature Conservancy, 1974-82, Hillel of Cin., 1980-86, adv. bd. dirs., Women's Def. Fund, 1977, Holmes House, 1978-80; sec. Arts Consortium, Cin., 1975-77, trustee, 1975-78; mem. exec. com. Cin. chpt. Am. Jewish Com., 1981—, v.p., 2000—; trustee Hillel House, Better Housing League; chmn. bd. Friends Cin. Parks, 1982-84, pres. 1977-79; chmn. bd. dirs. Washington Park Housing Co., 1997—; bd. dirs. Cin. Law Libr., Greater Cin./No. Ky. Apt. Assn., 1975-94, Chinese Music Festival, 1996-00, Greater Cin. Oral Health Commn., 2000—, United Jewish Cemetary, 1999, Friends of Spl. Treatment Ctr. for Juvenile Arthritis, Children's Hosp. Cin., 2000—, Opn. Smile, 1998. Mem. Ohio State Bar Assn., Ky. Bar Assn., Cin. Bar Assn., No. Ky. Bar Assn., Fed. Bar Assn., U. Coll. Life Scis. and Agr. Alumni Assn. (dist. dir. 1977-79), Ohio Apt. Assn. (bd. dirs. 1986-87), Cin. Apt. Assn. (bd. dirs. 1983-90, pres. 1986-87), U. Cin. Law Sch. Alumni Assn. (bd. dirs. 1973-76), Cornell Club Cin. (bd. trustees 2000—). Home: 231 Oliver Rd Cincinnati OH 45215-2638 Office: Cohen Todd Kite and Stanford 525 Vine St Ste 16 Cincinnati OH 45202-3121

COBHAM, VANESSA ELISE, psychologist; b. Melbourne, Victoria, Australia, Nov. 2, 1971; d. George Walter and Barbara Florence (Muncey) C.; m. Thomas Richard Fletcher, Sept. 4, 1993. BA, U. Queensland, 1991, degree with honors in psychology, 1992, PhD in Psychology, 1997. Lectr., rschr. in clin. psychology U. Queensland, 1996-99; pvt. practice, 1997-99; clin. psychologist Portsmouth (Eng.) Health Care Trust, 1999-2000, Mater Children's Hosp., Queensland, 2000—. Contbr. articles to profl. jours., chpt. to book. Recipient postgrad. rsch. award Australian Govt., 1993-96; grantee Nat. Health and Med. Rsch. Coun., 1996-97, U. Queensland, 1998. Mem. Australian Psychol. Soc., Australian Assn. for Cognitive and Behavioral Therapies, Brit. Psychol. Soc. Avocations: tennis, roller blading, eating out, theater. Office: Mater Children's Hosp, Brisbane Queensland 4072, Australia

COBLE, PAUL ISHLER, advertising agency executive; b. Indpls., Mar. 17, 1926; s. Earl and Agnes Elizabeth (Roberts) C.; m. Marjorie M. Trentanelli, Jan. 27, 1951; children: Jeffery Mansfield, Sarah Anne Davis, Douglass Paul Coble. A.B., Wittenberg U., 1950; postgrad., Case-Western Res. U., 1950-53. Reporter Springfield (Ohio) Daily News, 1944; reporter, feature writer Rockford (Ill.) Register-Republic, 1947-48; account exec. Fuller & Smith & Ross, Inc., Cleve., 1949-57; dir. sales promotion McCann Erickson, 1957-63; dir. sales devel. Marschalk Co., 1963-65, v.p., 1965-70, sr. v.p., 1970-73; pres. Coble Group, 1973—; chmn. bd., sec.-treas. Hahn & Coble, Inc., advt., mktg. and pub. relations, 1977—; pub. Islander mag., Hilton Head Island, S.C., 1973-83; asst. prof. advt. W.Va. U., 1982-83. Chief instr. Cleve. Advt. Club Sch., 1961-73. Contbr. articles to profl. pubs. Active fund raising drives for various charitable and youth orgns.; bd. dirs. The Deep Well Project Inc. Served with AUS, 1944-46. Mem. Sales and Marketing Internat., Assn. Indsl. Advertisers, Cleve. Advt. Club, Newcomen Soc., Woodside Country Club, Sea Pines Country Club, Cleve. Rotary. Home: 106 Longwood Green Ct Aiken SC 29803-2751

COBURN, NIALL FRANCIS, lawyer, educator, author; b. Luton, Eng., Apr. 4, 1959; arrived in Australia, 1964, naturalized, 1982; s. Bernard Duffy and Margaret Mary (O'Rourke) C.; m. Eileen Anna Wray-McCann, Feb. 18, 1989; children: Harrison, Christian, Gabriel. LLB, U. Tasmania, Australia, 1984, BA, 1984; LLM, U. Melbourne, Australia, 1996. Bar: Supreme Cts. and High Ct. of Australia 1986. Solicitor Legal Aid Commn. of Victoria, Melbourne, Australia, 1987-89; barrister Victorian Bar, Melbourne, 1989-92; prin. lawyer Australian Securities and Investments Commn., Brisbane, 1992—; sr. tutor Queens Coll., Melbourne U.; tutor Griffith U., Brisbane; mem. com. Queensland sect. corps. Law Coun. Australia; lectr. Cambridge, U.K. Author: Insolvent Trading, 1998, Poems of a Modern World; contbr. articles to profl. jours. Surf life saver Surf Life Saving Assn. Australia, Victoria, 1985-87; mem Amnesty Internat., Melbourne, 1978. Recipient Bronze award Surf Life Saving, 1986, Legal Writing prize U. Tasmania, 1983, Pub. Spkg. award Australian Securities Commn., 1993; Australian Securities and Investment Commn. grantee, 1999. Roman Catholic. Avocations: surfing, horseback riding, running, reading and writing. Office: Australian Sec/Inv Commn, 240 Queens St, Brisbane QLD, Australia

COBURN, RICHARD JOSEPH, company executive, electrical engineer; b. N.Y.C., Nov. 4, 1931; s. Elmer Roswell and Maria Veronica (Greenan) C.; m. Catherine Elizabeth Wilkinson (div. 1992); children: Jenifer, Catherine, Steven; m. Elizabeth A. Semmler, Jan. 1993. BSEE, Yale U., 1954. Devel. engr. Hamilton Standard, Windsor Locks, Conn., 1954-59; chief engr. Dynamic Controls Corp., South Windsor, Conn., 1959-66; mgr. digital logic Fairchild Industries, Germantown, Md., 1966-68; pres. Scan Optics, East Hartford, Conn., 1968-72, Coburn Tech., East Hartford, 1972-77, KCR Tech., East Hartford, Conn., 1977-91; chmn. Accent Color Sciences, Inc., East Hartford, Conn.; bd. dirs. Scan Optics, Manchester, Conn. Inventor electronic back pressure control, radio noise free switch, apparatus for image reproduction. Mem. Yale Club, Franklin & Eleanor Roosevelt Inst. Republican. Roman Catholic. Office: Accent Color Scis Inc 800 Connecticut Blvd East Hartford CT 06108-7303

COCCHI, ALESSANDRO, education educator; b. Bologna, Italy, Mar. 12, 1936; s. Massimo Cocchi and Maria Pia Fantoni; m. Emanuela Ercolani, Sept. 4, 1963; children: Nicola, Alberto, Giovanni. Engr., U. Bologna, 1959, Pharmacist, 1962. Tchr. U. Bologna, 1962-69, prof., 1970—; cons. in field. Author: (books) Thermophysics for Engineers, 1976, Applied Acoustics, 1968, Italian Law on Noise Pollution, 1995; editor: Noise Pollution, 1989. Mem. ASHRAE, ASA, INCE, IAAU, Italian Assn. of Acoustics (pres. 1981-85), Acad. of Scis. of Bologna. Office: Dienca Dept/Engring Faculty, Risorgimento 2, 40136 Bologna Italy

COCCIA, MARIA ELISABETTA, gynecologist, researcher; b. Foligno, Perugia, Italy, Feb. 2, 1960; d. Luciano and Mariella (Santini) C.; m. Gian Luca Bracco, June 2, 1985; children: Niccolò, Tommaso, Francesco. MD, U. Perugia, Italy, 1984, PhD in Perinatology, 1994. Cert. in Ob-gyn., U. Florence (Italy), 1989. Rschr., dept. of obstetrics/gynecology U. Florence, Italy, 1995—; bd. dirs. Italian Soc. Fertility and Sterility. Contbr. numerous articles to profl. jours. Mem. CECOS. Roman Catholic. Avocations: basketball, skiing. E-mail: mecoccia@tin.it. Home: Via Ippolito Nievo no 2, 50129 Florence Italy

COCHÉ, JUDITH, psychologist, educator; b. Phila., Sept. 2, 1942; d. Louis and Miriam (Nerenberg) Milner; m. Erich Coché, Oct. 16, 1966 (dec.); 1 child, Juliette Laura; m. John Anderson, Jan. 1, 1994. BA, Colby Coll., 1964; MA, Temple U., 1966; PhD, Bryn Mawr Coll., 1975. Diplomate Am. Bd. Profl. Psychology; lic. Psychologist, Pa., Md., N.J.; cert. in group psychotherapy Nat. Registry Group Psychotherapists. Rsch. asst. Jefferson Med. Coll., 1965-66; diagnostician Law Ct., Aachen, Germany, 1967-68; staff psychologist N.E. Community Mental Health Ctr., Phila., 1969-74; family clinician Inst. Pa. Hosp., 1974-76; instr. psychology Drexel U., 1976-77; lectr. Med. Coll. Pa., 1977-78; asst. clin. prof. Hahnemann Med. Coll., Phila., 1979—; pvt. practice Phila., 1974—, N.J., 1985—; assoc. prof. psychiatry U. Pa., 1985—; assoc. clin. prof. psychology in psychiatry U. Pa. Med. Coll., 1986—; mem. faculty Family Inst. of Phila., 1990—; sr. cons. Phila. Child Guidance Clinic, 1992-96; assoc. clin. prof. psychology in psychiatry U. Pa. Med. Coll., 1986—; clin. cons. Hilltop Prep Sch., 1977-86; clin. supr. Am. Assn. Marriage and Family Therapy. Co-author: Couples Group Psychotherapy, A Clinical Practice Model, 1990, Co. author Powerful Wisdom: Voices of Distinguished Women Psychotherapists, (1993); contbr. chpts. to books, articles to profl. jours. Bd. dirs. Whitemarsh Art Ctr., 1977-78, Please Touch Museum, 1982-89; mem. prof. adv. bd. Parents Without Ptnrs., 1977-86; mem. adv. com. Pa. Ballet/Shirley Rock. Grantee Del. Children's Bur. Bryn Mawr Coll., 1974-75, Pa. Hosp., 1975-77. Fellow Am. Group Psychotherapy Assn.; mem. APA, Am. Assn. Marriage and Family Therapy (approved supr.), Am. Family Therapy Assn., Phila. Soc. Clin. Psychologists (pres. 1980-81), Family Inst. Phila., Pa. Psychol. Assn. (chmn. legis. com. 1982), Soc. Rsch. in Psychotherapy. Address: Acad House 1420 Locust St Ste 410 Philadelphia PA 19102-4202

COCHENOUR, MARK DAVID, nuclear electronics; b. Pitts., Pa., June 25, 1975; s. Mark David and Donna Elizabeth C. Grad., Naval Nuclear Power Sch., 1998. Instr. Camp Takajo, Naples, Maine, 1994; mgr. Radio Shack, Pitts., 1994-95; nuclear reactor operator US Navy, Groton, Conn., 1995—. With USN, 1995—. Recipient Good Conduct award Sec. of Navy, 1998, Admiral Commendation, 1999, Captain Commendation, USS City of Corpus Christi. Mem. US Subvets. Republican. Presbyterian. Avocations: archery, reading, sports. Home: 40 South St Biddeford ME 04005-2421 Office: USS City of Corpus Christi SSN 705 FPO AE 09566

COCHETEUX, PHILIPPE AUGUSTE LOUISE, physician; b. Roubaix, France, Nov. 18, 1950; s. Jacques and Anne-Marie (Lucion) C.; m. Annie Perales, Oct. 31, 1975; children: Perrine, Julien. MD, U. Lille, 1980. Intern Cen. Hosp. of Roubaix, 1976-80; attaché Hosp. of U. Lilly, 1980—. Served as capt. with Reserves, 1985. Roman Catholic. Avocations: tennis, cycling. Home: 7 Rue Gambetta, Villers-Outréaux Nord, France 59142

COCHRAN, EARL VERNON, retired manufacturing company executive; b. Poplar Bluff, Mo., May 14, 1922; s. Earl J. and Bertha M. (Merrit) C.; m. Eleanor J. Greene, July 20, 1950; 1 child, Tara Lang. BS, R.P.I., 1947. Registered profl. engr., Ohio. Test lab. engr. Stromberg-Carlson, Rochester, N.Y., 1947-48; dir. elec. engring. dept. Commonwealth Rsch. & Devel., Dayton, Ohio, 1948-52; sales mgr. Dayton Precision Mfg. Co., Dayton, Ohio, 1952-57, v.p. sales, 1957-60; v.p. sales Kirkwood Industries, Cleve., 1960-78, dir., exec. v.p., 1978—; ret., 1994; dir. Aoyama Kirkwood, 1976-94; dir., pres. Kirkwood Can. Ltd., 1978-90. Bd. mem. Fairview Luth. Hosp. Found., Cleve., 1980-97. Ensign USN, 1941-46. Fellow IEEE; mem. Ohio Soc. Profl. Engrs. Avocations: tennis, computing, skiing, diving, golf. Home: 12550 Lake Ave Lakewood OH 44107-1575

COCHRAN, GEORGE CALLOWAY, III, retired bank executive, lawyer; b. Dallas, Aug. 29, 1932; s. George Calloway and Miriam (Welty) C.; m. Jerry Bywaters, Dec. 9, 1961; children—Mary, Robert. BA, So. Meth. U., 1954; JD, Harvard U., 1957; cert., La. State U. Sch. Banking, 1969. Bar: Tex. 1957. Assoc. Leachman, Gardere, Akin and Porter, Dallas, 1960-62; with Fed. Res. Bank of Dallas, 1962-76, sr. v.p., 1976-92, ret., 1992; adv. com. Bank Ops. Inst., Tex. A&M U., Commerce, 1982—; mem. task force on truth in lending regulation Bd. Govs. of Fed. Res. System, Washington, 1968-69; bd. dirs. Am. Inst. Banking., Dallas, 1986-90. Hist. landmark survey task force City of Dallas, 1974-78. Capt. USAF, 1958-60. Recipient Warner award for svc. to dance The Dance Coun., Dallas, 1999. Mem. State Bar Tex., Phi Beta Kappa (pres. North Tex. Assn. 1998-2000), Harvard Club. Methodist. Home: 3541 Villanova St Dallas TX 75225-5008

COCHRAN, GLORIA GRIMES, pediatrician, retired; b. Washington, June 24, 1924; d. Paul DeWitt and Muriel Ann (Quackenbush) Grimes; m. Winston Earle Cochran, June 10, 1950; children: Edith Ann, Winston Earle, Jr., Donald Lee, Robert Edward. BS in Zoology, Duke U., 1945; MD, 1949; MPH, Johns Hopkins Sch. Hygiene, Balt., 1979. Diplomate Nat. Bd. Med. Examiners, 1950, Am. Bd. Pediatrics, 1958. Clinic pediatrician, sch. med. advisor health dept. Montgomery County, 1955-65; fellow in pediat. habilitation St. Christopher Hosp. for Children, Phila., 1965-66; assoc. dir. Child Development Clinic Baylor Med. Sch., Tex. Children's Hosp., 1966-72; dir. Northern Va. Child Devel. Field Svcs. Bur. Child Health State Health Dept. Commonwealth Va., 1972-76; coord. Handicapped Svcs. Children's Hosp. Nat. Med. Ctr., Washington, 1976-78; acting chief Divsn. of Svcs. to Children with Spl. Needs Bur. Sch. Health Svcs., Washington, 1982-89; retired, 1989; cons. Head Start Program, Md., Va., Tex., Pa., D.C., 1965-89; bd. mem. Ctrs. for Handicapped, Silver Spring, Md., 1982-89; Child Health com. Med. Soc. D.C., Washington, 1976-91. Producer, editor: (teaching film) Challenge for Habilitation: The Child with Congenital Rubella Syndrome, 1976. Steering com. Rock Days Inter-Church Camp, Washington, 1978-82; bd. mem. Open Door Cmty. Ctr., Columbus, Ga., 1993-94; co-chair curriculum com. Columbus Coll. Acad. of Life Long Learning, Columbus, 1994. Mem. Am. Assn. Mental Retardation, Am. Med. Women's Assn., Assn. for Retarded Citizens, Am. Acad. Cerebral Palsy, Am. Acad. Pediatrics, Phi Beta Kappa, Delta Omega. Democrat. Methodist. Avocation: travel. Home: 1605 Greenbriar Dr Norman OK 73072-6717

COCHRAN, JACQUELINE LOUISE, management executive; b. Franklin, Ind., Mar. 12, 1953; d. Charles Morris and Marjorie Elizabeth (Rohrbaugh) C. BA, DePauw U., 1975; MBA, U. Chgo., 1977. Fin. analyst Pan Am World Airways, N.Y.C., 1977-79, Gen. Bus. Group W. R. Grace & Co., N.Y.C., 1979-80; sr. fin. analyst Gen. Bus. Group div. W. R. Grace & Co., N.Y.C., 1980-81, mgr. fin. analysis, 1981-82; dir. fin. planning and analysis Gen. Bus. Group div. W. R. Grace & Co., N.Y.C., 1982-85; v.p. fin. Am. Breeders Svc. div. W. R. Grace & Co., DeForest, Wis., 1985-87, v.p. feed ops. Grace Animal Svc. div., 1987-89; gen. mgr., chief ops. officer SoftKat div. W. R. Grace & Co., Chatsworth, Calif., 1990; pres. SoftKat div. W.R. Grace & Co., Chatsworth, Calif., 1990-92; vice-chmn., chief adminstrv. officer Baker & Taylor, Inc., Chatsworth, Calif., 1992, pres. SoftKat div., 1992; exec. cons. Jacqueline Cochran Cons., Westlake Village, Calif., 1993, 94; gen. mgr. Attica Cybernetics, Inc., Chatsworth, Calif., 1995; pres., owner CorporateLinks, Westlake Village, Calif., 1996—. Bd. visitors DePauw U., 1993-96. Recipient Women of Distinction award Madison (Wis.) YWCA, 1987; named to Acad. Women Achievers YWCA N.Y., 1984. Mem. Omicron Delta Epsilon, Phi Beta Kappa, Alpha Lambda Delta, Delta Delta Delta (advisor scholarship com. Madison chpt. 1985-89, treas. 1986-89, ho. corp. bd. dirs. 1986-89, fin. advisor 1986-89). Republican. Methodist. Avocations: reading, golf.

COCHRAN, JOHN M., III, lawyer; b. N.Y.C., June 26, 1941; s. John M. Jr. and Mildred Lee (Ford) C.; m. Véronique Bouchet du Val Jolie de Bonneau. AB, Coll. William and Mary, 1963; JD, George Washington U., 1967; Doctorat de l'Université, U. Paris, 1971. Bar: N.Y. 1967, Calif. 1974, France 1973; avocat à la Cour d'Appel de Paris 1992-98. Barrister Chambers of Lord Rippon of Hexham, London, 1974-98; ptnr. Willkie, Farr & Gallagher, Paris, 1984-93, Curtis, Mallet-Prevost, Colt & Mosle, Paris, 1993-98. Editor Butterworth's Jour. of Internat. Banking and Finance Law, 1986. Mem. Soc. Sportive du Jeu de Paume et des Raquettes (Paris). Home: Chateau Falfas, 33710 Bayon France also: 16 rue Montevideo, 75116 Paris France Home: Chateau Falfas, 33710 Bayon France also: 16 rue Montevideo, 75116 Paris France

COCHRAN, JOHN P., economics educator; b. Ft. Collins, Colo., Dec. 22, 1949; s. Ira Williams and Elizabeth Ann C.; m. I. Ann Cochran, Aug. 23, 1977. BA in Econs., Met. State Coll. of Denver, 1978; MA in Econs., U. Colo., 1981, PhD in Econs., 1985. Intern as sr. economist Colo. Pub. Utility Commn., summer 1986; asst. prof. econs. Met. State Coll. of Denver, 1986-90, chair of econs., 1990-94, assoc. prof. econs., 1990-96, prof. of econs., 1996-97, chair and prof. econs., 1997—; vis. lectr. econs. Met. State Coll. of Denver, 1981-82, vis. asst. prof., 1982-86, adj. asst. prof. econs. Regis U., Denver, 1986-90; presenter in field. Co-author: (book) The Hayek-Keynes Debate: Lessons for Current Business Cycle Research, 1999; contbr. articles to profl. jours.; editor books/publs. in field.

COCHRANE, BETSY LANE, state senator; b. Asheboro, N.C.; d. William Jennings and Bobbie (Campbell) Lane; m. Joe Kenneth Cochrane, 1958; children: Lisa, Craig. BA cum laude, Meredith Coll., 1958. Tchr. for eleven yrs.; mem. N.C. Ho. of Reps., Raleigh, 1980-88; house minority leader N.C. Ho. of Reps., Raleigh, N.C., 1985-88; mem. N.C. Senate, Raleigh, 1988—, chmn. Commn. on Aging, 1989-99, vice chmn. higher edn. com., 1991-92; senate minority whip, 1993-94, senate minority leader, 1995-96; tchr. Winston-Salem Sch. System, Highland Presbyn. Ch. Sch.; mem. Nat. Rep. Platform Com., So. Regional Edn. Bd., 1987—; chmn. Joint Legis. Ethics Com., 1989, N.C. Parks Com., 1986-90. Trustee Davie County Hosp.; bd. advisors Z. Smith Reynolds, 1995-99, Meredith Coll., 1995; chmn. pres.'s adv. coun. Meredith Coll., 1999—. Recipient Woman in Govt. award N.C. Jaycees, 1985; named One of 10 Outstanding Legislators in Nation, 1987, Disting. Citizen of Yr. N.C. Libr. Dirs., 1991, Legislator of Yr. N.C. Divsn. Aging, 1991, N.C. Assn. for Home Care, 1992, Citizen of Yr. N.C. Health Facilities Assn., 1993, Legislator of Yr. award N.C. Wildlife Fedn., 1995, Legislator of Yr. award Austism Found., 1995, Myers-Honeycutt award for excellence in pub. svc., 1996, Disting. Alumnae of the Yr. Meredith Coll., 1996, Dr. Ewald W. Busse award Aging Advocates of N.C., 1997. Baptist. Home and Office: 122 Azalea Cir Advance NC 27006-9582 Office: NC Senate 1119 Legislative Bldg Raleigh NC 27601

COCHRANE, JAMES LOUIS, economist; b. Nyack, N.Y., Aug. 31, 1942; s. Thomas and Anna (Yaroscak) C.; m. Katherine Prince Schirmer, Mar. 24, 1984; 1 child. BA, Wittenberg U., 1964; PhD, Tulane U., 1968. Instr. Tulane U., New Orleans, 1967-68; asst. prof. U. S.C., Columbia, 1968-70, assoc. prof., 1970-72, prof., 1972-77; sr. staff mem. NSC, Washington, 1978-79; directorate of intelligence CIA, Washington, 1980-83; sr. v.p., chief economist Tex. Commerce Bancshares Inc., Houston, 1984-88, N.Y. Stock Exch., 1988—; assoc. staff Brookings Instn., Washington, 1972-76, 76-78; 1st v.p. So. Econ. Assn., U. N.C., 1976-77; vis. prof. U. Melbourne, Australia, 1972, U. Tex., Austin, 1973-74; mem. adv. bd. White Ctr. Fin. Rsch., U. Pa., Fin. Markets Rsch. Ctr., Vanderbilt U.; mem. bd. advisors N.Y. Assembly; bd. dirs. Catalyst Inst., Columbia U. Ctr. Law and Econ. Studies; mem. emerging econs. program bd. U. Pa. Wharton Sch.; mem. deans adv. bd. Hofstra U. Sch. Bus.; mem. study equities markets Pace U.; mem. internat. adv. com. Ctr. for Internat. Affairs, Harvard U., U.S. Nat. Com. for Pacific Econ. Cooperation. Author: Macroeconomics Before Keynes, 1970, Macroeconomics Analysis and Policy, 1974, Industrialism and Industrial Man in Retrospect, 1977; editor: Multiple Criteria Decision Making, 1975; mem. editl. bd. History Polit. Economy, Duke U., 1974-80, So. Econ. Jour., U. N.C., 1976-79. Mem. History of Econs. Soc. (treas. 1974-80), Asia Soc. (adv. dir. 1986), Am. Econ. Assn., Western Fin. Assn. Avocations: tennis, singing, writing. Office: NY Stock Exch 11 Wall St Fl 7 New York NY 10005-1974

COCHRANE, ROBERT LOWE, biologist; b. Morgantown, W.Va., Feb. 10, 1931; s. Thomas Joseph and Isabelle Durston (Lowe) C. BA, W.Va. U., 1953; MS, U. Wis., 1954, PhD, 1961. Rsch. asst. genetics U. Wis., Madison, 1953-55, 1953-55, rsch. asst. zoology, 1957-60; with Fur Animal Exptl. Sta., Petersburg, Alaska, 1955; agt. in animal husbandry U.S. Dept. Agr., Madison, Wis., 1955-61; biologist FDA, Washington, 1961-62; sr. research fellow dept. anatomy U. Birmingham (Eng.), 1962-65; project assoc. dept. physiology U. Pitts., 1965-66; sr. endocrinologist Eli Lilly & Co., Indpls., 1966-80; rsch. assoc. G.D. Searle & Co., Skokie, Ill., 1980-81; with Short's Fur Farm, Granton, Wis., 1981-83; rsch. assoc. Marshfield (Wis.) Med. Found., 1983-84; biologist Northwood Fur Farms, Inc., Cary, Ill., 1984; cons. for FAO to Wildlife Inst. India, Dehra Dun, 1985; adj prof. div. animal and vet. sci., W.Va. U., Morgantown, 1987—. Ad hoc reviewer various sci. jours.; ad hoc reviewer U.S. Dept. of Agr. Competitive Rsch. Grants; participant Internat. Mink Show, Wis., 1976-99, W. Va. State Fox Show, Morgantown, 1989. Rsch. bd. advisors The Am. Biog. Inst., 1988-98; mem. adv. coun. Internat. Biog. Centre, 1989-98; mem. Golden Horseshoe Reunion Com., W.Va. Homecoming '96. Recipient Knight of Golden Horse Shoe award W.Va. Pub. Sch. System, 1945, W.Va. Boy's State, 1948; U. Birmingham (Eng.) sr. rsch. fellow, 1962-65. Mem. AAAS, Am. Inst. Biol. Scis., Soc. Exptl. Biology and Medicine, Soc. for Study of Fertility, Soc. Study of Reproduction, Am. Soc. Animal Sci., Endocrine Soc., N.Y. Acad. Sci., Soc. Endocrinology, Coun. Agrl. Sci. and Tech., NRA (life), Sigma Xi, Pi Kappa Alpha, Gamma Sigma Delta. Presbyterian. Achievements include major contributions to the establishment of the hormonal requirements for ova-implantation and embryonic diapause in the rat, the elucidation of the role played by prostaglandins in corpus luteum function, parturition and ductus arteriosus closure in the rat; the development of steroid synthesis inhibitors for controlling reproduction in mammals; the documentation of the timing, duration and pattern of reproductive cycles in martens; the dissemination of scientific information on fur farming to the commercial fur trade and public. Home: 404 Junior Ave Morgantown WV 26505-2208

COCHRANE, WALTER E., education administrator, writer; b. Phila.; s. Earl and Martha (Binder) C. BS, U. Pa., Phila., MS; grad. study, Columbia U., 1959-60. Cert. adminstr., N.Y., Pa., Mass., N.J., Maine; supt. schs., N.Y., Mass.; sch. prin., N.Y., Pa., Mass. Clarinet soloist Phila. Brahms Cycle, 1950; dir. bands Upper Darby Pa. Schs., 1950-51; prof. clarinet and chamber muisc Phila. Musical Acad., 1950-52; solo clarinetist Phila. Symphonic Band, 1950-58; dir. music Alexandria Va. City Schs., L.I., N.Y., 1951-58; clarinet soloist Alexandria String Quartet, 1952; dist. dir. Sch. Dist. II, L.I., N.Y., 1958-60; supr. music N.Y. State Edn. Dept., Albany, 1960-67; conductor NY State Bands, 1960-67; v.p. Found. Am. Art Song N.Y. State Edn. Dept., Albany, 1965-70; supr. music Hartford (Conn.) City Schs., 1967-69; asst. supt. Sch. Dist. 5, L.I., N.Y., 1970-78; supt. schs. Maine Sch. Adm. Dist. 19, Lubec, Maine, 1978-80; v.p. and dean Inst. Security and Tech., Phila., 1980-87; corp. dir. edn. PTC Career Insts., Phila., 1987; pres. Career Guidance Corp., 1988-91, dir. GED home study program N.Y. State, 1992—. Author: GED Home Study Program, Meet The Great Composers, The Gulf War, World Wars I and II, Mathematics Mastery Manual, Science Mastery Manual, Understand Music, Women Composers, Literature Mastery Manual, Who Was the Killer Composer?. Recipient Humanitarian award Chgo. PTC. Mem. ASCD, NEA, MENC, SAR, NYSSMA (adjudicator, all-

state conductor), NASSP, Am. Assn. Sch. Adminstrs., N.Y. Assn. Supr. and Curriculum Devel., Phila. Musical Soc.

COCILOVO, LUIGI, member European parliament; b. Palermo, Italy, Oct. 7, 1947. Mem. European Parliament, Italy, 1999—; mem. Group of the European People's Party (Christian Democrats) and European Democrats, mem. of bur.; mem. com. on employment and social affairs; substitute mem. com. on regional policy, transport and tourism; chmn. delegation to the EU-Malta Joint Parliamentary Com.; substitute mem. Delegation to the EU-Turkey joint Parliamenty Com. Office: Via Pignatelli Aragona 84, I-90100 Palermo Italy*

COCIU, VASILE, agriculture researcher; b. Hâncesti, Lâpusna, Romania, Feb. 10, 1924; s. Gheorghe and Elena (Tanase) C.; m. Teodora Stancescu; children: Dana, Alina-Craita. Degree in agr., Inst Agronomic N.Bălcescu, Bucarest, Romania, 1949; degree in psychology, U. Bucharest, Bucarest, Romania, 1949. Rschr. Inst. Pomology, Bucarest, 1949-57; rschr. II Horticultural Inst., Bucarest, 1957-67; rschr. I Pomology INst., Pitesti, Romania, 1967-95; scientific counselor Agrl. Acad. of Sci., Bucharest. Author: Romanian Pomology, Vols. 6 and 8, 1967, New Fruit Tree Varieties Like Progress Factor, 1990, The Apricot, 1993, The Plum, 1997. Grantee Romanian Acad., 1956. Mem. Acad. Agr. and Forest Sci., N.Y. Acad. Scis. Home: Hrisovului 5/28, 78406 Bucarest Romania Office: Acad Agr and Forest Scis, Mărăsti 61, 71331 Bucarest Romania

COCKBURN, JILL, behavioral epidemiologist, researcher; b. Newcastle, Australia, June 28, 1956; d. George Buchanon and Joy (Telfor) C.; m. Craig Douglas Wilson, Mar. 7, 1992. BS with honors, U. Newcastle, NSW, 1980, PhD, 1986; MS, London Sch. Hygiene and Tropical Medicine, 1993. Rsch. acad. faculty medicine and health scis. U. Newcastle, 1986-87; rsch. acad. Sch. Pub. Health U. Sydney, NSW, 1987-88; sr. behavioural scientist Anti-Cancer Coun. Victoria, 1988-95; head discipline of behavioural sci. in relation to medicine U. Newcastle, 1996—, head Sch. of Population Health Scis., 1999—; dir. rsch. Hunter Ctr. for Health Advancement, NSW, 1998—; bd. dirs. NSW Cancer Coun.; mem. exec. com. Newcastle Inst. Pub. Health, 1997-98. Contbr. articles to profl. jours. Mem. psychosocial working party Nat. Breast Cancer Ctr., Sydney, 1996—; chair Cervical Screening Adv. Network, Hunter Region, 1997—; mem. adv. com. Nat. Heart Found., Newcastle, 1997—. Recipient fellowship Victorian Health Promotion Found., 1992. E-mail: jillc@wallsend.newcastle.edu.au. Fax: 61-2-49-246209. Office: Hunter Ctr Health Advance, Locked Bag 10, Wallsend 2287, Australia

COCKCROFT, SHAMSHAD, physiology educator, researcher; b. Zanzibar, Tanzania, Nov. 26, 1951; arrived in Eng., 1970; d. Salehbhai Hassanbhai Jafferji and Zehra Gulamhussein; m. Frank Laurence Cockcroft, July 16, 1977; children: Jasmine, Jacob, Joshua. BS with honors, U. Manchester (Eng.), 1974; PhD, U. Birmingham (Eng.), 1977. Rsch. fellow U. Coll. London, 1977-84, lectr., 1985-91, reader, 1991-94, prof. cell physiology, 1994—. Editor: Biochem. Jour.; contbr. articles to profl. jours. Mem. Brit. Soc. Cell Biology, Lister Inst., Biochem. Soc. Avocations: swimming, walking, theatre, music. Home: 101 Riverside Rd, London N5 2SU, England Office: U Coll London dept physiolo, Univ St Rockefeller Bldg, London W4E 6SS, England

COCKE, WILLIAM MARVIN, JR., plastic surgeon, educator; b. Balt., Aug. 2, 1934; s. William M. and Clara E. (Bosley) C.; m. Sue Ann Harris, Apr. 25, 1981; children: Gregory William. Laura Marie, Julie Ann; children by previous marriage: William Marvin III, Catherine Lynn, Deborah Kay, Brian Thomas. B.S. with honors in Biology, Tex. A&M U., 1956; M.D., Baylor U., 1960. Diplomate: Am. Bd. Plastic Surgery (guest examiner 1978). Intern surgery Vanderbilt U. Hosp., Nashville, 1960-61; fellow gen. surgery Ochsner Clinic and Found. Hosp., New Orleans, 1961-64; chief resident surgery Monroe (La.) Charity Hosp., 1963-64; resident reconstructive surgery Roswell Park Meml. Inst., Buffalo, 1965-66; chief resident plastic surgery VA Hosp., Bronx, N.Y., 1966; practice medicine specializing in plastic surgery Nashville, 1968-75, Sacramento, 1976-79; pvt. practice medicine specializing in plastic surgery Bryan, Tex., 1980-92; prof. surgery, head div. plastic/reconstructive surgery Marshall U. Sch. of Medicine, Huntington, W.Va., 1992—; mem. staff St. Mary's Hosp., Cabell-Huntington Hosp., Huntington Vets. Med. Ctr.; asst. prof. plastic surgery Vanderbilt U. Sch. Medicine, Nashville, 1968-69, asst. clin. prof. plastic surgery, 1969-75; assoc. prof. plastic surgery Ind. U. Sch. Medicine, Indpls., 1975-76; chief plastic surgery service Wishard Meml. Hosp., Ind. U., 1975-76; assoc. prof. surgery U. Calif. Sch. Medicine, Davis, 1976-79, chmn. dept. plastic surgery, 1976-79; prof. surgery, chief div. plastic surgery Tex. Tech. U. Sch. Medicine, Lubbock, 1979-80, dir. Microsurg. Research Lab., 1979-80; clin. prof. surgery Tex. A&M U. Sch. Medicine, 1983-92; prof. plastic surgery, 1986-89; chief plastic surgery svc., dept. surgery, Olin Teague VA Med. Ctr., Temple, Tex., 1986-92; prof. head surgery divsn. plastic and reconstruction Marshall U. Sch. Medicine, 1992—. Author textbooks on plastic surgery; contbr. articles to profl. jours. Served with M.C. USAF, 1966-68. Recipient Dean Echols award Ochsner Hosp. Found., 1963. Mem. ACS, Am. Assn. Plastic Surgeons, Soc. Head and Neck Surgeons, Assn. for Acad. Surgery, Alton Ochsner Surg. Soc. Episcopalian. Home: 45 Olde Farm Rd Ona WV 25545-9747 Office: Marshall U Sch Medicine Dept Surgery 1600 Medical Center Dr Huntington WV 25701-3656

COCKERHAM, KIMBERLY PEELE, ophthalmologist, educator; b. Bellevue, Wash., Apr. 10, 1961; d. Fred Arthur and Dorothy Anne (Cooper) Piontkowski; m. Glenn Cooper Cockerham, Feb. 22, 1997. BA in Biology, U. Calif., San Diego, 1983; MD, George Washington U., 1987. Commd. 2nd lt. U.S. Army, 1983, advanced through grades to maj.; surg. intern Letterman Army Ctr., San Francisco, 1987-88; chief emergency svcs. McDonald Army Hosp., Newport News, Va., 1988-89; neuro-ophthalmology cons. Fitzsimons Army Med. Ctr., Denver, 1993-94; resident in ophthalmology Walter Reed Army Med. Ctr., Washington, 1989-92, neuro-ophthalmology fellow, 1992-93, mem. neuro-ophthlamology staff, 1993-94, 95—; orbital disease fellow Allegheny Gen. Hosp., Pitts., 1994-95; dir. orbital disease and oculoplastics Walter Reed Army Med. Ctr., Washington, 1995-98; ret., 1998; ophthalmologist Cockerham Eye Cons., Lock Haven, Pa., 1997—; dir. oculoplastics, orbital disease and reconstrn. Allegheny Gen. Hosp., Pitts., 1999—; asst. clin. prof. Uniformed U. Health Scis., Bethesda, Md.; instr. neuro-ophthalmology Harvard's Lancaster and Stanford basic ophthalmology courses, 1994—; oral bd. examiner Acad. Ophthalmology, 1998—. Contbr. articles to profl. jours., chpts. to books. Eye camp doctor Charitable Trust, New Delhi, India, 1996; mem. Surg. Eye Expedition Internat., 1997-99. Fellow Am. Acad. Ophthalmology; mem. N.Am. Soc. Neuro-Ophthalmology, Assn. Rsch. in Vision and Ophthalmology, Rotary Internat., Alpha Omega Alpha. Avocations: running, in-line skating, writing. Office: Allegheny Ophthalmic & Orbital Assocs 320 E North Ave Ste 116 Pittsburgh PA 15212-4756 also: Cockerham Eye Cons 930 Bellefonte Ave Lock Haven PA 17745-2749

COCKERHAM, WILLIAM CARL, sociologist, professor; b. Oklahoma City, Mar. 31, 1939; s. Carl Reese and Eva Louise C.; m. Frances Louise Coates, Jan. 20, 1960 (div. April 1964); children: Laura, Bruce; m. Cynthia (Ross) Cockerham, April 2, 1969; children : Geoffrey, Sean, Scott. BA, U. Okla., 1962; MJ, U. Calif. (Berkeley), 1969, PhD, 1971. Prof. Sociology U. Wyo., Laramie, Wyo., 1971-75; prof., Sociology, Medicine U. Ill., Urbana, Ill., 1975-91; prof. Sociology, Medicine, chair Sociology U. Ala., Birmingham, Ala., 1991—. Author: Medical Sociology, 7th ed., 1998, Health and Social Change in Russia and Eastern Europe, 1999, Sociology of Mental Disorder, 5th ed., 2000. Major Gen. U.S. Army Reserve, 1962-95 (legion of merit, 1993, disting. svc. medal, 1997). Fulbright Scholar, Germany, 1985.

COCKERILL, IAN DAVID, mining executive; b. Romford, Essex, Eng., Aug. 4, 1954; arrived in South Africa, 1975; s. Herbert Edward and Jean Elizabeth Diana (Hutchings) C.; m. Iona Beverley Heinemann; 3 children. BSc with honors, London U., 1975; MDP, UNISA, South Africa, 1980; MSc in Mining, Royal Sch. Mines, U.K., 1981; postgrad., Templeton Coll., Oxford, Eng., 1996. Geologist Union Corp., South Africa, 1975-78; tech. asst. AAC-DeBeers, Namaqualand, 1979-80; prodn. mgr. AAC-Free State Geduld & Saaiplaas Mine, South Africa, 1980-90; sr. divsl. mining engrng. Minorco, London, 1990-92; mine mgr. AAC South Africa Elandsrand & Westein Deep Mines, 1992-96; tech. dir. AAC South Africa Gold Divsn., 1996-98; exec. officer bus. devel. Anglogold Ltd., South Africa, 1998-99; mng. dir. Gold Fields Ltd., Johannesburg, South Africa, 1999—. Mem. Inst. Dirs., Assn. Mine Mgrs., SAIMM. Avocations: reading, fly fishing, travel, collecting wines, collecting motor cars. Home: Morningside 40, 17 Gardenia St, Sandton South Africa Office: Gold Fields Ltd, 24 St Andrews Rd Parktown, 2193 Johannesburg South Africa

COCKRILLE, STEPHEN, art director, business owner; b. Washington, Jan. 19, 1945; s. Donald Herbert and Dorothy Charolette (Hoover) C.; m. Éva Vágréti, May 17, 1987; children: Christopher Lewis, Micki Lee. BA, W.Va. State Coll., 1968; MA, U. N.D., 1972. Grad. tchg. asst. U. N.D., Grand Forks, 1971; design asst. Thomas Clayton Printing, N.Y.C., 1974-75; art dir. West Side Printing & Graphics, N.Y.C., 1975-76; studio mgr. Graphic Concern, Inc., N.Y.C., 1976-78; ind. art dir. N.Y.C., 1978-84; pres. Textart, Inc., N.Y.C., 1984-97; ret., 1997; judge New Eng. Book Show, Boston, 1987; selected for presentation to the Jordanian Min. of Edn. and staff on the U.S. textbook industry, N.Y.C., 1995. Prodr. numerous basal ednl. programs for nat. distbn., 1984-97. With U.S. Army, 1968-70, Vietnam. Recipient hon. mention New Eng. Book Show, Boston, 1992, Pupil's Edit. and Theme Posters, Boston, 1992, bronze award Dimensional Illustrators Awards Show, N.Y.C., 1992, 1st place award Ednl. Sch. Divsn. N.Y. Book Show, N.Y.C., 1994. Republican. Avocations: painting, reading, skiing, investing. Home: 1150 Kings Crown Rd Woodland Park CO 80863-7731

COCKRUM, WILLIAM MONROE, III, investment banker, consultant, educator; b. Indpls., July 18, 1937; s. William Monroe C. II and Katherine J. (Jaqua) Moore; m. Andrea Lee Deering, Mar. 8, 1975; children: Catherine Anne, William Monroe IV. AB with distinction, DePauw U., 1959; MBA with distinction, Harvard U., 1961. With A.G. Becker Paribas Inc., L.A., 1961-84, mgr. nat. corp. fin. div., 1968-71, mgr. pvt. investments, 1971-74, fin. and adminstrv. officer, 1974-80, sr. v.p., 1975-78, vice chmn., 1978-84, also bd. dirs.; prin. William M. Cockrum & Assocs., L.A., 1984—; mem. faculty Northwestern U., 1961-63; vis. lectr. grad. sch. mgmt. UCLA, 1984-88, adj. prof., 1988—. Mem. Monterey Club (Palm Desert, Calif.), Deke Club (N.Y.C.), UCLA Faculty Club, Alisal Golf Club (Solvang, Calif.), Bel-Air Country Club (L.A.), Delta Kappa Epsilon.

COCKTON, GILBERT, computer sciences researcher and educator; b. Newcastle Upon Tyne, England, Aug. 2, 1958; s. John and Irene (Foster) C.; m. Rosamund Eileen Stansfield, June 20, 1986; children: Jennifer Alice, John Samuel. BA, U. Cambridge, 1981, MA, 1990; PhD, Heriot-Watt U., 1993. Tchr. history and social studies Derbyshire County Coun., England, 1981-83; rsch. assoc. Scottish HCI Ctr., Edinburgh, 1986-88; from rsch. assoc. to lectr. U. Glasgow, Scotland, 1988-96; reader U. Northumbria at Newcastle, England, 1996-97; rsch. chair U. Sunderland, Eng., 1997—; sr. cons. Mari Computer Sys., Ashington, England, 1995-96; sec. IFIP Working Group 2.7, 1993-99, mem., 1988—; expert Commn. European Cmty., Brussels, 1992-97; project dir. Digital Media Network, N.E. of Eng., 1999—. Editor: Design Principles for Interactive Systems, 1996; dep. editor Interacting with Computers. hon. vis. rsch. fellow U. Newcastle Upon Tyne, Eng., 1995-98; hon. vis. lectr. U. Glasgow, Scotland, 1996-98. Fellow Royal Soc. of Arts; mem. Brit. Human Computer Interaction Group (SIGCHI liaison 1998—, HCI 2000 chair), Assn. Computing Machinery (Spl. Interest Group on Computer-Human Interaction internat adv. task force 1997—, software sys. award com. 1999—). Avocations: gardening, hiking, wine, history, art, gymnastics. Office: U Sunderland Sch Computing, PO Box 299, Sunderland SR6 0YN, England

COCOLIS, PETER KONSTANTINE, business development executive; b. Stamford, Conn., Sept. 22, 1942; s. Gus and Agnes (Vender) C.; m. Lorraine Patricia Marut, July 2, 1966; children: Peter Konstantine Jr., William Jonathan. BS in Engring., Boston U., 1964; MBA, Auburn U., 1976; cert., Def. Sys. Mgmt. Coll., 1973; cert. in nat. and internat. security mgmt., Harvard U., 1996. Commd. 2d lt. USAF, 1964, advanced through grades to lt. col., 1980, ret., 1984; mktg. mgr. N.Am. Aircraft Rockwell Internat., Washington, 1984-87, dir. mktg. and govt. affairs, 1987-89; dir. bus. devel. and govt. affairs Rocketdyne divsn. Rockwell Internat., Washington, 1989-95; sr. dir. bus. and govt. affairs N.Am. Aircraft divsn. Rockwell Internat., Washignton, 1995-96; sr. dir. bus. and govt. affairs The Boeing Co., Washington, 1996—. Contbr. articles to profl. jours. Bd. dirs. Lakeforest Home Owners Assn., Springfield, Va., 1985-88; v.p. Morwood Estates Home Owners Assn.; swimming ofcl. U.S. Swimming Orgn., No. Va., 1981-91. Decorated DFC, Air medals. Mem. AIAA (sr., coun. mem., com. chmn., bd. dirs.), Am. Mgmt. Assn., Nat. Space Club, Air Force Assn., Navy League, Emeritus Found. (bd. dirs., com. chmn.), Clifton Lions. Avocations: racquetball sailing, reading, swimming. Office: The Boeing Co 1200 Wilson Blvd Arlington VA 22209-2305

CODD, HENRY WALLACE, JR., finance executive; b. Easton, Pa., Apr. 17, 1966; s. Henry Wallace and Mary Patricia Codd; m. Kim Debra Codd, Sept. 2, 1995; children: Zoe Rachel, Naomi Leah. BSBA, Indiana (Pa.) U., 1988; MBA, U. Pitts., 1998. Contract mgr. Univ. Support Svcs., Herndon, Va., 1990-91; ops. supr. PNC Bank, Pitts., 1991-96, analyst, 1996-98; ops. mgr. Chevy Chase (Md.) Bank, 1998-99; dir. fin. and adminstrn. Griffin & Co., Inc., Washington, 1999—. Treas. Glenmont Assn., Columbia, Md., 1999. Mem. Georgetown Bus. Owners. Republican. Avocations: golf, skiing. Home: 5271 Golden Sky Ct Columbia MD 21045-2318 Office: Griffin & Co Inc Ste 310E 1025 Thomas Jefferson St NW Washington DC 20007-5232

CODNIA, JUAN PABLO, writer, teacher, technician; b. Buenos Aires, Jan. 29, 1964; came to the U.S., 1988; s. Basilio Codnia and Estela Araceli Larumbe; m. Maria Lourdes Lucena, June 14, 1991 (div. March 2000); 1 child, Michelle Codnia. Grad. electronic technician, Nat. Sch. Electronics, Buenos Aires, 1985; grad. computer operator, M. Moreno Inst., Buenos Aires, 1988. Equipment control staff Oceanwide USA, New Orleans, 1988-89, N.Y.C., 1989-91; equipment control staff Kerr Steamship Co., New Orleans, 1991-93. Author: Sunshine: Adventures of a Little Indian Chief, 1997, Sunshine (Spanish version), 1997, Lizzy & Wanda's Calendar I, 1997, Lizzy & Wanda at School, 1998, Lizzy & Wanda-A Summer Tour, 1998, Lizzy & Wanda-Faith in the Future, 1998, Lizzy & Wanda-Special Assignment, 1998, Lizzy & Wanda's Calendar II, 1999, Lizzy & Wanda-Permanent Memory, 1999, Lizzy & Wanda-Celebration Day, 1999, Lizzy & Wanda's Alphabet Album, 2000; writer (pop album) Afterimage, vol. I, 1996, vols. II and III, 1997, (song) Children, 1997. Vol. tchr. aide Paul Habans Elem. Sch., New Orleans, 1996-98; vol. tchr. St. Jude Cmty. Ctr. Sch. Religion, New Orleans, 1998—. Mem. Down Syndrome Assn. New Orleans. Avocations: family activities, reading, writing, drawing, playing bass guitar. E-mail: pablo@salemlutheranschool.com. Home: 2103 Cobblestone Ln Apt M New Orleans LA 70114-8946

CODOBAN, ALEXANDRU, science educator; b. Balnaca, Bihor, Romania, Sept. 21, 1933; s. Teodor and Floarea (Groza) C. Engr., U. Politehnica, Bucharest, Romania, 1957, PhD, 1979. Lic. pilot, gliding pilot. Asst. lectr. U. Politehnica, Bucharest, 1958-74, lectr., 1975-89, reader, 1990-92, prof., 1993—. Author: (book) Elements of Analytical Mechanics with Applications, 2000; co-author: (book) Problems of Mechanics, 1983; contbr. articles to profl. jours. Mem. Romanian Soc. of Acoustics, Am. Romanian Acad. Arts and Scis. Avocations: tennis, gliding, reading, concerts. Office: Politehnica Univ, Splaiul Ind nr 313, Ro-77206 Bucharest Romania

CODRON, MICHAEL VICTOR, theatrical producer; b. June 8, 1930; s. I.A. and Lily (Morganstern) C. Ed., St. Paul's Sch.; BA, Worcester Coll., Oxford U. Dir. Hampstead Theatre; adminstr. Aldwych Theatre; Cameron Mackintosh prof. contemporary theatre Oxford U., Eng., 1993. Prodns. include: Breath of Spring, 1957; The Birthday Party, 1958; Pieces of Eight, 1959; The Caretaker, 1960; The Tenth Man, 1961; Rattle of a Simple Man, 1962; Next Time I'll Sing to You, Private Lives, The Lovers and the Dwarfs, Cockade, 1963; Poor Bitos, The Formation Dancers, Entertaining Mr. Sloane, 1964; Loot, The Killing of Sister George, Ride a Cock Horse, 1965; Little Malcolm and His Struggle Against the Eunuchs, The Anniversary, There's a Girl in My Soup, Big Bad Mouse, 1966; The Judge, The Flip Side, Wise Child, The Boy Friend, 1967; Not Now Darling, The Real Inspector Hound, 1968; The Contractor, Slag, The Two of Us, The Philanthropist, 1970; The Foursome, Butley, A Voyage Round My Father, The Changing Room, 1971; Veterans, Time and Time Again, Crown Matrimonial, My Fat Friend, 1972; Collaborators, Savages, Habeas Corpus, Absurd Person Singular, 1973; Knuckle, Flowers, Golden Pathway Annual, The Norman Conquests, John Paul George Ringo...and Bert, 1974; A Family and a Fortune, Alphabetical Order, A Far Better Husband, Ashes, Absent Friends, Otherwise Engaged, Stripwell, 1975; Funny Peculiar, Treats, Donkey's Years, Confusions, Teeth 'n' Smiles, Yahoo, 1976; Dusa Stas, Fish & Vi, Just Between Ourselves, Oh, Mr. Porter, Breezeblock Park, The Bells of Hell, The Old Country, 1977; The Rear Column, Ten Times Table, The Unvarnished Truth, The Homecoming, Alice's Boys, Night and Day, 1978; Joking Apart, Tishoo, Stage Struck, 1979; Dr. Faustus, Make and Break, The Dresser, Taking Steps, Enjoy, 1980; Hinge & Bracket, Rowan Atkinson in Revue, House Guest, Quartermaine's Terms, 1981; Season's Greetings, Noises Off, Funny Turns, 1982, The Real Thing, 1982; The Hard Shoulder, 1983; Look, No Hans!, Benefactors, 1984; Jumpers, Who Plays Wins, Clockwise (film), 1985, Made in Bangkok, 1986, Woman in Mind, 1986; Hapgood, Uncle Vanya, Re Joyce!, The Sneeze, Henceforward, 1988; The Cherry Orchard, 1989; Man of the Moment, Look, Look, Hidden Laughter, Private Lives, 1990, What the Butler Saw, 70 Girls 70, The Revengers Comedies, 1991, The Rise and Fall of Little Voice, 1992, Time of My Life, 1993, Jamais Vu, 1993, Dead Funny, 1994, Arcadia, 1994, The Sisters Rosensweig, 1994, Indian Ink, 1995, The Killing of Sister George, 1995, Dealer's Choice, 1995, The Shakespeare Revue, 1995, A Talent to Amuse, 1996, Tom and Clem, 1997, Silhouette Heritage, 1997, Things We Do For Love, 1998, Elton John's Glasses, 1998, Alarms and Excursions, 1998, The Invention of Love, 1998, Copenhagen, 1999 (Tony award, 2000), Quartet, 1999, Comic Potential, 1999, Peggy For You, 2000. Recipient Michael Victor Codron CBE. Mem. Garrick Club. Office: Aldwych Theatre, London WC2B 4DF, England

CODY, AELRED JOSEPH, editor, priest; b. Oklahoma City, Feb. 3, 1932; s. Joseph Francis Cody and Frances Margaret Tucker. BA, St. Meinrad Coll., 1956; Sacrae Theologiae Licentiatus, U. Ottawa, Ont., Can., 1958, Sacrae Theologiae Doctor summa cum laude, 1960; Sacrae Scripturae Licentiatus, Pontifical Bibl. Inst./Commn., Rome, 1962, Sacrae Scripturae Doctor summa cum laude, 1968; diploma, French Bib. and Archaeol. Sch., Jerusalem. Ordained priest, 1957; professed Benedictine, 1952. Prof. Old Testament and ancient Near East studies S. Anselmo, Pontifical Biblical Inst., Rome, 1968-78; organist Abbazia di S. Anselmo, Rome, 1968-76; procurator gen. in Roman Curia Am.-Cassinese & Swiss-Am. Benedictine Congregations, Rome, 1975-78; master of novices and juniors St. Meinrad (Ind.) Archabbey, 1978-92; mem. pres.'s coun. Swiss-Am. Benedictine Cong., 1981-96, mem. legal com., 1984—, chmn. legal com., 1990—; assoc. editor Cath. Bib. Quar., Washington, 1987-92; gen. editor Cath. Bib. Quar., St. Meinrad, 1993—; mem. ofcl. Oriental Orthodox-Roman Catholic Consultation in U.S., Nat. Conf. of Cath. Bishops and Standing Conf. of Oriental Orthodox Bishops, 1981—; consultor for Holy See, Mixed Commn. Roman Cath. Ch. and World Alliance Ref. Chs., 1970. Author: Heavenly Sanctuary and Liturgy in the Epistle to the Hebrews, 1960 (prize of Christian Rsch. Found. Harvard U. 1960), A History of Old Testament Priesthood, 1969, Ezekiel, 1984; contbr. to profl. jours. and encycs.; mem. editl. bd. Biblica, Rome, 1968-73; mem. editl. com., consultative com. Concilium, Nijmegen, 1969-91. Mem. Royal Coll. Music (assoc., London), Royal Coll. Organists (assoc., London), Internat. Orgn. for Study of Old Testament, Internat. Assn. for Coptic Studies, Am. Oriental Soc., Soc. Bib. Lit., Cath. Bib. Assn. Am. (life, trustee 1984-87, exec. bd. 1993—). Avocations: reading, hiking, Renaissance and baroque keyboard music. Office: The Cath Bib Quar St Meinrad Archabbey Saint Meinrad IN 47577

CODY, ALAN MORROW, financial consultant; b. Huntington, WV, June 7, 1947; s. Peer John and Nancy (Speer) C.; m. Elisabeth Anne Allen, Nov. 29, 1969; 1 child, David Miles. AB, Cornell U., 1969; SM, MIT, 1974. Economist Data Resources Inc., Lexington, Mass., 1974-76; dir. indls. mktg., v.p. Data Resources Inc., Lexington, 1976-79; v.p. The Planning Economics Group, Woburn, Mass., 1979-81; sr. mgr. Mitchell and Co., Cambridge, Mass., 1982-84; sr. cons. Arthur D. Little, Inc., Cambridge, 1984-93; dir. valuation svcs., group Coopers & Lybrand, 1993-98; prin. Corp. Value Consulting Group Pricewaterhouse Coopers LLP, Boston, 1998—. Editor: Sloan Mgmt. Rev., Cambridge, 1973-74. Active Ripon Soc., Boston, 1982—; dir. bd. investment First Unitarian Soc. Newton (Mass.), 1984-92, chmn. bd. trustees, 1993-94; bd. dirs. Fgn. Film Soc. of Montgomery (Ala.), 1971-72, Newton Conservators, 1988-91, Newton Taxpayers Assn., 1988—, Newton Citizens Commn. on Energy, 1990-97. 1st lt. USAF, 1969-72. Mem. Inst. Chartered Fin. Analysts, Assn. Investment Mgmt. and Rsch., Boston Security Analysts Soc., Cornell Club (N.Y.). Republican. Unitarian. Office: PricewaterhouseCoopers LLP One Post Office Sq Boston MA 02109

CODY, DANIEL SCHAFFNER, lawyer; b. Columbus, Ohio, Nov. 21, 1948; s. Ralph Eugene and Grace (Schaffner) C.; m. Susan Ragsdale, Mar. 27, 1992; 1 child, Sean. Student, Kent State U., 1977; BA, Ohio State U., 1970, BSEd, 1973; JD, U. Akron, 1990. Bar: Ohio 1990, U.S. Dist. Ct. (no. dist.) Ohio 1990, U.S. Ct. Appeals (6th cir.) 1990, U.S. Ct. Appeals (4th cir.) 1992. Tchg. Archbishop Hoban H.S., Akron, Ohio, 1973-88, athletic dir., 1980-84; rsch. asst. Hon. Arthur Goldberg (ret.) U.S. Supreme Ct., U. Akron, 1989, staff intern Appellate Rev. Office, 1990-91; jud. clk. Ohio Ct. Appeals (9th dist.), Akron, 1990-91; assoc. Jacobson, Maynard, Tuschman & Kalur, Cleve., 1991-93; pvt. practice Akron, 1993—. Trustee U. Akron Law Alumni Assn., 1992—, Archbishop Hoban H.S., 1995—. Mem. Ohio State Bar Assn., Akron Bar Assn. Democrat. Roman Catholic. Office: 17 S Main St Ste 201 Akron OH 44308-1803

CODY, HIRAM SEDGWICK, JR., retired telephone company executive; b. Nov. 1, 1915; s. Hiram Sedgwick and Harriett Mary (Collins) C.; m. Mary Vaughn Jacoby, Oct. 4, 1941; children: Margaret Vaughn, Harriett Mary, Hiram Sedgwick III, Henry Jacoby, William Collins. BS cum laude, Yale U., 1937, LLB, 1940. Bar: N.C. 1940. With Western Electric Co., Inc., 1946-71; regional mgr. engring. and installation Western Electric Co., Inc., Chgo., 1961-64; dir. orgn. planning Western Electric Co., Inc., N.Y.C., 1964-65, sec., treas., 1965-71; asst. treas. AT&T, N.Y.C., 1971-80. V.p. Morris-Sussex coun. Boy Scouts of Am., 1970-80; vice-chmn. Zoning Bd. Adjustment Mountain Lakes, N.J., 1968-80; boro councilman, Mountain Lakes, 1960-61; trustee, treas. Asheville (N.C.) Sch., 1974-84; trustee Asheville Symphony Orch., 1981-91, Asheville Cmty. Concert Assn., 1981-91; bd. advisors Warren Wilson Coll., 1983—, chmn., 1987-90. With USN, 1941-45, MTO, comdr. USNR, 1946. Mem. N.C. State Bar, Tel. Pioneers Am. (v.p. 1969-71, treas. 1971-78), Tau Beta Pi. Home: 64 Wagon Trl Black Mountain NC 28711-2563

COE, JUDITH ANNE, music educator, composer, performer; b. Denver, June 11, 1955; d. James Arnold and Sonya Diane (Regnier) Hall; m. Loren R. Coe, June 14, 1975 (div. Dec. 1993); children: Jared, Joshua, Jessica. BM, Colo. State U., 1981, MM, 1983; DMA, U. Colo., 1991. Rsch. intern Denver Ctr. for Performing Arts Voice Lab., 1984-91; vis. artist Denver Sch. of Arts, 1991-92; vocal coach, vis. artist Denver Ctr. Theatre Co., 1991-92; instr. Front Range C.C., Ft. Collins, Colo., 1988-91; designer Vestige Pub. Co., Ft. Collins, 1994-96; asst. prof. dept. music Miss. U. for Women, Columbus, 1996—; adj. prof. Colo. State U., Ft. Collins, 1990-94. Author: Report on the Status of Women in College Music, 2000; assoc. editor: (ency.) Women Musicians in America, 2000; author/compiler: (webliography) Cyberspace Music Resources, 1999. Performing arts roster Miss. Arts Coun., 1999—; cmty. outreach affiliate Columbus Arts Coun., 1999—. Miss. U. for Women Faculty Devel. grantee, 1996, 97, 98, 99, 2000; Nat. Inst. for Deafness and Other Comm. Disorders grantee, 1990, 91, Columbus Arts Coun. grantee, 1999, 2000, Blas Internat. Sch. Traditional Irish Music and Dance grantee, 1999. Mem. AAUW (Leadership award 1999), NOW, Internat. Alliance for Women in Music (coord. of pub. advocacy 1999—, bd. dirs. 1996—), Am. Soc. Composers, Authors and Pubs., Coll. Music Soc. (co-chair com. on music, women and gender 1999—, profl. devel. com./ann. planning com. 1999—), Acad. and Rec. Industry Alliances (team organizer 2000), Nat. Assn. Tchrs. Singing (v.p., adjudications chair 1983-85), Southeastern Composers League, Internat. Assn. for Study of Popular Music. Democrat. Avocations: web design and development, photography, architecture, popular culture, travel. E-mail: jcoe@muw.edu. Office: Mississippi Univ for Women W-70 Columbus MS 39701

COE, MALCOLM JAMES, retired animal ecologist, consultant; b. Leyton, London, Nov. 20, 1930; s. Henry Herbert and Ada Selina (Powell) C.; m. Unity Anne Borlase Harris, July 9, 1960; 1 child, Christopher Falcon. BSc, U. London, 1955, PhD, 1964; MA, U. Oxford, Eng., 1969. Lectr. biology Royal Tech. Coll., Nairobi, Kenya, 1956-60; lectr. zoology Royal Coll., Nairobi, 1960-65; sr. lectr. U. Coll., Nairobi, 1965-68; lectr. animal ecology U. Oxford, Eng., 1968-95; tutorial fellow St. Peter's Coll., Oxford U., 1969-95. Author: Ecology of the Alpine Zone of Mt. Kenya, 1967, Islands in the Bush, 1985; co-author: Field Guide to the Acacia's of Kenya, 1985; editor: Oxford Illustrated Encyclopedia: The Natural World, 1985; co-editor: Mkomazi: The Ecology, Biodiversity & Conservation of a Tanzanian Savanna, 1999. With RAF, 1950-55. Recipient Gold medal Zool. Soc. So. Africa, 1989; emeritus fellow St. Peters Coll., Oxford U., 1995. Fellow Royal Geog. Soc. (sci. dir. mkomazi ecological rsch. program, Busk medal 1988). Avocations: cooking, gardening, broadcasting (radio and TV), travel. Office: St Peters Coll, Oxford OX1 2DL, England

COE, MARGARET LOUISE SHAW, community service volunteer; b. Cody, Wyo., Dec. 25, 1917; d. Ernest Francis and Effie Victoria (Abrahamson) Shaw; m. Henry Huttleston Rogers Coe, Oct. 8, 1943 (dec. Aug. 1966); children: Anne Rogers Hayes, Henry H.R., Jr., Robert Douglas II. AA, Stephens Coll., 1937; BA, U. Wyo., 1939. Asst. to editor The Cody Enterprise, 1939-42, editor, 1968-71. Bd. trustees Buffalo Bill Historical Ctr., 1966—, chmn., 1974-98, chmn. emeritus, 1998—; trustee emeritus Ctrl. City Opera House Assn., Millicent Rogers Found.; commr. Wyo. Centenniel Commn., Cheyenne, 1986-91. Recipient The Westerner award Old West Trails Found., 1980, Gold Medallion award Nat. Assn. Sec. of State, 1982, disting alumni award U. Wyo., 1984, exemplary alumni award, 1994, Gov.'s award for arts, 1988; inducted Nat. Cowgirl Hall of Fame, 1983. Mem. P.E.O., Delta Delta Delta. Republican. Episcopalian. Avocation: duplicate bridge. Home: 1400 11th St Cody WY 82414-4206

COECKE, BOB, physics, mathematics and philosophy researcher; b. Willebroek, Belgium, July 23, 1968; s. Robert and Yolanda (Jansens) C. Lic. in Physics with highest distinction, Free U. Brussels, 1992, DSc with highest distinction, 1996. Rsch. asst. Nat. Fund for Sci. Rsch., Brussels, 1992-96; postdoctoral rschr. Leo Apostel Interdisciplinary Rsch. Ctr., Brussels, 1996-97, Nat. Fund for Sci. Rsch., Brussels, 1997—; head rsch. unit music as sci. and art L. Apostel Int. Disc. Rsch. Ctr.; sci. collaborator rsch. unit Free U. Brussels, 1992—; founder pres. student orgn. music and experiment, 1994; organizer internat. workshops "Current Rsch. in Operational Quantum Logic"; lectr. in field. Contbr. articles to profl. jours. Mem. Internat. Quantum Structures Assn. Avocations: music, writing, painting, multi-media performances. Home: Luchtvaart Square 7/B6, 1070 Brussels Belgium Office: Free Univ Brussels, Fund-Dwis Pleinlaan 2, 1050 Brussels Belgium

COELLO VALADEZ, CARLOS ANTONIO, principal, researcher; b. Mexico City, Mex., Apr. 4, 1951; s. Antonio and Blanca Evelia (Garza) Coello; m. Beatriz Eugenia Villarreal, June 22, 1973; children: Carla, Antonio. Degree in edn., Centro de Estudios U., Monterrey, Mex., 1975, degree in engring., 1978; degree in pub. adminstrn., INAP, Mexico City, 1979. Dir. H.S. Divsn., Monterrey, 1972-79; vice rector Centro de Estudios U., Monterrey, 1979-80, rector, 1981—; instr. Dale Carnegie Inst., Monterrey, 1981. Pres. 10th Dist. Fed. Election Commn., Monterrey, 1988; assessor Mcpl. Pres. Monterrey, 1980-83. Recipient Support Recognition awards Nuevo Leon Assn. History, Geography and Statistics, 1995, Red Cross, 1993, Nuevo Leon Pub. Security State Office, 1998. Mem. L.Am. Coun. Internat. Assn. U. Pres. (v.p. 1994), Interam. U. Coun. for Social and Econ. Devel., Nat. Assn. Univs. and Instns. Edn. Office: Centro de Estudios U, Hidalgo 524 Pte, Monterrey 64000, Mexico

COENRAETS, ANDRE JEAN, psychosociologist; b. Brussels, Oct. 2, 1930; s. Philippe Coenraets and Jeanni Hendrick; children: Philippe, Colette, Christophe. Analyzer Mecar, Nivelles, 1953-61; mktg. dir. Graham, Ruisbroek, 1961-71, gen. mgr., 1972-77; pres. Quota Rsch. S.A., Brussels, 1977-94, Go Effective Skills Europe, Brussels, 1988—; adminstr., group therapist Centre European d'Etudes et de Formation Aux Relations Humaines, Linkebeek, 1967—. Author, editor Go Manager, 1986, Go Sales, 1988, Go Communication, 1989, GO-M, 1992, GO-M Quality, 1993, GO-M First Line, 1995, GO-PRO, 2000; inventor Eclosive pedagogy, 1991. With Artillery, 1953-54. Mem. C. of C. Home: Grand Rte 6, B-1630 Linkebeek Brabant, Belgium Office: Go Europe, av des Quatre Saisons 26, Waterloo B1410, Belgium

COETZER, AMANDA, tennis player; b. Hoopstad, South Africa, Oct. 22, 1972. Profl. tennis player, 1996—; winner tournament title WTA Tour Family Circle Championship, 1998; winner Budapest Ladies Open, 1997. Named Most Improved Player and recipient Diamond ACES award and Karen Krantzcke Sportsmanship award, 1997; title holder Benelux Open, 2000. Office: c/o WTA Tour 133 1st St NE Saint Petersburg FL 33701-3352*

COETZER, MARKUS WYNAND, engineering executive; b. Parys, South Africa, Apr. 22, 1952; s. Johannes Petrus and Jacomina Johanna (Blignaut) C.; m. Correne Erasmus, July 21, 1988. PhD in Engring., U. Stellenbosch, South Africa, 1983. Lectr. U. Stellenbosch, 1974-83, prof., 1983-89; co-owner, co-founder, v.p., product arch. Datafusion Systems, Stellenbosch, 1989-98, non-exec. v.p., 1998—; ind. cons. in high tech. industry, 1998—. Contbr. articles to profl. jours.; patentee in field. Mem. IEEE, South African Inst. Elec. Engrs., Engring. Coun. South Africa, Stellenbosch Flying Club. Avocations: history, archeology, music, reading. E-mail: coetzerw@iafrica.com. Fax: 27 21 887 2253. Office: 70 Brandwacht St, 7600 Stellenbosch South Africa

COEUR, PIERRE, medical education, biologist; b. Lyon, France, Nov. 12, 1935; s. André and Jeanne (Folliet) C.; m. Hélene Silberman, Dec. 21, 1974; children: Alain, Bernard, Henri, Brigitte, Sylvie, Valérie, Sabrina, Carole. Lic. of Sci., U. Sci., Grenoble and Lyon, France, 1958; MD, U. Sci. and Medicine, Lyon, 1968. Intern Hospices Civils, Lyon, 1964-68; asst. CHU, Lyon, 1968-70; prof. U. Lovanium, Kinshasa, Zaire, 1970-72; prof. medicine U. Lyon, 1972—; biologist hematology lab. Centre Hosp. Lyon Sud, Pierre Bénite, France, 1972—; pres. Fedn. Nationale des INternes Etanciens Internes CHU, France, 1983, Union Nationale des Medecins pour la Dissolution de l'ordre, France, 1984-94. Author: Demain la Santé, 1990, Une Vie...aw Laboratoire d' Hematologie, 1999. Mem. Internat. Soc. Hematology, Internat. Soc. Thrombosis Haemostasis, Syndicat Médecine Hospitalière France. Avocations: reading, travel, gardening. Home: Domaine des Contamines, 15 Allée des Prunus, 69140 Rillieux la Pape France Office: Centre Hosp Lyon Sud, Lab of Hematology, 69310 Pierre Bénite France

COFFEY, DAVID THOMPSON, guidance and counseling educator, consultant; b. Newtownards, Northern Ireland, May 6, 1936; s. Alexander and Sarah Elizabeth (Thompson) C.; m. Barbara Margaret Cole, July 1, 1971; children: Sara Ellen, Lisa Ruth. BA, Queen's U., Belfast, Northern Ireland, 1957, diploma in edn., 1960, diploma in advanced edn., 1975, PhD, 1986. Tchr. Annadale Grammar Sch., Belfast, 1957-76; sr./prin. lectr. Ulster Poly., Jordanstown, Northern Ireland, 1976-84; sr. lectr. U. Ulster, Jordanstown, Northern Ireland, 1984-95; freelance lectr., cons., 1995—; mem. econ. history panel Northern Ireland Exams. Bd., Belfast, 1970-76; mem. careers edn. and counseling panel Coun. Nat. Acad. Awards, London, 1978-83; mem. bd. Royal Coll. Nursing, Northern Ireland, 1984-87. Author: Schools and Work: Developments in Vocational Education, 1992; contbr. articles to profl. jours. Chmn. sch. govs. Movilla H.S., Newtownards, 1990—. Avocations: rugby football, walking, browsing. Home and Office: 3 Bladon Ave, Newtownards BT23 7BD, Northern Ireland

COFFEY, HELEN ELIZABETH, physicist; b. Chelsea, Mass., Nov. 17, 1944; d. Timothy Patrick and Helen Williamina (Stevens) C. BS, Merrimack Coll., 1966; MS, U. Colo., 1969. Mem. staff MIT, Cambridge, 1969-70; physicist NOAA, Boulder, 1972—, br. chief solar and high atmosphere br., 1977—; sec. Internat. Space Environment Svc., 1981—. High Altitude Obs. Astrogeophysics fellow, 1966-67. Recipient Silver medal U.S. Dept. Commerce, 1997. Mem. AAUW, Internat. Astronom. Union (commn. X working group internat. programs), Am. Geophys. Union (treas. Front Range br. 1985-87), Am. Meteorol. Soc., Am. Astron. Soc., AAAS, Colo. Coordinating Council of Women's Orgns. (corr. sec. 1983-84), Sigma Xi (treas. Boulder chpt. 1985-86, sec. 1986-87, v.p. 1987-89). Democrat. Roman Catholic. Club: Zonta of Boulder County (v.p. 1981-82, pres. 1983-84, bd. dirs. 1994-96). Editor: Solar-Geophysical Data, 1977—; geomagnetic and solar data table Jour. Geophys. Research, 1981—. Home: PO Box 21346 Boulder CO 80308-4346 Office: World Data Ctr A Solar- Terrestrial Physics NOAA E/GC2 325 Broadway St Boulder CO 80305-3337

COFFEY, MARK WILLIAM, theoretical physicist, applied mathematician; b. Lincoln, Nebr., Oct. 24, 1957; s. William Davis and Patricia Avalon (Morgan) C. BS, U. Iowa, 1980; MPhil, N.Y. U., 1983, PhD in Math., 1983; PhD in Physics, Iowa State U., 1991. Math. instr. N.Y. U., 1980-82; sci. programmer IBM Corp., Palo Alto, Calif, 1983-85; engr., programmer IBM Corp., Poughkeepsie, N.Y., 1985-88; rsch. asst. Iowa State U., Ames, 1989-91; NRC postdoctoral fellow Nat. Inst. Stds. and Tech., Boulder, Colo., 1992-94; applied math. instr. U. Colo., Boulder, 1994-95, vis. prof., 1995-97; physicist, sr. systems engr. Gen Dynamics Info. Sys., 1997; sr. scientist TRW, 1998—; lectr. U. Colo. physics dept., Boulder, 1992—; vis. prof. Ecole Normale Superieure, Paris, 1994. Contbr. over 60 articles to profl. jours. Recipient Sanxay prize, Davies Meml. Physics award: U. Iowa Honors Found. scholar. Mem. Am. Phys. Soc., Am. Math. Soc., Math. Assn. Am., Soc. Indsl. and Applied Math., Phi Beta Kappa, Sigma Xi, Phi Kappa Phi, Phi Eta Sigma. Achievements include rsch. of electrodynamic and thermodynamic properties of type II superconductors, static and dynamic properties of vortices, inverse problems in magnetic force microscopy, symmetries and exact solutions of nonlinear partial differential equations and cell discretization algorithm for the numerical solution of partial differential equations. Office: Univ Colo Dept Physics Cb 390 Boulder CO 80309-0001

COFFEY, NANCY ANN, real estate broker; b. Palm Springs, Calif.; d. Arthur Johnson and Joan (Hunter) C. BA, Stanford U., MS in Engring. Indsl. real estate broker Coldwell Banker, Houston, 1977-79; comml. broker Coldwell Banker, San Francisco, 1980-87, Cushman & Wakefield, N.Y.C., 1987-90; model Gilla Roos, N.Y.C., 1991-96; self-employed real estate broker, 1990-96; comml. real estate broker The Rolfe Group, N.Y.C., 1997-98, Cushman & Wakefield, Inc., N.Y.C., 1998-2000. Active Jr. League, San Francisco, 1981-87, N.Y.C., 1987-2000, sustainer, 1999-2000; active Palo Alto (Calif.) Jr. League, 2000—; mem. exec. com. spl. projects bd. Meml. Sloan Kettering Cancer Ctr., N.Y.C., vice chair Mem. Soc. of MSKCC; mem. parish life com. St. James Ch.; v.p. Class of 1967, Stanford U. Mem. Meml. Sloan-Kettering Cancer Ctr., Rockaway Hunting Club.

COFFIELD, CONRAD EUGENE, lawyer; b. Hot Springs, S.D., Nov. 26, 1930; s. Eugene M. and Alice (Hotvet) C.; children: Conrad Eugene, Michael, Megan, Edward, Philip; m. Mona L. Enfield, May 2, 1992. Student S.D. Sch. Mines and Tech., 1948-49; BBA, Washington U., St. Louis, 1952; LLB, U. Tex., 1959. Bar: Tex. 1959, N.Mex. 1959. Mem. Hervey, Dow & Hinkle, Roswell, N.Mex., 1959-64; gen. ptnr. Hinkle, Cox, Eaton, Coffield & Hensley, Roswell, 1964-66, resident ptnr., Midland, 1966-94, resident ptnr., Santa Fe, N.Mex., 1994—. Trustee Petroleum Mus., Library and Hall of Fame; bd. govs. Midland Community Theatre; bd. dirs. Santa Fe Pro Musica. Served with USCGR, 1952-56. Fellow Tex. Bar Found.; mem. ABA, Tex. Bar Assn., N.Mex. Bar Assn. (mem. bd. dirs. sr. lawyers), Santa Fe County Bar Assn., N.Mex. Oil and Gas Assn. Episcopalian. Office: Hinkle Cox Eaton Coffield Hensley 218 Montezuma Ave Santa Fe NM 87501-2625

COFFIN, ROBERT PARKER, architect, engineer; b. Chgo., Aug. 6, 1917; s. Charles Howells and Irene (Parker) C.; m. Emily Elizabeth Magie, Jan. 7, 1944; children: Betsy, Robert Jr., Barbara, John. BEngring., Yale U., 1939. Registered profl. engr., Ill., architect, Ill., Wis., Minn., Mo., Ind., Mich., Ky. Field engr. Commonwealth Edison, Chgo., 1939-50; architect Shaw Metz and Dolio, Chgo., 1950-56; ptnr. Coffin, Scherschel & Shaffer, Barrington, Ill., 1956—. Pres., sec. Long Grove (Ill.) Sch. Bd. Dist. 96, 1950-56; trustee Long Grove Village, 1956-59, pres., 1959-81, chmn. plan commn., 1981-98, mem. plan commn., 1998—. Lt. (j.g.) USN Air Corps, 1942-46. Recipient 5 Gold Key awards Nat. Home Builders Assn. Mem. AIA (emeritus), ASCE (life), Am. Soc. Archtl. Historians, Interfaith Forum on Ch. Architecture. Avocations: sailing, gardening, archeology, anthropology. Office: Coffin Scherschel and Shaffer Ltd 119 North Ave Barrington IL 60010-3299

COFFMAN, PATRICIA JOANNE, school nurse, counselor; b. Hagerstown, Md., Sept. 7, 1944; d. Glen Franklin and Hope LouEmma (Mellott) Smith; m. James Lee Coffman Sr., June 17, 1962; children: James Lee, Joel, Daniel, Julie. ADN, Hagerstown Jr. Coll., 1973; BS in Health Care Adminstrn., St. Joseph's Coll., North Windham, Maine, 1983; MS in Psychology, Shippensburg (Pa.) U., 1993; PhD in Counseling summa cum laude, LaSalle U., Mandeville, La., 1995. RN, Pa. Staff nurse Fulton County Med. Ctr., McConnellsburg, Pa., 1973-75; sch.nurse Tuscarora Sch. Dist., Mercersburg, Pa., 1975—, dept. head of nursing; sec. Nursing Home Bd. Dirs., Coshocton, Ohio, 1973-94, Jacob's Dwelling Nursing Home; chmn. Ctrl. Banking Sys., Hagerstown, 1989-95, Supreme Coun. of the House of Jacob; part-time tchr. Hagerstown Bus. Coll. Author policy manual and articles. Co-facilitator victims group, 1994-95, children of divorce, 1994-95, others; developer "at risk" program Caring for Kids vol. tutoring program and classes. Mem. Psi Chi. Avocations: travel, reading, family activities, church activities, crocheting. Home: 10809 Etter Ave Mercersburg PA 17236-9604

COFFMAN, RENEE ELISE, pharmacy educator, pharmacist; b. Columbus, Ohio, Aug. 5, 1964; d. Daryl Eugene and Susan Kay Coffman; m. Harry Rosenberg, Dec. 24, 1999. BS in Pharmacy, Ohio No. U., 1987; PhD in Pharmaceutics, Purdue U., 1995. Pharmacist Revco Drug Stores, Bucyrus, Ohio, 1987-88, Piqua (Ohio) Meml. Med. Ctr., 1988-90; tchg./rsch. asst. Purdue U., West Lafayette, Ind., 1990-96; asst. prof. Western U. Health Scis., Pomona, Calif., 1996-99; prof., facilitative officer for student svcs. So. Nev. Ednl. Svcs., Henderson, 1999—; pharmacy tech. program advisor Riverside (Calif.) County Office Ednl. Regional Occupation Program Adv. Com., 1999. Contbr. articles to profl. jours. Am. Assn. Pharm. Scientist-Am. Found. for Pharm. Edn. fellow, 1993-95. Mem. AAAS, Am. Assn. Pharm. Scientists, Am. Assn. Colls. Pharmacy, Nev. Pharmacy Alliance. Avocations: hiking, golf. E-mail: rcoffman5@lv.rmci.net. Office: So Nev Ednl Svcs 1701 Whitney Mesa Dr Ste 8 Henderson NV 89014-2046

COFFMAN, VANCE D., aerospace company executive; b. Kinross, Iowa, Apr. 3, 1944. BS in Aerospace Engring., Iowa State U.; MS in Aeronautics/Astronautics, Stanford U., PhD in Aeronautics and Astronautics. Guidance and control sys. analyst Space Sys. divsn. Lockheed Martin, 1967, v.p., 1985-87, divsn. v.p., asst. gen. mgr., 1987-88, pres. Space Sys. divsn., 1988, exec. v.p.; pres., COO Missiles sector Lockheed Martin, Bethesda, Md., CEO and vice chmn. bd. dirs., 1997-98, chmn., CEO, 1998—; bd. dirs. Bristol-Myers Squibb. Recipient Profl. Progress in Engring. award Iowa State U., 1989. Fellow AIAA, Am. Astron. Soc.; mem. Nat. Acad. Engring., Am. Def. Preparedness Assn., Nat. Security Indsl. Assn., Security Affairs Support Assn. Office: Lockheed Martin 6801 Rockledge Dr Bethesda MD 20817-1877

COGĂLNICEANU, DAN, ecology educator; b. Bucharest, Romania, Mar. 31, 1960; s. Alexandru and Maria Corina (Dudău) C.; m. Gina Carmen Radulian, July 10, 1985; children: Alexandru, Andrei. BS, Bucharest U., 1985, MS, 1986, PhD, 1997. Biochemist Ctr. of Hematology, Ploiesti, Romania, 1986-89; immunologist V. Babes Inst., Bucharest, 1989-90; ecologist Inst. Biology, Bucharest, 1990, Bucharest U., 1990—; DAPTF/SSC/IUCN, Romania, 1994—; referee sci. jours., 1995—; project mgr. Environ. Documentation Ctr., Bucharest, 1993-96. Author: Methods and Techniques for the Study of Ecology of Amphibians, 1997; co-author: Energy, Economy, Ecology, 1998, Management of Natural Capital, 1999; contbr. articles to profl. jours. Lt. Romanian Army, 1980-81. Grantee European Cmty., 1993, TEMPUS, 1993, 97, TEMPRA, 1998. Mem. Societas Europaea Herpetologica (editl. bd. Amphibia-Reptilia 1996-99), Romanian Ecol. Soc. (steering com. 1996—). Avocations: hiking, camping, Aiki-do, basketball. Home: Apt #13, Str Gr Manolescu 2 SC A, 78176 Bucharest Romania Office: Bucharest U Fac Biology, Spl Independentei 91-95, 76201 Bucharest Romania

COGDELL, RICHARD JOHN, botanist, biochemist, educator; b. Guildford, Surrey, Eng., Feb. 4, 1949; s. Harry William Frank and Evelyn (Passmore) C.; m. Barbara Lippold, June 25, 1970; children: Jesse Simon, Lucy Miriam. BSc in Biochemistry with hons., U. Bristol, Eng., 1970; PhD in Biochemistry, U. Bristol, 1973. Rsch. fellow Cornell U., Ithaca, N.Y., 1973-76; sr. rsch. fellow U. Wash., Seattle, 1974-75; from lectr. to Hooker prof. U. Glasgow, Scotland, 1975-93; Hooker prof. U. Glasgow, 1993—; vis. prof. UCLA, 1986; vis. fellow U. Stuttgart, Germany, 1994; guest rsch. prof. Max Planck Inst. Radiation Chem., Mulheim, Germany, 1996; gov., dir. Scottish Crops Rsch Inst., Invergowrie, Tayside, Scotland. Contbr. articles to profl. jours. Royal Soc. Edinburgh fellow, 1991; recipient Humbolt Rsch. prize, 1996. Mem. Biochem. Soc., Am. Soc. Photobiology, Internat. Photsynthesis Soc. (mem. internat. com. 1995—, sec. 1998—). E-mail: R.Cogdell@bio.gla.ac.uk. Office: Divsn Biochem/Molec Biology, U Glasgow, Glasgow G12 8QQ, Scotland

COGERT, HARMON IAN, management executive; b. Bklyn., Sept. 25, 1929; s. Jack D. and Deborah Bowie Cogert; m. Isabel Bragin (div. July 1970); children: Alton, Mitchell, Robyn; m. Barbara Helen Alex, Aug. 1, 1970; children: Valerie, Gregory. Student, NYU, 1950-53, L.A. State U., 1950-53. Regional dir. Sears, Roebuck & Co., 1954-59; pres. Parents Mag., N.Y.C., 1959-70, Comml. Funding of Calif., Woodland Hills, 1970-97, Union Pacific Telephone Co., Canoga Park, Calif., 1993-97, Web Booth Corp., Oxnard, Calif., 1997—; dir. Better Reading Found., N.Y.C., 1959-64. Inventor video greetings booth, 1980, voice/fax machine, 1994, pub. Internet access unit Web booth, 1996. With U.S. Army, 1948-50;. E-mail: harmon@cogert.com.

COGGINS, RICHARD JAMES, electrical engineering educator; b. Sydney, Nov. 13, 1964. BSc, U. Sydney, 1986, BSEE with honors, 1988, PhD, 1997. Rsch. engr. U. Sydney, Australia, 1990-95, rsch. fellow, 1996-99, sr. lectr., 2000—. Author: Adaptive Analog VLSI Systems, 1995; contbr. articles to profl. jours. Grantee Australian Rsch. Coun., 1999, 2000. Mem. IEEE. Avocations: golf, sailing, German language. Office: U Sydney Sch Elec Info Engr, J03, Sydney 2006, Australia

COGHILL, DAVIS GAROLD, chiropractic physician, counselor, psychotherapist, educator; b. Gallup, N.M., Mar. 25, 1948; s. Donald Garold and June Elizabeth (Davis) C.; m. Dianna H. Glick, Jan. 26, 1991; children: Matthew Donald, Anna Janell. BA in Psychology, Calif. State U., L.A., 1973, MA in Spl. Edn., 1975, MA in Psychology, 1981; PhD in Counseling Psychology, U. Santa Barbara, 1985; D in Chiropractic cum laude, Life Chiropractic Coll. West, 1990; PsyD, Am. Behavioral Studies Inst., 1998. Lic. marriage and family therapist; lic. doctor of chiropractic. Instr., counselor L.A. County Office Edn., 1976—; acad. counselor, drug/alcohol abuse prevention coord. Life Chiropractic Coll. West, San Lorenzo, Calif., 1987-90; pvt. practice So. and No. Calif., 1982—; oral commr. Bd. Behavioral Sci. Examiners, Calif., 1987—; counselor Montebello Unified Sch. Dist., 1993—; mem. med. team Humanitarian Med. Mission, Trinidad and Tobago, 1996, 97; lectr. in field. Patentee in field. Fellow Nat. Grief Counselors Assn., Nat. Poetry Therapy Assn., Soc. Traumatic Stress Studies, Intergenerational Psychotherapy Soc. (founding mem.). Avocations: martial arts, woodworking, music, lapidary and metal work.

COGLIANESE, KARA ANN, elementary education educator, consultant; b. Anaheim, Calif., Nov. 29, 1966; d. Charles Samual and Shirley Mae Newton; m. William Attilio Coglianese, Feb. 11, 1995. BA, Nat.-Louis U., Lombard, Ill., 1989; MEd in Curriculum and Instrn., Nat.-Louis U., Evanston, Ill., 1992. Cert. tchr., Ill. Tchr. Naperville (Ill.) Sch. Dist. 203, 1989-95, Buffalo Grove (Ill.) Sch. Dist. 96, 1995-97; instrn. design specialist and trainer ABACO Corp., Naperville, 1997-98; tchr. Prospect Heights (Ill.) Sch. Dist. 23, 1998—; instr. grad. courses Skylight Tng. and Pub., Arlington Heights, Ill., 1998—; quality assurance reviewer Ill. Bd. Edn., Springfield, 1998—; instrnl. design specialist and trainer Lake County Coll., Grayslake, Ill., 1999—. Mem. editl. bd. Tng. Today, 1997. Election judge, Wheeling Twp., Ill., 1997-98; program vol. Spl. Olympics, Schaumburg, Ill., 1998. Mem. ASCD, Phi Theta Kappa. Avocations: travel, cooking, reading, photography, hiking.

COGNARD, JACQUES JEAN, chemist; b. Toulouse, France, Oct. 24, 1941; arrived in Switzerland, 1972; s. Jean Joseph and Zlata (Pirnat) C.; divorced; children: Frederic, Madeleine. B, Lycée Francois 1er, Fontainebleau, France, 1960; M in Chemistry, U. Paris, 1966; PhD, U. Grenoble, France, 1971. Cert. engr. Ecole Nat. Chimie de Paris. R & D chem. engr. Ebauches S.A., Neuchâtel, Switzerland, 1972-74; head polymer group Asulab S.A., Marin, Switzerland, 1974—; speaker in field. Author: Science et Technologie du Collage, contbr. articles to profl. jours.; patentee in field. Pres. Mouvement Condition Paternelle, Neuchâtel, 1989—. Mem. Am. Chem. Soc., Adhesion Soc., Polymer Group Switzerland (bd. dirs.), Amnesty Internat., Ligue des Droits de l'Homme. Avocations: mycology, skiing, swimming. Home: Serroue 17, CH 2006 Neuchâtel Switzerland Office: Asulab S A, Rue des Sors 3, CH 2074 Marin Neuch, Switzerland

COGNE, MICHEL CLEMENT, immunologist, educator; b. Chatellerault, France, May 23, 1957; s. Guy and Bernadette (Degenne) C.; m. Christine Delumeau, Oct. 3, 1981 (div. Apr. 1994); children: Clement, Antoine, Etienne; m. Nadine Peyruchaud, Sept. 1996. MD, Poitiers U., 1982; PhD, U. Paris, 1988. Researcher Nat. Ctr. Scientific Rsch., France, 1988-92; prof. biochemistry U. Poitiers, France, 1992-94; prof. immunology U. Limoges, France, 1994—; dir. lab. immunology and immunogenetics U. Limoges, 1994—. Laureate Académie nationale de Médecine, 1997; grantee Found. Med. Rsch., 1987, Nat. Assn. Cancer, 1989, Nat. Cancer League, 1994. Mem. Institut Universitaire de France. Avocations: swimming, scuba diving. Home: Le Caillaud, 87170 Isle France Office: Lab Immunology & Immunogenetics, UFR Medecine, 87042 Limoges France

COGSWELL, FREDERICK WILLIAM, English language educator, poet, editor, publisher; b. East Centreville, N.B., Can., Nov. 8, 1917; s. Walter Scott and Florence (White) C.; m. Margaret Hynes, July 3, 1944 (dec. May 1985); children: Carmen Patricia Cogswell Robinson (dec.), Kathleen Mary Cogswell Forsythe; m. Gail Fox, Nov. 6, 1985 (div. Aug. 1997); m. Adele Bartlett, Sept. 20, 1997. BA with honors, U. N.B., 1949, MA, 1950; PhD (Imperial Order Daus. Empire fellow), U. Edinburgh, Scotland, 1952; LLD (hon.), St. Francis Xavier U., 1982; DCL (hon.), King's Coll., 1985; LLD (hon.), Mt. Allison U., 1988. From asst. to assoc. prof. dept. English U. N.B., Fredericton, 1952-64; prof. U. N.B., 1964-83, prof. emeritus, 1983—; exchange writer in residence, Scottish Arts Council, 1983-84. Editor: The Fiddlehead, 1952-66, Humanities Assn. Bull, 1967-72; pub. Fiddlehead Poetry Books, 1956-82; author: Charles G.D. Roberts, 1983, Charles Mair, 1986; poetry The Stunted Strong, 1954, The Haloed Tree, 1957, Descent From Eden, 1959, Lost Dimension, 1960, Star People, 1968, Immortal Plowman, 1969, In Praise of Chastity, 1970, The Chains of Liliput, 1971, The House Without A Door, 1973, Light Bird of Life, 1974, Against Perspectives, 1977; collected poems A Long Apprenticeship, 1980, Selected Poems, 1982, Pearls, 1983; Meditations: 50 Sestinas, 1986, An Edge To Life, 1987, The Best Notes Merge, 1988, Black and White Tapestry, 1989, Watching an Eagle, 1991 When the Right Light Shines, 1992, In Praise of Old Music, 1992, In My Own Growing, 1993, As I See It, 1994, The Trouble With Light, 1996, Folds, 1997, A Double with Vision Added, 2000; translator: The Testament of Cresseid, 1958, One Hundred Poems of Modern Quebec, 1970, 71, A Second Hundred Poems of Modern Quebec, 1971, The Poetry of Modern Quebec, 1976, Confrontation, 1973, The Complete Poems of Emile Nelligan, 1983, (with Jo-Anne Elder) Unfinished Dreams: Contemporary Poetry of Acadie, 1991, anthologies Five New Brunswick Poets, 1961, (with W.S. MacNutt and Robert Tweedie) The Arts in New Brunswick, 1967, (with Thelma Reid Lower) The Enchanted Land, 1968, One Hundred Poems of Modern Quebec, A Second Hundred Poems of Modern Quebec, The Poetry of Modern Quebec; Atlantic Anthology, Vol. 1 (prose), 1983, Vol. 2 (poetry), Climates by Herménégilde Chiasson (translator with Jo-Anne Elder), 1999; contbr. poems, articles to profl. jours. Mem. sr. arts fellowship awards com. Can. Council, 1972, mem. centennial poetry awards com., 1968; mem. Leave fellowship awards bd. humanities sect., 1973, 74; mem. poetry sect. Gov. Gen.'s award bd., 1973, chmn., 1974; bd. dirs. Can. Found., 1983—. Served with Canadian Army, 1940-45. Decorated mem. Order of Can., 1981; recipient Bliss Carman medal for poetry, 1945, 47, Douglas Gold medal, 1949, Gold medal for svc. to poetry as mag. editor Republic of

Philippines, 1956, Gold medal as disting. poet, 1956, medal for 125 Can. anniversary, 1992, Alden Nowlan awa: for excellence in the arts N.B. Gov., 1995; Nuffield fellow, 1959-60, Can. Coun. Sr. fellow, 1967-68. Mem. League Canadian Poets (regional exec. 1973-80, 1st v.p. 1985-86 , hon. life mem.), Canadian Authors Assn., Internat. P.E.N., Assn. Can. Pubs. (hon. life, Honors for Contrbns. to Can. Lit. and Publs. 2000), Ind. Pubs. Assn., Atlantic Pubs. Assn. (pres. 1979-80), Assn. Can. and Que. Lits. (pres. 1978-80), N.B. Writers' Fedn. (hon. life.; pres. 1983-85). Home: 31 Island View Dr, Douglas, NB Canada E3A 7R7

COHALAN, JOHN ROBERT, educator; b. Kilmichael, Cork, Ireland, May 13, 1939; s. John Robert and Mary Agnes (Dromey) C.; m. Margaret Mary Skuse, Jan. 14, 1967; children: Karen, John Keith, Lisa, Karl. BA, U. Coll., Dublin, 1970; MS in Econs., Trinity Coll., Dublin, 1971; MSc in Info. Tech., Queen Mary Coll., London, 1990. Govt. statis. Ctrl. Statistics Office, Dublin, Ireland, 1971-73; head econ. rsch. FAS, Dublin, Ireland, 1973-74; group economist Dunkeld Holdings, Dublin, Ireland, 1974-75; dir. Confedn. Irish Industry, Dublin, Ireland, 1975-81; prin. adminstr. European Commn., Brussels, 1981-83; sr. lectr. U. Limerick, Ireland, 1983—; cons. in field. Mem. Castleroy Golf Club, Ballybunion Golf Club. Roman Catholic. Avocations: golf, sailing, swimming, walking. Home: Brook Hall Newtown, Limerick Ireland Office: U Limerick, Dept Computer Sci, Limerick Ireland

COHEN, AARON, aerospace engineer; b. Tex., Jan. 31, 1931; s. Charles and Ida (Moloff) C.; m. Ruth Carolyn Goldberg, Feb. 7, 1953; children—Nancy Ann Santana, David Blair, Daniel Louis. BS, Tex. A&M U., 1952; MS in Applied Math., Stevens Inst. Tech, 1958, D Engring. (hon.), 1982. Microwave tube design engr. RCA, Camden, N.J., 1954-58; sr. research engr. Gen. Dynamics, San Diego, 1958-62; mgr. Apollo command and service module lunar module guidance nav. and control NASA, Houston, 1962-70, mgr. command and service module project, 1970-72, mgr. shuttle orbiter project, 1972-82, dir. research and engring., 1982-86, dir. Johnson Space Ctr., 1986-93; prof. Tex. A&M U., College Station, 1993—. Editor Astronautics sect. Marks Mechanical Engineer's Handbook, 9th edit.; contbr. articles to profl. jours. Vice chmn. engring. task force Target 2000 Tex. A&M U., College Station, 1981-83. Served to lt. C.E., U.S. Army, 1952-54, Korea. Recipient Exceptional Service medal NASA, Houston, 1969, Disting. Service medal, 1973, 81, 88, 93—, Goddard Meml. trophy, 1988; Presdl. Rank of Meritorious Exec., U.S. Govt., Washington, 1981, Presdl. Rank of Disting. Exec., 1982, 88; Named NASA Engr. of Yr., Washington, 1982, Engr. of Yr. Nat. Acad. Engring., 1988. Fellow Am. Astron. Soc. (W. Randolph Lovelace II award 1982), AIAA (Von Karman lectureship 1984, Von Braun award 1993, Hon. Fellow, 1995, Robert H. Goddard Astronautics award 1996), ASME (medal 1984), AJAA, Tau Beta Pi. Jewish. Avocation: tennis. Office: Texas A&M U Dept Mech Engring Ms 3123 College Station TX 77843-0001

COHEN, ALAN BARRY, educator, former foundation executive; b. Bklyn., Nov. 3, 1952; s. Max B. and Blanche (Katz) C.; m. Helaine Francine Hartman, Dec. 22, 1973; children: Jeremy Todd, Bradley Daniel, Melanie Ann, Brandon Adam. BA, U. Rochester, 1973; MS, Harvard U., 1975, ScD, 1983. Rsch. asst. Beth Israel Hosp. and Harvard Med. Sch., Boston, 1974-75; sr. analyst Urban Systems Rsch. & Engring. Inc., Cambridge, Mass., 1975-79; rsch. assoc. Harvard Sch. Pub. Health, Boston, 1979-81; rsch. assoc. Johns Hopkins Sch. Hygiene and Pub. Health, Balt., 1981-82, asst. prof., 1982-84; assoc. dir. John Hopkins Ctr. for Hosp. Fin. and Mgmt., Balt., 1983-84; program officer Robert Wood Johnson Found., Princeton, N.J., 1984-87, sr. program officer, 1987-88, v.p., 1988-92; rsch. prof. Heller Grad. Sch. Brandeis U., 1992-94; prof. health policy and mgmt. Boston U. Sch. Mgmt., 1994—, dir. health care mgmt. program, 1994—; nat. program dir. Robert Wood Johnson Found. Scholars in Health Policy Rsch. Program, 1992—; mem. nat. adv. com. Robert Wood Johnson Found. Info. for State Health Policy Program, 1994-98; cons. N.J. Dept. Health, 1993; chmn. commr.'s cardiac svcs. com. State of N.J., Trenton, 1990-92; mem. Inst. Medicine, Tech. Monitoring Panel on Access to Care, 1989-91; cons. D.C. State Health Planning and Devel. Agy., 1984, Nat. Ctr. Health Svcs. Rsch., 1984. Mem. editorial bd. Inquiry, Health Affairs; contbr. articles to profl. jours. Recipient Charles F. Wilinsky award Harvard Sch. Pub. Health, 1979; Kaiser fellow in health policy and mgmt., 1973-74; Dissertation grantee Nat. Ctr. Health Svcs. Rsch., 1979-80. Fellow Assn. Health Svcs. Rsch.; mem. APHA, AEA, APSA, NASI, Soc. for Med. Decision Making, Internat. Soc. for Tech. Assessment in Health Care, Zeta Beta Tau (pres. Gamma Pi chpt. 1972-73, treas. 1970-72), Beta Gamma Sigma. Jewish. Avocations: reading, travel, cinema, basketball, gardening. Office: Boston U Sch Mgmt 595 Commonwealth Ave Boston MA 02215-1704

COHEN, BENJAMIN JERRY, political economy educator; b. Ossining, N.Y., June 5, 1937; s. Abraham and Rachel (Grossman) C.; m. Jane DeHart, Sept. 20, 1986. BA, Columbia U., 1959, PhD, 1963. Economist Fed. Res. Bank N.Y., 1962-64; asst. prof. econs. Princeton (N.J.) U., 1964-71; assoc. prof. Tufts U. Fletcher Sch. of Law and Diplomacy, Medford, Mass., 1971-78; William L. Clayton prof. Internat. Econ. Affairs Fletcher Sch. Law and Diplomacy Tufts U., Medford, Mass., 1978-91; Louis G. Lancaster prof. Internat. Polit. Economy U. Calif., Santa Barbara, 1991—. Author: Organizing the World's Money, 1976, Banks and the Balance of Payments, 1981, In Whose Interest?, 1986, Crossing Frontiers, 1991, The Geography of Money, 1998. Mem. Am. Econ. Assn., Am. Polit. Sci. Assn., Coun. Fgn. Rels., Internat. Studies Assn., Pacific Coun. Internat. Policy. Jewish. Office: U Calif Dept Polit Sci Santa Barbara CA 93106

COHEN, CARL I., psychiatry educator, researcher; b. N.Y.C., Aug. 7, 1947; s. Louis and Louise Cohen; m. Katherine A. Henry, Sept. 12, 1987; children: Sara, Zachary. BA, CUNY, 1967; MD, SUNY, Buffalo, 1971; MA, NYU, 1974. Diplomate Am. Bd. Psychiatry and Neurology, Am. Bd. Psychiatry and Neurology with Added Qualifications in Geriatric Psychiatry. Intern Med. Coll. Pa., 1971-72; resident NYU Bellevue Med. Ctr., 1972-74; fellow NYU Med. Ctr., 1974-75; asst. prof., dir. social and cmty. psychiatry NYU Med. Ctr., N.Y.C., 1976-81; prof. psychiatry, dir. divsn. geriatric psychiatry SUNY Health Sci. Ctr., Bklyn., 1981—; dir. Downstate Mental Hygiene Assocs., Bklyn., 1983—, Bklyn. Alzheimer's Disease Assistance Ctr., 1988—; mem. adv. b.d L.I. Alzheimer's Found., N.Y., 1998—; spl. advisor White House Conf. on Aging, Washington, 1980; advisor to various coms. NIMH, 1985-99; presenter N.Y.C. Mayor's Conf. on Alzheimer's Disease, 1992-99. Author: Old Men of the Bowery, 1989; mem. editl. bd. Internat. Jour. Geriatric Psychiatry, London, 1983-99, Am. Jour. Geriatric Psychiatry, 1994-00; spl. editor Cmty. Mental Health Jour., 1993; contbr. over 150 articles to med. jours., chpts. to books. Bd. dirs. St. Francis Friends of Poor, N.Y.C., 1983—. Named One of Best Doctors in N.Y., New York Mag., 1996, 98; over 30 grants, cindluging NIMH, N.Y. State Dept. Health, pvt. founds. Fellow Am. Psychiat. Assn.; mem. Am. Assn. Geriatric Psychiatry, Am. Assn. Cmty. Psychiatrists (Psychiatrist of Yr. award 1991), Internat. Assn. Geriatric Psychiatry. Avocation: handball. E-mail: cohen c@hscbklyn.edu. Office: SUNY Health Sci Ctr Bklyn 450 Clarkson Ave # 1203 Brooklyn NY 11203-2056

COHEN, CHERYL DIANE DURDA, communications executive; b. Mpls., Jan. 26, 1947; d. Joseph and Dolores Catherine (Monahan) Durda; m. Miles Jon Cohen, June 24, 1967; children: Christopher, Michael, Brian, Katherine Kelly. BA, U. Minn., 1978; grad. Owner/Pres. Mgmt. program, Harvard U., 1992. Writer Aeration Industries Internat. Inc., Chaska, Minn., 1982-85, communications asst., 1985-86, communications mgr., 1986-88, v.p. pub. rels., 1988-93, v.p. mktg. and pub. rels., 1993-97; environ. mktg. cons. Aeration Industries Internat. Inc., Chaska, 1997—; bd. dirs. Aeration Industries Internat., Inc. Editor AIRE-02 News, 1985—, AQUA-02 News, 1988—; contbr. articles on water restoration and aquaculture to U.S. and internat. profl. jours., also conf. proc.; film editor, producer, 1986—. Bd. dirs. Minn. Assn. Retarded Citizens, Mpls., 1984-85, The Joseph Durda Found., 1990—; St. David's Sch. for Exceptional Children, Minnetonka, 1980-85; mem. adv. bd. Minnetonka Schs. CARE, Minn., 1982-92; dir. communications Minnetonka Football Assn., 1986-92, founding mem., 1986; mem. adv. coun. U. Minn. Women's Intercollegiate Athletics; founding mem. Minnetonka Basketball Club, 1984; active legis. testimony, lobbying, pub. speaking Adv. for Severely Disabled, 1981—; mem. U. Minn. Gopher Football Team's Parent Club, 1988-92; mem. USAF Acad. Parents Club, 1992-93, Harvard-Radcliffe Club Minn., 1992-96; co-facilitator Devel. Capable Young People series for Minnetonka community, 1983-84. Mem. Water Pollution Control Fedn., World Aquaculture Soc., Asian Fisheries Soc., Chesapeake Bay Found., Clean Water Found., U. Minn. Alumni Assn., U. Minn. Presidents Club (chartered), Minn. Press Club, Booster Club (producer cable TV sports show 1988-92, co-chair publicity 1988-92), Harvard Bus. Sch. Club Minn. (alumni mem.). Roman Catholic. Avocations: reading, sports, music. Office: Aeration Industries Internat Inc 4100 Peavey Rd Chaska MN 55318-2353

COHEN, CYNTHIA MARYLYN, lawyer; b. Bklyn., Sept. 5, 1945. AB, Cornell U., 1967; JD cum laude, NYU, 1970. Bar: N.Y. 1971, U.S. Ct. Appeals (2nd cir.) 1972, U.S. Dist. Ct. (so. and ea. dists.) N.Y. 1972, U.S. Supreme Ct. 1975, U.S. Dist. Ct. (cen. and no. dists.) Calif. 1980, U.S. Ct. Appeals (9th cir.) 1980, U.S. Dist. Ct. (so. dist.) Calif. 1981, U.S. Dist. Ct. (ea. dist.) Calif. 1986. Assoc. Simpson Thacher & Bartlett, N.Y.C., 1970-76, Kaye, Scholer, Fierman, Hayes & Handler, N.Y.C., 1976-80; assoc. Stutman, Treister & Glatt, P.C., L.A., 1980-81, ptnr., 1981-87; ptnr. Hughes Hubbard & Reed, N.Y.C. and L.A., 1987-93, Morgan, Lewis & Bockius, LLP, L.A., Phila., N.Y.C., 1993-98, Jeffer, Mangels, Butler & Marmaro LLP, L.A. and San Francisco, 1998—. Bd. dirs. N.Y. chpt. Am. Cancer Soc., 1977-80. Recipient Am. Jurisprudence award for evidence, torts and legal instns., 1968-69; John Norton Pomeroy scholar NYU, 1968-70, Founders Day Cert., 1969. Mem. ABA, Assn. Bar City N.Y. (trade regulation com. 1976-79), Assn. Bus. Trial Lawyers, Fin. Lawyers Conf., N.Y. State Bar Assn. (chmn. class-action com. 1979), State Bar Calif., Los Angeles County Bar Assn., Order of Coif, Delta Gamma. Avocations: tennis, bridge, rare books, wines. Home: 4531 Dundee Dr Los Angeles CA 90027-1213 Office: Jeffer Mangels Butler Marmaro LLP 2121 Ave Of Stars Fl 10 Los Angeles CA 90067-5010

COHEN, DAVID WALTER, academic administrator, periodontist, educator; b. Phila., Dec. 15, 1926; s. Abram and Goldie (Schlein) C.; m. Betty Axelrod, Dec. 19, 1948 (dec. Mar. 1992); children: Jane Ellen, Amy Sue, Joanne Louise. DDS, U. Pa., 1950; DSc (hon.), Boston U., 1975; PhD (hon.), Hebrew U., Jerusalem, 1977, U. Athens, 1979; Dr Honoris Causa, U. Louis Pasteur, Strasbourg, France, 1986; DHL (hon.), U. Detroit, 1989. Diplomate: Am. Bd. Periodontology (chmn. 1972). Research fellow pathology and periodontia Beth Israel Hosp., Boston, 1950-51; mem. faculty U. Pa. Sch. Dentistry, Phila., 1951—, prof. periodontics, 1962-86, chmn. dept., 1962-73; dean Sch. Dental Medicine U. Pa., Phila., 1972-83; dean emeritus U. Pa. Sch. Dentistry, Phila., 1983—; pres. Med. Coll. Pa., 1986-93; chancellor Allegheny U. of Health Scis., 1993-98, chancellor emeritus, 1998—; mem. staff Albert Einstein Med. Center, Phila., Children's Hosp., Phila.; pres. Jewish Publ. Soc., 1993-96; vis. prof. Boston U. Sch. Grad Dentistry, 1972—; nat. cons. periodontics USAF, 1965-70; bd. govs. Hebrew U., Jerusalem, Betty and Walter Cohen chair in periodontal rsch., 1986; D. Walter Cohen endowed chair in periodontics U. Pa., 1995. Author: (with H.M. Goldman) Periodontia, 1957, (with others) An Introduction to Periodontia, 1959, Periodontal Therapy, 1960, (with R. Genco and Goldman) Contemporary Periodontics, 1990, (with Genco, L. Rose and B. Mealey) Periodontal Medicine, 1999; also numerous articles and chpts. V.p. Jewish Publ. Soc., 1985-89, pres., 1993-96; pres. Nat. Mus. Am. Jewish History, Phila., 1996—. Served with USN, 1944-45. Named to Ctrl. H.S. Hall of Fame, 1976; 1st Presdl. scholar U. Calif., San Francisco, 1985-86; named for him Hebrew U. Betty and D. Walter Cohen Chair in Periodontal Rsch., 1986, U. Pa. D. Walter Cohen Endowed Chair in Periodontics, 1995; D. Walter Cohen Mid. East Ctr. for Dental Edn. dedicated by Hebrew U. of Jerusalem, 1997. Fellow AAAS, Am. Acad. Oral Pathology, Am. Acad. Periodontology, Inst. of Medicine of Nat. Acad. Scis.; mem. Am. Soc. Periodontists (pres. 1967), Friends of Nat. Inst. Dental Rsch. (pres. 1998—). Office: Med Coll Pa 3300 Henry Ave Philadelphia PA 19129-1191

COHEN, EDWIN SAMUEL, lawyer, educator; b. Richmond, Va., Sept. 27, 1914; s. LeRoy S. and Miriam (Rosenheim) C.; m. Carlyn Labenberg, June 27, 1936 (dec. 1942); m. Helen Herz, Aug. 31, 1944; children: Edwin C., Roger, Wendy. B.A., U. Richmond, 1933; J.D., U. Va., 1936. Bar: Va. 1935, N.Y. 1937, D.C. 1973. Assoc. Sullivan & Cromwell, N.Y.C., 1936-49; ptnr. Root, Barrett, Cohen, Knapp & Smith (and predecessor firm), N.Y.C., 1949-65; counsel Root, Barrett, Cohen, Knapp & Smith, 1965-69; prof. law U. Va., Charlottesville, 1965-68, Joseph M. Hartfield prof., 1968-69, 73-85, prof. emeritus, 1985—, professorial lectr. law, 1994—; asst. sec. treasury for tax policy, 1969-72, under sec. treasury, 1972-73; of counsel Covington & Burling, Washington, 1973-77, ptnr., 1977-86, sr. counsel, 1986—; vis. prof. Benjamin N. Cardozo Sch. Law, Yeshiva U., 1987-92, U. Miami Law Sch., 1993, 95-99, chmn. grad. program in taxation and estate planning, 1995-98; mem., counsel adv. group on corp. taxes ways and means com. U.S. Ho. of Reps., 1956-58; spl. cons. on corps. fed. income tax project Am. Law Inst., 1949-54; mem. adv. group Fed. Estate and Gift Tax Project, 1964-68; mem. Va. Income Tax Conformity Study Commn., 1970-71; cons. Va. Income Tax Conformity Study Commn., 1966-68; mem. adv. group to commr. IRS, 1967-68. Author: A Lawyer's Life Deep in the Heart of Taxes, 1994. Recipient Alexander Hamilton award Treasury Dept. Mem. Am. Judicature Soc., ABA (chmn. com. on corporate stockholder relationships 1956-58, mem. council 1958-61, chmn. spl. com. on substantive tax reform 1962-63, chmn. spl. com. on formation tax policy 1977-80, Disting. Svc. award taxation sect. 1997), Va. Bar Assn., D.C. Bar Assn., N.Y. State Bar Assn., Va. Tax Conf. (planning com. 1965-68, 85-95, trustee emeritus 1995—), C. of C. of U.S. (bd. dirs., chmn. taxation com. 1979-84), Assn. Bar City N.Y., N.Y. County Lawyers Assn., Am. Law Inst., Am. Coll. Tax Counsel, Order Coif, Raven Soc., Colonnade Club, Boar's Head Club, Farmington Club, City Club, Phi Beta Kappa, Omicron Delta Kappa, Pi Delta Epsilon, Phi Epsilon Pi (Nat. Achievement award). Home: 104 Stuart Pl Ednam Forest Charlottesville VA 22903

COHEN, GEORGE SOL, engineering consultant; b. N.Y.C., Jan. 10, 1925. BSEE, U. Dayton, 1953; MSEE, U. Mich., 1955, PhD in Elec. Engring., 1962. Registered profl. engr., Calif. Engr. U. Mich. Rsch. Inst./Electronic Def. Group, Ann Arbor, 1953-55; instr. U. Kans., Lawrence, 1955-56; engr. Electronic Def. Group, Ann Arbor, 1956-59, Bendix Sys. Divsn., Ann Arbor, 1959-61; rsch. engr. radio astronomy U. Mich., Ann Arbor, 1961-67; sr. mem. technical staff GTE Sylvania, Mountain View, Calif., 1967-69, 74-84; prof. elec. engring. U. Akron (Ohio), 1969-74; prin. engr. ARGO Sys., Sunnyvale, Calif., 1984-90, Space Sys./Loral, Palo Alto, Calif., 1990-94; cons. comm. space sys. Loral, Santa Rosa, Calif., 1994—. Rsch. Inst. fellow U. Mich. Rsch. Inst., 1955, fellow NSF, 1971. Mem. IEEE (sr.). Avocation: photography. Home: 1811 Palisades Dr Santa Rosa CA 95403-5706

COHEN, GORDON S., health products executive; b. N.Y.C., May 18, 1937; s. Leon Lewis and Irene (Lipton) C.; m. Marjorie Rennick, June 12, 1960; children: Terri Susan, Lisa Michelle, Bonnie Lynne. AB, Brown U., 1959; MD, Yale U., 1963. Diplomate Am. Bd. Pathology, Anatomic Pathology and Clin. Pathology. Instr. dept. pathology Yale U., New Haven, 1967-70, asst. prof. pathology, 1970-71, asst. clin. prof. pathology, 1971-76; pres. Jeneric Industries, Wallingford, Conn., 1975-86; chmn. Pentron Corp., Wallingford, 1977-87; pres. Jeneric/Pentron, Inc., Wallingford, 1987—; chmn. Customedix Corp., Wallingford, 1987—; attending pathologist Yale-New Haven Hosp., 1970-71, Hosp. St. Raphael, New Haven, 1971-76; pathologist The Charlotte Hungerford Hosp., Torrington, Conn., 1967-70. Author numerous articles in field. Sr. edn. officer Milford (Conn.) U.S. Power Squadron, 1987; mem. Congressman DeNardis's Small Bus. Adv. Com., 1982. Capt. (M.C.) USAR, 1964-70. Mem. Internat. Acad. Pathology, N.Y. Acad. Scis., Phi Beta Kappa, Sigma Xi, Alpha Omega Alpha. Avocations: sailing, shooting, book collecting. Office: Jeneric Pentron Inc 53 N Plains Industrial Rd Wallingford CT 06492-5841

COHEN, HARVEY JAY, physician, educator; b. Bklyn., Oct. 21, 1940; s. Joseph and Anne (Margolin) C.; m. Sandra Helen Levine, June 1964; children: Ian Mitchell, Pamela Robin. BS, Bklyn. Coll., 1961; MD, Downstate Med. Coll., Bklyn., 1965. Diplomate Am. Bd. Internal Medicine, Am. Bd. Hematology. Intern, then resident internal medicine Duke U. Med. Ctr., Durham, N.C., 1965-67, fellow hematology and oncology, 1969-71; chief hematology-oncology VA Med. Ctr., Durham, N.C., 1975-76, chief med. service, 1976-82, assoc. chief of staff-edn., 1982-84, now dir. geriatric research, edn. and clin. ctr.; assoc. prof. medicine Duke U. Med. Ctr., Durham, 1976-80, now prof. medicine, chief geriatric div., also dir. Ctr. for Study of Aging; chair bd. scientific counselors Nat. Inst. Aging, 1999. Author: Medical Immunology, 1977; editor: Cancer I and II, 1987, Jour. Gerontology: Med. Scis., 1988-92, Geriatric Medicine, 1997; contbr. numerous articles to profl. jours. Served as surgeon USPHS, 1967-69. Fellow ACP, Am. Geriatrics Soc. (bd. dirs. 1987-96, chair bd. dirs. 1995-96, sec. 1991-93, ethics com. 1992-96, pres. 1994-95), Gerontology Soc. Am. (clin. sec., rsch. com. 1987-92, chair publs. com. 1996-98, program chair 1994, pres.-elect 1999); mem. Am. Soc. Clin. Oncology, Am. Soc. Hematology, Am. Assn. Cancer Rsch. (cancer and acute leukemia group B, chair cancer in the elderly com.), Assn. Am. Physicians. Home: 2811 Friendship Cir Durham NC 27705-5521 Office: Duke U Med Ctr for Study Aging & Human Devel PO Box 3003 Durham NC 27710-0001

COHEN, IRWIN, economist; b. Bronx, N.Y., Feb. 29, 1936; s. Samuel and Gertrude (Levy) C. BS in Accounting, N.Y. U., 1956, MBA in Finance, 1964, MA in Econs., 1969; BS in Math., CCNY, 1970. Financial analyst U.S. SEC, N.Y.C., 1965-67, Fed. Res. Bank N.Y., N.Y.C., 1967-72, Prudential Ins. Co. Am., 1973-74, SEC, 1974—. Life Fellow Internat. Biog. Assn., Am. Biog. Inst. Research Assn. (dep. gov.), World Acad. Scholars, World Literary Acad., World Inst. Achievement; mem. Internat. Biographical Ctr. (dep. dir. gen.), Internat. Platform Assn. (life), Math. Assn. Am., Am. Finance Assn., Econ. History Assn. Home: 372 Central Park Ave Apt 2K Scarsdale NY 10583-1308

COHEN, JACK JOSEPH, religious educator, rabbi, retired; b. Bklyn., Mar. 21, 1919; arrived in Israel, 1961; s. Isidor Elkin and Helen (Grossman) C.; m. Rhoda Levine, Dec. 23, 1945; children: Michal Merav, Jeremy Micah, Adeena Chava. BHL, MHL, Jewish Theol. Sem., 1940, DD, 1968; BA, Blkyn. Coll., 1940; PhD, Columbia U., 1958; DD, Reconstructionist Rabbinical C, 2000. Ordained rabbi, 1943. Ednl. dir. Park Synagogue, Cleve., 1943-45; ednl. dir. Soc. Advancement Judaism, N.Y.C., 1952-54, rabbi, 1954-61; dir. Jewish Reconstructionist Found., N.Y.C., 1945-54, B'nai Brith Found. Hebrew U., Jerusalem, 1961-84; instr. philosophies religion & edn. Jewish Theol. Sem., N.Y.C., 1955-61; faculty mem. Reconstructionist Rabbinical Coll., Jerusalem, 1972-84, ret., 1984. Author: The Case for Religious Naturalism, 1958, Jewish Education in Democratic Society, 1965, The Reunion of Isaac & Ishmael, 1987, (in Hebrew) Guides in an Age of Confusion, 1993 (in English, 1999), Major Philosophers of Jewish Prayer in the 20th Century, 2000; mem. editl. bd. The Reconstructionist, Edn. & Democracy. Chmn. edn. commn. United Synagogue Am., N.Y.C.; vice chmn. placement commn. Rabbinical Assembly Am., N.Y.C.; bd. dirs. Religion & Labor Found., Labor Zionist Orgn., Com. Edn. & Culture Ministry Edn. Israel, Internat. Coun. Conf. Religion & Peace, Israel Interfaith Assn. Recipient Armstrong prize Intercultural Ctr. Youth, Jerusalem, 1969. Mem. Kehillat Mevakshei Derech (former chmn., bd. dirs.), Coll. Pluralistic Judaism (acad. com.), Rainbow Club (chmn. 1983). Avocations: music, walking, reading. E-mail: rhojac@netvision.net.il. Home: 8 Rabbi Tarfon, 93592 Jerusalem Israel

COHEN, JEFFREY MICHAEL, lawyer; b. Dayton, Ohio, Nov. 13, 1940; s. H. Mort and Evelyn (Friedlob) C.; m. Betsy Z. Zimmerman, July 3, 1966; children: Meredith Sue, Seth Alan. AB, Colgate U., 1962; JD, Columbia U., 1965. Bar: Fla. 1965, U.S. Supreme Ct. 1969; cert. civil trial lawyer Fla. Bar Bd. Cert., diplomate Nat. Bd. Trial Advocacy. Asst. pub. defender Dade County (Fla.), 1968-70, asst. state's atty., 1970-72, spl. asst. state's atty., 1973; ptnr. Fromberg Fromberg Gross Cohen Shore & Berke, P.A., 1972-84, Cohen, Berke, Bernstein, Brodie & Kondell, P.A., Miami, Fla., 1984—; adj. prof. litigation skills U. Miami Sch. Law, 1989—, chmn. Fla. bar com. on civil trial cert. Mem. ABA, Dade County Bar Assn. (bd. dirs.), Acad. Fla. Trial Lawyers, Assn. Trial Lawyers Am., Am. Judicature Soc., Nat. Inst. Trial Advocacy (chair and faculty mem.), Fla. Criminal Def. Attys. Assn. Home: 3628 Saint Gaudens Rd Miami FL 33133-6533 Office: Cohen Berke Bernstein Brodie & Kondell PA 2601 S Bayshore Dr Fl 19 Miami FL 33133-5419

COHEN, JOHN ARTHUR, retired library science educator, editor; b. Mudgee, Australia, Jan. 14, 1939; s. Howard George and Edna Percival (Johnston) C.; m. Hilary Anne Harris, Aug. 22, 1964; children: Simon, Katherine, Nicholas, Patrick. BA, U. New Eng., Armidale, Australia, 1972; MEd, U. Saskatchewan, 1973; PhD, Ohio State U., 1975; MLitt, U. New Eng., 1993. Ordained priest Anglican Ch. of Australia, 1987. Tchr. NSW Dept. of Edn., 1958-67; lectr. Armidale Teachers'Coll., Armidale, 1968-72, Armidale C.A.E., Armidale, 1975-76; sr. lectr. Goulburn C.A.E., Goulburn, NSW, 1976-83, Charles Sturt U., Wagga Wagga, NSW, 1983-98; ret., 1998; past pres. Kooringal. Author: Children's Literature, 1984; editor: Reading Time, 1986-2000. Sr. active Rotary Club of Kooringal, 1983; justice of peace State of New South Wales, 1960. Fellow Australian Coll. Edn., Royal Soc. Arts, English Speaking Bd. Avocations: classical music, reading. Office: Reading Time, P O Box 62, Ashmont 2650, Australia

COHEN, JOSHUA ROBERT, lawyer; b. East Patchogue, N.Y., Aug. 20, 1963; s. Abraham Cohen and Elizabeth Joan Caufield; m. Robin Renee Conlon, Feb. 28, 1967. BA, Hartwick Coll., 1985; JD, Fordham U., 1991. Bar: Conn. 1991, N.Y. 1992, U.S. Dist. Ct. (so. and ea. dists.) N.Y., 1992. Sr. assoc. Belair & Evans LLP, N.Y.C., 1991-99; ptnr. Garson, Gerspach, DeCorato & Cohen, LLP, N.Y.C., 1999—. Office: Garson Gerspach De Corato & Cohen LLP One Whitehall St New York NY 10004

COHEN, LAURENCE JONATHAN, philosopher, science association administrator; b. London, May 7, 1923; s. Israel and Theresa Cohen; m. Gillian M. Slee, 1953; 4 children. Student, St. Paul's Sch., London; MA, Balliol Coll., Oxford; DLitt. Asst. dept. logic and metaphysics Edinburgh U., 1947-50; lectr.in philosophy U. St. Andrews, Dundee, 1950-57; fellow, praelector Queen's Coll., Oxford, 1957-90; fellow emeritus Queen's Coll., 1990; vis. lectr. Hebrew U., Jerusalem, 1952; Commonwealth Fund fellow Princeton U. and Harvard U., 1952-53; vis. prof. Yale U., New Haven, Conn., 1972-73; vis. fellow Australian Nat. U., 1980; hon. prof. North Western U., Xian, China, 1987; vis. prof. Columbia U., N.Y.C., 1967-68; vis. prof. law Northwestern U., Chgo., 1988. Author: The Principles of World Citizenship, 1954, The Diversity of Meaning, 1962, The Implications of Induction, 1970, The Probable and the Provable, 1977, The Dialogue of Reason, 1986, An Introduction to the Philosophy of Induction and Probability, 1989, An Essay on Belief and Acceptance, 1992; contbr. articles to profl. jours. Mem. nat. exec. com. Coun. Protection of Rural Eng., 1992-95. Served with Brit. Naval Intelligence to Lt. (sp.) RNVR, 1942-45. Mem. Brit. Soc. Philosophy of Sci. (pres. 1977-79), Internat. Union History and Philosophy (co-pres. 1987-91), Brit. Acad. (fellow 1973, chmn. philosophy sect. 1993-96), ICSU (sec.-gen. 1993-96, mem. nat. com. for philosophy 1992—). Avocations: gardening, walking. Office: The Queen's College, Oxford OX1 4AW, England

COHEN, LEONARD (NORMAN COHEN), poet, novelist, musician, songwriter; b. Montreal, Que., Can., Sept. 21, 1934; s. Nathan B. and Marsha (Klinitsky) C. B.A., McGill U., 1955; postgrad., Columbia.; LLB (hon.), Dalhousie U., 1971; LLD (hon.), McGill U., 1992. Author: (poetry) Let Us Compare Mythologies, 1956, The Spice Box of Earth, 1961, Flowers for Hitler, 1964, Parasites of Heaven, 1966, Selected Poems, 1956-68, 1968, The Energy of Slaves, 1972, Death of a Lady's Man, 1979, Book of Mercy, 1984, Stranger Music: Selected Music and Songs, 1993, Dance Me to the End of Love, 1995, (novels) The Favorite Game, 1963, Beautiful Losers, 1966, also articles, songs including music for McCabe and Mrs. Miller, 1971, Natural Born Killers, 1994; rec. artist for Sony Music; albums include I'm Your Man, 1988, The Future, 1992, Cohen Live, 1993, More Best Of, 1997. Decorated Order of Can., 1992; recipient McGill Lit. award, 1956, Que. Lit. award, 1964, Gov. Gen.'s Performing Arts award, Can., 1993; Can. Coun. grantee, 1960-61. Office: c/o Kelley Lynch Stranger Mgmt Inc 419 N Larchmont Blvd Ste 88 Los Angeles CA 90004-3013

COHEN, MARC MAURICE, physician, consultant; b. Melbourne, Australia, Mar. 20, 1964; s. Maurice Marc and Eva Vera (Vogel) C. B in Med. Sci. with honors, Monash U., Melbourne, Australia, 1986, B in Med. Surgery with honors, 1991; PhD, Internat. U. Complementary Medicine, Sri, Lanka, 1994. Resident Alfred Hosp., Melbourne, 1991-92; lectr. Monash U., Melbourne, 1993-97, dir. complementary medicine unit, 1997—; cons. Cybele Herbal Labs., Melbourne, 1999. Author: (with others) Medicine of the Mind, 1999; contbr. articles to profl. jours. including Complementary Therapies in Medicine, Acupunctuer and Electrotherapeutics Rsch., Alternative Therapies in Health and Medicine. Chief med. officer Down to Earth Co-op, Melbourne, 1995-98. Recipient Australian Postgrad. Rsch. award Com-

monwealth Govt., 1996-98. Fellow Australian Med. Acupuncture Soc.; mem. Australasian Integrative Medicine Assn. (v.p. 1998—), N.Y. Acad. Scis. Avocations: fire twirling, clowning, yoga, rollerblading. E-mail: marc.cohen@med.monash.edu.au. Office: Monash U/Complem Med nit, 247 Clayton Rd, Clayton VIC 3168, Australia

COHEN, MARGARET ANNE, literature educator; b. N.Y.C., May 9, 1958; d. Bernard and Phoebe (Freeman) C. BA, Yale U., 1980; MA, NYU, 1982; PhD, Yale U., 1988. Instr. comparative lit. Yale U., New Haven, 1987-88; prof. comparative lit. NYU, 1988—. Author: Profane Illumination: Walter Benjamin and Surrealism, 1993, The Sentimental Education of the Novel, 1999; contbr. articles to profl. jours. Fellow in the Humanities, Yale U., 1986-87, Am. Coun. Learned Soc., 1991-92, NYU, 1992. Mem. MLA. Office: Dept Comparative Lit 19 University Pl Fl 4 New York NY 10003-4556

COHEN, MARK N., business executive; b. Camden, N.J., July 14, 1947; s. Morris and Esther (Sobel) C.; m. Rhoda Posner, Dec. 19, 1971; children: Michele Rebecca, Gregory Leighton. BS, U. Mo., Kansas City, 1969; postgrad., N.Y. Med. Coll., 1969-70; MS, Am. Western U., Tulsa, 1972, PhD, 1976. Cert. state advisor U.S. Congl. Adv. Bd. Founder, pres., chmn. Nat. Recall Alert Ctr., Marlton, N.J., 1973—; founder Acad. Guidance Svcs., Marlton, 1975-88; founder, pres., chmn. Nat. Corp. Svcs., Marlton, 1977—, Nat. Pub. Corp., Marlton, 1979—; pres. Am. Bus. Opportunity Commn., N.J., 1975; bd. dirs., chmn. Health Sytems Agy., Bellmawr, N.J., 1982; treas., bd. dirs. Perinatal Coop./South N.J., Camden, 1983; mem. bd. advisors Free Enterprise, Marlton, 1985; pres. Cohenterprises, Inc., Marlton, 1986, Am. Profl. Copy-Quick Printing Corp., Marlton, 1985, Nationwide Wats Telephone Answering Service, Inc., Marlton, 1985-88, Slim Scents, Inc., 1993, On Air-Everywhere, Inc., 1994, In-Press Express, Inc., 1994. Author: 100 Best Spare Time Business Opportunities Today, 1990, Win Your Weight, Loss War, 1998, Mindstrings and How to Pull Them, 1998. Bd. dirs. Beth Israel Synagogue; trustee Cooper Found./Cooper Hosp. U. Med. Ctr.; assoc. advisor post 65 Explorer Scouts. Recipient Young Exec. of Yr. award Jim Walter Corp., Tampa, Fla., 1972, Disting. Leadership award Am. Security Council Found., 1984, Annual Register award Esquire mag.; named one of 50 Bus. People to Watch, N.J. Bus. Jour. Mem. Am. Hosp. Assn., U.S. C. of C., Am. Assn. Fin. Profls., Nat. Council on Patient Info. and Edn., Nat. Health Lawyers Assn., N.J. Assn. Commerce and Industry (chmn. 1974), Am. Assn. Sch. Adminstrs., Am. Assn. Univ. Adminstrs., Am. Assn. Indiv. Investors, Internat. Coun. Computers Edn., MENSA. Republican. Jewish. Home: 6 Alluvium Lakes Dr Kirkwood Voorhees NJ 08043-4816

COHEN, MARTIN DAVID, lawyer; b. N.Y.C., Aug. 25, 1942; s. Julius and Eleanor Berkowitz Cohen; m. Marilyn Tobin, June 21, 1964 (div.); m. Susan Rae Cohen, May 27, 1984; children: Jason, Julie, Sarah. BS, Pa. State U., 1964; JD, Temple U., 1967. Sr. ptnr. Cohen & Feeley, Easton, Pa., 1967—; bd. dirs. Fulton Bank, Lancaster, Pa., Lafayette Amb. Bank, Lehigh Valley, Pa. Bd. dirs. Northampton County C.C. Found. Bd., Bethlehem, Pa., 1991—, Valley Youth House, Pa., 2000; devel. dir. Pa. State U. Adv. Bd., State College, Pa.; mem. adv. bd. Easton Boys & Girls Club. Recipient Pres.'s award Sales & Mktg. Execs. of Easton, Man & Youth award Boys & Girls Club of Easton, Martin Zippel award. Mem. Pa. Bar Assn., Pa. Trial Lawyers Assn., Northampton County Bar Assn., Judge Clinton Budd Palmer Am. Inn of Ct. Avocations: hiking, tennis, biking. Office: Cohen & Feeley 2940 William Penn Hwy Easton PA 18045-5227

COHEN, MILDRED THALER, art gallery director; b. N.Y.C., Oct. 30, 1921; d. William and Dora (Snow) Intner; m. Seymour R. Thaler, June 17, 1945 (dec. 1976); children: Frederic I., Joan Thaler Zimmer; m. Sidney Cohen, Mar. 20, 1982. BA, Hunter Coll., 1942; BLS, Pratt Inst., 1943. Librarian Queens Borough Pub. Libr., N.Y.C., 1943-44, Mus. of French Art, French Inst., N.Y.C., 1944-46; dir. Marbella Gallery, Inc., N.Y.C., 1971—. Author: (catalogues) Women Students of William Merritt Chase, 1973, Robert Hallowell, 1983, Eliot Clark, 1990, Tonalism, America's Gift to Landscape Painting, 1993, (brochures) Ethel Paxson, 1976, Three Generations of Wiggins, 1981, Samuel Rothbart, 1989, Rachel V. Hartley, 1991, Frank Kleinholz, 1992, Anthony Springer, 1996, Joseph Margulies, 1997, Allen Blagden, 1998, Hildegarde Hamilton, 1999, Samuel Brecher, 1999, James Consor, 2000. Bd. dirs. Lenox Hill Settlement House, N.Y.C., 1955-77. Mem. Appraisers Assn. Am., Hunter Coll. Alumni (pres. Queens chpt. 1951-54, past bd. dirs., pres. scholarship and welfare fund 1958-60, mem. coll. art adv. com., named to Hall of Fame 1973). Democrat. Jewish. Home and Office: 28 E 72nd St New York NY 10021-4234

COHEN, MOSES ELIAS, mathematician, educator; b. U.K., Nov. 30, 1937; s. Elias Moses and Katie (Hey) C.; m. Odette Jockel, Sept. 12, 1963; 1 son, Uri Elie. B.S., London U., 1963; Ph.D., U. Wales, 1967. Research fellow French AEC, 1968; asst. prof. Mich. Tech. U., 1968-69; asst. prof. math. Calif. State U., Fresno, 1969-70; asso. prof. Calif. State U., 1970-74, prof., 1974—; adj. prof. radiology Univ. Calif., San Francisco, 1992—. One-man show Phebe County Gallery, Calif. State U., Fresno; contbr. articles to profl. jours. Univ. scholar Phi Kappa Phi, 1997; co-recipient Best Paper award (research in pattern recognition) Am. Assn. Med. Systems and Informatics, 1985, Outstanding Research (in expert systems) award U. Calif. San Francisco, Fresno campus, 1987, 96, Outstanding Prof. award, 1991. Fellow Am. Inst. Med. Biol. Engring.; mem. AAUP, IEEE (engring. in medicine and biology soc.), Internat. Soc. Computers and Their Applications (bd. dirs.). Home: 7131 N Briarwood Ave Fresno CA 93711-0311

COHEN, MYRON LESLIE, business executive, mechanical engineer; b. N.Y.C., Mar. 7, 1934; s. Henry and Minnie (Pechenik) C.; m. Sally Claire Gilman, June 19, 1955; children: Amy Beth, David Lawrence, Hilary Ann. BSME, Purdue U., 1955; MSME, U. Ala., 1958; PhD, Poly. Inst. Bklyn., 1966. Registered profl. engr., N.J. Rsch. engr. Allegany Ballistics Lab., Hercules, Inc., Cumberland, Md., 1955-56; sr. thermodynamics engr. Rep. Aviation Corp., Farmingdale, N.Y., 1958-60; instr. mech. engring. Poly. Inst. Bklyn., 1960-66; asst. prof. mech. engring. Stevens Inst. Tech., 1966-69, assoc. prof. mech. engring., 1969-77, prof. mech. engring., 1977-78, dir. Med. Engring. Lab., 1975-78; prof. Inst. fur Biokybernetik und Biomedizinische Technik Universitat Karlsruhe, West Germany, 1974-75; dir. R&D hosp. products Chesebrough-Ponds's Inc., Trumbull, Conn., 1978-83; pres. CAS Med. Sys., Inc., Branford, Conn., 1983-91, chmn. bd., exec. v.p., 1991—; v.p. Freshet Press, Rockville Centre, N.Y., 1970-78; pres. C.A.S., Inc., Upper Montclair, N.J., 1975-78; adj. assoc. prof. surgery Coll. Medicine and Dentistry N.J., Newark, 1978-92. Contbr. articles on heat transfer, thermodynamics, tech. applied to medicine, phys. properties human skin, biomed. engring. to profl. jours.; rsch. in rocket propulsion, biomed. engring. V.p. Temple Beth Tikvah, Madison, Conn., 1980-82. Lt. U.S. Army, 1956-58. Recipient Humboldt prize, Sr. U.S. Scientist award Govt. West Germany, 1974, old master Purdue U., 1996; Outstanding Mech. Eng., Purdue U., 1998, Alumni Achievement award Poly. U., 2000. Fellow N.Y. Acad. Medicine; mem. ASME (chmn. stds. com. on med. devices 1982), Assn. Advancement Med. Instrumentation, AAUP, Soc. Biomaterials, Cardiovasc. Sys. Dynamics Soc., AIAA (chmn. N.Y. sect. 1971-72), N.Y. Acad. Scis., Theodore Gordon Flyfishers Club, Conn. River Salmon Assn. (bd. dirs. 1987—), Sigma Xi, Pi Tau Sigma. Home: 401 Three Corners Rd Guilford CT 06437-2523 Office: 44 E Industrial Rd Branford CT 06405-6507

COHEN, OREN SHLOMO, neurologist, researcher; b. Jerusalem, Dec. 13, 1962; s. Avraham and Geula (Spinner) C.; m. Sari Alfi, Mar. 18, 1965; children: Elad, Ofir. MD, Hadassah U., Jerusalem, 1987. Intern Hadassah U. Hosp., 1987, resident in neurology, 1992-97, sr. neurologist, 1997—; instr. Hebrew U. Med. Sch., 1994, lectr., 1999. Contbr. articles to profl. jours. including European Jour. Pharmacology, Neuropharmacology, Brain Rsch., Neurosci. Letters, Harefuah, Jour. Neurol. Scis., Jour. Neurology, Jour. Virology, European Jour. Clin. Pharmacology, Clin. Pharmacology and Therapeutics, Muscle and Nerve, Arthritis and Rheumatism, Neurology, European Jour. Neurology, Jour. Neuro-Oncology. Maj. Israel Def. Forces, 1988-92. Mem. Israeli Med. Assn., Israeli Neurol. Assn., Am. Acad. Neurology, European Neurol. Soc. Home: 27 Moshe Kol, 93715 Jerusalem Israel Office: Hebrew U Hosp, PO Box 12000, 91100 Jerusalem Israel

COHEN, PATRICIA TOWNSEND WADE (LADY PATRICIA TOWNSEND WADE COHEN), molecular biologist; b. Worsley, Lancashire, U.K., May 3, 1944; d. Charles Henry Townsend Wade and Elfrida Robertson; m. Philip Cohen, Feb. 17, 1969; children: Suzanne, Simon. BS, Univ. Coll., London, 1966; PhD, Univ. Coll., 1969. Postdoctoral rsch. fellow dept. genetics U. Wash., Seattle, 1969-71; sci. rsch. coun. fellow dept. biochemistry U. Dundee, Scotland, 1971-72, rsch./tchg. fellow, 1972-83, lectr. biochemistry, 1983-90; sr. scientist Med. Rsch. Coun., Dundee, 1991-93; spl. appointments scientist Dundee, 1994—; hon. reader dept. biochemistry U. Dundee, 1995—; head molecular biology Med. Rsch. Coun., Protein Phosphorylation Unit, Dundee, 1991—. Contbr. numerous articles to profl. jours. Mem. Biochem. Soc. U.K., Genetical Soc. U.K. Avocations: reading, skiing, golf. Office: U Dundee Dept Biochem, MRC Protein Phosphorylation Unit Tayside, DD1 5EH Dundee Scotland

COHEN, PERRY D., management consultant; b. Atlanta, May 27, 1946; s. Bernard W. and Rae Alice Cohen; m. Rosalie Mandelbaum, Aug. 16, 1975; children: Shayna K., Jonah B. BS, Carnegie-Mellon U., 1968; MS, MIT, 1971, PhD, 1979. Assoc. engr. Lockheed Ga. Co., Marietta, 1968-69; rsch. analyst Blue Cross-Blue Shield of Mass., Boston, 1971-72; instr. bus. MIT, Cambridge, 1972-75; rsch. assoc. Assn. Am. Med. Colls., Washington, 1975-77; sr. assoc. Urban Systems Rsch., Washington, 1977-79; pres. Perry Cohen Assocs., Washington, 1979—, Unison Corp., Bethesda, 1987-89; adj. assoc. prof. U. Md., 1991—; dir. health svcs. rsch. Parkinsons Disease Found., 1998—. Contbr. articles to profl. jours. Trustee Group Health Assn., Washington, 1986-92, Consumer Health Found., 1995-96, Medlantic Rsch. Inst., 1998—; trustee Nat. Capital chpt., Am. Parkinson's Disease Assn., 1996-98, v.p., 1997-98. MIT Spl. Rsch. fellow, 1972-75; grantee NIH, 1986-87, Nat. Cancer Inst., 1985-86. Mem. Am. Pub. Health Assn., Manpower Analysis and Planning Soc. (from v.p. to prs. 1981-83), Assn. Health Svcs. Rsch., Acad. Mgmt., Soc. for Health Care Planning and Mktg. Home: 3914 Harrison St NW Washington DC 20015-1938

COHEN, PHILIP, biochemistry educator; b. London, July 22, 1945; s. Jacob Davis and Fanny (Bragman) C.; m. Patricia Townsend Wade, Feb. 17, 1969; children: Emma Suzanne, Simon Daniel. BSc, Univ Coll., London, 1966, PhD, 1969; DSc (hon.), U. Abertay, 1998, U. Strathclyde, 1999. Postdoctoral fellow U. Wash., Seattle, 1969-71; lectr. in biochemistry U. Dundee, Scotland, 1971-78, reader in biochemistry, 1978-81, prof. enzymology, 1981-84, Royal Soc. rsch. prof., 1984—, dir. MRC protein phosphorylation unit, 1990—; mem. discovery adv. bd. Smith-Kline Beacham Pharm. Co., Phila., 1993-96; dir. Wellcome Trust Biocentre, 1997—. Author: Control of Enzyme Activity, 1976, 2d edit., 1983; series editor: Molecular Aspects of Cellular Regulation, 1980—; contbr. more than 400 articles and revs. to sci. jours. Recipient Colworth medal Brit. Biochem. Soc., 1977, Ciba medal, 1992; Prix Van Gysel, Belgian Royal Acads. Medicine, 1992, Louis Jeantet prize for Medicine, 1997, Pfizer Awd. for Innovative Sci., 1999, Dundee City of Discovery Rosebowl, Dundee City Coun., 1993, Anniversary prize European Biochem. Socs., 1977, named Knight Batchelor, 1998, hon. fellow Hannah Rsch. Inst.; fellow Univ. Coll., London. Fellow Royal Soc. Arts, Acad. Med. Scis., Royal Soc. London (Croonian lectr. 1998), Royal Soc. Edinburgh, Royal Coll. Pathologists (hon.); recipient Royal Soc. Edinburgh (Bruce Preller prize 1993). Home: Inverbay II, Invergowrie, Dundee DD2 5DQ, Scotland Office: U Dundee, Dept Biochemistry, Dundee DD1 5EH, Scotland

COHEN, PHILIP HERMAN, accountant; b. Bklyn., Dec. 4, 1936; s. David J. and Toby (Jaeger) C.; m. Susan Rudd; children: Davina Ellen, Tobias Samuel Dory. BS, NYU, 1957. From acct. to ptnr. Touche Ross & Co., N.Y.C., 1957-81; exec. v.p. fin., CFO Integrated Resources, Inc., N.Y.C., 1981-86, sr. exec. v.p. fin., CFO, 1986-90; fin. and real estate cons. Philip H. Cohen & Co., Cedarhurst, N.Y., 1990—; chmn. bd. dirs., pres., CEO FRMT Ltd. (A Bermuda Mut. Ins. Co.), 1996-99, chmn. exec. com., 1999—; bd. dirs. Diwal Corp., Mitcor Corp., Odin Mgmt. Corp., Sy Sims Sch. Bus. Yeshiva U.; chmn. bd. dirs. Fraternity Risk Mgmt. Trust, 1994-99, chmn. exec. com., 1999—; lectr. in field. Bd. dirs. Alpha Epsilon Pi Found., Inc., 1976—, Nat. Interfrat. Conf., 1975-86, Nat. Interfrat. Found., 1996—, State of Israel Bonds, N.Y.; bd. dirs. Sutton Pl. Synagogue, 1984-99, v.p., 1993-99; bd. dirs. joint purchasing com. Fedn. Jewish Philanthropies, 1977-78; mem. Cmty. Bd. Manhattan, N.Y., 1992—; internat. bd. dirs. Hillel Found. for Jewish Student Campus Life, 1999—. Recipient State of Israel Bond Peace award 1983, Accts. Bankers and Fin. award Am. Jewish Congress, 1984, Gold medal Nat. Interfraternity Conf., 1994, Disting. Svc. award Fraternity Exec. Assn., 1999. Mem. Found. Acctg. Edn., Am. Inst. CPA's (real estate com. 1987-90), N.Y. State Soc. CPA's (admissions com. 1968-69, chmn. fin. and leasing com. 1972-74, com. on rels. with the bar 1974-76, com. on real estate acctg. 1976-79, com. ins. 1980-81, fin. acctg. standards com. 1983-86, chmn. mem.-in-industry com. 1981-83, chief fin. officers com. 1984-86, furtherance com. 1986, annual conf. com. 1985-87, com. on ops. 1987-88, bd. dirs. 1983-86, v.p. 1985-86, Outstanding CPA in Industry award 1986), Fin. Execs. Inst., Am. Acctg. Assn., Nat. Assn. Accts., Soc. Ins. Accts., Alpha Epsilon Pi (supreme gov. 1966-73, nat. pres. 1974-76, mem. fiscal control bd. 1977-81, vice chmn. 1981-92, chmn. 1992—), Beta Alpha Psi, Areopagus. Jewish. Club: N.Y. Alumni of Alpha Epsilon Pi. Lodge: Masons. Home: 30 Beekman Pl New York NY 10022-8060 Office: 123 Grove Ave Cedarhurst NY 11516-2302

COHEN, ROBERT, medical device manufacturing and marketing executive; b. Glen Cove, N.Y., Sept. 23, 1957; s. Alan and Selma (Grossman) C.; m. Nancy A. Arey, Jan. 17, 1981. BA, Bates Coll., 1979; JD, U. Maine, 1982. Bar: N.Y. 1983, U.S. Dist. Ct. (so. and ea.) N.Y. 1983. Atty. Pfizer Inc., N.Y.C., 1982-86; asst. corp. counsel, asst. sec. Pfizer Hosp. Products Group, Inc., N.Y.C., 1986-88; v.p. bus. devel., dir. for med. device mfr. and marketer Deknatel Inc., Fall River, Mass., 1988-92; pres., CEO GCI Med., Braintree, Mass., 1992-93; v.p. bus. devel. Sulzermedica USA, Inc., Angleton, Tex., 1993-94, group v.p., 1994-98; v.p. bus. & tech. devel. St. Jude Med., Inc., St. Paul, Minn., 1998—; dir. Horizon Med. Products, Inc., Atlanta, 1998—, CardioFocus, Inc., Boston, 1999—; bd. dirs. Horizon Med. Products, Inc., CardioFocus, Inc. Author: 19th Century Maine Authors, 1978. Mem. ABA, Am. Corp. Counsel Assn. Republican. Home: 18683 Bearpath Trl Eden Prairie MN 55347-3476 Office: St Jude Med Inc One Lillehei Plz Saint Paul MN 55117

COHEN, ROBERT L., film producer; b. N.Y.C., July 7, 1936; s. Edward I. and Shirley (Schiff) C. BA, Pratt Coll., 1959. Baseball player Pitts. Pirates, 1961-63; advt. photographer Ladies Home Journal, N.Y.C., 1963-67; unit prodn. mgr. ABC Network, N.Y.C., 1967-74; producer, pres. Duo Prodns., Inc., N.Y.C., 1974-77; prodn. mgr. various major motion picture orgns., N.Y.C., 1977-80; dir., producer Robert L. Cohen, Inc., N.Y.C., 1980-98; pres., CEO Prodn. Link Internat., 1998—. Producer TV commls., 1967— (4 Clio awards); prodn. mgr. feature film, 1978 (Cannes Best Acting award). Dir. Clean Water Cou8n. N.J.; East Pa. rep. Monmouth County N.J. to Aberdeen N.J., 1998—. Sgt. U.S. Army, 1959-62. Mem. Dirs. Guild Am., Theodore Gordon Flyfishers (dir.), Atlantic Salmon Fedn. Club: Friars. Avocations: fly fishing, sailing, golf. Home and Office: 120 Warren Dr Matawan NJ 07747-1844

COHEN, ROBERT STEPHAN, lawyer; b. N.Y.C., Jan. 14, 1939; s. Abraham and Florence C.; children: Christopher, Ian, Nicholas; m. Stephanie J. Stiefel, Jan. 29, 1998. BA, Alfred U., 1959; LLB, Fordham U., 1962. Bar: N.Y. 1963, U.S. Dist. Ct. (so. and ea. dists.) N.Y. 1964, U.S. Ct. Appeals (2d cir.) 1965. Assoc. Saxe, Bacon & O'Shea, N.Y.C., 1963-68; mng. ptnr., chmn. Morrison, Cohen Singer and Weinstein and predecessor firms, N.Y.C., 1968—; lectr. in field; mem. faculty Am Acad. Psychiatry and the Law, 1984—. Contbr. articles to legal jours. Bd. dirs. N.Y. Pops, 1983—. 1st lt. JAG, USAR, 1965-67. Fellow Am. Coll. Family Trial Lawyers; mem. ABA, FBA, ATLA, N.Y. State Bar Assn., N.Y.C. Bar Assn., N.Y. Acad. Matrimonial Lawyers, Univ. Club (N.Y.C.). Office: 750 Lexington Ave New York NY 10022-1200

COHEN, RONALD J., lawyer; b. Englewood, N.J., Dec. 16, 1950; s. Irwin and Shirley (Kushel) C.; m. Jeanne K. Houser, June 22, 1981; children: Shay, Emily. BA, U. Fla., 1973; JD, U. Miami, 1976. Asst. city atty. City of Miami, 1979-83; assoc. Paul, Landy, Beiley & Harper, Miami, 1983-87; ptnr. Klausner & Cohen, PA, Hollywood, Fla., 1987-97, Ronald J. Cohen, PA, Miami, 1997—. Office: 8100 Oak Ln Ste 403 Miami Lakes FL 33016-7051

COHEN, SELMA, reference librarian, researcher; b. N.Y.C., Mar. 14, 1930; d. George and Rose (Cohen) Unger; m. Irwin H. Cohen, Nov. 19, 1950; children: Barbara Katzeff, Joel. Grad. high sch., William Howard Taft High Sch., 1948. Asst. bookkeeper acctg. dept. Severud, Perrone et al, N.Y.C., 1970-75; asst. bookkeeper acctg. dept. Russell Reynolds Assocs., Inc., N.Y.C., 1976-77, rsch. asst., 1977—, reference libr., 1985—. Chairwoman Scott Tower Charity Com., Bronx, 1976-84, Scott Tower Property Improvement Com., Bronx, 1983-84. Home: 3400C Paul Ave Bronx NY 10468-1042 Office: Russell Reynolds Assocs 200 Park Ave New York NY 10166-0005

COHEN, SOLLY, publishing and exhibition company executive; b. Alexandria, Egypt, May 26, 1946; s. Abraam and Rakelin C.; m. Marina Carafa, Mar. 5, 1988; 3 children. Degree in econs., Hautes Etudes Commls. Bus. Sch, Paris, 1969. Chmn. editl. group Masson, Milan, Italy, 1974-94; chmn. Miller Freeman Group Italy, Milan, 1994—; mng. dir. Fiera Milano Internat., 1994—; chmn. Amic Mostra Convegno, Milan, 1994—. Mem. Italian Assn. Bus. Press. (chmn.). Office: Fiera Milano Internat SpA, Lrgo Domodossola 1, 20145 Milan Italy

COHEN, STANLEY, biochemistry educator; b. Brooklyn, N.Y., Nov. 17, 1922; s. Louis and Fannie (Feitel) C.; m. Olivia Larson, 1951 (div.); children: Burt Bishop, Kenneth Larson, Cary; m. Jan Elizabeth Jordan, 1981. BA, Bklyn. Coll., 1943; MA, Oberlin Coll., 1945, PhD, 1989; PhD in Biochemistry, U. Mich., 1948; PhD, U. Chgo., 1985, Washington U., 1993. Instr. dept. biochemistry and pediatrics U. Colo., Denver, 1948-52; Am. Cancer Soc. fellow in radiology Washington U., St. Louis, 1952-53, assoc. prof. dept. zoology, 1953-59; asst. prof. biochemistry, sch. medicine Vanderbilt U., Nashville, 1959-62, assoc. prof., 1962-67, prof. biochemistry, 1967-86, disting. prof., 1986-2000, Am. Cancer Soc. rsch. prof. biochemistry, 1976, disting. prof. emeritus, 2000—; Charles B. Smith vis. rsch. prof. Sloan Kettering, 1984; Feodor Lynen lectr. U. Miami, 1986, Steenbock lectr. U. Wis., 1986. Mem. editorial bd. Abstracts of Human Developmental Biology, Jour. of Cellular Physiology. Cons. Minority Rsch. Ctr. for Excellence. Recipient Research Career Devel. award NIH, 1959-69, William Thomson Wakeman award Nat. Paraplegia Found., Earl Sutherland Research Prize Vanderbilt U., 1977, Albion O. Bernstein MD award Med. Soc. State N.Y., 1978, H.P. Robertson Meml. award Nat. Acad. Sci., 1981, Lewis S. Rosentiel award Brandeis U., 1982, Alfred P. Sloan award Gen. Motors Cancer Research Found., 1982, Louisa Gross Horwitz prize Columbia U., 1983, Disting. Achievement award UCLA Lab. Biomed. and Environ. Scis., 1983, Lila Gruber Meml. Cancer Research award Am. Acad. Dermatology, 1983, Bertner award MD Anderson Hosp. U. Tex., 1983, Gairdner Found. Internat. award, 1985, Fred Conrad Koch award Endocrine Soc., 1986, Nat. Medal Sci., 1986, 89, Albert and Mary Lasker Found. Basic Med. Research award, 1986, Nobel Prize in physiology or medicine, 1986, Tennessean of Yr. award Tenn. Sports Hall of Fame, 1987, Franklin Medal, 1987, Albert A. Michaelson award Mus. Sci. and Industry, 1987. Fellow Jewish Acad. Arts and Sci.; mem. Nat. Acad. Sci., Am. Soc. Biol. Chemists, Am. Chem. Soc., AAAS, Internat. Inst. Embryology, Internat. Acad. Sci. (hon. internat. coun. for sci. devel.).

COHEN, STEVEN ARTHUR, writer; b. Wichita, Kans., Sept. 9, 1951; arrived in the Netherlands, 1982; s. William Cohen and Celia (Friedman) Cohen. BS in Journalism, U. Kans., 1973. Reporter Wichita Eagle newspaper, 1973-75, Hollywood (Fla.) Sun-Tattler newspaper, 1975-77; communications cons. Phoenix, 1977-79; editor Salt River Project pub. utility, Phoenix, 1979-81; writer Steven Arthur Cohen Communications, Amsterdam, The Netherlands, 1982—; scriptwriter Fiesta Bowl Parade, Phoenix, 1978, 79, 80. Author: (exhbn. catalogue) Anne Frank in the World: 1929-1945, 1985. Publicity dir. Sta. KAET-TV (ednl.), Phoenix, 1980, 1st Annual Am. Heart Assn. Golf Classic, Scottsdale, Ariz., 1978, Ad 2 Phoenix, 1978-81, nat. mem. chmn., 1980, Internat. Green Cross, 1993, Comml. Anglo Dutch Soc., 1996—, John Adams Inst., 1997—. Mem. Am. C. of C. in the Netherlands (newsletter columnist 1989—), U. Kans. Alumni Assn. (life, Phoenix chpt.. pres. 1980), Comml. Anglo Dutch Soc., John Adams Inst. Jewish. Avocations: swimming, traveling, education. E-mail: sacohen@x-s4all.nl. Office: S A Cohen Comm, Cliostraat 18/2, 1077 KH Amsterdam The Netherlands

COHEN, STEVEN MICHAEL, orthodontist; b. Queens, N.Y., Mar. 18, 1966; s. Martin and Joan Cohen; m. Karen D. Cohen, July 20, 1991; children: Rachel, Derek. BA in Biology, Rutgers Coll., 1988; DMD, UMDNJ-NJDS, 1992; MS in Dentistry, cert. in orthodontics, Temple U., 1994. Assoc. program dir. Albert Einstein Med. Ctr., Phila., 1997—. Mem. Am. Assn. Orthodontists, Mid. Atlantic Soc. Orthodontists, So. Dist. Dental Soc. (pres. 1999—). E-mail: phillybraces@juno.com. Office: 2517 S Broad St Philadelphia PA 19148-4309

COHEN, WARREN JARED, journalist; b. N.Y.C., Mar. 5, 1967; s. Abbe and Irene Cohen; m. Alison Meures, Aug. 29, 1998. B Govt., Conn. Coll., New London, 1989. Prof., instr. Northwestern U., Evanston, Ill., 1997-99, Columbia Coll., Chgo., 1998-99; editor U.S. News and World Report, Chgo., 1999—. Contbr.: Merchants of Misery, 1996. Recipient Benjamin Fine award honorable mention, Washington, 1991, award Nat. Press Found., Madison, Wis., 1995, Arthur Burns fellowship Internat. Ctr. Fgn. Journalists, Hamburg, Germany, 1999. Mem. Investigative Reporters and Editors, Chgo. Headline Club. Avocations: ultimatee frisbee, basketball, reading, curling. E-Mail: wjcohen@yahoo.com. Home: 1448 W Evergreen #2 Chicago IL 60622-3213 Office: US News and World Report 2 Prudential Plaza Ste 2310 Chicago IL 60601

COHEN, WILLIAM SEBASTIAN, federal official, former senator; b. Bangor, Maine, Aug. 28, 1940; s. Reuben and Clara (Hartley) C.; children: Kevin, Christopher. AB cum laude, Bowdoin Coll., 1962; LLB cum laude, Boston U., 1965; LLD, St. Joseph's Coll., Windham, Maine, 1974; LL.D., U. Maine, 1975, Western New Eng. Coll., 1975, Bowdoin Coll., 1975, Nasson Coll., 1975, Thomas Coll., 1988, Colby Coll., 1988. Bar: Maine, Mass., D.C. Ptnr. Paine, Cohen, Lynch, Weatherbee & Kobritz, Bangor, 1966-72; instr. U. Maine, 1968-72; asst. county atty. Penobscot County, Maine, 1968-70; U.S. Senator from Maine, 1979-96; sec. defense The Pentagon, 1997—; Mem. Bangor Sch. Com., 1970-71, Bangor City Council, 1969-72, mayor, Bangor, 1972; Trustee Unity Coll.; bd. overseers Bowdoin Coll., 1973-85. Author: Of Sons and Seasons, 1978, Roll Call, 1981, Getting the Most Out of Washington, 1982, A Baker's Nickel, 1986, One-Eyed Kings, 1991, (with Gary Hart) The Double Man, 1985, (with George Mitchell) Men of Zeal, 1988, (with Thomas B. Allen) Murder in the Senate, 1993. Recipient Alumni award for disting. pub. service Boston U., 1976; named to N.E. Hall of Fame Basketball Team, 1962, Silver Anniversary award Nat. Collegiate Athletic Assn., 1987; Outstanding Young Man of Yr. Nat. Jaycees, 1975; James Bowdoin scholar, 1961-62; Alumni Fund scholar, 1962, selected for Balfour Silver Anniversary All-Am. Team, Nat. Assn. Basketball Coaches U.S., 1987. Office: Sec of Def 1000 Defense Pentagon Washington DC 20301-1000

COHEN ADDAD, JEAN-PIERRE, physicist, educator; b. Dieppe, France, Mar. 27, 1939; s. Robert Charles and Suzanne (Hodencq) Cohen A.; m. Claudine Franckel, Dec. 20, 1960 (div. 1994); children: Sylvie, Nicolas; m. Annie Viallat, Feb. 13, 1999; children: Vincent, Jade. DSc, U. Grenoble, 1966. From asst. to maitre-asst. U. Grenoble, France, 1966-67; tech. staff Bell Labs., Murray Hill, N.J., 1967-69; prof. U. Grenoble, 1970—; cons. Rhone-Ponlenc Co., France, 1985—, DSM Co., The Netherlands, 1995—, Pirelli, 1998—. Author: NMR and Fractal Properties on Polymeric Liquids, 1993, Physical Properties of Gels, 1996. Mem. Am. Phys. Soc., French Phys. Soc., N.Y. Acad. Scis. Avocations: skiing, paintings. Office: Lab Spectrometry & Physics, Domaine U, 38402 Saint-Martin d'Heres France

COHEN-SABBAN, NESSIM, auditor, accountant; b. Cairo, Aug. 4, 1930; came to U.S., 1984; s. Haim and Zakia (Baredes) C.-S.; m. Klemy Rodriguez, Apr. 7, 1960 (div. Mar. 1988); children: Haim, Nava, Shimon; m. Liliane Mann-Khasky, Sept. 8, 1988; children: Toufik, Elie, May. Grad., Cairo U., 1956, Tel Aviv U., 1964; postgrad., Touro Coll., 1991-92. CPA. Chief acct. David Ades & Son, Cairo, 1950-57; acct. Lodzia, Holon, Israel, 1957-61, Bank Leumi, Jaffa, Israel, 1961-64; internal auditor Head Office, Bank Le Melakha, Tel Aviv, 1964-78; auditor, acct. 1st Internat. Bank Israel, Tel Aviv, 1979-84, Greatway Co., N.Y.C., 1985, 88; internal auditor Play Knits Inc., N.Y.C., 1988—. Mem. Rabbinical of Bat-Yam, Israel, 1980-84; judge Bat-Yam City Ct., 1982-84. Officer Israel Army, 1961-84. Avocations:

reading poems in English, French, Hebrew and Arabic, helping weak and poor people. Home: 1013 Avenue Y Brooklyn NY 11235-5013 Office: Play Knits Inc 240 W 40th St Fl 3 New York NY 10018-1592

COHEN-TANNOUDJI, CLAUDE NESSIM, physics educator; b. Constantine, Algerie, France, Apr. 1, 1933; s. Abraham and Sarah (Sebba) Cohen-T.; m. Jacqueline Veyrat, Nov. 24, 1958; children: Alain, Joelle, Michel. Student, Ecole Normale Superieure, Paris, 1953-57; PhD in Physics, U. Paris, 1962. Researcher Centre Nat. La Recherche Scientifique, Paris, 1960-64; prof. U. Paris, 1964-73, Coll. de France, Paris, 1973—. Author 5 books. Recipient Julius Edgar Lilienfeld prize Am. Phys. Soc., 1992, Charles Hard Townes medal Optical Soc. Am., 1993, Harvey prize in sci. and tech. Technion, Israel, 1996, Gold medal CNRS, 1996; co-recipient Nobel prize for physics, 1997. Mem. Académie des Sciences, Am. Acad. Arts and Scis., Nat. Acad. Scis., Accademia dei Lincei, Pontitical Acad. Scis. Home: 38 Rue Des Cordelieres, 75013 Paris France Office: Lab Kastler Brossel, 24 Rue Lhomond, 75005 Paris France

COHN, DANIEL ROSS, physicist; b. Berkeley, Calif., Nov. 28, 1943; s. Roy Wolfsohn and Betty (Black) C.; m. Helen Desfosses, Aug. 25, 1967 (div. 1974); 1 child, Adam Robsohn; m. Joanne Brecker, June 10, 1978. BA, U. Calif., Berkeley, 1966; PhD, MIT, 1971. Rsch. scientist, gp. leader Francis Bitter Nat. Magnet Lab., MIT, Cambridge, Mass., 1971-80; div. head Plasma Fusion Ctr., MIT, Cambridge, 1980—; sr. rsch. scientist Nuclear Engring. Dept., MIT, Cambridge, 1980—; acting asst. dir. plasma fusion ctr. MIT, Cambridge, 1992-96; pres., CEO Integrated Environ. Techs., 1996—, vice chmn., 2000—; cons. in field. Editor Jour. of Fusion Energy, 1984-92; contbr. more than 150 articles to profl. jours.; patentee on monitoring and environ. tech. Recipient Discover award for Technol. Innovation, Discover Mag., 1999. Mem. Fusion Energy Div., Am. Nuclear Soc., Am. Phys. Soc., Phi Beta Kappa. Achievements include devel. of new energy and environmental technology. Home: 26 Walnut Hill Rd Chestnut Hill MA 02467-3125 Office: MIT Plasma Fusion Ctr 167 Albany St Cambridge MA 02139-4213

COHN, DAVID V(ALOR), oral biology and biochemistry educator; b. N.Y.C., Nov. 8, 1926; s. Ralph and Clara (Schenkman) C.; m. Evelyn Turner, 1947; children: Robert Warren, Emily. BS, CCNY, 1948; PhD, Duke U., 1952; postgrad., Western Res. U., 1953. Faculty U. Kans. Sch. Medicine, Kansas City, 1953-84, prof. biochemistry, assoc. dean rsch., 1974-82; assoc. chief staff for rsch. devel. VA Med. Ctr., Kansas City, Mo., 1953-82; prof. biochemistry U. Mo., Kansas City, 1971-82; v.p. R&D Immuno Nuc. Corp., Stillwater, Minn., 1982; sci. cons. Immuno Nuc. Corp., Stillwater, 1983—; rsch. prof. oral biology and biochemistry U. Louisville Sch. Medicine, Sch. Dentistry, 1984—, chmn. dept. oral health, 1989-91, chmn. dept. biol. and biophys. scis., 1992-97, univ. dir. tech. devel., 1996-99, asst. v.p. econ. devel. and indsl. rels., 1999—; asst. to v.p. rsch. U. Louisville, 1992-95, asst. v.p. econ. devel. and indsl. rels., 1999—; pres. Internat. Conf. on Calcium Regulating Hormones, 1980-86, exec. sec., 1986-89; mem. bd. sci. counselors Nat. Inst. Dental Rsch., Bethesda, Md., 1980-84; chmn. bd. sci. advisors Endotronics, Inc., 1983-85; bd. dirs. Cambridge Med. Tech., Inc., 1985-86. Editor: Hormonal Control of Calcium Metabolism, 1981, Endocrine Control of Bone and Calcium Metabolism, 1984, Calcium Regulation and Bone Metabolism: Basic and Clinical Aspects, 1987, Calcium Regulating Hormones and Bone Metabolism: Basic and Clinical Aspects, vol. II, 1992; editor in chief Bone and Mineral, 1986-94; contbr. articles to profl. jours. With USN, 1945-46. Grantee USPHS, 1957—, Am. Cancer Soc., 1959-60, VA, 1975-82, Ky. Heart Assn., 1991-93. Mem. AAAS, Am. Soc. Molecular Biology and Biochemistry, Am. Chem. Soc., Gordon Rsch. Conf. Chem. and Biol. of Bones and Teeth (chmn. 1974). Achievements include research on calcium metabolism, parathyroid gland parathormone/ chromogranin biosynthesis and secretion, bone cell growth, differentiation and hormone responsivity, economic development, entrepreneurship. Home: 5709 Apache Rd Louisville KY 40207-1715 Office: U Louisville Health Scis Ctr Dept Bioland Biophys Scis Ctr Louisville KY 40292-0001

COHN, ELLEN GAIL, criminologist; b. Bklyn., Apr. 14, 1963; d. Edgar M. and Marilyn Ruth (Fabricant) C.; m. James Roy Odza, May 29, 1995. BA in Law Enforcement, U. Md., 1984; MPhil in Cirminology, Cambridge (Eng.) U., 1988, PhD in Criminology, 1992. Lectr. U. Md. European Divsn., London, 1990; vis. asst. prof. Ind. U.-Purdue U., Indpls., 1991-93; asst. prof. Fla. Internat. U., Miami, 1993-98, assoc. prof. criminology, 1998—; cons., bd. dirs., mem. steering com. Miami-Dade Police Dept. Citizens' Vol. Program, 1996—; bd. dirs. Youth Crime Watch of Am., Miami, 2000—. Co-author: Evaluating Criminology and Criminal Justice, 1998; mem. editl. bd. Jour. Contemporary Criminal Justice, 1995—; contbr. articles to profl. jours. Recipient Cert. of Achievement, Coll. Urban and Pub. Affairs/Fla. Internat. U., 1997; grantee Nat. Inst. Justice, 1989-91, Fla. State Supreme Ct., 1997-98. Mem. Am. Soc. Criminology, Acad. Criminal Justice Scis. Democrat. Jewish. E-mail: cohne@fiu.edu. Office: Fla Internat U Ecs Rm 411 Miami FL 33199-0001

COHN, LAWRENCE STEVEN, physician, educator; b. Chgo., Dec. 21, 1945; s. Jerome M. an Francis Cohn; m. Harriett G. Rubin, Sept. 1, 1968; children: Allyson and Jennifer (twins). BS, U. Ill., 1967, MD, 1971. Diplomate Am. Bd. Internal Medicine. Intern Mt. Zion Hosp., San Francisco, 1971-72, resident, 1972-73; resident U. Chgo., 1973-74; practice medicine specializing in internal medicine Paramount, Calif.; pres. med. staff Charter Suburban Hosp., 1981-83; mem. staff Long Beach Meml. Hosp., Harbor Gen. Hosp.; clin. prof. medicine UCLA. Maj. USAF, 1974-76. Recipient Disting. Tchg. award Harbor-UCLA Med. Ctr., 1980, 90. Fellow ACP; mem. AMA, Calif. Med. Assn., L.A. County Med. Assn., Am. Heart Assn., Soc. Air Force Physicians, Phi Beta Kappa, Phi Kappa Phi, Phi Lambda Upsilon, Phi Eta Sigma, Alpha Omega Alpha. Home: 6608 Via La Paloma Palos Verdes Peninsula CA 90275-6449 Office: 16415 Colorado Ave Ste 202 Paramount CA 90723-5054

COHN, LINKIE SELTZER, professional speaker, author; b. Dallas, Nov. 22, 1925; d. Nathan A. and Ann (Ravkind) Levine; m. Marcus Seltzer (dec. 1973); children: Adrienne Lithman, Cathy Brenda Negrel, Robert Michael; m. Henry Cohn, 1994. Student So. Methodist U., 1943-44, 76, U. Tex., 1944-45. Profl. dancer Starlight Operettas, Dallas, 1943-44; exec. dir. SW region Am. Friends of Hebrew U., Dallas, 1973; prin. Linkie Seltzer and The Exercise Co., Dallas, 1981, founder Anderson-Cohn Inc., DBA Winners for Life Found.; columnist Achievement Mag., 1985; profl. speaker Love in Business Makes Dollars and Sense, 1981-84; pres. Speakers Source Internat. Speakers Bur., 1989-98; co-owner pubs. Winners for Life. Author: (with Donny Anderson) Winners For Life: A Success Guide for Teenagers Using the Proven Power of Goal Setting, Dallas Community Coll., 1978-85, How to Love & Be Loved, Communicate With Confidence; producer TV series: Covenant, 1972-73; choreographer Turtle Creek Chorale, 1997. Campaign chmn. women's div. Jewish Fedn. Dallas, 1970, pres. women's div., 1972-73; chmn. human rels. commn. Dallas Ind. Sch. Dist., 1968, pub. rels. Greater Dallas Cmty. Rels. Commn., 1983—; judge Dallas Morning News ann. contest Teenage Citizen Tribute, 1984. Named Campaigner of Yr., Jewish Fedn. Dallas, 1969. Democrat. Office: PO Box 12161 Dallas TX 75225-0161

COHN, LUCILE, psychotherapist, nurse; b. Kokomo, Ind., Apr. 17, 1924; d. Jacob and Anna (Kaplan) Kohn; m. Norman Cohn; children: Richard Alan, Robert Irving. PhD, Marquette U. Cert., registered clin. med. hypnotherapist; registered clin. hynotherpist, hosp. hospice grief counsel; diplomate Am. Psychotherapy Assn. Employee counselor Mt. Sinai Med. Ctr., Milw., 1965-70; adminstr. of patient care svcs. Milw., 1970-72; chmn. psychiat. nursing Milw. Region Med. Complex, 1972-82; cons. psychotherapist Cardinal Stritch Coll., Milw., 1982—; pvt. practice psychotherapy Milw., 1980—; prof. nursing Columbia Coll. Nursing, Milw., 1976—, Carroll Coll. Nursing, Waukesha, Wis., 1976—; profl. vol. dying patients and grieving families, nursing homes and hosps.; vol. counselor Alzheimer's and AIDS victims and their families, 1990—; frequent commencement spkr. for registered nurses' graduation. Contbr. chpts. in textbooks. Bereavement counselor St. Mary's Hosp. Hospice, Milw., 1996—; life mem. Women's Am. Orgn. Rehan. Through Tng., Mt. Sinai Med. Ctr. Aux., Jewish Home and Care Ctr., Hadassah; mem. Urban League, Temple Shalom, Pub. Libr. Lit. Soc., Milw. Heart Assn. 1st lt. Nurse Corps, U.S. Army. Named 1 of 2000 women of Achievement, London, 1972, Nurse of Yr., Wis. Nurses Assn., 1977. Mem. ANA, Am. Med. Psychotherapists Assn. (diplomate and fellow), Women's Assn. Orgn. Rehab. Through Tng. (life; pres. Beal chpt., regional v.p.), Am. Assn. Grief Counselors, U. Wis. Union (life). Democrat. Jewish. Avocations: swimming, painting, gardening, world travel, volunteering. Home: 929 N Astor St Unit 2406 Milwaukee WI 53202-3438

COHN-BENDIT, DANIEL MARC, foreign diplomat; b. Montauban/ Frankreich, France, Apr. 4, 1945. Mem. European Parliament, 1999—, mem. com. fgn. affairs/human rights/common security/def. pol, substitute com. on budgets; mem. Group of the Greens/European Free Alliance; chmn. delegation to the EU-Turkey Joint Parliamentary Com. Office: Parlement européen, 288 bd Saint Germain, F-75007 Paris France*

COIA, RAY, foreign currency trader; b. Glasgow, Scotland, Mar. 2, 1965; s. Vincent and Margaret (Quigg) C. MBA, Strathclyde U., Glasgow, 1999. Corp. exec. Nat. West Bank, U.K., 1982-93; corp. mgr. Dun & Bradstreet, U.K., 1993-95; dir. Scotia Capital Markets, U.K., 1996—. Avocations: shooting, car racing. Home: Waukers Farm, Eaglesham, Glasgow G76 ONT, Scotland Address: Burnbank Craigbet Rd, Bridge of Weir, Renfrewshire G76 ONT, Scotland

COIL, SUZANNE MAGDALENA, writer, artist; b. Elizabeth, N.J., Feb. 19, 1935; d. Michael and Magdalena Armbrusht Wolf; m. Jesse Lynell Coil, Sept. 16, 1959; children: Rene Matthias, Astrid Teresa Magdalena. BA, U. Chgo., 1955. Dir. promotion and publicity Houghton Mifflin Co., Chgo., Boston and Geneva, 1955-60; copy chief, dealer and with libr. sales dept. McGraw-Hill Book Co., N.Y.C., 1967-70; advt. mgr. trade books dept. Harcourt, Brace & World Inc., N.Y.C., 1970; mgr. ednl. advt. and promotion Dell Pub. Co. Inc., N.Y.C., 1970-76; mng. dir. ednl. advt. and promotion Bantam Books, N.Y.C., 1976-77, Avon Books, N.Y.C., 1977-83; mgr. ednl. advt. and promotions Franklin Watts Pub. Co., N.Y.C., 1983-89; ind. writer, 1999—; part-time faculty asst. U. Chgo., 1957-58; exam. proctor and grader, U. Colo. Psychology Dept., 1960-61; mem. faculty, chmn. dept. English, asst. to dir. pub. rels. Shimer Coll., Mt. Carroll, Ill., 1961-62. Author: Florida, 1987, George Washington Carver, 1990, The Poor in America, 1989, Poisonous Plants, 1991, Robert Hutchings Goddard: Pioneer of Rocketry and Space Flight, 1992, Harriet Beecher Stowe, 1993 (Notable Book of Yr. NCSS), Campaign Financing, 1994, Mardi Gras, 1994, Mabel, 1994, Christmas on the Gulf Coast, 1994. Named Hon. Citizen New Orleans, 1978. Mem. Ednl. Paperback Assn. (co-founder, past bd. dirs.), Soc. Children's Book Writers and Illustrators, Internat. Guild of Miniature Artisans, The Authors Guild. Avocations: oil painting, miniatures, crafts, jazz piano, literary fiction.

COISNE, HENRI PAUL, electrical wholesaling executive; b. Armentieres, Nord, France, June 21, 1923; s. Henri C. and Marie (Dufour) C.; m. Marie Louise Colombier, Oct. 28, 1947; children: Henri, Martine, Sylvie, Marie-Christine, Laurence. Grad., Air Force Acad., Salon, France, 1943. Cert. engr. Col. French Air Force, Paris, 1943-62; chief executive officer Societe Industrielle Cellulose Alizay, 1962-67; chmn., chief executive officer Sonepar, Paris, 1967—; adminstr. OTRA, The Netherlands, 1982—, SONEDIEL, Spain, 1986—. Decorated Croix de Guerre, Commandeur de la Legion d'Honneur. Mem. Movement des Enterprises de France Internat., Franco-Netherlands C. of C. (adminstr. 1983—), Maison de la Chasse, Tir aux Pigeons. Avocations: skiing, shooting. Office: Sonepar, 37 rue de Liege, 75008 Paris France

COJUANGCO, ANTONIO, telecommunications executive. Pres., CEO Philippine Long Distance Telephone Co., Manila, chmn. Fax: 63-2-818-6800. Office: Ramon Cojuangco Bldg 7th Fl, Makati Ave, Makati Metro Manila The Philippines*

COKER, GURNELLE SHEELY, retired secondary education educator; b. Ballentine, S.C., Nov. 17, 1915; d. George Johnston and Vennie Blanche (Amick) S.; m. Theron Hemingway Coker, Sr., Apr. 10, 1938; 1 child, Theron Hemingway Jr. BA, Winthrop Coll., 1936; M Edn., U. S.C., 1953. Cert. tchr., S.C. Tchr. 5th grade Hebron Consolidated Sch., Cades, S.C., 1936-38; elem. prin. Lexington County, Gilbert, S.C., 1938-41; jr. stock tracer 21st Sub Depot, Columbia (S.C.) Army Air Base, 1942-43; med. technician Station Hosp. Lab., Ft. Jackson, S.C., 1944-46; English tchr. Chapin (S.C.) High Sch., 1948-55; English tchr. Brookland-Cayce High Sch., West Columbia, S.C., 1955-69, English tchr., counselor, 1958-69, dir. guidance, 1969-81, ret., 1981. Author: Reflections of a Soon to be Forgotten Generation, 1998. Sec. Earlwood Little Boys Baseball League, Columbia, 1954-55; mem. Lexington (S.C.) County Mental Health, 1970-75; active fund dr. Am. Heart Assn., Columbia, 1975—. Recipient Life Svc. award Ascension Luth. Ch. Women, 1955, Our Saviour Luth. Ch. Women of Evang. Luth. Ch. Am., 1990; appreciation So. Interscholastic Press Assn., 1964, Meritorious Svc. award Brookland-Cayce Sch. Bd. Trustees, 1981; Spl. Study scholar Lexington Sch. Dist. II, 1959; named Tchr. Yr. Lexington County Dist. II, 1968; portrait hung in Lexington Dist. Wall of Fame, 1992. Mem. Lexington County Ret. Educators Assn. (pres. 1985-87, chmn. com. selects and awards scholarships to H.S. srs.), S.C. Ret. Educators Assn. (coun. dels. 1981-98, sec. 1989-90, S.C. ret. asst. cert. counselor, 1992-98), Gen. Fedn. Womens Clubs Sc.C. (v.p. West Columbia 1992-94, pres. 1994-96, Best Creative Writing award 1995-96, 1st pl. essay, 1995-96, cert. award for Outstanding Accomplishment in Legacy Writing Contest), U. S.C. Alumni Assn., S.C. Classroom Tchr. Assn. (pres. 1964-66), Alpha Delta Kappa (chpt. pres. 1984-86), Delta Kappa Gamma (editor, composer S.C. Alpha Eta State Hist. vol. II 1946-90, contbr. articles and editorials to Alpha Eta state digest 1966-71, pres. chpt. 1994-96, Svc. award 1971, 2d v.p. Alpha Eta state S.C. 1987-89, chmn. com. to write vol. III Alpha Eta state internat. state history 1997—, Internat. Svc. award 1989), Order Eastern Star (worthy matron Earlwood chpt. 1959-60). Republican. Lutheran. Avocations: spectator sports, fishing, reading, family birthday parties, church activities. Home: 1440 Cardinal Dr West Columbia SC 29169-6016

COKER, SALLY JO, sociology educator; b. Springfield, Ill., Aug. 24, 1956; d. Charles D. and Barbara J. (Bailey) Bozeman; m. Joel Dwain Coker, Nov. 7, 1974; 1 child, Corey Alan. BS, U. Houston, 1992, MA, 1995. Rsch. asst. to prof. psychology U. Houston, 1991; student asst. to dean administrn. Lee Coll., Baytown, Tex., 1992; instr. sociology, Am. minorities, social problems, marriage and family, San Jacinto C.C., Pasadena, Tex., 1995—; instr. sociology, Am. minorities, social problems, marriage and family Alvin (Tex.) C.C., 1995-97; instr. sociology, Am. minorities, social problems, orgnl. behavior Lee Coll., 1992—; instr. social inequality, prins. of sociology Am. minorities U. Houston, 1999—; human resource mgmt. spkr. H.B. Zachry, Houston, 1995; tng. cons. H.B. Zachry Co., 1999; human resources cons. Mem. AAUP, Am. Sociol. Assn., Tex. C.C. Tchr.'s Assn., Phi Kappa Phi. Democrat. Home: 3607 Trailwood Dr Baytown TX 77521-4835 Office: U Houston Downtown One Main Houston TX 77002

COKER, WILLIAM SIDNEY, historian, educator; b. Des Moines, July 18, 1924; s. William McKinnon and Myrtle (Spurgeon) C.; m. Hazel Pauline Gaskin, May 27, 1944 (dec. 1990); children: Judy, Nancy, Elizabeth, Terri; m. Frances Camferdam, April 9, 1992 (dec. 1997). BA with distinction, U. Okla., 1959, PhD, 1965; MA, U. So. Miss., 1962. From asst. to assoc. prof. U. So. Miss., Hattiesburg, 1966-69; from assoc. prof. to prof. U. West Fla., Pensacola, 1969-87, chmn. dept. history, 1987-91, prof. emeritus, 1992; dir. Papers of Panton, Leslie & Co. U. West Fla., 1973-87. Author: Spanish Censuses of Pensacola, 1981, (with others) Indian Traders of the Southeastern Spanish Borderlands, 1986 (Patrick award 1986, Phi Alpha Theta award 1986), Florida from Beginning to 1992. Recipient Rsch. award Nat. Historic Pubis. and Records Commn., 1973-87. Mem. Fla. Hist. Soc. (pres. 1997-2000). Home: 615 Bayshore Dr Apt 401 Pensacola FL 32507-3565

COL, PHILIPPE ROBERT, nuclear engineer; b. Diego-Suarez, Madagascar, July 15, 1962. Diploma Engr. Arts and Trades, Ecole Nat. Supérieure, 1986; B, Lycée A. Lumiére, La Ciotat, Bouches du Rhône, France. Engr. in charge Electricité de France Direction de l'Equipement Centre d'Ingénierie Gén.; engr. responsible for tech. group Electricité de France-Gaz de France Svcs. Lot en Garonne; jr. officer mixed tech. svc. Electricité de France-Gaz de France Ctr. d'Agen. Mem. Caisse Mutuelle Complémentaire d'Action Sociale (treas. equestrian sect.). Avocations: tennis, all terrain motorcycles and bikes, photography. Office: EDF-CIG-HM, 140 Ave Viton, Marseille 13401, France

COLACINO, MICHELE, physicist; b. Rome, Mar. 18, 1940; s. Nicola and Marcella (Nicotera) C.; m. Mariarosaria Valensise, Sept. 30, 1972; children: Nicola, Marcella. Degree in Physics, U. La Sapienza, Rome, 1964; Specialization Degree, Ser. Meteo/Nat. Rsch. Coun., Rome, 1966. Fellow Ist Fisica Atmosfera, Rome, 1966-67, scientist, 1968-70, sr. scientist, 1971-90, dir., 1982-94, rsch. dir., 1991—; dir. sub-project P.F. Environment, CNR, Rome, 1979-83; chmn. InterDivsnl. Commn. on History-Internat. Assn. of Geomagnetism and Acronomy, Edinburgh, 1991-95; coord. sub-project Phys. and Chem. Ant. Ath., PNRA, Rome, 1986—. Editor: Series of Proc. of Workshops Italian Research on Antarctic Atmosphere, 1989, 90, 92, 94, 96, 98, Exploring the Earth, 1992, Geophysics: Past Achievements and Future Challenges, 1996, Global Change and History of Geophysics, 1996, Meteorologia, 1995, Climatologia Della Calabria, 1997; contbr. over 180 articles to profl. jours. Lt. Italian Air Force, 1965-66. Mem. Italian Phys. Soc., Italian Soc. Applied Meteorology, Deutschen Geophysikalischen Ges., Italian Geophys. Assn. (chmn. 1996—). Roman Catholic. Avocations: classical music, philosophical reading, soccer, swimming.

COLAIANNIA, LOUIS MARIO, construction executive, dentist, composer, pianist; b. Denver, Jan. 28, 1955; s. Louis Andrew and Rose Marie Colaiannia; 1 child, Louis Adam. DDS, U. Colo., 1980. Lic. dentist, Colo. Dentist Denver, 1980-98; dental dir., exec. dir. Safeguard Health Plans, Anaheim, Calif., 1996; pres. Colaiannia Enterprises Inc., Wheatridge, Colo., 1998—; CEO Dun-Rite Enterprises Inc., Wheatridge, 2000—; advisor Songs Across the Sea, Littleton, Colo., 1998—. Composer, pianist (music CD) Corners of the Soul, 1996, Sailing on a Dream, 1998, (symphony) Colaiannia's First Symphony, 2000; internat. concert pianist. Bd. dirs. Evergreen (Colo.) Music Festival, 2000; presenter numerous benefit concerts, nationwide, 1996—. Mem. Sons of Italy Lodge. Avocations: mountain climbing, various sports. Home: 5753 W 61st Dr Arvada CO 80003-5158 Office: Colaiannia Enterprises Inc 4800 Wadsworth Blvd Ste 400 Wheat Ridge CO 80033

COLAK, DILEK, researcher; b. Aksehir, Turkey, May 29, 1970; d. Halil and Ulfet Colak; m. Namik Kaya, Aug. 31, 1997; 1 child, Ibrahim Hamza. BS, Bilkent U., Ankara, Turkey, 1991, MSc, 1993; PhD, Ohio State U., 2000. Grad. rsch., tech. assoc. Bilkent U., 1991-93; grad. rsch. asst. U. Mich., Ann Arbor, 1993-94; grad. rsch. assoc. Ohio State U., Columbus, 1994-2000; mem. organizing com. Bilcon Internat. Conf. on Lightwave Tech. and comms., ankara, 1991; tchr. asst. Bilkent U., 1991-93. Contbr. articles, papers to profl. publs.; author 24th Gen. Assembly Internat. Union Radio Sci., 1993 (Young Scientist award). Mem. IEEE Antennas and Propagatio Soc., Soc. Women Engrs. Avocations: reading, teaching, biking, tennis. Fax: (614) 292-7297. E-mail: colak.1@osu.edu. Home: 700 Cuyahoga Ct Columbus OH 43210-1076 Office: Electrosci Lab 1320 Kinnear Rd Columbus OH 43212-1156

COLAKOGLU, NURI M(EHMET), television broadcasting executive, publisher; b. Izmir, Turkey, June 19, 1943; s. Hasan and Bertil (Mutafoglu) C.; m. Ayse Iffet Akmen, 1981; children: Hasan, Fatma, Bertil. BA in Polit. Sci., Ankara U., Turkey, 1967. Prodr. BBC, London, 1981-87, Milliyet, Istanbul, 1987-88; dep. gen. mgr. TRT, Ankara, 1988-89; pres. Show TV, Istanbul, 1991-95; chmn. Intermedia, Istanbul, 1989—; CEO, chmn. NTV, Istanbul, 1996—. Mem. TV Broadcasters Assn. (chmn. 1998—). Office: NTV, Eski Buyukdere Cad 61, 80560 Maslak, Istanbul Turkey

COLANDER-RICHARDSON, LATASHA, Olympic athlete; b. Portsmouth, Va., Aug. 23, 1976. Degree in comms., U. N.C., 1998. Winner Gold Medal 4x400 meter relay U.S.A. Track and Field Team, Sydney, 2000. Office: USA Track and Field Team One RCA Dome Ste 140 Indianapolis IN 46225*

COLANGELO, JAMES JOSEPH, psychotherapist; b. Jamaica, N.Y., Jan. 8, 1950; s. Joseph and Amalia (Bove) C.; m. Kathy DeGuardi, Nov. 12, 1983; children: Nicole, Steven, Christina. BA, Manhattan Coll., 1971; MSEd, St. John's U., 1974; PD, L.I. U., 1987, cert. in marriage, family therapy, 1987; postgrad., So. Calif. U. Diplomate Am. Bd. Sexology; cert. clin. mental health counselor; nat. cert. counselor; registered profl. hypnotherapist; bd. cert. sex therapist; cert. sex counselor. Ind. community mental health counselor Queens, N.Y.; caseworker N.Y.C. Dept. Social Svcs., Queens; clin. cons. Ea. Met. Counseling and Consulting Svcs., Queens; supr. Dept. Health & Human Svcs., Adminstrn. Children & Families, N.Y.C.; specialist Children and Families Program (DHHS/ACF); adj. faculty C.W. Post Ctr., L.I. U.; EEO counselor; mem. Region II AIDS com., DHHS. Recipient C. Eugene Morris award in mental health counseling L.I. U., 1992; named to Nat. Disting. Svc. Registry in Counseling, 1990. Mem. ACA, Am. Assn. Marriage and Family Therapists (clin., approved supr.), Am. Assn. Profl. Hypnotherapists, Am. Assn. Sex Educators, Counselors and Therapists (cert.), Am. Psychotherapy Assn. (diplomate), Internat. Assn. Marriage and Family Counselors, N.Y. Assn. Marriage and Family Counselors, N.Y. Mental Health Counselors Assn. (v.p. N.Y.C. area).

COLANGELO, ROCCO, JR., sales executive; b. Hazleton, Pa., Sept. 8, 1964; s. Rocco and Blanche (Farace) C. BSBA summa cum laude, Ind. (Pa.) U., 1986; MBA, U. Rochester, 1988. Mktg. coord. Quality Beverage Distbr. Hazleton, Inc., 1988—; tng. for intervention procedures by servers of alcohol trainer Health Communications, Inc., Washington, 1990—. Mem. Beta Gamma Sigma. Republican. Roman Catholic. Home: 1609 N Lee Ct Hazleton PA 18201-9495 Office: Quality Beverage Distr 695 S Poplar St Hazleton PA 18201-7793

COLARDYN, FRANCIS ACHILLE, physician; b. Kortrijk, Belgium, Dec. 3, 1944; s. Evariste and Carolina (Tarkanyi) C.; m. Michelle Fauconnier, July 10, 1967 (div. 1989); children: Gregory, Anouk; m. Marie-Antoinette Van Den Berghe, Sept. 10, 1989 (div. 1993). MD, State U., Ghent, Belgium, 1970, postgrad., 1973-76, specialist in internal medicine degree, 1975. Asst. in internal medicine Univ. Hosp., Ghent, 1970-75, asst. prof. intensive care unit and emergency room, 1976-86, head dept. intensive care, 1981—, prof. intensive care, 1986—; full prof. U. Ghent, 1997—; head physician Ghent Univ. Hosp., 1999—; pres. dept. medicine Internat. Faculty Schelde, 1994—; mem. Nat. Coun. on Blood, 1995—; pres. Commn. of Recognition in Intensive Care, 1996; bd. dirs. Aurora-Av Hosp. Mem. med. adv. bd. Internal Medicine Digest, 1983-87. Mem. Commn. to the Ministry of Health for med. urgencies, 1976-85. Mem. Belgium Soc. Ultrasonagraphy, Belgian Soc. Med. Informatics, Belgian Soc. Intensive Care (bur., mem. tchg. commn., pres. 1993-94), Belgian Assn. Burn Injuries, Belgian Soc. Oxygen Metabolisms, European Soc. Intensive Care Medicine (mem. coun. 1996—), Toxicological Soc. Belgium and Luxembourg, Belgian Working Group on Cardiac Pacing and Electrophysiology, Am. Soc. Microbiology, Dutch-Belgian Soc. for A.R.D.S. (bd. dirs. 1990—), Soc. Critical Care Medicine, European Soc. Parenteral and Enteral Nutrition, Reanimation Soc. French Lang., Flemish Soc. Clin. Nutrition Metabolism (founding), N.Y. Acad. Scis. Office: Univ Hosp, De Pintelaan 185, B 9000 Ghent Belgium

COLAS, GILLES F., company executive; b. Avignon, Vaucluse, France, Dec. 2, 1948; s. Philippe and Françoise (Pellequer) C.; m. Françoise Pouzenc, June 22, 1972; children: Antoine, Julie, Louis. Degree in civil engring., Ecole Nat. Ponts et Chaussees, Paris, 1971; MS in Indsl. Engring., Stanford U., 1972. With Flat Glass br. Saint-Gobain Group, Paris, 1973-80, indsl. v.p. Flat Glass br., 1982-86; CEO Saint-Gobain de Colombia, Bogota, 1980-82; Vegla CEO Saint-Gobain Group, Aachen, Germany, 1986-92; sr. v.p. corp. planning Compagnie de Saint-Gobain, Paris, 1992—. Officer French Army Air Res. Decorated chevalier Nat. Order of Merit (France). Mem. Polo Club Paris, Golf Club Joyenval. Home: 16 rue de la Ferme, 92200 Neuilly France Office: Compagnie de Saint-Gobain, Les Miroirs 18 Ave D'Alsace, 92096 La Defense France

COLBATH, BRIAN (BRIAN COLBATH WATSON), actor, script and live performance writer; b. Port Washington, N.Y., July 14; s. H. Desmond Watson and Mary (Colbath) Watson Haynes. BS in Speech and Drama, Ithaca Coll., 1965. Cert. tchr., N.Y. Tchr. speech Canandaigua (N.Y.) Acad., 1965-67; speech pathologist West Seneca (N.Y.) Ctrl. Schs., 1967-70; v.p. Projects Plus, Inc., N.Y.C., 1994—; mem. Blue Ribbon panel Daytime Emmy Awards, N.Y.C., 1985-91. Appearances include daytime TV programs, Tony Awards show, N.Y.C., 1989-99, various prodns. Studio Arena Theatre, Buffalo; scripwriter indsl. films; writer night club acts. Named one of Outstanding Young Men of Am., 1970. Mem. AFTRA,

SAG, Actors' Equity. Home: 15 W 67th St Apt 2RW New York NY 10023-6226 Office: Projects Plus Inc 145 W 45th St Ste 300 New York NY 10036-4008

COLBERT, BENJAMIN, English educator; b. Detroit, Oct. 30, 1961; arrived in U.K., 1994; s. Edward and Shirley Mae (Silverstein) C.; m. Hilary Clare Weeks, Sept. 4, 1993. BA summa cum laude, Tulane U., 1983; MPhil, Oxford (Eng.) U., 1988; PhD, UCLA, 1996. ESL instr. Enosi Sch. Fgn. Langs., Athens, Greece, 1987-89; tchg. fellow UCLA, 1989-93; sr. lectr. English U. Wolverhampton, Dudley, U.K., 1994—; adj. instr. Southeastern Coll., Athens, 1988-89. Overseas Grad. scholar St. Catherine's Coll., Oxford, 1985-87. Mem. Keats-Shelley Assn. (sustaining mem., conf. fellow N.Y. Pub. Libr. 1992), Brit. Assn. Romantic Studies, Phi Beta Kappa. Office: U Wolverhampton, Castle View, Dudley DY1 3HR, United Kingdom

COLBERT, EDWARD JAMES M., astronomer; b. Bklyn., Dec. 5, 1966; s. Edward Paul and Elaine (Messore) C.; m. Pamela Quattro, June 29, 1996. BS, U. Ill., 1987, MS, 1988; PhD, U. Md., 1997. Spacecraft thermal design engr. Johns Hopkins U. Applied Physics Lab., Laurel, Md., 1988-91; grad. rsch. fellow Space Telescope Sci. Inst., Balt., 1994-97; rsch. fellow NASA, Greenbelt, Md., 1997-99; sr. sci. software mgr. Space Tel Sci. Inst., Balt., 1999—. Grantee NASA, 1999. Mem. Am. Astronomical Soc., AIAA. Avocations: ceramics, writing, reading. Office: Space Telescope Sci Inst 3700 San Martin Dr Baltimore MD 21218-2464

COLBERT, MARGARET MATTHEW, artist; b. N.Y.C., Apr. 18, 1911; d. William Diller and Kate (Lee) Matthew; m. Edwin Harris Colbert, July 8, 1933; children: George, David, Philip, Daniel, Charles. BFA, Calif. Coll. Arts and Crafts, 1931. Sci. illustrator Am. Mus. Natural History, N.Y.C., 1931-33. Contbr. numerous illustrations to books; executed murals of extinct life for Mus. No. Ariz., Big Bend Nat. Pk., Petrified Forest Nat. Pk., Albuquerque Natural History Mus.; one-person show Mus. No. Ariz., 1984; exhibited in group shows Mus. No. Ariz., 1984. Recipient engraved crystal award Soc. Vertebrate Paleontology, plaque Dinosaur Soc. Avocations: watercolor and oil portraits, ceramics, various crafts.

COLBERT, SALLYANN, anaesthetist; b. Galway, Ireland, June 4, 1964; d. Dominic and Doreen (Hoade) C.; m. David Patrick Farrell; 1 child, Conor Sebastian Colbert Farrell. MB Bch Bao, U.C.G., 1988; FFA, R.C.S.I., 1993. Intern Canberra Hosp., Australia, 1988-89; anaesthetic house officer Dublin, Ireland, 1990-93; rsch. registrar Paris, 1994-95; sr. registrar E.H.B., Dublin, 1996-98; sr. lectr. Mater Hosp., Dublin, 1998—; mem. Faculty of Anesethshists. Contbr. articles to profl. jours. Mem. Goethe Inst. Choral Orgn. Medal winner Glaxo Wellcome, 1994. Roman Catholic. Avocations: sing writing, mountain climbing, playing piano, reading. Home: 61 Nutley Ln, Dublin 4, Ireland

COLBEY, RICHARD, barrister, writer; b. Watford, Eng., May 3, 1960; s. Philip and Daphne (Matthews) C.; m. Emma Prinsley, May 24, 1994; children: Sarah Adele, James Samuel, Melanie Victoria. LLB, Exeter (Eng.) U., 1982. Barrister, 1984. In ind. practice London and Portsmouth, Eng., 1985—. Contbr. articles to The Guardian, The Daily Telegraph, The Ind., The New Statesman, The New Law Jour., The Solicitors' Jour. Avocations: soccer, cricket, travel, dinghy sailing. Office: Francis Taylor Bldg, Francie Taylor Bldg, Temple, Tanfield Chambers, London EC4Y7BB, England

COLBURN, DAVID DUNTON, investment manager; b. San Mateo, Calif., Aug. 18, 1958; s. Richard Dunton and Joan Francis (Garber) C.; m. Carolyn Louise Hadley, Sept. 30, 1989; children: Margaret Hadley, Ethan Dunton. BA, Harvard U., 1980; MBA, U. Pa., 1989. V.p. Bank of Am., L.A., 1981-87; investment mgr. CED Mgmt. Svcs. Inc., Northbrook, Ill., 1989-91; mng. ptnr. Lincolnshire Assocs., Ltd., 1991—, Dunsinane Capital Ptnrs., Ltd., 1995—; dir. Atchison Casting Corp., Haskel Internat., Inc. Mem. Harvard Club Chgo., Wharton Club Chgo. Office: 555 Skokie Blvd Ste 555 Northbrook IL 60062-2854

COLBURN, RICHARD DUNTON, business executive; b. Carpentersville, Ill., June 24, 1911; s. Cary R. and Daisy (Dunton) C.; children: Richard Whiting, Carol Dunton, Keith Whiting, Christine Isabel, David Dunton, McKee Dunton, Daisy Dunton. Student, Antioch Coll., 1929-33. Pres. Consol. Foundries Mfg. Corp. (and predecessors), 1944-64; underwriting mem. Lloyds of London. Home and Office: 1120 La Collina Dr Beverly Hills CA 90210-2616 also: 30 Chester Sq, London SW1W 9HT, England

COLCHESTER, CHARLES MEREDITH HASTINGS, charitable trust executive; b. London, Jan. 12, 1950; s. Halsey Sparrowe and Rozanne Felicity Hastings (Medhurst) C.; m. Serena Laura Peabody North, July 3, 1976; children: Alexander, Benjamin, Tamara, Zachary, Chloe, Zoe. BA with honors, Magdalen Coll., Oxford U., 1972. Dir. Well Trust, U.K., 1978, Initiative Project Trust, U.K., 1980; gen. dir., exec. dir. Christian Action Res. & Edn., U.K., 1987-94; gen. dir. CARE for the Family, U.K., 1997; dir. Well Marine Reinsurance Advs. Ltd., U.K., 1986-94, Tear Fund, U.K., 1989-94; exec. dir. CARE, U.K., 1995—; dir. Ctr. for Bioethics and Pub. Policy, U.K., 1998—, World Transformers Miny, 1998—; chmn. Dolphin Sch. Trust, U.K., 1988—, Ctr. for Bioethics and Pub. Policy, U.K., 1995—, P&P Trust, 1998—; trustee Swinfen Charitable Trust, 1999—. Editor Light and Salt Mag., 1990, CARE Mag., 1985-95. Ch. warden Holy Trinity Brompton, London, 1978-93, St. Paul's Anglican Fellowship, 1999-2000, St. Mary's Bryanston Sq., 2000. Arden scholar, 1969. Mem. Travellers Club. Anglican. Avocations: family, water colouring, travel, reading. Fax: 020 7233 0983. Home: 59 Mayford Rd, London SW12 8SE, England Office: CARE, 53 Romney St, London SW1P 3RF, England

COLDEWEY, WILHELM GEORG, geologist, educator; b. Lüdinghausen, Germany, Oct. 22, 1943; s. Georg and Ilse Wilhelmine (Blömker) C.; m. Angelika Finger, Aug. 22, 1987; 1 child, Linda. Diploma in geology, U. Muenster, 1970, D, 1975. Head of dept. Deutsche Montan Tech., Germany, 1990-99; prof. applied geology U. Muenster, Germany, 1999—; lectr. Ruhr-Univ., Bochum, 1981-91, Technische univ., Clausthal-Zellerfeld, 1987; sec. Fachsection Hydrogeologie, hannover, 1988-92; mem. adv. bd. Deutsche Geologische Gesellschaft, Hannover, 1997—. Author: Hydrogeologie, Hydrochemie und Wasserwirtschaft im mittleren Emschergebiet, 1976, Leitfaden zur Grundwasseruntersuchung im Festgestein bei Altablagerungen und Altstandorten, 1991; editor DMT Berichte Forschung und Prufung, 1990; assoc. editor Grundwasser, 1996-99. Mem. Internat. Assn. Hydrogeologists, Internat. Minewater Assn., Berufsverband Deutscher Geologen. Office: U Muenster Dept Geology, Corrensstr 24, 48149 Muenster Germany

COLDITZ, PAUL BERNARD, perinatal medicine educator, medical researcher; b. Australia, Dec. 30, 1951; s. Bernard Trevor and Doris (Wright) C.; m. Rhonda Kathleen Jarrett, Dec. 30, 1972; children: Stephen, Michael, Jennifer. MB BS, U. NSW, 1977, M in Biomed. Engring., 1985; PhD, Oxford (Eng.) U., 1988. Registrar The Children's Hosp., Sydney, 1980-83, neonatal fellow, 1984; rsch. scholar Oxford U., 1985-88; dir. Neonatal Care Unit King George V Hosp./, Sydney, 1989-91; prof. perinatal medicine U. Queensland, Brisbane, 1992—. Author: Obstetrics and the Newborn, 1997, (interactive CD ROM) Clinical Examination of the Newborn, 1998; contbr. articles to profl. jours. Bd. dirs. SIDS, 1994%; mem. sci. com. Bonnie Babes Found. Fellow Royal Coll. Paediatrics and Child Health, Royal Australasian Coll. Physicians; mem. Internat. Soc. Perinatal Medicine, Paediatric Rsch. Soc. Australia and New Zealand (pres. 1994-97), Perinatal Soc. Australia and New Zealand, Neonatal Soc. (Eng.), Australian Soc. Med. Rsch. Office: Perinatal Rsch Ctr, Royal Womens Hosp, Brisbane QLD 4029, Australia

COLDWELL, DAVID ALASTAIR, business administration educator; b. Calcutta, India, June 21, 1948; s. Newcombe Spence and Shiela Houston (Thomson) C.; m. Kathryn Jill McBride, Dec. 21, 1974; children: Jennifer, Alastair, Sarah. BSc with honors, London U., 1970; MA, U. South Africa, Pretoria, 1977, D Lit. and Philosphy, 1980, BA, 1984, BA in Econs., 1987. Tng. officer Road Transport Industry Tng. Bd., London, 1971-74; rschr., sr. rschr. NIPR, Johannesburg, South Africa, 1974-81; sect. head, rsch. cons. Chamber Mines Rsch. Orgn., Johannesburg, 1981-91; sr. lectr., assoc. prof., then prof. U. Natal, Durban, South Africa, 1991—. Contbr. articles to profl. jours. Recipient Merit award Union Carbide, 1983. Mem. Inst. Pers. and Devel., Internat. Inst. Social Econs. Anglican. Avocations: swimming, safaris, militaria. Office: U Natal, King George V Ave, 4000 Durban Natal Republic of South Africa

COLE, CAROL ALMA TOMLINSON, classical musician; b. San Francisco, Dec. 30, 1954; d. Frank Jack Tomlinson and Alma Georgina Jenkins; m. David Wallace Cole, Aug. 17, 1975; children: Philip Alphaeus, Tatiana Rosa. Artist diploma, Curtis Inst. Music, 1974. Concertmaster I Solisti Aquilani, L'Aquila, Italy, 1985-89; assoc. concertmaster Fla. Philharm. Orch., Ft. Lauderdale, Fla., 1991-98; chamber music coord. Summer String Acad. Ind. U., Bloomington, 1995—; artist in residence Dreyfoos Sch. Arts, W. Palm Beach, Fla., 1999—. Solo violinist Bernstein Serenade, 1971; 1st violinist La Scala Orch., Milan, Italy, 1975, Vancouver (Can.) Symphony Orch., 1975-79; (CD) The Florida Philharmonic - Music by Walton, 1992; concertizing violinist, 1976—; founder, performer 1807 & Friends Chamber Music Series, Phila., 1980—, Pocono Chamber Music Festival, Stroudsburg, Pa., 1980-87; founding mem., violinist Sagee Piano Trio, Miami, 1997—; violinist (CD) Sagee Trio - First Release, 2000. Vol. performer State Hosp. Tours, Marin County, Calif., 1968-69, Concerti per Tutti, Abruzzo, Italy, 1984-89, Fla. Philharm. Outreach Concerts, S. Fla., 1991—; bd. dirs., musical adv. Young Artist Chamber Orch., Ft. Lauderdale, 1999—. Recipient 1st place San Francisco Young Artists Competition, 1967, 1st pl. Internat. Violin Competition of Stresa, Italy, 1984; named finalist Internat. Violin Competition Romano Romanini, 1984, II Concorso Internat. Violin Lipizer, 1985. Mem. NARAS (voting), Am. String Tchrs. Assn. (state chair nat. competition 1998—), Music Tchrs. Nat. Assn., Suzuki Assn. Am. (voting), Curtis Inst. Music Alumni Assn. (class rep. 1998—), Fla. Fedn. Music Clubs. Avocations: painting, dancing, biking, cooking. Office: Dreyfoos Sch Arts Tamarind Ave Palm Beach FL 33480

COLE, CHARLES DEWEY, JR., lawyer; b. Lower Merion Twp., Pa., Aug. 12, 1952; s. Charles Dewey and Margaret Ann (Leach) C. AB, Columbia U., 1974; JD, St. John's U., Jamaica, N.Y., 1979; ML Info. Sci., U. Tex., 1982; LLM, NYU, 1988; LLM in Environ. Law, Pace U., 1993; LLM in Trial Advocacy, Temple U., 1999. Bar: N.Y. 1980, Tex. 1980, N.J. 1986, D.C. 1988, U.S. Dist. Ct. (we. and ea. dists.) Tex. 1980, U.S. Dist. Ct. (so. and ea. dists.) N.Y. 1980, U.S. Dist. Ct. (no. dist.) Tex. 1982, U.S. Dist. Ct. (no. dist.) N.Y. 1983, U.S. Dist. Ct. (we. dist.) N.Y. 1984, U.S. Dist. Ct. N.J. 1986, U.S. Dist. Ct. D.C. 1994, U.S. Ct. Internat. Trade 1980, U.S. Tax Ct. 1984, U.S. Ct. Appeals (5th and 11th cirs.) 1981, U.S. Ct. Appeals (Fed. cir.) 1982, U.S. Ct. Appeals (2d cir.) 1984, U.S. Ct. Appeals (D.C. cir.) 1987, U.S. Ct. Appeals (3d cir.) 1993, U.S. Supreme Ct. 1984; solicitor, Eng. and Wales, 1995. Law clk. to chief judge U.S. Dist. Ct. (ea. dist.), Beaumont, Tex., 1979-80, U.S. Ct. Appeals (5th cir.), Austin, Tex., 1981-82; assoc. Moore, Berson, Lifflander & Mewhinney, Garden City and N.Y.C., N.Y., 1982-85; assoc. and ptnr. Newman Schlau Fitch & Burns P.C., N.Y.C. and Mineola, N.Y., 1985-88; assoc. Meyer, Suozzi, English & Klein, P.C., Mineola and N.Y., 1988-95; of counsel Newman Fitch Altheim Myers, P.C., N.Y.C. and Newark, 1995—; instr. trial techniques program Hofstra Law Sch., 1994—; instr. intensive trial advocacy program Widener Law Sch., 1999—. Author: Law Books as a Charitable Contribution, 1975, The EPA Lender Liability Regulations: EPA's Questionable Authority to Promulgate the Regulations as Part of the National Contingency Plan, 1993; contbr. book revs. to profl. publs. Mem. The Law Soc., N.Y. State Bar Assn. (comml. and fed. litigation sect., sec. com., appellate practice com.), N.J. State Bar Assn., D.C. Bar, N.Y. County Lawyers Assn. (com. on fed. cts.), Maritime Law Assn. U.S. (proctor), Bar Assn. 5th Fed. Cir., Am. Assn. Law Librs., Law Libr. Assn. Greater N.Y., Brit. and Irish Assn. Law Librs., Osgoode Soc., Am. Soc. for Legal History, Soc. Advanced Legal Studies, Supreme Ct. Hist. Soc., Selden Soc., Federalist Soc. for Law and Pub. Policy, Scribes (bd. dirs., chair brief-writing competition com.), Clarity. Republican. Home: 16 94th St Apt 3B Brooklyn NY 11209-6643 Office: Newman Fitch Altheim Myers PC 14 Wall St New York NY 10005-2101

COLE, CHARLES DUBOSE, II, law educator; b. Monroeville, Ala., May 14, 1938. BSBA, Auburn U., 1960; JD cum laude, Samford U., 1966; LLM, NYU, 1971; D (hon.), Faculdade Marcelo Tupinamba, Sao Paulo, Brazil, 1991. Bar: Ala. 1966, U.S. Supreme Ct., 1971, U.S. Ct. Appeals (fed. cir.) 1997, U.S. Ct. Internat. Trade, 1997. Law clk., assoc. atty. Porterfield & Sch., Birmingham, Ala., 1965-66; prof. law Cumberland Sch. Law Samford U., Birmingham, 1966-75, 81—; Lucille S. Beeson prof. law and dir. internat. programs, master comparative law degree program Cumberland Sch. Law, Birmingham, Ala., 1993—; dir. permanent study commn. Ala. Jud. System, 1972-74; dir. Ala. Jud. Conf. Criminal Justice Survey, 1973; dir. adv. com. Ala. jud. article implementation Ala. Dept. Ct. Mgmt., 1974-75; dir. so. regional office Nat. Ctr. for State Cts., Atlanta, 1975-79; adminstrv. dir. cts. Commonwealth of Ky., Frankfort, 1979-81; lectr. Cumberland Inst. for Continuing Legal Edn., Ala. Continuing Legal Edn., Josephson/Kluwer Bar Rev. Ctr. Am., Inc., 1967-87; law and social sci. adv. coun. Coll. Liberal Arts/Auburn U., 1991-96, chmn. 1992-94, dean's coun., 1996—; chmn. profl. adv. com. Office Advancement Auburn U., 1992-93; reporter civil justice adv. group Middle Dist. Ala., 1991-93; del. Moscow Conf. on Law and Econ. Coop., The Kremlin Palace, 1990; legal specialist (pro bono) Parliament of Ukriane, 1993; v.p. faculty Samford U., 1989-90; policy com. mem. Cumberland Sch. Law, 1989-92, 2000—; mem. faculty exec. com. Samford U., 1988-89; del. U.S./Japan Bilateral Session, 1988; presenter U.S. Info Agy., Internat. Meeting Brazil/U.S., 1988; participant seminar Claremont McKenna Coll./NEH, 1986. Author: (with Brewer) Alabama Constitutional Law, 1992, 2d edit., 1997; contbr. articles to profl. jours.; mem. editl. bd. Ala. Lawyer, 2000—. Bd. dirs. Auburn U. Bar Assn., 1991—. Named Outstanding Prof. Student Bar Assn./Cumberland Sch. Law, 1972-73, 83-84, Outstanding Alumnus, Phi Alpha Delta, 1973, Samford U. Cumberland Sch. Law, 1998. Mem. ABA (lectr. appellate judges seminar 1977-78), Am. Judicature Soc. (bd. dirs. 2000—), Supreme Ct. Hist. Soc., Am. Trial Lawyers Assn. (faculty mem.), Ala. Bar Assn. (action group mem. 1984-85, chmn. 1985-88, reporter task force on jud. selection 1988-89, com. on the future of the profession 1990-91, task force on legal edn. 1992—, com. on judicial and legal reform 1994-95, chmn. 1995-96), Ukrainian Legal Found. (bd. fgn. advisors 1993-98), Birmingham Bar Assn. (mem. civil ct. rules com. 1998-99), Auburn U. Bar Assn. (adv. bd. 1992—), Phi Alpha Delta. Home: 2337 Star Lake Dr Hoover AL 35226

COLE, DANIEL, music educator, conductor, clinician; b. Portland, Oreg., May 22, 1946; s. John Virgle and Barbara Jean (Johnson) Cole; 1 child, Erika Kristine. BA in Music, Marylhurst Coll., 1984; MMus in Conducting, U. Portland, 1987; MAT, Lewis and Clark Coll., 1996; PhD in Music Edn., Hamilton U., 1999. Cert. music tchr., Oreg., Wash. Music instr., orch. condr. Clark Coll., Vancouver, Wash., 1975-89; music instr. Marylhurst (Oreg.) Coll., 1985-94; prof. music edn., dir. bands Warner Pacific Coll., Portland, Oreg., 1993-97; condr., music dir. Pacific Crest Wind Ensemble, Marylhurst, 1988-97; prof. music U. Ala., Fairbanks, 1997-98; cons. music edn., conducting, 1998—; guest condr. Pres.'s USCG Band, 1994, Mercer U. Band, 1996. Author: Mardsan Guitar Method, 1979; editor Oreg. Music Educators Assn. mag., 1994-97. With USAR, 1966-73. Recipient Clark County Theater Art award, 1988, Disting. Svc. to Music Edn. award Oreg. Music Educators, 1994. Mem. Music Educators Nat. Conf., World Assn. Symphonic Bands and Ensembles, Coll. Music Soc., Coll. Band Dirs. Nat. Assn., Nat. Band Assn., Phi Mu, Tau Kappa Epsilon. Avocations: horseback trail riding, golf. E-mail: professor.dan@excite.com. Fax: 360-993-0046. Home: 6715 NE 63d St #227 Vancouver WA 98661-1980

COLE, DONALD POWELL, anthropology educator; b. Bryan, Tex., Mar. 21, 1941; s. Donald Putnam and Edna Lee (Powell) C. BA, U. Tex., 1963; MA, U. Calif., Berkeley, 1968, PhD, 1971. Asst. prof. Am. U. Cairo, 1971-75, assoc. prof., 1975-86, prof., 1986—, dept. chmn., 1987-89; vis. asst. prof. U. Calif., Berkeley, 1973-74; vis. assoc. prof. U. Chgo., 1976, U. Tex., 1983; cons. World Bank, Washington, 1977—. Author: Nomads of Nomads, 1975, Arabian Oasis City, 1989, Bedowin, Settlers and Holiday-Makers, 1998; contbr. numerous articles to profl. jours. Recipient Middle East Research award Population Council, Cairo, 1986; Ford Found. grantee 1987, 92. Democrat. Presbyterian. Office: Am U Cairo, 113 Kasr El-Aini, Cairo Arab Republic of Egypt

COLE, JOHN ADAM, insurance executive; b. Odessa, Tex., May 6, 1951; s. Alling and Millicent (McWilliam) C.; m. Karen Elisabeth Jones, June 28, 1974; children: J. Adam Jr., Robert H., Kathryn E. A in Occupational Studies in Acctg., Bus.i, Utica (N.Y.) Sch. Commerce, 1973; postgrad., New Sch. Social Rsch., 1984, Am. Coll., Bryn Mawr, Pa. ChFC, CLU. Sales mgr. Mohawk Frozen Foods, Marcy, N.Y., 1973-77; sole propr. From the C's, Inc., Rome, N.Y., 1975-77; agt., dist. asst. Equitable Fin. Svcs., Rome, 1978-83; advanced mktg. specialist Farm Family Ins. Cos., Albany, N.Y., 1984, dir. agt. and mgr. devel., 1985-87, dir. devel. and advanced life sales, 1987-96, dir. advanced markets, 1996-97, dir. life sales, 1997—; mem. mktg. com. Farm Bur. Bank, 1998—; adj. instr. various profl. tng. orgns., Rome, Utica & Albany, 1981—. Pres. Rome Cmty. Concerts Assn., 1978-80, Voorheesville (N.Y.) Ctrl. Sch. Bd., 1990—; cubmaster Boy Scouts Am.; mem. Holland Patent (N.Y.) Ctrl. Sch. Bd., 1982-85; mem. parents adv. bd. Pine Bush Little League, New Scotland Pop Warner, Guilderland Babe Ruth League; coach Ea. N.Y. State Champions team Babe Ruth Allstars, 1995; found. dir. Voorheesville Cmty. Schs. Found., 1999—. Mem. Ea. N.Y. Soc. CLUs & ChFCs (bd. dirs. 1986-91), Albany Assn. Life Underwriters (bd. dirs. 1987-92), Mohawk Valley Life Underwriters (pres., chmn. 1980-84), Kiwanis, N.Y. State Newsletter award 1992), Masons. Republican. Methodist. Home: 102 Woodview Ct Voorheesville NY 12186-9573 Office: Farm Family Ins Co PO Box 656 Albany NY 12201-0656

COLE, JOYCE MACKLIN, mathematics educator; b. Nashville, Aug. 3, 1944; d. Willie Clearence and Martha Virginia Macklin; children: Janine, Joe N, Jolandra. BS, Tenn. State U., 1967. Sec. Agrl. Ext. Svc., Nashville, 1973-75, Tenn. State U., Nashville, 1975-82; tchr. Spencer Youth Ctr., Nashville, 1982-83, Metropolitan Davidson County Schs., Nashville, 1983—. Mem. Nat. Coun. Tchrs. Math., Tchrs. Edn. Assn. Avocations: reading, listening to music, looking at movies, exercising, tutoring.

COLE, JULIO HAROLD, economics educator; b. Ancon, Canal Zone, Panama, June 5, 1955; s. Chester Harold and Victoria Elena (Bowles) C.; m. Ana Gina Vacadiez, Nov. 28, 1981; children: Joseph Harold, Janet Ruby. Lic., U. Francisco Marroquin, Guatemala, 1978; postgrad., U. Rochester, 1980-81. Credit analyst Bank of Am. Nat. Trust and Savings Assn., Santa Cruz, Bolivia, 1981-82; adminstrv. mgr. La Bélgica Sugar Mill, Santa Cruz, 1983-84; prof. econs. U. Francisco Marroquin, Guatemala City, Guatemala, 1985—; mem. acad. adv. bd. Ency. Brittanica, Inc., Mexico City, 1990—. Author: Latin American Inflation, 1987, Elementos de Econometria Aplicada, 1996; translator: Adam Smith: The Man and His Works, 1989, The Genius of the West, 1999, The Essays of Warren Buffett, 2000; contbr. articles to profl. jours. Recipient Ludwig von Mises Prize, Inst. Cultural Ludwig von Mises, Mexico City, 1990, Stillman Prize, U. Francisco Marroquin, Guatemala, 1990, Disting. Svc. Prof., 1990. Roman Catholic. Avocations: recreational reading. Home: 18 Ave A 8-40, Zona 15 VH I, Guatemala Guatemala Office: U Francisco Marroquin, Apartado 632-A, Guatemala City Guatemala

COLE, KRISTINE LOUISE, human resources professional; b. Stoneham, Mass., July 21, 1952; d. John James and Marie Louise (Juel) Bax; m. Donald Gerhard Cole, Mar. 3, 1973. BS with honors, Bath U., Eng., 1974; Grad., Tech. Coll., Eng., 1975. Grad. cert. Mng. dir. Bax Assocs. Pty Ltd., 1983—. Author publs. in field including: Office Administration and Supervision, 1992, How to Succeed at an Interview, 1982, How to Succeed at a Job Interview, 1991, Crystal Clear Communication, 1993, 2000, Supervision: Management in Action, 1998, 2000; contbr. articles to profl. jours. Fellow Australian Inst. of Co. Dirs., Australian Human Resources Inst. (assoc.); mem. ASTD, Nat. Spkrs. Assn. of Australia (accredited), Australian Inst. Devel.. E-mail: KrisCole@bax.com.au.

COLE, LEONARD AARON, political scientist, dentist; b. Paterson, N.J., Sept. 1, 1933; s. Morris and Rebecca (Harelick) Cohen; m. Ruth L. Gerber, July 7, 1957; children: Wendy Marcia, Philip Arthur, William Edward. Student, Ind. U., 1951-53; DDS, U. Pa., 1957; BA with highest honors in Polit. Sci., U. Calif., Berkeley, 1961; MA, Columbia U., 1965, PhD, 1970. Dental extern Children's Hosp. East Bay, Oakland, Calif., 1960; pvt. dental practice Hawthorne, N.J., 1961—; lectr. polit. sci. William Paterson Coll., Wayne, N.J., 1970-85; lectr. community dentistry Fairleigh Dickinson U., Teaneck, N.J., 1981-87; adj. prof. New Sch. Social Rsch., N.Y.C., 1986-88; adj. prof. pol. sci., faculty assoc. Program Sci., Tech. and Soc., Rutgers U., Newark, 1987—; vis. rsch. scholar U. Helsinki, summer 1991. Author: Blacks in Power, 1976, Politics and the Restraint of Science, 1983, Clouds of Secrecy, 1988, Element of Risk: The Politics of Radon, 1993, The Eleventh Plague: The Politics of Biological and Chemical Warfare 1996; contbr. articles to profl. jours.; item writer in polit. sci. Ednl. Testing Service. Pres. Glen Rock Human Rels. Coun., 1969-70; chmn. Jewish Community Rels. Coun. No N.J., 1986-89; bd. dirs. Jewish Coun. for Pub. Affairs, 1987—, vice chair, 1991-99, chair, 2000—; bd. dirs. Columbia U. Grad. Sch. of Arts and Scis. Alumni, 1999—. Capt. Dental Corps, USAF, 1957-59. Recipient Ben-Gurion award State of Israel Bonds, 1981, citation for acad. and community leadership N.J. Senate, 1988; fellow NEH, 1981; Rockefeller Found. Scholar-in-Residence, Bellagio, Italy, 1996. Fellow Phi Beta Kappa Soc.; mem. ADA, AAAS, N.Y. Acad. Scis., Am. Polit. Sci. Assn. Home: 381 Crest Rd Ridgewood NJ 07450-2436 Office: 723 Lafayette Ave Hawthorne NJ 07506-2348

COLE, MICHAEL WILLIAM HENRY, aerospace executive; b. Keresley, Eng., Aug. 16, 1949; s. Barry William Makepeace and Clara Alba Maria (Baiocco) C.; m. Giuliana Lucia Di Matteo, June 5, 1974; children: Maximilian Barry Joseph, Michaela Vanessa Audrey. BSc in Physics, U. Sussex, 1970. Sales mgr. SISTEL, Rome, 1970-76, Siai Marchetti, Sesto Calende, Italy, 1976-80; rep. Asia Siai Marchetti, Singapore, 1980-85; rep. N.E. Asia Agusta, Hong Kong, 1985-88; regional sales mgr. Shorts, Hong Kong, 1988-94; regional dir. Shorts Missile Systems, Kuala Lumpur, Malaysia, 1994-95; dir. sales Bombardier Aerospace, Kuala Lumpur, 1995-99; comml. dir. Fokker Svcs. Asia, Singapore, 1999—; dir. Agusta Aviation Pte Ltd., Singapore, 1983-85; cons. Caradas, Hong Kong, 1993-94. Roman Catholic. Avocations: scuba diving, boating, motorcycling, swimming. Office: c/o Fokker Svcs Asia, Bldg 139, Piccadilly E Camp, Seletar Airport 798378, Singapore

COLE, PHILLIP ALLEN, lawyer; b. Washington, D.C., Mar. 3, 1940; s. Gordon Harding and Dorothy Barbara (Jugel) C.; m. Mary Jo Ruff, July 2, 1994; children: Jennifer Leigh, Christopher Harding, Catherine Anne. BA, U. Maryland, 1961; JD, Georgetown U., 1964. Bar: Md. 1964, Minn. 1968, U.S. Supreme Ct. 1967, U.S. Ct. Appeals (8th cir.) 1968, U.S. Dist. Ct. Minn. 1965, U.S. Ct. Military Appeals 1965; cert. civil trial specialist. Assoc. Beatty & McNamee, Hyattville, Md., 1968; founder, sr. mem. Lommen, Nelson, Cole & Stageberg, Mpls., 1969—; special counsel Md. House of Dels., 1968. Contbr. articles to profl. jours. Capt. USMC, 1965-67. Mem. Minn. Def. Lawyers, Am. Bd. Prof. Liability Attys., Internat. Assn. Def. Counsel. Avocations: golf, reading. Office: Lommen Nelson Cole & Stageberg 1800 IDS Ctr Minneapolis MN 55402

COLEBUNDERS, ROBERT, internist, researcher; b. Wilrijk, Antwerp, Belgium, Apr. 19, 1949; s. Jules and Maria (Huygens) C.; m. Vera Boeynaems, Mar. 20, 1982; children: Ken, Britt. MD, Free U. Brussels, 1973, Specialist in internal medicine, 1981; PhD, U. Antwerp, 1990. Head clin. AIDS rsch. Project Sida, Kinshasa, Zaire, 1985-88; vis. scientist Ctrs. for Disease Control, Atlanta, 1988-89; head clin. AIDS rsch. Inst. Tropical Medicine, Antwerp, 1989—. Contbr. articles on clin. aspects of AIDS to sci. jours., chpts. to books. Recipient Wro Goslings prize Infectious Disease Soc. Flanders and The Netherlands, 1993. Office: Inst Tropical Medicine, Nationalestraat 155, 2000 Antwerp Belgium

COLEMAN, ANNE LOUISE, physician, ophthalmologist; b. Richmond, Va.; d. Custis and Janet (McCeachy) C.; m. Thomas R. Belin; 1 child, Janet Constance. BA in Chemistry magna cum, Duke U., 1980; MD, Med. Coll. Va., 1984; MS in Epidemiology, UCLA, 1994, PhD in Epidemiology, 1997. Asst. prof. UCLA Sch. Medicine, 1990-97; attending ophthalmologist Sepulveda (Calif.) VA Hosp., 1990-95; assoc. prof. UCLA, 1997—, Charles Drew U., L.A., 1998—; cons. UCLA Med. Ctr., 1991—, Kaiser Permanente, Woodland Hills, Calif., 1995—. Fellow Am. Acad. Ophthalmology (chair interspecialty edn. com. 1997—, Honor award 1997); mem. AAAS, AAUW, APHA, Am. Coll. Epidemiology, Am. Coll. Eye Surgeons, Am. Glaucoma Soc., Am. Med. Women's Assn., Am. Statis. Assn., Assn. Rsch. in Vision and Ophthalmology, Bay Surg. Soc., Calif. Assn. Ophthalmology, Calif. Med. Assn., Glaucoma Soc. So. Calif., John Hopkins Med. and Surg. Assn.,

L.A. Soc. Ophthalmology (program chair 1999-2000), L.A. County Med. Assn., L.A. Rsch. Study Club, N.Y. Acad. Scis., Pan Am. Assn. Ophthalmology, Rsch. Study Club L.A., Soc. Epidemiologic Rsch., UCLA Dept. Ophthalmology Assn., West Coast Glaucoma Soc., Wilmer Residents Assn., Women in Ophthalmology (treas., bd. dirs. 1997-2000), Ecuadorian Soc. Ophthalmology (hon.), Nat. Honor Soc., Phi Eta Sigma, Phi Lambda Upsilon, Sigma Zeta Laude, Alpha Omega Alpha, Delta Omega Soc., Phi Kappa Phi. E-mail: colemana@ucla.edu. Office: 100 Stein Plz Ste 118 Los Angeles CA 90095-7065

COLEMAN, BERNELL, physiologist, educator; b. Jefferson County, Miss., Apr. 26, 1929; s. Percy and Julia (Nailor) C.; m. Annie C. Richardson, Jan. 30, 1962; children—Rochelle, Ronald. BS, Alcorn A&M Coll., 1952; Ph.D. (Univ. fellow), Loyola U. Stritch Sch. Medicine, Chgo., 1964. Research asst. in biochemistry U. Chgo., 1956-57; research in cancer Hines (Ill.) VA Hosp., 1957-59; instr. St. Louis U. Sch. Medicine, 1963-65, asst. prof. physiology, 1965-67; asst. prof. Chgo. Med. Sch., 1967-69, asso. prof., 1969-76, prof., 1976; prof. Howard U. Coll. Medicine, Washington, 1976—; chmn. dept. physiology and biophysics Howard U. Coll. Medicine, 1979—; lectr. Cook County Grad. Sch. Medicine, U. Ill. Med. Sch.; vis. prof. Rush Med. Coll.; external examiner Godfrey Huggins Sch. Medicine, U. Zimbabwe, Salisbury, 1981; mem. cardiovascular and pulmonary study sect. Nat. Heart, Lung and Blood Inst./NIH, 1982-83, rsch. tng. rev. com., 1990-94. Peer rev. com. Am. Heart Assn., 1988-93, 95—, rsch. com., 1993—. With U.S. Army, 1953-56, Korea. Recipient research award Chgo. Med. Sch. Bd. Trustees, 1975; NIH research fellow, 1960-61; NIH grantee, 1966-68, 69-74, 74-76, 79—; USPHS fellow, 1961-63; Dept. Def. grantee, 1965-67. Mem. AAUP, Am. Physiol. Soc. (cardiovascular fellow 1985), Am. Heart Assn. (basic sci. coun.), AAAS, Fedn. Am. Socs. Exptl. Biology (vis. scientist for minority instns. programs 1982-83, 1989-90), N.Y. Acad. Scis., Am. Soc. Hypertension (charter), Sigma Xi, Phi Rho Sigma. Democrat. Achievements include research numerous publs. in cardiovascular physiology. Home: 14200 Myer Ter Rockville MD 20853-2350 Office: 520 W St NW Washington DC 20001-2337

COLEMAN, BRENDA FORBIS, gifted and talented educator; b. Dallas, May 17, 1951; d. Thomas Carlyle and Dorothy Jean (Tillerson) Forbis; m. Rufus Andrew Coleman, July 2, 1971; 1 child, Christopher Andrew. BS, Dallas Bapt. U., 1972; MEd, East Tex. State U., 1979; cert. gifted and talented, Tex. Woman's U., 1990. Elem. tchr. Plano (Tex.) Ind. Sch. Dist., 1972-79; elem. tchr. Lewisville (Tex.) Ind. Sch. Dist., 1983-86, gifted and talented facilitator, 1986-89; elem. tchr. Lake Dallas (Tex.) Ind. Sch. Dist., 1989-91, gifted and talented EXCEL program coord., 1991-97, 6th grade phys. sci. tchr., 1997-98, gifted and talented specialist, 8th grade yearbook advisor, 1998—; presenter in field, Univ. Interscholastic League acad. coach, 1995-96, 1997-98, judge, 1996-97. Organizer canned food dr. Lake Dallas Families, 1989. Mem. Tex. Assn. for Gifted and Talented, Assn. of Tex. Profl. Educators, Phi Delta Kappa. Republican. Methodist. Avocations: traveling, researching family history, collecting antiques, attending theatrical events. Home: 109 Woody Trl Lake Dallas TX 75065-3123 Office: Lake Dallas Ind Sch Dist 190 Falcon Dr Lake Dallas TX 75065

COLEMAN, CLAIRE KOHN, public relations executive; b. New Castle, Pa., Nov. 19, 1924; d. Louis and Florence (Frank) K.; m. Frederick H. Coleman, Mar. 10, 1957; children: Franklin, Elliot. BA, Pa. State U., 1945. Market editor Fairchild Publs., N.Y.C., 1945-48; asst. home editor N.Y. Times, 1949-50; pub. rels. dir. United Wallpaper, Chgo., 1950-53, Assoc. Am. Artists, N.Y.C., 1953-54; dir. Wallpaper Info. Bur., N.Y.C., 1954; dept. head Roy Bernard, Inc., N.Y.C., 1955-58; pub. rels. dir. The Siesel Co., N.Y.C., 1972—, sr. v.p., 1981-88; pres. Tisch Trask Comm. Resources Pub. Rels. Group, 1988-89; sr. v.p. Anthony M. Franco, N.Y.C., 1989-90; pres. Coleman Comm., N.Y.C., 1990—. Mem. ctrl. steering com., Sch. Dist. Critical Assessments, New Rochelle, N.Y., 1969-71; bd. dirs., v.p. Beechmont Assn., 1960-74, mem. adv. bd., 1990-2000; mem. Mayor's Adv. Coun. on Aging, 1966; mem. Mayor's Adv. Com. on Bd. Edn. Appointments, 1969; v.p. Coun. of PTAs, 1969-70; chmn. women's divsn. United Jewish Appeal, New Rochelle, 1971. Fellow Internat. Furnishings and Design Assn. (formerly Nat. Home Fashions League: founder 1947, nat. treas. 1977-78, nat. pres. 1980-81, N.Y. chpt. v.p. 1994, v.p. mktg. 1998-2000, Cir. of Excellence award 1994, Internat. Hon. Recognition award 1998); mem. Women Execs. Pub. Rels. (bd. dirs. 1983-84, sec. 86-87, pres.-elect 1994-95, pres. 1996-97), Woman Execs. Pub. Rels. Found. (v.p. 1992-93, pres. 1993-94, bd. dirs. 1998-2000).

COLEMAN, DALE LYNN, engineering executive, educator; b. Topeka, June 17, 1958; s. Dale R. Coleman and Linda C. (Parks) Meiergerd; m. Patricia Bermudez, Nov. 20, 1982; 1 child, Athena C. AS in Electronic Engrng. Tech. with honors, Cleve. Inst. Electronics, 1987, BS in Electronic Engrng. Tech. summa cum laude, 1993, MS in Engrng. and Tech. Mgmt. summa cum laude, 1998. Cert. quality engr., regulatory affairs cert. Electronic engrng. technician Litton G & CS, L.A., 1979-82; sr. electronics technician Cedars-Sinai Med. Ctr., L.A., 1982-85; svc. engr. Litton AMS, San Diego, 1985-86; elect. engr. tech. IMED Corp. R & D, San Diego, 1987-93, regulatory affairs engr., 1993-98; mgr. regulatory affairs Laborie Med. Technologies, Williston, Vt., 1998—, dir. RA/QA, 1999—; participant Space Life Scis. mission Space Sta. Freedom, NASA; project mgr. Internat. Space Sta. Infusion Pump Project, 1995-98; adj. prof. engrng. and tech. mgmt. So. Calif. U. for Profl. Studies, 1999—. Co-author: The Art of Hsin Hsing Yee Ti Kenpo Kung Fu, 1991; contbr. articles to profl. jours. Active UN Assn., 1979—, bd. dirs., 1994-98; sr. officer USCG Aux., 1980—, aviator, flotilla comdr., 1994-95; USCG liaison U.S. Naval Sea Cadet Corps., NAS Miramar, 1985-98; sr. officer USAF Aux., 2000—. With USN, 1976-79. Recipient Outstanding Achievement Gold medal U.S. Dept. Transp; named Outstanding Citizen Exch. Club, 1989, Outstanding Grad. Cleve. Inst. Electronics, 1990. Mem. IEEE, Am. Soc. for Quality, Regulatory Affairs Profl. Soc., Alpha Beta Kappa. Achievements include contributions to patents for improved switching power supply and medical device interunit interface connector system; research in H2 generation of reversed biased capacitors, and in lead-acid battery life prolongation. Office: Laborie Medical Techs 310 Hurricane Ln Williston VT 05495-2081

COLEMAN, DEBORAH ANN, electronics company executive; b. Central Falls, R.I., Jan. 22, 1953; d. John Austin and Joan Mary Coleman. BA, Brown U., 1974; MBA, Stanford U., 1978; PhD in Engrng. (hon.), Worcester (Mass.) Poly., 1987. Mfg. supr. Tex. Instruments, Attleboro, Mass., 1974; with fin. mgmt. tng. program Gen. Electric, Providence, 1975-76; with fin. mgmt. Hewlett-Packard, Cupertino, Calif., 1978-81; contr. Macintosh/Apple 32 group Apple Computer, Cupertino, 1981-84, dir. ops., 1984-85, v.p. worldwide mfg., 1985-87, CFO, 1987-89, CIO, 1990-92; v.p. materials ops. Tektronix Inc., Wilsonville, OR, 1992-94; chmn., CEO Merix Corp., Forest Grove, OR, 1994—; CIO Apple Computer, Cupertino, 1990-92; v.p. materials ops. Tektronix Inc., Wilsonville, Oreg., 1992-94; chmn., CEO, pres. Merix Corp., Forest Grove, Oreg., 1994—; Mem. U.S. Dept. Def. Mfg. Sci. Tech. Bd., 1988-91; bd. dirs. VMX, Inc., Software Pub Corp., Octel. Mem. adv. coun. Stanford Inst. Mfg. Automation, 1985-87; mem. Harvard U. Bus. Sch. Vis. Com., 1987—, Com. of 200, 1987—; trustee San Jose/Cleve. Ballet, 1989-92, Brown U., 1994—. Mem. Internat. Women's Forum. Democrat. Roman Catholic. Office: Merix Corp 1521 Poplar Ln Forest Grove OR 97116-0300•

COLEMAN, EDWARD LAWRENCE, councilman; b. Albany, Ga., Oct. 15, 1922; s. Lawrence and Ollie Mae (Green); m. Rosemary Premmer Thomas, Sept. 1942 (divorced); children: Randall, Cheryl, Sandra; m. Juanita Sarah Lancaster, June 6, 1962. Student, Ky. State U. Press operator Ford Motor Co., Canton, Ohio; Ward 2 precinct committeemen Canton City Coun., coun. mem., 1974—; chmn. cmty. and econ. devel. com. Canton City Coun.; adv. bd. mem. Total Living Ctr., Canton. Past treas. Canton Tomorrow; bd. dirs. Canton Cmty. Clinic; mem. United Auto Workers, Nat. Black Elected Officials Caucus, exec. com. Stark County Dem. Party. Inducted into Football, Basketball & Umpiring Amateau Sports Hall of Fame, Canton; named Outstanding Citizen of Yr. NAACP, Man of Yr. Phillip Randolph Orgn. Mem. Canton Negro Oldtimers (bd. dirs., Originators award). Democrat. Baptist. Avocations: watching sports, reading newspapers. Office: Canton City Coun Office PO Box 24218 Canton OH 44701-4218

COLEMAN, ERIC NORMAN, pediatrician, cardiologist; b. Ayr, Scotland, June 22, 1925; s. Philip Norman and Marion (Nisbet) C. MBChB, U. Glasgow, Scotland, 1948, MD, 1961. Ho. physician Royal Hosp. for Sick Children, Glasgow, 1948-49, registrar, 1954-58, sr. registrar, 1958-59, head cardiology svc., 1961-90; ho. surgeon Hairmyres (Scotland) Hosp., 1949; sr. ho. officer City Hosp., Nottingham, Eng., 1951-52, So. Gen. Hosp., Glasgow, 1952-54; lectr. in child health U. Glasgow, 1959-61; sr. physician Royal Hosp. for Sick Children, Glasgow, 1988-90; regional postgrad. advisor Com. on Medicine and Pediatrics, Glasgow, 1975-90; Leonard Gow lectr. in child health U. Glasgow, 1988-90. Contbr. articles to profl. publs., chpt. to book. Capt. RAMC, 1949-51. Fellow Royal Coll. Physicians, Royal Coll. Paediatrics and Child Health, Soc. Cardiol. Sci. and Tech.; mem. Brit. Pediatric Assn. (hon.), Brit. Cardiac Soc., Scottish Pediatric Soc., New Club. Roman Catholic. Avocations: music, art, theology.

COLEMAN, GARY WILLIAM, elementary school educator, retired; b. Davenport, Iowa, Dec. 16, 1945; s. Robert Earl and Mildred Margaret (Mast) C.; m. Janice Marie Coleman, Dec. 29, 1973; children: Heidi Marie, Sean Robert. BS in Elem. Edn., U. S.D., 1987; BSBA, Ariz. State U., 1969. Cert. elem. tchr., EMT, S.D. Tchr. Marty (S.D.) Indian Sch., 1987-91; tchr. Parkston (S.D.) Elem. Sch., 1991-2000, ret., 2000; acct./bookkeeper Ulland Bros Constrn., Austin, Minn.; realtor assoc. Myre-Sorenson Real Estate, Albert Lea, Minn.; bldg. constrn. contractor, landscaper, Alcester, S.D. Sgt. USAF, 1969-73. Mem. NEA, Parkston Edn. Assn. (v.p. 1995-96, pres. 1996-97, founder scholarship fund 1997). Office: Parkston Schs Box D Parkston SD 57366

COLEMAN, HENRY JAMES, JR., management educator, consultant; b. Cleve., Nov. 28, 1947; s. Henry James and Kathryn Adele (Ketchum) C.; m. Sharon Ann Boothe, Sept. 12, 1971 (div. Jan. 1975). AB, Dartmouth Coll., 1969, MBA, 1970; PhD, U. Calif., Berkeley, 1978. Employment mgr. Lima (Ohio) Meml. Hosp., 1977-78; strategic planner NCR Corp., Dayton, Ohio, 1980-81; vis. asst. prof. Calif. Poly. State U., San Luis Obispo, 1983-85; dean Sch. Mgmt., Columbia Pacific U., San Rafael, Calif., 1985-92; assoc. prof. mgmt. St. Mary's Coll. Calif., Moraga, 1992-2000; mgmt. cons. Lafayette, Calif., 2000—; adj. prof. Holy Names Coll., Oakland, Calif., 1987, 90-92; mgmt. cons. Orgn. Dynamics, Berkeley, 1970, Comm. Workers Am., San Francisco, 1971, Exide Corp., Reading, Pa., 1988-89, Retirement Fin. Ctrs. Am., Las Vegas, Nev., 1996. Contbr. articles to profl. jours. Nat. Def. Grad. fellow, 1971. Mem. Western Acad. Mgmt., Phi Beta Kappa. Episcopalian. Avocations: color photography, music appreciation.

COLEMAN, JAMES JULIAN, lawyer; b. New Orleans, May 5, 1915; s. William Ballin and Millie (Davis) C.; m. Dorothy Louise Jurisich, July 30, 1940; children: James Julian, Thomas Blaise, Peter Dee, Dian Judith. B.A., Tulane U., 1934, J.D., 1937; LL.D. (hon.), Hampden-Sydney Coll., 1982. Bar: La. 1937. Sr. ptnr. Coleman, Johnson & Artigues, New Orleans; past pres. Internat. Trade Mart, New Orleans Philharmonic Symphony; hon. consul gen. Republic of Korea; vice-chmn. La. Jud. Compensation Commn. Past pres. New Orleans C. of C., Jr. Achievement New Orleans, Adult Edn. Ctr.; past bd. dirs. U.S. C. of C., Internat. House, Fed. Rels. Assn.; past chmn. New Orleans coordinating com. NASA; founder Peoples League; trustee emeritus Principia Coll.; past chmn. Tulane U. Bus. Sch. Coun.; chmn. bd. trustees Crimestoppers. Decorated Order of Oranje-Nassau Diplomatic Service Merit Republic Korea; recipient Nat. Achievement award Jr. Achievement, Loving Cup award New Orleans Times-Picayune, 1980, Joseph W. Simon, Jr. award, 1981, Disting. Alumnus award Tulane U., 1982, New Orleans Activist award, 1984, C. Alvin Bertel award, 1985; named to Bus. Hall of Fame, 1984; named Pres. Emeritus, World Trade Ctr., N.Y.C., Chmn. Emeritus, The City Energy Club, Humanitarian of Yr. ARC, 2000; recipient Benemerenti Papal Honor, 1989. Mem. ABA, Internat. Bar Assn., La. Bar Assn., New Orleans Bar Assn., Am. Judicature Soc. (past dir.), Beta Gamma Sigma (hon.). Christian Scientist (1st reader 1953-56). Home: 10 Audubon Pl New Orleans LA 70118-5526 Office: 321 Saint Charles Ave New Orleans LA 70130-3145

COLEMAN, JAMES JULIAN, JR., lawyer, industrialist, real estate executive; b. New Orleans, May 7, 1941; s. James Julian Sr. and Dorothy Louise (Jurisich) C.; m. Carol Campbell Owen, Dec. 19, 1970 (dec. Sept. 1979); 1 child, James Owen; m. Mary Olivia Cochrane Cushing, Oct. 12, 1985. BA, Princeton U., 1963; postgrad. in law, Oxford (Eng.) U., 1963-65; JD, Tulane U., 1968. Bar: La. 1969, U.S. Supreme Ct. 1969. Chmn. Internat.-Matex Tank Terminals, New Orleans, 1969—; pres. Coleman Devel. Co., New Orleans, 1969—, IMTT, Quebec, 1993—, Nfld. Transhipment Terminal Inc.; ptnr. Coleman, Johnson & Artigues, New Orleans, 1972—; chmn. DownTown Parking Service, New Orleans, 1978—; pres. City Ctr. Properties, New Orleans, 1980—; chmn. East Jersey R.R. and Terminal Co., 1993; trustee Loving Found., New Orleans, R.L. Blaffer Found., Houston; dir. U.S. Coast Guard Found. Author: Gilbert Antoine de St. Maxent: The Spanish Frenchman of New Orleans, 1975. Mem. history coun. Princeton U., 1982—; mem. N.J. Commn. on Sci. and Tech., 1992—; bd. dirs. N.J. Mfg. Extension Program, 1998—, Liberty Sci. Ctr., Liberty State Park, N.J., 19999—; bd. overseers N.J. Inst. Tech., 1999—. Named H.M. Hon. Brit. Consul for La., Brit. Consulate, New Orleans, 1975—, to Order of Brit. Empire, Queen Elizabeth II, London, 1986. Mem. ABA, La. Bar Assn., N.Y. Yacht Club, N.Y. Racquet Club, Newport Reading Room, So. Yacht Club, New Orleans Lawn Tennis Club, USN League (bd. dirs. New Orleans), Union League Club. Republican. Mem. Ch. of Christ Scientist. Office: Coleman Johnson & Artigues 321 St Charles Ave 10th Fl New Orleans LA 70130-3145

COLEMAN, JOHN WILLIAM, urologist; b. Jersey City, Jan. 26, 1939; s. John William and Marion Cecille (McAuliffe) C.; m. Rosemary Elizabeth Romano, July 13, 1963 (div. 1984). AB, Georgetown U., 1960, MD, 1964. Diplomate Am. Bd. Urology. Intern, resident surgery NY Hosp., 1964-66, resident in urology, chief resident in urology, 1968-72, asst. attending surgeon urology, 1972-75; assoc. attending urologist N.Y. Hosp./Cornell Med. Ctr., 1975—; chief med. officer 21st Princeton LPH5, 215 Marines U.S. Navy, Vietnam, 1964-66; assoc. prof. urology Cornell Med. Coll., 1975—; cons. Rockefeller U. Hosp., N.Y.C., 1985—; Vets. Gen. Hosp., Taipei, Taiwan, 1987; bd. dirs. Am. Bur. for Med. Advancement in China. With USMC, 1966-68. Recipient John K. Lattimer award, 1997, N.Y., N.J. sect. Nat. Kidney Found. award, 1997. Fellow ACS, Am. Acad. Pediatrics; mem. Asian Surg. Soc., Chinese Am. Med. Soc., Soc. Pediat. Urology, Soc. Urologie Internat. Roman Catholic. Avocations: golf, study of southeast Asia. Office: 53 E 70th St New York NY 10021-4941 also: 254 Canal St Rm 3001 New York NY 10013-3501

COLEMAN, LEWIS WALDO, bank executive; b. San Francisco, Jan. 2, 1942; s. Lewis V. and Virginia Coleman; m. Susan G.; children: Michelle, Gregory, Nancy, Peter. BA, Stanford U., 1965. With Bank Calif., San Francisco, 1965-73; With Wells Fargo Bank, San Francisco, 1973-86, exec. v.p., chmn. credit policy com., until 1986; vice chmn., CFO, treas. Bank Am., San Francisco, 1986-95; sr. mng. dir. Montgomery Securities, San Francisco, 1995-98; CEO Nations Bank Mongomery Securities, San Francisco, 1998—.

COLEMAN, MICHAEL CHRISTOPHER, educator; b. Dublin, Ireland, June 19, 1946; arrived in Finland, 1970; s. Michael Sidney and Beatrice (McGreevy) C.; m. Sirkka Helinä Makkonen, Sept. 27, 1970; children: Michael Donagh, Heli Kristiina, Markus Kevin. BA in History, U. Coll. Dublin, 1970; MA in History, U. Pa., 1974, PhD in Am. History, 1977. Comml. artist various Irish advt. agys., 1964-66; lectr. English U. Jyvaskyla, Finland, 1970-72, 72-81, 1981—, dir. N.Am. studies program, 1990—. Author: Presbyterian Missionary Attitudes Toward American Indians, 1837-1893, 1985, American Indian Children at School, 1850-1930, 1993; contbr. articles to profl. jours. With Irish N.G., 1960s. Teaching fellow U. Pa., Phila., 1973-76, Newberry Libr. short-term fellow, Chgo., 1988, 89, Smithsonian Instn. short-term fellow, Washington, 1989, sr. rsch. fellow Finnish Acad., 1996-97. Mem. Am. Hist. Assn., Orgn. Am. Historians, Am. Soc. Ethnohistory. Avocations: miniature models, football, swimming, gardening. Office: U Jyväskylä, Dept English, Jyväskylä Finland

COLEMAN, PAUL JEROME, JR., physicist, educator; b. Evanston, Ill., Mar. 7, 1932; s. Paul Jerome and Eunice Cecile (Weissenberg) C.; m. Doris Ann Fields, Oct. 3, 1964; children: Derrick, Craig. BS in Engrng. Math., U. Mich., 1954, BS in Engrng. Physics, 1954, MS in Physics, 1958; PhD in Space Physics, UCLA, 1966. Rsch. scientist Ramo-Wooldridge Corp. (name now TRW Systems), El Segundo, Calif., 1958-61; instr. math. U. So. Calif., L.A., 1958-61; mgr. interplanetary scis. program NASA, Washington, 1961-62; rsch. scientist UCLA, 1962-66, prof. geophysics, space physics, 1966—; asst. lab. dir., mgr. Earth and Space Scis. divsn., chmn. Inst. Geophysics and Planetary Physics Nat. Lab., Los Alamos, N.Mex., 1981-86; dir. Inst. Geophysics and Planetary Physics UCLA, 1989-92; dir. Nat. Inst. for Global Environ. Change, 1994-96; pres. Univs. Space Rsch. Assn., Columbia, Md., 1981-2000; bd. dirs. Axcess Inc., Dallas, Quantrad Corp., Madison, Wis., Scyld Comp. Corp., Columbia, Md., others; mem. adv. bd. San Diego Supercomputer Ctr., 1986-90, chmn., 1987-88, others; trustee Univs. Space Rsch. Assn., Columbia, Md., 1981-2000, Am. Tech. Initiative, 1990—, Internat. Small Satellite Orgn., 1992-96; vis. scholar U. Paris, 1975-76; vis. scientist Lab. for Aeronomy Ctr. Nat. Rsch. Sci., Verrieres le Buisson, France, 1975-76; com. mem. numerous sci. and ednl. orgns., cons. numerous fin. and indsl. cos. Co-editor: Solar Wind, 1972; co-author: Pioneering the Space Frontier, 1986; mem. editorial bd. Geophysics and Astrophysics Monographs, 1970—; assoc. editor Cosmic Electrodynamics, 1968-72; contbr. revs. to numerous profl. jours. Apptd. to Nat. Commn. on Space, Pres. of U.S., 1985, apptd. to Space Policy Adv. Bd., Nat. Space Coun., v.p. of U.S., 1991; bd. dirs. St. Matthew's Sch., Pacific Palisades, Calif., 1979-82, v.p., 1981-82. 1st lt. USAF, 1954-56, Korea. Recipient Exceptional Sci. Achievement Medal NASA, 1970, 1972, spl. recognition for contributions to the Apollo Program, 1979; Guggenheim fellow 1975-76, Fulbright scholar, 1975-76, Rsch. grantee NASA, NSF, Office Naval Research, Calif. Space Inst., Air Force Office Sci. Research, U.S. Geol. Survey. Mem. AAAS, AIAA, Am. Geophys. Union, Am. Phys. Soc., Internat. Acad. Astronautics, Bel Air Bay Club (L.A.), Birnam Wood Golf Club (Montecito, Calif.), Cosmos Club (Washington), Valley Club (Montecito, Calif.), Eldorado Country Club (Indian Wells, Calif.), Tau Beta Pi, Phi Eta Sigma. Avocations: flying, skiing, racquetball, tennis, golf. Home: 1323 Monaco Dr Pacific Palisades CA 90272-4007 Office: UCLA Inst Geophysics & Planetary Physics 405 Hilgard Ave Los Angeles CA 90095-9000

COLEMAN, REXFORD LEE, lawyer, educator; b. Hollywood, Calif., June 2, 1930; s. Henry Eugene and Antoinette Christine (Dobry) C.; m. Aiko Takahashi, Aug. 28, 1953 (dec.); children: Christine Eugenie, Douglass Craig; m. Sucha Park, June 15, 1978. Student, Claremont McKenna Coll., 1947-49; A.B., Stanford U., 1951, J.D., 1955; M. in Jurisprudence, Tokyo U., 1960. Bar: Calif. 1955, Mass. 1969. Mem. faculty Harvard U., 1959-69; mem. firm Baker & McKenzie, 1969-83, income ptnr., 1971-73, capital ptnr., 1973-83, mng. ptnr. Tokyo office, 1971-78; sr. ptnr. The Pacific Law Group, L.A., 1983—; adj. prof. McGeorge Sch. Law, U. Pacific, 1989—; lectr. Gray's Inn, The Inns of Ct. Sch. Law, London, 1989; cons. U.S. Treasury Dept., 1961-70; counselor Japanese-Am. Soc. for Legal Studies, 1964—; guest lectr. Ford Seminar on Comparative History, MIT, 1968; lectr. Legal Tng. and Research Inst., Supreme Ct., Japan, 1970-73; guest lectr. Colloquium Scholars, Calif. Luth. U., 1989; chmn. fgn. bus. customs consultative com. Bur. Customs, Ministry of Fin., Govt. of Japan, 1971-72; chmn. fgn. bus. consulatative commn. Japanese Ministry of Internat. Trade and Industry, 1973-76; mem. U.S. Del., U.S.-Japan Income Tax Treaty Negotiations, 1961, internat. bd. advisors, McGeorge Sch. Law, U. Pacific, 1989—. Author: Am. Index to Japanese Law, 1961, Standard Citation of Japanese Legal Materials, 1963, The Legal Aspects Under Japanese Law of an Accident Involving a Nuclear Installation in Japan, 1963, An Index to Japanese Law, 1975; editor: Taxation in Japan, World Tax Series, 1959-70; founding chmn. bd. editors: Law in Japan: An Ann., 1964-67; mem. bd. editors Stanford Law Rev., 1954-55, Japan Ann. Internat. Law, 1970-92; mem. Internat. Adv. Bd., The Transnational Lawyer, 1988—; contbr. articles to profl. jours. Participant in Japanese-Am. Program for Cooperation in Legal Studies, 1956-60; co-chmn. Conf. on Internat. Legal Protection Computer Software, Stanford Law Sch., 1986, Tokyo, Japan, 1987. Served to 1st lt., Inf. AUS, 1951-53; lt. col. Ret. Ford Found. grantee, 1956-60. Mem. ABA, State Bar Calif., Mass. Bar Assn., Japanese-Am. Soc. for Legal Studies, Internat. Fiscal Assn. Japan, Res. Officers Assn. (v.p. army dept. Far East 1974-75), Ret. Officers Assn., Internat. House Japan (Tokyo), Stanford U. Alumni Assn., Gakushi Kai (grads. of former Japanese Imperial Univs. Assn.), Internat. Law Assn. Japan, Japan-Western Assn., Pacific Basin Econ. Council, (U.S. exec. com. 1985-87), Nihon Shihō Gakkai, Nihon Kokusai Hō Gakkai, Nihon Kokusai Shihō Gakkai, Sozei Hō Gakkai, Phi Alpha Delta. Episcopalian (vestryman 1966-69, del. Conv. Episcopal Diocese Mass. 1968, Conv. Episcopal Diocese L.A., 1989-91, Bishop's com. 1983-87, 91-93). Clubs: Tokyo Am; Harvard (N.Y.C.), North Ranch Country. Home: 32314 Blue Rock Rdg Westlake Vlg CA 91361-3912 Office: The Pacific Law Group 12121 Wilshire Blvd Ste 205 Los Angeles CA 90025-1164

COLEMAN, ROBERT J., lawyer; b. Phila., Dec. 24, 1936; s. Francis Eugene and Mary Veronica (McCullough) C.; m. Mary Patricia Coleman, June 26, 1955; children: Debra, Robert P., Linda, Martin S. AB, Villanova U., 1959; JD, Temple U., 1964. Bar: Pa., U.S. Dist. Ct. (ea. dist.) Pa., U.S. Ct. Appeals (3d cir.), U.S. Supreme Ct. With First Pa. Bank, Phila., 1955-57; underwriter Employer's Mut. Co., Phila., 1957-59; claim adjuster Safeco Ins. Co., Phila., 1959-62; claim supr. Gen. Accident Ins., Phila., 1962-64; assoc. Rappaport & Lagakos, Phila., 1964; trial atty. Allstate Ins. Co., Phila., 1964-67; chmn., CEO Marshall, Dennehey, Warner, Coleman & Goggin, Phila., 1967—; chmn. hearing com. Pa. Disciplinary Bd., Phila., 1986-94; mem. Pa. Bd. Law Examiners. Assoc. editor Phila. County Reporter, 1984-96; contbr. articles to legal publs. Bd. dirs. Ins. Soc. Phila.; dir. HERO Scholarship Fund Delaware County; bd. visitors Temple U. Law Sch. With USAR, 19654-62. Mem. ABA, Pa. Bar Assn., Phila. Bar Assn., Phila. Bar Found. (trustee), Pa. Def. Inst., Internat. Assn. Def. Lawyers, Def. Rsch. Inst. Republican. Roman Catholic. Avocations: tennis, boating, travel. Home: 908 Penn Valley Rd Media PA 19063-1652 Office: Marshall Dennehey Warner Coleman & Goggin 1845 Walnut St Philadelphia PA 19103-4708

COLEMAN, RODERICK FLYNN, lawyer; b. Washington, Pa., Sept. 20, 1958; s. Harry Sullivan and Marlyn Hope (McAninch) C.; m. Gale Faith Zeisel, July 28, 1984; children:, Tara, Lindsey. BA, Oglethorpe U., 1980; JD, Stetson U., 1983. Bar: Fla. 1983, U.S. Dist. Ct. (so. dist.) Fla. 1984, U.S. Ct. Appeals (11th cir.) 1984, U.S. Dist. Ct. (mid. dist.) Fla. 1988. Assoc. Law Offices of Richard Ralph, Miami, Fla., 1983-85, Schwartz and Assocs., Miami, 1986-87; ptnr. Marlow, Connell, Valerius, Abrams, Lowe & Adler, Miami, 1988-96, Stettin & Coleman, P.A., Miami, 1996-97, Coleman & Assocs., P.A., Coral Gables, Fla., 1997—. Mem. ABA, Fla. Bar, Dade County Bar Assn., Fla. Trial Lawyers Assn., Am. Judicature Soc., Riviera Country Club, Kiwanis. Republican. Avocations: golf, sailing. Home: 1470 Mendavia Ave Coral Gables FL 33146-1608 Office: 122 Minorca Ave Coral Gables FL 33134-4510

COLEMAN, RONALD LEE, insurance claims executive; b. Danville, Va., June 10, 1941; s. Raymond Lee and Mildred Sue (Floyd) C.; m. Stephanie Walther Barton Ewalt; children: Ronald Lee, Christopher Brent. BSBA summa cum laude, Va. Poly. Inst. and State U., 1964; BS in Pub. Adminstrn. summa cum laude, U. Richmond, 1964, postgrad., 1971; postgrad. law sch., U. Va., 1980. Pres. Johnson & Coleman, Ltd., Richmond, 1974-79, Ron Coleman & Assocs., Ltd., Richmond, 1981—; v.p. Schnell, Johnson & Coleman, Ltd., Richmond, Va., 1979-81; adj. prof. U. Tex., Austin, Pa. State U., State College; adv. coun. Pamplin Bus. Sch., Va. Tech. Author: Investigation and Handling of Aviation Claims, 1981, Presentation of Evidence in Accident Reconstruction Cases, 1989, others; editor-in-chief Claimsman mag., 1971-76; contbr. articles to profl. jours. Mem. U.S. Senatorial Bus. Adv. Bd., 1988; mem. adv. coun. Paplin Coll. Bus., Va. Tech.; mem. Rep. Presdl. Task Force, 1988; mem. Va. Rep. Com., Chesterfield County, 1984; mem. The Pres.'s Coun., 1990, Pres. Club Rep. Party; bd. dirs. Va. Tech. Found., Va. Tech. Athletic Fund. Mem. ABA (tort and ins. practice sect.), Richmond Claims Assn. (pres. 1971-72, Man of Yr. award 1971), Va. Claims Assn. (Bob Anderson Humanitarian award), Def. Law Inst., Atlanta Claims Assn., Profl. Claims Assn. Richmond, Truck Ins. Def. Assn., 1872 Soc. at Va. Poly. Inst. and State U., Assn. Lloyds Mems. (London), Ut Prosim Soc. at Va. Poly. Inst. and State U., Va. Tech. Found., 1789 Soc. at Hampdon-Sydney Coll., Soc. of Founders Hampden-Sydney Coll., Va. Hist. Soc., Rotunda Soc. U. Va., Reform Club (London), St. James Club (London), Salisbury Country Club, Hurlingham Club (London), Sloane Club (London), Quinnipiack Club (New Haven), Yale Club N.Y.C. Methodist. Avocations: jazz, golf. Office: 13807 Village Mill Dr Midlothian VA 23113-4361

COLEMAN, WANDA, poet, writer; b. L.A., Nov. 13, 1946; d. George and Lewana Evans; m. Austin Straus, May 1, 1981; children: Anthony, Luanda, Ian Wayne Grant. Author: (books) Imagoes, 1983, Heavy Daughter Blues, 1987, A War of Eyes & Other Stories, 1988, African Sleeping Sickness, 1990, Hand Dance, 1993, Dicksboro Hotel, 1995, Native in a Strange Land: Trials and Tremors, 1996, Bathwater Wine, 1998, (novel) Mambo Hips & Make Believe, 1999. NEA fellow in poetry, 1981, Guggenheim fellow in poetry, 1984, Calif. Arts Coun. fellow in fiction, 1989; named writer's resident Djerassi Found., 1990; recipient Lenore Marshall Poetry prize, 1999. Mem. PEN Ctr. West, Writers Guild Am. Fax: 310-641-6806. E-mail: wcoleman44@hotmail.com. Office: Black Sparrow Press 24 10th St Santa Rosa CA 95401-4714

COLEN, FREDERICK HAAS, lawyer; b. Pitts., May 16, 1947; married, 1972. BSChemE, Tufts U., 1969; JD, Emory U., 1975. Bar: Pa. 1975, Ga. 1975, U.S. Patent Office 1976, U.S. Dist. Ct. (we. dist.) Pa. 1975, U.S. Dist. Ct. (no. dist.) Ga. 1975, U.S. Ct. Appeals (fed. and 3d cirs.) 1975, U.S. Supreme Ct. 1980. Chem. engr. Shell Oil Co., New Orleans, 1969-71; san. engr. USPHS, Morgantown, W.Va., 1971-73; patent atty. Mobay Chem. Corp., Pitts., 1975-79; assoc. Reed Smith Shaw & McClay, Pitts., 1979-86, ptnr., 1986—. Contbr. articles to profl. jours. Mem. ABA, Allegheny County Bar Assn., Pa. Bar Assn., Ga. Bar Assn., Am. Intellectual Property Law Assn. Home: 4940 Ellsworth Ave Pittsburgh PA 15213-2807 Office: Reed Smith Shaw & McClay 435 6th Ave Ste 2 Pittsburgh PA 15219-1866

COLER, MYRON A(BRAHAM), chemical engineer, educator; b. N.Y.C., Mar. 30, 1913; s. Marcus and Bertha (Bebarfald) C.; m. Viola Ethel Buchbinder, Nov. 15, 1942 (dec. Jan. 1993); children: Mark D., Sandra Coler Carson; m. Lena Amark, Feb. 16, 1996 (div. Mar. 1998). AB, Columbia U., 1933, BS, 1934, ChE, 1935, PhD, 1937; postgrad., NYU, Bklyn. Poly. Inst. With NYU, N.Y.C., 1941-75, prof., dir. surface tech. program dir. creative sci. program; supr., rsch. scientist Manhattan Project, 1943-45; founder, pres., dir. chmn. bd. Markite Co., Markite Corp., Markite Engring. Co., 1948-67, Coler Engring. Co., 1967—, The Vulcan Press Divsn., Valmath, 1988—; sponsor-in-residence Franklin Inst. Rsch. Labs., 1975-81; cons. numerous cos. and govt. agys. Author: Aircraft Engine Finishes, 1941; editor, contbg. author: Essays on Creativity in the Sciences, 1963, Essays on Invention and Education, 1977; numerous articles to profl. jours.; patentee in field. Bd. dirs. Woodward Envicon, Marcus and Bertha Coler Found.; mem. adv. com. dept. phys. and engring. metallurgy Polytechnic Inst. N.Y.; mem. pres.'s com. for Sch. Continuing Edn., NYU; appointee Nat. Inventors Coun., 1966-74; mem. state tech. svc. com. Dept. Commerce; with divsn. cultural studies UNESCO-Dept. State, 1982. Named hon. prof. Polytechnic Inst. N.Y.; Weston fellow Electrochem. Mem. AAAS, Am. Math. Soc., Materials Rsch. Soc., Am. Nuclear Soc., N.Y. Acad. Sci., Electrochem. Soc., Am. Ceramic Soc., Am. Chem. Soc., Am. Soc. for Metals, Am. Def. Preparedness Assn., Internat. Precious Metals Inst., Sigma Xi, Phi Beta Kappa, Phi Lambda Upsilon, Tau Beta Pi, Epsilon Chi. Address: Empress Hotel 7766 Fay Ave La Jolla CA 92037-4309

COLES, BERTHA SHARON GILES, visual information specialist; b. Paris, Tenn., Aug. 13, 1949; d. Charles Ray and Etter Bell (Lightfoot) Giles. Student, Profl. Edn. Divsn. Dallas, 1979, Dynamic Graphics Ednl. Found., 1980, No. Va. C.C., 1981. Typesetter, illustrator Def. Printing, Washington, 1979-83; editl. asst. Exec. Office of Pres., Washington, 1983; visual info. specialist Naval Media Support Ctr., Washington, 1983—. Design, layout, paste-up specialist for various publs., including USN Medicine, 1981, 83, Bull., 1983, Playbook, 1995; cover design July 1996 issue All Hands Mag.; design, layout Posture Statement Mag., 1997; cover design USN-(Joint Civilian Orientation Conf.)-Dept. Def.; cover design and layout of Dept. Navy Posture Statement, 1998. Bd. dirs. London Woods Cmty. Assn., Capitol Heights, Md., 1995. Democrat. Avocations: painting, gardening, interior decorating, collector. Home: 5634 Onslow Way Capitol Heights MD 20743-3059 Office: Navy Media Support Ctr 2511 Jefferson Davis Hwy Arlington VA 22202-3926

COLES, BRYONY JEAN, archaeologist, educator; b. Longton, Eng., Aug. 12, 1946; d. John and Jean (Harris) Orme; m. John Morton Coles, Feb. 28, 1985. BA with honors, U. Bristol, Eng., 1968; postgrad. diploma, Inst. Archaeology, London, 1970; MPhil, U. Coll., London, 1972. Lectr. archaeology U. Exeter, Eng., 1972-89; sr. lectr. archaeology U. Exeter, 1989-91, reader archaeology, 1991-96, prof. prehistoric archaeology, 1996—; dir. Somerset Levels Project, U.K., 1973-89, Wetland Archaeology Rsch. Project, 1986—; chair North West Wetland Survey, U.K., 1994—; dir. Ctr. Wetland Rsch., 1997—; mem. humanities rsch. bd. Brit. Acad., U.K., 1994-96; mem. archaeology and history panel Nat. Mus. and Galleries of Wales, 2000—. Author: Anthropology for Archaeologists, 1981, Wetland Management, 1995, (with J. M. Coles) Sweet Track to Glastonbury, 1986 (Archaeology Book of Yr. 1986), (with J.M. Coles) People of the Wetlands, 1989, (with J.M. Coles) Enlarging the Past, 1996; contbr. articles to profl. jours. Recipient George Stephenson medal Instn. Civil Engrs., 1995, Brit. Archaeol. award, ICI award for best project, 1975-98; named Rsch. reader Brit. Acad., 1991-93. Fellow Soc. Antiquaries London; mem. Prehistoric Soc. (v.p. 1994-98, Baguley prize 1990, 98). Office: Univ Exeter, Exeter EX4 4QE, England

COLES, GERALD VIVIAN, occupational hygienist; b. Cardiff, Wales, Apr. 5, 1924; arrived in Australia, 1976; s. Charles and Olive (Randell) C.; m. Ruth Mary Crowe Robinson, July 18, 1953 (div. June 1976); children: David, Christine; m. Ingrid Rutishauser, July 1976. BSc, U. Wales, 1949. Asst. chemist AngloIranian Oil Co., Abadan, Iran, 1944-47, 49-51; rsc. asst. Long Ashton Rsch. Sta., Bristol, England, 1952-55; from factories inspector to occupl. hygienist Uganda Govt., Kampala, 1955-71; occupl. hygienist Br. Railways, 1971-74; sr. lectr. London Sch. Hygiene & Tropical Medicine, 1974-76; scientific officer Pub. Health Dept., Perth, Australia, 1976-78; advisor in occupl. hygiene Shell Co. Australia, Melbourne, 1978-84; cons. in field Werribee, Victoria, Australia, 1984—. hon. fellow Deakin U., 2000—. Avocations: sailing, swimming, mountain hiking, cross country skiing. Fax: 03 9741 9495. Office: 2 Highview Rise, PO Box 317, 3030 Metung VIC 3904, Australia

COLESSIDES, NICK JOHN, lawyer; b. Kavala, Greece, Jan. 14, 1938; came to U.S., 1958; s. John T. and Maroula (Karakas) C.; m. Sophia Simons Symeonidis, Oct. 5, 1970. BS in Polit. Sci., U. Utah, 1963, MS Polit. Sci., 1967, JD, 1970. Bar: Utah 1970, U.S. Dist. Ct. Utah 1970, U.S. Ct. Appeals (10th cir.) 1970, U.S. Dist. Ct. (so. dist.) Ohio 1975, U.S. Ct. Appeals (9th cir.) 1976. Chief deputy county atty. Salt Lake County (Utah) Atty.'s Office, 1970-74; city atty. West Jordan (Utah) City Atty.'s Office, 1971-78, Park City (Utah) Atty.'s Office, 1976-80; atty. pvt. practice, Salt Lake City, 1970—; bd. dirs. Merrill Lynch Bank, U.S.A., Salt Lake City City. Trustee Greek Orthodox Ch., SaltLake City, 1976, 77, 87, 88, 98, 99, Utah Cmty. Reinvestment Corp. Mem. Assn. Trial Lawyers Am., Utah Trial Lawyers Assn., U. Utah Coll. of Law Alumni Assn. (trustee 1995-98), Utah State Bar Assn., Salt Lake County Bar Assn., Am. Inn of Ct. VII (master of the bench, pres. 1997, 98). Greek Orthodox. Avocations: gardening, cooking, reading. Home: 32 Haxton Pl Salt Lake City UT 84102-1410 Office: 466 S 400 E Ste 100 Salt Lake City UT 84111-3301

COLETTA, GERARD CHARLES, management consultant; b. Cambridge, Mass., Dec. 9, 1944; s. Gerard Charles and Eileen Gertrude (Barrett) C.; m. Pamela S. Wight, June 30, 1984; children: Nadine, Sean. BSChemE, Tufts U., 1966; MSChemE, MIT, 1968; postgrad., U. Calif., Berkeley, 1969-71. Design engr. Standard Oil of Calif., San Francisco, 1968-71; staff cons. Arthur D. Little, Inc., Cambridge, 1971-78; corp. dir. of safety and health Nat. Semiconductor Corp., Santa Clara, Calif., 1978-81; sr. cons. Risk Planning Group, Darien, Conn., 1981-83; pres. Risk Control Services, Tiburon, Calif., 1983-86; prin. and practice mgr. Tillinghast div. Towers Perrin Co., San Francisco, 1986-91; sr. v.p., nat. practice mgr., bus. continuity cons. Marsh USA (formerly Sedgwick of Calif.), San Francisco, 1991-2000; v.p., nat. practice leader, bus. continuity cons. Palmer & Cay, Boston, 2000—; spkr. in field. Contbr. articles to profl. jours. Mem. ASTM (chmn. com. 1980-85, bd. dirs. sub-com. 1987-91, Spl. Service award 1985, Achievement award 1986), Am. Soc. Safety Engrs., Nat. Safety Mgmt. Soc., Tufts U. Chem. Engring. Alumni Council, Tau Beta Pi. Republican. Avocations: tennis, skiing, jogging. Office: Palmer & Cay 189 State St Boston MA 02109-2647

COLETTI, GIUSEPPE, surgeon, consultant; b. Citta'di Castello, Perugia, Italy, Sept. 7, 1955; s. Gino and Palma (Bartoccioni) C.; m. Fulvia Costa, Apr. 25, 1992; children: Matteo, Martina. Med. degree, U. Perugia, 1981; cardiac surgery degree, U. Bari, Italy, 1987. Fellow U. Bari, 1982-85; fellow in cardiothoracic surgery St. Antonius Hosp., Nieuwegein, The Netherlands, 1985-86; sr. house officer in cardiothoracic surgery Papworth Hosp., Cambridge, Eng., 1986-87; resident in cardiac surgery Pinna Pintor Clinic, Torino, Italy, 1987-89; sr. resident in cardiac surgery U. Leuven, Belgium, 1989-90; cons. in cardiac surgery Spedali Civili, Brescia, Italy, 1990—; tchr. cardiac surgery Nurse Sch., Brescia, 1991-93. Contbr. articles to med. jours. Mem. Soc. Italian Cardiologists, European Assn. Cardio-Thoracic Surgery. Roman Catholic. Avocations: jogging, tennis. Office: Cardiochirurgia, Ple Spedali Civili 1, 25125 Brescia Italy

COLETTI, JOHN ANTHONY, lawyer, furniture and realty company executive; b. Cherry Point, N.C., Sept. 22, 1952; s. Joseph Nicholas and Gloria Lucy (Fusco) C.; m. Barbara Nancy Carlotti, July 20, 1975; children: Lisa M., Kristen B. Student, Biscayne Coll., 1970-72; BA summa cum laude, Boston Coll., 1974, JD, 1977. Bar: R.I. 1977, U.S. Dist. Ct. R.I. 1977. Assoc. Resmini, Fornaro, Colagiovanni & Angell, Providence, 1979-81; ptnr. Coletti & Tente, Cranston, R.I., 1981—; pres. Coletti's Furniture, Inc., Johnston R.I., 1983-95, Coletti's Realty, Inc., Johnston, 1983-96. Legal counsel Cranston Housing Authority, 1988—; interviewer alumni admissions coun. Boston Coll., 1980—. Mem. ABA, R.I. Bar Assn., R.I. Conveyancers Assn., Nat. Assn. Retail Collection Attys., Phi Beta Kappa. Roman Catholic. Avocations: horseback riding, golf, figure skating. Office: Coletti & Tente 311 Doric Ave Cranston RI 02910-2903

COLFIN, BRUCE ELLIOTT, lawyer, video producer; b. Bklyn., June 9, 1951; s. Abraham and Sylvia (Laykin) C.; m. Virginia Mary Faszczewski, Sept. 27, 1981. BA, CUNY, 1977; JD, N.Y. Law Sch., 1980. Bar: N.Y. 1982, U.S. Dist. Ct. (so., ea. dists.) N.Y., 1987, U.S. Ct. Internat. Trade, 1990. Audio engr. Snowball Sound Systems, N. Bergen, N.J., 1974-77; producer, dir. cable TV program What's On, N.Y.C., 1976-84; stage mgr. Peter Tosh U.S. tour Rolling Stones Records, 1978; v.p., producer Upswing Artists Mgmt., N.Y.C., 1979-86; pres., producer, dir. LegalVision, Inc., N.Y.C., 1982-87; ptnr. Jacobson & Colfin, N.Y.C. and Washington, 1985-90; mem. Jacobson & Colfin, P.C., N.Y.C. and Washington, 1990—; pres. Fifth Ave. Media, Ltd., N.Y.C., 1996—; assoc. prof. music bus. and tech. Five Towns Coll., 1999; spkr. Discovery Ctr., N.Y., 1st Ann. Musicians Seminar, L.I., N.Y. Law Sch. Media Law Soc., 1986; vis. lectr. SUNY, Oneonta, 1988—; panelist New Eng. Music Orgn. Conf., 1998, Emerging Artists and Talent in Music, 1999. Assoc. producer music video Blues Alive, 1982; exec. prodr., dir. video series Entertainment Law Video Primer, 1984; exec. prodr. (CD) Zen Tricksters, 1999; monthly columnist Ind. Music Producers Soc. Jour., NARAS N.Y. chpt. newsletter; contbr. articles to profl. jours.; columnist: Replication News, 1998, Medialine, 2000. Mem. ABA (com. on entertainment sports law, subcom. chmn. patent, trademark and copyright com. 1989, subcom. chmn. internat. law and practice, internat. intellectual property rights com., spl. subcom. on multimedia 1994—, editl. advisor pubs. com. internat. law sect. 1990-92, exec. com. entertainment law cir. 1989-91), NATAS (N.Y. chpt.), N.Y. State Bar Assn. (entertainment, arts and sports law sect., com. on talent agys. and talent mgmt., com. on rights of publicity 1994—), Nassau County Bar Assn., Speaker's Bureau (entertainment and sports law comm.), Copyright Soc. U.S.A. (editl. bd. 1986-88), Nat. Acad. of Recording Arts and Scis. (N.Y. chpt.). Jewish. Avocations: traveling, writing, stamp collecting, hockey. E-mail: BRUCE@Thefirm.com. Office: Jacobson & Colfin PC 19 W 21st St Rm 603A New York NY 10010-6805

COLGAN, GEORGE PHILLIPS, real estate developer, real estate analyst; b. Tokyo, June 3, 1947; s. Jack Phillips and Kimiko (Furukawa) C.; m. Ann Elizabeth Dickerson, Sept. 1, 1968; 1 child, Matthew Seth. Student, Ga. Tech. U., 1965-66; BS in Biology, Ga. State U., 1970. Credit mgr. C&S Nat. Bank, Atlanta, 1969-74; statewide credit mgr. GE Credit Corp., Atlanta, 1974-76; regional v.p. A.L. Williams & Assocs., Atlanta and Houston, 1977-81; dir. sales and mktg. Hooker Barnes Homes, Inc., Atlanta, 1982-84, Brayson/Am. Homes, Atlanta, 1984-87; real estate markets analyst, pres. Whitehall Homes, Inc., Atlanta, 1987-95, residential developer, cons., 1995—. Contbr. articles to profl. jours. Asst. scoutmaster, unit commr. Troop 525 Boy Scouts Am., Norcross, Ga., 1989-94; del. So. Bapt. Conv., Atlanta, 1985; precinct del. Rep. Nat. Party, 1986, 88; pres. Norcross H.S. Wrestling Boosters Club, 1994-96. Mem. Nat. Assn. Home Builders (Cert. of Appreciation 1986). Republican. Presbyterian. Avocations: angling, paleontology, motorcycling. Home: 1590 Keylake Dr Suwanee GA 30024-4263 Office: 3245 Peachtree Pkwy Ste D214 Suwanee GA 30024-1097

COLGATE, STEPHEN, small business owner; b. N.Y.C., June 25, 1935; s. Gilbert Colgate and Nina (King) Heiner; m. Doris Eleanor Horecker, Dec. 17, 1969. BA, Yale U., 1957. CEO, owner Offshore Sailing Sch., Ltd., Ft. Myers, Fla., 1964—, Offshore Travel, Inc., N.Y.C., 1978-88, On and Offshore, Inc., Captiva Island, Fla., 1975—, Cafe Offshore Inc., City Island, Fla., 1981-84. Author: Colgate's Basic Sailing Theory, 1973, Fundamentals of Sailing, Cruising and Racing, 1978, The Yachtsman's Guide to Racing Tactics, 1981, Steve Colgate on Sailing, 1991, Steve Colgate on Cruising, 1991, Steve Colgate on Racing Rules, 1991. Served to capt. USAF, 1958-60. Mem. U.S. Sailing Assn., Internat. Sailing Fedn. (vice chair tng. and devel. com.), Internat. Sailing Schs. Assn. (pres.), U.S. Olympians (Fla. chpt.), Nat. Marine Mfrs. Assn., N.Y. Yacht Club (N.Y.C.), Royal Ocean Racing Club (London), Royal Bermuda Yacht Club, Cruising Club of Am. Republican. Episcopalian. Avocations: bicycling, sailing.

COLIBAR, OLIMPIA MIHAELA, nutritionist; b. Arad, Romania, Mar. 27, 1961; d. Liviu Vasile and Elisabeta Margareta (Baier) Marincas; m. Dorin Leon Colibar, Feb. 22, 1962; 1 child, Sebastian. DMV, Fac. Vet. Medicine, Timisoara, Romania, 1985. Veterinarian IAS ScÂnteta, Arad, 1985-89; rschr. ICUB Pasteur, Arad, 1989-91; asst. U. Agrl. Sci. and Vet. Medicine Banatul, Timisoara, 1991-95, lectr., 1995-98, lectr., asst. prof., 1999—. Author: Nutrition of Domestic Carnivores, 1995; contbr. articles to profl. jours. Mem. Acad. Sci. Bucharest, Nat. Vet. Med. Assocs. Avocation: pathology of reptiles. Office: Univ Agr Sci/Vet Medicine, Calea Aradului nr 119, 1900 Timisoara Romania

COLIN, BLAKEMORE, physiology educator; b. Stratford-on-Avon, Eng., June 1, 1944; s. Cedric Norman and Beryl Ann (Smith) B.; m. Andree Elizabeth Washbourne, Aug. 11, 1965; children—Sarah Jayne, Sophie Ann, Jessica Katy. B.A., Corpus Christi Coll., Cambridge, 1965, M.A., 1969; Ph.D., U. Calif.-Berkeley, 1968; M.A., Magdalen Coll., Oxford, 1979. Univ. demonstrator physiol. lab. U. Cambridge, 1968-72, lectr., 1972-79; fellow, dir. med. studies Downing Coll., 1972-79; Locke research fellow Royal Soc. Eng., 1976-79; Waynflete prof. physiology Oxford U., Eng., 1979—, professorial fellow Magdalen Coll., 1979—; vis. prof. NYU, 1970, MIT, Cambridge, 1971, Salk Inst., San Diego, 1982-83. Mem. scientific adv. bd. Cognitive Neurosci. Inst. N.Y., 1981—. Author: Mechanics of the Mind, 1977. Editor: Handbook of Psychobiology, 1975; Mindwaver, 1986. Mem. editorial bd. Perception, 1971—, Behavioural and Brain Scis., 1977—, Exptl. Brain Research, 1979—, Jour. of Developmental Physiology, 1978—, News in Physiol. Scis., 1985—. Mem. Internat. Brain Research Orgn., Physiol. Soc., Exptl. Psychology Soc., European Brain and Behaviour Soc., Soc. for Neurosci. Avocations: running; broadcasting. Office: Univ Lab of Physiology,, Parks Rd,, Oxford OX1 3PT, England

COLIN, CYRILLE JEAN, epidemiologist; b. Lyon, France, May 18, 1958; s. Marcel and Micheline (Flory) C.; m. Isabelle Chevalier, April 23, 1994; children: Eugenie, Paul-Remi, Lucie. MD, Claude Bernard, Lyon, 1990, PhD, 1993. Lectr. U. Claude Bernard, Lyon, 1990-95, asst. prof., 1995-98, prof. epidemiology and health econs., 1998—; cons. Rhone Pouleuc Rohrer, Paris, 1988-90. Editor in chief: Jour. D'Economie Medicale, 1990—. Home: 14 rue Laurencin, 69002 Lyon France Office: Dept Med Info, Hotel Dieu, 69002 Lyon France

COLIN, JEAN-PIERRE, law educator; b. Neuves-Maisons, Lorraine, France, Feb. 28, 1937; s. Marc and Jeanne (Vermion) C. D in Droit, U. Nancy, France, 1963; degree in polit. sci., U. Paris, 1966. Prof. U. Nancy, France, 1964-66, U. Algiers, Algeria, 1967-69, U. Reims, France, 1969—; spl. adv. to Min. Culture, France, 1981-86, 88-93. Author: Le Mandarin Etranglé, Reflexions sur la Fonction Sociale de L'Art, 1993, L'acteur et Le Roi, Portrait en Pied de Jack Lang, 1994. Served in French military, 1963-64. Mem. Internat. Assn. Polit. Sci., French Inst. Internat. Rels., French Inst. Comparative Law. Avocation: theater. Home: 1 Rue de la Fontaine, F-51300 Heiltz-Le-Hutier France Office: U Reims, 57 rue Pierre Taittinger, 51100 Reims France

COLIN, RALPH FREDERICK, JR., retired executive; b. N.Y.C., Jan. 17, 1933; s. Ralph Frederick and Georgia (Talmey) C.; m. Catherine Meacham, Jan. 24, 1965 (div. June 1980); m. Carolyn Endres, Oct. 6, 1982; stepchildren: Leslie Van Breen, Pamela D'Antonio, Melissa Loughlin, Philip. AB, Harvard Coll., 1954. Investment banker W.E. Hutton & Co., N.Y.C., 1957-64; in various positions, then sr. v.p. bus. and govt. affairs The Columbia House Co., N.Y.C., 1964-95. Bd. mem. Bennington (Vt.) Mus., Vt. Symphony Orch., Green Mountain Coll., Poultney, Vt., Vt. Chpt. The Nature Conservancy, Maple St. Sch., Manchester, Vt., Dorset Ednl. Found., Bennington County Regional Commn., Northshire Civic Ctr., Manchester, Manchester Music Festival, 1995-96. Pilot USAF, 1954-57, Res. to 1980. Mem. NARAS, Nat. Acad. TV Arts Scis., Harvard Club NYC (admissions com. 1984-87). Avocations: music, fine arts, mil. history. Address: PO Box 1759 Manchester Center VT 05255-1759

COLL, JOHN CHARLES, university administrator, chemist; b. Manly, N.S.W., Australia, July 24, 1944; s. James and Esmé (Reid) C.; m. Frances Maria Quiggin, May 24, 1968; children: Eamon James, Joseph Robert. BSc with 1st class honors, U. Sydney, 1966, PhD, 1969, DSc, 1987. Rsch. assoc. U. Ill., Urbana, 1969-71; lectr. Imperial Coll., London, 1971-72; lectr./reader James Cook U., Townsville, Australia, 1972-90; pro-vice chancellor Ctrl. Queensland U., Rockhampton, 1991-96; pro vice-chancellor Australian Cath. U., Sydney, 1996—; bd. dirs. Tropical Beef Ctr., Rockhampton, 1993-95; dep. chmn. Coral Reef Rsch. Inst., Sydney, 1995-96. Contbr. over 150 articles to profl. jours. Bd. dirs. Belmont Bd. Govs., Rockhampton, 1993-95. Roman Catholic. Avocations: scuba diving, underwater photography, swimming, travel, singing. Home: 8/55 Carter St, Cammeray NSW 2062, Australia Office: Australian Cath U, 40 Edward St, North Sydney NSW 2060, Australia

COLLAN, YRJÖ URHO, medical educator, researcher, physician; b. Helsinki, June 23, 1941; s. Yrjö Johannes and Toini Lahja (Sederholm) C.; m. Eira Kyllikki Lehto, Oct. 9, 1971; children: Y. William Mikael, Lauri Urho, Anni Toini. Candidate in medicine, U. Helsinki, 1963, lic. in medicine, 1968, DMS, 1972. Bd. cert. pathologist. Registrar dept. pathology U. Helsinki, 1968-73; registrar dept. surgery U. Cen. Hosp., Helsinki, 1973-74; assoc. prof. dept. pathology U. Helsinki, 1976-77, cons. dept. pathology, 1977-78; lab. supr. Inst. Occupational Health, Helsinki, 1978-80; prof., chmn. pathology U. Kuopio, Finland, 1980-88; dir. histopathology U. Cen. Hosp., Turku, Finland, 1988-89; prof. U. Turku, 1989—; chmn. com. for postgrad. edn. U. Kuopio, 1982-88; dir. pathology service U. Cen. Hosp., Kuopio, 1980-88; contract prof. U. Ancona, Italy, 1985-87; expert cons. Nat. Bd. Health, Helsinki, 1987—; chmn. Prognostication and Cancer Rsch. Group, Turku, 1991—; coord. cancer rsch. program, Turku, 1994—. Author: Medical English, 1975; editor: Morphometry in Morphological Diagnosis, 1982, Stereology and Morphometry in Pathology, 1984, Annals of Clinical Research, Annales Chirurgiae et Gynecologiae, 1969-74; edtl. bd. Acta Sterologica, 1981—, Analytical and Cellular Pathology, 1987—, Forma, 1989—, Electronic Jour. Histology and Histopathology, 1994—, Polish Jour. Pathology, 1995—, Analytical and Quant Cytol Histol, 1996—, others. Mgr. Soc. Young Friends of Nature in Finland, Helsinki, 1961-62; bd. dirs. student union Helsinki U., 1966; v.p. North Savo Cancer Soc., Kuopio, 1982-88. Lt. Finnish mil., 1964. Fogarty internat. fellow, 1974-75, NSF/Acad. Finland grantee, 1988-89; recipient Class I medal Order of White Rose of Finland, 1982, Symbol of Accademia Medico Chirurgica del Piceno, Italy, 1986, Medal City Milan, 1986, Ancona, 1991. Fellow Royal Coll. Pathologists; mem. Internat. Acad. Pathology (internat. councillor 1982-88, pres. Finnish sect. 1986-88), Internat. Union Against Cancer (roll of honour 1997—), Internat. Soc. Stereology (Scandinavian rep. 1983-87), European Soc. Pathology (chmn. com. for diagnostic quantitative pathology 1988-92), Internat. Soc. Diagnostic Quantitative Pathology (pres. 1988-92), European Soc. Analytical Cellular Pathology (coun. 1986-93, 97—), Soc. for Cytometry and Morphometry in Finland (chmn. 1982-87, 90—), Finnish Cancer Soc. (bd. dirs. 1992—), Soc. for Cancer Rsch., Turku (chmn. 1993-94). Lutheran. Avocations: ornithology, languages. Office: U Turku Dept Pathology, Kiinamyllynkatu 10, FIN20520 Turku Finland

COLLARD, EUGENE ALBERT, clergyman, publisher; b. Liège, Belgium, July 1, 1915; s. Jules Marie and Eugenie Marie (Deronchêne) C. Student philosophy and theology, Diocesan Sem., Tournai, Belgium, 1933-40; DCL, U. Cath. Louvain, Belgium, 1942, diploma in social and polit. scis., 1943. Ordained priest Roman Cath. Ch., 1940. Curator Our Lady Parish, Farciennes, Belgium, 1942-44; dir. media orgn. Diocese of Tournai, Mons, Belgium, 1945-88; pub. weekly Dimanche, Mons, 1946-90; lectr. sociology of religion Université Catholique de Louvain, 1951-80; dir. Instituto Pastoral Conf. dos Bispos do Northeast Brazil, Natal, 1964-65. Mem. M.N.B. (resistance orgn.), occupied Belgium, 1943-44. Served with Belgian Health Svc., 1937, 39-40. Decorated chevalier de l'Ordre de Leopold, Belgium, 1956; hon. canon Diocese of Tournai, 1965. Mem. Union des Editeurs de la Presse Périodique Belge (adminstr. 1955-88, pres. 1974-75). Home: Place de Vannes 20, B 7000 Mons Hainaut, Belgium

COLLARD, GUY EUGÈNE, chemical civil engineer; b. Liège, Belgium, Jan. 12, 1949; s. Paul C. and Eva Beylkens. Chem. Civil Engr., U. Liège (Belgium), 1971. Researcher SCK-CEN, Mol, Belgium, 1971-75, head project, 1975-85, program mgr., 1985-89, head rsch. unit, 1989-95, head divsn., dir. radioactive waste and cleanup, 1995—. Office: CEN/SCK Belgium Nuc Rsch, Boeretang 200, 2400 Mol Antwerp, Belgium

COLLEC, JEAN-CLAUDE, group treasurer; b. Langres, Champagne, France, Sept. 25, 1959; s. Robert and Jeanine (Le Fur) C. BAC C, Coll. St. Sauveur, Redon, France, 1977; HEC 82, Hautes Etudes Commerciales, Paris. Correspondent Riyadh Groupe Bouygues, Riyadh, Saudi Arabia, 1983-85; contract mgr. Groupe Bouygues, Jijel, Algeria, 1985; treas. Groupe SCREG, Paris, 1986; asst. treas. Group Financiere Agache, Paris, 1987-89; group treas. Yves Saint Laurent, Paris, 1989—. Mem. Assn. HEC, Groups HEC Luxe, Groupe HEC Banque Fin, Groupe HEC Consommation. E-mail: jccollec@cybercable.fa. Home: 30 Au de Versailles, 75016 Paris France Office: Groupe Yves Saint Laurent, 5 Ave Narceau, 75016 Paris France

COLLEN, MORRIS FRANK, medical association administrator, physician; b. St. Paul, Nov. 12, 1913; s. Frank Morris and Rose (Finkelstein) C.; m. Frances B. Diner, Sept. 24, 1937; children: Arnold Roy, Barry Joel, Roberta Joy, Randal Harry. BEE, U. Minn., 1934, MB with distinction, 1938, MD, 1939. Diplomate Am. Bd. Internal Medicine. Intern Michael Reese Hosp., Chgo., 1939-40; resident Los Angeles County Hosp., 1940-42; chief med. service Kaiser Found. Hosp., Oakland, Calif., 1942-52; chief of staff Kaiser Found. Hosp., Oakland, 1952-53; med. dir. Permanente Med. Group, West Bay Div., 1953-79, dir. med. methods research, 1962-79, dir. tech. assessment, 1979-83, cons. div. research, 1983—; chmn. exec. com. Permanente Med. Group, Oakland, 1953-73; dir. Permanente Services, Inc., Oakland, 1958-73; lectr. Sch. Pub. Health, U. Calif., Berkeley, 1966-78; lectr. info. sci. U. Calif., San Francisco, 1970-85; lectr. U. London, 1972, Stanford U. Med. Ctr., 1973, 75, 84-86, Harvard U., 1974, Johns Hopkins U., 1976, also others; adj. asst. prof. biomed. informatics Uniformed Svcs. U. Health Scis., 2000—; cons. Bur. Health Services, USPHS, 1965-68, chmn. health care systems study sect., 1968-72, mem. adv. com. demonstration grants, 1967; advisor VA, 1968; cons. European region WHO, 1968-72; cons. med. fitness program U.S. Air Force, 1968; cons. Pres.'s Biomed. Research Panel, 1975; mem. adv. com. automated Multiphasic Health Testing, 1971; discussant Nat. Conf. Preventive Medicine, Bethesda, Md., 1975; mem. com. on tech. in health care NAS, 1976; mem. adv. group Nat. Commn. on Digestive Diseases, U.S. Congress, 1978; mem. adv. panel to U.S. Congress Office of Tech. Assessment, 1980-85; mem. peer rev. adv. group TRIMIS program Dept. Def., 1978-90; program chmn. 3d Internat. Conf. Med. Informatics, Tokyo, 1980; chmn. bd. sci. counselors Nat. Libr. Medicine, 1985-87, mem. lit. selection tech. rev. com., 1997—, chmn., 2000; cons. Nat. Libr. Med., 1985-88, Nat. Cancer Inst., 1999-00. Author: Treatment of Pneumococcic Pneumonia, 1948, Hospital Computer Systems, 1974, Multiphasic Health

Testing Services, 1978, Medical Informatics: A Historical Review, 1995; editor: Permanente Med. Bull., 1943-53; mem. editl. bd. Preventive Medicine, 1970-80, Jour. Med. Sys., Methods Info. Medicine, 1980-97, Diagnostic Medicine, 1980-84, Computers in Biomed. Rsch., 1987-94; contbr. articles to med. jours., chpts. to books. Recipient Computers in Health Care Pioneer award, 1992; Johns Hopkins Centennial scholar, 1976; fellow Ctr. Advanced Studies in Behavioral Scis., Stanford U., 1985-86; scholar-in-residence Nat. Libr. Medicine, 1987—. Fellow ACP, Am. Coll. Cardiology, Am. Coll. Chest Physicians, Am. Inst. Med. and Biol. Engring.; mem. AMA, Inst. Medicine of NAS (chmn. tech. subcom. for improving patient records 1990, chmn. workshop on informatics in clin. preventive medicine 1991), Am. Fedn. Clin. Rsch., Am. Coll. Med. Informatics (pres. 1987-88, Morris F. Collen medal named in his honor 1993), Salutis Unitas (v.p. 1972), Soc. Adv. Med. Sys. (pres. 1973), Nat. Acad. Practice in Medicine (chmn. 1982-88, co-chmn. 1989-91), Am. Med. Informatics Assn. (bd. dirs. 1985-96), Internat. Health Evaluation Assn. (pres. 1995-96, Lifetime Achievement award 1992, David E. Morgan award for achievement in health care info. 1998), Internat. Med. Informatics Assn. Sr. Officers Club, Alpha Omega Alpha, Tau Beta Pi. Home: 4155 Walnut Blvd Walnut Creek CA 94596-5834 Office: 3505 Broadway Oakland CA 94611-5714

COLLENETTE, DAVID M., Canadian government official; b. London, 1946; m. Penny Hossack, Oct. 11, 1975; 1 child, Christopher. BA, York U., 1969; postgrad., Carleton U. Exec. v.p. Mandrake Mgmt. Cons., Toronto and Ottawa, Can.; adminstrv. officer Int. Life Ins. Co., London, 1970-72; coord. 41st Ann. Couchiching Conf., 1972; exec. dir. Liberal Party of Ont., 1972-74; M.P. from Don Valley East dist. Ho. of Commons, Ottawa, Ont., Can., 1974-79, 80-84; min. state multiculturalism, 1983-84; sec. gen. Liberal Party Canada, 1985-87; min. nat. def., min. vets. affairs Govt. of Can., Ottawa, 1993-97; min. transport Govt. of Can., 1997—; del. NATO, Brussels, UN, N.Y.C., EEC, Strasbourg, S.Am.; party sec. to Postmaster Gen., Dep. Govt. House Leader; chmn. Standing Com. Energy Legis.; vice chmn. External Affairs and Nat. Def., Subcom. on Van. Rels. with L.Am. and Caribbean, 1982-83. Vol. overseas dem. devel. work; monitor elections in Haiti, Chile, Romania, Czech Republic. Mem. Univ. Club (Toronto), Nat. Liberal Club (London). Anglican. Avocations: squash, swimming, classical music, theatre. Office: Transport Can, 330 Sparks St, Ottawa, ON Canada K1A ON5

COLLET, PIERRE GEORGES, computer scientist; b. Santiago, Chile, June 10, 1966; s. Georges Henri and Jeanne Lucie (Huron) C.; m. Valérie Blanc, July 26, 1997. BSc in Computer Sci., U. Paris VII, 1987, BA in English, 1989, MSc in Computer Sci., 1989; PhD in Computer Sci., U. Paris SUD, 1997. Computer programmer Rank-Xerox-France, Paris, 1986-87; lectr. U. paris VII, 1987-88; cons. Nat. Semiconductor European Rsch. Ctr., Reading, Eng., 1988; lectr. École Nationale Supérieure de Techniques Avancées, Paris, 1990-92; asst. prof. Ecole Nationale Superieure de Techniques Avancees (ENSTA), Paris, 1993—, U. Paris VIII, Saint-Denis, 1990-94; asst. mgr. Euroways, Paris, 1993-94; dir. rsch. PICSEL, Antony, France, 1994-95, Magellan: Computer Aided Surgery, Antony, France, 1995-98; asst. prof. Conservatoire National des Arts et Métiers (CNAM), Versailles, 1992-98; rschr. INRIA 1998-2000, École Polytech., 2000—, DREAM European Project, 2000—. Translator: Mastering C++, 1993; contbr. articles to profl. jours. Mem. NY Acad. Sci., Exptl. Aircraft Assn., Fedn. Nationale Aeronautique, Mensa, Internat. Aerobatic Club. Avocations: aviation, aerobatics, old English (West Saxon). Office: Centre de Math Appliquees, Ecole Polytechnique, 92128 Palaiseu Cedex, France

COLLETTE, JEAN-PAUL MARIE ALBERT, civil engineer, educator; b. Liege, Belgium, May 25, 1951; s. Paul and Anne-Marie (Penders) C.; m. Gabrielle E. de Neuville, Dec. 20, 1975; children: Sebastien, Maureen. Civil engr. in physics, U. Liege, Belgium, 1975; MBA, Ecole de Perfectionnement au Mgmt., Liege, 1984. Cert. engring. mgmt. Rsch. engr. Euratom-Ceng, Brussels, France, 1975-78; vice mgr. engring. office, R&D mgmt., nuclear equipment Cockerill Mech. Industries, Seraing, Belgium, 1978-89; head engring. dept., bd. dirs. Centre Spatial de Liege (Belgium)-ESA Facilities, 1989—; lectr. IBM Edn. Ctr., Brussels, 1981-84; prof. Ecole de Perfectionnement au Mgmt., Liege, 1986, Inst. Gramme, Liege, 1990—; cons. various orgns., Embourg, Belgium, 1987—. Author: Nuclear Decontamination, 1976, Physics, 1987; co-author: High Efficiency AFBC Combined Cycle, 1985; contbr. articles to profl. jours. Mem. city com. Polit. Party, Embourg, 1991—. Comdt. H.Q. staff officer, 1980, Liege. Grantee Rotary Found., 1975, Euratom, Grenoble, 1975. Mem. ASME, Assn. des Ingenieurs de L'universite de Liege, Soc. d'Astronomie de Liege, Kiwanis, EPM Alumni. Avocations: tennis, yachting.

COLLIER, DUAINE ALDEN, manufacturing and distribution company executive; b. Chambersburg, Pa., Aug. 19, 1950; s. Clyde Alden and Etta Jean (Browell) C.; m. Trudy Jean Shoap, Aug. 22, 1970; children: Patrick, Crystal. BS in Math., Shippensburg U., 1972. Product specialist ITT Domestic Pump, Shippensburg, 1972-77; pres., CEO College Town, Inc., Shippensburg, 1971—; gen. mgr. Shippensburg Pump Co., Inc., 1985—; bd. dirs., sec.-treas. Beidel Printing House, Inc., Shippensburg, 1975—, White Mane Pub. Co., Inc., Shippensburg, 1987—. Committeeman Franklin County Rep. Party, 1989-92; pres. Shippensburg Area Devel. Corp., 1983-84, bd. dirs., 1982-84; bd. dirs. Shippensburg Midget Football Assn., Inc., coach, 1984-94, head coach, 1991-94; pres. Maroon & Grey Football Club, 1991-94; bd. dirs. Shippensburg U. Found., 1995—; bd. dirs., pres. Shippen Place, Inc., 1996-99; mem. adv. bd. Orrstown Bank, 1998—; v.p. Main St. Non-profit Redevel. Corp. Mem. The Wednesday Club, Masons (master Orrstown lodge 1979), Shippensburg Lions Club (pres. 1989-90), Sons of the Am. Legion. Methodist. Avocations: hunting, fishing, skiing, photography, painting. Office: College Town Inc PO Box 337 17 W Burd St Shippensburg PA 17257-1223

COLLIER, JOYCE ANN, budget analyst; b. Oak City, N.C., July 23, 1947; d. Amos and Arrena Estella Spruell; m. Walter Columbus Collier, Aug. 21, 1970 (dec. June 1990). BA, N.C. Ctrl. U., 1970; MA, Maple Springs Bapt. Bible Coll. and Sem., 1994. Bookkeeper Boys and Girls Homes of Md., Silver Spring, 1979-81; acctg. technician Naval Med. Command, Bethesda, Md., 1981-83; budget analyst Naval Med. Command, Washington, 1983-86, Naval Security Group, Ft. Meade, Md., 1986—; asst. prof. Maple Springs Bible Coll. and Sem., 1986-97. Chair fin. Maple Springs Bapt. Ch., Capitol Heights, Md., 1972—; cons. Mt. Calvary Free Will Bapt. Ch., Washington, 1997—, New Testament Deliverance Ch., Washington, 1997—. Mem. Am. Assn. Christian Counselors, Nat. Notary Assn., West Martin Alumni. Avocations: reading, exercising. E-mail: jcollier@prodigy.net.

COLLIER, NATHAN MORRIS, musician, music educator; b. Clinton, Okla., July 23, 1924; s. Lotan Morris and Annie Carlletta (Willsey) C.; m. Frances Aleta Snell, June 24, 1955; children: Susan Aleta Kowalski, Ray Morris. MusB, U. Okla., 1949; MusM, U. Rochester, 1951. String music cons. Lincoln (Nebr.) Pub. Schs., 1951-68; asst. concertmaster Lincoln Symphony Orch., 1953—; first violin Omaha (Nebr.) Symphon, The Nebr. Sinfonia, 1956-79; assoc. concertmaster, 1977-78, acting concertmaster, 1978; concertmaster Lincoln Symphony, Lincoln Little Symphony, 1977-78; asst. prof. violin, theory Nebr. Wesleyan U., Lincoln, 1968-84; string tchr. St. John Luth. Sch., Seward, Nebr., 1983-89; asst. concertmaster Nebr. Chamber Orch., 1973-91; acting concertmaster on occasion; prin. second violinist Des Moines Symphony, 1979—; concertmaster Omaha Pops Orch., 1988-90; 1st violinist Avanti String Quartet, 1990; asst prof. music, condr. symphony orch. Kans. State U., Manhattan, 1980-81, pvt. tchr., 1st violinist Resident String Quartet, 1980-81; vis. instr. music Concordia U., Seward, 1985, 90; guest prin. violinist Des Moines Symphony, 1979, 87; guest violinist, violist Myron Cohen Met. and the Midlands String Quartets, Omaha, 1988—, Hastings (Nebr.) Symphony, 1990—, Met. String Quartet; violist and solo violinist with Collegium Musicum Concordia, 1999—; viola instr. chamber music coach summer course U. Nebr., Lincoln, 1991; concertmaster, soloist Nebr. Camerata-Orch. Berlin tour, 1992; mem. adv. bd. Rocky Ridge Music Ctr., 1972—; cons., lectr. in field. Composer various mus. pieces; arranger numerous compositions for string quartet, 1980. Tchr., co-organizer Brownville (Nebr.) Summer Music Festival, 1972-77. With USN, 1943-46. Grantee U.S. Govt., 1966-67. Mem. Am. String Tchrs. assn. (nebr. Pvt. Studio Tchr. of Yr. 1994), Music Tchrs. Nat. Assn. (nationally cert. 1994—), Music Educators Nat. Conf., Violin Soc. Am., Chamber Music Am., Lincoln Music Tchrs. Assn., Nat. Sch. Orch. Assn., NEA, Nebr. State Edn. Assn., Lincoln Musicians Assn., Omaha Musicians Assn., Lincoln Arts Coun. (co-recipient Lincoln Mayor's Arts award 1995), Pi Kappa Lambda. Democrat. Methodist. Home: 4544 Mohawk St Lincoln NE 68510-4838

COLLIÈRE, MARIE-FRANÇOISE, nursing educator, ethnohistory researcher; b. Oran, Algeria, Apr. 6, 1930; d. Emile Edouard Colliere and Henriette Marie-Lucie (Potier) C. BA, U. Paris, 1950, Degree in Psychology, 1951; Cert. Nurse, Paris, 1954, Cert. Social Worker, 1958; MSc in Pub. Health Nursing, Wayne State U., Detroit, 1965; postgrad., U. Lyon, France, 1968-70; Diploma in History of Civilization, U. Paris VII, 1982. Cert. nurse and social worker. Prof., rschr. U. Lyon II, 1965-94; prof. continuing edn. workshops and seminars Ecole Internationale, Lyon, 1965-94; nat. cons. dist. and home nursing, 1968-95; cons. hist. rsch. various univs., 1980-2000; permanent cons. to bd. experts WHO Geneva, 1974-96. Author: Promote Life: from women care practice to nursing care, 1982, The First Art of Life: Caring, 1996; contbr. articles to profl. jours.; leader workshops and seminars with video Anthrop. and Hist. Approach of Care, 1988-90, 91. Leader in cmty. health devel., Lyon, 1970-94. Decorated Order Acad. Palms (France). Mem. Sigma Theta Tau. Avocation: trekking in the Sahara. Office: 15 Rue Professeur Morat, 69008 Lyon France

COLLIGNON, STEF G., recording company executive; b. Rotterdam, The Netherlands, Nov. 10, 1965; s. Ton A. and Coby F.H. (Meijer) C.; m. Antoinette F. Smit Sibinga, June 27, 1998; 1 child, Merijn A. MA, U. Leiden, The Netherlands, 1990. Product mgr. Philips Classics, Baarn, 1990-92, artist and repertoire mgr., 1992-94; gen. mgr. Polygram Classics, Hilversum, 1994-96; v.p. mktg. Philips Music Group, Amsterdam, 1996-99; mng. dir. Polydor BV, Hilversum, 1999—. Chmn. Netherlands Theatre Orch., Amsterdam, 1996; mem. adv. bd. Classic FM, 1995-97; chmn. Nat. Student Orch., 1987-88; condr. Chamber Orch. Concerts, 1994—. Office: Polydor BV, Mozartlaan 25, 1217 CM Hilversum The Netherlands

COLLIGON, JOHN SMALLWOOD, electronics engineering educator; b. Middlesbrough, Eng., Feb. 3, 1937; s. James and Isabel Mary (Pickering) C.; m. Angela Postlethwaite, July 25, 1962; children: Judy Louise, Stuart Jeffrey. B in Electronics Engring. with honors, U. Liverpool, Eng., 1958, PhD, 1962. Chartered engr.; chartered physicist. Rsch. fellow Royal Aircraft Establishment, Farnborough, Hants, Eng., 1961-64, sr. sci. officer, 1964-68; lectr. U. Salford, Lancs, Eng., 1968-71, sr. lectr., 1971-93, prof., 1993—; sec. gen. Internat. Union for Vacuum Sci., Technique and Applications, Brussels, 1989-98. Editor in chief Jour. Vacuum, 1981-89, co-editor, 1998—; contbr. over 100 articles to profl. jours. Royal Soc. Indsl. rsch. fellow, 1988-89. Fellow IEEE, Inst. Physics, Am. Vacuum Soc. Avocations: Russian language, tennis, table-tennis, music. Office: U Salford, The Crescent, Salford M5 4WT, England also: Manchester Met U, Chester St, Manchester M1 5GD, England

COLLIN, BRUCE EDWARD, investor; b. N.Y.C., Apr. 11, 1956; s. Robert William and Maryann (Nathan) C. BA magna cum laude, Conn.. Coll., 1978; Cert. in Spanish with highest honors, U. Salamanca, Spain, 1973; MS, Fordham U., 1999. Brand asst. Procter & Gamble, Cin., 1978-80; coll. field rep. Prentice-Hall/Simon & Schuster, Englewood Cliffs, N.J., 1981-93; acquisitions editor Simon & Schuster, Plano, Tex., 1993-94; account exec. McGraw-Hill, Plano, 1995-97. Co-founder, pres. Com. to Award Miss Piggy the Oscar (CAMPO), Cin., 1979-80. Mem. Phi Beta Kappa. Republican. Jewish. Avocations: swimming, politics, softball. Home: 170 Prospect Ave Apt 9F Hackensack NJ 07601-1873

COLLINA, KATHLEEN ALICE, corrugated box company executive; b. N.Y.C., Oct. 24, 1938; d. Louis Orville and Evelyn Dorothy (Cosgrove) Seawood; m. Nido Edward Collina, Sept. 14, 1957; children: Susan B. Collina Schulte, Gary E., Jill A. Collina Labar, Douglas J., Steven J. Grad. high sch., Easton, Pa. Svc. rep. Bell Telephone Co. of Pa., Easton, 1956-59, Stanley Home Products, Westfield, Mass., 1962-78; exec. asst. MA 500, Inc., Nazareth, Pa., 1973-86, Century Packaging Inc., Whitehall, Pa., 1987—. Capt. leadership team capital campaign Notre Dame High Sch., Easton, 1991-92. Mem. Ladies Ancient Order of Hibernians (pres. 1993-96, treas. 97—, Anna Malia Ruddy award 1997). Home: 3825 Church Rd Easton PA 18045-2909 Office: Century Packaging Inc 5217 Kemmerer St Whitehall PA 18052-1848

COLLINET, PIERRE ALAIN, research associate; b. Brussels, Aug. 13, 1965; s. Lucien and Jeanne (Piret) C. Degree in Info. Scis., Inst. D'Enseignement Superieur en Scis. de L'Info. et de la Documentation, Brussels, Belgium, 1986. Corp. documentalist Union Miniere, Brussels, 1987-88; rsch. asst. Spencer Stuart Mgmt. Cons., Brussels, 1988-92; head of rsch. Russell Reynolds Assocs., Brussels, 1992—. Author, editor: Directory of Documentation Centers of Museums for Brussels and Walloon Brabant, 1986; co-author, editor: Directory 1982-1992 of I.E.S.S.I.D. Alumni, 1993. Avocations: chess, internet, tennis. Home: Place des Bienfaiteurs 4, 1030 Brussels Belgium Office: Russell Reynolds Assocs, Blvd Saint-Michel 27, 1040 Brussels Belgium

COLLINS, ALLEN HOWARD, psychiatrist; b. Washington, Sept. 6, 1942; s. Murray and Bertha (Baccalman) C.; m. Stephanie Evelyn Awn, May 22, 1976; children: Sasha Marie, Matthew Allen, Alyssa Beth. AB, Columbia Coll., 1964; MD, Tufts U., 1968; MPH, Columbia U., 1974. Diplomate Am. Bd. of Psychiatry and Neurology; Nat. Bd. of Med. Examiners; cert. psychoanalysis. Mental health career develop. fellow NIMH, Rockville, Md., 1968-74; staff psychiatrist Region II NIMH, N.Y.C., 1972-74, psychiat. cons., 1974-90; chief psychiat. consultation liaison svcs. Lenox Hill Hosp., N.Y.C., 1974-76, chief psychiat. inpatient svc., 1976-78, chief of psychiatry svc., 1978-86, dir. dept. of psychiatry, 1986—, pres. med. bd., 1994-96, 2000—; examiner in psychiatry Am. Bd. of Psychiatry and Neurology, Evanston, Ill., 1979—, chief proctor, 1991—; clin. prof. of psychiatry N.Y. Med. Coll., Valhalla, 1988-90; tng. and supervisory psychoanalyst divsn. of psychoanalytic tng., 1986-90; assoc. clin. prof. psychiatry Cornell U. Med. Coll., 1990-93; clin. prof. psychiatry NYU Med. Ctr., 1993—; vis. prof. psychiatry SUNY/Downstate Health Sci. Ctr., 1998—. Author: (with others) Provider's Guide To Hospital-Based Services, 1986; contbr. articles to profl. jours. With USPHS, 1968-74. Fellow Am. Psychiatr. Assn., Am. Acad. of Psychoanalysis, N.Y. Acad. Medicine. Avocations: tennis, golf, reading biographies, history.

COLLINS, ALMA JONES, English educator, writer; b. New London, Conn., June 14, 1921; d. Walter Melville Jones and Anne Teresa Harrington; m. Daniel Francis Collins, Apr. 9, 1994. BA, Conn. Coll., 1943; MA, Trinity Coll., 1952, U. Conn., 1962. Tchr., counselor W. Hartford (Conn.) Bd. Edn., 1947-72; pres. Arts Universal Rsch. Assocs., Inc., 1978—; cons. for corp. product devel.; rep. for artists. Contbr. articles and monographs in nat. and internat. publs. Mem. Phi Beta Kappa, Delta Kappa Gamma. Avocations: writing poetry and fiction. Home and Office: 275 Steele Rd A318 West Hartford CT 06117-2763

COLLINS, CHRISTOPHER CARL, manufacturing executive; b. Schenectady, N.Y., May 20, 1950; s. Gerald Edward and Constance (Messier) C.; m. Margaret Elizabeth Busby Cox, May 20, 1972 (div. Apr. 1978); 1 child, Carly Elizabeth; m. Mary Sue Kuhn, Jan. 9, 1988; children: Caitlin Christine, Cameron Christopher. BSME, N.C. State U., 1972; MBA, U. Ala., 1975. Sales engr. Westinghouse Elec. Corp., Birmingham, Ala., 1972-76; market rsch. analyst Westinghouse Elec. Corp., Buffalo, 1976-77, mgr. market planning, 1978-79, mgr. gearing divsn., 1980-82; pres., chmn., CEO Nuttall Gear Corp., Niagara Falls, N.Y., 1983-97; pres. Nuttall Gear, LLC, Niagara Falls, 1997-98; v.p. corp. devel. Wilson Greatbatch Ltd., Clarence, N.Y., 1999; chmn. bd., CEO Bloch Industries LLC, Rochester, N.Y., 1999—, Zepto Metrix Corp., Buffalo, 1999—; mem. small bus. adv. coun. Fed. Res. Bank N.Y., 1992-95; chmn. bd. ZeptoMetrix Corp., Buffalo, 1999—. Bd. dirs. Kenmore Mercy Hosp., 1986-93; mem. ho. of dels. United Way, Buffalo, 1986—; mem. Buffalo Fin. Planning Com., 1994; exec. bd. dirs. Greater Niagara Frontier coun. Boy Scouts Am., 1998—; Rep. and Conservative candidate for U.S. Congress, 1998; mentor Ctr. for Entrepreneurial Leadership, SUNY, 1999—. Mem. Chief Execs. Orgn., World Pres.'s Orgn., Young Pres. Orgn. (chmn. edn. com. 1988-89, chpt. chmn. 1989-90, chmn. membership 1990-91, chmn. exec. com. 1991-96), Brookfield Country Club, Holimont Ski Club. Republican. Roman Catholic. Avocations: golf, skiing, aviation. Home: 9660 Cobblestone Dr Clarence NY 14031-1576 Office: Bloch Industries LLC 140 Commerce Dr Rochester NY 14623-3592

COLLINS, DAVID JOHN, chemistry educator, researcher; b. Lismore, NSW, Australia, July 2, 1931; s. David Albert and Elsie Jane (Stratford) C.; m. Berenice Norma Keough, July 27, 1963; children: John Leslie, Delwyn Leanne, Narelle Bronwyn, Grant Andrew. MS, U. Sydney, Australia, 1954, PhD, 1958. Rsch. officer Royal Hosp. for Women, Paddington, NSW, 1956-58; postdoctoral fellow Ohio State U., Columbus, 1958-59; Glaxo postdoctoral fellow Imperial Coll., South Kensington, Eng., 1959-60; dir. rsch. lab. Royal Hosp. for Women, Paddington, NSW, 1961-63; sr. rsch. fellow chemistry sect. dept. vet. physiology U. Sydney, 1963-70; sr. rsch. fellow dept. chemistry Monash U., Clayton, Victoria, Australia, 1971-76, reader dept. chemistry, 1976-96, hon. sr. rsch. fellow dept. chemistry, 1997—; assoc. dept. history and philosophy of sci. U. Melbourne, Australia, 1998—; vis. prof. dept. chemistry U. Auckland, New Zealand, 1990. Co-author: Plants for Medicines: A Chemical and Pharmacological Survey of Plants in the Australian Region, 1990; contbr. numerous sci. papers to profl. publs. Fellow Royal Australian Chem. Inst.; mem. Am. Chem. Soc., Royal Soc. Chemistry. Avocations: bookbinding, tennis, crafts. Office: Monash U Dept Chemistry, Monash U Dept Chemistry, Wellington Rd, Clayton VIC 3168, Australia

COLLINS, DENNIS GLENN, mathematics educator; b. Gary, Ind., June 26, 1944; s. Glenn and Irene Martha (Richman) C.; m. Barbara Jean Hamilton, July 14, 1979; 1 child, Glenn H. BA, Valparaiso U., 1966; MS, Ill. Inst. Tech., 1970, PhD, 1975. Temp. instr. Mich. State U., East Lansing, 1975-76; instr. U. New Orleans, 1976-79; asst. prof. Valparaiso (Ind.) U., 1979-82; from asst. prof. to prof. math. U. P.R., Mayaguez, 1982—, chmn. math. dept. pers. com., 1994-95; vis. assoc. prof. dept. math. Mich. State U., 1988-89; judge computer sci. 38th Internat. Sci. and Engring. Fair, San Juan, P.R., 1987; presenter econ. modelling World Bank, 1994; presenter optical echo theory of quasars Seminario Interuniversitario de Investigación Matematica, Rio Piedras, P.R., 1995, organizer 15th conf., 2000, Am. Math. Soc., Orlando, Fla., 1996; presenter 8th Quadrennial Internat. Conf. on Graph Theory, Kalamazoo, 1996, 9th, 2000, 1st Biennial Energy Analysis Conf., U. Fla., Gainesville, 1999. Created copyrighted set postcards of mathematicians and physicists, 1983; composed short Columbus Cantata and short Spaceship Cantata. NSF fellow, 1966-67; vis. scholar Mich. State U., 1988-89, 96-97. Mem. Internat. Soc. for Sys. Sci. (presenter 42nd meeting Atlanta 1998, 19th conf. on Entropy, Boise, Idaho, 1999), presenter and organizer, 15th SIDIM (Sem. Int. de Inv. Mat.), 2000, Soc. Photo-optical Instrumentation Engrs., Internat. Soc. for Optical Engring., Am. Math. Soc. (presenter ann. meetings 1985-87, invited address 5th Internat. Conf. on info. rsch., informatics and cybernetics 1990, presenter Internat. Symposium on Econ. Modelling, World Bank 1994, Detroit meeting 1997, dialog com. to rector 1997—, poster session 10th internat. math. conf. Chgo. 1998), Soc. Indsl. and Applied Mathematicians, N.Y. Acad. Scis., Sigma Xi. Lutheran. Home: 7108 Grand Blvd Hobart IN 46342-6628 Office: U PR Dept Math Mayaguez PR 00681

COLLINS, DON CARY, lawyer; b. Sept. 10, 1951; s. Everett Hugh Jr. and Evelyn Loriene (Wootton) C.; m. Kimberly Diane Collins. Student, Western Ky. U., 1969-70; BA, Ill. State U., Normal, 1972; JD, So. Ill. U., 1976. Bar: Ill. 1976, Mo. 1977, U.S. Supreme Ct., U.S. Ct. Appeals (7th cir.), U.S. Dist. Ct. (so. dist.) Ill. Pub. rels./media chmn. S.W. Ill. Regional Spl. Olympics, 1979; bd. dirs. Children's Ctr. for Behavioral Devel., Edgemont, Ill., 1989-91. Mem. ABA, ATLA, Ill. Bar Assn., Mo. Bar Assn., St. Clair County Bar Assn., East St. Louis Bar Assn., Met. St. Louis Bar Assn., Ill. Trial Lawyers Assn., Am. Judicature Soc., So. Ill. U. Sch. Law Alumni Assn. (bd. dirs. 1984—, v.p. 1986-87, pres. 1987-88). Fax: 618-234-4015. Office: 126 W Main St Belleville IL 62220-1502

COLLINS, FRANCIS WINFIELD, chemical company executive; b. N.Y.C., Jan. 5, 1927; s. Francis W. and Lillian A. (Schaeffler) C.; m. Rhoda Henry Collins, May 30, 1952; children: Sharon, Russell, Margaret, Cynthia, Wayne. BA cum laude, Amherst Coll., 1948; MA, Columbia U., 1949. From control chemist to asst. dept. head Merck and Co., Rahway, N.J., 1949-60; tech. rep. E.I. DuPont de Nemours, Wilmington, Del., 1960-65; from supt. to sr. market rschr. E.I. DuPont de Nemours, Gibbstown, N.J., 1965-85; ret., 1985; pres. Brandywine Cons., Inc., Wilmington, Del., 1985—; tchg. and tutoring, 1985—. Chair Hanby Civic Assn., Wilmington, 1978-80, West Milford (N.J.) Adv. Commn., 1969; chpt. chair Svc. Corps Ret. Execs., 1991-93, regional mktg. coord., 1994-95, regional computer coord., 1994-96 (spl. award 1996, Platinum award 1997); counselor Internat. Exec. Svc. Corps, 1993—; asst. chmn. bd. trustees Minikin Opera, Wilmington, 1985-94. Recipient Platinum award for outstanding svc. Svc. Corp. Ret. Execs., 1998. Avocations: world travel, sailing, camping, gardening. Home and Office: 614 Loveville Rd Apt C2G Hockessin DE 19707-1607

COLLINS, FUJI, clinical psychologist; b. Tokyo, Nov. 3, 1954; s. Boyd Leslie and Kimiko (Terayama) C.; 1 child, Lacey Nichole. BS, Ariz. State U., 1977; MS, Ea. Wash. U., 1989; MA, The Fielding Inst., 1993, PhD, 1994. Cert. clinical therapist. Commd. 2d lt. U.S. Army, 1978, advanced through grades to maj., 1989, lt. platoon leader, adminstrv. officer, 1978-79; lt. bat. adjutant 509th Airborne Bat. Combat Team, 1977-80; capt., air def. fire coordination officer U.S. Army, 1981-83, capt. battery comdr., 1983-85, capt., 1985-86; clin. therapist Wash. State Patrol, 1985-95; dir. of adminstrn., Japanese Counseling Program Richmond Area Multi-Svcs., Inc., San Francisco, 1995-97, dir. children and youth svcs., 1995-97; prof. psychology Ctrl. Wash. U., Ellensburg, 1997-2000; assoc. dir., asst. dean dept. multicultural programs/svcs., U. Ariz., Tucson, 2000—, dir. Asian Pacific Am. Student Affairs, 2000—; assoc. prof. psychology and sociology N.Mex. Mil. Inst., 2000—; adj. prof. John F. Kennedy U.; coord. Wash. State Patrol Critical Incident/Peer Support Team, Wash. State Hostage Negotiator; mem. Thurston/Mason County Critical Incident Stress Debriefing Team; dir. Richmond Counseling Ctr., 1995—; vis. lectr. Georgetown U., 1996—; faculty Nat. Asian Am. Psychology Tng. Ctr., San Francisco, 1996—, cons. Disaster Mental Health Inst., 1999—. Vol. Thurston/Mason County Crisis Clinic; mem. steering com. Thurston/Mason County Critical Incident Team. Ariz. Humanities scholar, 2000—. Mem. ACA, APA, Wash. State Psychol. Assn., Asian Am. Psychol. Assn., Soc. for Psychol. Study of Ethnic Minority Issues, Am. Critical Incident Stress Found., Wash. State Hostage Negotiation Assn., Assn. Police Planning and Rsch. Officers. Home: 104 Linda Cir Roswell NM 88201 Office: U Ariz MLK Bldg Rm 320 PO Box 210128 Tucson AZ 85721-0128

COLLINS, (JAMES) GERARD, Irish government official; b. Abbeyfeale, Ireland, Oct. 16, 1938; m. Hilary Tattan. Ed., Univ. Coll. Dublin, Ireland. Former vocat. tchr.; acting gen. sec. Fianna Fail Party, 1964-67; mem. Dail, 1967-97; parliamentary sec. to min. for industry and commerce, 1969-70, also to min. for Gaeltacht, 1969-70, min. for posts and telegraphs, 1970-73; mem. Limerick County Coun., 1974-77; min. for justice, 1977-81, 87-89, min. fgn. affairs, 1982, 89-92, spokesman fgn. affairs, 1983-87; v.p. Fianna Fail Party, 1992—; M.P., leader Fianna Fail group European Parliament, 1994—, v.p., 1998—; chmn. parliamentary com. Secondary Legis. European Cmtys., 1983—; pres. del. to South Africa, European Parliament, 1994—; v.p. European Parliament.

COLLINS, GORDON DENT, recording company executive; b. Berkeley, Calif., Mar. 27, 1924; s. Edward Everett and Dorothy Janet C.; m. Louise Norma Krivicich, July 23, 1960; children: Daniel Edward, Patrick Doyle, Christine Anne, Gordon Jr. Student, U. Maine, 1943-44; BSEE magna cum laude, U. Wash., 1948; postgrad., Stanford U., 1960-63. Registered profl. engr., N.Y. Founder, chief executive officer Collins Rec. Co., Los Altos, Calif., 1968—; assigned to Comissariat à l'energie Atomique, Ctr. Nuclear Studies, France. Served to lt. U.S. Army Signal Corps, 1943-52. Named Man of Yr. Elfun Soc., San Jose, Calif., 1980. Mem. Soc. Engrs. and Scientists of France, Phi Beta Kappa, Tau Beta Pi, Phi Kappa Psi, Sigma Xi. Club: No. Calif. Golf Assn. (Pebble Beach). Achievements include rec. on location in divers venues, 13 states, 19 countries, 5 continents; pioneer in atomic power development; first co. to record ann. awards ceremony of Nat. Acad. Rec. Arts and Scis. Patentee in field. Avocations: playing golf, travel, photography, genealogy. Office: PO Box 934 Los Altos CA 94023-0934

COLLINS, HARVEY ARNOLD, art educator, retired; b. High Springs, Fla., Aug. 22, 1927; s. Harvey Arnold and Pansy Henrietta (Bugg) C.; m. Thelma L. Haufler, Apr. 22, 1951; children: Cheryl, Patty, Marc. BFA, U. Fla., 1951, MFA, 1952; LLD (hon.), Olivet Nazarene Coll., Kankakee, Ill., 1982. Assoc. prof. Olivet Nazarene Coll., Kankakee, 1953-58; instr. art Largo (Fla.) Jr. High Sch., 1958-60, Oak Grove Jr. High Sch., Clearwater, Fla., 1960-71; assoc. prof., chair dept. art Olivet Nazarene U., Kankakee, 1971-91, ret., 1991; adj. instr. art history Sante Fe C.C., Gainesville, Fla., 1994—. painter murals various univs., hosps., librs. Cpl. Signal Corps, U.S. Army, 1946-47, Korea. Recipient George Washington Tchr. medal Freedoms Found., Valley Forge, Pa., 1962, Disting. Svc. award Coll. Ch., Bourbonnais, Ill., 1986. Mem. Coll. Art Assn., Kappa Delta Pi. Democrat. Avocations: travel, tropical plants, model bldg. Home: 13310 NW 39th Ave Gainesville FL 32606-4719

COLLINS, JAMES DUFFIELD, marine engineer, editor; b. Logansport, Ind., Dec. 20, 1919; s. Louis Duffield and Gaynelle May (Mobley) C.; m. Barbara Cook, Mar. 12, 1949; children: Barbara Cook Jr., James Duffield II. BS in Marine Engring., U.S. Mcht. Marine Acad., 1946. Process engr. Gen. Motors Corp., Indpls., 1940-44; marine engr. Moore McCormack Lines, N.Y.C., 1946; sr. project engr. rsch. and devel. Gen. Motors Corp., Indpls., 1946-82; editor-at-large Marcel Dekker, Inc., N.Y.C., 1986—. Contbr. author: Materials and Processes, 1985; author: Bowline Knot, 1972; contbr. articles to profl. jours; patentee in field. Lt. (j.g.) USNR, 1946-57, ret. Mem. Soc. Naval Architects and Marine Engrs., Masons. Avocations: music, concert master, orchestra and symphony member. Home and Office: 5228 Bevedere Dr Indianapolis IN 46228-2137

COLLINS, JAMES FRANKLIN, ambassador; b. Aurora, Ill., June 4, 1939. AB cum laude, Harvard Coll., 1961; MA, Ind. U., 1964, postgrad., 1964-67; postgrad., Moscow State U., 1965-66. Dir. for intelligence policy Nat. Security Coun., Washington; dep. exec. sec. for Europe and L.Am. U.S. Dept. of State, Washington; vice counsel U.S. Dept. of State, Izmir, Turkey; polit. counselor U.S. Dept. of State, Amman, Jordan; dep. chief of mission Am. Embassy U.S. Dept. of State, Moscow, 1990-93; coord. for regional affairs for New Ind. States U.S. Dept. of State, 1993-94; sr. coord. Office of Ambassador-at-Large for New Ind. State U.S. Dept. of State, Washington, 1994-95; amb.-at-large, spl. advisor to sec. State for the New Ind. States, 1995-97; U.S. amb. to Russian Fedn. Moscow, 1997—. Office: Am Embassy Moscow Russia Dept State Washington DC 20521-0001

COLLINS, JAMES SLADE, II, lawyer; b. St. Louis, June 9, 1937; s. James Slade and Dolma Ruby (Neilsen) C.; m. Neva Frances Guinn, June 27, 1959; children: Shari, Camala Ann. BSBA, Washington U., 1958, JD, 1961. Bar: Mo. 1961, U.S. Supreme Ct. 1969, U.S. Dist. Ct. (ea. dist.) Mo. 1972, U.S. Ct. Appeals (8th cir.) 1972. Assoc. Whalen, O'Connor, Grauel & Sarkisian, St. Louis, 1961-70, ptnr., 1970-72; ptnr. Whalen, O'Connor, Collins & Danis, St. Louis, 1972-75; assoc. Hullverson, Hullverson & Frank, Inc., St. Louis, 1975-78; pvt. practice St. Louis, 1979—. Trustee Village of Hanley Hills, Mo., 1966-69, mayor, 1967, mcpl. judge, 1967-68, 69-70. Mem. ABA, ATLA, Mo. Trial Lawyers Assn., Bar Assn. Met. St. Louis, Lawyers Assn. St. Louis, Phi Delta Phi. Republican. Baptist. Home: 916 Parkwatch Dr Ballwin MO 63011-3640 Office: 6654 Chippewa St Saint Louis MO 63109-2527

COLLINS, JOAN HENRIETTA, actress; b. London, May 23, 1933; came to U.S., 1938; d. Joseph William and Elsa (Bessant) C.; m. Anthony Newley (div.); children: Tara, Sacha; m. Ronald S. Kass, Mar., 1972 (div.); 1 child, Katy; m. Peter Holm (div.); m. Maxwell Reed. Ed., Francis Holland Sch., London; student, Royal Acad. of Dramatic Art. Films include: Cosh Boy, Our Girl Friday, I Believe in You, Girl in the Red Velvet Swing, Sea Wife, Rally Round the Flag Boys, Island in the Sun, Seven Thieves, Road to Hong Kong, Sunburn, The Stud, Game for Vultures, The Bitch, The Big Sleep, The Good Die Young, Land of the Pharoahs, The Bravados, Esther and the King, Warning Shot, The Executioner, Subterfuge, Revenge, Quest for Love, Tales From the Crypt, The Bawdy Adventures of Tom Jones, The Opposite Sex, The Virgin Queen, Quest for Love, Decadence, 1994, In the Bleak Mid-Winter, 1995, The Clandestine Marriage, 1998, The Flintstones-Viva Rock Vegas, 1999, Joseph and His Technicolor Dreamcoat, 1999; theater appearances include: Jassey, Claudia, The Skin of Our Teeth, The Praying Mantis, The Last of Mrs. Cheyney, The 7th Veil, A Doll's House, Private Lives, 1990 (London, Broadway, also tour), Love Letters, 2000; TV films include: Drive Hard, Drive Fast, 1973, The Man Who Came to Dinner, Paper Dolls, 1982, The Wild Women of Chastity Gulch, 1982, The Cartier Affair, The Making of a Male Model, 1983, Her Life as a Man, 1984; miniseries: The Moneychangers, 1976, Sins, 1986, Monte Carlo, 1986, Tonight at 8:30, 1991, Dynasty: The Reunion, 1992; appeared in Faerie Tale Theater (Showtime TV), 1982; star TV series: Dynasty, 1981-89; other TV appearances: Roseanne (ABC), 1993, Mama's Back spl., 1993, Annie: A Royal Adventure (TV Movie), 1995, Hart to Hart spl., (TV movie), 1995, Pacific Palisades, (TV Series), 1997, Sweet Deception (TV Movie), 1998, Will and Grace, 2000; video spl. Secrets of Fitness and Beauty, 1994; author: Past Imperfect (autobiography), 1978, Katy, A Fight for Life, Joan Collins Beauty Book, (novels) Prime Time, 1988, Love and Desire and Hate, 1991, My Secrets, 1994, Too Damn Famous, 1995, Second Act (autobiography), 1996, My Friends Secrets, 1999. Decorated Order of Brit. Empire; recipient Emmy nomination, Golden Globe award, Ace award, People's Choice award; named to Order Brit. Empire. Avocations: travel, 18th Century art.

COLLINS, JOHN CLEMENTS, physicist, educator; b. Colchester, Eng., Dec. 8, 1949; s. Hugh C. and Florence E. (Seymour) C.; m. Mary A. Brown, Oct. 24, 1991. BA, U. Cambridge, Eng., 1971, PhD, 1975. Postdoctoral fellow Princeton (N.J.) U., 1975-76, asst. prof., 1976-80; from asst. prof. to prof. Ill. Inst. Tech., Chgo., 1980-90; prof. Pa. State U., State College, 1990—. Author: Renormalization, 1984; contbr. articles to profl. jours. Guggenheim fellow, 1986; recipient Humboldt award, 2000. Mem. Am. Phys. Soc. Avocations: music, Scottish country dancing, hiking. Office: Pa State U 104 Davey Lab University Park PA 16802-6300

COLLINS, KENNETH JOHN, physician, researcher; b. London, Feb. 19, 1929; s. George William John and Edith Clara (Fairhall) C.; m. Adèle Mary Fox, Sept. 25, 1954; children: Sarah Louise, Nicholas Justin, Joanna Simone. BSc with honors, Univ. Coll., London, 1954; DPhil, Merton Coll., Oxford, Eng., 1960; MB, BS, Guy's Hosp., London, 1974. Grad. asst. Med. Rsch. Coun., Oxford, 1954-63; asst. dir. MRC unit London Sch. Hygiene and Tropical Medicine, 1963-69; sci. coord. Internat. Biol. Program, London, 1969-74; ho. surgeon, ho. physician Royal Surrey County Hosp., Guildford, Eng., 1973-75; sr. mem. external staff Med. Rsch. Coun., London, 1975-93; cons. geriat. physician, sr. clin. lectr. St. Pancras Hosp., London, 1975-93; mem. med. examining bds. U. London, 1974-94; cons. heat illness Army Pers. Rsch. Establishment, Farnborough, Eng., 1980-94, Ministry of Health, Saudi Arabia, 1980-84; cons. heat and nutrition Esso, Bahrain and Mid. East, 1965-67; cons. schistosomiasis Edna McConnell Orgn., Sudan, 1974-80, Edna McConnell Clark Found., N.Y.; cons. aging and effects of cold Dept. of Environ., London, 1989-94. Co-author: Human Adaptability, 1977, Hypothermia the Facts, 1983 (Henderson award 1983), The Biology of Human Aging, 1986, Capacity for Work in the Tropics, 1988, Handbook of Methods for Measurement of Working Capacity, Physical Fitness and Energy Expenditure in Tropical Populations, 1990, The Thermal Environment, 1990, 2nd edit., 1996; also many book chpts. and numerous sci. articles. Fellow Royal Coll. Physicians; mem. Soc. for Study of Human Biology (treas. 1982-87), Physiol. Soc., Royal Hort. Soc., Guildford Golf Club. Avocations: horticulture, golf, music, opera. Home: Windhover, 12 Albury Rd, Guildford GU1 2BU, England Office: St Pancras Hosp, St Pancras Way, London NW1 0PE, England

COLLINS, MARGARET HELEN, pathologist; b. Bronx, N.Y., July 5, 1950; d. Michael Robert and Catherine (Murray) C. BS cumma cum laude, Fordham U., 1972; MD, Georgetown U., 1977. Diplomate Am. Bd. Pathology. Intern in pathology Cornell U.-N.Y. Hosp., N.Y.C., 1977-78, resident in pathology, 1978-80; chief resident in pediatric pathology Columbia-Presbyn. Med. Ctr., N.Y.C., 1980-82, rsch. resident in pediatric pathology, 1982-83, asst. prof. clin. pathology, 1983-91; assoc. prof. pathology Ind. U., Indpls., 1991-95; pathologist Children's Hosp. Phila., Phila., 1995-98, Children's Hosp. Med. Ctr., Cin., 1999—; assoc. prof. pathology U. Cin., 2000—. Contbr. rsch. articles to med. jours. Rsch. fellow N.Y. Lung Assn., 1983-85, Am. Lung Assn., 1985-87. Mem. AMA, AAAS, Am. Med. Women's Assn., U.S.-Can. Acad. Pathology, Am. Thoracic Soc., Soc. Pediatric Pathology, Phi Beta Kappa. Democrat. Roman Catholic. Office: Children's Hosp Med Ctr 3333 Burnet Ave Cincinnati OH 45229-3026

COLLINS, RICHARD STRATTON (DICK COLLINS), retired public relations executive; b. Smith Center, Kans., Dec. 11, 1929; s. Edgar Wesley and Rosina Ann (Allbert) C.; children: Ann Michelle, Jennifer Lee, Logan Reed. BA, U. Tex., 1952. Editor of Lookout Look Mag., N.Y.C., 1952-53, asst. circulation promotion mgr., 1953-57, circulation promotion mgr., 1957-64, pub. rels. mgr., 1964-67; v.p., dir. corp. pub. rels. Cowles Communications, N.Y.C., 1967-74; assoc. The Jonathan Rinehart Group, N.Y.C., 1974-76; dir. pub. rels. ABA, Chgo., 1976-80, dir. comms., 1980-89, dir. comms./pub. affairs, 1989-94; ret., 1994. Writer, producer audio/visual prodns. and speeches; writer mag. advts. (award of Excellence Communication Arts Mag. 1971); contbr. articles to jours.; newspaper columnist. Bd. dirs., pres. Family Counseling Svcs., Bergen County, N.J., 1968-76. Recipient Silver Screen award U.S. Indsl. Film Festival, 1979, The Chris Plaque, Columbus Film Festival, 1979. Mem. Pub. Rels. Soc. of Am. (Silver Anvil award 1964). Avocations: golf, gardening, reading history, civil liberties organizations, recording for the blind.

COLLINS, RONALD LEE, information scientist, securities dealer; b. Hampton, Va., May 4, 1962; s. Rudolph and Ida Mae Collins; m. Lea Ann, Mar. 19, 1994; 1 child, Matthew Lewis. BS in Mgmt Sci. and Info. Tech., Va. Tech., 1985. Broker Lawson Fin., St. Petersburg, Fla., 1985-99; pres., CEO Distance Matters, Inc., Clearwater, Fla., 1996-99. Webmaster. First to swim Tampa Bay U.S. Masters Swimming, 1998. Mem. Clearwater Masters Swimming. E-mail: president@distancematters.com. Home and Office: 1920 Cobblestone Way Clearwater FL 33760-1622

COLLINS, ROSE ANN, minister; b. Pitts., July 5, 1935; d. Joseph and Rochelle (McCrary) Covington; m. Frank Collins, June 30, 1960 (div. 1978); children: Gar Andre, Guy Tracy. BA, Ctrl. Bible Coll., Springfield, Mo., 1987; MDiv, Assemblies of God Theol. Sem., Springfield, Mo., 1989. Ordained to ministry, 1990. Assoc. minister Deliverance Temple World Outreach Ministries, Springfield, 1988-90; evangelist Deliverance Temple World Outreach Ministries, Springfield and Pitts., 1991-93; chaplain Western Ctr., Canonsburg, Pa., 1993-96; trustee Northside Ch. of God in Christ, Pitts., 1982-87, bd. dirs., 1983-87. Vol. Ctr. Victims Violent Crime. Mem. Soc. Chaplains (Western chpt.), Pa. Coun. Chs., Ret. Enlisted Assn. (hon., Steel City chpt. 72 chaplain 1994-96). Avocations: reading, walking. Home: 6290 Auburn St Apt 622 Pittsburgh PA 15206-3136

COLLINS, S(ARAH) RUTH KNIGHT, education educator; b. Northumberland, Pa., May 13, 1939; d. Walter Brown and Alice Marie (Neighbour) Knight; m. Frank Gibson Collins, June 13, 1960; children: James, Pamela Collins Williams. BA, Wheaton Coll., 1960; MA, U. Tex., Austin, 1974; PhD, Vanderbilt U., 1980. Tchr. various levels Evanston, Ill., 1960-61, Berkeley, Calif., 1961-71; demonatration tchr. for head start and kindergarten U. Tex., Austin, Tex., 1969-74; tchr. in early childhood U. Tex., Austin, 1972-74; tchr. reading Motlow State C.C., Tullahoma, Tenn., 1977-91, coord. of English, 1979-81, prof. edn., 1982-93, coord. social scis., 1986-93; mem. state-wide adv. coun. for tchr. edn. and cert., 1987-90, state-wide adv. coun. for minorities in tchr. edn., 1990-91; pres. faculty coun. Motlow C.C., 1979-80, tchr. 1978; adj. prof. edn. Mid. Tenn. State U., 1979-89; presenter at profl. confs. Writer and proofreader for religious publ. sci. tech. editor, Tullahoma Telesis, 1980—, columnist, 1996—; writer for HealthWise, 1998—; contbr. articles to profl. jours. Actress Cmty. Playhouse, Tullahoma, 1973-87; storyteller various librs. and pub. schs., 1974—; violinist Mid. Tenn. Symphony Orch., Murfreesboro, 1987-89; presenter programs on grief and loss at various profl. confs. and cmty. orgns., 1973—; bd. mem., yearly speaker Compassionate Friends, 1985—; active Unitarian Universalist Ch., Tullahoma, 1993—; home vol. Hospice Highland Rim.; tchr. competitve swimming, diving, water ballet, program dir., 1949-68; panelist (TV series) How to Combat Juvenile Delinquency, Chgo., 1956; vol. Harton Regional Med. Ctr., 1997—, Hands-On Sci. Ctr., 1999—. Recipient Gov. Ned McWherter's cert. of recognition Tenn. Collaborative Leadership Acad., 1991. Mem. NEA, ASCD, AAUP (v.p. 1986-87, sec. 1990-91), Assn. Tchr. Educators, Bus. and Profl. Women's Club, Tenn. Edn. Assn., Internat. Reading Assn., Nat. Assn. for Edn. of Young Children (pres.-elect local chpt. 1972-73), Phi Delta Kappa, Kappa Delta Pi. Avocations: reading, sewing, playing and teaching violin/fiddle, public speaking. Home and Office: 1703 Country Club Dr Tullahoma TN 37388-4831

COLLINS, THOMAS WILLIAM, caterer, consultant; b. Lewiston, Idaho, Nov. 4, 1926; s. William James and Mary (Egan) C.; m. Mary Charlene Tracy, Aug. 1, 1947 (dec. Apr. 1984); children: Kathleen, William, Charles. Grad. high sch., Staples, Minn., 1944. Owner Collins Cafe, Park Rapids, Minn., 1947-63, Tom Collins Restaurant, Walker, Minn., 1963-83, Tom Collins Catering, Walker, 1983—. Author: Collins Cooking Secrets, 1981. Fundraiser DFL, 1976-83; adv. bd. Lake Country Food Bank, Mpls., 1981-86. Served with USN, 1945-46, 51-52. Recipient Recognition award Mont. Gov., 1978, cert. of Spl. Congl. Recognition, 1995; Tom Collins Day proclaimed by Minn. Gov., 1977. Mem. Assn. Great Lakes Outdoor Writers, Am. Legion. Lodge: Masons (sr. warden 1958), Shriners. Avocations: hunting, fishing, photography. Home and Office: PO Box 33 Walker MN 56484-0033

COLLINS, WALTER LLOYD GEORGE, editor; b. Broken Arrow, Okla., Dec. 6, 1917; s. Dow Otho and Myrtle Hester (Campbell) C.; m. Ruth Leona Hamilton, Sept. 3, 1935; children: Mary, Walter, Alvin, Shirley. BA, Pan Am. U., 1966; MA, U. Tulsa, 1975. Aviation cadet USAAF, 1942; advanced through grades to maj. USAF, 1962; exec. in charge C-E Installation Project NATO, Europe, North Africa, Mid. East, 1956-57; sr. editor radar and missiles project USAF, 1957-58; ops. officer C-E divsn. Def. Atomic Support Agy., Alburquerque, 1959-63; dir. comm.-elec., spacetrack NORAD, Colorado Springs, 1963-64; ret., 1964; gen. mgr. Desert Lodge, Moab, Utah, 1967-68; design engr., planner Beech Aircraft Corp., Wichita, Kans., 1968-72; dir. internat. student affairs Spartan Sch. Aeronautics, Tulsa, 1979-83; pres. R&W Internat., Tulsa, 1984-88, Alpha-Omega Press, Tulsa, Ponca City, Okla., 1990—; adv. bd. Higher Edn. Com. Okla. Acad. State Goals, 1977-95. Author: On the Razor's Edge, 1990. Mem. Kay County (Okla.) Rep. Com., 1993—; mem. Ponca City Traffic Commn., 1997-2000. Mem. Acad. Am. Poets, Nat. Author's Registry, Nat. Order Battlefield Commns., Am. Air Mus. in Great Britain, Air Force Assn., Ret. Officers Assn. Avocations: writing, editing, photography. Office: Alpha-Omega Press PO Box 2163 Ponca City OK 74602-2163

COLLINS, WILLIAM LEIGHTON, engineering educator; b. Highland, Ill., Jan. 8, 1906; s. William Alvin and Clara Lucy (Lauener) C.; m. Anita Blanche Wood, Feb. 3, 1938; children: Kathryn Janet, William Wood. BS, U. Ill., 1928, MS, 1932. Instr. U. Ill., Urbana-Champaign, 1930-37, assoc., 1937-39, asst. prof., 1939-45, assoc. prof., 1945-49, prof., 1949-65, prof. emeritus, 1965—. Co-author: Statics and Strength of Materials, 1959, Educating Engineers for World Development, 1979; contbr. articles to profl. publs. Pres. Champaign County Coun. Social Agencies, 1950, Champaign County Cmty. Chest, 1949; mem. cmty. coun. Leisure World of Md., Silver Spring, 1988-95. With U.S. Army, 1942-45, ret. lt. col. AUS. Fulbright grantee short programs (3); recipient Diploma de Heresped de Honor U. Central de Venezuela, 1961; Alumni Honor award U. Ill. Coll. of Engring., 1969; W. Leighton Collins faculty award established in his honor U. Ill., 1997. Fellow ASCE, Am. Soc. for Engring. Edn. (exec. dir. 1965-70, exec. dir. emeritus 1971—, sec. 1955-65, gen. coun. 1954, Hall of Fame 1993, Disting. and Unusual Svc. award 1971); mem. ASTM, U. Ill. Coll. Engring. Acad. for Excellence in Engring. Edn., Rotary Internat., Cosmos Club, Gamma Alpha (nat. pres. 1936). Republican. Methodist. Avocations: bowling, gardening, stamps, rocks. Home: 5400 Vantage Point Rd Columbia MD 21044-2681

COLLINS, WILLIAM LEROY, telecommunications engineer; b. Laurel, Miss., June 17, 1942; s. Henry L. and Christene E. (Finnegan) C. Student, La Salle U., 1969; BS in Computer Sci., U. Beverly Hills, 1984. Sr. computer operator Dept. Pub. Safety, Phoenix, 1975-78, data communications specialist, 1978-79, supr. computer ops., 1981-82; mgr. network control Valley Nat. Bank, Phoenix, 1979-81; mgr. data communications Ariz. Lottery, Phoenix, 1982-85; mgr. telecommunications Calif. Lottery, Sacramento, 1985—; Mem. Telecomm. Study Mission to Russia, Oct. 1991. Contbr. to profl. publs. Served as sgt. USAF, 1964-68. Mem. IEEE, Nat. Sys. Programmers Assn., Centrex Users Group, DMS Centrex User Group, Accunet Digital Svcs. User Group, Telecomms. Assn. (v.p. edn. Sacramento Valley chpt. 1990-94, pres. 1995, chpt. assn. dir. 1996-97, chpt. past pres. 1996, Prestigious Svc. award 1997), Telecom. Assn. (chmn. corp. edn. com. 1994-95, conf. com. 1994-95, co-chair conf. program com. 1996, program dir. edn. 1996, corp. dir. edn. 1996-97, pres.-elect 1998, pres. and ceo, 1999), SynOptics User Group, Timeplex User Group, Assn. Data Comm. Users, Soc. Mfg. Engrs., Data Processing Mgmt. Assn., Am. Mgmt. Assn., Assn. Computing Machinery, Am. Soc. for Quality Control, Bldg. Industry Cons. Svc. Internat., Assn. for Quality and Participation, KC, Calif. Integrated Svcs. Digital Network User Group, Computer Security Inst., Assn. Pub. Comms. Officials, Armed Forces Comms. and Electronics Assn., Assn. Info. Tech. Profls., H.P. Open View Forum. Roman Catholic. Home: 116 Valley Oak Dr Roseville CA 95678-4378 Office: Calif State Lottery 600 N 10th St Sacramento CA 95814-0393

COLLUFIO, HECTOR FERNANDO RAMON, company executive; b. Buenos Aires, Dec. 4, 1934; s. Vicente and Amelia (Loffredo) C.; m. Iris Susana Ferrazzoulo, Feb. 10, 1965; 1 child, Dino Pablo. Pub. acct., Sch. Econ. Scis., Buenos Aires, 1961, lic. in econs., 1969, D of Econ. Scis., 1977. Prof. acctg. Pub. Schs., Buenos Aires, 1964-90; prof. polit. econs. Superior Nat. Inst. Professorship, Buenos Aires, 1968—; fin. sect. Inst. Internat., Paris, 1971-72; chief rng. devel. DGI, 1979-87, chief legis. dept., 1990—; cons. in field. Author: Income Tax, 1979, Taxes/Capital and Net Patrimony, 1979, Tax-Eventual Profits, 1979; contbr. articles to profl. jours. Mem. Profl. Coun. Econ. Socs. Home: Dellepiane 4264-9o B, 1407 Buenos Aires Argentina Office: H Yrigoyen 370, Buenos Aires Argentina

COLMAN, CHARLES KINGSBURY, academic administrator, criminologist; b. Nashua, N.H., May 14, 1929; s. Charles David Colman and Lela (Bessey) Sproul; m. Marjorie Gertrude Bahe, Aug. 19, 1950; children: Charles David, Cathleen Ann. Diploma, Yale U., 1961; BA, U. Md., 1963; MEd, Stetson U., 1972; EdD, Fla. Atlantic U., 1978. Spl. agt. USAF, U.S. Army, 1947-67; asst. prin. Satellite High Sch., Satellite Beach, Fla., 1969-81, dean acad. edn., 1981-85; ctr. dir. Brevard C.C., Patrick AFB, Fla., 1985-92; provost Brevard C.C., Palm Bay, Fla., 1992-94; pres. emeritus, 1994—; Mem. Fla. State Adv. Com. on Mil. Edn., Patrick AFB, 1985—; edn. rep. Semiconductor Mfg. Tech., Dallas, 1985—. Author: Formative Years, 1970; author computer software. Co-founder Boys Club Am., Melbourne, Fla, 1968. Grantee Fla. Dept. Edn., 1987, 89, 90, 91, U.S. Dept. Edn., 1991-92; recipient Ace award Fla. Dept. Edn., 1991. Mem. Retired Officers' Assn., Assn. for Supervision and Curriculum Devel., Assn. Former Intelligence Officers (v.p. 1998—, Fla. chpt.), Assn. Former OSI Spl. Agents (sec. 1998—, Space Coast chpt.), Phi Delta Kappa (chpt. pres. 1983-84). Avocations: golf, computer programming. Home: 1230 Seminole Dr Ind Hbr Bch FL 32937-4123 Office: Brevard Community Coll Palm Bay Campus 250 Grassland Rd SE Palm Bay FL 32909-2206

COLN, WILLIAM ALEXANDER, III, pilot; b. Los Angeles, Mar. 20, 1942; s. William Alexander and Aileen Henrietta (Shimfessel) C.; m. Lora Louise Getchel, Nov. 15, 1969 (div. July 1979); 1 child, Caryn Louise. BA in Geography, UCLA, 1966. Cert. airline transport pilot, flight engr. Commd. USN, Pensacola, Fla., 1966; pilot, officer USN, Fighter Squadron 102, 1969-71, Port Mugu, Calif., 1975-77; pilot, officer USNR, Port Mugu, Calif., 1971-75, advanced through grades to lt. comdr., 1978; ret. USNR, 1984; capt. Delta Airlines, Inc. (formerly Western Airlines Inc.), Los Angeles, 1972—. Recipient Nat. Def. medal USN, 1966. Mem. Nat. Aero. Assn., Airline Pilots Assn., Aircraft Owners and Pilots Assn., UCLA Alumni Assn., Am. Bonanza Soc., Internat. Platform Assn., Santa Barbara Yacht Club. Democrat. Club: Santa Barbara (Calif.) Athletic, Santa Barbara Yacht. Avocations: sailing, scuba diving, flying, computers, electronics. Home: 486 Cota Ln Montecito CA 93108-1210 Office: Delta Air Lines Inc LA Internat Airport Los Angeles CA 90009

COLOE, PETER JOHN, biotechnology educator; b. Maffra, Victoria, Australia, Jan. 2, 1952; s. Martin Maxwell and Rita Irene (Chown) C.; m. Susan Valerie Beale, Oct. 6, 1979; children: Daniel, Matthew. BSc with honors, Monash U., 1972, PhD, 1976. Sr. tutor Monash U., Australia, 1976-78; sr. scientific officer Vet. Rsch. Inst., Melbourne, 1978-85; sr. lectr. RMIT U., Melbourne, 1985-89, prin. lectr., 1989-91, prof. biotech., head dept. applied biology and biotech., 1992—; cons. lectr. Swinburne Inst. of Tech., Australia, 1975-85; hon. sr. lectr. Monash U., 1980-85. Contbr. articles to profl. jours.; 3 patents in field. Fellow Australian Soc. Microbiology; mem. N.Y. Acad. Sci., Am. Soc. of Microbiology, Australian Vet. Poultry Assn. Roman Catholic. Avocations: sports, fishing, reading, music. Office: RMIT U Dept Applied Biology, and Biotech 124 LaTrobe St, Melbourne 3000, Australia

COLOGLU, MUSTAFA GOKMEN, natural gas company executive, consultant; b. Istanbul, Dec. 23, 1937; s. Mesut and Saime (Bilge) C.; m. Zehra Cologlu, Sept. 17, 1965. BS, Istanbul U., 1964; MBA, Ankara Econ. & Bus. Sci. Acad., 1977. Rsch. asst. Kandilli Obs., Istanbul, 1962-68; expert on longterm planning Turkish Petroleum Corp., Ankara, 1970-76; head of planning dept. Turkish Aerospace Industries, Ankara, 1976-79, Istanbul Gas Co., 1994—; cons., Istanbul, 1979-94. Lt. Turkish Army, 1968-70. Muslim. Office fax: 00 90212 5743353. Office: Istanbul Gas Distbrn Co, Istasyon Cd #81, Yesilkoy Istanbul Turkey

COLOGNE, GORDON BENNETT, lawyer; b. Long Beach, Calif., Aug. 24, 1924; s. Knox M. Cologne; m. Patricia Cologne; children: Steven J., Ann Maureen Meyer. BS, U. So. Calif., 1948; LLB cum laude, Southwestern U. Sch. of Law, L.A., 1951. Bar: Calif. 1951, U.S. Supreme Ct. 1961. Trial atty. U.S. Dept. of Justice, Jacksonville, Fla., 1951-52; pvt. practice Indio, Calif., 1952-61; mayor Indio City Coun., 1954; mem. state assembly Calif. Legis., Sacramento, 1961-65; mem. senate Calif. State Senate, Sacramento, 1965-72; justice Ct. of Appeal, San Diego, 1972-84; govt. rels. atty. Sacramento, 1984-99. With USN, 1944-46. Named one of Outstanding Young Men of Calif., Calif. Jr. C. of C., 1961; recipient Freedom Found. award, 1965.

COLOM, NYANI IISHA, payments company executive; b. Washington, May 19, 1970; d. Wilbur O'Neil Colom and Audrey Rowe; m. Sory Ibrahim Diaby, Aug. 29, 1998. BS, Fisk U., 1993; MBA, European U., Paris, 1997, M in Pub. Rels. and Bus. Comms., 1999. Editor Genesis Press, N.Y.C., 1992-96; mgr. mktg. and comm. MasterCard Internat., Brussels, 1997—. Big Sister Big Bros./Big Sisters, Nashville, 1991; mem. Dems. Abroad, Paris, 1998. Mem. Am. Club of Brussels, Delta Sigma Theta. Avocations: reading, squash, belly dancing, golf. Office: Master Card Internat, 10A rue Colonel Chaltin, 1180 Brussels Belgium

COLOMBINI, FABIANO, economist, educator, consultant, researcher; b. Crespina, Pisa, Italy, Jan. 21, 1950; s. Marino and Silvana (Ferrini) C.; m. Clori Giannini, June 20, 1988; 1 child, Lorenzo. Diploma di Ragioniere, Tech & Comml. Inst., A. Pacinotti, Pisa, Italy, 1969; Laurea in Econs. & Commerce, U. Pisa, Italy, 1974. Asst. prof. banking and fin. U. Pisa, Italy, 1977-83, assoc. prof. corp. fin., 1983-87, prof. econs. of fin. intermediaries, 1988-89; rsch. scholar London Sch. Econs., 1982-83; dir. inst. Econs. of Fin. Intermediaries, U. Cagliari, Italy, 1987-88, full prof. medium and long term lending, 1987-88; cons. Cassa per il credito alle imprese artigiane, Rome, 1991-94; lectr. econs. of fin. intermediaries U. Luiss G. Carli, Rome, 1997—. Author: Economia della Cassa depositi e prestiti, Pisa, 1978, Banche e ist. speciali nel finanziamento delle aziende agricole, 1985, Gli ist. di credito speciale. Aspetti strutturali e tendenze evolutive, 1990, Gli intermediari finanziari. Elementi essenziali, 1993; co-author (with R. Ricci), La finanza delle piccole e medie aziende, 1987, (with R. Malavasi, A. Landi) Innovazioni e ristrutturazione negli istituti di credito speciale in F. Colombini, Innovazioni e strategie negli istituti di credito speciale in Italia, 1994, Intermediari bancari, mobiliari e assicurativi, Principi gestionali, 1997, (with M. De Simoni, A. Mancini) La gestione dei portafoghi asionari. Modelli e tecniche per l'altività di asset management, 2000, (with M. De Simoni, A. Mancini) Intermediari e mercati finanziari. Teoria e gestione, 2000; contbr. numerous articles to profl. jours. Recipient scholarships Consiglio Naz. delle Ricerche, Rome, 1975, 1981; prize Banca Toscana, Florence, 1977. Fellow European

Fin. Assn., Italian Accad. Econ. Aziendale, Italian Soc. Storia della Ragioneria, Italian Alumni Assn. of London Sch. Econs. Office: U Pisa Fac Econs Aziendale, Via C Ridolfi 10, 56124 Pisa Italy

COLOMBO, ARMANDO WALTER, manufacturing automation researcher, educator; b. Maipu, Mendoza, Argentina, Aug. 7, 1960; arrived in Portugal, 1999; s. Cayetano Armando and Angela Cecilia (Bertolo) C.; m. Fabiola Angelica Espinoza, June 4, 1987; 1 child, Gianfranco Paolo. BS in Electromechanics, Nat. Tech. Coll., Mendoza, 1979; engr. electronics, Nat. Poly. U., Mendoza, 1990; MSc in Control Sys. Engring., Nat. U. San Juan, Argentina, 1994; D of Engring. in Mfg. Automation, U. Erlangen, Germany, 1998. Cert. in engring. Project engr. Electra S.A., Mendoza, 1982-86; asst. Nat. Poly. U., Mendoza, 1986-90, asst. prof., 1990-91; asst. prof. Nat. U. San Juan, 1991-94; asst. rschr. Inst. Automation, San Juan, 1991-94; rschr. U. Erlangen-Nürnberg, Germany, 1995-98; prof. New U. Lisbon, Portugal, 1999—; vis. rschr. U. Maribor, Slovenia, 1988, U. Zaragoza, Spain, 1992; vis. trainee Siemens A.G., Erlangen, 1988. Author: Modeling and Analysis of Flexible Production Systems, 1995, Hierarchical Control of Flexible Production Systems, 1998; co-contbr. chpt., R. Carelli, to: Computer-Assisted Management and Control of Manufacturing Systems, 1996, Simulationsbasierte Planungssysteme für Organisation und Produktion, 1999; contbr. articles to profl. publs.; patentee in field. Grantee Internat. Assn. for Exch. Students for Tech. Exp., 1988, rsch. grantee Argent Sci.-Technol. Coun., 1992-94, grantee German Acad. Exch. Svc., 1995-96. Mem. IEEE, Gesellschaft für Informatik. Roman Catholic. Avocations: classical music, mountain biking, football. Home: Botequim, Rua Luis de Camões 20-1, 2815-147 Charneca de Caparica Portugal Office: New Univ Lisbon, Quinta da Torre, 2825 Monte da Caparica Portugal

COLOMBO, ARRIGO, philosophy educator; b. Busto Arsizio, Varese, Italy, Sept. 11, 1921; s. Francesco and Maria (Ghioldi) C.; m. Marie-Josèphe Beauchard, June 30, 1979. Lic. in scholastic philosophy, Aloisianum Faculty, Gallarate, Italy, 1948; lic. in theology, S. Luigi Faculty, Naples, 1952; PhD, State U., Milan, Italy, 1956. Asst. U. Genoa, Italy, 1959-65; prof. U. Lecce, Italy, 1966-81, assoc. prof., 1981-91, founder, dir. Rsch. Ctr. for Utopian Studies, 1982—, founder, dir. Lab. of Poetry, 1986-00. Author: Le Società del Futuro Saggio Utopico Sulle Società Postindustriali, 1978, Utopia e Distopia, 1987, L'utopia Rifondazione di un'idea e di una storia, 1997, Materiali per l'Utopia Il Diavolo, 1999, Materiali per l'Utopia La Societè Amorosa, 2000; editor: L'Utopia—Per Una Società Giusta e Fraterna, 18 vols., 1991—. Founding mem. Cristiani per il Socialismo, Rome, 1974-76, founder-dir. Movimento per la Società di Giustizia e per la Speranza, 1998—; active Democrazia Proletaria, Lecce, 1986-91, Rifondazione Comunista, Lecce, 1991-93. Mem. Soc. for Utopian Studies (U.S.), Internat. Assn. for Utopian Studies (Rome). Roman Catholic. Avocations: art, music, movies. Home: Via Monte S Michele 49, 73100 Lecce Italy Office: Ctr Interdipart Ricr Utopia, v Stampacchia, Plzo Parlang, 73100 Lecce Italy

COLOM I NAVAL, JOAN, foreign diplomat; b. Barcelona, Spain, July 5, 1945. V.p. European Parliament, 1999—, vice-chmn. bur., mem. com. on budgets, substitute com. on econ. and monetary affairs; mem. of bur. Group of the Party of European Socialists; mem. delegation for relations with the People's Republic of China. Mem. Socialist Party of Catalonia. Office: PSC-OPE, Carrer Nicaragua 75-77, E-08029 Barcelona Spain*

COLONNA, DENIS AUGUSTE, tourism business executive, consultant; b. Salon, Provence, France, Feb. 17, 1963; arrived in Vietnam, 1987; s. Auguste Claude and Ginette (Botti) C. Technician cert., Pigier U., France, 1983. Cert. acct. Vietnam mgr. Exotissimo, Thailand, 1987; v.p. Majonc Assn., Vietnam, 1988-91; mng. dir. Exotissimo, Ho Chi Minh City, Vietnam, 1992—. Home: 6/49 Tran Nao Dist 2, Hochi Minh City Vietnam Office: Exotissimo, 37 Jon Duc Thang Dist 1, Ho Chi Minh City Vietnam

COLONNA, JEAN-FRANÇOIS JACQUES, computer scientist, computer artist; b. Paris, Sept. 14, 1951; s. Marie-Angele C.; m. Daniele Bouillerot, Mar. 27, 1953 (div. 1981); 1 child, Olivier. Grad. in Engring., Nat. Sch. Telecomm., Paris, 1970; PhD, Nat. Poly. Inst., Grenoble, France, 1985. Chief engr. France Telecom, Paris, 1971—; cons. Ministry Industry, Paris, 1985-87; dir. Groupe Synthese Video-Lactamme, Palaiseau, France, 1976—; Y2K bug specialist; lectr. in field. Author: Images Du Virtuel, 1996; contbr. over 200 articles to profl. jours. Lt. Telecom., Paris, 1970-71. Recipient 3d prize Seymour Cray Contest, Paris, 1987, 1st prize Paris-Concours Internat. des Tech. Creation, 1990. Mem. IEEE. Avocations: U.S. model railroading, Flemish painting. Fax: 33(0)1 69 33 30 11. E-mail: colonna@cmapx.polytechnique.fr. Home: 14 rue de la Vieille Poste, 78350 Jouy en Josas France Office: CMAP, Ecole Polytechnique, 91128 Palaiseau Cedex, France

COLP, NORMAN BARRY, photographic artist, curator; b. Bronx, N.Y., Sept. 3, 1944; s. Joseph Johnny Colp and Martha (Berman) Colp Levine; m. Marsha Stern, July 18, 1981. BA in Art, CUNY, 1967; postgrad., Pratt Inst., 1967, Parsons Sch. Design, 1971. Archtl. modelmaker Milton Glaser Inc., N.Y.C., 1978-80; assoc. curator Alternative Mus., N.Y.C., 1979-80; curator exhibits Ctr. for Book Arts, N.Y.C., 1980-83, exhbn. coord., 1983; instr. Pratt Graphics Ctr., N.Y.C., 1983-84; instr. Sch. Visual Arts, N.Y.C., 1982-86, acad. advisor, 1984-87; photog. artist, curator N.Y.C., 1978—; cons. curator Anchorage Mus. History and Art, 1990, Golden & Dresnin Design, Phila., 1990, Islip Art Mus., East Islip, N.Y., 1990, Boca Raton (Fla.) Mus. Art, 1991; cons. on book Exploring Color Photography, 1991, 97, The Girls' Guide to Hunting and Fishing, 1999-2000; artist-in-residence Pub. Sch. 1, Long Island City, N.Y., 1977-78, Cabin Creek Ctr. for Work and Environ. Studies, N.Y.C., 1979; workshop presenter-in-residence Mus. Holography, N.Y.C., 1985; cons. Artists Found., Inc., Boston, 1986, juror, 1989; lectr. in field. Author: Freud's Recipe, Crazy Hair, A Primer on Art Criticism, 1983; one-man shows include Victoria and Albert Mus., London, 1991, Islip Art Mus., 1993, UCLA, 1994, Coll. of Charleston, 1997, Hugo de Pagano Gallery, N.Y.C., 1998; exhibited in group shows at Mus. Modern Art Libr., Mus. Fine Arts, St. Petersburg, Fla., Boca Raton Mus., Corcoran Galley of Art, Washington, U. Art Mus., U. Calif., Berkeley, Wadsworth Atheneum, Hartford, Conn., The Ralls Collection, Washington; represented in permanent collections Nat. Libr., Paris, Victoria and Albert Mus., Corcoran Gallery, Libr. Congress, Mus. Modern Art Libr., N.Y.C., N.Y. Pub. Libr., Queens Mus. of Art, Flushing, N.Y., Islip Art Mus., East Islip, N.Y., Bklyn. Mus. of Art, Archives of Am. Art, Smithsonian Instn., Washington, Whitney Mus. Am. Art. Grantee Com. for Visual Arts, 1980, Met. Transit Authority, 1991, Fieldcrest Cannon Inc., 1991. Avocations: collecting American art and Japanese redware pottery and gutta-purcha frames. Home and Studio: 180 W End Ave Apt 3R New York NY 10023-4913

COLPAERT, ROGER ACHILLE JACQUES, steel wire/steel cord company executive; b. Waarmaarde, Belgium, Oct. 3, 1928; s. Alfons and Alice (Messeeuw) C.; m. Marie-Therese Soens, Oct. 6, 1955; children: Ann, Carl, Chris, Tom. Lic. in bus. adminstrn., U. Leuven, Belgium, 1950. With NV Bekaert SA, various locations, 1952—; corp. v.p. MBU Steelcord, Zwevegem, Belgium, 1982—; pres. Bekaert U.K., Eng.; dir. B.S.W.C., USA, UBISA, Spain, B.S.B., Japan, B.B.S.C., Australia, Beksa, Turkey. Served to lt. Belgium Arty., 1950-52. Home: Senator Bossuytstraat 12, 8500 Kortrijk Belgium Office: N V Bekaert SA, Bekaertstraat 1, 8550 Zwevegem Belgium

COLQUHOUN, KEITH, writer; b. London, Aug. 5, 1937. Asia cons. The Economist, London, 1980—. Author of 8 novels. Home: The Old Rectory East Mersea, Essex CO5 8SZ, England

COLQUHOUN, PETER LLOYD, artist, educator; b. N.Y.C., Dec. 1, 1955; s. Harvey Edward Colquoun and Janet Olive Gurge. BFA, Pratt Inst., 1989. Tchr. painting New Bklyn. Sch., 1979-81, N.Y. Acad., N.Y.C., 1981-83, Centro del Arte Verrochio, Casole d'Elsa, Italy, 1985-86, Crosby Painting Studio, N.Y.C., 2000—. Bd. dirs., columnist N.Y. Artists Equity, 1998—. Max Beckmann scholar Bklyn. Mus. Art Sch., 1974-76, Adolph & Esther Gottlieb Found. grantee, 1993, Helene Wurlitzer Found. residency, Taos, N.Mex., 2000. Mem. Audubon Artists (giulia Palermo prize 1994), Orgn. Ind. Artists, Fedn. Modern Painters and Sculptors. Home: 105 Duane St #4C New York NY 10007

COLSON, EARL MORTON, lawyer; b. Bklyn., Mar. 8, 1930; s. Abraham and Rebecca (Hecker) C.; m. Helen Theresa Austern, Apr. 24, 1960; children: Adam Thomas, Amy Esther, Deborah Austern. BS magna cum laude, Syracuse U., 1950; LLB magna cum laude, Harvard U., 1957. Bar: N.Y. 1958, D.C. 1960. Assoc. Chadbourne, Parke, Whiteside & Wolff, N.Y.C., 1957-60, Arent, Fox, Kintner, Plotkin & Kahn, Washington, 1960-68; partner Arent, Fox, Kintner, Plotkin & Kahn, 1968—; adj. prof. law Georgetown U., 1970—; lectr on tax subjects. Author: Capital Gains and Losses, 1975; co-author: Federal Taxation of Estates, Gifts and Trusts, 1975. Bd. dirs. Washington Hebrew Congregation, 1979—, v.p., 1984-90, pres., 1990-92; trustee Kingsbury Ctr., 1978-81; mem. N.Y. bd. overseers Hebrew Union Coll., 1995-97; bd. dirs. D.C. chpt. Am. Jewish Com., 1995-98. Mem. ABA (chmn. estate and gift tax com. sect. taxation 1972-73), D.C. Bar Assn. (chmn. tax com. 1971-72, treas., bd. govs. 1974-76), Am. Law Inst., Assn. of Bar of City of N.Y., Cosmos Club Washington. Office: 1050 Connecticut Ave NW Washington DC 20036-5303

COLTA, ONISIM, painter, stage designer, educator; b. Baia Sprie, Romania, June 10, 1952; s. Gheorghe and Ileana (Cernestean) C.; m. Rodica Elena Ardelean; 1 child, Ioan Paul. Grad., Ion Andreescu Fine Arts Inst., Cluj, Romania, 1972-76; postgrad., Post U., Bucharest, Romania. Stage designer State Theatre, Arad, Romania, 1976—; prof. Acad. Visual Arts, Oradea, Romania, 1998—. One-man shows include Philo Gallery, Cluj, 1976, Alpha Gallery, Arad, 1978, Union Plastic Artists Gallery, Cluj, 1980, Internat. Diogenis Gallery, Athens, Greece, 1982, Arts Home Gallery, Bucharest, 1986, Halios Gallery, Timisoara, 1987, Severin Rattenberg Gallery, Aachen, Germany, 1988, Rosengarten Gallery, Bielefeld, Germany, 1989, Art Gallery, Arad, 1992, Rom. Cult. Ctr. Budapest, Hungary, 1994, Nat. Art Mus., Cluj, 1996, Art Mus., Oradea, 1998, Erkel Ferenc Mus., Gyula, Hungary, 1999, Art Mus., Arad, 2000; exhibited in numerous group shows. Pres. Youth Profl. Artists Assn., Arad, 1978-81, 86-89. Mem. Profl. Artists Assn. Romania (pres. 1994-98), Internat. Artists Assn. Greek Catholic. Avocation: harmony of the universe. Home: Splai Praporgescu, Bloc 18 Apt 34, 2900 Arad Romania Office: Nat Art Gallery Delta, Eminescu 2, 2900 Arad Romania

COLVIN, CLARK SHERMAN, educator, management consultant; b. Seattle, Oct. 26, 1958; s. Henry Alfred and Dorothy Angie (Tigner) C.; m. Patricia Ann Stanford, Mar. 12, 1989. BA, U. Wash., 1984; MPA, Seattle U., 1986; DPA, Golden Gate U., 1988; MBA, Oxford U., 1991; PhD, Eurotech. Rsch. U., 1992; diploma, U.S. Naval War Coll., 1993, U. London, 1994; DLitt, St. Clements U., 1995. Owner, mgr. COMCAR Computerized Auto Network, Bellevue, Wash., 1981-82; spl. asst. Wash. State Senate, Olympia, 1983-84; state chmn., pres. Wash. State Pub. Lands Assn., Seattle, 1984-86; master tchr. Independent Learning High Sch., Berkeley, Calif., 1986-87; gen. ptnr. Armand E.R. Mulden & Assoc., Livermore, Calif., 1987—; chmn., sr. ptnr., CEO Clark Sherman Colvin Inc., Salem, Oreg., 1992—; gen. ptnr. Colvin Land and Investment LLC, 1998—; founder, chmn. E.B. Consult, 1999—; adj. prof. Chapman Coll., Vallejo, Calif., 1987-88; legis. liaison Ken Selander, Atty., Burien, Wash., 1984; faculty assoc. Intercollegiate Studies Inst., Bryn Mawr, Pa., 1988; lectr. Am. U., Washington, 1989-90. Author: Where Jurisdictions Meet, 1984, (with others) Conflict Analysis and Resolution, 1988. Mgr. Danville (Calif.) City Coun. campaign, 1987; mem. Rep. Nat. Com., Washington; mem. Woodrow Wilson Internat. Ctr. for Scholars. Lt. USNR, 1987-95. Mem. Soc. for U.S. Constitution, Assn. Mil. Surgeons U.S. (medal), Nav. Res. Assn., Ctr. for Study of Presidency, As. Soc. Pub. Adminstrn., Oxford Ctr. Mgmt. Studies Assn. Methodist. Avocations: archaeology, philosophy, sailing. Office: 3040 Comml St SE Ste 200 Salem OR 97302

COLWELL, GENE THOMAS, engineering educator; b. Chattanooga, Aug. 3, 1937; s. William Clarence and Mary Virginia (Smith) C.; m. Peggy Ann Fletcher, June 1, 1973. BSME, U. Tenn., 1959, MSME, 1962, PhD, 1966. Rsch. engr. Oak Ridge (Tenn.) Nat. Lab., 1959-62; instr. U. Tenn., Knoxville, 1962-65; rsch. engr. Oak Ridge Nat. Lab., 1965-66; asst. prof. Ga. Inst. Tech., Atlanta, 1966-71, assoc. prof., 1971-77, prof., 1977-95; prof. emeritus, 1995—; assoc. dir. Ga. Inst. Tech., Atlanta, 1984-87; vis. prof. U. Carabobo, Venezuela, 1971; cons. in field. Patentee in field; contbr. articles to profl. jours. Recipient numerous Rsch. grants. Fellow ASME (life); mem. Sigma Xi, Pi Tau Sigma. Avocations: tennis, golf, hiking. Home: 9145 Prestwick Club Dr Duluth GA 30097-2442

COLWELL, RITA ROSSI, microbiologist, molecular biologist, educator, federal agency administrator; b. Nov. 23, 1934; m. Jack H. Colwell, May 31, 1956; children: Alison E.L., Stacie A. BS in Bacteriology with distinction, Purdue U., 1956, MS in Genetics, 1958; PhD, U. Wash., 1961; DSc, Heriot-Watt U., Edinburgh, Scotland, 1987; DSc (hon.), Hood Coll., 1991; DSc, Purdue U., 1993; LLD, Notre Dame Coll., 1994; DSc (hon.), U. Surrey, Eng., 1995, U. Bergen, Norway, 1999, Coastal Carolina U., 1999, U. Md. Balt. County, 1999, E. Carolina U., 1999, St. Mary's Coll., 1999. Rsch. asst. genetics lab. Purdue U., West Lafayette, Ind., 1956-57; rsch. asst. U. Wash., Seattle, 1957-58, predoctoral assoc., 1959-60, asst. rsch. prof., 1961-64; asst. prof. biology Georgetown U., Washington, 1964-66, assoc. prof. biology, 1966-72; prof. microbiology U. Md., 1972—, v.p. for acad. affairs, 1983-87; dir. Ctr. Marine Biotech., 1987-91; pres. Md. Biotech. Inst. U. Md., 1991-98; dir. NSF, 1998—; hon. prof. U. Queensland, Brisbane, Australia, 1988, Quindao U., China, 1995; cons., advisor Washington area comms. media, congressman, legislators, 1978—; external examiner various univs. abroad, 1964—; mem. coastal resources adv. com. dept. natural resources State of Md., 1979; NAS ocean scis. bd., 1977-80, vice-chair polar rsch. bd., 1990-94; mem. Nat. Sci. Bd., 1984-90, sci. adv. bd. Oak Ridge Nat. Labs., 1988-90, 93-96, adv. com. FDA, 1991-92, food adv. com., 1993-96, sci. bd., 1996—. Author 18 books including (manual numerical taxonomy) Collecting the Data, 1970, (with M. Zambruski) Rodina-Methods in Aquatic Microbiology, 1972, (with L. H. Stevenson) Estuarine Microbial Ecology, 1973, (with R. Y. Morita) Effect of the Ocean Environment on Microbial Activities, 1974, (with A. Sinsky and N. Pariser) Marine Biotechnology, 1983, Vibrios in the Environment, 1985, Nucleic Acid Sequence Data, 1988, (with others) Marine Biotechnology, 1995, Microbial Diversity, 1996; mem. editorial bd. Microbial Ecology, 1972-91, Applied and Environ. Microbiology, 1969-81, Oil and Petrochemical Pollution, 1980-91, Jour. Washington Acad. Scis., 1981-87, Johns Hopkins U. Oceanographic Series, 1981-84, Revue de la Fondation Oceanographique Ricard, 1981—, Estuaries, 1983-89, Zentralblatt fur Bacteriologie, 1985—, Jour. Aquatic Living Resources, 1987—, System. Applied Microbiology, 1985—, World Jour. Microbiology and Biotechnology, 1988-95; contbr. more than 500 articles and revs. to profl. jours. including Can. Jour. Fisheries and Aquatic Scis., Soc. Gen. Microbiology, Jour. Bacteriology, Applied & Environ. Microbiology, others. Recipient Gold medal Internat. Biotech. Inst., 1990, Purkinje Gold medal Achievement in Scis. Czechoslavakian Acad. Scis., 1991, Civic award Gov. Md., 1990, Woman of the Yr. award Women Legislators of Md., 1996, Cert. Recognition NASA, 1984, Alice Evans award Am. Soc. Microbiol., 1988, Andrew White medal Loyola Coll., 1994, medal of distinction Barnard Coll./Columbia U., 1996; named Prof. Extraordinairo, U. Catolica Valparaiso, Chile, 1976, one of Outstanding Women on Campus, U. Md., 1979, Scholar of Yr., Phi Kappa Phi, 1992. Fellow AAAS (chmn. sect. biol. scis. 1993-94, pres. 1995, chmn. bd. 1996), Grad. Women Sci., Can. Coll. Microbiologists, Am. Acad. Microbiology (chmn. bd. govs. 1989-99), Washington Acad. Scis. (bd. mgrs. 1976-79, pres. 1996-98), Marine Tech. Soc. (exec. com. 1982-88), Sigma Delta Epsilon; mem. Am. Soc. Microbiology (various sci. coms. 1961—, pres. 1985, chmn. program com. REGEM-1 1988, Fisher award 1985), World Fedn. Culture Collections, Internat. Union Microbiol. Soc. (v.p. 1986-90, pres. 1990-94), Am. Inst. Biol. Scis. (bd. govs. 1976-82), Am. Soc. Limnology and Oceanography, Internat. Coun. Sci. Unions (gen. com., exec. bd. 1993-96), U.S. Fedn. Culture Collections (governing bd. 1978-88), Soc. Indsl. Microbiology (bd. govs. 1976-79, Charles Thom award 1998), Classification Rsch. Group Eng. (charter), Soc. Gen. Microbiology, French Soc. Microbiology, (hon.), Israeli Soc. Microbiology (hon.), Soc. Applied Microbiology (hon.), Bangladesh Soc. Microbiology (hon., fgn.), Australian Soc. Microbiology (hon.), Phi Beta Kappa, Sigma Xi (Ann. Achievement award 1981, Rsch. award 1984, nat. pres. 1991), Omicron Delta Kappa, Delta Gamma (Delta Gamma Rose award, 1989). E-mail: rcolwell@nsf.gov. Achievements include research in marine biotechnology, marine and estuarine microbial ecology, survival of pathogens in aquatic environment, ecology of Vibrio cholerae and related organisms, microbial systematics, marine microbiology, antibiotic resistance, environmental aspects of Vibrio cholerae in transmission of cholera, global climate and cholera transmission. Office: NSF Office of the Dir 4201 Wilson Blvd Ste 1205 Arlington VA 22230-0001

COLY, LISETTE, foundation executive; b. N.Y.C., Apr. 6, 1950; d. Robert Raymond and Eileen (Lyttle-Garrett) C.; children: George Robert Damalas, Anastasia Eileen Damalas. BA cum laude, Hunter Coll., 1973. Sec. Parapsychology Found., Inc., N.Y.C., 1972-75, assoc. editor, 1975—, v.p., 1978—, exec. dir., 1999—. Assoc. editor Parapsychology Rev. and Procs. Ann. Internat. Parapsychology Found. Confs., 1978—; editor, conf. coord. Procs. Ann. Internat. Confs., 1989—; editor-in-chief Internat. Jour. Parapsychology. Office: Parapsychology Found Inc 228 E 71st St New York NY 10021-5136

COMBALDIEU, JEAN-CLAUDE, trade organization executive; b. 1935. Degree in law, Ecole Ctr. de Paris. Bar: Paris Civil Ct. 1967, Paris Ct. Appeal 1967, Ct. Cassation 1975. Mng. dir. Inst. Nat. de la Propriété Industrielle, 1983-94; pres. Office for Harmonization in the Internal Market, Alicante, Spain, 1994—. Named Officer Legion of Honour, Officer of Nat. Order of Merit, Grand Officer Order of Merit Spain & Germany. Office: OHIM, Avda de Aguilera 20, 03080 Alicante Spain

COMBE, MICHEL, lawyer; b. Aubenas, France, Mar. 6, 1959; s. Gaston Combe and Noelle Duffaud; m. Rose Marie Orsoni, Sept. 7, 1959; 1 child, Hadrien. Diplome d'Etudes Appofondie, Droit Affaires, Aix en Provence, France, 1982; MBA, Inst Superieur des Affairs, Paris, 1984. Registered lawyer, France. Staff asst. Coopers & Lybrand, Paris, France, 1984-92; ptnr. Price Waterhouse Coopers Landwell, Paris, France, 1992—. Office: Price Waterhouse Coopers, 10 Place de la Joliette, 13002 Marseille France

COMBES, FRANSOISE MARIE, astronomer; b. Montpellier, France, Aug. 12, 1952; s. André and Aline (Gely) C.; m. Denis Bottaro, Mar. 25, 1978; children: Bottaro André, Thierry, Sylvain. Physician diploma, 1973, physician agregation, 1975; PhD, U. Paris, 1980. Asst. prof. Ecole Normale Superieure, Paris, 1975-78, assoc. prof., 1978-83, dir. physician lab, 1985-89; prof. U. Paris, 1983-85; astronomer Observatoire de Paris, 1989—; Author: Galaxies and Cosmology, 1991; editor: Dynamics of Galaxies and Molecular Clouds, 1991; also articles. Author: Galaxies and Cosmology, 1991; editor: Dynamics of Galaxies and Molecular Clouds, 1991; contbr. articles to profl. jours. Recipient IBM prize in physics, 1986, Petit Ormoy prize Acad. Sci., 1993. Mem. Am. Astron. Soc., Internat. Astron. Union, European Astron. Soc. Avocation: oil painting. Office: Observatoire de Paris, 61 Ave de l'Observatoire, F-75014 Paris France

COMBESCURE, MONIQUE, physics researcher; b. La Tronche, France, Apr. 23, 1950; d. Claude and Marinette (Molmerret) Moulin; m. Alain Combescure, Aug. 30, 1974; children: Claire, Etienne, Mireille, Christelle. Grad., ENS, Paris, 1974, U. Paris VI, 1974; PhD, U. Paris VI, 1979. Rschr. Nat. Ctr. Sci. Rsch., France, 1974—. Office: LPT Batiment 210, 91405 Orsay France

COMBEST, LARRY ED, congressman; b. Memphis, Tex., Mar. 20, 1945; s. Lawrence Nelson and Callie (Gunter) C.; m. Sharon McCurry, Sept. 10, 1981. BBA, W. Tex. State U., 1969; JD, Lubbock Christian U. Farmer, stockman Memphis, 1965-71; county trainee Dept. Agr., Graham, Tex., 1971; spl. asst. Senator John Tower, Washington, 1971-78; owner Combest Distbg., Lubbock, Tex., 1978-85; mem. 99th-106th Congresses from 19th Tex. dist., Washington, 1985—; chmn. agriculture com. Recipient Santa Fe award Future Farmers Am., 1962, Gerald W. Thomas Outstanding Agriculturalists award for pub. svc., 1989, Lubbock Area Found. Hero of Yr. award, 1999. Republican. Methodist. Lodges: Rotary, Lions. Office: US Ho of Reps 1026 Longworth Bldg Washington DC 20515-4319

COMBS, SEAN, record company executive, producer; b. N.Y.C., 1971; 1 child. Promoter hip-hop events Howard U., Washington, 1980s; intern Uptown Records, 1991, head A&R dept., 1991; pres., CEO Bad Boy Entertainment, 1994—. Prodr.: Forever My Lady (Jodeci), 1991, Diary of a Mad Band (Jodeci), 1993, What's the 411? (Mary J. Blige), 1993, My Life (Mary J. Blige), 1994, Project: Funk Da World (Craig Mack), 1994, Ready to Die (The Notorious B.I.G.), 1994, Think of You (Raymond Usher), 1994, Faith (Faith Evans), 1995; also prodr. records by Supercat, 7669, Keith Sweat, Caron Wheeler, Mix Tape Volume 2, 1997, Money Talks, 1997, In Tha Beginning...There Was Rap, 1997, Diana, Princess of Wales: Tribute, 1997, Chef Aid: The South Park Album, 1998; artist: No Way Out, 1997. Office: Bad Boy Entertainment 3311 Kensington Ave Ph Philadelphia PA 19134-1401

COMBS, STEPHEN PAUL, pediatrician, health facility administrator; b. Bristol, Tenn., Feb. 11, 1966; s. Paul Willis and Janis Rose C. BS, East Tenn. State U., 1988, MD, 1992. Diplomate Nat. Bd. Med. Examiners, Am. Bd. Pediat., Am. Bd. Forensic Examiners, Am. Bd. Forensic Medicine. Resident in pediat. Duke U., Durham, N.C., 1992-95; asst. chief pediat. residents Duke Children's Hosp. Duke U., 1994-95; ptnr. Mountain Region Pediats., Kingsport, Tenn., 1995-98, sec., 1999—; pediatrician Gray (Tenn.) Sta. Pediat., 1996—; dir. pediat. intensive care, chmn. pediat. critical care Wellmont Health Sys., quality oversight com., Holston Valley Med. Ctr., Kingsport, Tenn., 1996—; chmn. dept. pediat. Indian Path Med. Ctr.; mem. med. adv. bd. Am. Homepatient, Nashville, 1995—; regional faculty PALS Tenn. chpt. AHA, 1995—; mem. child fatality rev. bd. jud. dist. II State of Tenn., 1995—; asst. prof. family medicine, asst. prof. internal medicine E. Tenn. State U., James H. Quillen Coll. of Med.; chmn. Quality Improvement, Wllmont; bd. dirs. Mountain Region Speech and Hearing. Contbr. articles to profl. jours. Recipient Forty Under 40 award Bus. Jour. Fellow AAP (resident rep. 1993-95); mem. AMA, Tenn. Med. Assn., N.C. Med. Assn., Duke Med. Alumni Assn., East Tenn. State U. Med. Alumni Assn. (rep. 1992—), History of Appalachia Soc. Republican. Baptist. Avocations: Civil War, Revolutionary War, gardening, snow skiing, golf. Home: 405 Westfield Pl Kingsport TN 37664-6410 Office: Gray Sta Pediat 2103 Forest Dr Ste 5 Gray TN 37615-8423

COMBS, STEVEN PAUL, orthopedic surgeon; b. Ft. Dodge, Iowa, Apr. 9, 1944; s. Eugene Charles and Marie Wilhelmina (Mack) C.; m. Penelope Ann Calvey, July 6, 1974; children: Patrick, Mary Katherine, Meaghan, Bridget. BS, U. Iowa, 1966, MD, 1970; MBA, Lake Erie Coll., 1991. Diplomate Am. Bd. Orthopedic Surgery; cert. physician exec. Intern Robert Packer Hosp., Sayre, Pa., 1970-71; resident in orthopedics Cleve. Clinic, 1971-75; orthopedic surgeon Drs. DeMarco & Irwin, Willoughby, Ohio, 1979—; pres. med. staff Lake Hosp. Sys., 1998—. Served to maj. USAF, 1975-79. Fellow ACS; mem. AMA, Am. Acad. Orthopedic Surgeons, Orthopedic Rsch. Soc., Coll. Physician Execs., Lake County Med. Soc. (pres. 1991), Lake Hosp. Found. (chmn. 1993-96), Ohio State Med. Assn. (alt. del. AMA 1997—, chmn. legis. com. 1997—). Republican. Roman Catholic. Home: 8685 King Memorial Rd Mentor OH 44060-7960 Office: Lake Orthopaedic Assn 36100 Euclid Ave Ste 170 Willoughby OH 44094-4475

COMBS, W(ILLIAM) HENRY, III, lawyer; b. Casper, Wyo., Mar. 18, 1949; s. William Henry and Ruth M. (Wooster) C.; divorced; 1 child, J. Bradley. Student, Northwestern U., 1967-70; BS, U. Wyo., 1972, JD, 1975. Bar: Wyo. 1975, U.S. Dist. Ct. Wyo. 1975, U.S. Ct. Appeals (10th cir.) 1990, U.S. Supreme Ct. 1990. Assoc. Murane & Bostwick, Casper, 1975-77, ptnr., 1978—. Mem. com. on resolution of fee disputes, 1988-92. Mem. ABA (tort and ins. practice, law office mgmt. sects.), Natrona County Bar Assn., Def. Rsch. Inst., Am. Judicature Soc., Def. Lawyers Assn. of Wyo., Assn. Ski Def. Attys., Nat. Bd. Trial Advocacy (cert.), U.S. Handball Assn., Waterski USA, NRA, Casper Boat Club, Casper Petroleum Club, Porsche Club Am., BMW Club Am. Republican. Episcopalian. Avocations: handball, waterskiing, snow skiing, climbing, driving. Office: Murane & Bostwick 201 N Wolcott St Casper WY 82601-1922

COMEGYS, ETHEL BLANCHE, brokerage house administrator; b. Balt., Sept. 11, 1961; d. Elmer Anthony and Ethel Blanche Weber; m. Mark Steven Comegys, Apr. 26, 1989. BA with honors, Johns Hopkins U., 1983. Bank teller Augusta Fed., Balt., 1984-89; from funds processing svc. rep. to client svc. rep. Legg Mason, Balt., 1992-98, client svc. asst. supr., 1999—. Active Nat. Trust, D.C., 1997, Balt. Preservation, Inc., 1998. Md. State Ho. of Dels. scholar, 1979. Democrat. Lutheran. Avocations: antiques, gardening, old house restoration.

COMELLINI, ENRICO, engineering executive; b. Bologna, Italy, Apr. 10, 1934; s. Roberto and Giulia (Gnudi) C.; m. Ivana Landini, July 18, 1966; children: Roberto, Elena. D of Engring., U. Bologna, 1959. Engr., mgr. Italian Electricity Industry, 1959-75; dir. distbn. engring. ENEL, Rome, 1975-95; pres. CISE Spa, Milan, Italy, 1995-96, CESI Spa, Milan, 1996-99; treas. Internat. Elec. Commn., 1997—; pres. CEI Italian Elec. Commn., 1998—. Contbr. articles to profl. jours. Fellow IEEE. Office: CESI, viale Monza 259, 20126 Milan Italy

COMER, DOUGLAS EARL, computer science educator, consultant; b. Vineland, N.J., Sept. 9, 1949. BS, Houghton (N.Y.) Coll., 1971; PhD, Pa. State U., 1976. Asst. prof. computer sci. Purdue U., West Lafayette, Ind., 1976-81; assoc. prof. computer sci. Purdue U., West Lafayette, 1981-84, prof. computer sci., 1984—; mem. tech. staff Bell Labs., Murray Hill, N.J., 1982-83; dean Interop Grad. Inst., Foster City, Calif., 1996-98, instr. seminars on Transmission Control Protocol/Internet Protocol and networking, 1989—, cons., 1987—; cons. networking Softbank Corp., 1987—. Author 11 books in networking field and 4 books in operating system design, including: Operating System Design, Vol. 1, 1984, Vol. 2, 1987, Internetworking with TCP/IP, 3 vols. and rev. edits., 1991-2000, The Internet Book, 1994, rev. edit., 2000, Computer Networks and Internets, 1999; contbr. articles to profl. jours. Recipient Lifetime Achievement award Software Tools Users Group USENIX, 1996; rsch. grantee NSF, Sun, Digital Equipment, AT&T, Def. Advanced Rsch. Projects Agy., 1983—. Fellow Assn. for Computing Machinery (Outstanding Tchg. award Purdue chpt. 1995); mem. Sigma Xi, Upsilon Pi Epsilon. Avocation: postscript drawings. Office: Purdue U Dept Computer Sci University St R 156 Lafayette IN 47907-1398

COMISSIONA, SERGIU, conductor; b. Bucharest, Romania, June 16, 1928; came to U.S., 1969; naturalized, 1976; s. Isaac and Jean L. (Haufrecht) C.; m. Robinne Florin, July 16, 1949. Studied with Constantin Silvestri and Eduoard Lindenberg, 1928; ed. music conservatoire, Bucharest; Mus.D. (hon.), Peabody Conservatory Music, 1972; LHD (hon.), Loyola Coll., Balt., 1973, Towson State U., 1980; D.F.A. (hon.), Washington Coll., Chestertown, Md., 1980, Western Md. Coll., 1977, U. Md., 1981, Johns Hopkins U., 1982. Operatic conducting debut in Faust at Sibiu, 1945, conducting debut Bucharest Opera Orch., 1946; violinist Bucharest Radio Quartet, 1946, Rumanian State Ensemble Orch., 1947, asst. condr., 1948, music dir., 1950-55; prin. condr. Rumanian State Opera, 1955-59, Asian Youth Orch., 1995; founder, condr. Ramat Gan (Israel) Chamber Orch., 1960-67; music dir. Haifa (Israel) Symphony, 1960-66, Israel Chamber Orch., 1960-67, Goteburg (Sweden) Symphony Orch., 1966-67, Balt. Symphony Orch., 1969-84, condr. laureate, 1995—; music dir. Houston Symphony Orch., 1983-88, N.Y.C. Opera, 1987-89, Helsinki Philharm. Orch. (also chief condr.), 1990-93, Vancouver Symphony, 1990—, Orquesta Sinfonica de RTVE, Madrid, 1990-97, Asian Youth Orch., 1995—, Vancouver Symphony Orch., 1990—; Am. debut with Phil. Orch., 1965; mus. adviser, condr. No. Ireland Orch., 1967-68; artistic dir. Temple U. Music Festival, 1976-80, music advisor, prin. condr., 1977-80; music dir., prin. condr. Chautauqua Symphony Orch. Summer Festival, 1976-80; music adviser Am. Symphony Orch., 1978-82; artistic advisor Houston Symphony Orch., 1980-83; permanent guest condr. Radio Philharm. Orch. of Netherlands, 1982-83, chief condr., 1983-89; with London Symphony, Stockholm Philharm., Swedish Radio Orch.; founder Joseph Meyerhoff Hall, Balt. Decorated Order Merit 2d Class Rumania; winner internat. competition for young condrs. Besancon, France, 1954; recipient Gold medal award City of Goteborg, 1973, Ditson Condr.'s award Columbia U., 1979. Mem. Royal Swedish Acad. Music (hon.); Knight Order Arts Letters (France). Home: ICM Artists Classical Divsn 10 W 66th St Apt 20F New York NY 10023-6210 Office: Hemsing Assocs c/o Josephine Hemsing 401 E 80th St Apt 14H New York NY 10021-0650*

COMPAGNA, DONNA J., preschool administrator, primary school educator; b. Manchester, N.H., Apr. 24, 1951; d. Raoul Real and Yvette Therese (Bailard) C.; m. July, 1973 (div. 1982); children: Monicca Cay Ouellette, Nathant Jacob Ouellette. B in Sci. and Human Svcs., N.H. Coll., 1981; AMS Cert., Boston Coll., 1984. Cert. ct. mediator Rock County Mediation. Adminstr., founder REACH, Derry, N.H., 1976-82; adminstr., founder, exec. dir. Derry Montessori Children's Ctr., 1982—. Mgr. Gordon Humphrey State Senator Campaign, 1988, Campaign for Reagan. Mem. Am. Montessori Soc., Beaver Lake Improvement Assn. (dir. 1988-98), Nutfield Coun. Arts. Avocations: stained glass, calligraphy, sewing, mediation, homeopathy. Home: 42 Pond Rd Derry NH 03038-4015 Office: Derry Montessori Children's Ctr 65 E Broadway Derry NH 03038-2405

COMPAGNON, JEAN GEORGE ANDRE, writer; b. St. Germain, Yvelines, France, Oct. 26, 1916; s. Marcel and Lucie (Dehesdin) C.; m. Jacqueline Terlinden, Sept. 27, 1947 (dec. 1964); children: Anne, Antoine, Madeleine, Bernard, Odile, Isabelle; m. Sylvie Palewski, July 2, 1964; 1 stepchild, Benedicte Chenneviere. Student, St. Cyr Mil. Acad., St. Cyr, France, 1934-36; diploma, War Coll., Paris, 1955; student, Inst. Controle Gestion, Paris, 1973. Commd. French Army, 1934; lt. 4th Hussards Fgn. Legion, France, N. Africa, 1937-43; capt. 2d Armored Div., French Indochina, Franch, Indochina, 1943-47; major NATO, London, 1948-53; col. 1st Airborne Hussards, Algeria, 1956-60; brigadier gen. Mil. Attache, U.S. Embassy, Washington, 1962-65; brigadier gen., comdr. 2nd Armored Brigade, Paris, 1968-1970; major gen., comdr. 11th Airborne Div., Pau, 1971-73; lt. gen., comdr. 3rd Area Command, Rennes, France, 1973-75; lt. gen., writer French Reserves, Paris, 1976—; tchr. War Coll., Paris, 1960-62; chief staff French Army, Baden Baden, Fed. Republic Germany, 1965-67; cons. Audit by Ganide, Paris, 1976-81. Author: The Strategic Victory of the Second War, 1984 (Foch prize), Landing in Normandy, 1984, The Strategic Victory of the Second War, 1984 (Foch prize), General Leclerc, Marechal ai France, 1994. Active Acad. Overseas Scis., Paris, 1989. Decorated Great Cross French Legion Honor, 1974, Great Cross French Order Merit, 1989, Officer Legion Merit (U.S.A.), 1965, citations French Cross War, 1940-60. Mem. Internat. Fedn. Fgn. Legions (hon. chmn.), Assn. Hereditary Honors (hon. chmn.), Nat. Union Armor (hon. chmn.), Gentlemen-Riders Club. Roman Catholic. Home: 36 Rue de Moscou, 75008 Paris France Office: Acad Overseas Sci, 15 Rue Laperouse, 5016 Paris France

COMPAGNONI, DEBORAH, Olympic athlete; b. Bormio, Sondrio, Italy, June 4, 1970. Winner gold medal women's giant slalom XVII Winter Olympic Games, Lillehammer, Norway, 1994, XVIV Winter Olympic Games, Nagano, Japan, 1998. Winner 3 gold medals World Ski Championship, 1987, 96, 97, 3 gold medals Olympic Winter Games, Albertville, 1992, Lillehammer, 1994, Nagano, 1998; named Most Popular Woman of the Yr., Grazia Women Mag., Italy, 1997. Office: Comitato Olimpico Nazionale Italiano, Foro Italico, 00194 Rome Italy*

COMPAORE, BLAISE, Burkina Faso government official; b. Ziniare, Feb. 3, 1951. Comdr. Nat. Training Ctr. for Commandos, 1983; mem. Nat. Revolutionary Coun., 1983; min. state to pres., 1984, min. justice, 1984-87; chmn. Popular Front, 1987-91; first pres. Fourth Republic, 1991; pres. Orgn. African Unity, 1998. Office: Office of the Pres, 03 B P 7030, Ouagadougou Burkina Faso

COMPER, TONY, banker; b. Toronto, Ont., Can., Apr. 24, 1945; m. Elizabeth Comper. BA in English, U. Toronto, 1966; DHL (hon.), Mt. St. Vincent U. With Bank of Montreal, 1967—, with ops. and sys. group, 1971-82, sr. v.p. personal banking, 1982, sr. v.p., sr. ops. officer treasury group, 1982-84, sr. v.p., mgr. London br., 1984-86, sr. v.p., sr. mktg. officer corp. and govt. banking, 1986-87, exec. v.p. ops., 1987-89, pres., chief gen. mgr., COO, 1989-90, pres., COO, 1990-99, pres., CEO, 1999, chmn., CEO, 1999—, also bd. dirs., now CEO; bd. dirs. Bank of Montreal and its subs., Harris Bankcorp, Inc., Harris Trust and Savs. Bank, BMO Nesbitt Burns Inc. Bd. dirs. C.D. Howe Inst., BMO Nesbitt Burns Inc., C.D. Howe Meml. Found., Catalyst, N.Y., Can. Club Toronto; hon. chair bd. govs. Yee Hong Ctr Geriatric Care; chair Capital Campaign U. Toronto; past chair governing coun. U. Toronto; past vice-chair St. Michael's Hosp. Recipient Human Rels. award Can. Coun. Christians and Jews, 1998. Avocations: golf, classical music, theater, art. Office: Bank Montréal, 1st Canadian Pl 100 W King St, Toronto, ON Canada M5X 1A1

COMPERE, PIERRE, retired psychologist; b. Aywaille, Belgium, Nov. 6, 1934; s. Henri and Jeanne (Close) C.; m. Gerda Hilgers, July 8, 1965; children: Muriele, Thomas. Lic. bot., Univ., Liege, Belgium, 1956. Rsch. asst. I.N.E.A.C., Belgian Congo, 1958-60, I.B.E.R.S.O.M., Belgium, 1961-62, Min. Nat. Edn., Belgium, 1963; scientific officer Nat. Bot. Garden, Belgium, 1964-70, sr. scientific officer, 1970-93, head dept., 1993-99; ret., 1999. Author: Vegetation Map of Lower Congo, 1970, Algae From Lake Chad I-VII, 1974-77, Flore Pratique Algues d'eau de Belgique, 1986; co-editor: Studies on Aquatic Vascular Plants, 1982. 2d lt. Belgian Army, 1957-58. Mem. Internat. Assn. Theoretical & Applied Limnology, Internat. Phycological Soc., Internat. Soc. Diatom Rsch. Roman Catholic. Avocations: orienteering sports. Home: Rue Des Cottages 131, B-1180 Brussels Belgium Office: Nat Bot Garden, Domein Van Bouchout, B-1860 Meise Belgium

COMPTON, CHARLES DANIEL, chemistry educator; b. Elizabeth, N.J., Jan. 8, 1915; s. Charles Daniel and Janie (Little) C.; m. Ida Lightman, Dec. 19, 1953. AB cum laude, Princeton U., 1940; PhD in Chemistry, Yale U., 1943. Rsch. chemist Calco Chem. Co., 1943; instr. Princeton, 1944-46; rsch. assoc. Manhattan Dist. Project, Princeton, 1943-45; faculty Williams Coll., 1946—, prof., 1957—, chmn. chemistry dept., 1964-74, Halford R. Clark prof. natural sci., 1966-72, Ebenezer Fitch prof. chemistry, 1972-77, Ebenezer Fitch prof. chemistry emeritus, 1977—; lectr. chemistry New Coll., U. South Fla., 1979-81. Author: Introduction to Chemistry, 1958, Inside Chemistry, 1979, Japanese transl., 1982; contbr. articles to profl. jours. Allied Chem. and Dye Co. fellow, Yale U., 1942-43. Fellow AAAS; mem. Am. Chem. Soc., Phi Beta Kappa, Sigma Xi. Home: 1050 Riverside Dr Apt A304 Palmetto FL 34221-5056

COMPTON, DALE LEONARD, retired space agency executive, consultant; b. Pasadena, Calif., June 18, 1935; s. John Leonard and Gladys Imnachuck (Foster) C.; m. Marilyn Doris Garland, June 21, 1959 (dec. Mar. 1997); children: David, Debora; m. Doris Bost Martin, Aug. 6, 2000. BSME, Stanford U., 1957, MS in Aero. Engring., 1958, PhD, 1969; MMS in Mgmt. Sci., MIT, 1975. Rsch. scientist NASA-Ames Rsch. Ctr., Moffett Field, Calif., 1957-72, Tech. asst. to dir., 1972-73, dep. dir. astronautics, 1973-74, chief space sci. div., 1974-80, mgr. IRAS Project, 1980-81, dep. dir. astronautics, 1981-82, dir. engring. & computer systems, 1982-85, dep. dir., 1985-88, dir., 1988-94; Sloan fellow MIT, Cambridge, Mass., 1974-75. Recipient NASA's Outstanding Leadership and Disting. Svc. medals, SES Presdl. Ranks of Meritorious and Disting. Exec. Fellow AIAA (named Outstanding Engr./Astro. 1983-84), AAAS; mem. Internat. Acad. Astronautics, Tau Beta Pi, Sigma Xi. Avocations: woodworking, reading, sailing, bird watching. Home: 10131 Phar Lap Dr Cupertino CA 95014-1113

COMPTON, JENNIFER LEE, writer; b. Wellington, New Zealand, Oct. 12, 1949; arrived in Australia, 1972; d. William John Suter Maughan and Dorothy Mary (Lee) C.; m. Matthew John O'Sullivan, July 31, 1971; children: Harvey, Alexandra. Student, Cen. Theatre Drama Sch., Auckland, New Zealand, 1968-69; student, NIDA Playwrights' Studio, Sydney, Australia, 1974. Writer in residence U. Canterbury, Christchurch, New Zealand, 1980—. Playwright, Crossfire (No Man's Land), 1976, Julia's Song, 1991, Barefoot, 1994, The Big Picture, 1997, The Quick Brown Fox Jumps Over the Lazy Dog, 2000; author: (poems) From the Other Woman, 1993, Aroha, 1998, Blue, 2000. Recipient AWGIE award Australian Writers' Guild, 1976, Katharine Mansfield & Bank New Zealand award, 1977, Robert Harris Poetry prize, 1995; New Zealand State Literary Fund grantee, 1977; fellow NSW Ministry for the Arts, 1995. Avocations: knitting, horse riding, gardening. Home: Verona Bumballa Rd, Wingello 2579, Australia

COMPTON, WILLIAM THOMAS, real estate investor; b. Bedford, Ind., Dec. 1, 1945; s. Thomas Franklin and Dorothy Jane (Smith) C.; m. Nancy Marie Radocchia, Sept. 13, 1969 (div. Aug. 1994); children: Kimberly Dawn, Lindsay Ann; m. Kathleen Ann Berrigan, Feb. 14, 1997. BS in Mgmt., MIT, 1968, Postgrad., 1968-70. Cert. data processor. Sr. systems analyst First Nat. Bank Boston, 1970-73; systems analyst Gen. Computer Systems, Wellesley, Mass., 1973-76; bus. systems analyst Fram Corp., East Providence, R.I., 1976-78; v.p. Span Mgmt. Systems, East Providence, 1978; project leader Prime Computer Inc., Natick, Mass., 1979-81; owner Compton Software Solutions, Tiverton, R.I., 1981-88; prodn. foreman Tillotson Rubber Co., Inc., Fall River, Mass., 1988-89. Author several computer software programs, 1982-85. Loaned officer United Fund Boston, 1970. Mem. Data Processing Mgmt. Assn. (cert. data processing instr. 1985-86). Republican. Methodist. Lodge: Kiwanis (local v.p. 1985, pres. 1985-86). Avocation: stained glass. Home and Office: 250 Ash St Brockton MA 02301-4140

COMSTOCK, ROBERT DONALD, JR., real estate executive; b. Miami, Fla., Sept. 28, 1921; s. Robert Donald Sr. and Gertrude (Quigg) C.; m. Mary Evans, Oct. 12, 1949; children: Carol Frances, Robert Donald III (dec.). BS in Commerce, U. Miss., 1943. Lic. real estate broker. Acct. New Orleans Pub. Service Co., 1946-47; salesman, br. mgr. Capitol Records, Inc., New Orleans and Charlotte, N.C., 1948-51; regional v.p. Atlanta, 1952-57; owner, pres. Comstock Distbg. Co., Atlanta, 1957-74, Comstock and Assocs., Atlanta, 1968-74, Cartridge Control Corp., Atlanta, 1968-80, Comstock Properties, Atlanta, 1980—; pres. Ctr. for Rehab. Tech., Ga. Tech. U., Atlanta, 1987-91, chmn. bd., 1991—. Mem. Atlanta Arts Alliance, 1970—, Atlanta Symphony, 1970—; bd. dirs. Christian Council Met. Atlanta, 1975-77; trustee So. Ctr. for Internat. Studies; mem. Atlanta Hist. Soc. Served to exec. officer USN, 1943-46, PTO. Named #1 Distbr. CBS Records, Columbia Broadcasting, N.Y.C., 1965, 69, Outstanding Distbr. Columbia Phonographs, Columbia Broadcasting, 1968, 70-72. Mem. Atlanta Bd. Realtors, Capital City Club, Commerce Club, Breakfast Club (pres. 1970-71), Trinity Presbyn. Ch. Men's Club (pres. 1977, Rotary (pres. Atlanta Midtown 1978-79), Omicron Delta Kappa. Avocations: golf, swimming, foreign affairs. Home: 3400 Ridgewood Rd NW Atlanta GA 30327-2418 Office: 1447 Peachtree St NE Ste 804 Atlanta GA 30309-3029

COMUNIAN, ANNA LAURA, psychologist, educator; b. Conselve, Italy, Feb. 19, 1940; d. Eugenio and Maria (Baldoni) C. PhD, Padova U., Italy, 1964, 68. Prof. Padova U., Italy, 1968—; vis. prof. U. Crakow, Poland, 1985, 89, U. Zagreb, 1986, 89, U. Warsaw, 1989, U. Seville, Spain, 1992, U. Bratislava, Slovakia, 1995, U. Constanz, Germany, 1995, U. Freiburg, Germany, 1997, U. Boston, 1999, Concepcion, Chile, 2000; rschr., presenter in field. Contbr. articles to profl. jours., chpts. to books. Mem. Italian Psychol. Assn., Italian Assn. Study Non-Verbal Comm. (bd. dirs. 1994-96), APA, Internat. Soc. Study Behavioral Devel., Internat. Assn. Cross-Cultural Psyology, Internat. Coun. of Psychologists (bd. dirs. 1993-96), Internat. Acad. Family Psychology, Stress and Anxiety Rsch. Soc. (nat. rep. 1994—), Soc. Personality Assessment, Assn. Moral Edn. Roman Catholic. Avocations: music, poetry. Home: Via Terrassa 81, 35026 Conselve Italy Office: Dept Psychology, Via Venezia 8, 35100 Padua Italy

CONAND, CHANTAL, biologist, educator; b. Cracovie, Poland, Apr. 10, 1943; arrived in France, 1947; d. Louis and Irène (Melnikoff) Kurtz; m. François Conand, Sept. 23, 1968; children: Favot Claire, Gabrielle, Hélène. DEA in Oceanography, U. Marseille, France, 1965, Lic. Sci. Naturelles, 1966, D in Oceanography, 1974; D d'Etat es Sci., U. Brest, France, 1988. Assoc. prof. U. Marseille, 1964-68, U. Dakar, Senegal, 1970-76, U. Brest, 1976-77, 84-92; detached scientist ORSTOM, Noumea, France, 1979-84; prof. U. St. Denis La Réunion, France, 1995—, dir. lab. ecologie marine, 1994—. Author: Holothurians of Pacific Islands, 1990; editor bull. Beche-de-mer, 1990—; contbr. articles to profl. publs. Mem. Assn. Française Halieumétrie, Coral Reef Assn., Vie Océane Ong La Réunion, Tropical Fisheries Soc. Pac. Sci. Avocations: diving, choral singing, hiking. Home: Rte du Piton Bois de Nefles, 97490 Sainte Clotilde France Office: U de la reunion, Lab Ecologie Marine, 97715 Saint Denis France

CONAWAY, CHARLES, retail company executive. Exec. v.p., chief operating officer Reliable Drug Stores, Inc., 1989-92; sr. v.p. pharmacy CVS Corp., Woonsocket, R.I., 1992-95, exec. v.p., CFO, 1995-99, pres., chief operating officer, 1999—; chmn., CEO Kmart Corp., Troy, MI; bd. dirs. Linens 'n Things. Office: CVS Corp 1 Cvs Dr Woonsocket RI 02895-6146*

CONCES, RORY JOSEPH, philosophy educator; b. East Chicago, Ind., Aug. 8, 1954; s. Dewey and Shirley Conces; m. Ann Marie C., May 28, 1977; children: Christopher D., Colin P., Daniel T. BA in Psychology and Philosophy, Creighton U., 1976; MA in Philosophy, DePaul U., 1980; PhD in Philosophy, U. Mo., Columbia, 1991. Instr. Columbia (Mo.) Coll., 1985, Moberly (Mo.) Area Jr. Coll., 1990; vis. asst. prof. U. Nebr., Omaha, 1992—; lectr. Creighton U., Omaha, 1994—; vis. asst. prof. South China Normal U., Guangzhou, 2000; program chair Nat. 3d World Studies Conf., Omaha, 1994—; coord. Nebr. Ctr. Critical Thinking, Omaha, 1994—; bd. mem. Coalition for Ecodevel. and Cmty. Action in Haiti, Lincoln, Nebr., 1992-96. Author: Blurred Visions: Philosophy, Science and Ideology in a Troubled World; editor: Internat. Third World Studies Jour. and Rv., 1994—. Mem. Am. Philos. Assn., Ctrl. States Philos. Assn., Soc. Social and Polit. Philosophy, Phi Beta Delta. Avocations: mountain climbing, travel, photography. E-mail: rconces@unomaha.edu. Home: 12311 Wirt St Omaha NE 68164-2593 Office: U Nebr at Omaha Dept Philos and Religion 60th And Dodge Sts Omaha NE 68182-0001

CONDAT, JEAN-BERNARD, computer security specialist, consultant; b. Béziers, Hérault, France, Nov. 26, 1963; s. Jacques and Gisèle (Aubry) C. Miage, U. Lyon I, France, 1985; D in Music Edn., U. Lyon II, France, 1991. Cert. confidential accreditate. CEO's pvt. cons. SVP, S.A., Paris, 1985—; with Proteasy S.A., Paris. Author: Nicolo Paganini, 1987; editor: L'Art du Facteur d' Orgues, 1985, Golden Section and Music, 1986; translator The Little Black Book of Computer Viruses, 1993. With French Mil., 1988-89. Recipient Golden Sect., Chevalier, 1988. Mem. Chaos Computer Club France (gen. sec. 1990—, pres. 1990—). Roman Catholic. Avocations: squash, naturism. E-mail: condat@proteasy.org. Office: Proteasy SA, 42 bd Sebastopol, 75003 Paris France

CONDÉ, HENRI PAUL LOUIS, retired physicist; b. Stockholm, Sept. 2, 1930; s. Louis Fredrik and Elisabeth (Bergman) C.; m. Siv Berit Kahl, May 16, 1959; children: Carina, Johan. M Engring., Royal Inst. Tech., Stockholm, 1955, Lic. in Tech., 1963, DSc in Tech., 1965. Laborator Swedish Nat. Def. Establishment, Stockholm, 1955-95; assoc. prof. Royal Inst. Tech., Stockholm, 1965; prof. dept. neutron rsch. Uppsala (Sweden) U., 1986-95; neutron nuclear data expert; mem. nuclear data com. OECD/Nuclear Energy Agy., 1968-91, Paris, 1970-77, chmn. group of experts on nuclear data internat. nuclear data com. Internat. Atomic Energy Agy., Vienna, Austria, 1971-97; chmn. Swedish Nuclear Data Com., 1972-95; mem. Swedish com. on data for sci. and tech. Internat. Coun. Sci. Unions/Swedish Acad. Scis., Stockholm, 1974—; mem. expert group on accelerator-driven transmutation of nuclear waste, Swedish Nuclear Power Inspectorate, 1996—, adv. European Union Fusion Tech. Programme, European Com., Brussels, 1999-2000. Contbr. over 80 articles to profl. jours. and internat. confs. Fellow Swedish Phys. Soc. Home: Lomvägen 549, SE-19256 Sollentuna Sweden Office: Uppsala U Angstrom Lab, Dept Neutron Rsch Box 525, SE-75120 Uppsala Sweden

CONDE DE SARO, JAVIER, diplomat, NATO official; b. Spain, Mar. 13, 1946; married; 3 children. LLM, U. Madrid, 1967; grad., Diplomatic Sch., 1971. With Directorate Gen. for Internat. Econ. Rels. Ministry of Fgn. Affairs, Spain, 1971-76; asst. dir. gen. for Internat. Rels, Directorate Maritime Fisheries, Ministry of Fgn. Affairs, 1976-78; dir. polit. affairs on Africa and Asia Ministry of Fgn. Affairs, 1978; counsellor Ministry of Transport, Tourism and comm., 1978-79; econ. and comml. counsellor Embassy of Spain, Rabat, 1979-83, Buenos Aires, 1983-86; gen. dir. for juridical and instnl. coord. Secretariat State European Cmtys., Ministry of Fgn. Affairs, 1986-90, chief of cabinet, 1990; amb. Embassy of Spain, Algeria, 1990-94; sec. gen. for European Cmtys. Ministry of Fgn. Affairs, 1994-96; amb., permanent rep. of Spain to NATO Ministry of Fgn. Affairs, Brussels, 1996-2000; amb. permanent rep. to Spain European Union, Brussels, 2000—. Office: NATO Hdqrs, 52 Bd du Régent, B-1110 Brussels Belgium*

CONDE MONTERO-RIOS, FRANCISCO PEDRO, physician, researcher; b. Vigo, Pontevedra, Spain, Oct. 10, 1945; s. Fernando Conde and Josefina Montero-RÚos; m. Gabriella Bermani, Feb. 14, 1976 (dec. 1987); 1 child, Alberto; m. Stephanie Salvarelli, Jan. 30, 1995. Grad. in medicine and surgery, U. Santiago de Compostela, Spain, 1969, MD in Medicine and Surgery, 1973; MD in Medicine and Surgery, U. Genoa, Italy, 1983. Resident Hosp. Nuestra Señora del Perpetuo Socorro, Vigo, Spain, 1967-69; predoctoral fellow Centro de Investigaciones Biológicas, Madrid, 1970-72; postdoctoral fellow in immunology Agrl. Rsch. Coun., Cambridge, 1973-74; postdoctoral fellow immunology U. Cambridge, 1974-75; scientist Inst. Nat. dei Tumori, Milan, 1975-76; scientist Inst. de Bioquímica de Macromoléculas Univ. Autónoma Madrid, 1977-79; dir. immunochem. unit in rsch. dept. Hosp. Ramón y Cajal, Madrid, 1979—; prof. microbiology U. Autónoma Madrid, 1977-78, prof. immunology, 1978-79, prof. membrane biochemistry, 1981-82; prof. del curso monográfico del doctorado U. Complutense, Madrid, 1980-81, prod. continuous tng. in medicine, 1980-81, fundamental immunochemistry, 1980-81; pres. rsch. com. Hosp. Ramón y Cajal, Madrid, 1988-89, Hosp. Ramón y Cajal Med. Assn., 1993-95; com. of workers Hosp. Ramón y Cajal, 1995; dir., founder Shift S.A. Founder Concon mag., 1984; contbr. 150 scientific, political, technical articles to jour. Dir. Labor Union Sección Sindical CSI CSIF Hosp. Ramón y Cajal, Madrid, 1995-96; mem. Nat. Health Com. Popular Party, 1993—; dir., founder trade union ASI, Madrid, 1996-98; founder, v.p. trade union ASADE Assn. Sanitaria Dem., Madrid, 1999—. Mem. nat. and internat. scientific socs. Partido Popular. Roman Catholic. Avocations: trees, photography, computers, knowledge. Fax: 349-137-31158. Home: Nueva Zelanda 52, 28035 Madrid Spain Office: Hosp Raman y Cajal, Crta Colmenar Km 9, 28035 Madrid Spain

CONDER, JIMMIE LEE, commercial pilot, farmer; b. San Antonio, Nov. 24, 1934; s. William Thomas and Kathryn Louise Conder; m. JoNell Conder, Jan. 27, 1962 (div. Dec. 23, 1983); children: Laurie A., Troy E.; m. Bernice A. Conder, June 8, 1998. AA in Liberal Arts, Coll. So. Idaho, 1982. Lic. comml. pilot, multi-engine land, single engine land, instrument, DC-3. Commd. 2d lt. USAF, 1960, advanced through grades to maj., 1969; aerial gunner 90th Bomb Squadron, Korea, 1952-53; aviation cadet Air Tng. Command, Bainbridge, Ga., 1957-60; pilot, aerial tanker USAF Tactical Air Command, Biggs AFB, Tex., 1960-64; air commando pilot 315th Air Commando Group, Vietnam, 1964-65; pilot Mil. Airlift Command, Travis AFB, Calif., 1966-68; airlift coord./emergency actions officer 513th Tactical Airlift Wing, RAF Mildenball, Eng., 1968-70; civil air patrol liaison USAF, Twin Falls, Idaho, 1971-75; charter pilot Reeder Flying Svc., Twin Falls, Idaho, 1975-77; asst. safety and info. officer/pilot Idaho Bur. Aeronautics, Boise, 1977-79; corp. pilot Nielson, Twin Falls, 1983; safety and info. officer/chief pilot Idaho Bur. Aeronautics, Boise, 1984-88; pilot Corp. Air, Billings, Mont., 1988—; adminstr. Idaho Bur. Aeronautics, 1995-96; pilot/program mgr. AirServ Internat., Ethiopia, 1991-92, 93, Sudan, 1995, Mozambique, Uganda and Congo, 1996-97, Uganda, Congo, 1998; airlift coord., pilot Flood Disaster Relief, Mozambique, 2000. Decorated D.F.C., 3 Air Force Commendation medals, 20 Air medals. Mem. Gideons, Alpha Eta Rho (hon.). Republican. Avocations: farming, antique clock restoration, political science. E-mail:comet@cyberhighway.net. Home: Bird-in-Hand Farm 3623 N 2000 E Filer ID 83328-5667

CONDIE, VICKI COOK, nurse, educator; m. Michael J. Condie; children: Jennifer, Jamie, Stephen. Diploma, Deaconess Hosp. Sch. Nursing, 1969; BSN summa cum laude, SUNY, 1983; MS, Syracuse U., 1986; cert. advanced study in nursing edn., Widener U., 1991. RN, N.Y. Dir. nursing edn. Cayuga C.C., N.Y., 1987—, prof. nursing; SIDS educator Western N.Y. SIDS Ctr., 1987—; chmn. utilization rev. com. Cayuga County Dept. Health, 1985—, profl. adv. com. for Cert. Home Health Agy., 1987—; adj. prof. SUNY Health Sci. Ctr., Syracuse.; active N.Y. State Coun. ADN Programs. Active Florence Nightingale Mus. Assn., London. Recipient Chancellors' award for excellence in profl. svc. SUNY, 1998. Mem. ANA, N.Y. State Nurses Assn. (mem. coun. nursing edn., 1994-99), Omicron Alpha, Sigma Theta Tau.

CONDIT, DORIS ELIZABETH, retired historian; b. Balt.; d. Harlan Whitney and Dorothy Elizabeth (Witte) Morgan; m. Kenneth W. Condit, Aug. 22, 1953; children: Caroline Walbridge, Victoria Whitney. Student, Johns Hopkins U., 1945-46; AB, George Washington U., 1949, MA, 1952. Historian U.S. Corps of Engrs. Hist. Divsn., Balt., 1949-51; ops. analyst Johns Hopkins U. Ops. Rsch. Office, Chevy Chase, Md., 1952-56; rsch. scientist, sr. rsch. scientist Am. Univ. Ctr. for Rsch. in Social Sys., Washington, 1956-69; sr. rsch. scientist Am. Inst. for Rsch., Kensington, Md., 1969-74; cons. Office of Sec. of Def., Washington, 1974-77, 85-87, contract historian, 1977-85; cons. Braddock, Dunn & McDonald, 1973-74, Am. Insts. for Rsch., 1974, Ops. Rsch. Office, 1956-57; assoc. prof. rsch. Am. U., 1960-

69; rsch. area chmn. Ctr. for Rsch. in Social Sys., 1966-70; mem. ad hoc group for Sci. and Tech. Info., 1962. Author: Allied Supplies for Italian Partisans During World War II, 1954, A System for Handling Data on Unconventional Warfare, 1956, Case Study in Guerrilla War: Greece During World War II, 1961, Modern Revolutionary Warfare: An Analytical Overview, 1973, The Test of War, 1950-53, History of the Office of the Secretary of Defense, Vol. II, 1988, (with Bert H. Cooper, Jr. and others) Challenge and Response in Internal Conflict, 3 vols., 1967-68, U.S. Military Response to Overseas Insurgencies, 1970, Strategy and Success in Internal Conflict, 1971, Population Protection and Resources Management in Internal Defense Operations, 1971. Recipient Gardiner G. Hubbard Meml. prize in Am. history George Washington U., 1949. Mem. Soc. for History in Fed. Govt., Phi Beta Kappa. Episcopalian.

CONDIT, PHILIP MURRAY, aerospace executive, engineer; b. Berkeley, Calif., Aug. 2, 1941; s. Daniel Harrison and Bernice (Kemp) C.; m. Madeleine K. Bryant, Jan. 25, 1963 (div. June 1982); children: Nicole Lynn, Megan Anne; m. Janice Condit, Apr. 6, 1991. BS MechE, U. Calif., Berkeley, 1963; MS in Aero. Engring., Princeton U., 1965; MS in Mgmt., MIT, 1975. Engr. The Boeing Co., Seattle, 1965-72, mgr. engring., 1973-83, v.p., gen. mgr., 1983-84, v.p. sales and mktg., 1984-86, exec. v.p., 1986-89, exec. v.p., gen. mgr. 777 divsn., 1989-92, pres., 1992-96, chmn., CEO, 1996—; adv. coun. Dept. Mech. and Aerospace Engring., Princeton (N.J.) U., 1984—; chmn. aero. adv. com. NASA Adv. Coun., 1988-92; bd. dirs. The Fluke Corp., Nordstom, Inc. Co-inventor design of a flexible wing. Active Mercer Island (Wash.) Utilities Bd., 1975-78; bd. dirs. Camp Fire, Inc., 1987-92; exec bd. chief Seattle coun. Boy Scouts Am., 1988-90; trustee Mus. of Flight, Seattle, 1990—. Co-recipient Laurels award Aviation Week & Space Tech. magazine, 1990; Sloan fellow MIT, Boston, 1974. Fellow AIAA (Aircraft Design award 1984, Edward C. Wells tech. mgmt. award 1982, Wright Brothers Lectureship Aeronautics 1996), Royal Aero. Soc.; mem. NAE, Soc. Sloan Fellows (bd. govs. 1985-89), Soc. Automotive Engrs., Rainer Club, Columbia Tower Club (Seattle). Clubs: Rainier, Columbia Tower (Seattle). Office: The Boeing Co 7755 E Marginal Way S Seattle WA 98108-4000

CONDITT, MARGARET KAREN, scientist, policy analyst; b. Mobile, Ala., Aug. 7, 1953; m. David Joseph Bruno, Feb. 13, 1988; 2 stepchildren: Josh, Holly. BS in Chemistry, U. Ala., Tuscaloosa, 1975; PhD in Chemistry, U. Colo., 1984. Field hydrologist U.S. Geol. Survey, Tuscaloosa, 1975; sci. aide II Geol. Survey Ala., Tuscaloosa, 1975-77; tchg. asst. U. Ala., Tuscaloosa, 1977-79; rsch. asst. U. Colo., Boulder, 1979-84; sr. scientist Procter & Gamble, Cin., 1984—; reviewer sci. edn. grant proposals NSF, Washington, 1988; mem. water sci. and tech. bd. com. Nat. Acad. Scis., Washington, 1989-91. Author: (chpt.) Advanced Techniques in Synthetic Fuels Analysis, 1983; contbr. articles to profl. jours. Intern Colo. Gov.'s Sci. and Tech. Adv. Coun., 1981-83; appointee Liberty Twp. Bd. Zoning Appeal, 1994-97, elected trustee Liberty Township, 1998—; trustee, sec. Woodmoor Ter. Homeowner's Assn. Bd., 1993-97, pres. 1996-97. Recipient fellowship Mining and Mineral Resources and Rsch. Inst., 1980, Rsch. fellowship U. Colo. Grad. Sch., 1981, Browns-Rickett grant AAUW, 1982. Mem. Am. Chem. Soc. Roman Catholic. Avocations: collecting antiques, Boy Scouts. Home: 6959 Rock Springs Dr Liberty Township OH 45011-9376

CONDO, JAMES ROBERT, lawyer; b. Somerville, N.J., Mar. 2, 1952; s. Ralph Vincent and Betty Louise (MacQuaide) C.; m. Rhonda H. King, June 7, 1997. BS in Bus. and Econs., Lehigh U., 1974; JD, Boston Coll., 1979. Bar: Ariz. 1979, U.S. Dist. Ct. Ariz. 1979, U.S. Ct. Appeals (9th cir.) 1982, U.S. Ct. Appeals (D.C. cir.) 1989, U.S. Ct. Appeals (10th cir.) 1989, U.S. Supreme Ct. 1983, U.S. Ct. Appeals (6th cir.) 1991, U.S. Ct. Appeals (4th cir.) 1994. Assoc. Snell & Wilmer, Phoenix, 1979-84, ptnr., 1985—; judge pro tem Ariz. Ct. Appeals. Bd. dirs. Ariz. Town Hall. Fellow Ariz. Bar Found.; mem. ABA, State Bar Ariz., Maricopa County Bar Found. E-mail: jcondo@swlaw.com. Office: Snell & Wilmer One Arizona Ctr Phoenix AZ 85004-2202

CONDOM, PIERRE PHILIPPE, periodical editor and publisher; b. Toulouse, France, Nov. 30, 1941; s. Joseph and Gabrielle (Brochon) C.; m. Mariele Nicaud, Apr. 2, 1971; children: Raphael, Chloe. Speciales in Math., Lycée Chaptal, Paris, 1963. Avionics editor Aviation Mag. Internat., Paris, 1967-75, def. editor, 1969-75, editor-in-chief, 1975-81; editor-in-chief Interavia Aerospace Rev., Geneva, 1982—; dir. aerospace pubs. Interavia S.A., Geneva, 1982—, pub. dir., 1988—, pres., chief exec. officer, 1989-90; pres., chief exec. officer Aerospace Media Pub. S.A., Geneva, 1990-99; mng. dir. Air X Cosmos SA, Paris, 1999—. Active Nat. French Fencing Team. Served with French army, 1965-66. Fellow Royal Aero. Soc.; mem. Assn. des Journalists, Profls. de l'Aeronautics et de l'Espace, Acad. Nat. de l'Air et l'Espace (corr.), Aviation Space Writers Assn. (chmn.), Internat. Found. Airline Passengers Assn. Avocations: fencing, tennis. Home: 288 Les Mannessières, Collonges/Saleve France 74160 Office: 33 Route de l'aeroport, Box 56, 1215 Geneva 15, Switzerland

CONDON, FRANCIS EDWARD, retired chemistry educator; b. Abington, Mass., Oct. 12, 1919; s. Maurice Francis and Eva Isabel (Cole) C.; m. Mary Anna Medvetz, Jan. 9, 1943; children: Francis E., Mary Ellen (Mrs. George Laessig III), John M., Arthur T., Dorothy A. (Mrs. Ronald G. Waldt), James M., Rita C. A.B., Harvard, 1941, Ph.D., 1944. Research chemist Phillips Petroleum Co., Bartlesville, Okla., 1944-52; asst. prof. chemistry CCNY, 1952-61, assoc. prof., 1962-66, prof., 1967-82, ret., 1982, Louis J. Curtman prof., 1976-78; founder, chmn. Seven Siblings Found., Ltd., 1977-94; vis. prof. Purdue U., 1960. Author: (with H. Meislich) Introduction to Organic Chemistry, 1960, Study Projects in Physical Chemistry, 1963, Chess monographs, 1992—, also articles; contbr. chpt. to Catalysis, 1958. Mem. planning bd. Borough of Bogota, N.J., 1963; Trustee, pres. Bogota Swim Club, Inc., 1967-71. Petroleum Research Fund grantee, 1967-70; NSF Sci. Faculty fellow U. So. Calif., 1964-65. Mem. Am. Chem. Soc. (dir. N.Y. sect. 1967-68), U.S. Chess Fedn. (life), Glen Rock (N.J.) Chess Club (pres. 1975-79, Washington Twp. (N.J.) Chess Club (pres. 1990-92), Dumont (N.J.) Chess Mates (sec. 1992-99), St. Joseph's Holy Name Soc. (pres. 1974-75, sec. 1992—), Alpha Chi Sigma, Sigma Xi. Home: 471 Larch Ave Bogota NJ 07603-1058

CONDON, JOSEPH DENNIS, broadcasting executive; b. Albany, N.Y., Apr. 12, 1946; s. Joseph O. and Loretta (Halleran) C.; m. Kathleen M. Sullivan, Jan. 25, 1969; 1 child, Daniel J. Assoc. Degree in Bus. Adminstrn., Hudson Valley C.C., Troy, N.Y., 1966; BA in Mktg. and Acctg., Siena Coll., 1969; Degree in Pub. Rels., Albany Bus. Coll., 1975. Cert. TV prodn. specialist, USARNG, 1970. Announcer, disc jockey WTRY Kopps/Monahan Corp., Troy, 1963-67; announcer, news and weathercaster WAST-TV RKO Gen., Albany, 1967-68; announcer, disc jockey WABY Radio, Albany, 1967-69; announcer WTEN/WROW Capital Cities Comm., Albany, 1969-83; with WROW/WYJB Radio Albany Broadcasting, 1969—, pub. affairs dir., 1982—; owner Radio Albany.com, Albany, 2000—; N.E. corr. Voice of Am., Washington, 1983-87; cons. in field, 1991—. Pub. rels. chmn. bicentennial com. St. Mary's Ch. Sgt. N.Y. Nat. Guard, 1969-75. Recipient first place for best pub. affairs show N.Y. State Broadcasters, Albany, 1995, second place Nori award Ad Club, Albany, 1995, Best Sta. Event award N.Y. State Broadcasters, Albany, 1996, Best Pub. Affairs Series, 1997, 1998, Best Pub. Affairs Show, 1998, awd. Albany Broadcasting Co., 1998, cmty. svc. award for pub. affairs Nat. Broadcast Assn., 1998, 99, Proclamation, N.Y. State Senate, 1999, Proclamation, N.Y. Senator Neil Breslin, 1999; nominee Marconi award 1997, 98; recipient awards N.Y. State Broadcasters, 1999, silver microphone nat. finalist award, 1999, Best Pub. Affairs show award, 2000, Best Pub. Affairs Series award, 2000. Mem. AFTRA, NAACP, Am. Broadcast Pioneers Broadcast Found., N.Y. State Broadcasters (advisor job fair com.), Holocaust Survivors and Friends, R.R. Hist. Soc., Ad Club, Nat. Music Found. Avocations: broadcast historian, WWII historian, photographer, railroad historian. Home: 48 Glenwood Rd Menands NY 12204-2407 Office: Albany Broadcasting 6 Johnson Rd Latham NY 12110-5638

CONDON, STANLEY CHARLES, gastroenterologist; b. Glendale, Calif., Feb. 1, 1931; s. Charles Max and Alma Mae (Chinn) C.; m. Vaneta Marilyn Mabley, May 19, 1963; children: Lori, Brian, David. BA, La Sierra Coll., 1952; MD, Loma Linda U., 1956. Diplomate Nat. Bd. Med. Examiners, Am. Bd. Internal Medicine, Am. Bd. Gastroenterology; cert. nutrition support physician. Intern L.A. County Gen. Hosp., 1956-57, resident gen. pathology, 1959-61; resident internal medicine White Meml. Med. Ctr., L.A., 1961-63, attending staff out-patient clinic, 1963-64; active jr. attending staff L.A. County Gen. Hosp., 1964-65; dir. intern-resident tng. program Manila Sanitarium and Hosp., 1966-71, med. dir., 1971-72; chief resident internal medicine out-patient clinic Loma Linda U. Med. Ctr., 1972-74; fellow in gastroenterology Barnes Hosp./Wash. U., 1974-76; attending staff, asst. prof. medicine Loma Linda U. Med. Ctr., 1976-91, assoc. prof. medicine, 1991—, med. dir. nutritional support team, 1984—. Contbr. articles to profl. jours. Capt. U.S. Army, 1957-59. Fellow ACP; mem. AMA, Am. Soc. for Parenteral and Enteral Nutrition, Am. Gastroent. Assn., Calif. Med. Assn., So. Calif. Soc. Gastroenterology, Inland Soc. Internal Medicine, San Bernardino County Med. Soc. Republican. Seventh-day Adventist. Avocations: trombone, choral singing, camping, hiking, gardening. Home: 11524 Ray Ct Loma Linda CA 92354-3630 Office: Loma Linda U Med Ctr 11370 Anderson St Loma Linda CA 92354-3450

CONDRATE, ROBERT ADAM, SR., spectroscopy educator; b. Jan. 19, 1938; s. Adam Vincent and Angela Marian (Talacka) C.; m. Judith Campbell, Aug. 13, 1960; children: Barbara Louise, Robert Adam, Laura Angela. BS, Worcester Poly. Inst., 1960; PhD, Ill. Inst. Tech., 1965. Rsch. assoc. U. Ariz., Tucson, 1966-67; from asst. prof. spectroscopy to assoc. prof. N.Y. State Coll. Ceramics, Alfred (N.Y.) U., 1967-78, prof., 1978—; vis. prof. Los Alamos Sci. Lab., 1972, GTE, Towanda, N.Y., 1980; summer lectr. Korea Inst. Sci. & Tech., Seoul, 1989; cons. ceramic cos.; spectroscopy cons. Statue of Liberty/Ellis Island Found., 1984-86. Co-editor: Advances in Materials Characterization, 1983, Vol. II, 1985; mem. editl. bd. Nat. Forum, Asian Jour. Spectroscopy; assoc. editor Am. Ceramic Soc., 1989—; contbr. articles to profl. jours. Mem. parents adv. bd. secondary edn. Alfred-Almond Cen. Sch., 1975-80; Danforth Found. assoc. for higher edn, 1976-85. Recipient Spectroscopy award Chgo. Sect. Soc. Applied Spectroscopy, 1964, Scholes award Alfred U., 1972, commendation Statue of Liberty/Ellis Island Found., 1984-86; grantee Inland Steel-Ryerson Found., 1963-64, NSF, 1966-67, 84-86, 86-87, Coll. Ctr. Finger Lakes, 1969, Alfred U. Rsch. Found, 1975; NIH fellow, 1964-65; SUNY faculty exch. scholar, 1988—. Fellow Am. Inst. Chemists, Royal Soc. Chemistry, Am. Ceramic Soc.; mem. AAAS, Can. Ceramic Soc., Am. Chem. Soc., Soc. Applied Spectroscopy, Am. Phys. Soc., Coblentz Soc., N.Y. Acad. Scis., Clay Minerals Soc., Materials Rsch. Soc., Keramos, Sigma Xi, Phi Kappa Phi, Psi Lambda Upsilon, Sigma Alpha Epsilon, Tau Beta Pi, Mason. Home: 5761 Random Rd Alfred Station NY 14803-9793

CONDREN, CONAL STRATFORD, political science educator; b. London, Apr. 1, 1944; arrived in Australia, 1970; s. William Joseph and Beatrice Elizabeth (Deal) C.; m. Averil Claire Burgess; children: Aoise, Allegra. BSc in Econs., London Sch. Econs., 1965, MSc in Econs., 1966, PhD, 1969. Asst. lectr. London U., Rhodesia, 1967; lectr. U. NSW, Sydney, 1970-77, sr. lectr., 1977-85, assoc. prof. polit. sci., 1985-90, prof. polit. sci., 1990—, dir. humanities rsch. program, 1997—; vis. fellow Cambridge (Eng.) U., 1990, 95-96. Author: The Status and Appraisal of Classic Texts, 1985, George Lawson's Politica and the English Revolution, 1989, The Language of Politics in 17th Century England, 1995, Satire, Lies and Politics: The Case of Dr. Arbuthnot, 1997, Thomas Hobbes, 2000; author, editor: Politica Sacra et Civilis, by George Lawson, 1992. Fellow Australian Acad. Humanities; mem. Clare Hall Cambridge, Churchill Coll. Cambridge. Avocations: sailing, pottery, writing fiction. Office: Univ NSW, Dept Political Sci Sydney NSW 2052, Australia

CONE, JAMES ELMER, physician; b. Eugene, Oreg., July 3, 1949; s. Elmer and Eleanor (Scott) C.; m. Blanche Grosswald, June 30, 1991. AB, Stanford U., 1971; MD, U. Calif., San Francisco, 1978; MPH, U. Calif., Berkeley, 1978. Internship/residency Cook County Hosp., Chgo., 1978-80; epidemic intelligence svc. Ctrs. for Disease Control, Cin., 1980-82; resident internal medicine Worcester (Mass.) Meml. Hosp., 1982-83; chief, Occupational Health Clinic San Francisco Gen. Hosp., 1983-91; dir. health effects Carpenters Health and Safety, Washington, 1992-93; asst. clin. prof. U. Calif., San Francisco, 1983—; acting chief Hazard Evaluation System and Info. Svc./State of Calif., Berkeley, 1994-98; chief Occupational Health Branch State of Calif., Oakland, 1999—. Editor: Problem Buildings, 1989, Occupational Medicine Secrets, 1999. Bd. dirs., pres. Assn. Occupational Health Clinics, Washington, 1992-93. With USPHS, 1980-82. Mem. Am. Pub. Health Assn. (chmn. sect. 1985-86), Am. Coll. Occupational and Environ. Medicine. Avocation: sailing. Home: 1517 Henry St Berkeley CA 94709-2007 Office: Occupational Health Branch 1515 Clay St Ste 1901 Oakland CA 94612-1423

CONE, MICHAEL MCKAY, venture capitalist; b. Washington, Oct. 14, 1947; s. Montie Fowler and Eleanor Newcomb (Faulk) C.; m. Constance Anne Hennessy, July 21, 1971. AB, Princeton U., 1969; MPhil, Yale U., 1973, PhD, 1976. Chemist E.I. DuPont de Nemours, Wilmington, Del., 1977-81; area supt. E.I. DuPont de Nemours, LaPlace, La., 1981-84; bus. analyst E.I. DuPont de Nemours, Wilmington, 1984-85, tech. svc. specialist, 1985-86; devel. mgr. E.I. DuPont de Nemours, Parlin, N.J., 1986-89; cons. E.I. DuPont de Nemours, Wilmington, 1989-94; mgr. new bus. devel. E.I. DuPont de Nemours, Deepwater, N.J., 1994-98; ptnr. Crossway Ventures, Toms River, N.J., 1998—; bd. dirs. Wayn-Tex Inc., Waynesboro, Va., F.T. Industries, LLC, Franklinville, N.J., Gen. Econopak, Inc., Phila. Patentee in field. Mem. AAAS, Am. Chem. Soc., Product Devel. & Mgmt. Assn. (dir. sponsor devel. 1994-97), Sigma Xi, Princeton Club N.Y., Corinthian Yacht Club Phila. Avocations: sailing, skiing, music. Home: 1910 Spruce St Philadelphia PA 19103-6613 Office: Crossway Ventures 864 Rte 37 W Ste 16 Toms River NJ 08755-5033

CONG, JASON JINGSHENG, computer scientist, educator, consultant, researcher; b. Beijing, Feb. 20, 1963; came to U.S., 1986; m. Jing Chang, Jan. 28, 1995. BS, Peking U., China, 1985; MS, U. Ill., 1987, PhD, 1990. Intern Xerox Palo Alto (Calif.) Rsch. Ctr., summer 1987, Nat. Semiconductor Co., Santa Clara, Calif., summer 1988; rsch. asst. U. Ill., 1986-90; asst. prof. UCLA, 1990-94, assoc. prof., 1994-98, prof., 1998—; cons. Intel Corp., Santa Clara, 1994—; tech. adv. bd. Mentor Graphics, San Jose, Calif., 1994-96, Magma Design Automation, Palo Alto, 1997—. Author: Yield Enhancement of Reconfigurable VISI Systems, 1992; contbr. over 130 articles to profl. jours. Recipient Young Investigator award NSF, 1993. Mem. IEEE (sr. mem., assoc. editor 1999—, Best Paper award 1995), Assn. Computing Machinery (adv. bd. 1993—, assoc. editor 1995—, Meritorius Svc. award 1998). Office: UCLA 4711 Boelter Hl Los Angeles CA 90095-0001

CONGALIDIS, JOHN PETER, chemical engineer; b. Athens, Greece, Aug. 22, 1953; s. Peter J. and Melpomeni (Frangouli) C. Diploma in chem. engring. with highest honors, Nat. Tech. U., Athens, 1976; ScD in Chem. Engring., MIT, 1981. Registered profl. engr., Del. Rsch. asst. MIT Energy Lab., 1976-81; area engr. polymer products dept. Exptl. Sta. E. I. DuPont de Nemours & Co., Wilmington, Del., 1981-84, divsn. engr. polymer products dept. Exptl. Sta., 1985-87; divsn. engr. polymer products dept. Chambers Works E. I. DuPont de Nemours & Co., Deepwater, N.J., 1988-89, sr. engr. polymer products dept. Chambers Works, 1989-92; sr. rsch. engr. ctrl. sci. and engring. European Tech. Ctr. Du Pont de Nemours Internat. S.A., Meyrin, Switzerland, 1992-95; rsch. supr. ctrl. R&D DuPont de Nemours Internat. S.A., Meyrin, Switzerland, 1995-99; Six Sigma project leader DuPont Ctrl. R&D Exptl. Sta., Wilmington, Del., 1999—; invited lectr. Tech. U. Eindhoven Symposium on Process Control in Chem. Industry, 1993, N.J. Inst. Tech., 1988. Contbr. articles to profl. jours. and conf. procs. Recipient Prize of Tech. Chamber of Greece, 1974-76, 2d prize Hellenic Math. Soc., 1970; deptl. fellow MIT, 1981. Mem. AIChE, Del. Assn. Profl. Engrs. Avocations: opera, music, traveling. Home: 112 Talleyrand Dr Wilmington DE 19810-3948 Office: DuPont Ctrl R&D PO Box 80356 Wilmington DE 19880-0356

CONGALTON, CHRISTOPHER WILLIAM, lawyer; b. N.Y.C., Apr. 8, 1946; s. William Alexander and Jacqueline Rose (Ryan) C.; m. Susan Tichenor, May 29, 1971. AB, Fairfield (Conn.) U., 1968; JD, Georgetown U., 1971. Bar: N.Y. 1972, U.S. Dist. Ct. (so. dist.) N.Y. 1974, U.S. Ct. Appeals (2d cir.) 1974, U.S. Supreme Ct. 1976, Ill. 1988, Colo. 1990. Assoc. Dunnington, Bartholow & Miller, N.Y.C., 1971-78; asst. gen. counsel Diamond Internat. Corp., N.Y.C., 1978-82; gen. counsel, v.p. Children's TV Workshop, N.Y.C., 1987-88; chmn. and ceo Moffitt Co., Schiller Park, Ill., 1988—. Mem. ABA, (corp. banking & bus. sect.), Am. Corp. Counsel Assn., N.Y. State Bar Assn., Assn. of Bar of City of N.Y., Chgo. Bar Assn., Eagle Springs Golf Club. Home: 1500 N Lake Shore Dr Chicago IL 60610-6657 Office: Moffitt Co 9347 Seymour Ave Schiller Park IL 60176-2206

CONGER, CYNTHIA LYNNE, financial planner; b. Omaha, Dec. 8, 1948; d. Bob Bruce Ashton and Cleo (Artz) Ashton Taplin; m. Terry H. Conger, Dec. 21, 1969 (div. June 1989); children: Cynthia T., Scott A. BA in Acctg., U. Ark., Little Rock, 1980, MBA in Fin. and Econ., 1983. CPA, Ark.; cert. fin. planner. Staff acct. Leaseway Ark., Inc., Little Rock, 1981-83; rsch. asst. Indls. Rsch. and Econ. Com., Little Rock, 1983; agt. Conn. Mutual Life, Little Rock, 1983-84; v.p., fin. planner Ark. Fin. Group, Inc., Little Rock, 1984-94, pres., 1995—; pres. Cynthia L. Conger, CPA, PA, Little Rock, 1989—. Mem. Civitan, Little Rock, 1985-89. Mem. LWV (adv. bd. 1997—), Internat. Assn. Fin. Planning (Ark. chpt., v.p. 1986-87, pres. 1987-89, nat. bd. dirs. 1994-98, Delphi rsch. task force 1991), Ret. and Sr. Vols. (adv. bd. 1995—), Registry Fin. Planning Practitioners. Methodist. Avocations: reading, crewel embroidery, cooking. Office: Ark Fin Group Inc 225 E Markham St Ste 275 Little Rock AR 72201-1634

CONIDI, DANIEL JOSEPH, private investigation agency executive; b. Chgo., Mar. 11, 1957; s. Joseph Frank and Gloria (Zimmerman) C. BS, SUNY, Albany, 1983; MA, Chgo. State U., 1987. Lic. pvt. detective, Ill. Owner, mgr. Conidi Enterprises, Chgo., 1979-81; pres. Daniel J. Conidi-Assocs., Chgo., 1981—; cons. Office Cook County Sheriff, Chgo., 1983-90; freelance lectr., 1983—. Author: Professional Investigative Methods, 1984, Private Investigators Training Manual, 1986. Del. Cook County Rep. Conv., 1987. Recipient cert. of appreciation Boys Town, 1982; named Ky. col. State of Ky., 1987. Mem. World Assn. Detectives, Internat. Police Congress, Coun. Internat. Investigators, Nat. Assn. Investigations and Security, Fraternal Order Police, NRA (life), Navy League (life), Univ. Club, Masons, Shriners. Presbyterian. Avocations: flying, writing. Home: 500 Ashland Ave River Forest IL 60305-1825 Office: 734 N La Salle Dr Ste 1082 Chicago IL 60610-3530

CONKEL, ROBERT DALE, lawyer, pension consultant; b. Martins Ferry, Ohio, Oct. 13, 1936; s. Chester William and Marian Matilda (Ashton) C.; m. Elizabeth A. Cargill, June 15, 1958; children: Debra Lynn Conkel McGlone, Dale William, Douglas Alan; m. Brenda Jo Myers, Aug. 2, 1980; 1 child, Chelsea Ashton. BA, Mt. Union Coll., 1958; JD cum laude, Cleve. Marshall Law Sch., 1965; LLM, Case Western Res. U., 1972. Bar: Ohio 1965, U.S. Tax Ct. 1974, U.S. Supreme Ct. 1974, Tex. 1978, U.S. Ct. Appeals (5th cir.) 1979. Supr., Social Security Adminstrn., Cleve., 1958-65; trust officer Harter Bank & Trust Co., Canton, Ohio, 1965-70; exec. v.p. Am. Actuaries, Inc., Grand Rapids, Mich., 1970-73, pension cons., southwest regional dir., Dallas, 1974-88; mgr. plans and rsch. A.S. Hansen, Inc., Dallas, 1973-74; pvt. practice, Dallas, 1973—; sr. cons., Coopers & Lybrand, Dallas, 1989; pres. Robert D. Conkel, Inc., 1989—; mem. devel. bd. Met. Nat. Bank, Richardson, Tex.; instr. Am. Mgmt. Assn., 1975, Am. Coll. Advanced Pension Planning, 1975-76. Sustaining mem. Rep. Nat. Com., 1980-88. Enrolled actuary, Joint Bd. Enrollment U.S. Depts. Labor and Treasury. Mem. ABA (employee benefit com. sect. taxation), Ohio State Bar Assn., Tex. Bar Assn., Dallas Bar Assn., Am. Soc. Pension Actuaries (dir. 1973-81), Am. Acad. Actuaries. Contbr. articles to legal publs.; mem. editl. adv. bd. Jour. Pension Planning and Compliance, 1974-83. Office: 100 N Central Expy # 519 Richardson TX 75080-5332

CONLEY, SUSAN, art director, writer; b. N.Y., Sept. 30, 1967; d. John Hames and Nancy Anne (Connolly) C. BFA, N.Y Inst., 1986; Cert in film, N.Y.U., 1988; M in philosophy, Trinity Coll., Dublin, Ireland, 1999. Freelance designer N.Y.C., 1984-92; creative dir. Guitar World Mag., N.Y.C., 1992-94; art dir. N.Y. Mag. Entertainment Weekly, N.Y.C., 1995-98, Roger Black Cons., N.Y.C., 1998; One of Everything Design, Dublin, Ireland, 1999—; bd. mem. Irish Theatre Mag., Dublin, 1999—, Yankee Rep. Theatre Co., 1995-98. Writer, dir. True Love Speaketh, 1997, Love Life Work, 1993; dir. Hat Blocking By Herace, 1989. Recipient Silver Medal design Soc. Publication Design, 1997, Merit Design award Typography 17, 1996, Soc. Publ. Design, 1996. E-mail: susanellen 1@yahoo.com. Office: One of Everything Design, 24 Saint Joseph's Rd, Dublin D7, Ireland

CONLON, BRIAN THOMAS, promotion executive; b. Oceanside, NY, Mar. 19, 1958; s. Thomas James and Joan Anna (Erickson) C.; m. Mary Jane Lewis, Nov. 12, 1988; children: Brendan Lewis, Ryan Bradshaw Erickson, Emily Rose Mary. BA in English, Hofstra U., 1979. Asst. account exec. DR Group, N.Y.C., 1981-82, account exec., 1982-83; account exec. D.L. Blair, Inc., Garden City, N.Y., 1983-85, v.p./account supr., 1985-90, sr. v.p., 1990-91, exec. v.p., 1991—. Roman Catholic. Office: DL Blair Inc 1051 Franklin Ave Garden City NY 11530-2931

CONLON, MICHAEL NOEL, gas company executive; b. Athlone, Ireland, Dec. 15, 1936; s. James Anthony and Margaret Mary (Poynton) C.; m. Kathleen Josephine McDonald, Apr. 12, 1956; children: Bryan, Deirdre, Niamh, Rory, Orla Cloda. LLD, Nat. U., Dublin, 1995. Sr. exec. local govt., 1950-60; county mgr. Cork County Coun., 1960-79; chief exec. Irish Bacon Export Bd., Dublin, 1962-64; CEO T.S.B., Cork, Ireland, 1979-89; chmn. Irish Gas Bd., Cork, 1989—; chmn. Alexander and Alexander (Ireland) Ltd., B.G.E. (U.K.) Ltd., London, Mercy Hosp., Cork. Contbr. articles to profl. jours. Active Nat. Econ. and Social Coun., Dublin, 1989-94. Recipient Medal of Honor European Savs. Bank Group, 1992. Fellow Inst. Chartered Secs., Irish Mcpl. Inst., Irish Mktg. Inst., Irish Bankers Inst. Roman Catholic. Avocations: golf, tennis, fishing, gardening, travel. Office: Bord Gais Eireann, Cork Ireland

CONNAUGHTON, DAVID MICHAEL, management consultant; b. Youngstown, Ohio, Feb. 19, 1943; s. James M. and Dorothy Edith Roberts C.; m. Marilyn Jane Goscewski, Dec. 31, 1966; children: Erin, James. BS in Math., USAF Acad., 1965; MBA, Harvard U., 1973. Asst. to COO Burton Duenke Constrn. Co., St. Louis, 1973-74; sr. cons. Cambridge (Mass.) Comm. Group, 1975-77; fin. mgr. IBM, Armonk, N.Y., 1980-91; prin. Gemini Cons., Morristown, N.J., 1991-96; ptnr. Organizational Dynamics, Burlington, Mass., 1997-98; dir. Benchmarking Ptnrs., Cambridge, 1998-2000; founder, mng. ptnr. ROI Team, Lexington, Mass., 2000—; cons. in field. Mem. Sabre Soc. Avocations: pilot, artist, triathlete. E-mail: dconnaugton@rcn.com. Office: ROI Team 2 Laurel St Lexington MA 02421-4212

CONNELL, ANNIE MAHAN, educator; b. Damariscotta, Maine, Dec. 30, 1956; d. Clifton R. and Geraldine (McFarland) M. BS, U. So. Maine, Gorham, 1979, MS in Edn.l Adminstrn., 1988. Cert. tchr. K-8, spl. edn. tchr. K-12, prin. K-12. Tchr. 3d grade York (Maine) Sch. Dept.; tchr 1st grade Union 74, Damariscotta; chair bldg. staff devel. com., chair/coord. sch. improvement com., playground com./project; chair K-5 health edn. support team, union 74 health edn. com.; rep. sec. union staff devel. com.; rep. early childhood com. Union 74, leadership design team; mem. Citizen Adv. Task Force on Teen and Young Adult Health; mem. Student Assistance Team Bristol Consol. Sch.; rep. Healthy Me-Healthy Maine Com., Dept. Edn., Augusta, Maine. Rep. Maine Assessment Portfolio Project Dept. Edn., Augusta, Maine; bd. dirs. Shoreline Cmty. Mental Health Svcs., Brunswick, Maine, chair program com. Mem. Delta Kappa Gamma, Phi Kappa Phi. Home: 275 Pemaquid Harbor Rd Pemaquid ME 04558-4311

CONNELL, DESLEY WILLIAM, chemist, educator, administrator; b. Monto, Australia, July 31, 1938; s. William Eugene and Alva Caroline (Dowse) C.; m. Patricia Ann Wright, Jan. 17, 1960; children: Luke Daulton, Melissa Tace. BS, U. Queensland, Brisbane, Australia, 1961, MS, 1964, PhD, 1968; DSc, Griffith U., Brisbane, Queensland, Australia, 1991. Dir. Gippsland Lakes Environ. Study Ministry for Conservation, Melbourne, Victoria, Australia, 1973-76; dean, prof. Sch. of Australian Environ. Studies Griffith U., Brisbane, Queensland, 1976-89; dir. Govt. Chem. Lab., Brisbane, 1989-95; prof. faculty environ. scis. Griffith U., Brisbane, 1995—, prof. Sch. of Pub. Health; vis. prof. SUNY, Stonybrook, N.Y., 1981, 87, City U. Hong Kong, 1997; mem. Great Barrier Reef Consultative Com., Townsville, Qld Australia, 1976-82. Author: Experiments in Environ. Chemistry, 1980, Water Pollution: Causes and Effects in Australia and New Zealand, 1981, Chemistry and Ecotoxicology of Pollution, 1984, Bioaccumulation of Xenoiobiotic Compounds, 1990, Basic Concepts of Environmental Chemistry,

1997. Mem. Water Quality Coun. of Queensland, Brisbane, Qld. Australia, 1979-89, Australian Conservation Found. Coun., 1978-81; chairperson Queensland Water Quality Task Force, 1991—. Recipient Commonwealth scholarship, Australian Govt., Brisbane, 1957-58, Commonwealth Postgrad. award, Australian Govt., Brisbane, 1964-68, Australian Inst. Food Sci. and Tech. award, 1969, Churchill fellowship, Churchill Found., 1975. Fellow Royal Australian Chem. Inst. (inaugural chmn. environ. divsn. 1987-90, inaugural environ. medal, 1993). Achievements include a major contribution to the devel. of an understanding of the behavior of chemicals in the environment. Home: 39 Pinecone St Sunnybank QLD 4109, Australia

CONNELLAN, WILLIAM WESLEY, higher education administrator; b. Detroit, Apr. 25, 1945; s. Thomas Kennedy and Florence Irene Connellan; m. Mary Emma Solonika Simms, Aug. 17, 1969 (div. Jan. 1979); 1 child, Brian Patrick; m. Catherine Joanne Marine, Oct. 12, 1985. BA, Oakland U., Rochester, Mich., 1967; MA, U. Mich., 1971, PhD, 1981. Reporter Detroit News, 1965-70; acting v.p., assoc. provost, dir. pub. rels. Oakland U., 1970-97, vice provost, 1997—; vis. scholar U. Mich., Ann Arbor, 1987, Harvard U., 1999-2000; participant Inst. for Edn. Mgmt., Harvard U., Cambridge, Mass., 1993. Mem. exec. com. Met. Detroit Conv. and Visitors Bur., 1979—, chair, 1999-2000; mem. Rochester Hills (Mich.) Bldg. Authority, 1981-97; mem. Avon Twp. Charter Commn., Rochester Hills, 1982-84; active Habitat for Humanity. Mem. Am. Assn. Higher Edn., Earthwatch Inst., Detroit Econ. Club, Sigma Xi. Democrat. Presbyterian. Avocations: international research projects, recreational sports. Home: 804 Augusta Ct Rochester MI 48309-1500 Office: Oakland U 205 Wilson Hall Rochester MI 48309-4422

CONNELLY, MARK, writer, educator; b. Phila., July 8, 1951; s. Edward James and Hilda Virginia (Pfleger) C. BA in English and History, Carroll Coll., 1973; MA in Creative Writing, U. Wis., Milw., 1974, PhD in English, 1984. Instr. English Milw. Area Tech. Coll., 1986—; cons. Great Lakes Precision Products. Author: The Diminished Self: Orwell and the Loss of Freedom, 1987, The Sundance Reader, 1997, Orwell and Gissing, 1997, The Sundance Writer, 1999. Treas. Irish Cultural and Heritage Ctr. of Wis., 1993—. Recipient Ann. Fiction award Milw. Mag., 1982, 1st Place Fiction award Ind. Mag., 1982. Presbyterian. Avocations: reading, travel, Irish studies. Office: Milw Area Tech Coll 700 W State St Milwaukee WI 53233-1419

CONNELLY, THEODORE SAMPLE, communications executive; b. Middletown, Conn., Oct. 15, 1925; s. Herbert Lee and Mabel Gertrude (Wells) C. BA, Wesleyan U., 1948, postgrad., 1951; postgrad., U. Paris, 1950. Sec. nat. com. edn. Am. Trucking Assn., Inc., Washington, 1952-54; dir. pub. affairs Nat. Automobile Club, San Francisco, 1955-62; pres., chmn. Connelly Corp., San Francisco, 1963—; treas. Ednl. Access Cable TV Corp.; dir. Mission Neighborhood Ctrs., Inc., Neighborhood Devel. Corp.; mem. adv. com. Calif. motor vehicle legis., 1955-62, Calif. State C.of C. com. hwys., 1958-62; trustee, sec., v.p. Lincoln U.; sec. Lincoln U. Found., 1968-82; mem. USN Treasure Island Restoration Adv. Bd., 2000—; bd. dirs. San Francisco Program for Aging, founder, dir. Comm. Libr., 1963—, Comm. Inst., 1977—; founding mem. Calif. Coun. UN U., 1976; organizer Internat. Child Art Collection; co-founder African Rsch. Commn., 1970; established Connelly Fund, 1981; mem. founding regents Am. Pan-Pacific U., 1991; co-established awds. for excellence in writing about comm., 1981—; mem. steering com. Mesopotamian Exhibit, 1993—. Author/compiler: BCTV: Bibliography on Cabletelevision, 1975—, 13,500 References on Cable-TV, 1975—, Electromagnetic Radiation, 1976; editor: An Analysis of Joint Ventures in China, 1982, CINCOM-2000: Worldwide Communications Courses and Degrees, 2000; contbr. articles to profl. jours.; prodr., writer, dir. numerous cable-TV programs. Co-founder computer Learning Ctr. for Srs., St. Francis Meml. Hosp., 1998; founder Cyber Rsch. Ctr., Palmyna@toll.org., 2000. With USNR, 1943-54. Recipient cert. of merit San Francisco Jaycees, 1959, award of merit USPHS, 1980, citation U.S. Dept. H&HS, 1981, commendations U.S. Coun. World Comm., 1983. Mem. AAAS, AAUP, NAACP, SAR, Pub. Rels. Round Table San Francisco,, Atlanta Hist. Soc., Asian Mass Comm. and Info. Ctr. (Singapore), UN Assn. USA, Dolphin Swimming and Boating Club (San Francisco), Golden Gate Swimmer, Hawaii Theatre Ctr. (Honolulu), Marines' Meml. Assn. E-mail: palmyraAtoll@aol.com. Office: Lock Box 472139 Marina Sta San Francisco CA 94147-2139

CONNER, JAMES HOYT, trade association executive; b. Atlanta, Nov. 10, 1937; s. Joseph Hoyt and Vernell (Lee) C.; m. Wanda Lee Crowe, Mar. 20, 1966; 1 child, Meredith Lee. BA, Ga. State U., 1962, MBA, 1968. Mktg. rep. Armstrong World Industries, Greenville, S.C., 1962-66; sec. Ga. Textile Mfrs. Assn., Atlanta, 1966-72; exec. v.p. Am. Yarn Spinners Assn., Gastonia, N.C., 1972—; sec. Textile Edn. Found., Atlanta, 1967-72, Am. Textile Emport Co., Inc., Gastonia, 1988—; sec., treas. Craft Yarn Coun. Am., Inc., Gastonia, 1982—, AYSA Self-Insurers Fund, Gastonia, 1984—. Contbr. articles to mags. and newspapers. Tres. AYSA Polit. Action Com., Gastonia, 1987-91. Named One of Top 10 Textile Leaders Textile World Mag., 1985, 88, Top 50 Textile Leaders of Century, 1999. Mem. Univ. Club Washington D.C., Gaston Country Club, Oasis Shrine Temple, Mason. Baptist. Avocations: camping, boating, fishing, hunting. Office: Am Yarn Spinners Assn PO Box 99 Gastonia NC 28053-0099

CONNER, MICHAEL TIMOTHY, lawyer; b. Berkeley Heights, N.J., Oct. 6, 1947; s. Joseph H. and Marion C.; m. Carol Ann Mann, July 4, 1981; children: Kelly, Lindsay, David. BA in Polit. Sci., Am. U., 1969, JD, 1976. Bar: D.C. 1977, U.S. Ct. of Appeals (D.C. cir.) 1979, U.S. Ct. of Appeals (1st cir.) 1986, U.S. Ct. of Appeals (4th cir.) 1983. Staff atty. Nat. Oceanic & Atmospheric Adminstrn., Washington, 1977-81; staff atty. U.S. Dept of Commerce, Washington, 1981-85, chief, gen. litig. divsn., 1985—. Named Atty. of the Year, Dept. Commerce Gen. Coun., 1989. Home: 12588 Cross Hollow Ct Herndon VA 20170-5741 Office: US Dept Commerce Office Gen Counsel Rm 5890 Washington DC 20230-0001

CONNER, WARREN WESLEY, lawyer; b. Cat Spring, Tex., Aug. 14, 1932; s. George William and Frieda Johanna (Kollatschny) C.; m. Suzanne Rosser, Oct. 29, 1955; children: Connie Suzanne, Cathy Lorrane; m. Sharon Ann Welch, July 28, 1978. BBA, So. Meth. U., 1959, JD, 1963. Bar: Tex. 1963, U.S. Dist. Ct. (so. dist.) Tex. 1971. Ptnr. Sheehan & Conner, Friona, Tex., 1963-65; founder, ptnr. Conner & Clover, P.C., Sealy, Tex., 1965-95; with Conner, Cantey & Clover, Sealy & Brenham, Tex., 1995, ret., 1996; bd. dirs. Citizens State Bank, Sealy, Industry Telephone Co.; past pres. Austin County (Tex.) chpt. Am. Cancer Soc.; past v.p. Sealy Area Hist. Soc. Served with U.S. Army, 1953-55. Mem. State Bar Tex., Austin County Bar Assn. (past pres.), Masons, Shriners (past pres.), Rotary (past pres.), Lions (past pres. New Ulm chpt.). Presbyterian. Office: RR 1 Box 68-f Cat Spring TX 78933-9604

CONNERY, SEAN (THOMAS CONNERY), actor; b. Edinburgh, Scotland, Aug. 25, 1930; s. Joseph and Euphamia C.; m. Diane Cilento, 1962 (div.); 1 son, Jason; m. Micheline Roquebrune, 1975; 1 stepdaughter. D.Litt. (hon.), Heriot-Watt U., 1981. Dir. Tantallon Films Ltd., 1972—; first theater appearance in road show co. of South Pacific, Eng., 1953, also in Macbeth, Judith; films include: Let's Make Up, 1955, No Road Back, 1956, The Hill, 1956, Action of the Tiger, 1957, Another Time, Another Place, 1957, Hell Drivers, 1958, Tarzan's Greatest Adventure, 1959, Darby O'Gill and the Little People, 1959, On the Fiddle, 1961, The Longest Day, 1962, The Frightened City, 1962, Woman of Straw, 1964, Marnie, 1964, A Fine Madness, 1966, Shalako, 1968, The Molly Maguires, 1968, The Red Tent, 1969, The Anderson Tapes, 1970, The Offence, 1973, Zardoz, 1973, Ransom, 1974, Murder on the Orient Express, 1974, The Wind and the Lion, 1975, The Man Who Would be King, 1975, Robin and Marian, 1976, A Bridge Too Far, 1977, The Great Train Robbery, 1979, Cuba, 1979, Meteor, 1979, The Outland, 1981, Time Bandits, 1981, Sword of the Valiant, 1982, Wrong is Right, 1982, Five Days One Summer, 1982, The Name of the Rose, 1986, The Untouchables, 1987 (Acad. award for best supporting actor), The Presidio, 1988, Indiana Jones and the Last Crusade, 1989, Family Business, 1989, The Hunt for Red October, 1990, The Russia House, 1990, Highlander 2: The Quickening, 1991, Robin Hood: Prince of Thieves, 1991, (also exec. prodr.) Medicine Man, 1992, Rising Sun, 1993, A Good Man in Africa, 1994, Just Cause, 1995, First Knight, 1995, The Rock, 1996, (voice) Dragon Heart, 1996; actor, co-exec. prodr.: Medicine Man, 1992; James Bond films include: Dr No, 1963, From Russia with Love, 1964, Goldfinger, 1965, Thunderball, 1965, You Only Live Twice, 1967, Diamonds are Forever, 1971, Never Say Never Again, 1983; TV appearances include Requiem For a Heavyweight, 1957, Anna Karenina, The Crucible; prodr., dir.: The Bowler and the Bonnet (film documentary), I've Seen You Cut Lemons (London stage); prodr.: Something Like the Truth, Playing by Heart, 1998, (narrator) Macbeth, 1999; exec. prodr. Finding Forrester, 1999; exec. prodr., actor The Avengers, 1998, Entrapment, 1999. Served with Brit. Royal Navy. Named Star of the Yr., Nat. Assn. Theater Owners, 1987, Commander of Arts, France; recipient Tribute award Brit. Acad. Film and Television Arts, 1990, Cecil B. DeMille Golden Globe award Hollywood Fgn. Press Assn., 1996; recipient Lifetime Achievement award ShoWest Conv., 1999, Career Achievement award Nat. Bd. Rev., 1993. Office: CAA 9830 Wilshire Blvd Beverly Hills CA 90212-1804

CONNOLLY, JANET ELIZABETH, retired sociologist and criminal justice educator; b. New Rochelle, N.Y., June 28, 1929; d. Michael A. and Vincentia (Bonitatibus) Dandry; m. Edward C. Connolly, June 7, 1952; children: Michael, Matthew, Christopher, Benedict, Andrew. BA, Chestnut Hill Coll., Phila., 1951; MA, Temple U., Phila., 1970, PHD, 1975; hon. degree, Rilski Neofit U., Blagoevgrad, Bulgaria, 1992. Intelligence clk. CIA, Washington, 1951-52; tchr. Prince George's County Bd. Edn., Hyattsville, Md., 1952-53; rsch. assoc. Pa. Prison Soc., Phila., 1974-76; field dir. rsch. Georgetown U. Law Sch., Washington, 1976-77; rsch. dir. Phila. Commn. for Effective Criminal Justice, 1977-78; mem. faculty dept. criminal justice Temple U., Phila., 1980-91; mem. faculty dept. sociology Am. U. in Bulgaria, Blagoevgrad, 1991-96; guest lectr. Sch. Law Kiril E Metodi Univerzitet, Skopje, Macedonia, 1993; cons. Bucks County Correctional Facility, Doylestown, Pa., 1987-91; evaluator Phila. Prison System, 1973. Campaign chairperson, Doylestown, Pa., 1980, 82, 84, 86, 90; pres. Bucks County Assn. for Corrections and Rehab., Doylestown, 1988-91; trustee Bucks County Community Coll., Newtown, Pa., 1989-91; bd. dirs. ARC, Bucks County chpt., Doylestown, 1980-82; mem. New Hope (Pa.) Civil Svc. Commn., 1986-91; bd. dirs. Planned Parenthood, 1986-88. U.S. Justice Dept. dissertation grantee, Washington, 1972. Mem. ACLU, LWV, Law and Soc. Assn., Am. Correctional Assn., Balkan Ednl. and Sci. Assn. (mem. sci. senate). Democrat. Avocations: gardening, embroidery, oil painting. Home: 130 N Main St New Hope PA 18938-1317

CONNOLLY, K. THOMAS, lawyer; b. Spokane, Wash., Jan. 23, 1940; s. Lawrence Francis and Kathleen Dorothea (Hallahan) C.; m. Laurie Samuel, June 24, 1967; children: Kevin, Megan, Amy, Matthew. BBA, Gonzaga U., Spokane, Wash., 1962; JD, Gonzaga U., 1966; LLM in Taxation, NYU, 1972. Bar: Wash. 1966, U.S. Ct. Mil. Appeals 1967, U.S. Tax Ct. 1983. Assoc. Witherspoon, Kelley, Davenport & Toole, Spokane, 1972-77; ptnr./prin. Witherspoon, Kelley, Davenport & Toole, 1977—; assoc. prof. law Gonzaga Sch. Law, 1973-77. Bd. overseers Gonzaga Prep. Sch., Spokane, 1988-89; bd. trustees Spokane Guild Sch. for the Handicapped, 1975-78, Wash. State U. Found. Bd., 1992-97, Whitman Coll. Planned Giving Coun., 1994—. Capt. U.S. Army, 1966-70. Recipient Wall St. Jur. award, 1962; decorated Bronze Star medal. Mem. Wash. State Bar Assn. (founder, chmn. health law sect. 1989-92, health law coun. 1989-94, pres. tax sect. 1987-88, mem. tax coun. 1984—), ABA (chmn. health care subcom. 1990-94). Republican. Avocations: tennis, astronomy. Office: Witherspoon Kelley Davenport & Toole 1100 Old National Bldg Spokane WA 99201

CONNOLLY, MICHAEL EDWARD, municipal official, waste management administrator; b. Woonsocket, R.I., Dec. 17, 1952; s. Edward Thomas and Barbara Ellen (Sawyer) C. BA, R.I. Coll., 1977. Lic. wastewater operator. Lab. technician City of Woonsocket, 1978-86, chemist, 1986-91, wastewater pretreatment coord., 1991—; labor union pres. AFSCME, Woonsocket, R.I., 1994—; v.p. Narragansett Water Pollution Control Assn., 1978—, pres. 1998. Mem. Elks. Roman Catholic. Home: 1 Lamoureux Blvd North Smithfield RI 02896-7513 Office: Woonsocket Pretreatment Div 11 Cumberland Hill Rd Woonsocket RI 02895-4819

CONNOLLY, THOMAS EDWARD, judge; b. Boston, Nov. 7, 1942; s. Thomas Francis and Catherine Elizabeth (Skehill) C. AB, St. John's Sem., Brighton, Mass., 1964; JD, Boston Coll., 1969. Bar: Mass., 1969. Assoc. Schneider & Reilly, Boston, 1969-73; ptnr. Schneider, Reilly, Zabin, Connolly & Costello, P.C., Boston, 1973-85, Connolly Leavis & Rest, Boston, 1986-90; judge Mass. Superior Ct., Boston, 1990—; regional adminstrv. justice Norfolk County, 2000—; instr. law Northeastern Law Sch., Boston, 1975-76. Mem. governing coun. Boston Coll. Law Sch. Alumni Coun., 1980-82. Fellow Am. Coll. Trial Lawyers; mem. ABA (vice chmn. products liability sect. 1978-80), Trial Lawyers Assn. Am. (nat. gov. 1977-80), Mass. Acad. Trial Lawyers (gov. 1976-90), Univ. Club (Boston), Algonquin Club (Boston). Democrat. Roman Catholic. Home: 253 Marlborough St # 4 Boston MA 02116-1731 Office: The Superior Ct Dedham MA 02026

CONNOLLY, THOMAS JOSEPH, retired bishop; b. Tonopah, Nev., July 18, 1922; s. John and Katherine (Hammel) C. Student, St. Joseph Coll. and St. Patrick Sem., Menlo Park, Calif., 1936-47, Catholic U. Am., 1949-51; JCD, Lateran Pontifical U., Rome, 1952; DHL (hon.), U. Portland, 1972. Ordained priest Roman Cath. Ch., 1947. Asst. St. Thomas Cathedral, Reno, 1947, asst., rector, 1953-55; asst. Little Flower Parish, Reno, 1947-48; sec. to bishop, 1949; asst. St. Albert the Gt., Reno, 1952-53; pastor St. Albert the Gt., 1960-68, St. Joseph Ch., Elko, 1955-60, St. Theresa's Ch., Carson City, Nev., 1968-71; bishop of Baker, Bend, Oreg., 1971-2000, bishop emeritus, 2000—; Tchr. Manogue High Sch., Reno, 1948-49; chaplain Serra Club, 1948-49; officialis Diocese of Reno; chmn. bldg. com., dir. Cursillo Movement; moderator Italian Cath. Fedn.; dean, mem. personnel bd. Senate of Priests; mem. Nat. Bishops Liturgy Com., 1973-76; region XII rep. to adminstrv. bd. Nat. Conf. Cath. Bishops, 1973-76, 86-89, mem. adv. com., 1974-76; bd. dirs. Cath. Communications Northwest, 1977-82. Club: K.C. (state chaplain Nev. 1970-71). Office: Bishop of Baker PO Box 5999 911 SE Armour Dr Bend OR 97702-1489

CONNOR, JOHN MURRAY, agricultural economics educator; b. Attleboro, Mass., July 7, 1943; s. John Murray Sr. and Victoria Rose (Moro) C.; m. Ulla Maija Niemelä, Apr. 3, 1972; 1 child, Timo. BA cum laude, Boston Coll., 1965; MA, U. Fla., 1974; MS, U. Wis., 1974, PhD, 1976. Vol. U.S. Peace Corps, Nigeria, Uganda, 1966-68; agrl. economist Econ. Rsch. Svc. USDA, Madison, 1976-79; head food mfg. rsch. Econ. Rsch. Svc. USDA, Washington, 1979-83; assoc. prof. agrl. econs. Purdue U., West Lafayette, Ind., 1983-89; prof. Purdue U., West Lafayette, 1989—, asst. dept. head, 1985-88; ajd. prof. Catholic U. Sacred Heart, Piacenza, Italy, 1991—; vis. prof. Åbo (Finland) Akademi U., 1994; cons. subcom. on multinats. U.S. Senate, Washington, 1974-76, select com. on nutrition, 1977-78; cons. UN Ctr. on Transnats., 1981-82, U.S. Dept. Justice, 1999; chair Orgn. and Performance World Food Systems, 1988-93. Author: Market Power of Multinationals, 1977, Food Processing: An Industrial Powerhouse in Transition, 1988, 2d edit., 1997, (with others) Food Manufacturing Industries, 1985; contbr. articles to profl. jours., chpts. to books. Grantee U.S. Office Tech. Assessment, 1984-85, Inst. Food Technologists, 1986-88, 94-95, Ind. Dept. Commerce, 1987-91, Econ. Rsch. Svc., USDA, 1988-89, Coop. State Rsch. Svc., USDA, 1989—. Mem. AAUP (pres. Purdue U. chpt. 1988-90, exec. bd. ind. conf. 1990-94, nat. coun. 1991-92), Am. Agrl. Econs. Assn. (policy award 1980, comm. award 1985, Disting. Extension Program award 1993), Indsl. Orgn. Soc., Am. Econs. Assn., ACLU. Home: 4355 Creekside Pass Zionsville IN 46077-9292 Office: Purdue U Dept Agrl Econs West Lafayette IN 47907-1445

CONNOR, JOSEPH E., accountant; b. N.Y.C., Aug. 23, 1931; s. Joseph E. Connor; m. Cornelia B. Camarata, Apr. 17, 1958 (dec. Oct. 11, 1983); children: Anthony, Cornelia, David; m. Sally Howard Johnson, Dec. 27, 1992. AB summa cum laude, U. Pitts.; MS in Bus., Columbia U.; DHL (honoris causa), Georgetown U., 1989. Joined Price Waterhouse & Co., N.Y.C., 1956; ptnr. Price Waterhouse & Co., 1967-92, ptnr. in charge So. Calif., 1973-76; mng. ptnr. Western region Price Waterhouse & Co., Los Angeles, 1976-78; chmn. policy bd. U.S. Price Waterhouse & Co., 1978-88, chmn. World Firm, 1988-92, ret., 1992; Disting. prof. bus. Georgetown U., 1992-94; under-sec. gen. UN, N.Y.C., 1994—; cons. fgn. direct investment program U.S. Dept. Commerce; project adv. rsch. study AICPA; lectr. in field.; mem. adv. coun. Columbia U. Grad. Sch. Bus.; bd. visitors U. Pitts. Grad. Sch. Bus., Georgetown U. Sch. Bus.; chmn. U.S. Coun. for Internat. Bus., 1987—; mem. Pres.'s Mgmt. Adv. Coun., Pres.'s Pvt. Sector Survey on Cost Control. Contbr. articles to profl. lit. Trustee YMCA Greater N.Y.; bd. overseers Meml. Sloan Kettering Cancer Inst.; bd. dirs. Georgetown U., 1982-92; mem. coun. Brookings Instn. Served to 1st lt. U.S. Army, 1954-56. Mem. N.Y. State Soc. CPAs (chmn. internat. ops. com., mem. acctg. and auditing com., real estate acctg. com.), Calif. Soc. CPAs (legis. com.), Internat. C. of C. (exec. bd. 1989-94, pres. 1990-92), Met. Club (Washington), Links Club, Univ. Club. Office: UN UN Plz New York NY 10021

CONNOR, LEO EDWARD, special education administrator; b. Phila., Sept. 5, 1922; s. Leo A. and Margaret (McMahon) C.; m. Frances Partridge, June 7, 1952. BA, LaSalle U., 1945; MA, U. Pitts., 1949; EdD, Columbia U., 1955. Cert. tchr. spl. edn., adminstr., audiologist. Tchr. Pitts. and Phila. schs., 1945-49; elem. prin., dir. elem. edn. Clarkstown Cen. Sch. Dist., New City, N.Y., 1950-57; ednl. dir. Lexington Sch. for the Deaf, N.Y.C., 1957-68, exec. dir., 1968-85; exec. dir. Lexington Ctr. for Hearing Impaired, N.Y.C., 1985-88; chmn. N.Y. Schs. for Deaf and Blind, Albany, N.Y., 1968-83, Coun. on Edn. of Deaf, Washington, 1976-78, Nat. Adv. Com. on Media for Handicapped, Washington, 1978-80; adj. prof. edn. Columbia U., N.Y.C.; instr. NYU, N.Y.C. Author: Administration of Special Education, 1960, History of Research, 1978, History of the Lexington School for the Deaf, 1988, Review of Oral Education, 1980; editor: Speech for the Deaf Child, 1971, Lexington Education Series, 1965-80; contbr. articles to profl. jours. Chmn. Bd. Zoning Adjustment, Borough of Spring Lake, N.J., 1989-96, chmn. lake com., 1990-95; trustee New Rochelle (N.Y.) Coll. Recipient annual award N.Y. Coun. Exceptional Children, Albany, 1988. Fellow Am. Speech/Hearing/Lang. Assn. (clin. cert. competency); mem. Alexander Graham Bell Assn. (Honors of the Assn. award 1986, pres. 1970-72), Coun. for Exceptional Children (pres. 1968-69). Roman Catholic. E-mail: franle-o@att.net. Home: 23343 Blue Water Cir Boca Raton FL 33433-7035

CONNOR, PAUL EUGENE, social worker; b. Atchison, Kans., Aug. 11, 1921; s. Samuel Walters and Juanita Marie (Fry) C.; m. Louise Dorothy Schiddel, June 28, 1959 (div. 1964). BS in History with honors, Columbia U., 1962, MA, 1963; grad. cert. in social work, Fordham U., 1973; postgrad. summer history program, Cambridge U., 1990-96. Lectr. Am. History Rutgers State U., 1966-67; lectr. S.E. Asian history New Sch. Social Rsch., 1967-68; caseworker Bergen Ctr., South Bronx, N.Y., 1970-73; caseworker Protective Svcs. Bur. of Child Welfare, Bronx, N.Y., 1973-76; caseworker preventive svcs. Spl. Svcs. for Children, N.Y.C., 1976-83; supr. I family program Crisis Intervention Svcs., N.Y.C., 1983-87; tchr. The Internat. Ctr., N.Y.C., 1977-86. Rec. sec. Bronx Coun. for Environ. Quality, 1981-83, bd. dirs., 1983—; docent Mus. of City of N.Y., 1988-91, Abigail Adams Smith Mus., 1993-95, South St. Seaport Mus., 1993-96. Mem. Internat. Coun. Social Welfare, Asia Soc., Am. Hist. Assn., S.C. Hist. Soc., N.C. Lit. and Hist. Assn., Soc. of Boonesborough, Clan Buchanan Soc. in Am., English Speaking Union, Benjamin Franklin Reform Dem. Club. Democrat. Home: 2755 Reservoir Ave Apt 5A Bronx NY 10468-2730

CONNOR, THOMAS BYRNE, JR., ophthalmologist; b. Balt., Apr. 18, 1959; s. Thomas Bryne and Eleanor (Rulls) C.; m. Susan Rose, Sept. 1, 1991. BS, Haverford Coll., 1981; MD, Johns Hopkins, 1988. Diplomate Am. Bd. Ophthalmology. Instr. ophthalmology Johns Hopkins, Balt., 1993-94; asst. prof. ophthalmology Medical Coll. Wis., Milw., 1994-99, assoc. prof. ophthalmology, 1999—. Mem., bd. dirs. Bel Conto Chorus, Milw., 1997—. Recipient Iris Innovation award Wisecraft, Inc., 1999, Best Doctors in Am., 1996. Mem. Am. Acad. Ophthaomology (Honor award 1998), Assn. Rsch. Vision Ophthalmology, AMA, Vitrucus Soc., Milw. Ophthalmological Soc. Roman Catholic. Avocation: classical music. E-mail: tconnor@mcu.edu.

CONNORS, RICHARD F., judge; b. N.Y.C., Mar. 20, 1930; s. Patrick Francis and Marie (Goss) C.; m. Jacqueline M., June 16, 1956; children: Maureen, Patricia C., Richard F. Jr. BA, St. Peter's Coll., 1951; JD, Seton Hall U., 1956. Trial atty. Sam Lieberman, Newark, 1957-59; ptnr. Lieberman, Gorrin, Connors, Newark, 1959-71, Gorrin, Connors & Ironson, 1971-73; judge Hudson County Ct., Jersey City, N.J., 1973-78, Superior County Ct., Jersey City, N.J., 1978—. With USN, 1948-53. Mem. ABA, Am. Trial Attys. Assn., N.J. Bar Assn., Essex County Bar Assn., Trial Attys. N.J. Office: Superior Ct NJ 583 Newark Ave Jersey City NJ 07306-2301

CONOBY, JOSEPH FRANCIS, chemist; b. Albany, June 12, 1930; s. Joseph Francis and Helen Emma (Brucker) C.; m. Mary Joan A. Ryan, June 21, 1958; children: James Francis, Mark Joseph. BS, Union Coll., 1952. Sr. tech. svc. engr. Allied Chem. Corp., Syracuse, N.Y., 1956-66; rsch. chemist Conversion Chem. Corp., Rockville, Conn., 1966-69; environ. engr., indsl. hygienist Honeywell Bull, Billerica, Mass., 1969-87, mgr. environ. and health engring., 1969-87; mgr. environ. engring. Bull HN Worldwide Info. Sys., 1987-95; sr. scientist Concorp, Inc., Acton, Mass., 1996—; adv. bd. Mass. Water Resources Authority Sewer Use (rules and regulations, policy and procedures, and facilities planning task forces); cons. exptl. project course Mass. Inst. Tech., 1977-78. Contbr. articles to profl. jours.; patentee in field. Lt. USN, 1952-56. Mem. Am. Indsl. Hygiene Assn., Nat. Assn. Environ. Mgmt. Home: 5 Samuel Parlin Dr Acton MA 01720-3206 Office: Concorp Inc PO Box 2766 Acton MA 01720-6766

CONOLE, RICHARD CLEMENT, management consultant; b. Binghamton, N.Y., Dec. 7, 1936; s. Clement V. and Marjorie E. (anable) C.; children: Margaret Ann Dutton, Linda Elizabeth Fandel; m. Sharyn Stafford, Apr. 18, 1969; 1 child, Samantha Erin. Student, U. Pa., 1955, 60, Clarkson Coll., 1956-57. With data processing dept. Campbell Soup Co., Inc., Camden, N.J., 1954; draftsman Gannett, Fleming, Corddry & Carpenter, Inc., Ardmore, Pa., 1955-56; plant mgr., office mgr. Tabulating Card Co., Inc., Princeton, N.J., 1957-59, asst. to pres., asst. sec.-treas., sec., 1959; pres., dir. Data Processing Supplies Co., Inc., Princeton, 1959; sec., dir. Whiting Paper Co., Inc., Princeton, 1959, pres., 1961-62; pres., dir. Mercer-Princeton Realty Co., Inc., Princeton, 1959-61; pres. Am. Bus. Investment Co., Inc., Princeton, 1960; pres., dir. Business Supplies Corp. Am., Skytop, Pa., 1962-65, Gen. Bus. Supplies Corp., Ardmore, 1965-71; chmn. bd. Nat. Productive Machines, Inc., Elkridge, Md., 1965-71; v.p., chmn. finance com., dir. Pocono Internat. Raceway Inc., 1964-74; pres. Gen. Automotive Supplies Co., 1971-72; pres., dir. Autoberfest, Inc., 1973, Promotional Printing Ltd.; pres. The World Series of Auto Racing Corp., 1973-78, Tex. Internat. Raceway, Inc., College Station, 1976—, Speedway Mgmt. Corp., 1978—; pres., chief exec. officer Gt. Tex. Truckstop, Tex. World Affordable Homes; pres., dir. Tex. Internat. Raceway Inc., 1991—; sales cons. Hess & Barker, 1972-76; mem. competition com. U.S. Auto Club, 1976—; treas., chmn. fin. com. Tex. Pvt. Sch. Found., Inc.; trustee Allen Acad.; founder Tex. 500, Tex. Grand Prix, Tex. Race of Champions; owner Camelot Farms and Camelot Sires, 1987—; featured speaker N.Am. Vet. Conf., 1994, Nat. Greyhound Assn. Conf., 1994, World Greyhound Racing Fedn. Conf., Dublin, 1994, Internat. Borzoi Conv., Calgary, Can., 1995. Patentee magnetic printing cylinder. Mem. Am. Mgmt. Assn., Tex. Manufactured Housing Assn., Phila. Dist. Squash Racquets Assn. (life), U.S. Squash Racquets Assn., Nat. Coursing Assn. (Australia), Nat. Greyhound Assn., Tex. Greyhound Assn. (bd. dirs. 1991—), The Kennel Club (Eng.), Canine Control Coun. (Australia), Tex. Horse Race Assn., Tex. Thoroughbred Breeders Assn., Am. Quarter Horse Assn., Skytop (Pa.) Club, Phila. Country Club, Merion Cricket Club (Haverford, Pa.), Manor Club (Pocono Manor, Pa.), Springdale Golf Club (Princeton, N.J.), Brazos Valley Kennel Club (affiliate Am. Kennel Club, Can. Kennel Club. Home: PO Box 9191 College Station TX 77842-9191 also: 16512 E Glenbrook Blvd Fountain Hls AZ 85268-2333 Office: Tex World Speedway Inc PO Box 11000 College Station TX 77842-1000

CONOVER, DOROTHY NANCY LEVER, medical practice administrator, nurse; b. Abington, Pa., Jan. 11, 1941; d. Charles Ambler and Dorothy Nancy (Greenway) Lever; m. Albert Paul Conover, Dec. 23, 1960 (div. Aug. 1981); 1 child, Hollie Marie. Degree in nursing, Phila. Gen. Hosp. Sch. Nursing, 1960. Staff and pvt. duty nurse Morton Plant Hosp., Clearwater, Fla., 1963; med. asst., sec. Office of E.E. Wilkison, MD, Tallahassee, 1966-69; med. sec. Urology Clinic Assocs., Houston, 1977-78; adminstr. Glenn A. Helwig, M.D.-Coastal Women's Ctr., Clearwater, 1979-98, Digestive Disease Assn. Clearwater, 1998-99, Northeast Family Practice, St. Petersburg, Fla., 1999—. Editor (newsletter) People with AIDS, 1995. V.p. Meadows Swim

Team Booster Club, Stafford, Tex., 1974, Meadows Cmty. Improvement Assn., Stafford, 1975; ruling elder Presbyn. Ch., 1976—. Mem. Assn. Healthcare Mgrs., Profl. Assn. Healthcare Office Mgrs., Am. Acad. Procedural Coders (adv. bd. 1994-95), Med. Group Mgmt. Assn. (mem. ob-gyn. assembly, sec.-treas. 1996, pres.-elect 1997, pres. 1998, newsletter editor ob-gyn. assembly 1995-96, adv. bd. Ob Prac Mgmt Newsletter 1997-98, gastroenterology adminstrn. assembly 1998-99, Med. Group Mgmt. Assn. primary care assembly 1999—), Clearwater Bus. and Profl. Womens Club (treas. 1985-86), Am. Coll. Medical Practice Execs. Republican. Presbyterian. Avocations: gardening, needlepoint, depression era glassware. Home: 246 Temple Ln Belleair Blf FL 33770-1966 Office: Northeast Family Practice 8730 4th St N Saint Petersburg FL 33702-3186

CONOVER, ROBERT WARREN, retired librarian; b. Manhattan, Kans., Oct. 6, 1937; s. Robert Warren and Grace Darline (Grinstead) C.; BA, Kans. State U., 1959; MA, U. Denver, 1961. Librarian, supervising librarian County of Fresno, Calif., 1961-66; county librarian County of Yolo, Woodland, Calif., 1967-68; dir. City of Fullerton (Calif.) Pub. Library, 1968-73, City of Pasadena (Calif.) Pub. Library, 1973-80, Palos Verdes Library Dist., Palos Verdes Peninsula, Calif., 1980-85, City of Commerce (Calif.) Pub. Library, 1985-97, ret. Pres. Kapalua Bay (Hawaii) Villas, Inc. Recipient Pres.'s award Fresno Jaycees, 1963. Mem. ALA, Orange County Libr. Assn. (pres. 1971), Spl. Librs. Assn., Calif. Libr. Assn. (pres. Yosemite chpt. 1965, mem. coun. 1981), Santiago Libr. System Coun. (pres. 1972), Met. Coop. Libr. System (exec. com. mem., 1994, vice chair 1995, chair 1996), Univ. Club, Pi Kappa Alpha. Episcopalian. Home: Kapalua Bay Villas 500 Bay Dr # 17g-5 Lahaina HI 96761-9034

CONRAD, DANIEL EDWARD, physician; b. Chgo., Aug. 30, 1935; s. Benjamin Edward and Dorothy Elizabeth Esther (Sonne) C.; m. Jane Ellen Parker; children: Kristin Anne, Carol Patricia, Mary Catherine. BS in chem., Univ. Ill., 1956, MB, 1958, MD, 1960. Diplomate Am. Bd. Internal Medicine, Am. Bd. Preventive Medicine in Occupl. Medicine. Pvt. practice internal medicine Swedish Covenant Hosp., Chgo., 1966-78; medical dir. central region AT & T Long Lines, Chgo., 1971-81; corp. medical dir. GTE Automatic Elec., Northlake, Ill., 1981-84, West Suburban Hosp., Oak Park, Ill., 1984-86, Lockheed Martin Energy Systems, Oak Ridge, Tenn., 1986-97; ptnr. Conrad & Conrad Cons., Knoxville, Tenn., 1997—; vice-chmn. dept. medicine Swedish Convenant Hosp., Chgo., 1973-79. Contbr. numerous articles to profl. jours. and news media. Pres. United Lutheran Ch., Oak Park, Ill., 1977-79, River Forest Tennis Club, 1977; mem., bd. dirs. Youth Svcs. Youth Haven, Oak Ridge, Tenn., 1991—, Knoxville Opera Co., 1995—; pres. Tenn. Coll. Occupational Medicine, 1990-91. Recipient First Annual Corp. Health Achievement award Am. Coll. Occupational & Environ. Medicine, 1997. Fellow Am. Coll. Occupational & Environmental Medicine (dir. 1981-84, sec. 1984-87), Am. Coll. Physicians, Am. Coll. Preventive Medicine, Cen. States Occupl. Med. Assn. (pres. 1982-83), Rotary Internat. Republican. Lutheran. Avocations: sailing, music, woodworking. Home: 11409 Berry Hill Dr Knoxville TN 37931-2804

CONRAD, DAVID PAUL, business broker, retired restaurant chain executive; b. Greensboro, N.C., Jan. 11, 1946; s. Lucas Lee and Elizabeth Gertrude (Kincaid) C.; 1 child, Lucas Wilfong. BSBA, East Carolina U., 1970; cert. in real estate, Forsyth Tech. Coll., 1979. From cashier to cook Libby Hill Seafood, Greensboro, N.C., 1962-64; plant mgr. Libby Hill Seafood Restaurants, Inc., Greensboro, N.C., 1970-76; mgr. Libby Hill Seafood Restaurants, Inc., Winston-Salem, N.C., 1976-85; v.p., dir. ops. Libby Hill Seafood Restaurants, Inc., Greensboro, N.C., 1985-93, also bd. dirs., 1985-93; comml. real estate broker Allied Comml. Real Estate, Kernersville, N.C., 1993; franchise owner Swisher Maids of West Greensboro, N.C., 1994-99, regional dir., 1996-98; broker-in-charge VR Bus. Brokers; broker VR Bus. Brokers. Mem. Greensboro Jaycees, 1973-81; vol. St. Jude's Children's Rsch. Hosp. Staff sgt. N.C. N.G., 1968-74. Mem. Masons, Inst. Cert. Bus. Counselors. Republican. Methodist. Avocation: family. Fax: (336) 854-2202. Office: VR Business Brokers Four Seasons Exec Ctr 9 Terrace Way Ste A Greensboro NC 27403-3667

CONRAD, EDGAR WILLIAM, educator; b. Lancaster, Pa., Sept. 15, 1942; came to Australia, 1977; s. Amos Kreider and Violet May (Reese) C.; m. Linda Mae Slonaker, Aug. 29, 1964. BA, Lebanon Valley Coll., 1964; M.Div., United Theol. Sem., 1968; Th.M., Princeton Theol. Sem., 1969, PhD, 1974. Asst. prof. La Salle Coll., Phila., 1974-75; sr. lectr. Univ. of Queensland, Brisbane, Australia, 1977-90; prof. Univ. Queensland, 1990—. Author: Reading Isaiah, 1991, Fear Not Warrior, 1985, Zechariah, 1999; contbr. articles to profl. jours. Com. mem. subject adv. com. Bd. of Secondary Schs., Brisbane, 1979-93; producer Australian Broadcasting Corp., 1994. Recipient Mellon fellowship Mellon Found., 1976, rsch. grant Australian Rsch. Coun., 1997. Mem. Australian Assn. for Study of Religions (pres. 1987-89), SOc. of Biblical Lit., Am. Acad. of Religion. Home: 67 Clewley St, 4075 Corinda Australia Office: Univ Queensland Studies in Religion, 4072 Saint Lucia Australia

CONRAD, HAROLD THEODORE, psychiatrist; b. Milw., Jan. 25, 1934; s. Theodore Herman and Alyce Barbara C.; m. Elaine Marie Blaine, Sept. 1, 1962 (dec.); children: Blaine, Carl, David, Erich, Rachel. AB, U. Chgo., 1954, BS, 1955, MD, 1958. Diplomate Am. Bd. Psychiatry. Intern USPHS Hosp., San Francisco, 1958-59, commd. sr. asst. surgeon, 1958, advanced through grades to med. dir., 1967; resident psychiatry USPHS Hosp., Lexington, Ky., 1959-61, Charity Hosp., New Orleans, 1961-62; chief of psychiatry USPHS Hosp., New Orleans, 1962-67, clin. dir., 1967; dep. dir. div. field investigation NIMH, Chevy Chase, Md., 1968; chief NIMH Clin. Rsch. Ctr., Lexington, 1969-73; cons. psychiatry region IX USPHS, HEW, San Francisco, 1973-79; dir. adolescent unit Alaska Psychiat. Inst., Anchorage, 1979-81, supt., 1981-85; clin. assoc. prof. psychiatry U. Wash. Med. Sch., 1981-85; med. dir. Bayou Oaks Hosp., Houma, La., 1985—. Contbr. to publs. in field. Recipient Decorated Commendation Medal, various community awards for contbns. in field of drug abuse and equal employment opportunity for minorities. Fellow Royal Soc. Medicine, Am. Psychiat. Assn.; mem. AMA, Alpha Omega Alpha, Alpha Delta Phi. Office: 855 Belanger St Houma LA 70360-4463

CONRAD, JOHN REGIS, lawyer, engineering executive, consultant; b. Bloomington, Ind., Feb. 23, 1955; s. John Francis and Patricia Ann (English) C.; m. Paula Jane Vessels, July 4, 1980; children: William Celestine Vessels, John Paul Vessels, M. Alexander Vessels, David Thomas Kelamalamalamanokeakua Vessels, Rachel Elizabeth Ho'ouluolaikealoha Vessels. AB cum laude, Harvard U., 1977; MBA, JD, Ind. U., 1981. Bar: Hawaii 1981, Fla. 1994, Tex. 1994, N.C. 1995, U.S. Dist. Ct. Hawaii 1981, U.S. Ct. Appeals (9th cir.) 1981, U.S. Ct. Claims 1981, U.S. Tax Ct. 1981. Assoc. Cades, Schutte, Fleming & Wright, Honolulu, 1981-85, 89-90, Thompson & Chan, Honolulu, 1985-89; ptnr. Cades Schutte Fleming & Wright, Honolulu, 1991-94; regional bus. mgr. Kimley-Horn and Assocs., Inc., West Palm Beach, Fla., 1994-96, regional prodn. mgr., 1996-98; regional bus. mgr. Kimley-Horn and Assocs., Inc., Phoenix, 1999—; lectr. law Kapiolani C.C., Honolulu, 1984-86; adj. prof. Richardson Sch. Law, U. Hawaii, 1989-90. Author: A Conrad Genealogy, 1979, Hawaii Probate Sourcebook, 1985, rev. 1986, rev. 1992; co-author: Beyond the Basics: Hawaii Estate Planning & Probate, 1985, Hawaii Wills & Trusts Sourcebook, 1986, Hawaii Guardianship Sourcebook, 1988; editor HICLE Fin. and Estate Planning Manual, vol. II, 1989, vol. I, 1990. Planned giving com. Hawaii Heart Assn., Honolulu, 1983-86; arbitrator Hawaii Ct. Annexec Arbitration Program, 1989-94; sch. bd. Star of the Sea Sch., Honolulu, 1992-94, pres., 1993-94, chair Carnival, 1992; chair Cub Scout Pack Aloha Coun. Boy Scouts Am., den leader Cub Scout Pack, Gulf Stream Coun., Grand Canyon Coun.; lector Good Shepherd of the Hills Ch., Cave Creek, Ariz. Fellow Am. Coll. Trust and Estate Coun.; mem. ABA, Am. Arbitration Assn., Hawaii Bar Assn. (chmn. estate and gift tax com. 1984-85, CFO probate and estate planning sect. 1989-90), Hawaii Bar Found. (bd. dirs. 1985-92, v.p. 1989, pres. 1989-91), Ancestral Trails Hist. Soc., Sons of Am. Legion, John T. Reilly Hist. Soc., Hawaii Estate Planning Coun. (bd. dirs. 1991-94, sec. 1993). Roman Catholic. Avocations: running, genealogy, coin collecting, scouting. Home: 33214 N 61st St Cave Creek AZ 85331-5206 Office: Kimley-Horn and Assocs Inc 7600 N 15th St Ste 250 Phoenix AZ 85020-4335

CONRAD, JOSEPH HENRY, animal nutrition educator; b. Cass County, Ind., Dec. 7, 1926; s. Ferdinand M. and Marie E. (Hubenthal) C.; m. Frances Ash, June 18, 1950; children: Kenneth A., Leonard J., Carol Ann, Joseph C. BS, Purdue U., 1950, MS, 1954, PhD, 1958; prof. (hon.), Fed. U. Viçosa, Brazil, 1965. Asst. prof. Purdue U., West Lafayette, Ind., 1958-63, assoc. prof., 1963-68, prof., 1968-71; animal scientist Fed. U. Viçosa, 1961-65; prof., coord. tropical animal sci. programs U. Fla., Gainesville, 1971-95. Co-author: Swine Production, 1982; contbr. monographs and numerous articles on animal nutrition and tropical animal prodn. to profl. jours. Served with USN, 1944-46. Recipient Disting. Nutritional award Distillers Feed Rsch. Coun., 1964; Moorman fellow, 1989. Fellow Am. Soc. Animal Sci. (Internat. Animal Agrl. award 1985, Bohstedt award 1987, Internat. Mktg. award 1989); mem. World Assn. Animal Prodn. (v.p.), Latin Am. Soc. Animal Prodn., Sociedade Brasileira de Zootecnia, Purdue U. Alumni Assn. (life, pres.'s coun.), Sigma Xi, Gamma Sigma Delta. Republican. Lutheran. Home: 1824 NW 10th Ave Gainesville FL 32605-5312 Office: PO Box 110910 Gainesville FL 32611-0910

CONRAD, MARCEL EDWARD, hematologist, educator; b. N.Y.C., Aug. 15, 1928; s. Marcel Edward and Lulu Marie (Geraghty) C.; m. Marcia Louise Grove; children: Marcel Edward, III, Mark E., Carol J., Erin E., Julia P. BS, Georgetown U., 1949, MD, 1953. Diplomate Am. Bd. Internal Medicine, Am. Bd. Hematology. Intern Walter Reed Gen. Hosp., Washington, 1953-54; resident, then chief resident in internal medicine Walter Reed Gen. Hosp., 1955-60; mem. staff Walter Reed Army Inst. Rsch., 1961-74, chief dept. hematology, 1965-74; chief clin. investigation svc. Walter Reed Army Med. Ctr., 1971-74; clin. asst. prof., then clin. assoc. prof. medicine Georgetown U. Med. Sch., 1964-74; prof. medicine U. Ala. Med. Sch., Birmingham, 1974-83, also dir. div. hematology and oncology, 1974-83; prof. medicine, pathology, dir. divsn. hematology, oncology U. South Ala., Mobile, 1983—, dir. USA Cancer Ctr., 1985—. Contbr. numerous articles to med. publs. Commd. 1st lt. M.C. U.S. Army, 1953; advanced through grades to col. 1968. Decorated Legion of Merit with oak leaf cluster; recipient Skinner medal U.S. Army, 1955, Hoff medal, 1962, John Shaw Billings award, 1967, William Beaumont award, 1972, Walter Reed award, 1974. Fellow Internat. Soc. Hematology, ACP (Laureate award 1989); mem. AAAS, Assn. Am. Physicians, Internat. Soc. Hematology, Am. Soc. Clin. Investigation, Am. Physiol. Soc., Internat. Soc. Blood Transfusion, Am. Soc. Hematology, Am. Soc. Clin. Oncology, Am. Chem. Soc., Soc. Exptl. Biology and Medicine, So. Soc. Clin. Investigation, Am. Fedn. Clin. Rsch. Roman Catholic. E-mail: mconrad@usamail.usouthal.edu. Home: 28451 Perdido Pass Dr Orange Beach AL 36561-3602 Office: U South Ala Usa Cancer Ctr Mobile AL 36688-0001

CONRAD, MELVIN LOUIS, biology educator; b. Kiowa, Kans., Mar. 10, 1927; s. Marvin Bearl and Elsie Louise (Murphy) C.; m. Eula Montes Vieira, Apr. 3, 1954; children: Albert Vieira Conrad, Celia Conrad Theiler, Daniel Vieira Conrad. BA in Biology, Southwestern Coll., 1950; MA, George Peabody Coll. Tchrs., 1956; PhD, U. Mo., 1980. Ednl. missionary Meth. Ch., Brazil, 1950-54; tchr. biology and gen. sci. McLeansboro (Ill.) Twp. High Sch., 1956-58; asst. prof. biology Oxford (Ga.) Coll. Emory U., 1958-67; from asst. prof. to prof. plant taxonomy N.E. Mo. State U. (name changed to Truman State U.), Kirksville, 1967-91, prof. emeritus, 1991—; vis. instr. botany U. Ga., Athens, 1967; mem. teaching staff Reis Biol. Sta., St. Louis U., nr. Steelville, Mo., 1988—; reviewer Army C.E., 1985. Bd. dirs. ARC, Kirksville, 1984-93, chmn. Adair County chpt. 1985, dir. blood svcs., 1993; bd. dirs. The Border Line Theatre, Inc., v.p., 1997-99; chmn. Kiowa City Tree Bd., 1996—; bd. dirs. Kiowa Alumni Assn., chmn., 1997—; lay leader Kiowa United Meth. Ch., 1996, 97. Mem. Mo. Native Plant Soc. (pres. 1983-85), Am. Soc. Plant Taxonomists, Kans. Wildflower Soc., Am. Legion (post comdr. 1997—), Lions Internat. (dist. gov. 1983-84, other offices), Beta Beta Beta, Phi Sigma. Republican. Avocations: gardening, carpentry, photography, family genealogy. Home: 1014 Dickinson St Kiowa KS 67070-1726

CONRAD, PETER, sociology educator; b. N.Y.C., Apr. 12, 1945; s. George and Gertrude (Rosenthal) C.; m. Ylisabeth Bradshaw, Apr. 12, 1975; children: Rya, Jared. BA, SUNY, Buffalo, 1967; MA, Northeastern U., 1970; PhD, Boston U., 1976. From instr. to asst. prof. sociology Suffolk U., Boston, 1971-75; asst. prof. sociology Drake U., Des Moines, Iowa, 1975-78; from asst. prof. to prof. Brandeis U., Waltham, Mass., 1979—, Harry Coplan prof. social scis., 1993—; vis. asst. prof. NYU, N.Y.C., 1978. Co-author: Deviance and Medicalization, 1980, Having Epilepsy, 1983; editor: Sociology of Health and Illness, 1997; co-editor: Health and Health Care Developing Countries, 1992, Qualitative Sociology, 1982-87. Bd. dirs. Codman Cmty. Farm, Lincoln, Mass., 1987-92; commr. Conservation Commn., Lincoln, 1992—. Shannon grant NIH, 1994-96; vis. scholar Harvard Med. Sch., Boston, 1986, Godjah Mada U., Yogyakata, Indonesia, 1989-90, Disting. Fulbright scholar Queen's U., Belfast, Ireland, 1997; recipient Charles Horton Cooley award, 1981. Mem. Am. Sociol. Assn. (chair med. sociology 1987-89), Soc. for Study of Social Problems (pres. 1995-96), Eastern Sociol. Soc. Avocations: biking, hiking, films, cooking Greek food, travel. Office: Brandeis U Dept Sociology Waltham MA 02454-9110

CONRAD, RICHARD A., opera singer, educator; b. N.Y.C., Aug. 12, 1935; s. Lester Alexander and Mildred Lillian (Murley) C. AAS, N.Y. State U., 1955; BFA, Boston U., 1957. artistic dir. Boston Acad. of Music, 1980—. Opera debut Am. premiere of Mozart's La Finta Semplice, Boston, 1961; recital debut Philips Collection, Washington, 1961; opera appearances with cos., orchs. on radio, TV in U.S., Can., Europe, Gt. Britain, Africa, 1961—; opera recordings on Decca/London, Pearl, CRI, Teldec, Westminster, Video of Bel Canto, among others.

CONRAD, STEVEN ALLEN, critical care and emergency physician, biomedical engineer, educator; b. St. Martinville, La., Aug. 23, 1953; s. Karl Donovan and Dolores Beatrice (Bienvenu) C.; m. Mona Theresa Hollier, Aug. 9, 1974; children: David, Lesley, Taylor. BS, U. S.W. La., 1974; MD, La. State U., Shreveport, 1978; MS, Case Western Reserve, Cleve., 1980, PhD, 1985; MS in Engring., La. Tech. U., 1981. Diplomate Am. Bd. Internal Medicine, Critical Care Medicine, Am. Bd. Emergency Medicine; cert. nutritional support physician. Postdoctoral trainee in biomed. computing Case Western Res., 1979-80; resident internal medicine La. State U., Shreveport, 1981-84; fellow in critical care medicine Mayo Grad. Sch. Medicine, Rochester, 1984-86; asst. prof. medicine La. State U. Med. Ctr., Shreveport, 1986-91, assoc. prof. medicine, 1991—, dir. crit. care medicine tng. program, 1987—, dir. med. ICU, 1986—, assoc. prof. emergency medicine, 1996-97, chmn. dept. emergency medicine, 1996—; instr. in computer sci. Winona State U., 1985-86, asst. prof. physiology, 1988-91; adj. assoc. prof. biomed. engring. La. Tech. U., Ruston, 1989—, adj. prof. human ecology, 1996—, prof. emergency medicine and internal medicine, 1997—; adj. assoc. prof. mech. engring. Inst. for Micromanufacturing, 1994—; cons. physician critical care VA Med. Ctr., 1986—, dir. extracorporeal life support program, 1993—, co-dir. nutritional support svc., 1994—, transplant intensivist Willis Knighton Regional Heart Transplant Program, 1994—, attending physician in pediat. ICU, 1994—; mem. emergency med. svcs. task force Shreveport Fire Dept., 1992—; prin. investigator in multiple device and drug trials. Editor: Pulmonary Function Testing: Principles and Practice, 1984; manuscript reviewer ASAIO Jour., Artificial Organs; abstract reviewer Critical Care Medicine; contbr. chpts. to books and articles to profl. jours. Grantee Am. Heart Assn. Fellow ACP, Am. Coll. Crit. Care Med., Am. Coll. Chest Physicians, Am. Coll. Emergency Physicians; mem. IEEE, Biomed. Engring. Soc., Shock Soc., Am. Soc. Artificial Internal Organs, Internat. Soc. for Artificial Organs, Soc. for Acad. Emergency Medicine, Am. Soc. for Parenteral and Enteral Nutrition, Alpha Omega Alpha, Sigma Xi, Phi Kappa Phi, Beta Gamma Sigma, Sigma Iota Epsilon. Office: La State U Med Ctr 1501 Kings Hwy Shreveport LA 71103-4228

CONRADER, CONSTANCE RUTH, artist, writer, librarian; b. Vandalia, Mo., Apr. 13, 1919; d. Gilbert Fordyce and Elizabeth Florence (Cleghorn) Stone; m. Jay Merten Conrader, Nov. 29, 1941 (dec. 1996). Student, Carroll Coll., 1938-40, North Park Coll., 1940-41. Cert. pub. libr. Artist, author Oconomowoc, Wis., 1940—; libr. Oconomowoc Pub. Libr., 1947-82, vol. 1982—; illustrator Turtox classroom charts Gen. Biol. Supply House, Chgo., 1940-60; manuscript critique Baha'i Pub. Trust, Wilmette, Ill., 1970-89, editor, 1988. Author, illustrator: Blue Wampum, 1958; co-editor: Tokens From the Writings of Baha'u'llah, 1973, Baha'i newsletter, 1997—; illustrator: Northwoods Wildlife Region, 1983; co-author, illustrator articles to profl. jours.; co-editor regional Baha'i Newsletter, 1997—. Chair UN Day, Oconomowoc, 1976-86. Avocations: gardening, music, reading, cooking. Home: 738 E Washington St Oconomowoc WI 53066-3110

CONRADI, ERWIN, retail executive. CEO, pres. gen. mgmt. bd. Metro Internat. AG, Zug, Switzerland, Metro Deutschland subs. Metro Internat. AG, Germany; pres. Metro Holding AG; vice chmn. supervisory bd. Allianz Versicherungs-AG, Munich; chmn. supervisory bd. Kaufhof AG, Cologne. Office: Neuhofstrasse 4, 6340 Baar Germany*

CONRADIE, MURRAY NEIL, financial executive; b. Pietermaritzburg, South Africa, Jan. 9, 1966; came to U.S., 1992; s. Joseph William and Yvonne Huntley (Elliott) C. Diploma in acctg., Natal Technikon, Durban, South Africa, 1988; LLB, Natal U., Durban, 1985. CEO, Century Clocks, Durban, 1987-92, Quantum Time, San Diego, 1992-93, Authentic Apparel, San Diego, 1993-95, Global Entertainment Network, Inc., Incline Village, Nev., 1996—, Nutek, Inc., Lake Forest, Calif., 1998—; also bd. dirs. Avocations: computers, waterskiing, outdoors, snowskiing. Fax: 714-799-5466. E-mail: ceo@nutk.com. Office: Nutek Inc 15722 Chemical Ln Huntington Beach CA 92649-1509

CONRADS, BERNHARD WILHELM, management executive, editor; b. Bamberg, Bavaria, Germany, Sept. 12, 1944; s. Joseph and Martha Conrads; m. Dorothea Albine Müller, Dec. 19, 1970; children: Florian, Julian. MBA, U. Würzburg, 1970, D in Polit. Sci., 1974. Mgmt. cons. Mgmt. Ptnr., Stuttgart, 1974-79; head dept. social mktg. and pub. rels. Bundesvereinigung Lebenshilfe, Marburg, 1979-89, nat. dir., 1989—; bd. dirs. Deutsche Behindertenhilfe Aktion Mensch, Mainz, 1992—. Head editor Lebenshilfe-Zeitung, 1989—; editor rep. Geistige Behinderung, 1989—. V.p. Spl. Olympics Germany, Würzburg, 1992—. Mem. McCusion Internat. Coun., Rotary (Marburg). Home: Weidenhäuser Strasse 89, 35037 Marburg Germany Office: Bundesvereinigung, Lebenshilfe fü Menschen, 35043 Marburg Germany

CONRADSEN, KELD OLE, associate lawyer; b. Sydney, Australia, June 3, 1964; arrived in Japan, 1985; s. Ole Conradsen and Bernice Ann Brown; m. Junko Kanamori, Aug. 4; children: Kaya, Pia. LLB, Keio U., Tokyo, 1992, Bond U., Queensland, Australia, 1994; LLM, Melbourne (Australia) U., 2000. Solicitor: Supreme Ct. England and Wales, all Australian Jurisdictions, High Ct. Australia. Clerk Minter Ellison, Melbourne, Australia, 1994-95; assoc. Hori Law Office, Tokyo, 1995-98, White & Case LLP, Tokyo, 1998-2000; atty. Budiardjo, Nugroho & Reksodiputro, Jakarta, Indonesia, 2000—. Office: Budiardjo Nugroho & Reksodiputro, Graha Niaga 24th Fl Jalan Jenderal, Sudriman Kav 58 Jakarta 12190, Indonesia

CONRATH, UWE, plant physiologist, educator; b. Neunkirchen, Saarland, Germany, Dec. 28, 1961. MS, U. Kaiserslautern, 1989, PhD, 1992. Postdoctoral fellow U. Kaiserlautern, Germany, 1992-93, Rutgers U., New Brunswick, N.J., 1993-95; asst. prof. U. Kaiserlautern, 1995—, venia legendi, 1999—. Contbr. articles to profl. jours. Recipient Freundeskreises der U. prize, 1993, Honor State Govt. Rheinland-Pfalz, 1993. Mem. AAAS, Am. Soc. Plant Physiologists, German Bot. Soc., Internat. Soc. Plant Molecular Biology, Soc. Biochemistry and Molecular Biology. Office: Univ Kaiserslautern, Paul Ehrlich Strasse 22, 67663 Kaiserslautern Germany

CONRICH, IAN PHILIP, film studies lecturer, publisher; b. London, Mar. 5, 1969; s. Samuel and Gilda Barbara (Conway) C. BA with 1st-class honors, U. Kent, Canterbury, Eng., 1991; MA, U. East Anglia, Norwich, Eng., 1992. Diploma in Tchg. English as a Fgn. Lang. Lectr. U. North London, 1994-97, Nottingham (Eng.) Trent U., 1997-2000, U. Surrey, Roehampton, 2000—; vis. lectr. Inst. Commonwealth Studies, U. London, 1996—, Aarhus (Denmark) U., 1997—; chair New Zealand Study Group, U.K., 1996—, organizer ann. New Zealand conf., London, 1997—; pub. Kakapo Books, Nottingham; mem. editl. bd. Jour. Popular Brit. Cinema, 1997—. Co-author: (monograph) Views from the Edge of the World: New Zealand Film, 1997; contbr. articles to profl. jours. Recipient sponsorship The Link Found., London, 1999; Brit. Acad. scholar, 1994-97. Mem. Soc. Cinema Studies, Internat. Assn. Media and History, New Zealand Arts Soc., Asian Cinema Studies Soc. (regional coord. for Britain). Avocations: reading, cinema, meeting friends, Norwich City Football Club matches. Home: 15 Garrett Grove, Clifton Village, Nottingham NG11 8PU, England Office: U Surrey Roehamptoin, Roehampton Ln, London SW15 5PU, England

CONROY, RICHARD TIMOTHY, writer, retired foreign service officer; b. Copperhill, Tenn., Dec. 20, 1927; s. Edward Hubert and Elizabeth Lowry (Scruggs) C.; m. Sarah Jane Booth, Dec. 31, 1949; children: Camille Booth, Sarah Claire. BA, U. Tenn., 1950. Fgn. svc. officer U.S. Dept. State, Washington, 1956-72; fgn. affairs staff Smithsonian Instn., Washington, 1972-88; ret., 1988. Author: The India Exhibition, 1992, Mr. Smithson's Bones, 1993, Old Ways in the New World, 1994, Our Man in Belize, 1997, Our Man in Vienna, 2000. Mem. Diplomatic and Consular Officers, Retired, Nat. Press Club. Democrat. Avocations: painting, sculpting, making jewelry, architectural photography, piano. Home: 5016 16th St NW Washington DC 20011-3842

CONSTAIN, ALBERTO, food products executive; b. Barcelona, Cataluna, Spain, May 16, 1924; s. Alberto and Alicia Constain; m. Maria Alicia Cinzano; children: Dora, Alicia, Fiona, Alberto. BBA, Nat. Sch. Commerce, Bogota, Colombia, 1942; degree in law, Ctrl. U. Ecuador, Quito, 1947. Pres. Constain S.A., Quito, 1946-54, Bogota, 1954—; pres. Licoresa S.A., Quito, 1980—, Coloma, Bogota, 1984—, Mercantil Licores, Quito, 1993—. Recipient Merit award Govts. Ecuador-Colombia, 1986. Mem. Met. Club (Bogota), Club Guaymaral (Bogota), Club de la Union (Guayaquil, Ecuador). Mem. Conservative Party. Roman Catholic. Avocations: golf, navigation. Office: Licoresa, Ave Amazonas 239, 2040 Quito Ecuador

CONSTANCE, BARBARA ANN, financial planner, small business owner, consultant; b. Springfield, Mass., Dec. 24, 1945; d. Edward F. and Margaret E. (Price) Corcoran; m. Thomas F. Tiedgen, Apr. 27, 1968 (div. 1975); m. G. Lawrence Gadsby Jr., May 5, 1978 (div. 1991); m. F. David Constance, Dec. 6, 1991. AA, Vt. Coll., Montpelier, 1965. CLU; chartered fin. cons. Adminstrv. asst. Mass. Mut. Life Co., Springfield and Hartford, Conn., 1965-75; office mgr. Am. Nat. Life Ins. Co., Springfield, 1976; traveling trainee Conn. Gen. Life Ins. Co., Bloomfield, 1976; sales rep. Conn. Gen. Life Ins. Co., Springfield, 1976-77; dir. mktg. NN Life Ins. Services, Johnston, R.I., 1978-80; sales rep. New Eng. Mut. Life Co., Providence, 1980-82; pvt. practice fin. planner Tiverton, R.I., 1982-97; pres., founder Heritage Prodns., Ltd., Tiverton, R.I., 1988-91; cons. Northwestern Mutual Life Ins. Co., Providence, 1986-87; co-founder, bd. dirs. Career Connections, Inc.; co-capt. SV/Nootka, 1997—. Bd. dirs. YWCA of Greater R.I., Big Sister Assn. of R.I. Mem. Am. Soc. CLUs and ChFC (past pres. R.I. chpt.), Nat. Assn. Life Underwriters, R.I. Life Underwriters, Assn. Health Ins. Agts., Newport County Women's Network (co-founder), R.I. Woman's Career Network, R.I. Bus. Esch., R.I. Estate Planning Coun. Republican. Episcopalian. Home: 434 Bliss Rd Longmeadow MA 01106-1548

CONSTANCE, MERVYN, utility executive; b. Trinidad, May 9, 1950; s. Julius and Winifred (William) C.; m. Kathleen McCleta Browne, Dec. 26, 1975; children: Mark Kevin, Marlon Jason, Davida Alexandre. Trade man asst. Water Sewage Authority, 1973, pipe fitter, 1979-83, water works foreman I, 1983—. Avocations: reading, cycling, basketball, travel, engring. drawing. Home: 8 John William Rd, Tabaquite, Trinidad and Tobago West Indies

CONSTANTIN, DANIEL, French government official; b. Thonon-les-Bains, France, Sept. 8, 1940; s. Jean and Germaine (Premat) C.; m. Maeva Haerer-aaroa, 1967; children: Emmanuel, Vaitiare. Prefect Drôme, 1987-89, Reunion Island, 1989-91, Sarthe, 1991—, Region Franche-Comté, 1997, Region Languedoc-Roussillon, 1998; dir. gen. Ville de Paris, 1994. Awarded Officer de la Légion d'honneur, Officier de l'ordre nat. du Mérite, Chevalier des Palmes académiques et du Mérite agricole, Médaille d'or de la Jeunesse et des Sports. Office: Pref région Languedoc-Roussillon, 34 pl Martyrs Résistance, 34062 Montpellier Cédex, France

CONSTANTINESCU, EMIL, president of Romania; b. Tighina, Nov. 19, 1939; m. Nadia Ileana, 1963; children: Dragos, Norina. Grad., U. Bucharest; DSc., 1979. Judge Ct. of Pitesti; lectr. faculty geology U. Bucharest, Romania, 1966—, rector, 1992—; pres. Nat. Bd. Rectors, Romania, 1992—, Govt. Romania, Bucharest, 1996—. Mem. N.Y. Acad. Scis. Christian Orthodox. Office: Office Pres, Geniului nr 1 Sect 6, 76238 Bucharest Romania*

CONSTANTINESCU, VALENTIN DAN, computer engineer, neuroscientist; b. Pitesti, Romania, May 6, 1928; arrived in Germany, 1978; s. Dan and Elena (Mandru) C.; m. Maria Victoria Constantinescu, Apr. 1, 1958; children: Mihai Adrian, Dan Andrei. Diploma in engring., Poly. U. Bucharest, Romania, 1952, DSc in Engring., 1996. Rschr. Inst. Neurology, Bucharest, 1964-70; group leader Inst. for Control Engring. R & D, Bucharest, 1960-68, Inst. for Machine Tools R & D, Bucharest, 1970-78; product specialist Computervision Co., Munich, 1979-93. Editor (books) in Control Engring., Logical Algebra, and Robot Programming; contbr. articles to sci. jours.; patentee in field logic circuits. Home and Office: Schaeftlarnstr 170, D-81371 Munich Germany

CONSTANTINESCU, VIRGILIU-NICULAE G., Romanian diplomat, mechanical engineer; b. Bucharest, Romania, Mar. 27, 1931; s. Gheorghe G. and Natalia N. (Manescu) C.; m. Monica-Elena Nicolau, Apr. 8, 1960; 1 child, Stefan-Nicolae. MS in Engring., Poly. Inst., Bucharest, 1952, DSc (hon.), 1974; PhD, Applied Mechanics Inst., Bucharest, 1956; D Hon Causa, U. porters, 1993, U. Liege, 1999. Rschr. Applied Mechanics Inst., 1952-56, head gas lubrication lab., 1956-69; asst. prof. Poly. Inst., 1954-59, assoc. prof., 1959-70, prof., 1970—, rector, 1990-92; pres. Romanian Acad., 1994-98; Romanian amb. to Belgium, Romanian Embassy, Brussels; vis. scientist Mech. Tech. Inc., Latham, N.Y., 1969-70; vis. prof. Rensselaer Poly. Inst., Troy, N.Y., 1972-74; pres. Rectors' Conf., Romania, 1990-92, Romanian Space Agy., Bucharest, 1991—; amb. of Romania to Belgium, 1997—; invited prof. U. Liege, 1999—. Author: Gas Lubrication, 1963, (ASME award 1969), Turbulent Lubrication, 1965, (A.E.C. award 1968), Sliding Bearings, 1980, (Allerton Press award 1985), 15 others; contbr. over 200 articles in field. V.p. Romania Cultural Found., Bucharest, 1990—. Recipient State prize Coun. of State, 1964, Sci. Merit medal, 1965, Brit. Tribology Gold medal, 1996. Mem. Romanian Acad. Scis. (corr., titularly, Aurel Vlaicu award 1959), Internat. Acad. Astronautics (corr., titularly), Royal Acad. of Belgium (assoc. mem.), Internat. Tribology Coun. (founding), Geselschaft Angewandte Mathematik and Mechanik. Mem. Greek Orthodox Ch. Avocations: swimming, tennis, bridge. Home: 7 Paris St, 71249 Bucharest Romania Office: Embassy of Romania, Rue Gabrielle 105, 1180 Brussels Belgium*

CONSTANTINIDES, LAMBIS GEORGE, import/export company executive; b. Nicosia, Cyprus, Sept. 2, 1935; s. George Charalambous and Maria George (Papapetrou) C.; m. Helena Lambis Joannides, Jan. 16, 1966; children: Maria-Christina, George. Grad., Am. U., Beirut, 1956; Diploma of german Lang., Inst. auf dem Rosenberg, St. Gallen, Switzerland, 1957; student, Handelshochschule, St. Gallen, Switzerland, 1957-58; Diploma of French Lang., Centre Culturel Français, Nicosia, Cyprus, 1970. With corr. dept. St. S. Loucaides & Co., Nicosia, 1958-60, with bookkeeping dept., 1960-62, sales/mktg./advt. staff, 1962-66; dir. M & L Constantinides Ltd., Nicosia, 1966-68; mng. dir. Lambis G. Constantinides Ltd., Nicosia, 1968—. Pres. Cyprus-Swiss Assn., Nicosia, 1992—. Chevalier (Knight) de l'Ordre National du Merite, French Pres. Mitterrand and French Govt., 1993, Officier de l'Ordre Nat. du Merite, 1999. Mem. Planetary Soc., Nat. Geographic Soc. Avocations: reading, music, sports, swimming, jogging. Home: 4 St Paul's St, Nicosia Cyprus Office: Lambis G Constantinides Ltd, 1 Timocharous St Box 1586, Nicosia Cyprus

CONSTANTINOU, CLAY, dean, lawyer; b. N.Y.C., Sept. 4, 1951; s. Dan and Helen (Maouris) C.; m. Eileen Calamari, Mar. 6, 1976; children: Jennifer, Dan. BA, N.J. City U., Jersey City, 1973; JD, Seton Hall U., Newark, 1981; LLM, NYU, N.Y.C., 1987; DHL (hon.), N.J. City U., 1999. Prin. Clay Constantinum, West Orange, N.J., 1981-91; ptnr. Wilenz, Goldman & Spitzer, Woodbridge, N.J., 1991-93; amb. U.S. Dept. State, Luxembourg, 1994-99; dean Sch. Diplomacy and Internat. Rels., South Orange, N.J., 1999—; bd. mem. HMO Blue, Newark, 1992-93. Nat. co-chair fin. Dukakis Presdl. Campaign, 1987-88; del. Dem. Nat. Conv., 1988, 92; commr. N.J. Turnpikes Assn., New Brunswick, 1989-93; bd. mem. Essex County Utilities Authority, Newark, 1992-93; fin. chmn. N.J. Clinton Presdl. Campaign, 1992; co-fin. chmn. Presdl. Inaugural Gala, 1993. Recipient Presdl medal Pres. Clerides of Cyprus, 1999, St. Barnabas medal Archbishop of Cyprus, 1999. Avocations: tennis, soccer, jogging. Home: 31 Orchard Ln Colts Neck NJ 07722-1569 Office: Seton Hall U McQuaid Hall Sch Diplomacy Internat Rels 400 S Orange Ave South Orange NJ 07079-2646

CONSTANZA, JEAN-LOUIS, aerospace engineer; b. Paris, Apr. 16, 1961. Diploma in engring., Nat. Sch. Aeronautics and Space, France, 1983; M in Internat. Strategy, Paris U., France, 1984; MBA, European Inst. Adminstrn. of Affairs, Fontainebleau, France, 1989. Mission chief Aerospatiale, Paris, 1984-86, project mgr., 1986-88; strategy dir. Framatome, Paris, 1989-91; mgr. JSA Internat., Boston and Paris, 1991-92; mgr. Arthur D. Little, Paris, 1992-93, sr. mgr., 1993-94, assoc. dir., 1994-98; mng. dir. Tele2, 1998—; chmn. everyday.com, 1999—. Mem. Racing Club France. Avocations: international downhill skiing, fencing, horseback riding, literature. E-mail: jean-louis@everyday.com. Home: 16 Rue Fernand Pelloutier, 92100 Boulogne France Office: Tele2, 14 Rue Des Freres Caudron, 78143 Velizy France

CONTALDO, FRANCO, medical educator; b. Pagani, Italy, Dec. 15, 1948; s. Salvatore Contaldo and Teresa Staiano; m. Immacolata Veneziano, Oct. 3, 1974; 1 child, Andrea G. MD, U. Napoli, Italy, 1972. Asst. prof. U. Napoli, 1974-76, rsch. assoc., 1976-79, 80-87, full prof., 1990—; rsch. assoc. U. Cambridge, Eng., 1979; assoc. prof. U. Lecce, Italy, 1987-90; rsch. assoc. Med. Rsch. Coun., London, 1988; prof. clin. nutrition U. Federico II, Napoli, 1990—; dir. Postgrad. Sch. Nutrition, 1994-97. Editor: Medical Complications of Obesity, 1979; chief editor Italian Jour. Clin. Nutrition and Metabolism, 1997—; contbr. articles to profl. jours. Recipient awards Nat. Rsch. Coun., 1980-85, Ministry Pub. Health, 1983, Ministry Univ., 1997. Roman Catholic. Avocation: anthropology. Office: Clin Nutrition Policlinico, Via Pansini, 80131 Napoli Italy

CONTE, JULIE VILLA, nurse, administrator; b. Manila, July 4, 1951; came to U.S., 1970; d. Gregorio Cortes and Lourdes (Villa) Dirige; m. Michael Don Conte, Jan. 22, 1983. BSN, Calif. State U., L.A., 1974; MBA, U. Phoeniz, San Diego, 1993. RN, Calif. Staff nurse Santa Monica (Calif.) Hosp., 1976-78; pub. health nurse Kaiser Found. Hosp., Panorama City, Calif., 1978-85; nursing supr. Nat. Med. Homecare, L.A., 1985-86; dir. home health Holy Cross Hosp., Mission Hills, 1986-88; dir. profl. svcs. Care Home Health, San Diego, 1988; dir. nursing Health Prime Home Health Svcs. of San Diego, Inc., 1988-92; dir. home health svcs. Alvarado Home Health Agy., San Diego, 1993-94; expert consulting Home Health and Bus. Cons., San Diego, 1994—; dir. patient care svcs. Unlimited Care, Inc., 1995-96; CEO, pres., adminstr. We Care Home Health Svc., Inc., 1996—; pub. health nurse cons. Able Home Health Care, Wilmington, Calif., 1984; bd. dirs. nursing Health Prime, Inc. Mem. NAFE, Nat. Assn. Home Care, Bapt. Nursing Fellowship (pres. Calif. chpt. 1997—, nat. pres.-elect 1999—), Alpha Delta Chi. Republican. Avocations: travel, foreign language, collecting, piano, organ. Home: 7982 Mission Center Ct Unit I San Diego CA 92108-1469

CONTE, LANSANA, president Republic of Guinea; b. 1944. Army officer, former comdr. Boké Region; pres. Republic of Guinea; pres. of Republic of Guinea, 1984—, prime minister, from 1984, former minister of def., security, planning, cooperation and info.; chmn. Comité militaire de redressement nat., 1984—. Office: Office of President, Conakry Guinea*

CONTI, INDALICIO PALOMAR, accountancy educator; b. Dinas, Philippines, Dec. 22, 1953; s. Ismael Hernandez Conti and Irenea Demit Palomar.. BS in Mgmt., Philippine Coll. of Commerce, Manila, 1976, BSC in Acctg., 1977; LLB, U. of the East, Manila, 1985; MBA, Polytechnic U. of Philippines. CPA. Jr. acct. Gen. Textile Mills, Inc., Libis, Quezon City, Philippines, 1978; dir., acct. Supreme Traders, Inc., Manila, 1978-79; auditor PUP Credit Union, Manila, 1978-83; legal rschr. Polytechnic U. of Philippines, Manila, 1992, prof., 1993—; fin. cons., bd. trustees Fieldridge Learning Ctr., Brgy. San Felipe, Batangas, 11999; tax cons., legal rschr. V.C. Ramirez Law Office, Quezon City, 1997—; external auditor N.F.K. Constrn., Merto Manila, 1998—, Vincent Mark Security Agy., Quezon City, 1998—, Psychol. Ext. Evaluation Rsch. Svcs., Quezon City, 1999—; assoc. prof. CBIBE Philippine Womwn's U., Manila, 1999; mem. faculty Colegio San Lorenzo Project 6, Quezon City, 2000—; mgr. Suntay, Matti, Dela Cruz & Assocs. Law Offices, Quezon City, 2000—. Author: (textbooks) Income Taxation Law, 1984, Transfer and Business Taxes, 1986, Fundamentals of Transfer and Business Taxes, 1987, Fundamentals of Income Tax, 1988. Mem. PICPA, GACPA, CALFCI. Roman Catholic. Avocations: martial arts, dancing, playing chess, bowling, reading. Office: Suntay Matti Dela Cruz & Assocs, 162 Roosevelt Ave Matti Bldg, Quezon City The Philippines

CONTI, MASSIMO, career officer, consultant; b. Rome, Italy, July 30, 1965; s. Alessandro and Maria (Panfili) C. Diploma in indsl. chemistry, Chem. Sch. S. Cannizzaro, Colleferro, Rome, Italy, 1984; D Indsl. Chemistry, U. Rome la Sapienza, 1993; diploma in Chem. Synthesis, U. Milan, 1997. Indsl. expert, chief technician Chemistry Lab. Fire Brigade, Rome, 1984-85; rsch. asst. U. Rome la Sapienza, 1991-93; cons. T.T.S. Tech. Trade Svc., Rome, 1996-97; rsch. chemist Menarini Ricerche, Pomezia, 1995-96; flying officer, chem. lab. supr., 1st lt. Italian Air Force, Pomezia, 1997—. Mem. Royal Soc. Chemistry (grad.), Nat. Chemistry Order, Am. Chem. Soc. Avocations: sailing, soccer. E-mail: maxconti@pcg.it. Home: Via L Longo 27, 00045 Genzano di Roma Italy Office: Italian Air Force/Chem Dept, Aeroporto Pratica di Mare, 00040 Rome Italy

CONTI, TOM, actor, writer, director; b. Paisley, Scotland, Nov. 22, 1941; s. Alfonso and Mary (McGoldrick) C.; m. Kara Drummond Wilson, July 2, 1967; 1 child, Nina. Appeared in plays on London's West End, Jesus My Son, 1998, Chapter Two, The Ride Down Mount Morgan, Savages, Other People, The Black and White Minstrels, Don Juan, The Devil's Disciple, Romantic Comedy, Chapter Two, Jesus My Boy: Broadway debut in Whose Life Is It Anyway, 1979 (Tony award), Jeffrey Bernard is Unwell, 1990; appeared in They're Playing Our Song, 1980; dir. Before the Party, 1980; dir., star Present Laughter, 1993; film appearances include Galileo, Eclipse, Merry Christmas Mr. Lawrence, Reuben, Reuben, 1983, American Dreamer, 1984, Saving Grace, Miracles, Heavenly Pursuits, Beyond Therapy, The Dumb Waiter, White Roses, Shirley Valentine, Someone Else's America, 1995, Sub Down, Something To Believe In, 1996, Don't Go Breaking My Heart, 1998, Out of Control, 1997, The Enemy, 2000; appeared in TV plays including the Beaux Strategem; appeared in American TV prodns. Princess and the Pea, Faerie Tale Theatre, the Beate Klarsfeld Story, The Quick and the Dead, Fatal Dosage, When Rabbit Howls, Wright Verdicts, The Inheritance, Friends, Deadline; appeared in Brit. TV prodns. The Glittering Prizes, Norman Conquests, Madame Bovary. Club: Garrick (London). Address: Chatto & Linnit, 123 A Kings Rd, London NW3 4PL, England

CONTOLI, LONGINO, biodiversity researcher, educator; b. Rome, Mar. 23, 1941; s. Adolfo and Lina (Amante) C.; m. Daniela Penko, Apr. 27, 1971; children: Antonio, Flora, Susanna. Grad. in Biol. Scis. cum laude, U. Rome, 1966. Expert Ctr. Genetic Evolution, Rome, Italy, 1969-73, rschr., 1973-76; collaborator Ctr. Genetic Evolution, Rome, 1976-88, top rschr., 1988—; pres. Assn. Teriologica Romana, Rome, 1981-90; chmn. biodiversity group Soc. Italiana di Ecologia, Parma, Italy, 1988-93; rsch. leader Ctr. Genetic Evolution, 1983—; prof. U. Viterbo, Italy, 1996—. Author: Tolfa Hills Natural Park Project, 1980; contbr. articles to profl. jours.; mem. sci. com. Hystrix jour., 1986—. Mem. Nature Conservation Group-Soc. Botanica Italiana, Italy, 1972—; mem. fauna and hunting com. Agr. DPT, Italy, 1993—; mem. nature conservation com. Ctr. Genetic Evolution, 1995—. Fellow UZI (referee 1994—), Legambiente (sci. com. 1980—). Avocations: cultural events, poetry, field trips, sport, romp with my children. Home: Via Arno NR 38, 00198 Rome Italy Office: Ctr Genetic Evolution, Via Lancisi NR 29, 00161 Rome Italy

CONTRERAS, DEE (DORTHEA CONTRERAS), municipal official, educator; b. Kansas City, Mo., Nov. 13, 1945; d. Robert MacGregor Hubsch and Dorothea Ann (Bauer) Wilson; m. Michael Raul Contreras, May 1969 (div. Nov. 1979); 1 child, Jason Michael Raul. BA in Anthropology, UCLA, 1967; JD with honors, Western State U., 1979. Bar: Calif. 1979. Sr. social worker San Diego County, 1968-80; sr. field rep. Svc. Employees Internat. Union Local 535, San Diego, 1980-88; bus. rep. Stationary Engrs. Local 39, Sacramento, 1988-90; sr. employee rels. rep. City of Sacramento, 1990-95, dir. labor rels., 1995—; mem. exec. bd. San Diego Imperial County Labor Coun., 1985-88; tchr. labor history U. Calif. Davis Ext., Sacramento, 1989—. Recipient Bread and Roses award Coalition of Labor Union Women, San Diego, 1981. Mem. Indsl. Rels. Assn. No. Calif. (mem. exec. bd. 1988-94, pres. exec. bd. 1994-96). Democrat. Avocations: reading, writing. Office: City of Sacramento Ste 601 921 10th St Sacramento CA 95814-2711

CONTU, MARCO ENRICO, judge; b. Cagliari, Sardinia, Italy, Aug. 17, 1961; s. Enrico and Licia (Scanu) C.; m. Lucia Pittorru, Apr. 24, 1966. Law Degree, U. Cagliari, 1988. Criminal judge Tribunale Tempio Pausania, Sardinia, 1991—; rschr. U. Sassari, Italy, 1998—. Editor Mycologia e Vegetazione Mediterranea, 1997; contbr. over 200 articles to Italian, French, Spanish, Am. jours., 1984—. Tchr. spl. sch., Tempio Pausania, 1998. Mem. Assn. Italian Magitrates. Avocation: research in mycology and criminal law. Office: Tribunale Tempio Pausania, Officio GIP Via Limbara, 07029 Tempio Pausania Sardinia, Italy

CONWAY, DAVID MARTIN, theologian; b. Formby, Liverpool, Eng., Aug. 22, 1935; s. Geoffrey Seymour and Elsie (Phillips) C.; m. Ruth Fairey Daniel, Mar. 10, 1962; children; Ann Conway-Jones, Moira Conway-Zheng, John. BA/MA, Cambridge (Eng.) U., 1957; DLitt, Lambeth, 1994. Internat. sec. Student Christian Movement of Great Britain and Ireland, 1958-61; study sec. World Student Christian Fedn., Geneva, 1961-67; sec. for chaplaincies in higher edn. Ch. of Eng., London, 1967-70; publs. editor World Coun. Chs., Geneva, 1970-74; asst. gen. sec. for ecumenical affairs Brit. Coun. Chs., London, 1974-83; tutor on ch. and soc. Ripon Coll. Cuddesdon, Oxford, Eng., 1983-86; pres. Selly Oak Coll., Birmingham, Eng., 1986-97; vice-chmn., chmn. Friends of the Ch. in China, London, 1987-90, 94—; treas. Internat. Assn. for Mission Studies, Birmingham, 1988-97. Author: The Undivided Vision, 1966, Seeing Education Whole, 1971, Look, Listen, Care, 1984, That's When the Body Works, 1991, God's Word and Our Many Worlds, 1997, Journeying Together Towards Jubilee, 1999; editor Christians Together, 1983-89, Oxford and Southwell Papers on Church and Society, 1984-86. Founder Assn. des Habitants de la Gradelle-Residence, Geneva, 1965; trustee Archbishops' China Appeal Fund, London, 1988—; mem. Coun. of St. Mary's Hospice, Birmingham, 1994-97. Anglican. Home: 303 Cowley Rd, Oxford OX4 2AQ, England

CONWAY, DOROTHY JEAN WILLIAMS, economist; b. Elizaville, Ky., Apr. 13, 1927; d. John Downing and Maud (Knight) Williams; m. Gene Farris Conway, Sept. 1, 1950; children: Lisa Ann Conway Allen, Janet Lee Conway Fleenor, Linda Knight Conway Hensley. Student, Ky. Wesleyan Coll., Winchester, 1945-46; BS, U. Ky., Lexington, 1949; student, Drexel Inst. Tech., Phila., 1952. Extension svc. agt. U. Ky., Maysville, 1949-52; tchr. home econ. Dayton (Ky.) H.S., 1952; therapeutic dietitian Doctor's Hosp., Phila., 1952-53; R&D lab. asst. Pillsbury Ballard, Louisville, Ky., 1953-54; home svc. adv. Indpls. Power and Light, 1954, The Gas Svc. Co., Topeka, Kans., 1954-56; lectr. home mgmt. U. Cin., 1963. Bd. mem. Mary P. Shelton Pub. Libr., Georgetown, Ohio, 1979-93; bd. United Way. Allocations Com. Cin., 1985-94; bd. mem., chmn. Georgetown United Meth. Ch., 1981-87; mem., pres., sec. U. Cin. Women's Club, 1958-98. Mem. DAR, Am. Home Econ. Assn., Brown County Gen. Hosp. Aux., Cin. Women's Club, Phi Epsilon Omicron. Methodist. Home: 315 E State St Georgetown OH 45121-1416

CONWAY, EARL CRANSTON, business educator, retired manufacturing company executive; b. Asbury Park, N.J., Nov. 14, 1931; s. Earl Cranston and Alda Evelyn (Hendrickson) C.; m. Nancy Lou Schucker, Oct. 23, 1954; children: Karen Marie, Anne Margaret, Earl Edward, Nancy Maureen. BA in Polit. Sci. and Internat. Rels., U. Pa., Phila., 1954. Sales-mktg. rep. Procter & Gamble, Phila., 1957-59; unit mgr. Procter & Gamble, Balt. and Chgo., 1960-64; dist. mgr. Procter & Gamble, Minn., Pa., 1964-69; divsn. mgr., nat. sales mgr. Procter & Gamble, Cin., 1970-81; gen. sales mgr. Europe Procter & Gamble, Brussels, 1981-85; corp. dir. world-wide quality Procter & Gamble, Cin., 1985-92; pres., COO, Innovative Foods Tech., Inc., 1998-99, also bd. dirs.; co-chmn. U.S. Quality Coun. of Conf. Bd., N.Y.C., 1989-92; adj. prof. U. Cin., 1990—; adj. faculty Indian River C.C., Indian River County, Fla., 1996—; lectr. quality and strategic planning Ministry of Light Industry, China, 1992—, Moscow and Kirov, Russia, 1994—; vis. lectr. bus. and engring. schs.; advisor quality mgmt. V.P. Gore, U.S. and Gov. Jim Hunt, N.C., 1992-93, 93-94. Vice chmn. nat. bd. dirs. Vols. of Am., New Orleans, 1991-96; mem., bd. trustees Ursuline Acad., Cin., 1992-93; mem. planning and zoning bd. City of Vero Beach, Fla., 1995-99; bd. dirs. Civic Assn., Indian River County, Fla., Vero Beach, Fla., 1995—; bd. dirs. Indian River Meml. Hosp., Indian River County, 1999—. 1st lt., inf. U.S. Army, 1955-56. Recipient Taguchi Quality Engring. award Am. Supplier Inst., 1989, Recognition by Ministry of Light Industry, People's Republic of China, Guangzhou and Wuxi, 1992-93. Mem. Am. Soc. Quality. Republican. Roman Catholic. Home: 1020 Olde Doubloon Dr Vero Beach FL 32963-2449

CONWAY, EILEEN, quality manager; b. Washington, DC, Apr. 12, 1960; d. Paul Thomas and Kathryn Ann C.; m. Eric Howard Kueckels, Feb. 14, 1994. BSME, Virginia Tech., 1984; MSME, Texas A&M, 1991. Mechanical engineer Evaluation Rsch. Corp., Arlington, Va., 1984-87; rsch. asst. Texas A&M Dept. Mechanical Engineer, College Station, 1987-89; rotor dynamics engineer GE Aircraft Engines, Evandale, OH, 1989-92; engine team leader GE Aircraft Engines, 1992-93; lead engineer, rotor design GE Power Generation, Schenectady, N.Y., 1993-94; mgr. test operations GE Power Generation, 1994-95; mgr. quality, technology, test GE Engine Svcs., California, 1996-98; sourcing quality gen. mgr. GE Power Systems, Schenectady, 1998-2000, e-engring. gen. mgr., 2000—; com. mem. Reliability and Maintainability Symposium Mgmt. Com., 1986-1988. Author: Effect of Straight Through Labyrinth Seals on Rotor Dynamics, 1993. Recipient Engineer Achievement awards GE Aircraft Engines, 1991, 93, Test Operations Financial Strategy award GE Power Systems, 1995, GE Exec. awds., 1992, 95, 97, 99, 2000, Six Sigma Certified Master Black Belt, 1999, Outstanding Young Women of Am. award, 1987. Mem. Am. Soc. Mechanical Engineers (sect. treas., co-chair, 1985-87). E-mail: eileen.conway@ps.ge.com. Office: GE Power Systems 1 River Rd Bldg 40 Schenectady NY 12345-6000

CONWAY, GORDON RICHARD, foundation executive; b. Birmingham, Eng., July 6, 1938; s. Cyril G. and Thelma (Goodwin) C.; m. Susan M. Mumford, Mar. 2, 1965; children: Simon G., Zoe M., Katherine E. BS, U. North Wales, 1959; diploma in agrl. sci., Cambridge (Eng.) U., 1960; diploma in tropical agr., U. West Indies, 1961; PhD, U. Calif., Davis, 1969; LLD (hon.), U. Sussex, 1998; DSc (hon.), U. West Indies, 1999. Rsch. scientist Agrl. Rsch. Ctr., Sabah, Malaysia, 1961-66; lectr., then reader dept. zoology Imperial Coll., London, 1970-80; prof., Ctr. Environ. Tech. Imperial Coll., 1980-88; rep. Ford Found., New Delhi, 1989-92; vice chancellor U. Sussex, Brighton, Eng., 1992-98; chair governing body Inst. Devel. Studies, Brighton, 1992-98; pres. Rockefeller Found., N.Y.C., 1998—; program dir. Internat. Inst. for Environ. Devel., London, 1986-88; co-chmn. Nat. Cmty. Devel. Initiative, N.Y.C., 2000—. Author: (with others) Unwelcome Harvest: Agriculture and Pollution, 1991, After the Green Revolution, 1990; The Doubly Green Revolution, 1997. Hon. fellow U. Wales, Bangor, 1997. Fellow Am. Acad. Arts and Sci.; mem. Reform Club. Office: Rockefeller Found 420 Fifth Ave New York NY 10018

CONWAY, JAMES DONALD, internist, educator; b. Newark, May 2, 1946; s. James M. and Dorothy (Kelly) C. Home and Office: 4300 Houma Blvd Ste 205 Metairie LA 70006-2924

CONWAY, JOHN BELL, environmental biologist, educator; b. Madison, Wis., Apr. 5, 1936; s. John Edward and Barbara (Bell) C.; m. Susan Jane Hawley, Sept. 1, 1961; children: Julie Anne, Steven Douglas. BS in Biology, San Diego State U., 1964, MS in Biology, 1967; MPH in Pub. Health, U. Minn., 1970, PhD in Environ. Biology, 1973. Asst. prof. bio. scis. Wright State U., Dayton, Ohio, 1972-76; asst. prof. bacteria and pub. health Wash. State U., Pullman, 1976-78, assoc. prof., 1978-81; prof. divsn. occupl. and environ. health Grad Sch. Pub. Health, San Diego State U., Calif., 1981-92; head divsn. occupl. and environ. health Grad Sch. Pub. Health, San Diego State U., 1984-87, assoc. dir., prof., 1987-92; assoc. dean, dir. profl. edn. program, prof. U. at Albany, N.Y., 1993-97, prof. Dept. Environ. Health and Toxicology, 1993—, interim dean, 1998—; cons. NBS/Lowry Engrs. and Planners, San Diego, 1984-95, Congressman Duncan Hunter, San Diego, 1991-92, Compliance Consultants, N.Y.C., 1993-95; pub. health officer Grand Teton Nat. Park, Moose, Wyo., summers, 1996, 97. Editl. reviewer Jour. Environ. Health, 1978— (Harry Bliss award 1985), Cancer Prevention Internat., 1994—. Recipient Outstanding Faculty award San Diego State U. Alumni, 1986. Mem. Nat. Environ. Health Assn. (chair air and water sect. 1979-80), Nat. Environ. Health Sci. and Protection Accreditation Coun. (chair 1994-96), Am. Pub. Health Assn. (Disting. Svc. award sect. on environ. 1997). Office: Univ at Albany One University Pl Rensselaer NY 12144-3456

CONWAY, LESLEY, psychologist; b. Cape Town, South Africa, Jan. 8, 1963; d. Ian Arthur and Elizabeth Janet (McGill) M.; m. Barry John Conway; 1 child, Caitlin. BA, U. Port Elizabeth, South Africa, 1983; M in Clin. Psychology, U. South Africa, Pretoria, 1988; D of Clin. Psychology, Rand Afrikaans U., Johannesburg, 1994. Cons. sel. & assessment JHB City Coun., Johannesburg, South Africa, 1989-95; clin. psychologist pvt. practice, Johannesburg, South Africa, 1989-95; dir., owner Lee Morrall Cons., Inc., Johannesburg, South Africa, 1996—. Mem. South African Psychol. Soc. Office: Lee Morrall Cons Inc, PO Box 156, Hurlingham View 2070, South Africa

CONWAY, RICHARD FRANCIS, investment company executive; b. Greenwich, Conn., Jan. 4, 1954; s. Francis Xavier and Marie (Bohan) C.; m. Greta Weil, Oct. 29, 1988; children: Signe Charlotte Weil, Anna Augusta Weil. BA, Harvard Coll., 1976; MBA, Yale U., 1981. Mgmt. trainee Citibank, N.Y.C., 1976-79; assoc. L.F. Rothschild, Unterberg, Towbin Inc., N.Y.C., 1981-83, v.p., 1983-86, prin., 1986-88; v.p. Salomon Bros. Inc., N.Y.C., 1988-90, Security Pacific Mcht. Bank, N.Y.C., 1990-91; sr. v.p. Needham and Co. Inc., N.Y.C., 1992-94; v.p. Smith Mgmt. Co., N.Y.C., 1994-97, Lone Star Securities Mgmt., Inc., N.Y.C., 1998-99; ptnr. Lampe, Conway & Co., LLC, N.Y.C., 1999—. Trustee Choate Rosemary Hall Sch., Wallingford, Conn., 1974-78; class com. Harvard Coll. Fund, Cambridge, Mass., 1991. Mem. Harvard Club (N.Y.C.), Knickerbocker Club (N.Y.C.), Georgica Assn. (Wainscott, N.Y.). Roman Catholic. Home: 1361 Madison Ave New York NY 10128-0713 Office: Lampe Conway & Co LLC Ste 2102 730 5th Ave New York NY 10019-4105

CONWAY, SAMUEL ANTHONY, retired chiropractor; b. Dallastown, Pa., Jan. 19, 1917; s. Clarence C. and Coletta Elizabeth (Smith) C.; student Lebanon Valley Coll., 1947-48; D.C., Nat. Coll. Chiropractic, 1951; m. Irene May Runkle, Feb. 6, 1944; 1 son, Samuel A. Gen. practic chiropractic medicine, Hanover, Pa., 1951-83; chmn. bd., pres. Golden Age Nursing Home, Inc., Hanover, 1961-82; trustee Nat. Coll. Chiropractic, 1960-80, mem. exec. bd. dirs., 1969-80, ret., 1982, chmn. bldg. fund com. 1961-64; participant internat. profl. confs. With Signal Corps, U.S. Army, 1942-46. Recipient Disting. Svc. award Nat. Coll. Chiropractic, 1972; lic. nursing home adminstr., Pa. Mem. VFW, DAV, Nat. Coll. Alumni Assn., Am. Chiropractic Assn., Pa. Chiropractic Assn., Pa. Assn. Drugless Therapists (pres. 1968-69, bd. dirs., Disting. Svc. award 1969), Health Care Facilities of Pa., Am. Nursing Home Assn., York County (Pa.), Hanover Area hist. socs., Antique Automobile Club, Am. Legion, Hanover Area C. of C., Masons, Shriners, Elks. Democrat. Mem. United Ch. of Christ (trustee). Address: 434 Deerfield Dr Hanover PA 17331-5203

CONWELL, HALFORD ROGER, physician; b. Cin., Jan. 28, 1924; s. Halford Fredrick and Erma Pearl (Cornelius) C.; m. Margaret Ann King, Dec. 15, 1965; children: Mark A., Sherri L., John H. BA, U. Wooster, 1948; MA, U. Louisville, 1950; MD, U. Cin., 1955. ATP; diplomate crew coordination tng. Continental Airlines. Practice in aviation medicine Huntsville, Tex., 1959—; mem. staff Huntsville (Tex.) Meml. Hosp., chief of staff, 1974-75, chief medicine, 1976-80, bd. trustees, 1991—; sr. U.S. med. officer Brit.

Caledonian Airways, 1977-89; cons. Aeromexico; chief flight surgeon Continental Airlines, 1996—; mem. Walker County Hosp. Dist., 1975-79, chmn., 1976-79; asst. dean of men, instr. psychology Heidelberg U., Tiffin, Ohio, 1950-51; instr. psychology Cin. Coll.; sr. med. examiner FAA; sr. examiner C.A.A. (U.K.), C.A.A. (Australia); newspaper columnist, 1992—. Trustee Biol. Analysis and Rsch. Found.; capt. (hon.) Tex. Internat. Airline; founder Bomber Command Mus. (R.A.F.) Lt. USNR, 1942-46. Recipient safe pilot award Nat. Pilots Assn., Pilot Proficiency award FAA, Profl. Svc. Citation. Mem. Brit. Assn. Aerospace Medicine, Latin Am. Aviation Med. Assn., Scottish Assn. Aviation Med. Examiners, Airline Med. Dirs. Assn., Civil Aviation Med. Assn. (v.p. 1968-80, dir. 1968—, pres. 1980-81, Award of merit 1994, 97), Mitchell Pediatric Soc., Academie Internationale de Medicine Aeronatque et Spatiale, Aircraft Owners and Pilots Assn. (med. adv. panel), Confederate Air Force (founding mem.), Airline Transp. Assn. (med. com.), Order Ky. Cols., Aerospace Med. Assn. (John A. Tamisiea award 2000), Quiet Birdmen, Masons, Psi Chi, Alpha Psi Omega (hon.). Office: 2800 Lake Rd Huntsville TX 77340-5632

CONYERS, CLAUDE BRUNSON, retired publishing executive; b. Cartersville, Ga., June 19, 1934; s. Claude Brunson and Rachel Keith (Stephens) C. BA, Vanderbilt U., 1956; MA, Columbia U., 1962; dance tng., New Dance Group, N.Y.C., 1959, Sch. of Am. Ballet, N.Y.C., 1960, Ballet Russe Sch., N.Y.C., 1961-64. Sr. editor Prentice-Hall, Inc., Englewood Cliffs, N.J., 1960-64; dancer PACT Ballet, Johannesburg, South Africa, 1965-66, Les Grands Ballets Canadiens, Montreal, 1967; editl. dir. Greystone Press, N.Y.C., 1968-70; editl. cons. N.Y.c., 1970-74; spl. projects editor Praeger Pubs., N.Y.c., 1975; sr. projects editor Macmillan Pub. Co., N.Y.c., 1975-87; editl. dir., scholarly and profl. reference Oxford U. Press, N.Y.c., 1988-98, v.p., 1995-99; mem. publs. com. N.Y. Acad. Scis., 1990-95. Bd. dirs. The George Balachine Found., 1999—; project dir. Popular Balanchine, 2000—. Lt. (j.g.) USNR, 1956-58. Recipient R.R. Hawkins award Profl. and Scholarly Pub./Assn. Am. Pubs., 1991, 93, 96, 98, Dartmouth medal ALA, 1987, 99. Mem. ASPCA, Internat. Assn. History Religions, Am. Acad. Religion, Am. Soc. for Theatre Rsch., Am. Studies Assn., Congress on Rsch. in Dance, Dance Critics Assn., Sacred Dance Guild, Soc. Archtl. Historians, Soc. Dance History Scholars (advisor, editl. bd. 1988—), Clan Keith Soc., Columbia Club, World Dance Alliance, Soc. for Scholarly Pub. Democrat. Episcopalian.

CONYERS, JOHN, JR., congressman; b. Detroit, May 16, 1929; s. John and Lucille (Simpson) C.; m. Monia Estes; children: John Jr., Carl Edward. B.A., Wayne State U., 1957, J.D., 1958; LL.D., Wilberforce U., 1969. Bar: Mich. 1959. Legis. asst. to Congressman John Dingell, 1959-61; sr. ptnr. firm Conyers, Bell & Townsend, 1959-61; referee Mich. Workmen's Compensation Dept., 1961-64; mem. 89th-106th Congresses from 1st (now 14th) Mich. dist., 1964—; former chmn. Govt. Ops. Com., former chmn. subcom. on legis. and nat. security; ranking mem. Judiciary Com.; Past dir. edn. Local 900, United Auto Workers; mem. adv. council Mich. Liberties Union; gen. counsel Detroit Trade Union Leadership Council; vice chmn. nat. bd. Ams. for Democratic Action; vice chmn. adv. council ACLU; an organizer Mems. Congress for Peace through Law; bd. dirs. numerous other orgns. including African-Am. Inst., Commn. Racial Justice, Detroit Inst. Arts, Nat. Alliance Against Racist and Polit. Repression, Nat. League Cities. Sponsor, contbg. author: Am. Militarism, 1970, War Crimes and the American Conscience, 1970, Anatomy of an Undeclared War, 1972; contbr. articles to profl. jours. Trustee Martin Luther King Jr. Ctr. for Non-Violent Social Change. Served to 2d lt. U.S. Army, 1950-54, Korea. Recipient Rosa Parks award SCLC. Mem. NAACP (exec. bd. Detroit), Kappa Alpha Psi. Democrat. Baptist. Office: 2426 Rayburn Bldg Washington DC 20515-2214

COOGAN, FRANK NEIL, health and social services administrator; b. Watertown, Wis., June 14, 1929; s. Neil Christopher and Lilian (Nelson) C.; m. Mary Louise Block, Apr. 14, 1951; children: Michael, Thomas, Karen. BS, U. Wis., 1951, MSW, 1955. Psychiatric social worker VA, 1955-62; dist. mental health cons. Wis. State Div. Mental Hygiene, 1962-65; dir. Bur. Alcohol and Other Drug Abuse, Wis. Dept. Health, 1965-77; v.p. DePaul Health Corp., 1977-90; behavioral health cons. Corphealth, West Allis, Wis., 1990-94; psychotherapist Am. Behavioral Clinics S.C., Milw., 1994—. With U.S. Army, 1951-53. Fellow Am. Coll. Addiction Treatment Adminstrs.; mem. Alcohol and Drug Problems Assn. N. Am. (chmn. membership com.), Wis. Alcohol and Drug Treatment Providers Assn. (bd. dirs.), Wis. Assn. Alcohol and Other Drug Abuse (bd. dirs., Outstanding Profl. award 1990, Pres.'s award 1999), Am. Legion. Lutheran. Avocations: hiking, golf, fishing, cycling, cross country skiing. Home: 2127 S 99th St Milwaukee WI 53227-1452

COOK, CATHY WELLES, state senator; b. New London, Conn.. BA, Conn. Coll. Mem. Conn. State Senate, Hartford, 1993—; ranking mem. tourism subcom.; mem. commerce and com.; ranking mem. appropriations com., human svcs. com.; mem. subcoms. on govt., transp. and conservation and devel.; gov.'s appointee Conn. Bd. of Protection and Advocacy for Persons with Disabilities; mem. Pres.'s Commn. of Nat. Acad. of Mental retardation. Republican. Office: Conn State Senate State Capitol Rm 3400 Hartford CT 06106

COOK, CHARLES EDWARD, JR., editor, political analyst; b. Shreveport, La., Nov. 20, 1953; s. Charles Edward and Mary Elizabeth (Hudgens) C.; m. Lucy Gerald, Apr. 17, 1982. Student, Georgetown U., 1972-77. Rsch. dir. Dem. Senatorial Campaign Com., Washington, 1977-79; so. regional desk person Kennedy for Pres. Campaign, Washington, 1979-80; pub. opinion analyst, polit. cons. William R. Hamilton & Staff, Washington, 1980; asst. dir. for polit. affairs Nat. Assn. of Home Builders, Washington, 1981-82; mem. profl. staff Senate Dem. Policy Com., Washington, 1982-84; editor The Cook Polit. Report, Washington, 1984—; election night analyst C-Span, 1986, 88, NBC News, 1988, CBS News, 1990, 92, NBC, 1994, 96, 98, CNN, 1996—. Columnist Roll Call, 1986-98, Nat. Jour., 1998—. Methodist. Home: 4002 E West Hwy Chevy Chase MD 20815-5915 Office: 1501 M St NW Ste 300 Washington DC 20005-1700

COOK, CHRISTOPHER CHARLES H., psychiatrist, educator, consultant; b. Ilford, Essex, Eng., Mar. 5, 1956; s. Cyril Christopher and Margaret Elizabeth (Holland) C.; m. Ruth Elizabeth Hopkins, July 22, 1978 (dec. 1985); children: Andrew, Beth; m. Joy Michelle Bowerman, Feb. 15, 1986; children: Rachel, Jonathan. BSc in Physiology, King's Coll., London, 1977; MB BS, St. George's Hosp. Med. Sch., London, 1981, MD, 1994. House officer St. James Hosp., London, 1981-82, Royal Cornwall (Eng.) Hosp., 1981-82; registrar United Med. & Dental Schs., London, 1982-87; drug and alcohol dependence lectr. U. Coll. and Middlesex Sch. Medicine, London, 1987-90; cons. psychiatrist Royal Air Force, 1991-94; sr. lectr. in addictions Inst. Psychiatry, London, 1994-97; prof. psychiatry of alcohol misuse Kent Inst. Medicine U. Kent, Canterbury, 1997—; trustee Addiction Recovery Found., London, 1990-93; chmn. mgmt. com. Willows Christian Counseling Svcs., Swindon, 1992-94; dir. Yeldall Christian Centres, Reading, 1993-97. Co-author: Treatment of Drinking Problems, 1997; media rev. editor Addiction Biology, 1995-99; asst. editor Addiction, 1995-99. Non-stipendiary curate Otham & Langley, Kent; dean Ch. of Eng. With RAF, 1990-94. Travel grantee Dr. Robert Malcom Trust, 1988; rsch. grantee Middlesex Hosp. Spl. Trustees, 1990-91, Med. Rsch. Coun., 1993-95. Mem. Royal Coll. Psychiatry, Soc. for the Study of Addiction (exec. com. 1996—), European Soc. for Bio-Medicine Rsch. on Alcohol. Anglican. Avocations: photography, gardening, computing. Office: Kent Inst Med & Hlth Sci, U Kent at Canterbury, Canterbury CT2 7PD, England

COOK, COLIN BURFORD, psychiatrist; b. London, Jan. 20, 1927; came to U.S., 1952, naturalized, 1975; s. Bertram William and Anna Marie (Forster-Jones) C.; M.D., London U., 1951. Diplomate Am. Bd. Psychiatry and Neurology, 1979. Rotating intern Bridgeport (Conn.) Hosp., 1952-53; resident Goodmayes Hosp., Warlingham Park Hosp., London, 1955-57; gen. med. practitioner, London, 1960-66; resident in psychiatry Marquette Sch. Medicine, Wis., 1968-69; resident in psychiatry Cornell U., White Plains, N.Y., 1969-71; fellowship Nat. Hosp. Neurol. Disease U. London, 1973; practice medicine, specializing in psychiatry, Stamford, Conn., 1975—; prof. psychiatry, Columbia U., N.Y.C., 1992-95; attending physician, psychiatrist Regional Network Programs, Inc., Conn., 1995-96. Author (as Alan Phillips) Jazz Improvisation and Harmony, 1965, 4th edit., 1998. Served with Brit. Navy, 1953-55, 57-59. Mem. AMA, Authors League. Club: Masons (32 degree). Address: 373 Strawberry Hill Ave Stamford CT 06902-2512

COOK, EDWARD DAVID, institute executive director; b. Newcastle on Tyne, Eng., Mar. 3, 1947; s. David Robert and Margaret Falconer (Watson) C.; m. Kathleen Hay, July 11, 1970; children: Simon, Kenneth. BA, Ariz. State U., 1968; MA, Edinburgh U., 1970; PhD, New Coll., Edinburgh, 1973; MA (hon.), Oxford (Eng.) U., 1984; DLitt, Gordon Coll., Wenham, Eng., 1999. Lectr. St. John's Coll., Nottingham, Eng., 1973-79; head of theology Westminster Coll., Oxford, 1979-87; fellow, chaplain Green Coll., Oxford, 1979-83; dir. Whitefield Inst., Oxford, 1987—; broadcaster BBC Radio/TV, London, 1987—; dean Oxford Centre for Mission Studies, 1982—; med. ethics advisor Archbishops, U.K., 1995—; advisor Xenotransplantation Authority, U.K., 1997, mem. coun. of Europe, 1999—; Templeton lectr. Mpls., Chgo. and Austin, 1994. Author: The Moral Maze, 1983, latest reprint, 1994, Blind Alley Beliefs, revised edit., 1996, Living in the Kingdom, 1992, Patients' Choice, 1993; cons. editor Ethics and Medicine, 1987, Humane Medicine, 1995, Dilemmas of Life (reprint), 1997. Advisor to select com. on genetics Ho. of Commons, London, 1994, select. com. on med. ethics Ho. of Lords, London, 1993. Recipient Bruce of Grangehill and Falkland prize Edinburgh U., 1970; Sir David Baxter scholar, Edinburgh U., 1970. Mem. Tyndale Fellowship. Scottish Baptist. Avocations: reading, theatre. Office: Whitefield Inst, Frewin Ct, Oxford OX1 3HZ, England

COOK, EUGENE AUGUSTUS, lawyer; b. Houston, May 2, 1938; s. Eugene A. and Estelle Mary (Stiner) C.; m. Sondra Attaway, Aug. 27, 1968; children: Laurie Ann, Eugene A. BBA, U. Houston, 1961, JD, 1966; LLM, U. Va., 1992. Bar: Tex. 1966, U.S. Dist. Ct. (so. dist.) Tex. 1967, U.S. Ct. Appeals (5th cir.) 1969, U.S. Supreme Ct. 1971, U.S. Ct. Claims 1972, U.S. Tax Ct. 1974, U.S. Ct. Appeals (11th cir.) 1982, U.S. Dist. Ct. (no., we. and ea. dists.) Tex. 1983. Ptnr. Butler & Binion, Houston, 1966-85; founding ptnr. Cook, Davis & McFall, 1985-88; justice Tex. Supreme Ct., Austin, 1988-93, chmn. jud. edn. exec. com., chmn. professionalism com., 1988-92; sr. ptnr. Bracewell & Patterson, Houston, 1993—; adj. asst. prof. law U. Houston, 1971-72, 74. Editor in chief, contbg. author: Creditors Rights in Texas, 2d edit., 1981; bd. dirs. U. Houston Law Rev., 1978-79; contbr. articles to profl. jours. Vice-chmn. bd. YMCA, 1977; bd. dirs. Spl. Olympics Tex., 1989-95, chmn. bd. dirs., 1994. Recipient Disting. Alumnus award U. Houston Law Ctr., 1990, Am. Inns of Ct.-Lewis F. Powell Jr. award, 1992. Fellow Am. Coll. Trial Lawyers, Am. Acad. Matrimonial Lawyers, Internat. Acad. Matrimonial Lawyers, Am. Bar Found., Tex. Bar Found. (Outstanding Pub. Svc. award 1990); mem. ABA, Am. Inns of Ct. (pres. Austin Inn 1990-91), Tex. Bar Assn. (chmn. grievance com. 1971-72, vice chmn. consumer law sect. 1976-77, chmn. consumer law sect. 1979-80, Presdl. Citation 1979, dir. family law sect. 1984-88, Presdl. Cert. Merit, 1983, 84, 86, Pres.'s award as most outstanding lawyer in Tex., 1989, chmn. pubs. com. 1981-82, Achievement award 1982, chmn. litigation sect. 1982-84, chmn. CLE, 1988-89), Houston Bar Assn. (seminar com. 1976-77, Chmn. of Yr. award, 1976-77, chmn. insts. com. 1977-78, Outstanding Svc. award 1977-78, chmn. CLE com. 1978-79, Pres.'s award, 1978-79, 96-97; chmn. consumer law sect. 1978-79, vice-chmn. family law sect. 1981-82, chmn. family law sect. 1982-83, Officers award 1983, chmn. staff and staffing com. 1985-86, chmn. Spl. Oympics Com. 1987-88, chmn. long range planning and devel. com. 1988-89, dir. 1984-86, 2d v.p. 1986-87, 1st v.p. 1987-88, pres. elect 1988-89, pres. 1989-90, chmn. profl. com. 1996-97), Texas Bd. Legal Specialization (cert.), Civil Trial and Family Law, Nat. Bd. Trial Advocacy (bd. cert. civil trial law), Tex. Assn. Cert. Civil Trial Law Lawyers, Gulf Coast Family Law Specialists Assn., Tex. Acad. Family Law Specialists, ABA, State Bar Tex., Phi Kappa Phi, Phi Theta Kappa (chmn. bd. dirs. 1966-71, 87-88, Most Disting. Alumnus in Nat. award, 1988), Omicron Chi Epsilon, Omicron Delta Kappa, Phi Rho Pi, U. Houston Alumni Assn. (bd. dirs. 1996—). Office: Bracewell & Patterson LLP S Tower Pennzoil Pl 711 Louisiana St Ste 2900 Houston TX 77002-2781

COOK, FRANCES D., diplomat; b. Charleston, W.Va., Sept. 7, 1945; d. Nash and Vivian Cook. BA, Mary Washington Coll. of U. Va., 1967; MPA, Harvard U., 1978; LLD, Shenandoah U., 1998. Certificats d'Etudes, Université d'Aix-Marseille (France), 1966. Commd. fgn. svc. officer Dept. State, 1967; spl. asst. to R.S. Shriver amb. to France, Paris, 1968-69; mem. U.S. Del. Paris Peace Talks on Viet-Nam, 1970-71; cultural affairs officer, consul Am. Consul Gen., Sydney, Australia, 1971-73; cultural affairs officer, first sec. Am. Embassy, Dakar, Senegal, 1973-75; personnel officer for Africa USIA, Washington, 1975-77; dir. office public affairs African Bur. Dept. State, Washington, 1978-80; amb. to Republic of Burundi Dept. State, Bujumbura, 1980-83; consul gen. Dept. State, Alexandria, Egypt, 1983-86; dep. asst. sec. of state for refugees Dept. State, Washington, 1986-87, dir. Office of West African Affairs, 1987-89; amb. to Cameroon Dept. State, Yaoundé, 1989-93; U.S. coord. for Sudan Dept. State, 1993; dep. asst. sec. of state for political-military affairs Dept. of State, Washington, 1993-95; amb. to Oman Dept. of State, Muscat, 1996-99. Recipient various honor awards Dept. State. Mem. AAUW, Am. Fgn. Svc. Assn., Coun. of Fgn. Rels., Harvard Club of N.Y.C., Army-Navy Club/Washington, Phi Beta Kappa (alumni). Home: 767 NW 18th St Homestead FL 33030-4051

COOK, FRANK RICHARDSON, aeronautical engineer, social scientist; b. Miss., Dec. 23, 1910; s. William Felder and May (Richardson) C.; m. Lois Lorton, June 24, 1935 (div. 1984); children: William L., Grady R.; m. Berty Cook, Dec. 9, 1989. BS in Aero. Engring., MIT, 1932; MA in Social Scis., U. Calif., Irvine, 1978, PhD, 1980. Dir. aero. engring. Honeywell, Inc., Mpls., 1950-55; founder, pres. Sci. Mgmt. Corp., Denver, 1956—, Tustin, Calif., 1956—; founder, pres. Frank R. Cook, 1955-62; cons. in over 30 countries demographic projects to measure 70 countries' relationships between 36 social and econ. variables. Col. USAF, 1933-49; PTO. Decorated Legion of Merit with 3 oak leaf clusters. Assoc. fellow AIAA. Republican. Episcopalian. Office: Sci Mgmt Corp PO Box 102312 Denver CO 80250-2312

COOK, HARRY CLAYTON, JR., lawyer; b. Washington, Mar. 25, 1935; s. Harry Clayton and Lillian June (A'harrah) C.;m. Jane Clare Melius, 1963 (div. 1974); children: Christianne Pier, Nicole, Harry Clayton III; m. Judith Ann Tabler, 1994; children: Rebecca Lyeth Kelsey, Parker Burr Kelsey. BSChemE, Princeton U., 1956; LLB, U. Va., 1960. Bar: Colo. 1960, N.Y. 1961, Pa. 1966, D.C. 1973. Assoc. Sullivan & Cromwell, N.Y.C., 1960-63, Holme Roberts & Owen, Denver, 1964, Pepper Hamilton & Scheetz, Phila., 1965-69; ptnr. Pepper Hamilton & Scheetz, 1969-70, 73; on assignment as sr. tax counsel Sun Oil Co., Phila., 1970; ptnr. Cadwalader Wickersham & Taft, Washington, 1974-87, Bishop, Cook, Purcell & Reynolds, Washington, 1988-90; pvt. practice Langley, Va., 1991—; of counsel Bastianelli, Brown and Kelley, Washington, 1992—; page to U.S. Sen. E.D. Millikin, Colo., 1950-52; gen. counsel Maritime Adminstrn.; mem. Maritime Subs. Bd., U.S. Dept. Commerce, Washington, 1970-73; U.S. del. to Soviet Union for Maritime Agreement between U.S. and USSR, 1971-73; mem. Adminstrv. Conf. U.S., 1980-90, chmn. com. on jud. rev., 1982-88, sr. fellow, 1988-90; mem. Nat. Def. Exec. Res., U.S. Mil. Sealift Command, 1983-91, mem. emeritus, 1991—, U.S. Office of Tech. Assessment; mem. citizens adv. panel on U.S. Maritime Ind., 1982-85, cargo policy workshop participant, 1984-85. Mem. editorial bd. Va. Law Rev., 1958-59, exec. editor, 1959-60; contbr. articles to profl. jours. Dir. Com. on the Present Danger; bd. dirs. Inst. for Fgn. Policy Analysis; bd. govs. United Svcs. Orgn., 1997—; maritime adv. bd. Rep. Liberia. Mem. ABA, D.C. Bar Assn., Fed. Bar Assn. (com. gen. counsels 1970—), Am. Law Inst. (life), Maritime Law Assn. U.S. (marine fin. com., proctor in admiralty), Chevy Chase (Md.) Club, Cosmos Club (Washington), Fishers Island Club (N.Y.), Hay Harbor Club (N.Y.), Met. Club (Washington) Racquet Club Phila., Univ. Club (N.Y.C.) (San Francisco), Order of Coif, The Raven Soc. Phi Delta Phi. Home: 1011 Langley Hill Dr McLean VA 22101-1709 Office: Two Lafayette Centre 1133 21st St NW Ste 500 Washington DC 20036-3331

COOK, HARVEY CARLISLE, law enforcement official; b. Cambridge, Md., June 19, 1936; s. John Morrison and Lula Arbelia (Warfield) C.; m. Shirley Marie Cox, Aug. 4, 1973; children: Brenda, Claudine, John, Anne. AA in Police Sci., Charles Ct. Community Coll., LaPlata, Md., 1973; BBA, U. Md., 1979, cert. in paralegal, 1980; cert. in criminal justice, FBI Nat. Acad., Quantico, Va., 1983. USCG Masters lic., 1988. Inspector Tidewater Fisheries Dept., Hughesville, Md., 1958-61, dist. inspector, 1962-64; lt. Md. State Marine Police, Hughesville, 1965-69; capt. Md. State Marine Police, LaPlata, 1970-72, Md. Natural Resources Police, LaPlata, 1973-75; maj. Md. Natural Resources Police, Annapolis, 1976-86, dep. supt., 1986-88; dir. Hovercraft tng. and ops. Hover Systems, Inc., 1988-93; dir. health & indsl. safety Mech. Constrn. Inc., 1994—; dir. marine & indsl. safety & security Cook & Assocs., 1995—; liaison officer Emergency Mgmt. Agy., Pikesville, Md., 1974-86, USCG Aux., Balt., 1982-86. Bd. dirs. Charles County Fair, LaPlata, 1985. Recipient Ann. Safe Boating award USCG Aux., 1975, Disting. Svc. award Gov. of Md., 1987, C.G. Aux. Pub. Educator award, 1999, C.G. Sustained Aux. Svc. award, 2000; named Best Engring. Soldier Md. N.G. 121st Engr. Battalion, 1967, Disting. Citizen, Mass. Gov.'s Office, 1983; commd. Ky. Col., Gov. Ky., 1983. Mem. FOP, NRA (life), Nat. Police Officers Assn. Am. (charter), Hoverclub Am., U.S. Hovercraft Soc. Inc. (bd. dirs. 1987, v.p. 1990-92, pres. 1993), USCG Auxiliary (vice flotilla comdr. 1996, comdr. 1997-98, flotilla staff officer 2000), Dr. Samuel A. Mudd Soc. Inc. (treas. 1987), So. Md. Bd. Realtors, Md. Chiefs Police Assn., Charles County Cmty. Coll. Alumni Assn. (pres. 1984). Republican. Methodist. Avocations: hunting, fishing, power boating, antiques. Office: Cook & Assocs 408 Briarwood Rd Wallingford PA 19086-6503

COOK, HELENA MARY, lawyer, researcher; b. London, Sept. 8, 1956; d. Leonard George and Hilda Mary (Storey) C.; m. Laurens Francois Fransman, July 9, 1994; children: Lindsey Aidan, also son. BA with honors, Cambridge (Eng.) U., 1978, MA, 1982; LLM, Harvard U., 1984. Cert. solicitor, 1979. Solicitor Clifford Chance, London, 1981-83; staff atty. Lawyers Com. for Human Rights, N.Y.C., 1984-87; legal advisor Amnesty Internat., London, 1987-90, head legal office, 1990-94; cons., lectr. U. Essex, Colchester, Eng., 1994-95, U. Nottingham, Eng., 1994-95, 99; dir. policy and rsch. Pub. Law Project, London, 1995-98; mem. exec. bd. Internat. Svc. Human Rights, Geneva, 1994-2000; with Interights, London, 1994—. Contbr. articles to profl. jours., chpts. to books. Harkness fellow Commonwealth Fund, Harvard Law Sch., 1983-84. Avocations: playing classical guitar, theatre, skiing and swimming, creative writing.

COOK, IAN AINSWORTH, psychiatrist, researcher, educator; b. N.Y.C., May 1, 1960; s. Charles David and Bobette Cook. BS in Engring. magna cum laude, Princeton U., 1982; MD, Yale U., 1987. Diplomate Nat. Bd. Med. Examiners, Am. Bd. Psychiatry and Neurology. Resident in surgery U. Colo., Denver, 1987-88; resident in psychiatry Neuropsychiat. Inst. UCLA, 1991-94, chief resident in liaison psychiatry, 1993-94, instr. dept. psychiatry, 1995-96, assoc. dir. residency edn. dept. psychiatry, 1995-96, asst. prof psychiatry, 1996—; registrar Neuropsychiat. Inst., 1999—; dir. NPI Acad. Info. Tech. Core, 1999—; assoc. dir. Office of Profl. and Cmty. Edn., 1998—; examiner Am. Bd. Psychiatry and Neurology, 1998—. Mem. editl. bd. Jefferson Jour. Psychiatry, 1992-94; contbr. articles to profl. jours. Rsch. fellow Nat. Inst. Mental Health, 1993-96; recipient Young Investigator award Nat. Alliance Rsch. Schizophrenia and Depression, 1995, 97. Mem. Am. Psychiat. Assn. (Burroughs-Wellcome fellow 1992, mem. com. of resident and fellows 1992-94, mem. steering com./practice guidelines 1994—), Nat. Eagle Scout Assn., Sigma Xi, Tau Beta Pi. Achievements include four patents in biomed. devices and methods. Office: UCLA Neuropsychiat Inst & Hosp 760 Westwood Plz Los Angeles CA 90095-8353

COOK, JAMES JUNIOR, academic administrator; b. Pryor, Okla., Oct. 25, 1946; s. Paul Amos and Gladys Blanche (Davis) C.; m. Stephanie Karlene Schneidewent, May 6, 1967; children: Adrian Leigh, Shaun Michael. BA in Edn., Northeastern State U., 1970; MA in History, S.W. Tex. State U., 1973; EdD in Higher Edn., Tex. Tech. U., 1977. Asst. prof. history Schreiner Coll., Kerrville, Tex., 1972-76; dir. student activities Midland (Tex.) Coll., 1977-78; asst. campus dir. N.Mex. State U., Alamogordo, 1978-81; dir. acad. and student svcs. East Tex. State U., Texarkana, 1981-82; v.p. student affairs Seminole (Okla.) Jr. Coll., 1982-84, v.p. acad. affairs, 1984-89, pres., 1987-96; exec. v.p. Rose State Coll., Midwest City, Okla., 1996—; chmn. East Cen. Okla. Edn. Consortium, 1989-91; pres. Bi-State Athletic Conf., 1989-90. Contbr. articles to profl. jours. Alumni v.p. Leadership Okla., Oklahoma City, 1990; active Seminole Spl. Edn. Found., 1989-96; mem. troop com. Boy Scouts Am., Seminole, 1989-95, chmn. Big Teepee dist., 1998—; v.p. Jasmine Moran Children's Mus., Seminole, 1989-96; grad. Leadership Midwest City, 1997. Named Citizen of Yr., Seminole C. of C., 1989. Mem. Okla. Acad. for State Goals, Coun. Pres. Okla. (chmn. 1995-96), Seminole Hall of Fame, Phi Theta Kappa. Avocations: tennis, reading. Home: 10201 SE 55th St Oklahoma City OK 73150-4532 Office: Rose State Coll 6420 SE 15th St Midwest City OK 73110-2704

COOK, JEANNE GARN, historian, genealogist; b. Wadsworth, Ohio; d. Ralph D. and Rose M. Garn; m. William A. Cook; children: William Jeffrey, Julie L. Cook Boatwright, James A. BA, Hiram Coll., 1947. Woman's supr. City Recreation Dept., Wadsworth, 1947-51; libr. Cleve. City Schs., 1953-55; physician's office receptionist Cleve., 1978-81; self-employed genealogist, historian various orgns., Parma Heights, Ohio, 1982—; lectr. in field. Editor Cleve. Colony Mayflower Newsletter, 1991-95, 97—; author: (poetry) The Blue of Autumn, 1990 (Golden Poet award), also numerous genealogies and slide programs. Vol. craft instr. City of Parma Heights, 1968-75. Mem. Western Res. Hist. Soc. (vol. libr. 1980—, mem. geneal. com. 1981—, com. mem. 1989), Ohio Geneal. Soc., Parma-Cuyahoga Genealogy Soc. (pres. 1986-97, v.p. and editor newsletter 1997—), Daus. Am. Colonists (state sec. 1993-99, regent local chpt. 1979-81, 91-95, state 1st vice regent 1999—), 1st Families of Ohio (lectr. 1982—), Cleve. Colony Mayflower Descs. (bd. assts., pub. rels. com. 1987—), Hiram Coll. Club of Women, Parma Heights Book Discussion Club, Flagon and Trencher. Avocations: composing music, displays, crafts, sewing, travel. Home: 6428 Nelwood Rd Parma Heights OH 44130-3211

COOK, JENIK ESTERM (JENIK ESTERM COOK SIMONIAN), artist, educator; b. Rezaieh, Iran, July 7, 1940; came to U.S., 1964; d. Sameual Amijon and Nanajan (Amreh Sarkissian) Simonian; m. Carrol Ross Cook, Sept. 28, 1961; children: Fiona Gitana Cook Anderson, Herold H. Studied with Hossein Delrish, Iran, 1968-70; studied with Barbara Lae, Scotland, 1970-78; studied with Chalita Robinson, 1981-87, studied with Jake Lee, 1987-90, studied with Dr. Alex Vilumsons, 1988-94. Tchr. art; resident artist Orlando Gallery, L.A.; art tchr. U. Judaism, Bel Air. One-woman shows include Pacific Design Ctr., L.A., 1996, Orlando Gallery, 1997, 98, Bakery Digital Post Prodn. Ctr., L.A., West Wood Fed. Bldg., L.A., 1999, Hilton Hotel, L.A., 1999; exhibited in groups shows at Orlando Gallery, 1998, L.A. Conv. Ctr., 1998. Rheinfelden (Germany) Town Hall, 1998, Gallery Merkel, Grenzack, Germany, 1998, L.A. Art Expo, 1998, MGM Conf. Ctr., 1999, Long Beach Conv. Ctr., 1999, Art 21, Las Vegas MGM Conv. Ctr., 1999, Art Expo, N.Y., 2000; set designer, scenic artist North Hollywood Ch. of Religious Sci., 1999. Office: Everywomans Village 5650 Sepulveda Blvd Van Nuys CA 91411-2981

COOK, JUDITH RUTH, administrative nursing supervisor; b. Washington, Dec. 14, 1942; d. John Thomas and Merle Moore (Davidson) Ridge; m. Stanley Blaine Cook, Aug. 1, 1964; children: Christopher, Sarah Ann Cook Westfall. RN, Washington Hosp. Sch. Nursing, 1963; BSN, Waynesburg Coll., 1991. RN, Pa. RN Montefiore Hosp., Pitts., 1963-64, Washington (Pa.) Hosp., 1964-71, 73-90; real estate agt. N.F. Johnson Real Estate, Washington, 1978-81; adminstrv. nursing supr. Washington Hosp., 1990—. Mem. planning com. South Franklin Twp., Washington, 1985-86. Mem. Pa. Assn. Adminstrv. Nursing Suprs., Sigma Theta Tau. E-mail: cook@m-lynk.com. Office: Washington Hosp 155 Wilson Ave Washington PA 15301-3398

COOK, JULIAN ABELE, JR., federal judge; b. Washington, June 22, 1930; s. Julian Abele and Ruth Elizabeth (McNeill) C.; m. Carol Annette Dibble, Dec. 22, 1957; children: Julian Abele III, Peter Dibble, Susan Annette. BA, Pa. State U., 1952; JD, Georgetown U., 1957, LLD (hon.), 1992; LLM, U. Va., 1988; LLD (hon.), U. Detroit, 1996, Wayne State U., 1997. Bar: Mich. 1957. Law clk. to judge Pontiac, Mich., 1957-58; pvt. practice Detroit, 1958-78; judge U.S. Dist. Ct. (ea. dist.) Mich., Detroit, 1978, chief judge, 1989-96, sr. judge, 1996—; spl. asst. atty. gen. State of Mich., 1968-78; adj. prof. U. Detroit Sch. Law, 1971-74; gen. counsel pub. TV Sta. WTVS, 1973-78; labor arbitrator Am. Arbitration Assn. and Mich. Employment Rels. Commn., 1975-78; mem. Mich. State Bd. Ethics, 1977-78; instr. trial advocacy workshop Harvard U., 1988—, trial advocacy program U.S. Dept. Justice, 1989-90; com. on fin. disclosure Jud. Conf. U.S., 1988-93, chmn., 1990-93; screening panel NYU Root-Tilden-Snow Scholarship Program, 1991, 96—; mem.

U.S. Sentencing Commn. Judicial Adv. Group, 1996-98; mem. nat. bd. trustees Am. Inn Ct., 1996—; mem. adv. com. Nat. Publs., 1994-96, chmn. nat. nominations and election com., 1994-95; pres. chpt. XI, Master of Bench, 1984-95. Contbr. articles to profl. jours. Exec. bd. dirs. Child and Family Svcs. Mich., 1968-89, past pres., 1975-76; bd. dirs. Am. Heart Assn. Mich., 1968-89, Hutzel Hosp., 1984-95; chmn. Mich. Civil Rights Commn., 1968-71; co-chair exec. com. Walter P. Reuther Libr. Labor and Urban Affairs, Wayne State U.; mem. bd. visitors Georgetown U. Law Ctr., 1992—. With Signal Corps, U.S. Army, 1952-54. Recipient Merit citation Pontiac Area Urban League, 1971, Pathfinders award Oakland U., 1977, Svc. award Todd-Phillips Home, Inc., 1978, Disting. Alumnus award Pa. State U., 1987, Georgetown U., 1989, Focus and Impact award Oakland U., 1985; resolution Mich. Ho. of Reps., 1971, Outstanding Community Svc. award Va. Park Community Investment Assocs., 1992, 1st Ann. Trailblazers award D. Augustus Straker Bar Assn., 1993, Renowned Jurist award Friends of African Art, 1993, Brotherhood award Jewish War Vets. U.S., 1994, Paul R. Dean award Georgetown U. Law Sch., 1997; named Boss of Yr., Oakland County Legal Secs. Assn., 1974, one of Mich. Most Respected Judges, Mich. Law Weekly, 1990-91; named one of the Best Judges, Detroit Monthly, 1991; named Disting. Citizen of Yr., NAACP Oakland County, Mich., 1970. Fellow Am. Bar Found., Mich. Bar Found. (vice-chmn. 1992-93, chmn. 1993—); mem. NAACP (mem. state constl. revision and legal redress com. 1963, Disting. Citizen of Yr. 1970, Presdl. award North Oakland County, Mich. chpt. 1987), ABA, Fed. Bar Assn. (fed.-state ct. seminar lectr. Detroit chpt. 1981—), Mich. Bar Assn. (chmn. constl. law com. 1969, vice-chmn. civil liberties com. 1970, co-chmn. profl. devel. task force 1984-87, U.S. cts. com. 1988-95, com. on professionalism 1991—, Champion of Justice 1994), Mich. Tribunal Assn. (bd. dirs. 3rd cir. 1992-98), Detroit Bar Assn. (Bench-Bar award 1987), Oakland County Bar Assn. (chmn. continuing legal edn. com. 1968-69, jud. liaison Dist. Ct. com. 1977, unauthorized practice law com. 1977), Wolverine Bar Assn. (Bench-Bar award 1987, D. Augustus Straker award 1988), Mich. Assn. Black Judges, Am. Inn of Ct. (founder Met. Detroit chpt., pres., master of bench, chmn. 6th cir. com. on standard jury instructions 1986—), Am. Law Inst., Union Black Episcopalians (Detroit chpt., Absalom Jones award 1988), Justice Frank Murphy Honor Soc.

COOK, LEWIS ANDERSON, physician, anthropologist; b. Beckley, W.Va., June 22, 1942; s. Wilson and Anne (Legato) C.; m. Vicki Miles, May 23, 1966; children: Wilson, Tiffany Anne. BA, W.Va. U., 1968, MD, 1973; MS, U. Coll. London, 1999. Diplomate Am. Bd. Family Practice, Nat. Bd. Med. Examiners. Resident in family practice Med. Coll. Va., Va. Commonwealth U., Richmond, 1973-76; family practice physician Fayetteville, W.Va., 1976-97; clin. asst. prof. W.Va. Sch. Medicine, 1990-99; cons., reviewer W.Va. Med. Inst., 1980-86; chmn. dept. family practice Raleigh Gen. Hosp., 1984-97, pres. bd. trustees, 1988, chief of staff, 1985, 91. Author: History of Fayetteville; contbr. articles to profl. jours. Chmn. pk. bd. City of Fayetteville, W.Va., 1981-84; pres. Keep Am. Beautiful, Fayette County, 1900-98; chmn. Fayetteville Hist. Bd.; chmn. Fayette County Litter Control, 1992-97; physician Fayetteville Sports, 1976-97; mem. W.Va. Gov.'s Adv. Bd. for State Health Policy, 1996; mem. Regional Health Adv. Com. for State of W.Va., 1990-95; mem. Fayette Fine Arts Coun., 1990-97. With U.S. Army, 1962-65. Fellow Am. Acad. Family Practice; mem. W.Va. State Med. Assn., Raleigh County Med. Soc., Fayette County Med. Soc. (pres. 1980), Am. Anthrop. Assn., W.Va. Archaeol. Soc., Soc. Primitive Tech., Early Am. Industries Assn. (bd. dirs. 1995-98), Sci. Instrument Soc. (Eng.), Surveyors Hist. Soc., Med. Collectors Assn., Mid-West Tool Collectors Assn. (v.p. 1994-97), Oughtred Soc., Ohio Tool Collectors Assn., Astron. Soc. of Pacific, Kanawha Valley Astron. Soc., Astron. League, Rotary (W.Va. chpt. pres. 1984). Avocations: woodworking, astronomy, architecture, tennis, golf. E-mail: miles@inetone.net and l.cook@ucl.ac.uk. Home: RR 3 Box 4-a Fayetteville WV 25840-9502 Office: Univ Coll London, 44 Amhurst Rd Flat C, London E8 1JN, England

COOK, MARY GOOCH, elementary school educator; b. Columbus, Ga., May 1, 1943; d. Joe Lee and Ella Mae (Crimes) Gooch; m. Robert James Cook Sr.; children: Robert James Jr., Kevin Scott. BS, Ala. State Coll., 1965, M in Edn., reading spl., 1973; cert. in elem. edn., Tuskegee U., summer 1968; cert. reading specialist, Ga. State U., 1973; cert. edn. specialist, Troy State U., 1991. Cert. tchr., Ga. Tchr. Fox Elem. Sch., Columbus, Ga., 1973-94, Gentian Elem. Sch., Columbus, Ga., 1994—. Arbitrator BBB, Columbus, 1989-95; cmty. leader tchr. Combined Cmty. South Columbus, 1988-91; mem. voter registration com. Bd. Registration, Columbus, 1990-95; mem. support youth activities com. Columbus Cmty. Ctr., 1994. Mem. AAUW, Nat. Coun. Tchrs. Math., Internat. Reading Assn., Muscogee Assn. Educators (faculty rep. Fox Elem. Sch. 1973-94, Gentian Elem. Sch. 1994-96), Sigma Rho Sigma (pres. Montgomery, Ala. chpt. 1964—), Kappa Delta Pi. Home: 4655 Illini Dr Columbus GA 31907-6613 Office: Cusseta Rd Elem Sch 4150 Cusseta Rd Columbus GA 31903-4499

COOK, SISTER M(ARY) MERCEDES, educator, educational administrator; b. Hagerstown, Md., Dec. 18, 1939; d. Garland and Anita Rideoutt (Willis) C. Student, Fordham U.; BA, Ea. Conn. State U., 1974, MS, 1983; grad., Norwich Dicocesan Prins. Acad., Conn., 1991. Joined Sistes of Charity of Our Lady of Mother of the Ch., Roman Cath. Ch.; cert. tchr., Conn. Tchr., prin. St. Joseph Sch., Baltic, Conn., 1959-61; tchr. Sacred Heart Sch., Byram, Conn., 1961-63, Bloomfield, Conn., 1963-66, Taftville, Conn., 1966-67; tchr. Acad. of Holy Family, Baltic, 1967-84; tchr., vice prin. Assumption Sch., Manchester, 1984—; tchr., chair dept. English Acad. of the Holy Family, Baltic, 1990—, vice-prin., guide counselor, 1990—; mem. Project To Increase Mastery Math. and Sci. Mem. ASCD, Nat. Assn. Math., Nat. Coun. Tchrs. English, Math. Assn. Am., Nat. Cath. Ednl. Assn., Conn. Assn. Math. Tchrs. Democrat. Avocations: reading, writing, painting, cooking, interior decorating.

COOK, PAMELA MARGARET, French educator; b. Gateshead, Eng., Apr. 11, 1955; came to U.S., 1983; d. John Andrew and Doreen Cook; m. Philip Edward Mirowski, June 14, 1986; 1 child, Alexander John Daniel Mirowski. BA with honors, U. Nottingham, Eng., 1977; MA, Tufts U, 1985, Yale U., 1991; MPhil, Yale U., 1991, PhD, 1991. Tchr. Sawston Coll., Cambridge, Eng., 1978-83; asst. head dept. Hitchin Sch., Herts, Eng., 1983-85; part-time asst. prof. French St. Mary's Coll., Notre Dame, ind., 1990—. Mem. Hoosier Environ. Coun., Indpls., 1997—; mem. Ind. Opera North. Christine Jankowski fellow, 1984. Mem. MLA. Avocations: singing, flute, piano, theater.

COOK, PAUL FABYAN, chemistry educator; b. Ware, Mass., Aug. 2, 1946; s. Fabyan Henry and Almina Carrie (Dragon) C.; m. Sandra Joanne Urban, May 17, 1969; 1 child, Karen Michelle. BA, Our Lady of the Lake, San Antonio, 1972; PhD, U. Calif., Riverside, 1976. Postdoctoral fellow U. Wis., Madison, 1976-80; asst. prof. biochemistry La. State U. Med. Ctr., New Orleans, 1980-82; asst. prof. Tex. Coll. Osteo. Med., Ft. Worth, 1982-84; assoc. prof. U. North Tex. Health Sci. Ctr., Ft. Worth, 1984-86, prof., 1986-88, prof. and chair dept. microbiology and immunology, 1988-94; Grayce B. Kerr prof. biochemistry, prof. chem./biochem. Okla. U., 1996—; vis. prof. U. Wurzburg, Germany, 1987, 95; mem. adv. bd. Life Sci. Advances, 1986-95; mem. adv. bd. biochemistry study sect. NIH, Bethesda, Md., 1987-92; co-chair Gordon Conf. on Enzymes, Coenzymes and Metabolic Pathways, 1993. Contbr. chpts. to Heavy Atom Isotope Effect in Enzyme-Catalyzed Reactions, 1991, Kinetic and Regulatory Mechanisms from Isotope Effects, 1991, Isotope Effects in Transferase Reactions, 1991, pH Dependence of Isotope Effects, 1991, Isotopes in Organic Chemistry, 1992, Molecular Oncology and Clinical Applications, 1993, Modern Engineering, 1994, Enzymes Dependent on Pyridoxal Phosphate and Other Carbonyl Compounds, 1994, 99, Steenbock Symposium on Enzymatic Mechanisms, 1999, Advances in Enzymology, 2000; editor: Enzyme Mechanism from Isotope Effects, 1991; mem. editl. bd.: Jour. Biol. Chemistry, 1984-90, Jour. Theoretical Biology, 1988-89, Protein and Peptide Letters, 1994—, Biochimica Biophysica Acta, 1997—; contbr. articles to Biochemistry, Jour. Biol. Chemistry, others. With USAF, 1966-70. Recipient Rsch. Career Devel. award NIH, 1983-88; grantee Robert A. Welch Found., 1985-96, NIH, 1981-99, NSF, 1989—, NATO Sci. Affairs, 1990-97; NIH fellow, 1977-79, Alexander von Humboldt rsch. fellow, 1987, 95. Mem. Am. Chem. Soc. (mem. nominating com. 1991-92, sec. 1992-94 divsn. biol. chemistry, councilor 1996-2000), Biophys. Soc., Am. Soc. Biol. Chemists, N.Y. Acad. Scis. Achievements include development of theory on isotope effects applied to enzyme-catalyzed reactions and determination of enzyme mechanisms. Office: Okla U Dept Chemistry/ Biochemistry 620 Parrington Oval Norman OK 73019-3050

COOK, PETER JOHN, geologist, foundation executive; b. Oct. 15, 1938; s. John and Rose (Mitchell) C.; m. Norma Irene Walker, Sept. 16, 1961; children: John Rowan, Julian Peter. BSc with honors, Durham U., U.K., 1961; MSc, Australian Nat. U., 1966; PhD, U. Colo., 1968; DSc, Durham U., 1986. From geologist to sr. geologist Bur. Mineral Resources, Canberra, Australia, 1961-76; sr. rsch. fellow Australian Nat. U., Canberra, Australia, 1976-82; chief scientist to assoc. dir. Bur. Min. Resources, Canberra, 1982-90; dir. British Geol. Survey, Nottingham, U.K., 1990-98; pres. Euro Geo Survey, Brussels, 1994-96; non-exec. dir. Bd. Minerals Industry Rsch. Orgn., 1993-2000; v.p. Global Sedimentary Geology Program, 1996—; exec. dir. Australian Petroleum Coop. Rsch. Ctr., Canberra, 1998—, PJC Internat., 1998—; non-exec. dir. MineXchange, 1999—; pres. Forum European Geol. Surveys, 1996-97; chmn. UNESCO-IOC Ocean Sci. and Resources, 1985—; dir. PJC Internat. Pty. Ltd., 1998—. Author, co-author papers, monographs, books, articles including sci. in a market economy. Decorated Comdr. Brit. Empire for svcs. to sci. and industry, 1996. Fellow Australian Acad. Tech. Sci. and Engring. (chair internat. rels. com. 2000—); mem. Geological Soc. London (Maj. John Coke medal 1997), Australian French Assn. Scientists (chair 2000—), Commonwealth Club. Office: APCRC, GPO Box 463, Canberra ACT 2601, Australia

COOK, ROBIN, author; b. N.Y.C., May 4, 1940; s. Edgar Lee and Audrey (Koons) C.; m. Barbara Ellen Mougin, July 18, 1979. BA, Weslyan U., 1962; MD, Columbia U., 1966. Resident in gen. surgery Queen's Hosp., Honolulu, 1966-68; resident in ophthalmology Mass. Eye and Ear Infirmary, Boston, 1971-75, mem. staff, from 1975; clin. instr. Harvard U. Med. Sch., 1972. Author: The Year of the Intern, 1972, Coma, 1977, Sphinx, 1979, Brain, 1981, Fever, 1982, Godplayer, 1983, Mindbend, 1986, Outbreak, 1987, Mortal Fear, 1988, Mutation, 1989, Harmful Intent, 1990, Vital Signs, 1990, Blindsight, 1991, Terminal, 1992, Fatal Cure, 1994, Acceptable Risk, 1995, Invasion, 1997, Chromosome 6, 1997, Toxin, 1998. Lt. comdr. USN, 1969-71. Avocations: skiing, surfing, painting, cooking. Home: 4601 Gulf Shore Blvd N # P4 Naples FL 34103-2221 Office: care Putnam Pub Berkley Pub Group 200 Madison Ave New York NY 10016-3903

COOK, ROBIN, United Kingdom federal official; b. Feb. 28, 1946; married; two children. Student, U. Edinburgh. Tutor-organizer Workers' Ednl. Assn., 1970-74; councilor Edinburgh Town Coun., 1971-74, chmn. Edinburgh housing com., 1973-74; sec. Edinburgh City Labour Party, 1970-72; elected M.P. for Edinburgh Ctrl., 1974-83, elected M.P. for Livingston, 1983—; sec. state for fgn. and commonwealth affairs London; opposition front bench spokesman on treasury and econ. affairs, 1980-83, European and cmty. affairs, 1983-84, the city, 1986-87; shadow sec. of state for health and social security, 1987-92, trade and industry, 1992-94, fgn. and commonwealth affairs, 1994-97; sec. of state for fgn. and commonwealth affairs, 1997—. Mem. Labour Party. Office: Fgn & Commonwealth Affairs, Downing St, London SW1A 2AL, England*

COOKE, CARLTON LEE, JR., mayor; b. Marion, Ala., July 12, 1944; s. Carlton Lee and Willie (Rinehart) C.; divorced; 1 child, Kimberly Ann. Student, U. Hawaii, 1962-65; BA, La. Tech. U., 1966; postgrad., U. Tex., 1970-72. Mfg. engr. Tex. Instruments, Austin, 1972-75, site personnel mgr., 1975-81, mktg. mgr., 1981-83; pres., CEO Greater Austin C. of C., 1983-87; mayor City of Austin, Austin, 1988—; pres., CEO good2CU.com, Inc., 1999-2000; chmn., CEO Habitek Internat., Inc., 1991—; pres., CEO, U.S. Med. Systems, Inc., 1992—; bd. dirs. Bill Concepts Corp., U.S. Long Distance Corp., Tanisys Tech. Corp., Sharps Compliance, Corp., Med. Polymers Tech., Inc., CUville.com, Inc., FIData.com, Inc.; adv. dir. M2K Corp.; participant U.S. Conf. Mayors, Washington, 1991; mem. Anthony Commn., U.S. Congress. Contbr. editor to mags. Mem. Austin City Coun., 1977-81, mayor pro tem, 1979; co-chmn. Jerry Lewis Telethon, Austin, 1986-87; chmn. United Negro Telethon, 1991, Tex. Housing Fin. Corp., 1992, Austin Charter Com., 1993-94, Tex. Walk of Stars, 1991—. Capt. USAF, 1966-72. Decorated Bronze Star (Vietnam); recipient Carl Burnett Cmty. award, 1981, Disting. Austin Citizen's award, 1992, Excellence award Real Estate Coun. of Austin, 1992; named Jaycee of Yr. Austin Jaycees, 1976, one of Five Outstanding Young Texans Tex. Jaycees, 1979. Mem. Nat. League Cities (chair fin. steering com.), Tex. Mcpl. League (pres. 1991), Austin-San Antonio Corridor Coun. (pres. 1988, 91), VFW. Baptist. Avocations: travel, reading, civic work, movie history, art. E-mail: usmedsys@onr.com. Home: PO Box 50442 Austin TX 78763-0442 Office: Office of Mayor 515 Congress Ave Ste 2520 Austin TX 78701-3509

COOKE, CHANTELLE ANNE, writer; b. Denver, Apr. 9, 1971; d. Frederick Blaize and Claire Gail (Jones) C. Student, Collin County C.C., Plano, Tex., 1989-93. Author: (poetry chapbook) Songs From Stars, 1995, (poetry chapbook) Wild Irises on God's Mountainside, 1999, (poetry cassette tape) Visions, 1997; contbg. editor tech. articles for computer industry, 1994-96; freelance writer articles and poems. Recipient Star of Loyalty, Paralyzed Vets. Am., 1996. Mem. Internat. Soc. Poets, Acad. Am. Poets, Poetry Connection, Magic Cir. Democrat. Roman Catholic. Avocations: mosaic art, home interior decorating, pistol target shooting, needlepoint. Home: 3862 Spring St S Salem OR 97302-6064

COOKE, EVELYN KATHLEEN CHATMAN, retired elementary education educator; b. Jackson, Tenn.; d. Charles Elijah and Josie (Bond) Chatman; m. James T. Cooke, Apr. 21, 1954 (div. Aug. 1970); 1 child, Madelyn LaRene. BA cum laude, Lane Coll., 1955; MEd, Xavier U. Tchr. pub. schs. Chattanooga, 1957-67, Cin., 1967-93; ret., 1993; cons. career edn. Cin. Pub. Schs. Pres., reader, cons. Hymnal Revision com. United Meth. Ch.; chmn. com. on edn. Gaines United Meth. Ch., chair commn. on religion and race, coord. global concerns, chair spiritual growth, chair ecumenical action, program Beatrice Rowe subgroup, life mem. United Meth. Women; chair Christian global concerns, nat. Top Ladies of Distinction, Inc., program designer; mem. upper grade sch. study coun.; bd. dirs. Wesley Child Care Ctr.; mem. program com. Dist. Ethnic Minority Laity Coun.; organizer, founder Young Adult ensemble; mem. Beyer Music Soc.; chair Commn. Religion and Race; ch. sch. leader, cert. lay spkr. United Meth. Ch.; mem. Cin. Dist. Social Witness Ministry United Meth. Ch. Recipient Spirit of Detroit award, 1981, Outstanding Educator award Phi Delta Kappa, Outstanding Contbns. to the City, Chattanooga, 1989, City of Springdale, Ohio citation, 45th Dist. Ohio Ho. of Reps. citation, 25th Dist. Ho. of Reps. citation, 85th Dist. Mich. Ho. of Reps. citation, Mayor of Toledo citation, 1991, Lucas County Commrs. citation, 1991. Mem. NAACP (life), Fellowship United Methodists in Music, Worship and the Arts, Coun. Co-Op Action, Am. Fedn. Tchrs., Ohio Fedn. Tchrs., Cin. Coun. Educators, Nat. Coun. Negro Women (life), Nat. Caucus Black Aging (life), Top Ladies of Distinction, Inc. (life, outstanding svc. award 1981, nat. chair 1987—, nat. 2d v.p. chmn. info. com., pres. Cin. chpt., chair adv. com. nat. membership chair, contbr. Protocol Primer, Outstanding Svc. award Area V 1993, Spl. Tribute award Cin. chpt., Nat. pres.'s citation 1995, cert. of merit), AARP, Ohio Ret. Tchrs. Assn. (life), Hamilton County Ret. Tchrs. Assn. (life), Status of Women (nat. chair 1987-89, area V dir. 1989-93), Black Meths. for Ch. Renewal, West Ohio Conf. Commn. Christian Unity and Interreligious Concerns, Sigma Gamma Rho (life, nat. constn. and by-laws com., antibasileus Epsilon Lambda Sigma chpt., contbr. pearls of Protocol, Spl. Tribute award), Gamma Theta Sigma, Sigma Rho Sigma. Methodist (dir. music ch., chair com. on worship). Home: 6748 Elwynne Dr Cincinnati OH 45236-4022

COOKE, FRED CHARLES, real estate broker; b. Winchester, Tenn., Dec. 3, 1915; s. Warner Cleveland and Emma (Lancaster) C.; m. Pamela Burr, Dec. 27, 1942; children: Gary Donald, David Charles, Pamela Ann, Alexander Campbell. AB, Lincoln Meml. U., 1939; grad., Realtor's Inst., 1988. Commd. USAF, 1942, advanced through ranks to lt. col.; project officer, R & D engr. specialist USAF, Eglin AFB, Fla., 1951-53; resigned USAF, 1953; realtor Ft. Walton Beach, Fla., 1956—. With USAF Res. Decorated DFC, Air medal with oak leaf cluster; inducted into Alumni Athletic Hall of Fame, 1987. Mem. Ft. Walton Beach Bd. Realtors (pres. 1959-60, 65), Fla. Assn. Realtors (dist. v.p. 1965, pres. Diamond Pin Club 1988), Nat. Assn. Realtors (bd. dirs. 1983-86, realtor emeritus 1993), Fla. Real Estate Exchangors (founder 1972), Greater Ft. Walton Beach C. of C. (chmn. waterways and reefs com. 1983-87, Award of Excellence), Fla. Waterways Adv. Bd., Ft. Walton Yacht Club (vice commodore 1984, commodore 1989, dir. 1990-95), Ft. Walton Power Squadron (commdr. 1972-73), Civitan (pres. 1961-62, dist. v.p. Birmingham 1963), Emerald Coast Sailing Assn. (founder 1992). Republican. Episcopalian. Home: 227 Alconese Ave SE Unit F Fort Walton Beach FL 32548-2803 Office: 79 Beal Pky NE Fort Walton Beach FL 32548-4822

COOKE, SIR HOWARD, Jamaican government official; b. Goodwill, St. James, Jamaica, Nov. 13, 1915; s. David Brown Cooke and Mary Jane Minto; m. Ivy Sylvia Lucille Tai, July 22, 1939; children: Howard Fits-Arthur, Richard Washington McDermott, Audrey Faith. Cert. in teaching, Mico Coll. Tchr. Mico Tng. Coll., 1936-38; headmaster Belle Castle All Age Sch., Port Antonio Upper Sch., Montego Bay Boys' Sch., 1952-58; br. mgr. Standard Life Ins. Co., 1960-71; mem. West Indies Fed. Parliament, 1958-62; unit mgr. Jamaica Mut. Life Assurance Soc., 1971-81; br. mgr. Alico Jamica, 1982-91; min. of govt. Jamaica, Kingston, 1972-80; pres. of senate Jamaica, 1989-91; gov. gen. Jamaica, Kingston, 1991—. Former chmn. People's Nat. Party; sr. elder, lay pastor United Ch. Jamaica and Grand Cayman. Decorated Knight Grand Cross of the Most Disting. Order of St. Michael and St. George, Queen of Eng., 1991, Knight Grand Cross of Royal Victorian Order, 1994. Mem. Masons. Mem. United Ch. Jamaica & Grand Cayman. Avocations: football, cricket, gardening, reading. Home: 20 Peter Pan Ave, Montego Bay Saint James, Jamaica Office: Office of Gov Gen, King's House Hope Rd, Kingston 10, Jamaica*

COOKE, IAN DOUGLAS, obstetrics and gynecology educator, researcher; b. Sydney, Australia, Mar. 19, 1935; arrived in Eng., 1962; s. Douglas and Mary (Pickles) C.; m. Sheila Margaret Middleton, May 15, 1965; children: Jennifer Alison, David George. MB, BS, Sydney U., 1958, D Gynecology and Obstetrics, 1962. Jr. med. tng. Royal Prince Alfred Hosp., King George V Meml. Hosp., Sydney, 1958-62; MacIlrath vis. prof. Royal Prince Alfred Hosp., Sydney, 1995; rsch. fellow obstet. medicine rsch. unit Aberdeen, Scotland, 1963-65; Wellcome travelling fellow Hormone Inst., Karolinska Hosp., Stockholm, 1965-66; NIH rsch. fellow dept. reproductive biology Case Western Res. U., Cleve., 1966-68; sr. lectr. ob-gyn Welsh Nat. Sch. Medicine, Cardiff, 1968-72; prof. U. Sheffield, Eng., 1972-2000; mem. Human Fertilisation and Embryology Authority, London, 1991-95. Co-editor: Donor Insemination, 1993; contbr. articles on fertility and sterility and human reprodn. to sci. jours. Grantee Harris Trust (Birthright), 1986. Fellow Royal Coll. Obstetricians and Gynaecologists (coun. 1980-92, Sims Black vis. prof. West Africa 1996, Simpson orator 1998); mem. Brit. Fertility Soc. (coun. 1991—, chmn. 1996-99), Soc. for Study Fertility, Endocrine Soc., Brit. Med. Assn. Mem. United Reform Ch. Avocations: reading, skiing, music. Office: Jessop Hosp for Women Univ Dept, Leavygreave Rd, Sheffield S3 7RE, England

COOKE, JOHN P., judge; b. 1944. Bar: Ireland. Pvt. practice specializing and European Cmty., internat. law; judge Ct. of First Instance of European Communities, Luxembourg, 1996—; advocate in cases before Ct. of Justice of European Communities, Commn. and Ct. of Human Rights of Coun. of Europe. Mem. Coun. of Bars and Law Socs. of European Cmty. (pres. 1985-86). Office: Ct of First Instance EC, Blvd Konrad Adenauer, L-2925 Luxembourg Luxembourg*

COOKE, KEVIN GEORGE, lawyer, consultant, executive; b. Melbourne, Victoria, Australia, Apr. 21, 1931; s. George Joseph and Honor Beatrice (Henwood) C.; m. Anne Leonore Young, Mar. 4, 1978. LLB, Melbourne U., Australia, 1953. Cert. Barrister, Solicitor. Ptnr. Cooke & Cussen Solicitors, Melbourne, Australia, 1953-75, sr. ptnr., 1975-86, sr. cons., 1986-91; dir. various real estate devel., banking and trade cos. U.S., Eng., France, Portugal, 1965-91; dir., cons. various real estate devel, investment, and trade cos. Australia, 1991—; sr. advisor Beihai govt., China, 1994—; mem. internat. rels. adv. com. Gold Coast City Coun., 1997—. Chmn. Corps of Commissionaires, Brisbane, 1992—; chmn., trustee Totally & Permanently Disabled Soldiers Assn., Melbourne, 1986-97; trustee Royal Australian Inf. Mus., Singleton, 1988-98, Limbless Soldiers Assn., Melbourne, 1980-96; pres. Royal United Svc. Inst., Queensland, 1998—. Maj. Gen. Chief of Army Res., 1985-88, Canberra. Decorated Mil. Officer of the Order of Australia, Mil. Efficiency Decoration, Reserve Force Decoration. Fellow Australian Inst. Co. Dirs., Soc. Sr. Execs.; mem. Internat. Bar Assn., Law Inst. Victoria, Chinese Australian C. of C. (mgmt. com. 1998—). Avocations: sailing, tennis, military history. Home: 47 Admiralty Dr, Paradise Waters QLD 4217, Australia

COOKE, LOUISE RENE, plant pathologist, educator; b. Carshalton, Surrey, Eng., Aug. 20, 1953; d. Lewis Butler and Doris Rene (Coles) C. BSc in Biochemistry, U. Bristol, Eng., 1974, PhD, 1978. Rsch. asst. Long Ashton Rsch. Sta., Bristol, 1978-80; plant pathologist Dept. Agr. for No. Ireland, Belfast, 1981—; lectr. Queen's U. Belfast, 1987—. Editor, author: Phytophthora infestans, 1995; contbr. articles to sci. jours., including Potato Rsch., Plant Pathology, Crop Protection, Pesticide Sci., Annals Applied Biology; patentee in field. Grantee U.K. Home-Grown Cereals Authority, 1998—, 2000—. Mem. Soc. Irish Plant Pathologists (pres. 2000—), Brit. Soc. for Plant Pathology, European Assn. Potato Rsch., Assn. Applied Biologists. Avocations: singing with university choir, attending concerts and theatre. Office: Dept Agr and Rural Devel, App Pl Sci Div, Newforge Ln, Belfast BT9 5PX, Northern Ireland

COOKE, PHILIP HOWARD, television director, producer; b. Charlotte, N.C., Aug. 31, 1954; s. Bill Howard and Thelma (Blackwelder) C.; m. Kathleen Rene Paille, Mar. 22, 1977; children: Kelsey Taylor, Bailey Christine. BA, Oral Roberts U., 1976; MA in Journalism, U. Okla., 1986. Dir. Oral Roberts TV, Tulsa, 1978-90; exec. prodr. Phil Cooke Pictures, Inc., Burbank, Calif., 1990—; cons. various TV prodn. facilities, 1983—. Producer, dir. numerous TV programs. Recipient Addy award Am. Advt. Fedn., 1981, 82, 83, Angel awards Religion in the Media, Los Angeles, 1985, 86, 96, 97, 98, 99, 2000, 3 awards Okla. Film Festival award 1982, Videography award, 1998, Covenant award, 1997, 98, Crystal Comm. award, 2000. Mem. Acad. TV Arts and Scis., Am. Film Inst., Nat. Religious Broadcasters (bd. dirs.). Republican. Office: Phil Cooke Pictures Inc PO Box 1515 Burbank CA 91507-1515

COOKE, R(ICHARD) CASWELL, JR., architect; b. Richmond, Va., Dec. 19, 1935; s. Richard Caswell and Caroline (Kellock) C.; m. Mary Gibson, June 6, 1962; children: Richard, Frederick, Gordon, Molly. BArch, U. Va., 1962; MArch, Yale U., 1967. Registered architect, Mass., Conn., Va., N.C., S.C., Ill., N.J., Pa., N.S., Colo., R.I. Project mgr. Clinch Crimp Brown & Fischer, Boston, 1962-64, Paul Rudolph Architect, New Haven, 1964-65; prin., dir. Geotactics, Inc., New Haven, 1965-82; gen. mgr. Gulf Consult Architects, Al Khobar, Saudi Arabia, 1982-86; prin. Fellows, Read, Leoncavallo & Cooke, Princeton, N.J., 1986-89; v.p., dir. arch. Washington Group (formerly Raytheon Engrs. & Constructors), Phila. and London, 1989—; pres. Washington Architects LLC (formerly Raytheon Architects), Princeton, Phila., London; lectr. Quinnipiac Coll., New Haven, St. Paul's Ch., Kiwanis Club; juried design Yale U. Prin. works include design of Petromin Corp. Bldg., Riyadh, Saudi Arabia, Baxter Health Care Facility, Calif., Roche Carolina Campus, S.C., Can. Red Cross Facility, N.S., Derby (Conn.) Elderly Housing, The Mus. at Fort Bliss, El Paso, Tex. Chmn. New Haven Harbor Commn., 1976, Conn. Regional Planning Com., 1976; bd. dirs. Am. Businessmen's assn., Saudi Arabia, 1986; pres. Yale Alumni Assn. Sch. Architecture, 1978; past bd. dirs. Conn. Soc. Architects. Recipient Christchurch Sch. Alumni award, 1975, first design award Milford Yacht Club, 1977, Alpha Rho Chi award U. Va., 1962. Mem. AIA, N.J. Soc. Archs., Nat. Coun. Archtl. Registration Bds., Assn. of Yale Alumni, Yale Club of Princeton (past pres.), Constrn. Specification Inst., Illuminating Engrs. Soc., Am. Soc. Landscape Archs., Sons of the Revolution (N.J. bd. dirs.), Henry Found. for Bot. Rsch. Episcopalian. Office: Washington Architects LLC 510 Carnegie Ctr Princeton NJ 08540-6241

COOKE, ROBIN BRUNSKILL (LORD COOKE OF THORNDON), judge; b. Wellington, New Zealand, May 9, 1926; s. Philip Brunskill and Valmai Digby (Gore) C.; m. Phyllis Annette Miller, 1952; 3 children. LLM with honors, Victoria U., Wellington, 1949, LLD (hon.), 1989; LLD (hon.), U. Cambridge, 1990; MA, PhD, Gonville & Caius Coll., Cambridge, Eng., 1954; DCL (hon.), U. Oxford, 1991. Barrister Wellington, 1955-72, queen's counsel, 1964; judge New Zealand Supreme Ct., Wellington, 1972-76, New Zealand Ct. of Appeal, 1976-86; pres., 1986-96; mem. House of Lords, Eng., 1996—; mem. adv. bd. Justice All-Souls Rev. of Adminstrv. Law, U.K., 1979-88; vis. fellow All Souls Coll., Oxford, 1990, disting. vis. fellow Victoria

U. Wellington, 1996—; pres. Ct. Appeal Western Samoa, 1982, 94—, Cook Islands, 1981, 82; judge Supreme Ct. Fiji, 1995—, overseas judge Hong Kong Ct. of Final Appeal, 1997—. Editor: Portrait of a Profession Centennial Book of N.Z. Law Soc.; editor-in-chief The Laws of New Zealand; contbr. articles to profl. jours. Chmn. Commn. of Inquiry into Housing, 1970-71. Decorated Knight Bachelor, 1977, Knight of Brit. Empire, 1986; Caius Coll. Hon. fellow, 1982; named Privy counsellor, 1977. Mem. Internat. Commn. of Jurists (commn. mem.), Am. Law Inst., Law Asia (life), Inner Temple (hon. bencher 1985—), Wellington Club, Oxford & Cambridge U. Club. Mem. Ch. Eng. Avocation: theatre, cricket. Home: 4 Homewood Crescent, Wellington New Zealand Office: PO Box 1530, Wellington New Zealand also: House of Lords, London SW1A 0PW, England

COOKE, STEVEN JOHN, chemical engineer, consultant, scientist; b. Grand Rapids, Mich., Oct. 1, 1954; s. Edward G. and Annette M. (Minnema) C.; m. Marguerite K. Oldenburger, June 18, 1977; children: Allison, Jonathan. BS in Chemistry, Calvin Coll., 1977; M in Chem. Engring., Ill. Inst. Tech., 1987; postgrad. in Engring., Calif. Coast U. Registered profl. engr., Ill.; cert. profl. chemist, quality engr., quality auditor. Chemist, lab. supr. Matheson Gas Products, Joliet, Ill., 1977-80; chief chemist Cardox, Countryside, Ill., 1980-85; scientist Am. Air Liquide, Countryside, 1985-92; asst. quality mgr. Alphagaz Divsn. of Liquid Air, Countryside, 1992-93; quality assurance/quality control mgr. Am. Air Liquide, Countryside, 1993-95; quality mgr. Carbonic Industries Corp., 1995-98, Airgas Carbonic, Duluth, Ga., 1998—. Contbr. articles on quality systems to profl. jours. Group leader Hazardous Materials Emergency Response Team; treas. Christian Reformed Ch. Mission, Western Springs, Ill., 1982-93, Chicagoland Diaconal Task Force Bd., Palos Heights, Ill., 1989-92. Fellow Am. Inst. Chemists; mem. Am. Soc. Quality Control, Am. Chem. Soc. (publicity chair I&EC divsn. 1989-95, chair I&EC divsn. 1999—), Compressed Gas Assn. (CO2 task force, gas specifications com.). Achievements include patent for portable gas analyzer.

COOKSEY, RAY WAGNER, human resource management educator; b. Hamilton AFB, Calif., Aug. 30, 1954; arrived in Australia, 1982; s. James Wagner Cooksey and Jean Elizabeth (Blowers) Barrows; m. Christie Anne Christopher, Dec. 19, 1976; children: Sarah Anne, Aaron James. BSc, Colo. State Univ., 1976, MSc, 1978, PhD, 1981. Engring. psychologist Bendix Corp., Denver, 1981-82; lectr. in edn. Univ. New England, Armidale NSW, Australia, 1982-90, sr. lectr. in psychology, 1990-94, assoc. prof., 1994-99; prof. Univ. New England, Armidale NSW, 2000—; statistical cons. U.S. Dept. Agriculture, Ft. Collins, Colo., 1977-81; external assessor Australian Rsch. Coun., 1993—; editorial bd. mem. Jour. of Behavioral Decision Making, 1997—. Author: Judgment Analysis: Theory, Methods & Applications, 1996; contbr. articles to profl. jours. V.p., federal state councillor UNE Tchr.'s Assn., Australia, 1986-88. Recipient Vice-Chancellor's award for Teaching Excellence, Univ. New Eng., 1995. Mem. The Brunswik Soc., System Dynamics Soc., Soc. Judgment and Decision Making, Australian and New Zealand Acad. Mgmt., Phi Beta Kappa. Avocations: reading science fiction, ten pin bowling, astronomy, fractal mathematics. Office: Univ New Eng, Sch Mktg & Mgmt, 2351 Armidale Australia

COOKSLEY, WILLIAM GRAHAM EARNSHAW, liver disease physician, educator, researcher; b. Brisbane, Australia, May 30, 1940; s. Leslie Graham and Marjorie (Earnshaw) C.; m. Enid Vivienne Tindale, Mar. 28, 1964; children: Graham Andrew, Anna Katrina. MBBS, Queensland U., Brisbane, 1963, MD, 1978. Fellow Royal Australasian Coll. Physicians, 1974. Med. officer Royal Brisbane Hosp., 1964-70; med. postgrad. rsch. scholar U. Queensland, 1971-72; vis. rsch. fellow (Nuffield) Clin. Rsch. Ctr., Harrow, Eng., 1973-74; asst. prof. medicine U. Queensland, 1975-79; vis. scientist NIH, Bethesda, Md., 1981; assoc. prof. medicine U. Queensland, 1979-88; dir. Royal Brisbane Hosp. Found., 1988-98; cons. Govt. Queensland, 1982-97, Govt. Australia, 1994, prof. biochemistry U. Queensland, 1988-98; mem. regional grants com. Nat. Health and Med. Rsch. Coun., Australia, 1988-97; convenor 3d Internat. Meeting on Hepatitis C and Related Viruses, 5th Internat. Meeting on Hepatitis D Virus, 1995, 7th Internat. Meeting on Hepatitis C and Related Viruses, 2000; invited lectr. internat. meetings Chgo, London, Madrid, India, Hong Kong, Indonesia, Thailand. Contbr. over 150 articles to med. and scientific jours.; mem. editl. bd. Jour. Viral Hepatitis, Jour. Hepatology, Jour. Gastroenterology and Hepatology. Cons. internat. devel. program, Indonesia, 1982-86; chmn. steering com. control of infectious diseases in southeast Asia, 1995-2000; mem. Pan-Pacific Working Party on Control of Hepatitis B, South Pacific, 1985-87; mem. Australian Viral Hepatitis Prevention Bd., 1995-2000. Recipient postgrad. rsch. scholarship Nat. Health and Med. Rsch. Coun. Australia, 1971, program grant, 1982-97, traveling fellowship Nuffield Found., 1973. Mem. Am. Assn. Study Liver Disease, Internat. Assn. Study of Liver, Asian-Pacific Assn. Study of Liver (hon. sec. 1982-86), European Assn. Study of Liver. Avocations: antiques, horticulture, Victorian literature, classical history. Home: 13 Sefton Rd, Clayfield QLD 4011, Australia Office: Royal Brisbane Hospital, Brisbane QLD 4027, Australia

COOLEY, ANDREW LYMAN, corporation executive, former army officer; b. St. Louis, Oct. 14, 1934; s. Andrew L. and Algretta R. (Carr) C.; m. Joan Lynn Wheatley, Jan. 9, 1958; children: Cathleen Wheatley, Caroline Carr. BA, George Washington U., 1964, MA, 1967; MS, U.S. Army Command and Gen. Staff Coll., 1966; postgrad., U.S. Army War Coll., 1972-73. Commd. 2d lt. U.S. Army, 1955; advanced through grades to maj. gen. U.S. Army, Continental U.S. and Hawaii, 1955-64; bn. adv. Vietnam, 1964-65; aide to chief of staff SHAPE, Belgium, 1967-69; tank bn. comdr. Germany, 1969-70; mem. staff Dept. of Army Pentagon, 1970-72; brigade comdr. and div. chief of staff Korea, 1975-77; exec. to comdr. in chief Pacific Hawaii, 1978-79; asst. div. comdr. 101st Airborne Div., 1979-81; asst. dep. dir. for politico-mil. affairs, plans and policy directorate Joint Chiefs of Staff, Washington, 1981-83; mil. adviser Habib-Draper Mission, Lebanon, 1982-83; dir. strategy, plans and policy Dept. Army, Washington, 1983-85; comdg. gen. 24th Inf. Div. (Mech.) and Fort Stewart, Hunter Army Air Field, Fort Stewart, Ga., 1985-87; chief Office Military Cooperation, Cairo, 1987-89; ret., 1989; program mgr. Vinnell Brown Root, Turkey Base Maintenance Agreement, 1989-91; project mgr. ops. and maintenance Brown and Root Svcs. Corp., Houston, 1991-94; program mgr. Project Restore Hope Somalia, 1993; ind. cons. with expertise in Africa, Croatia, Bosnia and Haiti, 1994-97; dir. ops. Dyncorp Internat. Tech. Svcs., 1998—. Author: Diplomatic Significances of the Great White Fleet, 1966, Realistic Deterrence in NATO, 1973. Decorated Def. D.S.M. with oak leaf cluster, Legion of Merit with oak leaf cluster, Bronze Star, Air medal, others; Fed. Exec. fellow Brookings Instn., 1977-78; named to Officer Candidate Sch. Hall of Fame, 1979. Mem. Assn. U.S. Army, Armor Assn. Episcopalian. Home: 17202 De Chirico Cir Spring TX 77379-6269

COOLEY, FANNIE RICHARDSON, emeritus educator, consultant; b. Tunnel Springs, Ala., July 4, 1924; d. Willie C. Richardson and Emma Jean (McCorvey) Stallworth. BS, Tuskegee (Ala.) Inst., 1947, MS, 1951; PhD, U. Wis., 1969. Cert. counselor. Asst. inst. Tuskegee Inst., 1947-48, prof. counseling, 1969-2000, prof. emeritus, 2000—; instr. Alcorn A&M Coll., Lorman, Miss., 1948-51; asst. prof. Ala. A&M Coll., Normal, 1951-62, assoc. prof., 1964-65; grad. fellow Purdue U., West Lafayette, Ind., 1962-64; house fellow U. Wis., Madison, 1965-69; cons. VA Med. Ctr. Tuskegee, 1969—. Mem. AAUW, AAUP, ASCD (bd. dirs., Disting. Svc. award 1985), Ala. Assn. Counseling and Devel. (pres. 1976-77, Svc. award 1978-79), Ala. Assn. for Counselor Edn. (pres. 1985-86), Aassn. Specialists in Group Work (pres. 1989-90, Career award 1998), Internat. Platford Assn., Chi Sigma Iota. Episcopalian. Home: 802-C Avenue A Tuskegee Institute AL 36088-2402 Office: Tuskegee Inst Dept Counseling and Student Devel Thrasher Hall Tuskegee Institute AL 36088

COOLEY, JOHN KENT, journalist, author; b. N.Y.C., Nov. 25, 1927; arrived in Greece, 1999; s. John Landon and Ruth (Robinson) C.; m. Edith Stoegermayer, Mar. 21, 1951 (div. 1970; 1 child, Katherine Anne; m. Eugenia Katelani, May 22, 1970; 1 child, Alexander Anthony. BA, Dartmouth Coll., 1952; postgrad., U. Vienna, 1953, Columbia U., 1965. Editorial rschr. U.S. High Commn., Vienna, 1950-51, 52-53; freelance reporter Paris edit. N.Y. Herald Tribune, Morocco, 1953-55; translator, press attache U.S. Army C.E., Casablanca, Morocco, 1955-57; freelance journalist Christian Sci. Monitor, NBC News, others, Algeria, Tunisia, Libya, 1957-64; Middle East corr. Christian Sci. Monitor, Beirut, 1965-78; def. corr. Christian Sci. Monitor, Washington, 1978-80; corr., Middle East specialist ABC News, London, 1981-91, Nicosia, Cyprus, 1991-98; occasional lecturing in U.S. and abroad, 1967—. Author: Baal, Christ and Mohammed, 1965, East Wind Over Africa, 1966, Green March, Black September, 1973, Libyan Sandstorm, 1981, Payback, 1991, Unholy Wars, 1999, rev. edit., 2000; also numerous mag. and jour. articles, ency. articles on Middle East. Served with Signal Corps, U.S. Army, 1946-47, Austria. Recipient Overseas Press Club citations, 1967, 69, 74, 82, George Polk Career award L.I. U., 1995; Fgn. Corr. fellow Coun. on Fgn. Rels., N.Y.C., 1964-65; Carnegie Endowment for Internat. Peace sr. assoc., 1980-81. Mem. Internat. Inst. for Strategic Studies, Royal Inst. Internat. Affairs (assoc.), Phi Beta Kappa. Avocations: swimming, reading, listening to classical music, short wave radio. Home and Office: 3 Korai St, Kifissia 14561, Greece

COOLEY, REGINA KAE, educational administrator; b. Dalhart, Tex., July 29, 1956; d. James Lee and Virginia Lee (Cagle) Ferguson; m. Danny Ray Cooley, Oct. 18, 1975; children: Keenan DeWaine, Kyle Lee. Grad. high sch., Dalhart; grad. tchr. aid, Internat. Corr. Schs., 1995. Tchr. aide Dalhart Elem. Sch., 1988-90; libr. aide, hearing, vision and spinal screener Hartley (Tex.) Sch., 1990—; saleswoman Alco Dept. Store, Dalhart, 1989; mgr. Photo Kwick, Dalhart, 1990. Vol. Phandle Cmty. Svcs. Avocations: reading, making jewelry, needlepoint. E-mail: kae.cooley@pintz.net. Office: Hartley Sch PO Box 56 Hartley TX 79044-0108

COOLEY, ROBERT EARL, religion and archaeology educator; b. Kalamazoo, Sept. 12, 1930; m. Eileen H. Carlson; children: Robert Carl, Gerald Earl. BA in Bibl. Studies and Archaeology, Wheaton Coll., 1955, MA in Religious Edn., 1957; PhD in Hebrew Studies and Near Ea. Archaeology, NYU, 1968. Grad. asst. in archaeology Wheaton (Ill.) Coll., 1955-57, dir. archaeol. studies, asst. prof. archaeology, 1965-68; dean of men Cen. Bible Coll., Springfield, Mo., 1957-59, dean of students, 1959-64, acad. dean, 1964-65; asst. prof. Bilbe and archaeology Wheaton (Ill.) Coll., 1965-68; dir. religious activities NYU, 1962-63; asst. to pres. Dropsie U., Phila., 1967-68; assoc. prof. Evangel Coll., Springfield, 1968-70, dean of coll., 1970-73; vis. prof. Drury Grad. Sch., Springfield, 1971-73; prof. anthropology and religious studies, dir. Ctr. for Archaeol. Rsch. S.W. Mo. State U., Springfield, 1973-81; pres., prof. Bibl. studies and archaeology Gordon-Conwell Theol. Sem., South Hamilton, Mass., 1981-97, chancellor, 1997—; area supr., architect Dothan Archaeol. Expdn., Israel, 1959, 60, 64; mem. staff Oyster Bay Site 7, N.Y., 1963; site supr. joint expdn. to Ai, Khirbet Haiyan and Khirbet Raddana, Israel, 1969; field dir. expdn., Raddana, Israel, 1970, 72, 74; dir. field schs. various sites, Mo., 1971-81; with Phase I surveys, 1974-81; field archaeologist Tell Retaba Expdn., Arab Republic of Egypt, 1977-78; dir. publs. project Dothan II, 1978—; field dir., prin. investigator Smith Cabin site, Mo., 1979; lectr. various profl. confs., Brazil, Belgium, Israel, Portugal, Korea, 1972-88. Asst. issue editor spl. edit. Jour. Ednl. Sociology, 1963; sr. editor Christianity Today, 1990-92; contbr. articles to profl. jours.; creator concept film, 1968. Bd. dirs. Hist. Site Bd., City of Springfield, 1970-78, chmn., 1974-78; bd. dirs. Mo. Heritage Trust, 1977-81, Appalachian Ministries Edn. Resource Ctr., 1985—, World Relief, Wheaton, Ill., 1985-94; mem. Gov.'s Adv. Coun. on Hist. Preservation, State of Mo., 1977-81, interfaith adv. coun. Harvard Semitic Mus., Harvard U., 1985—; mem. planning bd. Bicentennial Commn.; corporator Beverly (Mass.) Hosp., 1985—. Founder's Day award NYU, 1969. Mem. Am. Schs. Oriental Rsch. (trustee 1978-80), Archaeol. Inst. Am., Evang. Theol. Soc. (pres. 1970), Near East Archaeol. Soc. (v.p. 1972-78), Soc. Bibl. Lit., Nat. Assn. Profs. Hebrew (treas. 1968-73), Am. Anthrop. Assn., Soc. Am. Archaeology, Soc. Profl. Archaeologists, Assn. Field Archaeology, Israel Exploration Soc., Mo. Archaeol. Soc. (site preservation bd. 1975-81, pres. Ozarks chpt. 1969-75), Mo. Assn. Profl. Archaeologists (v.p. 1978-79, pres. 1980-81), Assn. Theol. Schs. (sec. 1986-88, pres. 1991-94), Nat. Assn. Evangs. (bd. adminstrn. 1982—), World Relief (pres. 1990-94), Rotary (program com. Springfield 1970-81). Avocations: fishing, golf, photography, outdoor activities. Home: 1408 Ferncroft Towers Danvers MA 01923-4058*

COOLEY, WILLIAM CROCKETT, mechanical engineer, retired educator; b. Lakeland, Fla., Dec. 19, 1924; s. Sumner Dewey Cooley and Kate Lilah Crockett; m. Anne Waterman, June 4, 1949 (div.); children: Jean, Brian, Stuart, Laura. ME, MIT, 1944, ScD, 1951; MS in Aeronautics, Calif. Inst. Tech., 1947. Student engr. on nuclear propulsion Fairchild project Nuclear Energy for Propulsion of Aircraft, Oak Ridge, Tenn., summer 1947; staff engr. Lexington project MIT, summer 1948; rsch. engr. N.Am. Aviation, L.A., 1951-53, 58-61; nuc. propulsion engr. GE, ANPD, Cin., 1953-58; chief space propulsion and aux. power program NASA, Washington, 1961-63; v.p., tech. dir. Exotech, Inc., Alexandria, Va., 1963-68; pres. Terraspace Inc., Rockville, Md., 1968-84; assoc. prof. engring. George Mason U., Fairfax, Va., 1985-91, ret., 1991. Patentee water jet tech.; contbr. articles to rsch. publs. Lt. USNR, 1952-61. Recipient Pioneer award U.S. Nat. Water Jet Conf., Pitts., 1985. Mem. ASME (life), Water Jet Tech. Assn. (opening lectr. 5th Pacific Rim Internat. conf. 1998). Democrat. Unitarian. Avocations: swimming, skiing, ballroom dancing, writing poetry, tutoring. Home: 10604 Kitty Pozer Dr Apt A Fairfax VA 22030-4261

COOLEY, WILLIAM EMORY, JR., radiologist; b. Charlottesville, Va., Jan. 28, 1941; s. William Emory Sr. and Madelle Elizabeth (Fullen) C.; m. Janella Mahoney Haney, Dec. 26, 1966; children: Angela Janette, William Emory, James Haney. BA, Emory U., 1963; MD, U. Va., 1967. Diplomate Am. Bd. Radiology. Rotating intern. U.S. Naval Hosp., Phila., 1967-68; resident radiology U.S. Naval Regional Med. Ctr., Phila., 1972-75; radiologist U.S. Naval Regional Med. Ctr., Portsmouth, Va., 1975-76, asst. chief radiology, 1976-77; radiologist Bloomington (Ill.) Radiology S.C., 1977-79, pres., 1979—; chief radiologist Brokaw Hosp., Normal, Ill., 1979-85, St. Joseph Hosp., Bloomington, Ill., pres. med. staff, 1981, med. dir. radiology, 2000—; med. dir. radiology Bromen Health Care System, Bloomington, 1985—, pres. med. staff, 1990. Mem. citizens adv. coun. Sch. Dist. 87, Bloomington, 1981-84; v.p. McLean County unit Am. Cancer Soc., 1989-90, pres., 1990-94. Comdr. USN, 1966-77. Fellow Am. Coll. Radiology (alt. councillor 1987-92, councillor 1993-99, mem. commn. on small and rural practices 2000); mem. AMA, Radiol. Soc. N.Am., Am. Roentgen Ray Soc., Am. Inst. Ultrasound Medicine, Ill. Radiol. Soc. (exec. com. 1986-99, pres. 1994-95), Ctrl. Ill. Radiol. Soc. (pres. 1990-91), Clin. Magnetic Resonance Soc., Bloomington Country Club, Masons. Republican. Presbyterian. Avocations: book collecting, tennis, personal computers. Office: Bloomington Radiology SC 200 S Towanda Ave Normal IL 61761-2155

COOLIDGE, ROBERT TYTUS, deacon, historian, educator; b. Boston, Mar. 30, 1933; s. Lawrence and Victoria Stuart (Tytus) C.; m. Ellen Osborne, Sept. 10, 1960 (div.); children: Christopher, Miles, Matthew. Grad., Groton (Mass.) Sch., 1951; AB, Harvard U., 1955; MA, U. Calif. at Berkeley, 1957; BLitt, U. Oxford, Eng., 1966. Ordained deacon Episcopal Ch., 1967. Non-stipendiary min. Christ Ch. Cathedral, Montreal, Que., Can., 1967-69, 71—, dir. Montreal Fund for the Diaconate, 1984—; non-stipendiary min. St. Marylebone Ch., London Clin., 1969-71; mem. faculty Loyola Coll. (now Concordia U.), Montreal, 1963—, assoc. prof. history, 1968-88, adj. assoc. prof., 1988—; historian Monticello Assn., 1975—. Contbr. to hist. vol. Fellow Royal Hist. Soc.; mem. Am. Soc. Ch. History, Ecclesiastical History Soc., Medieval Acad. Am., Am. Hist. Assn., Soc. d'Histoire de l'Eglise de France, Montreal Amateur Athletic Assn., Oxford and Cambridge Club (London), Univ. Club (Montreal), Royal St. Lawrence Yacht Club. Home: POB 4070, Westmount, PQ Canada H3Z 2X3

COONEY, J(OHN) GORDON, JR., lawyer; b. Alexandria, Va., Mar. 22, 1959; s. John Gordon Sr. and Patricia Ruth (McEwen) C.; m. Gretchen Smith Millspaugh, July 17, 1999. BA, Wesleyan U., 1981; JD magna cum laude, Villanova U., 1984. Bar: Pa. 1984, U.S. Dist. Ct. (ea. dist.) Pa. 1986, U.S. Ct. Appeals (5th cir.) 1997, U.S. Ct. Appeals (3d cir.) 1988. Law clk. to hon. judge J. William Ditter Jr. U.S. Dist. Ct. (ea. dist.) Pa., Phila., 1984-86; assoc. Morgan, Lewis & Bockius, LLP, Phila., 1986-92, ptnr., 1992—; adj. lectr. Villanova U. Sch. of Law, 1993—, master Inn of Ct., 1999—; barrister U. Pa. Law Sch. Inn of Ct., 1994-96. Editor-in-chief Villanova U. Law Rev., 1983-84; mem. lawyer's editl. bd. The Legal Intelligencer, 1997—. Trustee Rosemont Sch. of the Holy Child, 1997—; alumni bd. mgrs. Episcopal Acad., 1996—. Mem. ABA (com. on class actions and derivative suits), Pa. Bar Assn., Phila. Bar Assn. (profl. guidance com., fed. cts. com.), Union League Phila., Merion Cricket Club, Pyramid Club, Wesleyan U. Alumni Assn. (pres. Phila. area 1993-96), Arthritis Found. (bd. dirs Ea. Pa. chpt. 1993-96), Order of Coif. Republican. Roman Catholic. Office: Morgan Lewis & Bockius LLP 1701 Market St Philadelphia PA 19103-2903

COONEY, PATRICK LOUIS, writer; b. Bellflower, Calif., Apr. 7, 1947; s. Jack William and Lauretta (Jenkins) C.; m. Rosemary Santana Cooney, Sept. 10, 1967; 1 child, Carl. BA in Sociology, Fla. State U., 1969; MA, PhD, U. Tex., 1976; MBA, Fordham U., 1979; cert. in Field Botany, N.Y. Bot. Garden, Bronx, 1993. Asst. prof. sociology Coll. Mount St. Vincent, Bronx, 1975-77; mktg. exec. pub. firms, 1980-89; Cert. in Field Botany; spkr. Martin Luther King Jr. Inst. for Non-Violence, Westchester County, N.Y., 1994; presenter in field. Author: Discovering the Mid-Atlantic: Historical Tours, 1991, Seeing the United States as the South and the World Community of the North: Using the Approach of Martin Luther King Jr. to Invigorate the Next Civil Rights Movement, 1994, The Role of Multiculturalism in Establishing A New Period of Separate but Equal Segregation in the United States: A Comparison of the Periods After and First and Second Civil Wars, 1997. Civil rights activist. With Army Nat. Guard, 1966-73. Dissertation fellow Sweden-Am. Inst., N.Y.C., 1973-74. Mem. Torrey Bot. Club (chairperson field com.). Democrat. Mem. Soc. of Friends. Home: 221 Mount Hope Blvd Hastings Hdsn NY 10706-2509

COONEY, PATRICK RONALD, bishop; b. Detroit, Mar. 10, 1934; s. Michael and Elizabeth (Dowdall) C. B.A., Sacred Heart Sem., 1956; S.T.B., Gregorian U., Rome, 1958, S.T.L., 1960; M.A., Notre Dame U., 1973. Ordained priest Roman Cath. Ch., 1959 ordained bishop, 1983. Assoc. pastor St. Catherine Ch., Detroit, 1960-62; asst. chancellor Archdiocese of Detroit, 1962-69, dir. dept. worship, 1969-83; rector Blessed Sacrament Cathedral, 1977-83; regional bishop Roman Cath. Ch., Detroit, 1983-89; apptd. bishop Diocese of Gaylord, Mich., 1989—. Office: Diocese of Gaylord Pastoral Ctr 611 W North St Gaylord MI 49735-8349

COONS, BARBARA LYNN, public relations executive, librarian; b. Peoria, Ill., June 1, 1948; d. Harold Leroy and Norma (Brauer) C. BA, Stephens Coll., Columbia, Mo., 1970; MA, U. N.C., 1972; MLS, Cath. U., 1982. Research asst. Am. Revolution Bicentennical Office Library of Congress, Washington, 1974-76, editorial asst., office of the Asst. Librarian, 1976-78; ednl. liaison specialist Library of Congress, Washington, 1978-82; dir. rsch. svc. Gray and Co., Washington, 1982-85, v.p., 1985-86; v.p., dir. rsch. svcs. Hill and Knowlton Pub. Affairs Worldwide, Washington, 1986-92, sr. v.p., 1992-95, sr. mng. dir., 1996—; dir. rsch. svcs. Hill and Knowlton USA, 1997—; pres. Library of Congress Profl. Assn., 1982. Mem. Spl. Libraries Assn., Stephens Coll. Alumnae Club of Greater Washington (pres. 1987). Lutheran. Home: 709 Arch Hall Ln Alexandria VA 22314-6208 Office: Hill & Knowlton Pub Affairs Worldwide 600 New Hampshire Ave NW Washington DC 20037-2403

COOPER, ALAN BRUCE, psychiatry educator; b. Aug. 19, 1928. BA in Biochemistry, Wesleyan U., Middletown, Conn., 1949, MA in Immuno Genetics, 1951; MD, N.Y. Med. Sch., 1955; postgrad., Armed Forces Inst. Pathology, 1964; cert., Flight Surgeon Sch., 1964. Diplomate Nat. Bd. Med. Examiners. Gen. rotating intern Lenox Hill Hosp., N.Y.C., 1955-56; resident anatomic and clin. pathology N.Y. Med. Coll., N.Y.C., 1956-58; chief resident pathology Boston Lying-In Hosp., 1958-59, Free Hosp. for Women, Brookline, Mass., 1958, Harvard U. Med. Sch., Boston, 1958-59, Mass. Meml. Hosp., Boston U. Med. Sch., 1959-60; resident psychiatry Baylor Coll. Medicine, Houston, 1965-68, asst. instr. psychiatry, 1965-68, clin. instr. psychiatry, 1968-73, clin. asst. prof. psychiatry, 1974-78, clin. assoc. prof., 1978-95; clin. asst. prof. psychiatry U. Tex. Med. Sch., Houston, 1973-85, asst. prof. dept. psychiatry and behavioral scis., 1986-88, assoc. prof., 1986-98, prof. dept. psychiatry and behavioral scis., 1999—; instr. biology Wesleyan U., Middletown, 1949-51; instr. anatomic and clin. pathology N.Y. Med. Coll., N.Y.C., 1956-58; instr. dept. pathology Harvard U. Med. Sch., Boston, 1958-59, Boston U. Med. Sch., 1959-60; fellow NIMH, Washington, 1965-68; candidate, fellow New Orleans Psychoanalytic Inst., 1966-72, advanced candidate, 1972-75; cons. psychiatry Rice U. Student Health Program, Houston, 1967-68; instr. New Orleans Psychoanalytic Inst., 1975-78; asst. instr. Houston/Galveston Psychoanalytic Inst., 1975-76, instr., 1976-78, tchg. analyst, 1978-81, tng. and supervising analyst, 1982-98, tng. and supervising analyst emeritus, 1998—; staff Meth. Hosp., Houston, 1965-95, Hermann Hosp., Houston, 1986—, Harris County Psychiat. Ctr., Houston, 1987-96; presenter in field. Contbr. chpts. to books and articles to profl. jours. Maj. USAFMC, 1963-65. Fellow Am. Psychiat. Assn. (life), Tex. Soc. Psychiat. Physicians (life, govt. affairs 1991-95, ethics edn. 1991-95), Houston Acad. Medicine; mem. AAAS, AMA, Internat. Psychoanalytic Assn., Am. Psychoanalytic Assn. (life, cert. psychoanalysis, tng. and supervising analyst 1982, resources com. 1984, COPE curriculum com. 1984-90, natural history insts. com. 1984-86, com. on psychoanalytic practice 1984-85, founds. com. 1991-97, others), Am. Chem. Soc., Aerospace Med. Assn. (space medicine br. 1960-65), Baker-Channing Soc., Mass. Meml. Hosp. Med. and Surg. Soc., Med. Assn. S.W., Tex. Med. Assn., Boston Pathology Residents Soc. (exec. com.), Harris County Med. Soc. (mental health com. cons. 1970, 73-78), Harris County Mental Health Assn. (profl. adv. com. 1968-72), Houston/Galveston Psychoanalytic Found. (founder, treas., vice-chmn. 1975-78), Houston/Galveston Psychoanalytic Inst. (admissions com. 1978-93, bull. and candidates manual com. 1982-86, chmn., 1984-90, edn. com. 1982—, fin. com. 1998, others), Houston/Galveston Psychoanalytic Soc. (ethics com. 1979-86, program chmn. 1982-84, pres.-elect 1982-84, pres. 1984-86, program com. 1992-94, others), Houston Psychiat. Soc. (ethics com. 1980-82, com. to develop direct care to cmty. 1984-85, others), Lenox Hill Hosp. Alumni Assn., Phi Delta Epsilon (life), Sigma Xi. Fax: 713-500-2746. E-mail: acooper@msi.uth.tmc.edu. Home: 1111 Caroline St Apt 3012 Houston TX 77010-3046 Office: U Tex Med Sch Mental Scis Inst 1300 Moursund St Houston TX 77030-3406

COOPER, ALAN MICHAEL, psychiatrist; b. Balt., Mar. 14, 1950; s. William I. and Barbara (Stein) C.; m. Elizabeth Ann Mumper, May 31, 1980; children: William, Leigh. SB, MIT, 1972; MD, Med. Coll. Va., 1976. Diplomate Am. Bd. Psychiatry and Neurology. Intern Med. Coll. Va., 1976-77, resident in psychiatry, 1977-78; resident in psychiatry U. Va. Hosps., 1978-79, fellow pain clinic, 1979-80, fellow child and adolescent psychiatry, 1981; instr. psychiatry Harvard Med. Sch., Boston, 1980-81; assoc. in anesthesia (psychiatry) Brigham & Women's Hosp., Boston, 1980-81; dir. diagnostic and evaluation unit David C. Wilson Hosp., Charlottesville, Va., 1982-84; clin. adminstr. psychiatry Va. Bapt. Hosp., Lynchburg, 1984-85; chief psychiatrist Ctrl. Va. Cmty. Svcs., Lynchburg, 1985-92; cons. psychiatrist Ctrl. Va. Tng. Ctr., Lynchburg, 1992—; asst. prof. clin. family medicine U. Va. Sch. Medicine, Charlottesville, 1997—; faculty Lynchburg Family Practice Residency Program, 1997-2000. Bd. dirs. First Unitarian Universalist Ch. of Lynchburg. MIT Nat. scholar, 1968. Mem. Am. Psychiat. Assn., Am. Soc. Clin. Hypnosis, Psychiat. Soc. of Va., Lynchburg Acad. Medicine, Nat. Assn. for the Dually Diagnosed. Office: Central Virginia Tng Ctr PO Box 1098 Lynchburg VA 24505-1098

COOPER, CHESTER LAWRENCE, research administrator; b. Boston, Jan. 13, 1917; s. Israel and Hannah (Levenson) C.; m. Orah Pomerance, July 23; children: Joan Laurence Gould, Susan Louise Cooper. BS, NYU, 1939, MBA, 1941; PhD, Am. U., Washington, 1960. Asst. dep. dir. CIA, Washington, 1947-62; sr. staff White House/NSC, Washington, 1962-66, U.S. Dept. State, Washington, 1966-70; dir. internat. div. Inst. Def. Analysis, Arlington, Va., 1970-72; fellow Woodrow Wilson Internat. Ctr. Scholars, Washington, 1972-75; dep. dir. Inst. Energy Analysis, Oak Ridge, Tenn., 1975-83; dep. dir., acting dir. Internat. Inst. Applied Systems Analysis, Laxenburg, Austria, 1983-85; coord. internat programs Resources for the Future, Washington, 1985-92; dep. dir. Battelle Pacific N.W. Labs., Washington, 1992—; cons. Aspen Inst., Sci. Policy Assocs., Washington, Screenscope Films, Washington. Author: The Lost Crusade, 1971 (award 1971), The Lion's Last Roar, 1977; editor: Growth in America, 1976, Science for Public Policy, 1987. Nat. War Coll. scholar, Washington, 1952-53, Internat. Inst. Applied Systems Analyses hon. scholar, Laxemburg, Austria, 1986. Mem. Coun. Fgn. Rels., Poets, Essayists, Novelists, Cosmos Club. Avocations: fishing, gardening, sculpting, 18th Century Furniture and Silver. Home: 7514 Vale St Chevy Chase MD 20815-4004 Office: Battelle Pacific NW Labs 901 D St SW Washington DC 20024-2169

COOPER, CHRISTOPHER DONALD, educator; b. Sydney, Australia, June 14, 1942; s. Ronald Walter and Florrice Elsa (Brabin) C.; m. Elisabeth

Francisca Valkenburg, Feb. 6, 1965; children—Christopher, Timothy, Louise, Simone. B.Sc. with honors, Sydney U., 1962, M.Sc., 1965; Ph.D., U. London, 1968. Lectr., sr. lectr. Macquarie U., Sydney, Australia, 1969—. Author: Computer Programming, 1968; Infinite Numbers, 1974; Numbers, their Personalities and Properties, 1974; Permutations, 1974. Avocation: cathedral bell ringing. Home: 31 Epping Ave, Eastwood 2122, Australia Office: Macquarie U, North Ryde 2112, Australia

COOPER, EDWARD SAWYER, cardiovascular internist, educator; b. Columbia, S.C., Dec. 11, 1926; s. Henry Howard and Ada Crosland (Sawyer) C.; m. Jean Marie Wilder, Dec. 2, 1951; children: Lisa Marie Cooper Hudgins, Edward Sawyer Jr. (dec.), Jan Ada, Charles Wilder. AB, Lincoln U., Pa., 1946; MD, Meharry Med. Coll., Nashville, 1949; MS, U. Pa., 1972. Diplomate Nat. Bd. Med. Examiners, Am. Bd. Internal Medicine. Intern Phila. Gen. Hosp., 1949-51, resident in medicine, 1951-54, NIH fellow in cardiology, 1956-57, pres. med. staff, 1969-71; co-dir. Stroke Rsch. Ctr., 1968-74, chief med. svc., 1973-76; prof. emeritus medicine U. Pa., Phila., 1973—; bd. dirs. Independence Blue Cross; mem. adv. bd. Hypertension Detection and Followup Program, Phila., 1974—. Trustee Am. Found. Negro Affairs, 1969—, Rockefeller U., 1992—. Served to cpt. USAF, 1954-56. Fellow Phila. Coll. Physicians (coun.); mem. ACP (master), Am. Heart Assn. (chmn., bd. dirs., past nat. pres.), Alpha Omega Alpha. Democrat. Methodist. Achievements include research on stroke and hypertension. Home: 6710 Lincoln Dr Philadelphia PA 19119-3155 Office: University of Pa Hosp 3400 Spruce St Philadelphia PA 19104-4206

COOPER, ELVA JUNE, artist, writer; b. Wilmore, Ky., Mar. 18, 1933; d. Scott Combs and Rhoda Mae (Hundley) Bishop; m. Lowell Howard Cooper, Nov. 29, 1952; children: Lowell Scott, Linda Janet, Candace Lea, Connie Lynn, June Roxanne. Student, Georgetown Coll., 1952-53, Southwestern Jr. Coll., 1961, U. West Fla., 1994, Pensacola Jr. Coll., 1998. Owner June Bug Art and Gifts, Pensacola, Fla., 1973-94, The Studio, Pensacola, Fla., 1986-94. Cons. editor Church Recreation, 1993-95; contbr. articles to mags. Drama writer, dir. Myrtle Grove Bapt. Ch., Pensacola, Fla., 1977-96, artist in residence, 1973-96, discipleship tng. dir., 1973-79, 88-97; sec. Lillian (Ala.) First Bapt. Ch., 1984-95; writer Bapt. Sunday Sch. Bd., Nashville, Tenn., 1987-98; state recreation counselor Fla. Bapt. Conv., Jacksonville, 1994-98; discipleship tng. dir. Pensacola Bay Bapt. Assn., 1994-96. Three time winner of Peggy award Popular Ceramics Mag., 1970; numerous other awards in art shows. Mem. Quayside Art Gallery (asst. publicity, 1984), Foley Art Assn., Art Study Club. Baptist. Avocations: porcelain doll making, sewing, flower arranging, stained glass artist.

COOPER, JAMES MELVIN, healthcare executive, consultant; b. Prescott, Ariz., Oct. 29, 1940; s. Audrey Louise Cooper; m. Marlene Kitay, Oct. 29, 1960; children: Jamie Lynn Hill, David Paul. BS in Adminstrn., George Washington U., 1976, MBA, 1979. Cert. healthcare exec. Enlisted USN, 1959, advanced through grades to capt.; officer-in-charge pers. support detachment Naval Hosp., San Diego, 1979-81; dir. for ambulatory care Naval Hosp., Camp Pendleton, Calif., 1981-83; manpower analyst The Pentagon, Washington, 1983-85; dir. for adminstrn. Naval Med. Clinics, San Diego, 1985-88; exec. officer Naval Hosp., Long Beach, Calif., 1988-91; comdg. officer U.S. Naval Hosp., Naples, Italy, 1991-93; ret. USN, 1993; v.p. Capital Health Svcs., San Diego, 1994-97; treas. Ramona/Julian Health Care Adv. Coun., 1996—. Bd. dirs., chmn. Ramona (Calif.) Food and Clothes Closet, 1995—. Decorated Legion of Merit, Meritorious Svc. medal (3). Fellow Am. Acad. Med. Adminstrs.; mem. Am. Coll. Healthcare Execs. (diplomate), Am. Coll. Managed Care Execs., San Diego Women in Health Adminstrn., Fed. Health Care Execs. Inst. (life), DAV (life), Assn. Med. Svc. Corps Officers (chmn. mentoring com. 1996—), Kiwanis of Ramona (pres. 1996-97), VFW (life). Avocations: jogging, horseback riding, leather tooling. Office: Ambulatory Care Cons PO Box 1912 Ramona CA 92065-0925 Address: 1221 Cook St Ramona CA 92065-3211

COOPER, JAMES ROBERT, III, computer software company executive, mobile communications consultant; b. Mobile, Ala., Nov. 21, 1938; s. James Robert Jr. and Mary Nell (McMichael) C.; m. Marion Griser (div.); m. Nina Jessica Dotterer; children: Jessie Cameron, Charles Dotterer. BS in Sociology and Psychology, Spring Hill Coll., 1965. With sales and mktg. Proctor & Gamble, 1963-69; cons. to marine industry, 1969-79; pres., founder BCI Utilities Constn., Clearwater, Fla., 1979-84; v.p. aviation and navigation, co-founder ComGrafix, Inc., Clearwater, 1984-94; pres. Satellite Data, LLC; CEO Cooper Rsch., SP, Newport, R.I., 1994—; former mem. com. Radio Tech Commn., Washington, Cooper Rsch.; mem. mgmt. systems coun. ATA, interstate truckload corriers conf. Patentee in field. Bd. dirs. Mus. Yachting, Ida Lewis Yacht Club, Seaman's Ch. Inst. With USAR, 1958-63. Fellow Royal Inst. Navigation; mem. Nat. Marine Election Assn., Wild Goose Assn., U.S. Yacht Racing Assn. (contbg. mem.). Republican.

COOPER, JOHN AMBROSE, management coordinator, international marketer; b. Freetown, Sierra Leone, Mar. 5, 1948; s. Daniel Philip and Nancy Etta Cooper; children: John Ambrose, Daniel Kalen. AA in Humanities, Onondaga C.C., SUNY, Syracuse, 1979; AA in Bus., Columbia (Mo.) Coll., 1984, BA in Individual Studies, 1986; MSc in Internat. Mktg., Syracuse U., 1988; BS in Indsl. Mgmt., Empire State Coll., SUNY, 1992; MBA, Syracuse U., 1996. Acct. gen. dept. City of Freetown, Sierra Leone, 1969-71; quality assurance insp., inventory control coord. Joseph Schlitz Brewing Co., Baldwinsville, N.Y., 1976-80; prin. clk. J.A. Jones Constrn. Co., Baldwinsville, 1980-82; mgmt. coord. Anheuser-Busch, Inc., Baldwinsville, 1982—. Mem. editing staff Baldwinsville (N.Y.) Eagle Newsletter. Tng. participant Resolve: A Ctr. for Dispute Settlement, Inc., Syracuse, 1982, Muscular Dystrophy Assn., Baldwinsville, N.Y. (lock-up fundraiser participant for children summer camp, 1996). Mem. Am. Mktg. Assn., Indsl. Rels. Rsch. Assn., West Indian Cultural Assn. (exec. com. 1990), Internat. Stars Soccer Orgn. (gen. sec., coach), Internat. Exhibitors Assn., Anheuser-Busch Employee Assn. (exec. bd. 1983), Hon Appointment to the rsch. bd Advisors, Am. Biographical Inst., Internat. Platform Assn., Soc. Competitive Intelligence Profls., Am. Mgmt. Assn., Eagle Club Crystal Cathedral Ministries. Roman Catholic. Avocations: competitive sports (soccer), debate, travel. Home: 111 Lafayette Rd Apt 625 Syracuse NY 13205-2936 also: One Busch Pl Saint Louis MO 63118

COOPER, JOHN RICHARD, electro-forensic engineer, consultant on standards; b. Hutchinson, Kans., June 16, 1926; s. Charles Dudley and Mabel (Fletcher) C.; m. Sophia Jane McDonald, Sept. 18, 1949; children: Mary Alice, Elizabeth Jane Cooper Peek, Melissa Ann. BSEE, Kans. State U., 1949. Registered profl. engr., Ill. Sales engr. Allis-Chalmers Mfg. Co., Chgo., 1949-59, Marathon Electric Mfg. Co., Chgo., 1959-60; dir. application svcs. S&C Electric Co., Chgo., 1960-91; pres. John Cooper Cons. Svcs., Inc., Wilmette, Ill., 1991—; chmn. book IEEE Recommended Practice for Protection and Coordination of Industrial and Commercial Power Systems, 1986. Fellow IEEE (stds. medal 1992, achievement award 1997), Industry Application Soc. of IEEE (chmn. exec. bd. long range planning com. 1995-99). Episcopalian. Avocation: traveling, fishing. E-mail: jcooper120@cs.com. Office: 1918 Wilmette Ave Apt C Wilmette IL 60091-3288

COOPER, JULIA CLARE, medical writer executive; b. Blackpool, Lancashire, Eng., Nov. 19, 1964; d. Terrance and Daphne Irene (Waine) C. BA in Natural Scis., U. Cambridge (Eng.), 1986, PhD, 1990. Chartered chemist; cert. in editing, writing. Bio-chem. researcher Technische U., Munich, 1990-92; electrophysiologist Bayer, Leverkusen, Germany, 1993-94; med. writer Hoechst Marion Roussel, Frankfurt, Germany, 1995-98; sr. med. writer Parexel, Uxbridge, U.K., 1998-99; assoc. dir. med. writing Europe Parexee, Uxbridge, U.K., 1999—; guest researcher Physikalisch-Technische Bundestalt, Berlin, 1992; leader seminar Mgmt. Forum, Eng., 1996—; free-lance translator, 1994—. Contbr. articles to profl. jours. Mem. Am. Med. Writers Assn., European Med. Writers Assn. (edn. officer 1998—), Royal Soc. Chemistry, Brit. Inst. Regulatory Affairs. Avocations: belly dancing, single malt whisky. Office: Parexel Internat Ltd, 50 Oxford Rd, Uxbridge Middlesex UB9 4DL, England

COOPER, KATHLEEN BELL, economist; b. Dallas, Feb. 3, 1945; d. Patrick Joseph and Ferne Elizabeth (McDougle) Bell; m. Ronald James Cooper, Feb. 6, 1965; children—Michael, Christopher. B.A. in Math. with honors, U. Tex., Arlington, 1970, M.A. in Econs, 1971; Ph.D. in Econs, U. Colo., 1980. Research asst. econs. dept. U. Tex., Arlington, 1970-71; corp. economist United Banks of Colo., Denver, 1971-79, chief economist, 1980-81; v.p., sr. fin. economist Security Pacific Nat. Bank, Los Angeles, 1981-83, 1st v.p., sr. economist, 1983-85, sr. v.p., economist, 1985-86, sr. v.p., chief economist, 1986-87, exec. v.p., chief economist, 1988-90; chief economist Exxon Corp., Irving, Tex., 1990—. Trustee Scripps Coll., Com. for Econ. Devel.; mem. Dallas Com. on Fgn. Rels., Internat. Women's Forum. Mem. Nat. Assn. Bus. Economists (past pres. Denver and L.A. chpts.; bd. dirs. 1975-78, pres. 1985-86), Nat. Bur. Econ. Rsch. (bd. dirs., exec. com.), Am. Bankers Assn. (econ. adv. com. 1979-81, 86-90, chmn. 1989-90), U.S. Assn. Energy Econs. (pres. 1996), Am. Econ. Assn., Conf. Bus. Economists (tech. cons. to bus. coun. 1993-94). Office: Exxon Corp 5959 Las Colinas Blvd Irving TX 75039-2298*

COOPER, LEON N., physicist, educator; b. N.Y.C., Feb. 28, 1930; s. Irving and Anna (Zola) C.; m. Kay Anne Allard, May 18, 1969; children: Kathleen Ann, Coralie Lauren. AB, Columbia U., 1951, AM, 1953, PhD, 1954, DSc, 1973; DSc hon. degrees; DSc, U. Sussex, Eng., 1973, U. Ill., 1974, Brown U., 1974, Gustavus Adolphus Coll., 1975, Ohio State U., 1976, U. Pierre et Marie Curie, Paris, 1977. NSF postdoctoral fellow, mem. Inst. for Advanced Study, 1954-55; rsch. assoc. U. Ill., 1955-57; asst. prof. Ohio State U., 1957-58; assoc. prof. Brown U., Providence, 1958-62, prof., 1962-66, Henry Ledyard Goddard U. prof., 1966-74, Thomas J. Watson Sr. prof. sci., 1974—; dir. brain sci. program Inst. for Brain and Neural Sys., Providence, 1978-91; dir. Inst. for Brain and Neural Systems Brown U., Providence, 1991—; lectr. pub. lectures, internat. conf. and symposia; vis. prof. various univs. and summer schs.; cons. indsl., ednl. orgns.; sponsor Fedn. Am. Scientists; mem. Def. Sci. Bd., 1989-93; co-chair Nester Inc., assoc. Neurosci. Rsch. Program. Author: Introduction to The Meaning and Structure of Phsyics, 1968, Structure and Meaning, 1992, How We Learn, How We Remember: Toward an Understanding of Brain and Neural Systems, 1995; Contbr. articles to profl. jours. Recipient Nobel prize (with J. Bardeen and J.R. Schrieffer), 1972, award of Excellence, Grad. Faculties Alumni of Columbia U., 1974, Descartes medal Acad. de Paris, U. Rene Descartes, 1977, John Jay award Columbia Coll., 1985, award for Disting. Achievement Columbia U., 1990, Alexander Hamilton award Columbia Coll., 1995; Alfred P. Sloan Found. rsch. fellow, 1959-66, John Simon Guggenheim Meml. Found. fellow, 1965-66. Fellow AAAS, Am. Phys. Soc., Am. Acad. Arts and Scis.; mem. Am. Philos. Soc., Nat. Acad. Scis. (Comstock prize with J.R. Schrieffer 1968), Soc. Neurosci., Internat. Neural Network Soc., Phi Beta Kappa, Sigma Xi. Office: Brown U Box 1843 Dept Physics and Neurosci Providence RI 02912-1843

COOPER, MARGARET LESLIE, lawyer; b. Geneva, N.Y., Apr. 13, 1950; d. Jack Frederick and Barbara Ann (Hitchings) C. BA in Math., Rollins Coll., 1972; JD, Mercer U., 1976. Bar: Fla. 1976, U.S. Dist. Ct. (so. dist.) Fla. 1977, U.S. Ct. Appeals (5th cir.) 1977, U.S. Ct. Appeals (11th cir.) 1981; bd. cert. civil litigation and bus. litigation. Assoc. Jones, Foster, Johnston & Stubbs, PA, West Palm Beach, Fla., 1976-81, ptnr., 1981—; assoc. prof. Palm Beach Jr. Coll., West Palm Beach, 1985-86. Pres. Young People's Pres.'s Coun., Norton Gallery Art, West Palm Beach, 1982-84; chmn. campaign Lou Frey for Gov., Palm Beach County, 1986; bd. dirs. Planned Parenthood of Palm Beach; bd. trustees Ann Norten Sculpture Gardens. Named to Sports Hall Fame, Rollins Coll., 1986, 88, Winter Park H.S. Sports Hall of Fame, 1998. Fellow Am. Bar Found.; mem. Palm Beach County Bar Assn., Exec. Women Palm Beach, Palm Beach Jr. League, Women's Internat. Tennis Assn. (disciplinary rev. bd. 1985), Adult Tennis Coun., U.S. Tennis Assn. (vice chair grievance com., capt. Maria Bueno Cup Team), The Beach Club. Republican. Avocations: tennis, snow skiing. Home: 2121 S Flagler Dr West Palm Beach FL 33401-8005 Office: Jones Foster Johnston & Stubbs PA PO Box 3475 West Palm Beach FL 33402-3475

COOPER, MARTIN, education educator; b. London, Mar. 7, 1934; arrived in Australia, 1956; s. William Todunter and Kathleen Machell (Ward) C.; m. Lois Hung, June 1, 1966; 1 child, Nicole. BSc, Manchester U., U.K., 1955; Diploma in Edn., Sydney U., Australia, 1957; MA, Dalhousie U., Nova Scotia, Can., 1970; PhD, Ottawa U., Can., 1972. Tchr. Knox Grammar Sch., Sydney, 1958-67; lectr. Dalhousie U., 1969-70; assoc. prof. U. Ottawa, 1971-78; prof. U. New South Wales, 1978-2000; prof. emeritus U. NSW, 2000—. Author: Higher School Certificate Physics, 1988, also various texts on statis. methods. Found. mem. Australia Ensemble adv. com., 1979-2000. Mem. Sydney Mozart Soc. (pres.).

COOPER, MARTIN CHARLES, computer scientist, educator; b. Manchester, Eng., Dec. 3, 1959; arrived in France, 1987; MA, Oxford U., Eng., 1980; PhD, Sheffield U., 1987. Prof. computer sci. U. Toulouse III, France, 1993—. Author: Visual Occlusion and the Interpretation of Ambiguous Pictures, 1991; contbr. articles to profl. jours. Office: Univ Toulouse III IRIT, 118 Route de Narbonne, 31062 Toulouse France

COOPER, MICHAEL LEE, lawyer; b. Roseburg, Oreg., July 9, 1958; s. Leroy Everrett Cooper and Mattie Verline Orrell. BS with honors, U. Oreg., 1979, JD, 1984. Bar: Oreg. 1984, U.S. Dist. Ct. Oreg. 1986, U.S. Ct. Appeals (9th cir.) 1988, U.S. Supreme Ct. 1988. Pvt. practice Eugene, Oreg., 1984—. Spkr. seminar Clergy and the Law, 1992-93. Deacon 1st Landmark Missionary Bapt. Ch., Springfield, Oreg., 1984—, treas. 1997—; trustee Union Roque Bapt. Camp, Springfield, 1985-98; tchr. Bapt. history Springfield Sch. of Bible, 1992-96, tchr. ancient history, 1984-96. Mem. Oreg. State Bar. Home: 1465 Cottonwood Ave Springfield OR 97477-7661 Office: 895 Country Club Rd Ste C175 Eugene OR 97401-6006

COOPER, NORTON J. (SKY COOPER), liquor, wine and food company executive; b. Phila., Aug. 16, 1931; s. Maurice J. and Elsie (Goldstein) C.; divorced; children: John Amos, Rob. BA, Cornell U., 1953. With Charles Jacquin et Cie Inc., Phila., 1955—, pres., CEO, prin. owner, 1979—; pres., CEO, prin. owner Chambord et Cie, France, Doumen Canton Liquer Co. Ltd., Guandong, People's Republic of China, St Dalfour et Cie, Marmande, France; pres. Lost Horizons Wines Pty, Capetown, South Africa. Author: off-Broadway prodn. Ballad of Jazz Street, 1959. Served to 1st lt. AUS, 1953-55. Decorated Ordre de Chevalier de Provence. Mem. Confrerie des Chevalier, du Tastevin.

COOPER, PENNY, retired administrative assistant, writer, artist; b. Bklyn., Dec. 4, 1942; d. S. Oliver Stone and Elaine Bernhard. BA in English Lit., Queens Coll., 1964. Sec., adminstrv. asst. various orgns.; adminstrv. assoc. Planned Parenthood Fedn. Am., N.Y.C., 1987-93; ret., 1993. Editor W. 71 St. Block Assn. Newsletter, 1970's, Friends and Advs. of the Mentally Ill Newsletter, 1980's, Planned Parenthood Fedn. Am., 1988-93; installation artist, 1994-99. Jewish. Avocations: writing poetry, photography, reading, singing.

COOPER, RICHARD ALAN, lawyer; b. Hattiesburg, Miss., July 19, 1953; s. H. Douglas and Elaine (Reece) C. BA, BS, U. Ark., Little Rock, 1976; JD, Washington U., St. Louis, 1979. Bar: Mo. 1979, Ill. 1980, U.S. Dist. Ct. (ea. dist.) Mo. 1980, U.S. Dist Ct. (so. dist.) Ill. 1988. Law clk. U.S. Dist. Ct., St. Louis, 1979-80; assoc. William R. Gartenberg, St. Louis, 1980-81; assoc. Danis, Reid, Murphy, Tobben & Cooper, St. Louis, 1983-87, ptnr., 1987-88; ptnr. Law Office Terry Sharp, P.C., 1988-89; pvt. practice, 1989-90; ptnr. Danis & Boyce, 1990-93, Davis, Cooepr, Cavanagh & Hartweger, L.C., 1994-98; CFO MedCard Am., Inc., 1997-99; liaison to Washington U. Sch. Law, Mo. Assn. Trial Attys., St. Louis, 1983-85; presenter in field. Bus. mgr. Urban Law Jour., 1978-79; editor Bankruptcy Law Reporter, 1983-88, co-mgr., editor, 1984-88; co-author seminars including Fair Debt Collection Practices, Collecting Judgments and Non UCC Liens. Recipient Milton F. Napier trial award Lawyers Assn. St. Lois, 1979, Outstanding Sr. Bus. Major award Wall St. Jour., 1976. Mem. Mo. Bar Assn., Boulder Yacht Club (commodore 1998-99). Avocation: sailint. Office: Law Offices Richard Alan Cooper 2379 Cedar Dale Ct Maryland Hts MO 63043-4163

COOPER, ROBERT ALFRED, electrical engineer; b. Rotherham, Yorkshire, England, Feb. 24, 1938; came to the U.S., 1983; s. Douglas Dentith and Ann (Duffy) C.; m. Carol Hawkhead, Aug. 12, 1961; children: Mark Anthony, Richard John. BS in Engring., RAF Coll., 1969; BA in Physics, Open U., 1979; postgrad., Cambridge U., 1971, Cambridge U., 1976. Commd. 2d lt. RAF, 1953, advanced through grades to squadron leader, 1977, ret., 1983; mgr. European programs mil. scis. group Sci. Applications Internat. Corp., McLean, Va., 1983-89; chief engr. space physics div. Sci. Applications Internat. Corp., Washington, 1989-94; pres. Cooper Engring. Cons., Annapolis, Md., 1994-96; dir. NASA Inst. Advanced Aerospace Concepts, Allied Tech. Group, Lanham, Md., 1996—; chmn. NASA Space Physics Tech. Panel, Washington, 1989-90; co-chmn. U.S./United Kingdom Space Assets Working Group, 1979-82. Author: Space Physics Handbook, 1991; editor: Engring. Coll. Jour., 1968. Flight safety officer CAP, Fairfax, Va., 1984—. Fellow British Interplanetary Soc.; mem. IEEE, AIAA, Inst. Elec. and Electronic Inc. Engrs. (North Am. rep. 1984—), Royal Yachting Assn., Rotary (dir. programs Dulles, Va. chpt. 1991). Roman Catholic. Avocations: yacht racing, shooting, swimming, philately, astronomy. Home: 920 Yachtsman Way Annapolis MD 21403-3481 Office: Allied Technology Group 4200 Forbes Blvd Ste 106 Lanham Seabrook MD 20706-6303

COOPER, STEPHANIE R., lawyer; b. Phila., Sept. 8, 1944; d. Eli Louis and Dvora (Wolinsky) C.; 1 child, Joshua Cooper Olesker. BA, Sarah Lawrence Coll., 1965, MFA, 1976; JD, Yeshiva U., 1986. Bar: Conn. 1987, N.Y. 1988, U.S. Dist. Ct. (so. and ea. dists.) N.Y. 1988. Assoc. Edwards & Angell, N.Y.C., 1986-88, Burrows, Poster & Franzblau, N.Y.C., 1988-90, Janvey Gordon, N.Y.C., 1990-95; of counsel Moses & Singer LLP, N.Y.C., 1995—. Author: Get Your Back in Shape, 1984. Mem. ABA, Assn. of Bar of City of N.Y., Bus. Coun. Lincoln Ctr. Corp. Fund. Avocations: chamber music, fiction and non-fiction writing, painting. Office: Moses & Singer LLP 1301 Avenue of The Americas New York NY 10019-6022

COOPERMAN, ALVIN, television and theatrical producer; b. Bklyn.; s. Nathan and Marietta (Steinmann) C.; m. Marilyn Frances Fisher; Children: Karen Lynn, Audrey Joan, Margot Jane. Exec. dir. booking Shubert Theatre Enterprises, N.Y.C., 1963-68; v.p. spl. programs NBC, N.Y.C., 1967-68; exec. v.p. Madison Sq. Garden Ctr., Inc., N.Y.C., 1968-72; pres. Madison Sq. Garden Prodns., N.Y.C., 1968-72; CEO Athena Comms. Corp., N.Y.C., 1972—. Developed and produced spl. program Wide Wide World, 1955; exec. prodr. Producer's Showcase, 1955-56, Big Event, 1976-77, Screen Gems, 1957-58; prodns. include Dodsworth, Rosalinda, Jack and the Beanstalk, Shirley Temple Storybook, 1956-57, The Untouchables, 1962-63, Bolshoi Ballet Romeo and Juliet (Emmy award nomination 1976), Pele's Last Game, Amahl and the Night Visitors, A Tribute to Toscanini (Emmy award 1980), An Evening with Jerome Robbins (Emmy award 1981), The Life of Pope John Paul II, Ain't Misbehavin, 1985 (Emmy award, Best Musical of the Year award NAACP), My Two Loves, 1986, Safe Passage, 1987, Family Album, 1987, Witness to Survival, 1988-90; prodr./writer animated spl. NBC-TV Fourth King, 1984; prodr./dir./writer TV spl. Mobs and Mobster, 1993; prodr. cable TV show The Higgins Boys and Gruber Show, 1993 (Ace award nominee), ABC movie: Follow the River, 1994; writer: (stage musical) Honky Tonk Heaven, 1995, (ABC spl.) Susan B. Anthony Slept Here, 1995 (Am. Women in Radio and TV Best Documentary award), (feature film) Charity Royall, 1997-98; (play) Thrall, 1999; creator, writer: (websites) The Stork Club, Platinum, 1996; writer, lyricist (musical) The Life and Adventures of Santa Claus, 1998, weathertainment.com, 1999; established Infotainment Internat., Inc., 1999; website developer (with Herman Rush) Weathertainment.com, 1999. Creative cons. Rep. Nat. Conv., 1972; mem., trustee Judy Holliday Meml. Com. for Am. Med. Ctr., Denver; chmn. N.Y. chpt. Arthritis Found.; pres. Broadway Walk Stars Found., 2000. Recipient Peabody award, 1957, Christopher award, 1957, Judy Holliday Humanitarian award, 1972. Mem. Newcomen Soc. N.Am., Am. Theatre Planning Bd., Players Club. Home: 146 Central Park W New York NY 10023-2005

COOPERRIDER, TOM S., botanist; b. Newark, Ohio, Apr. 15, 1927; s. Oscar Harold and Ruth Evelyn Cooperrider; m. Miwako Kunimura, June 13, 1953; children: Julie Ann, John Andrew. BA, Denison U., 1950; MS, U. Iowa, 1955; PhD, 1958. Instr. biol. scis. Kent (Ohio) State U., 1958-61, asst. prof., 1961-65, assoc. prof., 1965-69, prof., 1969-93, emeritus prof., 1993—, curator herbarium, 1968-93, dir. bot. gardens, 1972-93; mem. editl. bd. Univ. Press, 1976-79; on leave as asst. prof. dept. botany U. Hawaii, 1962-63; NSF rschr. Mountain Lake Biol. Sta., U. Va., summer 1958; faculty mem. Iowa Lakeside Lab., U. Iowa, summer 1965; cons. endangered and threatened species U.S. Fish and Wildlife Svc. Dept. Interior, 1976-83; cons. Davey Tree Expert Co., 1979-85, Ohio Natural Areas Coun., 1983, regional reviewer Flora of North Am., 1993—. Author: Ferns and Other Pteridophytes of Iowa, 1959, Vascular Plants of Clinton, Jackson and Jones Counties, Iowa, 1962, The Dicotyledoneae of Ohio, Part 2, 1995; editor, co-author: Endangered and Threatened Plants of Ohio, 1983. Active YMCA-YWCA Students in Govt., Washington, 1950; personnel placement U.S. Census Bur., Washington, 1950-51; Quaker Internat. Vol., Fed. Republic Germany, 1951. Served with U.S. Army, 1945-46. Recipient Osborn award Ohio Biol. Survey, 1994, Alumni Citation award, Denison U., 2000; dedicatee Kent Bog State Nature Preserve, Ohio Dept. Natural Resources, 1995; NSF predoctoral fellow, 1957-58. Fellow AAAS, Ohio Acad. Scis. (chair Ohio flora com. 1969-97), Explorers Club; mem. Internat. Assn. Plant Taxonomists, Bot. Soc. Am., Nature Conservancy, Wilderness Soc., So. Appalachian Bot. Soc., Blue Key, Sigma Xi. Home: 548 Bowman Dr Kent OH 44240-4512

COOPERSMITH, JEFFREY ALAN, distribution corporation executive; b. N.Y.C., Mar. 23, 1946; s. Jack J. and Anita S. (Selikoff) C.; m. Marjorie Myers, July 5, 1987; children: Jarred, Aubrey, Lorie, Julie. B in Mgmt. Engring., Rensselaer Poly. Inst., 1967; MBA, Ohio State U., 1979. Security arbitrage Arnhold and S. Bleichroeder, Inc., N.Y.C., 1967-70; with Pfizer, Inc., N.Y.C., 1970-72, asst. contr. Minerals, Pigments and Metals divsn.; with Distbn. Ctrs., Inc. subs. Distek, Inc., Westerville, Ohio, 1972-87; v.p., contr. Distbn. Ctrs., Inc. subs. Distek, Inc., Westerville, 1975-77, v.p., treas., 1977-78, v.p. fin., 1978-80; exec.v.p. Distek, Inc., Westerville, 1980-83, pres., COO, 1983-87, also bd. dirs.; pres. Directel, Inc., 1981-93; pres., CEO Triplefin, Inc., 1993—; bd. dirs. Axis Advt. Bd. dirs. Columbus Jewish Cmty. Ctr. Mem. World Pres. Orgn., CEO Orgn., Direct Mktg. Assn. (contbg. author handbook). Office: 250 Civic Center Dr S Ste 500 Columbus OH 43215-5088

COOPERSTOCK, FRED ISAAC, physics educator, researcher; b. Winnipeg, Man., Can., Aug. 20, 1940; s. Thomas and Sima (Lipen) C.; m. Ruth Claire Bellan, Aug. 26, 1962; children: Jeremy, Ramona. BSc, U. Man., Winnipeg, 1962; PhD, Brown U., 1966. Prof. physics U. Victoria, Can., 1967—; Can.-France sci. exch. visitor Inst. Henri Poincaré, Paris, 1973-74, 80-81; Lady Davis vis. prof. Technion, Haifa, Israel, 1987-88; vis. prof. Tata Inst., Bombay, 1995, U. del Pais Vasco, Bilboa, Spain, 1995. Co-editor Developments in Relativity, Astrophysics and Cosmology, 1990, Procs. of the 3rd Can. Conf. on Gen. Relativity and Relativistic Astrophysics World Sci., 1990; apptd. reviewer Math. Revs., 1997; contbr. articles to profl. jours. Rsch. grantee Natural Scis. and Engring. Rsch. Coun. Can., 1968—. Mem. Internat. Soc. on Gen. Relativity and Gravitation, Am. Phys. Soc. Avocations: badminton, photography. Office: Dept Physics and Astronomy, Univ Victoria, Victoria, BC Canada V8W 3P6

COOUVREUX, JEAN CLAUDE, physician; b. St. Maure, France, Apr. 11, 1946; s. Luc and Myriam (Le Du) C.; m. Marie France Bezancon, Sept. 16, 1968 (div. 1974); children: Jean Christophe, Olivier; m. Laurence Seilles, Feb. 25, 1989. B Math., France, 1963; postgrad., Tours, France, 1969; PhD, CHU, Tours, 1973. Pvt. practice internal medicine France, 1972-94; head medicine dept. Hosp. Buzancais, France, 1974-92; mgr. Med. Clinic, United Arab Emirates, 1993-98, Med. Store, United Arab Emirates, 1993-98; co-owner, ptnr. army supplies med. divsn. Nashwan, Abu Dhabi, United Arab Emirates, 1999—. Author: Mandragore and Anaesthesiology, 1973; contbr. articles to profl. jours.; developer emergency treatment in desert. Dep. mayor Buzancais, France, 1982-92; pres. Sports Club, Buzancais, 1979-85; treas. Blind People Assn., Indre, 1969-72; bd. dirs. Papillons Blancs, Tours, France, 1964-69. Recipient Civic Merit medal France, 1957. Avocations: golf, hunting, aviation, defense territory research. Office: Nashwan Med Divsn, PO Box 70373, Abu Dhabi United Arab Emirates

COPANS, KENNETH GARY, accountant; b. Stamford, Conn., Dec. 6, 1946; s. Lawrence W. and Rosaline (Davidoff) C.; m. Jo Ellen Silbert, Apr. 25, 1971; children: Richard Harris, Mark Adam. BS in Acctg., Bucknell U., 1968. CPA, N.Y. With Arthur Andersen & Co., N.Y.C., 1968; with Copans, Copans & Piccone, N.Y.C., 1971-74, ptnr., 1974-84, mng. ptnr.,

1984—; instr. Long Island U., Found. for Acctg. Edn. Bd. dirs. Congregation Aqudas Israel, Newburgh, N.Y., 1980—. Served with U.S. Army, 1968-70. Mem. AICPA, N.Y. State Soc. CPAs, S.C. Soc. CPAs, N.J. Soc. CPAs, Am. Assn. Personal Fin. Planners, Pencor. Republican. Avocations: fishing, golf, tennis. Home: 43 Parkhill Dr New Windsor NY 12553-6437 Office: Copans & Co 540 Gidney Ave Newburgh NY 12550-3129

COPE, EDWIN, surgeon; b. Rokiskis, Lithuania, June 29, 1926; arrived in South Africa, 1930; s. David Copelowitz and Olga (Beder) C.; m. Carmel Hyman, July 24, 1950 (dec. Nov. 1981); 1 child, Gary Bentley. MBBCh, U. Witwatersrand, Johannesburg, South Africa, 1950, DS, 1962. Intern Teaching Hosps., Johannesburg, South Africa, 1951-52, registrar, 1953-61, cons., 1962—. Avocations: reading, swimming, athletics, walking. Home: Porter Ave, Grauleng 2196, South Africa Office: 195 Jeppe St, Grauleng 2001, South Africa

COPE, KATHLEEN ADELAIDE, critical care and parish nurse, educator; b. Bethlehem, Pa., Sept. 12, 1926; d. Harry Raymond and Mabel Eva (Newhard) Stine; m. Robert Clayton Cope, Aug. 9, 1951; children: Debra Kathleen Howard, Terry Faye Cicero. BA in Psychology summa cum laude, Bellevue (Nebr.) Coll., 1972; diploma, St. Luke's Hosp., Bethlehem, 1951; student, Whitworth Coll., Spokane, 1989, Wash. State U., Spokane, 1989. RN, Pa., Wash.; cert. nutrition support nurse; cert. critical care nurse, quality improvement, health promotion specialist. Pvt. duty nurse Exeter (N.H.) Hosp., 1957-60; nurse Red Cross Blood Mobile, Portsmouth area, N.H., 1961-65; staff nurse Clarkson Hosp., Omaha, 1966, asst. head nurse, 1966-67, head nurse, 1967-68, supr., organizer coronary care ctr., 1968-70; staff nurse ICU/critical care Sacred Heart Med. ctr., Spokane, 1973—; founder, dir. nutritional risk/identification network Health Improvement Partnership, Spokane, Wash., 1997—; mem. adv. coun. edn. com. Nutrition Screening Initiative, Washington, 1992—, Nutrition Inst. La., New Orleans, 1993—; apptd. del. by U.S. Senate to White House Conf. on Aging, 1995; developer Body Mass Index awareness cmty. action project through Leadership Spokane Class 1999. Author booklet, manual; author resolution: Ensuring the Future of the Medicare Program presented to White House and Congress; contbr. articles to newsletter and jours. Apptd. Silver Senator by U.S. Senate for Wash. in Nat. Silver Haired Congress, 1997. Recipient Cmty. Leadership Recognition award YWCA, Spokane, 1993, commendation for developing a model for nation from former U.S. surgeon gen., 1999. Mem. ANA, Wash. State Nursing Assn., Nat. Coun. on Aging, Am. Soc. for Critical Care Nursing (founding), Am. Soc. for Parenteral and Enteral Nutrition, U.S. apptd. Silver Senator for Wash. State in Nat. Silver Haired Congress, Sigma Theta Tau. Avocations: reading, walking, hiking, bicycle, cooking, crafts. Home: 8315 N Lucia Ct Spokane WA 99208-9654

COPELAND, JACQUELINE TURNER, music educator; b. Birmingham, Ala., Mar. 22, 1939; d. Charles Smith and Julia (Northrop) Turner; m. William Edward Copeland, Apr. 20, 1962; children: Denise Arlene, Dawn Alane. B in Music Edn., Birmingham-So. Coll., 1960; M in Music Edn., Wichita State U., 1977. Cert. music tchr. grades K-12, Ala., Ga., Kans., La., Va. Music tchr. Jefferson County Bd. Edn., Birmingham, 1960-62, 63-64, DeKalb County Bd. Edn., Decatur, Ga., 1965-68; choral music tchr. Fairfax (Va.) County Bd. Edn., 1968-69, Derby (Kans.) Unified Sch. Dist. #260, 1977-80, Maize (Kans.) Unified Sch. Dist. #266, 1980-84; music tchr. Montgomery (Ala.) County Pub. Schs., 1984-85; instr. voice and piano Acad. Performing Arts, Montgomery, 1985-95, Studio of Jacqueline T. Copeland, Montgomery, 1995—; accompanist County-Wide Music Festivals, Birmingham, 1960-65; sect. leader Dekalb Cmty. Chorus, Decatur, Ga., 1965-68; sect. leader, exec. bd. New Orleans Concert Choir, 1970-74; asst. dir., dir. chorale Wichita Choral Soc., 1974-84; dir. opening ceremony Bicentennial Fair, Wichita, 1976; mem. Montgomery (Ala.) Civic Chorale, 1984-87; musical dir. for theatre depts. Performing Arts Jr. High, Performing Arts H.S., Faulkner U., 1986—. Author: Music Teacher Handbook, 1967; editor, contbg. author: Teacher Advisement Handbook, 1980. Secret svc. wife White House Wives, Washington, 1968-70; leader, trainer, area chmn. Camp Fire Girls, New Orleans, 1970-74; leader, membership com., exec. bd. Camp Fire Girls, Wichita, 1974-82; elected ofcl. Citizens Participation Orgn., Wichita, 1984; area chmn. Am. Heart Assn., Montgomery, 1988-94; vol. DA Election, Montgomery, 1994. Recipient Groovey Tchr. award WQXI Radio, Atlanta, 1967, Gov.'s commendation Revolutionary Bicentennial Com., Wichita, 1976; named Outstanding Young Women of Am., New Orleans, 1971. Mem. NOW, AAUW, Music Tchrs. Nat. Assn., Ala. Music Tchrs. Assn., Montgomery Music Tchrs. Forum, Alpha Chi Omega (Montgomery chpt. treas. 1995-99, pres. 1999—), Alpha Chi Omega Alumnae (del. to 4 nat. convs., pres., v.p.). Democrat. Baptist. Avocations: searching for collectibles for country decor. Home: 6121 Bell Road Mnr Montgomery AL 36117-4362

COPELAND, JAMES E., lawyer; b. Indpls., July 17, 1954; s. Donald E. and Lorene Ellen (Fine) C.; m. Catherine Elena Hurst, July 15, 1989; children: Caitlin, Kendon; 1 stepchild: Amanda Collins. BA, U. Fla., 1977, JD, 1981. Bar: Fla. 1981; U.S. Dist. Ct. (so. dist.) Fla. 1990, U.S. Dist. Ct. Trial Bar Fla. 1991. Assoc. Roger C. Hurd, P.A., North Palm Beach, Fla., 1981-84; ptnr. Hurd & Copeland, P.A., Palm Beach Gardens, Fla., 1984-92, Hurd, Copeland & Horvath, Palm Beach Gardens, 1992-94; pvt. practice Palm Beach Gardens, 1994—; adv. bd. Leasing Technology, Inc., West Palm Beach, 1992-96; seminar lectr. Lorman Edn. Svcs., Eau Claire, Wis., 1996. Author publs. in field. Mem. Palm Beach County Bar Assn. (chmn. blood bank com. 1988-91, lectr. Law Week 1985-89), Assn. Trial Lawyers of Am., ABA, No. Palm Beach County C. of C., Fla. Blue Key Honor Soc., Masons (lodge officer 1999), Habitat for Humanity. Republican. Methodist. Avocations: boating, scuba diving, golf, fishing. Office: 8895 N Military Trl Ste 302D Palm Beach Gardens FL 33410-6267

COPELAND, JOHN HOWARD, communications executive, television producer; b. San Diego, Oct. 13, 1950; s. Glenn H. and Luella Louise (Schmid) C.; m. Shannon Gloria Casey, Nov. 20, 1987. BA, Chapman U., 1973. Asst. to exec. prodr. Evan Lloyd Prodns., London, 1974-76; mem. TV and audio visual staff Chapman U., Orange, Calif., 1977-78; asst. to prodr. Media Prodns., Inc., L.A., 1978-79; post prodn. supr. Rattlesnake Prodns., Inc., L.A., 1979-81, assoc. prodr., 1986-88, prodr., 1988-95; post prodn. supr. Walt Disney Pictures, Burbank, Calif., 1981-82; assoc. prodr. Walt Disney Pictures/Rattlesnake Prodns., Burbank, 1983-85; prodr., exec. v.p. Netter Digital Entertainment Inc., L.A., 1995—, also sec. bd. dirs. prodr. (TV documentary) The Wild West, 1993 (Emmy nomination 1994), (TV show) Babylon 5, 1993-98, (TV movie) Siringo, 1994; co-prodr. (TV pilot) Babylon 5 - The Gathering, 1993; supervising prodr. (TV show) Hypernauts, 1995-96; prodr. (TV movies) Babylon 5: In the Beginning, 1997, Babylon 5: Third Space, Babylon 5: The River og Souls, 1998, Babylon 5: A Call to Arms; prodr. (TV series) Crusade, 1998-99; exec. prodr. (TV series) Voltron: The Third Dimension, 1998-99. Named Alumni of the Yr. Chapman U., Orange, 1996; Recipient Hugo award World Sci. Fiction Soc., 1996, E. Pluribus Unum award Am. Cinema Found., 1997; recipient Hugo award World Sci. Fiction Soc., 1997, Best Cable Series award Acad. Sci. Fiction and Horror, 1999. Mem. NATAS (Emmy 1994, 95), Dir.'s Guild of Am. Office: Netter Digital Entertainment Inc 5200 Lankershim Blvd Ste 290 North Hollywood CA 91601-3100

COPELAND, ROBERT BODINE, internist, cardiologist; b. Arab, Ala., Jan. 24, 1938; s. Haden Paul and Jimmie Alice (Bodine) C.; m. Jenny Trammell, June 26, 1960; children: Robert Theodore, Haden McTieyre. BS, Auburn U., 1960; MD, U. Ala., Birmingham, 1963. Diplomate Am. Bd. Internal Medicine; cert. internal medicine, cardiovascular diseases and geriatrics. Intern then resident, clin. rsch. fellow in cardiology Mass. Gen. Hosp., Harvard Med. Sch., Boston, 1963-67; physician Clark Holder Clinic, LaGrange, Ga., 1967-77; founder, dir. Ga. Heart Clinic, LaGrange, 1972—; founder, pres. So. Cardiopulmonary Assocs., LaGrange, 1977—; clin. prof. med. U. Ala., Birmingham, 1980—, Emory U., Atlanta, 1980—; bd. govs. Am. Bd. Internal Med., Phila., 1980-86, Joint Commn. on Accreditation of Healthcare Orgns., Chgo., 1991-97. Contbr. articles to profl. jours. Trustee LaGrange Coll.; chmn. bd. trustees ACP-ASIM Found., 1999-2001. Recipient Disting. Alumni award U. Ala., Birmingham, 1985. Fellow ACP (gov. Ga. chpt. 1987-91, Master 1993, regent 1993, chair bd. regents 1998-99), Royal Coll. Physicians, Am. Coll. Cardiology; mem. Am. Heart Assn. (pres. Ga. affiliate 1985-86), Nat. Acad. Sci., Inst. of Medicine. Office: 1551 Doctors Dr Lagrange GA 30240-4139

COPELAND, ROY WILSON, lawyer; b. Ft. Knox, Ky., Jan. 2, 1957; s. George Wilson and Mary Lou Copeland; m. Cheryl LaFayne Smith, June 17, 1989; children: Roy II, Rachelle, Kelleigh, Kameron. AB, U. So. Calif., L.A., 1979; JD, U. Ga., 1983. Bar: Ga. 1984, U.S. Dist. Ct. (mid. dist.) Ga. 1984, U.S. Ct. Appeals (11th cir.) 1984. With Drew, Eckl & Farnham, Atlanta, 1983-84, Copeland & Haugabrook, Valdosta, Ga., 1985—; adj. prof. bus. law Ga. State U.; prof. pub. law Valdosta State U., 1984-92. Contbr. articles to UCLA Black Law Rev., Howard Law Jour. Counsel NAACP, Valdosta, 1988-94; chmn. of bd. Georgians United, Atlanta, 1994-96; bd. dirs. Valdosta State Coll. Found., 1992-94; pres., bd. dirs. 100 Black Men of Valdosta, 1994-96; bd. dirs. 100 Black Men of Am.; v.p. Ga. Legal Svcs., Atlanta, 1996-98. Recipient Comty. Svc. award NAACP, 1993, Outstanding Svc. award 100 Black Men of Valdosta, 1997. Mem. Nat. Bar Assn., Ga. Assn. of African Am. Attys., State Bar Ga., Valdosta Bar Assn., Phi Beta Kappa. Office: Copeland & Haugabrook 102 E Adair St Valdosta GA 31601-4506

COPLEY, GORDON, executive search company administrator; b. Huddersfield, Eng., Apr. 22, 1942; s. Frank and Maria Agatha (Bruce) C.; m. Maureen Anne Carter, Jan. 10, 1966 (div. July 1986); children: Susan Jennifer, Simon Scott. BS in Physics with honors, Edinburgh (Scotland) U., 1966, MS in Nuclear Physics, 1967, PhD in Nuclear Physics, 1970. Indsl. engr. Procter & Gamble Ltd., U.K., 1970-71, plant mgr., 1971-73, salesman, 1973, brand mgr., 1973-75; mng. dir. J.S. Vallis & Co. Ltd., Bermuda, 1975-80; cons., dir. Wrightson Wood, U.K., 1980-90; dir., prin. Copley Wall & Assocs. Ltd., U.K., 1991—; dir. Mfg. Mgmt. Ltd., U.K., 1982-96, Bus. West Pubs. Ltd., U.K., 1982-86. A. Pilot officer Scotland Royal Air force Vol. Res., 1962-65. Mem. Burnham and Berrow Golf Club (chmn. 1991-93, 94-97). Avocations: golf, flying, keeping fit. Office: Copley Wall and Assocs Ltd, 100 Jermyn St, London SW1Y 6EE, England

COPLEY, IAN BRUCE, neurosurgeon consultant; b. Mirfield, Eng., Jan. 22, 1934; s. Frank and Maria Agatha (Bruce) C.; m. Jennifer Mary Forster, Apr. 19, 1991; 1 child, Oliver. MB BChir, Med. Sch., Leeds, 1959. Med. officer Her Majesty's Forces, Kenya, Africa, 1960-64; registrar neurosurgery Natal Provincial Adminstrn., Durban, South Africa, 1965; sr. lectr. anatomy U. Natal, Durban, South Africa, 1972-81; cons. Med. Univ. of So. Africa, 1981-82; head neurosurgery South African Defence Force, Pretoria, South Africa, 1982-88; prof., head neurosurgery med. U. So. Africa, 1988-99; cons. neurosurgeon No. Province U. So. Africa, Pietersburg, 1999—. Contbr. numerous articles to profl. jours. Lt. col. South African Defence Force Med. Svcs., 1982-88, Pretoria. Recipient Gen. Svc. medal Rhodesian Govt., Salisbury, 1979. Fellow Royal Coll. Surgeons (Ireland); mem. Royal Coll. Surgeons (Eng.), Royal Coll. Physicians London (lic.), South African Mil. History Soc. (nat. chmn. 1990-92), Nat. Monuments Coun. (N.W. Province), 1996-99, South African Coll. Medicine (assoc.). Avocations: aviation, sailing, piano, book collection. Home: Lincolnshire Lodge, Kommando NEK Box 573, Hartbeespoort 0216, South Africa Office: Med U of So Africa, Box 226, Medunsa 0204, South Africa

COPPENS, FILIP, publishing executive; b. Sint-Niklaas, Belgium, Jan. 25, 1971; s. Leon Anna and Anita (Carmeliet) C. Degree in Journalism, Ready Press Agy., Mechelen, Belgium, 1990-91. Journalist Bouwmag., Ghent, Belgium, 1994; prodn. mgr. SMK Publ., Ghent, Belgium, 1994-95, Fotek NV, Sint-Niklaas, 1995-99, Sweet & Maxwell, London, 1999—; spkr. and cons. in field. Author: Pre-Atlantis, 1994, Sind Wir Allein?, 1996; editor Frontier 2000, 1995—; contbr. articles to profl. jours. Dir. Frontier Scis. Found., Dronten, The Netherlands, 1995—. Mem. FUO, Ancient Astronauts Soc., Mut. UFO Network, Internat. Assn. Near Death Experiences. Avocations: films, musicals. Home: The Old Station House, Dirleton, East Lothian EH39 5LR, Scotland

COPPENS, PHILIP, chemist; b. Amersfoort, Holland, Oct. 24, 1930; s. Alexander and Sophie (Berkeley) C.; m. Marguerite Louise Anholt, Aug. 6, 1957; children: Alon, Eldad, Daniel David. PhD, U. Amsterdam, Netherlands, 1960; Dr. honoris causa, U. Nancy, France, 1989. Chemist Weizmann Inst. Sch., Rehoboth, Israel, 1957-60, 62-65, Brookhaven Nat. Lab., Upton, L.I., N.Y., 1960-62, 65-68; prof. chemistry SUNY, Buffalo, 1968—; adj. prof. applied physics and engring. sci. Cornell U., 1982-87; disting. prof. SUNY, Buffalo, 1992—, H. M. Woodburn chair chemistry, 1999—; vis. prof. Fordham U., 1966-67, Aarhus U., Denmark, 1973, U. Grenoble, France, 1974-75, 87, U. Calif., Santa Barbara, 1992; gov. consortium of advanced radiation sources U. Chgo., 1994—; materials rsch. adv. com. NSF, 1980-82; exec. com. Nat. Synchotron Light Source User, 1983-85, adv. com. High Flux Beam Reactor Program, Brookhaven Nat. Lab., 1985-90; steering com. Advanced Photon Source Argonne Nat. Lab, 1991-94. Recipient Harker award Hauptman-Woodward Med. Inst., 1995, George Aminoff award Swedish Acad. Scis., 1996. Fellow AAAS; mem. Internat. Coun. of Sci. Unions (gen. com. 1996-99), Am. Crystallographic Assn. (v.p. 1977, pres. 1978, Buerger award 1994), Internat. Union Crystallography (exec. com. 1987-99, pres. 1993-96), Internat. Coun. Sci. Unions (gen. com. 1996-98), Am. Chem. Soc. (Schoelkopf award Western N.Y. sect. 1996), Materials Rsch. Soc., Royal Dutch Acad. Scis. (corr.). Office: Suny Dept Chemistry Buffalo NY 14260-0001

COPPER, JOHN FRANKLIN, Asian studies educator, consultant; b. Omaha, Oct. 30, 1940; s. Russell B. and Ina Belle (Townsend) C.; m. Lei Wang, Mar. 1, 1996; 1 child, Royce Wellington. BA, U. Nebr., 1961; MA, U. Hawaii, 1965; postgrad., U. Calif., Berkeley, 1966-68; PhD with Distinction, U. S.C., 1975. Lectr. U. Md., Tokyo, 1971-76; rsch. fellow Hoover Instn., Stanford, Calif., 1976-77; assoc. prof. Southwestern Coll., Memphis, 1977-83; exec. dir. Asian Studies Ctr., Washington, 1983-84; grad. prof. J.F.K. Ctr., Ft. Bragg, N.C., 1984-85; Stanley J. Buckman disting. prof. internat. studies Rhodes Coll., Memphis, 1985—. Author: A Matter of Two Chinas, 1979, China's Global Role, 1980 (Clarence Day Found. award 1981), Taiwan's Elections, 1984, Human Rights in Post-Mao China, 1985, A Quiet Revolution, 1988, Taiwan: Nation-State or Province?, 1990, 2d edit., 1996, China Diplomacy, 1992, Historical Dictionary of Taiwan, 1993, Taiwan's 1991 and 1992 Non-Supplemental Elections, 1994, The Bamboo Gulag: Human Rights in the People's Republic of China, 1991-92, 94, Words Across the Taiwan Strait, 1995, The Taiwan Political Miracle, 1997, Coping with a Bad Global Image, 1997, Taiwan's Mid-1990s Elections, 1998, Taiwan Nation-State or Province?, 3d edit., 1999, As Taiwan Enters the New Millennium, 1999, Historical Dictionary of Taiwan, 2d edit., 2000; contbr. articles to profl. jours. Bd. govs. East-West Ctr., 1983-89. Winner Internat. Comms. award, 1997. Mem. Am. Assn. Chinese Studies (bd. dirs.), Internat. Studies Assn., Assn. Asian Studies, Am. Mensa Ltd. Republican. Presbyterian. Office: Rhodes Coll Dept Internat Studies 2000 N Parkway Dept Internat Memphis TN 38112-1690

COPPERFIELD, DAVID (DAVID KOTKIN), illusionist, director, producer, writer; b. Metuchen, N.J., 1956. Student, Fordham U. prof. magic NYU, 1974; creator, founder Project Magic, 1982. Levitated across Grand Canyon, 1984; walked through Great Wall of China, 1986; escaped from Alcatraz prison, 1987, vanished Statue of Liberty, 1989, survived bldg. implosion challenge, 1989; went over Niagara Falls, 1990; vanished Orient Express, 1991, introduced flying illusion, 1992; escaped from burning ropes 13 stories above ground before 15,000 people, Caesar's Palace, 1993; performer, dir., producer, writer (TV spls.) The Magic of David Copperfield annually since 1978; presdl. command performance, 1981, 82, 85, 87, 92; performer (musical) Magic Man, 1974; appeared in film Terror Train, 1980. Nat. spokesperson at Olympics U.S. Orgn. Disabled Athletes, Seoul, Republic of Korea, 1988. Recipient Emmy awards and/or nominations, 1979, 80, 81, 83, 84, 85, 86, 88, 89, 90, 91, 92, Golden Rose award Montreux Film Festival, 1987, Bambi award-European equivalent of Oscars, 1993; named Magician of Yr. Acad. Magical Arts, 1980, 87; named Entertainer of Yr. Am. Guild Variety Artists, 1981, City of Atlantic City, 1986, Nat. Assn. Campus Activities, 1987; named one of Ten Outstanding Young Men in Am. U.S. Jaycees, 1985; named one of Top Ten Entrepreneurs (age 30 or under) Young Entrepreneur Orgn., 1987; named America's Fastest Rising Star by Forbes Mag., 1993. Achievements include Am. producer to premiere Am. TV spl. in Peoples Republic of China, 1986; Broke box office attendance records Miami Knight Ctr., 1984, Warner Theater, Washington, 1985, Caesars Palace, Las Vegas, Nev., 1985, Taipei Sports and Cultural Stadium, 1987, Premier Theater, Mexico City, 1987, Coliseum, Hong Kong, 1988, World Trade Ctr., Singapore, 1988, Putra World Trade Ctr., Kuala Lumpur, 1988, Giganto Arena, Porto Allegre, Brazil, 1988, Fox Theatre, Detroit, 1989, 92; broke European attendance record Dortmond, Germany, 1993. *

COPPERMAN, ALAN BARRY, obstetrician-gynecologist; b. Queens, N.Y., Jan. 20, 1963; s. Stuart Morton and Renee (Stein) C.; m. Kira Phillips, May 5, 1995. BA, U. Pa., 1985; MD, N.Y. Med. Coll., 1989. Diplomate Am. Bd. Ob-Gyn. Intern Yale New Haven Hosp., 1989-90, resident ob-gyn., 1990-93; fellow Mount Sinai Med. Ctr., N.Y.C., 1993-95; dir. divsn. reproductive endocrinology dept. ob-gyn. Mt. Sinai Med. Ctr., N.Y.C., 1997—. Fellow ACOG, Am. Soc. Reproductive Medicine (assoc.). Office: Mt Sinai Med Ctr 1212 5th Ave New York NY 10029-5210

COPPERMAN, STUART MORTON, pediatrician; b. Bklyn., June 5, 1935; s. Irving and Anne (Reisfield) C.; m. Renee Stein, Aug. 17, 1958; children: Beth, Alan, Cara. BA cum laude, Bklyn. Coll., 1956; MD, SUNY-Bklyn., 1960. Diplomate Am. Bd. Pediat. Rotating intern. L.I. Jewish Hosp., New Hyde Park, N.Y., 1960-61, resident in pediat., 1961-63; practice medicine specializing in pediat. Merrick, N.Y., 1965—; mem. staff L.I. Jewish Hillside Med. Ctr., Schneider Children's Hosp., New Hyde Park, Nassau County Med. Ctr., East Meadow, Winthrop U. Hosp., Mineola, North Shore Univ. Hosp., Manhasset; clin. assoc. prof. pediat. SUNY Med. Sch., Stony Brook, 1972—; asst. prof. clin. health studies SUNY Sch. Allied Health, Stony Brook, 1977—; clin. instr. physicians asst. program Stony Brook Med. Ctr., 1972—; prof. pediat. St. George's Med. Coll., St. Vincent, W.I., acting chmn. pediat., 1979-80; med. advisor Assn. Children with Downs Syndrome, 1971-98; mem. com. for handicapped Bellmore Sch. Dist., 1976-86; mem. ad hoc com. on cmty. as sch. Merrick-Bellmore Schs., 1976-90; bd. dirs. North Shore-L.I. Jewish I.P.O., L.I. Sch. Health Edn. Coalition, North Shore Physicians Orgn., North Shore - L.I. Jewish PHO; mem. Nassau County Sch. Health Edn. Commn., 1990-93; mem. ad hoc com. on prevention of birth defects March of Dimes; preceptor in pediat. Physicians Asst. Program, Cath. Med. Ctr.; mem. doctor's adv. com. Shaare Zedek Hosp., Jerusalem, 1974-98; med. cons. Matchbox Toys, 1985-88, Proctor & Gamble, 1988, Carnation Co., 1989-90, Disney Ednl. Svcs., 1990-95, vaccine divsn. Merck Corp., 1997—, Sepracor, 1999—; cons., mem. spkrs. bur. N.Y. State Med. Soc., N.Y. State Senate Com. Mental Hygiene, 1988—, Lederle Labs., 1989-95, Merck Labs., 1996—, Wallace Labs., 1996—, ucb Pharma, 1999—, Connaught, 1999—, Abbott Labs., 1996—, Pfizer, 1998—, Sepracor, 1999—; author, co-founder, pres., bd. dirs. Child Health Imagery Prodns., 1997—. Appearance TV shows on Downs Syndrome, learning disabilities, CPR, first aid, infant exercise programs, TV's effects on children, infectious disease, parent-infant bonding, immunizations, enuresis, toilet training, prevention of cigarette smoking among children, 1972—, also on HealthLinks (Life Time TV), 1990-93; mem. editl. adv. bd. Jour. Assn. for Physician Assts., 1987—; editl. cons. Jour. Pediat. Mgmt., 1991—; contbr. chpt. to Textbook Pediat. Sports Medicine; developer Babycise (infant parent interactive program in video tape and book form), 1985; rschr. on hetacillin, 1966, pyridoxine effect on serotonin level and performance in children with Down's Syndrome, 1970-75, Alice in Wonderland syndrome as presenting sympton of infectious mononucleosis, 1966-77, on transmission of group A Beta hemolytic strep infection from pet reservoirs to children, 1963-81; med. editor Air Fair Mag., 1991-93, L.I. Parent Mag., 1985-93, L.I. Family Mag., 1994-95; contbr. articles to profl. jours. Mem. sch. bd. Temple Beth Am., Merrick, 1972-78, mem. exec. com., 1973-74, chmn. com. Israel and World Affairs, 1976-78, mem. sch. com., 1976-78, mem. ritual com., 1976-93; mem. N.Y. State Senate com. on mental hygiene, 1990—; mem. profl. adv. bd. So. Shore divsn. YM-YWHA; benefactor Merrick Libr., 1992—. With U.S. Army, 1963-65. Recipient Physician Recognition award AMA, 1966—, testimonial dinner and plaque Assn. Children with Down Syndrome, 1972, Best Clin. Tchrs. of Pediat. award Nassau County Med. Ctr., 1981-82; named Merrick Profl. of Yr., 1994. Fellow Am. Acad. Pediat. (chmn. com. TV effects on children 1976—, mem. nat. com. comm. and pub. info. 1984-85, mem. nat. com. on substance abuse 1998-2001, media spokesperson 1988—, tobacco, alcohol and drug-free generation coord. 1988-98, chmn. substance abuse com. 1992—, N.Y. state chmn. substance abuse com. 1992-94, managed care com. chpt. 2 1993-95), Internat. Coll. Pediat.; mem. AMA, N.Y. State Med. Soc. (com. on alcohol 1997—), Nassau County Med. Soc. (com. on mental health 1980—, project assist 1992—, Nassau Acad. Medicine Pub. Health com. 1991—, libr. com. 1993—, chmn. pediat. sect. 1995—), Nassau Pediat. Soc. (mem. exec. bd. 1972—, chmn. com. on mental health 1972-88, v.p. 1994-95, pres. 1996-97). A Non-Smoking Generation Internat. (organizer, med. dir. Am. divsn.), Am. Lung Assn., Nassau-Suffolk Lung Assn. (life mem., dir. 1982-84), Am. Physicians Fellowship for Israel Med. Assn., Assn. Children with Learning Disabilities (mem. profl. adv. bd.), La Leche League, Latin Am. Parents Assn., L.I. Sch. Health Edn. Coun. (bd. dirs. 1989-92), Alpha Epsilon Pi (chancellor Phi Theta chpt. 1955-56), Phi Delta Epsilon (consul Zeta chpt. 1960), B'nai Brith. Office: 3137 Hewlett Ave S Merrick NY 11566-5328

COPPIETERS, KRISTIAAN HENDRIK JUSTIN, computer company executive; b. Aalst, Belgium, Sept. 29, 1959; s. Willy Karel Antoon and Godelieve Elodia Adelina (LeCompte) C.; m. Kristel Adrienne Couck, Sept. 6, 1985; children: Joris, Elien, Wouter. Lic in Math., Ryksuniversiteit, Gent, Belgium, 1982; MS in Math. with great distinction, U. Gent, 1982. Tchr. math. Aalst, 1982-83; civil svc. position State U. Gent, 1983-84; sci. cooperator U. Gent, 1984-85, sci. asst., 1985-86, informaticus, 1986-88; informaticus Software House, Kortryk, Belgium, 1988-90; product mgr. Apple Centre, Gent, 1990-93; gen. mgr. Computer Cons., Kortryk, 1993-95; exec. Elemensa, Wellington, New Zealand, 1995—. Contbr. articles to Dr. Dobb's Jour. Avocations: bike riding, walking, music, photography. Home and Office: 34 the Track, Plimmerton, Porirua, Wellington New Zealand

COPPIN, POL R., spatial data sciences educator; b. Kortrijk, Flanders, Belgium, June 3, 1953; s. Jan and Maria (Vanlerberghe) C.; m. Ann G. Germonprē, Jan. 13, 1977; children: Sten, Jan, Matti. Student, U. Canterbury, Christchurch, New Zealand, 1971-72; BS in Agrl. Engring., U. Gent, Belgium, 1975, MS in Forestry Engring., 1977; PhD in Forestry, U. Minn., St. Paul, 1991. Dist. mgr. Belgian Forest Svc., Gent, 1977; assoc. expert Food and Agriculture Orgn. of UN, Santa Cruz, Bolivia, 1977-79; tech. officer Food and Agriculture Orgn. of UN, Rome, 1979-81; expert Food and Agriculture Orgn. of UN, Rangoon, Burma, 1982-84; rsch. coord. IWONL Eurosense NV, Brussels, 1981-82; project leader Deutsche Forstinventur Svc. Gmbh, Manila, 1984-86; sr. cons. Swedforest Consulting AB, Managua, Nicaragua, 1986-88; instr., doctoral fellow U. Minn., St. Paul, 1988-91; prof. Purdue U., West Lafayette, Ind., 1991-96; prof. U. Leuven, Belgium, 1996—, head dept. of land mgmt., 1998—; rsch. asst. U. Canterbury, 1971-72; short-term cons. various internat. agys., 1979-92. Contbr. articles to tech. jours. Scoutmaster Boy Scouts, Belgium, 1972-76, soccer coach Tippecanoe (Ind.) Soccer Assn., 1992-95, volleyball coach various teams and locations, 1977-81. Mem. IEEE (geosci. and remote sensing soc. 1992—), Am. Soc. Photogrammetry of Remote Sensing, Remote Sensing Soc. (U.K.), Internat. Soc. Tropical Foresters, Commonwealth Forestry Assn., Royal Flemish Engring. Soc., Agrl. Engring. Faculty Soc. Gent, Flemish Forestry Assn. Roman Catholic. Avocations: scuba diving, mountaineering, tennis, hiking, traveling. Office: U Leuven, Vital Decosterstraat 102, B-3000 Leuven Belgium

COPPLESTONE, DAVID WESLEY, artist, small business owner; b. Newton, Mass., Feb. 29, 1952; s. Wesley and Elizabeth (Winchell) C. Diploma, Art Inst. of Boston, 1975. Owner Landscape Design, Wellesley, Mass., 1967-73, Home Improvement Contractor, Wellesley, 1973—, Copplestone Artworks, Wellesley, 1975—; product design, graphic artist Fun-N-Safe Inc., Natick, Mass., 1991; owner gourmetgames.com, 1998—. Inventor of games: Lots, C.A. Hoopster, Geronimo and Stackm. Mem. Mus. of Fine Art, Boston. Mem. Wellesley Artist Assn., Cambridge Art Assn., Coply Soc., Italo Am. Ednl. Club. Avocations: golf, tennis, windsurfing, classic films, billiards. Home and Office: 6 Shadow Ln Wellesley MA 02482-4311

COPPOCK, JANET ELAINE, mental health nurse; b. Tipton, Ind., June 2, 1954; d. Jack Donavon and Bonnie Ruth (Luse) Weismiller; divorced; children: Jonathan Andrew, Daniel Jason. Student, Ball State U., 1972-73; ASN, Ind. U., Kokomo, 1977. RN, Ind., Mich.; cert. psychiat./mental health nurse ANCC. RN charge staff and med.-surg. Tipton County Meml. Hosp., Ind., 1977-79; RN psychiat. staff Howard Cmty. Hosp., Kokomo, 1987-89; pvt. nurse Kokomo, 1989-95; RN psychiat. and addiction treat-

ment, instr. Koala Hosp. & Counseling Ctr. Behavioral Healthcare Corp., Kokomo, 1995-98; RN psychiat. and addiction treatment Lafayette (Ind.) Behavioral Health System, 1998-99; RN psychiat. staff Home Hosp. of Greater Lafayette Health Svcs., Inc., Lafayette, 1999—; instr. parenting edn. Kinsey Youth Ctr., Kokomo, 1995-96; co-developer Koala Halfway House, Behavioral Healthcare Corp., Kokomo, 1996, house mgr., 1996-98. Author: Poetic Reflections, Expressions and Inspirations, 1986, Faithful Resolutions, 1993, Coming to Terms, 1998. Recipient Golden Poet award World Poetry Orgn., 1987, 88. Mem. Ind. State Nurses Assn., Internat. Platform Assn., Nurses Svc. Orgn., Writers' Ctr. Indpls., Ind. U. Alumni Assn. (life), Kokomo H.S. Band Boosters, Rose-Hulman Parent's Assn. Avocations: musical instruments, art, movies, basketball. Home: 2711 President Ln Kokomo IN 46902-3066

COPPOLECCHIA, ROSA, internist; b. Hoboken, N.J., Mar. 28, 1964; d. Sergio and Maria Corrada (Annese) C. BS in Biology, St. Peter's Coll., 1986; DO, U. Medicine & Dentistry N.J., 1992. Diplomate Nat. Bd. Osteo. Med. Examiners, Am. Bd. Internal Medicine. Intern Union Hosp., U. Medicine and Dentistry of N.J., 1992-93; resident in internal medicine Overlook Hosp., Summit, N.J., 1993-96; post-doctoral fellow environ. and occupl. medicine UMDNJ-Robert Wood Johnson Med. Sch., Piscataway, N.J., 1996-98; asst. dir. employee health svcs. Schering Plough Corp., Kenilworth, N.J. Mem. AMA, ACP (assoc.), Am. Coll. Preventive Medicine, , Am. Women Med. Assn., Am. Coll. Occupl. and Environ. Medicine, Am. Osteo. Assn., N.J. Med. Soc.

COPPS, SHEILA, Canadian government official; b. Hamilton, Ont., Can., Nov. 27, 1952; d. Victor Kennedy and Geraldine (Guthro) C.; m. Austin Thorne; children: Jacqueline, Susan, Steven, Danelle. BA in French, English with hons., U. Western Ont., London; postgrad., U. Rouen, France, McMaster U., Hamilton. Reporter Ottawa Citizen, 1974-76, Hamilton Spectator, 1977; asst. to Ont. Liberal leader Stuart Smith, Hamilton, 1977-81; mem. Legis. Assembly Ont., Toronto, 1981-84, House of Commons, Ottawa, 1984-97; apptd. dep. leader Liberal Party Can., Ottawa, Ont., 1990—; dep. prime min. Govt. of Can., Ottawa, 1993-97, min. environ., 1993-96, min. of Can. heritage, 1996—. Author: Nobody's Baby, 1986. Mem. Liberal Party. Office: Dept Can Heritage 12th Fl, 15 Eddy St care Diane Anka, Hull, PQ Canada K1A OM5

COPSETTA, NORMAN GEORGE, real estate executive; b. Pennsauken, N.J., Mar. 11, 1932; s. Joseph J. and Mary P. (DeMello) C.; m. Patricia Fitzpatrick, Mar. 5, 1971; children: Gregory, Margaret, Andrew, Norman G. Jr.; stepchildren: Samuel Sassano, James Sassano. Cert. real estate, Rutgers U. Extension, Camden, N.J., 1952; AA, Internat. Accts. Soc. Schl. Acctg., Chgo., 1968. Lic. title insurance agent, N.J. Settlement clk. Market Street Title Abstract Co., Camden, 1949-53; settlement administrator West Jersey Title & Guaranty Co., Camden, 1953; title examiner, abstract adminstr. Realty Abstract Co., Cherry Hill, N.J., 1954-64; mcpl. treas., tax collector Borough of Somerdale, N.J., 1961-65; title examiner, legal adminstr. Davis, Reberkenny & Abramowitz, Cherry Hill, 1974-97; pres., title officer Cooper Abstract Co., Cherry Hill, 1974-99, chmn. bd., 1997—; N.J. fgn. commr. of deeds in and for Pa., 1959—; mem. faculty Title Acad. N.J. Custodian of funds Somerdale Bd. Edn., 1960-64. Mem. ABA (assoc.), N.J. Title Ins. Agts. Assn., Haddonfield (N.J.) Hist. Soc., Camden County Hist. Soc. Avocation: local history. Office: Cooper Abstract Co 401 Cooper Landing Rd Ste C6 Cherry Hill NJ 08002-2598

COQUERY-VIDROVITCH, CATHERINE M., educator; b. Paris, Nov. 25, 1935; d. Remi and Marcelle (Weill) Vidrovitch; m. Michol L. Coquery, June 31, 1958; children: Natacha, Marina, Sarah, Julien. BA, U. Sorbonne, Paris, 1964, MA, 1969. ENS France, 1959-61; chef Travaux Ecole Pratique Hautes Etudes, Paris, 1962-69; maitre asst. Ecole Hautes Etudes Scis., Paris, 1969-71; maitre asst. U. Paris-7, 1971-72, prof., 1972-73, full prof. history, 1973—; Afrique, U. Paris 7/CNRS, 1983-95; adj. prof. SUNY, Binghamton, 1981—. Author: Brazza et la Mission de l'Ouest Africain, 1966, Le Congo au temps des grandes C concession naires, 1972; author: L'Afrique Noire de 1800 nos jours, 1976, Afrique Noire Permanences et Ruptures, 1984, Histoire des villes d'Afriqus noir, 1993, Les Africaines, 1994, L'Afrique et les Africains du 19e, 1999, others; contbr. articles to profl. jours.; mem. editl. bd. Cahiers d'Etudes Africaines. Mem. French Commn., UNESCO, 1986-95, v.p. commn. on racism and apartheid. Recipient Disting. Africanist award African Studies Assn., 1999; decorated Legion d'Honneur, Etat Francais, 1985, 96. Mem. Fellow W. Wilson Ctr. Washington; mem. Soc. Francaise d'Histoire d'Outremer (v.p. 1984—), Internat. African Inst. (cons. dir. 1986-92), Am. Coun. Learned Soc., Social Sci. Research Coun. (mem. joint com. on African studies), Internat. Hist. Studies Bureau, 2000-2004. Avocations: swimming, hiking. Office: Lab SEDET U Paris 7, 2 Place Jussieu, 75005 Paris France

CORAN, ARNOLD GERALD, pediatric surgeon; b. Boston, Apr. 16, 1938; s. Charles and Ann (Cohen) C.; m. Susan Myra Williams, Nov. 17, 1960; children: Michael, David, Randi Beth. AB, Harvard U., 1959, MD, 1963. Diplomate Am. Bd. Surgery, Am. Bd. Thoracic Surgery, Am. Bd. Pediat. Surgery. Intern in surgery Peter Bent Brigham Hosp., Boston, 1963-64, resident in general and thoracic surgery, 1964-69; resident in pediatric surgery Children's Hosp., Boston, 1966-68; chief pediat. surgery, assoc. prof. surgery U. South Calif. Med. Sch., L.A., 1972-74; chief pediat. surgery, prof. surgery U. Mich., Ann Arbor, 1974—; surgeon in chief C.S. Mott Childrens Hosp., Ann Arbor, 1981—. Contbr. articles to profl. jours. Lt. comdr. USN, 1970-72. Avocations: skiing, golf, running. Home: 505 E Huron St Apt 802 Ann Arbor MI 48104-1553 Office: CS Mott Childrens Hosp Rm F3970 Ann Arbor MI 48109-0245

CORBET, PHILIP STEVEN, zoology educator, consultant ecologist; b. Kuala Lumpur, Malaysia, May 21, 1929; s. Alexander Steven and Irene (Trewavas) C.; divorced; 1 child, Katarina Alexandra Kjellström. BS, U. Reading, Eng., 1950, DS, 1962; PhD, U. Cambridge, Eng., 1953, ScD, 1976. Zoologist East African Freshwater Fisheries Rsch. Orgn., Jinja, Uganda, 1954-57; entomologist East Africa Virus Rsch. Orgn., Entebbe, Uganda, 1957-62; rsch. scientist Entomology Rsch. Inst., Can. Dept. Agriculture, Ottawa, Ont., 1962-67; dir. Rsch. Inst., Can. Dept. Agriculture, Belleville, Ont., 1967-71; prof., chmn. dept. biology U. Waterloo, Ont., 1971-74; prof., dir. Joint Ctr. Environ. Scis. U. Canterbury and Lincoln Coll., New Zealand, 1974-78; prof. dept. zoology U. Canterbury, Christchurch, New Zealand, 1978-80; prof. zoology dept. biol. scis. U. Dundee, Scotland, 1980-90; head dept. U. Dundee, 1983-86; prof. emeritus zoology U. Dundee, Scotland, 1990—; hon. prof. U. Edinburgh, Scotland, 1996—; Commonwealth vis. prof. dept. applied biology U. Cambridge, Eng., 1979-80. Author: A Biology of Dragonflies, 1962, reprinted 1983, Dragonflies: Behavior and Ecology of Odonata, 1999; co-author: Dragonflies, 1960, rev. edit., 1985, The Odonata of Canada and Alaska, vol. 3, 1975, rev. edit., 1978. Recipient Gold medal Entomol. Soc. Can., 1974. Fellow Inst. Biology (London), Royal Soc. Edinburgh, Entomological Soc. Can., Royal Entomological Soc. Avocations: natural history, music. Fax: 01736 810 056. E-mail: pscorbet@creanmill.u-net.com. Home and Office: Crean Mill St Buryan, Cornwall TR19 6HA, England

CORBET, RICHARD HUGH, trade policy specialist, educator, writer; b. Perth, Australia, Nov. 18, 1936; came to U.S., 1990; s. John Arthur and Freda Marian (Sherwood) C.; m. Rosalind Mary Willett Bevan, June 10, 1961 (div. Oct. 1978); children: Zoe Mary Louisa, John Llewelyn Guy Sherwood. BA, U. Adelaide, Australia, 1960; postgrad., U. Keele, Eng., 1990-93. Cert. journalist Brit. Inst. Journalists. Rsch. asst. Cazenove & Co., stockbrokers, London, 1961-62; rsch. asst. conservative backbench com. on European cmty. Brit. Ho. of Commons, London, 1962-63; econs. corr. Thomson Newspapers on internat. econ. affairs, London, 1963-65; specialist writer The Times, London, 1965-68; dir. Trade Policy Rsch. Ctr., London, 1968-89; mng. editor The World Economy, Boston and Oxford, Eng., 1977-89; guest scholar Woodrow Wilson Internat. Ctr. for Scholars and the Brookings Inst., Washington, 1990-92; sr. fellow Manhattan Inst., N.Y. and Washington, 1992-93; dir. trade policy program Sigur Ctr. for Asian Studies George Washington U., Washington, 1993-97; pres. Cordell Hull Inst., Washington, 1998—; spl. advisor Opposition Spokesmen on Trade, Brit. Ho. of Commons, London, 1978-79; cons. on trade policy Internat. C. of C., Paris, 1979-83; mem. adv. com. on studies in internat. trade policy U. Mich. Press, Ann Arbor, 1989—; mem. adv. bd. The World Economy, Oxford and Boston, 1990—; cons. European Inst. Japanese Studies, Stockholm, 1994-97; cons. Swiss-Asia Found., Lausanne, 1996-99. Co-author: Trade Strategy for the Asia-Pacific Region, 1970; co-editor: Europe's Free Trade Area Experiment, 1970, Commonwealth Policy in a Global Context, 1971, In Search of a New World Economic Order, 1974; rapporteur various profl. reports, including Economic Policy for the European Community, 1974, Trade Routes to Sustained Economic Growth, 1987, Public Scrutiniy of Protection, 1987; contbr. articles to profl. jours. Served with Australian Army, 1955-56; with Citizen Mil. Forces Australian Army, 1957-61; with Royal Ulster Rifles Brit. Territorial Army, 1961-62. Fax: 202-338-0327. Home: 2400 Pennsylvania Ave NW Washington DC 20037-1729

CORBETT, JOHN ANTHONY, psychiatry educator; b. Leeds, Eng., May 26, 1936; s. Benjamin and Constance (Lucas) C.; m. Julia Margaret Nelson, June 20, 1963. MB BS, London U., 1960, D in Psychol. Medicine, 1963. Cons. psychiatrist St. Georges Hosp., London, 1967-69; physician Bethlem Royal & Maudsley Hosp., London, 1969-86; prof. devel. psych. U. Birmingham, Eng., 1986—. Editor: Scientific Basis of Mental Retardation, 1984, Training and Professional Development, 1994; editor Jour. Mental Handicap Rsch., 1990-94. Recipient gold medal Burden Found., 1979. Fellow Royal Coll. Physicians (Eng.), Royal Coll. Psychiatrists (Eng.), Royal Coll. Paediatricians & Child Health; mem. Br. Inst. Learning Disability (chmn. 1990-95), World Psychiat. Assn. (sec. child and adolescent sect. 1970-99). Avocation: gemology. E-mail: J.a.corbett@bham.ac.uk. Home: U Ashridge 88 Holtye Rd, East Grinstead RH19 3HU, England Office: U Birmingham, Lea Castle, Kidderminster DY103PP, England

CORBETT, LENORA MEADE, community college educator; b. Reidsville, N.C., Aug. 1, 1950; children: Kenneth Russell Johnson, Ralph Nathaniel Brown. AAS in Electromechanics, Tech. Coll. of Alamance, 1985, AAS in Electronics, 1986; BS in Indsl. Tech., Electronics, N.C. A&T State U., 1996. Cloth inspector Burlington (N.C.) Industries, 1971-74; electrician's helper Williams Electric, Greensboro, N.C., 1978, Nobility Mobile Homes, Reidsville, N.C., 1979; instr. math. and physics Alamance C.C., Graham, N.C., 1985—, chmn. learning resources, 1993. Contbr. poems to profl. publs. (Golden Poet award 1991, Merit award 1990, 92). Mem. sr. choir Jones Cross Rd. Ch., Reidsville, 1988-94, pastor's aide mem., 1988-90, jr. Sunday sch. tchr., 1989-91, asst. choir sec., 1988-94. Mem. AAUP, AAUW, Alamance C.C. Alumni Assn., Golden Key, N.C. A&T State U. Alumni Assn. Baptist. Avocations: cooking, reading, writing poetry, drawing, singing. Office: Alamance CC 1247 Jimmie Kerr Rd Graham NC 27253

CORBETT, MELANIE CAROLINE, ophthalmologist; b. London, June 19, 1963; d. Francis Roger Derek and Diana Caroline (Herman) C.; m. Simon Harold Wood, July 11, 1987. BSc with honors, Royal London Hosp. U. London, 1984, MBBS, 1987, MD, 1997. House officer Royal London, St. Bartholomew's and Moorfields Eye Hosps., 1987-90; registrar Oxford (United Kingdom) Eye Hosp., 1990-92; registrar St. Thomas' Hosp., London, 1992-93, Williams rsch. fellow, 1993-95; sr. registrar Moorfields Eye Hosp., London, 1996, Kings Coll. Hosp., London, 1996-97, St. Thomas' Hosp., London, 1997-98; Corneal fellow Moorfields Eye Hosp., London, 1998-99; cons. Western Eye Hosp., London, 1999—. Contbr. articles to profl. jours. Fellow Royal Coll. Surgeons, Royal Coll. Physicians and Surgeons (Watson prize lectureship 1996); mem. United Kingdom and Ireland Soc. of Cataract and Refractive Surgeons, Royal Coll. Ophthalmologists (chmn. ophthalmic trainees group 1996-98), Hurlingham Club London. Avocations: hockey, squash, tennis. E-mail: melanie@corbwood.demon.co.uk. Home: 2 Tredegar Sq, Bow, London E3 5AD, England Office: The Western Eye Hosp, Marylebone Rd, London NW1 5YE, England

CORBETT, MICHAEL MCGREGOR, retired judge; b. Pretoria, Transvaal, South Africa, Sept. 14, 1923; s. Alan Frederick and Johanna Sibella (McGregor) C.; m. Margaret Murray Luscombe, July 9, 1949; children: Margaret Joan, Felicity Anne, Andrew William, Peter Alan. BA, U. Cape Town, 1942, LLB, 1946, LLD (hon.), 1982; BA, U. Cambridge, Eng., 1947, LLB, 1948; LLD (hon.), U. of the Orange Free State, South Africa, 1990, U. Rhodes, South Africa, 1990, U. Pretoria, South Africa, 1993, U. Witwatersrand, South Africa, 1994, U. Stellenbosch, 1996. Queens counsel Cape Bar, 1961—; judge Cape Provincial div. The Supreme Ct., 1963-74, judge of appeal Appellate div., 1974-89, chief justice, 1989-96, ret., 1996. Co-author: (books) Law of Succession in South Africa, 1980, The Quantum of Damages in Bodily and Fatal Injury Cases, 4th edit., 1995. Lt. (1st Royal Natal Carbineers) South African Army, Egypt and Italy, 1942-45. Named Hon. Bencher Lincoln's Inn., 1991; recipient Order for Meritorious Svc., Pres. Mandela, 1996; hon. fellow Trinity Hall, Cambridge, 1992. Mem. ABA (hon.), City and Civil Svc. Club, Kelvin Grove Club. Presbyterian. Avocations: tennis, roaming table mountain.

CORBETT, RICHARD GRAHAM, parliament member; b. Southport, Merseyside, England, Jan. 6, 1955; s. Harry Graham and Kathleen Zita (Bryant) C.; m. Inge Elisabeth Van Gaal, July 1984 (div. 1989); 1 child, Tom; m. Anne Marguerite De Malsche, Dec. 28, 1989; children: Hannah, Laura. BA in Philosophy, Politics and Econ., U. Oxford, 1976; D in Polit. Sci., U. Hull, 1995. Trainee European Cmty., Luxembourg, 1976-77; sec. gen. European Coordination Bur. Internat. Youth Orgn., Brussels, 1977-81; civil servant European Parliament, Brussels, 1981-89; policy advisor Socialist Group, European Parliament, Brussels, 1989-94, dep. sec. gen., 1995-96; M.E.P. from Merseyside West constituency, 1996-99, M.E.P. from Yorkshire and Humber constituency, 1999—; v.p. Instl. Affairs Com., 1997-99; mem. Environment and Consumer Protection Com., 1997-99; mem. Econ. and Monetary Affairs Com., Animal Welfare Com., Disability Com., GLOBE; ambassador Mersey Partnership, Liverpool, Eng., 1997. Author: The European Parliament, 1995, 4th edit., 2000, A Socialist Policy for Europe, 1985, The Treaty of Maastricht: From Conception to Ratification, 1992, The European Parliament's Role in Closer EU Integration, 1998; contbr. articles to profl. jours. Pres. Jeunesse European Fedn., 1979-81; sec. GMB Trade Union, Brussels, 1990-93. Mem. Oxford U. Labour Club (sec. 1975), Fabian Soc. (br. chmn. 1984-85). Mem. Labour Party. Avocations: walking, football, skiing. Home: 22 William Henry St, W Yorks Saltaire BD18 4PP, England Office 2: 2 Blenheim Terr, Leeds L52 9JG, England

CORBIER, PHILIPPE, physiologist educator; b. Amiens, France, Mar. 2, 1947; m. Colette Fuzillier, Feb. 28, 1976; children: Christophe, Benoit. DSc, U. Paris XI, 1971. Rsch. scientist in devel. endocrinology and lab endocrinology Ctr. Nat. Recherche Scientifique, Orsay, France, 1972-94; instr. physiology U. Paris XI; rsch. scientist lab. neuroendocrinology UCLA, 1983. Contbr. articles to sci. jours. Mem. N.Y. Acad. Scis. Home: 18 rue Charles de Gaulle, 91400 Orsay France Office: U Paris XI Fac Pharmacy, rue Jean Baptiste Clement, 92290 Chatenay-Malabry France

CORBIN, CHARLES PAUL, cable television executive; b. Eureka, Calif., Feb. 18, 1943; s. Charles Paul and Louise F. (Hanson) C.; m. Marlyce Olsen, Feb. 2, 1963; children: Shelley, Matthew. BA, Humboldt State U., 1967; postgrad., U. Kans., 1971-72, Boise State U., 1973-74. Lic. 1st class radiotelephone operator. Announcer, engr. Stas. KRED/KIEM-TV, Eureka, 1960-62; ground flight service agt. Pacific Air Lines, San Francisco, 1962-65; prodn. mgr. Sta. KIEM-TV, Eureka, 1965-67; chief. engr., program dir. Sta. KTWU-TV, Topeka, 1967-72; program dir. Sta. KAID-TV, Boise, Idaho, 1972-74; sr. v.p. programming Sta. KOCE-TV, Huntington Beach, Calif., 1974-81; v.p., chief operating officer Sta. KQED/Golden Gate Prodns., San Francisco, 1981-83; dir. TV programming The Nashville Network/Opryland U.S.A., Inc., 1983-94, v.p., 1994—; v.p. TNN and CMT CBS Cable, 1997. Mem. State of Tenn. Film, Entertainment and Music Comm., Nashville, 1987—; pres. W.O. Smith Nashville Cmty. Music Sch., 1996—; bd. dirs. Nashville chpt. ARC, 1985—, chmn. exec. com., chmn. bd. dirs., 1991—, nat. conv. chmn., 1993; bd. dirs. Second Harvest, 1994—, Nashville 2d Harvest Food Bank, 1995—; mem. bd. advisors Belmont U., Nashville, 1996—; pres. W.O. Smith Cmty. Music Sch., 1996—. Recipient (with Willie Nelson) TV Spl. of Yr. award Music City News, 1985, Who's Who award Humboldt State U. Alumni Assn., 1989, Leonard T. Rambeau Internat. award Can. Country Music Assn., 1996, L.A. Area Emmy award, 1979, L. Rambeau award Canadian Country Music Assn. Internat., 1996, Hubert Long award NATD, 1997. Mem. NARAS (bd. govs., bd. dirs. Nashville chpt., Grammy awards TV com. 1998—), NATAS (bd. dirs. 1987—, pres. 1995—, pres. Mid-South chpt. 1994-97, trustee 1997—, Emmy award 1979, pres. leadership music 1999—), Country Music Assn. (bd. dirs. 1986—, pres. 1993, chmn. bd. dirs. 1994), Nat. Cable Acad., Nat. Assn. TV Program Execs., EAR Found. (chmn. bd. dirs. 1999—), Nashville Talent Dirs. Assn. (v.p. 1987—), Acad. Country Music, Nashville Area C. of C. (tourism task force 1991—), Center Hill Yacht Club, Nashville Yacht Club. Republican. Episcopalian. Avocations: boating, camping, traveling. Home: 1231 Knox Valley Dr Brentwood TN 37027-7150 Office: CBS Cable 1 Music Cir S Nashville TN 37203-4312

CORBIN, KRESTINE MARGARET, manufacturing company executive, fashion designer, columnist; b. Reno, Apr. 24, 1937; d. Lawrence Albert and Judie Ellen (Johnston) Dickinson; m. Lee D. Corbin, May 16, 1959 (div. 1982); children: Michelle Marie, Sheri Karin. BS, U. Calif., Davis, 1958. Asst. prof. Bauder Coll., Sacramento, 1974—; columnist Sacramento Bee, 1976-81; owner Creative Sewing Co., Sacramento, 1976—; pres., chief exec. officer Sierra Machinery Inc., Sparks, Nev., 1984, also bd. dirs.; nat. sales and promotion mgr. Westwood Retail Fabrics, N.Y.C., 1985—; bd. dirs. Sierra Pacific Resources, Sierra Pacific Power Co., NEWTRAC; cons. in field. Author: Suede Fabric Sewing Guide, 1973, Creative Sewing Book, 1978, (audio-visual) Fashions in the Making, 1974; producer: (nat. buyers show) Cream of the Cream Collections, 1978—, Style is What You Make It!, 1978-83. Named Exporter of Yr. State of Nev., 1989. Mem. Crocker Art Gallery Assn., 1960-78, Rep. Election Com., Sacramento, 1964, 68; apptd. by Gov. of Nev. to Internat. Program Adv. Com.; elected head Bd. Federal Reserve Bank 12th Dist., 1995—. Mem. Home Economists in Bus., Am. Home Econs. Assn., Internat. Fashion Group, Women's Fashion Fabrics Assn., Nat. Machine Tool Builders Assn. (mem. internat. export com.), Nat. Fluid Power Assn., Nev. World Trade Coun. (bd. dir.), Omicron Nu. Office: Sierra Machinery Inc 1651 Glendale Ave Sparks NV 89431-5912 also: PO Box 435 Reno NV 89504-0435

CORBITT, EUMILLER MATTIE, education educator, special education educator; b. Detroit, Jan. 7; d. Harrison and Arnetha (Tatum) Jones; m. Luther Corbitt (div. Dec. 1976); children: Tonya, Stephen. BS, Wayne State U., 1969, MEd, 1976, EdS, 1995. Cert. elem. and secondary sch. tchr., cert. tchr. spl. edn. emotionally and mentally impaired, grades K-12, elem. secondary sch. and central office administration. Tchr. mentally impaired Detroit Pub. Schs., 1969-72, tchr. emotionally impaired, 1972-75, spl. edn. tchr. cons., 1975—, Title I tchr. math. and sci., summers 1993-96; mediator Spl. Edn. Mediation Svcs., Lansing, Mich., 1986-96, Spl. Edn. Mediation Svcs. State Project PL 94-142, Lansing, Mich., 1985—; spl. edn. hearing officer Mich. Dept. Edn., Lansing, 1985—; developer at-risk program for emotionally impaired, socially maladjusted and ADHD students 12-17 yrs. Wolverine Human Svcs., Detroit, Mich. 1998—; mem. U.S. del. educators and attys. to South Africa for evaluation of schs. and govtl. agys. under leadership of Nelson Mandella Citizen Amb. program People to People, Spokane, Wash., 1996; mem. citizens alliance to uphold spl. edn. study adv. com. Emotionally Impaired Children in Mich./Lansing, 1986; mem. North Ctrl. Assn. accreditation com. Grand Rapids (Mich.) Pub. Schs., 1981; presenter profl. devel. conf. Detroit Fedn. Tchrs. and Det. Pub. Sch. Adminstrs., 1996. Chairperson Met. Detroit chpt. March of Dimes, 1987; chairperson Women Who Dare to Care com. United Negro Coll. Fund, Detroit, 1987-89; gen. coord. Mus. African Am. History, Detroit, 1987; tutor, usher, chairperson Hartford Meml. Bapt. Ch., Detroit, 1979—. Recipient Mayor's award of merit for Cmty. Svc., City of Detroit, 1987, plaque and cert. March of Dimes, 1987; recognized as outstanding educator Detroit Tchr., Detroit Fedn. Tchrs., 1987, 94. Mem. Coun. for Exceptional Children (presenter nat. conv. 1983, cert. 1983), Soc. Profls. in Dispute Resolution, Wayne State U. Alumni Assn., Delta Sigma Theta (chairperson 1965—), Phi Delta Kappa (chairperson). Avocations: golf, writing poetry, racquetball, painting, reading. Home: 1249 Navarre Pl Detroit MI 48207-3014 Office: Detroit Pub Schs Office Specialized Std Svcs 5057 Woodward Ave Rm 1010 Detroit MI 48202-4050

CORBITT, GRETCHEN JOHNSON, music educator; b. Delway, N.C., Dec. 20, 1920; d. Leondias Lafayette Johnson and May Picolo Garner; m. John Calvin Corbitt, Dec. 22, 1949 (dec. Aug. 1995); children: Nathan, Alzada, Gretchen, Rebekah. AB, Meredith Coll., 1943. Music tchr. McDowell Sch. System, Marion, N.C., 1969-80; dir. theatre Foothills Children's, Marion, N.C., 1973-74; dir. boys choir Cmty. Boys Choir, Marion, N.C., 1974-75; v.p. McDowell N.C. Symphony, Marion, N.C., 1974; columnist McDowell News, Marion, N.C., 1980-84; writer, 1979-98. Author: No Woman Had Gone, 1979, Journey Back to God, 1998. V.p. McDowellNorth Carolina Symphony, 1974. Mem. State Music Assn., Nat. Music Educators Conf., Nat. Pen Women League. Republican. Baptist. Avocations: reading, board games, camping. Home: 25 Cardinal Dr Asheville NC 28806-9726

CORBRIDGE, STUART EDWARD, geography educator; b. Blackpool, Lancashire, Eng., Apr. 11, 1957; s. Edward and Barbara Mary (Jamieson) C.; m. Joan Mary Simms, Apr. 18, 1981; 1 child, Joanne Elizabeth. BA, Cambridge (U.K.) U., 1978, PhD, 1986. Lectr. Huddersfield (U.K.) U., 1981-85, London U., 1985-87; assoc. prof. Syracuse (N.Y.) U., 1987-88; lectr. Cambridge U., 1988—; prof. U. Miami, Fla., 1999—; vis. prof. Jawaharcal Nehru U., New Delhi, 1993; cons. dept. internat. devel. Govt. U.K., 1998—, Econ. and Social Rsch. Coun., Govt. U.K., 1996-99; fellow Sidney Sussex Coll., Cambridge, 1988—. Author: Debt and Development, 1993; co-author: (with J. Agrew) Mastering Space, 1995; (with J. Harriss) Reinventing India, 2000; contbr. articles to profl. jours. Recipient awards U.K. Natural Resources Internat., 1997-99, U.K. Dept. Internat. Devel., 1998—, U.K. Econ. and Social Rsch. Coun., 1998-2000. Mem. Assn. Asian Studies, Devel. Studies Assn. Avocations: running, soccer, soul music, contemporary fiction. Office: U Miami Sch Internat Study PO Box 8067 Coral Gables FL 33124-2060

CORBUCCI, GIAN GIACOMO, medical educator; b. Gubbio, Italy, Jan. 1, 1947; s. Domenico and Licia (Massi) C.; m. Irene Ottavi, Aug. 1, 1983; 1 child, Leonardo. MD, U. Perugia, Italy, 1973. Physician anesthesia dept. Civil Hosp., Gubbio, 1974-88; rsch. fellow U. London, 1986-88; assoc. prof. U. Cagliari, Italy, 1988-99; prof. sport medicine, dir. Sch. Anesthesia/Intensive Care U. Cagliari, 1996—; dir. rsch. program in intensive care in collaboration with Columbia U., N.Y.C.; dir. rsch. program on cellular metabolism. Author 2 books and more than 150 papers in field. Mem. Rotary. Mem. Democratic Party. Roman Catholic. Avocations: running. Home: Via Dante 70, 06024 Gubbio Perugia Italy Office: Ospedale S Giovanni di Dio, V Ospedale, 09100 Cagliari Italy

CORBY, SIR BRIAN, insurance company executive; b. Raunds, Northants, Eng., May 10, 1929; s. Charles Walter and Millicent Corby; m. Elizabeth Mairi McInnes, 1952; children: Fiona, Jane, Nicholas. MA, St. John's Coll., Cambridge, Eng., 1952; DSc (hon.), City U., London, 1989; D.Litt. (hon.), Coun. for Nat. Acad. Awards, 1991; DSc (hon.), U. Hertfordshire, 1996. Mgr. O'seas Life Prudential Assurance Co. Ltd., London, 1966-68, asst. gen. mgr., 1968-73, dep. gen. mgr., 1974-75, gen. mgr., 1976-79; chief actuary Prudential Corp. Plc., London, 1980-81, group chief exec., 1982-90; chmn. Prudential Corp. Plc, London, 1990-95, Montanaro Smaller Cos., Investment Trust Plc, London, 1995-99, Moorfield Estates Plc, London, 1996—, The Brockbank Group, London, 1997-2000; chmn. South Bank Bd., U.K., 1990-98; bd. dirs. XL Capital Ltd. Pres. Geneva Assn., 1990-93, Nat. Inst. Econ. & Social Rsch., 1994—; chancellor U. Hertfordshire, 1993-96. Created knight bachelor Order of Brit. Empire. Fellow Inst. Actuaries; mem. Confedn. Brit. Industry (pres. 1990-92). Office: The Brockbank Group, 10 St Mary Ave, London EC3A 9BS, England

CORCHON, LUIS CARLOS, economics educator, researcher; b. Madrid, Mar. 28, 1949; s. Justo and Amparo (Diaz) C.; m. Maria Del Mar Lopez, Oct. 26, 1984. B degree, Colegio del Pilar, Madrid, 1967; lic., U. Complutense, Madrid, 1973, D degree, 1978; PhD, London Sch. Econs., 1986. Asst. prof. U. Complutense, Madrid, 1974-76, assoc. prof., 1978-84; prof. U. Alicante, 1988-97, U. Pompeu Fabra, Barcelona, 1997-98, U. Carlos III, Madrid, 1998—; cons. Bellore, Morristown, N.J.; head Commn. for Evaluating Rsch. in Econs., Spain, 1992; mem. com. Congress on Resource Allocation, Montreal, 1996, European meeting Econometric Soc., Istanbul, 1996, European Workshop on Gen. Equilibrium, Barcelona, 1998. uthor: The Theory of Implementation, 1996, Theories of Imperfect Competitive Markets, 1996, 2d. edit., 2000; assoc. editor Jour. Pub. Econ. Theory, 1997, Revista

Espanola de Economia, 1991-97; contbr. articles to profl. jours. including Jour. Econ. Theory and Quar. Jour. Econs. Fulbright scholar, 1989; recipient Deutcher Akademischer Austauschdienst award, 1991-94, Internat. Assn. for Cooperation with Scientists from Newly Ind. States award European Commn., 1995—. Avocations: history, novels, travel, movies. Office: U Carlos III, C/Madrid 126, 28903 Getafe, Madrid Spain

CORCOS, THIERRY, physician, cardiologist; b. Tunis, Tunisia, Oct. 8, 1954; s. Victor and Elyane (Krief) C.; m. Laure Dehen, Mar. 22, 1991; children: Léa, Lise. Intern, H Paris, 1978; MD, U. Paris-VII, 1982, diploma in echocardiography, 1982, specialist in cardiology, 1983. Cert. statis. methodology, U. Paris-South, 1982; cert. cardiovasc. pharmacology, U. Montreal, Que., Can., 1983; certs. of stats., U. Montreal, 1984. Intern in medicine, emergency dept. Lariboisière Hosp., Paris, 1977-78; resident in medicine and cardiology Paris Hosps., 1978-82; resident in cardiology Montreal Heart Inst., 1982-83, clin. and rsch. fellow, 1983-84; chef de clinique des univs. U. Paris Sch. Medicine, 1984-87; asst. Paris hosps., dept. thoracic and cardiovasc. surgery La Pitié U. Hosp., 1984-87; co-dir. interventional cardiology Ctr. Médico-Chirurgical Parly-Grand Chesnay, Le Chesnay, France, 1987-99, Clinique Turin, Paris, 1999—; invited lectr. and presenter in field; lectr. interventional cardiology U. Paris, 1997—; dir. Francophone meeting on interventional cardiology, 1997—. Reviewer Arch. Mal. Coeur, European Heart Jour., Am. Heart Jour., Cathet Cardiovascular Intervent; contbr. over 100 articles to med. and scientific jours.; co-author (audio-visual ednl. film) Outpatient Coronary Angiography, 1994. Fellow French Soc. Cardiology, European Soc. Cardiology, Am. Coll. Cardiology, Am. Heart Assn. Coun. on Clin. Cardiology, Soc. for Cardiac Angiography and Interventions; mem. Am. Heart Assn. Coun. on Basic Sci., Interventional Cardiology Group, European Working Group on Coronary Circulation. Jewish. Avocations: music, history, religion, calligraphy. Home: 20 rue des Ecoles, 75005 Paris France Office: Clinique Turin Dept Cardio, 9 rue de Turin, 75008 Paris France

CORCOSTEGUI, ANGEL, bank executive. Dep. chmn., chief exec. Banco Santander Ctrl. Hispano, Madrid. Office: Banco Santander Ctrl Hispan, Plaza Canalejas 1, 28014 Madrid Spain

CORD, STEVEN B., foundation administrator; b. N.Y.C., July 22, 1928; s. Mandel E. and Bertha T. Cord; children: Emily, Louise, Daniel. EdD, Columbia U., 1962. Prof. Indiana U. of Pa., 1962-86; pres. Henry George Found. Am., Columbia, Md., 1986—; dir. Henry George Sch., N.Y.C., 1980—, Robert Schalkenbach Found., N.Y.C., 1981—; dir. rsch. Ctr. for the Study of Econs., 1980—. Author: Henry George: Dreamer or Realist?, 1965, rev. edit., 1984, Catalyst, 1979, Evidence for Land Value Taxation, 1987. Home: 6167 Llanfair Dr Columbia MD 21044-3848 Office: Henry George Found Am 2000 Century Plz # 238 Columbia MD 21044-3273

CORDANI, UMBERTO GIUSEPPE, geosciences educator; b. Milan, Italy, May 17, 1938; arrived in Brazil, 1949; m. Luigi and Beatrice Angela (Colnaghi) C.; m. Lisbeth Kaiserlian, July 3, 1965; children: Marina, Renato. Degree in Geology, U. São Paulo, Brazil, 1960, DSc, 1968. Instr. U. São Paulo, 1961-68, asst. prof., 1968-73, free-docent, 1973-77, assoc. prof., 1977-80, prof., 1980—, dir. Inst. of Geoscis., 1987-91; dir. Inst. Advanced Studies, U. São Paulo, 1993-97; vis. prof. U. Brussels, 1971, U. Chile, 1972, U. Tex., 1974, U. Oxford, 1981, U. Calif., 1984, U. Milan, 1987. Author books; contbr. articles to profl. jours. Decorated medal of merit Regional Coun. Engring., 1993, Gt. Cross of Sci. Merit, Brazilian Ministry Sci., 1994, Gold medal Jose Bonifacio, Brazilian Geol. Soc., 1998, French Govt. Chevalier dans; 'Ordre des Palmes Academiques, 1999; Gulbenkian Found. prof., Portugal, 1996; Chevalier/Ordre des Palmes Academiques, French Min. Edn. Fellow Brazilian Acad. Sci., Latin Am. Acad. Sci., Third World Acad. Sci. (Medal lecture 1996); mem. Internat. Union Geol. Scis. (officer, exec. com., pres. 1988-92). Home: Av Caxingui 283/71, 05579000 Sao Paulo Brazil Office: Inst Geoscis/U Sao Paulo, Rua do Lago 562, 05508-900 São Paulo Brazil

CORDARO, ROBERT ANTHONY, financial analyst; b. Phila., Feb. 18, 1954. BS, Phila. U., 1976, MBA, 1984. CFA. Asst. treas. VF Corp., Reading, Pa., 1989-92; CFO Wrangler Europe, London, 1992-94, VF Europe, Brussels, 1994-96; pres. VF Asia Pacific, Hong Kong, 1996—. Mem. Assn. for I, Am. C. of C. (Hong Kong). E-mail: cordarb@vfc.com. Fax: 852 2318 1825. Office: VF Asia Ltd, 22 Kai Cheung Rd, Kowloon Hong Kong

CORDEIRO, CECILIA, chemist, educator; b. Havana, Cuba, Oct. 6, 1944; arrived in Costa Rica, 1994; d. Vicente Cordeiro and Maria Naranjo; m. Ricardo López, Apr. 29, 1968 (dec. Apr. 1998); children: Ricardo, Lianne. Lic. in chemistry, U. Havana, 1969, M in Chemistry, 1976; PhD, 1981, U. Costa Rica, 1997. Mem. faculty U. Havana, 1969-77, asst. prof. analytical chemistry, 1977-83, prof. analytical chemistry, 1983-94, rsch. scientist Inst. Materials and Reagants for Electronic Industry, 1985-94; tchr. chemistry Lincoln H.S., San Jose, Costa Rica, 1995—; dir. dept. analytical chemistry Havana U., 1971-75; cons. Cuban Nickel Industry, 1971-85; invited prof. Moscow U., 1977, 79, 82, Tech. U., Budapest, Hungary, 1985, 87, U. Autonoma Madrid, 1987, 90, 92, 93. Author: (textbooks) Analytical Chemistry, 1985-91; contbr. articles to profl. jours.; patentee in field. Mem. N.Y. Acad. Sci. Home: Pavas, 310-1000 San Jose Costa Rica Office: Lincoln Sch, Moravia, 1919-1000 San Jose Costa Rica

CORDELL, BEULAH FAYE, special education educator; b. Clifty, Ark., Mar. 5, 1939; m. Jack Cordell; children: Dennis, Kevin. B in English and Social Studies, U. Ark., 1987, M in Spl. Edn. and Reading, 1994. Cert. tchr. K-12, Ark. Tchr. Benton County Alternative Sch., Rogers, Ark., 1988-90, Job Tng. Partnership Act at Fayetteville, Ark., 1990-91; reading and study skills tchr. N.W. Ark. C.C., Rogers, 1991-94; dir. spl. edn. tutoring The One-Room Sch., Springdale, 1993—; kindergarten tchr. Springdale, 1994-96; tchr. ESL and GED N.W. Tech. Inst., 1996—. Contbg. writer The Mailbox Mag., 1999—. Bd. dirs. Ozark Literacy, Inc., Fayetteville, 1984-90; contbg. mem. Beaver Lake Lit., Inc., Rogers, 1994—. Recipient Tchg. Excellence award Gamma Beta Phi, 1993, Outstanding Achievement cert. Internat. Biog. Inst., Cambridge, Eng., 1998. Mem. Coun. for Exceptional Children, Am. Assn. Mentally Retarded, Poets and Writers Assn., Am. Biog. Inst. (rsch. bd. of advisors 1999). Avocations: oil painting, writing poetry and children's fiction. Home: 1100 N Monitor Rd Springdale AR 72764-9024 Office: 807 C Bailey St Springdale AR 72764-4247

CORDELL, HILARY MARGARET, solicitor; b. Birmingham, Eng., Aug. 3, 1960; arrived in Hong Kong, 1987; d. Reginald Terence and Rose Elizabeth Curley; m. Edward Ki Fung Ng, Dec. 28, 1988; children: Edward Christian, Elise Catherine, Laurence James. LLB, Leicester U., 1981. Asst. solicitor Herbert Smith, London, 1985-87, Slaughter & May, Hong Kong, 1987-90, Wragge & Co., Birmingham, Eng., 1990-94; ptnr. Baker & McKenzie, Hong Kong, 1994—. Contbr. Hong Kong New Gazette, 1994-96. Mem. Hong Kong Law Soc. Anglican. Avocations: walking, ornithology, literature. Office: 12th Fl Hutchison House, 10 Harcourt Rd, Hong Kong China

CORDER, STEVEN LEE, non-profit organization executive; b. Sacramento, Sept. 24, 1958; s. Donald Leon and Betty Jean C.; m. Thea Marie, Feb. 4, 1960; children: Erica, Jamie. BSBA, U. Denver, 1981, MBA, 1982. Fin. reporting mgr. Norwest Banks, Denver, 1987-90; v.p., controller Christian Booksellers Assn., Colorado Springs, 1990-96; fin. mgr. Cook Comms., Colorado Springs, 1996-97; dir. fin. Focus on the Family, Colorado Springs, 1997—. Republican. E-mail: Steve.Corder@juno.com.

CORDERO, MANUEL RAUL, ophthalmologist; b. Lima, Peru, Oct. 29, 1931; s. Manuel Nicolas and Josefina Domitila (Cossi) C.; m. Emma Aida Garcia-Zapatero, June 21, 1958; children: Raul, Manuel. MD, U. San Marcos, Lima, 1957, Cavetano Heredia, Lima, 1972. Diplomate Am. Bd. Ophthalmology. Rotating intern St. Bernard Hosp., Chgo., 1958-59; resident in ophthalmology Chgo. ENT Hosp., 1959-62; asst. ophthalmologist Social Security Hosp., Lima, 1962-66, chief ophthalmologist, 1966-69; ophthalmologist Anglo Am. Hosp., Lima, 1969-85; pvt. practice Lima, 1985—. Ophthalmologist Summer Inst. Linguistics, Peruvian jungle, 1964-82, Orphans of Terrorism, Ayacucho, Peru, 1996-97. Served with Peruvian Army med. corps, 1957-59. Fellow ACS, Am. Acad. Ophthalmology; mem. Peruvian Ophthalmol. Soc. (past pres.). Home: Jose Antonio 170, 12 La Molina Peru Office: Tudela y Varela 138, San Isidro Peru

CORDESS, CHRISTOPHER CHARLES, consultant forensic psychiatrist, psychoanalyst; b. London, Apr. 28, 1945. MB, Dublin (Ireland) U., 1970, MA, 1972; MPhil, U. London, 1984. Cons. forensic psychiatrist St. Bernard's Hosp., London, 1987-96; prof. forensic psychiatry U. Sheffield, Eng., 1997—; vis. prof. psychotherapy Kyushu U., Fukuoka, Japan, 1996-97; pvt. practice psychoanalyst, London. Editor: Forensic Psychotherapy, Crime Psychodynamics and the Offender Patient, 1996; contbr. chtps. to books and articles to profl. jours. Fellow Royal Coll. Psychiatrists, Royal Coll. Physicians, Savile Club, Hurlingham Club, Marylebone Cricket Club. Avocations: literature, travel, motorbikes, broadcasting on professional and related subjects, music. Office: Rampton Hosp, Retford Notts, York DN22 0PD, England

CORDINER, WILLIAM LAWSON, retired diplomat; b. Peterhead, Aberdeen, Scotland, Mar. 9, 1935; s. Alexander Lamb and Jessie Lawson (Browlie) C.; m. Annie Milton, Oct. 7, 1935; 1 child: Neil Stuart. Cert., Scottish Higher Learning, Boroughmuir, Edinburgh, 1952. Sr. collector of income tax East African Common Svcs., Nairobi, Kenya, 1960-67; exec. officer H.M. Diplomatic Svc., London, 1967-68; acct. H.M. Diplomatic Svc., Saigon, 1968-70; vice consul H.M. Diplomatic Svc., Addis Ababa, Ethiopia, 1971-74; econ. sec. H.M. Diplomatic Svc., Kuwait, 1974-75; comml. sec. H.M. Diplomatic Svc., Baghdad, 1975-77; Middle East advisor DHSS Export Divsn., London, 1977-79; Rhodesia desk H.M. Diplomatic Svc., London, 1979-80; Brit. Govt. rep. H.M. Diplomatic Svc., Antiqua, Barbada and St. Kitts Nevis, 1980-83; consul for Pacific Northwest, U.S. H.M. Diplomatic Svc., Seattle, 1983-87; asst. commonwealth coord. dept. H.M. Diplomatic Svc., London, 1988-90; sec. to Brit. delegation Commonwealth Heads of Govt. Mtg., Kuala Lumpur, 1989; high commr., consul for Pacific islands under Am. sovereignty south of equator H.M. Diplomatic Svcs., Nuku'Alofa, Kingdom Tonga, 1990-94. Named Hon. Citizen of Wash. State, 1987, Hon. Ambassador of Goodwill, Wash. State, 1987; decorated Order of the Brit. Empire, HM The Queen, London, 1995. Mem. Chateau des Vigiers Golf and Country Club/France. Avocations: golf, gardening, travel, painting, writing.

CORDINI, GIOVANNI, Italian and law educator; b. Castelsangiovanni, Italy, Aug. 2, 1950; s. Ettore and Luisa (Lattuada) C. Degree in polit. sci., U. Pavia, Italy, 1974. Lectr. U. Pavia, 1981-92, prof., 1993—; presenter in field. Author: The Compulsory Vote, 1988, Environmental Law, 1995, Environmental Comparative Law, 1997, Legal Studies on Citizenship, 1998, Theoretical Constitutional Perspectives on Citizenship, 1998; editor: Towards the World Governing of the Environment, 1996. Mem. Internat. Assn. Water Law, Internat. Ct. of the Environment Found. (mem. sci. coun.), European Acad. Arts, Scis. and Humanities (corres. mem.). Roman Catholic. Office: U Pavia, Strada Nuova N 65, 27100 Pavia Italy

CORDOBA, RICARDO, medieval history educator, researcher; b. Cordoba, Spain, Nov. 18, 1960; s. Ricardo an d Magdalena (De La Llave) C.; m. Maria Trinidad Conde, Oct. 1, 1993; children: Purificacion, Blanca. D of History, U. Cordoba, 1986. Asst. prof. U. Extremadura, Caceres, Spain, 1988-89; asst. prof. U. Cordoba, 1989-90, sr. lectr., 1990—; adv. editor Meridies Review, Cordoba, 1994—, Molinum Review, Madrid, 1998—; mem. cons. tech. team Cordoba Restoration of Cordoba Water Mills, 1996—; dir. rsch. project The Fountains of Cordoba, 1997—. Author: The Medieval Industry of Cordoba, 1990, Sexual Assaults in Medieval Castile, 1994; co-author: Kinship, Authority and Thought. The Castilian Nobility (12-15 Centuries), 1990, Fountains From Cordoba Province, 1999. Recipient Rsch. fellowship Ministerio Ed. Yciencia, 1984-87, Postdoctoral Rsch. fellowship Centro De Estudios Historicos, 1988-89. Mem. Soc. History of Tech., Spanish Soc. History of Scis. and Techniques, Spanish Soc. Medieval Studies. Avocations: footing, photography, travels. Home: Tomas De Aquino 12 2o1, 14004 Cordoba Spain

CORDÓN, LUIS FRANCISCO, mechanical engineer, educator, consultant; b. Houston, Feb. 7, 1964; s. Luis Alfredo and Vilma Beatriz (Rodas) C. BS in Mech. Engring., Texas A&M U., 1989; MA in Bus. Adminstrn., U. Francisco Marroquin, 2000. Prodn. asst. Orenstein & Koppel, Hattingen, Germany, 1990; design engr. Ascensores Universales, Guatemala City, Guatemala, 1990-92; prodn. supt. Tabacalera Nacional, Guatemala City, 1992-93; tech. mgr. Productos Electricos, Guatemala City, 1993-2000; orgn. and methods mgr. Xanadu Corp., 2000—; prof. catedratico Universidad del Valle de Guatemala, 1991-97; prof. econs. Universidad Francisco Marroquin, 2000—; cons. Ascensores Universales, 1993-94; thesis admnstrv.-fin. cons., 1999—. Treas. Club Ecuestre Vista Hermosa, Guatemala, 1992-94; vocal II Assn. Nat. de Ecuesties de Guatemala, 1993-97. Mem. ASME. Roman Catholic. Avocation: horseback riding. Home: 18 av B 7-69 z 15 VH 1, 01015 Guatemala City Guatemala Office: Calz Aguilar Batres 42-21 z 12, Guatemala City Guatemala

CORDONNIER-PRATT, MARIE-MICHÈLE, molecular biologist, researcher; b. Sallanches, France, Sept. 28, 1951; came to U.S., 1985; d. Gérard Anatole Cordonnier and Odile Marie Genoyer; m. Lee Herbert Pratt, Aug. 4, 1990. Degree, U. Rouen, France, 1975, PhD, 1977; D, U. Paris, 1987. Postdoctoral scholar U. Rouen, 1977-78; rsch. assoc. Vanderbilt U., Nashville, 1978-79, USDA, Beltsville, Md., 1979-80; maitre asst. U. Geneva, Switzerland, 1980-85; staff scientist Ciba-Geigy Biotech., Research Triangle Park, N.C., 1985-90; rsch. assoc. Inst. Nat. Rsch. Agronomique, Versailles, France, 1991-92; rsch. sci. U. Ga., Athens, 1992-99, sr. rsch. scientist, 2000—; cons. Gene Machines, San Carlos, Calif., 1999—; sci. cons. Univ. Pky. Alliance, Athens, 1999—; tech. developer U. Ga., 1997—; econ. developer Applied Genetic Tech. Resource, Athens, 1996—. Contbr. articles to profl. jours.; patentee in field. Rsch. grantee Roussel-Uclaf, 1977-79, Marc Birkigt Funds, 1982, Swiss Nat. Funds for Sci. Rsch., 1983-86, Ciba-Geigy AG, Basel, Switzerland, 1983-85, USDA, 1991-92, 93-96, 98-2000, NSF, 1996-99, 98—, S & K Seeds (Novartis), Enkhuizen, The Netherlands, U. Ga. Rsch. Found., 1998-2000, Ga. Rsch. Alliance/Gene Machines, 1999. Roman Catholic. Avocations: painting, sculpture, dancing, skiing, music. Office: U Ga Dept Botany Athens GA 30602

CORDWELL, ARTHUR G., county official; b. Portage, Pa., Sept. 29, 1938; s. Jacob and Cora Cordwell; m. Mary Ann Cordwell, June 29, 1957; children: John, James, Toni. BSME, Point Park Coll., Pitts., 1985. Coord. econ. devel. svcs. Consol. Nat. Gas Co., Pitts., 1981-86; mgr. econ. devel. Peoples Natural Gas Co., Pitts., 1986-95; exec. dir. econ. devel. County devel. Corp. of Butler, Pa., 1996—. Chmn. Butler County Tourism, 1999; bd. dirs. Tri-County Pvt. Industry Coun., Butler, 1998-99, Pa. Econ. Devel. Coun., 1997-98; mem. Am. Econ. Devel. Coun. Mem. Butler County C. of C. (bd. dirs. 1998-99).

CORDWELL, NIGEL MARTIN, advocate, solicitor; b. Douglas, Isle of Man, Oct. 26, 1961; s. Norman and Leonora (Barrow) C.; m. Karen Jayne Price; 3 children. Degree in Latin, Liverpool (Eng.) U., 1983; degree in law, Manchester (Eng.) Met. U., 1986. Lic. solicitor Eng., 1989, advocate Isle of Man, 1996, solicitor Ireland, (Eire), 2000. Prin. NM Cordwell & Co., 1983-86; asst. Gregson & Ashton, Liverpool, 1987-91; ptnr. Prickett Partnership, Manchester, 1991-94; pupil advocate Simcocks, Isle of Man, 1994-96; ptnr. Callow & Cordwell, Douglas, Isle of Man, 1996—; mem. notarial faculty Office of Archbishop of Canterbury, 1994. Author: The Civil Investigation Handbook, 1996. Fellow Inst. Profl. Investigators, Coll of Personal Injury Lawyers; mem. Assn. Personal Injury Lawyers, Isle of Man Law Soc., English Law Soc., Irish Law Soc. Office: Callow & Cordwell, 6 Hill St, Douglas IM1 1EF, Isle of Man

CORE, HARRY MICHAEL, psychiatric social worker, mental health therapist and administrator; b. Core, W.Va., Oct. 7, 1933; s. Earl Lemley and Freda Bess (Garrison) C.; m. Jane Ann Boggs, Oct., 1976; children: Kevin M., Brian D., Jennifer T. BS, W.Va. U., 1955; MSW, U. N.C., 1957. Psychiat. social worker Lake County Mental Health Ctr., Mentor, Ohio, 1960-67, asst. dir., 1967-72, exec. dir., 1972-87; psychiat. social worker Simon & Bertschinger MDs, Inc., Eastlake, Ohio, 1966-92; clin. assoc. Kent A. Young, PhD & Assocs., Mentor, Ohio, 1992—; trustee Tri-Care, Inc., Westlake, Ohio, 1986-87. Trustee Western Res. Counseling, Inc., 1988—, Point One Behavioral Health Svcs., 1997—; mem. adv. bd. Lakeland C.C. Sch. Nursing, 1983—. 1st lt., U.S. Army, 1957-60. Fellow Am. Orthopsychiat. Assn. (life); mem. Acad. Cert. Social Workers, NASW, Ohio Coun. Cmty. Mental Health Agys. (trustee 1981-84, v.p. 1984). Democrat. Mem. Christian Ch. (Disciples of Christ). Home: 6707 Stratford Rd Painesville OH 44077-1533 Office: Lake Ambulatory Care Ctr 9500 Mentor Ave Ste 320 Mentor OH 44060-8712

CORELL, HANS, Swedish judge, diplomat; b. Västermo, Sweden, July 7, 1939; s. Alf Corell and Margit Norrman; m. Inger Peijfors, 1964; 2 children. LLB, U. Uppsala, 1962; LLD (hon.), U. Stockholm, 1997. Ct. clk. Eksjö Dist. Ct. and Göta Ct. of Appeal, 1962-67; asst. judge Västervik Dist. Ct., 1968-72; legal adviser Ministry of Justice, 1972, 74-79; assoc. judge of appeal Svea Ct. of Appeal, 1973; asst. under-sec. divsn. constitutional and adminstr. law Ministry of Justice, 1979-81; appointed judge of appeal, 1980; under-sec. Ministry of Justice, 1981-84; amb., under-sec. for legal affairs Ministry of Fgn. Affairs, 1984-94; under sec.-gen. for legal affairs The Legal Counsel of the UN, 1994—; mem. Permanent Ct. of Arbitration, The Hague, 1990—. Co-author: Sekretesslagen, 1992; contbr. articles to profl. jours. Avocations: art, music, ornithology. Office: Office of Legal Affairs UN United Nations Plz New York NY 10017

COREN, LANCE SCOTT, consulting firm executive; b. Inglewood, Calif., Dec. 19, 1949; s. Melville and Shirley Ann (Ehrlich) C.; m. Susan Hodges; 1 child, Amy Elizabeth. BSBL, Van Norman U., L.A., 1973; cert. ins. law, UCLA, 1975; cert. comparative psychology, The Calif. Grad. Inst., 1975; MBA, Cal-Western U., 1976; cert. automotive analysis, UCLA Traffic Inst., 1991, UCLA Traffic Inst., 1991. Cert. automotive expert, Calif., Nat. Inst. Automotive Svc. Elegance. Auto claims adjustor Gulf & Western Cos., L.A., 1974-77; western regional mgr., field ops. Guaranty Nat. Ins. Group, L.A., 1977-80; pres., chief exec. officer L.S.C. Enterprizes, Inc., Torrance, Calif., 1980—; pres., CEO L.S.C. Ent., Inc./Corenco Corp., N.Y.C./Torrance, Calif., 1980—; ptnr. C&H Racing Team U.S.A., 1989—; bd. dirs. Capital Investment Trust, N.Y., L.S.C. Investment Co., L.A., N.Y.C., Palm Springs Ann. Rd. Races-Concours D'Elegance, Newport Invitiational Concours D'Elegance, Palos Verdes Concours D'Elegance; cons. Auto Assn. Am., L.A., 1984-88, State Farm Inst. Co., L.A., 1984-92, U.S.A.A. Ins. Co. L.A., 1986-92, Inst. Inst. Hwy. Safety, 1987-92; mem. Internat. Orgn. of Experts to UN, 1992-93; adv. bd. dirs. Nat. Automobile Dealers Assn., 2000. Author: The International Firm, 1976, Exotic Automotive Investments, 1985; adv. bd. Vehicle Values, 1999-2000. Fund raiser Children's Hosp., Orange County, 1987, Soroptimist Internat., Newport Beach, 1983, Children's Hosp. Soc. of Calif., Fresno, 1985; mem. govs. coun. Ins. Practices, 1987-91, Carroll Shelby Heart Fund, L.A., 1990; vice chmn. The Coren Found., Fresno, Calif., 1998-2000. Named One of Outstanding Young Men in Am., U.S. Jaycees, 1986; recipient Presdl. Sports award (skiing), Washington, 1973, Internat. Man of Yr. Automotive Internat. Fedn. of Automotive Analysts, London, 1992. Mem. Internat. Soc. Automotive Appraisers (pres. 1983-84), Am. Assn. Auto Appraisers (pres. 1984-85), Soc. Automotive Engrs., Internat. Soc. Automotive Analysis. Democrat. Jewish. Avocations: tennis, snow skiing, auto racing. Office: L S C Enterprizes Group Inc 20545 Eastwood Ave Torrance CA 90503-3611

CORETH, JOSEPH HERMAN, bank executive; b. San Antonio, Jan. 14, 1937; s. Rudolph C. and Eltha (Zipp) C.; m. Margaret Nowell Graham, June 18, 1960; 1 child, Elizabeth Coreth Bowden. BS, U.S. Mil. Acad., 1959; MA, Cornell U., 1966; JD, George Washington U., 1989. Bar: Md. 1989, Tex. 1990, D.C. 1990, N.H. 1991, U.S. Supreme Ct. 1993. Commd. 2d lt. U.S. Army, 1959, advanced through grades to maj., 1967; assoc. prof. English U.S. Mil. Acad., West Point, N.Y., 1966-69; chief plans officer 4th Inf. Div., An Khe, Vietnam, 1969-70; resigned U.S. Army, 1970; exec. v.p. Nat. Mortgage Corp., Washington, 1970-78; pres. Stannard's, Inc., Silver Spring, Md., 1979-84; v.p., trust officer Riggs Bank NA, Washington, 1985—. Former trustee, assoc. Grads. U.S. Mil. Acad.; mem. Order of St. Johns. Clubs: Metropolitan (Washington); Chevy Chase (Md.). Avocations: golf, birding. Home: 5508 Park St Chevy Chase MD 20815-7107 Office: Riggs Bank NA 808 17th St NW Washington DC 20006-3910

CORETTE, LOUIS, obstetrician/gynecologist, educator; b. Estreès, Aisne, France, Oct. 6, 1930; s. Charles Corette; m. Bernadette Lefevre, April 19, 1955; 4 children. MD, U. Lille, 1958, grad. in Obstetrics and Gynecology, 1961. specialist in gynecological oncology. Head svc. ob.-gyn. Hosp. Armentières, France, 1962-78, Hosp. St. Philipert, Lomme, France, 1977-96; ret., 1996; hon. prof. Free Med. Faculty, Lille. Mem. French Soc. Gynecology, French Soc. Ob-gyn. Roman Catholic. Home: 6 rue Henri Loyer, 59800 Lille France

COREY, ELIAS JAMES, chemistry educator; b. Methuen, Mass., July 12, 1928; s. Elias and Tina (Hashem) C.; m. Claire Higham, Sept. 14, 1961; children: David, John, Susan. BS, MIT, 1948, PhD, 1951; AM (hon.), Harvard U., 1959; DSc (hon.), U. Chgo., 1968, Hofstra U., 1974, Colby Coll., 1976, Oxford U., 1982, U. Liege, 1985, U. Ill., 1985, Kenyon Coll., 1989, Helsinki Coll., 1990, Ariz. U., 1990, Merrimac Coll., 1990, Hokkaido U., 1991, Boston Coll., 1992. From instr. to asst. prof. U. Ill., Champaign-Urbana, 1951-55, prof., 1955-59; prof. chemistry Harvard U., Cambridge, Mass., 1959—, Sheldon Emory prof., 1968—. Contbr. articles to profl. jours. Bd. dirs. phys. sci. Alfred P. Sloan Found., 1967-72; mem. sci. adv. bd. dirs. Robert A. Welch Found. Recipient Intrasci. Found. award, 1968, Ernest Guenther award in chemistry, 1968, Harrison Howe award, 1971, Ciba Found. medal, 1972, Evans award Ohio State U., 1972, Linus Pauling award, 1973, Dickson prize in sci. Carnegie Mellon U., 1973, George Ledlie prize in sci. Harvard U., 1973, Nichols medal, 1977, Buchman award Calif. Inst. Tech., 1978, Franklin medal in sci. Franklin Inst., 1978, Sci. Achievement award CCNY, 1979, J.G. Kirkwood award, Yale U., 1980, C.S. Hamilton award U. Neb., 1980, Chem. Pioneer award, Am. Inst. Chemists, 1981, V.D. Mattia award Roche Inst. Molecular Biology, 1985, Wolf prize (chem.), Wolf Found., 1986, Silliman award, 1986, Japan prize, 1989, Nat. Med. Sci., 1988, Nobel prize in chemistry, 1990, Gold Medal Award, AIC, 1990, Roger Adams award Am. Chem. Soc. 1993, numerous others; fellow Swiss-Am. Exch., 1957, Guggenheim Found., 1957-58, 68-69, Alfred P. Sloan Found., 1956-59. Mem. Am. Acad. Arts and Scis., AAAS, Am. Chem. Soc. (hon., award in synthetic chemistry 1971, Pure Chemistry award 1960, Fritzche award 1968, Md. sect. Remsen award 1974, Arthur C. Cope award 1976, Roger Adams award organic chemistry 1993, Madison Marshall award 1985), Nat. Acad. Sci., Franklin Inst., Chem. Soc. Japan (hon.), Sigma Xi. Office: Harvard U Dept Chemistry Rm 319 12 Oxford St Dept Cambridge MA 02138-2902

COREY, GORDON RICHARD, financial advisor, former utilities executive; b. Osceola, Wis., Sept. 27, 1914; s. Ralph Watson and Bessie Mabel (Simpson) C.; m. Margarete Moeller Grenn, 1967; children by previous marriage: Eleanor Corey Tatge, Margaret Corey Amundson, Gordon Ralph, Martha Elizabeth. BA, U. Wis., 1936; MBA, Northwestern, 1940. CPA, Ill. V.p. Commonwealth Edison Co., 1952-62, exec. v.p., 1962-64, chmn. fin. com., 1964-73, vice chmn., from 1973; now ret., now pvt. fin. adv. Clubs: Commercial, Wayfarers, Ridge and Valley Tennis. Home: 2511 Park Pl Evanston IL 60201-1315

COREY, JUDITH ANN, educator; b. Peoria, Ill., Dec. 1, 1937; d. Lyle William and Eileen A. (Zigrang) Springston; m. Thomas W. Corey, Aug. 12, 1961; children: John William, Jeffrey Michael, Gregory Lyle, Mark Andrew. BA in Bus., English, Marycrest Coll., 1960; MA in Counseling, Bradley U., 1972. Lic. tchr. K-12, Ill.; lic. clin. profl. counselor. Tchr. Riverview Sch., Spring Bay, Ill., 1960-61, Lincoln Sch., East Peoria, Ill., 1963-64; counselor Bradley U., Peoria, 1972-73; clin. psychologist intern Zeller Zone Ctr., Peoria, 1973; dean students Morton (Ill.) High Sch., 1974-85; tchr. Jefferson Sch., Morton, 1985—. Contbr. poem to Worlds Greatest Contemporary Poems, 1981 (Hon. Mention). Campaign work Grace Bunn Lievens Ill. Rep., 89th Dist. Ill., Morton, 1994; mem. exec. bd. Ill. State Deans' Assn., 1980-84, historian, 1980-82, membership com., 1982-84. Named to Outstanding Young Women in Am., 1973. Mem. NEA, Ill. Edn. Assn., Morton Edn. Assn. (newsletter editor 1987-90, mem. exec. com. and maj. negotiator, 1987—, v.p. 1993-95), Assn. Play Therapy, Phi Kappa Phi (life), Kappa Gamma Pi, Pi Lambda Theta. Roman Catholic. Avocations: reading, writing, photography, music, nature. Home: 20432 Tennessee Ave

Morton IL 61550-9777 Office: Jefferson Sch 220 E Jefferson St Morton IL 61550-2003

CORFIELD, PENELOPE JANE, historian, educator; b. York, Yorkshire, England, Sept. 4, 1944. MA, Oxford U., 1970; PhD, London U., 1976. Lectr. in history Bedford Coll., London, 1969-85; lectr. in history Royal Holloway, London, 1985-95, prof. history, 1995—; vis. prof. Japan Soc. for Promotion of Sci., 1994. Author: The Impact of English Towns 1700-1800, 1982, Power and the Professions in Britain 1700-1850, 1995; editor: Language, History and Class, 1991, Youth and Revolution in the 1790s, 1996. Fellow Royal Hist. Soc., Soc. Antiquaries of London. Office: Royal Holloway, Dept History, Egham Surrey TW20 0EX, England

CORGIER, MONIQUE MARIE-CLAUDE, chemistry/biology researcher; b. Lyon, France, Oct. 10, 1947; d. Antoine Alexandre and Marie Germaine (Rochet) C. Masters degree, U. Lyon, 1968, PhD, 1974. Rsch. worker Nat. Ctr. for Sci. Rsch., Lyon, 1968; univ. asst. U. Lyon, 1968-69; rschr. Nat. Inst. Sci. Appliquées, Lyon, 1969-74, Pharmuka, Paris, 1975-88; expert rschr. Aventis, Lyon, 1988—; mem. adv. bd. Rhône-Poulenc S.A., Courbevoie, France, 1987-93. Contbr. articles to profl. jours. Avocations: travel, cycling, skiing. Home: 302 rue Garibaldi, 69007 Lyon France Office: Rhone Poulenc Agro, Aventis CS, 14-20 rue Pierre Baizet, 69009 Lyon France

CORIGLIANO, ALBERTO, structural engineer; b. Milan, Italy, Feb. 16, 1963; s. Vincenzo and Carla (Fabbiocchi) C.; m. Claudia Comi, July 29, 1989; children: Silvia, Gabriele. M in Structural Engring., Poly. Milan, 1988. Asst. prof. Poly. Milan, 1991-98, assoc. prof., 1998—. 2d lt. Mil. Corps Engrs., Italy, 1988-89. Avocations: photography, skiing. Home: Via Mossotti #2, 20159 Milan Italy Office: Politecnico Milan Dept Structural Engring, Piazza L da Vinci 32, 20133 Milan Italy

CORINALDESI, MARCELO RUBEN, accountant; b. Bahia Blanca, Argentina, Mar. 21, 1958; s. Ruben Corinaldesi and Maria Ana Sepulveda; m. Maria Julia Amestoy, Sept. 16, 1981 (div. 1989); children: Maria Ana, Alfredo Luis, Paula Julia; m. Maria Leticia D'Annunzio, Apr. 20, 1990; 2 children, Nicole and Ailin. Degree in acctg., U. Nacional del Sur, Bahia Blanca, 1984, specialist in bankruptcy, 1992. Summary instr. Direccion Gen. Impositiva, Bahia Blanca, 1981-84; assoc. Oliva & Corinaldesi, Coronel Dorrego, 1984—; cons. Municipalidad Coronel Dorrego, 1987-88; prof. C. Nacional Superior, Coronel Dorrego, 1989-95. Mem. Club San Martin (Col. Dorrego 1999—). Avocations: running, aerobics. Office: Estudio Oliva & Corinaldesi, Maciel 743, 8150 Coronel Dorrego Argentina

CORIO, MARK ANDREW, electronics executive; b. Buffalo, July 18, 1961; s. Anthony Jack and Gertrude Irene (Nordin) C.; m. Lisa Marie Mitchell, May 18, 1985; 1 child, Joshua Robert. BSEE, SUNY, 1983. Elec. engr. Monarch Machine Tool Co., Cortland, N.Y., 1983-85; electronic des. engr. Landis Tool Co., Waynesboro, Pa., 1985-87; controls engr. The Gleason Works, Rochester, N.Y., 1987-88; sr. lab. engr. U. Rochester, 1988-91; sr. devel. engr. Eastman Kodak Co., Rochester, N.Y., 1991-95; pres. Rochester MicroSystems, Inc., 1994—, chmn. bd., 1994—. Patentee in field. Mem. IEEE, Planetary Soc., Internat. Soc. for Analytical Cytology, Internat. Soc. for Optical Engring. Home: 37 Bucky Dr Rochester NY 14624-5407 Office: Rochester MicroSystems Inc 400 Airpark Dr Ste 60 Rochester NY 14624-5729

CORK, ALAN LESLIE, business editor; b. Hatfield, Eng., Mar. 25, 1944; s. Joyce Doris Desbois; m. Margaret Elizabeth Coleman; children: Emma, James. Dep. editor Sports Trader Benn Bros., Tonbridge, Kent, Eng., 1976-78; editor Solid Fuel Harper Trade Jours. Ltd., London, 1978-83; editor Refrigeration and Air Conditioning EMAP plc, London, 1983-85; editor Shoe and Leather News, 1986-95; mng. editor Hosp. Equipment, Hosp. Development Wilmington plc, Dartford, Kent, Eng., 1995—. Author: Mr. Fear, 2000. Mem. Med. Journalists Assn., Nat. Union Journalists. Mem. Conservative Party. Avocation: family. Home: 52 Cambridge Rd, London SE20 7XL, England Office: Wilmington plc, Church Hill, Dartford Kent DA2 7EF, England

CORLEY, JENNY LYND WERTHEIM, elementary education educator; b. Lincoln, Ill., June 18, 1937; d. Robert Glenn and Nancy Lynd (Hoblit) Wertheim; m. William Gene Corley, Aug. 9, 1959; children: Anne Lynd Corley Baum, Robert William, Scott Elson. BS in Music Edn., U. Ill., 1959, MS in Music Edn., 1961; postgrad., U. Ill., Loyola U., 1985—. Tchr. choral music Mahomet (Ill.)/Seymour K-12, 1959-61; supr. music Fairfax County (Va.), 1961-63; Tchr. music Highland Park (Ill.) 107, 1969, dir. gifted edn., 1969-70; tchr. music Glenview (Ill.) 34, 1981—; v.p. Corley Agroleum Properties, 1993—; water safety instr./trainer ARC; lifeguard instr./trainer Cmty. First Aid & Safety, 1995. Dir. mid-Am. bd. ARC, Chgo., 1980-86; mem. Chgo. Symhony Orch. Chorus, 1965-75. Recipient Heart of Gold United Way, 1992, Cmty. Svc. award Ill. Park & Recreation Assn./Ill. Assn. Park Dists., 1994, Disting. Svc. award Boys and Girls Swimming Ofcl., Ill. High Sch. Assn., 1994. Mem. Music Edn. Nat. Conf., North Shore Music Tchrs. Assn. (treas. 1987-90), Jr. League Chgo. (treas. 1978-81), Sigma Alpha Iota, Phi Delta Kappa (found. chmn. 1994—), U. Ill. Music Alumnae (pres. bd. dirs. 1995-97). Presbyterian. Home: 744 Glenayre Dr Glenview IL 60025-4411 Office: Springman Sch 2701 Central Rd Glenview IL 60025-4134

CORLEY, ROSE ANN MCAFEE, government official; b. Lawton, Okla., Aug. 21, 1952; d. Claude James and Mary Margaret (Holman) McAfee; m. Gary Michael Griffin, Feb. 14, 1973 (div. Oct. 1984); m. Terry Joe Corley, July 31, 1988; stepson Troy Justin Corley. BS, Cameron U., Lawton, Okla., 1970; diploma, Army Command and Staff Coll., Ft. Leavenworth, Kans., 1989; MCJA, Oklahoma City U., 1990; cert., Army Mgmt. Staff Coll., Ft. Belvoir, Va., 1991. Cert. in Distbn. Mgt. Supply clk. Dept. of Army, Ft. Sill, Okla., 1972-80, supply mgmt. asst., 1980-82; supply systems analyst Dept. of Army, Ft. Lee, Va., 1982; supply tech. Dept. of Army, Ft. Sill, Okla., 1982-83, supr. inventory mgmt. specialist, 1983-86, manprint program mgr., 1986-91; weapon system advisor Def. Logistics Agy., San Antonio, 1991-96; customer svc. rep. Def. Logistics Agy., Robins AFB, Ga., 1996-98; dir. supply mgmt. NIH, Rockville, Md., 1998—; equal employment counselor USA Field Artillery Sch., Ft. Sill, Okla., 1976-82; mentor Fed. Women's Program, Kelly AFB, Tex., 1991-96. Active Md. Citizen Foster Care Rev. Bd., 1999—. Recipient Cert. of Appreciation, Sec. of Def., Washington, 1984, Cert. of Appreciation, Directorate of Engring. and Housing, Ft. Sill, 1986; decorated Order of St. Barbara, U.S. Army Arty. Sch., Ft. Sill, 1991. Mem. Fed. Women's Program, Soc. Logistics Engrs., Fed. Mgrs. Assn., Kelly Mgmt. Assn., World Affairs Coun. of San Antonio, Internat. City Mgmt. Assn., Tex. Corvette Assn. Avocations: autocrossing, reading, golf, crafts. Home: 11706 Balsamwood Ter Laurel MD 20708-3175 Office: NIH Office Logistics Mgmt 6011 Executive Blvd Rockville MD 20852-3804

CORLUY, WALTER JOSEPHUS, retired bank senior executive; b. Borgerhout, Belgium, Apr. 8, 1938; s. Louis and Helena (Lauwers) C. PhD in Law, Cath. U., Louvain, Belgium, 1961, MA in Econs., 1962. Jr. Bank van Antwerpen, Antwerp, Belgium, 1964-65, Generale Bank Antwerp (formerly Bank van Antwerpen), Antwerp, 1965-76; credit dept. Generale Bank, Brussels, 1976-79; dep. mgr., mgr., regional gen. mgr. Generale Bank, Aalst, Belgium, 1979-85; regional gen. mgr. Generale Bank Antwerp (formerly Bank van Antwerpen), 1985-89; advisor Generale Bank, Brussels, 1989-98; ret., 1998; exec. mgr. Corluy Mgmt. and Cons. Ltd., 1987—; univ. tchr. financing U. Antwerp, EHSAL, Brussels, IPO, Antwerp, Vlekho Business Sch., Brussels. Author: Finance and Risk Management in International Trade, 1990, 2d edit., 1995; co-author: Practical Guide for Financial Management, 1995. With Belgian Mil., 1963-64. Mem. Rotary Club. Roman Catholic. Avocations: cycling, mountain climbing, walking, languages, jogging. Home: Prins Albertlei 5 Box 1, 2600 Antwerp Belgium

CORMAN, JULIE ANN, producer, director; b. Omaha, June 22, 1942; d. Gordon Francis Halloran and Mary Julia (Corcoran) Halloran-Ferrier; m. Roger William Corman, Dec. 26, 1970; children: Catherine, Roger, Brian, Mary. BA, UCLA, 1964. V.p. New World Pictures, L.A., 1971-83; exec. v.p. Concorde-New Horizons Pictures, Inc., L.A., 1984—; pres. Trinity Pictures, Inc., L.A., 1984—; conf. chmn. UCLA Extension, 1991; chair grad. film and TV dept. NYU, Maurice Kanbar Inst. Film and TV, Tisch Sch. Arts, 2000. Producer (films) Boxcar Bertha, 1972, Crazy Mama, 1975, Lady in Red, 1976, The Dirt Bike Kid, 1985, DA, 1988, A Cry in the Wild (Silver medal Houston Internat. Film Festival 1990), (TV movie) Drop Out Mother, 1988, White Wolves series, 1990-95, Max is Missing, 1995, Legend of the Lost Tomb, 1996, The Westing Game, 1997; chmn. Grad. Film and TV Dept. N.Y. U., 2000, Maurice Kanbar Inst. Film and Television, 2000, Tisch Sch. Arts, 2000. Mem. Air Resources Bd., Calif., Internat. Women's Forum, 1990. Named Prodr. of Yr. Acad. Family Film, 1996. Mem. Women in Film. Roman Catholic. Office: Trinity Pictures 11600 San Vicente Blvd Los Angeles CA 90049-5102

CORMIE, DONALD MERCER, investment company executive; b. Edmonton, Alta., Can., July 24, 1922; s. George Mills and Mildred (Mercer) C.; m. Eivor Elisabeth Ekstrom, June 8, 1946; children: John Mills, Donald Robert, Allison Barbara, James Mercer, Neil Brian, Buce George, Eivor, Robert. BA, U. Alta., 1944, LLB, 1945; LLM, Harvard U., 1946. Bar: Alta. 1947. Queens counsel, 1964; sessional instr. faculty law U. Alta., 1947-53; sr. ptnr. Cormie, Kennedy, Edmonton, Barristers, 1954-87; instr. real estate law Dept. of Extension, U. Alta., 1958-64; pres., bd. dirs. Collective Securities, Ltd., Cormie Ranch, Inc., Sea Investors Corp.; With Can. Mcht. Marine, 1943-44. Recipient Judge Green Silver medal in law. Mem. Dean's Coun. of 100 Ariz. State U., World Pres.'s Orgn., Chief Execs. Orgn. (bd. dirs. 1976-79), Can. Bar Assn. (mem. coun. 1961-76, chmn. adminstrv. law 1963-66, chmn. taxation 1972-82, v.p. Alta. 1968-69), Found. Legal Rsch. Can. (hon. life). Home and Office: 5101 N Casa Blanca Dr Unit 314 Scottsdale AZ 85253-6989

CORMIER, JACQUES, manufacturing executive; b. West Bathurst, Can., July 24, 1948; arrived in Australia, 1992; s. Alphonse and Antoinette (Rioux) C. Cert. prodn. and inventory mgmt. Mfg. systems mgr. Philips Info. Systems, Montreal, 1984-86; dir. logistics Burroughs Wellcome Canada, Montreal, 1986-88; mfg. cons. Qantel Canada Inc., Montreal, 1988-90; product mgr. Qantel Corp., San Francisco, 1990-92; dir. mktg. Qantel Bus. Systems Ltd., Sydney, 1992-95; mng. dir. Asia Pacific Astea Internat. Inc., Sydney, 1995—. Editor: Small Manufacturing Tools, 1992. Mem. Am. Prodn. and Inventory Control Soc. (chmn. SM sigs 1991-92, pres. Montreal chpt. 1986-87), Assn. for Svc. Mgmt. Internat. Avocations: gardening, walking. Office: Astea Internat Inc, 39-41 Chandos St Level 1, Saint Leonards NSW 2065, Australia

CORNA, MARK STEVEN, construction company executive; b. Columbus, Ohio, July 21, 1949; s. Albert and Ann Elizabeth (Amicon) C.; m. Margaret Ann Igoe, July 18, 1970 (div. Apr. 1986); children: Joshua Daniel, Sophia Ann; m. Marti Cordray, Dec. 3, 1999. With Corna and Di Cesare Builders, Inc., Columbus, 1970-76, pres., 1985-95; pres. The M.S. Corna Co., Columbus, 1976-85, Corna/Kokosing Construction Co., 1995—; bd. dirs. Commerce Nat. Bank of Columbus, 1990—. Parochial sch. soccer, basketball coach, 1982-85, 89-91; mem. Devel. Com. for Greater Columbus, 1989—, chmn., 1995-97; bd. dirs. ProMusica, 1991-97, pres., 1995-96. Named Exec. of Yr., Nat. Assn. Women in Constrn., 1992; recipient Cen. Ohio State of Israel Bonds Dorl'Dor award, 1997. Mem. Assn. Gen. Contractors of Cen. Ohio (bd. dirs. 1980-87, pres. 1986), Assn. Gen. Contractors of Ohio (bd. dirs. 1994—, treas. 1997—), Builders Exch. Cen. Ohio (bd. dirs. 1981-90, pres. 1989, Cornerstone award 1995), Greater Columbus C. of C. (bd. dirs. 1996-98), Athletic Club Columbus. Democrat. Roman Catholic. Avocations: reading, music, golf, sailing, motorcycles. Office: Corna/Kokosing Constrn Co 2500 Harrison Rd Columbus OH 43204-3510

CORNABY, KAY STERLING, lawyer, former state senator; b. Spanish Fork, Utah, Jan. 14, 1936; s. Sterling A. and Hilda G. Cornaby; m. Linda Rasmussen, July 23, 1965; children: Alyse, Derek, Tara, Heather, Brandon. AB, Brigham Young U., 1960; postgrad. law, Heidelberg, Germany, 1961-63; JD, Harvard U., 1966. Bar: N.Y. 1967, Utah 1969, U.S. Patent and Trademark Office 1967. Assoc. Brumbaugh, Graves, Donahue & Raymond, N.Y.C., 1966-69; ptnr. Mallinckrodt & Cornaby, Salt Lake City, 1969-72; sole practice Salt Lake City, 1972-85; mem. Utah State Senate, 1977-91, majority leader, 1983-84; shareholder Jones, Waldo, Holbrook & McDonough, Salt Lake City, 1985—. Mem. Nat. Commn. on Uniform State Laws, 1988-93; mem. adv. bd. U. Mich. Ctr. for Study of Youth Policy,1990-93; mem. Utah State Jud. Conduct Commn., 1983-91, chmn., 1984-85; bd. dirs. KUED-KUER Pub. TV and Radio, 1982-88; bd. dirs. Salt Lake Conv. and Visitors Bur., 1985—. Mem. N.Y. Bar Assn., Utah Bar Assn., Utah Harvard Alumni Assn. (pres. 1977-79), Harvard U. Law Sch. Alumni Assn. (pres. 1995—). Office: Jones Waldo Holbrook & McDonough 1500 Wells Fargo Bank Plz 170 S Main St Salt Lake City UT 84101-1605

CORNARO, CHRISTOPH, retired Austrian diplomat; b. Vienna, Oct. 8, 1931; s. Franz and Erna (Schwind) C.; m. Gail Macmahon, Oct. 1, 1955; children: Andrea, Markus, Pia, Katharina, Antonia, Johannes. Dr. Law, U. Vienna, 1955; postgrad., Swarthmore Coll. With Austrian Fgn. Svc., 1955—; mem. Austrian Embassy, London, 1957-62, Brussels, 1965-70; head Sec. Gen.'s Office, Brussels, 1972-76; amb. to Iran, 1976-79, Arab Republic of Egypt, Sudan and Somalia, 1979-82; chief protocol Fgn. Ministry, Vienna, 1982-88; amb. to India, 1988-93; amb. to Holy See Rome, 1994-96; ret.

CORNEANU, GABRIEL CONSTANTIN, science educator; b. Craiova, Dolj, Romania, Sept. 28, 1942; s. Constantin Ion and Ioana Ilie (Georgescu) C.; m. Cecilia Gheorghe Sarbu, Apr. 28, 1979 (div. Aug. 1987); 1 child, Lavinia-Mihaela; m. Mihaela Mihai Carbunaru, Dec. 12, 1987; 1 child, Mihai-Alexandru. Biology diploma, U. Bucharest, Romania, 1965; specialist in med. genetics, U. Medicine and Pharmacy, Bucharest, 1969; D in Biology-Genetics, Romanian Acad., Cluj-Napoca, Romania, 1974. Sci. rschr. A.I. Cuze U., Iasi, Romania, 1965-67; from asst. prof. to assoc. prof. U. Craiova, 1967-93, prof., 1993—; mem. senate U. Craiova, 1990-92; dep. mgr. Postgrad. Inst. Biomath., Craiova, 1990-93; sci. cons. Craiova br. Romanian Acad., Bd. for Sci. History, 1993—. Author: (book) Biological Synthesis, 1997; editor, author: (monograph) Elements of Vegetal Radiobiology, 1989; inventor in field. Fellow Inst. Ecology Acad. Sci., Rep. Moldova, Chisinau, European Cell Biology Orgn., Internat. Radiation Protein Assn., Internat. Assn. for Plant Tissue Culture; mem. N.Y. Acad. Scis. Orthodox. Avocations: civilization culture, history, travel. Home: Stirbej Vodă D2/3, R-1100 Craiova Dolj, Romania Office: U Craiova, A I Cuza 13, R-1100 Craiova Dolj, Romania

CORNEANU, MIHAELA MIHAI, engineering educator, researcher; b. Hunedoara, Romania, July 12, 1961; d. Mihai Stefan and Maria Ovidiu (Popescu) Carbunaru; m. Eugen Ion Ples, Sept. 28, 1984 (div. Mar. 1987); m. Gabriel Constantin Corneanu, Dec. 12, 1987; 1 child, Mihai-Alexandru. Agrl. engr., U. Agrl. Scis., Timisoara, Romania, 1984; D in Biology-Genetics, U. Babes-Bolyai, Cluj, Romania, 1998. Cert. in engring. Agr. engr. Coop. Farm, Sânmihaiu-Român, Romania, 1984-88; rsch. engr. U. Agron. Scis., Timisoara, 1988, U. Craiova, Romania, 1988-92; asst. prof. Craiova U., 1992-96, assoc. prof., 1996—. Inventor in field; contbr. sci. papers to profl. jours. Fellow Internat. Assn. for Plant Tissue Culture, European Cell Biology Orgn., European Soc. for New Methods in Agrl. Rsch. Orthodox. Avocations: animals, literature, traveling. Home: Stirbei Vodă D2/3, R-1100 Craiova Dolj, Romania Office: U Craiova, A I Cuza 13, R-1100 Craiova Dolj, Romania

CORNEGLIANI, LUISA, veterinarian, researcher; b. Milan, July 4, 1965; d. Vincio Michele Cornegliani and Enrica Dorina Sartirana. Grad. in vet. medicine, U. Milan, 1991, profl. abilitation, 1991. Asst. Clinica Vet. S.Siro, Milan, 1988-91, veterinarian, 1991-93; veterinarian Clinica Vet. Malpensa, Samarate, Italy, 1992-99; vet. rschr. Bayer, Milan, 1997-99, Internet, Milan, 1999, Arcoblu, Milan, 1989-99; with Ambulatorio Vet. M. Gioia, Milan; cons. Le Point Vet. Italie, Milan, 1996-99, I.C.F. svl, Cremona, Italy, 1989-99. Mem. Eugopean Soc. Vet. Dermatology, Nat. Conf. on Small Animal Vet. Specialists (assoc.), SCIVAC. Roman Catholic. Avocations: ice skating, snowboarding, mountain biking. Office: Ambulatorio Vet M Gioia, Via M Gioia 67, 20124 Milan Italy

CORNELIA, VASILE, chemist, researcher; b. Homorâciu, Romania, Sept. 12, 1942. BS, Valeii de Munte, Romania, 1960; degree in Chemistry, Bucharest (Romania) U., 1965; PhD, Al I. Cuza U., Iasi, Romania, 1971. Chemistry diplomate. Asst. prof. Medicine and Pharmacy U., Iasi, Romania, 1965-66; rschr. Poni Inst. Macro-Molecular Chemistry, Iasi, Romania, 1966-71, sr. rschr., 1971—; asst. prof. Laval U. Quebec, Can., 1995—, Gh. Asachi Tech. U., Iasi, Romania, 1999—; rsch. program dirs. Romanian Acad., Iasi, Romania. Author, editor: Handbook of Polyolefins, 1993, 99. Fulbright scholar, 1995. Mem. IUPAC. Orthodox. Office: Romanian Acad, 41A Gr Ghica Voda Alley, RO6600 Iasi Romania

CORNELIS, FRANÇOIS, oil industry executive. Degree in mech. engring., U. Louvain, Belgium. Systems engr. Petrofina S.A., Brussels, coord. supply and refining ops.; supply and shipping mgr. Petrofina S.A., London; vice chmn. bd. dirs., CEO, mng. dir. Petrofina S.A., Brussels, 1990—; v.p., spl. asst. to pres. Am. Petrofina, Dallas, 1983-90; vice chmn., exec. v.p., pres. Trading, Gas and Power; chmn. Elf Atochem, Total Fina Elf S.A. Office: Total Fina Elf SA, 2 place de la Coupole, 92400 Courbevoie Defense 6, France*

CORNELISSEN, ELISABETH, pediatrician; b. Terheyden, The Netherlands, Dec. 8, 1962; d. Harrie and Elisabeth (Hessels) B.; m. Ferdinand Voors, May 17, 1997. B of Medicine, U. Nymegen, The Netherlands, 1988, MD, 1992. Med. rschr. U. Hosp., Nijmegen, The Netherlands, 1988-92, trainee pediatrician, 1992-97, trainee pediatric nephrologist, 1997-99, pediat. nephrologist, 1999—. Office: U Hosp Nijmegen, PO Box 9101, NL6500HB Nijmegen The Netherlands

CORNELISSEN, REINERUS LOUWRENTIUS, engineering company executive; b. Opsterland, The Netherlands, Aug. 28, 1969; s. Cornelius and Jacoba (Boonman) C.; m. Christine Helene Urbach, July 31, 1998. M in Engring., U. Groningen, 1993; PhD, U. Twente, 1997. Dir. CCS, Enschede, 1997—. Office: U Twente Chair Energy Tech, Dept Mech Engring Box 217, 7500 AE Enschede The Netherlands

CORNELIUS, HELENA EVELYN SUSAN, psychologist, consultant; b. Sydney, NSW, Australia, Nov. 27, 1944; d. Max and Stella Cornelius; m. Malcolm Rex Turnbull, Feb. 16, 1970 (div. 1980); children: Deborah, Kerry, Martin. BA, U. Sydney, 1965. Publicist Cornelius Furs, Sydney, 1966-67, dir., 1968-80; psychology tutor U. Sydney, 1967-68; counselor New Awareness Centre, Sydney, 1980-83; pvt. practice Sydney, 1980-86; psychology lectr. Self-Transformation Centre, Sydney, 1980-86; dir. programs Conflict Resolution Network, Sydney, 1986—; dir. CR Essentials Tng. video, 1994. Author: The Gentle Revolution, 1998, Everyone Can Win (translated into Russian, Chinese, Spanish, Indonesian and Romanian), 1989, Conflict Resolution Trainers' Manual, 1987, 93. Mem. NSW Psychologists Registration Bd., Australian Psychol. Soc., Australian Soc. Authors, Bd. Counseling Psychologists. Avocations: creative writing, tennis, reading, theatre. Office: Conflict Resolution Network, PO Box 1016, Chatswood NSW 2057, Australia

CORNELIUS, JACQUELYN H., high school principal, educator; b. Jacksonville, Fla., Feb. 26, 1948; d. Jack Allen and Dorothy Mae Henson; m. Carey Michael Cornelius, May 21, 1982; children: Amber, Heather. BA, U. Fla., 1970; MEd, U. No. Fla., 1984. Eng. tchr. Forrest High Sch., Jacksonville, 1970-84, asst. prin., 1984-87; arts dir. Douglas Anderson Sch. of the Arts, Jacksonville, 1988-95, prin., 1996—; vis. evaluation team mem. So. Accreditation of Colls. and Schs., 1989—; dir. Fla. Edn. Found., 1991-95; spkr. in field; bd. dirs. Fla. Women's Consortium, Duval County Assn. Secondary Sch. Adminstrs., Fla. Fedn. Bus. and Profl. Women, Inc., The Fla. Women's Alliance. Choreographer, host pub. TV. programs Inside Your Schs., The Hearing Impaired: The Creative Tchr., Testing: Pros and Cons. Active Jacksonville Symphony Edn. com., 1999—, Theatre Jacksonville, 1991—; mem. Mayor's Insight com., 1993-94, Mayor's Task Force on Domestic Violence, 1997-98; bd. dirs. Gateway Girl Scout Coun., 1991-94, Youth Leadership Jacksonville, 1992-94, Cultural Coun. Greater Jacksonville, 1998—. Recipient Excellence award Fla. Commr. of Edn., 1988, Arts Educator award Jacksonville Arts Assembly, 1995. Mem. Nat. Network of Performing and Visual Arts Schs. (treas., nominating chair arts advocacy com., arts achievement chair, southeast regional publicity chair), Nat. Assn. Secondary Sch. Prins. (Fla. chpt.), Jacksonville Women's Network, Bus. and Profl. Women's Club (First Coast, River City chpts., pres. 1995, vol. chair, jr. civitan com., mem. chair, program chair, ace com.), Jacksonville Rotary (internat. edn. chair, publicity com., charity com.). Avocations: travel, reading. E-mail: cornelius@educationcentral.org. Home: 4103 Cedar Rd Orange Park FL 32065-6903 Office: Douglas Anderson Sch of Arts 2445 San Diego Rd Jacksonville FL 32207-3699

CORNELL, ANNA CLAIRE, advertising executive; b. Lafayette, La., Sept. 9, 1968; d. Robert Kirk and Phyllis Claire (Schiller) C. BS in Advertising, U. Tex. Austin, 1990. Media planner The Richards Group, Dallas, 1991-94; media supr. Wieden & Kennedy, Portland, Oreg., 1994-96; assoc. media dir. Wieden & Kennedy, Amsterdam, Netherlands, 1996—. Avocations: travel, running. Office: Wieden & Kennedy, Keizersgracht 125-127, 1015CJ Amsterdam The Netherlands

CORNELL, HUGH JAMES, biochemist, researcher; b. Albury, NSW, Australia, Oct. 17, 1930; s. Hugh James and Dorothy Isobel (Murray) C.; m. Margaret May McKinnon, Nov. 20, 1954; children: Ross, Pamela, Merrin. BSc, U. Melbourne, Australia, 1965, MSc, 1968, PhD, 1972. Chartered chemist Royal Australian Chem. Inst. Sr. polymer chemist Glazebrooks Paints Ltd., Melbourne, Australia, 1951-59; chief chemist H.P. Products Party Ltd., Melbourne, Australia, 1960-68; sr. rsch. fellow Royal Childrens Hosp., Melbourne, Australia, 1969-75; sr. lectr. Royal Melbourne Inst. Tech., Australia, 1976-90, assoc. prof., 1991-97, adj. prof., 1998—; rschr. various industries and med. facilities, 1951-75; tchr., rschr. various univs., 1976—; vis. prof. Karolinska Inst., Sweden, 1985, U. Munich, 1990. Author: Wheat: Chemistry & Utilization, 1997, Mostly Mozart, 1997; contbr. articles to profl. jours. Recipient silver medal City and Guilds of London, 1953; fellow Royal Childrens Hosp., Melbourne, 1969, Coeliac Soc. Great Britain, London, 1974. Fellow Royal Australian Chem. Inst.; mem. N.Y. Acad. Scis. Mem. Ch. of Christ. Achievements include devel. process for manufacture of silicone modified alkyds, elucidated factors required for high quality wheat syrup prodn., discovery of new evidence for an enzyme deficiency in celiac disease and components in wheat which cause the symptoms; co-discoverer of the major bound fatty acid in wool, 18-methyleicosanoic acid. Office: RMIT Dept Applied Chemistry, GPO Box 2476V, Melbourne Victoria 3001, Australia

CORNELSSEN, INSE, economics educator; b. Kaiserslantern, Germany, Feb. 12, 1940; s. Friedrich August and Hertha Sophie (Erb) C.; divorced; children: Heike, Christian, Derek. Diploma-Volkswirt, Free U., Berlin, 1987, Dr.rer.pol., 1991. Stage prodr. Berliner Arbeitskreis Film, Germany, 1965-81; sec. of BAF Berliner Arbeitskreis Film, Berlin, 1975-80; journalist Germany, 1981-82; rsch. asst. WZB, Berlin, 1987-93; prof. econ. policy FH Hannover, Germany, 1994—. Author: Der Fall Japan, 1991, Kultur als Triebkraft Wirtschaftlicher Entwicklung, 1991; editor, translator Wang Meng: Lauter Fuersprecher, 1989, Der Bueffel ist schwarz, 1981. Del. Feie Demokratische Partei, Berlin, 1979—. Mem. European Assn. Devel. and Tng. Insts., Soc. for Internat. Devel., Transparency Internat. Avocations: cats, dogs, sailing, theatre. Office: Fachhochschule Hannover, Ricklinger Stadtweg 120, 30459 Hannover Germany

CORNESS, SIR COLIN (ROSS), business executive; b. Chorlton, Eng., Oct. 9, 1931; s. Thomas and Mary Evlyne (Lovelace) C. MA, Cambridge U., 1958; advanced mgmt. diploma, Harvard U., 1970. Dir. Taylor Woodrow Constrn. Ltd., London, 1961-64; mng. dir. Redland Tiles Ltd., 1965-70; group mng. dir. Redland PLC, 1967-82, chmn., 1977-95; chmn. Glaxo Wellcome plc, 1995-97; chmn. Nationwide Bldg. Soc., 1991-96; non-exec. dir. Union Camp Corp., 1991-99, Chubb Security plc, 1992-97, Taylor Woodrow plc, 1997—. Served lt. 3d Dragoon Guards, Brit. Army, 1950-51. Mem. United Oxford and Cambridge Club. Office: 54 Chesterfield House, South Audley St, London W1K 1HB, England

CORNET, ALBERT, physics educator; b. Gironella, Barcelona, Spain, Apr. 27, 1955; s. Isidro Cornet and Carme Calveras; m. Rosa Lladós, July 23, 1978; children: Anna, Estel. PhD, U. Barcelona, 1982, U. Paul Sabatier, Toulouse, France, 1983. Lectr. U. Barcelona, 1982-90, prof., 1990—; acad. coor. U. Barcelona, 1994—, post-grad. coord. sci. courses, 1994—. Contbr. articles to profl. jours. Pres. Ball de Gitanes, Castellar Valles, Spain, 1991—,

Found. of the Sch. El Cajal, Castellar Valles, 1997—. Mem. Materials Rsch. Soc., Real Sociedad Española de Fisica. Avocations: football, traditional dancing. Office: U Barcelona Dept Electronic, Diagonal 647, 08028 Barcelona Spain

CORNETT, GREGG, newspaper publisher, newspaper editor, computer company executive; b. Dayton, Ohio, May 12, 1954. PhD in Computer Sci. Pres. Computer Commuter, Batesville, Ark., 1982-87, Gregg Cornett Assocs., Batesville, Bald Knob, Searcy, Ark., 1984—; pub., editor Bald Knob Banner, 1987—; CEO G.C.A. Computer Svcs., 1993—; v.p. Wood Nursery, Inc., 1995-96; systems analyst Arkansas Pub., 1996—; police photographer Bald Knob Police Dept., 1988—; computer cons. Gregg Cornett Assocs., 1984—, freelance journalist, Bald Knob, 1987—. Author (booklet) Neighborhood Crime Prevention, 1989; contbr. articles to newspapers. Area coord. City Crime Prevention, Bald Knob, 1988—; assoc. KARK-TV Community Network, Little Rock, 1990—; acting city clk. City of Bald Knob, 1991; rural community cons. City of Bald Knob, 1988—; founding bd. dirs. Rsch. Internat., Aruba. Recipient Better Newspaper Advt. award Ark. Press Assn., 1988; Gregg Cornett Day proclaimed by City of Bald Knob, 1990. Fellow Rotary; mem. C. of C. (bd. dirs. 1988—). Avocations: writing, photography, electronics.

CORNETTE DE SAINT-CYR, BERNARD, plastic surgeon; b. Meknes, Morocco, May 27, 1944; s. Cornette de Saint-Cyr; children: Guillaume, Faustine. MD, U. Paris, 1976. Intern Hopitaux de Paris-Ambroise Paré-Necker-St. Louis-Pitie, 1975-76; resident Hopital Jean Rostand, Paris-Iury, 1977-80; practice medicine specializing in plastic surgery Paris, 1980—. Mem. Internat. Soc. Aesthetic Plastic Surgery (prof. postgrad. edn. in aesthetic plastic surgery), Assn. de la Noblesse Franç aise, Sociéte Française de Chirurgie Plastique, Reconstructice et Ethetique, Golf Joyeuval, Maxim Bus. Club, St. James Club (Paris). Address: 15 Rue Spontini, 75116 Paris France

CORNFORTH, SIR JOHN WARCUP, chemist; b. Sydney, Australia, Sept. 7, 1917; s. John William and Hilda (Eipper) C.; m. Rita H. Harradence, Sept. 27, 1941; children: Brenda (Mrs. David Osborne), John, Philippa (Mrs. William Horder). BSc, U. Sydney, 1937, MSc, 1938; DPhil, Oxford U., 1941, DSc (hon.), 1976; DSc (hon.), E.T.H. Zurich, 1975, Trinity Coll., Dublin, Univs. Liverpool, Warwick, Aberdeen, Hull, Sussex, Kent and Sydney. Mem. sci. staff Med. Rsch. Coun., London, 1946-62; dir. Milstead Lab. Chem. Enzymology, Shell Rsch. Ltd., Sittingbourne, Kent, Eng., 1962-75; Royal Soc. rsch. prof. Sch. Chemistry and Molecular Scis. U. Sussex, Brighton, Eng., 1975-82. Contbr. articles on chemistry of penicillin, total synthesis of steroids and other biologically active natural products, chemistry of heterocyclic compounds, biosynthesis of steroids, enzyme chemistry to profl. jours. Decorated comdr. Brit. Empire; knighted, 1977; apptd. Companion of the Order of Australia, 1991; recipient Stouffer prize, 1967, Prix Roussel, 1972, Nobel Prize in Chemistry, 1975. Fellow Royal Soc., 1953 (Davy medal 1968, Royal medal 1976, Copley medal 1982), Royal Soc. Chemistry (Corday-Morgan medal 1953, Flintoff medal 1966), Am. Chem. Soc. (Ernest Guenther award 1969); mem. Biochem. Soc. (CIBA medal 1966), Am. Soc. Biol. Chemists (hon.), Am. Acad. (hon. fgn. mem.), Australian Acad. Sci. (corr.), Netherlands Acad. Sci. (fgn.), NAS (fgn. assoc.). Home: Saxon Down, Cuilfail, Lewes BN7 2BE, England Office: U Sussex Sch Chemistry, Physics & Environ Sci, Falmer Brighton BN1 9QJ, England

CORNICK, MICHAEL F(REDERICK), accounting educator; b. Evansville, Ind., Apr. 15, 1940; s. Isadore John and Belle (Wigdor) C.; m. Charlotte Bozovich, Mar. 2, 1985; children; Elizabeth Ann, Ann Elliott. BS in Indsl. Mgmt., Purdue U., 1963; MBA, U.N.C., Chapel Hill, 1970, PhD, 1980. CPA, N.C. Stockbro. Thomson and McKinnon, Winston-Salem, N.C., 1965-68; bank officer 1 st. Nat. Atlanta, 1970-72; assoc. prof. acctg. U. N.C., Charlotte, 1985—; adv. Internat. Bus. Club, Charlotte, 1987— ; leader Internat. Acctg. Overseas, Fed. Rep. Germany, London, 1988—. Author: Bank Accounting, 1984; contbr. articles to profl. jours. Mem. British Am. Bus. Coun. 1st lt. U.S. Army, 1963-65. Recipient cert. appreciation, Retarted Citizens Greensboro, 1983. Mem. AICPA, Inst. Mgmt. Accts. (dir. 1985-88), Am. Acctg. Assn., N.C. Soc. CPAs, Charlotte World Trade Assn. Avocations: reading, tennis, basketball. Home: 1409 Biltmore Dr Charlotte NC 28207-2556 Office: U NC Dept Acctg Charlotte NC 28223

CORNICK, ROGER COURTENAY, asset management company executive; b. Derby, England, Feb. 13, 1944; s. William and Cynthia (Courtenay) C.; m. Susie Mary Laing; two children. Grad., Queen Elizabeth's Sch. Mgr. Abbey Life Assurance Co., England, 1968-70; asst. dir. Hambro Life Assurance Co., England, 1970-77; dir. Crown Fin. Mgmt., England, 1977-80; ptnr. Courtenay Mng. Group, England, 1980-82; dir. Perpetual Mng. Group, England, 1982-87; dep. chmn. Perpetual Plc, England, 1987—. Home: Mill Barn Farm Drift Rd, Winkfield, Berkshire SL4 4RP, England

CORNILLET, THIERRY, foreign diplomat; b. Montelimar, France, July 23, 1951. Mem. European Parliament, 1999—, mem. com. citizens' freedoms/rights, justice, home affairs, substitute com. on regional policy, transport and tourism; mem. Group of the European People's Party (Christian Democrats) and European Democrats; mem. delegation for relations with Australia and N.Z. Mem. Union for French Democracy. Office: Parlement européen, Rue Wiertz ASP 13E154, B-1047 Brussels Belgium*

CORNISH, BRIAN ALEXANDER, retired university dean; b. Sydney, Australia, May 4, 1938; s. Allan McNeil and Gwendoline Anne (Peacock) C.; m. Margaret Patricia O'Connell, Mar. 30, 1964; children: Peter, Felicity, Nicholas. BEngring, U. Sydney, 1959; MEngring., U. New South Wales, 1971, PhD, 1978. Chartered engr., Australia. Rsch. engr. U. New South Wales, Sydney, 1960-70; lectr. New South Wales Inst. Tech., 1970-76, sr. lectr., 1978-81, dep. head Sch. Civil Engring., 1982; prof. Calif. State U., Sacramento, 1977; dean Sch. Info. Studies, Riverina-Murray Inst. Higher Edn., Wagga, Australia, 1983-89, praelector, mem. coun., 1986-90; prof. info. mgmt. Charles Sturt U., Wagga, 1991-98; mem. bd. govs., mem. Riverina adv. coun., 1994—, asst. dep. vice-chancellor, 1994—. Author: (with A. Pattison, E. Laurenson and others) Australian Rainfall and Runoff, 1977; contbr. articles to profl. jours. Mem. New South Wales Govt. Bd. Sr. Sch. Studies. Mem. Am. Geophys. Union. Avocations: designing and hand crafting furniture, gardening, fishing. Home: 26 Kars St, Beechworth VIC 3747, Australia Office: Charles Sturt U, Locked Bag 675, Wagga NSW 2678, Australia

CORNISH, LEONARD SOUTHWARD, biomedical engineer; b. Kingston upon Thames, England, June 8, 1944; s. Henry Willie Southward and Nina Mary (Riddle) C.; m. Rosemary Bertha Matheson, Sept. 9, 1967; children: Helen, Andrew, Annie, Neil, David. BS in Engring., U. London, 1966; MPhil, U. Hong Kong, 1978. Chartered elec. engr., Eng.; chartered bioeng., Eng. Jr. design engr. Brit. Aircraft Corp. Ltd., Weybridge, 1967-68, electronic devel. engr., 1968-72, dep. head voltage transient testing lab., 1971-72; electronics engr. electronics svcs. unit U. Hong Kong, 1972-92; tech. svcs. contr. ECHO Internat. Health Svcs. Ltd., Coulsdon, Surrey, Eng., 1993-98, head dept. biomed. engring., 1998—. Contbr. articles to profl. jours. Founder, mem. Hong Kong Oxfam Group, 1975, vice chmn., 1980-81, 83-84, chmn., 1981-83; coun. mem. Oxfam Hong Kong, 1988-92. Mem. IEEE (sr.), Instn. Elec. Engrs., Instn. Physics and Engring. in Medicine. Avocations: golf, gardening. Home: 58 Oakfield Goldsworth Pk, Woking Surrey GU21 3QS, England

CORNISH, LINDA SOWA YOUNG, children's books writer and illustrator, educator; b. Woodburn, Oreg., May 14, 1943; d. Cecil Edward and Marian Regina (Nibler) Sowa; m. Edmund Y.W. Young, June 11, 1966 (div. July 1988); children: Laura Young Engelmann, Amy L.H. Young, Kimberly Young Brummund; m. H.T. Cornish, Oct. 6, 1991. BA, U. Portland, 1966; EdM, Temple U., 1968. Tchr. spl. edn. Phila. Sch. System, 1966-69; tchr. elem. and spl. edn. North Clackamas Dist. 12, Search & Rescue Unit Post 989, Milwaukie, Oreg., 1974-92; author, illustrator Dahlia Pub. Co., Hillsboro, Oreg., 1994—. Author, illustrator: Pong and the Birthday Journey, 1984, Pong's Visit, 1994, Pong's Ways, 1995, Bobby's Story: A Family's Struggle with Mental Illness, 1997. Adv. for homeless mentally ill; mem. Love Circle, chancel choir United Meth. Women. Mem. AAUW, ASCD, Assn. for Childhood Edn. Internt., Oreg. Coun. Tchrs. English, Northwest Assn. Book Publishers. Republican. Methodist. Avocations: watercolor painting, classical music, volunteer work with elderly and mentally ill, community writing and craft classes. Home: 1295 SW Brookwood Ave Hillsboro OR 97123-7593 Office: Dahila Pub Co PO Box 1123 Hillsboro OR 97123-1123

CORNISH, RICHARD JOSEPH, international affairs consultant, retired diplomat; b. Omaha, Nov. 7, 1925; s. Lebbeus Morrison and Lydia Christine (Herrmann) C.; m. Beverly Anne Cormier, July 28, 1958; children—Pamela Anne, Allyson Juillette, Carolyn Lydia. B.A., Yale U., 1949; M.A., Am. U., 1965; diploma U.S. Air War Coll., 1976. Commd. fgn. service officer Dept. State, 1959; 2d sec., vice consul U.S. Embassy, Rangoon, Burma, 1959-62; 2d sec., consul U.S. Embassy, Lome, Togo, 1964-66; regional dir. AID, Savannakhet and Vientiane, Laos, 1967-71; polit. adviser Dept. Def., Frankfurt, Germany, 1973-75; dir. mil. assistance Dept. Def., Addis Ababa, Ethiopia, 1975-77; 1st sec. for polit. and econ. affairs U.S. embassy, Yaounde, Cameroon, 1979-81; 1st sec., polit. affairs, U.S. Embassy, London, 1981-85; ret., 1985; cons. London Diplomatic Assn., 1985-87, The Parvus Co., 1985-90, Trefoil Partnership, Ltd., London, 1987-90; chmn. bd. dirs. Cornish Assocs., 1987—. Author: The Development of Nationalism in Burma, 1966, The National Decision Making Process, 1975, Deployment of Military Forces, 1975. With USAAF, 1944-46, Asia Pacific Theater; served to lt. col. USAFR, 1949-77. Mem. Diplomatic and Consular Officers Ret., Am. Fgn. Service Assn., Assn. Diplomatic Studies, Assn. Asian Studies, Royal Commonwealth Soc., Kipling Soc. Clubs: Chevy Chase (Md.); Travellers, RAF (London); University (Washington); Yale (N.Y.C.). Lodges: Rotary (bd. dirs. 1976-77), Masons.

CORNSTUBLE, HERMAN LOGAN, retired industrial engineer; b. Wayne City, Aug. 20, 1921; s. Logan Stephen and Mary Cathern (Feeny) C. A in Indsl. Engring. Mgmt., Washington U., St. Louis, 1966, BS in Indsl. Mgmt., 1988. Mfg. indsl. engr. Boring Mfg. Corp., St. Louis, 1956-91; cons. to univ. students Boring Mfg. Corp., St. Louis. Cpl. U.S. Army, 1943-45, WWII, China, Burma, India; USN, 1952, Korea. Mem. Assembly of God Ch. Achievements include the manufacturing of the first Mercury Space Capsule used in the first American orbital space flight piloted by Lt. Col. John Glenn who completed three orbits around the world which was considered the forerunner of current Moon flight. Home: 2107 Wente Pl Florissant MO 63031-8546

CORNWALL, JOHN MICHAEL, physics educator, consultant, researcher; b. Denver, Aug. 19, 1934; s. Paul Bakewell and Dorothy (Zitkowski) C.; m. Ingrid Linderos, Oct. 16, 1965. AB, Harvard U., 1956; MS, U. Denver, 1959; PhD, U. Calif., 1962. NSF postdoctoral fellow Calif. Inst. Tech., Pasadena, 1962-63; mem. Inst. Advanced Study, Princeton, N.J., 1963-65; prof. physics UCLA, 1965—; vis. prof. Niels Bohr Inst., Copenhagen, 1968-69, Inst. de Physique Nucléaire, Paris, 1973-74, MIT, 1974, 87, Rockefeller U., N.Y.C., 1988; faculty RAND Grad. Sch., 1999; cons. Inst. Theoretical Physics, Santa Barbara, Calif., 1979-80, 82, bd. dirs., 1979-83; assoc. Ctr. Internat./Strategic Affairs, UCLA, 1987—; cons. MITRE Corp., Aerospace Corp., Los Alamos Nat. Labs., RAND Corp.; mem. dir.'s adv. com. Lawrence Livermore Labs., 1991—; mem. Def. Sci. Bd., 1992-93, mem. task force, 1996; chmn. External Rev. com. Accelerator Oper. and Technol. Divsn., Los Alamos Nat. Labs., 1995-97; chmn. external rev. com. Ctr. for Internat. Security and Arms Control, Stanford U., 1996; adv. commn. Accelerator Prodn. Tritium Project, 1997—; cons. John D. and Catherine T. MacArthur Found.; prof. sci. and policy analysis RAND Grad Sch., 1998—; mem. sci. and tech. panel Def. Threat Reduction Agy., 2000. Author: (with others) Academic Press Ency. of Science and Technology, Union of Concerned Scientists Report on Nat. Missile Def., other encys. and books; contbr. numerous articles to profl. jours. With U.S. Army, 1956-58. Grantee NSF, NASA; NSF pre/postdoctoral fellow 1960-63, A.P. Sloan fellow, 1967-71. Fellow AAAS; mem. Am. Phys. Soc., Am. Geophys. Union, N.Y. Acad. Sci. Avocations: jogging, bicycling, golf, bridge. Office: UCLA Dept Physics Los Angeles CA 90095-0001

CORNWELL, DAVID JOHN MOORE See LE CARRÉ, JOHN

CORP, LESTER DESMOND, financial executive; b. London, Apr. 17, 1946; s. Ernest Arthur and Constance Mabel (Strickland) C.; m. Mary Ann Robbins, Apr. 6, 1974. BSc in Econs., London U., 1967. From trainee to mgr. Coopers & Lybrand, London, 1967-75; fin. acct. Sun Life Assurance, London, 1975-78; dir. fin. and resources Conservative Party Ctrl. Office, London, 1978-84; fin. contr. Leeds Castle Found., Maidstone, Eng., 1985-88; dir. fin. Zool. Soc. London, 1988-94, Royal Albert Hall, 1994—; fin. dir. Grant Leisure Group Ltd., London, 1985-94. Vice chmn. Conservative Party, Midsussex, Eng., 1975-84; trustee Brooke Hosp. for Animals, 1994—. Fellow Inst. Chartered Accts. in Eng. and Wales; mem. Brit. Inst. Mgmt. Episcopalian. Avocations: architecture, travel, classical music, motor industry, archaeology. Office: Royal Albert Hall, Kensington Gore, London SW7 2AP, England

CORRADA DEL RIO, BALTASAR, supreme court justice; b. Morovis, P.R., Apr. 10, 1935; s. Romulo and Ana Maria (del Rio) Corrada del R.; m. Beatrice Betances, Dec. 24, 1959; children: Ana Isabel, Francisco Javier, Juan Carlos, Jose Baltasar. BA in Social Scis., U. P.R., 1956, JD, 1959. Bar: P.R., 1959. Ptnr. McConnell Valdes Sifre & Ruiz Suria, San Juan, 1959-75; atty., chmn. Civil Right Commn., P.R., 1970-72; mem., resident commr. from P.R. 95th-98th Congress; mayor City of San Juan, P.R., 1985-89; atty. Baltasar Corrada Law Office, 1989-92; sec. of state Govt. of P.R., 1993-95; assoc. justice P.R. Supreme Ct., 1995—; pres. New Progressive Party, 1986-89. Pres. editorial bd. P.R. Human Rights Rev., 1971-72. Bd. dirs. P.R. Teleradial Inst. Ethics. Recipient Great Cross of Civil Merit of Spain King Juan Carlos I, 1987. Mem. ABA, Fed. Bar Assn., P.R. Bar Assn. Roman Catholic. Club: Exchange, San Juan Rotary. Office: P R Supreme Ct PO Box 9022392 San Juan PR 00902-2392

CORRAO, SALVATORE, internist; b. Gela, Sicily, Italy, May 25, 1963; s. Giacomo and Lucia (Tagliarino) C.; m. Licia Miceli, Sept. 4, 1995; 1 child, Giacomo Andrea. MS, Liceo Scientifico Leonardo, Agrigento, Italy, 1980; MD, U. Palermo, 1986. Cert. echocardiography, mesotherapy. Rschr. Palermo U., Italy, 1987-94, prof. Specialization Sch. Internal Medicine, 1996—; sr. attending physician Civico E Benfratelli Hosp., Palermo, 1994—, first level dir., 1996—; prof. nursing sch. U. Palermo, 1997—; chief of health info. system and stats. Unit of Civico e Benfratelli, G di Cristina and Ascoli Hosp., 1999—. Contbr. articles to profl. jours. Pres. Rotaract Club, 1980-82. Grantee Am. Soc. Hypertension, 1994. Mem. Soc. Italiana Medicina Interna (Nat. Young Rschr., 1991), Soc. Italiana Cardiologia (Young Rschr., 1991), Soc. Italian VRG, Soc. for Med. Decision Making. Avocation: piano, keyboard, guitar, music composition. Home: Via Dei Nebrodi 67, 90144 Palermo Sicily, Italy Office: U Palermo Inst Internal Med, Via Carmelo Lazzaro 2, 90100 Palermo Sicily, Italy

CORREA, ALONSO VELEZ, neurosurgeon; b. Copacabana, Colombia, Feb. 12, 1939; s. Bernardo and Bertha (Valez) C.; children: Sonya, Yvonne, Lara. Degree, Javeriana U., 1963. Intern Maimonides Hosp., Bklyn., 1964-65; resident in neurology Bronx (N.Y.) Hosp., 1967-68; resident in surgery N.Y. Med. Coll., Valhalla, N.Y., 1968; resident in neurosurgery Mt. Sinai Hosp. and Sch. Medicine, N.Y.C., 1969-74; dir. neurosurgery USPHS, 1975-82; asst. prof. clin. neurosurgery Mount Sinai Sch. of Medicine, N.Y.C., 1984-91. Officer U.S. Army, 1965-67. Office: St Joseph's Hosp and Med Ctr 703 Main St Ste J243 Paterson NJ 07503-2621

CORREA, CHARLES M., architect; b. Hyderabad, India, Sept. 1, 1930; m. Monika Sequeira, 1961; 2 children. Grad. U. Mich., MArch, MIT. Pvt. practice architecture, 1958—; chief architect New Bombay, 1971-74; chmn. Nat. Commn. Urbanisation Govt of India, 1985-88 , Housing Urban Renewal and Ecology Bd. (BMRDA), 1975-94; mem. steering com. Aga Khan Award for Architects, 1977-86; Padma Shri, Pres. of India, 1972. Works include: Mahatma Gandhi Meml. Mus., Sabarmati Ashram, Ahmedabad, Kanchanjunga apts., Bombay, Hotel Cidade de Goa, Brit. Coun. Hdqs., Delhi Nat. Crafts Mus., Delhi, State Assembly for Madhya Pradesh Govt., Bhopal, Jawahar Kala Kendra Mus., Jaipur, Delhi, Previ low-income housing, Peru, others. Recipient Gold medal RIBA, 1984, Gold medal Indian Inst. Architects, 1987, Gold medal Internat. Union Architects, 1990, Praemium Imperiale Japan Art Soc., 1994, Aga Khan award for architecture, 1998. Fellow AIA (hon.), Am. Acad. Arts and Sci. (hon.); mem. UAP (hon.), French Acad. d'Architecture, Internat. Acad. Architects, Finnish Assn. Architects, Am. Acad. Arts and Letters (hon.). Office: 9 Mathew Rd, Bombay 400 004, India*

CORRÊA, IRAN CARLOS STALLIVIERE, marine geology educator; b. Caxias do Sul, Brazil, Sept. 24, 1950; s. Ernani Aguiar and Libera (Stalliviere) C.; m. Helma Borngraber, Nov. 26, 1976; children: Ana Paula, Luciana. MS, UFRGS, 1979; specialization in remote sci., U. Bordeaux, 1989, PhD, 1990. Aux. prof. UFRGS, Porto Alegre, Brazil, 1974-80, asst. prof., 1981-84, prof., 1987—, prof. grad. course marine geology, 1982—; adj. prof. UFRGS, Porto Alegre, 1985-87, dept. mgr., 1983-85, vice dir. Geosci. Inst., 1985-88; dir. CECO, 1993-97, vice dir., 1997-99; vis. prof. U. Concepcion, Chile, 1993—; mem. scientific com. of the sea, 1994-99; chmn. FAPERGS, 1990-96; vice chmn. OSNLR, Brazil, 1997-99. Author maps and atlas. Mem. SBG, ABEQUA. Roman Catholic. Avocations: beach, music, theatre, movies. E-mail: correa@if.ufrgs.br. Office: Inst Geosci UFRGS, Av Bento Concalves 9500, 91501970 Porto Alegre Brazil

CORREA, JAIME MONTALVO, university administrator; b. Madrid, Spain; married; 2 children. PhD in Labour Law, Univ. Complutense de Madrid, Spain, 1970. Dir. Spanish Inst. Social Studies, Spain, 1982-84; pres. Nat. Inst. Pub. Adminstrn., Spain, 1984-86; vice-rector, rector Univ. Estatal a Distancia, Spain, 1986-89. Author books on social politics and labour law. Mem. com. and parliamentary group's spokesman Socialist Spanish Party, 1976-79; leader Labour Union of Madrid, 1976-79; mem. European Inst. Social Security, 1976-79; pres. Asturia's Regional Com., 1979-82. Office: Univ Para La Paz, Apartado 138, Ciudad Colon Costa Rica

CORREA, NESTOR ROLANDO, civil engineer, educator; b. San Juan, Argentina, June 13, 1957; arrived in Germany, 1984; s. Francisco and Luisa Mafalda (Fochi) C.; m. Susanne Kirsebauer, Mar. 18, 1994. D in Engring., U. Hannover, 1988. Asst. hydraulics Nat. U. San Juan (Argentina), 1983-84; engr., group leader Regional Ctr. Groundwater, San Juan, 1983-90; rsch. asst. U. Hannover (Germany), 1984-88, rsch. assoc., 1988-90; project mgr. hydrology Nat. Coop. for Disposal of Radioactive Waste, Wettingen, Switzerland, 1990-94; lectr. hydrology and water resources Tech. U., Cottbus, Germany, 1994-95; advisor tng. in civil and water engring. WAPDA Engring. Acad., Faisalabad, Pakistan, 1995-99; head GRDC (Global Runoff Data Ctr., Fed. Inst. Hydrology), Germany, 2000—; vis. prof. Fed. U. Paraiba, Campina Grande, Brazil, 1989-90. Editor: Modeling of Groundwater Flow at the Subregional Scale: Boundary Conditions, Transient and Thermal Effects, Inverse Modeling, 1994. Mem. ASCE, Deutscher Vereinigung fü Wasserwirtschaft, Abwasser und Abfall, Internat. Assn. Hydrological Scis. Achievements include development of groundwater management strategies for sustainable development of irrigation systems; development of fluid-logging technology for quantitative determination of transmissivity profiles in boreholes; integrated policy and strategy for abatement of antropogenic pollution on water and soil resources. Avocations: jogging, concerts, music. Home: Grosse Barlinge 63, D-30171 Hanover Low-Saxony, Germany Office: Global Runoff Date Ctr Fed Inst Hydrology, PO Box 200253, D-56002 Koblenz Germany

CORREALE, ERNESTO, cardiologist, consultant; b. N.Y.C., Sept. 7, 1926; arrived in Italy, 1937; s. Antonio and Teresa (Rossano) C.; m. Srinart Suriya, Nov. 11, 1967. Medicine, U. Naples, 1953, Specialist Cardiology, 1960, Professorship in Semeiology, 1968. Rotating intern N.Y. Polyclinic Med. Sch. and Hosp., N.Y.C., 1954-55; asst. resident, resident medicine Goldwater Meml. Hosp. NYU, 1955-57; asst. in internal medicine U. Naples, 1963-69; chief of cardiology dept. internal medicine Hosp. Caserta (Italy), 1969-93, primario emeritus cardiology dept. internal medicine, 1993—; mem. monitoring com. Gissi-Prevention Trial, 1993—; lectr. phys. and instrument semeiology Sch. Cardiology U. Naples, 1968-86. Contbr. numerous articles to profl. jours. Mem. monitoing and ethical bd. Hosp. Caserta. Decorated Commendatore al Merito della Republica (Italy); Fulbright scholar, 1954-57; named Grande ufficiale al Merito della Republica Govt. Italy; Paul Harris fellow Rotary. Fellow Am. Coll. Cardiology; mem. Assn. Nat. Medici Cardiologi Ospedalieri, Cardiologists (investigator Mario Negri rsch. group 1984—, regional del. 1983-84, mem. nat. directory 1984-86, sec. gen. 1986-88), European Collaboration on Low Dose Aspirin in Polycytemia Vera (mem. safety and monitoring bd. internat. trial). Roman Catholic. Avocations: reading, gardening. Home: Via Giotto 13, 81100 Caserta Caserta, Italy Office: Palazzo Anto, Via G M Bosco, 81100 Caserta Caserta, Italy

CORREALE, GIVLIO, public administrator educator, lawyer; b. Nocera, Italy, May 16, 1932; s. Francesco and Maria (Torre) C.; m. Concetta Giuffré Correale, Apr. 28, 1962; children: Ivo, Francesca. Degree in Law, U. Federico II, 1955. Judge Pretura, Naples, 1959-63, Procura della Republic, Crema, 1963, Acctg. Ct., Rome, 1963-81; prof. U. Camerino, 1974-86; prof. Pub. Adminstrn. Sch., Caserta, 1970-81, Rome, 1979-81; prof. U. La Sapienza, Rome, 1986—. Author: Preambles to the Study of Adminstrative Nisure, 1969, Contribution to the Study of Concert, 1974, Structure of the Administrative Trial, 1979, The Autonomy of the University, 1979. Recipient Prize of the Culture, Presidency of Cabinet, 1996; named Commendatore of the Italian Rep., 1981. Roman Catholic. Avocations: classical music, poetry, journalism. Home: Giulio Venticinque, Street 23, 00136 Rome Italy Office: Giuseppe Pisanelli Str 4, 00196 Rome Italy

CORREA SUTIL, SOFIA, historian; b. Santiago de Chile, Chile, Sept. 1, 1953; d. Jorge Correa-Montt and Sofia Sutil-Alcalde; m. Alfredo Jocelyn-Holt L., Aug. 23, 1986; 1 child, Emilia. PhD, Oxford U., 1994. Dir. history dept. U. Blas Cañas, Santiago, Chile, 1988-90; dir. Centro Barros Arana Nat. Lib., Santiago, 1990-93; dir. Nat. History Mus., 1993-96, head project new permanent exhbn., 1997-2000; lectr. U. Santiago de Chile, 1995—, dir. doctoral program Am. studies, 2000—; vis. fellow The Ctr. Lat. Am. Studies Cambride U., Eng., 1994, cons. Min. Edn. for design of hist. curriculum for secondary schs., 1996—. Co-author: (book) Chile en el Siglo XX, 1985; columnist Hoy Jour., 1978-80; columnist El Metropolitano newspaper, 1999. Dir. women's studies project Alternative Project for Democracy, Santiago de Chile, 1984-85. Roman Catholic. Home: Toledo 1940, Providencia Santiago Chile Office: U Santiago de Chile, Dept History, Alameda 3363 Santiago Chile

CORREIA, JOAO PEDRO SANTOS, marine biologist; b. Santarem, Portugal, June 9, 1972; s. Antonio and Maria do Rosario (Santos) C.; m. Leonor Teresa Sousa, May 15, 1996. Grad., U. Algarve, 1994; MSc, Tech. U. Lisbon, 1997. Biologist Lisbon Zoo, Portugal, 1995, Ipimar, Lisbon, 1995-97; biologist, curator fo collections Oceanario Lisbon, 1997—. Mem. Portuguese Biologists Assn., N.Y. Acad. Scis. Home: Rua Jorge Castilho 1613 7C, 1900-272 Lisbon Portugal Office: Oceanario de Lisboa SA, Esplanada D. Carlos I, 1998 Lisbon Portugal

CORRELL, ALSTON DAYTON, JR., forest products company executive; b. Brunswick, Ga., Apr. 28, 1941; s. Alston Dayton and Elizabeth (Flippo) C.; m. Ada Lee Fulford, June 23, 1963; children: Alston Dayton, Elizabeth Lee. BSBA, U. Ga., 1963; MS in Pulp and Paper Tech., U. Maine, 1966, MS in Chem. Engring., 1967. Tech. svc. engr. Westvaco, 1963-64; instr. U. Maine, Orono, 1964-67; various pulp and paper mgmt. positions Weyerhaeuser Co., 1967-77; pres. paperboard divsn. Mead Corp., Dayton, Ohio, 1977-80, group v.p. paperboard, 1980, group v.p. paper, 1981, group v.p. forest products, 1981-83, sr. v.p. forest products, 1983-88; sr. v.p. pulp and printing paper Ga.-Pacific Corp., Atlanta, 1988-89, exec. v.p. pulp and paper, 1989-91, pres., COO, 1991-93, pres., CEO, 1993, CEO, chmn. bd. and pres., 1993—; dir. Ga. Kraft Co., Rome, Brunswick Pulp & Paper Co., Ga., Northwood Pulp & Timber Ltd., Prince George, B.C., Can., B.C. Forest Products Ltd., Vancouver; pres., CEO, dir. Gr. Nd. Nekoosa Corp.; pres. Mead Tumber Co.; bd. dir. Sears, Roebuck & Co., SunTrust Banks, Atlanta, SunTrust Banks Inc., SunTrust Banks Ga., Inc., The Southern Co.; chmn. Inst. Paper Sci. and Tech., Inc.; bd. trustees Robert W. Woodruff Arts Ctr., U.S. Coun. Internat. Bus. Trade, U. Ga. Found.; bd. councilors The Carter Coun.; bd. govs. The Nature Conservancy. Bd. dirs. Miami Valley (Ohio) Boy Scouts, Nature Conservancy, Keep Am. Beautiful Inc., Ga. Rsch. Alliance; trustee U. Ga. Found., Robert W. Woodruff Arts Ctr.; chmn. United Negro Coll. Fund, vice chmn. Atlanta Campaign; mem. Atlanta coun. Boy Scouts Am., Atlanta Action Forum; bd. dirs. Ctrl. Atlanta Progress, chmn. 1995-97; mem. exec. com. Nat. Coun. Paper Industry for Air and Stream Improvemt, Inc., past chmn. bd. Recipient Nat. Brotherhood award, 1991, Disting. Alumnus award U. Ga., Terry Coll. Bus., 1994, Inst. Human Rels.

award Am. Jewish Com., 1995, Salute to Greatness award, The King Ctr., 1999; named one of 100 Most Influential Georgians, Ga. Trend Mag., 1994, 95, one of 25 Most Influential Georgians, 1996, 97, 98, CEO of Yr., Atlanta Bus. League, 1998, Exec. Papermaker of Yr., PaperAge, 1999. Mem. Ga. C. of C. (bd. dirs.), Atlanta C. of C. (bd. dirs., Forward Atlanta Policy Group, chmn. 1997-98), Commerce Club (Atlanta, bd. dirs.), Am. Forest & Paper Assn. (bd. dirs., forest resource product group exec. com.). Republican. Presbyterian. Office: Ga-Pacific Corp PO Box 105605 133 Peachtree St NE Fl 51 Atlanta GA 30303-1808

CORRETJA, ALEX, tennis player; b. Barcelona, Spain, Apr. 11, 1974. Profl. tennis player, 1991—. Recipient 4 tournament titles including Indian Wells, Gstaad Open, Legg Mason Tennis Classic, Generali Open. Avocations: music, basketball, soccer, golf. Office: c/o ATP Tour 201 Atp Tour Blvd Ponte Vedra Beach FL 32082-3211*

CORREU, SANDRA KAY, special education educator; b. Crowley, La., Aug. 24, 1938; d. Edward Dorsey and Elizabeth Mays (Wiggins) Peckham; m. Donald Audrey Correu, Sept. 5, 1959; children: Lisa G., Donald Andrew. BS in Edn., Mo. Western State Coll., 1976; postgrad., N.W. Mo. State Coll., 1980-86. Cert. in learning disabilities, behavior disordered, educable mentally handicapped, trainable mentally handicapped. Tchr. Autistic children Helen Davis State Sch., St. Joseph, Mo., 1976-78; tchr. behavior disordered St. Joseph (Mo.) Sch. Dist., 1978—; pres., v.p., mem. Assn. for Retarded Citizens, St. Joseph, 1976-86; bd. mem. United Cerebral Palsy, St. Joseph, 1980-86; devel. dir. summer program for MRDD youth in cooperation with Mo. Western State Coll.; presenter in field. Elder Presbyn. Ch. Mem. Nat. Dem., Coun. for Exceptional Citizens, Assn. for Retarded Citizens, Mo. State Tchrs. Assn., Greenpeace, Gorilla Found., World Wildlife Fund, Humane Soc. U.S., Common Cause, People for Ethical Treatment of Animals, Habitat for Humanity, Assn. Handicapped Artists. Avocations: reading, sewing, crafts. Home: 3228 Seneca St Saint Joseph MO 64507-2027 Office: St Joseph Sch Dist 10th and Edmond Saint Joseph MO 64507

CORRIGAN, E(DWARD) GERALD, investment banker; b. Waterbury, Conn., 1941. BS, Fairfield U.; MA, PhD, Fordham U. Group v.p. mgmt. and planning Fed. Res. Bank of N.Y., 1976-80; spl. assignment to chmn. bd. govs. Fed. Res. Sys., 1979-80; pres. Fed. Res. Bank of Mpls., 1981-84, Fed. Res. Bank of N.Y., N.Y.C., 1985-93; chmn. internat. advisors Goldman, Sachs & Co., N.Y.C., 1994-96, mng. dir., 1997—; Trustee The Am. Ditchley Found., The Bretton Woods Com., The Chgo. Mercantile Exch., Program on the World Economy, The Per Jacobsson Found., Fairfield U., fin. svcs. vol. corps steering com. The Group of Thirty, The Inst. for Fin. Stability, Bank for Internat. Settlements, The Trilateral Commn.; co-chmn. Aspen Inst. Mem. Aspen Inst. (co-chmn.), Econ. Club of N.Y. Office: Goldman Sachs and Co 85 Broad St New York NY 10004-2456

CORRIGAN, FAITH, journalist, educator; b. Cleve., Oct. 16, 1926; d. William John and Marjorie (Wilson) C.; m. Sigvald Matias Refsnes, Sept. 18, 1957 (dec. Feb. 1994); children: Marjorie Refsnes, Sunniva Collins, Stephen Refsnes. BA, Ohio State U., 1948; MAT, Kent State U., 1987. Cert. tchr. English, reading, Ohio. Staff writer women's news N.Y. Times, N.Y.C., 1953-57; investigative reporter Cleve. Plain Dealer, 1962-66; dir. pub. info. Cuyahoga County Bd. Commrs., Cleve., 1966-69; dir. news, publs. Huron Rd. Hosp., East Cleveland, Ohio, 1970-73; lectr. II U. Akron, Ohio, 1990-91; adj. prof. Kent State U., North Canton, Ohio, 1996-97, Kent State U., Ashtabula br., Geauga/Twinsburg, Ohio, 1999—; lectr. Fordham U., N.Y.C., 1956; expert witness U.S. Senate Medicare Hearings, Cleve., 1965; mgr. Cuyahoga County Welfare Levy Campaign, Cleve., 1966. Contbr. articles to newspapers. TESOL, Lit. Vols. Am.; mem. bd. mgrs. Eleanor B. Rainey Meml. Inst., Cleve., 1966-78; officer, trustee Lake County Cmty. Svcs. Coun., 1984-90; mem. adv. bd. Lake Geauga Legal Aid Soc., Painesville, Lake County, 1984-87; chair Initiative Petition Campaign on Environ. Waste Plant Issue, Willoughby, Ohio, 1991; officer, founder Ohio State U. chpt. Am. Newspaper Guild, 1947-48; del. rep. assembly N.Y. Newspaper Guild, 1954-57; poll judge Lake County Bd. Elections, 1984-98; field rep. U.S. Census Bur., 1989—; recruiter, crew leader U.S. Census 2000; disaster vol. Lake County chpt. ARC. Recipient award of achievement Press Club of Cleve., 1964, Pulitzer nominee Cleve. Plain Dealer, 1964, 1st in state Ohio Newspaper Women's Assn., 1964, 1st in state Pub. Contest of Am. Heart Assn., 1972, 1st pl. publs. award Internat. Assn. Bus. Communicators, 1971-72. Mem. VFW (Ladies Aux.), Willoughby Hist. Soc. (v.p. 1997—), Ohio Bicentennial Hist. Markers Rsch. Democrat. Roman Catholic. Avocations: expert on American china, glass, American labor history. Home: 37550 Euclid Ave Willoughby OH 44094-5622

CORRIGAN, PAULA ANN, career officer, internist; b. Cheyenne, Wyo., Feb. 17, 1961; d. Patrick Joseph and Eleanor Marie (Kasun) C. BS, U. Notre Dame, 1983; MD, U. N.Mex., 1987; M in Pub. Health in Tropical Medicine, Tulane Sch. Pub. Health, 1999. Diplomate Am. Bd. Internal Medicine, Am. Soc. Tropical Medicine and Hygiene. Advanced through ranks to lt. col. USAF; chief internal medicine clinic USAF, Holloman AFB, N.Mex., 1990-93, flight surgeon Hosp. 48 RQS, 1993-94; flight comdr. 18 AMDS/SGPF USAF, Kadena AB, Japan, 1996-98; res., Aerospace Med. Brooks AFB, TX, 1999—. Mem. ACP, AMA, Am. Heart Assn. (coun. mem. 1992-93), Am. Soc. of Tropical Medicine and Hygiene, Aerospace Med. Assn., N.Mex. Med. Soc., Soc. USAF Flight Surgeons. Roman Catholic. Avocation: scuba diving. Home: 1334 Arrow Spg San Antonio TX 78258-3233 Office: USAF SAM/GE 2602 W Gate Rd Brooks AFB TX 78235-5252

CORRIGAN-MAGUIRE, MAIREAD, peace worker; b. Belfast, Northern Ireland, Jan. 27, 1944; d. Andrew and Margaret C.; m. Jackie Maguire, Sept. 8, 1981; children: John Francis, Luke; stepchildren—Mark, Joanne, Marie-Louise. Grad., Miss Gordon's Comml. Coll., 1967; LL.D. (hon.), Yale U., 1976. Various secretarial positions in Belfast, 1959-76; co-founder Community of Peace People (No. Ireland Peace Movement), Belfast, 1976, chmn., 1980-81; hon. chair Peace People. Lay mem. Legion of Mary, Roman Cath. Ch., 1959—. Co-recipient Nobel prize for peace, 1976; recipient Carl von Ossietzky medal for courage, 1976. Fax: 01232 683 947. E-mail: peacepeople@gn.apc.org. Office: care Community of the Peace People, 224 Lisburn Rd, Belfast BT9 6GE, Northern Ireland*

CORRIN, CHRISTOPHER BRIAN, mining company executive; b. Godalming, Surrey, Eng., Sept. 8, 1953; s. Eric Stanley and Hazel Adrienne (Daukes) C.; m. Juliette Rose Womersley, Jan. 4, 1986; children: Emma Louise, Richard Julian. BA with honors, U. London, 1975; PGCE, U. Oxford, 1976; MBA, U. Cape Town, South Africa, 1982. Asst. divsn. mgr. Anglo Am. Corp., 1977-86; investment banker Schroders, 1987-88; mgr. De Beers (CSO), 1989-96; v.p. Minorco, 1997-98; exec. v.p. Anglo Am. Plc, London, 1999—; dir. Anglo Am. Internat. Ltd. Mem. Oxford and Cambridge Club. Office: Anglo American Plc, 20 Carlton House Ter, London SW1y 5AN, England

CORRIS, PAUL ANTHONY, physician, consultant; b. Bebington, Eng., May 20, 1953; s. Ronald George and Gladys (Ruffler) C.; m. Elizabeth Ann Hill, May 24, 1980; children: James Oliver, Katherine Elizabeth. MBBS, Westminster Medical Sch., London, 1976; MRCP, London, FRCP. House physician Westminster Hosp., London, 1976-77; house surgeon St. Richards Hosp., Chichester, 1977; sr. house officer Westminster Hosp., London, 1977-78, Leicester Teaching Hosp., 1978-79; registrar Freeman Hosp., Newcastle, 1980-81, rsch. fellow, 1981-83; sr. registrar Newcastle Teaching Hosp., 1983-86; cons. physician Newcastle Univ, Freeman Hosp., 1986-96, Freeman Hosp., Univ. Newcastle, 1996—; vis. prof. McGill Univ., Montreal, 1994-95; reader in Thoracic Medicine, U. Newcastle, 1996-2000, prof. thoracic medicine, 2000—. Contbr. articles to profl. jours. Mem. Coun. of British Lung Found. Grantee Scientific Rsch. grant Newcastle Univ. Hosp., 1996, numerous grants Brit. Lung Found., 1988—. Mem. Assn. Physicians of Great Britain and Ireland, British Thoracic Soc., Internat. Soc. for Heart and Lung Transplantation (sec.). Avocations: soccer, football, skiing. Office: Freeman Hosp, Freeman Rd, NE7 7DN Newcastle upon Tyne England

CORRY, CHARLES ELMO, geophysicist, consultant; b. Salt Lake City, May 15, 1938; s. Elmo Leigh Corry and Sylvia Birch; children: Christopher Charles, Matthew Lee. BS in Geology, Utah State U., 1970; MS in Geophysics, U. Utah, 1972; PhD in Geophysics, Tex. A&M U., 1976. Electronic missile checkout GD Convair-Astronautics, San Diego, 1960-64; rsch. assoc. Scripps Inst. Oceanography, La Jolla, Calif., 1965-68, Woods Hole (Mass.) Oceanographic Inst., 1968; mgr. geophys. rsch. AMAX, Golden, Colo., 1977-82; v.p. Nonlinear Analysis, Inc., Bryan, Tex., 1982-84; vis., adj., assoc. prof. geophysics Tex. A&M U., College Station, 1983-87; assoc. prof. geophysics U. Mo., Rolla, 1984-89; coord. world ocean circulation experiment Woods Hole Oceanographic Inst., 1990-95; cons. Golden, Denver, Colorado Springs, 1995—. Author: Laccoliths, Mechanics of Emplacement and Growth, 1988, Geology of the Solitario, Trans-Pecos Texas, 1990, Domestic Violence Against Men, 1999, (award); contbr. articles to profl. jours. and conf. procs., including Trans. Am. Geophys. Union, Jour. Applied Geophysics, others. Cpl., USMC, 1956-59, Calif. Fellow Geol. Soc. Am.; mem. ACLU, Am. Geophys. Union, Soc. Exploration Geophysicists. Buddhist. Achievements include overturning of paradigm that had existed for over 150 years, regarding galvanic current flow in ore bodies; discovery that ore minerals are commonly ferroelectrics and that ore bodies behave as a polarized dielectric medium, or solid plasma, in electrical surveys; development of the controlled source audiomagnetotelluric method for electrical exploration; field and theoretical studies of magmatic intrusions; terrestrial heat flow studies in the North Pacific; coordination of hydrographic program of World Ocean Circulation Experiment; relational database design and data modeling; civil liberties. E-mail: ccorry@pcisys.net. Home: 455 Bear Creek Rd Colorado Springs CO 80906-5820

CORSETTI, RENATO, psychologist; b. Rome, Mar. 29, 1941; s. Domenico Corsetti and Natalina Marzilli; m. Anna Michal Lowenstein, Dec. 28, 1981; children: Gabriele, Fabiano. MA in Econs., U. Rome, 1964; MA (hon.), U. Turin, Italy, 1972. Dir. CREDIOP, Rome, 1970-91; psycholinquist U. Rome, 1992—. Author: Lingua e Politica, 1977; editor: Diskriminacio, 1981; contbr. articles to profl. jours. Lt. Italian Army, 1964-66. Mem. Esperanto Assn. (bd. dirs. 1970—). Avocation: Esperanto language. Home: Colle Rasto, IT-00039 Palestrina Italy

CORSON, KIMBALL JAY, lawyer; b. Mexico City, Sept. 17, 1941; came to U.S., 1942; s. Harland Jerry and Arleen Elizabeth (Jones) C.; m. Ann Dudley Wood, May 25, 1963 (div. Apr. 1978); 1 child, Claudia Ring; m. Joy Lorann Sligh, June 16, 1979; children: Bryce Manning, Jody Darlene. BA, Wayne State U., 1966; MA, U. Chgo., 1968, JD, 1971. Bar: Ariz. 1972, U.S. Dist. Ct. 1971, U.S. Supreme Ct. 1991. Assoc. Lewis & Roca, Phoenix, 1971-74, ptnr., 1974-90; ptnr. Horne Kaplan & Bistrow, Phoenix, 1990-99; of counsel Shields and Andersen, 1999—. Co-author: Document Control: Organization, Management and Production, 1988; co-author: Litigation Support Using Personal Computers, 1989. Co-founder Desert Hills Improvement Assn., Phoenix, 1988—. With U.S. Army, 1961-64. Fellow Woodrow Wilson Found., 1966-67. Mem. ABA (civil practice and procedures com. antitrust sect. 1988—), Ariz. Bar Assn. (spkr. 1991—), Maricopa County Bar Assn., Internat. Trademark Assn. (editl. bd. The Trademark Reporter 1993-94, 99-2000, mem. publs. com. 1995-96), INTA Speaker, Am. Sailing Assn., Phi Beta Kappa. Avocations: music, computers, sailing, photography, first century history. Home: Summit Ranch 35808 N 15th Ave Phoenix AZ 85086-7228 Office: Shields and Andersen 7830 N 23rd Ave Phoenix AZ 85021-6808

CORSON, THOMAS HAROLD, manufacturing company executive; b. Elkhart, Ind., Oct. 15, 1927; s. Carl W. and Charlotte (Keyser) C.; m. Dorthy Claire Scheide, July 11, 1948; children: Benjamin Thomas, Claire Elaine. Student, Purdue U., 1945-46, Rensselaer Poly. Inst., 1946-47, So. Meth. U., 1948-49. Chmn. bd. dirs. Coachmen Industries, Inc., Elkhart, 1965-97, chmn. emeritus, dir., 1997—; bd. dirs. 1st State Bank, Middlebury, R.C.R. Sci. Inc., Goshen, Ind., Micrology Labs., Inc., Goshen, Great Lakes Capital, L.L.C., Morristown, N.J.; chmn., sec. Greenfield Corp., Middlebury. Adv. coun. U. Notre Dame; past trustee Ball State U.; dir., past trustee, past vice chmn. Interlochen (Mich.) Arts Acad. and Nat. Music Camp. With U.S. Naval Air Force, 1945-47. Mem. Ind. Mfrs. Assn. (past dir.), Elkhart C. of C. (past dir.), Ind. C. of C. (bd. dirs.), Ind. Hist. Soc. (dir.), Royal Poinciana Golf Club, Elcona Club (past dir.), Masons, Shriners. Methodist. Home: PO Box 340 Middlebury IN 46540-0340 Office: Coachmen Industries Inc PO Box 3300 Elkhart IN 46515-3300

CORSONELLO, PASQUALE, electronics engineering researcher, educator; b. Cosenza, Italy, May 4, 1964; s. Franco and Franca Lupi. MEE, U. Naples, Italy, 1988. Rschr. Nat. Coun. Rsch., Naples, 1988-91; lectr. U. Calabria, Cosenza, 1991-96; asst. prof. dept. electronics, computer sci. and sys. U. Reggio Calabria, Italy, 1997—, dir. Electronic Lab. Contbr. articles to sci. jours. Mem. IEEE, Soc. Computer Simulation. Avocation: flying. Fax: +39-984-494713. E-mail: pascor@nwdeis1.unical.it. Office: U Calabria Dept Elec CompSc, Loc Arcavacata, 87036 Rende CS, Italy

CORTAZAR, OSVALDO DANIEL, physicist, educator; b. Rosario, Santa Fe, Argentina, Dec. 11, 1960; s. Luis Alberto and Yolanda Juana (Perez) C.; m. Gabriela Raquel Gallicchio, May 2, 1986; 2 children. MS in Physics, U. Buenos Aires, 1986; PhD of Physics, U. Mar del Plata, 1990. Asst. prof. U. Mar del Plata, Argentina, 1986-90; vis. scientist Colo. State U., Fort Collins, 1991-94; assoc. prof. U. Mar del Plata, 1995—; invited prof. U. Navarra, Spain, 1997; mem. Nat. Coun. Sci. and Technol. Rsch. of Argentina (CONICET), 1998. Contbr. articles on laser and plasma physics to profl. jours. Achievements include participation in development of new x-ray-lasers sources, developing new sensors for detection of partial breaks in mechanical cables by fiber optics and laser technology. Home: Gral Paunero 2477, 7600 Mar del Plata BA, Argentina Office: Nat U Mar del Plata Fac Eng, Av Juan B Justo 4302 Eng, 7600 Mar del Plata Argentina

CORTÉS, CARLOS ELISEO, history educator; b. Oakland, Calif., Apr. 6, 1934; s. Carlos Federico and Florence Frieda (Hoffman) C.; m. Laurel Vermilyea, Apr. 26, 1978; 1 child, Alana Madrugada. BA in Comm. and Pub. Policy, U. Calif., Berkeley, 1956; MS in Journalism, Columbia U., 1957; B in Fgn. Trade, Am. Inst. for Fgn. Trade, 1962; MA in Portuguese and Spanish, U. N.Mex., 1965, PhD in History, 1969. Lab. asst. Jensen-Salsbery Chem. Co., Kansas City, Mo., 1952; cable splicer Whitaker Cable Corp., North Kansas City, Mo., 1953-54; editor Univ. Calif. yearbook Blue and Gold, Berkeley, 1955-56; gen. asst. Boxoffice Mag., Kansas City, Mo., 1956; asst. to dir. of pub. relations Am. Shakespeare Festival, Stratford, Conn., 1957; exec. editor Phoenix Sunpapers, 1959-61; proofreader Am. Men of Sci., Tempe, Ariz., 1961; reporter AP, Phoenix, 1961; asst. to dir. area studies Am. Inst. Fgn. Trade, Phoenix, 1961-62; teaching machine programmer Learning Inc., Tempe, 1961-62; acting asst. prof. history U. Calif., Riverside, 1968-69, asst. prof. history, 1969-72, chmn. Latin Am. Studies, 1969-71, asst. to vice chancellor for acad. affairs, 1970-72, assoc. prof. history, 1972-76, 1972-76, chmn. Chicano Studies Program, 1972-79, prof. history, 1976-94, prof. emeritus, 1994—, chmn. dept. history, 1982-86; cons. in field to govt. agys., sch. systems, univs., mass media and pvt. bus.; lectr. Smothsonian Inst., 1993-94. Author: The Children are Watching: How the Media Teach About Diversity, 2000; numerous books and articles to profl. jours. Served with U.S. Army, 1957-59. Kraft scholar; recipient numerous grants and fellowships, Vernon J. Scott award, Hubert Herring Meml. award, Pacific Coast Council on Latin Am. Studies, 1974, Disting. Teaching award, U. Calif.-Riverside, 1976, Eleanor Fishburn award, Washington EdPress Assn., 1977 Disting. Calif. Humanist award, Calif. Council for Humanities, 1980, Keys to the City, Kansas City, Mo. and Kansas City, Kans., 1982, Nat. Multicultural Trainer of Yr. award Am. Soc. for Tng. and Devel., 1989, Hilda Toba award Calif. Coun. Social Studies, 1995; named Bildner Fellow, Assn. Am. Schs. in South Am.; fellow Japan Found., 1986, Rockefeller Found., 1986-87. Mem. Calif. Coun. for Social Studies, Historians Film Com., Immigration History Soc., Internat. Assn. Audio-Visual Media in Hist. Rsch. and Edn., Nat. Assn. Chicano Studies, Nat. Coun. Social Studies, Soc. for Study of Multi-Ethnic Lit. of the U.S., So. Calif. Social Sci. Assn., Phi Beta Kappa, Phi Alpha Theta, Phi Kappa Phi. Home: 3088 Pine St Riverside CA 92501-2364 Office: U Calif Dept History Riverside CA 92521-0001

CORTES, DINA, pediatrician; b. Aarhus, Jylland, Denmark, Mar. 16, 1959; d. Per and Kirsten (Petersen) C.; m. Jorgen Mogens Thorup, May 28, 1988; children: Sebastian Cortes Thorup, Thomas Cortes Thorup. MD, U. Copenhagen, Denmark, 1986, PhD, 1998. Resident dept. pediatric surgery Rigshospitalet U. Copenhagen, 1986, resident dept. pathology Herlev Hosp., 1990-91, rsch. fellow dept. pediatric surgery Rigshospitalet, 1992-96, resident dept. pediat. Glostrup Hosp., 1997-2000; resident dept. orthopedics Frederikborg Amts Sygehus Hillerod, Denmark, 1987-88, resident dept. medicine, 1988-89, resident dept. surgery, 1988-90, resident dept. pediat., 1996-97; specialist registrar, lectr. dept. pediat. Glostrup Hosp. Univ. Copenhagen, 2000—. Contbr. numerous articles on cryptorchidism to profl. jours.; contbr. workshops, symposiums. Mem. Internat. Children's Continence Soc., Nordic Assn. for Andrology, Danish Paediatric Soc., Danish Soc. for Reproduction and Fetal Devel. Home: Bukkeballevej 60, 2960 Rungsted Kyst Denmark

CORTES, JOHN EMMANUEL, botanical garden administrator, consultant; b. Gibraltar, Sept. 11, 1956; s. Joseph Charles and Carmen (Bruzon) C.; m. Valerie Diane Pearce, Aug. 28, 1980; children: Mark, Zoë. BSc (1st class hon.), Royal Holloway Coll., U. London, 1979; DPhil, Magdalen Coll., Oxford, Eng., 1983. Exec. officer pers. Govt. of Gibraltar, 1983-86, higher exec. officer pers., 1986-88; hosp. mgr. Gibraltar Health Authority, 1988-90; gen. mgr., 1991; dir. Gibraltar Bot. Gardens, 1991—; mng. dir. Wildlife (Gibraltar) Ltd., Environ. Cons., 1991—; gen. sec. Gibraltar Ornithol. and Natural History Soc., 1976—; gov.'s trustee Gibraltar Heritage Trust, 1986—; mem. Gibraltar Sci. Authority and Nature Conservancy Coun., 1980—; v.p. Consejo Ibericao para la Defensa de la Naturaleza, 1995—; bd. dirs. Parque Natural de los Alcornoquales, Cadiz, Spain, 1998—. Author: The Birds of Gibraltar, 1980; co-author, editor: The Flowers of Gibraltar, 1996; editor: Aves Rapaces del Parque Natural de la Sierra de Grazalema, 1996, editor: Aves de la Bahia de Cadiz, 1998; co-editor: Statistics and Environment, 1999; editor, chief contbr. Gibraltar Nature News, 1992—; editor Alectoris, 1980-97. Justice of the Peace Gibraltar Judiciary, 1994—; bd. dirs. Gibraltar Health Authority, 1991—; mem. Devel. and Planning Commn., Gibraltar, 1990—; mem. CemeteriesBd., Gibraltar, 1996—. Recipient Gibraltar Heritage corp. award Gibraltar Heritage Trust, 1997. Fellow Linnean Soc. London; mem. Brit. Ornithologists' Union, Inst. Biology (chartered biologist 1979—), Inst. Ecology and Environ. Mgmt. Roman Catholic. Avocations: amateur dramatics, popular music, weight training. Home: 8/8 Buena Vista Rd, Gibraltar Gibraltar Office: Gibraltar Botanic Gardens, Red Sands Rd PO Box 843, Gibraltar Gibraltar

CORTEZ, ALFREDO DURVAL VILLELA, food products executive; b. Maceió, Alagoas, Brazil, July 14, 1934; s. Durval da Rocha Cortez and Consuleo Albuquerque Villela Cortez; m. Maria Inez Toledo Carnaúba, Feb. 1, 1959; children: Manoel, Alfredo Jr., Claudia. Degree in chem. engring., Fed U. Pernambuco, Recife, Brazil, 1958; degree in petroleum engring., Fed. U. Bahia, Salvador, Brazil, 1962; grad. econ. engring., Fed. U. Alagoas, Maceió, 1964. Various positions, also rep. to Soviet Govt. Brazilian Petroleum SA, Alagoas and Sergipe, 1958-70; chmn. Caila, Viçosa, Brazil, 1971-75; dir. Planal, Maceió, Brazil, 1975-76, Georena, Maceió, 1976-77; tech. supt. Asplana, Maceió, 1978-88; dir. Assucal, Maceió, 1989—; chmn. Apqeal, Maceió, 1977-78, Ceal, Maceió, 1986-87, Polo Cloro-Químico, Maceió, 1988. Contbr. articles to profl. jours. Decorated Brazilian Navy, Recife, 1965, Bolivian Sugar Industry, 1982, Honour medals Confea, Rio de Janeiro, 1997. Mem. Brazilian Soc. Sugar and Alcohol Technologists (vice chmn. 1981-84), Engring. and Archs. Regional Coun., Engrs. Syndicate Alagoas. Roman Catholic. Avocations: swimming, sailing, horse riding, fishing. Home: Apt 101, Av Alvaro Otacilio 6889, 57037270 Maceió Alagoas, Brazil

CORTEZ, RICARDO LEE, investment management executive; b. N.Y.C., Mar. 9, 1950; s. Eddie Adam and Marian Ruth (Lee) C.; children: Vanessa, Natalie, Rebecca; m. Harriet Anne Howard, Jan. 16, 1993. BA cum laude, CUNY, 1971; postgrad., Columbia U., 1971-73; cert. investment mgmt. analyst, U. Pa., 1993. Sr. stock market analyst Merrill Lynch, N.Y.C., 1971-76; exec. v.p. Trident Investment-Grace Capital, N.Y.C., 1976-78; pres. Liberty Capital Mgmt., N.Y.C., 1978-84, Cortez Capital Mgmt., N.Y.C., 1984-89; v.p., dir. fixed income Summit (N.J.) Trust Co., 1985-86; 1st v.p., dir. programs and communications Prudential Securities, N.Y.C., 1989-96, nat. sales dir. investment mgmt. svcs., 1996—; No. divsn. dir. Prudential Investments, 1998—, nat. dir. investment mgmt. svcs. divsn.; v.p. global multi-mgr. strategies Goldman Sachs, N.Y.C., 2000—; lectr. stock market analysis N.Y. Inst. Fin., N.Y.C., 1973-75. Author: (with Edson Gould) Industry and Stock Forecast, 1976. Named Spkr. of Yr., Mcpl. Treas.'s Assn. Calif., 1981. Avocation: former lead guitar for Mitch Ryder, Jay and the Americans, Coasters, other musical rock groups. Office: Goldman Sachs 1 New York Plz Fl Conc18 New York NY 10004-1950

CORTI, GIUSEPPE, soil scientist, researcher; b. Montespertoli, Tuscany, Italy, Feb. 24, 1961; s. Giovacchino Corti and Pierina Barnini. Diploma in accountancy, Enrico Fermi Sch., Empoli, Italy, 1980; degree in agr. and agronomy, U. Florence, Italy, 1989, PhD in Soil Sci., 1993. Grantee Nat. Rsch. Coun. Rome, Florence, 1989-90; grantee U. Florence, 1990, rschr. in soil sci., 1994—; cons. Emilia-Romagna Region, Bologna, Italy, 1990-91; cons. on guide Dolce Campagna, Antiche Mura. Author: The History of Karate, 1993. Fellow Internat. Soil Sci. Soc.; mem. Italian Soc. Agrarian Chemistry, Italian Soc. Pedology. Avocations: tai chi chuan (master), instructing karate. Home: Via Taddeini 54, 50025 Montespertoli Florence, Italy Office: U Florence Dept Soil Sci, Piazzale delle Cascine 28, 50144 Florence Italy

CORTRIGHT, BARBARA JEAN, writer; b. Oxford, Miss., Dec. 29, 1927; d. Lewis Stephen and Lucile (Chevalier) Grandy; m. Lem R. Cortright, Aug. 19, 1946; children: Lewis Stephen, Clyde Kenneth, Eric Allen, Barbara Edith. BFA with honors, Ariz. State U., 1949, MA in Humanities, 1977, MA in German Lang., 1979; PhD in Art History, U. N.Mex., Albuquerque, 1993. Instr. in art history Scottsdale (Ariz.) Coll., 1974-78; newsletter editor Heard Mus., Phoenix, 1978-79; lectr. in non-fiction Ariz. State U., Tempe, 1979-80; publicist O.K. Harris West Gallery, Scottsdale, 1981-84. Author: The Reach of Solitude, 1984; contbr. articles to profl. jours. NEA fellow, 1976. Mem. Phi Kappa Phi, Alpha Mu Gamma. Democrat. Episcopalian. Home: 516 E Erie Dr Tempe AZ 85282-3713

CORTS, KENNETH S., business educator; b. June 14, 1968; s. Paul R. and Diane S. Corts. BA, Furman U., 1990; PhD, Princeton U., 1994. Asst. prof. Harvard U., Cambridge, Mass., 1994—. Grad. rsch. fellow NSF, 1990-93, Dissertation fellow Sloan Found., 1993-94. Mem. Am. Econs. Assn. E-mail: kcorts@hbs.edu. Office: Harvard Bus Sch Soldiers Field Rd Boston MA 02136

CORUN, RONALD LEWIS, asphalt refining executive; b. Balt., Nov. 17, 1952; s. John Grebe and Cleo Hazel (Cornwell) C.; m. Mary Ann Hack, July 9, 1977; children: Mary Frances, Ronald Lewis. BSCE, U. Md., 1974. V.p., gen. mgr. Corun & Gatch, Inc., Fallston, Md., 1965-94; v.p. T.C. Simons, Inc., Fallston, Md., 1994-96; mgr. tech. support Citgo Asphalt Refining Co., Blue Bell, Pa., 1997—; pres. RLC Cons., Inc., Fallston, 1997—. Mem. Harford County Environ. Adv. Bd., Bel Air, Md., 1982-95. Recipient Sheldon G. Hayes award Nat. Asphalt Pavement Assn., 1994. Mem. Assn. Asphalt Paving Techs. Republican. Lutheran. Avocations: golf, skiing, fishing. Office: Citgo Asphalt 1900 Bel Air Rd Fallston MD 21047-2724

CORWIN, BERT CLARK, optometrist; b. Rapid City, S.D., Oct. 4, 1930; s. Meade and Adeline (Clark) C.; m. Lydia M. Forehand; children: B. Clark II, Kelley Linette Fromm. AS, S.D. State U., 1952; BS, Ill. Coll. Optometry, Chgo., 1956, OD, 1957. Pvt. practice Rapid City, 1957—; projects chmn. S.D. Lions Sight and Svc. Found., 1964; chmn. med. adv. com. to S.D. Dept. Pub. Welfare, 1968-76; mem. S.D. Adv. Coun. for Regional Med. and Health Planning, 1971; cons. S.D. Dept. Human Svcs., 1989—; adv. bd. S.D. Dept. of Svc. to Visual Impaired; bd. dirs. Super 8 Motel Developers, Rapid City Regional Airport, v.p., 1999-2000, pres., 2000—; chmn. bd. dirs. Transaction Network, Inc., 1997—; mng. ptnr. Right Line Lake, 1999—. Contbr. articles to profl. jours. Pres. Cleghorn PTA, Rapid City, 1968-70; bd. dirs. Am. Optometric Found., 1989-90, v.p., 1990-94, pres., 1994-96. Recipient Presdl. medal of honor Pres. of Ill. Coll. of Optometry, 1999, Spl. honor Am. Optometric Found. Fellow Am. Acad. Optometry (diplomate contact lens sect., sec.-treas. 1985-86, pres.-elect 1987-88, pres. 1988-90, chmn. 1st internat. meeting 1992); mem. Am. Optometric Assn. (exec. com. 1974-76, Am. Optometrist of the Yr. 1993), S.D. Optometric Soc. (pres. 1970-71), North Ctrl. State Optometric Conf. (bd. dirs. 1970-71), Black Hills Optometric Soc. (sec.-treas. 1958-69), S.D. State Bd. Examiners (pres. 1982-85), Nat. Acad. Practice Optometry (sec.-treas. 1990-94, Disting. Practi-

tioners award, co-chmn. 1994-96). Republican. Methodist. Club: Black Hills Water Ski (pres. 1963). Lodges: Masons, Elks, Lions (pres. Rushmore chpt. 1961-62, Robert Tyler award 1998). Avocations: skiing, water skiing, hunting, piloting, public speaking. Home: 5436 Timberline Trl Rapid City SD 57702-1806 Office: 810 Mountain View Rd Rapid City SD 57702-2520

CORWIN, JOYCE ELIZABETH STEDMAN, construction company executive; b. Chgo.; d. Cresswell Edward and Elizabeth Josephine (Kimbell) Stedman; m. William Corwin, May 1, 1965; children: Robert Edmund Newman, Jillanne Elizabeth McInnis. Pres. Am. Properties, Inc., Miami, Fla., 1966-72; v.p. Stedman Constrn. Co., Miami, 1971—; owner Joy-Win Horses, Gray lady ARC, 1969-70. Guidance worker Youth Hall, 1969-70; sponsor Para Med. Group of Coral Park H.S., 1969-70; hostess, Rep. presdl. campaign, 1968; aide Rep. Nat. Conv., 1972. Mem. Dade County Med. Aux. (chmn. directory com. 1970), Marion County Med. Aux., Fla. Psychiat. Soc. Aux., Fla. Morgan Horse Assn., Fla. Thoroughbred Breeders Assn. Clubs: Coral Gables Jr. Women's (chmn. casework com.), Golden Hills Golf and Turf, Heritage, Royal Dames of Ocala. Home: Windrift Farm 8500 NW 120th St Reddick FL 32686-4513

CORY, WALLACE NEWELL, retired civil engineer; b. Olympia, Wash., Mar. 10, 1937; s. Henry Newell and Gladys Evelyn (Nixon) C.; m. Roberta Ruth Matthews, July 4, 1959; children: Steven Newell, Susan Evelyn Cory Carbon. BS in Forestry, Oreg. State U., 1958, BSCE, 1964; MSCE, Stanford U., 1965. Registered profl. engr., Idaho, Oreg. Asst. projects mgr. CH2 M/Hill, Boise, Idaho, 1965-70; environ. mgr. Boise Cascade Corp., 1970-78, dir. state govt. affairs, 1978-82; dir. indsl. group JUB Engrs., Boise, 1982-84; chief engr. Anchorage Water & Wastewater, 1984-90; dir. pub. works City of Caldwell, Idaho, 1990-92; prin. engr. Montgomery Watson, Pasadena, Calif., 1992-95; adminstr. Idaho Divsn. Environ. Quality, Boise, 1995-98; planning and assessment leader Alexandria Wastewater Project Chemonics Interna., 1998-99. Precinct committeeman Idaho Rep. Com., Boise, 1968-72, region chmn., 1973-77. Capt. USAF, 1958-62. Fellow ASCE; mem. NSPE, Idaho Soc. Profl. Engrs. (pres. 1976-77, Young Engr. of Yr. award 1971), Air Pollution Control Assn. (chmn. Pacific N.W. sect. 1977-78), Idaho Assn. Commerce and Industry (chmn. environ. com. 1974-75). Avocations: hunting, fishing, shooting. Home: 7247 Cascade Dr Boise ID 83704-8635

CORYELL, GLYNN HEATH, financial service executive; b. Lexington, Ky., May 8, 1929; s. Glynn Lawrence and Allie May (Heath) C.; m. Diane Garnett Dobyns, Dec. 27, 1955 (div. Aug. 1981); children: Heather Diane, Holly. Grad., Culver (Ind.) Summer Cavalry Sch., 1947; AB, Harvard U., 1951; student, Harvard Law Sch., 1951-52, 54-55; MBA, Northwestern U., 1957. Supr. cost acctg. Procter & Gamble Co., Cin., 1957-60; sr. fin. analyst Socony Mobil Oil Corp., N.Y.C., 1961-62; dir. corp. profit planning, corp. economist Libby, McNeill & Libby, Chgo., 1962-67; treas. Lyntex Corp., N.Y.C., 1968-69; asst. treas. Std. Brands, Inc., N.Y.C., 1969-71; v.p. adminstr. and ops. Std. Brands Foods Co., N.Y.C., 1971-73; fin. v.p. Grand Union Co., Elmwood Park, N.J., 1973-76; exec. v.p., CFO, dir. Cramer Electronics, Inc., Newton, Mass., 1976-79; sr. v.p., CFO, dir. Kuhn's-Big K Stores Corp., Nashville, 1979-81; v.p. fin. and adminstrn., sec. Sunmark, Inc., St. Louis, 1981-83; corp. fin. cons. Lemoyne, Pa., 1984-88; pres. Glynn H. Coryell & Assocs. Inc. doing bus. as Travel Agts. Internat., Falls Church, Va., 1988-94; corp. fin. cons. Alexandria, Va., 1994—. Served with Intelligence U.S. Army, 1953-54. Mem. Alumnus Kellogg Grad. Sch. Mgmt. Northwestern U., Alexandria Consumers Affairs Commn. (vice chmn.), Korean War Vets. Assn. Republican. Baptist. Home and Office: 1105 Quaker Hill Ct Alexandria VA 22314-4742

COSANDEY, DAVID ANTOINE, financial risk specialist; b. Boston, Aug. 15, 1965; arrived in Switzerland, 1966; Diploma in physics, U. Lausanne, Switzerland, 1989; PhD in Physics, U. Berne, Switzerland, 1994. Sci. journalist Cedos, Geneva, 1989-91; rsch. asst. Lausanne Inst. Tech., 1991-95; bus. analyst Union Bank Switzerland, Geneva and Zurich, 1996-98; risk analyst Credit Suisse Group, Zurich, 1998—. Author: Le Secret de l'Occident, 1997, L'Europe et la Science, 1998. Co-founder Tibet Support Group Switzerland, Geneva, 1989.

COSANDEY, MAURICE ROGER, chemistry educator; b. Lausanne, Switzerland, Apr. 24, 1937; s. Henri and Marthe (Schertenleib) C.; m. Francine Tenthorey Apr. 4, 1964 (div. 1981); children: David, Denis; m. Francine Muller, Jan. 6, 1982. Degree in chem. engring., U. Lausanne, 1959, PhD, 1964. Postdoctoral fellow Harvard U., 1965-66; lectr. in phys. chemistry U. Lausanne, 1966-76; h.s. tchr. Gymnase de Chamblandes, 1976—; nat. del. Internat. Union Pure and Applied Chemistry-Com. on Tchg. of Chemistry, London, 1985-2000; head nat. team Internat. Chemistry Olympiad, 1986—. Editor Swiss rev. Chemistry and Biology, 1985—; contbr. articles to newspapers. Organizer recycling courses for Swiss chemistry tchrs., 1985—. Mem. Swiss Chemistry Olympic Com. (pres. 1996—), Swiss Assn. of French Spkg. Chemistry Tchrs. (sec. 1982—). E-mail: mcosandey@caramail.com. Home: Etourneaux 1, 1162 St-Prex Switzerland Office: Gymnase de Chamblandes, Desertes 29, 1009 Pully Switzerland

COSBY, RITA KAREN, newscaster; b. Bklyn., Nov. 18, 1964; d. Richard Roger and Adda Otilia (Arenfeldt) C. Honors degree, Conn. Sch. Broadcasting, 1983; BA in Broadcast Journalism, Spanish, U. S.C., 1989. Nat. sales mgr. Basic Wallpaper, Inc., Stamford, Conn., 1983-86; bus. cons. Lin-Gor, Inc., Clifton, N.J., 1986-89; announcer, control operator Sta. WACH-TV, Columbia, S.C., 1989; intern, asst. CBS Evening News, N.Y.C., 1989; anchor, reporter Sta. KERO-TV, Bakersfield, Calif., 1989-92, Sta. WBTV-CBS, Charlotte, N.C., 1992-95; sr. corr. FOX News, Washington, 1995—; news anchor S.C. Pub. Radio, Columbia, 1988-89; host, interviewer, prodr. Bus. and Fin. Shows, Bakersfield, 1989-92; host, interviewer Community Affairs Show, Bakersfield, 1989-92, Take One Prodns., N.Y.C., 1989—, Spanish Cable TV Show, Charlotte, 1993-95. News editor (newspaper) The Gamecock, 1987-89; writer (newspaper) The State, 1988-89; columnist (Hispanic newspaper) El Progreso Hispano, 1993—. Mem. adv. bd. Youth Involvement Coun., Charlotte, 1992-95; host, fundraiser United Negro Coll. Fund, Charlotte, 1993-95, Children's Miracle Network Telethon, Charlotte, 1993-95, Muscular Dystrophy Assn., Bakersfield, 1990-92; spkr., reader Charlotte-Mecklenburg Schs., Charlotte, 1992-95; vol., spkr. Girl Scouts U.S., 1989—; motivational spkr. anti-drug program DARE. Recipient Outstanding Sr. award U. S.C., 1989, Best Reporting award Kern County Press Club, 1991. Mem. NATAS (Emmy 1992, 95, listed as Outstanding Young Am. 1989, mem. nominating bd. 1997—), L.Am. Coalition (spkr. 1993—), L.Am. Women's Assn. (spkr. 1994—), Soc. Profl. Journalists (student pres. 1987—), Alpha Epsilon Rho (pub. info. officer 1987-89), Omicron Delta Kappa. Avocation: foreign languages. Office: Fox Network News 400 N Capitol St NW Ste 550 Washington DC 20001-1502

COSCARELLI, PEDRO GUIMARCES, physician; b. Rio de Janeiro, Aug. 3, 1971; s. Antonio Braga Coscarelli and Gilcina Guimarces E Silva. MD, Fed. U. Rio de Janeiro, 1995; MS/SUS, Hosp. de Ipanema, Rio de Janeiro, 1998. Physician IPPMG/Fed. U. Rio de Janeiro, 1996—, Hosp. Estadual Anchieta/SES/SUS, Rio de Janeiro, 1999—; rschr. med. biochemistry HU/Fed. U. Rio de Janeiro, 1996—; rschr. IPUB/Fed. U. Rio de Janeiro, 1998—. Contbr. articles to sci. jours. Mem. N.Y. Acad. Scis.

COSCAS, GABRIEL JOSUE, ophthalmologist, educator; b. Tunis, Mar. 1, 1931; s. Jules Joseph and Gilda (Guez) C.; m. Gisele Nataf, Mar. 23, 1957; children: Florence, Brigitte. MD, U. Paris, 1963. Chief ophthalmology clinic Hotel Dieu, Paris, 1963-70; maitre conf. agrege Univ. Paris-Val de Marne, 1970-79; prof. ophthalmology, chmn. dept. Univ. Eye Clinic de Creteil, 1979—; founder Conf. Angiographic de Creteil, 1972—; ophthalmologist, educator; b. Tunis, Mar. 1, 1931; s. Jules Joseph and Gilda (Guez) C.; M.D., U. Paris, 1963; m. Gisele Nataf, Mar. 23, 1957; children—Florence, Brigitte. Chief ophthalmology clinic Hotel Dieu, Paris, 1963-70; maitre conf. agrege Univ. Paris-Val de Marne, 1970-79, prof. ophthalmology, chmn. dept. Univ. Eye Clinic de Creteil, 1979-99 ; founder Conf. Angiographic de Creteil, 1972—. Served as med. lt. French Army, 1958-60. Author books, articles in field. Served as med. lt. French Army, 1958-60. Decorated Ofcl. de l'Ordre de Palmes Academiques, 1996, Ofcl. de l'Ordre Nat. de la Legion d'Honneur, 1999. Mem. Internat. Orgn. Against Trachoma (pres. 1977—), French Soc. Photocoagulation (pres. 1988), Acad. Internat. Ophthalmology (gen. sec. 1996—), Coll. Prof. Ophthalmology of France (pres. 1994-97), Joint European Soc. Rsch. Ophthalmology and Vision (pres. 1993-96). Home: 203 Vaugirard, 75015 Paris France Office: 40 Ave Verdun, 113 Blvd Saint-Jamaica, 75006 Paris France

COSENTINO, MICHELE, navy officer, researcher; b. Catania, Sicily, Italy, July 18, 1954; s. Orazio and Agatina (Catasta) C.; m. Maria Elena Vitiello, July 13, 1980; children: Marco, Claudia, Adriana. Grad. marine engring., State U., Naples, Italy, 1981. Commd. Italian Navy, 1974, advanced through grades to comdr., 1993; chief engring. officer Naval Ships and Submarines, Taranto, Italy, 1989-91; chief sect. submarine procurement MOD/Navy, Rome, 1991-93; chief sect. plans and policy Joint Staff/NATO, Brussels, 1993-96; chief sect. internat. programs MOD, Rome, 1997-99; chief sect. fin. programming MOD/Navy, Rome, 1999—. Co-author: The Soviet Navy (in Italian), 1990, The Italian Navy (in Italian and English); contbr. articles to profl. publs. Roman Catholic. Home: Via E Fieramosca 17A, 00012 Guidonia Italy Office: Navarm 3 Divisione, Piazzale D Marina 1, 00196 Rome Italy

COSENZA, GUSTAVO ENRIQUE, neurologist, neurophysiologist; b. Guatemala, Guatemala, June 24, 1948; s. Francisco Cosenza and Emma Concepcion (Chacon) De Cosenza; Socorro Mora, Oct. 15, 1983; children: Ellen, Thomas, Ana Lucia, Gustavo. MD, San Carlos U., Guatemala, 1973; degree in Neurology, U. Minn., 1978. Diplomate Am. Bd. Psychiatry and Neurology. Med. dir. Centro Neurologico, Guatemala, 1978—; pres., founder Asociacion Guatemalteca Neurologia, Guatemala, 1987-88; pres. Fedn. Centro Americana Ciencias Neurologicas, Guatemala, 1989-90. Dir. Aeroclub Guatemala, 1992-94; pres. Fundacion Preventiva Drogadiccion, 1986-92; v.p. IX Panam. Congress Neurology, Guatemala, 1995; del. World Fedn. Neurology, 1990. Fellow Am. Acad. Neurology; mem. Rotary (dir. 1990-91, Rotarian of Yr. 1982). Roman Catholic. Avocations: flight instruction, aircraft mechanics, guitar. Office: Centro Neurologico Cosenza, 3 Calle A 8-51 Zona 10, Guatemala 01010, Guatemala

COSGRIFF, PETER FRANCIS, retired physician; b. Melbourne, Australia, Feb. 28, 1928; s. Victor Francis and Mary Evelyne (White) C.; m. Patricia Bernadette Cooney; children: Michael, David, Brian, Peter, Anne, Jane, Paula. MBBS, U. Melbourne, 1952. Registered med. practitioner. Resident med. officer St. Vincent's Hosp., Melbourne, 1953, pathology registrar, 1955-56; resident med. officer Royal Children's Hosp., Melbourne, 1954; gen. practice physician Brighton, Victoria, Australia, 1957-97. Commodore Blairgowrie Yacht Squadron, Victoria, 1985-86. Avocations: music, theatre, literature, yachting. Home: 2/41 Linacre Rd, Hampton Victoria 3188, Australia

COSKUN, TAMER, engineering educator, researcher; b. Beysehir, Turkey, Oct. 27, 1967; s. Hasan and Mumine C.; m. Hacer Ozbek Coskun, June 15, 1995; children: Bukre Cenan, Hasan Bera. BS, Dokuz Eylul U., Izmir, Turkey, 1989, MS, 1993; PhD, Lehigh U., Bethlehem, Pa., 2000. Tech. staff Baris Electronics, Izmir, Turkey, 1988-89; rsch. and teaching asst. Pamukkale U., Denizli, Turkey, 1989-94; rsch. and teaching asst. dept. elec. engring. & comp. sci. Lehigh U., Bethlehem, Pa., 1994-99, vis. rsch. scientist dept. elec. engring. & comp. sci., 1999—. Contbr. papers in field. Recipient Scholarship for grad. edn. in U.S., Pamukkale U., Denizli, Turkey, 1994, Rsch. Assistantship, NSF, 1998, Vis. Scientist award P.C. Rossin Coll. of Engring. and Applied Sci., Bethlehem, Pa., 1999. Mem. Optical Soc. Am. Avocations: poetry, painting, swimming. E-mail address: tac6@lehigh.edu. Fax: 610-758-6279. Office: Dept Elec Engring and Computer Sci 19 Memorial Dr W Bethlehem PA 18015-3006

COSKUNER, SIBEL, bank executive; b. Ankara, Turkey, Feb. 23, 1962; d. Akif and Azize (Aykut) C. BS in Indsl. Engring., Mid. East Tech. U., Ankara, 1984; MS in Indsl. Engring., Bosphurs U., Istanbul, Turkey, 1986. Cert. prof. engr. Exec. trainee credit and mktg. Citibank N.A., Istanbul, 1986-87, asst. mgr. corp. fin., 1987-88, relationship mgr. credit and mktg., 1988-89; local corp. group head (asst. v.p.) credit and mktg. Citibank N.A., 1989-92, br. mgr. (v.p.) Izmir (Turkey) br., 1992-95; v.p. pvt. banking Turkey (v.p.) Citibank N.A., Istanbul, 1995-99; v.p., country head Turkey Deutsche Bank Pvt. Bank, 1999—; mem. various mgmt. coms. Mem. Young Businessmen and Profls. Assn., Propeller Club, Rotary. Avocations: painting, reading, swimming, snow skiing, tennis. Home: Hakki Sehit Han Sok, No 8/6 2 Ulus, 80600 Istanbul Turkey Office: Deutsche Bank Ceudet Pasa, Cad No 288 Bebek, 80810 Istanbul Turkey

COSMAS, GEORGES, legal administrator; b. 1932. Bar: Athens. Jr. mem. Greek State Coun., 1963, mem., 1973, state counsellor, 1982-94; mem. Spl. Supreme Ct., High Coun. of Judiciary, High Coun. of Min. Fgn. Affairs; pres. Trademark Ct. of Second Instance; chmn. spl. legis. drafting com. Min. of Justice; advocate gen. European Ct. of Justice, Luxembourg, 1994—. Office: European Ct of Justice, Blvd Konrad Adenauer Kirchberg, L-2925 Luxembourg Luxembourg*

COSOVLIU, OCTAVIAN IOAN, civil and structural engineer; b. Braila, Muntenia, Romania, Sept. 18, 1927; s. Ioan-Iordan Florea and Aurora Apostol (Dancovici) C.; m. Magdalena-Minerva Anastase Hâciu, Sept. 22, 1957; 1 child, Lavinia-Antonia. Degree in Civil & Structure Engr., Poly. Inst., Iassy, Romania, 1950; D in Tech. Scis., Constrns. Inst., Bucharest, Romania, 1986; diploma in concrete, steel & timber, 1992. Chief bldg. site Braila Constrns. Enterprises, 1950-55, dir., 1955-58; chief engr. Galatz (Romania) Constrns. Trust, 1958-60; chief engr. Project Galatz Inst., 1960-70, tech. dir., 1970-90, tech. councilor, 1990—; assoc. lectr. Poly. Inst., Galatz, 1960-65, Low-Danube U., Galatz, 1975-80, 98—. Author: Constructions Basement on Loess Soils, 1984; contbr. articles to profl. jours. Hon. chmn. Assn. for Sci., Culture and Def. of the Human Rights, Galatz, 1997. Mem. Internat. Soc. Soil Mechanics and Founds. Engring., Gen. Assn. Romanian Engrs. (gen. coun. 1990), Assn. of the Structure Bucarest Project Engrs., Nat. Commn. Insitu Behaviour Constrns., N.Y. Acad. Scis. Avocations: classic jazz, lawn tennis, mountains excursions. Home: Albatros Nr 1 Bloc M ap 24, 6200 Galatz Moldova, Romania Office: Project Galatz Inst, Str Navelor Nr 3, 6200 Galatz Moldova, Romania

COSPER, SAMMIE WAYNE, educational consultant; b. Greggton, Tex., Oct. 8, 1933; s. Sammie Hampton and Mabel Viola (Byrd) C.; m. Shirley Ann Aguillard, May 13, 1954; children: Ann Caprice, Michelle Marie, Renée Elizabeth. BS in Physics, U. La. at Lafayette, 1960, DSc (hon.), 1991; PhD in Nuclear Physics, Purdue U., 1965. Postdoctoral appointee Lawrence Radiation Lab. U. Calif. Berkeley, 1965-67; head Dept. Physics, dean Coll. Liberal Arts, Acad. v.p. U. La. at Lafayette, 1967-89; commr. higher edn. La. Bd. Regents, Baton Rouge, 1990-94; cons. higher edn. Lafayette, 1994—; com. mem. State Hi-Ed Exec. Officers, Denver, 1990—; com. mem. La. Assn. Bus., Industry Edn. Coun., Baton Rouge, 1986—; bd. dirs. La. Coun. Econ. Edn., Baton Rouge. Contbr. articles to profl. jours. Named Communicator of Yr. La. Pub. Rels. Assn., 1993; fellow Woodrow Wilson Found., 1960. Mem. Coun. for Better La. (bd. dirs.), Krewe Gabriel Mardi Gras Assn., Krewe Triton Mardi Gras Assn. (bd. dirs.), Krewe Zeus Mardi Gras Assn. (bd. dirs.). Republican. Roman Catholic. Avocations: hunting, fishing, reading. Home: 240 Thibodeaux Dr Lafayette LA 70503-4442

COSSA, DANIEL JACQUES, research oceanographer, educator; b. Aubenas, Ardèche, France, Dec. 24, 1947; arrived in Can., 1973 (French and Can. citizen); s. Noel Cossa and Henriette Girard; m. Anne-Marie Martine Tabard, Nov. 1, 1972; 1 child, Vincent. Grad. in pharmacy, U. Paris, 1970, DSc in Marine Biogeochemistry, 1987; D Natural Sci., U. Nantes, France, 1973. Prof. U. Que., Rimouski, Can., 1977-80; head chem. oceanography Fishers and Oceans Can., Quebec City, 1980-85; dir. dept. chem. pollutants French Inst. for Exploitation of the Sea/Ifremer, Nantes, 1985—; project coord. Dept. Environ., Montreal, Que., 1994-96; symposia organizer, including Symposium on Model Estuaries. Contbr. over 100 articles to profl. jours. including Can. Jour. Fisheries and Aquatic Scis., Marine Chemistry, chpts. to books; patentee sea water sampler. French-Can. exch. postdoctoral grant, Victoria, B.C., Can., 1977, NATO grant U. Conn., 1989. Office: IFREMER, BP 21105, F-44311 Nantes Cedex 3, France

COSSACK, ROGER, newscaster. Bar: Calif. U.S. Dist. Ct. (ctrl. dist.) Calif., U.S. Supreme Ct., U.S. Ct. Appeals (2d, 9th and 10th cirs.). Anchor CNN, Atlanta; corr. Burden of Proof (CNN), Atlanta.

COSSÉ, R. PAUL, realty company executive; b. Nashville, July 11, 1956; s. Xavier B. and Irene E. (Amburgey) C.; 1 child, Michelle Reneé. Student, Belmont Coll., 1974-75, Aquinas Jr. Coll., 1975-76, U. Tenn., Knoxville, 1976—, Middle Tenn. State U., 1980-81. Mktg. dir. First Tenn. Bank, Murfreesboro, Tenn., 1980-83; exec. v.p. First Federal, Columbia, Tenn., 1983-88; exec. v.p., mng. officer Security Trust Fed., Knoxville, 1988-89; pres., CEO Prudential Vol. Realty, 1989-98; pres. Home Mortgage Brokers, Inc., Knoxville, 1990-98; pres., CEO Fin. Investor Svcs. of Tenn., Inc., Knoxville, 1992-98, Ins. and Fin. Svcs. Group, Inc., Knoxville, 1992-98; realtor Realty Execs., 2000—; pres./CEO Southeastern Holdings of Tenn., Inc., 1995-98; bd. dirs. YMCA, Knoxville; realtor, Prudential Vol. Realty, 1998-2000, Realty Execs., 2000—; cons. in field. Pres. Big. Bros. and Big Sisters Maury County, Columbia, Tenn., 1987-88; bd. dirs. YMCA, Columbia, 1988; chmn. Saturn Run, Columbia, 1987-88; chmn. realtor divsn. Am. Heart Assn. and United Way, Knoxville. Mem. Tenn. League Savs. (leadership bd., publicity com.), Exch. Club. Republican. Avocations: golf, tennis. Office: Realty Execs PO Box 647 Powell TN 37849-0647

COSSÉE DE MAULDE, GUY JEAN, education educator, consultant; b. Maulde, Hainaut, Belgium, Apr. 19, 1935; s. Edouard and Emilie (van Zeebroeck) Cossée de M. BA in Philosophy, Jesuit Faculties, Louvain, Belgium, 1960; BA in Theology, Jesuit Faculties, Louvain, 1968; BA in Econs., Cath. U., Louvain, 1966. Cert. Jesuit Priest, 1967. Econs. researcher U. Catholique, Mons, Belgium, 1968-72; adviser Association Chrétienne des Dirigeants et Cadres, Brussels, 1968—; prof. Inst. d'Edn. Physique, Brussels, 1969-2000, Ecole Pratique des Hautes Etudes Commerciales, Brussels, 1974-2000; fellow Centre Avec., Brussels, 1985—. Mem. Pax Christi, Brussels; founding mem. Convergence Libertés Démocratiques, Brussels, Vivre Ensemble, Brussels, Commn. Justice et Paix, Brussels. Roman Catholic. Home: Rue de la Poste 130, 1030 Brussels Belgium

COSSI, PAULIN LAURENT, bank executive, economics educator; b. Porto-Novo, Benin, June 22, 1942; m. Andrée Chung, Apr. 8, 1972; children: Mèdegnissè, Dèlomè, Angelo. DSc in Econs., U. Grenoble, France, 1973. Diploma du Centre Technique et de Perfectionnement de la BCEAO, 1975; diploma Inst. FMI/Cours d'analyse et politique financière, 1980. Head rsch. dept. West African Ctrl. Bank, Cotonou, Benin, 1976-81; head internal audit West African Ctrl. Bank, Cotonou, 1981-86, dep. nat. dir., 1986-91, nat. dir., 1991—; alt. gov. IMF. Mem. Bénin Nat. Assn. Economists (pub. rels. officer Assn. Grad. Students of Grenoble), Lions (past sec.). Roman Catholic. Avocation; music. Office: BCEAO, CU BP 1111, Cotonou BP325, Benin*

COSSON, LOUIS, retired botany educator; b. Saint-Fargeau, France, July 16, 1937; s. Emile and Jeanne (Juery) C.; m. Françoise Thieulin; 3 children. Pharmacist, Pharm. Faculty, Paris, 1960; grad. in biol. scis., Paris, 1961, PhD in Biol. Scis., 1972. Asst., faculty of scis. Paris, 1962-69; maitre-asst., 1969-81; prof. botany, pharm. faculty U. Paris XI, Châtenay-Malabry, France, 1981-98; ret., 1998. Co-author book. Avocation: gardening. Home: Gobertier, F-07790 Saint Alban France

COSSONS, SIR NEIL, museum director; b. Nottingham, Eng., Jan. 15, 1939; s. Arthur and Evelyn Edith (Bettle) C.; m. Veronica Edwards; children: Nigel, Elisabeth, Malcolm. BA, U. Liverpool, Eng., 1961; MA, U. Liverpool, 1968, DLitt (hon.), 1989; Doctorates (hon.), U. Birmingham, Eng., 1979, Open U., 1984, U. Bradford, Eng., 1991, Nottingham Trent, 1994, Leicester, 1995, Sheffield Hallam, 1995, U. West of Eng., 1995, Bath, 1997, De Montfort, 1997, U. York, 1998. Curator of technology Bristol (Eng.) City Mus., 1964-69; dep. dir. City of Liverpool Museums, 1969-71; dir. Ironbridge Gorge Mus. Trust, Shropshire, Eng., 1971-83, Nat. Maritime Mus., London, 1983-86, Nat. Mus. Sci. and Industry, London, 1986—. Author: Industrial Archaeology, 1975, Ironbridge-Landscape of Industry, 1977; editor: (5 vols.) Rees's Manufacturing Industry, 1975, Making of the Modern World, 1992. Commr. English Heritage, 1989-95; mem. Design Coun., 1990-94; mem. comité scientifique Conservatoire Nat. des Arts et Mètiers, France, 1991—; mem. coun. Found. for Mfg. and Industry, 1993-98; mem. Brit. Waterways Bd., 1995—. Decorated Order Brit. Empire, companion Instn. Elec. Engrs., companion Inst. of Mgmt., hon. companion Royal Aero. Soc.; recipient Norton Medlicott medal Hist. Assn., 1991, Pres.'s medal Royal Acad. Engring, 1993. Fellow Soc. Antiquaries, Museums Assn. (pres. 1981-82), Tourism Soc.; mem. Assn. Ind. Museums (chmn. bd. dirs. 1978-83, pres. 1983—), Athenaeum Club (London). Avocations: traveling, industrial archaeology. Office: Sci Mus, Exhibition Rd, London SW7 2DD, England*

COSSUTTA, ARMANDO, member European Parliament; b. Milan, Sept. 2, 1926. Mem. European Parliament, Brussels, 1999—; mem. com. on constl. affairs, substitute mem. com. on fgn. affairs, human rights, common security and def. policy, mem. del. to European Union-Russia parliamentary cooperation com. Mem. Confed. Group of European United Left/Nordic Green Left. *

COSTA, ANDREW MICHELE, geotechnics technologist, consultant; b. Hackensack, N.J., Jan. 11, 1965; s. Andrew Louis and Joan Deloris (Del Masteo) C. Lab. technician Mt. Hope (N.J.) Rock Products, 1987-91; quality control and lab. mgr. Hamilton, Hinkle, & Ruth, Georgetown, Ky., 1991-94; lab. technician Asphalt Inst., Lexington, Ky., 1994; quality control and lab. mgr. Nally & Haydon Surfacing, Lebanon, Ky., 1994-96; field rep. L.E. Gregg & Assocs., Lexington, 1996; owner DBC Testing Labs., Lebanon, 1996—; mem. PAJKY Tech. Com., 1993-96, KCSA Tech. Com., 1994-96, N.J. SAT, 1987-96. Mem. ASTM, Pavement Industry Assn. Ky., Ky. Crushed Stone Assn., Soc. Asphalt Technologists. Republican. Roman Catholic. Home and Office: 745 Helm School House Rd Lebanon KY 40033-9741

COSTA, CLEIDE, biologist, researcher; b. São José do Rio Preto, Brazil, Oct. 22, 1940; d. José Joaquim and Vincentina De Faria C. Bachelor, Inst. Biociências UNESP, Brazil, 1963; PhD, Inst. Biociências USP, Brazil, 1972. Biologist Museu Zoologia/USP, S. Paulo, Brazil, 1966-98; head of entomology Museu Zoologia/USP, S. Paulo, 1974-98; prof. dept. zoology, USP, S. Paulo, Brazil, 1973—, Depto. Entomol. Univ. Fed. Paraná, Curitiba, Brazil, 1980—, dept. zoology, UNESP Botucatu, Sao Paulo, Brazil, 1979-99; reviewer CNPq, Brazil, 1987—, FAPESP, Brazil, 1988—; editl. bd., Revista Bras. Entomol., Brazil, 1995-96. Author (with others) Larvas de Coleoptera do Brasil, 1988 (Alexandre Rodrigues Ferreira award 1989); contbr. articles to profl. jours. Recipient Bunka award of rsch., Sumitomo Bank, Soc. Brasil de Cultura Japonesa, 1994. Mem. Sociedade Brasil Ent., Coleopterists Soc., Sociedade Brasil Zoologia Curitiba. Roman Catholic. Achievements include building a Neotropical collection of over 15,000 immatures stages of Coleoptera collected and reared in Laboratory, studying systematics, phylogeny and biodiversity of Coleoptera in general (immatures and adults) and Elateridae in particular. Office: Museu de Zoologia USP, Av Nazaré 481, 04263000 São Paulo Brazil

COSTA, GEORGE GEORGE (ADEL GEORGE COSTANDY), physician; b. Cairo, Jan. 27, 1951; came to U.S., 1981; s. George Toma Costandy and Elain R. Mosa. MD with honors, Cairo U., 1975. Cert. Ednl. Commn. for Fgn. Med. Grads. Rotating intern Cairo U. Hosp., 1975-76, Army Hosp., 1976-77; lab. technician, phlebotomist N.Y. labs., 1977-79; ear, nose and throat resident Cairo, 1978-79, 82-83, 1984-86; respiratory therapist trainee Mt. Vernon (N.Y.) Hosp., 1989; pediatric clk. Interfaith Med. Ctr., Bklyn., 1990; resident in internal medicine Woodhull Hosp., Bklyn., 1991. Mem. N.Y. Acad. Sci. Address: 23099 Barton Rd Grand Terrace CA 92313-4949

COSTA, JEFFERSON LUIS DA SILVA, agronomer; b. Teresina, Piauí, Brazil, May 16, 1960; s. Walter Vitório and Aury (Silva) C. BS, U. Brasilia (Brazil), 1981; MS, U. Viçosa (Brazil), 1984; PhD, U. Calif., Riverside, 1995. Researcher Embrapa, Goiânia, Brazil, 1984—; prof. Fed. U. Goiás, Goiânia, 1997—. Author: Soilborne Fungal Diseases on Dry Beans, 1999; contbr. over 140 articles to profl. jours., 13 chpts. to books. Recipient award Klotz Found., 1993, Storkan Hannes Found., 1994. Mem. Brazilian Plant Pathology Soc. (pres. 1989-90, pres. consultive coun. 1990-91), Brazilian Researchers Labour Union (pres. Goiânia 1988-90), Am. Plant Pathology Soc., Phi Beta Kappa. Avocations: aerobics, volleyball, speedboating, jet skiing. Office: Embrapa, Rice and Beans Rsch Inst, 75375000 Goiânia Goiás, Brazil

COSTA, PAOLO, rector, educator; b. Venice, Italy, July 23, 1943; s. Marion and Giuseppina (Baruffaldi) C.; widowed; children: Alessandro, Elena. Degree in econs., Ca' Foscari U., Venice, 1968. Vice rector Ca' Foscari U., Venice, 1989-92, rector, 1992—, prof. regional econs., 1980—; mem. European Parliament, Brussels, Belgium. Editor: Il trasporto merci e l'economia italiana Modelli di interazione e scenari oltre il 2000; co-author: Economia delle interdipendenze produttive Una introduzione all'analisi input-output; contbr. articles to profl. jours. Mem. European Sci. and Tech. Assembly of European Union, Coun. UN U. (Tokyo), Venice Sci. and Tech. Gateway. Office: Ca' Foscari U, Dorsoduro 3246, 30123 Venice Italy

COSTA, PAULO ROBERTO, military officer, engineer, educator; b. São Paulo, Brazil, Jan. 25, 1961; s. Agenor Silva and Luiza (Bartolo) C.; m. Maria Cristina Cardozo, July 19, 1986; children: Felipe, Bruno, Paulo Victor. Grad., Indsl. Engring. Coll., Sao Bernardo, Brazil, 1986; MS, Mil. Engring. Inst., Rio de Janeiro, 1992. Cert. automotive mech. engr. Head quality engring. divsn. Wapsa-Robert Bosch do Brasil, São Paulo, 1984-87; commd. lt. Brazilian Army, Rio de Janeiro, 1988, advanced to maj., 2000, head product engring. divsn., 1988-91, project mgr. R&D Inst., 1993—; prof. Severino Sombra U., Vassouras, Brazil. E-mail: procosta@ig.com.br. and cpaulo@ipd.eb.mi.br. Fax: 055-21-410-1421. Office: R&D Inst Brazilian Army, Av das Americas 28705, 23020470 Rio de Janeiro Brazil

COSTA, RAFFAELE, Italian government official; b. Mondovì, Cuneo, Italy, Sept. 8, 1936; 2 children. D in Polit. Sci. Councillor Mondovì, 1960—; provincial councillor Cuneo, 1975—; dep. Parliament, Cuneo-Alessandria-Asti, 1976, re-elected dep., 1979, 83, 87; v.p. Com. Agriculture and Forrests; under sec. of state, min. of justice Cossiga Govt.; under sec. of labour and social security Spadolini Govt.; under sec. of interior 1st and 2d Craxi Govt.; senator Mondovì Constituency; under sec. of pub. works Goria Govt.; min. without portfolio of community affairs and regions; min. of health Rome, 1994—; mem. European Parliament, Brussels, Belgium; dir. Provincia 2000. Mem. PLI Party. Office: Camera dei Deputati, Palazzo Marini via del Tritone 17, I-00100 Rome Italy*

COSTA, SILVANO, physician, consultant, researcher; b. Imola, Bologna, Italy, May 26, 1949; s. Ugo Costa and Francesca Martelli; m. Francesca Giuliani (div. 1998); 1 child, Francesco. B in Humanities, Liceo Rambaldi, Imola, Italy, 1968; MD, U. Bologna, 1974, grad. in Ob/Gyn, 1978. Diplomate Ob/Gyn. Med. officer Family Planning Clinic, Bologna, 1978-80; asst. prof. ob/gyn U. Bologna, 1980-89, assoc. prof. ob/gyn, 1989-99, prof. gynecology, oncology, 1996-99; cons. Cervical Cancer Screening Program, Emilia Region, 1997-99. Author: Chlamydia Trachomatis and Other STD's, 1983, Pelvic Inflammatory Disease, 1988, Laser Surgery in Gynecology, 1990; author, editor: Sexually Transmitted Disease, 1988. Rep. Med. Union, 1996-99. Mem. Italian Soc. Ob/Gyn, Internat. Soc. Vulvar Disease, Internat. Gynecology Soc. Avocation: fishing. Office: Dept Ob/Gyn, Via Massarenti 13, 40138 Bologna Italy

COSTA, XAVIER, architect, curator; b. Barcelona, Spain, Sept. 7, 1959. BA, U. Barcelona, 1984; Degree in Arch., Barcelona Sch. Arch., 1984; MS, U. Pa., 1988, PhD, 1990. Guest prof. Columbia U., N.Y.C., 1993-94; chief curator arch. Mus. Contemporary Art, Barcelona, 1995-98; chief curator Mies van der Rohe Found., Barcelona, 1998—; guest prof. Archtl. Assn., London, 1999-2000. Author: Situationists, 1996, Fabrications, 1998. Fulbright scholar Inst. Internat. Edn., N.Y., 1985, Gilbert Chinard scholar Inst. Français, Washington, 1989. E-mail: costa@coac.es. Fax: 34 93 410 2459. Home and Office: Xavier Costa Arch, Muntaner 155, 08036 Barcelona Spain

COSTACURTA, ALESSANDRO, professional soccer player; b. Oragolvaj, Italy, Apr. 24, 1966. Defender AC Milan, Italy, 1986—; soccer player Team Italy. Office: AC Milan Giuseppi Meazza San Siro, Via Piccolomini 5, 20151 Milan Italy*

COSTA-GAVRAS (KONSTANINOS GAVRAS), director, writer; b. Athens, Greece, Feb. 13, 1933; naturalized French citizen; m. Michele Ray, Sept. 12, 1968; children: Alexandre, Helene, Romain. Student, U. Sorbonne, Paris. Diplomate Inst. Higher Cinematic Studies. Ballet dancer Greece; asst. to film dirs. Yves Allegret, Jacques Demy, Rene Clair, Rene Clement, Jean Giorno; pres. Cinematheque francaise, 1982—. Dir., screenwriter films The Sleeping Car Murders, 1964, Z, 1969 (Acad. award for best fgn. lang. film, 1970, Jury Prize, Cannes Film Festival 1969, Raoul-Levy prize 1969, Golden Globe award 1970), Missing, 1982 (Golden Palm award Cannes 1982, Acad. Award for best screenplay 1982); dir. films Un Homme de Trop, 1966 (Moscow Film Festival prize), L'Aveu (The Confession), 1970, State of Siege, 1973 (Louis Delluc prize 1973), Special Section, 1975 (Cannes Film Festival award 1975), Madame Rosa (also actor), 1978, Clair de Femme, 1979, Hanna K, 1983, Conseil de Femme, 1986, Family Business, 1986, Betrayed, 1988, Music Box, 1990 (Golden Bear award Berlin film festival 1990), Little Apocalypse, 1992, Mad City, 1996; dir. opera Il Mondo Dela Luna (Joseph Haydn), 1994, Mad City, 1997; co-dir. A Propos de Nice, 1995, Lumiere and Compagnie, 1995. Named Best Dir., Cannes Film Festival 1975, Officier Ordre National du Merite; decorated Comdr. Arts and Letters, France, Chevalier Legion d'Honneur; recipient Life Achievement award De l'Academie Francaise, 1998, Gold medal of Bellas Artes King of Spain.

COSTAGLIOLA, FRANCESCO, former government official, macro operations analyst; b. Cranston, R.I., Aug. 24, 1917; s. Luigi and Rose (Lubrano) C.; m. Agnes Mary Ross, June 14, 1952 (dec.); children: Francesca Gensler, Marisa Costagliola, Antonia Burns, Roseanne Rubin. Student U. R.I., 1935-37; BSEE, U.S. Naval Acad., 1941; postgrad. Naval Postgrad. Sch., 1946-47, MIT, 1947-49, Cath. U. Am., 1967-71; MBA, Am. U., Washington, 1974. Commd. ensign U.S. Navy, 1941, advanced through grades to capt., 1960; served in U.S.S. Phoenix in 24 ops. PTO, 1941-46; comdg. officer U.S.S. Halsey Powell, Korea, 1951-52; various positions naval sea and shore assignments involving atomic energy, 1952-64; mil. asst. to asst. to Sec. Def., 1964-67; ret., 1968; commr. AEC, 1968-69; engr. RCA, 1974-76; staff mem. Joint Congressional Com. on Atomic Energy, Washington, 1967-68, 69-71, 76-77; staff mem. Office of Sec. of Senate, Washington, 1977-86; mem. Md. Radiation Control Adv. Bd., 1973-81. Contbr. articles to profl. jours. Decorated Legion of Merit, Bronze Star with Combat V (2). Mem. AAAS, Inst. Ops. Rsch. & Mgmt. Scis., Am. Nuc. Soc., U.S. Naval Inst., Pearl Harbor Survivors Assn., Naval Acad. Alumni Assn., Mil. Order World Wars, Mil. Order Carabao, Army and Navy Club (Washington). Roman Catholic. Home: 307 Gibbon St Alexandria VA 22314-4129

COSTANDY, ADEL GEORGE See COSTA, GEORGE GEORGE

COSTANETO, ERALDO MEDEIROS, biologist, educator; b. Maceio, Alagoas, Brazil, May 19, 1972; s. Rui Rodrigues Câmara Filho and Laura Nice Leite (Medeiros) Câmara. MS, UFAL, Maceio, 1998. Prof. Feira de Santana (Brazil) State U., 1995—. Contbr. articles to profl. jours. Mem. Brazilian Soc. Ethnobiology and Ethnoecology (founding), Soc. Ethnobiology, Soc. Human Ecology. Avocations: gardening, trekking, collecting insects, movies. Office: Feira de Santana State U, KM 3 BR116, 44031-460 Feira de Santana Brazil

COSTANTINI, MICHEL HENRI, humanities educator, researcher; b. Cannes, France, Feb. 11, 1949; s. Louis Marcel and Marie Jeanne (Botton) C.; m. m. Anne Marie Delatour (div. 1984); children: Gilles, Serge; m. Geneviève Alix Cittanova; 1 child, Else. Agregation de Grammaire, U. Paris, 1970, D State in Semiotics, 1993. Tchr. C.E.S. Dorval, Orly, France, 1972-77; asst. François Rabelais U., Tours, France, 1977-95, prof., 1995-96; prof. U. Paris VIII, 1996—; cons. editor The Semiotic Web, 1992-93, Advances in Visual Semiotics; co-organizer numerous confs. Author: Lire Les Acharniens d'Aristophane, 1988; editor: La mort en ses miroirs, 1990, La génération Thalès, 1992, Blois, la ville en ses images, 1994, Presenting of the Berkeley Conference IAVS, 1998; editor-in-chief Archipel égéen, 1986-96, EIDOS, internat. bull. visual semiotics, 1989—. With French Nat. Marine, 1974-75. Decorated chevalier Palmes Académiques (France). Mem. Internat. Assn. for Visual Semiotics (v.p.), Internat. Assn. for Spect. Semiotics, Franz Kafka Soc. Prague, Nikos Kazantzakis Soc. Home: E La Neus Verdura, 113 rue Haute d'Aulnay Mer, 41500 Loir et Cher France Office: U Paris VIII, 2 rue de la Liberte, 93 Saint-Denis France

COSTANZA, VICENTE, science educator, researcher; b. Rosario, Santa Fe, Argentina, Jan. 3, 1950; s. José C. and Francisca Di Benedetto; m. Liliana Margarita Devic, Jan. 4, 1972; children: Pedro, Juan Bautista, Margarita, Santiago, Roque, Violeta. Chem. Engr., Nat. Tech. U., Rosario, Argentina, 1973; PhD, Princeton U., 1980. Asst. prof. Facultad Ingeniería Química, Santa Fe, Argentina, 1974-76; rsch. fellow Calif. Inst. Tech., Pasadena, 1980-81; prof. INTEC(UNL-Consejo Nacional Investigaciones Científicas), Santa Fe, 1981—; vis. prof. Eidgenössische Tech. Hochschule, Zürich, Switzerland, 1989, Ecole Poly. Fed., Lausanne, Switzerland, 1991, Facultad de Ingeniería U. Buenos Aires, 1998—, Fac. Ingeniería, U. San Antonio Abad, Cusco, Peru, 1998 ; bd. dirs. Wood Tech. Group-INTEC, Santa Fe, Argentina, 1982—, Process Control Area INTEC, 1981—; project leader Interam. Bank for Devel.-Consejo Nacional Investigaciones Científicas, Santa Fe, 1993-96; fgn. cons. INFOCAL, La Paz and Santa Cruz, Bolivia, 1994; cons. Imperial Chem. Industries, Brussels, 1998-99; scientific rep. planning secretariat Govt. of Santa Fe Province, 1988; scientific advisor Proteger (NGO), Santa Fe, 1992—; mem. Centro de Estudios y Propuestas, Paraná, Entre Ríos, Argentina, 1998—; rschr. Consejo Nacional Investigaciones Científicas, 1982—, ind. researcher, 1986; cons. to Ministry of Agr. and Industry Province of Santa Fe, 1996; cons. sci. and tech. commn. Nat. Deputy Chamber, 2000—. Contbr. numerous articles to profl. jours. Grantee rsch. project on wood tech. Internat. Found. Sci., 1984, 85, Taking Nature Into Acct. Conf. European Parliament, 1995, rsch. project on wood tech. FONCYT, 1998—. Mem. Internat. Soc. Ecol. Econs. (reviewer 1997—). Avocations: piano, woodworking, gardening, horticulture, mathematics. Home: Rivadavia 1745, 3000 Santa Fe Argentina Office: INTEC, Güemes 3450, 3000 Santa Fe Argentina

COSTA PICAZO, ROLANDO, education educator, translator; b. Santa Fe, Argentina, Oct. 1, 1934; s. Antonio and Victoria (Picazo) Costa; m. Amalia Luisa Cortina Aravena, Dec. 4, 1958; children: Marcela, Mariana Victoria, Roland. Diploma in English, U. Nottingham, Eng., 1961; PhD, Mich. State U., 1970. Prof. Inst. Superior del Profesorado, Paraná, Argentina, 1954-59, 1962-68; asst. prof. Ohio U., Athens, 1970-72; exec. dir. Fulbright Commn., Buenos Aires, 1973-93; prof. U. Buenos Aires, 1984—. Author: W.H. Auden: Los Primeros Años, 1994; translator: Nick Adams (Ernest Hemingway), 1974, Musica Para Camaleones (Truman Capote), 1981, El Fantasma De Harlot (Norman Mailer), 1992, others. Mem. Argentine Assn. Am. Studies (pres. 1988-96, 99—), Buenos Aires English Profs. Assn. (pres. 1979-84). Avocations: reading, music, crossword puzzles, film theory, history. Home: Victorino de la Plaza 1570, 1428 Buenos Aires Argentina

COSTE, JEAN GEORGES, physicist; b. Paris, Nov. 12, 1930; s. Florent François and Denise Lucienne (Claude) C.; m. Bernadette Madeleine Saucier; children: Bertrand, Florent, Mathilde. Dir. rsch. CNRS, Nice, France. Avocations: music, mountain activities. Home: 3 Ave Albert 1er, 06320 La Turbie France Office: Lab Phys & Matiere Condense, Parc Valrose, Nice France

COSTE, MARION LOUISE, author, educational consultant; b. Neptune, N.J., Oct. 21, 1938; d. Archibald Murray and Esther Marion Fitz-Randolph; m. James William Coste, Nov. 27, 1959; children: Michael, David, Sandra, Elizabeth. BA, Conn. Coll., 1960. Cert. tchr., Va., Conn., Calif., Hawaii. Tchr. 2d grade Fountain Valley Calif.) Sch. Dist., 1975-77; tchr. sci. East Lyme (Conn.) Sch. Dist., 1978-79; curator of edn. Mystic (Conn.) Mcpl. Aquarium, 1979-81; tchr. trainer/cons. Kamehameha Schs., Honolulu, 1983-87; ednl. cons. Bishop Mus., Honolulu, 1987-89; pub. rels. coord. Honolulu Acad. of Arts, Honolulu, 1989-90; instr., lectr. Coll. of Edn., U. Hawaii, Honolulu, 1991-96; ednl. cons. Read Alana Am., 1997—. Author: Nene, 1993, Honu, 1993, Kolea, 1998 (Ka Polapala Po'okela award 1999). Bd. dirs., steering com. Children's Lib., Hawaii, 1988—. Anna Cross Giblin grantee Soc. of Children's Book Writers and Illustrators, 1992. Mem. ASCD, Internat. Reading Assn., Soc. of Children's Book Writers and Illustrators (steering com. 1985—). Avocations: golf, crafts, Chinese brush painting.

COSTE, RENÉ JEAN-H., theologian; b. St. Genest-Lerpt, France, Sept. 29, 1922; s. Henri and Rosine (Monchal) C. D of Civil Law, State U., Toulouse, France, 1962; D of Canon Law, Cath. U., Toulouse, France, 1962; ThD, Cath. U., Lille, France, 1969. Prof. Holy Scripture Seminaire de la Mission de France, Lisieux, France, 1948-52; prof. canon law CAth. U., Toulouse, 1956-68; prof. social ethics Cath. U., Toulouse, 1968-92; gen. del. Pax Christi-France, Paris, 1989-95, pres., 1995-99. Author 33 books including The Problem of the right of War in the Thought of Pius XII, 1962, International Ethics, 1964, Theology of Religious Freedom, 1969, Theology of Peace, 1997, The Social Dimensions of Faith, 2000. Recipient Malipiero prize for theol. rsch. Faculty Theology, Bologna, 1983; hon. prelate The Holy See, 1992. Home: 6 rue du Regard, 75006 Paris France Office: Pax Christi, 58 Ave de Breteuil, 75007 Paris France

COSTE, THIERRY, bank executive. Dep. CEO Caisse Nat. de Credit Agricole, Paris. Office: Caisse Nat Credit Agricole, 91-93 Blvd Pasteur, 75710 Paris France*

COSTELLO, JOHN H., III, business and marketing executive; b. Akron, Ohio, June 2, 1947; s. John H. Jr. and Lia Costello; children from previous marriage, Michael, Jeffrey, Matthew. BS in Indsl. Mgmt., Akron U., 1968; MBA, Mich. State U., 1970. Mktg. dir. Procter & Gamble Co., Cin., 1971-84; sr. v.p. Pepsi-Cola USA, Purchase, N.Y., 1984-86; exec. v.p. Wells, Rich, Greene, Inc., N.Y.C., 1986-88; pres., chief oper. officer Nielsen Mktg. Rsch. U.S.A., Chgo., 1988-93; sr. exec. v.p. Sears, Roebuck & Co., Hoffman Estates, Ill., 1993-98; pres. Auto Nation, Inc., Ft. Lauderdale, Fla., 1999—; CEO MVP.com, 1999—; sr. mktg. execs. panel Conf. Bd., N.Y.C., 1985-87; industry speaker on bus. trends and issues, 1985—; bd. dirs. The Quaker Oats Co, Sears Can. Mem. exec. bd. N.E. Ill. coun. Boy Scouts Am., 1993-97; trustee Multiple Sclerosis Soc., Chgo., 1990—, vice chmn., 1995—; bd. dirs. Nat. Multiple Sclerosis Soc., 1989—, chair fundraising, 1990-94, mem. exec. com., 1990—, chair nominating com., 1996—. Mem. Assn. Nat. Advertisers (bd. dirs. 1995—, vice chmn. 1998, chmn. 1999), Direct Ad Coun. (bd. dirs. 1996—, vice chmn. 1998), Direct Retail Advt. and Mktg. Assn. (bd. dirs. 1995—, Retail Mktg. Hall of Fame 1997), Lake Forest Club, Econ. Club Chgo., Conway Farms Golf Club. Episcopalian. Avocations: skiing, golf, travel. Home: 860 Gloucester Xing Lake Forest IL 60045-4902 Office: Republic Industries Auto Nation Inc 110 SE 6th St Fort Lauderdale FL 33301-5000

COSTELLO, KELLY LYNN, lawyer; b. Cin., Nov. 30, 1973; d. Patrick Michael and Vicki Lynn Costello. BSBA, Boston U., 1995; JD, George Washington U., 1998. Bar: Ill. 1998. Assoc. Katten Muchin Zavis, Chgo., 1998—. Mem. ABA, Chgo. Bar Assn. E-mail: kelly.costello@kmz.com. Office: Katten Muchin Zavis 525 W Monroe St Ste 1500 Chicago IL 60661-3693

COSTELLO, KENNETH R., lawyer; m. Janet Costello: children: Quinn, Ian. BA, Loyola U., L.A., 1975; JD magna cum laude, U. Santa Clara, 1978. Ptnr. Thelen, Marrin, Johnson & Bridges, L.A., 1986-92, Loeb & Loeb LLP, L.A., 1992-98, Jenkens & Gilchrist, L.A., 1998—; speaker in field. Co-author: Franchising Law: Practice and Forms, 1996, Franchising: Legal Compliance Check-Ups: Business Clients, 1985; contbr. articles to bus. and profl. jours.; mem. bd. editors Law Rev., U. Santa Clara, 1978. Office: Jenkens & Gilchrist 12100 Wilshire Blvd Fl 15 Los Angeles CA 90025-7120

COSTELLO, ROBERT MICHAEL, public relations executive; b. Scranton, Pa., Feb. 11, 1940; s. Peter Francis and Catherine C. (Meehan) C.; m. Anne Elizabeth Dempsey, June 8, 1968; children: Colleen A. McGraw, Ellen M. Student, Girard Coll., 1948-58; BS in English and Philosophy, U. Scranton, 1963. Reporter, editorial asst. Cath. Light, Scranton, 1966-67; press sec. Mayor James J. Walsh, Scranton, 1968-70; pub. rels. dir. Scranton (Pa.) Redevelopment Authority, 1970-72; reporter The Scranton (Pa.) Times/The Sunday Times, 1972-73; dep. press sec. Pa. Gov. Milton J. Shapp, Harrisburg, Pa., 1973-75; press sec. Pa. Health Sec. L. Bachman, MD, Harrisburg, 1975-78; pub. rels. dir. Pa. Turnpike Commn., Harrisburg, 1978-79; pub. info. dir. U.S. Dept. Health & Human Svcs., Phila., 1979-80; pub. rels. dir. Mercy Hosp. Scranton, Pa., 1980-95; sr. staff writer Mercy Hosp. Scranton, 1996—; blood svcs. coord. ARC, Scranton (Pa.) chpt., 1980-95; chmn. communications Diocesan Synod II, Scranton, 1982-85; vice chmn. Diocesan Communications Com., Scranton, 1986-89. Dep. press sec. Pa. Gov. Milton Shapp for Re-election Campaign, Harrisburg, 1973; press spokesman Pa. Health Dept., Harrisburg, 1976; bd. dirs. Lackawanna United Way, Scranton, 1982-85; pub. rels. cons. Judge James J. Walsh for Pa. Supreme Ct. Justice Election, 1988. With U.S. Army, 1963-66. Recipient citation of appreciation Diocese of Scranton (Pa.) Synod II, 1985, Patriotic Svc. award U.S. Savs. Bonds, Sec. of the Treasury, Washington, 1990; named Outstanding Community Blood Svcs. Coord., ARC, Scranton, 1990. Mem. Am. Soc. for Hosp. Mktg. and Pub. Rels. (cert.), Univ. Scranton Alumni, Girard Coll. Alumni. Democrat. Roman Catholic. Home: 1404 Delaware St Dunmore PA 18509-2022 Office: Mercy Hosp 746 Jefferson Ave Scranton PA 18510-1697

COSTENBADER, CHARLES MICHAEL, lawyer; b. Jersey City, Dec. 9, 1935; s. Edward William and Marie Veronica (Danaher) C.; m. Barbara Ann Wilson, Aug. 1, 1959; children: Charles Michael Jr., William E., Mary E. BS in Acctg., Mt. St. Mary's Coll., 1957; JD, Seton Hall U., 1960; LLM in Taxation, NYU, 1968. Bar: N.J 1960; U.S. Tax Ct. 1961, U.S. Ct. Appeals (3d cir.) 1973, U.S. Supreme Ct. 1983. Trial atty. office regional counsel IRS, N.Y.C., 1961-69; tax assoc. Shanley & Fisher, Newark, 1969-76; tax ptnr. Stryker, Tams & Dill, Newark, 1976-98; spl. counsel McCarter & English, Newark, 1998—. Mem. N.J. State and Local Expenditure and Revenue Commn., 1985-88. Mem. ABA, N.J. Bar Assn. (chmn. taxation sect. 1984-85), N.J. State C. of C. (chmn. cost of govt. com. 1988—), Am. Coll. Tax Counsel. Republican. Roman Catholic. Avocations: gardening, reading, sports. Home: 8 Neptune Pl Colonia NJ 07067-2502 Office: McCarter & English Gateway Four Ctr 100 Mulberry St Newark NJ 07101-4096

COSTER, HANS GERARD LEONARD, biophysicist, educator; b. Jakarta, Java, Indonesia, Mar. 11, 1939; arrived in Australia, 1951; s. Leonardus Andritus and Catharina (Oudendorp) C.; m. Marjorie Tillie Eakin, Jan. 4, 1964; children: Leonard A. G., Adelle C. F. MSc, U. Sydney, 1964, PhD, 1967. Exptl. officer Commonwealth Sci. and Indsl. Rsch. Orgn., Sydney, 1962-65; from lectr. to sr. lectr. U. NSW, Sydney, 1967-76; vis. prof. Kernforschung Anlage, Juelich, Germany, 1974-75; prof. physics U. NSW, Sydney, 1984—; councilor Australian Inst. Nuclear Sci. and Engring., Sydney, 1989—; chmn. bd. FuCell Pty. Ltd., Sydney, 1991—; dir. UNESCO Ctr. for Membrane Sci. & Tech., Sydney, 1988—; head dept. biophysics U. NSW, Sydney, 1984-87, 91-94. Author: (books) Experimental Physics, 1968, Thermodynamics of Life Processes, 1981, Membrane Science and Technology, 1994, Biophysics and Medical Physics, 1996, (book chpts.) Bioelectrochemistry, 1970, 73, Approach to Physical Sciences, 1970, 73, Membrane Transport in Plants, 1974, Topics in Bioelectrochemistry and Bioenergetics, 1977, Plant Membrane Transport: Current Conceptual Issues, 1980, Membrane Transport in Plants, 1984, Inorganic Carbon Uptake by Aquatic Photosynthetic Organisms, 1985, Plant Membrane Transport: The Current Position, 1989, Electropharmacology, 1990; inventor and patentee in field; contbr. papers and articles to profl. jours. Recipient medal for sci., UNESCO, 1998. Fellow Australian Inst. Physics (chmn. biophysics group 1979-81, pres. 1982-84); mem. Inst. Physics (London), Australian Acad. Sci. (mem. nat. com. for biophysics 1976-79, 95—), Australian Soc. for Biophysics (sec., treas., past pres. 1982-84). Avocations: house restoration, electronics/computing. Home: 34 Cook St, 2031 Randwick NSW, Australia Office: U NSW, Barker St-Kensington, 2052 Sydney NSW, Australia

COSTERMANS, JEAN, psychology educator, researcher; b. Kampenhout, Belgium, Aug. 5, 1935; s. Edward and Maria (De Putter) C.; m. Eliane Kottgen, Sept. 4, 1963; children: Isabelle, Philippe, Denis. PhD in Psychology, U. Louvain, Belgium, 1965. Lectr. U. Louvain, Belgium, 1967-73, prof., 1973-76, ordinary prof., 1976—; head Lab. for Cognitive Psychology, 1973-92; dean Faculty Psychology and Edn., 1980-85; pres. Dept. Exptl. Psychology, 1986-91; prorector U. Louvain, 1991-96. Author: Psychologie Du Langage, 1980, Les Activities Cognitives, 1998; co-editor: Processing Interclausal Relationships, 1997. Rsch. fellow NSF, Belgium, 1961-67. Mem. APA, Belgian Psychol. Soc. (pres. 1979-82), Belgian Fedn. Psychologists (pres. 1983-86), European Soc. Cognitive Psychology, Assn. French Lang. Psychology (pres. 1998—). Home: Rue Mataise 13, B-1450 Chastre Belgium Office: Dept Exptl Psychology, Place Cardinal Mercier 10, B-1348 Louvain-La-Neuve Belgium

COSTES, CLAUDE ROGER, biochemistry educator, consultant; b. Bougival, Yvelines, France, Apr. 26, 1933; s. Robert and Gabrielle Virginie (Raynal) C.; m. Marie-Claire Andree Prieur, Dec. 29, 1956 (dec. Apr. 1981); children: Patricia, Hélène, Vincent; m. Jacqueline Georgette Berroyer, Feb. 15, 1986. Degree in biochem. engring., I.N.A., Paris, 1956; degree in scis., U. Paris, 1957, DSc, 1965. Rsch. asst. INRA, Versailles, France, 1957-62, chargé de rsch., 1962-66; dept. head INRA, Versailles, 1971-72; prof. biochemistry Inst. Nat. Agronomique, Grignon and Paris, 1966-93, prof. emeritus, 1993—, dept. head, 1983-93; cons. Nat. Coun. Rsch., Paris, 1971-79, dep. dir. life scis., 1978-80; sci. advisor Bongrain Industry, Paris, 1980-96. Contbr. numerous articles to sci. and profl. jours. Mem. City Coun., Plaisians, France, 1995; pres. Maison de la Culture, Neauphle, France, 1972-76. Sgt. French Army, 1958-60. Fellow French Soc. Biochemistry; mem. French Soc. Vegetable Physiology (pres. 1980-81). Avocations: cinema, music, internat. travel, gardening. Home: 29 Residence Bois du Four, 78640 Neauphle le Chateau France

COSTIGLIO, LAWRENCE U., lawyer; b. Aug. 8, 1916; s. Angelo and Adalgisa C.; children: Christina, Peter, Eugene, Teresa. BL, Fordham U., 1941. Atty. N.Y.C., 1946-51, asst. U.S. atty., 1951-55; atty. Finley, Lileiwthel, N.Y.C., 1955-57; counsel N.Y. Banking Dept., N.Y.C., 1957-59; atty. Olive and Donnally, N.Y.C., 1959-61; exec. v.p. N.Y. Savings Banks Assn., N.Y.C., 1961-86; atty. Riukin, Radler & Babuer, Uniondale, N.Y., 1984-94, ret., 1994; dir. Fed. Housing Financial Bd., Washington, 1990-98. With U.S. Army, 1943-46. Home: 60-11 Broadway Woodside NY 11377

COSULICH, ANTONIO FELICE, shipping company executive; b. Trieste, Italy, June 4, 1939; s. Mario Augusto and Emma (Luzzatto Fegiz) C.; m. Patrizia Pesci, Dec. 4, 1965; children: Sabina, Marta, Alice, Orsola, Lucia, Natalia. Student publ schs., Genoa, Italy. Ship master cert. 3d officer various ships, 1961-62, 2d officer, 1962-64, chief officer, 1964-65; mng. dir. Fratelli Cosulich (HK) Ltd., Hong Kong, 1983-86, Fratelli Cosulich Spa, Genoa, 1968-83, 86—. With Italian Navy, 1959-61. Mem. Internat. Bunker Industry Assn. (chmn. 1996-98), Genoa Ship Agts. and Shipbrokers Assn. (chmn. 1996-2000). Avocations: cross-country skiing, mountain climbing, gardening. Office: Fratelli Cosulich SpA, Ponte Morosini 41, 16126 Genoa Italy

COTCHETT, JOSEPH WINTERS, lawyer, author; b. Chgo., Jan. 6, 1939; s. Joseph Winters and Jean (Renaud) C.; children—Leslie F., Charles P., Rachael E., Quinn Carlyle, Camilla E. BS in Engring., Calif. Poly. Coll., 1960; LLB, U. Calif. Hastings Coll. Law, 1964. Bar: Calif. 1965, D.C. 1980. Ptnr. Cotchett, Pitre & Simon, Burlingame, Calif., 1965—; mem. Calif. Jud. Coun., 1975-77, Calif. Commn. on Jud. Performance, 1985-89, Commn. 2020 Jud. Coun., 1991-94; select com. on jud. retirement, 1992—. Author: (with R. Cartwright) California Products Liability Actions, 1970, (with F. Haight) California Courtroom Evidence, 1972, (with A. Elkind) Federal Courtroom Evidence, 1976, (with Frank Rothman) Persuasive Opening Statements and Closing Arguments, 1988, (with Stephen Pizzo) The Ethics Gap, 1991, (with Gerald Uelmen) California Courtroom Evidence Foundations, 1993; contbr. articles to profl. jours. Chmn. San Mateo County Heart Assn., 1967; pres. San Mateo Boys and Girls Club, 1971; bd. dirs. U. Calif. Hastings Law Sch., 1981-93. With Intelligence Corps, U.S. Army, 1960-61; col. JAGC, USAR, ret. Fellow Am. Bar Found., Am. Bd. Trial Advs., Am. Coll. Trial Lawyers, Internat. Acad. Trial Lawyers, Internat. Soc. of Barristers, Nat. Bd. Trial Advs. (diplomate civil trial adv.), State Bar Calif. (gov. 1972-75). Clubs: Commonwealth, Press (San Francisco). Office: 840 Malcolm Rd Burlingame CA 94010-1401 also: 12100 Wilshire Blvd Ste 1100 Los Angeles CA 90025-7124

COTE, LOUISE ROSEANN, creative director, designer; b. Quincy, Mass., Sept. 16, 1959; d. John Anthony and Theresa Janet (Oriola) Burke; m. Robert Andrew Cote, Aug. 6, 1983. BA, Bridgewater State Coll., 1981. Advt. asst. Dunnington Super Drug, Brockton, Mass., 1978-81; bus. forms and graphic design artist Shawmut Bank of Boston, N.A., 1981-86; artist

AlliedSignal Inc., East Providence, R.I., 1986-92, adminstr. creative svcs., 1992-94, supr. creative svcs., 1992-94, supr. computer graphics svcs., 1994-95; owner, design dir. Katmandu Studio, North Attleborough, Mass., 1995—. Mem. Advt. Club Southeastern New Eng., North Attleboro and Plainville C. of C. (chmn. bd. 2000). Roman Catholic. Avocations: music, crafts. Office: Katmandu Studio 885 Mount Hope St North Attleboro MA 02760-1807

COTE, RICHARD JAMES, pathologist, researcher; b. L.A., May 10, 1954; s. Richard Patrick and Kathrine (Bisbas) C.; m. Anne Louise Foxen, Feb. 8, 1992; children: Nicholas Foxen, Juliet Anne, Grace Elizabeth. BS in Biology, U. Calif., Irvine, 1976, BA in Chemistry, 1976; MD, U. Chgo., 1980. Diplomate Am. Coll. Pathologists. Intern in surgery U. Mich. Hosp., Ann Arbor, 1980-81; rsch. fellow, immunology Meml. Sloan-Kettering Cancer Ctr., N.Y.C., 1981-83; rsch. assoc., immunology Meml. Sloan-Kettering Hosp., N.Y.C., 1983-85, fellow, pathology, 1987-88, chief fellow, pathology, 1988-90; resident, pathology Cornell U. Med. Ctr., N.Y.C., 1985-87; asst. prof., pathology U. So. Calif., L.A., 1990-95, assoc. prof., 1995-99, prof., 1999—; attending pathologist Kenneth Norris Cancer Ctr., L.A., 1990—; dir. genitourinary program U. So. Calif./Norris Cancer Ctr., 1997—; founder, dir. Impath, Inc., N.Y.C., 1987-2000; sci. dir. Neoprobe Corp., Columbus, Ohio, 1992-97; sci. cons. Abbott Labs., Chgo., 2000—; sci. dir. ChromaVision Med. Sys., Inc., San Juan Capistrano, Calif., 2000—; sci. cons. Abbott Labs., 2000—; sci. dir. John Wayne Cancer and Rsch. Inst., Santa Monica, Calif.; mem. numerous nat. and internat. adv. bds. in field. Author: Immunomicroscopy, 1994; editor Modern Surg. Pathology; assoc. editor Applied Immunohistochemistry; contbr. sci. papers to profl. jours., book chpts. Patentee in field. Am. Cancer Soc. fellow, 1988; recipient rsch. grants, awards NIH, ACS, others, 1981—. Mem. Soc. for Basic Urologic Rsch., Internat. Soc. for Hematotherapy, Phi Beta Kappa. Avocations: golf, photography, skiing, writing. Office: U So Calif 1441 Eastlake Ave Los Angeles CA 90033-1048

COTHER, ERIC JOHN, plant pathologist; b. Ayr, Australia, Apr. 28, 1948; s. Jack and Gwenda (Suthers) C.; m. Norma Joan Cantrill, Dec. 1, 1973; children: Melanie, Elouise. BS in Agriculture with honors, U. Sydney, 1970; PhD, Australian Nat. U., 1973. Plant pathologist NSW Agr., Yanco, Australia, 1973-75, rsch. scientist, 1975-87; sr. rsch. scientist NSW Agr., Orange, Australia, 1989-95; supr. rsch. NSW Agr., Orange, 1993-97; key rschr. Coop. Rsch. Ctr. for Weed Mgmt. Systems and Coop. Rsch. Ctr. for Sustainable Rice Prodn., prin. rsch. scientist, 1995—. Contbr. articles to profl. jours., confs., and books; patentee mycoherbicide; editor in chief Australasian Plant Pathology. Life mem. Australian Conservation Found. Fellow Govt. of Netherlands, 1979; recipient numerous rsch. grants. Mem. Australasian Plant Pathology Soc., Am. Phytopathol. Soc., Australian Conservation Found. (life), Australian Inst. Agrl. Sci. and Tech., Australian Soc. Microbiology, Rotary Club of Orange Daybreak, Apex Australia (life). Avocations: gardening, haute cuisine. Office: Agrl Rsch Vet Ctr, Forest Rd, Orange 2800, Australia

COTLER, JEROME MARVIN, orthopaedic surgeon; b. Bridgeton, N.J., July 26, 1928; s. Mitchell George and Elizabeth (Shapiro) C.; m. Florence, Aug. 19, 1951; children: Howard Bruce, Michelle Gail. BS, Ursinus Coll., 1948; MD, Jefferson Med. Coll., 1952. Intern Jefferson Med. Coll. Hosp., Phila., 1952-53, resident, 1953-57; orthop. surgeon pvt. practice, Bridgeton, N.J., 1957-73; instr. orthop. surgery Jefferson Med. Coll., Phila., 1957-70, clin. asst. prof., 1970-73; orthop. surgeon Jefferson Orthop. Assocs., Phila., 1973-95; clin. prof. Jefferson Med. Coll., 1973-81, prof., 1981—, Dr. Everett J. and Marian Gordon prof., 1991—; orthop. surgeon Jefferson Orthops. and Sports Medicine, Phila., 1995—. Co-editor: Spinal Fusion: Science and Techniques, 1990, Spinal Instrumentation, 1992; contbr. articles to profl. jours. Mem. Union League Phila., 1974—. Fellow ACS (mem. bd. govs. 1985-90, 93-99, mem. adv. coun. 1985-90, 93-99), Am. Acad. Orthop. Surgeons (bd. dirs. 1972-76); mem. Am. Orthop. Assn. (v.p. 1993-94), Masons. Home: 4 E Kings Hwy Haddon Heights NJ 08035-1430 Office: 130 S 9th St Ste 106 Philadelphia PA 19107-5233

COTÓN, EDUARDO, science researcher, educator; b. Buenos Aires, Jan. 12, 1962; s. Jose Lisardo Cortón and Maria Dorinda Perez; m. Silvia Adriana Fernandez, Aug. 23, 1991; children: Alejandro, Sebastian. Comml. Bachelor's, Inst. Dulcisimo Nombre Jesu, Buenos Aires, 1980; BS, La Plata (Argentina) U., 1989; PhD in Scis., Buenos Aires State U., 1999. Cert. biologist. Scholar Atomic Energy Nat. Bd., Ezeiza, 1991-92; chair in biology Buenos Aires State U., 1990-93, chair biol. instrumentation, 1992-95, chair biol. chemistry, head projects, 1995—; prof. ecology U. Salvador, Pilar, 1998—. Contbr. articles to profl. jours. Mem. Soc. Argentina de Investigaciones Bioquimicas. Avocations: computer games, swimming, cinema. Fax: 454232251. E-mail: eduardo@qb.fcen.uba.ar. Home: Av Ruiz Huidobro, Buenos Aires 1430, Argentina Office: U Buenos Aires, Pabellon 2 4to piso, 1428 Buenos Aires Argentina

COTRUBAS, ILEANA, opera singer, retired lyric soprano; b. Galati, Romania; d. Vasile C. and Maria C. m. Manfred Ramin, 1972. Student, Scoala speciala de Musica, Bucharest, Ciprian Porumbescu Conservatory, Bucharest, Musikakademie, Vienna, Austria. tchr. master-classes, interpretation and operatic roles. Debut as Yniold in Pelleas et Melisande, Bucharest Opera, 1964; appeared with Frankfurt (Fed. Republic Germany) Opera, 1968-71, Staatsoper, Vienna, 1970—, Covent Garden, London, 1971—, Staatsoper, Munich, 1973—, Lyric Opera Chgo., 1973-75, 83—, Opera Paris, 1974—, La Scala, Milan, 1975—, Met. Opera, N.Y.C., 1977—, San Francisco Opera, 1978, Ehrenmitglied Vienna Staats oper, 1991; major roles include: Zerlina, Susanna, Pamina, Norina, Gilda, Violetta, Elisabetta (Don Carlos), Mimi, Tatyana, Micaela, Manon, Antonia, Melisande; ret., 1990; author: Truth About Opera, 1998. Recipient 1st prize Internat. Singing Competition, Hertogenbusch, Netherlands, 1965; 1st prize Munich Radio Competition, 1966; Kammersängerin Vienna Staatsoper, 1981; Great Officer of the Order Sant' Iago da Espada, Portugal, 1990.

COTTA, RENATO MACHADO, mechanical engineer; b. Niteroi, Brazil, Mar. 5, 1960; s. Enéas Machado and Claudette (Oliviera) C.; m. Marcia Cristina Pires, June 3, 1982 (div. 1993); 1 child, Bianca Pires. BS, U. Fed. Rio de Janeiro, 1981; PhD in Mech. and Aerospace Engring., N.C. State U., 1985. Asst. prof. Inst. Tecnologico de Aeronautica, Brazil, 1985-87; assoc. prof. U. Fed. do Rio de Janeiro, 1987-94, prof., 1994—; adj. prof. U. Miami, Fla., 1994—; head heat transmission and tech. lab. U. Fed. do Rio de Janeiro, 1993—; head mech. engring. com. CNPQ, 1994—; cons. Nat. Commn. Nuclear Energy, Brazil, 1993—, Inst. Aeronautics and Space, Brazil, 1986—; mem. scientific coun. Internat. Ctr. Heat and Mass Transfer, 1994. Author: Integral Transforms in Computational Heat and Fluid Flow, 1993, The Integral Transform Method in Thermal and Fluids Science and Engineering, 1998; co-author: Heat Conduction: Mixed Formulations and Hybrid Computation; hon. mem. editl. adv. bd. Internat. Jour. Heat and Mass Transfer, 1994; editor-in-chief Hybrid Methods in Engineering. Fellow Brazilian Assn. Mech. Scis.; mem. Assembly Internat. Heat Transfer Confs. (del. 1992—). Roman Catholic. Achievements include development of the generalized integral transform technique. Office: PEM/COPPEUFRJ Cidade Univer, Cx Postal 68503, 21945970 Rio de Janeiro Brazil

COTTER, JAMES MICHAEL, lawyer; b. Providence, May 12, 1942; s. James Henry and Marguerite Louise (Clark) C.; m. Melinda Irene Tighe, Feb. 6, 1971; children: Elizabeth, Heather, Kathryn. AB, Fairfield U., 1964; LLB, U. Va., 1967. Bar: N.Y. 1967. Assoc. Simpson Thacher & Bartlett, N.Y.C., 1967-75, ptnr., 1975—. Trustee Fairfield U., 1995—; bd. dirs. M.G.A. Found., 1990—, chmn., 1990-92. Mem. ABA, N.Y. State Bar Assn., N.Y. Law Inst. (bd. dirs. 1984—, chmn. exec. com. 1993-98, pres. 1997—), Met. Golf Assn. (bd. dirs. 1974—, pres. 1990-92), Greenwich Conn. Country Club, Hudson Nat. Golf Club. Office: Simpson Thacher & Bartlett 425 Lexington Ave Fl 15 New York NY 10017-3954

COTTER, LAWRENCE, cardiologist, consultant; b. Cardiff, Wales, July 21, 1947; s. Lawrence and Mary (Jones) C.; m. Jennifer Lynne Jones, May 29, 1973; children: Lucy Claire, Daniel Owain. MB ChB, Manchester (Eng.) U., 1971; MBA, Keele U., Manchester, 1993. Profl. houseman Manchester Royal Infirmary, 1971-72; with cardiology staff Hammersmith Hosp., Manchester, 1972-73; registrar cardiologist Royal Infirmary, Edinburgh, 1975-77, Brompton Hosp., London, 1977-81; lectr. in cardiology Oxford (Eng.) U., 1981-84; cons. cardiologist, undergrad. hosp. dean Manchester Royal Infirmary, 1984—. Contbr. articles to profl. jours. Fellow Royal Coll. Physicians (Edinburgh, London; examiner, councillor, censor); mem. Royal Coll. Physicians. Avocations: family, rugby, books, birds, usquaebae research. Office: Cardiology Dept Oxford Rd, Manchester Royal Infirmary, Manchester M13 9WL, England

COTTER, MICHAEL WILLIAM, retired ambassador, business consultant; b. Madison, Wis., Aug. 1, 1943; s. Patrick William and Lois Katherine (Schaus) C.; m. Joanne Marie Miller, Aug. 30, 1974. BSFS, Georgetown U., 1965; JD, U. Mich., 1968; MS, Stanford U., 1976. Polit.-mil. affairs officer Am. Embassy, Ankara, Turkey, 1980-82; sr. Turkish desk officer U.S. Dept. State, Washington, 1982-84; polit. officer Am. Embassy, Kinshasa, Zaire, 1984-86, polit. counselor, 1986-88; mgmt. analyst sec. of mgmt. U.S. Dept. State, 1988-90, office dir. politico-military affairs, 1990-92; dep. chief of mission Am. Embassy, Santiago, Chile, 1992-95; U.S. amb. to Turkmenistan, 1995-98; internat. bus. cons., Washington, 1999—. Mem. Am. Fgn. Svc. Assn. (sec. 1989-91, bd. govs. 1988-89), Wis. Bar Assn. Home and Office: 4415 Springdale St NW Washington DC 20016-2715

COTTER, RICHARD TIMOTHY, lawyer; b. Chgo., Sept. 2, 1948; s. Edward Timothy and Julia Maria C.; m. Janet M. Sorrentino, Dec. 3, 1977 (div. Jan. 1993); children: Mary Julia, Carol Ann; m. Kimberly A. Morris, Sept. 11, 1993; children: Kathleen, Julia Ann. Bar: Fla. 1975, Ill. 1976, U.S. Supreme Ct. 1982. Ptnr. Echols & Cotter, Ft. Myers Beach, Fla., 1978-85, Echols, Cotter & Shenko, Ft. Myers Beach, Fla., 1985-95, Echols & Cotter, Ft. Myers Beach, 1995—; prof. Internat. Coll. Paralegal Instrn., Ft. Myers, 1992. Contbr. articles to profl. jours.; newspaper columnist Legal Eagle, 1995—. Pres. Cmty. Assn. Inst., South Gulf Coast chpt., Ft. Myers, 1984; dir. United Way of Lee County, Inc., Ft. Myers, 1990-92; dir. Chamber of S.W. Fla., Ft. Myers, 1989-91, vice-chmn. legal affairs, 1990-94; del. Fla. Democratic State Conv., 1995. Mem. Ill. Bar Assn., Fla. Bar (condo. and planned devel. com. 1993—, real property professionalism com. 1993—), Lee County Bar Assn., Fla. Assn. Realtors (local bd. attys. com. 1986-94), Ft. Myers Beach Lodge 362, Araba Shrine Temple, U.S. C. of C. (coun. mem. small bus. coun. 1994—, mem. social security com. 1995—). Avocations: golf, flying. Office: Richard T Cotter PA 6100 Estero Blvd Fort Myers Beach FL 33931-4347

COTTERILL, RODNEY MICHAEL, biophysics researcher; b. Bodmin, Cornwall, Eng., Sept. 27, 1933; arrived in Denmark, 1967; s. Herbert Harold and Aline Ivy (Le Cerf) C.; m. Vibeke Ejler Nielsen, Feb. 7, 1959; children: Marianne, Jennifer. BSc, U. Coll., London, 1957; MS, Yale U., 1958; PhD, Cambridge (Eng.) U., 1962; DSc, London U., 1973. Assoc. physicist Argonne (Ill.) Nat. Lab., 1962-67; prof. Danish Tech. U., Lyngby, 1967—; vis. prof. U. Tokyo, 1978, 85. Author: The Material World, 1985, No Ghost in the Machine, 1989, Enchanted Looms, 1998. Cpl. Royal Air Force, 1952-54. Recipient Hermer Meml. prize, Copenhagen U., Denmark, 1978; named Knight of the Danebrog, Denmark, 1979. Fellow Royal Danish Acad. Scis. and Letters, Inst. Physics U.K. (chartered physicist). Avocations: sailing, choral singing, chess, writing. Office: Danish Tech Univ, Bldg 307, 2800 Lyngby Denmark

COTTERRELL, ROGER BRIAN MELVYN, law educator; b. Birmingham, Eng., Nov. 30, 1946; s. Walter Leslie and Hilda Margaret (Randle) C.; m. Ann Zillah Poyner, Oct. 22, 1969; children: David Roger, Linda Ann Margaret. LLB, U. London, 1968, LLM, 1969, MSc, 1977, LLD, 1988. Lectr. U. Leicester, U.K., 1969-74; lectr. to sr. lectr. Queen Mary Coll. U. London, 1974-85, reader in legal theory, 1985-90, prof. legal theory, 1990—; head of dept. law Queen Mary and Westfield Coll. Queen Mary and Westfield Coll., U. London, 1989-91, dean faculty of laws, 1993-96; vis. prof. U. Tex. Austin, 1989, U. Lund, Sweden, 1996, Cath. U., Brussels, 1996, 97. Author: The Sociology of Law, 2d edit., 1992, The Politics of Jurisprudence, 1989, 92 (nominated Scribes Book award), Law's Community, 1995, Emile Durkheim: Law in a Moral Domain, 1999; contbr. numerous articles to profl. pubs. Panel mem. U.K. Nat. Univs. Rsch. Assessment, 1999—; mem. com. Heads of Univ. Law Schs., 1993-96. Recipient Vis. Scholars award British Coun., 1995. Mem. Law and Soc. Assn. (trustee 1996-99, chair articles prize com. 1999-2000), Soc. of Pub. Tchrs. of Law. Mem. Labour Party. Methodist. Avocations: exploring cities, listening to and writing about music. Office: Queen Mary/Westfield Coll, Dept Law Mile End Rd, London E1 4NS, England

COTTER-SMITH, CATHLEEN MARIE, art educator, artist; b. Dallas, 1950; d. Robert Jay and Betty Ann Cotter; 1 child, Ryan Patrick Holt; m. Jack Glendon Smith, Jr., 1991. BS, East Tex. State U., 1974; MS, Tex. A&M U., Commerce, 1977. Freelance artist, Garland and Plano, Tex., 1976—; assoc. prof. art Grayson County Coll., Dennison, Tex., 1981-85; prof. art Collin County C.C., Plano, Tex., 1986—, coord. art dept., 1986-97; cons. on book Equine Images, 1992. One-woman shows include Cultural Art Ctr., Plano, 1990, Collin County C. C. Gallery, Plano, 1994; exhibited in group show S.W. Watercolor Soc., Dallas, 1990, juried show S. Watercolor Soc., 2000; represented in permanent collection Farmerville C. of C.; illustrator for nat. card line, 1997—. Mentor Boles Children's Home, Quinlan, Tex., 1996-99. Recipient award S.W. Watercolor Soc. Mem. S. Watercolor Soc. (award in group 1999). Republican. Mem. Ch. of Christ. Avocation: nature lover. Office: Collin County CC 2800 E Spring Creek Pkwy Plano TX 75074-3300

COTTI, ELISABETTA, endodontist, educator, researcher; b. Cagliari, Italy, Apr. 6, 1962; d. Marino and Maria Irne (Dore) Cotti; m. Brunello Acquas, June 25, 1994; 1 child, Andrea. DDS, U. Cagliari, 1980; MS, Loma Linda U., 1990. Cert. in endodontics. Dentist in pvt. practice, Cagliari, 1985-88; pvt. practice as endodontist, Cagliari, 1991—; prof. U. Cagliari, 1992—. Contbr. chpt. to textbook, articles to profl. jours. Mem. Italian Endodontic Assn. (exec. com. 1993—), European Assn. Endodontology (country rep. 1997—). Avocations: skiing, water skiing, travel. Home: Via Romas 14S, 09124 Cagliari Italy Office: Endodontic Office, Via Memeli 66, 09124 Cagliari Italy

COTTING, PATRICK, marketing professional, consultant; b. Tafers, Fribourg, Switzerland, Feb. 28, 1970; s. Anton and Lillian Cattilaz. M in Bus. Econs., U. Fribourg, 1994; PhD in Bus. Econs., Johannes-Kepler-U. Linz, Austria, 1999. Mktg. asst. Kraft Jacobs Suchard, Neuchâtel, Switzerland, 1991, Credit Suisse, Zurich, Switzerland, 1996-97; sponsorship mgr. Credit Suisse, Zurich, 1997—; vis. prof. Schweitz Ausbildungszentrum Mktg., Kommunikation und Werburg, Biel, Switzerland, Verbandsmgmt.-Inst. U. Freiburg. Sgt. Swiss Army. Avocations: playing the flute, cycling, track and field, shooting. Home: Oberdorfstr 12, 1712 Tafers Fribourg, Switzerland Office: Credit Suisse, Postfach 100, Zurich 8070, Switzerland

COTTINGHAM, RICHARD SUMNER, paper company executive; b. Columbus, Ohio, May 7, 1941; s. Robert E. and Lee Alice (Gasaway) C.; m. Sheila L. Robertson, Dec. 20, 1980. BA in History, Ohio State U., 1964. Pres. Cottingham Paper Co., Columbus, 1968—. Bd. dirs. Network Svcs. Co., 1984-90, chmn., 1986-88. Served as lt. (j.g.) USN, 1964-67, Vietnam. Recipient Ernst & Young Master Entrepreneur of Yr. award for Columbus and Ctr. Ohio, 1998. Mem. Nat. Paper Trade Assn. (young exec. com. 1976), Am. Mgmt. Assn., Nat. Assn. Wholesale Distbrs., Internat. Sanitary Supply Assn., Chief Exec. Bds. Columbus, Econ. Club Columbus, Columbus C. of C., Ohio C. of C., Worthington Country Club. Republican. Address: Cottingham Paper Co 324 E 2d Ave PO Box 163579 Columbus OH 43216-3579

COTTON, JEAN-PIERRE AIMÉ, physicist; b. Lyon, France, June 10, 1941; s. Eugene and Marie-Louise Cotton; m. Claude-Marie Brigitte Cabotte, Oct. 10, 1964; children: Christine, Antoine. Lic. in physics, U. Marseille, France, 1964; grad., Ecole Superieure d'Electricite, Paris, 1966; DSc, U. Paris, 1973. Rsch. assoc. Commissariat à l'Energie Atomique, Saclay, France, 1968-72, physicist, 1972—. Editor Jour. Physique, 1979-83; contbr. articles to profl. jours. Lt. French Navy, 1966-68. Mem. Soc. Fransaise de Physique, European Phys. Soc., Am. Phys. Soc. Avocations: bicycle, movies. Home: 5 Allee du Bois Comtesse, 91440 Bures Sur Yvette France Office: Lab Leon Brillouin, CE Saclay, 91191 Gif Sur Yvette France

COTTRAUX, JEAN ANTOINE, psychiatrist; b. Montrottier, France, Feb. 27, 1942; s. Louis and Monique (Joly) C.; m. Francine Gobert; children: Muriel, Xavier. Baccalaureat, Lycée Ampère, Lyon, France, 1958; MD, U. Lyon, 1971; PhD in Med. Psychology, U. Lyon I, 1979, postgrad., 1986. Resident Univ. Hosp. Lyon, 1967-71, chief of clinic, 1971-76, adj. cons. psychiatrist, 1976-81, cons. psychiatrist, 1981-91, head anxiety disorder unit, 1991—; lectr. U. Lyon 1, 1976—, dir. cognitive behavior therapy diploma, 1980—. Co-author: Annual Series of European Research in Behavior Therapy, 1990, Which Psychotherapies for the Year 2000?, 1992, 14 others (in French), Cognitive-Behavior Therapies, 3rd edit., 1998, The Inside Enemies: Obsessions and Compulsions, 1998; contbr. numerous articles to profl. jours., chpts. to books. With French Navy, 1966-67. Grantee Inst. Nat. Rsch. et Santé Médicale, 1978-81, 81-82, 90-92, Unité de Formation et Rsch., 1980, 85, Conseil Recherche d'Ottawa, 1981, Programme Hosp. de Rsch. Clinique, 1994-96, 95-97, 97-99, Programme Hospitalier de Recherche Clinique, 1996; Duphar-France, 1982-85, Eli Lilly, 1989, Bristol-Myers-Squib, 1980-85, 97, Synthélabo, 1991-92, Smithkline-Beecham, 1992-93, Pfizer, 1994, Lundbeck, 1996. Fellow Acad. Cognitive Therapy Philosophia (founding fellow); mem. Am. Assn. for Advancement of Behavior Therapy, Internat. Assn. for Cognitive Therapy, N.Y. Acad. Scis., European Assn. Cognitive Behavior Therapy (pres. 1990), French Assn. Cognitive Behavior Therapy (pres. 1984-89). Avocation: piano. Fax: 33 (0) 4 723573 30. E-mail: cottraux@univ lyon1.fr. Office: Hopital Neurologique, 59 Blvd Pinel, 69394 Lyon France

COTTRELL, THOMAS SYLVESTER, pathology educator, university dean; b. Chgo., Feb. 2, 1934; s. Sylvester Vincent and Cleo (Medley) C.; m. Jane Chichester, July 3, 1959; children: Matthew Thomas, Anne Medley, Sarah Jane. AB, Brown U., 1955; MD, Columbia U., 1965. Diplomate Am. Bd. Pathology. Asst. prof. N.Y. Med. Coll., Valhalla, 1968-79; assoc. prof. pathology SUNY Sch. Medicine, Stony Brook, 1979—, assoc. dean clin. affairs, 1979-88, exec. assoc. dean, 1988-97; interim exec. dir. U. Hosp. SUNY, Stony Brook, 1983-84, interim chmn. dept. ob-gyn. Sch. Medicine, 1991-92, interim chmn. dept. surgery Sch. Medicine, 1996, vice dean, 1997—. Lt. USNR, 1957-60. Scholar John and Mary R. Markle Found., 1969-73. Fellow Coll. Am. Pathologists, N.Y. Acad. Medicine; mem. AAAS. Home: PO Box 1292 3775 Skunk Ln Cutchogue NY 11935-1541 Office: SUNY Sch Medicine Office Of Dean Stony Brook NY 11794-0001

COUCHEPIN, PASCAL, Swiss government official; b. Apr. 5, 1942; married; 3 children. Grad. in law, U. Lausanne. Lawyer; exec. state coun. Martigny, 1968, v.p., 1976, pres., 1984; fed. councillor, min. fgn. affairs Govt. of Switzerland, Berne, 1998—. Radical-Democrat. Office: Fed Dept Econ Affairs, Bundeshaus Ost, CH 3003 Berne Switzerland

COUCOUZIS, DEMETRIOS A. See IAKOVOS

COUDERT, DALE HOKIN, real estate executive, marketing consultant; b. Chgo., Nov. 29, 1941; d. Sidney and Ruth (Brower) Manowitz; m. Frederic R. Coudert (div.); children Dana, Alexandra. BA, Northwester U., 1964. V.p. Cross & Brown, N.Y.C., 1975-86; dir., sec. First Women's Bank, N.Y.C., 1980-87; head bus. devel., office of pres. 1st N.Y. Bank for Bus., 1988-91; mktg. dir. Lafer Mgmt., N.Y.C., 1993-94; pres., CEO Coudert Assocs. Ltd., N.Y.C., 1991—; broker Brown Harris Stevens Palm Beach Real Estate, Pal, 1999—; dir. Hosp. Tak Co., Long Island, N.Y., 1979-98. Pub., editor: (book) Business and Pleasure, 1986-87. Bd. dirs. Women's Rep. Club, N.Y.C., 1994, N.Y. Drama League, N.Y.C., 1975—; mem. nat. bd. dirs. Aspen Art Mus., Kennedy Ctr., 1996-98; trustee, treas. Zoo of the Palm Beaches at Dreker Park, 1996-98, bd. dirs., 1996—; regent St. John the Divine, N.Y.C., 1988. Fellow Aspen Inst. (life); mem. Internat. Womens Forum, Met. Opera Club, Women's Forum Fla. Avocations: piano, voice, dance, golf, tennis. Home: 485 Park Ave New York NY 10022-1228 also: 163 Seminole Ave Palm Beach FL 33480-3732 Office: Coudert Assn Ltd 485 Park Ave Ste 7A New York NY 10022-1228 also: Brown Harris Stevens Palm Beach Real Estate Ste 329 340 Royal Poinciana Plz Palm Beach FL 33480-4048

COUFAL, JAN, mathematician; b. Havl. Brod, Bohemia, Czech Republic, May 14, 1949; s. Josef and Hana (Ullmannova) C.; m. Eva Chalupska, Feb. 7, 1974; children: Petra, Ctibor, Ctirad. Mgr., Charles U., Prague, 1972, RNDr, 1981; PhD, U. Econs., Prague, 1991. Asst. U. Econs., Prague, 1971-75, prof.-asst., 1975-92, assoc. prof., 1992—; vice chief dept. math. U. Econs., 1990—. Author: Matematika-Efektivní vyčíslitelnost, 1989 (Rector's prize 1990); (with J. Klufa) Matematika I (Pro VŠE), 1994 (Rector's prize 1995), Matematicke struktury, 1995 (Rector's prize 1996), Učebnice matematiky I, 1996 (Rector's prize 1996), Matematika pro ekonomy, 1997 (U. Econ. prize 1998), Matematika pro Ekonomické Fakulty, 2000; author articles on complexity, history of math., stats. and computer sci. Mem. Am. Math. Soc., European Math. Soc., Union Czech Mathematicians and Physicists. Avocations: computer science, history. Office: U of Econs, Ekonomicka 957, 148 00 Prague Czech Republic

COUFOUDAKIS, VAN, political science educator; b. Athens, Greece, May 27, 1938; came to U.S., 1955.; s. Fotios and Helen (Voutopoulos)C.; m. Marion Mason, Dec. 26, 1964; 1 child, Helen. BA in Pub. Adminstrn., Am. U. of Beirut, 1962; MPA, U. Mich., 1964, PhD in Polit. Sci., 1972. Prof. Polit. Sci. Ind. U./Purdue U., Ft. Wayne, 1967—, interim dean Sch. Bus., 1983-94, interim dean Sch. Edn., 1994-95, dean Sch. Arts & Scis., 1996—; assoc. vice chancellor for acad. affairs, Ind. U./Purdue U. Ft. Wayne, 1986-96. Editor: (book) Greece and the New Balkans, 1999; contbr. articles to profl. jours. Chair Found. for Hellenic Studies, Washington, 1995—, AHEPA Ednl. Found., Washington, 1999—. Recipient Comdr. of Order of Phoenix pres. of the Greek Republic, 1998; hon. consul Republic of Cyprus Govt. Republic of Cyprus, 1985—. Mem. Modern Greek Studies Assn. (pres. 1995-99), Internat. Studies Assn. Greek Orthodox. Avocations: classical music, stamp collecting. E-mail: coufouda@ipfw.edu. Home: 2402 Oakridge Rd Fort Wayne IN 46805-3215 Office: Ind U Purdue U Sch Arts & Scis 2101 E Coliseum Blvd Fort Wayne IN 46805-1445

COUGHLAN, JAMES ERIC, sociology educator; b. Creswick, Victoria, Australia, Oct. 23, 1955; s. Eric and Sylvia Ida (Moralee) C.; div. BS in Maths. and Physics, Australian Nat. U., 1975, BA in Sociology, 1978; PhD in Asian and internat. studies, Griffith U. Postgrad. scholar Griffith U., 1990-93. Rsch. officer population census and demography br. Australian Bur. Statistics, Canberra, 1980-87; rsch. cons. Ctr. Study Australia-Asia Rels. Griffith U., Nathan, Queensland, Australia, 1987-89; rsch. assoc. Ctr. Study Australia-Asia Rels. Griffith U., Nathan, 1990-93; lectr. B in sociology Sch. Psychology and Sociology, Faculty Social Scis. James Cook U., Townsville, Queensland, 1993-98; sr. lectr. C in sociology James Cook U., Townsville, 1999—; vis. prof. Inst. Population and Social Rsch. Mahidol U., Salaya, Thailand, 1996-97; casual lectr. in Asian studies Faculty Arts Australian Cath. U., Brisbane, Queensland, 1993; vis. researcher Ctr. Asian and Pacific Studies Seikei U., Tokyo, 1992; cons. Bur. Immigration Rsch., 1990-92, Ethnic Cmties. Coun. Queensland, 1994; presenter in field. Co-author: Asians in Australia: Patterns of Migration and Settlement, 1997, The Diverse Asians: A Profile of Six Asian Communities in Australia, 1992; contbr. numerous articles to profl. jours., chpts. to books. Grantee numerous orgns., 1989-97. Fellow Internat. Ctr. Asian Studies; mem. Australian Inst. Internat. Affairs, Australian Pop. Assn., Nat. Assn. Edn. and Advancement of Cambodia, Laotian and Vietnamese Ams., Asian Studies Assn. Australia, Asian Am. Studies Assn., Chinese Studies Assn. Australia, European Assn. S.E. Asian Studies, Internat. Sociol. Assn., Japanese Studies Assn. Australia, Philippine Studies Assn. Australia, Refugee Rsch. Network Oxford U., Siam Soc., Vietnam Studies Assn. Australia. Avocations: gardening, swimming, travel, music. Office: James Cook U, Dept Sociology, Townsville 4811 Queensland, Australia

COUGHLIN, WILLIAM JAMES RAYMOND, administrative associate; b. L.I., N.Y., July 8, 1937; s. William James and Anna Miriam Coughlin. Student, St. Joseph's Coll., 1944-51, De La Salle Inst., 1951-55, St. John's U., 1956-60. With Western Union, N.Y.C., 1955-59, Interchem. Corp., N.Y.C., 1959-62; city register/fin. City of N.Y., 1959—; ret., 1999. Mem. Ancient Order of Hibernians, Collectors of Religion on Stamps, Varican Philatelic Soc., Eire Philatelic Assn., Am. Philatelic Soc., Emerald Soc. Republican. Roman Catholic. Avocations: postage stamps, geneology,

photography, autographs, travel. Home: 200 W Historic St Pittsfield MA 01201-6041

COUGHTREY, PETER JOHN, environmental consultant; b. Berkhamsted, Eng., Sept. 1, 1953; s. William Cecil John and Phyllis (Hobson) C.; m. Kathleen Joy Rixon, May 25, 1980; children: Anna Elizabeth, Louisa Jane. BSc in Botany and Zoology with honors, U. Bristol, Eng., 1975, PhD in Environ. Chemistry, 1978. Chartered biologist. Postdoctoral rsch. asst. U. Bristol, 1978-80; cons. Assoc. Nuclear Svcs. Ltd., Epsom, Eng., 1980-82; mgr. biol. scis. ANS Cons. Ltd., Epsom, 1982-91; chief scientist, biol. scis. W.S. Atkins Group, Epsom, 1991-93; prin. scientist Mouchel Cons., West Byfleet, Eng., 1993-94; divsional dir. environ. consultancy Mouchel Cons., West Byfleet, 1994—; mgr. environ. consultancy L.G. Mouchel & Ptnrs. Ltd., West Byfleet, 1996—; cons. U.K. Ministry Agr. Fisheries and Food, 1980—, Her Majesty's Inspectorate of Pollution, 1980—, Commn. of the European Cmtys., 1980—; exec. dir. Mouchel-IRE Ltd., Russia, Ukraine, Belarus, Uzbekistan, 1980—; gen. sec. Internat. Union Radioecologists, 1994-98. Co-author textbooks on contaminants in the environment; editor textbooks and symposium procs.; contbr. some 60 articles to profl. jours. Named Brit. Cons. Bur. Individual Cons. of Yr., 1996. Fellow Internat. Union of Radioecologists; mem. The Inst. of Biology, Brit. Ecol. Soc., Soc. Radiol. Protection. Avocations: gardening, stamp collecting, do-it-yourself. Home: West View, Stonards Brow Shamley Green, Surrey Guildford GU5 0UX, England Office: Mouchel Consulting Ltd, Parvis Rd West Hall, West Byfleet Surrey KT14 6EZ, England

COUIG, MARY PATRICIA, federal agency administrator; b. Evanston, Ill.; d. J. Dalton Jr. and Patricia Mae Couig; m. Merton Vincent Smith II, May 26, 1991; children: M. Vincent, Madeline Mae. AS, Berkshire C.C., 1977; BSN, Fitchburg State Coll., 1979; MPH, Johns Hopkins U., 1986. RN, Mass. Clin. nurse emergency/outpatient dept. Phoenix Indian Med. Ctr., Indian Health Svc., 1981-84, quality assurance/infection control specialist, 1984-85; pub. health educator Wis. Dept. Health and Social Svcs., Madison, 1986; investigator FDA, Boston, 1986-88; assoc. dir. nursing affairs office health affairs FDA, Rockville, Md., 1989-98; dir. edn. and outreach MedWatch FDA, Rockville, 1999—; spl. asst. to chief nurse officer USPHS, Rockville, 1992-96; mem. RN stds. of practice com. Md. Bd. Nursing, Balt., 1997-99. Contbr. articles to profl. jours. Fellow Am. Acad. Nursing; mem. ANA (Nurses in Congress and Exec. Br. 1998), Md. Nurses Assn. (mem. HIV/AIDS task force 1993), Commd. Officers Assn. (pres. 1998-99), Sigma Theta Tau. Avocations: hiking, antiques. Fax: (301) 827-7241. E-mail: mcouig@oc.fda.gov. Office: FDA HF-2 5600 Fishers Ln Rockville MD 20857-0001

COUKIS, PETER GEORGE, musician, composer; b. Waterbury, Conn., Jan. 15, 1955; s. George Peter and Antoinette (Kachulis) C.; m. Lucrecia Monje, Aug. 20, 1998. BA, Western Conn. State U., 1978; AS, Mattatuck C.C., Waterbury, 1987. Musical arranger, composer Waterbury Children's Found., 1977-78; arranger, songwriter Youth Theatre Ensemble, Watertown, Conn., 1985-87; producer, performer Laurel Cablevision, Litchfield, Conn., 1988-91; solo recording artist Waterbury, Wallingford, Conn., 1990—; founder Blue Plum Records, 1993—. Composer, keyboardist The Nutmeg Ballet, Torrington, Conn., 1988; songwriter World Star Prodns., New Haven, 1988; keyboardist South Mich. Ave, Wolcott, Conn., 1980-86; synthesizer player Angels and Co. (Nunsense), N.Y.C. and Waterbury, 1989; artist, prodr. cable In Performance, 1988, Repertoire, 1989 (Laurel award 1989), Kaleidoscope, 1991, 13-week cable series, 1991, cable spl., 1992; released cassette single Girl, 1992; rec. artist Stick Bride, 1994, Strange Beauty, 1995, Believe in Me, 1995, Midgetmajority, 1997, Tournament, 1997, Stephania in Orange, 1997, Blossoms of Beauty, 1999. Talk show guest Barbara Davitt's Coffee Break, Sta. WATR, Waterbury, 1990; feature guest Lifestyles with Dr. Kotler, Sta. WCAT-13, Waterbury, 1990. Mem. Conn. Songwriters Assn. (Three-year award 1985, Five-year award 1987), Nat. Acad. Recording Arts & Scis. (N.Y. chpt.). Democrat. Avocations: reading, traveling, outdoors, environmental awareness.

COUKOS, STEPHEN JOHN, lawyer; b. Boston, July 23, 1959; s. John Stephen and Agnes (Liakos) C.; m. Jody Isselbacher, June 23, 1985; children: Jennifer Ashley, Andrew Jay; m. Marie J. Buttarazzi, Sept. 17, 1994; children: Allison Marie, John Stephen. AB, Trinity Coll., Hartford, Conn., 1981; postgrad., Harvard U., 1985-86; JD, Stanford U., 1986. Assoc. Sullivan & Worcester, Boston, 1986-88; assoc. Bingham, Dana & Gould, Boston, 1988-94, ptnr., 1994-95; ptnr. Sullivan & Worcester, Boston, 1995-2000, Edwards & Angell, Boston, 2000—. Mem. ABA (banking law com., subcom. bank holding co. activities; bank and bank holding company acquisitions and dispositions), Mass. Bar Assn. (banking law com.), Boston Bar Assn. (banking law com.). Avocations: sports, physical fitness. Home: 819 Watertown St Newton MA 02465-2127 Office: Edwards & Angell 1 Post Office Sq Ste 2300 Boston MA 02109-2129

COULIC, VERY, emergency physician, researcher; b. Monceau, Hainaut, Belgium, Sept. 10, 1936; s. Paul Coulic and Gilberte Aurore Crevieaux; m. Yvette Germaine Messe, May 16, 1997. Grad., First Inst. Medicine, Moscow, 1960, sci. candidate for surgery, 1963; DSc in Surgery, People's Friendship U., Moscow, 1971. Med. diplomate. Sr. technician First Med. Inst., Moscow, 1959-61; jr. rschr. Transplantation Lab., Moscow, 1961-63; asst. in surgery and anatomy People's Friendship U., Moscow, 1963-71, docent, lectr. in anatomy, 1971-75, prof. in charge, 1975-84, sr. rschr., chief sci. group in exptl. clin. surgery, 1984-92; rschr. Jumet Civilian Hosp., 1992-97; emergency supernumerary physician, rschr. Brugman Hosp., Brussels, 1994—. Author: Function and Morphology of Intestinal Graft, 1974, Transplantation of Digestive Organs, 1986, Digestive Glands, 1987; patentee in field. Mem. Belgian Soc. for Gastroenterology (corr.), European Soc. for Analytical Cellular Pathology, Belgian Soc. for Internal Medicine. Avocation: music (classical and folk). Office: Brugman Hosp, 4 Place van Gehuchten, 1020 Brussels Belgium

COULIER, PATRICK, television executive; b. Nieuwpoort, Belgium, Aug. 28, 1958; s. Armand and Godelieve (Lefevere) C. Lic. agogiek, Vyre U., Brussels, 1982. Lector asst. Vyre U., Brussels, 1983-84; asst. gen. mgr. Inbelco, Poperinge, Belgium, 1983-85; gen. mgr. Media and Communication Svcs., Brugge, Belgium, 1985—; asst. prof. Belgian Radio and TV, Brussels, 1990. Mem. Oudstudentendkond VOB, West Aviation Club, Yacht Club Luchtmacht. Avocations: sailing, flying. Home: Grote Thems 116, 8490 Varsenare Belgium

COULSON, ALAN JAMES, electronics engineer, communications researcher; b. Christchurch, New Zealand, Nov. 20, 1962; s. Eric Thomas and Norma Beryl (Fee) C.; m. Carole Ann Michie, Mar. 26, 1988; 1 child, Patrick Fergus Michie. B in Elec. Engring., U. Canterbury, New Zealand, 1985; PhD in Elec. Engring., U. Auckland, New Zealand, 1999. Asst. engr. Civil Aviation, Wellington, New Zealand, 1985-87; systems engr. Airways Corp., Wellington, 1987-88; design engr. Solid State Logic Ltd., Oxford, Eng., 1988-90; rsch. engr. Indsl. Rsch. Ltd., Lower Hutt, New Zealand, 1991—. Contbr. articles to profl. jours. Mem. IEEE, Internat. Union of Radio Sci. (corr.). Office: Indsl Rsch Ltd, PO Box 31-310, Lower Hutt New Zealand

COULTER, JOHN RICHARD, retired senator; b. Perth, Australia, Dec. 3, 1930; s. John W.S. and Constance Amelia (Braddock) C.; m. Phyllis Ford Johnstone, Dec. 15, 1984. MBBS, U. Adelaide, 1956. Med. resident Royal Adelaide Hosp., 1956; gen. med. practice Adelaide, 1957-58; rsch. officer Inst. Med. and Vet. Sci., Adelaide, 1959-65, rsch. pathologist, 1966-80; univ. lectr. U. Adelaide, 1981-86; senator Fed. Parliament, Australia, 1987-95; ret. Fed. Parliament, 1995; leader Australian Dems., 1991-93; chmn. senate standing com. on environment, 1994-95, senate select com. on loan coun., 1992-93. Contbr. articles to profl. jours. Pres. Conservation Coun. of South Australia, Adelaide, 1983-84; v.p. Australian Conservation Found., Melbourne, 1977-81. Mem. Australian, New Zealand Environ. Mutagen Soc., Australian Conservation Found. Avocations: sailing, bushwalking, music. Home: Box 29, Longwood 5153 SA, Australia

COULTHARD, DAVID, race car driver; b. Twynholm, Scotland, Mar. 27, 1971. Profl. race car driver McLaren Mercedes-Benz Team, 1989—. 3-time Scottish karting champion, 1982-88, 2-time winner Scottish Open Championship, Brit. Super 1 Jr. Championship, Sr. Scottish Open Championship; 1st pl. Jr. FF1600 Championships, 1989, 3d pl. Brands Hatch Formula Ford Festival, 1989, runner-up Brit. F3 Championship, 1991, winner European Marlboro Masters of F3, Macau Grand Prix, 1991, 3d pl. F3000 Championship, 1993, GT Class winner Le Mans 24 Hour Race, 1993, 1st pl. Grand Prix Portugal, 1995, 3d pl. Drivers Championship, 1995, 2d pl. F1, Monaco, 1996, 3d pl., Europe, 1996, 1st pl. Australia and Italy, 1997, 2d pl. Austria and Europe, 1997, 3d pl. Drivers' World Championship, 1997; recipient Young Driver of Yr. award McLaren Autosport, 1990; named Scottish Sports Personality of Yr., 1994, ITV Young Sports Personality of Yr., 1994. Office: McLaren Internat Ltd, Albert Dr Woking Unit 22, Wokings Surrey GU21 5JY, England*

COUNCILMAN, RICHARD ROBERT, product development engineer; b. L.A., Apr. 25, 1922; s. Frank Dwight and Gladys Vera (Clark) C.; m. Louise Perry Spalding (div.); children: Richard Martin, Robert Gordon; m. Barbara McCollough (div.); 1 child, Scott Richard; m. Shirley Ann DeVries, Apr. 25, 1964; 1 child, Marc Wayne. Chief draftsman USN, Pasadena & China Lake, Calif., 1944-49; engring. supr. USAF, Edwards AFB, Calif., 1949-51; sr. design specialist Bill Jack Sci. Inst., Solana Beach, Calif., 1951-52; head optical mech. rsch. Hughes Aircraft Flight Test, Culver City, Calif., 1952-56; group supr. R & D LTV Elecs., Garland, Tex., 1956-64; sr. engring. specialist R & D Conductron Divsn. McDonald Douglas, St. Louis, 1965-70; sr. project engr. Sr. Scientist Lab. Brunswick Corp., St. Louis, 1968-75; dir., chmn. bd. Imperial Gen. Life Ins. Co., St. Louis, 1970-75; sr. project R & D Brunswick Corp., Tulsa, 1975-87; cons. product devel. pvt. practice, Collinsville, Okla., 1987—; cons. in field. Fellow Internat. Soc. Optical Engring., Soc. Photo-Optical Instrumentation Engrs. (pres. 1955-56). Achievements include patentee in field. Home: 17001 N 137th East Ave Collinsville OK 74021-4415

COUPER, ALASTAIR DOUGAL, geography educator; b. Aberdeen, Scotland, June 4, 1931; s. Daniel Alexander and Devina (Rilley) C.; m. Norma Milton, Aug. 30, 1958; children: Callum, Rona, Katrina, Roderick. MA, U. Aberdeen, 1962; PhD, Australian Nat. U., Canberra, 1967; DSc (hon.), U. Plymouth, Eng., 1995. Rsch. scholar Australian Nat. U., Canberra, 1963-66; lectr. U. Durham, Eng., 1967-70; prof. U. Wales, Cardiff, 1970-98, dean applied scis., 1972-77, prof. emeritus, 1999—; dir. Seafarers Internat. Rsch. Ctr., Eng., 1997-99; cons. UN, Geneva, London, 1971-90; prof. World Maritime U. (UN), Malmo, Sweden, 1986-88. Editor: Times Atlas of the Oceans, 1983 (U.S. Dartford medal 1983), The Shipping Revolution, 1992: author: New Cargo Handling and Employment, 1986, Voyages of Abuse, 1999; editor Internat. JNL, Maritime Policy and Mgmt., 1973-83. Trustee Nat. Maritime Mus. London, 1983-2000; mem. Brit. Commn. Maritime History, London, 1998—; advisor Greenwich Maritime Inst., London, 1999—. Fellow Nautical Inst., Italian Geographic Soc. Avocations: hill walking, organic gardening, books, theatre. Home: 112 Ely Rd, Cardiff CF5 2DA, Wales

COUPER, IAN DOUGLAS, family physician, medical educator; b. Port Elizabeth, Ea. Cape, South Africa, Aug. 25, 1961; s. John Laurence and Patricia (Cuthbert) C.; m. Jacqueline Du Berrand, Dec. 14, 1985; children: Timothy David, Michael John. BA, U. Witwatersrand, Johannesburg, South Africa, 1983, MB, BCh, 1987; M in Family Medicine, Med. U. South Africa, Pretoria, 1995. Cert. family physician South Africa. Intern Livingstone Hosp., Port Elizabeth, South Africa, 1988; med. officer Dora Nginza Hosp., Port Elizabeth, 1989; vol. Anglican Ch. Paraguay, Asuncion, 1989-90; med. officer Manguzi (South Africa) Hosp., 1991-93, med. supt., 1993-99; sr. family practitioner Odi Dist., sr. lectr. Northwest Province/Family Medicine Dept./Med. U. So. Africa, 2000—; adj. sr. lectr. Med. U. of Southern Africa, 1996-99; vis. sr. lectr. Monash U. Ctr. for Rural Health, Victoria, Australia, 1998. Author Poetry South Africa Jour. of Family Practice, 1994-97; contbr. articles and editorials to profl. jours. Treas. Manguzi Comty. Program, Kwangwanase, 1992-97. Conscientious objector 1991-93. Mem. South African Med. Assn., South Africa Acad. Family Practice and Primary Care, Rural Doctors' Assn. Southern Africa (chmn.). Episcopalian. Avocations: reading, fiction, nature, candle making. E-mail: couper@lantic.net. Office: PO Box 222, Medunsa 0206, South Africa

COUPLAN, FRANÇOIS JEAN-MARIE, ethnobotanist, writer; b. Paris, Jan. 5, 1950; arrived in Switzerland, 1995; s. Henri and Marie-Louise Henriette (Garban) C.; m. Françoise Renée Marmy; children: Sylvain, Melissa. PhD, Mus. Nat. History Naturelle, Paris, 1996. Tchr., 1975—, journalist, 1981—, writer, 1983—; food cons. Marc Veyrat, Annecy, France, 1996—, Jean-Georges Vongerichten, N.Y., 1996—; cons. in field; tchr. courses on edible uses of plants, 1975—. Author: Mangez vos soucis-Guide des Plantes Ornamentales Comestibles, 1983, reedition, 1999, Encyclopédie des Plantes Comestibles de l'Europe, 1984, Vol. 1-3, 1990, Plantes Sauvages Comestibles, 1985, Retrouvez les Légumes Oubliés, 1986, Vivre en Pleine Nature-le guide de la Survie Douce, 1987, Les Plantes Sauvages Comestibles-Promenades Gastronomiques, 1992, L'Herbier de la Gruyère, 1994, Jardiner au naturel, 1995, Herbier Gourmand, 1997, Essbare Wildpflanzen, 1997, Encyclopedia of the Edible Plants of North America, 1998—, Guide Nutritionnel des Plantes Sauvages et du Jardin, 1998; columnist FLD, Terre Sauvage, Nature & Progrès, Plantes et Santé, Le Chef, La Liberté, La Salamandre, Vie et Santé, Terre et Nature, Wild Food Forum; contbr. articles to profl. jours., mags. Mem. Assn. Journalists Spécialisés, Journalistes écrivains Nature l'Ecologie. Avocations: nature, music. Home: CH 1692 Massonnens Switzerland

COUPLES, FREDERICK STEVEN, professional golfer; b. Seattle, Oct. 3, 1959; m. Thais; 2 children: Gigi, Oliver. Student, U. Houston. mem. U.S. Ryder Cup golf team, 1989, 91, 93, 95, 97; mem. nat. teams USA vs. Japan, 1984, Asahi Glass Four Tours World Championship of Golf, 1990, 91, Dunhill Cup, 1991, 92, 93, 94, World Cup, 1992, 93, 94, 95, Pres.'s Cup, 1994, 96, 98. Named All-Am., 1978, 79; winner numerous golf tournaments including Kemper Open, 1983, Tournament Players Championship, 1984, Byron Nelson Golf Classic, 1987, French PGA, 1988, Nissan L.A. Open, 1990, 92, Tournoi Perrier de Paris, 1991, B.C. Open, 1991, Federal Express St. Jude Classic, 1991, Johnnie Walker World Championship, 1991, Nestle Invitational, 1992, The Masters, 1992, (with Jan Stephenson) J.C. Penney Classic, 1983, (with Mike Donald) Sazale Classic, 1990, (with Raymond Floyd) RMCC Invitational, 1990, Buick Open, 1994, World Cup, 1994, Dubai Desert Classic, 1995, Johnnie Walker Classic, 1995, The Player's Championship, 1996, Bob Hope chrysler Classic, 1998, Memorial Tournament, 1998; recipient Vardon trophy, 1991, 92; named PGA Player of Yr. Golf World Mag., 1991, 92, Golf Writers Assn., 1991, 92, PGA Tour Player of Yr, 1993, 94. Achievements include being the leading money winner PGA, 1992. Address: c/o PGA Tour 100 Ave of The Champions PO Box 109601 Palm Bch Gdns FL 33410-9601

COUQUE, HERVÉ RAOUL ANDRÉ, mechanical engineer, researcher; b. Chantilly, Oise, France, Sept. 1, 1956; s. Raymond Georges Jules and Denise Germaine Madeleine (Lemonnier) C. Diploma in tech., Amiens (France) U., 1977; French cert. engr. degree, Nantes (France) U., 1980; MSc, Brown U., 1984, PhD, 1987; MDR, Metz U., France, 1998. Postdoctoral S.W. Rsch. Inst., San Antonio, Tex., 1987-88, rsch. engr., 1988-89, sr. rsch. engr., 1989-94, cons., 1994-95; dynamic behavior of materials specialist Groupement Industriel d'Armement Terrestres Industries, Bourges, France, 1995—. Contbr. articles to sci. jours. and conf. publs., including Metall. Trans. A, Jour. Materials Sci., ASTM Spl. Tech. Pub., Metal Powder Report, Jour. Physics III, Internat. Jour. Powde Metallurgy, Engring. Fracture Mechanics, Jour. Materials Sci. Letters, Internat. Jour. Impact Engring. Mem. ASME, Am. Soc. for Metals, Soc. Automotive Engrs., Metallurgy Powder Industries Fedn. (organizing com. 1997 Internat. Conf. on Tungsten and Refractory Metals and Alloys 1996—), Dynamic Behaviour Materials European Assn. (bd. dirs. 1996—, mem. 1997 internat. conf. organizing com. 1996—). E-mail: h.couque@wanadoo.fr. Home: 3 Rue Mably, 18000 Bourges France Office: GIAT Industries, 7 Route de Guerry, 18005 Bourges France

COURBIS, RAYMOND PAUL, economist; b. Algiers, Algeria, Dec. 22, 1937; s. Jean Paul Courbis and Hélène Jacqueline de Bridiers de Villemor; m. Michèle Françoise Dussy, Nov. 8, 1963; 1 child, J. Paul. Grad. in engring., Sch. Mines Paris, 1961; PhD in Econs., U. Paris, 1971, Agrégé, 1971; D honoris causa, Tech. U. Lisbon, Portugal, 1991. Rsch. fellow French Ministry Fin., Paris, 1964-71; assoc. prof. U. Tours, France, 1972-73; assoc. prof. econs. U. Paris X, Nanterre, 1974-77, prof., 1977—, dir. Group for Applied Macroecon. Analysis, 1972—; assoc. prof. Ecole Poly., Paris, 1972-83; econ. adviser Nat. Sch. Adminstrn., Paris, 1972-82; sci. advisor Nat. Inst. Stats. and Econs., Paris, 1972-75. Author: Competitiveness and Growth in a Competitioned Economy, 1975; co-author: The Fifi Model, 1973 and 1975, The Method of Surplus Accounts, 1975, The MOGLI Model, 1980, also others; contbr. articles to sci. jours. and revs. Lt. arty. French Army, 1962-64. Decorated knight Legion of Honor, Nat. Order of Merit (France), Order of St. John (Baillage of Brandeburg). Mem. French Assn. Economists, European Econ. Assn., Internat. Regional Sci. Assn., Internat. Inst. Pub. Fin., Internat. I-O Assn., Internat. Assn. Rsch. in Income and Wealth, Soc. of Cincinnati. Office: U Paris X GAMA, 200 Ave de la République, 92001 Nanterre France

COURCIER, JEROME CLAUDE, banker; b. Fontenay-Le-Comte, France, June 28, 1960; s. Philippe and Jacqueline (Monnier) C.; m. Catherine Dilhac, Sept. 12, 1987; children: Tanguy, Romain, Ariane. Student, Inst. D'Etudes Polit., Paris, 1982. Acct. mgr. Credit Lyonnais, Paris, 1984-88, project mgr., 1989, br. group mgr., 1990-92; 1st v.p., ea. region mgr. Credit Lyonnais, Can., 1992-95; corp. & instl. mktg. mgr. Credit Lyonnais, Paris, 1995-97, head internat. financing, 1997—. With French Mil., 1983. Avocations: jogging, skiing, golf, hockey, soccer. Office: Credit LyonnaiseFin Divsn, 1 Rue Des Italiens, 75009 Paris France

COURDI, ADEL, radiotherapist; b. Cairo, Egypt, Sept. 11, 1947; arrived in France, 1976; s. Dimitri and Nadia (Jabbour) C.; m. Jociane Baracat, July 11, 1976; children: Stephane, Celine. MB, BChir, Cairo (Egypt) U., 1970, diploma in radiotherapy, 1974; diploma in rsch. in human biology, Paris, 1980. Resident Cairo Cancer Inst., 1971-74, asst. lectr., 1974-76; radiobiology researcher Gustave-Roussy Inst., Villejuif, France, 1976-80; asst. Ctr. Antoine-Lacassagne, Nice, France, 1980-87, specialist, 1987—, chief radiobiology unit, 1990—; tchr. in field, 1979—. Contbr. articles to profl. jours. Mem. European Soc. Radiation Biology, European Soc. Therapeutic Radiology and Oncology. Roman Catholic. Avocations: classic music, backgammon. Home: Borgheas, 06440 Peillon France Office: Ctr Antoine Lacassagne, 33 Ave Valombrose, 06189 Nice France

COURET, KEIRON LEIGH, performing arts presenter; b. New Orleans, June 29, 1970; d. William Earl Couret Jr. and JeanMarie Boudreaux. BA in Mgmt., Southeastern LA U., 1993, MBA, 1994. Grad. asst. Southeastern La. U., Hammond, 1993-94; asst. dir. Fanfare, Southeastern La. U., Hammond, La., 1996—; asst. mgr. Internat. Mktg. Sys., Metairie, La., 1995; asst. dir. Fanfare, Southeastern La. U., Hammond, La., 1996—; adminstrv. asst. Shared Med. Sys., Metairie, La., 1995-96; bd. dirs. Hammond Reginal Arts Ctr. Active Hammond Rep. Women, 1997-99, Hammond C. of C., 1996—. Mem. Am. Bus. Women's Assn. (woman of yr. award 1999), Nat. Assn. Female Execs., Assn. Performing Arts Presenters, Assn. Am. Univ. Women. Republican. Avocations: attending cultural events, cooking. E-mail: kcouret@selu.edu. Office: Fanfare Southeastern LA Univ Slu 10797 500 Western Ave Hammond LA 70402-0001

COURGEAU, DANIEL GUSTAVE, engineer; b. Antananarivo, Democratic Madagascar, Jan. 12, 1937; arrived in France, 1948; s. Daniel and Marie-Marcelline (Ravaomalala) C.; m. Hella Constant, Dec. 11, 1964; children: Christophe, Cyril. Engr., Paris Poly., 1956; D of Demography, Inst. Demography, Paris, 1969. Engr. Seita, Paris, 1959-66; sr. researcher Ined, Paris, 1966—; prof. Inst. Study Demographics, Paris, 1969—. Author: Les Champs Migratoires en France, 1970, Analyse Quantitative des Migrations Humaines, 1980, Three Centuries of Spatial Mobility in France, 1982, Méthodes de mesure de la mobilité spatiale, 1988, Analyse démographique des biographies, 1989, Event History Analysis in Demography, 1992, multilevel analysis in the social sciences, 1998; editor European Jour. of Population. Served as lt. Algerian Army, 1958-59. Mem. Internat. Union for Sci. Study Population, European Assn. for Population Studies. Avocation: drawing. Office: Nat Inst Study Demographics, 133 Bd Davout, 75 980 Paris France

COURNIER, MICHEL LOUIS, chemical engineer; b. Tarare, France, Nov. 7, 1947; s. Rene and Celine Elise (Martin) C.; m. Nicole Gabrielle Avignon Cournier, June 1, 1974; children: Bruno, Isabelle. Degree in Chem. Engring., Ecole Nat. Superieure, Nancy, France, 1971; degree in Ins., Ctr. of Study of Ins., Paris, 1987. Engr. Ctr. of Industry Rsch., Lubumbashi, Zaire, 1971-73, Rhone Progil, Aubervilliers, France, 1973-74, Schlumberger, Delft, The Netherlands, 1974; loss prevention engr. Factory Mutual Engring., Cleve., 1975; ins. underwriter Factory Mutual Internat., Paris, 1976-86; risk mgr. Alcatel, Paris, 1986—; co-chmn. Risk Mgmt. Forum, Monte Carlo, Monaco, 1995. Winner European Most Innovative Risk Financing Program award Internat. Risk Mgmt. Mag., 1997. Mem. AMRAE (v.p. 1995-98). Avocations: tennis, skiing, nature walking, economics reading. Home: 12 Ave Auguste Renoir, 78160 Marly Le Roi France Office: Alcatel, 30 Ave Kleber, 75116 Paris France

COURSHON, CAROL BIEL, civic worker; b. Cleve., Sept. 5, 1923; d. Maurice and Rita (Glueck) Biel; student Wesleyan Coll., Macon, Ga., 1941-42; m. Arthur Howard Courshon, Feb. 20, 1943;children: Barbara, Deanne. Chmn. hotel-motel divsn. Mothers March Dimes, 1948-53;co-chmn. bus. divsn. Greater Miami Heart Fund campaign, 1977-78; bd. dirs. Children's Svc. Bur. of Dade County, 1960-70, Family Svc. Assn. Am., 1977-84, United Family and Children's Svc. (now Family Counseling Svcs.), Dade County, 1970-96; mem. adv. com. U. Miami-Jackson Meml. Children's Hosp. Ctr., 1983-93; vol. tchrs. aide handicapped Dade County (Fla.) pub. schs., 1956-81; del. Dem. Nat. Conv., 1968; mem., chmn. adv. bd. Washington Savs. and Loan Miami Beach., 1979-82; mem. adv. bd. Jefferson Nat. Bank, Miami Beach, 1981-96; trustee Fla. House, 1978-96. Mem. Nat. Savs. and Loan League (exec. women's group 1979-83), Nat. Coun. Jewish Women (v.p. Bay div. 1953-55), Hadassah. Office: 100 SE 2nd St Ste 2800 Miami FL 33131-2124

COURSON, MARNA B.P., public relations executive; b. Waynesboro, Pa., Feb. 22, 1951; d. Eugene Perry and Charlotte Mae (Sherman) Roschli; m. Sydney E. Courson, May 24, 1982; 1 child, Sydney Alexandra. BA, Franklin and Marshall Coll., 1973; postgrad., U. Kans., Kansas City. Reporter Beach Haven Times/The Beacon, Manahawkin, N.J., 1973-74, Dailey Observer Newspaper, Toms River, N.J., 1974-76; comm. mgr. Frick India Ltd., New Delhi, 1976-77; reporter, dictationist UPI, Washington, 1978-80; reporter UPI, Richmond, Va.; reporter, editor AP, Balt., 1980-84; comm. coord. St. Luke's Hosp. Found., Kansas City, Mo., 1986-88; exec. v.p. pub. rels. Spaw and Assocs., Inc., Overland Park, Kans., 1988-89; exec. v.p. CCI Pub. Rels. & Mktg. Comm., Inc., Shawnee Mission, Kans., 1990-92; pres. CCI Pub. Rels. & Mktg. Comm., Inc., Kansas City, Mo., 1992—. Mem. Children's Mus., Vol. Leadership Coun.; vol. bd. dirs. Ctr. for Mgmt. Assistance; bd. dirs., exec. com. Silicon Prairie Tech. Assn.; exec. com. Mid Am. Youth Aviation Assn. Recipient Prism award for fund raising, numerous awards and honors for reporting, 1973-80; also pub. rels. awards, 1988-99. Mem. Internat. Assn. Bus. Communicators, Pub. Rels. Soc. of Am. (Pres.'s award with GKC), Nat. Assn. Women Bus. Owners, Nat. Soc. Fund Raising Execs., Kansas City C. of C., Mid Am. Youth Aviation Assn. (exec. com.). Office: Kansas City Downtown Airport 250 NW Richards Rd Ste 269 Kansas City MO 64116-4275

COURTAUD, BERNARD JEAN-JACQUES, human resource consulting executive; b. Massy, France, June 22, 1945; s. Paul and Simone (Mustel) C.; m. Bailleul Jocelyne; children: Sebastien, Alexandre, Stanilas. Engring. degree, Ecole Centrale, Paris, 1968; MBA, Insead, Fontainebleau, France, 1972. Cons. Commissariat a l'energie Atomique, 1968-72; cons. Port N.Y. Authority, N.Y.C., 1970-71, Peat Marwick Mitchell & Co., 1972-74; chmn. Groupe Courtaud, Paris, 1974-98, H.R. Cons. Network, 1998—. Chmn. Insead Alumni Assn., France, 1983-88. Office: HR Cons Network, 31 Rue des Poissonniers, 92200 Nevilly Seine France

COURTEAU, GIRARD ROBERT, prosecutor; b. St. Paul, Aug. 21, 1942; s. Robert William and Laura Gertrude Courteau; m. Mary Linda Lucas, Apr. 3, 1964 (div. May 1997); m. Susan Frances DeBaca, Aug. 8, 1997; children: Steven, Girard, Devin, Heather. AA, Coll. Marin, 1965; BA, U. Calif., Berkeley, 1967; JD, U. Calif., 1970. Bar: Calif. 1971, U.S. Dist. Ct. (ctrl. dist.) Calif. 1971, U.S. Dist. Ct. (no. dist.) Calif. 1983. Dep. dist. atty. Monterey County, Calif., 1971, Marin County, San Rafael, Calif., 1972—.

Assoc. editor Hasting's Law Jour., 1970; editor (monthly newsletter) Marin Law Enforcement Newsletter, 1974-89. Named Prosecutor of the Yr., Marin County Dist. Attys. Office, San Rafael, Calif., 1987. Mem. Calif. Dist. Attys. Assn., Marin County Bar Assn., Order of the Coif, Thurston Soc. Roman Catholic. Avocations: gardening, reading. Home: 1307 Park St Santa Rosa CA 95404-3542 Office: Marin Dist Attys Office Rm 130 Hall of Justice San Rafael CA 94903

COURTÉS, JOSEPH JEAN-MARIE, humanities educator, writer, semiotician; b. Hérault, France, Feb. 6, 1936; s. Jean and Marthe (Carles) C.; m. Annie Joullié, June 22, 1974; children: Sophie, Jean-Noël, Benoît. Lic., Paris U., 1964, doctorate, 1965; doctorate, Paris U., 1971, Paris U., 1983. Dir. Internat. Ctr. Semiotics and Linguistics, Urbino, Italy, 1971-73; asst. prof. Ecole de Hautes Études en Scis. Soc., Paris, 1973-84; prof. semiotics Toulouse (France) U., 1985—; pres. of commn. of semiotics and linguistics Toulouse U., 1986-92, 98—; internat. cons. EHESS, 1985—; mem. Sci. Coms. of Revs., France, 1986—. Author: Lévi-Strauss et les contraintes de la pensée mythique, 1973, Introduction à la sémiotique narrative et discursive, 1976, Sémiotique, dictionnaire raisonné de la théorie du langage, vol. I, 1979, vol. II, 1986, Le conte Populaire: poétique et mythologie, 1986, Sémantiques de lénancé, 1989, Sémiotique du discours: de l'énoncé à l'énonciation, 1991, Du signifié au signifiant, 1992, Sémiotique narrative et discursive, 1993, Du lisible au visible: analyse sémiotique d'une nouvelle de Maupassant, d'une bande dessinée de B. Rabier, 1995, Éthnolittérature, rhétorique et sémiotique, 1995, Stratégies d'écriture et instabilité du sens, 1996, Des motifs ethno-litteraines aux to poi, 1997, L'énonciation comme acte sémiotique, 1998. Mem. Assn. for Devel. Semiotics (pres. 1988—), Semio-Linguistics Soc. Ctr. (pres. 1991-93). Office: Toulouse II Univ, 31058 Toulouse France

COURTILLON, ALAIN JOSEPH, rheumatologist; b. Paris, Mar. 19, 1946; s. Maurice I. and Marguerite (Besnard) C.; m. Celia Thammavong, Aug. 17, 1970; children: Richard, Damien. Diploma, U. Paris, 1967; MD, U. Paris VII, 1975. Practice medicine specializing in physiotherapy Paris, 1967-73, gen. practice medicine, 1975-77; leader rehab. unit La Chataigneraie, Menucourt, France, 1978-88; med. mgr. Ctr. Reeducation Beaulieu, Rennes, France, 1988—; cons. in rheumatology Hosp. Cochin, Paris, 1975-88, burns unit, 1975-88, Hosp. Pitie, Paris, 1979-83, Ecole de Kinesitherapie, Paris, 1977-88; assoc. prof. Ecoles Kine, Ergo, 1989—. Contbr. articles to profl. jours. Mem. mid.-term care nat. taskforce Ministry Health. Served to capt. French Mil., 1973-74. Mem. ANMSR, Soc. Francaise de Reeducation, Soc. Francais de Rheumatologie. Avocations: mineralogy, natural life, communication, linguistics. Office: Ctr Reeducation, 41 Ave des Buttes de Coesmes, 35700 Rennes France

COURTILLOT, VINCENT EMMANUEL, geophysics educator, consultant; b. Neuilly, France, Mar. 6, 1948; s. Emmanuel Pierre and Francoise (Heulin) C.; m. Michèle Consolo, July 7, 1971; children: Carine, Raphaël. Diploma in mining civil engrng., Ecole Nationale Supérieure des Mines, Paris, 1971; MS in Geophysics, Stanford U., 1972; PhD in Geophysics, U. Paris 6, 1974; DSc in Geophysics, U. Paris 7, 1977. Asst. prof. U. Paris 7, 1973-77, assoc. prof., 1978-83, full prof., 1994—; full prof. Inst. Physique Du Globe, Paris, 1983-94; dir. dept. earth scis. Univ. Paris 7, 1980-83; dir. acad. rsch. and grad. studies Ministry of Edn., Paris, 1989-93; dir. dept. geomagnetism Inst. Physique du Globe, Paris, 1993-97; cons. Bur. Rsch. Geol. Min., Orléans, France, 1993-97; spl. advisor to Minister of Nat. Edn., Rsch. and Tech. in charge of higher edn., rsch. and tech., 1997-98; dir. Inst. Physique du Globe, Paris, 1996-98; dir. rsch. Ministry Edn., Rsch. and Tech., Paris, 1998—. Author: La Vie en Catastrophes, 1995, Evolutionary Catastrophes: The Science of Mass Extinctions, 1999; European editor: Geophysical Rsch. Letters, AGU, Washington, 1993-96; contbr. over 150 articles to profl. jours. Lt. Air Force, 1971-72, Paris. Recipient Geoscience prize Acad. of Scis., Paris, 1981, Franco-Brittanic prize Acad. Scis./Royal Soc., Paris, London, 1985, Silver medal CNRS, Paris, 1993; named Officier Ordre Nat. Du Mérite, Paris, 1999, Chevalier Légion d'Honneur, 1996, Comdr. Palmes Académiques, 1999. Fellow Am. Geophys. Union, Royal Astron. Soc. (assoc.); mem. European Union of Geoscis. (v.p. 1993, pres. 1995-97), Academia Europaea, Inst. Universitaire de France (sr.). Office: Inst de Physique du Globe, 4 Place Jussieu, 75252 Paris Cedex 05, France

COURTIN, ALFRED, environmental management consultant; b. Basel, Switzerland, Apr. 28, 1937; s. Alfred Franz-Hans and Helene Sophie (Disler) C.; m. Lieselotte Fischer, Apr. 18, 1964; children: Dominik, Caroline. DPhil, U. Basel, 1965. Postdoctoral rsch. assoc. Cornell U., Ithaca, N.Y., 1965-67; rsch. chemist Sandoz AG, Basel, 1968-73, jr. rsch. fellow, 1973-84; jr. fellow Sandoz Tech. AG, Basel, 1985-91, sr. fellow, 1991-97; ret., 1997; cons. environ. mgmt., 1997—. Contbr. over 20 articles to profl. jours.; German patentee in field of organic chemistry. Candidate for state parliament, Basel-Stadt, 1992, 96. Sgt., Swiss Army, 1957-87. Mem. Am. Chem. Soc., New Swiss Chem. Soc., Eco Swiss (pres. tech. com. 1998—). Liberal-Democrat. Episcopalian. Avocations: hiking, stamps, wine. Home: Schützenmattstr 54, CH-4051 Basel Switzerland

COURTNEY, THEODORE KRAFT, safety engineer, health research scientist; b. Atlanta, Jan. 8, 1965; s. Francis E. and Mary E. (Watson) C.; m. Sherri F. Forrester, Dec., 1987; children: Mary Ann, Michelle Faith. BS in Applied Psychology, Ga. Tech., 1987; MS in Indsl. Engrng., U. Mich., 1991. Design engr. GTE Govt. Systems, Needham, Mass., 1987-88; staff scientist Courtney Consultants, Atlanta, 1988-89; rsch. engr. Ga. Tech. Rsch. Inst., Atlanta, 1989-93; sr. rsch. assoc. Liberty Mutual Rsch. Ctr., Hopkinton, Mass., 1993-97; assoc. dir. Liberty Mutual Rsch. Ctr., Hopkinton, 1997—; vis. lectr. Harvard Sch. Pub. Health, Boston, 1995—; mem. com. on cumulative trauma disorder control Am. Nat. Standards Inst., 1993—; maritime medicine and partnership U.S. Coast Guard, Washington, 1996-99. Contbr. over 20 articles to profl. jours. including Ergonomics, Safety Sci., others; guest editor Am. Jour. Indsl. Medicine, 1995, 97; writer, producer TV program Ergonomics: The New Era in Performance, 1995; mem. editl. bd. Am. Indsl. Hygiene Assn. Jour., 1998—. Deacon, Sunday sch. tchr., choral mem., Bapt. Ch., Northboro, Mass.; sci. advisor safety and health, Ga. Republican Gubernatorial Campaign, 1988; co-founder, strategist, rschr., Citizens for Safer Highways, Charlton, Mass., 1996—. Pres. scholar Ga. Tech., 1983-87; Niosh fellowship U. Mich., Ann Arbor, 1990-91. Mem. Assn. Cert. Safety Profls. (cert.), Am. Soc. Safety Engrs., Human Factors and Ergonomics Soc. Avocations: film criticism, basketball. Office: Liberty Mutual Rsch Ctr 71 Frankland Rd Hopkinton MA 01748-1231

COURTNEY, WILLIAM HARRISON, diplomat; b. Balt., July 18, 1944; s. Wilbur Harry Courtney and Mary Lee (Mitchell) Fleming; children: William Jr., Mary Alison. BA in Econs., W.Va. U., 1966; PhD in Econs., Brown U., 1980. Fgn. svc. officer Dept. State, Washington, 1972-99; dep. exec. sec. NSC, The White House, Washington, 1987-88; dep. U.S. negotiator U.S.-Soviet Def. and Space Talks, Geneva, 1988-91; amb. Nuclear Testing & Nuclear Weapons Safety, Security, and Dismantlement,ACDA, Washington, 1991-92; amb. to Kazakhstan, 1992-95, amb. to Georgia, 1995-97; spl. asst. to pres. for Russia, Ukraine and Eurasia, White House, Washington, 1997-98; sr. advisor Fgn. Affairs Reorgn., U.S. Dept. State, Washington, 1998-99; sr. advisor U.S. Commn. Security & Coop. in Europe, 1999; pres. DynMeridian, Alexandria, Va., 2000—. Mem. Coun. Fgn. Rels. E-mail: courtneywmh@mindspring.com. Home: 3722 48th St NW Washington DC 20016-3213 Office: 6101 Stevenson Ave Alexandria VA 22304-3540

COURTOIS, ANDRÉ GEORGES, microbiologist; b. Stanleyville, Belgium, Feb. 5, 1942; s. Ghislain and Ghislaine (Blondiaux) C.; m. Berit Bjerke Nilsen, Nov. 13, 1970 (div. June 1994); children: Erik, Kari. MD, U. Catholiq., Louvain, Belgium, 1966. Chief svc. bacterio Hosp. Mama Yemo, Kinshasa, Zaire, 1971-73; microbiologist Clinique N.D. Bruyeres, Liege, Belgium, 1973-81, chief svc. lab., 1981—. Mem. Soc. Belge Biologie Clinique (mem. bur. 1986-95, 98-99). Home: Ave J Wautrs 4/11, 4130 Tieff Belgium Office: Clinique N D Bruyeres, Rue de Gaillarmont 600, 4032 Liege Belgium

COURTOIS, BERNARD PIERRE, electronic engineer, consultant; b. Paris, Apr. 17, 1948; s. Louis Adolphe and Raymonde Alice (Froissart) C.; m. Martine Marthe Robin, July 1, 1978; children: Sophie, Julie. Engr., ENSIMAG, Grenoble, France, 1973; D in Engring., Nat. Inst. Poly. Grenoble, 1976; DS, Inst. nat. polytechnique de Grenoble, 1981. Chargé de recherche Nat. Ctr. for Sci. Rsch., Grenoble, 1981—; dir. rsch. Centre nat. de la recherche sci., Grenoble, 1984—, head dir. rsch., 1993—; cons. in field. Editor 10 books; author more than 250 sci. papers; chmn. 10 confs. Recipient numerous rsch. grants. Mem. IEEE (Meritorious Svc. award 1993), Assn. for Computing Machinery. Home: Chemin de Beauplan, 38340 Voreppe France Office: Inst Nat Polytechnique Grenoble, 46 Ave Félix Viallet, 38031 Grenoble France

COURTY, PHILIPPE ROBERT, chemist, petroleum association professional; b. Paris, Dec. 17, 1938; s. Clément François and Simone Irma (Ferry) C.; m. m. Jacqueline Palau, Aug. 20, 1962 (dec.); children: Patrice, Marie-Christine; m. Yvonne Saccomani, Aug. 22, 1970 (div.); children: Jean-Philippe, Floriane; m. Raphaëlle Patus, 2000. Grad. in indsl. chemistry, Nat. Inst. Applied Scis., Lyon, France, 1962; PhD In Applied Scis., U. Chimie, Lyon, 1966. Rsch. engr. Soc. d'Etudes Chimiques l'Industrie l'Agriculture, Argenteuil, France, 1962-65, Nat. Ctr. Sci. Rsch., Paris, 1965-66, La Radio Technique, Evreux, France, 1966, Inst. Français du Pétrole, Rueil Malmaison, France, 1967—; sr. rsch. engr. Inst. Français du Pétrole, Rueil Malmaison, 1978-79, project mgr., 1979-84, chief rsch. engr., 1984-89, dep. mgr., 1989-90, dir., 1990—. Co-author: Applied Heterogeneous Catalysis, 1978; inventor patents for chlorine prodn. method, synthesis of alcohols, 100 patents in chemistry; contbr. articles to profl. jours. Recipient Prix Menier, Soc. des Arts Chimiques, Paris, 1991. Avocations: jogging, hiking, skiing. Office: Inst Français Pétrole, Inst Francais Petrole, PO Box 311, 92506 Rueil Malmaison France

COURY, MAXIME, executive managing director; b. Alexandria, Egypt, Mar. 18, 1925; s. Georges C.; m. Antoinette Marnier-Lapostolle, July 4, 1952; 1 child, Gilles. Student, Ecole Superieure de Chimie, 1946-48; Diploma Ingenieur, E.S.F.M., 1951. Asst. purchasing mgr. Sté Marnier-Lapostolle, Paris, 1952, purchasing mgr., 1953-55, asst. export dir., 1956-60, export dir., 1961-72, mng. dir., export dir., 1973-88, vice chmn. and exec. mng. dir., export dir., 1989—. Recipient Officier de l'Ordre Nat. du Merite. Office: Societe Marnier-Lapostolle, 91 Blvd Haussmann, 75008 Paris France

COUSINEAU, PHILIP ROBERT, writer, filmmaker; b. Columbia, S.C., Nov. 26, 1952; s. Stanley Horace and Rosemary Marie (La Chance) C.; 1 child, Jack Philip Blue Beaton-Cousineau. BA cum laude, U. Detroit, 1974. Writer-in residence Shakespeare and Co. Bookstore, Paris, 1987; script judge Bay Guardian Scriptwriting Contest, 1987-89; judge Nat. Ednl. Film and Video Festival, 1990; mem. adv. bd. Joseph Campbell Archives and Libr., 1991—; documentary film judge Emmy Awards, 1992; dir. mythological tours Joseph Campbell Found., 1993-96; documentary judge San Francisco Film Festival, 1993-95. Author: Deadlines, 1991, UFOs: Manual for the Millenium, 1995, German edit., 1997, Soul Moments: Marvelous Stories from the World of Synchronicity, 1997, Spanish edit., 1998, The Art of Pilgrimage, 1998, Portuguese edit., Spanish edit., 1999 (Quality Paperback Book Club selection 1998); editor: The Hero's Journey: Joseph Campbell on His Life and Work, 1990, Portuguese edit., 1995, rev. edit., 1999, The Soul of the World, 1993 (Quality Paperback Book Club selection 1993, Book of Yr. award Contemporary Photography 1994), Soul: An Archaeology, 1994, Chinese edit., 1997, Turkish edit., 1999, Prayers at 3 A.M., 1995, Design Outlaws, 1997, Riddle Me This: A World Treasury of Folk Riddles, 1999, Spanish edit., 2000, Chinese edit., 2000, The Soul Áflame, 1999, The Book of Roads, 2000, contbr. to 12 other books; co-dir., screenwriter documentary films: The Peyote Road, 1993 (best documentary award Gt. Plains Film Festival, Cine Golden Eagle award, Bronze Telly award, silver award Chgo. Film Festival, award Mill Valley Film Festival); screenwriter: Presence of the Goddess, 1987, Ecological Design, 1994 (Golden Gate ward, Cine Golden Eagle award, Sundance Film Festival); co-writer: Wayfinders: A Pacific Odyssey, 1999 (Gold Apple, Nat. Ednl. Media Network Festival, Hawaii Film Festival), The Red Road to Sobriety, 1995 (Cine Golden Eagle award 1995, Gold award Red River Film Festival 1998), Your Humble Serpent: The Legacy of Reuben Snake, 1996 (Silver Apple award Nat. Ednl. Film Festival, Gold award Red Earth Film Festival), The 1932 Ford V8, 1986, Balcorman Films, 1987, (film) Eritrea: A Portrait of the Eritrean People, 1989; co-writer (video) Wiping the Tears of Seven Generations, 1991 (Best Video award Am. Indian Film Festival, Silver Telly award, Gold Apple award Nat. Ednl. Film Festival; co-writer, assoc. prodr. The Hero's Journey: The World of Joseph Campbell, 1987 (Silver Apple award Ednl. Film and Video Festival); co-writer film Forever Activists: Stories from the Veterans of the Abraham Lincoln Brigade, 1990 (Acad. Award nomination, jury prize San Francisco Film Festival); co-writer: Eritrea: A Portrait of the Eritrean People, 1989; co-writer: The Hero's Journey: The World of Joseph Campbell (Silver Apple award ednl. film and video festival 1987), The 1932 Ford V8, 1986. Trustee Native Land Found., 1993-96. Recipient award Nat. Assn. Ind. Pubs., 1991; fellow Calif. Inst. Integral Studies, 1991-95. Avocation: travel. Office: Harper San Francisco Pubs 353 Sacramento St San Francisco CA 94111-3620

COUSINO, JOE ANN, sculptor; b. Toledo, Nov. 17, 1925; d. George Carl and Lucille Caroline (Kocher) Bux; m. (div.); children: Paula Rene, Richard Nils. BA in Art, U. Toledo, 1947; stud., U. of Mex., 1948, U. Ill., 1953; attended, Internatl. Wkshp., Pietra Santa, Italy, 1980. Art tchr. Ctrl. YMCA & YWCA, Toledo, 1945-47; sculptor tchr. U. Tex. Jr. Coll., Gainesville, 1965, Defiance (Ohio) Coll., 1970, Bowling Green (Ohio) State Univ., 1971; profl. sculptor worldwide, 1963—; founder and pres. Toledo Potter's Guild, 1951-55; Ohio rep. Am. Craft Coun., N.Y.C., 1960-62; pres. Fedn. Art Socs. North Ohio, 1965-67, trustee 1963; co-chair midwest Kefauver com. Art in the Embassies Program, Dept. of State, Washington, 1966. One-woman shows include Toledo Mus. Art, Frank Ryan Gallery, Chgo., Forsythe Gallery, Mich., Mount St. Joseph Gallery, Cin., Arndt Mus. Art, Elmira, N.Y., Button Gallery Ltd., Saugatuck, Mich., Bowling Green State Univ. Grad. Ctr. Gallery, Ohio State Gallery, Kent State Univ. Gallery, Exhbn. Bangkok, 1990; prin. sculptures include Rio de Janeiro Brazil Dept. of Commerce, 1963, the John Leslie Stevens Meml., Oak Harbor, Ohio, Mame Gordon Meml., United Ch., Sylvania, Ohio, Greek Orthodox Holy Cathedral, Christ the King Ch., Toledo Hosp., Riverside Hosp., Univ. Toledo, Med. Coll. Ohio, Toledo Botanical Gardens, U. Toledo Student Union Bldg., 1994, Way Libr., Perrysburg, Ohio, 1986, U. Toledo McMaster Astronom Bldg., 1989, Sister of St. Francis, Mother House Commons, Tiffon, Ohio, 1999, Toledo Opera Sculpture Honor Opera Condrs. Presentation, 1999; works featured in numerous mags. and jours. Eagle Pitcher Bearing divsn. of Bunting Brass of U.S.A., Engring. Soc. of Ohio, featured spkr. UNICEF, Madras, India, 1984; recipient Woman of Toledo civic award, 1987; bd. dirs. Toledo Arts Commn., 1978-84. Recipient Outstanding Svc. in Field of Art award Fedn. of Arts, Toledo, 1967. Mem. Internat. Sculpture Ctr., Pan Pacific S.E. Asia Women's Assn.; Scandinavian Club of Toledo. Episc. Avocations: internat. travel, folk dancing, jazz, photography, lectr. on art. Home and Studio: 3717 Indian Rd Toledo OH 43606-2408

COUSINS, ANTHONY DOUGLAS, English literature educator; b. Sydney, NSW, Australia, May 8, 1950; s. Douglas Edward and Valerie (Green) C.; m. Carolyn Joy Pankhurst, June 28, 1951; children: David, Matthew. BA, Syndey U., 1972, MA, 1975; PhD, Monash U., Australia, 1980. Sr. tutor Monash U., 1976-78; lectr. Macquarie U., North Ryde, NSW, 1979-82, sr. lectr., 1983-91, assoc. prof. English lit., 1992—; vis. adj. prof. Renaissance Studies Ctr. U. Mass., 1995; vis. scholar Pa. State U., 1997; vis. fellow Princeton U., 1999. Author: Shakepeare's Sonnets and Narrative Poems; editor jours. So. Rev., 1981-83, Jour. Jane Austen Soc. of Australia, 1995—, Morreana, 1996—; contbr. articles to profl. publs.; author: The Catholic Religious Poets from Southwell to Crashaw; co-author, co-editor: Political Identity of Andrew Marvell, 1990; co-editor: More's Utopia and the Utopian Inheritance, 1995; editor: Quarles' Emblemes, 1990, Greville's Certaine Learned and Elegant Works, 1991. Grantee Macquairie U., 1993, Sir Ian Potter Found., 1995; rsch. scholar Humanities Rsch. Ctr., Australia, 1993. Mem. MLA, Amici Thomae Mori, Australia & New Zealand Medieval & Renaissance Soc., Australian Univs. MLA, Renaissance Text Soc. Avocations: music, kung fu. Office: Macquarie U, Sch of English, North Ryde NSW 2109, Australia

COUSINS, WILLIAM JOSEPH, lawyer, litigation consultant; b. New Haven, Conn., Sept. 28, 1917; s. Salvatore Colombieri and Mary (Arpaia) C.; m. Betty Jean Collins, June 25, 1954; children: Mimi Causey, Anna Maria, William J. Jr. BA, Yale U., 1940, LLB, 1943. Bar: Conn., U.S. Dist. Ct. Conn., U.S. Ct. Appeals (2d cir.) 1946. Law clk. New Haven (Conn.) Superior Ct., 1946-48; pvt. practice New Haven, 1946-52; ptnr. Arpaia & Cousins, New Haven, 1952-56; sr. ptnr. Cousins, Dooley & Barnston, Conn., 1956-68, Cousins, Ritter & Silverstone, New Haven, 1968-81, Carmody & Torrance, New Haven, 1981-87; dir. William J. Cousins & Assoc., Woodbridge, Conn., 1987; ret., 1987; apptd. spl. master and parajud. officer U.S. Dist. Ct. Conn.; sr. ptnr. conflict resolution svc. Cousins and Cooper; prosecutor Woodbridge Town Ct., 1948-60, town counsel Town of Woodbridge, 1948-76, chmn. Citizens Action Commn., 1952-55. Chmn. New Haven County Reps., 1960-64; chmn. Cath. Interracial Council, 1952-56. Served as sgt. USAAF 1943-46, PTO. Mem. ABA (lawyers conf. of jud. adminstrn. divsn.), Fed. Bar Assn., Am. Judicature Soc., Soc. Profl. Dispute Resolution, Nat. Inst. for Dispute Resolution (assoc.), Law and Soc. Assn. Republican. Roman Catholic. Clubs: Yale, Mory's, The Graduate. Home and Office: 24 Barberry Ln Woodbridge CT 06525-1326

COUSSEMENT, ROMAIN, physicist, educator; b. Beveren-Leie, Belgium, July 21, 1935; s. Georges and Maria (Coorevits) C.; m. Olga De Boiserie. BS in Math. and Physics, Cath. U. Leuven, Belgium, 1957, Licentiate, 1959, PhD, 1964; PhD, U. Leuven, 1965. Assoc. prof. Cath. U. Leuven, 1965-70, prof., 1970-72, ord. prof., 1972—. Recipient Laureate, Koninklijke Vlaamse Academie, Klasse der Wetenschappen, 1962, Prize of the Alumnu, U. Stichting, Brussels, 1971, De Leeuw-Damray-Boulart prize Belgian Sci. Found., 1995. Mem. Am. Phys. Soc., European Phys. Soc., Koninklijke Vlaamse Academie van Belgie, Wetenschappen en Kunsten, Letteren en Schone Kunsten van België. Home: Av Fernand Labby 43, B-1390 Bossut-Gottechain Belgium Office: Inst Kern Stralingsfysica, Celestijnenlaan 200D, 3001 Leuven Belgium

COUTARD, OLIVIER, research scientist; b. Montelimar, France, Feb. 28, 1965; s. Christian and Josette (Baccot) C.; m. Agnes Sander, Apr. 11, 1998; children: Nathan, Zoe. DEA in Transport, Ecole Nat. Ponts Chaussees, Paris, 1988, degree in engring., 1988, PhD, 1994. Rsch. assoc. Ecole Nat. Ponts Chamsses, 1994-96; rschr. Ctr. Nat. Rsch. Sci., Marne-La-Valle, France, 1996—; sec. Com. for Assessment of Transport Policy in Paris Region, 1995-98. Mem. editl. bd. Jour. Urban Tech., 1998—, Flux, 1990—; editor: The Governance of Large Technical Systems, 1999. Avocation: movies. Office: LATTS ENPC, 6 Ave Blaise Pascal, F-77455 Marne la Vallee France

COUTAZ, JEAN-LOUIS, optical sciences educator; b. Aix-les-Bains, France, May 7, 1956; s. Charles and Denise (Roulet) C.; m. Catherine Ferroud, Aug. 27, 1984; children: Claire, Magali. M in Physics, Université Scientifique, Grenoble, France, 1978, Thèse d'État, 1981; Thèse d'Etat, Institut Nat. Polytechnique, Grenoble, 1987. Asst. prof. U. Blida, Algeria, 1981-82; rschr. Centre National de la Recherche Scientifique, Grenoble, 1983-93; postdoctoral rschr. Royal Inst. Tech., Stockholm, 1988-89; prof. U. Savoie, Le Bourget du Lac, France, 1993—; coord. project FOA, Brite-Euram EEC Programme, Grenoble, 1993-95, DUO INCO-Copernicus EEC Programme, 1998—; dir. Lab. of Microwaves and Characterization, 1995-99. Author about 130 publs. and comms. in sci. jours. and comms. in sci. confs. Mem. Optical Soc. Am. Office: LAHC-U de Savoie, Campus Scientifique, 73376 Le Bourget du Lac France

COUTEAU, MARIE-JOSÉ, sociologist; b. Pecquencourt, Nord, France, Mar. 15, 1961; d. René and Cécile (Lukaszewski) C.; m. Max Chlebowski. B in Philosophy and Sociology, U. Nanterre, 1983, M in Philosophy and Sociology, 1984, D.E.A. in Sociology, 1985. Sociologist Agy. Nat. de Recherche sur Le Sida Centre Nat. de la Recherche Scientifique, Paris, 1990-94; sociologist CERSES-CNRS, Paris, 1994—. Contbr. articles to profl. jours. Laureate of Vocation's Found., Sociologist of Med. Ethics, 1988. Fellow Recherche en Scis. Sociales. Office: CNRS, 59 rue Pouchet, 75849 Paris Cedex 17, France

COUTEAU, PAUL, astronomer; b. La Roche-Sur-Yon, France, Dec. 31, 1923; s. René Couteau and Marie Antoinette Lelièvre; m. Marie Madeleine Le Sueur, June 20, 1952; children: Florence, François Xavier, Pascaline, Jean Charles, Natalie, Oliver. Lic. in math., Rennes, France, 1947; M in Math., Paris, 1947; Doctor, U. Sorbonne, Paris, 1986. Eschr. Nat. Ctr. Sci. Rsch., Nice, France, 1956-59; asst. Ensci. Superior, Nice, 1951-56, adj. astronomer, 1959-69, titular astronomer, 1969—. Author: Observing Visual Double Stars, 1981, Ces astronomes fous du ciel, 1981, Le Grand Escalier, 1992, Les reves de l'infini, 1996, Le Ciel Est Mon Jardin, 2000. Roman Catholic. Home: 3 Ave Brown-Sequard, 06000 Nice France Office: Observ Cote Azur, URA 13661 BP 229, 06304 Nice France

COUTEAUX, PAUL, foreign diplomat; b. Paris, July 31, 1956. Mem. European Parliament, 1999—, mem. com. on devel. and coop., substitute com. fgn. affairs/human rights/common security; mem. Union for Europe of the Nations Group; mem. delegation for relations with the Palestinian Legis. Coun. Home: Le Fournay, F-18320 Jouet Sur L'Aubois France*

COUTERMARSH, EVA MARINA, personnel executive; b. Salisbury, Md., Oct. 29, 1967; d. Ernest Richard Jr. and Marina (Hernandez) C. BA in English and Comms., Mass. Coll. Liberal Arts, 1997. Cert. personnel cons. Nat. Assn. Personnel Svcs. Area coord. Experiment in Internat. Living, Brattleboro, Vt., 1992; adminstrv. asst. Nathan & Co., Pittsfield, Mass., 1992-93; personnel asst. Assoc. Staffing, Inc., Phoenix, 1993-94, staffing coord., 1994-95, sr. staffing coord., 1995-97; staffing mgr. Assoc. Staffing, Inc., Mesa, Ariz., 1997-98; sr. pers. cons. KNF&T, Boston, 1998—. Mem. Ariz. dist. 28 Republican Com., Scottsdale, 1997-98. Mem. NAFE, New Eng. Human Resources Assn., Mass. Assn. Pers. Cons. Republican. Roman Catholic. Avocations: reading, travel, entertaining, outdoors. Fax: (617) 574-8222. E-mail: EVA@KNFT.COM. Home: 35D Richardson Ave Wakefield MA 01880-2912 Office: KNF&T 133 Fed St Boston MA 02110

COUTINHO, EVANS CLIFTON, chemist, educator, researcher; b. Mangalore, Karnataka, India, Jan. 17, 1961; s. Edwin Cyril and Celine Josephine (Monteiro) C.; m. Susan Joseph, June 9, 1996. BSc in Chemistry, Parle Coll., Mumbai, India, 1981; BSc in Tech., Bombay U., 1984, MSc in Tech., 1986; PhD in Tech., Bombay Coll. Pharmacy, 1989. Lectr. pharm. chemistry Bombay Coll. Pharmacy, Mumbai, 1986-91, asst. prof. pharm. chemistry, 1991-97, prof., 1997—; cons. TATA Elxsi, Mumbai, 1995—. Contbr. 34 articles to profl. jours. Recipient Dr. M.K. Rangnekar Meml. medal Bombay U., 1984, Best tchr. award for pharmacy colls. Pamdal, Mumbai, 1993, Career Award for Young Tchrs., All India Coun. Tech. Edn., New Delhi, 1995, Rsch. award scheme Univ. Grants Commn., 1999. Mem. Indian Biophys. Soc., Nat. Magnetic Resonance Soc. Avocations: music, hockey, reading. Home: 6C-303 Alica Nagar, Lokhandwala twp, Kandivili(E) Mumbai 400 101, India Office: Bombay Coll of Pharmacy, Kalina Santa Cruz (E), Mumbai 400 098, India

COUTRELIS, ANDRÉ, lawyer; b. Cairo, Apr. 15, 1944; arrived in France, 1965; s. Camille Nemer and Catherine Coutrelis; m. Nicole Françoise Merceron, Oct. 6, 1979. Licence en Droit, U. Paris, 1969, postgrad., 1971; LLM, U. Calif., 1973. Admitted conseil juridique, Paris, 1982, avocat, 1987. Founder law firm Coutrelis & Associes, Paris and Brussels, 1982—; specialist in community law. Mem. Am. Hosp. of Paris. Mem. Internat. Bar Assn., Internat. Assn. of Boalt Alumni, Assn. Internationale des Juristes pour le Droit de la Vigne et du Vin, Assn. Européenne pour le Droit de l'Alimentation, Assn. Juristes Europeens. Avocations: chess, swimming, movies, art, classical music. Home: 52 Ave de la Renaissance, Brussels 1040, Belgium Office: Coutrelis & Associes, Rue de la Loi 235, Brussels 1040, Belgium

COUTROT, PHILIPPE, chemist, researcher; b. Paris, Nov. 19, 1941; s. Robert and Eliane (Forgeot) C.; m. Denise Delmas, Mar. 29, 1966; children: Jean-François, Anne, Frédéric. Lic. in scis., Sorbonne, Paris, 1963; diploma in higher studies, Sorbonne, 1964, CAPES, 1964; agrégé in chemistry, Paris, 1965; PhD, U. Paris VI, 1973; postgrad., Nat. Sci. Rsch. Ctr. (CNRS), Gif/Yvette, France, 1978-79. Student prof. IPES, Paris, 1961-65; asst. Faculty of Scis., Paris, 1965-69, asst. master, 1969-70; asst. master U. Paris VI/Pierre et Marie Curie, 1970-81; prof. organic chemistry U. Henri Poincaré Nancy (France) 1, 1981—; dir. lab. organic chemistry 2 U. Henri Poincaré, 1981—, dir. dept. chemistry, 1981-83, pres. specialty and establishment com. 27, 32d sect., 1987-83, dir. rch. ctr. PSP, 1991-93, dir. Nancy Inst. Molecular

Chemistry, 1994—; chemistry cons. French Ministry Superior Edn. and Rsch., 1989-93, rep. at French Nat. Sci. Rsch. Com. sects. 16 and 20, 1989-95, chemistry expert doctoral studies and rsch. bd., 1994-95; dir. Regional Tech. Pole Phys. and Molecular Chemistry, Nancy, 1994. Contbr. numerous articles to profl. jours. Mem. French Nat. Com. of Univ., Sect. 32, Paris, 1999; sci. attaché French Embassy, Amsterdam, The Netherlands, 1968-69. Chevalier des Palmes Académiques. Mem. French Chem. Soc. (bd. dirs. organic chemistry divsn. 1995). Office: U H Poincaré Nancy 1, PO Box 239, 54506 Vandoeuvre les Nancy, France

COUTTS, ALISTER WILLIAM, government executive; b. Aberdeen, Scotland, Dec. 21, 1950; s. Alexander Taylor and Charlotte Willamena (Knowles) C.; m. Sheelagh Anne Smith, Sept. 25, 1975; children: Callum, Fionagh, Moyra. DQS Abertay Dundee, U. Scotland, 1975; BA with honors, Open U., Eng., 1979; MBA with distinction, Hong Kong U., 1989; MSc, Heriot-Watt U., Scotland, 1989, PhD, 1997. Asst. quantity surveyor Armour & Ptnrs., Aberdeen, 1969-71, quantity surveyor, 1975-76; sr. quantity surveyor Anderson Morgan Assocs., Aberdeen, 1976-78; profl. officer Govt. of Hong Kong, Hong Kong, 1978-81; project coord. Hong Kong Mass Transit Rlwy. Corp., Hong Kong, 1981-89; dir. project mgmt. and devel. DCI (Holdings) Ltd., Glasgow, Scotland, 1989-93; dir. ops. Fife Healthcare NHS Trust, Leven, Scotland, 1993-98; dir. property & architecture Highland Coun., Inverness, Scotland, 1998—; lectr. U. Hong Kong, 1978-79, Hong Kong Polytechnic U., 1984-89; tutor Open U., 1993—, Dundee U., 1991-92. Mem. Children's Panel, Aberdeen, 1976-78. Fellow Royal Instn. Chartered Surveyors, Chartered Inst. of Bldg., Inst. Mgmt.; mem. Scottish Football Assn. Referees (pres. 1994-96), Hong Kong Football Referees Assn. Scottish National Party. Avocations: soccer refereeing, hiking, travel. Office: The Highland Coun, Glenurquhart Rd, Inverness IV3 5NX, Scotland

COUTURE, ARMAND, civil engineer; b. Quebec City, Can., 1930. BSc in Civil Engring., Laval U., Quebec, Can., 1953, MSc in Structures and Found., 1955; postgrad., U. Calif., Berkeley, 1958; Doctorate honoris causa, U. Quebec á Montrél. Structural engr. Nat. Ports Coun., Ottawa, Ont., Can., 1953-55, Fenco, Montreal, 1955-61; ptnr., dir., then chmn. and CEO Gen. Engring. Co., Ltd., Montreal, 1962-67; ptnr., dir. tech. and econ. studies Lamarre Valois Internat. Lavalin, Montreal, 1967-72, v.p., mem. mgmt. com., 1972-85, pres., CEO Shawinigan Lavalin Inc., 1983-87, sr. group v.p., 1988-91; sr. v.p. SNC-Lavalin, Inc., Montreal, 1991-92; pres., COO Hydro-Quebec, Montreal, 1992-96; chmn., bd. dirs. Societe D'Energie de la Baie James, Montreal, 1992-96; pres. La Soc. Bedelmar Ltee, Laval, Quebec, 1996—; chmn. bd. dirs. Institut Nat. de la Recerche Scientifique, 1998—. Recipient Can. Commemorative 125 medal, 1992, Julian C. Smith medal Engring. Inst. Can., 1995. Mem. Ordre des Ingenieurs du Quebec, Assn. Profl. Engrs. Ont., Can. Inst. Profl. Engrs., Can. Acad. Engring., Club Saint-Denis, Club de Golf Laval-sur-le-Lac. Office: 244 Bazin, Laval, PQ Canada H7N 4R5

COUTURE, JEAN GUY, bishop; b. Quebec, Que., Can., May 6, 1929; s. Odilon and Eva (Drolet) C. BA, Laval U., Quebec, 1949, PhB, 1949, L.Theol., 1953, L.Sc.Phys., 1959. Ordained priest Roman Cath. Ch., 1953; prof. math. and scis. St. Georges H.S. and Coll., Beauce, Que., 1953-65; adminstr. coll. St. Georges H.S. and Coll., 1961-68; mem. adminstrn. Roman Cath. Diocese Quebec, 1968-75; bishop of Hauterive Que., 1975-79, of Chicoutimi, 1979—. Mem. Order of Can., Order of Red Cross (officer). Home and Office: 602 E Racine, Chicoutimi, PQ Canada G7H 1V1

COUTURE, MAURICE, archbishop; b. Saint-Pierre-de-Broughton, Qué., Can., Nov. 3, 1926. Ordained priest Roman Cath. Ch., 1951; ordained titular bishop of Talattula and aux. bishop of Québec, 1982. Bishop Baie-Comeau, Qué., 1988-90; archbishop of Qué, primate of Can., 1990—. Home: CP 459 HV, 2 Port-Dauphin, Québec, PQ Canada G1R 4R6 Office: Archdiocese of Québec, 1073 René-Levesque Ouest, Sillery, PQ Canada G1S 4R5

COUTURIER, MAURICE SERGE, language and literature educator; b. Breuil-Barret-Vendée, France, July 10, 1939; s. Maurice D. and Rachel F. (Jaulin) C.; m. Yvonne M. Guillotin, Oct. 25, 1965; children: Anne, Françoise. MA in English, Sorbonne U., Paris, 1970, Doctorate 3rd Cycle, 1972, Agrégation, 1973, Doctorat d'Etat, 1976. Asst. Cath. U. of Angers, France, 1966-67, 68-70; instr. Loras Coll., Dubuque, Iowa, 1967-68; asst. prof. U. Notre Dame, Ind., 1970-72; assoc. prof. Sorbonne U., 1974-78; prof. U. Nice, France, 1978—; fellow Claremont Calif., 1989; vis. prof. San Diego State U., 1981, 88. Author: La Polka Piquée, 1982, Textual Communication, 1991, Nabokov ou la Tyrannie de l'auteur, 1993, La Figure de l'auteur, 1995, Roman et censure, 1996, others; contbg. editor Fiction Internat., 1981—, French Rev. of Am., 1991—, Nabokov Studies, 1993—; editor Am. Lit. Col. L'Age d'Homme, 1980-83; chief editor Nabokov's works in French; translator Nabokov and David Lodge. Vice pres. French Assn. Am. Studies, 1976-78. Chief cpl. French inf., 1961-63. Avocations: music, photography, hiking. Office: U Nice, 98 bd E Herriot, 06204 Nice France

COUVE DE MURVILLE, MAURICE NOËL LÉON, archbishop; b. June 27, 1929; s. Noël and Marie (Souchon) Couve de Murville. MA, Trinity Coll., Cambridge, Eng.; STL, Inst. Catholique, Paris; MPhil, U. London; DU (hon.), Open U.; DD (hon.), U. Birmingham. Ordained priest Roman Catholic Ch. 1957. Curate St. Anselm's, Dartford, England, 1957-60; priest in charge St. Francis, Moulsecoomb, England, 1961-64; Catholic chaplain U. Sussex, England, 1961-77, U. Cambridge, England, 1977-82; archbishop Birmingham, England, 1982-99; Grand cross conventual chaplain Sovereign Mil. Order of Malta, 1982. Author: John Milner 1752-1826, 1986; co-author (with Philip Jenkins) Catholic Cambridge, 1983, Karl Leisner Priest in Dachau, 1988, Slave From Haiti The Life of Pierre Toussaint, 1995, Marcel Callo, 1999, The Man Who Founded California Blessed Junipero Serra, 2000. Avocations: walking, gardening. Office: 54 Sutton Rd, Seaford East Sussex BN25-1SS, England

COVAULT, LLOYD R., JR., retired hospital administrator, psychiatrist; b. Troy, Ohio, Feb. 3, 1928; s. Lloyd R. and Anne Marie (Grisez) C.; m. Janet Eileen Davidson, June 12, 1951; children: Sheryl Ann, Jane Helen, Michael Lee, Roger Ken. BA, Miami U., Oxford, Ohio, 1950; MD, Ohio State U., 1954. From extern to asst. supt. Orient (Ohio) State Inst., 1953-70; pvt. practice, Columbus, 1968-75; psychiat. trainee Ctrl. Ohio Psychiat. Hosp., Columbus, 1966-68, psychiatrist, 1982-85; supt. Columbus State Inst., 1970-74; med. dir. North Ctrl. Cmty. Mental Health Ctr., Columbus, 1974-79, cons. psychiatry, 1985-90; assoc. prof. psychiatry Ohio State U. Med. Sch., 1975-76; cons. psychiatry North Ctrl. Cmty. Mental Health Ctr., Columbus, 1985-90; from dir. to cons. psychiatrist S.E. Mental Health Ctr., Columbus, 1979-97, cons. psychiatrist, 1986-97; med. dir. Charles B. Milles Mental Health Ctr., Marysville, Ohio, 1989-95; psychiat. cons. Union Manor Nursing Home, Marysville, Ohio, 1996-98; ret., 1999; mem. Franklin County Mental Health and Retardation Bd., 1970-74, Ohio Dept. Mental Health, ret. 1984; cons. psychiatrist Madison County Mental Health Ctr., London, 1984-85, Chillecothe VA Hosp., 1995-99; staff psychiatrist Ohio Correction Complex, Orient, 1988-89; 1st med. coord. Netcare Admission Unit Ctrl. Ohio Psychiat. Hosp., 1985-87; founding father Physicians Assn. Ohio Dept. Mental Health, 1956-68, pres. 1957; psychiatrist, cons. Buckeye Ranch for Children and Adolescents, Grove City, Ohio, 1998-99. Recipient Union County Pillar award, 1991; named Ohio's Disting. Rural Practitioner, Ohio State Dept. Health, 1993. Fellow Am. Assn. Mental Retardation (life, chmn. adminstrn. state chpt. 1974-75), Am. Psychiat. Assn. (life); mem. Ohio Psychiat. Assn., Neuropsychiat. Soc. Ctrl. Ohio (pres. 1973-74), Mental Health Supts. Assn. (pres. Ohio chpt. 1973-74). Home: 11092 Darby Creek Rd Orient OH 43146-9797

COVER, NORMAN BERNARD, retired electronic data processing administrator; b. Ephrata, Pa., Mar. 25, 1935; s. Barney Blaney and Chelta V. (Huff) C.; m. Violet Hurmagene Winouski, Nov. 26, 1960; children: Brian Lee, Keith Alex. Student, Jacksonville U., 1955. Cert. in data processing. Tabulator operator State Farm Fire & Casualty Co., Bloomington, Ill., 1952-53; programming operator State Farm Mut. Auto Ins. Co., Jacksonville, Fla., 1954-56, shift supr. EDP, 1957-61; asst. supt. EDP State Farm Mut. Auto Ins. Co., Winter Haven, Fla., 1962-67, EDP supt., 1968-78, data processing mgr., 1979-97, ret., 1997. Chmn. data processing adv. com. Polk C.C., 1976-92; sponsor Winter Haven H.S. Cotillion Club, 1982-88; chmn. stamp out crime com. Cypress Gardens, 1975-80, dir.1980-82, v.p. 1984, sec. 1985, pres. 1986, chmn. bd., 1987, 91; dist. gov. Sertoma Lake Ridge, 1988-89, sec.-treas., 1990-91; dir. Sertoma Camp Endeavor Inc., 1989, sec. 1990, 93-95, v.p. devel. and pub. rels., 1991-92, pres., 1996, chmn. bd. dirs., 1997-99, v.p. devel., 2000—. Mem. Data Processing Mgmt. Assn. (S.E. regional treas. 1974-75, S.E. regional v.p. 1975-77, internat. v.p. 1977-78, dir. spl. interest group cert. data processors 1978-80, v.p. 1981, pres. 1982, internat. dir. Polk County chpt. 1982-83, chmn. bylaws com. 1983-97, past. pres.'s com. 1970—, Individual Performance awards 1972-91), SAR. Democrat. Home: 70 Greenfield Ct Winter Haven FL 33884-1302

COVEY, GEOFFREY HAROLD, chemical engineer; b. Guildford, Surrey, Eng., May 28, 1949; s. William Harold and Audrey Laura (Bright) C.; m. Virginia Anne Covey, Aug. 15, 1971 (div. Dec. 1992); children: Timothy Eadward, Emma Jane, Alexander Edmund; m. Brenwyn Glenice Laycock, Sept. 1997; 1 child, Nathan William. BSc in Chem. Engring., U. Surrey, 1972; PhD, U. Melbourne, Victoria, Australia, 1978. Rsch. engr. Laporte Industries Ltd., Grimsby, Eng., 1972-74; rsch. scientist, tech. supt., mgr. DARS tech. Australian Paper Mfrs., Melbourne, 1977-86; sect. leader process tech. Assoc. Pulp and Paper Mills, Burnie, Tasmania, 1986-90; gen. mgr. and cons. Covey Consulting, Somerset, Tasmania, 1990—; sr. lectr. U. Melbourne, 1992—. Contbr. articles to profl. jours.; patentee on chem. recovery. Recipient Benjamin medal Australian Pulp and Paper tech. Assn., 1983. Avocations: coin collecting, bushwalking, English history. Office: U Melbourne, Parkville, Melbourne VIC 3052, Australia

COVI, LINO, psychiatrist; b. Trento, Italy, Mar. 19, 1926; came to U.S., 1956, naturalized, 1965; s. Giuseppe and Giuseppina (Mariotti) C.; m. Beverly A. Yeutsy, Dec. 30, 1958 (dec.); children: Lisa Martina, Michelle Peppina, Gina Albina, Tina Maria. Student in philosophy, U. Florence, Italy, 1945-47, Sch. Social Work, Trento and Rome, 1949-51; MD, U. Rome, 1955. Asst. U. Rome Neuropsychiat. Clinic, 1955-56; intern Albert Einstein Med. Ctr., Phila., 1956-57; resident fellow psychiatry Johns Hopkins Hosp., Balt., 1957-60, dir. outpatient clin. rsch. unit, 1968-83, dir. Cognitive Therapy Clinic, 1982-98, dir. treatment assessment rsch. unit, 1983-94; assoc. clin. prof. U. Md. Med. Sch., Balt., 1986-92; instr. psychiatry Johns Hopkins U., 1960-67, asst. prof., 1967-72, assoc. prof., 1972—; vis. psychiatrist Balt. City Hosp., 1960-80; vis. scientist Nat. Inst. Drug Abuse-Addiction Rsch. Ctr., Balt., 1988-94, guest rschr., 1996—; psychiatrist Francis Scott Key Med. Ctr.-Hopkins Bayview Med. Ctr., Balt., 1988—; med. dir. Friends Health Svcs., 1994-97; cons. Friends Rsch. Inst. Epoch Ctrs., Balt., 1997—; staff psychiatrist Patuxent Instn., Jessup, Md., 1960-62; chief out-patient dept. Gundry Hosp., Balt., 1962-86, pres. bd. dirs., 1972-84, rsch. dir., 1973-86; mem. bd. govs. Cen. Md. Health Systems Agy., 1978-83; rsch. psychiatrist NIMH Collaborative Studies, 1962-64, co-prin. investigator, 1964-65, prin. investigator, 1965-83, prin. investigator clin. trials of new drugs for depression and anxiety, 1970-94, studies of group cognitive therapy in depression, 1980-94; tchg. assoc. Sheppard and E. Pratt Hosp., 1973-79; cons. Pharm. Rsch. Labs., 1971-96, Centro Psicologia Clinica, Milan, 1981—. Editor: The Md. Psychiatrist, 1974-80, Today's Psychiatry, Md. Med. Jour., 1985-95; contbr. articles to profl. jours. Mem. human rights com. Coop. Studies Program, VA, 1981-84. Mem. AMA (prof. staff drug evaluation coun. on drugs 1968-71), Am. Coll. Neuropsychopharmacology (coms.), Md. Psychiat. Soc. (coms.), Am. Psychiat. Assn. (nat. coms., dep. rep. Md., Newsletter award 1977), Am. Soc. Clin. Psychopharmacology, World Fedn. Mental Health, Johns Hopkins Med. Soc., Assn. Advancement Behavior Therapy, Md. Med. Soc., Balt. Med. Soc. (chmn. coms.), Collegium Internat. Neuropsychopharmacologicum, Italian-Am. Hist. Assn. Democrat. Roman Catholic.

COVIELLO, ALFREDO, physiology educator; b. San Miguel de Tucuman, Argentina, Dec. 6, 1932; s. Alfredo and Elvira (Martinez Castro) C.; m. Luisa Angela Orce Remis, July 11, 1967 (dec. Mar. 1975); children: Ana Luisa, Alfredo; m. Ana Maria Gonella, Aug. 1, 1980. MD, U. Nacional Tucuman, Argentina, 1960; PhD, U. Nacional Tucuman, 1972. Diplomate in Medicine. Rsch. fellow U. Cath., Louvain, Belgium, 1963-65; instr. of physiology U. Tucuman, 1966-70, asst. prof. of physiology, 1971-73, prof. of physiology, 1974-92; dir. Fundación Inelco, Tucuman, 1992; career investigator Conicet, Argentina, 1973; dir. Inst. of Physiology, Tucuman, 1974-92; cons. Coun. of Rsch., Tucuman, 1972-89. Author, editor: Advances In Renal Physiology, 1984, Elements of Human Physiology, 1995, Human Physiology Cingolani-Houssay, 1988. Recipient Acad. award Acad. Ciencias Medicas, 1976, Acad. Nacional de Medicina, 1990, N.Y. Acad. Scis., 1994. Mem. Consejo Argentino Hipertension, Interam. Soc. Hypertension. Roman Catholic. Avocation: swimming. Home: Pasaje Oncativo 682, 4000 Tucuman Argentina Office: Fundacion Inelco, Av Mitre 35, 4000 Tucuman Argentina

COVIN, CAROL LOUISE, computer consultant; b. Chgo., July 2, 1947; d. Raymond Lincoln and Elizabeth Day (Notley) Frederick; m. David William Covin, Jan. 24, 1968; children: David William Jr., Jonathan Michael. BA, George Washington U., 1972. Data base adminstr. USN, Alexandria, Va., 1973-77; cons. Data Base Mgmt., Inc., Springfield, Va., 1977-79, 82-87; pres. Covin Assocs., Falls Church, Va., 1987-90; cons. Electro-Tech. Internat., Annandale, Va., 1990-91, Abacus Tech., Chevy Chase, Md., 1991-93, Tech. Internat., Fairfax, Va., 1993-95; with Xybernaut Corp., Fairfax, 1995—. Author: The Computer Professional's Job Guide to Washington, D.C., 1989, Covin's New England Computer Job Guide, 1991, Covin's Washington Computer Job Guide, 1993, Covin's Midwest Computer Job Guide, 1995, Covin's Southeast Computer Job Guide, 1998. Mem. Assn. Systems Mgmt. (pres. 1990-92, v.p. 1992-93, treas. 1993-96), Data Adminstrn. Mgmt. Assn., Washington Apple Pi.

COVINGTON, MICHAEL AARON, computer scientist; b. Valdosta, Ga., Sept. 14, 1957; s. Charles Gordon and Hazel (Roberts) C.; m. Melody Mauldin, July 25, 1982; children: Catherine Anne, Sharon Elizabeth. BA summa cum laude, U. Ga., 1977; MPhil, Cambridge U., 1978; PhD, Yale U., 1982. Postdoctoral fellow U. So. Calif., L.A., 1982-84; rsch. assoc. U. Ga., Athens, 1984-85, asst. rsch. scientist, 1985-90, assoc. rsch. scientist, 1990-2000, sr. rsch. scientist, 2000—; contbg. editor Visual Developer Mag., Scottsdale, Ariz., 1990-2000. Author: Syntactic Theory in the High Middle Ages, 1984, Astrophotography for the Amateur, 1985, 2d edit., 1999, Dictionary of Computer Terms, 1986, Natural Language Processing for Prolog Programmers, 1993; contbg. editor Poptronics (formerly Electronics Now Mag.), Farmingdale, N.Y., 1995-2000; contbr. articles to profl. jours. Named U.S. Pres.'s scholar Internat. Sci. Sch., 1973; recipient First prize humanities/social scis., IBM Supercomputer Competition, 1989-90. Mem. IEEE (sr.), Assn. for Computational Linguistics, Linguistic Soc. of Am., N.Y. C.S. Lewis Soc., Am. Radio Relay League, Assn. for Logic Programming. Baptist. Avocations: astronomy, electronics, amateur radio, languages, ch. work. Office: U Ga Artificial Intelligence Ctr Athens GA 30602-7415

COVINGTON, VERONICA PRO, librarian, educator; b. Laredo, Tex., Nov. 14, 1949; d. Gilberto and Herminia (Esquivel) Pro; m. Billy C. Covington, Jan. 3, 1980; children: Christina, Jennifer, Elizabeth. BS in Edn., Tex. A&I U., 1971; MEd, Sam Houston State U., 1986; PhD in Curriculum and Instruction, Tex. A&M U., 1996. English tchr. Martin H.S., Laredo, Tex., 1970-73; English tchr., chair Dunbar H.S., Lubbock, Tex., 1973-75; asst. dir. Upward Bound Tex. Tech. U., Lubbock, 1975-77; English tchr. Matthews Jr. High, Lubbock, 1977-80; English tchr., chair Mance Park Jr. High, Huntsville, Tex., 1980-90; head libr. Huntsville H.S., 1990-95; coord., testing and program evaluation Huntsville Ind. Sch. Dist., 1995-98; libr. Austin Ind. Sch. Dist., 1998—; cert. translator Tex. Dept. Criminal Justice, Huntsville, 1989—; adj. prof. children's lit. U. Tex., Austin. Contbr. articles to profl. jours. Active Huntsville Leadership Inst., 1996-97; ambassador Huntsville-Walker County C. of C., 1997-98; mentor at-risk students Huntsville Ind. Sch. Dist., 1985-97. Elected del. The White House Conf. on Libr. and Info. Svcs., Washington, 1991. Mem. Nat. Assn. for Bilingual Edn., Tex. Assn. for Bilingual Edn., Tex. Assn. of Sch. Adminstrs., Coun. for Exceptional Children, Nat. Assn. for Gifted Children, Tex. State Tchrs. Assn. (pres. 1986-89), Delta Kappa Gamma (bd. dirs. com. chair 1985). Avocations: reading, travel, writing. Office: Austin Ind Sch Dist Baily Mid Sch 4020 Lost Oasis Holw Austin TX 78739-5501

COVINO, CHARLES PETER, chemicals executive; b. West New York, N.J., Dec. 9, 1923; s. Isaac L. and Rose (Luongo) C.; m. Sylvia A Covino, Dec. 27, 1947; 1 child, Candida. Student, U. Ala., 1941-43; BBA, Manhattan Coll., 1951; MBA, NYU; DHL (hon.), Philathea U., Can., 1963; DS (hon.), Manhattan Coll., 1995. Chmn. bd., CEO Gen. Magnaplate Corp., Linden, N.J.; mem. Hoover Inst. Coun. for Global Polit. and Econ. Transition, 1994; lectr. in field. Contbr. over 28 articles to profl. jours. Bd. dirs. Peoples Bankcorp, 1990. Recipient Air Force Assn. N.J. Wing award for space contbns., 1960, Royal Cross Austria Prince Rudolph, 1964, Eloy Alfaro Found. of Panama award, 1965, Manhattan Coll. Outstanding Alumni award, 1972, Vaaler award Chem. Engring. Inst., 1976, Indsl. Rsch. 100 award for Material Devels. of Yr., 1964, 68, 78, ASM award for Disting. Svc. and Contbns. to Metals Industry, 1967, Cookware Design of Yr. award Housewares Mfr.'s Assn., 1967, award of yr. Packaging Inst., 1967-68, Outstanding New Product award Popular Sci. mag., 1967, Packaging Design award Design Inst., 1968, Outstanding USA Design award U.S. Info. Agy., 1968, Italian-Am. Man of Sci. award 1978, Churchill Medal of Wisdom award, 1995, Heros of Chemistry award Am. Chem. Soc., 1996, Am. Chem. Soc. award, 1996, Thomas Alva Edison award for best N.J. invention of Yr., 1999; named to N.J. Inventors Hall of Fame, 1994-95, Manhattan Coll. Athletics Hall of Fame, 1998, N.J. Corp. Inventors Hall of Fame, 1999. Achievements include over 93 patents and trademarks; invention of non-destructive testing method for thick lead shielding in nuclear reactors, ultrasonic test method for nuclear tubing used for condensors, various metal surface enhancement processes; featured in Guinness World Book of Records for world's slipperiest solid lubricant. Office: Gen Magnaplate Corp 1331 Route 1 & 9 N Linden NJ 07036

COVITZ, AKIBA J., law educator; b. Providence, R.I., June 17, 1967; s. Howard H. and Marsha R. Covitz; m. Miriam B. Spectre, July 22, 1991. BA, St. John's Coll., 1991; MSL, Yale U., 1997; PhD, U. Pa., 1999. Assoc. dir. undergrad. counseling U. Pa., Phila., 1994-96, lectr., 1994-96; sr. rsch. assoc. Yale Law Sch., New Haven, Conn., 1997—, lectr., 2000—; cons. on legal confidentiality to numerous orgns., 1998—. Author: (book) E-Law, 2000; contbr. articles to profl. jours. Democrat. Jewish. Avocations: hiking, social justice, vegetarianism, constitutional interpretation. E-mail: akiba.covitz@yale.edu. Office: Yale Law Sch PO Box 208215 New Haven CT 06520-8215

COWAN, DALE HARVEY, internist, lawyer; b. Cleve., Jan. 25, 1938; s. Milton Jerome and Clara (Umans) jC.; m. Deborah Wolowitz, Jan. 28, 1967; children: Rachel, Morris Benjamin, William Ezra. AB, Harvard U., 1959, MD, 1963; JD, Case Western Res. U., 1981. Diplomate Am. Bd. Internal Medicine with subspecialty cert. in hematology and med. oncology. Bar: Ohio 1981. Intern Cleve. Met. Gen. Hosp., 1963-64, resident, 1964-65, 67-70; practice medicine specializing in internal medicine, hematology and oncology; dir. hematology and oncology Marymount Hosp., Cleve., 1982—; asst. prof. medicine Case Western Res. U., Cleve., 1970-75, assoc. prof., 1975-84, clin. prof. environ. health scis., 1985—; assoc. Health Sys. Mgmt. Ctr., 1982-90; of counsel Burke, Haber & Berick, 1984-86; pres. med. staff Parma (Ohio) Cmty. Gen. Hosp., 1997-98; med. dir. Cmty. Oncology Group Cleve. Clinic Found., Cleve., 1999—; spl. cons. President's Commn. on Bioethics, Washington, 1981-82; mem. nat. adv. coun. Nat. Heart Lung and Blood Inst., Bethesda, Md., 1982-85. uthor: Preferred Provider Organizations, 1984; co-editor Human Organ Transplantation, 1987; contbr. articlesIt o profl. jours. Bd. dirs. Bur. Jewish Edn., 1977-87, Northeast Ohio affiliate Am. Heart Assn., 1982-86; pres. Ohio/W.Va. Oncology Soc., 1990-94; trustee No. Ohio Cancer Resource Ctr., 1998—, chmn. 1999—. Lt. comdr. USPHS, 1965-67. Fellow ACP, Am. Coll. Legal Medicine; mem. AMA, ABA, Am. Soc. Hematology, Am. Soc. Clin. Oncology, Am. Assn. for Cancer Rsch., Am. Health Lawyers Assn. (bd. dirs. 1988-94), Am. Soc. Law and Medicine, Acad. Medicine Cleve. (pres. 1997-98). Home: 19600 Shaker Blvd Cleveland OH 44122-1830 Office: 6100 W Creek Rd Ste 15 Cleveland OH 44131-2133

COWAN, HENRY JACOB, architectural engineer, educator; b. Aug. 21, 1919; s. Arthur and Erna (Salisch) C.; m. Renate Proskauer, June 22, 1952; children: Judith Anne, Esther Katherine. BS with honors, U. Manchester, Eng., 1939, MS, 1940; PhD, U. Sheffield, Eng., 1952; DEng, U. Sheffield, 1963; MArch, U. Sydney, Australia, 1984, DArch (hon.), 1987. Mem. faculty dept. archtl. sci. U. Sydney, 1953—, prof., 1953—, head dept., 1953-84, dean arch., 1966-67, pro-dean, 1968-84; vis. prof. Cornell U., 1962, Kumasi (Ghana) U., 1973, Trabzon (Turkey) U., 1976; pres. Bldg. Sci. Forum of Australia, 1969-71. Author 25 books, including: The Master Builders, Science and Building, Architectural Structures, Environmental Systems, The Science and Technology of Building Materials, Handbook of Architectural Technology, Structural Systems; editor: Archtl. Sci. Rev., 1958—, Vestes, 1966-78. With Royal Engrs., 1941-45. Decorated officer Order of Australia, 1983. Fellow ASCE, Royal Australian Inst. Archs. (hon. 1979), Royal Soc. Arts (Hartnett medal 1998), Inst. Structural Engrs. (Spl. Svc. award 988), Instn. Engrs. Australia (R. W. Chapman medal 1956, J. Monash medal 1994). Home: 6 Hale Rd Apt 57, Mosman NSW 2088, Australia Office: U Sydney, Dept Archtl Sci, Sydney NSW 2006, Australia

COWAN, REBECCA GAIL, artist, illustrator; b. Ottawa, Ont., Can., Feb. 28, 1955; d. Robert Charles and Mildred Claire (Lifshitz) Shnay; m. Jerold Cowan, Oct. 8, 1978. Student, Dawson Coll., 1972-74, Ryerson Poly. Inst., 1974-76; BA, York U., 1981; postgrad., Toronto Sch. Art, 1983-85. lectr. Malaspina Printmakers' Studio, 1991; instr. Open Studio, lectr., 1992; artist mem., bd. dirs. Open Studio, 1992-94, chair 100 print com., 1993. One-woman shows include Here and Now Gallery, Toronto, 1990, Malaspina Printmakers Soc., Vancouver, 1991, Open Studio Gallery, Toronto, 1992, Holy Blossom Temple, Toronto, 1994, Saints and Sinners, 1997; group exhbns. include North York Colour and Form Soc., 1986, Aviva Art Show, 1989, Soc. Can. Artists, 1990, Open Studio Gallery, Innovations in Printmaking, Saskatoon, Internat. Women's Day Exhbn., Toronto, 1992, Toronto Indoor Art Show, 101 Prints, Vancouver, 1993, Angels, Opperthauser Gallery, Alta., The Sukkah Project Koffler Gallery, Toronto, Buch of Printmakers U.W.O., Toronto Outdoor Art Exhbn., 1994, Nat. Libr. Can., 1995, ARA Internat. Book Arts Exhbn., Montreal, 1996, Confronting Cancer through Art, Philadelphia, 4th Ore. Book Biennial, 1996, Art of the book 98', Toronto, 1998, Southern Graphics Coun. Conf., 1999, Tempe Calcutta Book Fair, India, 1999, La. U. Artists Books, 1999, others; represented in permanent collections Can. Coun. Art Bank, Peat Marwick Thorne, CIBC, Nat. Libr. Can., Newmarket Pub. Libr. Mem. Can. Bookbinders and Book Artists Guild, Visual Arts Ont., So. Graphics Guild, Am. Print Alliance. Home: 363 Dovercourt Rd, Toronto, ON Canada M6J 3E5

COWAN, RUSSELL EDGAR, gastroenterologist; b. London, Oct. 3, 1944; s. Francis George and Doris Hilda (Lack) C.; m. Gillian Talbot, Sept. 11, 1971; children: Elliot, Ashley, Abigail. MB BS, U. London, 1969, MD, 1979. European specialist register in gen. medicine and gastroenterology. House officer Guy's Hosp., London, 1969-71, med. registrar, 1971-73; MRC clin. rsch. fellow St. Thomas Hosp., London, 1973-76; clin. rsch. fellow U. So. Calif., 1977-78; sr. med. registrar Royal London Hosp., 1976-81; cons. physician Essex Rivers Healthcare Trust, Colchester, Eng., 1981—; cons. physician Oaks Hosp., Colchester, 1981—; chmn. locally organized rsch. scheme, N.E. Thames Regional Health Authority, 1990-92. Author: (book chpt.) Wright's Liver and Biliary Disease, 1992; contbr. articles and reports to profl. publs. Rsch. and travel grantee Astra Found., 1995. Fellow Royal Coll. Physicians (bd. examiners 1998—, regional assessor 2000—), Royal Soc. Medicine (coun. mem. 1990-93, v.p. coloproctology sect. 1994-97), Brit. Soc. Gastroenterology (hon. treas. endoscopy sect. 1989-95), Assn. Coloproctology Great Britain and Ireland (gastroenterology rep. coun. 1995-98). Anglican. Avocations: theater, gardening, rearing ducks and geese, photography. Fax: 01206 742384. E-mail: cowans@btinternet.com. Office: Colchester Gen Hosp, Turner Rd, Colchester Essex C04 5JL, England

COWAN, STUART MARSHALL, lawyer; b. Irvington, N.J., Mar. 20, 1932; s. Bernard Howard and Blanche (Hertz) C.; m. Marilyn R.C. Toepfer, Apr., 1961 (div. 1968); m. Eleanor Schmerel, June, 1953 (dec.); m. Jane Alison Averill, Feb. 24, 1974 (div. 1989); children: Fran Lori, Catherine R.L., Erika R.L., Brownen P.; m. Victoria Yi, Nov. 11, 1989. BS in Econs., U. Pa., 1952; LLB, Rutgers U., 1955. Bar: N.J. 1957, Hawaii 1962, U.S. Supreme Ct. 1966. Atty. Greenstein & Cowan, Honolulu, 1961-70, Cowan & Fewy, Honolulu, 1970-89; pvt. practice, 1989—; of counsel Price Okamoto

Himeno & Lum, 1993—; arbitrator Fed. Mediation & Conciliation Svc., Honolulu, 1972—, Am. Arbitration Assn., Honolulu, 1968—, Hawaii Pub. Employee Rels. Bd., 1972—. Pres. Hawaii Epilepsy Soc., 1984-86; acquisition chair Hawaii Family Support Ctr., 1995-97. Lt. USN, 1955-61. Mem. ABA, Hawaii Bar Assn., Am. Judicature Soc., Assn. Trial Lawyers Am. (state committeeman for hawii 1965-69, bd. govs. 1972-75), Consumer Lawyers Hawaii, Hawaii Trial Lawyers Assn. (v.p. 1972-78), Japan-Hawaii Lawyers Assn., Soc. Profls. in Dispute Resolution, Inter Pacific Bar Assn., Honolulu Symphony Soc. (bd. dirs. 1989-99), Hawaii Epilepsy soc. (pres. 1984-86), Royal Order of Kamehameha, Order of St. Stanislas, Sovereign Order of St. John of Jerusalem Knights Hospitallen, Waikiki Yacht Club, St. Francis Yacht Club, Hawaii Yacht Club, Plaza Club, Honolulu Club, Hawaii Scottish Assn. (chieftain 1983-88), St. Andrews Soc., Caledonian Soc. (vice chieftain 1983-85), Honolulu Pipes and Drums (sec.-treas. 1985-90), New Zealand Police Pipe Band, Masons (York Rite, Scottish Rite no. and so. jurisdictions, Grand Lodge Hawaii, grand orator 1992, sr. grand steward 1993, jr. grand warden 1994, sr. grand warden 1995, grand master 1997), Red Cross of Constantine, Royal Order Scotland, Pearl Harbor (master 1971, chaplain 1992-96), Hawaiian Koolau, Masonic Kilties N.J., Masada (#51 N.J.), USS Missouri Meml. Assn., Elks, Chinese Acacia Club, Royal Hawaiian Ocean Racing Club. Jewish. Home: 47-339 Mapumapu Rd Kaneohe HI 96744-4922 Office: 707 Richards St Honolulu HI 96813-4616 also: 47-653 Kamehameha Hwy # 202 Kaneohe HI 96744-4965

COWAN, THOMAS DAVID, emergency medical services professional; b. Asheville, N.C., Jan. 5, 1957; s. Richard Eugene and Mary Virginia (Jacobs) C.; m. Elaine Hyatt, June 22, 1986. AAS in Nursing, Asheville Buncombe Tech. Inst., 1977, diploma in emergency med. sci., 1982; cert. in emergency med. svc., Mgmt. Inst. U. N.C., Charlotte, 1985. RN, N.C., Tenn. Field technician Buncombe County EMS, Asheville, 1978-82, ops. supr., 1982-91; emergency med. svcs. liaison Meml. Mission Med. Ctr., Asheville, 1991-94, regional EMS mgr., 1994-96, regional EMS dir., 1996—; mem. adv. com. Emergency Sci. Med. Curriculum Asheville Buncombe Tech. Coll., 1983—; mem. Region B EMS Coun., 1996—. Mem. N.C. Assn. Emergency Med. Svc. Adminstrs., Am. Trauma Soc. Office: Mission St Josephs 509 Biltmore Ave Asheville NC 28801-4690

COWARD, SIR JOHN, former lieutenant governor of Guernsey; b. Oct. 11, 1937; s. Reginald John and Isabelle (Foreman) C.; m. Diana Taylor, 1963; 2 children. Joined Royal Navy, 1959, advanced through grades to vice adm., 1989, with submarines, 1959-76, naval asst. to first sea lord, 1978-80; HMS Brilliant, 1980-82; dir. naval operational requirements, 1984, flag officer sea tng., 1987-88; adm. Flotilla One, 1988-89, Submarines Ea. Atlantic, 1989-91; commdt. RCDS, 1992-94; ret., 1994; lt. gov. Guernsey, Channel Islands, 1994—; ret.; underwriting meml. Lloyds. Decorated Disting. Svc. Order, knight of Bath. Avocations: sailing, gardening, golf, cricket.

COWART, T(HOMAS) DAVID, lawyer; b. San Benito, Tex., June 12, 1953; s. Thomas W. Jr. and Glenda Claire (Miller) C.; children: Thomas Kevin, Lauren Michelle, Megan Leigh; m. Greta E. Gerberding, Aug. 12, 1995. BBA, U. Miss., 1975, JD, 1978; LLM in Taxation, NYU, 1979. Bar: Miss. 1978, Tex. 1979; CPA Tex., Miss. Assoc. Dossett, Magruder & Montgomery, Jackson, Miss., 1978, Strasburger & Price, Dallas, 1979-87; ptnr., assoc., shareholder Johnson & Gibbs, Dallas, 1988-90; shareholder Jenkens & Gilchrist, Dallas, 1991—; adj. prof. law So. Meth. U. Sch. Law, 1988; mem. key dist. adv. coun. IRA, Dallas, 1989-95, chmn., 1990-93; mem. Coll. State Bar Tex.; lectr. in field. Mem. editl. bd. Flexible Benefits, 1993—, 401k Advisor, 1994—, COBRA Adv., 1996—. Mem. adv. com. Goals for Dallas, 1984-85; vol. Children's Med. Ctr., 1992-96. Mem. ABA (sect. taxation, employee benefits com., vice-chmn. 1995-97, chmn. elect 1997-98, chmn. 1998-99, sect. 83 issues task force, chmn. health plan designs issues subcom. 1992-95, health care task force 1991-98, chmn.-designate joint com. on employee benefits 1997-99, chmn. joint com. employee benefits 1999-2000), Am. Coll. Employee Benefits Counsel (charter, founder, 1st chair), State Bar Tex. (sect. taxation, com. compensation and employee benefits, fed. legislation, regulations and revenue rulings subcom. 1986-87, chmn. fiduciary stds. for trustees subcom. 1987-88), Dallas Bar Assn. (lectr. 1985—, coun. mem. employee benefits sect. 1989-92, treas. 1992, sec. 1993, v.p. 1994, pres. 1995), S.W. Benefits Assn. (bd. dirs. 1994-97), Dallas Benefits Soc. (co-moderator 1991-92, bd. dirs. 1991-93), Omicron Delta Kappa, Beta Alpha Psi, Phi Alpha Phi. Office: Jenkens & Gilchrist 1445 Ross Ave Ste 3200 Dallas TX 75202-2785

COWDEN, JERE LEE, management consultant; b. Canonsburg, Pa., Apr. 3, 1947; s. Clair V. and Elizabeth B. (Boyle) C.; m. Sharon Noreen Tahl, Oct. 15, 1971; children: Michael C., Alissa L. BA in Econ., Ind. U. of Pa., 1969. Cert. employee benefit specialist. Acct. exec. Master Plan, Inc., Pitts., 1969-70, Babb, Inc., Pitts., 1970-78; acct. exec., mgr. Babb, Inc., Wayne, Pa., 1978-79; owner, pres., cons. Innovative Benefit Concepts, Inc., Pitts., 1979-83; owner, cons. Mockenhaupt, Mockenhaupt, Cowden & Parks, Inc., Pitts., 1983-96; pres., owner Spectrum Benefit Options, Inc., Pitts., 1996—; active Pitts. Total Compensation Network. Contbr. numerous articles to profl. jours. and newspapers. Mem. diocesan coun. Episcopal Diocese Pitts., 1974-76; mem. fin. and stewardship com. Ch. the Ascension, Pitts., 1985—. Mem. Internat. Soc. Cert. Employee Benefit Specialists (bd. dirs. 1986-88, governing coun. 1986-88, long range planning com. 1986-92, pres. 1988, program and edn. chmn. Pitts. chpt.), Am. Compensation Assn., Inst. Mgmt. Cons. (cert. mgmt. cons.), Pitts. Assn. Group Execs., Assn. Corp. Growth, Planning Forum. Avocations: gardening, snow skiing, theater. Home: 210 Chaucer Ct S Sewickley PA 15143-8726 Office: Spectrum Benefits Optinos 1 Gateway Ctr Fl 11 Pittsburgh PA 15222-1435*

COWDEN, ROGER HUGH, II, systems engineer; b. Dayton, Ohio, Jan. 26, 1955; s. Roger Hugh and Beverly Eileen Cowden. BS in Systems Engrng., Wright State U., 1979. Engr. Steve R. Rauch Inc., Dayton, 1979—; sec. Dayton Inventors Coun., 1994—. Mem. NSPE, Heartland Vintage Thunderbird Club (v.p.). Achievements include patent for secondary containment for underground storage tanks. Home: 9985 Ainsworth Ct Miamisburg OH 45342-4571 Office: 1550 Soldiers Home West Car Rd Dayton OH 45418-2146

COWEN, BRIAN, government official; b. 1960; married; 2 children. Student, U. Coll., Dublin. Elected to Dail, 1984; min. Ministry Labor, 1992-93; min. Ministry Transport, Energy & Comm., 1993-94, opposition spokesman, 1994-97; min. Dept. Health, Dublin, 1997—, Fgn. Affairs. Office: Iveagh House, 80 St Stephens Green, Dublin 2, Ireland*

COWEN, ZELMAN, former governor general of Australia, educator; b. St. Kilda, Victoria, Australia, Oct. 7, 1919; s. Bernard and Sara (Granat) C.; m. Anna Wittner, June 7, 1945; children: Simon, Nicholas, Katherine, Benjamin. Ed., Scotch Coll., Melbourne, Australia, BA, 1939, LLB, 1941, LLM, 1942; LLD (hon.), U. Melbourne, 1973, MA, 1947, BCL, 1947, DCL, 1968; LLD (hon.), U. Hong Kong, 1967, U. Queensland, 1972, U. Western Australia, 1981, U. Turin (Italy), 1981, U. Tasmania, 1990, Victoria U. of Tech., 1998; D.Litt. (hon.), U. New Eng., 1979, U. Sydney, 1980, James Cook U. of North Queensland, 1982, Oxford, 1983; D.H.L. (hon.), Hebrew Union Coll., Cin., 1980; D.Univ. (hon.), U. Newcastle, 1980, Griffith U., 1981, Sunshine Coast U., 1999; D.Phil. (hon.), Hebrew U., Jerusalem, 1982, U. Tel Aviv, 1985; LLD (hon.), Australian Nat. U., 1985; D.H.L. (hon.), U. Redlands, 1986. Hon. master of bench Gray's Inn; Queen's counsel of Queensland Bar; mem. Victorian bar; privy counsellor, 1981; fellow Oriel Coll. Oxford U., 1947-50, hon. fellow, 1977, provost, 1982-90; hon. fellow New Coll., 1978; prof. public law, dean Faculty of Law U. Melbourne, 1951-66, emeritus prof., 1967—; vice-chancellor U. New Eng., 1967-70, U. Queensland, 1970-77; gov. gen. Australia Canberra, 1977-82; acad. gov. of bd. govs. Hebrew U., Jerusalem, 1969-77, 82—, Tel Aviv U., 1987—; mem. council U. Lesotho, 1976-77; pres. Australian Inst. Urban Studies, 1973-77; law reform commr. Commonwealth of Australia, 1976-77; chmn. Australian Vice-Chancellor's Com., 1977; mem. Chief Justice's law reform com., 1951-66; vis. prof. U. Chgo., 1949, Harvard Law Sch., 1953-54, 63-64, Fletcher Sch. Law and Diplomacy, 1953-54, 63-64, U. Utah, 1954, U. Ill., 1957-58, Washington U., St. Louis, 1959; Tagore Law Prof. U. Calcutta, 1975; disting. vis. fellow hon. law prof. Griffith U., 1992—; disting. vis. prof. Victoria U. Tech., 1994—. Specialist editor: Dicey: Conflict of Laws, 1949, Australia and the United States: Some Legal Comparisons, 1954; (with P.B. Carter) Essays on the Law of Evidence, 1956; American-Australian Private International Law, 1957; Federal Jurisdiction in Australia, 1959, (with Leslie Zines), 2d edit., 1978; (with D. Mendes da Costa) Matrimonial Causes Jurisdiction, 1961; The British Commonwealth of Nations in a Changing World, 1964; Sir John Latham and Other Papers, 1965; Sir Isaac Isaacs, 1967, 2d edit., 1993; Introduction to 2d edit., Evatt: The King and His Dominion Governors, 1967, The Private Man (A.B.C. Boyer Lectures, 1969); Individual Liberty and The Law (Tagore Law Lectures, 1975), Reflections on Medicine, Biotechnology and the Law, 1985, Pound Lectures U. of Nebraska, A Touch of Healing, 1986; contbr. chpts., articles, essays on legal, polit., social and univ. subjects to Australian, U.K., U.S., Can. and European publs. Pres. Asthma Found. Victoria, 1963-66, Adult Edn. Assn. Australia, 1970-86; bd. dirs. Australian Opera, 1969-77; chmn. bd. govs. Utah Found., 1975-77; chmn. Australian Studies Centre Com., London, 1982-90; chmn. Press Council (U.K.), 1983-88; chmn. Nat. Coun. Australian Opera, 1983-95; chmn. council Victoria League for Commonwealth Friendship, 1987-90; chmn. trustees, Visnews, 1986-91; trustee Van Leer Inst., Jerusalem, 1985—, chmn. bd., 1988-95, hon. chmn., 1995—; mem. Weizmann Inst., 1988—; trustee Sir Robert Menzies Meml. Trust, 1987—; trustee Winston Churchill Meml. Trust, 1987-89; bd. dirs. Sir Robert Menzies Meml. Found., 1990-97; chmn. Australian Nat. Acad. Music, 1995-2000. Decorated knight Order of Australia; knight grand cross Order St. Michael and St. George; knight bachelor Order St. John of Jerusalem, then assoc. knight of justice; knight grand cross Royal Victorian Order; companion Order St. Michael and St. George; knight grand cross of Order of Merit of Italian Republic, 1990; hon. fellow Trinity Coll., Dublin, Robb & Wright Coll., U. New England, St. John's Coll., U. Queensland; Rhodes scholar, 1940, Menzies scholar U. Va., 1983; Lee Kuan Yew Disting. Visitor, Singapore, 1987; recipient Supreme Ct. prize, Melbourne, 1941; Vinerian scholar, Oxford U., 1947. Fellow Royal Soc. Arts, Acad. Social Scis. in Australia (hon.), Univ. House of Australian Nat. U. (hon.), Royal Australian Inst. Architects (hon.), Australia-Britain Soc. (nat. pres. 1993-95), Order Australia Assn. (nat. pres. 1992-95), Australian Acad. Tech. Scis. (hon.), Inst. Chartered Accts. in Australia (hon.), Royal Australian Coll. Physicians (hon.), Royal Australian Coll. Med. Adminstrs. (hon.), Royal Australian Coll. Ob-Gyn (hon.), Australian Acad. Humanities (hon.), Australian Soc. Accts. (hon.), Australian Coll. Rehab. Medicine (hon.), Australian and N.Z. Assn. Advancement of Sci.; mem. N.S.W. Bar Assn. (life), Am. Acad. Arts and Scis. (fgn. hon. mem.). Office: 4 Treasury Pl, East Melbourne VIC3002, Australia

COWIE, MARTIN RICHARD, cardiologist, epidemiologist; b. Edinburgh, Scotland, July 1, 1966; s. Alan and M. Eleanor M. (Hill) C.; m. Helen Barbara Gunn, July 15, 1989; children: Alasdair George, Laura Anne. B in Med. Biology, U. Aberdeen, Scotland, 1988, MB, BChir, 1989, MD, 1999; MSc, U. London, 1997. Registrar in cardiology Univ. Coll. Hosps., London, 1992-95; rsch. fellow Imperial Coll., London, 1995-97; specialist registrar in cardiology Hillingdon Hosp., London, 1997-98; hon. lectr. Imperial Coll., 1997-98; clin. sr. lectr. cardiology U. Aberdeen, 1998—. Contbr. articles to profl. jours., chpts. to books. Gov. Primary Sch., Ealing, London, 1995-98. Wellcome Truste fellow, 1995; project grantee Brit. Heart Found., 1994, 95, 97. Fellow Royal Soc. Medicine; mem. Royal Coll. Physicians (London), Med. Soc. of London, Brit. Cardiac Soc., Med. Rsch. Soc. (com. mem.). Avocations: piano, pipe organ, gardening, opera. Office: U Aberdeen Med Sch Dept Med, Polwarth Bldgs Foresterhill, Aberdeen AB25 2ZD, Scotland

COWLES, ELIZABETH HALL, program consultant; b. Wichita Falls, Tex., Aug. 27, 1936; d. Eugene DeWitt and Lorena (Perry) Hall; m. James Edgar Cowles, Dec. 26, 1957 (div. Jan. 1989); children: Gary Randall, Jan Alison Cowles Sendker, Richard Scott. BS in Edn., North Tex. State U., Denton, 1958; MAIS, U. Tex., Dallas, 1994. Elem. tchr. Long Beach (Calif.) Ind. Sch. Dist., 1958-59; tchr. 6th grade Austin (Tex.) Ind. Sch. Dist., 1960-62; statewide project dir. Rainbow Days, Inc., Dallas, 1989-90; LIFESPAN exec. dir. Dallas County Hosp. Dist., Dallas, 1990-94; Dallas Healthy Start exec. dir. Fed. Initiative Dallas County Hosp. Dist., Dallas, 1994-98; nat. cons. cmty. collaboration, program devel., resource devel. Concensus Bldg., 1999—; state pres. Tex. Coalition for Juvenile Justice, Dallas, 1983-84; mem. adv. com. Tex. Juvenile Probation Commn., Austin, 1987-88. Author: Early Influences on Development of English Language, 1994; initiated Listener Project, 1981. Pres. bd. dirs. Lone Star coun. Camp Fire, Dallas, 1986-87; mem. nat. steering com. Camp Fire, Inc., Kansas City, Kans., 1989; bd. dirs. United Way of Met. Dallas, 1988-89; pres. bd. dirs. Women's Coun. Dallas County, 1988-89; mem. pub. affairs com. Mental Health Assn.; mem. cmty. leaders forum Ctr. for Non-Profit Mgmt., 1996-97; mem. cmty. action com. Dallas Coun. on Alcohol and Drug Abuse, 1996-97; chair adminstrv. bd. Lovers Lane United Meth. Ch., 1997; dir. Juvenile Justice. Recipient Cmty. Advocacy award Dallas County Juvenile Dept., 1985, Gulick award for cmty. svc. Camp Fire, Inc., 1989, Women Helping Women award Women's Ctr. of Dallas County, 1995, Susan B. Anthony award United Meth. Ch., 1997, Award for Ednl. Excellence in Programming Planned Parenthood of Dallas, 1998. Mem. LWV (bd. dirs. 1982-85), Nat. Assn. Healthy Start (founding mem. bd. dirs. 1998). Avocations: travel, reading, swimming, tennis, family.

COWLES, FREDERICK OLIVER, lawyer; b. Steubenville, Ohio, Oct. 18, 1937; s. Oliver Howard and Cornelia Blanche (Regal) C.; m. Christina Monica Muller, Sept. 9, 1961; children: Randall, Eric, Gregory, Cornelius. AB magna cum laude, Yale U., 1959; JD, Harvard U., 1962. Bar: R.I. 1963, Mich. 1967, Ill. 1969, N.Y. 1998, Conn. 1998. Assoc. Hinckley, Allen, Salisbury & Parsons, Providence, 1962-67; internat. atty. Upjohn Co., Kalamazoo, Mich., 1967-69; chief internat. atty. Am. Hosp. Supply Crp., Evanston, Ill., 1969-71; internat. atty. Kendall Co., Boston, 1971-73; chief internat. counsel Colgate Palmolive Co., N.Y.C., 1973-86, assoc. gen. counsel, asst. sec., 1986-90, assoc. gen. counsel, asst. sec., v.p. legal ops., 1990-94, sr. assoc. gen. coun., asst. sec., v.p. legal ops., 1994-97, multinat. estate planning, 1997—; dir. various cos. Deacon South Salem Presbyn. Ch.; mem. com. Lewisboro Boy Scouts; co-founder Internat. House R.I. Inc.; group leader Operation Crossroads Africa, Gambia. Mem. ABA, Am. Corp. Coun. Assn., Internat. Bar Assn., Westchester Fairfield Corp. Csl. Assn., Yale Alumni Assn. Westchester, Internat. Lawyers Assn., Phi Beta Kappa. Fax: 914-276-7853. E-mail: focowles@bestweb.net. Home: 111 Oscaleta Rd South Salem NY 10590-1003 Office: Multinational Estate Planning PLLC 358 Route 202 Somers NY 10589-3207

COWLES, ROBERT LAWRENCE, lawyer; b. Jacksonville, Fla., Feb. 5, 1942; m. Barbara Bearden; children: Robert L., Kelli R. McMullin. BS, U. N.C., 1964; JD, Emory U. Law Sch., 1969. Bar: Fla. 1969, Ga. 1969. Claims adjuster, supr. Travelers Ins. Co., Jacksonville, Atlanta,, N.Y.C., 1964-68; assoc. Neely, Freeman & Hawkins, Atlanta, 1968-69, Swift, Currie, McGhee & Hiers, Atlanta, 1969-71; dir. Howell, Kirby, Montgomery, D'Aiuto, Dean & Hallowes PA, Jacksonville, 1971-76; pres. Cowles, Coker & Myers, Jacksonville, 1976-83, Cowles, Coker, Myers, Schickel & Pierce PA, Atlanta, 1982-83, Cowles, Hayden, Facciolo, McMorrow & Barfield PA, Jacksonville, 1984-87; judge Fourth Judicial Cir. Ct., Atlanta, 1987-90; comdr. Legler, Werber, Dawes, Sadler & Howell PA, Jacksonville, 1990-91; pvt. practice Law Offices of Robert L. Cowles, 1991-93; ptnr. Cowles & Shaughnessy PA, Jacksonville, 1993-2000; pvt. practice The Cowles Law Firm, Jacksonville, 2000—. Bd. dirs. Boys Home of Jacksonville, 19895. Mem. Am. Bd. Trial Advocacy, Fla. Bar Assn. (chmn. bd. cert. civil trial lawyers com. 1998-99), State Bar Ga. Avocations: golfing, gardening, travel. Office: The Cowles Law Firm 1930 San Marco Blvd Ste 203 Jacksonville FL 32207-1200

COWLES, WALTER CURTIS, naval architect; b. Chgo., Aug. 25, 1919; s. Harry Samuel and Blanche Lee (Gates) C.; m. Betty Ann McDuff, July 28, 1945; children: Mark Allan, Garry Stephen, Kent Edward, Joy Elizabeth. BS in Engring., U. Mich., 1942. Draftsman Am. Ship Bldg. Co., Cleve., 1942-51, chief hull draftsman, 1951-57, naval architect, 1951-63; marine designer Esso/Exxon, N.Y.C. and Morristown, N.J., 1963-84; ret., 1984. Contbr. paper to Transactions of Soc. Naval Architects and Marine Engrs., 1980; coord. publ. of centennial hist. vol., 1993; pub. Antrim Steamers A Brief History of Steam Navigation on the Inland Lakes of Antrim County Michigan, 1997. Mem. Soc. Naval Architects (life), U.S. Naval Inst. (life), Am. Soc. Naval Engrs. Home: 55 Fieldstone Dr Morristown NJ 07960-2634

COWLES, WILLIAM STACEY, newspaper publisher; b. Spokane, Wash., Aug. 31, 1960; s. William Hutchinson 3rd and Allison Stacey C.; m. Anne Cannon, June 24, 1989. BA in Econs., Yale Coll., 1982; MBA in Fin., Columbia U., 1986. V.p., pub. The Spokesman Rev., Spokane, Wash. Office: Cowles Publishing Co PO Box 2160 Spokane WA 99210-2160

COWLEY, NIEL LESTER ORR, computer science educator, consultant, researcher; b. Port Elizabeth, Ea. Cape, South Africa, Mar. 31, 1951; s. Thomas Niel and Franscina Margaretha (Kruger) C.; m. Iona Hockly, Dec. 14, 1974; children: Bruce Niel, Bridget. BSc in Chemistry and Math., U. Port Elizabeth, South Africa, 1974, BEd, 1977, BSc in Computer Sci. with hons., 1983, MSc in Computer Sci., 1989. Secondary asst. Marist Bros. Coll., Port Elizabeth, South Africa, 1975-77, Lawson Brown H.S., Port Elizabeth, 1977; dept. head Theodor Herzl H.S., Port Elizabeth, 1978-81; jr. lectr. dept. computer sci. U. Port Elizabeth, 1981-86, lectr., 1986-95, sr. lectr., 1995—; mem. control bd. Inst. Sci. and Math. Edn., U. Port Elizabeth, S. Africa, 1986-98, primary math. programme com., 1996—, info. tech. adv. bd. student learning ctr. task team, U. Port Elizabeth distance edn. adv. bd., acting head U. Port Elizabeth unit Ctr. Excellence in Distributed Multimedia Applications, 1997—. Contbr. rsch. and articles to ednl. jours. Lay minister Anglican Ch., Port Elizabeth, S. Africa. Grantee: U. Port Elizabeth and Human Sci. Rsch. Coun., Washington, 1994, U. Port Elizabeth, Ga. Tech. U. and U. Ga., 1995, Ctr. for Sci. Devel. Human Scis. Rsch. Coun. Ea. Cape, South Africa, 1996/97. Mem. S. African Inst. of Computer Scientists and Info. Technologists, Computer Soc. S. Africa (com. mem. Ea. Cape chpt. 1986-90, Finalist for Computer Person of Yr. 1986, Computer Person of Yr. 1987 Ea. Cape chpt.), Southern African Computer Lectrs. Assn., Assn. Math. Educators So. Africa (com. mem. E. Cape Br., 1978-98). Avocations: art and literature, cinema, gardening, music, travel. Office: U Port Elizabeth Dept CSc/, Info Systems PO Box 1600, Port Elizabeth 6000, South Africa

COWLEY, ROBERT WILLIAM, editor, writer, lecturer; b. N.Y.C., Dec. 16, 1934; s. Malcolm and Muriel (Maurer) C.; m. Blair Phillips (div.); children: Elizabeth Blair Roberts, Miranda Phillips Heller; m. Edith Pray Lorillard, June 24, 1978; children: Olivia Lorillard, Savannah Caroline Lorillard. AB, Harvard U., 1956. Assoc. editor Am. Heritage, N.Y.C., 1956-64; mng. editor Sky, N.Y.C., 1964; asst. editor The Reporter, N.Y.C., 1965-66; articles editor, mng. editor Horizon, N.Y.C., 1966-72; co-editor The Saturday Review of the Arts, N.Y.C. and San Francisco, 1972-73; sr. editor, exec. editor Houghton Mifflin, Boston, 1973-77; sr. editor Random House, N.Y.C., 1977-84, Henry Holt, N.Y.C., 1984-88; founding editor, editor-in-chief MHQ: The Quarterly Jour. of Military History, N.Y.C., 1988-98; cons., writer, 1998—. Author: The Rulers of Britain, 1982; editor, introducer, contbr.: Experience of War, 1992; co-editor: (with Malcolm Cowley) Fitzgerald and the Jazz Age, 1966, (with Geoffrey Parker) The Reader's Companion to Military History, 1996; contbg. author: A Weekend with the Great War: Proceedings of the Fourth Annual Great War Inter-Conf. Sem., 1997, "To the Best of My Ability": The American Presidents, 2000; editor, contbr. What If?: The World's Foremost Military Historians Imagine What Might Have Been, 1999. Fellow Soc. Am. Military Historians; mem. Soc. Mil. History. Democrat. Episcopalian. Avocation: jazz collecting, military archaeology. Home: PO Box 268 5 Church Rd Sherman CT 06784-1334 Office: Am Hist Publications 37 W 39th St New York NY 10018-3886

COWLEY, STANLEY WILLIAM HERBERT, solar-planetary physics educator; b. Coventry, Eng., Apr. 11, 1947; s. Leslie and Jenny (Clarke) C.; m. Lynn Doreen Moore, Aug. 15, 1970; children: William, James, Emma. BSc, Imperial Coll., London, 1968; PhD, U. London, 1972; DIC, Imperial Coll., 1972. Assoc. Royal Coll. Sci., U.K., 1968. Rsch. asst. Imperial Coll., 1975-77, SERC advanced fellow, 1977-82, lectr., 1982-85, reader in space physics, 1985-88, prof. physics, head space & atmospheric physics group, 1988-95; prof., head radio & space plasma physics group Leicester (Eng.) U., 1996—; chmn. Internat. Assn. Geomagnetism and Aeronomy/divsn. III Internat., 1991-95; mem. European Incoherent Scatter (Radar Assn.) Coun. Internat., 1990-95, Particle Physics and Astronomy Rsch. Coun., Swindon, U.K., 1994-96; Birkeland lectr. Norwegian Acad. Sci. and Letters, 1994. Editor-in-chief Annales Geophysicae, 1992-99; contbr. over 290 scientific articles on space plasma physics to internat. profl. jours., including Jour. Geog. Rsch., Geophys. Rsch. Letters, others. Fellow Royal Astron. Soc. (Chapman medal 1991), Am. Geophys. Union (Van Allen lectr. 1994); mem. Inst. Physics, European Geophys. Soc. Avocations: painting, drawing. Office: U Leicester Dept Phys Astro, University Rd, Leicester LE1 7RH, England

COWLISHAW, MICHAEL FREDERIC, electronic engineer; b. Bath, Eng., Aug. 27, 1953; s. Mervyn George and Hilda Antonia Elizabeth (Gil) B.; m. Kittredge Cary, Dec. 31, 1982; 1 child, Mark. BSc in Electronic Engring., U. Birmingham, Eng., 1974. Chartered engr., U.K. Electronic engr. IBM U.K., Hursley, 1974-81; scientist IBM U.K. Sci. Centre, Winchester, 1982-85; programmer IBM U.K., Hursley, 1986-89, IBM Fellow, 1990—; cons. Oxford (Eng.) English Dictionary, 1987—; vis. prof. U. Warwick, 1999—. Author: The Rexx Language, 1985, 90, The NetRexx Language, 1997. Fellow Instn. Elec. Engrs., Brit. Computer Soc., Royal Acad. Engring. Achievements include patents in color display apparatus and in improvements in text processing. Avocations: caving, potholing, hiking, programming, curiosity. Office: IBM UK Ltd, PO Box 31 Birmingham Rd, Warwick CV34 5JL, England

COWPERTHWAIT, LINDLEY M., lawyer; b. Abington, Pa., Mar. 13, 1933; s. Lindley Murray Cowperthwait and Ruth Bronde Nicholas; m. Suzanne Dewees, Nov. 26, 1955 (div. July 1976); children: Murray, Mary Ruth, Edward, Linda, Tom, Suzanne; m. Karin Schmid Cowperthwait, Apr. 1, 1989. BA, Calif. State U., 1957; LLB, U. Pa., 1960, JD, 1970. Assoc. Wisler, Pearlstine, Talone Craig & Garrity, Norristown, Pa., 1960-68, ptnr., 1968-80; pvt. practice Norristown, 1980-96; of counsel High, Swartz, Roberts & Seidel, LLP, Norristown, 1997—. Prodr., author, dir. (video) Medicine for Lawyers, 1980-93; author: Damages-Delay and Punitive 1999. Bd. dirs. ARC, Norristown, 1993-95, Big Bros./Big Sisters, Norristown, 1985-92. Recipient Citizenship award Big Bros./Big Sisters, 1992. Mem. Pa. Trial Lawyers Assn. (pres. 1974-75), Montgomery County Trial Lawyers (founder, sec. 1965-74), Assn. Trial Lawyers of Am., Pa. Bar Assn., Pa. Soc. Republican. Episcopalian. Avocation: sailing. Home: 22116 Reeses Corner Rd Rock Hall MD 21661 Office: High Swartz Roberts & Seidel LLP 40 E Airy St Norristown PA 19401-4803

COWSER, DANNY LEE, lawyer, mental health specialist; b. Peoria, Ill., July 7, 1948; s. Albert Paul Cowser and Shirley Mae (Donaldson) Chatten; m. Nancy Lynn Hatch, Nov. 11, 1976; children: Kimberly Catherine Hatch Cowser, Dustin Paul Hatch Cowser. BA, No. Ill. U., 1972, MS, 1975; JD, DePaul U., 1980. Bar: Ill. 1980, Wis. 1981, U.S. Dist. Ct. (no. dist.) Ill. 1981, U.S. Ct. Appeals (7th cir.) 1983, U.S. Dist. Ct. (ea. and we. dists.) Wis. 1984, U.S. Supreme Ct. 1984, Ariz. 1985, U.S. Ct. Appeals (9th cir.) 1987, U.S. Dist. Ct. Ariz. 1989, U.S. Tax Ct. 1990, U.S. Ct. Claims 1990. Adminstr. Ill. Dept. Mental Health, Elgin, 1972-76, psychotherapist, 1976-79; assoc. Slaby, Deda & Henderson, Phillips, Wis., 1982-83; ptnr. Slaby, Deda & Cowser, Phillips, 1983-86; asst. atty. City of Flagstaff, Ariz., 1986-88; pub. defender Coconino County, Flagstaff, 1988-89; pvt. practice Flagstaff, 1989-97; atty. City Park Falls, Wis., 1983-86; spl. dep. Mohave County capital def., 1989-90; instr. speech comms. No. Ariz. U., 1992-93; adminstrv. law judge Ariz. Dept. Econ. Security, 1997—. Bd. dirs DeKalb County (Ill.) Drug Coun., 1973-75, Counseling and Personal Devel., Phillips, 1985-86, Northland YM-WYCA, 1990-91. Reginald Heber Smith fellow, 1980-81; C.J.S. legal scholar, 1979. Mem. ABA, Ariz. Bar Assn., State Bar Ariz. (cert. specialist in criminal law 1993-98), State Bar Wis., Nat. Assn. of Criminal Def. Lawyers. Democrat. Avocations: skiing, photography, bicycling. Office: PO Box 22329 Flagstaff AZ 86002-2329

COX, ALMA TENNEY, retired English language and science educator; b. Sand Run, W.Va., Apr. 6, 1919; d. Albert Law and Viola Columbia (Gooden) Tenney; m. James Carl Cox Jr., Sept. 8, 1945; children: James Carl III, Joseph Merrils II, Alma Lee, Elizabeth Susan, Albert John. BA, W.Va. Wesleyan Coll., 1946; MEd, West Tex. State U., 1975. Elem. sch. tchr. Floyd (Va.) County Schs., 1940-42, Nicholas County Schs., Summersville, W.Va., 1942-43; high sch. English tchr. Harrison County Schs., Lewisburg, W.Va., 1943-45; English tchr. am. Embassy, Baghdad, 1956-58; high sch. English and Sci. tchr. Tulsa Sch. System, 1965-68; high sch. English and Sci. tchr. Plainview (Tex.) Ind. Sch. System, 1969-86, ret., 1986. Author: Birds in

Plainview, 1998. Pres. Plainview Federated Women's Club, 1988-90, Hale County Retired Tchrs., 1990-91, Hale County Hist. Com., 1985-91, United Meth. Women; sec. Disable Am. Vet. Aux., 1990. Named Woman of Yr. Plainview Federated Women's Club, 1991, Hale County Retired Tchrs., 1990-91, Disable Am. Vet. Aux., 1991, Hale County Hist. Com., 1991; recipient Woman of Distinction AAUW, 1997. Mem. Delta Kappa Gamma (pres. Gamma Iota chpt. 1990-92, pres. Epsilon Alpha chpt. 1998—). Republican. Avocations: oil painting, reading, travel, tatting, crocheting, flower gardening. Home: 5105 Stacey Ave Fort Worth TX 76132-1628

COX, BERRY GORDON, rancher; b. Garden City, Tex., Mar. 6, 1923; s. Sam W. and Thelma (Berry) C.; m. Edna Earle Jonas, Dec. 21, 1941; children: Karen, Berry S. Grad. high sch., Martin County, Tex. Rancher Andrews, Tex.; pres. Andrews Livestock Show, West Tex. Livestock Show; bd. dirs. Commerce State Bank, Andrews, Soil and Water Dist., Andrews; chmn. USDA Agr. Stablzn. Conservation Svcs. Com., Andrews, Andrews Tax Revue; life career counselor Andrews Sch. System. Bd. dirs. Permian Gen. Hosp. Mem. West Tex. Cattle Raisers Assn. (pres.), Goldenspread Chaolais Cattle Raisers Assn. (bd. dirs.), Andrews C. of C. (life; bd. dirs.), Masons, Chambership Gold Coats. Baptist. Avocation: quarter horse racing. Home and Office: PO Box 27 Andrews TX 79714-0027

COX, CHARLES C., economist; b. Missoula, Mont., May 8, 1945; m. Monica Lewis, 1984. BA magna cum laude, U. Wash., 1967; AM, U. Chgo., 1970, PhD, 1975. Asst. prof. econs. Ohio State U., Columbus, 1972-80; nat. fellow Hoover Instn., 1977-78; asst. prof. mgmt. Tex. A&M U., College Station, 1980-82; chief economist SEC, Washington, 1982-83, commr., 1983-89, acting chmn., 1987; prin., sr. v.p. Lexecon, Inc., Chgo., 1989—. Nat. fellow Hoover Institution, 1977-78. Mem. Am. Econ. Assn., United Shareholders Assn. (chmn. 1990-93), Mt. Pelerin Soc., Phi Beta Kappa. Office: Lexecon Inc 332 S Michigan Ave Ste 1300 Chicago IL 60604-4397*

COX, CLARICE ROBINSON, writer; b. Helena, Mont., May 11, 1914; d. William Mont and Adelia Anne (Geier) Robinson; m. Gene H. Cox, June 11, 1938 (dec. June 1996); children: William Edward, James Laurence (dec. Aug. 1999), Willa Margaret. BA in English, Intermountain Union, 1935; MEd in Comms., U. Hawaii, 1968. H.S. tchr. Mont., Oreg. and Hawaii schs., 1936-60; asst. base edn. adviser 408th Fighter Group USAF, Klamath Falls, Oreg., 1960-61; writer, demonstrator Maui Project NIMH, Wailuku, Hawaii, 1965-67; instr. Honolulu C.C., 1967-73, 75-79; freelance writer Roseburg, Oreg., 1995—; cons., lectr. Mont. Pers. Devel. Ctr., Helena, 1979-88; cons., lectr. Queen's Med. Ctr., Honolulu, 1980-89, Am. Soc. Ind. Security, Honolulu, 1981, Honolulu Police Dept., 1980-88; presenter in field. Author: Criminal Justice: Improving Police Report Writing, 1977, Instant Teaching Skills, 1995; (with Jerrold G. Brown) Report Writing for Criminal Justice Professionals, 1991, 2d edit., 1998; contbr. articles, poems, short stories to profl. jours. and popular mags. Mem. Oreg. Com. on Aging, 1996-98, Hawaii Com. on Aging, 1973-78; mem. panel John Jay Coll. Criminal Justice, N.Y.C., 1996, Acad. Criminal Justice Scis., Albuquerque, 1998; vol. Mercy Hosp., Roseburg, Oreg., 1995—. Recipient Lifetime Achievement award Police Writers Club, 1997. Mem. Acad. Criminal Justice Scis., Am. Soc. Criminology, Am. Soc. Indsl. Security, Internat. Assn. Women Police (assoc.), Police Writers Club (panelist). Home: 16925 Hierba Dr Apt 242 San Diego CA 92128-2662

COX, COREY LYNN, urban planner; b. Edmonton, Alta., Can., Nov. 9, 1955; d. John Nicholas Polonuk and Barbara Marion Gowda; m. Thomas Hamilton Cox, June 24, 1987; children: Jeffrey John, Brian Thomas. BS in Geography, Ariz. State U., 1988, MPA, 1995. Cert. urban planner Am. Inst. Cert. Planners. Planner City of Phoenix, 1988-99; regional devel. planning mgr. Maricopa Assn. Govts., Phoenix, 1999—; cons. drafting com., tech. advisor Gov.'s Growin Smarter Commn., Phoenix, 1999. Columnist Ariz. Planning, 1989—. Mem. Ariz. Planning Assn. (v.p. legis. affairs, 1995—, mem. exec. bd.). Unitarian. Avocation: gardening. Office: Maricopa Assn Govts 302 Noert 1st Ave Ste 300 Phoenix AZ 85003

COX, DAVID A., rail transportation executive; b. Tipton, Ind., Feb. 21, 1936. BA, Purdue U. Chainman Nickel Plate R.R., Frankfort, Ind., 1956; rodman Nickel Plate R.R., Brewster, Ohio, 1956-59; asst. structural engr. Nickel Plate R.R., Cleve., 1959-62, draftsman, 1962-64; draftsman Norfolk and Western Rlwy., Cleve., 1964-65; real estate agt. Norfolk and Western Rlwy., Roanoke, Va., 1965-71, dir. real estate, 1971-82; dir. indsl. devel. Norfolk (Va.) So. Corp., 1982-90, asst. v.p. indsl. devel., 1990-95, v.p. properties, 1995-99, sr. v.p. properties and devel., 1999—; dir. Forward Hampton Rds. Office: Norfolk So Corp 3 Commercial Pl Norfolk VA 23510-2108

COX, DONALD C., economics educator; b. Lawrence, Mass., Jan. 6, 1954; s. Donald C. and Mary T. Cox. BS in Econs., Boston Coll., 1975; MA in Econs., Brown U., 1977, PhD in Econs., 1980. Economist Fed. Res. Bank of N.Y., 1980-81; fellow Hoover Inst./Stanford (Calif.) U., 1984-85; asst. prof. Wash. U., 1981-87; assoc. prof. Boston Coll., 1987-95, prof., 1995—; presenter confs. in field; cons. The World Bank, 1986—. Contbr. articles to profl. jours., publs.; referee profl. jours. Grantee NIH, 1989-91, 96-2000, NSF, 1986-89, U.S. Wis. Inst. for Rsch. on Poverty, 1986, Dept. Labor, 1979, Instl. Reform and the Informal Sector, 1994, Nat. Coun. for Soviet and E. European Rsch., 1995. Home: 101 Summit Ave Apt D Brookline MA 02446-2305 Office: Boston Coll Dept Econ Chestnut Hill MA 02167

COX, FRANK D. (BUDDY COX), oil company executive, exploration consultant; b. Shreveport, La., Dec. 20, 1932; s. Ohmer M. and Beulah O. (Scott) C.; m. Betty Jean Hand, June 19, 1956; children: Cynthia Dell, Carolyn Diane, Frank D. Jr. BS in Bus. Adminstrn., La. Tech. U., 1956; postgrad., Centenary Coll., 1958-59. Cert. profl. landman; lic. real estate, Fla. Various positions Exxon Corp., Houston, 1955-86, chief landman, v.p. coal resources, 1980-86; pvt. practice Houston, 1986-89; sr. v.p. Energy Exploration Mgmt. Co., Houston, 1989-94; v.p., mgr. T-Bar-X Ltd. Co., Houston, 1994-2000; v.p., dir. Power Exploration Internat., Houston, 1994-2000; ptnr. East Tex. Reef Fund, Ltd., 1994-2000; land mgr. Thomson-Barrow Corp., 1994-2000; land mgr. Tecolotita, Inc., 1994-2000, ret., 2000; exploration cons. Houston, 2000—. Active Second Bapt. Ch., Houston. Capt. USAF, 1956-58. Named disting. mil. grad. La. Tech. U., Ruston, 1955. Mem. Am. Assn. Profl. Landmen, Houston Assn. Profl. Landmen, W. Houston Assn. Profl. Landmen, W. Houston Exxon Annuitant Club, 100 Club of Greater Houston, La. Tech. U. Found., Crimestoppers Inc., Pi Kappa Alpha Ednl. Found., Omicron Delta Kappa Found., Delta Sigma Pi. Republican. Avocations: golf, tennis, amateur radio. Home and Office: 14830 Carolcrest St Houston TX 77079-6312

COX, GARY WALTER, political science educator; b. Patuxent River, Md., Sept. 23, 1955; s. Dale William and Patricia Broadway Cox; m. Diane Christine Lin, June 18, 1988 (dec. Jan. 1999); 1 child, Dylan Gregory. BS, Calif. Tech. U., 1978, PhD, 1982. From asst. prof. to assoc. prof. U. Tex., Austin, 1982-86; assoc. prof. U. Calif., La Jolla, 1986-90, prof., 1990—. Author: (books) The Efficient Secret, 1987, Making Votes Count, 1997 (Woodrow Wilson Found. award 1998; co-author: (book) Legislative Leviathan, 1993 (Fenno prize 1994). Guggenheim fellow, 1995, Am. Acad. Arts and Scis. fellow, 1996. E-mail: gcox@weber.ucsd.edu.

COX, GREGORY STEVENS, educator, lecturer, publisher, broadcaster; b. Ilchester, Somerset, Eng., Feb. 14, 1947; s. James Stevens and Helen (Whitton) C.; m. Rosemary Rossiter, June 24, 1969; children: Emma, Andrew. BA with honors, Oxford U., 1969, MA, 1972; MEd with distinction, Exeter (Eng.) U., 1994; PhD, Leicester (Eng.) U., 1995. Bookseller, pub. Toucan Press, St. Peter Port Guernsey, Channel Islands, 1969—; schoolmaster Blanchelande Coll., Guernsey, Channel Islands, 1972-89, Grammar Sch., Guernsey, 1989-98; head 6th form Blanchelande Girls' Coll., 1998—; lectr. States of Guernsey, 1972—. Author: Victor Hugo aux îles de la Manche, 1996, St. Peter Port 1680-1830 The History of an International Entrepot, 1999; editor: Thomas Hardy Year Book, 1970—. Recipient Travel Scholarships Gilbert Murray Fund, Athens, 1977, Coun. of Europe, Sweden, 1994. Fellow Royal Asiatic Soc. Roman Catholic. Avocations: book collecting, chess, hill walking, researching history. Home and Office: Toucan Press White Cottage, Rue de Carteret, Castel Guernsey GY5 7YG, Channel Islands

COX, HOWARD ELLIS, JR., venture capitalist; b. N.Y.C., Feb. 1, 1944; s. Howard Ellis and Anne Delafield (Finch) C.; m. Julia Bolton Dempsey, Oct. 31, 1970. BA, Princeton U., 1964; JD, Columbia U., 1967; MBA, Harvard U., 1969. Bar: N.Y. 1967. Co-mng. ptnr. Greylock, Boston, 1971—; bd. dirs. Amisys, Rockville, Md., Arbor Health Care, Lima, Ohio, Greylock Mgmt. Corp., Boston, Stryker, Kalamazoo, Pryon Corp., Milw., HPR, Boston, Centene, St. Louis, Landacorp, Chico, Calif., Vincam, Miami, Carinstone, Miami, Managed Comp., Boston. Bd. dirs. Preuss Found., San Diego, 1986—, Nat. Venture Capital Assn., Washington, 1997—; trustee Dana Farber Cancer Inst., 1987—; v.p., trustee Assn. Relief of the Elderly, N.Y.C. Capt. U.S. Army, 1969-71. Mem. New England Venture Capital. Bus. Assocs. Club Boston (pres. 1979-80). Episcopalian. Home: 225 Sargent Rd Brookline MA 02445-7517 Office: Greylock 1 Federal St Boston MA 02110-2012

COX, JOHN SAMUEL TWEEDALE, surgeon; b. Jamestown, Australia, Aug. 8, 1931; s. Robert Malcolm Tweedale and Irene Anne (Poling) C.; m. Carola Ray McAuley, Sept. 24, 1963; children: Henry, Simon, Henrietta, Julius, Naomi. MB BChir, Adelaide (Australia) U., 1955, M of Surgery, 1964. Cert. specialist surgeon. Vascular fellow Harvard U., Boston, 1960-61; sr. surg. registrar Queen Elizabeth Hosp., Adelaide, 1963-66; clin. asst. Royal Adelaide Hosp., 1966-72; sr. vis. surgeon Modbury Hosp., Adelaide, 1972-98; chmn. staff soc. Modbury Hosp., Adelaide; clin. tutor Adelaide U., 1980-98. Contbr. articles to profl. jours. Fellow Royal Coll. Surgeons (London), Royal Australian Coll. Surgeons; mem. Australian Med. Assn., Royal Adelaide Golf Club. Roman Catholic.

COX, JOHN THOMAS, JR., lawyer; b. Shreveport, La., Feb. 9, 1943; s. John Thomas and Gladys Virginia (Canterbury) C.; m. Tracey L. Tanquary, Aug. 27, 1966; children: John Thomas, III, Stephen Lewis. BS, La. State U., 1965; JD, 1968. Bar: La. 1968, U.S. Dist. Ct. (we., mid. and ea. dist.) La., U.S. Dist. Ct. (ea. dist.) Tex., U.S. Ct. Appeals (5th and 8th cir.), U.S. Tax Ct., U.S. Supreme Ct. Assoc. Sanders, Miller, Downing & Keene, Baton Rouge, 1968-70, Blanchard, Walker, O'Quin & Roberts, Shreveport, La., 1970-71; ptnr., 1971—; tchr. bus. law Centenary Coll. La. Served to lt. USAR, 1963-69. Lt. USAR, 1963-69. Recipient George Washington Honor medal Valley Forge Freedoms Found. Mem. ABA, La. Bar Assn., Caddo parish Bar Assn., Am. Assn. Def. Counsel, La. Assn. Def. Counsel, Shreveport Club. Presbyterian. Address: 555 Dunmoreland Dr Shreveport LA 71106-6124

COX, KENNETH LEE, medical educator; b. Klamath Falls, Oreg., Jan. 27, 1946; m. Kathleen Cox. BS, Seattle U., 1968; MD, U. Wash., 1971. Diplomate Am. Bd. Pediat., Am. Bd. Pediat. Gastroenterology, Nat. Bd. Med. Examiners. Assoc. prof. pediat. U. Calif., Davis, 1978-89; chmn. pediat. Calif. Pacific Med. Ctr., San Francisco, 1989-95; prof. pediat. Stanford U., Palo Alto, Calif., 1995—. Contbr. over 100 articles to profl. jours. Office: Stanford U 750 Welch Rd Ste 116 Palo Alto CA 94304-1508

COX, MICHAEL DAVID, chief internal auditor; b. Sittingborne, Kent, Eng., Sept. 18, 1945; m. Heather Mary Raven, Aug. 6, 1966; children: Jeannette, Jo Anne. Diploma in Bus. Studies, Massey U., New Zealand, 1989. Various positions BBC, London, 1963-77; asst. internal audit dept. BBC, 1977-82; sr. mgmt. auditor Broadcasting Corp. of New Zealand, Wellington, 1982-89; group internal audit mgr. Television New Zealand, Auckland, 1989-99, chief internal auditor, 1995—. Recipient Prize in Internal Auditing, Massey U, 1989. Fellow Inst. Internal Auditors (pres. 1987-89, dist. dir. South Pacific region 1988-90, regional dir. South Pacific Region 1990-92, bd. dirs. 1992-97, Richard Ratliff award 1993), Inst. Chartered Accts. of New Zealand (acctg. technician). Office: TVNZ, POB 3819 100 Victoria St W, Auckland New Zealand

COX, PAT, artist; b. Pasadena, Calif., Mar. 6, 1921; d. Walter Melville and Mary Elizabeth (Frost) Boadway; m. Dale William Cox Jr., Feb. 19, 1946; children: Brian Philip, Dale William III, Gary Walter. BA, Mills Coll., 1943, MA, 1944. Graphic artist Pacific Manifolding Book Co., Emeryville, Calif., 1944-45; tchr. art to adults China Lake, Calif., 1957-63; tchr. art to children Peninsula Enrichment Program, Rancho Palos Verdes, Calif., 1965-67; graphic artist Western Magnum Corp., Hermosa Beach, Calif., 1970-80; tchr. art workshop Art at Your Fingertips, Rancho Palos Verdes, 1994-95. One-woman shows include Palos Verdes Art Ctr., Rancho Palos Verdes, Calif., 1977, 79, 83, 92, Thinking Eye Gallery, L.A., 1988, Ventura (Calif.) Coll. Art Galleries, 1994, Mendenhall Gallery, Whittier (Calif.) Coll., 1995, The Gallery at Stevenson Union, So. Oreg. Coll., Ashland, 1996, Fresno Art Museum, Fresno, Calif., 1999; two person exhibits Laguna Art Mus., Laguna Beach, Calif., 1971, Creative Arts Gallery, Burbank, Calif., 1993; group exhibits include Long Beach Mus. Art, Art Rental Gallery, 1979, L.A. County Mus. Art, Art Rental Gallery, 1979, Palm Springs Mus. Art, 1980, Laguna Art Mus., 1981, N.Mex. Fine Arts Gallery, 1981, Pacific Grove Art Ctr., 1983, Phoenix Art Mus., 1983, Riverside Art Mus., 1985, Laguna Art Mus., 1986, Zanesville Art Ctr., Ohio, 1987, The Thinking Eye Gallery, L.A., 1987, 89, Hippodrome Gallery, Long Beach, 1988, N.Mex. State Fine Arts Gallery, 1988, Long Beach City Coll., 1989, Newport Harbor Art Mus., 1988, Downey Mus. Art, 1990, 92, Rachele Lozzi Fine Art Gallery, L.A., 1991, Internat. Contemporary Art Fair L.A., 1986, 87, 88, 92, U. Tex. Health Sci. Ctr., 1992, Long Beach Arts, 1991, 92, 93, Young Aggressive Art Mus., Santa Ana, 1993, U. Ark. Fine Arts Gallery, Fayetteville, 1994, Laura Knott Art Gallery, Bradford Coll., Mass., 1994, Bridge Street Gallery, Big Fork, Mont., 1994, St. John's Coll. Art Gallery, Santa Fe, 1995, L.A. Harbor Coll., Calif., 1995, Walker Art Collection, Garnett, Kans., 1995, San Francisco State U., 1996, Coleman Gallery, Albuquerque, 1996, Loyola Law Sch., L.A., 1996, San Bernardino County Mus., 1996, Prieto Gallery, Mills Coll., Oakland, Calif., 1996, U. So. Calif. Hillel Gallery, L.A., 1997. Trustee L.A. Art Assn., 1972-79; bd. dirs. Palos Verdes Art Ctr., 1966-70, 87-89, chair exhbn. com., 1982-85, co-chair Art for Fun(d)s Sake, 1966; judge Tournament of Roses Assn., Pasadena, 1975; mem. strategic planning Palos Verdes Art Ctr., 1988; mem. Pacific Pl. Planning Commn. Percent for Art, San Pedro, Calif., 1989; juror Pasadena Soc. Artists, 1973, 81, Women Painters West, 1984-85. Recipient Silver Pin award Palos Verdes Art Ctr., 1988, Calif. Gold Discovery award V.I.P. Jury Panel, L.A., 1994. Mem. Nat. Watercolor Soc. (juror 1981, 1st v.p. 1980, 4th v.p. 1984), Nat. Mus. Women in the Arts, Oakland Mus. Art, Mus. Contemporary Art, L.A. County Mus. Art, Palos Verdes Cmty. Art Assn. (cert. appreciation 1981). Avocations: gardening, reading.

COX, ROBERT HAMES, chemist, scientific consultant; b. Toronto, Mar. 23, 1923; came to U.S., 1951; s. Giffard and Lavinia Sarah (Hames) C.; m. Dora Maria Forstrom, Sept. 5, 1953; children: William H., Frederick G., Irene M. PharmB, U. Toronto, 1946; BSP, U. Sask., Saskatoon, Can., 1948, MSc, 1950; PhD in Medicinal Chemistry, U. Mich., 1954. Lic. pharmacist, Ont. Head dept. pharm. chemistry U. B.C., Vancouver, Can., 1949-51; asst. to mgr. product devel. Mallinckrodt Chem. Works, St. Louis, 1954-56; tech. dir. Vick Internat. div. Richardson-Merrell, N.Y.C., 1956-60, assoc. dir. tech. svcs., 1960-64; v.p. rsch. and devel. Walker Labs. Richardson-Merrell, Mt. Vernon, N.Y., 1964-66; dir. new products Winthrop Labs. div. Sterling Drug, N.Y.C., 1966-75; co-founder, pres. New Eng. Pharms., Inc., Randolph, Mass., 1978-82; pres. Robert H. Cox & Co., Scarsdale, N.Y., 1975—, Cox & Fay, Inc., Scarsdale, 1991—; cons. Drug Enforcement Adminstrn., Washington, 1976-78, Nat. Cancer Inst., Bethesda, Md., 1980-81, Indonesian Govt., Jakarta, Java, 1991—. Co-editor-in-chief: Medicinal Chemistry, Vol. III, 1956, Vol. IV, 1959. Leader Jamaica Mission, UN Adv. Svcs., 1988; mem. U.S. Exchanges del. to China, 1990. Recipient Roberts medal Ont. Coll. Pharmacy, 1955, George E. Parke medal, 1957. Fellow Am. Inst. Chemists (pres. N.Y. 1986-87, leader sci. del. to China 1986, coleader to USSR 1989); mem. Am. Chem. Soc. (treas. medicinal chemistry div. 1962-63), Parenteral Drug Assn., Cen. Atlantic States Assn. Food and Drug Ofcls., Chemists Club (trustee). Episcopalian. Achievements include patents for drugs (sympatholytics/cycloplegics) and medical devices including hemodialysis; conducted practical synthesis of suberone precursor of early antihypertensive, guanethidine; early evaluation (1940s) of oxidized cholesterols in etiology of experimental atherosclerosis. Office: 99 Litchfield Ponds Dr Litchfield CT 06759-3310

COX, STEPHEN JAMES, educator; b. Blackburn, Lancashire, U.K., Dec. 5, 1946; s. Harold and Norah C.; m. Pauline Victoria Cox, July, 1970; children: Rachel, David. BA with honors in Geography, Birmingham U., 1969; PDESL in English, Leeds U., 1970; MA in Edn., Sussex U., 1977. Tchr. Brit. Vol. Svc. Overseas, Bolivia, 1965-66; overseas career svc. profl. Brit. Coun., London, Warsaw, Accra, 1969-84; edn. attache Brit. Embassy, Washington, 1984-85; asst. sec. Royal Soc., London, 1985-91, exec. sec., 1997—; dir. gen. Commonwealth Inst., London, 1991-97; chief exec. Westminster Found. for Democracy, London, 1995-97; chair Brit. Coun., Whitley Coun., London, 1981-84; mem. exec. com. GB Ea. Europe Ctr., London, 1988-91. Editl. bd.: Round Table, London, 1994—. Active Brit. Labour Party, U.K., 1973—; coun. mem. Parlimentary and Sci. Com., 1997—. Decorated comdr. Royal Victorian Order (U.K.). Fellow Royal Geog. Soc. (mem. various coms. 1995—), English Speaking Union; mem. Brit. Assn. for Advancement Sci. (coun. mem. 1997—). Avocations: cricket, travel, art, architecture. Office: The Royal Soc, 6 Carlton House Terr, London SW1Y 5AG, England

COX, WILLIAM ANDREW, cardiovascular thoracic surgeon; b. Columbus, Ga., Aug. 3, 1925; s. Virgil Augustus and Dale Jackson C.; m. Nina Recelle Hobby, Jan. 1, 1948; children: Constance Lynn Cox Rogers, Patricia Ann Cox Brown, William Robert, Janet Elaine Cox Sidewater. Student, Presbyn. Coll., 1942, Harvard U., 1944-45, Cornell U., 1945; BS, Emory U., 1950, MD, 1954; MS in Surgery, Baylor U., 1961. Diplomate Am. Bd. Surgery, Am. Bd. Thoracic Surgery. Active duty USN, 1943-46; lt. (j.g.) USNR, 1946-54; commd. 1st lt. M.C. U.S. Army, 1954, advanced through grades to col., 1969; intern Brooke Army Med. Ctr., San Antonio, 1954-55, resident gen. surgery, 1956-60; resident cardiovasc. thoracic surgery Walter Reed Army Med. Ctr., Washington, 1960-62, staff cardiothoracic surgeon, 1962; asst chief cardiothoracic surgery Letterman Gen. Hosp., San Francisco, 1962-65; chief dept. surgery and cardiothoracic surgery 121 Evacuation Hosp, Seoul, Korea, 1965-66; cons. cardiothoracic surgery Korean Theatre, 1965-66; asst. chief cardiothoracic surgery Brooke Army Med Ctr., 1966-69, chief, 1969-73, bd. dirs. thoracic surgery residency programs, 1966-73, ret., 1973; Brooke Tower, on call for Pres. Lyndon B. Johnson when he visited his Tex. Ranch, 1967-72; clin. prof. cardio-thoracic surgery U. Tex. Sch. Medicine, San Antonio, 1971—; practice specializing in cardiovasc. thoracic surgery, Corpus Christi, Tex., 1973-93; cons. cardio-thoracic surgery Brooke Army Med. Ctr., San Antonio, 1977—; chief staff Meml. Med. Ctr., 1980; dir. disaster med. care region 3A Tex. State Dept. Health, 1973-88; mem. Coastal Bend Coun. Gov.'s Emergency Med. Svc. Commn., 1979-88; mem. adv. bd. on congenital heart disease Tex. Dept. Health, 1980-88; participant joint confs. on cardiovasc. surgery and thoracic surgery Am. People Amb. Program, Leningrad, Moscow, Bucharest, Romania, Belgrade, Yugoslavia, Prague, Czechoslovakia, 1987; del. Vanderbilt U. Joint conf. vascular surgery Dublin, Ireland, Edinburgh, Scotland, London, 1986; participant joint confs. cardiovasc. surgery and thoracic surgery Am. Amb. People to People Program, Singapore, Kuala Lumpur, Malaysia, Hanoi, Vietnam, DaNang, Vietnam, Hue, Vietnam, Saigon, Vietnam, Hong Kong, 1992, People to People Am. Amb. Program, Eng., Scotland, Wales, 1996, 13th worldwide conf., Chester, England, 1998, 14th worldwide conf., Hong Kong, 2000, Denton A. Cooley Cardiovasc. Surgery Soc. mtg. Coeur d'Alene, Idaho, 2000; spkr. symposium Controversies in Cardiology, Dr. Willis Hurst, Holland Am. Lines Veendam, 1997. Contbr. numerous articles to profl. jours. Ruling elder Presbyn. Ch., 1960—. Decorated Legion of Merit, Army Commendation medal; recipient A Prefix award Surgeon Gen. U.S. Army, commendation Surgeon Gen. South Korea, commendation Eighth U.S. Army Commdg. Gen. for Emergency Surgery on Adm. Blackburn U.S. Negotiator for Peace, Pan mun jom, North Korea; named hon. citizen Phila. by Mayor Edward G. Rendell, 1995. Fellow Am. Coll. Chest Physicians; mem. AMA, Soc. Thoracic Surgeons, Denton A. Coley Cardiovasc. Surgery Soc., Tex. Med. Assn. (del. conf. infectious diseases Bangkok, Hong Kong, Beijing, Shanghai, 1983), So. Thoracic Surgery Assn., Nueces County Med. Soc., Corpus Christi Surg. Soc., 38th Parallel Med. Soc., U.S. Power Squadron, People to People Internat., Internat. Platform, USN League (life), Retired Officers Assn. (life), Navy Meml. Yacht Club (past commodore presidio San Francisco), T-Bar-M Racquet Club, Corpus Christi Country Club, Corpus Christi Athletic Club, Corpus Christi Town, Ft. Sam Houston Officers Club. Republican. Home: 5214 Wooldridge Rd Corpus Christi TX 78413-3833

COX, WILLIAM MARTIN, lawyer, educator; b. Bernardsville, N.J., Dec. 26, 1922; s. Martin John and Nellie (Fotens) C.; m. Julia Sebastian, June 14, 1952; children: Janice Cox Trautman, William Martin, Joann Cox Cahoon, Julieann Cox Allen. AB, Syracuse U., 1947; JD, Cornell U., 1950. Bar: N.J., U.S. Dist. Ct. Mem. Dolan & Dolan, Newton, N.J., 1950—; mem. faculty, tchr. zoning admintrn. Rutgers U., 1968-98; gen. counsel emeritus N.J. Planning Ofcls.; pres. N.J. Inst. Mcpl. Attys., 1982-84, mem. Land Use Law Drafting Com., 1970— (chmn. 1993-98), dir., sec. Equip, Inc., Marion, N.C.; v.p. Newton Century Co., 2000—. Author: Zoning and Land Use Administration in New Jersey, 19th edit., 2000. With U.S. Army, 1943-45. Recipient Resolution of Appreciation award N.J. Senate and Gen. Assembly, 1994,Pres.'s Disting. Svc. award N.J. League Municipalities, 1999. dem. ABA, N.J. Bar Assn., Sussex County Bar Assn., Am. Planning Assn., Newton Cemetary Assn. (bd. dirs., v.p. 2000—), Monarchist League, Rotary (pres. 1978-79, Vocat. award 1996), Am. Legion, VFW. Baptist. Office: 1 Legal Ln Newton NJ 07860-1827

COXAM, VERONIQUE MARTINE, physiologist, researcher; b. Thiers, France, Dec. 17, 1961; d. Yves and Annie (Benard) Desprez; m. Jean-Yves Michel Coxam, Sept. 1, 1984; children: Emmanuel, Caroline. BS with honors, U. Nantes, France, 1983; MS with honors, U. Clermont, France, 1985, PhD with honors, 1990; postdoctoral degree, U. Utah, 1992-93. Cert. scientist. Fellow Nat. Inst. Agrl. Rsch., France, 1985-90; rsch. asst. Nat. Inst. Agrl. Rsch., 1990-92, rsch. assoc., 1993-97, head mineral metabolism unit, 1997—; vis. prof. U. Utah, 1992-93. Author: Fetal and Neonatal Development, 1988; contbr. articles to profl. jours. mem. Am. Soc. for Bone and Mineral Rsch., Nat. Inst. Agrl. Rsch. (mem. sci. com.). Avocations: skiing, hiking. Office: Inst Nat Rsch Agronomique, 63122 Saint Genes Champanelle Auvergne, France

COXON, ANN YVONNE, physician, consultant; b. Saigon, Indochina, Oct. 11, 1940; arrived in Eng., 1947; d. James Stanley and Elizabeth Ann (Traute) C. MB, BS, London U., 1963, DCH, 1965; MRCS, 1961. MRCP. Gen. med. tng. Guy's Hosp., Hammersmith Hosp., Great Ormond St. Childrens, 1963-70; specialist tng. Hammersmith Hosp., Nat. Hosp. Queen Square, 1971-83; cons. physician Portman Clinic, London, 1983—; ind. physician London, 1983—; dir. medicine and rsch. Howard Found. Rsch., 1983—; founder Age Power, 1997; founder Brit. Islamic Ctr. Contbr. articles to profl. jours. Mem. Harveian Soc., Med. Soc. of London. Muslim. Avocations: comparative religion, physical fitness. Office: 78 Harley St, London W1N 1AE, England

COY, DORIS RHEA, counselor, educator; b. Portsmouth, Ohio, Sept. 7, 1938; d. Haldor Ellsworth and Dorothy Evelyn (Weese) Rhea. BS, U. Rio Grande, Ohio, 1963; MA, Ohio State U., 1966, PhD, 1996. Nat. cert. counselor, nat. cert. career counselor, nat. cert. sch. counselor; lic. prof. counselor; cert. elem. prin., supr., pupil pers., sch. counselor, elem. tchr., Ohio. Sales clk. Morris 5&10, Jackson, Ohio, 1954-58; tchr. Jackson County Schs., Jackson, 1958-59; tchr. Whitehall (Ohio) City Schs., 1959-66, sch. counselor, 1966-92, chair dept., 1982-92; pres. Am. Sch. Counselor Assn., Alexandria, Va., 1989-90, ACA, Alexandria, 1994-95; pvt. practice Doris Rhea Coy & Assocs., Pickerington, Ohio, 1979—; lectr. U. North Tex., Denton, 1996-97, asst. prof. counselor edn., 1997—; co-dir. ERIC/CASS Ctr. for Sch. Counseling, 1998—. Editor: Toward the Transformation of Secondary School Counseling; author booklet, articles and book chpts.; author conflict mgmt. and crisis mgmt. programs. Recipient numerous awards, honors and grants. Mem. ASCD, ACA, Am. Sch. Counselor Assn., Ohio Counseling Assn. (pres. 1992-93), Ohio Sch. Counselor Assn. (pres. 1984-85), Tex. Counseling Assn. (chair profl. devel. com. 1997—), Tex. Career Guidnce assn. (sec./newsletter editor 1997-98, pres.-elect 1998—), Tex. Sch. Counselor Assn., Tex. Assn. for Counselor Educators and Suprs., League for Profl. Women, AAUW, Nat. Career Devel. Assn., Assn. for Counselor Educators and Suprs., Delta Kappa Gamma, others. Office: U North Tex Dept Counseling PO Box 311337 Denton TX 76203-1337

COYLE, JOSEPH THOMAS, psychiatrist; b. Chgo., Oct. 9, 1943; s. Joseph Thomas and Mercedes (Sartor) C.; m. Genevieve Sansoucy, Aug. 19, 1968; children: Andrew, Peter, David. AB, Coll. of the Holy Cross, 1965;

MD, Johns Hopkins U., 1969; MA (hon), Harvard U., 1991. Diplomate Am. Bd. Psychiatry and Neurology. Asst. prof. pharmacology Johns Hopkins Sch. of Medicine, Balt., 1974-76, asst. prof pharmacology and psychiatry, 1976-78, assoc. prof pharmacology and psychiatry, 1978-80, prof of neurosci., psychiatry and pharmacology, 1980-91, dir. div. of child psychiatry, 1982-91, Disting. Svc. prof. of child psychiatry, 1985-91; Eben S. Draper prof. of psychiatry and neurosci. Harvard U., Boston, 1991—; chair consol. dept. psychiatry Harvard Med. Sch., Boston, 1991—; co-dir outpatient pharmacotherapy clinic Johns Hopkins Hosp., Balt., 1977-82; mem. sci. adv. bd. Pfizer Scholars Program, N.Y.C., 1989-94 John F. Merck Found., Boston, 1990—, Abbott Pharms., North Chgo. Ill., 1990—, Guilford Pharms., Balt., 1992-98. Contbr. articles to profl. jours. Mem. adv. bd. NIMH, Washington, 1990-94. Recipient AE Bennett award, 1978, Gold Medal award, 1991, EA Strecker award Inst. Pa. Hosp., 1991, McAlpin award, Mental Health Assn., Washington, 1992, Salmon Medal of N.Y. Acad. of Medicine, 1993. Fellow Am. Psychiat. Assn. (Found. Fund prize 1985, Adolph Meyer award 1994, Kemp Fund award 1996), Am. Acad. of Arts and Scis.; mem. Soc. Neurosci. (pres. 1991-92), Am. Coll. Neuropsychopharmacology (pres.-elect 2000, Efron award 1982), Am. Acad. Child and Adolescent Psychiatry, Am. Soc. Pharmacology and Exptl. Therapeutics (John Jacob Abel award 1979), Inst. of Medicine of the Nat. Acad. Sci. (Pasarow Found. award 1997). Avocations: reading, fishing. Office: Harvard Med Sch Dept Psychiatry 115 Mill St Belmont MA 02478-1041

COYNE, EDWARD JAMES, international business educator; b. St. Louis, Sept. 25, 1930; s. Horace John and Bessie (Stinebaker) C.; m. Kathleen (Hayman), Sept. 9, 1952 (dec. April 1985); children: Edward James, Kevin Patrick, Shawn Thomas, Colin Mark, Kathleen Patrice; m. Beulah (Shelton), April 19, 1986. BS, La. State U., 1952; MBA, Nova U., 1992; PhD, U. Bradford (Yorkshire, U.K.), 1994; LHD (hon.), Nova U., 1980. Gen. mgr., dir. Comalco Products, Pty., Sydney, Australia, 1966-73; pres. Kaiser Bauxite Co., Discovery Bay, Jamica, 1974-86; v.p., gen. mgr., Rod, Bar, Wire Kaiser Aluminum & Chem., Oakland, Calif., 1986-90; exec., residence Nova U., Ft. Lauderdale, Fla., 1991-93; dir. MIBA program Nova Southeastern U., Ft. Lauderdale, 1993-96; acad. dean Am. Coll. Dublin, Dublin, Ireland, 1997-98; vis. prof. Samford U., Birmingham, Ala., 1999—; adv. bd. Inst. Internat. Edu., Southeastern Region, 1983-86, Ctr. Internat. Bus., U. Leeds, U.K., 1995—; vis. fellow U. Bradford, U.K., 1996—. Author: Targeting the Foreign Direct Investor, 1995, (chapt.) International Business Org., 1999; contbr. articles to profl. jours. Vice-chmn. Agr. Mktg. Corp., Jamaica, 1981-86; chmn. Discovery Bay Water Co., Jamaica, 1974-80; vice-chmn. Aboukir Edu. & Industl. Inst., Jamaica, 1976-85; adv. bd. World Trade Council Ft. Lauderdale, 1995-96. Recipient Comdr. Order of Distinction, Govt. Jamaica, 1980; Sports Hall of Fame, Jackson-Madison County, Tenn., 1997. Mem. Acad. Internat. Bus., HR Devel. Internat. Jour. Republican. Roman Catholic. Avocations: reading, travel, teaching. Home: 2752 Berkeley Dr Birmingham AL 35242-4105 Office: Sch Bus Samford U 800 Lakeshore Dr Birmingham AL 35229-0001

COYNE, JOHN MICHAEL, artist, educator; b. St. Stephen, N.B., Can., May 23, 1950; s. John Joseph and Marie Eleanor (Dennison) C. BFA, Mt. Allison U., 1975; MFA, U. Regina, 1977. Prof. visual arts Sir Wilfred Grenfell Coll., Meml. U. Nfld., 1991—; lectr. Acadia U., 1977-78, asst. prof., 1978-84, assoc. prof., 1984-86, head dept. art, 1983-86, senate mem., 1981-84, bd. govs., 1985-86, art gallery adv. bd., 1978-86; founding head dept. visual arts Sir Wilfred Grenfell Coll., Meml. U. Nfld., 1986-92, assoc. prof., 1986-91, prof., 1991—, senate mem., 1991-92, 98—, head Divsn. of Arts, 1999—; mem. art procurement com. Govt. Nfld. and Labrador, 1986-92; bd. dirs. Arts Atlantic mag. One-man shows include Owens Art Gallery, Mt. Allison U., 1983, U. Coll. Cape Breton Art Gallery, 1983, St. Mary's U. Art Gallery, 1983, Acadia U. Art Gallery, 1983, 84, U. N.B. Art Ctr., 1984, Sir Wilfred Grenfell Coll., 1987, 89, Meml. U. art Gallery, 1990, Emma Butler Gallery, St. John's, 1990, Arts and Culture Ctr. Corner Brook, 1997; group exhbns. include Mackenzie Gallery, 1978, Newfoundland Artists Gallery, 1978, Art Gallery N.S., 1980, Edmonton Art Gallery, 1984, U. N.B. Art Ctr., 1985, Mira Godard Gallery, 1985, 91, Fredericton, N.B., 1988, Meml. U. Art Gallery, 1994; represented in permanent collections Govt. Nfld. and Labrador, Art Gallery N.S., Mt. Allison U., N.S. Art Bank, U. Regina, St. Mary's U. Art Gallery, Sir Wilfred Grenfell Coll., Husky Oil, Labatt's Breweries, Bank N.S., Midland-Doherty, Placer Dome, Inc., Davies, Ward and Beck, Xerox Can., Faskin-Colvin, Abitibi-Price, Toshiba Can., Air Can. and pvt. collections. Greenshields Found. grantee, 1976. Avocations: reading, photography, running, digital imaging. E-mail: mcoyne@swgc.mun.ca. Home: 31 Central St, Corner Brook, NF Canada Office: Meml Univ Nfld, Corner Brook, NF Canada A2H 6P9

COZEN, LEWIS, orthopedic surgeon; b. Montreal, Aug. 14, 1911; came to U.S. 1922; AB, U. Calif., San Francisco, 1929, MD, 1934. Diplomate Am. Bd. Orthopedic Surgery. Intern San Francisco Hosp., 1933-34; resident orthopedic surgeon U. Iowa, 1934-35; resident and fellow orthopedic surgery San Francisco County Hosp., 1935-36, Children's Hosp. and Mass. Gen. Hosp., Boston, 1936-39; pvt. practice orthopedic surgery L.A., 1939-40, 45—; clin. prof. orthopedic surgery UCLA, 1965-93; assoc. clin. prof. emeritus Loma Linda Med. Sch., 1963—; attending orthopedic surgeon, emeritus Cedars Sinai Med. Ctr., 1939—, Orthopaedic Hosp., 1939—; chief orthopedic surgery City of Hope, 1948-67; sr. attending orthopedic surgeons, emeritus Unit One L.A. County Hosp., 1950-63; vis. lectr. U. Santo Tomas, Manila, U. Madrid, Spain; Far East Sch. of Medicine, Manila, 1994, Hadassah Med. Ctr., Jerusalem, 1994, U. Brussels; lectr. in field; vis. lectr. Brussels, U. London, Stammore, Eng., U. Guadalajara, Mexico, others. Author: Office Orthopedics, 1955, 4th edit. 1973, Operative Orthopedic Clinics (with Dr. Avia Brockway), 1960, Atlas of Orthopedic Surgery, 1966, Difficult Orthopedic Diagnosis, 1972, Plannings and Pitfalls in Orthopedic Surgery, Natural History of Orthopedic Disease, 1993, Supplement Book, 1996; mem. editl. bd. Resident & Staff Physician; contbr. numerous articles to profl. jours. Vol. physician Internat. Children's Program, Orthopedic Hosp., Mexicali, Mexico. Lt. col. U.S. Army, 1940-45. Fellow ACS, Internat. Coll. Surgeons, Am. Coll. Rheumatology, Royal Soc. Medicine; mem. Am. Rheumatism Assn., Internat. Orthopedic Assn., Am. Orthopaedic Assn. (sr.), Am. Acad. Orthopaedic Surgeons, So. Calif. Rheumatism Assn. (pres. 1979), Western Orthopaedic Assn., Phi Beta Kappa, Alpha Omega Alpha. Avocations: swimming, golf, dancing, travel.

COZIER, JEFFREY PATRICK, management professional; b. Bridgetown, Barbados, July 23, 1950; s. Frederick Lloyd and Leila Granville (Griffith) C.; m. Paula Ann Smith; children: Jason J.F., Russell J. MBA, Internat. Mgmt. Ctr., Buckinghamshire, U.K., 1992. Adminstr. Mfrs. Life Ins. Co., Barbados, 1970-79; regional supr. Am. Internat. Group, Barbados, 1979-84; mgr. sales and mktg. Colonial Life Ins. Co., Barbados, 1984-87; gen. mgr. Barbados Mktg. Corp., 1987-89; mktg. mgr., gen. mgr. Sissons Paints Ltd., 1989-95; sec. gen. Caribbean Broadcasting Union, St. Michael, Barbados, 1996—. Bus. Adminstrn. fellow Can. Sch. Mgmt., Toronto, 1991, Life Mgmt. Inst. fellow, Ga., 1979, Inst. Commerce fellow, London, 1979. Mem. Inst. Mgmt., Barbados Mfrs. Assn., Barbados Hotel Assn., Barbados C. of C., Bridgetown Club, Wanderers Cricket Club, Thistle (past master). Methodist. Avocation: international affairs. Home: Capri Skeete's Hill, Rockley, Christ Church Barbados Office: Caribbean Broadcasting Union, Waterford House, Waterford Saint Michael Barbados

COZON, STANISLAS MARIE, information technology and management consultant; b. Casablanca, Marocco, May 30, 1957; s. Etienne and Françoise (Nebout) C.; m. Emmanuèle Consigny, Oct. 5, 1985. Degree, Inst. d'Etudes Politiques, Paris, 1977, Ecole Nat. Adminstrn., France, 1981. Inspecteur des Fin. France, 1981-85; sr. advisor to CEO Credit Nat., France, 1985-89; bus. unit mgr. Cap Gemini Soc., Paris, 1989-90, corp. devel. exec., 1991-92; dep. to COO Cap Gemini Soc. (now Cap Gemini), Paris, 1993—. With French Navy, 1979. Avocations: golf, wine, riding. Office: Cap Gemini, 76 ave Kleber, 75016 Paris France

COZZA, EDUARDO NESTOR, university executive, researcher; b. Moron, Argentina, May 12, 1956; s. Jose and Gabriela Adela (Buccaro) C.; m. Maria Del Carmen Vila Cozza, Dec. 16, 1983; children: Julia, Ezequiel. Chemist, U. Buenos Aires, 1979, PhD, 1986; postdoc. trainee, U. South Fla., Tampa, 1990. Cert. chemist. Profl. staff U. Buenos Aires, 1980-87; assoc. in rsch. U. South Fla., Tampa, 1987-90; profl. staff CONICET, Buenos Aires, 1990-92, investigator, 1992-96; sec. acad. affairs U. de Moron, Argentina, 1996—; cons. Blogen, Buenos Aires, 1991-95, World Bank, Washington, 1999; fellow investigator, Fulbright Commn., Columbia, 1995-96; dir. univ. studies U. de Moron, Argentian, 1993-96. Author: Endothelins in Endocrinology: New Advances, 1995; contbr. articles to profl. jours. Mem. Soc. Argentinian Investigation, Soc. Argentina Investigation Clinic, N.Y. Acad. Scis. Avocations: stamp collecting, paddle, soccer, small bottle collecting, guitar playing. Home phone: 54-11-4797-3933. Office: Univ Moron, Cabildo 134, 1708 Moron Argentina

CRABTREE, BEN C., home health care agency administrator; b. Las Vegas, Sept. 11, 1964; s. Ben C. and Jaynelle (Felix) C.; m. Virginia Kathryn Vance, Feb. 7, 1988 (div. Nov. 1989); m. Tania Oylan Tason, May 5, 1992; children: Greta, Bryan. AS, Panama Canal Coll., La Boca, Rep. of Panama, 1993, Austin Peay State U., 1995; BBA, Our Lady of the Lake U., 1995. Cert. firearms instr., range officer; registered massage therapist. Software tech., adminstr. asst. Ace Personal Health Care, Inc., San Antonio, 1994-95; dir. info. systems River City Fin. Health Group/Home Health Care Solutions, San Antonio, 1995; chief fin. officer, alt. adminstr. A&E Quality Home Health Care, San Antonio, 1996-99; pres. Oylan, Inc., San Antonio, 1997-99; pres., owner Antonian Bodyworks, 1999—; profl. adv. com. Silver Days Home Health Care, San Antonio, 1996-97, Responsive Health Svcs., 1997-99. Mem. Dist. 128 State Budget Adv. Com., San Antonio, 1995. Ssgt. U.S. Army, 1984-92. Mem. U.S. Practical Shooting Assn., Tex. Action Shooting Club, Internat. Defensive Pistol Assn., Nat. Range Officers' Inst., Nat. Assn. Home Care, Am. Masage Therapy Assn. Avocations: practical shooting, web page design. Office: Antonian Bodyworks PO Box 790911 San Antonio TX 78279-0911

CRACIUN, CONSTANTIN, geologist, researcher; b. Marasesti, Romania, July 10, 1943; s. Anghel and Anica (Margineanu) C.; m. Lidia Ecaterina Pirchner, Apr. 18, 1968. Diploma in geology, U. Bucharest, 1966, PhD in Geology, 1984. Geologist Inst. for Soil Sci., Bucharest, Romania, 1967-70, rschr., 1970-84, sr. rschr., 1984—, head mineral. group, 1986—, head soil genesis and ecopedology dept., 1999—; cons. U. Bucharest, 1978-82, 96-97; cons. U. Agronomy Land Improvement Faculty, Bucharest, 1992-95, mem. agrl. faculty, 1997-98. Author: Clay Minerals in Soils: Implications for Agriculture, 2000; co-author: Methods of Chemical Analyses of Soil, 1986, Physical Methods of Minerals and Rocks Analysis, 1986, Pollution with Petroleum and Brine of Soils in Romania, 1999; contbr. articles to profl. jours.; patentee in field. Fellow Romanian Soc. Soil Sci. (gen. sec. 1997), Romanian Clay Group (vice-chmn. 1992-97); mem. European Nuclear Soc., Romanian Soc. Geology, Romanian Assn. Nuclear Energy. Avocations: music, literature, collecting picture postcards. Home: ScD Apt #51, Drumul Taberii 105 Bl A9, 77461 Bucharest Romania Office: Inst for Soil Sci, B-dul Marasti 61 Sector 1, 77331 Bucharest Romania

CRAIG, ANNA MAYNARD, financial educator, consultant; b. Columbus, Ohio, Sept. 2, 1944; d. David Stuart and Ann (Armstrong) C.; m. John D. Hogan, Nov. 26, 1976. BA cum laude, Smith Coll., 1966; MA, U. Wis., 1970, PhD, 1972. Chartered fin. analyst; cert. fin. planner, accredited tax advisor; enrolled treasury agt. Asst. prof. U. Ill., Chgo., 1971-75; vis. asst. prof. Ohio State U., Columbus, 1974-76; asst. prof. Cen. Mich. U., Mt. Pleasant, 1976-79; cons. Am. Productivity Ctr., Houston, 1979-81; adj. prof. Houston Bapt. U., 1980-86, Jones Grad. Sch. Adminstrn., Rice U., Houston, 1984; adj. prof. dept. fin. U. Ill., Champaign-Urbana, 1987-91; adj. faculty Goizueta Bus. Sch. Emory U., Atlanta, 1992—; faculty exec. and concentrated MBA programs Ga. State U., 1992-93; CMBA, 1995—; bd. advisors Assn. for Internat. Exch. Students in Econs. and Commerce, U. Ill., 1987-91; advisor U. Ill. FMA Nat. Honor Soc., Fin. Club. Editor: (with John D. Hogan) Dimensions of Productivity Research, Vol. 1, 1980, Vol. II, 1981. Bd. dirs. Champaign-Urbana Symphony, 1987-91; mem. trust mgmt. com. Univ. YWCA, Champaign, 1987-91. Ford fellow, U. Wis., 1970-72, NSF fellow, Stanford U., 1972; Fulbright scholar, 1966-67; named Outstanding Prof. Fin. U. Ill. Commerce Coun., 1987-88. Mem Am. Econ. Assn., Atlanta Soc. Fin. Analysts, Assn. for Investment Mgmt. and Rsch., Fin. Mgmt. Assn., Smith Coll. Alumnae Assn. (chmn. spl. gifts 1983-86, class fund agt.), Fulbright Alumni Assn., Phi Beta Kappa, Beta Gamma Sigma. Office: Emory Univ Goizueta Business School Atlanta GA 30322-0001

CRAIG, ARTHUR DEWITT, JR., neurosurgeon, research scientist; b. Lansing, Mich., Aug. 31, 1951. BS, Mich. State U., 1973; PhD, Cornell U., 1978. Rsch. assoc. in phys. biology N.Y. State Coll. Vet. Medicine Cornell U., Ithaca, N.Y., 1977-78; postdoctoral fellow in physiology and biophysics Wash. U. Sch. Medicine, St. Louis, 1978-80, rsch. assoc. in anatomy and neurobiology, 1980-81; rsch. assoc. in physiology U. Kiel, Germany, 1981-83; instr., rsch. asst. prof. in physiology U. Würzburg, Germany, 1983-86; James R. Atkinson pain rsch. scientist Barrow Neurol. Inst., St. Joseph's Hosp. and Med. Ctr., Phoenix, 1986—, assoc. staff scientist, 1993—, sr. staff scientist, 1996—, staff scientist divsn. neurosurgery, 1998—; grad. asst. in comparative physiology Cornell U., 1976; postdoctoral asst. in med. neuroanatomy Wash. U. Sch. Medicine, 1980; lectr. in neurosci. Barrow Neurol. Inst., 1987—, U. Ariz. Coll. Medicine, 1992; vis. prof. neurosci. McGill U., 1993, U. Calif., San Diego, 1993-95; vis. prof. Sch. Dentistry McGill U., Montreal, 1996-97; ad hoc reviewer NIH, 1991—, NSF, 1981—, Neurosci. Letters, 1983—, Exptl. Brain Rsch., 1983—, Jour. Neurophysiology, 1985—, Neurosci., 1987—, Jour. Comparative Neurology, 1987—, Jour. Neurosci., 1990—, Brain Rsch., 1990—, Pain, 1992—, Nature, 1994—, Nature Medicine, 1997—, European Jour. Neurosci., 1997—, Sci., 1998—, Nature Neurosci., 1998—; adj. rsch. assoc. prof. cell biology and anatomy U. Ariz. Coll. Medicine, 1991-96, rsch. prof., 1996—; mem. faculty NIH Motor Control Tng. Program, dept. physiology U. Ariz., 1990—, mem. selection com., 1995-2000, chair 1999; spl. project assoc. Scottsdale (Ariz.) Mayo Clinic, 1994-95; mem. rsch. coord. com. Barrow Neurol. Inst., 1989-94; external reviewer Ctr. for Study Persistent Pain U. Md., 1998-99, U. N.C., Chapel Hill, 1997, Johns Hopkins Med. Sch., Balt., 1999—. Author: (with others) Somatosensory Integration in the Thalamus, 1983, Sensory Receptor Mechanisms, 1984, Development, Organization and Processing in Somatosensory Pathways, 1985, Basic Mechanisms and Clinical Applications, 1985, Thalamus and Pain, 1987, Pain and Central Nervous System Disease: The Central Pain Syndromes, 1991, The Midbrain Periaqueductal Gray Matter: Functional, Anatomical and Neurochemical Organization, 1991, Touch, Temperature and pain in Health and Disease: Mechanisms and Assessments, 1994, Forebrain Areas Involved in Pain Processing, 1995, The Emotional Motor System, 1996, Anesthesia: Biologic Foundations, 1997, Textbook of Pain, 1999; contbr. more than 50 articles to profl. jours. including Jour. Neurophysiol., Neurosci. Letters, Brain Theory Newsletter; mem. editl. bd. Jour. Comparative Neurology, 2000—, Jour. Pain, 1991—. Recipient nat. merit scholarship Chrysler Corp., 1968-73; grantee NIH, INSERM. Mem. AAAS, Internat. Assn. for the Study of Pain, Am. Physiol. Soc., Am. Pain Soc., N.Y. Acad. Scis., Soc. for Neurosci. Office: Barrow Neurol Inst 350 W Thomas Rd Phoenix AZ 85013-4409

CRAIG, CHARLES SAMUEL, marketing educator; b. Atlantic City, May 6, 1943; s. Charles Hays and Catherine Sara (McMullen) C.; m. Elizabeth Anne Coyne, Aug. 10, 1985; children: Mary Catherine, Caroline Elizabeth. BA, Westminster Coll., 1965; MS, U. R.I., 1967; PhD, Ohio State U., 1971. Mktg. rep. IBM, Providence, 1966-68; asst. dir. Mechanized Info. Ctr., Columbus, 1971-73; asst. prof. lib. adminstrn. Ohio State U., Columbus, 1971-73, asst. prof. mktg., 1972-74; asst. prof. mktg. Grad. Sch. Bus. and Pub. Adminstrn. Cornell U., Ithaca, N.Y., 1974-77, assoc. prof., 1977-79; assoc. prof. mktg. Stern Sch. of Bus. N.Y.U., 1979-81, assoc. prof. mktg., 1981-84, prof. mktg., 1984-88, assoc. dean acad. affairs, 1984-88, prof. mktg. internat. bus., 1988—, chmn. mktg. dept., 1991-98, dir. entertainment media and tech. program, 1998—; dir. Presbyn. and Reformed Pub. Co., Phila., 1973—; mem. exec. bd. Jour. Retailing, 1985—. Co-author: Consumer Behavior: An Information Processing Perspective, 1982; International Marketing Research, 1983, 2d edit., 2000, Global Marketing Strategy, 1995; co-editor: Personal Selling: Theory, Research and Practice, 1984, The Development of Media Models in Advertising, Repetition Effects over the Years, The Relationship of Advertising Expenditures to Sales, 1986; mem. editl. bd. Jour. Mktg. Rsch., 1978-85, Jour. Retailing, 1980-85, Jour. Advt. Rsch., 1994—, Internat. Jour. of Advt., 1997—; contbr. articles to profl. jours. NDEA fellow, 1969-71. Mem. Am. Mktg. Assn., Assn. Consumer Rsch., Acad. Internat. Bus., Phi Kappa Phi, Omicron Delta Epsilon, Psi Chi. Presbyterian. Home: 100 Bleecker St Apt 28D New York NY 10012-2207 Office: NYU 44 W 4th St New York NY 10012-1106

CRAIG, CYNTHIA MAE, mathematics educator; b. Brownsville, Tex., Jan. 22, 1951; d. Richard Virgil and Mae Margaret (Phillips) Cole; m. Daniel Baxter Craig, Jan. 15, 1971; children: Tammy Michelle Craig Black, Heather Elizabeth Craig Rios. BA, Augusta (Ga.) Coll., 1985, MEd, 1989, specialist in edn., 1993. Cert. devel. specialist; cert. tchr., Ga. Tchr. 5th-6th grade tchr. Blessed Sacrament Sch., El Paso, Tex., 1981-82; tchr. 4-8th grade honors math. St. Mary on the hill Cath. Sch., Augusta, Ga., 1985-87; tchr. Aquinas H.S., Augusta, 1987-88; asst. prof. of math. in learning support Augusta State U., 1989—, asst. chair learning learning support, 1998—; presenter at profl. confs. in field. Contbr. articles to profl. jours. Mem. ASCD, Ga. Assn. of Devel. Educators, Nat. Assn. for Devel. Edn., Phi Delta Kappa (newsletter editor 1990-93, v.p. membership 1993-94, newsletter editor 1989-92, 94-96, 97-98, found. rep. 1996-97, newsletter editor 1997-98, rsch. rep. 1998—). Avocations: reading, hiking, traveling, Office: Augusta State U Learning Support 2500 Walton Way Augusta GA 30904-4562

CRAIG, DAVID PARKER, retired chemistry educator; b. Sydney, NSW, Australia, Dec. 23, 1919; s. Andrew Hunter and Mary Jane (Parker) C.; m. Veronica Bryden-Brown, Aug. 29, 1948; children: Andrew, David, Mary Louise, Douglas. BSc with honors, U. Sydney, 1940, MSc, 1941; PhD, U. Coll. London, 1949, DSc, 1956; DChem (hon.), U. Bologna, Italy, 1985; DSc (hon.), U. Sydney, 1989. Lectr. chemistry U. Sydney, 1945; Turner and Newell rsch. fellow and lectr. U. Coll. London, 1946-52; prof. phys. chemistry U. Sydney, 1952-56; prof. theoretical chemistry U. Coll. London, 1956-67; prof. theoretical and physical chemistry Australian Nat. U., Canberra, Australian Capital Ter., 1967-85; pres. Australian Acad. Sci., Canberra, 1990-94; exec. mem. Commonwealth Sci. & Indsl. Rsch. Orgn., Canberra, 1980-85. Author: Excitons in Molecular Crystals, 1968, Molecular Quantum Electrodynamics, 1984; contbr. articles to profl. jours. Named officer Order of Australia, Govt. of Australia, 1985; fellow Royal Soc. London, 1968, Australian Acad. Sci., 1969. Home: 199 Dryandra St, O'Connor ACT2602, Australia Office: Australian Nat U, Rsch Sch Chemistry, Canberra ACT 0200, Australia also: Australian Acad Sci, GPO Box 783, Canberra ACT 2602, Australia

CRAIG, DAVID VICTOR, archivist; b. Dublin, Oct. 13, 1951; s. Victor Howard and Kathleen Joyce (McGilligan) C.; m. Sarah Ward-Perkins, Dec. 2, 1994. BA, Dublin U. (Trinity Coll.), 1973, PhD, 1984. Archivist Pub. Record Office of Ireland (now named Nat. Archives), Dublin, 1973-80, sr. archivist, 1980-89; dir. Nat. Archives, Dublin, 1989—; mem. Irish Manuscripts Commn., Dublin, 1989—, Irish Com. of Hist. Scis., Dublin, 1991-98. Mem. Soc. Archivists (chmn. Irish region 1984-87), Irish Soc. for Archives (com. mem. 1976-90), Econ. and Social History Soc. Ireland (sec. 1991—). Avocations: current affairs, reading, sailing. Office: Nat Archives, Bishop St, Dublin Ireland

CRAIG, ELIZABETH COYNE, marketing executive; b. N.Y.C., Jan. 7, 1956; d. John Thomas and Mary Ellen (O'Sullivan) Coyne; m. Charles Samuel Craig, Aug. 10, 1985; children: Mary Catherine, Caroline Elizabeth. BS in Occupl. Therapy, NYU, 1980, MBA, 1986. Occupl. therapist Jacobi Hosp., N.Y., 1980-81, St. Vincent's Hosp., N.Y., 1981-85; mktg. intern worldwide consumer banking Citibank U.S. and Europe Consumer Bank, Citicorp Ins., N.Y.C., 1985-86, mgmt. assoc., 1986-87, asst. mgr., 1987-88, mktg. mgr. new product devel., 1988-90, asst. v.p. life acquisitions and relationship mktg., 1990-93, v.p. life and health acquisitions and relationship mktg., 1993-94, v.p. 3d party direct response, retail ins. sales pilots, 1994-96, v.p. annuity product mgmt., 1996-99; sr. v.p. e-commerce investment and ins., product mgr. Citi fi Interactive Fin. Network, Long Island City, N.Y., 1998-99; v.p. customer relationship mgr. Citibank Online, Long Island City, 1999—; bd. dirs. First Citicorp Life Ins. Co. Mem. Am. Occupl. Therapy Assn., Fin. Women's Assn., Direct Mktg. Assn. Avocations: antiques, bicycling. Office: Citibank One Court Sq Long Island City NY 11120

CRAIG, HAROLD KENT, systems analyst; b. Columbus, Ohio, Nov. 21, 1956; s. Harold Harding and Mildred Annie (King) C.; m. Cathy M. Preslar, Nov. 19, 1979; 1 child, Brian Scagel. Student, Goddard Coll., 1979. Lic. plumbing, boiler making, air conditioning, forced warm air heating; spl. elec. lic.; cert. exam proctor. V.p., project mgr. Craig Plumbing Co., Inc., Raleigh, N.C., 1972-95; v.p., project mgmt. Confluence Tech., Raleigh, N.C., 1976—; sr. systems analyst Datasonix Inc., Smithfield, N.C., 1982-84; heating, ventilation, air cond., plumbing and mech. cons. Valley Constrn. Co., Inc., Koslusco, Miss., 1985-86; sr. project mgr. and estimator Sneeden Mechanical Contractors, Inc., Wilmington, N.C., 1986-88; U.S. bus. agent The Circle Group, Arusha, Tanzania, 1974—; sr. estimator Bay Mech. Inc., Raleigh, N.C., 1996-97; sr. project mgr., estimator Atlantic Coast Mech., Inc., Raleigh, 1997-98; sys. cons. Consulting, Tech., and Design, Inc., Research Triangle Park, N.C., 1988-94. Author: Yes, the Sun Will Rise, 1979; assoc. editor: (periodical) In the Steps, 1976-81; contbr. articles to profl. jours.; contbg. editor, Contractor mag., 1998—. Mem. bd. adjustments Town of Cary (N.C.), 1981; mem. bd. Raleigh Artists' Cmty., 1974-79. E-mail: hkentcraig@yahoo.com. Home: 101 Sweet Spire Way Apt 1C Cary NC 27513-3389

CRAIG, JONATHAN, petroleum geologist, researcher; b. Swindon, Wiltshire, Eng., Jan. 31, 1958; s. Harold and Winifred Georgine (Dolling) C.; m. Susan Elizabeth Dale, May 19, 1984. BSc in Geology/Geography with 1st class honors, U. Nottingham, Eng., 1979; PhD in Structural Geology, Univ. Coll. Wales, Aberystwyth, 1985. Geologist Geomorphological Svcs. Ltd., Marlow, U.K., 1980-85; contract geologist Shell Petroleum Devel. (Tanzania) Ltd., Dar-es-Salaam, 1983-85; project geologist, staff geologist Lasmo North Sea Plc. and Lasmo Internat. Ltd., London, 1985-93; structural specialist Lasmo Oil (Colombia) Ltd., Bogota, 1993; sr. staff geologist, new ventures coord. Lasmo Internat. Ltd., New Ventures, London, 1994-95; group chief geologist Lasmo Plc, London, 1996—; guest lectr. U. Coll. Wales, Aberystwyth, 1985, rsch. supr., 1988—; guest lectr. U. Nottingham, 1985-90, U. Coll., London, 2000—. Author: Tectonic Evolution of the British Isles, 1997; contbr. articles to profl. jours. Tower capt. St. Peter's Ch., Harrold, Bedfordshire, Eng., 1989-92; mem. coun. Bedfordshire Assn. Ch. Bellringers, 1990-91; dir. Clifton Reynes Archaeol. Excavation, Buckinghamshire. Hon. fellow Univ. Coll. Wales, Aberystwyth, 1996—. Fellow Geol. Soc. London; mem. Am. Assn. Petroleum Geologist, Geologists' Assn., Petroleum Exploration Soc. Gt. Britain. Anglican. Avocations: bellringing, philately, railway history, natural history, conservation. Office: Lasmo Plc, 101 Bishopsgate, London EC2M 3XH, England

CRAIG, ROY PHILLIP, writer, educator, rancher; b. Durango, Colo., May 10, 1924; s. Philip Howard and Anna Dorothea Craig. BA, U. Colo., 1948; MS, Calif. Inst. Tech., 1950; PhD, Iowa State U., 1952. Group leader Dow Chem. Co., Denver, 1952-60; assoc. prof., coord. phys. scis. U. Colo., Boulder, 1961-66, rsch. assoc. UFO study, 1966-67; vis. prof. U. Hawaii, Honolulu, 1968-69; writer, lectr., rancher La Plata County, Colo., 1969—; cons. Dow Chem. Co., Midland, Mich., 1959; vis. prof. Clarkson Coll. Tech., Potsdam, N.Y., 1962-65, Colo. Coll., Colorado Springs, 1979, State of Ponape, 1981; curriculum cons. U. Hawaii, Honolulu, 1969; spkr. Foresters, Soil Conservationists, Cattlemen's Assn., Bur. Indian Affairs, Colo. LWV, Colo. Edn. Assn., 1971-84; pres. Four Corners Rsch. Inst., Durango, 1975-86. Co-author: Scientific Study of UFOs, 1969; author: UFOs: An Insider's View of the Official Quest for Evidence, 1995; contbr. articles to profl. jours. Pres. La Plata County Landowners Assn., 1974-92. With U.S. Army, 1943-46, ETO. Mem. Four Corners Llama/Alpaca Owners Assn., Phi Beta Kappa, Sigma Xi. Avocations: skiing, white-water rafting, chess. Home and Office: PO Box 335 23808 Hwy 172 Ignacio CO 81137

CRAIG, SANDRA KAY, sales executive; b. Willoughby, Ohio, Nov. 21, 1962; d. Charles Soloman and Lacey Marie (Webb) Eggers; m. Robert Joseph Craig, June 28, 1986 (div. Jan. 1993); 1 child, Misty Marie Mangus; m. Robert David Del Tiempo, Feb. 14, 1995; stepchildren: Jaime Brandon, Joseph David Del Tiempo. AAB cum laude, Shawnee State U., 1985; BBA summa cum laude, Ohio U., 1987; postgrad., Pepperdine U., 1998-2000. From ter. mgr. to sales mgr. ARA Cory, San Diego, 1988-90; sales rep. Rsch. Inst. Am., Riverside, Calif., 1990-92, 96-00; regional sales mgr. So. Calif., Rsch. Inst. Am., L.A., 1992-95; leader's coun. Rsch. Inst. Am., Culver City, 1996-2000, pres. bd. dirs., 1996-97, asst. mgr., 1997, 1999-2000, corp. acct. mgr., 1997-2000; mem. sales adv. bd. RIA/CLR Group (formerly Rsch. Inst. Am.), Culver City, 1998-2000; sr. v.p. Media Strategy

Lawnmower Media, Culver City, 2000; sr. account exec. SAP Am., Irvine, Calif., 2000—; cons. Video Ave., Paradise Pizza, Chillicothe, Ohio, 1987-88; sales rep. to corp. account mgr. Rsch. Inst. Am. Orange County, L.A., 1990-2000. Active Girl Scouts U.S., Menifee, 1988-92, Jr. All Am. Football. Mem. NAFE, NOW, PTA, Phi Kappa Phi, Phi Theta Kappa, Delta Mu Delta. Democrat. Avocations: travel, reading, jazz, karate. Home: 5360 Via Vopapo Yorba Linda CA 92887-3130 Office: SAP America 18101 Von Karman Ave #900 Irvine CA 92612

CRAIG, WILLIAM EMERSON, lawyer; b. Springfield, Mass., July 6, 1942; s. W. Emerson and Vera L. (Platt) C.; m. Susan Hart Ryan; children: Lathrop B., Linsley G. BA, Dartmouth Coll., 1964; LLB, Yale U., 1967. Assoc. Wiggin & Dana, New Haven, 1967-73, ptnr., 1974-97, sr. counsel, 1997—; sec. HGT Fund, Inc., New Haven, 1972-90, pres., bd. dirs. 1990-93; sec. Pomperaug Woods, Inc., Southbury, Conn., 1986-91; sec. bd. dirs. Fairbank Corp., New Haven, 1975—. Mem. New Haven Rep. Town Com., 1969-75, New Haven Bd. Fin., 1976-81, New Haven Environ. Adv. Coun., 1988-91; bd. dirs., treas. Planned Parenthood Coun., 1988-93, Planned Parenthood Conn. Found., 1991-95. Fellow Conn. Bar Found. (bd. dirs. 1987-97, treas. 1987-91); mem. ABA, Conn. Bar Assn. (exec. com. of real property and banking law sects.), New Haven County Bar Assn., Quinniplack Club, The Quechee Club (Vt.). Congregationalist. Avocations: skiing, tennis, squash, bicycling. Home: PO Box 411 Quechee VT 05059-0411 Office: Wiggin & Dana One Century Tower New Haven CT 06508-1832*

CRAIK, DAVID JAMES, drug chemistry research scientist; b. Melbourne, Australia, Apr. 18, 1955; s. James Alexander and Joan (Veitch) C.; m. Robyn Beverly Gosbell, Dec. 5, 1977; children: Andrew, Peter, Jennifer. BS with honors, La Trobe U., Melbourne, 1977, PhD, 1981. Postdoctoral rsch. fellow Fla. State U., Tallahassee, 1980-81, Syracuse (N.Y.) U., 1981-82; lectr. Victorian Coll. Pharmacy, Melbourne, 1983-87, dean Sch. Pharm. Chemistry, , 1988-94; prof. drug design and devel. U. Queensland, Brisbane, Australia, 1995—. Editor: NMR in Drug Design, 1996, (jour.) Current Medicinal Chemistry. Fellow Royal Australian Chem. Inst. (Adrien Albert lectr. 1993); mem. Am. Chem. Soc., Australian and New Zealand Soc. Magnetic Resonance (bd. dirs. 1996—). Office: U Queensland, Ctr Drug Design & Devel, Brisbane QLND4072, Australia

CRAIK, WENDY JEAN, farm federation administrator; b. Canberra, ACT, Australia, Dec. 5, 1949; d. Duncan Robert and Audrey Mavis (Ion) C.; m. Grant Hawley, Dec. 22, 1979. BSc with hons., Australian Nat. U., Canberra, 1973; PhD in Zoology (fisheries), U. Brit. Columbia, Vancouver, Can., 1978; grad. diploma in Mgmt., Capricornia Inst. Advanced Edn, Queensland, Australia, 1986. Various positions Great Barrier Reef Marine Park Authority, Townsville, Australia, 1978-95, exec. officer, 1992-95; exec. dir. Nat. Farmers' Fedn., Barton, ACT, Australia, 1995—; mem. numerous coms.including East Coast Tuna Mgmt. Adv. Com., 1987-92, Australian com. of the Internat. Union for Conservation of Nature and Natural Resources, Marine subcom. 1992, chair 1994-95), Queensland Fisheries Policy Coun., 1993-95, Great Barrier Reef Aquarium adv. bd., 1993-94, adv. bd. Australian Inst. Maritime Law, 1994, mgmt. com. Nat. Farmers Fedn., 1995-99, Trustee Australian Farmers' Fighting Fund, 1995—; adv. com. Nat. Landcare, 1996-99, AIMS Coun., 1997—, Inst. Land and Water Resource Bd., 1997—; chair, mem. adv. Land and Water Svc., 1996-2000; mem. Nat. Info. Econ. Adv. Bd., 1998-2000. Contbr. numerous articles to various environ. and popular publs. Recipient Nat. Undergrad. scholarship, 1968-70, Canberra scholarship, 1967, CSIRO postgrad. studentship, 1973-77. Fellow Acad. Tech. and Sci. Engring.; mem. Inst. Pub. Adminstrn. Australia, Environment Inst. Australia, Australian Coral Reef Soc., Australian Women in Agrl. Avocations: reading, hiking, golf. Office: Nat Farmers Fedn, 14-16 Brisbane Ave, Barton ACT 2603, Australia

CRAILSHEIM, KARL EBERHARD RICHARD, biologist, researcher, educator; b. Graz, Styria, Austria, Nov. 17, 1950; s. Rolf and Erika (Kusterle) C.; m. Ingeborg Luise Heger; children: Eberhard, Hartwig, Dietmar. PhD, Karl-Franzens U., Graz, Austria, 1976. Asst. zoology Karl-Franzens U., Graz, 1977-78, asst. prof., 1978-88, assoc. prof., 1988-97, prof., 1997—, lectr. psychology, 1984—, dean of studies, 1998—. Mem. internat. sci. bd. Apiddopic, 1997—. Mem. Internat. Union for the Study of Social Insects (chmn. 1996—). Avocation: photography, music, literature. Home: Merangasse 42, A-8010 Graz Styria, Austria Office: Karl-Franzens U, Univ Pl 2, A-8010 Graz Styria, Austria

CRAIN, RAY, statistician, consultant; b. St. Louis, Apr. 17, 1944; s. Chester Raymond and Mary Louise Crain; m. Barbara Hope Fagnan, Sept. 2, 1967; 1 child, Michelle Wigmore. AB, Knox Coll., 1965; MA, U. Calif., Riverside, 1967; PhD, U. N.Mex., 1974. Mgr. stats. McNeil Pharm., Spring House, Pa., 1980-81; sr. biostatistician Miles Pharms., West Haven, Conn., 1981-83; dir. statis. svcs. Boots Pharms., Shreveport, La., 1983-84; mgr. biometrics DuPont Co., Wilmington, Del., 1984-85, cons. dept. cen. R & D, 1985-90; dept. coord. Corp. Electronic Info. Security Com., 1987-90; sr. statistician Baxter Hyland Div., Glendale, Calif., 1990-91, Advanced Micro Devices, Sunnyvale, Calif., 1991-93; ind. cons., 1993-97, 99—; with LifeScan, Milpitas, Calif., 1997-99. Author: Scientific Computing Division's Enhanced Statistical Products Product Plan; contbr. articles to profl. jours. Mem. Am. Soc. Quality (chmn-elect local sect. 1995), Am. Statis. Assn., Soc. Clin. Trials, Orgn. Devel. Network, Phi Beta Kappa, Sigma Xi. Democrat. Unitarian. Home: 1038 Sandalwood Ln Milpitas CA 95035-3232

CRAIS, DAVID R., healthcare consultant; b. New Orleans, June 12, 1965; s. Ronald R. and Beverly D. C.; m. Maria Eugenia Hartman, Sept. 27, 1997. BA in History, BS in Bus., Loyola U., 1988. Ptnr. Black & Co., New Orleans, 1988-92; terr. mgr. i Stat Corp., Princeton, N.J., 1992-99; region v.p. Careside, Inc., Culver City, Calif., 1999—; chmn. Import/Export Trust Authority, Baton Rouge, 1992-98; bd. dirs. ElChisme.com, CubaMedical.com, TheRights.com. Author: Selling to VITA, 1999; contbr. article to Miss. Med. News; patentee for lab cost analysis. Dir. Edwards for Gov., La., 1991; campaing mgr. Tsongas for Pres., Gulf states, 1992. Fellow Inst. Politics; mem. C. of C. New Orleans (bd. dirs. 1996-97), VNA (bd. dirs. 1996-99). Roman Catholic. Avocations: hunting, mountain biking, furniture design, antiquarian books. Home: 340 W Diversey Pkwy Apt 2716 Chicago IL 60657-6245 Office: Careside Inc 6100 Bristol Pkwy Culver City CA 90230-6604 also: ElChisme.com CubaMedical.com 54 Crane St New Orleans LA 70124

CRALL, DALE EUGENE, accountant; b. Midland, Mich., Mar. 30, 1936; s. Maurice Wilson and Dorothy May (Tucker) C.; Janice Louise Sterling, Sept. 8, 1956; children: Carrie Lou, Michael David, Thomas Lee (dec.). BA, Olivet Nazarene U., 1961; BDiv, Nazarene Theol. Sem., 1965; M of Christian Edn., Western Theol. Sem., 1967. Cert. info. sys. auditor; cert. computer profl. Computer operator IBM, Kansas City, Mo., 1961-62; computer ops. supr. Trader's Nat. Bank, Kansas City, 1962-65; pastor West Ch. of the Nazarene, Grand Rapids, Mich., 1965-66; computer programmer analyst Lear Siegler Inc., Grand Rapids, 1966-67; EDP acct., mgr. Seidman & Seidman CPA Firm, Grand Rapids, 1967-69; dir. data processing Pa. Ho. Furniture, Lewisburg, Pa., 1969-70; divsn. chief fiscal and sys. Pa. Dept. of Transp., Harrisburg, Pa., 1970-91; prin. Seidel & Assocs., Harrisburg, 1991—; with Armstrong, Burke & Co., P.A., Holmes Beach, Fla.; computer cons. Seidman & Seidman, Grand Rapids, 1967-69; spl. asst. for EDP Sec. of Transp., Harrisburg, 1978-79. Sec. Jenison (Mich.) Sch. Bd., 1968-69; 4 gallon blood donor Ctrl. Pa. Blood Bank, Harrisburg, 1993. With USNR, 1953-61. Mem. Electronic Data Processing Auditor's Assn. (chpt. pres. 1983-84, bd. dirs. 1980-86), Nat. Assn. of Tax Preparers. Avocations: reading, travel, fishing. Office: Armstrong Bruk & Co PA 214 54th St Holmes Beach FL 34217-1701

CRAM, DONALD JAMES, chemistry educator; b. Chester, Vt., Apr. 22, 1919; s. William Moffet and Joanna (Shelley) C.; m. Jane Maxwell, Nov. 25, 1969. BS, Rollins Coll., 1941; MS, U. Nebr., 1942; PhD, Harvard U., 1947; PhD (hon.), U. Uppsala, 1977; DSc (hon.), U. So. Calif., 1983, Rollins Coll., 1988, U. Nebr., 1989, U. Western Ontario, 1990, U. Sheffield, 1991. Rsch. chemist Merck & Co., 1942-45; asst. prof. chemistry UCLA, 1947-50, assoc. prof., 1950-56, prof., 1956-90, S. Winstein prof., 1985-95, univ. prof., 1988-90, univ. prof. emeritus, 1990—; chem. con. Upjohn Co., 1952-88, Union Carbide Co., 1960-81, Eastman Kodak Co., 1981-91, Technicon Co., 1984-92, Inst. Guido Donegani, Milan, 1988-91; State Dept. exch. fellow to Inst. de Quimica, Nat. U. Mex., 1956; guest prof. U. Heidelberg, Fed. Republic Germany, 1958; guest lectr. S. Africa, 1967; Centenary lectr. Chem. Soc. London, 1976. Author: From Design to Discovery, 1990, (with Pine, Hendrickson and Hammond) Organic Chemistry, 1960, 4th edit., 1980, Fundamentals of Carbanion Chemistry, 1965, (with Richards and Hammond) Elements of Organic Chemistry, 1967, (with Cram) Essence of Organic Chemistry, 1977, (with Cram) Container Molecules and Their Guests, 1994; contbr. chpts. to textbooks, articles in field of host-guest complexation chemistry, carbanions, stereochemistry, mold metabolites, large ring chemistry. Named Young Man of Yr. Calif. Jr. C. of C., 1954, Calif. Scientist of Yr., 1974, Nobel Laureate in Chemistry, 1987, UCLA medal, 1993; recipient award for creative work in synthetic organic chemistry Am. Chem. Soc., 1965, Arthur C. Cope award, 1974, Richard Tolman medal, 1985, Willard Gibbs award, 1985, Roger Adams award, 1985, Herbert Newby McCoy award, 1965, 75, Glenn Seaborg award, 1989, Nat. Medal of Science, Nat. Sci. Found., 1993; award for creative rsch. organic chemistry Synthetic Organic Chem. Mfrs. Assn., 1965; Nat. Rsch. fellow Harvard U., 1947, Am. Chem. Soc. fellow, 1947-48, Guggenheim fellow, 1954-55. Fellow Royal Soc. (hon. 1989); mem. NAS (award in chem. scis. 1992), Am. Acad. Arts and Scis., Am. Chem. Soc., Royal Soc. Chemistry, Surfers Med. Assn., San Onofre Surfing Club, Sigma Xi, Lambda Chi Alpha. Office: UCLA Dept Chemistry Los Angeles CA 90095-0001

CRAMER, BRIAN STARKWEATHER, electrical engineer; b. Phila., Aug. 15, 1955; s. Arthur A. and Mary S. (Starkweather) C.; m. Colette C. Kolondra, May 20, 1979; children: Brian Alex, Arielle Nicole, Corinne Elizabeth. BSEE, Lehigh U., 1977. Registered profl. engr., Ill. Engr. AIL Sys., Deer Park, N.Y., 1977-81; sr. engr. Lockheed Electronics, Plainfield, N.J., 1981-84; pres. EPP, Inc., Plainfield, Ill., 1984-90; prin. engr. ComEd, Chgo., 1991-96, tech. expert inductive coordination and elec. effects, 1996—. Contbr. articles to profl. jours. Youth soccer coach Manhattan (Ill.) Soccer Assn., 1992-96; asst. scoutmaster Boy Scouts Am., Manhattan, 1996—. Mem. IEEE (sr., mem. insulated conductor com. magnetic fields working group 1996—), Am. Railroad Engring. & Maintenance-of-way Assn. (assoc., consulting mem. comm. & signal subcom. F 1994—), Conference Internationale des Grands Reseaux Electriques a Haute Tension. Office: ComEd 1319 S 1st Ave Maywood IL 60153-2405

CRAMER, DOUGLAS SCHOOLFIELD, broadcasting executive; b. Louisville, Aug. 22; s. Douglas Schoolfield and Pauline (Compton) C.; m. Joyce Haber, Sept. 25, 1966 (div. 1973); children: Douglas Schoolfield, III, Courtney Sanford. Student, Northwestern U., 1949-50, Sorbonne, Paris, 1951; B.A., U. Cin., 1953; M.F.A., Columbia U., 1954. Prodn. asst. Radio City Music Hall, N.Y.C., 1950-51; with script dept. Metro-Goldwyn-Mayer, 1952; mng. dir. Cin. Playhouse, 1953-54; instr. Carnegie Inst. Tech., 1955-56; TV supr. Procter & Gamble, 1956-59; broadcast supr. Ogilvy, Benson & Mather, 1959-62; v.p. program devel. ABC, 1962-66, 20th Century-Fox-TV, Los Angeles, 1966-68; exec. v.p. in charge prodn. Paramount TV, 1968-71; ind. producer, pres. Douglas S. Cramer Co., 1971—; exec. v.p. Aaron Spelling Prodns., 1976-87, vice-chmn., 1988-90. Exec. prodr.: Bridget Loves Bernie, CBS-TV, 1972-73, QB VII, 1973-74, Dawn: Portrait of a Teenage Runaway, NBC-TV, 1976, Danielle Steel's Fine Things, Kaledescope, 1990, Changes, Daddy, Palomino, 1990-91, Secrets, 1991, Heart Beat, 1992, Star, Message to Nam, 1993, Vanished, Family Album, 1994, Zoya, 1993, Perfect Strangers, No Greater Love, 1995, Family of Cops I & II, CBS-TV, 1995-96, The Ring, Remembrance, Full Circle, NBC-TV, 1996; co-exec. prodr.: Love Boat, ABC, 1977-86, Vegas, ABC, 1978-81, Wonder Woman, ABC, 1975-77, CBS, 1977-78, Dynasty, 1981-89, Hotel, 1983-87, Trade Winds, 1993; prodr.: (feature film) Sleeping Together, 1995; author: (plays) Call of Duty, 1953, Love Is A Smoke, 1957, Whose Baby Are You, 1963, Last Great Dish, 1994, Lust For Murder, 1995. Pres. Mus. Contemporary Art, L.A., 1990-93, 1st vice-chair, 1993-96: bd. trustees, 1983-96; Internat. Coun. Mus. Modern Art, N.Y.C., 1993—; pres., bd. trustees Douglas S. Cramer Found., 1993—; trustee M.O.M.A. N.Y., 1993—. Mem. Univ. Club of N.Y.C., Beta Theta Pi. Address: PO Box 713 Lakeville CT 06039-0713 Office: 160 E 72d St New York NY 10021

CRAMER, DUNCAN, educator in psychology; b. Rotterdam, The Netherlands, May 30, 1948; arrived in Eng., 1958; s. Hans and Mary Eileen (Sargent) C.; m. Susan Elizabeth Rees, Aug. 24, 1973 (div. 1981). BSc with Hons., U. Coll., London, 1969; PhD, Inst. Psychiatry, London, 1973. Chartered psychologist, Eng. Lectr. in psychology Queen's U., Belfast, No. Ireland, 1973-76; lectr. in social psychology Loughborough (Eng.) U., 1977-90, sr. lectr., 1991-96, reader, 1996—. Author: (books) Close Relationships, 1998, Fundamental Statistics for Social Research, 1997; co-editor Brit. Jour. of Med. Psychology, 1995-2000; also profl. jour. articles. Fellow Brit. Psychol. Soc. Avocations: current affairs, cooking, reading, writing. Home: 14 Hill Top Rd, Lcstrshr Loughborough LE11 3LW, England Office: Loughborough U, Ashby Rd, Lcstrshr Loughborough England

CRAMER, ESTHER RIDGWAY, author, historian, retired supermarket executive; b. La Habra, Calif., Jan. 17, 1927; d. Claude Arthur and Ida Alma (Leutwiler) Ridgway; m. Stanley Edward Cramer, June 17, 1948; children: Cynthia Ann Cramer Freeman, Melinda Cramer Ching, Janet Cramer Esguerra Buddle. BA, Pomona Coll., Claremont, Calif., 1948; postgrad., U. So. Calif., 1949, Calif. State U., Fullerton, 1960-67. Cert. secondary sch. tchr., Calif. Supr. phys. edn. Fullerton Schs., 1948-51; city historian City of La Habra, Calif., 1965—; v.p. cmty. rels. Alpha Beta Co., La Habra, 1979-86, dir. consumer affairs, 1973-79; author, historian Orange County, Calif., 1965—; mem. Orange County Hist. Commn., Santa Ana, Calif., 1973—; commr. USDA Meat and Poultry Inspection Bd., Washington, 1982-84; v.p. Orange County Centennial, Santa Ana, 1987-89. Author: La Habra, The Pass Through the Hills, 1970, The Alpha Beta Story, 1973, Brea, The City of Oil, Oranges and Opportunity, 1992, A Bell in the Barranca, 1996; editor: A Hundred Years of Yesterdays, 1989, 2d edit., 2000, Early Business History of Orange County, 1992, others; numerous oral histories in collection at Calif. State U., Fullerton. Mem. adv. bd. Orange County coun. Boys and Girls Club, 1978—, past pres.; mem. adv. bd. La Habra Boys and Girls Club, 1987—, past pres.; mem. adv. bd. La Habra Children's Mus., 1980—. Recipient Donald Pfleuger award for local history Hist. Soc. So. Calif., 1992, Outstanding Author award U. Calif., Irvine, 1970, Outstanding Contbn. award Orange County Hist. Conf., 1999, Women Helping Women award Brea/La Habra Soroptimists, 2000; named to Hall of Fame, So. Calif. Grocers, 1985, Hall of Fame, Fullerton Union H.S., 1994, Citizen of Yr., City of La Habra, 1978. Mem. Orange County Hist. Soc. (pres. 1971-72), Orange County Pioneer Coun. (pres. 1993-94), La Habra Old Settlers Hist. Soc. (historian 1973—), Mortar Board, Phi Beta Kappa. Republican. Methodist. Avocations: writing, travel. Home: 600 Linden Ln La Habra CA 90631-3124

CRAMER, FRANK BROWN, engineering executive, combustion engineer, systems consultant; b. Long Beach, Calif., Aug. 29, 1921; s. Frank Brown and Clara Bell (Ritzenthaler) C.; m. Hendrika Van der Hulst, 1948 (div. 1962); children: Frieda Hendrika, Eric Gustav, Lisa Monica, Christina Elena; m. Paula Gil, Aug. 3, 1973; children: Alfred Alexander, Consuelo F., Peter M. BA, U. So. Calif., 1942, postgrad., 1942-43, 46-51. Rsch. fellow U. So. Calif., L.A., 1946-51; supr. engring. Rocketdyne, Canoga Park, Calif., 1953-63; pres. Multi-Tech, Inc., San Fernando, Calif., 1960-69; systems cons. Electro-Optical Systems, Pasadena, Calif., 1969-70, McDonnell-Douglas Astronautic, Huntington Beach, Calif., 1971-72; pres. Ergs Unltd. Inc., Mission Hills, Calif., 1973-89; pres. Acquisition, Mission Hills, 1988—, sr. prin. in applied tech. assoc., 1999—; instr. engring. stats. U. So. Calif., L.A., 1955-57, sys. cons. dept. medicine, 1959-68; sys. cons. Jet Propulsion Lab., Pasadena, 1964-68; mem. coun. Realtors Coun. Comml. and Investment Brokers. Author: Statistics for Medical Students, 1951, Combustion Processes/Liquid Rocket Engring., 1968; contbr. articles to profl. jours.; patentee in field. Committeeman Libertarian Party, San Fernando Valley, Calif., 1966, Rep. Party, Mission Hills, 1967-68; dir. realtor's com. on the air quality mgmt. plan So. Calif. Air Quality Control Dist., treas. realtor com. for air quality, 1994-95, vice chmn., 1996; pres. San Fernando Rep. Club, 1967-68; dir., mem. exec. com. Los Angeles County Bd. Realtors. Office: Acquisition 14800 Alexander St Mission Hills CA 91345-1210

CRAMER, MARK CLIFTON, lawyer; b. St. Petersburg, Fla., July 20, 1954; s. WIlliam Cato and Alice J. Cramer; m. Carol Balnkenship, Aug. 6, 1977; children: Ryan Albert, Philip Rogers. BA, U. N.C., 1976; JD, U. Va., 1979. Bar: D.C., 1979, Fla. 1982, N.C. 1986. Assoc. Cramer & Lipsen, 1979-80; ptnr. Cramer & Cramer, 1980-81; dir. congl. rels. U.S. Govt. Printing Office, Washington, 1981, dep. gen counsel, 1981-83; gen. counsel, 1983-85; vice pres., gen. counsel Blankenship-Cramer Devel. Corp., Charlotte, NC, 1985—; legis. cons. N.C. Drug Cabinet, 1990; pvt. practice, 1991—; sec. N.C. Global TransPark Authority, 1991—; vice pres. Found. for Transportation Trade and Commerce, 1998—; exec. dir. Real Estate and Bldg. Industry Coalition, 1995—. Editor: Legislative Histories of the Laws Affecting the U.S. Govt. Printing Office as Codified in Title 44 of the U.S. Code. Liaison mem. Adminstrv. Conf. U.S., 1984-85; chmn. Mecklenburg County Zoning Bd. of Adjustment, 1986-92; commr. N.C. Gen Statutes Commn., 1988-93; mem. Mecklenburg Planning Dist., 1989, Charlotte Mecklenburg Consolidation Charter Study Commn., 1990, Mecklenburg County Redistricting Com., 1991; Transportation Comm. of 100, 1994; Charlotte Mecklenburg Citizens Transit Advisory Grp., 1999—; Surface Water Improvement & Mgmt. Task Force, 1997-99; Charlotte Mecklenburg Smart Growth Task Force, 1999—; vice chmn. Mecklenburg County Reps., 1989-93; founder, moderator Rep issues Forum; co-chmn. Mecklenburg CountyCom. to re-elect Gov. Jim Martin, 1988. Recipient Pub. Printer's G.'d medal for disting. svc., U.S. Govt. Printing Office, Long Leaf Pine award Gov. State of N.C. Mem. N.C. Bar Assn. Mecklenburg County Bar Assn., Urban Land Inst., N.C. Citizens for Bus. and Industry, Phi Beta Kappa, Sigma Nu (recipient Sr. Scholarship award 1976).

CRAMP, DAVID CHRISTOPHER, agriculturist, consultant; b. Hamburg, Germany, Feb. 27, 1952; arrived in Spain, 1993; s. Cecil and Gladys Millicent (Gordon) C.; m. Annabel Margaret Osborne, Oct. 14, 1990; 1 child, Lucy Virginia. BSc with honors, London U., 1972; postgrad. diploma in biology, U. Wales, Cardiff, 1993. Flight lt. Royal Air Force, worldwide, 1972-92; rschr. U. Wales, Cardiff, 1992-93; freelance cons. Aracena, Spain, 1994—. Author: The Beekeepers Field Guide, 1999; contbr. articles to profl. jours. Mem. Internat. Bee Rsch. Assn. (rep. for Spain 1998—), Old Cranwellian Assn. Roman Catholic. Avocations: beekeeping, sailing, reading, tennis. Home: Molino El Bombo, 21200 Aracena Spain

CRANBORNE, VISCOUNT ROBERT MICHAEL JAMES GASGOYNE CECIL, British government official; b. Sept. 30, 1946; m. Hannah Ann Stirling, 1970; 5 children. Degree in History, Oxford U. Mem. parliament for Dorset S. House of Commons, 1979-87; mem. House of Lords, 1992-99, Lord Privy Seal and Leader, 1994-97; parliamentary under-sec. State for Defence Ministry of Defence, 1992-94; leader of opposition House of Lords, 1997-98. Office: House of Lords, Westminster, London SW1A OPW, England*

CRANDELL, K(ENNETH) JAMES, management and strategic planning consultant, entrepreneur; b. Ajax, Ont., Can., July 12, 1957; s. James Bauder Butterill and Barbara Joy Gillard; m. Christine Josephine McElhenney, July 28, 1984. B in Adminstrn. and B in Commerce, U. Ottawa, 1980; MBA, Fla. Atlantic U., 1982. CPA, Fla., Calif. Assoc. dir. entrepreneurial svcs. div. Ernst & Young, Ft. Lauderdale, Fla., 1982-88; founder, chmn., CEO NBS Cons. Group, Inc. (d/b/a New Bus. Strategies), Los Gatos, Calif., 1988—; guest lectr. State Univ. System. Writer, co-producer TV series Florida Business Advisor, 1988; contbr. articles to mags. Recipient Up and Comer award, 1988. Mem. AICPA, Fin. & Adminstrn. Mgmt. in Entertainment, Fla. Inst. CPAs, Calif. Soc. CPAs, Am. Assn. Accts. (MAS divsn. 1980-93), Inst. Mgmt. Accts. (bd. dirs. Ft. Lauderdale 1983—, pres. 1988-89, bus. planning com. 1987-89), Can.-Am. Bus. Alliance (co-founder), U. Miami Venture Coun. Forum, Gold Coast Venture Capital Club (v.p., bd. dirs. 1987-91, treas. 1987-88, co-editor newsletter 1987-89), Ft. Lauderdale C. of C. (chmn. venture capital activities 1986-88, small bus. coun. 1985-90), others. Avocations: ice hockey, published songwriter, reading. Office: NBS Cons Group Inc PMB #J 245 Mount Hermon Rd Ste M Scotts Valley CA 95066-4045 also: 14125 Capri Dr Ste 7 Los Gatos CA 95032-1516

CRANE, ALFRED CHARLES, JR., scientist; b. Phila., Nov. 4, 1943; s. Alfred Charles Sr. and Anne Mary (Voder) C.; m. Linda Louise Moore, Nov. 30, 1968; 1 child, Alfred Charles Crane III. BS in Physics, The Citadel, 1965. Commd. 2d lt. USAF, 1965, advanced through grades to lt. col.; chief quality control divsn. Hdqr. Air Force Spl. Projects Fac., Westover AFB, Mass., 1967-71; staff photographic/intel officer Hdqr. USAF, Washington, 1971-76; chief reconaisance divsn. USAF in Europe, Ramstein AB, Germany, 1976-79; program mgr. reconnaissance systems Rome Air Devel. Ctr., Griffies AFB, N.Y., 1979-83; ch. collection mgmt. divsn. 6 TIG, Osan AB, Korea, 1983-84; divsn. chief intel systems Hdqr. Air Command, Langley AB, Va., 1984-87; ret. USAF, 1987; sr. scientist Autometric Inc., Tabb, Va., 1987—; mem. bd. dirs. ASPRS, 1990-92; rsch. assoc. Va. Inst. for Marine Sci., Gloucester, 1992-94. Editor: Airborne Reconnissance XVII, 1994, Airborne Reconnissance XIX, 1995. Bd. trustees Va. Aerospace Bus. Roundtable, Hampton, 1993—; advisor Opportunity Va.: Developing a Strategic Plan, Richmond, 1994, Remote Sensing-A High Tech Tool for Virginia, 1989. Decorated Bronze star Pacific Air Forces, 1967. Mem. Am. Soc. Photogrammetry Remote Sensing, Va. Aerospace Bus. Roundtable, Nat. Mil. Intelligence Assn. (chpt. pres. 1984-88), Air Force Assn. Republican. Episcopalian. Home: 104 Winder Rd Tabb VA 23693-3222

CRANE, DIANA MARILYN, sociology educator; b. Toronto, Ont., Can., Apr. 5, 1933; d. John Halliday and Lorna Margaret (Somerville) Crane; m. Michel E.A. Herve, Sept. 13, 1965; 1 child, Adrienne Marcelle. AB, Radcliffe Coll., 1953; MA, Columbia U., 1961, PhD, 1964. Asst. prof. sociology Yale U., New Haven, 1964-68; asst. to assoc. prof. Johns Hopkins U., Balt., 1968-72; assoc. to full prof. sociology U. Pa., Phila., 1973—; vis. prof. sociology U. Poitiers, France, 1989-90; cons. Orgn. for Econ. Coop. and Devel., Paris, 1971-72, 74. Author: Invisible Colleges, 1972, The Sanctity of Social Life, 1975, The Transformation of the Avant-Garde, 1987, The Production of Culture Media Industries and Urban Arts, 1992, Fashion and Its Social Agendas, 2000; editor: Sociology of Culture: Emerging Theoretical Perspectives. Guggenheim fellow, 1974-75, Fulbright grantee, 1987-88. Mem. Am. Sociol. Assn., Internat. Sociol. Assn., Sociology of Culture Sec. of Am. Sociol. Assn. (chair 1991-92). Democrat. Avocations: photography, travel. Home: 13 rue Cassette, 75006 Paris France Office: U of Pa Dept Sociology 113 McNeil Philadelphia PA 19104-6299

CRANE, KENT BRUCE, international investments executive; b. North Hornell, N.Y., July 25, 1935; s. Willard L. and Elizabeth (Ewart) C.; divorced; children: Jeffrey Stuart, James Andrew. BA cum laude, Dartmouth Coll., 1957; postgrad. in internat. econs., Am. U., 1958. Third sec. polit. sect. U.S. Embassy, Jakarta, Indonesia, 1960-62; with U.S. Dept. State, Washington, 1963-64; vice consul in charge econ. sect. U.S. Consulate, Zanzibar, 1964-65; 2d sec. polit. sect. U.S. Embassy, Accra, Ghana, 1965-67; sr. rsch. assoc. for fgn. affairs, sec. to task force on conduct of fgn. rels. Rep. Nat. Com., 1967-68; spl. asst. to Senator George Murphy, 1968-69, nat. security affairs adv. to V.P. of U.S., 1969-72; asst. dir. for East Asia and Pacific USIA, 1972-74; adminstrv. asst. to Rep. Peter H.B. Frelinghuysen, 1974-75; project dir. U.S. Commn. on Orgn. of Govt. for Conduct of Fgn. Policy, 1974-75; chmn. bd. Crane Pub. Co., Ridgewood, N.J., 1975-80; co-chmn. Africa subcom. Rep. Nat. Com., 1978-80; pres., mng. dir. Crane Group Ltd., Washington, 1978-87; pres. Ranch Devel. and Mgmt., Inc., Tex., 1980-90; officer, dir. various cos. U.S. and abroad including Corona Co., Harrow Corp., 1984-92, Beliz-Orient Corp., Nepal Wildlife Corp., 1986—, Crane (Africa) Ltd., 1994—, Galamuka (Zambia), 1996—; real estate joint ventures U.S., N.Z., Spain, Turkey, Africa; mgr., dir. resort devels. Nepal, Belize, Namibia, South Africa, Ukraine, Zambia; assoc. developer Amanresorts Ltd., Hong Kong, Geneaal Hotel Mgmt. Ltd., Singapore. Served to 1st lt. U.S. Army, 1957-59, to capt. USAR. Mem. Inst. Strategic Studies (London), Nat. Rifle Assn. (dir.), Explorers Club, Game Conservation Internat., Met. Club (N.Y.C.), Internat. Club (Washington), Capitol Hill Club (Washington), Internat. Economists Club, Mt. Kenya Safari Club, Safari Internat. Club. Fax: 27-31 709-0564. Address: 701 Old Main Rd, Cowiew Hill Durban 3610, South Africa

CRANE, PHILIP MILLER, congressman; b. Chgo., Nov. 3, 1930; s. George Washington III and Cora (Miller) C.; m. Arlene Catherine Johnson, Feb. 14, 1959; children: Catherine Anne, Susanna Marie, Jennifer Elizabeth, Rebekah Caroline, George Washington V, Rachel Ellen, Sarah Emma, Carrie Esther. Student, DePauw U., 1948-50; BA, Hillsdale Coll., 1952; postgrad.,

U. Mich., 1952-54, U. Vienna, Austria, 1953, 56; MA, Ind. U., 1961; PhD, 1963; LLD, Grove City Coll., 1973, Nat. Coll. Edn., 1987; Doctor en Ciencias Politicas, Francisco Marroquin U., 1979. Advt. mgr. Hopkins Syndicate, Inc., Chgo., 1956-58; tchg. asst. Ind. U., Bloomington, 1959-62; asst. prof. history Bradley U., Peoria, Ill., 1963-67; dir. schs. Westminster Acad., Northbrook, Ill., 1967-68; mem. 91st-106th Congresses, 12th (now 8th) Ill. Dist., 1969—; vice chmn. Ways and Means Com. Author: Democrat's Dilemma, 1964, The Sum of Good Government, 1976, Surrender In Panama: The Case Against the Treaty, 1978; contbr.: Continuity in Crisis, 1974, Crisis in Confidence, 1974, Case Against the Reckless Congress, 1976, Can You Afford This House?, 1978, View from the Capitol Dome (Looking Right), 1980, Liberal Cliches and Conservative Solutions, 1984. Dir. rsch. Ill. Goldwater Orgn., 1964; mem. nat. adv. bd. Young Ams. for Freedom, 1965—; bd. dirs. Am. Conservative Union, 1965-82, chmn., 1976; bd. dirs., chmn. Intercollegiate Studies Inst.; bd. advisors Ashbrook Ctr., Ashland U., 1983—; univ. trustee, 1988-93; founder Rep. Study Com., 1972—, chmn., 1984; commr. Commn. on Bicentennial U.S. Constn., 1986-91; trustee Hillsdale Coll. Recipient Distinguished Alumnus award Hillsdale Coll., 1968, Independence award, 1974, William McGovern award Chgo. Soc., 1969, Freedoms Found. award, 1973; named Ill. Statesman's Father Yr., 1979. Mem. ASCAP, VFW (award 1978), Am. Hist. Assn., Orgn. Am. Historians, Acad. Polit. Sci., Am. Acad. Polit. and Social Scis., Am. Legion, Phila. Soc., B'nai B'rith (award 1978), Phi Alpha Theta, Pi Gamma Mu. Office: US Ho of Reps 233 Cannon House Bldg Washington DC 20515-0001

CRANE, ROGER RYAN, JR., lawyer; b. Washington, Mar. 28, 1946; s. Roger Ryan Crane and Jeanette (Hurlbut) Rosar. AB, Coll. of Holy Cross, 1968; JD, Fordham U., 1973; LLM, NYU, 1980. Bar: N.Y. 1974; U.S. Dist. Ct. (so. and ea. dist.) N.Y. 1974; U.S. Ct. Appeals (2nd cir.) 1974, (1st cir.) 1994. Assoc. Dunnington Bartholow & Miller, N.Y.C., 1973-79, Trubin Sillcocks Edelman, N.Y.C., 1979-81; ptnr. Trubin Sillcocks Edelman, N.Y.C., 1981-84; ptnr., head litig. dept. Bachner Tally Polevoy & Misher, N.Y.C., 1984-2000; ptnr. McCarter & English, N.Y.C., 2000—. Contbr. articles to profl. jours. Mem. N.Y.C. Bar Assn. (prof. discipline com. 1996-99), Univ. Club N.Y., Tuxedo Club. Avocations: golf, tennis, fly fishing, riding. Office: McCarter & English 300 Park Ave New York NY 10022-7402

CRANE, STEVEN, financial company executive; b. Los Angeles, Jan. 21, 1959; s. Roger D. and Violet (Heard) C.; m. Susan Jean Perea June 27, 1998; 1 child Allison Nicole. Grad. h.s. With Mobar Inc., Torrance, Calif., 1976-78; v.p. internat. Fluid Control Internat., Marina del Rey, Calif., 1978-79; pres. Energy Devel. Internat., Torrance, 1979-85; pres., CEO Kaempen USA, Inc., Anaheim, Calif., 1985-91; founding ptnr., chmn. Western Fin. Group, Inc., Redondo Beach, Calif., 1991-95; CEO Artist Network, Huntington Beach, Calif., 1993-95; chmn., bd. dirs. EVP BusinessMall.com Inc. (merged with CorpHQ Inc.), Long Beach, 1995—; bd. dirs. Artist Network; chmn. bd. dirs. We. Finance Group, Inc.; bd. dirs. Source Capital Inc., 1999 . Avocations: kickboxing, photography, basketball, bird hunting. Office: EVP BusinessMall.com Inc 110 W Ocean Blvd Ste 604 Long Beach CA 90802-4628

CRANFILL, VIRGINIA MAY, retired nursing administrator; b. Winfield, Kans., Jan. 28, 1931; d. Archie Lewis and Eva Dell (Martin) Fisher; m. B. Charles Smith, Aug. 3, 1949 (div. Nov. 1978); children: Charles David Smith, Terry Lee Smith (dec.), Bruce Wayne Smith, Nancy Ann Smith Barnhurst; m. Bert D. Cranfill, Oct. 1, 1981. Grad. with honors Sch. Practical Nursing, Hinsdale (Ill.) Hosp., 1964; student, South Fla. C.C., Avon Park, 1971-73; AS with honors, Polk C.C., Winter Haven, Fla., 1975; student, Fla. So. Coll., Lakeland, 1983-84. RN, Fla., Ga., Tenn., Calif.; LPN, Ill., Tenn., Fla.; cert. instr. CPR, cert. instr. BLS, Am. Heart Assn.; lic. EMT, Tenn.; cert. profl. in healthcare quality Healthcare Quality Certification Bd. of Nat. Assn. for Healthcare Quar.; cert. case mgr., cert. internal auditor. Emergency rm. nurse Hinsdale Hosp., 1964-65; office receptionist, dental asst. Dr. J.C. Trivett, DDS, Madison, Tenn., 1965-66; staff nurse Little Creek Sanitarium and Hosp., Concord, Tenn., 1966-68; office nurse Dr. S.A. King, Gen. Practice, 1973-75; asst. DON Hillcrest Nursing Home, Avon Park, 1975; charge nurse med./surg. unit Smyrna (Ga.) Hosp., 1976; insvc. dir. Jellico (Tenn.) Cmty. Hosp., 1976-77; charge nurse maximum security infirmary Avon Park Correctional Instn., 1978-79; charge nurse med./surg./orthop. unit Med. Ctr. Hosp., Punta Gorda, Fla., 1979; circulating surg. nurse St. Helena Hosp., Deer Park, Calif., 1981-82; DON Lake Wales (Fla.) Convalescent Ctr., 1987-88; medicine nurse Fla. Hosp. Heartland Divsn., Avon Park, 1968-69, surgery technician, 1969-73, circulating nurse, 1975-76, charge nurse med./surg. unit, 1979-81, supervisory positions, coord. nursing quality assurance, 1982-87, 88-91, coord. med. quality assurance and utilization rev., 1992, case mgmt. coord., 1993, physician liaison, 1994-95, internal auditor, 1996-97, ret., 1997; mem. adv. bd. Home Health Agy., Sebring, Fla.; asst. to physicians regarding rules and guidelines of Fed. Govt. Health Care Fin. Adminstrn., 1990—; participant various profl. seminars and workshops. Cmty. instr. ARC; past vol. EMT and nurse Jellice Ambulance Svc.; spiritual mentor Walker Meml. Jr. Acad.; deaconess, hostess, active in evangelism outreach Seventh-Day Adventist Ch. Mem. Am. Bd. Quality Assurance Utilization Rev. Physicians (diplomate), Case Mgmt. Soc., Nat. Assn. Health Care Quality (cert.), Assn. Seventh-Day Adventist Nurses (bd. dirs., pres.-elect), Fla. Assn. Health Care Quality, Fla. Utilization Rev. Assn. Republican. Avocations: reading, crafts, sewing, music, writing. Home: 1417 W Avon Blvd Avon Park FL 33825-9511

CRANFORD, JAMES MICHAEL, lawyer; b. Washington, Jan. 26, 1946; s. Jack and Wanda C.; m. Teresa, July 23, 1994; children: William Bodie, James Michael, Heather, Christopher. BA, Mercer U., 1978; JD, Woodrow Wilson U., 1984. Atty. pvt. practice, Macon, Ga., 1985—. Mem. city coun. Macon, 1995-99. Mem. Ga. Bar Assn., Ga. Trial Lawyers Assn., Ga. Assn. Criminal Defense Lawyers, Macon Bar Assn., Macon Assn. Criminal Justuce Lawyers, Middle Ga. Trial Lawyers Assn. Episcopalian. Avocations: family, motorcycle racing, scuba diving, boxing, fishing. Home: 1842 Williamson Rd Macon GA 31206-3342 Office: 913 Washington Ave Macon GA 31201-6720

CRANKSHAW, JOHN HAMILTON, mechanical engineer; b. Canton, Ohio, Aug. 29, 1914; s. Fred. Weir and Mary (Lashels) C.; m. Wilma Chaffee Thurlow, June 5, 1940; children: Wilma Jean, John H., Geoffrey Thurlow. B.S. in Mech. Engring., MIT, M.S., 1940. Rotating engr. Gen. Electric Co., 1940-41, sect. engr., mech. design sect. Motor Engr. divsn. Locomotive Car Equipment, Erie, Pa., 1946-52; exec. engr. J.A. Zurn Mfg. Co., Am. Flexible Coupling Co., 1952-54; v.p. engring., 1954; exec. v.p., dir. Zurn Industries, Inc., mng. dir. Zurn R & D. Divsn., until 1957; pres., dir. Dynetics, Inc., Erie, 1957—, Dynetic Sys., Inc., Erie, 1970—; expert witness numerous product liability cases. Mem. adv. coun. Gannon Coll.; chmn. Erie Sewer Authority. Served to maj. Ordnance Dept., AUS, 1941-46. Registered profl. engr., Pa. Mem. ASME, Soc. Automotive Engrs., Assn. Iron and Steel Engrs., Soc. Exptl. Stress Analysis, Soc. Naval Architects and Marine Engrs., Am. Soc. Metals, ASTM, Am. Soc. Lubricating Engrs. Erie Engring. Socs. Coun. (pres. 1955-57), Pa. Soc. Profl. Engrs., MIT Club (N.Y.), Sigma Xi. Author several tech. papers. Achievements include 25 US and 5 fgn. patents; invention and design of main propulsion couplings and clutches for nuc. powered submarines and Navy and Coast Guard surface ships. Home and Office: Dynetics Inc 439 Shawnee Dr Erie PA 16505-2433

CRANLEY, WILLIAM PATRICK, insurance executive; b. Balt., Apr. 11, 1960. Diploma, U. Dijon, France, 1981; BA, Brown U., 1982; MA in Chinese Studies, U. Mich., 1988, MBA, 1988; diploma, Hopkins-Nanjing Ctr., China, 1987. Mng. dir. China Cigna Corp., Shanghai, 1998—. Fgn. Affairs Conf. scholar U.S. Naval Acad., 1982. Mem. Am. C. of C. Shanghai (treas. 1998, vice chmn. 1999), Shanghai Hist. House Assn. (founder). Office: Cigna Corp China Merchants, 66 Lujiazui Rd Ste 2612, 200120 Shanghai China

CRANOIS, NICOLE SIMONE, communications executive; b. Aurillac, France, Apr. 2, 1949; d. Mouchel Cranois; children: Julien, Marie. Diploma, Commonwealth Sch., Sydney, 1967; Maitrise Littres, Sorbonne U., 1970. Press officer Elf Aquitaine, Paris, 1974-81, Family Ministry, Paris, 1981-83; press officer Sanofi, Paris, 1984-85, exec. v.p. corp. comms., 1986—. Avocation: swimming. Office: Sanofi-Synthelabo, 174 Avenue de France, 75013 Paris France

CRAPON DE CAPRONA, COUNT NOËL FRANÇOIS MARIE, lawyer, historian; b. Chambery, Savoie, France, May 23, 1928; s. Denys and Eleanor Worthington (Mather) C. de C.; Baccalaureats, Coll. St. Martin, Pontoise, France, 1947; LL.B., U. Paris, 1952, Diploma, Inst. Comparative Law, 1951, postgrad. Sch. Polit. Scis., 1952-54; m. Barbro Sigrid Wenne, 1954; children—Guy, Yann. Asst. mgr. Sta. Catalina Estancias, Argentina, 1947-48; editor dept. gen. affairs and info. FAO, UN, Rome, 1954-57, liaison officer for UN and various orgns. FAO Office Dir. Gen., 1957-65, chief reports and records, 1966-72, chief conf. ops. br., 1972-74, sec. gen. FAO Conf. and Council, 1974-78, dir. FAO Conf., Council and Protocol Affairs, Rome, 1974-83. Served with French Army, 1944. Recipient 25 Years of Service award, Silver medal FAO, 1979. Mem. Alumni Assn. Coll. St. Martin, Alumni Assn. Ecole des Sciences Politiques; Soc. in France of SAR. Roman Catholic. Research on early medieval history, especially Longobards. Home: Lojovägen 73, S-18147 Lidingo Sweden

CRASSWELLER, ROBERT DOELL, retired lawyer, writer; b. Duluth, Minn., Sept. 17, 1915; s. Arthur Hallifax and Mary Elizabeth (Doell) C.; m. Mildred Elizabeth Clarke, Mar. 21, 1942; children: Peter, Karen Farbman, Pamela Baldino. BA, Carleton Coll., 1937; LLB, Harvard U., 1941. Bar: Minn. 1941, N.Y. 1960. Pvt. practice Duluth, Minn., 1942-43; econ. warfare posts U.S. Dept. State, Washington, 1943-45; ptnr. McCabe, Gruber, Clure, Donovan & Crassweller, Duluth, Minn., 1946-51; mining exec. West Indies Mining Corp., San Juan, P.R., 1951-53; counsel Pan Am. Airways, N.Y.C., 1954-67; vis. fellow Coun. Fgn. Rels., N.Y.C., 1967-70; vis. prof. Bklyn. Coll., Sarah Lawrence, N.Y.C., 1969-70; staff atty. ITT, N.Y.C., 1970-74, gen. coun. Lat. Am., 1975-81. Author: Trujillo: Life and Times of a Caribbean Dictator, 1966, The Caribbean Community, 1972, Perón and the Enigmas of Argentina, 1986; reviewer (books) for Fgn. Affairs, 1968-81. Dir. Forum for World Affairs, Stamford, Conn., 1986-87. Mem. Internat. Assn. Torch Clubs (Chapel Hill Club v.p. 1994-95), Soc. Automotive Historians. Republican. Avocations: gardening, travel, reading, writing, antique cars. Home: 101 York Pl Chapel Hill NC 27514-6521

CRAVEN, JAMES MICHAEL, economist, educator; b. Seattle, Mar. 10, 1946; s. Homer Henry and Mary Kathleen Craven; 1 child, Christina Kathleen Florindo-Craven. Student, U. Minn., 1966-68; BA in Sociology, U. Manitoba, Winnipeg, Can., 1971, BA in Econs., 1971, MA in Econs., 1974. Lic. pilot; cert. ground instr. Instr. econ. and bus. Red River C.C., Winnipeg, 1974-76; lectr. rsch. methods of stats. U. Manitoba, Winnipeg, 1977-78; instr. econ. and bus. Big Bend C.C., Moses Lake, Wash., 1980-81; planning analyst Govt. P.R., San Juan, 1984; prof. econs. and bus. Interam. U. P.R., Bayamon, 1984-85; instr. econs., lectr. history Green River C.C., Auburn, Wash., 1988-92; prof. dept. chair econs. Clark Coll., Vancouver, Wash., 1992—; vis. prof. St. Berchman's U., Kerala, India, 1981, 83, 86, 91; instr. econs. Bellevue (Wash.) C.C., 1988-92; cons. Bellevue, 1988—, Irwin Pubs., 1995—. Inventor in field; contbr. articles to profl. jours. Platform com. mem. Wash. State Dem., Seattle, 1992; cons. Lowry for Gov. Campaign, Seattle, 1992; mem. (assoc.) Dem. Party Nat. Com., 1994-99; mem. Nat. Steering Com. for Re-election of Pres. Clinton, 1995-96; mem. Pres.'s Second Term Com., 1996-99; tribunal judge Inter-Tribal Tribunal on Residential Schs. in Can., Vancouver, 1998; mem. Blackfoot Nation. With U.S. Army, 1963-66. Recipient pilot wings FAA, 1988-92; Govt. Can. fellow, 1973-74. Mem. Assn. Northwest Econ. Educators, Wash. Edn. Assn., Assn. Nat. Security Alumni, Blackfoot Confederacy. Avocations: flying, languages, tennis, hiking. Home: 904 NE Minnehaha St Apt C9 Vancouver WA 98665-8732 Office: Clark Coll Dept Econs 1800 E Mcloughlin Blvd Vancouver WA 98663-3598

CRAVER, CHARLES HENRY, illustrator; b. Eldon, Mo., Dec. 6, 1909; s. Charles Henry and Sylvia (John) C.; m. Nadia Aileen Palmer, Nov. 5, 1950. Student, St. Louis Sch. Fine Art, 1927-30, 34-36; AB, Washington U., 1933. Freelance mag. illustrator Capper Publs., Topeka, Kans., 1933-36; freelance mag. illustrator So. Agriculturist, Nashville, Tenn., 1936-42, Christian Bd. of Publ., St. Louis, 1945-1948; staff artist Mo. Dept. Health, Jefferson City, 1948-79, bur. chief, 1957; bur. chief Mo. Dept. Health Edn., Jefferson City, 1959; instr. art dept. Lincoln U., Jefferson City, 1991-94. Works include mural at Christian Ch., 1937, Bapt. Ch., 1945, exhibit at Am. Pub. Health, 1955 (2 awards), Mo. state seal, 1949, numerous landscapes, 1950-97. Mem. Capital City Coun. on the Arts, Jefferson City; advisor Nichols Ctr., Jefferson City. Staff Sgt. U.S. Air Corps, 1942-45, Africa. Recipient presdl. citation Mo. Pub. Health Assn., Jefferson City, 1984. Mem. St. Louis Artists Guild, Co. of Mil. Historians, Soc. for Army Hist. Rsch., Mil. Hist. Soc. Republican. Disciples of Christ. Home: 1305 Moreland Ave Jefferson City MO 65101-3734

CRAW, FREEMAN (JERRY CRAW), graphic artist; b. East Orange, N.J.; s. Stanley Reston and Mildred (Godfrey) C.; m. Janet Secor Johnson (dec.); children: Peter (dec.), Stephanie (dec.). Grad., Cooper Union, hon. degree, 1967. Artist Am. Colortype, Clifton, N.J., 1940-44; art dir. Tri-Arts Press, N.Y.C., 1944-65, art dir., v.p., 1956-65; prin. Freeman Craw Design, N.Y.C., 1965-81; mgr. graphics and prodn. Rockefeller U. Press, N.Y.C., 1981-86; prin. Freeman Craw, graphist, Millburn, N.J., 1986—. One-man shows include: Am. Type Founders, U. Ala., BBDO, N.Y.C., Carnegie-Mellon U., Cooper Union, Royal Coll. Art, London, Soc. Typog. Designers, London, Soc. Typog. Arts, Chgo., Rochester Inst. Tech., N.Y.; represented in permanent collections: Mus. Modern Art., N.Y.C., Cooper-Hewitt Mus., Smithsonian Instn., N.Y.C.; created 10 type faces. Mem. alumni adv. bd. Cooper Union, 1969-71. Recipient Goudy award Rochester Inst. Tech., 1981, Type Dirs. Club medal, 1988, Lernhardt award, 1966. Mem. Type Dirs. Club (bd. dirs. 1983-86), Art Dirs. Club, Guttenberg Mus. (hon.), Essex Skating Club (West Orange, N.J., hon.). Avocations: Japanese prints, lectures.

CRAWFORD, CINDY, model, actress; b. Dekalb, Ill., Feb. 20, 1966; d. Dan and Jennifer C.; m. Richard Gere, Dec. 12, 1991 (div.); m. Rande Gerber; 1 child. Student, Northwestern U. Model for Victor Skrebneski, 1984-86; signed with Elite Modeling Agy., 1986; spokesperson Revlon, 1989—, JH Collectibles, Pepsi Cola, Kay Jewelers; host MTV's House of Style, 1989-95. First featured on cover Vogue, 1986; exercise videos: Cindy Crawford's Shape Your Body Workout, 1992, The Next Challenge Workout, 1993; film appearances include: Fair Game, 1995; host TV special, 1995, also Sex with Cindy Crawford; feature corr. MTV. Supporter breast cancer rsch.; active Leukemia Soc. of Am. Office: Wolf-Kasteler 132 S Rodeo Dr Ste 300 Beverly Hills CA 90212-2414

CRAWFORD, FELIX CONKLING, dentist; b. Jan. 11, 1938. DDS, U. Tex. Dental Br., Houston, 1963. Pvt. practice Plainview, Tex. Pres. Rotary, Plainview, 1971-72, Plainview Country Club, 1973-74, Plainview C. of C., 1984; chmn. Tex. Dental Found., 1990-92. Named Outstanding Alumnus, U. Tex. Dental Br., 1996. Fellow Internat. Coll. Dentists, Acad. Gen. Dentistry, Am. Coll. Dentists (chmn. Tex. sect. 1994); mem. ADA (vice-chmn. Coun. Govt. Affairs 1999—, chmn. ADPac 1994-95), Tex. Dental Assn. (chmn. DenPac 1982-85, pres. 1988, Pres. award 1991, Disting. Svc. award 1994). Office: 2615 W 24th St Plainview TX 79072-1809

CRAWFORD, JOE JAY, real estate company executive; b. Nagoya, Honsu, Japan, Oct. 27, 1954; came to U.S., 1954; s. Charles B. and Betty K. (Wilson) C.; m. Kimberly R. Glover, Aug. 13, 1977; children: Taylor Garrett, Kimberly Faith. BBA in Econ. and Finance, Baylor U., 1976; MBA in Finance, U. Tex., 1978. Comml. credit analyst InterFirst Bank Dallas, 1979, banking officer, 1979-80, asst. v.p., 1980-83; asst. v.p. CitiCorp Real Estate, Dallas, 1983-85, v.p., area dir., 1985-90, v.p., sr. banker, team leader, 1990-93; sr. exec. officer Amstar Group, Ltd., Dallas, 1993-98; COO Amstar Group, Ltd., 1998—; cons. in field; bd. dirs. Nat. Multi-Housing Coun., Sycor Internat., Inc. Adult choir pres. 1st Bapt. Ch., Mesquite, Tex., 1984, Sunday sch. dir., tchr., 1986-87, chmn. budget com., 1986-88, deacon, 1982-89, vice chmn. deacons, 1984; dir., tchr. Sunday sch. Lakeridge Bible Ch., Mesquite, 1991-93. Named Outstanding Young Men of Am., U.S. Jaycees, 1980. Mem. Dallas Young Mortgage Bankers Assn. (sec.-treas. 1983), Sigma Phi Epsilon (life), Alpha Kappa Psi (treas., v.p. 1973-76, nat. conv. del. 1975, life 1976—), Omicron Delta Epsilon. Republican. Avocations: fly fishing, golf, hunting, camping, antique automobile restoration. Office: Amstar Group Ltd 1050 17th St Ste 1220 Denver CO 80265-1050 Address: PO Box 17361 Missoula MT 59808-7361

CRAWFORD, JOHN FORT, lawyer; b. N.Y.C., Sept. 23, 1937; s. Alfred Ross and Barbara (Fort) C.; m. Elisabeth Tjerneld, June 6, 1962 (div.); 1 child, Alexander Olaf; m. Anne-Gabrielle Laurent, May 19, 1989; children: Cyril David, William Franklin. BA, Haverford Coll., 1958; MA, Tufts U., 1959; postgrad., Inst. d'Etudes Politiques, Paris, 1959-61; JD, Columbia U., 1964. Bar: D.C. 1965, U.S. Ct. Appeals D.C. 1965, Paris 1970. Assoc. Surrey & Morse, Washington, 1964-68; spl. asst. to dir. gen. ILO, Geneva, 1968-70; assoc. Surrey & Morse, Paris, 1970-71, ptnr., 1971-85; ptnr. Jones, Day, Reavis & Pogue, Paris, 1986—, vice chmn. Bd. govs. Am. Hosp. Paris, 1983—; vice chmn. internat. bd. overseers Tufts U., 1988—; mem. adv. coun. U.S. and fgn. comml. svc. U.S. Dept. Commerce, 1988-91; bd. dirs. Aspen Inst. France, 1985—; trustee Carnegie Instn., Washington, 1994—; chmn. Global Peace Initiatives Found., Geneva. Decorated chevalier Legion of Honor (France); L.J. Palmer scholar, 1957-58; Noble Found. fellow, 1958-60. Mem. ABA, Bar Assn. D.C., Assn. Bar City N.Y., Internat. Bar Assn., Am. C. of C. in France (dir. 1976—, pres. 1985-88), European Coun. Am. C. of C. (chmn. 1987-90), Internat. C. of C. (coun. 1976—), U.S. Coun. for Internat. Bus. (trustee 1988—), Institut pour l'Arbitrage Internat. (treas., dir. 1985—), Coun. Fgn. Rels., Cercle de l'Union Interalliee (Paris; bd. dirs.), Polo de Paris, Nouveau Cercle de l'Union, Maxim's Bus. Home: 9 Ave Emile Deschanel, 75007 Paris France Office: 120 Rue Faubourg St Honore, 75008 Paris France

CRAWFORD, R. GEORGE, investment manager, educator; b. Mpls., Oct. 30, 1943; s. Robert John and Agnes C.; m. M. Holly Shissler, May, 17, 1980; 1 child, Katherine Barnes. BA, Harvard U., 1965, JD, 1968. Bar N.Y. 1974, DC 1970, Calif. 1972, Ohio, 1969. Law clk. to Hon. Byron R. White U.S. Supreme Ct., Washington, 1968-69; staff asst. to President Washington, 1970-72; v.p. Archon, Inc., L.A., 1972-74; chair pvt. capital sect. Jones Day Reavis & Pogue, L.A., 1974-93; prof. Stanford U., Calif., 1993—; pres. AII, Palo Alto, Calif., 1997—; rsch. fellow Hoover Instn., Stanford, Calif., 1994-97. Author: Derivatives for Decision Makers, 1996; contbr. articles to profl. jours. Dir. Fiduciary Found., Incline Village, Nev., 1992—; mem. supr. coun. Internat. Ctr. Not-for-Profit Law, Washington, 1998—. Mem. Internat. Corp. Governance Network (London) (com. on governance stds. 1997—). Fax: 775-832-9772. E-mail: geo@stanford.edu.

CRAWFORD, RUDY, emergency physician; b. Glasgow, Scotland, May 5, 1949; m. Jane Saunders, Sept. 21, 1973; children: Peter Rudy, Sarah Jane. BSc with hons., U. Glasgow, 1976, MBChB, 1978. House officer Royal Infirmary, Glasgow, 1978-79, registrar in surgery, 1980-85, registrar, 1985-87; sr. registrar Royal Infirmary, Aberdeen, 1987-90; cons. in accident and emergency medicine Royal Infirmary, Glasgow, 1990—; lectr. in anatomy Glasgow Univ., 1979-80; mem. working group accident emergency svcs. Scottish Office, Edinburgh, 1991-94, health bd. emergency planning com. Greater Glasgow, 1990—; hon. sr. lectr. Univ. Glasgow, 1990. Contbr. articles to profl. jours. Mem. commandent in chief St. Andrew's Ambulance Corps., Scotland. Fellow Royal Coll. Physician Surgeons (chmn. subcom. 1996—), Faculty Accident Emergency Medicine; mem. Royal Coll. Surgeons (instr. advanced trauma life support program 1992—), British Assn. Accident Emergency Medicine, St. Andrew's Ambulance Assn. (mem. coun., v.p. 1997), Rotary Internat. Avocations: running, photography, Karate, hillwalking, travel. Office: Glasgow Royal Infirmary, 84 Castle St, Glasgow G4 0SF, Scotland

CRAWFORD, SHEILA JANE, education educator, consultant; b. Beckley, W.Va., Mar. 1, 1943; d. Roger and Ruth (Ashworth) Crawford; m. Lloyd E. Johnston, June 4, 1966 (dec. Dec. 1988); 1 child, Jacqueline De Vries; m. James E. Toomey, Feb. 10, 1989 (div. 2000); m. Troy Thomason, 2000. BA, Tenn. Tech. U., 1963; MA in Christian Edn., Seabury Western Theol. Sem., 1965; MS in Curriculum and Instrn., U. Tenn., Martin, 1989; EdD in Instrn. and Curriculum Leadership, U. Memphis, 1994; postgrad., San Jose State U., U. Calif., Berkeley, U. Utah, Tex. Woman's U. Cert. tchr., Tenn; passed profl. in human resources profl. exam Soc. Human Resource Mgmt. Dir. Christian edn. St. Luke's Episcopal Ch., Rochester, Minn., 1965-66; elem. tchr. Santa Catalina Sch. Girls, 1967-69, Rowland-Hall St. Mark's Sch., Salt Lake City, 1968-69, Union City (Tenn.) Christian Sch., 1984-87; libr. Dept. Edn. U. Tenn. at Martin, 1987-89; rsch. asst. U. Memphis, 1989-92, adj. prof., 1996; prof., edn. dept. chair Lane Coll., Jackson, Tenn., 1992-94; reading tchr., drama club sponsor Ashland (Miss.) Mid. Sch., 1994-95; workshop presenter Jackson, Tenn., 1989-96; ednl. cons. Delta Faucet of Tenn. divsn. Masco Corp., Jackson, 1995—; homebound tchr. Jackson-Madison County Schs., 1996-97; instr., libr. LaGrange-Moscow (Tenn.) Sch., 1997-99; libr. Lauderdale Sch., Memphis; mem. campus All Stars, Honda, Jackson, 1992-93. Contbr. articles to profl. jours. Mem. Am. Counseling Assn., Tenn. ASCD, Assn. for Case Method Rsch., DAR, Nat. Libr. Assn., Ch. and Synagogue Libr. Assn., AAUW, Order Eastern Star (worthy matron 1980-81), Sch. Libr. Assn., Sigma Tau Delta, Kappa Delta Pi. Anglican. Achievements include research in the effect of chess on predicting and summarizing skills. Home: 3207 Thirteen Colony Mall Apt 1 Memphis TN 38115-2972

CRAWFORD, SUSAN A., realtor, artist; b. Phila., May 10, 1942. BA, Hollins U., 1964; CHC, Inst. Transformational Studies, 1994. Tchr. Conn., 1964-71; retail buyer, mgr. Norwegian Craft Shop/Lucretia L. Interiors, Farmington, Conn., 1971-78; owner Frog Pond, Farmington, Canton, Conn., 1978—; artist, 1978—; realtor Realty Execs., Canton, Avon, Conn., 1996—. Mem. Pk. and Recreation Commn., Canton, 1993-95, Econ. Devel. Commn., Canton, 1995-98, Dem. Town Commn., Canton, 1997—; founder, mem. Sam Collins Day Commn., 1995—. Mem. Conn. Women Artists, Canton Artists Guild (bd. dirs., pres. 1984-86, 97—), Canton C. of C. (Bus. Person of the Yr. 1995), Art Guild Farmington (bd. dirs.). Avocations: crafts, theater, music, reading, collectibles. Office: Frog Pond PO Box 352 Canton CT 06019-0352

CRAWFORD-MASON, CLARE WOOTTEN, television producer, journalist; b. Durham, N.C., July 22, 1936; d. Charles Thomas and Clare (Erly) Wootten; m. Robert Watts Mason; children: Victor Lawrence Crawford Jr., Charlene Elizabeth Crawford; stepchildren: John Mason, Robert Mason 3d. BA, U. Md., 1958. Reporter, columnist Washington Daily News, 1961-72; columnist Washington Star News, 1972-74; Washington bur. chief People mag., 1974-82; reporter, sr. prodr. NBC-TV, 1969-80; pres. CC-M Prodns. Inc., Washington, 1981—. Prodr. 1st network documentary on spouse abuse NBC-TV, 1975 (blue ribbon San Francisco Film Festival), 1st network documentary on child sexual abuse NBC, TV, 1977, People of the Year (CBS), 1982, If Japan Can, Why Can't We, 1980 (Dupont award Columbia U. Sch. Journalism), It's Up to the Women, 1984, The Issues Hit Home, 1986, Windows on Women, 1986, How To Fix Up a Little Old American Town, 1987, Work Worth Doing, 1987 (Golden Eagle award Coun. on Internat. Non-theatrical Events), The Deming Library: Vols. I-27, Implementing Deming, vols. 1-4; co-author: Thinking About Quality, Progress, Wisdom and the Deming Philosophy, 1994; prodr., dir. documentary series Quality of Else, 1991, W. Edwards Deming: The Prophet of Quality, 1994; co-author: Quality or Else: The Revolution in World Business, 1991, How Everyone Wins: Joy, Meaning and Profit in the Workplace, 1997, The Enneagram Nine Paths to a Productive and Fulfilling Life, 1999. Recipient Bill Pryor Meml. award, 1st prize Washington Newspaper Guild, 1966; Disting. Pub. Affairs Reporting award Am. Polit. Sci. Assn., 1967; Nat. Assn. Broadcasters award, 1971, 2 Emmy awards Nat. Acad. TV Arts and Scis., 1972, award for broadcast investigative reporting AAUW, 1972, award for investigative reporting Chesapeake Press Assn., 1971, Douglas Southall Freeman award for pub. service Va. Assn. Press Broadcasters, 1972; Washington Newspaper Guild award, 1974, Blue Ribbon Am. Film Festival, 1977, 1st place award Nat. Edn. Film Festival, 1985, documentary award Am. Women in Radio and TV, 1986, Golden Eagle award, 1986, 87, Award of Excellence Soc. Tech. Communication, 1988. Mem. AFTRA, SAG. Democrat. Roman Catholic. Office: 7755 16th St NW Washington DC 20012-1460

CRAWLEY, FREDERICK WILLIAM, banker, real estate company executive; b. London, June 10, 1926; s. William Clement and Elsie Florence (Valentine) C.; m. Ruth Eva Jungman, 1951; children—Nicola Carol, Fiona Ruth. With Lloyds Bank Plc, London, 1942-87, chief acct., 1969-73, asst. gen. mgr., 1973-75, joint gen. mgr., 1975-77, asst. chief gen. mgr., 1977-78, dep. chief gen. mgr., 1978-82, 83-84, chief exec., Calif., 1982-83, chief gen. mgr., 1984-85, dep. chief exec., 1985-87, also dir.; dep. chmn. Alliance &

Leicester Bldg. Soc., London, 1990-91, chmn., 1991-94, also bd. dirs.; dep. chmn. Girobank PLC, 1990-92, chmn., 1992-94, also bd. dirs., 1990-95; bd. dirs. Barratt Devels. PLC, 1988-96; chmn. Black Horse Agys., Ltd., 1985-88, Betta Stores, 1990-92, Legal & Gen. Recovery Investment Trust PLC, 1994—; bd. dirs. Legal & Gen. Bank Ltd. Mem. coun., mem. fin. and gen. purposes com. RAF Benevolent Fund, hon. treas., 1988—, bd. dirs., 1988—; bd. dirs. Battle Britain Appeal, 1988-91; dep. chmn. Royal Air Force Benevolent Fund Enterprises, 1990—. Fellow Chartered Inst. Bankers, St. Andrews Mgmt. Inst.; companion Inst. Mgmt, Army Flying (Middle Wallop) Club, Royal Air Force Club. Avocations: aviation, photography, shooting.*

CRAWSHAW, ALWYN, painter; b. Mirfield, Yorkshire, Eng., Sept. 20, 1934; s. Fred and Doris Letitia Gertrude (Brannon) C.; m. June Eileen Bridgman, Mar. 16, 1957; children: Natalie, Donna, Clinton. Student, Hastings Sch. Art, 1949-51. Founding ptnr. Russell Artists Mcdg. Ltd., Kingston-upon-Thames, Surrey, 1958-80; lectr., demonstrator acrylic and watercolor painting Daler-Rowney & Co. Ltd., Bracknell, Berkshire, Eng., 1972—; guest on BBC-TV, BBC radio, ind. radio. Exhibited work at Royal Soc. Brit. Artists, 1981, 82, 83, 84, 85, 86; author: Painting with Acrylic Colours, 1974, Learn to Paint with Acrylic Colours, 1979, Learn to Paint with Watercolours, 1979, Learn to Paint Landscapes, 1981, Learn to Paint Boats and Harbours, 1982, Learn to Sketch, 1983, Learn to Paint Still Life, 1984, The Artist at Work: Alwyn Crawshaw, 1984, Learn to Paint Outdoors in Watercolour, 1986, Learn to Paint in Oils for the Beginner, 1987, Sketch with Alwyn Crawshaw, 1988, The Half-Hour Painter, 1989, A Brush with Art, 1991, Alwyn Crawshaw's Watercolour Painting Course, 1991, Alwyn Crawshaw's Oil Painting Course, 1992, Alwyn Crawshaw Paints on Holiday, 1992, Alwyn Crawshaw Paints Oils, 1992, Crawshaw's Watercolour Studio, 1993, Alwyn Crawshaw's Acrylic Painting Course, 1994, Crawshaw Paints Acrylics, 1994, Crawshaw's Sketching and Drawing Course, 1995, Crawshaw Paints Constable Country, 1996; (video) Learn to Paint with Watercolour, 1986, Learn to Paint with Watercolor II, 1987, Farmhouse Landscape in Watercolour, Small Harbour Boats in Watercolour, 1989, Learn to Paint Oils, 1990, Learn to Paint Oils II, 1990 (TV series) A Brush with Art, Crawshaw Paints on Holiday, 1992, Crawshaw Paints Oils, 1992, Crawshaw's Watercolour Studio (TV) 1993, Crawshaw Paints Acrylics, 1994, Crawshaw's Sketching and Drawing Course, 1995, Crawshaw Paints Constable Country, 1996, Crawshaw's Outdoor Painting Course, 1997; also articles. Fine art print Wet and Windy included in top 10 prints, 1975; named One of Top 10 Video Tchrs. in U.S., 1991. Fellow Royal Soc. Arts; mem. Soc. Equestrian Artists, British Watercolour Soc., Nat. Assn. Painters in Acrylics (pres.), Soc. Amateur Artists (pres., founder). Mem. Ch. of England. Home: The Hollies, Stubb Rd Hickling, Norwich Norfolk NR12 OYS, England

CREAGAN, JAMES FRANCIS, diplomat; b. Elyria, Ohio, Dec. 28, 1940; s. James Malcolm and Mareta Creagan; m. Cherry Gwyn Jonsson, Jan. 29, 1966; children: Kevin James, Sean Malcolm Alan. BA in History, U. Notre Dame, 1962; PhD in Polit. Sci., U. Va., 1965. Asst. prof. govt. St. Mary's U., San Antonio, 1965-66; asst. prof. polit. sci. Tex. A&M U., Bryan, Tex., 1970-71; joined fgn. svc. Dept. State, Washington, 1966; labor and polit. officer Am. Embassy, Mex., 1967-69; labor attache Am. Embassy, San Salvador, El Salvador, 1969-70; 2nd sec., labor officer Am. Embassy, Rome, 1971-74; 1st sec. Am. Embassy, Lima, Peru, 1974-77; U.S. consul Am. Consulate Gen., Naples, 1977-80; officer-in-charge, Italian and Vatican affairs U.S. Dept. of State, 1980-82; polit. counselor Am. Embassy, Lisbon, 1982-86, Brasilia, 1986-88; dep. chief of mission Am. Embassy to the Holy See, 1988-91; consul gen. Am. Consulate Gen., Sao Paulo, 1991-92; sr. advisor for Latin Am. U.S. Mission to UN, 1992; dep. chief mission Am. Embassy, Rome, 1993-96; Am. amb. to Honduras, 1996-99; pres. John Cabot U., Rome, 1999—. Mem. adv. coun. U. Notre Dame. Mem. Am. Fgn. Svc. Assn., Cosmos Club, InterAm. Dialogue Club. Roman Catholic. Avocations: tennis, biking. Office: John Cabot Univ, Via Lungara 233, 00165 Rome Italy

CREAN, MAUREEN ROSE, educational consultant; b. Rockville Centre, N.Y., Oct. 8, 1949; d. Patrick Joseph and Drusilla (Donnelly) C. AAS, Hudson Valley C.C., Troy, N.Y., 1977; AB, Radcliffe Coll./Harvard U., 1979; MBA, U. Albany, N.Y., 1988. Dir. instl. planning Hudson Valley C.C., Troy, 1988-92; assoc. dir. C.D. Ednl. Opportunity Ctr., Troy, 1992-94; dir. instl. planning Regents Coll., Albany, 1994-96; pres. Productivity Ptnrs., Niskayuna, N.Y., 1990—. Pres., bd. dirs. Niskayuna Cmty. Daycare, 1995—, Girls, Inc., 1996; vol. Farano House, Albany, 1992—; bd. dirs. Our Bros. Keepers Found., Rsch. for Rett, Inc. JTPA grantee, 1991; N.Y. Sci. and Tech. Found. grantee, 1990. Mem. Harvard Club of Northeastern N.Y., Soc. Coll. and Univ. Planners. Office: Regents Coll 1038 Palmer Ave Niskayuna NY 12309-5811 Address: 904 1st St Apt 2 Hermosa Beach CA 90254-5312

CREASIA, DONALD ANTHONY, toxicologist, researcher; b. Milford, Mass., Mar. 28, 1937; s. Dominic and Minnie (Bufalo) C.; m. Joan La Belle, June 29, 1963; children: Karen Joan, Tracey Dawn. BS in Biology, U. Vt., 1961; DSc, Harvard U., 1967; PhD, U. Tenn., 1981. Rsch. assoc. Sch. Pub. Health, Harvard U., Cambridge, Mass., 1963-69; toxicologist Oak Ridge (Tenn.) Nat. Lab., 1970-77; program dir. Frederick (Md.) Cancer Rsch. Ctr., 1977-83; rsch. chemist U.S. Army R&D, Frederick, 1983-98; cons. Knoxville, Tenn., 1998—; cons. toxicology, 19635. Author: (chpts. in books with others) Internat. Symposium on the Biological Effects of Ozone and Related Photochemical Oxidents, 1983, Trycothecine Mycotoxicosis: Pathophysiological Efffects, 1989; contbr. over 120 articles to profl. jours. NSF scholar, 1965-67; NRC fellow, 1981-83. Mem. AAAS, Soc. Toxicology, Am. Coll. Toxicology, Soc. Govt. Toxicologists, Internat. Soc. Toxicology, Sigma Xi. Achievements include patents pending for use of castor bean protein as an immunological adjuvant, for nose-only and body plethismograph animal holder used in inhalation toxicology studies, and for discovery that insulin is equally effective in lowering blood glucose when inhaled into deep lung as when it is administered intramuscularly. Home: 605 Scotswood Cir Knoxville TN 37919-7457

CREATES, MARLENE RUTH, artist; b. Montreal, Que., Can., Apr. 18, 1952; d. Sydney Leslie and Margaret Isabel (Layte) C. BA in Art Edn., Queen's U., 1974. Tchr. visual arts dept. Algonquin Coll., 1975-82, U. Ottawa, 1982-85; program dir. photography Banff Ctr. for the Arts, summer 1991, N.S. Coll. Art and Design, 1998; vis. artist, guest lectr. various univs., art schs. and galleries, Can., Glasgow (Scotland) Sch. Art, U. Oxford, Eng. Solo and group exhbns. Can., Eng., Scotland, Ireland, France, Denmark and USA; represented in permanent collections Meml. U. Nfld., St. John's, Can., Can. Coun. Art Bank, Ottawa, Can. Mus. Contemporary Photography, Ottawa, City of Montreal, Air Canada, Montreal, Can. Mus. Civilization, City of Ottawa, Nat. Gallery Can., Ottawa, Can. Dept. Fgn. Affairs, Govt. of Nfld. and Labrador, Mt. St. Vincent U., Halifax, N.S., numerous others; author: The Diary Exhibition/Journaux Intimes, 1987, City and Sea, 1988, Don Wright 1931-1988: A Retrospective, 1990, Nature is a Verb to Me, 1992, Language and Land Use, Alberta, 1993, 94, The Distance Between Two Points is Measured in Memories, 1988, 99, Marlene Creates: Landworks, 1979-91, 1993, Language and Land Use, Newfoundland, 1994, Places of Presence, Newfoundland, 1989-1991, 1997. Co-founder, mem. bd. dirs. Ea. Edge Gallery, St. John's, 1986-94. Recipient Artist of the Yr. award Nfld. and Labrador Arts Coun., 1996. E-mail: marlene.creates@nf.sympatico.ca. Home: 132 Bond St, Saint John's, NF Canada A1C 1T9

CRECELIUS, DANIEL NEIL, history educator; b. St. Louis, Jan. 15, 1937; s. Wilson John and (Imhof) R.; m. Anahid Tashjian, July 21, 1963; 1 child, Gia Maria. BA, Colo. Coll., 1959; MA, Princeton U., 1962, PhD, 1967. Asst. prof. Calif. State U., L.A., 1964-68, assoc. prof., 1968-73, prof. Mid. East history, 1974—, chairperson, 1980-83, 98—; vis. lectr. UCLA, 1966-67, Colo. Coll., 1990, Cairo U., 1992. Contbr. numerous articles to profl. jours., chpts. to 11 books. Trustees' scholar Colo. Coll., 1955-59; Woodrow Wilson Nat. fellow, 1959-60, Princeton U. Near East fellow, 1961-62; grantee U. Mich., 1960, Princeton U., 1961, Fulbright Found., 1962-63, 91-92, 92, 95-96, 96, Nat. Def. Fgn. Lang. grantee, 1963-64, Am. Rsch. Ctr., 1972, 79, 96, Am. Philos. Soc., 1975, 80, 89, Social Sci. Rsch. Coun., 1973, Dept. HEW Office Edn., 1973, Calif. State U., L.A., 1975, NEH, 1980-82, 83-84, 87, 91-92, 92, Calif. State U. L.A. Found., 1979, 81, others; Joseph P. Malone fellow, 1998. Mem. Mid. East Studies Assn., Turkish Studies Assn., Phi Beta Kappa, Pi Gamma Mu. Lutheran. Avocations: travel, hiking, bird watching. Office: Calif State U LA 5151 State University Dr Los Angeles CA 90032-4226

CREED, CHRISTIAN CARL, lawyer, investigator; b. Alexandria, La., Oct. 31, 1963; s. George Alton and Mickey (Svebek) C.; m. Catherine Campball, Aug. 12, 1995. BA, La. State U., 1985; JD, Loyola U., New Orleans, 1995. Bar: La. 1995, U.S. Dist. Ct. (we., mid., and ea. dists.) La. 1995, U.S. Dist. Ct. (no. and so. dists.) Miss. 1998, U.S. Ct. Appeals (5th cir.) 1995. Assoc. Boles, Boles & Ryan, Monroe, La., 1995-98; mng. ptnr. Creed & Creed, Monroe, La., 1998—. Author, contbg. editor (newsletter) Young Lawyers Newsletter, 1997-98. Mem. adv. bd. Salvation Army, Monroe, 1997—; mem. cabinet United Way, Monroe, 1998-99, bd. dirs., 2000—; mem. fundraising com. Boy Scouts Am. Mem. ABA, La. Bar Assn., 4th Jud. Dist. Ct. Bar Assn. (exec. com.), Baton Rouge Bar Assn., La. Trial Lawyers Assn. (bd. govs.), Am. Inns of Ct. (Fred Fudickar chpt. 1995—), Monroe C. of C. (state and fed. govt. com.), Kiwanis Internat., Ducks Unlimited (sponsorship com.), Rotary Internat., Phi Delta Phi (life mem.). E-mail: law@creed-law.com. Office: Creed & Creed 1805 Tower Dr Monroe LA 71201-4964

CREEDE, MICHAEL DAVID, nursing administrator; b. Montclair, N.J., Dec. 2, 1946; s. Rodney Ballard and Betty Jean (Ross) Cole; m. Joanne Kay Williams, July 31, 1993 (div. Oct. 1997); children: Brenda Montgomery, Jeanette Rae Williams. BS in History, Ctrl. Mich. U., 1976; ADN, Northwestern Mich. Coll., 1991. Cert. ACLS. Asst. wardmaster Darnall Army Cmty. Hosp., Ft. Hood, Tex., 1982-84; skilled nursing staff nurse Reed City (Mich.) Hosp., 1985-91, acute care staff nurse, 1991-92, staff nurse critical care unit, emergency rm., 1992-94, nursing supr. skilled nursing facility, 1994-99; camp nurse Interlochen (Mich.) Ctr. Arts, 1999—; case mgr. Area Agy. on Aging of N.W. Mich., Traverse City, Mich., 1999—. Mem., sect. leader Cadillac Symphony Orch. Recipient Ray Tunney Meml. award, 1997. Mem. Am. Mensa Ltd., Internat. Biographical Ctr. (adv. coun.),Phi Theta Kappa. Episcopalian. Avocations: running, playing baritone and euphonium and valve trombone, deer hunting, building handcrafted furniture, collecting musical instruments. Home: 434 Elmrest St Cadillac MI 49601-9260

CREEL, SUE CLOER, secondary education educator; b. Columbus, Miss., July 4, 1943; d. Ducler Cornelius Cloer and Verna Sarah (Shackelford) Cloer Mackie; children: Ricky (dec.), Ronny. BA, Harding U., 1982, MEd, 1986; specialty degree in edn., Jackson (Miss.) State U., 1996. Tchr. 8th grade English Alfh Jr. H.S., Searcy, Ark., 1982-87; part-time editor, writer for neurosurgery Miss. Med. Ctr., Jackson, 1987-89; adminstrv. asst. to dean of nursing U. Miss. Med. Ctr., Jackson, 1988-89; tchr. advanced placement English and creative writing Jackson Pub. Schs., 1990—; adj. instr. world lit. and Brit. lit. Holmes C.C.; adj. prof. Holmes C.C., 1999—; adj. instr. English Hinds C.C., Raymond, Miss., 1987-89; cons. Nat. Writing Project, 1985, Univ. Ctrl. Ark., Conway, Ark., Nat. Writing Project; session chair Writing-Across-the-Curriculum K-12, Charleston, S.C., 1997; tchr. long distance learning interactive video ETV, 1998-99, 00—. Contbg. poet: Moments in the Garden, 1998, Miss. Musings, Miss. Poetry Soc., 1997, The Drifting Sands, 1999. With USN, 1962-63. Grantee Entergy, Jackson, 1994-96; fellowship Jackson (Miss.) State U., 1996; recipient 3 Editor's Choice awards, Beyond Call of Duty award JPSD, 1999; named tchr. excellence Calloway H.S., 2000. Mem. AAUW, Nat. Coun. Tchrs. of English, Am. Acad. Poets, Miss. Poetry Soc., Magnolia Romance Writers, The Poetry Guild (poetry included Best Poems of the 90s, 1998), Phi Kappa Phi, Beta Sigma Phi, Alpha Chi, Kappa Delta Pi, Sigma Tau Delta, Phi Alpha Theta. Mem. Ch. of Christ. Avocations: reading, writing, theater, gardening, competitions.1 of 522 candidates nationwide, for adolescent and Young Adulthood Natl. Bd. Cert. for Eng. Lang. Arts (AYA/ELA), 1998-99. Home: 625 Choctaw Rd Jackson MS 39206-5325

CREENAN, KATHERINE HERAS, lawyer; b. Elizabeth, N.J., Oct. 7, 1945; d. Victor Joseph and Katherine Regina (Lederer) Petervary; m. Edward James Creenan; 1 child, David Heras. BA, Newark State Coll., 1968; JD, Rutgers U., 1984. Bar: N.J. 1984, Maine, 1996, U.S. Dist. Ct. N.J. 1984, U.S. Ct. Appeals (3d cir.), 1998. Various tchg. positions including, Union and Stanhope, N.J., 1968-81; law clk. to presiding judge Superior Ct. of N.J. Appellate Div., Newark, 1984-85; assoc. Lowenstein, Sandler, Kohl, Fisher & Boylan, Roseland, N.J., 1985-88, Kirsten, Simon, Friedman, Allen, Cherin & Linken, Newark, 1988-89, Whitman & Ranson, Newark, 1989-93; sr. atty. Whitman Breed Abbott & Morgan LLP, Newark, 1993-99; assoc. Skadden, Arps, Slate, Meagher & Flom LLP, Newark, 1999—. Mem. ABA, N.J. State Bar Assn., Union County Bar Assn., Essex County Bar Assn. Office: Skadden Arps Slate Meaghar & Flom LLP 1 Newark Ctr Newark NJ 07102-5297

CREGER, DAVID LEE, financial planner, insurance executive; b. Bristol, Tenn., Mar. 20, 1957; s. Bobby Gene and Mary Nell (Goodman) C.; children: Joshua A., Sarah R. Student, Va. Highlands C.C., Abingdon, Va., 1975-76. Cert. agt./continuing edn. instr., Tenn., Va.; Life Underwriter Tng. Coun. fellow; registered fin. planner. Ins. agt. Home Beneficial Life Ins. Co., Bristol, Va., 1984-85, staff sales mgr., 1985-89; personal producing gen. agt./owner The David L. Creger Co., Bristol, 1989-91; agt. and mktg. svcs. mgr. Settlers Life Ins. Co., Bristol, 1991-96; pres. Pinnacle Fin. Svcs., Inc., Bristol, 1994—; v.p., gen. mgr. Ally-ance Mktg. Group, Inc., Bristol, 1996-97; disability income ins. course moderator Life Underwriter Tng. Coun., 1989-90; N.E. Tenn. (regional) Sales Conf. chmn. 1990; mem. adj. faculty Va. Highlands C.C., 1999-2000; lectr. in field. Contbr. articles to profl. jours. Pres. Bristol affiliate Am. Heart Assn., 1993-95, chmn. bd., 1995-96, chmn. Queen of Hearts Fundraiser, 1992, 93; vol. Appalachia region March of Dimes, 1992-93; account exec. United Way of Bristol, 1992-93, team capt., 1994, bd. dirs., 1995—, treas., chair fin. com., 1996-97, investment com. chmn., 1996-97, v.p., pres.-elect 1998; chmn. Profl. Div. Campaign Chmn. 1998—, Small Bus. Divsn. Campaign, 1999; pres. bd. dirs. 1999, immediate past pres., 2000; bd. dirs., The Janie Hammitt Meml. Children's Home, 1997; trustee, treas. Janie Hammitt Meml. Inc., 1998; mem. Tri-Cities Estate Planning Coun., 1998—; chmn. TALU Edn. Found. Com., 1997-98. Recipient Ernest E. Cragg Amb. award Life Underwriting Tng. Coun., 1994; named to Tri-Cities Bus. Jour. Regional 40 Under Forty, 1995, United Way of Bristol Vol. of Yr., 1996; named one of Outstanding Young Men of Am., 1998. Mem. Nat. Assn. Ins. and Fin. Advisors (polit. action com. 1989—), Tenn. Assn. Ins. and Fin. Advisors (N.E. Tenn. regional v.p. 1992-95, chair state profl. devel. com. 1994-95, sec. 1995-96, pres.-elect 1996-97, pres. 1997-98, past pres. 1998-99, state nat. committeeman 1999-2002), Bristol Assn. Ins. and Fin. Advisors (Queen of Hearts program com. 1986-97, pres. 1990, chair edn. com. 1991-93, exec. sec. 1993-94, chair state law and legis. com. 1993-95, sec. and treas., 1998-99, 2d v.p. 1999-2000, Louis I. Dubin Pub. Svc. award, Robert L. Rose Edn. and Assn. Achievment awards), Bristol C. of C. (VA legis. com. chair 1994, fed. issues com. chair 1995, govtl. rels. coun. vice-chair 1996, vice chair cmty. and govtl. rels. coun. 1997, exec. com. 1997, chmn. govtl. rels. divsn. 1998), vice-chmn. presdl. appointment bd. dirs. exec. com., 1999, Assn. Health Ins. Advisors (charter), Fin. Planning Assn. (charter), Nat. Assn. Ins. and Fin. Advisors (charter), Registered Fin. Planners Inst., Tri-Cities Estate Planning Coun., Tri-Cities Regional Chamber Coalition (bd. dirs. 1998), Bristol C. of C. (bd. dirs. 1995-99), Optimist, Rotary (Tenn.-Va. Sustaining Paul Harris fellow, bd. dirs.). Republican. Avocations: reading, computers, billiards. Office: Pinnacle Fin Svcs Inc 1913 Lee Hwy Ste 1A Bristol VA 24201-1623

CREGGY, STUART, retired lawyer; b. London, May 27, 1939; s. Leslie and Fay (Schneider) Creggy. MA, Western U., 1990. chmn. Sussex County Freeholds Plc, London and Brighton, Eng., 1971—. Magistrate, Marylebone Magistrates' Ct., West London, 1979; bd. dirs. Brighton & Hove Jewish Home for the Aged. Fellow Royal Philatelic Soc.; mem. Inst. Fin. Accts., The Law Soc., N.Y. County Lawyers Assn., Legal Friends of Haifa U., Variety Club Gt. Britain, Royal Automobile Club. Avocations: swimming, philatelic, reading. Office: 70 Grand Parade, Brighton BN2 2JA, England

CREHALET, YVES, advertising executive; b. Paris; m. Anne-Marie Crehalet; 4 children. Asst. brand mgr. Procter & Gamble, Paris, 1963-65; account dir. Publicis Advt. Agy., Paris, 1966-72; mgr. Crehalet Pouget Poussielgues Agy., Paris, 1973—; founder e-cpp group svcs., french-paradox.com, 1999. Author: Le Masque et la Marque, 1999—. Avocations: modern art, primitivism. Office: CPP, 61 Rue de Turenne, 75003 Paris France

CRÉHANGE, MARION, computer science educator, researcher; b. Nancy, Lorraine, France, Nov. 14, 1937; d. Etienne and Gilberte (Braun) Caen; m. Bernard Créhange, July 1, 1960; children: Catherine, Alain. MS, U. Nancy, 1958, DSc, 1975; PhD, Sci. U., Nancy, 1961. Asst. Faculty of Sci., Nancy, 1959-63; conf. instr. U. Nancy, 1963-71; prof. U. Nancy II, 1976-91, 1st class prof., 1991—; rschr. CNRS, Nancy, 1971-76; guest prof. U. Laval, Quebec, 1994. Co-author Programming: From Problem to Algorithm, From Algorithm to Program, Image and Videodisk: Image Based and Artificial Intelligence; contbr. articles to profl. jours. including Info. Processing and Mgmt., Information Expertise. Avocations: music, photography, hiking, skiing, tennis. Office: CRIN-CNRS Batiment LORIA, Campus Sci BP239, 54506 Nancy Cedex, France

CREIGHTON, ALYSSA MICHELE, investment company executive, consultant; b. Weldon, Calif., Sept. 18, 1974; d. William Dale and Deborah Diane C. BA in Bus., Calif. State U., Fullerton, 1998. Cert. Calif. tax preparer, CBEST lifetime. Spl. projects coord. Schwan's Sales Enterprises, Santa Ana, Calif., 1995-98; fin. asst. Robinson Ins., Irvine, Calif., 1998-99; assoc. Pacific Investment Mgmt. Co., Newport Beach, Calif., 1999—. E-mail: alicreight@aol.com. Office: Pacific Investment Mgmt Co 840 Newport Center Dr # 300 Newport Beach CA 92660-6310

CREIGHTON, WILLIAM BREEN, lawyer, educator; b. Belfast, No. Ireland, June 18, 1947; s. Robert John and Evelyn Margaret (Henderson) C.; m. Carolynn Muir Mackie, Sept. 3, 1976; children: Katharine Mackie, Rebecca Breen. LLB, Queens U., Belfast, 1969; PhD, Cambridge (Eng.) U., 1975; LLB, U. Melbourne, 1998. Sr. lectr., reader in law U. Melbourne, 1977-88; legal officer Australian Coun. Trade Unions, Melbourne, 1986-88; prin. legal officer Internat. Labour Orgn., Geneva, 1988-91; cons. Dept. Indsl. Rels., Commonwealth of Australia, Canberra, 1991-92; prof. law and legal studies La Trobe U., Melbourne, 1992-96; professorial fellow U. Melbourne, 1998—; spl. counsel Corrs Chambers Westgarth, Melbourne, 1997-99, ptnr., 1999—; mem. Adminstrv. Rev. Coun., Canberra, 1987-88; mem. adv. com. on distbn. of powers Constl. Commn., Canberra, 1986-88; mem. com. on indsl. legislation Nat. Labour Coun., Canberra, 1986-88; mem. Occupational Health and Safety Commn. of Victoria, Melbourne, 1985-86. Co-author: Labour Law: An Introduction, 3d edit., 2000, Labour Law: Text and Materials, 2d edit., 1993; joint editor Australian Jour. Labour Law, 1992—; author acad. study. Avocations: food, wine, bush walking, reading. Home: 444 Park Street, Carlton North VIC 3054, Australia Office: Corrs Chambers Westgarth, 600 Bourke St, Melbourne VIC 3000, Australia

CREMER, THOMAS GERHARD, music educator; b. New Brunswick, N.J., May 23, 1961; s. Gerhard Josef and Lois Elaine (Cottrell) C.; m. Eva Almira Vivanco Vargas, Feb. 8, 1986. MusB magna cum laude, U. Mass., 1983; MusM, U. Ky., 1989. Cert. music tchr., Mass., N.Y., Va., Ky., Ga., S.C. Music tchr. Athol-Royalston (Mass.) Schs., 1983-84; music tchr., band dir. Am. Sch. Lima, Peru, 1984-87; instr. tuba, euphonium U. Ky., Lexington, 1988-89; hon. asst. conductor Fitchburg (Mass.) State Coll., 1989-90; dir. bands, music instr. Warwick Acad., Bermuda, 1990-95; dir. nat. band Columbia Columbia Inst. Culture, Bogota, 1995; low brass instr. Augusta State U., 1996—; brass instr., asst. band dir. U. S.C., Aiken, 1998—; music dir. Jenkins County Middle Sch. and H.S., Millen, Ga., 1996-98; vis. prof. music, dir. faculty quintet Nat. Conservatory, Lima, 1985-87; tubist Nat. Symphony Peru, Lima, 1985-87; mem. Bermuda Secondary Sch. Curriculum Com., Warwick, 1991-94; asst. band dir. South Aiken High Sch., 1998—. Contbg. editor: Tuba Reference Guide, 1993; contbg. reviewer T.U.B.A. Jour., 1988, 94. Adv. All-City Music Fest, Lima, 1985-87; asst. band dir. South Aiken H.S., Aiken, 1999—. Recipient Diploma of Honor, West German Embassy in Peru, 1986; Acad. Excellence fellow U. Ky., 1988. Mem. Tubists Universal Brotherhood Assn., World Assn. Symphonic Bands Ensembles, Internat. Trombone Assn., Music Educators Nat. Conf., Masons, Phi Delta Kappa (Bermuda chpt., v.p., pres. 1992-94). Roman Catholic. Avocations: golf, reading, motorcycling, travel. Home: 3328 Tanglewood Dr Augusta GA 30909-2455

CREMERS, GEORGES ALEXIS, botanist, researcher; b. Brussels, Aug. 3, 1936; s. Raymond Cremers and Jeanne (Clothilde) Van Beesen; m. Marie-Jeanne Fontaine, May 26, 1973; 1 child, Sandrine. Grad., Vilvoorde, Belgium, 1959, Anderlecht, Belgium, 1960; M in Natural History, U. Abidjan, Ivory Coast, 1970; D in Plant Biology, U. Strasbourg, France, 1983. Curator herbarium Orstom, Abidjan, Ivory Coast, 1962-70, Tananarive, Madagascar, 1970-75, Cayenne, France, 1976-98; regional scientific com. Guyana, 1990; spkr., cons. in field. Contbr. articles to profl. publs. mem. Botanical Soc. France. Home: 10 rue des Fonds Thirel, 76 130 Mont-Saint-Aignan France Office: IRD Lab of Phanerogamu, 16 rue Buffon, 75005 Paris France

CREMIN, SUSAN ELIZABETH, lawyer; b. Chgo., July 2, 1947; d. William Amberg and Rosemary (Brennan) C. AB cum laude, Vassar Coll., 1969; JD, Northwestern U., Chgo., 1976. Bar: Ill. 1977. Assoc. Winston & Strawn, Chgo., 1976-83, ptnr., 1983-93, capital ptnr., 1993—. Co-author: Registration and Reporting Under the Exchange Act, 1995, 2nd edit., 1996. Trustee The Shedd Aquarium, Chgo., The Masters Sch., Dobbs Ferry, N.Y. Office: Winston & Strawn 35 W Wacker Dr Ste 4200 Chicago IL 60601-1695

CRENSHAW, BEN, professional golfer; b. Austin, Tex., Jan. 11, 1952; m. Julie Ann; children: Katherine Vail, Claire Susan, Anna Riley. Grad., U. Tex. Mem. U.S. World Amateur Cup Team, 1972; mem. U.S. Ryder Cup, 1981, 83, 87, 95; profl. golfer, 1973—; U.S. team capt. Kirin Cup, 1988; team capt. Ryder Cup Team, 1999. Winner San Antonio Open, 1973, Western Amateur open match and medal plan champion, 1973, Bing Crosby Nat. Pro-Am., Ohio Kings Island Open, Hawaiian Open, 1976, Colonial Nat. Invitational, 1977, NCAA Championship, 1971, 72, 73, Irish Open, 1976, Phoenix Open, 1979, Walt Disney World Team Championship, 1980, AnheuserOBusch Classic, 1980, Tex. State Open winner, 1980, Ryder Cup, 1981, 83, 87, Byron Nelson Classic, 1983, Masters tournament, 1984, PGA Sr. Event Jeremy Ranch Shoot-Out teameed with Miller Barber, 1985, Buick Open, 1986, Vantage Championship, 1986, USF&G, 1987, Doral Ryder Open, 1988, World Cup, 1988, Western Open, 1992, Masters winner Augusta Nat. Golf Club, 1995, Masters Tournament, 1995, Ryder Cup, 1999. Mem. Profl. Golfers Assn. Am. Office: 2905 San Gabriel St Ste 213 Austin TX 78705-3541

CRENWELGE-DEVALCK, DENISE YVONNE, freelance editor, writer, administrative assistant, language professional; b. San Antonio, Nov. 11, 1958; d. Joe Edward and Elizabeth Ann (Meurer) Crenwelge; m. Eddy DeValck, Aug. 7, 1992. AA, Howard Coll., 1978; BS in Journalism, Tex. A&M U., 1980. News dir. KBYG-AM, Big Spring, Tex., 1981-82; news anchor, reporter KTPX-TV, Midland, Tex., 1982-84; news dir. KBST AM/FM, Big Spring, 1984-89; comm. dir. to U.S. Rep. Charles Stenholm, Washington, 1989-92; freelance editor/writer Belgium, 1992-96; adminstrv. asst. Lovell White Durrant, Brussels, 1996-98; lang. specialist Lernout & Hauspie, Ieper, Belgium, 1998-2000, corp. comm. specialist, 2000—; vice chmn. Tex. AP Broadcasters State Bd., 1988-89; radio pres. Tex. AP Broadcasters State Bd., 1987-88; stringer Lubbock (Tex.)-Avalanche Jour., 1981-89; team mem. Rotary Internat. Group Study Exch., Tex. to Belgium, 1989. Mem. Tex. Press Women, 1987-89; pub. chmn. Symphony Guild, Big Spring, 1986-89; mem. March of Dimes Bd., Big Spring, 1987-89; chmn. Big Spring H.S. Reunion, 1987. Recipient Edn. award Tex. Assn. Broadcasters, 1988, Best Reporter award Tex. AP, 1987, Gavel award State Bar of Tex., 1987. Roman Catholic. Avocations: quilting, piano, swimming, baking, travel. Home: Parklaan 10, B-1852 Beigem Belgium

CREPS, PHILP LLOYD, child psychiatrist; b. Bowling Green, Ohio, Dec. 16, 1951; s. Wayne LeRoy and Elsie Marie (Frank) C.; m. Barbara Dawn Keller, Dec. 11, 1976(div. March 1991); children: Jesse Jean, Sarah Marie; m. Diane Ruth Cook Bostwick, Nov. 11, 1993. BS, Bowling Green (Ohio) State U., 1973; BA, U. Toledo, 1980; AS, Aurora (Colo.) C.C., 1986; DO, Mich. State U., 1991. Cert. psychiatry, child and adolescent psychiatrics, Am. Coll. Neurology and Psychology. Rsch. project dir. Mich. State U., East Lansing, 1984-85; instr. Lansing C.C., 1984-85; environ. scientist Ohio EPA, Bowling Green, 1985; rsch. chemist Fitzsimmons Med. Ctr., Aurora, 1985-

86; quality assurance chemist Pine Bluff (Ark.) Army Arsenal, 1986-89; extern Coll. Osteo. Medicine Mich. State U., Okemos, 1989-91; intern Riverside Osteopathic Hosp., Trenton, Mich., 1991-92; resident in psychiatry Case Western Reserve U., Cleve., 1992-95; fellow in child psychiatry Ind. U., Indpls., 1995-97; child psychiatrist Otis R. Bowen Ctr., Warsaw, Ind., 1996-2000; pres., CEO Creps Med. Corp., Pierceton, Ind., 1997—; child psychiatrist Madison Ctr. Counseling Assoc., Warsaw, Ind., 2000; psychiatrist Madison Ctr. for Children, South Bend, Ind., 2000—; chemist Pine Bluff Arsenal SMCPB, Quality Assurance Lab., 1986-89. Youth dir. Assembly of God Ch., Fostoria, Ohio, 1969-71; music dir. 1st Assembly of God Ch., Toledo, 1977-79; sec. Citizen's Council #3, Lansing, 1980-83. With USN, 1980-83. Recipient Alfred award South Counties Council, Newport, R.I., 1981, Mayor's Commendation City of Toledo, 1980. Mem. AMA (Ind. State chpt.), Am. Chem. Soc., Am. Osteopathic Assn., Am. Assn. Orthopsychiatry, Am. Acad. Child Adolescent Psychiatrists, Am. Coll. Osteopathic Neurologists and Psychiatrists, Assn. Osteopathic Physicians and Surgeons (Mich., Ind. chpts.), Am. Assn. Cmty. Psychiatrists, Am. Acad. Osteopathy, Cranial Acad.,Am. Assn. Social Psychiatry, Am. Group Psychotherapy Assn., Am. Acad. Clin. Psychiatrists, Practice Rsch. Network, Initiative Social Anxiety Assessment Care, Tri-State Group Psychotherapists, Charles F. Meninger Soc., Alpha Epsilon Delta, Psi Chi, Beta Beta Beta. Republican. Avocations: dairy farming, gardening, singing.

CRESCIMANNO, GIUSEPPINA MARIA GIULIA, agricultural studies educator; b. Palermo, Sicily, Italy, Sept. 15, 1955; d. Guglielmo and Nunzia (Aiello) C.; 1 child, Bosco Alessio. Degree in Agrl. Scis., U. Palermo, 1980. Rschr. U. Palermo, 1982-91, assoc. prof. agro-hydrology, 1992—; expert European Union, Brussels, 1998, coord. rsch. project, 1998—. Mem. Am. Soil Sci. Soc. Avocations: tennis, music, travel, cinema. Home: Via Catania 146, 90141 Palermo Sicily, Italy Office: U Palermo Dept ITAF, Viale Delle Scienze, 90128 Palermo Sicily, Italy

CRESPO, HERNAN, soccer player; b. Florida, Argentina, July 5, 1975. Forward Parma Italy Football Club; ctr., forward Lazio, 2000—. Address: Soc Sportiva, Corso d Italia 19/21, 00194 Rome Italy*

CRESPO, JOSÉ, electrical engineer, information scientist; b. Madrid, Sept. 13, 1966; s. José C. and María A. Del-Arco. Degree in telecomm. engring., Polytech. U. Madrid, 1989; MS in Elec. Engring., Ga. Inst. Tech., 1990, MS in Mgmt., 1993, PhD in Elec. Engring., 1993. Rschr. Ga. Inst. Tech., Atlanta, 1989-93; official-engr. Ministry of Industry, Paris, 1994; engr. Armines, Fontainebleau, France, 1994; asst. prof. engring. U. Alfonso X, Villanueva de la Canada, Spain, 1994-95; asst. prof. engring. Polytech. U. Madrid, 1995-98, assoc. prof. engring., 1999—, rsch. dir. artificial intelligence lab.; co-dir. Med. Informatics Group, Polytech. U. Madrid, 1996—. Contbr. articles to profl. jours. and papers to confs. Advisor Canalejas-Espros Found., Madrid, 1995-96. Rsch. grantee Spanish govt., 1989-93, E.N.S. des Mines de Paris, 1992, Hewlett-Packard, 1996; recipient Spanish award Med. Informatics, 1997, Ministry of Health Rsch. Project award 1998—. Mem. IEEE, AAAS, N.Y. Acad. Scis., Assn. Computing Machinery. Office: Poly U Madrid, Faculty Info, 28660 Boadilla Del Monte Madrid, Spain

CRESS, CECILE COLLEEN, retired librarian; b. Colorado Springs, Colo., Feb. 26, 1914; d. John Leo and Elizabeth Veronica (Rouse) Haley; m. Arthur Henry Cress, May 8, 1937 (div. 1960); children: Ronnie Lou Kordick, Dan, Elaine. BA, Adams State Coll., 1936; MA in English, Colo. Coll., 1964; MLS, Denver U., 1970. 5th grade tchr. Westcliffe (Colo.) Elem., 1953-56; English tchr. Penrose (Colo.) H.S., 1956-59; English-social studies tchr. Excelsior Jr. H.S. Dist. 70, Pueblo, Colo., 1959-64; libr. Pueblo County H.S. Dist. 70, Pueblo, 1964-80, Nat. Coll./Pueblo Br., 1980-91; cataloger in libr. Pueblo C.C., 1992-95. Tutor adult literacy program South Cen. Bd. Coop. Svcs., 1991. Recipient Ace of Clubs award Am. Contract Bridge League, 1988, 89. Mem. Pueblo Ret. Sch. Employees (v.p. 1990-92, pres. 1982-84, state bd. 1982-86, sec. 1995-97), Colo. Libr. Assn., Unit 367 Am. Contract Bridge Assn., Irish Club Pueblo (pres. 1995-96), Welsh Terrier Club Colo., Alpha Delta Kappa (Pueblo chpt., pres. 1976-78, state historian 1980-82, state bd. 1980-82, rec. sec. 1994-98), Am. Contract Bridge League (v.p. unit 367 1998-2000). Democrat. Roman Catholic. Avocations: duplicate bridge, Welsh Terriers, travel. Home: 901 Jackson St Pueblo CO 81004-2425

CRESSEY, BRYAN CHARLES, venture capitalist; b. Seattle, Sept. 28, 1949; s. Charles Ovington and Alice Lorraine (Serry) C.; m. Christina Irene Petersen, Aug. 19, 1972; children: Monique Joy, Charlotte Lorraine, Alicia Lin. BA, U. Wash., 1972; MBA, Harvard U., 1976, JD, 1976. Bar: Wash. 1976, Ill. 1977. Sr. investment mgr. First Chgo. Investment Corp., Chgo., 1976-80; prin. Golder, Thoma, Cressey, Fauner, Inc., Chgo., 1980—; prnt. Thoma, Cressey Equity Ptnrs., 1998—; chmn., bd. dirs. Cable Design Techs., Inc.; bd. dirs. Am. Habilitation, Inc., Houston, Assistive Tech., Ill., Clarion tech., Ill., Select Med., Harrisburg, Pa., Boston. Author: (theatrical play) Explosions. Bd. dirs. Infant Welfare Soc., Chgo., 1984—, Jr. Achievement, Chgo. Inductee Entrepreneurial Hall of Fame, 1998. Home: 500 W County Line Rd Barrington IL 60010-9629 Office: Thoma Cressey Equity Partners 9200 Sears Tower Chicago IL 60606

CRESSON, PIERRE-ARNAUD F. J., manufacturing executive; b. Malo-les-Bains, France, Sept. 29, 1956; s. René and Claude (Bourbonnaud) C.; m. Laure Berloty, Feb. 3, 1990; children: Paul, Delphine, Guillaume, Malo. Diploma, Ecole Sup. Sci. Econs./Comml., Cergy, France, 1979; M in Econs., U. Paris X, Nanterre, France, 1979; postgrad., Inst. Hautes Etudes Def. Nat., Paris, 2000. Fully qualified chartered acct., France. Asst. to sr. Peat Marwick (KPMG), Paris, 1979-84; various positions Schlumberger, 1986-88; contr. Africa and South Europe region Schlumberger Dowell, Paris, 1988-91; contr. Latin Am. unit Schlumberger Wireline, Venezuela, 1991-95; regional fin. dir. Benelux, Brussels, 1995-96; dir. canmaking and spares operation CMB Group (CarnaudMetalbox), Paris, 1997—, European svcs. project dir., 2000—; lectr. cost acctg. and internat. taxation Haute Etudes Commerciales, Paris, 1987-91; lectr. audit and acctg. French U. Paris XII, 1978-82. Officer French Army, 1982-83. Avocations: horse riding, skiing, jogging, theater. Fax: 33 1 49 18 45 04. Home: 22 Ave de l'Impératrice Josephine, 92500 Rueil-Malmaison France Office: CarnaudMetalbox, rue Fructidor, 75830 Paris Cedex 17, France

CRESSWELL, HELEN, children's writer; b. 1936. Author: Sonya-by-the-Shore, 1960, Jumbo Spencer, 1963, The White Sea Horse, 1964, Jumbo Back to Nature, 1965, Pietro and the Mule, 1965, Where the Wind Blows, 1966, A Tide for the Captain, 1967, The Signposters, 1968, The Sea Piper, 1968, Jumbo and the Big Dig, 1968, Rug is a Bear, 1968, Rug Plays Tricks, 1968, The Night Watchmen, 1969, A Game of Catch, 1969, A Gift from Winklesea, 1969, A House for Jones, 1969, Rug Plays Ball, 1969, Rug and a Picnic, 1969, The Outlanders, 1970, The Wilkses, 1970, Rainbow Pavement, 1970, John's First Fish, 1970, Up the Pier, 1971, The Weather Cat, 1971, The Bird Fancier, 1971, At the Stroke of Midnight, 1971, The Beachcombers, 1972, Jane's Policeman, 1972, The Long Day, 1972, Short Back and Sides, 1972, Blue Birds Over Pit Row, 1972, Roof Fall, 1972, Lizzie Dripping series, 5 vols., 1972-74 (2 TV series), The White Sea Horse and Other Tales of the Sea, 1972, The Bongleweed, 1973, The Bower Bird, 1973, The Key, 1973, The Trap, 1973, The Beetle Hunt, 1973, The Two Hoots series, 6 vols., 1974-77, Cheap Day Return, 1974, Shady Deal, 1974, Butterfly Chase, 1975, The Winter of the Birds, 1975, Two Hoots and the King, 1977, Bagthorpe series, 7 vols., 1977-78, Donkey Days, 1977, Absolute Zero, 1978, The Flyaway Kite, 1979, My Aunt Polly by the Sea, 1980, Dear Shrink, 1982, The Secret World of Polly Flint, 1982, Ellie and the Hagwitch, 1984, Whodunnit?, 1986, Moondial, 1987, Time Out, 1987, Dragon Ride, 1987, Fox in a Maze, 1988, Greedy Alice, 1989, Rosie and the Boredom Eater, 1989, The Story of Grace Darling, 1989, Whatever Happened in Winklesea?, 1989, Almost Goodbye Guzzler, 1990, Meet Posy Bates, 1990, Posy Bates Again, 1991, Lizzie Dripping and the Witch, 1991, The Bagthorpe Saga, 1992, Posy Bates and the Bag Lady, 1993, The Watchers: Mystery at Alton Towers, 1993, Classic Fairy Tales Retold, 1994, Polly Thumb, 1994, Stonestruck, 1995, Giant, 1995, The Little Sea Horse, 1995, Mystery in Winklesea, 1995, Mister Maggs, 1995, Bagthorpes Besieged, 1995, Bag of Bones, 1996, Sophie and the Seawolf, 1996, The Little Grey Donkey, 1997, Snatchers, 1998, Garlunk, Rumpelstiltskin (retold), 1998; tv dramas: Lizzie Dripping, 1972, Lizzie Dripping Again, 1974, Jumbo Spencer, 1976, The Secret World of Polly Flint, 1986, Moondial, 1988, Five Children & It, 1991, The Return of the Psammead, 1993, The Demon Headmaster, 1995, The Famous Five, 1995, In the Grip of the Demon Headmaster, 1996, The Phoenix & The Carpet 3, 1996, The Demon Heamaster 3, 1997; (TV drama) Little Grey Rabbit; editor: The Puffin Book and Funny Stories, 1992. Mem. Soc. of Authors, Brit. Acad. Film and TV Arts, Internat. PEN. Office: Old Church Farm, Eakring Newark Notts NG22 0DA, England

CRESWELL, CHARLES ALEXANDER, process engineering and management consultant; b. Balt., Mar. 9, 1952; s. Curtis Bennett and Carol Eugenia (French) C.; m. Diane Marie Foster, Mar. 2, 1974; 1 child, Elizabeth Foster. BSChemE, U. Va., 1975; MBA, Pa. State U., 1989. Process engr. Hershey (Pa.) Chocolate Co., 1979-81; process/mech. engr. Hershey Chocolate Co., Stuarts Draft, Va., 1981-83; sr. process engr. Hershey (Pa.) Chocolate USA, 1983-91; v.p. engring. Savannah (Ga.) Cocoa, Inc., 1991-92; owner Design Alternatives, Hummelstown, Pa., 1990-99; pres. DA Holdings Ltd., Hummelstown, 2000—. Editor Jour. Microcomputer Systems Mgmt., 1989-91. Lt. USN, 1975-79. Mem. Am. Inst. Chem. Engrs., Nat. Soc. Profl. Engrs., U. Va. Alumni Assn. (life). Avocations: astronomy, electronics. Office: DA Holdings Ltd 26 Merion Ln Hummelstown PA 17036-9263

CRESWELL, JOHN LEWIS, agricultural studies educator; b. Muscatine, Iowa, Feb. 21, 1940; s. John Stanley and Emma Mildred (Elliott) C.; m. Dorothy Anne Mefford, Aug. 28, 1965. AA, Burlington (Iowa) C.C., 1963; BS in Agronomy, Iowa State U., 1965; MS in Botany, Western Ill. U., 1971; PhD in Agrl. Edn., Iowa State U., 1990. Scientist Mason & Hanger-Silas Mason Co., Inc., Burlington, 1966, agronomist, 1967-73; county ext. dir. Iowa State U. Ext., Rockwell City, Iowa, 1974-79; ext. crop prodn. specialist Iowa State U. Ext., Cedar Rapids, 1980-99; nutrient mgmt. edn. coord. Iowa State U. Ext., 2000—; profl. and sci. coun. mem. Iowa State U., 1996-99. Contbr. articles to profl. jours. Mem. Am. Soc. Agronomy (cert. profl. agronomist), Iowa State U. Coun. Ext. Profls. (pres. 1995), Gamma Sigma Delta, Epsilon Sigma Phi. Avocations: photography, hiking. Home: 906 SE Wanda Dr Ankeny IA 50021-3811 Office: Iowa State Univ Extension Outreach Ctr 10861 Douglas Ave Urbandale IA 50322-2042

CREUTZBURG, REINER, education educator; b. Wismar, Germany, Dec. 25, 1953; s. Theo and Sylvia (Franck) C.; m. Britta Ahnfeldt, Aug. 7, 1989; children: Marcus, Carsten. Diploma Math., Univ. Rostock, 1976, Dr.rer.nat., 1985. Asst. prof. U. Rostock, 1977-85; head, intern lab. Acad. of Scis., Berlin, 1985-89; asst. prof. U. Karlsruhe, 1990-92; prof. FH - Univ. Brandenburg, Germany, 1992—; dir. Inst. for Networking and Multimedia Brandenburg e.V., 1994—; pres. Creutzburg Cons., Brandenburg, 1996—; prof. Multimedia Sys., Tampere U. of Tech., Tampere, Finalnd, 2000—. Co-author: (books) Memory Architecture and Parallel Access, 1994, Speicherarchitektur und Parallelzugriff, 1989. Mem. Rotary., SPIE. Avocations: reading, travel. E-mail: creutzburg@fh-brandenburg.de. Office: FH Brandenburg, Magdeburgerstr.50, Brandenburg D-14737, Germany

CREVELT, DWIGHT EUGENE, computer company executive; b. Kansas City, Mo., Jan. 16, 1957; s. James Robert and Louise Gwendolynn (Wolchek) C.; m. Jean Anne Cassens, Aug. 11, 1979; children: William Michael, Michelle Anne, Matthew Henry, Megan Louise. Student, U. Las Vegas, 1973-74, U.S. Naval Acad., 1975-77; BS in Computer Engring., Iowa State U., 1979. Computer engr., cons. Las Vegas, Nev., 1972-73; software engr. Gamex Industries, Las Vegas, 1973-74, United Audio Visual, Las Vegas, 1977; computer engr. Sircoma, Las Vegas, 1979-80; dir. research Mills-Jennings, Las Vegas, 1981; pres., chmn. Crevelt Computer, Las Vegas, 1977—; mgr. spl. projects Electronic Data Techs., 1988-91; dir. engring., quality assurance mgr. Internat. Game Techs., 1991-96; ptnr. Footraffic Promotional Gaming LLC, 1998—; lobbyist Nev. Legis. Author: (computer programs) CDC160/NCR310 Disassembler, 1971, Computer Networking, 1983, Telephone Access Control, 1984, Fiber Optic Network, 1984; co-author: Slot Machine Mania, 1987, Video Poker Mania, 1991. Former corr. sec. Clark County Rep. Cen. Com.; mem. U.S. Congl. Adv. Bd. Mem. NRA, Eagle Scout Assn., Soc. Naval Engrs., Am. Philatic Soc., U.S. Naval Acad. Alumni Assn., USN League, Las Vegas Exch. Club. Achievements include patentee on automated electronic casino gaming system, progressive gaming systems, electronic funds transfer. Office: Crevelt Computer System Inc 5391 Aston Ave Las Vegas NV 89142-1818

CREW, AUBREY TORQUIL, aerospace inspector; b. London, May 9, 1926; came to U.S. 1968; s. Thomas Alfred and Phyllis Sibil (Ibbetson) C.; m. Sally-Marie Thompson, Dec. 22, 1979; children: Clare Violet, Mark Ernest, Karen Audrey. Student, London Tech. Coll., 1956, Oslo State U., Norway, 1965-67. Marine radio officer Marchessini & Co., London, N.Y.C., 1956-57; flight radio officer Hunting Clan Aircraft Co., London, 1957-59; radio and TV engr. Radionette, Oslo, 1960-68; avionics tech. flight Lockheed Aircraft Co., Palmdale, Calif., 1971-82; aerospace inspector Rockwell Internat., Palmdale, 1983—. Appeared in film The Sundowners, 1959; extra in movies, TV commls. Vol. blood donor Viking Group Charities, Beverly Hills, Calif., 1969—; capt. USAF Civil Air Patrol, 1978—. With Royal Navy, 1941-56. Fellow Royal Soc. St. George; mem. Air Force Assn. Republican. Episcopalian. Avocations: flying, opera, orchestral concerts, swimming, church organ playing. Home: 2064 W Avenue J # 286 Lancaster CA 93536-5913

CRIADO, JOSE FERNANDO, business executive; b. Madrid, Jan. 25; s. Pedro and Matilde (Juarez) C.; m. Pilar Martin del Barrio, June 30, 1973; children: Guillermo, Marta. Degree agrl. engring., U. Politecnica, Madrid, Spain; degree history and geography, U. Autonoma, Madrid. Product and market mgr. Madrid; R&D deve. mng. dir. Mecanicas Asociadas, Madrid, 1981-89; comml. dir. Hella, Madrid, 1989-93; pres. Harden/Summit, Madrid, 1993-96, ERF Europe, Madrid, 1996—. Avocations: writing, reading, walking, gardening. Office: ERF Europe, Rosa de Lima 1 Bis, 28290 Las Matas/Las Rozas Madrid, Spain

CRIBBET, JOHN EDWARD, law educator, former university chancellor; b. Findlay, Ill., Feb. 21, 1918; s. Howard H. and Ruth (Wright) C.; m. Betty Jane Smith, Dec. 24, 1941; children: Carol Ann, Pamela Lee. BA, Ill. Wesleyan U., 1940, LLD, 1971; JD, U. Ill., 1947. Bar: Ill. 1947. Pvt. practice in law Bloomington, Ill., 1947—; prof. law U. Ill., Urbana, 1947-67, dean. Coll. Law, 1967-79; chancellor Urbana-Champaign Campus, U. Ill., 1979-84, Corman prof. law, 1984-88, prof. emeritus, 1988—. Author: Cases and Materials on Judicial Remedies, 1954, Cases on Property, 7th edit., 1996, (with others) Principles of the Law of Property, 1975, (with Prof. Corwin Johnson), 3d edit., 1989; editor: U. Ill. Law Forum, 1947-55; contbr. articles to profl. jours. Chmn. com. on jud. ethics Il. Supreme Ct.; pres. United Fund Champaign County, (Ill.), 1962-63; trustee Ill. Wesleyan U.; mem. exec. com. Assn. Am. Law Schs., 1973-75, pres., 1979. Served to maj. AUS, 1941-45. Decorated Bronze Star; decorated Croix de Guerre. Mem. ABA, Ill. State Bar Assn., Champaign County Bar Assn., Order of Coif. Lodge: Rotary. Home: 306 E Sherwin Cir Urbana IL 61802-7137 Office: U Ill Coll of Law 504 E Pennsylvania Ave Champaign IL 61820-6909

CRICHTON, MICHAEL (JOHN CRICHTON), author, film director; b. Chgo., Oct. 23, 1942; s. John Henderson and Zula (Miller) C. A.B. summa cum laude, Harvard U., 1964, M.D., 1969. Postdoctoral fellow Salk Inst., La Jolla, Calif., 1969-70; vis. writer MIT, Cambridge, 1988; creator, co-exec. prodr. TV show ER, 1994. Author: (as Jeffrey Hudson) A Case of Need, 1968 (Edgar award Mystery Writers of America 1968); (as John Lange) Odds On, 1966, Scratch One, 1967, Easy Go, 1968, Zero Cool, 1969, The Venom Business, 1969, Drug of Choice, 1970, Grave Descend, 1970, Binary, 1972; The Andromeda Strain, 1969, Five Patients, 1970 (Writer of the Year award Assn. American Medical Writers 1970), (with Douglas Crichton) Dealing: Or, The Berkeley to Boston Forty-Brick Lost-Bag Blues, 1971, The Terminal Man, 1972, The Great Train Robbery, 1975 (Edgar award Mystery Writers of America 1979), Eaters of the Dead, 1976, Jasper Johns, 1977, Congo, 1980, Electronic Life, 1983, Sphere, 1987, Travels, 1988, Jurassic Park, 1990, Rising Sun, 1992, Disclosure, 1994, Lost World, 1995, Airframe, 1996, Timeline, 1999; screenwriter, dir. film Westworld, 1973, Coma, 1978, The Great Train Robbery, 1979, Looker, 1981, Runaway, 1984; dir. film Pursuit, 1972, Physical Evidence, 1989; co-screenwriter Jurassic Park, 1993, Rising Sun, 1993; co-screenwriter, co-writer Twister, 1996; co-prodr. (film) Disclosure, 1994, Sphere, 1998, Eaters of the Dead, 1999. Mem. bd. overseers Harvard U. Recipient George Foster Peabody award ER, 1995, Emmy Best Dramatic series ER, 1996. Mem. Authors Guild, Writers Guild, Am. West, Dirs. Guild Am., Prodrs. Guild, PEN Am. Ctr. Acad. Motion Picture Arts and Scis., Phi Beta Kappa. Office: Constant C Prodns 282 Katonah Ave # 246 Katonah NY 10536-2110

CRICHTON, PAUL, psychiatrist, researcher; b. Dundee, Scotland, Feb. 4, 1946; s. Albert and Jessie Barbara (McKenzie) C. MA, Oxford (Eng.) U., 1973; MD, Munich U., 1984. Hon. asst. house physician Nat. Hosp. for Neurology and Neurosurgery, London, 1986; sr. house officer, registrar Charing Cross Hosp., London, 1986-92; sr. registrar Maudsley Hosp., London, 1992-96; cons., sr. lectr. Guy's Hosp., London, 1996-97, Royal Marsden Hosp., London, 1997—. Contbr. articles to profl. jours. Recipient Essay prize Mental Health Found. and Royal Soc. Medicine, 1996; Lincoln Coll./Oxford scholar, 1965-69. Mem. Royal Coll. Psychiatrists. Office: Royal Marsden NHS Trust, Fulham Rd, London SW3 6JJ, England

CRICK, FRANCIS HARRY COMPTON, science educator, researcher; b. June 8, 1916; s. Harry and Anne Elizabeth (Wilkins) C.; m. Ruth Doreen Dodd, 1940 (div. 1947); 1 son; m. Odile Speed, 1949; 2 daus. B.Sc., Univ. Coll., London; PhD, Cambridge U., Eng. Scientist Brit. Admiralty, 1940-47, Strangeways Lab., Cambridge, Eng., 1947-49; with Med. Rsch. Coun. Lab. of Molecular Biology, Cambridge, 1949-77; Kieckhefer Disting. prof. Salk Inst. Biol. Studies, San Diego, 1977—, non-resident fellow, 1962-73, pres., 1994-95; adj. prof. psychology U. Calif., San Diego; vis. lectr. Rockefeller Inst., N.Y.C., 1959; vis. prof. chemistry dept. Harvard U., 1959, vis. prof. biophysics, 1962; fellow Churchill Coll., Cambridge, 1960-61; Korkes Meml. lectr. Duke U., 1960; Henry Sidgewick Meml. lectr. Cambridge U., 1963; Graham Young lectr., Glasgow, 1963; Robert Boyle lectr. Oxford U., 1963; Vanuxem lectr. Princeton U., 1964; William T. Sedgwick Meml. lectr. MIT, 1965; Cherwell-Simon Meml. lectr. Oxford U., 1966; Shell lectr. Stanford U., 1969; Paul Lund lectr. Northwestern U., 1977; Dupont lectr. Harvard U., 1979, numerous other invited meml. lectrs. Author: Of Molecules and Men, 1966, Life Itself, 1981, What Mad Pursuit, 1988, The Astonishing Hypothesis: The Scientific Search for the Soul, 1994; contbr. papers and articles on molecular, cell biology and neurobiology to sci. jours. Recipient Prix Charles Leopold Mayer French Academies des Scis., 1961; (with J.D. Watson) Rsch. Corp. award, 1961, Warren Triennial prize, 1959, (with J.D. Watson & Maurice Wilkins) Lasker award, 1960, Nobel Prize for medicine, 1962; Gairdner Found. award, 1962, Royal Medal Royal Soc., 1972, Copley medal, 1975, Michelson-Morley award, 1981, Benjamin P. Cheney medal, 1986, Golden Plate award, 1987, Albert medal Royal Soc. Arts, London, 1987, Wright Prize VIII Harvey Mudd Coll., 1988, Joseph Priestly award Dickinson Coll., 1988, Order of Merit, 1991, Disting. Achievement award Oreg State U. Friends of Libr., 1995, Liberty medal, 2000. Fellow AAAS, Univ. Coll. London, Royal Soc., Indian Nat. Sci. Acad., Rochester Mus., Indian Acad. Scis. (hon.), Churchill Coll. Cambridge (hon.), Royal Soc. Edinburgh (hon.), Caius Coll. Cambridge (hon.), John Muir Coll. U. Calif., San Diego (hon.), Tata Inst. Fundamental Rsch., Bombay (hon.), Inst. Biology London (hon.); mem. Acad. Arts Scis. (fgn. hon.), Am. Soc. Biol. Chemists (hon.), U.S. Nat. Acad. Scis. (fgn. assoc.), German Acad. Sci., Am. Philos. Soc. (fgn. mem.), French Acad. Scis. (assoc. fgn. mem.), Royal Irish Acad. (hon.), Hellenic Biochemical and Biophysical Soc. (hon.), Academia Europaea. Office: Salk Inst Biol Studies PO Box 85800 San Diego CA 92186-5800

CRICK, RONALD PITTS, ophthalmologist, consultant; b. Toronto, Ont., Can., Feb. 5, 1917; arrived in U.K., 1919; s. Owen Pitts and Margaret (Daw) C.; m. Jocelyn Grenfell Robins, Mar. 22, 1941; children: Martin, Gillian, Jonathan, Adrian, Humphrey. MRCS LRCP, King's Coll. Hosp. Med. Sch., 1939. DOMS, FRCS (Eng.), FRCOPhth. Registrar ophthalmic, cons. ophthalmic surgeon King's Coll. Hosp., London, 1946-82, hon. cons. ophthalmic surgeon, 1982—; cons. ophthalmic Royal Eye Hosp., London, 1950-69, Belgrave Hosp. for Children, London, 1950-66; tchr. ophthalmology U. London, 1960-82; chmn. ophthalmic tng. com. South East Thames Regional Hosp. Bd., London, 1973-82. Co-author: (with R.B. Trimble) A Textbook of Clinical Ophthalmology, 1987, (with P.T. Khaw), 3rd edit., 2000; contbr. chpts. in books. Hon. chmn. Internat. Glaucoma Assn., London, 1974-2000, pres., 2000—. Surgeon lt. Royal Naval Vol. Res., 1939-46. Recipient Duke-Elder Glaucoma award Internat. Glaucoma Congress, 1985, Alim Meml. lectr. Ophthalmol. Soc. Bangladesh, 1992. Fellow Royal Coll. Surgeons (examiner ophthalmology), Royal Soc. Medicine (v.p. ophthamology); mem. Am. Soc. Contemporary Ophthalmology (charter, medal of Achievement 1985), European Glaucoma Soc., Royal Motor Yacht Club, Royal Automobile Club Pall Mall. Avocations: swimming, sailing, reading, motoring. Office fax: 171 346 5929. Home: 10 Golden Gates, Sandbanks Poole, Dorset BH13 7QN, England Office: Internat Glaucoma Assn, Kings Coll Hosp Denmark Hil, London SE5 9RS, England

CRIDER, ROBERT AGUSTINE, international financier, law enforcement official; b. Washington, Jan. 3, 1935; s. Rana Albert and Terasa Helen (Dampf) C.; student law enforcement U. Md., 1959-63; m. Debbie Ann Lee, Feb. 1960. Police officer Met. Police Dept., Washington, 1957-67; substitute tchr., bldg. trades instr. Maries R-1 Sch., Vienna, Mo., 1968-70; vets. constrn. tng. officer VA Dept. Edn., Mo., 1968-70; constrn. mgr. Tectonics Ltd., Vienna, 1970-79; owner, dir. R-A Crider & Assocs., St. Louis, 1979—; bd. dirs. TI-CO Investment Corp., Langcaster Corp. Served with USAF, 1952-56. Mem. Assn. Ret. Policemen, Internat. Conf. Police, Internat. Assn. Chiefs of Police, Nat. Police Assn., World Future Soc., Internat. Platform Assn., Mo. Police Chiefs Assn., Mo. Sheriff's Assn., Am. Correctional Assn., Law Enforcement Intelligence Assn., Internat. Drug Enforcement Assn., Nat. Assn. Fin. Cons., Internat. Soc. Financiers, Am. Legion, St. Louis Honor Guard. Roman Catholic. Clubs: Lions, K.C. (4th deg.). Home: PO Box 109 Vienna MO 65582-0109 Office: R-A Crider & Assocs PO Box 3459 2644 Roseland Ter Saint Louis MO 63143-2304

CRILLEY, JOSEPH JAMES, artist; b. Phila., Jan. 8, 1920; s. James John and Anna (Spoerl) C.; m. Marion Gertrude Haly, Jan. 31, 1948 (div.); children: Pamela, Geraldine, Candace, Joseph; m. Suzanne Corlette, Aug. 16, 1982. Student, Phila. Coll. Art, 1938-61. Art tchr. New Hope (Pa.)-Solebury High Sch., 1955-61; photographer William J. Keller, Inc., Buffalo, 1960-71. Photographer: New York, Island of Islands, 1965; one-man exhibn. Lambertville (N.J., 1976-80, 82-85, Coryell Gallery, Lambertville, 1981, Kiski Sch., Saltsburg, Pa., 1985, Genest Gallery, Lambertville, 1986-90, Phila. Sketch Club, 1990; exhibited in group shows at Nat. Acad. of Design, N.Y.C., Phila., Art and Alliance, Phila. Mus. of Art, Michener Art Mus., Doylestown, Pa., Mystic, Conn., others; represented in permanent collections at Kiski Sch., Atlantic Salmon Mus., Cape Breton, N.S., Can., Australia, France, others. Capt. AUS, 1942-45, ETO. Recipient 64 awards including Best of Show, 1983, New Hope Bar Seal, 1984, New Hope Arts Commn. Competition, 3 Gold medals, 1980-95, DaVinci Art Alliance Phila., Award of Excellence, 1991, 29th Mystic Internat., Conn., Anthony Cirino award 1992, Grumbacher Gold medal, 1996, Audubon Artists, N.Y., 15 awards 1962-95 Salmagundi Club, N.Y., 3 awards 1985-95, Phila. Sketch Club, Pa. Mem. Audubon Artists, Phila. Sketch Club, DaVinci Arts Alliance. Avocations: fly fishing, skiing.

CRILLY, JAMES A., retired accountant, tax specialist; b. Mt. Blanchard, Ohio; s. Andrew Dill and Fairy Gertrude G.; m. Doris L., May 16, 1956; children: Liz Ann, Peggy Sue. BCS in Commerce and Fin., Tiffin U., 1960. Accounts receivable supr. Cooper Tire & Rubber Co., Findlay, Ohio, 1958-66; contr. Stone Container Corp., Franklin, Ohio, 1966-68; asst. contr. E.I. Fisher Constrn., Forest Park, Ohio, 1969-70, Kanter Corp., Forest Park, Ohio, 1970-72; contr. Consolidated Foods, Cin., 1973-75; group contr. Consolidated Foods, St. Petersburg, Fla., 1975-76; owner Crilly's Acctg. Svc. Inc., Seminole, Fla., 1977—. A/1C USAF, 1952-56. Mem. Mem. Automobile License Plate Collectors Assn. (3d v.p. 1963-64, sec. treas. 1966-72, newsletter editor 1966-72, treas. 1972-74, pres. 1979-81, 89-91, Long Island Region award 1990). Democrat. Baptist. Avocations: license plates, camping, hunting, fishing. E-mail: jascrilly@aol.com. Office: Crillys Acctg Svc 8261 141st St Seminole FL 33776-2835

CRINO, MARJANNE HELEN, anesthesiologist; b. Rochester, N.Y., Aug. 18, 1933; d. Michael Jay and Helen Barbara (Kennedy) C.; m. Michael Anthony La Iuppa, Nov. 12, 1960 (dec. Feb. 1996); children: James Michael, Barbara Anne, John Christopher. BS, Coll. St. Teresa, 1955; MD, Med. Coll. Wis., 1959; MA in Theology, St. Bernard's Inst., 1991. Diplomate Nat. Bd. Med. Examiners. House staff Genesee Hosp., Rochester, 1959-61; per-

inatal mortality rsch., resident in anesthesiology Jackson Meml Hosp.-U. Miami, 1962-65; attending staff in anesthesiology Genesee Hosp., Rochester, N.Y., 1969—; mem. exec. com., med. staff sec., 1980, 82; acting chmn. dept. anesthesiology Genesee Hosp., Rochester, N.Y., 1989, 91, chmn. pain control com., 1989-95; clin. instr. anesthesiology U. Rochester Sch. Medicine, 1983—; cons. anesthesiology Rochester Psychiat. Ctr., 1975-85; instr. anesthesiology U. Miami Sch. medicine, 1966, 67; attending staff anesthesiology Jackson Meml. Hosp., Miami, 1966, 67. Mem. adv. bd. Isaiah House Hosp., 1994—, com. Pittsford (N.Y.) Rep. Party, 1970's-80's; vol. chaplain Genesee Hosp. Mem. N.Y. State Soc. Anesthesiologists (bd. dirs., vice spkr. 1983-86, del. 1971-82, 87—), Am. Soc. Anesthesiologists (del. 1979-86, 97), AMA, N.Y. State Med. Soc., Med. Soc. County of Monroe, Rochester Acad. Medicine, Cath. Physicians Guild Rochester (bd.dirs., pres. 1988-89), Margaret Roper Guild (pres. 1975-76), Cath. Women's Club (Diocese of Rochester). Roman Catholic. Avocations: reading, gardening, music. Office: Genesee Hosp Dept Anesthesiology 224 Alexander St Rochester NY 14607-4055

CRIPPA, DANIELE, modern art critic, lawyer; b. Milan, Italy, July 31, 1949; s. Guiseppe and Iole (Ricci) C.; m. Cristina Gentili, 1999. D in Law, Universita de Urbino, Italy, 1986. Lic. in law, Italy. Dir. Mus. Modern Art of Sculpture of Portofino, Italy, 1977—; expert for orgn. of sale of modern art, Semenzato S.A.S., Venice, Italy. Mem. Directtivo Liguria, Italy, 1985. Avocations: boating, skiing. Office: Via Telesio 19, 20145 Milan Italy

CRIPPS, ALLAN WILLIAM, immunologist, medical educator; b. Tamworth, Australia, Apr. 11, 1950; s. Roy William and Lucy Lillian (Steel) C.; children: Nathan, Dane, Natasha, Zachary. BSc, U. New England, Armidale, Australia, 1972, BSc with honours I, 1973; PhD, U. Sydney, Australia, 1976. Scientist Flinders Med. Ctr., Adelaide, Australia, 1976-78; scientific dir. Hunter Immunology Unit, Newcastle, Australia, 1978-88; found. dir. Australian Inst. Mucosal Immunology, Newcastle, Australia, 1988-90; chief scientist Hunter Area Pathology Svc., Newcastle, Australia, 1990-92, dir., 1992-95; dean, prof. health sci. U. Canberra, Australia, 1995-99, pro vice-chancellor Divsn. Sci. and Design, 1999—; bd. dirs. Coop. Rsch. Ctr. Freshwater Ecology, Canberra, 1995—, Coop. Rsch. Ctr. Landscape Evolution and Mineral Exploration, Perth, Australia, 1996—, ACT Innovation Ctr., Canberra, 1995-97; co-dir. 9th Internat. Congr. Mucosal Immunology Sydney, 1995-97. Contbr. over 200 articles to prof. jours. in fields of immunology and microbiology. Bd. dirs.. Nat. Health Scis. Ctr., 1996—. Fellow Australian Inst. Med. Scientists, Australian Soc. Microbiology; mem. Am. Soc. Microbiology, Soc. Mucosal Immunology. Avocations: Australian bush and high country. Office: U Canberra Faculty Appl Sci, U Canberra, Faculty Applied Scis, Canberra ACT 2601, Australia

CRIQUI, FERNAND, scientific writer; b. Strasbourg, France, May 14, 1921; s. Fernand and Alice (Sigle) C.; m. Margot Westermann, Sept. 1, 1949. Grad., U. Strasbourg, 1945. Prof. Univ. Centre for Teaching of Journalism, Strasbourg, 1959-83. Contbr. to many French and fgn. sci., med. & cultural periodicals, 1946—; author numerous monographs & books, over 2000 articles. Laureat de l'Acad. Française, 1970. Mem. AAAS, N.Y. Acad. Scis., Mouvement Universel de la Responsabilité Scientifique, Soc. des Ecrivains d'Alsace et de Lorraine. Avocations: chess, tennis, music. Home: 35 rue Dietterlin, F-67100 Strasbourg France

CRISMAN, MARY FRANCES BORDEN, librarian; b. Tacoma, Nov. 23, 1919; d. Lindon A. and Mary Cecelia (Donnelly) Borden; m. Fredric Lee Crisman, Apr. 12, 1975 (dec. Dec. 1975). BA in History, U. Wash., 1943, BA in Librarianship, 1944. Asst. br. libr. in charge work with children Mottet br. Tacoma Pub. Libr., 1944-45, br. libr., 1945-49, br. libr. Moore br., 1950-55, asst. dir., 1955-70, dir., 1970-74, dir. emeritus, 1975—; mgr. corp. libr. Frank Russell Co., 1985-96, ret., 1997; chmn. Wash. Cmty. Libr. Coun., 1970-72. Hostess program Your Libr. and You, Sta. KTPS-TV, 1969-71. Mem. Highland Homeowners League, Tacoma, 1980—, incorporating dir. 1980, sec. and registered agt., 1980-82; mem. Denham West Condominium Assn., Sun City, Ariz., 1995—, chairperson by laws com., 1999. Mem. ALA (chmn. mem. com. Wash. 1957-60, mem. nat. libr. week com. 1965, chmn. libr. adminstrn. divsn. nominating com. 1971, mem. ins. for librs. com. 1970-74, vice chmn. libr. adminstrn. divsn. personnel adminstrn. sect. 1972-73, chmn. 1973-74, mem. com. policy implementation 1973-74, mem. libr. orgn. and mgmt. sect. budgeting acctg. and costs com. 1974-75), Am. Libr. Trustee Assn. (legis. com. 1975-78, conf. program com. 1978-80, action devel. com. 1978-80), Pacific N.W. (trustee divsn. nominating com 1976-77), Wash. Libr. Assn. (exec. bd. 1957-59, state exec., dir. Nat. Libr. Week 1965, treas., exec. bd. 1969-71, 71-73), Urban Librs. Coun. (editl. sec. Newsletter 1972-73, exec. com. 1974-75), Ladies Aux. to United Transp. Union (past pres. Tacoma), Friends Tacoma Pub. Libr. (registered agt. 1975-83, sec. 1975-78, pres. 1978-80, bd. dirs. 1980-83), Smithsonian Assocs., Nat. Railway Hist. Soc., U. Wash. Alumni Assn., U. Wash. Sch. Librarianship Alumni Assn. Roman Catholic. Club: Quota Internat. (sec. 1957-58, 1st v.p. 1960-61, pres. 1961-62, treas. 1975-76, pres. 1979-80) (Tacoma). Home: 6501 N Burning Tree Ln Tacoma WA 98406-2108 also: 9054 N 109th Ave Sun City AZ 85351-4676

CRISP, ARTHUR HAMILTON, psychiatrist, educator; b. London, June 17, 1930; s. John William and Elizabeth Lillian (Clarke) C.; m. Irene Clare Reid, Feb. 1, 1958; children: Simon John, Timothy James, Toby Benjamin. MB, BS, U. London, Westminster, 1956; MD, U. London, Middlesex, 1967; DSc, U. London, 1979. Registered med. practitioner, London. Prof. psychiatry U. London, St. Geo Med. Sch., 1967-95; dean faculty of medicine U. London, 1976-80, prof. emeritus psychol. medicine, 1995—; chmn. edn. com. Gen. Med. Coun., U.K., 1982-88; chmn. adv. com. on med. tng. European Cmty., 1983-86. Author: Sleep, Nutrition and Mood, 1976, Anorexia Nervosa: let me be, 1980; contbr. articles to profl. jours. and chpts. to books in field. Fellow Royal Coll. Physicians, Royal Coll. Physicians Edinburgh, Royal Coll. Psychiatrists (sr. v.p. 1991-93, chmn. Stigma campaign); mem. Brit. Assn. for Social Psychiatry (chmn. 1988-95), Athenaeum. Avocations: tributories of the River Thames, golf, wood carving. Home: 113 Copse Hill Wimbledon, London SW20 ONT, England

CRISPIN, ANDRE ARTHUR, international trading company executive; b. Brussels, Belgium, Aug. 23, 1923; came to U.S., 1947; naturalized Am. citizen; m. Sylvia Clevenger; 5 children. Ed., U. Louvain, Belgium, 1943. V.p. Am. Supply and Equipment Co., Houston, 1947-48; chmn. Crispin Co., Houston, 1949—; hon. consul-gen. Belgium. Past chmn. bd. trustees so. region Inst. Internat. Edn.; mem. Citizens Environ. Coalition; past pres. Music Guild Houston; chmn. bd. trustees Awty Internat. Sch., Houston; mem. external internat. bd. advs. Tex. A&M U., College Station. liaison officer with Belgian Army, 1940-46. Decorated officier Ordre de Leopold II, Civic Cross 1st class, officier Ordre de Leopold ler (Belgium); chevalier Legion d'Honneur (France), Commdr.'s Cross Order of the Crown (Belgium), 1997; named one of 5 Outstanding Young Texans, 1953; recipient Houston Internat. Svc. award, 1986. Mem. Nat. Assn. Steel Pipe Distbrs. (past pres., bd. dirs.), Academie Internationale du Vin, Alliance Française de Houston (past pres., dir., exec. com.), Am. Inst. Imported Steel (past dir.), Commanderie de Bordeaux d'Amerique (grand maitre, gov.), Commanderie de Bordeaux du Texas à Houston (past maitre, commandeur), Commanderie du Bontemps, de Medoc et de Graves (France, commandeur d'honneur), German Wine Soc., Prodhomme, Jurade de St. Emilion Stylobate, Piliers Chablisiens, Compagnon de Loupiac, Echevin, Lussac Puisseguin St. Emilion, Lalande de Pomerol, Hospitaliers de Pomerol, Downtown Houston Assn., Belgian-Am. C. of C. (past bd. dirs.), French-Am. C. of C. (past pres. Houston chpt., dir.), Houston C. of C. (now named Greater Houston Partnership, bd. dirs. world trade divsn., internat. bus. com., past chmn.), World Trade Assn. (past pres., dir.), Petroleum Club of Houston (past dir., past 1st v.p.). Home: One Crestwood Dr Houston TX 77007 Office: Crispin Co 2929 Allen Pkwy Ste 2222 Houston TX 77019-7101

CRISPIN, JAMES HEWES, engineering and construction company executive; b. Rochester, Minn., July 23, 1915; s. Egerton Lafayette and Angela (Shipman) C.; m. Marjorie Holmes, Aug. 5, 1966. AB in Mech. Engring., Stanford U., 1938; MBA, Harvard U., 1941; grad., Army Command & Gen. Staff Sch., 1943. Registered profl. mech. engr., Calif. With C.F. Braun & Co. Alhambra, Calif., 1946-62; treas. Bechtel Corp., San Francisco, 1962-73, v.p., mem. fin. com., 1967-75, mgr. investment dept., 1973-75; retired, 1976; investment cons., Santa Barbara, Calif., 1978—. Trustee Santa Barbara Mus. Art, 1979-91, 97-98, pres., 1986-88, life. hon. trustee, 1992—. Lt. col. Ordnance Corps, AUS., 1941-46. Decorated Army Commendation medal with oak leaf cluster. Mem. Mil. Order World Wars, S.R., Soc. Colonial Wars, Colonial Wars Calif., Baronial Order Magna Carta, Mil. Order Crusades, Am. Def. Preparedness Assn., World Affairs Coun. No. Calif. (trustee 1968-75), Santa Barbara Mus. Art (trustee 1979-91, 97-98, pres. 1986-88, life hon. trustee 1992), Calif. Hist. Soc. (trustee 1979-86), Valley Club of Montecito (pres. 1987-90, bd. dirs. 1981-91), Calif. Club L.A., World Trade Club San Francisco (pres. 1977-78, bd. dirs. 1971-78), Santa Barbara Club (pres. 1995-96, bd. dirs. 1991-96), Pacific Union Club, San Francisco, Beta Theta Pi. Republican. Home fax: 805-565-9077. Office fax: 805-966-2081. Home: 470 Eastgate Ln Santa Barbara CA 93108-2248 Office: La Arcada Bldg 1114 State St Ste 220 Santa Barbara CA 93101-6712

CRISPIN, SAM, property services administrator, researcher; b. London, Feb. 7, 1969; s. Michael Julian and Janice Caroline (Munday) C. Grad., Leeds U., England, 1992. Sales exec. Evergreen Marine, London, 1992-94; chief rep. Brooke Hillier Parker, Shanghai, China, 1994-96; dir. rsch. PDSAVIUS, Shanghai, China, 1996—; dir. FTZ Football Club, Shanghai, 1999—. Office: 381 Huaihai Middle Rd, Shanghai 200020, China

CRIST, BAINBRIDGE, volunteer; b. Boston, Dec. 19, 1916; s. Lucien Bainbridge and Florence Libbey Crist; m. Elizabeth Green, Ag. 26, 1944 (dec. Aug. 1963); children: Anne Whitaker, William Bainbridge; m. Madeleine Mercier, May 16, 1964 (dec. Jan. 1994). BS, Harvard Coll., 1939. Reporter Washington Star, 1939-45; assoc. editor Nat. Aeronautics, Washington, 1945-46; Washington corr. Tide, Washington, 1946-50; chief Trade Press, news divsn. Office Price Stabilization, Washington, 1951; mem. staff, then v.p. Newmyer Assocs., Washington, 1951-74. Bd. mem. Legal Aid Soc., Washington, 1960-62; pres. South Yarmouth (Mass.) Libr., 1981-94; mem. Yarmouth Hist. Commn., 1979-81. Mem. Bass River Yacht Club (chmn. membership com. 1997—), Hyannis Yacht Club (assoc.), Harvard Club (sec. Washington 1964-73), Hist. Soc. Old Yarmouth (pres. 1980-83), Cape Islands Hist. Assn. (pres. 1986-90), Harvard Alumni Assn. (regional dir. 1980-83). Democrat. Home: 50 Pleasant St South Yarmouth MA 02664-4545

CRISTESCU, ROMULUS, mathematician, educator, science administrator; b. Ploiesti, Romania, Aug. 4, 1928; s. Ioan and Ecaterina (Georgescu) C.; m. Eufrosina Barbu, May 20, 1957. D of Math., U. Bucharest, Romania, 1955. Asst. prof. math. U. Bucharest, 1950-55, lectr. math., 1955-60, assoc. prof., 1960-66, prof., 1966—, dir. Inst. Math., 1973-75; now chmn. math. Academia Română, Bucharest. Author: Functional Analysis, 1965, 4th edit., 1983, Ordered Vector Spaces and Linear Operators, 1976, Topological Vector Spaces, 1977, others; contbr. articles to profl. jours. Mem. Romanian Math. Soc., Romanian Acad. (prize 1966). Home: Intrarea Dridu 2, 78416 Bucharest Romania Office: Academia Română, Calea Victoriei 125, 71102 Bucharest Romania also: U Bucharest Inst Math, Str Academiei 14, Bucharest 12, Romania

CRISTOFER, MICHAEL, actor, screenwriter, playwright; b. Trenton, N.J., Jan. 22, 1945; s. Joseph Peter and Mary (Muccioli) Procaccino. Student, Catholic U. Am., 1962-66, Am. U., Beirut, 1968-69. Repertory actor Arena Stage, Washington, 1967-68, Theatre of Living Arts, Phila., 1968, Beirut Repertory Co., 1968-69, N.Y. Shakespeare Festival, 1970, Mark Taper Forum, L.A., 1972-75; stage performance in Chinchilla, 1979, No End of Blame, 1983, Hamlet, 1993; TV appearances in The Entertainer, 1975, The Last of Mrs. Lincoln, 1975, Knuckle, 1976; film appearance in Enemy of The People, 1976, Little Drummer Girl, 1983; author plays The Mandala, 1967, Rienzi, 1968, Dorian, 1969, Plot Counter Plot, 1971, Americomedia, 1972, The Shadow Box, 1972 (L.A. Drama Critic award for best play 1975, Pulitzer prize drama 1977, Antoinette Perry award 1977, Tony award, 1977), Ice, 1974, Black Angel, 1976, The Lady and the Clarinet, 1980, C.C. Pyle and the Bunyan Derby, 1978, Breaking Up, 1986, Casablanca (adaption), 1985, Love Me or Leave Me, 1990, Amazing Grace, 1993; screenplays include Falling in Love, 1986, Witches of Eastwick, 1987, Bonfire of The Vanities, 1990, Boys on the Side, 1994, Breaking Up, 1997; author screenplay, dir.: (HBO original movie) Gia, 1998 (Dirs. Guild Am. award); dir.: (film) Body Shots, 1999, Original Sin, 2000. Recipient Theatre World award for performance, 1977, L.A. Drama Critics award for acting, 1973, OBIE award for acting, 1979. Office: CAA/Richard Lovett 9830 Wilshire Blvd Beverly Hills CA 90212-1804

CRITCHFIELD, SCOTT A., investment broker; b. Defiance, Ohio, Dec. 20, 1962; s. HH and Hilary (Moore) C.; m. Kathryn Barker, May 30, 1992; children: Thomas, Sarah, Anne. BS in BA, Valparaiso (Ind.) U., 1986. CFP. Floor salesperson Bachrach, Decatur, Ill., 1986-87, auditor, 1987-88, catalog mgr., 1988; ins. salesperson United Trust, Springfield, Ill., 1988-90, tng. dir., 1990-96; assoc. v.p., new broker trainer A.G. Edwards, St. Louis, 1996—; v.p. Roosevelt Equity, Springfield, 1992-96, fin. prin., 1992-96, bd. dirs., 1993-96. Vocal soloist Nat. Ch., Washington, 1991, Powell Hall, St. Louis, 1982, Opera House, Chgo., 1982, Air Force Acad. Cathedral, Boulder, Colo., 1983. Mem. Inst. of Cert. Fin. Planners. Avocations: sailing, skiing, travel, tennis, singing. Home: 1229 Du Motier Dr Ballwin MO 63011-3612 Office: AG Edwards & Son 100 N Jefferson Ave Saint Louis MO 63103-2207

CRITCHLOW, DONALD THOMAS, history educator; b. Pasadena, Calif., May 18, 1948; s. Patrick B. Critchlow and Anne Dawson Marchinton; m. Patricia Elizabeth Powers Feb. 18, 1978; children: Angieszka A., Magdalena D. BA magna cum laude, San Francisco State U., 1970; MA, U. Calif., Berkeley, 1972, PhD, 1978. Asst. prof. North Central Coll., Naperville, Ill., 1978-81, U. Dayton, Ohio, 1981-83; assoc. prof. Notre Dame U., South Bend, Ind., 1983-91; prof., dept. chair St. Louis U., Mo., 1991—; grad. dir. Phi Alph Theta, U. Dayton, U. Notre Dame; mem. Ill. steering com. OAH Conf. on the Promotion of History, Wesleyan U., Bloomington, Ill., 1980; program co-dir. Conf on Evolution of Fed. Social Policy, U. Notre Dame, South Bend, Ind.; guest scholar The Brookings Instn. 1976-77, Woodrow Wilson Internat. Ctr. Scholars/Guest Scholars, 1984-85, fellow 1996-97; vis. prof. U. Warsaw, 1988-89; summer fellow NEH, 1980, Rockefeller, 1983, 94. Author: (monographs) Brookings Institution 1916-1952 Expertise and Public Interest in a Democratic Society, 1985, Studebaker: The Life and Death of an American Corporation, 1852-1963, 1996, Intended Consequences: Birth Control, Abortion and the Federal Government in Modern America, 1999; co-author (with William Rorabaugh) America: A Concise History; editor: Socialism in the Heartland: The Midwestern Experience, 1986, A History of the United States I-V, 1995, The Politics of Abortion and Birth Control in Historical Perspective, 1996; co-editor (with Ellis Hawley), Federal Social Policy: The Historical Dimension, 1989, Poverty and Public Policy in Modern America, 1989, With Us Always: Private Charity and Public Welfare in Historical Perspective, 1998; contbr. chpts. to books and revs. and articles to profl. jours, presented papers at profl. confs., nat. and internat., 1981—; founding editor Jour. of Policy History; gen. editor Critical Issues in Policy History, Critical Issues in History. Named USIA Disting. Lectr., 1988-89, grantee, 1995; fellow Fulbright Scholars Program, 1997-98, USIA China Spkrs. Program, 1999. Home: 7175 Washington Ave University Cy MO 63130-4313 Office: St Louis U History Dept 221 N Grand Blvd Saint Louis MO 63103-2006

CRITELLI, GIUSEPPE, cardiologist, educator; b. Tiriolo, Catanzaro, Italy, Sept. 14, 1937; s. Raffaele and Maria (Custo) C.; m. Maria Giuseppina Panetta, July 20, 1967; 1 child, Alessandra. MD, U. Rome, 1962, postgrad., 1965, 69. Diplomate Italian Med. Orgn. Prof. medicine U. Naples, 1973-86; asst. prof. medicine U. Rome, 1962-69, prof. medicine, 1969-73, prof. cardiology, 1986—. Author: Preventive Cardiology, 1977, Transesophageal Electrogram and Pacing, 1984, Electrical Treatment of Arrhythmias, 1986. Fellow Am. Coll. Cardiology, European Soc. Cardiology, N.Am. Soc. Pacing and Electrophysiology. Home: Via Ceresio 11, 00199 Rome Italy Office: Univ Rome, Viale Policlinico 155, 00165 Rome Italy

CRITTENDEN, SOPHIE MARIE, communications executive; b. Mansfield, Ohio, Apr. 14, 1926; d. Joseph S. and Mary Ellen (Hagerman) Wojcik; m. Robert Eugene Crittenden, Aug. 24, 1946 (dec. 1987); children: Robert J., Mark A., Christopher E., Laura Ann. Student, Coll. St. Francis, 1944-45, Ohio U., 1945-46, North Central Tech. Coll., 1976-78. Substitute tchr. Mansfield City Schs., 1956-62; lab. technician The Ohio Brass Co., Mansfield, 1962-68, draftsman, 1968, mgr. internal publs., 1969-78, mgr. advt., 1978-83, mgr. comm., 1983-88; cons. comm. EFE N.Am., Inc., Mansfield, 1989-90; account coord. D & S Creative Advt., Inc., Mansfield, 1990—. Creator and shower of quilts. Com. chmn. United Way Campaign, Mansfield and Richland, Ohio, 1978; pub. relations chmn. Tribute to Women and Industry Project, Mansfield, 1986 (award 1985). Named Mrs. Mansfield Mrs. Am. Contest, 1961. Mem. Millennium Quilt Guild, Altrusa (pres. 1976, internat. chmn. mktg. and pub. rels. 1991-93). Republican. Roman Catholic. Avocations: fiber arts, antiques, quilting. Home: 84 Wildwood Dr Mansfield OH 44907-1621 Office: 140 Park Ave E Mansfield OH 44902-1830

CRITTO, SARA, broadcast executive; b. Corning, N.Y., June 17, 1946; d. Enrique Shaw; m. Adolfo Critto, May 11, 1968; children: Adolfo, Sara, Florencia, Elena, Enrique. Student, Cath. U., Buenos Aires, 1967. Rsch. asst. CEUPS Inst. Social Devel., Nat. U. Cordoba, 1974-76; mem. spouse program Eisenhower Found., U.S., 1984; pres. Accion Solidaria Radio Am., Buenos Aires, 1985-88, 2000, Accion Solidaria Radio Cultura, Buenos Aires, 1989—. Co-author (book): Voluntariado una Forma de Hacer y de Ser, 1998; co-author handbook: Health of Illness, Your Choice, 1990. Pres. Ednl. TV Found., 1992-2000. Mem. Jr. Svc. League Buenos Aires (bd. dirs. 1988-91). Roman Catholic. Avocation: choral singing. Home: Tagle 2872, 1425 Buenos Aires Argentina Office: Radio Cultura, Copernico 2306, 1425 Buenos Aires Argentina

CRNIC, JADRANKO, judge. Pres. Constitutional Ct. of Croatia, Zagreb. Office: Constitutional Ct of Croatia, Trg svetog Marka 4, 10000 Zagreb Croatia*

CRNKOVIC, ANISE ELAINE, marriage and family therapist; b. Alamogordo, N.Mex., Dec. 18, 1970; d. Vernon Eugene Sr. and Gloria Elaine (Hairston) C. AA, N.Mex. State U., 1993, BA, 1993, MS, 1995, PhD, 1998. Lic. marriage and family therapist. Marriage and family therapist Mesilla Valley Hosp., Las Cruces, N.Mex., 1994—, intensive outpatient program dir., 1995—, dir. clin. svcs., 1999—, dir. outpatient svcs., 1999—; dir. outpatient svcs. Mesilla Valley Hosp., Las Cruces, 1999—; dir. clin. svcs. Mesilla Valley Hosp., Las Cruces, N.Mex., 1999—; tchg. asst., rsch asst. N.Mex. State U., Las Cruces, 1993-95; doctoral fellow N.Mex. State U., Las Cruces, $D, 1995-98; treatment foster care program dir. N.Mex. State U., Las Cruces, 1998—, instr. marriage and family therapy program, 1998—; instr. marriage and family therapy program N.Mex. State U., Las Cruces, N.Mex., 1998—; cmty. counselor Cmty. Svcs., Oro Grande, Hill Rolls, N.Mex., 1986—; marriage and family therapist Assocs. for Marriage and Family Therapy, Las Cruces, 1997—; ptnr., profl. clown Somer, Sault & Co., Las Cruces, 1990-98. Counselor, dir. Vacation Bible Sch., Oro Grande, High Rolls, 1987—; counselor Aurora Diabetic Camp for Kids, Ft. Worth, 1987-89. Mem. Am. Assn. for Marriage and Family Therapy, Nat. Coun. Family Rels. Republican. Baptist. Avocations: piano, writing, teaching. Home: Ste 158 2001 E Lohman Ave 110 Las Cruces NM 88001-3167 Office: Mesilla Valley Hosp 3751 Del Rey Blvd Las Cruces NM 88012-8526

CROCE, PAUL W., lawyer; b. Pitts., May 13, 1968; s. William D. and Clara L. Croce; children: Thomas, Jack. JD, U. Louisville, 1995. Bar: Ind. 1996, U.S. Dist. Ct. (so. dist.) Ind., Ky. 1995, U.S. Dist. Ct. (we. dist.). Lawyer Fischer & Greene, Louisville, 1995-97, Boehl, Stopher & graves, Louisville, 1997—; bd. mem. Louisville Orch., 1997, Plainview, Louisville, 1997-99. Mem. ABA, Ind. State Bar Assn., Ky. Bar Assn., Louisville Bar Assn., Ky. Acad. Trial Attys., Def. Rsch. Inst. Office: Boehl Stopher Graves 2300 Aeson Ctr 400 W Market Louisville KY 40202

CROCHET, DOMINIQUE PIERRE, cardiologist, radiologist, educator; b. Vairé, France, July 20, 1948; s. Pierre and Marie Josephe (Thomas) C.; m. Marie Edith Hilleriteau, May 19, 1949; children: Valerie, Olivier. MD, Nantes U., France, 1976. Resident Hosp. Univ. Nantes, 1971-76, fellow, 1977-79; rsch. asst. Montreal Heart Inst., 1982-85; med. staff Hosp. U. Nantes, 1979-90, dir. hemodynamics ctr., 1987; prof. U. Nantes, 1990—. Mem. Cardiovascular Internat. Radiol. Soc. Europe, French Cardiovascular Imaging Soc. (pres. 1995), European Soc. Cardiology. Roman Catholic. Avocations: tennis, skiing, fishing. Office: Ctr Hemodynam Hosp U Nantes, 44035 Nantes France

CROCKER, BARBARA JEAN, infection control practitioner; b. Worcester, Mass., Oct. 13, 1942; d. Roy A. and Mildred E. (Ewing) Benson; m. David L. Crocker, Aug. 29, 1964; children: Beth, Mark, Matthew. Diploma, Henry Heywood Meml. Hosp., Gardner, Mass., 1963; BS, Anna Maria Coll., Paxton, Mass., 1982, MS in Nursing, 1985. Cert. infection control nurse. Staff nurse Worcester Hahnemann Hosp., 1965-72, nursing supr., 1972-81, infection surveillance nurse, 1981-85; nurse epidemiologist The Med. Ctr.-Hahnemann, Worcester, 1985-92; infection control practitioner U. Mass. Meml. Health Care, 1992—. Mem. Assn. Profls. in Infection Control and Epidemiology, Inc., Henry Heywood Meml. Hosp. Alumnae Assn.

CROCKER, IAN, Olympic athlete; b. Portland, Maine, Aug. 31, 1982. Recipient Gold medal 4 x 100-meter medley (team) Sydney Olympics, 2000; youngest man in U.S. history to break 1 minute, 50 seconds in 200-meter freestyle. Office: USA Swimming 1 Olympic Plz Colorado Springs CO 80909-5746*

CROCKER, JOY LAKSMI, concert pianist and organist, composer; b. San Antonio, June 12, 1928; d. Hugo Peoples and Anna Kathryn (Ball) Rush; m. Richard Lincoln Crocker, July 24, 1948 (div. July 1977); children: Nathaniel Homer, Martha Wells, David Laramie. MusB, Yale U., 1950; MS, Yale U., Berkeley, Calif., 1956; postgrad., Grad. Theol. Sem., 1978-81. Min. music First Congl. Ch., Branford, Conn., 1949-62; dir. music therapy West Haven (Conn.) VA Hosp.; min. music St. Stephen's Episcopal Ch./Sch., Orinda, Calif., 1963, First Bapt. Ch., Oakland, Calif., 1964-66, Greek Orthodox Cathedral, Oakland, 1969, San Quentin (Calif.) Protestant Chapel, 1976-78, Plymouth United Ch. of Christ, Oakland, 1977-84; pianist, assoc. dir. First Bapt. Ch., Managua, Nicaragua, 1984-94; organist, pianist Mills Grove Christian Ch., 1995; organist St. Andrews Presbyn. Ch., Pleasant Hill, Calif., 1996; prof. organ San Francisco Conservatory Music, 1962-69; chmn. piano dept. Nicaraguan Nat. Conservatory Music, 1984-93; founder-dir., prof. Bapt. Conservatory of Music, Managua, 1989—; instr. Yogalayam Yoga Ashram; creator, dir. diverse low-budget innovative music edn. programs, 1969—; mem. adjudicator Nat. Guild Piano Tchrs., Music Tchrs. Assn. Calif.; invited lectr. 3d Encuentro Iberoamericano de Profesores y Estudiantes de Musica, Cuba; piano concert and master class tours, Cen. and South Am., 1995. Pianist, Internat. Symposium of Universal Articulate Understanding of Sci., 1999; concert/presentation World Parliament of Religions South Africa, 1999; pianist Balboa Park Pause for Peace Millennial Concert, 1999-2000. Civic and legislation coord. Ch. Women United, Oakland unit and state unit, 1996—, chairperson for global concerns; pianist, organist Ch. Women United State Unit; San Francisco Bay area coord. for Hague Appeal for Peace; commr. World Summit on Peace and Time, Costa Rica, 1999. Named Woman of Yr., Bus. and Profl. Women's Club, Inc., 1995; recipient prizes for compositions San Francisco Concerto Orch., 1997, Music Tchrs. Assn. Calif., 1998, 2000. Mem. Am. Guild Organists, Am. Coll. Musicians, Music Tchrs. Assn. Mem. United Ch. of Christ. Avocation: traveling. Home: 3065 Monterey Blvd Oakland CA 94602-3559

CROCKER, RAY DEAN, musician, musical director; b. Ft. Worth, Nov. 1, 1949; s. Ben Raglin and Nancy Mahota (Potts) C.; m. Emily Janice Holt. Student, Tex. Christian U., 1967-69; MusB, North Tex. State U., 1974, MusM, 1977. Pianist Casa Manana Musicals, Ft. Worth, 1979-83; mus. asst. Opera Theatre U. North Tex. (formerly North Tex. State U.), Denton, 1980-81, instr. music, 1983-84; staff accompanist Tex. Womans's U., Denton, 1982-85; mus. dir. Surflight Summer Theatre, Beach Haven, N.J., 1984-85; asst. condr. 42nd St., nat. tour, 1985-86; mus. dir. Dallas Repertory Theatre, 1986-89, Sacramento Music Circus, 1988-90, Oscar's Place Dinner Theatre, Milw., 1990, 42d St. European Tour Co., 1991-97, Great Lake Opera, Milw., 1992; bd. dirs. Paint It Yellow Prodns., Inc., pres., 1999—. Composer: (mus.) Twas the Night Before Christmas, 1983, Frosty the Snowman, 1985, numerous instrumental, vocal, electronic chamber works; condr. mus. Dreamgirls, 1988. Mem. ASCAP, Am. Fedn. Musicians, Dramatists Guild, Phi Mu Alpha, Kappa Kappa Psi, Alpha Psi Omega. Home: 2764 N 90th St Milwaukee WI 53222-4609

CROCKER, RYAN C., ambassador; b. Spokane, Wash., June 19, 1949; married. BA, Whitman Coll., 1971; postgrad., Univ. Coll., Dublin, Ireland. Various positions with Am. embassies, Iran, Qatar, Tunis, Iraq, from 1971; chief polit. sect. Am. Embassy, Beirut, 1981-84; dep. dir. Office Israel and Arab-Israeli Affairs, Dept. State, Washington, 1985-87; polit. counselor Am. Embassy, Cairo, 1987-90; amb. to Lebanon, Am. Embassy, Beirut, 1990-93; amb. to Kuwait, Am. Embassy, Kuwait City, 1994-97; amb. to Syria, Am. Embassy, Damascus, 1998—. Office: Am Embassy Damascus c/o Dept State Washington DC 20521-6110

CROCKER, SAONE BARON, lawyer; b. Bulawayo, Zimbabwe, Jan. 11, 1943; came to U.S., 1963; d. Benjamin and Rachel (Joffe) Baron; m. Chester Arthur Crocker, Dec. 18, 1965; children: Bathsheba Nell, Karena Wynne, Rebecca Masten. BA, U. Cape Town, 1961, BA with honors, 1962; MA, Johns Hopkins U., 1966; JD cum laude, Georgetown U., 1983. Bar: D.C. 1983, U.S. Ct. Appeals (D.C. cir.) 1985, U.S. Dist. Ct. D.C. 1990, U.S. Supreme Ct. 1990, U.S. Ct. Appeals (7th cir.) 1991, U.S. Ct. Appeals (4th cir.) 1998. Adminstr. Guinea program African Am. Inst., Washington, 1965-66, author Africa Report, 1966; writer fgn. affairs div. Am. U., Washington, 1967-68; freelance writer Washington, 1968-80; atty. firm Wilmer, Cutler & Pickering, Washington, 1983-84; clk. to judge U.S. Ct. Appeals for D.C. Circuit, 1984-85; atty. firm O'Melveny & Myers, Washington, 1985-90, Beveridge & Diamond, Washington, 1990-92, Wright & Talisman, P.C., Washington, 1992—. Contbg. author: Zambia Handbook, 1967. AAUW fellow, 1963-65; Fulbright fellow, 1963; Johns Hopkins U. fellow, 1964-65; recipient Lawyers Coop. Pub. Co. awards, 1980. Mem. ABA, AAUW (state pres. 1992-94), Fulbright Assn. Office: Wright & Talisman PC 1200 G St NW Ste 600 Washington DC 20005-3838

CROCKETT, ANDREW DUNCAN, banker; b. Mar. 23, 1943; s. Andrew and Sheilah (Stewart) C.; m. Marjorie Hlavacek, 1966; 3 children. Ed., Queens' Coll., Cambridge U., Eng., Yale U. Exec. dir. Bank of Eng., 1989-93; with IMF, 1972-89; gen. mgr. Bank Internat. Settlements, Basel, Switzerland, 1994—; chmn. Fin. Stability Forum, 1999—. Contbr. articles to profl. jours. Avocations: reading, golf, tennis. Office: Bank Internat Settlements, Centralbahnplatz 2, 4002 Basel Switzerland

CROFF, DAVIDE, bank company executive. CEO Banca Naz. Del Lavoro, Rome; bd. dirs. Banca Naz. Del Lavoro, Rome. Office: Banca Naz Del Lavoro, Via Veneto 119, 00187 Rome Italy

CROFT, JONATHAN MAXWELL, publisher; b. Bath, Somerset, Eng., Aug. 6, 1953; s. John and Nikki (Geal) C.; m. Sarah Bridget Moore, May 2, 1981. BA in Theology, Bristol U., 1976. Scriptwriter British Broadcasting Corp., London, 1977-79, Ind. TV, London, 1979; pub. Absolute Press, Bath, Eng., 1979—; cons. Oberon Books, London, 1996—, U.K. arts del. European Cmty., Brussels, 1994. Pub. Absolute Classics, 1989-96, Outlines, 1996—; contbr. numerous articles to profl. publs. Publishing grant Arts Coun. of Great Britain, 1989-96; recipient Translation award Queen's U., 1995, Strindberg award Swedish Embassy, 1990, Ind. Pub. of Yr., Sunday Times, 1990, 91, Pub. award French Inst., 1996. Home: 7 Rode Hill, Bath England Office: Scarborough House, 29 James St West, Bath BA1 2BT, England

CROFT, JULIAN CHARLES BASSET, English language educator, poet, author; b. Newcastle, NSW, Australia, May 21, 1941; s. Jack Croft and Florence Helena (Champion) Brown; m. Loretta Ruth Amelia de Plevitz, Oct. 23, 1967 (div. 1979); 1 child, Laurence James; m. Caroline Margaret Ruming, Dec. 12, 1987; 1 child, Robertson Ruming. BA, U. NSW, Newcastle, 1961; MA, U. Newcastle, 1967. Prodn. asst. Australian Commonwealth, Sydney, 1961-62; lectr. English U. Sierra Leone, Freetown, South Africa, 1968-70; lectr., sr. lectr., assoc. prof., now prof. U. New Eng., Armidale, NSW, 1970—. Author: (poetry) Breakfasts in Shanghai, 1985, Confessions of a Corinthian, 1991, (novel) Their Solitary Way, 1986. Mem. Assn. for Study of Australian Lit. (life). Home: 3 Caroline Crescent, Armidale NSW 2350, Australia Office: U New Eng, Dept English, Armidale NSW 2351, Australia

CROGHAN, GARY ALAN, cancer research scientist, physician; b. Ft. Wayne, Ind., Oct. 2, 1954; s. Robert Thomas and Catherine Marie (Krantz) C.; m. Ivana Tallerico, July 3, 1982. BA, Wabash Coll., Crawfordsville, Ind., 1977; PhD, SUNY, Buffalo, 1982; MD summa cum laude, Buffalo Sch. Med., 1990. Rsch. asst. dept. diagnostic immunology rsch. and biochemistry Nat. Breast Cancer Project Lab., Roswell Park Meml. Inst., SUNY, Buffalo, 1980-82, rschr., 1982-84, rschr. cancer rsch. sci., 1984—, prin. investigator ovary and breast cancer lab, Diagnostic Immunology Rsch., 1985-90, asst. rsch. prof. pathology, 1986-87; intern gen. internal medicine Millard Fillmore Hosp., Buffalo, 1990-91; resident internal medicine Mayo Grad. Sch. Medicine, Rochester, Minn., 1991-94; clin. investigator Mayo Clinic, Rochester, 1994-97, sr. assoc. cons., med. oncology and internal medicine, 1997—; physician investigator nicotine rsch. Mayo Found., 1997—; asst. prof. med. oncology Mayo Grad. Sch. of Medicine, Rochester, 1996—; cons., lectr. in field. Contbr. articles in field. N.Y. State Cancer Predoctoral fellow, 1978-82, postdoctoral fellow, 1983-84, Cancer Immunology fellow Cancer Research Inst., 1984-86. Mem. AAAS, AMA, N.Y. Acad. Sci., Am. Assn. Clin. Chemists, Internat. Assn. Breast Cancer Rsch., Med. Soc. N.Y. State, Am. fertility Soc., Assn. Scientists RPMI, Union Concerned Scientists. Am. Soc. Microbiology, Minn. Med. Assn., Am. Assn. Cancer Rsch., Am. Soc. Clin. Oncology, Am. Soc. Preventive Oncology, Soc. for Rsch. on Nicotine and Tobacco, Am. Soc. for Addiction Medicine, Sigma Xi, Alpha Omega Alpha. Democrat. Office: Mayo Grad Sch Medicine Dept Med Oncology Rochester MN 55905-0001

CROIS, JOHN HENRY, local government official; b. Chgo., Jan. 13, 1946; s. Henry F. and Dorothy M. (Priebe) C. BA, Elmhurst Coll., 1969; MA, U. Notre Dame, 1972. Asst. village mgr. Village of Oak Lawn, Ill., 1975-85; village mgr. Village of Westchester, Ill., 1985; dir. West Cook County Solid Waste Agy., 1990—; coord. Oak Lawn Swine Flu Immunization Program, 1976; bd. dirs. Ill. Met. Investment Fund. Mem. ASPA, West Ctrl. Mcpl. Conf. (chmn. intergovtl. com. 1991, exec. bd. 1991—), Ill. Met. Investment Fund (dir. 1996—), Chgo. Area Transp. Study Coun. Mayors (North Ctrl. region), Internat. City Mgmt. Assn., Ill. City Mgmt. Assn., Metro-Mgrs. Assn., St. Germaine's Men's Club. Home: 10233 Karlov Ave Oak Lawn IL 60453-4235 Office: 10300 W Roosevelt Rd Westchester IL 60154-2568

CROISY, ALAIN, pharmacology researcher; b. St. Alban, France, Oct. 27, 1945; s. Edouard and Rose (Lesage) C.; m. Martine Jane Delcey, June 7, 1969; children: Cecile, Xavier. M in Chemistry, Superior Sch. Chemistry, Paris, 1966; PhD, U. Pierre & Marie Curie, Paris, 1974. Rsch. assoc. CNRS, Gif Sur Yvette, France, 1966-75; attache rsch. INSERM, Gif Sur Yvette, France, 1976-77, charge rsch., 1978-80; charge rsch. INSERM-Inst. Curie, Orsay, France, 1981-91, dir. rsch., 1992—; vis. assoc. Nat. Cancer Inst., Bethesda, Md., 1977-78. Contbr. rsch. papers to profl. jours. With French Air Force, 1968-69. Recipient Italian Ministry Scientific Rsch. Golden medal, Rome, 1974. Mem. European Assn. Cancer Rsch., Environ. Mutagen Soc., Soc. Cellular Pharmaco-Toxicology, Internat. Soc. Antiviral Rsch. Office: Inst Curie, Bat 110-112 Ctr Univ, 91405 Orsay France

CROMBACH, GERD, obstetrician-gynecologist; b. Cologne, Germany, Mar. 20, 1954; s. Wilhelm and Elisabeth (Werners) C.; m. Hetty Hülden, Mar. 26, 1980; children: Verena, Björn. Med. degree, U. Cologne, Germany, 1979, MD, 1982. Registrar dept. ob-gyn. U. Cologne, 1980-86, sr. registrar, 1986-87, cons. dept. ob-gyn., 1987-93; cons. dept. ob-gyn. U. Düsseldorf, Germany, 1993-98; chief sect. prenatal diagnosis and gynecol. ultrasound U. Düsseldorf, 1993-98; chief dept. ob-gyn. Marien Hosp., Dueren, 1998—; mem. editl. bd. Jour. Tumordiagnostik & Therapie. Contbr. numerous articles to med. jours. Recipient award Niederrheinisch-Westfälische Gesellschaft, 1992, 94, 96, 97. Mem. Deutsche Gesellschaft Gynäkologie und Geburtshilfe (award 1993), Deutsche Gesellschaft Ultraschall in Medicine, Deutsche Krebsgesellschaft. Roman Catholic. Avocations: sports, skiing, tennis, football. Office: Dept Ob-Gyn Marien Hosp, Dueren Hospital Str 44, 52353 Dueren Germany

CROMLEY, JON LOWELL, lawyer; b. Riverton, Ill., May 23, 1934; s. John Donald and Naomi M. (Mathews) C. BS, U. Ill., 1958; JD, John Marshall Law Sch., 1966. Bar: Ill. 1966. Real estate title examiner Chgo. Title & Trust Co., 1966-70; pvt. practice, Genoa, Ill., 1970—; mem. firm O'Grady & Cromley, Genoa, 1970-96; bd. dirs. Citizen's First Nat. Bank, 1984-92, Kingston Mut. Ins. Co., Genoa Main St., Inc. Mem. ABA, Am. Judicature Soc., Am., Ill. State Bar Assn., Chgo. Bar Assn., DeKalb County Bar Assn. Home: 130 Homewood Dr Genoa IL 60135-1260

CROMLEY, RAYMOND AVOLON, syndicated columnist; b. Tulare, Calif., Aug. 23, 1910; s. William James and Grace Violet (Bailey) C.; m. Masuyo Marjorie Suto (dec. Apr. 1946); m. Helen Sue Holcomb (dec. July 1967); children: Donald Stowe, Helen Sue, Jessica Lynn, Linda Grace, William Holcomb, Mary Ann, John Austin. BS in Physics, Calif. Inst. Tech., 1933; student, Japanese Lang. Inst., Tokyo, 1936-39, Strategic Intelligence Sch., Washington, 1954. Reporter Pasadena (Calif.) Post, 1928-34, Honolulu Advertiser, 1934-35, Flintridge Sch., Pasadena, 1935-36; reporter, then financial editor Japan Advertiser, Tokyo, 1936-40; editor Trans Pacific (econ. and financial weekly), 1938-40; with Wall St. Jour., 1938-55; Far Ea. corr., 1938-47, Washington corr., 1947-55; sci. editor radio program Monitor, 1955-56; econ. and financial commentator NBC radio, 1956-57; asst. producer CBS Radio, 1957-58; mil. analyst Newspaper Enterprise Assn., 1958-64; pres. Cromley News-Features, 1976—; syndicated columnist, 1964—; Asst. logic, freshman English Calif. Inst. Tech., 1928-30; lectr. Air War Coll., 1952, 54, Dept. State Fgn. Service Inst., 1955, 65-67; cons. guerilla war, Asian politics, 1952—. Author: Veterans Benefits, 1966, 2d edit., 1970, 3d edit., 1973, rev. edit., 1975, Educational Benefits, 1968, Ariwara Narihira and Japanese Poetry of the Heian and Nara Periods. Chmn. dist. bds. charter rev. Boy Scouts Am., 1956-60; sec. bishop's com. pastoral benefits Va. Conf. Meth. Ch., 1967-68; organizer com. estatlishment Martha Washington Libr., Mt. Vernon, Va., 1954; chmn. Inter-ch. Coun. Teen Activities and Teen Clubs, Mt. Vernon, 1955-57, World Coun. Youth, 1932-35. Prisoner of war, 1941-42; col. AUS, 1943-46; comdg. officer U.S. Mil. and Dept. State mission to Mao-Tse-tung's hdqs., Yenan, Communist China. Decorated Legion of Merit, Bronze Star medal. Mem. Nat. Trust for Historic Preservation, Asiatic Soc. Japan, State Dept. Corrs. Assn. (pres. 1954-55), White House Corrs. Assn., Ret. Officers Assn., Smithsonian Assocs., Nat. Archives Assn., Nat. Press Found., Am. Fgn. Svc. Assn., Nat. Press Club Washington, Assn.Corcoran Gallery Art, Sigma Delta Chi, Pi Kappa Delta. Republican. Methodist (lay spkr., Sunday sch. tchr.). Clubs: Tokyo Correspondents (exec. com. 1947); Overseas Writers (Washington). Home: Hollin Hills 1912 Marthas Rd Alexandria VA 22307-1952 Office: PO Box 46989 Washington DC 20050-6989

CROMMELIN, MARIE ADRIANUS, radiation oncologist; b. The Hague, The Netherlands, Nov. 13, 1942; s. Jacob Willem Hendrik and Laurine (Van Nieukerken) C.; m. Elske Albertha van Dyken, Mar. 7, 1975; children: Michiel Bonno Jacob, Jeroen Tjeerd Jouke. MD, State U., Groningen, The Netherlands, 1968; specialization in radiation oncology, U. Leyden, The Netherlands, 1975. Intern State U., Groningen; resident State U., Utrecht/Leyden, The Netherlands, 1969-75; radiation oncologist Catharina Hosp., Eindhoven, The Netherlands, 1975-99; sr. staff cons. Comprehensive Cancer Ctr. South, The Netherlands, 1975-99, chmn . regional breast cancer working group; treas. Nat. Dutch Breast Cancer Coun., 1995-99. Contbr. over 30 articles to profl. jours. in field of breast cancer, Hodgkins disease and cancer care. Capt. Med. Corps., Dutch Air Force, 1968-69. Avocations: history, genealogy, philosophy, archaeology, freemasonary and cancer care organizations. Home: Kastanjelaan 2, 5671 AN Nuenen Holland, The Netherlands Office: Catharina Hosp, RadOnc PO Box 1350, 5602 ZA Eindhoven Holland, The Netherlands

CROMMELIN, MICHAEL, law educator, university dean. BA, LLB with honors, U. Queensland; LLM, PhD, Br. Coll. Barrister, solicitor Victoria; pvt. practice law No. Territory; Zelman Cowen prof. law U. Melbourne, dean Sch. Law. Contbr. articles to profl. jours. *

CROMPTON, GRAHAM KENNETH, physician; b. Salford, Lancashire, Eng., Feb. 14, 1935; s. Bernard Humphrey and Clarice (Ridsdale) C.; m. Dorothy Margaret Graham, Dec. 6, 1966 (dec. 1992); children: Andrew Graham, Douglas Ewan; m. Jane Anne Robertson, Oct. 21, 1994. MBChB, Edinburgh (Scotland) U., 1959. Jr. hosp. physician U.K. Nat. Health Svc., Edinburgh, 1959-62, sr. registrar, 1966-69, cons. physician, 1969-99; registrar in medicine U.K. Nat. Health Svc., Salford, 1963-64; cons. Astra Clin. Rsch. Unit, Edinburgh, 1981-99; mem. task force Nat. Asthma Campaign, London, 1991-99; mem. ethics com. Smith Kline Beechams, London, 1986-91; cons. Quintiles Scotland Ltd., 2000—; part-time med. mem. Lord Chancellor's Dept., 1999—; clin. tchg. fellow medicine U. Edinburgh, 2000—. Author: Diagnosis and Managment of Respiratory Diseases, 2d edit., 1987; mem. editl. bd. Jour. Thorax, 1987-91; contbr. 13 chpts. to books, over 150 articles to profl. jours. Med. Rsch. Coun. fellow, 1964-66. Fellow Royal Coll. Physicians, Am. Coll. Chest Physicians; mem. Brit. Thoracic Soc. (coun. 1987-91, pres. 1994-95), British Thoracic Soc. (pres. 1994-96), Assn. Physicians, Nat. Panel Specialists. Socialist. Avocations: sports, fishing. Home and Office: 14 Midmar Dr, Edinburgh EH10 6BU, Scotland

CROMPTON, KENNETH CHARLES, lawyer; b. Mackay, Australia, July 19, 1948; s. Charles Frederic and Margaret Joan C.; m. Elizabeth Anne Meek, Aug. 21, 1971; children: Jodi, Alex, Anna. LLB, Melbourne U., Australia, 1970. Solicitor Morris, omesaroff and AArons Solrs, Melbourne, 1971-75, Setpn Williams and Smyth Solicitors, Melbourne, 1975-79; legal officer Australia Chamber Mfrs., Melbourne, 1979-87, from dir. ind. rels. to dir. Victoria, 1987-88, chief. exec. Victoria, 1988-92; with Corporate Counsel Pty Ltd., Melbourne, 1992—. Author: WorkCare Manual, 1974. Mem. Athenaeum, Royal Automobile Club of Victoria, Melbourne Cricket Club, Victorian Amateur Turf Club. Avocations: golf, tennis, photography, windsurfing. Home: 104 Scenic Crescent Eltham, Melbourne 3095, Australia Office: Australian Chamber Mfrs, Corp Counsel Pty Ltd, 30 Collins St Level 5, Melbourne 3000, Australia

CROMWELL, OLIVER DEAN, investment banker; b. Cleve., Sept. 19, 1950; s. Oliver and Mildred Jeanette (Galko) C.; m. Sheila Lea Terry, May 19, 1984; children: Ashley Melissa, Oliver Spencer. AB, Brown U., 1972; MBA, Harvard U., 1976. CFA. Trust adminstr. Bankers Trust, N.Y.C., 1973-74; assoc. Donaldson, Lufkin & Jenrette, N.Y.C., 1976-79, v.p., 1980-84, sr. v.p., 1985-87; sr. v.p. Oppenheimer & Co. Inc., N.Y.C., 1987-88; 1st v.p. Paine Webber, N.Y.C., 1988-90; founder, sr. mng. dir. Bentley Assocs. L.P., N.Y.C., 1990—; sr. mng. dir. Bentley Securities Corp., N.Y.C., 1991—. Exec. com., bd. dirs. Assoc. Alumni Brown U., 1985-87, bd. govs., 1987-88, co-head class agt. ann. fund, 1983-87, steering com. 5-yr. reunion fund, 1976-77, 10-yr. reunion fund, 1985-87, co-chmn. 20-yr. reunion fund, 1991-92, co-chmn. 25-yr. reunion fund 1996-97; ann. fund exec. com., 1991-93, co-chmn. N.Y. met. area com. Brown Campaign, 1992-94; class '72 v.p. Brown U., 1997—; major gifts com. Harvard Bus. Sch. 20th Reunion, 1995-96. Recipient Alumni Svc. award Brown U., 1990. Mem. Assn. for Investment Mgmt. and Rsch., N.Y. Soc. Security Analysts, Securities Industry Assn. N.Y. (exec. com. 1987-90), N.Y. Capital Roundtable (adv. bd. 1998—), Assn. Corp. Growth, Aston Martin Owners Club-East, Maserati Club Am., Rolls Royce Owners Club (bd. dirs. 1992-93), Bentley Drivers Club (U.K.), Brown U. Club N.Y.C. (bd. dirs. 1983-95, treas. 1984-89, v.p. 1989-91, pres. 1991-93), Harvard Bus. Sch. Club. N.Y. Home: 4 Eastway Bronxville NY 10708-4302 Office: Bentley Assocs LP 21st Fl 101 Park Ave Fl 21 New York NY 10178-0002

CROMWELL, RONALD R., educator; b. Roswell, N.Mex., Aug. 5, 1952; s. Edward Charles and Theresa (Dominick) C. MA, U. Colo., 1982; MM, Seattle U., 1984, EdD, 1988. Prin. St. Raphael Sch., El Paso, Tex., 1981-84, Seattle Cath. Schs., 1984-90; dir.clin. experiences Ind. U., Richmond, 1990-92; dir. tchr. edn. Marist Coll., Poughkeepsie, N.Y., 1992-97; prof., chair edn. SUNY, Oneonta, N.Y., 1997-99; dean Sch. Edn. and Allied Studies, Bridgewater (Mass.) State Coll., 1999—. Co-author: (chpts.) Promising Practices, 1994, Theories of Learning, 1996. Mem. Assn. Ind. Liberal Arts Colls for Tchr. Edn. (exec.com. 1996-97). Avocations: walking, cooking, theater.

CRON, THEODORE OSCAR, writer, editor, educator; b. Newton, Mass., June 20, 1930; s. Jacob and Anna Ruth (Siegel) C.; m. Rosalie Heilpern, Jan. 17, 1954 (dec. Dec. 1998); children: Elizabeth Daryl Koozmin, Adam David. AB, Harvard U., 1952, MAT, 1954. Asst. commr. FDA, Washington, 1965-68; cons., writer Cron Comm., Chevy Chase, Md., 1969-77, 91—; dir. info. FTC, Washington, 1977-79; speech writer Office of Surgeon Gen., Washington, 1979-89; dir. info. Nat. Assn. Elem. Sch. Prins., Alexandria, Va., 1989-91; editor Better Ways to Health, Chevy Chase, 1995-96; adj. prof. journalism George Washington U., Washington, 1979-96; writer, editor NIH, Bethesda, Md., 1991—, Nat. Health Svc. corps., Bethesda, 1992—, NSF, Washington, 1993—, Cardiology Rsch. Found., Washington, 1995—, Nat. Acad. Scis., 1996—. Author: Portrait of Carnegie Hall, 1966; contbr. articles to profl. jours. Chmn. bd. dirs. Edn. Study Ctr., Washington, 1968-73; trustee Intermet, Washington, 1971-75; bd. dirs. Nat. Coalition Consumer Edn., Madison, N.J., 1989-94. Recipient Spl. award Assn. Am. Indian Physicians, 1985, Freedom Found. at Valley Forge award 1989. Mem. Washington Ind. Writers, D.C. Sci. Writers Assn. Avocation: watercolor painting. Home: 5517 Trent St Chevy Chase MD 20815-5511

CRONE, DAVID LLOYD, horse racing industry executive; b. Hayfield, Eng., May 27, 1941; s. Walter and Irene (Simpson) C.; m. Caroline Ann Rhodes, Sept. 18, 1965; children: Charlotte Jane, Rachel Louise, Jasper Thomas. BSc, U. Bristol, 1962, PhD, 1966. Chartered chemist; registered analytical chemist, European chemist. Lectr. U. Hong Kong, 1965-70; sr. racing chemist The Hong Kong Jockey Club, 1970-98; sec. adv. coun. Internat. Fedn. of Horseracing Authorities on Doping Control, 1989 ; convenor working group on racehorse testing Internat. Lab. Accreditation Cooperation. Editor: Procs. of the Sixth Internat. Conf. of Racing Analysts and Veterinarians, 1987; co-editor: Testing for Therapeutic Medications, Environmental and Dietary Substances in Racing Horses, 1995; contbr. articles to profl. jours. Mem. lab. accreditation bd. govt. of the Hong Kong S.A.R., 1991-98, mem. appeal bd. panel toys and children's products safety ordinance, 1993-98, consumer goods safety ordinance, 1995-98. Fellow Royal Soc. of Chemistry, Assn. Ofcl. Racing Chemists (v.p. 1983-85, exec. bd. 1985-88, Award 1992). Anglican. Office: Irish Equine Centre, Johnstown Naas, County Kildare Ireland

CRONENBERG, DAVID, film director; b. Toronto, Ont., Can., Mar. 15, 1943. Ed., U. Toronto. Dir.: (films) Stereo, 1969, Crimes of the Future, 1970, They Came From Within, 1976, Rabid, 1977, The Brood, 1979, Fast Company, 1979, Scanners, 1981 (Internat. Fantasy Film award for Best Film), Videodrome, 1983 (Best Sci. Fiction Film), The Dead Zone, 1983, The Fly, 1986, Dead Ringers, 1988, Naked Lunch (NSFC award, NYFCC award), 1992, M. Butterfly, 1993, eXistenZ, 1998 (Silver Berlin Bear 1999); dir., writer, prodr., actor: Crash, 1997 (Cannes Jury Spl. prize); actor: To Die For, 1995, Extreme Measures, 1996, The Stupids, 1996. Office: William Morris Agy c/o John Burnham 151 S El Camino Dr Beverly Hills CA 90212-2775

CRONIN, DANIEL ANTHONY, archbishop; b. Newton, Mass., Nov. 14, 1927; s. Daniel George and Emily Frances (Joyce) C. S.T.L., Gregorian U., 1953, S.T.D. summa cum laude, 1956; LL.D., Suffolk U., Boston, 1969, Stonehill Coll., North Easton, 1971. Ordained priest Roman Cath. Ch., 1952; attache Apostolic Internunicature, Addis Ababa, Ethiopia, 1957-61, Secretariat of State, Vatican City, 1961-68; named Monsignor by His Holiness Pope John XXIII, 1962; named titular bishop of Egnatia and aux. bishop of Boston, 1968-70; Episcopal ordination from Richard Cardinal Cushing (archbishop of Boston), 1968; pastor St. Raphael Ch., Medford, Mass., 1968-70; bishop Fall River, Mass., 1970-92; archbishop of Hartford (Conn.), 1992—. Recipient Father Michael J. McGivney award K.C., 1999. Club: K.C. (4). Office: 134 Farmington Ave Hartford CT 06105-3723

CRONIN, JAMES WATSON, physicist, educator; b. Chicago, Ill., Sept. 29, 1931; s. James Farley and Dorothy (Watson) C.; m. Annette Martin, Sept. 11, 1954; children: Cathryn, Emily, Daniel Watson. A.B., So. Methodist U. (1951); Ph.D., U. Chgo.; D (hon.), U. Paris, 1995, U. Leeds, 1996, Univ. Pierre & Marie Curie, 1994; DSc (hon.), U. Leeds, 1996. Asst. physicist Brookhaven Nat. Lab., 1955-58; asst. prof. Princeton, 1958-65, prof. physics, 1965-71; prof. physics and astronomy U. Chgo., 1971—, prof. emeritus physics and astronomy; Loeb lectr. physics Harvard U., 1967; participant early devel. spark chambers; co-discoverer CP-violation, 1964; lectr. Nashima Found., 1993. Recipient Research Corp. Am. award, 1967, John Price Wetherill medal Franklin Inst., 1976, E.O. Lawrence award ERDA, 1977, Nobel prize for physics, 1980, Nat. Medal of Sci., 1999; Sloan fellow, 1964-66, Guggenheim fellow, 1970-71, 82-83. Mem. Am. Philos. Soc., Am. Acad. Arts and Scis., Nat. Acad. Sci. (coun. mem.), Am. Phys. Soc. Office: U Chgo Enrico Fermi Inst 5630 S Ellis Ave Chicago IL 60637-1433

CRONIN, PAUL DAVID, physical education educator, director; b. Dover, Mass., May 26, 1938; s. Jeremiah and Bridgit Fahy C.; m. Harriet Richmond McCormick, Aug. 26, 1964 (div. Mar. 1977); children: Peter Fleming, David Richmond; m. Elizabeth Ann Swift, Dec. 23, 1993. AB in History, Stonehill Coll., 1960; MSW cum laude, U. Pitts., 1967. Dir. riding program Sweet Briar (Va.) Coll., 1967—, from asst. prof. to assoc. prof. phys. edn., 1967-78, prof. phys. edn., 1978—; judge, cons. in riding Affiliated Nat. Riding Commn., Sweet Briar, 1967—; bd. dirs. Old Dominion Athletic Conf. Riding Com.; cons. cmty. planning Va. State Dept. Welfare, Richmond, Va., 1967; chmn. dept. phys. edn. and athletics Sweet Briar Coll., 1983-86, exec. com., 1995-98, presdl. search com., 1995-96, strategic planning com., land use com.; cons., instr. in field. Bd. dirs. Va. Horse Ctr. Found., Lexington, Va., 1996-99. Lt. USN, 1961-65. Sweet Briar Coll. grant, 1993-95; recipient 1st pl. Bedford Hunt Hunter Pace, 1995, Individual Champion award Orange County Hunt Team Chase, 1997. Mem. AAHPERD (newsletter editor 1975, bd. chair, chmn. 1976-77, chmn. bd. dirs. 1976-77, bd. dirs. 1980-83, dir. at large 1999-2000), Affiliated Nat. Riding Com., Am. Horse Coun., Am. Horse Show Assn. (recognized sr. judge 1965-87, ad hoc com. 1978-80, zone III rep. 1976-78), Ea. Competitive Trail Ride Assn., Intercollegiate Horse Show Assn. (pres. zone VII 1974-76), Mus. Hounds and Hunting, Nat. Sporting Libr., Nat. Steeplechase and Hunt Assn., Piedmont Environ. Coun., Royal Dublin Soc., S.W. Va. Hunter Jumper Assn. (bd. dirs. 1992-94, named to Hall of Fame 1997), U.S. Combined Tng. Assn., U.S. Equestrian Team Assn., Va. Horse Coun. (bd. dirs. 1981-82, Educator of Yr. 1997), Va. Horse Show Assn. (equitation com. 1974-80, dir., zone com. 1980-83), Bedford Hunt Club (bd. dirs. 1977-78), Farmington Country Club, Farmington Hunt Club, Nantucket Yacht Club, Nat. Beagle Club, North Am. Foxhound Club, Va. Foxhound Club. Avocations: sporting art, schooling horses, riding to hounds. E-mail: cronin@sbc.edu. Home: Farm House Rd Sweet Briar VA 24595 Office: Riding Program PO Box 4 Sweet Briar VA 24595-0004

CRONIN, TERENCE MICHAEL, computer scientist; b. Olean, N.Y., Jan. 12, 1949; s. John Michael and Rita Marie (Conlon) C. BS in Math., SUNY, Brockport, 1976, MA in Math., 1977. Mathematician USN, Mechanicsburg, Pa., 1979; math. statistician U.S. Army, Warrenton, Va., 1979-85, computer scientist, 1985-97; computer scientist U.S. Army, Ft. Monmouth, N.J., 1997—. Contbr. articles to profl. jours. Mem. IEEE, Assn. Computing Machinery, Photogrammetric Engring. and Remote Sensing, Mensa. Office: I2WD Bldg 600 Fort Monmouth NJ 07703

CRONKITE, WALTER, radio and television news correspondent; b. St. Joseph, Mo., Nov. 4, 1916; s. Walter Leland and Helen Lena C.; m. Mary Elizabeth Maxwell, Mar. 30, 1940; children: Nancy Elizabeth, Mary Kathleen, Walter Leland III. Student, U. Tex., 1933-35; LL.D., Rollins Coll., 1966, Bucknell U., Syracuse U.; L.H.D., Ohio State U.; hon. degree, Am. Internat. Coll., Harvard U. News writer, editor Scripps-Howard, also UP, Houston, Kansas City, Dallas, Austin, El Paso, Tex., N.Y.C.; UP war corr., 1942-45, fgn. corr., reopening burs. in Amsterdam, Brussels, chief corr. Nuremberg war crimes trials, bur. mgr., Moscow, 1946-48, lectr., mag. contbr., 1948-49, CBS-News corr., 1950-81, spl. corr., 1981—; mng. editor CBS Evening News with Walter Cronkite, 1962-81; chmn. The Cronkite Ward Co., 1993—. Host spl.: Universe, CBS, The Holocaust: In Memory of Millions, The Discovery Channel, 1993 (Cable Ace award, Best Program Interviewer); anchor for: TV news spls. Vietnam: A War That Is Finished, 1975, In Celebration of US, 1976, Our Happiest Birthday, 1977, The President in China, 1975, Solzhenitsyn: 1984 Revisited; Author: Challenges of Change, 1971, A Reporter's Life, 1996; co-author: South by Southeast, North by Northeast, Westwind; producer/host: The Cronkite Reports (12-episode series for Discovery Channel), 1994-96, Cronkite Remembers (8-part series for CBS and Discovery Channel), 1996. Recipient Peabody award, 1962, 81, several Emmy awards; William A. White award for journalistic

merit, 1969; George Polk Journalism award, 1971; Gold medal Internat. Radio and TV Soc., 1974; Alfred I. DuPont-Columbia U. award in Broadcast Journalism, 1978, 81; Presdl. medal of Freedom, 1981. Mem. Acad. Arts and Scis. (pres. nat. acad. N.Y. chpt. 1959, Govs. award 1979), Assn. Radio News Analysts, Nat. Press Club, Overseas Press Club, N.Y. Yacht Club, Explorers Club, Bohemian Club, Chi Phi. Office: CBS Inc 51 W 52nd St Ste 1934 New York NY 10019-6119

CRONSTRÖM, CHRISTOFER EIGESON, physicist, educator; b. Helsinki, Dec. 24, 1940; s. Nils-Erik Eige and Ingegerd (Lunden) C.; m. Britta Liisa Koskiaho, Feb. 21, 1994; 1 child, Carl Michael. PhD, U. Helsinki, 1967. Asst. U. Helsinki, 1962-64, rsch. fellow, prof., 1976—; rsch. fellow NORDITA, Copenhagen, 1965-66; with Inst. Advanced Study, Sch. Natural Sci., Princeton, N.J., 1969-71; assoc. prof. U. Jyvaskyla, Finland, 1971-73; sr. rsch. fellow Rsch. Inst. Theoretical Physics, Helsinki, 1973-75; sci. dir. Rsch. Inst. Theoretical Physics, 1975-76; Bd. dirs. NORDITA, 1979-89. Contbr. articles to profl. jours. Vice chmn. Profs. Union, Finland, 1980-85. Decorated knight 1st class Order of Lion (Finland); recipient gold medal Comenius U., 1993. Mem. Swedish Phys. Soc. in Finland (chmn. 1978-82), Finnish Phys. Soc. E-mail: christofer.cronstrom@helsinki.fi. Office: U Helsinki Dept Physics, PO Box 9, 00014 Helsinki Finland

CRONYN, HUME, actor, writer, film director; b. London, Ont., Can., July 18, 1911; came to U.S., 1932; s. Hume Blake and Frances Amelia (Labatt) C.; m. Jessica Tandy, Sept. 27, 1942 (dec.); children: Susan Cronyn Tettemer, Christopher, Tandy. Grad., Ridley Coll., 1930; student, McGill U., 1930-31; grad., Am. Acad. Dramatic Art, 1934; LL.D. (hon.), U. Western Ont., 1974; LHD (hon.), Fordham U., 1985. Lectr. drama Am. Acad. Dramatic Arts, N.Y.C., 1938-39, Actors' Lab., Los Angeles, 1945-46; bd. govs. Stratford Festival, Can. Author: Rope (screen version), 1947, Under Capricorn (screen version), 1948, also various short stories and mag. articles; author (with Susan Cooper) play Foxfire and ABC teleplay The Dollmaker (Christopher and Writers Guild awards 1985), (autobiography) A Terrible Liar, 1991. First profl. theatre appearance, Nat. Theatre Stock Co., Washington, 1931; appeared in Hippers Holiday, N.Y.C., 1934, various plays, N.Y.C., including High Tor, Room Service, The Three Sisters, The Weak Link, Retreat to Pleasure, The Survivors (star); motion pictures include Shadow Of A Doubt, 1943, Life Boat, 1944, The Seventh Cross, 1944, The Postman Always Rings Twice, 1946, The Green Years, 1946, A Letter for Evie (star), 1945, Brute Force (star), 1947, Top O' The Morning, People Will Talk (star), 1951, Sunrise at Campobello, 1960, Cleopatra, 1963, Gaily Gaily, 1968, The Arrangement, 1968, There Was a Crooked Man, 1969, Conrack, 1974, Parallax View, 1974, Honky Tonk Freeway, 1980, The World According to Garp, 1981, Roll Over, 1981, Impulse, 1983, Brewster's Millions, 1985, Cocoon, 1985, Batteries Not Included, 1987, Cocoon: The Return, 1988, The Pelican Brief, 1993, Camilla, 1994, Marvin's Room, 1996, Alone, 1999, (animated) People, 1995; (TV movies) An African Love Story, 1996, 12 Angry Men, 1997; starred in ANTA touring prodn. of Hamlet, 1949; co-starred with Jessica Tandy in ANTA touring prodn. of The Little Blue Light, Brattle Theatre, Cambridge, Mass., 1950, The Fourposter, 1951-53, Madame Will You Walk, 1953-54, The Honeys; A Day by the Sea, 1955, The Man in the Dog Suit, 1958; dir.: ANTA touring prodn. of Portrait Of A Madonna, Los Angeles, 1946, Now I Lay Me Down To Sleep, 1949-50, Hilda Crane, 1950, The Egghead, 1957, all N.Y.C.; appears in major network dramatic shows TV, including Show of the Week; TV appearances include Foxfire, A Hallmark Prodn., 1987, Day One, 1988, Age Old Friends, 1988, Broadway Bound, 1991, Christmas on Division Street, 1991, To Dance with the White Dog, 1993 (Emmy award, Lead Actor - Special, 1994); appeared in: Big Fish, Little Fish, 1961, Tyrone Guthrie Prodns., Mpls., 1963; played Polonius in Hamlet, N.Y.C., 1964; producer: Slow Dance on the Killing Ground, 1964; produced and starred: (with Jessica Tandy) comedy prodn. The Marriage (a dramatic series), 1954, Triple Play, 1958, 59; appeared title role: (with Jessica Tandy) Richard III, 1965; in: (with Jessica Tandy) Cherry Orchard, 1965; as Harpagon in: comedy prodn. The Miser, Mpls., 1965; as Tobias in A Delicate Balance, 1966, 67; as Harpagon in: revival The Miser, Mark Taper Forum, Los Angeles, 1968; as Frederick William Rolfe in: revival Hadrian VII, Stratford Nat. Theatre Co., Can., 1969, tour, 1969-70; as Capt. Queeg in: Caine Mutiny Court Martial, Los Angeles, 1971-72; appeared in: Promenade All, N.Y.C., 1972; dir., appeared in tour, 1972-73; appeared in: (with Jessica Tandy) Samuel Beckett Festival, Lincoln Center, N.Y.C., 1972; and tour Krapp's Last Tape in Samuel Beckett Festival, Toronto, Washington, other cities, 1973, (with Jessica Tandy) Noel Coward in Two Keys, 1974, tour, 1975, Many Faces of Love, 1974, 75, 76; appeared as Shylock in The Merchant of Venice; as Bottom in: (with Jessica Tandy) A Midsummer Night's Dream, Stratford (Ont., Can.) Festival, 1976; co-producer: (with Mike Nichols and star) The Gin Game (Pulitzer prize 1978), Golden Theatre, N.Y.C., 1977; tour The Gin Game, U.S., Can., Eng., USSR, 1978-79; star: tour Foxfire, Stratford (Ont.) Festival, 1980, Guthrie Theatre, Minn., 1981, Ethel Barrymore Theatre, N.Y.C., 1983; Traveler in the Dark, Am. Repertory Theatre, Loeb Drama Ctr., Cambridge, 1984; limited run of Foxfire, Ahmanson Theatre, Los Angeles, 1985; (with Jessica Tandy) The Petition, Golden Theatre, N.Y.C., 1986. Decorated Order of Canada; recipient Comodedia Matinee Club award for Fourposter, 1952, Barter Theatre award for outstanding contbn. to theatre, 1961, Delia Austria medal N.Y. Drama League for Big Fish, Little Fish 1961, Antoinnette Perry (Tony) award, also Variety N.Y. Drama critics poll of performance as Polonius, 1964, 9th ann. award Am. Acad. Dramatic Art 1964, Straw Hat award for best dir. 1972, Obie award for outstanding achievement, disting. performance Krapp's Last Tape 1973, Brandeis U. Creative Arts award 1978, nominee Tony award for The Gin Game 1979, winner Los Angeles Critics award 1979, named to Theatre Hall of Fame 1979, Nat. Press Club award 1979, Commonwealth award for disting. service in dramatic arts, 1983, Humanitas Prize, 1985, Kennedy Ctr. Honors, 1986, Alley Theatre award, 1987, Franklin Haven Sargent award Am. Acad. Dramatic Arts as disting. alumnus for quality of acting, 1988, Nat. Medal of Arts, 1990; Emmy award supporting actor Broadway Bound, 1992, Antoinette Perry Lifetime Achievement Award, 1994 (with Jessica Tandy). Mem. AFTRA, Screen Actors Guild, Writers Guild Am., Actors Equity Assn., Soc. Stage Dirs. and Choreographers, Dramatists Guild. Office: 63-23 Carlton St Rego Park NY 11374-2826 also: ICM Samuel L Cohn 40 W 57th St New York NY 10019-4001

CROOK, DAVID PAUL, historian; b. Brisbane, Australia, Jan. 12, 1937; s. David Ernest and Alice May (Harris) C.; m. Monica Josephine Burke, May 7, 1960 (div. 1999); children: Lisa Mary, Peter Francis, Daniel Sebastian, Gabrielle Maria; m. Ann Leslie Wallin, Nov. 13, 1999. BA with honors, U. Queensland, Australia, 1958, DLitt, 1988; PhD, U. London, 1961. Lectr. U. Queensland, Brisbane, 1962-65, sr. lectr., 1965-69, reader, 1969-90, prof., 1990-99; ret., 1999; rsch. cons. in field, 1999—. Author: American Democracy in English Politics, 1965, Diplomacy During the American Civil War, 1975, Benjamin Kidd--Portrait of a Social Darwinist, 1984, Darwinism, War and History, 1994. Life mem. Clare Hall, Cambridge, Eng. Mem. Australian Hist. Assn. Avocations: squash, tennis. Home: 9 Clare Pl The Gap, Brisbane 4061, Australia Office: U Queensland, St Lucia, 6072 Brisbane Australia

CROOK, JOHN MARK, neuroscientist, educator, researcher; b. Dewsbury, Eng., July 13, 1957; s. Gerald Geoffrey and Joan (Priestley) C. BA with honors, U. Keele, Eng., 1980, cert. in edn., 1980, PhD, 1987; Habilitation, U. Bochum, Germany, 2000. Cert. tchr., U.K. SERC rsch. scholar U. Keele, 1980-83, demonstrator, resident tutor, 1981-83; lectr. in German Newcastle Coll. of Further Edn., U.K., 1983-84; Max-Planck rsch. fellow Inst. Biophys. Chemistry, Göttingen, Germany, 1984-88; lectr. neurophysiology U. Bochum, Germany, 1988-97; sr. rsch. fellow Leibniz Inst. Neurobiology, Magdeburg, Germany, 1998—. Contbr. articles to profl. publs., chpts. to books. Rsch. scholar Sci. and Engring. Rsch. Coun., 1980-83; Rsch. fellow Max-Planck Soc., 1984-88; grantee European Sci. Found., German Rsch. Orgn., U. Bochum, 1988-93. Mem. Physiol. Soc., Soc. for Neurosci. Avocations: chess, skiing, hiking. Home: Eschenring 3, D-39171 Osterweddingen Germany Office: Leibniz Inst Neurobiology, D-39118 Magdeburg Germany

CROOK, JOSEPH MORDAUNT, architectural historian; b. London, Feb. 27, 1937; s. Austin Mordaunt and Irene (Woolfenden) C.; m. Susan Mayor, Sept. 7, 1975. BA, Oxford U., Eng., 1958, DPhil, 1961, MA, 1961. Lectr. Bedford Coll. London U., 1965-75, reader, 1975-80, prof., 1981-85; prof. Royal Halloway Coll., 1985-99; Slade prof. Oxford U., 1979-80, Waynflete lectr., 1985-86; emeritus prof. archtl. history London U., 1999—. Author: The Greek Revival, 1972, rev. edit., 1996, The British Museum, 1972, William Burges and the High Victorian Dream, 1981, The Dilemma of Style, 1987, The Rise of the Nouveaux Riches, 1999; co-author: History of the King's Works, 1973, 76. Fellow Soc. Antiquaries, Brit. Acad. Home: 55 Gloucester Ave, London NW1 7BA, England

CROOKE, KENNETH WARREN, political party director; b. Brisbane, Queensland, Australia, Feb. 23, 1946; s. Andrew Tasman and Lyn Margaret Crooke; m. Alexis Ann Kenny, Apr. 11, 1969; children: Jon, Ben, Dan. Journalist ABC News, Queensland, 1965-69; editor Cumberland Newspapers, Brisbane, 1970-71; publicity officer Old Govt. Tourist, Brisbane, 1972-75, press sec., 1975-81; dir. Old Govt. News and Info. Svcs., Brisbane, 1981-88, Nat. Party Australia, Queensland, 1988—. Mem. Pub. Rels. Inst. Australia. Mem. Ch. of England. E-mail: ken@npa.org.au. Address: Queensland Nationals, PO Box 5940, West End 4101, Australia

CROOKE, ROBERT ANDREW, media consultant, writer, educator; b. Bklyn., Apr. 17, 1947; s. Henry A. and Theresa E. (Dougherty) C.; m. Angela Keller Lynch, Sept. 13, 1969; 1 child, Sean Peter. BA in English, Providence Coll., 1969; MA in English, Fordham U., 1974. Sports reporter, columnist L.I. Press, Jamaica, N.Y., 1969-75; profl. radio, TV, ednl. film script writer N.Y.C., 1976-79; assoc. editor Mag. Age, N.Y.C., 1979-81; reporter, contbg. editor L.I. Bus. Newsweekly, Ronkonkoma, N.Y., 1981-86; sr. acct. exec. Howard J. Rubenstein, N.Y.C., 1986-87; dir. media rels. Reuters Am., Inc., N.Y.C., 1987-94; v.p. comm. Reuters New Media, N.Y.C., 1994-96; v.p. media rels. Reuters Am. Holdings, Inc., N.Y.C., 1996-2000; mng. dir. Broadgate Consultants Inc., N.Y.C., 2000—; adj. instr. English Suffolk County C.C., Selden, N.Y., 1972-76; lectr. Sch. Journalism, U. Nebr., 1998-99, Sch. Journalism, U. S.C., 2000—; adj. prof. pub. affairs NYU, 1998—. Author of poems and books; contbr. articles to profl. jours., newspapers and mags. Bd. dirs. Walt Whitmen Birth Place Assn., Huntington, N.Y., 1985-87; bd. corp. trustees The Vanderbilt Mus., Centerport, N.Y., 1984-87. Office: PO Box 392 334 Main St S Bridgewater CT 06752-1537

CROOKE, ROSANNE M., pharmacologist; b. Pittsfield, Mass., Oct. 30, 1955; d. Myron Michael and Marian Geneva (Russell) Muzyka; m. Stanley T. Crooke, Sept. 5, 1986. BA, Williams Coll., 1978; PhD, U. Pa., 1986. Rsch. asst. endocrine sec. dept. medicine U. Pa., Phila., 1978-81; fellow Wistar Inst. Anatomy and Biology, Phila., 1986-89; assoc. dir. Liver Pharmacology ISIS Pharms., Carlsbad, Calif., 1989—. Contbr. articles to profl. jours. Mem. AAAS, Soc. for In Vitro Biology, Soc. Toxicology. Avocations: hiking, gourmet cooking, bicycling. Home: 3211 Piragua St Carlsbad CA 92009-7840 Office: ISIS Pharms 2280 Faraday Ave Carlsbad CA 92008-7208

CROOKE, STANLEY THOMAS, pharmaceutical company executive; b. Indpls., Mar. 28, 1945; m. Nancy Alder (dec.); 1 child, Evan; m. Rosanne M. Snyder. BS in Pharmacy, Butler U., 1966; PhD, Baylor Coll., 1971, MD, 1974. Asst. dir. med. rsch. Bristol Labs., N.Y.C., 1975-76, assoc. dir. med. rsch., 1976-77, assoc. dir. R&D, 1977-79, v.p. R&D, 1979-80; v.p. R&D Smith Kline & French Labs., Phila., 1980-82; pres. R&D Smith Kline French, Phila., 1982-88; chmn. bd., CEO ISIS Pharms., Inc., Carlsbad, Calif., 1989; chmn. bd. dirs. GES Pharms., Inc., Houston, 1989-91; adj. prof. Baylor Coll. Medicine, Houston, 1982, U. Pa., Phila., 1982-98; chmn. bd. dirs. GeneMedicine, Houston, 1996-98; bd. dirs. Calif. Healthcare Inst., Indsl. Biotech. Assn., Washington, Idun Pharms., San Diego 1997—, Epix Med., Cambridge, Mass., 1996—, BIO, Washington; mem. sci. adv. bd. SIBIA, La Jolla, Calif. 1992-99; adj. prof. pharmacology UCLA, 1991, U. Calif. San Diego, 1994; bd. dirs. Synsorb Biotech Inc., Calgary, Can., 1999—; bd. dirs. Axon Instruments, Inc., Foster City, Calif. 1999—, Valentis, Inc., Burlingame, Calif., 1999—. Mem. editl. adv. bd. Molecular Pharmacology, 1986-91, Jour. Drug Targeting, 1992; editl. bd. Antisense Rsch. and Devel., 1994; sect. editl. bd. for biologicals and immunologicals Expert Opinion on Investigational Drugs, 1995. Trustee Franklin Inst., Phila., 1987-89; bd. dirs. Mann Music Ctr., Phila., 1987-89; children's com. Children's Svcs., Inc., Phila., 1983-84; adv. com. World Affairs Coun., Phila. Recipient Disting. Prof. award U. Ky., 1986, Julius Stermer award Phila. Coll. Pharmacy and Sci., 1981, Outstanding Lectr. award Baylor Coll. Medicine, 1984. Mem. AAAS, Am. Assn. for Cancer Rsch. (state legis. com.), Am. Soc. for Microbiology, Am. Soc. Pharmacology and Exptl. Therapeutics, Am. Soc. Clin. Pharmacology and Therapeutics, Am. Soc. Clin. Oncology, Indsl. Biotech. Assn. (bd. dirs. 1992-93). Achievements include numerous patents in field. Office: ISIS Pharms Inc 2292 Faraday Ave Carlsbad CA 92008-7208

CROOKENDEN, SIMON ROBERT, barrister; b. Cambridge, Eng., Sept. 27, 1946; s. Spencer and Jean Phyllis (Dewing) C.; m. Sarah Anne Georgina Margaret Pragnell, Aug. 20, 1983; children: Rebecca Jean, Thomas Henry, Alice Lily. MA in Mech. Scis., Corpus Christi Coll., Cambridge, 1968. Bar: Gray's Inn, 1975; Queen's Coun., 1996. Brand mgr. Unilever, London, 1969-72, Express Dairies, London, 1972-74; barrister London, 1975—; recorder, 1999—. Fellow Chartered Inst. Arbitrators. Office: Essex Ct Chambers, 24 Lincolns Inn Fields, London WC2A 3EG, England

CROOKS, PATRICIA KAY, counselor; b. Dallas, Mar. 23, 1951; d. Robert Virgil and Billie Marie Jones; m. John D. Crooks, Sept. 25, 1970; children: Christopher, Chip. BA, U. Tex., Arlington, 1974; MEd, U. N. Tex., 1994. Lic. profl. counselor. Tchr. Christian Acad. Oakcliff, Dallas, 1988-89; reservations Am. Airlines, Ft. Worth, 1989-90; dir. guidance and counseling Dallas Christian Sch., Mesquite, Tex., 1990-00; crisis counselor Garland (Tex.) H.S., 2000—. Mem. Nat. Assn. Coll. Admissions Counselors, Am. Assn. Marriage/Family Therapist, Tex. Counseling Assn. Mem. Ch. of Christ. Avocations: sailing, scuba, golf, reading. Home: 105 France Ct Rockwall TX 75032-8400

CROPP, BEN, film producer; b. Bukais, Solomon Islands, Jan. 19, 1936; arrived in Australia, 1939; s. Allan Herbert and Louise (Taylor) C.; m. Lynn Mary Patterson, Feb. 24, 1979; children: Dean, Adam. Cert., Brisbane Tchrs. Coll., 1955. Mng. dir., producer Ben Cropp Prodns., Port Douglas, Australia, 1966—. Author: Shark Hunters, 1966; producer over 100 documentary films. Named Internat. Scuba Divers Hall of Fame, 2000. Mem. Australia Cinematographers Soc. (award 1966), Hon. Order of Australia A.M., 1999. Home and Office: Ashford Ave, Port Douglas 4871, Australia

CROSBIE, JOHN CARNELL, retired Canadian government official, university administrator, lawyer; b. St. John's, Nfld., Can., Jan. 30, 1931; s. Chesley Arthur and Jessie (Carnell) C.; m. Jane Furneaux, Sept. 8, 1952; children: Chesley, Michael, Beth. BA in Polit. Sci. and Econs., Queen's U., Kingston, Ont.; LLB, Dalhousie U., 1956; postgrad., London Sch. Econs. Bar: Nfld. 1957. Practice in St. John's, 1957-66; mem. St. John's City Coun., 1965-66, dep. mayor, 1966; min. Nfld. Dept. Mcpl. Affairs and Housing, 1966-67, Dept. Health, 1967-68; rep. Nfld. Ho. of Assembly from St. John's West, as Liberal, 1966-68; as Progressive Conservative, after 1971, govt. house leader, 1974-75; min. of fin., pres. Treasury Bd., also min. econ. devel. Nfld., 1972-74; min. fisheries, 1974-75, min. intergovtl. affairs Nfld., 1974-76, min. mines and energy, 1975-76; mem. Canadian Ho. of Commons for St. John's West, 1976-93, chmn. Progressive Conservative caucus on energy, after 1977, also parliamentary critic for industry, trade and commerce; min. of fin. for Can., 1979-80; min. of justice, atty. gen. Can., 1984-86, min. of transp., 1986-88, min. internat. trade, 1988-91; min. fisheries and oceans Atlantic Can. Opportunities Agy., 1991-93; ret., 1993; counsel Patterson Palmer Hunt Murphy, St. John's, Nfld., Can., 1993—; chancellor Meml. U. Nfld., 1994—; dir. Bell Can. Internat. Inc., others; hon. consul Mex. to HFLD, Labrador. Author: No Holds Barred, 1997. Mem. Order Can. (officer 1998). Office: Patterson Palmer Hunt Murph, 235 Water St PO Box 610, Saint John's, NF Canada A1C 5L3

CROSBY, IAN TRAVERS, chemistry educator and researcher; b. Melbourne, Victoria, Australia, Mar. 5, 1961; s. William Moncrieff and Jean Campbell (McDonald) C.; m. Fiona Caroline Fraser; 1 dau., Ella Florence. BSc with honors, U. Melbourne, 1982, PhD in Chemistry, 1987. Sr. tutor U. Melbourne, 1987; postdoctoral rsch. fellow U. Nottingham, U.K., 1987-89, Monash U., Melbourne, 1990-92; lectr. chemistry Victorian Coll. of Pharmacy, Monash U., Melbourne, 1992-98, sr. lectr., 1999—. Contbr. articles to profl. jours. Mem. Royal Australian Chem. Inst. (Pharm. Scis. Group Victorian br. sec. 1993—, chmn. 1994, Organic Group com. mem. 1990—), Victorian Nat. Parks Assn., Am. Chem. Soc., Melbourne Cricket Club. Avocations: sailing, bushwalking, golf. Office: Monash Univ Victoria Coll Pharm, 381 Royal Parade, Parkville Vic 3052, Australia

CROSBY, JOHN O'HEA, conductor, opera manager; b. N.Y.C., July 12, 1926; s. Laurence Alden and Aileen Mary (O'Hea) C. Grad., Hotchkiss Sch., 1944; BA, Yale U., 1950, DFA (hon.), 1991; LittD (hon.), U. N.Mex., 1967; MusD (hon.), Coll. of Santa Fe, 1968, Cleve. Inst. Music, 1974; LHD (hon.), U. Denver, 1977. pres. Manhattan Sch. Music, 1976-86. Accompanist, opera coach, condr., N.Y.C., 1951-56, founder, gen. dir., mem. conducting staff Santa Fe Opera, 1957-2000; guest condr. various opera cos. in U.S. and Can. and Europe, 1967—; condr. U.S. stage premiere Daphne, 1964; U.S. profl. premier Friedenstag, 1988; world premiere Wuthering Heights, 1958. With inf. AUS, 1944-46, ETO. Recipient Nat. Medal of Arts, 1991, Verdienstkreuz 1st klasse Bundesrepublik, Deutschland, 1992. Roman Catholic. Office: PO Box 2408 Santa Fe NM 87504-2408

CROSBY, LYNN A., business developer, owner. BS, Middle Tenn. State Univ., 1979. Registered massage therapist. Regional contract negotiator Fairchild Test Systems, Plano, Tex., 1979-87; regional sales GTE Directories, Irving, Tex., 1987-90; pres. Lynn A. Crosby Assocs., Dallas, 1990—; capital regional dir. Jaden Fabrics, Inc., Dallas, 1999—. Massage therapist Pan Am Games, Winnipeg, Can.,1999. Mem. Nat. Exec. Women in Hospitality (cfo 1999—), Am. Massage Therapy Assn. Avocations: equine, opera, theater, museums, charity. Office: PMB 441 5521 Greenville Ave Ste 104 Dallas TX 75206-2940

CROSBY, RALPH WOLF, communications executive; b. Annapolis, Md., Dec. 16, 1933; s. Raymond Thomas and Lillian Sylvia (Wolf) C.; m. Carlotta Stafford, June 16, 1958; children: Laura Crosby Avallone, Raymond, Belinda Crosby Butler. BS in Journalism, U Md., 1956. Reporter, editor Balt. News-Am., 1956-60; bur. editor Iron Age Mag., Washington, 1960-65, Med. Econs. mag., Washington, 1966-67; assoc. editor Kiplinger's Changing Times, Washington, 1967-70; exec. v.p. Annapolis Harbour House, Inc., 1970-86; pres. Crosby Mktg. Comm., Annapolis, 1972—; owner Severn Valley Racquet Club, Millersville, Md.; bd. dirs. Annapolis Bank and Trust Co. Editor (book) Person to Person Management, 1966; contbr. articles to numerous mags. including N.Y. Times Mag. Recipient Jesse H. Neal editorial award, 1966. Mem. Md. Direct Mktg. Assn., Advt. Assn. Balt., Greater Annapolis C. of C. (pres. 1975-76), Annapolis Bus. Coalition (pres. 1983-84), U. Md. Colonnade Soc. (nat. chair 1994-95), Nat. Press Club, Annapolis Touchdown Club (pres. 1976), U. Md. Dean's First Edit. Club (chmn. 1986—), Annapolitan Club. Democrat. Avocation: tennis. Home: 139 Wallace Manor Rd Edgewater MD 21037-1205 Office: Crosby Mktg Comms 705 Melvin Ave Ste 200 Annapolis MD 21401-1544

CROSBY, THOMAS W., computer scientist; b. Boston, Apr. 17, 1942; s. Thomas W. and Dorothy Crosby. AA, Dean Jr. Coll., 1962; BA, Mich. State U., 1964; MBA, Babson Coll., 1980. From software engr. to mgr. corp. advanced tech. lab. Data Gen., Westboro, Mass., 1974—. Mem. IEEE, VFW, Vets of Vietnam. Office: Data General Corp 4400 Computer Dr Westborough MA 01580-0001

CROSBY, WILLIAM DUNCAN, JR., lawyer; b. Louisville, Sept. 1, 1943; s. William Duncan and Lucille (Edwards) C.; m. Constance Elaine Frederick, June 2, 1973; children: William Duncan III, Lelia Margaret. BA, Yale U., 1965; JD, Columbia U., 1968. Bar: Ky. 1968, U.S. Dist. Ct. D.C. 1971, U.S. Supreme Ct. 1977. Minority chief counsel Com. on Rules U.S. Ho. of Reps., Washington, 1972-94, chief counsel Com. on Rules, 1995-99; v.p., COO The Solomon Group, Washington, 1999—. Chmn. Dranesville Dist., Fairfax County (Va.) Rep. Party, 1987-89; mem. Fairfax County Rep. Com., 1981—. Lt. (j.g.) USNR, 1968-71. Mem. ABA, FBA, Ky. Bar Assn., D.C. Bar, Columbia Law Sch. Alumni Assn. of Washington (pres. 1987-89). Baptist. Avocation: swimming. Home: 920 Mackall Ave Mc Lean VA 22101-1618 Office: The Solomon Group 801 Pennsylvania Ave NW Ste 750 Washington DC 20004-2670

CROSIGNANI, PAOLO, epidemiologist, researcher; b. Novara, Piedmont, Italy, July 21, 1948; s. Pietro Crosignani and Anna Cuciz; m. Enza Familiari; 1 child, Silvia. D Physics, U. Milan, 1972, D Medicine, 1987, PhD in Stats., 1992. Rschr. Inst. Physiology, U. Milan, 1972-76, rschr. Inst. Surgery, 1976-78; rschr. divsn. epidemiology Nat. Cancer Inst., Milan, 1978—. Editor: Tobacco Observatory, 1998. Lt. aeronautics br. Italian Army, 1975. Avocation: jurying sailing races. Office: Nat Cancer Inst, 1 Venezian Rd, I-20133 Milan Italy

CROSIO, STEFANO, lawyer; b. Genoa, Italy, May 1, 1969; s. Giovanni and Marisa (Zanotta) C. JD, U. Genoa, Italy, 1993. Atty. Alpa-Galletto Law Firm, Genoa, 1993; ensign Italian Navy, Rome, 1993-94; atty. Gianni, Origoni & Ptnrs., Rome, 1994—, acting in-house counsel, 1997-99; internat. assoc. Simpson Thacher & Bartlett, N.Y., 1999-2000. Mem. Italian Bar, Internat. Assn. Young Lawyers. Avocations: theater, cinema, golf, skiing. Office: Gianni Origoni & Ptnrs, Via Delle Quattro Fontane 20, 00184 Rome Italy

CROSS, DEWITTE TALMADGE, III, physician, neuroradiologist; b. Birmingham, Ala., Feb. 28, 1953; s. DeWitte T. Jr. and Virginia G. Cross; m. Anne Haney, Apr. 19, 1980; children: Courtney Elizabeth, Kevin Andrew. BA, Vanderbilt U., 1975; MD, U. Ala., 1980. Diplomate Am. Bd. Radiology. Commd. ensign USN, 1976, advanced through gardes to lt. commdr., 1987; intern, gen. med. officer USN, San Diego and N.Y.C., 1980-82; residency in radiology Nat. Navel Med. Ctr., Bethesda, Md., 1982-85; head radiology Naval Hosp., Memphis, 1985-87; fellow in neuroradiology N.Y. Med. Coll., N.Y.C., 1987-88; fellow in neuroradiology Columbia U., N.Y.C., 1988-89, asst. prof., 1989-91; dir. interventional neuroradiology Washington U., St. Louis, 1991—; chmn. radiation safety oversight com. Barnes-Jewish Hosp., St. Louis, 1998—. Contbr. author: Abram's Angiography, 1996; contbr. articles to profl. jours. Mem. coun. City of Clayton, Mo., 1998-2000, mem. neighborhood coun. Named one of the Best Doctors in Am., Ctrl. Region, Woodward and White, 1996-97, 1998-99. Mem. AMA, Am. Soc. Interventional and Therapeutic Neuroradiology, Am. Soc. Neuroradiology, Am. Coll. Radiology, Radiol. Soc. N.Am. Presbyterian. Avocations: exercise, classic movies, photography, shortwave radio, cars. E-mail: crossDE@mir.wustl.edu. Office: Washington U Med Ctr Dept Radiology 510 S Kings Hwy Saint Louis MO 63110

CROSS, EDWIN NORMAN, book publisher; b. London, Apr. 3, 1951; s. Gerald Norman and Hermana (von Bohlen) C.; m. Marylon Elizabeth Price, Oct. 28, 1972; children: Pieter Nathanael, Simon Bartholomew, Elizabeth. Indsl. therapist Local Authority, London; founder, pub., trustee Chapter Two, London, 1976—; evangelist, 1976—. Author, editor Truth & Testimony Mag., 1991—. Mem. Plymouth Brethren. Home and Office: Chapter Two, Fountain House 1a Conduit Rd, London SE18 7AJ, England

CROSS, KENDALL, Olympic athlete; b. Hardin, Mont., Feb. 24, 1968. BA in Bus. Econs., Okla. State U., 1992. mem. U.S. Olympic Team, 2000. Recipient Gold medal 125.5 freestyle wrestling Atlanta Olympics, 1996; winner NCAA Championships, 1989, Olympic Team Trials, 1992, U.S. Nats., 1992, 95-96, Sunkist Internat. Open, 1990-91, 94-95, Krasnoyarsk Tournament, 1992, Mich. Internat. Open, 1995, Roger Coulon Tournament, 1996, 3rd place Sunkist Internat. Open, 1993; named Outstanding Freestyle Wrestler U.S. Nats., 1992, 95. Avocations: mountain biking, rollerblading, reading, yoga. Office: USA Wrestling 6155 Lehman Dr Colorado Springs CO 80918*

CROSS, MILTON H., lawyer; b. Phila., July 28, 1942; s. Sidney B. and Edythe Cross; m. Joyce Volchok, June 4, 1966; children: Brian, Jonathon. BS, U. San Francisco, 1965; JD, Villanova U., 1968. Bar: Pa. 1968. Corp. counsel AEL, Inc., Phila., 1968-75; assoc. Cohen, Verlin, Sherzer & Porter, Phila., 1975-78; pvt. practice Phila., 1978-79; ptnr. Monteverde & Hemphill, Phila., 1980-96, Spector, Gadon & Rosen, Phila., 1996—; adj. prof. Phila. Coll. Textiles and Sci., 1970-73. Chmn. Cheltenham Twp. Sch. Bd. Authority. Mem. ABA (sect. corp., banking and bus. law), Pa. Bar Assn., Phila. Bar Assn. Home: 251 Ironwood Cir Elkins Park PA

19027-1315 Office: Spector Gadon & Rosen 7 Penn Ctr Fl 7 Philadelphia PA 19103-2200

CROSS, PIPPA JANE, film company executive; b. Ipswich, Eng., May 13, 1956; d. Robert Lionel and Jill Patricia (Abbott) Cross; m. Graham R. Lee, Apr. 12, 1982; children: Maisie, Pierrot. BA with 1st class honors in English, Oxford (Eng.) U., 1977. Entertainment mgr. Wembley Conf. Ctr., London, 1977-80; drama planning mgr. Granada TV, Manchester, Eng., 1980-85; factual dept. mgr. TVS, Maidstone, Eng., 1985-88; head of devel. Granada Prodns., London, 1988-93, head of film, 1993—; dir. Brit. Screen, London. Prodr. August, 1995, Jack and Sarah, 1998; exec. prodr. Rogue Trader, 1999, Essex Boys, 1999, House of Mirth, 1999, Longitude, 1999; prodn. exec. My Left Foot, 1990, The Field, 1991. Office: Granada Film, London TV Ctr/Upper Ground, London SE1 9LT, England

CROSS, RODNEY BRUCE, economics educator; b. Wigan, U.K., Mar. 27, 1951; s. Sydney and Phyllis (Sharrock) C. BSc in Econs., London Sch. Econs./Polit. Sci., 1971; BPhil, U. York, U.K., 1972. Rsch. asst. U. Manchester, Eng., 1972-74; temp. lectr. Queen Mary Coll. U. London, 1974-75; lectr. U. St. Andrews, Scotland, 1975-90; sr. lectr. U. Strathclyde, Scotland, 1990-95, prof. econs., 1995—; cons. Polish Nat. Bank, Warsaw, 1990-92; Her Majesty's Treas. Acad. Panel, London, 1996—. Author: Economic Theory and Policy in the U.K., 1982 (Martin Robertson); editor: Unemployment, Hysteresis and the Natural Rate Hypothesis, 1988 (Blackwell), The Natural Rate of Unemployment, 1995 (Cambridge U.P.). Avocations: hill walking, rugby league. Office: U Strathclyde Dept Econs Curran Bldg 100 Cathedral, Glasgow G4 0LN, Scotland

CROSS, THEODORE LAMONT, publisher, author; b. Newton, Mass., Feb. 12, 1924; s. Gorham Lamont and Margaret Moore (Warren) C.; m. Sheilah Burr Ross, Sept. 16, 1950 (div. 1972); children: Amanda Burr, Lisa Warren; m. Mary Warner, 1974. Grad., Deerfield Acad., 1942; AB, Amherst Coll., 1946; LLB, Harvard U., 1950. Bar: Mass. 1950, N.Y. 1953. With Hale and Dorr, Boston, 1950-52; chmn. bd., CEO Warren, Gorham & Lamont, Inc., 1980-83; chmn. Faulkner & Gray, Pubs., 1985-92, Hanover Pub., Inc., 1985—; editor in chief Bus. and Soc. Rev., 1971—; editor Jour. of Blacks in Higher Edn., 1993—; cons. HEW, Fed. Office Econ. Opportunity, 1964-69; pub. gov. Am. Stock Exchange, 1972-77; bd. dirs. Inst. for Sci. Info., 1988—; lectr. on inner city econs. and minority econ. devel. Harvard, Cornell U., U. Va. Author: Black Capitalism: Strategy for Business in the Ghetto (McKinsey Found. book award 1969), (with Mary Cross) Behind the Great Wall, 1979, The Black Power Imperative, 1984, Birds of the Sea, Shore and Tundra, 1989; founder: Atomic Energy Law Jour., 1959; editor Harvard Law Rev., 1948-50. Trustee Amherst Coll., chmn. investment com., 1976-88; trustee Folger Shakespeare Libr., Princeton U. Press, Inst. Advanced Study, Nat. Humanities Ctr., John Simon Guggenheim Meml. Found.; mem. Coun. Fgn. Rels.; dir. Legal Def. Fund, NAACP, Century Assn., N.Y.C. With USNR, 1945-46. Mem. Coun. on Fgn. Rels. (treas.), Am. Philos. Soc. Home: 233 Carter Rd Princeton NJ 08540-2104 Office: 200 W 57th St New York NY 10019-3211

CROSSA, JOSÉ, biometrician, researcher; b. Paysandu, Uruguay, Aug. 16, 1946; arrived in Mex., 1984; s. José Eduardo and Sara Margarita C.; m. Yolanda Niell, Feb. 10, 1973; children: Veronica, Nicolas, Aldo, Luciano, Mateo. BSc, U. Uruguay, Montevideo, 1974; PhD, U. Nebr., 1984. Postdoctoral fellow Internat. Maize and Wheat Improvement Ctr., Mex., 1984-86, assoc. scientist, 1986-89, scientist, 1989-90, sr. scientist, 1990—, head biometrics and stats., 1992—. Author chpts. to books; contbr. more than 90 articles to profl. jours. including Crop Sci., Euphytica, Biometrics, Maydica, among others.; assoc. editor Crop Sci., 1995—, Euphytica, 1994—. Mem. Am. Statis. Soc., Am. Soc. Agronomy, Classification Soc. Am., Internat. Biometrics Soc. Home and Office: Apdo Postal 6-641, 06600 Mexico City Mexico

CROSSAN, JOHN ROBERT, lawyer; b. Buchannon, W.Va., May 31, 1947; s. Thomas Benjamin Jr. and Margaret Windsor (Hicks) C.; m. Monique Margaretha Scheen, Dec. 22, 1973; children: Ashley Margaret, Aubry Kelly. BS with honors, U. Va., 1969; JD, U. Chgo., 1974. Bar: Ill. 1974, U.S. Dist. Ct. (no. dist.) Ill. 1974, (ctrl. dist.) Ill. 1998, U.S. Ct. Appeals (4th and 10th cirs.) 1978, U.S. Ct. Appeals (7th cir.) 1979, U.S. Ct. Appeals (fed. cir.) 1983, U.S. Supreme Ct. 1985, U.S. Ct. Appeals (6th cir.) 1989. Staff atty. Ill. Task Force N.E. Ill. Pub. Transp., Chgo., 1972-73; assoc. Hill, Van Santen, Steadman, Chiara, Chgo., 1973-77; assoc., then ptnr. Cook, Wetzel and Egan, Ltd., Chgo., 1978-88; counsel Willian, Brinks, Hofer, Gilson and Lione, Chgo., 1989-90; ptnr. Brinks, Hofer, Gilson & Lione, Chgo., 1991-97, Chapman and Cutler, Chgo., 1998—; dir. Va. Engring. Found., 1996—, v.p. 1998-2000, pres. 2000—. Author: Quick Guide to the Patent Law, 1994; contbr. articles to profl publs. Pres. aux. bd. Chgo. Architecture Found., 1983-85. Mem. ABA, Am. Intellectual Property Lawyers Assn., Chgo. Yacht Club. Home: 2825 N Cambridge Ave Chicago IL 60657-6018 Office: Chapman and Cutler 111 W Monroe St Ste 1700 Chicago IL 60603-4006

CROSSER, CARMEN LYNN, marriage and family therapist, clinical social worker, consultant; b. Iowa Falls, Iowa, Jan. 17, 1970; d. Gary Laverne Sr. and Karen Dorothy (Ulrich) C. AA, Ellsworth C.C., 1990; BS, Iowa State U., 1993; MSW, U. Iowa, 1995; postgrad., U. Chgo., 1998—. Lic. clin. social worker, marriage and family therapist, Ill.; cert. brief therapist, ACSW. Grad. teaching asst. U. Iowa, Iowa City, 1994-95; mental health therapy intern Mid-Eastern Cmty. Mental Health Ctr., Iowa City, 1994-95; clin. social worker Sinnissippi Ctrs., Inc., Dixon, Ill., 1995-97; family therapist Ctr. for Counseling, DeKalb, Ill., 1997—; cons. sexual abuse svcs. Sinnissippi Ctrs. Inc., 1997-98; rsch. asst. U. Chgo., 1998—, tchg. asst., 1999—; revs. asst. Jour. of Marital and Family Therapy, 1999-2000. Mem. DeKalb Area Women's Ctr., 1997—; mem. instnl. rev. bd. No. Ill. U., DeKalb, 1997—. All-Am. scholar, 1995. Mem. ACA, NASW, NOW, Am. Soc. Prevention Cruelty Animals (voting mem.), Am. Assn. Marriage and Family Therapy (clin. mem.), Am. Coll. Counselors, Internat. Assn. Marriage and Family Counselors, Ill. Soc. Clin. Social Work, Assn. Play Therapy, Nat. Fedn. Socs. for Clin. Social Work, Golden Key, Phi Kappa Phi, Phi Alpha. Office: Ctr for Counseling 14 Health Svcs Dr Dekalb IL 60115

CROSSLEY, RICHARD JULIAN SPENCER, retired mathematics educator; b. London, May 1, 1938; s. John Walter Haigh and Margery Phyllis (May) C. BA, Oxford (Eng.) U., 1960, PhD, 1964. Sr. rsch. assoc. Queen's U. of Belfast, Northern Ireland, 1962-64, 66-67; NSF rsch. fellow Harvard U., Cambridge, Mass., 1964-66; lectr. U. York, Eng., 1967-92; ret., 1992. Contbr. articles to profl. publs. Mem. concerts com. York U., 1982—. Mem. Inst. Physics, Royal Musical Assn., Brit. Music Soc. of York (various offices 1970—), Nat. Fedn. Music Socs. (mem. com. 1990—), London Math. Soc., Brit. Soc. History of Math. Avocations: public transport, history of science. Home: 9 Arncliffe Mews, York YO10 4EL, England

CROSSLEY, THOMAS ROGER, manufacturing systems engineer, consultant; b. London, Apr. 28, 1939; s. Thomas and Margery (Downham) C.; m. Beryl Jackson, July 12, 1963; 1 child, Anthony Martin. BSc (Engr.) in Aero. Engring., U. London, 1961; PhD in Control Sys., U. Salford, 1969. Apprentice Bristol (Eng.) Aeroplane Co., 1957-61; engr. Brit. Aircraft Corp., Preston, 1961-64; lectr. U. Salford, 1964-71, sr. lectr., reader, 1972-79, prof., 1980-97; dir. AMTeC, Macclesfield, 1984-88; mng. dir. Synektikos Ltd., Bolton, 1978—. Co-author: (with B. Porter) Modal Control: Theory & Application, 1972. Cadet Pilot Officer RAFVR, 1958-61. Fellow Royal Aero. Soc., Instn. Elec. Engrs. Avocation: golf. E-mail: roger.crossley@btinternet.com. Home: 18 St Leonards Ave Lostock, Bolton Greater Manchester BL6 4JE, England

CROSSLEY-HOLLAND, KEVIN (JOHN WILLIAM), poet, children's writer; b. 1941. Editor Macmillan & Co., Pubs., London, 1962-69; Gregory fellow in poetry, 1969-71; talks prodr. BBC, London, 1972; editorial dir. Victor Gollancz, Pubs., Ltd., London, 1972-77; editorial cons. Boydell and Brewer, Ltd., 1983-89; prof. humanities and fine arts U. St. Thomas, Minn., 1991-95; vis. prof. English St. Olaf Coll., Minn., 1987, 88, Fulbright scholar, 1989. Author: Havelok the Dane, 1964, King Horn, 1965, The Green Children, 1966, The Callow Pit Coffer, 1968, Beowulf, 1968, (with Jill Paton Walsh) Wordhoard, 1969, Norfolk Poems, 1970, The Pedlar of Swaffham, 1972, Pieces of Land: Journeys to Eight Islands, 1972, The Rain-Giver and Other Poems, 1972, The Sea-Stranger, 1973, The Fire-Brother, 1974, Green Blades Rising: The Anglo-Saxons, 1975, The Wildman, 1976, The Dream-House, 1976, The Norse Myths, 1981, Between My Father and My Son, 1982, The Dead Moon, 1982, Beowulf, 1982, Time's Oriel, 1983, (with Gwyn Thomas) Tales from the Mabinogion, 1984, Axe-Age, Wolf-Age: A Selection for Children from the Norse Myths, 1985, Storm, 1985, Waterslain and Other Poems, 1986, British Folk Tales, 1987, (with Gwyn Thomas) The Quest for Olwen, 1988, Wulf, 1988, Old English Elegies, 1988, The Painting-Room, 1988, Under the Sun and Over the Moon, 1989, Sleeping Nanna, 1989, East Anglian Poems, 1989, The Stones Remain, 1989, (with Gwyn Thomas) The Tale of Taliesin, 1992, The Labours of Herakles, 1993, New and Selected Poems, 1965-1990, 1991, Sea Tongue, 1991, Tales from Europe, 1991, Long Tom and the Dead Hand, 1992, (libretto) The Wildman, 1995, The Language of Yes, 1996, Short!, 1998, Poems from East Anglia, 1997, The Old Stories, Tales from East Anglia and the Fen Country, 1997, (Drama) The Wuffings, 1997, The King Who Was and Will Be, 1998, The Seeing Stone, 2000, Enchantment, 2000, Selected Poems, 2000; translator: The Battle of Maldon and Other Old English Poems, 1965, Storm and Other Old English Riddles, 1970, The Exeter Book of Riddles, 1978, The Anglo-Saxon World, 1982; editor: Running to Paradise: An Introductory Selection of the Poems of W. B. Yeats, 1968, Winter's Tales for Children 3, 1969, The Faber Book of Northern Legends, 1977, The Faber Book of Northern Folk-Tales, 1980, The Riddle Book, 1982, Folk-Tales of the British Isles, 1985, Oxford Book of Travel Verse, 1986, Northern Lights: Legends, Sagas and Folk-Tales, 1987, Medieval Lovers, 1988, Medieval Gardens, 1990, The Young Oxford Book of Folk Tales, 1998. Fellow Royal Soc. Lit. Office: Clare Cottage, Burnham Market, Norfolk PE31 8HE, England

CROTEAU, DENIS, bishop; b. Thetford Mines, Que., Can., Oct. 23, 1932. Ordained priest Roman Cath. Ch., 1958. Bishop Diocese MacKenzie/Ft. Smith, Yellowknife, N.W.T., Can., 1986—. Office: Evêché, 5117 52d St, Yellowknife, NT Canada X1A 1T7

CROTTI, DANIELE, medical microbiologist; b. Milan, Jan. 8, 1948; s. Argento and Serena (Luzzeri) C.; m. Giovanna Fonzo; children: Luca, Silvia, Marco. MD, U. Perugia, Italy, 1973, specialization in hygiene, pub. health, 1989; specialization in immuno-hematology, U. Pisa, Italy, 1977; specialization in microbiology, U. Milan, 1982. Asst. dir. Civil Hosp., San Severino, Italy, 1978, Matelica, Italy, 1978-79, asst. dir. Civil Hosp., Gorizia, Italy, 1979-81, assoc. dir., 1981-87; assoc. dir. Civil Hosp., Gualdo, Italy, 1987-88, Pub. Health Provincial Lab., Perugia, 1988-89; WHO agreement prof. U. Asmara-Eritrea, Italy, 1997-98; asst. dir. Regional Hosp., Perugia, 1974-78, assoc. dir., 1989-97, 98—. Author: Aspetti Attuali Nella Diagnosi delle Infezioni Intestinali, 1997; co-author: Element di diagnostica Parassitologica, 1994, Microbiologia per I Piccoli Laboratori, 1999; contbr. or co-contbr. over 200 articles to profl. publs. gen. practitioner Medicina Democratica, Lebanon, 1976; parasitologist UNICEF, Albania, 1997; vol. clin. microbiologist, Malawi, 1993-95; vol. parasitologist, Eritrea, 1997. Mem. ASM, ESCMID, Italian Assn. Clin. Microbiologists (nat. counsellor 1991-96, head COSP 1996—, award for Congress poster 1996). Home: Pianello, Via Pilonico Paterno 4, 06131 Perugia Italy Office: R Silvestri Hosp, San Sisto, Via 9 Dottori SNC, 06132 Perugia Italy

CROTTY, ROBERT BELL, lawyer; b. Dallas, Aug. 16, 1951; s. Willard and Betty (Bell) C.; m. Sarah Smith, Mar. 8, 1980; children: Robert Edwin, Rebecca Bell. BA, Va. Mil. Inst, 1973; JD, U. Tex., 1976. Bar: Tex. 1976, U.S. Dist. Ct. (no. dist.) Tex. 1977, U.S. Ct. Appeals (5th cir.) 1978. Assoc. Akin, Gump, Strauss, Hauer & Feld, Dallas, 1976-82, ptnr., 1983-92, hiring ptnr., 1988-91; prin. McKool Smith, P.C., Dallas, 1992-94; ptnr. Crotty & Johansen, L.L.P., Dallas, 1995—; bd. visitors Va. Mil. Inst., 1995-99. Mem. Leadership Dallas, 1981; dir. Salesmanship Club, 1989-90, 94-95, Va. Mil. Inst. Alumni Assn., 1991-95, Highland Park Ind. Sch. Dist. Edn. Found., 1991-97, pres. 1997—; chmn. GTE Byron Nelson Classic, 1995; pres. Dallas Bus. League, 1983, Big Bros./Big Sisters Met. Dallas, 1987-88; deacon North Dallas Bible Ch., 1989-95. 1st lt. U.S. Army, 1976, USAR, 1973-81. Fellow Tex. Bar Found. (life), Dallas Bar Found., Dallas Bar Found. Fellows (pres. 1999—); mem. Dallas Bar Assn., Tex. Law Rev. Assn. (life), State Bar Tex. Avocations: golf, reading, rock climbing, hiking. Office: Crotty & Johansen LLP 2311 Cedar Springs Rd Ste 250 Dallas TX 75201-7810

CROTTY GUILE, JULIANNE MARIE, musician, composer, writer; b. Omaha, Mar. 13, 1956; d. Richard and Beverly Ruth (Dillon) Crotty; m. Peter John Guile. BA, NYU, 1986; MA in Eng., U. Nebr., 1992. Singer Western Austrian Opera, Perth, 1987-88; prof. English and humanities Coll. St. Mary's, Omaha, 1989-92, U. Nebr., Buena Vista, Iowa, 1989-92, Metro C.C., Buena Vista, Iowa, 1989-96; dir. Noteworthy Music, Omaha, 1992—. Composer Crest of Cedar, 1994 (music award 1996); poet, author: Love From The Inside Out, 1988 (poetry award 1989). Counsel Boys Town Nat., Omaha, 1994; telephonist Pro Life, Omaha, 1998—; fund raiser New Cassel Retirement Home, Omaha, 1998—. Recipient Stuart Creativity award Duchesne Acad., Omaha, 1974. Mem. Nat. Music Tchrs. Assn. (Omaha chpt.), Crook House. Avocations: sailing, walking, swimming. E-mail: jcrottyg@aol.com.

CROUCHER, JOHN, statistician, educator; b. Sydney, NSW, Australia, Apr. 11, 1947; s. Sydney Ross and Phyllis May (Taylor) C.; m. Lynn Margaret Stevens, Dec. 4, 1970 (div. 1989); children: Joanne, Amy; m. Kay Amos, Sept. 9, 1989. BA with hons., Macquarie U., NSW, Australia, 1970; MS, U. Minn., 1972, PhD, 1973. Actuarial clk. M.L.C. Life Assurance Co., Sydney, 1963-67; teaching assoc. U. Minn., Mpls., 1971-73; prof. stats. Macquarie U., Sydney, 1974—; cons. various cos., Sydney, 1975—, Totalisator Agy. Bd., Sydney, 1985-93; sports journalist Fairfax Media Orgn., Sydney, 1984-86; TV presenter Channel 10 TV Network, Sydney, 1985—; dir. Croucher Cons. Svcs. pty., Ltd., 1992—; chmn. Responsible Gaming Com. of NSW. Author: Elementary Statistics for Business, 1977, Statistics: An Introduction, 1980, Operations Research: A First Course, 1982, Statistics: A Modern Introduction for Business and Management, 1986, Introductory Mathematics and Statistics for Business, 1989, Exam Scams, 1996, Great Frauds and Everyday Scams, 1997, Introductory Mathematics and Statistics for Business, 3rd edit., 1998; contbr. articles to profl. jours. Ruth Cumming scholar, English Speaking Union, 1970, travel scholar P&O Shipping Lines, Sydney, 1970; grantee NSW Dept. Sport and Recreation, 1986. Mem. Ops. Research Soc. Australia, Australian Math. Soc. Avocations: tennis, squash, cricket, bushwalking.

CROUCHER, PAUL HAROLD, optometrist, educator; b. Sydney, Australia, Feb. 19, 1960; s. Donald Gordon and Joan Mary (Milne) C. BS, U. Melbourne, 1984, BS in Optometry, 1984. Optometrist Melbourne, 1985—; clin. instr. Victorian Coll. Optometry, Melbourne, 1995-98; lectr. U. Melbourne, 1995—, U. NSW, Sydney, 1994—; Victorian State Dir., ACBO, Australia, 1990-93, nat. sec., 1994-98, nat. pres., 1998—. Fellow Victorian Coll. Optometry, Australia Coll. Behavorial Optometry, Coll. of Vision Devel. Home: 10 Nalinga Ct, 3134 Warranwood Australia Office: Howell Croucher & Assoc, 204 Canterbury Rd, 3135 Heathmont Australia

CROUÏGNEAU, FRANÇOISE, deputy editor; b. Chambery, France, Dec. 15, 1944; d. Pierre and Andrée Blanche (Valour) Henrion; m. Marc Crouïgneau, Apr. 16, 1966; children: Ivan, Nicolas. Propedeutique, Sorbonne, Paris, 1962; M in Communication, Sorbonne, 1966. Specialist internat. econs. Les Echos, Paris, 1968-85, dep. editor, 1989—; internat. econs. specialist Le Monde, Paris, 1985-89, 1985-89. Decorated Chevalier de l'Ordre Nat. du Mérite, 1995. Mem. Assn. Journalistes Économiques et Financiers (v.p. 1983-85). Avocations: music, gardening, theater, classic dance. Office: Les Echos, La Boétie 46, 75008 Paris France

CROUTHAMEL, THOMAS GROVER, SR., editor; b. Berkeley, Calif., Sept. 10, 1930; s. Martin Luther and Elizabeth (Grover) C.; m. Madalene Donati, Sept. 6, 1954; children: Thomas Grover Jr., Annalise. BS, Thiel Coll., 1953. Sr. drug investigator FDA, L.A. and Edison, N.J., 1958-81; pres. Thomas G. Crouthamel, Inc., Bradenton, Fla., 1981—; ptnr. Crouthamel & Crouthamel, Bradenton, 1983-93; treas. Crouthamel Enterprises, Inc., Liberty Hill, Tex., 1986-92; sr. editor Keystone Press, Bradenton, 1982—. Author: Auditing EtO, 1982, It's OK, 1986, A History of Trailer Estates, 1987; When the Unthinkable Happens, 1995; contbr. articles to profl. jours. Cubmaster Boy Scouts Am., Pomona, Calif., 1963, committeeman, Spotswood, N.J., 1968-76, adult adviser Explorer Post, 1976-79; trustee Spotswood Libr. Bd., 1970-79; co-leader Compassionate Friends, Sarasota, Fla., 1984-90, chpt. advisor, facilitator, Englewood, Fla., 1989-91. With U.S. Army, 1953-55. Mem. Parenteral Drug Assn., Internat. Narcotics Officers Assn., The Authors Guild, AAAS, Toastmasters (pres. 1969-71), Masons (high priest local chpt. 1967). Avocations: travel, reading, fishing. Office: PO Box 6163 Bradenton FL 34281-6163

CROUZET, JOËL JEAN, research scientist; b. Cauderan, France, July 12, 1958; s. Francois Marie and Francoise Marie (Dabert) D.; m. Benedicte Marie Semon, July 2, 1982; children: Timothee, Benjamin, Sixtine, Alix. Agrl. engr., Inst. Nat. Agronomique, France, 1982, PhD in Microbiology, 1987; entitled to supr. rsch., U. Paris VII, 1995. Cert. assoc. rsch. dir. Rsch. scientist Genetica, Joinville-Ce-Pont, France, 1983-85, sr. rsch. scientist, 1985-88; sr. rsch. fellow Rhône Poulenc Rorer, Vitry-sur-Seine, France, 1988-94, dept. mgr. molecular microbiology, 1994-96, dept. dir. vector devel., 1996-97, dir. vector devel., 1997-99; sr. rsch. fellow Rhône-Poulenc, Coubevoie, France, 1996-99, sr. rsch. adviser, 1987-96; dir. AP Cells, SA, 1999-2000; dir. of rsch. Neurotech S.A. Inventor in field; contbr. articles to profl. jours. Sci. officer French Navy, 1982-83. Recipient Doistau-Blutet award French Acad. Scis., 1992. Mem. Am. Soc. Microbiology, Soc. Indsl. Microbiology, French Soc. Microbiology. Avocations: gardening, jogging. Home: 12 Rue Michel Voisin, 92330 Sceaux France Office: Neurotech SA, 4 rue Pierre Fontaine, 91000 Enry France

CROUZET, M.-J. MICHEL, educator; b. Nantes, France, Jan. 7, 1928. Student, Ecole Normale Superieure, 1948. Prof. U. Sorbonne, 1983—. Author: Stendhal et le langage, La poétique de Stendhal, tomes I et II, Nature et Société chez Stendhal, Le héros fourbe chez Stendhal, Monsieur Moi-même, ou la vie de Stendhal, La Route et le noir, essai sur la romanesque stendhalien, La Chartreuse de Parme, le roman stendhalien, Lucien Leuwen, le mentir vrai de Stendhal; contbr. numerous books and articles on Stendhal, Modern French Lit. and critical theory. Office: U Sorbonne, 1 rue Victor Cousin, 75005 Paris France

CROVELLA, CARLO UMBERTO, financial markets analyst, consultant; b. Moncalieri, Turin, Italy, Aug. 7, 1961; s. Umberto and Rita (Turio) C.; m. Elena Barni, Aug. 10, 1968; children: Camilla, Giovanni. Degree in econs., U. Turin, 1987. Fin. analyst ERSEL, Turin, 1987-89; editor, analyst CFS/Econs., Milan, 1990-91; chief analyst, editor ARITMA, Turin, 1992—, also bd. dirs.; prof. fin. U. Herisaü., 1998—; prof. fin. investments and assets mgmt. U. Herisau, 1999—. Contbr. articles to profl. jours. including Rivista della Montagna. Mem. Italian Corp. Treasuries Assn., Italian Fin. Analysts Assn., Italian Climbing Club. Avocations: skiing, climbing, canyoning, kayaking. Home: via Principe Tommaso n 37, Turin Italy Office: ARITMA, Corso Galileo Ferraris n 71, 10128 Turin Italy

CROW, JOHN ARMSTRONG, writer, educator; b. Wilmington, N.C., Dec. 18, 1906; s. George Davis and Olive Lois (Armstrong) C.; m. Josephine Gorden, 1956; children: Diane O., John Armstrong. A.B., U. of N.C., 1927; M.A., Columbia, 1930; Ph. D., Litt.D., U. of Madrid, Spain, 1933. Instr. U. N.C., 1926-27, Davidson Coll., N.C., 1927-28, N.Y.U., 1928-37; instr. U. Calif., Los Angeles, 1937—; chmn. Spanish dept. U. Calif., 1949-54; Helped organize Internat. Inst. of Ibero-Am. Literature, Mexico City, 1938, sec., 1938-40; chmn. Sect. of Cultural Exchange, 1940—. Author: Federico Garcia Lorca, 1945, Panorama de las Americas, 1997, 8 other edits., Epic of Latin America, 1946, 4th edit., 1992, California As a Place to Live, 1953, Mexico Today, 1957, 92, Spanish American Life, 1963, Spain—The Root and the Flower, 1963, 85, Italy: a Journey Through Time, 1965, Greece: the Magic Spring, 1970, An Anthology of Spanish Poetry, 1979, others; editor Latin Am. entries and revs. to Ency. Americana, 1942; co-editor Jour. Revista Iberonamericana; contbr. articles on lit., history, art, dancing to leading mags. U.S. and Latin Am. also encys. Mem. Soc. Mayflower, Authors League Am., Desc. Knights of Garter, Order of Don Quixote, Phi Beta Kappa. Home: 218 N Bundy Dr Los Angeles CA 90049-2826

CROW, JOHN DOWNING, United States Army officer; b. Nov. 18, 1973. BS, U.S. Mil. Acad., 1996. Tank platoon leader U.S. Army, Camp Casey, Korea, 1996-97, battalion liaison officer, 1997; co. exec. officer U.S. Army, Ft. Knox, Ky., 1997—.

CROW, LAURA JEAN, design educator, costume designer; b. Hanover, N.H., Sept. 29, 1945; d. James Franklin and Rebecca Ann (Crockett) C.; m. Daniel Caine, Apr. 28, 1980 (div. Mar. 1987); children: Sarah Katherine, Matthew Jordan Caine. BFA, Boston U., 1967; MFA, U. Wis., 1969; postgrad., U. London, 1969-70, Courtauld Inst., 1969-70. Lectr. Brandeis U., Waltham, Mass., 1985; assoc. prof. U. Mass., Amherst, 1986-87, U. Mich., Ann Arbor, 1987-94; prof. U. Conn., Storrs, 1994—; active NEA Theatre Comms. Group, Washington and N.Y.C., 1998; adjudicator young designer's forum U.S. Inst. for Tech. Theatre, 1988-99; U.S. rep. to OISTAT, 1999—. Costume designer: (Broadway prodns.) Warp, Sweet Bird of Youth, The Water Engine, Fifth of July, Burn This, The Seagull, Redwood Curtain, (off-Broadway prodns.) The Farm, Winter Signs, Hamlet, A Tale Told, Orchards, Brilliant Traces, Raft of Medusa, Cakewalk, Sympathetic Magic, others, (films) Harry and the Hendersons, Fifth of July, The Lathe of Heaven, Charlie Smith & the Fritter Tree; designer regional theaters including Seattle Rep, ACT, Hartford Stage, Goodman Theatre, Milw. Rep., Berkeley Rep., Ariz. Theatre Co., Mark Taper Forum, Arena Stage, Alley Theatre, Long Wharf Theatre, Hartford Stage, Old Globe Theatre, Asolo Theatre, Ctr. Stage. Recipient Drama Desk award N.Y. Drama Critics, 1973, Joseph Jefferson award Jeff Com., Chgo., 1975, 76, 77, 78, 88, Obie award Village Voice, 1980, Am. Theatre Wing award, 1980, 97, Dramalogue award L.A. Drama Critics, 1988, 97, Backstage West award, 1997, San Francisco Bay Area Critics award, 1998, Zoni award Phoenix Drama Critics, 1998, 99. Mem. United Scenic Artists, U.S. Inst. Theatre Tech. Fax: 860-486-3110. E-mail: laura.crow@uconn.edu. Home: 88 Hillyndale Rd Storrs Mansfield CT 06268-1802 Office: U of Conn Dept Dramatic Arts 802 Bolton Rd Storrs Mansfield CT 06269-1127

CROWDER, GEORGE ERROL, political philosophy educator; b. Wellington, New Zealand, Feb. 27, 1956; arrived in Australia, 1995; s. Ernest Clifford and Gudbjorg (Arnadottir) C.; m. Maria Weston Merritt, Mar. 1, 1989 (div. 1994). LLB (hons), Victoria U., Wellington, New Zealand, 1977, BA, 1980, BA (hons), 1981; DPhil, U. Coll. Oxford, 1988. New Zealand law profl. cert. Investigating officer Wanganui Computer Ctr. Privacy Commr., Wellington, 1978; legal advisor Justice Dept., Wellington, 1978-80; tutor U. Coll. Oxford, 1985-90; adj. asst. prof. Calif. State U., Fullerton, 1991, Baruch Coll. CUNY, 1993-94, Hunter Coll. CUNY, 1994; lectr. Flinders U. South Australia, Adelaide, 1995—; instr. New Sch. Social Rsch., N.Y., 1994-95. Author: Classical Anarchism, 1991; contbr. articles to profl. jours. Recipient Commonwealth scholarship Assn. Commonwealth Univs., 1982-85; Rsch. grantee Brit. Acad., 1989. Mem. Australasian Polit. Studies Assn. (treas. 1996-98). Avocations: squash, swimming, cricket. Office: Flinders Univ S Australia Sch Pol Internat Studies, GPO Box 2100, 5001 Adelaide Australia

CROWE, WILLIAM JAMES, JR., educator, international consultant; b. La Grange, Ky., Jan. 2, 1925; s. William James and Eula (Russell) C.; m. Shirley Mary Grennell, Feb. 14, 1954; children: William Blake, James Brent, Mary Russell. BS, U.S. Naval Acad., 1946; MA in Edn., Stanford U., 1956; PhD in Politics (Harold W. Dodds fellow), Princeton U., 1965. Commd. ensign U.S. Navy, 1946, advanced through grades to adm.; comdg. officer U.S.S. Trout, 1960-62; comdr. Submarine Div. 31 San Diego, 1966-67; sr. adviser Vietnamese Navy, 1970-71; dep. to Pres.'s Spl. Rep. for Micronesian Status Negotiations, 1971-73; dep. dir. strategic plans CNO Staff, 1973-75; dir. East Asia and Pacific region Office of Sec. of Def. Washington, until 1976; comdr. Middle East Force Bahrain, 1976-77; dep. chief naval ops. plans and policy Washington, 1977-80; comdr.-in-chief Allied Forces So. Europe, 1980-83, comdr.-in-chief Pacific, 1983-85; chmn. Joint Chiefs of Staff, 1985-89; prof. geopolitics U. Okla., Norman, 1989-94; chmn. Fgn. Intelligence Adv. Bd., Washington, DC, 1993-94; U.S. amb. to U.K. London, 1994-97; counselor Ctr. for Strategic and Internat. Studies, Washington, 1989-94; prof. U. Okla., 1989-94. Author: Line of Fire, 1993; co-author: Reducing Nuclear Danger: The Road Away from the Brink, 1993; author supr. ops. plan for repatriation of U.S.S. Pueblo crew. Trustee Princeton U., 1995-2000; dir. USNA Found., 1998—. Decorated Defense DSM with three oak leaf clusters (Dept. Def.), Navy DSM with two oak leaf clusters (USN), DSM (U.S. Army, USAF, USCG), Legion of Merit, Bronze

Star with combat V, Air medal with six oak leaf clusters. Mem. U.S. Naval Inst., Am. Polit. Sci. Assn., Internat. Studies Assn., Coun. on Fgn. Rels., Washington Inst. Fgn. Affairs, Phi Gamma Delta, Phi Delta Phi. Office: Global Options 1615 L St NW Ste 1350 Washington DC 20036-5655

CROWE-HAGANS, NATONIA, manufacturing executive, engineer; b. Chgo., Feb. 10, 1955; d. Benjamin Kermit and Natalie (Williams) Crowe; m. Louis Fisher (div.); children: Sean Crowe, Tamara Fisher; m. William Hagans. AA, Vets. Hosp., Chgo., 1977; BSEE, U. Ill., Chgo., 1983; MS in Mgmt., Maryville U., 1988. Cert. mgr. Institute of Certified Professional Managers. Cert. mgr. Corning Glass Works, Bluffton, Ind., 1980; intern Corning (N.Y.) Glass Works, 1981-82; assoc. engr. McDonnell Douglas, St. Louis, 1983-84, engr., 1984-85, sr. engr., 1986-87, laser team leader, 1987-88; staff mgr. McDonnell Douglas, Huntington Beach, Calif., 1988-89; mgr. quick response ctr. Loral Electro-optical Sys., Pomona, Calif., 1989, mgr. mfg. svcs., 1989-91, mgr. material control svcs., 1991-92, program mgr., 1992-93; mgr. prodn. Loral Electro-optical Sys., Pomona, 1993-94; mgr. mfg. engr. Rockwell Automation, Allen Bradley, Milw., 1994-97, dir. electromech. ops., 1994-97; dir. ops. overhaul and repair United Techs.-Hamilton Std., Windsor Locks, Conn., 1997—; bd. dirs. Matarah Industries. Mem. Womens Aux., Yorba Linda, Calif., 1989, Illiteracy Com., St. Louis, 1984, PTA, Corona, Calif., 1991. Named to Acad. Women Achievers, 1999. Mem. NAFE, Nat. Soc. Black Engrs. (co-founding mem. Gateway chpt. 1987-88, Svc. award 1988), Nat. Mgmt. Assn. (sec., com. mem., numerous awards 1990), Profl. Dimensions, Assn. Mfg. Excellence, Assn. of Women Achievers. Avocation: writing science fiction. Home: 16 Krystal Ln Windsor CT 06095-2623

CROWELL, KENNETH E., lawyer, chemical engineer; b. Kearny, N.J., Dec. 29, 1957; s. Earl L.S. and Moira Parker (Foster) C.; m. Liliana Mino, June 24, 1990. BS in Biology, Allegheny Coll., 1979; BSChemE, N.J. Inst. Tech., 1984, MS in Chem. Engring., 1992; JD, Rutgers U., 1997. Registered profl. engr., N.J.; bar: N.J., N.Y. Tech. sales rep. Armak divsn. Akzo N.V., Chgo., 1979-82; prodn. mgr. Drew Chem. divsn. Ashland Oil, Kearny, N.J., 1984-87; sr. chem. engr. Jacobs Engring. Group, Mountainside, N.J., 1987-92; sr. environ. engr. Schering Plough Corp., Union, N.J., 1992-94; assoc. Milbank, Tweed, Hadley & McCloy LLP, N.Y.C., 1997—. Author: Handbook of Biotechnology, 1997. Mem. ABA, AIChE, N.Y. State Bar Assn., Essex County Bar Assn., Bar Assn. of City of N.Y., Order of the Coif, Tau Beta Pi. Avocation: fly fishing. Home: 40 Mitchell Rd Gillette NJ 07933-1428 Office: Milbank Tweed Hadley and McCloy LLP 1 Chase Manhattan Plz Fl 47 New York NY 10005-1413

CROWL, ROBERT MITCHELL, research scientist; b. Arkon, Ohio, Dec. 31, 1952; s. Robert Harold and Doris Jean Crowl; m. Jody Ann Hash, July 1, 1972; children: Jennifer, Lindsay, Jason. BA, Pfeiffer Coll., 1975; PhD, U. Fla., 1979. Postdoctoral fellow U. Calif., Berkeley, 1979-81; rsch. scientist Hoffmann-La Roche, Nutley, N.J., 1981-92; project mgr. Sphinx Pharms., Durham, N.C., 1992-94; sr. rsch. fellow Norvatis Pharms., Summit, N.J., 1994—. Damon Runyon-Walter Winchell Cancer Fund fellow U. Calif., Berkeley, 1979. Mem. AAAS, Phi Beta Kappa. Achievements include patent in Acquired Immune Deficiency Syndrome (AIDS) Viral Envolope Protein and Method of Testing for AIDS. Avocations: internet, genealogy. Office: Novartis Pharm 556 Morris Ave Summit NJ 07901-1398

CROWLEY, JAMES PATRICK, hematologist, medical educator; b. Birmingham, Eng., Oct. 13, 1943; came to U.S., 1947; s. Francis Michael and Rose Ann (Donaghy) C.; m. Carol Ann Crowley, Dec. 6, 1943; children: Jason W.F., James M. AB, Providence Coll., 1965; MD, Georgetown U., 1969; MA, Brown U., 1981. Intern Boston City Hosp./Harvard Med. Sch., 1969, resident, 1970; resident Mass. Gen. Hosp., Boston, 1971, Peter Bent Brigham Hosp., Boston, 1974; instr. medicine Harvard Med. Sch., Boston, 1974; asst. prof. medicine Brown U., Providence, 1975-81, assoc. prof., 1981-92, prof., 1992—; dir. hematology R.I. Hosp./Brown U., Providence, 1992-2000; chief hematology/oncology Meml. Hosp. of R.I., Pawtucket, 2000—; bd. dirs. Providence Ambulatory Health Care Found., Inc.; cons. Naval Blood Rsch. Program, USN, 1977—; adj. prof. medicine Tufts U. Sch. Vet. Medicine, 1986—. Author: Principles of Transfusion Medicine, 2nd edit., 1995; contbr. articles to profl. jours. Mem. Retirement Bd. City of Providence, 1993—; physician Camp Yawgoog Boy Scouts Am., 1992—. Capt. USNR, 1971-95, ret. Recipient Transfusion Medicine Acad. award NIH, 1984-89, award R.I. Blood Banking Soc., 1986. Mem. Am. Soc. Hematology, R.I. Med. Soc. (pres. 1992-93), Providence Med. Assn., (pres. 1992-92), Mt. Tom Club (v.p. 1994). Democrat. Roman Catholic. Achievements include important contbns. to the devel. of successful system for freezing blood and deglycerolizing blood for transfusion on Navy hosp. ships, successful demonstration that erythropoeitin could enhance autologous pre-donation prior to orthopedic surgery and the immunosuppressive effects of passenger leukocytes during allogeneic transfusion. Office: RI Hosp 593 Eddy St Providence RI 02903-4971

CROWLEY, MAURICE ANTHONY, bishop; b. Cork, Munster, Ireland, May 11, 1946; arrived in Kenya, 1972; s. Denis and Nora (Walsh) C. BS, Univ. Coll. Cork., Ireland, 1968. Rector Mother of Apostles Sem., El Doret, Kenya, 1983-98; vicar gen. El Doret Cath. Diocese, 1992-98; bishop Cath. Diocese, Kitale, Kenya, 1998—. Office: Catholic Diocese, PO Box 4656, Kitale Kenya

CROWLEY, MICHAEL NORMAN, stockbroker; b. Sydney, NSW, Australia, May 28, 1952; s. Brian Robert and Patricia (Fenner) C.; m. Christine Joan Anderson, Dec. 17, 1977; children: Sally Louise, Hugh Philip. B in Commerce in Acctg. and Fin. Mgmt., U. NSW, 1975. Dir. Ord Minnett Ltd., Sydney, 1983-89, Baring Securities Ltd., Sydney, 1990-92, BZW Australia Ltd., Sydney, 1992-98, ABN Amro Australia Ltd., Sydney, 1998—. Mem. Securities Inst. Australia (affiliate). Avocations: golf, swimming.

CROWLEY, MICHAEL RYAN, real estate appraiser/analyst, educator; b. Spring Valley, Ill., Oct. 18, 1943; s. William P. and Mary T. (Bergagna) C.; m. Diane T. Kujawa, Sept. 29, 1962; children: Michael R. Jr., Mary Frances. BA, U. Chgo., 1968, MBA, 1971. Exec. v.p. 1st Savs. and Loan, Spring Valley, 1963-77; owner Real Estate Cons., Spring Valley, 1977—; part-time faculty Ill. Valley C.C., Oglesby, 1980—; sr. resdl. appraiser, resdl. mem. Appraisal Inst., Chgo., 1981—; presenter seminars on touring Walt Disney World. Recipient Appreciation award St. Bede Acad., Peru, Ill., 1991. Mem. Ill. Assn. Real Estate Educators (charter), Illini Valley Realtors (affiliate), Ill. Valley Appraisers (past pres.). Home: 511 Ladd Rd Spring Valley IL 61362-1107

CROWLEY, THOMAS JAMES, psychiatry educator; b. Mpls., Aug. 10, 1937; s. Cornelius Thomas and Rose Crowley; m. Hildegard Heinrich, June 16, 1962; children: Christopher T., Devin P. BA, BS, U. Minn., 1960, MD, 1962. Lic. physician, Colo. Resident in psychiatry U. Minn. Sch. Medicine, Mpls., 1963-66; prof. psychiatry U. Colo. Sch. Medicine, Denver, 1968—; pres. T.J. Crowley Corp., Denver, 1996—; inventor ski safety equipment; cons. U.S. Nat. Inst. on Drug Abuse, Rockville, Md., 1975-98; mem. panel Inst. Medicine/Nat. Acad. Sci., Washington, 1996-98. Contbr. chpts. to books, articles to profl. jours.; patentee avalanche-victims air-from-snow breathing device. Mem. adv. panel on drug dependence WHO, Geneva, 1995—. Capt. USAF, 1966-68. Recipient MERIT grant award Nat. Ins. on Drug Abuse, 1997—. Fellow Am. Psychiat. Assn., Coll. on Problems of Drug Dependence (pres. 1991-92); mem. AAAS, Rsch. Soc. on Alcoholism, Am. Assn. Psychiatrists in Addiction, Am Assn. Avalanche Profls. Avocations: running, skiing (alpine and nordic), windsurfing, cooking. E-mail: Thomas.Crowley@uchsc.edu. Office: U Colo Sch Medicine Box C-268-35 4200 E 9th Ave Denver CO 80262

CROWLEY, TONY, linguist, educator; b. Liverpool, U.K., Dec. 1, 1960; s. Cornelius and Barbara (Fyldes) C. BA, Oxford U., 1981, Diploma in Gen. Linguistics and Comparative Philology, 1982, MA, 1986, PhD, 1987. Lectr. U. Southhampton, 1984-93, sr. lectr., 1993-94; prof. U. Manchester, 1994—, chair dept., 1996-98; reader Oxford U. Press, 1994, 96—; reviewer Oxford U., 1996-99. Author: (books) The Politics of Discourse, 1989, Proper English: Readings in Language, History and Cultural Identity, 1992, Language in History; Theories & Texts, 1997, The Politics of Language in Ireland, 1366-1922, 1999, The Routledge Language And Cultural Theory Reader, 2000; editor: The Politics of Language Series, 1991-99. Recipient Rsch. award, British Acad., Dublin, 1992, 94, Leverhulme, 1993. Mem. Assn. U. Tchrs., Assn. U. Profs. Labour Party. Avocation: soccer. Office: U Manchester Dept English, Oxford Rd, M13 9PL Manchester U.K.

CROWN, ALAN DAVID, liberal arts educator; b. Leeds, Yorkshire, Eng., Sept. 28, 1932; s. Abraham Wolfe and Sarah (Addlestone) C.; m. Sadie Rose, Feb. 10, 1959; children: Ann Jacqueline Lakos, Aviva Lesley Rosenfeld. BA, Leeds U., 1954, MA with Distinction, 1958; PhD, Sydney U., 1967. Lectr. U. Sydney, 1962-67, sr. lectr., 1968-83, assoc. prof., 1983-89, prof., 1990-97; acting pres. Oxford Ctr. for Hebrew Studies, Oxford, Eng., 1987; prof. emeritus U. Sydney, 1998—; chmn. Mandelbaum House, Sydney, 1990-95, Hebrew Examiner's Com., Bd. of Studies, NSW, 1990-94; advisory coun. World Union of Jewish Studies, Jerusalem, 1992-95. Editor: (book) The Samaritans; editor numerous books; contbr. articles to profl. jours. Sgt. Royal Army Ednl. Corps, Britan, 1954-56. Decorated Order of Australia, 1995. Fellow Oxford Ctr. for Hebrew and Jewish Studies (sr. assoc.). Jewish. Avocation: reading. Home: 1/24 Blaxland Rd, 2023 Bellevue Hill NSW Australia Office: U Sydney, Mandelbaum House H.67, 2006 NSW Sydney Australia

CROWN, DAVID ALLAN, criminologist, educator; b. Long Beach, N.Y., Sept. 13, 1928; s. John and Florence (Coe) C.; m. Maria Braml, Feb. 13, 1954; children: Ingrid, Eric. BS, Union Coll., 1948; M in Criminology, U. Calif., 1960, D in Criminology, 1969. Spl. agt. CIC, 1951-53; asst. dir. San Francisco Indentification Lab., U.S. Postal Inspection Service, 1957-67; dir. Questioned Document Lab., Records Analysis Group, Dept. Army, Washington, 1967-72, Questioned Documents Staff, INR/DDC, U.S. Dept. State, Washington, 1972-77; chief Questioned Documents Lab., Office of Tech. Services, 1977-82; lectr. Chabot Coll., Hayward, Calif., 1966-67, Georgetown U., Washington, 1973; adj. prof. Am. U., Washington, 1971-80; professorial lectr. George Washington U., 1973-77, Antioch Sch. Law, 1977-1981; guest lectr. FBI Acad., Quantico, Va.; pres. Crown Forensic Labs., Inc.; chmn. recert. com. Am. Bd. Forensic Document Examiners. Author: The Forensic Examination of Paints and Pigments, 1968; co-author: Forensic Science, 1982, Legal Medicine, 1985, Forensic Handwriting Examination, 1993; contbr. articles to profl. publs.; mem. editl. bd.: Jour. Forensic Scis., 1971-73, Internat. Jour. Forensic Document Examiners; book rev. editor, 1973-74, assoc. editor, 1974-84. Pres. Temple Bat Yam, Sanibel, Fla., 1996-98. Mem. Am. Acad. Forensic Scis. (chmn. questioned document sect. 1969-70, exec. com. 1970-74, pres. 1974-75), Am. Soc. Questioned Document Examiners (chmn. accreditation com. 1969-70, sec.-treas. 1976-78, pres. 1980-82), ASTM (chmn. questioned document com. 1970-71, vice chmn. 1972), Forensic Sci. Found. (dir. 1971-72, trustee 1973-75), Am. Coll. Document Examiners (dir. 1970—), Ft. Myers Officers Club. Home: 3344 Twin Lakes Ln Sanibel FL 33957-5528

CROWN, NANCY ELIZABETH, lawyer; b. Bronx, N.Y., Mar. 27, 1955; d. Paul and Joanne Barbara (Newman) C.; children: Rebecca, Adam. BA, Barnard Coll., 1977, MA, 1978; MEd, Columbia U., 1983; JD cum laude, Nova Law Sch., 1992. Cert. tchr.; Bar: Fla. 1992. Tchr. Sachem Sch. Dist., Holbrook, N.Y., 1978-82; v.p. mail order dept. Haber-Klein, Inc., Hicksville, N.Y., 1984-88; mgr. mdse., dir. ops. Sure Card Inc., Pompano Beach, Fla., 1988-89; legal intern Office U.S. Trustee/Dept. Justice, 1992; assoc. John T. Kinsey, P.A., Boca Raton, Fla., 1993-95; pvt. practice Nancy E. Crown, P.A., Boca Raton, Fla., 1995—; owner Crystal Title, Inc., 1999—. Recipient West Pub. award for acad. achievement, 1992. Mem. Fla. Bar Assn., Phi Alpha Delta. Democrat. Jewish. Avocations: theatre, walking, reading, jazz.

CROWSON, HENRY LAWRENCE, mathematician, educator; b. Okeechobee, Fla., Apr. 16, 1927; s. Ernest Hubbard and Mary Elizabeth Crowson; m. Betty Mae George, June 16, 1951; children: Lawrence George, James Maxwell, Timothy David. BChemE, U. Fla., Gainesville, 1953, MS in Math., 1955, PhD in Math., 1959. Cert. engr. in tng., Fla. Asst. prof. U. Fla., Gainesville, 1958-60; advisory mathematician IBM Corp., Gaithersburg, Md., 1960-72; sr. mathematician CACI Corp., Arlington, Va., 1975-77; assoc. prof. U. P.M., Saudi Arabia, 1977-79, U. Houston, 1982-86, TIEC/MUCIA, Shah Alam, Malaysia, 1986-89, Tex. A&M Internat. U., Laredo, 1990-98; cons. Bell Labs., CACI, Vitro Labs., Cornell U., others, 1955—. Reviewer books and math. texts, 1965-68. Mem. Am. Math. Soc., Sigma Xi, Pi Mu Epsilon. Republican. Avocations: reading, music, composing poetry. Home: PO Box 3038 Laredo TX 78044-3038

CROWSTON, CATHERINE MIYA, curator; b. Pitts., Nov. 20, 1963; d. Wallace Bruce and Taka (Okubo) C. BA with honors, U. Western Ont., 1986; MA, York U., 1989. Asst. curator Art Gallery York U., 1988-95; dir., curator Walter Phillips Gallery, Banff Ctr., 1995-97; sr. curator Edmonton Art Gallery, 1997—, now dir. exhbns. and programs, sr. curator. Author various contemporary art exhbn. catalogues and contbr. to arts periodicals. Office: 2 Sir Winston Churchill Sq, Edmonton, AB Canada T5J 2C1

CROWSTON, WALLACE BRUCE STEWART, management educator; b. Toronto, Ont., Can., Jan. 28, 1934; s. Arthur William and Clara Helena (Donnelly) C.; m. Taka Ohkubo, Sept. 15, 1961; children: Kevin, Cathy, Clare. BA Sc, U. Toronto, 1956; SM, MIT, 1958; MSc, Carnegie Mellon U., 1965, PhD, 1968. Asst. prof. U. Alta., 1960-62; asst. prof. MIT, 1966, assoc. prof., 1969-72; prof., faculty adminstrv. studies York U., 1972-87, dean, 1976-84; dean faculty mgmt. McGill U., Montreal, Que., Can., 1987-2000, dir. Ctr. Internat. Mgmt. Studies, 1990—. Mem. Univ. Club (Montreal). Office: McGill U Faculty Mgmt, 1001 Sherbrooke St W, Montreal, PQ Canada H3A 1G5

CROWTHER, G. RODNEY, III, television production company executive, writer, photographer; b. Asheville, N.C., Jan. 11, 1927; s. G. Rodney Jr. and Martha Maria (Lewis) C. Grad., Boys' Latin Sch., Balt., 1944; student, Sch. Modern Photography, N.Y.C., 1947-50. Fashion photographer Amos Parrish & Co., N.Y.C., 1950-53; ind. comml. photographer Chevy Chase, Md., 1956-61; free-lance writer Washington, 1962—; pres. The Carrollian Age, Washington, 1987—. Author: Surname Index to Sixty-Five Volumes of Colonial and Revolutionary Pedigrees, 1964; contbr. articles to Nat. Geneal. Soc. Quar., 1962—; photograph Sputnik and the Big Dipper in Modern Mus. Art, N.Y.C., Echo I satellite in Smithsonian Inst., Where 'KONG' Stood, UN, N.Y.C., 1951. Served with USN, 1945-46, PTO. Episcopalian. Avocations: miniature gardening, audio-video editing. Home: PO Box 134 North Beach MD 20714-0134 Office: PO Box 369 Ben Franklin Sta Washington DC 20044

CROZIER, BRIAN ROSSITER, journalist; b. Aug. 4, 1918; s. R.H. and Elsa (McGillivray) Crozier; m. Mary Lillian Samuel, 1940 (dec. 1993); four children; m. Kacqueline Marie Mitchell, 1999. Student, Lycee, Montpellier Colleges, Peterborough Coll., Harrow,, Trinity Coll. of Music, London. Music and art critic London, 1936-39; reporter and sub.-ed. Stoke-on-Trent, Stockport, London, 1940-41; aeronaut. inspection, 1941-43; sub.-ed. Reuters, 1943-44, News Chronicle, 1944-48; sub.-ed. and writer Sydney Morning Herald, Australia, 1948-51; corr. Reuters AAP, 1951-52; features editor Straits Times, Singapore, 1952-53; leader writer and corr. The Economist, 1954-64; commentator BBC, 1954-66; chair Forum World Features, 1965-74; editor Conflict Studies, 1970-75; co-founder and dir. Inst. for Study of Conflict, 1970-79; cons. in field, 1979—; columnist Now!, London, 1980-81, Nat. Rev., N.Y., 1978-99, The Times, 1982-84, The Free Nation, London, 1982-89; adj. scholar The Heritage Found., 1983-95; Disting. vis. fellow Hoover Inst., Stanford, Calif., 1996—. Publs. include: The Rebels, 1960, The Morning After, 1963, Neo-Colonialism, 1964, South-East Asia in Turmoil, 1965, The Struggle for the Third World, 1966, Franco, 1967, The Masters of Power, 1969, The Future of Communist Power (in U.S.A.: Since Stalin) 1970, De Gaulle (vol. 1), 1973, (vol. 2) 1974, A Thoery of Conflict, 1974, The Man Who Lost China (Chiang Kai-shek), 1977, Strategy of Survival, 1978, The Minimum State, 1979, Franco: Crepusculo de un hombre, 1980, The Price of Peace, 1980; co-author: Socialism Explained, 1984, This War Called Peace, 1984; author: The Andropov Deception, 1984; editor: The Grenada Documents, 1987, Socialism: Dream and Reality, 1987, The Gorbachev Phenomenon, 1990, Communism: Why Prolong its Death Throes?, 1990, Free Agent: The Unseen War, 1993, The KGB Lawsuits, 1995, others; contbr. articles to profl. jours. Avocations: taping stereo, piano. Home: 18 Wickliffe Ave, Finchley N3 3EJ, England

CROZIER, WALTER RAYMOND, psychology educator; b. Belfast, Northern Ireland, July 27, 1945; s. Walter Thomas and Elizabeth Jane Lavinia (McClintock) C.; m. Sandra Ann Hamilton, Aug. 19, 1972; children: John, Beth. BA with honors, Queens U., Belfast, 1968; MSc, Stirling U., Scotland, 1969; PhD, Keele U., Eng., 1974. Chartered psychologist. Sr. lectr. South Glamorgan Inst., Cardiff, Wales, 1972-83, Lancashire Poly., Preston, 1983-90; sr. lectr. U. Wales, Cardiff, 1990-98, reader, 1998—. Editor: Shyness and Embarrassment, 1990, Shyness: Development, Consolidation and Change, 2000; author: Manufactured Pleasures, 1994, Individual Learners, 1997; co-editor: (with R. Ranyard & O. Svenson) Decision Making, 1997; mem. editl. bd. Empirical Studies of Arts, 1995—. Fellow Brit. Psychol. Soc. (com. mem. Welsh br. 1994—); mem. Internat. Assn. Empirical Aesthetics (v.p. 1983-96). Mem. Labour party. Mem. Ch. of Wales. Avocations: rambling, reading, sports. Office: Cardiff U Sch Social Scis, King Edward VII Ave Flamorgan Bldg, Cardiff CF10 3WT, Wales

CRUCIOLI, PIERGIORGIO, air force officer; b. Teramo, Italy, Mar. 5, 1941; s. Corrado and Ida (Moser) C.; m. Enrica Pennarola, Sept. 18, 1966; children: Sabrina, Silvia, Samanta. Cert., Air Force Acad., Naples, Italy. Ofcl. test ctr. Air Force, Praticadi Mare, Italy, 1981-83; inspector, legal advisor NATO, Munich, 1987-90; non-commd. officer Italian Air Force, Caserta, 1990-91; chief of devel. and procurement Italian Air Force, Rome, 1991-96, gen. def. staff chief of planning and fin., 1996-97; 3d air region comdr. Italian Air Force, Bari, 1997—. Recipient Hon. career awards Min. Def., 1980, 81, 87, 90. Mem. Casa Dell'Aviatore. Roman Catholic. Avocations: scuba diving, fishing, mushroom picking, swimming. Office: Third Air Region, Via Dalmzaio 70D, 70121 Bari Italy

CRUICKSHANK, ARTHUR RICHARD IVOR, paleontologist; b. Nairobi, Kenya, Feb. 29, 1932; s. Arthur Alexander and Esme (Latimer-Saunders) C.; m. Enid Haddon, Mar. 30, 1963; children: Peter Arthur, Susan Mary, David Andrew. BSc, Edinburgh U., 1957, BSc with honors, 1958; PhD, Cambridge U., 1963. Asst. dir. Bernard Price Inst. Paleontology U. Witwatersrand, South Africa, 1967-78; tutor, assoc. lectr. Open U., Milton Keynes, Eng., 1979-96; hon. rsch. fellow Leicester U., Eng., 1991—; hon. rsch. assoc. Leicester City Mus., 1988—. Hon. v.p. Borders Liberal Party, Scotland, 1983-85; chair Bosworth Liberal Dems., Hinckley, England, 1986-92. Cadet RAF, 1951-53. Mem. Paleontol. Assn. England. Office: Natural Scis Geology, New Walk Mus, LE1 7EA Leicester England

CRUIKSHANK, DALE PAUL, astronomer; b. Des Moines, Aug. 10, 1939; s. Paul Cecil and Bette Helen C.; m. Yvonne Jean Pendleton, Jan. 1, 1997; children: Paul, Mark, Jeffrey. BS, Iowa State U., 1961; MS, U. Ariz., 1965, PhD, 1968. Astronomer U. Ariz., Tucson, 1969-70, U. Hawaii, Honolulu, 1970-88; rsch. scientist NASA Ames Rsch. Ctr., Moffett Field, Calif., 1988—; panelist ultraviolet, optical, infrared astronomy from space NAS, Washington, 1999-2000. Editor: Infrared Astronomy, 1981, Neptune and Triton, 1995; contbr. articles to profl. jours. Recipient Muhlmann prize Astronomical Soc. Pacific, 1982; grantee NASA, 1975-2000, Nat. Geographic Soc., Washington, 1972. Fellow Calif. Acad. Scis.; mem. Am. Astronomical Soc. (chmn. divsn. planetary scis. 1990-91), Internat. Astonomical Union (pres. commn. 16 2001-03). Office: NASA Ames Rsch Ctr MS 245-6 Moffett Field CA 94035-1000

CRUISE, TOM (TOM CRUISE MAPOTHER, IV), actor; b. Syracuse, N.Y., July 3, 1962; s. Thomas C. III and Mary Lee Mapother; m. Mimi Rogers, May 9, 1987 (div. 1990); m. Nicole Kidman, Dec. 24, 1990; adopted children: Isabella Jane Kidman, Connor Antony Kidman. Grad. H.S., Glen Ridge, N.J. Actor: stage prodn. Godspell; feature film appearances include Endless Love, Taps, 1981, Losin' It, 1981, The Outsiders, 1983, Risky Business, 1983, All the Right Moves, 1983, Top Gun, 1986, Legend, 1986, The Color of Money, 1986, Cocktail,1988, Rain Man, 1988, Born on the Fourth of July, 1989 (Acad. award nominee for best actor 1990, Golden Globe award Best Actor Drama, Chgo. Film Festival Critics award, Best Actor), Days of Thunder, 1990, Far and Away, 1992, A Few Good Men, 1992, The Firm, 1993, Interview with the Vampire, 1994, Mission Impossible, 1996, Jerry McGuire, 1996 (MTV Movie award Best Male Performance, Golden Globe award Best Performance Comedy/Musical, Blockbuster Entertainment award Favorite Actor-Comedy/Romance, nominated Oscar award Best Actor), Eyes Wide Shut, 1998, Magnolia, 1999 (Golden Globe, 2000), Mission Impossible 2, 2000; prodr. Without Limits, 1998.

CRUM, ALBERT BYRD, psychiatrist, consultant; b. Omaha, Nov. 17, 1931; s. J. Rufus and Alberta (McCreary) C.; m. Rosa Maria Hennessy y Sinclair; children: Rosa Maria Crum O'Brien, Elsie Crum McCabe, Alberta Crum Fousek. BS, U. Redlands, Calif., 1953; MD, Harvard U., 1957; MS, NYU, 1987; DS (hon.), U. Redlands, 1974. Med. intern Columbia U. div. Bellevue Med. Ctr., N.Y.C., 1957-58; rsch. fellow, psychiat. resident Creedmoor Inst. for Psychol. Studies, Queens Village, N.Y., 1958-59; chief, neuropsychiatric svcs., Continental Air Command USAF Hosp., 1959-61; psychiat. resident Columbia U. Psychiat. Inst. of Columbia-Presbyn. Hosp., N.Y.C., 1961-63; pvt. practice Brooklyn Heights, N.Y., 1963—; active attending staff Gracie Sq. Hosp., N.Y.C., 1963—; med. dirs. Psychiatric Svcs. Internat. P.C., Brooklyn Heights, 1980—; ednl. dir. med. and health seminars Internat. Inst. for Human Behavior, Inc., Brooklyn Heights, 1983—; advisor Office of Tibet, N.Y.C., 1984—; clin. prof. behavioral scis. NYU, N.Y.C., 1987—; pres., dir. behavioral scis. Way of Life/N.Y., Ltd., Brooklyn Heights, 1989—; pres. Y.F. One/N.Y., Ltd., Brooklyn Heights, 1991—, Y.F. Nationwide, Inc., Brooklyn Heights, 1991—, Immune Advantage Internat., Inc., Brooklyn Heights, 1995—; chmn., mem. Immune Products, L.L.C., Brooklyn Heights, 1996; co-chmn. U.S. Coordinating Commn. for Nomination of His Holiness the Dalai Lama of Tibet for the Nobel Peace Prize, Brooklyn Heights, 1986—; adj. prof. anatomy and neuroanatomy, NYU, 1987—; ptnr. Burdick Assocs. Investment Firm, Brooklyn Heights, 1976—; pres. Burdick Assocs. Owners Corp., Brooklyn Heights, 1983—; chmn. Human Behavior Found., Brooklyn Heights, 1968—; chmn. selection com. Human Behavior Found.'s Albert Schweitzer Humanitarian Award, Brooklyn Heights, 1986—. Author (chpt.) The Triumphant Person, 1989. Bd. dirs. Albert Schweitzer Fellowship, N.Y.C., 1982—; chmn. William James Found., Brooklyn Heights, 1989—; bd. dirs. Burdick Internat. Ancestry Library, Sarasota, Fla., 1985—; mem., chn., bd. advisors NYU's Coll. of Dentistry, N.Y.C., 1988—; mem. Brooklyn Heights Assn., 1970—. Capt. USAF, 1959-61. Recipient Disting. Svc. award Bklyn. Jr. C. of C., 1966, Bicentennial award Nat. Jogging Assn., 1976. Fellow Royal Coll. Physicians and Surgeons in Psychiatry; mem. Pan Am. Med. Assn., Nat. Bd. Med. Examiners, Med. Coun. of Can., Am. Acad. Clin. Psychiatrists, Am. Orthopsychiatric Assn., Am. Psychiat. Assn., AMA, Med. Soc. State of N.Y., Kings County (N.Y.) Med. Soc., World Med. Assn., World Fedn. Mental Health, Am. Physicians Art Assn., Harvard Med. Soc., English Speaking Union, Harvard Club of N.Y., Bklyn. Club, Heights Casino and Racquet Club, MENSA (life, nat. coord. 1980-84), Phi Beta Kappa (councillor 1981-84). Avocations: jogging, studying world religions, history, leadership. Home and Office: Psychiat Svcs Internat PC 77 Remsen St Brooklyn NY 11201-3401

CRUM, HENRY HAYNE, lawyer; b. Denmark, S.C., Oct. 1, 1914; s. J. Wesley Jr. and Priscilla (Hart) C.; m. Mary Bass, July 27, 1946; children: Elizabeth, J. Wesley III, H. Hayne III. AB, Wofford Coll., 1935; LLB, U. S.C., 1939. Bar: S.C. 1939, U.S. Ct. Appeals (4th cir.) 1953, U.S. Dist. Ct. S.C. 1959, U.S. Tax Ct. 1963, U.S. Supreme Ct. 1953. Ptnr. Crum & Crum Attys., Denmark, 1939-40, 45—; mem. S.C. Supreme Ct. Grievance and Discipline Com., 1978-81, S.C. Supreme Ct. Specialization Adv. Bd. for Taxation, 1982-84, S.C. Bar Resolution of Fee Disputation Bd., 1983-84; city atty. City of Denmark, 1946-76. With AUS, 1940-45, ETO, Col. USAR ret. Decorated Bronze Star, ETO Ribbon with 5 Campaign Stars, Bronze Arrowhead. Democrat. Methodist. Avocations: golf, tennis, reading. Home: 277 N Palmetto Ave Denmark SC 29042-1107 Office: Crum & Crum Attys PO Box 12B Denmark SC 29042-0012

CRUMBAUGH, JAMES CHARLES, psychologist; b. Terrell, Tex., Dec. 11, 1912; s. Charles Miller and Hallie Virginia (Dansby) C.; m. Edna Mae Bailey, 1938 (dec. 1946); 1 child, Charles; m. Teresa Amanda Croteau, June 14, 1975 (dec. Feb. 1989); m. Lois Dickson Hicks, Nov. 10, 1992. AB, Baylor U., 1935; AM, So. Meth. U., 1938; PhD, U. Tex., 1953. Lic. psychologist, Miss.; cert. logotherapist. Psychologist, tchr. Memphis State

U., 1947-56; chmn. Dept. Psychology MacMurray Coll., Jacksonville, Ill., 1957-59; rsch. dir. Bradley Ctr., Inc., Columbus, Ga., 1959-64; staff psychologist VA Med. Ctr., Augusta, Ga., 1964-65, Gulfport, Miss., 1965-80; so. regional dir. Inst. Logotheraphy, Berkeley, Calif., 1980—; rsch. cons. Internat. Graphoanalysis Soc., Chgo., 1968—. Author: Counseling for Graphoanalysts, 1970, Everything to Gain, 1973; co-author: Logotherapy, 1980; co-editor: Primer of Projective Techniques, 1990. With U.S. Army air Corps, 1941-45. Rsch. fellow Duke U., 1954-55. Mem. APA, Miss. Psychol. Assn. (Kinlock Gill award 1989), Southeastern Psychol. Assn., So. Soc. Philosophy and Psychology, Psi Chi. Roman Catholic. Avocation: writing. Home: 140 Balmoral Ave Biloxi MS 39531-4701

CRUMBLY, ISAAC J., biology educator; b. Widener, Ark., June 6, 1938; s. Isaiah and Edna Crumbly; married Nov. 27, 1965; children: Isaac O., Konata Ato. BS in Horticulture, U. Ark., Pine Bluff, 1961; MS in Horticulture, U. Ill., Champaign, 1963; PhD in Botany, N.D. State U., 1970. Instr. horticulture Alcorn A&M U., Lorman, Miss., 1963-65; instr. Ft. Valley (Ga.) State U., 1965-67, assoc. prof., 1970-76, prof., 1976—, assoc. dean Coll. Arts and Scis., 1994-99; rsch. assoc. N.D. State U., Fargo, 1967-70; summer rsch. faculty Tenn. Valley Authority, Muscle Shoals, Ala., 1973-75, Oak Ridge (Tenn.) Nat. Lab., 1983-84, Lawrence Livermore (Calif.) Nat. Lab., 1985-87; pub. affairs roundtable fellow So. Edn. Found., Atlanta, 1981-82. Recipient Letter commendation Pres. Ronald Regan, 1988, cert. Recognition Sec. Energy James Watkins, 1992, Spl. award Am. Assn. Petroleum Geologists, 1999. Mem. AAAS, Am. Assn. Higher Edn., Am. Assn. Black in Energy, Beta Kappa Chi. Office: Ft Valley State U 1005 University Dr Fort Valley GA 31030

CRUMLEY, LAURA LEE, literature educator; b. Pitts., Mar. 30, 1949; d. William Wolf and Laura Marie (Canning) C.; child from previous marriage, Stefan Gregory Perez-Crumley. BA, Indiana U. Pa., 1971; MA, U. Pitts., 1975, PhD, 1983. Tchr. Berlitz Sch. Langs., Pitts., 1971-73; educator U. San Buenaventura, Cali, Colombia, 1979-81; educator U. Valle, Cali, Colombia, 1980—, asst. prof., chairperson dept. lit., 1982-85, assoc. prof. lit., 1985-87, prof., rschr., 1987—, dir. spl. student programs, 1988-93, prof. grad. seminars, masters programs, 1988-90, 92, 1993—, assoc. dean rsch. humanities divsn., 1996—; prof. Native American culture and lit. U. Valle, 1992—; prof. grad. seminars U. Nariño, 1989-92, 98; free-lance translator, Pitts., 1971-77, Cali, 1977-81; spkr., lectr. ednl. instns., Cali, 1980—; participant poetry workshop with Leslie Ullman, Cali, 1984; dir. writing workshops U. Valle, 1988-89, 92-93, Colegio Bolivar, Cali, 1988-89, Inst. de Estudios del Pacifico, 1995-96; Maya Hieroglyphic Seminars, U. Tex., Austin, 1986, 87, 88, 89, 90, 92, 96; participant with La Tarumba Theater Workshop in Rsch. Group on Dramaturgy, 1989-91; mem. acad. adv. com. doctorate programs in humanities and social scis., U. Valle, 1994; founder, dir. rsch. group Amerindian Literatures and Cultures, 1995—; organizer (with Nersa Caballero) forum on Nat. Identity and African Culture in Am., 1995, (with Marcos Yule and Manuel Sisco) forum on Nasa Yuwe and World View of Nasa Culture, 1996; dir. poetry workshops for tchrs. Colegio Colombo-Britanico, Cali, 1998-99. Contbr. articles to lit. jours.; co-editor lit. jour. Revista Poligramas, 1985; contbr. poetry to Voces y Diferencias, 1997. Grantee U. Valle, 1984-87, Colombian Inst. Higher Learning, 1987-88; recipient rsch. bonus U. Valle, 1990, 91, 92, 93, 94, 95, rsch. grant group project Amerindian Narrative Traditions, 1997; named Disting. Prof. U. Valle, 1994. Mem. Latin Am. Indian Lit. Assn., Inst. Internat. Lit. Iberoamericana, Am. Translators Assn., Latin Am. Studies Assn., Rachel Carson Homestead Assn., Nat. Geog. Soc., Nat. Audubon Soc., Autenticos Baseball Sporting Club (pres. 1993—). Presbyterian. Avocations: writing poetry, songs and children's stories, horseback riding, swimming, travel. Home: Carrera 79 No 6-57, AA25493 Cali Colombia Office: U del Valle Dept Letras, Apartado Aereo 25360, Cali Valle, Colombia

CRUMLIN-PEDERSEN, OLE, archaeologist; b. Hellerup, Denmark, Feb. 24, 1935; s. Gunnar and Gudde (Jørgensen) Pedersen; m. Leni Voldby Jensen, 1959 (div. 1976); children: Jens, Tine; m. Ingeborg Christmas-Møller, Sept. 29, 1978; children: Jonas, Morten (dec.). Student, Tech. U. Copenhagen, 1960. Mus. curator Nat. Mus. Copenhagen, 1962-93, dir. rsch., 1993-2000; bd. dirs. Viking Ship Mus., Roskilde, Denmark; mem. Commn. F. Unterwasserarchaeologie, Germany, 1993-98; prof. Medieval Archaeology Aarhus U., 1997—. Author: The Skuldelev Ships, 1968, Viking-Age Ships of Hedeby, 1997; rschr. in field. Recipient K. Muckelroy Meml. prize, 1985, Chr.-Albrechts Univ. medal, 1986, E. Westerby prize, 1988, Festschrift Shipshape prize, 1995. Home: 3 Guldborgvej, DK-4000 Roskilde Denmark Office: Nat Mus Ctr Maritime Arch, Havnevej 7, DK-4000 Roskilde Denmark

CRUMMETT, WARREN BERLIN, analytical chemistry consultant; b. Moyers, W.Va., Apr. 4, 1922; s. Elmer and Virginia Maude (Smith) C.; m. Elizabeth Ann Stathers, Feb. 28, 1948; children: Allan Warren, Daniel David. BA, Bridgewater (Va.) Coll., 1943; PhD, Ohio State U., 1951. Control chemist Solvay Process Co., Hopewell, Va., 1943-46; chemist Dow Chem. Co., Midland, Mich., 1951-55, lab. supr., 1955-61, asst. lab. dir., 1961-71, rsch. scientist, 1971-84, rsch. fellow, 1984-88; cons. chemist, Midland, 1988—; mem. sci. adv. bd. EPA, Washington, 1976-78, cons., 1980; cons. USAF, Washington, 1981. Contbr. articles to sci. jours. Recipient H.H. Dow medal, 1980, Disting. Alumnus award Bridgewater Coll., 1983. Mem. Am. Chem. Soc. (chmn. analytical div. 1983, Midland sect. award 1987), Rsch. Soc. Am., N.Y. Acad. Scis. Achievements include research on hypothesis of trace chemistries of fire. Home and Office: 808 Crescent Dr Midland MI 48640-3434

CRUMPTON, CHARLES WHITMARSH, lawyer; b. Shreveport, La., May 29, 1946; s. Charles W. and Frances M. (McInnis) C.; m. Thu-Huong T. Cong-Huyen, Sept. 17, 1971; children: Francesca, Ian. BA, Carleton Coll., 1968; MA, U. Hawaii, 1974, JD, 1978. Bar: Hawaii 1978, U.S. Dist. Ct. Hawaii 1978, U.S. Ct. Appeals (9th cir.) 1982. Tchr. dept. edn. State of Hawaii, Honolulu, 1972-73, 75-77; Fulbright prof. U. Can Tho, Vietnam, 1973-75; assoc. John S. Edmunds, Honolulu, 1978-80, Ashford & Wriston, Honolulu, 1980-85, David W. Hall, Honolulu, 1985-88; dir. Hall & Crumpton, Honolulu, 1988-93; dir., shareholder Stanton Clay Chapman Crumpton & Iwamura, Honolulu, 1993—; pres./dir. Internat. Law Found., 1996—; barrister Am. Inn of Ct. IV, Honolulu, 1985-87; arbitrator Court-Annexed Arbitration program 1st Cir. Ct. State of Hawaii, 1987—; arbitrator, mediator Am. Arbitration Assn., 1988—, Arbitration Forums, 1990—, Mediation Specialists, 1994—, Dispute Prevention & Resolution, 1995—; mem. com. on lawyer professionalism Hawaii State Jud. Conf., 1988-89; arbitrator/mediator com. fee disputes Hawaii Bar Assn., 1990—, mem. com. jud. adminstrn., 1990—, mem. com. jud. performance, 1992-94, chair sect. on alternative dispute resolution, 1997—; prof. Hawaii Pacific U., 1995—; faculty/spkr. on ins. law, employment law, alternative dispute resolution, civil litigation, 1993—. Asst. dir. youth vols. Am. Cancer Soc., Honolulu, 1972-73. Fulbright grantee U.S. Dept. State, 1973-75. Mem. ATLA, ABA (torts and ins. practice sect., litigation sect., alt. dispute resolution sec.), Hawaii Bar Assn., Inter-Pacific Bar Assn. Avocations: sports, guitar. E-mail: crumpton@paclawteam.com. Home: 47-538 Hui Iwa St Kaneohe HI 96744-4658 Office: Stanton Clay Chapman Crumpton & Iwamura 700 Bishop St Ste 2100 Honolulu HI 96813-4120

CRUNDWELL, DUNCAN JAMES, electronics executive; b. Maidstone, Kent, Eng., Mar. 18, 1957; s. James Stanley and June (Reid) C.; m. Bridgette Grieve, Dec. 24, 1983 (div. Jan. 1995); 1 child, Ben; m. Natasha Shankova, May 12, 1995. BS in Mech. Engring., Brunel U., London, 1979; MBA, Henley Mgmt. Coll., Eng., 1996. Chartered Engr. Student engr. Dowty Group, Cheltenham, Eng., 1975-79; chief engr. Yamco, London, 1979-80; tech. mgr. Bandive, London, 1980-84; custom projects mgr. Solid State Logic, Oxford, Eng., 1984-86; systems mgr. Solid State Logic, 1986-88, product group mgr., 1988-90; mng. dir. Solid State Logic Organ Systems, Brandon, Eng., 1990-95; CEO, pres. Solid State Logic Organ Systems, Detroit, 1995—; tchr. Opening Windows on Engring., Oxford Schs., 1988-91. Prodr.: (radio program) Glad to Be Gay or Not?, 1977 (UK Local Radio award 1977); client/project mgr. new hdqs. bldg. Solid State Logic (Royal Inst. Brit. Architects award 1989); inventor in field. Recipient Dir. Gen.'s cert. Engring. Coun., London, 1990. Mem. Instn. Mech. Engrs. (chmn. YM panel 1988-89, sec. 1987-88, Outstanding Project Work award 1979), Assn. MBAs. Anglican. Avocations: photography, architecture, music, fine art. Home: 1766 Grant St Birmingham MI 48009-2036 Office: Solid State Logic Organ Sys 37545 Schoolcraft Rd Livonia MI 48150-1009

CRUSE, JULIUS MAJOR, JR., pathologist, educator; b. New Albany, Miss., Feb. 15, 1937; s. Julius Major and Effie (Davis) C. BA, BS with honors, U. Miss., 1958; DMS with honors, U. Graz, Austria, 1960; MD, U. Tenn., 1964, PhD in Pathology (USPHS fellow), 1966, USPHS postdoctoral fellow, 1964-67; DD (hon.), Gen. Theol. Sem., N.Y., 1999. Mem. faculty U. Miss. Med. Sch., 1967—; prof. immunology, biology Grad. Sch., 1967-74, prof. pathology, 1974—, asso. prof. microbiology, 1974—, dir. grad. studies program in pathology, 1974—, dir. clin. immunopathology, 1978—, dir. immunopathology sect., 1978—, dir. tissue typing lab., 1980—, assoc. prof. medicine, 1989—; lectr. pathology U. Tenn. Coll. Medicine, 1967-74; aj. prof. immunology Miss. Coll., 1977—; mem. sci. adv. bd. Immuno Tech. Corp., L.A.; active FDA Expert Panel on Alternatives to Silicone Breast Implants, 1994—. Author: Immunology Examination Review Book, 1971, rev. edit., 1975, Introduction to Immunology, 1977, Principles of Immunopathology, 1979; editor-in-chief Immunologic Rsch., 1981—, Pathology and Immunopathology Rsch., 1982-90, Concepts in Immunopathology, 1985—, The Year in Immunology, 1984—, Pathobiology: Jour. Immunopathology, Molecular and Cellular Biology, 1990-98, Exptl. & Molecular Pathology, 1999—, Transgenics: Biological Analysis Through DNA Transfer; contbns. to Microbiology and Immunology; editor Immunomodulation of Neoplasia, Antigenic Variation: Molecular and Genetic Mechanisms of Relapsing Disease, 1987, Autoimmunoregulation and Autoimmune Disease, 1987, The Year in Immunology, vol. 1, 1984-85, vol. 2, 1985-86, The Year in Immunology, vol. 3, 1987, The Year in Immunology, vols. 4, 5, 1988, vol. 6, 1989-90, Genetic Basis of Autoimmune Disease, 1988, Cellular Aspects of Autoimmunity, 1988, Therapy of Autoimmune Diseases, 1989, B Lymphocytes: Function and Regulation, Conjugate Vaccines, 1989, Molecules and Cells of Immunity, 1990, Immunoregulation and Autoimmunity, 1986, Organ-Based Autoimmune Diseases, 1985, Autoimmunity: Basic Concepts, Systematic and Selected Organ-Specific Diseases, 1985, Clinical and Molecular Aspects of Autoimmune Diseases, 1990, Immunoregulatory Cytokines and Cell Growth, 1989, Complement Profiles, 1992; co-editor: Self-Nonself Discrimination in the Immune System, 1992, Complement Profiles, vol. 1, 1992, Illustrated Dictionary of Immunology, 1995, 2d edit., 2000, Atlas of Immunology, 1998; contbr. chpts. to books and articles to profl. jours; editor-in-chief: Experimental and Molecular Pathology, 1999—. Recipient Pathologists award in continuing edn. Coll. Am. Pathologists-Am. Soc. Clin. Pathologists, 1976; Julius M. Cruse collection in immunology established in his honor Middleton Med. Libr., U. Wis., Madison, 1979, Julius M. Cruse collection of T.S. Eliot's works, St. Mark's Libr., Gen. Theol. Sem. (Episcopal), N.Y.C.; Wilson Found. grantee, 1990-95, 93-94, 95-98; B.S. Guyton lectr. on history of medicine, 1998; Fulbright scholar, 1958-60. Fellow AAAS, Royal Soc. Promotion Health, Am. Acad. Microbiology, Am. Soc. for Histocompatibility and Immunogenetics (chmn. publs. com. 1987-95, councillor 1997-99, historian 2000—), Intercontinental Biog. Assn.; mem. AMA (Physicians Recognition award 196-75), Clin. Immunology Soc., Am. Inst. Biol. Scis., Am. Soc. Clin. Pathologists, Can. Soc. Microbiologists, N.Y. Acad. Scis. Exptl. Biology and Medicine, Soc. Francaise d'Immunologie, Reticuloendothelial Soc., Transplantation Soc., Electron Microscopy Soc. Am., Am. Assn. History Medicine, The Paul Ehrlich Soc., Am. Assn. Pathologists, Am. Chem. Soc., Brit. Soc. Immunology, Can. Soc. Immunology, Am. Soc. Microbiology, Internat. Acad. Pathology, Am. Assn. Immunologists (historian 1990—), Sigma Xi, Phi Kappa Phi, Phi Eta Sigma, Alpha Epsilon Delta, Gamma Sigma Epsilon, Beta Beta Beta. Episcopalian. Office: U Miss Med Ctr Dept Pathology 2500 N State St Jackson MS 39216-4500

CRUTCHFIELD, ALEXANDER, investor, investment banker, venture capitalist; b. Tucson, Dec. 12, 1958; s. Alec Randall and Virginia Cushing (Smith) C. BA, Claremont McKenna Coll., Calif., 1980; MBA, Columbia U., 1984. Assoc. RRY Ptnrs., Buckingham, Pa., 1984-86; exec. v.p. 1st Colo. Corp., Denver, 1986-87, vice chmn., 1987-95; vice chmn. Am. Water Devel., 1987-95; pres. Crutchfield & Co., Denver, 1988-93; gen. ptnr., mng. dir. Oasis Ptnrs. (Mex.), Phoenix, 1993—, also bd. dirs.; pres. Baca Minerals Inc., Denver, 1985-90; prin. RRY Ptnrs., 1986-87, mng. dir., 1988; chmn. ATFAB Corp., Boca Raton, Fla., 1986—; vice chmn. The Water Exch., 1989-91, Weis, 1988-90; founder, ptnr. Ironwood Advisors, 1999—, Ironwood Energy, 1999—; founder, mem. inv. com. Washington Investments, 1999—; mem. adv. bd. N2Plus, Phoenix, 1999—, Intershipper, Phoenix, 1999—, Grants Online, N.Y.C., 2000—; bd. dirs. MEDAM SA, Buenos Aires. Mem. Nat. Cattleman's Assn., Econs. Club N.Y., Denver Petroleum Club, Mensa. E-mail: alexc@oasispartners.com. Office: Oasis Partners PO Box 7728 Phoenix AZ 85011-7728

CRUTCHFIELD, EDWARD ELLIOTT, JR., banking executive; b. Detroit, July 14, 1941; s. Edward Elliott and Katherine (Sikes) C.; m. Nancy Glass Kizer, July 27, 1963; children: Edward Elliott, III, Sarah Palmer. BA, Davidson Coll., 1963; MBA, U. Pa., 1965. With First Union Nat. Bank, Charlotte, N.C., 1965—, head retail bank svcs. group, 1970-72, exec. v.p. gen. adminstrn., 1972-73, pres., 1973-84, vice chmn., from 1984; pres. First Union Corp. (parent), Charlotte, 1983-86, CEO, 1984-96, chmn., bd. dirs., 1996—; bd. dirs. Bernhardt Industries, Inc., Charlotte, 1983—. Bd. deacons Myers Park Presbyn. Ch.; bd. dirs. United Cmty. Svcs., Salvation Army, Charlotte Bd., Charlotte Latin Sch.; trustee Mint Mus. Art, N.C. Nature Conservancy; bd. mgrs. Charlotte Meml. Hosp.; bd. visitors Davidson Coll. Mem. Charlotte C. of C., Assn. Res. City Bankers, Am., N.C. bankers assns., Am. Textile Mfrs. Assn., Young Pres.'s Orgn. Clubs: Charlotte City, Charlotte Country, Linville (N.C.) Golf. Office: 1st Union Corp One First Union Center 301 S College St Charlotte NC 28202-6000

CRUTCHFIELD, SUSAN RAMSEY, neurophysiologist; b. Pasadena, Calif., Oct. 7, 1941; d. Henry Colwell Ramsey and Rowena Ruth (Lockett) Banning; m. Ralph L. Crutchfield, Sept. 26, 1964 (div. Sept. 1973); children: Pamela Montague, Ashley Noland. AA, Pine Manor Coll., 1961; student, Sorbonne U., Paris, 1961-62; BA, George Washington U., 1964; MA, U. Calif., San Diego, 1978; PhD, Aston U., Birmingham, Eng., 1986. Research assoc. U. Calif. Med. Ctr., San Diego, 1978-80, researcher, 1986-89, clin. instr. dept. pediats. divsn. neonatology, 1989-94, asst. clin. prof. depts. ophthalmology and pediat., 1994-98, clin. prof. dept. pediat., 1998—; rschr. Birmingham (Eng.) U., 1980-86. Mem. San Diego Jr. League, Mingeii Internat., Stuart Collection, U. Calif., San Diego, Sangre de Cristo Audubon Soc.; trustee Foxcroft Sch., Middleburg, Va., 1994—, La Jolla Chamber Music Soc.; pres. arts coun. bd. San Diego State U. Mem. AAAS, N.Y. Acad. Scis., European Neurosci. Soc., Internat. Soc. Clin. Electrophysiology Vision, Assn. Rsch. Vision and Ophthalmology, Brit. Soc. Neurophysiology, La Jolla Beach and Tennis Club. Avocations: camping, horseback riding, hiking, photography, gardening. Home: PO Box 2129 Santa Fe NM 87504-2129 Office: Univ Calif San Diego Pediat Divsn San Diego CA 92103-0831 also: 227 E Palace Ave Ste M Santa Fe NM 87501-2043

CRUTZEN, PAUL JOSEF, research meteorologist, chemist; b. Amsterdam, The Netherlands, 1933. PhD in Meteorology, Stockholm U., 1973; hon. degree, York U., Can., 1986, Tel Aviv U., 1997, Oreg. State U., U. Bourgogne, Dijon, France, U. Liège, Belgium, 1997, U. Cath., Louvain-le-Neuve, Belgium, Aristotelian U., Thessaloniki, Greece, 1996, U. Athens, Greece, 1998, U. East Anglia, Norwich, Eng., 1994. Prof. Max-Planck-Inst. fur Chemie, Mainz, Germany. Recipient Nobel Prize for Chemistry, 1995. Mem. NAS (fgn. assoc.), Russian Acad. Scis. (fgn. assoc.), Royal Swedish Acad. Scis., Royal Swedish Acad. Engring. Scis., Academia Europea.

CRUZ, EMMANUEL MANUEL, scientist; b. San Antonio, Philippines, Apr. 4, 1943; s. Feliciano Liwanag and Conchita Manuel C.; m. Thelma Santos, Dec. 28, 1968; children: Charmaine, Cheryl, Charina. BS, Ctrl. Luzon State U., Munoz, Philippine, 1963; MS, Araneta U. Found., Manila, 1968; PhD, Auburn U., 1975. Instr., assoc. prof. CIS U., Munoz, Philippines, 1965-82; rsch. SEAFDEC, Tigbauan, Philippines, 1983-84; cons. USAID, P. Siantar, Indonesia, 1985-86; rsch. scientist KISR, Salmiya, Kuwait, 1986—; dean CLSU, Munoz, 1982, chmn., 1975-81; team leader SEAFDEC, 1984; project leader KISR, Salmiya, 1987-94. Contbr. articles to profl. jours. USAID/NEDA fellow, 1972-75. Mem. Asian Fisheries Soc., Internat. Assn. Aquatic Ecology & Mgmt., World Aquaculture Assn. Avocations: tennis, jogging, travel, reading, computer games. Office: Mariculture Fisheries Dept, Kiwait Inst Sci Rsch, Salmiya 22017, Kuwait

CRUZ, LUIZ DE CASTELLO, diplomat, lawyer; b. Rio de Janeiro, Mar. 11, 1938; s. Elmano da Costa and Anna Amelia (de Castello) C.; m. Anna Luiza de Almeida, Nov. 10, 1965 (div. Dec. 1978). JD, U. Brazil, Rio de Janeiro, 1960. Called to bar: Rio de Janeiro, 1960. Consul of Brazil San Francisco, 1967-71; asst. delegation of Brazil LAFTA, Montevideo, Uruguay, 1971-74; asst. to head, legal and consular dept. Ministry of Fgn. Affairs, Brazil, Brasília, 1976-81, head legal divsn., 1981-82; consul gen. of Brazil Rotterdam, 1987-91; dir. internat. law dept. Orgn. Am. States, Washington, 1982-86; legal advisor Ministry of Culture of Brazil, Brasília, 1993-94. Mem. Brazilian Soc. Internat. Law, Brazilian Lawyers Inst., Pan-Am. Inst. of Procedural Law. Home: SQS 110, bloco A Apto 501, 70373010 Brasilia Brazil

CRUZ-DIEZ, CARLOS, painter; b. Aug. 17, 1923. Student, Sch. of Plastic and Applied Arts, Caracas. Dir. art Venezuelan subs. of McCann-Erickson Advt. Agy., 1946-51; tchr. history of applied arts Sch. of Arts, Caracas, 1953-55; works on phys. qualities of color now named Physichromies, 1955-56; owner, mgr. Studio Vis. Arts and Indsl. Design, Caracas, 1957; prof., asst. dir. Sch. of Arts, Caracas, 1959-60; painter Paris, 1960—. One-man shows Caracas, Madrid, Genoa, Turin, London, Paris, Cologne, Oslo, Brussels, Ostwall Mus., Dortmund, Düsseldorf, São Paulo, N.Y.C., Bogota, Rome, Venice, Essen, Munich, Albers Mus., Bottrop, Germany; exhibited in numerous group shows; represented in permanent collections at Mus. de Bellas Artes, Caracas, Victoria and Albert Mus., Tate Gallery, London, Casa de las Americas, Havana, Städtisches Mus., Leverkusen, Germany, Mus. Ludwig, Cologne, Mus. Modern Art, N.Y.C., Mus. Contemporary Art, Montreal, Mus. des 20, Jahrhunderts, Vienna, Mus. Modern Art Lambert Collection, Dublin, Ireland. Recipient Grand Prix 3d Biennale, Cordoba, Argentina; Prix Internat. de Peinture a la IX Biennale de Sao Paulo. Home: 23 rue Pierre Semard, 75009 Paris France

CRUZ E SILVA, EDGAR FIGUEIREDO, biochemist, researcher; b. Lisbon, Portugal, May 17, 1958; s. Joaquim M. and Deolinda G.F. da Cruz e Silva; m. Odete Abreu Beirão, Sept. 2, 1984; children: Cristóvão, David. BSc, U. Essex, Colchester, U.K., 1983; PhD, U. Dundee, U.K., 1988, U. Coimbra, Portugal, 1996. Prin. investigator Rockefeller U., N.Y., 1991-95; guest assoc. prof. U. Aveiro, Portugal, 1996—, dir. Centro de Biologia Celular, 1997—, chmn. dept. biology, 1999—; external ptnr. CDC, 1997—; adj. sec. Rsch. Inst. U. Aveiro, 1998—. Contbr. chpts. to books in field. Grantee Ministry of Sci. and Tech., 1998. Mem. N.Y. Acad. Scis., Biochem. Soc. U.K., Soc. for Neurosci., Sociedade Portuguesa Bioquimica (v.p. 1997—). Roman Catholic. Home: Rua Clara Passos Esteves 19, 2135 Samora Correia Portugal Office: U Aveiro, Centro Biologia Celular, 3810 Aveiro Portugal

CRUZ E SILVA, JOAQUIM ALBERTO, science administrator; b. Fundão, Portugal, July 24, 1934; s. Aires Ferreira da Silva and Zulmira da Cruz e Silva. Diplome, Faculty of Vet. Medicine, Lisbon, Portugal, 1957; PhD, Tech. U. of Lisbon, 1972, Aggregation, 1973. Rsch. asst. Nat. Lab. Vet. Rsch., Lisbon, Portugal, 1959-64; rschr. Coun. of Overseas Sci. Rsch., Lisbon, Portugal, 1964-74; asst. Tech. U. of Lisbon, Portugal, 1964-72, prof. auxiliar, 1972-74, prof. extraordinary, 1974-79; sec. state higher edn. Portuguese Govt., Portugal, 1976-78; prof. cathedratic Tech. U. of Lisbon, Portugal, 1979; pres. Nat. Inst. for Sci. Rsch., Lisbon, 1978-80, Inst. for Tropical Sci. Rsch., Lisbon, 1980—; mem. Superior Coun. for Sci. and Tech., Lisbon, 1986-95, Econ. and Social Coun., Lisbon, 1994-95; pres. gen. assembly Portuguese Soc. Vet. Scis., Lisbon, 1989-97. Author: (book) Contribution for the Study of the Helmintes Parasites of Mozambique Vertebrates, 1971; contbr. articles to sci. jours. Vet. lt. Army, 1957-59, 63-64, Lisbon. Recipient Mendanha Jr. prize Tech. U. Lisbon, 1957, Pfizer prize Portuguese Soc. Vet. Scis., 1971; commendator of the Order of Infante D. Henrique, Portuguese Govt., 1985. Mem. N.Y. Acad. Scis., World Assn. for Advancement of Vet. Parasitology, Soc. Française de Parasitologie, Portuguese Soc. Vet. Scis., Portuguese Soc. Hidatidology (pres. 1997—), World Assn. Hidatidology. Roman Catholic. Avocation: sports. Home: Av do Brasil 44-3 F DTO, 1700-071 Lisbon Portugal Office: Inst for Tropical Sci Rsch, Inst for Tropical Sci Rsch, Rua da Junqueira 86, 1349-007 Lisbon Portugal

CRUZ-HERNANDEZ, ANGEL GUMERCINDO, computer research specialist; b. La Salud, Cuba, Jan. 13, 1946; s. Angel and Amparo (Hernandez) C.; m. Magaly Sobrino, July 5, 1969 (dec. 1992); children: Antuanet, Ahmed; m. Daniela Norat-Perdomo, Oct. 22, 1998. BS, U. Habana, 1969; MS, Centro Adiest. Computacion, 1981; PhD, ISPJAE, 1996. Prof. U. Habana, Havana, 1965-73; engr. Centro Inv. Digital, Havana, 1973-81; sr. rschr. Inst. Ctrl. Inv. Digital, Havana, 1981—; cons. EMCO, Havana, 1979-89; mem. Consejo Cientifico ICID, Havana, 1979—, mem. PhD nat. com. electronic and telecom. Author: Manual Circ. Integrados. Familia TTL, 1991; co-author: Dermatoglyphics: the Quiet Science, 2000; contbr. articles to profl. jours.; patentee in field. Sec. Consejo del Trabajo, 1973-76, 79-86. Recipient Bronze medal BAHX, Moscow, 1979, Jesus Menendez medal Cuban State Coun., 1991, Rafael Ma. de Mendive award SNTEC, Havana, 1991. Mem. Soc. Cubana Bioingenieria, Internat. Fedn. Med. & Biol. Engring. Avocations: collecting maps, photography, cats. Home: Cisneros Betancourt # 312, 11800 La Habana Cuba

CRUZ-HERNÁNDEZ, JUAN JOSE, English and American studies educator; b. Caracas, Venezuela, May 22, 1959; arrived in Spain, 1968; s. Juan Cruz and Maria Carmen Hernandez; m. Justa Suarez; children: Jorge, Eduardo. BA in Philology, U. La Laguna, Spain, 1982, PhD in Philology, 1986, BA in History, 1999. Dep. head dept. English and German U. La Laguna, 1991-92, dep. dir. grad. program, 1991-93, dir. grad. program, 1996-98, head grad. program, 1998—; cons. Ministry of Edn., Spain, 1998, Town Hall, Tegueste, Spain, 1998—. Author: Norman Mailer de Corea a Vietnam, 1988, Desnudos, Muertos, y Ofendidos, 1999; co-author: Culture and Power, 1995, Años de fuego lustros delluvia, 2000; contbr. revs. to profl. publs; mem. editl. bd. Revista Canaria de Estudios Ingleses, 1990, Atlantis, 1994, Miscelanea, 1994. Mem. Am. Studies Assn., Orgn. Am. Historians, Am. Hist. Assn., Assn. Española de Estudios Anglo-N.Am., European Assn. Am. Studies. Avocations: Am. cultural history, literature. E-mail: jcruz@ull.es. Home: Barbuzano 5, E 38280 Tegueste Spain Office: U La Laguna, Dept Philology, E-38071 La Laguna Spain

CRUZ-MAYOR, ANTONIO MANUEL, lawyer, real estate and shipping executive; b. Las Palmas, Spain, Jan. 31, 1940; s. Antonio and Manuela (Prendes) C.-M.; m. Elsa Gloria Suarez, Mar. 19, 1970; children: Silvia, Elsa, Antonio, Alejandro, Alberto. B, La Salle U., Las Palmas, 1958; lic. in law, Salamanca (Spain) U., 1963. Gen. dir. Sup. Cruz-Mayor, S.A., Las Palmas, 1965-96; owner Incrupe, S.L., Las Palmas, 1975—, Inmocruz Canarias, S.L., Las Palmas, 1996—, Prendelsa, S.L., Las Palmas, 1997—, Cruzpren, S.L., Las Palmas, 1999—, Internat. Shipping, Liberia, 1999—; atty., Las Palmas, 1965—. Mem. Law Sch. Avocation: art collecting. Office: Inmocruz Canarias SL, Paseo Tomas Morales 92-1, E-35004 Las Palmas Spain

CRYER, DENNIS ROBERT, pharmaceutical company executive, researcher; b. Dearborn, Mich., Mar. 30, 1944; s. Earl Wilton and Marguerite Gladys C.; children: Jonathan Eric, Catherine Grace, Laura Rose. BA in Biology, Johns Hopkins U., 1968; MD, Albert Einstein Coll. Medicine, 1977. Intern Children's Hosp. Phila., 1977-78, resident, 1978-79, 80-81; fellow in pathology and molecular biology U. Pa. Sch. Medicine, Phila., 1979-80; fellow in human genetics Sch. Medicine U. Pa., Phila., 1981-84, clin. asst. prof. pediatrics Sch. Medicine, 1983-84, asst. prof. pediatrics Sch. Medicine, 1984-87; assoc. clin. rsch. dir. E.R. Squibb and Sons, Princeton, N.J., 1987-89; assoc. med. devel. dir. Squibb U.S. Pharm. Group, Princeton, 1989-90, med. ops. dir., 1990-91, med. dir., 1991-94; sr. med. dir. cardiovascular/metabolism Women's Healthcare, 94-96, v.p. cardiovascular/metabolics, 1996; v.p. cardiovascular/metabolic advocacy programs Bristol Myers Squibb U.S. Pharm., Princeton, N.J., 1996—; corp. rep., corp. affairs com. Am. Soc. Hypertension, 1991—; mem. internat. adv. bd. Internat. Symposium on Drugs Affecting Lipid Metabolism, 1993-95, 99—; corp. rep. Pharm. Round Table, 1997—; mem. sci. and tech. com. Liberty Sci. Ctr., N.J., 1998—. Author: with others Cold Spring Harbor Symposium on Quantitative Biology, 1974, Methods in Cell Biology, 1975; contbr. articles Jour. of Molecular Biology, Jour. Lipid Rsch., Jour. Clin. Investigation. Grantee Nat. Heart, Lung, and Blood Inst., NIH, 1986, Am. Heart Assn., 1987; recipient Merck Faculty Devel. award Merck, Sharp, and Dohme,

1984. Fellow Am. Heart Assn. (arteriosclerosis coun., corp. rep. Pharm. Round Table, 1997—); mem. AAAS, Am. Diabetes Assn., Am. Fedn. Med. Rsch., Am. Soc. Human Genetics, Am. Soc. Hypertension (corp. rep., corp. affairs com.), Endocrine Soc., Fedn. Am. Socs. for Exptl. Biology, Internat. Atherosclerosis Soc., Molecular Medicine Soc., N.Y. Acad. Scis., Soc. Women's Health Rsch., Alpha Epsilon Delta. Achievements include pioneering development of evidence that eukaryotic chromosomes contain a single, double-stranded DNA molecule; demonstration of a gene dosage effect for mitochondrial DNA (using mating strains of yeast); development of methods using stable isotopes and gas chromatography-mass spectrometry to study human lipoprotein metabolism; demonstration of accurate measurement of hepatic lipoprotein synthesis using these methods; demonstration of a powerful autosomal dominant human gene which lowers cholesterol in a family with coexistent familial hypercholesterolemia. Home: 530 Aspen Woods Dr Yardley PA 19067-6314 Office: Bristol-Myers Squibb Co PO Box 4500 Princeton NJ 08543-4500

CRYMBLE, JOHN FREDERICK, chemical engineer, consultant; b. N.Y.C., Oct. 18, 1916; s. Hugh and Hannah (Knecht) C.; m. Mary Alenda Smith, June 24, 1944; 1 dau., Joanne Lee (Mrs. Donald L. Gilmore). BA, Columbia U., 1938, BS, 1939, MChemE, 1940. Prodn. supr. E.I. duPont de Nemours and Co., Chambers Works, Deepwater, N.J., 1940-73; sr. prodn. engr. E.I. duPont de Nemours and Co., Chambers Works, Deepwater, 1973-76; cons., 1977—. Past pres. Salem City Bd. Edn., also rep. N.J. Sch. Bds. Assn.; bd. dirs. Salem Free Libr. Mem. AIChE, Am. Chem. Soc., John Jay Assocs. Columbia, Thomas Egleston Assocs. Columbia Sch. Engring. and Applied Sci., Columbia U. Alumni Assn. (past exec. com., v.p. Phila., alumni medalist 1988), DuPont Country Club (Wilmington, Del.), Sigma Xi, Phi Lambda Upsilon, Tau Beta Pi. Methodist (trustee, past lay leader). Home and Office: 65 W Broadway Salem NJ 08079-1329

CRYSTAL, DAVID, linguist, writer; b. Lisburn, Ireland, July 6, 1941; s. Samuel Cyril and Mary Agnes (Morris) C.; m. Molly Irene Stack, Apr. 1, 1964 (dec. 1976); children: Steven David, Susan Mary, Timothy Joseph, Lucy Alexandra; m. Hilary Frances Norman, Sept. 18, 1976; 1 child, Benjamin Peter. BA, U. Coll., London, 1962; PhD, U. London, 1966; DSc, Queen Margaret Coll., Edinburgh, Scotland, 1996. Rsch. asst. Survey English Usage, London, 1962-63; asst. lectr. U. Coll. North Wales, Bangor, 1963-65; lectr. U. Reading, Eng., 1965-69; reader U. Reading, 1969-75, prof., 1975-85; hon. prof. U. Wales, Bangor, 1985—; non-exec. dir. W&R Chambers, Edinburgh, 1990-93; bd. dirs. British Coun., London, 1996—. Author: Linguistics, Language and Religion, 1965, What is Linguistics?, 1968, 5th edit., 1985, Linguistics, 1971, 2d edit., 1985, The English Tone of Voice, 1975, Child Language, Learning and Linguistics, 1976, 2d edit., 1987, Introduction to Language Pathology, 1980, 4th edit., 1998, A Dictionary of Linguistics and Phonetics, 1980, 4th edit., 1997, Clinical Linguistics, 1981, Directions in Applied Linguistics, 1981, Profiling Linguistic Disability, 1982, 2d edit., 1992, Language Handicap in Children, 1984, Linguistic Encounters with Language Handicap, 1984, Who Cares About English Usage?, 1984, 2d edit., 2000, Listen to your Child, 1986, The Cambridge Encyclopedia of Language, 1987, 2d edit., 1997, Rediscover Grammar, 1988, 2d edit., 1996, The English Language, 1988, Making Sense of English Usage, 1991, Nineties Knowledge, 1992, Introducing Linguistics, 1992, Cambridge Encyclopedia of the English Language, 1995, Discover Grammar, 1996, English as a Global Language, 1997, Language Play, 1998, The Penguin Dictionary of Language, 1999, Language Death, 2000, Happenings, 2000; co-author: Systems of Prosodic and Paralinguistic Features in English, 1964, Investigating English Style, 1969, Advanced Conversational English, 1975, Skylarks, 1975, Convent, 1989, Datasearch series, 1991, 1992, others; editor: Eric Partridge: In His Own Words, 1980, Linguistic Controversies, 1982, Cambridge Encyclopedia, 1990, 4rd edit., 2000, The Cambridge Concise Encyclopedia, 1992, 2nd edit., 1995, The Cambridge Paperback Encyclopedia, 1993, 3rd edit., 1999, The Cambridge Factfinder, 1993, 4rd edit., 2000, The Cambridge Biographical Encyclopedia, 1994, 2nd edit., 1998, The Cambridge Biographical Dictionary, 1995, John Bradburne: Songs of the Vagabond, 1996, John Bradburne's Mutemwa, 2000, others; co-editor: The English language, 1987, others; editor Linguistics Abstracts, 1985-96, Child Language Teaching and Therapy, 1985-96, Making Sense of English, 1990-93, others; assoc. editor Jour. Linguistics, 1970-73; cons. editor English Today, 1985-94; contbr. articles to profl. jours. dir. Ucheldre Ctr., Holyhead, U.K., 1991—; trustee Holyhead Opportunities Trust, 1989-92. Recipient OBE, Officer of the Order of the Brit. Empire, 1995. Fellow Brit. Acad., Coll. Speech Therapists, Royal Soc. Arts; mem. Soc. Indexers (hon. pres. 1992-95), Nat. Literacy Assn. (chmn. 1995—), Royal Coll. Speech Lang. Therapists (hon. v.p. 1995—), Nat. Assn. Profls. Concerned with Lang. Impaired Children (hon. pres. 1985—), Internat. Assn. Tchrs. English as a Fgn. Lang. (hon. pres. 1995—), Linguistics Assn. Great Britain (sec. 1965-70), Linguistics Soc. Am., Am. Speech Lang. Hearing Assn. Roman Catholic. Avocations: arts, book collecting, music, acting, cinema.

CRYSTAL, JAMES WILLIAM, insurance company executive; b. N.Y.C., Oct. 9, 1937; s. I. Frank and Evelyn G. Crystal; m. Jean Crystal; children: James F., Sanford F., Jonathan F. BS, Trinity Coll., 1958. With Royal Globe Ins. Group, N.Y.C., 1956; underwriter Home Ins. Co., N.Y.C., 1957; spl. agt. Home Ins. Co., San Francisco, 1958-59; chmn., chief exec. officer Frank Crystal & Co. Inc., N.Y.C., 1960—; chmn. bd. F.F.H. Ins. Co., Northeast Inst. Co.; bd. dirs. Atlantic Internat. Ins. Co. Bd. dirs. Auto Resources, Inc., Inst. for East-West Studies, Inc.; chmn. Internat. Space Brokers; trustee Mt. Sinai NYU Health Orgn. and Mt. Sinai Med. Sch., Trinity Coll. Mem. Nat. Assn. Casualty and Surety Agts., Harmonie Club, N.Y. Stock Exch. Lunch Club, India Ho. Club N.Y., Century Country Club, Wings Club N.Y. Republican. Home: 875 Park Ave New York NY 10021-0341 Office: Frank Crystal & Co 40 Broad St New York NY 10004-2315

CRYSTAL, STEPHEN, health care educator, researcher; b. Oct. 6, 1946. BA, U. Chgo., 1968; MA, Harvard U., 1975, PhD, 1981. 0chief div. health care svcs. U. Calif. Sch. Medicine, San Diego, 1985-87; dir. mgmt. sys., human svcs. rschr., program planner N.Y.C. Human Resources Adminstrn. Family and Adult Svcs., 1972-85; rsch. prof., chmn. divsn. on aging, dir. AIDS rsch. Inst. Health, Health Care Policy and Aging Rsch. Rutgers U., New Brunswick, N.J., 1987—, asst. dir. rsch. Ctr. for State Health Policy, 1999—; vis. prof. dept. health care policy Harvard Med. Sch., Cambridge, Mass., 1995-96; advisor N.J. Legislature, Trenton, 1998—; mem. study sects. NIH, Bethesda, Md., 1998—; investigator N.J. Dept. Health and Sr. Svcs., Trenton, 1999—. Recipient John Kendrick prize Internat. Assn. for Rsch. on Income and Wealth, women's health rsch. leadership award Jacobs Inst. for Women's Health, 1999. Fellow Am. Gerontol. Soc. Am.; mem. APHA, Am. Sociol. Assn., Am. Econ. Assn., Am. Statis. Assn. E-mail: scrystal@rei.rutgers.edu. Office: Rutgers U Inst Health Health Care Policy and Aging Rsch 30 College Ave New Brunswick NJ 08901-1283

CSABA, IMRE FERENC, obstetrician and gynecologist; b. Tolna, Hungary, Nov. 2, 1926; s. Imre Jenő and Rács C.; m. Tatjana Erzsébet, June 15, 1923; children: Imre, Tünde. MD, U. Pécs, Hungary, 1951; Habilitation, U. Pécs, 1965. Pvt. practice Pécs, 1951-55; asst. prof. ob-gyn. Med. U. Pécs, 1967-73, prof. ob-gyn., 1973—; dir. dept. ob-gyn. Med. U. Pécs, 1975-91. Mem. Coun. Pécs, 1980-90. Homored and Merited physician of the Hungarian Republic. Mem. Assn. Hungarian Ob-Gyn., Assn. Bulgarian and Germany Ob-Gyn. (hon.). Achievements include work in reproductive endocrinology, microsurgery and in vitro fertilization. Avocation: music. Home: Kis réti u 5, 7636 Pécs Hungary

CSABA, LASZLO, economist; b. Budapest, Mar. 27, 1954; s. Ede and Marta (Biro) C.; m. Gabriella Onody, Mar. 22, 1980; children: Zoltan, Orsolya. BA, Budapest U. Econs., 1976, MA, 1978; PhD, Hungarian Acad. Sci., 1984, postgrad., 1996; Dr.Habil., BUES, 1997. Fellow Inst. for World Economy, Budapest, 1976-87; sr. econ. Kopint-Datorg, Budapest, 1988-2000; sr. econ. IRES dept. Cen. European U., Budapest, 2000—; advisor Ministry of Fin., Budapest, 1991-93; lectr. Budapest U. Econs., 1978-91; prof. Coll. of Fgn. Trade, Budapest, 1991-97, Budapest U. Econs., 1997—, Kossuth U. Scis., Debrecen, 1999; mem. Reform Com. on Pub. Fin., Budapest, 1995-96; vis. prof. L. Bocconi U., Milan, Italy, 1991, U. Helsinki, 1993, Europa U. ViaDrina, Frankfort, Germany, 1997, Ctrl. European U., 1997-98, Free U. Berlin, 1998, 99, 2000. Author: The Capitalist Revolution in Eastern Europe, 1995, Eastern Europe in the World Economy, 1990; editor: Privatization, Liberalization & Destruction, 1994, Systemic Change and Stabilization in Eastern Europe, 1991, The Hungarian Small Business in Comparative Perspective, 1998; co-editor: (with M. Dimitrov, W. Andreff) Economies in Transition and the Varieties of Capitalism, 1999, (with Z. Bara) Small Country Adjustment to International Economic Disturbances, 2000. Mem. European Assn. for Comparative Econs. (v.p. 1990-94, 96—, pres. 1999-2000), Hungarian Acad. Scis. (com. on econs. 1985—, co-chmn. 1996—). Roman Catholic. Avocations: classical music, opera, soccer, tourism. Office: Kopint-Datorg, Cen European U, IRES Dept, 1051 Budapest Hungary

CSAKVARI, BELA, chemist; b. Stari Vrbas, Yugoslavia, May 30, 1924; arrived in Hungary, 1945.; MS, Eotvos U., 1950, PhD, 1960; DS, Hungary Acad. Scis., 1970. Asst. prof. Eotvos U., Budapest, Hungary, 1954-61, assoc. prof., 1962-69, prof., 1970-95, prof. emeritus, 1996—; head dept. gen. and inorganic chemistry Eotvos U., 1966-92. Editor Kemiai Kozlemenyek, 1964—, New Results in Chemistry, 1970—. mem. com. instrumentation Ministry of Edn., 1970-88; mem. state com. Sci. Policy, Budapest, 1990-94. Mem. Phys. and Inorganic Chemistry (mem. com. HAS 1964-92), Inorganic and Organometallic Chemistry (mem. com. HAS 1975—). Home: Torocko u 28, H-1026 Budapest Hungary Office: Eotvos Lorand U, Pazmany P setany 2, H-1518 Budapest Hungary

CSÁKY, MORITZ, history educator; b. Levoca, Slovakia, Apr. 3, 1936; s. Gustav and Vera (Normann-Ehrenfels) C.; m. Eva-Marie Loebenstein, Mar. 27, 1977; 1 child, Stefan. DPhil, U. Vienna, 1966, Habilitation, 1979; Master degree, St. Gabriel Coll., Vienna, Austria, 1961; lic. in ecclestical history, Gregorian U., Rome, 1963. Assoc. prof. history U. Vienna, 1979-84; prof. U. Graz, Austria, 1984—; v.p. Rsch. Coun., Vienna, 1988-97; pres. Internat. Rsch. Ctr. Cultural Studies, Vienna, 1992-95. Author: The Kulturkampf in Hungary, 1967, From Enlightenment to Liberalism, 1981, The Ideology of Operetta and Viennese Modernity, 199€; editor: Hermann Bahr Diary I-IV, 1994-2000, Europe in the Age of Mozart, 1995. Recipient Széchényi prize State of Hungary, 1989, prix-Europe Acad. Strasbourg, 1994, Karl von Vogelsang award Austrian Rep., 1998. Mem. Austrian Acad. Sci. (Wilhelm-Hartel award 1997). Office: U Graz, Heinrichstrasse 26, A-8010 Graz Austria

CSANAKY, GYORGY GEZA, pathologist; b. Pecs, Baranya, Hungary, Nov. 16, 1953; s. Gyorgy and Marta (Maurer) C.; m. Andrea Judit Kincses, Dec. 21, 1978; children: Tibor, Katalin. MD, Univ. Med. Sch. of Pecs, Hungary, 1978, PhD, 1994. Cert. specialist in pathology. Resident County Hosp. Somogy, Kaposvar, Hungary, 1978-80; mem. staff County Hosp. Baranya, Pecs, 1980-85; instr. Univ. Med. Sch. of Pecs, 1985-95; chief pathologist Markusovszky Tchg. Hosp., Szombathely, Hungary, 1995—. Contbr. articles to profl. jours. Mem. Soc. Hungarian Pathologists. Home: Petőfi u 68, 7623 Pécs Hungary Office: Markusovszky Tchg Hosp, Markusovszky u 3, 9700 Szombathely Hungary

CSANGO, THOMAS MICHAEL, health organization executive; b. Budapest, Hungary, Apr. 16, 1938; s. Alexander and Margaret Csango; m. Judy Joan Gosztonyi, Aug. 25, 1961; 1 child, Andrea. Technician, Tech. Coll. Budapest, 1956, biomed. engr., 1966; mktg., Coll. Commerce Budapest, 1972. Rschr. Medicorworks, Budapest, 1966-72, head med. dept., 1972-89; fin. supr. med. dept. St. Imre Hosp., Budapest, 1989—; cons. Sote U., Budapest, 1982-89. Contbr. articles to profl. jours. Avocations: travel, crossword puzzles, gymnastics. Home: Liszt Ferenc Square 6, 1061 Budapest Hungary Office: Saint Imre Hosp, Tetenyi ut 12-16, 1115 Budapest Hungary

CSÁNYI, VILMOS, biologist, researcher, educator; b. Budapest, Hungary, May 9, 1935; s. Vilmos and Margaret (Illés) C.; m. Éva Nádai, Sept. 4, 1988; children: Julia, Gabor. Masters, Eötvös U., Budapest, 1958; PhD, Semmelweis Med. Sch., Budapest, 1965, DSc, 1970. Rsch. chemist Chinoin Pharm. Co., Budapest, 1958; asst. prof. dept. med. chemistry Semmelweis U., 1958-73; prof., head dept. ethology Eötvös U., 1973—; associated editor World Future, USA, 1990-95; project lead com. edn. Internat. Union Biologists, 1989—. Author: General Theory of Evolution, 1982, Evolutionary Systems and Society, 1989, Ethology, 1994; contbr. over 200 articles to profl. jours. Mem. Hungarian Ethological Soc. Budapest (pres. 1990—), Hungarian Biol. Soc. Budapest (v.p. 1994—), Gen. Evolution Rsch. Group, Humanethology Soc., Lang. Origin Soc., Hungarian Acad. Sci., European Acad. Sci. and Arts. Avocation: gardening. E-mail: H1872csa@ella.hu. Office: Eotvos U Budapest Dept Ethology, Javorka S u 14, H-2131 God Hungary

CSAPÓ, BENŐ, education educator; b. Szentgál, Hungary, Mar. 5, 1953; s. Benő Csapó and Jolán Csefkó; m. Vilma Tóth, Oct. 27, 1979; children: Gergely, András. MS in Physics and Chemistry, Attila József U., Szeged, Hungary, 1977, PhD in Edn., 1979, Dr.Habil., 1996. Research asst. Attila József U., Szeged, Hungary, 1976-77, research fellow, 1977-79, asst. lectr., 1979-82, asst. prof., 1982-87, assoc. prof., 1987-97, vice chair dept. edn., 1987-90, full prof., 1997—, chair Inst. of Edn. and Psychology, 1990-95, head dept. edn., 1995-99; fellow Ctr. for Advanced Study in the Behavioral Scis., Stanford (Calif.) U., 1994-95. Humboldt Rsch. felllow U. Breman, 1999. Mem. ASCD, Internat. Soc. Study Behavioral Devel., World Assn. Ednl. Rsch., European Assn. Rsch. on Learning and Instrn. (nat. corr. 1987-97, mem. exec. 1997—), Am. Ednl. Rsch. Assn. Home: Fö fasor 132/B, H-6726 Szeged Hungary Office: U Szeged, Petőfi sgt 30-34, H-6722 Szeged Hungary

CSAPÓ, ZSOLT, obstetrician, gynecologist, educator; b. Kecskemét, Hungary, Feb. 26, 1938; s. Endre and Borbála (Szabó) C.; m. Éva Barthos, Sept. 10, 1940; children: Zsolt, Szabolcs. MD, Med. U. Szeged, Hungary, 1962; PhD, Semmelweis U., Budapest, Hungary, 1986. Cert. specialist in pathology, ob-gyn. Asst. prof. in pathology Med.U. Szeged, 1962-71; chief pathologist Gen. Hosp., Szeged, 1971-73; asst. prof. ob-gyn. Semmelweis U., 1973-85; assoc. prof. Semmelweis U. Med. Sch., 1985—, dep. dir., 1998—, head Histology Lab., 1989—, head prenatal and/or gynecology wards, 1986—, head tchg. of English speaking course in ob-gyn., 1993—. Contbr. articles to med. jours., including Arch. Pathology, Jour. Molecular Cellular Cardiology, Am. Jour. Pathology, Jour. Reproductive Medicine. Master sgt. Hungarian Army, 1963. Mem. Internat. Soc. Gynecol. Pathologists, Coll. Hungarian Ob-Gyn., European Assn. of Gynecologists and Obstetricians. Avocation: tennis, reading. Office: Semmelweis U I Dept, Ob-Gyn, Baross u 27, 1088 Budapest Hungary

CSÁSZÁR, GÉZA, geologist; b. Muraszemenye, Hungary, Feb. 28, 1943; s. János and Julianna (Nagy) C.; m. Mária Kellencz, Nov. 30, 1968; children: Ajna, Ilma, Gábor. Grad., Eötvös Loránd U., Budapest, Hungary, 1966, PhD in Geology, 1984; DSc, Hungarian Acad. Sci., 1999. Jr. scientist Hungarian Geol. Inst., Budapest, 1966-67, sr. scientist, 1967-70, project mgr., 1990—; in charge mineral resources Mongolian-Hungarian Geol. Expdn., Choibalsan, Mongolia, 1970-71; sci. sec. Hungarian Ctrl. Office Geology, Budapest, 1971-78; head dept. Hungarian Geol. Inst., Budapest, 1978-90, project mgr., 1990-99; head regional geol. dept. Eötvös Loránd U., Budapest, 1999—; sci. educator, 1989—; sec. Stratigraphic Commn. Hungary, Budapest, 1972-80, pres., 1990—; mem. Internat. Cretaceous Subcommn., 1984—; co-leader Tethyan Cretaceous Correlation, Internat. Geol. Correlation Program, 1987-93; rsch. lectr. Eötvös Loránd U., 1990-99; corr. Geol. Survey, Vienna, 1989; sec. Commn. Geol. Hungarian Acad. Sci., 1996—; v.p. Soc. Geol. Herit. Hungarian, 1997-99. Mem. editl. bd. Acta Geologica Hungarica, Slovak Geol. Mag.; editor-in-chief Bull. Hungarian Geol. Soc. Recipient decoration Work Coun. Mins., Budapest, 1976, Cestné uznání Czechoslovak Acad. Scis., 1986, Koch medal, 1994; Szechenyi Prof. scholar, 1999. Mem. Carpatho-Balkan Geol. Assn. (pres. Stratigraphic, Paleogeog. and Paleontologic Commn.), Coun. Nature Protection Hungary. Home: Szlacsányi F 180, H-1151 Budapest Hungary Office: Geol Inst of Hungary, Stefánia ut 14, H-1143 Budapest Hungary

CSASZAR, GYULA, psychiatrist; b. Szombathely, Hungary, Jan. 29, 1928; s. Gyula and Gyulane Ilona (Varadi) C.; m. Gyulane Elisabeth Levay, Aug. 2, 1952 (div. Mar. 1958); 1 child, Albert; m. Gyulane Emoke Bagdy, Apr. 1, 1961; children: (twins) Zsolt, Noemi. Internist Mcpl. Hosp., Budapest, Hungary, 1956-71, chief med. physician, 1971—. Author: Psychosomatic Medicine, 1980, Psychosomatic Praxis, 1989. Avocation: gardening. Home: Szt Istvan krt5, 1055 Budapest Hungary

CSÁTHY, LÁSZLÓ, neonatologist; b. Budapest, Hungary, Oct. 23, 1954; s. Károly and Julia (Egle) C.; m. Agnes Dézsi, Sept. 20, 1980; children: Anna, Zsuzsanna. MD, Univ. Med. Sch. Budapest, 1980; PhD, Acad. Sci. Budapest, 1993. Resident in pediats. County Hosp. Debrecen, Hungary, 1980-84, pediatrician, 1984-87, neonatologist, 1987—; head scientific coun. County Hosp. Debrecen, 1992. Br. Pediat. Assn. fellow, 1995, Hungarian Acad. Scis. fellow, 1988. Mem. ESPR, Hungarian Pediat. Assn., Hungarian Neonatology Assn., Royal Coll. Pediat. and Child Health, Hungarian Med. Assn. Am. Avocations: gliding, photography, computer, fishing. E-mail: lcsathy@mail.datanet.hu. Office: County Hosp Dept Pediat, Bartók B 2-26, H 4043 Debrecen Hungary

CSÉCSEI, GYÖRGY ISTVÁN, neurosurgeon, educator; b. Debrecen, Hungary, Aug. 27, 1948; s. Károly and Etelka (Varga) C.; m. Katalin Éva Módis, Aug. 1, 1975; children: Zsófia, György, Noémi. MD, Debrecen U. Medicine, 1972. Intern Dept. Neurosurgery, Giessen, Germany, 1981-82, 84, resident, 1985-87; asst. Debrecen U. Medicine, 1972-79, cons., 1979-85, 85-87, asst. prof. neurosurgery, 1988-92, prof., 1992—; dir. dept. neurosurgery Debrecen U. Medicine, 1992—. Mem. Hungarian Neurosurg. Soc. (gen. sec. 1995), German Neurosurg. Soc. Roman Catholic. Avocation: playing classical guitar. Home: Hajdu-Bihar, Akadémia u 97, 4032 Debrecen Hungary Office: Debrecen Univ Medicine, Nagyerdei Krt 98 Dept Neuro, 4012 Debrecen Hungary

CSENDE, FERENC, pharmacist, researcher; b. Debrecen, Hungary, June 14, 1965; s. Ferenc József and Ferencné Zsófia (Csuka) C.; m. Ferencné Andrea Porkoláb, Aug. 26, 1989; children: Gergely David, Kristóf Máté. BSc, Albert Szent-Györgyi Med.U., Szeged, Hungary, 1989. Rsch. pharmacist Alkaloida Chem. Co. Ltd., Tiszavasvári, Hungary, 1989-94; asst. Albert Szent-Györgyi Med. U., Szeged, 1994-96; rsch. pharmacist, mgr. Medikament Pharm. Trading Co., Ltd., Szeged, 1996-97; rsch. mgr. Taxus Pharms., Tiszavasvári, 1997—. Contbr. articles to profl. jours. Mem. Hungarian Pharm. Soc. Home: Vasvári Pál u 61, H-4440 Tiszavasvári Hungary Office: Taxus Pharmaceuticals, Vasvári Pál u 110, H-4440 Tiszavasvári Hungary

CSENDES, ERNEST, chemist, corporate and financial executive; b. Satu-Mare, Szatmár-Németi, Romania, Mar. 2, 1926; came to U.S., 1951, naturalized, 1955; s. Edward O. and Sidonia (Littman) C. m. Catharine Vera Tolnai, Feb. 7, 1953; children: Audrey Carol, Robert Alexander Edward. BA, Protestant Coll., Hungary, 1944; BS, U. Heidelberg (Ger.), 1948, MSc, 1950, PhD summa cum laude, 1951. Rsch. asst. chemistry U. Heidelberg, 1950-51; rsch. assoc. biochemistry Tulane U., New Orleans, 1952; rsch. fellow chemistry Harvard U., 1952-53; rsch. chemist organic chems. dept. E. I. Du Pont de Nemours and Co., Wilmington, Del., 1953-56, elastomer chems. dept., 1956-61; dir. rsch. and devel. agrl. chems. div. Armour & Co., Atlanta, 1961-63; v.p. corp. devel. Occidental Petroleum Corp., L.A., 1963-64, exec. v.p. rsch., engring. and devel., mem. exec. com., 1964-68; COO, exec. v.p., dir. Occidental Rsch. and Engring. Corp., L.A., London, Moscow, 1963-68; mng. dir. Occidental Rsch. and Engring. (U.K.) Ltd., London, 1964-68; pres., CEO TRI Group, London, Amsterdam, Rome and Bermuda, 1968-84; chmn., CEO Micronic Techs., Inc., L.A., 1981-85; mng. ptnr. Inter-Consult Ltd., Pacific Palisades, Calif.; internat. cons. on tech., econ. feasibility and mgmt., 1984—; pres., CEO, chief tech. officer Gen. Grinding Corp., L.A., 1991—; chmn., CEO Eden Mgmt. Ltd., L.A. and London, 1993—. Contbr. 250 articles to profl. and trade jours., studies and books. Recipient Pro Mundi Beneficio gold medal Brazilian Acad. Humanities, 1975; Harvard U. fellow, 1953. Fellow AAAS, Am. Inst. Chemists, Royal Soc. Chemistry (London); mem. AIAA, IEEE, SMME, AIChE, Am. Chem. Soc., German Chem. Soc., N.Y. Acad. Sci., Am. Concrete Inst., Am. Water Works Assn., AMS Internat., Acad. Polit. Sci., Nat. Def. and Indsl. Assn., Sigma Xi. Achievements include 44 patents; rsch. in area of elastomers, rubber chemicals, adhesives, dyes and intermediates, organometallics, organic and biochemistry, high polymers, antioxidants, superphosphoric acid and ammonium polyphosphates, plant nutrients, pesticides, process engineering, design of fertilizer plants, sulfur, potash, phosphate and iron ore mining and metallurgy, coal combustion and cleanup of acid gases and air toxics, self-cleaning micronized coal fuels, municipal water clean-up, methods for aerodynamic grinding of solids, particles technology, advanced building materials, petrochemicals, biomed. engring., consumer products; also acquisitions, mergers, internat. fin. related to leasing investments and loans, trusts and ins., new Eurodollar instruments; regional indsl. devel. related to agr. and energy resources; projects in western Europe, no. Africa, Russia, Japan, Saudi Arabia, India, China and the Philippines. Home: 514 N Marquette St Pacific Palisades CA 90272-3314

CSERHATI, TIBOR, chemical engineer; b. Kiskunfelegyhaza, Hungary, Nov. 11, 1938; s. Mihaly and Maria (Szluka) C.; m. Judit Nagy, 1971 (div. 1981); 1 child, Eva. Degree in Chem. Engring., Tech. U. Budapest, 1962, MD, 1968, PhD, 1973; DSc, Hungarian Acad. Scis., 1988. Rsch. fellow Dairy Rsch. Inst., Hungarian Acad. Scis., 1965-73; sr. rsch. scientist Plant Protection Inst., Hungarian Acad. Scis., 1975-88; sci. counsellor Ctrl. Rsch. Inst. for Chemistry, Hungarian Acad. Scis., 1989—. Author 3 books; contbr. chpts. to books, more than 400 articles to profl. jours. Home: Pillango Park 8/B, 1149 Budapest Hungary Office: Hungarian Acad Sci, Pusztaszeri u 57, 1525 Budapest Hungary

CSERNI, GÁBOR ZSOLT, pathologist, consultant; b. Kecskemét, Hungary, Jan. 27, 1966; s. Imre and Katalin (Kurucz) C.; m. Emese Csongrádi, Aug. 30, 1991; children: Bálint, Dorottya. MD, Szent-Gyorgyi Med. U., Szeged, Hungary, 1990, PhD. Med. diplomate. Cons. Bács-Kiskun County Hosp., Kecskemét, 1990-92, 94—; resident Szent-Gyorgyi Med. U., 1992-94. Contbr. articles to profl. jours. With Hungarian Army, 1993-94. Mem. Hungarian Med. Chamber, Hungarian Pathol. Soc., Internat. Acad. Pathology, Hungarian Soc. Senology, Hungarian Soc. Oncologists. Roman Catholic. Avocations: literature, theatre, film, music. Fax: 36-76-481219. Office: Bács-Kiskun County Hosp, Nyíri Út 38, H-6000 Kecskemét Hungary

CSERNY, TIBOR, geologist-engineer; b. Budapest, Hungary, Apr. 7, 1951; s. György and Ilona (Buday) C.; m. Katalin Cserny-Mészáros, Dec. 18, 1976; children: Peter, Aniko. MSc, Leningrad Mining U., 1974; degree, Budapest Tech. U., 1985; PhD, Miskolc U., Hungary, 1997. Cons. Internat. Geol. Expdn., Mongolia, 1978-79; project mgr. Hungarian Geol. Survey, 1979-95; rsch. fellow Geol. Inst. Hungary, Budapest, 1974-77, project mgr. limnogeological rsch., 1995—; sci. sec. Hungarian Geol. Inst., 1982-91; sec. VIII RCMNS Congress, Budapest, 1985; invited prof. environ. geology Miskolc U., 1997—, Sopron U., 1999—. Co-author: Geological and Landscape Conservation, 1994, Global Geological Record of Lake Basins, 1994, Lake Basins Through Space and Time, 2000; also articles. Rsch. grantee Ministry of Environ., Copenhagen, 1992, Hungarian Acad. Scis., Cambridge, Eng., 1993, 94; grantee Soros Found., China, 1996; Ministry of Edn. scholar, Munich, 1991. Mem. Hungarian Geol. Soc. (sec. 1981-94), IAEG, INQUA. Fax: 36-1-251 07 03. E-mail: csernyt@mafi.hu. Office: Geol Inst Hungary, 14 Stefania St, 1143 Budapest Hungary

CSIBA, LASZLO, neurologist; b. Sajoszentpeter, Hungary, May 10, 1952; s. Laszlo and Eva (Geressy) C. MD, Debrecen U., Hungary, 1976; neurologist, Postgrad. U., Budapest, 1980, psychiatrist, 1986; PhD, Hungary Acad. Sci., Budapest, 1990, Doctor of Acad., 1999. Resident dept. neurology Debreeen Hosp., Hungary, 1976-81; rsch. fellow Max-Planck Inst., Cologne, Germany, 1981-83, Chugoku Rousai, Kure City, Japan, 1986-87; rschr. INSERM, Toulouse, France, 1996; vis. prof. Tohoku U., Sendai, Japan, 1997; prof. and chmn. dept. neurology Debrecen U., 1997—; pres. neurological adv. bd., Budapest, 1996-99; mem. com. bd. cert., Budapest, 1995. Contbr. articles to profl. jours. Founder Maltesian Charity Orgn. Recipient Szechenyi grant, Hungarian Govt., 1997, Excellence in Stroke Rsch. award, European Stroke conference, 1994. Office: U Med Sch Debrecen, Nagyerdei Krt 98, 4012 Debrecen Hungary

CSIHA, KÁLMÁN, bishop; b. Érsemlyén, Bihar, Romania, Sept. 17, 1929; s. Sándor Kázmér and Erzsébet (Szilágyi) C.; m. Emese Nagy, Nov. 6, 1956 (dec. Feb. 1996); 1 child, Emese. MS, Protestant Theol. Inst., Kolozsvár, Romania, 1954, DS, 1975; D Honoris Causa, Reformed Theol. Acad., Debrecen, Hungary, 1993. Ordained minister Reformed Ch. Romania. Vicar Nagyvárad Dist. Reformed Ch. Romania, 1954-56, minister Nagyvárad Dist., 1956-57; minister Kolozsvár Dist. Reformed Ch. Romania,

Gógánváralja, 1964-70; minister Kolozsvár Dist. Reformed Ch. Romania, Marosvásárhely, 1970-80, dean, 1980-90; bishop Transylvanian Dist. Reformed Ch. Romania, Kolozsvár, 1990—; mem. ctrl. com. World Coun. Chs., Geneva, 1991-98; pres. Consultative Synod of Hungarian Reformed Chs., Budapest, 1995—; v.p. Hungarian Reformed World Fedn., Budapest, 1991-98. Author: Theological Studies, 3 vols., 1991-2000, Sermons, 6 vols., 1991-99, Light Through the Bars, 1992; contbr. articles to profl. jours. Polit. prisoner, Gherla and other camps, Romania, 1957-64. Office: Bishop's Office, Str I C Brătianu 51, 3400 Cluj Kolozsvár, Romania

CSIKY, BOTOND S., physician; b. TG-Mures, Romania, Nov. 13, 1967; arrived in Hungary, 1984; s. Csaba Csiky and Klara Nagy; m. Gabriella Orsi, 1995; children: Anna, Csiky. MD, U. Med. Sch. Pécs, Hungary, 1992. Resident U. Med. Sch. Pécs, 1992-94, 96-97, staff mem., 1997—; postdoctoral rsch. fellow U. Minn., Mpls., 1994-96. Contbr. articles to profl. jours. Mem. Hungarian Soc. Hypertension, Hungarian Soc. Nephrology. Office: U Med Sch Pécs, 2d Dept Med, Pacsirta 1, 7624 Pécs Hungary

CSILLAG, LASZLO, physicist; b. Budapest, Feb. 23, 1934; s. Jozsef and Jozsefne (Türr) C.; m. Janka Faggyas; children: Kristof, Dora, Lucia, Sara. Degree in physics and math., Roland Eotvos U., 1957, PhD, 1973. Rschr. Ctrl. Rsch. Inst. for Physics, Budapest, 1958-92, Rsch. Inst. for Solid State Physics, Budapest, 1992—; scientific sec. Rsch. Inst. for Solid State Physics, 1986-98, sec. emeritus, 1998—. Contbr. articles to profl. jours.; co-author: Experimental Spectroscopy, 1989. Recipient Petzval award Optical Soc., 1989. Roman Catholic. Avocation: gardening. Office: Rsch Inst Solid State Physi, Konkoly Thege M ut 29-33, H-1121 Budapest Hungary

CSILLIK, BERTALAN BERTRAM, anatomist; b. Szeged, Hungary, Nov. 10, 1927; s. Bertalan sen. and Alice (Csiky) C.; m. Elizabeth Knyihár, Apr. 30, 1972; children: Eva, Peter, Anita, Andrea. MD, U. Med. Sch., 1954; PhD, Hungarian Acad. of Scis., 1962, ScD, 1968. Demonstrator of anatomy U. Med. Sch., Szeged, Hungary, 1950-54, asst. prof. anatomy, 1954-62, assoc. prof. anatomy, 1964-68, prof. anatomy, 1968—; asst. prof. pharmacology U. Pa., Phila., 1962-63; project dir. Bay Zoltán Inst. Biotechnology, Szeged, 1993—; vis. prof. Harvard Med. Sch., Boston, 1974-74, 77-78, 93-94; vis. prof. neuroanatomy Yale Med. Sch., New Haven, Conn., 1982, 92-95; chmn. dept. anatomy Univ. Med. Sch., Szeged, 1968-93; Fogarty sr. rsch. fellow Yale Med. Sch., 1992-94; bd. dirs. of the presidium of the PhD com. Albert Szent-Györgyi Med. U. Author: The Post-Synaptic Membrane, 1965, 2d edit. 1967; co-author: The Protean Gate, 1986 (Pub. Niveau award 1988), Topographical Anatomy, 1988, 2d edit. 1992 (Pub. Niveau award 1991); patentee in field. Recipient Silver Order of Labour Hungarian Govt., 1986. Mem. Dugonics Soc. (pres. 1992—), Hungarian Acad. Sci. (bd. dirs. doctoral com. 1985—, Laureate 1993), European Fedn. for Exptl. Morphology (bd. dirs. of the presidium 1991—), Internat. Brain Rsch. Orgn., Hungarian Anatomical Soc. (past pres.), Szeged Acad. Com. (pres. 1983-93, hon. pres. of neurobiology sect.), Soc. Friends of the Albert Szent-Gyorgyi Med. U. (chmn. 1997—), Acad. Royale de Medicine de Belgique (corr.), Deutsche Akademie Naturforscher Leopoldina. Avocations: violin playing. Home: Pillich Kalman u 24, H-6726 Szeged Hungary Office: Bay Zoltan Inst Biotech, Derkovits fasor 2, H-6726 Szeged Hungary

CSISZÁR, ANTAL, mechanical engineer; b. Jánoshalma, Hungary, Nov. 20, 1946; s. Antal and Anges Varga (Antalné) C.; m. Katalin Fülöp, Dec. 29, 1973; 1 child, Antal. M.E., Tech. U. Budapest, 1970; spl. engr. for environ. protection, 1981; PhD, Tech. U. Budapest, 1986. Designing engr. Lang Machine Wks., Budapest, 1970-74; research engr. Inst. for Elec. Power Research, Budapest, 1974-82; specialist Inst. Tech. Cons., Budapest, 1982-84, Inst. Environ. Protection, Budapest, 1984-86, Vegyepszer Tech. Research Inst., Budapest, 1986-94; chief engr. '96 Kft. Ltd., Budapest, 1994—; cons. in field; expert Hungarian Indsl. and Comml. Ministry, Sci. Soc. Mech. Engrs., Sci. Soc. Energy, Hungarian Acad. Engring., ASME; mng. dir. KTTK Ltd.; auditor TÜV CERT. Author: Environmental Protection and Manufacturing, 1988, Ency. of Environmental Protection, 1990; contbr. over 60 articles to pofl. jours. Recipient award, Com. of Sci. Soc. of Mech. Engrs., 1984. Mem. Soc. Engery (com. of sci.), Sci. Soc. Mech. Engrs. (chmn. nuclear energy com. 1979, sec. energy and chem. machinery 1989), Sci. Soc. Hungarian Environ. Protection, Sci. Soc. Hungarian Engring. Important achievements include patentee for noise reduction of supersonical jet into the pipe in power plants; designer steam turbine blades and vanes, analyzinnd elements of conventional and nuclear power plants; with fault tree method recudtion of SO2 and NO8 emission in Hungary, noise reduction in power plants. Avocation: teaching special course in environmental protection. Home: Kecskemeti U 13, H-1053 Budapest Hungary Office: 96 Kft Ltd, Bogdány u 10/A, H-1117 Budapest Hungary

CSOLLANY, SZILVESZTER, Olympic athlete; b. Sopron, Hungary, Apr. 13, 1970. Winner Silver Medal rings World Championships, 1992, 96, 97, winner Gold Medal rings European Championships, 1998, winner Silver Medal rings World Championships, 1999; winner Gold Medal rings Sydney, 2000. Office: Magyar Torna Szoevetseg, Dosza György ut 1-3, 1143 Budapest Hungary*

CSONTOS, JÓZSEF GYÖRGY, minister, counselor; b. Örkény, Pest, Hungary, Jan. 30, 1954; s. János Csontos and Sarolta Hencz; m. Virginia Henriette Wuellner, Mar. 23, 1984 (div.); children: Flóra, Sarolta, János. Diploma, Theol. Acad., Budapest, Hungary, 1980; MA in Theol. Studies, McCormick Theol. Sem., Chgo., 1984. Ordained min. Reformed Ch., 1986. Min. Hungarian Reformed Ch., Dabas, Hungary, 1980—; rep. Hungarian Reformed Ch./European Conf. Pastoral Care and Counseling, 1993-97. Crisis counselor Telephone Crisis Ctr., Budapest, 1987-97; pres. Hungarian Dem. Forum, Dabas, 1988; mem. Hungarian Dem. Forum Coun., Budapest, 1989; leader, founder Amnesty Internat., Dabas, 1992. Soldier Hungarian Infantry, 1974-76. Mem. Hungarian Game Soc. Avocations: swimming, parashoot jumping, horseback riding, playing. Office: Reformed Ch, Ravasz László u 7, 2370 Dabas Hungary

CSOPAKI, GYULA, science educator; b. Kölcse, Hungary, Mar. 30, 1946; s. Karoly and Jolan (Balku) C.; m. Fock Ibolya. MSc, Tech. U., 1969; PhD, Acad. of Scis., 1987. Scientific assoc. Tech. U., Budapest, 1969-86, assoc. prof., 1986—; vis. prof. POSTECH, Pohang, Korea, 1992; project team expert ETSI, Sophia, Antipolis, France, 1993; scientific sec. Acad. of Scis., 1985-95; vice dean Faculty of Elec. Engring. and Informatics, 1993—. Office: Tech Univ, Budapest U Tech, and Economcis, 1521 Budapest Hungary

CSOREGH, INGEBORG, crystallographer; b. Budapest, Hungary, June 9, 1942; d. Vilmos and Gladys (Sebesta) Kieselbach; m. Sandor Csoregh, July 14, 1962; children: Anna-Marie, Peter Anders, Linda Alexandra. Phil Lic, U. Stockholm, 1972, PhD, 1983. Asst. Stockholm U., 1966-84, rsch. assoc., 1984-90, sr. lectr., assoc. prof. chemistry, 1990-99, prof. structural chemistry, 2000—; lectr. in field. Office: Dept Structural Chem, Arrhenius Lab/Stockholm U, Stockholm S 106 91, Sweden

CSÖRGÖ, TAMÁS, physicist, researcher; b. Gyöngyös, Hungary, Oct. 3, 1963; s. Tibor and Tiborné (Studer) C; m. Judit Bácsi; children: Tamás Jr., Judit, András. MSc, Elte U., Budapest, Hungary, 1987; PhD, Hungarian Acad. Scis., Budapest, Hungary, 1991, Doctorate, 2000. Postdoctoral fellow Nordita & Niels Bohr Inst., Copenhagen, 1991-92; sr. rsch. fellow Rsch. Inst. for Particle & Nuclear Physics Hungarian Acad. of Scis., Budapest, 1991—; guest scientist U. Lund, Sweden, 1994-95, Columbia U., N.Y.C., 1995-96, 98, 99, 2000; vis. Fulbright scholar, Columbia U., 1996-97; sec. Hungarian Nat. Sci. Fund Coll. Scis., Budapest, 1991. Co-editor: Proceedings of Strangeness in Hadronic Matter, 1996, Proceedings of Correlations and Fluctuations, 1998. Go West fellow, European Union, Brussels, 1994; recipient Acad. Juvenile prize, Hungarian Acad. Scis., 1997, Advanced Rsch. award Fulbright Found., 1996. Mem. Am. Phys. Soc., Eötvös Phys. Soc., European Ctr. for Theoretical Studies. Office: MTA KFKI RMKI, Konkoly-Thege M ut 29-33, H-1525 Budapest 114, Hungary

CUA-CHRISTMAN, FLORENCE TANSY, radiation and environmental protection consultant; b. Manila, Philippines, Aug. 3, 1953; d. Jose P. and Petra Tansy C.; m. Edward Christman, July 1, 1979. BS in Physics magna cum laude, Coll. Holy Spirit, Manila, 1973; MS, Rutgers U., 1978, 91, Purdue U., 1981. Health physicist Philippine Atomic Energy Commn., Philippines, 1973-80, Brookhaven Nat. Lab., N.Y., 1977-80; cons. in radiation and environ. protection Christman, Cua & Assoc., Princeton, 1980—. Fellow IAEA, 1975-77. Mem. Nat. H.P.S. Assn. Women in Sci., Nat. FEdn. Philippine-Am. Women, N.J. Health Physics Soc., Philippine-Am. Acad. Scis. and Engring. Democrat. Roman Catholic. Avocations: videotapes on radiation, science and technology. Office: Christman-Cua Assocs 443 Sayre Dr Princeton NJ 08540-5845

CUADRADO, JAVIER, mechanical engineering educator, researcher; b. San Sebastian, Guipuzcoa, Spain, Oct. 22, 1966; s. Diego Cuadrado and Consuelo Aranda. BS in Mech. Engring., U. Navarra, San Sebastian, 1990, PhD in Mech. Engring., 1993. Asst. prof. U. Navarra, 1990-93, assoc. prof., 1993-94; rsch. asst. CEIT, San Sebastian, 1991-92, rsch. assoc., 1993; assoc. prof. U. La Coruña, Ferrol, Spain, 1994-2000; prof., 2000—; mem. acad. senate U. La Coruña, Ferrol, Spain, 1996-2000; head technol. rsch. ctr. U. La Coruña, 1997-2000; mem. sci. policy selection com. Galician Govt., 1994-96, 99-2000. Grantee Spanish Ministry Edn. and Sci., 1991-92. Mem. ASME (assoc.). Roman Catholic. Office: U La Coruña (EPS), Mendizabal S/N, 15403 Ferrol Spain

CUATT, JOHN EDWARD, sales executive; b. Carmel, Calif., Oct. 10, 1958; s. Donald Ray and Shirley May C.; m. Elaine Sue Miller, Oct. 14, 1979 (div. Feb. 1, 1986); children: Collin James, Natonya Renell; m. Patricia Ann Cuatt, June 10, 1989; stepchildren: Randy Swearingen, Melissa McGee. Grad. H.S., Denton, Tex., 1977. Brickmaker Acme Brick Co., Denton, 1977-79; security officer Magnum Security, Dallas, 1979-81, Republic Security, Garland, Tex., 1981-88; correctional officer Miss. Dept. Corrections, Pearl, 1988-89; asst. mgr. Goodwill Industries, Jackson, Miss., 1989-93; fleet maintenance Crescent Uniform, Jackson, 1993-96; lease option specialist Watson Quality Ford, Jackson, 1996—; sales cons. Watson Quality Ford, 1996—. Sponsor Ms. Cattlemens Assn., Jackson, 1998-99. Mem. Mid-Miss. Mustang Club. Republican. Mem. Pentecostal Ch. Avocations: bowling, motorcycles, antique cars. Home: 260 Lowe Cir Ste 18B Richland MS 39218-9207 Office: Watson Quality Ford 6130 I 55 N Jackson MS 39211-2642

CUBA, IVAN, artist; b. Notts, Eng., 1920. Student, U. Auckland, New Zealand; DLitt, Editorial Poets Acad. India. Editor: International Poets India. Hon. rep., pres. Temple of Arts Mus., U.S.A., Centro Studi E Scambi Internat., Italy. Served in WWII, POW. Recipient Poet Laureate gold Medal Rome, 1979, Greek gold medal, 1941; named poet laureate Internat. Acad., 1995, silver medal Internat. Man of Yr., 1996. Fellow Internat. Poets Acad., Acad. Leonardo da Vinci Rome (life). Home: PO Box 5199, Auckland New Zealand

CUBA, STANLEY L., government official; b. Denver, Apr. 30, 1948; s. Frank I. Cuba and Wanda Helen Kugaczewska; m. Ewa Zofia Galkowska, Sept. 18, 1998. BA in Polit. Sci., Europe-Columbia U., 1970; cert. in East European studies, Inst. on East Cen., 1972; MA in History, Columbia U., 1978. Assoc. conf. coord. Polish Inst. Arts and Scis., N.Y.C., 1970-72; asst. to pres. Kosciuszko Found., N.Y.C., 1972-79; assoc. dir. Andre Zarre Gallery, N.Y.C., 1980-82; transl. Denver, 1983-90; ct. clk. II Denver County Ct., 1986-90; cert. investigator Mayor's Office of Contract Compliance, Denver, 1990-2000; prevailing wage investigator auditor's office Denver Internat. Airport, 2000—; Mayor's Office of Contract Compliance liaison to Asian C. of C., Denver, 1993-2000; presenter in field. Author: (exhbn. catalogs) Stefan Mrozewski (1894-1975) Wood Engravings: A Posthumous Exhibition, 1976, Jozef Pankiewicz (1886-1940): A Loan Exhibition of Oils, Watercolors, Sketches and Graphics, 1978, Hussars and the Crescent: The Polish Relief of Vienna, 1983, The Art of Jozef Bakos: An Early Modernist, 1891-1977, 1988, Colorado Women Artists, 1859-1950: An Unprecedented Exhibition of Women Artists Living or Working in Colorado from 1859 to 1950, 1989, Jan Sawka: A Selected Retrospective, 1990, The Art of Jozef Bakos: Selections from the Estate of Jozef Gabryel Bakos, 1992, Olive Rush: A Hoosier Artist in New Mexico, 1992, John F. Carlson and Artists of the Broadmoor Art Academy, 1999; co-author: (book) Great Drawings of the 20th Century, 1981, The Colorado Book, 1993, The Art of Charles Partridge Adams, 1993, (exhbn. catalogs) George Luks: An American Artist, 1987, Pikes Peak Vision: The Broadmoor Art Academy, 1919-1945, 1989, Hayes Lyon: A Colorado Regionalist (1909-1987), 1991; contbr. to Allgemeines Kunstler Lexikon, 1998-99, also to exhbn. catalogs and mags. Mem. Denver Cath. Archdiocesan Adv. Coun., 1999—; mem. mus./gallery com. Arvada (Colo.) Ctr. for Arts and Humanities, 1990—. Recipient Bicentennial Recognition of Exhbn. Curated on History of Polish Cmty. in Colo., 1859-1876, Colo. Bicentennial Commn./Denver Mayoral Bicentennial Commn., 1976; Interpreter grantee Ford. Found./Citizens Exch. Corps, 1969.i. Mem. Polish Nat. Alliance (lodge 134, v.p. 1990-96, fin. sec. 1996-98), Polish Am. Hist. Assn. (mem., chmn. award com. 1979-83, Rev. Joseph Swastek prize 1984), Polish Inst. Arts & Scis., Kosciuszko Found. Democrat. Roman Catholic. Avocations: collecting art, travel, attending art exhibitions, concerts, and theater, films. Home: 2643 Utica St Denver CO 80212-3007

CUBITT, SALLY ANNE, administrative assistant; b. Northampton, England, July 21, 1955; d. Leslie George and Margaret Anne (Edgar) C.; m. Christopher King; 1 child, Lucy Emily. Advt. mgr. Frames Travel, Northampton, England, 1980-86; mng. dir. Flip Presentations, London, 1987-92; asst. to chmn. HHCL & Ptnrs., London, 1995—. Inventor of footwear. Mem. Ch. of England. Avocations: running, cycling, horse riding. Home: 10 Compton Rd, London N21 3NX, England Office: Chime Comms plc, 14 Curzon St, London W1J 5HN, England

CUCCHI, GIUSEPPE, NATO official; b. Ancona, Italy, July 3, 1940; m. Guia Cipriani; 2 children. Grad., Mil. Sch. Nunziatella, 1960; LLM, U. Bologna, 1970; postgrad., French Army War Coll., 1978; MPA, Harvard U., 1984. Commd. lt. Italian Armed Forces, 1960, advanced through grades to lt. gen., 1999, arty. lt., comdr. 5th and 3d corps, then 4th Alpine corps, staff officer missile brigade, schs., tactics & logistics; staff officer internat. rels., mil. attaché Army Gen. Staff, dir. Mil. Ctr. for Strategic Studies, 1991-97, mil. advisor to Italian Prime Minister, 1996-99, dir. Coord. Office for Def. Materials Prodn., 1998-99; Italian mil. rep. to NATO Mil. Com. Brussels, 1999—; rep. with several working groups of NATO and FINABEL; instr. various univs. internationally. Author and contbr. to profl. publs. Office: NATO Hdqrs, Blvd Leopold III, 1110 Brussels Belgium*

CUCHACOVICH, MIGUEL TURTELTAUB, rheumatologist, medical educator; b. Santiago, Chile, Apr. 20, 1957; s. Ernesto Jait Cuchacovich and Sara Krugliag Turteltaub; m. Rina Steinsapir Francos, May 24, 1979; children: Alvaro, Stephanie, Gabriel, Rafael, Sharon. MD, U. Chile, Santiago, 1981. Med. diplomate. Fellow in internal medicine U. Chile, 1982-85, fellow in rheumatology, 1985-87; fellow in immuno-rheumatology U. Montpellier, France, 1989-90; staff physician sect. rheumatology Clin. Hosp. U. Chile, 1987-95, head sect., 1995—; instr. medicine U. Chile, 1987-92, asst. prof., 1992-96, assoc. prof., 1996—. Contbr. numerous articles to med. jours., including Arthritis and Rheumatism, Jour. Molecular Medicine, others. Recipient Internat. prize in Rheumatology, Govt. of Uruguay, 1989; Nat. Found. Sci. and Tech. grantee. Fellow Am. Coll. Physicians, Pan-Am. League Against Rheumatism, Internat. League Against Rheumatism, Chilean Soc. Internal Medicine, Chilean Soc. Immunology, Chilean Soc. Rheumatology, Med. Soc. Santiago (bd. dirs. 1997—). Jewish. Home: Roberto del Rio 978, Providen Santiago Santiago, Chile Office: Office 1104, Fidel Oteiza 1921, Santiago Santiago, Chile

CUDHEA-PIERCE, PETER WOODBURY, software architect; b. Nashua, N.H., Jan. 21, 1958; s. David W. and Joan (Prichard) C.; m. Karen Pearson, June 14, 1980 (div. Apr. 1989); m. Lee Pierce, Sept. 26, 1992; 1 child, Emily Bliss. BA, Harvard U., 1980; postgrad., MIT, 1985-89, MS, 1988. Satellite network programmer (BBN) Bolt Bearnek & Newman, Cambridge, Mass., 1980-85; seminar registrar Werner Erhard & Assocs., N.Y.C., 1989-90; sr. software engr. Intersys. Corp., Cambridge, 1990—, network devel. mgr., 1994-99, head performance, scalability group, 1999—; program leader Conn. tegrity Program Designs, Waltham, Mass., 1999—. Co-author: (broadside) Compact for a New Millennium, 1996. Mem. IEEE (Computer Soc.), Assn. Computing Machinery. Home: 11 Marlboro Rd Lexington MA 02421-7809

CUDKOWICZ, LEON, medical educator; b. Lodz, Poland, Jan. 18, 1923; came to U.S., 1956; s. Mauryce and Masza (Malynski) C.;m. Margaret Chandler, Mar. 14, 1950 (div. July 1981); children: Alexander, Penelope; m. Teresa Cuiza de Alfaro, Jan. 18, 1986. BS, U. London, 1946, MD, 1951. James Hudson fellow Yale U. Sch. Medicine, 1956-58; registrar St. Thomas Hosp., U. London, 1958-59; asst. prof. then assoc. prof. medicine Dalhousie U., Halifax, N.S., Can., 1960-69; prof. medicine Thomas Jefferson U., Phila., 1970-74; prof., chmn. Wright State U., Dayton, 1974-79, King Faisal U., Dammam, Saudi Arabia, 1979-81; prof. medicine U. Cin., 1981-95, prof. emeritus, 1995—. Author: Human Bronchial Circulation, 1970; contbr. 107 articles to profl. jours. Capt. RAMC, 1946-49. Capt. RAMC, 1946-49. Fellow RCP, Nat. Pediat. Soc. Bolivia (hon.), NIH (sr.). Avocations: writing, mountaineering, gardening, travel. Home: Yonder Hill Farm Highland OH 45132 Office: U Cin Sch Medicine 253 Bethesda Ave Cincinnati OH 45229-2827

CUENOD, CHARLES ANDRE, radiologist, researcher; b. Tunis, Tunisia, May 13, 1960; s. Daniel Cuenod and Elisabeth Petitpierre. MD, Paris V, 1985, PhD, 1996. Functional imaging, MRI specialist. Resident in radiology Paris Hosps. (AP-HP), 1985-91; vis. assoc. NIH, Bethesda, Md., 1991-93; clin. chief AP-HP, France, 1993-99; asst. prof., 1999—. Author: Cahiers d'IRM, 1991; editor RBM: Rev. Europeeune de Tech. Biomed., 1996-2000; contbr. articles to profl. jours., 1988—. Recipient 2000 award European Congress Radiology. Mem. French Radiological Soc. Avocations: art, rock climbing. Office: HEGP, 20 rue Leblanc, 75015 Paris France

CUETO, ADOLFO OMAR, history educator; b. San Rafael, Mendoza, Argentina, Jan. 26, 1955; s. Jose and Maria Dolores (Sanchez) C.; m. Liliana Zaragoza, Dec. 18, 1982; children: Maria Victoria, Maria Florencia, Francisco Javier. M in History, U. Nacional de Cuyo, Mendoza, Argentina, 1979, D in history, 1977. Prof. history U. Nacional de Cuyo, 1987-95, rschr., 1989—; dir. Ctr. Interdisciplinary Regional Studies, Mendoza, 1988—. Author: five Different Aspects in The History of Mendoza, 1991, Institutional History of Mendoza, 1992; dir. Regional Studies mag., 1988—, editor, 1989—; contbr. articles to profl. jours. U Nacional de Cuyo scholar, 1980. Office: Univ Nacional De Cuyo, CC 345 Revista de Estudioes Region, 5500 Mendoza Argentina

CUETO-MANZANO, ALFONSO MARTIN, nephrologist, researcher; b. Sayula, Mex., Nov. 14, 1964; s. Alfonso Cueto and Ana Maria Manzano; m. Maria Guadalupe Ramirez-Guzman. MD, U. Guadalajara, Mex., 1988; degree in internal medicine, Nat. Autonomous U. Mex., Mexico City, 1992, degree in nephrology, 1994, MSc, 1996. Resident in internal medicine Nat. Inst. of Nutrition, Mexico City, 1989-92, resident in nephrology, 1992-94, resident in clin. rsch., 1994-96, staff nephrologist, 1996-99, clin. researcher, 1997-99; clin. researcher Mex. Inst. Social Secirity, Guadalajara, 1999—. Contbr. chpts. to books and articles to profl. jours. Recipient award Nat. Coun. of Sci. and Tech., Mex., 1999. Mem. Mex. Inst. Nephrology Rsch., Internat. Soc. Nephrology (Fellowship award 1996), Internat. Soc. Peritoneal Dialysis. Avocations: sports, basketball, soccer, jogging. Office: Hosp Especial Ctr Med Occid, Belisario Dominguez #1000, 44320 Col Indep Guadalajara Mexico

CUEVAS, ENRIQUE GERMAN, electrical engineer; b. La Paz, Bolivia, Sept. 26, 1953. BEE, Tex. A&M U., 1976; MEE, U. Tex., 1978, D Elec. Engring., 1986. Prof. Univ. Mayor San Andres, La Paz, 1979-80; tech. mgr. Entel, La Paz, 1980-81; mem. of tech. staff AT&T Bell Labs., Holmdel, N.J., 1986-89, dist. mem. tech. staff, 1990-96, dist. mgr., 1998-99, tech. cons., 1997—; chmn. U.S. Working Party 4B, Satellite Performance Stds., 1994-99, ATM AOS Group, SAT, 1997-98, others. Inventor in field; contbr. articles to profl. jours. and publs. Mem. IEEE, AIAA. Achievements include being an expert in performance characteristics of digital satellite comms. systems; leader of satellite team that demonstrated first intercontinental of ATM via satellites. Office: AT&T 101 Crawfords Corner Rd Holmdel NJ 07733-1900

CUEVAS DE DOLMETSCH, ANGELA, lawyer; b. Cali, Valle, Colombia, Jan. 22, 1942; d. Elciario and Margarita (Gamboa) Cuevas; m. Francois Dolmetsch, Aug. 12, 1962; children: Angela Marie, Richard. Degree in law, U. San Buenaventura, Colombia, 1980; MA in Latin Am. Studies, London U., 1989; postgrad., London Sch. of Econs., 1989—. Pvt. practice; legal cons. Universal de Cambios, Cali, Colombia, 1965—. Author: La Otra Cara del Dolar, 1975, Of Government and Guerrillas, 1988. Founder first women's polit. party; candidate for Colombian Senate, 1991; prs. Women for Democracy. Mem. Mujeres por la Democracia (pres. 1991), Federacion Colombiana de Abogadas (pres. 1991), Internat. Fedn. Women Lawyers (regional v.p. 1986-88, internat. pres. 1988-90, internat. dir. 1990—), Internat. Fedn. Women's Lawyer. Home: Apartado Aereo 12-54, Cali Colombia

CUGNINI, ALDO GODFREY, electrical engineer; b. Buenos Aires, Apr. 26, 1956; came to U.S., 1956; s. Aldo Mario and Cecilia (Heitner) C.; m. Helen Van Zobler, Oct. 25, 1987; children: Charlotte, Elizabeth. BS, Columbia U., 1977, MS, 1979. Product specialist RCA Broadcast Sys., Camden, N.J., 1979-80; sr. project engr. CBS Labs., Stamford, Conn., 1980-87; dir. rsch. Broadcast Tech., Greenwich, Conn., 1987-89; from rsch. staff to prin. mem. Philips Labs., Briarcliff Manor, N.Y., 1989-96, head advanced TV rsch. dept., 1996-98; hardware design mgr., project mgr., digital video group Philips Consumer Electronics, Briarcliff Manor, N.Y., 1998—; specialist group mem. ATSC Tech. Group on Distbn., Washington, 1994-97; tech. oversight group Grand Alliance, 1994-97; bd. dirs. Advanced TV Tech. Ctr., Washington. Contbr. articles to profl. jours. Mem. IEEE, Audio Engring. Soc., Eta Kappa Nu. Achievements include 5 patents in field. Avocation: astronomy. Office: Philips CE 345 Scarborough Rd Briarcliff Manor NY 10510-2027

CUGOLA, GIANPAOLO, software engineer; b. Catania, Italy, July 15, 1970; s. Marco Cugola and Raffaella Sciuto. MS, Poly. U. Milan, 1994, PhD, 1997. Adj. prof. Poly. U. Milan, 1998—; asst. prof. U. Svizzera Italiana, Lugano, Switzerland, 1997—. Office: Poly U Milan, via Ponzio 34/5, Milan Italy 20133

CUHADAROGLU, BURHAN, mechanical engineer, educator; b. Trabzon, Turkey, July 2, 1961; s. Turhan Yilmaz and Nurhayat (Alioglu) C.; m. Nilufer Caglayan, Jan. 7, 1995; children: Turhan Can, Deniz. BS, Istanbul Tech. U., 1983; MSc, Karadeniz Tech. U., 1986, DSc, 1991. Assoc. prof. Karadeniz Tech. U., Trabzon, Turkey, 1999—. Mem. Mech. Engrs. Ch. Turkey, Soc. HVAC & Sanitary Engrs., World User Assn. Computational Dynamics. Avocations: hiking, history, nature. E-mail: burhan@ktu.edu.tr. Office: University, Ktu Makina Muh Bolumu, 61080 Trabzon Turkey

CUI, FUZHAI, materials scientist; b. Lianyungang, China, Nov. 4, 1945; s. Shou-Ren and Pei-Jie (Liu) C.; m. Wan-Lan Huang; 1 child, Han. MSc, Tsinghua U., 1982, PhD in Nuclear Materials, 1984. Postdoctoral fellow FOM Inst., Amsterdam, The Netherlands, 1987-89; from assoc. prof. prof. Tsinghua U., Beijing, China, 1989—; prin. scientist of biomaterials Tsinghua Sch. of Material Sci. and Engring., 1997—; rsch. fellow MIT, Boston, 1997; dir. rsch. Materials Physics Lab. Tsinghua U., 1990-93. Author: Biomaterials Scince, 1996; contbr. articles to profl. jours. Mem. Am. Materials Rsch. Soc., Am. Biomaterials Soc., Chinese Materials Rsch. Soc., China Ctr. for Advanced Sci. & Tech. Avocations: music, reading. Office: Tsinghua U, Dept Materials Sci, 100084 Beijing China

CUI, JISHENG, statistician; b. Jinan, China, Feb. 7, 1963; parents Yanqing Cui and Ailan Wu; m. Hongyan Wang, Aug. 18, 1987; children: Wanyuan, Wanping, Wanting. BSc, Shandong U., 1979; M in Medicine, Shanghai Med. U., 1990; PhD, La Trobe U., 1997. Lectr. Shandong Med. U., Jinan, China, 1990-94; statistician Nat. Ctr. HIV Epidemiology & Clin. Rsch., Sydney, 1997-98; rsch. fellow U. Melbourne, Victoria, Australia, 1999—. Office: U Melbourne, 200 Berkeley St, Melbourne Victoria, Australia

CUI, JUNYAN, editor, author; b. Tianjin, China, Dec. 26, 1942; s. Mingqiu and Shizhi (Wang) C.; m. Chen Yan, Sept. 20, 1972; children: Cui Yuli, Cui Yujie. Grad., Beijing Fgn. Lang. U., 1965. Officer Xinjiang (China) Mil. Region, 1965-69; technician East Wind Radio Factory, Beijing, 1969-78; editor China Film Assn., Beijing, 1978-84, sec. of secretariat, 1985—, editor-in-chief World Screen, China Film Press, 1991—; vis. scholar Sorbonne U. Paris, 1988-90; participant Internat. Visitor Program of the U.S. Govt., 1993;

guest prof. Beijing Film Acad.; vis. scholar Harvard U., 1997-98; assoc. rschr. Harvard-Yenching Inst. Author: Contemporary Film Theories, 1985; editor-in-chief: Dictionary of Film Art, 1986 (award 1987); translator: What Is Cinema?, 1987 (award 1990); editor and publisher: Dictionary of Modern Motion Picture and Video Technology, 1998, Current Terms of Image Technology, 1997; contbr. articles to Chinese Ency., 1987. Mem. coun. Chinese People's Assn. for Friendship with Fgn. Countries, Beijing, 1986—. Recipient spl. award for outstanding achievement State Coun. People's Republic China, 1994. Mem. Chinese Comparative Lit. Assn., Chinese Soc. World Cinema (coun. 1982—), Chinese Film Critic Assn. (coun.), Chinese Soc. Film and TV Technics. Avocations: martial arts, photography, philately. Home: Capital U Med Sci, Yo An Men, Beijing 100054, China Office: China Film Press, 22 Beisanhuan Donglu, Beijing 100013, China

CUI, ZHANFENG, chemical engineer, educator; b. Renqiu, Hebei, China, Nov. 16, 1962; arrived in U.K., 1988; s. Chun-Ting Cui and Su-E Li; m. Jing Yu; children: Jennifer Yan, Michael Tian-ao. BS, Inner Mongolia Inst. Tech., 1982; MS, Dalian U. Tech., 1984, PhD, 1987; MA (hon.), Keble Coll., 1994. Chartered engr., U.K. Lectr. Dalian (China) U. Tech., 1987-88; rsch. fellow Strathclyde U., Glasgow, Scotland, 1988-91; lectr. Edinburgh (Scotland) U., 1991-94; lectr. Oxford (Eng.) U., 1994—, Donald Pollock prof. chem. engring., 2000—; vis. faculty Ga. Tech., 1999. Contbr. articles to profl. jours. Esso fellow Royal Acad. Engring., 1994-97. Mem. Instn. Chem. Engrs., Inst. Physics and Engring. in Medicine. Avocations: bridge, basketball. Office: Oxford Univ Dept Engr Sci, Parks Rd, Oxford OX1 3PJ, England

CUIFFO, FRANK WAYNE, lawyer; b. Houston, Oct. 13, 1943; s. Richard and Helen (Giaco) C.; m. Barbara Joyce Streeter, Nov. 26, 1966; children: Karen, Deborah, Richard, Steven. BS, U. Notre Dame, 1964; JD, Fordham U., 1967. Bar: N.Y. 1967. Assoc. Pennie & Edmonds (formerly Pennie, Edmonds, Morton, Taylor & Adams), N.Y.C., 1967-69; sr. assoc. Emmet, Marvin, & Martin, N.Y.C., 1969-74, Golenbock & Barell, N.Y.C., 1974-78; mng. ptnr. Carro, Spanbock, Kaster & Cuiffo, N.Y.C., 1978-93; chmn. real estate dept., exec. com. Donovan, Leisure, Newton & Irvine, N.Y.C., 1993-98; ptnr. McDermott, Will & Emery, N.Y.C., 1998—. Mem. ABA, U.S. Patent Bar, N.Y. State Bar, Siwanoy Country Club, South Seas Club. Office: McDermott Will & Emery 50 Rockefeller Plz Fl 12 New York NY 10020-1600

CUISON, ROY JOCSON, physician; b. Manila, Philippines, Oct. 7, 1953; s. Rene Toledano and Felicidad (Jocson) C. BS, U. St. Tomas, 1974, MD, 1978; MBA, Ateneo U., 1989. Intern Vets. Meml. Hosp., Quezon City, Philippines, 1978-79; mcpl. health officer Dept. of Health, Binalbagan, Philippines, 1979-80; resident Singian Meml. Hosp., Manila, Philippines, 1980-82, chief resident, 1982-83, cons. staff medicine, sec. med. coun., 1983-90, asst. med. dir., 1989-90; cons. medicine/toxicology/gerontology St. Tomas U. Hosp., Manila, Philippines, 1990—; cons. gen. medicine St. Jude's Hosp., Manila, Philippines, 1990—; assoc. prof. U. St. Tomas, 1983—, chmn. dept. physiology; chmn. CME com. Coll. Pharm. Medicine, Manila, 1989—, dir. specialty bd., 1984—, course dir., 1992—, pres., 1997—, head med. and sci. affiliation Merck Inc. Phihlippines, 1981—. Instr. Philippines Nat. Red Cross, Manila, 1978. Recipient Ideal Filipino award Internat. Press Rsch. Inc., Manila, 1989; named Physician of Yr. Devel. Filipino Writers, Manila, 1989. Fellow Exptl. & Clin. Pharmacology; mem. Internat. Soc. Internal Medicine, Royal Colls. of Physicians, Philippine Canine Club, De La Salle U. Alumni Assn. Roman Catholic. Avocations: football, martial arts, tenpin bowling. Office: UST Faculty Medicine, Espana St, Manila The Philippines

CULEA, MONICA, physics educator; b. Turda, Cluj, Romania, July 8, 1951; d. Alexandru and Otilia (Campeanu) Sechel; m. Eugen Culea, 1974; chlidren: Cristina, Eugen. MSc, U. Cluj-Napoca, Romania, 1975, PhD, 1993. Physicist Inst. of Isotopic and Molecular Tech., Cluj, 1979-85, sr. scientist, 1985-97; assoc. prof. U. Babes-Bolyai, Cluj, 1999—; sr. scientist Sc. Natex S.R.L., Cluj, 1999. Author: Handbook of Water Analysis, 1998; contbr. articles to profl. jours. Mem. Romanian Soc. Physics, Romanian Soc. Mass Sepctrometry, Romanian Soc. Analytical Chemistry. Greek Catholic. Avocation: painting. Home: Mehendinti 80/13, 3400 Cluj-Napoca, Cluj Romania Office: SC Natex SRL PO Box 374, Sos Cluj-Oradea Km 8, 3400 Cluj-Napoca, Cluj Romania

CULER, LOUIS, consulting engineer; b. Gent, Belgium, June 21, 1925; s. Benjamin and Claire (Epstein) C.; m. Claire Culer, Aug. 21, 1951; children: Diane, Brigitte, Geraldine. BSCE, U. Brussels, 1951. Cons. engr. Bur. d'Etudes L. Culer, Brussels, 1956—; gen. mgr. Fire Control, Brussels, 1968—. Contbr. articles to profl. jours. Mem. Belgian Chamber Cons. Engrs., Royal Soc. Engrs., Gaulois Club, Lorraine Club, Rotary. Office: Ave des Villas 77, Bur Etudes Culer, 1190 Brussels Belgium

CULHANE, HIND RASSAM, psychologist, educator, film historian; b. Mosul, Iraq, Feb. 20, 1939; came to U.S., 1955; d. Noel Michael and Sophie (Bakhazy) Rassam; m. John William Culhane, Aug. 27, 1960; children: Michael Noel, T.H. AA, Cazenovia (N.Y.) Jr. Coll., 1957; BA, Rockford Coll., 1959, MA, 1963; MEd, Columbia U., 1988, EdD, 1992; M Pedagogy (hon.), Mercy Coll., 1998. Edn. coord. Head Start, Chgo., 1965-69, Westchester County, N.Y., 1969-77; assoc. dean grad. program L.I. U., Dobbs Ferry, N.Y., 1976-82; asst. prof. Mercy Coll., Dobbs Ferry, N.Y., 1982-92, assoc. prof., assoc. chair social scis. divsn., 1992—; adj. prof. Mercy Coll., Dobbs Ferry, 1970-76; guest lectr. The U. Baghdad (Iraq), 1981-84; campus coord. Woodrow Wilson fellows program Mercy Coll., 1990-97; group dynamics leader NAIM Found. Workshop, Washington, 1992-93; guest psychologist Mental Health Hour Arabnet radio, Washington, 19945; psychologist, admissions com. U. Poznań (Poland) Med. Sch., 1994—; commentator on Arab film, CUNY TV, 1998. Author (Arab film history) East/West, An Ambiguous State of Being, 1995; contbr. article to Ency. Modern Mid. East, 1996. Mem. Arab-Am. Anti-Defamation League, Washington, 19875. Nat. Multicultural Faculty Devel. fellow, 1995-97; Nat. fellow Tchg. for a Change, C.C. of Aurora, Colo., 1995; Fulbright Scholar to Syria, 2000—. Mem. Psi Chi, Delta Pi. Avocations: collecting Arab songs, world travel, environmental concerns. Office: Social Scis Bldg Mercy Coll 555 Broadway Dobbs Ferry NY 10522-1134

CULHANE, JOHN WILLIAM, journalist, author, film historian; b. Rockford, Ill., Feb. 7, 1934; s. John William and Isabel June (Fissinger) C.; m. Hind Noel Rassam, Aug. 27, 1960; children: Michael Noel, T.H. BS, St. Louis U., 1956; cert. in advanced internat. reporting, Columbia U., 1966. Reporter St. Louis (Mo.) Globe Dem., 1955; daily columnist, reporter Rockford Register-Republic, 1956-61; reporter, feature writer, fgn. corr. Chgo. Daily News, 1962-66; assoc. editor Newsweek mag., N.Y.C., 1966-71; freelance journalist N.Y. Times mag., others, N.Y.C., 1971-85; roving editor Reader's Digest, Pleasantville, N.Y., 1985-93; roving writer Johimith Robidoux Prodns., 1994—; artist in residence Disney Inst.; jury chmn. 2d N.Y. Internat. Animation Film Festival, 1974; lectr., Northwestern U., 1995, NYU, 1996; lectr. film festival, Mulhouse, France, 1990; moustro-of-ceremonies Mickey Mouse's 50th Birthday Retrospective and Whistle-Stop Train Tour Across the U.S., 1978; guest clown Ringling Bros., Barnum and Bailey Circus, 1974-84; instr. 1st course in history of animation for coll. credit Sch. Visual Arts, N.Y.C., 1972; sr. lectr. animation history U. Arts, Phila., 1997-98, NYU, 1997—, Fashion Inst. of Tech., N.Y.C., 2000—; vis. artist Disney Inst., Fla., 1999—; writer Richard Williams Animation, London, 1973. Author: (critical essays) Walt Disney, 1972, Special Effects in the Movies, 1981, Walt Disney's Fantasia, 1983, Backstage at Disney's, 1983, The American Circus: An Illustrated History, 1990 (Washington Irving Book Selection Westchester Libr. Assn. 1991), Disney's Aladdin: The Making of an Animated Film, 1992, (documentary) The Making of Aladdin: A Whole New World, 1992; co-author: The Art of the Muppets, 1980, (TV spls.) Noah's Animals, 1974, King of the Beasts, 1976, Last of the Red Hot Dragons, 1980; contbr. The 50 Greatest Cartoons, 1994; voice of cartoon dragon, moderator: (coll. tour) Disney on Film: A Forum on Animation and Fantasy Filmmaking, 1981; co-prodr. (documentary) Circus!, 1983; commentator (documentaries) Fantasia: The Making of a Masterpiece, 1991, Frank and Ollie, 1995, (TV spl.) The Flying Wallendas: Legends on the High Wire, 1998; writer (TV spl.) Illusionist David Copperfield Vanishes the Statue of Liberty, 1983, (feature film) The Thief and the Cobbler, 1995; (CD-ROM essay) Walt Disney's Snow White and the Seven Dwarfs, 1998, (essays) The Disney Century, Fantasia Set for a New Millennium, 1998, "Charlie Brown: A Boy for all Seasons" N.Y. Mus. of Broadcasting, 1984, "Fantasia 2000: Visions of Hope" N.Y. Hyperion, 1999; model for Mr. Snoops character Walt Disney's The Rescuers, 1977, model for 2nd Disney character, Flying John in "Rhapsody in Blue" in "Fantasia 2000". Master-of-ceremonies Winnebago County Sesquicentennial, Rockford, 1968; mem. Clearwater Assn. (author: PCBs: The Poison That Won't Go Away). Served with AUS, 1957-58. Recipient 4 1st Prize awards Ill. AP, 1960, 61, 63, 64, St. Louis U. Alumni Merit award as writer and film historian, 1982; Ford fellow Columbia U., 1965-66; Ill. Humanities Coun. grantee, 1991; Woodrow Wilson fellow in writing and film history, 1993. Mem. Writer's Guild Am., Clearwater Assn., Alpha Sigma Nu, Sigma Delta Chi (2 awards for pub. service journalism 1964, 69). Avocations: global travel, environment. Office: care Joelle Delbourgo Assocs 450 7th Ave Ste 3004 New York NY 10123-3004

CULIK, BORIS MICHAEL, marine zoologist; b. Munich, Dec. 29, 1958; s. Paul and Rosemarie (Limburg) C.; m. Barbara Susanne Wildhagen, June 12, 1961; children: Laura, Nicolai, Charlotte. BS, York U., Toronto, 1980; Doctor rerum naturalium, Christian-Albrechts U., Kiel, Germany, 1986, habilitation, 1994. Rsch. asst. Inst. Ecological Chemistry, Munich, 1979, York U., 1980; pharm. rep. Contacta Medica, Munich, 1980-81; rsch. asst. Inst. Water Mgmt., Munich, 1981-82; rsch. asst. Inst. Marine Scis., Kiel, Germany, 1982-84, scientist, 1984-88, scientific asst., 1989-94, asst. prof., 1994-98, assoc. prof., 1998—. Author: Die Welt Der Pinguine, 1993, Pinguine, 1995, 99, (several documentary films) Rsch. on Cormorants, 1994-97, Rsch. on Chilean Penguins, 1994—, Rsch. on Cetaceans, Aquatic and Semi-Aquatic Mammals, 1996—, Rsch. on Antarctic Penguins, 1982-97; contbr. numerous articles to profl. jours. German Forschungsgemeinschaft grantee, 1985—. Mem. German Zool. Soc., German Ornithol. Soc., European Cetacean Soc., Internat. Soc. of Biotelemetry. Avocations: biking, swimming, hiking, skating. Office: Abteilung Meereszoologie Institut Meereskunde, Düstenbrooker Weg 20, D-24105 Kiel Germany

CULLARI, SALVATORE SANTINO, clinical psychologist, educator, writer; b. Caroniti, Calabria, Italy, Apr. 1, 1952; came to U.S., 1955; s. Carmelo and Carmela (Cullari) C.; m. Kathryn Plesce, Apr. 26, 1985; children: Catherine, Dante. BA, Kean Coll., 1974; MA, Western Mich. U., 1976, PhD, 1981. Lic. psychologist, Pa., W.Va. Dir. psychology White Haven (Pa.) Ctr., 1982-83; psychologist Danville (Pa.) State Hosp., 1983-84; coord. of psychology Harrisburg (Pa.) State Hosp., 1984-86; prof., chair dept. psychology Lebanon Valley Coll., Annville, Pa., 1986—; cons. Bur. Disability Determination, Harrisburg, 1987—. Author questionaire acad. social evaluation scales, 1990, Treatment Resistance, 1996; editor Found. of Clin. Psychology, 1998; contbr. numerous articles to profl. jours. Mem. APA, Assn. Advancement of Behavior Therapy, Pa. Psychol. Assn., Soc. for the Exploration of Psychotherapy Integration. Office: Lebanon Valley Coll Psychology Dept Annville PA 17003

CULLEN, JAMES G., telecommunications industry executive; b. 1942; Married. B.A., Rutgers U., 1964; Postgrad., M.I.T. With N.J. Bell Telephone Co., Newark, N.J., 1964, pres., CEO, 1989-95; vice chmn. Bell Atlantic Corp., Phila., 1995-96, 1996-98, pres., CEO Telecom, 1998—. Office: Bell Atlantic Corp 1310 N Court House Rd Ste 1 Arlington VA 22201-2586

CULLEN, MARK KENNETH, lawyer; b. Springfield, Ill., Sept. 27, 1962; s. Richard W. and Ann (Orr) Carlson; m. Marica L. Heagy, Aug. 5, 1989; 1 child, Kristin Anne. BA with honors, Northwestern U., 1984; MBA/JD, U. Ill., Urbana-Champaign, 1988. Bar: Ill. 1988, U.S. Dist. Ct. (no. dist.) Ill. 1988, U.S. Dist. Ct. (ctrl. dist.) Ill. 1991. Rsch. analyst Fed. Res. Bank Chgo., Chgo., 1983-84; tchg. and rsch. asst. U. Ill., Urbana-Champaign, 1984-88; atty., asst. cashier The First Nat. Bank Chgo., Chgo., 1988-91; shareholder, dir. Sorling Northrup Hanna Cullen and Cochran Ltd., Springfield, Ill., 1991—. Vice-chmn., trustee First United Meth. Ch., Springfield, 1991-95; v.p. Boy Scouts Am., Springfield, 1994—. Mem. Springfield Lions Club (pres. 1996-97). Avocations: golf, scouting, computers, basketball, collectibles. Office: Sorling Northrup Hanna Cullen & Cochran Ltd PO Box 5131 607 E Adams St Ste 800 Springfield IL 62701-1623

CULLEN, PAULA BRAMSEN, author; b. May 12, 1942. BS in English, Washington U., 1967. Self-employed author Princeton, N.J., 1968—; pres. Opportunity Found., Princeton, 1992—; co-owner Spraying Sys. Co., Wheaton, Ill., 1989—. Author: Journey of Storms, 1994; author of poetry; contbr. articles to publs.

CULLEY-FOSTER, ANTHONY ROBERT, international business consultant; b. Londonderry, No. Ireland, July 31, 1947; came to U.S., 1971; s. Allen Foster and Eileen Louisa Culley; children: Joshua, Daniel, Valentina. Diploma, Reading U., 1969, Coll. Preceptors, U.K., 1971; BA magna cum laude, Roosevelt U., Chgo., 1973, MA, 1981. Cert. tchr., U.K. High sch. tchr. London, 1969-71; dir. Boys & Girls Clubs of Chgo., 1971-77; personal asst. to chmn. Combined Internat. Corp., Chgo., 1977-81; founding dir., chief exec. officer The Congl. Award, Washington, 1981-85; pres. Culley-Foster & Co. Internat., Washington, 1985—; cons. W. Clement Stone Enterprises, Chgo., 1978-86, Brit. and Am. Multinat. Corps., 1985—. Nat. organizer Run Across Am. program Am. Bicentennial Com., 1976, Run for Ireland program Olympic Coun., Ireland, 1980; co-founder Congl. Award U.S., 1979, Pres.'s Award for Youth, Ireland, 1983; founding chmn. No. Ireland Partnership U.S., 1990, No. Ireland-U.S. C. of C. Inc., 1993; mem. Nat. Boys Club U.K., 1966—; trustee Internat. Fedn. Keystone Youth orgns., World Meml. Fund for Disaster Relief, Boys and Girls Clubs Washington, Boys and Girls Clubs No. Ireland, Boys and Girls Clubs-Chgo. Alumni Assn. Recipient Duke of Edinburgh's Gold Award, 1966, Pub. Service commendations Office of Pres. of U.S., 1976, 79, 83, 91, 96, Congl. award U.S. Congress, 1981, Nat. Achievement award Pres.'s Coun. on Phys. Fitness and Sports, 1976, Nat. Achievement award Olympic Coun. Ireland, 1980. Mem. Brit.-Am. C. of C., C. of C. of the U.S., French-Am. C. of C., Brit.-Am. Bus. Assn. Washington D.C., Irish Rowing Union (hon. life), Royal Automobile Club (U.K.). Office: Culley-Foster & Co Internat PO Box 17370 Washington DC 20041-0370

CULLHED, INGEMAR ERIK ARNE, cardiologist; b. Jönköping, Sweden, Mar. 26, 1927; s. Eric Gottfrid Oliver and Nina Maria (Jonsson) C.; m. Inger Astrid Marianne Benjaminsson, May 31, 1952; children: Marie, Susanne, Thomas. Grad. in medicine, Uppsala (Sweden) U., 1947, MD, 1953, PhD, 1964. Asst. prof. internal medicine Uppsala U., 1964; intern, resident Univ. Hosp., Uppsala, 1954-68, chief physician dept. cardiology, 1968-92; ret., 1992. Rsch. com. Heart Lung Fund, Stockholm, 1976-84. Mem. Swedish Med. Assn., Swedish Med. Soc., Swedish Soc. Cardiology (chmn. 1979-81). Lutheran.

CULLINEY, JOHN JAMES, radiologist, educator; b. N.Y.C., Oct. 17, 1955; s. Michael and Marion (Dakowski) C.; m. Margaret Mary Steinhardt, Oct. 11, 1986. BS, Rutgers U., 1977, MS, 1981; MD, U Medicine and Dentistry N.J., 1984. Diplomate Am. Bd. Radiology, Nat. Bd. Med. Examiners. Intern physician Med. Coll. of Pa. Hosp., Phila., 1984-85; resident physician U. Medicine & Dentistry N.J., Newark, 1985-89; fellow body imaging, instr. diagnostic radiology Hahnemann U. Hosp., Phila., 1989-90, asst. prof. clin. diagnostic radiology, 1990-92; asst. prof. clin. diagnostic radiology, chief uroradiology U. Med. and Dentistry N.J., Newark, Pa., 1990-92; clin. instr. diagnostic radiology, chief cross-sect. imaging Mercy & Moses Taylor Hosps. affiliates Temple Med. Sch., Scranton, Pa., 1992—; pres. Radiol. Cons. Inc., 1999—; chief uroradiology U. Med. and Dentistry N.J., Newark, 1990-92; bd. dirs. Radiol. Cons., Inc., Dunmore, Pa., 1994—; co-dir. Phoenix Vascular Lab.; dir. radiology Mercy Hosp. Scranton, Clin. Vascular Lab. Mem. AMA, AAUP, Am. Coll. Radiology, Am. Soc. Breast Imagers, Roentgen Soc. N.Am., KC. Roman Catholic. Avocations: amateur radio technician class, skiing. Home: 210 Stevenson Rd Clarks Summit PA 18411-8900 Office: Radiol Cons Inc 751 Keystone Indsl Park Dunmore PA 18512-1530

CULLINGHAM, ANTHONY CHARLES, communications educator, advertising writer; b. Harrogate, Eng., July 9, 1957; s. Sebastian Finbar and Sheila (Foster) C.; m. Emma Claire Hancock. Degree in advt./mktg., Bristol (Eng.) Poly., 1977. Writer Saatchi & Saatchi, London, 1979-82; sr. writer Geers Gross, London, 1982-84; dir. Lintas Advt., London, 1984-88; course dir. West Herts Coll., Watford, Eng., 1988—; freelance tng. cons. BBC, Eng.; edn. advisor QRE Advt. Group Sri Lanka. Writer Ads Internat., 1994; script advisor (radio program) Education Matters Radio Work, 1996; tng. cons. for BBC, 1996; vocal leader Filbert Nutters Group. Recipient Creative Banana award Paul Gayter Soc., 1989, Silver award D & AD, 1990, Bronze award, 1990. Avocations: football, running, collecting ephemera, music. Office: West Herts Coll, Hempstead Rd, Watford WD1 3EZ, England

CULLMANN, WOLFGANG WALTER, microbiologist; b. Duesseldorf, Germany, Mar. 15, 1950; s. Walter and Dorothea (Abt) C. MD, Tech. U. Aachen, 1977; PhD, U. Bochum, 1986. Scientific asst. U. Cologne, 1977-78, U. Duesseldorf, 1978-79, U. Bochum, 1980-89; lab. head Hoffmann La Roche, Basel, 1990-93; cons. Mcpl. Hosp., Stuttgart, 1993—. Roman Catholic. Avocations: mountaineering, motorbiking. Home: Hauffstr 21, D-73614 Schorndorf Germany Office: Mcpl Hosp, Tunzhofer Str 14, D-70191 Stuttgart Germany

CULLOM, WILLIAM OTIS, trade association executive; b. Huntsville, Ala., Mar. 20, 1932; s. Otis McKinley and Elna (Reese) C.; m. Caryl James, May 26, 1956; children: Cheryl Ann Cullom Stewart, Jennifer James Cullom Barksdale. BS, Fla. State U., 1958. Finger-print expert FBI, 1950-52; asst. bus. mgr. Fla. State U., 1954-64; with Ryder Truck Rental Inc., Miami, Fla., 1964-79; exec. v.p. mktg., to Ryder Truck Rental Inc., 1979; pres., chief operating officer Jartran, Inc., Coral Gables, Fla., 1979-81; pres. Greater Miami C. of C., 1981—; v.p. Orange Bowl Com., 1992—. Sec., bd. dirs. Miami-Dade Coll. Found.; mem. cabinet exec. com. Beacon Coun. United Way, Miami, 1974-80; trustee Bethune Cookman Coll., Daytona Beach, Fla., Barry U., St. Thomas U., Miami-Dade C.C. Found.; past chmn. bd. trustees Fla. State U; chmn. adminstrv. bd. Kendall Meth. Ch.; mem. pres.'s adv. com. Fla. Meml. Coll., Miami; bd. dirs. Bapt. Hosp. Found., Coconut Grove Playhouse, Goodwill Industries, Salvation Army; v.p. Orange Bowl Com.; chmn. bd. trustees Fla. State U. Found., 1994-95; chmn. Greater Miami Chamber Coalition. With U.S. Army, 1952-54. Recipient Miami Black Bus. Cmtys. Econ. Unity award, 1984, Anti Defamation League Human Rels. award, 1992, Disting. Cmty. Svc. award, 1998, Cedars Found. Concern award, 1994, NCCJ Humanitarian award, 1995, Silver Medallion award Greater Miami NCCJ, Citizen of Yr. award Greater Miami Rotary Club; named South Fla. Scout of Yr., Scouts Internat. in South Fla., 1997. Mem. Am. Trucking Assn., Truck Leasing and Renting Assn. (pres. Fla. chpt. 1972-73), Fla. State U. Nat. Alumni Assn. (pres.), Miami Hist. Assn., Brickell Club, Univ. Club, Riviera Country Club, City Club, Bankers Club, Ocean Reef Yacht Club, Gov.'s Club (Tallahassee), Dearing Bay Yacht Club, Biscayne Bay Yacht Club, Mountain Air Country Club (Burnsville, N.C.), Rotary. Democrat. Methodist. Home: 8445 SW 151st St Miami FL 33158-1961 Office: Greater Miami C of C 1601 Biscayne Blvd Miami FL 33132-1224

CULLUM, LEE BROOKS, journalist; b. Dallas, Mar. 18, 1939; d. Charles Gillespie and Garland Chapman Cullum; m. James Howard Clark Jr., June 29, 1962 (div. June 1976); 1 child, James Howard Cullum Clark. Student, Sweet Briar Coll.; BA, So. Meth. U., 1961; DHL (hon.), Monterey Inst. Inter. Studies, 1997. Reporter, then exec. prodr. and on-air moderator Newsroom Sta. KERA-TV, Dallas, 1970-76, v.p. program devel., 1976-81; account exec. Hill & Knowlton, Dallas, 1981-82; editor D Mag., Dallas, 1982-85; dir. client svcs. Hill & Knowlton, Dallas, 1985-86; editor editl. page Dallas Times Herald, Dallas, 1986-91; commentator Newshour with Jim Lehrer (formerly Macneil-Lehrer Newshour), Washington, 1988—; columnist Dallas Morning News, Dallas, 1992—; bd. dirs. Coun. Fgn. Rels., N.Y., Pacific Coun. Internat. Policy, L.A. Bd. dirs. S.W. Legal Found., Dallas, 1995-99, The Hockaday Sch., Dallas, 1997—; bd. visitors Internat. Programs Ctr., Okla. U., 1997—. Recipient Matrix award Women in Comms., 1977, 85, J. B. Marryatt award Dallas Press Club, 1996. Mem. Nat. Conf. Editl. Writers. Episcopalian. Avocations: the arts, traveling, books.

CULP, JOE C(ARL), electronics executive; b. Little Rock, July 23, 1933; s. Charles Carl and Doris Evelyn (Jackson) C.; m. Norma Carol Kennan, Jan. 26, 1954; 1 dau., Karen Gay Culp Ashorn. BSEE, U. Ark., 1955. Staff asst. to exec. v.p. Collins Radio, Dallas, 1967-68; with Rockwell Internat., Dallas, 1968-88, dir. data sys. mktg., 1968-71, dir. mktg. transp. sys. divsn., 1971-78, v.p. Latin Am. divsn., 1978-80, v.p., gen. mgr. transp. sys. divsn., 1980-82, pres. telecomm. group, 1982-88; pres., CEO Lightnet, Rockville, Md., 1988-89; exec. v.p. Communications Transmission Inc., Austin, Tex., 1989—; pres. Culp Comm. Assocs. Inc., Austin, 1990—; bd. dirs. iMagic TV, Crosskeys Corp., Gen. Bandwidth Corp., March Telecomms.; mem. chmn. exec. coun. Newbridge Networks Corp. Chmn. engring. bd. U. Tex., Arlington, 1984; bd. advisors Coll. Engring. U. Ark., Fayetteville, 1982. Named Disting. Grad., Coll. Engring. U. Ark., 1981, Disting. Engr., U. Tex., Arlington, 1984. Mem. Electronic Industry Assn. (bd. govs. 1984-88), U.S. Telephone Suppliers Assn. (dir. 1984-88), Ind. Telephone Pioneers. Republican. Methodist. Office: Culp Communications Assocs Inc 5 Hedge Ln Austin TX 78746-3208

CULP, NATHAN CRAIG, lawyer; b. Camden, Ark., 1965; s. Harold Lloyd and Carole Culp; m. Clara M. Graves, 1995. BA, La. Tech. U., 1988; JD, U. Ark., 1991. Bar: Ark. 1991, U.S. Dist. Ct. Ark. 1992. Law clk. Walker, Roaf, Campbell, Ivory and Dunklin, Little Rock, 1989-91, assoc., 1991-94; staff atty. Pub. Employee Claims divsn. Ark. Dept. Ins., Little Rock, 1994-99, Ark. Hwy. and Transp. Dept., 1999-2000; asst. dir. pub. employee claims div. Ark. Dept. Ins., Little Rock, 2000—. Mem. Ark. Bar Assn., Pulaski County Bar Assn. Methodist. Avocations: computers, reading. Office: Pub Employee Claims Div Ark Ins Dept 1200 West Third St Little Rock AR 72201

CULPEPPER, WARREN LEIGH, management consultant; b. Atlanta, Jan. 30, 1942; s. Harry Stuart and Alma Elaine (Payne) C.; m. Suzanne Elizabeth Hooper, Nov. 28, 1964 (dec. June 1982); children: Warren Leigh, Jonathan Lane; m. Cathryn Lee Thrasher, Aug. 27, 1995. BA cum laude, U. of the South, 1964. CLU. Agt. Mass Mutual Life Ins. Co., Nashville, 1964-67; sys. engr. IBM, Atlanta, 1967-70; dir. customer svcs. Info. Sys. Am., Atlanta, 1970-79; CEO Culpepper and Assocs., Inc., Atlanta, 1979—; bd. dirs. Geac Computers, Ltd., Toronto, Ont., Can., Reaction Design, San Diego. Pub., editor The Culpepper Letter, 1979-98, Software Pricing Trends, 1981, 84, 87, 90, 93, Software Industry Compensation Library, annually 1982-99, Financial Operating Ratios for Software Companies, 1990, 92, 94, 96, 98. Vestry St. Patricks Episcopal Ch., Dunwoody, Ga., 1980-83. Staff sgt. Air Nat. Guard, 1964. Republican. Episcopalian. Avocations: hiking, genealogy. E-mail: warren@culpepper.com. Fax: 520-441-5114. Home: 10436 Big Canoe Big Canoe GA 30143-5125

CULTIAUX, DIDIER, New Caledonian government official. High commr. Govt. of New Caledonia, Nouméa; prefect de Seine-et-Maruc, Melvn, France; now gen. dir. Nat. Police, France. Office: Prefect Auragne, 18 Boulevard Desaix, 63000 Clermont-Ferrrand France

CULTON, PAUL MELVIN, retired counselor, educator, interpreter; b. Council Bluffs, Iowa, Feb. 12, 1932; s. Paul Roland and Hallie Ethel Emma (Paschal) C. AB, Minn. Bible Coll., 1955; BS, U. Nebr., Omaha, 1965; MA, Calif. State U., Northridge, 1970; EdD, Brigham Young U., 1981. Cert. tchr., Iowa. Tchr. Iowa Sch. for Deaf, Council Bluffs, 1956-70; ednl. specialist Golden West Coll., Huntington Beach, Calif., 1970-71, dir. disabled students, 1971-82, instr., 1982-88; counselor El Camino Coll., Via Torrance, Calif., 1990-93, acting assoc. dean, 1993-94; counselor El Camino Coll., Via Torrance, Caif., 1994-97; interpreter various state and fed. cts., Iowa, Calif., 1960-90; asst. prof. Calif. State U., Northridge, Fresno, Dominguez Hills, 1973, 76, 80, 87-91, L.A., 1999—; vis. prof. U. Guam, Agana, 1977; mem. allocations task force, task force on deafness, trainer handicapped students Calif. C.C.s, 1971-81. Editor: Region IX Conf. for Coordinating Rehab. and Edn. Svcs. for Deaf proceedings, 1970, Toward Rehab. Involvement by Parents of Deaf conf. proceedings, 1971; composer Carry the Light, 1986. Bd. dirs. Iowa NAACP, 1966-68, Gay and Lesbian Cmty. Svcs. Ctr., Orange County, Calif., 1975-77; founding sec. Dayle McIntosh Ctr. for Disabled, Anaheim and Garden Grove, Calif., 1974-80; active Dem. Cent. Com. Pottawattamie County, Council Bluffs, 1960-70; del. People to People N.Am. Educators Deaf Vis. Russian Schs. & Programs for Deaf, 1993.

League for Innovation in Community Coll. fellow, 1974. Mem. Registry of Interpreters for Deaf, Congress Am. Instrs. Deaf, Am. Deafness and Rehab. Assn., Calif. Assn. Postsecondary Educators Disabled, Am. Fedn. Tchrs., Am. Sign Lang. Tchrs. Assn., Nat. Assn. Deaf. Mem. Am. Humanist Assn. Avocations: vocal music, languages, community activism, travel, politics. Home: 2567 Plaza Del Amo Apt 203 Torrance CA 90503-8962

CULVER, DAN LOUIS, federal agency administrator; b. Savannah, Ga., Dec. 7, 1957; s. Louis Harry and Jean Marie Culver. BS in Mktg., U. Tenn., 1981; postgrad., Air Force Acad., 1982, Cornell U., 1985; BS in Edn. and Tng., U. West Fla, 1995; MEd in Orgnl. Devel. and Leadership, U. West Fla., 1998. Logistics support officer USAF, Ft. Walton Beach, Fla., 1982-86; mgmt. assoc. Barnett Bank, Ft. Walton Beach, Fla., 1987-89; program adminstr. for disaster relief SBA, Atlanta, 1989—; diplomatic observer, UN, N.Y.C.; promoter of lecturers, entertainers and authors who appear before live audiences. Pioneered automation of air force support ops., 1982-84. Served on bd. of dirs. to business and non-profit organizations. Vol. disaster relief for victims of Hurricane Hugo, Charleston, S.C., 1989, Hurricane Andrew, Miami, Fla., 1992, Miss. River flood, 1993, L.A. earthquake, 1994. With USAF, 1982-86. Recipient Commander-in-Chief's Spl. Recognition for Excellence award, Pres. Ronald Reagan, 1986. Mem. Internat. Platform Assn., Order of the Knight Templars, Maison Internat. des Intellectuels, Internat. Parliament for Safety and Peace. Avocations: flying, skiing, sailing. Office: PO Box 5453 Fort Walton Beach FL 32549-5453

CULYER, ANTHONY JOHN, economics educator; b. London, July 1, 1942; s. Thomas Reginald and Betty Ely (Headland) C.; m. Sieglinde Birgit Kraut, Aug. 26, 1966; children: Thomas Wolfgang, Alexandra Naomi. BA, Exeter (Eng.) U., 1964; D in Econs. (hon.), Stockholm Sch. Econs., 1999. Tutor, asst. lectr. U. Exeter, Eng., 1965-69; from lectr. to reader econs. U. York, Eng., 1969-79, prof., 1979—, pro vice chancellor, 1991-94, dep. vice chancellor, 1994-97, dir. health devel., 1997—, head dept. econs., 1986—; adj. prof. U. Toronto, Can., 1989—, vis. prof., 1991; vis. prof. Otago, U., New Zealand, 1979, Queen's U., Can., 1976, Trent U., Can., 1985-86, Cen. Inst. Tech., New Zealand, 1996; mem. Ctrl. R & D com. Nat. Health Svc., London, 1991—; chmn. Nat. Health Svc. Taskforce on R & D Funding, 1993-94; chmn. com. on guidelines in econ. evaluation of pharms. Dept. Health, 1997-98; vice chmn. North Yorkshire Health Authority, 1996-99, Nat. Inst. Clin. Excellence, 1999—; dep. chmn. Office Health Econs., 1998-99; adv. on R&D to High Security Psychiatric Svcs. Commn. Bd., 1996—, NHS dir. of R&D, 1997-99; mem. Overseas Trade Svcs. Healthcare Sector Group, 1998—, Brit. Coun. Adv. Com., 1996-98; mem. population health program adv. com. Can. Inst. Advanced Rsch., 1995—, Inst. Work and Health Rsch. Adv. Com., Can., 1997; chmn. N.E. Yorkshire Area of Royal Sch. of Ch. Music, 1996—; mem. Diocese of York Liturgy and Music Com. Co-editor Jour. Health Econs., 1981—; mem. editl. bd. Clin Effectiveness in Nursing, Med. Law Internat., British Med. Jour., Econ. Review, Jour. Med. Ethics; contbr. articles to profl. jours. Trustee Can. Health Svcs. Rsch. Found., 2000—. Decorated comdr. Order Brit. Empire. Fellow Acad. Med. Scis.; mem. Health Economists' Study Group (founding chmn. 1970—). Avocations: church music, gardening. Email: ajc17@york.ac.uk. Home: The Laurels, Barmby Moor, York Y042 4EJ, England Office: U York, Dept Econs, York Y01 5DD, England

CUMMING, THOMAS ALEXANDER, stock exchange executive; b. Toronto, Ont., Can., Oct. 14, 1937; s. Alison A. and Anne B. (Berry) C.; m. E. Mary Stevens, Mar. 12, 1965; children: Jennifer, Allison, Katy. BAS, U. Toronto, 1960. Registered profl. engr., Can. With Bank of Nova Scotia, 1965-88; spl. rep. Toronto, 1965-68; br. mgr. Dublin, Ireland, 1969-71, London, 1971-75; v.p. Calgary, Alta., Can., 1975-80; sr. v.p. Calgery, Alta., Can., 1980-85, Toronto, 1986-88; pres., CEO Alta. Stock Exchange, Calgary, 1988-99; mem. coun. Power Pool of Alta; bd. dirs. Calgary R&D Authority, YMCA of Calgary Found. Mem. Assn. Profl. Engrs., Calgary C. of C. (pres. 1991), Calgary Golf and Country Club, Calgary Petroleum Club. Home and Office: 2906 10th St SW, Calgary, AB Canada T2T 3H2

CUMMING, WILLIAM JAMES, orthopaedic surgeon; b. Sydney, Australia, Nov. 10, 1930; s. John and Alice Helena (Gaines) C.; m. Marion Fay Skillen, May 21, 1954; children: Christopher John, John William, Amanda Jane. MBBS (hon.), U. Sydney, 1953; FRACS, Royal Australian Coll. Surgeon, Melbourne, 1959; FA (Orth) A., Australian Orthopaedic Assn., 1992. Resident med. officer Royal Newcastle Hosp., Newcastle, Australia, 1953-56; orthopaedic registrar Royal Newcastle Hosp., Newcastle, 1957-59; orthopaedic surgeon St. George Hosp., Sydney, 1959-99, Royal Alexandria Hosp. for Children, Sydney, 1960-75, Sutherland Hosp., Sydney, 1962-84, Kareena/Pacific, St. George pvt. hosps., Sydney, 1961-99; assoc. prof. U. Sydney, 1989-99; external examiner Indonesian Orthopaedic Assn., 1984-99. Contbr. articles to profl. jours. Recipient Australian medal Order of Australia, 1998, medal Royal Australian Coll. of Surgeons, Melbourne, 1992. Fellow Australian Orthopaedic Assn. (pres. 1993-94, L.O. Betts medal 1987), Indonesian Orthopaedic Assn. (life hon. fellow). Presbyterian. Avocations: tennis, theatre, literature, travel. Home: 42 James Cook Island 2224, Sydney Australia Office: 50 Montgomery St, Kogarah, 2217 Sydney Australia

CUMMINGS, ANTHONY WILLIAM, lawyer, educator, banker; b. Port Jefferson, N.Y., Dec. 3, 1962; s. Leonard and Annie (Earl) C. Student, Tulane U., 1980-81; BS in Applied Econs., Hofstra U., 1985, JD, 1988; MBA, U. N.C., 1997. Bar: N.Y. 1988, D.C. 1990, U.S. Dist. Ct. (ea. and so. dists.) N.Y. 1990, U.S. Ct. Mil. Appeals 1990, U.S. Ct. Appeals (2d, 11th and fed. cirs.) 1991, U.S. Tax Ct. 1991, U.S. Supreme Ct. 1992, N.C. 1995. Assoc. Ronald J. Rosenberg, Garden City, N.Y., 1988-89; of counsel Costa & Bernsten, Hauppauge, N.Y., 1989-92; contract atty. Bernsten & Newman, Hauppauge, 1990-93; pvt. practice, Patchogue, N.Y., 1990-94, Raleigh, N.C., 1994-97; assoc. Fin. Instns. Group, 1995-97, First Union Securities, Inc., Charlotte, N.C., 1997-2000; v.p. Hales & Co., N.Y.C., 2000—; adj. instr. law Suffolk County C.C., Selden, N.Y., 1992-94; coord. adminstrv. svcs. N.C. Biotech. Ctr., Research Triangle Park, N.C., 1994-95; adj. instr. bus. Wake Tech. C.C., Raleigh, 1995-97; coord., lectr. CLE programs Suffolk Acad. Law. 1989-94; co-chmn. appellate practice com. Suffolk County Bar Assn.; judge Jessup Internat. Law Moot Ct. Competition, 1990-91. Editor-in-chief Hofstra Property Law Jour., 1988; assoc. editor Jour. Suffolk Acad. Law, 1992-94. Pres. U. N.C. MBA Student Assn., 1996-97. Recipient award of recognition Suffolk County Bar Assn., 1991, cert. of disting. merit Suffolk Acad. Law, 1991. Mem. ABA, Am. Coll. Forensic Examiners, N.C. State Bar Assn., D.C. Bar Assn., N.Y. State Bar Assn., Hofstra U. Alumni Orgn. (exec. coun. 1990-94), Scabbard and Blade, Phi Eta Sigma. Office: One First Union 250 Park Ave New York NY 10177-0001

CUMMINGS, JAMES WILLIAM, poet; b. Bangor, Maine, Mar. 9, 1960; s. Donald Ernest and Marjorie May (Condon) C. Grad., Nokomis Regional H.S., Newport, Maine, 1978. With Cianbro Corp., Pittsfield, Maine, 1979, Stinson Seafood Co., Belfast, Maine, 1987—. Contbg. author: (book anthology) Treasured Poems of America, 1990-92, Memories of Tomorrow, 2000 (Disting. Poet 1999); contbr. to The Maine Genealogist; author (song anthology): Stars and Stripes, 1991; songwriter: See You that Manger, After The Storm, Lights of the City. Mem. Internat. Soc. of Poets (various anthologies 1993-2000), Sparrowgrass Poetry Forum, Poetry Guild, Smithsonian Instn., Libr. Congress (charter).

CUMMINGS, JOHN PATRICK, lawyer; b. Westfield, Mass., June 28, 1933; s. Daniel Thoams and Nora (Brick) C.; m. Dorothy June D'Ingianni, Dec. 27, 1957 (div. May 1978); children: John Patrick, Mary Catherine, Michael Brick, Kevin Andrew, Colleen Elise, Erin Christine, Christopher Gerald; m. Marilyn Ann Welch, May 23, 1980. BS, St. Michael's Coll., 1955; PhD, U. Tex., 1969; JD, U. Toledo, 1973, MCE, 1977. Bar: Ohio 1973, U.S. Mil. Appeals 1974, U.S. Dist. Ct. (no. dist.) Ohio 1979. Mgr. Hamilton Mgmt., Inc., Austin, Tex., 1962-68; scientist Owens Ill., Toledo, 1968-73, risk mgr., 1974-76, staff atty., 1977-80, mgr. legis. affairs, 1981-84; pres. Hansa World Cargo Svc., Inc., Oakland, Calif., 1984-86; in-house counsel Brown Vence & Assocs., San Francisco, 1987-88; gen. counsel Pacific Mgmt. Co., Sacramento, 1986-88; pres. John P. Cummings & Assocs., Fremont, Calif., 1988—; cons. Glass Packaging Inst., Washington, 1970-83, EPA, Washington, 1970-74. Contbr. articles to profl. jours.; patentee in field. With USAF, 1955-62, 68-69, 75-76, 84-85, col. Res. ret. 1986. USPHS fellow, 1963-66. Fellow Royal Chem. Soc.; mem. ABA, VFW, Am. Chem. Soc., ASTM (chmn. 1979), Am. Ceramic Soc. (chpt. chmn. 1973), Res. Officers Assn. (legis. chmn. 1979-85), Am. Legion, KC (4th degree). Roman Catholic. Avocations: reading, travel, coin and stamp collecting. Home: 843 Barcelona Dr Fremont CA 94536-2607 Office: PO Box 2847 Fremont CA 94536-0847

CUMMINGS, NICHOLAS ANDREW, psychologist; b. Salinas, Calif., July 25, 1924; s. Andrew and Urania (Sims) C.; m. Dorothy Mills, Feb. 5, 1948; children: Janet Lynn, Andrew Mark. AB, U. Calif., Berkeley, 1948; MA, Claremont Grad. Sch., 1954; PhD, Adelphi U., 1958. Chief psychologist Kaiser Permanente No. Calif., San Francisco, 1959-76; pres. Found Behavioral Health, San Francisco, 1976—; chmn., CEO Am. Biodyne, Inc., San Francisco, 1985-93, Kendron Internat., Ltd., Reno, Nev., 1992-95; chmn. Nicholas & Dorothy Cummings Found., Reno, 1994—; chmn., pres. U.K. Behavioural Health, Ltd., London, 1996-98; Disting. prof. U. Nev., 1997—; chmn., CEO DynaMed Integrated Care, Inc., 1998—; co-dir. South San Francisco Health Ctr., 1959-75; pres. Calif. Sch. Profl. Psychology, L.A., San Francisco, San Diego, Fresno campuses, 1969-76; chmn. bd. Calif. Cmty. Mental Health Ctrs., Inc., L.A., San Diego, San Francisco, 1975-77; pres. Blue Psi, Inc., San Francisco, 1972-80, Inst. for Psychosocial Interaction, 1980-84; mem. mental health adv. bd. City and County San Francisco, 1968-75; bd. dirs. San Francisco Assn. Mental Health, 1965-75; pres., chmn. bd. Psycho-Social Inst., 1972-80; dir. Mental Rsch. Inst., Palo Alto, Calif., 1979-80; pres. Nat. Acads. of Practice, 1981-93. Served with U.S. Army, 1944-46. Fellow APA (dir. 1975-81, pres. 1979); mem. Calif. Psychol. Assn. (pres. 1968). Office: Nicholas & Dorothy Cummings Found 561 Keystone Ave PMB 212 Reno NV 89503-4331

CUMMINGS, SEAN SPENCER, oil and gas industry executive; b. Oklahoma City, Okla., Feb. 20, 1959; s. Douglas Raymond and Peggy Jane C.; m. Terri Lynn Cummings, Apr. 8, 1989; 1 child, Sean Conor Spencer Cummings. BBA in Fin., Okla. U., 1982. Controller Kirkpatrick Supply, Oklahoma City, 1977-81; v.p. Cummings Oil Co., Oklahoma City, 1982-98, pres., 1999—; owner Seacon Energy LLC, Oklahoma City, 1982—; v.p. Seabrea Gas Systems, Inc., Oklahoma City, 1988—. Past pres. Big Bros./Big Sisters, Oklahoma City, 1985-94; Okla. Children's Health Found. (dir., pres. 1991—), Okla City YMCA (dir., treas. 1996—). Mem. Okla. Ind. Petroleum Assn. (bd. dirs. 1996—), Petroleum Club of Oklahoma City (dir., pres. 1990-96). Avocation: golf. Office: Cummings Oil Company 4917 N Portland Ave Oklahoma City OK 73112-6113

CUMMINGS ROCKWELL, PATRICIA GUILBAULT, psychiatric nurse; b. Ludlow, Mass., June 22, 1939; d. Lee Allen and Mavis Isabella (White) Guilbault; m. Philip W. Cummings, Oct. 23, 1960 (dec. Jan. 1978); children: Sharon Ellen Timmons, Geoffrey Scott Cummings, Susan Mavis Lornitzo, Lee Millett Cummings, Mary Rockwell Thon; m. William Leonard Rockwell Jr., Aug. 18, 1990. ADN, Vt. Coll., 1982; BSN, Norwich U., 1987. RN, Vt. Staff nurse Ctrl. Vt. Hosp. Nursing Home, Berlin, 1982-84, 87—; staff psychiat. nurse Va. Hosp. Ground East, White River Junction, Vt., 1987-94; owner Globe Travel, Bradford, Vt., 1988-94; rschr. Norwich U., Northfield, Vt., 1988—; nurse-entrepeneur Globe Travel, 1988—. Tchr. adult edn. ARC, Bradford, Vt., 1988, 89. Mem. ANA (nat. and Vt. chpts.), AAUW. Avocations: writing, traveling, medical geneology. Home: 307 Godfrey Rd East Thetford VT 05043-9517

CUMMINS, JAMES DUANE, correspondent, media executive; b. Cedar Rapids, Iowa, Mar. 11, 1945; s. Dewey Homer and Dorothy Marie (Colgan) C.; m. Constance Marie Driscoll, July 27, 1968; children: Kimberly, Christine, Douglas, John, Molly, Bill. BS in journalism, Northwestern U., 1967, MS in journalism, 1968. News reporter Sta. KGLO-TV, Mason City, Iowa, 1969-70, Sta. WOOD-TV, Grand Rapids, Mich., 1970-73, Sta. WTMJ-TV, Milw., 1973-75, Sta. WMAQ-TV, Chgo., 1975-78; corr. NBC News, Chgo., 1978-89; corr./bur. chief NBC News, Dallas, 1989—. Corr. (news reports) Civil War-El Salvador, 1981, Korean Airline Disaster, 1983, Hurricane Hugo, 1989, Waco Standoff, 1993, Calif. Earthquake, 1994, Okla. City Bombing, 1995, Oklahoma Tornadoes, 1999. Recipient Nat. News Emmy award for "Floods", 1993, Emmy award Chgo. TV Acad., 1976, 1st place award Nat. Assn. Black Journalists, 2000, Nat. News Emmy award nomination for "Oklahoma Tornadoes," 2000. Mem. Northwestern U. Sch. Journalism Alumni Assn., Northwestern U. N Men's Club, Sigma Delta Chi (journalism soc.). Roman Catholic. Avocations: reading, swimming, golf, fishing. Home: 5815 Flintshire Ln Dallas TX 75252-5132 Office: NBC News 3100 Mckinnon St Dallas TX 75201-7003

CUMMINS, MICHELLE MARIE, otolaryngologist, head and neck surgeon; b. Windsor, Ont., Can., July 14, 1959; came to U.S., 1994; d. James Thomas and Helen Mary (Weiler) C.; m. Jerry Dean Pilkington. BS, U. Waterloo, Can., 1982; MD, U. Toronto, 1987, MS, 1994. Intern St. Joseph Health Ctr., Toronto, 1987-88; resident Santa Barbara (Calif.) Cottage Hosp., 1988-89, U. Toronto, 1989-92; otolaryngologist Dalhousie U., Nova Scotia, Can., 1992-94; lectr. in field. Contbr. articles to profl. jours. Otolaryngology & Profl. Voice fellow Bowman Gray Sch. Medicine, Winston-Salem, N.C., 1994-96. Mem. Am. Acad. Otolaryngology Head & Neck Surgery, Am. Rhinological Soc., European Laryngological Soc., Can. Soc. Otolaryngology. Roman Catholic. Avocations: fitness walking, pottery, skiing, swimming, biking. Office: 1300 N Virginia St Ste 112 Port Lavaca TX 77979-2512

CUMMINS, NANCYELLEN HECKEROTH, electronics engineer; b. Long Beach, Calif., May 22, 1948; d. George and Ruth May (Anderson) Heckeroth; m. Weldon Jay Cummins, Sept. 15, 1987; children: Tracy Lynn, John Scott, Darren Elliott. Student, USMC, Memphis, 1966-67. From tech. publ. engr. to engring. instr. Missile and Space divsn. Lockheed Corp., Sunnyvale, Calif., 1973-77; test engr. Gen. Dynamics, Pomona, Calif., 1980-83; quality assurance test engr. Interstate Electronics Co., Anaheim, Calif., 1983-84; quality engr., certification engr. Rockwell Internat., Anaheim, 1985-86; sr. quality assurance programmer Point 4 Data, Tustin, Calif., 1986-87; software quality assurance specialist Lawrence Livermore Nat. Lab., Yucca Mountain Project, Livermore, Calif., 1987-89, software quality mgr., 1989-90; from sr. constrn. insp. to sr. quality assurance engr. EG&G Rocky Flats, Inc., Golden, Colo., 1990-91, engr. IV software quality assurance, 1991-92, instr., developer environ. law and compliance, 1992-93; software, computer cons. CRI, Dabois, Wyo., 1993-97; contractor Dept. of Energy, Golden, Colo., 1997-98; test mgr. Keane Inc., Lakewood, Colo., 1998; project officer Keane Inc., Lakewood, 1998—; customer engr. IBM Gen. Sys., Orange, Calif., 1979; electronics engr. Exhibits divsn. LDS Ch., Salt Lake City, 1978; electronics repair specialist Weber State Coll., 1977-78. Author: Package Area Test Set, 6 vols., 1975, Software Quality Assurance Plan, 1989. Vol., instr. San Fernando (Calif.) Search and Rescue Team, 1967-70; instr. emergency preparedness and survival, Claremont, Calif., 1982-84, Modesto, Calif., 1989; mem. Lawrence Livermore nat. Lab. Employees Emergency Vols., 1987-90, EG&G Rocky Flats Bldg. Emergency Support Team, 1990-93, Dubois Search and Rescue, 1995-97. Mem. NAFE, NRA, Nat. Muzzle Loading Rifle Assn., Am. Soc. Quality, Job's Daus. (majority mem.). Republican. Avocations: living history, survival, weapons, camping, native Am. crafts.

CUMMINS, PATRICIA WILLETT, academic administrator; b. Worcester, Mass., Oct. 16, 1948; d. Warren Joseph and Mary (Shannon) Willett; m. Christopher J. Cummins, Oct. 4, 1975; children: John, Mary. BA cum laude, Smith Coll., 1970; MA, U. Rochester, 1971; PhD, U. N.C., 1974. Asst. prof. Lafayette Coll., Easton, Pa., 1973-74; from asst. prof. to prof. W.Va. U., Morgantown, 1974-84; prof., dept. chairperson No. Ariz. U., Flagstaff, 1984-89; dean Arts and Humanities SUNY, Buffalo, 1989-95; dean Arts and Scis. U. Toledo, Ohio, 1995-2000; prof. French U. Toledo, 1995-2000; vice provost acad. affairs. Va. Commonwealth U., Richmond, 2000—. Author: Commercial French, 1982; author, editor: Literary and Historical Perspectives of the Middle Ages, 1982, Le Regime Tresultile, 1976, Issues and Methods in French for Business and Economic Purposes, ; mem. editorial bd. Ars Lyrica 1980-86; editor-in-chief Fgn. Lang. Ann., 1983-85. Bd. dirs. Arts in Edn. Inst. Western N.Y., 1990-95, Buffalo-Lille Sister Cities,Pick of the Crop Dance Ensemble, 1992-95. Recipient Young Scholars award Mediaeval Acad. Am., 1977; NEH fellow, 1976-77; grantee French Govt. Bus., 1983, U.S. Dept. Edn., 1986, 87-89, Que. (Can.) Govt., 1979. Mem. MLA (del. assembly 1979-81), Internat. Courtly Lit. Soc. (chief bibliographer 1979, bibliographer 1974-83), Soc. for Text and Music, Am. Assn. Tchrs. French (v.p. 1985-91, chair pedagogical commn. 1985-91, co-chair proficiency commn. 1990-92, chair French Bus. commn. 1993—), Southeastern Medieval Assn. (v.p. 1981-83, pres. 1983-85), Am. Coun. Tchg. Fgn. Langs., Coun. Colls. Arts and Scis. (chair commn. on comprehensive instns. 1994-96, mem. com. on long term planning 1995-96, chair com. on metro. univs. 1996-98, mem. exec. bd. 1996-98). Democrat. Roman Catholic. Avocations: tennis, squash, softball, volleyball, bridge.

CUNEO, DENNIS CLIFFORD, automotive company executive; b. Ridgway, Pa., Jan. 12, 1950; s. Clifford Francis and Erma Theresa (Nissel) C.; m. Bonnie Frances Mish, Aug. 18, 1972; children: Corinne, Kyle, James. BS, Gannon U., 1971; MBA, Kent State U., 1973; JD, Loyola U., New Orleans, 1976. Bar: D.C. 1977. Trial atty. U.S. Dept. Justice, Washington, 1976-80; assoc. Arent, Fox, Kintner, Plotkin & Kahn, Washington, 1980-84; gen. counsel New United Motor Mfg. Inc. joint venture GM-Toyota, Fremont, Calif., 1984-88, v.p. legal and govt. affairs, 1988-90, v.p. corp. planning and legal affairs, 1990-92, v.p. corp. planning and external affairs, corp. sec., 1992-96; sr. v.p. legal, environ., external affairs Toyota Motor Mfg. N.Am., 1996-2000, sr. v.p., 2000—; chmn. Calif. Workside Rsch. Com., Sacramento, 1988-96; lectr. exec. program U. Calif., Davis, 1988-95; lectr. internat. motor vehicle program MIT, Berlin and Beijing, 1994; mem. Gov. Pete Wilson Trade Mission to Asia, 1993; bd. dirs. Toyota Motor Corp. Svcs., Inc., 1996-99. Campaign chmn. United Way, Alameda County, 1993-95, No. Ky. United Way, 2000; co-chmn. Blue Ribbon com. to Save the Oakland A's, 1994; vice chmn. Alameda County Econ. Devel. Bd., Oakland, 1990-96, Team Calif., Sacramento, 1994; bd. visitors Loyola Law Sch., 1987-95; mem. Calif. Select Com. on Jud. Retirement, 1993; mem. steering com. Bay Area Coun., San Francisco, 1990-95, Bay Area Dredging Coalition, San Francisco, 1991-96; mem. Statewide Pupil Assessment Rev. Panel, Sacramento, 1996-97; bd. dirs. Oakland-Alameda County Coliseum, 1995-97, Cin. United Way, 1997—, Bay Area Regional Tech. Alliance, Oakland, 94-96; mem. flood relief cabinet ARC, 1997; mem. Gov.'s Task Force on Child Devel., Frankfort, Ky., 1999—. Mem. ABA, Nat. Mfrs. Assn. (bd. dirs., exec. com., chmn. human resources policy group 1999—), Calif. Mfrs. Assn. (vice chmn. 1994-99, pres. Calif. manufactures svcs. corp. 1996-97), Oakland Football Mktg. Assn. (pres. 1995-96), No. Ky. C. of C. (bd. dirs. 1997-98), Greater Cin. C. of C. (bd. dirs. 1998—), Metro. Club (bd. dirs. 1999—), Assoc. Industries Ky. (bd. dirs. 1999—). Avocations: skiing, model trains. Office: Toyota Motor Mfg NAm 25 Atlantic Ave Erlanger KY 41018-3188

CUNEY, MICHEL LOUIS, geologist, researcher; b. Piney, France, May 21, 1948; s. Marcel and Renee (Cuney) C.; m. Liliane Legras Cuney, Aug. 1973; children: Helene, Guillaume, Christian. DSc, Nancy (France) U., 1981, PhD, 1976. Engr. Polytechnic Inst., Nancy, France, 1972-76; rsch. asst. C.R.P.G., Nancy, France, 1976-88; rsch. dir. CREGU, Nancy, France, 1989—; expert in U-Geology, IAEA, Vienna, Austria, 1992—. Author: L'Uranium, 1992, Regards sur l'Uranium III, Les Grands Types Digesements, 2000; contbr. articles to profl. jours. Mem. Geology Soc. France, Am. Geophys. Union, French Mineralogical Soc. Office: CREGU UMR G2R 7566, BP23, 54501 Nancy France

CUNHA, BURKE A., physician; b. Hartford, Conn., Mar. 25, 1942; s. Anthony S. and Philomena S. Cunha; m. Marie A. Boyer, Sept. 5, 1970; children: Zachary A., Cheston B. AB, U. Conn., 1965; MD, Pa. State U., 1972. Diplomate Am. Bd. Internal Medicine. Resident Hartford (Conn.) Hosp., 1973-75, fellow in infectious disease, 1975-77, asst. chief infectious disease divsn., 1977-79, chief med. svc., 1977-79; asst. prof. medicine U. Conn. Sch. Medicine, Farmington, 1977-80; chief infectious disease divsn., vice chmn. dept. medicine, epidemiologist Winthrop-Univ. Hosp., Mineola, N.Y., 1980—; asst. prof. medicine SUNY, Sch. Medicine, Stony Brook, 1980-82, assoc. prof. medicine, 1982-91, prof. medicine, 1991—; dir. arts and humanities series Winthrop-Univ. Hosp., 1994—, history of medicine series, 1995—, multicultural aspects of medicine, 1996—. Editor-in-chief Infectious Disease Practice, 1991—, Antibiotics for Clinicians, 1996—; editor 10 books, 1984—; author 50 chpts. to books and 800 articles to profl. jours. Vol. Peace Corps, Chile, 1965-68. Recipient Disting. Alumni Fellow award Pa. State U. Coll. Medicine, 1997. Fellow Am. Coll. Chest Physicians, Am. Coll. Clin. Pharmacology, Am. Acad. Microbiology, Infectious Disease Soc. Am., Am. Coll. Physicians (master). Avocations: classical studies, philosophy, history. Office: Winthrop Univ Hosp Infectious Disease Divsn 259 1st St Mineola NY 11501-3987

CUNNIGAIPUR, ANURADHA DHANASEKARAN, biochemist, researcher; b. Chennai, Tamilnadu, India, Dec. 16, 1968; parents Dhanasekaran Kuppuswami Cunnigaipur and Rani Dhanasekaran; m. Sivanesan Subramanian, May 23, 1995; 1 child, Sanjana Sivanesan. BSc, U. Madras, Chennai, 1988, MSc, 1990, MPhil, 1991, PhD in Biochemistry, 1995. Rsch. assoc. dept. biochemistry and molecular biology U. Madras, 1995-97; rsch. biochemist Inst. for Med. Microbiology and Hygiene, Mainz, Germany, 1997-98; sci. and tech. agy. rschr. Nat. Inst. for Environ. Studies, Tsukuba, 1998—; scientist regional environ. divsn. Nat. Inst. for Environ. Studies, Tsukuba, Inst. for Med. Microbiology and Hygiene, Mainz. Contbr. rsch. articles to sci. publs. Recipient Distinction award Directorate of Gen. Health Svcs., 1990; sr. rsch. fellow Coun. for Sci. and Indsl. Rsch., 1991, sci. fellow Inst. for Med. Microbiology and Hygiene, 1997-98, sci. and tech. agy. fellow Japanese Sci. and Tech. Agy., 1998-00. Mem. Japanese Biochem. Soc., Soc. Biol. Chemists, Soc. Toxicologists. Avocations: Indian classical music, violin, swimming, badminton. Fax: 0081 298 502512. E-mail: anuradha@nies.go.jp. Office: Nat Inst Environ Studies, 16-2 Onogawa, 305 0053 Tsukuba Ibaraki, Japan

CUNNINGHAM, ATLEE MARION, JR., aeronautical engineer; b. Corpus Christi, Aug. 17, 1938; s. Atlee Marion and Carlos Dean (Shepherd) C.; m. Diana Wahl Bonelli, July 17, 1976; children by previous marriage: Christopher Atlee Acie, Scott Patrick, Sean Michael. BS in Mech. Engring., U. Tex., 1961, MS in Mech. Engring., 1963, PhD, 1966. Rsch. scientist Def. Research Lab., Austin, Tex., 1965; engring. staff specialist Gen. Dynamics Corp., Ft. Worth, 1965-93, Lockheed Corp., Ft. Worth, 1993-95, Lockheed Martin, 1995—; vis. indsl. prof. So. Meth. U. Inst. Tech., Dallas, 1969-70; vis. assoc. prof. aero. engring. U. Tex., 1978—; lectr. in aeroelasticity Nat. Cheng Kung U., Taiwan, 1984, U. Tex., Arlington, 1990—; cons. NASA, USAF, USN, U. Tex. Vice pres. Tex. Fine Arts Assn., Fort Worth, 1972. Served with USN, 1962-64. Welding Rsch. Assn. fellow, 1961-62; NATO fellow, 1964-65; recipient NASA Cert. of Recognition for tech. publ., 1980, Extraordinary Achievement award Gen. Dynamics, 1980, 83, 89. Fellow AIAA (assoc.; tech. reviewer jours.); mem. Sigma Xi. Contbr. articles to profl. jours. and AGARD publs.; innovator in subsonic, transonic and supersonic steady and oscillatory aerodynamics method; developer new methods for predicting high angle of attack aerodynamics in subsonic and supersonic flows. Major contbr. to aeroelastic developments and improvements for Gen. Dynamics F-16 and F-111 aircrafts. Pioneer in new technology development for unsteady separated flows and buffeting on aircraft maneuvering at high angle of attack involving support of Air Force, Navy, NASA, National Aerospace Laboratory (Netherlands), General Dynamics, Lockheed and University of Texas at Austin. Developer of steady and unsteady force testing techniques for aerodynamic investigations using water tunnels, new concepts and methods for nonlinear aeroelasticity. Home: 4932 Black Oak Ln Fort Worth TX 76114-2936

CUNNINGHAM, CRAIG NEIL, lawyer; b. Uitenhage, South Africa, Dec. 28, 1962; s. Desmond Arthur and Denise Lavinia (Meyer) C.; m. Seonaid Margaret Douglas, Jan. 30, 1993 (div. Mar. 1995); m. Jane Prescott Heath Bevan, Mar. 28, 1998. B, U. Port Elizabeth, South Africa, 1986; LLB, U. Capetown, South Africa, 1988; LLM, U. Capetown, 1999. From atty. to assoc. Findlay & Tait The Cape Town Office Bowman Gilfillan Inc., Capetown, South Africa, 1989-96, dir., 1997—; examiner Sch. for Prac. Legal Training, Capetown, 1993-96. With South African Air Force, 1981—. Mem. South Africa Maritime Law Assn., Royal Cape Yacht Club, Clovelly Country Club. Avocations: water sports, snow skiing, walking, yachting, travel. Office: Findlay Tait The Cape Town, PO Box 248, 8000 Cape Town South Africa

CUNNINGHAM, EDWARD PATRICK, geneticist; b. Dublin, Aug. 4, 1934; s. Eugene Francis and Kathleen Agnes (Moran) C.; m. Catherine Dee, Mar. 20, 1965; children: Helen, Eoghan, John, Donal, Conor, Clare. BS in Agrl., Nat. U. Ireland, 1956, MS in Agrl., 1957; PhD, Cornell U., 1962.

Rsch. officer Agrl. Rsch. Inst., Dublin, 1962-70, head dept. animal genetics, 1970-80, deputy dir. rsch., 1980-88; dir. animal prodn. and health divsn. FAO, Rome, 1990-93; prof. animal genetics Trinity Coll., Dublin, 1974—; dir. RDI, Dublin, 1994—, IdentiGen, Dublin, 1996—; vis. prof. WorldBank, Washington, 1988. Author: Animal Breeding Theory, 1969, World Livestock Production, 1990; editor: The North African Screw Worm Program, 1993; contbr. over 100 sci. articles to profl. publs. Home: Vesington House, Dunboyne Ireland Office: Trinity Coll, Dept Genetics, Dublin Ireland

CUNNINGHAM, GARY H., lawyer; b. Grand Rapids, Mich., Jan. 11, 1953; s. Gordon H. and Marilyn J. (Lookabill) C.; m. Arlene M. Marcy, Apr. 23, 1983; children: Stephanie M., Gregory H. B.Gen. Studies, U. Mich., 1975, MA, 1977; JD, Detroit Coll. Law, 1980. Bar: Mich. 1980, U.S. Dist. Ct. Mich. 1983, U.S. Ct. Appeals (6th cir.) 1986, U.S. Ct. Appeals (Fed. cir.) 1990. Law clk. and estate adminstr. U.S. Bankruptcy Ct., Ea. Dist. Mich., Detroit, 1980-83; assoc./ptnr. Schlussel, Lifton, Simon, Rands, Galvin & Jackier, Southfield, Mich., 1983-90; ptnr./shareholder Kramer Mellen, P.C., Southfield, Mich., 1990-95; prin. shareholder Strobl Cunningham Caretti & Sharp, P.C., Bloomfield Hills, Mich., 1995—. Sr. staff mem. Detroit Coll. of Law Rev., 1978-80; contbr. articles to profl. jours. Mem. ABA (bus. law sect.), Fed. Bar Assn. (chmn. bankruptcy sect. 1989-91), Oakland County Bar Assn. (bus. law com.), State Bar of Mich. (mem. corp., fin. and bus. law sect.), Am. Bankruptcy Inst. (sponsor), Comml. Law League of Am., Detroit Econ. Club, Detroit Inst. Arts, Delta Theta Phi. Avocations: sailing, skiing, tennis. Home: 2959 Cedar Ridge Dr Troy MI 48084-2613 Office: Strobl Cunningham Caretti & Sharp PC 300 E Long Lake Rd Ste 200 Bloomfield Hills MI 48304-2376

CUNNINGHAM, JACK, British government official; b. County Durham, Eng., Aug. 4, 1939; married; 3 children. BS, Durham U., PhD in Chemistry. Elected M.P. Whitehaven, Eng., 1970-83, Copeland, Eng., 1983—; parliamentary pvt. sec. to James Callaghan, 1974-76, min. for energy, 1976-79, opposition front bench spokesman industry, 1979-83, elected shadow cabinet, 1983, shadow environment sec., 1983-89; shadow leader, campaigns coord. Ho. of Commons, 1989-92; mem. Privy Coun., 1992; shadow sec. state Dept. Fgn. and Commonwealth Affairs, 1992-94, Dept. Trade and Industry, 1994-95; min. fisheries and food, 1997-98; min. for the cabinet office, chancellor Duchy Lancaster, 1998-99. Rsch. fellow Durham U., 1966-68. Office: House of Commons, London SW1A 0AA, England

CUNNINGHAM, JAMES ARCHIBALD, bank executive; b. Bad Godesberg, Germany, Nov. 25, 1951; s. Francis and Marianne Dagmar (de Dardel) C.; m. Elisabeth Claudia Schiestl, Dec. 30, 1982; children: Alexander James, Benjamin Peter. Bachelors degree cum laude, U. Princeton, 1973; MBA, U. Pa., 1981; degrees in fin. asset mgmt. and engring., U. Lausanne, Switzerland, 1998. 2nd v.p. corp. fin. Smith Barney, London, 1983-86; portfolio mgr. Pictet & Cie, London, 1986-91; dir. instnl. mktg. Alliance Capital, London, 1991-93, AIG, London, 1993-95; regional head portfolio mgmt. Credit Suisse Pvt. Banking, Lausanne, 1995-99; head pvt. portfolio mgmt. Bank Sarasin, Basel, Switzerland, 1999—. Bd. dirs. Swiss Boy Scouts, Lausanne, 1997-99; councilor Protestant ch., LeMontsur-Lausanne, 1997-99. Mem. Ivy Club (Princeton U.), Cercle du Jardin (Neuchâtel, Switzerland). Avocations: riding, skiing, hiking, history. Office: Bank Sarasin and Cie, Elisabethenstrasse 62, CH-4002 Basel Switzerland

CUNNINGHAM, JOHN RANDOLPH, project manager; b. Alexandria, La., July 17, 1954; s. John Adolphus and Zelma Audrey (Cox) C.; m. Teresa Ellen Toms, Jan. 22, 1977. BS in Computer Sci., La. Tech. U., 1976; masters cert. in project mgmt., George Washington U., 1999. Cert. project mgmt. profl., 1999. Customer support specialist South Ctrl. Bell Tel. Co., New Orleans, 1977-81; data communication designer Weyerhaeuser, Tacoma, 1981-87, acct. rep., 1987-89, planning mgr., 1989-92, EDI project leader, 1992-2000; project mgr. Vision Compass, Inc., Seattle, 2000—; mem. adv. bd. U. Wash., Seattle, 1989-94; spkr. fin. EDI confs. Contbr. articles to profl. jours. Vol. Big Bros., Tacoma, 1989-99, Wash. State First Responder, 1989-2000; instr. CPR, 1990-2000, neighborhood emergency tng., 1999-2000. Mem. NRA, Computer and Automated Systems Assn. (treas. 1991-95, pres. 1995-99), Project Mgmt. Inst., Indsl. Computing Soc., Instrument Soc. Am., Toastmasters Internat., Upsilon Pi Epsilon. Republican. Baptist. Home: 319 SW 328th St Federal Way WA 98023-5645

CUNNINGHAM, JOSEPH NEWTON, JR., cardiothoracic and vascular surgeon; b. Selma, Ala., Mar. 10, 1940; s. Joseph N. and Velma (Greenfield) C.; m. Bonnie Halper; children: Teri, Lori, Stephanie, Jessica, Gaynor, Joseph, Daniel. BS, U. Ala., 1962; MD, Med. Coll. Ala., 1966. Attending surgeon divsn. thoracic surgery NYU Med. Ctr., N.Y.C., 1974-82, Bellevue Hosp., N.Y.C., 1974-82, Manhattan VA Hosp., N.Y.C., 1974-82, Beekman-Downtown Hosp., N.Y.C., 1977-83, St. Vincent's Hosp. and Med. Ctr., N.Y.C., 1977-90; chmn. dept. surgery Maimonides Med. Ctr., Bklyn., 1982—, chief divsn. cardiothoracic surgery, 1982-88, 99—; attending surgeon dept. surg. svcs. Coney Island Hosp., Bklyn., 1982—, Bklyn. VA Hosp., 1982—, Kings County Hosp., Bklyn., 1985—; attending surgeon, dir. divsn. cardiothoracic surgery SUNY Health Sci. Ctr., Bklyn., 1985—. Contbr. numerous chpts. to textbooks in field. Rsch. fellow in surgery Parkland Meml. Hosp./U. Tex. Southwestern Med. Sch., Dallas, 1966-72; dir. Berg Lab. for Cardiothoracic Rsch. NYU Med. Ctr., N.Y.C., 1975-82; dir. lab. for surg. rsch. Edward Neimeth Inst. Med. Rsch. Maimonides Med. Ctr., 1982—. Grantee USPHS, 1966-72, NIH, 1981-84, 93-96, Maimonides Med. Ctr. R&D Found., 1990-93, 94-95, N.Y. Cardiac Ctr., 1993-96. Fellow ACS (mem. com. on applicants L.I. dist.), N.Y. Acad. Medicine; mem. Am. Heart Assn., Soc. Thoracic Surgeons, Am. Surg. Assn., Am. Coll. Chest surgeons, Am. Assn. Thoracic Surgery, Internat. Soc. Cardiovascular Surgery, Am. Soc. Artificial Internal Organs, N.Y. Acad. Scis., N.Y. Surg. Soc., N.Y. Cardiovascular Soc., N.Y. Cardiol. Soc., N.Y. Heart Assn. Coun. on Rsch., N.Y. Soc. Thoracic Surgery (pres. 1990), N.Y. Soc. Surgeons, Bklyn. Surg. Soc. (pres. 1989). Office: Cardiothoracic Surg Assoc 4802 10th Ave Brooklyn NY 11219-2844

CUNNINGHAM, MARINA, university program director; b. Shanghai, Mar. 25, 1944; came to U.S., 1963; d. David Shlav and Bella Rogovina; m. Roger J. Cunningham; children: Mark, Larissa. BA, U. Ill., Chgo., 1969; PhD, Northwestern U., Evanston, Ill., 1976. Refugee resettlement caseworker Jewish Fedn. Chgo., 1978-80, Jewish Fedn. N.Y., 1980-83; dir. Russian sr. ctr. refugee resettlement West Orange, N.J., 1983-88; asst. dir. Ctr. for Continuing Edn. William Paterson U., N.J., 1988-96; dir. Global Edn. Ctr. Montclair (N.J.) State U., 1996—; adj. prof. Russian lit. and lang., William Paterson U., 1988-96. Trustee, mem. Internat. Inst. of N.J., Jersey City, 1995—; bd. dirs., mem. Montclair Shared Housing, 1995—; bd. dirs. Montclair Sister City, 1997—. Univ. partnership grantee USIA, Kirovograd, Ukraine, 1999—; fellow Woodrow Wilson Found., Princeton, N.J., 1972. Mem. Assn. Internat. Edn. Adminstrs., Nat. Assn. Fgn. Student Advisors. Jewish. Avocations: international affiliations, travel, reading. Office: Montclair State U Global Edn Ctr Upper Montclair NJ 07043

CUNNINGHAM, NANCY SCHIEFFELIN, business educator; b. Mobile, Ala., Sept. 14, 1951; d. William Orville and Burline (Livingston) Schieffelin; m. Donald Frank Cunningham, Aug. 18, 1975; children: Benjamin Grant, Paige Allison. BA magna cum laude, U. North Tex., 1975; MA, Ohio State U., 1982. Cert. Myers Briggs Type Indicator adminstr. Mem. English faculty Franklin U., Columbus, Ohio; English curriculum coord. Ctr. for Unique Learners, Rockville, Mo.; mem. English faculty McClennan C.C., Waco, Tex.; coord. bus. writing Baylor U., Waco. Contbr. articles to profl. jours.; created and administers a writing proficiency exam. for bus. students; sr. editor: The Perryman Report, 1991—, The Perryman Texas Letter, 1992—. Baylor U. summer rsch. grantee. Mem. MLA, Assn. for Bus. Communication (rep.), Nat. Coun. Tchrs. English, Soc. for Tech. Comm., Perryman Tex. Editors (editor newsletters).

CUNNINGHAM, PIERCE EDWARD, lawyer, city planner; b. Cin., Aug. 18, 1934; s. Francis E. and Adelaide (Kraus) C.; m. Roberta Roche, Sept. 6, 1958; children: Pierce E., Jr. James M., Sarah Ellen, Anna C. BA, Holy Cross, 1956; LLB, Georgetown U., 1959. Bar: Ohio 1960, U.S. Supreme Ct. 1977. Atty. Hartford Accident and Indemnity Co., Cin., 1960-61; pvt. practice Hamilton, Ohio, 1961-62; asst. atty. gen. Ohio State Atty. Gen.'s Office, Columbus, 1963-70; prin. Pierce E. Cunningham and Assocs., Cin., 1964-75; ptnr. Clark & Eyrich, Cin., 1975-81, Frost & Jacobs, Cin., 1981-97; of counsel Baker Hostetler, Cleve., 1997—; chmn. Riverfront Adv. Commn., Cin., 1970-72, Zoning Bd. Appeals, Cin., 1970-72; mem. Urban Design and Rev. Bd., Cin. 1970-72, City Planning Com., Cin., 1968-73, chmn. 1970-73. Contbr. articles to profl. jours. Mem. May Festival Com., Cin., 1972-74, Cin. Bar Assn. Vol. Lawyers for Poor. Named Lawyer of Yr. Cin. Bar Assn. Vol. Lawyers for Poor, 1982-83. Mem. Am. Bd. Trial Advs., Ohio Bar Assn. (faculty continuing legal edn.), Cin. Bar Assn. (panel of neutrals CPR 1998—), Am. Arbitration Assn. (midwest region adv. coun., large complex litigation panelist), Cin. Tennis Club (pres. 1976-78), Cin. Country Club (bd. govs. 1995—), Potter Stewart Inn of Ct., Inner Cir. U.S. Senate, 1999—. Avocations: tennis, sailing. Home: 8 Hill And Hollow Ln Cincinnati OH 45208-3317 Office: Baker & Hostetler 3200 312 Walnut St Cincinnati OH 45202

CUNNINGHAM, TOM ALAN, lawyer; b. Houston, Nov. 5, 1946; s. Warren Peek and Ellen Ardelle (Benner) C.; m. Jeanne Adrienne Moran, July 21, 1972; 1 child, Christopher Alan. BA, U. Tex., 1968, JD, 1974. Bar: Tex. 1974, U.S. Dist. Ct. (so. dist.) Tex. 1976, U.S. Ct. Appeals (5th and 11th cirs.) 1981, U.S. Dist. Ct. (no. dist.) Tex. 1982, U.S. Dist. Ct. (we. dist.) Tex. 1984, U.S. Ct. Appeals (8th cir.) 1991. Ptnr., Fulbright & Jaworski L.L.P., Houston, 1974-98; founding ptnr. Cunningham, Darlow, Zook & Chapoton, L.L.P., Houston, 1998—. Bd. trustee Childrens Charity Fund, Houston, 1983-88; mem. exec. com. bd. dirs. Assn. for Cmty. TV; active South Tex. Ctr. for Legal Responsibility. Lt. (j.g.) USNR, 1969-72. Fellow Am. Bar Found., Am. Coll. Trial Lawyers, Tex. Bar Found. (sustain life fellow, chmn. bd. trustees, adv. bd., chair 1995—), Houston Bar Found.; mem. CPR Inst. for Dispute Resolution (panel of disting. neutrals), ABA (litigation sect., discovery com., alternate dispute resolution com., forum com. constrn. industry, arbitration com. 1995—), Am. Arbitration Assn. (panel of arbitrators), Am. Coll. Trial Lawyers, Houston Bar Assn. (professionalism com., chmn. constn. bicentennial com., Pres.'s award 1988, arbitration com., membership com.), State Bar Tex. (chmn. dist. 4H grievance com. 1982-88, chmn. spl. com. on lawyer advt. and solicitation 1982, bd. dirs. 1989-92, chair bd. dirs. exec. com. 1991-92, chair com. for lawyer discipline, 1992-94, chair gen. counsel adv. com., Pres.'s award 1983, Pres.'s citation for meritorious svc. 1991, Pres.'s spl. recognition for meritorious svc. 1993, 94, nominee Outstanding Young Lawyer, 1981, exec. com., mem. ct. rules com.), Tex. Bar Found. (chair Lola Wright com., chair bd. trustee, adv. bd., mem. new fellows com., mem. awards com., mem. pub. com., mem. bd. dirs., mem. ct. rules com., chair bd. trustees 1995—), Tex. Bd. Legal Specialization, Tex. Assn. Def. Counsel, Tex. Ctr. Legal Ethics and Professionalism, Tex. Empowerment Network (bd. dirs.), Resolution Forum, Inc. (pres.), Coronado Club, Houston Club, Lakeside Country Club, Phi Delta Phi. Home: 10811 Pine Bayou St Houston TX 77024-3018

CUNNINGHAM, WILLIAM HUGHES, academic administrator, marketing educator; b. Detroit, Jan. 5, 1944; married; 1 child. BA, Mich. State U., 1966, MBA, 1967, PhD, 1971, LLD (hon.), 1993. Mem. faculty U. Tex., Austin, 1971—, assoc. prof. mktg., 1973-79, prof., 1979—, assoc. dean grad. programs, 1976-82, Foley/Sanger Harris prof. retail merchandising, 1982-83, acting dean Coll. Bus. Adminstrn. and Grad. Sch. Bus., 1982-83, dean, 1983-85, pres., 1985-92, Centennial Chair Bus. Edn. Leadership, 1983-85, Regents Chair Higher Edn. Leadership, 1985-92, Lee Hage and Joseph D. Jamail Regents Chair Higher Edn. Leadership, 1992—, James L. Bayless Chair for Free Enterprise, 1988—; chancellor U. Tex. Sys., Austin, 1992—; bd. dirs. Jefferson-Pilot Corp., John Hancock Funds, Golfsmith Internat. Inc.; mem. Corp. of the Conf. Bd. Author: (with W.J.E. Crissy and I.C.M. Cunningham) Selling: The Personal Force in Marketing, 1977, 2d edit. (with D.W. Jackson and Cunningham), 1988, Effective Selling, 1977, Spanish edit., 1980, (with S. Lopreato) Consumers' Energy Attitudes and Behavior, 1977, (with Cunningham) Marketing: A Managerial Approach, 1981, 2d edit. (with Cunningham and C. Swift), 1988, (with R. Aldag and C. Swift) Introduction to Business, 1984, 3d edit. (with R. Aldag and S. Block), 1992, 4th edit. (with R. Aldag and M. Stone), 1995, (with B. Verhage and Cunningham) Grondslagen van het Marketing Management, 1984, (with R. Aldag and S. Block) Business in a Changing World, 1992, also monographs and articles; editor Jour. Mktg., 1981-84. Bd. dirs. Houston Area Rsch. Coun., 1984; mem. Mental Health/Mental Retardation Legis. Oversight Com., 1984; mem. adv. bd. Found. for Cultural Exch./The Netherlands-U.S.A.; bd. dirs. Lyndon Baines Johnson Found. Recipient Teaching Excellence award Coll. Bus. Adminstrn., U. Tex., 1972, Alpha Kappa Psi, 1975, Hank and Mary Harkins Found., 1978, Disting. Scholastic Contbn. award Coll. Bus. Adminstrn. Found. Adv. Council, 1982, Disting. Alumnus award Coll. and Grad. Sch. Bus., Mich. State U., 1983, 93, Tree of Life award Jewish Nat. Fund, 1992; named among top 20 profs. Utmost Mag., 1982; rsch. grantee Univ. Rsch. Inst., 1971, 72-73, Latin Am. Inst., 1972, So. Union Gas Energy, 1975-76, ERDA, 1976. Mem. Am. Inst. for Decision Scis., Am. Mktg. Assn., Assn. Consumer Rsch., So. Mktg. Assn., S.W. Social Sci. Assn., Phi Kappa Phi, Omicron Delta Kappa. Office: U Tex Sys Office Chancellor 601 Colorado St Austin TX 78701-2904

CUNY, JEAN-PIERRE, engineering company executive; b. Menton, France, Apr. 8, 1940; s. Robert A. and Marie-Louise (Marchal) C.; m. Anne-Marie Fousse, Apr. 20, 1968; children: Florence, Cécile. MS, MIT, 1965. Project engr. Serete, Paris, 1965-68; dir. Fermin-Didot Etudes, Paris, 1968-73, DAFSA Documentation, Paris, 1973-76; project dir. CGA, Bretigny, France, 1976-77; prodn. dir. Placoplatre, Rueil, France, 1977-82, comml. dir., 1982-86, chmn., CEO, 1986-99; dep. chmn. Gypsum Divsn. BPB, London, 1988-94, CEO, 1994-99, dir., 1988-99; pres. Assn. Industries de Constrn. et des Components, Paris, 1990-93, Eurosypsum, Brussels, 1995-97, Coun. European Producers Materials for Constrn., 1990, 93, European Mfrs. Expanded Polystyrene, Brussels, 1992. Recipient Legion of Honor, France, 1994. Home and Office: 50 ave de Saxe, F-75015 Paris France

CUNY, STEPHANE FRANÇOIS, banker; b. Cognac, France, Nov. 3, 1963; s. Christian Stanislas and Joelle Marie-France (Lanxade) C.; m. Bénédicte Anne Lapicorey, Oct. 5, 1991; 1 child, Edouard. Student, Lycee Privé Saint Genevieve, Versailles, France, 1985; degree in engring., Ecole Nat. Supérieure d'Art et Métiers, Paris, 1988. Head info. systems Assurance Générale de France, Lisbon, Portugal, 1988-90; head French Franc Interest Rate Swapstrade Société Générale, Paris, 1990-92, head U.S. Dollars Global Book for Europe, 1993—; treas. Société Générale, Hong Kong, 1998—, head IRS trading in Ausa, head of bond trading in Asia, 1998—. Pres., founder. Club des Sveltes, Paris, 1992-93. Recipient Portuguese Rugby Cup, 1989, Nat. Rugby Fedn. Championship award, Portugal, 1989. Avocations: skiing, sailing, rugby, chess, bridge. Office: Société Gén, 3 rue Lafayette, Paris 75009, France

CUOMO, ANDREW, federal agency administrator. BA, Fordham U., 1979; JD, Albany Law Sch., 1982. Asst. dist. atty. Dist. Atty's Office, Manhattan; ptnr. Blutrich, Falcone and Miller, N.Y.C.; chmn. N.Y.C. Commn. on the Homeless, 1991-93; asst. sec. cmty. planning and devel. U.S. Dept. Housing and Urban Devel., Washington, 1993—, sec. Campaign mgr. Mario M. Cuomo for Gov. N.Y., 1982; founder, pres. H.E.L.P., 1986, founder Genesis, 1992. Recipient Good Neighbor award ARC, Outstanding Comty. Svc. award Latin Soul, 1988, Man of the Yr. award Coalition of Italian Am. Orgns., 1988, Ed Sulzberger award, Our Town newspaper, 1989, Pub. Svc. award Coun. of Jewish Orgns., 1989, Disting. Comty. Svc. award NYU, 1991, Bard award, 1992, Albert Einstein award, 1993, Encore Heart to Heart award, 1994, Innovation Am. Govt. award John F. Kennedy Sch. Govt. Harvard U., 1996. Office: Sec HUD 451 7th St SW Washington DC 20410-0001

CUPERS, JEAN-LOUIS GEORGES, philologist, musicologist; b. Brussels, June 19, 1946; s. Adolphe Nicolas and Nelly (Thiel) C.; m. Michèle Jenny Derixhon, Jan. 19, 1985; children: Dorothée, Aurore. Philosophy and Letters, Cath. U. Louvain, 1968, Archaeology and History of Art, 1972, BPh, 1971, DLitt, 1977. Asst. lectr. Faculties Univ. St. Louis, Brussels, 1968-77, lectr., 1977-78, sr. lectr., 1978—; sr. lectr. HEC, Liege, Belgium, 1977-92, prof., 1992—. Author: Aldous Huxley and Music, 1985, Euterpe and Harpocrates: The Literary Challenge to Music, 1988, (with Ulrich Weisstein) Musico-Poetics in Perspective: Calvin S. Brown in Memoriam, 2000; contbr. articles to profl. jours. Recipient Govt. Medal for Piano, Acad. Music, Brussels, 1966. Mem. Belgian Comparative Lit. Assn. (pres. 1994-96), Internat. Comparative Lit. Assn., European Soc. for Study of English (advisor 1993-94). Avocations: walking, reading, playing piano, writing poetry in French. Office: Facultés U St Louis, 43 Blvd du Jardin Botanique, 1000 Brussels Belgium

CUPP, MARILYN MARIE, sales executive; b. Coleman, Tex., Feb. 22, 1953; d. Kellum and Jean (Sheppard) Guthne: Johnson; m. David Allan Coyle (div. Aug. 1981); 1 child, Daniel Steven Jr. BBA, So. Meth. U., Dallas, 1976. Buyer Kelly's Childrens Shop, Dallas, 1982-90. Albums include I'm Walking On Sunshine; producer Nat. Dem. Conv., Stas. ABC, CBS and NBC, 1992. Mem. DeSoto Bapt. Ch. Recipient Grammy award as best singer of yr., 1996. Mem. So. Meth. U. Alumni Assn., 500, Inc. Democrat. Methodist. Avocations: swimming, gardening, exercising, reading. Home: 1024 Inez St Early TX 76802-2516

CUPP, STEVEN EUGENE, real estate executive; b. Knoxville, Tenn., July 1, 1950; s. Boyd Eugene and Katherine Sue (Chapman) C. BS, U. Tenn., 1973. Sales mgr. Towne and Country Assn., Roswell, Ga., 1973-75; sales assoc. Barton and Ludwig Realtors, Roswell, Ga., 1975-79; pres. C&C Properties, Roswell, Ga., 1979-85; broker/assoc. Ackerman and Co., Atlanta, 1985-95; pres. Brannen and Cupp Realty Advisors, Atlanta, 1995—; mem. Atlanta Bd. Realtors, 1990-95; realtor Atlanta Comml. Bd. Realtors, 1995—. Democrat. Baptist. Avocations: golf, jogging, travel, wine. E-mail: Brannen@onramp.net. Office: Branen and Cupp Realty Advisors 5784 Lake Forrest Dr NW Ste 235 Atlanta GA 30328-6206

CUPPENS, FRÉDÉRIC DANIEL ANDRÉ, computer science researcher, educator; b. Montpellier, Herault, France, Oct. 13, 1962; s. Roger Michel Paul and Marguerite-Marie Thérèse (Fasseur) C.; m. Nora Boulahia, May 18, 1989; children: Tania, Yohann. Engr. in computer sci., ENSEEIHT, Toulouse, 1985; PhD in Computer Sci., ENSAE, Toulouse, 1988; habil., U. Paul Sabatier, Toulouse, 2000. Rsch. engr. Office Nat. d'etudes Recherches en Aeronautique, Toulouse, 1989—; prof. Ecole Nat. Supérieure des Telecomm., Paris, 1989-2000, Ecole Nat. Supérieure de l'Aeronautique et de l-Espace, Toulouse, 1990-2000, U. Paul Sabatier, Toulouse, 1996-2000. Editor: Computer Security-Esorics, 2000; translator: An Introduction to Database Systems, 1998. Mem. Soc. des Electriciens et des Electroniciens, European Symposium Rsch. in Computer Security (programme com. chair 2000). Avocations: bridge, swimming, hiking. Office: Onera Ctr de Toulouse, 2 ave Edouard Belin, 31055 Toulouse France

CUPSTID, ROBERT JACK, JR., writer; b. Crystal Springs, Miss., Oct. 9, 1944; s. Robert Jack, Sr. and Eula Mae (Smith) C.; m. Margaret Ann Shirey, June 10, 1966 (div. 1985); children: Wilburn Conway, Matthew Jared. AA in Acctg., Santa Fe C.C., Gainesville, Fla., 1964; BA in Journalism, U. Fla., 1973; degree, Inst. paralegal Arts Scis., 1992. Cert. legal asst. Miss. Bar Assn. Criminal investigator Natchez (Miss.) Police Dept., 1967-70; staff writer Miss. Press Register, Pascagoula, 1974-77; freelance writer Natchez, 1977-88, 96—; feature writer Vicksburg (Miss.) Evening Post, 1992-94; legal asst. ACLU, Union Jackson, Miss., 1994-96; legal rep. VA, Jackson, 1994-96. Contbr. to mags. Pilot, Civil Air Patrol, 1975-77. Recipient Commendation, Natchez Police Dept., 1969, Pub. award Miss. Press Register, 1975, Gov. Staff award Jackson, Miss., 1978, Miss. News award River Cities Mag., 1993, Story of Yr., Raconteur Mag., 1995, 96. Mem. NRA (life), ACLU (bd. dirs., adv. bd. 1996—), Nat. Assn. Legal Assts., Writer's Guild Am. Republican. Pentacostal. Avocations: fly fishing, archery, antique cars. Home and Office: 26 Montgomery Rd Natchez MS 39120-5340

CURCIO, CHRISTOPHER FRANK, city official; b. Oakland, Calif., Feb. 3, 1950; s. Frank William and Virginie Theresa (Le Gris) C. BA in Speech/Drama, Calif. State U., Hayward, 1971; MBA in Arts Adminstrn., UCLA, 1974; MPA in Pub. Policy, Ariz. State U., 1982. Intern John F. Kennedy Ctr. for Arts, Washington, 1973; gen. mgr. Old Eagle Theatre, Sacramento, 1974-75; cultural arts supr. Fresno (Calif.) Parks and Recreation Dept., 1975-79; supr. cultural and spl. events Phoenix Parks, Recreation and Libr. Dept., 1979-87, budget analyst, 1987, mgmt. svcs. adminstr., 1987-97, dep. dir., 1997—; mgmt. and budget analyst City of Phoenix, 1985; grants panelist Phoenix Arts Commn., 1987, Ariz. Commn. on Arts, 1987-88; voter Zony Theatre Awards, 1991-92; freelance theater critic, 1987-89; theater critic Ariz. Republic, 1990-98, PHX Downtown, 1997-98, CityAZ, 1997-98, Ariz. Foothills Mag., 1998—, Sunday Showtunes Broadway's Biggest Hits, 1998-2000, In Theater Mag., 1999—, Variety, 1995—, KBAQ-FM Radio, 1999—, Broadway's Biggest Hits, 2000—. Active Valley Leadership Program, Phoenix, 1987—, Valley Big Bros./Big Sisters, 1980-94; chair allocation panel United Way, 1990-92; sec. Los Olivos Townhome Assn., Phoenix, 1986-92. Mem. Am. Soc. Pub. Adminstrn., Nat. Recreation and Park Assn., Am. Theatre Critics Assn., Internat. Theater Critics Assn., Ariz. Park and Recreation Assn. Republican. Avocations: theater history, writing, reading, cooking, gardening. Office: Phoenix Parks Recreation Libr Dept 200 W Washington St Fl 16 Phoenix AZ 85003-1611

CURCIO, EDGARDO, energy economics educator, researcher; b. Rome, Italy, Dec. 25, 1930; m. Carla Gorga. Gra. in Econs. and Polit. Sci., U. Rome, 1952. Mgr. import-export API, Rome, 1955-59; comml. mgr. BPD-Bombrini Parodi Delfino, Rome, 1959-68; mgr. in fin. programming ENI Holding, Rome, 1968-80; gen. mgr. for devel. and planning AGIP, Milan, Italy, 1981-90; v.p. Sogesta, Rome, 1991-93; chmn. AIEE, Rome, 1990—; sci. dir. Luiss U., Rome, 1996—; v.p. fin. IAEE, Cleve., 1997—. Office: AIEE, Via Giorgio Vasari 4, 00196 Rome Italy

CURE, GRAHAM LEWIS, food scientist; b. Southampton, Hampshire, Eng., Mar. 27, 1949; arrived in Ireland, 1986; s. Ronald William Lewis and Doreen Emily (Wright) C.; m. Margaret Joy Lee, May 6, 1978; 1 child, William Lewis. BSc, U. Reading, U.K., 1970, PhD, 1974. Chief microbiologist Cadbury Schweppes, U.K., 1975-78, group quality assurance mgr., 1982-86; tech. mgr. Cadbury Rathmore, Ireland, 1979-82; tech. dir. Cadbury Ireland Ltd., 1986—; non exec. dir. Texcell Ltd., Ireland, 1995—. Contbr.: Sampling-Microbiological Monitoring of Environments, 1973. Treas. Malahide Cmty. Coun., Ireland, 1990-98. Fellow Inst. Food Sci. and Tech. Avocations: cricket, tennis. Office: Cadbury Ireland Ltd, Malahide Rd, Coolock Dublin 5, Ireland

CURETON, BRYANT LEWIS, college president, educator; b. Hammonton, N.J., July 3, 1938; s. Charles Ladd and Laurie Evelyn (Harrell) C.; m. Jeanette Elaine Smith, Aug. 14, 1967; children: Elizabeth Ladd, Sarah McDaniel. BA, Maryville Coll., 1960; MA, Am. U., 1964; PhD, U. Pa., 1976. Customer rels. asst., internat. divsn. Irving Trust Co., N.Y.C., 1964-65; tchr. Bordentown (N.J.) Military Inst., 1965-67; instr. Hartwick Coll., Oneonta, N.Y., 1971-73, asst. prof., 1973-78, assoc. prof. polit. sci., 1978-89, prof., 1989-94, assoc. dean, 1978-80, v.p., dean of coll., 1980-86, provost, 1986-94; pres., prof. polit. sci. Elmhurst (Ill.) Coll., 1994—; vis. scholar Harvard U. Div. Sch., 1988. With USMCR, 1963-68. Mem. Am. Polit. Sci. Assn., Am. Assn. Higher Edn. Office: Elmhurst Coll Office of Pres 190 Prospect Ave Elmhurst IL 60126-3271

CURFMAN, DAVID RALPH, neurological surgeon, musician; b. Bucyrus, Ohio, Jan. 2, 1942; s. Ralph Oliver and Agnes Mozelle (Schreck) C.; m. Blanche Lee Anderson, June 6, 1970. Student, Capital U., 1960-62; AB, Columbia Union Coll., 1965; MS, George Washington U., 1967, MD, 1973. Diplomate Nat. Bd. Med. Examiners. Asst. organist, choirmaster Peace Luth. Ch., Galion, Ohio, 1956-62; bus. mgr. Mansfield/Galion Ambulance Svc., Galion, Ohio, 1962-66; with news divsn. Sta. WTOP-TV, Washington, 1965; choirmaster, assoc. organist Grace Luth. Ch., Washington, 1966-73, historian, curator, 1969—; tchg. fellow in anatomy George Washington U., Washington, 1966-67, gen. surgery intern, 1973-74, resident in neurol. surgery, 1974-78; resident in neuropathology Armed Forces Inst. Pathology, Washington, 1975; resident in pediatric neurol. surgery Children's Hosp. Nat. Med. Ctr., Washington, 1976; teaching fellow in anatomy Georgetown U., Washington, 1967-69, clin. instr. neurol. surgery, 1978—, neurol. surgeon, 1978—; chief divsn. neurol. surgery Jefferson Hosp., Alexandria, Va., 1989-93, Wash. Hosp. Ctr. Soc., 1992—, operating room com. 1998—; vice-chmn. bylaws com. Providence Hosp., 1987-95; panelist ann. meeting ethical issues in neurol. surgery Am. Assn. Neurol. Surgery; guest spkr. Nat. Youth Leadership Forum, 1996—. Chmn., chief author: Physician's Reference Guide for Medicolegal Matters, 1982. Elected mem. D.C. Rep. Com., 1988-94; bd. dirs., historian The Christmas Pageant of Peace, Inc., Washington, The Leo Sowerby Found.; pres., bd. govs. Nat. Columbus Celebration Assn. Hon. mem. Quiz Kid Show, 1953; recipient

Found. award Cathedral Choral Soc., 1997. Mem. AMA (Phys. Recognition award 1983—), Assn. Am. Med. Colls. (nat. student chmn. rules and regulations com. 1971-73), Am. Soc. Law, Medicine and Ethics, Med. Soc. D.C. (chmn. medicine and religion com. 1981-83, chmn. medico-legal com. 1986-88), Pan Am. Med. Soc. (mem. exec. bd. 1993-97, pres. 1997—), Congress Neurol. Surgeons (joint section on neuro-trauma and critical care), Am. Coll. Legal Medicine, Washington Acad. Neurosurgery, Assn. Mil. Surgeons U.S. (Continuing Edn. Neurosurgery award 1993—), Osler Soc., Galion Hist. Soc. (charter), Children Am. Revolution (pres. Ohio 1963-64, hon. pres.), Gen. Soc. Sons of the Revolution (chmn. bicentennial commemorative com. death of Gen. George Washington 1999), SR, Nat. Officers' Club, SR, bd., N.Y./D.C. Socs., 1997—, bd., Sons of the Amer. Revolution, Washington, 1996, U.S. Capitol Hist. Soc. (founding supporting mem., trust mem.), Nat. Cathedral Assn., Cathedral Choral Soc. (v.p. bd. trustees 1981-83, pres. 1984-86, repertoire chmn. 1981-92, found. award 1997), Am. Guild Organists (dean D.C. chpt. 1974-76, publicity chmn. nat. conv. 1982, state chmn. 1984-91, nat. com. long-range devel. 1990-96), Internat. Congress Organists (Washington program chmn. 1977), Royal Sch. Ch. Music (Eng.), St. Andrew's Soc. Washington D.C.- 1760, Soc. War 1812 (Md. chpt., 1st v.p. D.C. chpt., dist. dep. pres. gen.), Pilgrim Soc. (Plymouth chpt.), Hymn Soc. Am., Order Three Crusades (1096-1192), Mil. Hospitaller Order Saint Lazarus Jerusalem, Sovereign Mil. Order Temple of Jerusalem (grand chirurgeon), Sons & Daughters of Colonial & Antebellum Bench & Bar, Mil. Order Loyal Legion U.S., Sons of Union Vets. Civil War (chmn. historic Memorial Day observances), Lincoln Birthday Nat. Commemorative Com. (v-chmn., master of ceremonies 1995-99), Hospitaller Order of St. John (knight), Crawford County Coin Club (charter mem.), Columbus Philatelic Soc., Am. Polit. Items Collectors Assn., George Washington U. Club, Elks (Galion Lodge No. 1191, hon. founder Elks Nat. Found.), Ordo Sancti Constantini Magni, Sons/Daus. of the Pilgrims (historian gen.), Continental Soc. Sons Indian Wars, Order of Indian Wars in the U.S. (historian gen.), Soc. Colonial Wars (surgeon 1997—), Samuel Victor Constant Soc., Sons Am. Colonists (surgeon gen. 1997—), Nat. Soc. Children Am. Colonists (v.p. gen.), Colonial Order of the Acorn N.Y., Order of Wash., Vet. Corps Artillery State N.Y., Am. Revolution Soc., Soc. of 1812, Hereditary Order Descendants of the Loyalists and Patriots of the Am. Revolution, Sigma Xi (pres. George Washington U. chpt. 1981-82), Phi Delta Epsilon (life). Home: 4201 Massachusetts Ave NW Washington DC 20016-4701 Office: 3301 New Mexico Ave NW Ste 210 Washington DC 20016-3622

CURIA, EDUARDO LUIS, economist, researcher; b. Buenos Aires, Dec. 11, 1945; s. Luis Curia and Celia Silvain; m. Eliana Rosa Arena, Dec. 27, 1974; children: Eduardo Mariano, Fernand Alejo. High Studies of Econs., Cath. U. La Plata. Lawyer diplomate. Dir. econs. dept. Litoral U., Santa Fe, Argentina, 1974; dir. econs. career Salvador U., Buenos Aires, 1978; vice min. Ministry of Econ. Affairs, Argentina; pres. Econ. and Social Analysis Ctr., Buenos Aires, 1990; mem. acad. counsel Argentine Indsl. Union, 1992; mem. econ. com. Stock Exch. Bd., Argentina, 1993-99. Author: The Convertibility and It's Deviations, 1994, The Convertibility: The Crisis of Peronism?, 1996, Two Years of Menem's Economic, 1997. Mem. Argentine Economists Meeting. Avocations: chess, cinema. Office: CASE, Tucuman 326 P 3 of 25, 1049 Cap Fod Argentina

CURIC, MLADJEN B., meteorology educator; b. Zabljak, Montenegrin, Nov. 24, 1947; s. Blazo and Grana N. (Obradovic) C.; m. Natalija A. Milic Curic, Apr. 15, 1972; children: Jelena, Nikola. BS in Meteorology, U. Belgrade, Yugoslavia, 1968, MS, 1974. Cert. meteorologist. Teaching asst. U. Belgrade, Yugoslavia, 1972-78, asst. prof., 1979-83, assoc. prof., 1984-89, prof., 1990—; dir. Inst. Meteorology, Belgrade, Yugoslavia, 1979-82; vice dean Faculty of Physics, Belgrade, Yugoslavia, 1982-84. Author: Problems in Dynamic Meteorology, 1983, Meather Modification, 1998; contbr. papers in field. Recipient Vukov's award Sch. Coun., Belgrade, 1968, Award for best marks during studies, U. Coun., Belgrade, 1972, Charter of the Rep. Hydrometeorological Inst., Mng. bd., Belgrade, 1998. Orthodox. Avocation: skiing. Home e-mail: curic@rudjer.ff.bg.ac.yu. Office e-mail: curic@afrodita.rcub.bg.ac.yu. Fax: 381 11 3282 619. Home: Vinogradski venac 36, 11030 Belgrade Yugoslavia Office: Inst Meteorology, Dobracina 16, 11000 Belgrade Yugoslavia

CURIGER, BICE, magazine editor-in-chief, curator; b. Zürich, Switzerland, July 18, 1948; d. Werner and Livia (Roberti) C. Lic.Phil.I, U. Zürich, 1982. Art critic Tages-Anzeiger, Zürich, 1972-80; editor-in-chief, co-founder and co-pub. Parkett Pub., Zürich, 1984—; curator Kunsthaus, Zürich, 1992—. Author: Meret Oppenheim, Defiance in the Face of Freedom, 1989 (German 1982). Office: Parkett Publishers, Quellenstr 27, CH-8005 Zürich Switzerland

CURIR, ANNA, astronomer, researcher; b. Turin, Italy, Nov. 5, 1953; d. Luigi Valentino and Carla (Garrone) C.; m. Roberto Maria Ferraris, Dec. 27, 1979; children: Giulia, Federico. Degree in math., U. Turin, 1976. Astronomer Astron. Observatory of Turin, 1976-81, 83—, supr. libr., 1989—; vis. scientist astrophysics Oxford (Eng.) U., 1982, sr. mem. Linacre Coll., 1982—; prin. investigator Agenzia Spaziale Italiana project, 1995-97. Author: Collapsed Stars, 1983; contbr. articles to profl. jours. including Astrophys. Jour., Astron. Jour., and Astronomy and Astrophysics. Mem. Internat. Astron. Union., Internat. Soc. Gen. Relativity and Gravitation. Mem. Italian Green Party. Avocations: skiing, bridge. Office: Osservatorio Astronomico, Strada Osservatorio 20, 10025 Pino Torinese Turin, Italy

CURL, JAMES STEVENS (E. B. KEELING; ADYTUM), architect, educator, writer; b. Belfast, No. Ireland, Mar. 26, 1937; s. George Stevens and Sarah (McKinney) C.; m. Eileen Elizabeth Blackstock, Jan. 1, 1960; children: Astrid, Ingrid; m. Stanisława Dorota Iwaniec, May 29, 1993. Student, Campbell Coll., Belfast, 1946-54, Queens U. and Belfast Coll. of Art, 1954-58; diploma in architecture, Oxford Sch. of Architecture, 1964, Dip. T.P., 1967; PhD, Univ. Coll., U. London, 1981. Arch., planner Oxford, Eng., 1963-69; tutor in history of architecture Oxford Sch. Architecture, 1967-73; archtl. editor Survey of London, 1970-73; archtl. advisor European Archtl. Heritage Yr. Scottish Civic Trust, Glasgow, Scotland, 1973-75; prin. arch., planner Hertfordshire County (Eng.) Coun., 1975-78; sr. lectr. in history of architecture, course leader in archtl. conservation Leicester (Eng.) Sch. of Architecture, 1978-88; prof. archtl. history Centre for Conservation Studies De Montfort U., Leicester, 1988-98; emeritus prof., sr. rsch. fellow De Montfort U., 1998-2000; prof. archtl. history, sr. rsch. fellow Queen's U. Belfast, Ireland, 2000—. Writings include: European Cities and Society, 1970, The Victorian Celebration of Death, 1972, City of London Pubs, 1973, Victorian Architecture, 1973, The Erosion of Oxford, 1977, English Architecture: An Illustrated Glossary, 1977, The Egyptian Revival, 1982, The Life and Work of Henry Roberts (1803-76), Architect, 1983, The Londonderry Plantation 1609-1914: The History, Architecture and Planning of the Estates of the City of London and Its Livery Companies in Ulster, 1986, Victorian Architecture, 1990, The Art and Architecture of Freemasonry, 1991, Classical Architecture, 1992, Encyclopaedia of Architectural Terms, 1993, Georgian Architecture, 1993, A Celebration of Death, 1993, Egyptomania, 1994, Victorian Churches, 1995, Oxford Dictionary of Architecture, 1999, 2000, The Honourable The Irish Society, 1608-2000: The City of London and the Colonisation of County Londonderry in the Province of Ulster in the Realm of Ireland, 2000, The Victorian Celebration of Death: A Study in Thanatopsis, 2000. Recipient Sir Charles Lanyon prize for measured drawings, 1956, 58, Ulster Arts Club prize, 1958, Rsch. award Brit. Acad., 1982, 83, 92, 94, 98, RIBA, Sir Banister Fletcher award for Best Book of Yr., 1992. Fellow Soc. Antiquaries of London (Rsch. award 1979, 80, 81, 83), Soc. Antiquaries of Scotland; mem. Royal Town Planning Inst., Royal Inst. Brit. Archs., Royal Inst. of Architects of Scotland, Royal Inst. of Architects of Ireland, Oxford Civic Soc. (chmn. 1969-72), Art Workers' Guild, Royal Over-Seas League. Home: 15 Torgrange, Holywood BT18 0NG, Northern Ireland

CURL, ROBERT FLOYD, JR., chemistry educator; b. Alice, Tex., Aug. 23, 1933; s. Robert Floyd and Lessie (Merritt) C.; m. Jonel Whipple, Dec. 21, 1955; children: Michael, David. BA, Rice U., 1954; PhD, U. Calif., Berkeley, 1957; D (hon.), U. Buenos Aires, 1997. Rsch. fellow Harvard U., Cambridge, Mass., 1957-58; asst. prof. chemistry Rice U., Houston, 1958-63, assoc. prof., 1963-67, prof., 1967—, chmn. dept. chemistry, 1992-96, Harry C. and Olga K. Wiess prof. natural scis., 1996—; master Lovett Coll., 1968-72; vis. rsch. officer NRC Can., 1972-73; vis. prof. Inst. for Molecular Sci., Okazaki, Japan, 1977, U. Bonn, 1985, Erskine Fell., U. Canterbury, 1999. Contbr. articles profl. jours. Fellow NSF, Alfred P. Sloan fellow, 1961-63; NATO postdoctoral fellow, 1964; recipient Clayton prize Instn. Mech. Engrs., London, 1958, Internat. New Materials prize Am. Phys. Soc., 1992, Alexander von Humboldt sr. U.S. scientist award, 1984, Order of Golden Plate, 1997, Achievement Carbon Sci. award Am. Carbon Soc., 1997, co-recipient Nobel prize in chemistry, 1996, Tex. Disting. Scientist award, 1997, Johannes Marcus Marci award in spectroscopy, 1998, Madison Marshall award, 1998, Space Act award, 1998, Centenary medal Roy. Soc. of Chem., 1999. Fellow Am. Optical Soc., Am. Acad. Arts and Scis.; mem. NAS, Am. Chem. Soc., European Acad. Scis., Arts and Letters (titulaire mem.), Phi Beta Kappa, Sigma Xi. Methodist. Home: 1824 Bolsover St Houston TX 77005-1728 Office: Rice University PO Box 1892 6100 Main St Houston TX 77005-1892

CURLE, ROBIN LEA, computer software industry executive; b. Denver, Feb. 23, 1950; d. Fred Warren and Claudia Jean (Harding) C.; m. Lucien Ray Reed, Feb. 23, 1981 (div. Oct. 1984). BS in Bus. Comm., U. Ky., 1972. Systems analyst 1st Nat. BAnk, Lexington, Ky., 1972-73, SW BancShares, Houston, 1973-77; sales rep. Software Internat., Houston, 1977-80; dist. mgr. UCCEL, Dallas, 1980-82; v.p. and gen. mgr. Southeastern region Info. Sci., Inc., Atlanta, 1982-83; v.p. sales and mktg. TesserAct, San Francisco, 1983-86, Foothill Rsch., San Francisco, 1986; pres., founder Curle Cons. Group, San Francisco, 1986-89; mgr. strategic mktg. MCC, Austin, Tex., 1989-90; founder, exec. v.p. Evolutionary Tech., Inc., Austin, 1991-99; pres., CEO Journée Software, Austin, Tex., 1999—, also bd. dirs.; bd. dirs. Evolutionary Techs. Internat., Austin Software Coun., Tex. Property and Casualty, Journée Software, CEO, 1999—; dir. adv. bd. Vertec, U. Tex. Engring. Sch.; adv. bd. SWTS U. Recipient Ma Ferguson award Exec. Women Internat. 1997, Grad of Yr. award Nat. Bus. Incubator Assn. 1996, Profiles in Power award, 1999; feature in Forbes Mag., 1996, Entrepreneur Mag., 1997; named top 50 most prestigious people Digital South; profile documentary Entrepreneurial Revolution, 1997, Inc 500 List, 1997, 98. Mem. U. Ky. Alumni Assn., Women in Tech., Women of Austin, Software Exec. Com., Inc. 500 Cos., Austin C. of C., Delta Gamma (pres. 1969). Republican. Avocations: scuba diving, running, skiing, cooking. Home: 7009 Quill Leaf Cv Austin TX 78750-8306

CURLEY, ROBERT AMBROSE, JR., lawyer; b. Boston, June 5, 1949; s. Robert Ambrose and Terese M. (O'Hara) C.; m. Kathleen M. Foley, June 10, 1972; children: Christine, Elizabeth, Margaret. AB cum laude, Harvard U., 1971; JD, Cornell U., 1974. Bar: Mass. 1974, U.S. Dist. Ct. Mass. 1975, U.S. Ct. Appeals (1st. cir.) 1976. Prin. Curley & Curley, P.C., Boston, 1974—, pres.; lectr. Mass. Continuing Legal Edn., Mass. Def. Attys., Mass. Acad. Trial Attys., Flaschner Judicial Inst., Nat. Bus. Inst. Mem. ABA, Internat. Assn. Def. Counsel, Def. Trial Acad., Mass. Bar Assn. (lectr., chmn. civil trial practice sect., civil litig. com. 1990-91, Mass. Def. Lawyers Assn. (co-chmn. products liability sects. 1994-96, bd. dirs., sec. 1998-99, treas., v.p. 1999-2000, pres.-elect 2000—), Nat. Bus. Inst., Def. Rsch. Inst. (v.p., treas. 1999), Am. Trial Lawyers Assn. (assoc.), Harvard Club (Hingham, treas. 1983-84, v.p. 1984-85, pres. 1985-86), Clover (Boston). Roman Catholic. Office: Curley & Curley PC 27 School St Ste 600 Boston MA 02108-4391

CURLEY, WALTER JOSEPH PATRICK, diplomat, investment banker; b. Pitts., Sept. 17, 1922; s. Walter Joseph and Marguerite Inez (Cowan) C.; m. Mary Walton, Dec. 18, 1948; children: Margaret Cowan, Walter Joseph, Patrick III, John Walton, James Mellon (dec. 1994). BA, Yale U., 1944; cert., U. Oslo, 1948; MBA, Harvard U., 1948; LLD (hon.), Trinity Coll., Dublin, Ireland, 1976. Mgr. Caltex Oil Co., India, 1948-52, Italy, 1952-55, N.Y.C., 1955-57; v.p. San Jacinto Petroleum, 1957-60; ptnr. J.H. Whitney Co., 1961-75; bd. dirs. France Growth Fund, N.Y.C.; commr. pub. events, chief protocol City of N.Y., 1973-74; amb. to Ireland, 1975-77, amb. to France, 1989-93; prin. W.J.P. Curley, 1978-89; pres. Curley Land Co., Pitts., 1993—. Author: Letters From The Pacific, 1965, Monarchs in Waiting, 1974. Trustee Buckley Sch., 1960-75, Miss Porter's Sch., Farmington, Mass., 1965-74, Barnard Coll., 1966-75, N.Y. Pub. Libr., 1972-75, The Frick Collection, 1993—; hon. chmn. French-Am. Found., N.Y., 1993—. Decorated Bronze Star; Cloud and Banner (Republic of China); comdr. French Legion of Honor. Mem. Coun. Fgn. Rels., Yale Club, Knickerbocker Club, Links Club, Racquet and Tennis Club, Rolling Rock Club (Ligonier, Pa.), Kildare St. Club (Dublin), Bedford Golf and Tennis Club, St. Stephen's Green Club (Dublin), Traveller's Club (Paris). Office: 450 Park Ave Ste 2104 New York NY 10022-2605

CURLIN, WILLIAM G., bishop; b. Portsmouth, Va., Aug. 30, 1927. Student, Georgetown U., St. Mary's Sem., Balt. Ordained priest Roman Catholic Ch., 1957. Titular bishop Rosemarkie and aux. bishop Washington, 1988-93; bishop diocese of Charlotte Pastoral Ctr, Charlotte, N.C., 1994—. Office: Chancery Office PO Box 36776 Charlotte NC 28236-6776

CURLOOK, WALTER, management consultant; b. Coniston, Ont., Can., Mar. 14, 1929; s. William and Stephanie (Acker) C.; m. Jennifer Burak, May 28, 1955; children: Christine, William Paul, John Michael, Andrea. BA in Sci., U. Toronto, 1950, MA in Sci., 1951, Ph.D., 1953; D.Sc. (hon.), Laurentian U., 1983. Postdoctoral fellow Imperial Coll. Sci. and Tech., London, 1954; rsch. metallurgist Inco, Sudbury, Ont., Can., 1954-59; supr. rsch. sta. Inco, Port Colborne, Ont., 1959-60; supr. rsch. Inco, Copper Cliff, Ont., 1960-64, asst. to gen. mgr., 1964-69; dir. tech. COFIMPAC, Paris, 1969-72; v.p. adminstrv. and engring. svcs. Inco, Copper Cliff, 1973-74; v.p. Inco, N.Y.C., 1974-77; sr. v.p. prodn. Inco Metals Co., Toronto, 1977-80, pres., chief exec. officer, 1980-82; exec. v.p. Inco Ltd., Toronto, 1982-91, vice chmn., 1991-94; dir. Inco Ltd., 1989-94; pres. Inco Gold Co., Toronto, 1987-89; pres. commr. P.T. Inco, Indonesia, 1990-93; pres., dir. gen. Goro Nickel, S.A., Noumea, New Caledonia, 1992-97; disting. adj. prof. U. Toronto, 1999—; mem. Nat. Adv. Com. Mining Industry, 1980-94; mem. Premier's Coun. Econ. Renewal, 1991-94. Patentee in field. Bd. dirs. Foundation Cambrian Found., Sudbury, 1983; first chmn. bd. Cambrian Coll. Applied Arts and Tech., Sudbury, Ont., 1967. Recipient Mc Charles prize U. Toronto, 1989; inducted into Can. Mining Hall of Fame, 1997. Fellow Can. Acad. Engring.; mem. Assn. Profl. Engrs. of Ont., Metall. Soc. of Can. Inst. Mining and Metallurgy (Airey 1979, Platinum medal 1994), Mining Assn. Can. (bd. dir. and past chmn.), Sci. North (hon. life Sudbury chpt. 1988), Ont. Mining Assn. (past pres.), Order of Can. Home and Office: 25 Cluny Dr, Toronto, ON Canada M4W 2P9

CURNOW, PHILIP MICHAEL JOHN, financial planner; b. London, Nov. 25, 1952; arrived in Wales, 1983; s. George Earnest and Bridget Margaret (Hanafin) C.; m. Bronwyn Ellen Williams, June 6, 1981 (div.); children: Gweniver Ysella, Rhodri Bleddian. Student, City of London Sch., 1963-70, Cordwainers Coll., 1970-73. Dir. Curnowcraft Ltd., 1979-90; cons. Helm Jns. Brokers, London, 1990-92; compliance mgr. Investment Mktg. Internat., Liverpool, Eng., 1992-94; pvt. practice Llandrindad Wells, Wales, 1995—; with Homeowner Internet Svcs., Nexus Internat. Mem. Life Ins. Assn., Soc. Fin. Advisers, Chartered Ins. Inst., Ind. Fin. Adviser Promotions, Assn. Christina Ind. Fin. Advisors. Home: CWRT, LD1 6ET Llandrindod Wells Wales Office: Emporium House, Temple St, LD1 5DL Llandrindod Wells Wales also: Robson House, Robson St, Stroke on Trent ST1 4VER, England

CURRAN, AUDREY, psychologist, educator; b. Cleve., Dec. 12, 1943; d. Millard and Nora Maria Harwell; m. Robert Criste Curran, July 20, 1967; children: Robert Criste Jr., Michaela, Aline, Audrey. BA magna cum laude, Seaton Hill Coll.; MA, Fielding Inst., 1984, PhD, 1984. Lic. clin. psychologist, Calif., Ohio, internat. forensic psychologist. H.S. tchr., counselor Calif.; pvt. practice clin. psychologist, 1986—; chair psychology dept. Notre Dame Coll., Ohio, 1989—; adj. prof. psychology/grad. program John Carroll U., Ohio, 1994-98; cons. in field. Contbr. articles to newspapers and mags.; writer syndicated column, Curran Events, 1980-87, Headlines, 1980-87. Mem. APA, Ohio Psychol. Assn. Avocations: travel, snow and water skiing, snorkeling. Home: 27020 Cedar Rd # 61 Beachwood OH 44122-1163

CURRAN, MICHAEL WALTER, management scientist; b. St. Louis, Dec. 6, 1935; s. Clarence Maurice and Helen Gertrude (Parsons) C.; m. Jeanette Lucille Rawizza, Sept. 24, 1955 (div. 1977); children: Kevin Michael, Karen Ann, Kathleen Marie (dec.), Kimberly Elizabeth; m. Mary Jane Lemanek, Aug. 18, 1981. BS, Washington U., St. Louis, 1964. With Monsanto Co., St. Louis, 1953-65; supervisory positions dept. adminstrv. services Monsanto Co., 1956-64, research technician inorganic chems. div., 1964-65; sr. ops. research analyst Pet Inc., St. Louis, 1965-68; pres. Decision Scis. Corp., St. Louis, 1968—; also dir. Decision Scis. Corp. Co-author: Handbook of Budgeting, 1981, 4th edit., 1999, Effective Project Management Through Applied Cost and Schedule Control, 1996; editor: Professional Practice Guide to Risk, Vols. 1-3, 1998; contbr. articles to profl. jours.; developer theories of bracket budgeting and range estimating. Adviser Jr. Achievement, St. Louis, 1958-59; active United Way, 1958-62. Mem. Inst. Mgmt. Scis. (chmn. St. Louis chpt. 1971-72), Ops. Research Soc. Am., Assn. Advancement Cost Engring. (chmn. risk mgmt. com. 1991—, mem. editl. adv. com. 1997—, Tech. Excellence award 2000), Project Mgmt. Inst. (mem. editl. adv. com. 1997—), Soc. Cost Estimating and Analysis, Internat. Platform Assn., Mensa, Intertel, Sigma Xi, Alpha Sigma Lambda. Office: Decision Scis Corp PO Box 28848 Saint Louis MO 63123-0048

CURRAN, WILLIAM P., lawyer; b. Mpls., Feb. 27, 1946; s. William P. and Margaret L. (Killoren) C.; m. Jean L. Stabenow, Jan. 1, 1978; children: Patrick, Lisa, John. BA, U. Minn., 1969; JD, U. Calif., Berkeley, 1972. Law clk. Nev. Supreme Ct., Carson City, 1973-74, state ct. adminstr., 1973-74; assoc. Wiener, Goldwater & Galatz, Las Vegas, Nev., 1974-75; chief dept. dist. atty. Clark County Dist. Atty.'s Office, Las Vegas, 1975-79; county counsel Clark County, Las Vegas, 1979-89; pvt. practice Las Vegas, 1989-94; ptnr. Curran & Parry, Las Vegas, 1994—. Co-author: Nevada Judicial Orientation Manual, 1974. Recipient Educator Yr. award UNLV Internat. Gaming Inst., 1998. Mem. ABA (state del. 1994—), Internat. Assn. Gaming Regulators (chmn. 1992-94), Nat. Assn. County Civil Attys. (pres. 1984-85), State Bar Nev. (pres. 1988-89), Nev. Gaming Commn. (chmn. 1989-99). Democrat. Roman Catholic. Office: Curran & Parry 601 S Rancho Dr Ste C-23 Las Vegas NV 89106-4825

CURREY, CECIL BARR, history educator; b. Clarks, Nebr., Nov. 29, 1932; s. Cecil Chalmers Currey and Edith Estelle Barr; m. Laura Gene Hewett, Aug. 14, 1952; children: Samuel Bowman, Anne Estelle, Laura Alise. BA, Ft. Hays State U., 1958, MS, 1959; PhD, U. Kans., 1965. From asst. to assoc. prof. history Nebr. Wesleyan U., Lincoln, 1964-67; prof. mil. history U. So. Fla., Tampa, 1967—; vis. prof. U. Nebr., 1966-67; vis. prof. mil. history U. Hawaii, Honolulu, summers 1991, 92; ednl. cons., 1967-98; mil. analyst Desert Shield/Desert Storm, various T.V. stas., 1990-91; invited speaker Viet Nam Fgn. Ministry, Hanoi, 1988. Author: Road to Revolution: Benjamin Franklin in England, 1765-1775, 1968, Follow Me and Die: The Destruction of an American Division in World War II, 1984, Edward Lansdale: The Unquiet American, 1989, Victory at Any Cost: The Genius of Viet Nam's General Vo Nguyen Giap, 1996 (Pulitzer nomination 1997), Long Binh Jeil: An Oral History of the U.S. Army's Notorious Prison in Viet Nam, others; contbr. to books, encys., and dictionaries, also over 25 articles to profl. publs. Col. USAR, 1953-92. Grantee U. So. Fla. Rsch. Found., 1988, 89; recipient Disting. Alumni award U. Kans., 1975. Mem. Assn. 3d World Studies (book prize 1997). Avocation: travel. Home: 3330 Lake Crenshaw Lutz FL 33549 Office: U South Fla Dept History 4202 E Fowler Ave Tampa FL 33620-8000

CURRIE, CHRISTOPHER CHARLES, database administrator; b. Bridgeport, Conn., Feb. 20, 1943; s. Thomas Thoburn Currie; m. Kanjana Kumkoon, June 20, 1970 (div. Jan. 1986); 1 child, Gregory Lewis. BS, USAF Acad., 1965; MS, Ga. Inst. Tech., 1970. Commd. 2d lt. USAF, 1961, advanced through grades to maj., ret., 1985; computer sys. cons. Analytical Sys. Engring., Burlington, Mass., 1985-88, Digital Equipment Corp., Burlington, 1988; database adminstr. Arkwright FM Global, Johnston, R.I., 1988—. Contbr. articles to website www.onesalt.com, 1986—. Mem. ACLU, USAF Acad. Assn. Grads., World Federalist Assn., Am. Legion. Avocations: kayaking, sunfish sailing, Golden Retrievers. E-mail: curriec@tiac.net.

CURRIVAN, BRUCE JOSEPH, electronics engineer; b. Nicosia, Cyprus, Nov. 14, 1950; father Am. citizen; s. Eugene Ambrose and Rachel (Marash) C.; m. Annamaria Panunzio, Nov. 12, 1978; children: Joseph, Jean Anne, Peter. BSEE, Cornell U., 1972; MS in Engring., Princeton U., 1976. Assoc. engr., Astro-Electronics Div. RCA, Princeton, NJ, 1972-76; comms. sys. design engr. Stanford Telecom., Sunnyvale, Calif., 1977-81, 84-94, tech. dir., 1995-97; ingénieur d'études Thomson-CSF, Gennevilliers, France, 1982-83; tech. dir. modern devel. WaveSpan Corp., Mountain View, Calif., 1997-98; dir. sys. architecture Broadcom Corp., Irvine, Calif., 1998—. Presenter in field; contr. articles to profl. jours; patentee in field. Natural Law candidate for U.S. Ho. of Reps., 1996, 2000; chmn. Natural Law Party Central Com., Santa Clara County, Calif., 1996-98. Mem. IEEE (sr., chmn. 802.14 cable modem phys. layer subcom. 1995-97). Office: Broadcom Corp 16205 Alton Pkwy Irvine CA 92618-3616

CURRY, DANIEL FRANCIS MYLES, filmmaker; b. N.Y.C., Sept. 22, 1946; s. John Joseph Jr. and Florence Cecelia (Rattler) C.; m. Ubolvan Chaiwatana, July 27, 1972; children: Devin, Daniel. BA, Middlebury Coll., 1968; MFA, Humboldt State U., 1979. Vol. cmty. devel. U.S. Peace Corps, Khon Kaen, Thailand, 1969-71; writer-dir. ednl. TV Ministry of Edn., Govt. of Thailand, Bangkok, 1971-72; freelance filmmaker/artist/designer various clients Bangkok, 1972-74; instr. fine arts Cape Cod Community Coll., West Barnstable, Mass., 1974-77; instr. film and theatre Humboldt State U., Arcata, Calif., 1977-79; visual effects artist Universal Studios Hartland Facility, North Hollywood, Calif., 1979-80; art dir. Modern Film Effects, Hollywood, Calif., 1980-85; v.p., dir. creative svcs. Cinema Rsch. Corp., Hollywood, 1985-88; visual effects producer-dir. Star Trek, the Next Generation, Paramount Pictures, Hollywood, 1987—; pres. O.M.R. Prodns., Manhattan Beach, Calif., 1989—. Supr., title designer Star Trek IV, Top Gun, Flash Dance, Fatal Attraction, Cujo, The Blob, Rocky IV, Cobra, Staying Alive, Tootsie, Risky Business, Amadeus, The Right Stuff, Mommie Dearest, Uncommon Valor, Pure Luck, Back to School, Raging Bull, Class, Cool World, Captured, Christine, Body Double, Flashpoint, Tiger Town, Invasion U.S.A., Fast Forward, Bolero, Wild Thing, Pray for Death, Days of Thunder, Indiana Jones & The Temple of Doom, Star Trek, Generations; visual effects prodr. 6th season Star Trek, The Next Generation (best spl. visual effects Emmy award 1992), Star Trek Deep Space Nine, 1993—, Star Trek Voyager, 1995— (Emmy award). Recipient Emmy award for spl. visual effects Acad. TV Arts and Scis., 1992, 94, nominations, 1989, 90, Internat. Monitor award, 1996. Mem. Acad. TV Arts and Scis., Soc. Motion Picture and TV Engrs., Am. Film Inst., Am. Soc. Cinematographers. Avocations: painting, sculpture, world travel. Office: Paramount TV Group 5555 Melrose Ave Los Angeles CA 90038-3112*

CURRY, DAVID, guidance staff developer; b. Bklyn., Feb. 12, 1940; s. David and Ella (Washington) C.; m. Mary Elaine Cuthrell, Nov. 17, 1962; 1 child, Anjorin Sebastian. BA in Polit. Sci./Econs., CCNY, 1972; MS in Edn., Bklyn. Coll., 1990, adv. cert. in guidance and counseling, 1990. Cert. elem. tchr., N.Y. Asst. offic mgr. Elmo Roper & Assocs., N.Y.C., 1964-70; accounts investigator Citibank, N.Y.C., 1970-72; rsch. assoc. Nat. Urban League, N.Y.C., 1972-76; adminstrv. dir. Edn. Unltd., Bklyn., 1978-82; guidance counselor N.Y.C. Bd. of Edn., Bklyn., 1982—. County com. Polit. Club; area policy bd. #3 Cmty. Devel. Agy. City of N.Y.; mem. Unity Dem. Club; mem. block assn. With USAF, 1963. Impact II grantee N.Y.C. Bd. Edn., 1984, 86; N.Y. State Dept. Labor fellow, 1995; recipient Cmty. Svc. award HPD of N.Y.C., 1992, William F. Boyland Edn. award, 1996; named Father of Yr. Sisterhood of Single Black Mothers, 1984. Mem. ASCD, ACA, ASCA, Alpha Phi Alpha. Yoruba. Avocations: trombone, barritone horn, camping, writing. Home: 519 Macdonough St Brooklyn NY 11233-1511 Office: Cmty Sch Dist # 16 1010 Lafayette Ave Brooklyn NY 11221-2303

CURRY, EVERETT WILLIAM, JR., college official, minister; b. Glendale, Calif., Mar. 7, 1942; s. Everett William and Sylvia Pauline (Burkholder) C.; m. Barbara Kay Orman, June 13, 1964; children: Kimberly Suzanne Curry McSwain, Kevin Everett. BA, Calif. State U., Northridge, 1964; MDiv, Am. Bapt. Sem., Berkeley, Calif., 1967; cert. pub. rels., UCLA, 1971; Doctor of Ministry, San Francisco Theol. Sem., San Anselmo, Calif., 1977. CFP; chartered mut. fund counselor. Min. to youth First Bapt. Ch., San Fernando, Calif., 1960-62; assoc. pastor Valley Park Bapt. Ch., Sepulveda, Calif., 1962-66; dir., media ministries Coachella Valley Bapt. Found.,

Thermal, Calif., 1966-68; pastor Lakeview Terrace Bapt. Ch., Lakeview Terrace, Calif., 1968-71; dir., media ministries L.A. Bapt. City Mission Soc., 1971-74; pastor Cmty. Bapt. Ch., Pearl Harbor, Hawaii, 1974-78, First Bapt. Ch., Coos Bay, Oreg., 1978-86; planned giving counselor Am. Bapt. Found., Valley Forge, Pa., 1986-98; assoc. exec. min. Am. Bapt. Chs. Oreg., Portland, 1998-2000; dir. planned giving Linfield Coll., McMinnville, Oreg., 2000—. Editor: Oscillator, Oreg. Tualatin Valley Amateur Radio Club, 1999—. Chmn., bd. dirs. Coos Bay Sch. Dist., Coos Bay, 1988-89; chief, chaplain corps, Coos Bay Police Dept., 1979-85; pres. Hawaiian Islands Pub. Radio, Honolulu, 1977-78; bd. dirs. Rosevilla Found., 1998—. Named Alumnus of Yr., Am. Bapt. Sem. of the West, 1995. Mem. Am. Bapt. Ministers Coun. (sen. 1983-87, 92, 94-95), Western Commn. on Ministry (sec. 1988-91, chair 1992-94), Coos-Bay North Bend Rotary (Outstanding Citizen award 1985). Republican. Baptist. Avocations: amateur radio, backpacking, genealogy, travel. Home: 1546 NE Greensword Dr Hillsboro OR 97124-6139

CURRY, JOHN PATRICK, insurance company executive, management consultant; b. Logan, W.Va., May 3, 1934; s. Albert Bruce and Mary Naomi (Shugert) C.; m. Patricia Jean Blessington, Oct. 26, 1956; children: Joseph Patrick, Mary Patricia, Kathleen Anne, Carmen Frances, John Gregory. Student St. Charles Coll., Catonsville, Md., 1949-52; B.A., U. Notre Dame, 1956; M.S. in Ops. Research, Western Mich. U., 1976. Lic. profl. cons. Mich. Agt., Conn. Mut. Life Ins. Co., 1959-65; gen. agt. Occidental Life Ins. Co., Los Angeles, 1965-66; pres. Investment Assocs. Inc., 1966-69; gen. agt. Fed. Life Ins. Co., Peoples Home Life Ins. Co. and Home Assurance Cos., 1969-71; actuarial cons. Am.-Brit. Ins. & Annuity Co., Ltd. (Bermuda), Battle Creek, Mich., 1979-87; mgmt. cons., 1971-88; owner, mgr. Nat. Search Cons., exec. search firm, Kalamazoo; owner, operator Curry Supply Co., Portage, Mich., 1978-83; pres. The Consulting Group, Inc. (Del.), Kalamazoo, 1985—; pres. The Pilot Co., Turks and Caicos Islands, 1985-90; dir. Anglo-Am. Ins. Co., Ltd. (Bermuda), 1979-87. Served with U.S. Army, 1957-59. U. Notre Dame scholar, 1952-55; Pat O'Brien scholar, 1956. Republican. Roman Catholic. Clubs: Sertoma (charter dir. 1961-64) (Kalamazoo). Home: 7226 Rockford St Kalamazoo MI 49024-4122 Office: The Consulting Group Kalamazoo MI 49024

CURRY, MARY EARLE LOWRY, poet; b. Seneca, S.C., May 13, 1917; d. Ullin Sidney and Mary Sloan (Earle) Lowry; m. Peden Gene Curry, Dec. 25, 1941; children: Eugene Lowry, Mary Earle (dec.). Student, Furman U., Greenville, S.C., 1944-45. Author: (poetry books) Looking Up, 1949, Looking Within, 1961, reprinted, 1980, Hymn, 1973; contbr. to Yearbook of Modern Poetry, Poets of Am., Poetic Voice of Am., We the People, Poetry Digest, Poetry Anthology of Verse, Internat. Anthology on World Brotherhood and Peace, Parnassas of World Poets, others; weekly poetry columns in Inman Times, Fountain Inn Times, Fort Mill Times, Laurens Advertiser, Ware Shoals Life, others. Recipient World award for culture Centro Studi E Ricerche Delle Naioni, Italy, 1985. Mem. Centro Studi Scambi Internat. Roma, United Meth. Women's Orgns., United Meth. Ministers' Wives Clubs, various cmty. clubs. Avocations: music, photography, reading. Home: 345 Curry Dr Seneca SC 29678-1907

CURRY, THOMAS JAMES, manufacturers representative; b. New Brunswick, N.J., Sept. 8, 1921; s. Thomas Christopher and Leanore Margaret (Craven) C.; m. Mary Louise Bisaccio, Apr. 1, 1945. BA, Rutgers U., 1944. Export sales traffic mgr. Am. Cyanamid Corp., Bound Brook, N.J., 1945-47; sales coord. Interchemical Corp., Bound Brook, 1948-52; sales rep. Sun Chem. Corp., N.Y.C., 1953-67; pvt. practice mfrs. rep. Pa., 1968—. Pres. coun. Rutgers U. Mem. Col. Henry Rutgers Soc. Avocations: golf, geneaology, photography, history. Home: 10 Crestline Rd Wayne PA 19087-2607

CURT, DENISE MORRIS, artist, limner, photographer; b. New Haven, Nov. 15, 1936; d. Bertrand and Anna Geraldine (Fiak) Rocheleau; m. John Morris, Oct. 4, 1954 (dec.); children: Tyler John, Cynthia Leigh Morris Bell; m. Albert A. Curt, 1973 (div. 1981). Student of Louis Crescenti, Orange, Conn., 1950-52; student, Whitney Sch. Art, New Haven, 1950, Luchetti Sch. Art, New Haven, 1951, Paier Sch. Art, Hamden, Conn., 1951. Dir. Meet The Artists and Artisans, Milford, Conn., 1962—; interior designer State of Conn., Hartford, 1972-75. One-woman shows Gull Gallery, Provincetown, Mass., Chapelle Jean Cocteau, Villefranche Sur Mer, France, Garfield Galleries, Orange, Conn., Yale U., Stratford Gallery, Stevenson (Md.) Galleries, also others; represented in numerous pvt. and pub. collections throughout world. Lectr. to numerous civic orgns.; mem. Vis. Artists in Schs., 1970—; commr. Conn. Commn. on Arts, 1974-79; photography chmn. Milford Fine Arts Coun., New Haven Arts Coun.; bd. dirs. Milford Hosp. Aux.; mem. Literacy Vols., Milford. Recipient award Mystic Art Festival, 1969, Sterling House Art Show, 1985, Glastonbury Art Guild, 1988. Mem. Guilford Art League (bd. dirs. 1975-80), Nat. League Am. Pen Women (category painting, bd. dirs. Fairfield chpt., art chair), Conn. Classic Arts, Milford Hist. Soc., Yale U. Gallery, Met. Mus. Art. Republican. Congregationalist. Avocations: Renaissance and baroque music, antiques, foreign travel. Fax: 203-876-2322. E-mail: ctlimner@snet.net. Home and Studio: 41 Green St Milford CT 06460-4709

CURTIN, JOHN DORIAN, JR., chemical company executive; b. Tulsa, Dec. 30, 1932; s. John D. and Marie (Meyercord) C.; m. Nancy Clark, July 8, 1959; children: Maura, Margaret, John D. III. BA, Yale U., 1954; MBA, Harvard U., 1956. Exploration landman Pan Am. Petroleum Corp., Casper, Wyo., 1956-59; group v.p. Black, Sivalls & Bryson, Inc., Houston, 1959-67; pres., bd. dirs. Sage Engrng. & Valve Co., Houston, 1967-69; v.p., bd. dirs. 1st of Tex., Inc., Houston, 1969-73; v.p., mgr. corp. fin. Rauscher Pierce Securities Corp., Houston, 1973-74; founder, CEO Curtin & Co., Inc., 1975-89; exec. v.p., chief fin. officer Cabot Corp., Boston, 1989-95, also bd. dirs.; chmn., CEO, pres. Cabot Safety Corp. (now Aearo Corp.), 1994-98; bd. dirs. Aero Corp., 1994—; bd. dirs. Augat, INc., Imperial Holly Corp. Trustee Houston Ballet Found., 1979-89, bd. dirs. Bus. Arts Found., Houston, 1981-83, DaCamera Soc., Houston, 1987-89, Huntington Theatre, Boston, 1991-94. With U.S. Army, 1956-58. Mem. Somerset Club, The Country Club, The Comml. Club. Republican. Roman Catholic. Home: 60 Chestnut St Boston MA 02108-3507 Address: Aearo Corp 5457 W 79th St Indianapolis IN 46268-1675*

CURTIN, JOHN PAUL, JR., investment banker; b. Glen Ridge, N.J., Sept. 25, 1950; s. John Paul and Ann Dixon C.; m. Anne Nickel, June 17, 1972; children: Hayden, Thomas, Whitney. BA, Williams Coll., 1972; MBA, Harvard U., 1976. From assoc. to mng. dir. Goldman, Sachs & Co., N.Y.C., 1976-96, mng. dir., 1996—; dir. Cadillac Fairview, Toronto, Maxxcom Inc., Toronto. Trustee Art Gallery Ontario, Toronto, 1995-99, Royal St. Georges Coll., Toronto, 1998-00, Psalmodi Found.; dir. Brascan Corp., Toronto. Home: 9 E 92nd St New York NY 10128-0607

CURTIS, ANTHONY SAMUEL, journalist; b. London, Mar. 12, 1926; s. Emanuel and Eileen Phoebe (Freedman) C.; m. Sarah Myers; children: Job, Charles, Quentin. BA/MA, Merton Coll., Oxford, Eng., 1950. Lectr. Brit. Inst. Sorbonne, 1950-51; freelance journalist and critic TQ Times, New Statesman/BBC, 1952-55; dep. editor Times Lit. Suppt., 1955-58; Harkness fellow in journalism Yale, 1958-59; lit. editor Sunday Telegraph, 1960-70, Fin. Times, 1970-89; lit. corrs. and critic, 1989-95; feature writer for numerous BBC broadcasts and radio plays; lectr. for Brit. Coun., France and India, 1973-98. Author: New Developments in the French Theatre ÈSartre, Anouilh, De Beauvoir, Camus , 1949, (criticism) The Pattern of Maugham, 1974, (biography) Somerset Maugham, 1982; Lit Ed: on reviewers and reviewing, 1998; editor: The Rise and Fall of the Matinee Idol, 1977; co-editor: Maugham: The Critical Heritage, 1987, others. Mem. com. London Libr. With RAF, 1945-48. Fellow Royal Soc. Arts; mem. Garrick Club, Literary Soc., Traveller's Club, Beefsteak Club. Avocations: chess, backgammon, solitaire.

CURTIS, DAVID AMES, translator, writer; b. Winchester, Mass., May 15, 1956; s. Grant Edward and Elaine Constance (Chalberg) C. BA in Philosophy cum laude, Harvard U., 1979. Rsch. activist Va. Community Devel. Orgn., Petersburg, Va., 1974-75, Black and Reform Newspaper Indexing Project/Yale U., New Haven, 1978; community organizer Carolina Action/ACORN, Columbia, S.C., 1979-80, Greensboro, N.C., 1980-82; dir. rsch. Black Periodical Fiction Project/Yale U., New Haven, 1982-85; freelance translator, editor, writer Paris, 1985—. Rschr.: (book) Our Nig by. H.E. Wilson, 1983; translator/editor: (books) Cornelius Castoriadis Political and Social Writings, 3 vols. 1988, 92, Philosophy, Politics, Autonomy, 1991, Cleisthenes the Athenian, 1995, The Jews: History, Memory, and the Present, 1996, The Castoriadis Reader, 1997, World in Fragments, 1997, Writing: The Political Test, 2000; mem. bd. editl. advisors Thesis Eleven jour., 1992—. Union organizer Fedn. of Univ. Employees, New Haven, 1982-84; co-founder, Agora Internat., Paris, 1990—; conf. organizer, Paris, 1992.

CURTIS, JAMES L., psychiatrist; b. Jeffersonville, Ga., Apr. 27, 1922; s. Will and Francis (Hall) C.; m. Vivian Alzine Rawls, Dec. 11, 1948; children: Lawrence, Paul. BA, Albion Coll., 1943; MD, U. Mich., 1946; cert. psychoanalysis, Columbia U., 1954. Diplomate Am. Bd. Psychiatry and Neurology, Am. Bd. Addiction Psychiatry. Intern Wayne County Gen. Hosp., Eloise, Mich., 1947, resident in psychiatry, 1948; resident in psychiatry SUNY, Bklyn., 1949-50; from instr. to clin. asst. prof. SUNY Dowstate Med. Ctr., Bklyn., 1954-68; assoc. dean, assoc. prof. psychiatry. Cornell U. Med. Ctr., N.Y.C., 1968-80; clin. prof. psychiatry N.Y. Med. Coll., N.Y.C., 1980-82, Columbia U. Coll. Physicians & Surgeons, N.Y.C., 1982—; dir. dept. psychiatry Harlem Hosp. Ctr., N.Y.C., 1982-2000. Author: Blacks, Medical Schools and Society, 1971; contbr. articles to profl. jours. Capt. USAF, 1952-54. Fellow Am. Psychiat. Assn., Am. Orthopsychiat. Assn., Am. Psychoanalytic Assn., Am. Acad. Psychoanalysts. Democrat. Congregationalist.

CURTIS, JAMES RICHARD, flight engineer; b. Champaign, Ill., Feb. 2, 1930; s. John Wesley and Jessie May (Quackenbush) C.; m. Constance Ann Sticher, Jan. 10, 1954; children: Christie Lynn, James Richard Jr., Stephen Lawrence. Student, U. Ill., 1947-48. Profl. flight engr.; cert. airframe and power plant mechanic, comml. pilot. Plant mgr. Dean's Dairy, Champaign, 1947-50; draftsman C.S. Johnson Co., Champaign, 1955; aircraft mechanic Am. Airlines, Ft. Worth, 1955; flight engr. Chgo., 1956-95; trained flight crews Spantax Airlines, Madrid, 1966-69, Mid. East Airlines, Beirut, Lebanon, 1966-69; ret., 1995; check airman, flight engrng. instr. Am. Airlines, Chgo., 1964-86; examiner designee FAA, Chgo., 1966-67. Served as sgt. USAF, 1950-54.

CURTIS, JAMES THEODORE, lawyer; b. Lowell, Mass., July 8, 1923; s. Theodore D. and Maria (souliotis) Koutras; m. Kleanthe D. Dusopol, June 25, 1950; children: Madelon Mary, Theodore James, Stephanie Diane, Gregory Theodosius, James Theodore Jr. BA, U. Mich., 1948; JD, Harvard U., 1951; ScD (hon.), U. Mass., 1972. Bar: Mass. 1951. Assoc. Adams & Blinn, Boston, 1951-52; legal asst., asst. atty. gen. Mass., 1952-53; pvt. practice law Lowell, 1953-57; sr. ptnr. firm Goldman & Curtis, and predecessors, Lowell and Boston, 1957—. Chmn. Lowell and Greater Lowell Heart Fund, 1967-68; mem. adv. bd. Salvation Army, sec., 1956-58; mem. Bd. Higher Edn. Mass., 1967-72; elected mem. Lowell charter Commn., 1969-71; del. Dem. Party State Convs., 1956-60; trustee U. Mass., Lowell, 1963-72, chmn. bd., 1968-72; bd. dirs. U. Mass. Rsch. Found., Lowell, 1965-72, Merrimack Valley Health Planning Coun., 1969-72. Served with U.S. Army, 1943-46, spl. agt. Counter Intelligence Corps., 1945-46. Decorated Knight Order Orthodox Crusade Holy Sepulcher. Mem. ABA, ATLA, Mass. Bar Assn., Middlesex County Bar Assn., Mass. Acad. Trial Lawyers, Am. Judicature Soc., Harvard Law Sch. Alumni Assn., U. Mich. Alumni Assn., Lowell Hist. Soc., DAV, Harvard Club of Lowell (pres. 1969-71, bd. dirs.), Masons, Delta Epsilon Pi. Home: 111 Rivercliff Rd Lowell MA 01852-1471 Office: Goldman & Curtis PC] 144 Merrimack St Ste 444 Lowell MA 01852-1789

CURTIS, JOHN EDWARD, museum curator, archaeologist; b. London, June 23, 1946; s. Arthur Norman and Laura Letitia Ladd (Thomas) C.; m. Vesta Sarkhosh, July 1, 1977; children: Roxana Lily, Neil Edward. BA, U. Bristol, Eng., 1967; postgrad. diploma, U. London, 1969, PhD, 1979. Rsch. asst. dept. Western Asiatic antiquities The Brit. Mus., London, 1971-74, asst. keeper, 1974-89, keeper, 1989—. Author: Nush-i Jan III: The Small Finds, 1984, Excavations at Qasrij Cliff and Khirbet Qasrij, 1989, Ancient Persia, 1989, revised edit., 2000; co-author: (with A.R. Green) Excavations at Khirbet Khatuniyeh, 1997; editor: Fifty Years of Mesopotamian Discovery, 1982, Bronzeworking Centres of Western Asia, 1988, (4 books) Relations Between Mesopotamia and Iran: Proceedings of Lukonin Seminars, 1993, 95, 97, 2000, (with J. E. Reade) Art and Empire: Treasures from Assyria in the British Museum, 1995. Fellow Soc. Antiquaries; mem. Brit. Assn. Near Ea. Archaeology (chmn. 1996—), Brit. Sch. Archaeology in Iraq (vice-chmn. 1996—), Brit. Inst. Persian Studies (mem. exec. com. 1991—), Ancient Persia Fund (hon. sec. 1987—). Avocations: local history, genealogy. Home: 4 Hillfield Rd, London NW6 1QE, England Office: The Brit Mus, Dept Western Asiatic Antiq, London W1B 3DG, England

CURTIS, KAREN HAYNES, lawyer; b. Laurel, Miss., Sept. 15, 1951; d. John Travis Haynes Jr. and Jeannine Burkett Tanner; m. George Ware Cornell Jr., Nov. 10, 1978; children: Laurel Elizabeth Cornell, Jaime Rodriguez Cornell. BS in Biology, Tulane U., 1973; JD summa cum laude, Nova Law Ctr., 1978. Bar: Fla. 1978; U.S. Ct Appeals (5th cir.) Fla. 1980, U.S. Ct. Appeals (11th cir.) Fla. 1981; U.S. Dist Ct. (so. dist.) Fla. 1982, U.S. Dist Ct. (mid. dist.) Fla., 1986; U.S. Supreme Ct. 1994. Law clk. Steel, Hector & Davis, Miami, Fla., 1978; law clk. to Judge William M. Hoeveler U.S. Dist. Ct., Miami, Fla., 1978-80; assoc. Shutts & Bowen, Miami, Fla., 1980-84, ptnr., 1985-95; founding ptnr., pres. Gallwey, Gillman, Curtis, Vento & Horn P.A., Miami, Fla., 1995—. Treas., dir. Ch. by the Sea, 1994—. Listed in Leading Fla. for Civil Appellate Law. Mem. ABA, Fla. Assn. Women Lawyers, Fed. Bar Assn., Dade County Bar Assn. (ins. law com. 1990-91, banking and corp. litigation com. 1992-93, appellate ct. com. 1991—, appellate ct. rules com. 1993—, grievance com. 1988-91), Fla. Bar Bd. of Legal Specialization and Edn.(cert. in appellate practice), Acad. Fla. Trial Lawyers, Assn. Trial Lawyers of Am., Supreme Ct. Historical Soc., Am. Judiciary Soc. United Ch. of Christ. Avocations: reading, piano, computer. Home: 5300 La Gorce Dr Miami Beach FL 33140 Office: Gallwey Gillman Curtis Vento & Horn PA 200 SE 1st St Ste 1100 Miami FL 33131-1912

CURTIS, PAULA ANNETTE, elementary and secondary education educator; b. Natrona Heights, Pa., Apr. 16, 1953; d. Stephen John and Josephine Kathleen (Killian) C. BS in Edn., Geneva Coll., 1974; postgrad., U. Vt., 1975, Pa. State U., New Kensington, 1978. Cert. religious edn. tchr., Pitts. Diocese. Tchr. Transfiguration Sch., Russellton, Pa., 1979—, dir. religious edn., 1995-98; tchr. continuing edn. C.C. of Allegheny County, Pitts., 1992—, Pa. State U., New Kensington, 1988—; tchr. O'Mara Driving Sch., Lower Burrell, Pa., 1976—, Lenape Votech., 1990—; CCD tchr. Transfiguration Sch., Russellton, 1995-97, head tchr., head fine arts dept., 1995-97; chmn. vision and values in Pitts. Diocese, Transfiguration Sch., 1980-97; CCD tchr. St. Clement Parish, Tarentum, Pa., 1986-92, dir. religious edn., 1987-92; dir. religious edn. St. Joseph Parish, Natrona, Pa., 1992-93; product tester Nat. Family Opinion Poll, 1987—; model Van Enterprises, Cranberry, Pa., 1989-92; tchr. driver edn. Plum (Pa.) Sr. H.S., 1996-98. Vol. Help Beautify the Cmty. with Art, Russellton. Mem. Nat. Cath. Educators Assn., Nat. English Tchrs. Assn. Democrat. Roman Catholic. Avocations: craft designs, needle work, collecting reptiles, collecting and breeding tropical birds, breeding Shih-Tzus. Home: 211 W 9th Ave Tarentum PA 15084-1241 Office: Transfiguration Sch CCD Office 100 Mckrell Rd Russellton PA 15076-1100

CURTISS, ELDEN F., bishop; b. Baker, Oreg., June 16, 1932; s. Elden F. and Mary (Neiger) C. B.A., St. Edward Sem., Seattle, M.Div., 1958; M.A. in Ednl. Adminstrn, U. Portland, 1965; postgrad., Fordham U., U. Notre Dame. Ordained priest Roman Cath. Ch., 1958; campus chaplain, 1959-64, 65-68; supt. schs. Diocese of Baker (Oreg.), 1962-70; pastor, 1968-70; pres./rector Mt. Angel Sem., Benedict, Oreg., 1972-76; mem. bd. regents Mt. Angel Sem., Benedict, 1976-93; bishop of Diocese of Helena (Mont.), 1976-93; archbishop Diocese of Omaha, 1993—; mem. ecumenical ministries State of Oreg., 1972; mem. pastoral svcs. Oreg. State Hosp., Salem, 1975-76; bishop Diocese Helena, Mont., 1976-93, Archdiocese of Omaha, 1993; chmn. bd. Boys Town USA, Cath. Mut. Relief Soc. Am.; mem. Pontifical Coun. for Family (Rome); Episcopal advisor Serra Internat. Mem. Nat. Cath. Ednl. Assn. (Outstanding Educator 1972, bishops and pres's com. coll. dept.). Office: Archdiocese of Omaha 100 N 62nd St Omaha NE 68132-2702

CURTO, DANIEL ALBERTO, airline transport pilot, flight instructor; b. Comodoro Rivadavia, Chubut, Argentina, Oct. 12, 1962; s. Alberto Daniel Curto and Dominga Marino. Grad., Aeroclub 13 de Diciembre, C. Rivadavia, Argentina, 1983; degree as comml. pilot, Sch. Tech. Aviation Profl., Buenos Aires, 1985, degree first comml. pilot, 1989, degree as flight instr., 1991, degree as profl. pilot, 1992. Capt. Govt., Comodoro Rivadavia, Argentina, 1986-92; dir. Sudamericana de Aviation, Buenos Aires, 1993-96; capt. Kaiken Airlines, Rio Grande, Argentina, 1997, Southern Winds Airline, Cordoba, Argentina, 1998—; dir. Aeroandes Airline, Buenos Aires, 1998. Fellow Aeroclub Don Torcuato; mem. Association Pilot Airline (del. 1999—), Asociation Argentine Civil Pilots (dir. 1997—); diplomate Crew Mgmt Resource. Roman Catholic. Avocations: paraglading. Home: Av Rivadavia 6437, Piso 2 7, 1406 Buenos Aires Argentina Office: Southern Winds Airlines, Av Colon 54 PB, 5000 Cordoba Argentina

CURZI-DASCALOVA, LILIA, neurophysiologist, researcher, consultant; b. Pavlikeni, Bulgaria, Oct. 3, 1935; arrived in France, 1967; m. Lucien Curzi, May 23, 1963; children: Catherine, Muriel. MD, Med. Sch. Sofia, Bulgaria, 1961, splty. neurology, 1967; PhD of Neurophysiology, U. Paris 6, 1971; DSc, U. Paris 12, 1976; Habilitation Rsch. Direction, U. Paris 5, 1987. Med. dr. State Ry. Soc., Bulgaria, 1961-64; resident Inst. Postgrad. Med. Tng., Sofia, 1961-67; med. dr. U. Hosp. Cochin, Paris, 1967-70; rsch. fellow Inst. Nat. Santé et de la Recherche Med., Paris, 1971-76; sr. rschr. INSERM, Paris, 1976—; cons. Paris U. Hosp., 1980—; head rsch. staff U. Paris-INSERM, 1980—; bd. dirs. European club Sleep Rsch. in Infants and Children. Author: Manual of Methods for Recording and Analyzing Sleep-Wakefulness States in Preterm and Full-term Infants, 1996; co-editor: Sleep and Cardiorespiratory Control, 1991; mem. editl. bd.: Dev. Brain Dysf.; contbr. critical revs. to Pediat. Rsch., Jour. EEG Clin. Neurophysiol., Sleep, Acta Ped Scand.; contbr. sci. articles to profl. jours. Sci. grantee INSERM and corr. state rsch. direction, Belgium, Germany, Italy, Poland, Chile, 1983—. Mem. European Neuroscis. Assn., European Sleep Rsch. Soc., Am. Sleep Rsch. Soc., Neonatal Soc. London. Avocations: fine arts, music, reading, mountains, bridge. Office: Hosp R Debré INSERM, E9935 48 bd Sérurier, 75019 Paris France

CUSCHIERI, ALFRED, anatomy and genetics educator, researcher; b. Sliema, Malta, July 23, 1945; s. Joseph and Doris (Chapelle) C.; m. Monica Mufsud, May 25, 1969; children: Astrid, Thelma. MD, U. Malta, 1967; PhD, U. London, 1972. Med. house officer St. Luke's Hosp., Malta, 1967-69; lectr. dept. anatomy U. Malta, 1972-78, prof. dept. anatomy, cons. geneticist dept. health, 1983—, head dept. anatomy, 1992-96, dir. inst. gerontology, 1990-96; assoc. prof. dept. anatomy Kuwait U., 1978-83; cons. geneticist Kuwait Med. Genetics Ctr., 1978-83; mem. Nat. Bioethics Consultative Com., Malta, 1982-96; leader Malta Registry Congenital Anomalies, 1984—. Contbr. articles to profl. jours.; rschr. in congenital anomalics, cytogenetics and genetic diseases. Vice chancellor, knight comdr. Mil. and Hospitallier Order of St. Lazarus of Jerusalem, Malta Grand Priory, 1994—. Mem. Anatom. Soc. Gt. Britain and Ireland, Genetics Soc. Gt. Britain, Italian Assn. Anatomy. Avocations: collecting and restoring antiques. Home: Le Camee Triq L-Arznu, San Gwann SGN10, Malta Office: U Malta, Dept Anatomy, Msida MSD06, Malta

CUSHING, SARA ELIZABETH, English language educator, writer; b. Richmond, Va., July 7, 1950; d. William Routledge and Sara Margie (Williams) C. BA, Duke U., 1972; MS, SUNY, Cortland, 1978. Cert. tchr. secondary English, N.Y. Adminstrv. asst. Duke Players/Duke U., Durham, N.C., 1970-72; substitute tchr. Maine-Endwell and Union Endicott Schs., Endicott and Endwell, N.Y., 1972-73; tchr. English and drama John F. Kennedy High Sch., Richmond, Va., 1973-75; project coord. Alekna Constrn., Endicott, 1975-77; tchr. English Vestal (N.Y.) Sr. High Sch., 1977-78, Greene (N.Y.) Jr.-Sr. High Sch., 1978-88; writer, editor, writing cons., 1981—; instr. English, computer lab. mgr., weekend coord. coll. Piedmont Tech. Coll., Greenwood, S.C., 1988—; rental agt. Drucker and Falk, Richmond, 1974-75; liaison/amb. to Lander Coll., Greenwood, 1990-91, co-chmn. Praxis Conf., 1990-91; team leader S.C Advanced Technol. Edn. Exemplary Faculty Team, 1995-98, Ad-hoc Workplace Rsch. Team Leader, 1996-97. Author: (textbook) You, Too, Can Write, 1990, 4th edit., 1998. Recipient summer seminar stipend NEH, Atlanta, 1984. Mem. AAUW, Ea. Regional Competency-Based Edn. Consortium (bd. dirs., conf. chair 1999-2000), S.C. Tech. Educators Assn., South Atlantic MLA, Greene Tchrs. Assn. (pres. 1983-85, mem. negotiating team 1984-86), S.C. Tech. Educators Assn., Phi Theta Kappa (hon.). Avocations: writing, gardening, reading, dramatics. Home: 119 Parkwood Rd Greenwood SC 29646-8535 Office: Piedmont Tech Coll PO Box 1467 Greenwood SC 29648-1467

CUSHING, SIR SELWYN JOHN, electric power industry executive; b. Sept. 1, 1936; s. Cyril John and Henrietta Marjory (Belle) C.; m. Kaye Dorothy Anderson, 1964; 2 children. FCA, U. New Zealand1, 1957. ACIS, 1958; CMA, 1959. Ptnr. Esam Cushing & Co., sharebrokers, Hastings, 1960-86; exec. dir. Brierley Investments Ltd., 1986-93; dep. chmn. Air New Zealand, Auckland, New Zealand, 1988-98; chmn. Air New Zealand, 1998—, Electricity Corp. New Zealand, 1993—, Carter Holt Harvey Ltd., 1991-93. Mem. Wellington Club. Avocations: cricket, music. Office: Air New Zealand Ltd, 29 Customs St, West Auckland New Zealand*

CUSHING, STEVEN, linguist, educator, researcher, consultant; b. Brookline, Mass., June 25, 1948; s. Alfred Edward and Evelyn (Kaufman) C. SB, MIT, 1970; MA, UCLA, 1972, PhD, 1976. Rsch. asst. MIT, 1967-70, UCLA, 1973-74; instr. U. Mass., Boston, 1974-75, Roxbury C.C., Boston, 1975-77; rsch. staff Higher Order Software Inc., Cambridge, Mass., 1976-82; rsch. assoc. Rockefeller U., N.Y.C., 1979; instr. Northeastern U., Boston, 1983-86, 95-96; from master lectr. to assoc. prof. Boston U., 1986-94; rsch. fellow NASA-Ames Rsch. Ctr., Mountain View, Calif., 1987-88, Stanford U., Palo Alto, Calif., 1987-88, NASA-Langley Rsch. Ctr., Hampton, Va., 1989; asst. prof. St. Anselm Coll., Manchester, N.H., 1983-85, Stonehill Coll., North Easton, Mass., 1985-89; adj. prof. Union Inst. Grad. Sch., Cin., 1994—; mem. bd. editl. commentators The Behavioral and Brain Scis., 1978—; chmn. software design Internat. Conf. Sys. Scis., Honolulu, 1978; mem. 1st fgn. del. USSR Acad. of Scis., 1989; session chmn. sesson on internat. comm. Internat. Pragmatics Conf., Kobe, Japan, 1993; invited spkr. Internat. Conf. on Maritime Edn. and Tng., Rijeka, Croatia, 1999. Author: Quantifier Meanings: A Study in the Dimensions of Semantic Competence, 1982, Fatal Words: Communication Clashes and Aircraft Crashes, 1994, 1997, 2d edit., 2000; assoc. editor Language, 1998—; contbr. articles to profl. jours. and mags. Mem. nat. exec. coun. Nat. Ethical Youth Orgn., 1965-66; violist Cambridge (Mass.) Symphony Orch.; fiddler Boston Scottish Fiddle Club, Strathspey and Reel Soc. N.H. Recipient New Eng. Regional award Future Scientists of Am., 1965, 1st pl. award U.S. Nat. Scottish Fiddle Composition Competition, 1996; NSF grantee, 1965, 70-71, NIMH grantee, 1970-71, NDEA grantee, 1970-73; Woodrow Wilson Found. fellow, 1970-71, NASA Summer Faculty fellow, 1987-89; rsch. affiliate MIT, 1978-79, Boston U., 1986-88. Mem. N.Y. Acad. Scis., Linguistic Soc. Am., Nat. Ctr. for Sci. Edn., Internat. Pragmatics Assn. E-mail: stevencushing@alum.mit.edu. Home: 2000 Commonwealth Ave Apt 1508 Brighton MA 02135-5722

CUSHMAN, VALERIE JEAN, athletic director; b. Rome, N.Y., Oct. 25, 1962; d. Robert Harley and Peggy Ann C. BS in Edn., SUNY, Cortland, 1984; MS in Edn., East Stroudsburg U., 1988; PhD in Higher Edn., Syracuse U., 2000. Tchr. John Coleman H.S., Kingston, N.Y., 1984-87; tchr., coach Vassar Coll., Poughkeepsie, N.Y., 1988-97; athletic dir. Randolph Macon Woman's Coll., Lynchburg, Va., 1997—. Mem. Nat. Assn. Collegiate Women Athletic Adminstrs. (nominating com. 1996-97), Nat. Collegiate Athletic Assn. (nominating com. 1997—). Home: 105 Mullbury Pl Lynchburg VA 24502-5820 Office: Randolph Macon Womans Coll 2500 Rivermont Ave Lynchburg VA 24503-1555

CUSICK, FAY HOPE, English language educator, consultant; b. N.Y.C., Jan. 7, 1940; d. Lester and Julia Hope (Abbott) Funk; m. Vincent Cusick, Nov. 9, 1963; children: Patrick, Shaun, Daniel, Hope Elaina. BA, St. John's U., Jamaica, N.Y., 1963; MA, Adelphi U., 1978; MS, Hofstra U., 1986, cert. advanced study, 1991. Tchr. English, Seaford (N.Y.) H.S., 1978-95, dir. publs., 1981-95; prof. English, U. N.C., Wilmington, 1996—, also ednl. teleconferencing cons.; adj. prof. Adelphi U., Garden City, NY., 1981-93, Briarcliff Coll., 1994-95. Author numerous poems. Mem. Congressmen Lent and King's selection com. U.S. Mil. Acad., Massapequa, N.Y., 1983-95.

Named Outstanding Tchr. of Yr., Elks Club, Massapequa, 1994. Mem. ASCD, AAUW (v.p. 1995—), Nat. Coun. Tchrs. English, Lions (chmn. scholarship com. 1997—, Outstanding Tchr. of Yr. award Seaford 1994). Avocations: writing, travel, classical music, camping, canoeing. Home: 207 Lakeview Dr Hampstead NC 28443-2748 Office: Coastal Carolina Coll English Dept Western Blvd Jacksonville NC 27403

CUSSLER, EDWARD LANSING, JR., chemical engineer, educator; s. Edward Lansing and Eleanor Christine (Lloyd-Jones) C.; m. Elizabeth Campbell Beidler. BS in Chem. Engring., Yale U., 1961; MS in Chem. Engring., U. Wis., 1963, PhD, 1965. Rsch. asst. U. Wis., Madison, 1961-64, postdoctoral fellow, 1964-65; postdoctoral fellow U. Adelaide, Australia, 1965-66, Yale U., 1966-67; asst. prof. Carnegie-Mellon U., 1967-70, assoc. prof., 1970-73, prof., 1973-80; prof. U. Minn., Mpls., 1980—. Mem. editl. bd. Jour. Membrane Sci., 1976—, AIChE Jour., 1995—. Recipient William H. Frances S. Ryan award Carnegie-Mellon U., 1975, George Taylor Tchg. award U. Minn., 1987. Mem. AIChE (Alan P. Colburn award 1975, bd. dirs. 1989-92, v.p. 1993, pres. 1994), Am. Assn. Engrs. Soc. (chair 1996). Office: U Minn Chem Engring Dept 421 Washington Ave SE Minneapolis MN 55455-0373

CUSTODI, PAOLO ANTONIO, secondary education educator; b. Novara, Italy, June 13, 1957; s. Pietro and Livia Lucia (Volpi Spagnolini) C. Degree in Astronomy, U. Bologna, Italy, 1981. Tchr. Vocat. Tng. Sch., Omegna, Italy, 1982-83, Tech. Sch., Verbania, Italy, 1983-84, Jr. H.S., Suno, Italy, 1984-85; tchr. math. and natural scis. Jr. H.S., Fara Novarese, Italy, 1985—; translator Jackson Libri, Milan, 1989-91. Contbr. articles to profl. jours. Mem. Geol. Soc. Am., Brit. Mus. Assn., N.Y. Acad. Scis., Smithsonian Instn., Marine Biol. Assn. U.K., Astron. Soc. Pacific, Brit. Soc. Philosophy of Sci. Avocations: books, classical studies, cats. E-mail: pcustod@tin.it. Home: Via C Battisti 55, 28073 Fara Novarese Italy

CUTCHINS, CLIFFORD ARMSTRONG, IV, lawyer; b. Norfolk, Va., May 13, 1948; s. Clifford Armstrong III and Ann (Woods) C.; m. Jane McKenzie, Aug. 14, 1971; children: Sarah Helen, Ann Woods. BA, Princeton U., 1971; JD, MBA, U. Va., 1975. Bar: Va. 1975, U.S. Dist. Ct. (ea. dist.) Va. 1975, U.S. Ct. Appeals (4th cir.) 1975. Ptnr. McGuire, Woods, Battle & Boothe, Richmond, Va., 1975-90; sr. v.p., gen. counsel, sec. James River Corp. Va., Richmond, 1990-97, Ft. James Corp., Deerfield, Ill., 1997—; bd. dirs. Ft. James Europe N.V., Ft. James Operating Co. Bd. dirs. Arts Coun. Richmond, 1980-86, Richmond Heart Assn., 1980-83, St. Catherine's Sch., Richmond, 1983-86, Richmond Ballet, 1986-88, Richmond Children's Mus., 1986-94, Richmond on the James, 1986-88, Henrico Drs. Hosp., 1986—, Hist. Richmond Found., 1990-94, Richmond Met. Blood Svc., 1995-97, Kohl Children's Mus., Wilmette, Ill., 1998—; chmn. Fort James Found., 1997—. Mem. ABA, Va. Bar Assn., Country Club Va. (bd. dirs. 1990-93), Commonwealth Club (bd. dirs. 1983-86, 96-97), Conway Farms Golf Club, Kinloch Golf Clubs. Republican. Baptist. Avocations: golf, travel, photography. Home: 118 Tempsford Ln Richmond VA 23226-2319 Office: Fort James Corp PO Box 89 1650 Lake Cook Rd Deerfield IL 60015-4753

CUTIÉRREZ-CORTINES, CRISTINA, foreign diplomat; b. Madrid, Dec. 17, 1939. Mem. European Parliament, 1999—, mem. com. on environment, pub. health and consumer policy, substitute com. on culture, youth, edn., media and sport; mem. Group of the European People's Party (Christian Democrats) and European Democrats; mem. delegation for relations with S.E. Europe; vice-chair delegation to the EU-Lithuania Joint Parliamentary Com.; substitute delegation to the EU-Turkey Joint Parliamentary Com. People's Party. *

CUTINELLI-RENDINA, EMANUELE, humanities educator, journalist; b. Rome, July 8, 1959; s. Gioacchino Cutinelli-Rendina and Teresa Farano; m. Ornella Catteruccia, May 3, 1989; children: Maria, Olimpia. B, Liceo Visconti, Rome, 1978; PhD, U. Rome, 1985; LittD, U. Lausanne, Switzerland, 1997. Tchr. Liceo Classico G. Carducci, Rome, 1988-92; maître asst. U. Lausanne, 1992; freelance journalist, 1987. Author: (books in Italian) Church and Religion in Machiavelli, 1998, Guide to Machiavelli, 1999; editor: Croce-Th. Mann, 1991, Croce-Vossler, 1991; co-editor Storiografia, 1987, Biglli, 1991; contbr. articles to profl. jours. Fellow Collegium Romanicum. Home: Av de Montoie 37, 1007 Lausanne Switzerland Office: U Lausanne, Sect d Italien, 1015 Lausanne Switzerland

CUTISPOTO, GIUSEPPE, astronomer; b. Catania, Italy, Nov. 14, 1959; s. Domenico and Rosalia (Di Liberti) C. Diploma, G. Marconi, Catania, 1977; Laurea in Physics, U. Catania, 1982, PhD in Astrophysics, 1988. Cert. assoc. astronomer. Assoc. astronomer Catania Astrophys. Obs., 1983-86, rsch. astronomer, 1987-97, assoc. astronomer, 1998—. Contbr. sci. papers to profl. jours. Maj. cpl. Italian Army, 1986-87. Rotary Found. scholar, 1988. Mem. Italian Astron. Soc., European Astron. Soc. Avocations: soccer, tennis, music. Fax: 39-095-330592. E-mail: gcutispoto@alpha4.ct.astro.it. Office: Catania Astrophys Obs, V S Sofia 78, 95125 Catania Italy

CUTLER, BERNARD JOSEPH, editor-in-chief, writer; b. N.Y.C., May 26, 1924; s. Joseph Louis and Sophie (Appel) C.; m. Carol Ann Rataic, Mar. 6, 1948. BSME, Pa. State Coll., 1945. Reporter Pitts. Press, 1945-51; reporter N.Y. Herald Tribune, 1951-56, Moscow corr., 1956-58, chief Paris bur., 1958-60; mng. editor European edition N.Y. Herald Tribune, Paris, 1960; editor European edition N.Y. Herald Tribune, 1961-66; European corr. Scripps-Howard Newspapers, Paris, 1966-69; fgn. editl. writer Scripps-Howard Newspapers, Washington, 1969-72; chief editl. writer Scripps-Howard Newspapers, 1972-80, editor-in-chief, 1980-89, fgn. affairs columnist, 1989-95. Author: Reactionary! Sgt. Lloyd W. Pate's Story, 1956. Recipient Disting. Alumni award Pa. State U., 1972. Clubs: Gridiron, National Press. Office: 2735 P St NW Washington DC 20007-3065

CUTLER, DAVID HORTON, editor, publisher; b. Boston, May 26, 1934; s. Fred Abbott and Elizabeth Horton (Carnahan) C.; m. Martha Marie Emery, Dec. 6, 1959; children: Geoffrey, Gregory. BA in Journalism, U. Nev., 1959. Editor, publ. The Merchant mag., Newport Beach, Calif., 1962—; publ., founder Bldg. Products Digest, Newport Beach, 1982—. With U.S. Army, 1953-55. Mem. Masonic Lodge, Scottish Rite, Shriners. Office: The Merchant Mag 4500 Campus Dr Ste 480 Newport Beach CA 92660-1872

CUTLER, MORENE PARTEN, civic worker; b. Waxahachie, Tex., July 27, 1911; d. Bedford Taylor and Lofie Mae (Stockton) Parten; m. Robert Ward Cutler, Apr. 27, 1954 (dec. Dec. 1993). Student, Trinity U., 1929, U. Okla., 1931, U. Tex., 1933. Asst. to dir. N.Y. Sch. for Interior Decoration, N.Y.C., 1938; chief cons. Hilton Hotels Corp., Chgo., 1946-48; free-lance interior designer, 1948-54. Author: Stagecoach Inn--Iron Skillet and Velvet Potholder, 1981. 1st. pres., chmn. bd. dirs. Salado (Tex.) Bicentennial Com., 1974—, chmn. Salado Sesquitennial Com., 1984—; bd. dirs. Cen. Tex. Bicentennial Com., 1974; mem. Internat. Debutante Ball, N.Y.C., 1956—, Beautify Tex. Coun., 1976—; chmn. Beutify Salado Com., 1979-80; founder Tex. Bluebonnet Com., 1961; trustee Cen. Tex. Area Mus., Salado, 1968-75; hon. mem. Ellis County Mus., Waxahachie, 1967—. Recipient Tex Good Will awards, 1960—, Outstanding Dist. Gov. award Beautify Tex. Coun., 1984. Mem. AIA (founder N.Y. aux. chpt. 1958, citation 1966), Chautauqua Preservation Soc. (bd. dirs. Waxahachie chpt. 1975), Preservation Soc. Newport County, Salado C. of C. (bd. dirs. aux. chpt. 1974-75), Tex. Soc. Washington. Episcopalian. Club: Met. (N.Y.C.). Home: PO Box 26 Salado TX 76571-0026

CUTLER, SARAH TAYLOR, educator, enamelist, writer; b. N.Y.C., July 18, 1940; d. James Karr and Nedra Mary (Evans) Taylor; m. George Aylwin Otto, Aug. 31, 1963; (div. Aug., 1977) children: Sarah Perin Otto, Richard Talbot Otto; m. Robert Sumner Cutler, Aug. 31, 1986. BA, Duchesne Coll., 1962; MA, U. Nebr., 1982. Cert. prin. elem., secondary, Eng., Spanish, Nebr. Tchr. pub. and private schs. Omaha, N.Y.C., 1961-65; tchr. Am. Sch., Lima, Peru, 1971-72, Buffalo County Schs., Nebr., 1977-79, Cen. Tech. C.C., Grand Island, Nebr., 1977-79; asst. Ctr. for Leadership Devel. Am. Coun. on Edn., Washington, 1980-82; asst. to dep. dir. Coun. for Internat. Exchange of Scholars, Washington, 1982-85; adminstr. sci. and tech. courses AAAS and Confedn. Cen. Am. Nat. Univs., Washington, 1986-90; cons. Pacific War Project, NHK-TV, Japan, Washington, 1991-92; Interciencia observer AAAS, Bogota, Columbia, 1993, Trinidad, 1994. Group exhbns. include Enamelist Soc., Newport, Ky., 1989, Kennedy Ctr. Artist Gallery, Washington, 1991—, Fort Myers Women's Exhibit, Arlington, Va., 1994. Citizen lobbyist for War Clause of Constitution, 1990—; assoc. Women Strike for Peace, Washington, 1992; precinct chair Congl. Dist. 8 & Legis. Dist. 15, Precinct 23 & 33, Potomac, Md., 1994-99; mem. Sedona Intensive Clearing for Millenium, 1999; vol. Nat. Mus. Women in Arts. Grantee Nebr. Art Coun., 1978-80, Reading is Fundamental, Nebr., 1979-81; recipient 1st and 2d pl. medals U.S. Army Rec. Svc. Nat. Craft Contest, 1994. Mem. DAR, Washington-Tokyo Women's Club, Past Parents Assn. Washington Internat. Sch. (chair person), DAR (regent Great Falls chpt. 1998-99, vol. genealogist, mus. docent), DAR Mex. Soc. (assoc.), Colonial Dames C17. Spiritualist. Avocations: textile arts, theatre arts. E-mail: SarahTCutler@hotmail.com.

CUTLER, WALTER LEON, diplomat, foundation executive; b. Boston, Nov. 25, 1931; s. Walter Leon and Esther Dewey (Bradley) C.; m. Sarah G. Beeson, Mar. 16, 1957 (div. 1981); children: Allen Bradley, Thomas Gerard.; m. Isabel K. Brookfield, Nov. 28, 1981. BA, Wesleyan U., Middletown, Conn., 1953; MA, Fletcher Sch. of Law & Diplomacy, 1954. Joined U.S. Fgn. Service, 1956; vice consul Am. consulate Yaounde, Cameroon, 1957-59; fgn. affairs officer Dept. State, Washington, 1959-60; staff asst. to sec. of state Dept. State, 1960-62; 2d sec. Am. Embassy Algiers, Algeria, 1962-65; prin. officer Am. Consulate Tabriz, Iran, 1965-67; polit. officer, 1st sec. Am. Embassy Seoul, Korea, 1967-69, Saigon, Vietnam, 1969-71; spl. asst. for Vietnam Peace Negotiations U.S. Dept. State, 1971-73; mem. Sr. Seminar in Fgn. Policy, 1973-74; dir. Office Ctrl. African Affairs, 1974-75; amb. to Zaire, 1975-79; amb.-designate to Iran, 1979; prin. dep. asst. sec. for congl. rels. Dept. State, Washington, 1979-81; amb. to Tunisia, 1982-84, Saudi Arabia, 1984-87, 1988-89; rsch. prof. diplomacy Georgetown U., Washington, 1987-88; pres. Meridian Internat. Ctr., Washington, 1989—; spl. emissary for sec. gen. UN, N.Y.C., 1994. Served with U.S. Army, 1954-56. Recipient Disting. Alumnus award Wesleyan U., 1983, King Abdul Aziz award Saudi Arabia, 1986, Presdl. Performance award, 1986, 87, Wilbur J. Carr award U.S. Dept. State, 1989, Dir. Gen.'s Cup award, 1993; decorated Order of the Leopard, Zaire, 1979. Mem. Coun. Fgn. Rels., Am. Fgn. Svc. Assn., Am. Acad. Diplomacy (bd. dirs.), Washington Inst. Fgn. Affairs (bd. dirs.), Mid. East Inst., Am. Tunisian Assn. (hon. com. The Am. Coms. on Foreign Rels.), Met. Club. Office: Meridian Internat Ctr 1630 Crescent Pl NW Washington DC 20009-4004

CUTNAW, MARY-FRANCES, emeritus communications educator; b. Dickinson, N.D., June 15, 1931; d. Delbert A. and Edith (Calhoun-Pritchard) C. BS, U. Wis., 1953, MS, 1957, postgrad., to 1968. Life tchg. license in speech, English and French, Wis. Vol. tchr. Vocat. Sch. for World War II Displaced Persons, Stevens Point, Wis., 1951-52; speech tchr. Pulaski H.S., Milw., 1953-55; tchg. asst. dept. speech U. Wis., Madison, 1956-57, spl. asst. Sch. Edn., summer 1957; instr. speech U. Wis.-Stout, Menomonie, 1957-58, dean of women, 1958-59, asst. prof. speech, 1959-64, assoc. prof. speech, 1964-74, prof. emeritus, 1974—; comm. and pers. cons., St. Paul, 1974—; writer, editor, pub. New Legal Press, 1995—. Author: How to Settle a Living Trust, 1996. Organizer, past advisor Young Dems., Menomonie, 1959—; founder Edith and Kent Cutnaw Scholarship, U. Wis., Stevens Point, 1960—; bd. dirs. Blaisdell Place, Mpls., 1980-85. Hon. scholar U. Wis., Madison, 1959-60, 67-68. Mem. ACLU, NOW, Internat. Platform Assn., Wis. Acad. Arts and Scis., Wis. Women's Network, Progressive Roundtable (Mpls.), Calhoun Beach Club (Mpls.), Amnesty Internat., World Jewish Congress (charter), U. Club St. Paul, Greenpeace, Dunn County Humane Soc., Soc. for Prevention of Cruelty to Animals, Gamma Phi Beta, Phi Beta, Sigma Tau Delta, Pi Lambda Theta. Roman Catholic. Avocations: ecology, civil rights, animal rights, consumer protection, health and wellness. Office: New Legal Press PO Box 282 Menomonie WI 54751-0282

CUTOIU, DAN, state secretary, physicist, researcher; b. Bucharest, Romania, Nov. 6, 1953; s. Vasile Artenie and Rodica Aurora (Bulaceanu) C.; m. Georgia Alexandra Baltog, Feb. 12, 1993; 1 child, Ana. Diploma, U. Bucharest, 1977; PhD, Inst. Atomic Physics, 1990. Programmer Ministry of Def., Bucharest, 1977-79; physicist Inst. of Physics and Nuclear Engring., Bucharest, 1979-88, rschr., 1988-93, sr. rschr., 1993—; pres., state sec. Nat. Commn. for Nuclear Activities Control, Bucharest, 1997—. Contbr. articles to profl. publs. Mem. Inst. of Physics and Nuclear Engring. Br. Romanian Comunist Party, Bucharest, 1979-89, Nat. Peasant Christian Dem. Party, Bucharest, 1992—; mem. Strategy Dept. of Romanian Dem. Conv., Bucharest, 1993-96; parliamentary counsellor Commn. for Edn. and Rsch. of the Romanian Ho. of Reps., Bucharest, 1995, 96. Grantee Romanian Acad., 1995. Mem. Romanian Phys. Soc. Orthodox. Avocations: motoring, hiking, skiing, photography. Home: 19 N Racota, R-71312 Bucharest Romania Office: Romanian Govt Nat Commn, 14 Libertatii Blvd, R-76106 Bucharest Romania

CUTRONE, LUIGI CUTRONE, chemist; b. Ielsi, Italy, May 18, 1950; s. Pasquale and Giovanna (Passarelli) C.; m. Maria Teresa Maiorano, Aug. 8, 1976; children: Giovanna, Pasquale, Annarita. BSc in Chemistry, Loyola Coll., Montreal, Can., 1974; MS in Organic Chemistry, McGill U., Montreal, Can., 1980. Research and devel. chemist M.F. Paints 1972, Laval, Que., Can., 1977-81; application devel. Tioxide Can. Inc., Tracy, Que., 1981-85; section. mgr. Tioxide UK Ltd, Stockton-on-Tees, Eng., 1985-87; tech. service mgr. Tioxide Italia, Scarlino, 1987-90; tech. dir., 1990—; human resources and SHE mgr. Tioxide Italia, Scarlino, 1992-94, works mgr., 1994-96; mng. dir., 1996—. Contbr. articles to profl. jours. Fellow Oil and Colour Assn.; mem. Fedn. Coating Soc. Roman Catholic. Office: Tioxide Italia SPA, Contrada Casone CP 113, 58022 Follonica Italy

CUTSHALL, BRIAN ERVIN, radio news director; b. Fort Lee, Va., Nov. 24, 1962; s. Ervin Decator and Dorothy Gay (Willett) C. BS in Comm., U. Tenn., 1985. Writer U. Tenn., Knoxville, 1983-85; freelance writer, 1985-87; freelance journalist Knoxville News-Sentinel, 1992—; news dir. WSMG-AM-FM, Greeneville, 1987-2000; internet news dir. Greene County Online, 2000—; interviewer, presenter histories project, 1999—. Pub. Info. officer Greene County Civil Def., 1988—; bd. dirs. Greene County Am. Heart Assn., 1992—, USS Greeneville, Inc., 1989—, publicity chmn. Operation Playground, Greeneville, 1991—, Project SAVE, Knoxville and Greeneville, 1993—, summer festival Town of Tusculum, 1993-96, 1994, Max Douthat Meml. Golf Classic, Greeneville, 1993, USS Greeneville Com., 1988—, Takoma Hosp. Golf Classic and Gala, Greeneville, 1993-96; mem. Greene County Spl. Olympics Com., 1992; bd. dirs. Greene County Habitat for Humanity, 1997-99. Recipient awards Nat. Assn. Secondary Sch. Prins., 1980, Handicaps Unltd., 1988, Greeneville Pilot Club, 1988, Greeneville Schs., 1988, Greene Valley Devel. Ctr., 1989, 91, 93, 94, Greene County Sch. Sys., 1990, March of Dimes, 1991, Tenn. Dept. Employment Security, 1992, Keep Greene Clean, 1993. Mem. Tenn. Assn. Broadcasters, Cmty. Drug and Alcohol Prevention Network (past treas.). Office: Greene County Online 10 Decatur St Greeneville TN 37743-7702

CUTT, MALCOLM GEORGE, accountant; b. Edinburgh, Scotland, Feb. 14, 1961; s. Ronald Torrance and Sheila (Smith) C.; m. Alison Coyle, Mar. 10, 1990; children: Christina, Jamie. LLB, U. Edinburgh, 1981. Trainee acct. Whitelaw Wells & Co., Edinburgh, 1981-84; asst. acct. Scottish Life Assurance Co., Edinburgh, 1987-89; finance officer Queen Margaret Coll., Edinburgh, 1989-99; asst. mgr. Peat Marwick, Edinburgh, 1994-87; finance officer Queen Margaret U. Coll., Edinburgh, 1999—. Mem. Inst. of Chartered Accts. of Scotland. Mem. Ch. of Scotland. Avocations: scouts, golf, church. Office: Queen Margaret U Coll, Clerwood Ter, EHh128TS Edinburgh Scotland

CUTTS, STEPHEN PAUL, civil engineer, linguistics researcher; b. Detroit, Dec. 5, 1965; s. John Peter and Sonja Edla (Bealing) C.; m. Rebecca Angela Cotter, Oct. 24, 1998; 1 child, Christopher Anthony. BS, Oakland U., 1985; MS, Calif. Inst. Tech., 1988; MA in Linguistics, Calif. State U., Fullerton, 1993. Registered profl. engr., Calif. Engr. County Sanitation Dists. Los Angeles County, Whittier, Calif., 1988—. Contbr. articles to profl. jours., including Gen. Linguistics, Solid Waste Assn. N.Am. Ann. Landfill Gas Symposia. Earle C. Anthony fellow Calif. Inst. Tech., 1986-87. Mem. Solid Waste Assn. N.Am. Avocations: numismatics. E-mail: cuttssp@aol.com. Home: 585 Palo Verde Ave Pasadena CA 91107-2327 Office: County Sanitation Dists Los Angeles County 1955 Workman Mill Rd Whittier CA 90601-1415

CUYPERS, JOHAN PETER, physicist; b. Weert, Limburg, The Netherlands, May 18, 1963; s. Jan and Mia (Janssen) C.; m. Annelies Touw, Aug. 29, 1997. MS, U. Tech. Eindhoven, 1988; PhD, Stichting Fund. Onderzoek Mat., Utrecht, 1992. Clin. physicist-in-tng. Radiotherapeutisch Inst. Limburg, Heerlen, The Netherlands, 1993-96, clin. physicist, 1996-99; clin. physicist Univ. Hosp. Vrye Universiteit, Amsterdam, The Netherlands, 1999—. Avocations: music, reading, sport (squash, volleyball), movies. Office: Dept Clin Phys and Informatics, U Hosp Vrye Universiteit PO Box 7057, 1007 MB Amsterdam The Netherlands

CUYUGAN, JORGE HENSON, publishing executive, author; b. San Fernando, Pampanga, Philippines, Mar. 11, 1957; s. Felipe Santiago and Virgilia Miranda (Henson) C.; m. Alicia Lazatin Mesina, June 6, 1993. BS in Indsl. Engring., De La Salle U., Manila, 1979, BS in Chem. Engring., 1981. Tech. cons. Advantage Techs. Inc., Manila, 1982; cottage industry cons. Nat. Cottage Industries Devel. Authority, Pampanga, 1983-85; feasibility studies cons. Dept. Trade & Industry, Pampanga, 1992; coll. instr. U. Assumption, Pampanga, 1985-90; pres. Bright Concepts Printing House, Pampanga, 1990—; pres. Ctr. for Philatelic Rsch. and Studies, Inc., Pampanga, 1996—; editor, pub. Postage Stamps' Digest, Pampanga, 1994—; philatelic cons. Philippine Postal Corp., Pampanga, 1992—, La Union, 1996—. Author: A Business Planning Manual, 1992, A Guidebook on Starting Your Own Business, 1987, A Beginners' Pictorial Guide on Stamp Collecting, 1999; editor, pub.: The Postage Stamps' Digest, 1994—. Pres. U. Philippines Inst. Small Scale Industries Alumni Found., Ctrl. Luzon chpt., Pampanga, 1987-89. Recipient nat. svc. award U. Philippines-Inst. Small Scale Industries Alumni Found. Inc., Quezon City, 1988, nat. philatelic svcs. award Philippine Postal Corp., Manila, 1994. Mem. Am. Philatelic Soc., Pampanga Stamp Collectors Soc. (pres. 1998—), Rotary of Metro San Fernando (charter v.p. 1990), KC (grand knight Infant Jesus Coun. 1991-92). Roman Catholic. Avocations: social/civic trainings, philatelic writing/consulting, business and management consulting. Home: Purok 6, Baliti, 2000 San Fernando Pampanga, Philippines Office: Region 3 Philatelic Ctr, Angeles City PO, 2009 Angeles City Philippines

CVETKOVIC, ZORKO, secretary; b. Osijek, Croatia, Sept. 4, 1924; s. Gjuro and Olga (Cica) C.; m. Lijerka Rodonicic, Mar. 19, 1949. BEE, U. Zagreb, Croatia, 1950, DS, 1982. Engr. Elektrana, Zagreb, Croatia, 1950-57; engr. in chief Elektroprijenos, Zagreb, Croatia, 1957-90; sec. CIGRE, Zagreb, Croatia, 1989—. Pres. K.K. Mladost, Zagreb, 1962. Fellow CIGRE, AMSE. Avocations: tennis, skiing, bridge. Home: Medvescak 55, 10000 Zagreb Croatia Office: HK CIGRE, Berislaviceva 6, 10000 Zagreb Croatia

CYBULSKI, ZYGMUNT ALOJZY, chemist, educator; b. Milcz, Poland, June 17, 1935; s. Franciszek and Waleria (Krajniak) C.; m. Aleksandra Helena Kalka, Feb. 27, 1960; 1 child, Katarzyna. M of Chemistry, Higher Sch. Pedagogics, Gdansk, Poland, 1959; Doctorate, Higher Sch. Agr., Szczecin, Poland, 1972; DSc, Schiller U., Jena, Germany, 1989. Tchr. mid. schs. various cities, Poland, 1953-64; lectr. Coll. Pedagogics, Koszalin, Poland, 1964-67, Higher Sch. Engring., Koszalin, 1968-73; scientist Hohenheim U., Stuttgart, Germany, 1973-74; asst. prof. Higher Sch. Engring., Koszalin, 1975-84; rschr. Schiller U., Jena, 1985-88; asst. prof. U. Tech. and Agr., Bydgoszcz, Poland, 1989-90, chmn. dept. chemistry, 1989, prof. chemistry, 1990—; chmn. dept. chemistry Higher Sch. Engring., Koszalin, 1968-88; dir. Inst. Material Engring., Koszalin, 1975-78; mem. presidium All Poland Trade Unions Alliance, Warsaw, 1998—. Author: (books): Chemistry I, 1966, Chemistry II, 1966, Any Problems of Applied Chemistry, 1966, (with Z. Jablonski) Laboratory of General Chemistry, 1970, General Chemistry with Elements of Physical Chemistry, 1973, Some Problems of Chemistry, 1977, Practice of Chemistry, 1978, Some Question of Chemistry, 1986, Struktur und Eigenschaften von Chalkogeniden des Typs MABX4, 1988; patentee in field. Mem. Polish Parliament, Warsaw, 1993-97, vice-chmn. Europe agreement com., Warsaw, 1994-97; pres. Fedn. Polish Tchrs. Assns. Higher Schs. and the Sci., Warsaw, 1993—; mem. presidium All Poland Trad Unions Alliance, Warsaw, 1998—, mem. regional bd., Bydgoszcz, 1999—. Recipient Gold Cross of Poland Pres. Republic of Poland, 1977, Order Polonia Restituta IV Rang, 1983, III Rang, 1997, V Rang, 1983, IV Rang, 1997. Mem. Polish Chem. Soc., Polish Soc. Pedology (regional vice-chmn. 1964-85), Polish Fedn. H.S. Tchrs. Warsaw (pres. 1993—), Polish Hunting Soc. Social Democrat. Avocations: hunting, traveling, boating, fishing. Home: Bydgoskich, Olimpijczykow 6/45, 85-792 Bydgoszcz Poland Office: U Tech Agr, Kordeckiego 20, 85-225 Bydgoszcz Poland

CYKLIS, PIOTR, mechanical engineer; b. Cracow, Poland, Sept. 20, 1960; s. Jerzy and Romana (Dobosz) C.; m. Elzbieta Kaszowska, June 29, 1986; children: Dorota, Szczepan, Jacek. MSc in Applied Mechanics, Cracow U. Tech., 1984, MSc in Thermal Energy Sys., 1985, PhD, 1991. Asst. Cracow U. of Tech., 1984-91, adj., 1991—; head of lab. Cracow U. of Tech., 1993—. Contbr. articles to profl. jours. Mem. SIMP. Avocations: fishing, audio, music. Home: ul Królewska 29/2, 30-040 Cracow Poland Office: Cracow Univ of Tech, al Jana Pawła II 37, 31-864 Cracow Poland

CYLKE, FRANK KURT, librarian; b. New Haven, Feb. 13, 1932; s. Frank Anton and Helen Mary (Callahan) C.; m. Mary Elizabeth Newhouse, Dec. 28, 1962; children: Frank Kurt, Mary Amanda, Virginia Ann. B.A., U. Conn., 1954; M.L.S., Pratt Inst., 1957; postgrad., Fairfield U., Am. U., Georgetown U. Libr. Graham-Eckes Sch., Palm Beach, Fla., 1957-58; reference libr. Bridgeport (Conn.) Pub. Libr., 1958-62; head pub. svc. New Haven Pub. Libr., 1962-65; asst. libr. Providence Pub. Libr., 1965-68; chief libr. rsch. U.S. Office Edn., 1968-69; exec. dir. fed. libr. com. Libr. of Congress, 1970-73; dir. nat. libr. svc. for blind, physically handicapped Library of Congress, 1973—; instr. Grad. Libr. Sch. U. R.I., 1967-68; instr. Grad. Libr. Sch. Cath. U. Am., 1974—, bd. visitors, 1980—; exec. sec. panel edn. & tng. Com. Sci. and Tech. Inst.; chmn. librs. tech. com. Met. Washington Coun. Govts., 1970-71; sec. U.S. Book Exch., 1972-74; sec.-treas. Joint Venture Pub. Activity, 1970-74; mem. E. Greenwich (R.I.) Free Libr. Corp., 1967—; adv. bd. Ednl. Resources Info. Ctr./Clearinghouse Libr. and Info. Sci., 1970-72; bd. visitors Grad. Sch. Libr./Info. Sci., Pratt Inst., 1980—; pilot Mystic Seaport. Editor: Captains Shelf, 1964-66, FLC Newsletter, 1970-73, Library Service for the Blind and Physically Handicapped: An International Approach, 1979,. Recipient Va. Cultural Laureate, 1992, Dayton M. Forman Meml. award, 1996 (Can. Nat. Inst. for the Blind); grantee U.S. Office Edn., 1972. Mem. ALA (F.J. Campbell medal 1982, Joseph W. Lippincott award 1994), Spl. Librs. Assn. (chpt. pres. 1975-76), Am. Soc. Info. Sci. (sec. 1974-75), World Blind Union, Internat. Fedn. Libr. Assns. (founder, chmn. sect. for blind), Friends of Librs. for Blind in N.Am. (founder, ex-officio bd. dirs.), Shenandoah Natural History Assn., Manuscript Soc., Crow's Nest, Ancient Order Hibernians. Roman Catholic. Avocations: sailing, birding. Home: PO Box 192 Great Falls VA 22066-0192 Office: Libr of Congress Nat Libr Svc 1291 Taylor St NW Washington DC 20542-0002

CYPHERS, ANN MARIE, archaeologist, researcher; b. Canton, Ill., June 2, 1950; d. Lewis C. and Frances P. (Tomic) C.; m. José Jorge Rolando Guillén, Dec. 27, 1975 (div. 1996); children: José L., Jennifer C. BBA, U. Ill., 1972; MS, U. Wis., 1975; PhD in History, U. Nacional Autonoma de Mexico, Mexico City, 1987. Rsch. asst. U. Nacional Autonoma de Mexico, 1979-81, rsch. scientist, 1981—; dir. San Lorenzo Tenochtitlán Archeol. Project, Mex., 1990—; lab. dir. Chalcatzingo Project, Urbana, Ill., 1974-76. Author: Chalcatzingo, Estudio de Cerámica y Sociedad, 1992, Descifrando los Misterios de la Cultura Olmeca, 1995; co-author (with Kenneth Hirth): Tiempo y Asentamiento en Xochicalco, 1988. Recipient rsch. grants. Nat. Geographic Soc., 1992, 93, 95, 96, NEH, 1992-95, Am. Philos. Soc., 1990, Mex. Nat. Bd. Sci. and Tech., 1991-96, Nat. U. Mex., 1990-96. Mem. Soc. Am. Archaeology, Mex. Nat. Sys. Rschrs., Mex. Acad. Sci. Avocations: music, reading. Home: Tzinal/Sitilpech No 251, Residencial Jardines Ajusco, 14200 Mexico City Mexico Office: UNAM Inst Investigaciones, Circ Ext CU Coyoacan, 04510 Mexico City Mexico*

CYR, J. V. RAYMOND, telecommunications company executive; b. Montreal, Que., Can., Feb. 11, 1934; s. Armand and Yvonne (Lagace) C.; m. Marie Bourdon, Sept. 1, 1956; children: Helene, Paul Andre. Student, Ecole Poly.; BASc, U. Montreal, 1958; postgrad., Bell Labs., N.J., Nat. Def. Coll., 1972-73; LLD (hon.), Concordia U., Montreal, 1988. With Bell Can., 1992-96, BCE, Inc., 1987-93; engr. Bell Can., 1958-65; staff engr. Bell Can., Montreal, 1965-70; chief engr. Bell Can., Quebec City, 1970-73; from v.p.

ops. staff region to v.p. Bell Can., Montreal, 1973-75, pres., 1983-85, chmn., pres., CEO, 1985-87, chmn. bd., 1987-89; chmn., 1992-96; from exec. v.p. to v.p. adminstrn. Bell Can., Quebec, 1975-83; pres. Bell Can., Montreal, 1983-85, chmn., pres., CEO, 1985-87; chmn., 1992-96; chmn. bd. Bell Can., Montreal, 1987-89; pres. BCE Inc. (formerly Bell Can. Enterprises), Montreal, 1987-88; pres., CEO BCE, Inc. (formerly Bell Can. Enterprises), Montreal, 1988-89, also bd. dirs., chmn., pres., CEO, 1989-90, chmn., CEO, 1990-92; chmn. BCE, Inc. (formerly Bell Can. Enterprises), 1992-93, dir., sr. advisor to chmn.'s office, 1993-97; chmn. Montreal Trust, 1989-90; bd. dirs. Can. Nat., Air Can., SR Telecom, ART Advanced Rsch. & Techs. Inc., Polyvalor Inc., Cognicase Inc., G.T.C. Transcontinental Ltd., Manitex Inc., CESCOM Inc., Cable Satisfaction Internat. Inc., Fonds de Solidarité des Travailleurs du Que., Avestor Corp. Inc., Cogni-Sci. Inc., TransCanada PipeLines Investments (Que), Inc., Argo-Tech Inc.; bd. dirs. Transp. Can. Pipelines, chmn. bd., 1989-92; chmn. Telesat Can., 1992-98, TMI Comm., 1994-97, Geomatics Internat. Inc., 1995-2000, VISTAR Telecomms. Inc., 1998-99, Polyvalor Inc., 1997—; vice-chmn. Domtar Inc., 1994-96, Advanced Rsch. and Techs., 1998—. Assoc. gov. U. Montreal; past chmn. Jr. Achievement Can., Montreal Mus. Contemporary Art, Opera de Montreal; bd. dirs. Ecole Poly. de Montreal, Old Port of Montreal Corp. Inc. Decorated Officer Order of Can., 1988; recipient Can. Engrs. Gold medal, 1987, Ordre du Mérite des Diplômes, U. Montreal, 1988, Laureate of Prix des comm. du Que., 1990, Mgmt. Achievement award McGill U., 1991, Great Montrealer award, 1991, Commemorative medal for 125th ann. of Confedn. of Can., 1992, Personnalité du 125e Anniversaire de l'Ecole Poly, 1998; chair in mgmt. of tech. named in his honor Ecole Poly, named Laureate Personnalite du 125e Anniversaire de l'Ecole Polytechnique, 1998. Mem. Can. Acad. Engring. (founding), St. Denis Club, St. James Club, Mt. Bruno Golf Club, Islemere Club. Roman Catholic. Avocations: golf, swimming. Fax: (514) 870-4136. Office: Bell Canada, 1050 Beaver Hall Hill 19th, Montreal, PQ Canada H2Z 1S4

CYTRYCKI, SLAWOMIR WACLAW, bank executive; b. Lodz, Poland, Dec. 17, 1951; s. Ryszard and Emilia (Gosztyla) C.; m. Elzbieta Michel, Jan. 11, 1973; children: Michal, Andrzej. Grad., Lodz U., Poland, 1971; M of Econs., Leningrad Inst. Econs. & Fin., Russia, 1974. Asst. lectr. Lodz U., Poland, 1974; head internat. dept. Nat. Com. Polish Students Assn., Warsaw, Poland, 1974-77; deputy dir. internat. dept. Ministry Sci., Higher Edn. & Tech., Warsaw, Poland, 1977-82; spl.asst. to under-sec. gen. UN, N.Y.C., 1982-87; advisor to prime min. Office of Coun. of Mins., Warsaw, 1987-88, deputy chief of cabinet of prime min., 1988-89; deputy chief of cabinet of pres. Chancery of the Pres., Warsaw, 1989-90; dir., gen. sec. Bank Handlowy w Warszawie, Warsaw, 1991-95, mem. mgmt. bd., 1996-98, mng. dir., 1998—. Office: Bank Handlowy w Warszawie, ul Chalubinskiego 8, 00-950 Warsaw Poland

CYWAR, ADAM WALTER, management engineer; b. Kearny, N.J., Mar. 14, 1937; s. Adam Benjamin and Sophie Julia (Kurak) C.; m. Gloria Ella Beresford, Mar. 29, 1956 (div. May 1973); children: Victoria Fumagalli, Douglas A., Sophia; m. Rose Barter Tubb, May 11, 1973. BSME, N.J. Inst. Tech., Newark, 1960, MSMgtE, 1965. Design engr. Colgate-Palmolive, Jersey City, N.J., 1956-60; indsl. engr. Lionel Corp., Hillside, N.J., 1960-63; sr. engr. IBM Corp., Boca Raton, Fla., 1963-93; pres. Adam Cywar Indsl. Engr., Austin, Tex., 1993—; v.p. info. sys. RPM Assocs., Georgetown, Tex., 1993-97; founder IBM Worldwide Activity Based Mgmt. Competency Ctr. Author: Handbook of Industrial Engineering, 1982 (IBM Achievement award 1983). Chmn. Town of Poughkeepsie Rep. Com. to Elect Jim Buckley, 1968. Mem. ASME (sr. mem.), Inst. Indsl. Engrs. (sr., treas. 1975-90, dir. honors and awards 1970-75, Disting. Svc. award 1977). Avocations: writing, industrial engineering research. Home and Office: Adam Cywar Indsl Engr 4307 Las Palmas Dr Austin TX 78759-5062

CYWES, SIDNEY, pediatric surgeon, educator; b. Paarl, Cape Prov., South Africa, Jan. 1, 1931; s. Kolman and Ida (Shoolman) C.; m. Marlene Voges, Oct. 16, 1960; children: Robert, Colette. MB, ChB, U. Cape Town, Rondebosch, South Africa, 1953, MMed. in Surgery, 1958; DSc in medicine (hon.), U. Cape Town, 1999. Cert. pediatric surgeon South African Med. and Dental Coun. Lectr. surgery U. Cape Town, 1961-69, assoc. prof., 1969-75, Charles F.M. Saint prof. pediatric surgery, head dept., 1975-96, fellow, 1987—; emeritus prof. paediatric surgery, U. Cape Town, 1997—; chief pediatric surgeon Red Cross War Meml. Children's Hosp., Rondebosch, 1975-97, prin. paediatric surgeon, 1997—; founder Child Safety Ctr., U. Cape Town and Red Cross Children's Hosp.; Sir Arthur Sims Commonwealth prof., 1997. Author: (with Cremin and Louw) Radiological Diagnosis of Digestive Tract Disorders in the Newborn, 1973; mem. editl. bd. Paediatric Surgery Internat., 1985—, South African Jour. Physiotherapy, 1986, Jour. Pediatric Surgery, 1987—; guest editor Burns-Continuing Med. Edn., 1989, Jour. Pediatric Surgery Internat., 1990; editor for Africa Pediatric Surgery Internat., 1990—; editl. corr. Portuguese Jour. Pediatric Surgery, 1994; contbr. over 200 articles to med. jours., chpts. to books. Pres. Child Accident Prevention Found. So. Africa, 1989—. Decorated Order for Meritorious Svc. Class 1 (South Africa; recipient merit award CPA, 1968, Salus medal Dept. Nat. Health, 1993, Franco Soave medal Gaslini Inst., Genoa, Italy, 1996, Univ. Parma medal, 1996, J.H. Louw Gold medal SAAPS, 1996; Cecil John Adams scholar and travel fellow, 1963, Sir Arthur Sims Professorship to Comonwealth Countries, 1997. Fellow ACS,, Royal Coll. Surgeons (Eng.), Royal Coll. Surgeons (Edinburgh), Royal Coll. Physicians and Surgeons (Glasgow, hon.), Coll. Surgeons South Africa (hon.), Am. Acad. Pediatrics (hon.); mem. Med. Assn. South Africa (coun. Cape Western br. 1967-72, Hamilton Maynard medal 1968, 81, Andries Blignaut Meml. medal 1986), Brit. Assn. Paediatric Surgeons (hon., overseas mem. on coun. 1976), Royal Australasian Coll. Surgeons (hon. sect. paediatric surgery 1977), South African Assn. Paediatric Surgeons (sec.-treas. 1975-80, exec. mem., pres. 1980-84, 92, rep. to World Fedn. Assns. Paediatric Surgeons coun. meeting, Santiago, Chile 1986, Lima, Peru 1988), World Fedn. Assns. Paediatric Surgeons (exec. com. 1989—, v.p. 1992, pres. 1995-98), Pan African Pediatric Surg. Assn. (exec. coun. 1994—), South African Paediatric Assn., Coll. Medicine South Africa (assoc. founder, faculty surgery, examiner), Assn. Surgeons South Africa, South African Transplant Soc., Surg. Rsch. Soc. So. Africa, South African Oncology Assn., Eccuadorian Assn. Paediatric Surgeons (hon.), Brit. Assn. Paediatric Surgeons, Israeli Assn. Paediatric Surgeons (hon.), Am. Pediat. Surg. Assn. (hon.). Home: 24 Monterey Dr, Constantia WC 7800, South Arica Office: Red Cross Children's Hosp, Dept Pd Surg, Inst Child He, Rondebosch WC 7700, South Africa

CYWIŃSKI, ZBIGNIEW, structural engineering educator; b. Toruń, Poland, Feb. 12, 1929; s. Piotr Paweł and Irena (Mazurkiewicz) C.; m. Helena Wilczyńska, Apr. 11,1956; children: Ewa Kido, Iwona Cywińska-Suska, Piotr, Anna. BSCE, Tech. U. Gdańsk, Poland, 1953, MSCE, 1955, PhD in Engring., 1964; DS in Engring., Tech. U. Wrocław, Poland, 1968. Lic. engr. for bridges, bldgs., Poland. Instr., asst. prof. Tech. U. Gdańsk, 1953-65, asst. prof., 1966-70, assoc. prof., 1973-79, prof. structural engring., 1980-87, 88—, head postgrad. divsn. faculty civil engring., 1974-75, vice dean faculty civil engring., 1975-78, dean faculty civil engring., 1984-87, 93-99; consulting engr. U. Baghdad, Iraq, 1965-66; asst. prof. U. Mosul, Iraq, 1970-73; UNESCO expert Ministry Edn., Mogadishu, Somalia 1979-80; prof. U. Tokyo, 1987-88. Author: Structural Mechanics I, 6 edits., 1973 (Ministry award 1976), Structural Mechanics II, 2 edits., 1976; editor procs. Preservation of the Indsl. Heritage, 1993, 95, 99 (Rector award 1994); reviewer in field; contbr. numerous articles to profl. publs. 2d lt. Polish Armed Forces, 1950-52. Mem. ASCE, Polish Soc. Theoretical and Applied Mechanics (head regional coun. 1990-92), Internat. Assn. Bridge and Structural Engring. (alternate del. to permanent com. 1994—), Polish Soc. Bridge Engrs. Roman Catholic. Achievements include theory of thin-walled members of variable stiffness; bimoment distrubution method; the paradox of torsional buckling; perforated hybrid I-beams; architectural and civil engineering heritage; service life and aesthetics of bridges, construction sustainability, engring. edn. Avocations: archaeology, oriental studies, mushroom hunting, travel. Home: ul Mściwoja 50/32, 80-357 Gdańsk Poland Office: Tech U Gdańsk, ul G Narutowicza 11/12, 80-950 Gdańsk Poland

CZABÁN, JÁNOS, academic administrator; b. Miskolc, Borsod, Hungary, Nov. 16, 1935; s. János and Jánosné (Mária Heinemann) C.; m. Anna Szentbenedeki Székelyhidy, Nov. 24, 1959; 1 child, Ágnes. MBA, U. Econ. Scis., Budapest, Hungary, 1959, D in Bus. Econs., 1974; PhD in Economic Sci, Hungarian Acad. of Scis., Budapest, 1983, Habilitation, 1989. Head dept. fin. Tech. U. for Heavy Industry, Miskolc, Hungary, 1987-88, head dept. bus. econs., 1987—, vice-dir. Inst. of Econs., 1987-90, prof. bus. econs., 1989—; dean Sch. of Econ. Scis. U. Miskolc, Hungary, 1990-94, pro-rector, 1994-97; guest prof. Montan U., Leoben, Austria, 1992-93; mem. adv. bd. The Coll. for Fin. and Accountancy, 1993—, Hab. Coun. U. Budapest. Author: (textbooks) Industrial Management, 1970, Industrial Business Economics I-II, 1976, Organizational Prognostics I, 1991, The Theory of Cost Management: Cost and Profit Calculations, 1995, Chapters on the Different Subject Areas of Business Economics, 1996, Some Questions on Organizational Prognostics, 1998, Prognostics and Strategy of the Beginning of the 3rd Millenium, 1999. Recipient Karol Adamiecki prize, Poland, 1986, Hungarian Higher Edn. plaque, Budapest, 1994, Istvan Szechenyi medal, 1990, Signum Aurum Universitatis, 1993, St. George Cross Order, 1996, Pro Universitate, 1997. Mem. Econometric Soc., Internat. Coun. for Small Bus., Hungarian Acad. of Scis. (mem. com. for future prognostics, com. for indsl. econs., mgmt. and orgn. com., Miskolc com.), Nat. Coun. for Mgr. Tng., Hungarian Econ. Soc., Scientific Soc. for Orgn. and Mgmt., Hungarian Soc. for Small Bus., Internat. Acad. Scis. of Nature and Soc. Avocations: painting, driving, tennis. Office: U Miskolc, Miskolc-Egyetemváros, 3515 Miskolc Borsod, Hungary

CZACZKES, MORRIS, lawyer; b. Willimantic, Conn., Jan. 18, 1955; s. Harry and Eva (Wind) C. BA, Columbia Coll., 1977; JD, Northwestern U., 1980. Bar: Conn. 1981, U.S. Dist. Ct. Conn. 1981, Ill. 1982, U.S. Ct. Appeals (7th cir.) 1982. Ptnr. Czaczkes & Czaczkes, Norwich, Conn., 1981—. Mem. Citizen's Adv. Coun. for Housing Matters State of Conn., 1988—; chairperson Non-Housing Ct. Dists., 1988—. Mem. ABA (internat. law and bus. law and corps. sects.), Am. Trial Lawyers Assn., Inter-Am. Bar Assn., Conn. Trial Lawyers Assn., Conn. Bar Assn. (comml. law and bankruptcy and corps. sects.), Internat. Bar Assn. (bus. orgn. and internat. sales and related transactions sects.), New London County Bar Assn. Lodge: Elks, St. James. Avocations: skiing, sailing, bicycling, photography. Office: Czaczkes & Czaczkes 482 W Main St Norwich CT 06360-5443

CZAJKOWSKI, FRANK HENRY, lawyer; b. Bklyn., Jan. 7, 1936; m. Cecilia J. Artowicz, Sept. 3, 1955. BA, St. John's U., Bklyn., 1957; JD, St. John's U., 1959; LLM, George Washington U., 1966. Bar: N.Y. 1960, Pa. 1970, Conn. 1974, U.S. Supreme Ct. 1964. Claims adjustor Hartford Accident & Indemnity Ins. Co., N.Y.C., 1959-60; agt. Equitable Life Assurance Soc., N.Y.C., 1960; atty. Corp. Counsel's Office, N.Y.C., 1960-62, Fgn. Claims Settlement Commn., Washington, 1962-68; atty. Atlantic-Richfield Co., N.Y.C., 1968-70, Phila., 1970-72; assoc. gen. counsel Unilever U.S.A. Co., Greenwich, Conn., 1972-98; pvt. practice, 1998—; instr. Fairfield U. Ctr. Lifetime Learning, 1976, Sacred Heart U., 1983; arbitrator Am. Arbitration Assn. Mem. ABA, Conn. Bar Assn., Westchester-Fairfield Corp. Counsel Assn. Office: 7 Lafayette Dr Trumbull CT 06611-2751

CZAJKOWSKI, GERARD ZYGFRYD, physicist, educator; b. Neustadt, Germany, Oct. 11, 1944; m. Wiesława Krystyna Jędrzejewska, 1967; 1 child, Marcin. MS, Nicolaus Copernicus U., Toruń, Poland, 1967, PhD, 1971, DSc, 1975. Sci. asst. Nicholas Copernicus U., 1967-75; asst. prof. U. Tech. and Agr., Bydgoszcz, Poland, 1976-87, head dept. theoretical physics, 1977—, assoc. prof., 1987-94, prof. physics, 1994—; vis. prof. physics Scuola Normale Superiore, Pisa, Italy, 1987-88, 95-96, 99-2000. Contbr. articles to profl. jours. Fellow Alexander von Humboldt Found., Bonn, Germany, 1980-81, 84-85, Consiglio Nazionale Ricerche, Rome, 1996, NATO-CNR fellow, 1995. Mem. European Phys. Soc., N.Y. Acad. Scis., Polish Phys. Soc., Italian Phys. Soc. Avocations: history, history of art, foreign languages, traveling. Office: Inst Math Physics, S Kaliskiego 7 U Tech/Agr, PL 85796 Bydgoszcz Poland

CZAJKOWSKI-BARRETT, KAREN ANGELA, human resources management executive; b. Bklyn., Sept. 13, 1957; d. Frank Henry and Cecilia (Artowicz) Czajkowski; div. Mar. 1992; children: Jennifer Marie, Michael Joseph. BSBA, Fairfield U., 1979; MBA, Sacred Heart U., 1984. Office systems analyst Union Trust Co., Stamford, Conn., 1979-80, sr. office systems analyst, 1980-81; ops. analyst Homequity, Inc., Wilton, 1981-82, project leader human rels. dept., 1982-85, organization devel. cons., 1985-87; tng. and devel. cons. People's Bank, Bridgeport, Conn., 1987-90; mgr. human resource planning and devel. Pitney Bowes Mgmt. Svcs., Stamford, 1990-93, dir. human resources planning and devel., 1993-98; regional learning mgr. Hewitt Assocs. LLC, Rowayton, Conn., 1998—; adj. instr. Sacred Heart U., Bridgeport, 1987. Sec. Cub Scouts Adv. Com., 1991-92; mem. regional bd. Conn. Fedn. Cath. Sch. Parents, 1993-94; treas. St. Theresa Sch.-Home Sch. Assn., 1994-96. Recipient award Nash Engring., 1979; named Bus. Advisor of Yr., INROADS/Fairfield-Westchester Counties, Inc., 1993. Mem. ASTD, Am. Mgmt. Assn., Human Resource Planning Soc. Home: 28 Wendover Rd Trumbull CT 06611-1530 Office: Hewitt Assocs LLC 40 Highland Ave Norwalk CT 06853-1599

CZAKO, LASZLO, internist, gastroenterologist, health economist; b. Szeged, Hungary, Jan. 5, 1966; s. Laszlo Czako and Piroska Csomor. Diploma, Albert Szent-Gyorgyi Med. U., Szeged, 1990, Attila Jozsef U., Szeged, 1999. Fellow Albert Szent-Gyorgyi Med. U., 1990—; rschr. Occpl. and Environ. Health, Sch. Medicine, Kitakyushu, Japan, 1994-95. Grantee Matsumae Found., Japan, 1994, Japanese Coun. for Med. Tng., 1999. Mem. Hungarian Gastroenterol. Soc., European Pancreatic Club. Avocations: sports, music, movies, theatre. Office: 1st Dept Med U Szeged, Fac of Med, Koranyi 8, H-6722 Szeged Hungary

CZAPLEWSKI, LLOYD GEORGE, biotechnology educator; b. Harrogate, Yorkshire, Eng., July 5, 1963; s. Sylvester James Czaplewski and Christina Stodart Lilley; m. Karen Margaret Russell, July 26, 1997. BSc with honors, U. East Anglia, Eng., 1984; PhD, U. Glasgow, Scotland, 1989. Rsch. asst. U. Glasgow, 1984-87; postdoctoral scientist U. Leeds, Eng., 1988-90; rsch. scientist Brit. Biotech, Oxford, Eng., 1990-91, sr. scientist, 1991-93, group leader, 1993-96, sr. group leader, 1996-2000; dept. head biology Brit. Biotech, Oxford, 2000—; chair biol. safety com. Brit. Biotech, Oxford, 1998—, biol. safety officer, 2000—; vis. lectr. cancer studies U. Manchester (Eng.) Inst. Sci. and Tech., 1996-2000. Author: (book chpts.) Methods in Enzymology, 1997, Chemokines in Human Disease, 1998; patentee in field; contbr. papers to profl. jours. Avocations: scuba diving, cycling. Fax: 01865 781034. E-mail: czaplewski@brit.bio.co.uk. Office: Brit Biotech Ltd, Watlington Rd, Cowley Oxford OX4 5LY, England

CZAPLINSKI, KAZIMIERZ, civil engineer; b. Pulawy, Poland, Apr. 16, 1926; s. Tadeusz Czelaw and Jozefa Monika (Marcinowska) C.; m. Wanda Maria Komarska, Nov. 7, 1928; children: Jagienka, Przemyslaw, Krzysztof, Michal. MS in Engring., Gdansk U. Tech., Poland, 1952; PhD, Wroclaw Tech. U., Poland, 1967. Site mgr. Spoleczne Przeds Bud., Gdansk, Poland, 1949-52; main engr. Mostostal, Wroclaw, Poland, 1952-62; asst. prof. Wroclaw Tech. U., 1963-72, assoc. prof., 1972-89, prof., 1990—; deputy dir. Wroclaw Tech. U., 1972-81, 87-91, dean, 1993-96. Author: Realization of Construction Objects-Erection of Structures, 1990; co-author: Construction Design Methodology, 1980, Realization of Construction Objects-Theoretical Fundamentals, 1984, (manual) Rebuilding and Modernization of Houses, 1988. Pres. Cath. Inteligensia Club, 1966-84, Social Com. Panorama Raclawicka Mus., 1990—; pres. Nat. Coun. Lay Catholics, Poland, 1994-98, mem., 1998—. Mem. Polish Soc. Civil Engrs. (pres. 1990-93). Home: Szolc-Rogozinskiego 3, 53-209 Wroclaw Poland Office: Wroclaw Tech U, Wybrzeze Wyspianskiego 27, 50-370 Wroclaw Poland

CZAPOWSKI, GRZEGORZ, geologist, researcher; b. Warsaw, Poland, May 18, 1950; s. Zdzisław and Wanda (Lamowska) C.; m. Janina Starczewska, Jun 12, 1976. MSc, Warsaw U., 1973; DSc, Polish Geol. Inst., 1998. Lectr. in geology Warsaw U., Poland, 1973-79; rschr. Polish Geol. Inst., Warsaw, 1979—; head divsn. chem. resources, Polish Geol. Inst., Warsaw, 1992-97. Co-editor Geol. Quarterly, 1994, 99; contbr. more than 47 articles to profl. jours. Mem. Internat. Assn. Sedimentologists, Soc. for Econ. Paleontology and Mineralogy, Soc. for Sedimentary Geology, Polish Geol. Soc. Avocations: mountain trailing, reading, classical music. Office: Polish Geol Inst, Rakowiecka 4, 00-975 Warsaw Poland

CZÁRÁN, LÓRÁNT, geographer; b. Sighisoara, Romania, Jan. 4, 1969; s. István and Klára (Kiss) C.; m. Andrea Judith Szász, Aug. 4, 1990; 1 child, Viktória. MSc, U. Cluj, Romania, 1993. Geog. info. sys. coord. U. Cluj, 1992-93; environ. cons. Civitas Found., Cluj, 1993-94; rsch. fellow Collegium Budapest, 1994-95; vis. rschr. UN Environment Programme, Arendal, Norway, 1996—. Served with Romanian mil., 1987-88. Jr. Rsch. grant Collegium Budapest, 1994. Mem. Planetary Soc., Internat. Airline Passengers Assn. Roman Catholic. Avocations: skiing, caving, computers, mountain climbing, tennis. Home: Recoltei 7, 3130 Dumbraveni Romania

CZARNOWSKI, MARIAN, plant physiologist, researcher, educator; b. Swinna Poreba-Wadowice, Poland, Dec. 10, 1933; s. Jan and Marianna (Tumulik) Czopek; m. Anna Stepankova, July 21, 1966; children: Margitta, Milan. MSc, Jagiellonian U., Cracow, 1957, D in Natural Scis., 1962, DSc (habilitated), 1973, Professor (titular), 1988. Asst. in plant physiology Polish Acad. Scis., Cracow, 1956-62, sr. asst., 1962-74, assoc. prof., 1974-88, prof. extraordinarius, 1988-91, prof. ordinarius, 1991—, dep. head of sci. rsch., 1976-95, head dept. plant physiology, 1995-98, dir. dept. plant physiology, 1998-2000; lectr. Jagiellonian U., Cracow, 1957-60; Tchr. Tng. Coll., Cracow, 1968-81, 85-90; mem. com. physiology, genetics and breeding plants Polish Acad. Sci., 1996-1998. Author: Methods for Estimation of Plant Photosynthetic Production, 1973; editor-in-chief Monographs, 1996—; contbr. articles to profl. jours. Recipient Polonia Restituta-Knight's Cross, Polish. Rep. Pres., 1988, prize Polish Acad. Scis., 1989. Mem. N.Y. Acad. Scis., Internat. Biol. Programme (Polish com. 1964-73), Polish Soc. Hort. Sci. Roman Catholic. Avocations: phytospectroradiometry, gardening. Home: Krolewska 55/25, 30-081 Cracow Poland Office: Polish Acad Scis Inst Plant Physiology, Slawkowska 17, 31-016 Cracow Poland

CZAUDERNA, MARIAN, animal scientist; b. Piaseczno, Poland, Sept. 8, 1952; s. Antoni Stanislaw and Zofia (Huszoz) C.; married, Dec. 25, 1978; children: Maciek Marek, Krystztof Piotr. MSc in Chemistry, Warsaw (Poland) U., 1976, PhD in Chemistry, 1979. Asst. radiochem. lab. dept. chemistry Warsaw U., 1979-80, asst. lectr. chemistry, 1980-82, lectr., 1982-94, lectr. methods of activation analysis, 1982-94, supr. lab. radiochemistry, 1987-94; lectr. Kielanowski Inst. Animal Physiology and Nutrition, Jablonna, Poland, 1994—. Contbr. over 50 articles to profl. jours. Mem. NSZZ Solidarnose, 1980—. Roman Catholic. Avocations: theater, football. Home: Biatostocka 9 m 28, 03-741 Warsaw Poland Officde: Kielanoswki Inst, Polish Acad Sci, 05110 Jablonna Poland

CZÉKUS, JÁNOS, NATO official; b. Szigetszentmiklós, Hungary, Apr. 8, 1944; married; 2 children. Grad., Hungarian Mil. Acad., 1966; cert., War Coll., 1976; additional mil. strategy postgrad. work; PhD, Hungarian Acad. of Scis., 1989. Commd. 2d lt. Hungarian Army, 1966, advanced through grades to maj. gen., comdr. various air def. and radar units, incl. bn. comdr., 1966-76; dep. comdr., then comdr. radar unit, comdr. land forces divsn. Army Radioelectronic Reconnaissance Ctr., 1976-83; dep. head, head of chair Zrínyi Miklós War Coll., 1983-90, dep. comdr. Coll. for Scis., acting vice-rector Nat. Def. U., 1990-97; dep. chief def. planning directorate, Def. Staff Hungarian Army, 1997-99; mil. rep. from Republic of Hungary to NATO Mil. Com., 1999—; mem. Nat. Doctoral and Qualifying Com., 1993-96, Hungarian Accreditation Com., Expert Com. in Mil. Scis., 1994-97, Sci. Com. of Strategy and Def. Rsch. Inst., Min. of Def., 1991-96; pres. doctoral senate Zrínyi Miklčs War Coll., 1991-97, pres. edit. bd. Gazette, 1991-96, edtl. bd. Mil. Sci. Newsletter, 1994-96. Decorated Officer's Cross, Order of Hungarian Republic; recipient Szent-Györgyi Albert award, 1993. Mem. Assn. of Hungarian Mil. Sci. (v.p. 1995-98, pres. 1997), Hanns-Seidel found. (adv. bd. 1992-94). Office: NATO Hdqrs, Blvd Leopold III, 1110 Brussels Belgium*

CZEMPIEL, ERNST-OTTO, educator, researcher; b. Berlin, May 22, 1927; s. Franz and Annie (Ruether) C.; m. Christa Dahlhoff, Aug. 12, 1952; children: Benedikt, Laurenz. PhD, U. Mainz, 1956. Asst. prof. Tech. Hochschule, Darmstadt, Fed. Republic of Germany, 1957-64, assoc. prof., 1964-65; prof. U. Marburg, Fed. Republic of Germany, 1966-70; prof. internat. rels. U. Frankfurt, Fed. Republic of Germany, 1970-92, prof. emeritus, 1992—; co-dir. Hesse Found. Peace and Conflict Rsch., Frankfurt, 1970-96; chmn. Kuratorium Hessischer Friedenspreis, 1994—. Author: Das Amerikanische Sicherheitssystem 1945-1959, 1966; Macht und Kompromiss: Die Beziehungen der Bundesrepublik Deutschland zu den Vereinten Nationen 1956-1970, 1971; Amerikanische Aussenpolitik, 1979; Internationale Politik, 1981; Friedensstrategien, 1986, 2d edit., 1998; Machtprobe Die USA und die Sowjetunion in den achtziger Jahren, 1989; Weltpolitik im Umbruch, 1993, 2d edit.; Die Reform der UNO Moeglichkeiten und Missverstandnisse, 1994; Kluge Macht. Aussenpolitik fuer das 21. Jahrhundert, 1999; contbr. articles on internat. rels. and fgn. policy to profl. jours. Mem. Deutsche Vereinigung für Politische Wissenschaft, Internat. Studies Assn. Roman Catholic. Avocation: sailing. Home: Erfurter Str 14, D-35039 Marburg Germany Office: Peace Rsch Inst Frankfurt, Leimenrode 29, D-60322 Frankfurt Germany

CZERNER, OLGIERD WŁADYSŁAW, architect, educator; b. Świętochłowice, Poland, Apr. 15, 1929; s. Karol and Jadwiga Stanisława (Czerwińska) C.; m. Barbara Iwona Łuczko, Mar. 19, 1930; children: Rafał, Dorota. Master, Polytech. Sc., Wrocław, Poland, 1952, PhD, 1960, Habil., 1969. Rschr. Polytech. Sch., Wrocł, 1951-66, lectr., 1966-77, prof., 1977—; conservator of city's monuments Municipality of Wrocław, 1955-65; dir. Mus. of Arch., Wrocław, 1965-99. Author: Rynek Wrocławski, 1976, Wrocław-krajobraz i architektura, 1976, Wrocław na dawnej rycinie, 1989, Lwow na dawnej rycinie i planie, 1997; editor: Cemetery Art, 1995; author/editor: The Polish Avant-Garde, 1981. Vice pres. Internat. Coun. Monuments & Sites, Paris, 1990-93, pres. Polish Com., Warsaw, 1985-94. Recipient Prize of 1st step Ministry of Culture and Fine Arts, Warsaw, 1977; decorated Bachelor Cross of the Order of the Renaissance of Poland, Pres. of State, 1978. Mem. Union of Hist. Arts, Assn. of the Conservators (hon.), Assn. Polish Architects, Internat. Coun. Monuments Sites (hon.). Home: Bernardyńska #5/4, 50-156 Wroclaw Poland

CZERNILOFSKY, ARMIN PETER, biochemist; b. Puchberg, Noe, Austria, Mar. 28, 1945; came to U.S., 1976; s. Josef and Paula (Gut) C.; m. Barbara Baker, 1982 (div. 1989); children: Daniel Josef, Felix David; m. U. Weyer, 1994. Univ. Dozent, PhD, U. Vienna, 1974, 91. Biochemist U. Vienna, Austria, 1972-77; postdoctoral fellow, adj. asst. prof. U. Calif., San Francisco, 1976-77, 78-81; postdoctoral fellow U. Vienna, 1977-78; staff scientist Acad. Sci., Salzburg, Austria, 1981-82, Max Planck Soc., Köln, Federal Republic of Germany, 1982-87; cons. Cal-Bio and AGS, Calif., 1987-88; head external rsch. office Boehringer Ingelheim/Austria Gestiubh, Vienna, 1989—; prof. biochemistry Rheinisch-Westf. Tech. U., Aachen, Fed. Republic of Germany, 1986-87, pvt. dozent molecular biology, 1987—, dozent biochemistry, U. Vienna, 1991. Contbr. articles to profl. jours. on biochemistry and molecular biology. Rsch. grantee Am. Rsch. Fund, 1977, 81, Austrian Sci. Fund, 1981, European Community, 1986; fellow European Molecular Biology Orgn., 1973, 74-75, 81; recipient Honor award for Sci. and Arts The Körner Stiftung, 1974. Mem. AAAS, N.Y. Acad. Scis., Soc. Neurosci., Am. Microbiology Soc., Austrian Biochemistry Soc., German Cancer Soc. Office: Boehringer Ingelheim R&D, Dr Boehringer-Gasse 5-11, Vienna A-1121, Austria

CZERNUSZENKO, WLODZIMIERZ, environmental hydraulics professional; b. Warsaw, Poland, June 4, 1939; s. Wlodzimierz Czernuszenko and Zofia (Gorecka) C.; m. Victoria Wladyslawa Reiss Czernuszenko, Nov. 22, 1962; children: Marek, Jacek. BS, MS, Tech. U. Warsaw, Poland, 1962, PhD, 1973, Dr.Habil., 1984. Asst. Inst. Hydrology, Warsaw, Poland, 1964-67; assoc. prof. Inst. Meteorology, Warsaw, Poland, 1968-85; assoc prof. Inst. Geophysics, Warsaw, Poland, 1986-90; prof. U. Miss., Oxford, 1991-94, Inst. Geophysics, Warsaw, Poland, 1995—. Author: Encyclopedia of Fluid Mechanics, 1990; contbr. articles to profl. jours. Mem. Water Mgmt. Com. Polish Acad. Scis., 1995, Internat. Assn. Hydraulic Rsch., 1995. Avocations: travel, sports. E-mail address: wczer@igf.edu.pl. Fax: (48-22) 691 5915. Office: Inst Geophysics, Ks Janusza 64, 01-452 Warsaw Poland

CZERWINSKI, EDWARD JOSEPH, foreign language educator; b. Erie, Pa., June 6, 1929; s. Joseph and Anna (Branecka) C. BA, Grove City Coll., 1951; MA in Drama and English, Pa. State U., 1955; postgrad., Emory U., 1955-57, Ind. U., 1960-61; MA in Russian, U. Wis., Madison, 1964, PhD in Russian and Polish, 1965. Instr. English Ga. Tech. Inst., Atlanta, 1957-59; asst. prof. English and drama McNeese State Coll., La., 1959-60; assoc. prof. Russian and Polish lits. U. Pitts., 1965-66, SUNY at Buffalo, 1966-67; assoc. prof. Russian and Polish U. Kans., Lawrence, 1967-70; prof. Russian and

comparative lit. SUNY, Stony Brook, 1970-93, prof. emeritus, 1993—; ofcl. translator from Polish into English Interpress Pubs., Warsaw; founder, exec. and artistic dir. Slavic Cultural Center, Port Jefferson, N.Y., 1970—, pres. bd. trustees, 1970—. Editor: (with J. Piekalkiewicz) The Soviet Invasion of Czechoslovakia: The Effects on East Europe, 1972; editor, translator Pieces of Poland: Four Polish Dramatists, 1983, (with Mario Suško) Twenty Yugoslav Poets: the Meditative Generation, 1982, Bogdan Suchodolski's A History of Polish Culture, 1986, Bogdan Grzelonski's America Through Polish Eyes, 1988; editor: Alternatives: An Anthology of Slavic and East European Drama, 1983, (with Mario Susko) The Mythmakers: An Anthology of Contemporary Yugoslav Short Stories, 1984, (with Nicholas Rzhevsky) The Dramaturg and Dramaturgy, 1986, Chekhov Reconstructed: New Translations of Chekhov's Plays, 1987, Satire Cum Poesis: Three Bulgarian Plays, 1987, Contemporary Polish Theater and Drama (1956-84), 1988, (with Czeslaw Hernas) Alter-Altar Art: A Revolution of Silence in Contemporary Polish Art, 1989, Tadeusz Rozewicz's Bas-Relief and Other Poems, 1992, A Dictionary of Polish Literature, 1994; author numerous articles and revs.; mem. editorial bd. Books Abroad (now World Lit. Today), 1968—, 20th Century Lit., Comparative Drama, spl. editor, 1969-70; editor: Slavic and East European Arts Jour., 1982—, Polish lit. sect. Ency. Brit, 1975-78, 88-96; area editor ea. Europe Theatre Companies of the World, 1986—. Tour sponsor Poland's Studio Theatre, 1973, 76. Served to 2d lt. USAF, 1951-53. Kosciuszko Found. grantee, 1962-64; Wanda Rohr Found. grantee, 1963, Internat. Dimensions grantee, 1966, Fulbright grantee Yugoslavia, 1968-69; Inter-Univ. travel grantee USSR, 1968-69, Inter-Univ. travel grantee Czechoslovakia, 1969; Internat. Rsch. and Exch. Bd. fellow, Yugoslavia, 1983-84, summer seminar grantee, Bulgaria, 1985, IREX grantee Poland, 1987, 90-91; recipient Disting. Alumni award Grove City Coll., 1973, Chancellor's Excellence in Teaching award SUNY, 1973-74; Amicus Poloniae award Poland, 1974, Disting. Prof. award N.Y. State Tchrs. of Fgn. Langs., 1975; named Man. of Yr. in Culture and Arts, Am. coun. Polish Cultural clubs, 1986. Mem. MLA (exec. com. Slavic-Western lit. rels. 1970-72), AAUP, Polish Acad. Arts and Scis. Am., Am. Assn. Tchrs. of Slavic and East European Langs., Am. Assn. Advancement of Slavic Studies, PEN Am. Ctr. Home: 341 W 47th St Apt 4R New York NY 10036-2429

CZERWINSKI, THOMAS J., health facility administrator; b. Bklyn., Mar. 10, 1949; s. Thomas B. and Irene O. (Bobrek) C.; m. Christine U. Urbano, Mar. 31, 1979; children: Thomas L., Lauren R. AAS, Dutchess C.C., Poughkeepsie, N.Y., 1972; BS, SUNY, Albany, 1974; MPA, Cornell U., 1976. Cert. profl. in healthcare quality. Adminstr. dept. radiology Albany (N.Y.) Med. Ctr., 1976-78, v.p. diagnostic and profl. svcs., 1978-89, adminstr. end stage renal disease facility, 1978-91; health ctr. adminstr. Community Health Plan, Poughkeepsie, 1991-93; dir. ambulatory care svcs. King Khaled Eye Specialist Hosp., Riyadh, Saudi Arabia, 1994-96, dir. quality mgmt., 1996—; cons., lectr. Hosad Project Riyadh, 1998—; adj. lectr. health svcs. adminstrn. Russell Sage Coll., Albany, 1990-93; lectr. mgmt.-orgnl. devel. and comms. SUNY, Albany, 1977-80; field reviewer Joint Commn. Internat., Chgo., 1999. Author, presenter Leadership Devel. Program, QM Team Facilitator Workshop, 1996—; speaker 2d Internat. Nursing Symposium, 1998. Bd. dirs. End Stage Renal Disease Network of N.Y., Inc., 1988-91, Homer Perkins Ctr., Inc., 1989-91; mem. Renal Disease Svc. Agy., 1981-92, bd. dirs., 1982-92; mem. blood svcs. coun. N.E. N.Y. Region ARC, Albany, 1987-90; mem. Renal Disease Network 26 Coord. Coun., Syracuse, N.Y., 1980-88, mem. exec. com., 1983-88; mem. Mid-Hudson Valley Quality Network, 1991-93, Empire State Regatta Devel. Com., 1986-87, Capital Dist. Sleep/Wake Disorders Study Ctr. Joint Mgmt. Com., 1989-91; mem. alumni admissions interview com. Cornell U., 1977—; mem. planning com. Albany Med. Ctr. Acad. Facilities Redevel., 1988-91; mem. adv. com. Albany Regional Radiation Oncology Program, 1986-90; mem. adv. bd. Organ Procurement Orgn. of Albany Med. Coll., 1988-91; dir. Albany Red Cross, Blood Bank search com., 1986-89; chmn. Capital Dist. Clin. Lab. Project Task Force, 1986-88; mem. strategic long range planning com. N.E. N.Y. United Way, 1986-90; mem. com. AIDS issues Albany Med. Ctr., 1987-91, Radioisotope and Radiation Safety Com., 1979-88, mem. exec. com. 1987,88, co-chmn. Fund for 21/21 Employee campaign, sec. transfusion com., 1983-90, chmn. United Way Employee campaign, 1987-88, chmn. universal precautions task force, 1987-90; mem. AIDS adv. com. North Colonie Ctrl. Schs. Bd. Edn., 1988-91; coach Westland Hills Little League, 1987-89; den leader Gov. Clinton Coun. Boy Scouts. Am., 1988. SP5 U.S. Army, 1967-70. Named Alumni Interviewer of Yr. Johnson Grad. Sch. Mgmt., Cornell U., Ithaca, N.Y., 1990. Mem. Nat. Assn. for Healthcare Quality, Am. Coll. Healthcare Execs. (assoc.), Med. Group Mgmt. Assn. (mem. multispecialty group exec. assembly 1994—, mem. opthalmology assembly 1994—), Riyadh Quality Mgmt. Network (pres. 1997—), Am. Legion, Elks. E-mail: tomski@shabakah.com. Home: C-204/KKESH PO Box 7191, Riyadh 11462, Saudi Arabia Office: King Khaled Eye Specialist, PO Box 7191, Riyadh 11462, Saudi Arabia

CZETWERTYNSKI, MICHEL-FELIX, diplomat; b. Warsaw, Poland, Nov. 20, 1938; arrived in Belgium, 1946; s. George Vincent Czetwertynski and Rose Zoltowska; m. Kristina Sigurdson, Oct. 14, 1971; children: Alexandre Wladimir, Constantin Nicolas. M in Social Sci., U. Brussels, Brussels, 1964. Joined ministry fgn. affairs Belgium, 1968; attaché Belgian Embassy to Brazil, Rio de Janeiro, 1969-72, to Finland, Helsinki, 1973-74; 1st sec., del. NATO, Brussels, 1974-78; counselor Belgian Embassy to U.K., London, 1978-80; counselor Belgian Embassy to India, New Delhi, 1980-83; amb. to Bangladesh Dhaka, 1983-84; dep. chief of protocol ministry of fgn. affairs, Brussels, 1984-87; amb. to Nigeria Lagos, 1987-91; amb. to Brazil Brasilia, 1992-96; amb. to Lebanon and Cyprus, 1997-2000, amb. to Portugal, 2000—. Decorated comdr. Order of the Crown; comdr. Italian Order of Merit; comdr. Aztec Eagle Order (Mexico); Grand Cross of Rio Branco. Office: Ministry Fgn Affairs, 15 rue des Petits Carmes, 1000 Brussels Belgium

CZIGLER, ISTVAN, psychologist; b. Budapest, May 23, 1946; s. Imre and Katalin (Kovari) C.; m. Erika Safir; children: Balazs, Anna. MA, Eotvos Lorand U., Budapest, 1974; PhD, Eotvos Lorand U., 1984; DSc, Hungarian Acad. Scis., Budapest, 1994. Fellow Inst. Psychology/Hungarian Acad. Scis., Budapest, 1969-87; deputy dir. Inst. Psychology/Hungarian Acad. Scis., 1989—; assoc. prof. Eotvos Lorand U., Budapest, 1987-89; assoc. prof. Kossuth Lajos U., Debrecen, Hungary, 1976-86, prof. 1997—; assoc. prof. Eotvos Lorand U., 1987-97. Author: (book) Attention, 1994; contbr. articles to profl. jours. Mem. Hungarian Psychol. Assn. (pres. 1990-97). Avocations: music, art. E-mail: czigler@cogpsyphy.hn. Office: Inst for Psychology, Hungarian Acad Sci/POB 398, Budapest H-1394, Hungary

CZIHAK, GERHARD, biologist; b. Vienna, Austria, Nov. 10, 1928; s. Viktor and Johanna (Misa) C.; m. Ilse Zimmermann, Feb. 27, 1965; children: Elisabeth, Wolfgang, Christoph, Johanna, Valentin. DPhil, U. Vienna, 1952. Asst. prof. biology U. Tuebingen, Germany, 1954-61; rsch. fellow Max-Planck Inst., Tuebingen, 1961-65; mem. faculty U. Salzburg, Austria, 1970; prof. genetics and devel. biology U. Salzburg, 1971—. Author: Gr. Zoologisches Praktikum (Zoolog. Laboratory), 1959; author, editor: (textbook) Biology, 5th edit., 1992; editor: The Sea Urchin Embryo, 1975. Home: Akademiestrasse 15, A-5020 Salzburg Austria Office: Univ Salzburg, Hellbrunnerstrasse 34, A-5020 Salzburg Austria

CZINGER, KEVIN ROBERT, entrepreneur, venture capitalist; b. Cleve., Apr. 15, 1959; s. Kenneth Robert and Ethel Mac (Hudock) C.; m. Katrin Julia Blucher, Aug. 28, 1987; children: Antonia, Lukas. BA, Yale U., 1982, JD, 1987. Bar: N.Y. 1987. Asst. U.S. atty. Manhattan U.S. Atty's. Office, N.Y.C., 1988-90; exec. dir. Goldman Sachs Internat., London, 1990-94; exec. v.p., COO BMG Entertainment, N.Y.C., 1994-96; CEO, founder Volcano Entertainment, LLC, N.Y.C., 1996-98; mng. dir. Merrill Lynch & Co., Inc., 1998-99; COO Webvan.com, Foster City, 1999-2000; venture capitalist, entrepreneur-in-residence Benchmark Capital, 2000—. Office: Benchmark Capital 2400 Sand Hill Rd Menlo Park CA 94025-6941

CZIRÓK, EVA, microbiologist; b. Vereb, Fejér, Hungary, June 18, 1937; d. Ákos and Irén (Vincze) C.; m. Peter Lépes, July 24, 1965. MD with distinction, Med. U., Budapest, Hungary, 1964, DSc, 1988. Lic. physician, clin. lab., clin. microbiology. Jr. bacteriologist Pest County Pub. Health Sta., Budapest, 1964-69, sr. bacteriologist, 1969-78; head Nat. Escherichia Reference Lab. B. Johan Nat. Inst. Pub. Health, Budapest, 1978—, head bacteriological dept., 1996—, dep. dir., head divsn. microbiology, 1998—; sec. Nat. Microbiology Bd., Hungarian Ministry Health and Welfare, 1992-96, chmn., 1997—. Author: Guide Book for Bacteriology for Clinical Microbiologists, 1980, How to Attack Bacteria, 1996; editor-in-chief Manual of Clinical and Epidemiological Bacteriology, 1999; contbr. articles to profl. jours. Mem. Hungarian Soc. Microbiology (head bacteriol. sect. 1993—, exec. bd.), Hungarian Soc. Infectious Diseases, Hungarian Soc. Hygiene. Telephone: 361 476-1118. Home: Hollán Ernö 13-15, H-1136 Budapest Hungary Office: Nat Ctr Epidemiology, Gyáli u 2-6, H-1097 Budapest B Johan, Hungary

CZOBOR, FRANCISC, chemist, researcher; b. Arad, Romania, Sept. 1, 1962; s. Francisc and Elena C.; m. Iuliana Oprea, Mar. 22, 1986; children: Ilda, Anna. MS in Indsl. Chemistry, Poly. U., Bucharest, Romania, 1986; PhD Inst. Organic Chemistry, Romanian Acad. Scis., Bucharest, 1997. cert. engr., organic chemist. Engr. chem. fertilizers factory, Valea Calugareasca, Romania, 1986-89, Chimopar S.A., Bucharest, 1989-90; rsch. scientist Chem. and Pharm. Rsch. Inst., Bucharest, 1990-94; sr. rsch. scientist Cantacuzino Inst., Bucharest, 1994-99; specialty inspector I, World Bank Project Coord. Unit Ministry of Health, Bucharest, 1999—. Contbr. articles to sci. jours. Mem. Regional Assn. Antivral Rsch. Ctrl. and Ea. European, Romanian Fedn. Modern Karate.. Fax: 03040-1-4115672. E-mail: czobor@cantacuzino.ro. Office: Cantacuzino Inst, Spl Independentei 103, 70100 Bucharest Romania

CZOCHRALSKA, BARBARA, chemist, researcher, educator; b. Lodz, Poland; d. Jan and Wiktoria (Gradkowska) Kubiak; children: Tiaza Bem, Ewa Wisniewska; m. Jan Antoni Czochralski, May 15, 1960. MS, Poly. Sch., Lodz, 1955; PhD, Yagellonian U., Cracow, Poland, 1962; Habil, U. Warsaw, 1975. Diplomate in chem. engring. Asst. Yagellonian U., 1955-62; asst. prof. chemistry U. Warsaw, 1963-75, assoc. prof., 1975-90, prof. dept. biophysics, 1990—; dir. Lab. of Biophysics, Inst. Exptl. Physics, 1975-79. Author: Electroreduction of nucleic bases, 1975, Sensitivity of the Matter, 1998; contbr. 100 articles to profl. jours. Recipient award Ministry of Nat. Edn., 1970. Mem. Internat. Soc. Bioelectrochemistry, European Soc. Photobiology. Avocations: literature, theater. Office: U Warsaw Dept Biophysics, Al Zwirki & Wigury 93, 02-089 Warsaw Poland

CZOLCZYNSKI, KRZYSZTOF, mechanics educator; b. Łódź, Poland, Dec. 20, 1956; s. Miroslaw and Zofia (Iwan) C.; m. Teresa Elzbieta Kluk, Mar. 26, 1978. MS, Tech. U. Lodz (Poland), 1980, PhD, 1989, DSc, 1994. Mech. engr. Prof. mechanics Tech. U. Lodz (Poland), 1996—. Mem. European Mechanics Soc., Nat. Geographic Soc., N.Y. Acad. Scis. Roman Catholic. Avocations: astronomy, philosophy, numismatics. Office: Tech U Lodz Divsn Dynamics, Stefanowskiego 15, 90-924 Łódź Poland

CZON, SEUNG-GUL, English educator, translator; b. Mokpo, Chonnam, Korea, June 14, 1941; s. Dokkun Czon and Whasung Park; m. Hae-Won Chung, Oct. 12, 1970; children: Kyung-Hoon, Kyung-Hyo. BA, Seoul (Korea) Nat. U., 1962, MA, 1966; MA, U. Iowa, 1975; postgrad., Sogang U., Seoul, 1978-83. Lectr. Korea U., Seoul, 1968-70; instr. dept. English Seoul Nat. U., 1970-76, asst. prof., 1976-80, assoc. prof., 1980-85, prof., 1985—; dir. Am. Studies Inst., Seoul Nat. U., 1990-94. Author: American Literature and Its Tradition, 1985, Survey of American Literature, 1992; translator: Poems of Robert Frost, 1978, Short Stories of Isaac B. Singer, 1979, Short Stories of Nathaniel Hawthorne, 1998. Served with Korean Air Force, 1962-66. Fulbright scholar, 1973-75; fellow Am. Coun. Learned Assns., 1979-80. Mem. MLA (Am. lit. sect.), Am. Studies Assn., Am. Studies Assn. of Korea (v.p. 1987-89, pres. 1994-96), English Lang. and Lit. Assn. of Korea (dir. pub. rels. 1982-84). Avocations: trekking, baduk, tennis. Home: 1-203 Samho Villa, 179 Pyungchang-dong, Chongro-ku Seoul 110-012, Korea Office: Seoul Nat U, Shinrim-dong Kwanag-ku, Shinrimdong Seoul 151-742, Korea

CZORNIAK, ANDREW, artist; b. Tetylkiwci, Ukraine, Dec. 14, 1913; came to U.S., 1949; s. Michael and Mary Czorniak; m. Mary Czorniak, Nov. 8, 1952; children: Michael A. Czorniak, Elizabeth A. Malsick. Student, Nowakiwsky Sch. Art, Lviv, Ukraine, 1930-34, Pratt Inst., Bklyn., 1953-56, U. Conn. Asst. art dir. Prelle Advt. Agy., Hartford, Conn., 1956-58; art dir. Advt.-Art Agy., Hartford, 1958-62; art editor Aetna Life & Casualty, Hartford, 1962-81. Painter ch. murals Dibshche Lviv, OBL, Ukraine, 1935, Sokoliwka, OBL, Lviv, Ukraine, 1936, Borshchovichi, OBL, Lviv, Ukraine, 1939; exhibited in group shows at Ansbach, Ausburg, Ashafenburg, Bavaria, Germany, 1946; one man show in Hartford, Conn., 1954; illustrator Ukrainian newspapers; editor Ukrainian Historical Publ. Mem. Conn. Acad. Fine Arts, Wadsworth Atheneum, Hartford Advt. Club, Ukrainian Artists Assn. in U.S.A. Avocations: wood carving, stained glass, sculpting. Home: 76 Conestoga Way Glastonbury CT 06033-3304

CZUBAK, ANTONI, mechanical engineering educator; b. Piotrkow Trybunalski, Poland, Apr. 26, 1928; s. Michał and Franciszka (Dobrzelak) C.; m. Janina Pawlikowska, Feb. 1956; children: Maria Anna Polak, Piotr Czubak. B in Engring., Silesia Tech. U., Gliwice, Poland, 1952; MSc, U. Mining and Metallurgy, Cracow, Poland, 1954, PhD in Mech. Engring., 1960, DSc, 1966. Assoc. prof. to prof. U. Mining and Metallurgy, Cracow, 1952-74; prof. mech. engring. Coll. Sci. and Tech., Port Harcourt, Nigeria, 1974-79, Kielce (Poland) U. Tech., 1980-83, River State U. Sci. and Tech., Port Harcourt, 1983-86, U. Mining and Metallurgy, 1986-93, Kielce U. Tech., 1993—; dep. dir. Inst., U. Mining and Metallurgy, 1969-74; head mech. engring. dept. Coll. Sci. and Tech., Port Harcourt, 1974-79; dep. rector Kielce U. Tech., 1981-83; dean faculty engring. River State U. Sci. and Tech., 1984-86; mem. Coun. for Mining Industry, Polish Acad. Scis., 1987-92. Author: Vibratory Conveyors, 1964, (monograph) Analysis of Bulk Material Motion on Vibratory Conveyors, 1966; co-author: Transportation Machinery and Auxiliary Equipment for Open Pit Mining Industry, 1968 (Rectors award 1969); contbr. over 60 articles to nat. and internat. scientific jours. Polish Rsch. Coun. grantee, Warsaw, 1997. Mem. Polish Soc. Theoretical and Applied Mechanics, Polish Coun. Theory of Machines and Mechanisms. Avocations: volleyball, tennis, auto travel. Home: Szujskiego 11/4, 31-123 Cracow Poland Office: Kielce U Tech, Al Tysiaclecia P P 7, 25-314 Kielce Poland

CZUDEK, STANISLAV, surgeon; b. Cesky Tesin, Czech Republic, Nov. 14, 1958; s. Josef and Stepanka (Sikora) C.; m. Urszula Wawrosz, Sept. 20, 1986; children: Michal, Marcin. MD, U. Olomouc, Czech Republic, 1983, PhD, 1997. Intern U. Ostrava, 1986; resident U. Prague, Czech Republic, 1993; surgeon Nemocnice Podlesi, Trinec, Czech Republic, 1984—, chief dept. mini invasive surgery, 1993—, chief dept. of surgery, 1997; dir. Hosp. Podlesi, Trinec, 1992—. Author, editor: Miniinvasive Surgery, 1996; contbr. articles to profl. jours. Mem. European Assn. for Endoscopic Surgery, Czech Surg. Soc. (adminstrv. bd. 1996—), Soc. Am. Gastrointestinal Endoscopic Surgeons, Czech Soc. of Noninvasive and Endoscopic Surgery (pres. 1999). Avocations: skiing, football, music. Home: 545, 73998 Mosty Czech Republic Office: Hosp Podlesi, 73961 Trinec Czech Republic

CZYZ, ZBIGNIEW HENRYK, research scientist, educator; b. Wilno, Poland, Jan. 19, 1930; s. Czeslaw Jozef and Malwina (Skuracz) C.; m. Regina Smejlis, June 4, 1952. BSEE, Warsaw (Poland) U. Tech., 1952, MSEE, 1959, PhD in Elec. Engring., 1968, DSc, 1988. Mem. rsch. staff Telecomms. Rsch. Inst., Warsaw, 1952-59, head microwave antenna lab., 1959-70, ind. rsch. scientist, 1964-73, rsch. group mgr., 1970-76, sr. rsch. scientist, 1973-92, prof. antennas, radar polarimetry, 1992—; lectr. Tech. U., Warsaw, 1962-64, 73-74; rsch. scientist Mil. Acad. Tech., Warsaw, 1970-73; presenter, chair confs. in field; mem. internat. sci. com. Internat. Workshop on Radar Polarimetry, Nantes, France, 1992-95. Contbr. over 50 articles to profl. jours.; 7 patents in field of antenna design, measurements and on polarization fourspher method of canceling partially polarized radar clutter. Mem. IEEE (organizer, chpt. chmn. Poland sect. 1990-92), Assn. Polish Elec. Engrs. (organizer, 1st chmn. microwave techniques chpt. 1970-80), URSI (corr.), Polish Acad. Scis. (mem. electronics and comms. com. 1975—), Internat. Soc. Optical Engring. Avocations: travel, chess, classical music, science fiction. Home: Bartosika 4-45, PL 03982 Warsaw Poland Office: Telecomms Rsch Inst, Poligonowa 30, PL 04051 Warsaw Poland

CZYZAK, BOGDAN, historian; b. Lomazy, Podlasie, Poland, July 21, 1940; s. Edward and Maria (Szafranska) C.; m. Halina Augustynowicz, Apr. 19, 1975; 1 child, Radosław. Doctor, Poznań U., Poland, 1975. Asst. prof. Polish Acad. of Sci., Poland, 1979-93; prof. Olsztyn U., Poland, 1993-98, Elblag's Higher Sch. of Humanitic, Poland, 1998, Warsar's Higher Sch. of Journalism, Poland, 1999—; temporary worker Sci. Acad. of USSR, 1987-90. Author: Cultural Dilemas on Polish Coast, 1985, An Intimate Life of Toarina Katarina II, 1993, Polish-Lithuanian-Disputes About to be Published in XIX, XX; co-author: The History of Gdansk, Vol. IV, 1999. Mem. Solidarity, Poland, 1980. Scholarship Historische Commn. of Berlin, 1985. Roman Catholic. Avocation: research work. Home: Kameliowa 45, 81-591 Gdynia Poland

CZYZAK, STANLEY JOACHIM, astronomy educator, researcher; b. Cleve., Aug. 21, 1916; s. John J. and Sophia Jane (Jezierski) Czyzak; m. Ruth Louise Long, Sept. 10, 1942; children: Stanley Robert, James William, Patricia Ann, David Martin. BS in Chem. Engring., Fenn Coll. (Cleve. State U.), 1935, BS in Civil Engring., 1936; MS in Chemistry, John Carroll U., 1939; DSc in Physics and Math., U. Cin., 1948. Registered profl. engr., Ohio. Asst. to chief metallurgist Forest City Foundry, Cleve., 1935-36; asst. rsch. metallurgist Aluminum Co. of Am., Cleve., 1936-37; rsch. engr. Una Welding, Inc., Cleve., 1937-41; commd. 1st lt. USAF, 1941, advanced through grades to brig. gen., 1966, ret., 1976; Stephen H. Wilder fellow U. Cin., 1945-48; assoc. rsch. physicist Argonne (Ill.) Nat. Lab., 1948-49; rsch. physicist Batelle Meml. Inst., Columbus, Ohio, 1949-50; asst. prof. physics U. Detroit, 1950-51, assoc. prof. physics, vice chmn. dept., 1953-59, prof. of physics, 1959-60; prof. astronomy Ohio State Univ., Columbus, 1966-85. Contbr. approximately 160 articles to profl. jours. including: Am. Jour. Physics, Phys. Review, Jour. Optical Soc. Am., Jour. of Mechanics and Physics of Solids, Jour. of Chem. Physics, Astrophys. Jour. Supplement, Monthly Notices of the Royal Astron. Soc., Astron. Soc. of the Pacific, Astrophys. Jour., Jour. of Applied Physics, Memoirs of Royal Astron. Soc., Proceedings of Phys. Soc., Internat. Astron. Union Symposia. Recipient Disting. Svc. award Fenn Coll., (now Cleve. State U.), 1965. Fellow Royal Astron. Soc.; mem. Internat. Astron. Union, Am. Astron. Soc., Sigma Xi, Tau Beta Pi. Roman Catholic. Achievements include two U.S. patents: on a method for growing single crystals of Cds and Zns; an apparatus for growing single crystals of Cds and Zns. Avocation: flying (civilian flight instr. single, multi-engine aircraft, also instrument FAT flying). Office: Ohio State Univ Astronomy Dept 174 W 18th Ave Columbus OH 43210-1106 Address: Oakwood Village 2161 Willow Run Cir Enon OH 45323-9788

CZYZEWSKI, JERZY JULIAN, physicist; b. Lwow, Poland, July 27, 1939; s. Faustyn and Mieczyslawa C.; m. Danuta Kochan, June 23, 1962 (div. Jan. 1989); children: Joanna, Kinga; m. Grazyna Rogalska, Jul. 8, 1989; 1 child, Jacek. D, Univ. Wroclaw, Poland, 1971, habilitation, 1977. Asst. prof. Univ. Wroclaw, 1963-81, assoc. prof., 1981-92, prof., 1992—; head of surface science sect. Inst. of Experimental Physics, Wroclaw Univ., 1984—, deputy dir., 1993-96. Co-author: Invention of the Electron Stimulated Ion Angualr Desorption Method in Surface Sci., 1974; contbr. articles to profl. jours. Leader Solidarity Univ. Wroclaw, 1980. Lt. Antyaricraft artilery, Wroclaw, 1971-74. Recipient Welch Found. grant Internat. Union of Sci., Tech. and Application of Vacuum, 1973, Golden Cross Golden Cross of Merit Polish State Counsil, 1978, Knight Cross of Polania Restitute Order Pre. of Poland, 1996. Fellow Polish Vacuum Soc. (dep. dir. surface sci. sect.). Roman Catholic. Avocations: classical music, philosophy, politics, sports. E-mail: jerzy@zfpifd.uni.wroc.pl Fax number: 48 71 322 3365. Home: ul Slubicka 37/1, Wroclaw 53-615, Poland Office: Inst Experimental Physics, PL M Borna 9, Wroclaw 50-204, Poland

CZYZYK, ARTUR STANISLAW, internal medicine and diabetes physician; b. Bodzentyn, Poland, Feb. 6, 1927; s. Kazimierz and Franciszka (Piróg) C.; m. Teresa Jadwiga Kasperska, Aug. 17, 1961; children: Maria Czyzyk-Krzeska, Jan. MD, U. Med. Sch., Cracow, Poland, 1951. Rsch. scholar dept. pharmacology U. Med. Sch., Cracow, 1948-50; asst. dept. internal medicine U. Med. Sch., Warsaw, 1951-55, asst. prof., 1955-60, assoc. prof., 1961-67, prof., 1971—, head, chmn. dept. gastroenterology and metabolic diseases, 1968-97, prof. emeritus medicine, 1997—; mem. expert com. diabetes WHO, Geneva, 1967-92; v.p. European Assn. for Study of Diabetes, Düsseldorf, Germany, 1968-70, Internat. Diabetes Fedn., Brussels, 1976-82, Fedn. der Donau-Symposia über Diabetes Mellitus, Vienna, Austria, 1989-93. Author: (in Polish) Pathophysiology and Clinical Picture of Diabetes, 1987, 2d edit., 1997; discovered inhibition of intestinal absorption of glucose by anti-diabetic biguanides, hypocholesterolemic effect of salicylhydroxamic acids; contbr. articles to profl. jours. Mem. Soc. Scientiarum ac Litterarum Varsoviensis, Gesellschaft Endokrinologie und Stoffwechselkrankh (hon.), Hungarian Diabetes Assn. (hon.), Polish Diabetes Assn. (hon.). Home: ul Koszykowa 14 app 4, PL00-564 Warsaw Poland

DA, THIERRY, bank executive; b. Beziers, France, Apr. 4, 1944; d. Robert and Monique (Andrié) D.; m. Ruriko Tarusawa, June 1976 (div. 1986). Engr., ECP, France, 1967; ENA, France, 1972; AMP, Harvard U., 1993. Staff Caisse des Depots, Paris, 1972-78; fin. attache Ministry of France, Tokyo, 1978-81; dep. gen. mgr. Banque Indosvez, Tokyo, 1982-86; v.p. Asia Banque Indosvez, Paris, 1986-91; exec. v.p. fin. CNP, Paris, 1992; CEO Sedgwick SA, Paris, 1994-99; sr. banker Caisse de Depots, Paris, 1999—. 1st lt. French Cavalry, 1969-70. Recipient Sacred Treasury Order award Japanese Govt., 1982. Mem. Assn. Paris Brokers. Home: 8 rue du Boccador, 75008 Paris France Office: Caisse de Dépôts, 84 rue de Lille, 75008 Paris France

DABASY, EVA ANNA, educator, nutritionist; b. Tann, Germany, Apr. 10, 1946; d. Leo Charles Robb and Vilma Anna Baaden; m. Janos Geza Dabasy; 1 child, Julia. Cert., Tech. Tchrs. Coll., Australia, 1968; Diploma of Nutrition and Food Svc., Emily Mcpherson Coll., Australia, 1968; BEd, Latrobe U., Australia, 1978, MEd, 1984. Food sci. lectr. Emily Mcpherson Coll., 1968-70; head food sci. dept. William Angliss Inst., Australia, 1972-95, team coord. food sci. and nutrition, 1995-97, projects coord., 1997, coord. vocat. edn. and tng., degree studies, 1998—, sr. curriculum devel. officer tng. & rsch. devel. divsn., 1999—; cons. Asian Devel. Bank, Indonesia, 1993, Stds. Learning Materials and Assessment Adviser, Indonesia Australia Ptnrship for Skills Devel. Program, Travel and Tourism Project, 2000; mem. bd. of studies Edn. Dept. of Victoria, Australia, 1998-99; hon. prof. Albert Schweitzer Internat. U., Geneva, 2000—. Contbr. articles to Asean Food Jour., The Australian Runner, Jour. Home Econ. Assn. Australia. Mem. Australian Nutrition Found. (bd. dirs. 1985-89), Australian Inst. Food Sci. and Tech. (chair nutrition com. 1984-87), N.Y. Acad. Scis., London Diplomatic Acad. (mem. founding coun. 2000—). Home: 51 Buller Dr Glen Waverley, 3150 Melbourne Victoria, Australia

DABBAGH, ABDALLAH E., geology educator, research center administrator; b. Taif, Saudi Arabia, May 21, 1945; s. Eassa Abdallah and Omhani Dabbagh; m. Thuraya Ibrahim Al-Arrayed, Sept. 1969; children: May, Hashim, Noor, Layla. BSc in Geology, Am. U. Beirut, 1968; PhD in Structural Geology, U. N.C., 1975. Adminstrv. asst. Raytheon Corp., Jeddah, Saudi Arabia, 1964; rsch. asst. Coll. Petroleum and Minerals, Dhahran, Saudi Arabia, 1968-69; vis. lectr. Princeton (N.J.) U., 1975-76; asst. prof. geology U. Petroleum and Minerals, Dhahran, 1976-79; assoc. prof. geology King Fahd U. Petroleum and Minerals, Dhahran, 1980—, dir. rsch. inst., dean, 1978-97, advisor to rector, 1997—; leader sci. program of Prince Sultan bin Salman, astronaut on U.S. shuttle 51-G, 1985; advisor Min. Petroleum & Mineral Resources, 1997—; bd. dirs. Saudi Aramco, Dhahran. Mem. editorial bd. Arab Jour. for Gulf States, 1988—. Mem. Faculty Housing Devel., Dhahran, 1985-90. Scholar ARMCO, 1963-68, Gov. of Saudi Arabia, 1969-75; recipient Prince Mohammad bin Fahd award for ednl. excellence, 1989, award for scientific achievements in environment rsch., 1992. Mem. Am. Assn. Petroleum Geologists, Geol. Soc. Am. (King Faisal medal 1985), Water Scis. and Tech. Assn., Internat. Petroleum Congress (nat. standing com. 1984, nat. standing com. energy 1988—), Sigma Xi. Avocation: reading. Office: King Fahd U, Box 445, Dhahran 31261, Saudi Arabia

DABBOUSI, BASHIR OSAMA, research scientist; b. Oakland, Calif., July 15, 1969; s. Osama B. and Maysam Muwafaq (Al-Haffar) D.; m. Rasha Hisham Daadoush, Aug. 26, 1993; 1 child, Dana. Student, King Fahd U. Petroleum, Dhahran, Saudi Arabia; BS, U. Calif., Berkeley, 1991; PhD, MIT, 1997. Rsch. scientist Saudi Aramco - Lab Rsch. & Devel. Ctr., Dhahran, Saudi Arabia, 1997—. Contbr. articles to profl. jours. Predoctoral fellow MIT, Cambridge, Mass., 1991-97. Mem. Phi Beta Kappa. Avocations:

sports, travel, cuisine. Office: Saudi Aramco, PO Box 10125, Dhahran 31311, Saudi Arabia

DABBS RILEY, JEANNE KERNODLE, retired public relations executive; b. Corsicana, Tex., 1922; d. Robert and Anne (Forrest) McCluer; m. John David Kernodle, June 27, 1942 (div. 1968); 1 child, Elizabeth Kernodle Cabell; m. Jack Autrey Dabbs, Feb. 14, 1981 (dec. 1992); m. James J. Riley, Jr., June 28, 1997 (dec. 1999). BS in Sociology, Tex. Woman's U., 1970. Supr., writer pub. rels. St. Paul's Hosp., Dallas, 1974-76; dir., v.p. mktg. svcs. Fidelity Union Life Ins. Co., Dallas, 1976-81, ret., 1981. Author poetry book and greeting cards. Mem. comm. com. Mental Health Assn., Austin, Tex., 1991; pres. aux. Seton Med. Ctr., Austin, 1985-86; mem. Dallas Civic Chorus, Austin Choral Union. Recipient Editorial medal Freedoms Found. Valley Forge, 1973, Eddy award Internat. Assn. Bus. Communicators, 1974, 76, 79, Matrix award Women in Comm., Inc., 1975, Best of Show award Life Ins. Advts. Assn., 1980, Sr. Vol. award Retirees Coordinating Bd., 1989. Mem. Tex. Women's U. Alumnae Assn. (pres. Capital Area chpt. 1987-89), Tuesday Book Club Austin (pres. 1986), Austin Poetry Soc. Methodist. Avocations: book reviewer, singing. Home: 2806 Cherry Ln Austin TX 78703-2820

DABENGWA, DUMISO, Zimbabwean government official; b. Bulawano, Matebeleland, Zimbabwe, Dec. 6, 1939; s. Mavakatsha and Mahliki D.; m. Zodwa Khumalo, Aug. 8, 1980; children: Ijeoma, Sithembile, Dingumuzi, Nombulelo, Vusisizwe. Diploma, Inst. Admintrv. Mgmt., U.K., 1986. Sch. tchr. Cyrene Mission, Zimbabwe, 1958; clk. City Coun. Bulawayo, Zimbabwe, 1959-60, Barclay's Bank Bulawayo, Zimbabwe, 1961-62; with Zimbabwe African People's Union, 1963-79; with nat. army Govt. of Zimbabwe, 1980-81, 82-96, mem. parliament, dep. min. home affairs, 1990-92, min. home affairs, 1992—; mng. dir. Duze Enterprises, 1987-90; mem. Politburo Zanu Pf, 1994. Chmn. Bulawayo Province, mem. ctrl. com. ZANU P.F., 1989—; chmn. Mafela Trust, 1990; trustee Zimbabwe Devel. Trust, 1991, Edward Ndlovu Meml. Trust, 1991; active Matebeleland Zambezi Water Project-Trust, 1991, Matebeleland Devel. Found., 1992; detained Chikurubi Maximum Prison, 1984-86. Avocation: golf. Home: 39 Diamond Dr, Fourwinds Bulawayo Zimbabwe Office: Min of Home Affairs, Pvt Bag 7703, Causeway Zimbabwe

DABERKO, DAVID A., banker; b. Hudson, Ohio, 1945. BA, Denison U., 1967; MBA, Case Western Res. U., 1970. Mgmt. trainee Nat. City Bank, Cleve., 1968-72, asst. v.p., 1972-73, v.p. bank investment divsn., dept. head met. lending divsn., 1973-80, sr. v.p. corp. banking, 1980-82, pres., 1987-93; exec. v.p. corp. banking Nat. City Corp., Nat. City Bank, Cleve., 1982-85; pres., bd. dirs. Nat. City Bank (formerly BancOhio Nat. Bank), Columbus, 1985-87; dep. chmn. Nat. City Corp., Cleve., 1987-93, pres., CEO, 1993-95, chmn., CEO, 1995—; dir. Fed. Res. Bank, Cleve. Trustee Cleve. Tomorrow, Greater Cleve. Growth Assn., Case Western Res. U., Hawken Sch., Neighborhood Progress, Univ. Cir. Inc., Univ. Hosp. Health Sys.; co-chair Harvest for Hunger Campaign, 1992, 93. Mem. Bankers Roundtable. Office: Nat City Corp National City Center 1900 E 9th St Cleveland OH 44114-3401

DABINETT, DIANA FRANCES, visual artist; b. Bulawayo, Zimbabwe, Apr. 20, 1943; d. Leslie Frank and Ivy Annie (Eastwood) May; m. Patrick Dabinett, Aug. 1969; children: Emily Thomas. BA in fine arts, U. Cape Town, 1963. H.S. art tchr. Zimbabwe, 1965-66; H.S. English tchr. Eng., 1967-69; asst. curator London (Ont.) Art Gallery, 1969-73; visual arts advisor, adv. panel Fed.-Prov. Cultural Agreement, Newfoundland, Can., 1992-00; bd. mem. Ea. Edge Gallery, St. John's, 1993-99; Can. artists rep. Newfoundland and Labrador, 1980-97; artist in residence Hopedale, Labrador, 1998-99. One-woman shows St. John's, 1989-92, Lunenberg, N.S., 1992, Christine Parker Fine Art St. John's, 1994, 2000; two-person installation exhbn. Pathways, 1997-99; group exhbn. Discovery Travelling Maritimes, 1997; commd. works at Birthing Ctr. and Cancer Ctr., Cmty. Hosp. of the Monterey Peninsula, St. Lawrence Hosp., Newfoundland, N.S. Health and Welfare Dept. Halifax; illustrator book: Icebergs—Castles in the Sea, 2000. Avocations: reading, nordic skiing, hiking. Address: Box 1005, Torbay, NF Canada A1K 1K9

DABIRÉ, CHRISTOPHE JOSEPH, Burkina Faso government official; b. 1948; married; 3 children. Degree in econs. Economist-planner, chief of infrastructure and equipment dept. Govt. of Burkina Faso, 1981-84, dir. studies and projects ministry of planning, 1984-88, cons. and negotiator, 1988-92, minister of health and social affairs, 1992-94, minister of health, 1994—, min. higher edn. and sci. rsch. Office: Min Higher Education, 03 BP 704 7, Ouagadougou Burkina Faso*

DABROWSKI, EDWARD JOHN, television technical director; b. Chgo., Nov. 16, 1957; s. Edward J. and Justina J. (Grilc) D. BS in Elec. Engring., Ill. Inst. Tech., Chgo., 1979. Engr. Sta. WMAQ-TV, Chgo., 1976-83, tech. dir., 1983—; enrg.-in-charge The Jenny Jones Show, 1995. Tech. dir. (NBC afternoon spl.) The Sixth Street Kids, 1984, (WMAQ-TV docu-drama) Fast Break to Glory: Dusable Panthers, 1988, Chgo. Sisslin (Chgo. Emmy award 1989), Chgo. Bears Pre-Season football, 1993, Engring. Devel. Group, 1996—. Emmy nomination, Chgo. Chpt., 1998. Mem. IEEE, Soc. Broadcast Engrs., NATAS (Emmy nominations Chgo. chpt. 1986), Nat. Assn. Broadcast Employees and Technicians (steward Chgo. chpt. 1981-87, mobilization coord. Chgo. 1994-95), Natl. Assn. of Broadcast Employees and Technicians, Broadcasting and Cable Television Workers Sector of the Communications Workers of Amer., AFL-CIO Steward and Exec. Bd. Mem. Chgo. Local 41 1999—, Am. Radio Relay League (life), Chgo.-Suburban Radio Assn., Mus. Broadcast Comm. (charter), Am. Fraternal Union, Slovene Nat. Benefit Soc. (rec. sec. lodge 449). Democrat. Roman Catholic. Avocations: amateur radio, photography. Office: Sta WMAQ-TV NBC Tower 454 N Columbus Dr Chicago IL 60611-5514

DABROWSKI, OTTON JAN, engineering educator; b. Krosno, Poland, Dec. 13, 1922; s. Wojciech and Josepha (Forman) D.; m. Richarda Nowicka, Dec. 23, 1949; children: Lydia, Martha, Dorothy. M.Engring., Tech. U. Wrocław, Poland, 1949, Dr.Tech. Sci., 1957. Designer Design Office Engring. Constrn., Wrocław, 1950-62; lectr., sr. lectr. Tech. U. Wrocław, 1948-55, assoc. prof., 1955-66, prof., 1966—, head structural mechanics chair, 1966-68, dean civil engring. faculty, 1965-68, 71-73, 1990-93, vice-rector, 1981-82, dir. Civil Engring. Inst., 1987-90; prof. Ahmadu Bello U., Zaria, Nigeria, 1973-78. Author: Mechanics of Structures, 1961, 4th edit., 1997, Theory of Space Structures, 1987; contbr. articles to profl. jours. Decorated Gold Cross of Merit, knights cross Polonia Restituta, officers cross Polonia Restituta. Mem. Polish Assn. Theoretical and Applied Mechanics (chmn. Wrocław br. 1967-70), Polish Assn. Civil Engrs. (chmn. Wrocław br. 1967—, mem. com. of sci.), Wrocław Assn. Scis. (chmn. tech. scis. divsn. 1983-85). Avocations: tennis, skiing. Home: 144 Sudecka, 53-129 Wrocław Poland Office: Technical Univ Wrocław, 27 Wybrzeze Wyspianskiego, 50-370 Wrocław Poland

DACE, KAREN YVETTE, executive assistant, travel consultant; b. Lebanon, Ill., Feb. 18, 1957; d. Robert Daniel and Mary Frances (Gibbs) D. BA, U. Calif., Riverside, 1980. CFO Campus Crusade for Christ, Nairobi, Kenya, 1986-92, exec. sec., 1991-95, exec. asst., 1995—; travel cons. Mem. Alpha Kappa Alpha. Baptist. Avocations: mountain climbing, modeling. Home: PO Box BW 1335, Borrowdale Harare Zimbabwe Office: Campus Crusade for Christ, P Bag BW 6249, Borrowdale Harare Zimbabwe

DACEY, ROBERT FRANK, accountant, executive; b. Dayton, Ohio, Aug. 8, 1954; s. Frank Robert and Florence Helen (Duckro) D.; m. Lauri Solita Castillo, May 20, 1989. BBA magna cum laude, U. Cin., 1977; JD, George Mason U., 1996. CPA, Ohio. Sr. acct. Deloitte Haskins & Sells, Cin., 1977-79; bus. mgr., contr. United Press Internat., Inc., London, 1979-81; sr. mgr. Deloitte & Touche, Washington, N.Y.C., Cin., 1981-91; dir. GAO, Washington, 1991—. Editor GAO Financial Audit Manual, 1992. Instr. Junior Achievement, Cin., 1983-85; pres. Milford (Ohio) Area Jaycees, 1984. Mem. AICPA. (cert. info. systems auditor), Beta Gamma Sigma. Avocations: bicycling, hiking, scuba diving. Home: 1601 Wrightson Dr Mc Lean VA 22101-4418 Office: GAO 441 G St NW Washington DC 20548-0001

DACORONIAS, DIMITRI, physician, researcher; b. Rome, May 26, 1956; s. Antonio Dimitri and Adele (Guerrini) D. MBChB, State Med. Sch., Rome, 1982, diploma in vascular surgery, 1987. Asst. biomed. rschr. Coun. Nat. Rsch., Rome, 1978-79; intern State Med. Sch., Rome, 1979-82; house surgeon Addolorata Hosp., Rome, 1982-87; physician Italian NHS, Rome, 1986-87, asst. pub. medicine, 1988; clin. monitor, proj. team leader, clin. supr. Bracco Spa, Milan, 1988-2000; med. affairs mgr. CVS Drugs Chiesi Group, Parma, 2000—; head clin. rsch. cardiovascular drugs, project coord. Chiesi Spa, Parma, 2000—; vis. tchr. G.P. Assn., Rome, 1986-87; vis. prof. Med. Sch., Rome, 1996. With Italian Mil., 1982-83. Fellow Internat. Coll. Angiology, Royal Coll. Physicians (faculty pharm. medicine); mem. Ordine Dei Medici, Am. Heart Assn., Drug Info. Assn. Avocations: golfing, sailing, bridge. E-mail: d.dacoronias@chiesigroup.com. Home: Bainsizza Sq 10, 00195 Rome Italy Office: Chiesi Group R&D Divsn, Palermo 26/A, 43100 Parma Italy

DACOUTROS, JOHN GEORGE, food and drink technologist, business executive; b. Malta, July 5, 1941; s. George John and Virgnia Mary (Anastasi) D.; m. Yolanda Carm Ellul, Apr. 30, 1967; children: Diana, Cristina. Student, U. Bristol, Eng., 1960-62. Cert. food and drink technologist. Wine maker John Dacoutros & Sons, Malta, 1963-74; soft drinks bottler Dacoutros Group, Malta, 1964-89, fruit juice producer, 1990—; CEO, Malta Film Studios, 1980-82; water treatment cons. film producer, film dir.; patentee various purification and desalination processes. Pres. Local Residents Assn., 1986—. Recipient 56 film awards in 35 countries, 1970-89. Fellow Brit. Bottlers Inst.; mem. Malta C. of C., Lions Club of Malta, Casino Maltese, Knights of Malta, Malta Inst. Mgmt. Roman Catholic. Avocations: cinematography, photography, boating, tending vineyards. Home: Dar Joland, Triq Harrub, NXR 09 Madliena Malta

DACRE, PAUL MICHAEL, newspaper editor; b. Nov. 14, 1948; s. Peter and Joan Dacre; m. Kathleen Thomson, 1973; 2 children. Degree with honors in English, Leeds (Eng.) U. Reporter, feature writer, assoc. features editor Daily Express, 1970-76, Washington and N.Y.C. corr., 1976-79; N.Y. Bur. chief Daily Mail, 1980; news editor Daily Mail, London, 1981-85, asst. editor news and fgn., 1986, exec. editor features, 1987, assoc. editor, 1989-91, editor, 1992—; editor Evening Standard, London, 1991-92; dir. Assoc. Newspaper Holdings, London, 1991—, Teletext Holdings Ltd., 2000—; mem. Press Compaints Commn., 1998; bd. dirs. DMGT, plc. Office: Daily Mail, 2 Derry St Kensington, London W8 5TT, England

DACRE OF GLANTON, BARON **See TREVOR-ROPER, H(UGH) R(EDWALD)**

DA CRUZ VILAÇA, JOSÉ LUÍS, judge, government executive, law educator, legal counsel; b. Braga, Portugal, Sept. 20, 1944; married; 4 children. Law Degree, U. Coimbra, 1966, postgrad., 1967; DEA in Internat. Econs., U. Paris I, 1976, Doctorate in Internat. Econs., 1978. Asst. lectr. law, dept. polit. and econ. scis. U. Coimbra, 1966-72, lectr. polit. econs. law, 1972-73, prof. fin. econs. law, 1982-83; prof. tax law Adminstrn. Study and Tng. Ctr, U. Coimbra; prof. Centre European Studies; mem. Assembly of the Republic, Portuguese Parliament, 1980-86; state sec. Dept. Interior Ministry, Portugal, 1980, Prime Minister's Office, Portugal, 1981-82, Dept. European Integration, Portugal, 1982; full prof., dir. Inst. European Studies Lusiada U., Lisbon, 1988—; adv. gen. Court of Justice of European Cmtys., 1986-88; pres. Court of First Instance of European Cmtys., 1989-95, mem. com. wise men reform EU jud. sys.; ptnr. PLMJ & Assocs., Lisbon; speaker in Congress; exec. com. mem. Christian Democrat Group, 1983, v.p., 1985; v.p. CDS, 1985; adv. com. Acad. European Law, European U. Inst.; mem. scientific com. Rechts Akademie Univ. Trier; lectr. profl. and legal institutions in Portugal, Spain, France, Italy, Germany, United Kingdom, Belgium, Greece, Austria, Brazil, Morocco, U.S., Argentina, Colombia, Peru, Bolivia, and Ecuador. Nat. svc. as head Legal Dept., Ministry of the Marine, 1969-72. Recipient Special citation in the Naval Order; decorated Gran Croce del Ordine di Merito della Repubblica Italiana, Grand-Croix de l'Ordre de la C. de C., Luxembourg. Mem. European Air Law Assn. (com. mgmt. mem.), Comite d Orientation Found. for European Studies, Portuguese Assn. European Law (sec. gen.). Office: Pereira & Assocs, Ave Liberdade 224, 1250-148 Lisbon Portugal

DADÁK, VLADIMIR JAN, biochemistry educator; b. Starnov, Moravia, Czech Republic, Nov. 9, 1931; s. Jan and Augusta (Konecná) D.; m. Bozena Páleníková, Dec. 17, 1959; 1 child, Hana. B, Palacky U., Olomouc, Czechoslovakia, 1951; M, J.E. Purkyne U., Brno, Czechoslovakia, 1953, PhD, 1959; DSc, Czech Acad. Sci., Prague, 1976. Chemistry diplomate. Asst. faculty sci. J.E. Purkyne U., Brno, 1959-66, docent biochemistry, 1966-73, prof. extraordinarius, 1973-79, prof. ordinarius, 1979—, sr. rschr., 1991-98; rsch. fellow Alexander von Humboldt-Stifung, Bonn, Germany, Marburg, Germany, 1967-68, Frankfurt, Germany, 1992; vis. scholar Fulbright scholar program Washington, Phila., 1991; cons. prof., rsch. adviser Lab. Biophysics, Slovak Acad. Sci., Kosice, Slovakia, 1990-92; mem. coordinating com. for rsch. plans in biology and biochemistry, Prague, Czechoslovakia, 1981-90; mem. com. Coun. for East Europe Coordination of Rsch. of Experts, Moscow, 1983-89. Exec. editor Folia, Biologia/Bratislava, 1976-88; contbr. articles to profl. jours. Mem. Soc. for Popularizatin of sci. and Tourism, Czechoslovakia, 1974—, Assn. for Gymnastics, Brno, 1963—. 1st lt. Czechoslovakian mil., 1975-91. Recipient scholarship Swedish Inst., Stockholm, 1976, Silver medal faculty sci. Palacky U., Olomouc, 1979, Gold medal J.E. Purkyne U. Faculty Sci.,Brno, 1981. Mem. Czech Bioenergetics Group (rep., del. 1981-91), Czechoslovak Biochem. Soc. (chmn. Moravia br. 1977-87), Humboldt Club of Czech Republic (com. mem. 1990-93). Avocations: history, farming, gardening, tourism. Home: Udolní 43, 60200 Brno Czech Republic Office: Masaryk U Faculty Sci Dept Biochemistry, Kotlárská 2, 61137 Brno Czech Republic

DADEN, BRADLEY FRANCIS, geologist, petroleum engineer; b. London, Walthamsto, Eng., Oct. 8, 1967; Barry Edward and Kathleen Yvonne (Evans) D. BSc in Applied Geology with hons., U. Plymouth, Eng., 1989; MSc Computing in Earth Scis., U. Keele, Staffordshire, Eng., 1990. Logging geologist Baker Hughes Inteq., Aberdeen, Scotland, 1989-92, wellsite geologist, 1992-94, drilling fields engr., 1994—. Fellow Geology Soc. London; mem. Soc. Petroleum Engrs. Avocations: hiking, fishing, reading, music, car restoration. Home: 20 Pickford Walk Avon Dale, Essex Colchester CO4 3TJ, England Office: Baker Hughes Inteq, Denmore Rd Bridge of Don, Aberdeen AB23 8FZ, Scotland

DADGARI, FARZAD, soil scientist, environmental specialist; b. Tehran, Mar. 28, 1951; arrived in Canada, 1982; s. Khalis Dadgari and Badri Pes Aran; m. Zhanet Tabib, Sept. 12, 1974; 1 child, Darius. BSc in Geology, Pahlavi U., 1974; MS in Soil Science, Shiraz U., 1978; PhD in Soil Sci., N.C. State U., 1982. Profl. agrologist, Ont., Can.; cert. profl. soil scientist, U.S. Rsch. asst., tchg. asst. Shiraz (Iran) U., 1974-78; rsch. assoc. N.C. State U., Raleigh, 1978-82, rsch. scientist, 1982; sessional lectr. U. Guelph, Ont., 1983; sr. lead scientist Acres Internat. Ltd., Niagara Falls, Ont., 1983-95; sr. project scientist Acres Internat. Corp., Amherst, N.Y., 1996-99; pres., owner FD Cons., St. Catharines, Ont., 1999—; wetlands cons. Acres Internat. Corp. Author: Soil Survey Manual for Ethiopia, 1993, Soil Fertility Initiative, 1999; editor Soil Sci. Soc. of Am. Jour., 1992-93. Vol. Heart and Stroke Found., St. Catharines, 1999-2000; mem. adv. com. Fgn. Student Com. N.C. State U., 1979-82. Mem. Ont. Inst. Agrologists, Agr. Inst. of Can., Soil Sci. Soc. Am., World Soil Conservation Soc., Soil and Water Conservation Soc., Internat. Soc. Soil Sci., Gamma Sigma Delta.

DADLANI, DURUDARSHAN HIRANAND, securities trader; b. Eldoret, Kenya, May 7, 1956; s. Hiranand Ghanshamdas and Hari Hiranand (Chhugani) D.; m. Hansa Athwani, Feb. 26, 1989; children: Jaikishin, Holi. Student, Redbridge Tech., 1974. Accounts clk. Edward Lumley & Co., London, 1974; documentary credits clk. Rafidain Bank, London, 1975; sec., P.A. Markman Frysh Ltd., London, 1976-77, various cos., London, 1977; shipping asst. Laurie & Co. Ltd., London, 1978; sec., P.A. U. London, 1979, various cos., London, 1979-90; sales rep. Sun Alliance, Hornchurch, U.K., 1991-93; commodities trader Ilford, U.K., 1993-95; accounts exec. Euroforex Currencies, London, 1995-96; del. cons. Mackenzie Assocs., London, 1996; market rsch. interviewer MORI Ltd., 1998—. Author plays; contbr. poems to profl. publs. Avocations: financial markets, family, magnotherapy, yoga, religions. Office: Goodshow Trading, 47 Oaklands Park Ave, Ilford 161 1TG, United Kingdom

DAEHLIE, BJORN, Olympic athlete; b. Elverum, Norway, June 19, 1967. Winner gold medals men's 10 and 15 kilometer cross-country skiing, silver medal men's 30 kilometer cross-country skiing XVII Winter Olympic Games, Lillehammer, Norway, 1994. Winner 12 Olympic medals including 8 gold. Office: Norwegian Olympic Committee & Confederation of Sports, Idrettens Hus Hauger Skolevei 1, 1351 Rud Norway also: c/o Nordic World 140 Webster Rd Shelburne VT 05482*

DAEHNE, LARS SIEGFRIED, chemist; b. Berlin, Sept. 2, 1959; s. Siegfried and Anneliese (Kölling) D.; m. Grit Hübschmann, Apr. 20, 1985; children: Tim, Götz. Diploma, Humboldt U., Berlin, 1986, PhD, 1990; Habilitation, Free U., Berlin, 1997. Sci. asst. Humboldt U., 1986-90; postdoctoral rsch. fellow Ciba-Geigy Found., Nagoya, Japan, 1991-92, TU Braunschweig, Germany, 1992-93; guest rsch. prof. STA Japan, Tsukuba, 1998; rschr. Max Planck Inst., Golm, Potsdam, Germany, 1999—; vis. rschr. Wayne State U., Detroit, 1997, 98. Contbr. over 30 articles to internat. jours. With German Army, 1979-81. Rsch. grantee Japan Sci. and Tech. Corp., 1998; recipient Dr. Otto Röhm Gedachtnis prize Röhm Co., 1998. Mem. German Chem. Soc., German Bunsen Soc., European Photochemistry Assn. Christian-Evangelic. Avocations: sailing, wind surfing, cross-country skiing, bicycling, walking. Home: Stillerzeile 3, 12587 Berlin Germany Office: Max Planck Inst Colloids In, Am Mühlenberg 2, 14476 Golm Potsdam, Germany

DAEMS, DANIEL, civil engineer; b. Wilrijk, Antwerp, Belgium, Aug. 11, 1958; s. Leonard and Anna (Marien) D.; m. Hilde Wouters, Feb. 22, 1982; children: Anouk, Timen. M in Electro-mech. Engring., Vrije U., Brussels, 1982, Degree in Biomed. Engring., 1983. Asst. U. Brussels, 1983-85; devel. engr. Opticable, Huizingen, 1985-88; dept. mgr. Raychem, Kessel Lo, Belgium, 1988—. Mem. Koninklijke Vlaamse Ingenieurs-Vereniging. Achievements include patents in the field of fiber optic organizers and closures. Office: Raychem, Diestsesteenweg 692, 3010 Kessel-Lo Belgium

DAEPHENKHAE, PHITAK, hospital development company executive; b. Maechan, Thailand, May 4, 1952; s. Zenku and Mylan Daephenkhae; m. Siriya Thantakyl, Aug. 15, 1989; children: Natapong, Apichaya. MD, Sun Yet-Sen Med. U., Guangzhou, China, 1980; MSc in Social Sci., Ramkumhang U., Bangkok, Thailand, 1987; PhD (hon.), Payap U., Chiangmai, Thailand. Physician Monglay Hosp., Yunnan, China, 1980-82, chief surgery, 1982-83, dep. dir., 1983-84; mng. dir. Gold Source and Investment Co., Chiangmai, 1988-96, Internat. Hosp. Devel. Co. Ltd., Chiangmai, 1996—; organizer Parker Advance Med. Ctr., Guangzhou, 1997-99, Cina Urology Inst., Beijin, 1998-99; rsch. scientist S.E. Asia Dept., Wuhan Social Sci. Inst., 1988-90; cons. Lialdou Secondary Sch., 1995-99, Orphanage and Aged Home, 1995-99. Lt. Thailand armed forces, 1966-76. Recipient Best Svc. award Lialdou Secondary Sch., 1997, Best Donation award Bhudism Study Inst., 1998. Home: 411/17-18 M 5 Maejo Land, Sansai Rd, Chiangmai 50290, Thailand Office: Internat Hosp Devel Co Ltdf, 181 Rajvithi Rd Sriphoom, Chaingmai 50200, Thailand

DAESCU, CONSTANTIN, chemist, educator; b. Bucharest, Romania, May 21, 1943; s. Ioan and Ana (Teslea) D.; m. Ana-Elena Bob, Nov. 25, 1967; children: Dana-Voica, Mihai. Engr., Politech. U. Timisoara, 1966, D, 1977. Asst. Politech. U. Timisoara, Romania, 1966-77; prof. Politech. U. Timisoara, 1977—; cons. Industry, Romania, 1985—; expert Internat. Monetary Fund, Romania, 1996—. Author: Drug Chemistry and Technology, 1994; Drugs Industry, 1999. Patentee in field; contbr. articles to profl. jours. Capt. Romanian Army Res. Fellow Romanian Chem. Soc.; mem. N.Y. Acad. Scis. Orthodox Christian. Avocations: oenology, country ceramics, mountains. Home: 11-13 Take Ionescu, 1900 Timisoara Romania Office: Politehnica Univ, Piata Victoria 2, 1900 Timisoara Romania

DAESETY, VISHNUVARDHAN, biologist, researcher; b. Vellore, India, Jan. 2, 1966; s. Munirathnam and Vijayalakshmi Daesety; m. Geetha Srinivas, Aug. 5, 1996; 1 child, Vikram. BS, S.V. U., Tirupathi, India, 1986; MSc, S.K. U., Anantapur, India, 1989; PhD, Mysore U., India, 1995. Jr. rsch. fellow Ctrl. Food Technol. Rsch. Inst., Mysore, 1989-93, sr. rsch. fellow, 1993-95; rschr. Nat. Inst. Biosci. and Human Tech., Tsukuba, Japan, 1995-97; fellow Tufts U., Boston, 1997-99, rsch. assoc., 2000—. E-mail: dvishnuv@yahoo.com.

DAEUBLER-GMELIN, HERTA, government official; Mem. parliament Govt. of Germany, 1982—, now min. of justice. Office: Ministry of Justice, Postfach 200365 Heinemannstr 6, 53175 Bonn Germany*

DAFTUAR, CHITTRANJAN NARAIN, psychology educator; b. Patna, Bihar, India, Oct. 5, 1940; s. Jugal Kishor and Janki (Devi) D.; m. Mirdula Smiriti Manju, May 9, 1969; children: Soma C., Shalav C., Lucky C. BA with honors, Patna (India) U., 1960, MA, 1962; diploma, Indian Inst. Tech., 1964; DLitt, Magadh U., 1985. Prof. Maharaja Sayaji Rao U., Baroda, India, former head of psychology dept.; hon. dir. Salahkaar Cons., Baroda, 1983—, Coun. of Behavioral Rsch., India, 1972—. Author: Job Attitudes in Indian Management, 1980, Organizational Behaviour, 1992, Behavioral Quotient, 2000; editor Behaviorometric, 1971—; editor ASRAM newsletter, 1998—; contbr. articles to profl. jours. and editl. bd. 5 profl. jours. Mem. Indian Soc. for Tng. Devel. (chairperson Baradoa chpt. 1985-87, nat. coun. mem. 1987-97), Internat. Assn. of Applied Psychology, Am. Psychology Assn. (fgn. affiliate), Assn. Stress Rsch. and Mgmt. (founder chmn. 1998—), Indian Assn. of Applied Pscyh. (regl. chmn.). Hindu. Avocations: reading, meditation, watching TV, writing, management training. Office: Dept Psychol MS Univ, University Rd, Bardoa 390002, India

DAGAR, SURENDER, textile chemist; b. India, May 12, 1973. B in Tech. in Textile Chemistry, Guru Jambheshwar U., Hisar, India, 1996; MSc in Tech. in Textile Chemistry, U. Mumbai, Matunga, India, 1999. Shift in-charge prodn. sewing thread unit Vardhman Group, Mahavir Spinning Mills Ltd., Hoshiapur, India, 1996-97, exec. sewing thread unit, 1999; fabrics exec. Shahi Export Ho., Okhla-New Delhi, India, 1999—. Active, Nat. Svc. Scheme. Mem. Am. Chem. Soc., Textile Assn. India (life). Avocation: handball. Home: H # 338, Sector 16, Faridabad 121 002, India

DAGAS, CONNIE, publishing executive; b. Montagut, Spain, Apr. 30, 1956; d. Jaoquin and Pilar (Grabulosa) D. Head receptionist California Apts., Salou, Spain, 1985-86; overseas exec. Viajes Simon, Salou, Spain, 1986-87; incoming sr. exec. Iberian Svcs. Ltd., London, 1988-90; incoming mgr. Latin Travel Ltd., London, 1990-93; co-owner, Libreria Complices, Barcelona, Spain, 1994—; co-owner, gen. mgr. Egales, Barcelona, Spain, 1995—. Editor: Nadador Nocturno, 1997, Diario De Suzanne, 1998, Glamour En Antena, 1998, El Ultimo Verano, 1999, Six of One, 1999, Ahora y Entonces, 2000, Amigos y Amantes, 2000. Avocations: travel, theatre, cinema, photography, walking. Office: Egales, Cervantes 2, 08002 Barcelona Spain

DAGAUT, PHILIPPE, chemist, researcher; b. Chateauroux, France, May 4, 1960; s. Robert and Josette (Blanchard) D.; m. Edith Marthe Jacquet, June 20, 1988; children: Noé, Jérémie. Maitrise in Chemistry, U. Orleans, France, 1983; DEA, P.M. Curie U., Paris, 1984, PhD, 1986. Guest worker Nat. Bur. Stds., Gaithersburg, Md., 1987-88; rsch. chemist CNRS, Orleans, 1988—; reviewer Combustion Inst., Pitts., 1992—; prin. investigator E.C. contracts, 1995—; supr. PhD students, U. Orleans, 1990—. Co-author: Trends in Physical Chemistry, 1992, 99; co-author: Advances in reactor design and Combustion Science, 1990; contbr. articles to profl. jours.; editl. adv. bd. Internat. Jour. Chem. Kinetics, 1996-98. Mem. Combustion Inst. French Section (Prix de Thèse Paul Laffite 1987). Achievements include research on chemical kinetic model for natural gas combustion; chemical kinetic model for kerosene combustion and NOx, chemical kinetic model for NO-Reburning. Office: CNRS-LCSR, 1C Ave de la Recherche Sci, 45071 Orleans Cedex 2, France

DAG-ELLAMS, IDRIS, neurosurgeon; b. Agenebode, Edo, Nigeria, Oct. 2, 1949; s. Alhassan Garba Rekyia (Aigbona) E.; m. Ugonwa Okpara; children: aisha, Nkechi, Naema, Ayman. Grad., Christiana Albertina U., Kiel,

Germany, 1979, MD, 1982. Resident, rsch. fellow Justus Liebig U. Hosp., Giessen, Germany, 1979-85; cons., sr. lectr. Ahmadu Bello U. Hosp., Zaria, Nigeria, 1985-89; neurosurgeon King Khalid Hosp., Najran, Saudi Arabia, 1989-90; cons. Kign Abdul Aziz Hosp., Jeddah, Saudi Arabia, 1990-91; locum sr. cons. King Fahd Hosp., Hofuf, Saudi Arabia, 1991-92; sr. cons. Al-Noor Specialist Hosp., Makkah, Saudi Arabia, 1993—, head dept. neurosurgery, 1993—, chmn. surg. divsn., 1993-99, dep. chief med. dir., 1993-99; chmn., exec. dir. Nanfield Inc., Mississauga, Can., 1999. Contbr. articles to profl. jours. Fellow West African Coll. Surgeons; mem. AAAS, N.Y. Acad. Scis., Nigeria Med. Assn. (pres. 1982-85), Rotary. Avocation: reading.

DAGHIR, NUHAD JOSEPH, dean; b. Beirut, Feb. 22, 1935; s. Joseph Asad and Angel (Nahas) D.; m. Mona Nassar, July 24, 1965; children: Ramzi, Samir, Nabil. BS, Am. U. Beirut, 1957; MS, Iowa State U., 1959, PhD, 1962. Asst. prof. Am. U. Beirut, 1962-67, assoc. prof., 1967-75, prof., 1975-86, dean faculty agriculture, 1996—; dir. tech. svcs. Shaver Poultry Co., Cambridge, Ontario, Canada, 1986-92; dean faculty of agriculture U. Arab Emirates U., Al-Ain, 1992-96; agrl. cons. FAO, Amman, Jordan, 1972-73, ARAMCO, Saudi Arabia, 1968-69, various poultry cos., 1962—, Kuwait Inst. for Sci. Rsch., 1990, 92. Editor: Poultry Production in Hot Climates, 1995, Procs. 6th Symposium on Nutrition and Health in the Near East, 1971; author: Encyclopedia of Animal Production in Lebanon, 1984; contbr. articles to profl. jours. Commr. Lebanese Boy Scout Assn., Beirut, 1952-57. Mem. World Poultry Sci. Assn. (pres. Lebanese br. 1963-84), Am. Poultry Sci. Assn., Am. Inst. Nutrition, Gamma Sigma Delta, Sigma Xi. Avocations: swimming, reading, music. Home and Office: Am U Beirut, Beirut Lebanon

DAGIT, DEBORAH LYNNE, high technology executive; b. San Francisco; d. Daniel O'Neil Morris and June Lillis Read; m. Daniel F. Dagit, July 4, 1997; 1 child, Alexandra Isabelle. BS in Psychology with honors, Oreg. State U., 1982; postgrad., San Jose State U., 1988. Human resources generalist Signetics Corp. (now Philips Semiconductor), Sunnyvale, Calif., 1983-87; ops. mgr. Bridge-to-Jobs, Sunnyvale, 1987-91; sr. mgr. stratetic cultural initiatives Sun Microsystems, Inc., Mountain View, Calif., 1991-93; dir. performance support Silicon Graphics, Inc., Mountain View, 1993—; spkr. in field. Contbr. articles to profl. jours. Founding mem. conf. bd. Workforce Coun. in Diversity; mem. Equal Employment Adv. Coun., Pres.'s Com. on Employment of People with Disabilities; bd. vice chair Alliance for Cmty. Care; mem. Human Rights Campaign. Recipient No. Calif. Human Resources Coun. award for profl. excellence, 1992, Tribute to Women in Industry award, 1996, Gay & Lesbian Ctr. Corp. Vision award, 1998; named Advocate of Yr., Santa Clara County Com. for Employment of Disabled, 1998. Mem. PMAA, PABA, SHRM, NCHRC, ILG. Fax: (650) 932-0912. E-mail: dagit@sgi.com. Office: Silicon Graphics Inc MS 705 1600 Amphitheatre Pkwy Mountain View CA 94043-1351

DAGNINO-PASTORE, JOSE MARIA, economist, consultant; b. Buenos Aires, Nov. 19, 1933; s. Lorenzo Dagnino-Pastore and Elida Locci; m. Irene María Lipka, Sept. 11, 1959; children: Sandra, Silvia. CPA, Nat. U. of La Plata, Argentina, 1953, D of Econ. Sci., 1954; MA in Econs., U. Calif., Berkeley, 1960; AM in Econs., Harvard U., 1961, PhD in Econs., 1963. Sr. economist, rsch. dir. Di Telle Inst. Found. L.Am. Econ. Rsch., Argentina, 1963-65, 65-66; exec. sec. Nat. Devel. Coun., Argentina, 1968-69; Minister of the Economy Govt. of Argentina, 1969-70, 82; amb.-at-large Govt. of Argentina, Geneva, Switzerland, 1976-78; advisor, cons. 4 countries, 12 internat. orgns., 1978—; chmn. Econométrica, Argentina, 1978—, 25th ann. meeting World Bank, Washington, 1970; bd. dirs., chmn. Banespa, Argentina, 1991; bd. dirs., exec. dir. Fortabat Group of Cos., Argentina; bd. dirs. Air Liquide, Sudameris Bank, Pirelli Group of Cos. Author: Income and Money, Argentina, 1935-60 (O. Gimenez prize 1965), Economic Chronicles, Argentina 1969-88, The New Look of the Argentine Economy, 1995; contbr. over 60 articles to internat. books and jours. in field. Mem. Italo Argentina Coop., Argentina, 1990, 91—, Ginastera Found., 1991; bd. dirs. Fortabat Found., Argentina, 1989; mem., bd. dirs. Inter Am. Dialogue, Washington, 1981, 92—; bd. dirs, vice chmn. Nat. Endowment for the Arts, Argentina, 1992, 97—. Decorated medals, Govt. Bolivia, Govt. Belgium, 1970; recipient O Giménez Found. prize. Mem. Nat. Acad. Econ. Sci. (Argentina), Acad. Strategy (Argentina), Coll. Grads. in Econ. Sci., Argentine Assn. Polit. Econs., Argentine Coun. on Fgn. Rels. (counselor). Roman Catholic. Fax: 54-1-4815-9691. E-mail: dpastore@datamarquets.com.ar. Office: Cerrito 1136 EP, 1010 Buenos Aires Argentina

DAGOGO-JACK, SAMUEL E., medical educator, physician scientist, endocrinologist; b. Abonnema, Rivers, Nigeria, Mar. 17, 1954; came to U.S., 1990; s. Karibi Jim and Titty (Biribota) D.-J.; m. Agbani Ibinabo Iyalla, May 28, 1983; children: Karibi, Ibi, Alali, Tari. MBBS, U. Ibadan (Nigeria), 1978, MD, 1994; MSc, U. Newcastle Upon Tyne (U.K.), 1988. Diplomate Am. Bd. Internal Medicine, Am. Bd. Endocrinology, Am. Bd. Diabetes and Metabolism. Rsch. assoc. U. Newcastle Upon Tyne (U.K.), 1983-85; cons. physician U. Port Harcourt (Nigeria), 1985-89; chief resident endocrinologist King Faisal Specialist Hosp., Riyadh, Saudi Arabia, 1989-90; rsch. fellow Washington U. Sch. Medicine, St. Louis, 1990-92, instr. medicine, 1992-93, asst. prof. medicine, 1993-97, assoc. prof. medicine, 1998—; assoc. chief internal medicine svc. Barnes-Jewish Hosp., St. Louis, 1996-2000; prof. medicine, dir. diabetes program U. Miss. Med. Ctr., Jackson, 2000—; dir. minority health rsch. Montgomery VA Med. Ctr., Jackson, 2000—; lectr. St. Louis Acad. Scis., 1995, The Ethical Soc., 1996; lectr. Nat. Diabetes Edn. Initiative, 1997—; ad-hoc reviewer for numerous sci. jours.; extra-mural rschr. diabetes drugs devel. programs for the pharm. industry; chair Excellence Diabetes Mgmt. Symposium, 1998-99. Author: The Diabetes Guide, 1992, (with others) The Washington Manual, 1995, The Uncomplicated Guide to Diabetes Complications, 1999; internat. editl. adv. bd. Kuwait Med. Jour., 1995-98; mem. editl. adv. bd. Current Drug Targets; contbr. over 100 articles to profl. jours. Diabetes Prevention grantee NIH, 1994—, Diabetes Rsch. & Tng. Ctr. grantee, 1999—; recipient Young Investigator Travel award Internat. Soc. Endocrinology, 1987; grantee Diabetes Rsch. Tng. Ctr., 1999-2000. Fellow ACP (co-dir. workshop urban health 1998), Royal Coll. Physicians (London), Am. Fedn. Clin. Rsch.; mem. AAAS, Am. Diabetes Assn. (sec. St. Louis chpt. 1997-98, pres. 1998-00, mem. sci. and med. adv. group, rsch. fellow 1990-91, clin. rsch. award 1997—), Endocrine Soc., Am. Fedn. for Med. Rsch., Ctrl. Soc. for Clin. Rsch. (chmn. endocrinology sect. 2000—). Achievements include nat. and internat. diabetes edn. and rsch. programs, extra-mural research director diabetes drugs development programs. Office: Dept Medicine U Miss Med Ctr 2500 N State St Jackson MS 39216

DAGTOGLOU, PRODROMOS, lawyer, educator; b. Athens, Greece, Dec. 24, 1929; s. Dimitrios and Olga (Karipides) D.; m. Genette Malet de Carteret, Apr. 17, 1963; children: Miranda Olga, Ion Dimitris, Olivia. Law Diploma, U. Athens, 1951; JD, U. Heidelberg, Germany, 1959, Hon. Prof. Law., 1981. Bar: Athens, 1954. Asst. prof. law Sch., U. Heidelberg, 1962-67, assoc. prof., 1967-68; prof. law Law Sch., U. Regensburg, Germany, 1968-76; prof. law Law Sch., U. Athens, 1976-97, emeritus prof., 1998—; vis. fellow All Souls Coll., Oxford (Eng.) U., 1972-73, Sch. Law, U. Calif., Berkeley, 1978, 88, U. Dijon (France), 1987, Nat. U. Yokohama, Japan, 1992, others; hon. prof. law U. Regensburg, 1981—; hon. sr. lectr. Univ. Coll., U. London, 1981—; legal expert civil aviation European Commn., Brussels, 1994-97; pvt. practice law London, Athens. Author: Human Rights, 1991, Administrative Law, 4th edit., 1997, Administrative Courts Procedure, 2d edit., 1994, European Community Law, Vol. I, 2d edit., 1985, supplements, 1989, 93, Vol. II, 1998. Pres. Nat. Broadcasting Coun. of Greece, Athens, 1989-91. Mem. European Air Law Assn. London (pres. 1988—), Fedn. Internat. de Droit Europeen (pres. 1986-88), Hellenic Assn. European Law (pres. 1986-92, 94—). Office: Nat U Athens, Hippokratous 33, Athens 106 80, Greece

DAGUM, ESTELA BEE, statistician, researcher; b. Cordoba, Argentina, Nov. 30, 1935; arrived in Canada, 1972; d. Hector Ernest and Ida (Reolon) Bee; m. Camilo Dagum, Dec. 22, 1958; children: Alexander, Paul, Leonardo. PhD summa cum laude, Nat. U. Cordoba, 1960. Asst. prof. Nat. U. Cordoba, 1963-65, assoc. prof., 1966; sr. rschr. Mathematica, Princeton, N.J., 1967-68; prof. Nat. U. Mex., Mexico City, 1968-70, Coe Coll., Cedar Rapids, Iowa, 1971-72; head Statistics Canada, Ottawa, Ont., 1972-76, chief, 1977-80, dir. rsch., 1981-93; vis. prof. U. Bologna, Italy, 1994-98; full prof. U. Bologna, 1999—; sr. advisor U.S. Presdl. Commn. on Labor Statistics, Washington, 1978-79, U.S. Bur. Census, Bur. Labor, 1977, Australian Bur. Statistics, Canberra, 1985, Ctrl. Statis. Office, London, 1994-96, Ctrl Bur. Statistics, Jerusalem, Israel, 1996, Stats. New Zealand, 1998, Australian Bur. Stats., 1998; mem. U.S. Nat. Acad. Scis. Commn. on Energy Modeling, 1990-92; adj. prof. faculty engring. U. Western Ont., 1985-93. Contbr. articles to profl. jours. Recipient Julius Shiskin award Washington Statis. Soc., 1980. Fellow Am. Statis. Assn. (com. on energy 1987-90), Internat. Inst. Forecasters (pres. 1988-90, bd. dirs. 1985-90, Crystal Globe award 1996); mem. Internat. Assn. Rsch. in Income and Wealth, Statis. Soc. Can. (program chair 1989), InterAm. Statis. Inst. (v.p. 1997—). Achievements include author of XII-ARIMA seasonal adjustment method adopted by majority of statistical bureaus. Office: U Bologna Fac Statis Scis, Via delle Belle Arti 41, 40126 Bologna Italy

DAGUZAN, JACQUES JEAN EDMOND, research biologist, educator; b. Eure, France, Nov. 7, 1940; s. Jean and Gladyss (Piel) D.; m. Michèle Tronyo, Oct. 24, 1939; children: Elisabeth, Philippe. B in Biol. Scis., U. Rennes, France, 1963, M in Biol. Sics., 1965, PhD in Biol. Scis., 1967, DSc, 1975. Tchr. secondary sch. Rennes, 1961-63; rschr., lectr. U. Rennes, 1964-68, rsch. sr. lectr., 1968-82; prof. 2d class U. Rennes I, 1982-90, prof. 1st class, head of lab. of zoology and ecophysiology, 1999-2000, prof., 1997; v.p. bd. admission Natural Scis. Aggregation, Paris, 1993-96; cons. in field of molluscs, bioecology, ecophysiology, and heliciculture. Decorated Knight of Agr., 1989, Knight of Acad., 1990, Officer of Agr., 1996. Mem. French Malacol. Soc. (pres. 1986-88), French Zool. Soc., French Ecol. Soc., Malacol. Soc. London. Avocations: classical music, collecting famous vintage wines, genealogy. Home: 9 rue du champ Gaudois, 35510 Cesson-Sevigne France Office: U Rennes I Lab Zool & Ecophysiology, Ave General Leclerc, 35042 Rennes France

DAHABA, ASHRAF AZIZ, anesthesiologist; b. Cairo, May 4, 1959; arrived in Austria, 1991; s. Abdel Aziz and Atiat Dahaba. B Medicine B Surgery, Cairo U., 1982, MSc in Anesthesiology, 1988, MD, 1997; PhD in Anesthesiology, Karl Franzens U., Graz, Austria, 1994. Resident in anesthesia Cairo U., 1985-88, lectr. in anesthesia, 1988-91; rschr. dept. anesthesia Karl Franzens U., Graz, 1991-97, 98—; rschr. Ludwig Boltzmann Inst., Vienna, Austria, 1997-98; rschr. in field. Contbr. articles to profl. jours. Home: Lohnberg 27, 8181 St Ruprech/Raab Austria Office: Dept Anesthesiology, Auenbruggerplatz 29, A-8036 Graz Austria

DAHINDEN, JUSTUS, architect; b. Zurich, Switzerland, May 18, 1925; s. Joseph and Eugenie (Kraus) D.; diploma architect Fed. H.S. Tech., Zurich, 1949, Dr. sc. techn., 1956; Dr. (hon.) Tech. U., Sch. Architecture, Bratislava, Slovakia; m. Marta Arquint, Dec. 23, 1950; children: Zeno, Ivo, Delia. Pvt. practice architecture, Zurich, 1955—; prof. Vienna Tech. U., 1974; vis. prof. Faculty Architecture and Urbanism, Buenos Aires U. 1988—, prof. Internat. Acad. Architecture, 1988—; prof. honoris causa Archtl. Inst. Georgian Tech. U., 1995. Recipient 12 1st prizes nat. and internat. competitions; award for excellence in design of Uganda Martyrs' Shrine, Mityana, Uganda, from Guild for Religious Architecture at St. Louis Nat. Conf. on Religious Architecture, 1969; award for superlative achievement interior design for Hostellerie RigiKaltbad, Institutions mag., 1969; award for superlative achievement for interior design Tantris Restaurant, Institutions mag., 1959; Grand Prix Internat. d'Urbanisme et d'Architecture Paris/Cannes, 1979; Grand Prix d'Architecture, CEA, Paris, 1981; World Biennale of Architecture award INTERARCH for Huma 20000, 1983, INTERARCH Sofia award, 1981, 85, 87, 89. Fellow AIA (hon.); mem. Société Internationale des Artistes Chretiens (v.p., hon. pres.), NAUTILUS Found. (v.p., mem. HEPTAGON group 1989). Research on new urban structure, Akro-Polis. Outstanding works include: National Shrines of Mityana and Namugongo, Uganda, 1969; numerous Cath. Chs. in Switzerland, Italy, Germany, Africa, China; Pyramidal Office Bldg., Zurich, 1970; Swiss vacation village Twannberg, 1973; Trigon village, Doldertal, Zurich, 1975; project for Floating Hotels, Migros Ctr. Ostermundigen, CH, 1989, Holy Sergeij Cathedral for 2000 faithful, St. Petersburg, Russia, 1994—, touring exhbn., Paris, Milan, Sofia, Tokyo, Buenos Aires, Sao Paulo, Rome, Moscow, Tbilisi, 1981—; Leisure City at Munich, Germany, 1975; House of the Oriels, Zurich, 1983. Author: Standortbestimmung der Gegenwartsarchitektur, 1956; New Trends in Church Architecture, 1966; Urban Structures for the Future, 1971; Radio-City et Ville de Loisir, Centre d'Etudes Architecturale à Bruxelles, 1972; Thinking-Feeling-Acting, 1973, Justus Dahinden Architecture Monograph, 1987. Home: Kienastenwiesweg 41, 8053 Zurich Switzerland Office: Inst Raumgestaltung, Karlsplatz 13, A1040 Wien Austria*

DAHIYA, RAJBIR SINGH, mathematics educator, researcher; b. Rattangarh, Haryana, India, Dec. 3, 1940; came to U.S., 1968; s. Ram S. and Kesar (Devi) D.; m. Krishna Tavathia, Dec. 11, 1966; children: Madhu, Ranjan. PhD, Birla Inst. Sci. and Tech., Pilani, India, 1967. Lectr. Birla Inst. Sci. and Tech., 1967-68; asst. prof. math. Iowa State U., Ames, 1968-72, assoc. prof., 1972-78, prof., 1978—; reviewer math. revs. Zentralblat; referee applied math. jours. Contbr. over 140 rsch. papers on delay and advanced differential equations, transform theory and spl. functions to U.S., European and Australian profl. jours. Mem. Am. Math. Soc. Democrat. Hindu. Home: 3144 Sycamore Rd Ames IA 50014-4510 Office: Iowa State U Dept Math Ames IA 50011-0001

DAHL, ARLENE, actress, writer, designer, cosmetic executive; b. Mpls., Aug. 11, 1928; d. Rudolph and Idelle (Swan) D.; m. Marc A. Rosen; children: Lorenzo Lamas, Carole Christine Holmes, Stephen Andreas Schaum. Student, U. Minn., 1943-44, Mpls. Inst. Art, 1945, Minn. Coll. Music, 1944, Minn. Bus. Coll., 1944. Pres. Arlene Dahl Enterprises, 1952-67; v.p. Kenyon & Eckhart, 1967-72; pres. Woman's World divsn. Kenyon & Eckhart Advt. Agy., 1967-72; nat. beauty and health advisor Sears Roebuck Co., 1970-75; internat. dir. Sales and Mktg. Execs. Internat., 1972-75; fashion dir. O.M.A., 1975-78; pres. Dahlia Parfums, Inc., 1975-80, Dahlia Prodns., Inc., 1978-81, Dahlmark Prodns., 1981—, Scandia Cosmetics, Ltd., 1978-80; pres., chmn. Lasting Beauty Ltd., 1986—. Author: Always Ask a Man, 1965, 12 Beautyscope books, 1968, rev. edit., 1978, Arlene Dahl's Secrets of Hair Care, 1969, Arlene Dahl's Secrets of Skin Care, 1972, Beyond Beauty, 1980, Arlene Dahl's Lovescopes, 1983, Arlene Dahl's Weekly Astro Forecast, 1991, 92, 93, 94, 95, 96, 97, 98, 99, Arlene Dahl's Hollywood Horoscope internat. syndicated weekly column, 1994—; actress: (Broadway plays) including Mr. Strauss Goes to Boston, Questionable Ladies, Cyrano de Bergerac, Applause (Tony award musical), (films) including (debut) My Wild Irish Rose, The Bride Goes Wild, Reign of Terror, A Southern Yankee, Ambush, The Outriders, Three Little Words, Watch the Birdie, Scene of the Crime, Inside Straight, No Questions Asked, Desert Legion, Slightly Scarlet, Sangaree, Caribbean Gold, Jamaica Run, Diamond Queen, Here Come the Girls, Bengal Brigade, Kisses for My President, Woman's World, Journey to the Center of the Earth, Wicked as They Come, She Played with Fire, Les Poneyettes, Du Blé Enliases, The Land Raiders, The Way to Kathmandu, Fortune Is a Woman, The Big Bank Roll, Who Killed Maxwell Thorn?, Midnight Warrior, 1991, (TV shows) Lux Video Theatre, 1952-53, guest starring appearances on The Love Boat, Fantasy Island, Love American Style, One Life to Live, 1981-84, Night of 100 Stars, 1983, Happy Birthday Hollywood, 1987, All My Children, 1995, Renegade, 1995, 96, 97, Air America, 1999; hostess (TV series): Pepsi-Cola Theatre, 1954, Opening Night, 1958, Arlene Dahl's Beauty Spot, 1966, Arlene Dahl's Starscope, 1979-80, Arlene Dahl's Lovescope, 1980-82; played throughout U.S. in One Touch of Venus, The Camel Bell, Blithe Spirit, Liliom, The King and I, Roman Candle, I Married an Angel, Bell, Book and Candle, Applause, Marriage Go Round, Pal Joey, A Little Night Music, Forty Carats, Life with Father, Murder Among Friends, Dear Liar; nightclub acts Flamingo Hotel, Las Vegas, Latin Quarter, N.Y.C., musical stage appearances: Carnegie Hall, 1997, London Paladium, 1992, 1998, Salute to MGM Musicals; internat. syndicated beauty columnist Chgo. Tribune/ N.Y. News Syndicate, 1950-70, Arlene Dahl's Lucky Stars Column, Globe Communications, 1988-90, Arlene Dahl's Starscope Mag., 1991, 92, 93, 94, 95, 96, 97, Horoscope 2000, 1999; designer sleepwear for A.N. Saab & Co., 1952-57, In Vogue with Arlene Dahl (Vogue Patterns), 1980-85, Arlene Dahl Pvt. Collection Jewelry, 1989-94, Arlene Dahl's Jewels of Fortune Home Shopping Network, 1996. Hon. life mem. Father Flannagan's Boys Town; internat. chair Pearl Buck Found.; bd. dirs. Hollywood Mus.; chair, founder Broadway Walk of Stars Found., Inc. Recipient 10 Laurel awards Box Office mag., Hollywood Walk of Fame Star, 1952, Coup de Chapeau Deaville Film Festival award, 1982, 92; named Best Coiffed, Heads of Fame awards, 1967-72, 80, award Scandinavian Hall of Fame, 1997; named Woman of the Yr., Advt. Club of N.Y.C., 1969, Mother of the Yr., 1982, Lifetime Achievement award WorldFest, 1994, Leadership in the Arts, 1997. Mem. NATAS (trustee), Acad. TV Arts and Scis. (bd. govs., v.p.), Acad. Motion Picture Arts and Scis. (vice chair N.Y. spl. events), founder, pres., Broadway Walk of Stars Found., Inc., Author's Guild, Commanderie de Bontemps du Medoc et Graves, Commanderie de Bordeaux (N.Y.), Nat. Trust for Hist. Preservation, Sierra Club, Vesterheim Norwegian/Am. Found., Film Soc., Smithsonian Assocs., UNIFEM, Edward Grieg Soc. Office: Dahlmark Prodns PO Box 116 Sparkill NY 10976-0116

DAHL, CURTIS RAY, photographer; b. Valparaiso, Ind., Sept. 1, 1954; s. Ray Gustav and Vera Mae (Guse) D.; m. Bren Bennington, Mar. 18, 1990; children: Austin, Darren. BA, Principia Coll., 1996. Tennis instr. Westlake Tennis & Swim, 1976-80; co-owner, photographer Kaish Dahl Photography, 1980-99; owner, pres. Curtis Dahl Photography, 2000—. Bd. dirs. So. Calif. chpt. Tourette Syndrome Assn., L.A., 1995—, mem. Kodak Pro Team, 1996. Mem. Profl. Photographers of Am., Wedding and Portrait Photographers Internat. (spkr. 1997—), Ohr Hatorah Synagogue. Republican. Jewish. Avocations: tennis, philanthropies, movies, floral arranging. Home: 31962 Doverwood Ct Westlake Vlg CA 91361-4110

DAHLAN, AMMAR SADIK, Saudi Arabian provincial government official; b. Makkah, Saudi Arabia, Apr. 15, 1964; s. Abdullah Dahlan and Khayryah Mohammed Monenah; m. Nahlah Ezzat Mufti, Apr. 12, 1987; children: Rana, Khayryah, Renad. BS with 1st honors, King Abdulaziz U., Saudi Arabia, 1980; MS in Design, U. Miami, 1989; PhD in Arch., U. Strathclyde, Scotland, 1997. Lic. profl. arch. Gen. mgr. Bojyl Internat., Jeddah, Saudi Arabia, 1980-82, chmn., 1992-93; chmn. ASDECO Engring. Cons., Jeddah, 1994-97; cons. to mayor Jeddah Province Municipality, 1997—. Mem. Saudi Engring. Cmty., Ministry Trade, Ryadh, 1992. Named Outstanding Cons., GOCJ, 1996; recipient award for best design Office of Gov., Makkah, 1998. Mem. Saudi Archtl. Soc. (bd. dirs. 1987), Jeddah C. of C. and Industry (engring. com. 1986-98), Omran Soc. (bd. dirs. 1989-98), Assn. Cons. Archs. (U.K.), IFMA. Avocations: swimming, horseback riding, water skiing, camping, table tennis. Fax: 009662-6994125. Home: PO Box 6220, Jeddah 21442, Saudi Arabia

DAHLAN, ZULKARNAIN, internist, pulmonology consultant; b. Padang, Indonesia, Dec. 1, 1943; s. Dahlan and Nursiah Syarif; m. Dani Wardani; children: Yani Melani, Hanafi Dahlan, M. Ansari Dahlan. MD, Padjadjaran U., Bandung, Indonesia, 1972, postgrad., 1981, 89. Diplomate in internal medicine and pulmonology. Chief med. clinic Riau Regional Office Dept. Edn., 1973-77; asst. lectr. internal medicine Padjadjaran U., 1977-81, lectr., 1981-89, sr. lectr. in pulmonology dept., 1989—; postgrad. tng. Inst. Respiratory Medicine, Prince Alfred Hosp., Sydney, Australia, 1991, Dept. Medicine, State U., Groningen, Netherlands, 1990; chief Specialist Clinic An Nur, 1993—. Author: Guidelines of Dept. Pulmonology, 1987, Guidelines of Therapy and Study of Respiratory Infection, 1992, Guidelines in the Ambulatory Treatment of Asthma, 1994; chief editor Respirology, 1995. Mem. Indonesia Respirology Assn. (gen. sec. 1993—), Indonesian ImmunoAllergy Assn. (sec. Bandung br. 1995—), Bumi Sangkuriang Club. Islamic. Avocations: reading, tennis, travel, social activities, computer. Office: Med Fac Padjadjaran U, Hasan Sadikin Hosp, Bandung 40161, Indonesia

DAHLANDER, PIA YWONNE MARIA, bank executive; b. Stockholm, Sweden, Jan. 8, 1958; d. Sten Vidolf and Helny Gunborg (Gustafson) D.; James Maybery Bevan, July 19, 1992 (div. 1998); 1 child, James Wyndham. BS in Polit. Econs., U. London, 1982; acct., London Bus. Sch., 1983. Asst. mgr. S.G. Warburg, London, 1982-86; asst. dir. Enskilda Securities, London, 1986-89; dir. Usera y Morenes, Madrid, Spain, 1989-90; exec. dir. Nordic European Ltd., London, 1990-92; v.p. Chase Manhattan, Geneva, Switzerland, 1994-2000; mng. dir. head of Europe Deutsche Bank (Suisse) S.A., Geneva, 2000—. Avocations: dancing, tennis. Home: 15 Ave Eugene Pittard, 1206 Geneva Switzerland

DAHLBEN, SALIN ABRAHAM, neuropsychiatrist; b. Rio de Janeiro, Nov. 2, 1945; came to U.S., 1973; s. Abraham and Emilia D.; m. Sonia Sapolnik, July 8, 1971 (div. 1975); m. Jean Annette Leupold, Nov. 7, 1982 (div. 1996); children: Deborah, Rachael Emily, Lindsay Johanna, Joshua Robert, Brian Andre. BS, Hebrew Coll., Rio de Janeiro, 1963; MD, Fed. U., Rio de Janeiro, 1969. Cert. Bd. Med. Quality Assurance, Calif.; diplomate Am. Bd. Psychiatry and Neurology in gen. psychiatry with added cert. in geriatric psychiatry. Mem. med. staff Naval Hosp., Rio de Janeiro, 1970-71; intern Mt. Sinai Hosp. Svcs., N.Y.C., 1973-74; resident Boston City Hosp., 1974-75; fellow in neurosurgery Lahey Clinic, Boston, 1975-76; resident in neurosurgery U. Iowa Hosps., Iowa City, 1976-78, resident in psychiatry, 1979-80; chief resident Mt. Sinai Hosp. Med. Ctr., Chgo., 1981; med. unit dir. Bridgewater State Hosp., 1983-85; med. dir. Dorchester Mental Health Ctr., Mass., 1985-87; asst. psychiatrist McLean Hosp., Belmont, Mass., 1983—; clin. instr. psychiatry Harvard Med. Sch., Boston, 1983—; clin. assoc. Mass. Gen. Hosp., 1988-98, Mass. Mental Health Ctr., 1999—; assoc. Cambridge Hosp., 1990—. 1st lt. M.D. Brazilian Navy, 1970-71. Recipient prize Assn. Med. Students, Rio de Janeiro, 1968, 69; Nat. Coun. for Rsch. scholar, 1969-70; recipient Abbey Norman Prince award Mt. Sinai Hosp. Med. Ctr., Chgo., 1981. Mem. Am. Psychiat. Assn., Am. Acad. Psychiatry and the Law, Mass. Psychiat. Soc., Mass. Med. Soc., N.Y. Acad. Scis., Am. Mensa, Harvard Faculty Club, Sigma Xi (MIT chpt.). Office: 25 Mount Alvernia Rd Chestnut Hill MA 02467-1057

DAHLE, ARNE KRISTIAN, engineering educator; b. Sunndalsøra, Sunndal, Norway, Sept. 30, 1969; s. Olav Magne and Reidun B. (Dølehuset) D. MSc, Norwegian Inst. Tech., Trondheim, 1992; PhD, Norwegian U. Sci. and Tech., Trondheim, 1996. Program leader, sr. lectr. CAST U. Queensland, Brisbane, Australia, 1997—. Cpl. Royal Norwegian Air Force, 1997. Recipient Dr Ing Mathias Sems hon. prize Norwegian Metall. Soc., 1996. Mem. Am. Foundrymen's Soc., Minerals, Metals and Materials Soc. Avocation: soccer. Home: Indooroopilly, 3/73 Fairley St, Brisbane QLD 4068, Australia Office: U Queensland Dept Mining, Minerals Materials Engring, Brisbane QLD 4072, Australia

DAHLE, EGIL ODDVAR, brewmaster; b. Bergen, Norway, Sept. 28, 1930; s. Olav and Aasta (Kongsvik) D.; m. Laila Kleppan (div. Dec., 1988); children: Lillian, Torstein; life ptnr. Sonja Korsvold. Chem. Engr., Gøteborg Tech. Inst., Sweden, 1954; Brewmaster, Scandinavian Brewing H.S., Copenhagen, Denmark, 1986. Chem. engr. Falconbridge Nikkelverk, Kristiansand, Norway, 1955-57; lab. engr. Hansa Brewery, Bergen, Norway, 1957-82, plant engr., 1982-86; head brewer Hansa Brewery, Bergen, 1986-94; retired, 1994; lectr. Norwegian Soc. Brewmasters, 1979, 93. Mem. AAAS, The Planetary Soc., Norwegian Chem. Soc., Norwegian Orgn. Engrs., Norwegian Soc. Brewmasters, Norwegeian Defence Orgn, Norwegian Soldiers in Germany (Veterans), N.Y. Acad. Scis. Avocations: mountain walking tours, music, astronomy, cosmology.

DAHLEN, TOMMY STEFAN, anthropologist; b. Stockholm, Oct. 1, 1955; s. Stefan Hans and Sigbritt (Söderberg) D.; m. Karin Gauffin, Aug. 2, 1986 (div. Jan. 1989); m. Anna Karin Birgitta Jönhagen, May 6, 1989; children: Anton, Agnes. BD, Stockholm U., 1985, PhD, 1997. Tchr. dept. social anthropology Stockholm U., 1985-90, lectr. dept. social anthropology, 1997-2000; tchr. intercultural rels. program Lesley Coll., Cambridge, Mass., 2000—; tchr. dept. social anthropology Linkopny (Sweden) U., 1997. Author: Among the Interculturalists, 1997. Mem. Soc. for Intercultural Edn., Tng. and Rsch., Internat. Comm. Assn., European Assn. Social Anthropology. Avocations: playing piano, playing flute. Office: Dept Social Anthropology, Stockholm Univ, 10691 Stockholm Sweden

DAHLGAARD, JENS JØRN, business educator; b. Aarhus, Denmark; s. Hans and Ingrid (Rasmussen) D.; m. Su Mi Park, Mar. 7, 1982; children: Susanne, Johan. MSc, Aarhus Sch Bus., 1969, DBA, 1981. Sys. engr. IBM, Aarhus, 1969-70; asst. prof. Aarhus Sch. Bus., 1970-86, prof., 1986—; mem. exec. com. European Master Program on Total Quality Mgmt. Author: The Quality Journey, 1994, Fundamentals of TQM, 1998. Office: Linköping U, 58183 Linköping Sweden

DAHLGAARD, THOMAS, oil company executive; b. Copenhagen, Jan. 16, 1945; s. Poul and Johanne Marie (Junker) D.; m. Inge Elisabeth Laursen, June 16, 1967; children: Dorthe, Pernille. MSEE, Tech. U. Denmark, Copenhagen, 1968. Sci. engr. Danish TeleTech. Rsch. Lab., Copenhagen, 1968-73; project leader Kommunedata, Copenhagen, 1973-76; sys. analyst Serpro, Rio de Janeiro, 1976-77; tech. mgr. Kommunedata, Copenhagen, 1977-81; mgr. strategic planning, tech. planning, joint ventures Danish Oil and Natural Gas A/S, Horsholm, Denmark, 1981-91; tech. mgr. Denerco Oil A/S, Horsholm, 1991—. Home: 53A Bukkeballevej, DK-2960 Rungsted Kyst Denmark Office: Denerco Oil A/S, Christianshusvej 189 PO 353, DK-2970 Hørsholm Denmark

DAHLGREN, GORAN ERIK, public health expert; b. Stockholm, Sweden, May 14, 1938; s. Gunnar and Magnhild Emma (Aurelius) D.; m. Marita Antoinette Wienbeck Dahlgren, June 23, 1964. MA, U. Stockholm, 1964. Head Rsch. Divsn. Swedish Internat. Devel. Authority, 1968-72; head dept. for health sector studies County Coun., Stockholm, 1973-78; head planning and statistical dept. Nat. Bd. Health, Sweden, 1978-83; asst. under sec. state Min. Health, Sweden, 1984-87; advisor Min. of Health, Kenya, 1987-89; rschr. Inst. Future Rsch., 1990-92; chief adv. to dir. gen. Swedish Internat. Devel. Authority, 1992-95; asst. dir. gen. Nat. Inst. Pub. Health, Sweden, 1995—; policy advisor Ministry of Health, Vietnam, 1998—; vis. prof. U. Liverpool, 1999—; sec. to nat. commn. on Fgn. Aid, 1972-73; sec. to Nat. Com. on Health and Healthcare, 1980-84; adv. group to dir. gen. of WHO, 1994—; parliamentary com. on health care policies, Sweden, 1996—; adv., expert parliamentary com. on health devel., Sweden, 1997. Author: Health-care Markets of Tomorrow -- Winners and Loosers, 1994, Public Health Policies, 1995, (with Margaret Whitehead) Policies and Strategies to Promote Equity in Health, 1996. Mem. bd. Med. Rsch. Coun., Sweden, 1995—; mem. WHO task force on health in devel., 1995—; mem. task force for formulating a nat. rsch. strategy focusing on the social etiology of poor health Social Rsch. Coun., Sweden, 1997; mem., adv. group Regional Dir. of WHO, Euro Formulation of a revised health policy for the European region, 1997. Avocations: jazz music, exploring new cultures/countries. Home: Pokalvagen 4, 11740 Stockholm Sweden Office: Nat Inst for Public Health, Olol Palmesgata 17, Stockholm Sweden

DAHLGREN, HANS, ambassador; b. Uppsala, Sweden, Mar. 16, 1948; s. Eric and Eva (Svensson) D.; m. Helena Lindgren, June 16, 1973; children: Katarina, Cecilia. Economist, Stockholm Sch. Econs., 1971. Polit. reporter TV One News Prog., Stockholm, 1970-74, dep. fgn. editor, 1976-77; polit. adviser Fgn. Ministry, Stockholm, 1975-76; press sec. Swedish Social Dem. Party, Stockholm, 1977-82; press sec. Prime Minister's Office, Stockholm, 1982-83, asst. undersecretary of state, 1983-86, ambassador, 1986-91; permanent rep. to the UN UN, N.Y.C. Home: Karin Mansdotters Vag 7, 12235 Enskede Sweden Office: Permanent Rep to Sweden on the UN One Dag Hammarskjold Plaza 885 2nd Ave 46th Fl New York NY 10017-2201*

DAHLGREN, LARS FREDRIK RUDOLF, computer engineering researcher; b. Lund, Sweden, Jan. 7, 1966; s. Rolf and Birgitta (Ahlgren) D. MS, Lund (Sweden) U, 1990, PhD, 1994. Tchg. asst. Lund (Sweden) U., 1986-90, rsch. asst., 1990-94, rsch. assoc., 1995-96; programmer Lund (Sweden) U. Hosp, 1988; asst. prof. Chalmers U. Tech., Gothenburg, Sweden, 1996—; vis. rschr. MIT, 1995-96. Contbr. articles to profl. jours. Mem. IEEE Computer Soc., Assn. Computing Machinery (spl. interest group on computer arch., spl. interest group on measurement and evaluation, spl. interest group on micro arch. and programming). Office: Chalmers U Tech, Dept Computer Engring, SE-41296 Göteborg Sweden

DAHLIN, TORLEIF, engineering educator, researcher; b. Lund, Sweden, June 7, 1957; s. Lars and Kerstin (Johansson) D.; m. Anneli Håsteen, 1987 (div.); 1 child, Cecilia; m. Gunilla Sandell, Dec. 19, 1992; children: Erik, Björn. Degree in Remote Sensing, Lund U., 1982, MS in Civil Engring., 1984, Lic. Engring., 1990, PhD in Engring., 1993. Trainee Nat. Road Adminstrn., Malmö, Sweden, 1981-82; trainee/rsch. asst. dept. civil engring. Imperial Coll. Sci. and Tech., London, 1983; trainee VIAK AB, Malmö, 1984; tchg. asst., rsch. student dept. geotechnology Lund U., 1985-93, rschr. dept. geotechnology, 1993—; Swedish project coord. for bilateral project on groundwater together with U. Zimbabwe, 1989—; project coord. for rsch. project on elec. methods for mapping of aquifers, waste deposits and groundwater pollution, 1994-96, rsch. project on geophys. methods for mapping and monitoring waste deposits, 1995-98; coord. rsch./tng. project on environ. pollution Nicaragua, 1998—; supr. doctorate students U. Lund, U. Zimbabwe. Contbr. articles to profl. jours. Recipient Teknikbrostiftelsens grant for comml. application of rsch. results, 1995. Home: Skyttelinjen 41, S-22649 Lund Sweden Office: Dept Geotechnology, Lund U Box 118, S-221 00 Lund Sweden

DAHLMAN, ROLAND SVEN, advocate; b. Stockholm, Nov. 2, 1945; s. Carl Ludvig and Agnes Anna (von Axelson) Dahlman de Forstena; m. Gunilla Ulla Gordh, June 1, 1968; children: Roland Jr., Elisabet. LLB, U. Stockholm, 1970; LLM, Harvard U., 1974. Bar: Sweden. Assoc. Cleary, Gottlieb, Steen & Hamilton, Brussels, 1976-80; ptnr. Advokatfirman Södermark, Stockholm, 1980-91, Dahlman Advokatbra, Stockholm, 1992—; chmn. bd. dirs. Dow Agroscis. AB, Malmö, Sweden, Solvay Nordic AB, Täby, Sweden; bd. dirs. Erasteel Kloster AB, Söderfors, Sweden, Nortel Networks Nordic AB, Stockholm; consul gen. of Madagascar, Stockholm, 1991—; dean consular corps., Stockholm, 1997—. Author handbooks Internat. Taxation I and II, 1974; contbr. articles to legal jours. Pres. Kjellin Found., Karlstad, Sweden, 1990—; dir. Children's House Found., Stockholm, 1999—; auditor Nobility and Chivalry of Sweden, Stockholm, 1998—. Decorated Knight of the Order of St. John, Sweden, 1995, Knight of the Order of the Crown, His Majesty the King of the Belgians, 1991, Officer of the Order of Leopold, 1999, Knight of the Nat. Order of Merit, Pres. of Madagascar, 1997. Mem. Swedish-Belgian Assn. (pres. 1995—), Knickerbocker Club N.Y.C., Rotary. Office: Consul Gen, Box 7199, 103 88 Stockholm Sweden

DAHLMANN, NIELS FRIEDRICH, business executive, honorary consul; b. Shanghai, China, Oct. 22, 1937; s. Friedrich and Ruth (Carlsson) D.; m. Anne Hellsten, 1965 (div. 1979); m. Paula Margot Roth, Jan. 6, 1979; 1 child, Christian. Degree in Law and Econs., U. Uppsala, Sweden, 1956, U. Stockholm, 1961. Mem. staff Econ. Commn. for Europe, UN, Geneva, 1962; bus. cons. Accra, Ghana, 1962-65; regional mgr. Far East Saab-Scania, Hong Kong, 1965-71; v.p. GIA, Brussels, 1971-80, pres., 1980—. Author: (art book) Valdis Buss, 1992. Chargé d'affairs Ministry Fgn. Affairs, Riga, Latvia, 1992-93, hon. consul, 1991—. Office: GIA, 22 Ave I Gerard, Brussels 1160, Belgium

DAHLSTROM, BECKY JOANNE, journalist; b. Olympia, Wash., Sept. 24, 1957; d. Timothy Craddick and Shirleen (Stout) Roan; m. Kenneth W. Dahlstrom, Mar. 17, 1978 (div. Aug. 1984); children: Levi, Olivia; m. Robert Salley, Sr., Feb. 21, 1986 (div. Sept. 1994); 1 child, Robert, Jr. Student, Am. Coll., 1985-86. Writer Hospital, 1988-89; admitting clerk County Ventura (Calif.) Healthcare Agy., 1989—; writer, editor West Fork (Ark.) Elem. Sch., 1970-73. Author: (poem) My Authority, 1980 (Hon. mention 1980). Mem. Future Bus. Leaders Am. Republican. Baptist. Avocations: drawing, writing, horseback riding, racing cars, ceramics. Home: 9452 Telephone Rd Apt 114 Ventura CA 93004-2600

DAHLSTROM, JANE ESTHER, pathologist; b. Parramatta, N.S.W., Australia, Apr. 12, 1961; d. Peter Jon and Gyllian Summerfield (Cowell) Yeend; m. Stephen William Dahlstrom, Dec. 18, 1982 (div. 1991); children: Clare, Nicholas; m. Mark Llewellyn Bassett, Apr. 29, 1992; children: Hamish, Camilla, Katharine, Peter. M.B.B.S. with honors, U. Sydney, Australia, 1985; PhD, Australian Nat. U., Canberra, 1992. Cert. in family planning. Intern Concord (Australia) Repatriation Hosp., 1985-86; resident Woden Valley Hosp., Canberra, 1986-87; anatomical pathology registrar ACT Health, Canberra, 1992-99, coord. pathology breast cancer screening program, 1993-96; clin. tchr. U. Sydney, 1995-96; vis. fellow JCSMR, Australian Nat. U., 1992—; acad. pathologist conjoint appointment Canberra Clin. Sch., U. Sydney, The Canberra Hosp., Woden, ACT, Australia, 2000. Contbr. articles to profl. jours. Australian Nat. U. scholar, 1988-91. Fellow Royal Coll. Pathologists Australasia (David Nelson Meml. Trainee award); mem. Australian Soc. Cytology (state councillor 1999), Australian Vascular Soc., ACT Women's Med. Soc., Canberra Medico-Legal Soc. (pres. 1999). Avocations: music, sewing. Home: 14 Melbourne Ave, Deakin ACT 2600, Australia Office: ACT Pathology Anatomical Pathology, PO Box 11, Woden ACT, Australia

DAHM, ERIK, microbiologist; b. Thisted, Denmark, Jan. 25, 1953; s. Harald and Annelise (Rosenberg) D.; children: Christian, Louis, Sören. Degree in vet. sci., Royal Vet. U., Copenhagen, 1982. Animal practitioner Kolind, 1982-85; hygiene vet. Danish Vet. Directorate, 1985-88; microbiologist Foot Control, 1988-93; head lab. food and environ. control unit Aarhus Local Food Control, 1993-99; head regional lab. Danish Food Directorate, Aarhus, 2000—. Dep. mayor Local Cmty., 1997—. Conservative. Lutheran. Home: Vagtelvej 5, DK 8560 Kolind Denmark Office: Danish Food Directorate, Regional Office, DK 8200 Århus Denmark

DAHM, HELMUT JOHANNES, research institute administrator; b. July 8, 1925; s. Hans and Helene (Schwamm) D.; m. Annemarie Hermann, Aug. 6, 1955; 1 child, Andreas. PhD, U. Mayence, Fed. Rep. Germany, 1955; Habilitation, U. Munich, Fed. Rep. Germany, 1974. Mem. editl. bd. Problems of the East U.S. Embassy, Bonn., Fed. Rep. Germany, 1955-58; mem. editl. bd. Ost-Probleme Fed. Office for Press and Info., Bonn., Fed. Rep. Germany, 1958-69, editor-in-chief, 1960-62; head first dept. Fed. Inst. for East European and Internat. Studies, Cologne, Fed. Rep. Germany, 1962-89, prof. history of ideas and philosophy, 1983-89, ret., 1990; free publicist; head philosophy sect. 2d World Congress for Soviet and East European Studies, Garmisch-Partenkirchen, Fed. Rep. Germany, 1980. Author: (with A. Böhm) Heresies of the Time, 1961, Dialectics in the Change of Soviet Philosophy, 1963, German Opinion on Problems of Today: Man and Philosophy, 1964 (with Th. W. Adorno, K. Jaspers, J. Pieper, K. Löwith a.o.), Science in Communist Countries (with D. Geyer), 1967, Deterrence or People's War (The Military Doctrines of the Soviet Union and The People's Republic of China), 1968, Mutiny on the Knees: The Crisis of the Marxist Conception of World and Man, 1969, Democratic Socialism: the Czechoslavkian Model, 1971, (with F. Kool) Technique of Power, 1974, Vladimir Solovyev/Max Scheler, 1975, (with E.J.M. Kroker) Violence in Politics, Religion and Society, 1976, (with G. Katkov, E. Oberländer, N. Poppe and G.v. Rauch) Russia Enters the 20th Century, 1978, Main Features of Russian Thought, 1979, (with H. Vogel) The Soviet Intervention in Afghanistan, 1980, The Failed Escape, 1982, De-Ideologisation and Ideological Counter-Reformation in East Europe, (1960-80), 1982, (with J.J. Orourke, Th. J. Blakeley and F. Rapp) Contemporary Marxism, 1984, (with H.H. Hôhmannl, Alec Nove and H. Vogel) Economics and Politics in the USSR, 1986, Ethics: Critique of the Communist Justification of the Good, 1986, Socialist Theory of Crisis: The Soviet Turning-An Illusion, 1987, (with Th. J. Blakeley and George L. Kline) Philosophical Sovietology: The Pursuit of a Science, 1988, (with R. Bäumer and A.v. Stockhausen) Dismissal or Continuation of Metaphysics in the Sense of Natural Philosophy, 1990, Let Us Be Sober and Vigilant: Gustav A. Wetter and the Philosophical Sovietology, 1991 (with V.A. Lektorskij) Russia and Germany: Attempt at a Philosophical Dialogue, 1993, (with A. Ignatov) A History of the Philosophical Traditions of East Europe, 1996, (with R. Bäumer, J.H. Benirschke and T. Guz) In Fight for the Truth, 1997, (yearbook) The Soviet Union; Events, Problems, Perspectives, 1973-89; contbr. numerous articles to chpts., profl. publs. and encys.; editl. bd. Studies in Soviet Thought, 1961, Asian Thought and Soc., 1976, 1987, Studies in East European Thought, 1992; editl. bd. series: Sovietica, 1961—. Decorated Fed. Cross of Merit. Mem. German Assn. Sci. and Presence (head Philos. dept. 1979-92), East Acad. Koenigstein (head scholarly coun. 1983-93), Gustav-Siewerth Acad. Roman Catholic. Home: Im Tannenbusch 26, D-53119 Bonn Federal Republic of Germany

DAHM-DAPHI, JOCHEN, physician, researcher; b. Hamburg, Germany, Dec. 28, 1956; s. Hans George and Dietlinde (Bahrdt) Dahm; m. Dorothy Ilse Lotte Daphi, Dec. 16, 1989; 1 child, Priska. Grad., U. Hamburg, Germany, 1985, MD, 1992. Resident Gen. Hosp., Bergedorf, Germany, 1985-88; rsch. fellow U. Hamburg, 1992-96, head rsch. unit radio-oncology, 1996—. Contbr. articles to profl. jours. Mem., parent cons. Pub. Sch., Hamburg, 1997—. Avocation: music. Office: Univ Hosp Eppendorf, Martinistr 52, 20246 Hamburg Germany

DAHRENDORF, LORD RALF GUSTAV, social scientist, educator; b. Hamburg, Germany, May 1, 1929; s. Gustav and Lina (Witt) D.; m. Ellen de Kadt. PhD, U. Hamburg, 1952, London Sch. Econs., 1954; 24 hon. degrees from various univs. Privatdozent sociology U. Saar, Fed. Republic Germany, 1957; fellow Ctr. for Advanced Studies in Behavioral Scis., Palo Alto, Calif., 1957-58; prof. sociology U. Hamburg, 1958-60, U. Tubingen, 1960-66; prof. U. Constance, 1966-69, dean faculty social scis., 1966-67; mem. Fed. Parliament Govt. of Fed. Republic Germany, 1969-70; parliamentary sec. of state in German Fgn. Office, 1969-70; mem. Commn. of the European Cmtys., 1970-74; dir. London Sch. Econs., 1974-84; warden St. Antony's Coll., Oxford, 1987-97; trustee Ford Found., 1976-87; mem. Coun. of Brit. Acad., 1980-83; chmn. bd. Friedrich-Naumann Stiftung, 1982-87. Author: Marx in Perspective, 1953, Industrie-und Betriebssoziologie, 1956, Class and Class Conflict, 1959, Die angewandte Aufklä rung, 1963, Gesellschaft und Demokratie in Deutschland, 1965, Pfade aus Utopia, 1967, Essays in Theory of Society, 1968, Konflikt und Freiheit, 1972, Plä doyer für die Europä ische Union, 1973, The New Liberty, 1975, Life Chances, 1980, On Britain, 1982, Die Chancen der Krise, 1983, The Modern Social Conflict, 1988 (all transl. into many langs.), Reflections on the Revolution in Europe, 1991, LSE: A History of the London School of Economics 1895-1995, 1995, Morals, Revolution and Civil Society, 1997. Mem. Hansard Soc. of Electoral Reform, 1975-76; mem. Royal Commn. on Legal Svcs., 1976-79; mem. Com. to Rev. the Functioning of Fin. Instns., 1977-80; mem. German PEN Ctr., 1971—. Decorated Knight Comdr., Order Brit. Empire, also by govts. of Senegal, Luxembourg, Fed. Republic Germany, Austria, Belgium. Fellow Anglo German Soc. (presidium), British Acad., Royal Soc. Arts, Royal Coll. Surgeons (hon.); mem. AAAS (hon.), NAS (fgn. assoc.), Am. Philos. Soc., Royal Irish Acad. (hon.), others. Office: House of Lords, London SW1A 0PW, England*

DAI, IVAN NAP KWAN, interior design company executive; b. Hong Kong, Sept. 8, 1955; s. Hong Fan Dai and Lai Ching Tse; 1 child, Bessie Wing Ting. Higher Diploma in Design, Hong Kong Poly., 1977. Interior designer Spence Robinson Archs. Engrs. Interior Designers, Hong Kong, 1978-85; sr. designer Leese Robertson Freeman Designers Ltd., Hong Kong, 1985-90, assoc., 1990-92, ptnr., 1992—. Fellow Chartered Soc. Designers London; mem. Internat. Fedn. Interior Archs./Designers, Hong Kong Interior Design Assn. (profl., chmn.). Avocations: swimming, diving, badminton, photography, traveling. Home: South Horizons, Flat D 35 Fl Tower 2, Apleichau Hong Kong Office: Leese Robertsn Freemn Units 1-4, 8 Shum Wan Rd Marina Towr 1st Fl, Aberdeen Hong Kong

DAI, JINXIANG, materials scientist, electrochemist; b. Hebei, China, Apr. 23, 1963; came to U.S., 1999; s. Zhenqing and Xiuqin (Wang) D.; m. Ping Han, June 25, 1990; 1 child, Shurui. BSc, Nankai U., Tianjin, China, 1985; MSc, Nankai U., 1988. Engr. Tianjin Inst. of Power Sources, 1988-96, dir., 1992-96; asst. R&D dir. USNanocorp, Willington, Conn., 1999—; advisor USNanocorp, 1998-99. Recipient Best Article award Tianjin Inst. of Power Sources, 1994, Best Poster award The Inst. of Materials, East Asia, Singapore, 1999; scholar Nat. U. Singapore, 1996-99. Inventor secondary rechargeable electrochem. cell with a new cathode-active material, 1998. Avocation: soccer. Fax: 860-429-5911. E-mail: daixiang@hotmail.com. Home: 43 Burt Latham Rd Apt D1 Willington CT 06279-1905 Office: US-Nanocorp 156 River Rd Apt J Willington CT 06279-1626

DAI, LE RONG, chemistry educator; b. Cheng du, Sichuan, China, Dec. 6, 1938; d. An Bang Dai and Gui Zhen Wu; m. Shen Kang Ruan; children: Dai Sheng, Ruan Qian. B in Chemistry, Peking U., Beijing, 1960. Tchr. Peking U., Beijing, 1960-78, lectr., 1979-88, assoc. prof., 1989-95, prof., 1996—; vis. scholar U. Mo., Rolla, 1986, Clarkson U., Potsdam, 1987. Author: Surface Chemistry, 1994, Chemistry, 1998. Recipient Nat. Sci. and Technol. Progress awards State Sci. Commn., 1987; named Outstanding Tchr., Beijing Edn. Commn., 1997. Mem. Chinese Chem. Soc. (mem. edn. commn. 1992—), Chinese Microgravity Soc. Office: Inst Phys Chemistry, Peking Univ, Beijing 100871, China

DAI, LIMING, research scientist; b. Wenzhou, Zhejiang, China, Oct. 10, 1961; arrived in Australia, 1992; s. Ruichang Dai and Suinai (Jiang) M.; m. Lin Zhu, Aug. 1, 1986; children: Quanbin and Quanzhe. BSChemE, Zhejiang U., Hangzhou, China, 1983; PhD in Chemistry, Australian Nat. U., Canberra, 1991. Engr. Zhejiang Chem. Industry Rsch. Inst., Hangzhou, 1983-86, vice dir. rsch. divsn., 1984-86; postdoctoral rsch. fellow Cavendish lab. U. Cambridge, Eng., 1990-92; prin. rsch. scientist Commonwealth Sci. and Indsl. Rsch. Orgn., Melbourne, Vic., Australia, 1992—, mem. occupational health and safety com., 1993—; vis. fellow U. Ill., Urbana, 1992; mem. adv. coun. Internat. Biog. Ctr.; mem. rsch. bd. advisors Am. Biog. Inst. Contbr. articles to profl. jours.; inventor in field. Recipient World of English Jour. prize, 1984, Australia-Korea Found. award, 1994; IBC 20th Century award for achievement, 1995; Australian Nat. U. scholar, 1986-90. Mem. AAAS, Am. Chem. Soc., Australian Soc. Biomaterials, N.Y. Acad. Sci., Royal Australian Chem. Inst. Avocations: swimming, table tennis, philately, reading. Home: 23 Willow Ave, Glen Waverley Vic 3150, Australia Office: Commonwealth Sci & Indsl Rsch Orgn, Pvt Bag 10 Bayview Ave, Clayton Vic 3168, Australia

DAI, LI-XIN, chemistry researcher, educator; b. Beijing, China, Nov. 13, 1924; s. Chen-shui and Cui-yun (Wang) D.; m. Zhu-xin Dong, May 20, 1950; 1 child, Jing. BS, Zhejiang U., Hangzhou, China, 1947. Rsch. assoc. Shanghai Inst. Organic Chemistry, 1953-62, assoc. prof., 1962-84, prof., 1984—. Editor: (book) Advances of Organic Synthetic Chemistry, 1993; contbr. rsch. articles to profl. jours. Mem. Chinese Acad., Chinese Chem. Soc. Avocations: classical music, reading. Office: Shanghai Inst Organic Chemistry, 354 Fengling Rd, 200032 Shanghai China

DAI, PETER KUANG-HSUN, government official, aerospace executive; b. Shanghai, Republic of China, Dec. 14, 1934; came to the U.S., 1959; s. Ying Shen and Esther Ya-Ying (Huang) D.; m. Janie Ko-Tsen Chen; children: Diane P., Frederick J. BS in Engring., Cheng Kung U., Tainan, Taiwan, 1957; MS in Engring., U. Ill., 1960, PhD in Engring., 1963. Rsch. assoc. U. Ill., Urbana, 1962-63; rsch. engr. Air Force Materials Lab., Dayton, Ohio, 1963-65; sect. head TRW Systems, Redondo Beach, Calif., 1965-68, 69-74; prin. engr. Ralph M. Parsons Co., L.A., 1968-69; dept. mgr. TRW Def. and Electronics, Redondo Beach, 1974-80; asst. program mgr. ballistic missile div. TRW Def. and Space, San Bernardino, Calif., 1980-87, dep. program mgr., 1987-91; dir. nat. space program Republic of China, 1992-94; sr. advisor NSPO, 1994-97; ret., 1997; lectr. U. So. Calif., L.A., 1967-68, Calif. State U., Fullerton, 1968-69, Long Beach, 1971-72; tech. rev. panel mem. Underground Nuclear Test Def. Nuclear Agy., Washington, 1988-89. Mem. ASCE (chmn. subcom. 1978), AIAA, Chinese-Am. Engrs. and Scientists Assn. So. Calif. (pres. 1976, chmn. bd. 1977-79). Avocations: tennis, ballroom dancing.

DAI, WEI, research scientist; b. Nov. 7, 1957. MS, Purdue U., 1986, PhD, 1988. Rsch. assoc. Hipple Cancer Rsch. Ctr., Dayton, Ohio, 1990-92; asst. scientist Hipple Cancer Rsch. Ctr., Dayton, 1992-94; asst. prof. U. Cin., 1994-98, assoc. prof., 1998—. Office: U Cin Divsn Hematology-Oncology 231 Bethesda Ave Cincinnati OH 45229-2827

DAI, ZHENXUE, geologist, researcher, consultant; b. Xiantao, Hubei, China, June 11, 1962; s. Geshan Dai and Hongying Chen; m. Liying Gu Dongdong, Nov. 8, 1988; 1 child, Wei. B in Engring., Changchun U. Geology, China, 1984; MSc, Ctrl. Coal Mining Rsch. Inst., Xian, China, 1989; postgrad., U. La Coruna, Spain, 1997—. Asst. engr. Hydrogeological and Engring. Geology Inst. Hubei, 1984-86; engr. Ctrl. Coal Mining Rsch. Inst., Xian, China, 1984-94, assoc. rsch. prof., 1995-97; asst. rschr. U. La Coruna, Spain, 1997—; asst. rschr. U.S. Geological Survey, Lansing, Mich., 1994. Contbr. articles to profl. jours. Recipient Tng. scholarship Tech. U. Denmark, 1999; Rsch. fellowship UNDP, 1994. Mem. Nine-Three Scholar Soc., China Coal Soc. Avocations: table tennis, basketball, swimming, Chinese chess, go. Home: Hydrogeology Inst, 44 Yanta Rd, 710054 Xian Shaanxi, China Office: U La Coruna ETS Ingenieras, Campus de Elvina, 15192 La Coruna Spain

DAI, ZHONGNING, software engineer, materials scientist, researcher; b. Xiji, Ningxia, China, Apr. 28, 1966; s. Quanyong Dai and Xiuping Lee; m. Hongyun Xu, July 2, 1997. BS, Ningxia U., Yingchuan, China, 1990; MS, Fudan U., Shanghai, China, 1993, PhD, 1997. Tchr. Fudan U., Shanghai, 1992-93; postdoctoral rschr. Lisbon (Portugal) U., 1996-97; rsch. fellow Japan Atomic Energy Rsch. Inst., Takasaki, 1997-99; rsch. assoc. Ctr. for Sensor Materials, Mich. State U., East Lansing, 1999—; organizer internat. conf. Internat. Conf. on Nuc. Microprobe, Shanghai, 1994. Chmn. student union Ningxia U., China, 1987-90; leader student orgn. Fudan U., Shanghai, 1990-94. Mem. Am. Phys. Soc., Materials Rsch. Soc., Chinese Phys. Soc. Achievements include author of synthesis of epitaxial C60 films, synthesis of TiO2 by a new method, sysnthesis of FeTiO3, VN; designer and researcher nuclear microprobe. Avocations: music, sports, photographer. E-mail: zndai@pa.msu.edu and daiz@msu.edu. Fax: 760-284-5736. Home: 1115 University Vlg Apt G East Lansing MI 48823-6043 Office: Mich State Univ Ctr for Sensor Materials 16 Physics & Astronomy East Lansing MI 48824-1116

DAICHES, DAVID, retired English literature educator, author; b. Sunderland, Eng., Sept. 2, 1912; s. Salis and Flora (Levin) Daiches; m. Isobel Mackay, July 27, 1937 (dec. Aug. 1977); children: Alan Harry, Jennifer Rachel, Elizabeth Mackay; m. Hazel Margaret Newman, Dec. 22, 1978 (dec. Sept. 1986). MA, U. Edinburgh, Scotland, 1934; DLitt (hon.), U. Edinburgh, 1976; DPhil, U. Oxford, Eng., 1937; LHD (hon.), Brown U., 1964; Docteur de l'Université (hon.), Sorbonne, U. Paris, 1973; DLitt (hon.), U. Sussex, Brighton, Eng., 1978, U. Glasgow, Scotland, 1987, U. Guelph, Ont., Can., 1990; DUniv (hon.), U. Stirling, Scotland, 1980; Dottore 'ad honorem', U. Bologna, Italy, 1989. Bradley fellow Balliol Coll., Oxford U., 1936-37; asst. prof. English U. Chgo., 1940-43; 2d sec. Brit. Embassy, Washington, 1944-46; prof. English Cornell U., 1946-51; univ. lectr. English Cambridge U., 1957-61; fellow Jesus Coll., 1957-62; dean Sch. English Studies U. Sussex, 1961-67, prof. English, 1961-77, prof. emeritus, 1977—; dir. Inst. for Advanced Study in Humanities, Edinburgh U., 1980-86, Gifford lectr., 1983. Author over 40 books including The Novel and the Modern World, 1939, A Study of Literature, 1948, Robert Burns, 1950, Two Worlds, 1956, Critical Approaches to Literature, 1956, Literary Essays, 1956, Milton, 1957, A Critical History of English Literature, 1960, More Literary Essays, 1968, Scotch Whisky, 1969, Sir Walter Scott and His World, 1971, A Third World, 1971, Robert Burns and His World, 1971, Prince Charles Edward Stuart, 1973, Robert Louis Stevenson and His World, 1973, Moses, 1975, James Boswell and His World, 1976, Scotland and the Union, 1977, Glasgow, 1977, Edinburgh, 1978, Literature and Gentility in Scotland, 1982, Robert Fergusson, 1983, God and the Poets, 1984, A Weekly Scotsman and Other Poems, 1994; editor: Literature and Western Civilization, 6 vols., 1972-76, Fletcher of Saltoun: Selected Political Writings and Speeches, 1979, Edinburgh: A Traveller's Companion, 1986. Decorated Comdr. Brit. Empire. Fellow Royal Soc. Lit., Royal Soc. Edinburgh; mem. MLA (hon.), Assn. for Scottish Lit. Studies (hon. pres.), Saltire Soc. (hon. pres.), Scottish Arts Club (Edinburgh), New Club (Edinburgh).

DAIDONE, LEWIS EUGENE, financial services company executive; b. Perth Amboy, N.J., Aug. 6, 1957; s. Eugene John and Gertrude Rose (Sawyer) D.; m. Kathleen Eleanor Ward, May 11, 1985; children: Eugene Joseph, Brittany Nicole, Lewis Peter. BA, Rutgers U., 1979, MBA, 1980. CPA, N.Y., N.J. Sr. acct. Ernst & Young, N.Y.C., 1980-82; asst. controller Reserve Group, N.Y.C., 1982-84; mgr. commodity acctg. Dean Witter Reynolds, N.Y.C., 1984; v.p., treas., sec. Cortland Distbrs., Inc., Hackensack, N.J., 1984-89; sr. v.p., chief fin. officer Cortland Fin. Group, Inc., Hackensack, N.J., 1984-89; also bd. dirs. Cortland Distbrs., Inc., Hackensack, N.J.; mng. dir., chief fin. officer mutual funds Salomon Smith Barney, Inc., N.Y.C., 1990—; sr. v.p., chief fin. officer Mutual Mgmt. Corp., N.Y.C., 1990—; sr. v.p., treas. Smith Barney Funds., Inc., N.Y.C., 1990—, Smith Barney Money Funds, Inc., N.Y.C., 1990—, Smith Barney Muni Funds, N.Y.C., 1990—, Smith Barney Tax-Free Money Fund, N.Y.C., 1990—, Smith Barney Intermediate Mcpl. Fund, N.Y.C., 1992—, Smith Barney Mcpl. Fund, Inc., N.Y.C., 1992—, Smith Barney High Income Opportunity Fund, Inc., N.Y.C., 1993—; chmn. Global Horizon Investment Series, Brit. West Indies, 1992—, Smith Barney Internat. Funds, Luxembourg, 1993—; and exec. of 150 other investment cos. with Salomon Smith Barney; head global funds

adminstrn. SSB Citi Asset Mgmt., 1998—; v.p., treas. Cortland Trust, Inc., Hackensack, 1984-89; cons. in field. Trustee Wyndmoor Condominium Assn., Woodbridge, N.J. Named one of Outstanding Young Men Am., U.S. Jaycees, 1979. Fellow N.J. State Soc. CPAs; mem. AICPA, N.Y. State Soc. CPAs, Beta Gamma Sigma. Avocations: golf, racquetball. Office: Salomon Smith Barney Inc 388 Greenwich St New York NY 10013-2339

DAI-GIANG See NGUYEN, GIANG DAI

DAILEY, VICTORIA ANN, economist, policy analyst; b. San Antonio, Aug. 30, 1945; d. John Thomas and Helen (Bass) D. BA, Swarthmore Coll., 1967; PhD, U. Va., 1973. Economist FTC, Washington, 1972-79; economist U.S. Dept. Transp., Washington, 1979-95, ret., 1995. Econ. rsch. fellow Brookings Instn., 1971-72.

DAILY, FRANK J(EROME), lawyer; b. Chgo., Mar. 22, 1942; s. Francis Jerome and Eileen Veronica (O'Toole) D.; m. Julianna Ebert, June 23, 1996; children: Catherine, Eileen, Frank, William, Michael. BA in Journalism, Marquette U., 1964, JD, 1968. Bar: Wis. 1968, U.S. Dist. Ct. (ea. dist.) Wis. 1968, U.S. Dist. Ct. (we. dist.) Wis. 1971, U.S. Dist. Ct. (ctrl. dist.) Ill. 1990, U.S. Dist. Ct. (ea. dist.) Mich. 1994, U.S. Ct. Appeals (7th cir.) 1977, U.S. Ct. Appeals (3d and 5th cirs.) 1985, U.S. Ct. Appeals (4th, 6th, 8th, 9th, 10th, 11th cirs.) 1990, U.S. Supreme Ct. 1998, U.S. Dist. Ct. (no. dist.) Ill. 1999. Assoc. Quarles & Brady, Milw., 1968-75, ptnr., 1975—; lectr. in product liability law and trial techniques Marquette U. Law Sch., U. Wis., Harvard U. and seminars sponsored by ABA, State Bar Wis., State Bar S.D., State Bar S.C., Product Liability Adv. Coun., Chem. Mfrs. Assn., Wis. Acad. Trial Lawyers, Trial Attys. Am., Marquette U., Southeastern Corp. Law Inst., Risk Ins. Mgmt. Soc. Inc.; mem. bd. visitors Wake Forest U. Law Sch. Author: Your Product's Life Is in the Balance: Litigation Survival-Increasing the Odds for Success, 1986, Product Liability Litigation in the 80s: A Trial Lawyer's View from the Trenches, 1986, Discovery Available to the Litigator and Its Effective Use, 1986, The Future of Tort Litigation: The Continuing Validity of Jury Trials, 1991, How to Make an Impact in Opening Statements for the Defense in Automobile Product Liability Cases, 1992, How Much Reform Does Civil Jury System Need, 1992, Do Protective Orders Compromise Public's Right to Know, 1993, Developments in Chemical Exposure Cases: Challenging Expert Testimony, 1993, The Spoliation Doctrine: The Sword, The Shield and The Shadow, 1997, Trial Tested Techniques for Winning Opening Statements, 1997, Litigation in the Next Millennium -- A Trial Lawyer's Crystal Ball Report, 1998, What's Hot and What's Not in Non-Daubert Products Liability In the Seventh Circuit, 1998. Life mem. Pres.'s Coun., Marquette U., Pres.'s Cir., Boston Coll. Named Marquette U. Law Alumnus of Yr., 2000. Fellow Internat. Acad. Trial Lawyers; mem. ABA (past co-chair discovery com. litigation sect., vice chmn. products, gen. liability and consumer law com. of sect. tort and ins. practice, litigation sect. and mfrs. liability subcom.), ATLA, AAAS, Trial Atty. of Am., Wis. Bar Assn., Chgo. Bar Assn., Milw. Bar Assn., 7th Cir. Bar Assn., Am. Judicature Soc., Def. Rsch. Inst., Supreme Ct. Hist. Soc., Indsl. Truck Assn. (lawyers com.), Am. Law Inst., Product Liability Adv. Coun., Am. Agrl. Law Assn., Wis. Acad. Trial Lawyers, Assn. for Advancement of Automotive Medicine (life), Nat. I-Club U. Iowa, U. Ala. Nat. Alumni Assn., Circle of Champions. Roman Catholic. Office: Quarles & Brady 411 E Wisconsin Ave Ste 2550 Milwaukee WI 53202-4497

DAILY, LOUIS, ophthalmologist; b. Houston, Apr. 23, 1919; s. Louis and Ray (Karchmer) D.; B.S., Harvard U., 1940; M.D., U. Tex. at Galveston, 1943; Ph.D., U. Minn., 1950; m. LaVerl Daily, Apr. 5, 1958; children: Evan Ray, Collin Derek (dec.). Intern, Jefferson Davis Hosp., Houston, 1943-44; resident in ophthalmology Jefferson Davis Hosp., 1944-45, Mayo Found., Rochester, Minn., 1947-50; individual practice medicine, specializing in ophthalmology, Houston, 1950—; assoc. prof. ophthalmology U. Tex.-Houston, 1972-86, Baylor Med. Sch., Houston, 1950—. V.p. bd. dirs. Mus. Med. Sci., 1973-85, pres., 1980-82. Served as lt. (j.g.) USNR, 1945-46. Diplomate Am. Bd. Ophthalmology. Fellow A.C.S., Internat. Coll. Surgeons; mem. Soc. Prevention of Blindness (med. chmn. Tex. 1968-70), Contact Lens Assn. Ophthalmologists (exec. bd. 1976-78), Tex. Ophthal. Assn. (pres. 1963-64), Houston Ophthal. Soc. (pres. 1970-71), numerous other med. socs., Sigma Xi, Alpha Omega Alpha. Jewish. Clubs: Doctors, Harvard (dir. 1965-66) (Houston). Editl. bd. Jour. Pediatric Ophthalmology, 1964-68; assoc. editor Eye, Ear, Nose and Throat Monthly, 1962-65, Jour. Ophthalmic Surgery, 1970; contbr. numerous articles to profl. publs., also contbr. to books. Home: 2523 Maroneal St Houston TX 77030-3117 Office: 1517 Med Towers 1709 Dryden Rd Houston TX 77030-2400

DAILY, THOMAS V., bishop; b. Belmont, Mass., Sept. 23, 1927. Student, Boston Coll., St. John's Sem., Brighton, Mass. Ordained priest Roman Cath. Ch., 1952; missonary Peru as mem. Soc. St. James the Apostle; ordained titular bishop of Bladia and aux. bishop Boston, 1975-84; first bishop Palm Beach, Fla., 1984-90; bishop Diocese of Bklyn., 1990—. Address: Chancery Office PO Box C 75 Greene Ave Brooklyn NY 11238-1003 also: PO Box C Brooklyn NY 11202

DAIN, PHYLLIS, retired library educator, historian; b. N.Y.C., Nov. 29, 1929; d. Jacob Louis and Bessie Segal; m. Norman Dain, Mar. 10, 1950; 1 child, Bruce Russell. BA, Bklyn. Coll., 1950; MS, Columbia U., 1953, MA, 1957, DLS, 1966. From cataloger to chief med. cataloging Columbia U., N.Y.C., 1953-60; from lectr. to prof. libr. svc. Columbia U. Sch. Libr. Svc., N.Y.C., 1961-95, prof. emeritus, 1995—; adv. bd. Internat. Dictionary of Libr. Historians, 1999—. Author: The New York Public Library: A History of Its Founding and Early Years, 1972, The New York Public Library: A Universe of Knowledge, 2000; co-author: Civic Space/Cyberspace: The American Public Library in the Information Age, 1999; co-editor: Libraries and Scholarly Communication in the United States, 1990; co-editor issue Biblion, Library Trends; mem. editl. bd. Libr. & Culture, 1976—. Officer, bd. trustees Leonia (N.J.) Pub. Libr., 1976—, Flat Rock Brook Nature Assn., 1997—. Rsch. grantee NEH, 1973-75; Coun. Libr. Resources fellow, 1973-74; named Outstanding Vol. of Yr., Bergen County, N.J., 1998. Mem. ALA, Phi Beta Kappa, Beta Phi Mu. Jewish. E-mail: ndain@andromeda.rutgers.edu.

DAIN, STEPHEN JOHN, optometrist, educator, researcher; b. Wakefield, Yorkshire, Eng., Apr. 25, 1945; arrived in Australia, 1973; s. Sidney John and Margery (Impey) D.; m. Alison Theresa Wise, Aug. 9, 1969; children: Claire Elizabeth, Timothy Michael. BSc with honors, City U., London, 1968, PhD, 1972. Mng. optometrist G.C. Bateman Ltd., Guildford, Eng., 1972-73; research fellow dept. optometry U. Melbourne, Australian, 1973-75; lectr. Sch. Optometry, U. New S. Wales, Kensington, Kensington, Australia, 1976-82, sr. lectr., 1982-89, assoc. prof., 1990—, head of sch., 1998—; cons. to govt. and industry. Fellow Coll. of Optometrists, Am. Acad. Optometry, Illuminating Engring. Soc. of Australia and New Zealand, Metrology Soc. of Australia; mem. Internat. Colour Vision Soc. (mem. com.), Color Soc. Australia (treas. 1985-88, chair 1996-98). Mem. Uniting Chourch of Australia. Office: Univ of New South Wales, Sydney 2052, Australia

DAI XIANGLONG, banker; b. Yizheng City, 1944. Student, Ctrl. Inst. Fin. & Banking. Dep. sect. chief People's Bank of China, Jiangsu, Jiangsu Province, 1978; vice gov. People's Bank China, Jiangsu, 1993-95, gov., 1995—; dep. sect. chief, dep. head dept., vice-gov. Agrl. Bank China, Jiangsu, 1978-89; vice-magistrate Fengxian Co.; sec. CCP group Comm. Bank China, gen. mgr., vice chair bd., 1989; chair bd. China Pacific Ins. Co. Ltd., 1990-93; pres. Peoples Bank China. Office: People's Bank of China, 32 Chengfang Jie West Dist, Xichengu Beijing 100800, China*

DAIYA, PRAVIN CHATURBHUJ, marketing professional, consultant; b. Jaharsuguda, Orissa, India, May 31, 1944; s. Chaturbhuj Tejpal and Chaturbhuj Maniben Daiya; m. Rajani Pravin Tulpule, Oct. 6, 1976; 2 children. B Elec., VJTI, Mumbai, India, 1969; MMM, JBIM, Mumbai, 1980. Dir. Churning Mktg. Svcs., Mumbai, 1991—, Octopussy Travelling, Mumbai, 1994—; sec. gen. Indian Retailers Assn., Mumbai, 1997—. Mem. Nat. Ventre Performing Arts (life), Advt. Club India. Achievements include developing total process of new products and launching the same, development of scripts for advertising for various media. Home: 34 Vaibhav 876/877 SK, S K Bole Rd, Mumbai 400 028, India Office: Churning Mktg Svcs, Aundh, 8/12 Sakal Nagar Baner Rd, Pune 411 007, India

DAJANI, RAJAI MAHMOUD, obstetrician-gynecologist, consultant; b. Jerusalem, Mar. 17, 1939; s. Mahmoud Taher and Naheel Mustafa (Habboub) D.; m. Fadwa Jawdat Tuffaha, Aug. 27, 1972; children: Rami, Kareem, Naheel. BSc, Am. U. Beirut, 1960, MD, 1965. Diplomate Am. Bd. Ob-gyn. Resident ob-gyn. U. Chgo., 1965-68, chief resident ob-gyn., 1968-69, instr. dept. ob-gyn., 1969-70; head dept. ob-gyn. Makassed Hosp., East Jerusalem, 1971-78; dir., proprietor Dajani Hosp., East Jerusalem, 1979—; founding pres. Soc. Ob-gyn. West Bank Chpt., 1987-92. Trustee Bethlehem U., 1998—. Fellow ACOG (affiliate); mem. Palestinian Med. Coun., Nat. Soc. for Visually Handicapped (v.p., treas. 1981—), Arab Med. Welfare Assn. (v.p. 1998—). Avocations: travel, music, tennis. Office: Dajani Hosp for Women, PO Box 19355, 91192 East Jerusalem Israel

DAJANI, SAMI WAFA, chemist, economist, consultant; b. Jerusalem, Mar. 1, 1911; s. Namek Wafa and Asmeh A. (Imam) D.; m. Afaf Sulaiman W., 1937; 1 child, Salwa. Student, Am. U., Cahiro, 1928-29; BSc, Mont. State U., 1932, MSc in Chemistry, 1933; postgrad., London Sch. Econs., 1946; DSc (hon.), Mont. State U., 1982. Rsch. chemist Palestine Potash Ltd., 1934-35; sr. asst. statistician Palestine Govt., Jerusalem, 1936-46; sr. asst. commr. for commerce and industry, chief import and export controle Palestine Govt., 1947-48; tech. advisor Syro-Lebanese Higher Coun. of Common Interests, Damascus, Syria, 1948-50; tech. advisor and dir. stats., audit and rsch. Directorate-Gen. of Syrian Customs, Damascus, 1950-53; dep. min. of fin. and econ. advisor Govt. of Jordan, 1954-56; gen. mgr. Arab Potash Co., 1957-60; advisor to Libyan Govt. in statis. orgn. and gen. stats. UN, 1960-63; sr. statistician, dep. chief indsl. stats. sect. Office of Stats. UN, N.Y.C., 1963-64; regional advisor in stats. Econ. and Social Office UN, Beirut, 1965-69; asst. dir. Office Stats. UN, N.Y.C., 1969-72; statis. advisor to Govt. Kuwait UN, 1973-75, ret., 1995; tech. cons. to Ministry of Planning Govt. Kuwait, 1975-80; pvt. cons., Amman, 1981—. Home: Jebel Husein Al-Gharbi, PO Box 921523, Amman Jordan

DAJUN, DING, retired civil engineer, educator; b. Anhui, China, Apr. 28, 1923. B in Engring., Anhui U., 1948. From asst. prof. to prof. Nanjing Inst. Tech., 1948-93, ret., 1993; chmn. limit states design com. concrete & masonry bldgs. Group Coun. on Tall Bldgs. & Urban Habitat; lectr. in field. Mem. editl. bd. Internat. Chinese Jour. Bldg. Structures, Internat. English Jour. Advances in Structural Engring.; contbr. over 280 articles to profl. jours. Hon. dir. Internat. Fedn. Highrise Structures, India. Recipient Excellent Text prize 1st degree State Constrn. Ministry. Mem. Civil and Archtl. Engring. Soc. Nanjing (hon. pres.), Internat. Fedn. Highrise Structures (India), IABSE. Avocations: composing ancient Chinese poems, painting Chinese traditional pictures, Chinese calligraphy. Fax: (86)(025)-7713019. Office: Nanjing Inst Tech, No 2 Sipailou, Nanjing, Jiangsu 210096, China

DAKAS, CHRISTOS JOHN, pharmaceutical company executive; b. Athens, Greece, July 10, 1961; s. John C. and Amalia (Psarras) D.; m. Titika Maniati, Nov. 20, 1993; 1 child, Amalia. BSc, U. Toronto, Can., 1983; cert. in biochemistry, U. London, 1984; PhD in Pharmacy, U. Wales, Cardiff, 1989. Product mgr. P.N. Gerolymatos S.A., Athens, 1992-94, bus. devel. mgr., 1994-95; bus. unit mgr. Pierre Fabre Medicament, Athens, 1995-96; mktg. mgr. pharm. divsn. P.N. Gerolymatos S.A., Athens, 1997-98; dir. bus. unit Genesis Pharma S.A., Athens, 1999—; cons. CMM Hellas S.A., Athens, 1991-92, CCM Middle East, Athens, 1995-96. Contbr. articles to sci. publs. Founding mem. Sci. Pharm. Soc. Greece, 1992. Mem. Hellenic Soc. Medicinal Chemistry (gen. sec. 1991-92, pres. 1993-94), Panhellenic Union Pharmacists, Greek Soc. Pharm. Mktg., N.Y. Acad. Sci. Greek Orthodox. Avocations: tennis, squash, opera, theater, travel. Home: 11 Filopappou St, 11741 Athens Greece Office: Genesis Pharma SA, 24 Filellinon St, 152 32 Athens Greece

DAKIN, VLADIMIR IVANOVICH, radiation physics and chemistry researcher; b. Vyshniy Volochek, Russia, Mar. 5, 1935; s. Ivan Vladimirovich and Anna Yakovlevna (Artamonova) D.; m. Galina Nikonovna Tomashova, July 20, 1959 (dec. Aug. 1968); children: Sergei, Anna. Degree in chemistry, Moscow State U., 1959; postgrad., Karpov's Inst. Phys. Chemistry, Moscow, 1982. Rschr. Karpov's Inst. Phys. Chemistry, Obninsk, Russia, 1959-64; sr. rschr. Karpov's Inst. Phys. Chemistry, Moscow, 1964-93, Inst. Nuclear Rsch., Mexico City, 1993-95, State Acad. of Oil and Gas, Moscow, 1996—. Contbr. articles to profl. jours. Mem. Union of Oil and Chem. Industry. Avocation: computer programming. Home: korp 2 k 19, UL BDorogomilovskaia 14, 121059 Moscow Russia

DALAI LAMA (TENZIN GYATSO), supreme temporal and religious head of Tibet; b. Takster, Amdo province, Tibet, July 6, 1935; s. Chokyong and Diki Tsering. LittD (hon.), Banaras Hindu U., Varanasi, India, 1957; D in Buddhist Philosophy, Monasteries of Sera, Drepung and Gaden, Lhasa, 1959; DD, The Carroll Coll., Waukesha, Wis., 1979, Cen. Inst. for Higher Tibetan Studies, 1990; D of Buddhist Philosophy, U. of Oriental Studes, L.A., 1979; HHD, Seattle U., 1979; D (hon.), U. de Paris X Naterre Cedex, 1984. Enthroned Dalai Lama XIV Lhasa, 1940; was requested to assume full polit. power, 1950, fled to Chumbi in South Tibet on Chinese invasion, 1950, negotiated with China, 1951, fled to India after abortive revolt of Tibetan people against Communist Chinese, 1959; established govt.-in-exile Dharamsala, India; mem. nat. com. Chinese People's Polit. Consultative Conf., 1951-59; hon. chmn. China Buddhist Assn., 1953-59; del. Nat. Productivity Council, 1954-59, vice chmn. standing com.; chmn. preparatory com. Autonomous Region Tibet, 1955-59; announced Five-Point Peace Plan on future of Tibet in speech to U.S. Congl. Human Rights Caucus, 1987; speaker at European Parliament, Strasbourg, France, 1988. Author: My Land and My People, 1962, The Opening of the Wisdom Eye, 1963, An Introduction to Buddhism, 1965, Key to the Middle Way, 1971, Universal Responsibility and Good Heart, 1977, Four Essential Buddhist Commentaries, 1982, Kindness, Clarity and Insight, 1984, 87, A Human Approach to World Peace, 1984, Freedom in Exile, 1990, others. Recipient Magsaysay award, 1959, Admiral Richard E. Byrd Meml. award Internat. Rescue com., 1959, Lincoln award Rsch. Inst. Am., 1960, Plakett award Norwegian Refugee Council, Alber Schweitzer Humanitarian award, 1987, Special medal Asian Buddhist Council for Peace, 1979, Nobel Peace prize, 1989, Raoul Wallenberg Congl. Human Rights award Congl. Human Rights Found., 1989, Le Prix De La Memoire, Found. Danielle Mitterrand, 1989, Freedom award U.S.A., 1991. Address: Thekchen Choeling, McLeod Ganj, 176219 Dharamsala Himachal Pradesh, India*

DALAK, MIROSLAW ANTONI, mechanical engineering educator; b. Bydgoszcz, Poland, Feb. 11, 1958; s. Antoni and Czeslawa (Apczynska) D.; m. Elzbieta Walczak, Oct. 17, 1981; children: Dominik, Dalia. M in Engring., U. Tech. and Agr., Bydgoszcz, 1984; DSc in Engring., Tech. U. Poznan, Poland, 1993. Cert. engring. Instr. U. Tech. and Agr., Bydgoszcz, 1984-93, asst. prof., 1993—, head rsch. divsn. machining & cutting tools, 2000—; profl. experience improver Water and Sewage Co., Athens, Greece, 1983, Nokia (Finland) Rubber Industries, 1986; group mgr. Automobile Eisenach, Germany, 1987. Contbr. articles to profl. jours.; inventor in field. Fellow Polish Mech. Engrs. Assn., Sci. Soc. Orgn. and Mgmt.; mem. ASME. Avocations: traveling, music, tinkering, modern cutting. Home: 4/30 Mielczarskiego St, 85-796 Bydgoszcz Poland Office: Univ Tech and Agr, 7 Kaliskiego Ave, 85-796 Bydgoszcz Poland

DALAL, GANGADHAR GANPATRAO, electrical engineer; b. Thanegaon, India, Dec. 25, 1944; s. Ganpatrao Yashwantappa and Radhikabai Bakaramappa (Anwane) D.; m. Nirmala Balwantappa Deshmukh; m. Veena Gangadhar, Feb. 4, 1972; children: Sonali Basalingappa, Saraswati. B of Elec. Engring., Nagpur (India) U., 1968. Grad. pilot course in maintenance of large power plants, U.K.; grad. environ. impact assessment course USAID. Jr. engr. Maharashtra State Electricity Bd., Nagpur, 1968-69, dep. exec. engr., 1969-76, exec. engr., 1976-80; supt. engr. Maharashtra State Electricity Bd., Nashik, Koradi, India, 1980-86, dep. chief engr., 1987-96; chief engr. Maharashtra State Electricity Bd., Mumbai, 1996—; bd. examiners Govt. Maharashtra for Boiler Proficiency and Competency Exam., 1990-93; expert appraisal com. State Pollution Control Bd., Bombay, 1996; rep. state govt. Environ. Pub. Hearing, Maharashtra, 1997; mem. dist. accidents and crisis group Apex Body, Mumbai, 1998. Contbr. articles to profl. jours. Home: 3B Soudamini Haji Ali, MSEB Officer's Quarters, 400034 Mumbai India Office: Maharashtra State Elec Bd, Prakashgad Bandra (E) G-9, 400051 East Mumbai India

DALAL, MAYUR THAKORBHAI, charitable estate planner; b. Bombay, India, Apr. 1, 1958; came to U.S., 1988; m. Thakorbhai H. and Jaya T. (Rokadia) D.; m. Madhavi M. Shah, Dec. 8, 1985; children: Sagar, Reema. BS with honors, St. Xavier's, Bombay, 1978; B.Tech., Bombay U., 1981; MBA, Bajaj Inst. of Mgmt. Studies, Bombay, 1986. Mgmt. trainee A. Sarabhai Enterprises Ltd., Bombay, 1981-82, asst. mktg. exec., 1982-83; product mgr. Corn Products div. of CPC Internat., Bombay, 1983-86; mktg. mgr. Foods and Inns Ltd., Bombay, 1986-88; registered rep. Equitable Fin. Co., N.Y.C., 1988-91; asst. agy. mgr. The Equitable Cos., Lake Success, N.Y., 1991—; dist. mgr. The Equitable Cos., Lake Success, 1994-98; CEO Legacy Planning Group LLC, 1998—. Mem. Am. Mgmt. Assn., Internat. Assn. Fin. Planners, Inst. Cert. Fin. Planners, Am. Soc. CLU and ChFC, Nat. Assn. Life Underwriters, Estate Planning Coun., Assn. Indians in Am. (exec. com., v.p.), Masons, Am. Assn. Life Underwriters, Planned Giving Group N.Y. Home: 30 Hunt Ct Jericho NY 11753-1139 Office: Legacy Planning Group LLC PO Box 3709 New Hyde Park NY 11040-0800

DALAL, PRAFULCHANDRA M., neurologist, researcher; b. Ahmedabad, Gujarat, India, Jan. 29, 1932; s. Maganlal G. and Savitaben M. Dalal; m. Kumuda Rao; children: Manish, Ragini, Yamini, Anish. MB BS, U. Bombay, 1955, MD, 1958. Registrar in gen. medicine T.N. Med. Coll. and Nair Hosp., Bombay, 1956-58, tutor in medicine, 1958-62, asst. prof. medicine, 1962-65, prof. head of medicine, neurologist, 1965-69, prof. head of neurology/neurosci., 1963-90; mem. expert panel neurosci. WHO Internat., 1980-86; dir. rsch. Sir H.N. Med. Rsch. Centre, Bombay, 1983-87; vis. neurologist Sir N.H. Hosp. Rsch. Ctr., Bombay, 1983—, Li lavati Hosp. Rsch. Centre, Bombay, 1995—; vis. scientist NIH, Bethesda, Md., 1983; guest prof. Wayne State U., Detroit, 1968-69, Wake Forest U., 1978. Author: (with others) Handbook of Clinical Neurology, 1989, Infections and Subcortical Infarctions, 1995; editor: Medicine Update, Current Concepts in Internal Medicine, 1991; mem. editl. bd. Jour. Neuroepidemiology; contbr. articles to profl. jours. including Nature, Year Book of Neurology and Psychiatry, Lancet, Am. Heart Jour., JAMA, among others. Fellow Rockefeller Found., 1960-62, Wellcome Found., 1968-69; recipient Manorama Vijay Hazrat scholar Bombay U., 1955; Sr. commonwealth fellow Oxford (Eng.) U., 1967-68. Fellow Royal Soc. Medicine (London), Nat. Acad. Med. Scis. (India), Am. Heart Assn. (hon. stroke coun.); mem. Indian Acad. Med. Scis., Royal Soc. Medicine, Am. Coll. Chest Physicians, Internat. Coll. Angiology, Assn. of Physicians of India (pres. 1993), Indian Coll. Physicians (pres. 1993), Acad. Med. Specialists (chmn. 1996), Internat. Stroke Soc. (bd. dirs. 1995, Dr. B.C. Roy Nat. award in neuroscis. 1995). Avocations: chess, watching cricket, tennis, and football games, theatre. Home and Office: Clerk Rd Off Colony Ln, Mcpl Bldg No 3 Flat 18 2dFl, Bombay 400034, India

DALBERT, CLAUDIA, psychologist; b. Cologne, Germany, Aug. 9, 1954; d. Lambert and Klare (Schindler) D. Diploma in Psychology, U. Trier, Germany, 1979; Dr.rer.nat., U. Trier, 1987; Dr. rer. soc. habil., U. Tubingen, Germany, 1995. Rsch. asst. U. Trier, 1979-88, Coll. of Edn., Heidelberg, Germany, 1989; asst. prof. U. Tubingen, 1990-98; substitute prof. U. Ulm, Germany, 1995, U. Kaiserslautern, Germany, 1995-98; prof. U. Halle-Wittenberg, Germany, 1998—; vis. asst. prof. Washington U., St. Louis, 1993. Author: (book) Dealing With Injustice, 1996; contbr. articles to profl. jours. Mem. German Psychol. Assn. Home: Schillerstr 9, D-06114 Hallee Germany Office: U Halle-Wittenberg, D-06099 Halle Germany

DALBOGE, HENRIK, company executive; b. Aarhus, Denmark, Aug. 13, 1956; s. Erik and Inge Andersen; m. Birgitte Schjellerup Wulff; children: Louise, Christina. MS, U. Denmark, 1982, Lic. Sci., 1989. Project leader Nordisk Gentophs, Denmark, 1983-85; prin. scientist rsch. Novo Nordisk, Denmark, 1985-89, prin. scientist molecular biology, 1989-91, dept. head Gene Express, 1991-95; dir. SB Novo Nordisk, Denmark, 1995-99, EBO Novo Nordisk, Bagsvaerd, Denmark, 1999—. Contbr. articles to profl. jours.; patentee in field. Mem. Danish Rsch. Coun., European Coun. on Rsch., Devel. and Innovation. Avocations: sailing, fishing, skiing. Office: Novo Nordisk A/S, Novo Allé 8X, 2880 Bagsvaerd Denmark

DALBY, ALAN JAMES, pharmaceutical company executive; b. Glasgow, Scotland, Jan. 15, 1937; s. William J. P. and Elizabeth Jean (MacKenzie) D.; children: A. Royce, Mark. B.S., Paisley Coll., 1958. Analytical chemist Smith Kline & French Labs., Can., 1958; mgmt. trainee SK&F, Phila., 1960-61; gen. mgr. consumer products div. Menley & James Labs., Can., 1963-65; dir. mktg. SK&F, Can., 1966-71; v.p. comml. devel. Worldwide Pharms., Phila., 1971-72, v.p. Europe, Africa, India, Brussels, 1972-75, v.p. internat., 1975-80, pres., from 1980; exec. v.p. therapeutics products group Smith Kline Corp. (now SmithKline Beecham), Phila., 1980-87; pres. SmithKline and French Labs., Phila., 1980-87, also mem. corp. bd. dirs., 1987-94; bd. dirs., chmn. Reckitt & Colman, PLC (now called Reckitt Benckiser plc), 1995—; chmn. Reckitt & Colman, PLC, Immulogic Pharm. Corp., Alteon, Inc., Mass. Eye & Ear Infirmary. Mem. Hyannisport Golf Club, Somerset Club (Boston). Republican. Episcopalian. Office: Reckitt Benckiser plc, 67 Alma Rd, Windsor Berkshire 5L4 3HD, United Kingdom also: 67 Alama Rd, Windsor, Berkshire England*

DAL COVOLO, ENRICO, university dean; b. Feltre, Belluno, Italy, Oct. 5, 1950; s. Francesco and Brunilde (Monzardo) dal C. Dr. Classical Lit., Cath. U., Milan, 1974; ThM, Salesian Pontifical U., Rome, 1984; Dr. Theology and Patristics, Lateranense Pontifical U., Rome, 1989. Prin. Don Bosco H.S., Milan, 1981-86; prof. Salesian Pontifical U., Rome, 1986—; rector Pontificium Institutum Altioris Latinitatis, Rome, 1991—; dir. Salesian Jour., 1989—, Ricerche Teologiche Jour., 1992—. Author: Introduzione ai Padri Della Chiesa, 1990-96, I Severi e il Cristianesimo, 1987, Chiesa Società Politica, 1994; author/editor: Storia Della Teologia, 1995. Mem. Pontifical Internat. Acad. Mariology, Bessarione Acad. Patristic Studies, Commissione Teologico-Storica del Grande Giubileo, Pontificio Comitato de Scienze Storiche, Pontificia Accademia di Teologia. Avocations: skiing, Alpinism, classical music. Office: Univ Pontificia Salesiana, Piazza Dell'Ateneo Salesiano 1, 00139 Rome Italy

DALE, JOHN SORENSEN, investment company executive, portfolio manager; b. Mpls., Sept. 30, 1945; s. John Sorensen and Ruth Elaine (Bergstrom) D.; m. Cheryl Lee Woolley, June 19, 1965; children: John, Christopher. BA in Mktg. and Humanities, U. Minn., 1968. CFA. Securities analyst, portfolio mgr. Norwest Corp., Mpls., 1968-78, v.p., sr. trust investment strategist, 1978-84, sr. v.p., mgr. equity advisors, 1984-87; sr. v.p., sr. portfolio mgr. Peregrine Capital Mgmt., Mpls., 1987—. Fellow Inst. Chartered Fin. Analysts; mem. Assn. Investment Mgmt. and Rsch., Twin Cities Soc., Security Analysts, Internat. Soc. Fin. Analysts. Avocations: travel, fishing, hunting. Office: Peregrine Capital Mgmt LaSalle Plz Ste 1850 8th and LaSalle Minneapolis MN 55402-2018

DALE, ROGER GRAHAM, physicist; b. Gravesend, Kent, Eng., Dec. 5, 1946; s. Arthur Edmund and Joan (Graham) D.; m. Diana Mary Ruck, Sept. 6, 1969; children: Sarah Louise, Deborah Suzanne. BSc in Math. and Physics, U. London, 1966; MSc in Radiation Physics, St. Bartholomews Hosp. Med., Sch., London, 1969; PhD in Physics, Charing Cross Hosp. Med. Sch., London, 1980. Cert. FIPEM. Physicist Charing Cross Hosp., London, 1967-72, sr. physicist, 1972-80, prin. physicist, 1980-86, head of radiation physics, 1986-89; dir. radiation physics Riverside Health Authority, London, 1989-95; dir. radiation physics and radiobiology Hammersmith Hosps. NHS Trust, London, 1995—; hon. sr. lectr. divsn. medicine Imperial Coll. Sci., Tech. and Medicine, U. London, 1997—; physicist St. Williams Hosp., Rochester, Kent, Eng., 1966-67; specialist advisor Internat. Atomic Energy Agy., Vienna, 1995—; vis. prof. and spl. investigator Meml. Sloan-Kettering Cancer Ctr., N.Y.C., 1995. Contbr. articles to profl. jours., especially related to radiation biology applied to clin. practice. Recipient award Royal Coll. of Radiologists, London, 1990, Rontgen prize Brit. Inst. of Radiology, London, 1988. Avocations: history of sci., music. E-mail: r.dale@ic.ac.uk. Office: Charing Cross Hosp, Fulham Palace Rd, Hammersmith London W6 8RF, England

DALE, SHARER SUSAN, real estate agent; b. Walnut Creek, Calif., May 1, 1966; d. Robert Maurice and Susan (Warren) D. BS, U. Vt., 1988. Liaison, asst. to project mgr. Colchester (Vt.) Community Devel. Corp., 1988—; realtor Realty One, Pepper Pike, Ohio, 1995—. travel coord. Heritage Sports, 1989—; participant Modern Pentathlon, Gates Mills, Ohio,

1999. Mem. Cleve. Area Bd. Realtors, Orgn. Women Exemplifying Reason and Responsibility (pres. 1987-88), Shoreby Club, Club Corp. Am. (mem. devel. com.), Kappa Alpha Theta (pres. local chpt. 1986-87). Avocations: horseback riding, travel, bicycling, boating. Home: 9 E Summit St Chagrin Falls OH 44022-2709

DALE, TORBJØRN, marine biologist, educator; b. Molde, Norway, Sept. 4, 1949; s. Johannes and Dagfrid (Stokkedal) D.; m. Inger Sandlie, Sept. 15, 1975 (div. 1985); 1 child, Hans Petter; m. Anne May Skarpen, Aug. 18, 1990 (div. 1994); 1 child, Kjetil. BS, U. Bergen, Norway, 1974, MS equivalent, 1977. Fellow Århus (Denmark) U., 1977-78; substitute amanuensis U. Bergen, 1978-79, rsch. asst., 1979-82, 84; rschr. The Norwegian Rsch. Coun. Sci. & the Humanities, Bergen, 1985-87; asst. prof. Sogn & Fjordane Coll., Sogndal, Norway, 1987-88; assoc. prof. Sogn & Fjordane Coll., Sogndal, 1988—. Contbr. chpts. to books and articles to profl. jours. Chmn. Zool. Soc., Bergen, 1980; bd. dirs. Future in Our Hands, Bergen, 1981, Orgn. of Biologists, Bergen, 1984; treas. Venstre, Bergen, 1986. With Norwegian Army, 1969-70. Grantee Nansen Found., Bergen, 1980, 86, The Scandinavian Japan Sasakawa Found., Oslo, 1989; fellow Am. Scandinavian Found., Oslo, 1983, fellow U. Md., College Park, 1982-83. Mem. Norwegian Soc. Oceanographers (treas. 1995—), Norwegian Non-Fiction Writers, Soc. Limology and Oceanography, Soc. Protozoologists. Mem. Venstre Party. Lutheran. Avocations: jogging, hiking, fishing, gardening, photography. Home: Kongabergveien 4, 6856 Sogndal Norway Office: Sogn & Fjordane Coll, Faculty of Sci, 6856 Sogndal Norway

D'ALENE, ALIXANDRIA FRANCES, human resources professional; b. Buffalo, Oct. 21, 1951; d. Fern (Hill D'A. BA, Canisius Coll., Buffalo, 1973, MS, 1975, MBA, 1980. Tchr. Buffalo pub. schs., 1973-76; pers. cons. Sanford Rose Assocs., Williamsville, N.Y., 1976-78; mgr. benefits adminstrn. Svc. Sys. Corp., Clarence, N.Y., 1978-80; mgr. employee rels. Del. Monte Corp., Walnut Creek, Calif., 1980-82; human resource mgmt. cons. H.R.S., Inc., Winston-Salem, N.C., 1982-87; corp. pers. specialist Advance Stroes Co., Inc., Roanoke, Va., 1987-90; pers. dir. Alfred (N.Y.) U., 1990-94; dir. human resources Framtone Connectors USA, Inc., Norwalk, Conn., 1994—; mgr. Lord Corp., Shelton, Conn., 1994-96; dir. human resources Energy Scis., Inc., Wilmington, Mass., 1999—. Mem. Assn. Pers. Adminstrs., Indsl. Pers. Soc., Coll. and U. Pers. Assn., Phi Alpha Theta. Episcopalian. Home: 250 Lynnfield St # A Peabody MA 01960-4921 Office: 42 Industrial Way Wilmington MA 01887-4605

DALENS, BERNARD JACQUES, pediatric anesthesiologist; b. Petite Rosselle, France, 1949; s. Henri and Andree (Michel) D.; m. Helene Suzanne Assali, Mar. 15, 1974; children: Arielle, Luc, Charles, Violaine. MD, Faculty of Medicine, Clermont-Ferrand, France, 1979; PhD, Faculty of Sci., Clermont-Ferrand, France, 1986. Intern Univ. Hosps. Marseilles, France, 1971-74; resident Univ. Hosps., Clermont-Ferrand, 1975-80, asst. prof. anesthesiology, 1981-84; cons. anesthesiologist Univ. Hosp. Hotel-Dieu, Clermont-Ferrand, 1985—. Editor, author: Pediatric Regional Anesthesia, 1990, Anesthesie Loco-Regionale de la Naissance a' l'age Adulte, 1993, Regional Anesthesia in Infants, Children & Adolescents, 1995, Medicaments en Anesthesiologie, 1996. Recipient Edmond Lesne prize Nat. Com. on Childhood, Paris, 1979. Mem. French Soc. Anesthesiologists, Am. Soc. Anesthesiologists, French Lang. Soc. Pediat. Anesthesiology, Belgian Soc. Anesthesia & Reanimation (hon.). Roman Catholic. Avocations: medieval history, ancient theology. Home: 10 Rue Massillon, F-63000 Clermont-Ferrand France Office: Hotel-Dieu Pavillon Gosselin, Blvd La Garlaye, F-63000 Clermont-Ferrand France

D'ALESSANDRO, DOMINIC, financial executive; b. Italy, Jan. 18, 1947; arrived in Can., 1954; 3 children. BSc., Loyola Coll., 1967; postgrad., McGill U., 1971. Acct. Coopers & Lybrand, 1968-75, dep. mgr. Paris office, 1970-71; asst. contr. GenStar, Ltd., 1975; from dir. fin. to gen. mgr. GenStar, Saudi Arabia, 1976-79; v.p. Materials and Constrn. Group, San Francisco, 1979-81; dep. contr. Royal Bank of Can., Toronto, 1981, v.p. and contr., 1982, sr. v.p., 1983-87, exec. v.p. fin., 1987; pres., CEO Laurentian Bank of Can., 1988, Manulife Fin., Toronto, 1994—; also bd. dirs. ManuLife Fin., Toronto; adv. bd. Lazard Can., Ltd., Willis Inc.; past chmn. Canadian Life and Health Ins. Assn.; bd. dirs. Hudsons' Bay Co., Am. Coun. of Life Ins., Washington, TransCan. Pipe Lines. Mem. Bus. Coun. on Nat. Issues; chmn. United Way of Greater Toronto, 1998. Fellow Inst. Chartered Accts. (chartered). Office: Manulife Financial, 200 Bloor St E, Toronto, ON Canada M4W 1E5

DALESSIO, DONALD JOHN, physician, neurologist, educator; b. Jersey City, Mar. 2, 1931; s. John Andrea and Susan Dorothy (Minotta) D.; m. Jane Catherine Schneider, Sept. 4, 1954 (dec. Mar. 1998); children: Catherine Leah, James John, Susan Jane. BA, Wesleyan U., 1952; MD, Yale U., 1956. Diplomate Am. Bd. Internal Medicine. Intern in medicine N.Y.C. Hosp., 1956-57, asst. resident in medicine and neurology, 1959-61; resident in medicine Yale Med. Ctr., 1961-62; pres. med. staff Scripps Clinic, La Jolla, Calif., 1974-78; chmn. dept. medicine Scripps Clin., La Jolla, Calif., 1974-89, chmn. emeritus, 1989—, cons., 1982—, pres. med. group, 1980-81; clin. prof. neurology U. Calif., San Diego, 1973—; physician in chief Green Hosp., La Jolla, 1974-89; Musser-Burch lectr. Tulane U., 1979, Kash lectr. U. Ky., 1979; pres. Am. Assn. Study Headache, Chgo., 1974-76, Nat. Migraine Found., Chgo., 1977-79; chmn. Fedn. Western Soc. Neurology, Santa Barbara, Calif., 1976-77. Author: Wolff's Headache, 6th edit., 1993, Approach to Headache, 1973, 5th edit., 1992; editor: Headache jour., 1965-75, 79-84, Scripps Clinic Personal Health Letter; mem. editl. bd.: Jour. AMA, 1977-87; columnist San Diego Tribune. Capt. U.S. Army, 1957-59. Recipient Disting. Alumnus award Wesleyan U., Middletown, Conn., 1982. Fellow ACP; mem. Am. Acad. Neurology (assoc.), World Fedn. Neurology (Am. sec. 1980-90, rsch. group on migraine), La Jolla Country Club, La Jolla Beach/Tennis Club. Republican. Roman Catholic. Avocations: tennis, squash, piano. Home: 8891 Nottingham Pl La Jolla CA 92037-2131 Office: Scripps Clinic & Rsch Found 10666 N Torrey Pines Rd La Jolla CA 92037-1092

DALEY, ARTHUR STUART, retired humanities educator; b. Osceola, N.Y., Sept. 16, 1908; s. Kieran A. and Mary (Adams) D.; m. Jean Abendroth, Aug. 29, 1942; 1 child, Arthur Stuart. AB with honors in English, Syracuse U., 1932; postgrad., Harvard U., 1932-33; PhD, Yale U., 1942. Instr. English Syracuse (N.Y.) U., 1935-37, Ind. U., 1946-47, UCLA, 1947-49; asst. prof. English U. Nev., 1949-54; prof., chmn. dept. Coe Coll., 1954-59; prof. Drake U., Des Moines, 1959-76, chmn. dept., 1959-67, coord. humanities div., 1967-75, prof. emeritus, 1976—. Co-author: Private Charity in England, 1747-57, 1938; contbr. articles, especially on Shakespeare, to profl. jours.; contbr. articles to rev. Norton crit. edit. Wuthering Heights (Emily Bronte), Shakespeare Studies XXI, The Upstart Crow XIV. Served to lt. col. AUS, 1941-46, 51-53; lt. col. AUS ret. Decorated Bronze Star; hon. grant of English armorial bearings, 1978; mem. by right Ancient and Hon. Arty. Co. Mass. Mem. MLA, Soc. Mayflower Descs., Shakespeare Assn., Brontë Soc., Theta Alpha Phi, Sigma Nu. Home: 2705 Barnson Pl San Diego CA 92103-6103

DALEY, VETA ADASSA, educational administrator; b. St. Elizabeth, Jamaica, Jan. 14, 1953; came to U.S., 1981; d. Waldemar and Princess (Bartley) Solomon; m. Vincent Daley, Jan. 27, 1973; children: Yuland, Angelo. Cert. in edn., U. W.I., Jamaica, 1978; BS, Westfield (Mass.) State Coll., 1987, MEd in Adminstrn., 1991. Tchr. Ministry Edn., Jamaica, 1972-81, Forest Park Jr.-Mid. Sch., Springfield, Mass., 1987-92; grad. asst. Westfield State Coll., 1988-90; asst. prin. Duggan Mid. Sch., Springfield, 1992-94; prin. John F. Kennedy Mid. Sch., Springfield, 1994—; Mem. Mass. Curriculum Adv. Commn., Malden, 1992—. Advisor Jamaica Festival Commn., Mandeville, 1973-80, Jamaica 4-H Clubs, 1970-76; vice chmn. adminstrv. bd. Wesley United Meth. Ch., Springfield, 1988—, pres. Meth. Women, 1991-93; chmn. Liberian Christian Fund, Springfield, 1990, New Eng. Conf. United Meth. Women, 1994; mem. African Task Force-R.I., 1991—. Recipient Outstanding Achievement award Jamaica 4-H Clubs, 1975, Outstanding Achievement in Edn. award Jamaican Cmty., Springfield, 1992, citation Mass. Ho. of Reps., 1992. Mem. New Eng. League Mid. Schs., Springfield Adminstrv. Assn., Jack and Jill Am. (pres. Springfield chpt. 1992—, Disting. Mother of Yr. award ea. region 1994). Home: 81 Embury St Springfield MA 01109-1847 Office: John F Kennedy Mid Sch 1385 Berkshire Ave Indian Orch MA 01151-1819

DALEY, VINCENT RAYMOND, JR., real estate executive, consultant; b. Evanston, Ill., June 21, 1940; s. Vincent R. and Carole V. (Johnson) D.; m. Viola Elizabeth Bursiek, May 6, 1967; children: Kathleen Marie, Colleen Patricia. AA, Lincoln Coll., 1961; BS, Loyola U., Chgo., 1963; student in real estate, Roosevelt U., 1964. From salesman to store mgr. Sears Roebuck & Co., Chgo., 1962-73; v.p., cons. Kencoe Corp., Des Plaines, Ill., 1973-74; pres. Daley & Assocs., Chgo., 1974—; chmn. Wacker Real Estate Svcs., Chgo., 1997—; chmn. Wacker Mgmt. Corp., Chgo. Mem. Econ. Devel. Com., State of Ill., Springfield, 1985-88; state legis. asst. 8th Legis. Dist., Chgo., 1985-93. Men. Chgo. Bd. Realtors (life) (bd. dirs.), Nat. Assn. Realtors (bd. regents), Ill. Assn. Realtors (bd. dirs.), Realtors Land Inst. (bd. govs.), Realtors Nat. Mktg. Inst. (CCIM), Internat. Real Estate Fed. (sr. cert. valuerer, registered internat. mem., cert. investment finnancier). Democrat. Roman Catholic. Avocation: traveling. Home: 1807 N Orleans St Chicago IL 60614-5325 Office: Wacker Real Estate Svcs 400 N Michigan Ave Ste 415 Chicago IL 60611-4129

DALEY, WILLIAM M., federal government official; m. Loretta Daley; 3 children. BA, Loyola U.; LLB, John Marshall Law Sch., Chgo., LLD (hon.). Bar: Ill. 1975. With Daley and George, Chgo.; ptnr. Mayer, Brown & Platt; vice chmn. Amalgamated Bank, Chgo., 1989, pres., COO, 1990-93; sec. Dept. Commerce, Washington, 1997—; spl. counsel to Pres. for NAFTA. Recipient St. Ignatius award fro Excellence in the Practice of Law, 1975, World Trade award World Trade Ctr., Chgo., 1994. Office: Dept Commerce 14th St And Constitution Ave N rm 5854 Washington DC 20230-0001

D'ALFONSO, GIOVANNI, cardiologist, researcher; b. Palermo, Italy, Nov. 25, 1964; s. Angelo and Giovanna (Di Gregorio) D. Degree, Medicine Faculty, Palermo, Italy, 1990. Diplomate. Pvt. practice Palermo, 1992—; asst. FBF Hosp., Palermo, 1998—. Avocations: languages study, computers. Home: Corso Dei Mille N 704, 90123 Palermo Italy

DALGAARD, JØRGEN BREMS, retired educator, physician, medical examiner; b. Viborg, Denmark, June 11, 1918; s. Johannes N.B. and Laura (Brems) D.; m. Ena Bach, Sept. 30, 1944 (div. 1981); children: Lena, Lone, Lise; m. Anne Marie Jexner, Mar. 22, 1985; 1 child, Karin. MD, U. Copenhagen, 1943, PhD in Medicine, 1950. Intern and fellow various hosps., Sweden, 1943-45; prosector in anatomy and pathology U. Aarhus, Denmark, 1945-53, prof. in forensic medicine, 1959-88, dean faculty of medicine, 1964-65; asst. prof. pathology and forensic pathology U. Bergen, Norway, 1954-58; asst. prof. pathology Mayo Clinic, Rochester, Minn., 1958; ret.; cons. pathologist various hosps., Denmark, 1960-90; med. chmn. Copenhagen Clinic, Borup, Denmark, 1989-90; pathology Mcpl. and County Hosp., Molde, Norway, 1991-95. Author thesis on phosphatase and jaundice, 1950, monograph on carbon monoxide deaths, 1961, Forensic Medical Memoirs, 1997; contbr. numerous articles on forensic and traffic medicine to profl. jours.; editor reports in field. Med. officer various youth and scout camps. Lt. Med. Corps Finnish Army, 1941; capt. Med. Corps Danish Army, 1945, 51-55. Recipient Liberty Cross, Marshal Mannerheim of Finland, 1946; named to Order of Knighthood, King of Denmark, 1967, Queen of Denmark, 1983. Mem. Danish Assn. Traffic Medicine (hon., bd. dirs.), Scandinavian Assn. Traffic Medicine, Finnish Assn. Traffic Medicine (hon.), Swedish Assn. Traffic Medicine (hon.), Norwegian Assn. Traffic Medicine (hon.), Danish Assn. Forensic Medicine(hon.), German Orgn. Forensic Medicine, Brit. Orgn. Forensic Medicine, Internat. Assn. Traffic Medicine (Gerin medal 1989), Pan Orienteering Club. Home: Elmehøjvej 32, DK-8270 Højbjerg Denmark

DALGAARD-KNUDSEN, FRANTS, lawyer; b. Ringkjøbing, Denmark, Sept. 15, 1960; s. Knud and Lone D.-K.; m. Anne Marie Folkmar, Aug. 1, 1992; 2 children. LLB, U. Aarhus, Denmark, 1984; postgrad., U. Oslo, 1987; PhD in Law, European Univ. Inst., Italy, 1991. Bar: High Ct. Denmark, 1991, Supreme Ct., Denmark, 1996. Rschr. European Univ. Inst., 1984-87; nat. expert European Cmtys. Commn. Directorate Gen. XI, Belgium, 1987, Ctr. Electronic Documentation of the Supreme Ct. Cassazione, Italy, 1986-90; lawyer/adv. Koch-Nielsen & Grønborg, Denmark, 1988-96; ptnr. Plesner & Grønborg, Denmark, 1997—; NRC Coun. fellow, Denmark, 1990. Author: Mineral Concessions and Law in Greenland, 1991, (booklet) Utvindingskoncessioner, 1987; co-author: European Environmental Yearbook, 1988, International Legal Procedures in Denmark, 1995; contbr. articles to profl. jours. Mem. Am. Soc. Internat. Law, Danish Bar Assn., Internat. Bar Assn. Office: Plesner & Grønborg, Esplanaden 34, DK-1263 Copenhagen Denmark

DALGLEISH, ANGUS GEORGE, oncology educator; b. London, May 14, 1950; s. Ronald and Anna Eileen D.; m. Judy Ann Riley, Sept. 28, 1984; 1 child, Tristan Amadeus. BSc with honors, Univ. Coll., London, 1971, MB, BChir, 1974; MD, U. London, 1989. Cert. med. oncology. Med. officer Australian Flying Doctor Svc., Mt. Isa, Queensland, 1976-77; registrar Princess Alexandra, Brisbane, Australia, 1977-80, Queensland Radium Inst., 1980-81; oncology staff Royal Prince Alfred, Sydney, Australia, 1982-83; rsch. fellow ICR Royal Marsden Fulham Rd., 1984-86; cons. Clin. Rsch. Ctr., Northwick Pk. Hosp., 1986-91; found. chair oncology U. London, St. Georges Hosp. Med. Sch., 1991—; mem. sci. adv. bd. Progenics and Celgene, U.S.; sr. lectr., cons. virology Royal London Hosp., 1991; vis. prof. Inst. Cancer Rsch., 1997—; rsch. dir. Onyvax, 1997—. Co-editor: AIDS and the New Viruses, 1992, Tumor Immunology, 1995, HIV and the New Viruses, 1998; contbr. articles to profl. jours. Grantee Wellcome, MRC, CRC, LRF, EEC, Ralph Bates Cancer Trust. Fellow Royal Australian Coll. Physicians, Royal Coll. Physicians, Royal Coll. Pathologists. Avocations: music, flying, skiing, wind surfing. Office: St Georges Hosp Med Sch, Cranmer Terrace, London SW17 0RE, England

DALIGAND, DANIEL, engineer, association executive, expert witness; b. Lyon, France, June 14, 1942; s. Maurice and Pierina Maria (Grandelli) D.; m. Christiane Elisabeth H. Agobian, Dec. 17, 1966. M in Chem. Engring., Inst. Chimie et Physique Industrielles, 1965. Cert. engr. Engr. Syndicat Nat. des Industries du Plâtre, Paris, 1967-72, gen. sec., 1972—; adminstrv. sec. Eurogypsum, Paris, 1971—; sec. 13 mem. jury best craftsmanship in plaster work soc., Paris, 1982, 86; counsellor for technol. edn., 1986—; chmn. French Com. for Standardization of Gypsum and Gypsum Products, 1996; chmn. CEN/TC 241, European com. for standardization of gypsum products; chmn. French Commn. for Reaction to Fire Testing Methods, 1999. Author: (with J. Gibaru) Le Platre, 1981, (with others) Le Platre, Physico chimie, fabrication, 1982, Le Platre-Techniques de l'Ingenieur, 1994; editor Platre Info. Jour. Office: SNIP, 3 Rue Alfred Roll, 75017 Paris France

DALÍK, JOSEF, research mathematician, educator; b. Krnov, No Moravia, Czech Republic, Oct. 18, 1949; s. Jaromír and Melanie (Šušliková) D.; m. Terezie Knytlová, June 19, 1976; children: Hana, Josef, Klára. RNDr, Masaryk U., Brno, Czech Republic, 1975, CSc, 1979, docent, 1990. Stipendiary Math. Inst. Czech Acad. Sci., Brno, 1974-76; rschr., tchr. Brno U. of Tech., 1977—, head dept. math., 1997—; visitor Politechnika Poznan, U. Torun, Poland, 1980, NUI Maynooth, Ireland, 1998. Contbr. numerous articles to math. jours.; reviewer (jour.) Mathematical Reviews, 1980—. Mem. acad. senate, Technical U., 1990-99. Recipient rsch. grant Czech Republic, 1995. Mem. Am. Math. Soc., Assn. Czech Mathematicians and Physicians. Avocations: history, languages, sports. Office: Tech U Dept Math, Žižkova 17, 60200 Brno Czech Republic

DALINKA, MURRAY KENNETH, radiologist, educator; b. Bklyn., May 13, 1938; s. Joseph and Gertrude (Cohen) D.; m. Janice L. Kolber, Feb. 28, 1982; 1 son, Bradford Gordon; children by previous marriage: Ilene, Ian Scott. BS, U. Mich., 1960, MD, 1964. Diplomate Am. Bd. Radiology. Intern Pa. Hosp., Phila., 1964-65; resident in radiology Montefiore Hosp., N.Y.C., 1965-68; instr. radiology Harvard Med. Sch., 1970-71; from asst. prof. to assoc. prof. radiology Thomas Jefferson U. Hosp., Phila., 1971-76, prof., 1976—; chief orthop. radiology Hosp. U. Pa., 1976—; chief diagnostic radiology Thomas Jefferson U. Hosp., Phila., 1974-76; cons.hila. Naval Hosp., 1974-79, Walson Hosp., Ft. Dix Army Base, 1972-77. Author: Arthography, 1980, Symposium on Orthopedic Radiology, 1983; mem. editorial bd. Bone Syllabus IV, 1982—, Skeletal Radiology, 1982—, Conversations in Radiology, 1977-79; guest editor Emergency Medicine Clinics of North America, Vol. 3, 1985; editor: (with J.J. Kaye) Radiology in Emergency Medicine Clinics in Emergency, Vol. 3, 1984, (with J. Edeiken and D. Karasick) Edeiken's Roentgen Diagnosis of Diseases of Bone, 4th edit. Served to capt. USAF, 1968-70. James Picker research fellow, 1972-73. Mem. Internat. Skeletal Soc. (past pres.), Radiol. Soc. N.Am., Am. Coll. Radiology, Phila. Roentgen Ray Soc. (past pres.). Home: 318 S 21st St Philadelphia PA 19103-6531 Office: U Pa Hosp Dept Radiology 3400 Spruce St Philadelphia PA 19104-4206

DALLA MARIA, GABRIELE FELICE, water industry executive; b. Milan, Italy, July 10, 1953; s. Argia Margherita Pepe; m. Susanna Olivieri, June 9, 1984 (div. 1996); m. Grazia Monti, July 1997; children: Francesco Giacomo and Martina (twins). Degree in econs., Bocconi U., 1978. Qualified pub. acct., Tribunal Public Appraisal. Ct. apptd. expert for co.y appraisal Milan, 1997; auditor Arthur Young & Co., Milan, 1978-82; adminstrv. dir. Sim Brunt-Schlumberger, Milan, 1982-87, Braun Italy Gillette Group, Milan, 1987-90; adminstrv. and fin. mgr. Italseta, Como, Italy, 1990-92; fin. mgr. Sirtis Waste Mgmt. Group, Como, 1992-95; adminstrv. and fin. exec. Binda, Olgiate Olona, Italy, 1995-97; CFO USF Smogless, Italy, 1998; also bd. dirs. USF Italy; CFO FNAC Italia. Sgt. Italian Air Force, 1975-76. Avocation: collecting ancient books and coins. Home: Via Cosimo del Fante # 2, 20122 Milan Italy Office: FNAC Italia, Via Della Palla No 2, 20123 Milan Italy

DALLAS, DANIEL GEORGE, social worker; b. Chgo., June 8, 1932; s. George C. and Azimena P. (Marines) D.; B.A., Anderson (Ind.) Coll., 1955; B.D., No. Bapt. Theol. Sem., 1958; M.S.W., Mich. State U., 1963; M.Div., No. Bapt. Theol. Sem., 1972, D.Min., 1981; m. G. Aleta Leppien, May 26, 1956; children—Paul, Rhonda. Mem. faculty Mich. Dept. Corrections, Mich. State U., 1963-66; med. social adminstr. Med. Svcs. divsn. Mich. Dept. Social Svcs., 1966-68; cons. Outreach Ctr. of DuPage County, 1976—, also dir. social service Meml. Hosp. of DuPage County, Elmhurst, Ill., 1968—; therapist, lectr. Traffic Sch., Elmhurst Coll.; pvt. practice; indsl. cons. Mem. Elmhurst Sr. Citizen Commn., 1976—. Recipient Outstanding Service award Mental Health Assn. Ill., 1978. Mem. Nat. Assn. Social Workers, Soc. Hosp. Social Work Dirs., Am. Hosp. Assn., Nat. Registry of Health Care Providers, Mental Health Assn. Chgo. Club: Rotary. Contbr. articles to profl. jours. Office: 242 N York St Ste 203 Elmhurst IL 60126-2747

DALLAS, EUGENIA, artist, writer; b. Ukraine, Aug. 24, 1925; came to U.S., 1951; m. Stewart Dallas, Apr. 7, 1973 (div. Sept. 1993); 1 child, Gene Peter Elson. Author: The Destiny of Ukrainian Beauty, 1993, One Woman, Five Lives, Five Countries, 1998. Activist for independence of Dem. Ukraine, Calif. Aid to Ukraine. Mem. Press Club, Writers Club, Woman in Film, Motion Picture Coun. Fax: (323) 874-0761. E-mail: edallas1@aol.com. Home: 6702 Hillpark Dr Los Angeles CA 90068-2163

DALLEMAGNE-COOKSON, ELISE CAMILLE, writer; b. Tarrytown, N.Y., Mar. 31, 1933; d. Edmund Leo and Irene (Poisson) Cookson; m. Jeremy Gaige, June 6, 1951 (div. June 1955); m. Pierre Georges Dallemagne (dec. May. 1979); children: Pierre E., Paul C. AB, Katherine Gibbs Bus. Sch., 1951; student, NYU, 1951-52, Syracuse U., 1952-54, Fla. Inst. Tech., 1973-75. Publicist, prodn. asst. United Artists, 20th Century Fox, Columbia Pictures, N.Y., Hollywood, Calif., 1955-59; pub. affairs officer U.S. Fgn. Svc., Belgian Congo, 1959-60; farmer Congo and Argentina, 1959-68; internat. hi-tech sales rep. Harris Computers Fla., 1975-78; registered rep. Wall Street various internat. banks, N.Y.C., 1980-89; fgn. lang. tchr. Cherry Valley (N.Y.) Schs., 1989-93; freelance writer Cherry Valley, 1993—. Author: The Bearded Lion Who Roars, 1995, The Ombu Tree, 1998, The Filmmaker, 2000. Avocations: farming, teaching. Home and Office: 311 County Highway 34A Cherry Valley NY 13320-2404

DALLEN, RUSSELL MORRIS, JR., investment company executive, lawyer; b. Biloxi, Miss., Jan. 20, 1963; s. Russell Morris and Faye Annette (Werner) D.; m. Claire Lucia Hodgson, May 27, 1995; 1 child, Allegra Julia Faye. BA in Econs. and Polit. Sci., U. Miss., 1985; M in Internat. Affairs, Columbia U., 1987; Diploma in Internat. Law, Nottingham (Eng.) U., 1988; BA in Jurisprudence, Oxford (Eng.) U., 1990, MA in Law, 1994. Fgn. corres. Newsweek, London, 1990-91; sr. fellow, dir. UN Assn.-USA, N.Y.C., 1991-93; assoc. Morgan Stanley & Co., Inc., N.Y.C., 1994-96; ptnr. Stires, O'Donnell & Co., Inc., 1996-99, Brisbane, Mendez de Leon & Co., Fahnestock & Co. Inc., 2000—. Author: Revitalizing The United Nations, 1993; (with others) Issues Before the United Nations, 1989, A Global Agenda, 1992; contbr. articles to profl. jours. Mem. bd. govs. Harold W. Rosenthal Fellowship, Washington, 1985—; mem. exec. com. Manhattan coun. Boy Scouts Am., N.Y.C., 1992—; vol. Big Bros./Big Sisters, N.Y.C., 1992—. Recipient Ner Tamid Leadership award Nat. Jewish Com. on Scouting, 1979, Kluwer Internat. Law award, 1990, Article of Yr. award Common Market Law Rev.; named Century III Leader, 1981; Harry S. Truman scholar, 1983, U.K. Fgn. and Commonwealth Office scholar, 1987; Harold Rosenthal fellow, 1985, Am. fellow European Communities, 1986, Ctr. fellow Ctr. for Study of Presdy., 1985. Mem. N.Y. State Bar Assn., N.Y. County Lawyers Assn. (chmn. sub-com. 1992—), Oxford and Cambridge Club, Squadron A Club, Cornell Club, Landsdowne Club. Avocations: sailing, flying, riding. Home: M-365 PO Box 020010 Miami FL 33102-0010

DALLI, JOHN SAVIOUR, Maltese government legislator; b. Qormi, Malta, Oct. 5, 1948; s. Carmel and Emma (Bonnici) D.; m. Josette Callus, Sept. 21, 1975; children: Claire, Louisa. Fin. contr. Blue Bell Malta, 1977; mgr. MIS Blue Bell Europe, Brussels, 1977-79; pvt. cons. Malta, 1981-87; jr. min. for industry Malta Govt., 1987-89, min. econ. affairs, 1989-92, min. of fin., 1992-96, chmn. pub. accts. com., 1996-98, min. fin., 1998—; mem. Ho. of Reps. Malta Parliament. Fellow Chartered Assn. Cert. Accts. Roman Catholic. Avocation: reading. Home: 272 Main St, Balzan Malta Office: Cavalier House, Old Mint St, Valletta Malta

DALLÓ, JÁNOS, pharmacologist, researcher; b. Győr, Hungary, Mar. 7, 1936; s. Gyula and Gyuláné (Turóczi) D. MD, Med. U., Budapest, 1961. Asst. prof. pharmacology Med. U. Budapest, 1961-77; 1st asst. dept. pharmacology Semmelweiss U. Medicine, Budapest, 1977-82, assoc. prof., 1982—. C0-author: Pharmacology, 1987, 97; contbr. articles to profl. jours. Mem. N.Y. Acad. Scis., Hungarian Pharm. Soc., Hungarian Physiol. Soc., Hungarian Gerontol. Soc., Hungarian Neurosci. Soc. Avocations: composing and playing music. Home: Jégverem utca 8, H-1011 Budapest Hungary Office: Semellweiss U Pharm/Therap, Nagyvárad tér 4, H-1085 Budapest Hungary

DALLOS, GEORGE, electrical engineer, educator; b. Budapest, Hungary, Oct. 3, 1940; s. Ferenc and Etelka (Mikoczy) D.; m. Katalin Hajdu, Aug. 19, 1992. MS, Tech. U. Budapest, 1965; PhD, Hungarian Acad. Sci., 1987. Technician Hungarian TV, Budapest, 1958-60; from asst. prof. to assoc. prof. Tech. U. Budapest, 1965—. Co-author: Random Access Radio Channels, 1984; contbr. articles to profl. jours. Mem. IEEE. Office: Tech U Budapest, Sztoczek 2, H-1111 Budapest Hungary

DALMASSO, FILIBERTO, physician; b. Turin, Italy, Mar. 26, 1940; s. Giocondo and Ernesta (Germena) D. Degree in medicine, surgery, Italy, 1970. Tng. Turin U., Italy, 1968-72; asst. physician emergency dept. Osp. Mauriziano, Torino, Italy, 1972-75, asst. physician pulmonary divsn., 1975-77, vice head pulmonary divsn., 1977-82, head pulmonary divsn., 1982—; prof. sch. diseases of respiratory apparatus Milan U.; guest scientist and co-author Istituto Elettrotecnico Nazionale Galileo Ferraris of Turin; cons. pneumologist Inst. di Ricerca e Cura dei Tumori, Mauriziano Ordine, FIAT of Torino; leader sleep apnea group, Assn. Italiana Pneumologi Ospedalieri, 1996, WP4 European sci. project on respiratory sounds, 1995, 97. Contbr. of 100 articles to profl. jours. Recipient Respiratory Medicine prize of Ordine Mauriziano, Ordine del Cavalieri di Malta; grantee EDO Tempia Found., 1993. Fellow Centro Internat. Ricerche Giuridiche Iniziative Sci.; mem. AAAS, European Respiratory Soc., Assn. Italian Pulmonary Medicine, Am. Thoracic Soc., N.Y. Acad. of Scis., Respiratory Sounds European Club. Avocations: sailing, music, photography. Home: C Unione Sovietica 385, 10100 Turin Italy Office: Mauriziano, L go Turati 62, 10100 Turin Italy

DALMIA, JAI HARI, cement company executive; b. Lahore, India, Sept. 18, 1944; s. Jai Dayal and Krishna Devi (Jalan) D.; m. Kavita Seksaria, June 11, 1966; 1 child, Gautam. BEE, Jadavpur U., Calcutta, India, 1966;

MSEE, U. Ill., 1969. Trainee Detroit Edison, 1969-70; exec. dir. Orissa Cement, Rajgangpur, India, 1970-75; pres. Dalmia Cement (Bharat) Ltd., New Delhi, 1975—; mem. exec. com. Dalmia Inst. Sci. and Indsl. Rsch., New Delhi, 1972—. Patentee for concrete aggregates for manufacture of concrete articles, manufacture of cement with phospho-gypsum. Mem. IEEE, Cement Mfrs. Assn. (mng. com. 1972-75), Indian Refractory Makers Assn. (mng. com. 1978-84, chmn. mng. com. 1984-86). Avocations: photography, gymnastics, swimming. E-mail: jhdalmia@ieee.org. Home: 1 Tees January Marg, New Delhi 110011, India Office: Dalmia Cement (Bharat) Ltd, 15 Barakhamba Rd 12th Fl, New Delhi 110001, India

DALOZ, LUCIEN CHARLES GILBERT, archbishop; b. Syam, Jura, France, Oct. 9, 1930; s. Fernand and Gabrielle (Dobez) D. Licenciate in scholastic philosophy, Gregorian U., Rome, PhD in Theology. Ordained priest, 1955. Chaplain St. Louis des Français, Rome, 1955-57; vicar Morez, 1957-58; prof. Grand Seminaire de Montciel, Lons-le-Saunier, 1958-61, head, 1961-69; vicar gen. Diocese St.-Claude, 1969-75; bishop Langres, 1975-81; archbishop Besançon, 1981—; pres. Comm. Épiscopale du Clergé, 1982-88; mem. Conseil Permanent de l'Episcopat, 1988-94, Commn. Épiscopale de l'Enseignement Religieux, 1989-94; délégué de la C.E.F. á la Commn. Episcopale de la Communauté Européenne, 1993-99, pres. Comm. Justice et Paix, France, 2000—. Author: Le Travail Selon St. Jean Chrysostome, 1959, Soumettez La Terre, Le Travail et l'Homme d'Aujourd'hui, 1964, Qui Donc Est-il?, 1984, Dieu a Visité son Peuple, 1986, Nous Avons Vu Sa Gloire, 1989, Le Régne des Cieux s'est approché, 1994. Office: Archevêché, 5 Rue de la Convention, 25041 Besançon Cedex, France

DALRYMPLE, CHRISTOPHER GUY, chiropractor; b. Beaumont, Tex., Sept. 2, 1958; s. Guy H. and Betty Jane (Williams) D.; m. Angela Hackley, Dec. 15, 1979; children: Sarah E., William C., Clayton G. Student, Baylor U., 1976-78; D in Chiropractic Medicine, Tex. Chiropractic Coll., 1982. Diplomate Nat. Bd. Chiropractic Examiners, Tex. Bd. Chiropractic Examiners; ordained Baptist Deacon, 1988. Chiropractor Brassard Chiropractic Clinic, Beaumont, 1982-85; chiropractic physician, adminstr. Brenham (Tex.) Chiropractic Clinic, 1985—; host Back Talk, 1987-88; cons., lectr. in field. Author: Brenham & Masonry...150 Years Together, 1995; contbr. articles to profl. jours. Team chiropractor track team Blinn Coll., Brenham, 1987-94, Tex. track and field participants Olympics, 1992; Sunday sch. dir. First Bapt., 1986-87, 90-93, Sunday sch. tchr., 1987-89, bd. trustees Calvary Bapt. Ch., Brenham, 1992-94, Sunday sch. tchr. youth, 1993-94, actor, playwright ch. pageants, 1993-94, 96, 98, 99, deacon, chmn., 1994-98, chmn. pers. com., 1995-98, chmn. long range planning com., 1995-98, adult Sunday sch. tchr., 1995-99; treas. Brenham Ind. Sch. Devel.-PAC, 1994; participant Health Occupation Students of Am. Program, Brenham H.S., 1992—. Recipient State Sweepstakes Winner "Jake", Tex. Jaycees, 1984, Outstanding Officer, 1984. Mem. Am. Chiropractic Assn., Tex. Chiropractic Assn. (state com., labor rels. 1983, membership com. 1994-95, dist. 9 sec. 1983-84, chmn. publ. com. 1987-99, editor-in-chief 1987-99, dist. 8 state dir. 1996-99, state sec. 1999, pres.-elect 2000, Young Chiropractor award 1997, Pres.'s award 1999), Christian Chiropractors Assn., Tex. Chiropractic Coll. Alumni Assn., Baylor Alumni Assn. (life), K.T., Gideons Internat. (bible chmn. 1994—), Graham Masonic Lodge (various offices), Delta Sigma Chi (sec. 1981, bd. dirs. 1982). Republican. Baptist. Avocations: computers, reading, sevice work, arts, drama. Office: Brenham Chiropractic Clinic PO Box 2350 Brenham TX 77834-2350

DALRYMPLE, FREDERICK RAWDON, government educator; b. Sydney, NSW, Australia, Nov. 6, 1930; s. Frederick Sydney and Evelyn Jane (Nobbs) D.; m. Ross Elizabeth Williams; children: David, Laura. BA, U. Sydney, 1951; MA, Oxford (Eng.) U., 1954. Lectr. U. Sydney, 1955-56; fgn. affairs officer Dept. External Affairs, Australia, 1959-94; min. Australian Embassy, Jakarta, Indonesia, 1969-72; ambassador Australian Embassy, Israel, 1972-75, Jakarta, Indonesia, 1981-85, Washington, U.S., 1985-89, Tokyo, Japan, 1989-93; head econ. divsn. Dept. Fgn. Affairs, Australia, 1976-81; chmn. ASEAN Focus Group Pty., Ltd., Sydney, 1994—; vis. prof. U. Sydney, 1994—. Dep. chair Australia-Japan Found., 1994—. Named Officer, Order of Australia, 1987. Avocations: golf, gardening, philosophy. Office: ASEAN Focus Group Pty Ltd, 140 Sussex St Level 5, Sydney NSW 2000, Australia

DALRYMPLE, GLENN VOGT, radiologist, educator; b. Little Rock, Dec. 28, 1934; s. Clyde William and Sarah (Darnall) D.; m. Mary Jo June, Dec. 23, 1955; children: Anne Theresa, Mark Gregory. BS, U. Ark., 1956, MD, 1958. Diplomate Am. Bd. Radiology, Am. Bd. Nuclear Medicine. Rotating intern and resident in radiology U. Arks. Med. Ctr., Little Rock, 1959-60; resident in radiology U. Colo. Med. Ctr., Denver, 1960-61, chief resident in radiology and rsch. assoc., 1961-62, instr., 1962-63; asst. prof. to prof. radiology U. Ark. for Med. Scis., Little Rock, 1965-73, chmn. dept. radiology, 1973-76, clin. prof. radiology and biometry, 1976-87, prof. radiology, 1987-90; with Radilogy Cons., Little Rock, 1976-87; prof. radiology and internal medicine U. Nebr. Med. Ctr., Omaha, 1990-96, prof. radiology, radiation oncology, internal medicine, 1995-96, interim chair dept. radiation oncology, 1995-96, spl. asst. to vice chancellor acad. affairs, 1996—; mem. radiation adv. com. FDA, Washington, 1978-80; attending staff dept. radiology U. Nebr. Med. Ctr., Omaha, 1990-96; courtesy staff dept. radiology St. Joseph Hosp., Omaha, 1990-96, VA Med. Ctr., Omaha, 1990-96; adj. clin. prof. radiology, radiation oncology, internal medicine U. Nebr. Med. Ctr., 1996—, adj. prof. Coll. Info. Sci. & Tech., 1996—. Co-author: Medical Radiation Biology, 1972, Basic Science Principles of Nuclear Medicine, 1974, Radiology in Primary Care, 1975, Practical Radioimmunoassay, 1975; contbr. book chpts. and articles to profl. jours.; assoc. editor Radiation Research Soc., 1974-76. French horn Heartland Philharm. Orch., 1990—, extra player Omaha and Lincoln (Nebr.) Symphony, 1990—; french horn/trombone Ark. Symphony Orch., Little Rock, 1965-89, bd. dirs., 1979-83. Capt. USAF, 1963-65. Grantee NASA, USAEC, NIH, Am. Cancer Soc., VA Med. Rsch. Fellow Am. Coll. Radiology (commn. pub. health radiol. units and stds. 1984-90, Ark. chpt. pres. 1979); mem. AMA, Soc. Nuclear Medicine, Radiation Rsch. Soc., Health Physics Soc., Internat. Wound Ballistics Assn., Nebr. Med. Assn., Radiation Rsch. Soc., Radiol. Soc. of N.Am., Sigma Xi, Alpha Omega Alpha. Office: Univ Nebr Omaha 60th & Dodge St Omaha NE 68182-0001

DALTON, ROBERT ISSAC, JR., textile executive, consultant, researcher; b. Charlotte, N.C., Apr. 2, 1921; s. Robert I. and Edith (Gossett) D.; m. Gwin Barnwell, Nov. 16, 1946; children—Millie, Edith. B.S. in Textile Engring., N.C. State U. Vice pres. sales Whitin Machine Works, Whitinsville, Mass., 1946-67; pres. Cocker Machine and Foundry, Gastonia, N.C., 1967-70, Tech-Tex Inc., Charlotte, 1970—, Gossett-Dalton Co., Charlotte, 1973—, dir., 1955—; bd. dir. Cadmus Communication Co., Richmond, Va., 1983-96, Am.-Truetzschler, Charlotte, 1976-97, N.C. Nat. Bank, Charlotte, 1962-94. Pres. Charlotte Symphony Orch., 1979-80; mem. bd. edn. Mecklenburg County, Charlotte, 1957-58; chmn. nat. bd. dirs. Handicapped Orgn. Women, Inc., 1986; chmn. bd. trustees Brevard Coll, 1987-93, Brevard Music Ctr., 1998—. Served to maj. U.S. Army, 1943-46, ETO. Mem. Phi Psi. Methodist. Clubs: Charlotte City (pres. 1980-81), Charlotte Country. Avocations: tennis; photography. Home: 318 S Canterbury Rd Charlotte NC 28211-1838

DALWADI, THAKOR SHANKERBHAI, company executive; b. Anand, India, Oct. 30, 1959; s. Shankerbhai Ashabhai and Shantaben (Shankerbhai) D.; m. Daxaben Thakor, May 7, 1987; children: Samir Thakor, Snehal Thakor. Diploma in Elec., B&B Poly., VV Nagar, India, 1979; postdiploma in Refrigeration & A/C, L.D. Engring., Ahmedabad, India, 1980. Trainee engring. L.D. Engring., Ahmedabad, 1980-81, Air Control & Chem. Engring., Barejadi, India, 1980-81; jr. engr. elec. Jyoti Switchgear Ltd., Mogar, India, 1981-82; tech. exec. Power Build Ltd., Vallabh Vidyanagar, India, 1983—. Sgt. Nat. Cadet Corps, 1973-74. Mem. PBL (tech. exec. 1982—), Lions. Mem. Swaminarayan Satsang Mandle. Swaminarayan Religious. Avocations: Navrang Zerox Centre, Navrang Telecom Service, Navrang Lamination, Navrang Gruh Udyog. Fax: 0091-2692-40402. Home: Opp DN High Sch, Prajapati, Bhoovan, Station Rd, Anand, Anand 388001, India Office: Power Build Ltd, PB No 28 Anand Sojitra Rd, Gujarat 388 121, India

DALY, CAHAL BRENDAN CARDINAL, retired archbishop; b. Loughguile, Northern Ireland, Oct. 1, 1917. Student, St. Malachy's Coll., Belfast, Northern Ireland; MA, Queen's U., Belfast; DD, St. Patrick's Coll., Maynooth, Ireland, 1944; L.Ph., Institut Catholique, Paris, 1953; hon. doctorate, Queens U., Belfast, Trinity Coll., Dublin, Nat. U. Ireland, Notre Dame U., Ind., St. John's U., N.Y., Sacred Heart U., Conn., Exeter U. Ordained priest Roman Cath. Ch., 1941. Lectr., reader in scholastic philosophy Queen's U., 1946-67; bishop of Ardagh and Clonmacnois Roman Cath. Ch., Longford, Ireland, 1967-82; bishop of Down and Connor Roman Cath. Ch., Belfast, 1982-90; archbishop of Armagh, primate of all Ireland Roman Cath. Ch., 1990-96, cardinal archbishop, 1991-96, ret., 1996, archbishop emeritus, 1996—. Author: Morals, Law and Life, 1962, Natural Law, Morality Today, 1965, Violence in Ireland and Christian Conscience, 1973, Peace, the Work of Justice, 1980, The Price of Peace, 1991, Law and Morals, 1993, Peace, Now is the Time, 1993, Steps on My Pilgrim Journey, 1998. Office: ARD Mhacha 23 Rosetta Ave, Belfast BT7 3HG, Northern Ireland

DALY, COTTON, air transportation executive; b. Brewster, Mass., June 30, 1932; s. Howard and Catherien (Dimpfl) D.; m. Susan C., Jan. 27, 1956; children: Elizabeth Robin, Elaine, Christopher, Catherine. BA, Syracuse U., 1954; MBA, U. Md., 1955. Cargo sales rep. Am. Airlines, N.Y., 1959-61; mgr. freighter sked Am. Airlines, 1961-64; mgr. fleet rsch. Trans World Airlines, 1964-69, dir. cargo strategy, 1969-72, dir. airfreight sales, 1972-77; dir. cargo sales devel. PanAm, 1977-79, dir. cargo Lat. Am., 1979-80, dir. express svc., 1980-82; v.p. Airport Cons. Group, Jamaica, N.Y., 1982-86, Manhasset, N.Y., 1986-89; pres. Cargo Mktg. Group, Brewster, Mass., 1990—. Author: (tng. manual) Professional Air Freight Sales Skills, 1986; contbr. articles to profl. jours. Recipient Professionalism award Cargo Network Svcs., 1994. Mem. Air Transport Assn. Am. (chmn. cargo 1972), Internat. Air Cargo Fourm, Soc. World Air Cargo Profls. (pres. 1990), Air Cargo Assn. (program chmn. 1991). Office: Cargo Mktg Group 17 Scallop Way Brewster MA 02631-1147

DALY, HERMAN EDWARD, economist, educator; b. Houston, July 21, 1938; s. Edward Joseph and Mildred Herrmann Daly; m. Marcia Damasceno, July 19, 1963; children: Theresa Maria, Karen Denise. BA, Rice U., 1960; PhD in Econs., Vanderbilt U., 1967. Prof. La. State U., Baton Rouge, 1963-88; sr. economist World Bank, Washington, 1988-94; prof. U. Md., College Park, 1994—. Author: Steady State Economics, 1991, Beyond Growth, 1996; co-author: For the Common Good, 1994. Democrat. Office: Sch Pub Affairs Univ Md College Park MD 20742-0001

DALY, JOHN PATRICK, nurse educator and administrater, researcher, cons; b. Dublin, Ireland, June 30, 1958; arrived in Australia, 1968; s. Michael and Angela Mary (Hickey) D. BA in Edn., U. Wollongong, NSW, Australia, 1986, MEd with honours, 1989; B Health Sci. in Nursing, Riviera-Murray Inst. Higher Edn., NSW, 1987; PhD in Nursing, So. Cross U., Lismore, NSW, 1994. RN, Australia. Nurse, nurse educator hosps., Wollongong and Sydney, 1980-85; clin. instr. critical care Wollongong Hosp., 1985; lectr. nursing U. Tech., Sydney, 1986-88, U. Sydney Cumberland Coll., 1989; sr. lectr., head dept. U. Newcastle, NSW, 1989-92; assoc. prof. nursing, head sch. Charles Sturt U., Wagga Wagga, NSW, 1992-95; assoc. prof. nursing, sr. head divsn. nursing, faculty health U. Western Sydney, Macarthur, 1995-96, prof. nursing, head nursing divsn., 1996—; cons. Harcourt Brace, Sydney, 1987-93, Australian Soc. Hosp. Pharmacists, Sydney, 1994. Editor, author: Critical Care Nursing, 1994; contbg. author: Illuminations: The Human Becoming Theory in Practice and Research, 1995; co-editor, author: Contexts of Nursing, 2000; also articles. Grantee NSW Health Dept., 1993, 94, also others. Fellow NSW Coll. Nursing, Royal Coll. Nursing Australia, Inst. Nursing Execs.; mem. Australian Coun. Deans Nursing. Avocations: golf, opera, classical music, cooking, snow skiing. Office: U Western Sydney Faculty Health, PO Box 555, Campbelltown NSW 2560, Australia

DALY, PATRICK F., real estate executive, architect; b. Chgo., Jan. 25, 1949; s. John F. and Margaret M. (Gleason) D.; m. Shirley J. Kumis, June 25, 1971; children: Sean P., James P. BArch with honors and distinction, U. Ill., Chgo., 1972, BA in Archtl. History with honors and distinction, 1972. Cert. arch., Ill. Prin. Patrick F. Daly Archs. & Engrs., Chgo., 1975-77; chmn. bd. Armanco, Inc., Chgo., 1977—, PFDA, Inc., Chgo., 1975—, Daley Realty Corp., Chgo., 1980—, Dalan Devel. Corp., Chgo., 1986—; pres. Dalan/ Jupiter, Inc., Chgo., 1987—; mng. ptnr. Rising Sun Riverboat Casino and Resort, LLC, Chgo., 1995—; chmn. The Daly Group LLC, 1995—; bd. dirs. Internat. Marine & Gaming, Inc. (chmn. bd.) Empire Cruise Lines, Inc. Contbr. articles to profl. jours. Chmn. Ill. Ambs., Chgo., 1990-98; vice chmn. Met. Pier & Expn. Authority, Chgo., 1985—; commr. Nat. Adv. Commn. U.S. Dept. Labor, Washington, 1991-93; trustee Fund Am. Studies, 1993—, Univ. Ill. Found., 1993—, dir. emeritus 1999, Inst. Cmty. Empowerment, 1991-98; chmn. Chancellor's Corp. adv. com. U. Ill., Chgo., 1995—; adv. bd. mem. Ind. Univ. Ctr. Real Estate Studies, 1994—; dir. U.S. Com. for UNICEF/Chgo., 1996—; pres. U. Ill. Alumni Assn., 1997-99; leadership com. United Way, 1998; coun. mem. Brookings Instn. Recipient Alumni Achievement award U. Ill., 1993. Mem. Pres.'s Club, Chgo. Coun. on Fgn. Rels., Arts Club Chgo., Alpha Rho Chi. E-mail: pdaly@thedalygroup.com. Office: The Daly Group 20 N Wacker Dr Ste 1500 Chicago IL 60606-2903

DAMAN, HARLAN RICHARD, allergist; b. N.Y.C., Nov. 1, 1941; s. D. Leon and Frances (Weissler) D.; AB cum laude, Harvard U., 1963; MD, Albert Einstein Coll. Medicine, 1967. Diplomate Am. Bd. Pediatrics, Am. Bd. Allergy and Immunology. Intern, then resident Yale-New Haven Hosp./Med. Ctr., 1967-69; fellow in allergy and clin. immunology Nat. Jewish Hosp. Research Ctr./U. Colo. Med. Ctr., Denver, 1971-73, instr., 1974-81; clin. asst. prof. pediatrics Albert Einstein Coll. Medicine, N.Y.C., 1981—; dir. pediatric allergy clinic Bronx Mcpl. Hosp. Ctr., 1982-92; mem. Mt. Sinai Med. Ctr./Sch. Medicine, 1976-90. Co-editor: Psychobiologic Aspects of Allergic Disorders, 1986; contbr. chpt. to Outpatient Medicine, 1980; contbr. articles on pulmonary function testing in asthmatic disorders. Served to maj. M.C., USAF, 1969-71. Fellow Am. Acad. Pediatrics, Am. Coll. Allergy, Asthma, and Immunology, Am. Coll. Chest Physicians, Am. Acad. Asthma, Allergy, and Immunology; mem. N.Y. Allergy Soc., Westchester Allergy Soc. (ednl. program dir. 1978-89, treas. 1980-81, pres. 1982-83), Westchester Acad. Medicine. Office: 769 Kimball Ave Yonkers NY 10704-1534

DAMANIA, KAUSHIK M., physician; b. Mumbai, India, Nov. 3, 1939; s. Maneklal G. and Vimla M. (Broker) D.; m. Uma K. Mehta, Sept. 18, 1943; children: Sanjeev, Sameer. MB, BChir, U. Bombay, 1964. Diplomate internal medicine, med. oncology, hematology Am. Bd. Internal Medicine. Attending physician Brooks Hosp., Dunkirk, N.Y., 1972-97. Fellow ACP; mem. Am. Soc. Hematology, Am. Soc. Clin. Oncology. Home: 601 Temple Bells, 37 KM Munshi Rd, Mumbai 400007, India

DAMAS, JACQUES ALPHONSE M., medical educator; b. Seraing, Liege, Belgium, May 1, 1944; s. Hubert and Antoinette (Godefroid) D.; m. Christiane Pondant, Oct. 15, 1970. MD, U. Liege, Belgium, 1971, D of Biomed. Scis., 1976, Agrege de L'Enseignement Superieur, 1982. Post-doctoral fellow U. Liege, 1971-77, asst., 1977-83, master of confs., 1980-87, first asst., 1982-87, prof., 1987—; prof. Inst. Studies Paramedics. for the Province of Liege, 1971-77, 80-82; Contbr. numerous articles to sci. jours. Mem. Acad. Royale de Scis. (Theophile Gluge award 1977, Alvarenda award 1987, Fredericq award 1989). Home: Place d'Italie 4/051, B-4020 Liege Belgium Office: Univ Liege, Place Delcour 17, B4020 Liege Belgium

D'AMATO, ANTHONY ROGER, recording company executive; b. N.Y.C., Jan. 21, 1931; s. Agostino and Luisa (Galiani) D'A.; m. Gabrielle Hilton, June 26, 1958; children—Luisa, Jennie, Tania, Joanna, Antonia. B.A. in Music and English Lit. cum laude (Founders Day award 1956), N.Y. U., 1956; MI.A. (teaching fellow), Brandeis U., 1957. Artist and repertoire dir. stereophonic div. Decca Record Co., Ltd., Eng., 1958-78; pres. TDA Prodns. Ltd., N.Y.C., 1978—; exec. dir. Winnipeg (Man., Can.) Symphony Orch., 1979-80; v.p. artist and repertoire AudioFidelity Enterprises, N.Y.C., 1980-81; mng. dir. Mantovani Prodns., Mantovani Orch., N.Y.C., 1982—; mng. cons. Leopold Stokowski, 1964-72. Served with USMCR, 1951-53. Recipient Grand Prix du Disque, Charles Cros award rec., 1969. Mem. Assn. Cultural Execs. Can., Winnipeg C. of C., Phi Beta Kappa.

DAMAY, PIERRE LOUIS, physics and chemistry educator; b. Framerville, Picardy, France, Aug. 10, 1942. Diploma in Phys. Sci., Lille, 1964, Doctorate, 1968; Doctorate, Paris, 1972; postgrad., Cornell U., 1972-74. Rschr. Nat. Sci. Rsch. Ctr., Lille, France. Contbr. numerous articles to profl. jours. Mem. French Soc. Physics. Achievements include research on the structure and dynamics of molecular systems. Office: LASIR CNRS, 13 rue de Toul, 53046 Lille France

DAMBALKAR, KIRAN, infectious diseases physician; b. Adhalli, India, June 16, 1958; s. Arvind Tammaji and Shantabai Arvind (Khambaswadkar) Dambal; m. Sapna Kiran Kohli, June 5, 1982; children: Geetarjali, Arvind. MB BChir, Med. Coll. Bellary, Karnataka, India, 1980; diploma venerology of dermatology, Delhi (India) U., 1992; MD, U. Alt. Medicine, Calcutta, India, 1994. Resident Karnataka Cancer Rsch. and Therapy Ctr., Hubli, India, 1980-81; med. officer Delhi Adminstrn. Dispensary, 1981; sch. med. officer Delhi Adminstrn., New Delhi, 1981-87, SHS, DHS, Delhi Adminstrn., New Delhi, 1987-88; zonal coord. Cholera Control Ops., Delhi, 1988-90; cons. ASHA, New Delhi, 1992-93, Delhi Kannada Sch., New Delhi, 1991—; program officer Centralized Accident and Trauma Svcs., New Delhi, 1990; dep. dir. blood safety AIDS Control Cell, Delhi, 1994-97; lit. sec. Med. Coll., Bellary, 1978; chief med. officer GECU, 1997-99; dep. dir. health svcs., 1997-98; state leprosy officer Delhi Govt., 1997-99; chief med. officer Nat. Anti-Malaria Program, 1999—. Fellow Indian Assn. for Study of Sexually Transmitted Diseases and AIDS; mem. Indian Med. Assn., Indian Assn. Dermatologists. Mem. Bharatiya Dem. Party. Hindu Brahmin. Avocations: stamp collecting, reading about science, watching stars, music, swimming. Fax: (011) 3968329. E-mail: drkiram@mantraonline.com. Home: Flat # 48D Pocket B, Vikaspuri Ext Outer Ring Rd, New Delhi 110018, India Office: Directorate of Health Svcs Delhi Govt, Dir Health Svcs Delhi Govt, 22 Sham Nath Marg, New Delhi 110054, India

D'AMBOLA, LORI SUSAN, speech therapist; b. Belleville, N.J., Feb. 12, 1977; d. Joseph Toby and Patricia Ann D'Ambola. BS in Communicative Disorders, U. Ctrl. Fla., Orlando, 1999; postgrad., William Paterson U., Wayne, N.J. Phys. therapy aide Robert Ruffalo, PT, DC, CCSP, Bloomfield, N.J., 1994-2000; immunizations coord. U. Ctrl. Fla., 1997-99; speech therapist Bergen County Spl. Svcs., Paramus, N.J., 1999—. Mem. Golden Key, Order of Omega, Alpha Xi Delta. Avocations: reading, exercise, running. E-mail: lorid45@erols.com. Home: 134 Weaver Ave Bloomfield NJ 07003-4924 Office: Bergen County Spl Svcs 327 E Ridgewood Ave Paramus NJ 07652-4832

D'AMBROSIO, DANIELE ATTILIO, marketing professional; b. Milan, Italy, Oct. 5, 1957; s. Giordano Bruno and Maria (Garavaglia) D'A.; m. Marina Danna, June 29, 1987; children: Viola, Luca. Electronic Engr., U. Rome, 1981. Asst. brand mgr. Procter & Gamble Italy, Rome, 1983-85, brand mgr., 1985-87, mktg. dir., 1989-92, corp. mktg. dir., 1993—; brand mgr. Procter & Gamble U.S.A., Cin., 1987-88, assoc. advt. mgr., 1988-89; dep. gen. mgr. Eurocos (Procter & Gamble), Milan, 1992-93; prof. Luiss MBA, Rome, 1995-98, Luiss Mgmt., Rome, 1995-98, U. L'Aquila, Italy, 1997—. Co-author: The Electronic Commerce, 1999. Lt. Italian Navy, 1981-83. Avocations: motor boating, skiing, reading. Office: Procter & Gamble, Via Cesre Pavese 385, 00144 Rome Italy

DAME, CATHERINE ELAINE, acupuncturist; b. Holyoke, Mass., Oct. 1, 1951; d. Josaphat Charles and Lillian Geneva (Archer) Boulanger; m. William Henry Dame, Jan. 9, 1970 (div. May 1999); 1 child, Cristinna Lian. Acupuncture Diplomate, N.E. Sch. Acupuncture, Watertown, Mass., 1992; student, Ind. U., 1988-93; MEd, Cambridge Coll., 1994. Lic. acupuncturist, Mass.; nat. bd. cert. in acupuncture. Dept. mgr. Zayre Dept. Store, Chicopee, Mass., 1969; retail sales clk. Woodward & Lothrop Store, Alexandria, Va., 1971-72; dept. mgr. Steiger Dept. Store, Enfield, Conn., 1972-73; retail sales clk. Point Dept. Store, Ft. Walton Beach, Fla., 1973-74; assembly, repair mfg. Texas Instruments, Ft. Walton Beach, 1974-75; tller Third Nat. Bank, Springfield, Mass., 1975-81, customer svc. rep., 1981-82; teller Bank of N.E./Fleet Bank, Springfield, 1990-93; owner, mgr. Acupuncture Svcs., Chicopee, 1994—; cons. Cambridge Coll., Springfield, Mass., 1994-95; bus. office liaison Cambridge Coll., 1995-98. Mem. Am. Assn. Oriental Medicine, Nat. Commn. for Cert. of Acupuncturists Directory, Bus. and Profl. Trade Exch., Acupuncture Soc. Mass., Granby Regional Horse Coun., Kings Bridge Equine Rescue, Inc., Chicopee C. of C. Office: Acupuncture Svcs Chicopee 665 Prospect St Chicopee MA 01020-3047

DAMERON, KATHLEEN GAIL, communications specialist; b. St. Louis, Dec. 22, 1957; d. Carl T. and Barbara Clementine (Mathis) D.; m. Michel Alain Josselin, June, 1981 (div. 1986). BA in Comm., U. Redlands, 1979; Lic. Adminstrn. Econ. Social, U. Paris VIII, 1981. Trainer Acrea, Paris, 1981-88, Thomson Consumer Electronics, Paris, 1988-92; gerante Fashion Fair, Paris, 1993—. Mem. TESOL France (pres. Paris 1989-91), Soc. for Intercultural Edn., Tng. and Rsch. France (exec. com. 1992—), Soc. for Intercultural Edn., Tng. and Rsch. Europe (exec. com. 1993-95). Avocation: oriental dance. Office: Fashion Fair, KD Conseil, 271 Rue St Denis, 75002 Paris France

DAMGAARD, ERIK, political scientist, educator; b. Graasten, Denmark, Nov. 3, 1943; s. Anders Peder and Maria Anna (Moos) D.; m. Anneli Matthiesen, Nov. 5, 1965; children: Helle, Claus. Degree in polit. sci., Aarhus U., 1968, D in Polit. Sci., 1977. Asst. prof. Aarhus U., 1968-71, assoc. prof., 1972-85, prof., 1985—, chmn. dept. polit. sci., 1993-98; vis. fellow Yale U., New Haven, Conn., 1971-72; dir. Sandbjerg Estate, 1990-95. Editor Scandinavian Polit. Studies, 1985-87; contbr. articles to profl. jours. Mem. Danish Polit. Sci. Assn. (chmn. 1980-84). Home: Hvedebjergvej 19, DK-8220 Brabrand Denmark Office: U Aarhus, Dept Polit Sci, DK-8000 Århus Denmark

DAMIANOS, PANAYIOTIS, electronic engineer; b. Athens, Greece, June 15, 1954; s. Dimitrios and Aggeliki (Galanou) D.; m. Fotini Chatzaki Damianou, Feb. 10, 1983; children: Christine, Diane. MSc, U. Bradford, Eng., 1977; PhD in Philosophy, 1981. Post graduate Nuc. Rsch. Ctr., Athens, Greece, 1978-80; software and hardware support Greek Navy, Athens, Greece, 1982-83; svc. engr. Meditec SA, Athens, Greece, 1983-85; sales engr. Hewlett Packard Hellas, Athens, Greece, 1985-86; tech. dir. Info Quest Aebe, Athens, Greece, 1987-89, Scan Group Saic, Athens, Greece, 1989—; tech. dir. ITT Viometal Eskimo Abe, Athens, Greece, 1975—; tech. mgr. Mitsakis Ltd., Athens, Greece, 1975—; tech. supr. Grafico AE, Athens, Greece, 1975—. Author: An Inverter System for Solar Energy Applications, 1977, Microprocessor Control of Traction Motors, 1981; patentee in field. Avocations: computing, fishing, hunting, mechanical engineering. Home: 13 Olynthou St, 11143 Athens Greece Office: Scan Group SAIC, Messogion 2-4, 115-27 Athens Greece

D'AMICO, ANDREW J., lawyer; b. Phila., Feb. 18, 1953; s. Joseph J. and Alice H. (Falotica) D'A.; m. Georgiana R. Etheridge, Feb. 25, 1978; children: Andrew J. Jr., Joseph W., Jennifer T., Theresa J. BA, St. Joseph's U., Phila., 1975; JD, Villanova U., 1978. Bar: Pa. Supreme Ct. 1978, U.S. Dist. Ct. (ea. dist.) Pa. 1979, U.S Ct. Appeals (3d Cir.) 1981, U.S Supreme Ct. 1982. Sole practitioner Law Offices Andrew J. D'Amico, Media, Pa., 1979—. Coach Llanerch Hills Little League, Drexel Hill, Pa., 1986-96, St. Bernadette CYO Basketball, 1996-2000. Mem. ATLA, Pa. Trial Lawyers Assn., Del. County Bar Assn. (bd. dirs. 1991-92, 97, 98), Guy G. deFuria Am. Inn of Ct. (pres. 1995-96), Alpha Sigma Nu. Roman Catholic. Avocations: music, coaching sports, reading. Office: PO Box 605 115 N Monroe St Media PA 19063-3037

D'AMICO, GIUSEPPE, nephrologist; b. Messina, Italy, Sept. 6, 1929; s. Gaetano D'Amico and Gaetana Trifiletti; m. Anna Maria Allegri, July 11, 1957; 1 child, Stefano. MD, U. Milan, 1952. Diplomate Italian Bd. Internal Medicine. Trainee NIH, Chgo., 1957-58; tng. in internal medicine U. Milan, 1957, tng. in clin.pathology, 1962, prof. medicine, 1962; head divsn. nephrology San Carlo Hosp., Milan, 1967-95, dir. dept. nephrology and urology, 1995—. Author 35 books on nephrology; contbr. over 400 articles to internat. med. jours., over 15 chpts. to internat. textbooks. Recipient Internat. Ganassini award, Milan, 1961, Ambrogino d'Oro Mayor of City of Milan, 1974, Disting. Internat. medal Nat. Kidney Found., 1997. Fellow Royal Coll. Physicians (London), Royal Coll. Physicians (Edinburgh); mem. Internat. Soc. Nephrology (coun. 1984-93), European Soc. Nephrology (exec.

coun. 1981-84), Italian Soc. Nephrology (pres. 1981-83). Office: San Carlo Hosp, Via Pio II 3, 20123 Milan Italy

DAMIER, PHILIPPE GERARD, neurology educator; b. St. Marcellin, France, Feb. 21, 1963; s. Gerard P. and Annette J. (Jullin) D.; m. Florence J. Delamarre, June 22, 1991; children: Alexandre P., Ambroise. MD, Pitié-Salpêtrière, Paris, 1989; PhD, Pierre and Marie Curie U., Paris, 1995. Resident in neurology Paris, 1989-93; postdoctoral fellow MIT, Boston, 1993-95; asst. prof. Pitié-Salpêtrière, Paris, 1995—; head clin. rsch. ctr. Pitié-saltpetrière, 1996-98; prof. neurology CHU Nantes, 1999—; cons. Found. Pharma, Paris, 1994. Recipient Fauvert prize, Paris, 1993; Nat. Parkinson Found. grantee, 1994, Lavoisier grantee, 1993. Mem. Soc. for Neurosci., Am. Acad. Neurology, Movement Disorder Soc. Office: Clin Neurol Hosp Luennec, CHU Nantes, 44093 Nantes France

DAMINATO, VANDA, artist; b. Mezzolombardo, Trento, Italy, May 26, 1951; d. Giovanni Daminato and Candida Marinelli. Accademico, Accademia Arti Dell Incisione, Pisa, Italy, 1980. With Palazzo Grassi, Venice, Italy, 1979, Galerie Internat., N.Y.C., 1981, Museo Leonardo da Vinci, Milan, 1987, Villa Olmo, Como, Italy, 1987, Palazzo Della Gran Guardia, Verona, Italy, 1987, Museo d'Arte Moderna, Malta, 1988. Avocations: collecting modern art, animals. Office: Corso XXII, Marzo 28, 20135 Milan Italy

DAMOUR, THIBAULT, physicist; b. Lyon, France, Feb. 7, 1951; s. Georges and Andree (Ribes) D. Ecole Normale Superieure, Rue D'Ulm, Paris, 1974; PhD, U. Paris, 1974; Agregation de Scis. Physiques, France, 1974; Doctorate, U. Paris, 1979. Attache de rsch. Ctr. Nat. de la Rsch. Sci., France, 1977-81, charge de rsch., 1981-85, dir. of rsch., 1985-92; prof. Inst. des Hautes Etudes Scientifiques, Bures sur Yvette, France, 1989—. Contbr. more than 100 articles to profl. jours. Recipient Paul Langevin prize Soc. Francaise de Physique, 1984, Mergier-Bourdeix prize Acad. des Scis., Paris, 1990, Einstein medal Albert Einstein Gesellschaft, Bern, Switzerland, 1996. Mem. Acad. Scis. Office: Inst des Hautes Etudes Scis, 35 Route de Chartres, 91440 Bures-sur-Yvette France

DAMS, RICHARD, chemistry educator, researcher; b. Mol, Belgium, Aug. 25, 1938; s. Imelda Sambre, Sept. 29, 1962. MS, U. Gent, Belgium, 1960, D of Chemistry, 1964, D of Environ. Chemistry, 1974. Asst. U. Gent, 1960-77, asst. prof., 1977-84, full prof., 1984—, dir. Lab. Analytical Chemistry. Author: Gammaspectrometry, 1972; contbr. over 300 articles on analytical chemistry to profl. jours. Recipient Environ. prize Belgian Govt., 1975. Mem. Royal Flemish Chem. Soc. Office: Inst Nuclear Scis, Proeftuinstraat 86, B9000 Ghent Belgium

DAMS, RUDOLF, research and development chemist; b. Lier, Belgium, Apr. 1, 1956; s. Jozef and Martha (Van Elshocht) D.; m. Nadine Mertens, Oct. 21, 1983; children: Mellissa, Jessica. PhD in Chemistry, U. Antwerp, Belgium, 1982. Chemist 3M, Zwijndrecht, Belgium, 1981-83, sr. chemist, 1983-86, specialist, 1986-92, sr. specialist, 1992—. Contbr. articles to profl. jours.; holder 10 patents in field. Sgt. major, Belgian Army Arty., 1981-82. Avocations: soccer, running, reading, gardening. Office: 3M Belgium-EBC, Canadastraat 11, 2070 Zwijndrecht Antwerp, Belgium

DAMS, WALTER JOZEF AUGUST MARIA, computer engineer; b. Lier, Antwerp, Belgium, May 18, 1954; s. Jozef and Martha (Van Elshocht) D.; m. Marie-Louise Fransen, July 4, 1986; children: Robin, Sam. Tech. engr., Stedelijk Inst Tech. Onderwijs, Mechelen, Belgium, 1976, M.N.L.T. in Pedagogy, 1978; indsl. engr. electronics, Ctrl. Com., Brussels, Belgium, 1985. Installation and support coord. Computervision, Brussels, 1979-85; customer engr. Tandem Computers, Brussels, 1985-86; asst. svc. mgr. Ctr. Gen. Info., Brussels, 1986-87; tech. dir. Alfhabyte N.V., Vilvoorde, Belgium, 1988; internat. svc. support mgr. Agfa-Gevaert N.V., Berchem, Belgium, 1988-93; maintenance mgr. Agfa-Gevaert N.V., Mortsel, Belgium, 1993-97; adj. mgr. med/order support desk Agfa-Gevaert M.V. Mortsel, Belgium, 1997-99, logistics equipment mgr. total quality mgmt. and system support, 1999—.arbitrator Ctr. for Arbitration, Brussels, 1994—; mem. examining bd. final exams. dept. electro-mechanics tech. higher edn. short type S.I.T.O. Author: (Installation guide) Installing Computervision Cad/Cam Systems in Benelux, 1983; contbr. to V.I.K.-Engrs. Register, 1996-97; contbr. articles to engring. publs. Vice chmn. Pub. Libr., Lint, Belgium, 1988-94; bd. dirs. Sport Coun., Lint, 1994-96; mem. Milieu Adv. Coun., Lint, 1994—; mem. project and team MEIHOF-Lint (open reception ctr. for candidates and polit. refugees requesting right of asylum), 1997-98,. Mem. Flemish Engrs. Soc. (bd. dirs. 1991—, course leader 1992—). Avocations: football (referee), modern music. Home: Hoog Heibos 27, 2547 Lint Antwerp, Belgium

DAMUS, PAUL SHIBLI, cardiac surgeon; b. San Bernardino, Calif., Dec. 14, 1942; s. Shibli Shibl and Margaret Joan (Salia) D.; m. Karla Hilda Kuder, Aug. 28, 1971; children: Robert, Michael. BA, U. Colo., 1964; MD, UCLA, 1968. Intern, resident in gen. surg. UCLA, 1968-70; rsch. fellow Harvard U., Boston, 1970-72; resident in cardiothoracic surgery Columbis-Presbyn. Hosp., N.Y.C., 1979-80; resident in pediatric heart surgery Hosp. for Sick Children, Toronto, Ont., Can., 1979-80; dir. infant cardiac surgery St. Francis Hosp., Roslyn, N.Y., 1980-92, dir. cardiac thoracic surgery, 1992—. Creator cardiac operation Damus Procedure. Maj. USAF, 1975-77. Fellow ACS; mem. Soc. Thoracic Surgeons. Avocations: fly fishing, ancient history. Office: St Francis Hosp 100 Port Washington Blvd Roslyn NY 11576-1348

DAN, DOUGLAS KOSLOFF, geophysics educator; b. Jerusalem, Mar. 5, 1947; s. Israel Ray and Jean (Ball) K.; m. Ronot Kaufman, Apr. 4, 1996; children: Jonathan, Zeiner, Alan, Natalie, Ayelet. BSc, Hebrew U. Jerusalem, 1972; PhD, Calif. Inst. Tech., Pasadena, 1978. Lectr. Hebrew U. Jerusalem, 1978-80; prof. geophysics Tel Aviv U., 1981—; vis. prof. U. Houston, 1981, Fed. U. Bahia, Brazil, 1986; rschr. Geophys. Devel. Corp., Houston, 1990-92; chief scientist Paradigm Geophys. Herzlia, Israel, 1992—. Capt. Israel Def. Forces., 1965-68. Home: Harar Itzhak Nissin 2, 46423 Herzlia Israel Office: Tel Aviv U, Dept Geophysics, 69978 Tel Aviv Israel

DANAHER, MALLORY MILLETT (MALLORY JONES), actress, photographer, writer, poet; b. St. Paul, 1939; d. James Albert and Helen Rose (Feely) Millett m. Thomas C. Danaher, Mar. 1985; 1 child by previous marriage, Kristen Vigard. BA, U. Minn. CFO, Sheets & Co., N.Y.C., Happy Camper, N.Y.C., Everwarm a Del. Corp. Active with N.Y. Theatre 1971—; mem. original cos. of Annie and The Best Little Whorehouse in Texas, 1977; stage roles in Dodsworth, Berkshire Theatre Festival, Hedda Gabler, Kennedy's Children (dir. Olympia Dukakis), Edward Albee's Everything in the Garden (dir. Shelley Winters), House of Blue Leaves by John Guare, Berkshire Theatre Festival, Tornado, Lincoln Ctr. Libr. Theatre, Stella, Nat. Horn Theatre, N.Y.C., Cocteau's one-character play The Human Voice at Deutsches-Haus, NYU, Full Moon and High Tide (dir. Shelley Winters); off-Broadway prodn. Loose Connections, Judith Anderson Theatre; also (TV series) Love of Life, CBS-TV, Another World, NBC, Hunter, Thirtysomething, Superior Ct., Divorce Ct., The Judge, (NBC Movie of the Week) Eischied: Only the Pretty Girls Die, (motion picture) Tootsie, Columbia Pictures, Hell Hath No Fury with Barbara Eden, New Line Cinema: Alone in the Dark; exhibitor of photography: Third Eye Gallery, N.Y.C., 1974—, Modernage Discovery Gallery, N.Y.C., 1976-79, Gallery of St. Clement's, N.Y.C., 1979, 80; performer own poetry; author: Fatherless Child; co-producer, subject of film Three Lives and Broadway prodn. Epic Proportions; contbr. poetry to mags. Mem. Creative Coalition. Mem. Nat. Assn. TV Programming Execs., Women in Theatre, Nat. Assn. for Self-Employed, Actors Studio, Am. Women's Econ. Devel., The Friars Club, Legatus, Claremont Inst., Ctr. for Study of Popular Culture (bd. dirs.).

DANAS, ANDREW MICHAEL, lawyer; b. Redwood City, Calif., Apr. 25, 1955; s. Michael George and Marjorie Jean (Bailey) D. BA in Polit. Sci. and History, U. Conn., 1977; JD, George Washington U., 1982. Bar: D.C. 1982, U.S. Dist. Ct. (D.C. cir.) 1985, U.S. Dist. Ct. Md. 1987, U.S. Ct. Appeals (Fed. cir. 1984), U.S. Ct. Appeals (11th cir. 1987), U.S. Ct. Appeals (3d and 4th cirs.) 1988, U.S. Ct. Appeals (6th cir.) 1990, U.S. Ct. Appeals (2d cir.) 1998, U.S. Ct. of Claims 1984, U.S. Supreme Ct. 1994. Atty. Assn. Am. R.R.s, Washington, 1983-84; assoc. Grove Jaskiewicz & Cobert, Washington, 1984-90, Ptnr., 1991—. Contbg. author: Freewheeling; author legal column Intermodal Reporter, 1986-94; contbr. articles to profl. jours. Exec. com. Friends Assisting the Nat. Symphony, Washington, 1996-97. Mem. ABA, Internat. Bar Assn., Euro-Am. Lawyers Group (mgmt. com. 2000—), Transp. Law Inst. (chair 1993-94, mgmt. com. 2000—), Transp. Lawyers Assn. (chmn. legis. com. 1995-98, co-chmn. 1999-2000, Disting. Svc. award 1996), Phi Alpha Theta, Mensa. Avocations: skiing, music, travel. Home: 621 Tivoli Psge Alexandria VA 22314-1932 Office: Grove Jaskiewicz and Cobert 1730 M St NW Ste 400 Washington DC 20036-4579

DANCKERT, JOACHIM, engineering educator; b. Soroe, Denmark, Oct. 27, 1949; s. Kristen Joachim and Ebba (Winkel) D.; m. BEnte Esther Rasmussen Bjoern, Sept. 21, 1985; children: Bolette, Amalie. MS, Tech. U. Denmark, Lyngby, 1974, PhD, 1977. Rsch. asst. Tech. U. Denmark, Lyngby, 1977-78; sr. researcher, 1983-85; engr. Hellesens A/S, Gentofte, Denmark, 1978-79; head tooling group Technol. Inst., Taastrup, Denmark, 1979-83; prof. dept. production Aalborg (Denmark) U., 1985—; chmn. European Doctoral Sch. Tech. and SCi. Aalborg U., 1993-96, study dir., 1996—. Mem. Danish Acad. Tech. Sci., Internat. Instn. Prodn. Engring. Rsch. Home: Kong Christians Alle 63, Ålborg 9000, Denmark Office: Aalborg U Dept Prodn, Fibigerstraede 16, Ålborg 9220, Denmark

DANDAPANI, S., management consultant; b. June 23, 1921; B.A. with honors; M.A. in Sociology; cert. in bus. mgmt., social welfare, indsl. relations Calcutta U.; diploma in social policy Inst. Social Studies, The Hague; Ph.D. in Sociology. With Indian Rys., 1946-65, divisional comml. supt., until 1965; dep. dir. Ministry of Rys., Govt. of India, New Delhi, 1965-75; cons., adv. Internat. Labor Orgn. UN, N.Y.C., 1973-76, cons. FAO, 1979; UN cons. dept. internat. econ. and social affairs, 1980-81; also cons. to Govt. Liberia; joint chief Internat. Coop. Alliance, London, 1976-80; FAO cons. to Sultanate of Oman, 1980, now mgmt. cons. Recipient State award, Govt. of Bahrain, 2 awards Jet Air. Fellow Brit. Inst. Mgmt., Inst. Sales Mgmt., Inst. Adminstrv. Acctg.; mem. Inst. Rail Transport, Sociol. Assn. India, Anthrop. Assn. Bombay. Author: Sale A Profile: An Introduction to Sales Management in Retailing; Business Switch: An Introduction to Business Management in Retailing; Rationalization of Consumer Movement in Western Europe; Fundamentals of Social Survey and Research Methods; Facts From Figures; Research and Planning Methodology for Co-Op Enterprises; The Role of a Nominated Director in A Consumer Co-op Society; editor: (with K.P. Kornholz) Productivity in Retailing; Membership and Cooperative Effectiveness; (with G.V.J. Pratt) Statistics: A Management Tool. Home: 10 Holly Grove, Kingsbury, London NW9 8QU, England

DANDASHI, FAYAD ALEXANDER, operations research scientist, consultant; b. Damascus, July 20, 1959; came to U.S., 1982; naturalized, 1989; s. Ghada (Bahnasi) Dandashi; m. Mami Tazaki, Apr. 12, 1989; 1 child: Leonard Levi. BArch, U. Aleppo, 1982; BSCE, George Washington U., 1987, Applied Scientist in Gen. Ops. Rsch., 1992; MSME in Aeronautics, Astronautics and Rocket Propulsion, George Washington U. & NASA, 1989; MSc in Math., Oxford (Eng.) U., 1994. Designer-analyst, design div. George Washington U., Washington, 1985-89, head design div., 1989-91, doctoral fellow, 1992-93, applied scientist, sci. rsch. assoc., 1992-93; vice chmn. FANEX Australia Pty. Ltd., Brisbane, Australia, 1995-96, Japan, 1996-97, Europe, 1997-98; dir. FANEX Australia Pty. Ltd., Brisbane, 1994-98; pres., CEO Lynk Internat. Group, N.Y.C., Beverly Hills, Paris, 2000—; co-founder, dir. ICQA Pty. Ltd., Brisbane, Australia, 1995-98, pres., CEO, 1995-96, dir. mktg. and client rels. in Japan, 1996-97; vis. scientist Kyoto (Japan) U., 1996-97; advisor external, polit. rels. Establishment Le Jour. du Parlement, France, 1999—, bus. devel., pub. rels. BDA Comm., France, 2000—, internat. bus. rels. The Comm. Miss France, 2000—; mem. bd. dirs. FANEX Party Ltd., ICQA Party Ltd., FANEX USA, Inc., 1998—. Mem. AAAS, AIAA (sr.), Ops. Rsch. Soc. Am., Inst. Mgmt. Sci., Fedn. Am. Scientists, Am. Jewish Hist. Soc., Sigma Xi, Omega Rho (v.p. 1993-94), Sigma Gamma Tau. Achievements include studies in stochastic and mathematical modeling, mathematical programming and optimization, numerical analysis, nonlinear dynamics and complexity, design and analysis of aerospace, air-breathing single stage earth-to-orbit vehicles and rockets with APS/RAMJET/SCRAMJET/LACE propulsion systems using slush hydrogen and slush oxygen propellant, advanced aerospace technologies, science & technology policy, mathematical/statistical marketing models, mathematical and statistical theory of probability, co-founder and dir. Australian private college and its network worldwide. Fax: (212) 787-4359. Calif. phone: (310) 801-8585; Paris phone: +33) (0) 1.4222665. Office: Ste 4-A 48 W 68th St Apt 4A New York NY 10023-6015

D'ANDREA, ASTRID, archivist; b. Rome, Mar. 19, 1974; d. Giulio and Giuliana (Di Santo) D'A. Diploma in fgn. langs. and lit., U. Rome, 1996. Area mgr. Alba-Field Ednl. Italia, Rome, 1996; dealer Ency. Britannica, Rome, 1996; sec. Enterprise Oil Italia, Rome, 1997, archivist, 1998—. Mem. Assn. Italian Bibliotech. Avocations: playing piano and guitar, singing, travelling, reading, music. Home: Via Antonino Bongiorno 40, 00155 Rome Italy Office: Enterprise Oil Italiana, Via Del Due Macelli 66, 00187 Rome Italy

D'ANDRÉA-NOVEL, BRIGITTE, mathematics and systems control educator; b. Villerupt, France, Jan. 13, 1961; d. Emile and Yvette d'A.; m. Marc Jean-Marie Novel, Oct. 27, 1984; 1 child, Marc-Antoine. M in Math., U. Metz, France, 1983; diploma in Math. and Control, U. Paris, 1984; PhD in Math. and Control, École des Mines de Paris, 1987; DSc, U. Paris Sud-Orsay, 1995. Engr. diploma Ecole Superieure Info. Electronics Automatique. Asst. prof. École des Mines de Paris, 1988-92, prof., 1992—. Author: Commande Non Linéaire des Robots, 1988, Commande Linéaire des Systèmes Dynamiques, 1994; co-author: Theory of Robot Control, 1996; pianist who gives chamber music concerts (with flute or violin) at many festivals in France. Recipient Bronze medal Nat. Sci. Rsch. Ctr., 1989. Mem. IEEE, Club EEA. Avocations:. Home: 31 rue Guyton de Morveal, 75013 Paris France Office: Caor-École des Mines de Paris, 60 Blvd Saint-Michel, 75272 Paris France

DANDY, DAVID JAMES, surgeon; b. Southport, Lancashire, Eng., May 30, 1940; s. James and Margaret (Coe) D.; m. Stephanie Jane Essex, Sept. 17, 1966; children: James Edward Oliver, Emma Jane. BChir, Cambridge (Eng.) U., 1964, MB, 1965, MD, 1990, MChir, 1994. House physician and surgeon The London Hosp., 1964-65; demonstrator dept. anatomy U. Cambridge, Eng., 1965-66; surg. registrar various hosps., Eng., 1966-73; sr. fellow Toronto Gen. Hosp., 1973-74; sr. orthop. registrar St. Bartholomew's Hosp., London, 1974-75; cons. orthop. surgeon Addenbrooke's Hosp., Cambridge, 1975—; assoc. lectr. U. Cambridge, 1975—; civilian advisor RAF, Eng., 1976—, Royal Navy, 1978—. Author: (text books) Arthroscopic Surgery of the Knee, 1981, Essentials of Orthopaedics, 1989 (Glaxo award for med. writing 1990); author: Arthroscopic Atlas of the Knee, 1987; co-author (text book) Arthroscopy of the Knee, 1976. Recipient Robert Milne prize for surgery The London Hosp., 1965. Fellow Royal Coll. Surgeons of Eng. (mem. coun. 1994—, James Berry prize 1982), Brit. Orthop Assn. (pres. 1998-99, Robert Jones medal 1991); mem. Internat. Soc. of the Knee (chmn. edn. com. 1991-95), European Soc. for Knee Surgery and Arthroscopy (bd. dirs. 1992-96), Brit. Sports Trauma Assn. (pres. 1993-95), Brit. Assn. for Surgery of the Knee (pres. 1996—), Internat. Arthroscopy Assn. (pres. 1989-91), Brit. Orthopedic Assn. (pres. 1998-99). Office: Addenbrookes Hosp, Orthop Dept Hills Rd, Cambridge CB2 2QQ, England

DANE, STEPHEN MARK, lawyer; b. Chillicothe, Ohio, Mar. 27, 1956; s. Clyde and Rita M. (Murray) D.; m. Kim P. Piatt, July 7, 1979; children: Tara, Adam, Shannon, Alexandra, Courtney. BS with honors, U. Notre Dame, 1978; JD magna cum laude, U. Toledo, 1981. Bar: Ohio 1981, U.S. Ct. Appeals (6th and 10th cirs.) 1982, U.S. Dist. Ct. (no. dist.) Ohio 1983, U.S. Dist. Ct. (no. dist.) Tex. 1983, U.S. Ct. Appeals (5th cir.) 1984, U.S. Supreme Ct. 1985, U.S. Ct. Appeals (7th cir.) 1993. Law clk. U.S. Ct. Appeals (6th cir.), Cin., 1981-82; ptnr. Cooper, Walinski & Cramer, Toledo, 1986—; judge pro tempore Perrysburg Mcpl. Ct., 1990—. Mem. Charter Rev. Commn., Perrysburg, Ohio, 1988; pres. Perrysburg Dem. Club, 1987-88; mem. exec. com. Wood County Dem. Party, Bowling Green, Ohio, 1986-90; pres. St. Rose Peace and Justice Com., Perrysburg, 1987-92, St. John's H.S. Alumni Assn., 1988-89; chmn. Human Rights Commn. of Diocese of Toledo, 1991-93. Recipient Fair Housing award HUD, 1996, Spirit of Wood County award, 1988; named Lawyer of Yr. Lawyers Weekly, 1998; named to St. John's Jesuit H.S. Hall of Fame, 1991. Mem. ABA, Ohio State Bar Assn., Toledo Bar Assn. (chmn. fed. ct. com. 1987-89), Wood County Bar Assn., Roman Catholic. Home: 501 Hickory St Perrysburg OH 43551-2206 Office: Cooper Walinski & Cramer 900 Adams St Toledo OH 43624-1505

DANELL, GEORG CLAES VALDEMAR, holding company executive; b. Skinnskatteberg, Västmld, Sweden, Sept. 7, 1947; s. Claes and Brita (Drakenberg) D.; m. Ann-Liss Erika Nahlin, Apr. 4, 1975; children: Josef, Erika. Student, Stockholm U., 1973. Mem. Swedish Parliament, Stockholm, 1974-81; under sec. of state Ministry Transport and Comms., Stockholm, 1978; cabinet mem. Ministry of Housing, Stockholm, 1979-81; gen. sec. Moderate Party, Stockholm, 1981-86; sr. cons. Kreab AB, Stockholm, 1986-94; exec. v.p., mgr. office Kreab AB, Brussels, 1994—; advisor to Minister Econ. Affairs, Sweden, 1976-78; bd. dirs. J.M. Constrn. Co., 1982-88; dir. comm. and pub. affairs Nordstjernan AB, 1989-91; chmn. deregulated housing market and policy com., 1992; bd. dirs. Vasakronan Real Estate Group, Besqab Constrn. and Real Estate, Svenska Dagbladet Found. Vice chmn. Moderate Youth Orgn., Sweden, 1972-76; chmn. Moderate Party, Stockholm County, 1979-81; mem. steering com. European Dem. Union, 1982-86, chmn. Modrate Press Found., Stockholm, 1982-95. Capt. Swedish Artillery, 1973. Avocation: family travelling. Home: Avenue Bel Horizon 28, B-1640 Rhode St Genese Belgium Office: Kreab AB, Ave de Tervueren 13A, B-1040 Brussels Belgium

DANFORTH, ARTHUR EDWARDS, finance executive; b. Cleve., Jan. 23, 1925; s. Arthur Edwards and Jane (Hillyard) D.; m. Elizabeth Wagley, Mar. 17, 1956; children: Hillyard Raible, Nicholas Edwards (dec.), Jonathan Ingersoll, Elizabeth Wagley, Michael Stowe. B.A., Yale, 1949. With Hayden Miller Co., Cleve., 1949-54, First Nat. City Bank (predecessor to Citibank N.A.), N.Y.C., 1954-63; asst. mgr. Buenos Aires office First Nat. City Bank (predecessor to Citibank N.A.), 1959-61; treas. Bunge Corp., N.Y.C., 1963-65; sr. v.p., treas. Colonial Bank & Trust Co., Waterbury, Conn., 1965-70; chmn., chief exec. officer Farmers Bank of Del., Wilmington, 1970-76; prin. Danforth Group, New Canaan, Conn., 1976-98; ret., 1998. Former bd. dirs. United Way of Del., Boys Club of Wilmington, Grand Opera House Inc. of Del., NCCJ, Audubon Soc. Conn., Greater Wilmington Devel. Council. Served as ensign USNR, 1945-46. Mem. Sankety Head Golf Club, Nantucket Yacht Club, Yale Club. Home: 230 Bermuda Bay Ln Vero Beach FL 32963-3421

DANFORTH, WILLIAM HENRY, retired academic administrator, physician; b. St. Louis, Apr. 10, 1926; s. Donald and Dorothy (Claggett) D.; m. Elizabeth Anne Gray, Sept. 1, 1950; children: Cynthia Danforth Prather, David Gray, Maebelle Danforth Reed, Elizabeth D. Sankey. A.B., Princeton U., 1947; M.D., Harvard U., 1951. Intern Barnes Hosp., St. Louis, 1951-52; resident Barnes Hosp., 1954-57; now mem. staff; asst. prof. medicine Washington U., St. Louis, 1960-65, assoc. prof., 1965-67, prof., 1967—; vice chancellor for med. affairs Washington U., 1965-71, chancellor, 1971-95; chmn., bd. trustees Washington U., St. Louis, 1995-99, vice-chmn. bd. trustees, chancellor emeritus, 1999—; pres. Washington U. Med. Sch. and Assoc. Hosps., 1965-71; program coord. Bi-State Regional Med. Program, 1967-68; dir. Ralston Purina Co., Energizing Holdings; chmn. bd. dirs. Donald Danforth Plant Sci. Ctr. Trustee Danforth Found.; trustee Am. Youth Found., 1963—, Princeton U., 1970-74; pres. St. Louis Christmas Carols Assn., 1958-74, chmn., 1975—; co-chair Barnes/Jewish Hosp., 1996—; bd. dirs. BJC Health Systems, 1996—. Named Man of Yr. St. Louis Globe-Democrat, 1978. Fellow AAAS, Am. Acad. Arts and Scis.; mem. Inst. Medicine. Home: 10 Glenview Rd Saint Louis MO 63124-1308 Office: Washington U West Campus Campus Box 1044 7425 Forsyth Blvd Ste 262 Saint Louis MO 63105-2161

DANG, CHI VAN, hematology and oncology educator; b. Saigon, Vietnam, Nov. 2, 1954; came to U.S., 1967; s. Chieu Van and Nga Ngoc (Nguyen) D.; m. Mary Doreen Seeley, May 18, 1985; children: Eric Van, Vanessa Marie. BS in Chemistry, U. Mich., 1975; PhD in Chemistry, Georgetown U., 1978; MD, Johns Hopkins U., 1982. Diplomate Am. Bd. Internal Medicine, Am. Bd. Med. Oncology. Resident in internal medicine Johns Hopkins Hosp., Balt., 1982-85; fellow in hematology and oncology U. Calif., San Francisco, 1985-87; asst. prof. medicine Johns Hopkins U., 1987-91, assoc. prof., 1991-97, assoc. prof. oncol., pathology, molecular biology & genetics, 1995-97, dir. hematology, 1993—, prof. medicine, oncology, and pathology, 1997—, dep. dir. basic rsch., dept. medicine, 1996-99, co-dir. immunology and hematopoiesis, oncology, 1998-2000; vice dean rsch. Johns Hopkins Sch. Medicine, 2000—; mem. oncological scis. path B NIH, Bethesda, Md., 1993-97; cons. Novartis, East Hanover, N.J., 1993-98, Genentech, South San Francisco, Calif., 1995; sci. adv. bd. Lion Pharm. Corp., Balt. Contbr. articles to Nature, Molecular and Cellular Biology, Genes and Devel.; mem. editl. bd. Jour. Clin. Invest., 1998—, Neoplasia, 1999—. Scholar Leukemia Soc. Am., 1992-97, Stohlman scholar award Leukemia Soc. Am., 1996, Merit award NIH/NCI, 1999. Mem. Assn. Am. Physicians, Am. Soc. for Clin. Investigation (v.p. 2000), Phi Beta Kappa, Alpha Omega Alpha, Phi Lambda Upsilon. Avocations: India ink sketching, poetry. E-mail: cvdang@jhmi.edu. Home: 217 Upnor Rd Baltimore MD 21212-3425 Office: Johns Hopkins U Sch Med Ross 1025 720 Rutland Ave Baltimore MD 21205-2109

DANG, CHUANGYIN, operations research educator; b. Ruicheng, Shanzi, China, Aug. 25, 1963; arrived in New Zealand, 1993; s. Anwang Dang and Aixin Chang; m. Haijuan Zhang, Mar. 10, 1989; children: Michelle, Millie. BSc, Shanxi, China, 1983; MSc, Xidian, China, 1986; PhD cum laude, Tilburg, The Netherlands, 1991. Asst. prof. U. Calif., Davis, 1991-92, Delft U. Tech., Holland, 1992-93, Auckland U., New Zealand, 1993-98; asst. prof. City U. Hong Kong, 1998-2000, assoc. prof., 2000—. Author: Triangulations and Simplicial Methods, 1995; contbr. articles to profl. jours. Mem. INFORMS. Office: City U Hong Kong, 83 Tat Chee Ave, Hong Kong China

DANG, DUC CAN, biologist; b. Hanoi, Vietnam, July 15, 1931; arrived in France, 1950; s. Duc Kim and Thi Dam (Nguyen) D.; m. Thi Bach-Phung Chau, Sept. 25, 1965 (div. Oct. 1985); children: Duc Man, Duc Minh; m. Thi Anh-Tuyet Phan, June 17, 1989. BS, Faculty Scis., 1965, MS, 1969, D, 1971; DS, U. V, 1979. Tchr. Nat. H.S., Paris, 1955-65; biologist Nat. Ctr. Sci. Rsch., France, 1965-73; assoc. prof. U. Paris VI, 1974-87; rsch. scientist Nat. Ctr. Sci. Rsch., Paris, 1973-96, ret., 1996; cons. in field, 1993-96. Recipient Darolles prize Nat. Acad. Medicine, France, 1980. Mem. French Soc. Primatology (founder). Budhist. Avocations: violin, poetry, Chinese gymnastics. Home: 02 Monge St A25, 94110 Arcueil France

DANG, MARVIN S. C., lawyer; b. Honolulu, Feb. 11, 1954; s. Brian K.T. and Flora (Yuen) D. BA with distinction, U. Hawaii, 1974; JD, George Washington U., 1978. Bar: Hawaii 1978, U.S. Dist. Ct. Hawaii 1978, U.S. Ct. Appeals (9th cir.) 1979. Atty. Gerson, Steiner & Anderson and predecessor firms, Honolulu, 1978-81; owner, atty. Law Offices of Marvin S.C. Dang, Honolulu, 1981—; sr. v.p., bd. dirs. Rainbow Fin. Corp., Honolulu, 1984-95; bd. dirs. Foster Equipment Co. Ltd., Honolulu, Hawaii Cmty. Reinvestment Corp., 1994-96; bd. dirs. Hawaii Fin. Svcs. Assn., sec., 1991, treas., 1992, v.p., 1993, pres. 1994, lobbyist, 1996—; vice chmn. Hawaii Consumer Fin. Polit. Action Com., 1988-95, sec./treas., 1999—; hearings officer (per diem) Adminstrv. Drivers License Revocation Office, Honolulu, 1991-95. State rep., asst. minority floor leader Hawaii State Legislature, Honolulu, 1982-84; chmn., vice chmn., mem. Manoa Neighborhood Bd., Honolulu, 1979-82, 84-87; pres., v.p., mem. Hawaii Coun. on Legal Edn. for Youth, Honolulu, 1979-86; mem. Hawaii Bicentennial Commn. of U.S. Constn., Honolulu, 1986-88. Recipient Cert. of Appreciation award Hawaii Speech-Lang.-Hearing Assn., Honolulu, 1984; named one of Ten Outstanding Young Persons of Hawaii, Hawaii State Jaycees, 1983. Mem. ABA (standing com. on group and prepaid legal svcs. 2000—, coun. of fund for justice and edn. 1993-99, standing com. on law and electoral process 1985-89, spl. com. on youth edn. for citizenship 1979-85, 89-92, Hawaii membership chmn. 1981-93, exec. coun. young lawyers divsn. 1986-88), Hawaii State Bar Assn. (chair collection law sec. 1999—, bd. dirs. young lawyers divsn. 1990), Am. Prepaid Legal Svcs. Inst. (bd. dirs. 2000—). Avocations: family, law, politics. Office: PO Box 4109 Honolulu HI 96812-4109

DANG, NGUYEN DINH, physicist, painter; b. Hanoi, Vietnam, Sept. 3, 1958; s. Nam Nguyen Dinh and Chin Vu Thi; m. Thuy Mai Dinh Thi, Dec.

29, 1985; 1 child, Dong Nguyen Dinh. MS with distinction, Moscow State U., 1982, PhD in Physics, 1985, DSc in Phys. and Math. Scis., 1990. Jr. rschr. Vietnam Atomic Energy Commn., Hanoi, 1982; rschr. Inst. Theoretical Physics, Hanoi, 1986-87; sr. rsch. assoc. JINR Lab. Theoretical Physics, Dubna, Moscow, 1987-89; sr. rschr. Inst. Nuc. Sci. and Technique, VAEC, Hanoi, 1990—; contract rschr. Catania (Italy) sez. INFN, 1992-93; vis. scientist INS, U. Tokyo, RIKEN, Wako, Japan, Saitama U., Urawa, Japan, 1994—; dir. Computer Ctr. Nuc. Sci. (VAEC), Hanoi, 1997—. Editor: Perspectives of Nuclear Physics in the Late Nineties, 1995, RIKEN Symposium on Giant Resonances, 1997; contbr. over 65 articles to profl. jours. and conf. procs.; solo and group painting exhbns. in Vietnam, Russia, Japan; pvt. collections in Russia, France, Italy, Germany, U.S., Indonesia, Holland. Recipient DAAD award German Acad. Exch. Svc., Munich, 1992, Nishina Meml. fellowship, Tokyo, 1994, Sci. & Tech. fellowship, Tokyo, 1996, Japan Soc. Promotion Sci. fellowship, Tokyo, 1997. Mem. N.Y. Acad. Scis., Vietnam Physics Soc., Fine Arts Assn. Vietnam, Vietnam Assn. of Fine Arts. Avocations: painting, playing piano, classical music, photography. Office: Riken 2-1 Hirosawa, Wako City, Saitama 351-0198, Japan

D'ANGELO, ANDREA, business company executive; b. Milan, Apr. 21, 1966; s. Pasquale D'Angelo and Angela Capasso. MS, Federico II, Naples, 1990; MBA, Havard U., 1995. CPA, Italy. Cons. CRS, Naples, 1989-90, Booz Allen, Milan, 1990-93; asst. investment officer IFC, Washington, 1994; assoc. Booz Allen, N.Y.C., 1995-97; sr. assoc. Booz Allen, Rome, 1997-98; dir. Strategy & Bus. Devel., Brussels, 1998—; bd. dirs. Cantieru di Baia, Naples. Mem. HBS Alumni. Avocation: kayaking. Office: Lucent Techs, 161 Dreve Richelle Bldg M, 1410 Waterloo Belgium Address: 63 Avenue Bel Air, 1180 Brussels Belgium

D'ANGELO, DOMINIC, editor, writer; b. London, Nov. 5, 1954; s. Joseph and Barbara Gwendoline (Jarvis) d'A. MA, U. Glasgow, Scotland, 1985. Logistics dir., coord. New Beginnings Ltd., Scotland, 1989-92; programme editor Scottish Opera, 1992-97; editor Gay Scotland, Glasgow, 1993-97, pub., 1997-99; info. officer Dept. Internat. Devel., Glasgow, 1998—; freelance writer, critic, broadcaster, 1990—; dir. Personal Assistance, Ltd., Glasgow, 1990—, Calosa Pub. Ltd., Glasgow, 1995—; joint artistic dir. Glasgay! Lesbian & Gay Arts Festival, 1993. Author: The Glasgow Story, 1991; co-author: Glasgow City of Architecture & Design, 1999, Changing Glasgow By Design, 1994; designer: The Light of Truth and Beauty, 1999; rev., feature articles writer The Scotsman, The Herald. Pres. Glasgow U. Queen Margaret Union, 1981-82; hon. sec. The Alexander Thomson Soc., Glasgow, 1991—. Labour Party. Avocations: cinema and live performances, architecture. Fax: 0141 333 1949. Email: dominic@easynet.co.uk and d-dangelo@dfid.gov.uk. Home: 271 Sauchiehall St, Glasgow G2 3HQ, Scotland Office: 271 Sauchiehall St, Glasgow G2 3HQ, Scotland

DANGELO, EUGENE MICHAEL, elementary education educator; b. Greensburg, Pa., Oct. 6, 1955; s. Louis Anthony and Dolores Joan (Sylvester) D. BS in Music Edn., Duquesne U., 1977, MusM in Composition, 1979; PhD in Tchr. Devel., U. Pitts., 1985. Cert. music edn. grades K-12, elem. sch. prin. grades K-8, Pa. Music educator, choral & orch. dir. The Winchester-Thurston Sch., Pitts., 1985-88; music educator, choral dir. Mt. Pleasant (Pa.) Area Sch. Dist., 1988-99, elem. band dir., 1999—; mus. dir., prin. condr. Greensburg (Pa.) Mus. Soc. Philharm. Winds, 1990-95; adj. asst. prof. grad. edn. Seton Hill Coll., Greensburg, 1995—. Composer: All That I Might Be, 1987, Centennial Suite, 1987, The B. Cool Jingle, 1992, Millenium Fanfare and March, 2000. Dir. liturgical music St. Paul Ch., Greensburg, Pa., 1989-92, voting mem. parish coun., 1986-87; dir. music and liturgy St. Bede Ch., Bovard, Pa., 1993-98; dir. music St. Pius X Ch., Mt. Pleasant, 1998—; voting mem. St. Paul Elem. Sch. Bd. Edn., Greensburg, Pa., 1991-95; Westmoreland County Labor Conf. rep. Am. Fedn. Musicians Local 339, Greensburg, Pa., 1992; mem. devel. adv. bd. Holy Cross Elem. Sch., Youngwood, Pa., 1998; mem. adv. bd. exemplary tchr. database U.S. Dept. Edn., 1998— (Tchr. Excellence award finalist, 2000); dir., supr. liturgy and music Mt. Pleasant Cath. Chs., 2000—. Mem. ASCD, Am. Choral Dirs.' Assn., U. Pitts. Doctoral Assn. Educators (life), Pa. Music Educators' Assn., Music Educators' Nat. Conf. (dsignation as nat. registered music educator, 1991—), Pi Lambda Theta,. Democrat. Roman Catholic. Avocations: genealogy, numismatics, philately, radio communications, astronomy, antique auto restoration. Home: 260 Wyoming Ave Greensburg PA 15601-3980 Office: Mt Pleasant Area Sch Dist RR 4 Mount Pleasant PA 15666-9804

DANGER, PIERRE, humanities educator; b. Algiers, Sept. 9, 1939; 1 child, Alice. Prof., Univ., Poitiers, France. Author: Sensation et Objet Dans Le Roman De Flaubert, 1971, Eros Balzacien, 1989, Pulsion et Desir Chez Maupassant, 1993, Émile Augier ou le Théâtre de l'Ambiguité, 1998. Home: 20 rue des Ecoles, Paris France

DANGOOR, DAVID EZRA RAMSI, consumer goods company executive; b. Teheran, Iran, Aug. 3, 1949; arrived in sweden, 1950, came to U.S., 1987; s. Selim Eliaho and Ruth (Lehr) D.; m. Ida (Ide) Weitzen, May 24, 1992; children: Rebecca Frances, Diana Katherine, Louisa Faye, Selim Edward. Civilekonom (MBA), Stockholm Sch. Econs., Sweden, 1973. Asst. dir. Scandinavian Supplies AB, Stockholm, 1970-74; asst. corp. treas. AGA Group AB, Stockholm, 1974-76; asst. to. v.p. Philip Morris Europe, Middle East & Africa, Lausanne, Switzerland, 1976; dept. mktg. dir. Philip Morris Co. Germany, Munich, Fed. Republic Germany, 1977-80; area dir. No. Europe Seven Up Internat., London, 1980-84; pres. Benson & Hedges Can. Inc., Philip Morris Internat., Montreal, Que., Can., 1984-86; sr. v.p. mktg. Philip Morris USA, N.Y.C., 1987-92; exec. v.p. Philip Morris Internat., Rye Brook, N.Y., 1992—; bd. dirs. Rothmans, Benson & Hedges, Inc., Toronto, 1987—; mem. bd. dirs. and exec. com. Swedish Am. C. of C., N.Y., 1996—, chmn., 1998—; bd. dirs. Fgn. Policy Assn. N.Y., 1997—. Exec. v.p. Student Assn. Palmgrenska Samskolan, Stockholm, 1966-68; bd. dirs. Student Assn. Stockholm Sch. Bus. Adminstrn. and Econs., 1969-72, Am. Scandinavian Found., 1999—; officer Royal Swedish Coast Art; exec. bd. dirs. Raoul Wallenberg Com. of U.S., 1990-93; trustee Arthur F. Burns Fellowships, 1997—; mem. internat. devel. com. Internat. Fedn. Multiple Sclerosis Socs., 1993-95. Fellow Amaranten, Sweden, 1971. Mem. Swedish Am. C. of C. (bd. dirs. exec. com. 1996—), Sallskapet Club (Stockholm), Hurlingham Club (London), Hillside Tennis Club (Montreal), Southampton (N.Y.) Bath and Tennis Club, The Tuxedo Park (N.Y.) Club. Avocations: squash, tennis, sailing, bridge.

D'ANGORA, KENDRA MARIE, artist, preschool educator; b. Plymouth, Mass., July 4, 1968; d. Robert Joseph D'Angora and Marcia Leigh Nickerson; m. Christopher Michael Schopp, Sept. 26, 1998. BFA in Ceramics, Mass. Coll. Art, 1992; student, Aquinas Coll., 1997. Cert. lead tchr., Mass. Nanny Plymouth, Mass., 1985-87; clerical worker Charette Corp., Boston, 1990-95; freelance artist Allston, Mass., 1992—; preschool tchr. Clinton Path Preschool, Brookline, Mass., 1995-. Recipient Blue Ribbon, Boston Globe Scholastic Art, 1985, 86. Mem. Am. Craft Coun., Plymouth Art Guild (blue ribbon, 1985, 1986), Provincetown Art Assn., United South End Artists, Mus. of Fine Arts. Avocations: hiking, exercise, dancing, reading, skating. Home: 38 Brainerd Rd Apt 1R Allston MA 02134-4524

DANGREMOND, DAVID W., fine arts educator; b. Norristown, Pa., June 8, 1952; s. James L. and Joan O. (Kross) D.; m. Mary Plant Spivy, Oct. 18, 1980; children: Saumel Plant Chapin, Augustus Welles Ewing. BA cum laude, Amherst Coll., 1974; MA, U. Del., 1976, Yale U., 1987; MPhil, Yale U., 1990. Dir. Webb-Deane-Stevens Mus., Wethersfield, Conn., 1976-80, Bennington Mus., Vt., 1980-96; adj. prof. fine arts Trinity Coll., Hartford, Conn., 1996—; adj. prof. art history U. Hartford, Conn., 1977-80; tutor Historic Deerfield, Mass., 1975; trustee Williamstown (Mass.) Regional Art Conservation Lab., 1981-86, Florence Griswold Mus., Old Lyme, Conn., 1987—, v.p., 1992—; trustee Conn. Humanities Coun., 1997—; mem. adv. bd. Gunston Hall Plantation, Lorton, Va., 1985—, Nat. Trust Hist. Preservation; dir. Attingham Summer Sch., Shropshire, Eng., 1980—; profl. adv. bd. Victoria Mus., Portland, Maine, 1985—; bd. overseers Strawberry Banke Mus., Portsmouth, N.H., 1987—, v.p., 1988-90; mem. exec. com. Yale U. Art Gallery Assocs., 1987-93; mus. cons. various mus., 1993. Foreword author: Heritage Houses: the American Tradition in Connecticut 1660-1900, 1979; contbr. articles to jours. Bd. dirs. Hartford Architecture Conservancy, 1978-80; mem. adv. bd. Deacon John Grave Found.; mem. art and antiques coun. Conn. Pub. TV, Hartford, 1977-80; mem. concert com. Vt. Symphony Orch., 1980-86; trustee Musical Masterworks, 1992—, v.p. 1998—; div. head United Way Bennington County, 1982-84; del. Gov.'s Conf. on Future of Vt.'s Heritage, Montpelier, 1982; sr. warden St. Peter's Episcopal Ch., 1985—; bd. govs. Hill-Stead Mus., Farmington, 1990—; trustee Wadsworth Atheneum, Hartford, 1991—, exec. com., 1995—, chmn. curatorial com., 1995—, chmn. ethics com. 1996—, v.p. 1998—; trustee Conn. Hist. Soc., 1989—. Fellow Historic Deerfield, 1973; Winterthur fellow H.F. duPont Winterthur Mus., 1974-76; Sir George Trevelyan scholar Attingham summer sch., Shropshire, Eng., 1976. Mem. Am. Assn. for State and Local History (state awards chmn.), New Eng. Mus. Assn. (exec. com. 1985-86), Am. Assn. Mus. (accreditation vis. com., mus. assessment program cons.), Vt. Mus. and Gallery Alliance (pres. 1983-86), Greater Hartford Assn. of Historic Houses (bd. dirs.), Decorative Arts Soc., Am. Ceramics Circle, Coll. Art Assn., Soc. Archtl. Historians, Century Assn. (N.Y.C.), Knickerbocker Club (N.Y.C.), Grolier Club (N.Y.C.), Hartford Club, Old Lyme Country, Yale Club N.Y.C., Lawn Club (New Haven), Dauntless Club (Essex), Newport Reading Rm. Episcopalian.

DANGUE REWAKA, DENIS, diplomat. Permanent rep. of Gabonese Republic UN, N.Y.C. Office: UN Permanent Mission Gabon 18 E 41st St Fl 9 New York NY 10017-6222

DANIEL, CHARLES TIMOTHY, transportation engineer, consultant; b. N.Y.C., Aug. 3, 1958; s. John Carl and Eleanor (Sauer) D.; m. Melissa J. Sanft, Mar. 4, 1995. BA in Engring., Lafayette Coll., 1980; MS in Transp., MIT, 1982; MBA, NYU, 1991. Staff engr. George Beetle Co., Phila., 1983-84; project engr. Transamerica Leasing, Purchase, N.Y., 1984-87; mgr. tech. svcs. Transamerica Leasing, White Plains, N.Y., 1987-89, engring. cons., 1989—; treas. Midtown Daniel Corp., 1990—, pres., 1995—; mem. domestic freight container stds. subcom. Internat. Standardization Orgn. Tech. Com. on Freight Containers, 1986-88. Mem. alumni bd. Rutgers Preparatory Sch., Somerset, N.J., 1985—; county committeeman Middlesex County (N.J.) Dem. Orgn., 1992—. Mem. ASCE, Sigma Xi, Beta Gamma Sigma. Lutheran. Achievements include development of code structure for electronic data interchange of freight container chassis repair data. Home: 33 North Dr East Brunswick NJ 08816-1124 Office: Midtown Daniel Corp 20th Fl 645 Madison Ave Fl 20 New York NY 10022-1010

DANIEL, GEORGE FRANCIS, archbishop; b. Pretoria, Transvaal, Republic of South Africa, Apr. 23, 1933; s. Robert Francis and Catherine Mary (Pattison) D. Licentiate in Theology, St. Paul's Coll., Republic of South Africa, 1956; postgrad., St. John Vianney Sem., Republic of South Africa, 1961; BD, STL, Urbanianum, Rome, 1965. Ordained priest Roman Cath. Ch., 1964. Curate Archdiocese of Pretoria, 1965-67; parish priest Archdiocese of Pretoria, Waverley, 1967-69, Tembisa, 1969-75; archbishop of Pretoria, 1975—; with Mil. Ordinariate, Republic of South Africa, 1976—; coun. mem. Internat. Com. Mil. Ordinariates, Rome, 1985-87; v.p. II So. African Cath. Bishops' Conf., 1990-93; mem. Pontifical Coun. for Promoting Christian Unit, 1984—. Fax: 27 12 4602452. Home: Archbishop's House, 125 Main St, Waterkloof, Pretoria 0181, South Africa Office: Archdiocese of Pretoria, PO Box 17245, Groenkloof, Pretoria Gauteng 0027, South Africa

DANIEL, GEORGE PAUL, lawyer, consultant; b. Seremban, Malaysia, Sept. 4, 1953; s. Jebamoney Edward and Mary Arokiam; m. Paruvathy Suppiah, Apr. 18, 1982; 7 children. Cert. in Mass Comm., Malaysian Nat. U., Selangor, 1981; BA in Law with honors, U. Kent, Eng., 1985. Solicitor; corp. lawyer. Mng. ptnr. Daniel & Assocs., Internat. Law Office, Kuala Lumpur, 1992—; founder, dir. Humanist Advice and Liaison Ctr., Kuala Lumpur, 1993—; bus. cons. Malaysian Associated Indian C. of C. and Industry, Kuala Lumpur, 1995. Author: Politics of Malaysian Chinese Unity, 1995; contbg. author: Certified Management Digest, 1994-95; legal editor: Malaysian Current Law Jour., Indsl. Law Report, Malaysian Tax Cases, 1992. Mem. Malaysian Translators Assn., Malaysian Lit. and Lang. Orgn., Nat. Union Journalists, Law Assn. Asia-Pacific, Soc. Authors U.K., Nat. Writers Assn., Hakam-Malaysian Human Rights Soc. Avocations: activist for ethnic minority Indian activities, motivational speaking, reading, writing, travel. E-mail: tm.net.my.gpd. Fax: 603 242 6192. Office: Daniel & Assocs, 11th Fl, GPO Box 11917 Ste 11-03, Kuala Lumpur 50762, Malaysia also: Menara Promet, Jalan Sultan Ismail, Kuala Lumpur 50250, Malaysia

DANIEL, JOYCE TURNER, utility company administrator; b. Atlanta, Sept. 1, 1948; d. Joseph C. and Hazel (Wilkins) Turner; children: Lamont D. Hall, Lisa D. Hall; m. Sammie T. Daniel, Aug. 23, 1997. BA in Spanish and Secondary Edn., Clark Coll., Atlanta, 1970. Mgmt. trainee Sears, Atlanta, 1970-71, dept. mgr., 1971-72, asst. mdse. mgr. so. terr., 1972-77; supr. Oglethorpe Power Corp., Tucker, Ga., 1979-88, buyer II, 1988-93, sr. buyer, 1993-96; sr. buyer Ga. Transmission Corp., Tucker, 1996-97, 2000—, Intelisource, Atlanta, 1997-99, Ga. Transmission Corp., Tucker, 2000—; exec. on loan to Ga. Minority Supplier Devel. Coun. for Oglethorpe Power Corp., 1993, Buyer of Yr. nominee, 1994. Mem. NAACP. Recipient Youth Motivation commendation Nat. Alliance Bus., 1983; Communication Techniques award Eileen M. Higgins & Assocs., 1983. Mem. Nat. Assn. Purchasing Mgmt., Purchasing Mgmt. Assn. of Ga., Clark Coll. Alumni Assn., Atlanta AlphaBettes, Alpha Kappa Alpha. Democrat. Methodist. Avocations: reading, bike riding, needlepoint, bridal consultant. Fax: 770-724-7875. Home: 4230 Greentree Ln College Park GA 30349-1732 Office: Ga Transmission Corp 2100 E Exchange Pl Tucker GA 30084-5336

DANIEL, KENNETH RULE, former iron and steel manufacturing company executive; b. Milford, Conn., Oct. 13, 1913; s. Cullen Coleman and Margaret Estelle (Elliott) D.; m. Virginia Moody Simpson, June 11, 1938; children: Kenneth Rule, Cullen Coleman, Robert Tennent Simpson, William Francis McKemie. B.S., U. Ala., 1936, Profl. Degree in Mech. Engring., 1957, D.Sc., 1980. Registered profl. engr. Ala. With Am. Cast Iron Pipe Co., Birmingham, Ala., 1936-78; chief engr. Am. Cast Iron Pipe Co., 1948-55, v.p. engring., 1955-59, v.p. engring. and purchases, 1959-61, exec. v.p., 1961-63, pres., 1963-78, also dir., dir. various subsidiaries, 1963-78; vice chmn. bd. 1st Ala. Bank of Birmingham, 1977-86; Sesquicentennial hon. prof. U. Ala., 1981; bd. dirs. L&N R.R., Seaboard Coast Line R.R., CSX R.R. Mem. Ala. Bd. of Registration for Profl. Engrs. and Land Surveyors, 1967-87; mem. regional adv. council Conf. Bd., 1967-78, Ala. Export Council, 1966-69; bd. dirs. Community Chest, 1965-78, Jr. Achievement, 1964-78, Birmingham Centennial Corp., 1968-73, Warrior Tombigbee Devel. Assn., 1963-78, L and N RR-Seaboard Coast Line RR-CSX RR, 1969-78; gen. co-chmn. United Appeal, 1964, chmn. indsl. div., 1958; chmn. Radio Free Europe, Birmingham, 1966; mem. Jefferson County Judicial Commn., 1967-72; chmn. adv. bd. Salvation Army, 1968-69, mem. adv. council home and hosp., mem. nat. adv. council, 1976—; trustee Foundry Ednl. Found. (pres. 1964-65); trustee, mem. exec. com. So. Research Inst.; chmn. bd. trustees Jefferson County Cooper Green Hosp.; bd. visitors Berry Coll., Mt. Berry, Ga., 1968-78. Served to lt. col. AUS, 1941-46, ETO. Decorated Bronze Star, Legion of Merit; Croix de Guerre France; recipient Gold Knight of Mgmt. award Nat. Mgmt. Assn., 1965, William Booth award Salvation Army, 1967, Henry Laurence Gantt medal Am. Mgmt. Assn. and ASME, 1977, Exec. of the Yr. award Nat. Mgmt. Assn., 1978; named Engr. of the Yr., Birmingham Engring. Coun., 1967, Paladium medal Am. Engring. Soc. and Nat. Audubon Soc., 1986; elected to Ala. Acad. Honor, 1982, Nat. Mgmt. Assn. Hall of Fame, 1987, Ala. Engring. Hall of Fame, 1989. Fellow ASME (chmn. Birmingham sect. 1950-51, hon. mem. 1984); mem. NAM (dir. 1967-70), Am. Iron and Steel Inst. (bd. dirs. 1968-78), Assn. Industries Ala. (bd. dirs. 1963-78), Birmingham Area C. of C. (pres. 1969), Assn. Iron and Steel Engrs. (chmn. Birmingham sect. 1954, nat. dir. 1955), Am. Ordnance Assn. (pres. Birmingham post 1964), Am. Foundrymen's Soc. (Thomas W. Pangborn Gold Medal award 1974), Am. Soc. for Engring. Edn., Engring. Soc. Birmingham, Newcomen Soc. N. Am., Birmingham Country Club, The Club, Mountain Brook Club, Masons (knight comdr. Ct. of Honor), Kiwanis, Sigma Alpha Epsilon, Theta Tau, Tau Beta Pi. Methodist. Office: PO Box 2727 Birmingham AL 35202-2727

DANIEL, MILAN, parasitologist, researcher; b. Horazdovice, Klatovy, Czech Republic, June 14, 1931; s. Karel Daniel and Marie (Mayerova) D.; m. Vlasta Pacakova, Mar. 2, 1957; children: Milan, Jarmila. D in Natural Scis., Charles U., 1956; PhD, Czechoslovak Acad. Scis., Prague, 1959, DSc, 1987. Asst. prof. Charles U., Prague, 1954-55; fellow Czechoslovak Acad. Scis., Prague, 1956-59, rschr., 1960-86; sci. worker, head dept. Inst. Tropical Health, Prague, 1987-91, Postgrad. Med. Sch., Prague, 1992—. Author: Medical Entomology and Environment, 1989 (Czech Lit. Found. award 1990); co-author: Ecological Study of Toro Game Reserve (Uganda), 1984 (Czechoslovak Acad. Scis. award 1985) and 7 other sci. books, and 3 general audience books; acting editor Folia Parasitologica jour., 1970-73; mem. editl. bd. Jour. Med. Entomology, 1977-80; contbr. numerous articles to profl. jours. Recipient Merited Scientist award Czechoslovak Acad. Scis., 1981, E.N. Pavlovsky's medal Russian Acad. Scis., 1985. Mem. Internat. Congress of Acarology (exec. com., past pres. 3d congress 1971-74), Czech Soc. Parasitology (founding mem., sci. sec. 1960-71), Acad. Scis. Czech. Republic (permanent appraisal commn. 1994—), N.Y. Acad. Scis. Avocations: mountaineering, skiing, travel. Fax: 420 2 710 19335. Home: Tomanova 64, CZ-16900 Prague 6, Czech Republic Office: Postgrad Med Sch, Ruska 85, CZ-10005 Prague 10, Czech Republic

DANIEL, ROLF, microbiologist, researcher; b. Kassel, Hessen, Germany, Sept. 20, 1963; s. Horst Erich Otto and Erna Anna Hermine (Mörk) D. BS in Biology, U. Göttingen, Germany, 1991, PhD, 1994. Rschr. Inst. for Microbiology, Göttingen, Germany, 1990-95, lab. head, 1994-95, group leader, 1996—; rsch. fellow U. Calif, Berkeley, 1995-96. Author: Glycerinvergärung Durch Citrobacter Freundii, 1994; contbr. articles to profl. jours. With German Army, 1983-84. Recipient divsn. biology PhD award U. Göttingen, 1994; rsch. fellow Deutsche Forschungsgemeinschaft, 1995-96. Mme. AAAS, Am. Soc. for Microbiology, Vereinigung für Allgemeine Und Angewandte Mikrobiologie (Germany), Deutsche Gesellschaft für Hygiene und Mikrobiologie. Avocations: squash, swimming, soccer, cinema, biking. Office: Univ Göttingen, Grisebachstr 8, D-37077 Göttingen Germany

DANIEL, RONALD OVERTON, management consultant; b. Greenville, S.C., July 3, 1951; s. Hugh Rachford and Ruth (Hill) D.;. BME, U. Fla., 1973; MA, Am. U., 1977, PhD, 1983. Musician U.S. Army Band, Ft. Myer, Va., 1973-93; mem. faculty Duke Ellington Sch. Arts, Washington, 1980-93; music dir. Fillmore Arts Ctr., Washington, 1993-97; pres., CEO Daniel Mgmt. Group, Inc., Washington, 1993—; cons. Arts Edn. Partnership, Washington; curriculum devel. cons. D.C. Pub. Schs., Washington. Co-author: 112 Models for Education in the Arts, 1995; contbr. articles to profl. jours. Expert witness Nat. Endowment Arts, Washington, 1988; bd. dirs. Fillmore Arts Ctr., 1995-98, D.C. Coalition, Washington, 1997—. Mem. Greater Wash. Soc. Assn. Execs. (grantee 1994), Am. Soc. Assn. Execs., Winds & Rainbows Kite Club (co-founder, bd. dirs. 1998—, Flyer of Yr. 1998, 1999), Phi Delta Kappa (grantee 1984, dir. rsch. 1982-84). Democrat. Fax: 202-966-2283. E-mail: ceo@danielgrp.com. Avocations: cycling, running, sport kites.

DANIEL, SOMUAH, microbiology technician; b. Oda, Ghana, May 19, 1966; s. Kwabena and Akosua (Dora) Donkor; m. Deborah Agyei; children: Michael, Joshua. Grad., Sch. Med. Lab. Tech., Ghana, 1990; postgrad., U. Ghana, 1999—. Tech. officer Min. Health, Accra, 1988-93, Ashanti Goldfields Co., Accra, 1993—. Avocations: football, Bible reading. Home: Wawasi PO Box 583, Obuasi Ashanti Ghana

DANIEL, VOLKER RUEDIGER MARIA, immunologist, researcher; b. Hadamar, Hessen, Germany, Feb. 24, 1955; s. Oskar and Gertrud (Tkotz) D. MD, U. Giessen, Germany, 1981. Sci. asst. dept. internal medicine U. Giessen, 1980-81; sci. asst. dept. transplantation immunology Inst. Immunology, U. Heidelberg, Germany, 1982-94, lectr. dept. transplantation immunology, 1994-2000, prof. immunology, 2000—. Contbr. articles to profl. jours. Deutsche Forschungsgemein Schaft rsch. fellow, 1982-84. Mem. The Transplantation Soc., Internat. AIDS Soc. (advisor), New York Acad. of Sciences. Roman Catholic. Avocations: science, sports, history, music. Office: Inst of Immunology, Im Neuenheimer Feld 305, 69120 Heidelberg Germany

DANIEL, WILLIAM JOHN TREVOR, mechanical engineering educator, researcher; b. Lismore, NSW, Australia, May 5, 1951; s. William Charles and Hilda Wright (Wood) D.; m. Belinda Ann Bridge, July 7, 1984; children: Claire Frances, Gregory William. B Engring., U. Queensland, Australia, 1973, M Engring. Sci., 1975, PhD, 1979. Prof. mech. engring. U. Queensland, Brisbane, Australia, 1983—; vis. engring. analyst Ford Motor Co., Geelong, Australia, 1988, Compumod Pty. Ltd., Sydney, Australia, 1989; vis. lectr. U. Wis., Madison, 1995. Contbr. articles to sci. jours., including Internat. Jour. for Numerical Methods in Engring., Computer Methods in Applied Mechanics and Engring., Computers and Structures, AIAA Jour., Computational Mechanics. Sec. Queensland br. S.Am. Missionary Soc., 1998. Mem. Instn. Engrs. (Australia). Anglican. Office: U Queensland, Mech Engring Dept, Brisbane 4072, Australia

DANIELEWICZ, CLAUDIA ANNE, quality assurance engineer; b. Niagara Falls, N.Y., Aug. 8, 1964; d. Chester Albert and Florence Carolyn (Pasek) D. AS in Engring., Erie C.C., 1984; BS in Engring., Rochester Inst. Tech., 1987, MS in Engring., 1993. Cert. quality assurance/mech./process engr. Farm equipment oper. Danielewicz Dairy Farms, Sanborn, N.Y., 1984-93; intern mech. engring. Sohio Electro Mineral, Niagara Falls, N.Y., 1984-85, Vets. Hosp., Batavia, N.Y., 1985-86; sales assoc. Gold Circle, Niagara Falls, 1987-88; asst. planner Cambridge Instruments, Buffalo, N.Y., 1988; engr. mfr., quality Par Foam Products, Buffalo, N.Y., 1988-92; engr. quality assurance Avm (Arvin/Gabirel), Marion, S.C., 1992; quality assurance engr. GenCorp Automotive, Batesville, Ark., 1993-94; process/quality assurance engr. Courtaulds Thatcher Tubes, Woodstock, Ill., 1994-95; quality assurance engr. Statis. Resource Quality Network GM Corp., Pontiac, Mich., 1995-99; design release engr. chassis GM Corp., Pontiac, 1999—. Mem. ASME, Am. Soc. Quality, Nat. Soc. Profl. Engrs. Avocations: bowling, motorcross, stock car racing, farming, reading. Home: 4286 Saunders Settlement Rd Sanborn NY 14132-9411 Office: General Motors Corp Truck Group Code 483-511-7K5 2000 Centerpoint Pkwy Pontiac MI 48341-3146

DANIEL-LESUR, JEAN YVES, composer; b. Paris, Nov. 19, 1908; s. Robert and Alice (Thiboust) L.; student Paris Conservatoire, 1919-29; m. Simone Lauer, Mar. 30, 1943; children: Christian, Beatrice (Mrs. J. P. Brichant). Pianist, organist suppleant Basilica of Sainte-Clotilde, 1927-37; organist Benedictine Abbey, Paris, 1937-44; prof. counterpoint Schola Cantorum, 1935-57, prof. composition, 1957-64, dir., 1957-61, hon. dir., 1966—; composer music for films; mus. adviser Radiodiffusion-Television Franç aise, Paris, 1961-69, Administrateur Reunion des Theatres Lyriques Nationaux, 1971-73; insp. music Ministry Cultural Affairs, 1969-78, insp. gen. Mem. French commn. UNESCO, 1958—. Decorated grand officier Legion of Honor, comdr. Nat. Order of Merit, comdr. Order Arts and Letters; recipient Grand prize Gen. Council Seine, 1964, Ville de Paris, Conseil Municipal, 1969; grand prize Soc. Authors and Composers, Prix Samuel-Rousseau, Académie des Beaux-Arts, Prix Internat. Maurice Ravel, 1994, Grand prix du Disque, Nouvelle Acad. du Disque, 1994. Mem. l'Academie Charles Cros (prés d'honneur), l'Institut de France, Royal Acad. Belgium, Academie Européenne des Scis., des Arts et des Lettres. Composer numerous works, including Suite Francaise, 1935, Pastorale, 1938, Ricercare, 1939, Andrea Del Sarto (symphonic poem) 1949, Ouverture for a Festival, 1951, Song of Songs, 1953, Chamber Concerto for piano and orchestra, 1953; Cantique des Colonnes for voice and orch., 1954; Le Bal du Destin (ballet), 1954, Serenade, 1954; Elegie 2 guitars, 1956; Dance Symphony, 1956; Jubilee Mass, 1960; Fantasy for 2 pianos, 1962; Andrea del Sarto (opera), 1968; Symphonie, 1975; Ondine (opera) 1982, La Reine Morte, 1987 (opera); Dialogues Dans La Nuit (cantate) Encore un Instant de Bonheur (cantate), Le Voyage D'automne, 1991, A La Lisiere Du Temps, 1991, Permis De Sejour, 1991, Stele, flute and orch., 1991, Dialogues Imaginaires, 1991; Fantaisie Concertante for cello and orch., 1992, Vert Paradis, 1992, for voices and string quartet Quatre Nocturnes, 1993, La Nuit Reve, 1994, for flute, harp and orch. Impromptu, 1994, Lamento, 1995; contbr. articles to profl. jours. Office: Institut de France, 23 Quai de Conti, 75006 Paris France

DANIELOVÁ, VLASTA, biologist, researcher; b. Prague, Czech Republic, July 12, 1934; d. Oldřich and Růžena (Matysová) Pacák; m. Milan Daniel, Mar. 2, 1957; children: Milan, Jarmila. Rerum naturalim doctor, Charles U., Prague, 1957; PhD, Czechoslovak Acad. Scis., Prague, 1965, DSc, 1989. Rschr. Czechoslovak Acad. Sci., Prague, 1957-72, sr. rschr., 1972-84; sr. rschr. Nat. Inst. Pub. Health, Prague, 1984-87, leading rschr., 1987—; lectr., cons. Postgrad. Med. Sch., Prague, 1985. Author: Relationships of Mosquitos to Tahyňa Virus as Determinant Factors of Its Circulation in Nature, 1992; co-author: Tahyňa Virus Natural Focus in Southern Moravia, 1980,

Less Known Arboviruses in Central Europe: A New Arbovirus Lednice, 1986; contbr. 140 articles to profl. jours. Recipient award Czechoslovak Acad. Scis., Prague, 1966, 69, 74, award Czech Literary Found., Prague, 1979; named Merited Scientist, Czechoslovak Acad. Scis., Prague, 1976. Mem. Czech Soc. Parasitology (founder). Achievements include 3 patents for hybridoma lines producing monoclonals for diagnostic of HBsAg and Neisseria meningitidis non-typable strains. Avocations: touring, skiing. Home: Tomanova 64, CZ-16900 Prague 6, Czech Republic

DANIELS, FRANK EMMETT, mathematician, educator; b. Miami, Fla., Sept. 28, 1963; s. Dan and Jewell Rae (Morgan) D. BS, U. Fla., Gainesville, 1985, MS, 1987, PhD, 1994. Grad. teaching asst. math. dept. U. Fla., Gainesville, 1985-92; teaching asst. math. dept. Santa Fe Community Coll., 1992-94; prof. sys. adminstr. Great Basin Coll., Ely, Nev. Mem. Math. Assn. Am., Campus Advance (pres. 1988-91), Campus Christian Fellowship (pres. 1991-92), Phi Beta Kappa. Republican. Avocations: collecting comic books and Beatles items, Bibl. studies, role-playing games. Office: Great Basin Coll 2115 Bobcat Dr Ely NV 89301-3107

DANIELS, GERARD A.A., sports physician; b. Oostende, Belgium, Dec. 14, 1933; s. Louis-Eugeen and Elisabeth (Claes) D. D, K.U. Leuven, Belgium, 1961, licence physical edn., 1961; cert. cardiology, R.U. Gent, Belgium, 1973. Educ. School of Social Edn., De Haan, Belgium, 1971-79; doctor Basketball Of Ostend, Belgium, 1983-93, Football Team of Ostend, Belgium, 1963-95, Oylmpic Team, Belgium, 1972, 76, 84, Cycling Found., Belgium, 1964-84. Author: Trainen Voor Wielrenners, 1979, Voor Trainers Van Wielrenners, 1982, Sprinten Voor Wielrenners, 1983, Medische Begeleiding Van Wielrenners, 1986, Alles Wat De Wielertoerist Moet Weten, 1990, Op Pad Met Wielrenners, 1995; co-author: Encyclopedy of Sports Injurys; contbr. articles to profl. jours. Alderman of sports Mcpl. of Ostend, Belgium, 1979-89. Mem. Assn. De La Fedn. Internat. De Medicine Sportive, Fedn. Internat. De Medicine Sports, Internat. Assn. of Olympic Medical Officers, Internat. Assn. of Olympic Medical Officers. Avocation: expert of law-court. Office: Muscarstraat 25, 8400 Oostende Belgium

DANIELS, JOSEPH, neuropsychiatrist; b. Linden, N.J., Mar. 18, 1931; s. Bennie and Dora (Chese) D.; m. Shirley Perkins, July 20, 1996; children: Joan Marie, Jean Dorene. BA cum laude, Lincoln U., Oxford, Pa., 1953; MD, Howard U., 1957. Rotating intern Med. Ctr. Jersey City, 1957-58; resident in internal medicine Worcester (Mass.) City Hosp., 1958-59; resident in psychiatry Ancora (N.J.) Hosp., 1962-65; dir. outpatient clinic Christian Health Care Ctr., Wyckoff, N.J., 1966-70; dir. outpatient dept. Cmty. Mental Health Ctr., N.J. Coll. Medicine, Newark, 1970-79; med. dir., pres. Ctr. for Growth and Reconciliation, East Orange, N.J., 1979-87; sr. staff psychiatrist Pine Rest Christian Hosp., Grand Rapids, Mich., 1987-96; cons. Kent County Cmty. Mental Health Ctr., Grand Rapids, 1996—; mem. Healthy Kent 2000 Health Com., 1993-94; cons. psychiatrist Newark Bd. Edn., 1976-84, East Orange Bd. Edn., Victory House, Newark, 1976-82, Project Rehab, Grand Rapids, 1990-91. Author: The Urban Mission, 1974. Founder, pres., chmn. bd. Ministry Reconciliation Fellowship, 1980-87; bd. dirs. Grand Rapids Reach Inc., pres., 1991-93; selected mem. Leadership Grand Rapids, 1993-94. Capt. M.C., U.S. Army, 1959-62. Fulbright Sr. scholarship fellow U. Zimbabwe Sch. of Medicine, 1998-99. Mem. Beta Kappa Chi. Baptist. Avocations: sports, writing, reeading, volunteering. Office: Kent County Cmty Mental Health Ctr Lakeside Dr Grand Rapids MI 49501-0165

DANIELS, KATHLEEN A., educational administrator; b. Detroit, Jan. 24, 1945; d. Leondro Cardinez and Lillian Mary (Murray) Castro; m. Donald W. Daniels, Jan. 30, 1971 (div. May 1983); 1 child, Donald. BA in Environ. Design, Wayne State U., 1967; student, U. Calif., L.A., 1969. Photographic artist Jana Taylor & Co., Venice, Calif., 1985-88; rep., founder Am. Child Found., Venice, Calif., 1986-88; exec. dir. Cmty. Assns. Inst., L.A., 1989—. Recipient outstanding svc. award, 1989, exec. dir. of yr. award, 1992; inducted into Exec. Dir. of Yr. Hall of Fame, 1994. Mem. NOW, Nat. Woman's Political Caucus, Nat. Assn. Female Execs., Am. Soc. Assn. Execs., Sierra Club, Nat. Dem. Club, City of Hope Singles. Avocations: gardening, ceramic animal collector, reading. Home and Office: 2567 Wellesley Ave Los Angeles CA 90064-2737

DANIELS, MARCEL LUDOLPHE C.M., communications executive; b. St. Joris-Weert, Belgium, Feb. 14, 1952; s. Karel Lodewijk and Sylvia Johanna (Bollen) D.; m. Marie-Louise Vertongen, May 25, 1979; children: Thomas, Helene. MA in Interpreting cum laude, Leuven Cath. U., 1975. Freelance translator London, 1975-78; mgr. pub. relations Caterpillar Overseas, Brussels, 1978-80; mgr. mktg. communications Raychem Corp., Leuven, Belgium, 1980-86; dir. translations Crosby Assocs. Internat., Winter Park, Fla. and Brussels, 1986-87; communications mgr. Exxon Chem. Internat., Brussels, 1987-98; v.p. corp. affairs Alcan Europe, 1998—; founder, owner Lang. and Communication Systems, 1987—. Co-founder Boy Scouts Unit, St. Joris-Weert, 1966. Belgian Ministry Cultural Affairs scholar, Moscow, 1976-77. Mem. Internat. Assn. Bus. Communicators, Warande Bus. Club, Lions Club. Roman Catholic. Home: Vogelenzangstraat 151, B 3070 Kortenberg Belgium Office: Alcan Europe Ltd, PO Box 257, B 1950 Uxbridge UB8 7UF, Great Britain

DANIELSEN, SVEND-ERIK, bank executive; b. Copenhagen, Sept. 18, 1944; arrived in Greenland, 1975; s. Agner and Aase (Pedersen) D.; m. Mathilde Moeller, Aug. 11, 1982; children: Ditte, Heidi, Daniel, Mads. BCom, Sch. Econs. and Bus. Adminstn., Copenhagen, 1973. CPA. Ptnr. Deloitte & Touche, Nuuk, Greenland, 1975-82; mng. dir., CEO Grønlandsbanken A/S, Nuuk, Greenland, 1982—; cons. gen. to Norway. Decorated cross Order of Dannebrog (Denmark), cross Order of Merit (Norway), Cross Order of Merit (Greenland Home Rule). Mem. Rotary. Avocations: skiing, hunting, sailing, reading. Home: Nigerleq 55 PO Box 75, 3900 Nuuk Greenland Office: The Bank of Greenland, Po Box 1033, Nuuk Greenland 3900

DANIELSON, DEREK ARTHUR, lawyer, barrister; b. London, Eng., Nov. 9, 1950; came to U.S., 1996; s. John and Kitty (Friend) D.; 1 child, Tanis. B in Law, U. We. Ontario, London, Ontario, Can., 1974. Bar: Law Soc. Upper Can., 1976, Calif. 1994, U.S. Dist. Ct. (ctrl. dist.) Calif., 1996; cert trademark agt., Can., U.S., 1981. Ptnr. Solomon & Assocs., Toronto, Ontario, Can., 1976-79, Winton Altschuler, Toronto, 1979-81; sr. ptnr. Danielson & Assocs., Toronto, 1981-88, Danielson & Fox, Toronto, 1988-96; of counsel Law Offices Myles L. Berman, L.A., 1996—; area dir., com. mem. Ontario Legal Aid, Toronto, Can., 1985-96. Co-author: (book) Calif. DUI Trial Notebook, 1997, California Law Principles and Practice; contbr. articles to profl. jours. instr., coord., Can. Red Cross Instr.'s Sch., Toronto, 1968-78, Royal Life Saving Soc. Instr.'s Sch., 1968-78; bd. dirs. Toronto Can. Red Cross, 1973-78. Mem. Century City Bar Assn. (bd. govs., chmn. entertainment sect., co-chair criminal sect.), Beverly Hills Bar Assn., Calif. Deuce Defenders (cert. specialist), Criminal Cts. Bar Assn., Nat. Assn. Criminal Defense Lawyers (U.S.), Criminal Lawyers Assn. Can., Nat. Coll. DUI Defenders, The Canadian Acad. of Recording Arts and Scis., Can. Ind. Record and Prodrs. Assn. Avocations: squash, swimming, skiing. Office: Law Offices Myles L Berman 9255 W Sunset Blvd Ste 720 Los Angeles CA 90069-3304

DANIEWSKI, WLODZIMIERZ MARIA, chemistry educator, consultant; b. Solec-Zdroj, Poland, Feb. 15, 1933; s. Wlodzimierz Maria and Stefania (Piotrowski) D.; m. Jolanta Maria Schollenberger, Febr. 4, 1962; children: Dorothy, Christopher. MSc, Technical U., Warsaw, 1956; PhD, UMIST, Manchester, England, 1960; DSc, Inst. Org. Chemistry, Warsaw, 1972. Asst. Inst. Organic Chemistry, Warsaw, 1956-57; adj. ICHOPAN, Warsaw, 1960-73, asst. prof., 1973-89, assoc. prof., 1989-93, prof., 1993—; post doctoral rsch. fellow U. Pitts., 1964-66, 77-78, 83-84. Avocation: gardening. Home: Zamiany 15m45, 02-786 Warsaw Poland Office: Inst Org Chemistry Pol Acad Sci, Kasprzaka 44, 01-224 Warsaw Poland

DANILOV, GENNADY STEPANOVICH, physicist, researcher; b. St. Petersburg, USSR, Mar. 26, 1935; s. Ivan Danilovich Kozlovsky and Natalia Nicolaevna D.; m. Alisa Petrovina Ilyna, 1957 (div.1965); 1 child; m. Lidya Michaylovna Kotova, 1966; 1 child. Physicist, Petersburg State U., St. Petersburg, 1957; PhD, Inst. Theoret. and Exptl. Physics, Moscow, 1964, DSc, 1976. Researcher Phys. Tech. Inst., St. Petersburg, 1951-66, sr. researcher, 1966-71; sr. researcher Petersburg Nuclear Physics Inst., Gatehina, USSR, 1971-86; leading researcher Petersburg Nuclear Physics Inst., Gatehina, 1986—. Contbr. articles to profl. jours. Fax: 78127131963. E-mail: danilov@thd.pnpi.spb.ru. Office: Petersburg Nuc Physics Inst, 188350 Gatchina Leningrad District, Russia

DANILOV, VICTOR JOSEPH, museum management program director, consultant, writer, educator; b. Farrell, Pa., Dec. 30, 1924; s. Joseph M. and Ella (Tominovich) D.; m. Toni Dewey, Sept. 6, 1980; children: Thomas J., Duane P., Denise S. BA in Journalism, Pa. State U., 1945; MS in Journalism, Northwestern U., 1946; EdD in Higher Edn., U. Colo., 1964. With Sharon Herald, Pa., 1942, Youngstown Vindicator, 1945, Pitts. Sun-Telegraph, 1946-47, Chgo. Daily News, 1947-50; instr. journalism U. Colo., 1950-51; asst. prof. journalism U. Kans., 1951-53; with Kansas City Star, 1953; mgr. pub. rels. Ill. Inst. Tech. and IIT Rsch. Inst., 1953-57; dir. univ. rels. and pub. info. U. Colo., 1957-60; pres. Profile Co., Boulder, Colo., 1960-62; exec. editor, exec. v.p. Indsl. Rsch. Inc., Beverly Shores, Ind., 1962-69; pub., exec. v.p. Indsl. Rsch. Inc., 1969-71; dir., v.p. Mus. Sci. and Industry, Chgo., 1971-77; pres., dir. Mus. Sci. and Industry, 1978-87, pres. emeritus, 1987—; dir. mus. mgmt. program, adj. prof. U. Colo., 1987—; mem. rural industrialization adv. group Dept. Agr., 1967; mem. panel internat. transfer tech. Dept. Commerce, 1968; mem. sci. info. coun. NSF, 1969-72; chmn. Conf. on Implications Metric Change, 1972, Nat. Conf. Indsl. Rsch., 1966-70; chmn. observance Nat. Indsl. Rsch. Week, 1967-70; chmn. Midwest White House Conf. on Indsl. World Ahead, 1972, Internat. Conf. Sci. and Tech. Museums, 1976, 82; mem. task force on fin. acctg. and reporting by non bus. orgns., others. Author: Public Affairs Reporting, 1955, Starting a Science Center, 1977, Science and Technology Centers, 1982, Science Center Planning Guide, 1985, Chicago's Museums, 1987, rev. edit., 1991, America's Science Museums, 1990, Corporate Museums, Galleries, and Visitor Centers: A Directory, 1991, A Planning Guide for Corporate Museums, Galleries, and Visitors Centers, 1992, Museum Careers and Training: A Professional Guide, 1994, University and College Museums, Galleries, and Related Facilities, 1996, Hall of Fame Museums: A Reference Guide, 1997, Colorado Museums and Historical Sites, 2000; also articles; editor: Crucial Issues in Public Relations, 1960, Corporate Research and Profitability, 1966, Innovation and Profitability, 1967, Research Decision-Making in New Product Development, 1968, New Products--and Profits, 1969, Applying Emerging Technologies, 1970, Nuclear Power in the South, 1970, The Future of Science and Technology, 1975, Museum Accounting Guidelines, 1976, Traveling Exhibitions, 1978, Towards the Year 2000, 1981; editor profl. procs. Trustee Women of the West Mus., 1991-99, v.p., 1991-99; trustee La Rabida Childrens Hosp. and Rsch. Ctr., 1973-83; mem. U. Chgo. Citizens Bd., 1978-87. Mem. Am. Assn. Mus. (exec. com. 1976-77, bd. dirs. 1985-88, chmn. mus. studies task force 1988-89), AAAS, Assn. Sci.-Tech. Ctrs. (bd. dirs. 1973-84, sec.-treas. 1973-74, pres. 1975-76), Internat. Coun. Mus. (com. on sci. and tech. mus. 1972—, vice chmn. 1977-87, chmn. 1982-83, bd. dirs. 1985-88), Chgo. Coun. on Fine Arts (chmn. 1976-84), Ill. Arts Alliance (bd. dirs. 1983-86), Sci. Mus. Exhibit Collaborative (pres. 1983-86), Mus. Film Network (pres. 1984-86). Home: 250 Bristlecone Way Boulder CO 80304-0413 Office: Univ Colo Mus Mus Mgmt Program Campus Box 218 Boulder CO 80309-0218

DANILOW, DEBORAH MARIE, singer, songwriter, musician, rancher, realtor; b. Mineral Wells, Tex., Dec. 9, 1947; d. Stanton Byron and Irval Leona (Vanhoosier) D.; m. William Paul Cook Jr., June 1965 (div. Oct. 1967); m. Chance Gentry, Oct. 1971 (div. May 1974); m. Ellis Elmer Aldridge, Dec. 3, 1977 (div. Nov. 1984); children: Chandra Desiree, Anthony Ellis; m. Carl Graham Quisenberry, Feb. 7, 1992 (div. May 1997). Student, Brantley Draughon Bus. Coll., Ft. Worth, 1965-66, Tex. Christian U., 1965-67, U. Ariz., 1967-69. Asst. to pres. Hollywood Video Ctr., L.A., 1969-72; producer Western Inst. TV, L.A., 1972-77; owner Chanelde Ranch, Weatherford, Tex., 1977-84; band musician Bonnie Raitt, Jerry Williams, Malibu, Calif., 1984, Mick Fleetwood, Malibu, 1984; lead musician Jazz Talk, Ft. Worth, 1985-96; owner Brazos Valley Ranch Inc., 1987—, AAA Bail Bonds, Seymour, 1990-96. Composer numerous pub. songs, 1969—; lead musician Debbie Danilow and Soul Full o' Jazz, 1996—; debut solo CD Primordial Heart, 1999. Active Sheriffs Assn. Tex., Seymour, 1991-97, North Tex. Taxpayers League, Wichita Falls, Tex., 1991-96, Tex. State Notary Bd., Austin, 1990-99. Mem. NRA, Nat. Assn. Realtors, Tex. Realtors Assn., Greater Ft. Worth Bd. Realtors, Tex. Limousin Assn., Tex. Southwestern Cattle Raisers Assn., Tex. Cattlewomen's Assn., Am. Quarter Horse Assn. (life), Nat. Found. Quarter Horse Assn. (life), Dallas-Ft. Worth Profl. Musicians Assn., Ft. Worth Jazz Soc. (sec. 1987-89), N.Am. Limousin Found. (life), Australian Shepherd Club Am., Marchigiana Cattle Assn. (life). Avocations: music, horses and dogs, writing, performing. E-mail: star@debbiedanilow.com. Home and Office: Debbie Danilow Inc 3137 W 4th St Fort Worth TX 76107-2112

DANISI, JOHN J., philosopher, educator; b. Bklyn., Mar. 19, 1948; s. Jack F. and Mary (Kelly) D.; m. Carolyn S. Swallum, Sept. 30, 1989; children: Mary, Jacqueline. BA cum laude, St. Louis U., 1969; MA, NYU, 1974, PhD, 1993. Cert. secondary sch. tchr., Mo. Jr. high sch. tchr. Annunciation Sch., St. Louis, 1969-71; instr. St. Louis U., 1970; adj. asst. prof. dept. philosophy, NYU, 1982—. Contbr. articles to profl. jours. Invited del. Citizen Amb. Program People to People Internat.; Philosophy Edn. Del. to China, 1993, Edn. Delegation to Berlin, 1994, Spokane, 1994. Fellowship Andrew W. Mellon fellow, NYU, 1981, NYU fellow, 1978-82, A. Ogden Butler fellowship NYU, 1987; recipient William James Prize Essay Am. Philos. Assn. Eastern divsn. 1986. Mem. Am. Philos. Assn., Soc. for the Advancement of Am. Philosphy, Leibniz Soc. Home: 4445 Post Rd Apt 8H Riverdale NY 10471-3449 Office: NYU Dept Philosophy 503 Main Bldg. New York NY 10003-6688

DANJCZEK, DAVID WILLIAM, manufacturing company executive; b. Phillipsburg, N.J., Sept. 29, 1951; s. William Emil and Erna (Lob) D. BSFS, Georgetown U., 1973; postgrad., Waseda U., 1973-74, Loyola U., L.A., 1977-78. Contract adminstr. Aero Products, Woodland Hills, Calif., 1974-76, sr. contract adminstr., 1976-78; dir. internat. ops. Litton Industries, Washington, 1978-90, v.p. internat. bus., 1990-93; v.p. govt. and internat. affairs Western Atlas Inc., 1993-97; corp. v.p. Unova, Inc., 1997—; adj. prof. Georgetown U. Chair Industry sector adv. com. U.S. Dept. Commerce, chair; bd. dirs. Exec. Coun. Diplomacy. Mem. Mfrs. Alliance Productivity and Innovation (past chair global bus. coun.), Am. Countertrade Assn. (sec.), Univ. Club, Internat. Aviation Club. Roman Catholic. Avocations: squash, bridge. Home: 1300 Crystal Dr Arlington VA 22202-3234 Office: UNOVA 1660 L St NW Washington DC 20036-5603

DANJCZEK, MICHAEL HARVEY, social service administrator; b. Phillipsburg, N.J., May 9, 1949; s. William Emil and Erna (Lob) D.; m. Cynthia Ann Johanson, June 9, 1973; children: William Emil II, Liesel J., Rachel L., Peter L. BA in Urban Studies, Lehigh U., Bethlehem, Pa., 1972, MEd in Social Restoration, 1974, EdD in Ednl. Adminstrn., 1985; PhD (hon.), Lafayette Coll., 2000. Exec. dir. Lehigh Valley Opportunity Ctr., Bethlehem, Pa., 1972-74; pres., exec. dir. Children's Home, Easton, Pa., 1974—; adj. prof. Lehigh County C.C., 1987-91, Grad. Sch., Jersey City State Tchrs. Coll., 1989-92; treas. Pa. Coun. Children's Svcs., 1982-84; mem. Commn. on Accreditation, Nat. Assn. Homes for Children, 1982-87, chmn. bd. dirs., 1997-98; mem. authority bd. Northampton C.C., 1983-95; v.p. Pa. Coun. Children's Svcs., 1985-87, bd. dirs., 1987-89; bd. dirs. Lehigh Valley Drug Treatment Program, 1986-88; mem. Ea. U.S. Svc. Coun. of Coun. on Accreditation Svcs. for Families and children, 1987-92; treas. Nat. Assn. Homes and Svcs. for Children, 1988-93, chmn. bd. dirs., 1997-98; bd. dirs. Twin Rivers Cmty. Bank, 1991—; bd. dirs. Coun. on Accreditation Svcs. for Family and Children, 1993-98. Asst. wrestling coach Lafayette Coll., 1974-76; mem. exec. com. Rep. party of Northampton County, 1975-76; bd. advisors Jr. League Lehigh Valley, 1975-77; chmn. profl. adv. com. Family and Child Welfare of Lehigh Valley Cmty. Coun., 1976; mem. adv. bd. Cath. Social Svcs., Diocese of Allentown, 1976-81; mem. Wilson Boro Sch. Bd., 1980-83; bd. dirs. Pa. Coun. Vol. Child Care Agys., 1980-84; bd. dirs. Helen Beebe Speech and Hearing Ctr., 1980-89, pres. bd. dirs., 1987-89; bd. dirs. Parents Anonymous Pa., 1981-90, pres. bd., 1981-85; gen. campaign chmn. United Way of Northampton and Warren Counties, 1982-83; bd. dirs. Great Valley Girl Scout Coun., 1983-89; chmn. Minsi Trail Drug Abuse Prevention Rally for Forks of Del., Boy Scouts Am., 1987; mem. St. Bernard's Ch. Parish Coun., 1991-93; chmn. elect, v.p. econ. devel. Two Rivers Area Commerce Coun., 1991-92; chmn. Northampton County Sports and Spl. Events Com., 1994-97; mem. governing bd., CEO, chmn. BallYard, Inc., 1994; co-founder Pro Kids Alliance, 1994; mem. governing bd. St. Vincent's Home for Children, 1995—; bd. chair Children's Coalition of the Lehigh Valley, 1998-99, Pa. Coun. Children's Svcs., 1998-2000; bd. dirs. Families Internat., 1998—, Alliance for Children and Families, 1998—; co-founder Pro Kids Alliance, 1994—, CEO Alliance for Children and Families of the Lehigh Valley, 1999—. Recipient Disting. Cmty. Svc. award Easton Area Jaycees, 1975, Disting. Svc. award Pa. Com. on Internat. Yr. of Child, 1979, Coll. Edn., Lehigh U., 1983, Disting. Alumni award Lehigh U., 1987, Gafney award Lehigh U. Assn. Ednl. Adminstrs., 1988, Pres. award for cmty. svc. Easton Area Sales and Mktg. Execs., 1990, Svc. to Mankind award Sertoma Club, 1991; inducted to Notre Dame H.S. Athletic Hall of Fame, 1990. Mem. Lehigh U. Alumni Assn. Home Club (bd. dirs. 1990—), Lehigh U. Alumni Assn. (bd. dirs. 1987-90), Northampton Country Club (bd. govs. 1985-94), Nat. Fellowship Child Care Execs. (exec. sec. 1993-98, pres. 1992-93), Two Rivers Area C. of C. (chmn. 1993-95), Rotary (past pres. Easton). Republican. Roman Catholic. Avocations: private pilot, golf, skiing, travel. Home and Office: Childrens Home Easton 25th St and Lehigh Dr Easton PA 18042

DANJO, YUKITAKA, ophthalmologist; b. Fukuyama, Japan, Dec. 6, 1962; s. Takanobu and Yoshiko (Ando) D.; m. Yukiko Ishida, Sept. 8, 1991; children: Momoko, Rika Marie. BS, Osaka U., 1983, MD, 1987. Resident Osaka U. Med. Sch., Japan, 1987-89; asst. surgeon Osaka Seamen's Ins. Hosp., 1989-91; instr. Osaka Nat. Hosp., 1991-96; asst. prof. Osaka U. Med. Sch., 1996-99; dir. Osaka Seamens Hosp., 1999—. Mem. AAAS, Assn. for Rsch. in Vision and Ophthalmology, N.Y. Acad. Sci. Avocation: fishing. Office: Osaka U Med Sch Dept Oph, 2-2 Yamadaoka, Suita 565-0871, Japan

DANK, LEONARD DEWEY, medical illustrator, audio-visual consultant; b. Birmingham, Ala., Dec. 21, 1929; s. George and Ellen (Balsam) D.; B.A. in Zoology, Cornell U., 1952; grad. Sch. Med. Illustration, Mass. Gen. Hosp., 1955; m. Beryl Eileen Jealous, Sept. 30, 1961; 1 dau., Amelia Theresa. Staff med. artist, plastic surgery clinic Manhattan Eye, Ear & Throat Hosp., 1955-57, Eye Bank for Sight Restoration, 1957-59; owner Leonard D. Dank Med. Illustration Studio, 1959-79; pres. Med. Illustrations Co., 1979—(all N.Y.C.); cons. med. illustrator St. Luke's Hosp., 1961-83, trans-vision div. Milprint, Inc., 1965—, Woman's Hosp., 1963-83, H.S. Struttman, Inc., 1964—, Home Library Press, 1960-70 (all N.Y.C.), Synapse Communications, Inc. (Conn.), 1973-75, Contemporary Orthopaedics and Contemporary Surgery, 1981-85, P.W. Communications, Inc., 1982-89, Esquire Mags. Health and Fitness Clinic, 1985-88, Whittle Communications, 1988—. Recipient 1st prize certificate merit A.M.A., 1959, 1st prize citation of merit in motion picture program A.C.S., 1959, 62; Better Teller award Assn. Indsl. Advertisers, 1973, Outstanding Sci. Book award for Children Nat. Sci. Tchrs. Assn., 1982, Cert. of Merit Soc. of Illustrators, 1986. Mem. Assn. Med. Illustrators, Guild Natural Sci. Illustrators. Roman Catholic. Co-author: Gynecologic Operations, 1978; med. illustrator for numerous med. books, jours., elementary textbooks, juvenile books, encys. Home and Office: 800 Cox Ln Cutchogue NY 11935-1303

DANKO, GENE ANDREW, materials scientist; b. McKeesport, Pa., Mar. 10, 1958; s. Andrew John and Margaret Mary (Mosher) D.; m. April Jane Ludwig, Nov. 6, 1993 (div. Aug. 1996). BA in Biophysics, Johns Hopkins U., 1980, PhD in Materials Sci. and Engring., 1992. Rsch. staff Nat. Inst. Standards and Tech., Gaithersburg, Md., 1980-92; rsch. scientist Tech. Assessment & Transfer, Annapolis, Md., 1992-93; chief scientist Advanced Ceramics Rsch., Tucson, 1993-97; sr. materials scientist FM Techs., Fairfax, Va., 1997-99; pres. Exius Corp., Wilmington, Del., 1998—; sr. systems integration technologist Pratt & Whitney, East Hartford, Conn., 1999—; assoc. TEIN, Vienna, Va., 1998—. Mem. AIAA, Electrochem. Soc., Am. Ceramic Soc., Nat. Inst. Ceramic Engrs., U.S. Power Squadrons, Sigma Xi. Republican. Roman Catholic. Avocations: sailing, photography. Home: 125 South St #283 Vernon CT 06066-4439 Office: Pratt & Whitney 400 Main St # Ms163-23 East Hartford CT 06108-0968

DANKO, GEORGE, engineering educator; b. Budapest, Hungary, Apr. 3, 1944; came to U.S., 1986; s. Gyorgy and Ilona (Mihaly) D.; m. Eva Arvay, Dec. 14, 1976; 1 child, Reka. BSME, Tech. U. Budapest, 1968, PhD, 1976; MS in Applied Math., Eotovs U. of Scis., Budapest, 1975; PhD, Hungarian Acad. Scis., Budapest, 1985. Cert. Profl. Ski Instrs. Am. Assn. Asst. prof. Tech. U. Budapest, 1968-75, assoc. prof., 1979-86; fellow Hungarian Acad. Scis., Budapest, 1975-79; rsch. assoc. U. Nev., Reno, 1986-90, assoc. prof., 1990-95, prof. mining engring., 1995—; cons. Sierra Sci., Reno, 1990—; chmn. High-Level Radioactive Waste Mgmt. Conf., 1991, 92; portrait artist, Reno, 1987-92. Co-author: Methods for the Calculation of Pipeline Transients, 1976, Warming-up and Cooling of Electrical Machinery, 1982; contbr. articles to profl. jours. Com. rep. Truckee River Steering Com., Reno, 1993-94. Grantee U.S. Bur. Mines, 1986-97, U.S. Dept. Energy, 1991—, Clarkson Co., 1992-98. Mem. ASME, ISES (internat. organizing com. 1993-94), IFAC (internat. program com. 1995—), Soc. Mining Engrs., Am. Nuclear Soc. Achievements include patents for methods and apparatus for the determination of the heat transfer coefficient, process and apparatus for the determination of thermophysical properties, underground cooling enhancement for nuclear waste repository, method and apparatus for underground nuclear waste repository, others. Office: U Nev Reno Mining Engring Dept 173 Reno NV 89557-0001

DAŇKOVA, HELENA, chief librarian; b. Praha, Czech Republic, Apr. 3, 1934; d. Gustav and Milada (Srbková) D. Gymnasium grad., Praha. Libr. ÚVVL, Praha, Czech Republic, 1955-70; libr. Inst. Clin. and Exptl. Medicine, Praha, 1971-76, chief librarian, 1976—. Home: Krkonošská 2, 120 00 Praha 2, Czech Republic Office: Inst Clin & Exptl Medicine, Videňská 1958, Prague Czech Republic

DANN, ALEXANDER WILLIAM, JR., lawyer; b. Pitts., Mar. 20, 1923; s. Alexander William and Ella (Berry) D.; m. Alexander William III, Thomas Semmes, Elise Dann Oschwald, Katherine Dann Pruett. BA, Cornell U., 1948, LLB, JD, 1951. Bar: Tenn. 1951, U.S. Tax Ct. 1962, U.S. Ct. Claims 1965, U.S. Dist. Ct. (we. dist.) Tenn. 1971, U.S. Supreme Ct. 1972, U.S. Ct. Appeals (5th cir.) 1972, U.S. Ct. Appeals (6th cir.) 1980, U.S. Dist. Ct. Ark. 1981. Assoc. Canada, Russell & Turner, Memphis, 1950-55; from assoc. to ptnr. Tual Younger & Dann, Memphis, 1956-58; ptnr. Younger & Dann, Memphis, 1958-60, Dann, Hills & Blackburn, Memphis, 1961-78, Dann, Davis, Davis & Blackburn, Memphis, 1978-86; pres., sr. atty. Dann & Assocs., P.C., Memphis, 1986-95; ptnr., sr. atty. Dann, Allen & Murrell, Memphis, 1995—; legal counsel Miss. Valley Flood Control, Agc., Memphis, 1965—; cons. Western Dredging Assn., Seattle, 1988-97; cons., panelist Nat. Acad. Scis., Washington, 1987, 89. Contbr. 38 articles to profl. jours. Commr. elections Shelby County, 1965-67, 67-69, 69-71; chmn. Shelby County Rep. Party, Memphis, 1970-72; mem. civic com. Shelby County Charter Commn., Memphis, 1968-69; chmn. bd. trustees Memphis Brooks Mus. of Art, 1965-85, Memphis Front Street Theatre, 1966. Lt. (j.g.) USNR, 1943-46. Mem. ABA, Am. Arbitration Assn. (panelist 1993—), Tenn. Bar Assn., Memphis Bar Assn., Nat. Acad. Sci. (cons., panelist 1987-89, 90—), Memphis Country Club, Rotary, Alpha Delta Phi. Republican. Episcopalian. Avocations: waterfowl hunting, travel, oil painting, furniture woodworking, tennis. Home: 6246 Green Meadows Rd Memphis TN 38120-3101 Office: Dann Allen & Murrell 6263 Poplar Ave Ste 1103 Memphis TN 38119-4724

DANN, HANNS-DIETRICH, psychology researcher educator; b. Berlin, Sept. 16, 1939; s. Heinrich Ferdinand Richard and Jutta Annemarie (Hübner) D.; m. Erica Kunz,Feb. 23, 1968; children: Barbara, Evelyn Anja. Diploma in psychology, Free U., Berlin, 1965; D Social Scis., U. Constance, Germany, 1970, Habilitation in Psychology, 1975. Sci. asst., career advisor Inst. Psychology, U. Berne, Switzerland, 1965-67; sci. asst. dept. psychology U. Constance, 1967-74, asst. prof., 1974-76, assoc. prof., 1976-87, prin. investigator, dean Ctr. for Ednl. Rsch., 1971-85, dean faculty social scis., 1984-85; prof. psychology Inst. Psychology Friedrich Alexander U., Nürnberg, Germany, 1987—; head Inst. Friedrich-Alexander U., Nürnberg, Germany, 1989—; dir. Ctr. for Social Sci. Rsch. Friedrich Alexander U., Nürnberg, Germany, 1990—, dean faculty edn., 1993-95; lectr. pub. high schs., various cities, 1968-78; expert Swiss Nat. Rsch. Found., Berne, 1995—. Author: Aggression and Achievement, 1972, 3d edit., 1974; co-author: The Constance Training Model, 1987, 2d edit., 1990, The Observational System Bavis, 1988, Cooperative Learning at School, 1999. Bd. dirs. Sponsoring Assn. Windsbach Boys' Chorus, 1994—. Mem. APA (in-

ternat. assoc.), European Assn. Exptl. Social Psychology, Internat. Assn. on Tchrs. and Tchg. Avocations: music, theater, reading, sports. Office: Inst Psychology, Regensburger Strasse 160, 90478 Nürnberg Bavaria, Germany

DANN, OLIVER TOWNSEND, psychoanalyst, psychiatrist, educator; b. Mansfield, Ohio, Aug. 10, 1935; s. Edward William and Mary Virginia (Townsend) D.; m. Linda Marie Schweers, July 15, 1961; children: Sara Katharine, Jonathan William Jenner, Luke Nathan Townsend, Jesse Charles. AB, Columbia U., 1958; MD, Yale U., 1962. Diplomate Am. Bd. Psychiatry and Neurology. Resident in psychiatry Yale U. Sch. Medicine, New Haven, 1963-67, asst., assoc. prof. psychiatry, 1967-79; clin. prof. psychiatry U. Miami (Fla.) Sch. Medicine, 1980—; dir. Fla. Psychoanalytic Inst., 1997—; pvt. practice, Miami, 1979—. Contbr. articles to profl. jours. Mem. Mayflower Soc., Jamestowne Soc., Huguenot Soc. Fellow (life) APA, Ctr. for Advanced Psychoanalytic Studies; mem. SAR, Am. Psychoanalytic Assn., Internat. Psychoanalytic Assn., Western New England Inst. Soc. Psychoanalysis, Balt.-Washington Inst. Soc. Psychoanalysis, Fla. Psychanalytic Inst. Soc. Found., Phi Beta Kappa, others. Avocations: sailing, canoeing, hiking. Home and Office: 4550 SW 74th St Miami FL 33143-6271

DANNEELS, GODFRIED CARDINAL, archbishop; b. Kanegem, Belgium, June 4, 1933. Ordained priest Roman Cath. Ch., 1957; prof. liturgy and sacramental theology Cath. U. Louvain (Belgium), 1969-77; consecrated bishop of Antwerp, 1977; apptd. archbishop of Mechelen-Brussel (Belgium), 1979; elected mem. gen. secretariat Synod of Bishops, 1981; elevated to Sacred Coll. of Cardinals, 1983. Mil. bishop, Belgium; pres. Belgian Episcopal Conf. Mem. Congregation of Cath. Edn., Congregation of Evangelisation, Congregation of Divine Worship, Congregation for Oriental Chs., Coun. for pub. affairs of ch. Secretariate for non-believers., Pax Christi Internat. (pres. 1990-99). Address: Aartsbisdom, Wollemarkt 15, B-2800 Mechelen Belgium

DANNESKIOLD-SAMSOE, ULRIK OTTO HUBERT VIGGO, lawyer; b. Stege, Denmark, Feb. 20, 1965; arrived in Switzerland, 1985; s. Christian Viggo Danneskiold-Samsøe and Helene Carola (Kunzli) D.; m. Manuela Lundstrøm, Sept. 3, 1988; children: Philip, Niklas, Isabelle. Cand.Iur., U. Bern, Switzerland, 1989. Agt., advisor Product Internat., Beverly Hills, Calif., 1989; atty. Swigraph Ag, Zürich, Switzerland, 1990-91; mgr., lawyer Burgdorf, Switzerland, 1991—; advisor Gisselfeld Castle, Haslev, Denmark, 1993—. Bd. dirs. Fondation Guy Poirier, Montreal, Que.; mem. Royal Guard, Denmark. Mem. Parrot Soc. (Eng.), The Highlander Club (U.S.A.). Conservative Party. Avocations: family, sports, fishing, wildlife, travel. Home and Office: Lanzenen, 3800 Interlaken Switzerland also: Lettenvej 18, 4792 Askeby Denmark

DANON, AMBRA, costume designer; b. Rome. Student, Acad. Costume Design, Rome, Acad. Dramatic Art, Rome. Costume designer for theatre, films, opera, and TV. Mem. Acad. Motion Picture Arts and Scis. (art dir. br., Acad. award nomination 1980), European Film Acad. Berlin, Ente David Donatello Italy. Home: 4 Piazza Priscilla, 00199 Rome Italy

DANON, YEHUDA LEON, physician, researcher; b. Pazargik, Bulgaria, Sept. 9, 1940; arrived in Israel, 1948; s. Bencion and Fortune (Danon) D.; m. Ruth Hana Strauss, Jan. 29, 1967; children: Tal, Tamar, Michael. MD, Hebrew U., Jerusalem, Israel, 1967; postgrad., Weizman Inst. Sci., 1973-75; MB, Haifa (Israel) U., 1982. Diplomate Israeli Bd. Pediatrics, Israeli Bd. Immunology, Israeli Bd. Med. Mgmt., Israeli Bd. Pediatric Immunology and Allergy. Fogarty fellow NIH, Bethesda, Md., 1975-76; Fulbright fellow UCLA, 1976-77; dep. surg. gen. Israeli Def. Forces, 1982-83; dir. Beilinson Med. Ctr., Petah Tikva, Israel, 1985-87; surgeon gen. State of Israel, 1987-91; dir. Kipper Inst. Immunology/Tel Aviv U., 1991—, Children's Med. Ctr. of Israel, 1991—; vis. prof. medicine Albert Einstein Coll. Medicine, Bronx, N.Y., 1984-85; vis. prof. pediatrics Schneider Children's Hosp., L.I., N.Y., 1996-97; bd. dirs. Phenix Ins. Group; chief judge Coun. for Beautiful Israel, 1996-97. Editor: Medical Lessons of the War in Lebanon, 1985, Chemical Warfare Medicine, 1995, Pediatrics to 2000, 1996; editor Jour. pediatric Hematology. Chief scientist M.C., Israel Def. Forces, 1996—; mem. Nat. Helsinki Com., 1995—. Brig. gen. Israel Def. Forces, 1967-91. Recipient Granof award Israel Cancer Rsch. Found., 1983, Ambrouise Pare prize Med. Corps Inst., Bonn, Germany, 1988, Pinhas Sapir Med. award, Tel Aviv, 1992. Jewish. Avocations: horticulture, philately, art collecting, painting. Home: Farm # 61, 60991 Bney Atarot Israel Office: Tel Aviv U Sch Med, Schneider Childrens Med Ctr, 49202 Petah Tiqwa Israel

DANSE, ILENE HOMNICK RAISFELD, physician, educator, toxicologist; b. Bklyn., June 24, 1940; d. Jack and Henrietta (Poverstein) Homnick; m. James Atherton Danse, Aug. 10, 1982; children: Arthur Raisfeld, Robin Raisfeld. BS, CUNY, 1960; MD, NYU, 1964; student, Pratt Inst., Art Students League, Bklyn. Mus. Art Sch. Diplomate Nat. Bd. Med. Examiners, Am. Bd. Internal Medicine, Am. Bd. Toxicology. Assoc. prof. internal medicine SUNY, Stony Brook, 1975-83, assoc. prof. pharmacology, 1977-83, dir. clin. pharmacology and toxicology Sch. Medicine, 1978-83; acting chairperson clin. pharmacology Northport VA Hosp., L.I., N.Y., 1978-83; sr. advisor Chevron Environ. Health Ctr., San Pablo, Calif., 1982-84; prin. ENVIROMED Health Svcs., Inc., Novato, Calif., 1985—; ind. med. examiner toxicology and internal medicine Dept. Indsl. Rels., State of Calif., 1985—; assoc. clin. prof. dept. medicine div. occupl. and environ. medicine U. Calif., San Francisco, 1986—; assoc. clin. prof. dept. epidemiol. and preventive medicine U. Calif., Davis, 1991—; cons. in fields of toxicology, pharmacology, environ., occupl. and internal medicine, 1984—; mem. bd. sci. advisors Am. Coun. Sci. and Health; mem. sci. rev. panel Hazardous Substances Data Base, Nat. Libr. Medicine. Author: Common Sense Toxics In the Workplace, 1991; contbr. articles to sci. publs. Mem. bd. sci. advisors Am. Coun. on Sci. and Health; mem. sci. rev. panel Hazardous Substances Data Base, Nat. Libr. of Medicine. Fellow ACP, Am. Coll. Clin. Pharmacology; mem. AAAS, Am. Acad. Clin. Toxicology, Am. Chem. Soc. (environ. health and safety sect.), Am. Coll. Occupl. Medicine, Am. Indsl. Hygiene Assn. (occupational medicine sect.), Am. Coll. Toxicology, Am. Soc. Pharmacology and Therapeutics, Soc. Toxicology, Western Occupational Med. Assn. Achievements include patent for epithelial cell growth-regulating composition containing polyamines, and method of its use. Office: ENVIROMED Health Svcs Inc # 346 448 Ignacio Blvd # 346 Novato CA 94949-6085

DANSON, ANDREW, photographer; b. Bournemouth, Eng., Jan. 12, 1945; s. Bertram Wolfe and Theodora D.; 1 child, Akira. Student, U. Guelph, 1967. ofcl. photographer '76 Olympics; curator Yr. of the Child Show, Toronto, 1979, Documentary Styles Show Burlington, 1988; guest lectr. Meml. Univ. Nfld., 1983, Emily Carr Coll. Art and Design, 1987; part-time instr. digital imaging Humber Coll.; curator Cuban photographers exhbn. at U. Toronto, 2000, Canadian photographers exhbn. Fototeca de Cuba, Havana. Works exhibited in 17 solo exhbns., 1975—, 28 group exhbns. 1975— including Royal Ont. Mus., Photo Passage and Harbourfront, 80 piece Berlin survey exhbn. Friedrichshain Foto Galerie, 1999; represented in pvt. and pub. collections including City of Toronto Archives, Can. Mus. Contemporary Photography, Nat. Archives Can.; author: Unofficial Portraits, 1987, Face-Kao: Portraits of Japanese Canadians Interned During WWII, 1996; contbr. articles to mags.; works collected in Maison Europeene de la Photographie, Paris, Bibliotheque Nat. de France, Paris, Le Musee de La Photographie a Charleroi, Belgium, Scottish Nat. Portrait Gallery, Edinburgh, Can. Mus. of Contemporary Photography, Art Gallery of Ont., Nat. Archives of Can., City of Toronto Archives. Recipient Can. Coun. awards, Sec. of State award, Ont. arts Coun. award, Art Dirs. Club Toronto award, 1988, first prize color photo Internat. Assn. Bus. Commn., 1988; grantee Can. Coun. Project Cost, 1990, Ont. Arts Coun., 1990, Japanese Can. Redress Found., 1990, Can. Coun. B., 1991, 93, Tanenbaum Found., 1996, Can. Coun. Millennium, 1999, others. Mem. Toronto Photographers Workshop. E-mail: danson@nervebyte.com. Address: 186 De Grassi St, Toronto, ON Canada M4M 2K7

DANSON-SMITH, THEODORE CHALMERS, publisher, minister; b. Edinburgh, Scotland; s. James and Janet Isobel (Chalmers) Danson-S.; m. Heather Florence May Rainey. ThD in Theology with honors, Trinity Theol. Sem., 1986; BTh in Theology, Am. Bible Coll., 1979; DipTh, Evang. Inst. Theology, London, 1973; FME (hon.), Fellowship Evangelistic, Ministries, 1986; LittD (hon.), Am. Bible Coll., 1986. Mng. ptnr. B. McCall Barbour, Edinburgh. Fellow Evangelistic Ministries (Scottish leader, moderator 1999—). Office: 28 George IV Bridge, Edinburgh EH1 1ES, Scotland

DANTER, GLYN E., healthcare industry official; b. Cardiff, Wales, Sept. 19, 1944; arrived in Australia, 1987; s. Eric and Lila (Williams) D.; m. Linda M. Harris, Oct. 1, 1966; children: Sean, Joanne. Grad. high sch., Cardiff. Sys. devel. mgr. SiFO, Riyadh, Saudi Arabia, 1980-83; health cons. (info. tech.) SiFO, London, 1983-87; health industry cons., Sydney, Australia, 1987-91; mgr. profl. svcs. Digital, Sydney, 1991-93, health industry mgr., 1993-98; health industry mgr. Compaq Computer Australia, Sydney, 1998—. Mem. Brit. Computer Soc., Health Informatics Soc. Australia. Avocations: drummer in rock band, competition squash. Office: Compaq Computer Australia, 18-20 Orion Rd, Lane Cove, Sydney NSW 2066, Australia

D'ANTONIO, ENZIO, archbishop; b. Lanciano, Italy, May 16, 1925. Ordained priest to Roman Cath. Ch., 1949. Archbishop City of Boiano-Campobasso, Italy, 1977-79, City of Velebusdo and Lanciano, Italy, 1979-82, City of Lanciano-Ortona, Italy, 1982—. Office: Arcivescovado, CP 223 Via Gennaro Finamore 32, 66034 Chieti Lanciano, Italy*

DANTZIC, CYNTHIA MARIS, artist, educator; b. N.Y.C., Jan. 4, 1933; d. Howard Arthur and Sylvia Hazel (Wiener) Gross; m. Jerry Dantzic, June 15, 1958; 1 son, Grayson Ross. Student, Brooklyn Mus. Art Sch., Brooklyn, NY, 1947-50; Student, Bard Coll., 1950-52; BFA, Yale U., 1955; MFA, Pratt Inst., 1963. Tchr. art Baldwin Sch., Bryn Mawr, Pa., 1955-58; head art dept. Bentley Sch., N.Y.C., 1958-62; coord. art prog., instr. North Shore Commty. Arts Ctr., Roslyn, NY, 1962-64; instr. art CUNY-Bronx, N.Y.C., 1963-64; faculty L.I. U., Bklyn., 1964—, prof., 1975—, chair art dept., 1980-86; assoc. prof. art The Cooper Union, 1992-99, prof. art, 1999—; adj. prof., Cooper Union, N.Y.C., 1992—. One-woman shows include Resnick Gallery, L.I. U., Bklyn., 1983, 89, 95, 2000, East Hampton Gallery, N.Y.C., 1965-66, St. John's U. Gallery, 1995; exhibited in group shows at Blue Mountain Gallery, N.Y.C., 1984-85, 94-98, Hillwood Gallery, Greenvale, N.Y., 1985; commd. artist edit. of photo collages Bklyn. Arts and Culture Assn., 1983; represented in permanent collections Bklyn. Mus., N.Y., Rose Art Mus., Mass., Bard Coll., N.Y.; author, illustrator: Stop Dropping BreAdcrumBs on my YaCht, 1974, Sounds of Silents, 1976, Design Dimensions: An Introduction to the Visual Surface, 1990, Drawing Dimensions: A Comprehensive Introduction, 1999; contbr. numerous articles to profl. publs.; lectr., presenter in field. Trustee Park Slope Civic Coun., 1991—. Mellon grantee, 1984, L.I. Univ. faculty rsch. grantee, 1985—; recipient Newton Teaching Excellence award, 1988, Trustees award single work, 1990, Trustees lifetime award for Scholarly Achievement in art and art edn. L.I. Univ., 1999. Mem. AAUP, Internat. Soc. Copier Artists, L.I. U. Faculty Fedn. (exec. com. 1975—), Coll. Art Assn., Soc. Scribes. Avocations: piano; travel; collecting Americana and tribal and folk art. Home: 910 President St Brooklyn NY 11215-1604 Office: LI U Art Dept University Pla Brooklyn NY 11201

DANVERS, DAVID BELL, equity broker; b. Poughkeepsie, N.Y., Jan. 15, 1968; s. William David and Rachel (Bell) Rosenberg; m. Karen Minor, Sept. 24, 1994; children: Andrew Bennett, Erik Payson. BA in Econs, French, Union Coll., 1990. Cert. series 7 Nat. Assn. Securities Dealers. V.p. Salomon Smith Barney, N.Y.C., 1992—. Ptnr. in Edn., Bd. Edn., N.Y.C., 1995—; house capt. (repairs) Americares, New Canaan, Conn., 1996—. Mem. Nat. Assn. Securities Dealers, N.Y. Soc. Securities Analysts, Assn. for Investment Mgmt. and Rsch. Democrat. Methodist. Avocations: ice hockey, skiing, running. Fax: 212-723-8796. E-mail: dbellr@aol.com. Home: 34 Woodchuck Ln Norwalk CT 06854-3323

DANZIGER, GLENN NORMAN, chemical sales company executive; b. N.Y.C., Apr. 7, 1930; s. Victor and Freda (Lazar) D.; m. Florence Spielvogel, June 7, 1953; children: Jill Marla Danziger Hetson, Beth J. Danziger Keyes, Amy L. Tenenbaum. AB, Columbia U., 1952, BSCE, 1953. Chemist Breinig Bros., Hoboken, N.J., 1955-61; v.p., tech. dir. Flood and Conklin, Newark, 1961-65; tech. sales rep. Seabord Chem. Corp., Lodi, N.J., 1965-75; pres. Seaboard Sales Corp., Paterson, N.J., 1975—. Author: Formulation of Organic Coatings, 1967. Lt. (j.g.) USNR, 1953-55. Mem. NACD, N.Y. Met. Soc. Coatings Technology, Nat. Paint and Coatings Assn. Democrat. Jewish. Avocations: travel, golf, skiing, reading. Office: Seaboard Sales Corp 881 Market St Paterson NJ 07513-1126

DANZIGER, PETER, lawyer; b. N.Y.C., Jan. 5, 1949; s. Herbert and Eleanor (Rosner) D.; m. Joan Nelick, Aug. 15, 1970; children: Lisa, Carrie, Beth. BA, U. Vt., 1970; JD, Albany Law Sch., 1973; MS, SUNY, Albany, 1977. Bar: N.Y. 1974, U.S. Dist. Ct. (no. dist.) N.Y. 1974. Assoc. O'Connell and Aronowitz, Albany, N.Y., 1973-79, sr. ptnr., 1979—; instr. Albany Law Sch., 1972-73, SUNY at Albany, 1978-88. Author: (book) Special Education Litigation, 1989, Tapping Officials Secrets, 1989, 93, 97; author Albany Law Rev., 1972, (newspaper column) Legal Line, 1990-2000; contbr. Long Term Care Insurance in N.Y., 2000; editor: Representing People with Disabilities, 1989, 97, 2000. Legal counsel Jewish Family Svcs. of N.E. N.Y., Albany, 1977—. Named one of Best Lawyers in Am., Woodward/White Inc., 1991—. Mem. ABA, N.Y. State Trial Lawyers Assn., Am. Trial Lawyers Assn., Nat. Assn. of Elder Law Attys., N.Y. State Bar Assn. (chairperson com. on mental and phys. disabilities 1989-93). Office: O'Connell and Aronowitz 100 State St Ste 800 Albany NY 12207-1897

DANZIN, CHARLES MARIE, enzymologist; b. Paris, Sept. 8, 1944; s. Andre and Nicole (De Freminville) D.; m. Elisabeth Evrard, Aug. 25, 1970; 1 child, Claire. Degree in Engring., Ecole Speciale de Meca. Elec., Paris, 1966; PhD in Biochemistry, U. Paris, 1974. Fellow dept. biophysics Commissariat A L'Energie Atomique, Saclay, France, 1969-74; rsch. biochemist Merrell Dow Rsch. Inst., Strasbourg, 1975-87; group leader, head enzymology Marion Merrell Dow Rsch. Inst., Strasbourg, 1988-92, dir. dept. biochem. scis., 1993-96, acting dir. dept. pharm. scis., 1993-95; dir. dept. biotech. and biochemistry Rsch. Inst. Jouveinal/Parke Davis, Fresnes, France, 1996-98, dir. dept. biochemistry and enzymology, 1998-2000; dir. dept. biochemistry and enzymology Pfizer Global R & D, Fresnes, France, 2000—; overseas adv. bd. Internat. Symposia on Vitamin B6 and Carbonyl Catalysis, 1987-97, mem. French Bio-Organics Meeting com., 1999—; spkr. in field. Contbr. over 145 articles to profl. jours.; jour. reviewer Biochem. Pharmacology, Analytical Biochemistry, Bioorganic and Medicinal Chemistry Letters, Jour. Am. Chem. Soc., Eur. Jour. Med. Chemistry. Mem. AAAS, Am. Chem. Soc., N.Y. Acad. Scis., French chem. Soc., French Soc. Biochemistry and Molecular Biology, Biochem. Soc. Office: Inst Rsch Jouveinal/Pfizer, 3-9 Rue de la Loge BP 100, F-94265 Fresnes Cedex, France

DAOEDSYAH, TEUKU MOH, personnel director; b. Simpang Ulim, Indonesia, Nov. 24, 1924; s. Teuku Abu Achmad and Cut Nyak Meurah; m. Ratna Ayu Wada, Oct. 17, 1926; 3 children. Student, Kyoto Imperial U., 1943-45. Asst. gen. mgr. Ctrl. Trading Co., Tokyo, 1961-64; gen. mgr. PN Pnatja Niaga, Medan, Indonesia, 1965-69; personnel mgr. Mobil Oil Indonesia, Jakarta, 1970-85; advisor Satya Djaya Raya, Jakarta, 1986-88; mng. dir. Jabato Travel, Jakarta, 1989-90; advisor bd. dirs. Fuji Leasing, Jakarta, 1991-92; pvt. mgmt. cons., human rels. devel. Jakarta, 1992—; trade attache Indonesian Consulate, Hong Kong, 1959-60. Mem. IAPA, Indonesian Lawn Tennis Assn. (mgr. vet. tennis program), Planetary Soc. (sponsor). Moslem. Avocations: tennis, golfing, photography, gardening, classical music. Home: Jalan Delima Jaya III/50, Jakarta Indonesia

DAOUD, BASILE MOUSSA, archbishop; b. Maskane Homs, Syria, Sept. 18, 1930; s. Daoud Moussa and Kahla Elias (Dabbas) D. Lic. in Canon Law, S. Giovanni in Laterano, Roma, 1964. Bishop of couro Syrian Cath. Diocese of Cairo, Egypt; archbishop Syrian Cath. Archdiocese of Homs, Syria; now patriarch Syrian Cath. Ch., Homs, 1998—. Office: Archbishop Syrian Cath Ch, BP 368, Rue Hamidieh, Homs Syria*

DAOUD, MOHAMED, physicist; b. Tunis, Tunisia, Mar. 31, 1947; s. Hassen Dooud and Beya Bahri; m. Aicha Mehiri; children: Hassen, Taïeb, Maitrise. Maitrise, Ecole Normale Superieure, Saint Cloud, 1968-70, D.E.A., 1972, Agregation (hon.), 1971; These, U. Paris VI, 1977. Rsch. assoc. Commissariat a l'Energie Atomique C.E.A., Saclay, 1974-78, physicist, 1980—; physicist Boston U., 1978-80. Editor: Jour. de Physique, Fractals. Recipient Grand Prix, Groupement Français de Polymeres, 1978, prix Commissariat a l'Energie Atomique, 1986, Kuwait Found. for Advancement Scis. award, 1998. Mem. Societe Française de Physique, Am. Phys. Soc., N.Y. Acad. Scis. Office: CEN Saclay, Lab Leon Brillouin, 91191 Gif sur Yvette France

DAPELLO, JOSEPH J., lawyer; b. Bklyn., June 26, 1963. AB, Columbia Coll., 1985; JD, Harvard Law Sch., 1988. Bar: N.Y. 1989. lectr. N.Y.U. Stern Sch. Bus., 1997-99. Mem. N.Y. State Bar Assn., N.Y.C. Bar Assn. Home: 301 E 6U St Apt 9C New York NY 10021 Office: Schreck Rose & Dapello LLP 660 Madison Ave New York NY 10021-8405

DAPRON, ELMER JOSEPH, JR., communications executive; b. Clayton, Mo., Jan. 14, 1925; s. Elmer Joseph and Susanna (Kruse) D.; m. Sharon Kay Neuling, Feb. 22, 1977 (dec. Apr. 1987). Employed in constrn. Fairbanks, Alaska, 1947-48; tech. writer-editor McDonnell-Douglas Corp., St. Louis, 1948-57; freelance writer Paris, 1957; with Gardner Advt. Co., St. Louis, 1960-78, v.p., 1969-78; sr. v.p. Kenrick Advt. Inc., 1978-83; pres. Cornucopia Communications, Inc., 1979—. Producer syndicated radio and TV show Elmer Dapron's Grocery List; advt. and mktg. cons. to govt. and industry; daily commendator The Grocery List Armed Forces Radio Network (worldwide); contbr. articles to publs. Mem. Nat. Dem. Com., candidate for Gov. of Mo., 1992; nat. pres. Iwo Jima Task Force Two, 1994—; nat. chmn. Korea Task Force 2000, 1997—. With USMCR, 1943-45, PTO, 50-51, Korea. Recipient advt. awards including New Filming Techniques award Internat.-Film Festival; hon. fellow Harry Truman Libr. Inst. Mem. Nat. Agrl. Mktg. Assn., Miss. Valley Farm Mktg. (Man of Yr. 1974), Assn. R.R. Advt. and Mktg. (nat. membership chmn.), Marine Corps League (nat. vice comdt. 1967-69, nat. press officer 4th Marine Div. Assn. 1989—, publicity chmn.), Media Club, St. Louis Track Club. Democrat. Office: 119 Lakeview Estates Dr Warrenton MO 63383-5258

D'AQUINO, THOMAS, lawyer, business council chief executive; b. Trail, B.C., Can., Nov. 3, 1940; m. Susan Marion Peterson, 1965. BA, U. B.C., 1962, LLB, 1965; LhB, LLM, U. London, Ont., 1967; LLD (hon.), Queen's U., 1996. Adj. prof. law U. Ottawa, Ont., Can., 1975-83; chmn. Intercounsel Ltd.; pres., chief exec. Bus. Coun. on Nat. Issues, Ottawa, 1981—; former exec. asst. to Fed. Min., spl. asst. to Prime Min., Can., 1969-72; internat. cons. firm in London and Paris, 1972-75; frequent guest lectr.; mem. Chmn's Internat. Adv. Coun. of the Am.'s Soc.; adv. com. Can.-Japan Bus. Com.; founding mem. Pacific Coun. on Internat. Policy. Contbr. articles to profl. jours. Mem. World Econ. Forum Geneva, Inst. for Strategic Studies, London; assoc. Can. Corp. Higher Edn. Forum. Mem. Can. Bar Assn., Internat. Bar Assn., B.C. Law Soc. Office: Bus Coun on Nat Issues, 90 Sparks St Ste 806, Ottawa, ON Canada K1P 5B4

DARBIEU, MONIQUE RENÉE, translator, educator; b. Toulouse, France, Oct. 7, 1950; d. Ellen Marcel and Jeanne Julie (Marcou) D.; m. Patrick Andre Cayla, July 17, 1980; 1 child, Thomas. MBA, Toulouse Bus. Sch., 1972; BA in Russian Lang., Toulouse-Mirail U., 1973, MA in Russian Lang., 1980. Higher cert. in bus. Russian, France; higher cert. in bus. Spanish, Spanish C. of C., Paris. Tchr. sci., econs. and German, Toulouse, 1972-74; comml. attaché French Embassy, Moscow, 1974-76; adminstrv. asst. Interagra Co., Moscow, 1977-78; translator French Space Agy., Toulouse, 1978—; tchr. Russian, Toulouse Bus. Sch., 1989-90; temp. tech. translator Aérospatiale, 1991; translator Guide of Internat. Bus. Svcs. in the Haute-Garonne Toulouse C. of C. and Industry. Author: The Sun and the Past, Present and Future of Mankind, 1991. Mem. First Aid Assn., Toulouse. Home: 62 rue Maurice Be'canne, 31400 Toulouse France

DARBOURET, DANIEL, chemical engineer; b. Lorette, Loire, France, Mar. 19, 1963; s. Henri and Aimee (Rivat) D.; m. Danielle Grelet, July 8, 1989. Diploma in engring., Ecole Chimie Montpellier, France, 1986; PhD in Biochemistry, U. Lyon, France, 1990. Rschr. BioMerieux, Lyon, 1987-90, Millipore, Sunderland, U.K., 1990-91; application engr. Millipore, Paris, 1991-98, R&D application devel. mgr., 1998—. Contbr. articles to profl. jours. including Biochemistry Biophysics Rsch. Comm., Bioforum, Ultrapure Water, Jour. Analytical Atomic Spectrometry; patentee in field. Chief caporal Health Dept., France, 1986-87. Mem. Assn. Official Analytical Chemists, European Soc. Biochromatography (European first aid cert.). Avocations: travel, tennis. Home: BatB, 41 rue P Vaillant Couturier, 93130 Noisy-le-sec France Office: Millipore SA, BP 307, 78054 Saint Quentin Yvelines, France

DARBY, ANITA LOYCE, secondary school educator; b. Houston, May 16, 1964; d. Franklin Lile and Anita Florence (Carver) Keeling; m. Jim Steve Yarbray, June 20, 1987 (div. Nov. 1991); 1 child, Steven William; m. James C. Darby, Apr. 26, 1997; stepchildren: Brian Keith, Dustin Blaine. BA in Polit. Sci./Pre-Law, U. Houston, 1986, MEd, 1988. Cert. tchr. secondary social studies; cert. driver safety edn. Retail clk. Five and Ten Shoe Store, Houston, 1980-81; clothing retail clk. Weiner's Dept. Store, Houston, 1981-82; poll worker, phone analyst polit. surveys Houston, 1982-84; cashier, clk. inventory Carmona's Festival, Houston, 1984-86; sec., computer clk. Houston C.C. System, 1986-88; social studies tchr. MacArthur H.S., Houston, 1988—; mem. textbook selection com. Aldine Ind. Sch. Dist., Houston, 1989-91. Clean-up vol./sponsor Houston Galveston Coun. Cmty. and Environ. Planning, 1993-94; poll worker, phone surveyor polit. candidates, Houston, 1982—, Austin, Tex., 1983-84; vol. Rep. Nat. Conv., Houston, 1991; cons./sponsor Teen Ct., Mock City Coun., Youth and Govt., Houston, 1990—; sponsor Class 1998, 99; judge Speech and Debate Tournament, 1997-99; mem. vertical team curriculum writing, 1997-99; coach Fed. Challenge, 1999; Olympic coach cert. level I Youth Alliance Bowling Assn., 1998; mem. Sunshine Com., 1998-99; facilitator Ch. Campus Improvement; mem. Houston Coun. on World Affairs; vol. Metro Go Texan Houston Livestock Show and Rodeo Scholarship com.; tutor PSAT; test proctor TAP, TAAS; cert. Olypic Coach Level II, ABA, 2000; peer mediation supr., 2000. Scholar Nat. Tchr. Merit, 2000; finalist Tchr. of Yr., Houston, 1999-2000. Mem. Am. Fedn. Tchrs., Nat. Coun. for Social Studies, Adminstrn. and Supervision Assn., Tex. Coun. Social Studies, Aldine Coun. Social Studies, Internat. Order of Rainbow for Girls (past grand/state officer, Grand Cross), Order Ea. Star (past matron), Am. Polit. Sci. Assn., Tex. Coun. for Econ. Edn., Theatre Co. (actor, dir., asst. dir., tech. dir., stage mgr.), Kappa Delta Pi. Avocations: singing, reading, swimming, political activism, public relations. Fax: 281-985-6338. Office: MacArthur High Sch 4400 Aldine Mail Rd Houston TX 77039-5999

DARBY, BARBARA ANN-LOFTHOUSE, chemical technician; b. Phila., Sept. 15, 1961; d. Robert William and Lina Evelyn (James) Lofthouse; m. Joseph Francis Darby, Dec. 23, 1988; children: Robert Lofthouse, Joseph. GED, Phila., 1982. Cert. biocides operator; indsl. firefighter. Chem. operator Rohm & Haas, Phila., 1992-95; chem. technician Rohm & Haas, La Porte, Tex., 1995—; tng. coord. Bayport Biocides. Active World Wildlife Fund, Washington, 1994—, Clear Lake Ind. Sch. Dist. PTA, 1995—, Nature Conservancy, Tex., 1995; vol. United Way Campaign, Rohm & Haas Plants, 1992—; mem. Habitat for Humanity, 1996—, Natural Resources Def. Coun., 1996—; bd. dirs. Bay Area Sharks/Sharkettes, Tex. Intercity Football, Inc. Football League. Lutheran. Avocations: wildlife defense, environmental activities, cars. Home: 1749 Hialeah Dr Seabrook TX 77586-2938 Office: Rohm & Haas Bay Port Biocides 13300 Bay Area Blvd La Porte TX 77572

DARBY, MARIANNE TALLEY, elementary school educator; b. Adel, Ga., Nov. 8, 1937; d. William Giles and Mary (McGlamry) Talley; m. Roy Copeland Darby, Apr. 2, 1958; children: Susan, Leslie Darby Galifianakis, Allison Darby Davis. Student, Emory U., 1955-57; BS in Early Childhood Edn., Valdosta (Ga.) State Coll., 1973. Cert. early childhood and elem. edn. tchr., Ga. Tchr. 2d grade Adel Elem. Sch., spring 1973, tchr. 1st grade, 1973-98, ret., 1998. Pres. Cook County Jaycettes, Adel, 1962. Teacher of Year, Cook Elem. Sch., 1998—. Mem. Internat. Reading Assn. (South Cen. Ga. coun.), Profl. Assn. Ga. Educators, Adel Garden Club, Alpha Epsilon Upsilon, Alpha Delta Kappa (sec. 1980-82), Sigma Alpha Chi, Alpha Chi, Kappa Alpha Theta. Republican. Methodist. Avocations: sewing, piano, reading, African violets. Home: 710 S Forrest Ave Adel GA 31620-3523

D'ARCANGELO, MARCIA DIANE, educational media producer; b. Meadville, Pa., May 16, 1945; d. Terrence Benjamin and Eileene Marie

(Judy) Darcangelo; m. Thomas Brown Andrews V, Sept. 16, 1989. BS in Chemistry, Grove City Coll., 1967. Info. specialist Eastman Kodak Co., Rochester, N.Y., 1967-68; singer/dancer Kids Next Door-Young Ams. Orgn. (Katand Prodns.), L.A., 1968-69, Stand Up and Cheer TV Show, The Johnny Mann Singers, L.A., 1970-74; singer, dancer, actor John Brown's Body AEA Nat. Tour, Fitzgerald Prodns., L.A., 1975-76; singer, dancer The Perry Como Show-Roncom Prodns., 1977-82; med. news journalist Physicians Radio Network, N.Y.C., 1983-84; prodn. asst., prodn. coord. ASCD, Alexandria, Va., 1985-86, producer, sr. producer, 1987-88, mgr. media prodns., 1989—; cons. Holbrook & Kellogg, Falls Church, Va., 1990, Developmental Studies Ctr., San Ramon, Calif., 1991, Soc. for Preservation of Social Security and Medicare, Washington, 1991. Composer 4 mus. pieces (words and music); co-author 20 tng. manuals; author/co-author 46 video-based tchr. tng. programs, articles. Recipient award of merit VFW, 1971, Jack Kennedy Alumni Achievement award Grove City Coll. Alumni Assn., 1984, Clarion award Women in Comm., 1991, 6 Cine Golden Eagle awards Coun. on Internat. Nontheatrical Events, 1991, 92, 93, 94, Silver Apple award Nat. Ednl. Film and Video Festival, 1991, 93, 95, Bronze Apple award, 1993, 94, 99, Silver Screen award and Cert. for Creative Excellence U.S. Internat. Film and Video Festival, 1993, 94, 95, 96, Disting. Achievement award and Best of Category Ednl. Press Assn. Am., 1994, 95, 96, Telly Awards-Silver and Bronze, 1996, 98; award of excellence Nat. Sch. Pub. Rels. Assn., 1995, 96, Bronze award Columbus Internat. Film & Video, 1995. Mem. SAG, AFTRA, NAFE, ASCD, Am. Guild Variety Artists, Actors Equity Assn., Nat. Staff Devel. Coun., Internat. TV Assn., Internat. Interactive Comm. Soc., Women in Film and Video Internat. Avocation: singing.

D'ARCY, JOHN MICHAEL, bishop; b. Brighton, Mass., Aug. 18, 1932. Student, St. John's Sem., Brighton, 1949-57; ThD, Angelicum U., Rome, 1968. Ordained priest Roman Cath. Ch., 1957. Spiritual dir., prof. theology St. John's Sem., 1968-85; ordained titular bishop of Mediana and aux. bishop of Boston Archdiocese of Boston, 1975-85; bishop Diocese of Ft. Wayne-South Bend, Ind., 1985—. Office: Diocese of Ft Wayne-South Bend PO Box 390 1103 S Calhoun St Fort Wayne IN 46801

DARDE, JEAN DELPHIN, financial executive; b. Paris, Mar. 8, 1920; s. Robert René and Fernande Marie (Pierron) D.; m. Michéle Germaine de Demandolx, Nov. 15, 1947; children: Patrick, Guillemette, Christophe, Cecile, François, Xavier. Diploma, Ecole des Hautes études Commerciales, 1941. Mgr. LaRoche Fries Co., Paris, 1945-71; chmn. Soplaril, Paris, 1977-81, v.p., 1980; adminstr. Soplaril, Barcelona, Spain; pres. S.A. Deforges, Orleans, France, 1985; fin. mgr. Labs. SPS, Coulommiers, France. Recipient Chevalier of the Legion of Honour; decorated Mil. Cross, Mil. medal. Mem. Automobile Club of France. Home: 9 rue Adolphe Yvon N&G, 75116 Paris France Office: Labs SP5, 5 Rue de Montigny, 77120 Coulommiers France

DARDEN, BARBARA L., library director; b. Cleve., Apr. 6, 1947; d. Curley and Cora (Chambliss) Brown; m. Joseph S. Darden; children: Michelle, Crystal, Twilla. BS, Ohio State U., 1967; MS in Ednl. Media, Kent State U., 1971, MLS, 1971. Adminstrv. supr. Cleve. Pub. Schs., 1968-70; libr. Cuyahoga C.C., 1972-75, coord., 1975-77, interim dir., 1977-78, asst. dean, 1978-80, dir., 1980-84; dir. libr. Kean Coll., Union, N.J., 1984—; cons. Dembsy Assocs., Boston, 1967-81; editl. cons. Max Pub. Co., N.Y.C., 1967-81; cons. reader U.S. Office Edn., Washington, 1979-80; editl. cons. Jossey-Bass Pub. Co., 1979. Cons. editor Probe, 1976, Sch. Media Ctr., 1968, Booklist, 1969; contbr. articles to profl. jours. Bd. dirs. N.J. Adv. Bd. on Status of Women, 1988, Africana Studies, 1988; mem. N.J. State Libr. Adv. Bd.; bd. dirs. N.J. Ednl. Activities Task Force Libr. Com. Recipient Phillips award Kent State U., 1970. Mem. ALA (chmn. pay equity com. 1996, chair LAMA-COLA 1999), Higher Edn. Reps., N.J. Acad. Libr. Network (chmn. 1987, bd. dirs. 1995—), Coun. N.J. Librs. (prs. 1987—), N.J. Libr. Assn., Oral History Soc., N.J. Hist. Soc., Libr. Adminstrn. Mgmt. Assn. (chair 1997-99, bd. dirs. 1999), Coun. N.J. Coll. and Univ. Libr. Dirs. (pres. 1999—), Jr. League (Cleve. vice chmn. 1981, 83), Concerned Parents Club (pres. 1984), Women's City Club (adv. bd. 1997—). Avocations: music, reading. Office: Kean Univ Libr Morris Ave Union NJ 07083

DARDENNE, JEAN-PIERRE, film director; b. 1951. Dir. La Promesse, 1996 (Grand Prix, Internat. Critics Award at Valladolid, Prix Humanun, Assn. Belgium Critics, Best Film award at Potsdam, FIPRESCI award at Frankfurt, Audience award at Namur, Best Fgn. Film awards Am. Film Critics), Rosetta, 1999 (Golden Palm, Cannes Film Festival 1999); prodr. 60 documentaries and 5 feature films. Office: ARP, 75 Avenuedes Champs Elysees, 750008 Paris France*

DARDENNE, LUC, film director; b. 1954. Degree in philosophy. Dir. La Promesse, 1996 (Grand Prix, Internat. Critics award at Valladolid, Prix Humanun, Assn. Belgium Critics, Best Film award at Potsdam, FIPRESCI award at Frankfurt, Audience award at Namur, Best Fgn. Film award Am. Film Critics, Rosetta, 1999; prodr. 60 documentaries and 5 feature films. Office: ARP, 75 Ave des Champs Elysees, 75008 Paris France*

DAREVSKY, ILYA S., zoologist, herpetologist, researcher; b. Kiev, Ukraine, Dec. 18, 1924; s. Sergeus N. and Sofia I. (Russakovskaya) D.; m. Irine G. Bey-Bienko, June 18, 1958 (dec. 1979); 1 child, Alexandr; m. Vernata V. Grechko, Feb. 6, 1985. Grad., Moscow State U., 1952; DSc, Russian Acad. Scis., Leningrad, 1966. Sci. rschr., prof. Zool. Inst. Acad. Scis., 1958-61; head lab. Zool. Inst. Acad. Scis., Leningrad, 1962-96; leading scientist Zool. Inst. Acad. Scis., St. Petersburg, 1997—. Author numerous books; editor-in-chief Russian Jour. Herpetology, 1994—; contbr. more than 300 articles to profl. jours. Mem. Russian Acad. Scis. (corr.), Russian Nikolsky Herpetol. Soc. (pres. 1967—), Am. Soc. Ichtyologists and Herpetologists (hon.), Soc. for Integrative and Comparative Biology (hon.), European Herpetol. Soc. (hon.), N.Y. Acad. Scis. Avocations: philately, swimming. Home: Rashetov Str 7/33, 194017 Saint Petersburg Russia Office: Zool Inst Russian Acad Scis, Univ Emb 1, 199034 Saint Petersburg Russia

DARGAN, JOHN HENRY, business executive; b. Dublin, Ireland, Dec. 16, 1965; s. Peter Anthony and Cecilia (Blake) D.; m. Janet Tsai Dargan, Aug. 31, 1997. B Engring., Trinity Coll., Dublin, 1987; MBA, U. Pa., 1993. Bus. analyst McKinsey & Co., London, 1987-89; assoc. GE Capital Corp., London, 1989-91; cons. Oliver, Wyman & Co., London, 1993-95; head of strategy London Stock Exch., 1995-97; dir. spl. projects Warner Bros., L.A., 1997—; adviser Russian Privatization Inst., Moscow, 1992. Fulbright scholar, 1991, Palmer scholar, 1993. Roman Catholic. Home: 952 10th St Manhattan Beach CA 90266-5902 Office: Warner Bros 4000 Warner Blvd Burbank CA 91522-0002

DARGAN, PAMELA ANN, principal systems and software engineer; b. Norfolk, Va.; d. Thomas J. and Stana E. (Verich) Piazza; m. W. Scott Dargan, Dec., 1990. BS in Math., Va. Poly. and State U., 1979; MS in Computer Sci., George Mason U., 1993. Programmer Control Data Corp., Rockville, Md., 1979-80; tech. staff BDM Corp., Mc Lean, Va., 1980-81, TRW Fed. Sys. Group, Mc Lean, Va., 1981-87; dep. program mgr. Mystech, Inc., Alexandria, Va., 1987-89; lead engr. MITRE Corp., Mc Lean, 1989-98; prin. Litton Tasc, Inc., Chantilly, Va., 1998—; program chair East Coast Artificial Intelligence Work Sta. Users Group, 1984-85; author on open sys. for internat. confs. and publs. Contbr. chpts. to books and articles to profl. jours. Mem. IEEE, Assn. Computing Machinery, Internat. Coun. on Sys. Engring.

DARGAN, SURESH KUMAR, orthopedic surgeon; b. Kalka, Haryana, India, Nov. 27, 1961; s. Ved Parkash and Savitri Devi (Mehndiratta) D.; m. Seema Mehrotra, Apr. 14, 1993; 1 child, Shreya. B Medicine B Surgery, Govt. Med. Coll., Patiala, India, 1983, MS in Orthopedics, 1988. Resident Jankidas Hosp., Sonepat, India, 1986; sr. resident Govt. Med. Coll., Patiala, 1987-88; chief med. officer Deepak Hosp., Delhi, India, 1989-91; registrar E.S.I. Hosp., Delhi, 1991-94; specialist, chief orthopedics Govt. Gen. Hosp., Rafha, Saudi Arabia, 1994—; asst. dir. Sukhija Med. Ctr., Delhi, 1989; cons. in orthopedics Sukhija Nursing Home, Delhi, 1989-91, Wadhwa Med. Ctr., Delhi, 1989-94. Contbr. articles to profl. jours. Recipient award for excellence Ministry of Def. and Aviation, 1996, Best Doctor award Patients Friends Soc., 1997. Mem. Delhi Med. Assn., Indian Med. Assn., Internat. Med. Soc. Paralysis. Avocations: photography, reading, travel, music. Home: 265-A Pocket J&K, Dilshad Garden, Delhi 110095, India Office: Govt Gen Hosp, Rafha North Zone, Rafha North Zone, Saudi Arabia

DARIDAN, DOMINIQUE FRANÇOIS, bank executive; b. Paris, Nov. 26, 1944; s. Jean Henri and Marie-Odette (Nusse) D.; m. Myra El-Mahdy, Jan. 5, 1982; 2 children. Diploma, Inst. d'Etudes Politiques, Paris, 1966, lic. faculte de droit, 1968; MBA, Wharton Sch. of Commerce and Fin., 1970. Asst. mgr. Bank of Am., Paris, 1971-76; asst. v.p. Bank of Am., Athens, Greece, 1976-79; mgr. Bank of Am., Alexandria, Egypt, 1979-82; v.p. Bank of Am., London, 1982-87, Paris, 1987-91; dir., head credit mgmt. & credit rsch. CPR-Compagnie Parisienne de Reescompte, Paris, 1993-99; head credit rsch. Natexis Banques Populaires, Paris, 1999—. 2d lt. arty. French Army, 1970-71. Avocations: travel, reading, horseback riding. Home: 14 Rue des Saussaies, 75008 Paris France Office: Natexis Banques Populaires, 115 rue Montmartre, 75002 Paris France

DARIEN, STEVEN MARTIN, management consulting company executive; b. N.Y.C., Oct. 29, 1942; s. Leo and Laura Darien; m. Susan Ruth Kinsley, Nov. 29, 1942; children: Jodi Ellen, Andrew Todd. AB, Rutgers Coll., 1963; MBA, Columbia U., 1966. Claims settler Equitable Life, N.Y.C., 1963-64; mgmt. trainee Merck & Co., Inc., Rahway, N.J., 1966-69, mgr. coll. rels., 1969-74, exec. dir. pers. resources, 1974-79, exec. dir. U.S. Pers., 1979-85, v.p. employee rels., 1985-89, v.p. worldwide pres., 1989-90, v.p. human resources, 1990-96; pres. Darien Assocs., 1996-98; chmn., CEO The Cabot Adv. Group, Washington, 1998—; bd. dirs. Somerset Hosp. Chmn. Olin Inst. for Employment Practice and Policy; chmn. Olin Found. for Employment Policy and Practice. Mem. Columbia U. Bus. Sch. Alumni Assn. (v.p.).

DARION, JOE, librettist, lyricist; b. N.Y.C., Jan. 30, 1917; s. Isak and Rose (Nadelle) D.; m. Hellen Solomon, June 8, 1940. Student journalism, CCNY. Lyricist of popular songs including Ricochet, Changing Partners, Midnight Train, 1954-58; librettist opera, cantatas, song cycles including jazz opera Archy and Mehitabel; New Orleans Cantata, 1956-60; playwright, lyricist for Broadway prodns. Shinbone Alley, 1957; lyricist Broadway prodns. Man of La Mancha, 1965, Illya Darling, 1967; librettist for oratorio Galileo, 1967, cantata And David Wept, 1970, The Questions of Abraham, 1972, Christmas cantata A Handful of Souls, 1975, A Mass for Cain, 1978, opera Galileo Galilei, 1979; writer English sect. bilingual musical The Megilla, 1968; screenplay, lyrics Archy and Mehitabel, 1969; 72; writer play Better Than Wine, 1986, book and lyrics musical The Unicorn on Fashion Street, 1988, musical play Oswego, 1993. Served with USNR, World War II, PTO. Recipient Antoinette Perry award, 1965, 66, drama critics cir. award, 1965, 66, internat. broadcasting award, 1964, gold records award, Gabriel award, 1974, award Ohio State U. Telecomms. Ctr., 1975. Mem. ASCAP, Am. Guild Authors and Composers, Dramatists Guild, Nat. Acad. Rec. Arts and Scis. Jewish. Address: Pinnacle Rd PO Box 315 Lyme NH 03768-0315

DARIOTIS, TERRENCE THEODORE, lawyer; b. Chgo., Feb. 28, 1946; s. Theodore S. and Dorothy Mizzen (Thompson) D.; m. Jeanne Elizabeth Gibbons, Oct. 24, 1970; children: Sara Mizzen, Kristin Elizabeth, Jennifer Ann. BA in Philosophy, St. Joseph's Coll., Rensselaer, Ind., 1969; JD, Loyola U., Chgo., 1973. Bar: Ill. 1973, Fla. 1975, U.S. Tax Ct. 1993, U.S. Supreme Ct., 1978. Law clk. to presiding justice Appellate Ct. of Ill. (2d dist.), Waukegan, 1973-74; assoc. Keith Kinderman, Tallahassee, 1975-76; sole practitioner Tallahassee, 1976-82; ptnr. Kahn and Dariotis, P.A., Tallahassee, 1982-96, Warfel, Goldberg, Dariotis, Waldoch & Olive, P.A., Tallahassee, 1996-00; sole practice Tallahassee, 2000—; adj. prof. Fla. State U. Coll. Bus., 1987-93. Roman Catholic. Office: 1695 Metropolitan Cir Ste 6 Tallahassee FL 32308-3731

DARKE, MARJORIE (SHEILA), writer; b. Birmingham, Eng., Jan. 25, 1929; d. Christopher and Sarah Ann (Palin) D.; 3 children. Student, Leicester Coll. Art, Ctrl. Sch. Art, London. Textile designer London, 1951-54; writer. Author: Ride the Iron Horse, 1973, The Star Trap, 1974, Mike's Bike, 1974, What Can I Do?, 1975, A Question of Courage, 1975, Kipper's Turn, 1976, The Big Brass Band, 1976, The First of Midnight, 1977, My Uncle Charlie, 1977, A Long Way to Go, 1978, Kipper Skips, 1979, Carnival Day, 1979, Comeback, 1981, Tom Post's Private Eye, 1982, Messages, 1984, Imp, 1985, The Rainbow Sandwich, 1989, Night Windows, 1990, A Rose from Blighty, 1990, Emma's Monster, 1992, Just Bear and Friends, 1996. Mem. PEN, Soc. Authors. Office: care Rogers Coleridge & White Ltd, 20 Powis Mews, London W11 1JN, England

DARKE, RICHARD FRANCIS, lawyer; b. Detroit, June 17, 1943; s. Francis Joseph and Irene Anne (Potts) D.; m. Alice Mary Renger, Feb. 14, 1968; children: Kimberly, Richard, Kelly, Sean, Colin. BBA, U. Notre Dame, 1965; JD, Detroit Coll. Law, 1969. Bar: Mich. 1969. Atty. AAA, Detroit, 1969-72; assoc. Oster & Mollett P.C., Mt. Clemens, Mich., 1972-73; ptnr. Small, Darke, Oakes P.C., Southfield, Mich., 1973-77; v.p., gen. counsel, sec. Fruehauf Corp., Detroit, 1977-92; ptnr. Darke & Wilson, Grosse Pointe Woods, Mich., 1993—. Mem. ABA, Mich. Bar Assn., Detroit Bar Assn., Machinery and Allied Products Inst. (counsel), Mich. Gen. Counsel Group, Essex Country Club, Lockmoor Club. Roman Catholic. Avocation: golfing. Home: 23173 Alger Ln Saint Clair Shores MI 48080-2624

DARLING, ALISTAIR MACLEAN, British government official; b. Nov. 28, 1953; m. Margaret McQueen Vaughan; 2 children. Student, Aberdeen U. Mem. Lothian and Borders Police Bd., 1982-86; mem. Lothian Regional Coun., 1982-87, chmn. transp. com., 1986-87; mem. British Parliament, 1987—, chief sec. treas., 1997-98; sec. of state for social security, 1998—. Office: Sec of State Social Sec, 79 Whiteham Richmond House, London SWIA ZNS, England*

DARLING, JOHN ROTHBURN, JR., business educator; b. Holton, Kans., Mar. 30, 1937; s. John Rothburn and Beatrice Noel (Deaver) D.; m. Melva Jean Fears, Aug. 20, 1958; children: Stephen, Cynthia, Gregory. BS, U. Ala., 1959, M.S., 1960; Ph.D., U. Ill., 1967; Ph.D. (hon.), Chung Yuan Christian U., Taiwan, 1998. Divisional mgr. J.C. Penney Co., 1960-63; grad. teaching asst. U. Ill., Urbana, 1965-66; asst. prof. mktg. U. Ala., Tuscaloosa, 1966-68; assoc. prof. mktg. U. Mo., Columbia, 1968-71; prof. adminstrn., coord. mktg. Wichita State U., 1971-76; dean, prof. mktg. Coll. Bus. Adminstrn. So. Ill. U., Carbondale, 1976-81; v.p. acad. affairs and rsch., prof. internat. bus. Tex. Tech U., Lubbock, 1981-86; provost, v.p. acad. affairs, prof. mktg. and internat. bus. Miss. State U., Mississippi State, 1986-90; chancellor, disting. prof. internat. bus. La. State U., Shreveport, 1990-95; pres. Pittsburg (Kans.) State U., 1995-99, prof. mktg. and internat. bus., 1995-2000; vis. disting. prof. mktg. Rockhurst U., 2000—; mktg. rsch. cons. Southwestern Bell, 1970; sr. v.p. Boothe Advt. Wichita, 1972; pres. Bus. Rsch. Assocs., 1972-76; cons. Bus. Rsch. Assocs., 1976-82; spl. cons. FTC, Washington, 1972-75, U.S. Dept. Justice, 1973-74, Atty. Gen., State of Kans., 1972-76, Dist. Atty. 18th Jud. Dist., Wichita, 1972-76, Maya Internat. Inc., Houston, 1995—, Morrison and Assocs., Inc., Shreveport, 1995-97; vis. disting. prof. internat. mktg. Helsinki Sch. Econs. and Bus. Adminstrn., 1993—. Author: (with Harry A. Lipson) Marketing Fundamentals, Text and Cases, 1980, (with Raimo Nurmi) International Management Leadership: The Primary Competitive Advantage, 1997; mem. bd. cons. editors Jour. Advt., 1984—; mem. editl. rev. bd. Jour. Internat. Bus. Studies, 1991—, Jour. Entrepreneurship, 1997—; contbr. articles to profl. jours. Bd. dirs. Outreach Found., 1973-79, v.p., 1975-77; trustee Graceland Coll., Lamoni, Iowa, 1976-82; mem. mgmt. com. Park Coll., Kansas City, 1976-79. Dist. Eagle Scout Awd., Boy Scouts Amer., 1998. Mem. Internat. Coun. Small Bus., Am. Mktg. Assn., Am. Mgmt. Assn., Acad. Internat. Bus., Am. Econs. Assn., Am. Arbitration Assn., (mem. nat. panel arbitrators and mediators 1993—), Nat. Assn. Intercollegiate Athletics (mem. governing bd. 1994-95), So. Bus. Adminstrn. Assn., So. Mktg. Assn., So. Econs. Assn., So. Assn. Colls. and Schs. (chair reaccreditation com. 1982-95, chair faculty qualifications criteria com. 1989-90, com. to rev. criteria for accreditation 1990-92, commr. 1992-95, Nat. Assn. State Univs. and Land-Grant Colls. (chair regional accreditation rev. com. 1989-90), Sales and Mktg. Execs. Internat., Beta Gamma Sigma, Phi Kappa Phi, Omicorn Delta Kappa, Phi Delta Kappa, Kappa Delta Phi, Mu Kappa Tau, Pi Sigma Epsilon, Alpha Kappa Psi, Chi Alpha Phi, Alpha Phi Omega, Phi Eta Sigma, Delta Mu Delta, Alpha Mu Gamma. Home: 12705 E 37th Terr Ct Independence MO 64055-3179 Office: Office of the President Pittsburg State Univ 1701 S Broadway St Pittsburg KS 66762-5856

DARLING, SCOTT EDWARD, lawyer; b. Los Angeles, Dec. 31, 1949; s. Dick R. and Marjorie Helen (Otto) D.; m. Cynthia Diane Harrah, June 1970 (div.); 1 child, Smokie; m. Deborah Lee Cochran, Aug. 22, 1981; children: Ryan, Jacob. BA, U. Redlands, 1972; JD, U.S.C., 1975. Bar: Calif. 1976, U.S. Dist. Ct. (cen. dist.) Calif. 1976. Assoc. atty. Elver, Falsetti, Boone & Crafts, Riverside, 1976-78; ptnr. Falsetti, Crafts, Pritchard & Darling, Riverside, 1978-84; pres. Scott Edward Darling, A Profl. Corp., Riverside, 1984—; grant reviewer HHS, Washington, 1982-88; judge pro tem Riverside County Mcpl. Ct., 1980, Riverside County Superior Ct., 1987-88; bd. dirs. Tel Law Nat. Legal Pub. Info. System, Riverside, 1978-80. Author, editor: Small Law Office Computer Legal System, 1984. Bd. dirs. Youth Adv. Com. to Selective Svc., 1968-70, Am. Heart Assn. Riverside County, 1978-82, Survival Ministries, 1986-89; atty. panel Calif. Assn. Realtors, L.A., 1980—; pres. Calif. Young Reps., 1978-80; mem. GI Forum, Riverside, 1970-88; presdl. del. Nat. Rep. Party, 1980-84; asst. treas. Calif. Rep. Party, 1981-83; Rep. Congl. candidate, Riverside, 1982; treas. Riverside Sickle Cell Found., 1980-82, recipient Eddie D. Smith award; pres. Calif. Rep. Youth Caucus, 1980-82; v.p. Riverside County Red Cross, 1982-84; mem. Citizen's Univ. Com., Riverside, 1978-84, World Affairs Council, 1978-82, Urban League, Riverside, 1980-82. Calif. Scholarship Fedn. (life). Named one of Outstanding Young Men in Am., U.S. Jaycees, 1979-86. Mem. ABA, Riverside County Bar Assn., Speaker's Bur. Riverside County Bar Assn., Riverside Jaycees, Riverside C. of C. Lodge: Native Sons of Golden West. Avocations: skiing, swimming, reading. Office: 3697 Arlington Ave Riverside CA 92506-3938

DARLINGTON, DAVID WILLIAM, management consultant; b. Boston, Oct. 3, 1945; s. Horace and Maude Beatrice (Pfalzgraf) D.; m. Stacey A. Mitchell, May 24, 1986; children: Elizabeth Joy, Christine Rebecca. BS, Babson Coll., 1974; MBA, 1976; postgrad., Northeastern U., 1977-80. Planning engr. Stone & Webster Engring. Corp., Boston, 1974-75; project adminstr. Northrop Corp., Norwood, Mass., 1975-80; mgr. program adminstrn. internat. sys. dvisn. Sanders Assos., Inc., Nashua, N.H., 1980-82; bus. mgr.; cons., program mgr., contr. Arthur D. Little, Cambridge, Mass., 1982—. Served with USN, 1964-71. Mem. Am. Prodn. and Inventory Control Soc. (cert.), Inst. Cost Analysis (cert.), Inst. Mgmt. Accts., Appalachian Mountain Club, Betta Gamma. Home: 378 Charles Bancroft Hwy Litchfield NH 03052-8033

DARLINGTON, HENRY, JR., investment broker; b. N.Y.C., Jan. 8, 1925; s. Henry and Dorothy (Stone-Smith) D.; m. Frances Elizabeth Richardson, June 5, 1948 (div. Feb. 1965); children: Henry Darlington III, Elizabeth Aldrich, Victoria Wilde Darlington Yoder; m. Dorothea Fiske Page, July 1965 (div. Dec. 1973); m. Carla P. Barratt-Brown, June 1990. BA, Columbia U., 1949; LHD (hon.), St. Paul's Coll., Lawrenceville, Va., 1987. Salesman IBM, 1949-52; security salesman Cosgrave, Miller & Whitehead, 1952-55; gen. ptnr. Hill, Darlington & Co., 1955-62; v.p. B.J. Van Ingen & Co., Inc., 1956-59; registered rep. Cruttenden, Podesta and Miller, 1962; with syndicate dept. Loeb, Rhoades & Co., 1962-64, br. office adminstr., 1964-67, v.p., 1967-71, registered rep., 1972-79; investment exec. Shearson Loeb Rhoades, Inc. (now Salomon, Smith Barney), 1979-92. Trustee Hoosac Sch., Hoosick, N.Y., 1968-75, Ch. Heavenly Rest Day Sch., N.Y.C., 1968-74, Search and Care, N.Y.C., 1972-87, vestryman Ch. Heavenly Rest, 1969-75; bd. dirs. Fedn. Protestant Welfare Agys., 1962-89, asst. treas., 1971-79; bd. dirs. Episcopal Mission Soc., 1979-89, St. Paul's Ch., Rome, St. James' Ch., Florence, Italy; trustee Bd. Fgn. Parishes; warden Eglise Francaise du Saint Esprit, 1984-88. With USNR, 1943-46, lt. Res., 1946-65. Named to Order Ky. Cols. Mem. SAR, St. Nicholas Soc. (pres. 1976-78), S.R., St. Andrews Soc., St. George's Soc., The Huguenot Soc. (pres. 1986-89), Soc. Colonial Wars in the State of N.Y. (gov. 1991-93), Mil. Order of World Wars (N.Y. chpt.), N.Y. Soc. Mil. and Naval Officers World War, Navy League U.S. (past sec., treas. We. Conn. Coun.), Naval Order, Pilgrim Soc., St. George's Soc., Most Venerable Order of Hosp. of St. John of Jerusalem, Army and Navy Club, Union Club, Univ. Club, Everglades Club, Piping Rock Club, Delta Psi (trustee Alpha chpt. 1953-58). Home: 1115 5th Ave New York NY 10128-0100

DARLOW, GEORGE ANTHONY GRATTON, investor; b. Rochester, N.Y., June 16, 1938; s. Alfred Miltenberger and Lillian (Gratton) D.; m. Helen Julia Donovan, Mar. 2, 1971 (div.); 1 child, Gillian; m. Christiana Sewall Alden (div.). BA, Yale U., 1961; JD, Columbia U., 1971; LLD, Yale U., 1979, Columbia U., 1979, U. Rochester, 1979, Sweet Briar Coll., 1979. Trustee Am. Indian Archeol. Inst., Washington, Conn., 1973-93; chmn., trustee Inst. Am. Indian Studies, Washington, Conn., 1993—. With USN, 1961-64. Mem. Colony Found. (trustee 1995—), Ancient Free Accepted Masons (32nd Degree), Rotary Internat., Berzelius Soc., Beta Theta Pi, Lions Club. Republican. Episcopalian. Home: 35 Wykeham Rd Washington CT 06793-1308 Office: PO Box 1102 Washington CT 06793-0102

DARMAATMADJA, JULIUS RIYADI CARDINAL, archbishop; b. Muntilan, Dec. 20, 1934. Archbishop of Jakarta, Indonesia; created and proclaimed cardinal, 1994—. Office: Keus Kupan Agung, Jl Katedral 7, Jakarta 10710, Indonesia*

DARMANYAN, SERGEY, research physicist; b. Tashkent, USSR, Mar. 30, 1953; s. Arakel and Nina (Machkhelyants) D.; m. Marina Lyalina, Mar. 7, 1987; children: Nina and Marta (twins). MS with honors, Tech. U., Tashkent, 1975; PhD, Inst. Spectroscopy, Russian Acad. Scis., Moscow, 1982, sr. scientist diploma, 1989, DSc, Inst. Spectroscopy, 1992. Rschr. Inst. Electronics, Tashkent, 1975-78; sr. leading scientist Thermophysics Inst., Tashkent, 1982-93; head nonlinear spectroscopy sect. Inst. Spectroscopy, Russian Acad. Scis., 1993—; lectr. U. Tashkent, 1988-90; journal referee Phys. Letters, Phys. Rev.; dep. chmn. organizing com. Internat. Conf. Optical Solitons, Tashkent, 1989, Internat. Conf. Nonlineality and Disorder, Tashkent, 1990; vis. scientist Friedrich Schiller U., Jena, Germany, 1996-99. Author: Optical Solitons, 1987 (German edit. 1993); contbr. over 80 articles to sci. jours., including Phys. Rev., Optics Letters, Jour. Optical Soc. Am., Phys. Letters, Optic Comm. Grantee Internat. Sci. Found., 1992, NATO, 1996, German Rsch. Soc., 1997, Internat. Assn. for the Promotion of Cooperation with Scientists from the New Ind. States of the Former Soviet Union (INTAS), 1998, French Nat. Rsch. Ctr., 1999. Mem. Optical Soc. Am. (Vzbek state prize 1989). Avocations: soccer, chess. E-mail: darman@isan.troitsk.ru. Office: Russian Acad Scis, Inst Spectroscopy, 142190 Troitsk Moscow, Russia

DARMON, RENÉ YVES, dean, research educator; b. Constantine, Algeria, Sept. 10, 1938; arrived in France, 1990; s. Jacques and Elise E. (Tabet) D.; m. Nicole M. Schoenberger, July 26, 1963; children: Dominique, Henri. Diploma, Ecole Sup. Scis. Econs. Comml., Paris, 1961; MBA, Columbia U., 1963; PhD, U. Pa., 1973. Sales adminstrn. mgr. IBM, Paris, 1965-68; asst. prof. U. Laval, Que., Can., 1968-76; prof. McGill U., Montreal, Can., 1976-90; prof., dean of rsch. Ecole Supérieure Scis. Econs. et Commls., Cergy-Pontoise, France, 1990—; cons. various orgns., Can., France; presenter and spkr. in field. Author: Effective Human Resource Management in the Sales Force, 1992, La Vente: De la persuasion à la négociation commerciale, 1998, (with others) Advertising Management in Canada—Instructor's Manual, 1984, Canadian Marketing: A Management Perspective—Study Guide, 1981, 3d edit., 1989, Canadian Marketing: A Management Perspective, 1981, 3d edit., 1989, Advertising in Canada, 1991, others, (book chpts.) Communication de masse et consommation de masse, 1975, L'Administration, 1975, Contemporary Readings in Sales Management, 1977; mem. editl. bd.: Jour. Bus. Rsch., 1993—, Jour. Personal Selling and Sales Mgmt., 1980—, Can. Jour. Adminstrv. Scis., 1990—, others; contbr. articles and book revs. to profl. jours. and conf. procs. Recipient Bent Stidsen award of excellence Adminstrv. Sci. Assn. Can., 1992, Best Paper award EMAC Conf., 1993, award of best applied paper in mktg. Adminstrv. Sci. Assn. Can., 1993, Outstanding Paper award Nat. Sales Conf. in Sales Mgmt., 1997, 99; rsch. grantee FCAR, 1975-77, 81-84, 86-89, Ministries of Edn. and Comms., 1977-78, SSHRC, 1986-89, HEC-CERESSEC, 1993-94; rsch. fellow Assoc. Workshop for Bus. Rsch., U. Western Ont., 1974; SSHRC leave fellow, 1981-82. Mem. European Mktg. Acad. (coorganizer French-German workshop on mktg. models 1996), Acad. Mktg. Scis. (co-chmn. multicultral conf. 1998), French Assn. Mktg. (bd. dirs. 1992, 95, exec. com. 1992-96, chmn. sci. com. 1992-95, pres. 2000—), Adminstrv. Scis. Assn. Can., Am. Mktg. Assn. (exec.). Office: Ecole Sup Scis Econ Commls, Av Bernard Hirsch BP 105, 95021 Cergy-Pontoise France

DARNALL, ROBERTA MORROW, association executive; b. Kemmerer, Wyo., May 18, 1949; d. C. Dale and Eugenia Stayner (Christmas) Morrow; m. Leslie A. Darnall, Sept. 3, 1977; children: Kimberly Gene, Leslie Nicole. BS, U. Wyo., Laramie, 1972. Tariff sec., ins. adminstr. Wyo Trucking Assn., Casper, 1973-75; asst. clerical supr. Wyo. Legislature, Cheyenne, 1972-77, congrl. campaign press aide, 1974; pub. rels. dir. Casper, Wyo., Wyo. Rep. Ctr. Com., 1976-77; asst. dir. alumni rels. U. Wyo., 1977-81; exec. dir. Alumni Assn., 1981—. Bd. dir. Ivison Meml. Hosp. Found. Mem. St. Matthews Altar Guild (lector, usher, former acolyte, coord.), Higher Edn. Assn. Rockies, Am. Soc. Assn. Execs., Laramie C. of C. (past edn. com.), U. Wyo. Alumni Assn., Cowboy Joe Club, PEO (former courtesy com., officer). Republican. Episcopalian. Home: 15 Snowy View Ct Laramie WY 82070-5358 Office: PO Box 3137 Laramie WY 82071-3137

DARNELL, DORIS HASTINGS, storyteller, antique clothing collector, exhibitor; b. Chgo., Sept. 14, 1916; d. Willard Seth and Faith Emily (Olmstead) Hastings; m. Howard Clayton Darnell, Aug. 27, 1938; children: Elizabeth Loyd, John Hastings, Eric Allen. BA in Latin, Bryn Mawr Coll., 1939. Head resident, asst. to dir. Pendle Hill Grad. Sch. Religious and Social Concerns, Wallingford, Pa., 1939-40; libr. Res. Room and sci. Bryn Mawr (Pa.) Coll., 1950-52; acting head of library Westtown (Pa.) Friends Sch., 1952-53; head of library Westtown (Pa.) Sch., 1954-55; libr. Res. Room Haverford (Pa.) Coll., 1953-54; exec. dir., editor Westtown Alumni Assn., 1955-64; coord. of recruitment, then assoc. exec. sec. for personnel Am. Friends Svc. Com., Phila., 1964-78; creator, owner A Century of Elegance in Costume and Story, State College, Pa., 1980—; gov. com. Pendle Hill, Westtown Sch., Friends Select Sch. (Pa.), 1948-78; mem. Rufus Jones Assocs., Haverford Coll.; founding trustee Allen Hilles Fund (Phila.), 1982-91, trustee emerita, 1991—; lectr., exhibitor 19th and 20th century fashions, 1998—. Mem. AAUW, Costume Soc. Am., Palmer Art Mus., Women in the Arts, Internat. Costumers Guild. Quaker. E-mail: eleganztoo@aol.com. Home and Office: #C 36 500 Marylyn Ave State College PA 16801

DA ROCHA NETO, MIGUEL MAURICIO, construction executive, consultant; b. São Paulo, Aug. 7, 1958; s. Antonio Mauricio and Olga Mauricio (Pompeu de Camargo) Da R. Degree in bus. adminstrn., Faculdade Administração, São Paulo, 1987; degree in politics and strategy, Superior Sch. Way, São Paulo, 1987. Pres. Tenenge Engrng., São Paulo, 1981-86, Intertech Tech., São Paulo, 1986—; chief rschr. Tewewge Desenvolvimento e Engenharia, São Paulo, 1974-78. Contbr. articles to profl. publs. Mem., founder Rep. Party, São Paulo, 1990—. Pilot IV Air Force, 1974-77. Recipient Marechal Rondon award Geog. Soc., 1995. Mem. São Paulo Golf Club, São Paulo Tennis Club, Jockey Club. Social Democrat. Roman Catholic. Avocation: waterskiing. Office: Intertech Tech, Av Nacoe Unidas 13 797 8aII, 04974000 São Paulo Brazil

DAROFF, WILLIAM CLAYTON, lawyer; b. Miami Beach, Fla., Nov. 30, 1968; s. Robert Barry and Jane Linda (Abrahams) D.; m. Heidi Ilyse Krizer, Aug. 31, 1997. BA summa cum laude, Case Western Reserve U., 1995, JD, 1999, MA in Polit. Sci., 1999. Bar: Ohio 1999. Lead advanceman Kemp for Pres., Washington, 1986-88, Bush-Quayle '88, Washington, 1988; spl. asst. U.S. Dept. Energy, Washington, 1989-90; campaign mgr. Brachman for State Treas., Columbus, Ohio, 1990; spl. asst. to gov. State of Ohio, Columbus, 1990-92; dep. dir. Ohio Dept. Liquor Control, Columbus, 1992-93; pres. W. Daroff Consultants, Shaker Heights, Ohio, 1994-98; lead advanceman Dole-Kemp '96, Washington, 1996; assoc. Calfee, Halter & Griswold, LLP, Cleve., 1999-2000; dir. congl. affairs Rep. Jewish Coalition, Washington, 2000—. Sports editor East Side News, 1984-86; mem. editl. bd. Pub. Pers. Mgmt., 1991-92. Rep. nominee for Ohio State Rep., 11th Dist., 1994; mem. exec. com. Cuyahoga County Rep. Party, Cleve., 1987-88, 91-2000, mem. ctrl. com., 1987-88, 94-2000, exec. vice chmn. 1997-2000; alt. del. Rep. Nat. Conv., 1996; co-chmn. candidate endorsement com. Cuyahoga County Rep. Party, 1997-2000; mem. edn. com., bd. dirs. Young Leadership Divsn., Cleve. Jewish Cmty. Fedn., 1997-2000, mem. cmty. rels. com., 1999-2000; bd. dirs. Cleve. chpt. Am. Jewish Com., 1999-2000, exec. com., 2000; mem. leadership cabinet Cleve. Israel Bonds com., 2000; bd. dirs. Ohio Jewish Communities, Inc., 1999-2000, Bellfaire Jewish Children's Bur., 2000. Named to Honorable Order of Ky. Cols., 1992; recipient Meritorious Svc. award 4th Ward Rep. Club, 1989, 91, 93, Robert E. Hughes award Outstanding Svc., Cuyahoga County Rep. Party, 2000. Fellow Soc. for Am. Baseball Rsch.; mem. NRA (life), Cleve. Ripon Club, Columbus Athletic Club, Capital Club, Club at Key Ctr., Monday Thing Club (membership director 1989—), Case Western Res. U. Alumni Assn. (program com. 1998-2000). Republican. Jewish. Office: Rep Jewish Coalition 415 2d St NE Ste 100 Washington DC 20002

DAROWSKI, ROMAN, philosophy educator, historian; b. Szczepanowice, Poland, Aug. 12, 1935; s. Peter and Stanislawa Lesniak. M of Philosophy, Jesuit Faculty Philosophy, Cracow, Poland, 1958; M of Theology, Jesuit Faculty Theology, Warsaw, Poland, 1962; PhD, Gregorian U., Rome, 1966; postgrad., U. Munich, 1966-67; habilitation in philosophy, Pontifical Acad., Cracow, 1990. Assoc. prof. Jesuit Faculty Philosophy, Cracow, 1969-90, full prof., 1990—, dir. studies, 1968-73, dean faculty, 1973-82, 94-97; assoc. prof. Silesian Priests Sem., Cracow, 1970-76; assoc. prof. Pontifical Acad., Cracow, 1973-78, full prof., 1993—; rector Coll. Jesuits, Cracow, 1978-84; mem. Learned Coun. Polish Episcopate, 1973-82, 94-97. Author: Marxist Theory of Truth, 1973, Philosophy in Jesuit Schools in Poland in the 16th Century, 1994, Philosophy of Man, 1995, 2d edit., 1996, Studies in the Philosophy of the Jesuits in Poland in the 16th to 18th Centuries, 1999, Philosophy of the Jesuits in Poland in the 20th Century, 2000; editor, co-author: Man and World, 1972, Man: His Existence and Activity, 1974, Open in the Faith, 1974, Studies in the History of Philosophy, 1980; editor Forum Philosophicum, 1996—. Fax: 4812-4292095. E-mail: darowski@jezu-ici.krakow.pl. Office: Sch Philosophy & Edn, ul Kopernika 26, 31-501 Cracow Poland

DARR, ANN RUSSELL, poet, educator; b. Bagley, Iowa, Mar. 13, 1920; d. Henry Horton and Lessie Rebecca (Hooper) Russell; m. George Campbell Darr, Nov. 7, 1941 (div. Mar. 1981); children: Elizabeth Russell, Deborah Horton, Shannon Campbell. BA magna cum laude, State U. Iowa, 1941; postgrad., Harvard Coll., 1980, Am. U., 1981. Writer/actor NBC Radio, N.Y.C., 1941-43, 45-46; tape recs. for blind Libr. of Congress, Washington, 1950-60; instr. creative writing Poets in the Schs., Md., Va. and D.C., 1970-80, 92-93; co-dir. workshop Nethers (Va.) Arts Colony, 1979; poet/dir. Georgetown U., Washington, summer 1977-78; poet The Writers Ctr., Bethesda, Md., 1981—; adj. prof. dept. lit. Am. U., Washington, 1982—; fine arts seminar poet Montgomery (Ala.) Seminars, summer 1975; poet-in-residence Columbia (S.C.) Coll., spring 1975, 76, Am. Wind Symphony aboard Point Counterpoint II, U.S., 1976, 86, Jamaica, 1981, Europe, 1989, Eckard Coll., St. Petersburg, Fla., spring 1977; workshop poet St. Mary's (Md.) Coll., spring 1981, 82, 94, 95, 98, 99; judge for poetry Eckerd Coll., St. Petersburg, Fla., 1977, Nat. Endowment for Arts, Washington, 1979, Radcliff Coll., Cambridge, Mass., 1980, New Eng. Poetry Soc., Boston, 1981; mem. lit. panel Nat. Endowment for Arts, 1979-80; mem. adv. com. Folger Libr. Poetry Series, Washington, 1974-96. Author: St. Ann's Gut, 1971, The Myth of a Woman's Fist, 1973, Cleared for Landing, 1978, Riding with the Fireworks, 1981, Do You Take This Woman..., 1986 (Pub. award 1986), The Twelve Pound Cigarette, 1991, Confessions of a Skewed Romantic, 1993, Flying the Zuni Mountains, 1994, Gussie, Mad Hannah & Me, 1999, Love In the Past Tense, 2000; editor: Hungry As We Are, 1995; author numerous poems, 1961-99; translator (with others) Reading the Ashes, 1978, (with others) After the First Rain, 1997; featured poet Nat. Mus. Radio and TV, 1997. Mem. election com. Somerset (Md.) Town Bd., 1975-79; vol. Arena Stage, Washington, 1949-52. With U.S. Army Airforce (Women's Airforce Svc. pilot), 1943-44, WWII. Recipient Bunting fellowship Radcliffe Coll., 1979-80, Discovery 70 award Poetry Ctr., N.Y.C., 1970, Yaddo fellowship Yaddo, 1979, 86, MacDowell fellowship MacDowell Found., 1979. Mem. White House Conf. for Poets, Poetry Soc. Am., Acad. Am. Poets, Phi Beta Kappa, Zeta Phi Eta. Avocations: flying, traveling, acting, reading, collecting birds. Home: 4902 Falstone Ave Chevy Chase MD 20815-5540 Office: Am Univ 4400 Massachusetts Ave NW Washington DC 20016-8001

DARR, WALTER ROBERT, financial analyst; b. Phila., June 19, 1956; s. John Fluke Sr. and Lois Marilyn (Fry) D. BS in Commerce, Rider U., Lawrenceville, N.J., 1978; MBA, Rider U., 1991. Collateral analyst First Nat. Bank & Trust Co., Beverly, N.J., 1978-84; collateral analyst First Peoples Bank of N.J., Westmont, 1984-88, loan rev. analyst, 1988-92; loan acctg. tech. New Jersey Nat. Bank, Trenton, N.J., 1992-93; sr. credit analyst Carnegie Bank, N.A., Princeton, N.J., 1993-94, asst. cashier, sr. credit analyst, 1994-97; credit officer, credit dept. supr. Broad Nat./Independence Cmty. Bank, Newark, N.J., 1997-99; asst. sec., bus. banking divsn. ICB, Newark, N.J., 1999—. Treas. Cinnaminson Bapt. Ch., 1983-87, deacon, 1988-89, 93-94; mem. Lewis Shearer Chorale/Garden State Chorale, 1982-94; chmn.-treas. Mercer County chpt. Child Evangelism Fellowship of N.J., 1996-99. Recipient Sch. award Am. Legion Post, Medford, N.J., 1974. Republican. Baptist. Avocations: antique cars, bicycling, classical music, Victorian architecture. Home: 107 Manlove Ave Apt E-B Hightstown NJ 08520-3234 Office: Independence Cmty Bank 905 Broad St Newark NJ 07102-2622

DARRACOTT, STEPHEN LYNNE, editor; b. Kingaroy, Queensland, Australia, June 17, 1943; s. Herbert Claude and Rita Maurine (Groom) D.; m. Eunice Joan Mengel, Mar. 23, 1967; 1 child, James. ALCM, London Coll. Music, Kingaroy, 1961; postgrad., U. Queensland, Brisbane, 1969. Cadet journalist Kingaroy Herald, 1960-64; journalist Cumberland Newspapers, Brisbane, 1964-65; news editor Kingaroy Herald, 1965-71; journalist Courier Mail, Brisbane, 1971-73; editor Warwick (Australia) Daily News, 1973-84; editorial mgr. Western Pubs., Toowoomba, Australia, 1989-92, Star Newspapers, Toowoomba, 1992—; guest lectr. Darlin Downs Coll., Toowoomba, 1978; part-time tutor journalism Queensland U., Brisbane, 1985, 86; ESL tutor Slade Sch., Warwick, Queensland, 1987. Photographer Warwick Daily News, 1982 (Highly Commended award 1983). Sec. Road Safety Coun., Kingaroy, 1965-67; dep. contr. State Emergency Svc., Kingaroy, 1966-71; local preacher, elder Presbyn. Ch., Kingaroy, 1966-71, local preacher and session clk., Warwick, 1974-84; justice of the peace, Warwick, 1970—; mem. Disaster Relief Com., Warwick, 1973-84. Avocations: reading, teddy bears. Home: 24 Rowland St, Warwick Queensland 4370, Australia Office: Star Newspapers, Joseph St, Toowoomba Queensland 4350, Australia

DARRAS, DANIELLE, foreign diplomat; b. Carency, France, Dec. 22, 1943. Mem. European Parliament, 1999—, mem. com. on regional policy, transport and tourism, substitue com. on employment and social affairs, substitute com. on women's rights and equal opportunities; mem. Group of the Party of European Socialists; mem. Mems. from the European Parliament to the Joint Assembly of the Agreement between the African, Caribbean and Pacific States and the European Union. Socialist Party. Office: Hôtel de Ville, Rue Basly, F-62801 Lievin France*

DARRAS, DENNIS CONSTANTINE, power engineer; b. Athens, Greece, Oct. 26, 1922; s. Constantine Dennis and Hellen George (Mihopoulou) D.; m. Stella Rallou, June 17, 1953; children: Helen, Constantine. Grad., Coryalenios and Anargyrios Coll., Greece, 1939; MS in Mech. and Elec. Engring., Nat. Metsovion Polytech., Greece, 1949. With Socony-Vacuum Oil Co., 1949-50; With Pub. Power Corp., Athens, 1950, head power generating stations, operating dept., 1954-58, head prodn. and transmission sys., 1958-66, gen. mgr. prodn.-transmission, 1967-70, gen. mgr. prodn.-tramsmission and distbn., 1970-74; design and constrn. engr. PROMAFFAIRS AG; tech.-econ. cons., advisor to various enterprises and cos. worldwide, 1975—; designer/constructor energy networks, including 29 power generating stas., coal-oil-gas, hdyro and nuclear, high and super-high voltage transmission lines, switchyards and the assoc. equipment, 1950-96. Former pres. Hellenic Electromech. Soc. Served with Royal Hellenic Navy, World War II. Decorated chevalier Légion d'Honneur, officer Légion d'Honneur France; decorated Gallant Disting. Action Order, Navy War Cross, Convoy Escort medal with 6 stars, Nat. Resistance medal; recipient Pro Mundi Beneficio award Acad. Brasileira de Ciencias Humanas, 1975. Mem. IEEE, Tech. Chamber Greece (editor-in-chief Cronicles), Athenian Club, Glyfada Golf Club. Avocations: swimming, boating, photography, golf. Home: 76 Blvd de Tour Maubourg, 75007 Paris France

DARROUZET, JEAN-CLAUDE, home furnishings distribution business executive; b. Paris, Oct. 2, 1947; s. Albert Darrouzet and Odette Hanriat; m. Christine Pous; children: Sandrine, Nathalie. MBA, European Inst. Bus. Adminstrn., Fontainebleau, France, 1984; PhD in Mgmt., U. Lyon, France, 1980. Dir. sales and mtkg. BSN Emballage, France, 1980-85, mng. dir., 1985-92; pres. Graham Packaging, France, 1992-93, Evian, mineral water, 1993-97; chmn., CEO, Conforama Group, Marne La Vallee, France, 1997—; mem. mgmt. bd. PPR Group. Sub lt. Parachute Corps, French Army, 1972. Decorated chevalier Legion of Honor (France). Avocation: sports. Home: 22 Blvd Flandrin, 75116 Paris France Office: Conforama Group, 80 Blvd Mandinet, 77432 Marne La Vallee Cedex 2, France

DARROW, WILLIAM RICHARD, pharmaceutical company executive, consultant; b. Middletown, Ohio, Sept. 7, 1939; s. Richard William and Nelda Virginia (Darling) D.; m. Janet Elizabeth Swan, June 20, 1964; children: James William, Susan Elizabeth, Margaret Ellen. BA, Ohio Wesleyan U., 1960; MD, Western Res. U., 1964; PhD in Pharmacology, Case-Western Res. U., 1969. Intern Univ. Hosps., Cleve., 1964; sr. clin. rsch. assoc. CIBA Pharm. Co., 1969, asst. dir. clin. pharmacology, 1969-70; dir. clin. pharmacology CIBA-GEIGY Corp., 1970-75, exec. dir. clin. rsch., 1975-76; sr. v.p. rsch., med. dir. Wallace Labs. div. Carter Wallace, Inc., Cranbury, N.J., 1976-80; med. dir. Schering Labs. div. Schering-Plough Corp., Kenilworth, N.J., 1980, v.p. med. and regulatory affairs, 1981-82, sr. v.p. med. ops., 1982-94, sr. med. advisor, 1994—; chmn. rsch. com. N.J. Health Scis. Group, 1973-76, mem. exec. com., 1973-74, 76-86, treas., 1977-80, v.p., 1980-86, Bernards Twp. Bd. Health, 1979-93, v.p., 1980, pres., 1981-85, 86-93; chmn. Bernards Twp. Deer Study Task Force, 1999—; bd. dirs. N.J. Arthritis Found., 1990—, exec. com., 1991—, vice chmn., 1995-97, chmn. bd. dirs., 1997—; bd. dirs. Pharm. Rsch. Mfrs. Am. Ednl. and Rsch. Inst., 1993-2000, chmn. curriculum com., 1993-95; bd. dirs. Junior Achievement No. N.J., 1996; mem. sci. adv. bd. Clin. Rsch. Ctr. Robert Wood Johnson Med. Ctr., 1990-2000; mem. U.S. del. Internat. Conf. on Harmonization, 1991-99; mem. N.J. State Arthritis Adv. Coun., 2000—. Recipient Roche award, 1962, Humanitarian of Yr. award Arthritis Found. N.J., 1994; USPHS postdoctoral fellow, 1965-69. Fellow Royal Soc. Medicine, Am. Acad. Pharm. Physicians, Acad. Medicine N.J.; mem. AMA, Am. Acad. Pharm. Physicians (life), Drug Info. Assn., N.J. Acad. Scis., Pharm. Rsch. Mfrs. Am. (mem. steering com. med. section 1984-96, program chmn. 1988-89, vice-chmn. 1989-90, chmn. 1990-92, past chmn. 1992-96), Pharm. Rsch. Mfrs. Am. Found. (sci. adv. bd. 1990—, chmn. 1994—, chief sci. advisor 1997—), Phi Gamma Delta, Phi Rho Sigma, Omicron Delta Kappa, Pi Delta Epsilon, Basking Ridge Country Club (N.J.), Lakeside Country Club (Penn Yan, N.Y.). Republican. Presbyterian. Home: 42 Palmerston Pl Basking Ridge NJ 07920-2524 also: 521 E Lake Rd Penn Yan NY 14527-9422

DARSEY, JEROME ANTHONY, chemistry educator, consultant; b. Houma, La., Aug. 26, 1946; s. Elmer Joseph and Arline (Houghton) D.; m. Patricia Ann Bukowski, June 10, 1989; children: Brittany Angèle, Joseph Anthony, Mary Catherine. BS in Physics, La. State U., 1970, PhD in Chemistry, 1982. Asst. prof. chemistry and physics Gordon Coll. U. Ga. System, Barnsville, 1983-84; asst. prof. Tarleton State U./Tex. A&M U., Stephenville, Tex., 1984-88, assoc. prof., 1988-90; asst. prof. U. Ark., Little Rock, 1990-93, assoc. prof., 1993-96, prof., 1996—; univ. scholar natural scis. Tarleton State U., Tex. A&M U., 1989-90; cons. Oak Ridge (Tenn.) Nat. Lab., 1990-95; co-chmn. 1st workshop neural network applications to material scis. Dept. Energy, 1994; chmn. 1st APS Symposium on Applications of Artificial Neural Networks to Chemical Systems; invited lectr. 21st Australian Polymer Symposium, 1996. Sci. book reviewer Jour. Am. Chem. Soc.; contbr. articles to profl. jours. Grantee Am. Chem. Soc., 1986, 90, NSF, 1992, 96, NASA, 1994-2000; named Outstanding Univ. Researcher, U. Ark., 1995. Fellow AAAS; mem. Am. Chem. Soc. (chmn. Ark. sect. 1993), Am. Phys. Soc., Ark. Acad. Sci., S.W. Theoretical Chemistry Conf. (chmn. 1986-87), Tex. Acad. Sci. (vice chmn. chemistry divsn. 1986-87, chmn. 1987-88). Home: 1514 Alberta Dr Little Rock AR 72227-5803 Office: U Ark Dept Chemistry 2801 S University Ave Dept Little Rock AR 72204-1099

DARSONVAL, VINCENT ANDRÉ, plastic surgeon; b. Reims, France, Oct. 23, 1948; s. Guy and Gisele (Martinet) D.; m. Annie Lefebvre, June 15, 1971; children: Emmanuelle, Arnaud. BS, U. Paris, 1967; MD, U. Reims, 1980. Resident in otorhinolaryngology Regional Hosp. Angers, France, 1977-81; clinic chief Regional Hosp. Angers, 1981; chief clinic plastic and reconstructive surgery Regional Hosp. Tours, France, 1981-84; plastic surgeon, prof. Regional Hosp. Angers, 1984—. Author: Le Droit et la Chirurgie Esthetique, 1987. Office: CHR Angers, 1 Ave de l'Hotel Dieu, 49000 Angers France

DART, EDWARD CHARLES, biotechnology and bioscience consultant; b. Liverpool, Eng., Mar. 8, 1941; s. Arthur and Alice (Perkins) D.; m. Jean Ellen Long, Mar. 21, 1964; children: Gregory Charles, Leah Ellen, Katie Anna. BSc, Manchester (Eng.) U., 1962, PhD, 1965. Postdoctoral fellow UCLA, 1965-67, U. Calif., Berkeley, 1967-68; sr. rsch. scientist Imperial Chem. Industries PLC, Eng., 1968-72; group head biosci. Imperial Chem. Industries Corp. Lab., Eng., 1972-81; lab. mgr. Imperial Chem. Industries Corp. Lab., 1981-83; head Corp. Biosci. and Colloids Lab. Imperial Chem. Industries, Eng., 1983-85; assoc. rsch. dir. Imperial Chem. Industries Plant Protection, Eng., 1985-86; dir. R & D Zeneca Seeds (formerly Imperial Chem. Industries), Eng., 1986-97; CEO AdProTech Plc, 1997-99, Norwich Rsch. Park Partnership, 1997-98; chmn. Plant Biosci. Ltd.; chmn. Sci. and Engring. Rsch. Coun. Biotech. Directorate, Eng., 1984-89, U.K. Biotech. Joint Adv. Bd., 1992-94, Bioscis. and Biotech. Rsch. Coun. Tech. Bd., 1994-97, mem. coun., 1994-98; lectr. in field. Contbr. articles to profl. jours.; patentee in field. Mem. govt. adv. com. on genetic manipulation, 1984-96; pres. Berkshire & Oxfordshire Assn. for Sci. Edn., 1989-92; chmn. Govt. Foresight Panel on Agr., Horticulture and Forestry, 1997-99; mem. U.K. Agr. and Environ. Biotech. Commn., 2000. Decorated comdr. Order Brit. Empire, 1997. Fellow Inst. Biology; mem. Oxford Innovation Soc. Avocations: golf, gardening, music.

DARTNALL, TERENCE HAIG, philosopher, educator; b. Whitstable, Kent, Eng., Sept. 4, 1943; arrived in Australia, 1977; s. Douglas Haig and Eileen Philippa (Maflin) D.; m. Susan Marjorie Spiller, Dec. 22, 1975 (div. Feb. 1982); 1 child, Lisa Arwen; m. Wendy Elizabeth Miller, Feb. 30, 1982; 1 child, Adam. BA with hons., Bristol (Eng.) U., 1967; MLitt, Edinburgh (Scotland) U., 1969, Dip. Gen. Ling., 1970; PhD, Otago U., New Zealand, 1979; MSc, Sussex (Eng.) U., 1987. Head dept. philosophy U. Tonga, 1976; lectr. Adelaide (Australia) U., 1979-81, Nat. U. Singapore, 1981-85; sr. lectr., dir. artificial intelligence Griffith U., Queensland, Australia, 1988—. Editor: Artificial Intelligence and Creativity, 1994, (with Janet Wiles) Perspectives on Cognitive Science, 1999; cognitive sci. editor Metasci., 1996—; mem. editl. bd. AI Rev., 1997—, Dialogsin Psychology, 1997—; contbr. articles to profl. jours. Otago U. fellow, 1972-75, Australian Nat. U. fellow, 1977-78, Sussex U. fellow, 1992; recipient Best Contbn. Cognitive Sci. Australasia award Australasian Cognitive Sci. Soc., 1995; assoc. behavioral and Brain Scis., 1994—. Mem. Am. Assn. Artificial Intelligence, Australian Soc. History Philosophy Sci. Avocations: rock climbing, scuba, poetry, wine. Office: Faculty Info & Computing, Griffith U, Nathan 4111, Australia

DARVE, FELIX ANDRE, mechanical engineering educator; b. Chambery, Savoie, France, Dec. 28, 1947; s. Henri and Marie (Viard) D.; m. Dominique Mahaut, Nov. 1, 1971 (div.); 1 child, Eric; m. Francoise Grellety, Nov. 27, 1993; children: Luc, Estelle. Engr., Ecole Ctrl. Paris, 1971; D, U. Grenoble, France, 1974, DSc, 1978. Asst. prof. U. Grenoble, 1974-77, assoc. prof., 1977-84; prof. Inst. Nat. Poly. Grenoble, 1985—; dir. Greco Geomaterials, 1986-93, Ecole Nat. Supérieure d'Hydraulique et de Mécanique Grenoble, 1987-92, Alert Geomaterials, 1992—. Editor: Constitutive Relations for Soils, 1984, Manuel de Rheólogie des Géomatériaux, 1987, Geomaterials Constitutive Equations and Modelling, 1990, Mécanique des Géomatériaux, 1995. Recipient Palmes Académiques Chevalier, 1995. Home: 22 bis rue de Tournelles, 38000 Grenoble France Office: Lab Sols Solides Structures, INPG BP 53 Cedex 9, 38041 Grenoble France

DARWISH, AHMED M., engineering educator; b. Giza, Egypt, May 25, 1959; s. Mahmoud O. and Hoda H. (Hefny) D.; m. Nevine A. Khalil, Aug. 23, 1984; children: Hoda, Aly. BSc, Cairo U., 1981, MSc, 1984; PhD, U. Calif., Davis, 1988. Asst. prof. Cairo U., 1989-94, assoc. prof. computer engrng., 1994-99, prof. computer engrng., 1999—; vis. assoc. prof. Va. Tech., 1996; cons. Radio and TV Broadcasting, Cairo, 1989-92, Fairchild Imaging Sensors, Calif., 1988-89, UNESCO an FAO, 1999—. Assoc. editor Internat. Jour. Robotics and Automation, 1990—; contbr. articles to profl. jours. Mem. IEEE, ACM, Egyptian Soc. Engrs. Moslem. Avocations: football, soccer, travel. Office: Cairo Univ, Dept Engring Computer, Giza 12411, Egypt

DARWISH, EL SAYED YOUNIS, chemical company administrator, consultant; b. Tanta, Egypt, Oct. 15, 1924; s. Younis Mostafa and Zahira Mohammed (Mansi) D.; m. Ikbal Khedr El Kaissi, Mar. 16, 1950; children: Ahmed, Hosam, Ashraf. BS, Faculty Engring., Cairo, 1947; Master (hon.), Ecole des Poudres, Paris, 1954. Chem. engr. Shiffild Co., Cairo, 1947-48; plant mgr. L'Air Liquide Co., Cairo, 1948-49; commd. Arms and Ammunition Dept., Egypt, 1949, advanced through grades to maj., 1956; tech. mgr. Abu Zaabal Co. for Splty. Chems., Abu Zaabal, Egypt, 1956-67; chmn. Heliopolis Co. for Chem. Industry, Egypt, 1967-68, Abu Zaabal Co. for Splty. Chems., 1968-84, Universal Home Care Products, Nasr City, Egypt, 1984—; gen. mgr. L'Air Liquide Co., Cairo, 1956-57; chmn. Johnson Wax Egypt, Khankah, 1975-84; cons. for Arab Countries, 1958-88; Egypt rep. Internat. Labor Orgn., Geneva, 1995; cons. for Arab countries for devel. of chem. industries, 1976-88. Editor: Abu Zaabal Co. Mag., 1974-84. Bd. dirs. Chamber of Chem. Industries, Egypt, 1980—, Top Mgmt. Grads. Assn., Cairo, 1988—. Recipient 1st Class Appreciation award Pres. Sadat, Egypt, 1979, Tudor Vladimer award Pres. Chao Chesque, Romania, 1978, 79, Appreciation awards Engrs. Syndicate, Egypt, 1991-93. Mem. Heliopolis Club, Flowers Club. Mem. Nat. Party. Avocations: tennis, swimming, rowing, playing chess, poetry. Home: 16 Badr El Din El Aini St, Nasr City Cairo, Egypt Office: UNIPRO Egypt, 4 Salah Salem Rd, Nasr City Cairo, Egypt

DARY, MICHEL J.M., foreign diplomat; b. Marseille, France, Sept. 20, 1945. Mem. European Parliament, 1999—, mem. com. on agr. and rural devel.; substitute com. on devel. and coop.; mem. Group of the Party of European Socialists; chmn. delegation for relations with the Mashreq countries and the Gulf; substitute delegation to the EU-Malta Joint Parliamentary Com. Office: Conseil Gen des Bouches Rho, 52 Avenue de Saint-Just, F-13004 Marseille France

DAS, ANIBH MARTIN, pediatrician; b. Braunschweig, Germany, Jan. 17, 1961; s. Arabindo and Aparna (Sarkar) D.; m. Kathrin Glania, Dec. 3, 1993; children: Eileen, Martin Anselm, Miriam Rebekka, Jonathan Arvid. MD, Göttingen U., 1986, PhD, 1988. Intern Wolfsburg (Germany) Hosp., 1986; scholar Max-Planck Inst., Göttingen, 1987-88; postdoctoral rsch. fellow dept. biochemistry Oxford U., U.K., 1988-90; physician Hannover (Germany) Med. Sch., 1990-96; pediatrician Hamburg (Germany) U., 1996-2000. Contbr. articles to profl. jours. Recipient Rhone-Poulenc-Rorer prize for neuromuscular rsch., 1997. Mem. N.Y. Acad. Scis., Soc. for the Study of Inborn Errors of Metabolism, World Muscle Soc. Avocations: reading classical works, rowing. Office: Hannover Med Sch, Carl Neuberg Str 1, 30623 Hannover Germany

DAS, ANIRUDDHA MATHURANATH, veterinary microbiologist, educator; b. Darbhanga, Bihar, India, Nov. 17, 1952; s. Mathuranath Ramanchandra and Geeta Mathuranath Das; m. Dablina Aniruddha Sasaru, Nov. 29, 1993. B Vet. Sci. and Animal Husbandry, Bombay Vet. Coll., Mumbai, India, 1977, M Vet. Sci., 1982, PhD, 1988; postgrad., Auburn U., 1990. Vet. practitioner Clinic, Devlali, India, 1976-78; vet. inspector govt., Mumbai, 1981; vet. officer Bombay Vet. Coll., Mumbai, 1981-82, asst. prof., 1982-83, rsch. asst., 1983-87, asst. prof., 1987-92, sr. scientist, 1992-95, assoc. prof. vet. microbiology, 1995—; brucellosis expert govt., Mumbai, 1992—; clin. bacteriologist med. colls. and hosps., Mumbai, 1982-86; bacteriologist Nat. Svc. Scheme, Kolkewadi, 1987-88, Uchat, 1989; respondent Nat. Inst. Sci., Tech. and Devel. Studies, New Delhi, 1990-91. Contbr. articles to profl. jours. Mem. Indian Vet. Assn. (life), Indian Assn. Vet. Microbiologists, Immunologists and Specialists in Infectious Diseases (life), Bombay Vet. Coll. Alumni Assn. (life). Avocations: singing (Indian music), badminton, tennis, cooking, study of gems in relation to therapy, war/adventure movies. Home: Lic Colony, 25, A6-17, Yashdayini, Mumbai 400 103, India Office: Bombay Vet Coll, Parel, Mumbai 400 012, India

DAS, ARABINDA KUMAR, chemistry educator; b. Basirhat, India, May 20, 1947; s. Jogendra Nath and Kamala D.; m. Ruma Chakraborty. BS with honors, Calcutta U., India, 1967, MS, 1969; MS, Ohio State U., 1977; PhD,

Jadavpur U., India, 1982. Lectr. R.K.M. Residential Coll., Narendrapur, India, 1970-74, 77-79; teaching asst. Ohio State U., Columbus, 1974-77; lectr. Burdwan U., India, 1979-85, reader, 1985-91, prof., 1991-99, 99—, head chemistry dept., 1996-98; vis. prof. U. Valencia, India, 1994-95, 99. Author: Physical Science, 1974, General and Inorganic Chemistry, 1981, Techniques and Applications of Quantitative Analysis, 1987, Elements of Bioinorganic Chemistry, 1993; mem. editl. bd. Bulletin Indian Soc. Analytical Scientists, Mumbai, 1996—. Mem. Indian Chem. Soc., Indian Soc. Analytical Scientists, Paschim Banga Vigyan Mancha. Hindu. Avocations: reading, books, science, music. Home: Meghnad Saha Pally, I/1 Tarabag, Burdwan 713 104, India Office: U Burdwan Dept Chemistry, Golapbag, Burdwan 713 104, India

DAS, BAIDYA NATH, physics educator, researcher; b. Birbhum, India, Jan. 14, 1949; s. Adhar Chandra and Susama Das; m. Ila Biswas, Dec. 14, 1983; children: Aditi, Subhasri. BSc with honors, Calcutta (India) U., 1967; MSc in Physics, Indian Inst. Tech., Kharagpur, India, 1971, postgrad., 1972, PhD, 1978. Tchr. physics Godapiasal H.S., Midnapur, India, 1968-69; sr. rsch. asst. Indian Inst. Tech., Kharagpur, 1974-87; lectr. Indian Inst. Tech., 1987-91, asst. prof., 1991—; asst. warden B.C. Roy Hall Indian Inst. Tech., Kharagpur, 1993-95. Contbr. articles to profl. jours. Dir. Pub. Instrn. scholar Govt. West Bengal, India, 1964-67. Mem. Materials Rsch. Soc. India (life). Avocation: researching unconventional alternative medicines. Home: Qr No 2 BR-21 IIT Campus, Kharagpur 721302, India Office: Dept Physics IIT, Kharagpur 721302, India

DAS, DILLIP KUMAR, business executive; b. Samantarapur, Orissa, India, Jan. 26, 1948; s. Krutibas and Basanti Das; m. Geetishree Mohanty, Mar. 10, 1972; children: Debasis, Anindita, Paramita, Subhasis. Student, Ravenshaw Coll., Cuttack, Orissa, India; BSEE, U. Coll. Engring., Sambalpur, India, 1969. Asst. engr. Govt. Orissa, Hirakud Power House, Burla, India, 1971-73; jr. engr. OSEB, Bhubanesawr, India, 1969-71; asst. engr. OSEB, Bhubanesawr, 1973-74; proprietor Alfa Elecs. and Co., Cuttack, India, 1975-85; mng. dir. Alfa Transformers Ltd., Bhubaneswar, 1982—, Galaxy Medicare Ltd., Bhubaneswar, 1996—; bd. dirs. IDS (P) Ltd., Cuttack, OIC (P) Ltd., Dhenkanal, India, IPISteel Ltd., Cuttack. Editor Oasis, 1967-69. Sec. Orissa Small Scale Industries Assn., Cuttack, 1981-82, 82-83. Recipient Samaj Shree award Indian Coun. Mgmt. Execs., Bombay, 1992, Udyog Rattan awad Inst. Econ. Studies, Kathmandu, Nepal, 1993, Cert. of Merit, Nat. Coun. Small Industries, Madras, India, 1995. Mem. IEEE, Inst. Std. Engrs. Hindu. Avocation: poetry.

DAS, KALI PADA, engineering educator; b. Bengal, India, July 10, 1938; s. Anath Chandra and Renu Prova (Dutta) D.; m. Atreyee Pal, Mar. 13, 1970; 1 child, Nilanjan. BSc, Calcutta (India) U., 1958, MSc, 1960; PhD, Jadpaupur (India) U., 1972. Lectr. Bengal Engring. Coll., Sibpur, Howrah, India, 1961-62, Jalpaiguri (India) Govt. Engring. Coll., 1962-73, Kalyani (India) U., 1973-78; sr. scientist Eindhoven U. Tech., The Netherlands, 1979-81; lectr. Calcutta U., 1981-84, reader, 1984-93, prof., 1993—; vis. prof. U. Gent, Belgium, 1988. Author: Theory of Probability and its Applications, 1993; contbr. articles to profl. jours. Commonwealth Acad. Staff fellow Cambridge U., 1978-79, Vis. fellow Eindhoven U. Tech., 1987-88. Office: U Calcutta, 92 Acharya Prafulla Chandra, Calcutta 700 009, India

DAS, MAMOTA, education educator, researcher; b. Agra, India, Aug. 30, 1945; d. Kanai Lall and Aruna Barbara (Fleming) Chowdhury; m. Joy Das, Oct. 6, 1967. BA, St. John's Coll., Agra, 1963, MA, 1965; PhD, M.S. U., Baroda, India, 1984. Tchr. Queen Victoria, Agra, 1965-66, RMJ Sch., Agra, 1966-68; lectr. edn. Dahalbagh Ednl. Inst., Agra, 1971-84, reader edn., 1984-91; prof. edn. Annamalai U., Chidambaram, India, 1991—, dean edn., 1992—; dir. adult edn. Annamalainagar, India, 1992—, dir. environ. edn., 1995—. Inventor in field; contbr. articles to profl. jours. Recipient tchr. fellowship, U.G.C., Baroda, 1980, vis. professorship, Alagappa U., India, 1994, Exch. Program award, Khazakistan, 1995. Fellow Univ. Women's Assn. (pres. 1996-97), Annamalaluni (program dir. 1995—); mem. Psycho-Lingua. Congress Party. Christian. Avocations: reading, dramatics, gardening, light music. E-mail: auedu@usa.net. Home: Sudha Bagh Colony, Dayalbagh, Agra 282005, India Office: Annamalai U Dept Edn, Annamalainagar, 608002 Chidambaram Tamil Nadu, India

DAS, MRINAL KANTI, mechanical engineer; b. Jamshedpur, Bihar, India, Aug. 12, 1945; s. Harekrishna and Amiya D.; m. Gouri Dutta, Feb. 27, 1952; two sons. B Mech. Engring., U. Calcutta, 1967; M Technology/Machine Design, Indian Inst. Technology, 1970. Asst. engr. Motwane Mfg. Co., Nasik, India, 1970-72; sr. tech. officer Electronics Corp. of India, Ltd., Hyderabad, 1972-78; sr. exec. Hindustan Brown Boveri Ltd., Baroda, India, 1978-83; asst. mgr. Star Electronics, Baroda, 1983-86; sr. mgr., materials Elec. Rsch. and Devel. Assn., baroda, 1986—; mem. experts' com. on silver, technol. info. forecasting and assessment com., Govt. India, 1992—, mem. com. on renovation and modernisation of thermal power plants Ctrl. Bd. of Irrigation and Power, Govt. of India, 1999. Contbr. articles to profl. jours. Recipient cert. merit Cen. Bd. Irrigation and Power, New Delhi, 1994, N.K. Iyengar Meml. prize Instn. Engrs., 1985-86. Mem. Indian Soc. Non-Destructive Testing (exec. com. Baroda chpt.), Indian Inst. Metals (life). Office: Elec Rsch & Devel Assn, Makarpura Indsl Estate, 390010 Baroda India

DAS, MUKUL, toxicologist; b. Lucknow, India, July 9, 1956; s. Ghanshiam and Kamlesh (Rastogi); m. Sadhna Rastogi, Mar. 4, 1987; children: Ishan, Shanya. BSc, Lucknow Christian Coll., 1976; MSc, Lucknow U., 1978; PhD, Kanpur U., 1983. Rsch. fellow Indsl. Toxicology Rsch. Ctr., Lucknow, 1980-82; rsch. assoc. Wayne State U., Detroit, 1982-83; sr. rsch. assoc. Case Western Res. U., Cleve., 1983-86; scientist Indsl. Toxicology Rsch. Ctr., 1987-91, asst. dir., 1991-96, sr. asst. dir., 1996—. Burroughs Wellcome Fund Fell., 1985, Schering Plough Found. Fell., 1986, Internat. Union Biochemistry fellow, Czechoslovakia, 1988, Young Scientist Award, 1990. Mem. Am. Assn. Cancer Rsch. (corr.), Soc. Biol. Chemists India, Soc. Toxicology India, Indian Assn. Cancer Rsch., Indian Acad. Neurosci., Assn. Food Scientists & Technologists India, Food and Agriculture Div. Coun., India. Avocations: cricket, table tennis, music. Home: 215/19KA Kamal Sarovar, Subhash Marg, Lucknow India Office: Indsl Toxicology Rsch Ctr, Mahatma Gandhi Marg PO 80, Lucknow India

DAS, NACHIKETA, geochemist, consultant; b. Cuttack, Orissa, India, Feb. 20, 1956; s. Rajendra Prasad and Saudamini (Patnaik) D. BSc with honors, Utkal U., Orissa, 1976; MSc, Jawaharlal Nehru U., New Delhi, 1978; PhD, Glasgow (Scotland) U., 1986; Certificate IV in Workplace Trainer (category 2), 1998, Diploma of Bus., 1999, Diploma in Human Res. Mgmt., 1999. Lectr. in geology Utkal U., 1979-82; rsch. assoc. Pa. State U., State College, 1986; postdoctoral fellow in geochemistry Harvard U., Cambridge, Mass., 1986-88; sr. sci. officer Ministry of Sci. and Tech., Govt. of India, New Delhi, 1989-92; environ. chemist La Trobe U., Melbourne, Australia, 1992-93; geochemist CSIRO Divsn. of Petroleum Resources, Sydney, Australia, 1993-95; dir. NRI Enviro-Geo-Tech Australia, Sydney, 1995—; dir.-internat. Bridge Bus. Coll., Sydney, 1995—; cons. Dept. Fgn. Affairs and Trade, Govt. of Australia, Canberra, 1996, Dept. Sci. and Industry and Tourism, Canberra, 1996. Author: (in Oriya lang.) Berlin Berlin, 1995 (Raja Ram Mohan Roy award 1997), Kichhi Katha, 1995; contbr. articles to profl. jours. Pres. Dipti Coop. Housing soc., Ministry of Sci. and Tech., New Delhi, 1990-91. Natl. Scholarship by Ministry of Eucation and Soc. Welfare Govmt. of India, New Delhi, 1973, Natl. Scholarship by Ministry of Education and Culture Govmt. of India, New Delhi, 1976-78, Jr. Rsch. Fellowship of Counc. of Scientific and Indsl. Rsch., New Delhi, 1978-79; Assn. Commonwealth Univs. scholar, 1982-86; Asia in Australia Coun. fellow, 1995. Fellow Geol. Soc. India; mem. Australian Petroleum Cons.' Assn. (bd. dirs. 1995—). Avocations: photography, yoga, cricket. Home: 1/30-32 Coleridge St, Riverwood NSW 2210, Australia Office: Bridge Bus Coll, 83-85 Castlereagh St, Sydney NSW 2000, Australia

DAS, NIBARAN CHANDRA, mathematician, educator, researcher; b. Karimganj, Assam, India, July 2, 1954; s. Nirode Behari and Sohagmani Das; m. Saswati Purkayastha, July 12, 1986; children: Anirban, Nilanjana. Grad., Gauhati (India) U., 1975, MSc, 1977, PhD, 1995, Grad., 1975. Tchr. Kaliganj H.S., Karimganj, 1978-85; head dept. math. RS Girls' Coll., Karimganj, 1985—; rsch. guide Gauhati U., 1997—; head examiner Assam U., Silchar, India, 1996—. Contbr. articles to profl. jours. Univ. Grant Commn. Delhi Tchr. fellow, 1994, Internat. Conf., 1996. Mem. Assam Sci. Soc. (resource person math. tchg. 1997), Rabindrasadan T.C. Coop. Soc. (sec. 1988—), Assam Acad. Math. (exec. mem. 1990-96, 98—, sec. Karimganj bd. 1997—), Alahabad Math. Soc., Indian Soc. of Theoretical and Applied Mechanics, Siksha Sangrakshan Samity (ward 9 pres. 1994—). Avocations: computer programming. Home: Nilmani Rd, Karimganj 788710, India Office: RS Girls College, Main Rd, Karimganj 788710, India

DAS, NIRANJAN, engineering educator and researcher; b. Cuttack, Orissa, India, Aug. 14, 1942; s. Krishna Chandra and Soubhagini (Rath) D.; m. Manorama Das, Nov. 15, 1969; children: Bimelandu, Purnendu. BSc with honors, Ravenshaw Coll., Utkal U., 1962; BTech with honors, Indian Inst. Tech., Kharagpur, 1967; MSc in Engring., Sambalpur U., 1977; PhD in Engring., Jadavpur U., Calcutta, 1982. Jr. telecomms. engr. Talcher Thermal Power Sta., Orissa, 1967-71; asst. telecomms. engr., telecomms. divsn. Orissa (India) Pub. Svc. Commn., 1971-72; lectr. electronics U. Coll. Engring., Burla, Sambalpur U., 1972-77, reader electronics, 1977-90, prof. electronics, 1990—, dean planning and coordination, 1996-97; chief investigator Delhi Dept. Electronics sponsored tech. devel. project, 1986-89, 90-94. Contbr. articles to profl. jours. Expert, selection com. Union Pub. Svc. Commn., Delhi, 1992, Orissa Pub. Svc. Commn., Cuttack, 1986; mem. vis. team All India Coun. Tech. Edn., Delhi, 1998. Mem. IEEE, Inst. Electronics and Telecom. Engrs. Avocations: reading newspaper and booklets. Home: QR 5R/6 UCE, Burla, 768018 Burla India Office: UCE Burla, 768018 District-Sambalpur India

DAS, SAMIR KUMAR, software company executive; b. Calcutta, Bengal, India, Jan. 20, 1939; s. Susil Chitta and Sarasi Bala (Mohapatra) D.; m. Zeenat Neemuchwala, Mar. 8, 1972 (div.); children: Swagata, Saurav; m. Sangeeta Pillai, 1980; children: Sandeep, Sauvik. BA with hons., U. Calcutta, 1959, DSW, 1962; MBA, U. Hawaii, 1968. Personnel officer Hindustan Steel, Ltd., Durgapur, India, 1960-69, Air-India, Bombay, India, 1969-72; personnel mgr. The Metal Box Co. of India, Calcutta, 1972-74; gen. mgr. personnel and corp. planning Voltas, Ltd., Bombay, 1974-84; group v.p. personnel United Breweries Group, Bombay, 1984-89; group v.p. human resources devel. RPG Enterprises Ltd., Bombay, 1989-92; v.p. Deepak Fertilisers and Petrochems. Corp. Ltd., Pune, India, 1992-94, Voltas Ltd., Bombay, 1994-98; human resources dir. Softpros Inc., Atlanta, 2000—; ops. dir. Software Solutions Group, Atlanta; vis. prof. Jamnalal Bajaj Inst. Mgmt. Studies, Bombay, 1976-85; del. to world co. on behalf of Asia Pacific Fedn. Pers. Mgmt. Assn., World Fedn. Pers. Mgmt. Assn., 1988-92; adj. faculty, prof. orgn. behavior & HRM Spjain Inst. of Mgmt. and Rsch., Mumbai, India.cons. in field. Author: (presidential address) Personnel Profession in India, 1985. Fellow Brit. Inst. Mgmt., Nat. Inst. Pers. Mgmt. (pres. 1984-85, Profl. Excellence award 1986); mem. Indian Soc. Tng. and Devel., Nat. Human Resources Devel. Network (founding), Strategic Mgmt. Soc. U.S.A., Am. Soc. Tng. and Devel., Inst. Pers. Mgmt., Am. Alumni Assn. (pres. 1980), Indo-Am. Soc. (chmn. acad. programs 1991-94, 96-98, chmn. fin. adminstrn. Bombay chpt. 1995-96, exec. com.), Indian Soc. Human Resources Devel. (pres. 1997-98), Bombay Gymkhana Club, Royal Presidency Golf Club, Bombay Yacht Club, Karnataka Golf Assn. Baptist. Home: 5927 Myrtlewood Ct Tucker GA 30084-2073

DAS, SANTANU, engineering educator; b. Serampore, India, Oct. 3, 1965; s. Ajay Shankar and Gouri Rani (Sur) D.; m. Manimala Das, Jan. 15, 1998; 1 child, Sharadia. B Mech. Engring., Jadapur U., Calcutta, India, 1988, M Mech. Engring., 1990; PhD in Engring., Indian Inst. Tech., Kharagpur, 1996. Mgmt. trainee Projects & Devel. India Ltd., New Delhi, 1990-91; lectr. Dr. Babasaheb Ambedkar Technol. U., Lonere, India, 1994-98; asst. prof. Kalyani (India) Engring. Coll., 1998—. Fellow Indian Instn. Prodn. Engring. (life); mem. Instn. Engrs. India (life). Avocations: reading stories, novels, poetry. Home: B/1 195, Kalyani 741 235, India Office: Kalyani Engring Coll, Kalyani 741 235, India

DAS, SHANKAR PRASAD, physicist; b. Calcutta, W. Bengal, India, Mar. 16, 1959; s. Sudhir K. and Gita Rani (Mitra) D.; m. Soma Bhattacharyya, Apr. 15, 1990. BSc, Presidency Coll., Calcutta, India, 1979; MSc, Calcutta U., 1981; PhD, U. Chgo., 1986. Postdoctoral fellow U. Fla., Gainesville, 1986-88, 90-91, U. Utrecht, The Netherlands, 1988-90; vis. rsch. scientist Bhabha Atomic Rsch. Ctr. S.N. Bose Inst., India, 1991-93; vis. rsch. scientist Inst. Physik U. Mainz; reader Saha Inst., India, 1993; asst. prof. Jaharalal Nehru U., India, 1993-99, assoc. prof., 1999—; vis. rsch. scientist The Hahn Meitner Inst., Berlin, 1996. Contbr. over 30 articles to profl. jours. including: Phys. Rev., Phys. Rev. Letters, Jour. Chem. Physics, Jour. Stats. Physics. Recipient Award NSF, 1997—. Office: Jawaharlal Nehru U, Sch Phys Sci, New Delhi 110067, India

DAS, SUBHAJYOTI, hydrogeologist, consultant; b. Calcutta, India, Jan. 22, 1939; s. Byomkesh and Parulbala Das; m. Depali Karmakar, Nov. 24, 1969; 1 child, Dwaipayan. BSc with honors, Presidency Coll., Calcutta, India, 1959, MSc in Geology, 1961; cert., Colo. State U. Cert. merit U.S. Geol. Survey; cert. Am. Water Found, 1989-90. Jr. rsch. fellow Coun. Sci. and Indsl. Rsch., Calcutta, 1963; geologist Geol. Survey India, Calcutta, 1963-71, sr. geologist, 1971-72; sr. hydrogeologist Ctrl. Ground Water Bd., Faridabad, India, 1972-86; dir. Ctrl. Ground Water Bd., Bhubaneswar, India, 1986-97; ground water cons. Dept. for Internat. Devel., Govt. U.K., 1998; mem. sec. Orissa State Level Study Group on Estimation of Ground Water Resources, Bhubaneswar, 1986-94; mem. tech. coord. com. UNDP Kasai Subarnarekha Project, Jamsedpur, India, 1986-89; mem. sec. source finding com. Tech. Mission on Drinking Water, Bhubaneswar, 1987-97; dir., coord. conjuctive use studies in Hirakud command, mem. tech. adv. com. Ctrl. Ground Water Bd., Bhubaneswar, 1992-97; guest lectr. Indian Sch. Mines, Dhanbad, India, 1998. Prin. author: Hydrogeological Atlas of Orissa, 1996, Manual on Hydrograph Network Stations, 1996, National Perspective Plan for Recharge to Groundwater by Using Surplus Monsoon Runoff, 1996; author: Hydrogeological Features of Deltas and Estuarine Tracts in India, 1991, Aquifer Characteristics of Fractured Basement Rocks of Orissa, 1997. Recipient Fellowship award Indian Assn. Hydrologist; UN Devel. Project fellow, N.Y., 1989. Fellow Geol. Soc. India; mem. Assn. Geoscientists for Internat. Devel., N.Y. Acad. Scis. Hindu. Avocations: reading literature on arts, history, philosophy, music. Home and Office: c/o N Mohanty, 18 Madhusudan Nagar, Bhubaneswar 751001, India

DASBURG, JOHN HAROLD, air transportation executive; b. N.Y.C., Jan. 7, 1943; s. Jean Henry and Alice Etta Dasburg; m. Mary Lois Diaz, July 6, 1968; children: John Peter, Kathryn. AA, U. Miami, 1963; BS in Indsl. Engring., U. Fla., 1966, MBA, 1971, JD, 1973. Bar: Fla. 1974; CPA, Fla., Md. Staff Peat Marwick Mitchell & Co., Jacksonville, Fla., 1973-78, tax ptnr. in charge, 1978-80; v.p. tax Marriott Corp., Washington, 1980-82, v.p. fin., 1982-84, sr. v.p., 1984-85, exec. v.p., CFO, chief real estate officer, 1985-88, pres. lodging group, 1988-89; pres., CEO Northwest Airlines, 1990—; bd. dirs. St. Paul Cos., Owens Corning. Contbr. articles to profl. jours. Lt. (j.g.) USN, 1966-69, Vietnam. Republican. Roman Catholic.

DASCAL, MARCELO, philosophy educator, dean; b. São Paulo, Brazil, Nov. 11, 1940; arrived in Israel, 1965; s. Adolpho and Sarah (Schwartz) D.; m. Varda Ghilscher, Feb. 29, 1964; children: Hagit, Shlomit, Tamar. Lic. philosophy, U. São Paulo, 1963, grad. elec. engring., 1964; postgrad. in linguistics, U. Provence, Aix-en-Provence, 1965; PhD, Hebrew U., Jerusalem, 1973. Lectr. philosophy and linguistics U. Mass., Amherst, 1973-74; prof. linguistics State U. Campinas, Brazil, 1975-85; sr. lectr. philosophy Tel Aviv U., 1977-81, assoc. prof. philosophy, 1981-90, prof. philosophy, 1991—, dean humanities, 1995-2000; vis. assoc. prof. philosophy U. Calif., Berkeley, 1980-81. Author: Philosophy of Science, 1964, 2nd edit., 1966, Leibniz's Semiotics, 1978, Pragmatics and the Philosophy of Mind, 1983, Leibniz Language, Signs and Thought, 1987; editor: Methodological Foundations of Linguistics 4 vols., 1978-82, Dialogue--An Interdisciplinary Approach, 1985, Knowledge and Politics, 1989, The Institution of Philosophy, 1989, Cultural Relativism and Philosophy, 1991, Philosophy of Language: A Handbook of Contemporary Resarch, 2 books, 1992-96, Leibniz and Adam, 1993, Controversies, 1998, Pragmatics, 1999, Misunderstanding, 1999, others; editor Manuscrito, 177-99, Pragmatics and Cognition, 1991—. Fellow Rsch. Ctr. for Lang. and Semiotics, Bloomington, Ind., 1973, Netherlands Inst. for Advanced Studies, 1985-86, Inst. for Advanced Studies, Jerusalem, 1994-95. Mem. Internat. Assn. for the Study of Controversies (founder), Internat. Network for Econ. Method (founder), Internat. Soc. for the Study of Argumentation (Israeli rep.), Soc. d'Histoire et Epistemologie des Scis. du Lang. (mem. internat. com.), New Israeli Philos. Assn. (pres. 1996—), Jerusalem Philos. Soc., Leibniz Gesellschaft, Cognitive Sci. Soc., Internat. Assn. Dialogue Analysis. Avocations: singing in choir, playing clarinette. Office: Tel Aviv Univ, 69978 Tel Aviv Israel

D'ASCANIO, VINCENZO MARIA, chemical company executive; b. Milan, May 10, 1954; s. Luigi and Clara (Golato) D'A.; m. Daniela Polizzi, July 24, 1982; children: Margherita, Costanza. Degree in chem. engring., Poly. Inst., Milan, 1978; degree in bus. adminstrn., Bucconi U., Milan, 1988. Design engr. Chemint, Milan, 1978-80; technologist Exxon Chem., Vado Ligure, Italy, 1981-82, prodn. mgr., 1983-84; product mgr. Exxon Chem., Brussels, 1985-86; R & D mgr. Exxon Chem., Rouen, France, 1987-88; project mgr. Exxon, Florham Park, N.J., 1989; sales mgr. Exxon, Singapore, 1990; bus. unit mgr. Exxon, Paris, 1991-94, London, 1995; purchasing mgr. Exxon, Rome, 1996-97; indsl. dir. Air Liquide, Milan, 1998—. Mem. SAE, Engrs. Order. Roman Catholic. Avocations: sailing, cycling, skiing, golf, tennis. Office: Air Liquide Italia, Via Capecelatro 64, 20148 Milan Italy

DASCHUTA, MIGUEL ISMAEL ALEJANDRO, advertising executive; b. Buenos Aires, Nov. 9, 1943; s. Mauricio and Isabel (Hernando) D.; m. Norma Beatriz Meline; children: Alejandro, Vanesa, Patricio. Student Architecture, U. Buenos Aires, 1962-63. Jr. account exec. Yuste Publicidad, Buenos Aires, 1965-67, account exec., 1967-69; account exec. Ricardo de Luca Publicidad, Buenos Aires, 1969-73, account dir., 1973-75, ptnr., bd. dirs., account gen. dir., 1975-90, ptnr., v.p., gen. mgr., 1990-94, ptnr., pres., gen. mgr., 1994—. Mem. acad. coun. Pub. Affairs Sch. Mem. Argentine Assn. Adv. Agys. (mng. commn., acad. coun., bd. dirs.), Fundacion Empresaria Para La Calidad y La Excelencia (founder, adminstrv. coun.), Fundacion Premio Nat. a La Calidad (founder). Roman Catholic. Avocations: squash, fishing, running, sailing. Office: Ricardo De Luca Publicidad, Ricardo de Luca Publicidad, Alicia M deJusto 1930 3o, Buenos Aires 1107, Argentina

DASGUPTA, DIPANKAR KIRONCHANDRA, anesthesiologist, internist; b. Barishal, Bengal, India, Apr. 11, 1941; s. Kironchandra Satish and Savitri Kiron (Neogi) D.; m. Indrani D. Dutta, May 23, 1950; 1 child, Arijit. M.B.B.S., Calcutta (India) U., 1964; MS, Bombay U., 1969. Resident in anesthesiology Safderjang Hosp., New Delhi, 1965; registrar G.S.M. Coll., Bombay, 1965-68, lectr., 1968-69, reader, 1969-73; assoc. prof. B.Y.L.N. Med. Coll., Bombay, 1973-75, 1975-76; assoc. prof. G.S.M.C., Bombay, 1976-90; cons., prof., head. dept. Tata Meml. Hosp., Bombay, 1990—, in-chg. anesthesiologist ICU, Pain Clinic, 1996—; expert advisor Indian U.; guest lectr. in field internationally; examiner for postgrad. for 39 Indian univs. Contbr. articles to profl. jours.; editl. bd. Indian Jour. Anesthesiology, 1976—. Mem. Indian Soc. Anesthetists (pres. 1992, 93, gen. sec. 1980-86, mem. governing coun. 1976-79, 87-91, 92-95), Dr. G.S. Ambardekar Soc. (gen. sec. 1973-79), Indian Soc. Pain, Indian Soc. Trauma, Indian Soc. Anaesthesiologist (pres. 1992-93). Mem. Universal Brotherhood. Avocations: sports, music, performing arts, pneumismatic philately, social work. Home: Murari Ghag Marg, Prabhadevi, Bombay 400025, India Office: Tata Memorial Hospital, E Borges Marg, Bombay 400012, India

DASGUPTA, GOUTAM, physics educator; b. Raiganj, India, Mar. 8, 1963; s. Amaresh and Reba (Sensarma) D. BSc with honors, Raiganj U., 1985, BEd, 1992; MSc in Physics, North Bengal U., India, 1988, PhD in Thermal Diffusion, 2000. Asst. tchr. Sudarsanpur Dwarica Prasad Uchha, Vidyachakra, India, 1988—. Contbr. articles to profl. jours.; inventor in field. Avocations: literature, games, sports. Home: Milanpara, Raiganj 733134, India Office: Sudarsanpur Dwarica Prasad, Vidyachakra, Raiganj 733134, India

DASGUPTA, SAMIR, scientist; b. Barisal, India, Jan. 6, 1942; s. Surendralal and Sova D.; m. Banani; children: Anouska, Arijit, Surupa. BS with distinction, Calcutta U., India, 1961, BS in Tech., 1963; PhD, Massey U., Palmerston North, New Zealand, 1996. Asst. dir. chems. Indian Stds. Inst., New Delhi, 1966-72; tech. mgr. Azar Leather Co., Teheran, Iran, 1977-81; chemist Yorkshire Chems., Selby, England, 1972-77; tech. mgr. leather Yorkshire Chems., Selby, Eng., 1977-84; tech. dir. Atlas Refinery, Inc., N.J., 1984-90; scientist tanning tech. New Zealand Leather & Shoe Rsch. Assn., Palmerston North, 1991—. Contbr. articles to profl. jours; patentee in field. Fellow Soc. Leather Technologists and Chemists. Avocations: writing poems, short stories, trekking, gardening.

DASGUPTA, SANTANU, biological scientist, researcher, educator; b. Barisal, Bengal, India, Oct. 9, 1945; arrived in India, 1947; s. Sourendra Nath and Kamala (Sengupta) D.; m. Ryoko Kuriyama, May 1, 1983 (div. 1996); m. Anna Lena Aslund. BSc, Calcutta U., 1965, MSc, 1968, PhD, 1973. Lectr. Birla Inst. Tech. Scis., Pilani, India, 1973-75; postdoctoral fellow Oak Ridge (Tenn.) Nat. Lab., 1975-77, Inst. Biophys. & Molecular Biology, Madison, Wis., 1977-82, McArdle Lab. U. Wis., Madison, 1981-82; scientist NIDDKD NIH, Bethesda, Md., 1982-87, NCI NIH, Bethesda, Md., 1987-89; guest rschr. BMC Uppsala (Sweden) U., 1989-91; scientist NCI FCRDC, Frederick, Md., 1991-95; guest rschr. Stockholm U., 1995-97; rsch. scientist Uppsala U. BMC, 1997—. Contbr. articles to profl. jours. Mem. AAAS. Avocations: reading, film, photography, travel. Home: Norbyvagen 67AII, S-75239 Uppsala Sweden Office: Uppsala U BMC Inst Cell, Box 596, S-75124 Uppsala Sweden Address: U Uppsala Ctr Biomed, Dept Microbiol Box 581, 751 23 Uppsala Sweden

DASGUPTA, TARA PRASAD, chemistry educator; b. Calcutta, India, Jan. 29, 1941; s. Sushil Kumar and Tarubala (Roy) D.; m. Sibani Sen-Majumdar, May 30, 1970; children: Sutopa, Shuvra. BSc, Calcutta U., 1958, PhD, 1968; MSc, Bihar U., India, 1961. Rsch. fellow Univ. Coll., London, 1970-71; sr. rsch. assoc. SUNY, Buffalo, 1971-74; lectr. in phys. chemistry U. West Indies, Jamaica, 1974-77, sr. lectr. in phys. chemistry, 1977-80, prof. inorganic chemistry, 1980—, chmn. chemistry dept., 1992——; cons. Sci. Rsch. Coun., Jamaica, 1990-91. Editor Jamaican Jour. Sci. and Tech., 1990—; contbr. over 80 articles to internat. jours. Recipient Vice Chancellor's award U. W.I., 1996. Fellow Royal Soc. Chemistry, Caribbean Acad. Sci.; mem. Am. Chem. Soc., Caribbean Acad. Sci., Jamaican Soc. Scientists and Technologists (Natural Sci. award 1995). Home: 16 University Crescent, Kingston 6, Jamaica Office: U West Indies, Mona Chemistry Dept, Kingston 7, Jamaica

DASH, MADHAB CHANDRA, ecology educator; b. Puri, Orissa, India, Nov. 28, 1939; s. Harekrushna and Mukta Mani Dash; m. Sovita Hatial, Oct. 1, 1944; children: Sharmila, Dalia, Papiya (twins), Satya Prakash. BSc with hons., Utkal (India) U., 1961, MSc, 1963; PhD, U. Calgary, Alberta, Can. Lectr. zoology Orissa Govt. Ednl. Svc., 1963-67; rsch. asst. U, Calgary, Can., 1967-70, postdoctoral fellow, 1970; lectr. zoology Orissa Govt. Ednl. Svc., 1970-71, Berhampur U., India, 1971-73; reader ecology Sambalpur U. Sch. Life Scis., India, 1973-76, prof., 1976-99; mem. senate and acad. coun. U. Sambalpur, India, 1974-87, syndicate 1978-81, 85-86, 92-94; mem. bd. mgmt. Univ. Coll. Engring., Burla, India, 1992-95, G.M. Autonomous Coll. Sambalpur, 1992-95; mem. exec. body Orissa Sci. Acad., Bhubaneswar, India, 1992-95; v.p. Nat. Inst. Ecology, India, 1994-96; mem. nat. com. on Environ. Impact Assn. and environ. mgmt. of mining projects, Dept. Environment and Forests, Govt. India, New Delhi, 1995-97; mem. bd. govs. Regional Engring. Coll., Rourkel, India, 1996-2000. Author: Fundamentals of Ecology, 1993, Textbook of Higher Secondary Zoology, 1997; co-author: The Turtle Paradise, 1990, Brackish Water Prawn Culture, 1994; contbr. chpts to: Animal Energetics, 1987, Soil Biology Guide, 1990, Grassland Ecosystems of the World, 1979, Grasslands, System Analysis and Man, 1980, Soil Organisms and Litter Decomposition in Tropics, 1995. Mem. Orissa Bigyan Prachar Samiti, Burla, India, 1975—; founder, pres. Orissa Environ. Consciousness Soc., Jyoti Vihar, Sambalpur, 1981, life mem.; pres. Jyoti Vihar H.S. Mng. Com., 1985-86; mem. Orissa Environment Protection Com., 1993-96, Oriss Bigyan Acad., Bhubaneswar, India. Recipient Samanta Chandra Sekhar award, Orissa Sci. Acad. and Govt. of Orissa, Bhubaneswar, India, 1991, India Internat. Friendship award, India Internat. Friendship Soc., New Delhi, 1997, gold medal Zool. Soc. India, 1998. Fellow Nat. Acad. Scis. India; mem. Indian Sci. Congress (pres. zoology, entomology and fisheries sect. 1998-99). Avocations: popularizing sci., cards and indoor

games, comty. activities, family time, travel. Office: A-118 Nilakantha Nagar, Bhubanes Orissa 751012, India

DASHEVSKII, VENIAMIN YAKOVLEVICH, scinetist/metallurgist; b. Zaporozhie, Russia, Oct. 13, 1933; s. Yakov Veniaminovich and Sarra Michaylovna (Boruchovich) D.; m. Emma Vasilyevna Popenko, Nov. 28, 1968. Cert., Novokuznetsk, Russia, 1951; engr., Moscow Steel and Alloys Inst., Moscow, 1956; postgrad. student, Russian Acad. Sci., Moscosw, 1960-63; D in philosophy, Russian Acad. of Scis., Moscow, 1966; D in sci., Russian Acad. of Scis., 1993. Engr. Ferroalloy Plant, Chelyabinsk, Russia, 1956-60; researcher Inst. of Metallurgy Russian Acad. Scis., Moscow, 1963-77, sr. researcher, 1977-91, leading researcher, 1991-96, prin. researcher, 1996—. Scientific editor Russian Acad. of Scis. Publ., 1968-90; mem. editl. bd. Jour. Steel, Moscow, 1991—; inventor in field; contbr. numerous articles to profl. jours. Mem. Fed. Coun. and Resources Saving and Wastes Recycling Min. of Sci. & Tech. Russian Fedn., 1996—. Recipient Laureate of Premium of the USSR Soviet Ministries, 1991, Premium of the Gov. Russian Fedn., 1997; rsch. grants Internat. Sci. Found., 1994, 95. Mem. N.Y. Acad. Scis. Avocations: history of science and engineering development, literature. Home: Shvernika 9-4-48, 117449 Moscow Russia Office: Inst Metallurgy and Material Sci, Russ Acad Scis Leninsky Prospect 49, 117334 Moscow Russia

DASHO SONAM TOBGYE, judge. Chief justice High Ct. of Bhutan, Thimphu, Bhutan. Office: Kingdom of Bhutan, High Court, Thimphu Bhutan*

DASHTI, HUSSEIN MOHAMED, surgeon, educator, researcher; b. Kuwait, Kuwait, Feb. 16, 1948; s. Mohamed and Mariam Dashti; m. Zakyah Sahaf Alimohamed, 1976; children: Ali Hussain, Mohammed Hussein, Sadeq Hussein, Maryam H. MB BS, G.S. Med. Coll., Bombay U., 1975; MD, PhD, U. Lund, Sweden, 1986. House resident in gen. surgery and gen. medicine Amiri Hosp., Sabah Hosp., Psychiat. Hosp., Kuwait, 1975-77; asst. registrar in surgery Amiri Hosp., 1977-79; registrar in surgery Amimi and Farwaniya Hosp., 1979-82; registrar Farwaniah Hosp., 1987-88; acting sr. registrar in surgery Salmiya Clinic, 1988, sr. registrar in surgery, 1988-93; asst. prof. surgery Kuwait U., 1988-93, assoc. prof. surgery, 1993-97, prof. surgery, 1997—, vice dean adminstr., 1994—, mem. faculty coun., 1988—, mem. curriculum and assessment com., 1993—; cons. surgeon Salmiya Clinic, 1993—; participant, presenter numerous confs. Mem. editl. bd. Kuwait Med. Assn. Jour., 1993—, Jour. Med. Principles and Practice; mem. editl. adv. bd. Nutrition Jour., 1995; contbr. more than 85 articles to profl. jours. Recipient Best Sci. Rsch. award in med. scis. KFAS, 1995, Albert Schweitzer Golden Grand medal Polish Acad. Medicine. Fellow Internat. Coll. Surgeons (pres. elect Kuwait chpt. 1993—), ACS; mem. Kuwait Med. Assn., Afro-Asian Soc. for Advancement Trace Element Rsch., European soc. Surg. Rsch., Internat. Soc. Surgery. Office: Kuwait U Dept Surgery, PO Box 24923, Safat 13100, Kuwait

DA SILVA, DIONE BATISTA VILA-NOVA, plastic surgeon; b. Recife, Pernambuco, Brazil, July 25, 1948; parents Manoel Batista Silva and Antonia Vila-Nova Silva. Med. degree, U. Fed. Pernambuco, 1973; specialist in gen. surgery, Santa Casa de Misericórdia de Santos Hosp., São Paulo, 1976; specialist in plastic surgery, Serviço de Ciurgia Plástica de Santos, São Paulo, 1979. Med. and law diplomate. Staff Regional Hosp. Vale do Ribeira, Pariguera-Açu, 1974-76; staff emergency surgeon Pronto Socorro de Santos, 1975-98; chief dept. plastic surgery Hosp. Estivadores de Santos, 1982-90; chief and dir. dept. plastic surgery Hosp. Beneficencia Portuguesa Santos, 1990—; dir. dept. plastic surgery. Editor, contbr.: Manual do Residente de Pediatria, 1981, Cirurgia Plastica na Infancia, 1989; contbr.: VIII Internaional Congress of Plastic Surgery, 1983, Annals of the Brazilian Symposium on Facial Contourn, 1983. Recipient Silver Plate, Santa Cecilia dos Bandeirantes U., 1991, 92, 93, 94. Mem. Brazilian Soc. Plastic Surgery (titular mem., mem. ethics commn. 1994-95, examiner 1994-95), Ibero-Am. Fedn. Plastic Reconstructive Surgery (titular mem.). Roman Catholic. Avocations: swimming, running. Fax: 55-13-2895475. E-mail: jackdi@iron.com.br. Home: Ap 13, Tolentino Filgueiras 122, 11060471 São Paulo Brazil Office: Hosp Benefic Port Santos, Bernardino de Campos 47, 11065000 Santos Brazil

DA SILVA, JOAÓ EDUARDO NOVA FORTUNATO, engineering executive; b. Germiston, Gauteng, South Africa, Sept. 10, 1967; s. Manuel Joaó Fortunato and Eva Maria Milhazes (Nova) Da S.; m. Veronica Taurino, Sept. 18, 1993; children: Valentina, Bianca. BSc, Wits U., Gauteng, South Africa, 1992; MBA cum laude, Thames Valley U., London, 1999. Mng. dir. Cosira Group, Gauteng, 1992—. Avocations: equities, reading, squash. Home: 4 Talisman Pl Talisman Ave, 2008 Bedforduiew South Africa Office: Cosira Group, 38 Lower Germiston Rd, 2088 Heriotoale South Africa

DA SILVA, JOSE APARECIDO, psychology educator, consultant; b. Jaboticabal, Sao Paulo, Brazil, Sept. 25, 1952; s. Joaquim Rodrigues and Maria Jose Ferreira (Marques) Da S.; m. Deise Almeida, May 21, 1977; children: Daniel Almeida Da Silva, Juliana Almeida Da Silva. BA in Psychology with Honors, U. Sao Paulo, 1976, MA, 1979, PhD, 1981. Instr. U. Sao Paulo, Ribeirao Preto, 1977-79; asst. prof. U. Sao Paulo, 1979-81, asst. dr. prof., 1981-84, prof. psychology, 1984—; prof. Livre-Docente, 1984—, full prof., 1990, vice-chancellor, 1992-96, chancellor, 1996—; vis. prof. U. Calif., Santa Barbara, 1982-83; cons. reader Perceptual and Motor Skills, Missoula, Mont., 1983—, Psychol. Reports, 1983—, Psicologia, Sao Paulo, 1985—, Perception & Psychophysics, 1985—; cons. editor Nat. Rsch. Coun., Brazil, 1985—, CAPES, Brazil, 1985—; chmn. CNPq, 1999—. Author: Annual Research Report, 1984; contbr. articles to profl. jours. Recipient Emilio Myra y Lopez prize for monograph, 1982; grantee Nat. Rsch. Coun., 1979—, Fundacao de Amparo à Pesquisa do Estado de Sao Paulo, 1982—, Am. P sychol. Found., 1984—. Mem. APA, Psychol. Soc. Ribeirao Preto (officer 1977-78, 80-82), Psychonomic Soc., Brazilian Assn. Advancement of Sci., Ribeirao Preto Country Club, Sun Valley Club. Mem. Brazilian Dem. Party. Roman Catholic. Avocations: soccer, chess. Home: 465, Rua Antonio Ribeiro Rezende, 14 100 Ribeirao Preto SP, Brazil Office: 3900 Ribeirao Preto, Av dos Bandeirantes, 14 100 Sao Paulo Brazil

DA SILVA, LUIS FERNANDO, physicist and researcher; b. Santiago, Chile, Oct. 12, 1938; s. Fernando and Uberlinda Maria (Matus) Da S.; m. Rosa Eugenia Reveco, Aug. 4, 1960; children: Joao, Janio, Geir, Jilmara, Gilka. Licenciado, U. Chile, Santiago, 1971; M. Physics, Cath. U., Santiago, 1988. Prof. U. Técnica del Estado, Santiago, 1962-64, U. Chile, Antofagasta, 1964-65, U. de Concepción, Chile, 1965-71; prof. physics U. Técnica F. Santa Maria, Valparaiso, Chile, 1971—. Author: Elasticity, 1993; contbr. articles to profl. jours.; mem. editl. bd. Libertad 250, 1993-96. Grantee Sci. Coop. Program, Spain-Chile, 1994-96, CYTED, Spain, 1996-99. Mem. AAAS, Chilean Soc. Physics, Am. Phys. Soc., Indsl. and Applied Physics, Brazilian Soc. Physics, Chilean Writers Soc. (sec. 1994). Office: Univ Técnica Federico, Santa Maria Depto de Fisica, 110-V Valparaiso Chile

DA SILVA, PAULO AFONSO, engineering educator; b. Rio De Janeiro, Sept. 29, 1949; s. Washington L. and Rosa M. (Oliveira) Da S.; children: Mariana, Rafael. BS in Stats., Nat. Sch. Statis. Sci., Rio de Janeiro, Brazil, 1978; BS in Telecomm. Engring., Mil. Inst. Engring., Rio de Janeiro, Brazil, 1979; MSc, Fed. U. Rio de Janeiro, 1981; PhD, Fla. Inst. Tech., Melbourne, Fla., 1989. Cert. quality engr., reliability engr., quality auditor. Full prof. Mil. Inst. Engring., Rio de Janeiro, 1980-91, 92-94, chair Systems and Computer Grad. Program, 1991-92, chair rsch. grad. programs, 1994-95, dept. head systems engring., 1995-97, full prof., 1997—; publs. dir. Ops. Rsch. Brazilian Soc., Rio de Janeiro, 1986; v.p. Math. Edn., Rio de Janeiro, 1990-94; cons. Rsch. Nat. Coun., Brasilia, Brazil, 1993—. Author: Principles of Statistical Methods, 1998, Statistics for Engineers, 1997, Probabilities and Statistics, 1999, Probabilidad y Estadistica, 2000; assoc. editor: Interpersonal Computing and Technology, 1992—, The Electronic Jour. on Virtual Culture, 1992—; contbg. editor: Internat. Abstracts of OR; nat. corr. editor: Internat. Assn. Statis. Edn., 1999—. Recipient Marshall Hermes medal Brazilian Army, 1971, 1st Pl. in Telecomm. Engring. Graduation, Brit. Army, 1979, Peacemaker medal Brazilian Army, 1991. Mem. N.Y. Acad. Scis., Am. Soc. for Quality, Sigma Xi, Fla. Tech. Club. Avocations: keyboarding, running. Home: Rua Voluntarios Da Patria, 474/701 Humaitá, 22270010 Rio de Janeiro Brazil Office: Mil Inst Engring, Praca Gen Tiburcio 80, 22290270 Rio de Janeiro Brazil

DA SILVEIRA, GUILHERME, business consultant, actor; b. Rio de Janeiro, Oct. 16, 1942; s. Olympio Coutinho and Ilka Diniz Da Silveira. Civil Engr., Fed. U. Rio De Janeiro, 1967; MS, U. Calif., Berkeley, 1970; Diploma, Superior Sch. War, Rio de Janeiro, 1984. Cert. civil engr. Engr. Dept. Pub. Works, Rio de Janeiro, 1964-96; ret., 1996; chief tributary control svc. Dept. Pub. Works, Rio de Janeiro, 1994-96; pvt. bus. cons. Rio de Janeiro, 1996—; asst. prof. Fed. U. Rio de Janeiro, 1967-69; mem. staff Harvard U., Cambridge, Mass., 1969; prof. Cath. U. Rio de Janeiro, 1971-78; dep. supr. mineral engring. Brazilian Nucelar Enterprises, Inc., Rio de Janeiro, 1978-89; project mgr. Inst. Mcpl. Planning, Rio de Janeiro, 1989-92; chmn., pres. 10th Brazilian Symposium on Ops. Rsch., Rio de Janeiro, 1977; cons. in field. Author: Brazilian External Debt: Policy and Strategies Compatible With Economic Development, 1984; contbr. articles to profl. jours.; designer in field; actor working in: Romeo and Juliet, 1997, Crazy Encidity, 1997, What If in Spite of Everything We Love Each Other?, 1997, Villa-Lobos, A Life of Passion, 2000. Coord. polit. campaign Fed. Congressman/Dem. Labor Party, Rio de Janeiro, 1990; mem. suprapartisan com. Fernando Henrique Cardoso Presdl. Campaign, 1994; vol. Solazer-Leisure Handicapped Persons, Rio de Janeiro, 1990—; co-founder SorRio Soc. to Assist Poor Street Children, 1995; mem. regional exec. coun. Govt. of State of Guanabara, Brazil, 1968-69. Interam. U. Found. scholar, 1967; Orgn. Am. States fellow, 1969-70. Fellow Brazilian Soc. Ops. Rsch. (dr., 2d treas. 1975-83), Soc. Engrs. and Archs. Rio de Janeiro; mem. Am. Pub. Works Assn., U. Calif. Engring. Alumni Soc., Brazilian Jockey Club, Club dos Marimbas (fin. counselor 1993-97), Lions (Pres.'s Appreciation medal 1978, dir., 1st treas. 1977-79). Roman Catholic. Home: Block 1 Apt 603, Rua Santa Clara 431, 22.041-010 Rio de Janeiro Brazil

DA SILVEIRA, MARCOS AZEVEDO, mathematician; b. Rio de Janeiro, Brazil, Jan. 26, 1952; s. Mário-Marcos and Amélia da Silveira; m. Marlise A.V. de Araújo, June 12, 1994. B in Math., Pontificia U. Católica, Rio de Janeiro, 1974, M in Elec. Engring., 1976; DSc, U. Paul Sabatier, 1981. Assoc. prof. Cath. U. Rio de Janeiro, 1975—; rschr. CNRS, Toulouse, France, 1989. Office: EE Dept PUC-Rio #225, Rua Marques de Sao Vicente, Rio de Janeiro 22453900, Brazil

DASKALOV, GEORGI MIHAYLOV, scientist; b. Varna, Bulgaria, July 4, 1963; s. Mihail Georgiev Daskalov and Maria-Nona Filipova Chipeva-Daskalova; m. Elena Georgieva Balabanova, Aug. 3, 1991; 1 child, Mihail Georgiev. MSc, Sofia (Bulgaria) U., 1989; diplome d'etudes approfondies, U. d'Aix-Marseilles II, France, 1993, PhD, 1998. Specialist biologist Inst. Fish Resources, Varna, Bulgaria, 1989-90, rsch. scientist III, 1990-94, rsch. scientist II, 1994-98, rsch. scientist I, 1998—. Co-author: (book) Environmental Management of Fish Resources in the Black Sea and Their Rational Exploitation, 1997; contbr. sci. articles to profl. jours. Fellow Cen. European U., 1991-94, Open Soc. Fund, 1995-97, French Govt. fellow, 1992-93, 96-97. Mem. Union Dem. Forces. Fax: 359 52 257876. E-mail: gdaskalov@hotmail.com. Home: 38 Petko Karavelov Str, Varna 9002, Bulgaria Office: Inst Fish Resources, 4 Primorski Blvd, Varna 9000, Bulgaria

DASSARMA, SHILADITYA, geneticist, educator, research scientist; b. Calcutta, India, Nov. 11, 1957; arrived in U.S., 1966; s. Basudeb and Seba (Sen) DasS.; m. Priya Arora, Dec. 29, 1995; children: Satyajit, Anjali. BS in Chemistry with honors, Ind. U., 1979; PhD in Biochemistry, MIT, 1984. Postdoctoral fellow Harvard Med. Sch., Boston, 1984-86; asst. prof. U. Mass., Amherst, 1986-92, assoc. prof. dept. microbiology, 1992-97, prof. genetics, 1997—; vis. scientist Dept. Biochemistry and Molecular Genetics, Pasteur Inst., Paris, 1986, Dept. Microbiology, Cornell U. Med. Coll., N.Y.C., 1990; founder, adminstr. U. Mass. Amherst Molecular Biology/Biotech. Computer Ctr., 1987—; mem. adv. panel NSF, 1994-99, vis. program dir., 1997-98, mem. NIH study sect., 1999—; organizer Halobacterium Genome Consortium, 1999-2000. Editor: Archaea: A Laboratory Manual - Halophiles, 1995; mem. editl. bd. Jour. of Bacteriology, 1996-99; contbr. articles to profl. jours.; patentee expression of wild type and mutant glutamine synthetase in foreign hosts, recombinant gas vesicles and uses thereof, recombinant vector and process for flotation. Grantee NSF, 1987—, NIH, 1989-94, 97—, NATO, 1991-93. Mem. AAAS, Am. Soc. Microbiology. Avocations: biking, photography, travel, Indian classical music and culture. E-mail: dassarma@microbiology.umass.edu. Office: U Mass Dept Microbiology Amherst MA 01003

DASSIOS, GEORGE THEODORE, mathematician, educator, researcher; b. Patras, Greece, Jan. 22, 1946; s. Theodore and Helen (Kalliafas) D.; m. Eleni Dassios, Sept. 6, 1970; children: Constantine, Theodore. Diploma, U. Athens, Greece, 1970; MS, U. Ill., Chgo., 1972, PhD, 1975; Habilitation, Nat. Tech. U. Athens, 1980. Assoc. prof. Nat. Tech. U. Athens, 1977-81; asst. prof. U. Patras, 1975-77, prof., 1981—; vis. asst. prof. Brown U., Providence, 1978-79; vis. prof. U. Tenn., Knoxville, 1986-87. Rsch. grantee EEC, 1984—. Avocation: stamp collecting. Home: 186 Korinthou St, 262 21 Patras Greece Office: Univ Patras, 265 00 Patras Greece

DASSO, JEROME JOSEPH, real estate educator; b. Neillsville, Wis., Jan. 12, 1929; s. Henry J. and Frances (Schweickert) D.; m. Patricia Mary Conger, June 13, 1959 (div. 1978); children: James Daniel, Mary Cecilia, Nancy Ann, Wnedy Jo. BS, Purdue U., 1951; MBA, U. Mich., 1952; MS, U. Wis., 1960, PhD, 1964. Ptnr. Dasso Constrn. Co., Dubuque, Iowa, 1956-58; planner Franklin County, Columbus, Ohio, 1960-61; asst. prof. U. Ill., Urbana, 1964-66; vis. chairholder U. Hwawii, Honolulu, 1982-83; mem. faculty U. Oreg., Eugene, 1966-95, H.T. Miner chair in real estate, 1978-95, H.T. Miner chair emeritus, 1995—; vis. prof. U. Wis., Madison, 1984; cons. Internat. Assn. Assessing Officers, Chgo., 1972-75; ednl. cons. Hawaii Real Estate Commn., Honolulu, 1982-83. Co-author: (S. Kahn, R. Nesslinger et a)l Principle of Right of Way Acquisition, 1972, (with G. Kuhn) Real Estate Finance, 1983, (with A.A. Ring) Real Estate Principles and Practices, 8th edit., 1977, 9th edit., 1981, 10th edit., 1985, 11th edit., 1989, (with Jim Shilling) 12th edit., 1995, Computerized Assessment Adminstration, 1973; contbr. numerous articles to various publs. Lt (j.g.) USN, 1952-60. Vivian Stewart vis. fellow Cambridge U., spring, 1987. Fellow Am. Inst. Corp. Asset Mgmt. (bd. govs. 1988-91), Homer Hoyt Inst. ADv. Studies Real Estate & Urban Land Econs.; mem. Real Estate Educators Assn. (pres. 1980-81, Outstanding Svc. award 1981, Disting. Career award 1989), Am. Real Estate and Urban Econs. Assn. (bd. dirs. 1974-77, 80-83), Real Estate Ctr. Dirs. Chairholders Assn. (pres. 1987-88), Am. Real Estate Soc. (life, bd. dirs. 1985-86, v.p. 1988-89, pres. elect 1989-90, pres. 1990-91), Am. Fin. Assn. (life), Nat. Assn. Realtors (edn. com. 1970-76), Internat. Real Estate Soc. (pres. 1994-95), Elks, Eagles, Lions, KC. Roman Catholic. Avocations: golf, skiing, backpacking, photography. Address: PO Box 9103 Horseshoe Bay TX 78657-9103

DASTIDAR, MANISHA G., research scientist; b. Calcutta, India, Jan. 1, 1949; d. Sudhamaya and Usha Rani (Dey) Karkun; m. Indrajit Ghosh Dastidar, Dec. 2, 1970; children: Samanwoy, Somashree. BSc with honors, Calcutta U., 1969; MSc, Indian Inst. Tech., Delhi, 1971, MTech, 1973, PhD, 1979. Sr. sci. officer grade II Indian Inst. Tech., 1979-95, sr. sci. officer grade I, 1995-2000, assoc. prof., 2000—. Contbr. articles to profl. jours. Grantee GD Techno (P) Ltd., 1995, Ministry Environ. and Forests India, 1996, Ministry of Sci. and Tech., 1999. Mem. N.Y. Acad. Scis., Catalysis Soc. of India, Nat. Acad. Environ. Sci. Avocations: dramatics, Indian classical music, social work, travel. Office: Indian Inst Tech Hauz Khas, Ctr Energy Studies, New Delhi 110016, India

DASTRUP-HAMILL, FAYE MYERS, city official; b. Sanford, Colo., Dec. 15; d. Earl Dixon and Kady Florence (Cornum) Faucett; m. Sherly K. Myers (dec.); children: Carla Pearce, Susan Kitley (dec.), Mary Jane James, Elizabeth Ireland; m. Merrill E. Dastrup, Sept. 22, 1972 (dec. July 1987); m. Wayne A. Hamill, Mar. 23, 1991. Student, L.D.S. Bus. Coll., 1934-35; grad., Dale Carnegie Inst., 1953; degree in mcpl. works adminstrn., Mt. San Antonio Coll., 1960; student, Syracuse U. Inst., 1968; degree in tech. reporting, Chaffey Coll., 1970. Legal sec. W. W. Platt, City Atty., Alamosa, Colo., 1935-40; sec. pub. works dept. City of Ontario, Calif., 1957-60, dep. city clk., dep. city treas., 1960-64, city clk., 1964-93, city coun. mem., mayor and mayor pro tem, 1974-92; mem. part 150 implementation com. Ontario Airport, Calif., 1993—; chmn. noise adv. com., dept. trans. State of Calif. Ontario Airport, 1994—; sec. pers. dept. L.A. Housing Authority, 1948; mem. legis. subcom. So. Calif. Assn. Govts., chmn. hist. preservation and cultural arts com.; mem. revenue and taxation com. League of Calif. Cities, vice-chmn., chmn. Clks. Inst., gen. resolutions com., com. on environ. quality Inland Empire divsn.; chmn. San Bernardino County Planning Com., Criminal Justice; prese. So. Calif. City Clks. Assn., chmn. legis. com.; mem. exec. com. Valley Assn. of Cities; city coun. rep. Ontario Libr. Bd. Trustees. Escort sch. classes through City Hall; judge sci. fairs and sch. and comty. events; life mem. Friends of Ontario Libr.; mem., donor Friends of Mus. of History and Art, Ontario; pres., treas., trustee Ontario (Calif.) City Libr., 1993—; choir dir., life mem. Ch. of Jesus. Recipient plaque with gold gavel So. Calif. City Clks. Assn., 1972, Women Helping Women award Soroptomist Internat. of Ontario, 1981, 1990 Woman of Yr. award State Legislature, State of Calif., 1990, Woman of Achievement award 90s Women's Conf., 1990, 1994 YWCA Woman of Achievement award West End YWCA, 1994, Elizabeth S. Genee Lifetime Achievement award, West End YWCA, 1994, Bryce Denton award Mus. of History and Art, 1996, Outstanding Effort with Calif. Water plaque San Bernardino County Waterworks Dist. #8, 1986, Outstanding Svc. plaque Ontario Air N.G., 1990, Leadership plaque San Bernardino County Sheriff's Dept., 1993, Founding, Support and Encouragement of Crime Stoppers Spl. Recognition plaque Ontario Police Dept., 1993, Outstanding Comty. Svc. plaque U.S. Congressman Jay Kim, 1994, Plaque and Spl. Cert. congratulating receipt of Elizabeth Genee Lifetime Achievement award, 1994, Pub. Svc. Award trophy Adrian Meewis, 1972, plaque for dedicated and meritorious svc. to Ontario, as mayor City Coun. and City Clk., 1986, Lifetime Achievement plaque San Bernardino County Supr. Larry Walker, 1994, Svc. plaque South Coast Air Quality Mgmt. Dist., 1987, decorated plaque Salvation Army, 1992, others. Mem. Calif. Assn. Libr. Trustees and Commrs., Comty. Concert Assn. Pomona Valley (donor), Ontario C. of C. (life, Svc. Award plaque 1992), Musicians Club of Pomona Valley. Mem. Ch. of Jesus Christ of L.D.S. Avocation: vocal soloist. Home: 761 W Hawthorne St Ontario CA 91762-1510

DATCU, IOANA, visual artist; b. Bucharest, Romania, Apr. 22, 1944; arrived in U.S., 1981; d. Marin and Niculina (Chitescu) D; m. Vasile Porcisanu, Aug. 5, 1967 (div. 1983); 1 child, Isabelle Ioana. BA, Pedagogical Inst., Bucharest, 1967; BFA summa cum laude, U. Minn., 1987, MFA, 1991. Tchr. biology high sch., Argova, Preasna, Romania, 1967-74; photography asst. U. Minn., St. Paul, 1985-86; photographer civil rights dept. City Hall, St. Paul, 1986-87; darkroom supervisor Film in the Cities, St. Paul, 1987-88; gallery asst., curator Paul Whitney Gallery, St. Paul, 1987-91; art instr. Minn. Mus. Am. Art, St. Paul, 1993-94; instr. drawing & painting U. Minn., Mpls., 1996-97, adj. faculty, 1999—. One-person exhbns. include Flanders Contemporary Art, Mpls., 1994, Winona (Minn.) State U., 1995, Mont. State U., Billings, 1996, Ea. Washington U., Cheney, 1996, Indpls. Art Ctr., 1996, Kansas City (Mo.) Artists Coalition, 1997, Grants Pass (Oreg.) Mus. Art, 1997, Trinity Presbyn. Ch., Denton, Tex., 1998, South Bend (Ind.) Mus. Art, 1998, U. Dayton, Ohio, 2000; juried group shows include North Park Coll., Chgo., 1991, Historic Trinity, Detroit, 1993, 95, 96, Barrett House Galleries, Poughkeepsie, N.Y., 1994, 96, Coll. St. Catherine, St. Paul, 1995, Minot State U., N.D., 1995, St. John's U., N.Y., 1995, Katherine E. Nash Gallery, Mpls., 1992, 95, 96, Focal Point Gallery, N.Y.C., 1996, SoHo Photo Gallery, N.Y.C., 1997, Greater Lafayette Mus. Art., 1997, Truman State U., Mo., 1998, McNeese State U., La., 1998, Attelboro (Mass.) Mus. Art, 1998, 99, New World Art Ctr., N.Y.C., 1999, Ctrl. Mo. State U., 1999, Am. Bible Soc. Gallery, N.Y.C., 2000, Internat. Print Triennial, Cracow, Poland, 2000, New American Paintings Exhibit in Print, Open Studio Press, 1995, Images of the Spirit Traveling Exhibit, 1995-97, CIVA CODEX III traveling exhibit, 1997—; works represented in CD-Rom collections of Art Comms. Internat., 1995, Artmax Internat., 1995, Ency. Internat. Women Artists, Alliance Women Artists, 1997, New Art Internat., Book Art Press, 1997, Christianity and the Arts jour., 1999. Grantee Pollock-Krasner Found., 1992, Minn. State Arts Bd., 1994; Jerome Found. Residency fellow, 1994; McKnight Photography fellow, 1992, fellow Arts Midwest NEA, 1994-95, Clowes Fund regional residency fellow, Indpls., 1997; Vt. Studio Ctr. Residency award, Johnson, Vt., 1997. Mem. Christians in the Visual Arts, Nat. Assn. Women Artists, Inc. Mem. Eastern Orthodox Ch. Avocations: classical music, movies, yoga, books, animals. Home and Studio: 1202 E Justin St Pearce AZ 85625-4037

DATE, MAHESHWAR HARIHAR, medical education consultant, researcher; b. Pune, India, Mar. 2, 1946; s. Harihar Nilkanth and Malati Harihar (Tamhankar) D.; m. Aparna Maheshwar Date, Mar. 9, 1972; children: Kailas, Sonali. B of Ayurvesic Medicine and Surgery, Tilak Ayurved Coll., Poona, India, 1969, MASc, 1984; postgrad., Ayurved Coll. Sion East, Bombay, 1984. Registrar Seth-Tarachand-Ramanath Charitable Ayurvedic Hosp., Poona, 1970-71; jr. lectr. Tilak Ayurved Coll., 1971-79; prof. Ayurved Coll. Sion East, 1979—; prin. Ayurved Coll., Sion, India, 1998—; examiner New Delhi U., 1995-96; mem. faculty Ayuvedic medicine U. Bombay, 1980—, mem. acad. coun., 1982-85, 95—, chmn. bd. studies, 1982-85, 95-2000, senator, 1990—. Editor SWAYAM. Chmn. Brahman Seva Mandal, Dadar, India, 1999-2000; pres. Mumbai Marathi Granth Sangrahalaya, Dadar. Recipient Silver medal Fedn. Blood Banks, Mumbai, India, 1995. Mem. Nat. Integrated Med. Assn. (life, sec. 1993-96), Ayurved Adhyapak Mahasangh (v.p. 1989—). Avocations: writing scientific articles, poetry, stories. Fax: 022-4092562. E-mail: mhdate@yahoo.com, kailasmd@vsn.com. Home: 8/9 Indira Niwas, BS Rd, Dadar, Mumbai 400028, India Office: Ayurved Coll Sion, Nr Railway Station, Mumbai 400022, India

DATHE, MARGITTA ELSE ANNA, biophysicist, educator; b. Pasewalk, Germany, Jan. 6, 1952; d. Willi and Gisela (Bugdahn) Marx. Diploma in Physics, Humboldt U., Berlin, 1974; Dr.rer.nat., Acad. Scis. Germany, 1980. Sci. co-worker Ctrl. Inst. Molecular Biology, Berlin, 1974-76, Inst. of Drug Rsch., Berlin, 1976-91; leader rsch. group Inst. Molecular Pharmacology, Berlin, 1992—; lectr. Faculty of Pharm. Sci., Free U., Berlin, 1996—. Contbr. articles to profl. jours. Recipient Lessing prize, 1970, Leopoldina award, 1993. Avocations: architecture, mountain touring, historical literature, Ikebana. Office: Inst Molecular Pharmacology, Alfred-Kowalke-Str 4, 10315 Berlin Germany

DATILES, MANUEL BERNALDES, III, ophthalmologist, scientist; b. Manila, Feb. 26, 1951; came to U.S., 1979; s. Roberto Aguiling and Loretta (Bernaldes) D.; m. Jacqueline Romero, Mar. 13, 1976; children: Michelle, Joyce, Margaret, Jennifer, Manuel IV, Michael. BS cum laude, U. Santo Tomas, Manila, 1970; MD cum laude, U. Santo Tomas, 1974. Rsch. fellow Philippine Eye Rsch. Inst.-U. Philippines, Manila, 1975-76; resident in ophthalmology U. Philippines-Philippine Gen. Hosp., Manila, 1976-79; rsch. scholar, vis. scientist Lab. Vision Rsch. Nat. Eye Inst.-NIH, Bethesda, Md., 1979-82; clin. fellow corneal and cataract surgery Wilmer Eye Inst.-Johns Hopkins U. Hosp., Balt., 1982-83; sr. staff ophthalmologist Nat. Eye Inst.-NIH, Bethesda, 1983-88; acting chief cornea and cataract sect., clin. svc. br. Nat. Eye Inst.-NIH, 1989-92, chief cornea and cataract sect., clin. svcs. br., 1992—; chmn. surg. adminstrv. com. NIH Clin. Ctr. Hosp., 1994-95; vis. lectr. Wilmer Eye Inst.-Johns Hopkins U., Balt., 1984, Osaka (Japan) U., 1986, U. Munich, 1988, Harkness Eye Inst., Columbia U., N.Y.C., 1994-97. Editor cataract sect. Duane's Clinical Ophthalmology Textbook Series; guest editor Jour. Investigative Ophthalmology and Visual Sci., 1999, 2000; contbr. articles to profl. jours., chpts. to ophthalmol. books; reviewer jours. in field. Recipient Most Outstanding Silver Jubilarian in Med. Rsch. award U. Santo Tomas Alumni Assn. Am., 1999, Cert. Appreciation James Cardinal Hickey and Archdiocese of Washington. Mem. Assn. Rsch. in Vision and Ophthalmology, Am. Acad. Ophthalmology, Castroviejo Soc. Corneal Surgeons, Johns Hopkins Med. Surg. Assn., Internat. Assn. Ocular Surgeons, Washington Acad. Ophthalmology, Md. Soc. Eye Physicians and Surgeons. Roman Catholic. Avocations: drawing, soap carving, target shooting, guitar, chess. Office: NIH Nat Eye Inst Rm 10n226 Bethesda MD 20892-0001

DATIRI, BENJAMIN CHUMANG, soil and environmental scientist; b. Sho, Plateau, Nigeria, May 1, 1953; came to U.S., 1983; s. Chumang Dangyang and Antele (Pam) D.; m. Roseline Chundung Gwott, Apr. 5, 1980; children: Simidarwei, Teyeidarwei, Ninratdarwei, Yeipyeng, Noro. BSc, Ahmadu Bello U., Zaria, Nigeria, 1978, MSc, 1982; PhD, U. Wis., 1989. Mem. Nigerian Youth Svc. Program, Onicha-Olona, 1978-79; agrl. officer II Plateau State Ministry of Agr., Lafia, Nigeria, 1979; grad. asst. Ahmadu Bello U., 1979-80, asst. lectr., 1980-82; rsch. asst. U. Wis., Madison, 1983-84; rsch. assoc. Tuskegee (Ala.) U., 1990-93, rsch. technician, 1993-95; assoc. rsch. prof., rsch. coord. Selma (Ala.) U., 1996-98; rsch. assoc. prof. biomed. dept. Tuskegee U., 1998—. Contbr. articles to profl. publs.

Recipient Ch. Recreation League Leadership award Macon County of Ala., 1992, Basketball Coaches award Tuskegee-Macon County YMCA, 1994; Plateau State grad. scholar Govt. of Nigeria, 1983-86. Mem. Am. Soc. Agronomy, Soil Sci. Soc. Am., Sigma Xi (Tuskegee U. chpt. Outstanding leadership 1992, Dedicated Svc. award 1992). Achievements include discovery that chisel and no-till tillage systems do reduce surface runoff and increase infiltration, that wetting front migrations were found to be much deeper in soil profile than in conventional moldboard planting; hence, although surface water pollution may be reduced by conservation tillage, it could present a potential for groundwater pollution. Office: Biomed Dept Sch Vet Medicine Tuskegee Univ Tuskegee Institute AL 36088

DATKA, JERZY, chemistry educator; b. Zolynia, Poland, Sept. 12, 1942; s. Stanislaw and Regina (Wal) D.; m. Alina Smolinska, Oct. 8, 1977; 1 child, Datka Piotr. MSc, Jagiellonian U., Cracow, Poland, 1965, PhD, 1972. Asst. Jagiellonian U., Cracow, 1965-73, asst. prof., 1973-83, assoc. prof., 1983-92, prof., 1992—, head dept. inorganic chemistry. Contbr. more tha 110 articles to profl. jours. Recipient Min. of Sci. award, 1973, Polish Acad. Scis. award, 1983, Min. Edn. award, 1994. Mem. Internat. Zeolite Assn. Avocations: siteseeing, mountaineering, amateur photography. Home: Strzelcow 7A/34, 3I-422 Cracow Poland Office: Faculty Chemistry, Ingardena 3, 30-060 Cracow Poland

DATKIEWICZ, GREGORY, educator; b. Wroclaw, Poland, Nov. 5, 1955; s. Andrzej and Alina Krustyna (Komor) D. Grad., Wroclaw U., Poland, 1990; postgrad., Wroclaw Acad. Econs., Poland, 1990. Tchr. English lang. Telenia, Gora, Poland, 1979-80; factory worker Wroclaw, Poland, 1981-82; with Rokita Chem. Complex, Brzeg Dolny, Poland, 1982-86; clk. travel agy., Wroclaw, 1986-88; tchr. English Wroclaw, 1988-91; lectr. English ABB/Asea Brown Boveri, Wroclaw, 1991-92; tchr. Walbrzych, Poland, 1992-93, 93-95; mem. staff Tchr. Tng. Coll., Ostroleka, Poland, 1995—. Avocations: literature, history, philosophy, cycling, motorcycling. Home: Ul 11 Listopada 1/45, 07-400 Ostroteka Poland Office: Tchr Tng Coll, Ul Parkowa 6, 07-412 Ostroteka Poland also: PO Box 98, 07-400 Ostroteka Poland

DATO, VIRGINIA MARIE, public health physician; b. Jersey City, Sept. 6, 1957; d. Steven C. and Virginia R. Dato; m. Michael Chancellor, May 17, 1986; children: David, Katherine. BA, Rutgers U., 1979; MD, U. Pitts., 1983; MPH, Columbia U., 1992. Diplomate Am. Bd. Pub. Health and Gen. Preventive Medicine; diplomate Am. Bd. Pediat. Pediatric resident Bellevue Hosp., NYU Med. Ctr., N.Y.C., 1983-86; Infectious disease fellow Children's Hosp. Mich., Detroit, 1986-88; sr. pub. health physician N.J. Dept. Health and Sr. Svcs., Trenton, 1988-97, co-dir. preventive medicine and pub. health residency, 1995-97; sr. pub. health physician Ctr. Pub. Health Practice U. Pitts., 1997—; chair topics in pub. health N.J. Dept. Health, Trenton, 1991-93; chair instnl. rev. bd. N.J. Dept. Health and Sr. Svcs., Trenton, 1995-97; co-dir. Pa. and N.E. Regional Pub. Health Tng. Project, 1998-00. Mem. AMA, APHA, Am. Assn. Pub. Health Physicians (trustee 1997—, sec. 1998-2000, v.p. 2000—), Am. Coll. Preventive medicine, Pa. Med. Soc. (com. on pub. health 1998—), Pa. Pub. Health Assn. (trustee 1999—). Office: Ctr Pub Health Practice 125 Parran Hl Pittsburgh PA 15261-0001

DATTA, ANINDYA, computer science researcher; b. Calcutta, India, Aug. 10, 1964. B in Tech., Indian Inst. Tech., Kharagpur, 1986; MS in Computer Info. Scis., U. Md., 1990, PhD in Info. Scis. and Ops. Rsch., 1993. Tchg. asst. U. Md., College Park, 1987-90, grad. rsch. asst. Inst. Systems Rsch., 1990-93; asst. prof. Karl Eller Grad. Sch. Mgmt. U. Ariz., Tucson, 1993-98; CEO, founder Chutney Tech., Inc., Atlanta, 1998—; assoc. prof. DuPree Sch. Mgmt. Ga. Inst. Tech., Atlanta, 1998—; vis. rschr. AT&T Labs., Florham Park, N.J., 1996-97; dir. iXL Ctr. for Electronic Commerce, Ga. Inst. Tech., Atlanta, 1999-2000, Millennium Info. Systems, Pvt Ltd., Calcutta, 1996-2000; cons. AT&T, IBM, U.S. West; presenter in field. Contbg. author: Real-Time Database Systems, 1997, Integrated Network Management III, 1993; contbr. articles to profl. jours.; patentee in field. Grantee IBM, Digigraph Corp., USDA. Mem. IEEE, Assn. Computing Machinery, Inst. Ops. Rsch. and Mgmt. Scis., Assn. Info. Systems. Avocations: sports, reading, movies. Office: DuPree Coll Mgmt Ga Inst Tech 755 Ferst Dr Atlanta GA 30332-0001

DATTA, DEBATOSH, biotechnology and bioengineering educator; b. Diamond Harbour, India, Mar. 14, 1957; s. Pashupati and Ila Rani (Ghosh) D.; m. Rekha Ghosh, May 11, 1987; children: Deepanjan, Neelanjan. MBBS, Calcutta Nat. Med. Coll., 1981; MD, Univ. Coll. of Medicine, 1987. Lectr. Indian Inst. of Tech., Bombay, 1989-90, asst. prof., 1990-99, assoc. prof., 1999—; examiner in nuclear medicine, U. Bombay, 1992-96; reviewer Indian Coun. of Med. Rsch., Delhi, 1995-97, Indina Jour. Med. Rsch., New Delhi, 1995—; cons. Bombay Textile Rsch. Orgn., Mumbai, 1995—; expert Internat. Atomic Energy Agy., Vienna. Contbr. articles to sci. and profl. jours.; patentee in field. Grantee Bd. Rsch. in Nuclear Scis., India, 1997. Mem. Soc. Biomaterials and Artificial Organs (life), Internat. Soc. Artificial Organs. Hindu. Avocations: meditating, music, networking, reading. Office: Indian Inst Tech Sch, Biomed Engring, Mumbai 400076, India

DATTA, GOURANGA LAL, mechanical engineering educator; b. Barisal, Bangladesh, Dec. 1, 1943; arrived in India, 1950; s. Aswini Kumar and Indu Bala (Sen) D.; m. Runu Roy, Aug. 1, 1972; 1 child, Dalia. BSc, Burdwan U., West Bengal, India, 1963; BTech, Indian Inst. Tech., Kharagpur, West Bengal, 1966, MTech, 1968, PhD, 1974. Cert. mech. engr. Lectr. Indian Inst. Tech., Kharagpur, 1972-76; asst. prof. Indian Inst. Tech., Delhi, India, 1976-77; asst. prof. Indian Inst. Tech., Kharagpur, 1977-85, prof., 1985—; dean continuing edn. Indian Inst. Tech., Kharagpur, 1974-77, prin. coord. quality improvement program, 1977-90. Contbr. rsch. articles to profl. jours. Chmn. Tech. Coop. Poultry Soc., Indian Inst. Tech., Kharagpur, 1990-92; chmn. Green Swimmers Assn., Indian Inst. Tech., Kharagpur, 1989-92; vice chmn. governing body Hijli Coll., Kharagpur, 1996-99. Recipient The Corps of Engrs. Prize, The Inst. of Engrs., 1994-95, Sir L.P. Misra Meml. award, The Indian Inst. of Welding, 1999, Outstanding Acad. Yr. award, Indian Soc. Tech. Edn., 1998, Best Papers award. Fellow Indian Inst. of Welding (v.p. nat. coun. 1976-77), Instn. of Engrs. (chmn. local ctr. 1990-92); mem. Inst. Indian Foundrymen (chmn. Ctr. for Edn. and Tng. 1996—), Indian Soc. Tech. Edn. (chmn. sect. 1995-96). Avocations: reading, travel, social work. E-mail: gld@mech.iitkgp.ernet.in. Home: 206 Coop Housing Soc, 721306 Kharagpur India Office: Indian Inst Tech Kharagpur, Dept Mech Engring, 721302 Kharagpur India

DATTA, K. P., metallurgist, materials scientist; b. Calcutta, India, July 5, 1948; came to U.S., 1975; s. Dhirendra Nath and Kamala (Basu) D. BS in Metall. Engring., Indian Inst. Tech., Kharagpur, India, 1970, MS in Process Metallurgy, 1972; PhD in Materials Sci., Oreg. Grad. Inst., Beaverton, 1980. Metallurgist Alloy Steels Plant divsn. Sail, Durgapur, India, 1972-75; rsch. assoc. Oreg. Grad. Inst., Beaverton, 1980-81; vis. lectr. N.C. State U., Raleigh, 1982; sr. rsch. assoc. Baylor Coll. Dentistry, Dallas, 1983-84; metallurgist Spectrum Labs., Dallas, 1984-87; supr. materials lab. Poco Graphite divsn. Unocal, Decatur, Tex., 1987-90; edn. chair, cons. North Tex. chpt. Am. Soc. for Materials, Arlington, Tex., 1990-98; sr. R&D engr. Regal Ware, Inc., Kewaskum, Wis., 1998—; cons. Metall. Consulting Svcs., Decatur, Tex., 1990-98. Contbr. rsch. papers to profl. jours. Recipient Bronze award United Way, 1998; rsch. grantee Dept. Navy, 1977, Am. Iron & Steel Inst., 1980, NIH, 1983. Mem. ASTM, Am. Soc. for Materials Internat. (treas. Dallas chpt. 1987-90), Metall. Soc.-Am. Inst. Metall. and Petroleum Engrs. Achievements include findings in anomaly of toughness behavior with notch-root radius; sharp crack and blunt notch toughness behavior of quenched and tempered Aist 4340 steel; effects of material parameters on stretch formability of dual phase steel; estimation of ionic conductivity of copper iodide through tarnishing of copper in iodine atmosphere. Home: PO Box 143 Kewaskum WI 53040-0143

DATTA, PURNA CHANDRA, clinical psychologist, educator; b. Barisal, India, Jan. 1, 1943; came to U.S., 1980; s. Jogendra Kumar and Kanak (Ghosh) D.; m. Anita Rani, Feb. 7, 1969; children: Partha Michael, Aparna Kara. BA in Philosophy with honors, Dacca (Bangladesh) U., 1963, MA in Philosophy, 1964, MA in Psychology, 1967; PhD in Clin. Psychology, Newcastle U., NSW, Australia, 1979, M in Clin. Psychology, 1982. Lic. psychologist, Ga., Calif.; cert. eye movement desensitization reprocessing; diplomate Am. Bd. Forensic Examiners, Am. Bd. Forensic Medicine; diplomate-fellow Prescribing Psychol. Register. Psychologist Morisset (NSW) Hosp., 1974-80, clin. psychologist, 1983-84; psychologist Fairview State Hosp., Costa Mesa, Calif., 1980-83; psychologist Ctrl. State Hosp., Milledgeville, Ga., 1985-86, sr. psychologist, 1989-90; program dir. Gladesville (NSW) Hosp., 1984-85, So. Met. Devel. Disabilities Svc., Gladesville, 1986-88; staff psychologist Stockton (Calif.) Devel. Ctr., 1990-94, O.H. Close Sch. (Calif. Youth Authority), Stockton, 1994—; lectr. psychology Dacca Coll., 1968-69, Dacca U., 1969-73; tutor, demonstrator Newcastle U., 1973-74; lectr. psychiat. nursing Newcastle Tech. Coll., 1974-80; clin. instr. psychiatry U. Calif., Irvine, 1981-83; adj. prof. psychology U. Pacific, Stockton, 1992—; clin. psychologist mental health svcs. Perry Street Cmty. Ctr., Newcastle, 1976-77, 77; clin. psychologist pediatric unit Royal Newcastle Hosp., 1977-78; psychol. asst. Dr. F.M. Crinella, Costa Mesa. 1982-83; presenter in field. Contbr. articles to profl. jours. Talent scholar Commonwealth U. Dacca, 1960-64. Fellow Am. Coll. Forensic Examiners (diplomate in forensic medicine/forensic psychology); mem. APA, Assn. Therapists for Sexual Abusers, Calif. Psychol. Assn., Am. Assn. Clin. Hypnosis (cert. in hypnotherapy), Am. Coll. Forensic Examiners, Am. Coll. Forensic Counselors (diplomate in psychopharmacology, qualified med. evaluator, registrant Nat. Register of Health Svc. Providers in Psychology). Avocation: moving to different countries and visiting universities. Home: 7221 Shoreham Pl Stockton CA 95207-1224 Office: Behavior Therapy and Counseling Assocs 1652 W Texas St Ste 204 Fairfield CA 94533-5952

DATTA, RAMEN, metallurgist; b. Asansol, India, July 1, 1956; s. Mukunda Murari and Durga Dutta; m. Sumana Chakravertty, Aug. 5, 1982; 1 child, Sourabh. B of Engring., B.E. Coll., 1978; PhD in Material Sci., India Inst. Tech., 1982. Rsch. scholar India Inst. Tech., Delhi, 1978-82; rsch. engr. R&D Ctr. for Iron and Steel, Steel Authority of India Ltd., Ranchi, India, 1982-86, sr. rsch. engr., 1986-89, asst. rsch. mgr., 1989-93, prin. rsch. mgr., 1993-98, asst. gen. mgr., 1998—; vis. scholar U. Pitts., 1991; vis. scientist Tsniichermet, Moscow, 1989, 91. Assoc. editor Transaction of Indian Inst. of Metals, 1992-99, editor, 1999—; editor Proc. of Steel for the Automotive Sector, 1985, High Strength Steels, 1996; contbr. 50 articles to profl. jours.; patentee in field. Recipient Best Metallurgists award Govt. of India, 1994, Metallurgy and Material Sci. Gold medal Inst. of Engring., 1991-92. Mem. Indian Inst. of Metals (Young Material Scientist award 1991, Best Paper award 46th Ann. Tech. Meeting 1992, 51st Ann. Tech. Mtg. 1997). Avocations: light reading, music, cricket, tennis. Home: H-195 Shyamali, Ranchi 834002, India Office: R&D Ctr for Iron & Steel, Steel Authority of India, Ranchi 834002, India

DATTA, SUKDEB, anesthesiologist, pain management specialist; b. Jamshedpur, India, June 6, 1967; s. Kartik Chandra and Bela Datta; m. Koel Chatterjee, Sept. 27, 1997. MBBS, NRS Med. Coll., Calcutta, India, 1989. Postgrad. trainee in surgery Calcutta (India) U., 1992-94; resident in surgery Nassau County Med. Ctr., East Meadow, N.Y., 1994-95; resident in anesthesiology New Eng. Med. Ctr., Boston, 1995-96; resident in anesthesiology Cook County Hosp., Chgo., 1996-98, chief resident, clin. scientist, 1998-99, fellow pain mgmt. program, 1999-2000; asst. prof. U. Cin., 2000—; rschr., presenter in field. Author: Essentials of Practical Physiology and Viva in Physiology, 1987; contbr. articles to profl. jours. Recipient Midwest Anesthesiology Residents Conf. award Ohio State U., Columbus, 1999, Sigma Xi award, 1999. Mem. Am. Soc. Anesthesiologists, Internat. Anesthesia Rsch. Soc. (Best of Meeting award for sci. abstracts 74th Clin. and Sci. Congress 2000), Am. Soc. Regional Anesthesia, Ill. Soc. Anesthesiologists. Avocations: music, software. Fax: 773-469-0476. E-mail: sukdeb@hotmail.com., sukdeb.datta@uc.edu. Home: 8131 Village Dr Cincinnati OH 45242 Office: U Cin Hosps PO Box 670531 Cincinnati OH 45267-0531

DATTE, YAO JACQUES, pharmacologist; b. Tanda, Ivory Coast, Jan. 31, 1964; s. Kouakou and Dakrome (Abinan) D. MA, U. Abidjan, Ivory Coast, 1992; degree, U. Cocody, Abidjan, 1996; postgrad., Christian-Albrechts U., Kiel, Germany, 1998—; PhD, Paris XII U., 1999. Grad. asst. U. Abidjan, 1991-94, lectr. asst., 1997—; grad. asst. U. Kiel, 1995-98; mem. staff dept. nutrition and pharmacology Cocody-U. Mem. Soc. Gen. Physiology, N.Y. Acad. Scis. Roman Catholic. Avocations: football, walking. Office: Cocody-U UFR Bioscis, Dept Nutrition/Pharmacology, 582 Abidjan Ivory Coast

DATTILO, NICHOLAS C., bishop; b. Mahoningtown, Pa., Mar. 8, 1932. Educated, St. Vincent Sem., Latrobe, Pa., St. Charles Borromeo Sem., Phila. Ordained priest Roman Cath. Ch., 1958, apptd. Eighth Bishop of Harrisburg, 1989, ordained Bishop of Harrisburg, 1990. Bishop Diocese of Harrisburg, Pa., 1990—. Home and Office: PO Box 2153 4800 Union Deposit Rd Harrisburg PA 17105

DATZ, ISRAEL MORTIMER, information systems specialist; b. N.Y.C., Feb. 11, 1928; s. a. Mark and Lillian (Barkin) D.; m. Gerd Elin Alme-Torkildsen, Apr. 30, 1956. BS, CCNY, 1950; postgrad., U. Bergen, Norway, 1951-55. Chief programming group internat. Inst. Meteorology, Stockholm, 1958-59; head support svcs. sect. NASA Goddard Space Flight Ctr., Greenbelt, Md., 1959-61; mathematician Army Strategy and Tactics Analysis Group, Bethesda, Md., 1961-63; acting chief div. ops. analysis Dept. Commerce Maritime Adminstrn., Washington, 1963-64; head computer div. marine engring. lab. Annapolis (Md.) div. Naval Ship R & D Ctr., 1964-68, rsch. coord. math., 1968-72, tech. adv. ops. rsch., 1972-79; ind. cons., 1979-84; chief studies and analysis U.S. Army Engr. Sch., Ft. Leonard Wood, Mo., 1984-92; ind. cons., 1992—. Author: Planning In A Military Context: An Army Perspective, Power Transmission and Automation for Ships and Submersibles; Planning Tools For Ocean Transportation; contbr. articles to profl. jours. in U.S., Eng., Norway, Sweden, Germany. Recipient summer stipend Woods Hole Oceanographic Instn., 1949, rsch. stipend The Geophysics Inst., Bergen, Norway, 1953. Fellow AAAS; mem. N.Y. Acad. Scis., Inst. Ops. Rsch. and Mgmt. Sci., Assn. Computing Machinery, Nat. Def. Indsl. Assn., Am. Soc. Naval Engrs., Marine Tech. Soc., Soc. Naval Architects and Marine Engrs., U.S. Naval Inst. Home and Office: 1343 California Dr Rolla MO 65401-4529

DAUB, HENRIK HANNES, biochemist, researcher; b. Heilbronn, Germany, Sept. 8, 1968; s. Jörg Friedrich and Hannelore (Mehrmann) D. Diploma, U. Regensburg, Germany, 1994; PhD in Biochemistry, Max-Planck Inst. Biochemistry, 1998. Biochemist, rschr. Max Planck Inst. Biochemistry, Martinsried, 1994-98; postdoctoral rschr. MRC Lab. for Molecular Cell Biology Univ. Coll. London, 1998—. Contbr. articles to profl. jours. Fellow European Molecular Biology Orgn., 1998—. Office: MRC Lab Molecular Cell Biol, Gower St, London WC1E 6BT, England

DAUBEN, JOSEPH WARREN, history educator; b. Santa Monica, Calif., Dec. 29, 1944. AB, Claremont-McKenna Coll., 1966; AM, Harvard U., 1968, PhD in Hist. Sci., 1972. Tchg. fellow hist. sci. Harvard U., Cambridge, Mass., 1967-72; from asst. prof. to assoc. prof. Lehman Coll. CUNY, 1972-81, prof. hist. sci., 1981—; mem. Inst. for Advanced Study, Princeton U., 1977-78; vis. prof. ancient sci. Clark U., Worcester, Mass., 1971-72; vis. prof. hist. sci. Columbia U., N.Y.C., 1979-84, Oberlin (Ohio) Coll., 1980-81, N.Y. Bot. Garden, 1989—, NYU, 1989-93, Nat. Tsing-Hua U., Taiwan, 1991, Nat. Normal U., Taiwan, 1995, Inst. Hist. Nat. Sci., Chinese Acad. of Scis., 1999; vis. fellow Needham Inst. and Clare Hall, Cambridge U., fall 1999. Author numerous hist. vols., biographies of Georg Cantor and Abraham Robinson; editor Historia Mathematica, 1976-86. Humanist fellow NEH, 1973-74, Guggenheim fellow, 1980-81, NEH fellow, 1991-94, ACLS sr fellow, 1998-99; recipient Bolzano medal Czechoslovak Acad. Sci., 1978, Lenin medal U. Tashkent, USSR, 1986. Fellow AAAS, N.Y. Acad. Scis., Clare Hall (life); mem. Internat. Acad. Hist. Sci., Internat. Commn. History of Math. (chmn. 1985-94), Hist. Sci. Soc., Sigma Xi, Phi Beta Kappa. Office: CUNY Grad Ctr PhD Program in History 365 5th Ave at 34th St New York NY 10016-4309

DAUBERT, MADELINE J., accountant, educator; b. Norwich, N.Y., Aug. 22, 1941; d. Clifford T. and Marian A. Jones; m. Robert Louis Daubert, 1959; children: David, Lisa, Erik. BS, SUNY, Cortland, 1962; MLS, SUNY, Albany, 1969. CPA, N.C.; cert. libr., sch. media specialist, N.Y. Libr. various pub. schs. N.Y., 1966-78; mgr. mgmt. acctg. Peoples Security Life Ins., Durham, N.C., 1983-84; sys. acct. N.C. Ctrl. U., Durham, 1985-90; owner Madeline J. Daubert, CPA, Durham and Hendersonville, N.C., 1987—; adj. faculty Tex. Woman's U., Denton, 1990-91, U. South Fla., Tampa, 1993, U. N.C., Chapel Hill, 1995, 98; cons., workshop leader Libr. Congress, Washington, 1999; continuing edn. instr. Spl. Librs. Assn., Washington, 1995—; software cons. various univs., Tex., Tenn., Colo., N.C., 1990-91, U. N.C.-Asheville, 1987-89. Author: Financial Management for Small and Medium-Sized Libraries, 1993, Money Talk: Accounting Fundamentals for Special Librarians, 1995, Control of Administrative and Financial Operations in Special Libraries, 1996, Analyzing Library Costs, 1997. Trustee Keller (Tex.) Libr. Bd., 1991-92. Mem. AAUW (treas. Hendersonville, N.C. chpt. 1996-98). Office: 42 Oak Gate Dr Hendersonville NC 28739-9342

DAUDEL, RAYMOND, academic administrator, educator; b. Paris, Feb. 2, 1920; s. Georges and Jeanne (Plandé) D.; m. Pascaline Salzedo, June 30, 1944 (dec. 1976); children: Olivier, Sylvain. Degree in Engring., E.S.P.C.I., Paris, 1940; DSc, U. Sorbonne, Paris, 1944; PhD (hon.), U. Uppsala, Sweden, 1977, U. Louvain, Belgium, 1978, U. Barcelona, Spain, 1984. Asst. prof. Irene Joliot Curie U. Sorbonne, 1942-56, assoc. prof. Frederic Joliot, 1956-57, assoc. prof. Louis de Broglie, 1957-62, prof., 1962—. Author: (with R. Lefebvre and C. Moser) Quantum Chemistry (translated to Japanese), 1959, Chemical Carcinogenesis and Molecular Biology (translated to Japanese), 1966, The Realm of Molecules, 1993, (with L. Montagnier) AIDS, 1994, numerous others, translated into 12 langs. Named Officer of Légion d'Honneur, 1988; recipient Golden medal of Paris City, 1986. Home: 60 Rue Monsieur le Prince, 75006 Paris France Office: U Pierre et Marie Curie, 11 Rue Pierre & Marie Curie, 75005 Paris France

DAUDET, JEAN-LOUIS, pharmaceutical executive; b. Boulogne s/Seine, Paris, France, May 17, 1948; d. François and Therese (Suquet) D.; m. Isabelle Maître, June 21, 1972; children: Aurelien, Adrienne, Cecile, Sophie, Jean-Baptiste, Henri, Louis, Charles, Jeanne. Cert., Med. U., Paris, 1968. Med. rep. Lab. Biocodex, Montrouge, France, 1972-73, export mktg. supr., 1973-78, export asst. mgr., 1978-81, Europe dir., 1981-83; Latin Am. mgr. Solvay Pharma, Suresnes, France, 1983-94, Latin Am. dir., 1994-98, E. Africa dir., 1998-99; Latin Am. mgr. Lab Servier, Seine, France, 1999-2000. Home: 163 rue de Charenton, F-75012 Paris France Office: Lab Servier, 22 rue Garnier, F-92200 Nevilly Seine, France

D'AUDIFFRET, BRUNO-MARIE, engineering company executive; b. Guer, Brittany, France, Sept. 14, 1947; s. Francois Polycarpe and Agnes-Marie (de Pontbriand) D'A.; m. Sabine Elisabeth Turquet de Beauregard, May 19, 1972; children: Flavìen, Rodolphe, Pervenche, Maximin. MBA, Higher Sch. Comml. Studies, Paris, 1970; hon. degree, Institut Superieur De Gestion Des Entreprises, Tunis, Tunisia, 1972. Advt. mgr. Havas Conseil, Paris, 1971-72; mgmt. cons. Bossard Cons., Paris, 1972-81; mng. dir. Britool Ltd., Birmingham, Eng., 1989-91, bd. dirs., 1990—; v.p. logistics FACOM SA, Paris, 1981-86, v.p. mktg., 1986-89, v.p. bus. devel., 1992—. Sch.-parent advisor St. Jean de Bethune Champ, Versailles, France, 1985-89, Coll. ND du Grand, Versailles, 1991—, Blanche de Castille, Birmingham, 1990-91. Avocations: tennis, golf, skiing, family. Home: 44 Ave Jeanne Léger, F-78150 Le Chesnay France Office: FACOM SA, BP 99, F-91423 Morangis France

DAUDT, CARLOS EUGENIO, agronomist, educator; b. Sao Leopoldo, Brazil, Nov. 29, 1941; s. Eugenio Emilio and Maria Ida (Henemann) D.; m. Maria do Carmo Stabel, Dec. 21, 1963; children: Carlos Antonio Stabel, Christian S., Simone S. Agronomist (Engr.), U. Fed. Rio Grande do Sul, Brazil, 1964; MS, U. Calif., Davis, 1973, PhD, 1980. Postdoctoral fellow U. Calif., Davis, 1991; instr. Fed. U. Santa Maria, Brazil, 1966-69, asst. prof., 1970-73, assoc. prof., 1974-88, prof., 1989—; cons. Fed. Inst. for Rsch. in Grapes and Wines, Germany, 1986—; rschr. Nat. Coun. Rsch., Brasilia, Brazil, 1984—; sci. cons.FAPESP, Sao Paulo, Brazil, 1992—; sci. cons. Am. Vineyard Found., San Francisco, 1983. Author: The Dry Wine and its Home Production, 1981, also articles. Named Agronomist of Yr., Agronomist Soc., 1974; FAO fellow, Rome, 1971-73; C.A.P.E.S. fellow, Brasilia, 1977-80. Mem. N.Y. Acad. Sci., Am. Soc. Enology and Viticulture (profl.), Brazilian Soc. for Progress of Sci., Brazil Soc. Food Sci. and Tech., Rotary (pres. 1977). Roman Catholic. Avocations: soccer, music, reading, television, competetive sports. E-mail: ced.voy@zaz.com.br. Home: Rua Marques do Pombal 1938 #204, Porto Alegre RS 90540-000, Brazil Office: Fed U Santa Maria, Dept Food Sci/CCR, 97105-900 Santa Maria RS, Brazil

DAUFIN, GEORGES, chemical engineer; b. Paris, Feb. 18, 1941; s. Edmond and Josephine (Bihan) D.; m. Anne Lecerf, Jan. 26, 1966; children: Christine, Guillaume, Marion. B, Lycee Tours, France, 1958; MS, U. Rennes, France, 1964; PhD, U. Paris, 1974. Asst. INRA, Rennes, France, 1965-71, scientist, 1971-78, sr. scientist, 1978—; network coord. INRA, 1994-99. Editor: Membrane Operations in Food Processing, 1998. Avocation: volleyball. Office: INRA LRTL, 65 rue de St Brieuc, 35042 Rennes CEDEX France

DAUGAARD, HOLGER, food scientist; b. Copenhagen, Apr. 16, 1953; s. Peder Hansen and Tove Frida Daugaard (Johansen) Pedersen; m. Elsebeth Sørensen, June 7, 1978; children: Lisbet, Mikael. MSc in Biology, U. Copenhagen, 1978; MSc in Horticulture, Royal Vet. and Agrl. U., Copenhagen, 1981. Scientist Danish Inst. Agrl. Scis., Odense, 1981-82; tchr. Søhus Hort. Coll., Odense, 1982-86; extension horticulturalist Danish Assn. for Fruit growers, Odense, 1986-92, chief extension horticulturalist, 1992-97; scientist Danish Inst. Agrl. Scis., Årslev, 1997-2000, sr. scientist, 2000—. Contbr. articles to profl. jours. Seventh Day Adventist. Avocations: bird watching, camping, botany, religious activities. Home: Aertebjerggårdvej 75, DK 5270 Odense Denmark Office: Danish Inst Agrl Scis, Kirstinebjergvej 10, DK 5792 Årslev Denmark

DAUGHENBAUGH, TERRY LEE, steel industry executive; b. Latrobe, Pa., July 20, 1939; s. Gladys Idella Hollobaugh; m. Cristine Zubaty, May 1, 1999; children: Thomas, Todd, Tracey; stepchildren: Leslie, Neil. BS, U. Pitts., 1968; postgrad., Columbia U., 1985. With Kennemetal Corp., Latrobe, Pa., 1957-58; with Latrobe (Pa.) Steel Co., 1958-92, project engr., 1968-70, melt shop supt., 1970-73, mgr. primary ops., 1973-85, gen. mgr. mfg., 1985-88, gen. mgr. primary ops. and engring., 1988-92; pres. Innovative Water Tech., Inc. divsn. Innovative Group, Latrobe, 1992; pres., owner Spl. D Co., Latrobe, 1992-96; pres., chmn. bd. dirs. Baker Pyromet, Inc., Greenville, Pa., 1994-2000; gen. mgr. Baker Refractories BEC, Greenville, 2000—; cons. to steel industry, 1992-96. Chmn. bd. Ea. Westmoreland Devel. Corp., Latrobe, 1995-98, chmn. transp. com., 1989-99; mem. home rule commn. Borough of Latrobe, 1994-96; bd. dirs. Latrobe Area C. of C., 1995-98, Latrobe Area Devel. Coun., 1995—, Valley Players of Ligonier, 1997, Laurel Ballet, 1990-94, Westmoreland Blind Assn., 1987-89, Econ. Growth Connection, chmn. infrastructure com., 2000—; coach, mgr., commr. Latrobe-Derry Area Teener League, 1974-84. Mem. Am. Iron and Steel Engrs., Iron & Steel Soc., Assn. Iron and Steel Engrs., Loyalhanna Watershed Assn., Latrobe Area Devel. Coun., Alumni Elec. Metal Makers Guild, Ingot Metallurgy Forum, SPRPC Citizens Adv. Panel, Touchdown Club, Teutonia Mannechor. Republican. Lutheran. Avocations: skiing, golf. Fax: (home) 724-539-0799; (office) 724-646-3104. Home: 1129 Lauralynn Dr Latrobe PA 15650-4718

DAUGHERTY, J(AMES) PATRICK, oncologist; b. Athens, Tenn., May 17, 1948; s. James Larson and Dorothy Mae D.; m. Rebecca Poteet, Sept. 6, 1969; children: Lori, Andrea, Amy. BS in Natural Sci. cum laude, Lee Coll., 1969; postgrad., U. Chattanooga, 1967, Cleve. State C.C., 1968, E. Tenn. State U., 1969-70; PhD, U. Tenn., 1975; MD, U. Ala., 1981. Diplomate Am. Bd. Internal Medicine. Intern, resident Carrawy Meth. Med. Ctr., Birmingham, Ala., 1982-84; fellow med. oncology Fox Chase Cancer Ctr., Phila., 1985-87; staff physican Med. Ctr. Shoals, Muscle Shoals, Ala., 1987—; founder, dir., physician N.W. Ala. Cancer Ctr., Muscle Shoals, Florence, 1987—; staff physican Helen Keller Meml. Hosp., Sheffield, Ala., 1988—; staff physician Eliza Coffee Meml. Hosp., Florence, 1987—, Florence Hosp., 1987—; med. dir. Cumberland Valley Cancer Ctr., 1995—, North Ctrl. Ala. Cancer Ctr., 1996—; cons. physician Northwest Ala. Med. Ctr., Russellville, 1996; adj. prof. biomed. sci., co-dir. Lab. Applied Tech., U. North Ala.; grad. tech. asst. East Tenn. State U., Johnson City, 1969-70, U. Tenn., Knoxville, 1973-74; postdoctoral investigator Oak Ridge Grad. Sch. med. Sci. and Biology divsn. Oak Ridge Nat. Lab., 1974-76; vis. lectr. Lee Coll., Cleveland, Tenn., 1976-77; rsch. assoc. Lab. Molecular Biology, U. Ala., Birmingham, 1976-80, assoc. scientist Comprehensive Cancer Ctr., Newtown, 1980-84; mem. dir. Chandler Hall Hospice, Newton, Pa., 1986-87;

mem., chmn. several coms. Florence Hosp., ECM Hosp., Med. Ctr. Shoals, Helen Keller Meml. Hosp. Contbr. numerous articles to profl. jours. Bd. dirs. Lauderdale County chpt. Am. Cancer Soc., 1987—, pres., 1992—; bd. dirs. R&D coun. Riverbend Mental Health Ctr., Florence, 1992—, United Way of the Shoals, 1990—, Shoals Area C. of C., exec. com., vice chair pub. policy; chmn. bd. trustees Woodmont Christian Sch., Florence, 1994—; deacon Woodmont Bapt. Ch., 1994—; pres. cabinet U. No. Ala.; bd. dirs., investment com. U. No. Ala. Found.; steering com. Conf. Spiritual Renewal. Named Disting. Alumnus Lee Coll., Cleveland Tenn., 1992, Small Bus. of Yr. Shoals Area C. of C., 1994; NDEA fellow, 1971-73. Mem. ACP,AMA, Am. Soc. Internal Medicine, Am. Assn. Cancer Rsch., Am. Soc. Clin. Oncology, So. Assn. Oncology, Med. Assn. Ala. (alt. del 1989, del 1992), Lauderdale County Med. Soc., Colbert County Med. Soc., So. Med. Assn., Ala. Cattleman's Assn., Shoals Area C. of C. (bd. dirs., exec. com., vice chmn. pub. policy), Christian Booksellers Assn., Rotary, Sigma Xi. Avocations: woodworking, collecting southern crafts. Home: 1960 Jackson Rd Florence AL 35630-1833 Office: NW Ala Cancer Ctr 302 W Dr Hicks Blvd Florence AL 35630-6160 also: 101 Wh Blake Jr Dr Muscle Shoals AL 35661-2152

DAUGHERTY, KENNETH EARL, research company executive, educator; b. Pitts., Dec. 27, 1938; s. Thomas Hill and Laura Elizabeth (Schuda) D.; m. Joan Kay Ogrosky, Dec. 22, 1961; children: Brian Earl, Kirsten Kay. BS in Chemistry, Carnegie-Mellon U., 1960; PhD in Analytical Chemistry, U. Wash., 1964; M. Bus. Econs., Claremont Grad. Sch., 1971. Chemist Marbon Chem.-Borg Warner, Washington, W.Va., 1960; research chemist Rohm and Haas Corp., Bristol, Pa., 1964; group leader, sr. staff Amcord, Riverside, Calif., 1966-71; assoc. prof. chemistry U. Pitts., 1971-73; dir. research and devel. Gen. Portland Inc., Dallas, 1973-77; dir. energy and materials sci. Inst. Applied Scis. North Tex. State U., Denton, 1977-79; prof. chemistry North Tex. State U., 1979—, chmn. analytical divsn., 1980—; pres. KEDS Inc., KD Cons., 1977—; owner TRAC Labs., Denton, 1981—; adj. prof. chemistry U. Pitts., 1973—, N. Tex. State U., Denton, 1974—; adj. faculty Army Command and Gen. Staff Coll., 1983—; cons. in field. Author numerous publs. in field. Patentee in field. Served to col. AUS, 1964-66, Res., 1966—. Fellow DuPont, Shell Oil, Standard Oil, NSF, 1964. Decorated Army Commendation medal, Army Achievement medal, Army Meritorious Svc. medal. Fellow Am. Inst. Chemists; mem. Research Soc. Am., ASTM, Rilem, Nat. (transp. research bd.), N.Y. Acad. Scis., Am. Ceramic Soc. (program chmn. 1986), Am. Chem. Soc. (chpt. pres. 1960, chmn. Dallas-Ft. Worth 1986), Applied Spectroscopy Soc., Soc. Petroleum Engrs., Soc. Plastics Engrs., Sr. Army Comdrs. Assn., Sigma Xi, Pi Kappa Alpha, Omicron Delta Epsilon, Phi Lambda Upsilon, Alpha Chi Sigma, Masons (32 deg.), Shriners, Rotary. Republican. Methodist. Home: 1912 Hunskor Rd Oak Harbor WA 98277-8666

DAUGHERTY, LINDA HAGAMAN, private school executive; b. Denver, Jan. 25, 1940; d. Charles B. and Agnes May (Wall) Hagaman; m. Thomas Daniel Daugherty, Nov. 20, 1965; children: Patrick, Christina Marie. BS in Bus., U. Colo., 1961; postgrad., Tulane U., 1963-64, U. St. Thomas, 1990-91. Sr. systems analyst Lockheed Electronics NASA, Houston, 1966-73; sr. systems cons. TRW Systems Internat., Caracas, Venezuela, 1973-74; sy. systems cons. TRW Systems, L.A., 1974-75; sr. systems analyst Intercomp, Houston, 1979-80; cons. Daugherty Fin. Svcs., Inc., Katy, Tex., 1980-82, pres., 1979-91; mng. ptnr. Motivated Child Learning Ctrs., Katy, 1976—; pres. Williamsburg Country Day Sch., Katy, 1983—, Nottingham Country Day Sch., Katy, 1977—. Pres. Mason Creek Women Reps. Club, Katy, 1980; treas. Nottingham Country Civic Club, Katy, 1979; mem. adv. bd. Nottingham Country Club, 1982-85; co-founder Friends of Archaeology U. St. Thomas, pres., 1991-93; mem. Epiphany Ch. Social Works Commn.; asst. curator Archaeology Gallery, U. St. Thomas; mem., pres. Friends of Boerne Pub. Libr., 1997—; San Antonio World Affair Coun. Mem. Houston Archeology Soc., Tex. Archeology Soc., Archaeology Inst. of Am., Boerne Women's Club. Roman Catholic. Avocations: archaeology, bridge. Office: Nottingham Country Day Sch PO Box 489 Boerne TX 78006-0489

DAUGHTERY, VERGIL LACY, III, inventor; b. Valdosta, Ga., July 15, 1959; s. Vergil Lacy Jr. and Pearl Catherine (Tipton) D.; m. Elizabeth Marie Kramer, Dec. 28, 1982; children: Vergil Lacy IV, Sara Catherine. BS, Ga. Inst. Tech., 1990, MS, 1995. Mem. R&D staff Ga. Tech. Rsch. Corp., Atlanta, 1984-99; devel. officer Magnolia Manor, Americus, Ga., 1991—; founder Econ. Inventions LLC, Americus, Ga., 1997—; bd. dirs. Lawrence Capitol Mgmt., Inc., Richmond, Va. Author: Derivatives: Pricing and Application, 1999; inventor expirationless option; contbg. editor S.E. Jurisdiction United Meth. Newspaper. Del. South Ga. Conf. United Meth. Ch., 1998, mem. S.E. Jurisdictional Adminstrv. Coun.; bd. dirs. Morningside United Meth. Ch., Americus, SEMAR, Inc. With U.S. Army, 1978-84. Mem. Ga. Tech. Alumni Assn. Democrat. Avocation: bridge. Address: 29 Thomas Coke Dr Waynesville NC 28785-5911

DAUKANTAS, GEORGE VYTAUTAS, counseling practitioner, educator; b. Stolzenau, Germany, Dec. 20, 1946; came to U.S., 1949; s. Chester and Alexandra Daukantas. AA magna cum laude, Lesley Coll., 1973; BA in Psychology, U. Mass., 1976; MA in Counseling Psychology, U. No. Colo., 1982; MEd in Psychol. Studies, Cambridge Coll., 2000. Cert. computer programming/ops. Estate coord. St. Petersburgh, Fla., 1986-91; customer svc. rep., pc operator Applied Image Reprographics, Quincy, Mass., 1993-96; asst. tchr. severely challenged boys and girls Boston Pub. Schs., 1997—. Sgt. E-5 U.S. Army, 1964-67, USNG, 1975-82. Recipient Cold War Recognition Cert., U.S. Army, 1999. Mem. ACLU, Am. Counseling Assn./ACES, Assn. for Counselor Edn. and Supervision, Mass. Mental Health Counselor's Assn., Am. Civil Liberties Union, Amnesty Internat., Am. Legion. Democrat. Roman Catholic. E-mail: daukantas@hotmail.com. Home: 34 Mount Auburn St Apt 201 Cambridge MA 02138-6022

DAUKSHUS, A. JOSEPH, systems engineer; b. Tamaqua, Pa., Oct. 17, 1948; s. Anna N. Daukshus. BS in Aerospace Engring., Pa. State U., 1975. Devel. engr. Carl Zeiss Inc., Thornwood, N.Y., 1984-88; cons. Panasonic, Secaucus, N.J., 1988, Pratt & Whitney, E. Hartford, Conn., 1989; cons. AT&T, Largo, Fla., 1990, Somerset, N.J., 1990-91; cons. Torrington (Conn.) Co., 1990, Trecom Bus. Systems, Edison, N.J., 1990-91; systems engr. Canberra Industries, Meriden, Conn., 1991-93; sales assoc. Sears Roebuck and Co., Danbury, Conn., 1993-94; engr. EIS Internat., Stamford, Conn., 1995-96, Oxford Health Plans, Norwalk, Conn., 1996-98, Reuters, Stamford, 1998-2000; quality analyst Oxford Health Plans, Trumbull, Conn., 2000—; cons. Executone, Darien, Conn., 1994-95, NASDAQ Stock Market Inc., Trumbull, Conn., 1994-95. Mem. N.Y. Acad. Sci. Home: PO Box 8916 New Fairfield CT 06812-8916

DAUL, JOSEPH, foreign diplomat; b. Strasbourg, France, Apr. 13, 1947. Mem. European Parliament, 1999—, vice chmn. com. on agr. and rural devel., substitute com. on fgn. affairs/human rights/common security; mem. Group of the European People's Party (Christian Democrats) and European Democrats; mem. delegation for relations with Can.; substitute delegation to the EU-Romania Joint Parliamentary Com. *

DAUM, JOHANNES PETER, architecture educator; b. Bodenhofen, Austria, Oct. 10, 1920; s. Otto Franz and Ada Antonia (Czermak) D.; m. Eleonore Anna-Maria Pichler, July 15, 1953; children: Christoph, Andreas. Diploma in engring., Tech. Hochschule Wien, Vienna, Austria, 1949, D D Technischen Wissenschaften, 1957. Univ. asst. Institut for History of Architecture, 1950-67; univ. prof., dir. Inst. History of Architecture U. Innsbruck, Austria, 1968-90, prof. emeritus, 1991—, dean faculty of architecture, 1977-79; architect Vienna, 1955-69; permanent rep. faculty German, dean Conf. for Architecture, 1975-84; expert Fonds zur Förderung D. Wissenschaftl. Forschung, Vienna, 1969-90. Co-author: Forschungen und Funde, 1980, Sinngestalten, 1989, Echo, 1990, Von der Bauforschung zur Denkmalpflege, 1993, Velia Studi e Ricerche, 1994. Lt. Deutsche Wehrmacht, 1940-45. Recipient medal of merit for Old City Hall in Tirol, 1984, Golden Hon. Needle Soc. Mus. of Tirolein Farm-Houses, 1984, Cross of Honour for Sci. and Art, Austrian Pres. of State, 1985. Mem. German Archaeologic Institut (corr.), Koldewey-Gesellsahft, Archaeol. Soc. Innsbruck, Austrian Nat. Com. Icomos. Roman Catholic. Home: Tschiggfreystrasse 27, A6020 Innsbruck Austria Office: Inst Baukunst Denkmalpflege, Technikerstrasse 13, A-6020 Innsbruck Austria

DAUM, JULIE HAMBROCK, executive recruiter; b. Cin., Aug. 5, 1954; d. Vincent and Mary Hembrock; m. Robert Charles Daum; children: Alexandra, Schuyler, Bailey. BS, Pa. State U., 1976; MBA, Wharton Grad. Sch., 1979. Assoc. McKinsey & Co., L.A., 1979-81; v.p. Chase Manhattan Bank, London, N.Y.C., 1981-85, Citibank, N.Y.C., 1985-87; cons. Nordeman Grimm, N.Y.C., 1988-90; mng. dir. corp. bd. resources Catalyst, N.Y.C., 1991-98; mng. dir. U.S. board svcs. Spencer Stuart, N.Y.C., 1993—. Bd. dirs. City Harvest, 2000—, Student Sponsor Partnership, 2000—, Women's Forum, 2000—. Mem. Coloby Club, River Club, Tuxedo Club. Episcopalian. Home: 120 E End Ave New York NY 10028-7552 Office: Spencer Stuart 277 Park Ave Fl 29 New York NY 10172-2998

DAUMEN, GUSTAVO J., company executive; b. Caracas, Venezuela, May 2, 1942; s. Gustavo A. and Fronilde A. (Anzola) D.; m. Maria M. Kerdel, Nov. 6, 1970; children: Graciela, Guillermo, Gustavo. Engr., Cen. U., Caracas, 1966; degree in econ. devel. and planning, Cambridge (Eng.) U., 1974. Cert. in mech. engring. Gen. mgr. Epsilon Ite, Caracas, 1966-72; gen. dir. Environment Ministry, Venezuela, 1973-78; advisor Nat. Ports Inst., Venezuela, 1978-79, France Metro, Caracas, 1980-86; dir. Metro Mantenimiento C.A., Venezuela, 1980-86; pres. Grupo 986 C.A., Caracas, 1987—. Mem. Coll. Engrs. of Venezuela, Oxford and Cambridge U. Club. Roman Catholic. Avocations: jogging, golf, traveling. Office: Grupo 986 CA, Apartado 81170, 1080 Caracas Venezuela

DAUS, ARTHUR STEVEN, neurological surgeon; b. Louisville, Feb. 6, 1957; s. Arthur Theodore Daus Jr. and Marilyn Ann (McCord) Hanish; m. Victoria Lynn Schilla, July 10, 1982; children: Arthur S. Jr., Haley N. BS in Physics magna cum laude, Vanderbilt U., 1977; MD, St. Louis U., 1981. Diplomate Nat. Bd. Med. Examiners, Am. Bd. Neurol. Surgery, Fedn. State Licensing Examiners; lic. physician, Ky., N.Mex., Ariz., Mo., Calif. Rotating intern in surgery U. Ky. Med. Ctr., Lexington, 1981-82, resident neurosurgeon, 1982-88; pvt. practice Midwest Neurosurgery Ctr., Joplin, Mo., 1988—; instr. cervical spine instrumentation A.M.E. Med. Co., Kansas City, Mo., 1992. Mem. Nat. Coalition of Physicians Against Family Violence, Chgo., 1994—. Recipient Ky. State Residents award Am. Coll. Surgeons com. on trauma, 1985; named Ky. Col. State of Ky., 1985—. Mem. AMA (Physician's Recognition award 1990-94, 3 Physician's Recognition awards with spl. commendation, 1993-96, 96-2000, 2000—), So. Med. Assn., Jasper-Newton County Med. Soc., So. Neurosurg. Soc. (first honorable mention resident's competition 1984), Congress Neurol. Surgeons, Am. Assn. Neurol. Surgeons (3 continuing edn. awards 1990-92, 93-95, 96-98), Nat. Audubon Soc., Phi Beta Kappa, Phi Eta Sigma. Republican. Roman Catholic. Avocations: chess, swimming, archery, riflery, horseback riding. Home: 5 Teal Dr Joplin MO 64804-5816 Office: Midwest Neurosurgery Ctr 1111 McIntosh Cir Ste 305 Joplin MO 64804-3693

DAUS, VICTORIA LYNN, nurse midwife; b. Cleve.; m. Arthur Steven Daus; 2 children. RN, Luth. Med. Ctr., Cleve., 1975; BSN, St. Louis U., 1982; MSN, U. Ky., 1987; D of Nursing, Case Western Res. U., 1996; postgrad. in nursing, Francis Payne Bolton Sch. Nursing. RN, Mo., Ohio, Ky., NSW, Australia. Nurse newborn nursery, neonatal intensive care nurse, pediatrics nurse Fairview Gen. Hosp., Cleve., 1975-78; neonatal intensive care nurse, neonatal transport nurse Royal Alexandria Hosp. for Children, Sydney, NSW, Australia, 1978-79; midwife Crown Street Women's Hosp., Sydney, 1979-80; labor and delivery nurse, postpartum nurse Deaconess Hosp., Cleve., 1980; neonatal intensive care nurse Cardinal Glennon Meml. Hosp. for Children, St. Louis, 1981-82; labor and delivery nurse Chandler Med. Ctr. U. Ky., Lexington, 1982-83; labor and delivery nurse, tchr. childbirth edn., labor and delivery charge nurse Humana Hosp., Lexington, 1983-85; coord. quality assurance Prince of Wales Hosp. for Children, Sydney, 1986; hosp. floater for coronary care, neurosurg., orthopedics and med., surg. nurse Good Samaritan Hosp., Lexington, 1985-87; clin. instr. obstetrics and pediatrics Lexington C.C., 1988. Mem. Am. Assn. Neurosci. Nurses, Am. Coll. Nurse-Midwives (cert.), Nat. Assn. Nurse Practitioners in Reproductive Health, N.Am. Nursing Diagnosis Assn., Assn. Reproductive Health Profls., Assn. Women's Health, Obstet. and Neonatal Nurses, Sigma Theta Tau. Republican. Roman Catholic.

DAUSES, MANFRED ALBERT, law educator; b. Bamberg, Germany, Mar. 10, 1944; s. Baptist Johann and Margarete Sophie (Bosch) D. Dr.iur.utr, U. Würzburg, 1970; DES de droit comparé, U. Strasbourg, 1972; Ancien Elève, Ecole Nat. d'Adminstrn., 1973; Dr.h.c., World U., 1987, Australian Inst. Coord. Rsch., 1995. Govt. atty. Regional Ct., Essen, Germany, 1975-77; judge regional ct. Essen, 1977-78; asst. head of dept. Fed. Ministry of Justice, Germany, 1978-79; sr. law clk., dir. Ct. of Justice of the European Communities, Luxembourg, 1979-93; prof., Jean Monnet chair U. Bamberg, Germany, 1993—; vis. prof. internat. law Boston U., 1981-85; lectr. European law Europa-Inst., U. of Saarbrücken, Germany, 1985-88, Tech. U. of Aachen, Germany, 1988-92; hon. prof. German Law Charles U. of Prague, Czech Republic, 1998—; vis. lectr., prof. several univs., Switzerland, Poland, U.S., Japan; lead expert EU Phare Project in Czech Republic, 1994—, co-expert PHARE Projects in Poland, Hungary, Estonia, and Moldova, 1995—; dep. dir. gen. Internat. Biog. Ctr., Cambridge, Eng. Editor: Handbook of European Economic Law, 2 vols., 1993, 9th edit., 2000; editor, co-author: Osterweiterung der Europäischen Union, 1998; co-editor European Jour. of Econ. Law, 1990—; author, co-author 15 books; contbr. over 200 articles to profl. jours., transl. into 15 langs. Mem. Internat. Inst. for Strategic Studies, Internat. Inst. of Space Law, Internat. Law Assn. Avocations: jogging, bicycling. Office: Otto-Friedrich U Bamberg, D-96045 Bamberg Germany

DAUSSET, JEAN, immunologist; b. Toulouse, France, Oct. 19, 1916; s. Henri and Elizabeth D.; m. Rose Mayoral, Mar. 17, 1962. AB, Lycee Michelet, 1939; MD, U. Paris, 1945. Intern, then resident in internal medicine and hematology Paris Mcpl. Hosps., 1946-50; dir. lab. Nat. Transfusion Ctr., 1950-63; prof. immunohematology U. Paris, 1963-77; prof. exptl. medicine Coll. de France, Paris, 1977-87; dir. research unit on immunogenetics Hopital Saint-Louis, Paris, 1969-84; dir. Human Polymorphism Study Ctr., 1984—; researcher in field of man's histocompatibility system anbd human genome. Served to capt., World War II. Recipient Nobel prize in physiology or medicine, 1980, Honda prize Honda Found. Japan, 1987. Mem. Academie des Sciences de l'Institut de France, Am. Acad. Arts and Sci., NAS (Washington). Home: 44 Rue des Ecoles, 75005 Paris France Office: 27 Rue Juliette Dodu, 75010 Paris France

DAUTRESME, DAVID LUCIEN, bank executive; b. Marseille, France, Jan. 5, 1934; s. Paul Jean and Paulette Rosalie (Lang) D.; m. Michéle Pierrette Hugodot, Dec. 18, 1958; children: Bertrand, Aline, Marianne. PhD in Econs., U. Paris, 1955; grad. summa cum laude, Inst. d'Etudes Politics Paris, 1955; grad., Ecole Nationale d'Administration, Paris, 1962. Auditeur, conseiller référendaire Cour des Comptes, Paris, 1962-66; asst. to min. of fin. in charge of treas. affairs Paris, 1967-68; sr. exec. v.p. Credit Lyonnais, Paris, 1968-82; chmn., CEO, Credit du Nord, Paris, 1982-86; gen. ptnr. Lazard Freres et Cie, Paris, 1986—; bd. dirs. Compagnie de Credit, AXA, Casino, Immobiliere Marseillaise, Fonds Partenaires, Club Mediterranée, Assn. Francaise des Banques; bd. dirs., chmn. Credit Agricole Lazard Fin. Products Bank. Author: Economy and Capital Market, 1985. Lt. French inf., 1958-60. Decorated Mil. Cross, Legion of Honor. Mem. European Bankers Assn., Cercle Interalliee, Yacht Club France. Roman Catholic. Avocations: sailing, golf. Home: 67 rue de Miromesnil, 75008 Paris France Office: Lazard Freres & Cie, 121 Blvd Haussmann, 75008 Paris France

DAUVALTER, VLADIMIR, ecology researcher; b. Octyabrskiy, USSR, Sept. 24, 1957; s. Andrey and Amalia (Haberkorn) D.; m. Margarita Gapon, June 4, 1983; children: Anton, Maria. Geologist, Oil Coll., Octyabrskiy, USSR, 1976; Hydrogeologist, Mining Inst., Leningrad, 1983; PhD in Geography, Lake Rsch. Inst., St. Petersburg, 1994; DSc in Geography, Inst. Water Problems, Moscow, 2000. Engr. VNIIGIS, Octyabrskiy, USSR, 1983-86; hydrogeologist Apatite Co., Kirovsk, USSR, 1986-89; sr. engr. Inst. North Indsl. Ecology Problems, Apatity, Russia, 1989-94; researcher Inst. North Indsl. Ecology Problems, Apatity, 1994-97, sr. researcher, 1997-99, head lab., 1999—. Author: Quality Formation of Surface Waters and Sediments Under Conditions of Anthropogenic Loads of Water Catchments Within the Arctic Area, 1996, Geochemical Migration of Elements in Subarctic Freshwater Body, 1997, Ecosystem of the Pechora River in Modern Conditions, 2000; contbr. articles to profl. jours. Sr. lt. antiaircraft artillery, 1983. Fellow Interna. Arctic Sci. Com. Oslo. Lutheran. Avocations: gardenign, music, car driving and repair, physical training. Home: 54 Fersman St Flat 23, 184200 Apatity Murmansk, Russia Office: Inst North Indsl Ecology Problems, 14 Fersman St, 184200 Apatity Murmansk, Russia

DAUVRIN, THIERRY, researcher; b. Saint Josse, Belgium, Nov. 13, 1959; s. Jacques and Paule (De Greve) D.; m. Anne De Smet, Oct. 14, 1983; children: Marie, Elisabeth, Alice. PhD in Biochemistry, UCL, Belgium, 1988. Rsch. scientist Puratos, Belgium, 1987-95, rsch. mgr., 1995—. Mem. Am. Soc. Microbiology, Belgian Soc. Biochem. & Molecular Biology. Office: Frimond, Rue Bourrie 12, B-5300 Andenne Belgium

DAVALOS-GUEVARA, C. MAURICIO, agroindustrial company executive; b. Riobamba, Chimborazo, Ecuador, June 24, 1944; s. Clemente and Beatriz (Guevara-Merino) Davalos-Larrea; m. Rita Teran-Teran, Oct. 25, 1975; children: Ana Corina, Maria Clara, Isabel Maria, Irene. BA, Northwestern U., Evanston, Ill., 1970; MA, Vanderbilt U., 1973; Economista, Cath. U., Quito, Ecuador, 1974. Prof. Cath. U., Quito, 1973-75, dir. econ. rsch., 1973-74; mgr. Citibank, Quito, 1975-79; minister energy Govt. Ecuador, Quito, 1979; gen. mgr. Ctrl. Bank of Ecuador, Quito, 1979-81; chmn. bd. Nat. Devel. Bank, Quito, 1982; gov. Ecuador Internat. Monetary Fund, 1979-81; pres. Andea Res. Fund, 1980-81; CEO Agroflora C. Ltda, Quito, 1983, Rosel C. Ltda, Quito, 1990-94; pres. Florisol C. Ltda, Quito, 1984—; gen. mgr. Rimaco C. Ltda, Quito, 1989-98; gen. mgr., gov. Ctrl. Bank Ecuador, Quito, 1979-81; pres. Ecuador Com. for Pacific Basin, 1998. Author: A Fiscal History of Ecuador, 1975. Mem. Commn. to Write Current Constitution of Ecuador, Quito, 1977; nat. v.p. Democracia Popular, Quito, 1981-82; energy minister Govt. Ecuador, Quito, 1979; rep. to Nat. Constitl. Assembly, 1997-98; min. agriculture Govt. Ecuador, 2000—. Cadet Ecuador Army, 1960-62. Named Hon. Citizen of Tenn., Gov. Tenn., Nashville, 1970; recipient Medal of Honor Provincial Coun. Pinchincha, Quito, 1981, Pedro Vicente Maldonado medal Municipality of Riobamba, Ecuador, 1982, Profl. Merit medal Economists Assn. Quito, 1996, Labour Merit medal Govt. of Ecuador Labor Ministry, 1997. Mem. Assn. Productores y Exportadores de Flores (pres. 1990-94), Agrl. Chamber (mem. bd., pres. 1993-94), Centro de Estudios para el Desarrollo (mem. bd. 1989—), Empresa Ecuatoriana de Aviación (mem. bd. 1993-94), Exporters Fedn. Ecuador (v.p. 1997—), Quito Tennis and Golf Club. Roman Catholic. Avocation: horseback riding. Home: PO Box 17-07-9465, Quito Ecuador Office: Agroflora C Ltda Edificio Multicentro, 502, 6 de Diciembre y la Niña, Quito Ecuador

DAVE, HEMANT JAYANTILAL, textile engineer; b. Dakor, India, Jan. 24, 1959; s. Jayantilal Chandulal and Sarojben Jayantilal (Saroj) D.; m. Jagruti Hemant Dave; children: Parth, Aarsh. D in Textile Tech., M.S. Univ., Baroda, India, 1980, B in Textile Tech., 1985, M in Textile Engring., 1988; degree in mktg. and sales mgmt., Bhawans Coll., Bombay, 1989. Supr. The Surat (India) Cotton Mills, 1980-81; in charge of auto-shed Priyalaxoni Mill, Baroda, 1981-88; asst. mgr. Neomer Divsn. ACW Co. Ltd., Baroda, 1988-97; dir. Hi Tech Splty. Fabrics Ltd., Vadodara, India, 1997—. Mem. Textile Assn. India (hon. sec. 1988—). Avocations: reading, music, cricket. Office: Hi Tech Splty Fabrics Ltd, G/F-4 Trimurti Apt RC Dutt, Vadodara 390004, India

DAVENPORT, ANN ADELE MAYFIELD, home care agency administrator; b. New Orleans, Nov. 12, 1941; d. Henry Louis and Myrtie Iola (Cason) Mayfield; m. John Wayne Davenport, June 18, 1966; children: Steven Lyle, Daniel Ryan, Elaine Adele. BA, Southeastern La. Coll., 1963; MA in Edn., George Peabody C., 1965; MA in Sociology, Tex. Tech. U., 1971. Tchr. various schs., 1963-70; instr. of sociology Tex. Tech. U., Lubbock, 1970-74, James Madison U., Harrisonburg, Va., 1981-82, Ga. So. Coll., Statesboro, 1982-84; 5th grade tchr. Bulloch county Schs., Statesboro, Ga., 1985-87; gerontology project coord. Dept. of Nursing Ga. So. Coll., 1987-88; project dir. Sr. Companion Program Ctr. for Rural Health and Rsch., Ga. So. U., Statesboro, 1988-93; instr. dept. health sci. edn. Ga. So. Coll., Statesboro, 1993-95; exec. dir. Ogeechee Home Health Agy., Statesboro, 1995-96, Homebound Svcs., Statesboro, 1996—. Editor various newsletters, 1987—. Bd. dirs. Citizens Against Violence, Statesboro, 1987-88, Habitat for Humanity, 1990—; pres. Coun. on Children and Parents, Statesboro, 1988-89, 93-94; mem. steering com. Bulloch County Commn. on Human Svcs., 1989—; mem. adminstrv. bd. dirs., coun. on ministries, nominating com. Pittman Park United Meth. Ch.; pres. Ogeechee Wellness Coun., 1992—; bd. dirs. Ogeechee Home Health Agy., 1989-93. Mem. Ga. Rural Health Assn. (sec. 1988-89, editor state newsletter 1989—), So. Sociol. Soc., Ga. Gerontol. Assn., Ga. Sociol. Assn., AAUW (newsletter editor Statesboro 1987-89), Am. Soc. on Aging, Nat. Coun. on the Aging, Am. Rural Health Assn. Avocations: tennis, reading. Home: 1 Greenwood Ave Statesboro GA 30458-5032 Office: Homebound Svcs Inc PO Box 2473 Statesboro GA 30459-2473

DAVENPORT, JEFFREY PATON, financial planner, investment advisor; b. Clearwater, Fla., May 25, 1963; s. Joseph Pleasant Davenport and Jacquiline Claire Davis; m. Jenny Virginia Nunez, Oct. 25, 1996; children: Christian Michael, Lauren Ashley. AS, St. Petersburg Jr. Coll., 1983; BS in Bus., Fla. State U., 1985. CFP, Colo.; cert. fin. councilor for health care profls.; lic. series 7, gen. securities lic. Intern Investment Mgmt. & Rsch., Seminole, Fla., 1989-92; pres., founder Davenport PA, St. Petersburg, Fla., 1989—; sr. mgr. MPI Internat., St. Petersburg, 1986-89; registered securities rep. Fortis Fin. Group, St. Petersburg, 1992—; intern Xelan Inst., St. Petersburg, 1994-96; mng. ptnr. Xelan The Econ. Assn. of Health Profls., San Diego, 1994—; mem. adv. bd. J. Martin & Assoc., Inc., St. Petersburg, Oasis, U. South Fla., St. Petersburg, 1995—; chmn. bd. United Family Buyers, Inc., Orlando; cons., adminstr. Davenport Dental, P.A., Sarasota, Fla., 1998—. Com. mem. Am. Heart Assn., St. Petersburg, 1994, 95; bd. dirs. Stepping Stone, St. Petersburg, 1995; vol., counselor Oasis Children's Program, St. Petersburg, 19955. Mem. Inst. CFPs, Pinellas County Osteopathic Med. Soc., St. Petersburg Yacht Club, Phi Ro Pi, Delta Sigma Pi. Republican. Avocations: snow skiing, traveling, tennis, scuba diving. Office: Davenport PA 3839 4th St N Ste 350 Saint Petersburg FL 33703-6112

DAVENPORT, LINDSAY, professional tennis player; b. Palos Verdes, Calif., June 8, 1976. Profl. tennis player, 1993—. Ranked 3d Doubles (with Chanda Rubin), 1993; recipient 3 career pro singles titles (1) Lucerne, 1993, (2) Brisbane, Lucerne, 1994, 95; winner singles & doubles (with Jana Novotna) Bausch & Lomb Championships, 1997; named to Olympic Team 1996; gold medalist singles, 1996; ranked #1 1998, 99; winner Bank of the West, 1998, Toshiba Classic, 1998, Acura Invitational, 1998, U.S. Open, 1998, European Championships, 1998, Toray Pan Pacific (doubles) 1999, Sydney Internat., 1999; Wimbledon, 1999, Chase Championships, 1999, Madrid Internat., 1999, Stanford, 1999, Tokyo (Princess Cup), 1999, Phila., 1999; finalist New Haven, 1999; semifinalist Australian Open, 1999, U.S. Open, 1999, Grand Slam Cup, L.A., 1999; winner Australian Open, 2000. Office: US Tennis Assn 70 W Red Oak Ln White Plains NY 10604-3602*

DAVENPORT-HINES, RICHARD PETER TREADWELL, historian; b. Hampstead, Eng., June 21, 1953; s. John Hines and June Patricia (Treadwell) Pearson; m. Frances Jane Davenport, May 20, 1978; children: Hugo Denzil Rufus, Cosmo Rory Hector Albertyn. BA, Selwyn Coll., Cambridge, Eng., 1975, MA, 1979; PhD, Cambridge U., 1979. Rsch. officer Bus. History Unit London Sch. Econ., 1983-86; historian Glaxo Pharm. Group, London, 1983-89; rsch. assoc. New Dictionary Nat. Biography, 1995. Author: Dudley Docker, 1984, Speculators and Patriots, 1986, Markets and Bagmen, 1986, Business in the Age of Reason, 1987, British Business in Asia since 1860, 1989, Sex Death and Punishment, 1990, Business in the Age of Depression and War, 1990, The MacMillans, 1992, Glaxo, 1992, Vice, 1993, Auden, 1995, Gothic, 1998, The Pursuit of Oblivion, 2001. Treas. Pembridge Sq. Garden Trust, Kensington, Eng., 1981-83; mem. com. London Liberty, 1997-2000. Avocation: urban window-boxes. Home: Domaine du Meygris, 07200 Ailhon France

DAVEY, ALAN EDWIN, advanced composites and armour executive; b. Bristol, Eng., Nov. 25, 1935; s. Edwin and Doris (Jefferies) D.; m. Pamela Elsie Chard, Aug. 10, 1957; children: Andrew, Richard. MSc, Cranfield U., Bedfordshire, U.K., 1959. Chartered engr. Apprentice Bristol Aircraft Ltd., 1952-57, structural analysts, 1957-61; chief technologist Bristol Composite Materials Engring. Ltd., 1961-86; engring. mgr. Meggitt Composites, West Midlands, Eng., 1986—. Contbr. chpts. to books and articles to profl.

jours.; patentee in field. Scout leader, Bristol, 1962-86. Avocations: sculpture, painting. Home: Kantara Hanbury Rd, Droitwich Spa WR9 7DN, England Office: Meggitt Composites, New Rd Netherton, West Midlands DY2 9AF, England

DAVEY, ALISON, principal, educational consultant; b. Gunnedah, Australia, Dec. 20, 1938; d. Joseph Taylor and Winsome Dell (Baker) T.; m. Brian Arthur Davey, Dec. 17, 1960. Tchr.'s Cert. Tchr.'s Coll., Newcastle Tchr.'s Coll., 1957, Dept. Edn., New S. Wales, 1961; McGrath Tutor Cert. Kip McGrath Edn. Ctr., 1996. Asst. tchr. dept. edn. Telarah Sch., New South Wales, Australia, 1958-59, Parkes Sch., Maitland Girls H.S., New South Wales, 1960—, W. Cessnock Sch., New South Wales, 1961-68; dep. mistress dept. edn. E. Maitland Sch., New South Wales, 1969-73; prin. dept. edn. Ellalong Sch., New South Wales, 1974-77, Bellbird Sch., New South Wales, 1978—; mng. cons. Kip McGrath Edn. Ctr., Cessnock, 1996—. Councillor Cessnock City Coun., 1983—, dep. mayor, 1998—; treas. mgmt. com. Marthaville Arts and Cultural Ctr., Cessnock, 1988—; chairperson Cessnock Cmty. Ctr., 1993—; sec., treas. environ. issues Cessnock Tidy Town Com., 1986—; bd. dirs. Hunter Orch. Bd., 1990—. Recipient award New S. Wales Bicentennial Celebrations City of Cessnock, 1989. Mem. Cessnock Bus. and Profl. Women's Club (sec. women issues 1962—, cmty. welfare issues). Mem. Uniting Ch. Australia. Avocations: cycling, walking, reading, music, camping. Home: 12 Alfred Street, 2325 Cessnock NSW, Australia Office: Kip McGrath Edn Ctr, 37 Vincent St, 2325 Cessnock NSW, Australia

DAVEY, KENNETH JACKSON, government finance and management educator, consultant; b. Leigh-on-Sea, Essex, Eng., Dec. 7, 1932; s. Reginald Alfred and Vera Elizabeth (Jackson) D.; m. Beryl Joyce Herbert, Aug. 18, 1962; children: Guy Reginald, Julian Michael, Stephanie Mary. BA with hons., Merton Coll., Oxford, Eng., 1954; MA, Oxford U., 1956; M in Social Sci., Birmingham (Eng.) U., 1971. Adminstr. H.M. Overseas Civil Svc., Uganda, 1957-69; dir. studies E. African Staff Coll., 1970-72; lectr., sr. lectr. U. Birmingham (Eng.), 1972-81, prof., 1981—, dir. Inst. Local Govt. Studies, 1983-88, head Sch. Pub. Policy, 1988-89; mem. econ. and social rsch. com. Overseas Devel. Adminstrn., 1992-98, coord. internat. rsch. on urban mgmt., 1990-92; coord. Brit. Know How Fund Local Govt. Prs grammes, Czech Republic, Hungary, Slovakia, 1991—; cons. local govt. mgmt. World Bank, Bangladesh, Brazil, China, Hungary, Jordan, Kenya, Mexico, Pakistan, other countries. Author: Taxing a Peasant Society, 1974, Financing Regional Government, 1983, Urban Management: The Challenge of Growth, 1996. Vice chmn. Malvern Coll. Coun., 1994—; mem. Worcester Diocesan Synod, 1987-92. Lt. Royal Artillery, 1954-56. Decorated Order Brit. Empire. Fellow Royal Soc. Arts. Mem. Ch. of Eng. Avocations: choral music, walking. Home: Haymesbrook, Haymes Dr, Cleeve Hill, Cheltenham GL52 3QQ, England Office: U Birmingham, Sch Public Policy, Birmingham B15 2TT, England

DAVEY, RICHARD X., pathologist; b. Melbourne, Australia, July 26, 1945; s. Horace and Desma (Stewart) D.; m. Phillipa R. Davey, 1971; children: Catherine, Clare, Lucy. MA, U. Melbourne, 1968, PhD, 1974; BSc, Monash U., Melbourne, 1976, MB BS, 1981; M.Med.Sci., U. Newcastle, 1997. Clin. pathologist Western Hosp., Melbourne, 1990—; lectr. in field. Contbr. articles to profl. jours. Fellow Royal Coll. Pathologists Australia, Am. Soc. Clin. Pathologists (fgn.), Nat. Acad. Clin. Biochemists. E-mail: richard.davey@wh.org.au. Office: Western Hospital, Gordon St, Footscray 3011, Australia

DAVEY, THOMAS RONALD ALBERT, metallurgical engineer, educator, consultant; b. Melbourne, Victoria, Australia, Mar. 27, 1925; s. Thomas Raymond and Lillie Rose (Harris) D.; m. Kathleen Ann Bonython, July 24, 1954; children: David John, Lucy Ann, Julia Dianne. BSc, U. Melbourne, 1947, BMetE, 1958, MMetE, 1954, DAppSci, 1967. Rsch. metallurgist Broken Hill Assoc. Smelters, Port Pirie, South Australia, 1949-54; chief rsch. officer B.H.A.S., Port Pirie, 1958-59; works engr. Norddeutsche Affinerie, Hamburg, Germany, 1954-57; rsch. metallurgist Imperial Smelting Corp., Avonmouth, Eng., 1957-58; sect. leader, cons. Imperial Smelting Corp., Avonmouth, 1959-63; sr. prin. rsch. scientist div. chem. engring. CSIRO, Melbourne, 1963-69, rsch. planner minerals rsch. labs., 1972-79; prof. metall. Colo. Sch. Mines, Golden, 1969-72; prof. metall. engring. U. Melbourne, 1979-81; cons., mng. dir. Metacon, Melbourne, 1981—; cons. UN, Bolivia, 1970-72, numerous corps., N.Am., Europe, 1970-91; coun. mem. U. Melbourne, 1981-85, grad. coun. mem., 1975-87, chmn., 1981-82, v.p., 1984-87, 96-99. Contbr. some 68 articles to profl. jours.; holder 26 patents in field. Recipient Wilhelm Hofmann medal W. Hofmann Internat. Consortium, 1977, 87. Fellow Instn. Mining and Metall., Australian Inst. Mining and Metallurgy (Pres.' medal 1987); mem. AIME (Extractive Metallurgy Lectr. Award recipient 1988, best paper gold medal 1955), Australian Mineral Industry Cons. Assn. E-mail: rondavey@alphalink.com.au. Home: Unit 220, 57 Gloucester Ave, Berwick VIC 3806, Australia

DAVEZAC, BERTRAND, art historian; b. Paris, Apr. 27, 1930; came to U.S., 1954; s. Henry Paul and Solange (Carpentier) D.; m. Shehira Dora Doss, June 6, 1960; 1 chlid, Karim. PhD, Columbia U., 1971. Chief curator The Menil Collection, Houston, 1979-2000. Author: After the Fall of Constantinople, 1996. Decorated chavalier des Arts et Lettres (France). Mem. DaCamera Soc. of Houston (bd. dirs. 1988—). Democrat. Avocations: music, literature.

DAVID, BONNIE PREMKUMAR, veterinary microbiologist, researcher; b. Madras, Tamil Nadu, India, Oct. 24, 1955; s. Bonnie and Leela (Koilpillai) D.; m. Shoba Devanesan, Oct. 1, 1979; children: Preba, Abraham. B in Vet. Sci., Madras (India) Vet. Coll., 1978, M in Vet Sci., 1989, PhD in Veterinary Microbiology, 1995. Radiolog. Safety Officer,. Rsch. asst. Tamil Nadu Animal Husbandry Svcs., Madras, India, 1979-89; asst. prof. Tamil Nadu Vet. and Animal Scis. U., Madras, 1990—. Contbr. sci. articles to nat. and internat. jours. Avocations: choir singing, guitar. Home: 13 Rotler St, Taml Nad Madras 600 112, India Office: T Nadu Vet & Animal Scis U, Vepery High Rd, TamilNad Madras 600 007, India

DAVID, DAN, photojournalist, photographer; b. Bucarest, Romania, May 23, 1929; arrived in Israel, 1960; s. Alfred and Elize (Goldenthal) D.; m. Mia Fischer, March 17, 1963 (dec. Apr. 1978); m. Gabriela Fleischman, May 23, 1980; children: David, Ariel. BS in Econ. Scis., U. Bucarest, Romania, 1953; PhD (hon.), Tel Aviv U., 1996. Photo reporter various orgns., Romania, Israel, 1953-61; pres. DEDEM Automatica, Rome, 1962-68; dir. Photome Internat. PLC, Bookham, UK, 1968-92; chmn. Photome Internat. PLC, Bookham, 1992—; dir. Fomat, Tel Aviv, 1961—, Nippon Autophoto, Tokyo, 1968—, Tecnotron, Madrid, 1965-95, Autophoto Sys., Tustin, Calif., 1969-73. Inventor photographic high speed processor, automatic dispenser, automatic identification camera. Gov. Tel Aviv U., 1980. Jewish. Avocations: chess, cycling, hiking, swimming, music. Office: Via Marco Aurelio 37, Rome 00187, Italy also: Photome Internat PLC, Church Road, Bookham Surrey KT23 3EU, UK

DAVID, F. JORGE, food association executive; b. Los Andes, Aconcagua, Chile, Dec. 17, 1922; s. Francisco David and Matilde Lebon; m. Edith Eliana Ramirez, Mar. 17, 1946; children: Jorge A., Matilde C. Diploma, Kans. State U., 1976, Cargill Investor Svcs., Miami, 1985. Agt. Nat. Inst. of Trade, Buenos Aires, 1954-56; comml. attache ad hoc Buenos Aires, 1954-56; gen. mgr. Cen. Millers Assn., Santiago, 1974-85, Cereal and Trade Co., Santiago, 1985-87, So. Miller Assn., Santiago, 1987—; pres. Latin Am. Millers Assn., Chile, 1997-98, 99-00; pres., chmn. bd. Latin Am. Milling Sch., Venezuela, 1997-98; v.p. La Previsora Ins. Co., Santiago, 1976-80; mem. bd. dirs. Cotrisa, Santiago; mem. Wheat Commn., Santiago, 1974-80, Govt. Wheat Commn., 1996-2000; spkr. in field. Author: (books) Trigo un Legado de Ceres, 1980, Trigo en Chile: Una Historia Descondcida, 1994, World Grain, 1997. Mem./pilot Air Club, Los Andes, Chile, 1945. Mem. Polo and Equitation Club/Santiago. Roman Catholic. Avocation: writing. Fax: (56) 2-6397982, (56) 2-6391368. Home: Luis Carrera 2331/10, Vitacura-Santiago Chile Office: So Millers Assn, Huerfanos 757 of 502, Santiago Chile

DAVID, FRANÇOIS, company executive, sociologist, economist; b. Clermont-Ferrand, France, Dec. 5, 1941; s. Jean David and Rose Cabane; m. Monique Courtois, Sept. 9, 1967; children: Fabrice, Julien. Degree in sociology, Ecole Nat. d'Adminstrn.; grad., Inst. Polit. Studies, France, Coll. for Sr. Civil Servants. Civil adminstr. dept. fgn. econ. rels. Ministry of Fin., 1969-73; comml. advisor French Embassy, Gt. Britain, 1974-76; head agrl. policy office Ministry of Fin., 1976-78; asst. dir. of cabinet Min. of Fgn. Trade, 1978-80; from asst. mgr. to asst. dir. Ministry of Economy, Fin. and the Budget, 1981-86; dir. of cabinet of the min. Min. of the Fgn. Trade, 1986-87; dir. external econ. rels., 1987-90; internat. mng. dir. Aérospatiale Co., 1990-94; chmn., mng. dir. Coface, Puteaux, France, 1994—. Author: The Export Myth, International Trade Adrift, The Export War, International Economic Relations, Autopsy of Great Britain, others. Named Officier de la Légion d'Honneur, Chevalier de l'Ordre Nat. du Mérite, Officier du Mérite Agricole. Avocations: tennis, golf. Office: Coface, 12 Cours Michelet, 92065 Paris La Défense Cedex, France

DAVID, GEORGE ALFRED LAWRENCE, industrial company executive; b. Bryn Mawr, Pa., Apr. 7, 1942; s. Charles Wendell and Margaret (Simpson) D.; m. Barbara Osborn, Sept. 4, 1965; children: Eliza Pell, Hannah Lawrence, Henry Gibb. BA, Harvard U., 1965; MBA, U. Va., 1967. Asst. prof. fin. and acctg. U. Va., Charlottesville, 1967-68; v.p. The Boston Cons. Group, 1968-75; sr. v.p. corp. planning and devel. Otis Elevator Co., N.Y.C., 1975-77, sr. v.p., gen. mgr. Latin Am. ops., West Palm Beach, Fla., 1977-81, pres. N.Am. ops., Farmington, Conn., 1981-85, pres., CEO Otis Elevator Co., 1985-89, chmn., 1989-97; sr. v.p. (parent company) United Techs. Corp., 1988-89, exec. v.p. and pres. comml./indsl., 1989-92, pres., COO, 1992—, CEO, 1994—, chmn., 1997—. Chmn. Greater Hartford chpt. ARC, 1985-87, US-ASEAN Coun. Bus. and Tech., 1995—, Nat. Minority Supplier Devel. Coun., 1998—; trustee Wadsworth Atheneum, Hartford, 1984—; bd. dirs. Inst. Internat. Econs., Washington, 1996—. Republican. Episcopalian. Office: United Techs Corp 1 Financial Plz # Ms526 Hartford CT 06103-2608 also: Otis Elevator Co 10 Farm Springs Rd Farmington CT 06032-2526

DÁVID, IBOLYA, federal official; b. Baja, Aug. 12, 1954. Grad. in law, U. Arts Sci., Pecs, 1981. Lawyer; min. Ministry of Justice, Budapest, Hungary, 1998—. Hungarian Democratic Forum. Office: Ministry of Justice, Kossuth ter 4, 1055 Budapest Hungary

DAVID, J(AMES) BARRY, equine veterinarian; b. Ft. Collins, Colo., July 5, 1957; s. James T. and Shirley A. (Cahill) D.; m. Amanda Hamilton, May 31, 1994. BS, Colo. State U., 1983, DVM, 1987. Diplomate Am. Coll. Vet. Internal Medicine. Intern veterinarian Hagyard-Davidson-McGee Assocs., Lexington, Ky., 1987-88, assoc. veterinarian, 1988-91; assoc. veterinarian Georgetown Equine Hosp., Charlottesville, Va., 1992-94, Dubai (United Arab Emirates) Equine Hosp., 1994; resident in large animal internal medicine Tex. A&M U., College Station, 1994-97; assoc. veterinarian Hagyard-Davidson-McGee Assocs., Lexington, Ky., 1997-99, Blue Ridge Equine Clinic, Earlysville, Va., 1999—. Recipient clin. resident award Tex. Vet. Med. Assn. Aux., 1996. Mem. Am. Vet. Med. Assn., Am. Assn. Equine Practitioners. Avocations: fly fishing, squash. Office: Blue Ridge Equine Clinic 4510 Mockernut Ln Earlysville VA 22936-9698

DAVID, JOSEPH RAYMOND, JR., writer, periodical editor; b. Chgo., July 9, 1936; s. Joseph R. Sr. and Elsie (Sarakhan) D. BA, Lake Forest Coll., 1957. Freelance writer various pubs., 1970—; editor Education in Focus, Alexandria, Va., 1990; cons. Annenberg CPB Math & Sci. Project, 1993. Author: The Fire Within, 1981, Glad You Asked!, 1986, Teacher of the Year, 1996. Mem. Washington Press Club. Home: PO Box 2 Alexandria VA 22313-0002

DAVID, MORGAN RENAN, business consultant; b. St. Brieuc, France, Apr. 3, 1964; arrived in Denmark, 1992; s. Rene and Eliane (Lemoine) D. Diploma etudes politiques, Inst. D'Etudes Politiques, Paris, 1985, DEA in Econ., 1986. Cons. IDATE, Montpellier, France, 1986-87, Internat. Data Corp., France, Denmark, 1987-95; bus. devel. cons. Kommunedata, Copenhagen, Denmark, 1997-98, Mobilix Market Intelligence, Denmark, 1997, Aspect Comm., Strategic Mktg., San Jose, Calif., 1998—. Office: Aspect Telecomm 1730 Fox Dr San Jose CA 95131-2311

DAVID, PATHIKULANGARA JOSEPH, physicist, researcher; b. N. Parur, Kerala, India, May 7, 1964; s. Pathikulangara Varghese Joseph and Alappat Joseph Cicily. BS, U. Kerala, India, 1985; MS, Banaras Hindu U., Varanasi, India, 1988, PhD, 1996. Project scientist Inidian Inst. Tech., Kanpur, UP, India, 1997—. Contbr. articles to profl. jours. Mem. Internat. Soc. Optical Engring. (student). Syrian Roman Catholic. Avocations: making good friendships. E-mail: davidj@iitk.ac.in. Home: Thynothil Kadavu Ln, Kerala Aluva 683 101, India Office: Indian Inst Tech, Dept Physics, UP Kanpur 208016, India

DAVID, PAUL ALLAN, economist, economic historian; b. N.Y.C., May 24, 1935; s. Henry and Evelyn (Levinson) D.; m. Janet M. Williamson, May 24, 1958 (div.); m. Sheila Ryan Johansson, Sept. 19, 1982; children: Rachel, Matthew; step-children: Kenneth, Elizabeth. A.B. summa cum laude in Econs, Harvard U., 1956, Ph.D., 1973; postgrad., Pembroke Coll., Cambridge (Eng.) U., 1956-58; MA, Oxford (Eng.) U., 1994. Asst. prof. econs. Stanford U., 1961-66, asso. prof., 1966-68, prof., 1969—, prof. history (by courtesy), 1976—, William Robertson Coe prof. Am. econ. history, 1978-94, chmn. dept., 1979-83; sr. rsch. fellow All Souls Coll., Oxford, 1994—; prof. econ. and econ. history U. Oxford; sr. fellow Stanford Inst. Econ. Policy Research, Stanford U.; vis. prof. Harvard U., 1972-73; vis. professorial fellow Churchill Coll., Cambridge U., 1977-78; prof. Am. history and instns. U. Pitt.; vis. fellow All Souls Coll., Oxford (Eng.) U., 1967-68, 93-94; fellow Center for Advanced Study in Behavioral Scis., 1978-79; vis. prof. U. Paris-Dauphine, U. Maastricht, U. Ancona; cons. in field. Author: Nations and Households in Economic Growth: Essays in Honor of Moses Abramovitz, 1974, Technical Choice, Innovation and Economic Growth: Essays on American and British Experience in the Nineteenth Century, 1975, Reckoning with Slavery: A Critical Study in the Quantitative History of American Negro Slavery, 1976; founding editor Jour. Econ. of Innovations and New Tech.; contbr. numerous articles to profl. jours. Guggenheim fellow, 1975-76; Fulbright scholar, 1956-58. Fellow Am. Acad. Arts and Scis., Internat. Econometric Soc., Brit. Acad.; mem. Econ. History Assn. (v.p., pres. 1988-89), Coun. Royal Econ. Soc. (U.K.). Address: Stanford U Dept Econs Stanford CA 94305-6072

DAVID, REUBEN, lawyer; b. Baghdad, Iraq, June 12, 1928; came to U.S., 1951; s. Isaac Solomon David and Tefaha (Nisan) Solomon D.; m. Nesta Paley David; 1 child, Aram. License in Law, Iraq Law Coll., Baghdad, 1951; BA, NYU, 1958, JD, 1962. Bar: Iraq 1951, N.Y. 1969. Asst. corp. counsel City of N.Y., 1970-76, chief legal unit dept. personnel, 1976-78; dep. dir. for legal affairs N.Y.C. Employees' Retirement System, 1978—. Mem. ABA, N.Y. State Bar Assn. Home: 30 Fifth Ave New York NY 10011-8812

DAVID, RONALD BRIAN, child neurologist; b. Richmond, Va., Aug. 3, 1937; m. Candace M. Heiderich; children: Ronald Bryan, Susan D. Staub, Elizabeth D. Kurtz, Thomas Edwin, Whitney Sears, Jennifer Pund. BS, Ea. Mennonite Coll., 1960; MD, Med. Coll. Va., 1964. Diplomate Am. Bd. Psychiatry & Neurology, Am. Bd. Pediatrics, Nat. Bd. Med. Examiners, Am. Bd. Child Neurology. Fellow in pediat. Mayo Grad. Sch. Medicine, Rochester, Minn., 1965-67, fellow in child neurology, 1967-70; from asst. prof. to assoc. prof. Med. Coll. Va., Richmond, 1970—; vis. prof. Coll. William & Mary. Editor: Pediatric Neurology for the Clinician, 1992; series editor: Mosby Neurology-Psychiatry Access Series, 1996; editor: Child and Adolescent Neurology, 1996; contbr. articles to profl. jours., chpts. to books. Fellow Am. Acad. Neurology, Am. Acad. Cerebral Palsy and Child Devel., Am. Acad. Pediatrics; mem. Am. Neurol. Assn., Child Neurology Soc., Internat. Neuropsychol. Soc., Learning Disabilities Coun., Am. Epilepsy Found., Va. Neurol. Soc., Va. Pediat. Soc., Orton Soc. Office: Children's Neurol Svcs 5875 Bremo Rd Richmond VA 23226

DAVID, SERGE MICHEL, chemistry educator; b. Grenoble, France, Nov. 6, 1921; s. Joseph Jacques and Valerie (Séaume) D.; m. Georgette Emilie Potier, Sept. 7, 1949; children: Bruno, Dominique, Claire. Ancien elève, Ecole Normale Superieure Ulm, Paris, 1945, agrégation physique, 1945; DPhil, Oxford U., 1948; DSc, Sorbonne U., Paris, 1949. Lectr. U. Nancy, France, 1949-54, prof. organic chemistry, 1954-65; prof. organic chemistry, now prof. emeritus U. Paris-Sud, Orsay, France, 1965—. Author: The Molecular and Supramolecular Chemistry of Carbohydrates, 1995. Roman Catholic. Avocations: skiing, mountaineering. Home: 28 Rue Maginot, 91400 Orsay France Office: U Paris-Sud, Bât 420, 91405 Orsay France

DAVID, WARD S., bank officer, retired federal agency executive; b. Bertrand, Nebr., Nov. 29, 1934; s. Stanton S. and Helen M. (Gifford) D.; married Aug. 12, 1956; children: Kim, Teri, Mick, Stan, Rod. BS in Agriculture, U. Nebr., 1956. Conservationist USDA, North Platte, Nebr., 1957-59; work unit conservationist USDA, Holdrege, Nebr., 1959-68; dist. conservationist USDA, Alma, Nebr., 1968-75; area conservationist USDA, Tucumcari, N.Mex., 1975-83, Escondido, Calif., 1983-86; divsn. ops. mgr. USDA, Washington, 1986-93, ret., 1993; ops. mgr., v.p. Bank of Am., Fallbrook, Calif., 1994—. Author: Ask Not for Victory, 1991; contbr. articles to various publs. Mem. sch. bd. Alma, 1971-75. With USAFR, 1956-57. Mem. Soc. Conservation Soc. Am. (charter, pres. 1967-69), Am. Assn. Ret. Persons (officer). Republican. Methodist. Avocations: sports, writing, reading, jogging, movies. Address: 2321 Morro Rd Fallbrook CA 92028-4410 Office: Bank of Am 1125 S Main St Fallbrook CA 92028-3326 also: Morgan Stanley-Dean Witter 1615 S Mission Rd Fallbrook CA 92028-4155

DAVÍDEK, JIŘÍ, chemistry educator; b. Krásna Hora, Czech Republic, Apr. 23, 1932; s. Josef and Marie (Votlučková) D.; m. Eva Kopecká; children: Jiří, Tomáš. MSc, Inst. of Chem. Tech., 1954, PhD, 1958, DSc, 1970. Rsch. worker Inst. of Food Technology, Prague, 1954-60; assoc. prof. Inst. of Chem. Technology, Prague, 1960-65; rsch. worker Nat. Rsch. Coun., Ottawa, 1965-67; prof. Inst. of Chem. Technology, Prague, 1968—. Author books; contbr. over 300 articles to profl. publs. Recipient State Prize Acad. of Sci., 1973. Mem. Czech Chem. Soc. (bd. dirs., chmn. working group agrl. and food chemistry), Czech Biochem. Soc., Am. Inst. Food Technologists, Fedn. European Chem. Societies (nat. rep. food chemistry divsn.). Home: Obrovskeko 12, 14100 Prague Czech Republic Office: Inst of Chem Tech, Technicka 1905, 16628 Prague Czech Republic

DAVIDHAZY, ANDREW, photography educator; b. Budapest, Hungary, Dec. 27, 1941; came to U.S., 1957; s. Andras and Gabriella (Petracsek) D.; m. Lucille M. Root (div.); children: Jennifer, Andrew; m. Susan Rebecca Homan; 1 child, Cameron. BFA, Rochester (N.Y.) Inst. Tech., 1966, MFA, 1968. Assoc. dir. Sch. Photographic Arts and Scis., Coll. Continuing Edn., Rochester, 1972-76, dir. arts and graphic arts, 1976-78; prof., chmn. imaging and photo tech. Rochester Inst. Tech., 1989—. Contbr. articles to profl. jours. Mem. Internat. Soc. Optical Engring., Soc. Imaging Sci. and Tech., Photographic Soc. Am. (assoc.). Roman Catholic. Avocations: photography, sailing. E-mail: andpph@rit.edu. Home: 615 Phelps Rd Honeydye Falls NY 14472-9016 Office: Rochester Inst Tech 70 Lomb Memorial Dr Rochester NY 14623-5604

DAVIDOVICH, MICHAEL VLADIMIROVICH, computer science, electronics educator, consultant; b. Saratov, USSR, Feb. 18, 1950; s. Vladimir Rakhmielievich and Barbara Fedotovna (Altukhova) D.; m. Vera Alexandrovna Kustova, Apr. 20, 1988; 1 child, Evgenia. Diploma of Engr., Radiophysics Saratov State U., USSR, 1972; Postgrad. diplomae, Saratov State U., Russia, 1990; PhD, Saratov State U., 1991, DSc, 2000. Engr. Rsch. Inst. "Wave", Saratov, USSR, 1972-77; sr. engr. Tantal, Saratov, 1977-81, leader at group, 1981-87; sr. researcher Ctrl. Rsch. Inst. Measuring Equipment, Saratov, Russia, 1987-90; researcher, cons., 1987-97; leader sector Ctrl. Rsch. Inst. Measuring Equipment, Saratov, 1990-95; assoc. prof. Saratov State Tech. U., 1995—. Contbr. numerous articles to profl. jours. Mem. IEEE (organizer Microwave Theory & Techniques, Electron Devices, Antennas and Propagation, Components, Packaging & Mfg. Tech. Saratov-Penza chpt. 1994-95, chair, 95-97, 97). Avocations: music, literature, tennis, fishing. Home: Kirov sq 8 apt 169, 410600 Saratov Russia Office: Saratov State Tech U, Polytechnic Str 77, 410054 Saratov Russia

DAVIDOW, JEFFREY, ambassador to Mexico; b. Boston, Jan. 26, 1944; m. Joan Labuzoski; 2 children. BA, U. Mass., 1965; MA, U. Minn., 1967; postgrad., Osmania U., Hyderabad, India, 1968-69. Joined Fgn. Svc., Dept. State, 1969; polit. officer Santiago, Chile, 1974-76, Capetown/Pretoria, Republic of South Africa, 1976-78; desk officer Office So. African Affairs, Dept. State, 1978-79; Congl. fellow, 1979-82; head U.S. Liaison Office Am. Embassy, Harare, Zimbabwe, 1982-83; fellow Ctr. for Internat. Affairs, Harvard U., 1983-85; dir. Office Regional Affairs and Office So. African Affairs, Dept. State, 1985-86; dep. chief of mission Am. Embassy, Caracas, Venezuela, 1986-88; U.S. amb. to Republic of Zambia, Lusaka, Republic of Zambia, 1988-90; dep. asst. secy. for African affairs Dept. State, Washington, D.C., 1990-93; U.S. amb. to Venezuela Dept. State, Caracas, 1993-96; asst. sec. state for inter-Am. affairs Dept. State, Washington, 1996-98; amb. to Mex., 1998—. Fellow Ctr. Internat. Affairs, Harvard U., 1982. Fellow Am. Polit. Sci. Assn. (congrl. staff aide). Office: Am Embassy, Paseo de Ta Reforma 305, 06500 Mexico City Mexico

DAVIDOW, JOSEPH RUSSELL, psychologist; b. Vineland, N.J., Oct. 23, 1955; s. Israel and Angelica B. (Santoro) D. Student, Emerson Coll., 1973-74; BA, Glassboro State Coll., 1977, MA, 1980; MA, New Sch. Social Rsch., 1985; EdD, Indiana U. of Pa., 1998. Cert. sch. psychologist, N.J. Asst. dir. Mental Health Assn. N.Y. and Bronx Counties, N.Y.C., 1988-90; therapist Washington Sq. Inst., N.Y.C., 1989—, Bklyn. Mental Health Clinic, 1990—; psychologist Ocean City (N.J.) Pub. Schs., 1990—; cons. in field; adj. prof. psychology Ricard Stockton Coll. of N.J., 1996—. Contbr. to profl. publs. Mem. Nat. Assn. Sch. Psychologists, N.J. Assn. Sch. Psychologists, N.J. Psychol. Assn. Avocations: music, baseball, reading, cooking, travel. Home: 310 Frances Ave Linwood NJ 08221-1410

DAVIDS, CAROLUS AUGUSTINOS, economics educator; b. Voorburg, The Netherlands, Oct. 14, 1952; s. Hendricus Joannes Gerardus and Susanna Maria (Hoefsloot) D.; m. Marjolein Catherine St. Hart, Mar. 17, 1995; children: Michael Reinier, Judith Catherina. MA, U. Leiden, The Netherlands, 1976, PhD in History, 1986. Rsch. asst. U. Leiden, 1976-78; asst. prof. history Erasmus U., Rotterdam, 1978-88; rsch. fellow Royal Netherlands Acad. Arts and Scis., 1988-94; prof. econs. and social history Free U. Amsterdam, 1994—. Author: Zeewezen en Wetenschap de Wetenschap en de Ontwikkeling van de Nagigatieteckniek in Nederland Tussen, 1986; editor: (with Jan Lucassen) A Miracle Mirrored: The Dutch Republic in European Perspective, 1995. Grantee Neils Stensen Stichting, 1986; fellow Netherlands Inst. for Advanced Study, 1992-93; recipient Dirk Jacob Veegensprys, Hollandsche Maatschappt oer Wetenschappen Maarlem, 1985. Roman Catholic.

DAVIDS, EDGAR, professional soccer player; b. Paramaribo, Surinam, Mar. 13, 1973. Mid-fielder Ajax Football Club, Amsterdam, Holland, AC Milan Football Club, Italy; winner Ajax Club European Cup, 1995; now mid-fielder Juventus Football Club, Torino, Italy, 1997—. Office: Juventus Football Club SpA, Piazza Crimea 7, 10131 Turin Italy also: Stadio delle Alpi, Piazza Crimea 7, 10131 Torino Italy*

DAVIDS, ROBERT EDWARD, computer security specialist; b. Haarlem, The Netherlands, May 16, 1939; arrived in Australia, 1952; s. David Willem and Maria Ursula (van Ryn) D.; m. Marjorie Swanston, Apr. 24, 1969; children: Karin, Andrew. Degree in chem. engring., U. New So. Wales, 1966. Trainee chemist Unilever Australia, Sydney, 1957-60; exptl. officer Australian Atomic Energy Co., Sydney, 1960-69; sr. systems programmer British Columbia Hydro & Power, Vancouver, Can., 1969-71; software mgr. Bank of New So. Wales, Sydney, 1971-75; from sr. tech. cons. to sr. security cons. Westpac Banking Corp., Sydney, 1975—; mem. subcom. Australian Standards, Sydney, 1984—. Avocations: amateur radio, photography. Office: Westpac Banking Corp IBN11, 72 Christie St, Saint Leonards NSW 2065, Australia

DAVIDSEN-NIELSEN, NIELS, English educator; b. Arrild, Jutland, Denmark, Sept. 14, 1937; s. Laurids and Betty (Davidsen) Nielsen; m. Marianne Schlüter, Sept. 5, 1963; children: Mette, Hans, Marie. MA, Copenhagen U., 1966, Candidate in Phonetics, 1969, PhD, 1979. Asst. prof. Copenhagen U., 1966-71, assoc. prof., 1972-85; vis. prof. Tufts U., Boston, 1971-72; prof. Copenhagen Bus. Sch., 1985—; rep. Danish Cultural Inst., Copenhagen, 1986—; vis. fellow Lancaster (Eng.) U., 1988, Corpus Christi Coll., Cambridge, Eng., 1993-94; bd. mem. Danish Lang. Coun., Copenhagen, 1991-2000, vice-chmn., 2000—; cons. Danish Nat. Ency.,

Copenhagen, 1992—; chmn. European Baccalaureate Examining Bds., Schola Europae, 1998 session; mem. reference group on lang. politics Nordic Coun. Mins., 1999—, chmn., 2000—. Author: English Phonetics, 1977, Neutralization and Archiphoneme, 1978, Tense and Mood in English, 1990; co-author: Mastering English, 1997, Festschrift: Sounds, Structures and Senses, 1997; editor Copenhagen Studies in Language, 1986—. Vice-chmn. Danish Ednl. Coun., Copenhagen, 1993-98. Sgt. Royal Danish Airforce, 1956-58. Decorated knight Order of Dannebrog, 1999; grantee Danish Rsch. Coun., Copenhagen, 1993-97. Mem. Internat. Assn. Univ. Profs. English. Lutheran. Avocations: piano, tennis. Home: 50 Kronprinsensvej, 2000 Frederiksberg Denmark Office: Copenhagen Bus Sch, 15 Dalgas Have, 2000 Frederiksberg Denmark

DAVIDSON, ALASTAIR BROWNE, politics educator; b. Suva, Fiji Islands, Feb. 11, 1939; s. William Lambert and Celeste (Walker) D.; children: Francesca, Rurik. BA with honors, Australian Nat. U., 1963, PhD, 1966; LLB, Monash U., 1988. Clk. Dept. Prime Min., Canberra, Australia, 1958; lectr., reader Monash U., Clayton, Victoria, Australia, 1966-88, prof. politics, 1993—; prof. govt. U. Sydney, Australia, 1989-93; prof. Swinburn U. of Technology, 1997—; Wallenberg prof. human rights Rutgers U., N.J., 2000—; prof. stagiaire Coun. of Europe, Strasbourg, France, 1992; mem. Inst. for Advanced Study, Princeton, 1999-2000. Author: The Communist Party of Australia, 1969, Antonio Gramsci Towards an Intellectual Biography, 1977, The Invisible State: The Formation of the Australian State, 1990; co-editor: (with A. Spegele) Rights, Justice and Democracy in Australia, 1991. Advisor Commonwealth of Australia Strasbourg Conf. on Democracy, Canberra, 1992. Mem. Australian Coun. for Europe. Avocation: swimming. Office: ISR, Swinburne U Technology, Hawthorn VIC 3122, Australia

DAVIDSON, AMANDA MARGARET, financial advisor; b. London, Apr. 1, 1955; d. Ian Thomas and Györgyi Magdolna Davidson. BSc, U. London, 1976. Fin. cons. London, 1977-82, 86-88; dir. Chase de Vere, London, 1982-84, Holden Matthews Fin. Svcs., London, 1988-92, Holden Meehan, London, 1992—; membership and disciplinary coms. Personal Investment Authority, London, 1994—, disciplinary com.; dir., vice-chair U.K. Social Investment Forum, London, 1994—; vice-chair ctrl. London com. IFA Assn., 1993—, local dir. IFA promotion, 1987—. Contbr. articles to profl. jours. Gov. Channing Sch., London, 1996—. Unitarian. Avocations: violin, swimming, scuba diving, theater, holidays. Office: New Penderel House, 283-288 High Houbon, London WC1V 7HZ, England

DAVIDSON, BILL (WILLIAM JOHN DAVIDSON), entertainment journalist, author; b. Jersey City, Mar. 4, 1918; s. Louis J. and Gertrude (Platt) D.; m. Muriel Roberts, May 21, 1960 (dec. Sept. 1983); 1 child, Carol; m. Maralynne Beth Nitz, July 27, 1986. BA, NYU, 1939. Assoc. editor Collier's mag., N.Y.C., 1946-56; contbg. editor Look mag., N.Y.C., 1956-61; editor-at-large Saturday Evening Post, N.Y.C., 1961-69; radio commentator NBC, N.Y.C., 1968-71; TV writer Universal Studios, Universal City, Calif., 1971-76; contbg. editor TV Guide, Radnor, Pa., 1971-90, L.A. Mag., 1992-95; chmn. alumni communications com. NYU, 1959-64; freelance writer, 1992—. Author: The Real and the Unreal, Six Brave Presidents, 1962, Indict and Convict, 1971, (with Sid Caesar) Where Have I Been?, 1982, Spencer Tracy: Tragic Idol, 1988, Jane Fonda: An Intimate Biography, 1990, (with Danny Thomas) Make Room for Daddy, 1991; scriptwriter The Wednesday Woman, 2000. Mem. N.Y. County Dem. com., N.Y.C., 1948-50. Served as sgt. U.S. Army, 1941-45, ETO. Recipient Disting. Reporting award Sigma Delta Chi, 1951, 53, Albert Lasker Med. Journalism award, 1953, Disting. Journalism award Family Service Assn. Am., 1963. Mem. Writers Guild Am. West. Democrat. Home: 13225 Morrison St Sherman Oaks CA 91423-2156

DAVIDSON, BRUCE, Olympic athlete; b. Dec. 31, 1949. Recipient Silver medal U.S. Equestrian team Munich Olympics, 1972, Individual World Champion, 1974, Gold medal U.S. Equestrian team Montreal Olympics, 1976, L.A. Olympics, 1984, Atlanta Olympics, 1996, Bronze medal World Equestrian Games, 1990, Gold medal Pan Am. Games, 1995, Individual Gold medal, team Bronze medal World Three-Day Event Championship, 1978, 1st pl. De Broke Nat. Preliminary Championship, 1986, CCI Rolex Chesterland Three-Day Event, 1986, Ledyard Horse Trials, 1987, CCI, 1987, Rolex Little River Olympic Screening Trial, 1988, CCI Rolex/Ky. Internat. Three-Day Event, 1989, North Ga. Internat. Horse Trials, 1990, Land Rover World Three-Day Event, 1993, 95, Rolex/USET Spring Championship, 1993, Badminton CCI, 1995, Silver medal U.S. Equestrian team Atlanta, 1996; named U.S. Combined Tng. Assn. Rider of Yr. 15 times. Office: care Am Horse Shows Assn 220 E 42nd St Rm 409 New York NY 10017-5806*

DAVIDSON, CHRISTOPHER, cardiologist; b. Ilkley, Yorkshire, Eng., Nov. 24, 1944; s. Christopher Lynton and Elizabeth Mary D.; m. Dawn Davis, July 7, 1970; children: Christopher Lynton, Alexandra Sophie. BA, Cambridge (Eng.) U., 1965, MBChB, 1969. Cons. phys. Rochdale Dist. Hosp., 1976-89; cons. cardiologist Brighton (Eng.) Nat. Health, Care Trust, 4D, 1989—. Fellow Royal Coll. Physicians (Eng.), European Soc. Cardiology; mem. European Assn. Internal Medicine (v.p. 1994-96), European Fedn. Internal Medicine (sec. gen. 1997—). Liberal Democrat. Avocations: tennis, beekeeping. Home: 11 Royles Close, Rottingdean Brighton BN2 7DQ, England Office: Dept Cardiology, Royal Sussex County Hosp, Brighton BN2 SBE, England

DAVIDSON, CHRISTOPHER, special education consultant. Head Spl. Edn. Ctr. Geelong Grammar Sch., Victoria. Founding editor Australian Jour. Learning Disabilities; co-author: Wordswork.

DAVIDSON, (MARIE) DIANE, publisher; b. L.A., Mar. 6, 1924; d. Charles Casper and Stella Ruth (Bateman) Winnia; divorced, 1953; children: David William, Ronald Mark. AB, U. Calif., Berkeley, 1943; MA, Calif. State U., Sacramento, 1959. cert. secondary tchr., 1944. Tchr. Campbell (Calif.) High Sch., 1944-45; actress Pasadena (Calif.) Playhouse, 1945, U.S.O. Camp Shows, N.Y.C., 1946-47; tchr. El Camino H.S., Sacramento, 1954-85; illustrator, publisher, editor Swan Books, Fair Oaks, Calif., 1979-99. Author: Feversham, 1969; editor: History of Trinity Episcopal Church, Folsom, California, 1856-1994, 1996; contbr. articles to Shakespeare mag. Mem. NEA, PEN, Authors Guild, Calif. Writers Club, Calif. Tchrs. Assn., Phi Beta Kappa, Pi Lambda Theta. Democrat. Episcopalian. Avocations: gardening, writing. Home: 8146 Toyon Ave Fair Oaks CA 95628-7633

DAVIDSON, DONALD ALLEN, environmental sciences educator; b. Lumphanan, Scotland, Apr. 27, 1945; s. John Forsyth and Jane Cole (Morton) D.; m. Caroline Elizabeth Brown, Apr. 3, 1969; children: Louise, Lorna, Alan. BS, U. Aberdeen, Scotland, 1967; PhD, U. Sheffield, Eng., 1972. Lectr. U. Wales, Lampeter, 1971-76, U. Strathclyde, Glasgow, 1976-87; reader, prof. U. Stirling, Scotland, 1987—; mem. com. Natural Environment Rsch. Coun. Contbr. over 75 articles to profl. jours.; author/editor 9 books. Fellow Royal Soc. Edinburgh. Avocations: gardening, walking. Office: U Stirling, Dept Environ Sci, Stirling FK9 4LA, Scotland

DAVIDSON, ERNEST ROY, chemist, educator; b. Terre Haute, Ind., Oct. 12, 1936; s. Roy Emmette and Opal Ruth (Hugunin) D.; m. Reba Faye Minnich, Jan. 27, 1956; children: Michael Collins, John Philip, Mark Ernest, Martha Ruth. BSc, Rose-Hulman Inst. Tech., 1958, DEng (hon.), 1998; PhD, Ind. U., 1961; PhD (hon.), Uppsala U., 2000. NSF Postdoctoral fellow U. Wis.-Madison, 1961-62; asst. prof. chemistry U. Wash., 1962-65, assoc. prof., 1965-68, prof., 1968-84; prof. Ind. U., Bloomington, 1984-86, disting. prof., 1986—; disting. vis. prof. Ohio State U., 1974-75; vis. prof. IMS, Japan, 1984, Technion, Israel, 1985. Editor: Jour. Computational Physics, 1975-98, Internat. Jour. Quantum Chemistry, 1975—, Jour. Chem. Physics, 1976-78, 98—, Chem. Physics Letters, 1977-84, Jour. Am. Chem. Soc., 1978-83, Jour. Phys. Chemistry, 1982-90, Accounts of Chem. Rsch., 1984-92, Theoretica Chimica Acta, 1985-98, Chem. Revs., 1986—; contbr. numerous articles on density matrices and quantum theory of molecular structure to profl. jours. Union Carbide fellow Rose-Hulman Inst. Tech., 1958; NSF fellow Ind. U., 1961; recipient Hirschfelder prize in theoretical chemistry, 1997-98; Sloan fellow, 1967-68; Guggenheim fellow, 1974-75; laureate l'Academie Internationale des Sciences Moleculaires Quantiques, 1971. Fellow Am. Phys. Soc., Sigma Xi; mem. NAS, Am. Chem. Soc. (Computers in Chemistry award 1992, Theoretical Chemistry award 2000), Am. Acad. Arts and Scis., Ind. Acad. Sci. (Chemist of Yr. award 1999), Phi Lambda Upsilon, Tau Beta Pi. Home: 1013 Woodbine Ct Bloomington IN 47401-5445 Office: Ind U Chemistry Dept 800 E Kirkwood Ave Bloomington IN 47405-7102

DAVIDSON, FRANK PAUL, retired macroengineer, lawyer; b. N.Y.C., May 20, 1918; s. Maurice Philip and Blanche (Reinheimer) D.; m. Izaline Marguerite Doll, May 19, 1951; children: Roger Conrad, Nicholas Henry, Charles Geoffrey. BS, Harvard U., 1939, JD, 1948; DHL (hon.), Hawthorne Coll., 1987. Bar: N.Y. 1953, U.S. Dist. Ct. (so. dist.) N.Y. 1953. Dir. mil. affairs, gen. counsel Houston C. of C., 1948-50; contract analyst Am. Embassy, Paris, 1950-53; assoc. Carb, Luria, Glassner & Cook, N.Y.C., 1953-54; pvt. practice law N.Y.C., 1955-70; founding pres., counsel, bd. dirs. The Inst. for the Future, 1967-70; rsch. assoc. MIT, Cambridge, Mass., 1970-96; also chmn. system dynamics steering com. Sloan Sch. Mgmt., coord. macro-engring. Sch. Engring., MIT; semi-ret., 1984; pres. Tch. Studies Inc., N.Y.C., 1957-96, vice chmn. Inst. for Ednl. Svcs., Bedford, Mass., 1980-84, spl. lectr. Société des Ingénieurs et Scientifiques de France, 1991, NAS del. to Renewable Resources Workshop, Katmandu, Nepal, 1981, governing bd. Channel Tunnel Study Group, 1957-85, co-founder Channel Tunnel Study Group, London, Paris, 1957, apptd. to NASA Exploration Task Force, Washington, 1989, mem. internat. sci. and tech. com. Ocean Cities Symposium, Monaco, 1995. Author: Macro: A Clear Vision of How Science and Technology Will Shape Our Future, 1983, Macro: Big is Beautiful, 1986; editor: series of AAAS books on macroengring., Tunneling and Underground Transport, 1987; co-editor: Macro-Engineering, Global Infrastructure Solutions, 1992, Solar Power Satellites, 1993, 2nd edit., 1998, Festschrift, Macro-Engineering and The Earth: World Projects for the Year 2000 and Beyond, 1998; mem. editorial bd. Interdisciplinary Sci. Revs., 1985—; mem. adv. bd. Tech. in Soc., 1979—, Mountain R&D, 1981-2000, Project Appraisal, 1986-98. Bd. dirs. Internat. Mountain Soc., Boulder, Colo., 1981-2000, Assn. Prospective 2100, Paris, 1997; trustee Norwich (Vt.) Ctr., 1980-83, mem. steering com. Am. Trails Network, 1986-88, bd. dirs. Am. Trails Washington, 1988-90. RCAC, 1941-46, ETO; Troop Leader 10th Cdn., Armoured Rgt. (Fort Garry Horse), Intelligence Officer and Squadron Leader, GSO III (Intelligence) Second Armoured Brigade Group, maj. Tex. State Guard; apptd. to Senate Ft. Garry Horse, 1995. Decorated chevalier Legion of Honor (France), 1999; recipient Key to City Osaka, Japan, 1987, Twice the Citizen award Royal Mil. Inst. Can., 1999; elected Mem. Honoraire, Pres. d'Honneur Assn. Louis Armand, Paris, 1996-99; Lewis Mumford Fellow Rensselaerville Inst., 1982. Mem. ABA, Internat. Assn. Macro-Engring. Socs. (bd. dirs. 1987—, hon.chmn. 1997-2000), Am. Soc. Macro-Engring. (bd. dirs. 1982—, vice chancellor 1983-97, pres. 1997-98, chmn. 1998), Assn. Bar of City of N.Y. (internat. law com. 1959-62), Major Projects Assn. (mem. overseas adv. com. U.K. 1995—), Knickerbocker (N.Y.C.) Club, St. Botolph (Boston) Club, MIT Quarter Century Club. Home: 26A Parker St Lexington MA 02421-4907

DAVIDSON, JAMES JOSEPH, III, lawyer; b. Lafayette, La., July 27, 1940; s. James Joseph and Virginia Lee (Dunham) D.; m. Kay Cecile Holloway, Aug. 7, 1962; children: Kimberly Kay, James Joseph IV, Lynda Leigh, Virginia Holland. BA, U. SW La., 1963; JD, Tulane U., 1964. Bar: La. 1964, U.S. Dist. Ct. (we. dist.) La. 1965, U.S. Dist. Ct. (ea. dist.) La. 1979, U.S. Dist. Ct. (mid. dist.) La. 1986, U.S. Ct. Appeals (5th cir.) 1972 Us. Supreme Ct. 1975, U.S. Ct. Appeals (11th cir.) 1981. Ptnr. Davidson, Meaux, Sonnier, McElligott & Swift, Lafayette, La., 1964—. Mem. exec. bd. Evangeline Area coun. Boy Scouts Am., 1969-80; trustee U. La. Lafayette Found., 1980—, pres., 1988-91. Fellow Am. Bar Found. (life); mem. La. State Bar Assn. (del. 1970-96), La. Bar Found., La. Assn. Def. Counsel (dir. 1975-77), Nat. Assn. R.R. Trial Counsel, Am. Bd. Trial Advocates (adv. bd.), Am. Counsel Assn., Internat. Assn. Def. Counsel, Assn. Def. Trial Attys., Assn. Transp. Practitioners. Republican. Baptist. Home: 539 Girard Park Dr Lafayette LA 70503-2601 Office: PO Box 2908 Lafayette LA 70502-2908

DAVIDSON, MARK, writer, educator; b. N.Y.C., Sept. 25, 1928. BA in Polit. Sci., UCLA, 1948; MS in Journalism, Columbia U., 1950. Sci. writer U. So. Calif., L.A., 1980-90; prof. comm. Calif. State U., Dominguez Hills, Carson, 1985-99; freelance writer; faculty adviser Soc. Profl. Journalists, 1993-96; lectr. in field; writer for Steve Allen Show, 1964, Dinah Shore Show, 1978, CBS Mag. Show with Connie Chung, 1980. Author: Uncommon Sense, 1984, Invisible Chains of Thought Control, 1999, Watchwords: A Dictionary of American English Usage, 1999. Sackett scholar Columbia U.; recipient Nat. Emmy for writing Dinah Shore Show NATAS, 1978. Mem. PEN, Am. Soc. Journalists and Authors, Nat. Assn. Sci. Writers, Am. Med. Writers Assn., Authors Guild, Writers Guild Am., Calif. Faculty Assn. (v.p. Dominguez Hills chpt. 1992-96), Soc. Advancement Edn. (assoc. mass media editor 1997—).

DAVIDSON, PER, marketing professional, researcher; b. Stockholm, May 31, 1953; m. Uicui Davidson; children: Linda, Johan. Mng. dir. Sverige Barometer, Stockholm, 1995—. Home: Langstovagen 51, 12530 Alvsjo Sweden Office: Sverige Barometern, Gamla Brogatan 26, 10154 Stockholm Sweden

DAVIDSON, RICHARD ALAN, data communications company executive; b. Chgo., June 25, 1946; s. Jacob Aaron and Belle Rina (Feldman) D.; m. Sharyn Gail Ellman, Aug. 19, 1973; children: Kevin Scott, Caryl Elise. BSEE, U. Mich., 1970; MBA, Northwestern U., 1975. Project engr. Motorola, Inc., Schaumburg, Ill., 1967-74; ptnr. Feature Film Svcs., Skokie, Ill., 1974-77; mgr. planning Motorola, Inc., Schaumburg, Ill., 1977-78, mgr. mktg., 1978-79; tech. dir. Voice & Data Systems, Chgo., 1979-82; engring. mgr. Infolink Corp., Northbrook, Ill., 1982-84; pres. Davidson Data Communications, Lake Forest, Ill., 1984—; v.p. engring. Feature Film Svcs., Skokie, 1976—. Inventor pay TV system; contbr. articles to profl. jours. Unit commr. Boy Scouts Am., Lake County, Ill., 1989—; comms. officer USAF Aux. CAP, 1991—. Recipient Cert. of Appreciation Boy Scouts Am., 1990. MEm. IEEE, Assn. for Computing Machinery, Assn. for MBA Execs., North Shore Radio Club (tech. dir.), Tau Delta Phi. Republican. Jewish. Avocations: amateur radio, electronics, photography. Home and Office: 1900 S Millburne Rd Lake Forest IL 60045-4112

DAVIDSON, RICHARD K., railroad company executive; b. Allen, Kans., Jan. 9, 1942; s. Richard B. and Thelma (Rees) D.; m. Lynne P. Durham, July 11, 1998; children: Richard Byron, Elizabeth Ann. BA in History, Washburn U., 1965, D of Commerce (hon.), 1984. Brakeman, conductor Mo. Pacific R.R., St. Louis, 1960-66, transp. tng. program, 1966, asst. trainmaster, trainmaster, 1966-75, asst. supt. to asst v.p. ops., 1975-76; v.p. ops. Mo. Pacific Railroad, St. Louis, 1976-85; v.p. ops. Union Pacific R.R., Omaha, 1985-89, exec. v.p. ops., 1989-91, chmn., CEO, 1991—; pres. Union Pacific Corp., Omaha, 1994—, COO, 1995-97, chmn., pres., COO, 1997—. Mem. Happy Hollow Club. Office: Union Pacific RR 1416 Dodge St Omaha NE 68179-0002

DAVIDSON, ROBERT, religious studies educator; b. Mar. 30, 1927; s. George Braid Davidson and Gertrude May Ward; m. Elizabeth May Robertson, 1952; 8 children. MA in Classics with 1st class honors, U. St. Andrews, 1949, BD in Old Testament with distinction, 1952; DD (hon.), U. Aberdeen, 1985, U. Glasgow, 1993. From asst. lectr. to lectr. Biblical studies U. Aberdeen, 1953-60; lectr. Hebrew and Old Testament U. St. Andrews, 1960-66; lectr. Old Testament studies U. Edinburgh, 1966-69, sr. lectr., 1969-72; prof. Old Testament lang. and lit. U. Glasgow, 1972-91; prin. Trinity Coll., Glasgow, 1982-91; Edward Cadbury lectr. Birmingham U., 1988-89; moderator gen. assembly Ch. Scotland, 1990-91. Author: The Bible Speaks, 1959, The Old Testament, 1964, The Bible in Religious Education, 1979, The Courage to Doubt, 1983, Wisdom and Worship, 1990, A Beginner's Guide to the Old Testament, 1992, Go by the Book, 1996, Vitality of Worship, a Commentary in the Psalms, 1998, (with A.R.C. Leaney) Biblical Criticism, vol. 3 of Pelican Guide to Modern Theology, 1970, (with others) Cambridge Bible Commentary, 1973, 79, Daily Study Bible, 1983, 86; contbr. articles to profl. jours. Fellow Royal Soc. Edinburgh. Avocations: music, gardening. Office: 30 Dumgoyne Dr, Bearsden Glasgow G61 3AP, Scotland

DAVIDSON, RONALD CROSBY, physicist, educator; b. Norwich, Ont., Can., July 3, 1941; s. William Crosby and Annie Beatrice (Caley) D.; m. Jean Farncombe, May 18, 1963; children: Cynthia Christine, Ronald Crosby Jr. BSc, McMaster U., 1963; PhD, Princeton U., 1966. Faculty dept. physics U. Md., 1968-78; prof. physics MIT, 1978-91; prof. astrophys. scis. Princeton U., 1991—; vis. scientist Los Alamos Sci. Lab., 1974-75; asst. dir. for applied plasma physics Office of Fusion Energy Dept. Energy, Washington, 1976-78; dir. Plasma Fusion Center MIT, Cambridge, Mass., 1978-88; chmn. magnetic fusion adv. com., 1982-86; dir. Princeton Plasma Physics Lab., 1991-96. Author: Methods in Nonlinear Plasma Theory, 1972, Theory of Nonneutral Plasmas, 1974, 2d edit., 89, Physics of Nonneutral Plasmas, 1991. Recipient Disting. Assoc. award Dept. Energy, 1986, Leadership award Fusion Power Assocs., 1986, Kaul Found. Excellence award, 1993; Ford Found. fellow, 1963-64, Imperial Oil fellow, 1963-66, Sloan Rsch. Found. fellow, 1970-72. Fellow AAAS, Am. Phys. Soc. (chmn. div. plasma physics, 1983-84). Office: Princeton U Plasma Physics Lab PO Box 451 Princeton NJ 08543-0451

DAVIDSON, SALLY HOPE, anesthesiologist; b. Ft. Worth, Tex., June 17, 1938; arrived in Sweden, 1978; d. John Francis and Elizabeth Catherine (Hope) D.; m. Bengt Erik Alfred Lindgren, Apr. 26, 1980; 1 child, Birgitta Lindgren. BS, Oreg. State U., 1960, MD, 1964. Intern Milwaukee County, Milw., 1964-65; resident Portland, Oreg., 1965-67; instr. Portland, 1967-68; staff mem. Physicians & Surgeons, Portland, 1968; instr. Ulleual Hosp., Oslo, 1969-76; asst. prof. Drammen (Norway) Hosp., 1976-77; instr. St. Eriks Hosp., Stockholm, 1978-79, Norrtälje (Sweden) Hosp., 1979-81; instr. Danderyd Hosp., Sweden, 1981-85, head of gen. surgery anesthesia, 1985-87, head of orthopedic anesthesia, 1987—; asst. prof. Built Up Anesthesia Block Svc. Ortho. Surgery, Svensk. Contbr. studies to profl. pubs. Mem. Swedish Soc. for Anesthesia and Intensive Care, Swedish Med. Assn. Avocations: Nordic skiing, sailing.

DAVIDSON, SHIRLEY JEAN, elementary and secondary educator; b. DuQuoin, Ill., June 2, 1946; d. Richard Haley and Doris Jean Gaddis; m. Philip H. Davidson, Aug. 30, 1969; children: Susan Elizabeth, Matthew Philip. BS in Elem. Edn., So. Ill. U., Carbondale, 1969; MAT in Learning Disabilities and Reading, Rockford Coll., 1982; MA in Sch. Adminstrn., Concordia U., River Forest, Ill., 1997. Cert. in sch. adminstrn., learning disabilities, social emotion disorders, educable mentally handicapped, elem. edn., reading, Ill. Thcr. 4th grade Coulterville (Ill.) Elem. Sch., 1968-70; tchr. 2d grade Gifford (Ill.) Grade Sch., 1970-73, Rockton (Ill.) Grade Sch., 1973-85; reading/learning disabilities specialist Rockford (Ill.) Area Literacy Coun., 1988-93; spl. edn. tchr. Byron (Ill.) Sch. Dist., 1995-96, Dist. 47, Crystal Lake, Ill., 1993-95, 96—; ind. reading cons. Elco Industries, Rockford, 1991-92; mem. peacemaking com. Indian Prairie Sch., Crystal Lake, 1998-00, mem. tech. com., 1997-00, mem. social com., 1996-97. Active First Presbyn. Ch., Rockford, 1975—. Mem. ASCD, Crystal Lake Elem. Tchrs. Assn., Pi Lambda Theta, Phi Kappa Phi. Avocations: tennis, reading, cross stitch. Office: Indian Prairie Sch 651 Village Rd Crystal Lake IL 60014-2005

DAVIDSON, VICKY L., university administrator; m. Edward F. Maleszewski; children: Jesse, Adam. A, Sinclair Cmty. Coll., Dayton, Ohio, 1973; BS in adminstrn., Miami Univ., 1982, MBA, 1990. Architectural designer, 1973-76; sr. designer NDM Corp., 1976-79; mgr. facilities dept. Mead Data Ctr., Dayton, 1983-87; cons. Sand Hill, Inc., Franklin, Ohio, 1987-93; facilities planner Wright State Univ., Dayton, 1993-95, asst. v.p., 1995—. Mem. Soc. for College & Univ. Planning. Office: Wright State Univ 3640 Colonel Glenn Hwy Dayton OH 45435-0002

DAVIDSON-BURNET, GAIE, university administrator; b. Hay-on-Wye, Brecknock, Eng., Dec. 12, 1945; d. Robert and Ruth (Colbeck) Rowland; m. Robert John Spjut, Dec. 11, 1976 (div. Nov. 1990); children: Francesca, Nadine; m. Francis Robert Burnet, July 10, 1992. BSc, Queen's U., Belfast, No. Ireland, 1972, MSc, 1974; PhD, London Sch. Econs./Polit. Sci., 1988. Rsch. assoc. Social and Econ. Rsch. Coun., Khartoum, Sudan, 1974-75, Univ. Coll., London, 1975-77; grad. tchr. London Sch. Econs., 1978-81; sr. lectr. London Guildhall U., 1980-90; sr. rsch. fellow U. Kent, Canterbury, Eng., 1990-95; head of rsch. and stats. Univs. and Colls. Admissions Svc., Cheltenham, Eng., 1995—; cons. Brit. Telecom, London, 1976-77; hon. Darwin Coll. fellow U. Kent, 1983—; hon. rsch. fellow Westhill Coll., U. Birmingham, 1997—, U. Surrey, 1996—; hon. fellow Rutherford U. Kent, 1995—. Author: (book chpt.) The National Perspective: CAT and the Student Experience, 1992; contbr. reports to profl. publs. Mem. edn. policy com. Royal Soc. Arts, London, 1996-98; mem. com. vice-chancellors and prins. Profl. and Vocat. Higher Edn. Adv. Panel, London, 1995-97. Mem. Labor Party. Avocations: opera, traveling in Italy, renovating old barns and windmills. Office: Univs and Colls Admiss Svc, Rosehill New Barn Lane, Cheltenham GLS2 2LZ, England

DAVIER, MICHEL, physicist, educator; b. Bourg-en-Bresse, France, Mar. 6, 1942; s. Jean and Elise (Tarpin) D.; m. Francoise Gadot; children: Diane, Eve. PhD, U. Paris, Orsay, 1969. Rsch. asst. U. Paris, 1969-70; asst. prof. Stanford (Calif.) U., 1970-73, assoc. prof., 1973-75; prof. U. Paris, Orsay, 1975—, dir. Lab. de l'Accelerateur Lineaire, 1985-94. Author: Physique pour les Sciences de la Vie, 3 Vols., 1987-88; contbr. more than 375 articles to profl. jours. Recipient Abraham-Bloch-Bruhat prize Ecole Normale Superieure, Paris, 1991, Gentner-Kastler prize French and German Phys. Socs., 1994. Mem. French Phys. Soc., European Phys. Soc., French Acad. Scis. Office: Lab de l'Accelerateur Lin, U Paris-Sud, 91405 Orsay France

DAVIES, BRIAN MICHAEL, retired psychiatry educator; s. Thomas and Lilian (Drake) D.; m. Rona Audrey Waters, Dec. 26, 1951; children: Debra, Gareth. B in Llanelly, Welsh Sch. Medicine, 1950, MD, 1958. Intern, resident, physician Maudsley & Bethlem Hosp., London, 1956-64; prof. psychiatry U. Melbourne, Australia, 1964-90; prof. psychiatry emeritus U. Melbourne, 1990; cons. psychiatrist Royal Melbourne Hosp., Melbourne, 1964-90. Author student textbook on psychiatry, numerous books on psychiat. rsch. Capt. Royal Army Med. Corps, 1951-53. Fellow Royal Coll. Physicians, Royal Coll. Psychiatrists, Australian and New Zealand Coll. Psychiatrists. Avocations: golf, reading.

DAVIES, DAFYDD ALED, publishing executive; b. Carmarthen, Wales, Feb. 21, 1967; s. David Rees and Margaret Marian D.; m. Delyth Wyn Lloyd. Degree, Baptist Coll., Bangor, Wales, 1989. Dir. SAIN, Fflur, 1988—; min. religion, North Wales, 1988—; dir. Cyhoeddiadaur Gair, Wales, 1992—, Gair am Air, 1992—; cons. Cristion, 1993—. Author: Ein Tad, 1993, 3650 Weddiaui Blant, 1995, Gweddiau Cyhoeddus, 1996; editor Bwletin, 1988-97. Devel. officer Sunday Sch. Coun., Wales, 1989—; exec. mem. U.K. Children's Com., 1989—; chmn. Baptist Youth, Wales, 1993—; treas. Spectrum Project, U.K., 1995—. Mem. Consultative Group for Ministry to Children U.K. (treas. 1988-97). Plaid Cymru. Baptist. Avocations: reading, computers, fine dining. Home: Aely Bryn, Chwilog Pwllheli, Gwynedd LL53 3UD, Wales Office: Sch Edn Univ Coll, Cyhoeddiadaur Gair, Bangor LL57 2PX, Wales

DAVIES, DENNIS RUSSELL, conductor, music director, pianist; b. Toledo, Ohio, Apr. 16, 1944. BA, Juilliard Sch. Music, 1966, MA, 1968, DMA, 1972. Music dir. Norwalk (Conn.) Symphony Orch., 1968-72, St. Paul Chamber Orch., 1972-80, Cabrillo Music Fest, 1974-92, White Mountain Festival Arts, 1975-77; condr. Juilliard Ensemble, 1968-74, Flying Dutchman Bayreuth Festival, 1978-80; prin. condr. Bklyn. Philharm., 1991-95; now music dir. Am. Composers Orch., 1995—; regular guest condr. Netherlands Opera, 1973-82, Berlin Philharm., Vienna Radio Orch., Chgo. Lyric Opera; guest condr. Stuttgart (Germany) Opera, 1976-80, music dir., 1980-87; gen. music dir., Bonn, 1987-95; chief condr. Stuttgart Chamber Orch., 1995—, Vienna Radio Symphony Orch., 1996. Office: American Composers Orchestra 1775 Broadway Ste 525 New York NY 10019-1903*

DAVIES, GARETH, retired steels and engineering company executive; b. Feb. 13, 1930; s. Lewis and Margaret Ann Davies; m. Joan Patricia Prosser, 1953; 1 child. Student pub. schs., Aston, Birmingham, Eng. With Glynwed Group, 1957—, computer mgr., 1964-69, fin. dir., 1969-81, mng. dir., 1981-87; group chief exec., chmn. Glynwed Internat. plc, Birmingham, Eng., 1987-98. Avocations: music, gardening. Office: 4 Beech Gate Roman Rd, Little Aston Park, Sutton Coldfield B74 3AR, England

DAVIES, GILLIAN, judge, writer, educator; b. Abersoch, Wales, U.K., Apr. 5, 1940; d. Ninian Rhys and Gweneth Elizabeth (Griffith) D. Grad., Grenoble (France) U., 1958; Barrister at Law, Inns of Ct., London, 1961; PhD, U. Wales, 1997. Barrister-at-law Lincoln's Inn, Inn of Ct., London, 1962-63; legal asst. The De La Rue Co. Ltd., London, 1963-65; head legis. and periodicals sect. United Internat. Bur. Protection Intellectual Property, Geneva, 1965-70; legal asst., 1970-80; asst. dir. gen., chief legal advisor Internat. Fedn. Phonog. Industry, London, 1980-91; judge, mem. bd. appeals European Patent Office, Munich, 1991-97; presiding judge, chmn. bd. appeals EPO, Munich, 1997—; dir. Snowdon Mountain Railway, Llanberis, U.K., 1970-99; hon. prof. U. Wales, Aberystwyth, 1994—. Author: Piracy of Phonograms, 1981, 2d edit., 1986, Private Copying of Sound and Audiovisual Recordings, 1984, 2d edit., 1993, Copyright and The Public Interest, 1994, 2d edit., 1997; co-author: Challenges to Copyright and Related Rights in the European Community, 1983, Copinger and Skone James on Copyright, 14th edit., 1999. Avocations: travel, golf, painting. Fax: 0 89/23 99-30 14. Office: European Patent Office, Erhardstrasse 27, D-80331 Munich Germany

DAVIES, HUW CATHAN, physicist, educator; b. Wales, Feb. 5, 1944. BSc, U. Wales, 1965; DIC, Imperial Coll., 1969; PhD, U. London, 1969. Lectr. U. Reading, Eng., 1969-74, 75-82; rsch. scientist NASA, Langley, Va., 1974-75; prof. ETH, Zurich, Switzerland, 1982—; vis. prof. Imperial Coll., London, 1986, U. Karlsruhe, 1985, George Washington U., Washington, 1979. Mem. editl. bd. Contbns. Atmospheric Physics, Tellus; contbr. articles to profl. jours. Fellow Royal Meteorol. Soc.; mem. Academia Europae, Am. Meteorol. Soc., Am. Geophys. Union, Swiss Soc. Meteorology, European Geophys. Soc., Internat. Assn. Meteorology and Atmospheric Scis. (pres.), Internat. Commn. Dynamic Meteorology, European Ctr. Medium-range Weather Forecasting, Swiss Nat. Rsch. Coun. Office: Honggerberg HHP, ETH, 8093 Zurich Switzerland

DAVIES, JOHN HUW, science educator; b. Carmarthen, Wales, Feb. 16, 1962; s. James Lloyd and Tegwen Powys Davies; m. Glynis Ann Jones, Aug. 7, 1993; children: Megan Fflur Dafydd, Elen Mair Dafydd. BA, Cambridge (Eng.) U., 1983; MS, Calif. Inst. Tech., 1988, PhD, 1990. NERC postdoctoral fellow Inst. Theoretical Geophysics U. Cambridge, 1990-92; lectr. dept. earth scis. U. Liverpool, Eng., 1992—. Contbr. articles to sci. jours. Rsch. grantee Nuffield Found., 1993, Natural Environment Rsch. Coun., 1997; supercomputing resources Natural Environment Rsch. Coun., 1997. Fellow Royal Astron. Soc.; mem. Am. Geophys. Union, Nat. Sci. Soc. for Wales (chmn. 1998-00), Brit. Geophys. Assn. (sec. 1995-98). E-mail: davies@liv.ac.uk. Office: U Liverpool, 4 Brownlow St, Liverpool L69 7GP, England

DAVIES, JOYCE, business consulting executive; b. Rochester, N.Y., Aug. 8, 1923; d. Jenkin Henry and Hilda Irene (Lane) Davies; m. Steward Samuel Flaschen, April 21, 1949; children: John, Sheryl, David, Evan. BA in Chemistry, Queen's U., Kingston, Ont., Canada, 1946; MS in Chemistry, Miami U., Oxford, Ohio, 1949. Chmn., CEO Flaschen & Davies, New Canaan, Conn., 1986—; co-founder TranSwitch Corp., Shelton, Conn., 1988—. Avocations: family, travel, photography, Internet. Office: Flaschen & Davies 592 Weed St New Canaan CT 06840-6127

DAVIES, LAURA, professional golfer; b. Coventry, Eng., Oct. 5, 1963. Profl. golfer LPGA, 1987—; mem. European Solheim Cup Team, 1990, 92, 94, 96, 98. 15 career victories, including Circle K LPGA Tucson Open, 1988, Jamie Farr Toledo Classic, 1988, Lady Keystone Open, 1989, Inamori Classic, 1991, McDonald's Championship, 1993, Standard Register Ping, 1994, 95, 96, 97, Sara Lee Classic, 1994, Chick-fil-a Charity Championship, 1995, Star Bank LPGA Classic, 1996, LPGA Tour Championship, 1996, L.A. Women's Championship, 2000, The Philips Invitational, 2000; recipient Rolex Player of Yr. award, 1996; named Mem. Brit. Empire, Queen Elizabeth II, 1988. Office: care LPGA 100 International Golf Dr Daytona Beach FL 32124-1082

DAVIES, MERTON EDWARD, planetary scientist; b. St. Paul, Sept. 13, 1917; s. Albert Daniel and Lucile (McCabe) D.; AB, Stanford, 1938, postgrad., 1938-39; m. Margaret Louise Darling, Feb. 10, 1946; children: Deidra Louise Stauff, Albert Karl, Merton Randel. Instr. math. U. Nev., 1939-40; group leader Math. Lofting, Douglas Aircraft Co., El Segundo, Calif., 1940-48; sr. staff Rand Corp., Santa Monica, Calif., 1948-59, 62—, liaison USAF, Washington, 1959-62. U.S. observer inspected stas. under terms Antarctic Treaty, 1967; TV co-investigator Mariner Mars, 1969, 71, Mariner Venus/Mercury 1973 Mission, Voyager Mission, Galileo Mission, Magellan Mission, Mars Observer Mission, Clementine Mission, Mars Global Surveyor Mission. Fellow AIAA (assoc.); mem. AAAS, Am. Soc. Photogrammetry. Author: (with Bruce Murray) The View from Space, 1971; (with others) Atlas of Mercury, 1978. Patentee in field. Home: 1414 San Remo Dr Pacific Palisades CA 90272-2737 Office: Rand Corp 1700 Main St Santa Monica CA 90401-3297

DAVIES, NOEL WILLIAM, chemist, researcher; b. Sydney, Australia, Feb. 26, 1953; s. Arthur Nicol and Mary (Dennett) D.; m. Sharn Kathleen Cooper, Apr. 10, 1976; children: Stephanie, Christopher. BSc in Agr. (hons.), Sydney Univ., 1975; PhD, Univ. Tasmania, Tasmania, 1994. Profl. officer Univ. NSW, Sydney, 1975-79; rsch. fellow Univ. Tasmania, Hobart, Tasmania, 1979-84, OIC Mass Spectrometry, 1984—; scientific program chmn. Royal Australian Chem. Inst.'s 11th Analytical Conf., 1991; mem. ISO com. TC54, Madrid, 1994; convenor Australian & New Zealand Soc. Mass Spectrometry 16th Conf., Hobart, 1997. Contbr. articles to profl. jours. Recipient fellowship Winston Churchill Meml. Trust, 1988. Fellow Royal Australian Chem. Inst.; mem. Australian and New Zealand Soc. Mass Spectrometry (exec. com.), Am. Soc. Mass. Spectrometry. Avocations: choral singing, minerals. Fax: 61-3 62262494. E-mail: noel.davies@utas.edu.au. Office: Cen Sci Lab Univ Tasmania, PO Box 252 74, Hobart 7001, Australia

DAVIES, OMAR, Jamaican government official; b. May 28, 1947. BS, U. West Indies, 1968; MS, Northwestern U., 1970, PhD, 1973. Tchr. Glenmuir High Sch., Jamaica, 1963-69; asst. prof. food rsch. Stanford U., Calif., 1973-75; dir. regional and social planning Nat. Planning Agency, Kingston, 1975-80; sr. lectr. dept. econ. U. West Indies, 1980-89; dir. gen. Planning Inst. of Jamaica; min. without portfolio for planning, devel., and project implementation Govt. of Jamaica, Kingston, 1993, min. finance and planning, 1993—. Office: Ministry of Finance PO Box 512, 30 National Heroes Circle, Kingston Jamaica*

DAVIES, PETER JOSEPH, gastroenterologist; b. Terang, Australia, May 15, 1937; s. Thomas Hugh and Margaret (Sutton) D.; m. Clare Loughnan, Dec. 21, 1960; 1 child, Maria Eleanor. MBBS, U. Melbourne, Australia, 1961, MD, 1991. Resident med. office St. Vincent's Hosp., Melbourne, 1962, med. registrar, 1967-68; pvt. practice, 1971—; asst. physician to outpatients St. Vincent's Hosp., Melbourne, 1971-83, asst. physician gastroenterology unit, 1971-86. Author: Mozart in Person: His Character and Health, 1989, Beethoven in Person: His Deafness, Illnesses and Death, 2001; contbr. articles to profl. jours. Fellow Royal Australian Coll. Physicians, Gastroent. Soc. Australia, Royal Soc. Medicine; mem. Royal Coll. Physicians (U.K.), Am. Musicological Soc., Royal Musical Assn. Avocations: reading, music, hiking, travel, meditation.

DAVIES, SIR PETER MAXWELL, composer, conductor; b. Manchester, Eng., Sept. 8, 1934; s. Thomas and Hilda Davies; student Manchester U. MusB with honors, Royal Manchester Coll. Music, 1956; studied with Goffredo Petrassi, Rome, 1959-62; Harkness fellow Grad. Music Sch., Princeton U., 1962-64; MusD (hon.), Edinburgh U., 1979, Manchester U., 1981, Bristol U., 1984, Open U., 1986, Glasgow U., 1993, Durham U., 1994; LLD (hon.), Aberdeen U., 1981; LittD (hon.), U. Warwick, 1986; LLD (hon.), U. Salford, 1999. Dir. music Cirencester Grammar Sch., 1959-62; vis. composer Adelaide (Australia) U., 1966; founder, co-dir. Pierrot Players, 1967-71; founder, artistic dir. The Fires of London, 1971-87; founder, artistic dir. St. Magnus Festival, Orkney Islands, 1977-86, pres., 1986—; prof. composition Royal No. Coll. Music, Manchester, Eng., 1978-80; artistic dir. Dartington Summer Sch. Music, 1979-84; participant UNESCO Conf. Music Edn., Sydney, Australia, 1965; lectr. tours, Europe, Australia, N.Z., U.S., Can., Brazil; vis. prof. Fromm composition Harvard U., 1985; series sch. broadcasts BBC-TV; assoc. condr./composer Scottish Chamber Orch., 1985-94, composer laureate, 1994—; pres. North Eng. Edn. Conf., Chester, 1985, Nat. Fedn. Music Socs., 1989—, Cheltenham Arts Festivals, 1994-96, Composer's Guild Gt. Brit., 1986—, St. Magnus Festival, Orkney Islands, 1986—; conductor/composer BBC Philharm., 1992—; assoc. condr., composer Royal Philharm. Orch., 1992—. Composer, piano, orch. and solo instruments, also theater works including: quartet Movement for string quartet, 1952, Sonata for trumpet and piano, 1955, Alma redemptoris mater for ensemble, 1957, Five Motets for SATV Soli SATB chorus and ensemble, 1959, O Magnum Mysterim for SATB chorus, 1960, First Fantasia on an In Nomine of John Taverner for orch., 1962, Second Fantasia on John Taverner's In Nomine for orch., 1964, Revelation and Fall for soprano and ensemble, 1965, Antechrist for ensemble, 1967, Missa super L'Homme Arme for speaker and ensemble, 1968, St. Thomas Wake Foxtrot for orch., 1968, Worldes Blis for orch., 1969, Eight Songs for a Mad King music theater work for dancer and ensemble, Taverner opera, 1970, From Stone to Thorn for mezzo sporano and ensemble, 1971, Stone Litany for mezzo soprano and orch., 1973, Miss Donnithorne's Maggot music theater work for ensemble, 1974, Ave Maris Stella for ensemble, 1975, Symphony No. 1 for orch., 1976, The Martyrdom of Saint Magnus chamber opera, 1976, A Mirror of Whitening Light for ensemble, 1977, The Two Fiddlers opera for children to perform, 1978, Le Jongleur de Notre Dame music theater work for ensemble, 1978, Salmoe ballet in two acts, 1978, Black Pentecost for mezzo soprano, baritone and orch., 1979, Solstice of Light for tenor, SATB chorus and organ., 1979, The Lighthouse chamber opera, 1979, Cinderella opera for children, 1979, Symphony No. 2 for orch., 1980, Piano Sonata, 1981, Brass Quintet, 1981, Image, Reflection, Shadow for ensemble, 1982, Sinfonia Concertante for orch., 1982, Into the Labyrinth for tenor and orch., 1983, The No. 11 Bus music theater work for ensemble, 1984, Symphony No. 3 for orch., 1985, An Orkney Wedding with Sunrise for orch., 1985, Violin concerto for violin and orch., 1985, Strathclyde Concerto No. 1 for Oboe and orch., 1987, Resurrection opera, 1987, Strathclyde Concerto No. 2 for Cello and orch., 1988, Concerto for Trumpet and orch., 1988, The Great Bank Robbery music theater for children, 1989, Symphony No. 4, 1989, Strathclyde Concerto No. 3 for horn, trumpet and orch., Strathclyde Concerto No. 4 for Clarinet and orch., Caroline Mathilde ballet, 1990, Ojai Festival Overture for orch., 1991, Strathclyde Concerto No. 5 for violin, viola and string orch., Strathclyde Concerto No. 6 for flute and orch., 1991, Strathclyde Concerto No. 7 for double bass and orch., 1992, The Turn of the Tide for orch. and children's choir, 1992, Strathclyde Concerto No. 8 for Bassoon and Orch., 1993, A Spell for Green Corn: The MacDonald Dances for Orch., 1993, Symphony No. 5 for orch., 1994, Cross Lane Fair for Orch., 1994, Strathclyde Concerto No. 9 for six woodwind instruments and string orch., 1994, The Beltane Fire Choreographic Poem for orch., 1995, The Three Kings for chorus, orch. and soloists, 1995, The Doctor of Myddfai opera in two acts, 1995, Symphony No. 6, 1996, Strathclyde Concerto No. 10 concerto for orch., 1996, Conccerto for Piccolo, 1996, Job-Oratorio for chorus, orch. and soloists, 1997, Mavis in las Vegas theme and variations for orch., 1997, Sails in St. Magnus No.(1) 15 keels laid in Norway for Jerusalem-farers for orch., 1997, The Jacobite Rising for chorus, orch. and soloists, Concerto for Piano, 1997, A Reel of Seven Fishermen for orch., 1998, Sea Elegy, for chorus, orch. and SATB soloists, Rome Amor Labyrinthus, for orch., Sails in St. Magnus III: An Orkney Wintering. Stone poems in Orkahowe: great treasure, for alto, saxaphone and orch., 1999, trumpet Quintet, for string quartet and trumpet. Decorated Comdr. Order Brit. Empire, 1981, Knight Batchelor, 1987; recipient Corbett medal svcs. to chamber music, 1989, Outstanding Contbn. to Benefit Orchs. First award Assn. British Orchs., 1991, Gulliver award Performing Arts in Scotland, 1991, Charles Groves award Nat. Fedn. Music Socs., 1995. Fellow Royal No. Coll. Music, Royal Incorporation Archs. Scotland (hon.), Royal Scottish Acad. Music & Drama, Royal Coll. Music; mem. Nat. Fedn. Music Socs. (pres. 1989—), Royal Acad. Music (hon.), Accademia Filarmonica Romana, Royal Philharm. Soc. (hon., Large Scale Composition award 1995), Schs. Music Assn. (pres. 1983—), Composers Guild Gt. Britain (pres. 1986—), Guildhall Sch. Music & Drama (hon.), L'Ordre Arts et lettres (officier), Royal Swedish Acad. Music., Soc. Promotion New Music (pres. 1995—), Bayerische Akademie der Schonen Kunste. Office: care Mrs Judy Arnold, 50 Hogarth Rd Flat 3, London SW5 0PU, England

DAVIES, ROBERT KARL, British politician; b. St. Asaph, Wales, July 26, 1963; s. Robert Keith and Dilys Catherine (Hughes) D. BA, U. Coll. Wales, Aberystwyth, Wales, 1984. Acad. rschr. U. Coll. of Wales, Aberystwyth, Eng., 1984-86; parliamentary rschr. Ho. of Commons, London, 1986-89; radio prodr. BBC, Cardiff, Wales, 1989-90, polit. editor, 1990-93; chief exec. PLAID CYMRU, Wales, 1993—; dir. Mentrau PLAID CYMRU, Cardiff, 1995—. Parliamentary candidate PLAID CYMRU, Clwyd N.W., 1987. Mem. Welsh Language Soc. (chmn. 1984-85). Mem. PLAID CYMRU Party. Office: PLAID CYMRU-The Party of Wales, 18 Park Grove, Cardiff CF10 3BN, Wales

DAVIES, ROBIN HAVARD, quantum pharmacology and biology researcher; b. London, Jan. 12, 1934; s. William Eynon and Louise Adelaide (Copp) D.; m. Lysbeth Judy Throndsen, Dec. 24, 1964; children: Conrad, Walter, Benjamin. BA in Chemistry, Oxford (Eng.) U., 1958, PhD in Chemistry, 1963. Post-doctoral rsch. assoc. Inst. Molecular Physics, U. Md., 1963-65; rsch. Ctrl. Math. and Stats. Group, 1967-71, prin. theoretician pharms. divsn. Imperial Chem. Industries, 1971-84; sr. rsch. assoc. Welsh Sch. Pharmacy, U. Wales, Cardiff, 1984—; symposium leader Sanibel, Fla. Quantum Biology Symposia, 1985-94; prof. di contratto U. Pisa, Italy, 1993-94. 2nd lt. Royal Artillery, 1952-54. Mem. Internat. Soc. Quantum Biology. Avocations: rugby football, opera, literature. Home: 12 Belgrave Court, 25 Cowbridge Rd East, Cardiff Wales CF11 9BJ, United Kingdom Office: Welsh Sch Pharmacy, Univ Wales Cardiff, Cardiff CF11 3XF, Wales

DAVIES, ROGER, geoscience educator; b. London, Aug. 29, 1948; came to U.S., 1972, naturalized, 1985; s. Trevor Rhys and Gracie Rhys (Beaton) D.; m. Corinne Marie Scofield, Oct. 29, 1977 (div. 1999); children: Colin, Gavin. BS with honors, Victoria U., Wellington, N.Z., 1970; PhD, U. Wis., 1976. Meteorologist New Zealand Meteorol. Svc., Wellington, 1971-77; scientist U. Wis., Madison, 1977-80; from asst. prof. to assoc. prof. atmospheric sci. Purdue U., West Lafayette, Ind., 1980-87; assoc. prof. McGill U., Montreal, Que., Can., 1987-95; from assoc. prof. to prof. U. Ariz., Tucson, 1995—; mem. Earth Radiation Budget Expt. Sci. Team, 1980-92, First Internat. Satellite Cloud Climatology Project, Regional Exptl. Sci. Team, 1984-87, Internat. Radiation Commn., 1993—. Assoc. editor: Jour. Geophys. Rsch., 1987-92; contbr. articles and book revs. to profl. publs. Rsch. grantee NASA. Mem. Am. Meteorol. Soc., Am. Geophys. Union, Hungarian Meteorol. Soc. Avocations: sailing, tennis. Office: U Ariz Inst Atmospheric Physics Pas Bldg 81 Tucson AZ 85721-0001

DAVIN, HARRY MAURICE, internist; b. Hamilton, Ohio, Sept. 21, 1948; s. William Ambrose and Anna Marie (Buckley) D.; m. Margaret Marie Secrist, Oct. 24, 1948; children: Susan Marie, Anna Marie. BS cum laude, Xavier U., Cin., 1970; MD, U. Cin., 1974. Diplomate Am. Bd. Internal Medicine, Am. Bd. Geriatrics, Am. Bd. Hospice and Palliative Medicine. Intern Good Samaritan Hosp., Cin., 1974-75, resident in internal medicine, 1975-77; mem. staff Mercy Hosp. Hamilton, 1977—, med. chief of staff, 1996—; mem. staff Ft. Hamilton Hughes Meml. Hosp., 1977—; pvt. practice Hamilton, 1977—; med. dir. Vitas Hospice, Hamilton, 1996—; pres. Hamilton Acad. Medicine, 1981; sec. med. staff Mercy Hosp. Hamilton, 1984, pres. med. staff, 1985; sec. exec. com. Ft. Hamilton Hughes Meml. Hosp., 1988, pres. med. staff, 1990; trustee, co-dir. Hospice Miami Valley; med. dir. progressive care unit Joseph Ctr., Golden Yrs. Healthcare; pres. adv. bd. of health City of Hamilton; mem. adv. bd. St. Raphael Svc. Ctr. Mem. ACP, AMA, Am. Soc. Internal Medicine, Acad. Hospice Physicians (founding), Am. Geriat. Soc., Ohio Geriat. Soc., Ohio State Med. Assn., Cin. Geriat. Soc., Butler County Med. Soc. (treas. 1985-86, pres. 1988-89), Hamilton Acad. Medicine (pres.). Roman Catholic. Avocation: photography. Home: 680 Glenway Dr Hamilton OH 45013-3560 Office: MD Inc 532 Main St Hamilton OH 45013-3222

DAVIS, ADA ROMAINE, nursing educator; b. Cumberland, Md., June 7, 1929; d. Louis Berge and Ethel Lucy (Johnson) Romaine; m. John Francis Davis, Aug. 1, 1953; children: Kevin Murray, Karen Evans-Romaine, William Romaine. Diploma in nursing, Kings County Hosp., Bklyn., 1949; BSN, U. Md., Balt., 1973, MS, 1974; PhD, U. Md., College Park, 1979, postdoctoral student, 1985-89. Cert. editor in life scis. Asst. prof. grad. program U. Md., Balt., 1974-79; chmn. dept. nursing Coll. of Notre Dame, Balt., 1979-82; assoc. dean grad. program Georgetown U. Sch. Nursing, Washington, 1982-87; nurse cons. Health Resources and Svcs. Adminstrn., Rockville, Md., 1987-93, HHS, USPHS, Bur. Health Profls., Rockville, 1987-93; assoc. prof. and dir. undergrad. program Johns Hopkins U. Sch. of Nursing, Balt., 1993-98, prof. emeritus, 1998—; reviewer Choice, ALA; evaluator methodology and findings for rsch. studies; hist./med. biographer. Author: John Gibbon and His Heart-Lung Machine, 1992, Advanced Practice Nurses: Education, Roles and Trends, 1997; editor: Ency. of Home Care for the Elderly, 1995; contbr. articles to nursing jours.; assoc. editor Hopkins InteliHealth, Johns Hopkins Family Health Guide, 1999, Johns Hopkins Insider, 1998. Recipient excellent performance award HRSA; rsch. grantee U. Md. Grad. Sch. Mem. AAAS, ANA (cert. adult nurse practitioner), Soc. for Neoplatonic Studies, Nat. Orgn. Nurse Practitioner Faculties, Am. Acad. Nurse Practitioners, Am. Pub. Health Assn., Gerontol. Soc. Am., Nat. Trust for Hist. Preservation, Am. Geriat. Soc., Md. History of Medicine Soc., Soc. for the Social History of Medicine (Oxford U.), N.Y. Acad. Scis., Coun. Sci. Editors, Sigma Theta Tau. Office: 525 N Wolfe St Baltimore MD 21205-2110

DAVIS, ALAN JAY, lawyer; b. Phila., Feb. 4, 1937; s. Rudolph Alan and Adele (Saver) D.; m. Roslyn Kutcher, Oct. 4, 1939; children: Jennifer C., Michael R. BA, U. Pa., 1957; JSD, Harvard U., 1960. Bar: Pa. 1961, U.S. Dist. Ct. (ea. dist.) Pa. 1961, U.S. Ct. Appeals (3d cir.) 1961, U.S. Supreme Ct. 1979. Law clk. to chief judge U.S. Ct. Appeals (3d cir.), Phila., 1960-61; assoc. Wolf, Block, Schorr & Solis-Cohen, Phila., 1961-66; chief asst. dist. atty. Office Dist. Atty., Phila., 1966-68; ptnr. Wolf, Block, Schorr & Solis-Cohen, Phila., 1968-91, chmn. litigation dept., 1987-91; sr. litigation ptnr. Ballard Spahr Andrews & Ingersoll, Phila., 1991—; spl. master to investigate prison system and sheriff's dept. Ct. of Common Pleas, Phila., 1968-70; lectr. law U. Pa. Sch. Law, Phila., 1973-77; City Solicitor Phila., 1980-82; chief labor negotiator Southeastern Pa. Transp. Authority, Phila., 1982, Sch. Dist. Phila., 1984, 96, City of Phila., 1991-93. Chmn. met. adv. bd. Anti-Defamation League of B'nai B'rith, Phila., 1986-88; mem. sch. com. Germantown Friends Sch., Phila., 1986-88; trustee Free Libr. of Phila., 1995-98; pres. U. Pa. Law Sch. Am. Inns of Ct., 1998—. Fellow Am. Coll. Trial Lawyers; mem. ABA, Pa. Bar Assn., Phila. Bar Assn., Am. Law Inst., Legal Club, Jr. Legal Club. Democrat. Jewish. Office: Ballard Spahr Andrews & Ingersoll 1735 Market St Fl 51 Philadelphia PA 19103-7599

DAVIS, ALAN MARK, software executive; b. Bklyn., Jan. 6, 1949; s. Barney and Hannah (Slobodow) D.; m. Virginia Susan Zachary, Nov. 1976; children: Marsha Sydney, Michael Zachary. BS in Math., SUNY, Albany, 1970; MS in Computer Sci., U. Ill., 1973, PhD, 1975. Asst. prof. computer sci. U. Tenn., Knoxville, 1975-77; mem. tech. staff GTE Labs., Waltham, Mass., 1977-78; mgr. software engrng. dept. GTE Labs., Waltham, 1978-87, dir. software tech. ctr., 1981-83; dir. R&D GTE Comm. Systems, Phoenix, 1983-84; v.p. BTG, Inc., Vienna, Va., 1984-88; acting chair computer sci. dept. George Mason U., Fairfax, Va., 1990-91, prof. info. and software engrng., 1990-91; El Pomar prof. software engrng. U. Colo., Colorado Springs, 1991-2000; sole propr. Davis Co., Colorado Springs, 1991-95; pres. Omni-Vista, Inc., Colorado Springs, 1998—. Author: Software Requirements, 1993, 201 Principles of Software Development, 1995; assoc. editor Jour. Systems and Software, 1987—. Bd. dirs. Colorado Springs Symphony Orch., 1992-95. Recipient cert. of volunteer excellence So. Colo. AIDS Project, Colorado Springs, 1996. Fellow IEEE (editor-in-chief IEEE Software, 1994-98, cert. appreciation Computer Soc. of IEEE, 1984, 98); mem. Assn. Computing Machinery (recognition svc. award 1990, 92, assoc. editor Comm. ACM, 1981-91), Sigma Xi. Office: Omni-Vista 4350 Arrows West Colorado Springs CO 80907

DAVIS, ALVIN G., company executive; b. Post, Tex., Nov. 12, 1927; m. Barbara Ann Hext, July 28, 1955; children: Glen Robert Davis, Debra Ann Garland, Jay Todd Davis. Student, Tex. A&M, 1944; BS in Agr., Tex. Tech. Coll., 1951; postgrad., South Plains Coll., 1980; grad., Tex. Tech. U., 1983-84. Agrl. advisor, asst. cashier, asst. v.p. Brownfield (Tex.) State Bank and Trust Co., 1952-64; owner, mgr. Hub Specialty Co., Post and Brownfield, 1952-59, The Cowboy Stores, Tex., 1959-79; exec. v.p., dir. First Nat. Bank, Clovis and Melrose, N.Mex., 1964-65; exec. v.p., gen. mgr. Ranching Heritage Assn. and Endowment Fund Nat. Ranching Heritage Ctr., Tex. Tech. U., Lubbock, Tex., 1981-93; ret., 1994; owner, operator livestock farm; responsible for breeding, raising, showing, mktg. Quarter, Paint and Appaloosa horses, 1956-81; spkr. in field. Pub., writer numerous poems. Active Monterey Ch. of Christ, Lubbock, 1981—, elder, 1988-90; mem. Lubbock Heritage Soc., W. Tex. Hist. Assn., Tex. Mus. Assn.; mem. numerous 4-H Clubs; participant numerous livestock shows. With U.S. Army, 1946-47. Recipient Appreciation award San Juan Spring Roundup, 1995, Peter McCue award Petersburg, Ill., 1998, Lifetime Achievement award Am. Cowboy Culture Awards, 1999, numerous outstanding svc. awards. Mem. Am. Cowboy Culture Assn., Inc. (pres., founder), Am. Jr. Rodeo Assn. (adminstr., founder), Nat. Intercollegiate Rodeo Assn. (adminstr., life mem.), Nat. We. Artists Assn. (adminstr., founder), Former Tex. Ranger Assn. (life mem.), Old Trl. Drivers Assn. Tex. (hon. lifetime pres.), Ranching Heritage Assn. (chmn., adminstr., life mem.), Tex. Cowboy Reunion Old Timer's Assn. (life mem.), Tex. Tech. Animal Sci. Alumni Assn. (pres.), We./English Retailers Am. (chmn., founder, life mem.), We. Music Assn. (pres., Bill Wiley award 1995), Tex. Cowboy Poets Assn. (chmn., founder), Youth Rodeo Found. Am. (chmn., founder), Post C. of C. (mgr.), Brownfield C. of C. (pres.), Levelland C. of C. (pres.), Nat. Cowboy Symposium & Celebration (pres., chmn.), Am. Chuckwagon Assn. (pres.), Am. Legion. Fax: 806-795-4749. Home: 4124-62d Dr Lubbock TX 79413

DAVIS, ANDREW NEIL, lawyer, educator; b. Boston, Nov. 7, 1959; s. Gerald Stanley and Sarah Lee D.; m. Suzanne Frances DiBenedetto, Oct. 11, 1992; children: David R. Bray, Hannah M., Zachary G. BS in Biology, Trinity Coll., 1981; MS in Botany, U. Mass., 1983, PhD in Botany, 1987; JD, George Washington U., 1990. Bar: Conn. 1990, U.S. Dist. Ct. Conn. 1991, Mass. 1998. Atty. Pepe & Hazard, Hartford, Conn., 1990-93, Brown, Rudnick, Freed & Gesmer, Hartford, 1993-94; ptnr. LeBoeuf, Lamb, Greene & MacRae LLP, Hartford, 1994—; adj. prof. environ. studies Conn. Coll., 1994—. Sr. author/co-author: The Home Environmental Sourcebook, 1996, ISO 14001: Meeting Business Goals Through An Effective Environmental Management System, 1998; contbr. articles to profl. jours. Mem. Leadership Greater Hartford, 1997; chmn. lake adv. commn. Town Marlborough, 1992—, zoning commn., 1993-95. Recipient Hon. Sci. award Bausch & Lomb, 1977; Albert L. Deslisle Botany fellow, 1982. Mem. Am. Arbitration Assn. (environ. adv. com. 1993-95), Conn. Bar Assn. (exec. com. environ. law sect. 1996—), Conn. Bus. and Industry Assn. (environ. policies coun. 1991—), Internat. Coun. Shopping Ctrs., Conn. Groundwater Assn. Avocations: photography, sailing, scuba diving, arctic travel, reading. Office: LeBoeuf Lamb Greene & MacRae LLP 225 Asylum St Fl 13 Hartford CT 06103-1529

DAVIS, ANNALEE RUTH CONYERS, clinical social worker; b. Bentonville, Ark., July 8, 1944; d. Lloyd Milton and Jessie Alberta (Robe) Conyers; m. Rushton Eric Davis, Aug. 26, 1967 (div. Apr. 1980); children: Michelle Leigh, Rushton Kendrick. BA, Hendrix Coll., 1966; MSW, U. Okla., 1982. Internat. cert. alcohol and drug counselor; diplomate Internat. Acad. Behavioral Medicine, Counseling and Psychotherapy; lic. marriage and family therapist, Okla.; lic. clin. social worker, Okla.; diplomate in clin. social work; cert. critical incident debriefer; bd. cert. expert in traumatic stress. Psychiat. intern Tulsa Psychiat. Ctr., 1980-82, postgrad. intern, 1982-83; clin. social worker New Choice, Inc., Tulsa, 1983-85; pvt. practice Tulsa, 1985—; bd. dirs. Associated Ctrs. for Therapy; chairperson Quality Assurance and Program Devel. Coms. Head edn. com. Sunbelt Alliance, Tulsa, 1978-80; mem. Fgn. Policy Study Group, Tulsa, 1980-88, LWV, Tulsa, 1978—; mem., tchr. Meth. Ch., Tulsa, 1967-90; bd. dirs. Ctr. Christian Counseling, 1978-88; mem. Singles Available for Comty. Svc., 1999—. Mem. NASW (diplomate, clin. mem., bd. dirs. Okla. chpt. 1999-2001), Am. Acad. Experts in Traumatic Stress (diplomate, clin. mem.), Acad. Cert. Social Workers, Okla. Assn. Social Workers, Okla. Assn. Profl. Alcohol/Drug Counselors, Okla. Assn. Alcohol and Drug Abuse, Internat. Acad. Behavioral Medicine, Counseling and Psychotherapy, Singles Available for Cmty. Svc., Rotary Internat. Democrat. Methodist. Home: 6714 E 76th St Tulsa OK 74133-3422

DAVIS, ARTHUR COLUMBUS, health facility administrator; b. Albion, Mich., Nov. 22, 1948; m. Vivian A. Davis, June 24, 1974; children: Arthian A., Adrian A. BS, Savannah State U., 1970; MS, U. Wis., 1973; MPA, Western Mich. U., 1982. Emergency mgmt. coord. Mich. Dept. State Police; food technologist Phillip Morris Corp., Battle Creek, Mch.; enrivonr. health coord. Mich. Dept. Corrections, Jackson; health and safety officer Mich. Dept. Cmty. Health, Lansing. Mem. city coun., City of Albion, 1995—; mem. gov.'s fire safety task force com. Mich. State Police Dept., Lansing, 1994. Lt. col. USAR, 1970—. Mem. NAACP, Nat. Black Caucus, Am. Conf. Indsl. Hygienist, Am. Soc. Microbiologist. Democrat. Baptist. Avocations: physical fitness, carpentry. Home: 901 Huntington Blvd Albion MI 49224-9483 Office: Mich Dept Cmty Health 3423 N MLK Blvd Lansing MI 49224

DAVIS, BETTY BOURBONIA, real estate investment executive; b. Ft. Bayard, N.Mex., Mar. 12, 1931; d. John Alexander and Ora M. (Caudill) Bourbonia; children: Janice Cox Anderson, Elizabeth Ora Cox. BS in Elem. Edn., U. N.Mex., 1954. Gen. ptnr. BJD Realty Co., Albuquerque, 1977—. Bd. dirs. Albuquerque Opera Build, 1977-79, 81-83, 85-87, membership cochair, 1977-78; mem. Friends of Art, 1978-85, Friends of Little Theatre, 1973-85, Mus. N.Mex. Found.; mem. grand exec. com. N.Mex. Internat. Order of Rainbow for Girls; mem. Hodgin Hall Preservation com. U. N.Mex. Recipient Matrix award for journalism Jr. League. Mem. Albuquerque Mus. Assn., N.Mex. His. Soc., N.Mex. Symphonyy Guild, Jr. League Albuquerque, Alumni Assn. N.Mex., Mus. N.Mex. Found., Albuquerque Petroleum Cub, Albuquerque Knife and Fork Club, Internat. Platform Assn., Order Eastern Star, Order Rainbow for Girls (past grand worth adv. N.Mex., past mother adv. Friendship Assembly 50, state exec. com. N.Mex. Order 1989, chair pub. rels. com., co-chair gen. arrangements com. 1990-97), Tanoan Country Club, Albuquerque Mus. Found., Albuquerque Guild Santa Fe Opera, Alpha Chi Omega (chpt. advisor, bldg. corp. 1962-77). Republican. Methodist. Home: 9505 Augusta Ave NE Albuquerque NM 87111-5820

DAVIS, BLONDELL GILLIAM, business manager, evangelist, artist, author, poet; b. Ft. Pierce, Fla., Dec. 21, 1942; d. Fred Douglas and Mary Louise Gilliam; m. Levoid Davis, July 15, 1962; 1 child, Sherry Yvonne. AA, Lincoln Jr. Coll. Ordained to ministry Apostolic (Holiness) House of Prayer. State evangelist House of Prayer, Tampa, Fla., 1980—, mgr. bakery, 1987—. Author: Miracles on the Mind, 1993, Miracles Never Cease; editor Ho. of Prayer Gospel Press. Avocations: writing, cooking, drawing, painting, sewing. Home: 3210 E Lambright St Tampa FL 33610-3609 Office: The House of Prayer 3006 E Ellicott St Tampa FL 33610-2136

DAVIS, BRIAN LEE, finance company executive, consultant; b. Asheville, N.C., July 16, 1970; s. Evy Lee and Peggy (Margaret) D.; m. Anne-Marie Webster. BA in Acctg., Furman U., 1992; MBA, Queens Coll., 1998. Dir. Dun & Bradstreet, Charlotte, 1992-98; v.p. DeWolff, Boberg & Assocs., Inc., Richardson, Tex., 1999—. Republican. Avocations: running, tennis. E-mail: briandavis dba@msn.com. Office: DeWolff Boberg & Assocs Inc 601 Stevenson Ln Baltimore MD 21286-7602

DAVIS, BRIDGET D., film company executive, producer; b. L.A., Apr. 24, 1969; d. Lonell and Addie Rean (Moore) D. BA, UCLA, 1991. Asst. to Bill Duke L.A., 1993-95; dir. devel. Yagya Prodns., L.A., 1995-96; v.p. film and television Edmonds Entertainment, L.A., 1996—. Office: Edmonds Entertainment 3018 Stocker St Apt 8 Los Angeles CA 90008-4634

DAVIS, CECELIA GRACE, elementary and secondary education educator; b. Fairton, N.J., Apr. 16, 1937; d. Harry S. and Pearl (Cheesman) Grace; m. Kenneth L. Davis, Dec. 10, 1955; children: Michael, Diane (dec.), Sonja. BA, Glassboro State Coll., 1975. Cert. elem. edn. Substitute tchr. Lawrence Twp. Sch., Cedarville, N.J., 1968-76, Downe Twp. Sch., Newport, N.J., 1968-76; tchr. 1st grade Cumberland Christian Sch., Vineland, N.J., 1976-77; bus. mgr. K&M Diesel Services Inc., Cedarville, 1977-83; sales rep. The Real Estate Ctr., Ft. Pierce, Fla., 1984—; tchr. lang. arts St. Andrew's Sch., Ft. Pierce, 1986—; instr. adult edn. Indian River C.C., Ft. Pierce, 1991—. Author: The Ring of Fire: The Day All Hell Broke Loose, The Adventures of Jerry and Me, Jaime; author poetry and various songs. Area rep. counselor Youth for Understanding Internat. Student Exchange Program, Cedarville, 1979-83; talent searcher 1st Assembly, Millville, N.J., 1973-76, youth dir., 1980-82; host parent to 10 internat. students. Named Mother of Yr., 1st Assembly, 1961. Avocations: sport fishing, golfing, bowling, water skiing, writing. Home: 2491 SE Victory Ave Port Saint Lucie FL 34952-6774

DAVIS, CHARLES ELLIOT, accounting educator; b. Greenville, N.C., Sept. 18, 1959; s. Charles Cedric and Shirley (Newton) D.; m. Elizabeth Boozer, July 22, 1989; children: Charles Andrew, Claire Elizabeth. BBA, Coll. of William and Mary, 1981; MBA, U. Richmond, 1989; PhD, U. N.C., 1991. CPA, Va. Acctg. trainee Reynolds Metals Co., Richmond, Va., 1981-83, asst. cost acct., 1983, fin. sys. analyst, 1982-84; staff cons. Coopers & Lybrand, Richmond, 1985-86; fin. sys. acct. Investors Savs. Bank, Richmond, 1987; asst. prof. acctg. Baylor U., Waco, Tex., 1991-97, assoc. prof., 1997—, dir. grad. acctg. programs, 1998—. Author: OMAR: Online, Multimedia Accounting Review, 2000; contbr. articles to profl. jours. Chmn. parent adv. bd. Baylor Piper Ctr. for Child Devel., Waco, 1998; coach H.O.T. Soccer Assn., Waco, 1998—. Mem. AICPA (group of 100 1999—, chmn. acctg. careers subcom. 1998-99 chmn. acct. educator award task force 2000, grantee 1990), Am. Acctg. Assn. (webmaster ABO sect.). Baptist. Fax: 254-710-1067. E-mail: charles davis@baylor.edu. Office: Baylor U 500 Speight Ave Waco TX 76706-1458

DAVIS, CHARLES HARVEY, neurosurgeon, consultant; b. London, Apr. 6, 1949; s. Albert and R. (L.) D.; m. Dec. 18, 1973; 2 children. Trainee London, 1981-87; cons. neurosurgeon, 1987—. Contbr. chpt. to book Diseases of Spinal Cord. Fellow Royal Coll. Surgeons.; mem. Soc. British Neurosurgical Surgeons. Avocation: gardening. Office: Royal Preston Hosp, Sharoe Green Ln, PR2 4HT Preston England

DAVIS, CHARLES RAYMOND, political scientist, educator; b. Hampton, Va., Jan. 16, 1945; s. Cecil Raymond and Fronda Gail (Bradshaw) D.; m. Terry Lorraine Barr, Oct. 1, 1963 (div. July 1979); children: Kimberly Dawn Ingram, Charles Robert; m. Raymonda Carolyn Mays, Feb. 12, 1982. BA in Polit. Sci., U. Louisville, 1974; MA in Polit. Sci., U. Ky., 1975, PhD of Polit. Sci., 1985. Instr. Jefferson Community Coll., Louisville, 1976; claims rep. Aetna Casualty, Madisonville, Ky., 1977-78; rsch. asst. U. Louisville, 1979-80; rsch. analyst Ky. Health Svcs., Frankfort, 1981-85; asst. prof., masters degree program coord. U. So. Miss., Long Beach, 1986-89; asst. prof. U. So. Miss., Hattiesburg, 1989, assoc. prof., 1991-99, prof., 1999—; policy analyst Ky. Gov.'s Coalition on Health Costs, Frankfort, 1982; acting dir. grad. studies, U. So. Miss., Hattiesburg, 1990. Author: Organization Theories and Public Administration, 1996; editl. bd. Internat. Jour. Orgn. Theory & Behavior, 1997; contbr. numerous articles to profl. jours. Mem. AAUP, ASPA, Am. Polit. Sci. Assn., So. Polit. Sci. Assn., Northeastern Polit Sci. Assn., Miss. Polit. Sci. Assn., Miss. chpt. ASPA. Mem. Ch. of Christ. Avocations: photography, travel, reading, music, history of old West. Home: 417 Browns Bridge Rd Hattiesburg MS 39401-8703 Office: U So Miss Dept Polit Sci Southern Sta # 5108 Hattiesburg MS 39406

DAVIS, CHERRY DEAN, investigator, poet; b. Phila., Oct. 9, 1964; s. Duval Edgar Davis and Ruby Nell Chatman; m. Tina Jeanine Cole, June 28, 1997; 1 child, Catrina. Drug investigator U.S. Army, Ft. Hamilton, 1984-88; fraud investigator Caribbean Long Line Svc., Charlotte Amalie, V.I., 1988-89; claims adjudicator Colonial Claims, Inc., Mt. Laurel, N.J., 1989-90; sr. correction officer N.J. Dept. Corrections, Bordentown, 1990-96; sr. investigator N.J. Dept. Corrections, Trenton, 1996—. V.p. South Trenton Area Residents' Soc., 1994, pres. 1995-97. Sgt. U.S. Army, 1984-88, hon. discharge, 1988. Mem. Assn. Internal Affairs Investigators, Am. Correctional Assn., Affirmative Actions Officers Coun., Am. Legion. Avocations: body building, fishing, writing, horesback riding. Fax: 609-633-2237. E-mail: cdd@gateway.net.

DAVIS, CHRISTOPHER KEVIN, equipment company executive; b. Ogden, Utah, Apr. 8, 1959; s. James LaVerne and Margaret Mary (Brewer) D.; m. Christine Marie Davis, Oct. 27, 1984; children: Jennifer Lee, Christopher Kevin, Kelly Anne. A in Liberal Arts, Meremac Coll., St. Louis, 1979; B of Gen. Studies, U. Mo., St. Louis, 1988. Lic. in real estate sales. Prodn. supr. Survival Tech., St. Louis, 1982-84; salesman Cardinal Properties Real Estate Co., St. Louis, 1981-84; packaging supr. Sigma Aldrich Chem., St. Louis, 1984-85; sales mgr. Gen. Turf and Grounds Equipment Co., St. Louis, 1985-86; sales mgr. TNT Golf Car & Equipment Co., St. Peters, Mo., 1986-91, gen. mgr., 1991-93; pres., CEO Gateway Power Equipment, St. Louis, 1993—; v.p. Eco-Green Techs., Inc., St. Louis, 1996-2000; pres. Gateway power Comms., St. Louis, St. Peters and Springfild, Mo., 1999-2000, Lake Ozark, Mo., 2000—; v.p. Magic Melt, LLC, Silex, Mo., 2000—. Mem. Missouri Valley Turfgrass Assn., Missouri Valley Golf Course Supts., Profl. Grounds Maintenance Assn., So. Ill. Golf Course Supts., Ozark Golf Course Supts., Gateway Bassmasters. Roman Catholic. Avocations: hunting, fishing, golf. Office: Gateway Power Equipment Inc 11170 Dorsett Rd Maryland Hts MO 63043-3526

DAVIS, CLAYTON, writer, pilot; b. Portersville, Ala., Feb. 27, 1931; s. Horace Milton Davis and Agnes Zama Meadows; m. Irene Alice Brink, Apr. 8, 1952; children: Lynne, Keith Harold. AA in Math. and History, San Antonio Coll., 1966; BA in Russian and Russian Studies, Syracuse U., 1967; postgrad., U. Md., 1971-75. Cert. comml. pilot and airline transport pilot, Md. Enlisted USAF, 1947, advanced through grades to master sgt., 1966, ret., 1970; math. tchr. Anne Arundel County Schs., Annapolis, Md., 1970-77; pilot Met. Air Charter, Balt., 1977-89, dir. ops., 1981-87; freelance writer Severna Park, Md., 1989—; flight instr., Md. Author: Flying Secrets, 1992, Flying Stories, 1992, So, You Want to Be a Pilot, 1999, Amelia, 2000, Kindness, 2000; contbr. to Redfield (S.D.) Press, Golden Times, S.D., Severna Park Voice, Md., www.Themestream.com, aviation mags., others. Founding mem. Md. Aviation Hist. Task Force. Mem. Nat. Writers Assn. (founder, pres. Balt.-Washington chpt. 1993). Republican. Lutheran. Avocations: photography, flying, gardening. E-mail: cd19@erols.com. Home: 2 Brenda Ct Severna Park MD 21146-3604

DAVIS, SIR COLIN REX, conductor; b. Weybridge, Eng., Sept. 25, 1927; s. Reginald George and Lilian (Colbran) D.; m. April Cantelo, 1949 (div. 1964); 2 children; m. Ashraf Naini, 1964; 5 children. Student, Royal Coll. Music, London, 1944-49. Asst. condr. BBC, Scottish Orch., 1957-59; mus. dir. Sadler's Wells Opera Co., London, 1961-65; chief condr. BBC Symphony Orch., 1967-71; music dir. Royal Opera House, Convent Garden, London, 1971-86; prin. guest condr. Boston Symphony, 1972-84, London Symphony Orch., 1975-95; chief condr. Bavarian Radio Symphony Orch., 1983-92; prin. condr. London Symphony, 1995—; prin. guest condr. N.Y. Philharmonic, 1998; hon. condr. Dresden Staatskapelle, 1990. Decorated comdr. Brit. Empire, 1965, knight, 1980; comdr. Republic of Italy, 1976; Legion of Honor (France), 1982, Comdr.'s Cross Order of Merit Fed. Republic Germany, 1987, Comdr.'s Order of Arts and Letters France, 1990, Bayerischer Verdienstorden, 1992, Order of Lion 1st Class, Finland, 1992, Freedom of the City of London, 1992, Bavarian Order Merit, 1993, Gold medal Royal Philharm. Soc., 1995, Disting. Musician award Inc. Soc. Musicians, 1996, Sibelius Birthplace medal, 1998, Officier dans L'Ordre Nat. de Legion d'Honneur, 1999, Maximilians Orden of the Fed. Land Bavaria, 2000. Fax: 0207 609 5866. Office: 39 Huntingdon St, London N11BP, England

DAVIS, CONNIE WATERS, public relations and marketing executive; b. Gainesville, Ga., July 3, 1948; d. Starling Randolph and Evelyn Jeanette (Bonds) Waters; m. John W. Davis Jr., Sept. 24, 1971; 1 child, John Christopher. AA, Gainesville Jr. Coll., 1968; BA in Human Resources Mgmt., Brenau U., 1988; postgrad., Student Evaluation Inst. of Washington, 1988, U. Ga., 1972-73, 85—. Project evaluator Model Cities Program, Gainesville, 1970-74; pers. dir. Lanier Pk. Hosp., Gainesville, 1977-79; asst. dir. Ga. Mountains Ctr., Gainesville, 1979-83; owner, CEO Models by Davis and Davis, Gainesville, 1979—; dir. pub. rels. and sales Ramada Hotel, Gainesville, 1985—; dir. corp. devel. Chestatee Regional Hosp.; dir. Fashion Works, Gainesville; pres. Davis Consulting; owner Tastefully & Properly Growing Up, 1998, 99; cons. pub. rels. and mktg. Prodr., writer, implementor Tastefully Growing Up, Gracefully and Properly Growing Up; contbr. articles to mags. and newsletters; writer nat. poulty industry publ., 1990, 95. Publicity chmn. Cancer Soc., 1982, 83, 85; mem. Theatre Wings and Arts Coun.; bd. dirs., mem. mktg. com. Gainesville Jr. Coll., 1985—, trustee, 1995—; bd. dirs. ARC, 1978-79; co-chmn. Flag Com. for Olympics. Recipient Peach award Lions Club, 1979, Vol. award ARC, 1978, various modelling awards So. Models Assn., 1983, 2 Silver Shovel award 1993, 94, state vol. award, 1995; named Best Dressed Woman, Fashion Tour Group, 1984. Mem. Am. Heart Assn. (pres. 1995-96), Am. Lung Assn. (state bd. dirs., Vol. of Yr.), Greater Hall C. of C. (bd. dirs.), Gainesville C. of C., Gainesville Coll. Exec. Coun., Tourism and Conv. Bur. (chmn. 1983-84), N.E. Ga. Advt. Club, Pers. Adminstrs. Group, Ga. Hospitality and Travel Assn., Phoenix Soc., Rotary (cotillion dir. 1998—), Fashion Club (bd. dirs.). Avocations: exercising, skiing, boating, jogging, writing. Home: 1214 Chestatee Rd Gainesville GA 30501-2816

DAVIS, CRESWELL DEAN, lawyer, consultant; b. Abilene, Tex., Sept. 12, 1932; s. Emmett Dean and Marye (Creswell) D.; m. Mollie Villeret, Aug. 9, 1958; children: Addison Dean Davis, Kevin Tucker Davis. BA with honors, U. North Tex., 1953; JD, U. Tex., 1958. Bar: Tex. 1958. Asst. atty. gen. State of Tex., Austin, 1958-61; sr., mng. ptnr. Davis & Davis, P.C., Austin, 1961—; dir. Tex. Jr. Bar Conf., 1964-65. Author: Texas Legal and Consent Manual for Texas Hospitals, 1967-90; contbr. articles to profl. jours. Mem. U. North Tex. bd. regents, 1967-88, chmn., 1988; mem. U. North Tex. Health Sci. Ctr. and Tex. Coll. Osteopathic Medicine, 1967-88, chmn. 1988; adj. prof. hosp. law, Trinity U., San Antonio, 1967-90; adj. prof. pharmacy jurisprudence, U. Tex., 1969—. Recipient Disting. Svc. award Tex. Pharm. Assn., 1973, Outstanding Achievement award Tex. Assn. Life Underwriters, 1986, Outstanding Svc. award Tex. Assn. Child Care Facilities, 1984, Disting. Alumnus award U. North Tex., 1990. Mem. Rotary, Masons, Phi Alpha Delta. Episcopalian. Avocations: ranching, horses, education. Office: Davis & Davis PC 9442 N Capital Of Texas Hwy Austin TX 78759-7262

DAVIS, CRISPIN, publishing company executive; b. Mar. 19, 1949. Asst. brand mgr. Procter & Gamble, 1970-78, mktg. dir. U.K. ops., v.p. U.S. food ops., 1978-90; mng. dir. European ops. United Distillers, 1990-92; group mng. dir., bd. mem. Guinness (parent co.) United Distillers, Edinburgh (Scotland), London, 1992-94; CEO Aegis Group plc, London, 1994-99; exec. chmn. Reed Elsevier NV, Amsterdam, 1999-2000; co-chmn. Reed Elsevier plc, London, 1999-2000, CEO, 2000—. Office: Reed Elsevier NV, 25 Victoria St, London SW1H 0EX, England*

DAVIS, CRYSTAL MICHELLE, health association administrator; b. Havre de Grace, Md., Dec. 7, 1967; d. William Edward and Thelma LaBeatrix (Patterson) D. BA in Polit. Sci., U. Mass., 1989; postgrad., George Washington U., 2000. Exec. asst. Matshushita Electric Corp. of Am., Washington, 1989-94; adminstrv. asst. Ernst & Young LLP, Washington, 1991-94; staff asst. BP Amoco, Washington, 1995-99; program mgr. Providence Cmty. Health Ctrs., Inc., 1999—; health educator NOVAM, 1999. Vol. Clinton Presdl. Campaign, Washington, 1992; vol. emergency rm. Children's Nat. Med. Ctr., Washington, 1993-97; vol. enrollment and logistics teams The Experience Inc., Balt., 1993-94; vol. firefighter Arlington County Fire Dept., 1997-99. Recipient W.E.B. DuBois scholarship U. Mass., 1985-89. Mem. APHA. Avocations: horseback riding (dressage), reading, aviculture.

DAVIS, DAI, solicitor; b. Sunderland, Eng., Mar. 2, 1958; s. Austin and Edna (Getsof) D.; m. Beverley Ann Silverman, Feb. 28, 1993. MA in Physics, Oxford (Eng.) U., 1979; MSc in Computing Sci., U. Newcastle-Upon-Tyne, Eng., 1983. Mem. Instn. Elec. Engrs., Chartered Engr., Mem. Royal Soc. Arts, Mfr. and Commerce; solicitor Supreme Ct. Eng. and Wales, 1983. Solicitor, ptnr. Percy Crow Davis & Co., Sunderland, 1983-86; solicitor Eversheds, Leeds, Eng., 1986-92, ptnr., 1992—; head, IT Law North Nabarro Nathanson, Sheffield, Eng.; nat. chmn. Computer Law Practice Group, Eversheds, 1996-98; mem. Internat. Electrotechnic Com., Legal Action Group, 1991-96, convener, 1996—. Contbr. various internat. law conf. procs. Mem. Law Soc. Avocations: tennis, cooking, travel, reading, information technology. Office: Naboro Nathanson, Victoria Quays Wharf St, Sheffield South Yorkshire S2554, England

DAVIS, DARRELL L., automotive executive; b. Sharon, Pa., Aug. 8, 1939; s. Paul Darrell and Dorothy Jane (Snyder) D.; m. Jacqueline Donna Pain, July 18, 1986; children: Paul Darrell II, Robert Tod. BS, Youngstown State U., 1963; cert. Stanford Exec. Program, Stanford U., 1987; cert. Global Leadership Program, U. Mich., 1993. Svc. rep., warranty mgr., dist. mgr., asst. zone mgr. Chrysler Motors Corp., Orlando, Fla., 1966-77; zone mgr. Chrysler Motors Corp., Omaha, 1977-78, Troy, Mich., 1978-79; nat. distbn. mgr., regional mgr., gen. mgr. import export ops., gen. sales mgr. Chrysler Motors Corp., Detroit, 1979-88; pres., chief exec. officer Alfa Romeo Distbrs. N. Am., Orlando, 1988-91; gen. sales mgr. Chrysler Corp., Orange, Calif., 1991-93; v.p. Chrysler Internat. Corp., Detroit, 1993-95; gen. mgr. Europe Chrysler Corp., Detroit, 1993-95; pres., COO Chrysler Fin. Corp., Southfield, Mich., 1995-97, chmn., CEO, 1997-98; v.p. Chrysler Corp., 1997-99; sr. v.p. Daimler Chrysler Corp., 1998—; bd. mgmt. Daimler Chrysler Svcs. AG, 1999—; pres., CEO Daimler Chrysler Fin. Svcs. N.Am., LLC, 1999—. Bd. dirs. Boys and Girls Clubs of S.E. Mich., 1998—. Lt. U.S. Army, 1963-65. Republican. Avocations: auto collecting, American history.

DAVIS, DAVID BRION, historian, educator; b. Denver, Feb. 16, 1927; s. Clyde Brion and Martha (Wirt) D.; m. Toni Lisa Hahn, Sept. 9, 1971; children: Adam Jeffrey, Noah Benjamin; children by previous marriage: Jeremiah Jonathan, Martha Elizabeth, Sarah Brion. A.B. summa cum laude, Dartmouth Coll., 1950, Litt.D., 1977; A.M., Harvard, 1953, Ph.D., 1956; M.A., Oxford U., 1969; L.H.D., U. New Haven, 1986; Litt.D., Columbia U., 1999. Scheduler Cessna Aircraft Co., Wichita, Kan., 1950-51; instr. history Dartmouth, 1953-54; mem. faculty Cornell U., 1955-69, prof. history, 1963-69, Ernest I. White prof. history, 1964-69; prof. history Yale U., 1969—, Farnam prof. history, 1972-78, Sterling prof. history, 1978—, assoc. dir. Nat. Humanities Inst., 1975, dir. Gilder Lehrman Ctr. Study Slavery Resistance Abolition, 1998—; Fulbright lectr., Hyderabad, India, 1967, univs. Guyana and W.I., 1974; Walter Lynwood Fleming lectr. So. history La. State U., 1969; Harmsworth prof. Oxford (Eng.) U., 1969-70; fellow Center Advanced Study Behavioral Scis., 1972-73, Henry E. Huntington Library, 1976, Whitney Humanities Inst. Yale U., 2000— (sr. fellow 2000—); Benjamin Rush lectr. Am. Psychiat. Assn., 1976; French-Am. Found. chair in Am. civilization Ecole des Hautes Etudes en Sciences Sociales, Paris, 1980-81; Fulbright lectr., Israel, Holland, Italy, 1981; Patten lectr. Ind U., 1981; Hanes lectr. U. N.C., 1982; Thompson lectr. Vassar Coll., 1983; Robert Fortenbaugh Meml. lectr. Gettysburg Coll., 1983; disting. scholar in residence Ky. State U., 1984; mem. Internat. Conf. on Capitalism and Slavery, Bellagio, Italy, 1984; Phi Beta Kappa vis. lectr., 1984-85; disting. resident Westminster Coll., Salt Lake City, 1985; project dir. research grants NEH, 1980, 81; Gilbert Osofsky lectr. U. Ill., Chgo., 1986; Arnold Shankman lectr. Winthrop Coll., Rock Hill, S.C., 1987, William W. Cook lectr. U. Mich. Sch. Law, 1988; Elijah Lovejoy lectr. Colby Coll., 1989; James Neal Primm lectr. U. Mo.-St. Louis, 1989; Goltz lectr. Bowdoin Coll., 1989; William E. Massey Sr. lectr. Harvard U., 1989; Athearn lectr. U. Colo., 1990; Scofield lectr. U. Mo., Kansas City, 1991; lectr. Soc. Fellows NYU, 1991, U. Houston, 1991; participant conf. Hamilton Coll., 1992; tchr. summer course Gilder-Lehrman Inst., 1994-2000; John Hope Franklin lectr. Adelphi Coll., 1995; Paley lectr. Hebrew U., Jerusalem, 1995; lectr. Black History Month Coll. Charleston, 1995, Worcester State Coll., 1995; Taft lectr., U. Cin., 1996, lectr. Vanderbilt U., 1996, Conf. on Slave Trade U. Chgo., 1997, Ohio Hist. Soc., 1997, Coll. of Charleston, 1997, 98, 2000, Conf. on New World Slavery Rutgers U., 1997, N.J. Con. Hist. Edn., 1997, Cornell U., 1998, N.Y. Bar Assn., 1998, Omohundro Inst. Early Am. Hist. and Culture, Williamsburg, 1998, Villanova U., 1999, Inst. Hist. Rsch., London, 1999; Popkin lectr., UCLA, 1999, Conf. on Slavery Nottingham, England, 2000. Author: Homicide in American Fiction, 1790-1860, A Study in Social Values, 1957, The Problem of Slavery in Western Culture, 1966, rev. edit., 1988 (Italian,trans.), The Slave Power Conspiracy and the Paranoid Style, 1969, The Problem of Slavery in the Age of Revolution, 1770-1823, 1975, rev. edit. 1999, Slavery and Human Progress, 1984, From Homicide to Slavery: Studies in American Culture, 1986, Revolutions: Reflections on American Equality and Foreign Liberations, 1990 (German trans.); co-author: The Great Republic, 1977, 4th edit., 1992, The Antislavery Debate, 1992; editor: Ante-Bellum Reform, 1967, The Fear of Conspiracy, 1971, Ante-Bellum American Culture: An Interpretive Anthology, 1979, 97; co-editor: The Boisterous Sea of Liberty: A Documentary History of America From Discovery Through the Civil War, 1998; contbr. N.Y. Review of Books. Mem. Subcom. internal security Dem. Nat. Policy Coun., Pulitzer Prize Com., 1968, Bancroft Prize Com., 1989; co-chair adv. bd. Gilder-Lehrman Inst. Am. History, 1995—, tchr. summer sem., 1994-99. With AUS, 1945-46. Recipient Anisfield Wolf award in race relations, 1967, Pulitzer prize for nonfiction, 1967, Mass Media award NCCJ, 1967, Bancroft prize, 1976, Nat. Book award for history and biography, 1976, Presdl. medal Dartmouth Coll., 1991; Guggenheim fellow, 1958-59; Fulbright grantee, 1980; NEH fellow, 1983-84, Gilder-Lehram Inaugural fellow, 1996-97. Fellow Am. Acad. Arts and Scis., Brit. Acad. (corr.); mem. Am. Philos. Soc. (adminstrv. bd. Benjamin Franklin papers), Mass. Hist Soc., Am. Hist. Assn. (Albert J. Beveridge award 1975), Inst. Early Am. History and Culture (coun. 1976-79), Am. Antiquarian Soc., Soc. Am. Historians, Orgn. Am. Historians (pres. 1988-89, chair Frederick Jackson Turner award com. 1989, Lincoln prize com. 1992), Milan Group in Early U.S. Hist. Jewish. Home: 733 Lambert Rd Orange CT 06477-1806

DAVIS, DIANA FAGAN, creative arts and communications professional; b. Melbourne, Victoria, Australia; d. Joseph Lawrence and Nancy Breheny (Fagan) D. BA, U. Melbourne, 1963, Diploma in Edn., 1965, BEd, MA, 1968; PhD, Monash U., Victoria, Australia, 1973. Tchr. Kilbreda Schs., Victoria, 1963-64; psychologist Dept. Labor & Nat. Sci., Victoria, 1966; lectr. RMIT, Victoria, 1967-68; tutor Monash U., Victoria, 1968, sr. tutor, 1969-71, lectr., 1972-76, sr. lectr., 1977-88; prof. James Cook U., Townsville, Australia, 1988—, head Coll. of Music, Visual Arts and Theatre, dep. dean postgrad. studies. Office: James Cook U, Townsville Queensland 4811, Australia

DAVIS, EARON SCOTT, environmental health law consultant, lawyer; b. Chgo., Sept. 7, 1950; s. Milton and Grayce D.; m. Gilla Prizant, May 29, 1977; children: Jeremy Adam, Jonathan Michael, Daniel Benjamin. BA, U. Ill., 1972; JD, Washington U., St. Louis, 1975; MPH, UCLA, 1978. Bar: Ill. Asst. to chmn. Ill. Pollution Control Bd., Chgo., 1975-77; environ. cons. Fred C. Hart Assocs., Washington, 1979-80; atty. coord. Migrant Legal Action Program, Washington, 1980-81; environ cons. Evanston, Ill., 1981—. Editor, pub. Ecol. Illness Law Report, Evanston, 1982-89; author: Toxic Chemicals: Law and Science, 1982; contbr. articles and book chpts. to various publs. Exec. dir. Human Ecology Action League, Evanston, 1983-84; mem. nat. adv. bd. Environ. Task Force, Washington, 1984-88, Nat. Ctr. for Environ. Health Strategies (Recognition of Excellence 1991); mem. adv. com. D.C. Lung Assn. (spl. commendation 1981), Washington, 1980-82, Clean Air Coalition, Phila, 1983-85, U.S. EPA's Indoor Air Quality clearinghouse Planning Team, 1990-92. Recipient Presdl. award Am. Acad. Environ. Medicine, 1983, Carlton Lee award Am. Acad. Environ. Medicine, 1988, Gargoyle award Coun. for Disability Rights, 1992. Mem. Soc. Environ. Journalists. E-mail: earondavis@aol.com. Home: 643 Hibbard Rd Wilmette IL 60091-2042

DAVIS, EDGAR GLENN, science and health policy executive; b. Indpls., May 12, 1931; s. Thomas Carroll and Florence Isabelle (Watson) D. m. Margaret Louise Alandt, June 20, 1953; children: Anne-Elizabeth Davis Polestra, Amy Alandt, Edgar Glenn Jr. AB, Kenyon Coll., 1953; MBA, Harvard U., 1955. With Eli Lilly & Co., Indpls., 1958-91, mgr. budgeting and profit planning, 1963-66, mgr. econ. studies, 1966-67, mgr. Atlanta sales dist., 1967-68, dir. market research and sales manpower planning, 1968-69, dir. mktg. plans, 1969-74, exec. dir. pharm. mktg. planning, 1974-75, exec. dir. corp. affairs, 1975-76, v.p. corp. affairs, 1976-90, v.p. health care policy, 1990; pres., chmn. bd. dirs. Centre for Health Sci. Info., Boston, 1990—; fellow Ctr. for Bus. and Govt. Kennedy Sch. of Govt. Harvard U., 1991—; adj. prof. Butler U., Indpls.; exec. in residence Coll. of Bus., Butler U.; pres. Eli Lilly and Co. Found., 1976-88; mem. Inst. Ednl. Mgmt., Harvard U. Grad. Sch. Edn., 1987; mem. Inst. Medicine NAS, 1981—; chmn. staff Bus. Roundtable Task Force on Health, 1981-85; U.S. rep. UN Indsl. Devel. Orgn. Conf., Lisbon, 1980; participant UNIDO meeting of experts on pharms., 1981; rep. to UN Commn. on Narcotic Drugs, Vienna, 1981, UN Econ. and Social Coun., N.Y.C., 1981, UN Indsl. Devel. Orgn. Conf. Casablanca, 1981, Budapest, 1983, Madrid, 1987; trustee Boston Biomed. Rsch. Inst., 1991—; fellow Ctr. for Bus. and Govt., Kennedy Sch. Govt., Harvard U.; co-chmn. Harvard Conf. on Govt. Role in Civilian Tech., 1992,

Harvard Conf. Pharmaceutical Rsch., Innovation and Pub. Policy, 1993; co-chmn. Harvard Biotech. Roundtable, 1991—; vis. scholar and advisor Health and Welfare Unit, Inst. for Econ. Affairs, London, vis. scholar Green Coll. Oxford (Eng.) U., 1994—; chmn. Nat. Fund for Med. Edn., 1994—, San Francisco; lectr. in field.; dir. English Speaking Union, Indpls. Contbr. articles to profl. jours. Pres., chmn. bd. Indpls. Health Inst., 1988-91; trustee Kenyon Coll., Gambier, Ohio, Ind. Hist. Soc.; pres. bd. trustees Boston Biomed. Rsch. Inst.; chmn. Nat. Fund for Med. Edn., 1996—; bd. dirs. Carnegie Coun. on Ethics and Internat. Affairs and accredited nongovtl. observer rep. to UN, Goodwill Found. Ind. Inc., 1987-95, Sta. WFYI Pub. TV, Indpls., 1983-91, Indpls. Mus. Art, Am. Symphony Orch. League, 1987-92, Nat. Health Coun., 1984-91, Pub. Affairs Coun., Washington, Nat. Fund for Med. Edn.; bd. advisors Christian Theol. Sem., N.C. Schl Arts, Bishops Sch., LaJolla, Calif.; chmn. bd. dirs. Ind. Repertory Theatre, 1979-85; vice chmn., exec. com., bd. dirs. Indpls. Symphony Orch. and Ind. State Symphony Soc., 1977-91; chmn. task force on fine arts Commn. for Future of Butler U.; chmn. exec. com. Pan Am. Econ. Leadership Conf., 10th Pan Am. Games, Indpls.; mem. Chgo. Coun. on Fgn. Rels. Fellow The Hudson Inst. (sr. adj. Indpls.); mem. NAM (bd. dirs., vice-chmn. health policy com. 1987-91), Ind. Soc. Pioneers, Met. Club (Washington), Edgartown Yacht Club, Naples (Fla.) Yacht Club, Woodstock Club, Royal Poinciana Golf Club (Fla.), Contemporary Club, Lambs Club, Crooked Stick Golf Club, Chappaquiddick Beach Club, Edgartown Golf Club, N.Y. Yacht Club, Traders Point Hunt Club, Reform Club London. Fax: 317-940-9455. Office: Butler U Coll Bus Adminstrn 4600 Sunset Ave Indianapolis IN 46208-3487

DAVIS, E(DWARD) MARCUS, lawyer; b. Atlanta, Nov. 24, 1951; s. Edward Martin and Marcine (McConnell) D.; m. Sue Fouquet; children: Edward Clark, Hannah Morgan. AB in Econs., Duke U., 1973; JD, U. Ga., 1976. Bar: U.S. Supreme Ct. 1981. Ptnr. Davis, Zipperman, Kirschenbaum & Lotito, Atlanta, 1983—. Contbr. articles to profl. jours. Mem. ABA, ATLA, Ga. Trial Lawyers Assn., Ga. Criminal Def. Lawyers Assn., Nat. Bd. Trial Advocacy (cert.), Am. Bd. Profl. Liability Attys. (cert.), Lawyers Club of Atlanta. Presbyterian. Avocations: boating, painting, flying, horses. Office: Davis Zipperman Kirschenbaum & Lotito 918 Ponce De Leon Ave NE Atlanta GA 30306-4212

DAVIS, ESTHER YVONNE BUTLER, religious studies educator; b. Balt., June 15, 1955; d. Jake Robert and Harriet (Johnson) Butler; m. Glenn Edward Davis, June 20, 1987; 1 child, Glenn Edward Jr. Cert., U. Md., 1975; student, Coll. Notre Dame, Balt., 1984-86; grad., Baltimore Sch. Bible, 1991. Dep. clk. U.S. Dist. Ct., Balt., 1974-77; inventory control supr. Comcast Cable TV, Timonium, Md., 1982-86; installation mgr. Prime Cable TV, Lanham, Md., 1986-88; purchasing adminstr. United Artists Cable, Balt., 1988-93; substitute tchr. Kinder Praise Learning Ctr., Arlington Bapt. H.S., Balt. County Pub. Sch. Sys. Author: Spirit in Action, 1994, Call Upon the Lord, 1994, Assurance, the Anchor Relationship, 1994; prodr. (tape) Spirit in Action, 1995. Div., coord. Women's Ministry-C.O.G., Balt., 1970-72; vol. Women's Correctional Facility, Jessup, Md., 1993—, Men's Pre-Release Facilty, Jessup, 1983-87; vol. South Balt. Homeless Shelter, 1993-94; v.p. Christian Delights Ministry, Inc. Family Bible Inst. and Sem. scholar, 1993. Avocations: singing, reading, skating, walking, picture collecting. Home: 1 Courtland Woods Cir Pikesville MD 21208-2646

DAVIS, EVELYN MARGUERITE BAILEY, artist, organist, pianist; d. Philip Edward and Della Jane (Morris) Bailey; m. James Harvey Davis, Sept. 22, 1946. Student pub. schs., Springfield; student art, Drury Coll.; piano, organ student of Charles Cordeal. Sec. Shea and Morris Monument Co., before 1946; past mem. sextet, soloist Sta. KGBX; tchr. Bible, organist, pianist, vocal soloist, dir. youth choir Bible Bapt. Ch., Maplewood, Mo., 1956-69; pvt. instr. piano and organ, voice Croma Harp, Affton, Mo., 1960-71, St. Charles, Mo., 1971-83; Bible instr. 3d Bapt. Ch., St. Louis, 1948-54; pianist, soloist, tchr. Bible Temple Bapt. Ch., Kirkwood, Mo., 1969-71; asst. organist-pianist, vocal soloist, tchr. Bible, Bible Ch., Arnold, Mo., 1969; faculty St. Charles Bible Bapt. Christian Sch., 1976-77; organist for Dr. Jack Van Impe Crusades and Dr. Oliver B. Green Crusades; organist, pianist, soloist, Bible tchr., dir. youth orch., music arranger, floral arranger Bible Bapt. Ch., St. Charles, 1971-78; organist, vocal soloist, floral arranger, Bible tchr. Faith Missionary Bapt. Ch., St. Charles, 1978-82; organist, floral arranger, vocal soloist Belleview Bapt. Ch., Springfield, Mo., 1984-90; tchr. piano, organ, voice, organist, Springfield, 1983—; pianist Golden Agers Pk. Crest Bapt. Ch., Springfield, 1991; interior decorator, floral arranger, organist, vocal soloist for weddings and funerals. Composer: I Will Sing Hallelujah, (cantata) I Am Alpha and Omega, Prelude to Prayer, My Shepherd, O Sing unto the Lord a New Song, O Come Let Us Sing unto the Lord, The King of Glory, The Lord Is My Light and My Salvation, O Worship the Lord in the Beauty of Holiness, The Greatest of These Is Love, Prayer to the Lord Our God, We Will Sing Praises, His Name Is Jesus, From Bethlehem's Manger to the Cross, The King of Kings Is Coming! Alleluia! To the Throne You Go, also numerous hymn arrangements for organ and piano. Past pianist, Sunday sch. tchr., mem. choir East Ave. Bapt. Ch. Fellow Internat. Biog. Assn. (life), Am. Biog. Inst. Rsch. Assn. (life); mem. Nat. Guild Organists, Nat. Guild Piano Tchr. Auditions, Internat. Platform Assn. Home: 5135 E Farm Road 174 Rogersville MO 65742-8220

DAVIS, FERD LEARY, JR., law educator, lawyer, consultant; b. Zebulon, N.C., Dec. 4, 1941; s. Ferd L. and Selma Ann (Harris) D.; m. Joy Baker Davis, Jan. 25, 1963; children: Ferd Leary III, James Benjamin, Elizabeth Joy. BA, Wake Forest U., 1964, JD, 1967; LLM, Columbia U., 1984. Bar: N.C. 1967. Editor Zebulon (N.C.) Record, 1958; tchr. Davidson County Schs., Wallburg, N.C., 1966; ptnr. Davis & Davis and related law firms, Zebulon and Raleigh, N.C., 1967-76; asst. pros. Wake County Dist. Ct., Raleigh, 1968-69; town atty. Town of Zebulon, 1969-76; founding dean Campbell U. Sch. Law, Buies Creek, N.C., 1975-86, prof. law, 1975—; dir. Inst. to Study Practice of Law and Socioecon. Devel., 1985—; chmn. The Davis Cons. Group, Inc., Buies Creek, 1987—; pres. LAWLEAD, 1995—, Nat. Inst. to Enhance Leadership and Law Practice, 1998—; cons. U. Charleston, W.Va., 1979; vis. scholar Ctr. for Creative Leadership, 1993. Assoc. editor Wake Forest U. Law Rev. Trustee Wake County Pub. Librs., 1971-75, Olivia Raney Trust, 1969-71; mem. N.C. State Dem. Exec. Com., 1970-72, N.C. Gen. Statutes Commn., 1977-79, Commn. on the Future of N.C., 1980-83. 1st Lt. USAR, 1959-66. Babcock scholar Wake Forest U., 1963-67; Dayton Hudson fellow Columbia U., 1982-83. Fellow Coll. Law Practice Mgmt.; mem. ABA, N.C. Bar Assn., N.C. State Bar, Rotary, Phi Delta Phi, Delta Theta Phi, Omicron Delta Kappa. Democrat. Office: Nat Inst to Enhance Leadership and Law Practice Campbell U Sch Law PO Box 4280 Buies Creek NC 27506-4280

DAVIS, FRANCIS RAYMOND, priest; b. Washington, Feb. 10, 1920; s. Frank Raymond and Ruth Madeline (Donovan) D.; B.A., St. Bernard's Sem., Rochester, N.Y., 1941; M.L.S., Cath. U. Am., 1953. Ordained priest Roman Cath. Ch., 1945; asst. pastor St. Ambrose Ch., Rochester, 1945-50; prof. lit. St. Bernard's Sem., 1950-51, librarian, 1950-69, prof. speech., 1958-67; pastor Our Lady Lourdes Ch., Elmira, N.Y., 1969-78; pastor St. Mary's Ch., Dansville, N.Y., 1978-80, St. Patrick's Ch., Corning, N.Y., 1980-90. Mem. Chemung county gen. edn. bd. Diocese of Rochester, 1971-78; mem. exec. com. Chemung County (N.Y.) Council Aging, 1972-76; mem. adv. com. Chemung County Office for Aging, 1973-78; mem. exec. com. Ecumenical Preaching Mission, 1977-78; bd. dirs. All Saints' Acad., Corning, 1986-90, founder. Fellow Internat. Biog. Assn.; mem. ALA, Cath. Library Assn. (officer sem. sect. 1958-61), Ch. and Synagogue Library Assn. (nominating com. 1979), Elmira Vicinity Ministerial Assn. (officer 1972-73). Author articles and book revs. Address: 155 State St Corning NY 14830-2534

DAVIS, GLENN KEVIN, publishing executive; b. Enfield, Middlesex, Eng., Feb. 4, 1951; s. John Sydney and Joyce Evelyn (Salmon) D.; m. Brenda Phipps, Sept. 24, 1977; children: Gregory, Shelley. Acct. Graham & Gillies Ltd., London, 1970-73; account exec. Wilkinson, Scott-Turner, London, 1973-74; group mng. dir. Billington & Wright Ltd., London, 1974-84; mng. dir. MMS Publs. Ltd., Bishops Stortford, Eng., 1984-88; founder, pub., mng. dir. Today Mags. Ltd., Suffolk, Eng., 1988—. Editor, pub. Suffolk & Norfolk Life mag., 1989 (Best New Mag. award). Press officer Rotary, Edmonton, Eng., 1977-79; mem. exec. com. Enfield (Eng.) C. of C., 1977-80; press officer Roundtable, Huddesdon, Eng., 1984-86; vice chmn. Saxtead Parish Coun., Suffolk, 1988—. Fellow Brit. Inst. Mgmt.; mem. Inst. Journalists, Inst. Mtg. Avocations: squash, oil painting, walking, reading. Home: Barn Acre House, Saxtead Green, Suffolk IP13 9QJ, England Office: Today Mags Ltd Barn Acre, Saxtead Green, Suffolk IP13 9QJ, England

DAVIS, H. ALAN, retired airline captain, consultant; b. Knoxville, Tenn., Apr. 24, 1932; s. Fred Edwin Davis and Rose Lee (Perrin) Davis Williams; m. Betty Jean Carter, June 11, 1951; children: Cynthia Lynn Davis Roper, Linda Susan Davis Williamson, Scott Alan. BS, Jackson Coll., Honolulu, 1965; disting. grad., Indsl. Coll. of Armed Forces, 1970; M of Arts in Teaching, Rollins Coll., 1972; EdD, Nova U., 1980. Cert. FAA in airline transport. Commd. 1st sgt. USAF, 1951, advanced through grades to maj., 1972; dir. ops., chief pilot Sky Safari Air Travel Club, Orlando, Fla., 1972-73; co. check airman, capt. Rich Internat. Airways, Miami, Fla., 1979-85; dept. chmn., tchr. Maynard Evans High Sch., Orlando, 1973-85; co. check airman, line capt. Trans Air Link Corp., Miami, 1985-92; with ops. dept. Walt Disney World, Orlando, Fla., 1992-94; chief pilot Hemisphere Internat. Airlines, Miami, 1994-96; ret., 1996; entertainment ops. staff Walt Disney World, 1996—; Air Santo Domingo line capt. APA Internat., 1992-93. Recipient Nat. Achievement award, Am. Soc. Aerospace Edn., 1980. Mem. DAV (life), Aircraft Owners and Pilots Assn., Retired Officers Assn., Shriners, Masons, Quiet Birdmen. Republican. Avocations: golfing, hunting, fishing. Home: 8208 Banyan Blvd Orlando FL 32819-4145

DAVIS, J. ALAN, lawyer, writer; b. N.Y.C., Nov. 7, 1961. Student, Marlborough Coll., Eng., 1979; BA with distinction, So. Meth. U., 1983; JD with honors, U. Tex., 1987. Bar: Calif. 1988. Assoc. O'Melveny & Myers, L.A., 1987-89, Rosenfeld, Meyer & Susman, Beverly Hills, Calif., 1989-90; pvt. practice L.A., 1990-94; ptnr. Davis & Benjamin, L.A., 1995-98, Garvin, Davis & Benjamin, LLP, L.A., 1998-99; pvt. practice L.A., 1999-2000; sr. atty. legal and bus. affairs Warner Bros. Internat. TV Prodn., Burbank, Calif., 2000—. Mem. Calif. Bar Assn., Beverly Hills Bar Assn. (entertainment law sect. exec. com.), Brit. Acad. Film and TV Arts, L.A. (mng. dir. 1998, bd. dirs.), British Film Office (exec. com.). Avocations: skiing, scuba diving, tennis. Office: 4000 Warner Blvd Burbank CA 91522-0001

DAVIS, JEREMY MATTHEW, chemist; b. Bakersfield, Calif., Aug. 5, 1953; s. Joseph Hyman and Mary (Pavetto) D.; m. Bernadette Sobkiewicz, Aug. 28, 1976 (div.); children: Andrew Jeremy, Christopher Peter. BS in Biol. Scis., U. Calif., Irvine, 1974; M in Pub. Adminstrn., Calif. State U., Long Beach, 1983. Chemist I, II, Orange County Water Dist., Fountain Valley, Calif., 1977-84, chemist supr., 1984—. Papers in field. Lay eucharistic minister St. Margaret of Scotland Episcopal Ch., San Juan Capistrano, Calif., St. John the Divine Episcopal Ch., Costa Mesa, Calif. Named Lab. Person of Yr., Calif. Water Environment Assn., Santa Ana River Basin, 1984. Mem. MENSA, Am. Water Works Assn., Toastmasters Internat. (pres. Watermeisters club 1996, 99, gov. area C-5 founder's dist. 1999—). Office: Orange County Water Dist PO Box 8300 Fountain Valley CA 92728-8300

DAVIS, JOE DAVID, broadcast executive; b. Charleston, W.Va., Mar. 25, 1944; s. Maynard R. and Mary Jane (Entsminger) D.; m. Paulette Groves, July 2, 1966 (div. Jan. 1973); m. Carolyn Bradley, Apr. 19, 1975; children: Katherine Peterson, Jeff Davis, Sarah Dunn, Webb Davis. BS, Wheaton (Ill.) Coll., 1966; MS in Edn., U. So. Calif., 1969. Faculty assoc. Ariz. State U., Tempe, 1971-75; pres. Davis Eaton, Inc., Phoenix, 1975-85, Practice Resources, Inc., Scottsdale, Ariz., 1983-85; exec. dir. JAF Ministries, Agoura, Calif., 1985-89; v.p. Salem Media Corp., N.Y.C., 1992—, Salem Comm. Corp., N.Y.C., 1994—; gen. mgr. Sta. WMCA, N.Y.C., 1989—, Sta. WWDJ, Hackensack, N.J., 1994—. Mem. Manhattan adv. bd. Salvation Army, N.Y.C., 1993—, chmn. comm. com., 1992—; mem. organizing bd. N.Y. Urban Partnership, N.Y.C., 1992-93. With U.S. Armed Forces Radio and TV Svc., Athens, Greece. Fellow Am. Acad. Human Svcs.; mem. Nat. Assn. Broadcasters, Nat. Religious Broadcasters (contbr. articles to mag.), N.Y. Market Radio, Am. Broadcast Pioneer, Broadcast Found. Republican. Avocations: golf, gourmet cooking, computers. Office: Salem Media Inc 201 Route 17 Ste 601 Rutherford NJ 07070-2574

DAVIS, JOHN JAMES, religion educator; b. Phila., Oct. 13, 1936; s. John James and Cathryn Ann (Nichols) D.; m. Carolyn Ann. BA, Trinity Coll., Dunedin, Fla., 1959, DD (hon.), 1968; MDiv, Grace Coll. & Grace Theol. Sem., Winona Lake, Ind., 1962, ThM, 1964, ThD, 1967. Instr. Grace Coll. & Grace Theol. Sem., 1963-65, prof. of Old Testament, 1965—, exec. v.p., 1976-82, pres., 1986-93; exec. dean Near East Sch. Archaeology, Jerusalem, 1970-71; area supr. Tekoa Archeol. Expdn., Jordan, 1968, 70, Raddana Expdn., Jordan, 1974, Heshbon Expdn., Jordan, 1976, Abila Archeol. Expdn., Jordan, 1982, 84. Author: Paradise to Prison, 1975 (Book of Yr.), The Perfect Shepherd, 1979 (Book of Yr.) 14 other books. Chmn., bd. dirs. Kosciusko Comty. Hosp., 1994-95. Recipient Gold award United Way, 1980, Conservation award Barbee Property Owners Assn., 1983; named Outdoor Writer of Yr., Ind. Dept. Natural Resources, 1986, to the Kosciusko County Rep. Hall of Fame, 1992. Mem. Am. Schs. of Oriental Research, Near East Archeol. Soc., Outdoor Writers Assn., Hoosier Outdoor Writers Assn. (pres. 1984-86). Avocations: fishing, hunting, photography. Home: PO Box 557 Winona Lake IN 46590-0557 Office: Grace Theol Sem 200 Seminary Dr Winona Lake IN 46590-1224*

DAVIS, JOHN WARREN, investment company executive, program integrator; b. York, Pa., Feb. 14, 1946; s. Frank Asbury Jr. and Lillian Margaret (Billings) D. BA in Polit. Sci., Drake U., 1968; AA in Real Estate, San Diego City Coll., 1976; MS in Acquisition and Contract Mgmt., West Coast U., 1987; postgrad., Walden U., 1992—. Real estate sales staff, 1972-79; clk. GS 3 Naval Ocean Sys. Ctr., 1979-80; contract intern, contract adminstr. Office of Naval Rsch., 1980-84; contract specialist, warranted ordering officer Gen. Svc. 1102-11 Naval Weapons Sta., 1984-86; contract specialist Gen Svc. 1102-12 Navy Space Sys. Activity, 1986-88; procurement analyst Gen Svc. 102-12 COMNAVAIRPAC, 1988-98; def. contract mgr. Def. Contract Mgmt. Command, 1998—; CEO Claire de Lune Project 2000, 2000; del. San Diego State U. to the Nat. Acad. Conf. for Contract Mgmt. Educators, 1991, 92, 93; profl. cons. Computer Applications, Inc., 1992; mem. tech. program com., chairperson for electronic data interchange Soc. of Logistics Engrs., 1995; mem. Golden Hill planning com. City of San Diego; adj. instr. San Diego State U., chmn. curriculum rev. com. for acquisitiion. Author, Paperless Contracting, The EDI Revolution, 1995, contbr. articles to profl. publs. With U.S. Army, Vietnam, 1968-72. Fellow Nat. Contract Mgmt. Assn. (cert. profl. contract mgr.); mem. ABA (mem. sub-com. pub. law sector, sub-com. on intellectual property), SAR (nat., Calif. and San Diego chpts.), Am. Arbitration Assn. (nat. panel mem.), Soc. Govt. Meeting Planners (v.p. San Diego chpt.), Soc. Logistics Engrs., San Diego Athletic Club, San Diego Writers and Editors Guild, Author's Guild (past pres.). Episcopalian. Avocations: swimming, traveling. Home: PO Box 620657 San Diego CA 92162-0657

DAVIS, JOY LEE, English language educator; b. N.Y.C., Apr. 3, 1931; d. William Henry and Genevieve (Rhein) Belknap; m. Peter John King, Aug. 26, 1955 (div. Feb. 1985); children: William Belknap King, Russell Stuart King; m. John Bradford Davis, Jr., July 5, 1986. AB, Wellesley Coll., 1952, AM, 1953; PhD, Rutgers U., 1968; postgrad., Oxford (Eng.) U., 1978. Tchr. English Dana Hall Sch. for Girls, Wellesley, Mass., 1953-54; instr. English U. Mo., Columbia, 1954-55, Boston U., 1955-56; tchr. English Brookline (Mass.) High Sch., Spartanburg (S.C.) High Sch., 1956-60; prof. English Ohio Wesleyan U., Delaware, 1966-71, Hamline U., St. Paul, 1972-74, U. Minn., Mpls., 1974-77, Coll. St. Thomas, St. Paul, 1977-88; lectr., dir. Joy Davis Seminars, St. Paul, 1988—; prof. MA in Liberal Studies Program, Hamline U., 1993—. Author: Everything But: An Education Memoir, 1999; pub. poetry in New World Writing and Crisp Pine Anthology; lit. criticism in Midwest Quar., 1993, Jour. Grad. Liberal Studies, 1996. Bd. trustees Ramsey County Arts and Sci. Coun., St. Paul, 1974-80. Wellesley Coll. scholar, 1952. Mem. AAUW (dd. dirs., chair ednl. equity com. 1991, Svc. awrd St. Paul br. 1983), Midwest MLA, Mpls. Inst. Fine Arts, Minn. Club (bd. dirs. 1982-88), New Century Club (bd. dirs., spl. subjects chmn.) Schubert Club (bd. dirs., chmn. mus. com.), Wellesley Coll. Club (regional campaign com.), Delta Kappa Gamma. Republican. Presbyterian. Avocations: reading, travel, creative cuisine. Home and Office: 4312 Pond View Dr Saint Paul MN 55110-4155

DAVIS, JULIE KRAMER, communications executive; b. N.Y.C., Apr. 20, 1957; d. Jerome Kramer and Roberta Luttrell; m. Steven Curt Davis, Aug. 24, 1980; 1 child, Benjamin Herman. BA in English, Binghamton U., 1979; MS in Corp. Comm., Ithaca Coll., 1990; MA in Edn. and Human Devel., The George Washington U., 1996. Reporter Stas. WENE-AM-FM and WMRV-AM-FM, Endicott, N.Y., 1979; news dir. Sta. WINR-AM-FM, Binghamton, N.Y., 1979-81; prodr., reporter and personality Sta. WSKG-TV, Binghamton, 1981-89; multimedia specialist Westinghouse Savannah River Co., Aiken, S.C., 1990-96; corp. comm. dir. Cracker Barrel Old Country Store, Lebanon, Tenn., 1996—; instr. Broome C.C., Binghamton, 1988-90; presenter at various confs., 1992, 95-96. project mgr. and designer (CD-ROM) VOCs in Non-Arid Soil, 1995 (Gold prize Georgia VidFest 1995). Recipient Outstanding Achievement award The SIGCAT Found., 1996, Parthenon awardPub. Rels. Soc. Am., 1998, The Communicator award Print Media Competition, 1999, Crystal Obelisk award Women Execs. in Pub. Rels., 2000. Mem. Internat. Assn. Bus. Communicators, Internat. Soc. Performance Improvement, Coun. Comm. Mgmt., Women Execs. in Pub. Rels. (Social Responsibility award 2000), Phi Kappa Phi. Office: Cracker Barrel Old Country Store 307 Hartman Dr Lebanon TN 37087-2519

DAVIS, JUNE FIKSDAL, medical facility owner, floral designer; b. Alexnadria, Minn., June 18, 1944; d. Mads and Gladys Lillian Katherine (Engstrom) Fiksdal; m. Merrill Nathaniel Davis III, June 20, 1971; adopted sons: Kim Geoffrey, Marc Lee. Cert. with highest honor, Am. Sch. Floral Arts, Chgo., 1965. Floral designer Fiksdal Flowers, Rochester, Minn., 1960-70; prin. floral designer, nat. design tchr. Retail Florists, Kansas City, Mo., Houston, 1970-81; pres. owner, founder The Gables Found., Inc., Rochester, 1982—; floral designer, 1981—. Author: Floral Design, 1973 (Am. Inst. Floral Design award 1974). Cellist Rochester Symphony Orch., 1960-69; bd. dirs., fin. planner United Way, 1974; real estate placement Riverplace Devel., 1980; bd. dirs. Rochester Ballet, 1975; chair Symphony Ball, Rochester Symphony, 1975; coord. music program, new pipe organ, harpischord Unitarian Ch., 1975-81 (Outstanding Svc. award 1977), project pres. Walden Hill Bach Soc., 1975-82; vol. Mayo Clinic Visitors Bur. Mem. Am. Inst. Floral Design, Bus. and Profl. Women. Avocations: gourmet cooking, water sports, winter sports, skiing, European travel, camping, music.

DAVIS, KAREN ANN (KAREN ANN FALCONER), special education educator; b. Rockford, Ill., Sept. 24, 1948; d. Duane Fay and Vivian Marie (Milani) Falconer. BS in Edn., Ill. State U., 1971; MBA in Mgmt., Kennedy-Western U., 1994; MA in Tchg., Rockford Coll., 1996. Cert. Ill. assessing ofcl. Spl. edn. tchr. Winnebago Co-op, Rockton, Ill., 1971-76; assessor Winnebago Twp., Ill., 1977-85; program coord. Ill. Growth Enterprises, Rockford, Ill., 1977-87; substitute tchr. Rockford Pub. Schs., 1987-89, 92—; estate planner Bradford and Assocs., Rockford, 1988-89, A. Bergners, Rockford, 1989-91; spl. edn. tchr. Eisenhower Middle Sch., Rockford, 1992—. Pub. ofcl. Assessor-Winnebago Twp., 1977-85. Mem. Twp. Assessor's Assn. (treas. 1985), Nat. Audubon Soc. Roman Catholic. Avocations: photgraphy, bird watching, gardening, traveling, antiquing.

DAVIS, KEIGH LEIGH, aerospace engineer; b. Mitchell, S.D., Oct. 6, 1954; d. Clarence Ralph and Katherine Lee Schilling; m. Glenn Nickerson Davis, Nov. 24, 1992; 1 child, Tasha Clare Marie. BS in Aerospace Engring. & Mechanics, U. Minn., 1976; MS in Aerospace Engring., U. Dayton, 1983. Stability and control project engr. Flight Stability and Control Br., USAF, Wright Patterson AFB, Ohio, 1976-85, E-3/Joint Stars Program Office, Wright Patterson AFB, 1985-86; lead stability, control & flying qualities project engr. Advanced Tactical Fighter Program, Wright Patterson AFB, 1986-88, Advanced Tactical Fighter Sys. Program Office, Wright Patterson AFB, 1988-90; stability and control project engr. Joint Tactical Autonomous Weapon Sys. Program Office, Wright Patterson AFB, 1990-91; lead br. engr. Flight Stability and Control Br., Wright Patterson AFB, 1991-94; stability and control tech. specialist Flight Mechanics Br., Wright Patterson AFB, 1993—; chmn. MIL-STD-1797 pilot-in-the-loop oscillation update team ASC/ENFT, Wright Patterson AFB, 1992-95, responsible engr. for flying qualities of piloted aircraft mil. std., 1992—, mil. handbook, 1997—; co-chmn. USAF flying qualities devel. process team, 1995—. Mem. AIAA (sr.), Soc. Women Engrs. (life), Order of Ea. Star (pres.).

DAVIS, KENNETH WAYNE, English language educator, business communication consultant; b. Chariton, Iowa, June 22, 1945; s. Wayne Pitman and Jeanne Frances (West) D.; m. Bette Hargrove, Nov. 28, 1970; Cassandra Alice, Evan Thomas. BA, Drake U., 1967; MA, Columbia U., 1968; PhD, U. Mich., 1975. From asst. prof. English to assoc. prof. U. Ky., Lexington, 1975-88; assoc. prof. to prof. Ind. U.-Purdue U., Indpls., 1988—, dept. chair, 1998—; bus. cons., Lexington, 1977-88; pres. Komei, Inc., 1994—. Author: Better Business Writing, 1983, (with others) Business Communication for the Information Age, 1988, Rehearsing the Audience, 1988, (with others) Writing: Process, Product, and Power, 1993; prodr.: 2001: Lessons in Leadership videoconf., 1991; numerous other books and articles. Bd. dirs. Shepherd's House, Inc., Lexington, 1986-88, Waycross Camp and Conf. Ctr., 1995—, World Trade Club Ind., 1998—. Sgt. U.S. Army, 1968-71. Woodrow Wilson fellow, 1967; recipient Faculty Service award Nat. Univ. Continuing Edn. Assn., 1987. Mem. ASTD, Nat. Coun. Tchrs. English, Assn. Bus. Comm., Assn. Profl. Comm. Cons., Amnesty Internat. Episcopalian. Avocations: theater, travel. Office: Ind U-Purdue U Dept English 425 University Blvd Indianapolis IN 46202-5148

DAVIS, LAWRENCE WILLIAM, radiation oncologist; b. N. Braddock, Pa., Sept. 5, 1935; s. William Paul Davis and Julia Helen Zukas; children: James G., Karen E. BS, Juniata Coll., Huntington, Pa., 1957; MA, U. Pa., 1969; MBA, Temple U., 1984; MD, Georgetown U., 1961. Diploamte Am. Bd. Radiology (trustee 1981-95, asst. exec. dir. radiation oncology 1994—); lic. physician Pa., Md., N.Y., Ga. Asst. instr. radiology U. Pa., Phila., 1962-66, instr. radiology, 1966, 68-69, asst. prof. radiology, 1969-72, assoc. prof. radiology, 1972-75; prof. radiation therapy Thomas Jefferson Sch. Medicine, 1975-84; prof. and chmn. radiation oncology Albert Einstein Coll. Medicine, Bronx, 1984-91, Emory U., Atlanta, 1991—; cons. Armed Forces Radiobiology Rsch. Inst., Bethesda, 1968-70; exec. com. of med. staff Montefiore Med. Ctr., 1984-87, 1990-91, div. coun., 1988-89; prof. svc. com. Phila. div. Am. Cancer Soc., 1970-75. Contbr. numerous articles to profl. jours.; assoc. editor Internat. Jour. Radiation Oncology, 1986—; editorial bd. Neuro Oncology, 1989—, assoc. editor, 1991—; editorial bd Am. Jour. Clin. Oncology, 1991—. Capt. USAF, 1966-68. Fellow Am. Cancer Soc., Phila., 1963-64, NIH, 1964-66, Am. Cancer Soc. traineeship, 1968-71. Fellow Am. Coll. Radiology; mem. AMA, AAAS, Am. Assn. Cancer Rsch., Am. Coll. Radiology (commn. on radiation oncology 1981-90, bd. chancellors 1993-99), Am. Soc. Therapeutic Radiology and Oncology (chmn. bd. 1988-89, pres. 1987-88), Am. Coll. Hosp. Adminstrs., Am. Mgmt. Assn., Am. Radium Soc. (pres. 1992-93), Am. Soc. Clin. Oncology, Med. Assn. Atlanta, N.Y. Acad. Scis., Ga. State Med. Soc., Ga. State Radiol. Soc., Radiation Rsch. Soc., Radiol. Soc. N.Am., Alpha Omega Alpha. E-mail: davis@radonc.emory.org. Office: Emory Clinic 1365 Clifton Rd NE Atlanta GA 30322-1013

DAVIS, LEON, oil company executive; b. Arkansas City, Kans., Nov. 15, 1918; s. Miriam Kahan; m. Elene Meyer Davis, July 19, 1952; children: Lynn, Lance, Ross, Evan. BA, U. Okla., 1940. Co-owner Davis Bros., Tulsa and Houston, 1945—; chmn. bd. Alliance S.B.I.Co. Co., Tulsa. Chmn. Okla. Civil Rights Commn., 1966; co-founder, chmn. Interferon Found., Houston, 1979-90; pres. Urban League, Tulsa, 1964; bd. dirs. M.D. Anderson Hosp. Col. USAAF, 1940-48. Mem. Kiwanis (pres. 1965.). Avocation: tennis. Home: 502 Thamer Ln Houston TX 77024-6920 Office: Davis Bros 1221 Mckinney St Ste 3100 Houston TX 77010-2009

DAVIS, LOURIE IRENE BELL, computer education and information systems specialist; b. Las Vegas, N.Mex., Apr. 8, 1930; d. Currie Oscar and Minnie I. (Rodgers) Bell; m. Robert Eugene Davis, Aug. 21, 1950; children: Judith Anne, Robert Patrick, (adopted) Jaime Alleyn, (adopted) Flint Christopher. BS, West Tex. U., 1959; student, Ea. N.Mex. U., 1947-49, U. Tulsa, 1980-81. Cert. elem. tchr. Tchr. lang. arts, social studies, music grades 4-6 Okla., 1949-51, 66-73, Tex., 1959-65; programmer/analyst Blue Cross/Blue Shield Okla., Tulsa, 1972-75, mgr. sys., 1977-81, dir. info. sys., 1981-82, mgr. project control, 1983, mgr. info. ctr., 1984-85, mgr. profl. cons. and tng., 1985-87; faculty devel. coord. CAID Okla. State U., Okmulgee, 1987-90; adminstrv. officer Intertel, Inc., Tulsa, 1991-95; pres., CEO Intertel, Inc., 1995—, adminstrv. officer, 1991-95; pres., CEO, 1995—, sys. curriculum coord.; computer sci. instr. Tulsa Jr. Coll., 1975-76, mem. computer sci. adv.

bd., 1976-83, adj. instr., 1977-83, 93-94; computer bus. and edn. cons. Davis Cons., 1991—; mem. steering com. U.S. Senate bus. adv. bd., 1981-88; ind. cons., Tulsa, 1987; lectr. computer assisted instr. Success League of Innovation Conf., St. Louis, 1989, Music Users Group Conf., U. Tenn., Chattanooga, 1989, Pres.'s Day Des Moines Area C.C., 1990. Mem. budget panel United Way Tulsa, 1981-87, Allocations Exec. Com. Appreciation award, 1987; mem. U.S. Rep. Presdl. Task Force, 1982-93; mem. Holy Family Sch. Bd., 1991-95, nominating com. chair, 1993, sec., 1993-95. Winner League of Innovation for C.C.S. Competition, IBM, 1989. Mem. NAFE, AAUW, Assn. Sys. Mgmt. (regional dir. 1985-86, chpt. membership chair 1982-84, internat. merit awards 1980, 84), Tulsa Area Sys. Edn. Assn. (recorder 1980-81), Higher Edn. Acad. Coun. of Okla., Sierra Club, Arbor Day Found., Habitat for Humanity, Alpha Chi, Mensa, Intertel (nat. acceptance com. chair 1978, dir. region VIII 1987-91, membership officer 1991-95, chmn. bd. 1995-2000, pub. Integra, Jour. of Intertel 1992-2000, awarded lifetime mem. and appreciation award 1997). Republican. Mem. Unity Ch. of Christianity. Home and Office: Davis Cons 2403 W Oklahoma St Tulsa OK 74127-3027

DAVIS, LOWELL LIVINGSTON, cardiovascular surgeon; b. Urbanna, Va.. BS in Biology, Morehouse Coll., 1949; MS in Biology, Atlanta U., 1950; MD, Howard U., 1955; postgrad., U. Pa., 1959-60. Diplomate Am. Bd. Surgery, Am. Bd. Thoracic Surgery. Intern Jersey City (N.J.) Med. Ctr., 1955-56; resident Margaret Hague Maternity Hosp., Jersey City, 1956-57; resident ob-gyn. Elmhurst (N.Y.) Gen. Hosp., 1957-58, chief resident ob-gyn., 1958-59; resident in gen. surgery U.S. VA Hosp., Tuskegee, Ala., 1960-61; resident to chief resident in gen. surgery Nassau County Med. Ctr., Hempstead, N.Y., 1961-64; resident in cardiothoracic surgery Cook County Hosp., Chgo., 1967-68, sr. resident, 1968-69; pvt. practice N.Y.C., 1964-65, pvt. practice thoracic and cardiovascular surgery, 1975—; clin. assoc. prof. surgery L.A. County Gen. Hosp., U. So. Calif. Med. Sch., 1988—; fellow U. Oreg., Portland, 1972, St. Vincent Hosp., Portland, 1972, Med. Coll. Wis., Milw., 1973, Pacific Med. Ctr. Inst. of Med. Scis., San Francisco, 1974, Allen-Bradley Med. Scis. Rsch. Lab. Med. Coll. Wis., 1975, Hosp. for Sick Children, London, 1977-78, Tex. Heart Inst., Houston, 1983, Cardiac Surgery Rsch. Lab., Hadassah Med. Sch. and U. Hosp., Jerusalem, 1987; vis. surgeon NYU Med. Sch., 1991, Mayo Clinic, Rochester, Minn., 1991, U. Dusseldorf, Germany, 1991, Deutsches Herzzentrum, Berlin, 1991, Deutsches Herzzentrum, Munich, 1991, Klinik für Thorat-Herz-Und Gefab Chirurgie, Hanover, Germany, 1991, U. Vienna, Austria, 1992. Contbr. articles to profl. jours. With USN, 1943-46, USNR, 1965-71, comdr., 1965-67, capt. USNR, 1970. Recipient Asiatic Pacific Campaign medal with one Gold Star, Presdl. Unit citation. Fellow ACS, Internat. Coll. Angiology, Am. Coll. Angiology, Internat. Coll. Surgeons, N.Y. Acad. Medicine, Am. Coll. Chest Physicians, Am. Coll. Cardiology; mem. AAAS, Assn. Mil. Surgeons U.S., Am. Assn. for Thoracic Surgery, Soc. Thoracic Surgeons, Albert Starr Cardiac Surg. Soc. (founding), Am. Coll. Emergency Physicians, Lyman Brewer III Internat. Surg. Soc., Royal Soc. Medicine, Denton A. Cooley Cardiovasc. Surgery Soc., L.A. Surg. Soc. Home: 1200 N State St #10-250 Los Angeles CA 90033-1029

DAVIS, LOYD EVAN, defense industry marketing professional; b. Newark, Ohio, Apr. 10, 1939; s. Paul Edwin and Eleanor Amanda (Loyd) D.; m. Delores Madeline Wells, Nov. 10, 1959 (div. 1975); children: Mark Evan, Geoffrey Scott; m. Judith Ann Lambert, Sept. 15, 1977; 1 child, James Richard. BS in Elec. Engring., Okla. State U., 1963, MS in Elec. Engring., 1968. Commd. 2d lt. USAF, 1964, advanced through grades to maj., 1974; served in various locations, then ret. U.S. Air Force, 1979; mem. sr. profl. staff Dynatrend, Inc., Arlington, Va., 1979-82; mktg. mgr. govt. systems sector Harris Corp., Alexandria, Va., 1982-87; mktg. mgr. E-Systems Melpar Div., Falls Church, Va., 1987-90; mem. sr. profl. staff Adroit Systems, Inc., Alexandria, Va., 1990-95; sr. staff engr. L3 Comms Corp., Salt Lake City, 1996—. Mem. Assn. U.S. Army, Nat. Def. Indsl. Assn., Air Force Assn., Armed Forces Comm. Electronics Assn., Woodbridge Wireless Club (pres. 1972-73, 88-89), Davis County Amateur Radio Club (v.p. 1997), Mt. Vernon Amateur Radio Club (pres. 1987-88), Masons (sec. Bonneville lodge no. 31, F&AM 1999—). Republican. Methodist. Avocation: ham radio. Home: 1476 Madera Hills Dr Bountiful UT 84010-1523 Office: L3 Comms Corp Comm Systems West 640 North 2200 West Salt Lake City UT 84116-2925

DAVIS, LUANE RUTH, theatrical director, performer; b. Binghamton, N.Y., Sept. 10, 1960; d. Paul Joseph and Ruth Hardin (Wheeler) D., m. Jonathan Allen Fluck, (div. Dec. 1994). BA, Hunter Coll., 1983; MA, Goddard Coll., 1992; stage interpretation in ASL cert., The Juilliard Sch., 1994. Performer Broadway, regional, stock prodns., 1979—, Delta Queen Steamboat Co.; dir., choreographer showcase, cruise lines, children's shows, 1986—; adminstr. Maverick Theatre, N.Y.C., 1986-88; artistic dir. Interborough Repertory Theatre, N.Y.C., 1986—; writer self help, children's musicals, 1990—; pub. edn. specialist Dept. Mental Retardation Devel. Disabilities, N.Y.C., 1990-95; program coord. for deaf svcs. St. Vincent's Hosp., N.Y.C., 1997-98; prof. Nt. Tech. Inst. for the Deaf Rochester (N.Y.) Inst. Tech., 1998—; Am. Sign Lang. interpreter; creator Del-Sign acting technique, Interborough Repertory Theatre, N.Y.C., 1992—, spkr. in field; presenter Nat. Inst. Trial Lawyers. Author: (self-help) Taking Stage, 1995; (musical) Women of the American Revolution, 1991, The World in Her Hands: The Story of Helen Keller, 1993; author, prodr.: (musical) The Little Matchgirl, 1995. Active many accessibility issues for the disabled, N.Y.C. Recipient Women of Achievement award Gov. Pataki's Women Run N.Y.C., 1998. Mem. AFTRA, DAR, Actor's Equity Assn., League of Prof. Theatre Women, Registry of Interpreters of the Deaf, Deaf Entertainment Guild. Episcopalian. Avocations: sports, refinish furniture, teach children literacy. Home: 25 Mayapple Ln West Henrietta NY 14586-9518 Office: Interborough Theatre 154 Christopher St Ste 3B New York NY 10014-2840

DAVIS, LYNN HARRY, secondary education educator; b. Jamestown, N.Y., Mar. 6, 1949; s. Harry Lynn and Marjorie Ellen (Greenwood) D.; m. Patricia Ann Carapella; 1 child, Matthew Michael. BS, SUNY, Fredonia, 1971. Cert. tchr., N.Y. Sci. tchr. West Genesee Sch. Dist., Camillus, N.Y., 1972—; adult edn. computer tchr. West Genesee Sch. Dist., 1985-91, Syracuse U. Teaching Ctr., 1984-86; tech. support specialist Teaching Ctr. Syracuse U., 1991—; chmn. Sci. Bldg., West Genessee Sch. Dist., 1983-88, coord. sci. curriculum, 1988—. Contbr. numerous articles to profl. jours. Strategic planning com. mem. West Genesee Cen. Schs.; fundraiser United Way, Syracuse, 1978-81, YMCA, Syracuse, 1981; mem. Friends of Zoo, 1987-98. Mem. ASCD, N.Y. State United Tchrs. (del. 1980-85), Am. Fed. of Tchrs., Nat. Sci. Tchrs. Assn., West Genesee Tchrs. Assn. (v.p. for negotiations 1979-85, sec. 1986—, newsletter editor 1986—, webmaster 1997—). Avocations: golf, photography, computers. Home: 14 Blackwood Dr Liverpool NY 13090-3764 Office: West Genesee Cen Sch Dist Ike Dixon Rd Camillus NY 13031-9619

DAVIS, MARGARET THACKER, critical care, medical and surgical nurse; b. Greensboro, N.C., June 7, 1925; d. Tiller Foltz and Lucy Wright (Spencer) Thacker; m. Joe Southard Davis, Feb. 4, 1961; 1 child, Dana Lee. Diploma in nursing, Baylor U., Dallas, 1947; student, Ea. N.Mex. U., Roswell, 1978. RN, N.Mex., Tex., Fla. Office nurse Drs. Britt & Cafaro, St. Augustine, Fla., 1947-50, Dr. Robert J. Rowe, Dallas, 1950-61, Dr. F.A. English, Roswell, 1964-74; charge nurse post anesthesia care unit Ea. N.Mex. Med. Ctr., Roswell, 1990-91, ret., 1991. Named Employee of Month, Ea. N.Mex. Med. Ctr., 1985. Mem. ANA, Am. Soc. Post Anesthesia Nurses (charter), Post Anesthesia Nurses Assn. N.Mex. (bd. dirs. 1980-86, sec. 1986-87, legis. com. 1989-90), N.Mex. Nurses Assn. (dist. 5 sec. 1983-85, 91-93, pres. 1986-88, bd. dirs. 1988-90, 92-94, 96-98, membership chmn. 1988-90, chmn. nominating com. 1990, Nurse of Yr. award 1989, search for excellence award 1990, dist. 5 honored nurse 1995), Baylor U. Sch. Nursing Alumni Assn.

DAVIS, MARGERY HELEN, medical educator; b. Glasgow, Scotland, Nov. 2, 1947; d. James Alexander and Elizabeth Grey (Sanderson) Campbell; m. Brian Clive Davis, Dec. 26, 1973; children: Jocelyn, Campbell. MBChB, U. Glasgow, 1971. Sr. registrar in lab. and clin. hematology Western Gen. Hosp., Edinburgh, 1975-78; sr. lectr. med. edn. Ctr. for Med. Edn. U. Dundee, Scotland, 1994—; cons. Brit. Coun., Latvia, 1995-98, Malaysia, 1996-97, Kellogg Found., L.Am., 1994—. Contbr. articles to profl. jours. Mem. Royal Coll. Physicians, Brit. Med. Assn., Assn. for Study of Med. Edn. (coun. 1992—), Assn. for Med. Edn. in Europe. Office: Univ Dundee Ctr Med Edn, 484 Perth Rd, Dundee DD2 1LR, Scotland

DAVIS, MARGUERITE HERR, judge; b. Washington, Nov. 12, 1947; d. Norman Phillip and Margaretha Joanna Herr; m. James Riley Davis, June 20, 1970; children: Amy Marguerite, Christine Riley. AA with honors, St. Petersburg J. Coll., Clearwater, Fla., 1966; BA with honors, U. of South Fla., 1968; JD with honors, Fla. State U., 1971. Bar: Fla. 1971, U.S. Dist. Ct. (no. dist.) Fla. 1971, U.S. Dist. Ct. (mid. dist.) Md. 1985, U.S. Ct. Appeals (11th cir.) 1985, U.S. Supreme Ct. 1986. Atty. workers compensation div. U.S. Dept. Labor, Tallahassee, 1971; sr. legal aide Fla. Supreme Ct., Tallahassee, 1971-85, exec. asst. to Hon. Chief Justice Alderman, 1982-84; ptnr. Swann & Haddock, Tallahassee, 1985-87, Katz, Kutler, Haigler, Alderman, Davis & Marks, Tallahassee, 1987-93; judge Dist. Ct. of Appeal (1st dist.) Fla., Tallahassee, 1993—. Mem. editl. bd. Trial Advocate Quar., 1991-93; contbr. chpts. to books. Mem. ABA, Fla. Bar Assn. (Tallahassee chpt., appellate ct. rules com. 1995—, appellate ct. rules com. chair, 1995-97, grievance com., disciplinary rev. com., chmn. supreme ct. local rules adv. com., jud. cir. grievance com., rules of jud. adminstrn. 1995-99, chair 1997-98, chair jud. evaluation com. 1999-2000, exec. coun. appellate advocacy sect.), Fla. State Fed. Jud. Coun. (exec. dir. 1985—), Tallahassee Women Lawyers, Fla. Def. Lawyers Assn. (amicus curiae com.), Fla. Supreme Ct. Hist. Soc., Am. Arbitration Assn. (ad hoc com. stds. for appellate practice cert.), Altrusa Club of Tallahassee (treas. 1971-76), Fla. State U. Alumni Assn. (bd. dirs. 1975-76), Jud. Mgmt. Coun. (appellate ct. workload and jurisdiction com. 1996—, chair appellate rules liaison com., appellate practice and advocacy sect. 1996-98), Univ. So. Fla. (bd. dirs. Alumni Assn. 1999), Phi Theta Kappa. Methodist. Avocations: quilting, sewing, knitting, running, reading.

DAVIS, MARK HERBERT AINSWORTH, financial analyst, mathematician; b. Colne, Lancashire, Eng., May 1, 1945; s. Christopher Ainsworth and Frances Emily (Marsden) D.; m. Jessica Isabella Smith, Oct. 15, 1988. BA, Cambridge (Eng.) U., 1966, ScD, 1983; MS, U. Calif., Berkeley, 1968, PhD, 1971. Rsch. asst. Electronics Rsch. Lab., U. Calif., 1969-71; lectr. Imperial Coll., London, 1971-79, reader, 1979-84, prof., 1984-95; dir., head rsch. and product devel. Tokyo-Mitsubishi Internat. plc, London, 1995-99; prof. math. Imperial Coll., 2000—. Author: Linear Estimation and Stochastic Control, 1977, (with R.B. Vinter) Stochastic Modelling and Control, 1985, Markov Models and Optimization, 1993; editor-in-chief Stochastics and Stochastics Reports, 1978-95; assoc. editor Annals Applied Probability, 1994-96. Fellow Royal Statis. Soc., Inst. Math. Stats. Avocation: classical music (violin and viola). Home: 11 Chartfield Ave, London SW15 6DT, England Office: Imperial Coll, Dept Math, London Sw7 2BZ, England

DAVIS, MARTIN CLAY, lawyer, professor; b. Tulsa, Okla., Dec. 12, 1947; s. James William and Vera Ruby (Hatcher) D.; m. Rebecca Jo Strong, Aug. 22, 1970; children: Christopher James, Jennifer Alice. BA, U. Ark., 1970; JD, Vanderbilt U., 1973. Bar: Tex. 1973, U.S. Tax Ct. 1985, cert. specialist estate planning, probate law State Bar Tex. Assoc. atty. Gary, Thomasson, Hall & Marks, Corpus Christi, Tex., 1973-77, partner, 1977-94; partner Davis, Hutchinson & Wilkerson, LLP, Corpus Christi, Tex., 1994—; adj. prof. Corpus Christi (Tex.) State U., 1980-83, 87, Tex. A&M U.-C.C., 1993; bd. dirs. Corpus Christi Estate Planning Coun. (pres. 1985-86); pres. Am. Assn. Individual Investors, Corpus Christi subchpt., 1995-96; lectr. various profl. assns. Assoc. Editor: Vanderbilt Law Rev., 1972-73. Pres. Family Counseling Svc., Corpus Christi, 1984; trustee, chmn. United Meth. Ch., 1998. Recipient Leadership award, Corpus Christi C. of C., 1980. Fellow, Tex. Bar Found., Am. Coll. Trust & Estate Counsel; mem. ABA (subcom. chmn. taxation sect., 1975-80), State Bar Tex. (estate planning and probate law adv. commn., taxation sect.; planning com. advanced estate planning and probate course, 1982, 85, 91, planning com. wills and probate inst. 1985, 87, 88, com. to revise the Tex. Trust Act), Order of the Coif. Avocations: tennis, basketball, teaching. Office: Davis Hutchinson & Wilkerson LLP Frost Bank Plz Ste 1270 Corpus Christi TX 78470

DAVIS, MARY HELEN, psychiatrist, psychoanalyst, educator; b. Kingsville, Tex., Dec. 2, 1949; d. Garnett Stant and Emogene (Campbell) D.; m. Timothy Krenke, Oct. 3, 1992. BA, U. Tex., 1970; MD, U. Tex., Galveston, 1975; grad. in adult and child psychoanalysis, Inst. for Psychoanalysis, Chgo., 1982-92. Cert. Nat. Bd. Med. Examiners, Am. Bd. Psychiatry and Neurology, Child and Adolescent Psychiatry. Intern, then resident in psychiatry SUNY, Buffalo, 1975-78; fellow in child psychiatry U. Cin., 1978-80; asst. prof. Med. Coll. Wis., Milw., 1980-89, clin. assoc. prof., 1989-93; med. dir. adolescent treatment unit Milw. Psychiat. Hosp., 1981-86, Schroeder Child Ctr., 1986-89; pvt. practice, 1989-93; med. dir. Devereux-Victoria (Tex.) Psych. Residential Treatment Ctr., 1993-94; pvt. practice Lancaster, Pa., 1995—; cons. Milw. Mental Health Cons., 1980-93, Children's Svc. Soc., Milw., 1982-93, Cath. charities, Harrisburg, Pa., 1996—. Bd. dirs. Next Generation Theatre, Milw., 1988-90, Next Act Theatre, Milw., 1990-92. Mem. Am. Psychiat. Assn., Am. Soc. Adolescent Psychiatry, Am. Med. Women's Assn., Assn. for Child Psychoanalysis, Am. Psychoanalytic Assn. Baptist. Avocations: science fiction, music, computers, crochet.

DAVIS, MICHAEL C., law educator, commentator, activist, speaker; b. Columbus, Ohio; s. Charles and Esther Davis; m. Victoria T. Hui, Aug. 14, 1994; children: Maia K., Hana M. BA, Ohio State U., 1974; JD, U. Calif., San Francisco, 1980; LLM, Yale U., 1984. Bar: Hawaii 1980. Law clk. to Judge Martin Pence U.S. Dist. Ct., Honolulu, 1980-81; assoc. Carlsmith, Wichman & Case, Honolulu, 1981-83; lawyer Native Hawaiian Legal Svcs., Honolulu, 1984-85; prof. law Chinese U. Hong Kong, 1985—; vis. prof. Peking U., Beijing, 1988, 97; spkr. numerous confs. worldwide, 1990—. Author: Constitutional Confrontation in Hong Kong, 1990; author, editor: Human Rights and Chinese Values, 1995; contbr. articles to law jours., including Human Rights Quar., Harvard Human Rights Jour. Avisor Lawyers Com. for Human Rights, 1993—; mem. panel Hong Kong Rsch. Grants Coun., 1996—. With USN, 1968-71. Sr. fellow Schell Ctr. for Internat. Human Rights, Yale Law Sch., 1994-95. Mem. Am. Soc. Internat. Law (vice chmn. Pacific Rim group 1994—). E-mail: mcdavis@cukk.edu.hk. Home: Chinese U Hong Kong, Residence 4 Flat 7A, Shatin Hong Kong Office: Chinese U Hong Kong, Shatin Hong Kong

DAVIS, MICHAEL CHASE, aerospace industry executive, consultant, retired naval officer; b. Fullerton, Calif., Oct. 12, 1931; s. Arthur Elling Davis and Mary Stafford (O'Brien) Greene; m. Jacqueline L. Watkins, Dec. 6, 1976; children: Michael Chase, Jr., Mark Stafford. BS, U.S. Naval Acad., 1953; SM, MIT, 1961, ScD, 1961. Commd. ensign USN, 1953, advanced through grades to capt., 1971; design supt. Mare Island Naval Shipyard, Calif., 1966-68; sys. analyst Office Asst. Sec. Def., Washington, 1968-70; ship design dir. Trident Submarine and Aegis Warships, Naval Sea Sys. Command, Arlington, Va., 1970-75; comdg. officer David Taylor Naval Ship Rsch. and Devel. Ctr., Bethesda, Md., 1975-77; ret., 1977; program mgr. Sci. Applications, Inc., Arlington, 1977-79; program mgr., dir. Sea Shadow Stealth Ship and other marine programs, Lockheed Martin Missiles and Space Co., Sunnyvale, Calif., 1979-96; pub. Ovarian Cancer Internet Website, 1996-99. Decorated Legion of Merit, 1977; recipient DAR award for seamanship, 1953, D.W. Taylor award for sci. achievement, 1963, award for sci. achievement Bur. Ships, 1963, Joint Svc. commendation Sec. Def., 1970. Mem. IEEE, Am. Soc. Naval Engrs. (coun. mem. 1971-73), U.S. Naval Inst. Republican. Address: PO Box 505 Bakersville NC 28705-0505

DAVIS, MICHAEL JOHN EARLS, cardiologist; b. Launceston, Tasmania, Australia, July 26, 1952; s. Russell Earls and Irene Merle (Michel) D.; m. Wendy Paterson Manuel, Feb. 10, 1996; children from previous marriage: Rebecca, Timothy, Stephanie. MB, BS, U. Western Australia, Perth, 1976. Rsch. fellow in medicine Harvard U., Cambridge, Mass., 1984-86; clin. rsch. fellow Mass. Gen. Hosp., Boston, 1984-86; specialist lectr. Curtin U., Perth, 1986-89; sr. lectr. U. Western Australia, Perth, 1991—; cardiologist Royal Perth Hosp., 1985—, head dept. cardiology, 1996-99; vis. med. officer Repatriation Gen. Hosp., Perth, 1986-94, Hollywood Hosp., Perth, 1994—, head dept. cardiology, 1994—, mem. med. adv. com., 1994-98, deputy chmn., 1995; vis. specialist Mount Hosp., Perth, 1988—; cons. cardiologist Princess Margaret Hosp., Perth, 1989—. Rsch. grantee Commonwealth Australia, 1989-93; clin. fellow Nat. Heart Found., 1984-85. Fellow Royal Australian Coll. Physicians; mem. Cardiac Soc. of Australia and New Zealand (sec. electrophysiology working group 1990-91, 97-98), N.Am. Soc. Pacing and Electrophysiology, Am. Coll. Cardiology. Avocations: choral singing, water polo, golf. Office: GPO Box K823, Perth 6001, Australia

DAVIS, MICHAEL STEVEN, lawyer; b. Brookline, Mass., Aug. 1, 1947; s. Ralph and Beatrice (Levy) D.; m. Madelyn O. Davis, Aug. 16, 1970; children: Gregory, Adam, Bethany. AB, U. Rochester, 1969; JD cum laude, Boston U., 1972. Bar: N.Y. 1973, U.S. Dist. Ct. (so. and ea. dists.) N.Y. 1974, U.S. Ct. Appeals (2d cir.) 1974, U.S. Supreme Ct. 1979, U.S. Ct. Claims, 1980. Assoc. Chadbourne & Parke, N.Y.C., 1972-82; sr. counsel corp. litigation Am. Internat. Group, N.Y.C., 1982-88; ptnr. Zalkin, Rodin & Goodman, LLP, N.Y.C., 1988-99, Zeichner, Ellman & Krause, LLP, N.Y.C., 1999—; asst. adj. prof. C.W. Post Ctr., L.I. U., Glen Cove, N.Y., 1975-79. Editor Boston U. Law Rev., 1970-72. Mem. Citizens Ctr. for Children of N.Y., Inc., 1978-87; pres. Pelham (N.Y.) Jewish Ctr., 1986-88. Mem. ABA, Assn. Bar City of N.Y., Am. Arbitration Assn., Huguenot Bridge Club. Democrat. Office: Zeichner Ellman & Krause LLP 575 Lexington Ave New York NY 10022-6102

DAVIS, MULLER, lawyer; b. Chgo., Apr. 23, 1935; s. Benjamin B. and Janice (Muller) D.; m. Jane Lynn Strauss, Dec. 28, 1963 (div. July 1998); children: Melissa Davis Muller, Joseph Jeffrey; m. Lynn Straus, Jan. 23, 1999. Grad. with honors, Phillips Exeter (N.H.) Acad., 1953; BA magna cum laude, Yale U., 1957; JD, Harvard U., 1960. Bar: Ill. 1960, U.S. Dist. Ct. (no. dist.) Ill. 1961. Practice law Chgo., 1960—; assoc. Jenner & Block, 1960-67; ptnr. Davis, Friedman, Zavett, Kane, MacRae, Marcus & Rubens, 1967—; lectr. continuing legal edn., matrimonial law and litigation; legal adviser Michael Reese Med. Research Inst. Council, 1967-82. Author: (with Sherman C. Feinstein) The Parental Couple in a Successful Divorce, Illinois Practice of Family Law, 1995, 97, 98-99; mem. editl. bd. Equitable Distbn. Jour., 1984—; contbr. articles to law jours. Bd. dirs. Infant Welfare Soc., 1975-96, hon. bd. dirs., 1996—, pres., 1978-82; co-chmn. gen. gifts 40th and 45th reunions Phillips Exeter Acad., chair class capital giving, 1994-98. Capt. U.S. Army, Ill. N.G., 1960-67. Fellow Am. Acad. Matrimonial Lawyers (bd. mgrs. Ill. chpt. 1996-99), Am. Bar Found.; mem. ABA, FBA, Ill. Bar Assn., Chgo. Bar Assn. (matrimonial com. 1968-83, sec. civil practice com. 1979-80, vice chmn. 1980-81, chmn. 1981-82), Am. Soc. Writers on Legal Subjects, Chgo. Estate Planning Coun., Legal Aid Soc. (vice chmn. matrimonial bar 1991-95, vice chmn. 1995-97, chmn. 1997-99), Lawyers Club Chgo., Tavern Club, Lake Shore Country Club, Chgo. Club. Republican. Jewish. Home: 161 E Chicago Ave Chicago IL 60611-2601 Office: Davis Friedman Zavett Kane MacRae Marcus & Rubens 140 S Dearborn St Ste 1600 Chicago IL 60603-5288

DAVIS, PATRICIA M., educator; b. Lloydminster, Alberta, Can., Nov. 16, 1932; d. George E. and Edith May (Kent) McKerihan; m. Harold M. Davis, Dec. 17, 1958 (dec. Dec. 24, 1971); children: Harold Neal, Rosemary Anne. BA, Dallas Bapt. Coll., 1981; MA, U. Tex., Austin, 1988, PhD, 1994. From grass roots worker to materials cons., tchr. trainer Summer Inst. Linguistics/Min. Edn., Peruvian Amazon region, 1963-84; literacy trainer Summer Inst. Linguistics, England, 1979, 88, U. Oreg., 1985-88; internat. literacy educator and edn. cons. Summer Inst. Linguistics, Dallas, 1995—; literacy trainer, Ethiopia, 1992, Kenya, 1994, 97, U. N.D., 1995, 98, 99, Singapore, 1995, Asia, 1997, Peru, 1997-98, The Philippines, 1999, Dallas, 2000. Author: Cognition and Learning, 1991, La enseñanza del castellano como segunda lengua entre los grupos etnolingüísticos de la Amazonia, 1997; co-author: Bilingual Education: An Experience in Peruvian Amazonia, Spanish edit., 1979, English edit., 1981. Mem. Internat. Reading Assn., Comparative and Internat. Edn. Soc., Alpha Chi, Kappa Delta Pi, Phi Kappa Phi. Avocations: sewing, entertaining, reading anthropology. Office: Summer Inst Linguistics 7500 W Camp Wisdom Rd Dallas TX 75236-5639

DAVIS, PAUL ROBERT, investment manager, portfolio manager; b. Lynn, Mass., Mar. 17, 1964; s. Harold S. and Diane Aida Davis; m. Liane D'Alessandro, Oct. 12, 1991. AB, Dartmouth Coll., 1986; MBA, Harvard U., 1991. Assoc. cons. Monitor Co., Cambridge, Mass., 1985-86, cons., 1986-88, project mgr., 1988-89; v.p., prin. Yeager Wood & Marshall, N.Y.C., 1990-96, CFO, 1991-94; sr. v.p. Hagler, Mastrovita & Hewitt, Boston, 1996-98; sr. v.p., chief investment officer David L. Babson & Co., Cambridge, 1998—. Mem. Harvard Club N.Y., Assn. Investment Mgmt. and Rsch. (CFA, Chartered Investment Counselor), Dartmouth Alumni Assn. (leadership agt. 1988—). Avocations: offshore ocean yacht racing, animation art collecting, reading, Tonkinese cats. Office: David L Babson & Co One Memorial Dr Cambridge MA 02142

DAVIS, REX DARWIN, business consultant; b. Skiatook, Okla., June 11, 1924; s. Ivan Francis and Ruth Mae (Nabors) D.; m. Amelia Roberts Fry, Apr. 14, 1979; children by previous marriage: Deborah Ruth, Kathleen Marie. LLB, U. Okla., 1949; postgrad., Princeton U., 1966. Exec. asst. to asst. regional commr. Bur. Alcohol Tobacco and Firearms, Cin., 1962-66, asst. regional commr., 1966-70; dir. Bur. Alcohol Tobacco and Firearms, Washington, 1970-78; pres. Nat. Assn. Beverage Importers, Inc., Washington, 1978-85, Delta Cons., Inc., Washington, 1985-95; pres., chief exec. officer New Europe Wines, Inc., 1991-95; exec. dir. Pres.'s Forum of Beverage Alcohol Industry, 1990—; chmn. Lic. Beverage Info. Coun., Washington, 1981-85, Internat. Fedn. Wine & Spirits, Paris, 1982-85. Author: Federal Searches and Seizures, 1964. Vice chmn. Sky Ranch Found., Washington, 1983-85; pres. Treas. Hist. Assn., 1978-79. 1st lt. USAAF, 1943-45. Decorated Purple Heart, Air medal; recipient Chevalier de Merite Agricole French Gov., 1983, award for exceptional svc. Dept. Treasury, 1978, Meritorious Svc. award 1977; named Fed. Employee of Yr. Cin. chpt. Fed. Bus. Assn., 1965; Meritorious award William A. Jump Found., 1959. Mem. Am. Soc. Assn. Execs., Okla. Bar Assn., Pi Kappa Alpha, Internat. Club, Princeton Club. Avocations: golf, tennis, snorkeling, stamp collecting. Home and Office: Delta Cons Inc 311 10th St SE Washington DC 20003-2130

DAVIS, RICHARD CARLTON, rehabilitation consultant; b. Salem, Mass., June 10, 1948; s. William Montgomery and Ruth Wiley (Durkee) D.; m. Patricia Lynn Paquette, Apr. 6, 1974; children: Susannah, Amanda, Adam. BA, Concord Coll., 1969; postgrad., U. Iowa. Orientation tchr. Iowa Dept. for the Blind, Des Moines, 1971-73, rehab. tchr., 1973-77, rehab. counselor, 1977-80, sr. svc. specialist, 1980-86; so. area supr. N.Mex. Commn. for the Blind, Alamogordo, 1987-91, orientation ctr. adminstr., 1987-92; asst. commr. State Svcs. for the Blind, Minn. Dept. of Econ. Security, St. Paul, 1992-2000; cons. on blindness and rehab. Circle Pines, Minn., 2000—; cons. Nebr. Svcs. for the Visually Impaired, Lincoln, 1980, Am. Printing House for the Blind, Louisville, 1992. coord./vol. field svc. rep. Job Opportunities for the Blind, Balt., 1979-86; chair, vice chair Mayor's com. for the Handicapped, Alamogordo, 1990-92; bd. dirs. White Sands Press Club, Alamogordo, 1988-92. Recipient Silver award United Way, 1991, over 100% Goal award, 1990, Founders award N.Mex. Commn. for the Blind, 1992, Wayne E. Bonnell award Nat. Fedn. of the Blind, 1982, Gov.'s commendations, 1998, 2000, Cert. of Appreciation, Red Lake Nation's divsn. Rehab. Svcs. Mem. Nat. Coun. of State Agencies for the Blind (bd. dirs. 1994-98, treas. 1999-2000), Coun. of State Adminstrs. of Vocat. Rehab., Nat. Fedn. of the Blind (Des Moines Chpt. award 1983), Alamogordo Rotary Club. Avocations: camping, fishing, bicycling, canoeing, snowshoeing. Home: 136 Canterbury Rd Circle Pines MN 55014-1777

DAVIS, RICHARD LEE, chemist; b. Dexter, Iowa, Feb. 8, 1944; s. Clyde Edward and Linda Marie (Wilson) D.; m. Judith Marie Fread, Oct. 11, 1969; children: Julie, Kevin. BS in Chemistry, Northwest Mo. State U., 1966. Mgr. quality control Grain Processing Corp., Muscatine, Iowa, 1966-72, mgr. quality assurance, 1972-78; adminstr. regulatory affairs Inolex Pharm., Park Forsest South, Ill., 1978-81; mgr. product safety & compliance Ft. James Corp., Neenah, Wis., 1981-99, dir. product safety and compliance, 1999—. Mem. Am. Soc. Testing Materials (sub-com. chmn. 1981—, Merit award 1996), Am. Chem. Soc.

DAVIS, ROBERT LAWRENCE, lawyer; b. Cin., Apr. 5, 1928; s. Bryan and Henrietta Elizabeth (Weber) D.; m. Mary Lee Schulte, June 14, 1952; children: Gregory, Randy, Jenny, Bradley. BA, U. Cin., 1952; JD with honors, Salmon P. Chase Coll. Law, 1958. Bar: Ohio, 1958, U.S. Supreme Ct. 1966. Assoc. Trabert & Gay, Cin., 1958-62; ptnr. Trabert, Gay & Davis, Cin., 1962-68, Gay, Davis & Kelly, Cin., 1969-71; pvt. practice, Cin., 1972—; lectr. Mt. St. Joseph Coll, 1972-82; arbitrator Am. Arbitration Assn.; assoc. adj. prof. Salmon P. Chase Coll. Sch. Law, 1969-80; lectr. Good Samaritan Hosp. Sch. Nursing, 1960-71. Pres. bd. trustees Cmty. Ltd. Care Dialysis Ctr., 1978-86; mem. Hamilton County Ohio Hosp. Commn.,

1986, Kidney Found. Greater Cin., 1989, 1992. Capt. U.S. Army, 1946-48, 52-53. Decorated Bronze Star medal. Fellow Am. Coll. Trial Lawyers (state chmn. 1994-95); mem. Ohio Bar Assn., Cin. Bar Assn., Am. Bd. Trial Advs. (adv., pres. Cin. chpt. 1996), Lawyers Club (pres. 1962-63), Order of Curia, KC, Phi Delta Theta, Phi Alpha Delta, Sigma Sigma, Omicron Delta Kappa. Home: 9969 Voyager Way Cincinnati OH 45252-1962 Office: 3600 Carew Tower Cincinnati OH 45202

DAVIS, RONALD P., secondary school administrator; b. McKees Rocks, Pa., Dec. 15, 1970; s. Paul H. and Loretta M. (Crenshaw) D.; m. Gabrielle D. Teich, Feb. 14, 1998. BS in Edn., Slippery Rock U., 1992, MA in Student Personnel, 1994; EdD, Nova Southeastern U., 1999. Head camp counselor Boys and Girls Club, Pitts., 1989-93; resident advisor dept. residence edn. Slippery Rock (Pa.) U., 1991-94, grad. asst. Office Student Life, 1993-94; tchr. Stranahan H.S., Ft. Lauderdale, Fla., 1994-99, athletic dir., 1995-99; pres. Visions in Edn., Plantation, Fla., 1995-99; vice prin. Gateway Regional H.S., Woodbury Heights, N.J., 1999; prin. Palmyra (N.J.) Adult H.S., 2000—; speaker in field. Contbr. articles to profl. jours. Mem. Masons. Democrat. Lutheran. Avocations: baseball, football, animals, dancing, travel. Home: 26 Charles III Dr Glassboro NJ 08028-2836

DAVIS, SHIRLEY HARRIET, social worker, editor; b. Brookline, Mass., June 27, 1922; d. Jacob and Matilda (Goldberg) Freedman; m. Edward H. Davis, Nov. 11, 1943; children: Anita Maureen Davis Winn, Lawrence Paul. AB, Calvin Coolidge Coll., 1944; postgrad., Simmons Sch. of Social Work, 1944-45. Social worker Travelers Aid of N.Y., N.Y.C., 1944-48; dir. Community Svc. Workshop of Woodmere (N.Y.) Acad., 1966-70; v.p. for program and membership West End Aux. Peninsula Hosp. Ctr., Edgemere, N.Y., 1973-80; dir. Family Practice Playroom Coll. Medicine, Downstate Med. Ctr., Bklyn., 1977-83; officer mgr. Edward H. Davis, M.D., Loxahatchee, Fla., 1983-93; dir. publicity and pub. rels. Fla. Atlantic Region of Hadassah, 1994—; publ. com. Am. Jewish Congress Genetics of Breast Conf., 1997; publ. chair Walk for Better Health Fla. Atlantic Region Hadassah, 1998—, ann. spring conf. Fla Atlantic Region of Hadassah, 1995—. Editor: Hadassah of Wellington Fla., 1990-93. V.p. membership Hadassah of Wellington, 1992-94, bulletin bus. mgr.; dir. publicity and pub. rels., bd. dirs. Fla. Atlantic Region of Hadassah, 1994—; chair Fla. Atlantic Region of Hadassah Women's Health Symposium, 1996, 97, 98, 99, publicity chair Check It Out Breast Cancer Awareness Program, 1999—; chair Women's Health Symposium, 2000. Wellington chpt. honoree Fla. Atlantic Region of Hadassah ann. Woman of Valor awards, 1996, honoree Fla. Atlantic Region of Hadassah 13th Ann. Spring Conf. for Excellence in Publicity and Pub. Rels., 1998; recipient Nat. Hadassah Love of a Lifetime award, 1996, Nat. Hadassah Best Health Symposium Nation First Pl. award for Woman's Health Symposium, 1998. Republican. Jewish. Avocation: amateur radio. Home: 13604 Firewood Ct West Palm Beach FL 33414-8522

DAVIS, SHIRLEY ROSS See SULLIVAN, SHIRLEY ROSS

DAVIS, STEPHEN CLIVE, managment consultant; b. Petersfield, Hampshire, U.K., Oct. 1, 1950; s. William Davis and Agnes Beatrice Crowne; m. Susan Carol Ireson, 1978; children: Francesca, Alexandra. MBA, Bradford (U.K.) U., 1982. Master mariner. Chief officer P&O S.N. Co., London, 1969-81; ops. mgr. Neopetro (U.K.) Ltd., London, 1983-86; oil trader Klöckner und Co KgAA, Duisburg, Germany, 1987; fin. cons. Allied Dunbar, Guildford, U.K., 1988-91; cons. LS Cons., Farnborough, U.K., 1991-98, mng. cons., 1999—. Gov. Cove Sch., 1998. Mem. Assn. of MBA's, Royal Inst. of Navigation. Anglican. Avocation: sailing. Home: 23 The Birches, Cove GU14 9RP, United Kingdom Office: ES Cons, 30 A Cove Rd, Farnborough GU14 0EN, United Kingdom

DAVIS, SUSAN GLORIA, sales representative, consultant; b. St. Louis, Oct. 5, 1957; d. Victor Henry and Vivian Norma (Stille) D. BS, Maryville U., 1982; MBA, Oklahoma City U., 1983. Mktg. coord. HBE Bank Facilities, St. Louis, 1979-82; sales rep. NCR Corp., St. Louis, 1983-85; sr. sales rep. UNISYS, St. Louis, 1985-88; account exec. Gould Electronics, St. Louis, 1988-89; sales rep. Tandem Computers, St. Louis, 1989-94; acct. exec. Octel Comms., 1994-96; dir. acct. svcs. Bell Comms. Rsch., 1997—. Mem. NAFE, AAUW. Republican. Congregationalist. Avocations: golf, tennis, music, skiing, racquetball, swimming.

DAVIS, TERRI JUDITH, television producer, writer; b. Pitts., Feb. 9, 1961; d. Louis Jr. and Shirley Merle (Riley) D. Student, Columbia Coll., Chgo., 1979-80, UCLA, 1980-83, Fashion Inst. Tech., N.Y.C., 1983. Assoc. prodr. John & Leeza, 1993; exec. prodr. Manu Dibango and Hugh Masakela Live, 1994, In Their Eyes, 1996; show prodr. Marilu, 1995, The RuPaul Show, 1995, Loveline, 1996, Interior Motives, 1997-98, 99-2000 (Emmy award nomination for Best Show, Best Host 1997-98), The Christopher Lowell Show; writer Season to Taste, 1995, Interior Motives, others; talent and casting coord. various shows; involved in mktg. Pres. so. Calif. chpt. St. Jude Children's Rsch. Hosp., 1995-96. Mem. AFTRA, Emmy, NAFE. Democrat. Avocations: fundraising, fashion design, fiction. Office: Jude Entertainment 7940 Hollywood Blvd Apt 251 Los Angeles CA 90046-2698

DAVIS, TROY ARNOL, reflexologist, hypnotherapist; b. Quitman, Tex., Apr. 5, 1921. Student, Am. Inst. Reflexology, Am. Inst. Med. Hypnoanalysts. Cert. reflexologist; cert. hypnotherapist. Practice reflexology and hypnotherapy, Karnes City, Tex. Contbr. articles to profl. publs.; songwriter, poet. Served with USN, WWII. Recipient Presdl. medal of merit, Presdl. Task Force. Mem. Internat. Soc. Poets. Home: PO Box 295 Karnes City TX 78118-0295

DAVIS, TRUE, corporate executive; b. St. Joseph, Mo., Dec. 23, 1919; s. William True and Helen (Marstella) D.; m. Virginia Bruce Motter, Jan. 24, 1948 (dec. Sept. 1969); children—William True, Bruce Motter, Lance Barrow. Student, Cornell U., 1937-40; LHD, Tarkio U., 1963; JD, Mo. Western Coll., 1979. Salesman Anchor Serum Co., St. Joseph, Mo., 1940-41; v.p., sales mgr. Anchor Serum Co., 1945-50, pres., 1950-60; pres., dir. Research Labs., Inc., 1952-60, Pet's Best Co., 1954-60, World Health Inst., Ltd., 1958-60, Peters Serum Co., Kansas City, 1956-60, Wilke Labs., Inc., West Plains, Mo., Wilke Labs. of Tenn., Memphis, 1956-60, Peerless Serum Co., St. Joseph, 1956-60, Med. Industries, Inc., St. Joseph, 1957-60, Gothic Advt., Inc., St. Joseph, 1956-60, Certified Labs., Inc., St. Joseph, 1956-60, Davis Estate, Inc., St. Joseph, 1958-75, Carolina Vet. Supply, Inc., Charlotte, N.C., 1956-60, Anchor Serum Co. of Ind., Inc., Indpls., 1959-60, Anchor Serum Co. N.J., Camden, 1959-60, Anchor Serum Co. Minn., So. St. Paul, 1960; chmn., dir. Chemico Labs., Inc., Miami, Fla., 1960-63; chmn. Thompson Hayward Chem. Co., Kansas City, Mo., 1961-63; pres., dir. Philips Roxane, Inc., N.Y.C., 1959-63; v.p., dir. Philips Electronics and Pharm. Industries Corp., 1959-63; U.S. exec. dir. Inter-Am. Devel. Bank, 1966-68; ambassador to Switzerland, 1963-65, asst. sec. treasury, 1965-68; pres., chmn. bd. dirs. Nat. Bank of Washington, 1969-73; dir. Laurel Race Course, Md. 1970-84, Tri Ltd., Bahamas, 1976-98; trustee Riviere Realty Trust, Washington, 1972-83; Chmn. U.S. Port Security Com., 1965-68, N.Y. Pier Com., 1966-68, Pub. Adv. Com. Customs Adminstrn., 1966-68; mem. Fgn. Trade Zones Bd., 1965-68; U.S. del. Internat. Maritime Coord. Orgn., London, 1966, GATT Conf. Anti-Dumping Laws, Geneva, 1966; adviser U.S. delegation to World Bank and IMF, 1966; chmn. Dept. Commerce Export Expansion Coun., 1962-63, Washington Urban Coalition, 1971-72; mem. adv. bd. dirs. Washington Mut. Investors Fund, 1971-91. Contbr. articles to trade, farm pubs. Pres. Animal Health Inst., 1954-56, dir., 1946-59; mem. Nat. Serum Control Agy., 1947-58, chmn., 1954-55; exec. com. United Fund, 1960; bd. govs. Am. Royal, Kansas City, Mo., 1960-84; mem. Cornell U. Coun., 1962-68; bd. dirs. Washington Internat. Horse Show, 1975-85, pres., 1978-80, staff gov., Mo., 1949-54, 58-68, Ky., 1953-54; dir. Internat. Eye Found., Washington, 1995-98. Served to lt. USNR, 1943-45, chief test pilot Pearl Harbor. Recipient V.F.W. Outstanding Citizen award St. Joseph, 1960, St. Joseph Jr. C. of C. Boss Year award, 1960, Americanism Gold Medal, 1967, Exceptional Svc. award U.S. Treas., 1968. Mem. N.Y. Acad. Scis. (life), Am. Legion, VFW (nat. Americanization com. 1961-63, chmn. state com. 1960-63, Nat. Gold Medal for Americanization 1967, U.S. Treasury Exceptional Svc. award 1967), Mo. Acad. Squires, Phi Gamma Delta. Democrat. Clubs: Metropolitan (Washington), Fairfax Hunt. Home: 2510 Virginia Ave NW Washington DC 20037-1904

DAVIS, WILLIAM COLUMBUS, history educator, writer, lecturer; b. Birmingham, Ala., Aug. 28, 1910; s. William Columbus and Maude (Gray) D.; m. Mildred J. Dorman, July 24, 1948 (dec.); m. Dorothy A. Fleetwood, Feb. 14, 1987 (dec.). AB, U. Ala., 1931, MA, 1932; MA, Harvard U., 1943, PhD, 1948. Adminstrv. positions U.S. Senate, 1933-46; asst. prof. history U. Ga., 1948-51; faculty George Washington U., 1951-66, prof. Latin Am. history and govt., 1960-66, dir. Latin Am. studies, 1952-66; prof. internat. affairs, dir. Latin Am. studies, dir. lecture program, only permanent mem. faculty Nat. War Coll., Washington, 1963-74; dir., participant numerous radio, TV programs in field; lectr. various colls. and univs.; vis. prof. Samford U., 1983, 85. Author: The Last Conquistadores: The Spanish Intervention in Peru and Chile, 1863-1866, 1950, The Columns of Athens, 1951, Warnings from the Far South: Democracy versus Dictatorship in Uruguay, Argentina and Chile, 1995; co-author: Soviet Bloc Latin American Activities and Their Implications for United States Foreign Policy, 1960; editor: Index to the Writings on American History, 1902-1940, 1956, Am. Hist. Assn.'s Guide to Hist. Lit., 1960; contbr. articles on Latin Am. devels. to various publs. Mem. Phi Beta Kappa, Pi Kappa Phi. Baptist. Home: 1323 Darnall Dr Mc Lean VA 22101-3009

DAVISON, ELIZABETH JANE LINTON, education educator; b. Las Cruces, N.Mex., Mar. 9, 1931; d. Melvy Edgar Linton and Clara Virginia Hale; m. Curwood Lyman Davison, Jan. 29, 1954; 1 child, Lawrence. BS, N.Mex. State U., 1957; postgrad., U. N.Mex.; Grad., Norris Sch. Real Estate, Albuquerque, 1984. Cert. tchr., N.Mex., Oreg.; cert. real estate agt., N.Mex., appraiser. Sec., treas. C.L. Davison, Md., Pa., 1975-88, Clovis, N.Mex., 1975-88; ind. real estate contractor Century 21, Las Cruces, 1984-85; ret. Albuquerque Pub. Schs., 1957-60, 64-68; pres. Sun Dial Enterprises, 1984-95; tchr. Beaverton Pub. Schs., 1960-64. Mem. NEA, Legis. Coun., N.Mex. Albuquerque Classroom Tchrs. Inter-City Coun. (v.p.), AAUW, Phi Delta Kappa (Svc. key). Home: 3013 Cumberland Dr San Angelo TX 76904-6108

DAVISON, PETER HOBLEY, English language educator; b. Newcastle-upon-Tyne, England, Sept. 10, 1926; s. Thomas Mather and Doris (Hobley) D.; m. Sheila Mary Bethel, Mar. 5, 1949; children: Simon, John, Hugh. BA with hons., London U., 1954, MA, 1957; PhD, Sydney (Australia) U., 1963; LittD, U. Montfort, 1999, D. in Arts (hon.), 1999. Various positions, 1942-60; lectr. U. Sydney, 1960-64, Kathleen Robinson lectr., 1963; lectr., sr. lectr. Shakespeare Inst., Birmingham, Eng., 1964-73; prof. English St. David's U. Coll., Lampeter, Wales, 1973-79; prof. English, Am. Lit. Kent U., Canterbury, Eng., 1979-83; sec. to trustees Albany, London, 1983-92; prof., sr. rsch. fellow De Montfort U., Leicester, Eng., 1992—; cons. Ontario (Can.) Coun. Grad. Studies, 1982; selection com. Panizzi Found., British Libr., London, 1983-93; Cecil Oldman lectr. Leeds (Eng.) U., 1984; exec. sec. Econ. Rsch. Coun., London, 1992—. Author: Songs of the British Music Hall: A Critical Study, 1971, 2d edit., 1990, Popular Appeal in English Drama to 1850, 1982, Contemporary Drama and the Popular Dramatic Tradition in England, 1983, Hamlet: Text and Performance, 1985, Henry V: Masterguide, 1987, Othello: The Critical Debate, 1988, Orwell: A Literary Life, 1995; editor: Richard II, 1964, The Merchant of Venice, 1967, 1 Henry IV, 1968, The Dutch Courtesan, 1968, 2 Henry IV, 1977, Facsimile of the Manuscript of Nineteen Eighty-Four, 1984, Sheridan: A Casebook, 1986, The Complete Works of George Orwell, Vols. 1-9, 1986-87, Vols. 10-20, 1998, The Book Encompassed, 1992, The First Quarto of King Richard III, 1995; contbr. over 150 articles to profl. pubs. With Royal Navy, 1944-48. Recipient British Acad. award, 1982, Office of the Order of the British Empire, 1999. Mem. Bibliog. Soc. (mem. coun. 1971—, editor, 1971-82, pres. 1992-94). Mem. Ch. of Eng. Avocations: reading, music, walking. Office: Dept English, De Montfort U, Leicester LE1 9BH, England

DAVIS-THOMPSON, PAULINE, Olympic athletic. Winner Gold medal 4x100 meter relays Sydney, 2000. Office: Bahamas Amateur Athletic Assn, PO Box 55, Nassau 5517, Bahamas*

DAVLATOV, UBAIDULLO, judge. Chmn. Supreme Ct., Tajikistan. Office: Supreme Ct, Dushanbe Tajikistan

DAVOINE, FRANÇOISE, psychoanalyst; b. Bourg-Saint Maurice, France, June 18, 1943; d. Pierre Davoine and Georgette Bouchard; m. Jean Max Gaudilliere; children: Pierre, Brice, Gaudilliere. Grad., U. Paris, 1966. Maitre de conf. Ecole des Hautes Etudes en Sci. and Soc., Ctr. Etudes des Mouvements Sociaux, Paris. Editor: La Folie Witgenstein, 1992, Mere Folle, 1998. Mem. Ecole Freudienne. Office: EHESS-CEMS, 54 Bd Rospoil, 75006 Paris France

DAVY, DENIS, lawyer; b. Paris, June 18, 1946; s. André and Yvonne (Lefebvre) D.; m. Claude Leparmentier, June 28, 1975; 1 child, Christophe. Grad., U. Caen, France, 1970. Pvt. practice Law Offices of Davy, Cherbourg, France, 1972—. Served to lt. Marine Light Infantry, 1971-72. Mem. Yacht Club Cherbourg. Office: Law Offices of Davy, Rue de l'Alma 5, 50105 Cherbourg Cedex France

DAVY, JOHN LAURENCE, research scientist; b. Yea, Victoria, Australia, Mar. 14, 1949; s. Laurence William and Marjorie Joyce (Nattrass) D.; m. Elizabeth Anne Currer, Sept. 18, 1975; children: Claire Elizabeth, Jane Louise. BSc with honors, LaTrobe Univ., Melbourne, 1971; PhD, Australian Nat. U., Canberra, 1974. Rsch. scientist Commonwealth Sci. and Indsl. Rsch. Orgn., Melbourne, 1974-81, sr. rsch., 1981-88, scientist, prin. rschr., 1988—; applied physics course adv. com. Royal Melbourne Inst. of Tech., 1988-96. Contbr. articles to profl. jours. Recipient Sibyl Maud Cave Prize The Victoria League, 1966; rsch. fellowship GMH, Anu, Canberra, 1971-74. Mem. ASHRAE, Australian Math. Soc., Australian Acoustical Soc. (membership grading com. 1983-95), Acoustical Soc. of Am. Avocations: sailboarding, surfing, computing, bicycling, hiking. Home: PO Box 255, Carnegie VIC 3163, Australia Office: CSIRO, PO Box 56, Highett VIC 3190, Australia

DAVYDOV, YOURI ALEXANDROVICH, mathematician, educator; b. Kurgan, Russia, June 9, 1944; s. Alexandr Vladimirovich and Evdokia Nikolaevna (Sazykina) D.; m. Marina Leonidovna Zelvenskaia, Apr. 26, 1991; 1 child, Michel. PhD, U. Leningrad, 1970, DrSc (habil.), 1981. Asst. prof. U. Leningrad, 1966-75, assoc. prof., 1975-81, prof. math., 1981-93; prof. math. U. Lille I, France, 1993—. Co-author: Local Properties of Distributions for Stochastic Functionals, 1996; contbr. articles to profl. jours. Mem. St. Petersburg Math. Soc. (v.p. 1992, prize 1974). Office: Univ Lille I, Lab of Stats/Probabilities, 59655 Villeneuve d'Ascq France

DAWE, RICHARD ALAN, reservoir physics educator, petroleum engineering, educator, researcher; b. London, Nov. 2, 1943. BA in Chemistry, Oxford (Eng.) U., 1965, DPhil in Phys. Chemistry, 1968. Chartered engr. Inst. Energy. Lectr. in chem. engring. UMIST, Manchester, Eng., 1968-69; rsch. fellow in chem. engring. Leeds (Eng.) U., 1969-75; lectr. petroleum engring. Imperial Coll., London, 1975-86, sr. lectr., 1986-91, reader reservoir physics, 1991-97; 1st holder occidental chair in petroleum engring. U. Qatar, Arabian Gulf, 1997-99; 1st holder TTMC chair in petroleum engring. U. West Indies, Trinidad, 1999—. Founding mem. editl. bd. Transport in Porous Media Jour.; contbr. more than 150 articles to profl. jours.; editor, contbr. Modern Petroleum Tech. Inst. Petroleum, Eng., 2000. Fellow Inst. Petroleum (London; George Sells prize for best paper 1979), Royal Soc. Chemistry, Inst. Energy, Soc. Petroleum Engrs. (faculty sponsor). Office: UWI, Dept Chem Engring, St Augustine SW7 2AZ, Trinidad

DAWICKI, DOLORETTA DIANE, research biochemist, educator; b. Fall River, Mass., Sept. 13, 1956; d. Walter and Stella Ann (Olszewski) D. BS, S.E. Mass. U., 1978; PhD, Brown U., 1986. Rsch. assoc. Meml. Hosp. R.I., Pawtucket, 1986-92; asst. prof. Brown U., Providence, 1986-96; rsch. assoc. VA Med. Ctr., Providence, 1992-96; quality control sr. scientist Genzyme Corp., Framingham, Mass., 1996—. Contbr. articles to profl. jours. Mem. AAAS, Am. Soc. for Biochemistry and Molecular Biology, Parenteral Drug Assn. Achievements include research on in vivo antiplatelet mechanism of action of the clinical agent dipyridamole, endothelial cell injury, effects of nucleotides on leukocyte-endothelial cell interaction, assay development, optimization, and validation to monitor drug identity, safety, and efficacy. Home: 3 Odyssey Ln Franklin MA 02038-2460 Office: Genzyme Corp PO Box 9322 Framingham MA 01701-9322

DAWIDS, RICHARD GREENE, business executive; b. Copenhagen, Jan. 5, 1941; s. Adolf Carl and Barbara Greene (Gamwell) D. Student, Davidson Coll., 1960-61, U. Grenoble, France, 1966-67, U. Copenhagen, 1968. With Copenhagen Handelsbank, 1968-85, Tokyo, 1985-89; v.p. Surongo S.A., Brussels, 1982-90, pres., 1991—; bd. dirs. Cie Bois Sauvage, Brussels, Entreprises et Chemins de Fer en Chine, Brussels, Simonis Plastic S.A. ans, Belgium, I.R.M. S.A. Alleur, Belgium, Chocolats de Liris, Brussels, Belgium. Office: Surongo SA, 16-17 Rue du Bois Sauvage, 1000 Brussels Belgium

DAWIDSON, IRENA, dentistry educator; b. Wroclaw, Poland, Dec. 28, 1955; d. Adolf and Inga (Cukier) D. DDS, Karolinska Inst., Stockholm, 1980, PhD, 1999. Lectr. in forensic odontology Karolinska Inst., 1980—. Mem. European Orgn. for Caries Rsch., Internat. Orgn. for Forensic Odonto-Stomatology. Avocations: reading, writing, cinema, travel. Home: Götgatan 128 tr 2, 11862 Stockholm Sweden Office: Karolinska Inst/Foren Odont, PO Box 1352, 17126 Solna Sweden

DAWKINS, ANTHONY PETER, educational trust administrator; b. Birmingham, Eng., Nov. 12, 1945; s. David George and Jeanne Mary (Jefferies) D.; m. Sarah Wendy Hiscock, Mar. 31, 1973; children: John Anthony, Elene Rose, Samuel David. BA with honors, Cambridge (Eng.) U., 1967, diploma in architecture, part I, 1969; diploma in architecture, part II, Royal Inst. Brit. Architects, 1970, MA, 1971. Registered arch., U.K. Archtl. asst. A.G. Sheppard Fidler & Assocs., Birmingham, 1969-72; design arch., sr. asst. for rsch. bldg. Bidston Obs., Inst. Coastal Oceanography and Tides, Wirral, Birkenhead, Eng., 1971-72; asst. arch. Rowand Anderson Kininmouth & Paul, 1972-73; project arch. Rowand Anderson Kininmonth & Paul, 1973-76, Scottish Spl. Housing Assn., Edinburgh, 1976-78; pvt. practice Eng., 1979-80; contract project arch. Harper Fairley Partnership, Birmingham, 1988-90; founder, dir. Francis Bacon Rsch. Trust, Warwick, Eng., 1979-88, hon. dir., 1988—; founder, dir. Zoence Acad., 1988—; lectr., tchr. in field of Baconian-Rosicrucian founds. of modern sci. and soc., mythology, sacred landscape and wisdom traditions. Author: The Pattern of Initiation, 1981, The Virgin Ideal, 1982, Dedication to the Light, 1984, The Great Vision, 1985, Arcadia, 1988, A Commentary on the Great Instauration, Francis Bacon - Herald of the New Age, Bacon, 1997, The Master, 1993, The Grail Kingdom of Europe, 1995, The Temple Science, 1985, Zoence - Science of Life, 1995, A Commentary on the Great Instaunation, 1983, The Wisdom of Shakespeare in As You Like It, 1998, in The Merchant of Venice, 1998, in Julius Caesar, 1999, in The Tempest, 2000; contbr. articles to profl. jours. Hon. pres. Brit. Coun. Univ. for Peace, 1986; advisor London Theatre of Imagination, Daylight Theatre, New Shakespeare Globe Theatre; founder, elder Gatekeeper Trust, 1980—. Office: Roses Farmhouse, Epwell Rd Upper Tysoe, Warwick CV35 0TN, England

DAWKINS, JOHN SYDNEY, economist, consultant, company executive; b. Perth, Australia, Mar. 2, 1947; s. Alec Dawkins; m. Maggie Maruff, Mar. 2, 1987. Student, Scotch Coll.; Diploma in Agr., Roseworthy Agrl. Coll., Australia; B in Econs., U. Western Australia; DSc (hon.), U. South Australia, Queensland U. Technology. Former staff Australian Bur. Agrl. Econs.; mem. staff Australian Dept. Trade and Industry, 1971-72, trade union sec., 1973; mem. Australian Ho. of Reps., Canberra, 1974-75, 77-94, opposition spokesman for edn., 1980-83, opposition spokesman for industry and commerce, 1983; min. for fin. Govt. of Australia, 1983-84, min. assisting prime min. for pub. svc. matters, 1983, min. trade, 1985-87, min. assisting prime min. for youth affairs, 1984, min. employment, edn., tng., 1987-92, treas., 1992-93, rep. for spl. investment, 1994-95; press officer Australian Trades and Labor Coun., 1976-77; dir. Sealcorp Holdings Australia 1994—; chmn. John Dawkins & Co., 1994—, Med. Corp. Australasia, 1997—, Elders Rural Bank, 1998—; mem. adv. bd. Indian Ocean Centre; bd. dirs. Fred Hollows Found. Mem. nat. exec. Australian Labor Party, v.p., 1982; patron Menzies Sch. Health. Office: Level 25, 91 King William St, Adelaide 5000, Australia

DAWKINS, ROGER LETTS, immunologist, educator; b. June 25, 1941. B in Med. Sci., U. Western Australia, 1965, MBBS, 1966, MD, 1974; DSc, 1991. Clin. immunologist U. Western Australia, 1973-78, assoc. prof. immunopathology, 1978—, personal chair dept. pathology, 1991—; head dept. clin. immunology Royal Perth Hosp. and Queen Elizabeth II Med. Ctr., Western Australia, 1976-97; prof. immunology U. Western Australia, 1991—, dir. Ctr. Molecular Immunology and Instrumentation, 1994—; chmn., rsch. dir. Immunogenetics Rsch. Found., 1983—; dir. Inst. for Molecular Genetics and Immunology, 1993—; vis. prof. U. Leiden, The Netherlands, 1988; guest prof. Tongji Med. U., China, 1991; presenter in field. Contbr. chpts. to books: The Autoimmune Diseases, 2d edit., 1996, Textbook of Autoantibodies, 1995, Autoantibodies, 1995, Molecular Biology and Evolution of Blood Group and Mhc Antigens in Primates, 1995, Molecular Evolution of the Major Histocompatibility Complex, 1991, Progress in Immune Deficiency III, 1990, Autoimmune Disease II, 1989, Baillere's Clinical Endocrinology and Metabolism: Genetics of Diabetes, 1989; contbr. numerous articles to profl. pubs. including New Eng. Jour. Medicine, Nature, Lancet, others; mem. editl. bd. Muscle & Nerve, 1980-81, Australian & New Zealand Jour. of Medicine, 1980-81, Jour. of Neuroimmunology, 1981-83, Human Immunology, 1984—, Immunogenetics, 1988-98, others. Raine rsch. fellow U. Western Australia, 1970-72, Alexander von Humboldt Rsch. award Max Planck Inst., Germany, 1994; program and project grantee, 1986—. Fellow Royal Coll. Pathologists Australia, Royal Coll. Physicians London, Royal Australasian Coll. Physicians; mem. British Soc. Immunology, Australian Soc. Immunology, Australian Soc. Med. Rsch., Australasian and South East Asia Tissue Typing Assn., Am. Soc. Histocompatibility and Immunogenetics, Am. Assn. Immunologists, Internat. Soc. Animal Blood Group Rsch., Internat. Union Immunological Socs., others. Avocation: cattle breeding. Office: Ctr Molecular Immunology & Instrumentation, Queen Elizabeth II Med Ctr, Nedlands WA 6009, Australia

DAWOOD, MOHAMED YUSOFF, obstetrician, gynecologist; b. Singapore, Singapore, Sept. 13, 1943; came to U.S., 1974; s. Sheikh and Fatimah (Hussein) D.; m. Firyal Sultana Khan, July 14, 1978; children: Fatimah Sultana, Fauzia Sultana, Firdaus Sultana, Hassan Yusoff. MB, ChB, U. Sheffield, Yorkshire, Eng., 1968, MD, 1974; M of Medicine with gold medal, U. Singapore, 1972. Diplomate Am. Bd. Obstetrics and Gynecology, Am. Bd. Reproductive Endocrinology. First asst. in ob-gyn. U. Melbourne, 1974; from instr. to assoc. prof. ob-gyn. Cornell U. Med. Coll., N.Y.C., 1974-79; prof. ob-gyn. U. Ill., Chgo., 1979-90; Berel Held prof. ob-gyn. and reproductive scis. U. Tex. Med. Sch., Houston, 1990—; lectr. U. Singapore, 1973-74; cons., editorial cons., reviewer in field. Author: Green's Gynecology, 1990, Dysmenorrhea, 1981, Premenstrual Syndrome and Dysmenorrhea, 1985, Oxytocin, vol. 2, 1984, Prostaglandin Inhibition in Obstetrics and Gynecology, 1983; contbr. articles to profl. jours. Recipient Gold medal Jaycee Jr. C. of C. Singapore, 1973. Fellow ACS, ACOG, Am. Gynecol. & Obstet. Soc., Royal Coll. Ob-Gyn. (Edgar Gentilli prize 1974, Gold medal 1973); mem. Endocrine Soc. Achievements include research in prostaglandins in the causation of menstrual cramps and relief by blocking prostaglandins; role of oxytocin in human parturition, bone-depleting effect of GnRH agonists during treatment of endometriosis; presence of neurohypophyseal peptides in primate and human ovaries; regulation of primate corpus luteum. Office: Univ Texas Medical School 6431 Fannin St Ste 3204 Houston TX 77030-1501

DAWSON, ADAM, private investigator, former newspaper editor; b. N.Y.C., May 4, 1950; s. Martin and Renee D.; m. Constance Jo Stewart, Oct. 21, 1950. BA, Syracuse Univ., N.Y., 1972. Lic. private investigator, Calif. Press sec. U.S. Congressman M. Blouin, Washington, 1977-78; reporter Evening News, Annapolis, Md., 1978-79, Daily News, L.A., 1979-84; L.A. bureau chief Orange County Register, Santa Ana, Calif., 1984-88; city editor Journal Tribune, Biddeford, Maine, 1988-89; owner Dawson Ryan Assocs., L.A., 1989—; sr. instr. UCLA Extension, L.A., 1981-91. Mem. sports advisory coun. City Santa Monica, Calif., 1996—. Named Best Investigative Reporting Valley Press Club, L.A., 1982, named Best Investigative Series Orange County Press Club, 1986. Office: Dawson Ryan Assocs 12021 Wilshire Blvd # 846 Los Angeles CA 90025-1206

DAWSON, CHARLOE H.O., management consultant; b. Beckenham, England, Sept. 7, 1966; s. Michael H.O. and Dimity J. (Fry) D.; m. Nicola Hunt, June 6, 1998; children: Gina, Josh. Grad., Cambridge U., England, 1989. Engring. trainee Brit. Gas, 1984-87, Lucas, England, 1988; grad. trainee, acct. mgr. Santilii & Santilii Advt., London, 1989-92; acct. mgr. Duckworth Finn Grubb Waters Ltd., London, 1992-99; founding ptnr. the Found., London, 1999—; exec. dir. Duckworth Finn Grubb Waters, Ltd., 1999—. Mem. IPA (com. mem.). Avocations: football, old cars, golf, collecting music, whiskey and wine. Home: 33 St Georges Ave, London N7 0HB, England Office: The Found, 41 Great Pulteney St, London S1R 3DE, England

DAWSON, EDWARD JOSEPH, merger and acquisition executive; b. Rochester, Pa., Apr. 1, 1944; s. Ralph Edward and Evelyn May (Riggle) D.; m. Lynda Sue Weir, 1975; 5 children. BS in Indsl. Mgmt., Carnegie Mellon U., 1966; MBA in Fin., U. Chgo., 1968. Lic. security broker/dealer, real estate broker. Computer systems analyst, corp. fin. analyst Tex. Instruments Corp., Dallas, 1968-70, product planning mgr. digital systems divsn., 1970-72, mgr. comml. equipment bus. objective, 1972-74, mgr. mktg. electronic watch divsn., 1975-76, mgr. mktg. home video systems, 1976-77; sr. v.p. ops. and mktg. Capital Alliance Corp., Dallas, 1977-80, exec. v.p. merger ops., 1980-81, chmn. bd., CEO, pres., 1981—; sec. M&A Internat., 1988, v.p. 1989, 96, pres. 1990, 97. Pres. Marina del Rey Homeowners Assn., 1982-84. Mem. Omicron Delta Kappa, Beta Theta Pi. Mem. Ch. of Christ. E-mail: ed.dawson@cadallas.com. Home: 818 Stratford Dr Southlake TX 76092-7109 Office: Capital Alliance Corp 2777 N Stemmons Fwy Ste 1220 Dallas TX 75207-2293

DAWSON, EUGENE ELLSWORTH, university president emeritus; b. Kansas City, Kans., Jan. 23, 1917; s. Harold Lambert and Betty Ross Dawson; m. Arlene Wilburma Clark, May 7, 1935; children: Eugene Jr., Clark (dec.), LoLita, Edward, Brent, Deborah. BA, Pittsburg (Kans.) State U., 1940; STB, Harvard U., 1944; PhD, Boston U., 1949; postgrad., U. Chgo., 1953; DHL (hon.), U. Colo., 1967; HHD (hon.), Regis U., Denver, 1967; DLitt (hon.), Keuka Coll., Keuka Pk., N.Y., 1968; DD (hon.), U. Redlands, Calif., 1978; postgrad., St. Elizabeth's Hosp., Washington, 1978-79. Asst. prof. psychology Pittsburg State U., 1946-48, dean of adminstrn., prof. psychology, 1949-57; pres. Colo. Woman's Coll., Denver, 1957-70; pres. U. Redlands, 1970-78, pres. emeritus, 1978—; instr. summer sessions U. Chgo, Kent State U., U. Houston, Western Oreg. U., Iliff Sch. Theology; cons. higher edn. and human svcs., 1980—; evaluator grants to univs. and ednl. instns., 1990—. Contbr. articles to profl. jours., chpts. to books. Bd. dirs. Estes Pk. Ch. of the Air, 1980—, Qualife Wellness Cmty., Denver, 1982—, Samaritan Counseling Ctr., Denver, 1985—; sec. bd. trustees Temple Hoyne Buell Found., Englewood, Colo., 1990—; sec. bd. dirs. Buell Devel. Corp., Englewood, 1990—. Recipient Outstanding Alumni award Pittsburg State U., 1957, Meritorious Svc. award, 1977, Talmud Torah award Congregation Hebrew Edn. Alliance, Denver, 1969. Mem. Colo. Harvard Club, Nebr. PTA (life), Rotary Internat. (Paul Harris fellow So. Calif. divsn. 1972, pres. Denver chpt. 1964-65, dist. gov. 1967-68, Denver Rotary Found., 1985—), Phi Delta Kappa, Omicron Delta Kappa. Baptist. Avocations: tennis, hiking, reading, travel. Fax: (303) 744-1601. Home: 1361 Willow Ln Estes Park CO 80517-7359 Office: The Buell Found 1660 S University Blvd Denver CO 80210-2815

DAWSON, JAMES CLIFFORD, environmental science educator, geologist; b. Toronto, Ont., Can., Apr. 19, 1941; came to U.S., 1961; s. Clifford and Winifred Mary (Tadman) D.; m. Caroline Weiss, June 12, 1971. AA, Mt. San Antonio Coll., 1963; BA, UCLA, 1965, MS, 1967; PhD, U. Wis., 1970. Asst. prof. geology SUNY, Plattsburgh, 1970-74, assoc. prof., 1974-80, prof. environ sci., 1980-91, univ. disting. svc. prof., 1991—; pres. Nat. Assn. State Bds. Edn., 1998. Chmn. Adirondack Land Trust, Inc., Elizabethtown, N.Y., 1984-89; bd. dirs. Adirondack Coun., Elizabethtown, 1982—; pres. Assn. for Protection of Adirondack, Schenectady, N.Y., 1982-83; mem. exec. coun. Lake Champlain Com., Inc., Burlington, Vt., 1976-98, bd. regents N.Y. State, 1993—. Mem. AAA, Geol. Soc. Am., Am. Geophys. Union, Am. Assn. Petroleum Geologists, Soc. Am. Foresters, Sigma Xi. Home: 2 Birchwood Dr Peru NY 12972-2600

DAWSON, JEFFREY OWEN, forester, educator; b. Council Bluffs, Iowa, Aug. 12, 1949; m. Norine E. Dawson, June 2, 1974; children: Evan W., David O., Griffith P., Lauren E. Student, Creighton U., 1967-68; BS in Outdoor Recreation Resources, Iowa State U., 1971, MS in Forestry, 1973, PhD in Forestry, 1978. Park ranger, park planner Eastern Planning and Svc. Ctr., U.S. Nat. Park Svc., Washington, 1970; civil engring. technician Design Br., Mo. River Divsn., U.S. Army Corps Engrs., Omaha, Nebr., 1971; rsch. asst. dept. forestry Iowa State U., Ames, 1971-73, rsch. asst., rsch. assoc. forestry, 1974-77; nurseryman Iowa Conservation Commn. Nursery, Ames, 1973; forest hand Mensuration Sect. New Zealand Forest Svc., Kaingaroa Forest, Rotorua, 1973; asst. prof. forestry U. Ill., Champaign-Urbana, 1977-82, assoc. prof., 1982-89, prof., 1989—, prof., assoc. head dept. forestry, 1993-96, prof. dept. plant biology, 1998—, prof. Biotech Ctr., 1985—; vis. rsch. fellow dept. forestry Australian Nat. U., Canberra, 1985-86; lectr. in field; condr. seminars in field; proposal reviewer U.S. Sml. Bus. Adminstrn. Rsch. Grants Program, 1990—; mem. organizing com. N.Am. Symposium on Allelopathy, U. Ill., 1983; program reviewer Nat. Scis. and Engring. Rsch. Coun. Can., 1986, 87, Fonds pour la Formation de Chercheurs et l'Aide a la Rsch., Province of Que., 1989-91; mem. USDA Forest and Rangeland Renewable Resources Competitive Grants Program Rev. Panels, 1986-87, U.S. Dept. Energy Program on Woody Biomass Rev. Panel, 1985, 87, 89; rsch. and demonstration adv. com. Internat. Arid Lands Consortium, 1995—; proceedings editor and organizer Internat. Conf. on Frankia and actinorhizal plants, 1998. Contbr. numerous articles to profl. jours. including Can. Jour. Forest Rsch., Jour. of Arboriculture, Can. Jour. Botany, Ill. Arboriculture, Plant and Soil, Jour. Chem. Ecology; editl. bd. Ill. Arboriculture, 1981—; proceedings editor, organizer Ctrl. Hardwood Forest Conf., U. Ill., 1985, Proceedings of Internat. Conf. on Frankia and Actinorhizal Plants, Laval U., Que., 1984. Recipient Vis. Lectr. Travel award Forest Rsch. Inst., Fujian Province, China, 1987; 1st winner Forestry Club Outstanding Instr. award U. Ill., 1988, 91; grantee USDA Forest Svcs., 1978, 82, 86-90, 92-93, U. Ill., 1980, 86-88, Australian Nat. U., 1985-86, Argonne Nat. Lab., 1991, NSF/Soc. Am. Foresters, 1981; Creighton U. Acad. scholar. Mem. Am. Soc. Plant Physiologists, Soc. Am. Foresters, Nitrogen Fixing Tree Assn., Ill. Native Plant Soc., Walnut Coun., Sigma Xi, Xi Sigma Pi, Gamma Sigma Delta. Achievements include research in symbiotic nitrogen fixation by actinorhizal plants, tree physiology, forest ecology, silviculture, microbial ecology and physiology of the actinomycete Frankia. Avocations: fishing, photography, hiking, bicycling. Fax: 217-244-3469. E-mail: jdawson2@uiuc.edu. Office: Univ of Illinois 1316 Plant Scis Lab 1201 S Dorner Dr Urbana IL 61801-4720

DAWSON, MICHAEL, archeologist; b. Preston, Lancashire, Eng., July 15, 1955; s. William and Shirley (Jackson) D.; m. Judith Patricia Barton, Nov. 28, 1987. BA in Bus. Studies, Liverpool (Eng.) Poly., 1978; BA in Archeology, Univ. Coll., Cardiff, Wales, 1980; MPhil, U. Nottingham, Eng., 1992. Lectr. humanities Salford Tech. Coll., Eng., 1981-82; edn. officer in archeology Clwyd-Powys Archeol. Trust, Wales, 1982-84; freelance archeologist U.K. and Romania, 1984-85; archeol. field officer Chelmsford (Eng.) Archeol. Trust, 1985-87; sr. archeol. field officer Bedfordshire County Coun., Bedford, Eng., 1987-98; prin. archaeologist Samuel Rose Cottage Farm, Sywell, Northants, Eng., 1998—. Author: A Late Roman Cemetery at Bletsoe, 1994, Roman Sandy, 1997, Iron Age and Roman Settlement on the Stagsden Bypass, 2000; editor: The Accoutrements of War, 1987, Prehistoric, Roman and Post-Roman Landscapes of the Great Ouse Valley, 2000; contbr. numerous articles to profl. jours. Mem. Inst. Field Archeologists (chair South Midland group 1991-94, vice chmn. standing com. archeology unit mgrs. 2000—). Mem. Labour Party. Avocation: badminton. Office: Samuel Rose, Cottage Farm Sytell, Northamptonshire NN6 0BJW, England

DAWSON, NANCY ANN, hematologist, oncologist; b. San Francisco, Nov. 21, 1953; d. Malcolm Bryon and Helen Dorothy (Jones) D.; m. Neal Thomas Baron, Aug. 22, 1981; children: Blake Bryon Baron, Drew Randall Baron. AB, U. Calif., Berkeley, 1975; MD, Georgetown U., 1979. Diplomate Am. Bd. Internal Medicine, Am. Bd. Internal Medicine-Hematology, Am. Bd. Internal Medicine-Oncology, Nat. Bd. Med. Examiners; lic. MD, Md., Va. Commd. 2nd lt. U.S. Army, 1976, advanced through grades to col., 1997; intern in internal medicine Walter Reed Army Med. Ctr., Washington, 1979-80, residency internal medicine, 1980-82, fellowship hematology-oncology, 1982-85; tchg. fellow, instr. dept. medicine Uniformed Svcs. U. of Health Scis., Bethesda, Md., 1980-82, 83-85, asst. prof. dept. medicine, 1985-92, assoc. prof. dept. medicine, 1992-98, prof. dept. medicine, 1998-99; staff physician hematology-oncology svcs., asst. chief Walter Reed Army Med. Ctr., Washington, 1985-99, 88-90, asst. dir. intern tng. and transitional year program, 1990-91, dir. intern tng. and transitional year program, 1991-94, transitional program advsor to chief grad. med. edn., 1992-94, chief hematology-oncology, 1994-95, dir. clin. rsch., 1995-99; hematology-oncology cons. to Surgeon Gen. of U.S. Army, 1998, chief, hematology-oncology svc., 1999; dir. Genito-Urinary Med. Oncology, prof. dept. med. U. Maryland, Greenbaum Cancer Inst., 1999—. Editor: Prostate Cancer, 1994; contbr. chpts. to books and articles to profl. jours. Recipient Am. Med. Women's Assn. Disting. Student citation, 1979. Fellow Am. Coll. Physicians; mem. AMA, Am. Soc. Clin. Oncology, Assn. Mil. Surgeons of U.S., Am. Soc. Hematology, Women in Cancer Rsch., Am. Urol. Assn. Democrat. Roman Catholic. Home: 7721 Curtis St Chevy Chase MD 20815-4913 Office: Univ Md Greenebaum Cancer Ctr 22 S Greene St Baltimore MD 21201-1591

DAWSON, RAYMOND MURRAY, research scientist; b. Perth, Australia, Sept. 23, 1943; s. Frank Worth and Meryl Linley (Cohen) D.; m. Rosemary Joy Ackland, Dec. 11, 1971; children: Katherine Mary, Anne Christine. BSc with honors, U. Western Australia, 1965, PhD, 1972. Cadet Dept. Supply, Perth, 1962-64; scientific officer Dept. Supply, Melbourne, 1970-72; rsch. scientist Dept. Def., Melbourne, 1972-79, sr. rsch. scientist, 1979-88, prin. rsch. scientist, 1988—; attachment Austin Hosp. Melbourne U., 1979, Chem. Def. Establishment, Porton, Eng., 1986-87. Contbr. articles to profl. jours. Mem. Australasian Soc. Clin. and Exptl. Pharmacologists and Toxicologists, Austrlian Mil. Medicine Assn. Avocations: philately, gardening, travel, theatre. Office: Aeronautical/Maritime Rsch, GPO Box 4331, Melbourne VIC 3001, Australia

DAWSON, ROBERT EDWARD, SR., ophthalmologist; b. Rocky Mount, N.C., Feb. 23, 1918; s. William and Daisy (Wright) D.; m. Julia Belle Davis, Mar. 10, 1950; children: Dianne Elizabeth, Janice Elaine, Robert Edward, Melanie Lorraine. BS, Clark Coll., 1939; MD, Meharry Med. Coll., 1943. Diplomate Am. Bd. Ophthalmology (examiner 1979-82). Intern Homer G. Phillips Hosp., St. Louis, 1943-44, resident, 1944-46; preceptor Duke Hosp., Durham, N.C., 1946-50, hosp. instr., 1947-61, clin. instr. ophthalmology, 1968-70; pvt. practice Durham, 1946-55, 57-88; mem. attending staff ophthalmology Lincoln Hosp., Durham, 1946-55; cons. ophthalmology N.C. Cen. U. Health Svc., Durham, 1950-64; chief ophthalmology and otolaryngology Lincoln Hosp., Durham, 1959-76; mem. attending staff ophthalmology Watts Hosp., Durham, 1966-76; mem. attending staff ophthalmology, v.p. med. staff Durham County Gen. Hosp., 1976-88; med. dir. Lincoln Hosp., Durham, 1968-70; lectr. ophthalmology Lincoln Hosp. Sch. Nursing, Durham, 1948-56; clin. assoc. Duke U., Durham, 1969-75; clin. asst. prof. ophthalmology Duke U. Eye Ctr., Durham, 1975-87, scholar in residence, 1991—, cons. in ophthalmology, 1987-89; instr. ophthalmology Duke Hosp., 1948-67; chair dept. opthalmology 3310th Hosp., Scott AFB, Belleville, Ill., 1956-57; mem. N.C. Adv. Com. on Med. Assistance, 1972-85; mem. adv. bd. N.C. State Commn. for Blind, 1965-75; mem. Gov.'s Adv. Com. Med. Assistance; regional surg. dir. Eye Bank Assn. Am., Inc., 1968-79. Mem. Durham Coun. Human Rels., 1967-69; mem. Pres. Com. on Employment of Handicapped, 1971-79; bd. dirs. Durham County Tb Assn., 1950-54, Better Health Found., 1960-66, Durham Community House, 1966-68, Lincoln Community Health Ctr., Am. Cancer Soc., Durham United Fund, Durham County Mental Health Ctr., 1976-79, Found. for Better Health of Durham County Gen. Hosp., 1975-79; bd. dirs., v.p. Nat. Soc. Prevention of Blindness; trustee Durham Acad., 1969-72, Durham County Gen. Hosp.; life trustee Meharry Med. Coll.; trustee emeritus N.C. Cen. U., Mut. Savs. & Loan; mem. bd. mgmt. Meharry Med. Coll. Alumni Assn.; bd. assocs. Greensboro Coll., N.C.; co-founder, chmn. bd. dirs. Lincoln Pvt. Diagnostic Clinic; bd. visitors Clark Coll., Atlanta. Served as maj., M.C., USAF, 1955-57. Recipient Disting. Svc. award Clark Coll., 1984, Nat. Assn. Equal Opportunity in Higher Edn., 1985, Physician of Yr. award Old North State Med. Soc., 1981, Meritorious Svc. Highest award, 1991. Fellow ACS, Acad. Ophthalmology; mem. AMA, Nat. Soc. to Prevent Blindness (v.p.), Am. Assn. Ophthalmology, Soc. Eye Surgeons, Nat. Med. Assn. (trustee 1971-80, pres. 1979-80, Disting. Service award 1983), Pan Am. Med. Assn. (diplomate), Old North State Med. Soc. (pres. 1966-67), Durham Acad. Medicine (pres. 1967-68), NAACP (life), Durham Bus. and Profl. Chain, C. of C., Meharry Nat. Alumni Assn. (past pres.), Alpha Omega Alpha, Alpha Phi Alpha (past pres.), Sigma Pi Phi (pres.), Chi Delta Mu (pres.). Democrat. Mem. A.M.E. Ch. (stewards bd. 1968—). Mason (33d degree, Shriner). Club: Toastmasters (pres. 1969-70). Home: 817 Lawson St Durham NC 27701-4534 Office: 512 Simmons St Durham NC 27701-4334

DAWSON, TERANCE D., data processing specialist, city councilman; b. Montgomery, Ala., July 15, 1960; s. Ray L. and Emma J. (Fitzpatrick) D.; m. Darlett Lucy, Nov. 25, 1995. BS, Ala. State U., 1982. Programmer Ala. State U., Montgomery, 1980-82; computer clk. Dept. Def., USAF, Montgomery, 1983-85; programmer State of Ala., Montgomery, 1985-86, programmer analyst, 1986-90, programmer analyst II, 1990-97, data processing specialist, 1997—. Chmn. young Dems., Ala. Dem. Conf., MOntgomery, 1983; mem. Ala. Dem. Exec. Com., 1986. Methodist. Avocations: politics, karate, chess, computers. E-mail: tdawson@dhr.state.al.us. Home: 137 W Edgemont Ave Montgomery AL 36105-1640 Office: City of Montgomery PO Box 6050 Montgomery AL 36106-0050

DAXHELET, JEAN PAUL, anesthesiologist; b. Namur, Wallonia, Belgium, Oct. 27, 1958; s. Valere and Jenny (Laurent) D.; m. Francoise Magnette, Aug. 22, 1984; children: Laura, Sophie, Florence, Louise. MD, Cath. U. Leuven, Brussels, 1983, D in Anesthesiology, 1987, M in Hosp. Adminstrn., 1999. Asst. specialist Univ. Cath. Louvain, St. Luc Hosp., Brussels, 1987-88; titular anesthesiologist St. Elizabeth Hosp., Namur, Belgium, 1988—; asst. lectr. in obstet. anesthesia, St. Elizabeth and St. Philippe Hosps., 1990-96; med. dir. St. Elizabeth Hosp., Namur, 1995-2000. Mem. Belgian Group of Specialists, Belgian Soc. Anesthesiology and Reanimation, Belgian Med. Syndicate Assn. Avocations: toy collecting, oenology. Office: St Elizabeth Hosp, 15 Pl Louise Godin, B 5000 Namur Belgium

DAY, BRYAN PHILIP, aerospace engineer; b. Kenilworth, Warwickshire, Eng., May 1, 1938; s. Harold and Dorothy Margaret (Flint) D.; m. Rosalind Sanders, May 18, 1963; children: Christopher, Margaret, Richard. BS, Leeds U., 1959. Scientific officer Royal Aircraft Establishment, Farnborough, Eng., 1959-64, sr. rsch. fellow, 1964-71, prin. scientific officer, 1971-85; programme mgr. Ministry of Def., London, 1985-90, tech. dir., 1990-98; ret., 1998; bd. govs. Intelsat, Washington, 1982-85; vis. scientist APL Johns Hopkins U., Laurel, Md., 1992-94; mem. com. of experts European Space Rsch. Orgn., Nordweig-an-Zee, Holland, 1968-72. Contbr. articles to profl. jours. Councillor Parish Coun., Crondall, U.K., 1974-85; gov. Crondall Sch., 1980-85; chmn. Burial Bd., Crondall, 1980-85. Fellow IEE, Inst. Physics, Brit. Interplanetary Soc. Achievements include contbns. to design of U.K. satellites and launch vehicles, designer of U.K. 10 ion thruster and all U.K. spacecraft propulsion systems in 1960s and 70s; originator of use of liquified gases for small satellite propulsion. E-mail: bryan.day@lineone.net.

DAY, CHRISTOPHER MARK, lawyer; b. Atlantic City, N.J, May 24, 1968; s. Frederick Nicholes and Judith Lee Day. BA in Polit. Sci., Stockton State U., 1990; JD, Widener U., 1994. Bar: N.J. 1994, Pa. 1994, U.S. Dist. Ct. NJ 1994. Law clk. Hon. Richard J. Williams, Assignment Judge Superior Ct., Atlantic City, 1994-95; assoc. Cooper Perskie Law Firm, Atlantic City, 1995-98, Petro Cohen Law Firm, Atlantic City, 1998—. Bd. mem. Chief Arthur Brown Meml. Scholarship Found., 1992—, Chelsea Neighborhood Assn., 1995—; co-chmn. Attys. Reaching Others, 1995—. Mem. Atlantic County Bar Assn. (trustee 1998—), N.J. Workers Compensation Am. Inns Ct., Jr. C. of C. Home: 46 S Laclede Pl Atlantic City NJ 08401-5806 Office: Petro Cohen Law Firm 2111 New Rd Northfield NJ 08225-1512

DAY, IAN, genetics educator; b. Gloucester, England, Jan. 14, 1960; s. Cyril George and Emily Geraldine D.; m. Lorna Breindahl Schneider, Apr. 21, 1984; 1 child, Alexandra. BA with 1st class honors, U. Oxford, England, 1980; MB, B.Chir, U. Cambridge (Eng.), 1982, PhD, 1987. MRC tng. fellow Sch. Medicine U. Cambridge, 1984-87; clin. lectr., sr. registrar (hon.) Sch. Medicine Southampton (Eng.) U., 1987-92; prof. human genetics Sch. Medicine, 1997—; lectr. (hon.) U. Coll. London, 1993-95 , sr. lectr. (hon.), 1996-97; dir. MadgeBio Ltd., Eng., 1997—. Editor: Genetics of Common Diseases, 1997; contbr. articles, revs. to profl. jours.; patent for gel matrix electrophoresis, 1997. Intermediate fellow Brit. Heart Found., 1993-95, fellow Lister Inst., 1993; program grantee Med. Rsch. Coun., 1999—. Mem. Royal Coll. Pathologists, Brit. Soc. Human Genetics, European Soc. Human Genetics. Avocations: outdoor pursuits, fitness. Office: U Southampton Human Genetic, Duthie Bldg (MP808), SO16 64D Southampton Hants, England

DAY, JAMES SANDERS, history educator; b. Chitose AFB, Japan, Oct. 23, 1956; s. Herschel Harold and Edith Louise (Sanders) D.; m. Patricia René Davis, May 3, 1981; children: Abigail René, Mary Afton. BS in Engring., U.S. Mil. Acad., 1979; MA in History, U. Ga., 1989; diploma, U.S. Army Command Coll., 1993. Commd. 2d lt. U.S. Army, 1979, advanced through grades to maj.; asst. prof. history U.S. Mil. Acad., West Point, N.Y., 1989-92; ret. U.S. Army, 1995; instr. history Marion (Ala.) Mil. Inst., 1995-96, Judson Coll., Marion, 1996-99, U. Montevallo, 1997—, Auburn U., Montgomery, 1999—. Contbr. articles to profl. jours. Recipient Nat. Collegiate Edn. award, 1996. Mem. Am. Hist. Assn., Orgn. Am. Historians, So. Hist. Assn., Soc. for Historians Tech., Assn. Ala. Historians, Phi Kappa Phi, Phi Alpha Theta. Baptist. Avocations: running, handball, stock investments, tole painting, woodworking.

DAY, JOHN H., physicist; b. Savannah, Ga., June 5, 1952; s. John H. and Elsie M. (Gilliard) D.; m. Agnes A. Lasiter, Mar. 10, 1973; 1 child, Teresa D. BS in Physics, Bethune-Cookman Coll., Daytona Beach, Fla., 1973; MS in Physics, Howard U., Washington, 1976, PhD in Physics, 1982. Engr. Martin Marietta Aerospace Corp., Orlando, Fla., 1973; physicist Nat. Bur. Stds., Gaithersburg, Md., 1974-78, U.S. Geol. Survey, Reston, Va., 1979-82; engr. energy conversion sect. NASA/Goddard Space Flight Ctr., Greenbelt, Md., 1982-88, sect. head, 1988-90, asst. br. head space power br., 1990-92, br. head, 1992-98; chief technologist applied engring. and tech. directorate NASA/Goddard Space Flight Ctr., Greenbelt, 1998-99, chief elec. systems ctr., 1999—; mem. Interagy. Advanced Power Group, Washington, 1983—; mem. NASA Historically Black Colls. Working Group, Washington, 1991-92; mem. NASA/Goddard Space Flight Ctr. Recruitment Team, Greenbelt, 1990—; adv. coun. Auburn U. Comml. Ctr. Space Power & Advanced Electronics, 1996-99; adv. bd. Tex. A&M Ctr. for Space power, 1994-99. Mem. Pub. Schs. Math. Task Force, Prince George's County, Md., 1991-92. Grad. fellow Howard U., 1973, 74, 75, 79, NSF fellow, 1976, 77, 78; recipient Outstanding Performance cert. NASA, 1984-85, 87, 92-96, Internat. Cometary Explorer Group award NASA, 1985, Internat. Sun-Earth Explorer Group award NASA, 1987, NASA Performance Mgmt. and Recognition System awards 1989, 90, 91, 92, 93, Cosmic Background Explorer Group Achievement award NASA, 1990, Roentgen Satellite Group Achievement award NASA, 1991, Gamma Ray Observatory Group award NASA, 1992, Upper Atmosphere Rsch. Satellite Team award NASA, 1992, Goddard Exceptional Achievement award, 1993, Hubble Space Telescope Power System Anomaly Investigation Team award, 1994, Hubble Space Telescope Servicing Mission Sys. Rev. Team award, 1994, GGS Power Electronics Rev. Team award 1994, Landsat 7 Design Rev. Team Streamlining award, 1995, GOES-J NASA-Industry Team award, 1995, Xray Timing Explorer Power Sys. Team award, 1996, Exceptional Svc. medal NASA, 1998, Tropical Rainfall Measuring Mission Group Achievement award, 1998. Mem. AAAS, IEEE Power Engring. Soc., AIAA, Am. Phys. Soc. Forum on Physics and Soc., Nat. Soc. Black Physicists, Sigma Pi Sigma, Alpha Kappa Mu, Phi Beta Sigma. Achievements include design and development of solar electric power systems for numerous NASA sci. satellites. Home: 9711 Bald Hill Rd Mitchellville MD 20721-2881 Office: NASA Goddard Space Flt Ctr Elec Systems Ctr Mail Code 560 Greenbelt MD 20771-0001

DAY, KENNETH ARTHUR, consulting psychiatrist, educator, researcher; b. Hanwell, London, July 18, 1935; s. Arthur and Irene Laura (Pope) D.; m. Sheila Mary Torrance, June 27, 1959 (div. 1993); children: Caroline, Paul Vincent, Matthew Charles; m. Diana Ruth Robinson, Nov. 6, 1993. MB, ChB, Bristol (Eng.) U., 1961; DPM, Royal Coll. Surgeons, London, 1965. House physician/surgeon Bristol Hosps., 1961-62; registrar Bristol Mental Hosps., 1962-66; sr. registrar dept. psychiatry U. Newcastle-Upon-Tyne, Eng., 1966-69; sr. lectr. dept. psychiatry U. Newcastle-upon-Tyne, Eng., 1986-97; cons. psychiatrist Northgate and Prudhoe Nat. Health Svc. Trust, Morpeth, Eng., 1969-92, med. dir., 1992-96, hon. cons., 1996—; sci. adviser Dept. Health, London, 1981-87; Mental Health Act commr., Eng., 1987-95. Author books on mental retardation; contbr. articles to profl. jours.; photographer. Winston Churchill Trust fellow, 1972; WHO fellow, 1990. Fellow Royal Coll. Psychiatry (chair sect. for psychiatry of mental handicap 1983-87), Royal Soc. Medicine, Royal Soc. of Arts, Internat. Assn. for Sci. Study of Intellectual Disability (v.p. 1992-96, hon. officer), Royal Geog. Soc.; mem. European Assn. Mental Health and Mental Retardation (founder, v.p. 1992—), City Livery Club. Avocations: sports, the arts, photography, painting, natural history. Office: Northgate Hosp, Morpeth NE61 3BP, England

DAY, MARY JANE THOMAS, cartographer; b. Connors, New Brunswick, Can., Oct. 12, 1927; d. Angus and Delina (Michaud) Thomas; m. Howard M. Day, July 1, 1949; children: Laurie Anne Day Greene, Angus Howard. BS in Geography, U. Md., 1974, BS in Bus. & Mgmt., 1977. Meteorol. aide Hangar 8 Eastern Airlines, N.Y.C., 1946-47, U.S. Weather Bur., Washington, 1948-50; cartographic aide U.S. Navy Hydrographic Office, Suitland, Md., 1950-57, cartographer, 1957-62; cartographer U.S. Navy Oceanographic Office, Suitland, 1962-72, Def. Mapping Agy., Suitland/Brookmont, 1972-93; ret., 1994; cartographer USNS Harkness, 1978, Indonesian Naval Personnel, Jakarta, Indonesia, 1981-82. Compiled, wrote and published; The Descendants of John Thomas of Connors, N.B., 1988; author numerous poems. Mem. Andrews Officers Club (Md.). Avocations: traveling, genealogy, foreign languages. Home: 3532 28th Pky Temple Hills MD 20748-2922

DAY, MELVIN NORMAN, artist, art historian; b. Hamilton, New Zealand, June 30, 1923; s. Norman Darcy and Cora (Melvin) D.; m. Oroya McAuley, 1952. BA, U. New Zealand, 1960; BA with hons., Courtauld Inst. Art, U. London, Eng., 1966, MPhil, 1976. Cert. tchr. New Zealand. Tchr. New Zealand Schs., 1945-63; lectr. U. London Extension, Eng., 1964-68; lectr. in art history Walthamstow, Epsom Schs. of Art, Eng., 1966-68; dir. Nat. Art Gallery of New Zealand, 1968-78; art historian Govt. of New Zealand, 1978-83; mem. arts adv. panel Queen Elizabeth II Arts Coun., New Zealand, 1968-72; assessor in painting, art history, U. Canterbury, New Zealand, 1971-72, assessor in Art History U. Entrance Exams., 1970-76. Author: Nicholas Chevalier, Artist.; contbr. articles to art jours., catalogues; co-author (with others) Contemporary Artists, 1987, Contemporary Masterworks, 1991, Dictionary Australian Artists, 1992; artist: paintings in 25 one-man shows in New Zealand and Eng.; more group exhbns. in New Zealand, Eng. and U.S. With New Zealand Army, 1941-43, New Zealand Air Force, 1944-45. Recipient Queen's Silver Jubilee medal, 1977. Fellow Royal Soc. of Arts, Eng. Home: 6 Pinelands Ave, Seatoun Wellington 6003, New Zealand

DAY, MELVIN SHERMAN, information and telecommunications company executive; b. Lewiston, Maine, Jan. 22, 1923; s. Israel and Frances (Goldberg) D.; m. Louisa Walker; children: Cynthia Day Solganick, Wendy Day Young, Robert Marshall. BS, Bates Coll., 1943; postgrad., U. Tenn., 1953-54. Chemist Metal Hydrides Inc., Beverly, Mass., 1943-44, Tenn. Eastman Corp., Oak Ridge, 1944-46; sci. analyst AEC, Oak Ridge, 1946-48, asst. chief tech. info. svc. extension, 1950-56, chief, 1956-58; dir. tech. info. div. AEC, Washington, 1958-60; dep. dir. Tech. Info. and Ednl. Programs Office, NASA, Washington, 1960-61, dir. Sci. and Tech. Info. div., 1961-67, dep. asst. adminstr. tech. utilization, 1967-70; head Office Sci. Info. NSF, Washington, 1970-72; dep. dir. Nat. Libr. Medicine, HEW, Bethesda, Md., 1972-78; dir. Nat. Tech. Info. Svc. Dept. Commerce, 1978-82; v.p. Info. Tech. Group, 1982-84, Rsch. Publs., 1984-86; sr. v.p. Herner & Co., 1986-88; pres. M. Day Cons. Internat., Inc., Arlington, 1988—; exec. v.p. BIIS Corp., Herndon, 1991-94, GlobeNet Holding Corp., 1994-97; cons. IAEA, 1960;

adviser OECD, 1970, 75; U.S. mem. OECD info. policy group; U.S. mem. NATO Tech. Info. Panel, 1960-70, 79-82, chmn., 1970; chmn. com. on sci. and tech. info. Fed. Coun., 1970-72, chmn. com. on intergovtl. sci. rels., 1969-70, chmn. sci. info. exch. adv. bd., 1963-69, mem. chem. abstracts adv. bd., 1964-68; mem. Fed. Libr. Com., 1968-78, chmn. exec. bd., 1973-75; trustee Found. Ctr. 1972-78, trustee emeritus, 1991—; U.S. mem. adv. com. on librs., documentation and archives UNESCO; pres. abstracting bd. Internat. Coun. Sci. Unions, 1977-83; bd. dirs. Internat. Coun. for Sci. and Tech. Info., 1983—, Inst. for Internat. Info. Programs, 1985-88; trustee Engring. Info., Inc., 1981-84, bd. dirs., 1993-98; del. numerous panels; cons., adviser and lectr. in field; mem. adv. com. HHS Health Svcs. Rsch. Dissemination and User Liaison, 1990-92, also mem. dissemination com. Mem. editorial bd. Health Comm. and Informatics, 1977-80, Infomediary, 1990-93, Yearbook of the Database Info. Industry, 1990-91, Bull. of Am. Soc. Info. Sci., 1977-80. Bd. visitors U. Pitts. Grad. Sch. Info. Sci., 1977-83. With U.S. Army, 1944-46. Recipient Exceptional Svc. medal NASA, 1971, Superior Svc. award USPHS, 1976. Fellow AAAS, Nat. Fedn. Abstracting and Info. Svcs. (hon. fellow); mem. Am. Soc. Info. Sci. (chmn. internat. rels. com. 1972-75, pres. 1975-76, coun. 1975-77, editorial bd. bull.), Am. Chem. Soc., Spl. Libr. Assn., Am. Soc. Cybernetics (bd. dirs. 1975-79), Venezuelan Acad. Scis. (hon. corr.), Internat. Coun. Sci. and Tech. Info. (hon., disting. svc. award 1997), Cosmos Club. Home: 4309 Chesapeake St NW Washington DC 20016-4509

DAY, MICHAEL DENNY, entomologist, researcher; b. Sydney, Australia, Dec. 9, 1959; s. Philip Denny and Nancy Barbara (Merigan) D. BSc, U. Queensland, Brisbane, Australia, BSc with honors, 1993. Sci. asst. Dept. Lands, Brisbane, 1980-81; technician CSIRO, Brisbane, 1981-90, entomologist, 1990-96; entomologist Dept. Natural Resources, Brisbane, 1996—; entomologist Brisbane City Coun., 1995—, Landcare, Brisbane, 1996—, NSW Govt., Casino, 1997—, SPC, Suva, Fiji, 1996-98. Contbr. chpts. to books, articles to profl. jours. Mem. Queensland Entomol. Soc., Australian Entomol. Soc., IOBC. Avocations: sailboarding, touch football. Office: Alan Fletcher Rsch Sta, 27 Magazine St, 4075 Sherwood Australia

DAY, MICHAEL JOHN, actuary; b. Liverpool, England, Feb. 6, 1944; Children: Tanya Jane, Philip John. BSc (hons.), Liverpool Univ., 1965. Ptnr. Duncan C. Fraser & Co., Eng., 1970-86; dir. William M. Mercer Ltd., 1986-95; sr. ptnr. Michael J. Day, 1995—; dir. Pensions Communications Ltd., 1975-86; chmn. Heywood Ptnrs. Ltd., 1975-88; dir. William M. Merer Inc., 1992-95.

DAY, PETER RODNEY, geneticist, educator; b. Chingford, Essex, Eng., Dec. 27, 1928; came to U.S., 1963; m. Lois Elizabeth Rhodes, May 26, 1951; children: Susan Catherine, Rupert Peter, William Rodney. BS in Botany, Birbeck Coll., Eng., 1950; PhD, U. London, 1954. Sr. scientific officer John Innes Inst., Hertford, Eng., 1957-63; assoc. prof. Ohio State U., Columbus, 1963-64; chief, genetics dept. Conn. Agrl. Expt. Sta., New Haven, 1964-79; dir. Plant Breeding Inst., Cambridge, Eng., 1979-87; prof. genetics, dir. Rutgers U., New Brunswick, N.J., 1987—; sec. Internat. Genetics Fedn., 1984-93; trustee Internat. Ctr. for Maize and Wheat Improvement, Mexico City, 1986-92; chmn. Mng. Global Genetic Resources Bd. on Agrl., NAS, Washington, 1986-93. Author: Fungal Genetics, 1963, Genetics of Host-Parasite Interaction, 1974. Commonwealth Fund fellow U. Wis., 1954-56; Guggenheim Meml. fellow U. Queensland, 1972. Home: 394 Franklin Rd New Brunswick NJ 08902-2718 Office: Biotech Ctr 59 Dudley Rd New Brunswick NJ 08901-8520

DAY, PETER RUSSELL, telecommunications professional; b. Reading, Berkshire, Eng., Apr. 2, 1955; s. Albert Victor and Sylvie Marcelle (Clark) D. BS in Engring. with honors, Royal Mil. Coll. Sci., Swindon, Eng., 1980; mgmt. diploma, Henley, Eng., 1990; MBA, Henley, London, 1997. Chartered engr., U.K. Mil. advisor Zimbabwe Army, Bulawayo, 1981-82; 2 1/c parachute signal squadron 5 Airborne Brigade, Aldershot, Eng., 1982-85; mil. advisor Kenya Police, Nairobi, 1985; OC trials squadron Royal Signals, Blandford, Eng., 1986-87; head of radio sys. Ministry of Def., Muscat, Oman, 1987-92, tech. dir. telecomms., 1992—; dir. Boomer Ltd., Kampala, Uganda, 1994-96, Capital & Global Ltd., London, 1998—; cons. Rhino Rescue Trust, Nairobi, 1986-87. Author: Outback 80, 1981. Grand master Muscat Hash, 1995-97. Maj. Royal Signals, 1985; lt. col. Sultan's Armed Forces Signals, 1992. Recipient Disting. Svc. medal His Majesty Sultan Qaboos Bin Said, 1995. Fellow Royal Geographic Inst., Inst. Elec. Engrs. (U.K.); mem. Internat. Aircraft and Pilots Assn. Anglican. Avocations: private pilot, ice hockey, cross country running, traveling, cinema. Address: 1 Barons Lodge, 31 Ocean Wharf Westferry Rd, London E14 8LN, England

DAY, RALPH LAWRENCE, retired physician, abbot; b. Buenos Aires, Oct. 4, 1923; came to U.S., 1966, naturalized, 1975; s. Rafael Paniagua Tejefor and Maria Atanasia Diaz; m. Betty C. Day, Nov., 7, 1957. BA, U. Buenos Aires, 1952; PhD in Psychotherapy, Sequoia U., 1967, DO in Osteopathy, 1973; ND in Naturopathy, N.A.N.M., Portland, Oreg., 1970; ThD, Bernardean U., 1974; MD, United Am. Med. Coll., 1975; MD, MS, Ch. C. Homeopathy, 1976. Lic. naturopathic physician. With Min. Edn. and Welfare, Argentina, 1949-55; practicant medicine Inst. Burns and Plastic Surgery, Argentina, 1955-62; adminstr. Blood Bank Clinics Hosp., 1956-57; practicant medicine Aviation Mil. Ctrl. Hosp., 1957-58; practicant medicine Children's Ward Inst. Burns and Plastic Surgery, 1958-59, rschr., 1961; asst. prof. lab. techs. course Min. Health, 1961; criminal psychologist Dept. Police, Lima, Peru, 1963-66; founder, abbot Roman Cath. Ch. Soc. St. Benedict, Florence, Colo., 1990; chief pathologist Inst. for Bio-Social Rsch., Lima, 1963-66; dir., founder Family Clinic, Pocatello, Idaho, 1970-87; with S.S. Cosmas & Damian, Human Life Styling, Clinc, Boise, Idaho and Florence, Colo., 1971-89. Author: Stop Whining and Be a Man, 1996, Psychosomatic Medicine, 1996; co-author: Burns and Repair with Plastic Surgery, 1963; contbr. articles to profl. jours. With Argentinian Navy Aviation, 1942-48. Recipient 1st award, Gold medal Soc. Argentina Cirugia Plastica, 1961; fellow Geigy Labs., 1961. Mem. Am. Assn. Naturopathic Physicians, Am. Naturopathic Assn., Charles F. Menninger Soc., Toastmasters, Lions. Avocations: camera music, theology, psychotherapy, meditation. Home and Office: 628 E 3rd St Florence CO 81226-1213

DAY, RICHARD SOMERS, author, editorial consultant; b. Chgo., June 14, 1928; s. Milo Frank and Ethel Mae (Somers) D.; m. Lois Patricia Beggs, July 8, 1950; children: Russell Frank, Douglas Matthew, Gail Leslie. Student, Ill. Inst. Tech., 1946, U. Miami, 1947. Promotion writer, editor Portland Cement Assn., 1958-62, promotion writer, 1963-66; editor Am. Inst. Laundering, Joliet, Ill., 1962-63; free-lance writer Monee, Ill., 1966-69, Palomar Mountain, Calif., 1969-87. Cons. editor home and shop Popular Sci. mag., N.Y.C., 1966-89; editorial cons. St. Remy Multimedia, Montreal, Que., Can., 1987—; pres., exec. prodr. Vi-Day-O Prodns. Inc., Palomar Mountain, 1991-98; author numerous home improvement and repair books including: Patios and Decks, 1976, Automechanics, 1982, Do-It-Yourself Plumbing--It's Easy with Genova, 1987, Building Decks, Patios, and Fences, 1992 (Nat. Assn. Home and Workshop Writers Stanley Tools Do-It-Yourself Writing award 1992); editor: (newspaper) Powderlines, 1958; (mag.) Concrete Hwys. and Pub. Improvements, 1958-62; (mag.) Soil-Cement News, 1960-62, Fabric Care, 1962-63; prodr. videos: How to Cure Toilet Troubles, 1994, Mountain Man Horse packing, 1994; contbr. chpts. to books. Bd. dirs. Palomar Mountain Planning Orgn., 1984-91. Mem. Nat. Assh. Home and Workshop Writers (mng. editor newsletter 1982-96, 99—, bd. dirs. 1974—, pres. 1984-85). Home: PO Box 10 Palomar Mountain CA 92060-0010

DAY, ROGER WILLIAM, research executive; b. Starkville, Miss., Apr. 4, 1953; s. Augustine and W. Marzee Myers Day; m. Wendy Jan Gregor, Dec. 27, 1980; children: Ryan William, Ashley Anne. BS, Coll. of Charleston, 1977; PhD, U. Tenn., 1984. Sr. rsch. analyst Westvaco Corp., Charleston, S.C., 1973-76; sr. rsch. chemist Olin Corp., Pisgah Forest, N.C., 1983-86; rsch. assoc. Olin Corp., Cheshire, Conn., 1986-89, sect. leader, 1991-93; group leader Olin Corp., Brandenburg, Ky., 1989-91; assoc. dir. Praxair, Inc., Tarrytown, N.Y., 1993—. Contbr. numerous articles to profl. jours. Mem. Am. Chem. Soc. (com. on corp. assoc., chair subcom. 1996-98, chair 1998—, industry rels. adv. bd. 1998—), Coun. for Chem. Rsch. (govt. rels. com. 1997—). Avocations: chess, gardening, international travel, reading. E-mail: roger day@praxair.com. Office: Praxair Inc 777 Old Saw Mill River Rd Tarrytown NY 10591-6717

DAY, RONALD ELWIN, consulting executive; b. Randolph, Vt., Dec. 15, 1933; s. John Ellis and Esther Murle (Tabor) D.; m. Elizabeth Jean McKeage, June 26, 1955; children: Gary Alan, Kathi Ellen, Judy Anne, Jeffrey Evan. AA, Pasadena City Coll., 1958, student, 1958-59; BA, U. Calif., Santa Barbara, 1961; MBA, UCLA, 1962. Internal auditor North Am. Aviation, Downey, Calif., 1962-64; sys. and procedures mgr. Proto Tool Co., L.A., 1964-65; computer programmer First Nat. Bank, Boston, 1966-67, project mgr., 1967-73, sys. analyst, 1974-77, sys. planning com. chmn., trust divsn., 1977-89, trust info. mgmt. sys. adminstr., 1977-89; pres. Edge Sys. Projects, Inc., North Reading, Mass., 1990—. With USAF, 1952-56. Mem. Soc. Advancement of Mgmt., U.S. Ski Assn., Nat. Geog. Soc., Boston Computer Soc., Assn. Sys. Mgmt., Alpha Gamma Sigma. Republican. Home and Office: 2 Bigham Rd North Reading MA 01864-2904

DAY, RONALD RICHARD, financial executive; b. York, Pa., Nov. 14, 1934; s. Russell Aldinger and Rosa Ellenora (Reever) D.; m. Patricia Glee Duncan, Nov. 24, 1956. BS in Econs., Lebanon Valley Coll., Annville, Pa., 1956; postgrad., U.S. Army Fin. Sch., Indpls., 1957, Lehigh U., 1961. Mgr. cost control and sys. Mack Trucks, Inc., Allentown, Pa., 1963-67; mgr. cost acctg. Am. Chain divsn. Acco Babcock Co., York, 1967-70, divsn. contr., 1970-82; v.p. fin. and acctg. Chain and Forged Products Group Am. Chain divsn. Acco Babcock Co., 1982-89; pres., sr. v.p., contr., chief fin. officer AAA So. Pa., 1990—. Committeeman York County Rep. Party, 1972-74; bus. chmn. York County chpt. Am. Heart Assn., 1987-89. Served to 1st lt. U.S. Army, 1957-59. Mem. York Area C. of C., Internat. Platform Assn., Lafayette Club, Outdoor Country Club, Masons, Shriners, Order of DeMolay (mem. adv. bd. 1975-89), Rotary (sec. West York club 1988-92, pres. 1993-94). Lutheran. Avocations: golf, hunting, fishing, boating, travel. Home: 2430 Ramblewood Rd York PA 17404-3941 Office: AAA So Pa 2840 Eastern Blvd York PA 17402-2908

DAY, RUSSELL CLOVER, state agency administrator; b. Concord, N.H., June 29, 1943; s. Alan C. and Lois M. (Huntington) D.; m. Carol Ann Tasker, July 9, 1965; children: Jennifer Marie, Jeffrey Russell. BA, New England Coll., 1965; postgrad., Fairfield U., 1965, U. N.H., 1965-67; M in Human Svcs. Adminstrn., Antioch U., Keene, N.H., 1978. Examiner State of N.H. Soc. Security Disability Determination Svc., Concord, 1969-73, supr., 1973-81, dep. dir., 1981-85, adminstr., 1985—. Trustee New England Coll., 1987-89; mem. supervisory com. N.H. Fed. Credit Union, chairperson, 1995-97, bd. dirs., 1997—. Recipient Vol. Achievement award N.H. Credit Union League, Edward Filene award. Mem. Nat. Coun. Disability Determination Dirs. (exec. com. 1991-94), Masons, Lions Club (pres. 1983-84, chmn. region I, dist. 44-N 1995-96, Melvin Jones fellow 2000), New Eng. Coll. Alumni Assn. (chmn. 1987-89). Republican. Congregationalist. Avocations: fishing, boating, stamp collecting, photography. Home: PO Box 313 Hillsboro NH 03244-0313 Office: Social Security Disability Determination Svc PO Box 452 Concord NH 03302-0452

DAY, STACEY BISWAS, physician, educator; b. London, Dec. 31, 1927; came to U.S. 1955, naturalized 1977.; s. Satis B. and Emma L. (Camp) D.; m. Ivana Podvalova, Oct. 18, 1973; 2 children. MD, Royal Coll. Surgeons, Dublin, Ireland, 1955; PhD, McGill U., 1964; DSc, Cin. U., 1971. Intern King's County Hosp., SUNY Downstate Ctr., 1955-56; resident fellow in surgery U. Minn. Hosp., 1956-60; hon. registrar St. George's Hosp., London, Eng., 1960-61; lectr. exptl. surgery McGill U., Montreal, Que., Can., 1964; asst. prof. exptl. surgery U. Cin. Med. Sch., 1968-70; assoc. dir. basic med. rsch. Shriner's Burn Inst., Cin., 1969-71; from asst. to assoc. prof. pathology, head Bell Mus. Pathobiology U. Minn., Mpls., 1970-74; dir. biomed. comm. and med. edn. Sloan-Kettering Inst., N.Y.C., 1974-80; mem. Sloan-Kettering Inst. for Cancer Rsch., 1974-80; mem. adminstrv. coun., field coordinator, 1974-75; prof. biology Sloan Kettering divsn. Grad. Sch. Med. Sci. Cornell U., 1974-80; clin. prof. medicine divsn. behavioral medicine N.Y. Med. Coll., 1980-92; prof. biopsychosocial medicine, chmn. dept. community health U. Calabar (Nigeria) Sch. Medicine, 1982-85; prof. internat. health, dir. Internat. Ctr. for Health Scis. Meharry Med. Coll., Nashville, 1985-89, dir. WHO Collaborating Ctr. ICHS, 1987-89; founding dir. WHO Collaborating Ctr., Nashville, 1987-89, emeritus dir., 1989; adj. prof. family and cmty. medicine U. Ariz. Coll. Med. Scis., Tucson, 1985-89; univ. prof. internat. health U. Calabar, Nigeria, 1989—; permanent vis. prof. med. edn. Oita Med. Univ., Japan, 1992-99; Arris and Gale Lectr., Royal Coll. Surgeons, Eng., 1972; vis. lectr., Ireland, 1972; vis. prof. U. Bologna, 1977, Kyushu, Japan, 1990, U. Mauritius, 1991, Bratislava U., 1991, Japan, 1992, 1993, Beijing, China, 1993; vis. prof. health comm. U. Santiago, Chile, 1979-80, Colombo, Sri Lanka, 1996, South India, 1996, U. S.F. De Quito, Ecuador, 1996; vis. prof. Oncologic Rsch. Inst., Tallinn, Estonia, 1976, All India Insts. Health, 1976, U. Maiduguri, 1982, Kyushu, Japan, 1990; vis. acad. Oxford (Eng.) U., 1993-95; moderator med. cartography and computer health Harvard U., 1978, Acad. Scis., Czechoslovakia, 1987, Australia, 1988; Fulbright prof. Charles U., Czechoslovakia, 1989, hon. prof. Coll. of Health Sciences, Universad San Francisco De Quito (Ecuador) 1996; cons. Pan Am. Health Assn., 1974-90, U.S.-USSR Agreement for Health Cooperation, 1976, WHO Collaborating Centre Meharry Med. Coll., Nashville, 1985, NAFEO/AID, 1986-89; mem. expert com. for health, manpower devel., WHO, 1986-90; cons. Div. Strengthening Health Care Resources WHO, Geneva, 1987-90, UN-FSSTD, 1987, AID/Joint Memorandum of Understanding, W. Africa, Kenya, Sudan, So. Africa, 1985-89, to dean med. coll. faculty Med. and Health Scis., ABHA, Province of Asir, Saudi Arabia, 1981, to dir. High Tatras symposia Post Grad. Med. Inst., Bratislavia, 1990—, to rector Universidad Autonama Agraria Antonio Narro, Saltillo, Mexico, 1987-89; pres., chmn., Pub. Cultural and Ednl. Prodns., Montreal, U.S., 1966-85; bd. dirs. Internat. Health, African Health Consultancy Svc., Nigeria, Ekologia & Zivot, Slovakia; bd. dirs., v.p. Am. Sci. Activities Mario Negri Rsch. Found., 1975-80; hon. founding chmn., bd. dirs. Lambo Found. U.S.; v.p., trustee Cancer Relief Found., Calabar; pres., exec. dir. Internat. Found. for Biosocial Devel. and Human Health, 1978-86, chmn., 1986—; mem. Medzinárodny Poradny Vybor Nadácie Ekológia Zivot, Re. Slovakia, 1995—; cons. Inst. Health, Lyfford Cay, Bahamas, 1981, Govt. Cross River State, Nigeria, Itreto State and H.H. Obong of Calabar, Nat. Bd. Advs., Am. Biog. Inst., 1982—; cons. cmty. health and health comms. Navaho Nation, Sage Meml. Hosp., Ganado, Ariz., 1984; founder, cons. Primary Self-Health Clinics, Oban, Ikot Oku Okono, and Ikot Imo, Nigeraia, 1982-84; cons. High Tatras Internat. Health Symposia, Slovakia, 1990—; apptd. ambassador Gov. State of Tenn., 1986—; adj. clin. prof. medicine N.Y. Med. Coll.; hon. prof. Coll. Scis. Salud U. San Francisco, Quito, Ecuador, 1996; researcher in field. W-riter, 1965—; author: (verse) Collected Lines, 1966, (play) By the Waters of Babylon, 1966, (verse) American Lines, 1967, (play) The Music Box, 1967, Three Folk Songs Set to Music, 1967, Poems and Etudes, 1968, (novel) Rosalita, 1968, The Idle Thoughts of a Surgical Fellow, 1968, Edward Stevens-Gastric Physiologist, Physician and American Statesman, 1969, (novella) Bellechasse, 1970, A Leaf of the Chaatim, 1970, Ten Poems and a Letter from America for Mr. Sinha, 1971, Curling's Ulcer: An Experiment of Nature, 1972, Tuluak and Amaulik: Dialogues on Death and Mourning with the Innuit Eskimo of Point Barrow and Wainwright, Alaska, 1974, East of the Navel and Afterbirth: Reflections from Rapa Nui, 1976, Health Communications, 1979, The Biopsychosocial Imperative, 1981, What Is Survival: The Physician's Way and the Biologos, 1981, Developing Health in the West African Bush, 1995, Moudrost Samuraju (in Czech), 1998, Selected Poems and Embers of a Medical Life, 1999, In the Shadow of the Bush - Letters From Calabar, 1982-83, 2000; editor: Death and Attitudes Toward Death, 1972, Membranes, Viruses and Immune Mechanisms in Experimental and Clinical Disease, 1972, Ethics in Medicine in a Changing Society, 1973, Communication of Scientific Information, 1975, Trauma: Clinical and Biological Aspects, 1975, Molecular Pathology, 1975, (with Robert A. Good) series Comprehensive Immunology, 9 vols., 1976-80, Cancer Invasion and Metastasis-Biologic Mechanisms and Therapy, 1977, Some Systems of Biological Communication, 1977, Image of Science and Society, 1977, What Is a Scientist, 1978, Sloan Kettering Inst. Cancer Series, 1974-80, (with K. Inokouchi) Selections From the Chronicle of The Hagakure as Wisdom Literature: The Way of The Samurai of Saga Domain, 1993; editor-in-chief, mem. editl. bd.: Health Communications and Informatics, 1974-80; editor in chief: The American Biomedical Network: Health Care System in America Present and Past, 1978, A Companion to the Life Sciences, Vol. 1, 1979, A Companion to the Life Sciences, Vol. 2, Integrated Medicine, 1980, A Companion to the Life Sciences, Vol. 3: Life Stress, 1981, Advance to Biopsychosocial Health, 1984; editor in chief, mem. editorial bd. Health Communications and Biopsychosocial Health; editor: (with others) Cancer, Stress and Death, 1979, 2d edit., 1986, Computers for Medical Office and Patient Management, 1981, Readings in Oncology, 1980, Biopsychosocial Health, 1981; editor: Primary Health Care Guidelines: A Training Manual for Community Health, 2d edit., 1986, (with T.A. Lambo) Contemporary Issues in International Health, 1989; sr. editor (with Salat and others): Health and Quality of Life in Changing Europe in the Year 2000, 1992, Hagakure-Spirit of Bushido, (with H. Koga), 1993, (with K. Inokuchi) Selections from the Chronicles of the Hagakure as Wisdom Literature: The Way of the Samurai of Saga Domain, 1993, (with Salát) Health Management, Organization, and Planning in Changing Eastern Europe, 1993, The Medical Student and the Mission of Medicine in the Twenty First Century, (in Japanese, with M. Kobayashi and K. Inokuchi), 1995, The Wisdom of Hagakure, 1996, Developing Health in the West African Bush (2 parts), 1995, Letters of Owen Wagensteen to a Surgical Fellow: with a memoir, 1996, Man and Mu: The Cradle of Becoming and Unbecoming, 1997, Czech Caesura: Golden Prague and the Black Years (Notes from Diaries 1970-1990), 1998, Moudrost Samuraju Trigon, 1998 (in Czech), Selected Poems and Embers of a Medical Life, 1998, The Surgical Treatment of Ischaemic Heart Disease with An Account of The Coronary and Intercoronary Circulation in Man and Animals (Moynihan prize monograph), 1999, Introduction-Comprehensive Medicine (Oriental-Occidental Overview), 2000; mem. editl. bd.: Annual Reviews on Stress, Jour. Stress; cons. editl. bd. Comprehensive Medicine (Japan); also co-editor various publs.; contbr. articles to profl. lit.; producer TV and radio health edn. programs, Nigeria, TV film River Blindness (Onchocerciasis) in Africa, 1988. Served with Brit. Army, 1946-49. Recipient Moynihan medal Assn. Surgeons Gt. Britain and Ireland, 1960, Reuben Harvey triennial prize Royal Coll. Physicians, Ireland, 1957, Arris and Gale award Royal Coll. Surgeons, Eng., 1972, disting. scholar award Internat. Communication Assn., 1980, Sama Found. medal, 1982, disting. citation Hagakure Soc., 1992, Nat. Svc. medal Royal Brit. Legion, 1993; named to Hon. Order Ky. Cols., 1968; named Chieftan Ntufam Ajan of Oban Ejagham People, Cross River State, Nigeria, 1983; hon. prof. Del Colegio De Ciencas De La Salud De La Universidad San Francisco De Quito, 1996; recipient Chieftan Obong Nsong Idem Ibibio Nigeria, 1983, Mgbe (Ekpe) honor Nigeria, commendation WHO address Fed. Govt. Nigeria, Calabar, 1983, Leadership in Internat. Med. Health citation Pres. U.S., 1987, WHO medal, 1987, Agromedicine citation Commr. of Agr., State of Tenn., 1987, Assembly citation State of N.Y., 1987, Citation Congl. Record., 1987; Maestro Honorifo, U. Autonoma Agraria, Coahuila, Mex., 1987; presented Key to the City of Nashville, 1987; recipient Vice-Chancellor's Citation and Presentation for Primary Health Care Teaching in Nigeria, U. Calabar, 1988; Pamétni medal Postgrad. Med. Coll., Prague, 1991, Gold medal U. of Bratislava, 1991, Disting. Citation Hagakure Rsch. Soc., Japan, 1992, Nat. Svc. medal Royal Brit. Legion, 1993, Citation Commendation from Pres. Kyoto Prefectural U. Medicine, Japan, 1993, Citation Commendation on Contbn. to Med. Edn. from Pres. Oita Med. U., Japan, 1997; addresses presented by people of Ikot Imo, Nsit Anyang, Oban, 1982-84, Commendation from King of Calabar, 1984; Ciba fellow Can., 1965; Stacey Day Ward named in his honor by Fed. Min. and Gov. of Cross River State, Calabar Med. Ctr., Nigeria, 1986; charter mem. U.S. Normandy Com., 1988; 1st fgn. hon. mem. Hagakure Res. Soc. (Samurai), Kyushu, Japan, 1991. Fellow Zool. Soc. London Royal Micros. Soc., Royal Soc. Health, World Acad. Arts and Scis., Japanese Found. for Biopsychosocial Health (internat. hon. fellow and most disting. mem.), African Acad. Sci., African Acad. Med. Scis. (founder); mem. AAS, AMA, APHA, Am. Burn Assn., Internat. Burn Assn., Can. Authors Assn., N.Y. Acad. Scis., Am. Assn. History Medicine, Am. Inst. Stress (bd. dirs.), Am. Anthrop. Assn., Am. Rural Health Assn. (v.p. internat. sci. affairs, bd. dirs.), Soc. Med. Geographers USSR. Home: 6 Lomond Ave Chestnut Rdg NY 10977-6901

DAY, SUSAN, librarian, art historian; b. Hillingdon, Uxbridge, Eng., Apr. 3, 1943; arrived in France, 1968; d. Thomas Sydney and Irene Winifred (Hook) D. Ancienne Eléve, Ecole du Louvre, Paris, 1977, Elève diplômée, 1985. Rschr. L'Architecture d'aujourdhui, Paris, 1977-78; libr. Galerie Jean Soustiel, Paris, 1978-80; chief libr. Inst. Français d'Architecture, Paris, 1981—; prof. Inst. d'Etudes Techniques et Historiques de l'Objet d'Art, Versailles, France, 1988-89; guest lectr. Assn. Ali Baba, Paris, Oriental Rug Soc., Brussels; presenter in field. Author: Louis Süe Architectures, 1986, Jean-Charles Moreux, Architecte, dècorateur et paysagiste, 1999; author, gen. editor: Great Carpets of the World, 1996; contbr. articles to profl. jours; contbr. editor to the magazine HALI, 1997—. mem. Assn. des Bibliothécaires Français, Assn. des Historiens de l'Architecture Français. Anglican. Avocations: writing, drawing, traveling. Home: 15 villa Duthy, 75014 Paris France Office: Inst Français Arch, 6 rue de Tournon, 75006 Paris France

DAYA, SHERAZ MANSOOR, ophthalmic surgeon, health facility administrator; b. Nairobi, Kenya, Feb. 1, 1960; arrived in U.K., 1973; s. Mansoor Mohemadali and Sakerkhanoo (Tejani) D.; m. Marcela Milagros Espinosa-Lagana, Sept. 25, 1998; 1 child, Olivia Sheherezadh. BAO with honors, MB.B.Ch., Royal Coll. Surgeons, 1984. Diplomate Am. Bd. Internal Medicine, Am. Bd. Ophthalmology. Resident in internal medicine N.Y. Infirmary-Beekman, 1988-91; fellow in cornea U. Minn., Mpls., 1991-92; resident in ophthalmology Cath. Med. Ctr., N.Y., 1991-98, dir. corneal svcs., 1992-94; dir., cons. Corneoplastic Unit Eye Bank, Queen Victoria Hosp., 1994—; dir. Ctr. for Sight, East Orinstead, Eng., 1997—; mem. cornea adv. group U.K. Transplant Spl. Svcs., Bristol, Eng., 1994—; vis. prof. Mil. Hosp., Alexandria, Egypt, 1997. Contbr. to book: The Eye and Skin, 1995; contbr. articles to profl. jours. Recipient Achievement award Am. Acad. Ophthalmology, 1999. Fellow Royal Coll. Surgeons, Am. Coll. Surgeons, Am. Coll. Physicians; mem. Internat. Soc. Refractive Surgery (internat. coun. 1997—), European Soc. Cataracts/Refractive Surgery (refractive com. 1997—), U.K. Soc. Cataract and Refractive Surgery (coun. 1995—). Moslem. Avocations: squash, art, travel. Office: Ctr for Sight, 57 Harley St, WIN 1DD London England

DAYAL, RAM, retired science educator; b. Fatehpur, India, Oct. 12, 1930; s. Hira Lala Saxena and Jai Rani Devi. MS in Botany, U. Allahabad, 1952, PhD in Botany, 1958; postgrad., U. Guelph, Ont., Can., 1968-70. Lectr. botany C.M.P. Degree Coll., Allahabad, 1957-62; lectr. dept. mycology and plant pathology Banaras Hindu U., Vanarasi, India, 1962-73, assoc. prof. dept. mycology and plant pathology, 1973-83, prof., head dept. mycology and plant pathology, 1983-85, head dept. mycology and plant pathology, 1988-90, emeritus prof., 1992-95. Contbr. numerous papers to profl. jours. Fellow NAS, Indian Phytopathol. Soc. (Jeerasannidhi award and Gold medal 1992), Mycol. Soc. India. Avocations: music, playing Indian instruments, sitar, gardening. Home: Shiva Mandir Nagwa Rd Lanka, Varanasi 221005, India Office: Banaras Hindu U, Dept Mycololgy/Plant Pathol, Varanasi 221005, India

DAYME, MERIBETH G., business educator, consultant, voice educator; b. Aulander, N.C., Apr. 20, 1938; d. Luther E. and Edith (Wiley) B. BM and Voice, Salem Coll., 1960; M in Sacred Music in Voice and Choral, Union Theol. Seminary, 1962; PhD in Voice Sci., U. So. Calif., 1974. Instr. Wilson Coll., Chambersburg, Pa., 1963-66; Instr. voice, anatomy U. So. Calif., L.A., 1967-74; assoc. prof. music and life and health scis. U. Del., Newark, 1974-82; owner, consultant Bus. and the Arts, London, 1983—; instr. spl. anatomy interns and residents Huntington Meml. Hosp., Pasadena, Calif.; cons. Inst. Mgmt., 1987—, Royal Acad. Dancing, 1980—, Prudential Assurance, 1989—, Marks & Spencer, 1990—; CEO Comm. Arts and Assocs. Ltd.; lectr., spkr in field. Author: Dynamics of the Singing Voice, 1982, 4th edit., 1997, Speak with Confidence, 1988, Handbook of the Singing Voice, 1996, Creating Confidence, 1999; contbr. numerous articles to profl. jours., chpt. to The Hanbook of Management, 1996. Postdoct. fellow NIH, London, 1979-81. Fellow Royal Soc. Arts, Comet; mem. Residents Assn. Crediton Hill (chair). Avocations: reading, theatre, music, tennis. E-mail: meribeth@aol.com. Home and Office: 43 A Crediton Hill, London NW6 1HS, England

DAYNARD, RICHARD ALAN, law educator; b. N.Y.C., July 19, 1943; s. David M. and Sarah (Weidenbaum) D.; m. Carol S. Iskols, Aug. 9, 1975; children: David J., Gabriela C. BA, Columbia U., 1964, MA in Sociology, 1970; JD, Harvard U., 1967; PhD in Urban Studies and Planning, MIT, 1980. Bar: N.Y. 1967, U.S. Ct. Appeals (6th cir.) 1986, U.S. Supreme Ct. 1986, U.S. Ct. Appeals (11th cir.) 1987, U.S. Ct. Appeals (5th cir.) 1996. Law clk. 2d cir. U.S. Ct. Appeals, N.Y.C., 1967-68; teaching fellow Columbia U., N.Y.C., 1968-69; asst. prof. law Northeastern U., Boston, 1969-71, assoc. prof. law, 1971-73, prof. law, 1973—; lectr. Tufts Med. Sch.,

Boston, 1975-89; internat. lectr. and cons. Editor-in-chief Tobacco Products Litigation Reporter, 1985—; assoc. editor: Tobacco Control: An Internat. Jour., 1998—; contbr. articles in field to profl. jours. Chmn. Tobacco Products Liability Project, Boston, 1984—; pres. Group Against Smoking Pollution of Mass., Boston, 1983—, Clean Indoor Air Ednl. Found., Boston, 1983-92, Tobacco Control Resource Ctr., Inc., Boston, 1993—; pres. Stop Teenage Addiction to Tobacco, 1996-98. Mem. ABA, Am. Pub. Health Assn., Law and Soc. Assn., Phi Beta Kappa. Home: 90 Commonwealth Ave Boston MA 02116-3040 Office: Northeastern U Sch Law 400 Huntington Ave Boston MA 02115-5005

DAYOUB, ROBERT GEORGE, engineering agencies executive; b. Tanta, Egypt, Dec. 12, 1919; s. George Joseph and Marie George (Chammas) D.; m. Hoda Elias Ghadban, July 4, 1954; children: Raouf, Karim, Rafik. B-Commerce, U. Paris, 1938. Founder, gen. mgr. Egyptian Engring. & Automotive Supply Agys., Cairo and Alexandria, 1941—; founder, chmn. Comml. Engring. Agys., Damascus and Aleppo, Syria, 1959—, Egyptian Engring. Agys. S.A.E., Cairo, 1976—. Decorated knight Order of Merit (Italy). Mem. Gezira Sporting Club, Automobile Club. Avocations: swimming, golf. Home: 18 Saray El Gezira-Zamalek, Cairo 11211, Egypt Office: Egyptian Engring Agys SAE, 16 Naguib El Rihani, Cairo 11111, Egypt

DAYTON, DEANE KRAYBILL, translation company executive; b. Marion, Ind., May 24, 1949; s. Wilber Thomas and Donna Irene (Fisher) D.; m. Carol Mae Noggle, June 2, 1969; 1 child, Christopher Thomas. BA in Chemistry Edn., Ind. Wesleyan U., 1970; MS in Teaching, Randolph-Macon U., 1974; MS in Instrnl. Tech., 1976, PhD in Instrnl. Tech., 1976. Sci. tchr., chair sci. dept. Jessamine County Jr. High Sch., Nicholasville, Ky., 1970-73; asst. prof. instructional tech. sch. edn. U. Va., Charlottesville, 1976-77; grad. asst., teaching asst. Ind. U., Bloomington, 1973-76, asst. prof. instrnl. tech. Sch. Edn., 1977-83, dir. prodn. svcs. audio-visual ctr., 1979-83; dir. media div. CDC, Atlanta, 1981; v.p. cons. svcs. Ednl. Techs., Inc., Charlotte, N.C., 1983-85; exec. mgr. documentation and lang. transl. Intergraph Corp., Huntsville, Ala., 1985-98; v.p. ops. Berlitz GlobalNET, Princeton, N.J., 1998—; cons. trainer George Meany Ctr. Labor Studies, Silver Spring, 1978-82; cons., developer Discover Pl., Charlotte, 1984-86; tng. developer First Union Bank, Charlotte, 1982-85, United Carolina Bank, Monroe, N.C., 1984; cons. Anacomp, Sarasota, Fla., 1982-84. Co-author: Planning and Producing Instructional Media, 1985; producer (film) Computer Graphics for Communication, 1982; contbr. articles to profl. jours. Chairperson exhibits com. North Ala. Sci. Ctr., Inc., Huntsville, 1990-92. Recipient Young Scholar award AV Comm. Rev./Ednl. Resources Info. Ctr., 1977. Mem. ASTD, Nat. Soc. for Performance and Instrn., Soc. for Tech. Comm., Assn. for Ednl. Comm. and Tech. (pres. media design and prodn. divsn. 1982, James W. Brown award 1986). Avocation: developing computerized science museum exhibits. Home: 188 Carter Rd Princeton NJ 08540-2103 Office: Berlitz Internat 400 Alexander Park Princeton NJ 08540-6306

DAZEY, WILLIAM BOYD, retired lawyer; b. Chgo., Sept. 23, 1915; s. Alva William and Emma Mayo (Boyd) D.; m. Dolores Ann Melton, July 20, 1959; children: Barbara Ann Dazey Lantos, William Melton, Thomas Sumner, Daniel Putnam, Johnathan Mayo. Student, U. Ill., 1933; LL.B., Cumberland U., 1935. Bar: Tex. 1940. Ptnr. firm Godard & Dazey, Texas City, 1940-58; cons. Japan UN Assn., Tokyo, 1958-60; legal advisor Japan Consul Gen., Houston, 1960-86; ptnr. Dazey & Newey, Houston, 1970-80. Served to 2d lt. U.S. Army, 1942-46. Decorated Bronze Star with oak leaf cluster, Purple Heart; Third Order Sacred Treasure (Japan). Mem. ABA, State Bar Tex., Nat. Order Battlefield Commns., Japan-Am. Soc. Houston (founder, past pres.), Am. Inst. for Internat. Steel (emeritus), Torch Club, Phi Delta Theta. Democrat. Unitarian. Home: 419 E Hathaway Dr San Antonio TX 78209-6416

DAZLICH, DONALD ANTHONY, JR., atmospheric science researcher; b. Camden, N.J., Dec. 3, 1957; s. Donald Anthony and Mary Regina Dazlich; m. Angela Anne Dazlich, Aug. 16, 1980; children: David Andrew, Paula Jean. BS, Case Western Res. U., 1980; MS, U. Md., 1982. Grad. rsch. asst. U. Md., College Park, 1980-84; sci. programmer/analyst Centel Fed. Data Systems, Greenbelt, Md., 1984-88; rsch. assoc. Colo. State U., Ft. Collins, 1988—. Bd. dirs. Ft. Collins Right to Life, 1991-97; dist. capt. Larimer County Rep. Party, Ft. Collins, 1994—; adult leader Larimer County 4H, 1998—. Recipient Most Exceptional Performance award NASA Global Modeling and Simulation Br., 1987. Mem. Am. Meteorol. Soc. Evang. Presbyn. Avocations: hiking, model rocketry, reading history. E-mail: dazlich@atmos.colostate.edu. Office: Colo State Univ Fort Collins CO 80523

DCAMP, KATHRYN ACKER, human resources director; b. Hartford, Conn., Jan. 12, 1956; d. Donald Jalmer and Virginia Ruth (Wainman) Acker; m. Glenn William DCamp, July 17, 1978; 1 child, Kristen Louise. AA, Ball State U., 1976, BS magna cum laude, 1978. Cert. compensation profl., sr. profl. in human resources. Actuarial/analyst pensions Aetna Life & Casualty, Hartford, Conn., 1980-81, compensation analyst, 1981-82, compensation cons., 1982-84, compensation adminstr., 1984-85, exec. compensation cons., 1985-86, sr. adminstr./exec. compensation, 1986-88; compensation cons. The Assoc. Group, Indpls., 1988, compensation mgr., 1989-90, dir. exec. compensation benefits, 1990-93, dir. compensation, mgmt. edn. and exec. benefits, 1993-94; compensation leader GE Capital, Stamford, Conn., 1994-2000; global compensation leader Cisco Sys., San Jose, Calif., 2000—; ind. cons., 1986—, Motivation by Design, 1993—; spkr. on compensation topics; faculty advisor Univ. Evansville, Ind., 1990—; bd. dirs. Compensation and Benefits Profls. of Ind., 1992—; area rep. Ind. and Ky. Am. Compensation Assn., mem. nat. adv. bd. on exec. compensation, 1998—. Co-author: Spot Gainsharing Personnel Journal, 1989. Mem. Am. Compensation Assn., Soc. for Human Resources Mgmt. Lutheran. Office: 170 W Tasmarre San Jose CA 95113

DE, ABHIJIT, educational administrator; b. Calcutta, India, Apr. 4, 1955; s. Sudhansu Mohan and Fullara (Dutta) D.; m. Bandana Dutta, Feb. 9, 1988; 1 child, Abhinandan. BSc in Physics, Calcutta U., 1976; MSc in Applied Physics, Birla Inst. Technology, Ranchi, India, 1979; postgrad. diploma in mgmt., Sydenham Coll., Mumbai, India, 1982. Ptnr. Sett & De, Calcutta, 1982-86; from dir. to chmn. IIAS Sch. Mgmt., Calcutta, 1987—. Mrm. Rotary Internat. (sec. 1988-99, Paul Harris fellow 1994). Avocations: reading, photography, traveling. Home: CD-256 Salt Lake, 700064 Calcutta W Bengal, India

DE, SUBODH KUMAR, diplomat; b. West Bengal, India, Mar. 8, 1957; s. Sakti Pada and Sarama Bala D.; m. Putul Mondal, Apr. 21, 1986; children: Chandan Kumar, Subhayan Kumar. BS, Calcutta U., 1979, MS, 1982, PhD, 1990. Lectr. Visva-Bharati U., Santinikatan/W. Bengal, India, 1991-92; sr. lectr. Indian Assn. for Cultivation of Sci., Calcutta, 1992—. Avocations: reading, singing. Office: Indian Assn Cultivation/Sci, Jadavpur, Calcutta/W Bengal 700 032, India

DEA, DAVID YOUNG FONG, electrical engineer, consultant; b. Hong Kong, Mar. 6, 1924; came to U.S., 1937; s. Chun Fong and Teung Heung (Chow) D.; m. Mary Gin, Dec. 17, 1955; 1 child, George Hong. BSEE, U. Calif., Berkeley, 1950; postgrad., U. So. Calif., 1951-54. Mem. tech. staff Hughes Aircraft Co., Culver City, Calif., 1950; sect. mgr. Firestone Missile Div., Southgate, Calif., 1956-57; pres. Dea Electronics Co., L.A., 1957-59; dept. mgr. on missiles Hughes Aircraft Co., Culver City, 1959-63; project mgr. avionics Teledyne Corp., L.A., 1963-65; regional mgr. Bunker Ramo Corp., Canoga Park, Calif., 1965-66; project engr. LTV Corp., Dallas, 1966-73, Lear Siegler Corp., Grand Rapids, Mich., 1973-80; dir. engring. advanced battle tank devel. Nat. Water Lift Corp., Kalamazoo, 1980-82; cons. engr. McDonnell Douglas Corp., St. Louis, 1982-86; project mgr. Simmons Precision Corp., Vergennes, Vt., 1986-87; cons. engr. Control Data Corp., St. Paul, 1987-89; cons. M1 Tank Program Gen. Dynamics Corp., Sterling Heights, Mich., 1990-98; cons. weapon tech. United Defense LP, Mpls., 1998—; contbr. articles to profl. jours. Patentee in field. Violinist Inglewood (Calif.) Symphony. With USAF, 1943-46, Philippines, Japan. Mem. IEEE (sr.), Computer Soc. of IEEE. Republican. Avocation: swimming. Home: 2514 Normandy Dr SE Grand Rapids MI 49506-5471 Office: United Defense LP 4800 E River Rd Minneapolis MN 55421-1498

DE ABREU, SUE, elementary educator; b. Honolulu, Dec. 29, 1947; d. Lawrence and Mary (Jones-Howard) de Abreu-Morris; 1 child, Steven. AA, Gulf Coast Coll., Panama, 1967; BA, Fla. State U., 1971; BS, Harvard U., 1968; MS, Ga. So. Coll., 1984; MA, U. West Fla., 1985. Cert. art edn. tchr. K-12th, elem. tchr., sci. specialist 5th-6th grades, Fla. Reading specialist Craig Elem. Sch., Vail, Colo., 1980; tchr. sci. 7th-8th grade Ludowic County Schs., Jesup, Ga., 1981-84; tchr. sci. 5th-6th grade Gulf County Pub. Schs., Port St. Joe, Fla., 1985-98; state judge Fla. State Sci. and Engring., U. Fla., instr. Chmn. Gulf County-N.W. Fla. chpt. Nat. Dem. Com. Recipient Outstanding Fla. Artist award, Fedn. Fla. Women's Clubs Am. Mem. NEA, ASCD, Nat. Art Edn. Assn., Nat. Middle Sch. Assn., Nat. Wildlife Fedn. (Gulf County dir.), Wewahitchka Fedn. Women's Club (v.p. 1994-96).

DE ABREU ARRIMAR, JORGE MANUEL, library director; b. Chibia, Huíla, Angola, June 14, 1953; s. Andre de Sousa E. Silva and Aldina Bettencourt De (Abreu) A.; m. Maria Antónia Monteiro Giestas, Apr. 19, 1975 (div. July 1991); children: Cátia Solange, Patrícia Alexandra; m. Isabel Maria Peixoto Braga. Student, Faculdade De Letras, Lisboa/Azores, Portugal, 1975-82. With Hist. Archives of Macau, 1985; dir. libr. Macau Portuguese High Sch., 1986; sub-dir. Macau Nat. Libr., 1986-87, dir., 1987—; tchr. history high schs. in Angola, 1973-75, Azores, 1976-84, Portugal, 1984-85. Author poetry, history and library science books. Mem. Portuguese Librs. Assn., Portuguese Lang. and Culture Assn., Hist. Inst. Terceira Island. Avocations: painting, theatre. Office: Biblioteca Nacional, Av Conselheiro F de Almeida 89, Macau Macau

DEACON, NIGEL, chemistry educator, researcher; b. Leicester, L. Shire, Eng., Jan. 6, 1957; s. David and Barbara (Tomlinson) D.; m. Alison Margaret Glithero, Apr. 11, 1995,. BA in Natural Sci., St. Catharine's Coll., Cambridge, Eng., 1978, MA, 1981; grad., Royal Soc. Chemistry, 1979. Postgrad. Cert. Edn., 1979. Asst. chemist Wyggeston & Queen Elizabeth Coll., Leicester, Eng., 1979—; publisher music Sutton Elms Publs., Croft, Eng., 1988—. Composer over 100 musical scores for piano (fugues, folktune settings, preludes, minatures, chorales), 1986—; author (book of genealogy) The Deacon Family of Leicestershire, 1995, vol. II, 1998, vol. III, 2000; contbr. articles to Sch. Sci. Rev., 1984—. Civil defence warning officer UK Warning and Monitoring Orgn., Rugby, Warwickshire, Eng., 1982-93. Mem. Assn. Tchrs. and Lectrs. (coll. rep. 1979-93), Broughton Astley Conservative Club, Old-time Radio Show Collectors Assn., Vintage Radio Programme Collector's Circle. Avocations: radio dramas, piano, art, fine wines, chamber music. Home: 56 Arbor Rd, Leicshr Croft LE9 3GD, England Office: Wyggeston & Q Elizabeth Col, University Rd, Leicshr Leicester LE1 7RJ, England

DEAK, ISTVAN, mathematician, researcher; b. Budapest, Hungary, Sept. 21, 1945; s. Benjamin Deak and Klara Schlotzer; m. Istvanne J. Hajba, Feb. 16, 1972; children: Krisztian, Kinga, Sarolta, Emese. Degree in math., L. Eotvos U., Budapest, Hungary, 1969, Dr.rer.nat., 1971, Dr.habil., 1999. Asst. rschr. Tech. U. Budapest, 1969-72, sr. assoc. prof., 1991—; rschr. Computer and Automation Inst., Hungarian Acad. Scis., Budapest, 1972-91; vis. prof. Dalhousie U., Halifax, N.S., Can., 1984-86, U. Wis., Madison, 1989-90; vis. rschr. U. Zurich, Switzerland, 1997-98. Author: Random Number Generators and Their Applications, 1986 (Computer and Automation Inst. award 1987), Random Number Generators and Simulation, 1990. Recipient Gy. Farkas award Jour. Bolyai Math. Soc., 1976, award of dir. Computer and Automation Inst., 1982, 83. Fax: (36-1)463-1292. E-mail: deak@math.bme.hu. Office: OR Group Dept Diff Equation, Muegyetem rkp 3, H-1111 Budapest Hungary

DEAKYNE, WILLIAM JOHN, library director, musician; b. Harrisburg, Pa., June 25, 1936; s. William John and Hazel (Brown) D.; 1 child, Linda Tang Deakyne. MusB, U. Hartford, 1961; MLS, Villanova U., 1962; Diploma in French, Berlitz Sch., Phila., Stamford, Conn., 1967, 69. Cert. libr., N.J., Mass., N.Y., Wash. Dir. Meuser Meml. Libr., Easton, Pa., 1962-64; dir. Coyle Free Libr., Chambersburg, Pa., 1964-65, Free Libr. Springfield Twp., Phila., 1965-68, Darien (Conn.) Libr., 1968-78, East Lyme (Conn.) Libr., 1979—. Organist, pianist (composed Jeu de Clochette, 1964); contbr. articles to profl. jours. V.p. East Lyme C. of C., Niantic, Conn., 1985; mem. Am. Cathedral of the Holy Trinity, Paris, 1998—; charter mem. Planning Giving Soc., U. Hartford, 1996—. Mem. ALA (del. to Internat. Fedn. Libr. Assn. meetings Chgo., Copenhagen 1969), Les Amis de Vielles Maisons. Democrat. Avocation: promoting English pipe organs in the U.S., restoration of pipe organs in France. Home: Westchester Dr East Lyme CT 06333 Office: East Lyme Pub Libr 39 Society Rd Niantic CT 06357-1100

DEAL, LANCE EARL, Olympic athlete; b. Riverton, Wyo., Aug. 21, 1961; m. Nancy Deal; 1 child, Sarah Elizabeth. Student, U. Mont. mem. U.S. Olympic team, Seoul, 1988, 2000. Placed 1st in discus throw U.S. Jr. Championships, 1980, Pan Am. Jrs., 1980, 3rd place in hammer throw USA/Mobil Championship, 1986, 1st place, 1989, 1st place indoor championship, 1993, 2nd place World Cup, 1989, Silver medal, track and field, hammer throw Olympic Games, Atlanta, 1996. Mem. N.Y. Athletic Club. Office: USA Track & Field PO Box 120 Indianapolis IN 46206-0120*

DEAL, WILLIAM THOMAS, school psychologist; b. Canton, Ohio, Dec. 18, 1949; s. Richard Lee and Rheta Lucille (Gerber) D.; m. Paula Nespeca, Aug. 5, 1972. BS, Bowling Green State U., 1972; MA, John Carroll U., 1977; postgrad. Kent State U., 1979—. Sci. tchr. Westlake Schs., 1972-76, head bldg. sci. dept., 1974-76; intern sch. psychologist Garfield Heights Schs., 1976-77, sch. psychologist, 1977—; pvt. practice psychology, Parma Heights, Ohio, 1982-84. Alternate mem. adv. council Cuyahoga County Spl. Edn. Service Ctr., 1977—. Recipient Cert. of Recognition, Garfield Heights Bd. Edn., 1980; Outstanding Achievement award Cleve. Assn. for Children with Learning Disabilities, Inc., 1980; named Psychologist of Yr. Cleveland Sch., 1990. Mem. Nat. Assn. Sch. Psychologists, United Teaching Profession, Ohio Sch. Psychology Assn., Cleve. Assn. Sch. Psychologists, Phi Delta Kappa. Republican. Mem. Reformed Ch. Home: 5290 Kings Hwy Cleveland OH 44126-3059 Office: 4900 Turney Rd Cleveland OH 44125-2501

DE ALMEIDA, WAGNER BATISTA, chemistry educator, researcher; b. Juiz de Fora, Brazil, June 11, 1956; s. João B. and Maria D. (Souza) De A.; m. Marly A. B. Bonato, Dec. 20, 1978; children: Petrus, Matheus. MSc, U. Fed. Minas Gerais, Belo Horizonte, Brazil, 1982; postdoctorate, U. Manchester Inst. Sci./Tech., Eng., 1991; PhD, U. Manchester, 1991; postdoctorate, U. Fla., 1997. Cert. chemist. Sch. tchr. Assoc. Ed. Souza Ramos, Bicas, Brazil, 1976-77, Colégio Tiradentes, Juiz de Fora, Brazil, 1977-78, Colégio Pio XII, Juiz de Fora, 1976-78, Col. Estadual O. Progresso, Belo Horizonte, 1981-82; asst. prof. U. Itaúna, Brazil, 1982-83; assoc. prof. U. Fed. Minas Gerais, Belo Horizonte, 1983—; dir. phys. chemistry divsn. U. Fed. Minas Gerais, Belo Horizonte, 1985-86, headship Computational Chemistry Lab., 1994—; cons. Brazilian Agy. for Supporting Rsch., Belo Horizonte, 1995—, various sci. periodicals, 1995—. Author: (book) Memorial for Full Professor Position, 1997; mem. editl. bd.: Quimica Nova, 1996; contbr. rsch. articles to sci. jours. Rsch. assoc. fellow Agrl. Found. Rsch. Coun., U. Manchester, 1991, vis. prof. fellow Am. Chem. Soc., U. Fla., 1995, postdoctoral fellow Fundação Coordenação de Aperfeiçoamento de Pessoal de Nível Superior, 1997. Mem. Brazilian Soc. Chemistry, Royal Soc. Chemistry (London), N.Y. Acad. Scis. Roman Catholic. Avocations: playing guitar, football, listening to music, traveling, reading. Office: U Fed Minas Gerais, Av Antonio Carlos 6627, 31270901 Belo Horizonte Brazil

DEAN, CHRISTOPHER, ice dancer; b. Nottingham, Eng., July 27, 1958; s. Colin and Mavis (Pearson) D.; m. Isabelle Duchesnay, 1991 (div. 1993); m. Jill Trenary, 1994. MA (hon.), Nottingham Trent U., 1994. Police constable, 1974-80, pairs figure skater (with Jayne Torvill). Choreographer: Encounters for Eng. Nat. Ballet, 1996. Recipient (all with Jayne Torvill) Gold medal in ice dancing Olympic Games, 1984, Bronze medal, 1994; named (all with Jayne Torvill) Brit. Ice Dance Champion, 1978-83, 94, European Ice Dance Champion, 1981, 82, 84, 94, World Ice Dance Champion, 1981-84, World Profl. Ice Dance Champion, 1984, 85, 90, 95, 96, Personality of Yr., BBC Sportsview, 1983-84; inductee (with Jayne Torvill) World Figure Skating Hall of Fame, 1989; decorated Mem. Brit. Empire, 1981, Order Brit. Empire, 2000. Office: care Sue Young, PO Box 32 Heathfield, East Sussex TN21 OBW, United Kingdom

DEAN, COLIN LESLIE, philosopher, poet; b. Geelong, Victoria, Australia, Sept. 3, 1953; s. Ronald Clifford and Valerie June (Winter) D. BSc, Deakin U., Geelong, Australia, 1984, BA, 1988, BLitt with honors, 1991, MA, 1994; BLitt with honors, Deakin U., 1998. Cert. physics, social anthropology, historian religion, philosophy. Author: The Relationship Between Analysis and Insight in Madhyamika Buddhism, 1994, Evil Flowers: Poems by C. Dean, 1995, The Australian Aboriginal Dreamtime, 1996, Poisonous Flowers: Poems by C. Dean, 1997, Epistemology: A Guide to Philosophy, 1997, The religions of the Pre-Contact Victorian Aborigines, 1998, The Nature of Philosophy, 1998, A Moral Philosophy, 1998, Wet Flowers: Poems by C. Dean, 1999, A Conequence of the Epistemiological Holism of Quine, 1999, Cyber Sex, 2000, Xanadu: A Female Sexual Odyssey, 2000; contbr. articles to profl. jours. Mem. Australian Inst. Physics. Avocations: poetry, music, reading dialectics. Home: 72 Plume St, Norlane Geelong 3214, Australia

DEAN, DORSEY EDWARD, retired engineer; b. Akron, Ohio, Apr. 14, 1927; s. Clark Bolin and Cohen Lulu (Talbott) D.; m. Marian Louise Johns, Dec. 20, 1947; children: Linda Suzanne, Richard Thomas, Sheri Lynn, James Edward. BS with distinction, U. Akron, 1949. Registered profl. engr., Calif. Statis. quality control mgr. N.Am. tire plants Firestone Tire and Rubber Co., Akron, 1949-58; sr. quality/reliability engr. Canaveral ops. Martin Co., Cape Canaveral, Fla., 1958-60; rsch. mathematician RCA Internat. Missile Test Project, Patrick AFB, Fla., 1960-70; sr. quality engr., quality supr. Gen. Dynamics Space Sys. Divsn., Cape Canaveral, 1971-89; ret.; chmn. quality control and mgmt. adv. com. Brevard C.C., Cocoa, Fla., 1969-77; advisor Space Congress, Cocoa Beach, Fla., 1985-97. Author: (booklet) Firestone Quality, 1956. Pres. Convair Mgmt. Assn., Cape Canaveral, 1978; v.p. Merritt Towers Condo. Assn., Merritt Island, Fla., 1997-2000. With USN, 1945-46. Recipient Engr. of Yr. award Fla. Engring. Soc., 2000. Fellow Am. Soc. Quality (cert. quality engr., cert. reliability engr., regional bd. dirs. 1967-71, regional exec. dir. 1968-71, chmn. Cape Canaveral sect. 1977-78), Canaveral Coun. Tech. Socs. (chmn. 1984, 96, Engr. of Yr. 2000). Republican. Presbyterian. Achievements include development of statistical quality control and reliability engineering techniques in the tire, space, photographic, electronic and computer industries. Avocations: computers, photography, flying, swimming, scuba diving. Home: 300 S Sykes Creek Pkwy # 806 Merritt Island FL 32952-3313

DEAN, JOHN AURIE, chemist, author, chemistry educator emeritus; b. Sault Ste. Marie, Mich., May 9, 1921; s. Aurie Jerome and Gertrude (Saw) D.; m. Elizabeth Louise Cousins, June 20, 1943 (div. 1981); children: Nancy Elizabeth, Thomas Alfred, John Randolph, Laurie Alice, Clarissa Elaine; m. Peggy DeHart Beeler, Oct. 23, 1981; stepchildren: Diane Barbara, Lisa Lynn, James Edward, Jonathan Curtis. BS in Chemistry, U. Mich., 1942, MS in Chemistry, 1944, PhD, 1949. Tchg. fellow in chemistry U. Mich., Ann Arbor, 1942-44, 45-46, lectr. in chemistry, 1946-48; chemist X-100 Phase Manhattan Project Chrysler Corp., Detroit, 1944-45; assoc. prof. chemistry U. Ala., Tuscaloosa, 1948-50; asst. prof. chemistry U. Tenn., Knoxville, 1950-53, assoc. prof., 1953-58, prof. chemistry, 1958-81, prof. emeritus, 1981—; cons. Union Car Nuclear Div., Oak Ridge, 1953-74, Stewart Labs., Knoxville, 1968-81; vis. lectr. Peoples Republic of China, 1985. Author: Instrumental Methods of Analysis, 1948, 7th edit., 1988, Flame Photometry, 1960, Chemical Separation Methods, 1969, Flame Emission and Atomic Absorption Spectrometry, Vol. 1, 1969, Vol. 2, 1971, Vol. 3, 1975, Lange's Handbook of Chemistry, 15th edit., 1999, Handbook of Organic Chemistry, 1986, Solutions Manual for Instrumental Methods of Analysis, 7th edit., 1988, The Chemist's Ready Reference Handbook, 1990, Analytical Chemistry Handbook, 1995; contbr. articles to profl. jours., chpts. to books. Mem. Am. Chem. Soc. (Charles H. Stone award Carolina-Piedmont sect. 1974), Soc. Applied Spectroscopy (hon., chmn. S.E. sect. 1971-73, editor newsletter 1984-95, Disting. Svc. award 1991, Outstanding Svc. award 1995), Archaeol. Inst. Am., East Tenn. Soc. (pres. 1980-81), U.S. Naval Inst. (life), Sigma Xi, Phi Kappa Phi. Presbyterian. Address: 715 Garden Villa Way Knoxville TN 37909-2370

DEAN, JOHN FRANCIS, astronomer, researcher; b. Liverpool, Eng., Jan. 25, 1946; arrived in South Africa, 1948; s. Geoffrey Joseph and Norah Mary (Devlin) D.; m. Ann Maureen Wamsteker, Apr. 17, 1978; children: Geoffrey Richard, Pamela Mary. BSc, Capetown (South Africa) U., 1966; BSc in Physics with honors, Rhodes U., Grahamstown, South Africa, 1968; postgrad. in radio astronomy, Manchester U., Eng., 1969, PhD, 1973. Astronomer Coun. Sci. Indsl. Rsch., Capetown, 1973-80; sr. officer main office Electricity Supply Comm./ESKOM, Johannesburg, South Africa, 1981-86, sr. scientist modelling and devel., prodn. optimisation, system ops., 1987—. Contbr. articles to profl. jours. Mem. South African Inst. Physics, Ops. Rsch. Soc. South Africa, South African Coun. Natural Scientists. Achievements include development of method of determining interstellar absorption of light from stars using cepheid variables. Home: 15 Craig Ave, Randburg Transvaal 2194, South Africa

DEAN, MARTHA ANNE, lawyer; b. Phila., Mar. 31, 1959; d. Robert Charles Jr. and Edith Nancy Hayes Dean; m. Carlos Manuel Valinho, Sept. 8, 1984; 1 child, Elliot Charles Dean Valinho. Grad., Phillips Acad., 1977; BA, Wellesley Coll., 1982; JD, U. Conn., 1986. Bar: Conn. 1986, U.S. Dist. Ct. Conn. 1995, U.S. Appellate Ct. (2d cir.) 2000. Paralegal Tyler, Cooper & Alcorn, New Haven, 1982-83; assoc. Updike, Kelly & Spellacy, Hartford, Conn., 1986-88, Robinson & Cole, Hartford, 1990-94; pvt. practice Hartford, 1994—. Mem. law rev. U. Conn. Sch. of Law. Mem. ABA, ATLA, Conn. Bar Assn. (co-chair courtwatch com. 1996-98, mem. exec. com. 1995-99), Conn. Bus. and Industry Assn. (mem. steering com. environ. policies coun. 1996-99), Federalist Soc. (co-chair law and pub. policy studies, Hartford chpt. 1996—), Conn. Trial Lawyers Assn. (Avon chpt. rep. com.). Avocation: equestrian competition. Home: 75 Avon Mountain Rd Avon CT 06001-3904 Office: Law Offices of Martha A Dean 77 Buckingham St Hartford CT 06106-1703

DEAN, ODELL JOSEPH, JR., urologist, educator; b. Nashville, Mar. 9, 1958; s. Odell Joseph and Barbara Jean (Crowther) D. BS, Howard U., 1979; MD, La. State U., New Orleans, 1983. Diplomate Am. Bd. Urology. Resident in surgery and urology Howard U. Hosp., Washington, 1984-86; resident in urology Tulane U. Med. Ctr., New Orleans, 1986-89, fellow in renal transplantation, 1989-91; asst. prof. surgery and urology U. Mo., Columbia, 1991-93; asst. prof. urology Tulane U., 1993-95; attending urologist Columbia Healthcare Sys., Tex., 1996—; cons. Ellis Fischel Cancer Ctr., Columbia, 1991-93, Tulane Cancer Ctr., 1993-95; med. edn. adv. com. Tulane Med. Sch., 1994-95; residency program dir. Tulane dept. urology, 1994-95; assoc. rsch. fellow NIH, Bethesda, 1979-80; mem. prostate cancer adv. com. Tex. Dept. Health, 1996—. Contbr. articles to profl. jours. Advisor Neighborhood Youth Corps, New Orleans, 1980-91; sr. cons. Total Cmty. Action, New Orleans, 1993-95; pres. Am. Cancer Soc., Angelina County, Tex., 1998—. Grantee Atrium Med., 1989, Medtronic, 1989, Searle Pharms., Chgo., 1992, Pfizer Pharms., 1994. Fellow ACS; mem. Am. Urological Assn., Soc. Univ. Urologists, S.W. Oncology Group, Angelina County Med. Soc., Assn. Acad. Minority Physicians. Roman Catholic. Avocations: computer scis., tennis. Office: 710 Gaslight Blvd Ste C Lufkin TX 75904-3187

DEAN, PETER DUNCAN GOODEARL, molecular biologist; b. Princes Risborough, Bucks, U.K., Sept. 26, 1939; s. Hubert William and Evelyn Mary (Lewis) D.; m. Elizabeth Anne Harris, Aug. 13, 1966; children: Jonathan, Charlotte, Fiona. BA/MA in Chemistry, Oxford (U.K.) U., 1962, 66, BSc in Organic Rsch., 1963, DPhil in Biochemistry, 1966, DSc in Rsch., 1984. Chartered chemist. Reader U. Liverpool, U.K., 1968-84; dir. rsch. P&S Biochems., Liverpool, 1978-84; dir., founder Medesign Ltd., Southport, 1982-90; dir. R&D AGC Ltd., Cambridge, 1984-85; dir. new bus. CLS Ltd., Cambridge, 1985-87; CEO Cambio Ltd., Cambridge, 1987—; bd. dirs. Genesys Instruments, Ltd. Cambridge, Campod, Cambridge, Pringle House, Cambridge, NBS Biols., Ltd.; cons. Genentech, San Francisco, 1980-82, Amicon, Mass., 1975-84. Author: Affinity Chromatography, 1974, author/editor, 1984; contbr. articles to profl. jours. Recipient Merseyside Enterprise award City of Liverpool, 1980; finalist Prince of Wales award, 1982. Fellow Royal Soc. Chemistry. Avocations: collecting and rallying classic sports cars, jazz.

DEAN, ROBERT BERRIDGE, editor; b. San Francisco, Feb. 20, 1913; arrived in Denmark, 1977; s. Thomas Berridge and Margaret Beatrice (Postlethwaite) D.; m. Kirsten M. Jalmer, Apr. 4, 1939 (dec. 1975); children: Eric, Karen, Peter, Carl; m. Ebba Lund, June 8, 1978 (dec. 1999). BA, U. Calif., Berkeley, 1935; PhD, Cambridge (Eng.) U., 1938. Rsch. assoc. Cambridge (Eng.) U., 1938-39; rsch. asst. physiology U. Rochester, N.Y., 1939-40; teaching asst. physiology U. Minn., Mpls., 1940-41; rsch. assoc. chemistry Stanford (Calif.) U., 1941-44; asst. prof. chemistry U. Hawaii, Honolulu, 1944-47, U. Oreg., Eugene, 1947-52; mgr. sales devel. lab. Borden

Chem. Co., Bainbridge, N.Y., 1952-64; chief ultimate disposal EPA, Cin., 1964-75; jour. editor Waste Mgmt. & Rsch., Copenhagen, 1982—; cons. WHO, Copenhagen, 1975-85. Author: Modern Colloids, 1948; co-author: Water Reuse, 1981; editor: Incineration of Mcpl. Waste, 1988. Recipient Food Packaging Regulations Recognition award Adhesive Mfrs. Assn., 1960. Mem. AAAS. Avocations: mountain climbing, bicycling, gardening, woodworking, fixing things. Home: Dronningensgade 9, DK-1420 Copenhagen Denmark Office: WMR Editorial Office, Overgaden Oven Vandet 48E, DK-1415 Copenhagen K, Denmark

DEAN, ROBERT BRUCE, architect; b. Brockton, Mass., Jan. 15, 1949; s. Robert George and Marjorie Gertrude (O'Donnell) D.; m. Mary Hood Hoskinson, June 18, 1977; children: Robert Maxwell, Anne, Claire. BA, U. Pa., 1971; MArch, Columbia U., 1976. Registered architect, N.Y., Conn. Staff architect Skidmore, Owings & Merrill, Architects, N.Y.C., 1976-77; job capt. Stephen Jacobs & Assn., N.Y.C., 1977-78; staff architect Johnson-Burgee Architects, N.Y.C., 1978-79; pvt. practice architecture N.Y.C. and Syracuse, 1979-85; project architect Robert A.M. Stern Architects, N.Y.C., 1985-86; pres. Dean Design, Inc., New Canaan, Conn., 1986—; adj. assoc. prof. Columbia U., N.Y.C., 1978-83; asst. prof. Syracuse U., 1980-84. Contbr. articles to profl. jours. Bd. dirs. Redding Hist. Soc.; mem. Planning Commn. Town of Redding, Dem. Town com. Grantee Syracuse U., 1982, grantee Nat. Endowment Arts, 1983-84; William Kinne Fellow, 1976. Mem. AIA, Conn. Soc. Architects. Democrat. Congregationalist. Avocations: American cultural and commercial history. Office: Dean Design Inc 111 Cherry St New Canaan CT 06840-5530

DEAN, THOMAS JOSEPH, management educator; b. Allentown, Pa., Dec. 24, 1960; s. Theodore E. and Marie D.; m. Amanda Jane Brown, May 23, 1998. BS in Environ. Resource Mgmt., Penn. State U., 1982; MBA, Okla. State U., Stillwater, 1987; PhD in Strategic Mgmt., U. Colo., Boulder, 1992. Chemist Nat. Inst. Petroleum and Energy Rsch., Bartlesville, Okla., 1983-87; assoc. prof. U. Colo., Boulder, 1999—; Lundquist vis. prof. entrepreneurship U. Oreg., Eugene, 1997; assoc. prof. mgmt. U. Tenn., Knoxville, 1991-99. Author: (book) New Venture Formations in U.S. Manfacturing: The Role of Industry; contbr. articles to profl. jours. Recipient Best article award, Entrepreneurship Theory and Practice, 1992. Mem. Acad. Mgmt. (entrepreneurship divsn. program chair, dissertation award, 1993). Avocations: skiing, mountain biking. E-mail: deantj@colorado.edu.

DEAN, VIRGINIA AGEE, principal; b. Duff, Tenn., Oct. 15, 1945; d. Jack Harris and Edna Virginia Agee; m. Herman Ronald Dean, July 10, 1965; children: Virginia Renée, Ronald Craig. BEdin Elem. Edn., Lander Coll., 1967; MEd, Clemson U., 1974. 7th grade reading and maths. tchr. Ellen Woodside Elem. Sch., Pelzer, S.C., asst. prin.; head of guidance dept. Beck Mid. Sch., Greenville, S.C.; prin. Blythe Elem. Sch., Greenville, S.C., Fork Shoals Elem. Sch., Pelzer, S.C., Oakview Elem. Sch., Simpsonville, S.C.; curriculum cons. Greenville Sch. Dist., S.C.; proprietor, mgr. Basquettes, Inc., Greenville, S.C., cons., 1989, 90; spkr., cons. SCORE, Greenville, 1989, 90; mem. supt. adv. bd. Sch. Dist. Greenville County, 1975, 76. Recipient Small Bus. award of yr. Greenville SCORE chpt., 1985. Mem. S.C. DAR (Outstanding jr. mem. 1980). Home: 596 Reedy Fork Rd Piedmont SC 29673-9326 Office: Oakview Elem Sch 515 Godfrey Rd Simpsonville SC 29681-4927

DEANE, CHRISTOPHER PHILIP, company executive, corporate consultant; b. Sydney, NSW, Australia, Apr. 27, 1953; s. Philip Hobson and Diana Burfit (Walker) D.; m. Jan Robin Cropley, Nov. 28, 1975; children: Caroline, Jonathan, Elizabeth. B in Commerce, U. NSW, Sydney, 1974. Chartered acct. Australia. Acct. Peat Marwick, Sydney, 1973-80; group acct. Steetley Industries, Sydney, 1980-81; ptnr. KMG Hungerforas, Perth, Australia, 1981-84; mng. dir. TiOz Corp., Perth, 1984-87, Dilmet Investments Ltd., Sydney, 1985-87; CEO Rola Aust, Sydney, 1987-89; mng. dir. Beacon Engring. Products Pty Ltd., Sydney, 1998—; CEO Snowsay Pty Ltd., 1994—, Culligan Australia, 1999—; dir. Bmamedia Cons. Ltd., E-Club Australia Ltd., Credit Corp. Australia Ltd., Auscript Pty Ltd. Avocations: golf, swimming. Office: Culligan Australia, 35 Tebbutt St, Leichhardt NSW 2040, Australia

DEANE, DEBBE, psychologist, journalist, editor, consultant; b. Coatesville, Pa., July 30, 1950; d. George Edward and Dorothea Alice (Martin) Mays; widowed; children: Theo, Vonisha, Lorise, Voniece. AA in Psychology, Mesa Coll., 1989; BA Psychology, San Diego State U., 1993; MA in Psychology, Nat. U., 1995; postgrad., U.S. Internat. U., 1995—. Announcer Sta. KBPI, Denver, 1969-70, Sta. WKXI, Jackson, Miss., 1970-72; news anchor Sta. WNGE-TV, Nashville, 1973-76; news dir. Sta. KLDR, Denver, 1976-78; host, reporter Sta. KMGH-TV, Denver, 1978-81; news anchor, editor Sta. KHOW, Denver, 1978-79; news & pub. affairs dir. Sta. KLZ, Denver, 1979-80, Sta. KCBQ, San Diego, 1980-82; news anchor Sta. KOGO, San Diego, 1983-84; news anchor, reporter Sta. KCST-TV, San Diego, 1984-87; dir. comm. Omni Corp., San Diego, 1987—; news anchor Sta. KFI, L.A., 1990-91; sr. psychiat. therapist Behavioral Health Group, San Diego, 1993—; media liaison United Negro Coll. Fund, San Diego, 1990-92; dir. comm. United Chs. of Christ, San Diego, 1989-92; cons. San Diego Assn. Black Journalists, 1985-92, San Diego Coalition Black Journalists, 1985-92; cons. in field. Campaign fin. analyst San Diego County Registrar of Voters, San Diego, 1990; cons. San Diego County Office Disaster Preparedness, 1990-91, Nu Way Youth Ctr. & Neighborhood House, Inc., San Diego, 1991-92; counselor Project STARRT, San Diego, 1991-92; cons. United Way Home Start, Inc. Family Self-Sufficiency Program, 1996—; cons. and program coord. San Diego Healthy Start, Inc., 1997—, Samuel L. Gompers Secondary Inst. Math., Sci. & computer Tech., 1997—. Recipient San Diego Black Achievement award Urban League, 1989, Best News Show & Spot News award San Diego Press Club, 1985, Golden Mike award So. Calif. Broadcast Assn., L.A., 1986; named one of Top 25 Businesswomen Essence Mag., 1978, Outstanding Humanitarian Worldvision, 1993, Outstanding Humanities Alumna Mesa Coll., 1993, Woman of the Year. Mem. AFTRA, APA, Am. Women in Radio & TV, Women in Comm., Black Students Sci. Orgn. (sec. 1989-91), Africana Psychol. Soc. (media coord. 1990-92), Psi Chi. Democrat. Avocations: photography, fashion design, travel, volunteering, skiing. Home: 3545 Valley Rd Apt 1 Bonita CA 91902-4164

DEANE, LELAND MARC, plastic surgeon; b. N.Y.C., June 18, 1952; s. Maurice Allen and Barbara Elaine (Ushkow) D.; m. Danielle Anne Sheft, Nov. 21, 1993. BS, Union Coll., 1974; MD, SUNY, Bklyn., 1978. Diplomate Am. Bd. Surgery, Am. Bd. Plastic Surgery. Intern, then resident in surgery New Eng. Med. Ctr., 1978-83; resident in plastic surgery Ea. Va. Grad. Sch. Medicine, 1983-85; fellow in hand surgery Jefferson Med. Coll., 1986; pvt. practice L.I. Plastic Surg. Group P.C., Garden City, N.Y., 1986—; mem. surg. rev. com. Winthrop U. Hosp., Mineola, N.Y., 1986—, mem. resident edn. com., 1992—; instr. surgery Cornell Med. Coll., 1989—. Contbr. articles to profl. jours. Advisor Mothers of Super Twins, L.I., 1995—. Grantee So. Med. Assn., 1984. Fellow ACS, Am. Acad. Pediat.; mem. Am. Soc. Plastic and Reconstructive Surgeons, Northea. Soc. Plastic Surgeons, N.Y. Regional Soc. Plastic and Reconstructive Surgery, Seawanhaka Corinthian Yacht Club, N.Y. Yacht Club. Office: LI Plastic Surg Group PC 999 Franklin Ave Garden City NY 11530-2913

DEANE, RICHARD HUNTER, JR., federal judge; b. Oct. 18, 1952. BA, U. Ga., 1974, JD, 1977; LLM, U. Mich., 1979. Bar: Ga. 1977. Asst. U.S. atty. No. Dist. Ga., 1980-88; chief gen. crimes sect. U.S. Attys. Office, 1988-91, chief criminal divsn., 1991-94; magistrate judge U.S. Dist. Ct. (no. dist.) Ga., Atlanta, 1994-98; U.S. atty. No. Dist. Ga., Atlanta, 1998—. Office: 1800 US Courthouse 75 Spring St SW Atlanta GA 30303-3309

DEANE, SIMON CHARLES STUART, magazine editor; b. Edinburgh, Scotland, Dec. 4, 1962; s. Leon David and Anne Muriel (Hunter) D. BA, Stirling (Scotland) U., 1984; Diploma in Pub., London Sch. Printing, 1985. Asst. editor U.K. Holiday Guide, London, 1985-89; mng. editor, dir. The Travel & Leisure Mag., London, 1989—. Editor: Choice Villas and Apartments, Choice Museums and Attractions, Holiday!; past asst. editor Family Holidays in Britain, Holidays in Britain, Holiday Haunts, Go to Britain, others. Home: 11 St Stephens Rd, London E3 5JD, England Office: Travel & Leisure Mags Ltd, 114 Cranbrook Rd, Ilford IG1 4LZ, England

DEANE, SIR WILLIAM PATRICK, governor-general of Commonwealth of Australia; b. Jan. 4, 1931. Bar: N.S.W. 1957, Q.C. 1966. Judge Supreme Ct. N.S.W., 1977, Fed. Ct. Australia, 1977-82; pres. Australian Trade Practices Tribunal, 1977-82; Justice High Ct. Australia, 1982-95; Gov. Gen. Commonwealth of Australia, 1996—. Decorated Companion Order of Australia, Knight Brit. Empire. Office: Govt House, Canberra ACT 2600, Australia

DE ANGELIS, FRANCESCO, chemistry educator, consultant; b. Bari, Puglia, Italy, Oct. 19, 1949; s. Marsilio and Italia (Cáfaro) De A. Doctorate, U. Rome, 1974. Cert. chemist. Postdoctoral rschr. U. Rome, 1977-81, rschr., 1981-87; prof. organic chemistry U. L'Aquila, Italy, 1987—; vis. prof. U. Cambridge, Eng., 1981. Contbr. numerous articles to sci. jours. Mem. Royal Soc. Chemistry, Am. Chem. Soc., Italian Soc. Mass Spectrometry. Roman Catholic. Avocations: philately, photography, classical music. Office: U L'Aquila Dept Chemistry, COPPITO, I-67010 L'Aquila Abruzzi, Italy

DEANGELIS, PAULA MARY, cell biologist, researcher; b. North Tarrytown, N.Y., Dec. 3, 1956; arrived in Norway, 1989; d. Ralph F. and Anne E. (Fennell) DeA.; m. Trond Stokke, May 3, 1991. BS in Biology, Fordham U., 1978; MS in Cell Biology, NYU, 1981; PhD, U. Oslo, 1999. Rsch. technician Pub. Health Rsch. Inst., N.Y.C., 1979-82; rsch. asst. Meml. Sloan-Kettering, N.Y.C., 1982-89; cell biologist Nat. Hosp., Oslo, 1990—. Mem. Am. Assn. for Cancer Rsch., Internat. Soc. for Analytical Cytology, European Study Group for Cell Proliferation. Avocations: writing, photography, cooking, biking. Office: Rikshospitalet, Inst for Patologi, 0027 Oslo Norway

DEANS, PATRICIA HERRMANN, investment banker; b. Monmouth Beach, N.J., Oct. 28, 1956; d. Joseph Charles and Caroline (Hauck) Herrmann; m. Jamie Robertson Deans, Feb. 29, 1981 (div. Mar. 1992). BA, U. Mass., Boston, 1980; M Internat Fin, Rutgers U., 1984. Account mgr., media & telecomm. Bank Montreal, N.Y.C., 1984-86; v.p. Media corp. fin. Chase Securities, Inc., N.Y.C., 1986—, mng. dir., sr. ptnr. in global syndicated fin., 1996—, head media and telecom. Mem. Lawrence Beach Club, Phi Beta Kappa. Roman Catholic. Avocations: skiing, running, traveling, violin. Office: Chase Securities Inc 5th Fl 270 Park Ave Fl 5 New York NY 10017-2014 Address: 771 W End Ave Apt 4D New York NY 10025-5537 also: 57 Shepard Rd Norfolk CT 06058-1126

DEAR, RONALD BRUCE, social work educator; b. Phila., Sept. 23, 1933; s. John David and Margaret (McDade) D.; 1 child, Bruce. BA, Bucknell U., 1955; honors cert., U. Aberdeen, Scotland, 1955; MSW, U. Pitts., 1957; PhD in Social Work, Columbia U., 1972. Cert. social worker, N.Y., Wash. Chief social worker Mental Hygiene Cons. Svc., Aberdeen Proving Ground, Md., 1958-60; chief Neuropsychiat. Clinic, 7th Inf. Divsn., Korea, 1960-61; residence dir. Horizon House, Inc., Phila., 1961-64; prof. U. Wash., Seattle, 1970—; vis. prof. U. Bergen, Norway, 1984, U. Trondheim, Norway, 1996; faculty lobbyist U. Wash., 1983-85, 88-91, faculty pres., 1993-95; master tchr. Coun. on Social Work Edn., 1991, 93, 94, 97; mem. adv. bd. Internat. Population and Family Assocs., 1994—; bd. dirs. Wash. Future, 1994—. Editor: Poverty in Perspective, 1973; contbr. articles to profl. jours. and encys. Apptd. by gov. to income assistance adv. com., 1987-93, to adv. com. for Dept. S ocial and Health Svcs., 1980-83, Human Svcs. Policy Ctr., 1996—, adv. com. Wash. State Econ. Svcs., 1996—; mem. nat. adv. bd. Educating Students to Influence State Policy and Legislation, 1997—; appeared in centennial program of Columbia U. Sch. of Social Work, 1998. 1st lt. U.S. Army, 1957-61. Mem. NASW (Social Worker of Yr. Wash. chpt. 1981, mem. staff legis. N.Y.C. chpt. 1968-69), Acad. Cert. Social Workers, Coun. on Social Work Edn. Avocations: travel in over 45 countries, photography, hiking. Home: 7328 16th Ave NE Seattle WA 98115-5737 Office: U Wash Sch Social Work 4101 15th Ave NE Seattle WA 98105-6250

DEARBORN, MAUREEN MARKT, speech and language clinician; b. Brockton, Mass., Jan. 19, 1948; d. Francis Joseph and Marjorie Agnes (White) M.; m. James Clement Bovin, Nov. 6, 1970 (div. June 1973); m. David C. Dearborn, Jan. 14, 1989. BA in Speech Pathology and Audiology, U. Mass., 1970; MA in Ednl. Psychology, Am. Internat. Coll., Springfield, Mass. Speech and lang. clinician Holyoke (Mass.) Pub. Schs., 1970—. Chmn. Holyoke Cancer Crusade, 1985; voter registration chmn. Holyoke Dem. Com., 1987; chmn. deaconesses 2d Congl. Ch. Holyoke. Mem. Hampden County Tchrs. Assn. (pres. 1981, 87, sec. 1982, v.p. 1984-86, treas. 1988—), Holyoke Tchrs. Assn. (treas. 1989, DAR historian), Am. Speech, Hearing and Langs. Assn. (continuing edn. adv. bd. 1988-91, congl. action contact continuing edn. adv. bd. 1988-90), Mass. Tchrs. Assn., Mass. Speech, Hearing and Langs. Assn., New England Hist. and Geneal. Soc., Friends of the Lib. Coun. (treas. 1992—), Mass. Genealogical Soc., Assn. for Gravestone Studies, DAR (historian Eunice Day 1984), Wrentham Hist Soc., Dorchester Hist. Soc. Avocations: bicycling, antiques, genealogy, aerobics. Home: 257 W Franklin St Holyoke MA 01040-2210 Office: Holyoke Pub Schs 57 Suffolk St Holyoke MA 01040-5015

DEARNLEY, CHRISTOPHER HUGH, organist, choral director; b. Wolverhampton, Staff., U.K., Feb. 11, 1930; s. Charles and Gertrude (Smith) D.; m. Bridget Wateridge, Apr. 1, 1957; children: Mark, Rachel, Benjamin, Daniel. MA, DMus, Worcester Coll., Oxford, Eng., 1952; D Fine Arts, Westminster Coll., 1989. Organist, master of the choristers Salisbury Cathedral, U.K., 1957-68; organist, dir. of music St. Paul's Cathedral, London, 1968-90; dir. of music Christ Ch. St. Laurence, Sydney, Australia, 1990-91; organist St. David's Cathedral, Hobart, Australia, 1991; dir. of music Trinity Coll./U. of Melbourne, Australia, 1992-93; MMus St. George's Cathedral, Perth, Australia, 1993-94; organist, master of the choristers St. Andrew's Cathedral, Sydney, Australia, 1995; organist Christ Ch. Cathedral, Newcastle, Australia, 1996; chmn., v.p. Friends of Cathedral Music, U.K., 1970—; chmn., pres. The Harwich Festival, U.K., 1981—; hon. gov. Corp. of the Sons of the Clergy, U.K., 1989—; patron Organ Hist. Trust of Australia, 1990—. Editor: The Treasury of English Church Music, Vol. 3, 1965; author: English Church Music 1650-1750, 1970; performer (recordings) numerous organ and choral discs, 1963—. Doctor of Music, Archbishop of Canterbury, Lambeth, 1987, Lt. of the Royal Victorian Order, HM Queen Elizabeth II, Buckingham Palace, 1990. Avocations: sketching, gardening, bush walking. Home: PO Box 102, Wilberforce NSW 2756, Australia Office: Challacombe, Lower Marine Parade, Dovercourt Essex C012 3SR, England

DE ARRUDA CAMPOS, IVAN PERSIO, chemist, educator, researcher; b. São Paulo, Brazil, Aug. 20, 1962; s. Haroldo Eurico Browne de and Carmen (de Paula Arruda) Campos. BS, U. São Paulo, Brazil, 1986, PhD, 1992. Prof. U. Paulista, São Paulo, 1996—. Contbr. articles to profl. jours. Postdoctoral fellow U. São Paulo, 1992-95. Mem. AAAS, IUPAC, Brazilian Chem. Soc., Brazilian Assn. NMR Users, N.Y. Acad. Scis. Avocation: Roman and contemporary history. Office: Inst Quimica USP B12sup, Av Prof Lineu Prestes 748, 05508900 São Paulo Brazil

DEAUX, GEORGE RICHARD, language educator; b. Springfield, Mass., Feb. 23, 1931; s. Richard Edward and Elizabeth (Bessor) D.; m. Mieko Kitazawa, Nov. 7, 1985; children: Katherine, Christopher. BA, U. Minn., 1957; MA, Ind. U., 1961. Instr. English U. S.W. La., Lafayette, 1961-63; prof. English, dean Temple U., Phila., Tokyo, 1968-91; prof. Keio U., Tokyo, 1991-96, Musashi Inst. Tech., Tokyo, 1996—. Author: The Humanization of Eddie Clement, 1964, Exit, 1966, Superworm, 1968, The Black Death 1347, 1970; co-author: Activating College English, 1994. Capt. USMC, 1950-61. Fellow Woodrow Wilson Found., 1957; recipient Disting. Tchr. award Tianjin Normal U., 1982. Mem. Modern Lang. Assn., Japan Assn. Coll. English Tchrs. Avocations: motorcycle touring, boxing. Office: Musashi Inst Tech, Setagaya-ku Tokyo 158, Japan

DEAVER, PETE EUGENE, civil and aeronautical engineer; b. Ft. Worth, Mar. 8, 1936; s. Elmer Jack and Mattie Alline (Kelley) D.; m. Birdie Jo Foster, Apr. 30, 1954; children: Pete Eugene, Jr., Stephen Lewis, Mickey Jo, Robert. BS in Civil Engring., Cramwell Inst., 1957, BS in Geology, 1964; student, U. Tex., Arlington, 1954-61; MS in Engring. Mgmt., Pacific Western U., 1992, PhD in Mgmt., 1994. Aircraft engr. Gen. Dynamics Corp., Ft. Worth, 1957-61; project engr. ejection seat studies Kirk Engring. Co., Bethpage, N.Y., 1961-64; sr. engr. Ling Tempco Vought Aeros., Dallas, 1964-65; stress engr. Boeing Aircraft Co., Seattle, 1965-66; sr. aero. engr. Gen. Dynamics Corp., Albuquerque, 1966-74; owner, operator Deaver Engring. Co., Midland, Tex., 1974-84; cons. constrn. and petroleum industry. Served with USNR, 1952-54. Registered profl. engr., N.Mex., Tex. Mem. NSPE, Nat. Resource Conservation Commn., Soc. Exploration Geophysicists, Tex. Soc. Profl. Engrs., Masons (32 deg.). Baptist. Author: Basic Stress Analysis for Engineers and Draftsmen, 1967; Drilling Manual for Rotary Drilling, 1981, Rock Bit Design and Evaluation, 1992, Factors Affecting Rock Bit Penetration Rate, 1992, Solids Control in Drilling Muds, 1992, Drilling Management, 1994. Home: 2200 Sharpshire Ln Arlington TX 76014-3526

DE BACKER, CHRISTOPHE, securities company executive; b. Neuilly sur Seine, France, Nov. 1, 1962; s. Claude and Nicole (Barbier) de B.; m. Sadrine Currimjee, Sept. 12, 1997. Lic. in econs., U. Paris II, 1983; grad., Higher Inst. Mgmt., 1986. Salesman investment funds (Nat. Svc.) BIAO., Abidjan, 1987-88; salesman French equities ODDO, Paris, 1988-90; head French sales CCF Securities, Paris, 1991-94, head sales, 1991-95, mng. dir., 1995-98, chmn., CEO, 1998—. Home: 32 Ave Charles Floquet, 75007 Paris France Office: CCF Securities, 103 Ave des Champs Elysees, 75008 Paris France

DEBAKEY, LOIS, science communications educator, writer, editor; b. Lake Charles, La.; d. S. M. and Raheeja (Zorba) DeBakey. BA in Math., Tulane U., MA in Lit. and Linguistics, 1959, PhD in Lit. and Linguistics, 1963. Asst. prof. English Tulane U., 1963-64; asst. prof. sci. communication Tulane U. Med. Sch., 1963-65, assoc. prof. sci. communication, 1965-67, prof. sci. comm., 1967-68, lectr., 1968-80, adj. prof., 1981-92; prof. sci. comm. Baylor Coll. Medicine, Houston, 1968—; mem. biomed. libr. rev. com. Nat. Libr. Medicine, Bethesda, Md., 1973-77, bd. regents, 1981-86, cons., 1986—, co-chmn. permanent paper task force, 1987—, lit. selection tech. rev. com., 1988-93, chmn., 1992-93, outreach planning panel, 1988-89; dir. courses in med. comm. ACS and other orgns.; bd. trustees DeBakey Med. Found.; exec. coun. Commn. on Colls. So. Assn. Colls. and Schs., 1975-80; mem. nat. adv. coun. U. Soc. Calif. Ctr. Continuing Med. Edn., 1981, steering com. Plain English Forum, 1984, founding bd. dirs. Friends Nat. Libr. Medicine, 1985—, chmn. med. media award of excellence com. FNLM, 1992—, adv. com. Soc. for Preservation English Lang. Literature, 1986, Nat. Adv. Bd. John Muir Med. Film Festival, 1990-92, The Internat. Health and Med. Film Festival, Acad. of Judges, 1992-93; mem. adv. coun. U. Tex. at Austin Sch. Nursing Found., 1993—; cons. legal writing com. cons. ABA, 1983—; former cons. Nat. Assn. Std. Med. Vocabulary; pioneered instruction in sci. communication in meds. schs. Sr. author: The Scientific Journal: Editorial Policies and Practices, 1976; co-author: Medicine: Preserving the Passion, 1987; mem editorial bd.: Tulane Studies in English, 1966-68, Cardiovascular Research Center Bull., 1971-83, Health Communications and Informatics, 1975-80, Forum on Medicine, 1977-80, Grants Mag, 1978-81, Internat. Jour. Cardiology, 1981-86, Excerpta Medica's Core Jours. in Cardiology, 1981—, Health Comm. and Biopsychosocial Health, 1981-82, Internat. Angiology, 1985—, Jour. AMA, 1988—; mem. usage panel: Am. Heritage Dictionary, 1980—; cons. Webster's Medical Desk Dictionary, 1986, editl. adv. Encyclopedia Britannica; contbr. articles on biomed. communication and sci. writing, literacy, also other subjects to profl. jours., books, encys., and pub. press. Active Found. for Advanced Edn. in Sci., 1977—; trustee DeBakey Med. Found., 1995—. Recipient Disting. Svc. award Am. Med. Writers Assn., 1970, Bausch & Lomb Sci. award, 1st John P. McGovern award Med. Libr. Assn., 1983, Outstanding Alumna award Newcomb Coll., 1994; fellow Am. Coll. Med. Informatics, 1990, Royal Soc. for Encouragement of Arts Mfrs. and Commerce, 1991. Fellow Am. Coll. Med. Informatics; mem. Internat. Soc. Gen. Semantics, Med. Libr. Assn. (hon.), Coun. Biology Editors (dir. 1973-77, chmn. com. on editl. policy 1971-75), Coun. Basic Edn. (spl. com. writing 1977-79), Assn. Tchrs. Tech. Writing, Dictionary Soc. N.Am., Nat. Assn. Sci. Writers, Soc. for Health and Human Values, Com. of Thousand for Better Health Regulations, Golden Key, Phi Beta Kappa. Office: Baylor Coll Medicine 1 Baylor Plz Houston TX 77030-3411

DEBAKEY, MICHAEL ELLIS, cardiovascular surgeon, educator, scientist; b. Lake Charles, La., Sept. 7, 1908; s. Shaker Morris and Raheeja (Zorba) DeB.; m. Diana Cooper, Oct. 15, 1936; children: Michael Maurice, Ernest Ochsner, Barry Edward, Denis Alton; m. Katrin Fehlhaber, July 1975; 1 child, Olga Katerina. BS, Tulane U., 1930, MD, 1932; MD, U. Ottawa, Canada, 1970, Aristotelean U. Thessaloniki, Greece, 1972, U. Istanbul, Turkey, 1987, Karolinska Inst., 1997; MS, Tulane U., 1935, LLD (hon.), 1965; LLD (hon.), Lafayette Coll., 1965, U. Belgrade, Yugoslavia, 1967, McNeese State U., 1972, Southwestern U., 1978; Docteur Honoris Causa, U. Lyon, France, 1961, U. Brussels, 1962, U. Ghent, Belgium, 1964, U. Athens, Greece, 1964, U. Catholique Louvain, Belgium, 1971, Ljubljana U., Yugoslavia, 1976, U. Turin, Italy, 1965; DHC, U. Belgrade, Yugoslavia, 1967; LLD, Lafayette Coll., 1965; MD (hon.), Aristotelean U. of Thessaloniki, Greece, 1972; DSc, Hahnemann Med. Coll., 1973; D honoris causa, U. Buenos Aires, 1982; Docteur honoris causa, U. Louis Pasteur, Paris, 1991, Moscow State U., Russia, 1993, Tex. A&M U., 2000; D Mil. Medicine & Surgery honoris causa, Uniformed Svc. U. Health Scis., 1996; LittD in Medicine (hon.), U. Cin., 1969, Baylor Coll. Medicine, 1996, Siena Coll., 1999; D (hon.), Russian Mil. Med. Acad., 1996; D in Medicine (hon.), Karolinska Inst., 1997; DSc (hon.), Pa. State U., 1998; LHD, U. Tenn., Chattanooga, Quinnipiac Coll., 1989, Centenary Coll., 1993; HHD, Centenary Coll., 1979. Diplomate Nat. Bd. Med. Examiners, Am. Bd. Surgery, Am. Bd. Thoracic Surgery. Intern Charity Hosp., New Orleans, 1932-33, asst. surgery, 1933-35; asst. surgery U. Strasbourg, France, 1935-36, U. Heidelberg, Fed. Republic of Germany, 1936; instr. surgery Tulane U., New Orleans, 1937-40, asst. prof., 1940-46, assoc. prof., 1946-48; prof., chmn. dept. surgery Baylor Coll. Medicine, 1948-93, Disting. svc. prof., 1968—, v.p. med. affairs, 1968-69, CEO, 1968-69, pres., 1969-79, Olga Keith Wiess prof. of surgery, 1981—, chancellor, 1978-96, chancellor emeritus, 1996—; pres. The DeBakey Med. Found., 1961—; dir. Nat. Heart Blood Vessel Rsch. Demonstration Ctr. Baylor Coll. Medicine, 1975-85; dir. DeBakey Heart Ctr., Baylor Coll. Medicine, 1985—; surgeon-in-chief Ben Taub Gen. Hosp., 1963-93; sr. attending surgeon Meth. Hosp.; clin. prof. surgery U. Tex. Dental Br.; cons. surgery VA Hosp., U. Tex. M.D. Anderson Cancer Ctr., St. Luke's Hosp., Tex. Children's Hosp., Tex. Inst. Rehab. and Rsch. Brooke Gen. Hosp., Brooke Army Med. Ctr., Houston, Tex., Walter Reed Army Hosp., Washington, D.C.; mem. med. adv. com. Office Sec. Def., 1948-50, Ams. for Substance Abuse Prevention, 1984; mem. med. adv. bd. Internat. Brotherhood Teamsters, 1985—; mem. task force med. svcs. Hoover Commn., 1949; founding bd. dirs.Friends of Nat. Libr. of Medicine, 1985—, mem. bd. regents Nat. Libr. Medicine, 1956-60, 94-98, chmn., 1959, 98; past mem. nat. adv. heart coun. NIH; mem. Nat. Adv. Health Coun., 1961-65, Nat. Adv. Coun. Regional Med. Programs, 1965—, Nat. Adv. Gen. Med. Scis. Coun., 1965, Program Planning Com., Com. Tng., Nat. Heart Inst., 1961—; mem. civilian health and med. adv. coun. Office Asst. Sec. Def.; chmn. Pres.'s Commn. Heart Disease, Cancer and Stroke, 1964; mem. adv. coun. Nat. Heart Lung and Blood Inst., 1982-87; mem. Tex. Sci. and Tech. Coun., 1984-86; chmn. Found. Biomed. Rsch., 1988—, Physicians for Health in the Middle East, 1991—; trustee, v.p. Baylor Med. Found.; chmn., med. adv. bd. The DeBakey Heart Ctr. Health Letter; adv. bd. Family Cir.; internat. sci. coun. Fondation Cardiologique Princesse Liliane; adv. Dag Hammarskjöld Med. Sci. Prize Com.; mem. bd. visitors Uniformed Svcs. U. Health Scis., U. Calif.-Davis Sch. Medicine; mem. Baylor Coll. Med. Bd. Trustees, 1996; foreign adj. prof. Karolinska Inst., 1997. Author: (with Robert A. Kilduffe) Blood Transfusion, 1942; (with Gilbert W. Beebe) Battle Casualties, 1952; (with Alton Ochsner) Textbook of Minor Surgery, 1955; (with T. Whayne) Cold Injury, Ground Type, 1958, A Surgeon's Visit to China, 1974, The Living Heart, 1977, The Living Heart Diet, 1985, The Living Heart Brand Name Shopper's Guide, 1992, The Living Heart Guide to Eating Out, 1993, The New Living Heart Diet, 1996, The New Living Heart, 1997; editor: Yearbook of Surgery, 1958-70; chmn. adv. editl. bd. Medical History of World War II; founding editor Jour. Vascular Surgery, 1984-88; contbr. over 1500 articles to med. jours. Mem. Tex. Constl. Revision Commn., 1973. Col. Office Surgeon Gen., AUS, 1942-46; now Col. Res.; cons. to Surgeon Gen., 1946—; disting. mem. U.S. Army Med. Dept. Rgt., 1989. Decorated Legion of Merit, 1945, Independence of Jordan medal 1st Class, Merit order of Republic 1st Class Egypt, comdr. Cross of Merit Pro Utilitate Hominum Sovereign Order Knights of Hosp. of St. John of Jerusalem in Denmark; recipient Rudolph Matas award, 1954, Internat. Soc. Surgery Disting. Svc. award, 1958, Modern Medicine award, 1957, Leriche award Internat. Soc. Surgery, 1959, Great medallion U. Ghent, 1961, Grand Cross, Order Leopold, Belgium, 1962, Albert Lasker award for clin. research, 1963, Order of Merit Chile, 1964, St. Vincent prize med. scis. U. Turin, 1965,

Orden del Libertador Gen. San Martin, Argentina, 1965, Centennial medal Albert Einstein Med. Ctr., 1966, Gold Scalpel award Internat. Cardiology Found., 1966, Eleanor Roosevelt Humanities award, 1969, Meritorious Civilian Service medal Office Sec. Def., 1970, USSR Acad. Sci. 50th Anniversary Jubilee medal, 1973, Britannica Achievement in Life award, 1979, Medal of Freedom with Distinction Presdl. award, 1969, Disting. Svc. award Internat. Soc. Atherosclerosis, 1979, Centennial award ASME, 1980, Marian Health Care award St. Mary's U., 1981, Inst. Med. Nat. Acad. Sci., 1981, Soc. Biomaterials award for clin. rsch. in biomaterials Clemson U. and Soc. Biomaterials, 1983, Humana Heart Inst. award, 1985, Theodore E. Cummings award, 1987, Nat. Med. of Sci. award, 1987, First Issue Michael DeBakey medal ASME, 1989, Inaugural award Scripps Clinic and Rsch. Found., 1989, DeBakey-Bard Chair in Surgery, Baylor Coll. of Medicine, 1990, Disting. Svc. award Am. Legion, 1990, Lifetime Achievement award Found. for Biomed. Rsch., 1991, Jacobs award Am. Task Force for Lebanon, 1991, Maxwell Finland award Nat. Found. for Infectious Diseases, 1992, Lifetime Achievement award Acad. Med. Films, 1992, Order of Independence First Class medal United Arab Emirates, 1992, Academy of Athens award, 1992, Cmdrs. Cross Order of Merit (Fed. Germany), 1992, Pres. Disting. Svc. award Baylor Coll. Medicine, 1992, Gibbon award Am. Soc. Extracorporeal Tech., 1993, named in his honor Michael E. DeBakey Libr. Svc. Outreach award Friends of the Nat. Libr. Medicine, 1993, Alton Ochsner award relating smoking to health, 1993, Thomas Jefferson award AIA, 1993, Ellis Island Medal of Honor, 1993, Lifetime Achievement award Am. Heart Assn., 1994, Caring Spirit award Inst. Religion Tex. Med. Ctr., 1994, Samaritan Living Legend award Women's Internat. Ctr., 1994, Giovanni Lorenzini Med. Fedn. prize for basic biomed. rsch., 1994, Disting. Svc. award Tex. Soc. Biomedical Rsch., 1994, Heart Saver award Save A Heart Found., Cedars-Sinai Med. Ctr., 1994, Honor award United Meth. Assn. Health & Welfare Ministries, 1995, Michael E. DeBakey chair in Pharm. Baylor Coll. Med., 1995, Nat. Order of Vasco Nunez de Balboa (Panama), 1995, Health Care Hall of Fame Modern Healthcare, 1996, Sci. Rschr. of XX Century award govt. of Argentine Republic, 1996, Am. Inst. Aeronautics and Astronautics Pub. Svc. award, 1997, Boris Petrovsky Internat. Surgeons award, Inaugural honor for disting. physicians and scientists Med. Ctr. La. Found., 1997, Premio Giuseppe Corradi award, Bevagna, Italy, 1997, Rotary Nat. award, 1997, Tulane Coll. Sequicentennial medal, 1997, Fire of Genius award So. Utah U., 1997, Commonwealth Trust award for invention and sci., 1997; Michael E. DeBakey Heart Inst. Wis. named in his honor Kenosha Hosp. and Med. Ctr., 1992; Michael E. DeBakey, M.D. award for Excellence in Visual Edn. named in his honor, 1993; DeBakey Scholar in Cardiovasc. Scis. MD-PhD Program named in his honor Baylor Coll. Medicine, 1994; Michael E. DeBakey, MD Excellence in Rsch. award named in his honor Baylor Coll. Medicine, 1994, dedication of Northwestern U. Med. Sch. book, 1995, Michael E. DeBakey H.S. Health Professions named in his honor, 1996; named One of 200 Most Influential People in Telemedicine Telemedicine 200 Ctr. Pub. Svc. Comm., 1996, One of Top Ten Heroes, Millenium Soc., 1996, First Laureate of Boris Petrovsky Gold medal Russian Mil. Med. Acad., 1997, Rotary NASA Space Tech. Utilization Awd., 1997, Amer. Med. Assn., Leader in Med., 1997, Common Wealth Trust Awd. in Sci. and Invention, 1997, Hon. Doctor of the Russian Military Med. Acad., 1996, Southern Utah Univ. Fire of Genius Awd., Premio Giseuppe Corradi Awd. for Surg. and Scientific Rsch., 1997, Karolinska Inst. Hon. Doctor of Med. and Foreign Adj. Prof., 1997, Del Webb Corps. Legends of Tex. Bridge Honoree, 1997, Tulane Coll. Sesquicentennial Medal, 1997, Med. Ctr. of Louisiana Foundations inaugural Spirit of Charity Awd., 1998, Internat. Coll. of Angiology Hon. Fellowship and Lifetime Achievement Awd., 1998, Barney Clark award Artificial Heart Lab. and Medforte Rsch. Found. U. Utah, 1998, Legends of Cardiology award Assn. Black Cardiologists, 1998, John P. McGovern Lecture award Cosmos Club Found., 1998, Lifetime Achievement award Rsch. Am., 1998, Am. Legends award Nat. Ethnic Coalition Orgns. Found., Inc., 1998, Great Cross of Order St. James and Sword Govt. Portugal, 1998, Michael E. DeBakey Presdl. award named in his honor, 1998, Mus. Health and Med. Sci. Lifetime Membership award, 1999, Project ORBIS Internat. award, 1999, Soc. Vascular Surgery Disting. Svc. award, 1999, Am. Assn. Thoracic Surgery Sci. Achievement award, Am. Coll. Cardiology Puerto Rico chpt. Disting. Svc. award inaugural issues, 1999,Am. Inst. Archs. inaugural Michael E. DeBakey award contbns. to Am.'s Health, 1999, Children Uniting Nations inaugural Global Peace and Tolerance Lifetime Achievement award, 1999, John P. McGovern Compleat Physician award Houston Acad. Medicine and John P. McGovern, 1999, Am. Coll. Cardiology Presdl. citation, 2000, Inaugural Virtual Mentor award Am. Med. Assn., 2000, Jonathan Rhoads medal Am. Philos. Soc., 2000, Bicentennial Living Legends award Libr. Congress, 2000, Outstanding Alumnus award Tulane Med. Alumni Assn. Lifetime Achievement, 2000; Michael E. DeBakey Dept. Surgery Baylor Coll. Medicine named in his honor, 1999, Michael E. DeBakey Heart Inst. Kansas Hays Med. Ctr., 1999, Michael E. DeBakey Internat. Surg. Chair Uniformed Svcs. U. Health Scis., 2000, Michael E. DeBakey Isnt. Comparative Cardiovasc. Sci. and Biomedical DevicesTex. A&M U., 2000; inductee Sci. in Tex. Hall Fame, 2000. Fellow ACS (Ann. award Southwestern Pa. chpt. 1973), Inst. of Medicine Chgo. (hon.), Royal Coll. Physicians and Surgeons of U.S. (hon., disting. fellow 1992), Am. Inst. Med. and Biol. Engring. (founding fellow 1993), Biomaterials Sci. and Engr., Soc. Biomaterials, Am. Coll. Cardiology (hon.), Am. Coll. Health Care Execs. (hon.); mem. AAAS, Royal Soc. Medicine, Halsted Soc., Am. Heart Assn., So. Soc. Clin. Rsch., Southwestern Surg. Congress (pres. 1952), Soc. Vascular Surgery (pres. 1954), Soc. Vascular Surg. Lifeline Found. (pres. 1989), AMA (Disting. Svc. award 1959, Hektoen Gold medal 1954, 70), Am. Surg. Assn. (Disting. Svc. award 1981, pres. 1989), So. Surg. Assn. (pres. 1989-90, chmn. coun. 1995—), Western Surg. Assn., Am. Assn. Thoracic Surgery (pres. 1959), Internat. Cardiovascular Soc. (pres. 1958, pres. N.Am. chpt. 1964), Assn. Internat. Vascular Surgeons (pres. 1983), Mex. Acad. Surgery (hon.), Soc. Clin. Surgery, Nat. Acads. Practice Medicine, Internat. Coll. Angiology (hon. fellow), Soc. Univ. Surgeons, Internat. Soc. Surgery, Soc. Exptl. Bi.

DEBAKEY, SELMA, science communications educator, writer, editor, lecturer; b. Lake Charles, La.. BA, Newcomb Coll., Tulane U., New Orleans, postgrad. Dir. dept. med. communication Ochsner Clinic and Alton Ochsner Med. Found., New Orleans, 1942-68; prof. sci. communication Baylor Coll. Medicine, Houston, 1968—; editor Cardiovascular Research Ctr. Bull., 1970-84; mem. panel judges Internat. Health and Med. Film Festival, 1992. Author: (with A. Segaloff and K. Meyer) Current Concepts in Breast Cancer, 1967; past editor Ochsner Clinic Reports, Selected Writings from the Ochsner Clinic; contbr. numerous articles to sci. jours., chpts. to books. Named to Tex. Hall of Fame. Mem. AAAS, Soc. Tech. Communication, Assn. Tchrs. Tech. Writing, Am. Med. Writers Assn. (past bd. dirs.; publ., nominating, fellowship, constn., bylaws, awards, and edn. coms.), Council Biol. Editors (past mem. trn. in sci. writing com.), Soc. Health and Human Values, Modern Med. Monograph Awards Com., Nat. Assn. Standard Med. Vocabulary (former cons.). Office: Baylor Coll Medicine 1 Baylor Plz Houston TX 77030-3411

DE BARROS CONTI, THIBAUT R, chemical engineer; b. Ottignies, Belgium, Mar. 24, 1975; came to U.S., 1985; s. Gerard Oscar and Irene Maria (Cybulski) DeB.;. BD, Lycee Francais N.Y., N.Y.C., 1993; BSChemE, Carnegie Mellon U., 1997. Process safety engr. Air Products & Chems. Inc., Allentown, Pa., 1997-98, project devel. engr., 1998—. Advisor Lehigh Valley Jr. Achievement, 1998—. Mem. Carnegie Mellon U. Admission Coun.; Bucks County Acad. of Fencing. Avocations: tennis, dancing, skiing, competitive fencing. Office: Air Products & Chemicals Inc 7201 Hamilton Blvd Allentown PA 18195-1526

DE BARY, ETIENNE, artist, journalist; b. St. Avold, Moselle, France, Nov. 20, 1962; s. Jacques and Christiane (De Cazenove) De B.; m. Shayda Keliddarzadeh, Aug. 4, 1990; 1 child, Shad. Ed., Met de Penninghem, Paris, 1980-81, Beaux Arts de Paris, 1981-85. Layout designer, illustrator Femme Pratique, Paris, 1988; layout designer Création, Paris, 1989; art dir., layout designer Condé Nast, Paris, 1989, 92; creator, animator Velodrome a Parisian Cyberkunst halle; speaker, editor Fréquence Protestante, Paris, 1994, 95, 96. Exhibited in group shows 2&2-Le Studio Parisien, 1985, Galerie Brownstone, Paris, 1989, Galerie Basfroi, Paris, 1993, Albert Chanot Cultural Ctr. Clamart, 1994, 95; represented in permanent collection Lucie Weil-Seligmann. Avocations: playing go, roller blading. Home and Studio: 21 Rue Beccaria, 75012 Paris France

DEBBAGE, PAUL LAURENCE, anatomy educator, researcher, consultant; b. Norwich, Eng., Nov. 20, 1949; s. Herbert and Stella Grace (Larkman) D.; m. Ruth Beer, May 10, 1972; children: Katja, Miriam, Roy. BS, Durham (Eng.) U., 1971, MS, 1976; PhD, London U., 1980; Dr. rer. biol. hum. habil., Munich U., 1994; D Habilitation, Innsbruck (Germany) U., 1997. Tech. asst. Max Planck Inst., Tübingen, Germany, 1971-74, Med. Rsch. Coun., Carshalton, Eng., 1974-75; rsch. asst. Univ. Coll., London, 1975-82; sci. asst. Max Planck Rsch. Group, Würzburg, Germany, 1982-85, Georg-August U., Göttingen, Germany, 1985; sci. asst. Ludwig-Maximilians U., Munich, 1986-94, lectr., prof. anatomy, 1994-96; lectr., prof. histology Inst. Histology and Embryology, Leopold Franzens U., Innsbruck, 1996—; prof. Innsbruck U., 1997—. Patentee in field; contbr. articles to profl. jours. Mem. Anatomical Soc. Gt. Britain, Anatomische Gesellschaft, Gesellschaft für Neuropathologie und Neuroanatomie. Avocations: piano, history of ethics. Office: Leopold Franzens U Hist-Emb, Mullerstrasse 59, A-6020 Innsbruck Austria

DEBBANÉ, ANDREA, beverage company executive; b. Can., Aug. 13, 1965; d. Gabriel and E. Debbané; m. bruno Versavel. BA, Concordia U., Montreal; postgrad., Waseda U., Tokyo. Staff Dept. Comm. Can. Fed. Govt, 1986-87, Dentsu, Tokyo, 1990-91; exec. asst. Coca-Cola, Tokyo, 1991-93, mgr., 1993-94, head of pub. rels., 1994-95, v.p., 1995—. Govt. of Japan scholar. Mem. ACCJ, CCCJ, Tokyo Am. Club. Home: 3-14-24 Hiroo Shibuya Ku, Tokyo 150, Japan

DE BELIE, NELE MIETJE, agricultural engineering researcher; b. Sint-Niklaas, Oost-Vlaanderen, Belgium, Aug. 1, 1970; d. Firmin De B. and Simone De Bleeker; m. Koen Cochez, Sept. 12, 1998. Agrl. Engr., R.U.G., Ghent, Belgium, 1993, Aggregaat for tchg., 1994, PhD in Applied Biol. Scis., 1997. Asst. Fund Scientific Rsch. Gent U., Ghent, 1993-97; postdoct. fellow Fund Scientific Rsch. Katholieke U. Leuven (Belgium), 1997—; bd. dirs. Koninklijke Vlaamse Ingenieurs-vereniging, Flanders, Belgium, 1997—; scientific collaborator Faculté Universitaire des Scis. Agronomiques de Gembloux, 1997-99; mem. Sig15 EurAgEng, 1996—. Contbr. more than 40 articles to profl. jours. Office: Lab Agro-machinery & processing, Kard Mercierlaan 92, B 3001 Heverlee Oost-Vlaanderen, Belgium

DE BELLE, JOHN STEVEN COLE, biologist; b. Montreal, Que., Can., Oct. 1, 1957; s. John Charles and Nancy Ruth (Cole) de B. BSc, U. Western Ont., 1979; MSc, York U., Toronto, Can., 1987, PhD, 1991. Postdoctoral rsch. fellow U. Würzburg, Germany, 1991-94; rsch. scientist Max-Planck-Inst. for Biologische Kybernetik, Tübingen, Germany, 1994-97; asst. prof. biology U. Nev., Las Vegas, 1997—. Contbr. articles to profl. jours. Recipient W. Robert Thompson Meml. award Behavior Genetics Assn., 1987; postdoctoral fellowship Natural Scis. and Engring. Rsch. Coun., 1990, Long Term Rsch. fellowship Human Frontier Sci. Program Orgn., 1994; rsch. grantee NSF, 2000. Mem. Genetics Soc. of Am. Avocations: skiing, squash, badminton, tennis, cycling. Office: U Nev-Las Vegas Dept Biol Scis Box 454004 4505 S Maryland Pkwy Las Vegas NV 89154-9900

DEBENEDETTI, CARLO, entrepreneur; b. Turin, Italy, Nov. 14, 1934. Student, Polytech. U., Turin, Italy; PhD (hon.), Wesleyan U., 1986. Chmn., chief exec. officer Gilardini, Turin, Italy, 1972-76; chief exec. officer Fiat, Turin, 1976; vice chmn., chief exec. officer Ing. C. Olivetti and Co., Ivrea, Italy, 1978-83; chmn., chief exec. officer Ing. C. Olivetti and Co., Ivrea, 1983-96; bd. dirs., vice chmn., chief exec. officer Compagnie Industriale Riunite; founderEuromobiliare; chmn., chief exec. officer Confide; chmn. Cerus; chmn. Sogefi; dir. Ctr. Strategic Internat. Studies, Washington; mem. European Ady. Com., N.Y. Stock Exchange; bd. dirs. Valeo, Pirelli, Ed. L'Espresso. Named Cavaliere del Lavoro Republic of Italy, 1983, Officier, Légion d'Honneur Republic of France, 1987. Mem. Royal Swedish Acad. Engring. Scis., Confindustria (v.p. 1983). Office: CIR SpA, Via Ciovassino 1, 20121 Milan Italy*

DE BENEDETTI, ENZO, management consultant; b. Turin, Piedmont, Italy, July 25, 1935; s. Renato and Adriana (Valabrega) De B.; m. Margaret Vernon (div.); children: Anna, Charles, Elizabeth; m. Birte Jørgensen; 1 child, Luca. Degree in mech. engring., Polytech. U., Turin, 1959, D of Engring., 1960; degree in Mktg., Harvard U., 1970. Tech. dir. Perkins, Como, Italy, 1960-72; sr. tech. dir. Massey Ferguson, Rome, Italy, 1972-79; gen. mgr. Massey Ferguson, Paris, Europe, 1979-81; v.p. mfg. Internat. Harvester, Paris, Europe, 1981-84; v.p. ops. and planning Internat. Harvester, France, 1984-85; European pres. Premark Internat. Food Equipment Group, Rueil Malmaison, France, 1985-96, chmn., 1996-98; mgmt. cons. De Benedetti & Assocs., Rueil Malmaison, 1998—; mgmt. cons., 1998. Avocations: sailing, skiing. Office: De Benedetti & Assocs, 30 Bld Bellerive, 92500 Rueil-Malmaison France

DEBENEDETTI, PABLO GASTON, chemical engineering educator; b. Buenos Aires, Mar. 30, 1953; came to the U.S., 1980; U.S. citizen; s. Sergio Isaias and Francine Fanny (Lehmann) D.; m. Silvia Irene Strauss, July 11, 1987; children: Gabriel Alejandro, Dina Sonia. BS in Chem. Engring., Buenos Aires U., 1978; MS, MIT, 1981, PhD, 1985. Rsch. engr. O de Nora Impianti Elettrochimici, Milan, Italy, 1978-80; asst. prof. dept. chem. engring. Princeton (N.J.) U., 1985-90, assoc. prof., 1990-94, prof. chem. engring., 1994—, dept. chair, 1996—, class of 1950 prof., 1998—; Vaughan lectr. Calif. Inst. Tech., 1992; Katz meml. lectr. City Coll. CUNY, 1997; Wohl meml. lectr. U. Del., 1997; Cary lectr. Ga. Inst. Tech., 1998. Author: Metastable Liquids Concepts and Principles, 1996; mem. editl. bd. Jour. Supercritical Fluids, 1988—, Supercritical Fluid Sci. and Tech., 1995—, Jour. Chem. Engring. Data, 1996—, Revs. in Chemical Engring., 1999—, Chem. Engring. Edn., 2000—; contbr. articles to profl. jours. including Jour. Chem. Physics, Jour. Phys. Chemistry, Nature, Phys. Rev. Letters, Molecular Physics, Am. Inst. Chem. Engr. Jour., others. Named NSF Presdl. Young Investigator, 1987; European Econ. Cmty. fellow, 1978, Camille and Henry Dreyfus Tchr. scholar, 1989, Guggenheim fellow, 1991, Nat. Acad. Engring., 2000. Mem. AAAS, N.Y. Acad. Scis., Am. Inst. Chemical Engrs. (Profl. Progress award 1997), Am. Chemical Soc., Am. Physical Soc., Sigma Xi. Achievements include protein processing and separations with supercritical fluids; thermodynamics of supercritical fluids and mixtures; thermodynamics of supercooled and glassy water; thermodynamics and statistical mechanics of metastable systems; thermodynamics of polyamorphic phase transitions; structure, dynamics, and thermodynamics of glasses. Office: Princeton U Dept Chem Engring Princeton NJ 08544-0001

DEBENEDICTIS, RAFFAELE, Italian medieval literature educator; b. Miranda, Italy, July 19, 1964; came to U.S., 1984; s. Vincenzo and Ersilia DeBenedictis; m. Rita Filomena DeBenedictis, July 19, 1986; children: Dante Vincenzo, Davide Giulio, Diva Rafaella. BA, U. Windsor, Ont., Can., 1988; MA, Wayne State U., 1990; PhD, U. Toronto, 1996. Undergrad. asst. U. Windsor, 1985-87; grad. asst. U. Toronto, 1990-91; part-time instr. Wayne State U., Detroit, 1988-90, lectr., undergrad. coord., 1992—; ct. interpreter, Windsor, 1986—; journalist Corriere Canadese, Toronto, 1997—. Author: Pier Paolo Pasolini, 1990, Musica e Ordine Nella Divina Commedia, 2000. Translator, interpreter, Liberal Party of Can., Windsor, 1995—; translator Noi Found., Mich., 1998—; cons. culture and lang. Langua Tutor, Inc., Mich., 1998—. Mem. MLA, Am. Assn. for Italian Studies, Federazione Unitaria Stampa Italiana Estera, Agenzia Nazionale Stampa Associata, Caboto Club. Liberal. Roman Catholic. Office: Wayne State U 317 Manoogian Detroit MI 48202

DE BENOIST, ALAIN, writer, journalist; b. St. Symphorien, France, Dec. 11, 1943; s. Alain and Germaine (Langouet) deB.; m. Doris Christians, June 21, 1972; children: Frederik, Adrien. Lic. of Philosophy, Sorbonne, 1964; lic. of Law, U. Paris, 1965. Editor Nouvelle Ecole, Paris, 1969—; journalist Valeurs Actuelles, Paris, 1970-82, Le Figaro Mag., Paris, 1977-92, France Culture Radio, Paris, 1980-92; editor Krisis, Paris, 1988—; dir. Collections in various book pub. companies, Copernic, Pardes, Labyrinthe, 1977—. Author: Vu de Droite, 1977 (Great Prize of the Essay French Acad., 1978), Comment Peut-on Etre Paien?, 1981, L'Eclipse du Sacre, 1986, Europe, Tiers Monde, meme Combat, 1986, L'Empire Interieur, 1995, Famille et Societe, 1996, Ernst Jünger, 1997, Communisme et Nazisme, 1998, L'écume et les galets, 2000. Mem. Mouvement Normand, Club des Mille, Viking Soc. for Northern Rsch. Avocations: collecting books, travel, genealogy. Home and Office: 5 Rue Carriere Mainguet, 75011 Paris France

DE BETHUNE, GUY JACQUES, pediatrician; b. Marke, Belgium, Apr. 17, 1934; s. Jean Marie and Louise-Marie (de Vinck) de B.; m. Josephine-Marie van der Kelen, Sept. 5, 1959; children: Bernadette, Veronique, Elizabeth, Francis. MD, Cath. U. Louvain, Leuven, 1960; degree in paediatrics, Cath. U. Louvain, Leuven, Belgium, 1965. Chief dept. paediatrics Kliniek Maria's Voorzienigheid, Kortrijk, Belgium, 1965-99; retired. Contbr. articles to profl. jours. Avocations: ornithology, botany. Home: Patersmotestraat 40, B 8500 Kortrijk Belgium Office: Kliniek Maria's Voorzienigheid, Loofstraat 43, B 8500 Kortrijk Belgium

DE BETTIGNIES, BERTIN JEAN-MARIE, chemistry educator; b. Barlin, Pas De Calais, France, Jan. 7, 1944; s. Maximilien and Suzanne (Renard) de B.; m. Therese Marie Baron, Aug. 4, 1965; children: Etienne, Laurence, Philippe. Degree, U. Lille, 1968, D in Chemistry, 1971, D in Scis., 1978. Asst. prof. U. Lille, 1969-77, assoc. prof., 1977-87, prof., 1987—, dir. Inst. U. de Tech., 1984-97, dir. Ctr. de Formation par Apprentissage, 1992-2000; vice chancelor U. Scis. and Tech. Lille, 1997—; cons. Soc. Francaise d'Exportation des Resources Educatives, 1984—, Assn. Cons. for Inst. U. Tech., France, 1993—; referee Jour. Phys. Chemistry. Contbr. articles to profl. jours. Recipient Lievin Danel award Soc. Industrielle du Nord, 1990, Officier des Palmes Academiques, 1997, Fedn. Industries Mecanique award Soc. Industrielle du Nord, 1996; grantee R.A. Welsch Found., Tex. Christian U., Ft. Worth, 1976, Nato, U. Tex., 1974. Mem. Am. Chem. Soc., French Chem. Soc., N.Y. Acad. Scis., Rotary, Sigma Xi. Avocations: genealogy, civil association. Office: IUT Lille 1, BP 179, 59653 Villeneuve d'Ascq France

DEBEYSSEY, MARK SAMMER, molecular and cellular biologist; b. Putnam, Conn., Mar. 24, 1966; s. Ghaleb and Widad Debeyssey. BS cum laude, U. Conn., 1988, MS in Moleular and Cell Biology, 1992. Sr. toxicologist Ciba-Geigy, Farmington, Conn., 1988-89; rsch. scientist U. Conn. Health Ctr., Farmington, 1989-90; molecular and cellular biologist VA Med. Ctr., West Haven, Conn., 1990-94, Albert Einstein Sch. Medicine, Bronx, N.Y., 1994—; sr. lead analyst Bayer Pharm.-Wang Global, West Haven, Conn., 1998—. Contbr. articles to profl. jours. Chmn. Am. Druze Soc., Conn., 1990-91. Recipient Superior Performance award Dept Vets. Affairs, 1991. Mem. AAAS, Am. Chem. Soc., Planetary Soc. (assoc.), Am. Mus. Natural History, Archaeol. Inst. Am. (assoc.), Smithsonian Nat. Assocs. Office: Bayer Corp Wang Global 400 Morgan Ln West Haven CT 06516-4175

DE BIASI, RONALDO SERGIO, materials science educator; b. Rio de Janeiro, Mar. 11, 1943; s. Renato and Ruth Freitas (Pinho) de B.; m. Marilia Villa-Forte Coutinho, June 15, 1967; children: Sérgio, Cláudio. BSEE, Pontifical Cath. U., Rio de Janeiro, 1965; MSEE, PUC/RJ, 1967; PhD, U. Wash., 1971. Asst. prof. materials sci. Inst. Mil. Engring., Rio de Janeiro, 1971-74, prof., 1974—. Author: The World of Electronics, 1966, Fast Guide to DOS 6.2, 1994, also 6 others; mem. editl. bd. Materials Rsch., Revista Militar de Ciência e Tecn.; contbr. over 200 articles to profl. jours. Mem. Am. Phys. Soc., Brazilian Soc. Physics. Avocations: soccer, playing piano. Home: Rua Pinheiro Machado 99/901, 22231-090 Rio de Janeiro RJ, Brazil Office: Inst Mil Engring Pr Gen, Tiburcio 80, 22231090 Rio de Janeiro Brazil

DEBIEVE, JEAN-FRANCOIS, research scientist; b. Paris, Mar. 27, 1950; s. Roger and Cosette (Caillaud) D.; m. Eliane Bonanno, Jan. 15, 1983; children: Clara, Alexandra, Florence. 1st degree, U. Paris VI, 1969; Doctorat 3eme cycle, U. Aix/Marseille II, France, 1976, DSc, 1983. Rschr. Nat. Office Aerospace Studies and Rsch., Paris, 1975-80, Nat. Ctr. Sci. Rsch., Paris, 1980—; rschr. Inst. Statis. Mechanics and Turbulence, Marseille, 1980-95; rsch. supersonic group Inst. de Recherche sur les Phenomene hors d'equilibre, Marseille, 1995-97; tchr. Ecole Superieur d'Ingenieur Marseille, 1985-94. Contbr. articles to sci. jours. Home: 145 Ave des Chartreux, 13004 Marseille France Office: IRPHE, 12 Ave General Leclerc, 13003 Marseille France

DE BITTENCOURT, PAULO ROGÉRIO MUDROVITSCH, neurologist, researcher; b. Curitiba, Paraná, Brazil, Dec. 4, 1953; s. Paulo Orlando M. and Udine Vera Meri M. De Bittencourt; m. Lilian Dias Pereira, July 27, 1980 (div. 1984); m. Maristela Catarina Simioni, Mar. 18, 1989; children: Dante Paolo, Paulo Rogério, Sofia. MD, Fed. U. Paraná, 1976; PhD, U. London, 1981. Rsch. asst. Inst. Neurology, London, 1977-81; registrar Chalfont Ctr. for Epilepsy, Chalfont St. Peter, Eng., 1978-80; sr. house officer The Nat. Hosp., London, 1981; head of neurology and neurophysiology svc. Hosp. Nossa Senhora das Graças, Curitiba, 1982—; exec. dir. Unidade de Neurologia Clinica S/C Ltd., Curitiba, 1986—; vis. prof. UCLA, 1980, U. London, 1984, U. Wales, 1984, U. Cin., 1987; prof. neurology Fed. U. Parana, Curitiba, 1991; pres. Brazilian League of Epilepsy, Curitiba, 1986-90; 1st v.p. Internat. League against Epilepsy, Washington, 1989-93, chmn. commn., 1989-97; sec. gen. 19th Internat. Epilepsy Congress, Rio de Janeiro, 1991; sec.-gen., founder Inst. Amazon Studies, Curitiba, 1990-93; lectr. in field. Chief editor: Jour. Brazilian League of Epilepsy, 1986-91; mem. editorial bd. Epilepsia Jour., 1989-93, Acta Neurologica (Bogota), 1985-95, Archivos de Neurociencies (Mex.), 1993—; mem. editl. bd. Neurol. Infections and Epidemiology, 1996—; contbr. 150 papers to profl. jours. and books. Recipient Ednl. award Rotary Found., 1976, Amb. award Internat. League and Bur. for Epilepsy, 1991; rsch. grantee Thorn Epilepsy Rsch. Fund, 1979, Wellcome Found., 1980. Fellow Am. Acad. Neurology; mem. Brazilian Soc. Multiple Sclerosis (coun. mem. 1990—), Brazilian Acad. Neurology, NY Acad. Scis., Cuban Neurosci. Soc. Avocations: traveling, reading, rock and roll music. Office: Rua Padre Anchieta 155, 80410030 Curitiba Parana, Brazil

DEBIZE, JACQUES MARCEL, optical engineer; b. Jons, France, July 13, 1944; s. Gaston and Raymonde (Vernet) D.; m. Odile Jacquot, Apr. 25, 1969 (div. Dec. 1982); children: Christine, Alain; m. Genevieve Marguerite Marie Recoupe, June 4, 1983; 1 child, Laurent. Engring. degree, Ecole Superieure d'Optique, Paris, 1967. Registered engr., Europe. Optical designer II Angénieux, St. Héand, France, 1969-72, Sud Optique, Manosque, France, 1972-73; optical designer II Angénieux, St. Héand, 1973-76, head optical designer IIIA, 1976-90, dep.-mgr. IIIA, 1991-93, responsible optical study civil dept., 1994—. Achievements include patents for anamorphic zoom for television. Avocations: basketball, mineralogy, aquariophily, cinema video camera, UV printing optical device. Home: 13 Rue Périchon, 42570 Saint Heand France Office: Angénieux, 42570 Saint Heand France

DE BLASIO, MARIA P., physician; b. Naples, Italy, May 4, 1940; came to U.S., 1967; d. Agnello and Sophia (Recchia) de B. BA, St. Jeanne D'Arc Coll., Naples, 1958; MD, U. Naples, 1966; M in Piano and Composition, San Pietro A Maiella, Conservatory of Music, 1963. Resident Mt. Vernon (N.Y.) Hosp., 1967-72, Union Hosp., Bronx, N.Y., 1972, Misericordia Hosp., Bronx, 1968; fellow U. Pa., Phila., 1972; attending physician Our Lady of Mercy, Bronx, N.Y., 1982—, St. Barnabas Hosp., Bronx, N.Y., 1981—; med. dir. Jean Jugan Residence, Bronx. Named Best Physician of Yr., New Yorker mag., 1996. Mem. AMA, Bronx County Med. Soc., N.Y. State Med. Soc. Avocations: concerts, opera, reading. Home: 2226 Valentine Ave Bronx NY 10457-1106 Office: 3065 Grand Bronx NY 10468

DE BLAY, FREDERIC JOSEPH, pulmonologist, allergist; b. Laxou, France, July 11, 1958; s. Gabriel Jean and Marie Louise de Blay; m. Armelle Renee Prevôt, Sept. 10, 1983; children: Raphael, Axel, Alix, Roch, Arnaud. MD, Nancy U., 1989. Intern Ctr. Hospitalo Univ., Strasbourg, France, 1984-89, asst., chief clinic, 1990-94, mem. staff, 1994—; asst. prof. U. Va., 1989-90, prof. pulmonology, 1998—; expert on diseases related to environment European Parliament, 1992. Recipient Med. de la ville du Mont-Dore prize, 1992, Epidaure prize, 1998; Fulbright scholar, 1989. Mem. Am. Acad. Allergy and Clin. Immunology, European Respiratory Soc.. Avocations: sailing. Home: 11 Rue de Liepvre, 67100 Strasbourg France Office: Pavillon Laennec, Hosp Univ de Strasbourg, 67091 Strasbourg Cedex France

DE BLEECKER, JAN LEON, neurologist; b. Oudenaarde, Flanders, Belgium, Feb. 7, 1961; s. Georges and Paula (De Meester) De B.; m. Katrien I. De Keukelaere, Sept. 6, 1986; children: Emiel, Leonie, Henri. MD, Ghent State U., 1986, PhD, 1992. Neuromuscular disease rsch. fellow Mayo Clinic, Rochester, Minn., 1991-93; staff cons. Univ. Hosp., Ghent, 1994—; prof.

neurology Ghent Univ. Mem. Soc. Flemish Neuropsychiatrists, Belgian Soc. Neuropathology (vice pres. 1999—), Am. Acad. Neurology. Office: Univ Hosp, De Pintelaan 185, B-9000 Ghent Belgium

DEBNEY, GEORGE C., mathematical physicist; b. Beaumont, Tex., Feb. 19, 1939. BA, Rice U., 1961; PhD, U. Tex., 1967. Analyst TRW, Houston, 1966-68; prof. math. Va. Tech., Blacksburg, 1968-85; sr. mathematician ANSER, Arlington, Va., 1985-87; sr. scientist Schafer Corp., Arlington, Va., 1987-89, SAIC, Arlington, Va., 1989—. Contbr. more than 25 articles to profl. jours. Rsch. fellow Soc. for Engring. Edn., 1975, 76. Mem. Am. Phys. Soc., Math. Assn. Am. Achievements include research in defense techniques, performance, architecture, technology, and systems engineering. Office: SAIC/CSF 1901 N Moore St Ste 750 Arlington VA 22209-1717

DE BOER, FOKKE WANDER NICOLAAS, physicist, researcher; b. Amsterdam, The Netherlands, Apr. 3, 1942. B in Physics and Math., U. Amsterdam, 1964, M in Exptl. Nuclear Physics, 1968, PHD, 1974. Rsch. assoc. IKO, Amsterdam, 1969-77; sr. rsch. assoc. Free U., Amsterdam, 1977-78; faculty rsch. assoc. Paul Scherrer Inst., U. Fribourg, Villigen, Switzerland, 1981-83; prof. U. Cath. Louvain, Belgium, 1987-88, Goethe U., Frankfurt, 1989-92; guest scientist Kernfysisch Versneller Inst., Groningen, 1993-94; vis. prof. U. Colo., Boulder, 1978-80; prof. Inst. Kernphysik, Frankfurt, 1989-92; guest at NIKHEF, Amsterdam, 1994—; guest scientist Nat. Inst. Kernfysica Hoge Energiefysica (formerly IKO), Amsterdam, 1985-89. Contbr. articles to profl. jours. Heraeus Stiftung fellow, 1989-92. Address: Piraeusplein 3, 1019 NL Amsterdam The Netherlands

DE BOER, FRANK, soccer player; b. May 15, 1970. Defender Ajax (Netherlands) Football Club; mem. EURO 2000. Address: Ajax Supporter-svereniging, Postbus 22944, 1100 DK Amsterdam Netherlands*

DE BOER, PERRY H.G., data communications professional; b. Merksem, Antwerp, Belgium, Dec. 12, 1958; s. Robert de Boer and Maintje Vermeerbergen; m. Els Herbiest; children: Ineke, Joran, Jana. Elec. Engring. Diploma, VUB, Brussels, 1981; Advanced Mgmt. Diploma, Vlerick, Gent, Belgium, 1994. Rschr. Bell Telephone, Antwerp, Belgium, 1981-84; head engring. Sparnex, Antwerp, 1984-87; founder DATAX, Antwerp, 1988—. Mem. KVIV, ATM Forum, Vlerick. Avocations: sports, family, datacom.

DE BOER, RONALD, soccer player; b. Hoorn, May 15, 1970. Formerly with Twente; midfielder Ajax Football Club, Netherlands, 1993—; mem. Euro-2000, Barcelona Team. Office: Ajax Football Club, Supporter Sverenging POB 229444, 1100 DK Amsterdam The Netherlands*

DE BOER, UILKE F., contracting company executive; b. Dijken, The Netherlands, Sept. 27, 1941; s. Feike R. and Grietje (vanderKooy) DeB.; m. Antje Schurer, Nov. 18, 1965; children: Ingrid Greta, Lucien Feico Martin. BSCE, U. Leeuwarden, The Netherlands, 1965. Engr., area mgr. NBM Pipelines, Wolvega, The Netherlands, 1965-73; area mgr. NMB Pipelines, The Hague, 1986-92; constrn. mgr. Nacap B.V., Sliedrecht, The Netherlands, 1974-80; project mgr. Cogasco S.A., Buenos Aires, 1981-82, Kampsax-Nacap, Copenhagen, 1982-83, Nacap Algeria, Alger, 1984-85; pres. De Boer Pipeline Svcs. B.V., Terherne, The Netherlands, 1993—; bd. dirs. DeBoer Employment Svcs., Terherne. Deacon Dutch Reformed Ch.; commr. Ship Ctr. Lelystad B.V., 1994—. Mem. Buisleiding Indsl. Gilde, Pipeline Indsl. Guild. Liberal. Avocations: sailing, hunting, travel. Office: DeBoer Pipeline Svcs BV, Buorren 70, 8493LH Terherne The Netherlands

DEBONDT, JAN HENDRIK MARIA, bond dealer; b. Dendermonde, Belgium, Feb. 4, 1961; s. Frans and Laura (DeVidts) DeB.; m. Mia De Block, Aug. 14, 1984; children: Lauriem, Celine. Student, Heilige Maagd Coll., 1979. Clk. Cger Bank, Brussels, 1984-86; mktg. mgr. mutual funds Aslk Cyer Bank, Brussels, 1986-90, bond dealer, 1991-93; assoc. fixed income Goldman Sachs, London, 1993-95; v.p. fixed income sales Merrill Lynch, London, 1995-96, dir. fixed income sales, 1996-98; dir. fixed income sales Merrill Lynch, Frankfurt, 1998—; cons. Financieel Advies Bur. DeBondt, Merchtem, 1989-93; ptnr. Achilleus N.V., Brussels, 1991-92. Avocations: jogging, reading, music, theatre, gastronomy. Home: Peizegemstraat 94, B 1785 Merchtem Belgium

DEBONGNIE, JEAN-FRANÇOIS, mechanical engineer, educator; b. Brussels, Brabant, Belgium, Jan. 4, 1951; s. Paul and Berthe (Ertrijckx) D.; m. Quoc-Ha Duong-Hang, Feb. 8, 1975 (div. 1987); m. Marie-Anne Benoit, Mar. 1, 1991 (div. 1999). Engr. Civil Elec.-Mech., U. Liège (Belgium), 1973, PhD, 1978. Rsch. engr. U. Liège, 1973-78; prof. Ecole Mohammadia d'Ingénieurs, Rabat, Morocco, 1978-85; head computing ctr. Ecole Supérieure Interafricaine, Bingerville, Ivory Coast, 1986-89; prof. mech. engring. U. Liège, 1989—; cons. Comml. Ct., Liège, 1994—; prof. mech. engring. Pole U. Leonard de Vinci, Paris. Contbr. articles to profl. jours. Mem. ASME, Soc. Mfr. Engrs., Belgian Soc. Mech. Engrs. (mem. editl. bd.). Office: U Liège, U Liège, 1 Chemin dees Chemeuils, B-4000 Liège Belgium

DE BONT, ANTOON FRANS, biologist, educator, consultant; b. Turnhout, Belgium, Dec. 8, 1916; s. August De Bont and Marie-Louise De Clerck; m. Marie-José Hers, Oct. 27, 1945; children: Mady, Christine, Marie-Antoinette, Anne, Baudouin, Jan. MS in Biology, Cath. U., Leuven, Belgium, 1942, DSc, 1945. Dir. Govtl. Fisheries Rsch. Sta., Kipopo, Belgian Congo, 1947-56; prof. Lovanium U., Kinhasa, Zaire, 1957-71, vis. prov., 1971-76; extraordinary prof. Cath. U., Leuven, 1963-71, ordinary prof., 1971-84, emeritus prof., 1984—; sci. advisor Belgian Airforce Prevention against Birdstrikes, 1978—; participant internat. congresses of ICBP, IBP, SIL, ICSU, others. Contbr. more than 100 articles to sci. and profl. jours. Mem. Am. Ornithol. Union, Internat. Ornithol. congress, UNESCO, CITES (Belgian sci. com. 1984—). Avocations: bird ringing, consulting in international development projects. Home: Walenpotstraat Ia, B-3060 Bertem Belgium

DE BOOS, RODNEY MALCOLM, lawyer; b. Hastings, Victoria, Australia, June 18, 1949; s. Eric Meade and Joan Farrin (Webb) De B.; m. Narelle Kai Every, Feb. 9, 1975; children: Jonathon, Antony. LLB, Melbourne (Australia) U., Victoria, 1971. Articled clk. Corr & Corr, Melbourne, 1971-72; sr. legal officer ICI Australia, Melbourne, 1972-74, 1975-85; atty. Imperial Chem. Industries, London, 1973-74; prin. De Boos & Assoc., Melbourne, 1985-88; ptnr. Davies Ryan De Boos, Melbourne, 1988-98, Davies Collison Care Solicitors, Melbourne, 1998—. Contbr. articles to profl. publs. Mem. Trinity Grammar Sch. Coun.; v.p. Victorian InLine Hockey Assn. Mem. Licensing Exec. Soc. Australia and New Zealand (sec. 1992-95, pres. 1984-85), Licensing Exec. Soc. Internat. (sec. 1992-95, pres. 1998), Law Coun. Australia (chmn. intellectual property com. 1995-97, former dep. chmn. trade practices com.). Avocation: golf. Office: Davies Collision Cave Solic, 1 Little Collins St, Melbourne Victoria 3000, Australia

DE BORCHGRAVE, ARNAUD, editor, writer, lecturer; b. Brussels, Oct. 26, 1926; s. Count Baudouin and Audrey (Townshend) de B.; m. Dorothy Solon, Apr. 1950; 1 child, Arnaud; m. Eileen Ritschel, Mar. 31, 1959; 1 child, Trisha; m. Alexandra D. Villard, May 10, 1969. Student, Maredsous, Belgium, 1936-39, King's Sch., Canterbury, Eng., 1940-42. Free-lance writer Eastern Europe, 1946-47; staff United Press, Western Europe, 1947-51; mgr. Benelux Countries, 1949-51; European Corr. Newsweek, Paris, North Africa, Middle East, Indo-China, 1951-54; fgn. editor, sr. editor Newsweek, 1955-59, chief fgn. corr., 1959-62, mng. editor internat. edits., 1962-63, chief Newsweek Corr., 1964-80; columnist, TV host; sr. assoc. Ctr. for Strategic and Internat. Studies, 1981-85; editor in chief The Washington Times and Insight Mag., 1985-91; dir. Global Organized Crime Project, sr. advisor Ctr. for Strategic and Internat. Studies, Washington, 1991—; pres., CEO UPI, 1999—. Served with Brit. Royal Navy, 1942-46. Decorated commandeur de l'Ordre de Leopold II, Medaille Maritime Belge; recipient Medal of Honor Def. Council, 1980, Medal of Honor World Bus. Council, 1981, Washington Dateline award Soc. Profl. Journalists, also numerous awards for fgn. reporting. Mem. Am. Soc. Newspaper Editors, Internat. Press Inst., Inter-Am. Press Assn., Coun. on Fgn. Rels., Racquet and Tennis Club, Met. Club, Econ. Club of Washington, Nat. Press Club. Home: 2801 New Mexico Ave NW Washington DC 20007-3921 Office: Ctr for Strategic and Internat Studies 1800 K St NW Washington DC 20006-2202

DE BOSSCHERE, KOENRAAD O.M., computer scientist, educator; b. Oudenaarde, Belgium, July 29, 1963; s. Lucien C. and Georgette M. (Naessens) D.; m. Katrien Raphaella De Pryck, Aug. 26, 1989; 1 child, Liesbet. Electrotech. Engr., U. Ghent, Belgium, 1986, M.Computer Sci., 1987, PhD in Engring., 1992. Rsch. asst. U. Ghent, 1988-93, sr. rsch. asst., 1993-96, lectr., 1993—; rsch. assoc. FWO, Belgium, 1996—. Contbr. articles to profl. jours. Recipient Prize for Cultural Merits, Town of Melle, 1996. Mem. IEEE, Assn. Computing Machinery, KVIV. Avocations: gardening, music, reading, travel. Home: 3 Park Ter Linden, B-9090 Melle Belgium Office: Univ of ghent, St Pietersniewwstraat 41, B-9000 Ghent Belgium

DE BOUCHARD D'AUBETERRE, COUNT HUBERT GUY, former company executive, sculptor; b. Mercoeur, France, Nov. 10, 1912; s. Raoul Gaspard Savary and Vera Helene Marie (de Caprara de Montecucoli) B. d'A.; m. Alba Maria de Filkiewitch Beck, Nov. 28, 1944; children: Guy, Vera, Anne, Amaury, Yvan. Student schs., France, Monte Carlo. Chief of staff Apport-Rural Normandy, 1935-39; young officer French Army, 1939-40, WWII; Sec. Secours Nat. Nice, 1942; French Red Cross, 1943-44, Served in French resistance, WWII, Served in U.S. Army, 1944; mgr. Societe Transp. Industry, Nice, 1946-51; travel export mgr. Ste Camuscognac, Paris and Cognac, 1952-68; country mgr. Ste. Grand Marnier, Paris, 1967-74. Mem. Hunt Assn. Mercoeur (chmn. 1966-72), Football Assn. Mercoeur (chmn. 1969-85), War Vets. Assn. Mercoeur (chmn. 1969-85), Am. Legion. Roman Catholic. Clubs: Recherches Celtiques (Vichy); Saint Odilon (Mercoeur), Mythologie Française (Beauvais); Association entraide Noblesse Francaise (Paris). Home: Chateau de Fontaride, 43100 Mercoeur France

DE BOURBON BUSSET, JACQUES, writer, author; b. Paris, Apr. 27, 1912; s. Francois and Guillemette de B.; m. Laurence Ballande; children: Helene, Charles, Robert, Jean. Author of 40 books. Mem. Académie Française. Roman Catholic. Office: Institut De France, 23 quai de Conti, 75006 Paris France

DEBOW, THOMAS JOSEPH, JR., advertising executive; b. N.Y.C., May 18, 1936; s. Thomas Joseph DeBow and Evelyn Francis (Brooks) Menck; m. Rosalinda Angelini, Sept. 9, 1961; children: Yvette, Thomas J III, Walter Brooks. V.p. McCann Ericson, N.Y.C., 1965-69; dir. Young and Rubicam, N.Y.C., 1969-71; pres. Curry DeBow, N.Y.C., 1971-74; v.p. BBDO, N.Y.C., 1974-76; chmn. DeBow Comm. Ltd., N.Y.C., 1976-95, DeBow Comm., Ltd., 1995—. Mem. Cystic Fibrosis Found., dir., 1988—; vice chmn. Len Cariou Entreprolebrity Golf Tournament, 1990; vice chmn. children's legacy com. Franciscan Sisters of the Poor Found., 1996—. Mem. Friar's Sunshine Com. (chmn. 1987—, Friar of Yr. 1990), Knollwood Country Club, N.Y. Athletic Club. Home: 55 E 86th St New York NY 10028-1059 Office: DeBow Comm Ltd 850 7th Ave Ste 605 New York NY 10019-5230

DEBRABANDERE, FRANS JULES, linguist; b. Kortrijk, Belgium, May 18, 1933; s. André Debrabandere and Marie Louise Hubert; m. Monica Hartmann, Aug. 28, 1963; children: Peter, Koen, Joop. Diploma, Belgium Univ., Louvain, 1956, PhD, 1965. Tchr. Pedagogical Coll., Bruges, Belgium, 1958-94; ofcl. Dutch-Belgian Orgn., The Hague, The Netherlands, 1983-84; co-editor Etymol. Dictionary of the Dutch Lang., Amsterdam, The Netherlands, 1995—; founder, pres., chief editor De Leiegouw, Belgium, 1958—. Author: Study of Personal Names in the Region of Courtrai, 1350-1400, 1970, The Dialect of Courtrai, 1986, (dictionaries) Dictionary of Old Legal Terms, 1978, Etymological Dictionary of the Surnames in Belgium and North France, 1993, Dictionary of Courtrai dialect, 1999; contbr. articles to profl. jours. Mem. Commn. for Local History, 1965—, Commn. for Place Names, Bruges, 1971—, Royal Commn. for Place Names, 1978-93, Commn. for Langs. and Lit., 1986—; pres. Cultural Coun., 1995—; sec. gen. Royal Commn. Onomastics and Dialectology, 1984—. Recipient several awards. Mem. Internat. Svc. Club. Home: Keizer Karelstraat 83, B-8000 Bruges Belgium

DEBRECENI, LASZLO, physician, researcher, writer; b. Beremend, Baranya, Hungary, July 30, 1936; s. Lajos and Izabella (Tolnai) D.; m. Judit Sztarcsevich, Nov. 11, 1967 (div. Oct. 1980); children: Balazs, Andras. MD, Med. U., Pecs, Hungary, 1960, cert. in internal medicine, 1965, cert. in clin. laboratory, 1969; PhD, Sci. Qualificatory Com., Budapest, 1977. Resident Internal Medicine of Hosp., Mohacs, 1960-66, Clin. Lab. Hosp., Mohacs, 1967-69; head clin. lab. Hosp. Mohacs, 1969-97, dir., 1990-95, head internal medicine, 1991-96; scholar Heart Diseases Rsch. Found., N.Y.C., 1988; dir. Hosp. Siklos, 1999—. Author: Acupuncture in Clinical Medicine, 1988 (Nivo award 1989), Clear Consciousness, 1994, Theory and Praxis of Modern Acupuncture, 1996, Healing and Faith, 1997, How to Stay Forever Young, 2000; contbr. numerous articles to profl. jours. Chmn. Szili Laszlo Found., Mohacs, 1991-96; mem. Art Soc., Mohacs, 1995—. Grantee Soros Found., 1988. Fellow Internat. Coll. Acupuncture and Electro-Therapeutics; mem. Corps Hungarian Acad. Scis., N.Y. Acad. Scis. Avocations: travel, swimming. Home: Szabadsag stv 28, 7700 Mohacs Hungary Office: Hosp, Baross G str 6, 7800 Siklos Baranya, Hungary

DEBREU, GERARD, economics and mathematics educator; b. Calais, France, July 4, 1921; came to U.S., 1950, naturalized, 1975; s. Camille and Fernande (Decharne) D.; m. Françoise Bled, June 14, 1945; children: Chantal, Florence. Student, Ecole Normale Supérieure, Paris, 1941-44, Agrégé de l'Université, France, 1946; DSc, U. Paris, 1956; Dr. Rerum Politicarum honoris causa, U. Bonn, 1977; D. Scis. Economiques (hon.), U. Lausanne, 1980; DSc (hon.), Northwestern U., 1981; Dr. honoris causa, U. des Scis. Sociales de Toulouse, 1983, Yale U., 1987, U. Bordeaux I, 1988. Rsch. assoc. Centre Nat. De La Recherche Sci., Paris, 1946-48; Rockefeller fellow U.S., Sweden and Norway, 1948-50; rsch. assoc. Cowles Commn., U. Chgo., 1950-55; assoc. prof. econs. Cowles Found., Yale, 1955-61; fellow Ctr. Advanced Study Behavioral Scis., Stanford U., 1960-61; vis. prof. econs. Yale U., fall 1961; prof. emeritus U. Calif., Berkeley, 1962—, prof. Miller Inst. Basic Rsch. in Sci., 1973-74, prof. math., 1975—, univ. prof., 1985—; Guggenheim fellow, vis. prof. Ctr. Ops. Rsch. and Econometrics, U. Louvain, 1968-69, vis. prof., 1971, 72, 88; Erskine fellow U. Canterbury, Christchurch, New Zealand, 1969, 87, vis. prof., 1973; Overseas fellow Churchill Coll., Cambridge, Eng., 1972; Plenary address Internat. Congress Mathematicians, Vancouver, 1974; vis. prof. Cowles Found. for Rsch. in Econs., Yale U., 1976; vis. prof. U. Bonn, 1977; rsch. assoc. Cepremap, Paris, 1980; faculty rsch. lectr. U. Calif., Berkeley, 1984-85, univ. prof., 1985—, Class of 1958 Chair, 1986—; vis. prof. U. Sydney, Australia, 1987; lectr. in field. Author: Theory of Value, 1959, Mathematical Economics: Twenty Papers of Gerard Debreu, 1983; assoc. editor Internat. Econ. Rev., 1959-69; mem. editorial bd. Jours. Econ. Theory, 1972—, SIAM Jours. on Applied Math., 1976-79, Jours. of Complexity, 1985—, Games and Econ. Behavior, 1989—, Econ. Theory, 1991; mem. adv. bd. Jours. Math. Econs., 1974—; correspondent Math. Intelligencer, 1983-84. Served with French Army, 1944-45. Decorated Chevalier de la Légion d'Honneur, Commandeur de l'Ordre National du Mérite, Officier Le Légion d'Honneur; recipient Nobel Prize in Econ. Scis., 1983, Berkeley Citation, 1991; sr. U.S. Sci. awardee Alexander von Humboldt Found., 1977. Fellow AAAS, Econometric Soc. (mem. coun. 1964-72, 78-85, Fisher-Schultz lectr. 1969, exec. com. 1969-72, 80-82, pres. 1971), Am. Econ. Assn. (disting. fellow 1982, pres.-elect 1989, pres. 1990); mem. NAS (chmn. sect. econ. scis. 1982-85, com. human rights 1984-90, chair class V behavioral and social scis. 1989-92, mem. Coun. of NAS of USA 1993—), Am. Philos. Soc., French Acad. Scis. (fgn. assoc.), Berkeley Fellows.

DE BRIGARD, EMILIE, anthropologist, consultant; b. N.Y.C., Dec. 11, 1943; d. A. Lincoln and Ruth Emilie (Jaeger) Rahman; m. Raul de Brigard, June 11, 1966; 1 child, George. BA, Harvard Coll., 1963; MA, U. Calif., 1972. Guest curator dept. of film Mus. of Modern Art, N.Y.C., 1972-73; asst. to dir. human studies film archives Smithsonian Instn., Washington, 1975-77; prin. programmer Margaret Mead Film Festival Am. Mus. Natural History, N.Y.C., 1977-78; faculty Harvard Summer Sch., Cambridge, Mass., 1980-86; pres. Internat. Film Seminars, Inc., N.Y.C., 1981-83; vis. lectr. dept. anthropology Yale U., New Haven, Conn., 1989-91; pres. Soc. for Visual Anthropology, Washington, 1995-97, FilmResearch, Higganum, Conn., 1970—; cons. Choreometrics Project, N.Y.C., 1970-73; mem. Comité Internat. des Films de l'Homme, Paris, 1977—. Author: (books) The History of Ethnographic Film, 1971, Anthropological Cinema, 1973, Cine Antropológico, 1978; producer (film) Margaret Mead: A Portrait by a Friend, 1978. Elector Wadsworth Atheneum, Hartford, Conn., 1985-94, 1996—; corporator Conn. Inst. for the Blind-Oak Hill, Hartford, Conn., 1996—. Recipient scholarship Harvard U., Cambridge, Mass., 1963-64, fellowship, Yale U., New Haven, Conn., 1987-88; grantee: Wenner-Gren Found., N.Y.C., 1970-72, Tinker Found., N.Y.C., 1976. Fellow Am. Anthrop. Assn., Royal Anthrop. Inst.; mem. Soc. Woman Geographers, Town and County Club, Quinnipiack Club, Harvard Club of So. Conn. (v.p. 1995—), Saturday Morning Club. Avocations: costume and textiles. Home: 285 Riverside Dr Apt 7E New York NY 10025-5227 Office: FilmResearch 8 Christian Hill Rd Higganum CT 06441-4030

DE BRUIJN, INGE, olympic athlete; b. Barendrecht, The Netherlands, Aug. 24, 1973. Mem. swim team The Netherlands; participant Olympics, Barcelona, Spain, 1998; winner gold in 100 meter butterfly Olympics, Sydney, Australia, 2000, winner gold in 100 meter freestyle, 2000, winner gold in 50 meter freestyle, 2000; broke European record in 50 meter freestyle Goodwill Games, 1998; winner gold in 50 meter freestyle European Championship, 1999, winner gold in 100 meter butterfly, 1999, winner silver in 100 meter freestyle, 1999. Broke three world records, tied one world record, Sheffield, Eng., 2000. Office: Koninklijke Nederlandse Zwembond, Symfonielaan 13 PO 3438 EX, PO Box 7217 PO 3430 JE Nievwegein The Netherlands*

DE BRUIJN, JOOST DICK, biomedical engineer; b. Pijnacker, The Netherlands, Feb. 13, 1966; s. Dick Cornelis De Bruijn and Jannie Marie De Bruijn-Zorn; m. Yvonne Pearl Bovell, Aug. 19, 1994. BSc, Poly. Faculty, Delft, The Netherlands, 1988; PhD (hon.), U. Leiden, The Netherlands, 1993. Technician U. Amsterdam, Netherlands, 1988-89; technician U. Leiden, 1989, postdoctoral, 1993—; study dir., cons. Bioscan, Bilthoven, The Netherlands, 1995-96; study dir. biomaterials rsch. group, cons. U. Leiden, Bilthoven, 1996—; sr. rsch. scientist, mgr. IsoTis BV, Bilthoven, 1997—; scientist orthopedics dept. Utrecht (The Netherlands) U., 1998—. Contbr. over 40 articles to profl. jours.; patentee in field. European Cmty. grantee, Brussels, 1996, 98. Mem. Am. Soc. Biomaterials, Dutch Soc. Biomaterials, Bulgarian Soc. Oral Implantology (hon.), Tissue Engring. Soc. Office: IsoTis BV, Prof Bronkhorstlaan 10, 3723 MB Bilthoven The Netherlands

DE BRUN, SHAUNA DOYLE, industrialist, investment banker; b. Boston, June 3, 1956; d. John Justin and Marie Therese (Carey) Doyle; m. Seamus Christopher de Brun, July 24, 1982; children: Brendan Joseph, Kieran Christopher. Student, U. Salzburg, 1974-75; BA, Mt. Holyoke Coll., 1978; postgrad., Harvard U., 1981-82; M in Internat. Fin., Columbia U., 1984. Cert. fin. analyst. Assoc. Salomon Bros., N.Y.C., 1978; rsch. assoc. Kennedy Sch. Govt., Cambridge, Mass., 1979-80; faculty assoc. Harvard Bus. Sch., 1980-81; fgn. expert Beijing Normal U., Peoples Republic China, 1981-82; assoc. dir. N.Y. Capital Resources, N.Y.C., 1984-85; ptnr. Eppler & Co., Denver, 1985-87; pres. Eppler & Co., Teaneck, N.J., 1987-88; v.p. fin. Patten Corp., Stamford, Vt., 1988-91; pres. Serfimex USA, Inc., 1991-92; pres., CEO Pliana Holdings, Mexico City, 1992—. Columbia U. Internat. fellow, 1982; Sarah Williston scholar Mt. Holyoke Coll., 1975. Mem. AACCLA (v.p., treas.), Mex. Soc. Security Analysts, Am. C. of C./Mexico (past pres., dir.), Navy League U.S., Phi Beta Kappa, Harvard Club. Avocations: piano, horseback riding. Office: Pliana Holdings SA de CV, 275 Palmas 5th Fl, 11000 Mexico City Mexico

DEBS, RICHARD A., investment banker; b. Providence, Oct. 7, 1930; s. Abraham George and Madge (Fatool) D.; m. Barbara Knowles, July 19, 1958; children: Elizabeth Anderson, Nicholas. BA summa cum laude, Colgate U., 1952; postgrad. (Fulbright scholar), Cairo U., 1952-53; MA, Princeton U., 1956, PhD, 1963; LLB, Harvard U., 1958, grad. Advanced Mgmt. Program, 1973. Bar: N.Y. 1960. Researcher joint project Harvard-Princeton, 1958-59; with Fed. Res. Bank of N.Y., N.Y.C., 1960-76; legal dept. Fed. Res. Bank of N.Y., 1960-64, asst. counsel, 1964-69, sec. of bank, 1965-69, v.p. govt. bonds and securities, 1969-72, v.p. loans and credits, 1969-72, v.p. open market ops., 1972, sr. v.p., 1973, 1st v.p., chief adminstrv. officer, 1973-76; alt. mem. Fed. Open Market Com., 1973-76; mng. dir. Morgan Stanley & Co., Inc., 1976-87; pres. Morgan Stanley Internat. Inc., 1976-87; chmn. R.A. Debs & Co., 1987—; adv. dir. Morgan Stanley Group, 1987—; chmn. The Malaysia Fund Inc., 1987—; bd. dirs. IBJ Whitehall Bank & Trust Co., Aubrey G. Lanston & Co., Saudi Internat. Bank, London; advisor Bank Julius Baer, 1987—, United Gulf Group (Kuwait), 1987—, Dai-Ichi Mut. Life, Tokyo, 1988—, Nissho Iwai Corp., Tokyo, 1990—; chmn. com. fiscal agy. ops. Fed. Res. System, 1969-76; mem. Fed. Res. Steering Com. on Payments Mechanism, 1973-76, Fed. Res. Steering Com. on Internat. Banking, 1973-76; allied mem. N.Y. Stock Exchange, also chmn. adv. com. internat. capital markets; mem. com. multinat. enterprises U.S. coun. Internat. Bus.; mem. internat. capital markets adv. com. Fed. Res. Bank of N.Y.; mem. Nat. Commn. on Pub. Svc. (The Volcker Commn.); mem. Overseas Devel. Coun.; mem. U.S. Office Pers. Mgmt. Task Force on Pay Reform; mem. World Bank Adv. Group on Pvt. Sector Devel.; mem. bus. adv. coun. European Bank for Reconstrn. and Devel., Russian-Am. Banking Forum; mem. Take Stock in Am. Com., 1973-76; mem. Egypt-U.S. Bus. Coun.; mem. adv. coun. Near Eastern program Princeton U.; mem. N.Y. State Savs. Bond Com., 1973-76; adv. coun. Am. Inst. Banking, 1973-76. Contbr. articles on internat. banking to profl. publs. Chmn. emeritus, trustee Carnegie Hall; bd. dirs. Fedn. Protestant Welfare Agys.; trustee Carnegie Endowment for Internat. Peace, Am. Univs. Field Staff; trustee Am. U., Beirut, vice chmn., 1981-94, chmn., 1994—; bd. dirs. Am. Council on Germany; mem. vis. com. Middle East Center Harvard U., 1976-82, mem. vis. com. Ctr. for Internat. Affairs; mem. Group of 30, Reuters Carnegie Global Pub. Policy Group, 1999—; also mem. exec. com. Bretton Woods Com.; U.S. chmn. U.S.-Saudi Arabia Bus. Coun. Mem. ABA (com. Middle Eastern law), Assn. Bar City N.Y., Coun. Fgn. Rels., C. of C. U.S. (internat. policy com., chmn. subcom. on internat. econ. devel. 1979-87), Egyptian Am. C. of C. (chmn.), N.Y. C. of C. and Industry, Japan Soc., Asia Soc., Fgn. Policy Assn. (bd. govs.), Econs. Club, Century Assn. (N.Y.C.), Larchmont Yacht (N.Y.), River Club, Phi Beta Kappa Assocs. Office: Morgan Stanley & Co 1221 Ave of Americas New York NY 10020-1001

DE BURLO, COMEGYS RUSSELL, JR., investment advisor, educator; b. Phila.; s. Comegys Russell and Margaret (Whitehurst) de B.; m. Edith Power Thatcher; children: Jane Thatcher, Charles Russell, John Todd. BS, Swarthmore Coll.; MBA, U. Pa.; DBA, Harvard U. Past CFO Tufts U., v.p., prof., treas., hon. treas.; v.p. Ednl. Testing Svc., Princeton, N.J.; dir. UST Corp., NIH, Nat. Cancer Inst., Cancer Program Adv. Com., Cancer Rsch. Ctrs. Rev. Com., Am. Coun. on Edn., Com. on Taxation; pres., prin. The de Burlo Group Inc., 1987—. Past adv. com. No. Calif. Cancer Program; past mem. sci. adv. com. U. N.Mex. Cancer Treatment Ctr., Ohio State U. Comprehensive Cancer Ctr., 1983-97; pres. Mass. Assn. Schs. and Colls.; trustee Cambridge Friends Sch., Belmont Hill Sch., Moses Brown Sch., Lincoln Sch., BB&N Sch.; bd. mgrs. New Eng. Yearly Meeting; trustee Obadiah Brown/Sarah Swift Fund; commr. pub. trust funds. With USNR. Fellow Royal Hort. Soc.; mem. Assn. for Investment, Mgmt. and Rsch., Boston Security Analysts Soc., Internat. Assn. for Comparative Rsch. on Leukemia and Related Diseases (treas.), Am. Rhododendron Soc. (treas. Mass. chpt.), Swarthmore Coll. Alumni Coun., Harvard Club, Green Mountain Club, Appalachian Mountain Club, Am. Rhododendron Soc. (treas. Mass. chpt.), Tau Beta Pi. Office: 50 Federal St Boston MA 02110-2500

DEBUS, ELEANOR VIOLA, retired business management company executive; b. Buffalo, May 19, 1920; d. Arthur Adam and Viola Charlotte (Pohl) D. Student, Chown Bus. Sch., 1939. Sec. Buffalo Wire Works, 1939-45; home talent prodr. Empire Producing Co., Kansas City, Mo.; sec. Owens Corning Fiberglass Buffalo; pub. rels. and publicity Niagara Falls Theatre, Ont., Can.; pub. rels. dir. Woman's Internat. Bowling Congress, Columbus, Ohio, 1957-59; publicist, sec. Ice Capapdes, Hollywood, Calif., 1961-63; sec. to contr. Rexall Drug Co., L.A., 1963-67; bus. mgmt. acct. Samuel Berke & Co., Beverly Hills, Calif., 1967-75, Gadbois Mgmt. Co., Beverly Hills, 1975-76; sec., treas. Sasha Corp., L.A., 1976-92; former bus. mgr. Dean Martin, Eleanor Powell, Debbie Reynolds, Shirly MacLaine. Contbr. articles to various mags. Mem. Am. Film Inst. Republican.

DEBY, IDRISS, Chadian government official; b. Fada, Ennedi, Chad, 1952. Comdr. in chief armed forces; chmn. Interim Coun. State, Chad; head of state Chad, 1990-91; former mil. adviser to Pres. Hissene Habre; pres.

N'Djamena, Chad, 1990—. Office: Coun of State, Office of President BP74, N'Djamena Chad*

DEC, IGNACY, philosophy and theology educator, researcher; b. Hucisko, Poland, July 27, 1944; s. Wojciech Dec and Aniela Siuzdak. ThM, Pontifical Faculty Theology, Wrocław, Poland, 1971; PhD, Cath. U., Lublin, Poland, 1976, Dr. Habilitus in Humanities, 1991. Ordained priest Roman Cath. Ch., 1969. Rschr. Pontifical Faculty Theology, Wrocław, 1976-91; rector Priestly Sem., Wrocław, 1988-95; rector Pontifical Faculty Theology, Wrocław, 1992—, prof. docent, 1991-93, prof., 1993—. Author: Transcendence of a man in the world, 1994, Two Anthropologies: Thomas Aquinas' and Gabriel Marcel's Theories of Man, 1997, Why love? Philosophy of love in the thought of Gabriel Marcel, 1998, numerous others; editor: Holiness in contemporary times, 1990, In the splendor of the Eucharist. Themes from the congress: Eucharist in the history of the Church in Poland with a special regard to Silesia, 1996, Serve God with Joy, 2 vols., 2000, numerous others; editor: (jour.) Wrocławski Przeglad Teologiczny, 1993—. Mem. Episcopate Commn. for Sems., 1989-96, Episcopate Commn. for Edn., 1995—. Mem. Soc. Rectors of Univs. in Wrocław. Avocations: music, sports. Home and Office: pl Katedralny 14, 50-329 Wrocław Poland

DE CAIRES, CECIL FRANCIS, life insurance company executive; b. Georgetown, Guyana, Nov. 25, 1917; arrived in Barbados, 1962; s. Francis and Josephine (Gonsalves) de C.; m. Thelma Rosalind Elias, Jan. 28, 1942; children: Geoffrey Francis, Ian Francis. Grad. parochial sch., Georgetown. Founder, pres., CEO, Life of Barbados Ltd., Wildey, 1971-98, exec. chmn., 1998—; chmmn. Barbados Fire & Comml. Ins. Co. Ltd.; dept. chmn. GlobE Fin. Inc.; bd. dirs. Roybar Investment Corp. subs. Royal Bank Can., Sunbury Gt. House Inc., CGT Ins. Co. Ltd., Can. Pres. Barbados Assn. for Mentally Retarded Children, 1969-73, Caribbean Assn. for Mental Retardation, 1981-83; 1st chmn. Thelma Vaughan Meml. Home for Physically Handicapped Children in Barbados, 1973; chmn. fin., devel. and planning com. Nat. Children's Homd, 1983-87; chmn. Richmond Fellowship of Caribbean, 1987-89; hon. consul of Portugal for Barbados, 1996—. Decorated Companion of Honour (Barbados); named Master Entrepreneur, Ernst & Young and CIBC Entrepreneur of Yr., 1997; recipient award for 50 years outstanding contbn. to life ins. industry Life Underwriters assn. Barbados, 1997. Mem. Life Assurance Cos. Assn. Barbados (pres. 1963-65), Ins. Assn. Caribbean (hon. life, pres. 1976-78), Barbados Yacht Club, Lions (charter pres. Georgetown 1960-62, founder Barbados 1961, dist. gov. dist 60 W.I. and Guyanas 1963-64). Roman Catholic. Avocations: golf, community service. Fax: 246-436-8835. E-mail: cfdecaires@caribsurf.com. Home: St Anne, 27 Mt Clapham, Saint Michael Barbados Office: Life of Barbados Ltd, Life of Barbados Bldg, Wildey Barbados

DE CAIRES, DAVID FRANCIS, editor, lawyer; b. Georgetown, Guyana, Dec. 31, 1937; s. Francis Ignatius and Marie Celestine (Jardim) De C.; m. Doreen Sukhan, Dec. 3, 1966; children: Isabelle, Brendan. Qualified lawyer, U.K. Ptnr. de Caires and Fitzpatrick, Guyana, 1960-90; editor-in-chief Stabroek News, Georgetown, 1986—. Contbr. articles to profl. jours. Mem. various groups fighting for fair elections in Guyana. Mem. Commonwealth Press Union (Astor award 1992), Inter-Am. Press Assn. Avocations: reading, golf. Home: 239 Camp & Quamina Sts, Georgetown Guyana Office: Guyana Publs Ltd, 46-47 Robb St, Lacytown, Georgetown Guyana

DE CALLATAY, ETIENNE, economist, educator; b. Brussels, Belgium, Mar. 12, 1962; s. Thierry and Françoise (de Streel) de C.; m. Françoise Herbiet, Aug. 16, 1986; children: Charlotte, Olivia, Pierre. M in Econs., U. Namur, Belgium, 1985; MSc in Econs., London Sch. Econs., 1987. Economist Ctrl. Bank of Belgium, 1987-92, IMF, Washington, 1992-96; dep. chief of staff Prime Minister's Office, Brussels, 1996-99; chief economist Bank Degroof, Brussels, 1999—; prof. U. Louvain, Belgium, 1990—. Editor Reflets et Perspectives, 1999—. Adminstr., Belgian Inst. for Pub. Fin., Brussels, 1997—. Home: 272 Rue au Bois, 1150 Brussels Belgium Office: Bank Degroof, 44 Rue de l'industrie, 1040 Brussels Belgium

DE CAMPOS, LUIS MIGUEL, computer science educator; b. Granada, Spain, Apr. 12, 1961; s. Ramon and Elena (Ibanez) De C.; m. Carmen Lopez, Mar. 11, 1989. B in Maths., U. Granada, 1984, DSc, 1988. From asst. prof. to lectr. U. Granada, 1985—. Avocations: reading, cinema, travel, chess. Office: U Granada, Avda de Andalucia N 38, 18071 Granada Spain

DECAMPS, FREDDY, chemical engineer, educator; b. Halle, Brabant, Belgium, Mar. 16, 1940; s. Victor and Flore (Van Nerum) D.; m. Georgette Vandebotermet, July 5, 1966; children: Joëlle, Muriel. Degree in civil engring., KUL Louvain, Belgium, 1964. Rschr. Inichar, Liège, Belgium, 1966-67; rschr. SCK.CEN, Mol, Belgium, 1967-73, rschr., project leader, 1973-82; project leader Ecotecnic, Brussels, 1973-78; mng. dir. Recytec, Brussels, 1978-82; dep. gen. mgr. Ondraf/Niras, Brussels, 1983-92, gen. mgr., 1992—; vice chmn. Belgoprocess, Dessel, Belgium. With Belgium Mil., 1966. Mem. BNS (chmn. 1997-99), KVIV. Office: Ondraf Niras, Ave des Arts 14, 1210 Brussels Belgium

DE CASTRIES, HENRY, insurance company executive; married; 3 children. Grad. law degree, ENA. With French Fin. Ministry Inspection Office, 1980-84; dep. sec. Inter-Ministerial Com. on Indsl. Restructuring; with AXA, 1989—; corp. sec., 1991, sr. exec. pres., 1993; chmn. The Equitable Cos., U.S.; treas. AXS Atout Coeur. City councilor Abitain, Pyrenees, 1983. Recipient Chevalier de l'Ordre National du Mérite. Office: AXA Group, 25 Avenue Matignon, 75008 Paris France*

DE CASTRO, FRANCISCO JOSE BARNES, academic administrator. Rector Universidad Nacional Autonoma de Mexico, Mexico City. Office: U Nac Autonoma de Mex, Ciudad Universitaria, Del Coyoacan 04510, Mexico*

DE CASTRO, JOÃO JACOME, endocrinologist; b. Lisbon, Portugal, Mar. 28, 1963; s. Jorge E.T. and Maria (de Castro) Rodrigues; m. Mafalda de Arrochela, Sept. 12, 1987; children: Leonor, Matilde. MD with honors, U. Lisbon, 1987, postgrad., 1997. Diplomate Portuguese Bd. Endocrinology. Resident in medicine Santa Maria U. Hosp., Lisbon, 1987-89, registrar of endocrinology, 1990-93, sr. registrar of endocrinology, 1994-96; cons. endocrinologist Hosp. Militar, Lisbon, 1997—, dir. endocrine unit, 1998—; vis. endocrinologist St. Bartholomew's Hosp., London, 1994; sr. lectr. U. Lisbon, 1994—; asst. editor Endocrino Metab. Nutrition, Lisbon, 1996—. Contbr. articles to profl. jours. Maj. Med. Corps, Portuguese Army, 1990—. Recipient Epidemiology award Dept. Health, 1992, medal UN, 1997. Fellow Portuguese Endocrine Soc. (several awards); mem. Am. Endocrine Soc., Brit. Endocrine Soc. Roman Catholic. Avocation: riding. Office: Endocrine Unit Hosp Militar, Calçada da Estrela, 1249-075 Lisbon Portugal

DE CASTRO, PAOLO, former economics educator; b. South Pietro Vernotico, Italy, Feb. 2, 1958; s. Antonio and Beatrice (Moschettini) De C.; m. Marialuce Procacci, June 6, 1992. Degree in agril sci. and econ., U. Bologna, Italy, 1980. Asst. prof. U. Bologna, 1982-85, assoc. prof., 1992—; assoc. prof. U. Sassari, Italy, 1986-92; min. agr. Govt. Italy, Rome; agricultural advisor to EC pres., Romano Prodi European Commission, Brussels, 2000S; vis. prof. Wash. State U., 1985-86; sci. cons. Centre Internat. de Hautes Etudes Agronomiques Mediterraneennes, Paris, 1985-95, sci. bd., 1996—; sci. coord. Nomisma, Bologna, 1989—; sci. mag. dir. Genio Rurale, Bologna, 1989—; sci. bd. Sci. and Tech. Park, Palermo, Italy, 1993—; apptd. counsellor Italy's Prime Minister. Co-author: Rapporto 1994 Sull'agricultura Italiana, 1995, Rapporto 1995 Sull'agricultura Italiana, 1996. Served with Italian Army, 1992-93. Recipient Luigi Perdisa award U. Bologna, 1986; Nato Jr. fellow Nat. Rsch. Coun., Rome, 1987. Mem. European Agrl. Econ. Assn., Internat. Agrl. Econ. Assn. Office: European Commission, 200 rue de la loi/Wetstraat 200, 1049 Brussels Belgium*

DE CATALDO, MARK ANDREA A., science researcher; b. Milano, Italy, May 5, 1965; s. Francesco and Patricia (Murphy) de C.; m. Meeyoung Kim, Jan. 8, 1997. Laurea cum laude, U. Milan, 1989; MS, U. Notre Dame, 1992, PhD, 1995. Tchg. asst. U. Notre Dame, Ind., 1990-91; CNR fellow CNR of the Italian Govt., U. Notre Dame, Notre Dame, 1991-93, 1993-95; vis. asst. prof. Washington U. in St. Louis, 1995-97; rsch. fellow Max-Planck-Inst. for Mathematik, Bonn, Germany, 1997-98; vis. scholar Harvard U., Cambridge, 1998-99; asst. prof. SUNY Stony Brook, 1999—. Contbr. articles to profl. jours. Cpl. maj. Italian Army, 1989-90. Recipient fellowship CNR of Italian Govt., 1991-93, 93-95, rsch. grant NSF, 1997-2000, others; recipient award Am. Math. Soc., 1998. Mem. Am. Math. Soc. Office: Dept Math SUNY Stony Brook NY 11740

DECAUDAVEINE, MANUEL, investment company executive; b. Paris, Jan. 3, 1962; s. Yves and Florence (Gardette) D.; m. Sophie Letitia Ilbert, Oct. 16, 1959; children: Alice, Clementine, Francis. Diploma, ESCE, Paris, 1983. Fund mgr. B. A.-S. G. Warburg, Paris, 1986-93; sr. fund mgr. Credit Agricole Indosuez Ch. G., Paris, 1993-99; CEO ETNA Fin., Paris, 1999—; advisor B612, Paris, 1999. Contbr. articles to profl. jours. Comm. lead exec. Rassenblement Social Liberal; candidate Regional Assembly Paris, 1997-98. Home: 8 Rue de Florence, 75008 Paris France Office: ETNA Fin, 7 Rue D'Artois, 75008 Paris France

DE CELLES, CHARLES EDOUARD, theologian, educator; b. Holyoke, Mass., May 17, 1942; s. Fernand Pierre and Stella Marie (Shooner) De C. BA, U. Windsor, Ont., Can., 1964; MA in Theology, Marquette U., Milw., 1966; PhD, Fordham U., 1970; MA in Religion, Temple U., Phila., 1979. m. Mildred Manzano Valdez, July 17, 1978; children: Christopher Emanuel, Mark Joshua, Salvador Isaiah. Mem. faculty Dunbarton Coll. of Holy Cross, Washington, 1969-70; mem. faculty Marywood Coll. (became Marywood U., 1997), Scranton, Pa., 1970—, prof. religious studies, 1980—; mem. bd. examiners U. Calicut, Kerala, India, 1985-86; subject specialist Accrediting Commn. of Distance Edn. and Tng. Coun., 1995; moderator Students Organized to Uphold Life, Marywood Coll., 1982—, Task Force Social Justice and Environ., 1992-94, corrector off-campus degree program, 1977—, dept. scribe, 1995—. Author: Paths of Belief, Vol. 2, 1977, prin. coauthor rev. edit., 1987; The Unbound Spirit: God's Universal Sanctifying Work, 1985, Jesus: The Eternally Begotten of the Father as Human Being, 1993; editor Biographical Directory Cath. Acad. Scis. in U.S.A., 1994, Science and Religion in Dialogue, 1999; also pamphlets, articles, book revs., guest editorials, columns, letters, occasional columnist Nat. Cath. Register, 1983-87, The Dunmorean, 1996-97; regular columnist The Catholic Observer, 1996—; contbr. articles to profl. jours., mags. and newspapers. Mem. Ecumenism and Inter-faith Commn., Diocese of Scranton, 1992—, Ecumenical Leadership Com., 1999; bd. dirs. Scranton UN Assn., 1974-75, chmn. UN Day, 1974; mem. ProLife prep. Commn. Scranton Diocesan Synod, 1984-85; bd. dirs. Scranton chpt. Pennsylvanians for Human Life, 1983—, v.p., 1994—; leader Cath. Charismatic Prayer Group, Scranton, 1970-76; mem. com. local pack Cub Scouts, Scranton, 1990-95; Cath. religious emblems couns. Boy Scouts, 1993-96; chmn. prolife com. Immaculate Conception parish, 1994—. Fordham Univ. Presdl. scholar, 1966-68; recipient cert. of appreciation U.S. Cath. Conf., 1976, Disting. Svc. award UN Assn. U.S., 1974, cert. appreciation Boy Scouts Am., 1991, 92, 93, 94, 95, several athletic awards for rd. running yearly, 1987-96, multiple awards for speed walking, 1990-96; admitted to the Order Cor Mariae, Marywood Coll., 1990; invested Knight of the Equestrian Order of the Holy Sepulchre of Jerusalem, 1994. Mem. Cath. Acad. Sci. U.S.A. (pub. com. 1991—, chmn. program com. 1993-96, chmn. pub. com. 1997—, v.p. 1997—), Coll. Theology Soc. Am., Men of the Sacred Heart (Scranton chpt.), Scranton Organized Area Runners, Wyoming Valley Striders, Theta Alpha Kappa (chpt. moderator 1982—). Roman Catholic. Home: 923 E Drinker St Scranton PA 18512-2644 Office: Marywood U Dept Religious Studies Scranton PA 18509-1598

DE CERTAINES, JACQUES DONALD, biophysicist; b. Lyon, France, Apr. 10, 1946; s. Edme and Brigitte (Dillon) de C.; m. Madeleine Meunier, June 29, 1974; children: Gwenola, Olivier, Anne-Gaël. MS, U. Sorbonne, 1973; PhD, U. Rennes, 1977. Fellow Nat. Ctr. Sci. Rsch. (CNRS), Dakar, 1968-71, Ecole des Hautes Etudes en Sci. Sociales, Paris, 1971-74; asst. Med. Sch., Rennes, 1974-81; dir. NMR lab. U. Rennes, 1981-99; dir. dept. clin. biology Rennes Cancer Inst., 1995—; dir. Inst. Metabolic and Microvascular Imaging INSERM, U. Rennes, 2000—; rsch. asst. U. Copenhagen, 1989-90; adminstr. Rennes-Atalante Sci. Park, France, 1984-89, pres., 1998—; project mgmt. group European Projects in MRI and MRS, 1985-94; pres. Start-up Incubator Emergys, 1999—. Author: Resonance Magnetique Nucleaire, 1987, La Fievre des Technopoles, 1988, Magnetic Resonance Spectroscopy of Biofluids, 1989, Magnetic Resonance Spectroscopy in Biology and Medicine, 1992-96; chief editor Jour. Magnetic Resonance Analysis, 1995. Vice-mayor Rennes, 1983-89. Mem. Soc. Magnetic Resonance, European Soc. Magnetic Resonance in Biology and Medicine (bd. dirs. 1989-92). Avocations: parachuting, sailing. Home: 9 Cours Kennedy, 35000 Rennes France Office: U Rennes, Lab NMR, 35043 Rennes France

DECH, RUTH LYNN, academic administrator; b. London, Apr. 29, 1943; d. Josef Asher and Dora (Rosenfeld) Fraenkel; m. John Stewart Deech, July 23, 1967; 1 child, Sarah. BA with honors, Oxford U., England, 1965; MA, Brandeis U., 1966, Oxford U., 1969. Legal asst. Law Commn., London, 1966-67; asst. prof. U. Windsor, Can., 1968-70; lectr. law Oxford U., England, 1971-91; prin. St. Anne's Coll., Oxford U., 1991—; chmn. U.K. Human Fertilization and Embryology Authority, 1994—; Rhodes trustee, 1996—; mem. Human Genetics Commn., 2000—; vis. prof. Osgoode Hall Law Sch., Toronto, Can., 1978; vis. lectr. U. Cape Town, South Africa, 1994; gov. Oxford Ctr. Hebrew and Jewish Studies, 1994—, U. Coll. Sch., London, 1997—. Author: (booklet) Divorce Dissent, 1994; contbr. articles to profl. jours.; mem. editl. bd. Child & Family Law Quar., 1994—. Law fellow St. Anne's Coll., 1970-71. Fellow Royal Soc. Arts, Soc. Advanced Legal Studies (hon.); mem. Internat. Soc. Family Law (exec. councillor 1988—), United Oxford and Cambridge Club. Office: St Annes Coll, Woodstock Rd, Oxford OX2 6HS, England

DE CHADAREVIAN, SORAYA, history of science researcher; b. Rome, May 21, 1953; d. Etienne Sami de C. and Angelica Alice Giulini; m. Michael Cahn, Dec. 23, 1985; children: Livia Camilla, Flavia Celina. Abitur, German Sch. Rome, 1972; M in Biology, U. Freiburg (Germany), 1978; PhD in Philosophy, U. Konstanz, Germany, 1988. Rsch. asst. U. Freiburg, 1979; rsch. asst. U. Konstanz, 1980-85, part-time lectr., 1985-90; Walther-Rathenau fellow History of Sci., Berlin, 1989-90; rsch. fellow Wellcome unit for history of medicine U. Cambridge, Eng., 1991-96; researcher Hamburg (Germany) Inst. Social Rsch., 1997, sr. rsch. assoc., affil. lectr. dept. history & philos. sci., 1997—; ind. collaborator Oko-Inst., Freiburg, 1983-91. Author: Zwischen den Diskursen, 1990; co-author: (exhbn. catalogue) Representations of the Double Helix, 1995; co-editor: Molecularizing Biology and Medicine, 1998; adv. editor: Studies in History and Philosophy of Biological and Biomedical Sciences. Scholar German Acad. Exch. Svc., 1972-78; recipient Poste Rouge Nat. Ctr. Scientific Rsch., 1996. Mem. Brit. Soc. History Sci., Internat. Soc. History Philosophy and Social Studies of Biology, History Sci. Soc. Avocations: travel, yoga. E-Mail: SD10016@hermes.cam.ac.uk. Home: 77 Garden Walk, Cambridge CB4 3EW, England Office: U Cambridge Dept History & Philosophy of Sci, Free School Ln, Cambridge CB2 3RH, England

DE CHARETTE, HERVÉ, French political party executive; b. July 30, 1938; s. Helon de Charette and Jeanne de Nolhac; m. Michelle Delor, 1980. Student, Inst. Polit. Studies, Paris, Sch. Higher Comml. Studies, Sch. Nat. Adminstrn. Tech. adviser Ministry of Labor Govt. of France, Paris, 1973-74, cabinet dir. Ministry of Labor, 1976-78, dir. State Secretariat for Immigrant Labor, 1973-74, chief dept. Ministry of Fgn. Trade, 1978-80, dep. min. civil svc., 1986-88, min. housing, 1993-95, min. fgn. affairs, 1995-97; regional coun. v.p., Pays de La Loire, 1992; mem. Nat. Assembly Nievre, 1986, Nat. Assembly maine-et-Loire, 1988-93, 97; mayor St. Florent-le-Vieil, 1989; v.p. Union for French Democracy, 1989-98, dep. pres., 1998—. Office: Union French Democracy, 250 bd Saint Germain, 75007 Paris France

DE CICCO, FRANCIS, business consultant, religious administrator; b. San Francisco, Nov. 22, 1922; arrived in Germany, 1955; s. Alfonso and Anna Fedoronova (Golzeva) de C. AA, City Coll. San Francisco, 1942; student, U. Calif., Berkeley, 1943; BS, Trinity Coll., Dover, Del., 1991, MBA, 1993; D of Divinity (hon.), World Christianship Mins., Fresno, Calif., 1998. Cert. ultra high frequency engring. and radar War Dept., Signal Corps, U.S. Gen. agt. Webster Chgo. Corp., Paris, 1949-55; dist. mgr. for Germany Field Enterprises Edn. Corp., 1956-61; regional mgr. for Germany F.E. Compton & Co., Chgo., 1961-65; NATO forces agt. in Germany Deutscher Lloyd Vers. AG, 1966-95; internat. bus. cons. Stuttgart, Germany, 1995—; adminstr. Ch. of the Holy Grail, Stuttgart, 1998—; founder, dir. Am. Radio & Electronics Co., Paris, 1947-55; co-founder ednl. divsn. Ch. of Holy Grail, 1999, co-founder, Grand Master of Knights of Holy Grail, 1999. Contbr. tech. articles to profl. jours. Bd. trustees Pershing Hall, Paris, 1950; resident mem. Am. C. of C. France, 1950-55; master control engr. Armed Forces Network. Staff sgt. Supreme Hdqs. Allied Expeditionary Forces, 1943-46. Named Count de Vaux Moise, Lord Alexander II, Patriarchate of Antioch, 1991. Mem. NRA (life), VFW (sr. vice-commdr. 1951, life mem.), Am. Overseas Meml. Day Assn., Inc. Republican. Avocations: rare books, coins, engravings, psychic research. Home and Office: Fleckenweinberg 64, 70192 Stuttgart Germany

DE CIDRAC, CHARLES-ETIENNE, asset management executive; b. Neuilly, France, Sept. 14, 1964; s. Gérard and Claire (de Froberville) de C.; m. Marta Saada, July 28, 1990; children: Barthélemy, Eléonore, Alexandra. Diploma, Ecole Européenne Affaires, Paris, 1987. Contr. Matif SA, Paris, 1989-91, head mktg., 1991-97; head mktg. SG Asset Mgmt., Paris, 1997-99; global head cons. rels. Axa IM, Paris, 1999—; tchr. derivatives and acctg. U. Paris, 1990-91. Home: 38 rue de Tourville, 78100 Saint Germain France Office: Axa Investment Mgrs, 46 av de la Grande Armée, 75017 Paris France

DECIL, STELLA WALTERS (DEL DECIL), artist; b. Indpls., Apr. 26, 1921; d. William Calvin and Hazel Jean (Konkle) Smith; m. John W. Walters, June 19, 1940 (div. Sept. 1945); m. Casimir R. Decil, Feb. 6, 1965. Grad., Indpls. Acad. Comml. Art, 1939, John Heron Art Inst., Indpls., 1941. Staff artist William H. Block Co., Indpls., 1945-50, art dir., 1952-62; art dir. Frank R. Jelleff Co., Washington, 1950-51, Diamonds Dept. Stores, Phoenix, 1962-67; freelance artist Phoenix, Chgo., others, 1967-70; curator Mature Eye bi-ann. Prescott (Ariz.) Fine Arts Assn., 1996-2000; instr., lectr. Mountain Artists Guild, Prescott, 1995-97; mem. visual arts bd. Prescott Fine Arts Assn., 1990—; painting instr. Art Groups in Ariz.-N.Mex., 1970—, Phoenix Art Mus., 1975-77. Exhibited work in galleries in Phoenix, Scottsdale, Ariz., Las Cruces, N.Mex., Hoosier Salon, Folger Gallery, Indpls., Mammen II Gallery and Garelick Gallery, Scottsdale, Ariz.; 1-woman exhibits include Cave Creek, Carefree, Scottsdale, Ariz., N.Mex.; represented in pvt. collections in more than 20 states; in corp. collections including Continental Bank, Humana Hosp., Pueblo Grande Mus., VA Med. Ctr., Prescott, Mayo Ctr. for Women's Health, Scottsdale, Proctor Bank Vt., Bank of Rio Grande, Las Cruces, N.Mex. Past pres. Scottsdale Art League. Recipient Maxine Cherrington Meml. award Hoosier Salon, 1973; named Ad Woman of Yr., Indpls. Ad Club, 1958. Mem. No. Ariz. Watercolor Assn., Ariz. Artists Guild, Ariz. Watercolor Assn. (past pres.). Home: 9460 E Towago Dr Prescott Valley AZ 86314-7140

DECIUTIIS, ALFRED CHARLES MARIA, medical oncologist, television producer; b. N.Y.C., Oct. 16, 1945; s. Alfred Ralph and Theresa Elizabeth (Manko) de C.; m. Catherine L. Gohn. B.S. summa cum laude, Fordham U., 1967; M.D., Columbia U., 1971. Diplomate Am. Bd. Internal Medicine, Am. Bd. Med. Oncology. Intern N.Y. Hosp.-Cornell Med. Ctr., N.Y.C., 1971-72, resident, 1972-74; fellow in clin. immunology Meml. Hosp.-Sloan Kettering Cancer Ctr., N.Y.C., 1974-75, fellow in clin. oncology, 1975-76, spl. fellow in immunology, 1974-76; guest investigator, asst. physician exptl. hematology Rockefeller U., N.Y.C., 1975-76; practice medicine, specializing in med. oncology Los Angeles, 1977—; host cable TV shows, 1981—; med. editor Cable Health Network, 1983—, Lifetime Network, 1984—; mem. med. adv. com. 1984 Olympics; co-founder Meditrina Med. Ctr., free outpatient surg. ctr., Torrance, Calif., physician asst. supr., 1984; mem. fgn. policy leadership project Ctr. for Internat. Affairs, Harvard, Ill. Syndicated columnist Coast Media News, 1980's; producer numerous med. TV shows; contbr. articles to profl. jours.; author first comprehensive clin. description of chronic fatique syndrome as a neuro-immunologic acquired disorder. Founder Italian-Am. Med. Assn., 1982; co-founder Italian-Am. Legal Alliance, L.A., 1982—; mem. gov. bd. med. coun. Italian-Am. Found.; mem. Italian-Am. Civic Com., L.A., 1983, UCLA Chancellor's Assocs., Cath. League for Civil and Rel. Liberty, World Affairs Coun., L.A., Boston Mus. Fine Arts, Met. Mus. Served to capt. M.C., U.S. Army, 1972-74. Leukemia Soc. Am. fellow, 1974-76. Fellow ACP, Internat. Coll. Physicians and Surgeons; mem. AMA (Physician's Recognition award 1978-80, 82-85, 86-89, 89-91, 91-94, 94-96, 96—), Am. Soc. Clin. Oncology, N.Y. Acad. Sci. (life), Calif. Med. Assn., Los Angeles County Med. Assn., AAAS, Am. Union Physicians and Dentists, Internat. Health Soc., Am. Pub. Health Assn., Am. Geriatrics Soc., Chinese Med. Assn., Drug Info. Assn., Nat. Geographic Soc. (life), Internat. Platform Assn., Am. Soc. Hematology (emeritus), N.Y. Acad. Scis. (life), Fondazione Giovanni Agnelli, Smithsonian Instn., Nature Conservancy, Nat. Wildlife Fedn., Mensa, Phi Beta Kappa, Alpha Omega Alpha, Sigma Xi. Achievements include first comprehensive clinical description of chronic fatigue syndrome as a neuro-immunologic disorder probably caused by a retrovirus with multi-system complications. Avocations: collecting, reading, hunting, fishing, astronomy. The deCiutiis family was first ranked among the nobles of Italy in 893, designated a princely family and given the title of "Princes of the Holy Roman Empire" in 1629. Office: PO Box 384 Agoura Hills CA 91376-0384

DECK, RICHARD ALLEN, political scientist, consultant, writer, human rights activist; b. Concord, N.H., May 6, 1953; s. Herbert Heller Jr. and Eleanor DuVall (Deyo) D.; m. Jo Ann Marie Passariello, Nov. 15, 1986. Student, Ripon Coll., 1972-73, Waseda U., Japan, 1974-75; BA in Polit. Sci. and East Asian Studies summa cum laude with honors, Macalester Coll., 1977; cert. Urban and Regional Planning and Design, Harvard U., 1978; Grad. Cert. in Brit. Fgn. Policy, Oxford (Eng.) U., 1980; MA in Econs. in Pub. Policy & Adminstrn., U. Manchester (Eng.), 1982; M in City Planning, U. Calif., Berkeley, 1982; AM in Polit. Sci., Stanford U., 1985; MALS, Dartmouth Coll., 1994; PhD in Polit. Sci., Stanford U., 1997. Internat./intercultural rels. seminar leader Assn. of Current English Keio U., Japan, 1975; mag writer and interviewer The English Jour., Japan, 1975; rschr. writer Dem. Farmer Labor Party, Minneapolis, 1976; survey rchr. and analyst Project on Volunteerism Adelphi U., L.I., 1978; legis. analyst rschr. Assembly Edn. Com. New York St. Assembly, Albany, 1979; co-chair external affairs Grad. Assembly U. Calif., Berkeley, 1981-82; fellow internat. peace and security studies Social Sci. Rsch. Coun. and John D. and Catherine T. MacArthur Found., Southeast Asia, 1986-88; vis. joint fellow nat. and internat. security U. So. Calif. and UCLA, 1989; rsch. fellow and project coord. Asian Regionalization Asia/Pacific Rsch. Ctr., Stanford U. and The Asia Found. San Francisco, Calif., 1991-92; v.p. Catalyst Concepts, Berkeley, 1992—; founding dir. Asia/Pacific Reg. Policy Rsch. Inst., Berkeley and Emeryville, 1998—; social sys. dir. and bd. dirs. U. Calif. Space Working Group, U. Calif., Berkeley, 1979-80, 81-82; grad. rep. from Berkeley campus for the student body pres. coun. U. Calif. (systemwide), 1981-82; tchg. asst. Stanford (Calif.) U., 1983, 86, mem. grad. studies com., 1983-84, head tchg. asst., 1984, observer Project Peace and Coop. Asia-Pacific Region, 1984, mem. internat. rels. sr. faculty search com., 1985-86, co-instr., 1991; seminar group discussion leader, M.A.L.S. Colloquium on Ctrl. Amer., Darmouth Coll., 1984; lectr. and participant World Affairs Coun. No. Calif., study group on the Assn. of So. East Asian Nat., San Francisco, 1985; participant Project Soviet Internat. Behavior, U. Calif., Berkeley and Stanford U., 1985-86; lectr. Inst. S.E. Asian Studies, 1988, Nat. U. Singapore, 1988, Asean Insts. Conf. on U.S.-Asean Relations, Singapore, 1988; conf. participant and delegate 40th Anniv. Commemoration of the Signing of the United Nat. Charter in San Francisco, 1985; ofcl. observer U.S. del. Pacific Econ. Cooperation Coun., PECC Gen. Meeting/Conf., San Francisco, 1992; global media dir. U.S.-S.E. Asian Alliance for a Dem. Asia, Cambridge, Mass., 1998—; cons. Def. & Diplomacy, The Newshour with Jim Lehrer, PBS-TV, Washington and Arlington, Va., 2000. Author: U.S. official delegation "Dialogue Partners" session, First ASEAN Economic Congress, ASEAN Chambers of Commerce and Industry, and the Institute of Strategic and International Studies, 1987, Fourth ASEAN Institutes Conference on the Association of Southeast Asian Nations and the United States, 1988; (with others) Peace, Conflict, and Strategic Cultures in the Asia-Pacific Region, 1999 (nominee Kiriyama Pacific Rim book prize), (with others) The Singapore Puzzle, 1999 (nominee Kiriyama Pacific Rim book prize), Strategic Cultures in the Asia-Pacific Region, 1999 (paper edit., nominee Kiriyama Pacific Rim Book prize); contbr. to profl. articles; mem. editl. bd., editl. writer, polit. corr., and polit. feature writer The Stanford Daily, 1982-83; rschr. and writing cons. The Concept of Relationship in International Politics, 1989-90; contbr. papers to various organizations; interview subject (TV) Friday Background, Current Affairs Unit, Singapore Broadcasting Corp., 1987, Berita (Evening news), RTM (Malaysian govt. network), 1987,

Official Questionner of Malaysian Prime Minister Mahathir bin Mohamad, Iseas Singapore Lecture, Inst. of Southeast Asian Studies, 1988; (film) co-narrator and co-interviewer The Pennsylvania Underground: The Sanctuary Movement and Illegal Ctrl. Am. Refugees in Philadelphia, 1986; (newspaper) Internat. Herald Tribune, Republic of Singapore, 1987, (radio) The Michael Fay Caning Affair, The World Tonight with Phil Till Show, Radio Can., Vancouver, 1994; spl. contbr. Asiaweek newsmag., Hong Kong, 1998. Del. candidate N.H. Pres. Preferences Primary, Dem. Nat. Conv., Keene, 1972, Calif. Pres. Primary, Stanford, 1984, Berkeley, 1992; candidate N.H. Constl. Conv., Keene, 1974; city and campus chairperson Calif. Dem. Pres. Primary Campaign, Stanford U. and Palo Alto, Calif., 1984, 92; chmn. N.H. Govs.' Youth Hwy. Safety Adv. Com., 1972; staff intern Minn. Dem. Farmer Labor Party Hdqs., 1976; bd. dirs. U. of Manchester Postgrad. Soc. (UK), 1980-81; conf. participant and del. 40th Anniversary Commemoration of the Signing of the UN Charter in San Francisco: Conf. Assessing the UN After 40 Years, UN Assn. San Francisco and World Affairs Coun. No. Calif., 1985; spl. fellowship coord. Open Soc. Inst., N.Y.C., 1997-98, 2000; chairperson panel of experts and human resource persons Alliance of Asian Dems. Airman 3d class, USAF Aux., 1966. Recipient World Affairs Coun. Staff award, 1985; Nat. Forensics League scholar Ripon Coll., 1972-73; Harry Sherman scholar Macalester Coll., 1976-77; John W. Searle Meml. scholar Macalester Coll., 1976-77, Outstanding Sr. award, Minnesota Jaycees, College Court of Honor, 1977; N.Y. State Assembly Grad. Scholar fellow, 1979; Roothbert Fund fellow U. Calif., Berkeley, 1979-80, 81-82; Inst. Internat. Edn. scholar Oxford U., 1980; Rotary Internat. Grad. fellow U. Manchester, 1980-81; Lasker scholar U. Calif., Berkeley, 1981-82; Newhouse fellow U. Calif., Berkeley, 1981-82; Eisenhower Meml. Grad. scholar Stanford U., 1982-83; AMVETS scholar Stanford U., 1982-86; Stanford U. Grad. fellow 1982-86; MALS Grad. fellow Dartmouth Coll., 1984, 86; UN Assn. and World Affairs Coun. scholar, 1985; Fgn. Lang. and Area Studies grantee U.S. Dept. Edn., 1985; SSRC/MacArthur found. fellow in Internat. Peace and Security, N.Y.C., N.Y., and Chicago, 1986-88; USC-UCLA Visiting Joint fellowship in Nat. and Internat. Security, L.A., 1989; rsch. fellow Asia/Pacific Rsch. Ctr. Stanford U. and the Asia Found., San Francisco, 1991-92; co-nominee (with Dr. Chee Soon Juan, Singapore) Nobel Peace Prize, 1999-2000. Mem. Internat. Studies Assn. (presenter 1998), Asian Media Info. and Comm. Ctr., Assn. Asian Studies, Acad. Polit. Sci., Am. Polit. Sci. Assn., Pi Kappa Delta, Phi Alpha Theta, Pi Sigma Alpha, Phi Beta Kappa. United Ch. of Christ. Avocations: reading novels and screenplays, viewing films. Office: Catalyst Concepts PO Box 8393 Berkeley CA 94707-8393

DECKER, CHRISTIAN LUCIEN, research chemist; b. Guebwiller, Alsace, France, June 10, 1940; s. Lucien and Lucie (Kastler) D.; m. Danielle Freyss, Sept. 4, 1964; children: Luc, Sylvaine. M in Chemistry, Univ., Strasbourg, France, 1961, Dr es-Sci., 1967. Postdoctoral fellow Stanford Rsch. Inst., Menlo Park, Calif., 1961-72; rsch. asst. CNRS-Univ., Strasbourg, France, 1967-80; rsch. dir. CNRS-Univ., Mulhouse, 1981-2000; head of polymer photochemistry lab. U. Mulhouse; internat. adv. bd. RadTech-Asia, Tokyo, Polymer Internat. Author: (book chpts.) Degradation and Stabilization of PVC, 1984, Handbook of Polymer Science, 1989, Polymers for Microelectronics, 1990, Lasers in Polymer Science, 1990, Laser-Assisted Processing, 1991, Radiation Curing-Science and Technology, 1992, Processes in Photoreactive Polymers, 1995, Polymeric Materials Encyclopedia, 1996, Photopolymerization Fundamentals, 1997, Functional Polymers, 1998, MAcromolecules, 1999. Named Best Sci. paper RadTech Corp., 1985, 87, 92. Achievements include development of highly reactive monomers for radiation curing applications; study of laser-induced polymerization of acrylic resins; real time monitoring of ultrafast polymerizations; direct laser writing of microcircuits.; photostabilization of polymers photographting. E-mail: c.decker@univ mulhouse.fr. Office: CNRS Univ, 3 Rue Werner, 68200 Mulhouse France

DECKER, FRANZ PAUL, symphony conductor, educator; b. Cologne, Germany; s. Caspar and Elisabeth (Scholz) D.; m. Christa Terka, May 26, 1969; children: Arabella, Ariadne. Grad. high sch.; student, State Inst. for Mus. Edn., Cologne; M.Conducting, U. Cologne; Dr. honoris causa, Concordia U., Montreal, Que., Can. Choir dir., asst. condr., Municipal Theater, Giessen, 1945, condr. opera, Cologne, 1945, municipal dir. music, Krefeld, from 1946, prin condr., State Opera house, Wiesbaden, 1950-53, permanent dir., Municipal Symphony Orch., Wiesbaden, 1953-56, general music director, Bochum, 1956-64, chief condr., artistical dir., Rotterdam Philharmonic Orch., 1962-68, permanent condr., mus. dir., Montreal Symphony Orch., 1967-76, guest condr. opera and concerts worldwide; prin. guest condr. New Zealand Symphony, 1981-89, music dir., 1990-94; chief condr. and artistical dir. Orquestra Sinfonica de Barcelona, 1986—; prin. guest condr. Nat. Arts Ctr. Orch., Ottawa, 1991—; composer symphonies, opera, oratories, chamber music. Decorated Edgar Roquette Pinto medal Brazil, 1963, Herscheppend Schep Ik medal Netherlands, 1968; Order of Merit 1st class Fed. Republic of Germany; Jubilee medal Queen Elizabeth II. Address: 2 Kronenburgerstrasse, 50935 Koeln 41, Germany also: National Arts Centre Orchestra, 468B Mount Pleasant Ave, Westmount, ON Canada H3Y H3H

DECKER, HARLEY S., volunteer; b. Warwick, N.Y., Sept. 10, 1923; s. Seymour Andrew and Ethel Weeden Decker; m. Ruth Naomi Renish, Dec. 27, 1946 (div. June 1975); children: Rebekah, Paula, Lisa, Mark; m. Rozella Joan Decker, Oct. 14, 1988. Vol., desk scheduler, historian Friends Red Rock Canyon, Las Vegas; bd. mem. Palos Verdes Homeowners Assn., Las Vegas. Baptist. Avocations: stamps, photography, reading. Home: 3910 Visby Ln Las Vegas NV 89119-7182

DECKER, JAMES LUDLOW, management consultant; b. Batavia, N.Y., Nov. 5, 1923; s. James Ludlow and Ruth Adeline (Peard) D.; m. Bette Wilson Botzler, Jan. 31, 1997. B of Aero. Engring., Rensselaer Poly. Inst., 1944; postgrad. Textron Advanced Mgmt. Program, Harvard U., 1974. Registered profl. engr., Md. With The Martin Co., Balt., 1944-67; dep. mgr. Lunar Module, Apollo Office, NASA, Houston, 1963; program mgr. surface effect ship program U.S. Navy, Washington, 1967-72; v.p., gen. mgr. Bell Aerospace Can., Grand Bend, Ont., 1972-74; prin. J.L. Decker, Inc., Potomac, Md., 1974—; guest lectr. AIAA, 1972-79, Can. Aeros. and Space Inst., 1973-79, George Washington U., 1974, Royal Aero. Soc., 1972, Aero. Engring. Rensselaer Poly. Inst., 1990—; cons. USN, Maritime Adminstrn., USCG, NRC Can., Can. Coast Guard, various corps., 1972—. Contbr. articles to profl. jours.; patentee in field. Pres., Greenbrier Cmty. Assn., 1956-57; regional chmn. Rensselaer Fund, 1982; mem. Congl. Subcom. to Rev. NASA Adv. Com. Utilization, 1987; mem. pres.'s adv. coun. Meredith Coll., 1999. Buffalo Alumni scholar, 1941-44, N.Y. State Regents scholar, 1941-44, Rensselaer Alumni fellow, 1991. Fellow AIAA (assoc.); mem. Soc. Naval Archs. and Marine Engrs., Am. Soc. Naval Engrs., Rensselaer Soc. Engrs., N.Y. Acad. Sci., Patroons of Rensselaer, Cosmos Club (Washington), Towson Golf and Country Club, Sigma Xi, Tau Beta Pi. Republican. Baptist. Address: 1 Shawnery Ct Baldwin MD 21013-9657

DECKER, KATE DELANO CONDAX See DELANO-CONDAX, KATE

DECKER, SANDRA LYNN, economist, educator; b. Tiffin, Ohio, Apr. 15, 1964; d. John Erie and Sharon Rose Decker. AB, Dartmouth Coll., 1986; AM, Harvard U., 1990, PhD, 1993. Bus. analyst McKinsey & Co., N.Y.C., 1986-88; asst. prof. econs. NYU, N.Y.C., 1993—; faculty rsch. fellow Nat. Bur. Econ. Rsch., 1993—; cons. World Bank, Washington, 1985-96, U.S. VA, N.Y.C., 1992—, Montefiore Hosp., Bronx, 1994-95. Contbr. articles to profl. jours. Dartmouth Coll. fellow, 1988-89, Jacob J. Javits fellow U.S. Dept. Edn., 1988-92, Harvard Chiles fellow Chiles Found., 1992-93. Mem. Am. Econ. Assn., Internat. Health Econs. Assn., Population Assn. Am., Nat. Tax Assn., Assn. for Health Svcs. Rsch. Home: 1 Washington Square Vlg Apt 9K New York NY 10012-1606 Office: New York Univ 40 W 4th St Rm 602 New York NY 10012-1106

DE CLERCK, HERVÉ CHARLES, food products executive; b. Pau, France, Feb. 5, 1945; s. Jean de Clerck and Colette (de Courson) de la Villeneuve; m. Christine Zafiropulo, Mar. 6, 1968; children: Sophie, Isabel, Kurata, Guérinet. Diploma, Inst. Supérieur du Commerce Paris, 1968; internat. sr. mgmt. program, Harvard U., 1985. Brand mgr. Colgate Palmolive, France, 1970-72; devel. mgr. Colgate Food Div., France, 1972-74; gen. mgr. Synapse Consumer Research, France, 1974-77; owner/founder Maesina, France, 1974—; pres., chief exec. officer Benton & Bowles, Inc., France, 1977-85; also v.p. Benton & Bowles, N.Y.C.; chief operating officer Lesieur Cotelle, France, 1985-87; gen. mgr. Lesieur Alimentaire, France, 1987—; dir. RTL, France, 1991-96; mng. dir. IP France, 1991-96; v.p. internat. Havas Intermediation, 1997-98; founder MAYDREAM, Switzerland, 1999. Author: Relations Agences-Annonceur, 1976; founder, Marketing Mix mag., 1986. Served to lt. French armed forces, 1968-69. Mem. Colgate Bus. Club (co-founder, 1983). Roman Catholic. Avocations: yachting, polo. Home: 33 Blvd d'Angleterre, Les Pierres C13, CH 3962 Montana Switzerland

DECLERCK, PAUL JULES, pharmaceutical biology educator; b. Menen, Belgium, Feb. 5, 1958; s. Roland and Eveline (Lambeets) C.; m. Gerarda Jacobs, Aug. 23, 1980; children: Veerle, Steven, Marlies. Pharmacist, Katholieke U Leuven, Belgium, 1980, tchg. diploma, 1983, PhD, 1984. Cert. indsl. pharmacist. Fellow Belgian Am. Ednl. Found., N.Y.C., 1984-85; postdoctoral fellow Rockefeller U., N.Y.C., 1985-86; sr. rsch. asst. Nat. Fund Sci. Rsch., Belgium, 1986-90, rsch. assoc., 1990-93, sr. rsch. assoc., 1993-96; prof., rsch. dir. Katholieke U. Leuven, 1991—, vice-dean faculty pharm. scis., 1998—; Mem. Belgian Pharmacopoeia, Belgium, 1992—, Superior Coun. for Health, Belgium, 1994—; expert biotech. Ministry Health, Belgium, 1992—; founder mem. Alpro Found., Wevelgem, Belgium, 1996-2000; mem. gov. bd. Eurosci., Paris, 1997-98; mem. Commn. Drug R&D, Fwo, Belgium, 1997—. Recipient award for excellent contbn. Gordon Rsch. Conf., Ventura, Calif., 1992, prize Boehringer Ingelheim for Rsch. on Thrombosis and Haemostasis, 1993. Mem. INternat. Soc. Fibrinolysis and Thrombolysis, Internat. Soc. Thrombosis and Haemostasis (Travel Fund Young Scientists, 1989, Young Investigator's merit travel award, 1991), Internat. Soc. Pharm. Biotech. Avocations: bicycle riding, hiking. Office: Katholieke U Leuven, E Vanevenstraat 4, B-3000 Leuven Belgium

DE CLERCQ, GERRIT, editor-in-chief; b. Sint Agatha Berchem, Belgium, Aug. 15, 1951; s. Florent and Cecile (Otte) DeC.; m. Ann Neukermans, Dec. 15, 1978; 1 child, Robin. MA with distinction, State U., Ghent, 1977. Reporter Press Agy. Belga, Brussels, 1978-86, fgn. desk editor, 1986-88; cultural desk editor Het Nieuwsblad, Brussels, 1988-93; editor-in-chief UIT Mag., Antwerp, Belgium, 1993-95; editor Het Nieuwsblad, Brussels, 1999; prof. journalism, head dept. journalism Egon Coll., Ghent, 1999—. Avocations: music, books, karate, chess. Home: Warande 88, 9270 Laarne Belgium Office: Egon College, Savaanstraat 80, 9000 Ghent Belgium

DECLERCQ, GUIDO VICTOR ALFONS (BARON DECLERCQ), retired investment company executive; b. Ardooie, Belgium, Apr. 21, 1928; s. Gerard V. Declercq and Gabrielle Deboutte; m. Josine Ghekiere, Apr. 26, 1957; children: Dominik, Magda, Beatrijs, Philip, Pieter, Marijke. Student econs., U. Leuven, Belgium, 1946-50, student philosophy, 1950-53; student econs., Columbia U., 1951-52. Mng. dir. West-Flanders Devel. Council, Bruges, Belgium, 1954-57, Bank van Roeselare, Belgium, 1957-63; advisor Banque Lambert, Brussels, 1963-70; gen. adminstr. Katholieke U. Leuven, 1967-82; hon. gen. adminstr. Katholieke U. Leuven, Brussels, 1982—; chmn. Fidisco N.V., Brussels, 1982-94, hon. chmn., 1994—; chmn. Orda-B N.V., Leuven, 1970-98, hon. chmn., 1998—; bd. dirs. HSA-Spaarbank (Centea) N.V., Antwerp, GEVAERT N.V., Antwerp, Transurb Consult, Brussels, BeneVent, Brussels, MezzaFinance, Luxembourg, Leuven Rsch. Devel., U. Leuven; chmn. KB LuxLease, Luxembourg, MercaLease GmbH, Bremen, Germany, Investco NV, Brussels, 1982-94, hon. chmn., 1994—; sec. Stichting Amici Almae Matris Breda, Netherlands; chmn. investment com. Coll. Europe, Bruges. Author: Structurele Werkloosheid, 1954, Kust en Hinterland, 1956, Ieper, Economische Situatie, 1957. Pres. Internat. Assn. Cons. in Higher Edn. Instns., London, 1981-90; mem. Trilateral Commn. Recipient John Fraser Meml. award Australian Tertiary Inst. Cons. Cos. Assn., 1987.

DE CLERCQ, GUY MAURICE, psychologist, writer; b. Gent, Belgium, June 4, 1947; s. Gaston and Jeanne (De Jaeger) De C.; m. Anita Daes, Sept., 1970 (div. Dec. 1980); 1 child, Anouk. Grad. H.S., Gent, 1966. Employee travel agy., Brussels, 1969; barman Bar-Dancing, Gent, 1970; waiter Café-Restaurant, coast, Belgium, 1971; van driver parcel svc., Belgium, 1972-73; employee liquid gas factory, Gent, 1974-75; writer/journalist various newspapers, mags., 1976—; pvt. practice as trans-psychologist Gent, 1986-92. Author: (poem collection) Poems of Nature and Mysticism, 1992, (essays) Spirituality and the New Age, 1991, Holy, 1997, 1962-1997, 1997; (novels) The Horseman, 1995, Sacha, 1995, The Plot Against the Tulku, 1995, The Traveller, 1996, An Odyssea of Time, 1997, The Flower, 1998, Maya, 1998, Awaken in Paris, 1999, A Metaphysical Study: God, Man and the Worlds, 2000, others. Avocations: walking through the countryside, travel.

DE CLERCQ, WILLY C.E.H., member of European parliament, barrister; b. Ghent, Belgium, July 8, 1927; s. Frans and Yvonne (Catry) de C.; LL.D.; m. Fernande Fazzi, 1953; 3 children. Barrister, Ct. of Appeal, Ghent; with Gen. Secretariat UN, N.Y.C., 1952; mem. Chamber of Reps. Belgium for Ghent-Eekloo, Brussels, 1958-85, dep. prime minister in charge budget, 1966-68, dep. prime minister, 1973-74, minister fin., 1974-77, minister fin., 1981-85, vice prime minister, minister fin. and fgn. trade, 1981-85; mem. European Parliament, 1979-81; pres. Fedn. European Liberal and Democratic Parties, 1980-85, 89—. Commn. European Communities, 1985-89; pres. interim com. IMF, 1976-77, 83-85; prof. U. Ghent, U. Brussels. Pres. Partij voor Vrijheid en Vooruitgang, Belgium, 1971-73, 77-81; commr. for external rels. and trade Commn. European Community, 1985-89; mem. European parliament, pres. com. for external econ. rels., minister state, 1985—. Office: Cyriel Buyssestraat 12, B-900 Gent Belgium*

DECO, GUSTAVO RICARDO, physicist, computer scientist; b. Rosario, Santa Fe, Argentina, Nov. 7, 1961; arrived in Germany, 1987; s. Orlando and Norma (Campora) D.; m. Maria Eugenia Granitto, Dec. 31, 1994; children: Nikolas, Sebastian, Martin. M.Physics, Nat. U., Rosario, 1984, PhD in Physics, 1987; PhD and Habil. in Computer Sci., Tech. U., Munich, 1996. Fellow U. Rosario, 1984-87; postdoctoral fellow U. Bordeaux, France, 1987, U. Giessen, Germany, 1987-88; rschr. Siemens Corp. Rsch., Munich, 1989—. Author: An Information Theoretic Approach to Neural Computing, 1996, Information Dynamics; contbr. over 160 articles to profl. jours.; patentee in field. Avocations: literature, music, printing.

DE COEN, ANDRÉ, accounting educator; b. Gent, Belgium, May 18, 1950; s. Alois De Coen and Maria Vercauteren; m. Isabelle Moeyaert, Apr. 24, 1981; children: Lieven, Laurens, Miriam, Vincent. AA, Vlekho U., Belgium, 1974, BComm, 1976; MS, Columbia Pacific U., Calif., 1985, PhD, 1985. Asst. acct. Belgium, 1976-77; acct. Callens, Belgium, 1977, CMB, Belgium, 1978; coord. Vlekho, Belgium, 1978-83; coord. EHSAL, Belgium, 1983-84, lectr., 1984—. Author: (book) Organisatieleer, 1993; co-author: (book) Praktisch Vennootschapsboekhouden, 1984; contbr. articles to profl. jours. Mem. Am. Acctg. Assn., Accts. Vereniging LBC, European Acctg. Assn. Avocations: travel, cycling, family life. Home: Eikenstraat 1, 9620 Zottegem Belgium Office: EHSAL, Stormstraat 2, Brussels Belgium

DECONINCK, GEERT LEOPOLD, electrotechnical engineer; b. Oostende, Belgium, Feb. 6, 1968; s. August Renaat and Diomee (van Vooren) D.; m. An Magdalena Debbaut, Sept. 16, 1992. BSc in Engring., Kath. U. Leuven, Belgium, 1989, M. in Electrotech. Engring., 1991, PhD in Applied Scis., 1996. Rsch. asst. in electrotech. engring. Kath. U., Leuven, 1992-96, postdoctoral rschr., 1996-99, lectr., 1999—. Mem. IEEE (sr.), Royal Flemish Engrs. Soc. Home: Nazarethstr 4, B-9840 De Pinte Belgium Office: K U Leuven - ESAT, Kard Mercierlaan 94, B-3001 Leuven Belgium

DE CORTE, ERIK WILLY ALBERIC, educational psychology researcher; b. Blankenberge, Belgium, June 15, 1941; m. Rita Vanderheyde, Sept. 23, 1964; children: Emmanuel, Karolien. Degree in edn., U. Leuven, Belgium, 1964, D in Pedagogical Sci., 1970; Dr honoris causa, Rand Afrikaans U., Johannesburg, South Africa, 2000. Asst. FNRS U. Leuven, 1964-71, lectr. in ednl. psychology, 1971-72, prof. in ednl. psychology, 1976—, chmn. dept. ednl. scis., 1994-98; dir. Leuven Lang. Ctr., 1987-93; vis. scholar Sch. of Edn. Stanford U., 1998-99. Co-author: Foundations of School Learning and Teaching, 1972, (transl. German and French) Educational Objectives, 1973, 2d edit., 1976, Research on Teaching-Learning Processes: Present Trends and Issues, 1982, Growing in Teaching, 1990; editor: International Encyclopedia of Developmental and Instructional Psychology, 1996; co-editor Internat. Perspectives on the Design Technology-Supported Learning Environments, 1996; assoc. editor: (book series) Advances in Learning and Instruction; editor-in-chief jour. Learning and Instrn., 1990-93; editor Internat. Jour. Ednl. Rsch., 1986—; mem. editl com. for various jours in field. First laureate of Concours U. Belgium, 1965; recipient award for best publ. in edn. Ministry of Nat. Edn., 1973, award for outstanding rsch. articles U.S. Nat. Coun. Tchrs. Math., 1987. Mem. APA, European Assn. Rsch. on Learning and Instrn. (pres. 1985-89, Oeuvre award for outstanding contbns. to rsch. on learning and instrn. 1997), Belgian Psychol. Assn., Dutch Edn. Rsch. Assn., Am. Ednl. Rsch. Assn., Internat. Assn. Applied Psychology (pres. divsn. edn. instruction and sch. psychology 1994-98), Internat. Soc. for Study of Behavioral Devel., Royal Norwegian Soc. Scis. and Letters, Sect. Humanities (fgn.), Academia Europaea, Internat. Acad. Edn. (pres. 1998—). Avocations: music, painting, bicycling, belles-lettres. Home: Panoramalaan 5, B 3360 Bierbeek Belgium Office: U Leuven Dept Sci Pedag, Vesaliusstraat 2, B 3000 Leuven Belgium

DE COSMO, VITTORIO, physicist; b. Sepino, Italy, Dec. 17, 1946; s. Libero and Giuseppina (Colonna) de C.; m. Diana Rosa Gaio, Sept. 23, 1974; children: Amanda, Leonardo, Carolina. PhD, U. Florence, 1972. Prof. physics U. Cen. de Venezuela, Maracay, Venezuela, 1978-83; head of physics dept. IUPFAN, Maracay, 1977-83; project mgr. OMI-Agusta, Roma, Italy, 1986-88; hi-tech program mgr. Elettronica SpA, Roma, 1988-2000; remote sensing progrm mgr. ASI, Roma, 2000—; vis. scientist U. B.C., Vancouver, Can., 1983-85; temporary prof. physics, U. Lecce, Italy, 1992-93, U. La Sapienza, Roma, 1987-88. Contbr. articles to profl. jours. Pres. Amici di Sepino, Italy, 1994-95. Mem. N.Y. Acad. Sci. Avocations: orchids, cooking, fractals. E-mail: decosmo@asi.it. Office: Agenzia Spaziale Italiana, Vale Liegi 26, Roma 00198, Italy

DECOURRIERE, FRANCIS, foreign diplomat; b. Sars et Rosières, France, Nov. 22, 1936. Mem. European Parliament, 1999—, mem. com. on regional policy, transport and tourism, substitute com. on agr. and rural devel; mem. Group of the European People's Party (Christian Democrats) and European Democrats; vice chmn. Mems. from the European Parliament to the joint assembly of the Agreement between the African, Caribbean and Pacific States and the European Union. Mem. Union for French Democracy. *

DECRANE, ALFRED CHARLES, JR., petroleum company executive; b. Cleve., June 11, 1931; s. Alfred Charles and Verona (Marquard) DeC.; m. Joan Elizabeth Hoffman, July 3, 1954; children: David, Lisa, Stacie, Stephanie, Sarah, Jennifer. BA, U. Notre Dame, 1953; JD, Georgetown U., 1959; LHD (hon.), Manhattanville Coll., 1990. Bar: Va. bar 1959, D.C. bar 1959, Tex. bar 1961, N.Y. bar 1966. Legal dept. Texaco, Inc., Houston, 1959-64, N.Y.C., 1964-66; asst. to vice chmn. bd. Texaco, Inc., 1965-67, asst. to chmn. bd., 1967-68, gen. mgr. producing dept. Eastern hemisphere, 1968-70, v.p., 1970-76, sr. v.p., gen. counsel, 1976-77, sr. v.p., dir., 1977-78, exec. v.p., 1978-83, pres., 1983-86, chmn. bd. dirs., 1987-96, chmn., chief exec. officer, 1993-96; bd. dirs. CIGNA Corp., Bestfoods Corp, Harris Corp., Corn Products Internat., U.S. Global Leaders Growth Fund, Ltd. Trustee U. Notre Dame. 1st lt. USMCR, 1954-55. Mem. ABA (sect. sec. 1964-67, co-founder Natural Resources Law Jour. mineral law sect.). Office: PO Box 1247 Greenwich CT 06836-1247

DECRETON, MARC CAMILLE, electrical engineer, researcher; b. Ixelles, Belgium, Sept. 24, 1946; s. Andre Camille and Marie Claire (Buelens) D.; m. Anne Marie Boivin, Jan. 8, 1972; children: Cedric, Sandrine. Grad. in Electronic Engring., U. Louvain, Belgium, 1970; MS, U. Manitoba, Can., 1972; PhD, Ecole Poly., Lausanne, Switzerland, 1975. Rsch. asst. Ecole Poly., 1972-75, asst. prof., 1975-77; project engr. Centre D'Etude de L'Energie Nucleaire Studiecentrum Voor Kernenergie, Mol, Belgium, 1977-85; sect. head CEN-SCK, Mol, Belgium, 1985-90, project mgr., 1990-99; dept. head CEN-SCK, 1999—. Office: CEN SCK, Boeretang 200, Mol 2400, Belgium

DE CRISTOFARO, OSCAR RAFAEL, oncologist, educator; b. Buenos Aires, Mar. 11, 1954; s. Oscar Luis and Dora Ana (Arciprete) D.C.; m. Adriana Maria Sanchez Toranzo, Oct. 28, 1995. BS, Escuela Argentina Modelo, 1971; MD, Medicine Faculty Buenos Aires, 1978; splty. in oncology, Oncology Inst., Buenos Aires, 1989. Intern Oncology Inst. Angel Roffo-Faculty Medicine Buenos Aires U., 1980-81, resident in oncology, 1981-84, chief resident, 1984-85, resident, instr., 1985-86, 90-91, staff physician, 1991—; asst. prof. internal medicine Buenos Aires U., 1986-92, prof., 1992—. Author: Pautas Oncologicas Del Instituto de Oncologia Angel Roffo, 1988; contbr. articles to profl. jours. Fellow Nat. Cancer Ctr. Japan, 1986. Fellow Sociedad Argentina de Historia de la Medicine (sec. 1983-84); mem. AAAS, Sociedad Argentina de Cancerologia, Am. Soc. Clin. Oncology. Home: Azcuenaga 1487 10B, 1115 Buenos Aires Argentina Office: Instituto de Oncologia, U Buenos Aries, Av. San Martin 5481, 1417 Buenos Aires Argentina

DE CROO, HERMAN FRANCIS, government official; b. Brakel, Belgium, Aug. 12, 1937; s. Alfons and Germaine (Wauters) De C.; Doctorate in law, Université Libre de Bruxelles, 1961; m. Françoise Desguin, Sept. 16, 1961; children—Alexander, Ariane. Barrister at law, 1961—; mayor of Michelbeke (Belgium), 1964-71; rep. Belgian Parliament, 1968—; minister of Nat. Edn., 1974-77; minister of pensions, 1980; minister of communications and P.T.T., 1981-85; minister of transport, 1981-88; minister of and fgn. trade, 1985-88; pres. liberal faction Cultural Council, 1972-74; leader liberal faction Ho. of Reps., 1977-80; minister of communications and fgn. trade, 1985—; prof. Faculty of Law, U. Brussels, 1973—; chmn. European Council of Ministers of Transport, 1982, 86, Liberal Study Centre Paul Hymans, Brussels. Chmn. Princess Liliane Found., Mediatheek voor Vlaamse Gemeenschap musical found. Chmn. Autoworld (vet. cars) Collection, 1986—. Decorated comdr., grand officer Order of King Leopold; Grand Cross Order of the Crown; comdr. Nordstjarneorder (Sweden). Mem. Belgian Liberal Study Center (pres.), Found. for Pediatry (pres.), Belgian Tunesian Assn. (chmn.), Liberal Internat. Assn. (internat. v.p., vice-chmn.). Club: Rotary Internat. Author: numerous books; contbr. articles to profl. jours. Home: 57 Lepelstraat, Michelbeke-Brakel 9660, Belgium Office: House of Reps Cabinet of the Pres, Wetstraat 10, 1008 Brussels Belgium

DECROSTA, EDWARD FRANCIS, JR., former paper products company executive, consultant; b. Hudson, N.Y., Sept. 20, 1926; s. Edward F. and Anna Ruth (Crisci) DeC.; m. Annette Mae Powell, Sept. 20, 1953; children: Donna Marie, Lisa Ann. BCE, Rensselaer Poly. Inst., 1950; MS in Phys. Chemistry, Siena Coll., 1960; MBA, Rensselaer Poly. Inst., 1978. Plant chemist (process engr.) Universal Match Corp., Hudson, 1951-64; chemist Albany (N.Y.) Felt Co., 1965-69, mgr. tech. devel., 1969-72, dir. R&D, 1972-76; dir. rsch. and tech. devel. Papermaking Products Group, Albany Internat. Corp., N.Y.C., 1977-82, sr. scientist, 1982-93. Author (booklet) Chemical and Physical Properties of the Elements, 1956; contbr. articles to profl. jours.; patentee in field of thermocells. Served with USAAF, 1944-45, 1950-51. Fellow TAPPI (chmn. engring. divsn. 1982-84, E.H. Neese award engring. divsn. 1987); mem. Am. Chem. Soc., Internat. Assn. Sci. Papermakers, N.Y. Acad. Sci., Am. Legion, KC, Elks. Roman Catholic. Fax: 518-828-1635. Home and Office: 28 James St Hudson NY 12534-1310

DECSI, TAMAS, pediatrician; b. Pecs, Hungary, Oct. 27, 1957; m. Zsuzsanna Papp; 1 child, Agnes. MD, U. Med. Sch. Pecs, 1982, PhD, 1992, DSc, 1999. Intern U. Med. Sch., Pecs, 1982-86, registrar, 1987-94, sr. registrar, 1994-1999, reader and cons. pediatrician, 2000—. Office: Dept Pediatrics, Jozsef A 7, H-7623 Pécs Hungary

DE CURTIS, MAURO AUGUSTO, company executive; b. Sao Paulo, July 5, 1958; s. Ugolino Oreste Livino and Gilda (Ferraz) De C.; m. Taisa Adelia Collaco; 1 child, Andre Augusto. Student, Tecnico Em Eletronica, Mackenzie, Brazil, Engenheiro Eletronico, Mackenzie; degree in mktg., City U., Zurich, Switzerland; postgrad., U. Mich. Elevadores Schindler, Suica, Brazil, 1991—. Office: Elevadores Schindler, 23065480 Rio de Janeiro Brazil

DE CUYPER, FRANK ROGER FLORIMOND, translator, writer; b. Gent, Belgium, Mar. 30, 1957; s. Roger Frederik DeCuyper and Bertha Edmonda Ceunis. MA, U. Gent, 1981. Translator, 1992—. Contbr. (as Frank Roger) over 200 publs. to books, anthologies and mags., 1975—. Home: Voskenslaan 181, B-9000 Gent Belgium Office: Trierstraat 70, 1000 Brussels Belgium

DE DARDEL, JEAN-JACQUES PIERRE, diplomat; b. Neuchatel, Switzerland, Aug. 8, 1954; s. Gilbert Blaise and Yolanda (de Segadas Machado Guimaraes) d.; m. Marielle de Meyeres, Aug. 11, 1984; children: Guillaume, Alienor, Marine. Baccalaureat français c, Institut Florimont, Geneva, Switzerland, 1972; M in Econs., U. Geneva, 1975, Diploma of Higher Studies, 1979; PhD, Grad. Inst. Internat. Studies, Geneva, 1980. With Dept. Fgn. Affairs, Bern, Switzerland, 1981-89; head svc. Francophone affairs, 1987-89; counsellor Embassy of Switzerland, Washington, 1989-93; dep. chief of mission Embassy of Switzerland, Canberra, Australia, 1993-96; minister cultural affairs Embassy of Switzerland, Paris, 1996-98; ambassador Swiss Confederation to La Francophonie, Paris, 1998-2000; head Euro-Atlantic security sect. Dept. Fgn. Affairs, Bern, Switzerland, 2000—; pres. various coms. of Permanent Coun. of La Franco, 1997-99. Author: (books) La Cooperation au Developpement, Certitudes et Interrogations, 1981, Le Mont Athos: Itineraire d'une Decouverte, 1982, L'Art Aborigene Australien Contemporain, 1995, Aboriginal Art: An Immemorial Fountain of Youth, 2000; co-author: Swiss Neutrality and Security, 1990. Pres. Zofingue Student Soc., Geneva, 1973-74, com. mem. 1973-78; v.p. Cercle Richelieu Senghor. Mem. Cercle Richelieu Senghor, Cercle du Jardin, Cercle de la Grande Societe, Casino de la Grande Soc. Avocations: art, golf, tennis. Office: Fed Dept Fgn Affairs, 3003 Bern Switzerland

DEDEAUX, JULES A., city official; b. De Lisle, Miss., June 15, 1938; s. Louis and Leona (Roberteau) D.; m. Ruby Whitaker, Jan., 1960 (div. 1962); 1 child, Desiree; m. Jeraldine B. dedeaux, Mar. 22, 1963; children: Veronica, André, Jamila. BA, Tex. So. U., 1970; MSW, U. Houston, 1975. Case mgr. Neighborhood Ctrs., Inc., Houston, 1970-73; planner, mgr. City of Houston, 1975—. Mem. Black Orgn. for Leadership Devel., Houston, 1979-98. With USAF, 1956-59. Mem. NASW, Nat. Sociology Honor Soc. Avocations: music, fishing. Office: City of Houston 8000 N Stadium Dr Houston TX 77054-1823

DEDECKER, PAUL JEAN, mathematics educator, researcher; b. Ixelles, Brabant, Belgium, June 15, 1921; s. Jean Jospeh and Germaine Marie-Eugénie (Lengrand) D.; children: Marianne, Danielle, Martine, Guy, Roy-Mara. Lic. sci. math., U. Brussels, 1943, DSc, 1948; Agrégé de l'Enseignement Supérieur, U. Liège, Belgium, 1958. Asst. Royal Meteorol. Inst. Belgium, Brussels, 1946-53; chef de travaux U. Liège, Belgium, 1953-63; prof. U. Lille, France, 1963-71, U. Louvain, Belgium, 1963-79, U. Zulia, Maracaibo, Venezuala, 1980-81, Pedagogical Inst. Caracas, Venezuala, 1981-82; hon. prof. U. Cen. Venezuela, Caracas, 1965—; mem. Inst. for Advanced Study, Princeton, N.J., fall 1957, winter-spring 1984; fellow Wissenschaftskolleg zu Berlin, 1982-83; expert UNESCO, Santiago, Chile, 1959; lectr. U. Mich., Ann Arbor, fall. 1956, U. Rome, 1955; vis. prof. Acad. Scis. Cuba, La Habana, 1965, Fla. State U., Tallahassee, 1966, Fed. U. Rio de Janeiro, 1979, U. Puerto Rico, Mayagüez, 1985, Calif. State U., L.A., 1987-88, U. Puerto Rico, San Juan, 1995; founder Belgian Ctr. for Algebra and Topology, 1955; rsch. vis. scientist Mathematisches Forschungs Institut der ETH, Zürich, 1964, Steklov Inst. Math., Leningrad and Moscow, 1965, Aryah Mehr U. Tehran, Iran, 1975; lectr. numerous univs. Inventor new methods in multiple integrals of higher order calculus of variations, in noncommutative homological algebra and spl. methods for dealing with logical paradoxes in founds. of math. and hypertransfinite numbers. Editor underground press in Nazi occupied Belgium, 1943-44. Sgt. Belgian Air Force, 1945. Decorated Belgian medal of World War II, Belgian medal of Vol. War Svc.; recipient Adolphe Wetrems prize Royal Acad. Belgium, 1956, François Deruyts prize, 1962; grantee NATO, 1964, 73. Mem. French Math. Soc., Am. Math. Soc. Avocations: Latin American ethnology, pre-Columbian archaeology. Home: 12 Grand Rue, B-01341 Céroux-Mousty Belgium Office: U Ctrl Venezuela Fac Scis, Edificio A Doria # 16 Ave C, 1070 Caracas Venezuela also: U Brussels Campus Plaine, Chimie Physique II CP 231, 01050 Brussels Belgium

DEDEK, WOLFGANG, research scientist; b. Chemnitz, Germany, Aug. 13, 1930; s. Fritz and Margarethe (Rothling) D.; m. Hildegard, Leibnitz, June 10, 1961; children: Anke, Kerstin. Diploma in chemistry, U. Leipzig, 1956, Dr.rer.nat., 1959, Dr.rer.nat.habil, 1966. Head dept. Inst. Applied Radioactivity Deutsche Akademie der Wissenschaften, German Acad. Scis., Leipzig, 1957-64, head of dept. rsch. unit of chem. toxicology, 1964-90; rsch. scientist U. Leipzig, Inst. of Analystical Chemistry, 1991-95; retired, 1995. Contbr. articles to profl. jours. Avocations: gardening, classical music. Office: U Leipzig, Permoserstrasse 15, D-04303 Leipzig Germany

DE DEKEN, JEAN, marketing professional; b. Gent, Belgium, Feb. 16, 1954; s. Fernand and Agnes (Meirschaert) De D.; m. Joske Peleman, Sept. 26, 1979; children: Johanna, Judith. Student, Royal Acad. Art Sch., Gent. Asst. mktg. mgr., 1977-81; mktg. mgr. Prado Carpets, 1981-90; group mktg. mgr. Assoc. Weavers Europe, 1990—, Assoc. Weavers Internat., Prado Rugs, 1990—. With Belgium Mil., 1976-77. Mem. European Carpet Assn. Home: Karel van Manderstraat 12, 8510 Kortryk Marke, Belgium Office: Assoc Weavers, PO Box 148, 9600 Ronse Belgium

DEDEYAN, CHARLES, writer, literature educator; b. Smyrna, Apr. 4, 1910; arrived in France, 1919; s. Tigrane Pascal and Emma Elisabeth (Ekisler) D.; m. Phyllis Sivrisarian, Nov. 10, 1938. Student, Coll. Notre Dame Sainte Croi. Reader French lit. U. Rennes, 1942-45; prof. French and comparative lit. U. Lyon, 1945-49; prof. comparative lit. U. Paris Sorbonne, 1945—; vis. prof. various univs. Editor: (ency.) Clartes, 1958-92; author over 30 books on French lit. and comparative lit. Avocations: swimming, rare books, walking. Home: 90 bis rue de Varenne, 75007 Paris France

DEDMAN, BERTRAM COTTINGHAM, retired insurance company executive; b. Columbia, Tenn., Dec. 24, 1914; s. Bertram Cottingham and Mary Ella (Fariss) D.; m. Rainsford Bayard MacDowell, June 16, 1938; children: Rainsford Dedman Olson, Ella. A.B., U. of South, Sewanee, Tenn., 1937; J.D., George Washington U., 1941. Bar: Tenn. 1941, D.C. 1977. Trial atty. Antitrust Div., Dept. Justice, Washington, 1941-54, Texaco, Inc., Los Angeles, 1954-57; asst. counsel, asso. gen. counsel, gen. counsel Ins. Co. of N.Am., Phila., 1957-70; v.p., gen. counsel INA Corp. (now CIGNA Corp.), Phila., 1968-77; v.p., sec. INA Corp., 1975-79. Editor, contbr.: Merger of Insurance Companies, 1966. Served with USNR, 1944-47. Mem. Am., Fed., Tenn., Phila. bar assns., Am. Judicature Soc., Internat. Assn. Ins. Law (past pres. U.S. chpt.). Home: 500 Elmington Ave Nashville TN 37205-2513

DEDMAN, ROBERT HENRY, sales executive; b. Rison, Ark., Feb. 15, 1926; s. Robert Henry and Cornelia D.; m. Nancy McMillan, Dec. 6, 1952; children: Robert H. Jr., Patricia Dedman Dietz. BA, U. Tex., 1946, BS, 1948, LLB, 1948; LLM, So. Meth. U., 1953. Foun., chmn. ClubCorp Inc., Dallas, 1957—; mem. State Hwy. Commn., Austin, Tex., 1981-85, 87-91; adv. dir. Stewart Info. Svcs., 1989—. Chmn. bd. trustees, So. Meth. U., Dallas, 1993-96, active, 1976—. Named to Tex. Bus. Hall of Fame, 1987, Entrepreneur of Yr., Dallas, 1980, Marketer of Yr., Dallas, 1986; recipient Horatio Alger award, Washington, 1989. Republican. Methodist. Avocations: tennis, golf. Office: ClubCorp Inc Ste 700 3030 Lyndon B Johnson Fwy Dallas TX 75234-7763

DE DUVE, CHRISTIAN RENÉ, chemist, educator; b. Thames-Ditton, Eng., Oct. 2, 1917; s. Alphonse and Madeleine (Pungs) de D.; m. Janine Herman, Sept. 30, 1943; children: Thierry, Anne, Françoise, Alain. M.D., U. Louvain, Belgium, 1941, Ph.D., 1945, M.Sc., 1946; D honoris causa, U. Turin, 1969, U. Leiden, 1970, U. Sherbrooke, 1970, U. Lille, 1973, Cath. U. Santiago, Chile, 1974, U. René Descartes, Paris, 1974, State U. Liege, 1975, State U. Ghent, 1975, Gustavus Adolphus Coll., St. Peter, Minn., 1975, U. Rosario, Argentina, 1975, U. Aix-Marseille II, 1979, U. Keele, 1982, Katholieke U. Leuven, 1984, Karolinska Inst., Stockholm, 1986, U. Montreal, 1992, Rockefeller U., 1997. Lectr. physiol. chemistry faculty medicine Cath. U. Louvain, 1947-51, prof., head dept. physiol. chemistry, 1951-85, emeritus prof., 1985—; prof. biochem. cytology Rockefeller U., N.Y.C., 1962-74, Andrew W. Mellon prof., 1974-88, prof. emeritus, 1988—; vis. prof. Albert Einstein Coll. Medicine, Bronx, N.Y., 1961-62, Chaire Francqui State U. Ghent, 1962-63, Free U. Brussels, 1963-64, State U. Liège, 1972-73, Facultés Universitaires Notre-Dame de la Paix, Namur, 1990-91; Mayne guest prof. U. Queensland, Brisbane, Australia, 1972; pres. Internat. Inst. Cellular and Molecular Pathology, Brussels, 1974-91. Mem. editorial bd. Subcellular Biochemistry, 1971-87, Preparative Biochemistry, 1971-80, Molecular and Cellular Biochemistry, 1973-80. Mem. Conseil d'Adminstrn. du Fonds Nat. de la Recherche Scientifique, 1958-61; mem. Conseil de Gestion du Fonds de la Recherche Scientifique Médicale, 1959-61; mem. Commn. Scientifique du Fonds de la Recherche Scientifique Médicale, 1958-61; mem. Comité des Experts du Conseil Nat. de la Politique Scientifique, 1958-61; mem. adv. bd. Ciba Found., 1960-85; mem. adult devel. and aging research and tng. rev. com. Nat. Inst. Child Health and Devel., NIH, 1970-73; mem. adv. com. for med. research WHO, 1974-79; mem. sci. adv. com. Max Planck-Inst. für Immunbiologie, 1975-78, Ludwig Inst. Cancer Research, 1985-91 , Mary Imogene Bassett Research Inst., 1986-90, Clin. Research Inst. Montreal, 1986—; mem. biology adv. com. N.Y. Hall of Sci., 1986—; adv. sci. com. Basel Inst. for Immunology, 1989-93. Recipient Prix des Alumni, 1949, Prix Pfizer, 1957, Prix Francqui, 1960, Prix Quinquennal Belge des Sciences Médicales, 1967 (Belgium); Gairdner Found. Internat. award merit (Can.), 1967; Dr. H.P. Heineken prize (The Netherlands), 1973; Nobel prize for physiology or medicine, 1974; Harden award Biochem. Soc. (Gt. Britain), 1978; Theobald Smith award Albany Med. Coll., 1981; Jimenez Diaz award, 1985. Fellow AAAS; mem. NAS, Royal Acad. Medicine, Royal Acad. Belgium, Am. Chem. Soc., Biochem. Soc., Am. Philos. Soc., Am. Soc. Biol. Chemists, Pontifical Acad. Sci., Am. Soc. Cell Biology (coun. 1966-69, E.B. Wilson award 1989), Soc. Chimie Biologique, Soc. Belge Biochim. (pres. 1962-64), Deutsche Akademie der Naturforscher Leopoldina, Koninklyke Akademie voor Geneeskunde (Belgium), European Assn. Study Diabetes, European Molecular Biology Orgn., European Cell Biology Orgn., Internat. Soc. Cell Biology, N.Y. Acad. Scis., Soc. Belge de Physiologie, Sigma Xi; fgn. assoc. Am. Acad. Arts and Scis., Royal Soc. London, Royal Soc. Can., Académie des Sciences de Paris, Académie des Sciences d'Athénes, Academia Europaea, Deutsche Gesellschaft für Zellbiologie; numerous hon. memberships. Office: Rockefeller U 1230 York Ave New York NY 10021-6399 also: ICP, 75 Ave Hippocrate, B-1200 Brussels Belgium

DEDYSH, SVETLANA NICOLAYEVNA, scientist, researcher; b. Krasnogorsk, Moscow, Russia, July 25, 1963; d. Nicolai Ivanovich and Tatiana Grygorievna (Khmelevskaya) Suhov; m. Victor Victorovich Dedysh, Aug. 2, 1986; 1 child, Ekaterina. Master's degree, Moscow State U., 1985, PhD in Microbiology, 1990. Rschr. Inst. Microbiology Russian Acad. Scis., Moscow, 1990-98, sr. rschr. Inst. Microbiology, 1998—; vis. rschr. Ctr. for Microbial Ecology, Mich. State U., East Lansing, 1995, 97, 98, 99. Contbr. articles to profl. jours. Mem. Am. Soc. for Microbiology. Office: Inst Microbio Russ Acad Sci, Pros 60-Letya Octyabrya 7/2, 117811 Moscow Russia

DEE, JAMES PHILLIP, human resources consultant; b. Phila., Nov. 16, 1927; s. Nicholas M. and Lillian (Townsend) D'Addarie; m. Anneliese Zintel, June 30, 1958; 1 child, James P. Jr. AB, U. Fla., 1948; MA, U. Mo., 1950; PhD, Ohio State U., 1957. Asst. prof. Syracuse (N.Y.) U., 1959-63; assoc. prof. Pa. State U., 1963-67; prof. Bowling Green State U., 1967-69; dir. mgmt. devel. Ingersoll-Rand Co., 1969-72; project mgr. Internat. Labor Orgn., Nigeria, 1972-74; chief field ops. tng. br. UN Indstl. Devel. Orgn., Vienna, Austria, 1974-87; mng. dir. Human Resources Devel. Internat., Vienna, 1987—. Contbr. articles to profl. jours. Home and Office: Linke Wienzeile 158/33, A-1060 Vienna Austria

DEECKE, LUEDER, neurologist, educator; b. Lohe/Holstein, Germany, June 22, 1938; arrived in Austria, 1985; s. Hermann and Hildegard (Spieker) D.; m. Gertraud Flinspach, May 27, 1967; children: Ulf, Volker, Arved. MD, U. Freiburg, Germany, 1966; Habilitation in Neurology, U. Ulm, Germany, 1974. Intern U. Freiburg, 1968; resident U. Ulm, 1968-70; rsch. fellow Oto-Neurophysiol. Lab., U. Toronto, Ont., Can., 1970-71; resident U. Ulm, 1971-73, sr. resident, 1974-78, apl. prof. neurology, 1978-85; full prof. neurology U. Vienna, Austria, 1985—, head Clinic of Neurology, 1985—, head dept. clin. neurology, 1992—; head Ludwig-Boltzmann Inst. Functional Brain Topography, 1995—; mem. Intensive Care Neurology, WHO, 1986—; disting. vis. prof. dept. neurology U. Calif., Irvine, 1991, Simon Fraser U., Vancouver, B.C., Can., 1982. Contbr. 490 articles to profl. jours.; editor: Scientific American Medicine, German edit. "Neurologie", 1984—; mem. editl. bd. NeuroImage, 1995, European Arch. Psychiat. Neurol. Sci., Rev. EEG Neurophysiol. Clin., Electroenceph. Clin. Neurophysiol., Human Neurobiology, others. Lt. German Fed. Air Force Res., 1960—. Recipient award of City of Ulm, 1970, Dr. Herbert Reisner award, Vienna, 1989, Hoechst award, 1997. Mem. German Neurol. Soc., Germany Soc. Clin. Neurophysiology, Austrian Neurol. Soc., German EEG Soc. (pres. 1982-83), German Physiol. Soc., German Soc. Aerospace Medicine, Aerospace Med. Assn., Bárány Soc., Internat. Brain Rsch. Orgn., European Brain and behaviour Soc. (exec.), European Neuroscis. Assn. (exec.), Soc. of Austrian Neurologists and Psychiatrists (exec.), Internat. League Against the Epilepsies (Austrian sect. exec.), Austrian Parkinson Soc. (exec.), European Soc. Clin. Investigation, Vienna Soc. Pub. Health, Soc. for Promotion of Med. Rsch. (exec.), Soc. Physicians in Vienna (exec.), Austrian Soc. Against Muscle Diseases, Austrian Soc. for Neurorehab. (exec.), Austrian Soc. Child Neurology and Psychiatry (exec.), Austrian Soc. Neuroimaging (exec.), Austrian Soc. Tropical Medicine, Vienna Soc. Psychiatry and Neurology (exec.), Vienna Med. Acad. (exec.), Soc. for Internal and Gen. Intensive Care Medicine (exec.). Avocations: hiking, skiing, bicycling, hobbyist. Home: Himmelstr 44, A-1190 Vienna Austria Office: Univ Clinic of Neurology, Waehringer Guertel 18-20, A-1090 Vienna Austria

DEEG, EMIL WOLFGANG, manufacturing company executive, physicist; b. Selb, Germany, Sept. 20, 1926; came to U.S., 1967, naturalized, 1975; s. Fritz and Trina (Poehlmann) D.; m. Hedwig M.S. Kempf, Aug. 25, 1953; children: Wolfgang, Martin, Bernhard, Renate. Dipl. Physiker, U. Wuerzburg, 1954, Dr. rer. nat., 1956. Rsch. asst. Max Planck Inst., Wuerzburg, 1954-59; mem. tech. staff Bell Telephone Labs., Allentown, Pa., 1959-60; rsch. assoc. Jenaer Glaswerk Schott U. Gen., Mainz, Germany, 1960, dir. rsch., 1960-65; assoc. prof. physics and solid state sci. Am. U., Cairo, 1965-67; mgr. ceramic rsch. Am. Optical Corp., Southbridge, Mass., 1967-71, mgr. materials rsch., 1971-73, dir. process and materials rsch., 1973-75, dir. inorganic materials R&D, 1975-77, tech. adviser, 1977-78; sr. scientist Anchor Hocking Corp., Lancaster, Ohio, 1978-79, mgr. materials R&D, 1979-80; mgr. glass tech. Bausch & Lomb, Rochester, N.Y., 1980-82; mgr. glass and fiber devel. Mead Office Sys., Richardson, Tex., 1982-84; project mgr. AMP, Inc., Harrisburg, Pa., 1984-92; cons., Lemoyne, Pa., 1992—; mem. Internat. Commn. on Glass, 1963-81, Internat. Commn. for Optics, 1964-66; cons. NASA Spacelab Program, 1971-78; expert witness on glass product patent litigation German Patent Office, 1978-81. Author: (with H. Richter) Glas im Laboratorium, 1966; editor AMP Jour. Tech., 1993-98; patentee in field; contbr. chpts. to books, articles to profl. jours. Pres. PTA, Woodstock, Conn., 1970-71; committeeman Mohegan coun. Boy Scouts Am., 1967-73; trustee Woodstock Acad., 1971-78; overseer Old Sturbridge Village, Inc., 1972-81; chmn. Optical Info. Ctr., Southbridge, 1976-77. With German Army, 1944-45. Fellow Am. Ceramic Soc. (emeritus); mem. Optical Soc. Am. (emeritus), Nat. Inst. Ceramic Engrs., Internat. Tech. Inst. (inductee Hall of Fame for Engring., Sci. and Tech. 1988), ASM Internat., Engrs. Soc. Pa. (dir. 1996-98), Lions (pres. Woodstock chpt. 1975, zone chmn. dist. 23 C, Lions Internat. 1976-78). Home and Office: 501 Ohio Ave Lemoyne PA 17043-1525

DEEIK, KHALIL GEORGE, economist, financing company executive; b. Bethlehem, Nov. 12, 1937; s. George Said Diek and Wadiea (Jalil) Lama; m. Jalileh Mary Marzouka, Aug. 22, 1965 (dec.); children: George, Ramzi, Nader. BA, Sacramento State U., 1961, MA, 1964; PhD, U. So. Calif., 1972. Prin., adminstr. Manzanita Sch., Hyampom, Calif., 1964-65; mgr. Gen. Trading Co., Alkhobar, Saudi Arabia, 1966-69; program dir., instr. Krebs Coll., North Hollywood, Calif., 1969-72; chief investment officer, mng. dir., v.p., sr. advisor, exec. asst. to chmn. Olayan Saudi Investment Co., Olayan Financing Co., Jeddah, Saudi Arabia, 1973—, The Olayan Group of Cos.; bd. dirs. Saudi Polyester Products Co., Jeddah, 1984—; exec. com. mem. Saudi Arabian Constrn. and Repair Services Co., Jeddah, 1984—; hon. lectr. King Abdulaziz U., Saudi Arabia, 1979; faculty mem., program coord. Century U., Calif., 1978—. Mem. Internat. Educators Assn. (v.p. 1970-72), Marquis Club, Phi Delta Kappa, Phi Delta Epsilon. Club. Office: Olayan Fin Co, PO Box 8772, Riyadh 11492, Saudi Arabia

DEELSTRA, HENDRIK ANDRIES, chemistry educator; b. Genk, Limburg, Belgium, Apr. 5, 1938; s. Andries Hendrik and Antje (Meijer) D. PhD in Chemistry, U. Ghent, Belgium, 1963. Asst. U. Ghent, Belgium, 1959-63; lectr. U. Kinshasa, Zaire, 1963-64; prof. U. Kisangani, Zaire, 1964-67, U. Bujumbura, Burundi, 1967-72, U. Antwerp, Belgium, 1972—; scientific coord. Belgian Cooperation U., Bujumbura, 1978-95. Co-author: Xenobiotics in Food, Foods for Particular Use. Mem. Flemish Work. Party Food Scis., Royal Acad. Overseas Scis., Fedn. European Chem. Socs. (food working party 19984-92, chmn. working party on history of chemistry 1993-96). Fax: 32-3-8202734. E-mail: labrom@uia.ua.ac.be. Office: U Antwerp Dept Pharm Sci, Universiteitsplein 1, 2610 Wilrijk Belgium

DEEN, ALIEU SWARRAY, registrar; b. Freetown, Sierra Leone, Mar. 28, 1939; s. Muctarr Swarray and Adama Swarray (Baraka) D.; m. Asanatu Swarray Deen; children: Muctarr, Mohamed, Abubakarr, Alim. BA, Durham U., Freetown, Sierra Leone, 1963; diploma in edn., Durham U., 1964; M in Edn., U. Ibadan, Nigeria, 1979. Tchr. Sierra Leone Govt., Freetown, 1963-67; sr. rsch. officer West African Exam. Coun., Lagos, Nigeria, 1969-73; head nat. office, sr. dep. registrar West African Exam. Coun., Freetown, 1974-94; acting registrar West African Exam. Coun., Accra, 1995—; scholarship adv. com. Min. Edn., Freetown, 1996—. Contbr. articles to profl. jours. Master Boy Scouts, Freetown, 1968; chmn. med. ednl. bd. Ahmadiyya Mission, Freetown, 1996-98. Grantee Ford Found./Test Devel. and Rsch. Office, 1972, fellow, 1979, U.S. Aid Internat. Devel., 1989. Mem. Geog. Assn., African Assn. Edn. Assessment (pres. 1995). Moslem. Avocations: poetry, soccer, table tennis. Home: Pvt Mail Bag 254, 7 Babadori Hills, Freetown Sierra Leone Office: West African Exam Coun, PO Box 573 Tower Hill, Freetown Sierra Leone

DEERING, RONALD FRANKLIN, librarian, minister; b. Paxton, Ill., Oct. 6, 1929; s. Minor Franklin and Grace Gilmour (Perkins) D.; m. Geraldine Gibbons, June 27, 1953 (dec. Jan. 1965); m. Edith Ann Proctor, June 12, 1966; children: Mark David, Daniel Timothy. BA summa cum laude, Georgetown (Ky.) Coll., 1951; MDiv, So. Bapt. Theol. Sem., 1955, PhD, 1962; MLS, Columbia U., 1967. Ordained to ministry So. Bapt. Conv., 1950. Pastor 1st Hilltop Bapt. Ch., North College Hill, Ohio, 1949-50; instr. in Bible Georgeton (Ky.) Coll., 1950-51; pastor Blue River Bapt. Ch., Salem, Ind., 1954-59; instr. Greek, N.T. So. Bapt. Theol. Sem., Louisville, 1958-61, theol. libr., 1962-95, assoc. v.p. for acad. resources, 1995—; chmn. So. Bapt. Hist. Commn., Nashville, 1987-90; interim pastor 31 chs. in Ind., Ky., 1961-90; del. Bapt. World Alliance, Miami, Fla., Toronto, Ont., Can., L.A., 1965, 80, 85. Contbr. articles to profl. jours. Eli Lilly Theol. Librarianship grantee, 1967. Mem. AAUP, ALA, Southeastern Libr. Assn., Am. Theol. Libr. Assn. (nat. pres. 1984-85), Ky. Libr. Assn., Phi Alpha Theta, Beta Phi Mu, Sigma Tau Delta. Democrat. Home: 3111 Dunlieth Ct Louisville KY 40241-2937 Office: So Bapt Theol Sem 2825 Lexington Rd Louisville KY 40280-0001

DEERMAN, RUTH GILLETT, sales professional, flying instructor; b. El Paso, Tex., June 17, 1915; d. Otis Theodore and Katie Yvette (Textor) Gillett; m. Charlie Luther Deerman, Nov. 25, 1933 (dec. June 1992). Student, U. Tex., El Paso, 1966. Ccert. pvt. pilot, comml. instrument pilot, helicopter pilot, advanced ground sch. instr., flight instr. Flight instr. Border Aviation, El Paso, 1944; flight and ground instr. S.W. Air Rangers, El Paso, 1968; beauty cons. Mary Kay Cosmetics, El Paso, 1969-70, ind. sales dir., 1970-75, ind. sr. sales dir., 1975—; tchr. flying and ground sch., 1945—; accident prevention coucncilor FAA, 1972-80. Bd. dirs. Am. CCancer Soc.c, 1957-67; pres. Providence Meml. Hosp. Aux., 1960-61; past treas. Womans Coub El Paso; past bd. dirs. YWCA, El Paso; past pres. Women's Missionary Union, 1st Bapt. Ch. Named Tex. Flying Farmers State Queen, 1955; winner All Woman Transcontinental Air Race, 1954; inducted into El Paso Aviation Hall of Fame, 1983; honored with granite plaque Internat. Forest of Friendship, 1977; recipient Jimmie Kolp award for contbg. to aviation and 99s, 1975. Mem. NAFE, Nat. Assn. Flight Instr., 99s (lic. women pilots, past internat. pres.), Whirly Girls (Whirly Girl # 78), Silver Wings, El Paso Aviation Assn. (v.p. 1947), 66s (founder), Clowns of Am. Internat., El Paso C. of C. (coms. woman's dept.), PEO, Ladies Oriental Shrine Am. (FAA accident prevention councilor 1972-80), Daus. of Nile (queen 1951-52), Order Ea. Star (worthy matron 1945). Republican. Avocations: bowling, golf. Home and Office: 405 Camino Real Ave El Paso TX 79922-2003

DEETJEN, PETER HENRICH, physiology educator; b. Berlin, Dec. 22, 1932; s. Hanns and Eva M.L. (Merten) D.; m. Barbara H.M. Lenz, July 27, 1960; children: Katharina, Hanns, Annette, Christian. MD, U. Goettingen, Germany, 1957, PhD, 1963. Asst. prof. U. Goettingen, 1963; assoc. prof. SUNY, Buffalo, 1964-65, U. Munich, 1965-70; prof. physiology U. Innsbruck, Austria, 1971—; head dept. physiology U. Innsbruck, 1971—. Author 10 books on renal physiology; contbr. over 250 articles to profl. jours. Mem. Highest Med. Coun., Austria, 1975—. Mem. Academia Europaea, Acad. Sci. and Art Europe, Austrian Acad. Sci. Office: Univ Innsbruck, Dept Physiology, 3 Fritz Preglstr, Innsbruck A-6020, Austria

DEEV, ANATOLIYI STEPANOVICH, neurologist, consultant; b. Kamen, USSR, Mar. 2, 1941; s. Deev Stepan Dmitrievich and Efrosinia Ilinichna Barkova; m. Lilia Maksimovna Generalova, Apr. 7, 1972; children: Irina, Yulia. PhD in Med. Sci., Med. U., Leningrad, 1983, MD, 1991; prof., Med. U., Ryazan, 1994. Cert. in neurology. Neurologist City Hosp., Verhnya Salda, 1967-75; neurologist Regionl Hosp., Ryazan, 1975-82, dir. neurol. dept., 1982-85; asst. Med. U., Ryazan, 1985-91, docent, 1991-94, prof., 1994—; cons. Region Hosp., Ryazan, 1985—; dir. Treatment Ctr. of Brain Vascular Diseases, Ryazan, 1999; mem. sci. adv. group Med. U., Ryazan, 1998—, mem. problem commn., 1995—; mem. attestation commn. Dept. Healthcare, Ryazan, 1994—. Author: (book) Benign Intracranial Hypertension, 1997; editor: (books) Pathology of Neurosystem in Women of Reproductive Age, 1993, Diseases and Malfunction of Neurosystem in Women of Reproductive Age, 1995, Diseases and Malfunction of Neurosystem in Pregnant Women and in Postpregnant Period, 1994; mem. editl. group: (periodical) Pain and Its Treatment, 1995—). Mem. Soc. Neurologists (hon.). Avocations: classical music, literature, computer, painting. E-mail: dannover@mail.ru. Home: 1 Dzeleznodoroznaya 60kv 19, Ryazan 390005, Russia Office: Region Hosp Dept Neurology, Internationalnaya 3a, Ryazan 390039, Russia

DEFACIO, W. BRIAN, theoretical physicist; b. Palestine, Tex.; s. William Theodore and Nina Mary (Marlowe) DeF.; m. Maria Christine Martinez, Sept. 5, 1964; children: Patricia Ann, John Michael. BS, Tex. A&M U., 1963, MS, 1964, PhD, 1967. Asst. prof. Mo. U., Columbia, 1967-71, assoc. prof., 1971-83, prof. physics, 1983—; vis. physicist Ames Lab., Iowa State U., Ames, summer 1973, vis. assoc. prof. Iowa State U., 1974-75, vis. mathematician, 1979-81, Ames Lab., 1979-81; jubilee prof. Chalmers Tech. U., Göteborg, Sweden, 1983-84, vis. prof., summer 1987; vis. prof. U. Montpellier II, France, summer 1984; vis. prof. math. Tex. A&M U., 1997-98; lectr. in field. Assoc. editor Jour. of Math. Physics, 1979-81; internat. editl. bd. Nondestructive Testing and Evaluation, 1996—. Chair govering bd. Unitarian Ch., Columbia, Mo., 1989, 91; fin. chair Food Bank, Mo., 1990-92. Fellow Am. Phys. Soc.; mem. Am. Math. Soc., Soc. of Indsl. and Applied Math., Internat. Assn. of Math. Phys., Sigma Xi (chair 1992). Democrat. Achievements include research results on coherent states, noninertial observers, ambiguities and wavefront reconstructions in 3-D inverse problems, Feynman path functional, information theoretic wavelet nondestructive evaluation with acoustics, information theory for the global positions system, inverse problems for geodesy. E-mail: DeFacioB@missouri.edu. Office: Dept of Physics U Mo College And Rollins Sts Columbia MO 65211-0001

DEFAGO, ALFRED, Swiss ambassador. Amb. to U.S. Govt. of Switzerland. Office: Embassy of Switzerland 2900 Cathedral Ave NW Washington DC 20008-3499*

DE FARIA, TASSO FABIANO, economist, consultant; b. São João Del Rey, Brazil, Oct. 23, 1939; s. João Manoel and Lucy (Chaves) De F.; m. Luiza Ignez Teixeira Lopes, Jan. 16, 1966; children: Simone, Henrique. Student, Mil. Coll., Rio de Janeiro, 1960; degree in economy, U. Fed. de Minas Gerais, Belo Horizonte, Brazil, 1965; MSc, U. Fed. de Rio de Janeiro, Rio de Janeiro, 1969; PhD, COPPE-UFRJ, Rio de Janeiro, 1972. Economist Petrobràs, Rio de Janeiro, 1965-69, asst. to dir., 1970-73; fin. mgr. Fábrica Carioca je Catalisadores, Rio de Janeiro, 1974-75; comml. dir. Cia Bras. Estireno, Rio de Janeiro, 1976-81, Cia Petroq. Camaçari, São

Paulo, 1982-95; pres. Sanroda/R&D, São Paulo, 1996—; cons. D&D, São Paulo, 1996—. Author: Pipelines Transportation Prices, 1972, Transportation, 1976. Avocations: chess, lecturing. Home: Av Atlantica 514/602, 22010000 Rio de Janeiro Brazil Office: Av P Pereira de Andra-de, 545-21F Pinheiros, Sao Paulo 05469-000, Brazil

DE FARNEY, BARON See TESCHER DE CRANLEY, MICHEL

DE FAUCONVAL, BARON JEAN, retired companies director; b. Casteau, Belgium, June 30, 1921; s. Ferdinand and Héléne (d'Oultremont) de F.; m. Régine de Biolley, May 7, 1953; children: Oriane, Guillebert, Olivier, Jean Charles, Marie, Caroline. BA in Philosophy, Cath. U. of Leuven, Belgium, 1940, LLD, 1943, MA in Econs., 1945. Jr. exec. Nat. Bank of Belgium, Brussels, 1948-49; dept. head Ministry of Colonies, Belgium, 1950-54; mem. mgmt. various banks Soc. Generale De Belgique's Group, Brussels, Antwerp, Geneva, Amsterdam, 1954-67; exec. sec. Soc. Generale De Belgique's Group, 1968-78, exec. dir., sec., 1979-88; chmn. Compagnie Immobiliere de Belgique, 1979-88; dir., exec. com. Tractebel, Brussels, 1971-79, Assurances Genérales, Brussels, 1975-88, Union Miniere, Brussels, 1981-88; ret., 1988. Contbr. articles to profl. jours. Officer Armée Secréte, Belgium, 1943-44; vol. of war Belgian Army, 1944-45. Recipient War cross Belgian State; named Ordre de Léopold, Belgian State, Ordre de la Couronne, Belgian State. Mem. Cercle Royal Gaulois, Cercle Royal Du Parc, Royal Golf Club of Belgium, Harvard Club of Belgium. Roman Catholic. Avocation: golf. Home: Brabandtlaan 40, 3090 Overijse Belgium

DEFAYS, JULIEN HENRI, surgeon; b. Linkebeek, Belgium, Sept. 25, 1945; s. Michel Martin Defays and Helene Marie Hauben. MD, U. Catholique Louvain, Leuven, Belgium, 1975; degree in plastic surgery, U.C.L., Leuven, Belgium, 1981; degree in maxilofacial surgery, U. Marie et Pierre Curie, Paris, 1980. Surgeon CHU Moliere Longchamp, Brussels, 1981—, Clin. St. Etienne, Brussels, 1983-93, C.H.U. A. Vesale Charleroi, Belgium, 1981—, Clin. de Chatelet, Belgium, 1982-86, Clin. Reine Fabiola, Charleroi, 1981-86, Hosp. St. Jean, Brussels, 1996. Med. maj. Belgian Army Reserve, 1991. Mem. Groupement Belge des Specialistes, Belgian Soc. Plastic Surgery. Home: Kleiveld 29, 1630 Linkebeek Belgium Office: Ave De Messidor 158, 1180 Brussels Belgium

DEFERR, GERVASIO, Olympic athlete; b. Barcelona, Spain, Dec. 7, 1980. Placed 7th floor exercise World Championships, 1997, winner Gold Medal floor exercise European Jr. Championships, 1998, winner Silver Medal floor exercise World Championships, 1999; winner Gold Medal vault Sydney, 2000. Office: Fedn Espanola de Gimnasia, c/Maria de Molina No 60-1 derecha, 28006 Madrid Spain*

DE FEYDEAU DE SAINT-CHRISTOPHE, HENRI, lawyer; b. Saint-Junien, France, May 21, 1947; s. Michel de Feydeau de Saint-Christophe and Genevieve du Fontenioux; m. Alix de Laubespin, May 25, 1978; children: Francois-Pierre, Pauline, Humbert, Laure. Grad., Inst. Polit. Studies, Paris, 1969; degree in Bus. Law, U. Paris, 1970, M in Econs., 1971. Internat. Bar Assn., 1992. Head internat. tax dept. Compagne de Saint-Gobain, Paris, 1973-81; tax ptnr. Coopers and Lybrand, Paris, 1981-89; ptnr. BBLP-Moquet Borde & Assocs., Paris, 1989—. Contbr. articles to profl. jours. Mem. Internat. Fiscal Assn. (The Netherlands), Internat. Tax Planning Assn. (U.K.), Jockey Club (Paris), Soc. des Cin. (bd. dirs., French br.), Institut des Avocats Conseils Fiscaux (bd. dirs.). Roman Catholic. Avocations: geneaology, farming, forestry. Home: 29 rue de Grenelle, 75007 Paris France Office: Moquet Borde & Assocs, 30 Ave de Messine, 75008 Paris France

DEFFAA, CHIP, jazz critic; b. New Rochelle, N.Y., May 18, 1951; s. Louis Philip and Alberta (Saby) D. AB, Princeton U., 1973. Jazz critic N.Y. Post, N.Y.C., 1986—. Author: Swing Legacy, 1989, Voices of the Jazz Age, 1990, In the Mainstream, 1992, Traditionalists and Revivalists in Jazz, 1993, (with David Cassidy) C'mon Get Happy, 1994, Jazz Veterans, 1995, Blue Rhythms, 1996; editor F. Scott Fitzgerald: The Princeton Years, 1997. Trustee Princeton Tiger Mag., 1983—. Finalist for Excellence in Recorded Sound Rsch. award Assn. for Recorded Sound Collections, 1991; recipient Deems Taylor award ASCAP, 1993. Mem. Nat. Acad. Recording Arts & Scis., Am. Theatre Critics Assn., The Drama Desk. Avocations: music, theater, hiking, reading. Home: 50 Quartz Ln Paterson NJ 07501-3345

DE FLORA, ANTONIO CESARE, biochemistry educator; b. Genoa, Italy, Feb. 7, 1940; s. Giovanni C. and Enrichetta E. (Ardy) De F.; m. Patrizia Solange Bonavera, Oct. 7, 1967; children: Cristina, Alfredo, Giovanni, Donatella. MD with honors, Genoa U., 1964. Docent Ministry of Edn., Rome, 1968, 70; asst. prof. U. Genoa, 1970-73, assoc. prof. biochemistry, 1970-73, prof., 1973—, head biochemistry dept., 1981-90; vis. scientist Med. Rsch. Coun., Mill Hill, Eng., 1970; dir. target projects biotechnology Nat. Rsch. Coun., Rome, 1988-94, 98—; sci. coord. biology area Genoa U., 1995—; chmn. sci. com. Siena (Italy) consortium, 1992—; mem. bds. biotech., Brussels, 1985—. Editor-in-chief Italian Jour. Biochemistry, 1989-99; editor Biotech. Applied Biochemistry, 1988—; contbr. 210 articles to profl. jours.; patentee in field. Mem. Internat. Coun. Sci. Union, Fedn. European Biochemistry Socs., Biochem. Soc., Italian Biochem. Soc. (bd. dirs. 1975-80, Genova prize for sci. 1997). Avocations: symphonic music, swimming. Home: Via Caprera 4/11, 16146 Genova Italy Office: U Genova Dept Exptl Med, Viale Benedetto XV 1, 16132 Genova Italy

DEFOIS, GÉRARD, archbishop; b. Nueil-Sur-Layon, Maine-et-Loire, France, Jan. 5, 1931; s. Marcel and Denise (Boissinot) D. Diploma, Inst. Supérieur De Pastorale Caté-Chétique, Paris, École Pratique Des Hautes Études; PhD in Theology, Inst. Catholique, Paris. Chaplain Lycée De Cholet, 1957-63; dir. religious edn. Diocese Angers, 1965-67; dep. dir. Inst. Supérieur De Pastorale Caté Chétique, Paris, 1968-73; prof. sociology Inst. Supérieur De Culture Religieuse, Abidjan, 1971-76; sec.-gen. Frenca Episcopate, 1977-84; rector Catholic U., Lyon, 1984-90; prelate Sr Sainteté, 1985; asst. bishop Sens, 1990; archbishop Sens-Auxerre, Sens-Auxerre, 1990-95; archbishop Reims, France, 1995-98, Lille, France, 1998—; v.p. Union Des Établissements D'Enseignement Supérieur Catholique, 1985, pres., 1986-89, preacher during Lent Notre-Dame, Paris, 1989-91. Author: Le Sacrement de Réconciliation, 1970, Le Pouvoir Dans l'Eglise, 1973, Reélevélation et Société, 1974, Prendre Parti Pour l'Homme, 1977, Vulnérable et Passionnante Eglise, 1978, Jonas Ou l'Insurrection de Dieu, 1979, L'Occident en Mal d'Espoir, 1982, L'Europe et ses Valeurs, Une Question Pour l'Eglise, 1983, Pour Une Éthique de la Culture, 1987, Jean Paul II Pélerin de Dieu sur les Route des Hommes, 1989, Libres en Vérite, 1990, L'Enfant Promesse de Dieu, 1991, Avec Amour et Verité, 1995, Le Second Souffle de Vatican II, 1996, L'Eglise et les média, 1997. Decorated officer Legion of Honor. *

DE FRANCA, FRANCISCA PESSOA, biochemical engineering educator, researcher; b. Cedro, Brazil, July 28, 1948; d. Clovis and Juventina (Pessoa) de F. Degree in chem. pharmacy, Fed. U. Rio de Janeiro, 1970; DSc in Microbiology, Fed. U. Rio de Janeiro, Brazil, 1974. Prof. of graduation Sch. of Chemistry-Fed. U. Rio de Janeiro, 1971-95, coord. postgraduation, 1982-86, prof. for postgraduation, 1980—; rschr. NRC of Brazil, Rio de Janeiro, 1976—; divsn. head Ministry of Health, Rio de Janeiro, 1973-76. Contbr. articles to sci. jours. Mem. Brazilian Soc. Microbiology, Brazilian Pharm. Soc., N.Y. Acad. Scis. Roman Catholic. Avocations: travel, theatre, swimming. E-mail: fpfranca@h2o.eq.ufrj.br. Fax: 55-21-5904991. Office: FURJ Dept Biochem Engring, Bloco E Ilha do Fundao, 21949900 Rio de Janeiro RJ, Brazil

DEFRANCE, JÉRÔME, acoustics engineer, researcher; b. Rennes, France, May 28, 1967; s. André and Joëlle (Bouroullec) D.; m. Maryse Laurent, Oct. 10, 1993; 1 child, Énora. Diploma in engring., ENSAIS, Strasbourg, France, 1990; DEA in Acoustics, U. Maine, 1991, PhD in Acoustics, 1996. Acoustics engr. ITAC, Nantes, France, 1991-92, STBFT, Paris, 1992-93; rsch. engr. C.S.T.B., Grenoble, France, 1993—. With French armed forces, 1992-93. Mem. French Soc. Acoustics. Avocations: singing, playing flute, sailing, cinema. Home: 14 rue Alphonse Terray, 38000 Grenoble France Office: CSTB, 24 rue Joseph fourier, 38400 Saint-Martin-D'Heres France

DE FRANCHIS, AMEDEO, Italian diplomat; b. Naples, Aug. 9, 1939; married; 4 children. Degree in law, U. Rome, 1961. With East-West desk, Polit. Affairs Gen. Directorate Ministry of Fgn. Affairs, Italy, Rome, 1962-65; lt. Italian Army, 1965-67; vice consul, then dep. consul gen. Italian Consulate Gen., N.Y.C., 1967-70; counselor, then chargé d'affaires Italian Embassy, Tehran, 1976; dep. head, then head NATO Desk Ministry of Fgn. Affairs, Rome, 1976-79; at permanent delegation of Italy to NATO, 1979-83; dep. perm. rep. of Italy to NATO Brussels, 1983-84; amb. of Italy Pakistan, 1984-88; dep. sec. gen. of NATO, 1989-94; dir. gen. of polit. affairs Ministry of Fgn. Affairs, Italy, 1994-98; per. rep. of Italy to N. Atlantic Coun. Brussels, 1998—. Office: NATO Hdqrs, Blvd Leopold III, 1110 Brussels Belgium

DE FRONDEVILLE, ERIC CHARLES, portfolio manager; b. Nantes, France, Nov. 18, 1963; s. Bertrand Jean Maurice and Barbara Janice (Fuller) deF.; m. Nathalie Carole Bouvier; children: Christel, Nicolas, Elena. BS, Georgetown U., 1985. Completed 2-yr. program for Soc. Française des Analystes Financiers. Asst. credit mgr. Soc. Internat. de Banque, Paris, 1985-86; acct. exec. Banque Indosuez, Paris, 1987-88; fin. cons. Banque Pallas, Paris, 1988-90; equity fund mgr. Banque Colbert, Paris, 1990-95, Union des Assurances Parisiennes, Paris, 1995-97, Rothschild et Cie Banque, Paris, 1997—. Mem. Invalid Flying Disc de Paris (treas. 1991—), Pi Delta Phi. Democrat. Roman Catholic. Avocations: statistical collections, Ultimate Frisbee, backpacking, tennis, skiing. Home: 12 villa Médicis, 92270 Bois Colombes France Office: Rothschild et Cie Banque, 17 ave Matignon, 75008 Paris France

DE GAETANO, GIOVANNI M.D., biomedical researcher; b. Rodi Garganico, Foggia, Italy, Aug. 23, 1943; s. Vittorio and Antonietta (De Donato) de G.; m. Maria Benedetta Donati, Sept. 23, 1968; 1 child, Katleen. MD, Cath. U., Rome, 1968, cert. lab. and clin. hematology, 1971; PhD, U. Leuven, 1973; MD (hon.), Med. Sch., Debrecen, Hungary, 1995. Rsch. fellow Lab. Blood Coagulation U. Leuven, 1968-73; head lab. Mario Negri Inst., Milan, 1973-76, head lab. cardiovasc. clin. pharm., 1976-87; dir. Consorzio Mario Negri Sud, Santa Maria Imbaro, 1987—; invited prof. U. Bologna, 1985-87, U. Padua, 1992-94. Editor: Round Table Conference on Platelet Aggregation, 1971, Platelets: A Multidisciplinary Approach, 1978, Hemostasis, Prostaglandins and Renal Disease, 1980; editor Thrombosis Rsch., 1981-85, 92-96. Recipient Upjohn Achievement award Italian Soc. Pharmacology, 1981, Contbn. to Hemostasis award Internat. Thrombosis Soc., 1993. Mem. Italian Soc. Hemostatis (past pres.), European Thrombosis Rsch. Orgn. (sec. gen. 1988-96, pres. 1997—), N.Y. Acad. Scis., Royal Med. Acad. Brussels. Office: Consorzio Mario Negri Sud, Via Nazionale, I-66030 Santa Maria Imbaro Chieti, Italy

DE GAMARRA, AHNAL MARYNIKA CRIEGO, adult education educator; b. Calcutta, India, Oct. 19, 1947; d. Giovani and Ahnal Nadija (Patni) Criego; m. Jorge Edmundo Gamarra-Llanos, Jan. 25, 1975. AA, L.A. C.C., 1968; BA, Calif. State U., L.A., 1976; MA, Calif. State U., 1981; EdD, U.S. Internat. U., 1989. Medicare supr. Occidental Life Ins. Co., L.A., 1967-76; tchr. L.A. Unified Sch. Dist., 1974-89, adult educator, 1978—; adult educator Compton (Calif.) Unified Sch. Dist., 1978-89; prof. Calif. State U., L.A., 1980-85, coordinator Alternative Edn. Work Ctr., 1986-90; asst. prin. Adult Counseling Svcs. Manual Arts CAS, 1990-93; pvt. instrn., 1963-76; ednl. cons. Harlan L. Polsky Assocs., Los Angeles, 1980; literacy cons. State of Calif., 1979—; lectr. Bilingual Adult Literacy; asst. prin. ops. L.A. Unified Sch. Dist., 1993—. Author: Identifying and Teaching Adult and Juvenile Illiterates. Named Tchr. of Yr., Compton Unified Sch. Dist., 1981-82; nominee Calif State Tchr., 1986; recipient 1st pl. Native Spanish Interpretive Festival, 1965. Mem. ACSA, ASCD, NEA, Assn. Calif. Sch. Adminstrs., Assn. Mex.-Am. Educators, Assn. Asian-Pacific Adminstrs., Calif. Assn. Bilingual Edn., Coun. Mex.-Am. Adminstrs., Coun. Exceptional Children, Calif. Coun. Adult Edn., Nat. Literacy Coun., Am. Assn. Tchrs. of Spanish, Ednl. Toastmasters, Soroptomists, Pi Delta Kappa, Pi Delta Theta, others. Democrat. Avocations: reading, foreign languages. Office: PO Box PO Box 36371 Los Angeles CA 90036-0371

DE GASTINES, BRIGITTE, business executive; b. Paris, Mar. 22, 1944; d. Maurice Turckheim and Yvonne Weber; m. Bejitte Cachart, Aug. 31, 1994; children: Catherine, Nicelas, Elodie. Delegue apries-vaute SVP, St. Oven, France, 1964-66, attache, 1966-70, with pers., 1971-72, dir. gen. adjoint, 1973-76, chmn., 1976—; chmn. group SVP, France, SVP Internat., Suisse, SVP Suisse; mem. commn. Progress de Entrepries and MEDEF. Author: Passion SVP. Named Chevalier de le Legion d'Honneur, Officer de l'ordre Nat. Merit. Mem. Assn. Progress Mgmt. (pres.), Honneur du Mouvement Francais for le Qualite, Cons. Banque du France. Avocations: golfing, skiing. Office: SVP, 70 rue de Rosius, 33400 Saint Oven France

DE GAULLE, CHARLES, lawyer, politician; b. Dijon, France, Sept. 25, 1948. LLM, Faculty Law Paris, 1970; grad., Sch. of Polit. Scis., Paris, 1970. Mem. European Parliament, 1999—, mem. com. on econ. and monetary affairs, substitute com. on industry/external trade, rsch. and energy; atty. at law Paris, 1971-99; co-pres. Tech. Group of Ind. Mems. Mem. European Parliament, 1993—. Office: European Parliament, 60 rue Wiertz, 1047 Brussels Belgium

DEGAUQUE, PIERRE JULES, electronics educator; b. Lille, France, Sept. 19, 1946; s. Jules and Georgette (Menet) D.; m. Christine M. Martin, July 1, 1974; children: Emeline, Florence, Helene, Guillaume. Degree in elec. engring., U. Lille, 1967, DSc, 1970, PhD, 1976. From asst. prof. to prof. U. Lille, 1968 , dir. lab. radiopropagation and electronics, 1993—. Co-author, editor: Electromagnetic Compatibility, 1993; contbr. articles to profl. jours. Recipient Blondel medal Soc. Electricians et Electroniciens, 1990; fellow Summa Found., 1994. Mem. IEEE, Internat. Union Radio Sci. (v.p. exec. com. noise and interference). Home: 38 Rue Andre Messager, 59130 Lambersart France

DEGBEY, COLLINS EMMANUEL, investment company executive; b. Sokpoe, Ghana, Mar. 15, 1959; arrived in Thailand, 1994; s. Quao Degbe Klebeti Adeti and Akua Nenegbe Kunyehia; m. Vincentia Abla (div. 1993); children: Jeffrey Doe David, Mawuli Degbey. Accounts officer State Hotel, Accra, Ghana, 1979-85; health care nurse Akuse, Ghana, 1985-87; caretaker Elf Co., Accra, Ghana, 1991-94; web trader Health Products/Computer Programs, Thailand, 1995-98; CEO, owner Charlie House Inc., Thailand, Bahamas, 1997—; mktg. cons., 1997—; pres., CEO Noble Brands Inc., Tortola, British Virgin Islands; registered nurse Rightlife; CEO SID Network, 1998—, World Net Co., 1998—; sales rep. Family of Eagles, 1998—, Big Planet, 1998, Newbridge Networks, 1999; pres. Cdegbey Assocs., Inc., Computer Assocs. Silicon Valley, 1998-99, Global Investor World; pres./owner Volta Bus. Links, U.K., 1996; bd. dirs. AOL Time Warner, World Health Network, Hewlett Packard; mem. Interlotto Equity Transfer Sys., Internat. Players Guild, Freedom 2000. Mem. Prison Svc. Corrections Officers Assn., Pa., 1999; exec. Michigan Dancing Club, 1999, others. Mem. AAAS, Philantro Soc. Internat., Nat. Geographic Soc., Highlanders Club (fellowship), The Oxford Club, Angel Banker Club, Planetary Soc. Avocations: reading, music, wrestling, golf, tennis.

DEGEN, ROLF, child neurologist, researcher; b. Chemnitz, F Sachsen, Germany, July 25, 1926; Paul and Nella (Vogel) D.; m. Hanna-Elisabeth Schulz, June 18, 1955; children: Angela Plöger, Heike Eckardt. MD, U. Leipzig, Germany, 1954. Asst. Univ. Children's Hosp., Leipzig, Germany, 1956-66; head dept. child neurology Univ. Children's Hosp., Leipzig, 1966-73; head EEG dept. and dept. outpatient epileptic children Epilepsy Ctr. Bethel, Bielefeld, Germany, 1973-91, head practice for epileptic outpatients, 1991—. Author: Die Kindlichen Aufallsleiden, 1976, Praxis der Epileptologie, 2d edit., 1993; co-editor: (with Niedermeyer) Epilepsy, Sleep and Sleep Deprivation, 1981, rev. 2d edit., 1991, (with Niedermeyer) The Lennox Gastaut Syndrome, 1988, (with Dreifuss) The Benign Localized and Generalized Epilepsies in Early Childhood, 1992, Epilepsien und Epileptische Syndrome in Kindes-und Erwachsenenalter, Klinische und Elektroenzephalographische Differentialdiagnose, 1998, Epilepsien und Epileptische Syndrome im Kindes- und Erwachsenenalter, Elektroenzephalographie, 1999. Mem. German Neuropediatric Assn., Internat. League Against Epilepsy (hon.; German sect.), German EEG Assn. (mem. dir.). Christian Social Union. Lutheran. Avocations: classical music, psychology. Home: Telgter Str 42, 33619 Bielefeld Germany

DEGENER, JOHN EDWARD, medical microbiologist; b. The Hague, The Netherlands, July 19, 1950; s. Edward Henry Degener and Clementine Louise Petronella Maria Paijens; m. Wilhelmina Louisa Ruiter, Mar. 4, 1977; children: Loes, Clementine. MD, State U. Leiden, The Netherlands, 1976; registered med. microbiologist, U. Hosp. Rotterdam, The Netherlands, 1979, PhD, 1983. Mem. staff U. Hosp./Childrens Hosp. Sophia, Rotterdam, 1979-81, U. Hosp./Dijkzigt Hosp., Rotterdam, 1981-88; head dept. lab. med. microbiology Pub. Health Lab., Leeuwarden, Friesland, The Netherlands, 1988-96; head dept., prof. med. microbiology U. Hosp., Groningen, The Netherlands, 1996—. Contbr. articles and revs. to profl. jours. Mem. European Soc. Med. Microbiology and Infectious Diseases, Am. Soc. Microbiology, Netherlands Soc. Med. Microbiology, chmn. Netherlands Soc. of Microbiol., Rotary Internat. Avocations: french horn, bird watching. Office: Dept Med Microbiology U Hosp Groningen, Hanzeplein 1, 9713 GZ Groningen The Netherlands

DE GENNARO, RICHARD, retired library director, library advisor; b. New Haven, Mar. 2, 1926; s. Ralph and Acquilina (Pedicini) De G.; m. Birgit M. Erikson, June 12, 1953; children: Ralph, George, Christina. BA, Wesleyan U., 1951, MA, 1960; MS in LS, Columbia U., 1956; postgrad., Univs. Paris, Madrid and Perugia, 1951-55; grad. Advanced Mgmt. Program, Harvard U., 1971; DHL (hon.), Wabash Coll., 1991. Jr. acct. Atlas Constructors, Morocco, 1952-53; reference librarian N.Y. Pub. Libr., 1956-58, dir., 1987-90; successively reference librarian, asst. dir., assoc. univ. librarian systems devel., sr. assoc. univ. librarian Harvard U. Libr., 1958-70; dir. librs. U. Pa., 1970-86, adj. prof. English, 1979-86; libr. Harvard Coll., 1990-96; vis. prof. Grad. Libr. Sch., U. So. Calif., 1968-69; cons. libr. bldgs., tech. and mgmt.; mem. overseers com. to visit libr., Harvard U.; cons. MIT, Johns Hopkins U.; mem. adv. bd. Chem. Abstracts Svc., 1967-70; mem. Palinet bd. Union Libr. Catalogue, 1970—; mem. com. internat. sci. and tech. info. programs NAS-NRC, 1977-79; mem. Mellon Found. JSTOR Bd., 1995—; sr. libr. advisor JSTOR; mem. governing bd. Rsch. Librs. Group, 1979-89, sr. vis. fellow, 1980-81, chmn., 1984-95; Bowker lectr., 1979; Lazerow lectr., 1984. Author: Shifting Gears, Information Technology and the Academic Library, 1984, Libraries, Technology, and the Information Marketplace, Selected Papers, 1987; contbr. articles to profl. jours. Bd. dirs. Ctr. for Rsch. Librs., 1977-81; trustee U. Pa. Press, 1978-82. With USN, 1942-46. Recipient Disting. Alumnus award Wesleyan U., 1991; Hugh Atkinson award, 1993; named Acad. Rsch. Libr. of Yr., 1991; Coun. Libr. Resources fellow, 1971; Rockefeller Found. Ctr. fellow, Bellagio, Italy, 1981; info. tech. fellow U. Edinburgh, 1984. Mem. Assn. Rsch. Librs. (pres. 1975, dir. 1973-76), ALA (pres. info. sci. and automation div. 1975), Am. Soc. Info. Soc. (Melvil Dewey medal 1986), Century Assn. Club, Grolier Club, Harvard Club. Home: Unit 1414 988 Blvd Of The Arts Apt 1414 Sarasota FL 34236-4838

DE GENNES, PIERRE-GILLES, physicist, educator; b. Paris, Oct. 24, 1932. Ed. Ecole Normale Superieure, PhD. Rsch. scientist Centre d'Etudes Nucleaires de Saclay, 1955-59; prof. solid state physics U. Paris, Orsay, 1961-71; prof. Coll. de France, Paris, 1971—; dir. Ecole de Physique et Chimie, Paris, 1976—; sci. adv. for chem. physics Rhodia, France, 1999—. Author: Superconductivity of Metals and Alloys, 1965, The Physics of Liquid Crystals, 1973, Scaling Concepts in Polymer Physics, 1979, Simple Views on Condensed Matter, 1992-97, Les Objets Fragiles, 1994. Ensign French Navy, 1959-61. Recipient Nobel prize in physics, 1991. Mem. AAAS, Académie des Sciences, Dutch Acad. Scis., Royal Soc., Ukrainian Acad. Scis., Brazilian Acad. Scis. Nat. Acad. Scis. Avocations: skiing, drawing, hiking. Office: Ecole de Physique et Chimie, 10 rue Vauquelin, 75005 Paris France

DE GERENDAY, LACI ANTHONY, sculptor, educator; b. Budapest, Hungary, Aug. 17, 1911; came to U.S., 1912; s. László and Ilona (Jiraszek) de G.; m. Mary Ellen Lord, 1939 (dec. 1976); 1 child, Lynn; m. Elisabeth Gordon Chandler, May 12, 1979. Student, S.D. State Sch. Mines, Rapid City, 1929-30, Ursinus Coll., Collegeville, Pa., 1931-32, Nat. Acad. Design, N.Y.C., 1932-34, Beaux Arts Inst., N.Y.C., 1934-35. Prof. Lyme (Conn.) Acad. Fine Arts, 1979—; sculptor, 1936—. Exhbns. include Nat. Acad. Design, Pa. Acad., Boston Mus., Pa. Mus., Mus. San Francisco, Mus. Ariz., Cin. Mus., Mus. Rhode Island, Mus. Modern Art, Grand Ctrl. Galleries, Schonemann Gallery, Ferargil Gallery, Nat. Sculpture Soc., Arch. League, Corning Glass, N.J. Art Mus., N.Y. Coliseum, Salmagundi Club, Rockefeller Ctr., Loeb Ctr. NYU, Acad. Arts Letters, Lever House, Allied Artists, French Gallery, Smithsonian Inst., Nat. Arts Club, Sculpture Ctr., Am. Bible Soc., Hudson Valley Arts Assn., Nat. Collection Fine Arts, Washington, Mus. Fine Arts, Springfield, Mass., Foothills Art Ctr., Golden Colo., Florence Griswold Mus., Old Lyme, Conn., Madison (Conn.) Gallery, Old State House, Hartford, Conn., Cathedral St. John Divine, N.Y.C., Fedn. Medaille, British Mus., London, Am.'s Tower, N.Y.C., Brookfield Zoo, Chgo., Newington-Cropsey Found. Gallery, Hasting-on-Hudson, N.Y., Slater Mus., Nat. Acad. Mus., N.Y., 1998, Pub. Sculpture by Nat. Academicians, 1998; two man shows include Art Ctr, Old Lyme, Wall Focus Gallery, Chester, Conn., Art of The Animal Kingdom Bennington Ctr. Arts; prin. works include wood carving Courthouse, Aberdeen, S.D., bronze medal Hall of Fame Great Ams., NYU, bronze relief Torrington, Conn., sculpture Nat. Gallery Art, Washington, Gold medal Soc. Elec. Engrs., wood relief Post Office, Tell City, Ind., bronze relief Chgo., bronze equestrian relief Mus. Algiers, Algeria, mermaid fountain N.Y.C. Garden, bronze relief portrait Bklyn. C.C., N.Y.C., bronze archl. relief Modern Art Foundry, N.Y.C., silver coin Nat. Commemorative Soc., bronze medal Soc. Medallists, others. With U.S. Mil., 1943-46. Recipient Citation, City of N.Y., First prize N.J. Art Assn., Radding award Mus. Fine Arts, Springfield, 1977, Silver medal Allied Artists Am., 1977, Wendel Clinedinst award, 1982, 4 Battle Stars, Bronze Arrowhead U.S. Mil. Fellow Nat. Sculpture Soc. (mem. coun., Lindsey Morris Meml. award 1955, 81, 91, Bennett prize 1963, Roman Bronze Foundry award 1980, John Spring Art Founder award 1992); mem. Nat. Acad. Design (academician, Ellen Speyer prize 1947, 63, 91, Daniel Chester French Gold medal 1995), Nat. Arts Club (Salzman award 1994), Hudson Valley Arts Assn. (Mrs. John Newington award 1979, Elliot Liskin Meml. award 1995), Nat. Soc. Lit. Arts, Am. Medallic Soc., Fedn. Internat. Medaille. Republican. Avocations: golf, walking, hiking, horseback riding. Home & Studio: 2 Mill Pond Ln Old Lyme CT 06371-1118

DEGHENGHI, ROMANO, chemist; b. Rome, June 27, 1930; m. Ancilla Molinari Deghenghi, Sept. 7, 1957; children: Luigi, Paola. PhD Chemistry, U. Trieste, Italy, 1953. Asst. prof. Laval U., Quebec, Can., 1958-60; dir. chemistry Ayerst Labs., Montreal, Can., 1960-69, dir. rsch., 1970-79; scientific dir. Beaufour Labs., Paris, 1980-81, UPSA Labs, Paris, 1981-83, Debiopharm S.A., Lausanne, Switzerland, 1984-89; scientific dir., pres. Europeptides, Paris, 1990—. Home: 106 Chemin de Ronde, 78110 Le Vesinet France Office: Europeptides, 9 Ave Du Marais, 95100 Argenteuil France

DEGLISE, XAVIER MARCEL, science educator, researcher; b. Toulon, France, Aug. 20, 1941; s. Joseph Marcellin and Marie Yvonne (Jovet) D.; m. Genevieve Marie Gregoire, Mar. 30, 1967; children: Laure, Jean-Hugues, Guillaume. BSc in Chemistry, U. Nancy, France, 1963, MS, 1965, PhD, 1966, DS, 1968; BSc in Chem. Engring., Ecole Nat. Superieure des Industries Chimiques, Nancy, 1964. Asst. prof. E.N.S.I.C., 1964-67; postdoctoral fellow Laval U., Que., Can., 1968, asst. prof., 1969-70; asst. prof. U. Nancy, 1971-73, assoc. prof., 1974-85, prof., 1986—; dir. Sch. Wood. Sci. and Timber Engring. Ecole Nat. Superieure des Techs. et Industries du Bois, Epinal, France, 1985—; dir. Wood Material Rsch. Lab., 2000—; vis. prof. U. Nanjing, China, 1994, 96, 97; hon. prof. Warsaw Agrl. U., 1996—, Brasov U., Romania, 1999—; adminstr. Wood Tech. Ctr., Paris, 1982-97, Gillet Techs. Co., Casteljaloux, France, 1997—; mem. Nat. Bd. Univs., Paris, 1979-81, 86-97, Nat. Rsch. Coun., Paris, 1982-86; mem. coun. of orientation Banque Populaire de Lorraine, 1997—; co-dir. Eurofortech Ltd., Dublin, Ireland. Contbr. chpts. to books; patentee in field. Recipient chevalier Order of Palmes Academiques, 1989, officer, 1998, chevalier Nat. Order of Merit, 1996. Mem. Internat. Acad. Wood Sci., Am. Chem. Soc., Forest Products Soc., Soc. Chimique de France. Roman Catholic. Office: ENSTIB U Nancy I, BP 239, 54506 Vandoeuvre les Nancy Cedex, France

DE GOFF, VICTORIA JOAN, lawyer; b. San Francisco, Mar. 2, 1945; d. Sidney Francis and Jean Frances (Alexander) De G.; m. Peter D. Copelman, May 2, 1971 (div. Dec. 1978); m. Richard Sherman, June 16, 1980. BA in Math. with great distinction, U. Calif., Berkeley, 1967, JD,

1972. Bar: Calif. 1972, U.S. Dist. Ct. (no. dist.) Calif. 1972, U.S. Ct. Appeals 1972, U.S. Supreme Ct. 1989; cert. appellate law specialist, 1996. Rsch. atty. Calif. Ct. Appeal, San Francisco, 1972-73; Reginald Heber Smith Found. fellow San Francisco Neighborhood Legal Assistance Found., 1973-74; assoc. Field, De Goff, Huppert & McGowan, San Francisco, 1974-77; pvt. practice Berkeley, Calif., 1977-80; ptnr. De Goff and Sherman, Berkeley, 1980—; lectr. continuing edn. of bar, Calif., 1987, 90-92, U. Calif. Boalt Hall Sch. Law, Berkeley, 1981-85, dir. appellate advocacy, 1992; cons. Calif. Civil Practice Procedure, Bancroft Whitney, 1992; mem. Appellate Law Adv. Commn., 1995; apptd. applicant evaluation and nomination com. for State Bar Ct. by Calif. Supreme Ct., 1995; pvt. atty., clk. ct. com. Calif. Ct. Appeals, 1997-99; mem. com. on appellate practice ABA, 1997. Author: (with others) Matthew Bender's Treatise on California Torts, 1985. Apptd. to adv. com. Calif. Jud. Coun. on Implementing Proposition 32, 1984-85; mem. adv. bd. Hastings Coll. Trial and Appellate Adv., 1984-91; expert 20/20 vision project, commn. on future cts. Jud. Coun. Calif., 1993, apptd. to appellate standing adv. com., 1993-95; apptd. to Appellate Indigent Def. Oversight Adv. Com., State of Calif., 1995—; com. on appellate stds. of ABA Appellate Judges Conf., 1995-96; com. on appellate practice ABA, 1997; adv. bd. Witkin Legal Inst., Bancroft Whitney, 1996—; bd. dirs. Calif. Supreme Ct. Hist. Soc. (sec. 1999—), State Bar Calif., Appellate Law Cons. Group, 1994-95; appointee 9th Jud. Cir. Hist. Soc. Hon. Cecil Poole Biography Project, 1998. Fellow Woodrow Wilson Found., 1967-68. Mem. Calif. Trial Lawyers Assn. (bd. govs. 1988-88, amicus-curiae com. 1981-87, editor-in-chief assn. mag. 1980-81, Presdl. award of merit 1980, 81), Calif. Acad. Appellate Lawyers (sec.-treas. 1989-90, 2d v.p. 1990-91, 1st v.p. 1991-92, pres. 1992-93), Am. Acad. Appellate Lawyers, Edward J. McFetridge Am. Inn of Cts. (counsellor 1990-91, edn. chmn. 1991-92, social chmn. 1992-93, v.p. 1993-94, pres. 1994-95), Boalt Hall Sch. Law U. Calif. Alumni Assn. (bd. dirs. 1989-91), Order of Coif. Jewish. Office: 1916 Los Angeles Ave Berkeley CA 94707-2419

DEGOIX, CHRISTOPHE NICOLAS, manufacturing executive; b. Argenteuil, France, Feb. 5, 1972; s. Christian Raymond and Annie (Delille) D. Engring. Diploma, Ecole Centrale de Lyon, France, 1995; MS, Pa. State U., 1996; postgrad., Air Force Sch., France, 1997. Rsch. asst. CNRS, Lyon, 1994-95; tchr. Objectif Math, Paris, 1993-95; devel. engr. Fabrique Nationale Mfg. Inc., Columbia, S.C., 1995; rschr. Powder Metallurgy Lab. Pa. State U., State College, 1995-96; scientist, instr. French Air Force, Salon de Provence, 1997; project mgmt. group head R&D Procter & Gamble, Brussels, 1998—; cons. in field. Patentee in field. Founder, pres. Central Invest, Lyon, 1993-95. Recipient Rhones Alpes Region award, Lyon, 1995. Mem. Am. Soc. Materials, Ingecom. Avocation: judo (black belt). Home: Bd de Smet de Naeyer 42A, B-1090 Brussels Belgium Office: Procter & Gamble, Temselaan 100, B-1853 Strombeek-Bever Belgium

DEGONIA, MARY ELISE, government community relations executive, publisher; b. St. Louis, Sept. 23, 1954; d. Joseph Milton and Janice Doris (Walls) DeG. Student, Riverside Community Coll., 1971-73, Calif. State U., 1973-76. Dir., youth svcs. Los Padrinos, San Bernardino, Calif., 1975-78; chief, planning and evaluation Mayor's Office of Employment and Tng., San Bernardino, 1978-79; program mgr., v.p. Mondale Task Force on Youth, Washington, 1979-80; sr. policy analyst Nat. Youth Work Alliance, Washington, 1979-81; v.p. govt. rels. Youth Employment, Washington, 1981-88; pres. Capitol Perspectives, Washington, 1988—; pub. Capitol Perspectives Update; dir. pub. policy and legislation Nat. Youth Employment Ctr., N.Y.C., 1979-89; founding mem. Nat. Assn. for Community Base Orgn., Washington, 1979-83. Co-author: State Coordination Guide, 1987, Food for Thought, 1988, Stalking the Large Green Grant, 1979, Fund Diversification Guide, 1988. Founding chmn. Calif. Child, Youth and Family Coalition, Sacramento, 1976-78; nat. bd. dirs. Wider Opportunities for Women; sr. adv. Nat. Coun. La Raza Jobs for Youth, 1998—. Recipient Outstanding Performance award, U.S. Dept. Labor, Washington, 1980, Disting. Achievement award, U.S. Basics, Alexandria, Va., 1988. Mem. Nat. Youth Employment Coalition, State Issues Forum (exec. mem., bd. dirs.), Nat. Job. Tng. Partnership. Avocations: scuba diving, surfing, saxaphone playing, desert hiking. Office: Capitol Perspectives 1915 17th St NW # 200 Washington DC 20009-6202

DEGOS, CLAUDE-FRANCOIS, neurology professor; b. Villers sur Mer, Calvados, France, Oct. 12, 1939; s. Robert and Monique (Lortat-Jacob) D.; m. Catherine Anzani, Jan. 18, 1968; children: Louis, Thomas, Marie. MD, U. Paris, 1970; degree in med. edn., U. Paris VI, 1976. Cert. neurologist Nat. Me.d Council, 1974. Intern various hosps., Paris, 1965-70; sr. resident Faculty of Medicine, Paris, 1970-76; neurologist various hosps., Paris, 1976—; prof., chief neurology dept. U. Paris St. Joseph Hosp., 1976—; V.p. U. Paris, 1980-81; mem. med. bd. St. Joseph Hosp. (pres. 1986-87, 99—). contbr. numerous articles to profl. jours.,; mem editorial bd. La Revue du Praticien, 1972—. Decorated Chevalier de Legion d'Honneur, 1999. Mem. Intersyndicat. of Physicians, Surgeons, Biologists and Specialists of Paris Hosps. (pres. 1985-89), Nat. Syndicat of Physicians, Surgeons, Biologists and Specialists of Pub. Hosps. (pres. 1989—), French Nat. Soc. Neurology (bd. dirs., pres. 1990-2000), European Assn. Hosp. Physicians (v.p. 1995—), European Union of Med. Specialists (1980-97), Nat. Assn. French Physician Specialists of Nervous System Diseases (1980-96), French Soc. Neuropsychology. Roman Catholic. Avocations: music, painting. Home: 55 rue Geoffroy St-Hilaire, 75005 Paris France Office: Hosp St Joseph, 7 Rue Pierre Larousse, 75014 Paris France

DE GOSSON, MAURICE ALEXIS, mathematics educator, researcher; b. Berlin, Mar. 13, 1948; s. Alexis Arthur and Gerda Marita (Nylund) de G.; m. Charlyne Jocelyne Humblot, Jan. 10, 1970; children: Serge, Corinne, Samantha, Sven. BSc in Math., U. Nice, France, 1972, MSc in Math., 1973, PhD in Math., 1978; Habilitation, U. Paris VI, 1992. Sr. lectr. Wits U., Johannesburg, Republic of South Africa, 1985-87; asst. prof. U. Sask., Saskatoon, Can., 1987-89; assoc. prof. Cath. U. Lille, France, 1990-93, U. Kalmar, Sweden, 1993-98; prof. math. U. Karlskrona, Sweden, 1998—, rsch. dir., chair, 1999; sci. expert European Union, Brussels, 1997—. Author: Maslov Classes, Metaplectic Representation and Lagrangian Quantization, 1997, Mathematical Foundations of Semi-Classical Mechanics, 2000; contbr. articles to profl. jours. Avocations: karate, wine, philosophy. Office: U Karlskrona-Ronneby, IHN Math Dept, 37179 Karlskrona Sweden

DE GRAAFF, JAN, agricultural economist, educator, researcher; b. The Hague, The Netherlands, July 27, 1948; s. Arend Jacob and Johanna Maria (Rietdyk) De G.; m. Francoise Leguay, Jan. 12, 1980; 1 child, Florence. Degree in agrl. engring., Agrl. U. Wageningen, The Netherlands, 1974, PhD, 1996. Agrl. economist FAO, Nairobi, Kenya, 1976-78, Rome, 1978-80, Kingstown, Jamaica, 1980-82; lectr. U. Wageningen, 1982-84, sr. lectr., 1991—; mem. staff Royal Tropical Inst., Amsterdam, 1984-91. Author: The Economics of Coffee, 1986, Soil Conservation and Sustainable Land Use, 1993, The Price of Erosion, 1996. Avocations: tennis, badminton.

DEGRAFFENREID, JEFF GORDON, paramedic, educator; b. Oklahoma City, Feb. 12, 1970; s. Gordon Dean and JoAnn DeGraffenreid; m. Paula Ann Lash, Aug. 8, 1992; children: Faith, Isaac. BA, MidAm. Nazarene U., Olathe, Kans., 1996, MEd, 1999. Cert. paramedic, Kans. Paramedic Miami County Emergency Med. Svcs., Paolo, Kans., 1991-93; paramedic team leader Johnson County Med. Action, Olathe, 1993—, dir. emergency ops. team, 1995—; adj. prof. Johnson County C.C., Overland Park, Kans., 1995, MidAm. Nazarene U., 1999—; sch. safety advisor Olathe Sch. Dist., 1999—. Contbg. author: The Basic EMT, 1999; contbr. articles to profl. jours. Educator CPR for Life, Johnson County, 1991-2000; rep. MidWest Trauma Soc., Johnson County, 1998-99. Mem. Am. Acad. Med. Adminstrs., Nat. Assn. EMTs, Kans. Emergency Mgmt. Assn., Kans. Emergency Med. Svcs. Assn. (guest lectr. 1995-2000). Republican. Nazarene. Avocation: fly fishing. Fax: 913-715-1959. E-mail: jdegraffenreid@jocoems.org. Home: 15503 S Lindenwood Olathe KS 66062 Office: Johnson County Med Action 111 S Cherry Ste 300 Olathe KS 66061

DEGRAFFENRIED, JOHN WILLIE, chemist, researcher; b. Buffalo, N.Y., Mar. 20, 1957; s. John W. and Viola (Whitmore) D. BSc, SUNY, Fredonia, 1980; student, U. Ariz., 1980, U. Buffalo, 1981-82. Rsch. asst. SUNY, Fredonia, N.Y., 1982-83; chemist Red Wing Co., Inc., Fredonia, N.Y., 1983-85; analytical chemist Frontier Chemical, Niagra Falls, N.Y., 1989-92; vol. ARC, 1992-93; file clk. Child Care Coalition, 1993-94; writer, 1994; pres. City Curl Co., Inc., Buffalo, N.Y., 1998—; owner Quantum Photography Studio, Buffalo, N.Y., 1999—; analytical chemist Sorrento Cheese Co., Inc., Buffalo, N.Y., 1999—. Author: Intramolecular Quantum Chemistry & Physics Theory, 1993, Gas Chromatographic Theory, 1994, Solute Separation Science, 1997, Energy, Entropy & Enthalpy, 1995, Quantum Theory, 1997. Mem. NAACP (Buffalo chpt.), Am. Chemical Soc. (analytical chemistry award 1978), Assn. Ofcl. Analytical Chemists, N.Y. Acad. Scis., Libr. of Congress, Smithsonian Inst. Democrat. Avocations: chess, basketball, horseback riding, photography. Home: 31 W Balcom St Buffalo NY 14209-1407 Studio: 250 Delaware Ave Rm 10 Buffalo NY 14202-2014

DEGRAVE, ALEX G., computer engineer, consultant; b. Lokeren, Belgium, Aug. 3, 1957; came to U.S., 1988; m. Francine P. Leroy, Oct. 29, 1985; children: Aurelien, Colas, Jeremie. Post-grad. mgmt., Leuven U., Belgium, 1984, MBA in Fin. & Internat. Mgmt., 1986; MA in Ops. Rsch., Gent U., 1988. Industrial engr. Electronics Telecommunications, 1979; systems engr. IBM Belgium, Brussels, 1980-87; mktg. supr. IBM L.Am., Gaithersburg, Md., 1988-92; cons. IBM Consulting Group, Brussels, 1993-97, IBM Argentina, 1997-2000. Avocations: sailing, trekking, music, history. Home: Groeninglaan 13, 1933 Sterrebeek Belgium Office: IBM Consulting Group, Plantsoen 1 Victoria Regina, B-1210 Brussels Belgium

DE GRAVE, DANY MICHEL, biomedical engineer; b. Brussels, Apr. 29, 1965; s. Michel Maurice and Denise (Godderis) De G.; children: David, Paul. Grad. in chem. and agrl. scis. engring., Free U. Brussels, 1988; grad. in info. and comm. tech., Vlerick Sch., Ghent, Belgium, 2000. Asst. in human serology SmithKline Biols., Rixensart, Belgium, 1990-92; head clin. serology bacterial vaccines SmithKline Beecham Biols., Rixensart, 1993-96, head clin. immunology-bacterial vaccines, 1996—; mem. Nat. Com. for Clin. Lab. Stds., 1994—; presenter in field, Greece, Belgium, France, Italy, U.S. Contbr. articles to sci. jours. With Belgian Army, 1989-90. Mem. Am. Soc. for Microbiology, Am. Assn. for Clin. Chemistry, Assn. for Lab. Automation, Am. Soc. for Microbiology, ICT. Avocation: multimedia. Office: SmithKline Beecham Biols, Rue de L'Institut 89, 1330 Rixensart Belgium

DE-GRAVE, FRANK, federal official; b. Amsterdam, The Netherlands, June 27, 1955. Grad. law, U. Groningen, The Netherlands, 1979. With AMRO Bank, 1980-82; mem. Amsterdam Mcpl. Coun., 1982-86, Lower House, 1982-90; dep. mayor Amsterdam, 1990; state sec. Ministry of Social Affairs and Employment, 1996-98; min. of def. The Hague, 1998—. Mem. People's Party for Freedom and Democracy. Office: PO Box 20401, 2500 EK The Hague The Netherlands*

DEGROFF, RALPH LYNN, JR., investment banker; b. Balt., Oct. 23, 1936; s. Ralph Lynn and Marion (Day) D.; m. Marion Parsons Sinwell, Feb. 4, 1989. AB, Princeton U., 1958; MBA, U. Va., 1960. With Dillon, Read & Co. Inc., N.Y.C., 1961-81, v.p., 1970-74, sr. v.p., 1974-81; mng. dir. Donaldson, Lufkin & Jenrette, 1981-94; past bd. dirs. Interstate Gen. Corp., The Ryland Group, Regency Corp.; bd. dirs. Wagner Bros. Containers Inc., The Winthrop Trust Co.; trustee Holland Soc. N.Y. With U.S. Army, 1960-61. Mem. Soc. of the Cin., Colonial Wars, Md. Club, Elkridge Club, Hillsboro Club. Presbyterian. Address: 7 Gracie Sq New York NY 10028-8001 Home: 1002 Rolandvue Ave Baltimore MD 21204-6815

DE GROOF, CHRIS, electric company executive; b. Antwerp, Belgium, Feb. 13, 1953; s. Frans and Renee (Poucet) De G.; m. Myriam Maervoet; children Liesbeth, Annemie, Jan. MA in Econs., U. Louvain, 1977; MBA, U. Antwerp, 1979, PhD in Econs., 1982. Asst. prof. U. Antwerp (Belgium), 1976-80; head fin. modelling EBES/Electrabel, 1980-91; fin. officer Electrabel, 1992—; prof. U. Antwerp, 1986—. Roman Catholic. Avocations: music, books, skiing, biking, travel. Home: Sgt De Bruynestraat 27, 2140 Antwerp Belgium Office: Electrabel, Regentlaan 8, 1000 Brussels Belgium

DEGROOT, LOREN EDWARD, engineering executive, consultant; b. Grand Rapids, Mich., May 30, 1935; s. Edward and Edna May (Dykhuizen) DeG.; m. Joyce Elaine Swifink, June 15, 1956; children: Lori Robin, Cheryl Joy, Christine Linnae, Steven Benjamin. ASE, Grand Rapids Jr. Coll., 1955; BSME, U. Mich., 1957, MSME, 1961. Engr. Lear Siegler, Inc., Grand Rapids, 1961-65, mgr., 1965-68; dir. GM Corp., Milw., 1968-72; mgr. Rockwell Internat.-Cedar Rapids, Iowa, 1972-79, dir., 1979-84, v.p., 1984-86; v.p. Rockwell Internat., El Segundo, Calif., 1986-90; pres., chief exec. officer Windquest Internat. Industries, Inc., Grand Rapids, 1990-92; exec. v.p. Contour Roll Co., Grand Haven, 1992-95, pres., 1996; pres. Gabriel Entertainment Enterprises Inc., Branson, Mo., 1993—; pres. Inst. Navigation, Washington, 1972-73. Author numerous tech. papers; patents for Integrated Navigation Receiver, 1968, Doppler Compensated Navigation, 1968. Lt. (j.g.) USNR, 1957-60. Recipient Nat. Aviation Records Nat. Aero. Assn., Washington, 1983, World Aviation Records Fedn. Aeronautique Internationale, Paris, 1983, Significant Contbr. citation Aviation Week & Space Tech., Washington, 1983. Mem. Nat. Aviation Club, Inst. Navigation (Samuel F. Burka award 1966), Tau Beta Pi, Pi Tau Sigma. Avocations: cross-country skiing, racquetball, golf, tennis. Home: 229 Timbercrest Ct Holland MI 49424-2236

DE GROOT, PAUL FRANCISCUS, geophysicist; b. Enschede, Overijssel, The Netherlands, Apr. 10, 1956; s. Cor Franciscus and Gerdie Johanna (Lesscher) De G.; m. Mieke Hendrika Busch, June 18, 1981; children: Marieke, Michelle, Nadine, Bart. Rsch. geophysicist Shell, The Hague, The Netherlands, 1981-82; geophysicist Petroleum Devel. Oman, Muscat, Oman, 1982-86, Shell Petroleum Devel. Co., Port Hartcourt, Warri, Nigeria, 1986-90; sr. geophysicist Shell Internationale Petroleum Maatschappij, The Hague, 1990; project leader Technisch Natuurwetenschappelijk Onderzoek, Delft, The Netherlands, 1991-95; dir. De Groot-Bril Earth Scis., Enschede, The Netherlands, 1995—; cons. Technisch Natuurwetenschappelijk Onderzoek. Author: Seismic Reservoir Characterisation Employing Factual and Simulated Wells, 1995; co-author: Artificial Intelligence in the Petroleum Industry, 1996. Mem. European Assn. Geoscientists and Engrs., Petroleum Geologische Kring, Vereniging Artificiele Neurale Netwerken, Soc. Exploration Geophysicists, Koninklijk Nederlands Geologisch Mijnbouwkundig Genootschap. Achievements include co-invented method of seismic body recognition. Avocations: sports, reading, travel. Office: De Groot-Bril Earth Scis BV, Boulevard 1945-24, 7511 AE Enschede The Netherlands

DE GROOT, RUDOLF STEVEN, environmentalist; b. Voorburg, The Netherlands, Mar. 6, 1955; s. Peter Johannes and Christina Clarina (von Buytene) de G.; m. Sonja Maria Spenny, Aug. 29, 1986; children: Kira, Arjan. MSc, Utrecht U., 1981; PhD, Wageningen Agrl. U., 1994. Naturalist guide Met. Touring, Quito, Ecuador, 1978-79; sci. assoc. Nature Conservation Dept., Wageningen, The Netherlands, 1982-90; environ. cons., 1986—; assoc. prof. environ. scis. Wageningen U., 1991—; assoc. dir. Global Assessment Ctr. Maastricht U.; chmn. expert panel Internat. Union Conservation Nature & Natural Resources, Switzerland, 1990-93; mem. internat. com. on nature value Internat. Soc. Ecological Econs., Solomons, 1996—; mem. sr. adv. com. Inst. Rsch. Environ. & Economy, Ottawa, Ont., Can., 1992-97. Co-author: The Environment: Towards a Sustainable Future, 1994; author: Functions of Nature, 1992; editor Wetland Ecology and Mgmt., 1992; editor: Landscape - Ecological Impact of Climate Change, 1990; co-editor Environment and Devel. newsletter, 1983-91; editl. bd. Regional Environ. Change. Pres. Foudn. for Sustainable Devel., Wageningen, 1989—; mem. european Com. for Nat. Conservation Strategies, 1986-89. Rsch. grantee World Wildlife Fund, 1982-97, Prins Bernhard Found., 1980. Mem. World Conservation Union, Netherlands Royal Acad. Sci., Internat. Soc. Ecol. Econs. Green Party. Avocations: tennis, sailing, biking, drawing, photography. Home: Nwe Veenendaaleweg 229, 3911 MJ Rhenen The Netherlands Office: Environ Sys Analysis Group, PO Box 9101, 6700 HB Wageningen The Netherlands

DE GROOTE, ALEXANDRE G.Y., financial broker; b. Gent, Belgium, June 8, 1958; s. Guy and Christiane (Dumortier) De G.; m. Catherine Lebrun; children: Edouard, Charles. BBA, European U., Antwerpen, Belgium, 1981; MBA, U. Dallas, Irving, Tex., 1982. Sr. credit analyst Mfrs. Hanover Trust Co., N.Y.C., 1984-85; attaché de direction Mfrs. Hanover Bank Belgium, Brussels, 1985-86; mgr. Remy Freres & Fils, Brussels, 1986-89, dir., 1994-95; dir. Remy Internat., Luxembourg, 1990-93; mng. dir. Petercam Instnl. Bonds, Brussels, 1995—. Mem. De Warande, Brussels Bond Club (animator 1992-96). Home: rue des Fiefs 9, 1380 Lasne Belgium Office: Petercam Instl Bonds, 19 Pl Sainte-Gudule, 1000 Brussels Belgium

DE GROOTE, PATRICK, science educator; b. Hasselt, Limburg, Belgium, Jan. 13, 1958; s. Raymond De Groote and Claire Maldoy. Lic. in geography, Cath. U. Louvain, Belgium, 1979, PhD in Scis., 1986. Asst. Cath. U. Louvain, 1979-86; lectr. Coloma Inst., Mechelen, Belgium, 1983-86, Hoge Hotelschool, Maastricht, The Netherlands, 1986-96; lectr., prof. Economische Hogeschool Limburgs, Diepenbeek, Belgium, 1987-91; prof. Limburger Univ. Centrum, Diepenbeek, 1991—; cons., rschr. in demography, tourism, regional policy, tourism geography and transport. Author: The Belgian Hotel Industry, 1986, Geography of Belgian Tourism, 2 vols., 1993, A General Analysis of Tourism, 1995-96, 99, The Meetings and Conference Business in Belgium and The Netherlands, 1998, Tratlas Belgium, 2000, Iraq, 2000; editor rsch. papers., series Toeractua, 1997-2000. With Belgian mil., 1983-84. Roman Catholic. Avocations: reading, travel, walking, swimming, photography. E-mail: patrick.degroote@luc.ac.be. Home: Martelarenlaan 9/B10, 3500 Hasselt Belgium Office: Limburgs Univ Centrum, Universitaire Campus, 3590 Diepenbeek Belgium

DE GRUBEN, THIERRY, Belgian ambassador; b. Antwerp, Belgium, Nov. 17, 1941; m. Françoise Francq; 1 child, Christopher. PhD in Law. Mem. Belgian delegation to NATO, 1969-70; embassy sec. Belgian Embassy, Moscow, 1971-76; sec., then first sec. Belgian Embassy, London, 1976-80; consul gen. Belgian Embassy, Bombay, 1980-82; counsellor with Minister of Fgn. Affairs Belgian Embassy, 1982-85; amb. Belgian Embassy, Warsaw, 1985-90, Moscow, 1990-95; dep. dir. gen., Polit. Affairs, Spl. Envoy to Ea. Slavonia Belgian Embassy, 1996-97; amb., perm. rep. from Belgium to NATO Brussels, 1997—. Office: NATO Hdqrs, Blvd Leopold III, 1110 Brussels Belgium*

DEGUATEMALA, JOYCE, sculptor; b. Feb. 25, 1938; d. Cassius Albert and Martha (Prado Solares) Bush; m. Jason Leander Vourvoulias, Oct. 13, 1956; children: Albert Leander, Sabrina Marie, William Craig. Student in fine arts, U. Autonoma de Mex., 1958, U. Wis., 1959, Silpakorn U., Bangkok, 1960-62; Cert. in Physics, U. San Carlos, Guatemala, 1969. artist-in-residence Brandywine Workshop, Phila., 1993, also bd. dirs.; resident Djerassi Found., Woodside, Calif., 1994; invitational cultural specialist, lectr. workshops, juror Biannual, Honduras, 1999; cultural specialist U.S. Internat. Svcs., for Honduras, 1999. One-woman shows include Mus. Contemporary Latin Am. Art OAS, Washington, 1977, Marian Locks Gallery, Phila., 1979, 84, 85, 90, Barbara Gillman Gallery, Miami, Fla., 1982, 92, 93, 94, Northwood Inst., West Palm Beach, Fla., 1982, 14 Sculptors Gallery, N.Y.C., 1987, 88, 90, 92, Estela Shapiro Gallery, Mexico City, 1988, 90, 92, Djerassi Found., Woodside, 1994; exhibited in group shows Bienal Internat. do Sao Paulo, Brazil, 1975, 83, Marian Locks Gallery, Phila., 1979, 85, Macondo Gallery, Guatemala City, 1979, William Pa. Meml. Mus., Harrisburg, Pa., 1982, Mus. Latin Am. Contemporary Art, OAS, Washington, 1983, 90, Noyes Mus., Oceanville, N.J., 1983, Outdoor Sculpture/Fairmount Park, Phila., 1986, 14 Sculptors Gallery, 1987, 88, 89, 90, 91, 2d Internat. Ephemeral Sculpture Exhbn., Fortaleza, Brazil, 1989, Olympiad of Art, Seoul Olympic com. and the Guggenheim Mus., Seoul, Korea, 1988, Temple Gallery, Phila., 1987, Pub. Art on the Plaza, Phila., 1987, Inst. Contemporary Art U. Pa., Phila., 1991, Art Alliance, Phila., 1991, Lehigh U., Bethlehem, Pa., 1991, Exhbn. Fortaleza, Brazil, 1991, Kingsborough C.C., Bklyn., 1992, Abington Art Ctr., Jenkintown, Pa., 1992, 94, Phila. Coll. Textiles and Sci., Phila., 1992, Cen. Conn. State U., New Britain, 1992, Metro-Dade Art in Pub. Places, Miami, 1993, Barbara Gilman Gallery, Miami, 1993, 95, 96, 99, Brandywine Workshop, Phila., 1994, Internat. Art Exhbn., Miami Beach, 1995, Museo Am. Madrid, 1997, State Mus. of Pa., 1999, Open Space Gallery, Allentown, Pa., 1999, Barbara Gillman Gallery, 1999, numerous others; represented in permanent collections Nat. Mus. History and Fine Arts of Guatemala City, Mus. Contemporary Latin Am. Art, Washington, OAS, Ringling Bros. Mus. Art, Sarasota, Fla., Noyes Mus., Oceanville, N.J., Washington, Lehigh U., Bethlehem, Pa., Hershey Foods Corp. Tech. Ctr. (Pa.), Cedar Crest Coll., Allentown, Pa., Pan Am. Bank, Miami, Mus. Modern Art, Chapultepec, Mexico City, Hansen Properties, Ambler, Pa., Fed. Res. Bank, Phila., Please Touch Mus., Phila., Exmibal, El Estor, Guatemala, Olympiad Art, Art Pk., Seoul, Korea, Fla. Internat. U., Miami, others, and numerous private collections; sculpture commd. for Elkins Park Free Libr., Pa., 1985, AnnMarie Sculpture Garden, Prince Frederick, Md., 1998, State Mus. Pa., Harrisburg, 1998. Mem. adv. bd. Latin Am. and Caribbean Ctr., Fla. Internat. U., Miami; bd. dirs. Brandywine Workshop, Phila. Address: 320 Fairview Rd Glenmoore PA 19343-1402

DEGUCHI, YASUO, English literature educator; b. Mie Prefecture, Japan, Aug. 26, 1929; s. Ichiroemon and Kinue Deguchi; m. Sachiko Yasuoka, Oct., 1952; children: Kyoko, Hidemi. BA, Waseda U., Tokyo, 1953, MA, 1955. Asst. Waseda U., Tokyo, 1953-62, lectr., 1962-65, asst. prof., 1965-71, prof., 1971—; Brit. coun. fellow Oxford (Eng.) U., 1985, sr. guest scholar Campion Hall, 1989. Author: Keats, Man and His Works, 1974, Natsumesoseki in London, 1984, A History of Literary England, 1989, The Tower of London, 1993, Keats and His Age, 2 vols., 1997. Former pres. Assn. English Romanticism, Tokyo, 1975, Brit. Tea Assn., Tokyo, 1984; hon. pres. Soseki Mus. in London, Eng., 1985. Recipient Japan Translation award Japan Translater's Assn., Tokyo, 1974, Grand prize Internat. Acad., 1999. Mem. Brit. Soc. in Japan, Japan Author's Assn., Japan P.E.N. Club. Roman Catholic. Avocations: painting, angling, gardening. Home: 3-16-23 Zaimokuza, Kamakura 248, Japan Office: Waseda Univ, Nishi-Waseda, Tokyo Japan

DE GUENIN, JACQUES VINCENT, mayor; b. Libourne, France, May 2, 1931; s. Jean V. and Odette (Rozieres) De G.; m. Roseline Coquelin, Sept. 21, 1957 (dec.); children: Andre, Philippe; m. Odette Simon, June 17, 2000. Degree civil engring., Ecole Des Mines, Paris, 1954; MS, U. Calif., Berkeley, 1955. Engr. Esso France, Port Jerome, 1958-66; logistics dept. mgr. Esso France, Paris, 1971-72, contr., 1973-80; mgr. logistics div. Esso Europe, London, 1966-71; asst. fin. mgr. Peugeot S.A., Paris, 1980-84, mgr. non-automobile sector, 1984-93; mayor Saint-Loubouer, France; pub. (mag.) Lumieres Landaises; contbr. articles to profl. jours. Mem. Cercle Frederic Bastiat (pres.). Home: 40320 Saint Loubouer France

DE GUIO, ROLAND, electrical engineer, educator; b. Haguenau, Bas-Rhin, France, July 2, 1960; s. Robert and Gabrielle (Halter) De G.; m. Gabrielle Schmitt; children: Juliette, Jeanne, Louise. Engr., ESSTIN, France, 1983; degree in physics, France, 1985; PhD, U Strasbourg I, France, 1990. Prof. with agregation U. Monastir, Tunisia, 1985-87; prof. with agregation ENSAIS, France, 1987-90, assoc. prof., 1990-99; prof. ENSAIS, 1999—. Mem. IEEE, Soc. Elec. Engrs. Office: ENSAIS-LRPS, 24 bd de la victoire, 67084 Strasbourg France

DEGUTIS, MINDAUGAS, marketing research company executive; b. Vilnius, Lithuania, Dec. 8, 1971; s. Juozas and Stefanija (Rosinaite) D. BA, Vilnius U., 1993, MA, 1995. Rsch. asst. Inst. Internat. Rels. and Polit. Sci., Vilnius, 1993—; rsch. dir. SIC Market Rsch., Vilnius, 1994—; bd. dirs. SIC Gallup Media; nat. corr. Consultative Meeting on Youth Rsch. and Documentation of the Coun. of Europe, 1994—. Co-author: Political Parties in Lithuania, 1997. Polit. cons. Lithuanian Liberal Union, 1996, 2000. Mem. Am. Mgmt. Assn., European Soc. Opinion & Mktg. Rsch. Avocations: basketball, modern dance, travel. E-mail: mindaugas@sic.lt. Office: SIC Market Rsch, Raugyklo 15, 2001 Vilnius Lithuania

DEHAAN, PETER, educator; b. Utrecht, The Netherlands, Mar. 30, 1949; s. Peter G. and H. (Hettinga) D.; m. J. Arts, Oct. 10, 1982; children: Rosemarie, Caroline. Grad. high sch. Biochemist Free U., Amsterdam, The Netherlands, 1975-96, staff mem., 1996—. Home: Linnaeushof 61, 1098 KP Amsterdam The Netherlands Office: Free U, Boechorststraat 7, 1081 BT Amsterdam The Netherlands

DE HAAS, JAN HENDRIK DERK, management consultant; b. Leiden, The Netherlands, Dec. 29, 1960; s. Jan Hendrik and Maria Hilde (t'Hooft) de H.; m. Anne Simone Marie Auffret, Sept. 3, 1983; children: Helmert, Vivian, Vincent, Ariane. B in Econs., U. Rotterdam (The Netherlands), 1980, M in Econs., 1982, D in Bus. Mgmt., 1984. Mktg. researcher Philips, Eindhoven, The Netherlands, 1984-87; bus. unit mgr. VNU, Amsterdam, 1988; fin. mgr. Indumy, Dordrecht, The Netherlands, 1989-91; gen. mgr.

Indumy, Dordrecht, 1992—; gen. mgr. Auto Indumy, Dordrecht, 1994—, I.D.S., Rotterdam, 1997—, Indulease-GE Capital, Den Bosch, The Netherlands, 1999—. Mem. Jong Mgmt. Avocations: golf, hockey, skiing, piloting airplanes, travel. Home: Maaibeemd 47, 4824 NC Breda Noord Brabant, The Netherlands Office: BV Indumy, Mylweg 69, 3316 BE Dordrecht The Netherlands

DEHARENG, DOMINIQUE, chemist, researcher; b. Liege, Belgium, July 30, 1954; d. Andre and Micheline (joris) D.; children: Nicolas Dao, Laurence Dao. Lic. in Chem. Sci., U. Liege, 1976, DS in Chemistry, 1983. Rschr. in chemistry U. Liege, 1983—. Contbr. articles to profl. jours. Mem. AAAS, N.Y. Acad. Sci., Soc. Chemistry Belgium. Office: Cen D Ingenierie Proteines, Inst Chimie B 6/Sart Tilman, B-4000 Liege Belgium

DE HARTOG, JAN, writer; b. Haarlem, Holland, Apr. 22, 1914; s. Arnold Hendrik and Lucretia (Meyjes) de H.; m. Angela Priestley, 1946; children: Arnold, Sylvia, Nicholas, Catherine; m. Marjorie Mein, 1961; children: Eva, Julia. Student, Amsterdam Naval Coll., 1930. Staff mem. Amsterdam Municipal Theatre, 1932-37; writer-in-residence, lectr. creative playwriting U. Houston, 1962. Author: (plays) Mist, 1938, De Ondergang van de Vrijheid, 1939 (Gt. Nat. Drama prize 1939), Skipper Next to God, 1946, This Time Tomorrow, 1947, The Fourposter, 1951 (Tony award 1952), Death of a Rat, 1956, William and Mary, 1964, (novels) The Lost Sea, 1951, Mary, 1951, The Distant Shore, 1952, The Little Ark, 1954, A Sailor's Life, 1956, The Spiral Road, 1957, The Inspector, 1960, Waters of the New World, 1961, The Artist, 1963, The Hospital, 1964, The Call of the Sea, 1966, The Captain, 1966, The Children, 1968, The Peaceable Kingdom, 1971, The Lamb's War, 1979, The Trail of the Serpent, 1983, Star of Peace, 1984, The Commodore, 1986, The Centurion, 1989, The Peculiar People, 1992, The Outer Buoy, 1994, (mus.) I Do, I Do, 1966. Captain, Netherlands Merchant Marine. Recipient Netherlands Cross of Merit; named Officier de l'Academie, France, 1952, Commandeur of Netherlands Lion by Queen Beatrix of the Netherlands, 1996. Mem. Coun. of Am. Master Mariners. Mem. Soc. of Friends. Office: Lantz Office 200 W 57th St Ste 503 New York NY 10019-3211

DEHAYS, TAREK SAMIR ABU, company executive; b. Kuwait, Kuwait, Aug. 17, 1968; s. Samir M. and Khawla O. (Kamal) Abu-Dehays; m. Eman A. Afanah, Oct. 17, 1991; 1 child, Sarah. BS in Civil Engring., Jordan U., Amman, 1990; MS in Engring. Mgmt., U. Mich., 1990. Lic. engr. Site engr. Consolidated Contractors Inst., Muscat, Oman, 1991-92; projects mgr. Gulf Devel. Trading Enterprise, Muscat, 1992-95; founder, mng. dir. Aquatreat, Amman, 1995—; dir. Dehays Industries, Amman, 1995-96; cons. project Edgo Devel., Amman, 1995—. Fellow ASCE, ASME. Office: Middle East Environ Tech, PO Box 298, Amman 11512, Jordan

DE HEMPTINNE, JEAN B. CHARLES, research engineer, educator; b. Leuven, Belgium, June 15, 1962; s. Xavier and Françoise (Snoy) de H.; m. Colombe de Seze, May 2, 1992; children: Stella, Thérèse. Chem. engr., Cath. U. Leuven, 1985; PhD in Chem. Engring., MIT, 1990. Rsch. asst. MIT, Cambridge, 1985-90; environtl. mgr. Procter and Gamble, Brussels, 1990-91; rsch. engr. Inst. Francais du Petrole, Rueil Malmaison, France, 1991—; ast. prof. ENSPM, Rueil-Malmaison, 1994—. Fulbright Hays scholar. Mem. AIChE, Soc. Petroleum Engrs., Assn. Française des Techniciens du Pétrole. Home: 10 Avenue de General, de Gaulle, F-78110 Le Vésinet France Office: Inst Francais du Petrole, 14 Avenue de Bois Preau, F-92852 Rueil-Malmaison France

DE HERTOGH, HENDRIK PIETER WIM, outsourcing company executive; b. Elsene, Belgium, Mar. 11, 1966; s. Willy Fraçois De Hertogh and Maria Johanna Jonckheere; m. Ingrid Vercruysse; children: Evelyne, Liesbeth. Student, Hoger Inst., Belgium, 1987; degree in human resources mgmt., KVKH, Belgium, 1995, degree in mgmt., 1996. Sales exec. Exell, Brussels, Belgium, 1992-93, ORDA-S, Brussels, Belgium, 1993-94, Kodak, Brussels, Belgium, 1994-97; mgmt. cons. Graydon, Brussels, Belgium, 1993-94; dir. Danka, Brussels, Belgium, 1995-97; mng. dir. DSI, Brussels, Belgium, 1997—. Avocations: golf, reading. Home: Damstraat 110, 1800 Vilvoorde Belgium Office: DSI, Zandvoortstraat 4, 2800 Mecheuen Belgium

DEHEZ, PIERRE, educator; b. Ghent, Belgium, May 10, 1948; s. Andre and Ghislaine (de Pape) D.; m. Monique Delhaye, Aug. 26, 1972 (div. Mar. 1981); children: Nicolas, Bruno; m. Anne Francis, Jan. 16, 1982; children: Martin, Celine. MA, UCL, Louvain, Belgium, 1973, PhD in Econs., 1980. Rsch. assoc. core UCL, Louvain, Belgium, 1973-81; prof. European U. Inst., Florence, Italy, 1983-90, Erasmus U., Rotterdam, The Netherlands, 1991-92, UCL, 1990—; chmn. dept. of econs. European U. inst., 1985-87, 89, Cath. U. Louvain, 1994-2000. Contbr. articles to profl. jours. With Belgian Army, 1974-75. Mem. Union Belge Pschio Anstues, Am. Radiology League, Radio Soc. Gt. Brit. Avocation: amateur radio. Home: Rue D'Incourt 18, 1370 Dongelberg Belgium Office: Cath U Louvain, Place Montesquieu 3, 1348 Louvain Belgium

DEHLVI, ABDUL WADUD AZHAR, language educator; b. Dehli, India, Mar. 2, 1936; s. Abdul Malik Dehlvi and Amna Bi; m. Qudsia Azhar Qudsia Anwar, Sept. 23, 1967; children: M.M. Farrukh, M.M. Shahrukh. Degree, Punjab U., 1954, Delhi U., 1955; BA with honors, Delhi U., 1958, MA in Persian, 1960, cert. in French, 1960, diploma in Modern Arabic, 1964; DLitt in Persian, Tehran (Iran) U., 1970. Lectr. Delhi Coll./ Delhi U., 1962-71; assoc. prof. Jawaharlal Nehru U., New Delhi, 1971-78, prof., 1978—, chmn. Ctr. African and Asian Langs., 1971-75, 81-83, dean Sch. Langs., 1981-83; lectr. in field; mem. Bd. Studies of Persian in Punjab, Kashmir, AMU, Osmania, Bhagalpur and Calcutta Univs.; mem. seminar and lit. com. Shalib Inst., Delhi; mem. Rampur Raza Libr. Bd., 1991-97. Author: The Ramayana — The Holy Book of Hindus, 2 vols., 1973, Trends in Modern Persian Litarature, 1978; contbr. articles to profl. publs.; mem. editl. bd. various jours. in field. Recipient Nat. Lectr. award UGC, Delhi, 1985-87; UGC scholar, 1958-60; rsch. fellow Tehran U., 1967-70. Fellow Persian Acad. of India (bd. dirs.); mem. IndoArab Friendship Soc., Indian Congress of Asian and Pacific Studies, Assn. Indian Fgn. Lang. Tchrs., All India Oriental Conf. (life), Iran Soc. (life), Soc. of Promoters and Friends of Turkish and Ctrl. Asian Cultures (gen. sec. 1996—), Modern Fields Edn. Soc. (pres. 1995—), Crescent Edn. Soc. (gen. sec. 1988-94), All Indian Persian Tchrs. Assn. (joint sec. 1977-85, v.p. 1985-86), Eternal Divind Edn. Soc. Santinaketan (acting pres.). Mem. Indian Congress Party. Muslim. Home: 98 Haji Bhawan Sadar Bazar, Delhi 110006, India Office: JNU Sch Lang/ Lit/Cultural, New Mehrauli Rd, New Delhi 110067, India

DEHMELT, HANS GEORG, physicist; b. Germany, Sept. 9, 1922; came to U.S., 1952, naturalized, 1962; s. Georg Karl and Asta Ella (Klemmt) D.; 1 child from previous marriage, Gerd; m. Diana Elaine Dundore, Nov. 18, 1989. Grad., Graues Kloster, Berlin, Abitur, 1940; D Rerum Naturalium, U. Goettingen, 1950; D Rerum Naturalium (hon.), Ruprecht Karl-Universitat, Heidelberg, 1986; DSc (hon.), U. Chgo., 1987. Postdoctoral fellow U. Goettingen, Germany, 1950-52, Duke U., Durham, N.C., 1952-55; vis. asst. prof. U. Wash., Seattle, 1955; asst. prof. physics U. Wash., 1956, asso. prof., 1957-61, prof., rsch. physicist, 1961—; cons. Varian Assocs., Palo Alto, Calif., 1956-76. Contbr. articles to profl. jours. Recipient Humboldt prize, 1974, award in basic research Internat. Soc. Magnetic Resonance, 1980, Rumford prize Am. Acad. Arts and Scis., 1985, Nobel prize in Physics, 1989, Nat. Medal of Science, 1995; NSF grantee, 1958—. Fellow Am. Phys. Soc. (Davisson-Germer prize 1970); mem. Am. Acad. Arts and Scis., Am. Optical Soc., Nat. Acad. Scis., Sigma Xi. Achievements include co-discoverer (with Hubert Krüger) nuclear quadrupole resonance, 1949; inventor schemes using single trapped atomic particles as million-fold quantum amplifier, employed them as a leader of groups in for the first time permanently isolating and identifying at rest in vacuum an individual electron, a subatomic particle, a charged atom, ion Astrid, an antimatter particle, positron Priscilla, and in demonstrating spontaneous quantum jumps and measuring magnetism and size on single electron and positron with precisions 1,000 times higher than previously attained on millions of them. Home: 1600 43rd Ave E Seattle WA 98112-3205 Office: U Wash PO Box 35-1560 Seattle WA 98195-1560

DEHNERT, HANS GEORG, internist; b. Mainz, Germany, Oct. 4, 1961; s. Juergen Richard and Christa Rosemarie (Schmelzer) D.; m. Renate Schuetz, Sept. 30, 1994. MD, Heidelberg (Germany) U., 1987; doctor of medicine,

Mainz U., 1987. Sr. ho. officer nephrological unit St. John Hosp., Oberhausen, Germany, 1988; sr. ho. officer County Hosp. Gen. Medicine, Vaihingen, Germany, 1989-90; sr. ho. officer cardiology St. Mary's Hosp., Stuttgart, Germany, 1990-91, sr. ho. officer gastroenterology/oncology, 1991-92; registrar nephrology Kurpfalz Hosp., Heidelberg, Germany, 1991-94, sr. registrar, 1994-95. With 250th Airborne Med. Coy, 1988-96, with 260th Airborne Med Coy, 1997—. Mem. Bund Deutscher Internisten, Nephrologische Gesellschaft, Soc. of German Drs. for Emergency Medicine. Avocations: cycling, free-styling skiing, parachute jumping, glides-plane flying. Office: Nephrologische Praxis, 12 Jahn St, 56457 Westerburg Germany

DE HOLMSKY, DMITRY, lawyer; b. Neuilly, France, Oct. 22, 1932; s. Woldemar and Simone (Perthuis) de H.; m. Marie Le Barbier, Dec. 22, 1959; 1 child Rémi-Pierre. LLB, Faculty of Law, Paris, 1956. Pvt. practice law Paris. Author: La Lune Frousse, 1992. Capt. French Army. Home and Office: 36 rue Chalgrin, 75116 Paris France

DEHOUSSE, JEAN-MAURICE, federal official; b. Liège, Belgium, Oct. 11, 1936; 4 children. Faculty of law educator, U. Liège, 1960; cert. higher internat. studies, John Hoskins U., 1961; cert. higher fed. studies, U. Coll. Aoste, 1963, diploma higher fed. studies, 1964; diploma Am. Sec. Edn., LLD. Asst. faculty mem. law U. Liège, 1962; with Nat. Belgian Assn. Sci. Rsch., 1962-65; asst. Faculty of Law Inst. European Law, Liège, 1966-71; lectr. Higher Sch. Translators and Interpreters, Brussels, 1965-71; with Svc. for Polit. Sci. Policy, 1969-71; pres. Signs and Letters Ltd., Le Grand Liège Ltd.; from dep. leader to leader Cabinet for Minister Communal Rels., 1970, 71; Dep. Liège, 1971-81; 1972-81, 82-85; local cllr. Liège, 1977—; Minister of French Culture, 1977-79; pres. Regional Exec. for Walloon, 1979-81; senator Liège, 1981-91; Minister Walloon Economy, 1982—; minister pres. Walloon Region; with Fed. Ministry for Sci. Policy, Brussels, 1992—; member of European Parliament European Union, Brussels, Belgium; mem. senate commns. Walloon Regional Coun.; mem. PS Commn., Liège and Ctrl. Commn., USC, Liège, Fed. Assembly and Fed. Com. of PS; Brussels and PS exec. Grantee U. Liège, 1961. Mem. Socialist Party. Home: 17 Rue Saint-Pierre, B-4000 Liège Belgium Office: Ministry for Sci Policy, 155 rue de le loi, 1040 Brussels Belgium*

DEHOUSSE, MARTIN EUGENE, mathematics educator; b. Herstal, Liège, Belgium, Jan. 18, 1920; s. Pierre Lambert and Juliette (Francotte) D.; m. Geneviève Mathot, Feb. 25, 1946 (dec. Dec. 1988); children: Martine (dec. Nov. 1999), Marie-France. Licentiate sci. math., Free U. Brussels, 1946; PhD summa cum laude, Free U., Brussels, 1958. Tchr. Inst. du Arts et Metiers, Brussel City, Belgium, 1946-58; rational mechanic electronics theory Inst. Meurice-Chimie, Brussels, Belgium, 1950-58; CC math. stats. Offcl. U. Congo, Belgium, 1958-62; prof. U. Burundi, 1966-70; prof. of analytical and celestial mechs. Nat. U. Congo, Congo, 1962-91; mgr. Belgian acad. projects overseas brachistochrone for electron, 1960, vibration and gravity, 1964, 68, meteorite crater in Rwanda, 1973, effect earth's rotation on g and Eötvös's balance, 1958, 75, 80, colour photo Moon and comp. of surf, 1968, new function sagittal cross-section of human skull, 1970, 94, rocket's launching to east, 1973, 84, astron. determined time of Hesiode, 1973, 84, telescope collection cosmic rays, 1981, orbit determined minor planet, 1997, supernova 1054 and Constantin IX, 1999, comet of Julius Caesar 43 B.C., 2000. Contbr. chpts. to books and articles to scientific publs. Pres. Fedn. Internat. Deportes et Internes of Resistance, 1954. Decorated Grand Officier de l'Ordre la Couronne Cmmdr. O.C. glaives vermeil Croix de Guerre (Belgium), Medal of Merit Arts, Scis. and Letters (Zaire). Mem. The Biometric Soc., Nat. Stats. France, Soc. Math. Belgium, Club U. Found., C.A. Royal African Club, European Acad., Rotary. Avocations: piano, bridge. Home: Maeterlinck Ave 88, 1030 Brussels Brabant Belgium

DEHUI, SONG, engineering educator; b. Tian Jin, China, Feb. 19, 1939; d. Song Zhaokui and Chen Meijun; m. Wang Erqi, Sept. 30, 1965; children: Youtong Wang, Dahui Wang. Diploma, Beijing U. of Tech., 1960. Rschr. Xian Inst. Applied Optics, 1960-85; prof. Inst. of Tech./Xiamen U., 1986—. Contbr. articles to profl. jours.; inventor in field. Mem. China Instrument Soc., China Optics Soc., Xiamen Automation Soc. Office: Inst of Technology, Xiamen Univ, 361005 Xiamen/Fujian China

DEIGHTON, LEN, author; b. London, Feb. 18, 1929. Author: The Ipcress File, 1962 (motion picture U.S., 1963), Horse Under Water, 1963, U.S. edit. 1968, Funeral in Berlin, 1964 (motion picture U.S., 1965), Ou Est le Garlic/ Basic French Cooking, 1965, 2d edit., 1979, U.S. edit., 1977, Action Cook Book, 1965, Cookstrip Cook Book, 1966, Billion Dollar Brain, 1966 (motion picture U.S., 1966), An Expensive Place to Die, 1967, Len Deighton's Dossier, 1967, Only When I Larf, 1968 (motion picture U.S., 1968), Bomber, 1970 (radio drama U.S., 1970), U.S. Edit. of Declarations of War, 1971, Close-Up, 1972, Spy Story, 1974 (motion picture U.S., 1974), Eleven Declarations of War, 1975, Yesterday's Spy, 1975, Twinkle, Twinkle, Little Spy, 1976, Catch a Falling Spy, 1976, Fighter, 1977, U.S. edit., 1978, SS-GB, 1978, U.S. edit., 1979, Blitzkrieg, 1979, U.S. edit., 1980, XPD, 1981, Goodbye Mickey Mouse, 1982, Berlin Game, 1983, Mexico Set, 1984, London Match, 1985, Winter: A Berlin Family 1899-1945, 1987, U.S. edit., 1988, Spy Hook, 1988, Spy Line, 1989, Spy Sinker, 1990, Basic French Cookery Course, 1990, ABC of French Food, 1989, U.S. edit., 1990, MAMista, 1991, City of Gold, 1992, Violent Ward, 1993, Blood, Tears & Folly, 1993, Faith, 1994, U.S. edit., 1995, Hope, 1995, U.S. edit., 1996, Charity, 1996; co-author: The Assassination of President Kennedy, 1967, Airshipwreck, 1978, U.S. edit., 1979, Battle of Britain, 1980, 2d edit., 1990, U.S. edit., 1980; (13-part TV series) Game, Set & Match, 1985. Office: care Jonathan Clowes Ltd, 10 Iron Bridge House, Bridge Approach London NW1 8BD, England

DEINZER, RENATE IRENE, psychologist; b. Schweinfurt, Germany, Apr. 21, 1965; m. Gerold Jorg Deinzer; two children. PhD in Psychology, U. Trier, Germany, 1992. From rsch. asst. to asst. prof. U. Dusseldorf, Germany, 1991—. Office: U Dusseldorf Inst Med Psych, Postfach 101007, Düsseldorf 40001, Germany

DE IOHGH, HENDRIK HUIBERT, ecologist; b. The Hague, The Netherlands, Nov. 5, 1951; s. Willem and Elizabeth (Van Der Schrieck) De I.; children: Barbara Titia Meihuizen. MS, Wageningen u., The Netherlands, 1976, PhD, 1996. Head environ. dept. Haskoning, Nymegen, Holland, 1980-89; head CML, Leyden, Holland, 1990-98; deputy dir. Tropenbos, Wageningen, Holland, 1998—. Mem. IUCN (species survival commn., pres. NC 1990-2000). Avocations: sailing, hockey, nature photography, camping, travel. Home: POB 603, 6700 AP Wageningen Holland Office: PO Box 9518, 2300 RA Leiden The Netherlands

DEIPSER, ANNA, waste management engineer, researcher; b. Hamburg, Germany, Mar. 22, 1963. Diploma in engring., Coll. Tech., Hamburg, 1989. Rschr. Tech. U. Hamburg-Harburg, 1990—. Author: Waste Management & Research, 1994, Landfilling of Waste: Biogas, 1996, Environmental Science and Pollution Research, 1997, Waste Management and Research, 1998. Office: Tech U Hamburg-Harburg, Harburger Schlossstrasse 37, D-21079 Hamburg Germany

DEISENHOFER, JOHANN, biochemistry educator, researcher; b. Zusamaltheim, Bavaria, Germany, Sept. 30, 1943; came to U.S., 1988; s. Johann and Thekla (Magg) D.; m. Kirsten Fischer-Lindahl, June 19, 1989. Diploma in Physics, Technische U., Munich, 1971, PhD, 1974, Doctor habilis, 1987. Postdoctoral fellow Max-Planck Inst. Biochemie, Martinsried, Fed. Republic of Germany, 1974-76, staff scientist, 1976-88; investigator Howard Hughes Med. Inst., Dallas, 1988—; prof. biochemistry U. Tex., Dallas, 1988—. Contbr. over 75 sci. papers to profl. publs. Recipient Nobel prize for chemistry, 1988; co-recipient Biol. Physics prize Am. Phys. Soc., 1986, Otto Bayer prize, 1988; decorated The Knight Commander's Cross (Badge and Star) Of the Order of Merit of Germany, 1990, Bavarian Order of Merit, 1992. Mem. AAAS, Nat. Acad. Scis. U.S.A., Am. Crystallographic Assn., German Biophys. Soc., The Protein Soc., Biophys. Soc., Academia Europaea.

DEISS, ERICH, chemistry and physics researcher; b. Wädenswil, Switzerland, Mar. 23, 1948; s. Emil and Rosa (Jerusalem) D.; m. Christine Langford, May 22, 1976 (div. May 1989). BS in Chemistry, Swiss Fed. Inst.

Tech., Zurich, 1972, PhD, 1980. Tchg. asst. Swiss Fed. Inst. Tech., 1975-80; postdoctoral rschr. U. Fribourg, Switzerland, 1980-81; staff scientist Swiss Fed. Inst. Reactor Rsch., Würenlingen, 1981-87; sr. staff scientist Paul Scherrer Inst., Villigen, Switzerland, 1988—. Contbr. articles to sci. jours. Pres. Assn. for Social Assistance, Zurich, 1976-79. With Swiss Army, 1968. Mem. Astron. Soc. Baden (mem. exec. bd.). Avocations: choral singing, astronomy, philosophy, jogging. Home: Dachsweg 4, 5330 Zurzach AG, Switzerland Office: Paul Scherrer Inst, Dept Electrochemistry, 5232 Villigen AG, Switzerland

DEISS, JOSEPH, Swiss government official; b. Fribourg, Switzerland, Jan. 18, 1946; m. Elisabeth Müller; three children. Student, Coll. St. Michel, Fribourg; licence and doctorate econs. social sci., Fribourg U.; postgrad., U. Cambridge. Lectr. econs. Fribourg U., 1973-83, vis. prof. econs. and econ. policy, 1983-99, dean faculty econs. head Fed. Dept. Fgn. Affairs, Bern, 1993-96; elected mem. fed. coun., head Fed. Dept. Fgn. Affairs, 1995-, 1991; Switzerland, 1999—; mem. Grand Conseil fribourgeois, 1981-91, pres., 1991; mayor Barberêche, Switzerland, 1982-96; nat. councillor, 1991-99; vice chmn. Fgn. Affairs Commn., Nat. Coun., 1995-96; chmn. Commn. for the Total Revision of the Fed. Constitution, 1996; chmn. Raiffeisenbank, Haut-Lac, Courtepin, Switzerland, 1996-99; chmn. bd. dirs. Schumacher AG, Schmitten, Switzerland. Roman Catholic. Office: Fed Dept Fgn Affairs, Bundeshaus West, CH-3003 Bern Switzerland

DEISSLER, MARY ALICE, foundation executive; b. Oneanta, N.Y., Dec. 30, 1955; d. George W. and Carol (Zorda) Baker; m. James N. Deissler, Nov. 24, 1987; children: Benjamin, Eliza. BA, U. Mass., 1978; MBA, Babson Coll., 1982. Fin. analyst Digital Equipment Corporation, Maynard, Mass., 1978-82; devel. dir. Handel & Haydn Soc., Boston, 1984-89, gen. mgr., 1984-89, exec. dir., 1990—; pres., bd. dirs. Studebaker Movement Theatre Co., Boston, 1986-88. Bd. dirs. Early Music Am., N.Y.C., 1989—, v.p., 1991—, pres., 1996; bd. dirs. Babson Coll., 1990-94, Chorus Am., 1991—, v.p., 1992, pres.-elect, 1996, pres., 1997, pres. bd. dirs., 1997; mem. bd. Arts/Boston, 1994—, bd. dirs.; bd. dirs. Boston Ptnrs. in Edn., Berkshire Choral Soc., 2000—; treas. Handel House of Am. Found. Mem. Am. Symphony Orch. League. Office: Handel & Haydn Soc 300 Massachusetts Ave Boston MA 02115-4544

DEJACK, JACQUELINE ELVADEANA, artist, educator; b. St. Louis, Oct. 9, 1938; d. John Allen and Margie Louise (Cooksey) Williams; m. James Patrick DeJack (dec. June 1994); children: Jennifer Lynn, John Patrick. Student, St. Louis U, 1966-67, Webster Coll., 1978-79; AA, East Ctrl. U., 1979; student, U. Mo., 1998. Lic. real estate agt., Mich.; cert. broker sales and tchr. broker, Mo. Sales staff Hudsons Dept. Store, Detroit, 1957; with First Fed. Savs., Detroit, 1961-62; cons. to libr. dir. St. Louis U., 1965-66; bank cons., ins. mgr. Willston (Mo.) State Bank, 1967-68; co-founder, broker, cons. Tri County Real Estate, Pacific, Mo., 1971-89; pvt. practice artist and writer Jacquelinse's Affordable Graphics, Pacific, Mo., 1993—; fine art tchr., cons. Six Flags Over Mid-Am., Eureka, Mo., summer 1982. Supr. youth corp. St. Louis U., 1964; bd. mem. U. Mo., St. Louis, 1980; mem. Sears (Mich.) Writer's Guild, 1987. Mem. Cadillac Artis Guild, Phi Theta Kappa. Avocations: writing, art, history research, music, swimming.

DE JAGER, CORNELIS, retired astronomer; b. Texel, The Netherlands, Apr. 29, 1921; s. Jan and Cornelia (Kuyper) de J.; m. Duotje Rienks, Apr. 10, 1947; children: Els, Jan, Sieds, Corrie. PhD cum laude, U. Utrecht, 1952; Dr. (hon.), U. Wroclaw, Poland, 1975, U. Paris, 1976. Asst. theoretical physics and astronomy univs. Utrecht, Leiden, 1945-46; mem. faculty U. Utrecht, 1947-86, prof. space physics, 1960-86; ret., 1986; founder Lab. Space Rsch. U. Utrecht, 1961, mng. dir., then chmn. coun. Astron. Inst., 1963-83; extraordinary prof. astrophysics U. Brussels, 1961-73, founder Astrophysics Inst., 1961; hon. mem. Sci. Commn. Solar Terrestrial Physics, 1988. Author: Hydrogen Spectrum of the Sun, 1952, Structure and Dynamics of the Solar Atmosphere, 1959, The Solar Spectrum, 1963, Highlights of Astronomy, 1974, Image Processing Techniques in Astronomy, 1975, The Brightest Stars, 1980 (with Z. Svestka) The Physics of Solar Flares, 1987, (with J.I. Sakai) Solar Flares and Collisions Between Current-Carrying Loops, 1996 (with W.J. Kikkert) Van het Clyf tot Den Hoorn, 1998; contbr. articles to profl. jours. Recipient Karl Schwarzschild medal Astron. Gesellschaft, 1974, Hale medal Am. Astron. Soc., 1988, Cospar medal Internat. Cooperation in Space Sci., 1988, asteroid 3684 de Jager named in hon. Fellow Com. Sci. Investigation Claims Paranormal (Praise of Reason award 1990), mem. Internat. Acad. Astronautics (fgn., chmn. sect. basic scis. 1984-89, Von Karman award 1993), Internat. Union (asst. gen. sec. 1967-70, gen. sec. 1970-73), Internat., Coun. for Sci. (pres. com. space rsch. 1972-78, 82-86, world pres. 1978-80), European Coun. Skeptical Orgn. (chmn. 1994), Royal Netherlands Arts Sci. (fgn. sec. 1985-90, Hon. Silver medal 1990), SKEPSIS (chmn. 1987-98), Netherlands Soc. Astronomy Meteorology (hon., Silver medal 1955, Gold medal 1990), Royal Astron. Soc. London (assoc., Gold medal 1988), Royal Belgium Acad. (fgn.), Royal Acad. Liege (fgn.), Deutsche Akademie Leopoldina (fgn.), Indian Nat. Sci. Acad. (fgn.), Acad. Européene Paris (fgn.) Acad. Europaea London (fgn.).

DEJAMMET, ALAIN, diplomat. Perm. rep. of France to UN, N.Y.C., 1995—, pres. Security Coun., 1999—. Office: Perm Mission of France to UN 1 Dag Hammarskjöld Plz 245 E 47th St Fl 44 New York NY 10017-2201

DE JESUS, CARLITO GONZALES, financial services consultant; b. Manila, Philippines, Sept. 21, 1948; s. Ernesto and Rosario (Gonzales) de J.; m. Carmencita Camanag, Aug. 22, 1971; 1 child, Ayn C. AB English, Univ. of the Philippines, 1970. Cert. fin. planner. Gen. mgr. Makati Credit Bur., Inc., Manila, 1975-77; Primex Indsl. Corp., Manila, 1977-78; mng. dir. Omnibus Fin., Manila, 1978-82; pres. Vang Reins. Co. Ltd., Hong Kong, 1982—; mgr. Continental Pacific Bank & Trust Co., Hong Kong, 1982-83; pres. Bus. Plaza, Inc., Manila, 1992—; bd. dirs. Asiapac Fin., Ltd., London, World Commodities — Svcs. Corp, Timbol & Sons Realty & Transp. Corp; resident cons. Titan Group Cos., Asia World City, Manila, 1999—. Author: The Complete Guide to Making Money, 1988, The Secrets of Loan Abitrage, 1991 (Rotary award 1994), Loans & Capital, 1992, The Swiss Factor, 1995. Mem. St. James Club, Hilton/Vista Club. Avocations: writing books, painting, scale modeling, collecting cards, tennis. Home: 2169 Suter St Sta Ana, Manila Philippines 1009 Office: 9626 Kamagong St, Makati City 1200, Philippines

DE JESUS, JULIO ENRIQUE, science educator; b. Caguas, P.R., Nov. 6, 1964; s. Julio de Jesus Garcia and Ramonita Aponte; m. Luz Esther Rivera, May 28, 1989; 1 child, Gabriel Enrique. BS cum laude, U. P.R., 1986, MS magna cum laude, 1993; PhD suma cum laude, La Salle U., 1997. Cert. CPR instr. ARC. Wildlife photographer Biology Mus. U. P.R., Rio Piedras, 1982-91, prof. continuing edn. program, assoc. prof. biol. scis., 1995—; wildlife biologist U.S. Fish and Wildlife Svc., Cabo Rojo, P.R., 1984; prof. biochemistry/devel. biology Turabo U., Gurabo, P.R., 1987-91, 95-97; environmental instr., cons. U.S. Peace Corps, Washington, 1991-95; prof. zoology/environ. sci. InterAmerican U., Fajardo, P.R., 1995-97; program cons. P.R. Resource Ctr. Sci. and Engring., Rio Piedras. Author: Environmental Education Guides for Teachers and Non Formal Educators, 1995; (CD ROM) Puerto Rico, Island of Diversities, 1999. Educator Peace Corps Ecuador, Cuenca, 1991-95; vol. sci. tutor, Rio Piedras. Named Disting. Youngster in Sci. Govt. P.R., 1985, 88; grantee Smithsonian-Nat. Geographic Explorer, 1988, Smithsonian Inst. Latino Affairs Office, 1997-99; Rsch. Participation grantee Oak Ridge Associated Univs., 1988. Mem. N.Am. Assn. Environ. Edn., Assn. Tropical Biology, Nat. Peace Corps Assn., Assn. Am. Geographers. Achievements include discovery of three new species of land mollusks, new kind of symbiotic interaction between the snail Nenia tridens and the algae Chrococcus. Avocations: photography, reading, hiking, dowsing. Fax: 787-763-7305. Home: PO Box 418 Gurabo PR 00778-0418 Office: U PR Gen Studies Coll Rio Piedras PR 00936

DEJESUS-BURGOS, SYLVIA TERESA, information systems security manager; b. Rio Piedras, P.R., Puerto Rico, Jan. 13, 1941; came to U.S., 1961; d. Luis deJesus Correa and Maria Teresa (Burgos) deJesus. BA, Cen. U., Madrid, 1961. Sr. systems analyst H.D. Hudson Mfg. Co., Chgo., 1974-76; mgr. software engring. Morton Internat. Corp., Chgo., 1976-87; prodn. and dist. systems mgr. Kraft Foods divsn. Phillip Morris, Glenview, Ill., 1987-94; mgr. info. tech. svcs. Equate Petrochem. Corp. (Kuwait) joint ven-

ture Union Carbide and Petrochem. Industries Kuwait, 1994—. Editor U. Minn. Mgmt. Info. Systems Jour., 1984—. Pres. Chgo. chpt. Nat. Conf. Puerto Rican Women, 1980-83, nat. v.p. 1981-82; bd. dirs. Midwest Women's Ctr., 1980-82, YWCA, Chgo., 1982-84, Gateway Found. Substance Abuse Prevention and Rehab., 1986-87; v.p. communications Hispanic Alliance for Career Enhancements, 1986-87, bd. dirs. 1982-84, 91-92, chmn. bd., 1991-93; 1st v.p. Campfire Met. Chgo., 1982, bd. dirs. 1980-82; appointed to Selective Svc. Bd. by Ill. Gov. James Thompson, 1982; alt. del. Dem. Nat. Conv., N.Y.C., 1980; rep. Women in Mil. Svc. for Am. Meml., 1990-92. Served with USN, 1961-64. Recipient Youth Motivation award Chgo. Assn. Commerce and Industry, 1978-82, 86, YWCA Leadership award, 1980, 84, H.L. Kroft Achievement award, 1994. Mem. Women in Computing, Info. Systems Planners Assn., Navy League, Am. Legion. Republican. Roman Catholic. Office: Union Carbide 16055 Space Center Blvd Houston TX 77062-6251 Address: 16835 Middle Forest Dr Houston TX 77059-4033

DEJONCKERE, PHILIPPE HENRI, otolaryngologist; b. Ronse, Belgium, July 11, 1949; s. Edouard Dejonckere and Marthe Van Nerum; m. Suzanne Thiry, Sept. 2, 1978; children: Laurence, Aurélie. Grad., Conservatory of Music, Louvain, Belgium, 1971; degree in sexology, U. Louvain, 1971, MD, 1973, MA in Occupl. Medicine, 1975, PhD in Medicine, 1981; MA in Forensic Medicine, U. Liège, Belgium, 1986. Resident U. Hosp. St. Luc., Brussels, 1976-81; sr. resident U. Hosp. St. Luc., 1981-83; lectr. U. Louvain, 1983-86, assoc. clin. prof., 1986-89; assoc. prof. U. Utrecht, The Netherlands, 1989-91; prof., chmn. dept. phoniatrics U. Utrecht, 1991—; med. expert Fund Occupl. Diseases, Brussels, 1987—; invited lectr. U. Lille, France, 1984—; vis. prof. U. Kurume, Japan, 1996. Author 7 books; contbr. articles to profl. jours. Pres. Collegium Medicorum Theatri, 1999. Decorated officer Crown Order, knight Order of King Leopold (Belgium). Office: Inst Phoniatrics Utrecht U, PO Box 85500, 3508 GA Utrecht The Netherlands

DE JONG, JAN WILLEM, cardiochemist; b. The Hague, The Netherlands, Aug. 13, 1942; s. Willem and Johanna (Kuiper) De J.; m. Meiskelina Elizabeth van Lier, Oct. 9, 1968; stepchildren: Martha H., Harmanna M. BS, Leiden U., The Netherlands, 1964, MS, 1966; PhD, Erasmus U., Rotterdam, The Netherlands, 1971. Instr., asst. prof. Med. Faculty, Rotterdam/Biochem., Rotterdam, 1966-74; tchr. Adv. Analysis Sch./Biochem., Rotterdam, 1968-69; assoc. prof., dir. Cardiochem. Lab., Erasmus U., 1974—; established investigator Netherlands Heart Found., The Hague, 1975-80; vis. prof. U. Brescia, Italy, 1992-93; cons. Igen Inc., Rockport, Md., 1994-95; cons. U. Tex. Med. Ctr., Houston, 1982-83, European Space Agy., 1997-2000; mem. exec. com. Med. Faculty, Rotterdam, 1979-81; ad hoc advisor NATO Sci. Affairs, 1988, 94-95, Wellcome Trust Med. Rsch Coun., U.K., 1990-92, 96, Internat. Sci. Fedn., 1994, Netherland Orgn. Sci. Rsch., 1994, Brit. Cardiac Soc., 1994, Assn. Ricerca Cardiologica, Rome, 1995, Fedn. Rsch. Devel., Pretoria, South Africa, 1995; vice chmn. presidium Erasmus U., Rotterdam, 1991-98; evaluator European Commn. Biomed 2, 1995, 97, European Commn. 5th Framework, 1999; mem. sci. adv. bd. Netherlands Heart Found., 1992-96; referee Italian Ministry for Univ. and Sci. Rsch., 1998-2000; ad-hoc advisor U. Antwerp, 1998, U. Tel-Aviv, 1999; mem. NASA Life Sci. Peer Rev. Panel, 1999-2000. Editor: Myocardial Energy Metabolism, 1988, The Carmitine System, 1995; mem. editorial bd. Internat. Jour. Purine/Pyrim. Res., Lugano, Switzerland, 1989-93, Thoraxctr. Jour., Leiden, 1990—, Cardiovascular Drug Therapy, Norwell, Mass., 1994—; guest editor 14 sci. jours., Europe and U.S.; editor www.thoraxcenter.com, www.cardiofind.com. Inspector Birds Protection Act, The Hague, 1971-85. Fulbright fellow, 1973; recipient award Chris Barnard Fund, Cape Town, Republic of South Africa, 1986, 88, 92, German Acad. Exch. Svc., Berlin, 1981. Fellow European Soc. Cardiology (chmn. work group 1990-92, nucleus mem. 1983—); mem. Am. Heart Assn., Am. Physiol. Soc., Internat. Soc. Heart Rsch. (coun. 1984-93, chmn. European sect. 1989-90), Internat. Union Biochemistry and Molecular Biology. Avocations: tennis, ornithology, digital photography, bridge. Home: Stad en Landschap 51, 2923 BL Krimpen a/d IJssel The Netherlands Office: Erasmus U Thorax Ctr, PO Box 1738, 3000 DR Rotterdam The Netherlands

DE JONG, OLGA, sociologist, consultant, educator; b. Nogales, Mexico, Dec. 16, 1942; came to U.S., 1962; d. Alfonso and Viola (Garcia) Acosta; m. Remy Lucien de Jong, Dec. 18, 1966; children: Cristina, Michelle. BSBA, U. Ariz., 1966; MS in Fgn. Lang. Edn., U. Tenn., 1974; PhD in Ednl. Adminstrn., U. Ariz., 1986. Documentalist Tetra Tech Internat., Muscat, Oman, 1976-79; prin. Arab Unity Sch., Dubai, United Arab Emirates, 1979-81; ednl. cons. Al Ahliyah, Dhahran, Saudi Arabia, 1984-90, Al Khaligia Co., Riyadh, Saudi Arabia, 1987-88; field rep. U. Md., Riyadh, Saudi Arabia, 1988-90; sociological cons. GITEC Consulting, Kampala, Uganda, 1992; computer cons. Black & Veatch Internat., Lusaka, Zambia, 1994; socioeconomic cons. GOPA Cons., BadHomburg, Germany, 1994-95; socioeconomist Harza, Jordan, 1995; univ. lectr. Freiburg (Germany) Bus. Sch., 1997—; prin. Am. Internat. Sch. of Macedonia, 1999. Mem. Phi Lambda Theta, Phi Delta Kappa. Roman Catholic. Avocations: music, reading, golf, squash. Home: 24741 Crown Royale Laguna Niguel CA 92677-7441 Office: 23 rue de Rouffach, 68250 Westhalten France

DE JONG, RÉMY LUCIEN, water resources engineer; b. The Hague, The Netherlands, Aug. 2, 1933; came to U.S., 1958; s. Theo Johannes and Lucia Antonetta (Roest) de J.; m. Olga Acosta, Dec. 18, 1966; children: Cristina, Michelle. BSCE, Hogere Tech. Sch., 1958, U. Pa., 1960; PhD in Civil Engring., U. Ariz., 1969; LLB, Blackstone Coll., 1975. Asst. prof. U. Tenn., Knoxville, 1970-73; advisor Tetra Tech. Internat., Muscat, Oman, 1974-79; legal officer F.A.O., Dubai and Rome, Italy, 1979-82; assoc. prof. U. Petroleum and Minerals, Dhahran, Saudi Arabia, 1982-86; sr. water planner Ministry of Planning, Riyadh, Saudi Arabia, 1987-88; project mgr. Arriyadh Devel. Authority, Riyadh, Saudi Arabia, 1989-90; dir. gen. water mgmt. Ministry of Water Resources, Muscat, Oman, 1990-91; expert water mgmt. GOPA Cons., Badhomburg, Germany, 1991-94; sr. advisor water mgmt. German Agy. Tech. Coop., Amman, Jordan, 1994-97; water mgmt. cons., 1998—. Contbr. articles to profl. jours. Capt. Holland Mil., 1953-55. Fellow ASCE, Internat. Water Resources Assn., Internat. Assn. Water Law. Roman Catholic. Avocations: music, squash. Home: 535 N Stewart Ave Tucson AZ 85716-4447 Office: 23 rue de Rouffach, 68250 Westhalten France

DE JONGE, GERT FREDERIK, trading company executive; b. Steenwijk, Overijssel, The Netherlands, Sept. 21, 1965; arrived in Belgium, 1990; s. Gerrit and Frederika (Doldersum) De J.; m. Fiona Maria Neijndorff, May 12, 1995. MTS, Middelbare Technische Sch., Harderwijk, The Netherlands, 1986. Cert. application engr. gear pumps. Head calculation dept. AT&T and Philips Telecomm., Hilversum, The Netherlands, 1986-88; internal salesman Suurmond, Nunspeet, The Netherlands, 1988-90; br. mgr. Suurmond, Antwerp, Belgium, 1990-93, dir., 1993—; dir. Man Rollo Belgium, Antwerp, 1993-95; mem. mgmt. team Man Rollo, Zoetermeer, The Netherlands, 1991-95; dir. Jaycees, Lier, Belgium, 1992, 94, 96, Jeep VZW, Lier, 1991-94; trainer Jaycees Belgium, 1995—. Divers leader Jr. Chamber Internat., Lier, 1991—; bd. dirs. Jaycees, Lier, Belgium, 1992, 94, 96-98, pres., 1999-2000; bd. dirs. Jeep VZW, Lier, 1991-94; trainer Jaycees Belgium, 1995—. Recipient Werkpard award Best Mem., Lier, 1991, Paul Krick award Best Bd. Mem., 1996, Nethe award Best Dir., 1996, Henri Costa award, 1997. FEllow Jongekamer Lier. Avocations: photography, sailing, surfing. E-mail: Ferdie.deJonge@advalvas.Be. Home: Esmoreitlaan 7/41, B-2050 Antwerp Belgium Office: Noorderlaan 109, B-2030 Antwerp Belgium

DE JONGE, HENK JAN, New Testament educator, editor; b. Leiden, The Netherlands, Sept. 28, 1943; s. Marinus Izaäk and Maria Pieternella (Braun) de J.; m. Marianne Doelman, July 1, 1969; children: Hans L., Casper C., Lodew P. MA in Greek, Latin, Leiden U., 1969, PhD in Classical Philology, 1983. Jr. lectr. New Testament Amsterdam (Holland) U., 1970-77, sr. lectr. New Testament, 1977-84; sr. lectr. New Testament Leiden U., 1985-90, adj. prof. history of Bibl. exegesis, 1987-91, prof. New Testament, 1991—; mem. com. Soc. New Testament Studies, 1988-91; dir. bibl. studies Netherlands Sch. for Advanced Studies in Theology, 1991-94; dean faculty theology Leiden U., 1994-96; mem. adv. bd. Inst. for New Testament Textual Rsch., Münster, Germany, 1996—. Author: (textbook) Erasmus' Apologia Against Stunica, 1983; editor (essays) The Second Coming of Christ, 1994, Atonement or Kingdom of God, 1997, History of Leiden U., 2000; editor (quar. review) Novum Testamentum, 1979—. Deacon Église Wallonne, Leiden, 1975-88; regent Jean Pesynhof, Leiden, 1975-87; pres. Bibliothèque Wallonne, Leiden, 1978-87, 98—; sec. Rsch. Grants Com. of Leiden U. Fund, 1992—. Recipient Pres. d'honneur Bibliothèque Wallonne, 1988. Mem. Soc. New Testament Studies, Soc. Dutch Lit., Leiden Univ. Press (bd. dirs. 1990). Christian Democrat. Mem. Walloon Reformed Ch. Home: Zeemanlaan 47, 2313 SW Leiden The Netherlands Office: Leiden U Faculty Theology, PO Box 9515, 2300 RA Leiden The Netherlands

DE JONGH, WILHELMUS KAREL (WILLY K. DE JONGH), physicist; b. Eindhoven, The Netherlands, Jan. 25, 1931; s. Joseph and Maria Cornelia (Theelen) de J.; m. Gerda Johanna Lotte Herrmann, July 5, 1957; children: Linda, Wilhelmus Joseph, Heinz. BSc, H.T.S., Eindhoven, 1951. Asst. sales Willem Smit Transformers, Nijmegen, The Netherlands, 1953-54; R&D nuclear physics N.V. Philips, Eindhoven, 1954-55, project engr., 1955-65, X-ray lab. mgr., 1966-76, prin. sr. scientist, 1977-88; pres. R&D Omega Data Systems, Veldhoven, The Netherlands, 1989—; cons., lectr. N.V. Philips, 1966-88, Omega Data Systems, 1989—. Contbr. articles to profl. jours.; patentee in field; inventor in field. Achievements include invention of Uni-Quant method for standardless x-ray fluorescence analysis of elements, used world wide in science and industry. Avocation: writing.

DE JONG HENRICUS, CORNELIS JOHANNES, educator; b. Rotterdam, The Netherlands, Feb. 3, 1917; s. Gerardus Johannes and Cornelia Adriana (Bartelt) de J.; m. Ida Leijendekkers, Oct. 28, 1943. MD, Delft U., The Netherlands, 1940, D, 1953. Asst. prof. Delft U., The Netherlands, 1940-41; asst. to head high voltage networks Provincial Electricity Networks, Den Bosch, The Netherlands, 1941-43; elec. machine designer Heemaf, Hengelo, The Netherlands, 1943-63; prof. Eindhoven U., Hengelo, The Netherlands, 1960-84, Ghent U., Belgium, 1975-86; head tech. dept. Holec, Hengelo, The Netherlands, 1963-70, cons., 1970-74; lectr in field. Author: AC Motor Design, 1976, 89. Mem. Royal Inst. Engrs. Home: Antillenstr 3, 7556 AV Hengelo The Netherlands

DE JOUVENEL, HUGUES ALAIN, think-tank executive, consultant; b. July 2, 1946; s. Bertrand Edouard de Jouvenel and Helene Duseigneur; m. Beatrice de Bondy; children: François, Catherine; m. Christine de Guebriant; children: Helene, Charles. News editor French Ministry of Def., U.N., N.Y., 1971-72; prof. bus. schs. and us. Nat. Sch. Pub. Adminstrn., France, 1973-74; gen. dir. Futuribles Internat., Paris, 1974—. Co-author: The United Nations and the Future, 1976, Sciences, Technology and the Future, 1979, Le Point Critique, 1980, La fin des Habitudes, 1985, Protection sociale: trois scénarios contrastés, 1986, Les enjeux du vieillissement d=248mographique en Europe à l'horizon 2025, 1989, Europe's Aging Population: Trends and Challenges to 2025, 1989, Studies for the 21st Century, 1991, La Prospective des Déséquilibres Mondiaux, 1993, Catalunya a l'horitzo 2010, Catalan edit., 1994, Cataluna en el Horizonte 2010, Span. edit., 1994, Catalogne à l'horizon 2010, French edit., 1994, Le travail au XXIème siècle, 1995, Les sciences de la prévision, 1996, The Knowledge Base of Futures Studies, 1996, Victoria, DDM Media group, 1996, La France à l'horizon 2010, 1996, Changing Europe: An Overview of Broad Economic, Social and Cultural Trends, 1996, Vers une prospective des retraites en France à l'horizon 2030, 1998, (with Vincent Gollain and Alain Sallez) Emploi et Territoires en Ile-de-France: Prospective, 1999, La Tour d'Aigues, l'Aube edits., 1999, Décision, Prospective, Auto-organisation, 2000; editor-in-chief FUTURIBLES; contbr. numerous articles to newspapers and profl. jours. Mem. World Future Soc., Am. Acad. Arts and Scis. Fax: 33 0 1 42 22 65 54. E-mail: hjouvenel@futuribles.com. Home: 12 rue Falguiere-F, 75015 Paris France Office: Futuribles Internat, 55 rue de Varenne, 75341 Paris Cedex 07, France

DE JOUX, CHRISTOPHER JOSEPH BRIAN, consultant foreign affairs, library administrator; b. Pahiatua, Wellington, New Zealand, Nov. 15, 1960; arrived in Belgium, 1983; s. Brian Fonseca and Margaret Hellen (Saunders) de J.; m. Eliane Lucie Anciaux, July 19, 1986; children: David Brian Philippe, Alan Christopher Andrew. BA, Victoria U. of Wellington, New Zealand, 1982. Tchr. Brussels English Primary Sch., 1984-86; ministerial sec. Dept. Sci. and Indsl. Rsch., Wellington, 1986-88; mgmt. support officer New Zealand Embassy, Brussels, 1988-89; journalist East-West Publs., Brussels, 1990-91; rsch. asst. S.J. Berwin, Brussels, 1991-95; cons. Clifford Chance, Brussels, 1995-97, Simmons & Simmons, Brussels, 1997—. Environ. affairs officer Victoria U. Wellington, 1982; sec. VUW Tramping Club, Wellington, 1980-82. Recipient Gold Duke of Edinburgh medal N.Z. Gov.-Gen., 1978, Christian Doctrine prize St. Patricks Coll., 1978. Avocations: home repairs, mountaineering, squash, reading. Home: 11 Rue Saint Roch, B-4053 Embourg Belgium Office: Simmons & Simmons, 149 Ave Louise box 16, B-1050 Brussels Belgium

DEJOUX, CLAUDE, retired hydrobiologist; b. Niort, France, Dec. 18, 1939; s. Max and Yvonne (Chauvet) D.; m. Heidi Wohlert, Dec. 16, 1967; children: Judica Dejoux, Chantal Dejoux. BS, U. Toulouse, France, 1962; Degree in Agronomy Engring., Nat. Sch. Agronomy, Toulouse, 1962; PhD in Natural Scis., U. Paris VI, 1974. Cert. agronomy engr. Rschr. in hydrobiology Orstom, Paris, 1963-65; chief hydrobiology lab. Orstom, Ft. Lamy, Chad, 1965-72; dir. rsch. ctr. Orstom, N'Jamena, Chad, 1972-73; dir. rsch. mission Orstom, La Paz, Bolivia, 1985-89, Mexico City, 1992-95; internat. cons. hydrobiology, 1995—; cons. WHO, Geneva, Switzerland, 1973-91, Food & Agrl. Orgn., Rome, 1980, Global Environ. Monitoring Sys. Water, West and Ctrl. Africa, 1985, French Environment Ministry, La Martinique Island, 1983, Dutch Environment Ministry, West Africa (Mali, Guinea, Ivory Coast, Togo), 1990. Author: African Inland Waters Contamination, 1976, chpts. in other books; scientific editor: Lake Titicaca: Synthesis of Limnological Knowledge, 1992. Served with Chad mil. Mem. French Soc. of Limnology, Internat. Soc. of Limnology. Avocations: scuba diving, tennis, wild life photography. Home: 7A Rue du Moulin de Bordes, 33260 La Teste France

DEKA, DIBAKAR CHANDRA, organic chemist, educator; b. Village Kuriha, India, May 1, 1958; s. Lohit and Bhagyeswari D.; m. Krishna Sen, May 2, 1993; children: Jeechu, Ankur. BSc, Cotton Coll., 1979; MSc, Gauhati U., 1983; M in Technology, Indian Inst. Technology, Kharagpur, 1986, PhD, 1989; diploma in organic chem, Tokyo Inst. Tech., 1990. Analyst BRPL, Bongaigaon, India, 1983-84; lectr. Diphu Govt. Coll., India, 1987-91, Cotton Coll., Guwahati, India, 1991, Gauhati U., India, 1991-92; commonwealth rsch. fellow Univ. Manchester, U.K., 1997-998; sr. lectr. 1992-99, reader, 1999—. Mem. Soc. Chem. Edn. (joint sec. 1994—), Assam Sci. Soc. (life mem.). Hindu. Avocations: study, photography, playing chess, volleyball, badminton. Home: Village Dekapara, PO Azara 781 017, Guwahati Assam, India Office: Gauhati U, Dept Chemistry, 781 014 Guwahati Assam, India

DEKA, SURESH, microbiologist, educator; b. Sarthebari, Assam, India, June 11, 1955; s. Prasanna Kumar and Pratima (Bala) Deka; m. Jonali Kalita, May 2, 1989; 1 child, Kaustubh. BSc, Gauhati U., Guwahati, India, 1978, MSc, 1980, PhD, 1991. Asst. microbiologist Assam Agro Industries, Gwahati, 1983-85; sr. rsch. asst. Ctrl. Silk Bd., Boko, India, 1986-86; lectr. Dudhnoi (India) Coll., 1986-91; asst. prof. IASST, Guwahati, 1991—. Author: Chanekire Jivanar, 1978, Bhanga Dewal, 1982, Udvidar Katha, 1981, Dur Atitar Herowa Jiba, 1993. Mem. Assam Sci. Sic. (life; asst. gen. sec. 1995-97), Nat. Inst. Ecology, Soc. for Environ. Protection (life). Avocations: writing, gardening, computer. Home: Bashistha, Beltola, Guwahati Assam 781029, India Office: Inst Adv Study Sci and Tech, Khanapara, Guwahati, Assam 781022, India

DE KANTER, ELLEN ANN, English language professional, educator; b. Spokane, Wash., Mar. 10, 1926; d. George L. and Alison P. (Christy) Tharp; m. Scipio de Kanter, Feb. 2, 1949 (dec.); children: Scipio, Georgette, Robert, Adriana. BA, Mexico City Coll.-U. of Ams., 1947; MEd, U. Houston, 1972, MA in Spanish, 1974, EdD, 1979. Dir. bilingual edn., prof. U. St. Thomas, Houston, dir. bilingual edn., 1979—. Contbr. articles to profl. jours. Title VII grantee, 1986-89, 88-91, 89-92, 92-93, 92-95, 94-97, 95-98, 97-99, 98-2002. Mem. Nat. Assn. Bilingual Edn. (chmn. 1989 conf., program chair 1993 conf.), Houston Area Assn. Bilingual Edn. (pres. 1987-88), Inst. Hispanic Culture (bd. dirs. 1989-90). Home: 3015 Meadowview Dr Missouri City TX 77459-3308 Office: U St Thomas 3800 Montrose Blvd Houston TX 77006-4626

DE KEGHEL, ALAIN JEAN-MARIE, consul general of France, diplomat; b. Arcueil, Paris, Sept. 23, 1940; came to U.S., 1994; s. Guy de Keghel and Laure Vincent; m. Dominique N. Mijoule, Feb. 10, 1976; children: Isabelle, Francois, Florence, Thibault. M in Law, U. Strasbourg, France, 1966; M in German, U. Heidelberg, Germany, 1968. With French Fgn. Svc., Paris, 1968; attaché French Consulate Gen., Stuttgart, Germany, 1968-73; embassy counsellor French Embassy, The Hague, Netherlands, 1973-79, Bonn, Germany, 1979-81; German desk head office European Divsn., Paris, 1981-82; sr. advisor to pres. High Authority for the Media, Paris, 1982-86; dep. to the pres. and CEO RFO State Broadcasting, Paris, 1986-87; embassy counsellor Dakar, Senegal, 1987-89; consul gen. of France Tokyo, 1989-91; dep. dir. for info. French Dept. of Fgn. Affairs, Paris, 1991-94; dep. permanent rep. French Mission to the OAS, Washington, 1994-97, consul gen. of France, 1997—. Contbr. articles to profl. jours. Pres. bd. dirs. French Internat. Sch., Washington, 1997-98, v.p., 1998-2000. With Infantry, 1960-62, Algeria. Recipient Knight of German Merit Order, German Govt., 1981, Officer of Orange-Nassau Order Dutch Govt., 1979, Officer of French Merit Order French Grand Chancellor, 1998, Knight of Arts and Lettres French Sec. for Culture, 1993. Mem. French-Am. C. of C. (bd. dirs. 1997-2000). Avocations: history, tennis. Home: 8 rue J P Timbaud, F-75011 Paris France Office: French Consultate Gen, Bosmanslei 24, 2018 Antwerp Belgium

DEKENS, ALEXANDER LEON JEAN, computer company executive; b. Tongeren, Limburg, Belgium, Apr. 20, 1953; s. François Camille and Louisa Bernadine (Houbrechts) D.; m. Marie-Christine Julienne Jeanne Schampaert, Oct. 28, 1976; children: Kim, Wouter. Indsl. engr. degree, Hrito, Hasselt, 1976; burg. ingenieur, K.U., Leuven, 1973. Electronics engr. Ministry of Pub. Works, Brussels, 1976-77; customer svc. engr. Linotype Belgium, Brussels, 1978-83, Perkin-Elmer D.S., Brussels, 1983-84; sr. svc. engr. Prime Computer, Brussels, 1985; tech. supr. Concurrent Computer Belgium, Brussels, 1985-86, br. mgr., 1986-88, gen. mgr., 1988-91; gen. mgr. Chess Belgium, Kortenberg, 1991—; svc. mgr. LCI Belgium-Zayentem, 1996-99; gen. mgr. Impact Belgium, Aarschot, 2000—; mem. BIRA/ALT, Antwerp, 1991. Avocations: basket, squash. Office: Impact Belgium, Nieuwlandlaan B321, 3200 Aarschot Belgium

DE KERGORLAY, ROLAND MARIE, association executive; b. Paris, Oct. 5, 1926; s. Thibault Paul and Simone Isabelle (de Liedekerke Beaufort) de K.; m. Lavinia Ethel Zur Nedden, May 9, 1970; 1 child, Elisabeth. Student, U. Paris, 1946-47; BCom with honors, McGill U., Can., 1950; MPA, MA, Harvard U., 1953. Economist Nat. Bur. Econ. Rsch., Washington, 1953-54; adminstr. OEEC, Paris, 1954-57; head Benelux divsn. EEC, Brussels, 1958-61, sec. monetary com., 1962-69, dir. EC's dir. gen. external rels., 1969, dir. enlargement/negociation, 1970-72, dir. gen. external rels., 1973-76, head negotiating team, 1976-80; EEC amb. to U.S. EEC, Washington, 1980-82; v.p. Soc. Européenne des Satellites, Luxembourg, 1985-2000. Designated mem. Conseil Superieur des Francais de l'Etranger, 1989-97. Decorated grand officer Civil Merit (Spain); grand insignia Merit (Austria); grand officer Polar Star (Sweden); grand officer Order of Lion (Finland); comdr. Order La Couronne de Chene (Luxembourg), othrs. Roman Catholic. Avocations: music, shooting, fishing, master drawings, history. Home: 1 Ave des Sorbiers, 1180 Brussels Belgium

DE KESEL, TOON, safety, health and environmental executive; b. Beernem, Belgium, June 3, 1961; s. Gerard De Kesel and Jeannine Van Hyfte. Degree in tech. chem. engring., Inst. Tech. St. Lieven, Gent, Belgium, 1982; degree in edn., Inst. Tech. St. Antonius, Gent, 1983. Cert. in safety, health and environ. Mgr. health, safety and environ. Innogenetics NV, Gent, 1988—. Office: Innogenetics NV, Industriepark 7 Box 4, 9052 Gent Belgium

DE KEUKELEIRE, DENIS, chemist; b. Beerlegem, Belgium, July 28, 1943; s. Bernardus R. and Alice C. (Tuypens) De K.; m. Maria M. Gyselinck (dec. Sept. 1980); 1 child, Jelle D. Candidate chemistry, Ghent U., Belgium, 1964, B of Chemistry, 1966, PhD, 1971, habilitation organic chemistry, 1982. From rsch. fellow to rsch. assoc. Belgian Nat. Fund for Sci. Rsch., Belgium, 1966-92; prof., rsch. dir. Ghent U., 1992—, mem. rsch. coun., 1998—. Author: De Chemie van Hopbitterzuren, 1982, Chemistry and Analysis of Hop and Beer Bitter Acids, 1991; co-editor: Luminescence Techniques in Chemical and Biochemical Analysis, 1991; co-author: Hops and Hop Products, 1997; editor Chemie Mag., 1975-95. Recipient J. Stas award Royal Acad. Scis., 1971, L. Wielemans award Belgian Rsch. Fund. of Fermentation Industries, 1978, J. Gillis award Royal Flemish Chem. Soc., 1980. Mem. European Photochemistry Assn., Am. Chem. Soc., Phytochem. Soc. Europe. Avocation: sports. Home: Gontrode Heirweg 115, B-9090 Melle Belgium Office: Ghent U Faculty Pharm Scis, Harelbekestraat 72, B-9000 Ghent Belgium

DE KEYSER, JACQUES, neurologist, educator; b. Gent, Belgium, Apr. 8, 1954; s. P. and B. (Minnaert) De K.; m. M.B. De Jaeger; children: Bram, Roel. MD, Vrije U. brussels, 1981, Neurologist, 1986, PhD, 1989. Assoc. prof., staff neurologist Acad. Hosp. VUB, Brussels, 1986-94; sci. dir. CNS internat. Janssen Rsch. Found., Beerse, Belgium, 1994-95; prof. neurology, head dept. RUG/AZG, Groningen, The Netherlands, 1995—; cons. Orgn. Min. Health, Brussels, 1990-94, Marion Merrel Dow, Brussels, 1991-94. Recipient Galenus Prize for Pharmacology, 1988, prize for psychogeriatrics Soc. Psychogeriatrics, Belgium, 1989. Mem. Orde van de Prinse, Vereniging Vlaamse Zenuwartsen, European Stroke Coun. Home: Mernaweg 22, 9964 AS Wehe-den Hoorn The Netherlands Office: Acad Hosp Groningen, Postbus 30 001, 9700 RB Groningen The Netherlands

DEKHTYAR, YURI DAVID, physicist, biophysicist; b. Riga, Latvia, June 19, 1947; s. David Yudle and Basya Mendel (Skop) D.; m. Galina Boris Shnirman, Aug. 12, 1978; children: Eugenie, Darina. Engr., Riga Poly. Inst., 1971; PhD, Ural Poly. Inst., Sverdlovsk, Russia, 1982; DSc, U. Latvia, Riga, 1992. Designer Automation Design Bur., Riga, 1971-73; from rschr., group mgr. to assoc. prof. Riga Poly. Inst., 1976-93; prof. Riga Tech. U. (formerly Riga Poly. Inst.), 1993—, head inst., 1994—; mem. Med. Physics/Engring. European Network, 1995—. Author: Exoelectron Spectroscopy of Point Defects in Semiconductors, 1993; co-author: Exoelectron Spectroscopy of Defects in Solid States, 1981; mem. editl. bd. Physica Medica. Grantee Internat. Sci. Found., 1994, European Commn., Belgium, 1994, 98, 99; recipient Latvian State prize Govt. Latvia, 1989. Mem. N.Y. Acad. Scis., Material Rsch. Soc., Latvian Med. Engring. and Physics Soc. (pres. 1995—). Achievements include invention of method to record and read information, 1986. Office: Riga Tech Univ, 1 Kalku St, LV-1658 Riga Latvia

DEKKER, DAVID LINDSAY, geophysicist; b. Brisbane, Australia, July 1, 1951; s. John Andrew and Beryl Mavis (Kleindienst) D.; m. Catherine Ann Matheson, Dec. 18, 1981; 1 child, Andrew. BSc in Physics and Math., U. Papua New Guinea, Port Moresby, 1972; PhD in Geophysics, U. Queensland, Brisbane, 1983. Clk. Bur. Stats., Port Moresby, 1972-73; ptnr. David Rose Elec. Contracting, Brisbane, 1974; lectr. Mt. Isa (Queensland) Tech. and Further Edn. Coll, 1983-86; rsch. physicist Mt. Isa Mines Pty. Ltd., 1979-87, sr. rsch. physicist, 1987-89, supt. mine equipment, 1989-91, mgr. engring. rsch., 1991-95; rsch. group leader mine equipment automation Commonwealth and Sci. Indsl. Rsch. Orgn., 1995-99, mining sci. coord., 1996—; conf. presenter in field. Contbr. articles to profl. jours.; patentee in Australia, U.K., Germany, U.S. Mem. Australian Soc. Exploration Geophysicists, Am. Geophys. Union, Australian Inst. Mining and Metallurgy, Planetary Soc., Inst. Engrs. Australia (affiliate), Double Helix Club (Mt. Isa chpt. pres. 1994), Astronomy Group of Mt. Isa Inc. (pres. 1995), Rotary. Avocations: astronomy, cook, golf. Home: 137 Collingwood Dr, Collingwood Park QLD 4301, Australia Office: Queensland Ctr Adv Tech, 2643 Moggill Rd, Pinjarra Hills QLD 4069, Australia

DE KLERK, FREDERIK WILLEM, former state president; b. Johannesburg, Republic South Africa, Mar. 18, 1936; s. Jan de Klerk; m. Marike Willemse, Apr. 1969; 3 children; m. Elita Lanaras Georgiadis, Nov., 1998. BA, Potchefstroom U. for Christian Higher Edn., LLB cum laude, 1958. Assoc. law firm, Vereeniging, Republic South Africa; M.P. for Vereeniging, 1972-89, min. posts and telecommunications, social welfare-pensions, 1978, min. sport and recreation, 1978-79, min. mining and environ. planning, 1979-80, min. mineral and energy affairs, 1980-82, min. internal affairs, 1982-85, min. nat. edn., 1984-89; elected state pres. Cape Town, Republic South Africa, 1989; exec. state pres. Pretoria, Republic South Africa, 1989-1994; exec. deputy pres. Pretoria, Republic of South Africa, 1994-96; leader ofcl. opposition House of Assembly Parliament of Republic

of South Africa, Cape Town, 1996-97; chmn. mins.' coun. Ho. of Assembly, 1985-86, leader, 1986; leader Nat. Party in Transvaal, 1982-89, Nat. Party, 1989-97. Recipient Nobel Peace Prize, Nobel Foundation, 1993. Avocations: golf, reading, outdoors. Address: F W de Klerk Found, Private Bag X999, Cape Town 8000, South Africa Office: Pvt Bag X999, Cape Town 8000, South Africa

DE KLERK, JOSEPH ADRIAN, civil engineer; b. Pretoria, Gautang, South Africa, Apr. 4, 1972; s. Joseph Adrian and Gerda (Malan) DeK.; m. Juanita Duenage, Nov. 21, 1998. Nat. diploma in civil engring., Pretoria Tech., 1994, BA, 1996. Systems engr. Lesotho Highlands Project, 1995-97, site engr., 1997-98; estimator LTA Constrn., South Africa, 1998—. Mem. SAICE, ESCA. Avocations: model aircraft building, scuba diving. Office: LTA Constn, Jet Park Rd Jet Park S A, Johannesburg 1620, South Africa

DEKOK, DAVID, writer, reporter; b. Holland, Mich., July 17, 1953; s. Paul W. and Olga (Kilian) DeK.; m. Lisa W. Brittingham, Oct. 1, 1988; children: Elizabeth B., Lydia B. BA, Hope Coll., Holland, 1975. Reporter The News-Item, Shamokin, Pa., 1975-87, The Patriot-News, Harrisburg, Pa., 1987—; cons. PBS documentary Centralia Fire, 1982-83; guest lectr. Bucknell U., Lewisburg, Pa., 1988-97. Author: Unseen Danger: A Tragedy of People, Government and Centralia Mine Fire, 1986, republished, 2000. Del. Mich. Dem. Conv., 1972; mem. St. Stephen's Episcopal Sch. Bd., 1999—. Recipient Keystone Press award Pa. Newspaper Pubs. Assn., 1979, 86, 87, 90, 99, Pub. Svc. award AP Mng. Editors of Pa., 1981, Janus award Mortgage Bankers Am., 1992. Mem. Investigative Reporters and Editors, Nat. Press Club (Freedom of the Press award 1995), Soc. Profl. Journalists (pres. ctrl. Pa. chpt. 1989-91, Spotlight award 1995), Newspaper Guild, Nat. Writers Union. Episcopalian. Home: 113 Conoy St Harrisburg PA 17104-1608

DE KONING, CHARLES BERNARD, chemistry educator, researcher; b. Cape Town, South Africa, Nov. 1, 1961; s. Adriaanus Jan and Margaret Naomi (Hawkridge) deK. BSc, U. Cape Town, 1982, BSc with Honors, 1983, PhD, 1988. Post doctoral MIT, Boston, 1988-89, U. Hawaii, Honolulu, 1989-91; lectr. U. Witwatersrad, South Africa, 1992—. Mem. ACS, South Africa Chem. Soc. Office: Dept Chemistry, U Witwatersrand, 2050 Johannesburg South Africa

DE KONING, PETER HANS, marketing executive; b. Rotterdam, The Netherlands, Sept. 19, 1944; s. Matthijs Petrus and Violette Regina (Van Der Leide) De K. Doctorate, Erasmus U., Rotterdam, 1972. Asst. prof. Erasmus U., 1968-72; asst. to the v.p. ops., mktg. mgr., corp. planner Ferro Corp., Rotterdam, 1972-76; mng. planning and mktg. OGEM Bldg. & Constrn. Group, Rotterdam, 1976-80; gen. mgr. Westland Utrecht Real Estate Devel., Amsterdam, 1980-84; mktg. deve. mgr., pub. Elsevier Internat., Doetinchem, 1984-90; CEO, King Holding, King Pub. and Mktg. Cons., King Pensioen B.V. and Produkt Aanbod B.V. Hengelo-Gld, 1990—; founder Pub. Plaza, Worldwide Meeting Place of Pubs., 2000—; mem. mktg. and bldg. bd. NIMA, 1974-86; bd. dirs. De Achterpoorthe; lectr. mktg. comm. U. Lincolnshire and Humberside, Internat. Mktg. Acad. Dept. Enschede and U. Hertfordshire. Co-author: Polymarketing Zakboek; contbr. articles to profl. jours. V.p. Societas Studiosorum Reformatorum Roterodamensis; adv. com. Mark. Assn. of the EUR; mem. Investment Club 't Stockpaert, past pres.; mem. com. internat. trade C. of C., Ainhem. Mem. Mktg. Assn. (founder), Soc. of Internat. Rels., C. of C. Arnhem (mem. com. internat. trade.). Avocations: sailing, jogging, classical music and travelling. Fax: 00-31-575467492. E-mail: info@kingpmc.com and info@publishersplaza.com. Office: King Pub and Mktg Cons BV, Postbus 53 NL, 7255 ZH Hengelo Gld, The Netherlands

DE KRETSER, DAVID MORRITZ, research institute administrator, endocrinologist; b. Colombo, Sri Lanka, Apr. 27, 1939; arrived in Australia, 1949; s. Pervival Shirley and Iris Aileen (Ludekens) de K.; m. Janice Margaret Warren, Dec. 7, 1962; children: Steven, Mark, Ross, Hugh. MD, Monash U., Clayton, Australia, 1969; BM, U. Melbourne, Austraiia, 1962. Physician Prince Henry's Hosp. Victoria, Clayton, 1973-74, sr. rsch. fellow, 1974-78, assoc. dir. Med. Rsch. Ctr., 1977-78; sr. lectr. dept. medicine and anatomy Monash U., 1971-75, chmn. dept. anatomy, 1978-91, dir. Inst. Reprodn. and Devel., 1991—; mem. panel advisors Infertility Treatment Authority, 1999—; dir. Australian Ctr. Men's Reproductive Health, 1999—; Serono lectr. Am. Soc. for Andrology, 1985; numerous presentations in field at internat. meetings, including plenary lectures; mem. numerous nat. and internat. coms. Nat. Health and Med. Rsch. Coun.; mem. spl. program rsch. in reprodn. WHO. Editor numerous books; mem. editl. bds. numerous internat. jours.; contbr. over 600 articles to nat. and internat. med. jours. Bd. dirs. Bertarelli Found., 1999—. Recipient Wyeth award ann. meeting Pacific Coast Fertility Soc., 1970, Organon prize Australian and New Zealand Endocrine Soc., 1977; grantee Nat. Health and Med. Rsch. Coun. Australia, WHO, Ford Found. Fellow Royal Australian Coll. Physicians, Australian Acad. Sci., Internat. Acad. Human Reprodn. Mem. Uniting Ch. Achievements include research in field of reproductive biology, infertility and endocrinology; contributed to knowledge of electronmicroscopy of testes and male infertility; research on isolation and biology of inhibit which resulted in first isolation of inhibin; with colleagues established existence of paracrine regulatory mechanisms in testis and now exporing molecules involved. Home: 1 Leura St, Surrey Hills Vic 3127, Australia Office: Monash Med Ctr Inst Reprodn, 246 Clayton Rd, Clayton Vic 3168, Australia

DEKU, AFRIKADZATA, Afrikaan-centric scholar, researcher, writer, educator; b. Kadjebi, Ghana, Dec. 13, 1949; m. Yayra Deku; children: Mawunyo, Aku Sika, Mawulolo, Afrikamawuse, Afrikamawuedem. BA with honors, U. Cape Coast, Ghana, 1977; MSc, U. Ife, Nigeria, 1981; diploma, Inst. Internat. D'Adminstrn. Pub., Paris, 1983; MPhil, U. Paris XI, Sorbonne, 1983, PhD, 1985. Lic. mediator, arbitrator, negotiator. Ind. post-doctoral rsch. scholar U. Denver, 1986-87; founder, chief exec., prof. pan-Afrikan studies Afrikan Culture Inst., 1987—; vis. assoc. prof. Afrikan history Clark Atlanta U., 1990-91; vis. assoc. prof. Africana studies Morris Brown Coll., Atlanta, 1990; vis. assoc. prof. Afrikan culture, continuing edn. dept. Ga. State U., 1990; pub. The Afrikan Truth, 1994—, Continental Afrikan Pubs., 1990—; vis. prof. French and Afrikan lit. Wofford Coll., Spartanburg, S.C., 1988-89, Converse Coll., Spartanburg, 1989; trainer, guest speaker Clemson U. 4-H Operation Pride, 1994—; ACT ESL placement test fairness reviewer and cons., 2000; participant ACT ESL Teleconf., 2000; resident guest artist Kennedy Middle Sch., Aiken, S.C., 1997, Jackson (S.C.) Mid. Sch., 1998, S.C. Writers Ann. Workshop Conf. Faculty, Manuscript Evaluator; poetry judge Pan-Afrikan Poetry Recitals, Myrtle Beach, 1998; founder, bd. chmn. Afrikamawu Miracle Mission made up of: Continental Afrikan Devel. Authority, KADA, Continental Afrikan Govt. Implementation Authority, KAGO, and Continental Afrikan Culture Promotions Authority, KAFO; guest artist Spartanburg Internat. Festival, 1999, Ea. Lit. Fellowship, Clinton, S.C., 1999; guest author Lee County Young Authors Ann. Conf., Bishopville, S.C., 1999; lectr., spkr. and cons. in field. Author: (poetry) We Are All Continental Afrikans, 1991, Sacred Verses For My Afrikan Queens, 1992, Sacred Afrikan Spiritual Power From Within, 1993, Agbenoxevie Menye, Ablodesafui, Agbedefu (Ewe poetry), Courage, Mere Afrique, Cris de Tonnerre, Coups de Marteau, A Toi le Paradis de Ma Langue (Afrikan Poetry in French); (plays) No Where is Heaven, Breaking the Bloody Sword of Apartheid, (rsch. books) L'Union Continentale Africaine, vols. 1-3, 1986, Continental Afrikan Power Now, 1987, The Afrikan-Centric Perspective of the Afrikan World Crisis, 1988, Continental Afrikan Manifesto, 1999, Continental Afrikan Power in Figures, 1989, The Afrikan Gospel of Total Happiness Now and Always, 1991, The Power of Afrikan-Centricity, 1992, AFRIKAMAWUNYA or the Holy Afrikan Bible, 1997, Continental Afrika: From Two Hundred Million Seasons to the Present, 1994, The Power and Benefits of Continental Afrikan Culture, 1994, How to Be a Continental Afrikan Again, 1994, Positive Self-Knowledge Technology, 1994, Positive Goal Achievement Technology, 1994, Positive Problem-Solving Technology, 1996, Positive Decision-Making Technology, 1999, I Want To Tell You Why, 1995, From Eagle to Chicken and Back, 1995, Continental Afrikan Constitution of the Continental Afrikan Republic, 1998—; Why the World Bank /IMF/UN etc. Are a Curse Rather Than a Blessing to Afrika, 2000, The Afrikan Origin of Humanity, 2000, Behold Your Continental Afrikan Savior Afrikalela Is Born, 2000, Still Slaves in the "Land of the Free," 2000, Passing Our ABC Test of our African-Centricity, 2000, The Dates Western Powers do not want us to Know About, 2000, Authentic Continental Afrikan Name Book, 2000; spkr. in field. Founder Afrikan-Centricity Movement, Continental Afrikan Govt. Orgn., Continental Afrikan Found., Continental Afrikan Devel. Authority. Grantee S.C. Arts Commn., 1990-91; scholar Ghana Govt., 1970-72, 73-77, Commonwealth, 1975, 77, 78, French Govt., 1982-85; recipient OYO State Bursary award, 1980-81, Spartanburg, S.C. Arts Coun. award, 1989-90, S.C. Arts Commn. grant, 1990-91. Mem. ABA, Am. Arbitration Assn., S.C. Coun. for Mediation and Alternative Dispute Resolution, Internat. Biog. Assn., Internat. Platform Assn., French PhD Holders Assn., African Studies Assn., African Heritage Studies Assn., Am. Polit. Sci. Assn. E-mail: afrikalion@aol.com. Home: 182 Stribling Cir Spartanburg SC 29301-1651 also: Box 209, Dansoman Accra Ghana

DE LAAT, BASTIAAN, innovation policy analyst, consultant; b. Nijmegen, The Netherlands, Oct. 4, 1965. MA in Chemistry, U. Nijmegen, 1989; PhD in Environ. Sci., U. Amsterdam, The Netherlands, 1996. Rschr. Ctr. for Tech. Policy Studies/ Netherlands Orgn. Applied Sci. Rsch., Apeldoorn, 1990-92; rschr. U. Amsterdam, 1992-96, CSI Ecole Des Mines, Paris, 1992-98, Technopolis France, 1998—. Contbr. articles to profl. jours. Mem. Dutch Chem. Assn. (past pres. younger mems. com.), European Assn. for Study of Sci. and Tech., European Evaluation Soc. Office: 5 r Castiglione, 75001 Paris France

DE LAAT, GILBERT, automotive executive; b. Paterson, N.J., Apr. 2, 1957; s. Elmer Gilbert and Marjorie Lucille De Laat. BA, Columbia U., 1979; M of Pub. Policy, Harvard U., 1984. Adminstr. legal and regulatory affairs Isuzu Motors Am., City of Industry, Calif., 1985-93; mgr. govt. affairs Nat. Hwy. Traffic Safety Adminstrn. Subaru Am., Inc., Cherry Hill, N.J., 1995—. Congressional aid U.S. Congressman Andrew Maguire, Paramus, N.J., 1977-78. Mem. ABA, UN-USA, World Affairs Coun., Am. Trauma Soc., Am. Polit. Sci. Assn., Sonoma County Wine Growers Assn., N.Am. Riding Handicapped Assn. Republican. Roman Catholic. Avocations: sailing, martial arts, golf. Fax: 856-488-3255. E-mail: gdeLatt@subaru.com. Home: PO Box 1323 Ridgewood NJ 07451-1323 Office: Subaru Am Inc PO Box 6000 Cherry Hill NJ 08034-6000

DE LA BASTIDE, MICHAEL, judge. Chief justice Supreme Ct., Trinidad and Tobago. Office: Hall of Justice, Knox St, Port of Spain Trinidad and Tobago*

DE LA CAMPA, MIGUEL-ANGEL, entrepreneur, economist; b. La Habana, Cuba, Aug. 20, 1944; arrived in Can., 1993; s. Alberto de la Campa and Martha de la Torre; m. Marisela Ponce, Aug. 29, 1992; children: Ornella, Miguel-Angel, Rodrigo. BSFS, Georgetown U., 1969, MA, 1971. Pres., CEO, dir. Bolivar Goldfields, Toronto, Ont., Can., 1994—, Gran Colombia Resources, Toronto, 1995—; exec. dir., founder TechnoPetrol, Inc., Toronto, 1996—; bd. dirs. Venezuelan Mining Chamber, Caracas, Venezuela, Venezuelan-Am. C. of C., Caracas, Venezuelan Gold Assn., Caracas. Avocations: reading, sports.

DELACATO, JANICE ELAINE, learning consultant, educator; b. Bklyn., June 6, 1926; d. Frode Siegfried and Vilma (Rils) Gernstrom; m. Carl Henry Delacato, June 20, 1951; children: Elizabeth Delacato Putnam, Carl Henry, David Gernstrom. AB, Bryn Mawr Coll., 1948. Tchr. Rydal Hall, Ogontz Sch., Pa., 1948-49, The Spence Sch., N.Y.C., 1949-50, Chestnut Hill Acad., Phila., 1950-52; co-dir. The Chestnut Hill Reading Clinic, Phila., 1951-65, Delacato & Delacato Cons. in Learning, Phila., 1972-88; mgr. Morton (Pa.) Book Store, 1972-88; co-dir. The Delacato & Delacato Conf. Autism & Learning Disabilities, 1979-82. Editor newsletter Temple U. Med. Ctr. Women's Aux., Phila., 1953-65; class editor Bryn Mawr Coll. Alumnae Bull., 1966-79. Chmn. fund-raising com. Springside Sch., 1969-71; treas. Main St. Fair Antiques Booth, Chestnut Hill Hosp., 1965-77. Recipient Main St. Fair award Chestnut Hill Hosp., 1972. Mem. AAUW, Phila. Cricket Club. Republican. Unitarian. Home: The Glen 700 Thomas Rd Philadelphia PA 19118-4601

DE LA CONCHA, JOSE LUIS, pediatrician; b. Mexico City, Sept. 16, 1949; s. Jose De La Concha and Carmen Maria Palauos; m. Olga Margarita Zindel; children: Paola, Andres. MD, Nat. U. Mex., 1975. Asst. prof. Queretaro U., Mex., 1973; resident in anesthesia Michael Reese Hosp., Chgo., 1978; resident in pediats. Mt. Sinai Hosp., Chgo., 1979-81; fellow in infectious diseases Rush Med. Sch., Chgo., 1982-83, instr. pediats., 1983, head of pediat. infectious diseases, 1984-85, asst. prof. pediats., 1984-85; head inpatient pediat. dept. Columbus Hosp., Chgo., 1988-94; coord., prof. of infectious diseases Puebla U., Mex., 1996—. Author: On Your Marks, Set...1998. Mem. Colegio de Pediatria. Avocations: squash, paddle tennis.

DELA CRUZ, JOSE SANTOS, retired state supreme court justice; b. Saipan, Commonwealth No. Mariana Islands, July 18, 1948; s. Thomas Castro and Remedio Sablan (Santos) Dela C.; m. Rita Tenorio Sablan, Nov. 12, 1977; children: Roxanne, Renee, Rica Ann. BA, U. Guam, 1971; JD, U. Calif., Berkeley, 1974; cert., Nat. Jud. Coll., Reno, 1985. Bar: No. Mariana Islands, 1974, U.S. Dist. Ct. No. Mariana Islands 1978. Staff atty. Micro. Legal Svcs. Corp., Saipan, 1974-79; gen. counsel Marianas Pub. Land Corp., Saipan, 1979-81; liaison atty. CNMI Fed. Laws Commn., Saipan, 1981-83; ptnr. Borja & Dela Cruz, Saipan, 1983-85; assoc. judge Commonwealth Trial Ct., Saipan, 1985-89; state supreme ct. chief justice Supreme Ct. No. Mariana Islands, 1989-95; retired, 1995; mem. Conf. of Chief Justices, 1989-95, Adv. Commn. on Judiciary, Saipan, 1980-82; chmn. Criminal Justice Planning Agy., Saipan, 1985-95. Mem. Coun. for Arts, Saipan, 1982-83; chmn. Bd. of Elections, Saipan, 1977-82; pres. Cath. Social Svcs., Saipan, 1982-85. Mem. No. Marianas Bar Assn. (pres. 1984-85). Roman Catholic. Avocations: golf, reading, walking.

DE LA FUENTE RAMIREZ, JUAN RAMON, Mexican government official; b. Mexico City, Sept. 5, 1951; married; 3 children. MSc, U. Minn. Prof. Nat. Nutrition Inst.; rschr. Mex. Inst. Psychiatry; dir. health rsch. program U.N.A.M., dir. med. faculty, 1991—; sec. health Govt. of Mex., Washington, 1995—; vis. prof. several fgn. univs. Author books on health rsch. Vol. internat. health orgns. Office: Deleg Cuauhtémoc, Lieja 7-1 Piso Col Juarez, Mexico City 06696, Mexico

DE LAGABBE, ARNAUD, sales company executive, consultant; b. Paris, Oct. 13, 1962; s. Francois and Brigitte (Lecoeur) De L. Bachelor's degree, St. Louis de Gonzague, France, 1981; engring. degree, Sudria, France, 1986. Cert. electronic and computer engr. Project mgr. Credit Lyonnais, France, 1987-89, 3Com, 1989-91; sales exec. Bruno Rives, France, 1991-94, Gartner Group, France, 1994—; sales exec. for fin. and capital market Sun Microsystems, 1997—. With French Marines, 1986-87. Avocations: regatta sailing, rugby, skiing, chess. Home: 33 rue du Rocher, 75008 Paris France Office: Sun Microsystems, 13 av Morane Saulnier, 78120 Velizy Cedex France

DE LA GARZA, GERMAN, company executive; b. Mexico City, June 2, 1957; s. Angel De La Garza and Emma Estrada; m. Maria Pia De Vecchi, Sept. 6, 1980; children: Maria Pia, German. DVM, UNAM, Mexico City. Sales mgr. Veco, Mexico City, 1981-82; prodn. mgr. Broicers Frams, Morelos, Mex., 1982; pers. asst. to pres. Ministry of Health, Mexico City, 1983-85, purchasing dir., 1985-87; purchasing dir. Fertimex, Mexico City, 1988; pres. KCB Group, Mexico City, 1989—. Avocations: running, gym, tennis. Home: Nicolas San Juan 1326, 03100 Mexico City Mexico Office: KCB Group Oniente 229 # 70, Lol Agnicola Oriental, 08500 Mexico City Mexico

DE LA GARZA, LAURA, human resources professional; b. Mexico City, Nov. 25, 1964; d. Jose De La Garza and Laura Elena (Mendoza) Blanca. B of Indsl. Rels., Iberoamericana U., Mexico City, 1988. Gen. adminstr. Diseno y Concepto, Mexico City, 1988-90; personnel head Bristol-Myers Squibb, Mexico City, 1990-93; mgr. human resources Merrell Lepetit, Mexico City, 1993-95; dir. human resources Hoechst Marion Roussel, Mexico City, 1995-2000, AstraZeneca, Mexico City, 2000—. Mem. The Conf. Bd., Asociacion en Relaciones Industriales de Laboratorios Quimico Farmaceuticas, A.C. Avocations: horseback riding, reading, swimming, playing guitar. Office: AstraZeneca SA, Avenida Lomas Verdes # 67, 53120 Naucalpan Mexico

DE LA GARZA, LUIS ADOLFO, lawyer, energy company executive; b. Mission, Tex., Nov. 22, 1943; s. Adolfo and Carmen (Barrera) de la G.; m. Sherry Lynn Hatcher, Apr. 12, 1974; children: Miguel, Gabriel, Lucas. BBA, U. Tex., 1966; MBA, U. Hawaii, 1972; JD, U. Tex., 1975. Bar: Tex. 1975. Counsel El Paso Natural Gas Co., Tex., 1975-78; sr. counsel El Paso Co., Houston, 1978-81; sr. atty., asst. sec. Valero Energy Corp., San Antonio, 1981-87, v.p. corp. rels., 1987-97; v.p. corp. rels. PG&E Gas Transmission-Tex. Corp., San Antonio, 1997-2000. Chmn. March of Dimes San Antonio Walk Am., 1996, 97; bd. dirs., chmn. Latino leadership for the libr. campaign San Antonio Pub. Libr. Found.; bd. dirs. Tex. Equal Access to Justice Found., comms. com.; bd. dirs. Valero Polit. Action Com., San Antonio, 1984-97, chmn., 1987-97; bd. dirs. Valero Fed. Credit Union, 1987-88; bd. dirs. World Affairs Coun., San Antonio, 1987, exec. com., 1988-90; scout leader Boy Scouts Am., San Antonio, 1984; mem. Witte Coun., Witte Com., San Antonio Mus. Assn., 1985-90; bd. dirs., vice chmn. United Way Tex., mem. pub. policy com.; bd. dirs. Tex. Civil Justice League; mem. bus. adv. coun. U. Tex., San Antonio. Capt. USMC, 1966-72, Vietnam. Decorated Air medal with 15 oak leaf clusters; named One of the Hundred Most Influential Hispanics in Am. Hispanic Bus. Mag., 1990, One of the Corp. Elite in Am. Hispanic Mag., 1999-2000; recipient Breaking Barriers award Nat. Hispanic Employees Assn., 1993, Vol. of Yr. March of Dimes 1998. Fellow Tex. Bar Found.; mem. Tex. Bar Assn., San Antonio Bar Assn. (chmn. corp. counsel sect. 1986-88), Greater San Antonio C. of C. (govtl. affairs, edn. coun. steering com. 1987-90), Southside C. of C. (bd. dirs. 1989-90), San Antonio Hispanic C. of C. (bd. dirs. 1989-91). Democrat. Methodist. E-mail: luis.delagarza@gt.pge.com. Office: PG&E Gas Transmission-Tex Corp 7330 San Pedro Ste 400 San Antonio TX 78216-6235

DELAGE, GILLES PASCAL, international company sales executive; b. Paris, Apr. 23, 1953; s. Joseph and Raymonde (Lavie) D.; m. Dominique Jeanine M. Berna, Mar. 19, 1976; children: Thibault, Matthieu, Guillaume. MBA/Descaf, Ecole Supe rieure de Commerce, Amiens, France, 1976; DEUG, Bus. Rights U., Paris, 1977. Fin. exec. Creusot Loire Entreprises, Paris, 1977-79; export and fin. dep. mgr. Trindel, Paris, 1979-82; fin. mgr. Spie Batignolles, Velizy, France, 1983-86; internat. sales mgr. FECHOZ, Paris, 1986-87; Asia Pacific v.p. FECHOZ, Cergy Pontoise, France, 1987-95; gen. mgr. Acopex, Eragny, France, 1995-97; export v.p. Trophy/Trex Group, Marne la Vallie, France, 1997-2000; v.p. internat. sales Outinord, St. Amand Les Eaux, France, 2000—. Served with French Air Force, 1976-77. Mem. Association des Diplomes de L'ESCAE-Amiens (pres. 1976-87). Roman Catholic. Avocations: golf, skiing, tennis. Home: 16 Rue de la Treille, 95490 Vaureal France Office: Z I Mitry Compans B P 212, 77292 Mitry Mory France

DE LA GUARDIA, DULCIDIO JOSE, investment banker, financial consultant; b. Panama City, Panama, Mar. 28, 1964; s. Gilberto de la Guardia and Irma González Martinis; m. Nisla Viggiano, July 16, 1988; children: Dulcidio Emilio, Tomas Esteban. BS in Bus., Fla. State U., 1984; MBA, Loyola U., New Orleans, 1986. Asst. mgr. J.M., S.A., Panama City, 1984-85, Financiera Govimar, Panama City, 1987-88; fin. cons. Stotler & Co., Panama City, 1988-90; adminstrv. mgr. Bolsa de Valores Panama, Panama City, 1990-93, devel. mgr., 1993-95; mng. dir. Capital Traders Panama, Panama City, 1995—. Mem. Rotarac, 1984, MOLIRENA, 1985, Electoral Dels., 1991. Mem. Assn. Securities Dealers, Union Club, Kiwanis Club Panama (treas. 1995). Avocations: karate, tennis. Home: La Loma Calle 2a, Panama Panama Office: Capital Traders Panama, Box 7201, Panama 5 Panama*

DELAHANTY, CARLOS ANTHONY, industrial engineer; b. Scottsdale, Ariz., May 3, 1965; s. Carlos Victor and Mary Martha (Santa Marina) D. BS in Indsl. Engring., Ariz. State U., 1991. Indsl. engr. Intel Corp., Chandler, Ariz., 1993, Gaylord Container Corp., Glendale, Ariz., 1994; project scheduling engr., planning cons. Lockwood Greene Engrs., Phoenix, 1994-95; project scheduling engr. Honeywell Air Transp. Sys., Phoenix, 1996; indsl. engring. cons. Knight Architects Engrs. Planners, Inc., Phoenix, 1997; project and cost control engr. Honeywell Indsl. Automation and Control, Phoenix and Houston, 1997-99; project controls engring. dept. mgr. Goss Graphic Sys., Westmont, Ill., 1999-2000; indsl. engr., master scheduler Intel Corp., Albuquerque, 2000—. Mem. Inst. Indsl. Engrs., Project Mgmt. Inst., Alpha Pi Mu. Roman Catholic. Avocation: amateur bowling. E-mail: Anthony.Delahanty@gossgraphic.com and shotisdeep@aol.com. Home: 201 Country Club Dr SE Apt 1713 Rio Rancho NM 87124-0419 Office: Goss Graphic Sys 700 Oakmont Ln Westmont IL 60559-5551

DELAHANTY, REBECCA ANN, school system administrator; b. South Bend, Ind., Oct. 18, 1941; d. Raymond F. and Ann Marie (Batsleer) Paczesny; m. Edward Delahanty, June 22, 1963; children: David, Debbie. BA, Coll. St. Catherine, Minn., 1977; MA, Coll. St. Thomas, Minn., 1983; PhD, Ga. State U., 1994. Cert. in adminstrn. and supervision, Ga. Initiator, tchr. gifted kindergarten Dist. 284 Sch., Wayzata, Minn., 1977-83; gifted kindergarten coord. St. Barts Sch., Wayzata, 1983-85; prin. Dabbs Loomis Sch., Dunwoody, Ga., 1987-91; asst. to supt. Buford (Ga.) City Schs., 1993-98, supt., 1998-99; prof. Ga. State U., 1999—; mem. staff devel. adv. coun. Ga. Contbr. article to profl. publ. Mem. ASCD, Am. Ednl. Rsch. Assn., Nat. Assn. Gifted Children, Minn. Coun. Gifted and Talented, Phi Delta Kappa, Omicron Gamma.

DE LA HERAS, MARIA ELENA, dermatologist; b. Burgos, Spain, June 5, 1967; d. Jose Antonio de la Heras and Maria Elena Alonso. MD, Alicante U.; PhD, U. Alcala, 1996. Resident in dermatology Hosp. Ramon y Cajal, Madrid, 1992-95; rsch. fellow Alcala U., Madrid, 1996—; dermatologist Centro Medico Zarzuela, Madrid, 1996-98; participant at confs. U. Complutense, Madrid, 1994-97, Pharmacist Coll., 1993-97; sci. translator, Madrid, 1996-98. Co-author: Principles of Internal Medicine; redactor Dermatologia and Cosmetica, 1996—; contbr. articles to profl. jours. Recipient Nat. Medicine award Edn. Ministry, 1992, Nat. award Dermatol. Therapy Com., 1996. Mem. Madrid Dermatologists Assn. (sec. 1994—), German Dermatol. Soc. Roman Catholic. Avocations: reading, music, sailing, skiing, golf. E-mail: elasherasa@medynet.com. Home: Calle Embajadores 146-3 5oA, 28045 Madrid Spain Office: Hosp Ramon y Cajal Derm, Aptdo 31057, 28034 Madrid Spain

DE LA HOUSSAYE, BRETTE ANGELO-PEPE, electronics engineer, researcher; b. L.A., Aug. 20, 1960; s. Wilbert Joseph de la Houssaye and Paula Marie (Jones) Colby. BSEET, Devry Inst. Tech., 1989. Pvt. practice Calif., 1990—. Mem. IEEE, Libr. Congress Assoc., Nat. Trust Historic Preservation, Smithsonian Inst., Nat. Soc. Black Engrs., Am. Mus. Natural History. Achievements include discoveries of an alternate method for calculating work, using Newton's second Law of Motion and work energy theorem. Home and Office: 7719 Goodland Ave North Hollywood CA 91605-2041

DE LA HOYA, OSCAR, Olympic athlete, professional boxer; b. Bel Air, Calif., Feb. 4, 1973. Olympic boxer, lightweight divsn. Barcelona, Spain, 1992; champion jr. lightweight divsn. World Boxing Orgn., 1994, former champion lightweight divsn., 1994—; former champion lightweight divsn. Internat. Boxing Fedn., 1995—; champion lightweight divsn World Boxing Council, 1996—. Recipient Gold medal lightweight boxing divsn. Olympics, Barcelona, 1992; winner 4 championship titles in 4 different weight classes. Office: care Top Rank Boxing 3980 Howard Hughes Pkwy Ste 580 Las Vegas NV 89109-0995

DELAHUNT, BRETT, pathologist; b. Wellington, New Zealand, Feb. 20, 1950; s. John Joseph Delahunt; m. Susan Anne Kirk. BSc with honors, Victoria U., 1972; B of Med. Sci., U. Otago, New Zealand, 1976, MB ChB, 1978, MD, 1995. Resident med. officer Wellington Hosp., 1979-80; lectr. in pathology U. Otago, 1980-86, sr. lectr. in pathology, 1986-94, assoc. prof., 1994-96, prof., 1996—, chmn. dept. pathology Wellington Sch. Medicine, 1995—; dep. dean Wellington Sch. Medicine, 1998—; prin. med. advisor St. John Ambulance, New Zealand, 1993-97; bd. mgmt. Wellington Free Ambulance Svc., 1986-96; mem. nat. civil def. health planning com. Ministry of Civil Def., 1992—; mem. cancer reporting adv. group Ministry of Health, New Zealand; cons. pathologist New Zealand Cancer Registry Ministry of Health, 1997—; chair scientific adv. com. Wellington Med. Rsch. Found., 1997—, Ministry of Fgn. Affairs, NZ Com. for Dissemination of Humanitarian Law, 1998—. Editor: New Zealand Aid Manual, 1994, 2d

edit., 1995; contbr. over 100 articles to profl. jours. Recipient Svc. medal New Zealand Ambulance, 1991; created Knight Order of St. John, 1995, Knight of the Order St. Lazarus, New Zealand, 1999. Fellow Royal Coll. of Pathologists of Australia; mem. New Zealand Soc. of Pathologists (v.p. 1991-93, pres. 1996—), Internat. Soc. of Urol. Pathology (v.p. Australasia 1995-98, sec. 1998—), Cancer Soc. New Zealand (mem. scientific adv. group). Office: Wellington Sch Medicine, Sch Medicine PO Box 7343, Wellington South New Zealand

DELAITTRE, PIERRE ALAIN, oil company executive; b. Bergerac, Dordogne, France, Aug. 8, 1948; s. Xavier Marie and Jacqueline Marie (Vidal) D.; m. Marie Helene Colonna-De-Lega, June 18, 1976; children: Antoine, Caroline. BSc in Math. and Physics, U. Grenoble, France, 1969; student, Oceanographic Inst., Paris, 1972; mech. engr., École Supérieure Mécanique Électicite., Paris, 1974. Cert. mech. engr. Project engr. Doris, Paris, 1976-77; petroleum engr. Shell, various locations, 1971-91; project mgr. Elf, Pau, 1991-98, head internat. rels., 1999—; lectr. Inst. Francais du Pétrole, 1992—. Patentee in field of hydrocarbon technology. Lt. French Navy, 1974-75. Avocations: diving instructor, horseback riding. Office: Elf, CSTJF Ave Larribau, 64000 Pau France

DE LA LANZA ESPINO, GUADALUPE, chemist, researcher; b. Tlaxcala, Mex., July 20, 1941; d. Monterubio Antonio De la Lanza and González Guadalupe Espino. PhDBA, UNAM, Mexico City, 1981, BSc, 1964. Prof. UNAM, Mexico City, 1965-77, prof. Grad. Sch., 1978—&; advisor Direccion Gen. de Oceanografia Naval, 1983-89; rschr. in field. Author 10 books; reviewer for sci. jours.; contbr. more than 60 articles to profl. jours. Mem. Academia Mexicana de Ciencias, Wociedad Quimica Mexicana. Home: Odontologia # 6, 04360 Mexico City Mexico Office: Inst Biologia UNAM, Cd Universitaria, 04510 Mexico City Mexico

DELAMATER, WILLIAM DANIEL, underwriter; b. Atlanta, Apr. 13, 1972; s. William F. Jr. and Sharon McClure DeL.; m. Coreen Elise Genteman, June 3, 1995; 1 child, Amelia Elisabeth. BBA, Ga. State U., 1994, student, 1999—. Underwriter SAFECO Ins. Co., Stone Mountain, Ga., 1996-99; supr. underwriter SAFECO Ins. Co., Duluth, Ga., 1999-2000; underwriting mgr. So. Mut. Ins. Co., Athens, Ga., 2000—. Avocations: golf, investing. Office: So Mut Ins Co PO Box 7009 Athens GA 30604-7009

DE LA MORENA, JAVIER, engineering consultant; b. Granada, Granada, Spain, Sept. 27, 1963. Engr., Navarra U., San Sebastian, Spain, 1987; MBA, Inst. Estudios Superiores de la Empresa, Barcelona, Spain, 1989. Responsible for supply chain integration practice AT Kearney, Madrid, 1994-97, responsible consumer products, 1997—. Office: AT Kearney, Castellana 31, 28046 Madrid Madrid, Spain

DE LA MOTTE BOULOUMI, GUY NOËL, beverage company executive, mayor; b. Lyon, Rhone, France, Dec. 24, 1920; s. Jacques and Edith Marie (Bouloumié) de la Motte; m. Paulette Rouzeyrol, July 11, 1946 (div. Feb. 1952); children: Sophie, Catherine; m. Emilienne Bertani, Sept. 17, 1955; 1 child, Xavier. Diploma, Inst. Etudes Politiques, Paris, 1947. Gen. sec. Societe Eaux Minerales, Vittel, France, 1948-52, CEO, 1952-68, v.p., CEO, 1968-72, pres., CEO, 1972-92, hon. pres., CEO, 1992—. Mayor, City of Vittel, 1953-77, 95—. Lt. French Army, 1944-45. Decorated Cross of War, France, 1945, Officier Ordre Nat. Merite, France, 1976, Officier Legion d'Honneur, 1987. Mem. C. of C. (pres. 1980-86). Home: Ave Bouloumié, 88800 Vittel Vosges, France Office: City Hall, Place de la Marne, 88800 Vittel Vosges, France

DE LANEY, ALLEN YOUNG, retired surgeon; b. Arrington, Tenn., 1917; s. Joseph Peter and Mary Williams (Glover) D.; m. Margaret Duncan, May 30, 1947 (div. Jan. 1978); children: Allen G., Philip Andrew, Bruce Duncan, Mary Elizabeth Johnston; m. Thelma Lou House, Apr. 7, 1979; children: Stewart B. White, Joseph S. White. BS, U. Ark., 1937; MD, Tulane U., 1940. Diplomate Am. Bd. Surgery. Intern Grady Hosp., Atlanta, 1940-41; resident in pathology New Eng. Deaconess Hosp., Boston, 1941; resident in surgery New Orleans VA Hosp., 1948-52; fellow in surgery Tulane U., New Orleans, 1947-50; asst. chief surgeon USS Haven UASA Naval Hosp. Shop Inchon, Pusan, Korea, 1950-51; chief surgeon U.S. VA Hosp., Poplar Bluff, Mo., 1952-53; chief of staff Alachua Gen. Hosp., Fla., 1976-78; courtesy staff Alachua Gen. Hosp., 1987—; ret., 1988; chmn. Alachua County Emergency Medicine Coun., Gainesville, 1975-80. Pres. bd. dirs. Boys Club, Gainesville, 1955, Alachua County Thoracic Soc., Gainesville, 1956; bd. dirs. ARC, United Fund; mem. bus. coun. LWV, 1967-69; mem. Gainesville City Planning Cb., 1961-69; comdr. cons. Gainesville chpt. U.S. Power Squadron, 1985; Disting. mem. pres.'s coun. U. Fla.; founding trustee North Fla. Regional Hosp., Gainesville, 1969-76. Comdr. MC USNR, ret., 1985-86. Fellow ACS; mem. AMA, Fla. Thoracic Soc. (pres. 1961-62), Fla. Soc. Gen. Surgeons, Fla. Sheriffs Assn. (hon. life), Sigma Chi. Fax: 352-372-0818.

DELANEY, JOSEPH P., bishop; b. Fall River, Mass., Aug. 29, 1934. Student, Cardinal O'Connell Sem., Mass., Theol. Coll., Washington, N.Am. Coll., Rome, R.I. Coll. Ordained priest Roman Catholic Ch., 1960; ordained bishop of Fort Worth, 1981—. Office: 800 W Loop 820 S Fort Worth TX 76108-2936

DELANEY, MARY ANNE, pastoral educator; b. Waltham, Mass., Feb. 15, 1926; d. Thomas Joseph and Mary Teresa (Berry) D. BA, Regis Coll., 1953; MEd, U. Mass., Boston, 1973; MDiv, Andover Newton Theol. Sch., Newton Ctr., Mass., 1978. Tchr. various schs., Mass., 1953-73; pastoral counselor Boston City Hosp., 1974-76; dir. pastoral care Cape Breton Hosp., Sydney River, N.S., Can., 1978-81, Nova Scotia Hosp., Dartmouth, 1981-86, Misericordia Hosp., Edmonton, Alta., Can., 1986-91; pastoral counselor Assn. Pastoral Edn., Waltham, Mass., 1992-96, Emmanuel Coll., Boston, 1996—; supr. pastoral edn. Leland Retirement Home, Waltham, Mass., 1992—; vice chair bioethics consultative svc. Misericordia Hosp., Edmonton, 1987-91; vis. scholar Andover Newton Theol. Sch., 1991-92. Trustee Pastoral Inst., Halifax, N.S., Can., 1981-86; mem. commn. on ecumenism Archdiocese of Halifax, 1982-86; mem. of the Congregation of Sisters of St. Joseph, Boston, 1945—. Mem. Can. Assn. Pastoral Edn. (cert. com. 1987-91), Assn. for Clin. Pastoral Edn. (cert. supr., accreditation com. 1993-98, cert. com. 1998—). Roman Catholic. Avocations: international travel, classical music, art, reading. Home and Office: 16 Cutter St Waltham MA 02453-5911

DELANEY, MATTHEW SYLVESTER, mathematics educator, academic administrator; b. Ireland, Nov. 26, 1927; s. Joseph C. and Elizabeth M. (Bergin) D.; came to U.S., 1947, naturalized, 1952; student St. John's Coll., 1947-51; BA, Immaculate Heart Coll., L.A., 1958; MS, Notre Dame U., 1960; PhD, Ohio State U., 1971. Ordained priest Roman Cath. Ch., 1951; assoc. pastor L.A. Cath. Diocese, 1951-55; instr. math., physics Pius X High Sch., Downey, Calif., 1955-58, vice prin., 1960-62; instr. math. Immaculate Heart Coll., L.A., 1962-65, asst. prof., 1965-72, assoc. prof., 1972-76, prof., 1976—; asst. acad. dean, 1973-78; dean acad. devel. Mt. St. Mary's Coll., L.A., 1978-82, acad. dean, 1978-91; prof. math., 1991—, prof. emeritus, 1996—. NSF grantee, 1959-60, 61. Achievements include: Formal recognition of the eponyms, "Delaney Sets" and "The Delaney Symbol" in the disciplines of discrete geometry and math. crystallography, 1985. Mem. Internat. Union Crystallography, Am. Math. Soc., Math. Assn. Am., N.Y. Acad. Scis.. Democrat. Contbr. articles to math. publs., profl. jours. Home: Apt 32C 13700 El Dorado Dr Seal Beach CA 90740-3843 Office: Mount Saint Mary's Coll 12001 Chalon Rd Los Angeles CA 90049-1526

DELANGE, FRANÇOIS M., pediatrician; b. Brussels, June 6, 1935; s. Jacques and Louise (Miele) D.; m. Nicole Lavisse, Oct. 27, 1979; 4 children. MD, U. Brussels, 1960. Resident in pediatrics U. Brussels, 1965-72, dept., 1972-79, head clinics, 1979-82, prof. pediatrics, 1992—; exec. dir. Internat. Coun. for Control of Iodine Deficiency Disorders, Brussels, 1994—; cons. WHO, Geneva, UN Children's Fund, N.Y.C., European Cmty., Brussels, Internat. Atomic Energy Agy. Author: (with others) Endemic Goitre and Thyroid Function in Central Africa, 1974, Role of Cassava in the Etiology of Endemic Goiter and Cretinism, 1980, Nutritional Factors Involved in the Goitrogenic Action of Cassava, 1982, Cassava Toxicity and the Thyroid: Research and Public Health Issues, 1983, Pediatric Thyroidology, 1985, Research in Congenital Hypothyroidism, 1989, Iodine Deficiency in Europe: A Continuing Concern, 1993; contbr. over 300 articles to profl. jours. Mem. Belgian Soc. Pediatrics, Belgian Soc. Endocrinology, Belgian Thyroid Club, Am. Thyroid Assn., European Thyroid Assn., Asian and Oceania Thyroid Assn., Latin Am. Thyroid Soc., Société Française d'Endocrinologie, Internat. Coun. for Control Iodine Deficiency Disorders, Groupe de Recherches sur la Thyroïde, Assn. pour l'Etude du Goitre en Afrique et pays Francophones (v.p.). Home and Office: 153 Av.De la Fauconnerie, 1170 Brussels Belgium

DE LANGE, NORBERT HEINRICH, computer science educator, social science educator; b. Gelsenkirchen, Germany, July 15, 1953; s. Heinrich and Elisabeth (Wessel) de L.; m. Elisabeth Schütter, May, 1985; children: Johan, Dagmar. Grad., Ruhr U., Bochum, Germany, 1977; Dr.rer.nat., Westfälische Wilhelms U., Münster, Germany, 1979, habilitation, 1987. From asst. lectr. to lectr. Westfälische Wilhelms U., Münster, 1978-92, univ. prof., 1993-94; univ. prof. U. Osnabrück, Germany, 1994—. Office: Univ Osnabrück, Seminarstrasse 19, 49069 Osnabrück Germany

DE LANGE, PHILIP GERARDUS, mechanical engineer; b. Malang, Indonesia, Sept. 26, 1926; s. Arie Reinhard and Jaguilina Wilhelmina (Boer) De L.; m. Anthonina Aafje Van Der Berge, Apr. 6, 1950; children: Maria Wilhelmina, Victor Peter Anton. B of Mech. Engring., HTS, Rotterdam, 1950; DS, U. Leiden, 1991. Rsch. engr. Factory Small Arms, The Netherlands, 1957-60, Automobile Aircondition, Beyerland, The Netherlands, 1960-66; dir. Cons. Office, Haarlem, The Netherlands, 1966-69, Riswik, The Netherlands, 1969-73; sr. mech. engr. Fluor/Daniel, Haarlem, 1973-85. Co-author, editor: Orde en Vrede, 1997. Lt. Royal Dutch Navy, 1943-55. Mem. Internat. Inst. Asian Studies, Royal Inst. Linguistics and Anthropology, N.Y. Acad. Scis. Home: Diakenhuisney 112, 2033 AS Haarlem The Netherlands

DELANGHE, JORIS RICHARD, chemistry educator; b. Zelzate, Flanders, Belgium, July 22, 1957; s. Edward Jules Delanghe and Maria Josephina Verstraeten; m. Agnes Irma Vanhoof, July 4, 1984; children: Sigurd, Astrid. MD, U. Gent, Belgium, Clin. Pathologist, PhD. Hosp. physician City Hosp., Bruges, Belgium, 1982-83, Univ. Hosp., Louvain, Belgium, 1983-84; asst. U. Hosp., Gent, 1984-94, profl., 1994—. Patentee on early diagnosis of myocardial infarction, 1987. Mem. Belgian Soc. for Clin. Chemistry (pres. 1995—, Jr. Investigator award 1990), Am. Soc. Clin. Chemistry. Roman Catholic. Office: U Z Gent de Pintelaan 185, B-9000 Ghent Belgium

DELANNOY, ERIC, advertising executive; b. Libercourt, France, May 2, 1962; s. Rene and Jeannette (Zemmel) D.; m. Nicole Cabannes, Sept. 2, 1989; children: Alexis, Maxime. MBA, HEC, Jouy en Josas, France, 1984. Acct. exec. Leo Burnett, Paris, 1986-88, acct. dir., 1988-90, dep. mng. dir., 1990-93, mng. dir., 1993-97; mng. dir. BDDP, Paris, 1997-98; CEO BDDP@TBWA, Paris, 1999—; bd.d irs. TBWA Worldwide. Mem. Assn. French Advt. Agys. (bd. dirs. 1998—). Avocations: golf, scuba diving, rugby, internet. Home: 39 Ave du Roule, 92200 Nevilly/Seine France Office: BDDP TBWA, 162 164 Rue de Billancourt, 92700 Boulogne Billancourt France

DELANO, JIMMY GBOYEGA, business executive, accountant; b. Ibadan, Ogun State, Nigera, Dec. 29, 1953; s. Isaac Oluwole and Adepeju; m. Bolaji Bamidele (Sogbetun) Delano, July 11, 1981; children: Ladipo, Adepeju, Omorinsola, Oyedola. ACCA, London Sch. Acctg., 1982; MBA, South Bank U., London, 1982; MA, South Bank U., 1987. Bus. devel. mgr. Gillette Internat., 1983-90; gen. bus. mgr. Polaid Internat., 1990-93; v.p. internat. Soft Sheen Products divsn. L'Oreal; dir. treasury Immigration Adv. Svc., Longon, 1997-99. Home: 119 Graymoor Ln Olympia Fields IL 60461-1204

DELANO-CONDAX, KATE (KATE DELANO CONDAX DECKER), marketing and public relations executive; b. Phila., Mar. 23, 1945; d. John and Laura Foster (Delano) C. Student, Sweet Briar Coll., 1964-67, U. St. Andrews, Scotland, 1966-67, U. Pa., 1975-76. Legis. aide to Sen. Samuel J. Ervin, Jr. Subcom. Separation of Powers, Com. on Judiciary U.S. Senate, Washington, 1970-73; ptnr. U.S. Trade Trip to People's Republic China, 1973; assoc. producer, asst. dir. KYW-TV, Phila., 1973-74; account exec. Aitkin, Kynett Pub. Rels., Phila., 1975-77, ICPR Pub. Rels., N.Y.C., 1977-79; dir. pub. rels. Am. Heritage Pub. Co., Inc., N.Y.C., 1979-81; account exec. Howard J. Rubenstein Pub. Rels., Inc., N.Y.C., 1981-82; rsch. assoc. Nordeman Grimm Exec. Search Firm, N.Y.C., 1982-84; pres. Kate Delano Condax & Assocs. Mktg., N.Y.C., 1984-89; nat. dir. mktg. and pub. rels. Allmilmo Corp., Fairfield, N.J., 1989-92; mktg. and media cons.; exec. dir. Philadelphia 100; pres. Pet Bulls, Inc. Author: Horse Sense: Cause and Correction of Problems, 1979, 2d edit., 1990, Riding: A Guide for New Riders, 1995, 4th edit., 1999, 101 Training Tips for Your Dog, 1994, 6th edit., 1997. Probono housing counselor to elderly, N.Y.C., 1980—; bd. dirs., mktg. dir. Interfaith Caregivers, 1993—; dir. pub. affairs Recording for the Blind & Dyslexic, Princeton, N.J., 1995-97. Mem. Brit. Horse Soc. (instr.), Am. Horse Shows Assn. (ex-officio, judge), Soc. Mayflower Descendants, Nat. Soc. Colonial Dames Am., Acorn Club, Coffee House Club N.Y. Office: 314 E Central Ave Moorestown NJ 08057-3637

DELANO SMITH, CATHERINE, humanities researcher; b. Wallingford, Eng., Mar. 31, 1940. BA with honors, U. Oxford, Eng., 1962; BLitt, U. Oxford, 1965, DPhil, 1974. Asst. lectr. U. Durham, Eng., 1964-67; lectr. U. Nottingham, Eng., 1967-79, sr. lectr., 1979-89, reader, 1989-90; rsch. fellow U. London, 1993—. Author: Dauna Vetus, 1978, Western Mediterranean Europe, 1979; co-author: (catalogue) Maps in Bibles 1500-1600, 1991, (textbook) English Cartography, 1997, English Maps. A History, 1999; editor: Imago Mundi, 1994—; contbr. articles to profl. publs. Recipient Chevalier of Order of Merit of Grand Duchy of Luxembourg, 1971. Fellow Royal Geog. Soc., Soc. Antiquaries. Home and Office: 285 Nether St, London N3 1PD, England

DELAP, J. Q., JR., gas company executive; b. Liberal, Kans., May 29, 1948; s. J.Q. and Estella Fern (Cook) D.; m. Ellen Rubin, Oct. 22, 1983; children: J.Q. (Jake), Tiffani Jaye. BSME, Rose-Hulman Inst., 1970; MBA, Pepperdine U., 1978. Engr. Panhandle Eastern Pipeline Co., Kansas City, Mo., 1970-74; mgr. hydrocarbon sales Anadarko Prodn. Co., Houston, 1974-76; mgr. gas liquids acquisition No. Gas Products Co., Houston, 1976-77; mgr. gas supply Gulf Coast region Farmland Industries, Inc.; crude oil rep. Gulf Coast region CRA, Inc., Houston, 1977-79; pres. La. Energy and Devel. Corp., New Orleans, 1979-92, Loutex Energy Inc., 1980-92, Delta Gas Inc., 1980-92, La. State Gas Corp., 1981-92, Gas Systems Network, Inc., 1981-92, NorthCan Energy, Inc., 1981-92; founder, owner ENERGY Internat. Corp., 1992—. Bd. advisors Rose-Hulman Inst., 1980. Mem. ASME, Am. Gas Assn., La. Gas Assn. (bd. dirs.), Natural Gas Men of Houston, Am. Petroleum Inst., Ind. Prodrs. Assn. Am., Tex. Ind. Prodrs. and Royalty Owners, Pipeliners Assn. of Houston, Houston Energy Fin. Group, Houston Prodrs. Forum, Natural Gas Men of New Orleans, Petroleum Club (Houston). Presbyterian. Home: 2115 Forest Falls Dr Humble TX 77345-1778 Office: PO Box 6690 Kingwood TX 77325-6690

DELAPALME, BERNARD M.J., naval architect, engineer; b. Paris, May 23, 1923; s. Marcel and Simone (Gaveau) D.; m. Eveline Balay, May 5, 1956; children: Nathalie, Pauline, Pierre Louis, Matthieu, Charles. Engr., Ecole Poly., Paris, 1946, Ecole Nat. du Genie Maritime, Paris, 1949. Prof. elec. Ecole Nationale du Genie Maritime, 1951-56; dep. dir. Ctr. d'Etudes Nucleaire, Grenoble, France, 1956-64; gen. mgr. Rhone Alpes Cy, Lyon, France, 1964-72; from. v.p. rsch. to spl. advisor to pres. Elf Aquitaine, Paris, 1972-88; spl. advisor to pres. Lyonnnaise Des Eaux, Paris, 1988-93; cons. in field, 1988—; pres. Elf Techs., 1982-88. Fellow AAAS; mem. European Indsl. Rsch. Mgmt. Assn. (pres. 1974-77), Assn. Nat. Rsch. Tech. (pres. 1975-80), European Roundtable of Industrialists (assoc.). Avocations: golf, photography, gardening. Home: 28 Rue Scheffer, 75116 Paris France

DE LA PAZ, ADRIANO DE GUZMAN, internist, cardio-nephrologist, educator; b. Marikina, The Philippines, Sept. 16, 1935; s. Andres Eustaquio and Juliana Francisco (De Guzman) De La P.; m. Esperanza Reyes Querubin, Mar. 9, 1968; 1 child, Adrianne Marie Q. Med. degree, U. of The Philippines, 1961. Cert. career exec. svc. officer IV. Head dept. clin. rsch. Philippine Heart Ctr., 1975-86, asst. dir., 1996—; med. ctr. chief East Ave. Med. Ctr., The Philippines, 1986-92; asst. dean UERMMMC, The Philippines, 1981-83, asst. prof., 1985-95, assoc. prof. dept. medicine, 1995—. Editor-in-chief: Jour. Philippine Med. Assn., Clin. Update; assoc. editor: Philippine Jour. Cardiology, Philippine Jour. Nephrology. Pres. Marikina Jaycees, The Philippines, 1972, Rotary Club Marikina, The Philippines, 1977-78, Marikina Rotary Found., The Philippines, 1978-86, Marikina Heritage Found., The Philippines, 1985-88. Recipient Golden award in field of medicine Philippine Jaycees Senate, 1989, Most Outstanding Physician Philippine Med. Assn., 1973. Fellow Philippine Coll. Physicians (diplomate, pres. 1981-82, Disting. Fellow award 1994), Philippine Coll. Cardiology (diplomate, pres. 1982-83), Philippine Soc. Nephrology (diplomate, pres. 1984-86), Philippine Heart Assn. (pres. 1982-83, Disting. Scientist award 1994), Am. Coll. Cardiology, Rizal Med. Soc. (pres. 1972-73). Mem. Philippine Ind. Ch. Avocations: sports, reading, watching TV. Home: 198 E De La Paz, 1800 Marikina The Philippines Office: Philippine Heart Ctr, East Ave, 1104 Quezon City The Philippines

DE LA PEÑA, JOSE ABEL, plastic and reconstructive surgeon; b. Mexico City, Mex., Apr. 15, 1958; s. Abel and Rosa Martha (Salcedo) De La P.; m. Maria Barrigon, June 10, 1989. MD, U. Autonoma Metropolitana, 1976; plastic surgery, Hosp. Gen. Del Sur, 1986. Dir. Cleft Lip and Palate Clinic, Guanajuato, Mex., 1985-96; anatomy prof. Gen. Hosp., Mexico City, 1988-96, cons. physician, 1990-95; cons. physician Nat. Inst. of Cardiology, Mexico City, 1995-96; dir. Inst. for Plastic Surgery, Mexico City, 1995-96; pres. Asociacion de Residentes Y Ex Residentes, 1996; cons. physician Nat. Inst. Cardiology, Mexico City, 1995—; dir. Inst. plastic Surgery, Mexico City, 1995—. Contbr. articles to profl. jours. Fellow ACS; mem. Asociacion Mexicana de Cirugia Plastica Y Reconst., Internat. Soc. of Aesthetic Plastic Surgery. Avocations: golf, reading, travelling. Office: Acueducto Rio Hondo No 26, Lomas Virreyes, 11000 Mexico City Mexico

DE LA PEÑA, LUIS AUERBACH, physicist, educator; b. San Martin Puebla, Mex., July 23, 1931; s. Jose Antonio De La Peña and Blanca Auerbach; m. Valentina Campa, Nov. 20, 1957 (div. 1966); 1 child, Ireri; m. Ana Maria Cetto, Dec. 13, 1968; 1 child, Carolina. Elec. engr., Nat. Polytech. Mex., 1959; D of Math. Physics, State U. Moscow, 1964. Design engr. GAMSA, Mexico City, 1955-57; assoc. rschr., rsch. prof. Inst. de Fisica, Mexico City, 1958-94, emeritus prof., 1994—; cons. Nat. Inst. Nuclear Rsch., Mexico City, 1972-79, Light Mus. Sci. Ctr., 1994—; vis. prof. U. Rome, 1984-85, U. Santander, 1985, U. London, 1992-94, U. Paris VI, 1977-78. Author: Introduction to Quantum Mechanics, 1971, 91, Einstein, Lonely Sailor, 1987; co-author: The Quantum Dice: Introduction to Stochastic Electrodynamics, 1996, The Physical Sciences: Genesis and Evolution of Fundamental Concepts (Spanish edit.), 1999 ; editor: The Philosophy Behind Physics, 1993; contbr. articles to profl. jours. Nat. Rsch. fellow Ministry of Edn., 1984—; recipient Rsch. award UNAM, 1989. Fellow Third World Acad. Scis.; mem. Am. Phys. Soc., Mex. Phys. Soc. (v.p. 1967-69, Acad. medal 1984), Mex. Epistemology Soc. (pres. 1976-77), Mex. Acad. Scis. Home: Retorno Cerro Del Agua 98, 04360 Mexico City Mexico Office: Inst de Fisica UNAM, Apartado Postal 20-364, 01000 Mexico City Mexico

DE LA PIEDRA, JORGE, orthopedic surgeon; b. Peru, Feb. 11, 1923; came to U.S., 1960, naturalized, 1963; s. Luis G. and Rosa M. (Quinones) de la P.; m. June M. Daugherty, May 1, 1955; children: Ana Maria, Jorge Antonio, James Michael. Grad., U. de San Marcos, Lima, Peru, 1942, MD, 1960. Diplomate Am. Bd. Orthopedic Surgery, Am. Bd. Profl. Disability Cons. Intern Army Hosp., Lima, 1951-52; rotating intern Augustana Hosp., Chgo., 1952-53; resident in orthopedic surgery St. Francis Hosp., Peoria, Ill., 1953-54, Charlotte (N.C.) Meml. Hosp., 1954-57; fellow in orthop. divsn. Duke U. Hosp., 1956-57; acting chief orthopedic dept. Social Security Adminstrn. Hosp. 1, Lima, 1958-59; orthopedic surgen Mullens (W.Va.) Hosp., 1960-66; practice medicine specializing in orthopedic surgery, Princeton, W.Va., 1966—; mem. staff Princeton Cmty. Hosp., 1966—. Served with Peruvian Army, 1951-52. Recipient award Disting. Physicians of Am. Fellow Internat. Coll. Surgeons, Am. Acad. Disability Evaluating Physicians; mem. AMA (Physician's award 1969, 72-74, 77, 80, 84), W.Va. State Med. Assn., Mercer County Med. Soc., Am. Fracture Assn., So. Med. Soc., Latin Am. Soc. Orthopedic Surgeons, Orthopedic Rsch. and Edn. Found. (life), Peruvian Acad. Surgery, So. Orthopedic Soc., W.Va. Orthopedic Soc., Peruvian Am. Med. Soc., Nat. Assn. Disability Evaluating Physicians (charter), K.C. Roman Catholic.

DELAPLAINE, GEORGE BIRELY, JR., newspaper editor, cable television executive; b. Frederick, Md., Dec. 9, 1926; s. George B. and Ruth (Carty) D.; m. Elizabeth Barker, Aug. 12, 1955; children: George III, James, Edward, John. BBA, Johns Hopkins U., 1948. From reporter to publisher Frederick News-Post, 1949—; v.p. Frederick Brick Works, Inc., 1989—; chmn. bd. GS Communications. Named Honorary Am. Farmer Nat. Future Farmers Am., 1987; recipient Disting. Eagle Scout award, 1997. Mem. Kiwanis, Eagles, Jaycees, Masons. Republican. Episcopalian. Office: Frederick News-Post 200 E Patrick St Frederick MD 21701-5632

DELAPORTE, JACQUES, archbishop; b. Roye-Sur-Matz, Oise, France, Oct. 11, 1926; s. Fernand and Léonie (de Saint Quentin) D. Grad., Gregorian Pontifical U., Rome; diplome, École Des Hautes Études Commerciales. Cert. civil law, theology. Diocesian chaplain Beauvais, France, 1955-62; chaplain Paris, 1962-69; parish priest St. Jean Baptiste, Beauvais, 1969-71; arch-priest Compiègne, 1971-76; auxiliary bishop Nancy, France, 1976-80; archbishop Cambrai, France, 1980—; pres. Commn. Épiscopale des Migrations, 1982-88, Commn. Justice et Paix, 1988—. Author: Oser L'Espérance, 1989, L'Immigration, Le Coeur et La Raison, 1990, Le Coeur du Christ icone de Dieu, 1998. Avocation: tennis. Office: 11 rue du Grand Seminaire BP149, 59403 Cambrai France*

DE LA RENTA, OSCAR, fashion designer; b. Santo Domingo, Dominican Republic, July 22, 1932; s. Oscar and Maria Antonia (deFiallo) de LaR.; m. Francoise de Langlade, Oct. 31, 1967 (dec. 1983); 1 adopted child, Moises; m. Anne E. de la Renta, Dec. 26, 1989. Student, Santo Domingo U., Academia de San Fernando, Madrid. Mem. staff Balenciaga's AISA, Madrid; asst. to Antonio Castillo at Lanvin, Paris, 1961-63; chief designer Elizabeth Arden, N.Y.C., 1963-65; chief designer, chmn. bd. dirs. Oscar de la Renta, Ltd., N.Y.C., 1973—; designer Pierre Balmain, Paris, 1993—. Bd. dirs. La Casa del Nino Orphanage and Sch., Santo Domingo, Met. Opera, Carnegie Hall, Thirteen/WNET, Hispanic Designers, Spanish Inst. Decorated Order Juan Pablo Duarte, Order Cristobal Colon (Dominican Republic); recipient Coty awards, 1967, 68, Golden Tiberius award, 1968, Received Lifetime of Achievement award The Coun. of Fashion Designers of Am., 1990; Neiman-Marcus award, 1968; Fragrance Found. award 1978; Living Legend award Am. Soc. Perfumers, 1995; named to City Hall of Fame, 1973. Mem. Coun. Fashion Designers Am. (bd. dirs.). Office: Oscar de la Renta Ltd 550 7th Ave Fl 8 New York NY 10018-3207*

DELARGE, JACQUES ELIE, pharmacist, medical educator; b. Herstal, Belgium, Apr. 30, 1938; s. Arnold and Elisa (Cabolet) D.; m. Eva Anne Scheer, Apr. 24, 1962; children: Christian, Roger, Françoise. Diploma in Pharmacy, U. Liege, Belgium, 1961; diploma in Indsl. Pharmacy, U. Liege, 1965, D in Pharm. Scis., 1969. Asst. researcher U. Liege, 1961-68, sr. researcher, 1968-71, head of rsch., 1971-87, prof. medicinal chemistry, 1987—. Contbr. articles to profl. jours. Patentee in field. Recipient Specia award, 1961, Belgium Soc. of Pharm. Scis. award, 1973, Acad. of Medicine award, 1978. Mem. Drugs Registration Com (exec. com. 1989—), European Soc. Medicinal Chemistry. Office: U Liege, CHU Tour 4 Niv 5, Ave de L'Hopital 1, B-4000 Liege Belgium

DÉ LA ROCHA, JOSÉ JULIÁN, physician assistant; b. Santo Domingo, Dominican Republic, Nov. 14, 1952; came to U.S., 1965; s. Julio Ceasar dé la Rocha and Maria Altagracia (Cambero) dé la Rocha Guillandeaux; m. Jane Ann Grzanowski, Dec. 15, 1975 (div.); children: Tania Anayansi, Aliccia Francesca; m. Sevtap Buker, Feb. 14, 1996; stepchildren: Jasmine Lewis, Elcin Lewis. Student, Columbia U., 1973-77; AA, Anne Atundel C.C., Arnold, Md., 1983; BA, SUNY, Albany, 1985; BS with honors, U. Okla., 1992. ACLS; PALS. Enlisted USAF, 1979, advanced through grades to 1st lt., 1992; clin. specialist U.S. Army 10th MASH, Ft. Meade, Md., 1979-85; EMT U.S. Army Kimbrough Hosp., Ft. Meade, Md., 1985-87; combat medicine specialist Md. Army N.G., Balt., 1987-91; rsch. physician asst. Facilitator of Applied Clin. Trials, San Antonio, 1992-96; physician

asst. emergency med./family practice 6th Med. Group USAF, McDill AFB, Fla., 1992—; physician asst. Am. Health Choice/Rural Health Clinic, Von Ormy, Tex., 1996-97, U. Health Sys. Family Health Ctr./S.E., San Antonio, 1997; asst. clin. instr. health sci. ctr. U. Tex., San Antonio, 1997; physician asst. Folkman's Family Practice, Tampa, Fla., 1998-99, Brookins Internal Medicine, Tampa, 1998—, Jeffrey Miller MD, Tampa, 1999—; pres., CEO, JCorp Med. Mgmt. and Preventive Medicine Inst., Tampa; assoc. med. provider in family practice Gables Point Med. Group, Tampa; assoc. provider in emergency medicine EM-CARE, Inc., Clearwater, Fla. Rep. candidate from 28th Tex. dist. for Ho. of Reps., 1997-98. Med. officer USAFR. Decorated Expert Field Med. badge. FEllow Am. Acad. Physician Assts., Soc. Mil. Surgeons, Soc. Air Force Physician Assts. Home: 1108 W Indiana Ave Tampa FL 33603-4508 Office: James O Brookins MD Internal Medicine 4728 N Habana Ave Ste 202 Tampa FL 33614-7147 also: Jeffrey Miller MD Rheumatology/Internal Medicine 3218 W Azeelo St Tampa FL 33609 also: Gables Point Med Group 1914 W Martin L King Blvd Tampa FL 33607 also: EM-CARE Inc 18167 US Highway 19 N Clearwater FL 33764

DE LA ROCHA MARIE, JAVIER, bank executive; b. Lima, Peru, Dec. 16, 1944; s. Leoncio de la Rocha Zavaleta and Odette Marie Rousseau; children: Rumi de la Rocha Carbone, Miquel de la Rocha Carbone. BA in Econs., Catholic U. Peru, Lima, 1968; MA in Econs. of Fin., U. Toulouse, France, 1982. Asst. acctg. dept. Interna. Revenue Svc., Lima, 1962; asst. adminstrv. dept. Nat. Telecomm., Lima, 1963-68; analyst pub. fin. dept. Econ. Rsch. Bur. Ctrl. Reserve Bank Peru, Lima, 1968-76, chief dept. ctrl. govt. analysis, 1977-78, cons., 1979-81, chief dept. current affairs global analysis, 1982, v.p. global analysis, 1983-85, v.p. real sector analysis, 1986, sr. v.p. Econ. Rsch. Bur., 1987-89, sr. v.p. Treasury Bur., 1990, gen. mgr., 1991—; cons. World Bank, Lima, 1990, Macroconsult, Lima, 1990; dir. Fin. Devel. Corp. COFIDE, Lima, 1990-91. Author: Reaction Capacity and the Elasticity of the Peruvian Tax System, 1977, The International Monetary Fund's Economic Reordering Experiment in Peru, 1979. Home: Jr Jose R Valencia No 782 Magdalena, Lima Peru Office: Banco Ctrl Reserva del Peru, Miro Quesada 441, Lima 1, Peru*

DE-LA-ROSA, JORGE LUIS, biologist, researcher; b. Mexico City, Mar. 4, 1967; s. José Luis de-la-Rosa and Amalia Arana-de-De-la-Rosa; m. Raquel Tapia, Mar. 28, 1998. Degree in biology, Nat. Autonomous U. Mex., Mexico City, 1992, diploma in parasitology, 1995, MS, 1997. Chief of lab. Nat. Inst. Diagnostic Epidemiology, Mexico City, 1995-97, head zoonosis dept., 1997—. Author: Trichinellosis, 1992; contbr. articles to profl. jours. Verano de la Investigacion scholar, Baja California, Mex., 1991; Investigation Cientifica Rsch. grantee, Mexico City, 1998. Mem. Mex. Soc. Parasitology, Colegio Biol. Mex. Avocations: soccer, camping, swimming, squash. Office: Nat Inst Diagnost Epidemiol, Carpio 470 Colonia St Tomas, 11340 Mexico City Mexico

DE LAROSIÈRE DE CHAMPFEU, JACQUES MARTIN HENRI MARIE, bank executive; b. France, Nov. 12, 1929; m. France du Bos, 1960; 2 children: Henri, Laure. B Arts and Law, U. Paris; diploma, Inst. d'Etudes Politiques, Paris; student, Ecole Nat. d'Administration. Insp. fin. Govt. of France, 1958-61; chargé de mission Inspectorate-Gen. of Fin., 1961-63; chargé de mission Treasury, 1965-67, asst. dir., 1967; dep. dir., head dept. MInistry of Econs. and Fin., 1971-74; pvt. sec. to Minister Econs. and Fin., 1974; dir. Treasury, 1974-78, chmn. dps. of fin. Group of Ten, 1976-78, insp. gen. of fin., 1981—; mng. dir. IMF, Washington, 1978-87; chmn. com. of govs. Group of Ten, 1990; gov. Bank of France, 1987-93; pres. European Bank Reconstruction and Devel., London, 1993-98; Advisor to Paribas, 1998—; chmn. Per Jacobsson Found., 1999; trustee Reuters Founders Share Co. Ltd., 1999; pres. Observatoire de l'Epargne Européenne, 1999; dir. Renault, Banque Nationale de Paris, Air France, French Rys.; Société Nationale Industrielle Aerospatiale, 1974-78; Power Corp., 1998; Alstom, 1998; France Telecom, 1998. Decorated comdr. Legion of Honor, chevalier Nat. Order of Merit (France); Order of the Sacred Treasure (Japan); Order of Merit (Argentina); Order of Merit (Italy); Order of the Aztec Eagle (Mex.); cross grand officer Order of Merit (Germany); comdr. Order of Merit (Poland); Order of Friendship (Russia); comdr. Order of Merit (Hungary); knight comdr. Order Brit. Empire; Order of the Brilliant Star (Taiwan); Staria Platina (Bulgaria); Brazilian Order of the So. Cross, 1999.

DE LA RUA, FERNANDO, president of Argentina; b. Córdoba, Argentina, Sept. 15, 1937; m. Inés Pertiné; 3 children. LLD, U. Códoba. Advisor Ministry of Interior, Argentina, 1963-66; sen. Fed. Capital, Argentina, 1973-76; nat. sen. Argentina, 1983-89, 92-96; 1st chief of govt. Buenos Aires, 1996-99; pres. of Argentina, 1999—. Pres. bloc of nat. deps. Radical Civic Union, 1992—. Office: Office of Pres, Casa de Gobierno Balarce 50, 1064 Buenos Aires Argentina*

DE LA SELLE, ALBAN, banker; b. Lyon, France, May 2, 1966; s. Christian and Brigitte (Vollant) De La S.; m. Isabelle Saint Olive, July 20, 1991; children: Manon, Tristan. M in Econs. with highest distinction, U. Paris II, 1989; postgrad., Grad. Bus. Sch., Lyon, 1991. Fin. contr. Steelcase Strafor, London, 1992-94; mgr. Hill Samuel Bank, London, 1994-97; v.p. Dexia Internat., Paris, 1997—; cons., advisor Caravan, Paris, 1997—. Home: 114 rue Paul Vaillant, Couturier, 92240 Malakoff France Office: Dexia Internat Bank, 76 rue de la Victoire, F75320 Paris Cedex 09, France

DE LA TORRE, SATURNINO, education educator, researcher; b. Canalejas de Peñafiel, Valladolid, Spain, Oct. 16, 1941; s. Rufino and Rufina de la Torre; m. Rosario Frade, Apr. 14, 1973; children: Fernando, Ana. Degree in philosophy and letters, U. Barcelona, Spain, 1973, diploma in edn. tech., 1974, PhD in Edn. Scis., 1980. Elem. tchr. EGB, 1968-71; secondary tchr. BUP, 1971-74; prof. profl. tng. Poly. Inst., Barcelona, 1973-80, dir. dept. humanities, 1977-79, dir. dept. cultural ext., 1979-80; prof. Faculty Philosophy and Edn. Sci. U. Barcelona, 1974-80, temp. prof., 1980-85, prof. tchg. methodology and ednl. orgn., 1985—, dir. doctoral programs Faculty Edn. Sci., 1986—, prof. tchr. tng. and ednl. innovation, 1992—; cons. Inst. Leonardo Torres Quevedo, Madrid, 1984-87; sch. assessor, Barcelona, 1993—; internat. assessor creativity Foundator Internat. Creativity Network, 1997. Author: Educar en la creatividad, 1987, Evaluation of Creativity, 1991, Aprender de los errores, 1993, Didactics and Curriculum, 1993, Curriculum Innovation, 1994, Applice Creativity, 1995, Cine Formativo, 1996, For Creativity Research, 1996, Creatividad y Formación, 1997, Innovación Educativa, 1997; co-author: Manual of Creativity, 1991, Errores y Curriculum, 1994, Strategies of Simulation, 1997, Cine Para la Vida, 1998, Cómo Innovar Entos Centrós, 1998, also others; co-author: Estrategias didácticas innovadas, 2000. Mem. Spanish Edn. Soc., Catalan Edn. Soc., European Forum Acad. Orientation, Found. for Devel. Creativity (founding), Found. Internat. Creativity Network. Avocations: travel, art. Home: C/ Felipe de Paz 13 6 2a, 08028 Barcelona Spain Office: U Barcelona Faculty Edn, P Vall d'Hebron 171, 08035 Barcelona Spain

DELAUNAY, CHRISTIAN PIERRE ANDRÉ, orthopaedic surgeon, consultant; b. Tonnerre, France, July 1, 1953. MD, U. Paris, 1983, Orthopaedic Surgeon. Surg. intern Assistance Publique, Paris, 1979-83, clin. chief orthopaedic surgery, 1983-87, asst. in orthopaedic surgery, 1987-92; joint replacement fellow UCLA, 1986; orthopaedic surgeon Clinique de l'Yvette, Longjumeau, France, 1987—; cons. Sulzer Orthopedics, France, 1996—. Mem. French Orthopaedic Surgery Soc., European Hip Soc., Internat. Soc. Orthopaedic Surgery, Am. Acad. Orthopaedic Surgeons (internat. affiliate). Avocation: music. Office: Clinique de l'Yvette, 43 Route de Corbeil, 91160 Longjumeau France

DELAVEAU, PIERRE GEORGES, biologist, pharmacologist, educator; b. Charenton le Pont, France, June 4, 1921; s. Georges Delaveau and Suzanne Neuville; m. Christiane Gautier, June 18, 1949; children: Philippe, Jean, Françoise, Louis. B, Lycée Claude Bernard, Paris, 1939; D in Pharmacy, 1953; MD, Faculty Medicine, Paris, 1954; PhD, U. Paris, 1967; D.Honoris Causa, U. Liege, Belgium. Intern Hosp. Pub. Adminstrn., Paris, 1943-48; asst. in pharmacology Faculty Medicine, Paris, 1946-48; chargé rsch. Inst. Nat. Rsch., Agronomie, 1948-52; biologist Foch Hosp., Suresnes, 1952-77; agregate prof. Edn. Nat., Rouen, 1958-60; prof. Edn. Nat., Paris, 1960-87; expert pharmacology French Min. Health; chmn. commn. pharmacognosy Pharmacopoeia, 1963-88; mem. commn. authorization mktg. official drugs, 1980-88. Author/co-author 15 books for sci. broad edn.; dir. editor Dictionnaire des Sciences pharmaceutiques et biologiques of the Nat. Acad. Pharmacy, 3 vols., 1997. Mem. Internat. Group Polyphenols (chmn. 1982-84), Bot. Soc. France (chmn. 1987-89), Nat. Acad. Pharmacy (chmn. 1999), Nat. Acad. Medicine, Nat. Acad. Dental Surgery, Koninklijke Academie voor Geneeskunde van Belgium (hon. assoc.). Avocations: plant photography, gardening. Home: 13 rue Soufflot, 75005 Paris France

DELBEKE, FRANS T.M.C., chemistry educator; b. Poperinge, Flanders, Belgium, Sept. 6, 1945; s. Albert and Yvonne (Coutteure) D.; children: Barbara, Jochen. Dr Chemistry, State U. Ghent, Belgium, 1973. Asst. State U. Ghent, 1967-75, sr. asst., 1975-91, prof. chemistry, 1991—; ofcl. doping analyst, 1973—. Fellow Assn. Ofcl. Racing Chemists (v.p. 1992-94, sec./treas. 1998—, chmn. European sect. 1999-2000). Office: Dept Pharmacology Doping Lab, Salisburylaan 133, Merelbeke B-9820, Belgium

DELBOUILLE, PAUL, educator; b. Chenee, Belgium, Mar. 7, 1933; s. Maurice D.; m. Monique Mathot, Apr. 13, 1957 (dec. Oct. 1990); children: Catherine, Sylvie; m. Martine Willems, Jan. 30, 1999. D of Romance Philology, U. Liege, 1959. Asst. prof. U. Liege, Belgium, 1959-78, prof., 1978-98, dean Faculty Philosophy and Letters, 1980-86. Author: Poesie et Sonorites, 1984; editor: Complete Works of Benjamin Constant, 1993. Home: Thier de la Fouarge 14, B-4653 Bolland Belgium

DELBOURGO, ROBERT, physics educator; b. Bombay, Nov. 11, 1940; arrived in Australia, 1976; s. Sabatino and Yvette (Barki) D.; m. Elizabeth Mary Wilkinson; children: Tino, Daniel. BSc with 1st class honors, Imperial Coll., London, 1960, PhD, 1963; DSc, London U., 1976. Rsch. assoc. U. Wis., 1963-64; rsch. scientist ICTP, Trieste, Italy, 1964-65; guest scientist Weizmann Inst., Israel, 1965-66; lectr., reader Imperial Coll., 1966-76; prof. U. Tasmania, Australia, 1976—, dean Sci. Faculty,, 1989-91, dean grad. studies, 1992-96. Contbr. over 200 articles to profl. publs. Fellow Australian Acad. Sci. (chmn. nat. com. physics 1994-97, Thomas Ranken Lyle medal 1989), Australian Inst. Physics (Walter Boas medal 1988). Avocations: computing, table tennis, go. Office: U Tasmania Dept Physics, GPO Box 252-21 Sandy Bay, Hobart TAS 7001, Australia

DEL CASTILLO, JOSE MARIA, mechanical engineer, educator; b. Seville, Spain, Dec. 24, 1965; s. Jose Del Castillo and Purificacion Granados. MS in Engring., U. Seville, 1989, PhD in Mech. Engring., 1994. Rschr. U. Ruhr, Bochum, Germany, 1989-90, U. Seville, 1991-94; vis. scholar U. Calif., Berkeley, 1994-95; assoc. prof. mech. engring. U. Extremadura, Badajoz, Spain, 1995—; tng. engr. Aguas y Estructuras, Seville, 1990. Contbr. articles to profl. jours. European Union grantee, 1988-89; Spanish Ministry of Edn. scholar, 1995. Avocations: music, hiking, micology. Fax: 34-24-289601. E-mail: delcasti@unex.es. Home: Jesus Rincon 15 5-A, 06010 Badajoz Spain Office: Sch Indsl Engring, CRTA de Elvas s/n, 06071 Badajoz Spain

DELCROIX, JEAN-CLAUDE, management consultant; b. Kortrijk, Belgium, May 12, 1947; s. Jean Henri and Denise (Meulenbergh) D.; m. Genevieve Cambier, Sept. 27, 1969; children: Valerie, Nathalie, Marc. MCE, U. Louvain, 1970, B in Econs., 1972. Cert. civil engr. Researcher Credit Communal of Belgium, Brussels, 1972-74; adviser State Sec. for Economy, Brussels, 1974-75; operational dir. Prime Minister's Office, Brussels, 1975-85; dir. studies Bur. van Dijk, Brussels, 1985-92; pres. DECADE SA/NV, 1992-2000; rsch. dir. Gartner Group, Zaventem, Belgium, 2000—. Author: Solid Waste, 1974, The Car in the City, 1978, (French) Mastering Internet, 1997; contbr. articles to profl. jours. Bd. dirs. Effective Public Svc., Brussels, 1990. Mem. Soc. for Corp. Planners, European Internet Industry Assn. (bd. dirs. 1991—, pres. 1998-2000), Belgian Cons. Assn. (bd. dirs. 1991—). Avocation: sailing, art. Home: Rue Franz Merjay 117, B1050 Brussels Belgium

DEL DUCA, RITA, educator; b. N.Y.C., Apr. 1, 1933; d. Joseph and Ermelinda (Buonaguro) Ferraro; m. Joseph Anthony Del Duca, Oct. 29, 1955; children: Lynn, Susan, Paul, Andrea. BA, CUNY, 1955. Elem. tchr. Yonkers (N.Y.) Pub. Schs., 1955-57; tchr. kindergarten Sacred Heart Sch., Yonkers, 1962-64; tchr. piano, Scarsdale, N.Y., 1973-79; asst. office mgr. Foot Clinic, Hartsdale, N.Y., 1977-85; tchr. ESL, Linguarama Exec. Sch., White Plains, N.Y., 1985-89; ESL tutor, Scarsdale, 1989—. Dist. leader Greenburgh (N.Y.) Rep. Com., 1991-92. Mem. ASCAP. Avocations: oil painting, piano teaching, tennis, theatre arts. Home and Office: 10 Old Jackson Ave Unit 66 Hastings Hdsn NY 10706-3231

DELECOURT, PHILIPPE MAURICE, portfolio manager; b. Saint-Maixent Deux-Sevres, France, Nov. 14, 1947; s. Maurice and Yvonne (Darras) D.; m. Alix Marie Pierre Des Portes de la Fosse, Mar. 17, 1973; children: Agathe, Jeremie, Clemence, Matthias. Student, Inst. d'Etudes Politiques, Paris, 1969; Maitrise de Droit, Paris, 1969; diploma in history of law, 1970, diploma in pvt. law, 1970. Portfolio mgr. Credit Lyonnais, Paris, 1972-78, EBPF, Paris, 1995—; fund mgr. Banque Rothschild, Paris, 1978-82, L'Europeenne de Banque, Paris, 1982-90; head investment Barclays Bank, Paris, 1990-94; bd. dirs. Robinson Participations, Paris, Astek, Paris. Mem. Brancardier Hospitalite Nt. du Rosaire. Roman Catholic. Office: Lloyds Bank, 15 Ave D'iena, 75783 Paris Cedex 16, France

DE LEDINGHEN, VICTOR, gastroenterologist; b. Lille, France, Mar. 1, 1964; s. Arnauld and Annik (Bellouard) de L. MD, U. Poitiers, 1993. Intern Centre Hospitalier Universitaire, Poitiers, France, 1989-93; chief clinic U. Hosp. Poitiers, 1993-95; praticien hospitalier U. Hosp. Bordeaux, France, 1995—. Recipient award Inst. Recherche Maladies de l'Appareil Digestif, 1995; grantee Schering-Plough Inst., 1999; rsch. fellow N.Y.-Presbyn. Hosp.-Cornell U., N.Y.C., 2000. Mem. Assn. France Pour L'Etude du Foie, Club Franc de l'Hypertension Portale, French Nat. Soc. Gastroenterology. Office: Hopital Haut Leveque, Hepatogastroenterology Svc, 33604 Pessac Cedex, France

DE LENA, MARIO, physician; b. Orbetello, Italy, Mar. 11, 1940; m. Marina Stani; 1 child, Chiara. MD, Univ., Bari, 1966; postgrad., Ferrara Univ. Hematology, Ferrara, Italy, 1970, Pavia Univ. Med. Oncology, Pavia, Italy, 1973. Vol. asst. Inst. of Normal Human Anatomy, Bari, Italy, 1966-68; asst. Nat. Cancer Inst., Milan, 1968-77, assoc. physician in clin. oncology, 1977-81; chief physician of oncology divsn. Specialized in Cancer Rsch., Bari, Italy, 1981—; prof. by contract Faculty of Pharmacy, Bari, 1981-82; Italian rep. U.I.C.C., Geneva, 1989; scientific dir. Oncology Inst., Bari, 1986-93; v.p. Gruppo Oncologico Ctr., 1991; oncology rsch. expert Italian Health Min.; sci. dir. Oncology Inst., Bari, Italy, 2000—. Author: Interleukin 2, 1992; editor: Recent Advances in Lung Cancer, 1995; contbr. articles to profl. jours., over 320 publs. and 400 abstracts on oncological topics; mem. editl. bd. Internat. Jour. Oncology, Croation Jour. Oncology, Revisiones en Cancer, Tumori, Jour. Chemotherapy, Argomenti di Oncologia, others. Health Svc. officer LX Armoured Corps, 1967-68. Mem. ESMO (bd. dirs.), AACR, ASCO, Italian Medial Oncology Assn. (pres.). Home: Via Pende 15, 70100 Bari Italy Office: Oncology Inst, Via Amendola 209, 70126 Bari Italy

DELENA, OSCAR, industrial consultant; b. S. Giacomo, Campobasso, Italy, Apr. 20, 1944; s. Federico and Olga (Quinzii) D.; m. Egilda Ventrella; children: Federico, Guinluca. Perito elettronico, ITI, Fermo, Italy, 1963. Tchr. Nautical Inst., Termoli, 1963-64; jr. rschr. Borletti, Milan, 1967-68; sr. rschr. Soc. Ital. Vetro, South Salvo, 1969-94; cons. Termoli, 1995—. Patentee in field. Sergant Aeronautical, 1966—. Avocation: music. Home: Via Ticino, 86039 Termoli Italy

DE LEO, DIEGO, psychiatrist, researcher; b. Rovigo, Veneto, Italy, July 11, 1951; s. Vittorio and Bianca (Galli) De L.; m. Cristina Maria Trevisan, July 27, 1985; children: Nicola Ludovico, Vittorio Mattia. MD, U. Padua, Italy, 1977, specialist in psychiatry, 1981; PhD in Social and Behavioral Scis., U. Leiden, The Netherlands, 1988. Med. diplomate. From asst. prof. psychiatry to acting prof. psychiatry U. Padua, 1980-90, acting prof. mental hygiene, 1995—, head of psychogeriatric svc., 1989—, head of suicide unit, 1992—; guest prof. psychopathology U. Leiden, 1993—; cons. geriatric psychiatry Alzheimer Clinic, Fate Benefratelli Hosp., Brescia, Italy, 1990—, Ministry Pub. Health, Rome, 1994-95; temporary advisor for suicide, geriatric psychiatry, quality of life and care WHO, Geneva, Switzerland, 1988—; dir. WHO Collaborating Ctr. for Suicide Prevention, 1997—; prof. mental hygiene, dir. Australian Inst. for Rsch. and Prevention of Suicide, 1998—. Co-author: Disturbi Affettivi Nella Terza Età, 1987, Depression and Suicide in Late Life, 1990, Manuale di Psichiatria Dell'Anziano, 1994; editor: Preventive Strategies in Suicidal Behaviour, 1995; editor-in-chief: Italian Jour. Suicidology, 1991—; co-editor: Suicide Prevention: A Holistic Approach, 1998. Pres. Interact, Rovigo, 1967-70; mem. Rotaract, Rovigo, 1971-73, Jr. Chamber Internat., Padua, 1983-91. Lt. Italian Army, 1979-80. Recipient Nat. Rsch. award ICI-Pharma, 1985. Mem. Italian Assn. for Suicide Prevention (pres. 1993—), Internat. Acad. for Suicide Rsch. (founder, pres. 1995—), Internat. Assn. for Suicide Prevention (nat. rep. 1985—, Stengel award 1991, bd. dirs. 1997—, v.p. 1997—). Avocations: fencing, collecting antiques, music. Fax: 07 3875 3840. E-mail: d.deleo@mailbox.gu.edu.au. Office: Psychogeriatric Svc, Via Vendramini 7, 35137 Padua Italy

DE LEONARDIS, NICHOLAS JOHN, bank executive, financial lecturer, educator; b. Chgo., Nov. 13, 1929; s. John and Marie (Janik) De L.; m. Mary Ellen Kloss, Aug. 17, 1957; children: Deborah Marie, Valerie Ann, Nicolette Mary, Regina Ellen, John Paul. BS, De Paul U., 1951, MA, 1968. Salesman Asher J. Goldfine & Co., Chgo., 1953-55; mem. trust dept. staff First Nat. Bank, Chgo., 1955-63, with mcpl. sales dept., 1963-78, v.p. Money Market Ctr., 1978-80, v.p., chmn. money market com., 1980-85; sr. v.p., treas. La Salle Nat. Bank, subs. Algemene Bank Nederland, N.V., 1985-90; sr. v.p., chmn. asset and liability com. La Salle Nat. Corp.; exec. in residence dept. fin. De Paul U., Chgo., 1990—, lectr., 1968-78, dir. DePaul-People's Republic of China Project, 1990-95; lectr. MBA program De Paul, Hong Kong, 1997—; guest lectr. bankers' seminars, Poland, 1992—; grad. sch. banking U. Wis., Madison, 1980-87; mem. Dixon Assn. for Retarded Citizens, 1984, Gov.'s task force on Future of Mental Health in Ill., 1986-87; cons Polish Bankers, Warsaw, 1997; mem. com. specialist assignment and evaluation Chgo. Stock Exchange, 1993—; commn. review the state's mental health code, 1988; mem. adv. com. devel. disabilities Ill. Dept. Mental Health and Devel. Disabilities, 1993-2000. Contbr. articles to profl. publs. Trustee, past chmn. Found. Hearing and Speech Rehab., Chgo., 1968-92; pres. Dixon (Ill.) Assn. Retarded Citizens, 1984—. Mem. Union League Chgo., Heidelberg Club Internat., Delta Mu Delta, Beta Gamma Sigma. Office: De Paul U Dept Fin 1 E Jackson Blvd Ste 6126 Chicago IL 60604-2287

DELESPAUL, PHILIPPE A.E.G., psychologist, researcher; b. Mol, Belgium, June 27, 1958; s. Ignace A.E.G. and Marie-Antoinette (De Visscher) C.; m. Frieda J. Van Goethem, May 11, 1990. Diploma clin psychology, Katholieke Universiteit Leuven, Louvain, Belgium, 1981; PhD, U. Maastricht (The Netherlands), 1995. Ward head Psycho-Medisch Streekcentrum Vijverdal Psychiat. Hosp., Maastricht, The Netherlands, 1981; sr. acad. clinician Maastricht U., 1982—; sr. researcher Internat. Inst. Psycho-Social and Socio-Ecological Rsch. Found., Maastricht, 1985—; cons. Nat. Inst. Drug Abuse, Balt., 1992, World Fedn. Mental Health, Maastricht, 1987—, U. Utrecht, The Netherlands, 1992—. Co-author: Exp. of Psychopathology, 1992, Assessing Schizophrenia in Daily Life—The Experience Sampling Method, 1995. Recipient Young Scientist award, MRC, 1994. Mem. AAAS, Vereniging voor Gedragstherapie, Vlaamse Vereniging voor Gedragstherapie, Vlaamse Vereniging voor Klinische Psychologie, N.Y. Acad. Scis. Home: Daalstraat 33, B-3630 Maasmechelen Belgium Office: Maastricht U Dept Psychiat, PB 616, NL-6200 Maastricht The Netherlands

DELEST, PHILIPPE FRANCIS, retired food company executive, consultant; b. Paris, Dec. 28, 1933; s. Pierre and Marthe (Villar) D.; m. Christiane Dusart, Mar. 25, 1958; children: Alain, Brigitte; m. Genevieve Cousin, Jan. 5, 1967; children: Nathalie, Veronique, Bruno. Chem. Engr., ENSCP, Paris, 1956; MS, U. Paris, 1957. Rsch. engr. Kodak-Pathe, Paris, 1957-62; bus. engr. W.R. Grace, Paris, 1962-70; gen. mgr. Bartolac, Mantes La Jolie, France, 1970-73; devel. mgr. CECA S.A., Velizy, France, 1973-85; sci. coord. Systems Bio-Industries, Boulogne, France, 1985-96; ret.; pres. Adebio, Paris, 1990-94; lectr. in field. Patentee in field. With French Mil., 1959-61. Mem. Club Crin (pres. 1991—). Home & Office: 42 La Gaillarderie, 78590 Noisy le Roi France

DELEU, JOZEF HUGO MARIA, editor; b. Roeselare, Flanders, Belgium, Apr. 20, 1937; s. Louis Deleu and Germaine Demijttenaere; m. Annemarie Deblaere, Oct. 22, 1960; children: Lodewijk, Marjolein, Jeroen. Grad. h.s., 1956; Doctor Honoris Causa, U. Ghent, 1994. Tchr. Moeskroen-Menen, Belgium, 1956-70; founder, chief editor Ons Erfdeel, Rekkem, Belgium, 1957, Septentrion, Rekkem, 1972, De Franse Nederlanden-Les Pays-Bas Français, 1976, The Low Countries, 1993; founder, mng. dir. Stichting Ons Erfdeel, Rekkem, 1970—; bd. dirs. Maatschappij der Nederlandse Letterkunde, Leiden, Raad voor de Nederlandse Taal en Letteren, The Hague. Author numerous books of poetry and fiction. Recipient numerous prizes including Prize for Poetry, 1995, Taaluniepenning, 1995, Comdr. in de Orde van Oranje-Nassau, 1996, Chevalier dans l'Ordre des Arts et Lettres, 1997. Avocations: reading, walking. Home: Murissonstraat 220, 8930 Rekkem Flanders, Belgium Office: Stichting Ons Erfdeel, Murissonstraat 260, 8930 Rekkem Flanders, Belgium

DELEULE, DIDIER, philosophy educator; b. Paris, Jan. 24, 1941; s. Marcel and Marthe (Vieille) D.; m. Marie-France Antoine, Nov. 18, 1961; children: Sylvie, David-Emmanuel. Diploma in philosophy, Sorbonne, Paris, 1964, PhD in Philosophy, 1979. Asst. philosopher U. Franche Comté, Besançon, France, 1968-81; prof. philosophy U. Rennes (France), 1981-84, U. Paris X, Nanterre, 1984—; dir. U. Paris, Nanterre, 1991-93; pres. Conseil Nat. des Univs., France, 1992—. Author: La Psychologie, Mythe Scientifique, 1969, Le Corps Productif, 1972, Hume et la Naissance du Libéralisme Economique, 1979, The Living Machine; Psychology and Organology, 1992; mem. editl. staff Revue Philosophique, 1994—, Cités, 1999—. Pres. Ctr. Nat. des Lettres Philosophy, Paris, 1986-90. Home: 146 rue Legendre, 75017 Paris France Office: U Paris X, 200 Ave de la République, 92001 Nanterre France

DELEUZE, PHILIPPE HENRI, cardiothoracic surgeon, consultant; b. Toulouse, France, Nov. 6, 1958; s. René Charles and Michelle Suzanne (Arjac) D.; m. Corinne Michele Joyon, Sept. 30, 1988; 2 children. MD, U. Paris, 1982, DEA, 1988. Intern Hosp. de Paris, 1981-87, chief of clinic, 1987-91, physician, 1991-95; cardiothoracic surgeon St. Joseph Hosp., Paris, 1996—, Clinic Parly II, Versailles, 1996—; European clin. trials trainer for artificial heart Novacor, Baxter Co., Paris, 1991-95, cons., 1994-95, Medtronic Co., Paris, 1996—. Contbr. more than 100 articles to profl. jours. Gen. surgeon, officer French Mil., 1982-84. Mem. French Soc. Cardiothoracic Surgery, French Soc. Cardiology, Am. Soc. Artificial Internal Organs. Roman Catholic. Avocations: swimming, mountain biking, water and snow skiing, cinema. Office: St Joseph Hosp, 7 Rue Pierre Larousse, 75014 Paris France

DELFINO, LOUIS JOSEPH, sales representative; b. White Plains, N.Y., June 15, 1967; s. Joseph Conrad and Estelle Aida D.; m. Mary Patricia Delfino, Oct. 23, 1993; 1 child, Matthew. BS, Ithaca Coll., 1989. Mgr. Nike, Inc., various, 1989-97; regional mgr. Nike, Inc., Atlanta, 1997-98; sales rep. Nike Golf, Atlanta, 1998—. Home: 11055 Kimball Crest Dr Alpharetta GA 30022-6494

DEL FORNO, ANTON, classical guitarist, recording artist, composer, arranger, educator; b. Dumont, N.J., Aug. 17, 1950; s. Vito and Mildred (Casio) Del F. MusB, Mannes Coll. Music, N.Y.C., 1972. Musical debut Concrgebouw Hall, Holland, 1979; tchr. St. John's U., N.Y.C., 1973-75; pvt. tchr. N.Y. and N.J., 1975—; performer, lectr. numerous colls. and univs., 1973—. Debut Carnegie Recital Hall, N.Y., 1972, Concertgebouw Hall, Holland, 1979, Wigmore Hall, London, 1983, Alice Tully Hall, N.Y., 1983; composer mus. songs; sound recs. include Christmas Gifts, 1983, Anton Del Forno in Concert, Part I, 1985, Part II, 1988, Del Forno Plays Villa-Lobos, 1990. Mem. Broadcast Music, Inc. Roman Catholic. Avocation: vintage automobile collecting. Office: Juston Records PO Box 362 New York NY 10113-0362

DELGADO, RAMON LOUIS, educator, author, director, playwright, lyricist; b. Dec. 16, 1937; s. Eloy Vincent and Hildgard (Chapman) D. BA, Stetson U., 1959; MA, Baylor U., 1960; MFA, YAle U., 1967; PhD, So. Ill. U., 1976. Tchr. Lyman H.S., Longwood, Fla., 1960-62; mem. faculty Chipola Jr. Coll., Marianna, Fla., 1962-64, Ky. Wesleyan U., 1967-72, Hardin-Simmons U., 1972-74, So. Ill. U., 1974-76, St. Cloud (Minn.) State U., 1976-78; prof. speech and theater Montclair State U., Upper Montclair, N.J.,

1978—; evaluator N.J. Teen Arts Festival, 1980, 81; judge Am. Theatre Assn. Coll. Theater Festival, 1980, 82, 83, 84, 85, N.J. Teen Galaxy Competition, 1984. Playwright: Waiting for the Bus, 1968, Once Below a Lighthouse, 1972, The Jerusalem Thorn, 1979, A Little Holy Water, 1983, Stones, 1983, The Flight of the Dodo, 1990, Remembering Booth, 1997, The Iron Corset, 1999, Consider the Phoenix, 2000; editor: The Best Short Plays, 1981-89; author: Acting with Both Sides of Your Brain, 1986; contbr. articles to profl. jours. Sec. Forest St. Manor Condo Assn., 1997-99. Recipient Samuel French Play award, 1966, U. Mo. Play award, 1971, 75, playwriting awards Am. Coll. Theatre Festival, 1976, 77, 78, Grand prize Music City Song Festival contest, 1988, 7 hon. mentions, 1989; Midwest Profl. Playwrights fellow, 1978; Ford Found. grantee, 1961; playwright-in-residence INTAR, 1980. Mem. Dramatists Guild, Assn. for Theatre in Higher Edn., Nashville Songwriters Assn. Internat., Nat. Theatre Conf., Theta Alpha Phi, Phi Kappa Phi. Democrat. Home: 16 Forest St Apt 107 Montclair NJ 07042-3519 Office: Montclair State U Dept Theatre and Dance Upper Montclair NJ 07043

DELGADO BARRIO, FRANCISCO JAVIER, president supreme court of Spain. Pres. Tribunal Supremeo, Madrid, Spain. Fax: 341-319-4767. Office: Tribunal Supremo, Plaza de la Villa de Paris, 28004 Madrid Spain*

DELGADO RIVERA, FLAVIO, lawyer, consultant; b. Buga, Valle del Cauca, Colombia, May 21, 1944; s. Luis Alfonso Delgado Martinez and Rosa Elisa Rivera Plata; m. Sara Mejia Ospina, Dec. 19, 1981 (div.). JD, Javeriana U., Bogota, Colombia, 1969; LLD, Javeriana U., 1979. Recovery boss Nat. Impost Direction, Bogota, 1980, Regional Impost Direction, Cali, Valle, Colombia, 1981-83; mcpl. rental jefature Mayor of Cali, 1983-86; sec. lawyer Indsl. Nation Assn., Cali, 1987-88; litigator, lawyer Profl. Office, Cali, 1989—; interventor mgr. Banking Superintendence, Bogota, 1989; mediator, trade arbitrator C. of C., Cali, 1990-94. Mem. Permanent Com. Promotion, Valle of Cauca, 1988. Mem. Lawyers Club Javeriano. Conservative. Roman Catholic. Avocations: music, books. Office: Lawyer's Office, Calle 26 Norte 6N-13 Of 303, Cali Colombia

DELHAES, PIERRE VINCENT, engineer, researcher; b. Bordeaux, Arvitaine, France, May 17, 1939; s. Paul and Marthe (Courrouy) D.; m. Christiane Andree Normand-Seailles, Oct. 9, 1963; children: Vincent, Laurence, Fabien. Degree in chem. engring., U. Bordeaux, 1960, D in Phys. Chemistry, 1965. Rsch. assoc. CNRS, Bordeaux, 1965-70, head of rsch., 1970-82, rsch. dir., 1982——; assoc. rsch. dir. CNRS, 1990-94, 98—; pres. French Carbon Group, 1994—. Editor: World of Carbon, 1999; contbr. more than 300 articles to profl. jours. including Jour. Chem. Physics, Phys. Rev., among others. Mem. Soc. Francaise de Chimie (bd. dirs. 1998—), Groupe Francais des Carbones.

D'ELIA, GAETANO, journalist, educator; b. Bari, Apulia, Italy, July 5, 1949; s. Antonio and Emma (Boccardi) D'E.; m. Margherita Liuzzi, Dec. 26, 1974; children: Antonio, Emma. Degree in fgn. lang. lit., U. Bari, Italy, 1973. Postgrad. scholar Holder U., Bari, Italy, 1974-76; secondary sch. tchr. Sci. Sch. Conversano, 1976-81; rschr., lectr. U. Bari, 1982—; tchr. Istituto U. Orientale, Naples, 1992-95. Author: La Scrittura Multimediale di David Hare, 1990 (Spl. Mention award 1990); editor Godwin Club Italia, 1996; contbr. articles to profl. jours. Mem. Godwin Club Italia (pres. 1996-99). Roman Catholic. Avocations: theatre, movies, travel, reading, Roman history. Home: Piazza Moro 55, 70121 Bari Apulia, Italy Office: U Bari, V Garruba 7, 70125 Bari Italy

DELIBASIS, NICHOLAS DEMETRIUS, geoscientist; b. Lamia, Fthiotis, Greece, Jan. 26, 1935; s. Demetrius Nicolas and Panaghiotia Aglaia (Samara) D.; m. Helen John Peridou, Dec. 27, 1967; 1 child, Demetrius. Diploma in Geology, U. Athens, Greece, 1959, PhD in Seismology, 1969; postgrad., U. Frankfurt, Germany, 1973. Asst. Lab. Seismology, Athens, 1961-82; asst. prof. U. Athens, 1982-88, assoc. prof., 1988-94, prof. seismology, 1994—; cons. seismic safety during blasting operation, 1980; dir. geophysics-geothermy Divsn. Athens, 1998-99. Editor: Introduction of Plate Tectonic, 1999. Sub lt. Greek mil., 1960-61. Mem. Am. Geophys. Union. Home: Doukissis Plakentias Str, 152 34 Athens Greece Office: Dept Geophys Geothermy, Panepistimopolis-Ilisia, 157 84 Athens Greece

DELIBES, MIGUEL (MIGUEL DELIBES SETIEN), author; b. Valladolid, Spain, Oct. 17, 1920; s. Adolfo and Maria (Setien) D.; m. Angeles de Castro Ruiz, 1946 (dec. 1974); children: Miguel, Angeles, German, Elisa, Juan, Adolfo, Camino. LLD, U. Valladolid, Spain, 1944; Doctorate (hon.), U. Valladolid, U. Saarbrücken. Tchr. merchantile law U. Valladolid, Spain; vis. prof. U. Md., College Park, 1964; bd. dirs. El Norte de Castilla, Valladolid. Author: (fiction) La sombra del ciprés es alargada, 1948 (Nadal prize 1947), A'n es de dia, 1949, El camino, 1950 (pub. as The Path 1961), Mi idolatrado hijo Sisi, 1953, El loco, 1953, La partida, 1954, Los Railes, 1954, Diario de un cazador, 1955 (Cervantes prize Ministry of Information 1955), Siestas con viento sur, 1957, Diario de un emigrante, 1958, La Hoja roja, 1959, Las ratas, 1962 (pub. as Smoke on the Ground 1972), Cinco horas con Mario, 1966 (pub. as Five Hours with Mario 1988), La mortaja, 1969, Parábola del náufrago, 1969 (pub. as The Hedge 1983), El principe destronado, 1973 (pub. as The Prince Dethroned, 1986), Las guerras de nuestros antepasados, 1975, El disputado voto del señor Cayo, 1978, Los santos inocentes, 1981, El otro f'tbol, 1982, Tres pájaros de cuenta, 1982, Cartas de amor de un sexagenario voluptuoso, 1983, El tesoro, 1985, 377A, Madera de héroe, 1987 (pub. as The Stuff of Heroes 1990), Señora de rojo sobre fondo gris, 1991; (plays) Cinco horas con Mario, 1980, La hoja roja, 1987; (teleplays) Tierras de Valladolid, 1966, Castilla, esta es mi tierra, 1983; (other writings) Un novelista descubre América: Chile en el ojo ajeno, 1956, La barberia, 1957, Castilla, 1960 (pub. as Viejas historias de Castilla la Vieja 1964), La caza de la perdiz roja, 1963, Europa: parada y fonda, 1963, El libro de la caza menor, 1964, Obras completas (5 vols), 1964-75, USA y yo, 1966, Vivir al dia, 1968, La primavera de Praga, 1968, Con la escopeta al hombro, 1970, Un año de mi vida, 1972, La caza en España, 1972, Castilla en mi obra, 1972, S.O.S.: el sentido del progreso desde mi obra, 1975, Aventuras, venturas y desventuras de un cazador a rabo, 1977, Mis amigas las truchas, 1977, Castilla, lo castellano, y los castellanos, 1979, Un mundo que agoniza, 1979 (pub. as El mundo en la agonía, 1988), Las perdices del domingo, 1981, Dos viajes en automóvil: Suecia y paises bajos, 1982, La censura de prensa en los anos 40, y otros ensayos, 1985, Cinco horas con Mario, 1985, Castilla habla, 1986, Mi vida al aire libre: memorias deportivas de un hombre sedentario, 1989, Pegar la hebra, 1990, El conejo, 1991, El Ultimo coto, 1992, Diario de un jubilado, 1995, He Dicho, 1996, El hereje, 1998, Los Estragos Del Tiempo, 1999, Dos mujeres, 2000. Recipient Fastenrath prize, 1959, Nat. Critics prize (Spain), 1963, Prince of Asturias prize for literature, 1983, Castilla y León letters prize, 1984, City of Barcelona prize, 1987, Nat. letters award, 1991, Cervantes Lit. prize, 1993. Mem. Royal Acad. Lang. Office: Ediciones Destino, Provenza 260 4 planta, 08008 Barcelona Spain

DE LIEDEKERKE, CHARLES A., industrial company executive; b. Brussels, July 5, 1953; s. Charles A. de Liedekerke and Nicole M. Bekaert; m. Anne-Claire de Woot de Trixhe, Sept. 24, 1977; children: Chuck, Ariane, Isabelle. Student, Faculty N.D., Namur, 1974; lic. at law, Cath. U. of Louvain, 1977. Bar: Brussels, 1977. Sec.-treas. Amcar-Carmeuse, Fla., 1980-82; jr. exec. LaFarge Group, Paris, 1982-85, exec. v.p., 1998—; gen. mgr. LaForge Constrn. Materials, Dallas, 1985-89; v.p., gen. mgr. LaForge Constrn. Materials, Alberta, Can., 1989-92; CFO Bekaert Group, Kortrijk, Belgium, 1992-97; dir. Bekaert Group, Assubel A.T., Brussels, CDL & Co. Pres. ASBL Maison St. Thérèse, Brussels, 1997; dir. Inst. d'Etudes Theologiques, Brussels, 1997. Mem. Quarry Products Assn. (dir. 1998—), Cercle du Parc (founding mem. 1995—), A.N.R.B., Assn. Noblesse Royaume de Belgique. Avocations: tennis, mountaineering, skiing, sailing, music. Home: 8 Av Nestor Plissart, 1040 Brussels Belgium Office: LaFarge, 61 rue des Belles Feiilles, 75016 Paris France

DELIÈGE, IRÈNE JEANNE, music psychologist, researcher; b. Saintes, Brabant, Belgium, Jan. 15, 1939; d. Oscar Smisman and Madeleine Sergoris. 1st prices, Royal Music Conservatory, Brussels, 1954; Master's degree, Brussels U., 1985; PhD with highest distinction, Liege (Belgium) U., 1991. Prof. music State Sch., Brussels, 1959-79; prof. music psychology U. Liege, 1986—; head unit rsch. in music psychology U. Liege, 1986—. Coeditor: Music and Cognitive Sciences, 1989, Music and Cognitive Sciences, 1993, Musical Beginnings, 1995, Perception and Cognition of Music, 1997; chief editor Musicae Scientiae. Mem. APA, European Soc. for Cognitive Scis. of Music (permanent sec.), Psychonomic Soc. Office: U Liege, 7 Place Vingt Aout, B-4000 Liege Belgium

DELILLE, DANIEL, microbiologist, researcher; b. Paris, Oct. 26, 1944; s. Lucien and Raymonde (Fesquet) D.; m. Elisabeth Roule, Oct. 17, 1970; children: Nathalie, Bruno. Degree in Biochem. Engring., Inst. Nat. Scis. Applquées, Lyon, France, 1966; PhD, U. Claude Bernard, Lyon, 1977. Researcher TAAF, Paris, 1969-77; mgr. polar microbial investigation French Inst. Polar Rsch., Brest, France, 1978—; cons. in field. Contbr. over 50 articles to profl. jours. Avocation: photography. Home: 26 rue d'Orbais, 66000 Perpignan France Office: U Pierre et Marie Curie, UA 117 Laboratoire Arago, 66650 Banyuls Sur Mer France

DELIMA, LUTERO CARMO, engineering educator; b. São Paulo, Brazil, Mar. 17, 1952; s. Manoel Vieira DeLima and Maria do Carmo Lima; m. Lucia Setsuko Imamura, May 15, 1976; children: Maira Imamura, Lunie Imamura, Tanes Imamura. BSc, U. Santo Amaro, São Paulo, 1974; MSc, U. Santa Catarina, Florianopolis, Brazil, 1979; DSc, U. São Paulo, 1986; postgrad., U. Miami, 1990-91. Clk. Orion Co., São Paulo, 1967-70, Villanes Co., São Paulo, 1971-72; attendant Varig Air Line, São Paulo, 1973-74; lectr. physics Equipe H.S., São Paulo, 1975, U. Mato Grosso, Cuiaba, Brazil, 1976-87; lectr. mech. engring. U. Uberlandia, Brazil, 1987-98. Recipient Medallion and Cert., Beta Theta chpt. Phi Beta Delta, 1991, named hon. v.p., 1991; Fulbright fellow, 1990. Achievements include being the first person to propose a hydrogen system for the conservation of the Brazilian Amazonia. Avocations: reading, playing soccer, tennis, and chess. Home: Rua Cirineu Menezes 197 Vigilato, 38408-614 Uberlandia MG, Brazil Office: U Fed Uberlandia, Dept Mech Engring, 38403186 Uberlandia MG, Brazil

DELION, DORU SABIN, physicist; b. Bacău, România, June 5, 1951; s. Pavel and Victoria (Gavrileanu) D.; m. Ecaterina Daniela Roatis, Dec. 3, 1977; 1 child, Daniel Sabin. MSc, Fac. Physics, 1976; PhD, Inst. Atomic Physics, 1989. Rschr. Inst. Atomic Physics, Bucharest, 1979-93, sr. rschr., 1993-95, 1995; scientist sec. Internat. Summer Sch., Predeal, Romania, 1991, 95. Contbr. articles to profl. jours. Mem. Romanian Scientists Soc. Avocation: music. E-mail: delion@theor1theory.nipne.ro. Office: Inst Physic/ Nuclear Engring, Str Atomistilor 1, POB MG-6 Bucharest Romania

DELIRE, MARCEL JULIEN, pediatrician, immunologist; b. Brussels, July 17, 1942; s. Fernand and Elise (Dedecker) D.; m. Bernadette Serra, Mar. 31, 1969. Degree in humanities, Greek and Latin, U. Brussels, 1960, postgrad., 1975; MD, Louvain (Belgium) U., 1967, postgrad., 1972. Resident in pediatrics U. Marseille, France, 1967-69; mem. neonatology staff Namur, Belgium, 1969-71; head pediatric hematology St. Anne Hosp., Brussels, 1973-79; rschr. ICP, Brussels, 1974-79; med. dir. Hoechst, Brussels, 1981-86; clin. rschr. in immunology Behring Inst., Marburg, Germany, 1987-95; dir. cancer project SmithKline Beecham, Rixensart, Belgium, 1995—. Co-author: The Mast Cell, 1979, Advanced in Epileptology, 1989, The Medical Treatment of Epilepsy, 1992, Rationale for the Clinical Uses of Intravenous Polyvalent Immunoglobulin, 1995. Lt. Med. Svcs. Germany, 1971-73. Avocations: biology, music, piano. Office: SmithKline Beecham, Institut 89, B-1330 Rixensart Belgium

DELIRE, PHILIPPE, automotive engineer; b. Brussels, Belgium, Jan. 5, 1965; arrived in France, 1989; s. Richard and Claudine (Bulens) D. Sci. humanities, Cardinal Mercier Coll., Belgium, 1983; math., St. Gertrude Coll., Belgium, 1984; mech. civil engr., Cath. U. Louvain, Belgium, 1989. Cert. engring. Rsch. engr. IBM, Gironde, France, 1989-91, Hispano-Suiza, Normandie, France, 1992-93; ops. mgr. Geci Internat., Paris, France, 1993-97; chief project mgr. Valeo Thermal and Climate Control Divsn., Sarthe, France, 1994—; rsch. and advanced engring. mgr. Rockwell LVS, 1997—; program mgr. cockpit modules Sommer Allibert Siemens, 1999—. Coauthor: Superficial Tension, 1986; co-author (memoir) Radial Turbo-Generator for Internal Combustion Engine, 1989, (tech. publ.) Thermal Field Visualization in Power Modules, 1990; patentee in field. Officer Belgium Artillery, 1991-92. Mem. ASME. Avocations: jogging, swimming. Home: La Belie Alliance, Les Novis 72 1/0 Beaumont, Sarthe France

DELL, MICHAEL S., computer company executive; b. Houston, 1965; s. Alexander and Lorraine D.; m. Susan Lieberman, Oct. 23, 1989. Student, U. Tex., 1983-84. Founder Dell Computer Corp. (formerly PC's Ltd.), Austin, 1984—, now chmn., CEO. Recipient Entrepreneur of Yr. award Inc. Mag., 1990, Customer Satisfaction award JD Power, 1991, 93; named CEO of Yr. Fin. World Mag., 1993. Office: Dell Computer Corp 1 Dell Way Round Rock TX 78682-0001

DELL, PETER LAWSON, business educator; b. London, Oct. 24, 1934; s. Wilfred Lawson and Kathleen Anne (Jukes) D.; m. Marian Holt, May 9, 1959; children: Andrew Lawson, Helen Caroline, Michael John. MA, Cambridge (Eng.) U., 1958. Commd. Royal Engrs. (Army), 1955-73, advanced through grades to lt. col.; sr. exec. Courtaulds plc, U.K., 1973-78; chmn., CEO Courtaulds Engring. Ltd., U.K., 1978-82; mng. dir. Saiccor Pty. Ltd., South Africa, 1982-86, RK Carvill & Co., U.K., 1986-88; exec. cons. Ernst & Young, U.K., 1988-96; vis. prof. bus. Durham U., 1996—; bd. dirs. Inst. Customer Svc., 1997-99; cons. Robert Rummey Assocs., U.K., 1995—; mem. joint com. SERC:ESRC, U.K., 1978-82. Contbr. articles to profl. jours. Mem. bd. mgmt. Manchester Bus. Sch., 1993-98; vol. guide Henry Moore Found., 1996—. Decorated Mem. Order of Brit. Empire, 1971; Manchester Bus. Sch. vis. sr. fellow, 1975-96. Fellow Instn. of Civil Engrs., Instn. Engrs. Australia, Inst. Mgmt., Royal Soc. Arts; mem. Royal Automobile Club. Avocations: swimming, theater, art, opera. Home: 212 High St, Roydon Essex CM19 5EQ, England

DELLA FAILLE D'HUYSSE, CHRISTIAN, finance company executive; b. Bruges, Belgium, Mar. 8, 1931; s. Xavier and Marie-Anne (Coppieters Stochove) della Faille d'Huysse; m. Anouchka de Somer, Aug. 23, 1972; children: Savina, Amaury, Marie-Christine, Pauline. LLD, U. Leuven, Belgium, 1957, Degree in Econs., 1958. Trainee Bankers Trust, N.Y.C., 1960; mgr. WHK Bank, Brussels, 1961-65, pres., 1965-82; pres. CF Finance, Brussels, 1982—; fin. advisor and law cons. Lt. Belgium Air Force, 1952-55. Mem. Association de la Noblesse, American Club. Avocations: tennis, skiing, bridge, crossword puzzles, travel. Home: Avenue Empain 20, 1150 Brussels Belgium Office: SODEFIMO, Ave de Tervuren 61 Box 3, 1040 Brussels Belgium

DELLAGIARINO, GEORGE FRANCIS, geologist; b. Bklyn., Nov. 12, 1947; s. Joseph Francis and Mary Frances (Purpura) D.; m. Marguerite Frances Hansen, Aug. 17, 1974; children: Lisa, Amy. BS in Earth and Planetary Sci., U. Pitts., 1970; MS in Earth and Space Sci., SUNY, Stony Brook, 1972. Hydrol. field asst. Water Resources divsn. U.S. Geol. Survey, Mineola, N.Y., 1974; geologist Conservation divsn. U.S. Geol. Survey, New Orleans, 1975-78; staff geologist Conservation divsn. U.S. Geol. Survey, Reston, Va., 1978-82; staff geologist Minerals Mgmt. Svc., Reston, 1982-84, geologist, lease sale team leader, 1984—; geologist, geol. and geophys. data team leader Minerals Mgmt. Svc., Herndon, Va., 1988—; presenter in field. Contbr. articles to profl. jours. Cluster v.p. Saddler Oaks Cluster Assn., Reston, 1980-82, neighborhood watch coord., 1993—; religious edn. tchr. St. John Neumann Parish, Reston, 1988—; vol. scientist sci.-by-mail program Va. Mus. Sci., Richmond, 1994-95, Boston Sci. Mus., 1995—; mentor MentorNet program San Jose State U., 1999—. Recipient Quality Increase award Dept. of the Interior, 1981, 82. Mem. AAAS, Am. Geophys. Union, Am. Assn. Petroleum Geologists, Geol. Soc. Am. Roman Catholic. Achievements include establishing bureau guidelines for the preparation of geological reports and the formal identification of areas of hydrocarbon potential; service on Dept. of Interior task force to amend federal regulations to allow on-structure drilling of deep stratigraphic test wells on the outer continental shelf; assisted in authoring of prelease exploration and prelease prospecting regulations for minerals on outer continental shelf. Home: 2268 Gunsmith Sq Reston VA 20191-2325 Office: US Minerals Mgmt Svc MS 4070 381 Elden St Herndon VA 20170

DELL'ALBA, GIANFRANCO, member European Parliament; b. Livorno, Italy, May 24, 1955. Mem. European Parliament, Brussels, 1999—; mem. com. on budgetary control, substitute mem. com. on devel. and cooperation, com. on budgets, mem. mems. from European Parliament to Joint Assembly of Agreement between African, Caribbean and Pacific States and European Union. Co-pres. Tech. Group Ind. Mems. Office: European Parliament, Rue Wiertz ASP 7H153, B-1047 Brussels Belgium*

DELLA MUSSIA, JEAN PIERRE, editor-in-chief; b. Paris, Jan. 30, 1945; s. Louis Della Mussia and Marcelle Della Mussia-Devanz; m. Gerlinde Stoess, Aug. 17, 1974; children: Marc, Thomas. D in Engring., Ecole Nat. Supr. Arts, and Industries, Strasbourg, France, 1969. Journalist Newspaper: Inter Electronique, Paris, 1971-75, sect. editor, 1975-77, exec. editor, 1977-79; exec. editor Newspaper: Electronique Actualites, Paris, 1979-86; editorial dir. Newspaper: Electronique Puissance, Paris, 1983-86; editor-in-chief Processeurs et Systemes, Paris, 1985-86; to editor-in-chief Electronique Hebdo, Paris, 1986-90; editl. mgr. publs. Electronique Internat., Electronique, Mesures, Integration, Paris, 1990-2000. Editor-in-chief Electronique Internat. Hebdo. Avocations: wine, adventures. Office: Electronique Internat, 26 rue d Oradour sur Glane, Paris 75015, France

DELLA PAOLERA, GERARDO, rector, researcher; b. Feb. 22, 1959; s. Carlos Maria and Carmen (Geres) Della P.; m. Veronica Rosana Pipp, June 19, 1984; children: Marina, Carola, Martin. B in Econ., U. Catolica Argentina, Buenos Aires, 1982; MA in Econ., U. Chgo., 1985, PhD in Econ., 1988. Asst. rschr. macro econ. CEMA, Argentina, 1982; strategy and fin. rschr. Banco Rio de La Plata, Argentina, 1983-84; assoc. prof. U. Buenos Aires, 1984; lectr. U. Chgo., 1987; prof. U. Torcuato Di Tella, Buenos Aires, 1992, rector, 1991—; internal cons. Banco Rio de La Plata, 1983-84, internat. economist, 1988-89; fellow rschr. Inst. Torcuato Di Tella, 1990-91; econ. cons. Harvard U., 1991. Author: Desafios De La Educacion Superior, 1993. Marcos Garfunkel fellow Oxford (Eng.) U., 1994; recipient fellowship U. Chgo., 1984-88, grant Adeba, 1994, grant NSF, 1995. Mem. Am. Econ. Assn., Assn. Argentina Econ. Politics, Cliometric Soc., U. Chgo. Club in Argentina. Office: Univ Torcuato Di Tella, Minones 2177, 1428 Belgrano Chico, Argentina

DELLA ROCCA, GREGORY JOHN, orthopaedic surgeon; b. Albany, N.Y., Sept. 8, 1969; s. John Stephen and Marcia Rose Della Rocca. BS, Cornell U., 1992; PhD, Duke U., 1998, MD, 1999. Instr. Princeton Rev., Chapel Hill, N.C., 1995-98; orthopaedic resident Barnes-Jewish Hosp., St. Louis, 1999—; mem. med. policy action com., com. on minority affairs, med. adv. com. Duke U. Med. Ctr., Durham, 1995-96, instnl. rev. bd., 1994-95. Mem. Pi Kappa Phi (vice archon 1991). Avocations: soccer, downhill skiing. E-mail: rocco001@email.msn.com.

DELLA SALA, SERGIO F., neuropsychology educator, consultant; b. Milan, Sept. 23, 1955. MD, U. Milan, 1980, diploma in neurology, 1984, PhD in Neuropsychology, 1989. Sr. neurologist U. Milan, 1990-91; head of neuropsychology unit Veruno, 1992-93; prof. neuropsychology U. Aberdeen, Scotland, 1994—. Office: U Aberdeen Dept Psychol, William Guild Bldg, Aberdeen AB24 2UB, Scotland

DELLA VALLE, FRANCESCO, chemist; b. Rome, Dec. 13, 1937; s. Renato and Biancamaria (Guglielmi) Della V.; m. Beatrice Senepa, Oct. 16, 1962; children: Federica, Raffaella, Renato. PhD in Chemistry, La Sapienza U., Rome, 1961; Dr.Pharmacy (hon.), U. Padua, 1988; ScD (hon.), Georgetown U., 1989; D of Pharm. Techs. (hon.), U. Ferrara, 1993. Prodn. chemist Inst. Riuniti Biochem. Italy, Rome, 1962-65; tech. dir. Inst. Riuniti Biochem. Italy, 1965-67, Fidia Farmaceutici SpA, Abano Terme, 1968-77; mng. dir. Fidia Farmaceutici SpA, 1977-83, chief exec. officer, mng. dir., 1983-91; pres. Lifegroup SpA, Rome, 1991-96, Podolife Srl, Milan, 1995—; bd. dirs. Fidia Pharm. Corp., Washington, 1984-91, Fidia Rsch. Found., Washington, 1985-91, Bioiberica S.A., Barcellona, Spain, 1985-91; chmn. bd. Friuli Animal Rsch. SpA, Udine, 1986-91; pres. Inst. Studi Interesse Santiario SpA, Rome, 1988-91. Patentee in field. Mem. directive coun. Farmindustria, Rome, 1984-91, pres. commn. for sci. rsch., 1984-91; pres. Gestione Consorti srl, Rome, 1988-93, Inst. Formazione Operatori Sociali, Padua, 1986-93; mng. dir. Inst. Dermatol. Italiano Monselice Monselice (PD), 1992-96; v.p. Found. Cassa di Risparmio di Padova e Rovigo, Padova, 1992-93. Knight of Industry, Pres. of Italy, 1987, Knight of the Cross, 1985, Gold Medal for Civic Work, 1980. Mem. Italian Soc. Pharmacology, Italian Soc. Chemistry, Rotary. Roman Catholic. Office: Podolife Srl, Via Egadi 7, 20144 Milan Italy

DELLA VEDOVA, BENEDETTO, member European Parliament; b. Sondrio, Italy, Apr. 3, 1961. Mem. European Parliament, Brussels, 1999—; mem. com. on econ. and monetary affairs, substitute mem. com. on industry, external trade, rsch. and energy, mem. del. for rels. with Mashreq countries and the Gulf. Mem. Tech. Group of Ind. Mems. (mixed group). Office: care Partito Radicale, Via Torre Argentina 76, I-00186 Rome Italy*

DELLER, JUERGEN FRIEDHELM, psychology educator; b. Bielefeld, Germany, Mar. 15, 1960; s. Friedhelm and Margarete E. (Mueller) D.; m. Silvia Dahl, Dec. 18, 1992; children: Christoph, Jan Felix, Philipp Jonathan. Student, Judson Coll., Elgin, Ill., 1982-83; MA in Psychology, Kiel U., Germany, 1992; PhD, Bundeswehr U., Hamburg, Germany, 1998. Bank apprentice Commerzbank AG, Bielefeld, 1979-81; investment advisor Berliner Commerzbank AG, Berlin, Germany, 1981-82; mgmt. assoc. Daimler-Benz AG, Stuttgart, Germany, 1991-93, human resources specialist, 1993-95; sr. mgr. human resources DaimlerChrysler Svcs. (debis) AG, Stuttgart, Germany, 1996-97; sr. mgr. corp. leadership devel. DaimlerChrysler Svcs. (debis) AG, Berlin, Germany, 1997-99; prof. bus. psychology U. Applied Scis., Lueneburg, Germany, 2000—; dean bus. psychology dept. U. Applied Scis., Lueneburg, 2000—. Contbr. chpts. to books. Mem. APA, Soc. Indsl. and Org. Psychology, Deutsche Gesellschaft Psychologie. Avocations: running, hiking, cycling, music, politics. Office: U Applied Scis, Wilschenbrucher Weg 84, D 21335 Lueneburg Germany

DELLI COLLI, HUMBERT THOMAS, chemist, product development specialist; b. Utica, N.Y., July 8, 1944; s. Cyril Thomas and Carol Dolores (Fragola) D.; m. Judith Eleanor Maloney, June 24, 1967; 1 child, Kristin Anne. BS in Chemistry, Clarkson Coll., 1966, PhD, 1971. Physical chemist Edgewood Arsenal, Md., 1971-73; research scientist Westvaco Corp., Charleston, S.C., 1973-75, devel. mgr. agrichemicals, polychemicals dept., 1975-84, devel. mgr. new technology, polychemicals dept., 1984-91; mgr. agrl. chem. devel. Westvaco Polychems., Charleston, S.C., 1991—; commd. lt. col., 1991; deputy div. chief studies and analysis div. Operation Desert Storm, 1991; cons. U.S. Army Chem. Systems Lab., Aberdeen, Md., 1971—. Contbr. articles to profl. jours.; patentee in field. Pres. Mcpl. Bd. Health, Goose Creek, S.C., 1974-75; mem. Berkeley County (S.C.) Water and Sewer Authority, 1978-79; mem. vestry bd. St. Thomas Ch., North Charleston, S.C., 1986—; with Operation Desert Storm, 1991. With U.S. Army, 1970-73; capt. USAR, 19773-92. Grantee NDEA, 1966, Clarkson Coll., 1962, 66; Uniroyal Undergrad. scholar, 1962, N.Y. State Regents scholar, 1962. Mem. AAAS, N.Y. Acad. Sci., Am. Chem. Soc., So. Weed Sci. Soc., N. Cen. Weed Control Conf., S.C. Sci. Council (adv. bd. mem.), Weed Sci. Soc. Am. Republican. Roman Catholic. Lodges: KC, Ducks Unltd. Avocations: black powder firearms, hunting, fishing, woodworking, wine collecting. Fax: 843-746-8165. Home: 7 Campanella Ct Charleston SC 29406-8606 Office: Westvaco Polychems PO Box 70848 Charleston SC 29415-0848

DELLUC, BRIGITTE, museum curator; b. Angers, France, July 27, 1936; d. Jacques and Jeanne Jehier (de Chabalier) Antoine; m. Gilles Delluc, Sept. 15, 1962; 1 child, Sophie. BA, U. Paris, 1960; D in Prehistory, U. Paris I, 1975. Engr. IBM, Paris, 1960-65; rschr. Lab. d'Ethnologie Prehistorique, Paris, 1972-82, Musées de France, Les Eyzies, 1978-85; rschr. in prehistory Mus. Nat. d'Histoire Naturelle, Paris, 1982—; curator Musée de l'Abri Pataud, Les Eyzies, 1989-99. Author: Les manifestations graphiques aurifnaciennes des environs des Eyzies, 1978, L'art pariétal archaique en Aquitaine, 1991, Discovering Lascaux, 1990, Discovering Perigord Prehistory, 1991, Préhistoire de l'Art occidental, 1995, Visiter l'abri Pataud, 1998. Recipient Palmes Académiques, Min. de l'Education Nat., 1988; officer Palmes académiques, 1996. Mem. Soc. Historique et Archéologique du Périgord (sec. gen.), Soc. Préhistorique francaise, Spéléo-Club de Perigueux. Roman Catholic. Avocation: speleology in caves with prehistoric paintings and engravings. Home: Le Bourg, 2438 St Michel Villadeix France Office: Musée de l'Abri Pataud, 24620 Les Eyzies France

DELLUC, GILLES, physician, researcher; b. Périgueux, Dordogne, France, Aug. 22, 1934; s. Paul and Geneviève D.; m. Brigitte Antoine, Sept. 15, 1962; 1 child, Sophie. MD, Sch. of Medicine, Paris, 1967; D in Quaternary Geology, Anthropology, Prehistory, Paris VI Univ., 1985. Intern, asst. dr. various hosps., Paris, 1958-70; clinic chief Medical Sch., Paris, 1968-70; chief dept. of medicine Périgueux (France) Hosp., 1970—; researcher, lab. of prehistory Mus. of l'Homme, Paris, 1985—; dir. of clinic teaching Sch. of Medicine of Bordeaux, 1980—; v.p. Hist. Fedn. of the S.W. of France, 1988—, European Ctr. Prehistoric Researches, Vezere Valley. Author: Lascaux inconnu, 1979, Lascaux un nouveau regard, 1986, Les Chasseurs de la Préhistoire, 1979, Connaitre Lascaux, 1990, L'Art Pariétal archaique en Aquitaine, 1991, Connaitre la Préhistoire en Périgord, 1993, La Nutrition Préhistorique, 1995, Préhistoire de l'Artoccidental, 1995. Mem. Commn. des Sites (Dordogne), Périgueux, 1981—, Environmental Commn., Périgueux, 1981—. Lt. Navy, 1961-63. Named officer Palmes Académiques, 1997. Mem. Spéléoclub de Périgueux, Groupe de recherche pédagogique en diabétologie, Soc. Prehistorique francaise, Soc. History and Archeology Périgord, Fedn. francaise d'Archéologie, Historic and Archeologic Soc. of Perigord (pres. 1981—). Roman Catholic. Avocations: speleology, research of caves with prehistoric paintings or engravings, photography. Home: Le Bourg, 24380 Saint Michel France Office: Centre Hosp, 24000 Périgueux France

DELL'UTRI, MARCELLO, member European Parliament; b. Palermo, Sicily, Italy, Sept. 11, 1941. Mem. European Parliament, Brussels, 1999—; mem. com. on citizens' freedoms and rights, justice and home affairs, substitute mem. com. on legal affairs and the internal market, mem. del. for rels. with Switzerland, Iceland and Norway. Mem. Group of European People's Party (Christian Dems.) and European Dems. Mem. Forza Italia Party. *

DELMAS, MICHEL PIERRE, chemist, educator, researcher; b. Saint-Hippolyte, France, Aug. 28, 1947; s. Jean Casimir and Francine Marie (Friocourt) D.; m. Mau-Hoa Quach, Feb. 10, 1975; children: Guo-Fang, Guo-Hua. BS, U. Paul Sabatier, 1968, MS, 1969, PhD, 1971; DSc, Inst. Nat. Poly., 1980. Asst. prof. U., Phnom Penh, Cambodia, 1973-75, Sfax, Tunisia, 1975-81, Toulouse, France, 1981-83; assoc. prof. U. Inst. Nat. Poly., Toulouse, 1983-89, prof., 1989—; v.p. Inst. Nat. Poly. U. Toulouse, 1986-93. Contbr. articles to profl. jours.; patentee in field. With French mil., 1973-75. Decorated Chevalier Ordre Nat. du Merite. Fellow Inst. Francais des Relations Internationales,. Avocations: tennis, lecturing, painting. Home: 6 allee des Amazones, 31320 Auzeville-Tolosane France Office: Inst Nat Poly Ecole Nat Superieure Chimie, 118 Rt de Narbonne, 31077 Toulouse France

DELMON, BERNARD, chemistry educator; b. Le Havre, France, July 8, 1932; s. Andre and Paule (Delaplanche) D.; m. Brigitte Honore, Dec. 27, 1960; children: Xavier, Emmanuele, Elisabeth. Lic. Sci. Math. and Physics, U. Paris, 1954; Engr., Ecole Nat. Superieure Petrole, Paris, 1959; PhD, U. Cath. Louvain, Leuven, Belgium, 1959; DSc d'Etat, U. Grenoble, France, 1965. Asst. U. Cath. Louvain, Leuven, 1959-63; engr. Inst. Franc. Pétrole, Grenoble, 1963-68; maître de recherches Inst. Franc. Pétrole, Rueil Malmaison, France, 1969-70; chargé de cours U. Cath. Louvain, Louvain-la-Neuve, Belgium, 1970-74, prof., 1974-76, prof. ordinaire, 1976-97; prof. emeritus U. Cath. Louvain, Louvain-la-Neuve, 1997—; pres. dept. chimie et physique appliquées U. Cath. Louvain, Louvain-la-Neuve, Belgium, 1978-81, head Lab. Catalysis, 1984-97; chmn. working party on chem. engring. in the applications of catalysis European Fedn. Chem. Engring., 1991—; chmn. subcom. on advanced materials Internat. Union Pure and Applied Chemistry, 1993-97; mem. internat. adv. bd. State Key Lab. Chinese Acad. Sci., Dalian, 1999—; guest prof. State Key Lab. Coal Conversion, Taiyuan, 1999—. Author: Introduction à la Cinétique Hétérogène, 1969; co-author: The Control of the Reactivity Solids, 1979; co-editor Procs. Series of Congress, Preparation of Catalysts I, 1976, II, 1979, IV, 1987, V, 1991, VI, 1995, VII, 1998, Catalyst Deactivation, 1980, 87, 94, 99, Hydrotreatment and Hydrocracking of Oil Fractions, 1997, 99. Assoc. mem. Académie Royale de Belgique, Brussels, 1987; mem. Royal Belgian Acad. Coun. for Applications of Sci., Brussels, 1988. Recipient Humbolt Rsch. award Von Humbolt Stiftung, Germany, 1992. Mem. Am. Chem. Soc., Am. Ceramic Soc., French Chem. Soc., Belgian Chem. Soc. Roman Catholic. Achievements include 18 patents for catalysts, new materials. Home: 17 Ave des Merisiers, 1342 Limelette Belgium Office: U Catholique de Louvain, Pl Croix du Sud 2/17, 1348 Louvain-la-Neuve Belgium

DELMONT, JEAN PIERRE, gastroenterologist, educator; b. Bordeaux, France, Jan. 18, 1933; s. Pierre and Renee (Vallet) D.; m. Morita Mauri, Jan. 5, 1955; four children. BS, U. Marseille, 1955, MD, 1961. Resident, fellow Marseille Hosp., France, 1952-61; assoc. prof. Univ. Hosp., Marseille, 1966-70; prof. Univ. Hosp., Nice, France, 1970—; vis. prof. UCLA, San Francisco, 1976, U. Guadaljara, Mex., 1981. Author: La sprue non tropicale, 1961; editor: The Sphincter of Oddi, 1976, Cancer of the Exocrine Pancreas, 1986, Liver Transplantation, 1992. Pres. Internat. League Against Racism and Anti-Semitism, 1973-86. Decorated comdr. Academic Palms, chevalier d'honneur; recipient French Fedn. medal for rugby. Mem. French Gastroenterology Soc. (pres. 1993), Bockus Soc., Am. Gastroenterology Assn., Belgian Italian and Mexican Gastroenterology Assn., Omnisport Univ. Club (hon. pres.). Avocations: skiing, mountain hiking, pre-Colombian art. E-mail: jp.delmont@wanadoo.fr. Office: L'Archet Hosp, 06202 Nice France

DEL MORAL, AGUSTÍN, physics educator, researcher; b. Córdoba, Spain, Mar. 4, 1942; s. Agustín del Moral and Rosario Gámiz; m. María-Jesus Azanza, Sept. 5, 1967; children: Nerea, Victoria. M in Physics, U. Complutense, Madrid, 1965; PhD in Physics, U. Complutense, 1972; postgrad., Spanish Nuc. Ctr., Madrid, 1965. Rschr. Materials Lab., Ministry Pub. Works, Madrid, 1966; adj. prof. U. Navarra, San Sebastián, Spain, 1967-71, 73-75; vis. prof. U. Southampton, Eng., 1971-73; prof. agregated U. Granada, Spain, 1975-79; chair prof. condensed matter physics U. Zaragoza, Spain, 1979—; vis. rschr. Lab. L. Néel, France, 1975-76, U. Ill., Urbana, 1986, U. Southampton, 1976-87, Naval Surface Warfare Ctr., 1988, Brookhaven Nat. Lab, 1992, MIT, Cambridge, 1998—; internat. advisor Internat. Confs. on Magnetism (ICM, IUPAP), 1990-91, 96-97, mem. program com., 1993-94; expert large magnetic installations European Union, Brussels, 1990-91, mem. network for 100T magnet project, 1998-2000; head magnetism lab. Spanish Rsch. Coun. CSIC, Zaragoza, 1985-92, 98—; referee phys. rev., letters Am. Inst. Physics, N.Y.C., 1991—, others; mem. Concerted European Action on Magnets, 1988-94, So. European Pulsed Field Network, 1995-98, High Magnetic Field European Network, European Union, 2000-03; invited spkr. 20 magnetism meetings, 11 oral presentations. Contbr. about 30 chpts. to magnetism books, over 175 articles on magnetism to Phys. Rev. Letters, 1997, 98, Nature, 1997, others. Sublt., Spanish Army, 1966. Named Master on Physics Nat. award Spanish Govt., Madrid, 1965; grantee European Union, Brussels, 1985-96, Spanish-Am. Joint Rsch. Com., Washington and Madrid, 1986; Br. Coun.-Spanish Govt., 1990-95; exch. program MIT-Spanish MEC, 1998—; grantee NATO, 1998—. Fellow Inst. Physics (London) (chartered physicist); mem. Scis. Acad. Zaragoza (academician), European Magnetic Materials and Applications Confs. (internat. adv. mem. 1987-98, chmn. Zaragoza EMMA 1998, spkr.). Catholic. Achievements include involvement in Concerted European Action on Magnets, a network of 50 European Labs. targeting on very hard magnetic materials for tech. applications, European Union, 1988-94; also European Pulsed Field Network, a network of European magnetic labs., using strong pulsed magnet fields for rsch. in physics and advanced magnetic materials, European Union, 1999—. Avocations: mountaineering, philately, gardening, collecting lead soldiers. Fax: 34 976 761229. E-mail: demoral@posta.unizar.es. Office: U Zaragoza Fac Scis CM Phys, Ciudad Univ Pza S Francisco, E-50009 Zaragoza Aragon, Spain

DELO, ELLEN SANDERSON, lawyer; b. Nassawadox, Va., Nov. 29, 1944; d. Robert G. and Daisy B. (Hitchens) Sanderson; m. Arthur C. Delo Jr., Mar. 20, 1971; 1 child, Marjorie Cotton Delo. BA, U. Richmond, 1966; JD, Rutgers U., 1977; LLM, NYU, 1985. Bar: N.J., 1977, U.S. Dist. Ct. N.J., 1977, U.S. Tax Ct., 1987, U.S. Ct. Appeals (2nd cir.) 1997, D.C. 1999, N.Y. 1999. Law clk. to Hon. John J. Geronimo N.J. Superior Ct., 1977-78; assoc. Lamb Hutchinson Chappell Ryan & Hartung, Jersey City, 1978-80, Chasan Leyner Holland & Tarrant, Jersey City, 1980-84; assoc. Stryker Tams & Dill, Newark, 1985-92, ptnr., 1993-98; exec. compensation assoc. Bachelder Law Offices, N.Y.C., 1998—; lectr. on tax issues. Contbr. articles to profl. jours. Lay reader Ch. St. Andrew and Holy Communion, South Orange, N.J. Mem. ABA (tax sect., employee benefits com.). Democrat. Episcopalian. Avocation: animal welfare organizations and activities. Home: 340 Montrose Ave South Orange NJ 07079-2439

DELON, ALAIN, actor; b. Sceaux, France, Nov. 8, 1935; s. Fabien and Edith (Arnold) D.; m. Francine-Nathalie Canovas, Aug. 13, 1964 (div.); children: Anthony, Alain-Fabien. Student, Cath. Boarding Sch., Bagneux, France. Motion picture appearances include Quand la Femme S'en Mele, 1957, Sois Belle et Tais-Toi, 1957, Faibles Femmes, 1958, Le Chemin des Ecoliers, 1959, Plein Soleil, 1959, Rocco et Ses Freres, 1960, Quelle Joie de Vivre, 1961, Les Amours Celebres, 1961, L'Eclisse, 1961, Le Diable et Les Dix Commandements, 1962, Le Guepard, 1962, Melodie en Sous Sol, 1962, La Tulipe Noire, 1963, Les Felins, 1963, L'Insoumis, 1964, La Rolls Royce Jaune, 1964, Once a Thief, 1964, Les Centurions, 1965, Paris Brule-T-Il?, 1965, Texas Across the River, 1966, Les Aventuriers, 1966, Le Samourai, 1967, Histoires Extraordinaires, 1967, Diaboliquement Votre 1967, Adieu l'ami, 1968, Girl on a Motorcycle, 1968, La Piscine, 1968, Jeff, 1968, Die Boss, Die Quietly, 1970, Borsalino, 1970, Le Cercle Rouge, 1971, Madly, 1971, Doucement Les Basses, 1971, Red Sun, 1971, La Veuve Couderc, 1971, Assassination of Trotsky, 1971, Le Professeur, 1972, Scorpio, 1972, Traitement de Choc, 1972, Les Granges Brulées, 1973, Big Guns, 1973, Deux Hommes dans La Ville, 1973, La Race des Seigneurs, 1973, Les Seins de Glace, 1974, Borsalino and C, 1974, Zorro, 1974, Flic Story, 1975, Le Gitan, 1975, Mr. Klein, 1975, Comme un Boomerang, 1976, Le Gang, 1976, Armaguedon, 1976, L'Homme Pressé, 1977, Mort d'un Pourri, 1977, Attention Les Enfants Regardent, 1977, Airport 80, 1979, Trois Hommes a Abattre, 1980, Pour La Peau d'un Flic, 1981, Le Choc, 1982, Le Battant, 1982, Un Amour de Swann, 1983, Notre Histoire, 1984, Parole de Flic, 1985, Le Passage, 1986, Ne Re'veillez Pas un Flic qui Dort, 1988, Novelle Vague, 1989, Dancing Machine, 1990, Le Retour de Casanova, 1991, Un Crime, 1992, L'Ours en Peluche, 1993, Lejour Etlanuit, 1996, Une Chance Surdeux, 1997; stage appearances include Tis Pity She's a Whore, 1961, 62, Les Yeux Creves, 1996, Variations Énigmatiques, 1997. Served with French Marine Corps, 1953-55, Indo-China. Recipient Prix David de Donatello, Taormina Festival, 1972, Commandeur Arts et Lettres, 1986, Legion D'Honneur, 1991, Ours d'Or a Berlin, 1995, St. Georges a Moscow, 1999. Address: care Leda Prodns, 4 Rue Chambiges, 75008 Paris France

DELONAY, MICHAEL JOSEPH, insurance program specialist; b. San Jose, Calif., Apr. 21, 1952; s. Eugene L. and Ruth M. D.; m. Jessica Wilson, Aug. 24, 1974 (div. 1990); children: Mason, Braden; m. Catherine Evelyn Sullivan, Dec. 28, 1991. BA, U. Wis., 1976. Claims adjuster Commercial Union Ins., West Allis, Wis., 1979; claims supr. Commercial Union Ins., Oakbrook Terrace, Ill., 1979-83, Providence Washington, Elmhurst, Ill., 1983-86; from claims specialist to claims supr. Crum & Forster Mgrs., Chgo., 1986-89, claims supr., 1989-92; sr. claims specialist Coregis Ins., Chgo., 1992-98, program specialist, 1998—. Trustee Village of Carol Stream, Ill., 1993—; commr. DuPage Water Commn., Elmhurst, Ill., 1998—; bd. dirs. Bennington Homeowners Assn., Carol Stream, Ill., 1999—, No. DuPage Cable TV Consortium, Carol Stream, Ill., 1994—. E-mail: mdelonay@hotmail.com. Fax: 630-664-1064. Home: 1061 Rockport Dr Carol Stream IL 60188-4716 Office: Village of Carol Stream 500 N Gary Ave Carol Stream IL 60188-1899

DELORENZO, FERRUCCIO FRANCESCO, internist; b. Washington, Mar. 11, 1966; arrived in England, 1992; s. Francesco and Marinella (D'Aniello) D. MD, U. Naples, Italy, 1990, Cert. in Specialist Tng., 1995; PhD, Imperial Coll., London, 2000. Rscher. U. Naples, Milan, Italy, 1991-92; clin. asst. U. Coll. Hosp., London, 1992-93; sr. house officer Ashford Hosp., Middlesex, Eng., 1993-94; registrar Royal Brampton Hosp., London, 1994—; clin. rschr. Thrombosis Rsch. Inst., London, 1994—, lectr., 1996—; specialist registrar in internal medicine Ashford Hosp., London, 1999—. Author: (book) Deep Vein Thrombosis, 1997; contbr. over 50 articles to med. jours. Recipient fellowships European Molecular Biology Lab., Heidelburg, Germany, 1988, U. Naples, Italy, 1990. Avocations: tennis, classical music, travel. E-mail: dlorenzo@tri-london.ac.uk. Office: Thrombosis Rsch Inst, 1B Manresa Rd, Chelsea London SW3 6LR, England

DELORME, JACQUES, pediatrician; b. Antibes, France, Aug. 6, 1950; s. Georges and Odette (Bachelard) D.; m. Annie Merme, July 21, 1973; children: Arnaud, Xavier. MD, U. Marseille, 1973. Intern Martiques Hosp., France, 1975-78, attache de constultation en premier, 1979; practice medicine specializing in pediatrics Martiques, 1979—; charge d'enseignement clin. á la faculte Marseille, 1986—. V.p. Assn. des Parents d'eleve, Ecole de St. Pierre, Martiques, 1983-85, CES Pablo Picasso, Martiques, 1985—. Mem. Pediatrician Union. Roman Catholic. Avocations: tennis, skiing. Home: Lavigne de la Gravade, 13500 Martiques Saint Pierre France Office: 10 rue Jean Roque, 13500 Martiques France

DELORS, JACQUES, former government official; b. Paris, July 20, 1925; s. Louis and Jeanne (Rigal) D.; m. Marie Lephaille, Apr. 26, 1948; children: Martine Delors Aubry, Jean-Paul (dec.). Diploma, Ctr. Higher Studies of Banking, U Paris. Civil servant Banque de France, 1944-62; mem. Econ. and Social Coun., 1959-62; planning bd., chief of social affairs svc. Banque de France, 1962-69; gen. sec. permanent tng. and social promotion Econ. and Social Coun., 1968-73; spl. adviser on social and cultural affairs, Prime Minister Jacques Chaban-Delmas, 1969-72; mem. gen. council Bank of France, 1973-79; assoc. prof. U. Paris-Dauphine, 1973-79, dir. Center Research of Work and Health, 1975-79; Min. of Economy and Fin., 1981-84; mayor of Clichy, 1983-84; pres. European Commn., 1985-95; pres. UNESCO Internat. Commn. Edn. 21st Century, 1994—; pres. Groupement d'Études et de Recherches Notre Europe, 1996—. Author: Les Indicateurs Sociaux, 1971; Changer, 1975, (with others) En sortir Ou Pas, 1985, La France Par L'Europe, 1988, Le Nouveau Concert Européen, 1992, Pour Entrer dans le XXI Siècle, 1994, l'Unite d'un Homme, 1994, Combats pour l'Europe, 1996. Mem. steering com. French Socialist Party. Decorated Officier de la Légion d'honneur; recipient honorary doctorates from 24 univs.;Recipient Jean Monnet, Prince des Asturies, Onassis, Charlemagne, Carlos V and Erasmus prizes.. Office: Assn Notre Europe, 44 rue Notre-Dame des Victoires, F-75002 Paris France

DE LOS SANTOS, HECTOR JOSÉ, solid state device scientist, researcher; b. Santo Domingo, Dominican Republic, Dec. 15, 1957; came to U.S., 1968; s. Francisco José and Anadina (Hungria) De Los S.; m. Iris Violeta Santiago, June 12, 1982; children: Mara Iris, Hector Francisco, Joseph José. BS in Elec. Engring., U. P.R., Mayaguez, 1979; MS in Engring., UCLA, 1981; MS in Elec. Engring., Purdue U., 1985, PhD in Elec. Engring., 1989. Mem. tech. staff Hughes Aircraft Co., L.A., 1979-81; engr. Intel Caribbean, Inc., Las Piedras, P.R., 1981-84; scientist Hughes Space and Comms. Co., L.A., 1989—. Contbr. articles to profl. jours. Named Hispanic Engr. of Yr., Hispanic Engr. Nat. Achievement Awards Com., 1994. Mem. IEEE (sr.), IEEE Microwaves Theory and Techniques Soc. (chmn. L.A. chpt. 1990-92), Sigma Xi, Tau Beta Pi, Eta Kappa Nu. Achievements include patents for microwave active notch filter and operating method with photonic bandgap crystal feedback loop, tunable microwave network using microelectromechanical switches, photonic bandgap crystal frequency multipliers and pulse blanking filter for use therewith. Avocations: music, reading biographies, walking. Office: Hughes Space and Comms Co 1950 E Imperial Hwy El Segundo CA 90245-2701

DE LOUSANOFF, OLEG, lawyer; b. Frankfurt am Main, Germany, June 14, 1950; s. Oleg and Marianne (Idel) de L.; m. Christina Tuerck; children: Nadejda, Nikolaj, Anatol, Victor. First Legal State Exam, U. Freiburg, Breisgau, Germany, 1976, D summa cum laude, 1978; 2nd Legal State Exam, Stuttgart, 1980; student, London U. Econs., Keio U., Tokyo; LLM, U. Calif., Berkeley, 1981. Bar: Frankfurt 1981; notary pub. Asst. prof. Law Faculty U. Freiburg, Germany, 1976-80; assoc. Hengeler Mueller, Frankfurt am Main, Germany, 1981-83; ptnr. Hengeler Mueller, Frankfurt am Main, 1984—; pres. supervisory bds. OTIS Escalator GmbH, 1993-99; spkr., lectr. in field. Author: 3 books; contbr. over 50 articles to profl. jours. Trustee Dr. M. Lee Pearce Found., Lichtenstein, 1996—, Vorontzov Palace and Corps of Pages Meml. Trust. Mem. Internat. Bar Asn., Union Internat. Avocats., Union Noblesse Russe, German-French Soc. Frankfurt am Main. Russian Orthodox. Avocations: classical guitar, tennis, old books, Bordeaux wines. Home: Tannenwaldallee 11, 61348 Bad Homburg v.d.h Hessen, Germany Office: Hegeler Mueller Wietzel Wie, Bockenheimer Landstr 51, 60325 Frankfurt am Main Germany

DE LOUVILLE DE TOUCY, FRANCOIS-EUDES, fine art investment consultant, import executive; b. Paris, Aug. 29, 1947; s. The Marquis de Louville and The Baronne de Toucy. Degree in Bus. Mgmt., Unieco, Liège, Belgium, 1969; cert. in systems analysis, K.B.S. Computer Svcs., London, 1984. Singer, songwriter Phillips, Paris, 1970-71; dir. Artilands, London, 1970-75, Ebury Gallery, 1977-83, F. de Louville Fine Art, 1984—; chmn. de Louville Holdings, U.K., 1969—; launched co. Servus 2000 Ltd., 2000—. Author: The Male Nude, 1985. Avocations: art, music, sports. Office: De Louville Fine Art, 20 Brook Dr, London SW11 4TT, England

DELP, LUDWIG, solicitor, consultant; b. Darmstadt, Germany, Nov. 25, 1921; s. Friedrich and Frieda (Erbes) D.; m. Irmgard Roters, Apr. 12, 1954; children: Joachim, Gisela, Peter. Dipl-Vokswirt, U. Munich, 1949, DrJur, 1950. Solicitor Munich, 1951—; hon. prof. U. Erlangen, Germany, 1993; bd. dirs. Deutsches Bucharchiv, Munich, 1948—. Author: Die Kulturabgabe, 1950, Das Recht des geistigen Schaffens, 1993, Der Verlagsvertrag, 7th edit., 2000, Kleines Praktikum für Urheber-und Verlagsrecht, 4th edit., 2000, Buchwissenschaften-Dokumentation und Information, 1997; editor: Das gesamte Recht der Publizistik, 1954—. Recipient Bundesverdienstkreuz am Bande, Bonn and Munich, 1988. Mem. Rechtsanwaltskammer München, Börsenverein des Deutschen Buchhandels, Buchhändlerverbände Bayerns. Office: van-der-Tann Str 5, D-80539 Munich Germany

DELPACHITRA, SARATH BANDULA, economist; b. Colombo, Sri Lanka, Feb. 18, 1955; arrived in New Zealand, 1991; s. Sirisena and Leela (Randeniya) D.; m. Nayana Devika Domingo, Nov. 3, 1955; 3 children. BSc with honors, Peradeniya U., Sri Lanka, 1980; M of Comm. with honors, Lincoln U., Canterbury, New Zealand, 1990; PhD, U. So. Queensland, 1999. Asst. mgr. Plantations Corp., Sri Lanka, 1981-84; dep. dir. Gen. Treasury, Sri Lanka, 1984-92; sr. lectr. Open Poly., New Zealand, 1991—; economic educator U. So. Queensland, Australia, 1996—; convenor Econ. Tchrs. Australia, 1996-97. Contbr. articles to profl. jours. Rsch. fellow U. So. Queensland, 1995, UN Devel. Pprogram fellow, 1988. Mem. N.Y. Acad. Scis., Economists Soc., IEEA. Office: U So Queensland Sch Acctg & Fin, Open Polytech CAFI, Toowoomba QLD 4350, Australia

DELPECH, RENE GEORGES, science educator; b. Paris, July 29, 1920; m. Camille Theophile and Josephine Marie (Bouchardy) D.; m. Madeleine Marguerite Vallas, July 13, 1944; children: Claude, Bernard, Christiane. G-rad. in agronomist engring., Institut Nat. Agronomique, Paris, 1942, post-grad., 1943; D in Nature Scis., Paris SUD U., Orsay, France, 1975. Agrl. master Dept. of Agriculture, Toulouse, France, 1943-46; agrl. office engr. Dept. of Agriculture, Lille, France, 1946-48; works head Institut Nat. Agronomique, Paris, 1948-64, asst. chief, 1964-77, lectr., 1977-78, prof., 1978-85; gen. sec. Corn's Coops. Fedn., Toulouse, 1943-46; scientific adviser Nat. Park Vanoise, Chambery, France, 1975-99, Regional Scientific Coun. of Natural Patrimony, Lyon, France, 1995-99. Author: Typology of Forest Habitats-Vocabulary, 1985, Phytosociology and Pastoralism, 1989, Dictionary of Agriculture, 1999; contbr. articles to profl. publs. Recipient Gold medal French Agrl. Acad., 1975. Mem. French Bot. Soc. (v.p. 1996, Coun. prize 1989), French Ecol. Soc., Internat. Fedn. of Phytosociology (adminstr. 1992). Avocations: photography, gardening. Home: 40 Av Jean Jaures, F84290 Ste Cecile les Vigne France

DELPH, SHIRLEY COX, artist, designer, illustrator, consultant; b. Pasadena, Tex., Aug. 5, 1942; d. W. O. and Eula (Howell) Cox; m. Charles Robert Cox, July 12, 1964 (div. 1976); children: Robin Cox Schippel, Amy Cox Ecklund; m. Fred Kevin Delph, Apr. 15, 1978; 1 child, Nicolas Kevin. Student, Washington U., St. Louis, 1960-62; BFA, Chouinard Art Inst., 1964. Asst. Paramount Studios, L.A., 1963, design dept. Catalina Swimwear, L.A., 1964; designer Georgia Bullock, Inc., Santa Monica, Calif., 1964-65; adj. prof. textural design classes Sch. Internat. Studies Stanford U., Calif., 1966-67; owner, designer Cockamamy Needleart, Reno, Nev., 1968-76; tchr. needleart design Anderson Ranch Arts Found., Aspen/Snomass, Colo., 1977; owner, designer Needlepoint Whimsies Mfg., Austin, Tex., 1977-85; owner, artist Shirley Delph Design Art Licensing, Dripping Springs, Tex., 1985—; creative cons. Johnson Creative Arts, Townsend, Mass., 1973—, ThermoServ, Inc., Dallas, 1990— cons. design Royal Doulton USA, Somerset, N.J., 1993—, Hoffmaster Corp., 1993—, Recycled Paper Greetings, 1990—, Conimar Corp., 1995—, Am. Greetings, Cleve., 1996—, numerous others. Featured in Am. Home Crafts, Better Homes and Gardens mag.; contbr. article Better Homes and Gardens mag. Mem. adv. com. Paul Laxalt for US Senate, Reno, 1976, local Rep. candidates, Austin, 1985-89; del. Rep. leadership conf., Washington, 1976; spkr. enrichment programs Austin Area Schs., 1980-95. Recipient Tex. SesquiCentennial prize Austin Heritage Soc., 1986. Mem. Am. Quilters Soc., Nat. Trust, Lawyers Wives Assn. Stanford U. Law Sch. (program coord.), Putting Husbands Through Hon. Law Sch. Degree, Nat. Trust for Hist. Preservation. Avocations: sailing, gardening, quilting. Office: Shirley Delph Design Studio 606 Blue Hills Dr Dripping Springs TX 78620-3907

DELPIANO, MARCO ANTONIO, electrophysiologist, research scientist; b. Valparaiso, Chile, Nov. 4, 1940; arrived in Germany, 1969; s. Carlos Eduardo and Petronila Elsa (Robinson) D.; m. Sigrid Gertrud Uebel, Mar. 26, 1967; children: Bettina Antonia, Carlos Eduardo. Degree in biology, Chile U., Santiago, 1966; Biol. Diplomate, Giessen (Germany) U., 1971, Dr.sc., 1979. Biology asst. Chile U., Santiago, 1967-68, neurophysiologist, 1968-69; rsch. asst. Giessen U., 1970-78, Bochum (Germany) U., 1978-80; group leader Max Planck Inst., Dortmund, Germany, 1980—; rsch. scientist Max Planck Inst., Bad Nauheim, Germany, 1972-78; vis. rschr. SUNY, Bklyn., 1995-96; vis. prof. U. Valparaiso, Chile, 1999—. Author: Oxygen Sensing in Tissue, 1988, Arterial Chemoreception, 1993, Arterial Chemoreception Cell to System, 1994, Frontiers in Arterial Chemoreception, 1996, Oxygen Sensing: Molecule to Man, 1999; contbr. articles to profl. jours. Deutscher Akademischer Austauschdienst fellow, Bonn, Germany, 1969. Mem. AAAS, German Physiol. Soc., Arterial Chemoreception, N.Y. Acad. Sci., European Neurosci. Assn., Chilean Biol. Soc., Chilean Soc. Physiol. Sci. Roman Catholic. Avocations: classical music, photography, jogging, swimming. E-mail: marco.delpiano@mpi-dortmund.mpg.de. Home: Wallrabe Str 21, 44139 Dortmund Germany Office: MPI for Molecular Physiol, Otto-Hahn-str 11, 44227 Dortmund Germany

DEL PINO, GUSTAVO A., government official; b. Buenos Aires, Oct. 9, 1952; s. Guillermo R. and Delia Maria (Spallarossa) del P.; m. Irene L. Rodriguez, Dec. 13, 1980; children: Mariana Sofia, Maria Laura. BSEE, U. Buenos Aires, 1978; MS in Computer Sci., U. Ill., 1987; MBA, IAE, Buenos Aires, 1995. Sr. rschr. Brasil-Argentina Rsch. Program in Computer Sci., Buenos Aires, 1987-89; sr. cons. UN Devel. Program, Buenos Aires, 1989-90; staff of undersec. info. sys. Sec. of Pub. Affairs, Buenos Aires, 1990-91, nat. dir. audit and control of info. sys., 1991-92, nat. dir. info. sys., 1992-95, nat. dir. standardization and tech. assistance, 1995—; Argentinian rep. to Ibero-Am. Conf. Info. Tech. Authorities; prof. U. Austral, Buenos Aires, 1995-96. Editor: Technologie Standards for the Public Administration, vols. 1 to 3, 1997, 99, Technologie Standards for the Public Administration, vols. 1 to 10, 1995; author: RISC Architectures, 1988. U. Buenos Aires Peruilh fellow, 1984. Mem. IEEE (sr.), Assn. Computing Machinery, Internet Soc. Avocations: photography, hunting, snorkeling. Home: Juncal 1661, 1062 Buenos Aires Argentina Office: Secretary of Public Affairs, Av Roque Saenz Peña 511, 1035 Buenos Aires Argentina

DELPORT, VOLKER, telecommunications engineer; b. Suhl, Germany, Apr. 23, 1965; s. Wolfgang and Helgard (Fritzsche) D.; m. Elke Löffler. Telecomms. engr., Tech. U., 1991. Project mgr. XCom AG, Chemnitz, Germany, 2000—. Contbr. articles to profl. jours. With mil., 1984-86. Avocations: chess, piano. Home: Rochlitzer Strasse 39, D-09111 Chemnitz Germany Office: XCOM AG, Dresdner Strasse 40, D-09130 Chemnitz Germany

DEL RIO, JUAN LEGARRETA, plastic surgeon; b. Santiago, Chile, Oct. 20, 1949; s. Juan and Adela (Legarreta) del R.; m. Angeles Pulido Haba, Oct. 21, 1976; two children. BS, St. George's Coll., 1966; MD, U. Navarra, 1974. Resident in plastic surgery U. Madrid, Spain, 1974-78; plastic & reconstructive surgeon Ruber Internat. Hosp., Madrid, 1991—. Mem.

Spanish Soc. Plastic Reconstructive and Aesthetic Surgery, Internat. Soc. Aesthetic Plastic Surgery. Home: Camino Nuevo 65 La Moraleja, 28109 Alcobendas Madrid, Spain Office: Hosp Ruber Internat, La Maso, 38, 28034 Madrid Spain

DELRIO, PAOLO, surgeon; b. Naples, Italy, Apr. 23, 1964; s. Giovanni Delrio and Lidia Mercurio; m. Marialuisa Firpo, July 1, 1996; 1 child, Giovanni. Degree in Medicine, Federico II, Naples, 1988; MD, U. Naples. Clin. asst. U. Hosp., Naples, 1988-92; rsch. asst. U. Coll. London, 1993-94; clin. asst. City Hosp., Sessa Aurunca, Naples, 1994-95; sr. clin. asst. Villa Tasso, Naples, 1995-96; assoc. prof. surg. oncology Nat. Cancer Inst., Naples, 1996—. Astor fellow Univ. Coll. London, 1993. Avocations: swimming, reading, traveling. E-mail: delrio@mclink.it. Fax: 0039081418620. Office: Nat Cancer Inst Divsn Surg, Via M Semmola, 80131 Naples Italy

DEL RIO-HERRERA, SERGIO, banking executive; b. Tampico, Mexico, May 4, 1954; s. Sergio Del Rio and Graciela Herrera; m. Gabriela Mendoza, May 2, 1986; children: Sergio, Monica, Arturo. BS in Civil Engrng., U. Tamaulipas, 1978; M in Engrng., U. Mex., 1980; MA, The Am. U., 1984. Sr. cons. FOA Cons., Mex., 1979-81, 84-86; mktg. asst. Caribbeana Coun., Washington, 1983-84; investment advisor Operadora de Bolsa, S.A., Mex., 1986-89; fin. planning mgr. Columbia Labs., Mex., 1989; ptnr. Altec Cons., Mex., 1990-93; dir. Bancomer, S.A., Monterrey, Mex., 1994—. Mem. Mex. Inst. Fin. (v.p. 1992-94), Club San Agustin. Avocations: mountain biking, swimming. Office: Bancomer SA, Diagonal Sta Engracia 221, 64710 Monterrey Mexico

DEL SER, TEODORO, neurologist; b. Leon, Spain, Apr. 12, 1950; s. Teodoro Del Ser and Asunción Quijano; m. Maria Pilar Bartolome, Feb. 27, 1974; children: David, Pablo, Jaime Marcos. Licenciatura en psicologia, U. Complutense, Madrid, 1973, licenciatura en medicina, 1976, MD, 1987; grad. en sociologia politica, Escuela Estudios Politicas, Madrid, 1975. Resident Hosp. Iz de Octubre, Madrid, 1977-81; stagier Unité Izi INSERM, Paris, 1981-82; assoc. prof. psychology U. Complutense, Madrid, 1984-87; chief sect. Hosp. Severo Ochoa, Leganes, Spain, 1987—. Editor: Demencias Conceptos Actuales, 1992, Evaluacion Neuropsicologica y Funcionisl de la Demencia, 1994. Mem. Soc. Española Neurologia, European Neurol. Soc. Office: Hosp Severo Ochoa, Avda Orellana S/N, 28911 Leganès Madrid, Spain

DELSOL, MICHEL, biology educator; b. Montignac, France, Aug. 12, 1922; s. Louis and Marie-Louise (Peyrod) D.; m. Nicole Demay, June 29, 1946; children: Chantal, Jean Philippe, Marie Laure, Xavier, Marie. DSc, Etudes Secondaires, Paris, 1946. Asst. Faculty Scis., Paris, 1948-52; prof. Cath. U., Lyon, France, 1952-90, emeritus, 1990—; dir. Hautes Etudes, Paris, 1967—, hon., 1990—; mem. sci. counsel Dictionnaire du Darwinisme et de l'Evolution. Author Peut-on crér des Etres nouveaux?, 1968, Anatomie du système vasculaire des Têtards de Batraciens, 1972, Hasard-Ordre et Finalité en Biologie, 1973, Causes-Lois-Hasard en biologie, 1989, L'Evolution Biologique Quelques données actuelles, 1989, L'evolution biologque en vingt pro positions, 1991, L'origine des espèces aujourd'hui, 1995; editor Traité de Zoologie, vol. 14, 1986, 95; dir. collection Science-Histoire-Philosophie, 48 vols.; contbr. over 250 articles to profl. jours. Mem. French Zool. Soc., Societe Histoire Et Epistemologie Scis. Delavie. Roman Catholic. Home: 38 Quai Gailleton, 69002 Lyon France

DELTORT, BRUNO JEAN LOUIS, engineering executive; b. Nimes, France, Feb. 26, 1965; s. Louis and Paule (Gabeau) D.; m. Sophie Ferry, Aug. 11, 1990; children: Emilie, Adrien. Degree in engrng., Ecole Nat. Superieure, Brest, France, 1990; DEA, Ecole Centrale de Nantes, France, 1990; PhD, Ecole des Mines de Paris, 1993. Rsch. engr. Etablissement Technique Central de L' Armement, Paris, 1990-94; head vehicle design dept. Ecole Nat. Superieure Ingenieurs Etudes Techs. D'Armement, Brest, 1994-98; reliability engr., dept. mgr. asst. Centre Nat. d'Etudes Spatiales, Guyanais, 1999—. Contbr. articles to profl. jours. Mem. Soc. Automobile Engrng. Avocations: chess, boomerang. E-mail: bruno.deltort@cnes.fr. Office: Centre Spatial Guyanais, BP # 726, 97387 Kourou Cedex France Address: 11 Square Zulemaro, 97310 Kourou France

DEL TURCO, OTTAVIANO, minister of finance. Mgr. Socialist Youth Fedn. Rome, 1962-65; asst. sec. gen. Cgil, 1977; with Fiom, 1980-84; mem. Lower House, Italy, 1994-96, Senate, Italy, 1996; min. of finance Italy; head Nat. Anti-Mafia Commn., 1996—. Office: Ministry of Fin, Viale Europa 242, 00144 Rome Italy*

DE LUCA, ANTHONY JAMES, psychoanalyst, theologian; b. N.Y.C.; s. James Carl and Antoinette (Scarano) DeL. BA, St. John's U., 1957; STB, Cath. U. Am., 1961; BS, Queens Coll., 1963; MA, Fordham U., 1965, PhD, 1971; MA, St. John's U., 1973; DD, Lafayette U.; cert. psychoanalysis/psychotherapy, Postgrad. Ctr. Mental Health, 1975; postdoctoral studies, Georgetown U., 1997-98, Princeton U., 1999—. lic. clin. psychologist, Pa.; marriage counselor, N.J.; sch. psychologist, N.Y., N.J. Asst. prof. philosophy and psychology Notre Dame Coll., N.Y.C., 1967-71, Fordham U., N.Y.C., 1972-73; exec. dir. Am. Inst. for Creative Living, Inc. Bklyn., S.I., N.Y., Morrisville, Pa., East Brunswick, N.J., 1972—; assoc. pastor Bklyn Diocese, Roman Catholic Ch., 1961-67, cons. Marriage Tribunal, 1967—; UN rep. for Ch., spl. UN advisor to Kyrgyzstan at UN and Washington Embassy; chaplain to students, dean Internat. Sch. for Mental Health Practitioners, S.I. and Pa.; cons. N.Y.C. Police Dept., 1980—; dir., producer S.I. Cmty. TV; standing conf. for Oriental Orthodox Ch. and Oriental Orthodox Roman Catholic Cons., U.S.A., 1999—. Author: Freud and Future Religious Experience, 1976. Vicar gen. Malankara Syrian Orthodox Ch., 1998; mediator Civil Ct. City of N.Y., 1998; rector Ignatius U., Indpls. Fellow Am. Orthopsychiat. Assn.; mem. APA, Am. Philos. Assn., Am. Sociol. Assn., Am. Group Psychotherapy Assn., Am. Assn. Marriage and Family Therapists (supr.), Am. Found. Religion and Psychiatry, Alzheimer's Assn. (bd. dirs.), Coun. Register Health Providers in Psychology. Home: 2295 Victory Blvd Staten Island NY 10314-6625 also: 78 N Pennsylvania Ave Morrisville PA 19067-1110

DE LUCA, JEAN PIERRE, sales and marketing professional; b. Annecy, France, May 24, 1961; came to U.S., 1986; s. Jean De Luca and Angelina Tassan; married, Aug. 22, 1987 (div. Nov. 1999). Assoc., LTEGS, Annecy, 1982; Bachelor, Century U., Albuquerque, 1991, postgrad. Test mgr. quality control ALCATEL, Annecy, 1983-86; prodn. and svc. mgr. ALCATEL, Hingham, Mass., 1986-91, nat. sales and mktg. mgr. for helium leak detection, 1991—; dir. sales and mktg. helium leak detection ALCATEL, Hingham, 2000—. Contbr. articles to tech. jours., including R&D Mag., Vacuum and Thin Film, Assembly Mag. E-mail: jp.deluca@avp.alcatel.com. Home: 127R Glades Rd Scituate MA 02066-1145 Office: ALCATEL 67 Sharp St Ste 1 Hingham MA 02043-4348

DE LUCA, PATRICK, virtual manufacturing engineer, researcher; b. Marmande, France, Feb. 2, 1960; s. Pierre and Gisèle (Montsegur) De L.; m. Anne Khalef, Aug. 19, 1989; children: Théo, Apolline. BS, Bordeaux (France) U., 1979, MS, 1984, PhD in Applied Math., 1989; postdoctoral in applied mechanics, Stanford U., 1989-90. Product mgr. Engrng. Systems Internat., Rungis, France, 1991-92, composites thermoforming leader, 1993-96, composites virtual mfg. leader, 1997—; assoc. prof. École Centrale de Paris, Chatenay-Malabry, France, 1993-95. Contbr. chpt. to book, articles to profl. jours. V.p. Association des Docteurs Thésards, Arceuil, France, 1992-93. Scientist, Délégation Générale de l'Armement, 1985-86, Gramat, France, and SMAI in MEM section. Mem. SMAI, Adv. Scientific Com. of the Romanian Rsch. Ctr. in Sheet Metal Farming (CERTETA), AMAC (Assn. des Materiaux Comparits).

DELUCA, RONALD, former advertising agency executive, consultant; b. Reading, Pa., Oct. 28, 1924; s. Nicola and Grace (Carabello) DeL.; m. Lois Ann Hall, Nov. 27, 1952; children: Christine, Diane, Patricia, Maria, Lisa, Nicholas. Certificate comml. art, Pratt Inst., 1949; B.F.A., Syracuse U., 1951; B.A., New Sch. Social Research, 1966. Artist J.C. Penney, N.Y.C., 1951-52; designer Remington Rand, N.Y.C., 1952-53; art dir. Roy S. Durstine (advt.), N.Y.C., 1954-56, Kenyon & Eckhardt (advt.), N.Y.C., 1956-66; head creative group Grey Advt., N.Y.C., 1966-67; with Kenyon & Eckhardt Advt., N.Y.C., 1967-85; exec. v.p., vice chmn. Kenyon & Eckhardt Advt., 1976-85; pres. Bozell Jacobs, Kenyon & Eckhardt, N.Y.C., 1986-89, vice chmn., 1989-91; cons., 1991—. Home and Office: PO Box 551 Hancock NY 13783-0551*

DELUCIA, GENE ANTHONY, government administrator, computer company executive; b. Methuen, Mass., Feb. 20, 1952; s. Antonio Gitano and Carmen Theresa (Carpenito) DeL. BS, Boston Coll., 1973; MBA, Northeastern U., 1980. Project mgr. Delphi div. Arthur D. Little Inc., Lowell, Mass., 1975-78; gen. mgr. eastern region Arthur D. Little Inc., 1978-80; systems devel. mgr. Wang Labs. Inc., Lowell, 1980-83; pres., CEO Computer Innovations Inc., Lowell, 1983-86; pres. Corp. Investment Bus. Brokers, North Andover, Mass., 1986-88; v.p. Maximus Inc., Falls Church, Va., 1988-90, div. pres., 1990-96; pres. Strategic Visions Inc., Amesbury, Mass., 1996-97; mng. ptnr. Renaissance Govt. Solutions, Exeter, N.H., 1997—. Mem. AOPA. Avocations: skiing, racquetball, electronics, flying, golf. Home: 129 N End Blvd Salisbury MA 01952-2209 Office: GovConnect Inc Ste 306 One Hampton Rd Exeter NH 03833

DELUHERY, ALLISON, marketing specialist; b. Washington, Aug. 26, 1974; d. Patrick John and Margaret Morris D. BS, Cath. U. Am., 1996. Campaign fundraiser Sen. Tom Harkin, Des Moines, Iowa, 1996; mktg. asst. Biotech. Industry Orgn., Washington, 1997-98, mktg. coord., 1998-99, mktg. mgr., 1999—. Mem. Am. Soc. Assn. Execs. E-mail: adeluhery@bio.org. Office: Biotech Industry Orgn 1625 K St NW Ste 1100 Washington DC 20006-1621

DE LUIGI, MARIO, music journalist, magazine editor; b. Ivrea, Turin, Italy, Mar. 13, 1944; s. Aldo Mario De Luigi and Alessandra Bertot. Grad. high sch., Milan, 1962. Pub., editor Musica e Dischi, monthly mag., Milan, 1968—. Author: Musica e Parole, 1978, Cultura e Canzonette 1980, L'Industria Discografica in Italia, 1982. Office: Musica e Dischi, Via De Amicis 47, 20123 Milan Italy

DE LUMLEY-WOODYEAR, LIONEL, medical educator; b. Marseille, France, July 28, 1942; s. Athanase De Lumley-Woodyear and Eugenie Pascal; m. Marie Françoise De Martin De Vivies, May 29, 1969; children: Thierry, Thibault, Amaury, Ombline, Guilhem. D in Pediats., Limoges Med. Sch., France, 1971, prof. in pediats., 1985, D in Oncology, D in Hematology, 1997. Med. resident Limoges Med. Sch., 1971-76, asst. des hopitaux, 1976-81, medecin des hopitaux, 1981—, chief pediatrician, 1985—, dir. dept. pediats., 1999—; dir. Hemophilia Care Ctr., Limoges, 1985—, Cystic Fibrosis Care Ctr., Limoges, 1985—. Contbr. articles to profl. jours. Pres. Friends of the Nat. Mus. Adrien DuBouche, Limoges, 1991-98. Named Officier des Arts et Belles Lettres, Min. Culture, 1999. Mem. French Soc. Pediats., French Soc. Pediat. Oncology, World Fedn. Hemophilia. Avocation: decorative arts. Office: CHU Dupuytren, Service de Pediatrie, 87042 Limoges Cedex, France

DE LUNG, JANE SOLBERGER, independent sector executive; b. Anniston, Ala., July 9, 1944; d. Samuel and Margaret Polk (Oldham) S.; m. Harry Leonard De Lung, Apr. 23, 1965 (div. 1972); m. Charles F. Westoff, May 2, 1997. BA in History, Emory U., 1966; MA in Urban Planning, Roosevelt U., Chgo., 1972. Exec. asst. Cook County Legal Assistance, Chgo., 1967-69; asst. dir. family planning Am. Coll. Ob-Gyn, Chgo., 1969-71; v.p. Ill. Family Planning Coun., Chgo., 1971-80; asst. commr. Chgo. Dept. Pub. Health, 1981-82; pres. Pub. Solutions, Princeton, N.J., 1982-88, Population Resource Ctr., N.Y.C., 1988—. Bd. dirs. Princeton Area Cmty. Planning, 1983-85, Planned Parenthood Mercer County, Trenton, N.J., 1986-96, UN Assn. U.S.A.; mem. adv. bd. dept. sociology Princeton U., 1991—. Mem. APHA, AAUW, LWV, Population Assn. Am. Democrat. Episcopalian. Office: Population Resource Ctr 15 Roszel Rd Princeton NJ 08540-6248

DELVAL, ROBERT RICHARD, gynecologist, obstetrician, educator; b. Brussels, Jan. 29, 1947; s. Richard and Yvonne (Masquelier) D.; m. Martine van Griethuysen, Sept. 22, 1990; children: Isabelle, Sylviane, Renaud. MD, U. Libre Brussels, 1973. Asst. gynecologist Hosp. U. Brugmann, Brussels, 1973-75, Ctr. Hosp., U. C. DePaepe, Brussels, 1975-77; medecin militaire Hosp. Militaire Koln, Fed. Republic of Germany, 1977-78; responsible svc. echographie Clinique Antoine DePage, Brussels, 1977-86; with ob-gyn dept. Maternite Reine Astrid, Charleroi, Belgium, 1982-85, Ctr. Hosp. U. A. Vesale, Charleroi, 1985—, Hosp. Civil Charleroi, 1986—; pvt. cons. ob-gyn Bd. A. de Fontaine, Charleroi, 1979—. Mem. Groupement belge medecins Specialistes, Soc. Royale belge Gynecologie Obstetrique, Assn. Profl. Obstetriciens et Gyn. belges, Groupement Gyn. et Ob. de Langue Francaise de Belgique, Assn. belge Ultrasonologie Medicale. Avocations: music, reading, drawing, painting, photography. Office: Residence Anjou, Bd de Fontaine 21 16, B-6000 Charleroi Belgium

DEL VALLE, MARCELO GUSTAVO, information systems specialist, consultant; b. Buenos Aires, Jan. 10, 1955; s. Cecilio Arturo and Beatriz Mireya (Migliano) de V.; m. Patricia Monica Calabro, Apr. 20, 1958 (div. June 1989); m. Alicia Nilda Mayor, Dec. 26, 1956; children: Lorena Alejandra Facciorrusso, Augustín Nahuel del Valle. Cert. electronics technician, ENET No. 28, Buenos Aires, 1973; systems analyst, Nat. Tech. U., Buenos Aires, 1977; informatics lawyer, Nat. Tech. U., 1981. Systems analyst Armada Argentina, Buenos Aires, 1976-80; systems programmer leader U.B.D.S.S., Buenos Aires, 1980-86, FATE Soc. Anónima Indsl. Comercial Immobiliaria, Buenos Aires, 1986-91; project mgr. Antech S.R.L., Buenos Aires, 1991-95; health informatics project mgr. T.T.I.S.A., Buenos Aires, 1995—; health informatics cons. Antech S.R.L., 1989-91, Favolorós Found., Buenos Aires, 1982; nat. systems teaching leader, Belgrano U., Buenos Aires, 1982-83; data systems teaching leader, Nat. Tech. U., 1981-83. With Argentine Army, 1978-79. Mem. Informatics Scis. Profl. Coun. (sec. 1985-92). Roman Catholic. Avocation: Taekwondo. Home: UCRANIA 2137 CP Villa Adelina, Buenos Aires Argentina

DEL VALLE, TERESA, anthropology educator, researcher; b. Donostia-San Sebastian, Spain, Apr. 1, 1937; d. Julian del Valle and Maria Murga; children: Maider, Amagoia. BA in Art and History, St. Mary Coll., Leavenworth, Kans., 1966; MA in History, St. Louis U., 1969; MA in Anthropology, U. Hawaii, 1975, PhD in Anthropology, 1978. Cert. East-West Ctr., Hawaii, Methods in Cross-Cultural Analysis, 1978. Lectr. in Am. history U. Guam, 1969-72, rschr., 1969-72; rsch. asst., Comm. Inst. East-West Ctr., Honolulu, 1972-73; instr. anthropology U. del Pais Vasco, Donostia-San Sebastian, Spain, 1979-80, assoc. prof. anthropology, 1980-84, prof. anthropology, 1984—, chair, dept. anthropology, 1981-85, chair, Women's Studies Inst., 1991-94; rsch. assoc. U. Nev., Reno, 1985-86. Author: Social and Cultural Change in the Community of Umatac, Southern Guam, 1979, Korrika, a Ritual for Basque Ethnic Identity, 1993, Andamios para una nueva ciudad, Lecturas desde la Antropologia (Scaffolds for a New City: Readings From an Anthropological Perspective), 1997; editor: Gendered Anthropology, 1993, Perspectivas Feminístal desda la Antropologia Social, 2000; contbr. articles to newspapers, 1990—. Lectr. various social and cultural groups. Soc. Basque Studies grantee, 1981-83. Mem. European Assn. Social Anthropologists (v.p. 1988-89), European Soc. Oceanists (exec. com. 1992—), Antropologia Kultura Gizartea. Avocations: art appreciation, walking, cinema, yoga. Home: Nagusia 16, E-20159 Astesu Spain Office: U del Pais Vasco, Ave de Tolosa 70, E-20009 Donostia-San Sebasti Spain

DEL VECCHIO, LEONARDO, manufacturing executive. MA in Bus. Adminstrn., Venice U., 1995; M in Internat. Bus. (hon.), Mib Sch. Sgmt., Trieste, Italy, 1999. Chmn. bd., founder Luxottica Group SPA, Agordo, Italy. Recipient Silver award Fin. World Mag., 1994; apptd. Cavaliere del Lavoro della Repubblica, Italian Pres., 1986. Office: Luxottica Group SPA, Loc Valcozzena, Agordo Belluno BL 32021, Italy

DELVES, PETER JOHN, immunologist; b. Birmingham, Eng., Mar. 14, 1951; s. John Alfred and Miriam Eunice (Tudor) D.; m. Mary Jane Bishop, June 29, 1985; children: Joseph, Thomas, Jessica. BSc with honors, U. London, 1973, PhD, 1986; MSc, Brunel U., 1978. Rsch. officer Imperial Cancer Rsch. Fund, 1974-79; reader dept. immunology Univ. Coll. London, 1979—. Editor-in-chief: Ency. of Immunology, 1998; co-author: (CD-ROM) Interactive Core Tutorials in Immunology, 1996 (Cert. of Ednl. Merit Brit. Med. Assn. 1996), (slide atlas) Slide Atlas of Essential Immunology, 1992; author: (book) Antibody Production, 1997. Mem. Brit. Soc. Immunology. Avocations: travel, jazz, good food. Office: Univ Coll London Windeyer Inst, 46 Cleveland St, London W1P 6DB, England

DELVIG, ALEXEI ALEKSANDROVITCH, immunologist, researcher; b. Moscow, Apr. 5, 1959; s. Aleksandr Alekseevitch and Zoia Ivanovna (Simonova) D. m. Svetlana Valerjevna Glinianaia, Jan. 4, 1980; 1 child, Pavel.

DELVILLE, MICHEL E., research scientist; b. Ougree/Liege, Belgium, Apr. 30, 1969; s. Gilbert and Lucia (Furlanetto) D. BA, U. Liege, 1991, PHD, 1996. Cert. English and Am. lits. Belgian Nat. Fund for Sci. Rsch. Tchg. asst. U. Ill., 1991-92; rsch. asst. Belgian Nat. Fund for Sci. Rsch., 1992-96, sr. rsch. asst., 1996-98, assoc. prof., 1998—; vis. scholar U. Ill., 1992-93; cons. Ctr. des Paralitteratures et du Cinema, Chaudfontaine, Belgium, 1996-98. Author: The American Prose Poem, 1998, J.G. Ballard, British Council Writers and Their Work Series, 1998; contbr.: Trajectories of the Fantastic, 1997; contbr. articles to profl. jours. Recipient Prix Leon Guerin, Assn. des Amis de l'Universite, 1996, Studies award SAMLA, 1998, Choice Outstanding Academic Book award, 1998. Mem. European Assn. Am. Studies, Belgian Assn. Anglicists in Higher Edn., Assn. Belgo-Britannique (sec. 1996-98). Fax: 32-4366-57-21. E-mail: mdelville@ulg.ac.be. Home: 38 Allee du Beau Vivier, 4102 Seraing Liege, Belgium Office: Univ Liege, 3 Place Cockerill, 4000 Liege Belgium

DELWAIDE, JACOBUS LEONARD, lecturer, researcher; b. Antwerp, Belgium, Oct. 12, 1949; s. Leo H.J. and Josepha (Verlinden) D. BA, U. Calif., 1979; MA, Harvard U., 1984, PhD, 1992. Journalist De Standaard, Brussels, 1972-73; teaching fellow Harvard U., Cambridge, Mass., 1982-84; univ. lectr. Univ. Groningen, Groningen, 1990-92; sr. lectr. Cath. Univ. Brussels, 1992—; fellow-in-residence Netherlands Inst. for Advanced Studies in the Humanities and Social Scis., 1999-2000. Krupp Found. fellow, 1985, Fr. Ebert Found. Rsch. scholarship, 1986. Mem. Harvard Club Rhein-Ruhr. Office: KU Brussel, Vrijheidslaan 17, 1081 Brussels Belgium

DELY, MATTHIAS ALEXANDER, biologist, researcher; b. Kalocsa, Hungary, Jan. 5, 1937; s. Stephen Gabriel Dely and Helen Zwaller; m. Elizabeth Nagy, May 27, 1958 (div. Mar. 1974); 1 child, Gabriel; m. Valeria Kalucza, Aug. 10, 1989; 1 child, Matthias. Zoo technician, Agrl. Technicum, Pécs, Hungary, 1956; tchr. biology and geography, Tchrs. Tng. Coll., Pécs, Hungary, 1966; tchr. specializing in biology, Jozsef Attila U., Szeged, Hungary, 1969; candidate biol. sci., Hungarian Acad. Sci., Budapest, 1986. Cert. scientific expert in physiology and redox activation. Biologist Ctrl. Lab. Animal Rsch., Med. U. Pécs, 1970-80, cons., 1981-84, sr. mem., 1985-98; head Mecsek Zool. and Botanical Garden, Pécs, 1960-70; head Ctrl. Lab. Animal Rsch., Med. U. Pécs, 1990-98, councillor Med. Sch., 1995-99. Contbr. articles to scientific publs. Cons. environ. protection Green Party, Pécs, 1993. Recipient deptl. praise Min. Health, Budapest, 1989. Mem. Hungarian Soc. Physiology, Hungarian Assn. for Lab. Animal Sci., Hungarian Soc. Biology, Hungarian Soc. Ornithology and Nature Protection. Avocations: ecology, population biology, ornithology, fishing, swimming.

DEMACKER, PIERRE NICOLAAS, biochemist, researcher; b. Schimmert, Limburg, The Netherlands, Sept. 11, 1948; s. Nicolaas Marie and Maria Martha (Eerkens) D.; m. Helena Maria Janssen, Oct. 7, 1977; children: Susanne, Pauline, Lisette. D in Biology, U. Nijmegen, The Netherlands, 1973, PhD, 1978. Biochemist dept. internal medicine U Med. Ctr. Nijmegen, 1974-89, head lab. gen. internal medicine, 1989—. Contbr. more than 160 articles to sci. jours.; editl. asst. Biochem. Jour., 1995; mem. editl. bd. European Jour. Clin. Investigation, 1998, Netherlands Jour. Clin. Chemistry, 1999. Chmn. publicity commn. The Netherlands Assn. of Hard Hearing People, Utrecht, 1993. Mem. Netherlands Assn. Clin. Chemistry (Ortho award 1982), European Lipoprotein Club, Dutch Assn. Endocrinology. Avocations: tennis, volleyball, walking. Office: U Med Ctr Nijmegen, Dept Gen Internal Medicine, 6500 HB Nijmegen The Netherlands

DE MAEYER, EDWARD, virologist; b. Mechelen, Belgium, June 4, 1932; s. Pieter Jan. and Maria Louisa (Van Aken) De M.; M.D., U. Louvain, 1957; Agrege de l'Enseignement Superieur, 1964; m. Jaqueline Guignard, June 3, 1961. Rsch. fellow Children's Hosp., Boston and Harvard U., 1958-60; rsch. assn. Rockefeller Inst., 1960-61; lectr. virology U. Louvain (Belgium), 1961-65; maitre de recherche CNRS, France, 1966-74, dir., 1975-97, dir. rsch. em, 1998—; chef Laboratoire Institut Curie; tchr. microbiology Pasteur Inst. Fulbright fellow, 1958-61; mem. Nat. Com. Sci. Rsch., France, 1986-91; Prix Antoine Lacassagne de la Ligue Nationale Francaise Contre le Cancer, 1988; adv. bd. Internat. Soc. for Interferon and Cytokine Rsch., 1988—; expert viral diseases WHO, 1981—. Lederle Internat. fellow, 1959-60; recipient Jean-Louis Camus prize, Paris, 1971, Prix Gaston Rousseau de l'Academie des Sciences, Paris, 1976, Soc. de Microbiologie Francaise. Mem. Société de Microbiologie Française, Am. Soc. Microbiology, AAAS, Internat. Soc. for Interferon Rsch. (pres. 1984, 85, adv. bd. 1988—), World Health Orgn. (expert 1981), Sigma Xi. Contbr. numerous articles to sci. jours. Home: 34 Ave Saint Laurent, 91400 Orsay France Office: Inst Curie Bât, 110 Centre Universitaire, 91405 Orsay France also: Les Genievres, 45330 Augerville-la-Rivière France

DE MAEYER-GUIGNARD, JAQUELINE ATHÉNAIS, retired virologist, consultant; b. Geneva, Feb. 9, 1928; arrived in France, 1965; d. Charles Edmond and Lucie (Hakanauer) G.; m. Edward De Maeyer, June 3, 1961. MD, U. Geneva, 1953. Resident in internal medicine, pediatrics U. Hosp., Geneva, 1954-58; rsch. fellow in pediatrics and medicine Harvard Medical Sch., Boston, 1958-61; rsch. assoc. in virology U. Louvain, Belgium, 1961-63, fellow, 1963-65; dir. of rsch. CNRS, Paris, 1965-97; ret., 1997; cons. Ministry of Def., Paris, 1981-82, Ministry of Health, Paris, 1982-83. Co-author: Interferons and Other Regulatory Cytokines, 1988; mem. editl. bd. Jour. Interferon Rsch., 1983-96; contbr. over 125 articles to profl. jours. Recipient Laureate award Swiss Anti-Cancer League, Geneva, 1965, Rochas prize Found. Med. Rsch., 1969, Roberge prize French Acad. Sci., 1976, Lacassagne prize French Cancer League, 1988. Mem. Internat. Soc. Interferon Rsch. (hon.). Avocations: piano, yoga. Home: 34 Ave St Laurent B2, 91400 Orsay France Office: Les Genièvres, 45330 Augerville-la-Rivière France

DEMAISON, LUC, researcher; b. Evian, France, Jan. 26, 1958; s. Andre and Daisy (Monin) D.; m. Joëlle Meloche, Apr. 18, 1992; 1 child, Arvid. M Physiology, Grenoble (France) U., 1981, degree in cellular and molecular biology, 1985, postgrad., 1996. Postdoctoral rschr. Grenoble U., 1985-86; sci. assoc. U. Wis., Madison, 1986-87; rschr. Nat. Inst. Agronomical Rsch., Dijon, 1987—. Contbr. articles to profl. jours. Sec. ASC-Table Tennis, Chevigny St. Sauveur, 1995—. Quartier maitre French Navy, 1981-82. Recipient Jean Debiesse award Commissariat á l'Energie Atomique, Grenoble, 1985, Young Investigator award, Grenoble, 1986. Mem. Internat. Soc. for Heart Rsch. Avocations: fly fishing, table tennis. Home: 20 Impasse des Narcisses, 21800 Chevigny-St Sauveur France Office: INRA Unité Nutrition Lipid, 17 Rue Sully BV 1540, Dijon 21034, France

DEMAN, SURESH, educator; b. Bandikui, Rajasthan, India; s. Ram Narayan and Dakha (Gothwal) D.; m. Jennifer Mayo-Deman, Jan. 21, 1988; 1 child, Samantha India Deman. BSc, U. Rajasthan, Jaipur, India, 1971, MA, 1973; postgrad., Jawaharlal Nehru U., Delhi, 1977; MA, U. Pitts., 1986; ABD, 1987; MPhil, U. Bradford, U.K., 1998. Asst. prof. U. Rajasthan, Jaipur, 1974-88; tchg. fellow U. Pitts., Pa., 1983-87; rsch. fellow Australian Nat. U., Canberra, 1989-90; adj. faculty U. Conn., Hartford, 1990-92; vis. prof. econs. Fukuoka (Japan) U., 1992-94; faculty, postgrad. rsch. coord. U.K., 1994-95; hon. pres. Mayo-Deman Cons., Pitts., also hon. bd. dirs.; mem. senate Rajasthan U., 1973, U. Conn., 1990; UNEP/UNCTAD expert, 1995; vis. prof. U. Otago, New Zealand, 1996; sr. lectr. Fin. and Game Theory Greenwich U., 1997-99; lectr. in field. Contbr. numerous articles to profl. jours. Grad. rep U. Pitts., Pa., 1985-86; organizing sec. NI Asian Profls. Students Orgn., Belfast, 1995-97. Mem. Am. Econs. Assn., Royal Econ. Soc., Indian Econometric Soc. (life), Sigma Xi, India-Am. Soc. (hon. pres. 1988—). Avocations: music, creative art, movies, journalism and critique. Fax: 44181 859 4657. Home: 312 Chateau Ct

Pittsburgh PA 15239-2344 Office: Mayo-Deman Cons, c/o Sammy & Co PO Box 17517, London SE92ZP, England

DEMARCHI, ERNEST NICHOLAS, aerospace engineering administrator; b. Lafferty, Ohio, May 31, 1939; s. Ernest Constante and Lena Marie (Cireddu) D.; m. Sharon Titherley, 1996; children: Daniel Ernest, John David, Deborah Marie. BME, Ohio State U., 1962; MS in Engring., UCLA, 1969. Registered profl. engr., Ohio; registered profl. cert. mgr. With Boeing, 1962—; mem. Apollo, Skylab and Apollo-Soyuz missions design team in electronic and elec. systems, mem. mission support team for all Apollo and Skylab manned missions, 1962-74, mem. Space Shuttle design team charge elec. systems equipment, 1974-77, in charge Orbiter Data Processing System, 1977-81, in charge Orbiter Ku Band Communication and Radar System, 1981-85, in charge orbitor elec. power distbr., displays, controls, data processing, 1984-87, in charge space based interceptor flt. exper., 1987-88, kinetic energy systems, 1988-90, ground based interceptor program, 1990-97, dep. program mgr. Nat. Missile Def. Program, 1997—. Recipient Apollo Achievement award NASA, 1969, Apollo 13 Sustained Excellent Achievement Snoopy award, 1971, Exceptional Svc. award Rockwell Internat., 1972, Outstanding Contbn. award, 1976, NASA ALT award, 1979, Shuttle Astronaut Snoopy award, 1982, Pub. Svc. Group Achievement award NASA, 1982, Rockwell Pres.'s award, 1983, 87. Mem. AIAA, ASME, Nat. Mgmt. Assn., Varsity O Alumni Assn. Home: 8227 E Hillsdale Dr Orange CA 92869-2440 Office: 3370 E Miraloma Ave Anaheim CA 92806-1911

DE MARCO, ROLAND, chemistry educator; b. Melbourne, Australia, May 7, 1964; s. Candido and Angela (Tralli) De M.; m. Catherine Anne Rafferty, Apr. 18, 1992; 1 child, Sebastian Thomas. BS in Applied Chemistry, Melbourne, Australia, 1985, MS in Applied Chemistry, 1987, PhD in Chemistry, 1992. Rsch. scientist CSIRO Divsn. Minerals, Melbourne, Australia, 1990-92; lectr. U. Tasmania, Launceston, Australia, 1992-95, Curtin U., Perth, Australia, 1995—. Contbr. over 30 articles to profl. jours. Rsch. grantee Australian Rsch. Coun., 1993-94, 95, 96-97, 97—, Alternative Energy Devel. Bd., 1996-97, 99—, Minerals & Energy Rsch. Inst. Western Australia, 1997-98, Australian Inst. Nuclear Sci. and Engring., 2000—. Mem. RACI (mem. analytical chem. divsn. com.). Avocations: swimming, movies, family. Office: Curtin U Tech, GPO Box U1987, Perth 6845, Australia

DEMARCO, ROLAND R., foundation executive; b. Mt. Morris, N.Y., July 21, 1910; s. Marion and Mary (Scalzette) DeM.; m. Lydia Hees, June 23, 1934; children—Richard, Ronald, Lynn. Diploma, Geneseo State Tchrs. Coll., 1930; BS, N.Y. State Coll. Tchrs., 1934; AM, Columbia U., 1937, PhD, 1942; student, U. Munich, Germany, 1937, Shrivenham Am. U., Eng., 1945; postgrad., Officers Candidate Sch., 1944, Air Intelligence Sch., 1944; LLD, Chungang U., Seoul, Korea, 1959; DLitt, Sung Kyun Kwan U., Seoul, 1969; D.Litt., Hanyang U., Seoul, 1974. Instr. Gowanda Pub. Schs., 1930-34; dir. social studies East Islip H.S., N.Y., 1934-38; instr. social scis. Coll. Charleston, 1939, Columbia U., 1939-40; staff mem. Air Intelligence Sch., 1944-45; vis. prof. Columbia U., 1946-47; prof. history, head dept. social scis. Ala. State Tchrs. Coll., 1940-46, pres. dept., dean, 1949, from adminstrv. head to pres., 1949-52; pres. Finch Coll., 1952-70, pres. emeritus, cons., 1970-75; chmn., CEO Internat. Human Assistance Programs, Inc., N.Y.C., 1973-82, hon. chmn., 1982-84, 85-96, pres., CEO, 1984-85; head history dept. Finch Jr. Coll., 1947-49; curriculum cons. Jackson County Schs., Ala., 1940-43; mem. Nat. Adv. Coun. Edn. Disadvantaged Children, 1971-73; exec. vice chmn., chmn. ednl. adv. com. Am.-Korea Found., 1953-64, pres., 1964-68, 71-73, hon. chmn., 1968-71, chmn., chief exec. officer, 1973-75. Author: The Italianization of African Natives, 1943, The Comeback Country, Vol. I: Light of the East, an Insight into Korea, 1972. Contbr. articles to profl. jours. Founder Fathers of Am.-Korean Found., 1952; trustee Allen Stevenson Sch. Boys, pres., 1956-58; bd. dirs., treas. Council Higher Ednl. Instns., N.Y.C.; pres. All Am. Open Karate Championships, 1965-80, Karate Championships North Am., 1967-80; v.p. World Taekwan Do Fedn., 1973-82; trustee Universidad Politecnica de P.R., San Juan, 1974-85; bd. dirs. Am. Behavioral Scis., 1967-80; color commentator ABC-TV Wide World of Sports for Billiard Championship Match, 1962. Served to 1st lt. USAAF, 1943-46. Decorated Order Cultural Merit Nat. medal (Korea); named hon. citizen of Seoul, 1964; knight officer Order of Merit (Italy); recipient Disting. Alumni award SUNY, 1969, Disting. Alumni award Coll. Arts and Sci. at Geneseo, 1971. Home: 1400 East Ave Rochester NY 14610-1611

DEMARD, FRANCOIS GEORGES, otolaryngologist; b. Nice, France, Feb. 8, 1940; s. Auguste and Alice (Duhamel) D.; m. Danielle Velluti, Apr. 8, 1967 (div. 1999); children: Delphine, Nathalie. Student, U. Aix-Marseille. Asst. Univ. Hosp., Marseille, France, 1968-71; prof. Univ. Hosp., Nice, France, 1975-79, head, prof., 1979-85; head, prof. Ctr. Antoine Lacassagne, Nice, 1985-96. Pres. League Against Cancer, Nice, 1995—. Mem. French Soc. ENT, French Head & Neck Tumors Soc., Soc. Head & Neck Surgeons. Avocations: golf, skiing. Office: Ctr Antoine Lacassagne, 33 Ave de Valombrose, 06189 Nice cedex 2 France

DE MARGITAY, GEDEON, acquisitions and management consultant; b. Budapest, Hungary, Mar. 6, 1924; s. Joseph and Anne (de Bessenyei) de M.; came to U.S., 1953, naturalized, 1958; student U. Budapest Grad. Sch. Econs., 1941-44, Ecole des Scis. Politiques, Paris, 1946-48; m. Virginia Varet Martin, Dec. 30, 1963. With N.Y. Times, 1947-50, European info. div. Mut. Security Agy., 1950-53; with N.Y. Times, 1954-61; chief exec. Magnum Photos, Inc., N.Y.C., 1961-63; with Time Inc., 1964-75, dir. mktg. services Time/Life TV, 1975; dir. broadcast and corp. planning NBC, 1975-78; acquistions and mgmt. cons., N.Y.C., 1978—. Mem. Assn. for Systems Mgmt., Internat. Radio-TV Soc., World Future Soc., Am. Acad. Polit. and Social Sci. Republican. Presbyterian. Co-author: Broadcasting: The Next Ten Years, 1977. Address: 65 E 96th St New York NY 10128-0730

DE MARIA Y CAMPOS, MAURICIO, United Nations official. Head planning & policy unit Mex. Nat. Sci & Tech. Coun., 1971-72; dep. dir. evaluation dept. tech transfer Ministry Trade & Industry, 1973-74, dir. gen. fgn. investment, 1974-77, vice-min. indsl. devel., 1982-88; dir.-gen. tax incentives & fiscal promotion Ministry Fin., 1977-82; exec. v.p. Banco Mexicano SOMEX, Mexico City, 1989-92; dir.-gen. UN Indsl. Devel. Orgn., Vienna, Austria, 1993-97; amb.-at-large, adv. to UN Africa and Mid. East; amb. for spl. projects Secretariat Fgn. Affairs, Mexico. Mem. Club of Rome (pres. Mexican chpt.). Office: Secretariat Fgn Affairs, Ricardo Flores Magon 19, 06995 Mexico City Mexico*

DE MARINO, DONALD NICHOLSON, international business executive, former federal agency administrator; b. Greensburg, Pa., Sept. 28, 1945; s. Thomas C. and Sue Eleanor (Nicholson) De M.; m. Caroline Mack, Dec. 27, 1967 (div. 1981); children: Christopher Tyson, Benjamin Nicholson; m. Betsy Reiver, July 18, 1981; children: Alexander Reiver, William McCurdy. BA, U. Pa., 1967. Dir. Mack & Nicholson, West Chester, Pa., 1972-76; bus. cons. The Nicholson Group, Inc., N.Y.C., 1976-81; sr. project officer U.S.-Saudi Arabian Joint Commn. on Econ. Cooperation, Riyadh, Saudi Arabia, 1981-84, dir., 1985-87; mgr. Litton Industries Offset Investment Programs, Riyadh, 1984-85; sr. project adviser The Arab Investment Co., Riyadh, 1985; internat. bus. cons., prin. De Marino Assocs., Coatesville, Pa., 1987-88; dep. asst. sec. Africa, Near East and South Asia U.S. Dept. Commerce, Washington, 1989-90; U.S. advisor Tata Group of India, 1991—; chmn. Nat. U.S.-Arab C. of C., 1991—; pres. De Marino Assocs., Inc., 1992—; lectr. Wharton Sch. Advanced Mgmt. Program, 1994-96; nat. adv. com. Mid. East Policy Coun.; chmn. Arab-Fgn. C. of C., 1999-2000. Mem. nat. adv. bd. Mid. East Policy Coun. Decorated Chevalier, Sovereign Mil. Order of Temple of Jerusalem; recipient Disting. Svc. award Govt. of Saudi Arabia, 1987. Mem. Sovereign Mil. Order Temple Jerusalem (chevalier templars), Arab-Fgn. C. of C. (chmn. 1999-2000), Racquet Club, Mask and Wig Club. Republican. Presbyterian. Home: 43 Longview Rd Coatesville PA 19320-4311 Office: PO Box 791 Unionville PA 19375-0791

DE MARNEFFE, BARBARA ROWE, volunteer; b. Boston, June 2, 1929; d. H.S. Payson and Florence Van Arnhem (Cassard) Rowe; m. James Hopkins, Oct. 9, 1954 (div. 1969); m. Francis de Marneffe; stepchildren: Peter, Daphne, Colette. BA, Vassar Coll., 1952. Tchr. Chapin Sch., N.Y.C., 1952-54; adminstrv. asst. to dean Sch. of Indsl. Mgmt. MIT, Cambridge, Mass., 1959-60; asst. pub. rels. dir. Peter Bent Brigham Hosp., Boston, 1960-61, pub. rels. dir., 1961-63; pub. rels. cons. Diabetes Found. and Joslin Clinic, Boston, 1963-64; pub. rels. dir. McLean Hosp., Belmont, Mass., 1964-68; mgr. pub. affairs Cambridge (Mass.) C. of C., 1975-78; pres. de Marneffe Selections, Cambridge, 1978-90; bd. trustees Edith Wharton Restoration, Inc., 1999, co-chair, 2000. Contbr. articles to profl. jours. Trustee Archives of Am. Art of the Smithsonian Inst., Washington, D.C., 1983-99, trustee coun., 1999-2000; com. mem. Ellis Meml. Settlement House Antiques Show, 1968-89; bd. dirs. Friends of McLean Hosp., Belmont, Mass., 1967-89; officer, bd. dirs. Family Counseling Svc. of Cambridge, 1969-78; Mass. Rep. State Committeewoman, 1977-80; exec. sec. Cambridge Rep. City Com., 1956-57; pub. rels. dir. Peabody for Congress Campaign, Newton, Mass., 1968; bd. dirs. Nat. Com. on the Treatment of Intractable Pain, Washington, 1980-90; trustee Peterborough Players, N.H., 1983-89; docent N.C. Mus. of Art, Raleigh, 1992-93; chair Friends of the Pain Ctr. Mass. Gen. Hosp., Boston, 1995-99; corporator Brookline (Mass.) Savings Bank, 1995—; mem. adv. coun. Farnsworth Art Mus., Rockland, Maine, 1995-98; vestry Emmanuel Episcopal Ch., Dublin, N.H, 1995—. Mem. Jewelers of Am., Inc., Vassar Club (pres. Boston chpt. 1989). Avocations: medicine, business, politics, historical preservation, decorative arts, tennis. Home: 126 Coolidge Hl Cambridge MA 02138-5522

DEMARTINI, FRANK THOMAS, film company executive, lawyer; b. Oyster Bay, N.Y., Feb. 23, 1962; s. Frank Anthony and Grace Marie (Lombardi) DeM. AB, Syracuse U., 1983; JD cum laude, Touro Coll., Huntington, N.Y., 1986. Bar: Calif. 1986. Atty. Edwin J. Richards & Assocs., Santa Anna, Calif., 1986-88; prin. v.p. Pentalpha Film Group, Hollywood, Calif., 1987-89; atty. Lewis & Co., Santa Monica, Calif., 1988; owner Martin and DeMartini Law Firm, L.A., 1988-92; ptnr. Anderson & DeMartini, 1992-98; owner Palladin Film Group, 1994-98; ptnr. Barab, Anderson, Barton, DeMartini, Kline and Coate LLP, Beverly Hills, 1996-97; owner, CEO Frank DeMartini Prodns. (was DeMartini/Anderson Prodns.), L.A., 1998—; prodn. exec. NuImage, Inc., 1999—; cons. Dianne Bridget Beatty, L.A., 1987-89, Ashton Nolley, 1987-90, Dy Sharr Music Pub., 1988-92, Beholder Film corp., 1989-92, ALB Prodns., Inc., 1989—. Prodr. Motel Blue, 1997, The Replacement, 1999, aka The Alternate, Crocodile, 2000, Spiders, 2000, Crocodile 2 aka Death Roll, 2000; assoc. prodn. Crystal Lake, 1990, Loving Deadly, 1994; asst. prodr. TV show The Laughter Co., 1986. Asst. committeeman Nassau County Rep. Com., Salisbury, N.Y., 1985-86. Mem. ABA (tax entertainment com.). Roman Catholic. Avocations: music, theater. Office: Anderson & DeMartini 3765 Motor Ave # 710 Los Angeles CA 90034-6403

DE MARTINIS, UMBERTO, electrical engineering educator, consultant; b. Naples, Italy, June 10, 1944; s. Raffaele and Rachele (Vanacore) de M.; m. Anna Esposito, Oct. 24, 1972; children: Valerio, Claudio. MSEE, U. Naples, 1973. Rschr. Study Ctr. of Economy Applied Engring., Naples, 1974-84; assoc. prof. U. Salerno, Italy, 1984-93; prof. elec. engring. Inst. Elec. Tech. "Federico II", Naples, 1993—; mem. sci. coun. Italian Ctr. Aerospatial Rsch., Italy, 1996; elec. cons. Tobin, Tajikistan, 1997, China, 1997; mem. sci. com. Power Quality Europe. Contbr. articles to sci. jours., including IEEE-PAS, European Trans. on Elec. Power, Instn. Elec. Engring.-P.C. Energy mgr. Province of Caserta, Italy, 1993. Mem IEEE-Eletrotech. Italian Assn. (candidate to Europarliament 1999), Internat. Conf. Grands Réseaux Electriques, Circolo Canottieri Italia, Rotary. E-mail: martinis@unina.it. Office: Dept Elec Engring Federico, II, Via Claudio 21, 80125 Naples Italy

DE MARTINO, KENNETH, company executive; b. Sliema, Malta, July 11, 1960; s. Joseph and Josephine (Fenechsoler) De M.; m. Madeleine Busuttil, Nov. 18, 1990; children: Rachel, Stephanie, Martina. Cert. in modern mgmt., Brit. Careers TRG Coll., 1981; cert. in bus. mgmt., Alexander Hamilton Inst., 1984; cert. in mng. assertively, Guardian Bus. Svcs., Eng., 1988; cert. in fin. svcs., Thomas Cook Group, 1990. Asst. sales mgr. North Africa Thomas Cook Group, London, 1984-86, sales mgr. North Africa, 1986-88, area mgr. North Africa, 1988-91; mng. dir. Thomas Cook Malta, 1991-99; with KDM Group Companies including Guard & Warden Svc. House Ltd., Malta, Gozo, 1999—. Councillor local govt., Msida, Malta, 1996; sec. gen. Scout Assn. of Malta. Mem. Inst. Comml. Mgmt. (Eng.), Malta Inst. Mgmt. Roman Catholic. Avocation: scouting. Home: "Carina" V Denaro St, Msida MSD02, Malta Office: KDM Group Companies, Il Piazzetta Tower Rd, Sliema SLM16, Malta

DEMAS, SOPHIA PATTY, poet, former secondary education educator; b. Sparta, Greece, Mar. 10, 1934; came to U.S., 1951; d. Peter P. and Anastesia (Maravelia) Stamateas; m. 1954; 3 children. Grad. summa cum laude, L.I. U., 1972. Cert. tchr., N.Y. H.s. tchr. Nassau County, N.Y., 1960-80. Author: (poetry) Sophia's Anthology, 1995, Sophia's Autobiography, 1995. Campaigner Dem. Party, Suffolk, N.Y., 1990-94; vol. St. Joseph's Ch., Ronkonkama, N.Y., 1997—. L.I. U. scholar, Brookville, N.Y., 1968-72. Mem. Nat. Honor Hist. Soc. Democrat. Greek Orthodox. Avocations: sculpture, inventions, clothes design, architectural design, tennis. Office: Internat Poetry Hall of Fame 1 Poetry Plz Owings Mills MD 21117-6282

DEMATAKI, GLYKERIA J., federal official; b. Athens, Attiki, Greece, Sept. 11, 1964; arrived in Belgium, 1993; d. John S. and Chryssafia P. (Drossopoulou) D. Law degree, U. Athens, Greece, 1986; M of EC Law, U. Paris II Sorbonne, 1988, PhD in Law, 1992; LLM, Harvard U., 1991. Bar: N.Y., Athens. Atty. law firm, Athens, 1986-92; legal trainee Commn. of European Comtys., Brussels, 1994; atty. law firm, Brussels, 1994-95; law clk. Ct. of Justice of EC, Luxembourg, 1995-96; ofcl. Commn. European Comtys., Brussels, 1996—; vis. rschr. Harvard U. Law Sch., Cambridge, Mass., 1993. Co-author: (book) University Institute of Athens, 1985. Mem. 1st yr. coun. of students Faculty of Law, Athens, 1983. Scholar Greek Pub. Found., 1982-86, A.S. Onassis Found., 1988-90. Mem. N.Y. Bar, Athens Bar, Harvard Club Greece. Avocations: running cross-country, piano, ancient Greek.

DEMATTEIS, MASSIMILIANO, biology researcher, educator; b. Casale Monferrato, Italy, Nov. 11, 1970; arrived in Argentina, 1971; s. Humberto Dematteis and Maria Teresa Garcia; m. Laura Giuliana Vallejos, May 22, 1992; children: Bruno, Sofia. Licentiate in Genetics, U. Misiones, Argentina, 1994; D in Biological Scis., U. Cordoba, Argentina, 1999. Technician Ecology Ministry, Misiones, Argentina, 1992-93; rsch. auxiliar U. Misiones, Argentina, 1992-94; auxiliar prof. genetics U. Northeast, Corrientes, Argentina, 1995-98, prof. genetics, 1999—. Author: Flora of Paraguay-Vernonieae, 1999; contbr. articles to profl. jours. Mem. Soc. Argentiana de Botanica (rep. 1996). Office: Inst Botanica del Nordeste, Sargento Cabral 2131, 3400 Corrientes Argentina

DE MAURO, TULLIO, linguist; b. Torre Annunziata, Italy, Mar. 31, 1932; s. Oscar and Clementina (Rispoli) De M.; m. Annamaria Cassese, Apr. 20, 1963 (dec. July 1989); m. Silvana Ferreri, Mar. 1, 1998; children: Giovanni, Sabina. LLD, U. Rome, 1956. Asst. prof. Ist. Orientale, Napoli, Italy, 1958-62; prof. Faculty of Letters, Rome, 1962-67, Faculty of Magistero, Palermo, Italy, 1967-70; prof. Faculty of Letters, Salerno, Italy, 1970-74, Rome, 1974—; dir. dept. lang. scis. Faculty of Letters, Rome, 1982-88, 92. Author: Linguistic History of Italy, 1963, Wittgenstein: His Place in Semantics, 1966, Understanding Words, 1994, Saussure and Linguistics Today, 1995, Elementary Linguistics, 1998. Mem. Cercle Linguistique F. De Saussure, Academia Europaea. E-mail: t.demdueo&sll@let.unisoma1.it. Home: Via Garigliano 74A, I-00198 Rome Italy Office: Dept Sci Del Linguaggio, Via Cesalpino 14, I-00161 Rome Italy

DEMBERELTSEREN, DASHDORJIYN, judge. Chief justice Supreme Ct. Mongolia, Ulan Bator, Mongolian People's Republic. Office: Supreme Ct of Mongolia, Ulaanbaatar Mongolia*

DEMBIŃSKI, ARTUR BOGDAN, physiologist, urologist, researcher; b. Cracow, Poland, June 15, 1948; s. Edward and Maria (Matlak) D.; m. Barbara Magda Nagórzańka, Apr. 8, 1972 (div. June 4, 1996); 1 child, Marcin. MD, Med. Acad., Cracow, Poland, 1972. Asst. Med. Acad., Cracow, Poland, 1973-74; surgeon, 1974-84; older asst. Med. Acad., Cracow, Poland, 1975-77, asst. prof., 1978-88; urologist, 1985-92; assoc. prof. Med. Acad., Cracow, Poland, 1989-96; prof. Collegium Medicum Jagiellonian U., Cracow, Poland, 1996—. Inventor in field. Mem. Polish Physiol. Soc. (treas. 1980-89, sec. 1996—), Polish Urol. Soc. Avocations: fishing, skiing, walking in the country, model gliders. Office: Collegium Med Physiology, Grzegórzecka 16, 31-531 Cracow Poland

DEMBO, DONALD HOWARD, cardiologist, medical administrator, educator; b. Balt., Jan. 27, 1931; s. Sydney Harry and Yetta (Bank) D.; m. Leatrice Cohen, Aug. 10, 1952; children: Steven Jay, Michael Brian Dembo, Susan Ann Weinstein. BA, Johns Hopkins U., 1951; MD, U. Md., 1955. Diplomate Am. Bd. Internal Medicine, Am. Bd. Cardiovascular Disease. Internship Sinai Hosp., Balt., 1955-56; residency in medicine Univ. Hosp., Balt., 1956-58; asst. cardiologist in chief U.S. Army Hosp., Frankfurt, Germany, 1958-60; fellow in cardiology Univ. Hosp., 1960-61; chief of cardiology Md. Gen. Hosp., Balt., 1961-91, Good Samaritan Hosp., Balt., 1975-95; assoc. physician in chief, vice chair of medicine Sinai Hosp., 1995-99; asst. prof. medicine Univ. Md., 1970-91, Johns Hopkins Univ., 1991—; pres. Cen. Md. Cardiology, Balt., 1976-95; med. dir. Johns Hopkins Cardiology, Timonium, Md., 1999—. Contbr. articles to profl. jours. Bd. trustees Cardiopulmonary Resuscitation, Inc., 1975-77; chmn. adv. bd. Easton Waterfowl Festival, Easton, Md., 1990-93. Capt. U.S. Army, 1958-60. Recipient Bronze, Silver & Gold award Am. Heart Assn. (Md. affiliate), Svc. award Md. Gen. Hosp., Svc. award Good Samaritan Hosp., Disting. Physician award Sinai Hosp.; Cardiology tchg. scholar Hopkins/Sinai Internal Med. Program. Fellow ACP, Am. Coll. Cardiology (Md. chpt., trustee 1990-97, sec./treas. 1997-99, gov. elect 1999-00, gov. 2000-03), Am. Coll. Chest Physicians; mem. Am. Heart Assn. (Md. affiliate pres. 1971-72), Md. Soc. Cardiology (pres. 1976-78), Balt. City Med. Soc. (pres. 1996-97), Med. and Chirurgical Faculty (pres. 1994-95). Democrat. Jewish. Avocations: boating, swimming, tennis, fly fishing, photography. Home: 6103 Ivydene Ter Baltimore MD 21209-3521 Office: 110 W Timonium Rd Ste 2C Timonium MD 21093-7303

DEMBOWSKI, FREDERICK LESTER, educational administrator, educator, consultant; b. Syracuse, N.Y., July 17, 1948; s. Frederick L. and Jean Marie (Oswald) D.; m. Rhona Dembowski; children: Kirsten, Erika. BS, SUNY, Oswego, 1970, MS, 1972; EdD, U. Rochester, 1978. Asst. prof. SUNY, Albany, 1979-84, assoc. prof. ednl. adminstrn., 1984—, dir. Ednl. Mgmt. Inst., 1985—; prof., coord. PhD program Lynn U., Fla., 2000; cons. AID, Washington, 1984—; dep. chief party Somtad Project, Usaid/Somalia, Africa, 1988-90, chair, Dept. of Ed. Admin., 1995-2000. Author: School/Effective Sch. Dist. Mgmt., 1999, School Finance Management, 1983, Effective School District Management, 1999; editor: Administrative Uses of Microcomputers, 3 vols., 1984; contbr. articles to profl. jours., chpts. to books. Mem. Am. Sch. Bus. Ofcls. (chmn. mgmt. com. 1982—, outstanding rschr. award 1985), Am. Edn. Fin. Assn., Am. Ednl. Rsch. Assn., Am. Assn. Sch. Adminstrs., Phi Delta Kappa. Roman Catholic. Avocations: travel, fishing, diving. Office: Office Grad Studies Lynn Univ Ed 327 Boca Raton FL 33431

DEMBY, ALBERT JOE, Sierra Leone vice president. Dep. leader Sierra Leone People's Party Govt. of Sierra Leone; v.p. Govt. of Sierra Leone, Freetown, 1996—. Office: Office of VP, Independence Ave, Freetown Sierra Leone*

DEMEDTS, MAURITS, pneumology educator; b. Tielt, Belgium, June 11, 1941; s. Andre and Germaine (Ide) D.; m. Toan-Leng Tan, July 30, 1964; children: Ingrid, Karin. B in Thomistic Philosophy, U. Leuven, Belgium, 1961, MD, 1966, PhD (hon.), 1978. Prof. in pneumology U. Leuven, 1981—, head div. pneumology, 1990—, head rsch. lab. pneumology, 1988—; mem. directory bd. U. Hosp. Leuven, 1989-94. Co-editor 20 med. books; contbr. over 400 articles to profl. publs. Mem. Royal Acad. Medicine, nat. and internat. pneumologic socs. Home: Beatrijslaan 8, B-3110 Rotselaar Belgium Office: Univ Hosp GHB, Herestraat 49, B-3000 Leuven Belgium

DEMEESTER, FRANCKY, consulting company executive; b. Roeselare, Belgium, July 16, 1961; s. Raphael and Aline (Desimpelaere) D.; m. Ann Buyse, Aug. 22, 1987; children: Josefien, Louis. Mech. Engr., K.U. Leuven, Belgium, 1984, PhD in Mech. Engr., 1992; Cert. European Affairs and Lobbying, European Inst. Pub. Affairs & Lobbying, Belgium, 1994. Rsch. asst. K.U. Leuven, 1984-91, project coord., 1991-93; mng. dir. E-1 Cons. Group, Belgium, 1993—; mng. dir., owner Demeester & Ptnrs. Cons., Belgium, 1997—; expert EC Belgium, 1991-98. Cpl. Belgian army, 1986-87. Mem. Royal Inst. Internat. Rels. Avocations: travel, reading, cooking, gardening. Home: Mechelsesteenweg, 3071 Erps-Kwerps Belgium Office: E-I Cons Group, Ave des Arts 27, 1040 Brussels Belgium

DEMEESTER, JOSEPH MARIE, pharmacology educator; b. Ghent, Belgium, June 21, 1951; s. Gerard and Thérèse (Van Haute) D.; m. Rita Germana Debruyne, Nov. 8, 1975; children: Hadewich, Annelies, Marjolein, Floriaan. Candidate pharm sci., U. Ghent, 1971, pharmacist, 1974, PhD, 1980. Rsch. asst. U. Ghent, 1974-82, 1st asst., 1982-86, rsch. leader, 1986-89, prof., 1989—, dir. Lab. Gen. Biochemistry, 1991—; dir. Internat. Ctr. for Stds., Internat. Pharm. Fedn., 1994—. Contbr. articles to profl. jours. Lt. Medical Svc., 1978-79. Recipient sci. award Royal East-Flanders Pharm. Sci., 1975, laureate Royal Acad. Scis., Belgium, 1980; travel grantee Ministry Edn., 1981. Mem. AAAS, Biochem. Soc., Belgian Biophys. Soc. (v.p.). Avocations: playing piano, organ and harpsichord. Home: Sint-Baafskouterstraat 14, B-9040 Ghent Belgium Office: U Ghent Lab Biochemistry, Harelbekestraat 72, B-9000 Ghent Belgium

DE MEESTER, PAUL JOZEF AUGUST, nuclear engineering educator, construction company executive; b. Antwerp, Belgium, Apr. 13, 1935; s. Aimé and Maria (Lambrechts) De M.; m. Mia Van de Sande, July 11, 1961; children: Johan, Kristiaan. Burg. Metaalkundig ir., K.U. Leuven, Leuven, Belgium, 1958; MS, U. Pa., 1960; diploma, Inst Nat Scis Tech Nucleaires, Saclay, France, 1961; D Toegep. Wetensch., Cath. U. Louvain, Belgium, 1967. Rsch. scientist to sect. head Study Centre Nuclear Energy, Mol, Belgium, 1959-65; prof. U. Faculteiten Sint-Ignatius Antwerpen, Antwerp, 1961-2000; prof. nuclear engring. Cath. U. Louvain, 1965-2000, extra-ordinary prof., chmn. Ctr. for Nuclear Engring., 1995-2000, dean faculty engring., 1975-81, prof. emeritus, 2000—, pres. group exact sci., 1981-85, bd. dirs., 1981-85; pres. energy rsch. com. European Econ. Cmty., 1975-81; mem. European Com. for R&D, 1981-90; vis. prof. Inst. Tech., Bandung, Indonesia, T.U., Magdeburg; pres., chmn. bd. BESIX, also Belgische Betonmaatschappij-Soc. Belge des Bétons, 1985—; chmn. Betonimno, 1988—; v.p. Muller Trovaux Pubs., 1998—; mem. bd. Verbond van Belgische Ondermemingen-Fedn. des Entreprises Belges, 1993—; chmn. Stichting van de Onderneming-Fondation de l'Entreprise, 1997—, Assn. des Conseillers au Commerce Extérieur-Vereniging van Adviseurs van Buitenlandse Handel, 1997—, Internat. C. of C. Belgium, 1998—; bd. dirs. Paque, SEMA-Belgium, Centrum voor Overheidsinformatie, Groupe Inno-Bon Marché, ETEX, ANCORABEL, Amon; mem. jury Flanders Tech. Internat.; mem. sci. com. Inst. de Protection et de Sureté Nucléaire, Paris. Author several books; contbr. articles to profl. Counsellor City Coun., Leuven-Heverlee, 1972-76; v.p. Christian Dem. Party, Leuven-Heverlee, 1972-85, bd. dirs., exec. com. King Baudoin Found.; pres. Belgian Assn. for Nondestructive Testing. Decorated knight Order of the Crown, grand officer Order of the Crown, comdr. Order King Leopold II, comdr. Order of Leopold (Belgium); Hereditary nobility and title of Baron, 1990; named Laureate Universitaire Stichting, 1958; recipient award Non-Ferrous and Nuclear Fuel Metals, 1968; Fulbright fellow, 1958-59. Fellow Inst. Metals, Am. Assn. for Nondestructive Testing, Am. Nuc. Soc.; mem. ASTM, Internat. com. for Nondestructive Testing (hon. mem., Man of Yr. 1990), Soc. Engrs. Leuven, Soc. Flemish Profs., Russian Soc. for Nondestructive Testing and Tech. Diagnostics (hon.), Dutch Soc. for Quality Control Inspection and Nondestructive Technique, Assn. Civil Engring. Contractors in Belgium (pres. 1990-93), Alumni Lovaniensis, Fulbright Alumni, Royal Acad. Belgium (dir.), Internat. C. of C. Belgium (chmn. 1998—), Belgian Assn. Large Constrn. Cos. (hon. chmn.), Leuven U. Aero Club (pres.). Avocations: gliding, classical music, modern art. Home: Sint Jansbergsteenweg 211, B 3001 Heverlee Belgium Office: K U Leuven Dept MTM, de Croylaan 2, B 3001 Heverlee Belgium also: Besix, Mettewielaan 74-76, 1060 Brussels Belgium

DE MELLO, FERNANDO GARCIA, biophysics educator, researcher; b. Ubá, M.G., Brazil, July 23, 1944; s. Joaquim Garcia and Etelvina (Caffini) de M.; m. Maria Christina Fialho, Sept. 26, 1970; children: Leonardo, Marcos, Gabriella. BSc, UERJ, 1968; MD, Fed. U. Rio de Janeiro, 1972, MSc, 1973,

DSc, 1980. Fogary Found. assoc. fellow NIH, Bethesda, Md., 1973-76; rsch. assoc. prof. Northwestern U., Evanston, Ill., 1984-86; asst. prof. biophysics Carlos Chagas Filho Inst. Biophysics, Fed. U. Rio de Janeiro, 1976-80, assoc. prof., 1980-92, prof., 1992—, chief Lab. Neurochemistry, 1982—, chmn. molecular biophysics dept., 1991-92, vice dir. Carlos Chagas Filho Inst. Biophysics, 1992-93, dir., 1993-97. Contbr. articles to sci. jours., including Jour. Neurochemistry, Procs. NAS-USA, European Jour. Pharmacology. Decorated Nat. Order Sci. Merit (Brazil); Guggenheim fellow, 1984. Mem. Brazilian Acad. Sci., L.Am. Acad. Scis., Third World Acad. Sci. Avocations: reading, music. Office: Fed U Rio de Janeiro Inst, Biophysics, CCS-Ilha Fundao, 21949900 Rio de Janeiro Brazil

DEMENCHONOK, EDWARD VASILEVICH, philosopher, linguist, researcher, educator; b. Vitebsk, Belarus, Jan. 1, 1942; came to U.S., 1992; s. Vasiliy Ivanovich Demenchonok and Olga Stanislavovna Plovinskaya; m. Sondra Marisa Franceil, July 1, 1993; children: Anna, Leonid. BA in Music, Mus. Coll., Minsk, Belarus, 1961; MA in Russian and Spanish, Moscow State U. Lomonosov, 1969; PhD, Russian Acad. Scis., Moscow, 1977. Rschr., then sr. rschr. Inst. Philosophy Russian Acad. Scis., 1970-95; assoc. prof. Moscow State U. Lomonosov, 1982-84; prof. Moscow State Pedagogic U., 1991-92; prof. Spanish Am. dept. Acad. Slavic Culture, Moscow, 1991-92; assoc. prof. Spanish Brewton-Parker Coll., Mt. Vernon, Ga., 1994-95; assoc. prof. fgn. langs. Ft. Valley (Ga.) State U., 1995—; vis. rschr. Acad. Scis. Cuba, 1978, 79, 83; vis. prof. U. INCCA Colombia, Bogota, 1988-90; vis. prof. Spanish U. Ga., Athens, 1992-93; lectr. literature Spanish Am. thought and philosophy at various instns., including U. Cordoba, Argentina, 1987, Inst. Missionary Theology, Bogota, 1990, Nat. Inst. Sci. Rsch. Coord. Colombia, Bogota, 1989, 90, Inst. Faith and Secularity, Madrid, Spain, 1992, U. Complutense Madrid, 1992, others; participant profl. confs., most recently Internat. Congress of L.Am. Philosophy: Ethics in L.Am., Bogota, 1990, Internat. Congress: East and West, Dialogue of Cultures in Contemporary World, Moscow, 1992, 9th Internat. Congress in Galicia: Philosophy and Nation, Pontevedra, Spain, 1992, 2nd Internat. Congress L.Am. Philosophy, San Juan, P.R., 1993, 93rd Ann. Meeting Am. Philos. Assn., Chgo., 1995, 94th Ann. Meeting, Phila., 1997, Americas Coun. First Ann. Conf., Savannah, Ga., 1997, An Interdisciplinary Conf.: Hispanics: Cultural Locations, San Francisco, 1997, 45th Ann. Conf. of Southeastern Coun. on Latin Am. Studies, Savannah, Ga., 1998, 20th World Congress of Philosophy: Philosophy Educating Humanity, Boston, 1998, 3d World Congress Internat. Soc. Universalism, Wellesley, Mass., 1998, 13th Ann. Internat. Conf. in Lit., Visual Arts, and Cinema, Atlanta, 1998, Fulbright Seminar on Tradition and Transformation in Singapore and Malaysia, 1998, 38th Ann. S.E. Conf. of Assn. for Asian Studies, Athens, Ga., 1999, 14th Inter-Am. Congress of Philosophy, Puebla, Mex., 1999. Author: Contemporary Technocratic Thought in the U.S.A., 1984; (in Spanish) América Latina en la Época de la Revolución Científico-Téchnica, 1990, Filosofía en el Mundo Contemporaneo, 1990, Filosofía Latinoamericana: Problemas y Tendencias, 1990; editor: Problems of Philosophy and Culture in Latin America, 1983, Contemporary Catholic Philosophy, 1985, New Tendencies in Western Social Philosophy, 1988; contbr. articles to profl. jours., chpts. to books. Mem. MLA (participant convs. 1992, 93, 99), L.Am. Studies Assn. (participant XVIII congress 1994), Am. Philos. Assn., Internat. Soc. Universal Dialogue, Russian Philosophical Soc., Assn. Cultural Rschrs. Russia, Assn. for Philosophy and Liberation, Southeastern Coun. Latin Am. Studies, Soc. for Iberian and L.Am. Thought. Russian Orthodox. Avocation: music.

DE MENIL, LOIS PATTISON, historian, philanthropist; b. N.Y.C., May 15, 1938; d. Charles Krone and Julia Anne (Hasson) Pattison; m. Georges Francois Conrad de Menil, Aug. 3, 1968; children: John-Charles, Joy-Alexandra, Benjamin, Victoria. AB, Wellesley Coll., 1960; diploma, Inst. d'Etudes Politiques, Paris, 1962; Lic. in Law, U. Paris, 1962; PhD, Harvard U., 1972. Pres. D. M. Found., N.Y.C., 1986—; bd. dirs. AXA Nordstern Art Ins. Corp.; counsellor to Ministry of Culture, Romania, 1997—; mem. Coun. Fgn. Rels., 1976—, Inst. for Strategic Studies, London, 1978—, French Inst. Internat. Rels., Paris, 1980—, U.S. Coun. on Germany, N.Y.C., 1978—, Festival d'Automne, Paris, 1997—. Author: Who Speaks for Europe?, 1978; editor, translator: The African Unity Movement, 1965, French Foreign Policy under De Gaulle, 1967. Mem. internat. coun. Mus. Modern Art, N.Y.C., 1975—; mem. vis. com. to art mus. Harvard U., Cambridge, Mass., 1977—; vice-chair bd. dirs. Dia Ctr. for Arts, N.Y.C., 1985-96; vice-chair trustees coun. Nat. Gallery Art, Washington, 1988-97, Centre d'Art Contemporain, Geneva, 1995—; bd. dirs. World Monuments Fund, N.Y.C., 1990—, Groton Sch., 1991—. Fulbright scholar, France, 1960-62; Ford Found. fellow, 1966-68. Mem. Century Assn., Univ. Club, River Club, Harvard Club, Fishers Island Country Club, Phi Beta Kappa. Episcopalian. Avocations: art, skiing, tennis, adventure travel. Home: 120 E 70th St New York NY 10021-5007 Office: D M Found 149 E 63rd St New York NY 10021-7405

DEMENTIS, KATHARINE HOPKINS, retired interior designer; b. Indpls., Dec. 20, 1922; d. Stephen Francis and Margaret Bell (Yeager) Hopkins; m. Gilbert X. Dementis, Feb. 1, 1953; children: Mary Margaret Dementis O'Dwyer, Stephen Ezra Hall. Student, John Herron Art Sch., 1941-44; BS, U. Wis., 1971. Interior designer L.S. Ayres and Co., Indpls., 1945-51; pres. Ariz. Questers, Phila., 1991-93; ret., 1993. Mem. DAR, Lakes Club, Union Hills Country Club. Republican. Presbyterian. Avocations: artist, decorator, antique collecting. Home: 12830 Castlebar Dr Sun City West AZ 85375-3270

DEMÉNY, ATTILA, geologist, researcher; b. Budapest, Hungary, Sept. 14, 1962; s. István and Istránné (Lörincz) D.; m. Krisztina Takács, Mar. 12, 1988; children: András, Loránd. Degree in geology, Eötvös Loránd U., Budapest, 1986, Univ.Dr., 1991; PhD, Hungarian Acad. Scis., Budapest, 1994. Sci. fellow Hungarian Acad. Sci., 1986-89, rschr., 1989—. Contbr. articles to profl. jours. Recipient Youth award Hungarian Acad. Scis., 1995. Mem. Internat. Isotope Soc. (chmn. 1994-96), Internat. Assn. Geochemistry and Cosmochemistry (councillor), European Soc. for Isotope Rsch. Avocations: bicycling, travel. Office: Lab for Geochem Rsch, Budaörsi ut 45, H-1112 Budapest Hungary

DEMEOLA, RICHARD INGRAM, critical care nurse, emergency room nurse; b. Newark, N.J., Aug. 24, 1969; s. Richard and Jane Stevely (Wyness) D. ASN, U. Medicine & Dentistry NJ Sch. Nursing, 1992; BSN, Kean Coll., 1995; postgrad. CEN; cert. emergency trauma nurse splst., pediat. advanced life support, BCLS, ACLS, trauma nursing core course, emergency nursing pediatric course pre-hosp. trauma life support, emergency med. tech.-ambulance, emergency med. tech.-defibrillator, CCRN, flight RN; RN N.J., N.Y., Pa., Ariz. RN emergency dept. Robert Wood Johnson Univ. Hosp., New Brunswick, N.J., 1992-93; staff RN surgical trauma ICU U. Medicine & Dentristry NJ Univ. Hosp., Newark, 1993-94; chief flight RN Intensive Air Ambulance, North Brunswick, N.J., 1994 ; staff RN, relief charge nurse emergency dept. St. Vincent's Hosp. & Med. Ctr. of N.Y., 1995-96; flight nurse Statflight, Westchester Med. Ctr., 1996-99, MedCenter Air/Carolinas Med. Ctr., Charlotte, N.C., 1999—; dir. course in advanced trauma nursing. Capt. Old Bridge Vol. EMS, Old Bridge, N.J., 1990-94; active Old Bridge Vol. EMS, Old Bridge, 1986 . Named Mem. of Yr. Old Bridge Vol. EMS, 1987, 89. Mem. ANA, Emergency Nurses Assn., Am. Assn. Critical Care Nurses, Nat. Flight Nurses Assn., Nat. League of Nurses, N.J. State Nurses Assn., Am. Trauma Soc. Home: 903 Walnut Ave Northfield NJ 08225-1328

DEMERLY, MARK, architect; b. Lafayette, Ind., May 21, 1958; s. Francis George Demerly and Mary Jane Freeman. B in Environ. Scis., Ball State U., 1981, BArch, 1981. Lic. arch., Ind. Intern arch. James & Assocs., Lafayette, Ind., 1979-80, Woollen Molzan & Ptnrs., Indpls., 1983-85; project arch. Group Eleven Arch. & Planning, Indpls., 1985-92; project mgr. URS Greiner Woodward Clyde, Indpls., 1992-99; pres. Demerly Archs., Indpls., 1999—. Bd. mem. Ind. Film Soc., pres., 1987-92; com. mem. Indy Jazz Fest, 1998—. Recipient Citation award Soc. Landscape Archs., Indpls., 1994, Indpls. Monumental award City Indpls., 1998. Mem. AIA (treas. Indpls. chpt., Merit award 1992), Friends of Herron (bd. mem., pres. 1994—, Philanthropy award 1997). E-mail: mdemerly@netdirect.net. Fax: 317-251-1746.

DEMERY, DOROTHY JEAN, secondary school educator; b. Houston, Sept. 5, 1941; d. Floyd Hicks and Irene Elaine Burns Clay; m. Leroy W. Demery, Jan. 16, 1979; children: Steven Bradley, Rodney Bradley, Craig Bradley, Kimberly Bradley. AA, West L.A. Coll., Culver City, Calif., 1976; AS, Harbor Coll., Wilmington, Calif., 1983; BS in Pub. Adminstrn., Calif. State U., Carson, 1985; MS in Instructional Leadership, Nat. U., San Diego, 1991. Cert. real estate broker, tchr. math. and bus. edn., bilingual tchr., crosscultural lang. and acad. devel.; lang. devel. specialist. Eligibility social worker Dept. Pub. Social Svcs., L.A., 1967-74; real estate broker Dee Bradley & Assocs., Riverside, Calif., 1976—; tchr. math L.A. Unified Sch. Dist., 1985-91; math/computer sci. tchr. Pomona (Calif.) Unified Sch. Dist., 1991—; adj. lectr. Riverside C.C., 1992-93; mem. Dist. Curriculum Coun./Report Card Task Force, Pomona, 1994—; bd. dirs. Associated Pomona Tchrs. Chairperson Human Rights Com., Pomona, 1992—, sec. steering com., 1993—, adv. bd., 1993—; mem. polit. action com. Assoc. Pomona Tchrs., 1993-94. Recipient Outstanding Svc. award Baldwin Hills Little League Assn., L.A., 1972. Mem. Nat. Bus. Assn., Nat. Coun. Tchrs. Math., Aux. Nat. Med. Assn., Associated Pomona Tchrs. (bd. dirs.), Calif. Tchrs. Assn. (mem. state coun., 2000, chair site base, chair dept. math.). Avocations: hiking, tennis, walking. Home: PO Box 2796 Riverside CA 92516-2796 Office: Simons Middle School 900 E Franklin Ave Pomona CA 91766-5362

DEMETER, STEVEN, neurologist, internet publishing company executive; b. Budapest, Hungary, Jan. 12, 1947; came to U.S., 1957; s. Arpad and Ilona (Wiesner) D.; m. Diane Simkin, Jan. 8, 1984; children: Sara, Nikki. BS, CUNY, 1969; MD, N.Y. Med. Coll., 1973. Diplomate Am. Bd. Psychiatry and Neurology. Intern Beth Israel Med. Ctr., N.Y.C., 1973-74; neurology resident Albert Einstein Coll. Medicine, Bronx, N.Y., 1974-77; inst. neurology N.Y. Med. Coll., N.Y.C., 1977-79; fellow in behavioral neurology U. Iowa Coll. Medicine, Iowa City, 1979-81; fellow Ctr. for Brain Rsch., U. Rochester (N.Y.) Sch. Medicine, 1981-84, instr. neurology, 1982-84, asst. prof. Ctr. for Brain Rsch., 1984-87, asst. prof. neurology, 1987-89, clin. asst. prof., 1989-91, clin. assoc. prof., 1991-93; pres. Arbor Pub. Corp., San Diego, 1990—; assoc. clin. prof. neurosci. U. Calif., San Diego, 1995—; neurology cons. Rochester Psychiat. Ctr., 1985-91. Contbr. numerous articles to med. jours. Grantee Scottish Rite Schizophrenia Rsch. Found., 1987-90, Whitehall Found., 1990-93, NIH, 1991-94. Fellow Am. Acad. Neurology, Royal Soc. Medicine (London); mem. AAAS, Soc. for Neurosci., Tourette Syndrome Assn. (med. adv. bd. 1985-93, bd. dirs. 1987-93). Office: Arbor Pub Corp Ste 120 10393 San Diego Mission Rd San Diego CA 92108-2134

DEMETRIADES, ALECOS, geologist, geochemist, researcher; b. Larnaca, Cyprus, Aug. 8, 1947; arrived in Greece, 1976; s. Nicolaos and Christalla (Mappourides) D.; m. Stella Mavrommatis, Feb. 16, 1975; 1 child, Marina. BSc, U. London, 1974; MS in Mining Geology and Mineral Exploration, U. Leicester, Eng., 1975. Chartered geologist, engr. Rsch. asst. Rio Tinto Fin. & Exploration Ltd., London, 1972-73, sr. rsch. asst., 1974; exploration geochemist Inst. Geology and Mineral Exploration, Xanthi, Greece, 1976-81, Athens, Greece, 1981—; project mgr. Inst. Geology & Mineral Exploration, Xanthi, 1976-81, Athens, 1981—; sec. working group on regional geochem. mapping Western European Geol. Surveys, 1991-93, pub. rels. and fin. com. project Global Geochem. Baselines, Internat. Union Geol. Scis., 1996—. Co-author: Base Metal Sulfide Deposits in Sedimentary and Volcanic Environments, 1988, Mineral Deposits Within the European Community, 1988; contbr. articles to profl. jours. Dep. chmn. Parents Assn., Athens, 1994-95; chmn. Assn. of Friends of Music and Arts, Athens, 1992—; councilor Municipality of Zografou Music Sch., Athens, 1994-98. Fellow Geol. Soc. of London; mem. Instn. Mining and Metallurgy, Assn. Exploration Geochemists. Greek Orthodox. Avocations: photography, chess, sports. Home: PO Box 64047 Zografou, GR-15710 Athens Greece Office: Inst Geology & Mineral Exploration, 70 Messoghion St, GR-11527 Athens Greece

DEMETRIADI, PETER MICHAEL, commodities trader; b. Glasgow, Scotland, Jan. 4, 1953; s. Michael Anthony and Nancy Anna (Rodocanachi) D.; m. France Marie Ann Nicole Bodson, Sept. 10, 1980; children: Jennifer, Guy, James. Cert. in Finnish lang. and culture, Summer Univ., Finland, 1974; BA with honours, Univ. Coll., London, 1975. Grain trader Tradax, London, 1975-79; petrochems. trader Tradax-Cargill, Geneva, 1979-86; mgr. naphtha trading Cargill, Geneva, 1986, mgr. petrochems. trading, 1987; mgr. energy futures Cargill Investor Svcs., London, 1987-89; mgr. aromatics trading Mitsui and Co., Brussels, 1989-92; dir. Arden Chem. Ltd., Henley in Arden, Eng., 1992; gen. mgr. Sunkyong Chem. Trading Inc., 1992-97; mg. dir. Midland Petrochemicals Ltd, 1997—; chmn. Anglo-Danish Oil Co. Ltd, 1997—. Named Esquire, Venerable Order of St. John of Jerusalem. Mem. Marylebone Cricket Club, Army and Navy Club, Henley Royal Regatta, Inst. Petroleum. Avocations: cricket, tennis, music, riding.

DEMETRIOU, BASIL PHILIP, food products executive, consultant; b. Alexandria, Egypt, May 18, 1922; s. Philip and Marianthi (Marcou) D.; m. Eleanor Dakis Chondroudakis; 1 child, Philippa. BA with honors, U. Tex., 1951. Ind. explosives mfr. Limassol, Cyprus, 1941-45; indsl. trainer Gerber, Fremond, Mich., 1951; dir. Philippos Demetriou & Sons, Ltd., Limassol, 1952-58, pres., 1958-92; ret., 1992; pres. DHB, Ltd., Limassol, 1958-83; cons. in field, 1986—. Contbr. articles to profl. jours. Named Hon. TEx. Citizen Gov. State of Tex., 1951. Cyprus Am. Acad. Assn. (founder), Phi Etta Sigma, Phi Lambda Upsilon. Christian Orthodox. Clubs: Sporting (Limassol), Skii (Nicosia). Lodges: Rotary (sec. 1960-61, pres. 1967-68), St. Paul's, Zinon. Avocations: photography, skiing. Fax: 357 5 365688. Office: PO Box 99, PO Box 56099, Limassol CY-3304, Cyprus

DEMETRIOU, LEFTERIS, plastic and reconstructive surgeon; b. Athens, Nov. 7, 1943; s. Lycourgos and Katie (Markaki) D.; m. Pamela Bullock, Feb. 3, 1973; children: Katie, Christina, Rita, Thalia. MD, Med. Sch., Vienna, Austria, 1971; FRCSPr, Edinbourgh Coll., 1977. House officer Nat. Health Svc. Hosps., U.K., 1972-73; sr. house officer Nat. Health Svc., U.K., 1973-76; registrar gen. surgery Nat. Health Svc., Scotland, 1977-80, registrar plastic surgery, 1981-85; cons. plastic surgeon P.V.T., Nicosia, Cyprus, 1986—. Contbr. articles to profl. jours. Fellow Internat. Coll. of Surgeons; mem. Cypriot Surg. Soc., Internat. Soc. of Aesthetic Plastic Surgery, Internat. Fedn. of Sports Medicine. Avocations: sea sports, cactus gardening, mountaineering. Office: St Eleftherios Pvt Hosp, 64 Digenis Akritas Ave, Nicosia 1061, Cyprus

DEMEULDRE, MICHEL, sociologist, professor; b. Charleroi, Hainaut, Belgium, June 21, 1944; s. Maurice and Camille (Huart) D.; m. Isabelle Kabatu (div.); 1 child, Natasha. MS in Sociology, Free U. Brussels, Belgium, 1973, Phd in Social Scis., 1989. Journalist Le Peuple, Africa, Remarque Africaine,, Brussels, London, 1970-89; tchr. Athenee Royal de Gilly-Charleroi, Charleroi, Belgium, 1974-88; prof. Ctr. U. Charleroi, Belgium, 1988-91, U. Brussels, 1992—, U. du Travail Charleroi, 1992—; ombudsman social tourism European and African cities, 1974-77; researcher Nat. Found Sci. Rsch., Brussels, 1988—. Author: Tourism Policies, 1972, The Change in Urban Music, 1986, Logic of Aesthetics, 1989, Streets and Collective Styles Creations, 1997, Musical Pleasure and Body Techniques, 1998, Music and Sociology-Genetic Approach og Socio-Musical Process, 2000; contbr. articles to profl. jours. Mem. Ctr. Nat. d' Accueil, Ctr. Nat. Cooperation & Devel., Interculture (founder, pres. Charleroi, 1977—), Internat. Assn. for the Study of Popular Music (Belgian rep. 1986—) Internat. Fed. Settlements (Belgian rep. 1979-82). Avocations: music, fine arts. E-mail: demeuldre.michel@compagnet.be. Home: 59 Rue Saint Antoine, B-5651 Walcourt-Somzee Belgium

DE MEY, BART, integrated circuits expert; b. Mortsel, Antwerp, Belgium, Oct. 10, 1955. M in Exact Scis., U. Antwerp, 1978. Rsch. scientist U. Antwerp, 1978-83; ASIC design mgr. IMEC, Leuven, Belgium, 1983—; tng. network mgr. INVOMEC, Leuven, 1983; ASIC ECAD cons. Eurochip-Europractice, Leuven. Fax: 32-16-281 584. E-mail: bart.demey@imec.be. Office: IMEC, Kapeldreef 75, 3001 Leuven Belgium

DE MEYER, ARNOUD CYRIEL LEO, engineering educator, dean; b. Oudenaarde, Belgium, Apr. 12, 1954; s. Eugeen and Emma (De Winter) De M. Electrotech. Engr., U. Ghent, Belgium, 1976, Dr. in Mgmt., 1983. Instrumentation engr. Esso Chems., Belgium, 1977-78; rschr. Ministry of Sci. Policy, Belgium, 1978-79; rsch. assoc. U. Ghent, 1979-83, prof. tech. mgmt., 1989—; assoc. dean, 1990—; prof. INSEAD, Fontainebleau, France, 1983—; dir. gen. Euro Asia Ctr., Fontainebleau, 1995-99; bd. dirs. Videomgmt., Brussels, Option Internat., Lewe, Info. Coun. Devel. Authority, Singapore, Sentosa Devel. Corp., Singapore; vis. prof. Keil U., Tokyo, 1989-90, Germany, 1990. Author: Benchmarking Global Manufacturing, 1992, Creating Product Value, 1992; contbr. articles to profl. jours. Office: INSEAD, 87 Science Park Dr #03-01, Science Hub 118260, Singapore

DEMIĆ, MIROSLAV DRAGOLJUB, mechanical engineering educator; b. Rašanac, Serbia, Yugoslavia, Feb. 5, 1948; s. Dragoljub Stevan and Slobodanka Kuzman (Stojanović) D.; m. Zorica Miloš Lučić, Jan. 7, 1978; children: Ivan, Milan, Ivana. Grad. Mech. Engring., U. Kraqujevac, Yugoslavia, 1972, PhD in Mech. Engring., 1978; MSc in Mech. Engring., U. Belgrade, Yugoslavia, 1975. Designer Truck Factory, Priboj, Yugoslavia, 1972-77; rschr. Zastava, Kraqujevac, 1977-88; univ. prof. Faculty Mech. Engring., Kraqujevac, 1988—. Author: Powertrain Mounting, 1990, The Track Vehicles, 1992, The Truck Design, 1994, The Motorcycles, 1996, The Vehicle Oscillatory System Parameter Optimization, 1997, Vehicles Theory, 1999. Mem. Yugoslav Acad. Engring., Acad. Transport Russian Fedn. (academician), Acad. Quality Russian Fedn. (academician). Fax: 034 333192. E-mail: demic@knez.uis.kg.ac.yu. Home: Ljubise Jovanovica 7, 34000 Kraqujevac Serbia, Yugoslavia Office: Faculty Mech Engring, Kraqujevac, 34000 Kraqujevac Serbia, Yugoslavia

DEMICOLI, CHARLES, company director; b. Valletta, Malta, Aug. 8, 1946; s. Jack and Pauline (Vella) D.; m. Marlene Sultana, Jan. 12, 1970; children: Edward, Clive. Police supt. Malta, to 1981; personnel mgr. Forter Clark Products, Ltd., Malta, 1982-84; mgr. Independence Print, Malta, 1985-90; dir. Mimcol, Malta, 1988-92; mng. dir. Group 4, Malta, 1988-96; chmn. Kordin Grain Terminal, Malta, 1991—; bd. chmn. Federated Mills, Ltd., Malta, Sterling Parks, Ltd., Malta. Editor The People on Sunday, 1997-99. Local coun. mem. Msida, Malta, 1993-96. Mem. Nationalist Party. Avocations: philately, reading, travel. Home: 1 Ferrini Ct/University St, Msida MSD04, Malta Office: Sterling Parks Ltd, PO Box 50/Malta Intntl Air, Luqa Malta

DEMIDENKO, SERGE NIKOLAYEVICH, electronics educator, research manager; b. Molodechno, Minsk, Belarus, June 14, 1955; arrived in New Zealand, 1999; s. Nikolay Y. and Klara D. (Petrova) D.; m. Nina A. Kin, May 21, 1977 (div. Jan. 1996); children: Ann, Julia; m. Moi Tin Chew, June 17, 1997. MSc in Engring., Belarussian State U. Informatics and Radioelectronics, Minsk, 1977; PhD in Engring., Acad. Scis., Minsk, 1984. Chartered elec. engr.; cert. in higher edn. Sr. engr. Acad. Scis., Minsk, 1977-79, rsch. fellow, 1979-85, project mgr., 1985-87, head of dept., 1990-92; head of lab. Brest (Belarus) Computer Concern, 1987-90; hon. rsch. fellow Brunel U., London, 1990; vis. prof. Poly. of Milan, 1992-93; mgr. R & D Singapore Poly., 1993-99; assoc. prof. Massey U., New Zealand, 1999—; part-time assoc. prof. Belarussian State U. Informatics and Radioelectronics, Minsk, 1985—; program chair, mem. Asian Test Symposium Com., 1995—. Author: Generation and Application of Pseudorandom Sequences for Random Testing, 1988, Modular CAMAC-Systems for Research Automation, 1990; contbr. articles to profl. jours.; co-editor Jour. Electronic Testing Theory and Applications, 1990—; patentee in field. Recipient Bronze medal USSR Nat. Econ. Com., Moscow, 1984, USSR Rsch. Contest 1st prize A.S. Popov Sci.-Engring. Soc., Moscow, 1991; named Laureat, Nat. Young Rschrs. Contest, Ctrl. Com., Minsk, 1989, 91. Fellow Instn. Elec. Engrs. (internat. coun. rep. for Belarus 1992—); mem. IEEE (sr.). Avocations: canoeing, tourism, cars. Home: 28 Elmira Ave, Palmerston North New Zealand

DEMIDOVA, NADEJDA, engineering educator; b. Moscow, Dec. 17, 1945; d. Sergey and Elena (Gerasimova) D.; m. Gennady Malyshev. Student, Moscow, 1953-64; engr., Moscow Aviation Inst., 1964-70; PhD, 1976, DSc, 1991. Engr. Tsniimash, Moscow, 1970-71; engr. MAI, Moscow, 1971-72, asst., 1976-91, prof., 1991—. Author: Electrochemical System, 1992; contbr. articles to profl. jours. Office: Moscow Aviation Inst, Volokolamskdye Sh 4, 125871 Moscow Russia

DEMIDOW, MACIEJ ADAM, trade company executive, consultant; b. Kielce, Poland, Sept. 13, 1942; s. Vladimir Pavlovic and Anna Francesca (Polysevinci) D.; m. Maria Anna Domagala, Aug. 29, 1964; children: Beata, Agnieszka. MS, U. Cracow, Poland, 1965. Economist Coopexim, Katowice, Poland, 1965-67; dept. mgr. Centrozap, Katowice, Poland, 1967-77; mktg. mgr. HpH, Katowice, Poland, 1977-88; pres. BPC Ltd., Katowice, Poland, 1988—; dep. chief editor Hutmasz Quar., Katowice, 1978-88; v.p. Chamber of Fgn. Trade, Katowice, 1981-88; chmn. Simmex Internat. Fair, Katowice, 1983-85; dir. Arab-Polish Co. Ltd., Abu Dhabi, 1995—. Author: (manual) Negotiations in International Trade, 1985; contbr. articles to profl. jours. Recipient numerous Econ. Achievement awards. Mem. numerous bus. clubs. Avocations: travelling, geography, history. Office: Bus Promotion Ctr Ltd, Al W Korfantego 2, 40-956 Katowice Poland

DE MIGUEL, ADELIA, social sciences educator; b. Almazan, Soria, Spain, Aug. 9, 1962; d. Antonio de Miguel and Adelia Negredo; 1 child, Adelia Goretti. PhD in Psychology. Prof. U. La Laguna, Tenerife, Spain, 1986—. Co-author: Stress, Personality, and Health: A Non-Sexist Model on Stress, 1994. Fax: 03034-22317461. E-mail: admiguel@ull.es. Office: U La Laguna, Fac Psychology Guajara Camp, 38271 La Laguna S Cruz T, Spain

DE MIGUEL GONZALEZ, RAFAEL, avionics engineer, information systems consultant; b. Madrid, Sept. 9, 1957; s. Alfonso de Miguel Martinez and Agueda González Bermudez; m. Maria Soledad Caballero Pérez. Degree, Universitarian Studies Sch., Madrid, 1975; degree in aero. engring., Inst. Tech., Madrid, 1981; postgrad., INTA/Esteban Terradas Inst., Ajalvir, Spain, 1981-82. Engr. CESELSA, Madrid, 1983-84, design engr., 1985-87; tech. trainer Lanier, Madrid, 1987-88; tech. mgr. ATEL, Madrid, 1988-90; engring. dir. Data Finder, Madrid, 1990-99; corp. dir. A. Aerolog, Madrid, 1999—. Author: Stoll-Vtoll Airplane Technology, 1977, Manual de Instalación de Fax, 1987, Curso de Introducción a la Informática, 1991, Introducción al Faximil, 1997. Bd. dirs. Coll. Tech. Engrs. Aeronauticos, Madrid, 1988, Assn. Tech. Engrs. Aeronauticos, Madrid, 1988; pres. Bd. Gen. Elections, Madrid, 1993. Served with Spanish Air Force, 1981-83. Mem. Planetary Soc. Avocations: poetry, literature, musical composition. Office: A Aerolog, Vistalegre 51, 28270 Colmenarejo-Madrid Spain

DEMILLE, NELSON RICHARD, writer; b. N.Y.C., Aug. 23, 1943; s. Huron and Antonia (Lombardo) DeM.; divorced; children: Lauren, Alex.; m. Ginny Sindel Witte, 1988. BA in Polit. Sci. and History, Hofstra U., 1970, LHD (hon.), 1989; DLitt (hon.), L.I. U., 1993; LDH (hon.), Dowling Coll., 1997. Freelance writer Garden City, 1973—. Author more than 12 novels, including By the Rivers of Babylon, 1978, Cathedral, 1981, The Talbot Odyssey, 1984, Word of Honor, 1985, The Charm School, 1988, The Gold Coast, 1990, The General's Daughter, 1992, Spencerville, 1994, Plum Island, 1997, The Lion's Game, 2000; co-author: Mayday, 1998; contbr. short stories to mags. 1st lt. U.S. Army, 1966-69. Decorated Air medal, Bronze Star, Vietnamese Cross of Gallantry; recipient Estabrook award Hofstra U. Mem. Mystery Writers Am., Author's Guild, Mensa. Roman Catholic. Office: 61 Hilton Ave Ste 23 Garden City NY 11530-2813

DEMIN, DMITRY L'VOVICH, physics experimentalist, educator; b. Protva, Zhukov, Russia, Oct. 23, 1967; s. Lev Vasil'evich and Rosa-Alexandra Ivanovna (Krylova) D.; m. Ekaterina Eduardovna Kubatkina, Oct. 28, 1998. M of Natural Scis., Moscow Phys. and Tech. Inst., Dolgoprudny, Russia, 1993. Civil engr. Joint Inst. for Nuclear Rsch., Dubna, Russia, 1993-96, rsch. scientist, 1996—. Sgt. Armour Divsn. Soviet Army, 1986-88. Avocation: lawn tennis. Office: Joint Inst Nuclear Rsch, Lab Nuclear Problems, Dubna/Moscow Russia

DEMIRER, GOKSEL NIYAZI, environmental engineering educator; b. Corum, Turkey, Sept. 6, 1967; s. Kemal and Necla (Samsunlu) d.; m. Sibel Uludag, Oct. 28, 1999. BSc, Mid. East Tech. U., Ankara, Turkey, 1989, MSc, 1991; PhD, Vanderbilt U., Nashville, 1996. Rsch. asst. Mid. East Tech. U., Ankara, 1990-92, instr., 1997-98, asst. prof., 1998-99; assoc. prof. Mid. East Tech. U., Ankara, 1992-96, 1999—; rsch. asst. Vanderbilt U., Nashville, 1992-96; cons. Chamber of Environ. Engrs., Ankara, 1997—, Turkish Tech. Devel. Found., Ankara, 1999—; referee Jour. Cleaner Prodn., London, 1999—. Author: Fundamentals of Water Treatment, 1997. Mem. Chamber Environ. Engrs. (mem. adminstrv. bd. 1998—), Water Environ.

Fedn. Mem. Freedom and Solidarity Party. Avocations: reading, internet, travel, conferences, politics. Office: Mid East Tech U, Dept Environ Engring, 06531 Ankara Turkey

DEMIRKAN, HALIME, academic administrator; b. Izmir, Turkey, Sept. 18, 1954; d. Mustafa Lutfi and Muzaffer Cisko; m. Zafer Demirkan, Sept. 4, 1979; 1 child, Murat. BS in Indsl. Engring., Middle East Tech. U., Ankara, Turkey, 1978, MS in Indsl. Engring., 1981, PhD in Architecture, 1989. Instr. Middle East Tech. U., Ankara, 1979-84; researcher Bldg. Rsch. Coun. The Scientific and Tech. Coun. Turkey, Ankara, 1984-88; chairperson, vice-dean Bilkent U., Ankara, 1988—. Contbr. articles to profl. jours. Avocation: classical music. Office: Bilkent U, Dept Interior Arch & Environ Design, Ankara Bilkent 06533, Turkey

DEMIRKILIÇ, URUK, military career officer, surgeons, educator; b. Samsun, Turkey, Oct. 15, 1961; s. Kamil and Emine (Akbayrak) D.; m. Sibel Miskioglu, Nov. 4, 1985. MD, Gulhane Mil. Med. Faculty, Ankara, Turkey, 1985; cardiovasc. surgeon, Gulhane Mil. Med. Acad., Ankara, Turkey, 1993, asst. prof., 1995, assoc. prof., 1998. Commd. officer Turkish Army, 1985, advanced through grades to lt. col.; med. dir., ltd. Gulhane Mil. Med. Faculty, Ankara, 1985-86, chief med. sect. gen. hdqrs., 1986-88, gen. practitioner, doctor, 1988-93; cardiovasc. surgeon, capt. Mil. Hosp., Diyarbakir, Turkey, 1994-95; asst. prof. cardiovasc. surgery dept. Gulhane Mil. Med. Acad., Ankara, 1995-98, assoc. prof. cardiovasc. surgery dept., 1999—; chief med. sect. Turkish Gen. Hdqr., Ankara, 1986-88; chief cardiovasc. surgery dept. Mil. Hosp., Diyarbakir. Recipient First Degree award 100th Yr. Nat. Med. Rsch., Ankara, 1998. Mem. Internat. Soc. Cardiothoracic Surgery, Nat. Soc. Cardiovasc. Surgery, Nat. Soc. Vascular Surgery. Avocations: playing basketball, cinema, traveling. Home: Suleymanbey Sok 2379, 06570 Ankara Turkey Office: Gulhane Mil Med Acad, Cardiovasc Surgery Dept, 06010 Ankara Turkey

DE MITA, LUIGI CIRIACO, former prime minister Italy; b. Fusco, Avellino, Italy, Feb. 2, 1928. Mem. Chamber Deps., Benevento-Avellino-Salerno, Italy, 1963, 72—; nat. counsellor Christian Dem. Party, 1964, later vice sec.; under-sec. for the interior Italy, Rome, minister industry and commerce, 1973-74, minister fgn. trade, 1974-76, minister without portfolio with responsibility for the Mezzogiorno, 1976-79; sec. gen. Christian Dem. Party, 1982-88; prime minister Italy, Rome, 1988-89; mem. European Parliament, Brussels, Belgium. Office: Parlamento Europeo, Rue Wiertz, ASP 12E258 Bruxelles B-1047, Belgium*

DEMJANENKO, MILOS, physical chemistry researcher, consultant; b. Prague, Czechoslovakia, June 21, 1947; s. Nikolaj and Antonie (Benesovska) D. Student, Charles U., Prague, 1965-66, D Natural Scis. in Physics and Chemistry, 1974; CandSci, Czechoslovak Acad. Scis., Prague, 1979. Sci. rschr. Inst. Macromolecular Chemistry, Czechoslovak Acad. Scis., 1974-79, Nat. Rsch. Inst. for Protection Materials, Prague, 1979-91; leading sci. rschr. Lab. R & D, Prague, 1991—; participant internat. confs. and symposia. Contbr. articles to Macromolecules, Jour. Chromatography, Radiation Phys. Chemistry; patentee in field. Mem. European Phys. Soc., Union Czech Mathematicians and Physicists, Czech Chem. Soc. Home and Office: Dolni Počernice, Hrabačovská 223, 19012 Prague 9, Czech Republic

DEML, MAX, publishing company executive; b. Roding, Bavaria, Germany, Aug. 27, 1957; s. Konrad and Anna (Zollner) D.; m. Marianne Humer, Oct. 4, 1986; children: Tobias, Johannes. Student, U. Regensburg, 1977-79, U. Vienna, Austria, 1979-96. Dir. Forschungsinstitut fuer ethisch-oekologische Geldanlagen Rsch. Inst., Vienna, Austria, 1990—; mng. dir. EcoInvest Publ. Ltd., Vienna, Austria, 1991—. Co-author: (books in German) Against the Records, 1989, Green Money Handbook, 1990, Green Money Year Book, 2000; editor and author: (stock market newsletter), Eco Invest, 1991—. Rep. Internat. Fellowship of Reconciliation at UN in Vienna, 1986—. Grantee Cusanuswerk, Bonn, 1980-86. Avocations: bicycling, chess. Home: Schweizertalstr 8-10/5/1, A1130 Vienna Austria Office: Forschungsinstitut fuer ethisch-oekologische Geldanlagen, Tuerkenstr 9, A1090 Vienna Austria

DEMLING, JOACHIM HEINRICH, psychiatrist, psychotherapist; b. Fuerth, Bavaria, Germany, June 2, 1947; s. Ludwig and Elisabeth (Renner) D.; m. Antonie Staedele; 7 children. MD, U. Erlangen-Nürnberg, Germany, 1974, Prof., 1996. Intern depts. surgery, internal medicine and psychiatry Univ. Hosp, Wuerzburg, Germany, 1974-75; registrar State Mental Hosp.-U. Ulm, Günzburg, Germany, 1976-78, 3d Med. Clinic, Augsburg, Germany, 1978-79; registrar dept. neurology U. Saarbrücken, Homburg, Germany, 1979-81; scholar Max-Planck Inst. Biophys. Chemistry, Göttingen, Germany, 1982-83; staff physician dept. psychiatry U. Erlangen, 1983-98, acting dir., 1999-2000; med. cons. Pharmacia & Upjohn, Erlangen, Germany. Translator, reviser: Reactions to Psychotropic Medication, 1991; contbr. articles to med. jours., including Neuroendocrinology, Amino Acids, Biol. Psychiatry. Sgt. German Air Force, 1966-68. Mem. Soc. for Promotion Psychiatry (treas. U. Erlangen-Nürnberg chpt.). Lutheran. Avocations: psychotherapy, German and English literature, religion, psychopharmacology, philosophy of science. Office: U Erlangen Dept Psychiatry, Schwabachanlage 6, D-91054 Erlangen Germany

DEMMITT, JOYCE MILLER, library administrator; b. Pitts., Dec. 13, 1946; d. Kenneth William and Virginia (Booker) Miller; m. Paul Joseph Demmitt, Oct. 22, 1983; children: Louisa Dorothy, Daniel Kenneth. BA, Gettysburg Coll., 1968; MLS, U. Md., 1975. Reference libr. Howard County Libr., Columbia, Md., 1970-75, br. mgr., 1975-78, reader's adv. coord., 1978-81, head adult svcs., 1981-86, head info. svcs., 1986-96, assoc. dir. pub. svc., 1996—; mem. exec. bd. libr. assoc. tng. program Cooperating Librs. of Ctrl. Md., 1997—; spkr. in field. Contbr. chpts. to books. Pres. alumni chpt. U. Md. Coll. Libr. and Info. Sci., 1985-86; chair bd. dirs. Careerscope, Howard County, 1985-87; exec. bd. Assn. Cmty. Svcs., Howard County, Md., 1994-97; stakeholder Howard County United Vision, 1999; bd. dirs. Health Improvement Leadership Team, Howard County, 1996-99; chair Howard County Childcare Task Force, 1987. Grantee Md. Divsn. Libr. Devel. and Svcs., 1981—. Mem. ALA, Md. Libr. Assn. (pres. 1995-96). Democrat. Avocations: training, public speaking, child advocacy, piano. E-mail: demmittj@howa.lib.md.us. Office: Howard County Libr 6600 Cradlerock Way Columbia MD 21045-4912

DEMMLER, ALBERT WILLIAM, JR., retired editor, metallurgical engineer; b. Pitts., Feb. 21, 1929; Albert William and Hester Louisa (Dye) D.; m. Donna Lou Frederick, Feb. 16, 1957; children: Richard Frederick, Keith Alan (dec.), Diane Leslie, Debra Lynn. PhB in Liberal Arts, U. Chgo., 1948; BS in Metall. Engring., U. Mich., 1951, MS in Metall. Engring., 1952, PhD, 1955. Rsch. engr. Alcoa Rsch. Labs., New Kensington, Pa., 1955-68; registered rep. Butcher & Singer, Pitts., 1968-74; exec. searcher Reese Assoc., Pitts., 1974-76; assoc. editor Soc. Automotive Engrs. Inc. Mags., Warrendale, Pa., 1976-90, sr. editor, 1990-99; ret., 1999. Patentee in field. Mem. NRA, Soc. Automotive Engrs., Am. Soc. Metals Internat., Hypnotism Soc. Pa., Tarentum Dist. Sportsmens Club, Pa. Rifle and Pistol Assn., Pa. Gun Collectors Assn., Crowfoot Rod & Gun Club, Mensa, Tau Beta Pi, Phi Lambda Upsilon, Sigma Xi. Democrat. Presbyterian. Avocations: competitive rifle, pistol, hypnosis. Home: 132 Glenview Dr New Kensington PA 15068-4900

DEMMY, TODD LYLE, surgeon; b. Phila., May 29, 1960; s. Merlyn Ray and Claire Mildred D.; m. Maryellen Boyle, Oct. 19, 1985; children: Tara, Michael. BS, Pa. State U., 1981; MD, Jefferson Med. Coll., 1983. Diplomate Am. Bd. Thoracic Surgery, Am. Bd. Surgery. Assoc. prof. of surgery U. Mo., Columbia, 1991—; chief of thoracic oncology Ellis Fischel Cancer Ctr., Columbia, Mo., 1994—; co-dir. cardiac transplant program U. Mo., Columbia, 1991—. Recipient Thoracic Surgery Dirs. Assn. award Soc. Thoracic Surgeons, 1983. Mem. ACS (sec. Mo. chpt. 1989-99, v.p. 1999-2000, pres. 2000—). Republican. Roman Catholic. Avocations: piano, computer programming, tennis, swimming. Office: Univ Mo-Columbia 1 Hospital Dr Columbia MO 65201-5276

DÉMOGÉ, PAUL HUGH, orthodontist, educator; b. Paris, Apr. 3, 1925; s. Leon E. and Muriel (Tomasson) D.; children: Marc, Brice, Hugues. Diploma in Dental Surgery, U. Nancy, France, 1954; diploma in Orthodontics, Royal Coll. Surgeons, Eng., 1958; lic. in Sci., Sorbonne, Paris, 1961; DS in Odontology, U. Rene Descartes, Paris, 1973. Intern Forsyth Dental Ctr., Boston, 1954-55; clin. fellow Harvard U., Boston, 1955-57; pvt. practice orthodontist Paris, 1958-75; asst. prof. Ecole Dentaire De Paris, 1961-69; prof. orthodontics Faculty Dental Surgery, Paris, 1969-81; prof. U. Rene Descartes, Paris, 1981-94, prof. emeritus, 1994—; odontologiste chief of svc. Hosp. Paris, 1975-91; U. Rene Descartes. Co-author: (text book) Traite D'Orthodontie, 1960, 74, 80, 93. Coun. Order of Dentists, Paris, 1964-78; chmn. Nat. Comm. on Qualification for Orthodontists, France, 1979-94. With French Fgn. Legion, WWII; col. French Amred Forces Med. Corps. Decorated Chevalier, Legion D'Honneur, France, 1992, Officier, Ordre Nat. du Merite, France, 1980, Comrd., Ordre Du Ouissam-Alaouite, Morocco, 1994. Fellow Intern Coll. Dentists, Pierre Fauchard Acad.; mem. European Orthodontic Soc. (pres. 1980-81), Nat. Acad. Dental Surgeons (titulaire 1976—, pres. 1998), Am. Dental Club Paris (pres. 1986-88), N.Y. Acad. Scis. (life). Avocations: collecting and researching orders and medals.

DEMOLI, NAZIF, physicist, researcher; b. Pristina, Kosovo, Yugoslavia, Aug. 8, 1954; s. Bislim and Ranka (Kosijer) D.; m. Tatjana Elizabeta Komar, Nov. 6, 1976; children: Ivan, Hana. BSc, U. Zagreb, 1978, MSc, 1983, PhD, 1989. Postgrad. asst. Inst. Physics U. Zagreb, 1978-79, assoc., 1979-82, rsch. aux., 1982-84, rschr., 1984—. Contbr. over 50 articles to profl. jours. including Applied Optics, Optical Engring., Optics Commn., and Optics in Laser Tech. Grantee Deutscher Akademischer Austauschdienst (Germany), 1994. Mem. SPIE. Avocations: table tennis, chess. Home: Lea Mullera 14A, 10000 Zagreb Croatia Office: U Zagreb Inst Physics, Bijenicka C 46, 10000 Zagreb Croatia

DEMONSABERT, WINSTON RUSSEL, chemist, consultant; b. New Orleans, June 12, 1915; s. Joseph Francis and Davida Elizabeth (Gullett) deM.; m. Eleanor Ray Ranson, Aug. 8, 1955; 1 child, Winston Russel. BS in Chemistry, Loyola U., New Orleans, 1937; MA in Edn., Tulane U., 1945, PhD in Chemistry, 1952. Asst. prof. Loyola U., New Orleans, 1948-49, assoc. prof., 1949-55, prof., 1955-66; chief chemist Nat. Ctr. for Disease Control, Dept. Health and Human Svcs., Atlanta, 1966-69; chief contract liason br. Nat. Ctr. for Health Svcs. Rsch., 1969-73; chief extramural programs Bur. Drugs FDA, Rockville, Md., 1973-79; scientist adminstr. office of interagy. sci. coordination Office of Commr., FDA, after 1979; now cons., govt. liaison environ. chemistry and toxicology; assoc. prof. Tulane U., 1957-58; research chemist Am. Cyanamid Co., 1957-58; vice-chmn. Interagy. Testing Com., 1982. Contbr. to Ency. Americana, Ency. Chemistry, also profl. jours. Committeeman Boys Scouts Am., New Orleans and Atlanta; mem. curriculum coms. New Orleans Pub. Sch. Bd., 1965. Fellow AAAS, Am. Inst. Chemists (chmn. La. chpt. 1958-60, chmn. Ga. chpt. 1968-69, pres. D.C. chpt. 1982-83); mem. Am. Chem. Soc. (past chmn. La. sect.). Roman Catholic. Achievements include research in environmental effects (detection, prevention and treatment) of toxic wastes, pesticides and air pollution, and zirconium chemistry. Home and Office: 4317 Lake Trail Dr Kenner LA 70065-1541

DEMONTE, CYNTHIA MARIA, investor relations and management consultant; b. N.Y.C., May 23, 1956; d. Joseph James and Ammeda Ellan (Heiss) DeM.; m. Abraham Figueroa, Mar. 8, 1991. BA, NYU, 1978. Asst. dir. mktg. Tandem Computers, N.Y.C., Cupertino, Calif., 1978-82; v.p. corp. fin. Gruntal & Co., N.Y.C.; pres. DeMonte Assocs. Cons., N.Y.C., 1995—; v.p. Investor Access Corp., 1992-94; v.p. investor rels., corp. comm. Ruder Finn, 1994—; sr. v.p. investor rels. Fin. Rels. Bd., 1995; pres., founder Cynthia DeMonte Assocs Ltd./DeMonte Assocs., 1996—. Mem. Dinkin's Com., 1990—; Dem. nat. com. Women's Leadership Forum. Mem. NAFE, Nat. Investor Rels. Inst., Nat. Assn. Profl. Organizers, Am. Women's Econ. Devel. Corp., Am. Mgmt. Assocs., Ctr. for Entrepreneurial Mgmt., Am. Mgmt. Assn. Avocations: European travel, foreign language. Home: 138 Tatum Dr Middletown NJ 07748-3126 Office: Cynthia M DeMonte & Assoc 161 W 54th St New York NY 10019-5322

DE MONTEBELLO, PHILIPPE LANNES, museum administrator; b. Paris, May 16, 1936; came to U.S., 1951, naturalized, 1955; s. Roger L. and Germaine (de Croisset) de M.; m. Edith Bradford Myles, June 24, 1961; children: Marc, Laure, Charles. B.A. magna cum laude, Harvard U., 1961; M.A., NYU Inst. Fine Arts, 1963; LL.D. (hon.), Lafayette Coll., 1979; D.H.L. (hon.), Bard Coll., 1981; D.F.A. (hon.), Iona Coll., 1982. Assoc. curator European paintings Met. Mus. Art, N.Y.C., 1963-69; dir. Mus. Fine Arts, Houston, 1974-77; vice dir. for curatorial and ednl. affairs Met. Mus. Art, 1974-77, acting dir., 1977-78, dir., 1978—; mem. adv. coun. depts. art and archaeology Columbia U.; mem. Fogg, Fellow, Fogg Mus., Harvard U. Author: Peter Paul Rubens, 1969; mem. editorial bd. Internat. Jour. of Mus. Mgmt. and Curatorship. Trustee, NYU Inst. Fine Arts. Served to 2d lt. AUS, 1956-58. Decorated chevalier Legion d'Honneur (France), Encomienda de Numero de la Orden Isabel la Catholica (Spain), officier Ordre de Leopold (Belgium), Knight Commdr. Pontifical Order of St. Gregory the Great; recipient NYU Grad. Sch. Alumni Achievement award, 1978, gold medal Nat. Inst. Soc. Sci., 1989, The Spanish Inst., 1992, Rebekah Kohut award Nat. Coun. Jewish Women, 1993, NYU Alumni Assn. Disting. Alumni award, 1998; Woodrow Wilson fellow, 1961-62; Gallatin fellow, 1981. Mem. Assn. Art Mus. Dirs. (works of art com.), Mus. Coun. N.Y.C., Am. Fedn. of the Arts (trustee, exec. com.), Am. Assn. Mus. Avocations: collecting Old Master drawings, chess, tennis. Home: 1150 5th Ave New York NY 10128-0724 Office: The Met Mus of Art 1000 5th Ave New York NY 10028-0113

DE MONTLIBERT, CHRISTIAN ANNE PAUL, sociology educator; b. Orleans, France, July 28, 1937; m. Nadia Warlamow, Dec. 19, 1959; children: Catherine, Renaud, Ariane. BA in Psychology, U. Paris, 1959, Doctorat d'Etat in Sociology, 1973; postgrad., Sorbonne U., Paris, 1965. Asst. research Lab. Social Psychology, Sorbonne U., 1959-61; researcher Inst. for Adult Tng., Nancy, France, 1963-73; prof. sociology U. Strasbourg, France, 1973—, prof. Archtl. and Urbanism Sch., 1975—, researcher Sch. Social Arts, 1975—, mem. sci. and adminstrv. coms., 1978-83; dir. rsch. Cress U., Strasbourg, 1977—; prof. Inst. Social Scs., Athènes, 1988—, U. Lausanne, 1991-92, 94-95, Freiburg U., 1992—; cons. Council of Europe, Strasbourg, 1978-80; mem. sci. com. Regional Council Alsace, Strasbourg, 1984-86; dir. Doctoral Sch. of U. Strasbourg II, 1994-96. Author: Formation et analyse sociologique du travail, 1972, Youth and Employment in Europe, 1979, Crise économique et conflits sociaux, 1989, Introduction au raisonnement sociologique, 1990, Le Controle de la vie Privée, 1990, L'institutionnalisation de la formation permanente, 1991, L'impossible autonomie de l'Architecte, 1995, Maurice Halbwachs 1877-1945, 1997, La domination politique, 1997; dir. review Regards Sociologiques, 1991—; contbr. articles to profl. jours. Mem. French Sociol. Soc., Assn. Qualite de la Sci. Francaise. Office: U Strasbourg II, Rue Descartes, 67000 Strasbourg France

DE MOOR, BART L.R., researcher; b. Halle, Brabant, Belgium, July 12, 1960; s. A.J. and C. (Vagenende) De M.; m. Hilde E. Devoghel, July 9, 1988. Electrical engring., Cath. U. Leuven, Belgium, 1983, PhD in Electrical Engring., 1988. Rsch. assoc. Stanford U., Calif., 1988-89; prof. extra-ordinary Cath. U. Leuven, 1990—; rsch. assoc. Fund Sci. Rsch., Belgium, 1989—; main advisor on sci. and tech. Minister-Pres. of Flanders, 1994-99; mem. bd. Flemish Interuniv. Inst. for Biotech., Ctr. for Nuclear Energy; co-founder ISMC and Data45 NV. Assoc. editor several jours.; contbr. to book and more than 200 articles to profl. jours. Chief of cabinet Nat. Min. Sci., Brussels, 1991-92. Recipient several internat. sci. awards. Mem. Koninklijke Vlaamse Ingenieursvereniging, Soc. Indsl. Applied Math., IEEE. Home: Parklaan 5, B-3360 Lovenjoel Belgium Office: ESAT - KU Leuven, Kard Mercierlaan 94, 3001 Leuven Belgium

DE MORA, JUAN MIGUEL, indologist, educator, writer; b. Mexico City, Oct. 18, 1921; s. Miguel Magdaleno and Emilia Vaquerizo De M.; m. Maria del Carmen Morales, mar. 16, 1946 (div. Nov. 1978); 1 child, Carlos Miguel; m. Marja Ludwika Jarocka, Aug. 31, 1988. M Letters, U. Nat. Autonoma, Mexico, 1948; PhD, U. Latino-Americana, Havana, Cuba, 1951; PhD honoris causa, Ministerial Tng. Coll., Sheffield, Eng., 1960, Internat. Free Protestant, Episcopal U., London, 1962; Spl. Diploma in Sanskrit Studies, U. Paris, 1970. Sr. prof. Oriental Lit. U. Nat. Autonoma, Mexico City, 1965-73, permanent prof. Oriental Lit., 1973-98, assoc. rschr. in Sanskrit philology, 1972-78, part-time to full-time rschr. Sanskrit philology, 1978-91, permanent rschr. category C, 1991—; vis. prof. U. Salamanca, Spain, 1994, U. Delhi, India, 1982. Author: 21 novels including La Filosofia en la Literature Sanscrita, 1968, The Principle of Opposites in Sanskrit Texts, 1982, Solo queda el silencio, 2000; author/translator: (book) El Rig Veda, 1974 (4 edits.); contbr. more than 60 articles to profl. publs. Officer Mexican Red Cross, Mexico, 1943-59. Recipient Merit award Acad. U. Internat., Rome, 1961, Gold medal Mexican Red Cross, 1958. Mem. N.Y. Acad. Scis., Assn. Francaise pour Les Etudes Sanskrites, Kalidasa and Max Muller Internat. Sanskrit Soc., Vishwa Sahitya Sanskriti Sansthan, Internat. Inst. Indian Studies (mem. editl. adv. bd. 1993-98), Internat. Assn. Sanskrit Studies (regional dir. Latin Am. 1994-2000, v.p. 1981-94, cons. com. 2000), others. Avocations: collecting old and new films on videotape, reading, classical music.

DE MORAES, AFONSO HENRIQUE PASSOS, physician; b. Recife, Pernambuco, Brazil, May 26, 1960; s. Gilvan Antonio Henrique and Maria De Lourdes (Passos) de M.; m. Ana Cristina Nogueira, Oct. 19, 1998; children: Antonio Henrique, Carolina Zorzetto. Resident Mario Kroeff Hosp., Rio de Janeiro, 1986-87; physician pvt. clinic Sao Paulo. Mem. AAAS, Brazilian Assn. for Study of Obesity, Soc. Brasileira de Mastologia, N.Y. Acad. Scis., Am. Diabetes Assn. Roman Catholic. Avocation: music. Home: Travessa Meruipe 05, 04012020 Sao Paulo Brazil Office: Pvt Clin, Rua Mandel Borba 292 CJ 132, 04743011 Sao Paulo Brazil

DE MORAES, GEORGE SOARES, geriatrician, retired metallurgical engineer; b. Belo Horizonte, Brazil, Mar. 14, 1925; s. Amynthas Jacques and Albertina Woods (Soares) De M.; m. Gloria Muriel Hilf, Mar. 14, 1950; children: George, Ricardo, Rogério, Roberto, Barbara. BS in Metall. Engring., Carnegie Mellon U., 1949; student, U. Taubaté, São Paulo, 1980-82; MD, U. Mogi das Cruzes, São Paulo, 1985. Flight instr., pilot Brazilian Air Force, 1943-45; prodn. control engr., dir. maintenance São Paulo Air Force Depot, 1949-52, asst. to dir. gen. of Air Force material, 1952-55; pres. Commn. for Devel. of Aircraft, 1953-56; initiator, organizer, head Inst. for Cooperation with Industry, São José dos Campos, Brazil, 1955-56; head dept. materials rsch. Inst. Rsch. and Devel. CTA, São José dos Campos, 1956-63; dir. gen. Inst. R & D of Air Ministry, São José dos Campos, 1963-64; sec. Grupo Exec. Para O Desenvolvimento Da Industria Material Aeronáutico, Rio de Janeiro, 1963-64; ret. brigadier gen. Brazilian Air Force Res., 1964; consulting metall. engr., 1965; mng. dir. Mineração Ipanema, Fertimetal, S.A., Belo Horizonte, 1966-68; initiator, founder Minas Inst. Tech. (now U. Do Vale Do Rio Doce), 1967-68; sec. transp. Brazilian Govt., São Paulo, 1968-69, sec. transp., sec. welfare, 1969; cons. Inst. for Space Rsch., São Paulo, 1970-71; dir., cons. engr. Engenheiros Consultores Metminas, Rio de Janeiro, 1971, pres., 1977-79; dir. Clinica Moraes, 1985—; mem. bd. dirs. Matsulfur, S.A., Belo Horizonte, Brazil, 1980—; mem. joint joint Brazil-U.S. Commn. for Devel. of Indsl. Rsch., 1967-68; lectr. in field. Contbr. articles to profl. jours. Asst. to minister for aeronautics, Brazilian Govt., 1956-63. Recipient Cruz de Aviação medal Brazilian Govt., 1945, Atlantico Sul medal, 1946, Mérito Aeronáutico medal, 1963, Medalha de Prata, 1964; Troféu Serra Lima award Comml. Assn. Governador Valadares, Brazil, 1967; Indsl. Merit medal Govt. of State Minas Gerais, Brazil, 1968. Mem. Am. Inst. Mining and Metallurgy Engring., Gerontol. Soc. Am., Am. Aging Assn., Am. Coll. for Advancement of Medicine, Brazilian Soc. Geriat. and Gerontology, Brazilian Assn. Orthomolecular Medicine, Brazilian Soc. Oxidology, Brazilian Assn. Biomolecular Medicine, Mil. Club (Rio de Janeiro) (sr.), Air Force Club (Rio de Janeiro) (sr.), Brazilian Assn. for Metals (sr.). Roman Catholic. Avocations: soccer, swimming, tennis, golf. Home: Praca Bartolomeu Bueno 55, 12242-55 Sao Jose Dos Campos Brazil Office: PO Box 302, 12201-97 Sao Jose Dos Campos Brazil

DE MORAIS, PAULO CÉSAR, physics educator, researcher; b. Araguari, Minas, Brazil, Dec. 29, 1953; s. José Dias and Nair (Rangel) De M.; m. Rosana Ferreira de Godoy Morais, Dec. 29, 1977; children: Maria Teresa, Joao Paulo, Maria Fernanda. Degree in chemistry, U. Brasilia, Brazil, 1976, degree in physics, 1977, M in Physics, 1980; D in Physics, U. Minas Gerais, Belo Horizonte, Brazil, 1986. Asst. prof. physics U. Brasilia, 1978-84, assoc. prof., 1985—; cons. Bell Comm. Rsch., Red Bank, N.J., 1987-88. Contbr. over 60 articles to profl. jours. Grantee, Conselho Nacional de Desenvolvimento Científico e Tecnológico, Brazil, 1988, 90, 92, 94, 95, 97, Third World Acad. Scis.; Italy, 1991, Programa de Apoio ao Desenvolvimento Científico e Tecnológico, Brazil, 1992, Fundacao de Amparo a Pesquisa do Distrito Federal, 1994, 98. Mem. IEEE, Am. Phys. Soc., Brazilian Phys. Soc., Materials Rsch. Soc. Avocation: photography. Office: Univ Brasilia Inst Fisica, Campus Universitario, CPO4455 Brasilia 70919970, Brazil

DE MORI, RENATO, computer science educator, researcher; b. Milan, Aug. 5, 1941. PhD, Poly. U., Turin, Italy, 1967. Prof., chmn. U. Turin, 1977-79, prof., 1979-84; prof., chmn. Concordia U., Montreal, Que., Can., 1984-85; dir. Sch. Computer Sci. McGill U., Montreal, Que., Can., 1986-95; prof. Sch. Computer Sci. McGill U., Montreal, Que., 1995-96; v.p. rsch. Centre Recherche Informatique Montreal, 1987-94; prof. U. Avignon, France, 1997—; mem. Nat. Scis. and Engring. Council Can., 1983-89; assoc. Can. Inst. Advanced Rsch. Author: Computer Models of Speech, 1983; editor: Computer Perceptions, 1982, Spoken Dialogs with Computers, 1998; contbr. over 100 articles to profl. jours. Fellow IEEE Computing Soc.; mem. Assn. Computing Machinery, Can. Artificial Intelligence Soc. (v.p. 1986-88), Am. Assn. Artificial Intelligence. Office: U d'Avignon Lab Info BP1228, 339 Chemin Menajeries, 84911 Avignon CEDEX 9, France

DE MORSELLA, GUY CHRISTOPHER, economist; b. N.Y.C., Aug. 20, 1926; s. Julius Caesar and Ada (Villa) de M.; m. Karen Lunde, 1956 (div.); children: Christopher, Gregory, Julie, Camillo; m. Tanna Jiang, 1994. Student, U. Rome, 1945-49, Rensselaer Polytechnic Inst., Troy, N.Y., 1947; BS in Econs., Columbia U., 1955; postgrad., UCLA, 1962-63. Project dir. Litton Industries, Pitts., Venezuela and Philippines, 1968-71; pres. Franklin Mint Italia, Rome, 1971-72; agrl. industry cons. West Africa, 1972-74; project mgr. UN Food and Agriculture Orgn., Vietnam, Thailand, Afghanistan and Libya, 1974-80, Afghanistan; investor Mex., 1980-81; chief tech. adviser UN Dept of Tech. Cooperation for Devel., Micronesia, 1981-84; advisor U.S. Agy. for Internat. Devel., Tegucigalpa, Honduras, 1984-85; sr. ptnr. Agro-Indsl. Assocs., Rome, 1984; agrl. indsl. cons. Somalia, U.S., Liberia, 1964-68; devel. economist Lockheed Aircraft Internat., L.A., 1960-64; project mgr. CARE, Bolivia, Ecuador, Guatemala, 1957-59; pres. Chinese-Italian Cultural Assn., 1999—. Author: Reflections of a Disfranchised Voter, 1982, The Tetrahedron Conspiracy, 1986, Confessions of an International Bureaucrat, 1988, Interviews with Myself, 1996. Organizer, Dems. for Kennedy, Sausalito, Calif., 1960. With Engrs. Corps, 1946-47. Mem. Athletic Club (L.A.), Au Bord du Lac (Italy). Republican. Roman Catholic. Avocations: mountain climbing, swimming, hunting. Home: Bracciano, 00062 Rome Italy Office: AgroIndsl Assoc Chinese-Ita, Cult Assn Trevignano Romano, 00069 Rome Italy

DE MOUCHY, DUCHESSE, vineyard executive; b. N.Y.C., Jan. 31, 1935; citizen of Luxembourg; d. C. Douglas Dillon and Phyllis Ellsworth; m. James Brady Moseley, 1953; 1 child, Joan Moseley Frost; m. Prince Charles of Luxembourg (dec. July 1977); children: Princess Charlotte of Luxembourg (Mrs. Mark Cunningham), Prince Robert of Luxembourg; m. Duc de Mouchy, Aug. 3, 1978. Grad., Foxcroft Sch., Middleburg, Va., 1952. Asst. Paris editor The Paris Rev., 1956-65; pres. Union de Banque Suisse Luxembourg, 1977-81, Chateau Haut-Brion, Bordeaux, France, 1975—. Pres. Inner Wheel Club, Luxembourg, 1967-77, I.M.C. Kraizbierg, Luxembourg, 1977-98, Am. Luxembourg Club, 1967-78. Avocations: gardening, computers, golf. Office: Domaine C Dillon SA, 37 Ave Pierre 1er de Serbie, 75008 Paris France

DEMOULIN, PASCAL NOEL, astronomer; b. Clermont-Ferrand, Puy de Dome, France, Apr. 14, 1962; s. Henri and Rolande (Martin) Demoulin; m. Isabelle Pierron, Oct. 10, 1987; 1 child, Nicolas. Master, Paris 11, Orsay, France, 1983; Agregation of Physics, Nat., France, 1984; PhD in Astrophysics, Paris 7, 1989. Prof. student Ecole Normale Superieure, Cachan, France, 1981-85; asst. lectr. Ecole Normale Superieure, Ulm, France, 1986-89; researcher Paris Observatory, 1989—. Contbr. articles, reviews to profl. jours. Mil. svc., 1985-86. Mem. Internat. Astron. Union. Office: Paris Observatory, 5 Sq Jules Janssen, 92195 Meudon France

DEMOULIN, PHILIPPE ALBERT, telecommunications company executive; b. Antwerp, Belgium, Sept. 4, 1964; s. Albert Demoulin and Hilde Anné; m. Nilu Bharmal, June 12, 1993; children: Alexander, Caroline. BA

in Mgmt., Cath. U. Louvain, Belgium, 1986; diploma in internat. studies, Johns Hopkins U., Bologna, Italy, 1987. Trainee Generale Bank, Brussels, 1987; resident mgr. Alcatel, Dar es Salaam, Tanzania, 1989-91; project mgr. Alcatel, Antwerp, 1992-94, bus. devel. mgr., 1995-97; v.p. global bus. devel. SITEL, Brussels, 1997-99; dir. VKW, Antwerp, 1999—; mem. organizing com. Plato Project, C. of C., Antwerp, 1995-97. Lt. Logistics Corps., Belgium Army, 1987-88. Mem. Rotary (dir. internat. projects 1989-91). Home: Fourmentstraat 20, 2018 Antwerp Belgium

DEMOULIN, ROBERT-LÉON, retired educator; b. Huy, Belgium, May 8, 1911; s. Hubert Leopold and Louise Pélagie (Delmelle) D.; m. Colette Marique, July 25, 1942; children: Vincent, Agnès, Nathalie, Bruno. D. Phil. Lit., U. Liège, Belgium, 1932; Agrégé de l'Enseignement Superieur, U. Liège, 1938. Aspirant Fonds national Recherche Scientifique, Belgium, 1934-38; chargé de cours U. Liège, 1939-43, prof. ord., 1943-81; pres. Interuniv. Ctr. for Contemporary History, Belgium, 1972-87. Author: Les journées de Septembre 1830, 1934, Guillaume 1e et la transformation économique des provinces belges, 1938; editor: Liber Memorialis, L'Université de Liège, 1936-66, 1967. Lt. Belgian mil., 1939-45. Recipient Prix Chaix d'Est-Ange Inst. de France, 1939; decorated commandeur Order de la Couronne Grand Officier Order Léopold II. Roman Catholic. Home: 50 rue du Jardin Botanique, B 4000 Liège Belgium

DEMOYEN, CHRISTIAN ANDRÉ JEAN, lawyer; b. Chaumont, France, Dec. 29, 1939; s. André and Gilberte (Demarne) F.; m. Catherine Oliver, 1964; children: Renaud, Anne-Catherine, Marie-Mathilde. LLD, U. Paris, 1964. Prof. U. Paris; assoc., then ptnr. Lafarge, Flécheux Law Firm, Paris, 1970-79; ptnr. Demoyen & Assocs., Paris, 1979—. Mem. Soc. d'Avocats au Barreau de Paris. Fax: 33 1 45 24 47 08. Home: 67 Ave George Mandel, 75116 Paris France Office: Demoyen & Assocs, 17 Ave de Lamballe, 75016 Paris France

D'EMPAIRE, OSCAR EDUARDO, real estate executive; b. Maracaibo, Venezuela, Jan. 27, 1930; s. Carlos Julio and Consuelo Valentina (Belloso) d'E.; m. Maider Etcheberry, June 6, 1962; children: Luis Felipe, Alfredo, Julliette, Juan Carlos, Ana Maria. Student, St. Francis Coll., 1948-49. Sales rep. Carlos J. d'Empaire SA, Maracaibo, 1950—; bd. dirs. Comercial Belloso CA, Maraciabo, Seguros Occidental CA; pres. Centro Comercial del Sur, 1985—. Exhibited in numerous one-man and group exhbns., 1980—. Vice consul Denmark, Maracaibo, 1958-63, hon. gen. consul, 1973—. Recipient Order Ridder Af Dannebro Gordenen, Kingdom of Denmark, 1968, Order Andres Bello, Venezuela Ministry of Culture, 1985, Order Francisco de Miranda, Pres. of Venezuela, 1978. Mem. Rotary. Roman Catholic. Office: Carlos J d'Empaire SA, PO Box 301, Maracaibo Venezuela

DEMPSEY, BERNARD HAYDEN, JR., lawyer; b. Evanston, Ill., Mar. 29, 1942; s. Bernard H. and Margaret C. (Gallagher) D.; m. Cynthia T. Dempsey; children: Bernard H. III, Matthew B., Kathleen N., Rose Maureen G., Alexandra C., Anastasia M. BS, Coll. Holy Cross, 1964; JD, Georgetown U., 1967. Bar: Fla. 1968, D.C. 1979. Law clk. to chief judge U.S. Dist. Ct. (mid. dist.) Fla., 1967-69; asst. U.S. Atty. Mid. Dist. Fla., 1969-73; pvt. practice, 1973—; lectr. trial tactics seminars. Contbr. articles to legal jours. Recipient John Marshall award U.S. Dept. Justice, 1972, U.S. Atty's Outstanding Performance award 1970, 71, 72, 73. Mem. ABA, ATLA, Nat. Assn. Criminal Def. Lawyers, Nat. Employment Lawyers Assn., Fla. Bar Assn., Am. Judicature Soc., Fla. Bar Found., Univ. Club (Orlando), Winter Park (Fla.) Racquet Club, Delta Theta Phi. Republican. Roman Catholic. Office: Dempsey & Sasso Bank of America Ctr 390 N Orange Ave Ste 2700 Orlando FL 32801-1643

DEMPSEY, CECELIA See BYRNE-DEMPSEY, CECELIA

DEMPSEY, DONALD CHANDLER, stockbroker, financial planner; b. Detroit, Nov. 13, 1951; s. Donald Chandler Sr. and Phillippa E. D.; m. Karen Lynn Petroskey, Apr. 19, 1980; 1 child, Michael Patrick. B of Bus., Cleary Coll., 1975. CFP, Coll. Fin. Planning Denver. Sr. v.p. investments EF Hutton, Detroit, 1977-94, Prudential Securities, Detroit, 1994—. Roman Catholic. Home: 18134 Shelley Pond Ct Northville MI 48167-3543 Office: Prudential Securities 535 Griswold St Ste 1028 Detroit MI 48226-3692

DEMPSEY, EDWARD JOSEPH, lawyer; b. Lynn, Mass., Mar. 13, 1943; s. Timothy Finbar and Christine Margaret (Callahan) D.; m. Eileen Margaret McManus, Apr. 15, 1967; children: Kristen A. Stofi, Katherine B. Aydin, Shelagh E., James P. AB, Boston Coll., 1964; JD, Cath. U. Am., 1970. Bar: D.C. 1970, Conn. 1982. Assoc. Arent, Fox, Kintner, Plotkin & Kahn, Washington, 1970-72, Akin, Gump, Strauss, Hauer & Feld, Washington, 1972-75; supervisory trial atty. EEOC, Washington, 1975-79; assoc. Whitman & Ransom, Washington, 1979-81, Farmer, Wells, McGuinn & Sibal, Washington, 1981-82; ptnr. Farmer, Wells, Sibal & Dempsey, Washington, Hartford, Conn., 1983-84; dir. indsl. rels. and labor counsel United Technologies Corp., Hartford, 1985—. Capt. USNR (ret.). Mem. ABA. Office: United Techs Bldg Hartford CT 06101

DEMPSEY, JERRY EDWARD, retired service company executive; b. Landrum, S.C., Oct. 1, 1932; s. Adolphus Gerald and Willie Ceyattie (Lee) D.; m. Harriet Coan Calvert; children: Jerrie E., Harriet R., Margaret. BS, Clemson U., 1954; MBA, Ga. State Coll., 1968. With Borg-Warner Corp., Chgo., 1956-84, gen. mgr. York divsn., 1972-77, exec. v.p., 1977-79, pres., COO, 1979-84; sr. v.p. Waste Mgmt. Inc., Oak Brook, Ill., 1984-93; chmn., CEO PPG Industries, Inc., Pitts., 1993-97, chmn., 1997; bd. dirs. Navistar, PPG Industries, Inc., Eastman Chem. Co., Birmingham Steel. Dean's adv. coun. Sch. Engring. Clemson U., chmn. pres.'s adv. coun.; bd. dirs. Pitts. Theol. Sem., Greenville Symphony, Greater Greenville Forum. Named Bus. Leader of Yr., Oak Brook (Ill.) Jaycees, 1989; recipient Bronze award Fin. World, 1989, 90, Pres.'s award Clemson U., 1990, Disting. Svc. award, 1992, Horatio Alger award, 1995, Am. Heritage award Anti-Defamation League, 1995, Disting. Alumni award Ga. State U., 1999. Mem. ASHRAE, Melrose Club, Duquesne Club (dir.), Laurel Valley Golf Club, Greenville Country Club, Fox Chapel Golf Club. Office: PPG Industries Inc 1 Ppg Pl Pittsburgh PA 15272-0001

DEMPSEY, NOEL, administrator; b. Meath, Ireland, Jan. 1953; married; 4 children. Student, U. Coll., Dublin, St. Patrick's Coll., Maynooth, Ireland. Chmn. Trim Dist. Coun., 1981-82, 85-86, 91-92; chmn. Meath County Coun., 1986-87; elected to Dial, 1987; chief whip Dept. Sate and Govt., 1992; min. Dept. Environment & Local Govt., 1997—. Office: Dept Environment, Custom House, Dublin Ireland*

DEMPSTER, BARRY (EDWARD), writer, poet; b. Toronto, Ont., Can., Jan. 17, 1952; s. Albert Edward and Helen Florence (Robinette) D.; m. Karen Ruttan, Sept. 26, 1981. Student, Centennial Coll., 1972-75. lectr. poetry workshops League Can. Poets and Ont. Arts Coun. Artists in Sch. Program. Author: Fables for Isolated Men, 1982, Globe Doubis, 1983, Real Places and Imaginary Men, 1984, David and the Daydreams, 1985, Writing Home, 1989, Positions To Pray In, 1989, The Unavoidable Man, 1990, Letters From a Long Illness With the World, The D.H. Lawrence Poems, 1993, The Ascension of Jesse Rapture, 1993, Fire and Brimstone, 1997; co-author: Best Canadian Stories, 1980, Third Impressions, 1982; editor: Tributaries, An Anthology: Writer to Writer, 1978; contbr. to anthologies; book rev. and poetry editor. Recipient Confedn. Poets prize, 1995, Scarborough Bicentennial award of merit, 1996. Mem. League Can. Poets, Writers' Union Can. Avocations: writing film criticism, travel, music, gardening, bicycling. Address: 45 French Cres, Holland Landing, ON Canada L9N 1J8

DEMSKY, AARON, historian, educator; b. Bklyn., Dec. 23, 1938; arrived in Israel, 1965; s. Solomon and Sadie D.; m. Rosalind Shirley Gellis, June 20, 1961; children: Elisheva, Yonatan, Noam, Miriam, Shlomit, Seraya, Ariel. BS, Columbia U., 1961, MA, 1965; B in Religious Edn., Jewish Theol. Sem. Am., 1961; DHL (hon.), 1991; M in Hebrew Lit., Jewish Theol. Sem. Am., 1963; PhD, The Hebrew U., 1977. Prof. biblical history Bar-Ilan U., Ramat Gan, Israel, 1968—; epigrapher excavations at Tel Shiloh Bar-Ilan U., Ramat Gan, 1981-84, founder, dir. project for study of Jewish onomastics, 1991—, epigrapher excavations at Tel Gath of Philistines, 1997—. Editor: These Are the Names-Studies in Jewish Onomastics, vol. 1, 1997, vol. 2, 1999; contbr. articles to profl. jours. Fellow Meml. Found., 1966, 67, 78, 90-92, fellow NEH, 1978, Louis Ginzberg fellow, 1985. Office: Bar-Ilan U Dept Jewish Hist, Dept Jewish History, Ramat Gan 52900, Israel

DE MURAT DE LESTANG, HERVÉ, aeronautics general manager; b. Ziguinchor, Senegal, Sept. 10, 1953; s. Guy Joseph and Hélème (de Brauer) de M.; m. Marcella Dols, May 31, 1986; children: Valerie, Marc, Maxime, Victor. MBA, Ecole Superieure Sci. Econs., Paris, 1975, Inst. Adminstrn. Enterprises, Paris, 1996. Agy. mgr. Am. Express Travel, Paris, 1977-79; sales dir. Tabur Marine, Paris, 1979-81; trading dir. Gazocean, Paris, 1981-88; devel. dir. Thomson CSF, Paris, 1988-92; gen. mgr. Allia Real Estate Transaction Gmbh, Berlin, 1992-96, Soc. Nat. D'Etudes Constrn. de Moteurs D/Aviation, Paris, 1996—. Mem. Paris Country Club. Roman Catholic. Fax: 33-1-47953043. Home: 10 Rue Gustave Lambert, 92380 Garches France Office: 2 bd General Martial Valin, 75015 Paris France

DEMURO, PAUL ROBERT, lawyer; b. Aberdeen, Md., Mar. 21, 1954; s. Paul Robert and Amelia C. DeMuro; m. Susan Taylor, May 26, 1990; children: Melissa Taylor, Natalie Lauren, Alanna Leigh. BA summa cum laude, U. Md., 1976; JD, Washington U., 1979; MBA, U. Calif., Berkeley, 1986. Bar: Md. 1979, U.S. Dist. Ct. Md. 1979, D.C. 1980, U.S. Dist. Ct. D.C. 1980, U.S. Dist. Ct. (ea. dist.) Calif. 1986, U.S. Ct. Appeals (4th cir.) 1981, U.S. Tax Ct. 1981, Calif. 1982, U.S. Dist. Ct. (no. dist.) Calif. 1982; CPA, Md. Assoc. Ober, Grimes & Shriver, Balt., 1979-82; ptnr. Carpenter et al, San Francisco, 1982-89, McCutchen, Doyle, Brown & Enerson, San Francisco, 1989-93, Latham & Watkins, San Francisco, 1993—. Author: The Financial Managers Guide to Managed Care and Integrated Delivery Systems, 1995, The Fundamentals of Managed Care and Network Development, 1999; co-author: Health Care Mergers and Acquisitions: The Transactional Perspective, 1996, Health Care Executives' Guide to Fraud and Abuse, 1998; editor, contbg. author Integrated Delivery Systems, 1994; article and book rev. editor Washington U. Law Qrtly., St. Louis, 1975-76. Mem. San Francisco Mus. Modern Art, 1985—; bd. sch. health Calif. State U., 1992—. Fellow Healthcare Fin. Mgmt. Assn. (bd. dirs. No. Calif. chpt. 1990-93, 99—, sec. 1999—, nat. principles and practices bd. 1992-95, vice chair 1993-95, nat. bd. dirs. 1995-97, exec. com. 1996-97, chair compliance officers forum adv. coun. 1998-2000); mem. ABA (health law sect., chair transactional and bus. health care interest group 1998-2000, governing coun. 2000—), L.A. County Bar Assn. (health law sect.), Calif. Bar Assn., San Francisco Bar Assn., AICPA, Am. Health Lawyers Assn. (fraud and abuse and self-referral substantive law com. 1998—, task force on best practices in advising clients 1998-99), The IPA Assn. Am. (mem. legal adv. coun. 1996—), Med. Group Mgmt. Assn. Republican. Office: Latham & Watkins 505 Montgomery St Ste 1900 San Francisco CA 94111-2552

DEMUTH, PAVEL, pharmaceutical company executive, consultant; b. Prague, Czech Republic, May 17, 1962; s. Milan and Eva (Krizkova) D.; m. Zorka Hovorkova, Nov. 16, 1996; children: Tereza D., Jan D. MD, Charles U., Prague, 1986, neurology specialist, 1989, Degree in Neuropediat., 1992; MBA, Manchester (Eng.) Met. U., 1997. Asst. U. Pharm. Works, Prague, 1986-87; registrar U. Hosp., Prague, 1987-91; med. rep. Upjohn, Prague, 1992, sales trainer, 1992-93, dist. sales mgr., 1993-94, med. specialist mgr., 1994-96; sales mgr. Pharmacia-Upjohn, Prague, 1996; divsn. dir. Abbott, Prague, 1996; area gen. mgr. Beaufour, 1997—; internat. cons. Beaufour, 1998—. Mem. Assn. Pharmal Distributors, Internat. Assn. of Rsch. Baised Pharma. Co., Pharm. Network, France-Czech Bus. Cham. Avocation: off road racing.

DE MUYNCK, AIME, epidemiologist, researcher; b. Deinze, Belgium, May 1, 1942; s. Remi De Muynck and Germaine Lema; m. Rose Liefooghe; children: Bruno, Sofie. MD, Rijks U., Ghent, Belgium, 1968; MSc in Epidemiology, Harvard Sch. Pub. Health, Boston, 1981, MSc in Biostats., 1982; PhD, U. Instelling, Antwerp, Belgium, 1993. Med. dir. Bethania Hosp., Sialkot, Pakistan, 1969-71; gen. practice Couthuin, Belgium, 1971; asst. prof. Inst. Tropical Medicine, Antwerp, 1971-73, head dept., 1982-87; mem. staff Inst. Tropical Medicine Hosp., Kasongo, Zaire, 1973-74; mgr. Cenetrop, Santa Cruz, Bolivia, 1974-80; chief tech. advisor HSA, Islamabad, Pakistan, 1997—; cons. WHO, Geneva, 1978-79. Author: Ali En Fatima bij De Dokter, 1997, Atlas Etnische Minderheden, 1999; (software) Epitrop, 1986. Pres. Centrum Etnische Minderheden en Gezondheid, Brussels, 1986-90; coord. archeology study group ASG, Islamabad, 1998—. Recipient Laureat, ITM, 1973, Escudo de Honor, Santa Cruz Province, Bolivia, 1980, Huesped Illustre, City of Sucre, Bolivia, 1977. Mem. Belgian Soc. Tropical Medicine, Ctr. Rsch. Epidemiology Disasters. Roman Catholic. Avocations: hiking, archeological explorations. E-mail: adm@aime.sdnpk.undp.org. Home: 96/4 Str 76-H3, Islamabad Pakistan Office: Health Scis Acad, GPO Box 2993, Islamabad Pakistan

DE MUYNCK, JOHAN JULIEN LODEWYCK, construction company executive; b. Mortsel, Antwerp, Belgium; s. Louis De Muynck and Jozefine Tondeur; m. Mia De Grauwe; children: Johan Jr., Bart. Degree in civil engring., U. Ghent (Belgium), 1967. Engr. Ministry of Pub. Works, Belgium, 1967-72; CEO Van Roey, Belgium, 1973-98; chmn. Van Roey Co., Belgium, 1999—, Groep Van Roey, Belgium, 1989—; chmn. Europa Nostra Belgium; dir. Lessius. Lt. Belgian Army, 1968-69. Recipient Innovator award Insead. Home: Hof Ter Looy Looiweg 169, 2310 Rijkevorsel Antwerp, Belgium Office: Groep Van Roey, Sint-Lenaartsesteenwe 7, 2310 Rijkevorsel Belgium

DEMYANCHUK, ALEXANDER PETROVICH, political science educator; b. Lviv, Ukraine, June 11, 1950; s. Petro Panteleevich and Yevdokia Romanovna (Vinarchuk) D.; m. Valentina Ivanovna Kuscheva, July 5, 1975; children: Katherine, Olga. DSc in Physics, Inst. of Nuclear Rsch., Kiev, Ukraine, 1976; Tchr., Cherkassy State Pedagogical, Inst./Cherkassy, 1971. Tchr. of physics Secondary Sch., Malin, Ukraine, 1971; rschr. Inst. of Physics of Metals, Kiev, 1976-83; sr. rschr. Ukrainian Acad. Scis., Kiev, 1983-90; dep. dir. Fgn. Trade Co. Interan, Kiev, 1990-92; dir. on internat. affairs U. Kiev/Mohyla Acad., Kiev, 1992-95, assoc. prof., 1995-97, postdoctorate studies fellow, 1997—. Contbr. articles to profl. jours.; patentee in field. Sr. lt. Soviet Army, 1972-73. Recipient scholarships The Kennan Inst., 1996, Internat. Rschrs. Exch. Bd., 1998. Mem. Comparative and Internat. Edn. Soc., Ukrainian Phys. Soc. Avocations: classical music, computer games, poetry writing. Office: Univ Kiev-Mohyla Acad, 2 Skovoroda St, 04070 Kiev Ukraine

DEMYANOV, SERGEY EVGENIEVICH, physicist, researcher; b. Voronezh, Russia, Oct. 3, 1952; s. Evgeniy Alekseevich and Inna Ivanovna (Korosteliova) D.; m. Svetlana Petrovna Tsyplenkova, Sept. 6, 1975; children: Irina, Alexey. MSc, Poly. Inst., Voronezh, 1975; PhD, Inst. Solid State Physics, Minsk, Belarus, 1982, docent, 1986; DSc, Tech. Acad., Voronezh, Russia, 1988. Engr. Inst. Solid State Physics, 1975-79, jr. rschr., 1979-85, sr. rschr., 1985-89, head dept., 1989—; prof. Tech. Acad., Voronezh, 1999. Contbr. over 150 articles to profl. jours.; inventor in field. Recipient rsch. grant Internat. Sci. Found., 1994, 95. Mem. N.Y. Acad. Scis., The Planetary Soc. Avocations: sport, books, travelling. Home: Ya Kolas Str 57a-16, 220113 Minsk Belarus Office: Inst Solid State Physics, P Brovka Str 17, 220072 Minsk Belarus

DE NAPOLI, LORENZO, chemistry educator, researcher; b. Naples, Italy, Jan. 3, 1948; s. Achille and Iolanda (Marciano) De N.; m. Rosalia Morrone, Mar. 16, 1974; children: Achille, Iolanda. Lic. Elem., G. Mazzini, Naples, 1959; Lic. Media, F. D'Ovidio, Naples, 1962; Maturità Scientifica, V. Cuoco, Naples, 1968; Laurea Chimica, U. Naples, 1974, PhD, 1978. Lectr. U. Naples, 1978-80, lectr., rschr., 1980-84, prof., 1984—; cons. dept. organic chemistry U. Naples, 1980-96. Contbr. over 90 articles to profl. jours. Consiglio Nazionale Ricerche grantee Italian Rsch. Agy, 1994, 95, 96, 97, 98, 99, 2000. Home: Piazza Arenella 7/H, 80128 Naples Italy Office: U Naples Dept Organic Chem, Via Mezzocannone 16, 80134 Naples Italy

DENARO, ANTHONY THOMAS, psychiatrist; b. N.Y.C., Aug. 9, 1929; s. Joseph and Maria (DeGennaro) Denaro; m. Mitsuru Suzuki, Nov. 23, 1963. BS, CCNY, 1960; MD, U. Okla., 1969; MPA, U. Hartford, 1981. Diplomate Nat. Bd. Med. Examiners, Am. Bd. Psychiatry, Am. Bd. Gen. Psychiatry and Child Psychiatry, Adminstrv. Psychiatry. Intern Nassau County Med. Ctr., East Meadow, N.Y., 1969-70; resident in child psychiatry U. Pa., Phila., 1970-72, resident in gen. psychiatry, 1972-74; dir. child psychiatry U. Conn. Health Ctr., Farmington, 1974-78; dir. adolescent unit Natchaug Psychiat. Hosp., Willamantic, Conn., 1978-80; assoc. dir. child and adolescent service Mt. Sinai Hosp., Hartford, Conn., 1980-82; assoc. dir. child and adolescent psychiatry Elmcrest Psychiat. Inst., Portland, Conn., 1982-84; dir. outpatient psychiatry Woodhull Med. and Mental Health Ctr., N.Y.C., 1984-85; dir. child and adolescent psychiatry First Hosp. Wyoming Valley, Wilkes-Barre, Pa., 1985-98; med. dir. child and adolescent behavioral health svcs. Ea. Conn. Health Network, Inc., 1998-99; med. dir. Child Devel. Clinic, Scranton, Pa., 1999—; asst. prof. dept. psychiatry U. Conn. Sch. Medicine, Farmington, 1974-83. With U.S. Army, 1947-49. Fellow Am. Acad. Child and Adolescent Psychiatry; mem. AMA, Am. Psychiat. Assn., Am. Assn. Psychiat. Adminstrs., Northeastern Pa. Psychiat. Soc. (pres. 1990-91), Phi Beta Kappa. Republican. Office: Scranton Counseling Ctr Child Devel Clinic 326 Adams Ave Scranton PA 18503-1668

DEN BESTEN, JOHANNES BERNARDUS, linguist; b. Amsterdam, The Netherlands, Dec. 18, 1948; s. Adrianus Cornelis and Agnes F.E. (van der Wedden) den B.; m. PhD, Tilburg U., 1989. Rschr. Netherlands Organ. Pure Rsch., Amsterdam, 1974-78; asst. prof. U. Amsterdam, 1979-90, assoc. prof., 1991—. Author: Papers on Negerhollands, The Dutch Creole of the Virgin Islands, 1986, Studies in West Germanic Syntax, 1989, (with others) Afrikaans en Varieteiten van het Nederlands, 1998. Mem. Linguistic Soc. Am., Algemene Vereniging voor Taalwetenschap, Linguistic Soc. So. Africa. Home: Cornelis van der, Lindenstraat 22, 1071 TH Amsterdam The Netherlands Office: U Amsterdam Dept Linguist, Spuistraat 210, 1012 VT Amsterdam The Netherlands

DENCH, JUDITH OLIVIA, actress; b. York, England, United Kingdom, Dec. 9, 1934; d. Reginald Arthur and Eleanora Olave (Jones) D.; m. Michael Williams, Feb. 5, 1971; 1 child, Tara Cressida Frances. Student, Ctrl. Sch. Speech Tng.; LittD (hon.), Warwick U., 1978, York U., 1983. Theatrical appearances include: (Old Vic) Hamlet, Midsummer Night's Dream, Twelfth Night, 1957-58, The Importance of Being Earnest, As You Like It, Romeo and Juliet, 1959-61; (Venice Festival) Romeo and Juliet (Paladino d'Argentino), 1961; (Royal Shakespeare Co., Stratford) The Cherry Orchard, Measure for Measure, Midsummer Night's Dream, A Penny for a Song, 1961-62; (Oxford Playhouse) The Alchemist, The Three Sisters, Romeo and Jeanette, 1964; (Oxford and London) The Promise, 1966-67; (London) Sally Bowles in Cabaret, 1968; (Royal Shakespeare Co., London) Twelfth Night, A Winter's Tale, London Assurance, 1970; (Royal Shakespeare Co., Stratford) The Merchant of Venice, The Duchess of Malfi, 1971; tour of Japan with Twelfth Night, 1972; (London) London Assurance, 1973; (Oxford and London) The Wolf, 1974; (London) The Good Companions, 1974-75, The Gay Lord Quex, 1975; (Royal Shakespeare Co., Stratford) Much Ado About Nothing, The Comedy of Errors, Macbeth (SWET Best Actress award for Lady Macbeth), King Lear, 1976-77; Cymbeline, 1979; (Royal Shakespeare Co., London) Pillars of the Community, The Way of the World, 1977-78, (Aldwych) Juno and the Paycock (SWET Best Actress award, Evening Std. Drama award for best actress, Plays and Players award for Best Actress, Variety Club award Actress of Yr.), 1981, A Kind of Alaska, The Importance of Being Earnest (Std. Best Actress award, Plays and Players award for best actress), Pack of Lies (Plays and Players award, SWET Best Actress award), Mr. and Mrs. Nobody, 1988, Antony and Cleopatra (Olivier award, Evening Std. Drama award, Drama mag. award), Gertrude in Hamlet, The Cherry Orchard, 1989, 90, The Blough and the Stars, The Sea, Coriolanus, 1992, The Gift of the Gorgon, 1992-93, The Seagull, 1994, Filumena in London, 1998, Amy's View in New York, 1999; dir. plays Much Ado About Nothing, Look Back in Anger, The Boys from Syracuse, Romeo and Juliet; TV appearances include: Major Barbara, Talking to a Stranger (Best TV Actress of Yr. award 1967), Jackanory, Luther, Nieghbours, Marching Song, Days to Come, The Comedy of Errors, Macbeth, Village Wooing, Love in a Cold Climate, A Fine Romance, The Cherry Orchard, Going Gently, Saigon, Mr. and Mrs. Edgehill, 1988 (ACE award), Ghosts, Make and Break, Behaving Badly, Can You Hear Me Thinking, Torch, Absolute Hell (Oliver award Best Actress 1996), As Time Goes By: films: He Who Rides a Tiger, A Study in Terror, Four in the Morning (Brit. Film Acad. Most Promising Newcomer award 1965), A Midsummer Night's Dream, The Third Secret, Deat Cert, Wetherby, 1985, A Room with a View, 84 Charing Cross Road, A Handful of Dust (Brit. Acad. Film and TV Arts award 1989), Henry V, 1989, Jack & Sarah, 1994, Golden Eye, 1995, A Little Night Music, 1995 (Oliver award Best Actress in a Musical 1996), Mrs. Brown (Brit. Acad. Film and TV Arts Sctoland award 1997, Critics Circle Film award 1997, Golden Globe award for best actress 1997, Acad. award nomination 1997), Amy's View, 1997 (Critics Circle Drama award 1997), Tomorrow Never Dies, 1997, Shakespeare in Love, 1998 (Acad. award Best Supporting Actress 1998), Tea With Mussolini, 1999, The World is Not Enough, 1999, The Last of the Blond Bombshells, 2000, Chocolat, 2000. Recipient Rothermore award for lifetime achievement, 1997, Critics Circle award for outstanding svc. to the arts, Acad. Award for Best Supporting Actress for Shakespeare in Love, 1999, Tony Award for Best Actress in Amy's View; decorated Order Brit. Empire; Dame Comdr. Brit. Empire; named UK Entertainment Personality of Yr. Variety, 1999, Walpole medal, N.Y., 2000, Benjamin Franklin medal, Royal Soc. Arts, London, 2000. Mem. Religious Soc. Friends.

DE NEIJS, EDUARD OTTO, physicist; b. Rotterdam, Netherlands, Jan. 2, 1948; arrived in Republic S. Africa, 1963.; s. Frederik Hendkrik and Christina Dina (Stekelenburg) D.; m. Hendriena Francina Kruger, Jan. 26, 1974; children: Maurits, Francois, Rudolf. BS, U. Potchefstroom, S. Africia, 1968; MS, U. Potchefstroom, 1970, DSc, 1974. Rsch. fellow U. Potchefstroom, S. Africa, 1971-75; sr. lectr. U. of the North, S. Africa, 1976-84, prof., 1984—; head physics dept. U. of the North, 1979—. Contbr. articles to profl. jours. Mem. S. African Inst. Physics, Electron Microscopy Soc. S. Africa. Home: Unicorn Ave 2, 0699 Pietersburg S Africa Office: Dept Physics, U of the North, P/6X1106 Sovenga S Africa

DÉNES, JÓZSEF, industrial and scientific consultant; b. Budapest, Apr. 16, 1932; s. Sándor and Anna (Jokkel) D.; m. Éva Braun, Dec. 30, 1951; 1 child, Tamás. Diploma in math, Eötvös L. U., 1954, PhD in Math, 1961. Head of dept. Ctrl. Rsch. Inst. for Physics, Budapest, 1954-69, Inst. Coordination of Computer Techniques/SZKI, 1969-88; indsl. and scientific cons., 1988—; cons. Inst. for Telecomms., Budapest, 1968-75; vis. rsch. prof. Math. Rsch. Ctr., Madison, 1976; vis. rsch. fellow U. of Surrey, Guildford, U.K., 1986-87; vis. prof. Pa. State U. State Coll., 1989; cons. various Hungarian Banks, 1989—; assoc. prof. Eötvos L.U., 1961—; lectr. univs. in Europe, U.S., Can., Israel, Japan; exrerior rsch. fellow Rényi Math. Inst. Scientific Acad. Hungary, 1964—; rsch. fellow U. So. Calif., L.A., 1995-97. Co-author: Latin Squares and Their Applications, 1974 (Prize 1977), Theoretical and Practical Problems of Data Transmission, 1974, (in German) Latin Squares; co-editor: New Developments in the Theory and Applications, 1991; editl. bd. Moldovian Rsch. Jour., 2000—; contbr. articles and over 100 papers to profl. publs.; 4 patents in field. Mem. Bolyai Math. Soc., Am. Math. Soc., N.Y. Acad. Scis. Home: Csaba 10, 1122 Budapest Hungary

DE NEUFVILLE, PIERRE, retired brokerage house executive; b. Paris, Sept. 15, 1924; came to U.S., 1974; s. Andre and Jacqueline (de Villeneuve) de N.; 1 child, Oliver. BA, Sorbonne U., 1946. Asst. v.p. LaCruz, Linares, Spain, 1947-50; USAF liaison Coca-Cola Internat., Paris, 1950-54; mgr. sales promotion France-Presse, Paris, 1954-56; mgr. Hayden Stone, Paris, 1956-64; resident ptnr. Bache and Co., Paris, 1964-73; internat. v.p. Lehman Bros., N.Y.C., 1973-87; mgr. internat. dept. Balis, Zorn, Gerard Inc., N.Y.C., 1987-89; ret., 1989, writer. Author: The Half Wit, 1987, The Red Star, 1987. Counsel to co-chmn. U.S. Senate/Congress Peace Through Strength, Washington, 1987—. Served to brig. gen. Free French Army. Decorated Medaille Militaire, three Croix de Guerre, France, 1945. Sufi. Club: Yacht Club de France. Avocations: philosophy, writing, sailing.

DENEYS, KEITH DONALD, protective services official; b. Green Bay, Wis., Nov. 21, 1964; s. Donald Emil and Margaret Mary Deneys; m. Connie Lynn Pigeon, Dec. 16, 1964; children: Kyle Henry, Tamara Lynn, Anthony Keith. AS in Police Sci., N.E. Wis. Tech. Coll., 1986. Cert. firearms instr., sniper instr. trainer, Wis. Safety/security officer State of Wis., King, 1986-88; lt. Brown County Sheriff's Dept., Green Bay, 1988—; pres. Tactical Options, Inc., Pulaski, Wis., 1997—; owner, moderator Snipersonline Internet Email List, Pulaski, 1998—. Author, prodr.: Precision Decisions Sniper Video Training Series, 1997; co-author: National Tactical Officer As-

sa's Recommendations for SWAT Snipers, 1997; author: (newsletter) Tactical Option, 1998; contbr. articles to profl. publs. Mem. Am. Sniper Assn. (adv. bd.), Internat. Assn. Firearm Instrs., Law Envorcement Trainers Assn., Am. Soc. Law Enforcement Trainers, Assn. SWAT Personnel, Nat. Tactical Officers Assn. Avocations: hunting, fishing, web page construction, email list moderating. Office: Tactical Ops Inc 4274 Highview Cir Pulaski WI 54162-9723

DENG, JIUN-SHIOU, electronic engineer, educator; b. Tai-Chung, Taiwan, July 11, 1965; s. Li-Kuan and Lin-Wan (Lin) Deng. AS, Nat. Taipei Inst. Tech., 1986; BS, Nat. Taiwan Inst. Tech., Taipei, 1990; MS, Nat. Chioa-Tung U., Hsin-Chu, Taiwan, 1993, PhD, 1996. Cert. in digital electronical engring. Hardware design engr. Chain Tech. Computer, Taipei, 1986-87; tchr. Yio-Shu Vocat. Sch., Miao-Li, Taiwan, 1987-88, Che-Yon Vocat. Sch., Tai-Chung, 1990-91; teaching asst. Nat. Chiao-Tung U., 1991-92; lectr. electronics engring. Ming Hsin Inst. Tech. and Commerce, Hsin-Chu, 1993—. Contbr. articles to profl. jours. Mem. SPIE. Avocations: photography, theater, Chinese poetry, badminton, baseball. Office: Ming Hsin Inst Tech & Com, #1 Hsin-Hsing Rd, 304 Hsin-Feng Hsinchu Taiwan

DENG, MIN, materials scientist; b. Hengfeng, China, Mar. 21, 1965; s. Kunwen and Caie (Wang) D.; m. Junping Liu, May 15, 1969; 1 child, Sihao. BS, Nanjing Inst. Chem. Tech., 1986, MS, 1989, PhD, 1992. Functionary Nanjing (China) U. Chem. Tech., 1992-96, vice dir., 1996—. Contbr. articles to profl. jours. Recipient award of sci. and technology progress Govt. of Jiangsu Province, 1994, Chinese People's Liberation Army, Chinese Youth. Mem. Nanjing Silicate Assn., Chinese Ceramic Soc. (youth working com.). Office: Nanjing U Chem Tech, 5 Xin Mo Fan Rd, Nanjing 210009, China

DENG, MING-QI, microbiologist, researcher; b. Changsha, Hunan, China, Sept. 13, 1967; came to U.S., 1994; s. Yangsheng Deng and Ai Liang Long; m. Helen J. Liu, Jan. 20, 1991; children: Alice X., Frank. BS, Hunan Normal U., Changsha, 1989; PhD, U. Calif., Davis, 2000. Rsch. asst. Hunan Agrl. U., Changsha, 1989-94, U. Wis., Madison, 1994-95; postgrad. rschr. U. Calif., Davis, 1995-99; postdoctoral assoc. U. Minn., St. Paul, 2000—. Contbr. articles to profl. jours. Mem. AAAS, Am. Soc. Microbiology, Am. Soc. Parasitologists, Sigma Xi, Phi Sigma. Office: U Minn Dept Vet Pathobiology 1988 Fitch Ave Saint Paul MN 55108-6009

DENG, TIAN-BO, educator; b. DaLian, China, Sept. 12, 1963; arrived in Japan, 1985; B of Engring., DaLian U., 1984; M of Engring., Utsunomiya U., Japan, 1988; D of Engring., Tohoku U., Japan, 1991. Rsch. assoc. Toyohashi U. Tech., Japan, 1991-92; spl. rschr. Inst. Phys. & Chem. Rsch., Japan, 1992-94; asst. prof. Toho U., Japan, 1994-98, assoc. prof., 1998—. Contbr. papers to profl. pubs. Mem. IEEE (sr.), Inst. Electronics, Info. and Comm. Engrs. Home: Mimomi-cho 4-1098, Narashino 275-0002, Japan Office: Toho U Dept Info Scis, Faculty of Sci Miyama 2-2-1, Funabashi 274-8510, Japan

DENG, TIANQUAN, electrical engineering consultant, educator; b. Sichuan, China, Nov. 20, 1964; arrived in Singapore, 1994; BS, Sichuan Normal U., 1986; MS, U. Electronic Sci. and Tech., China, 1988; PhD, Nat. U. Singapore, 1996. Engr., lectr. U. Electronic Sci. and Tech. of China, 1989-93; chmn. Hongya Instn., Chengdu, China, 1993-94; rsch. scholar Nat. U. Singapore, 1994-96; sr. engr. OKI Tech. Ctr., 1997-98; founder, acting pres. DTQ Tech., 1999—; vice chair Nat. Com. Microwave Biomed. Engrs., Beijing, 1993—. Contbr. articles to profl. jours. Mem. AAAS, IEEE, Chinese Inst. Electronics. Avocations: playing football, playing badminton, dancing, painting.

DENG, ZHAOJING, physics educator; b. Yi Chang, Hu Bel, China, Mar. 17, 1932; s. Changhua Deng and Kalxiu Wang; m. Yongxiu Zhou; 1 child, Yulan. Student, Kun Ming (China) Normal U., 1952-54, S.W. Normal U., Chongqing, China, 1954-56. Asst. S.W. Normal U., Chongqing, 1956-78, lectr., 1978-81, assoc. prof., 1981-85, prof., 1985—; dir. Modern Rsch. Inst., S.W. China Normal U.; mem. coun. Edn.-Study Soc. Thermodynamics and Stats., Nanjing, China, 1984-96. Author: Classical and Quantum Theory of Ideal System, 1983, Ultrafine Particle and Fractal, 1993, Advance Quantum Mechanics, 1995, Ultrafine Particles and Their Aggregates, 1998. Recipient Secons Progressive Encouragement for Sci. and Technique of Sichuan Province. Mem. Condensed Matter Physics Assn. Avocation: drawing. Office: Dept Physics, SW China Normal U Beipei, Chongqing 400715, China

DENGEL, OTTMAR HUBERT, physicist; b. Kempten, Germany, Sept. 14, 1933. BS, Tech. U. Munich, 1954, MS, 1958, PhD, 1962. Rsch. asst. Tech. U. Munich, 1962-65; rsch. physicist Naval Surface Warfare Ctr., White Oak, Md., 1965-94; pres. Royal Systems, Front Royal, Va., 1994—. Achievements include 12 patents related to gas generators (hydrogen). Home: 6294 Browntown Rd Front Royal VA 22630-5133

DENGER, MICHAEL L., lawyer; b. Davenport, Iowa, Sept. 8, 1945; s. Ralph Henry and Bernice Marie (Cederberg) D.; m. Mary Elizabeth Colbert, Aug. 30, 1969; children: Lorna Marie, Mary Catherine, Rachel Anne. BS with highest distinction, Northwestern U., 1967; JD cum laude, Harvard U., 1970. Bar: D.C. 1970, U.S. Ct. Appeals (D.C. cir.) 1971, U.S. Supreme Ct. 1978. Assoc. atty. Sutherland, Asbill & Brennan, Washington, 1970-76, ptnr., 1976-92; ptnr. Gibson, Dunn & Crutcher LLP, Washington, 1992—; adj. prof. law Washington and Lee U., 2000—; speaker on antitrust, trade regulation numerous groups. Bd. editors Antitrust Report, 1992—; contbr. articles to profl. jours. Mem. nat. adv. coun. Northwestern U. Sch. Speech, Evanston, Ill., 1990—. 2d lt. USAR, 1970. Mem. ABA (vice chair antitrust law sect. 1985-86, sec. antitrust sect. 1988-91, chair-elect antitrust law sect. 1991-92, chair antitrust law sect. 1992-93, chair edit. bd. antitrust sect. Federal and State Price Discrimination Law 1991, co-editor in chief antitrust sect. State Antitrust Practice and Statutes 3 vols. 1990, vice chair edit. bd. antitrust sect. Antitrust Law Devels. 2d edit. 1984), Columbia Country Club (Chevy Chase, Md.). Republican. Roman Catholic. Avocations: tennis, collecting military miniatures, military history, bridge. Home: 5802 Kirkside Dr Chevy Chase MD 20815-7118 Office: Gibson Dunn & Crutcher LLP 1050 Connecticut Ave NW Ste 900 Washington DC 20036-5306

DENGIZ, MURAT, physics engineer, consultant; b. Ankara, Turkey, Jan. 15, 1957; s. Cebbar A. and Sukran Degiz; m. Yasemin Alpman, Jan. 17, 1983; children: Efe, Özgecan. BS in Physics, Middle East Tech. U., Ankara, 1981. Project engr. ASELSAN, Ankara, 1983-87, planning specialist, 1987-92, project mgr., 1992-97, project coord., 1997-98; project and engring. mgr. Marconi Com, Ankara, 1998—. Author: Project Management, 1998; contbr. articles to profl. jours. Res. officer Land Forces, 1981-83, Ankara. Mem. Nat. Project Mgmt. Assn. (founder, pres. 1995), Project Mgmt. Inst. (founder, pres. Turkey chpt. 1996). Socialist. Muslim. Avocations: biking, astronomy. E-mail: mdengiz@superonline.com. Home: Sogutozu Cad 51/C-3, 06520 Ankara Turkey Office: AND Proje Yonetim Danisman, Kulilay Sok 19/10 Tandogan, Ankara Turkey

DEN HEYER, MARTIN, internist; b. The Hague, The Netherlands; s. Arie Jacobus and Aagie (Van der Twan) d.; m. Wilma Derboam, Apr. 27, 1988; 1 child, Arca. MD, 1992, PhD, 1997. House officer Heyenburg Hosp., The Hague, 1992-93; rschr. Heyenburg Hosp., Tilburg, 1993-95; trainee internal medicine Troee Steden Hosp., Tilburg, 1995-97, U. Hosp. Nymegen, 1998-99. Contbr. articles to profl. jours. Lt. of artillery, Teh Netherlands, 1985-86. Recipient Fleehinury of Yselstein prize, The Hague, 1995. Home: v Kellstr 1, 6721 VT Benneleom The Netherlands Office: U Hosp Nymege dept IM, PO Box 9101, 6500 HB Nymege The Netherlands

DEN HOLLANDER, FRANK, mathematician, educator; b. Voorburg, The Netherlands, Dec. 1, 1956; s. Kees and Henny (Duport) Den H.; m. Lucia Marrucci, July 24, 1993. MSc, Leiden U., 1980, PhD, 1985. Postdoctoral Delft U., 1985-91; assoc. prof. Utrecht U., The Netherlands, 1991-94; prof. Nijmegen U., The Netherlands, 1994—. Contbr. articles to profl. jours. Travel award Royal Dutch Shell, 1984. Mem. Dutch Assn. for Math. Physics (chmn. 1996—), Dutch Assn. for Math., Internat. Statis. Inst., Bernoulli Soc. Avocation: pianist. Office: Math Inst U Nijmegen, Toernooiveld 1, 6525 ED Nijmegen The Netherlands

DENIARD, PHILIPPE ANDRE, chemist, researcher; b. Saint Sebastien Sur Loire, France, Mar. 23, 1957; s. Francois Amand and Andree Fernande (Chouin) D.; m. Sylvie Andree Courant, May 25, 1985; children: Estelle, Celine. BS, U. Nantes, France, 1979, MS, 1980; PhD, U. Nantes, 1989. Rschr. Nat. Ctr. Scientific Rsch., Nantes, 1985—; mem. sci. com. Inst. Sics. Ingemeir Thermique Energitiwus Nat., Nantes, 1991-95. Author: Progress in Intercalation Research, 1994, Molecular Crystal and Liquid Crystal, 1994; contbr. articles to profl. jours. Mem. Soc. Francaise Chimie. Home: La Haie, 44240 Suce Sur Erdre France Office: Inst Materiaux Jean Rouxel, 2 Rue de la Houssiniere, 44322 Nantes France

DENIAU, ISABELLE, delivery service executive; b. Strasbourg, Alsace, France, June 4, 1960; d. Jean and Monique (Aubree) Schwartz; m. Benoit Henri Pierre Deniau; children: Iris, Germain, Mathilde. Degree, Brevet Technicien Superieur, Strasbourg, France, 1981; MBA, Inst. Superieur Gestion, 1984; Mktg. Svc., INSEAD, France, 1990. Product mgr. Avis Rent-a-Car, Paris, 1984-86; mktg. mgr. Avis Lease, Paris, 1986-88; product mgr. DHL Internat., Roissy, France, 1988-91, 91-93; advtsg. and comm. mgr. DHL Internat., Roissy, 1993—. Home: 12 Ave Benoit Levy, 94160 Saint Mande Valde Marne, France Office: DHL Internat, 241 rue de la Belle Etoile, 95957 Roissy CDG Vald'oise, France

DENIOUS, SHARON MARIE, retired publisher periodical; b. Rulo, Nebr., Jan. 27, 1941; d. Thomas Wayne and Alma (Murphy) Fee; m. Jon Parks Denious, June 17, 1963; children: Timothy Scot, Elizabeth Denious Cessna. Grad. high sch. Operator N.W. Pipeline co., Ignacio, Colo., 1975-90; pub. The Silverton Standard & The Miner, Colo., 1990-99. Avocations: reading, hiking.

DE NIRO, ROBERT, actor; b. N.Y.C., Aug. 17, 1943; s. Robert and Virginia DeNiro; m. Diahnne Abbott; children: Raphael Eugene, Drina. Studied acting with, Stella Adler, Lee Strasberg. Motion pictures appearances include The Wedding Party, 1969, Hi, Mom!, 1970, Jennifer On My Mind, 1971, Bloody Mama, Born to Win, 1971, The Gang That Couldn't Shoot Straight, 1971, Bang the Drum Slowly, 1973, Mean Streets, 1973, The Godfather, Part II, 1974 (Acad. award best supporting actor), The Last Tycoon, Taxi Driver, 1976, New York, New York, 1900, 1977, The Deer Hunter, 1978, Raging Bull, 1980 (Acad. award best actor), True Confessions, 1981, The King of Comedy, 1982, Once Upon a Time in America, 1984, Falling in Love, 1984, Brazil, 1984, The Mission, 1985, Angel Heart, 1987, The Untouchables, 1987, Dear America: Letters Home From Vietnam, 1987 (documentary), Midnight Run, 1988, (also exec. prodr.) We're No Angels, 1989, Jacknife, 1989, Stanley & Iris, 1990, Goodfellas, 1990, Awakenings, 1991 (Acad. award nomination), Backdraft, 1991, Cape Fear, 1991, Guilty By Suspicion, 1991, Mistress, 1992, Night and the City, 1992, Mad Dog and Glory, 1993, This Boys Life, 1993, (also dir.) A Bronx Tale, 1993, Mary Shelley's Frankenstein, 1994, Casino, 1995, Heat, 1995, The Fan, 1996, Marvin's Room, 1996, Sleepers, 1996, (also prodr.) Wag the Dog, 1997, Copland, 1997, Great Expectations, 1998, 15 Minutes, 1999, Analyze This, 1999, Flawless, 1999 (also prodr.), The Adventures of Rocky and Bullwinkle, 1999 (also prodr.), Lenny Bruce: Swear to Tell the Truth, 1998 (TV, voice); prodr.: Entropy, 1999; co-prodr. Thunderheart, 1992; theater roles include Strange Show, 1982; exec. prodr.: (TV) Tribeca, 1993, (film) Faithful, 1996, Navy Driver, 2000, Meet the Parents, 2000, Conjugating Niki, 2000. Recipient Hasty Pudding award Harvard U. 1979, D.W. Griffith award for best actor, 1990. Office: Creative Artists Agy 9830 Wilshire Blvd Beverly Hills CA 90212-1825

DENIS, LOUIS J., oncology urologist; b. Antwerp, Belgium, Jan. 20, 1933; s. Karel M. and Elisabeth J. (Mertens) D.; m. Carmen M. Gomez, Apr. 9, 1965; children: Peter, Johan, Christine, Louis, Margaret. MD, U. Ghent, 1957; cert. in urology, Richmond Med. Coll., 1963. Chmn. urology dept. Antwerp City Hosps., 1978-98; prof. urology Vrye U. Brussels, 1978-98; pres. European Orgn. Rsch. and Treatment Ctr., Brussels, 1988-91. Chmn. adv. comm. Flemish Cancer Prevention, Brussels, 1983-96; sec. gen. Internat. Union Against Cancer, 2000. Fellow ACS; mem. Numerous Urology Assn., Rotary. Office: AZ Middelheim, Oncology Centre Antwerp, 2000 Antwerp Belgium

DENISON, JAMES DICKEY, broadcasting executive; b. Clarendon, Tex., July 1, 1926; s. Dallas D. and Gladys (Condron) D.; m. Jo Beth Huser, June 27, 1965; children: Jack D., P. Dianne, Robert Ladd, Kathryn Anne Denison (Kit). Student, McMurry Coll., 1943, 46, U. Tex., 1947-49; BArch, U. Houston, 1952. Contracting engr. Am. Bridge div. U.S. Steel, Houston, 1952-60; co-owner, v.p. Globe Equipment Rental, Houston, 1961-67; owner, operator B & B Steel, Hobbs, N.Mex., 1967-73; co-owner, chief exec. officer VLA Fabrication div. Structures, Inc., Hobbs, 1973-79; owner, operator Denison's Photography, Kingwood, Tex., 1979-82, Sta. KKTC-FM, Brownfield, Tex., 1985-96. Chmn. N.Mex. State Highway Commn., 1974-79; congl. aide U.S. Congressman Harold Runnels, N.Mex., 1971-72. Served with USN, 1944-46, PTO. Mem. Brownfield C. of C. Democrat. Methodist. Lodge: Rotary (v.p. Hobbs club 1971-72). Avocations: photography, fishing. Home: 10006 W Bolivar Dr Sun City AZ 85351-2303

DENISOV, ALEXANDER PAVLOVICH, financial company executive; b. Rybinsk, Yaroslavl, Russia, Nov. 30, 1945; s. Pavel Yefimovich and Maria Pavlovna (Nikolyukina) D.; m. Galina Alexandrovna Zhuravlyova; children: Igor Alexandrovich, Vladimir Alexandrovich. Tchr., Pedagogical Inst., Smolensk, Russia, 1972; Economist, All Union Inst. Fin. and Econ., Moscow, 1982; Dr.Econ. Sci., Russian Govt. Acad., Moscow, 1995. Phys. tng. instr. Rybinskkabel, Rybinsk, Russia, 1964-76, head of material and tech. dept., 1976-83; gen. mgr. Rybinskkabel, Rybinsk, 1991—; dep. dir. gen. questions Verhnevolzhskkabel, Andropov, 1983-87; dir. Verhnevolzhskkabel, Rybinsk, 1987-91. Author: The Questions of Administration of Joint Stock Companies, 1993, Joint Enterprise in Russian Economy: Problems of theory and Practice, 1995. Chmn. Cable Plant Mgrs., Russia, 1996—; mem. Internat. Assn. "Intercable", Moscow, 1997—, Elektrokabel of CIS Countries, 1992—. Recipient Birmingham Torch award Internat. Fin. and Econ. Partnership Inst., 1995. Mem. Club of Internat. Leaders. Orthodox Ch. Avocations: hunting, sport. Office: Rybinskkabel, 50th Anniversary of Oct, 152916 Rybinsk Russia

DENISOV, DMITRI ALEXEEVICH, chemical engineering educator; b. Moscow, Feb. 28, 1945; s. Alexey Alexeevich and Veronika Sergeevna D.; m. Tatjana Valdimirovna Lachtionova, Apr. 22, 1983; (div. Dec., 1990); 1 child, Darya. Engr in Tech., Mendeleev Chem. Tech. Inst., 1969; postgrad. studies, Inst. Inorganic Materials, Russia, 1970-71; Cert. in Alpinism tng., Sch. Trainers in Alpinism, Bezengy, 1978; translator, Moscow Linguistic U., Advanced Lang Tng. Ctr., 1995. Engr. Inst. Chem. Tech., 1969, Inst. Inorganic Materials, Russia, 1971-74; rschr. Moscow Mendeleev Inst. Chem. Tech., 1974-92, sr. rschr., 1992-96; scientist D. Mendeleev U. Chem. Tech., Russia, 1996—; asst. in biol. chemistry Moscow Dentist Inst., 1993-95. Contbr. articles to Russian Jour. Phys. Chemistry, Meteorol. Zeitschr., High Temperature, and jours. in acoustical field. Mem. Democratic Russia Movement, Moscow, 1991. Grantee: Internat. Sci. Found., 1993, 94. Mem. Russian Acoustical Soc., European Acoustics Assn. Avocations: skiing (alpinese trainer), painting. Home: Marshal Katukov ul 2 app322, 123592 Moscow Russia Office: Mendeleev U Chem Tech, Miuskaja pl 9, 125047 Moscow Russia

DENISOV, EVGUENII TIMOFEEVICH, chemist; b. Kaluga, Russia, June 19, 1930; s. Timofey Arsentievich and Olga Nikolaevna (Barsheva) D.; m. Zoya Alexeevna Shmeleva, Jan. 8, 1954 (div. Jan. 1980); children: Oleg, Vladimir; m. Taissa Grigorievna Lupenko, Feb. 9, 1980. Diploma, U. Moscow, 1953, PhD, 1957; Doctorate, Inst. Chem. Physics, Moscow, 1966. Jr. rschr. Inst. Chem. Physics, Chernogolovka, Russia, 1956-60, sr. rschr., 1960-67, head of lab., 1967—; mem. commn. IUPAC, 1979-89, chmn. 1989-91; chmn. sect. sci. coun. Acad. USSR, 1972-97; chmn. sci. coun. Inst. Chem. Physics, 1977—. Author: Liquid-Phase Reaction Rate Constants, 1974, Handbook of Antioxidants, 1995, 2000; co-author: Oxidation of O-Containing Compounds, 1977. Mem. Acad. of Creative Endeavours, Internat. Acad. of Sci. Avocations: philosophy and history books, travel, skiing. Office: Inst Problems Chem Phys, 142432 Chernogolovka Russia

DENISOV, NIKOLAY ALEXANDER, optical engineer; b. Morozovsk, Rostov, Russia, Dec. 18, 1950; s. Alexander and Evgenia D.; m. Lyudmyla Fomchenko, Feb. 8, 1975; children: Oleksandr, Artem. MS, Poly. Inst., Kyiv, Ukraine, 1973, PhD, 1987. From engr. to rsch. scientist Poly. Inst., Kyiv, 1973-88, sr. rsch. scientist, 1988—; asst. prof. Nat. Tech. U., Kyiv, 1995—. Inventor in field. Mem. Internat. Soc. Optical Engring. Office: Nat Tech Univ, Peremohy 37, 03056 Kyiv Ukraine

DENIZ, GÜNNUR, science educator; b. Sinop, Ayancik, Turkey, July 3, 1964; d. Nazmi and Nurten (Kutnu) D. BSc, Istanbul (Turkey) U., 1985, MSc, 1989; PhD, U. Liverpool, Eng., 1994. Rsch. asst. dept. immunology Istanbul U., Inst. Exptl. and Med. Rsch., 1986-90, 94-95, asst. prof. dept. immunology, 1995-98, assoc. prof. dept. immunology, 1998—; guest scientist SIAF, Davos, Switzerland, 1998. Author: (book) HLA, 1991, OUP, 1992, Reproductive Immunology, 1992, Drug Resistance in Leukemia and Lymphoma III, 1999; contbr. articles to profl. jours. Recipient Meliha Terzioglu award Basic Sci., 1997. Mem. Internat. Union of Immunol. Socs. (rep. 1998—), Turkish Soc. Immunology (gen. sec. 1998—), BSI. Avocations: squash, badminton, skiing, aerobics, traveling. Home: Sok No 29, Tunusbagi cad Namik Pasa, 81130 Üsküdar Istanbul, Turkey Office: Istanbul U, Vakij Guraba cad Sehremini, Istanbul 34280, Turkey

DENIZTEKIN, OSMAN ÇETIN, publisher; b. Istanbul, Turkey, Mar. 9, 1949; s. Nedim and Saadet (Esin) D.; m. Filiz Nayir, May 13, 1982; 1 child, Ece. Student, Dartmouth Coll., 1968-71. Fgn. news editor Yeni Ortam Gazetesi, Istanbul, Turkey, 1974-75, Politika Gazetesi, Istanbul, Turkey, 1975-76; export officer Pasabahce Ltd, Istanbul, 1976-79; mng. editor E Yayinlari, Istanbul, 1979-81; publisher CEP Kitaplari, Inc., Istanbul, 1982—; co-publisher Varlik Yayinlari, Inc., Istanbul, 1994—; translator. Mem. Turkish Publ. Assn., Alumni Assn. Robert Acad.

DENKE, CONRAD WILLIAM, motion picture producer; b. Cottonwood, Ariz., July 23, 1947; s. Lee Ernest and Barbara Ann (Russell) D.; m. Laura Lee Nielson; children: Alexander, Elisabeth. BA in Radio-TV Communications and Psychology, U. Wash., 1969. Dir. Sta. KCTS-TV, Seattle, 1967-69; dir. producer Cinema Assocs., Seattle, 1973-78; pres. Am. Motion Pictures, Seattle, 1978—, Am. Prodn. Svcs., Seattle, 1978—; bd. dirs. Am. Cinema Found., Whidbey Island Films. Dir., producer: (indsl. documentary) Tunnels Under Chicago, 1981 (Chris award 1981, Gold award, Silver award, Cine Golden Eagle award, 1981); dir. (ednl. documentary) More Than Bows and Arrows, 1978 (Best Western Documentary 1978); producer: (TV series) Adventures on Sinclair Island, 1986, (talk show series) Teens Talk, (PBS documentary) Educations Wars, 1996, National Desk, 1997, 99. Mormon bishop, stake presidency. With USAF, 1969-73. Recipient Cine Golden Eagle award Council on Internat. Nontheatrical Events, 1977, 79, 89, 95, Silver Cindy award Info. Film Producers Am., 1977, 98, Gold Camera award U.S. Indsl. Film Festival, 1978, Telly award, 1989, 95, 97, 2 Telly's, 1998, 2 Gold awards Emerald City awards, 1997, World medal N.Y. Film Festival, 1998, 2 Aegis awards, 1998, 2 Aurora awards, 1998. Mem. Internat. TV Assn. (dir. Seattle chpt. 1980-90, chpt. pres. 1983-84, Silver Reel, 1986, Gold Reel 1997), Wash. Motion Picture Coun. (pres. 1992-96), Assn. Ind. Comml. Producers (v.p. N.W. chpt. 1985-87, pres. 1987-90), Am. Cinema Found. in L.A. (bd. dirs., v.p. 1994—). Republican. Office: Am Motion Pictures 2247 15th Ave W Seattle WA 98119-2417

DENKE, PAUL HERMAN, retired aircraft engineer; b. San Francisco, Feb. 7, 1916; s. Edmund Herman and Ella Hermine (Riehl) D.; m. Beryl Ann Lincoln, Feb. 10, 1940; children: Karen Denke Mottaz, Claudia Denke Tesche, Marilyn Denke Oliver. BCE, U. Calif.-Berkeley, 1937, MCE, 1939. Registered profl. engr., Calif. Stress engr. Douglas Aircraft Co., Santa Monica, Calif., 1940-62; mgr. structural mechanics Douglas Aircraft Co., Long Beach, Calif., 1962-65, chief sci. computing, 1965-71, chief structures engr. methods and devel., 1972-78, chief scientist structural mechanics, 1979-84, staff mgr. Boeing fellow, 1985-2000; ret.; mem. faculty dept. engring. UCLA, 1941-50. Author numerous tech. papers. Assoc. fellow AIAA; mem. Soc. Automotive Engrs. (Arch T. Colwell merit award 1966, IAE Outstanding Engr. merit award 1985), Sigma Xi, Chi Epsilon, Tau Beta Pi. Democrat. Achievements include pioneering and developing finite element method of structural analysis. Home: 1800 Via Estudillo Palos Verdes Peninsula CA 90274-1908

DENKER, HENRY, playwright, author, director; b. N.Y.C., Nov. 25, 1912; s. Max and Jennie (Geller) D.; m. Edith Rose Heckman, Dec. 5, 1942. LL.B., N.Y. Law Sch., 1934. Bar: N.Y. 1935. Practiced law N.Y.C., 1935-38; exec. Research Inst. Am., N.Y.C., 1936-37; tax cons. Standard Stats. subs. Standard and Poor, N.Y.C., 1937-39; lectr. dramatic writing Am. Theatre Wing, 1961-63, Coll. of the Desert. Writer, dir., prodr.: (radio series) The Greatest Story Ever Told, N.Y.C., 1947-57; author: (Broadway plays) Time Limit, 1956, A Far Country, 1961, Venus at Large, 1962, A Case of Libel, 1964, What Did We Do Wrong, 1968, Something Old, Something New, 1976, Horowitz and Mrs. Washington, 1979; (off-Broadway) The Name of the Game, 1967, A Sound of Distant Thunder, 1969, The Headhunters, 1974, CurtainCall, 1999; (screenplays) The Heartfarm, 1970, The Hook, Twilight of Honor, Time Limit, A Time for Miracles, 1980, Outrage, 1984; writer, dir., prodr. numerous TV dramas, 1950-66; TV spls. include Give Us Barrabas, 1964, Neither Are We Enemies, 1971, The Choice, The Court Martial of Lietenant Calley, Mother Seton, 1980, Love Leads the Way, 1985, Outrage, 1986, Case of Libel, 1986; author: I'll be Right Home Ma, 1949, My Son, The Lawyer, 1950, Salome, Princess of Galilee, 1954, That First Easter, 1956, The Director, 1970, The Kingmaker, 1972, A Place for the Mighty, 1973, The Physicians, 1975, The Experiment, 1976, The Starmaker, 1977, The Scofield Diagnosis, 1977, The Actress, 1978, The Error Judgement, 1979, Horowitz and Mrs. Washington, 1979, The Warfield Syndrome, 1981, Outrage!, 1982, The Healers, 1983, Kincaid, 1984, Love Leads the Way, 1985, A Case of Libel, 1985, Robert, My Son, 1985, Judge Spencer Dissents, 1986, The Choice, 1987, The Retreat, 1988, A Gift of Life, 1989, Payment in Full, 1990, Doctor on Trial, 1991, Labyrinth, 1994, This Child is Mine, 1995, To Marcy, With Love, 1996, A Place for Kathy, 1997, The Third Day, 1999, Benjie, 1999, Class Action, 2000. Recipient Peabody award, 1949; Christopher award, 1953; Emmy award, 1948. Mem. Acad. TV Arts and Scis. (coun.), Authors League (coun.), Dramatists Guild (coun. 1967-69), Authors Guild, Writers' Guild. Jewish. Address: 241 Central Park W New York NY 10024-4530

DENKO, JOANNE D., psychiatrist, writer; b. Kalamazoo, Mich., Mar. 29, 1927; d. John S. and Marian Mildred (Boers) Decker; m. Charles Wasil Denko, June 17, 1950; children: Christopher Charles, Nicholas Charles, Timothey Charles. BA summa cum laude, Hope Coll., 1947; MD, Johns Hopkins U., 1951; MS in Psychiatry, U. Mich., 1963. Lic. psychiatrist Md., Ill, Mich., Ohio. Pvt. practice Columbus, Ohio, 1961-68; staff psychiatrist Fairview Hosp., Cleve., 1968-97, Cleve. Clinic Health Systems, 1997—, Luth. Hosp., Cleve., 1998—; pvt. practice Rocky River, Ohio, 1968—; cons. Juvenile Diagnostic Ctr., Columbus, 1967-68, VA Hosp., Cleve., 1968-72, Cmty. Mental Health Ctrs., Greater Cleve., 1974-80; clin. instr. Case Western Res. U., Cleve., 1981-83. Author: Through the Keyhole at Gifted Men and Women, 1977, (monograph) The Psychiatric Aspects of Hypoparathyroidism, 1962; contbr. articles to profl. jours.; author poetry, 1960—. Mem. AAAS (reviewer children's books), Cleve. Astron. Soc. (bd. dirs. 1984-86, 96-98), Mensa (Cleve. area br. pres. 1986-87), Great Books Discussion Group (Rocky River, chmn. 1985-92, 94—), Kiwanis Internat. Russian Orthodox. Achievements include naming sexual deviance klismaphilia; research in special problems of adults of high intelligence, educating gifted girls, teenage alcoholism, mental illness in pre-literate peoples, psychiatric aspects of lupus. Home and Office: 21160 Avalon Dr Cleveland OH 44116-1120

DENMAN, HUGH, foreign language educator; b. London, Oct. 20, 1936; s. Frederick and Vera (Gutteridge) D.; m. Sylvia Elaine Yarde, Dec. 21, 1962 (div. Jan. 1970); m. Edith Maier, Apr. 7, 1987. BA, Oxford (Eng.) U., 1961, diploma in social sci., 1963, MA, 1965. Lectr. U. Reading, Eng., 1969-71, Queen's U., Belfast, No. Ireland, 1972-87; Benzion Margulies lectr. in Yiddish studies U. Coll. London, 1989—. Contbr. articles to profl. jours. Avocation: mountain walking. E-mail: h.denman@ucl.ac.uk. Office: Univ Coll London Hebrew Dep, Gower St, London WC1E 6BT, England

DENMARK, FLORENCE HARRIET LEVIN, psychology educator; b. Phila., Jan. 28, 1931; d. Morris and Minnerva (Sharkis) L.; m. Stanley J. Denmark, June 7, 1953 (div. Apr. 1973); children: Valerie, Pamela (dec.) and

Richard (twins); m. Robert W. Wesner, Sept. 5, 1973; stepchildren: Kathleen, Michael, Wendy. AB, U. Pa., 1952, AM, 1954, PhD, 1958; DHL, Mass. Sch. Profl. Psychology, 1985, Cedar Crest Coll., 1988; D of psychology, Ill. Sch. Profl. Psychology, 1995; DHL, Alleghany Coll., 1998. Lectr. psychology CUNY, Queens, 1959-66; instr. to prof. CUNY, N.Y.C., 1964-90, doctoral faculty psychology, 1967-87, prof. psychology, 1984-90; Robert Scott Pace Disting. prof. psychology, chair Pace U., N.Y.C., 1988—; adj. prof. CUNY, N.Y.C., 1990—. Editor: Who Discriminates Against Women?, 1974, Psychology: The Leading Edge Into the Unknown, 1980, (with L.L. Adler) Violence and the Prevention of Violence, 1995, (with M.B. Nadien) Females and Autonomy: A Life-span Perspective, 1999, (with V. Rabinowitz and J. Sechzer) Engendering Psychology, 2000, others; co-editor: Women: Dependent or Independent Variable?, 1975; contbr. various chpts. to books and numerous articles to profl. jours. Mellon scholar St. Olaf Coll., 1977; grantee Ctr. Human Rels. U. Pa., U.S. Office Edn., Rsch. Found. State of N.Y., N.Y. Cmty. Trust, Nat. Sci. Found., Ford Found., Nat. Endowment for Humanities, Nat. Inst. Mental Health, Muskowini Fund, Pace U. Fellow APA (com. on accreditation 1998—, pres. divsn. 52 internat. psychology 1999, pres. 1980, mem. various coms.; Centennial award 1992, disting. contbns. to psychology in pub. interest 1993, disting. contbns. to internat. psychology award 1996, 99), Am. Psychol. Soc. (charter); mem. Internat. Coun. Psychologists (pres. 1989-90), Interamerican Soc. Psychology (Interamerican award in Psychology 1997), Internat. Orgn. for Study of Group Tensions (v.p.), N.Y. State Psychol. Assn. (pres. divsn. social psychology 1989-90, acad. divsn. 1990-91; Kurt Lewin award 1978, Wilhelm Wundt award 1988, Carolyn Wood Sherif award 1992, Allen V. Williams Jr. Meml. award 1994, Margaret Floy Washburn award 1996), N.Y. Acad. Scis. (fellow 1966, v.p. 1984-87, Psychology Adv. Com. 1971—), Eastern Psychol. Assn. (pres. 1986, bd. dirs. 1988-91), Coun. Sci. Pres. (sec., exec. bd. mem. 1983-84), Internat. Coun. Psychologists, Assn. Women in Psychology (Outstanding Women in Sci. award 1980, disting. career award 1996), Soc. for Advancement of Social Psychology, Nat. Coun. of Chairs of Grad. Depts. Psychology, Soc. for Psychol. Study of Social Issues (mem. Otto Klineberg Intercultural and Internat. Rels. Award. Com.), Century Club, Chemists Club, Psi Chi (nat. pres. 1978-80). Avocations: opera, ballet, theatre, travel, sports. E-mail: Fdenmark@pace.edu. Office: Pace U 41 Park Row Fl 13 New York NY 10038-1508

DENNEHY, LEISA JEANOTTA, pharmaceutical executive; b. Fairfield, Ohio, May 30, 1961; d. Will Robert and Rethel Jeanotta (Russell) Fights. BA in Chemistry, Miami U., Oxford, Ohio, 1982; BS in Med. Tech., Miami U., 1983; MBA, Duke U., 1991. Registered med. technologist. Med. technologist Mercy Hosp., Hamilton, Ohio, 1982-85; analytical chemist Procter & Gamble Co., Cin., 1985-87, products rsch. chemist, 1987-88; new products anlyst GlaxoWellcome, Research Triangle, N.C., 1988-90; internat. product mgr.-dermatology GlaxoWellcome, Research Triangle Park, N.C., 1990-91, mgr. new product market devel., 1991-95, sr. product mgr., 1995-96, internat. comml. strategy dir., 1996-99, dir. mktg., 1999—. Co-author: Supercritical Fluid Extraction and Chromatography, 1988; contbr. articles to profl. jours. Named Women of the Day, 1979; recipient many acad. scholarships, 1980-82. Avocations: music, sports, cooking, reading, travel.

DENNICK, LORI ANN, artist; b. Cannonsburg, Pa., Feb. 8, 1962; d. Albert William and Mary Alice (Baldwin) D. AS, Pa. Comml. Bus. Coll., Washington, 1987; BA, U. Md., 1992; MFA, Hunter Coll., N.Y.C., 1999. Freelance artist Pitts., 1992—; editor, art dir. Common Ground, Pitts., 1995-96; house artist Artists for Good Works, Pitts., 1998—; talent developer Main Line Models, McKeesport, Pa., 1999—; plus size model Main Line Inc., McKeesport, 1999—; art exhibitor St. Art, Pitts., 1993—. Artist Free to Do Anything, 1999, Flying Goddess, 1999, Heart Attack, 1999 (Best of Show 1999), Content Goddess, 1999. Mem. daffodil days com. Am. Cancer Soc., Pitts., 1999; pet advocate Animal Friends, Pitts., 1999. Named Miss 16 Plus-Model of Yr., Miami, Fla., 1995, Charity in Arts award, Pitts., 1999, Main Line Woman of 1999, McKeesport, 1999. Mem. Internat. Models Assn., Assn. Bus. and Profl. Women, Am. Legion Aux. Democrat. Presbyterian. Avocations: theater arts, travel, painting, jewelry design.

DENNING, SAMANTHA, advertising executive; b. London, Apr. 18, 1975; d. Gordon Albert Denning and Deborah Nichols. Degree in astrophysics, U. London, 1996. Acct. exec. TCS Advt., London, 1996—; comms. cons. TCS Advt.; founder, propr., chairwoman SLM, London; spkr. in field. Inventor Leeson-B-Phone. Spalding High Polit. candidate Monster Raving Loony, 1991. Mem. Order of Molloy (grand pubar 1999). Avocations: astronomy, philosophy, lecturing. Home: Goodfellows Hall, The Raceground, Spalding PE11 3AP, England Office: TCS Advt High Holborn, New Penderel House, London WC1V 7HG, England

DENNINGHOFF, KURT RICHARD, medical educator; b. Denver, Dec. 24, 1958; s. George William and Patricia Ann (Elledge) D.; m. Amy Jo Smith, May 12, 1984; children: Lara, Kurt Jr., Sarah. BE in Biomed. & Elec. Engring., Vanderbilt U., 1983, MD, 1987. Diplomate Am. Bd. Emergency Medicine. Asst. prof. U. Ala., Birmingham, 1992—. Contbr. articles to profl. jours. Recipient $1.5 million grant U.S. Army, 1997-99. Fellow Am. Acad. Emergency Medicine, Am. Coll. Emergency Medicine. Achievements: determined that retinal venous oxygen saturation correlates with blood loss and mixed venous oxygen saturation during blood loss. Avocations: sailing, fishing. Office: Dept Emergency Medicine UAB 619 19th St S Birmingham AL 35233-0001

DENNIS, JOHN HUGH, occupational hygiene and environmental science educator, consultant; b. Edinburgh, Scotland, Nov. 30, 1960; s. Clive Anthony Richard and Joan Cairns (Paterson) D.; m. Cora Anna Pieron, July 28, 1989; children: Drew Cameron, Leoni Anne, Rhys Anthony. BSc in Biochemistry, U. Regina, 1985; MSc in Occupational Hygiene, U. Newcastle, 1987, PhD in Medicine, 1993. Cert. occupational hygienist. Rsch. asst. Regina (Sask., Can.) Univ., 1984-86; rsch. assoc. Newcastle (Eng.) Univ., 1987-92; lectr. Bradford (Eng.) Univ., 1992—; cons. VCB Ltd., Bradford, 1992—; dir. Leazes Arcade Ltd., Newcastle, 1987—. Contbr. articles to sci. and profl. jours. Mem. Inst. of Occupational Hygiene (coun. 1996—). Avocations: sailing, racquet sports, mountain biking, gardening, children.

DENNIS, WAYNE ALLEN, graphic designer, photographer, advertising executive; b. Muskegon, Mich., Sept. 15, 1941; s. Allen Wesley and Gladys (Kruger) D.; m. Sherry Lynn Cross, Oct. 10, 1962 (div. 1978); children: Jeri Ann, Bradford, Craig; m. Marjorie Nan Karsten, Nov. 28, 1980. AS, Ferris State U., Big Rapids, Mich., 1961. Staff artist James River Corp., Kalamazoo, 1961-62; designer, prodn. mgr. Graphic Arts Svcs., Grand Rapids, Mich., 1962-67; art dir. Skeketee-Van Huis Inc., Holland, Mich., 1967-74; pres., creative dir. Dennis/Mokma Assocs., Holland, Mich., 1974-86; account spr. William R. Biggs/Gilmore Assocs., Grand Rapids, 1986; owner/mgr. Wayne Dennis Photography, Zeeland, Mich., 1987; dir. mktg. S2 Yachts, Inc., Holland, 1987-88; v.p. mktg. Celebrity Boats Inc., Benton, Ill., 1988-89; owner/mgr. Dennis Communications, Zeeland, 1989-95, Dennis Creative, 1995—; advisor Careerline Tech. Ctr., Holland, 1980-95. Photographer book cover: Michigan, 1980, 10th ann. cover, Crusing World mag., 1984, others. Recipient Gold Addy award, Am. Advt. Fedn., 1982, Silver Addy award, 1988; recipient Excellence award, Printing Industry of Am., 1984, Silver-Golden Quill award, Gilbert Paper Co., 1989, others. Mem. Assn. Great Lakes Maritime History. Avocations: maritime history, backpacking, bird watching, sailing, model ships. Address: PO Box 191 Pullman MI 49450-0191

DENNISON, DANIEL WAYNE, television news executive; b. Gunnison, Colo., Mar. 12, 1957; s. Milton Ira and Mary Ruth (Butler) D. BA, Colo. State U., 1979. News dir. Sta. KGUC-AM, Gunnison, 1971-75, Sta. KSTR Radio, et al, Grand Junction, Colo., 1975-79; reporter Sta. KMGH-TV, Denver, 1979-82; reporter, bur. chief KUSA-TV, Denver, 1982-95; news dir. Sta. KRDO-TV, Colorado Springs, 1995-96, Sta. KOAA-TV, Colorado Springs, 1996—; spkr. civic journalism workshops. Bd. dirs., treas. Western State Coll. Found., Gunnison, 1987-93; participant newsroom mgmt. Poynter Inst., St. Petersburg, Fla., 1996, participant power reporting, 1994. Named Nat. Communicator of Yr., Easter Seals Soc., 1983, 85, Broadcaster of Yr., Internat. Spl. Olympics, 1985; recipient Lowell Thomas award Colo. Ski Country USA, 1994, Regional Emmy award nominations, 1989, 94, 95. Mem. Radio TV News Dirs. Assn. (participant civic journalism 1997, 98, presenter 2000), Western Slope Press Assn. (pres. 1987-89), N.Am. Ski Journalists, Colo. Mountain Club (bd. dirs. 1988), Colorado Springs Press Assn. (bd. dirs. 2000). Lutheran. Avocations: climbing, skiing, hiking. Home: 5730 Dalton Dr Colorado Springs CO 80919-2487 Office: Sta KOAA-TV 530 Communication Cir Colorado Springs CO 80905-1744

DENNISON, GERARD FRANCIS, economic analyst; b. Lewiston, Maine, Aug. 3, 1948; s. Alfred Alexandre Jr. and Regina Violet (Routhier) D.; m. Patricia Elaine Potter, June 24, 1989; stepchildren: Rochelle Elizabeth Riordan, Melanie Lois Wentworth. BS BA, Thomas Coll., 1970, MBA, 1986. Lic. stockbroker, Maine. Sr. econ. analyst Maine Dept. Labor, Lewiston, 1971—; mem. confs. in field. City councilor City of Auburn, Maine, 1994—; corporator, bd. dirs., mem. various coms. Auburn-Lewiston Boys/Girls Club; corporator Auburn Pub. Libr.; bd. dirs. Lewiston-Auburn Econ. Growth Coun., Lewiston-Auburn R.R.; mem. cmty. bldg. com. United Way; mem. Kittyhawk Indsl. Park Com.; chair Enhanced Cmty. Policing Com.; mem. adv. coun., planning com. Lewiston-Auburn Coll; chair Auburn Indsl. Park Site Selection Com.; mayor's rep. Auburn Sch. Com., Lewiston Auburn Edn. Coalition, dir. Auburn Exch. Club, dir. exec. com. Androscoggin Valley Coun. of Govts.; coord. Androscoggin County campaign for Gov. Angus S. King Jr., 1998; mentor Togolese Refugee Family Resettlement Program; treas. Franco Am. Heritage Ctr.; mem. preservation com. St. Mary's Ch., Lewiston, Mo. Mem. USA Forum Francophone des Affaires, Auburn Exch. Club, Auburn Bus. Devl. Corp., New Auburn Amer. Legion Post #153 Son's, Poland Spring Country Club, Prospect Hill Country Club. Democrat. Roman Catholic. Avocations: golf, reading, bowling. Home: 28 7th St Auburn ME 04210-5633 Office: Maine Dept Labor 5 Mollison Way Lewiston ME 04240-5805

DENNISON, STANLEY SCOTT, retired lumber company executive, consultant; b. Mitchelville, Md., Sept. 1, 1920; s. Ralph Stanford and Cora Adeline (Scott) D.; m. Sharon Lee Johnson, June 1, 1983; 1 stepchild, Whitney C. Maddox; children by previous marriage: Judith Dennison Tucci (dec.), Joan Dennison Daffron, Joyce Dennison Bischoff. Ed., Columbia Union Coll., 1938; BS, MBA, Calif. Western U., 1979, PhD, 1982. Operative builder Dennison Co., 1939-43; traffic rep. U.P. R.R., 1943-49; v.p. Arlington Millwork, Va., 1949-52, Internat. Filling Machine Co., Petersburg, Va., 1952-57, Atlanta Oak Flooring Co., 1957-62; regional mgr. Ga.-Pacific Corp., Portland, Oreg., 1962-70; v.p. Ga.-Pacific Corp., 1970-78, sr. v.p., 1978-82, exec. v.p., 1982-85; exec. mgmt. cons., 1985—. Past trustee Stonehill Coll., U. Portland, Calif. Western U.; bd. dirs. Aquinas Ctr. Theology at Emory U., Atlanta. Mem. Capital City Club (Atlanta), Commerce Club (Atlanta), Alpha Kappa Psi. Democrat. Roman Catholic. Home: 5255 Glenridge Dr NE Atlanta GA 30342-1353

DENNISS, ALAN ROBERT, cardiologist; b. Brisbane, Queensland, Australia, Sept. 30, 1952; s. Alan Fergus and Dorothy Jean (Smith) D.; m. Wendy Jane Fisher, Nov. 14, 1992; children: Amelia, Dominique, Michael, Jeremy. BSc in Medicine, U. Sydney, Australia, 1974; MB, BChir, U. Sydney, 1977, MSc, 1978, MD, 1987. Registered med. practicioner, Australia, U.K. Med. registrar St. Vincent's Hosp., Sydney, 1979; cardiology registrar Westmead Hosp., Sydney, 1980-81, cardiology fellow, 1982-84, cardiologist, 1988—; cardiology fellow St. Thomas' Hosp., London, 1985, Brigham and Women's Hosp., Boston, 1986-87; clin. assoc. prof. U. Sydney, 1999. Contbr. articles to profl. jours. Recipient Ralph Reader prize Cardiac Soc. Australia and New Zealand, 1982; Overseas fellow Nat. Heart Found. Australia, 1985-87; rsch. grantee Nat. Health and Med. Rsch. Coun. Australia, 1994-97. Fellow Am. Coll. Cardiology, Coun. on Clin. Cardiology-Am. Heart Assn., European Soc. Cardiology; mem. Australian Med. Assn., Cardiac Soc. Australia and New Zealand. Office: Specialist Med Ctr, 202/151 Hawkesbury Rd, Westmead Sydney NSW 2145, Australia

DENNY, RICHARD WILLIAM GEOFFREY, writer, lecturer; b. Burwash, Sussex, Eng., Feb. 4, 1940; s. Henry Lytellton Lyster and Joan Dorothy Lucy Denny; m. Andreé Susanne Raymount, Feb. 25, 1961 (div. 1977); 1 child, Parrott; m. Linda May Holmes, Sept. 8, 1984; children: Lyster, Walter, Giles, Julius, Stephen. Mng. dir. Denny Farms Ltd., U.K., 1960-74; dir. Leadership Devel. Ltd., U.K., 1974-79; chmn. Man Mgmt. Ltd., Moreton-in-Marsh, Eng., 1979—, Denny Pub. Ltd., 2000—; motivational spkr. in field. Author: Selling to Win, 1988, Motivate to Win, 1992, Speak for Yourself, 1993, Succeed for Yourself, 1997, Wise Words for Management, 2000. Mem. Inst. Sales Mktg. Mgmt. (v.p. 1996—). Avocations: hunting, beekeeping, sailing, skiing. Home: Foxcote Ct, Moreton-in-Marsh, Gloucestershire GL56 0NJ, England Office: Richard Denny Orgn, PO Box 16, Moreton-in-Marsh GL56 0NH, England

DENNY, WILLIAM MURDOCH, JR., investment management executive; b. Schenectady, N.Y., June 10, 1934; s. William Murdock and Ione Elizabeth (Lundy) D.; m. Delores Gay Shillady, June 11, 1966; children: Ellen Gay, Nancy Beth, Linda Ann. ScB in Chemistry, Brown U., 1958; MBA in Fin., Drexel U., 1974. Mem. mgmt. staff chem. spltys. divsn. Pennwalt Corp., Phila., 1961-73; pres. Denny Fin. Enterprises, Paoli, Pa., 1974—; chmn. mgmt. com. Houston-Leon County Coal Co. Interests, Crockett, Tex., 1987—; winegrower Clover Mill Farm Vineyards & Winery, Chester Springs, Pa., 1998—. Bd. dirs. United Way of North Central Chester County, 1980-83. Lt. comdr. USN, 1959-61. Mem. Fin. Analysts Fedn., Fin. Analysts Phila., Navy League U.S., Corinthians Assn. (Phila. fleet capt. 1996-97), Phi Kappa Psi, Brown U. Club (pres. 1979-81, Phila.), Aronimink Golf Club (Newtown Square, Pa.), Yacht Club of Hilton Head Island (S.C.), Sea Pines Club. Home: Clover Mill Farm Chester Springs PA 19425 Office: PO Box 458 Paoli PA 19301-0458

DENOBLE, ROBERT, business executive; b. Ismaïlia, Egypt, Jan. 31, 1937; French citizen; s. Gilles and Françoise (Lo Rizzo) D.; m. Eliane Yvette Simon; children: Eric, Sylvie. Baccalaureat, Lycée Francais de Port-Said, Egypt, 1954; engr., Ecole D'Electricité et de Mécanique Industrielles, Paris, 1958. Rschr. R&D divsn. Electricité de France, Clamart, France, 1960-65; switchgear expert distbn. dept. Electricité de France, Paris, 1966-71, head equipment and planning divsn. distbn. area, 1972-77, head tech. svcs., 1978-81, head ctrl. equipment and tech. divsn., 1982-85; gen. comptr. R&D dept. Electricité de France, Clamart, 1986-96; v.p. Electricité de France, Paris, 1997-99; pres. standardization com. Union Internat. de Producteurs et Distbn. d'Electricité, Paris, 1990-93; pres. Com. Europeen de Normalisation Electrotechnique, Brussels, 1994-95. Mem. Union Technique de l'Electricité (pres. 1997—), Internat. Electrotechnical Commn. Geneva (v.p. 1996—). Office: UTE, 33 Ave du Gen Leclerc, 92262 Fontenay aux Roses France Home: 93 rue de Fontenay, 92262 LePlessis-Robinson France

DENOEUX, JEAN-PAUL, dermatologist; b. Amiens, Somme, France, Apr. 26, 1942; s. Pierre and Therese-Marie (Debouverie) D.; m. Michele Plouchart, Mar. 26, 1966; children: Olivier, François. MD, U. Picardy, Amiens, 1969. Interne U. Regional Hosp., Amiens, 1967-72; chef de clinique Faculty Medicine, Amiens, 1972-78; asst. U. Regional Hosp., Amiens, 1972-78; prof. dermatology and venereology Faculty Medicine, Amiens, 1978—; head dermatology and venereology dept. U. Regional Hosp., Amiens, 1981—; expert Ct. Appeal; founder, chmn. Picardy study group on AIDS, H.I.V. infection, 1985-93; pub. service physician anti-venereal diseases, Amiens, 1974—. Contbr. numerous articles to profl. jours. Mem. Assn. French-Speaking Dermatologists and Syphiligraphists, French Soc. Dermatology and Syphiligraphy, European Soc. Pediatric Dermatology, Dermatol. Research Soc., European Acad. Dermatology and Venereology, Nat. Trade Assn. Hosp. and Univ. Profs. (v.p. 1999—). Roman Catholic. Lodge: Lions. Office: Univ Regional Hosp, South Hosp, 80054 Amiens Cedex 1 France

DENOON, DAVID BAUGH HOLDEN, economist, educator, consultant; b. Toledo, Apr. 12, 1945; s. Clarence E. and Eleanor (Kratz) D. B.A., Harvard U., 1966; M.P.A., Princeton U., 1968; Ph.D., MIT, 1975. Asst. to chmn. Pa. State Bd. Edn., 1968; program economist U.S. AID, Dept. of State, Jakarta, Indonesia, 1969-71; asst. to pres. Nat. Bur. Econ. Research, N.Y.C., 1971-72; asst. prof. politics and econs. NYU, 1975-78, 79-80, assoc. prof. politics and econs., 1982—; v.p. U.S. Export-Import Bank, Washington, 1978-79; dep. asst. sec. U.S. Dept. Def., Washington, 1981-82, cons., 1982-91; cons. U.S. Dept. State, Washington, 1992-93. Author: Devaluation Under Pressure: India, Indonesia, and Ghana, 1986, Real Reciprocity-Balancing U.S. Economic and Security Policies in the Pacific Basin, 1993, Ballistic Missile Defense in the Post-Cold War Era, 1995; editor, contbr.: The New International Economic Order: A U.S. Response, 1979, Constraints on Strategy: The Economics of Western Security, 1986, Changing Capital Markets and the Global Economy, 1988. Active Bucks County Land Use Task Force, 1975-78, Bucks Rep. Party, 1976—. Mem. Asia Soc., Am. Econ. Assn., Am. Polit. Sci. Assn., Coun. Fgn. Rels., Internat. Studies Assn., Internat. Inst. for Strategic Studies, Harvard Club (N.Y.C.), Cosmos Club (Washington). Home: 3609 Creamery Rd Wycombe PA 18980 Office: NYU 715 Broadway New York NY 10003-6860

DENOON DUNCAN, RUSSELL EUAN, solicitor, consultant; b. Johannesburg, Transvaal, South Africa, Mar. 3, 1926; arrived in Eng., 1961; s. Douglas and Ray Evelyn (Reynolds) Denoon Duncan; m. Caroline Jane Lloyd Lewin, Jan. 28, 1956; children: James, Angus. Student, Michaelhouse, Natal, South Africa. Atty. and notary pub., South Africa; solicitor, Eng. Ptnr. Webber Wentzel, Johannesburg, 1952-61; ptnr. Cameron McKenna (formerly Cameron Markby Hewitt), London, 1963-87, sr. ptnr., 1987-90, cons., 1990-98; chmn. Nat. Australia Group Ltd., London, 1987-91. Lance bombardier South African Artillery, 1943-46. Decorated Order of Merit (officers class) Pres. Poland, 1995; named Freeman, Worshipful Co. Solicitors, 1987. Fellow Inst. of Dirs.; mem. Brit. Polish Legal Assn. (chmn. 1989-95, pres. 1995-2000), Brit. Hungarian Law Assn. (v.p. 1991-93), City of London Club, Royal Tennis Ct., Rand Club. Avocations: mountain walking, tennis, painting. Home: Rose Cottage Watts Rd, KT7 0BX Thames Ditton Surrey, England

DENSMORE, DOUGLAS WARREN, lawyer; b. Jan. 30, 1948; s. Warren Orson and Lois Martha (Ery) D.; m. Janet Roberta Broadley, Oct. 26, 1973; children: Bradley Wythe, Andrew Fitz Douglas. AB, Coll. of William and Mary, Williamsburg, Va., 1970; JD cum laude, U. Toledo, 1975. Bar: Ohio 1976, U.S. Dist. Ct. (no. dist.) Ohio, Va. 1980, U.S. Dist. Ct. (ea. and we. dists.) Va. 1980, U.S. Ct. Appeals (4th cir.) 1980, U.S. Supreme Ct., 1997. Assoc. Gertner, Barkan & Robon, Toledo, 1975-77, Shumaker, Loop & Kendrick, Toledo, 1977-79; corp. counsel Dominion Bankshares Corp., Roanoke, Va., 1979-80; assoc. Woods, Rogers, Muse, Walker & Thornton, Roanoke, Va., 1980-84; ptnr. Woods, Rogers & Hazlegrove, Roanoke, Va., 1984-96, Flippin, Densmore, Morse and Jessee, Roanoke, Va., 1996—. Coauthor: Examining the Increase in Federal Regulatory Requirements and Penalties: Is Banking Facing Another Troubled Decade?, 1995; contbr. articles to profl. jours. Bd. dirs. New Century Tech. Coun.; Vet. Corps of Arty. N.Y., Army-Navy Union. Decorated Venerable Order St. John (Eng.), Companion of the O'Conor Don (Ireland), knight grand cross Royal Order of Don Carlos I (Portugal), knight grand cross Order of St. Catherine, knight comdr. of justice Order of St. Lazarus, first class Order of Polonia Restituta (Poland), knight grand cross Order St. Stanislas (Poland), knight grand cross Order of the Temple, knight comdr. Order of Crown of Thorns, knight grand cross Order of St. Michael and St. George, knight grand cross Orthodox Order St. John, knight Order of St. John, Knights of Malta, knight grand cross Order of Holy Cross of Jerusalem, knight grand cross with collar Order of St. Gregory, knight grand cross Order of St. Stephen, Royal Ukranian Order of St. Vladimir the Great, knight grand cross Greek Order of St. Denis of Zante, Order of the White Eagle with collar. Fellow Baskerville Soc. (U.K.); mem. ABA (banking law com. 1988—, uniform comml. code com. 1988—), Va. Bar Assn. (corp. code com. 1984—), Bar Assn. City of Roanoke (bd. dirs. 1998—), Am. Corp. Counsel Assn., Roanoke Regional C. of C. (bd. dirs. 1999—), Scottish Soc. Va. Highlands (v.p. 1994-95, pres. 1995-96, bd. dirs. 1992—), Brit. Manorial Soc. (Lord of Stratford St. Andrew), Augustan Soc., English Speaking Union (bd. dirs.), Soc. of St. George, Kiwanis Internat., Masons (32 degree, master, jr. deacon 1992), Shriners, Royal Order of Scotland, Shenandoah Club (Roanoke), Roanoke Country Club, Farmington Country Club (Charlottesville, Va.). Episcopalian. Avocations: golf, gardening, reading. Office: 2625 S Jefferson St Roanoke VA 24014-3315

DENTEN, CHRISTOPHER PETER, lawyer; b. Oakland, Calif., Apr. 23, 1964; s. Richard and Waltraud Denten; m. Mary McLaughlin, May 18, 1996. BA, U. Calif., Berkeley, 1986; JD, U. San Francisco, 1990. Bar: Calif. 1991, U.S. Dist. Ct. (no. dist.) Calif. 1991, U.S. Ct. Appeals (9th cir.) 1991; CPA, Colo. Tax profl. KPMG Peat Marwick, Oakland, 1988-92; sr. tax analyst Cisco Sys., Inc., San Jose, Calif., 1992-97; dir. legal affairs and taxation Network Assocs., Inc. (formerly McAfee, Inc.), Santa Clara, Calif., 1997—; bd. dirs. Network Assocs. fgn. subs., 2000—. Named to Outstanding Young Men of Am., 1982; Brother Gary Stone Meml. scholar, 1982. Mem. AICPA, Santa Clara Bar As, U. Calif. Berkeley Alumni Assn., U. San Francisco Law Sch. Alumni Assn., Network Assocs. Pres. Club. Republican. Roman Catholic. Avocations: marathons, golf, art, travel. Home: PO Box 117932 Burlingame CA 94011-7932 Office: Network Assocs Inc 3965 Freedom Cir Santa Clara CA 95054-1203

D'ENTREMONT, EDWARD JOSEPH, infosystems engineer, educator; b. Lynn, Mass., June 25, 1954; s. Joseph Albenie and Gertrude Grace (Flattery) D'E. BA in Math., Salem State Coll., 1976; MS in Applied Math., Northeastern U., 1982. Floor supr. Jordan Marsh co., Peabody, Mass., 1972-76; sci. programmer Electronics Corp. Am., Cambridge, Mass., 1977, Sulivan and Cogliano, Waltham, Mass., 1977; software engr. Raytheon Svc. Co., Burlington, Mass., 1977-86, Baytheon Missile Sys. divsn., Bedford, Mass., 1986-96, Desktop Data Inc., Burlington, Mass., 1995-98; prin. software engr. Newsedge Corp., Burlington, 1998—; part-time instr. Fitchburg State at Raytheon Inst., Tewksburg, Mass, 1986-96, U. Lowell, Mass., 1991—; sr. software engr. Raytheon Co.; part-time instr. continuing edn. Salem State Coll., 1993-95. Campaign worker presdl. campaigns, 1968-72, city coun., state rep., Lynn, 1976, Dukakis for Gov., Lynn, 1982; vol. tech. com. Aborn Elem. Sch. Mem. IEEE, Am. Math. Soc., Math. Assn. Am., Soc. for Indsl. and Applied Math., IEEE Computer Soc., N.Y. Acad. Scis., Assn. Computing Machinery, St. Mary's H.S. Alumni Assn., Salem State Coll. Alumni Assn., Northeastern U. Alumni Assn., Lexington Racquet and Swim Club. Democrat. Roman Catholic. Home: 50 York Rd Lynn MA 01904-1130

DENUIT, MICHEL MARCEL, statistics educator; b. Kinshasa, Congo, Aug. 21, 1972; s. Christian Etienne Denuit and Danielle Josée Waltens. Degree in math./statistics, Free U. Brussels, 1994, degree in actuarial scis., 1996, PhD in Statistics, 1997. Lectr. Free U. Brussels, 1994-99; prof. Cath. U., Louvain-La-Neuve, Belgium, 1999—. Contbr. articles to profl. jours. Recipient Olbrechts-Tyteca award, 1997; grantee Communauté Francaise de Belgique, 1995-98, Acad. Royale des Sciences de Belgique, 1998. Fellow Belgian Actuarial Assn., Belgian Statis. Soc.

DENZLER, JAMES WYATT, pharmacist; b. Marion, Va., Jan. 30, 1958; s. Roger Vincent Denzler and Helen Margaret Lambert Williams. BS in Biology, East Tenn. U., 1981, U. Minn., 1988. Registered pharmacist, Va., Calif., N.Y. Pharmacist Longs Drugs, Santa Barbara, Calif., 1988-90, Thrifty Drugs, Santa Barbara, 1990-91, Eckerd/Revco, Virginia Beach, Va., 1991-2000, Norfolk (Va.) Gen. Hosp., 1998—; pharmacist mgr. Rite Aid, Virginia Beach, Va., 2000—; pres., owner Denzler Corp., Norfolk, 1996—. Mem. Am. Pharm. Assn., Audubon Soc., U.S. Table Tennis Assn., Pi Kappa Alpha (chpt. pres.), Phi Delta Chi (chpt. pres.). Avocations: birding, table tennis, weightlifting, photography. E-mail: jamz9260@aol.com.

DEO, BRAHMA, metallurgist, educator; b. Sultanpur, India, Mar. 18, 1946; s. Baijnath Prasad and Urmila Devi Shukla; m. Surabhi Upadhyaya; children: Sudhindra, Ishani. B in Technology, Indian Inst. Technology, Khuragpur, 1967; M in Technology, BHU, Varanasi, India, 1969; DPhil, U. Burdwan, 1975. Rsch. engr. Rsch. & Devel. Steel Auth. India, Rauchi, 1970-77, Creusot Loire Enterprises, France, 1977-80; rsch. assoc. Imperial Coll., London, 1980-83; from asst. prof. to prof. Indian Inst. Technology, Kanpur, 1983—; vis. prof. Hoogovens Ijmuiden, The Netherlands, 1988-91. Co-author: Fundamentals of Steelmaking Metallurgy, 1993; contbr. articles to profl. jours. Avocations: music, sports, hiking in Himalayas. Office: Indian Inst Technology, Dept Materials/Metallurgy, Kanpur 208016, India

DEO, SUDHA SHRIKANT, immunologist, researcher; b. Kalyan, India, Dec. 29, 1954; d. Ramchandra Pralhad and Sushila Ramchandra Ghogale; m. Shrikant Vaman Deo; 1 child, Swanand Shrikant. BSc with honors, St. Xavier's Coll., Mumbai, India, 1976; MSc, Haffkine & Cancer Rsch. Inst., Mumbai, 1984; postgrad., Seth Gordhandas Sundardas Med. Coll., Mumbai, 1994-99. Rsch. asst., Lady Tata fellow Cancer Rsch. Inst., Mumbai, 1977-

80, 80-83; sr. sci. officer B.J. Wadia Hosp., Mumbai, 1984—. Contbr. articles to profl. jours. Avocations: painting, classical music, embroidery, games, reading. Office: Bai Jerbai Wadia Hosp, Parel, Mumbai 400 012, India

DE OLAZABAL, EUGENIA, commercial photographer; b. Mexico City, Sept. 4, 1940; d. Rendón Victor and Eulalia (Orendain) De O.; m. Alejandro Olazabal, Apr. 24, 1964; children: Ximena, Alejandro. Diploma in photography, Iberoamericana U., Mexico City. Recipient Ariel award for Best Documentary of Yr., Mex., 1975, Excellence award for Best Ednl. T.V. series, 1985. Avocations: cinema, museums, concerts, art.

DE OLIVEIRA, JOÃO SERPA, retired biology educator; b. Bom Sucesso, Brazil, Oct. 26, 1926; s. Modesto and Carmelita Luiza (Do Nascimento) De O.; m. Maria Luiza Gomes, July 9, 1974 (dec. 1987); children: Susan Joyce, Hermann John. Acct., Academia Comercio, 1947; biologist, Univ Fed Minas Gerais, 1960, sanitary engring., 1961, lic. Nat. History, 1962. Acct. Instituto Nacional de Previdencia Social, Belo Horizonte, Brazil, 1953-78; prof. Colé Estadual M. Gerais, Belo Horizonte, 1968-73; rep. Ind. Comp. Neo Life Amazônia Ltda., Belo Horizonte, 1982-86. Contbr. articles to profl. jours. Mem. The Planetary Soc., Internat. Ozone Assn. (colaborator, rep.), Internat. Assn. on Water Pollution Rsch. and Control (rep. ind. comp.). Avocations: music, astronomy, writing. Home: R Fernando Magalhaes Gomes, 225-Itapoa, 31710250 Belo Horizonte Brazil

DE OLIVEIRA MACIEL, MARCO ANTONIO, Brazilian vice president; b. 1940; married; 3 children. BA in Juridical and Social Scis., Catholic U., Pernabuco, Brazil. Pres. Pernambuco Union of Students, 1962; fed. dep., 1966; pres. Chamber of Deps., 1977-79; gov. Pernambuco, 1979-82; PDS Senator, 1982, 90, min. of edn., 1994; now v.p. Govt. of Brazil, Andar. Office: Palacio Planalto, Prado Tres Poderes, 70150900 Andar Sala 129, Brazil*

DE ORLEANS-BORBON, ALVARO JAIME, investment company executive; b. Rome, Mar. 1, 1947; arrived in Monaco, 1980; s. Alvaro and Carla (Parodi-Delfino) De Orleans-Borbon; m. Giovanna San Martino, May 22, 1974; children: Pilar, Andres, Alois. B.Elec. Engring., Rome U., 1974. Cert. engr., Italy. With SMAE Spa, Rome, 1973-82; self-employed Monte Carlo, Monaco, 1982—; v.p. Torrebreva S.A., Sanlucar, Spain, 1982—; bd. dirs. Agregados Livianos C.A., Caracas, Venezuela; mem. exec. com. Fundación COTEC para Innovación Technólogica, Madrid, 1993—. Decorated Civil White Cross, 1st class, Spanish Air Force, Madrid, 1980. Mem. Royal Aero Club of Spain (1st v.p. 1993—), Internat. Aeronautic Fedn. (v.p. 1995—). Roman Catholic. Avocation: competitive gliding.

DEOUL, KATHLEEN BOARDSEN, executive; b. New London, Conn., May 5, 1944; d. Harry Kostrope Boardsen and Elizabeth (Conti) Dunham; m. Barry Melvyn Davis, May 21, 1966 (div. Jan. 1977), m. Neal Deoul, June 20, 1982; 1 child, Shannon Rae. Grad. high sch., New London, Conn. Br. mgr. Qwip Systems (divsn. Exxon), Balt.; br. ops. mgr. Exxon Office Systems, Pitts., 1977-82; owner, pres. Bus. Quars., Crystal City, Va., 1983-95, Wellness Alternatives, Balt., 1993—. Mem. adv. bd. Network Mktg. Lifestyles Mag.; mem. Team Diamond; co-chair chmn. Found. for Alternative Cancer Treatments. Mem. President's Club Exxon, President's Club Nikken, Inc. (Distbr. of Yr. 1999-00). Avocations: venture capitalist, travel, writing, interior decorating, public speaking.

DEOUL, NEAL, electronics company executive; b. N.Y.C., Feb. 27, 1931; s. George and Pearl (Hirschfield) D.; m. Bernice Kradel, Dec. 25, 1955 (div.); children: Cara Jan, Stefani Neva, Evan Craig; m. Kathleen B. Davis, June 20, 1982; 1 child, Shannon Rae. BS in Physics, CCNY, 1952; JD, Bklyn. Law Sch., 1959. Bar: N.Y. 1960. Engr. Signal Corps., U.S. Army, Evans Signal Lab., Belmar, N.J., 1952-55, Airborne Instruments Lab., Deer Park, N.Y., 1955-56; sales mgr. FXR, Inc., Woodside, L.I., 1956-60; pres. Microwave Dynamics Corp., Plainview, L.I., 1960-61, Paradynamics, Inc., Huntington Station, N.Y., 1961-64; mgr. Servo Corp. Am., Hicksville, N.Y., 1964-66; v.p. Trio Labs., Inc., Plainview, 1966-69; exec. v.p. Microlab/FXR, Livingston, N.J., 1969-74; pres. Neal Deoul Assocs., Balt., 1974—. Chmn. Found. for Alternative Cancer Treatments, Balt., 2000—. Mem. IEEE (sr.), N.Y. State Bar Assn., Md. Bar Assn., Young Pres.'s Orgn., Profl. Group Engring. Mgmt., Am. Arbitration Assn. Home and Office: 2 Bellchase Ct Baltimore MD 21208-1300

DEOULINE, EUGENY ALEXEEVITCH, engineer, educator; b. Moscow, Russia, July 9, 1938; s. Alexey Konstantinovitch and Sophia Nikolaevna (Golubkova) D.; m. Violetta Alexeevna Stakchanova, Feb. 23, 1963; 1 child, Natalia Machurova. Degree in engring., Bauman Moscow Tech. U., 1962, DSc, 1971, PhD, 1988. Engr. Engring. Plant, Moscow, 1962-64; lectr. asst. Bauman Moscow Tech. U., 1964-70, docent, 1970-98, dep. prof., 1988-90, prof., 1990—, supr. student sci. bur., 1977—. Contbr. articles to profl. jours. including Applied Surface Sci., Surface Sci.; patentee in field. Recipient dance prize Moscow Adult Championships, 1996, 98, medal 850th Ann. Moscow, 1997. Mem. Russian Vacuum Soc. (adv. coun. 1994-99), Am. Vaccum Soc., Moscow Figure Skating Club. E-mail: deulin@nuk-mt.bmstu.ru. Office: Bauman Moscow Tech U, 2d Baumanskaya 5, 107005 Moscow Russia

DE PABLO, LUIS, composer; b. Bilbao, Spain, Jan. 28, 1930; s. Seravín and Victoria (Costales) De P.; m. Marta Cárdenas, Apr. 7, 1975. Student, U. Madrid, 1952; D Honorus Causa, U. Complutense Madrid, 1996. Founder Tiempo y Musica, 1959; pres. Spanish Juenesses Musicales; mem. jury various competitions at Amiens, Siena, others. Composer numerous orchestral and instrumental works, including Monos y liebres for brass clarinet and marinba, Flessuoso string quartet, Relampagos for tenor and orch., concerto for violin and orch., Retratos y transcripciones for piano, Trimalchio for bassoon and horn, quintet for clarinte and strings, concerto for guitar and chamber orch., 4 operas; works commissioned by Festivals of Royan, Darmstadt, Palermo, Donaueschingen, Zagreb, Shiraz, Norddeutscher Rundfunk, Bremen, Radio France, Radio Limoges, Found. Gulbenkian, City of Munich, J. March Found., Goethe Inst., Radio Nacional de España, Orquesta Nacional de España, Montecarlo Orch, City of Bonn, U. Ottawa, others; contbr. articles to profl. jours., books. Address: Relatores 22 5, 28012 Madrid Spain

DE PÁDUA, FERNANDO PARAISO, cardiology educator, internist; b. Faro, Algarve, Portugal, May 29, 1927; s. Carlos Paraiso and Irene Archer (Moreira) De P.; m. Maria Mauela Vieira Pinto, June 2, 1952; children: Josè Manuel, Fernando Manuel, João Manuel Pinto. Grad. in Medicine, U. Lisbon, Portugal, 1950; grad. student in Cardiology, Harvard U., Boston, 1952-53; specialist in Cardiology, Med. Assn., Lisbon, 1954; PhD, U. Lisbon, 1959. Intern Univ. Hosps. St. Marta, Lisbon, 1950-53; asst instr. U. Hosp. St. Maria, Lisbon, 1952-59, asst. prof., 1959-63, assoc. prof., 1963-67, dir. dept. medicine, 1964; full prof. internal medicine, 1967, full prof. cardiology, 1988, pres. sci. coun. faculty of medicine, 1989-91, dean faculty of medicine, 1991-97, ret., 1997; dir. Ctr. Studies of Preventive Cardiology, Lisbon, 1976-88, Nat. Inst. Preventive Cardiology, Lisbon, 1986—; pres. Portugese Heart Found., Lisbon, 1979-87. Editor: Electrocardiology New Frontier, 1980, Update, 1992; author and editor: Cindi-Portugal 2nd Quinquenium, 1994, Cindi Portugal 3rd Quinquenium, 1998; dir. Rev. Portugese Terapeutica Medica, 1967, Rev. Portugese Clin. Terapeutics, 1972. Lt. Portugese Army Med. Forces 1951-52. Named Hon. Pres. Soc. Cardiology, 1983, Hon. Mem. Soc. Rheumatology, 1991, Hon. Pres. Portuguese Heart Found., 1994; recipient Gold medal Min. Health. Fellow European Heart Assn., Internat. Soc. and Fedn. Cardiology-Epidemiology and Prevention; mem. Cindi-European WHO Program, Acad. Medicine, Portugese Soc. Cardiology (pres. 1977-80), Internat. Coun. Cardiology (bd. dirs., pres. 1992-94), Internat. Soc. Electrocardiology (founder). Achievements include leadership in nat. fight against hypertension and stroke and in countrywide integrated non-communicable diseases intervention program (Cindi-Euro-WHO), founding of World Movement Heart and Health in Portugese in 1995. Home: R Das Amoreiras 72-E-4 DTO, 1250-024 Lisbon Portugal Office: Ave Fontes Pereira de Melo 35-2C, 1050-118 Lisbon Portugal

DE PALACIO DEL VALLE-LERSUNDI, LOYOLA, government official; b. Madrid, Sept. 16, 1950. Degree in law, Complutense U., Madrid. Founder, pres. Popular Group party, 1983-86; mem. Coun. Europe, 1987-90; dep. chmn. Popular Group Parliament, 1989-86; senator Sergovia Spanish Parliament, 1986-89, nat. mem., 1989-99, min. agriculture, fishing and food, 1996-99; v.p., commr. transport, energy and rels. European Commn., 1999—; mem. Coun. Europe, 1987-90; asst. spokeswoman Popular Group. Avocations: sailing, skiing, fishing, music. Office: European Commn, Rue de la Loi 200, B-1049 Brussels Belgium

DEPAN, MARY ELIZABETH, civic volunteer, nurse; b. Boston, Oct. 5, 1927; d. Frank and Josephine Madeline (Lennon) Natter; m. Harry McCarthy Depan, Apr. 26, 1952 (div. Aug. 1981); children: Harry, Madeline, Mark, Andrew. Student, Notre Dame Acad., 1945; diploma in nursing, St. Elizabeth Hosp., Boston, 1948; student, Skidmore Coll., 1960—. RN, Mass. Oper. rm. supr. Gt. Lake Naval Sta., Chgo., 1949; staff nurse Beth Israel Hosp., Boston, 1949. Monitor, leader Gt. Books Found., Glens Falls, N.Y., 1960—, Adirondack C.C., Glens Falls, 1960—; vol., bd. dirs. Literacy Vols., Glens Falls, 1983—; vol. nurse ARC, Glens Falls, 1985—; active area sr. citizen's orgn., 1992—. Lt. (j.g.) USN, 1949-52. Recipient cert. for porcelain painting, 1991. Mem. Women in Arts (chartered), Porcelain Artists, Nat. Mus. Women in the Arts (charter), Women's Meml. (charter). Roman Catholic. Avocations: painting, travel, museums, volunteering. Home: 43 Quade St Glens Falls NY 12801-2706

DEPANGHER, MICHAEL LEON, accountant; b. Sydney, NSW, Australia, Apr. 9, 1960; s. Leo and Mary Louise (Carnovale) D.; m. Amanda Kathleen Nesbitt, Dec. 10, 1983; children: Jacqueline Kathleen, Nathan Michael. B in Econs., Macquarie U., Sydney, Australia, 1985; MBA, U. NSW, Sydney, Australia, 1998. Assoc. Chartered Acct., Australia. Auditor KPMG Peat Marwick, Sydney, 1985-88; adminstrn. mgr. MLC Investments, Ltd., Sydney, 1988-94; chief acct. MLC Ltd., Sydney, 1994-95; gen. mgr. adminstrn. MLC Investments Ltd., Sydney, 1995-96; relationship mgr. MLC Ltd., Sydney, 1996-98, bus. devel. and projects mgr., 1998—; project mgr. Three Sixty Ltd., 1998—. Hon. treas. Muscular Dystrophy Assn. NSW, Sydney, 1999. Home: 66 Provincial Rd, Lindfield, Sydney NSW 2070, Australia Office: MLC Ltd, 105-153 Miller St, Sydney NSW 2060, Australia

DEPAOLO, ROSEMARY, college dean, university president; b. Bklyn., July 17, 1947; d. Nunzio and Edith (Spano) DeP.; m. Dennis B. Smith, 1977 (div. 1983); m. T. Frederick Wharton, 1984. BA, CUNY, Flushing, 1970; MA, Rutgers U., 1974, PhD, 1979. Asst. prof. to prof., dir. Ctr. for Humanities Augusta (Ga.) Coll., 1975-90; asst. dean Coll. Arts and Sci. Ga. So. U., Statesboro, 1990-93; dean Coll. Arts and Scis. Western Carolina U., Cullowhee, N.C., 1993-97; pres. Ga. Coll. and State U., Milledgeville, 1997—. Office: Ga Coll and State U CBX 020 Milledgeville GA 31061*

DEPARDIEU, GÉRARD, actor; b. Dec. 27, 1948; s. Renè and Alice (Marillier) D.; m. Elisabeth Guignot, Apr. 11, 1970; children: Guillaume, Julie. Ed. Ecole Communale, Cours d'art Dramatique de Charles Dullin, Ecole d'art Dramatique de Jean Laurent Cochet. Pres. jury Cannes (France) Internat. Film Festival, 1992. Performances include: (theatre) Les Garcons De La Bande (Jean-Laurent Cochet), 1968-69, Une Fille Dans Ma Soupe (Terence Frisby), 1970, Galapagos (Jean Chatenet), 1971, Saved (Edouard Bond), 1972, Home (David Storey), 1972, Isme (Nathalie Sarraute), 1973, Isaac (Manuel Puig), 1973, La Chevauchee Sur Le Lac De Constance (Peter Handke), 1974, Les Gens Deraisonnables Sont En Voie De Disparition (Handke), 1977, Les Insenses Sont En Voie d'Extinction, 1978, Tartuffe (Molière), 1983; (musical comedy) Lily Passion (Barbara), 1986, Les Portes Du Ciel, 1999; (feature films) Le Beatnik Et Le Minet, 1965, Nathalie Granger, 1971, Le Cri Du Cormoran Le Soir Au Dessus Des Jonques, 1971, Le Tueur, 1971, L'Affaire Dominici, 1972, Un Peu De Soleil Dans L'Eau Froide, 1972, Au Rendez-Vous De La Mort Joyeuse, 1972, La Scoumoune, 1972, Deux Hommes Dan La Ville, 1972, Le Viager, 1972, Rude Journee Pour La Reine, 1973, Les Gaspards, 1973, Les Valseuses, 1973, Stavisky, 1973, Vincent Francois, Paul Et Les Autres, 1974, Pas Si Mechant Que Ca, 1974, 1900, 1975, Maitresse, 1975, La Dernière Femme, 1975, Sept. Morts Sur Ordonnance, 1975, Barocco, 1976, Renè La Canne, 1976, Baxter, Verra Baxter, 1976, Dites-Lui Que Je L'Aime, 1977, Le Camion, 1977, La Nuit Tous Les Chats Sont Gris, 1977, Preparez Vos Mouchoirs, 1977, Rê De Singe, 1977, Le Sucre, 1978, Les Chiens, 1978, Le Grand Embouteillage, 1978, Loulou, 1979, Mon Oncle D'Amerique, 1979 (spl. prize of the Cannes Festival, prize of French Cinema), Le Dernier Metro, 1980 (Cesar award for Best Actor, France 1981), Je Vous Aime, 1980, Inspect. Decorated chevalier Order of Merit (France); recipient Gérard Philipe Grand prize, 1973, Fellowship award Brit. Film Inst., 1989; named Best Fgn. Actor 1980-90, Am. Critics Assn., 1990. Office: care CAA 9830 Wilshire Blvd Beverly Hills CA 90212-1804

DE PAULA DIAZ, ANDES JULIAO DAVID, Telecommunications executive, consultant; b. Havana, Cuba, May 5, 1968; arrived in Sweden, 1973.; s. Anacleto Juliao and Lourdes Jane Jonsson (Diaz) D. Coll. of Katedralskolan, Uppsala, Sweden, 1987; MS, Polytechnic U. of Valencia, Spain, 1993-94, Linköping Inst. Tech., Sweden, 1994. Market rschr. IBM, Stockholm, 1993; area mgr. Ericsson Radio Syss., Stockholm, 1994-96; sales and mktg. mgr. Ericsson Telecom., Sao Paulo, Brazil, 1987-98; gen. mgr. Netcom Conss. of Brazil, Sao Paulo, 1998-99; sales and mktg. dir. Netcom Conss. USA, Miami, Fla., 1999; coord., mem. exec. com. Group Ops. Ericsson Latin Am., Stockholm, 1994-95; bd. mem. Ericsson Mercosur Alliance, Sao Paulo, 1997-98. Editor Facts and News, 1994-95. 2d Lt., Swedish Army, 1988-89. Erasmus scholar, 1993. Avocations: golf, scuba diving, foreign languages. Home: 6767 Collins Ave Apt 2009 Miami FL 33141-3268

DE PAUW, DANIELLA AUGUSTA, company executive; b. Leuven, Brabant, Belgium, July 16, 1956; arrived in South Africa, 1982; d. Filecien De Pauw. Bus. mgmt. diploma, Damelin Bus. Sch., South Africa, 1989, fin. mgmt. diploma, 1995; nat. diploma in freigh forwarding, South African Assn. Forwarders, 1996. Mng. dir. Pro Freight Aircargo, Johannesburg, South Africa, 1987-96, AEI, Johannesburg, South Africa, 1996-99, Danzas AEI So. Africa Party Ltd., Gauteng, South Africa, 1999—. Mem. Toastmasters. Avocations: horse riding, reading. Office: Danzas AEI SA Pty Ltd, Box 558 Kempton Pk, Gauteng 1620, South Africa

DE PAUW, GOMMAR ALBERT, priest, educator; b. Stekene, Belgium, Oct. 11, 1918; came to U.S., 1949, naturalized, 1955; s. Desiré and Anna (Van Overloop) De P. Diplomate Classical Humanities, Coll. St. Nicholas, Belgium, 1936; JCB, U. Louvain, 1943, JCL, 1945; Juris Canonici Dr., Catholic U. Am., 1953. Ordained priest Roman Cath. Ch., 1942. Parish priest, chaplain Cath. Social Action, Ghent, Belgium, 1945-49, N.Y.C., 1949-52; successively prof. moral and fundamental dogmatic theology and canon law sem. div., assoc. prof. philosophy coll. div. Mt. St. Mary's Coll., Emmitsburg, Md., 1952-65, dean studies maj. sem. div., 1954-64, mem. council adminstrn., 1957-65; Theol. adviser II Vatican Ecumenical Council, 1962-65; founder-pres. Cath. Traditionalist Movement, Inc., 1964—. Author: The Educational Rights of the Church, 1953, The Rebel Priest, 1955, The Traditional Roman Catholic Mass, 1977, Bishops on War and Peace, 1983, The Traditional Requiem Mass, 1989, The Challenge of Peace Through Strength, 1989, Keep The Faith-Reagan Dicta, 2000; co-author: New Catholic Ency.; Dictionary of the Bible, Ephemerides Theologicae Lovanienses; editor: Sounds of Truth and Tradition, Quote... Unquote; producer Latin radio mass, various religious phonograph records, audio and video cassettes. With Belgian Army inf. M.C., 1939-45, World War II Resistance and Free Polish Forces. Decorated Honor Cross (Free Polish Forces); recipient Achievement Citation, U.S. Army. Mem. AAUP, Internat. Platform Assn., Cath. Theol. Soc., Am. Canon Law Soc. Am., Am. Security Coun., Am. Cath. Philos. Assn., Nat. Cath. Ednl. Assn., Univ. Prof. for Acad. Order. Fax: 516-333-7535. Home and Office: Cath Traditionalist Movement 210 Maple Ave Westbury NY 11590-3117

DEPAUW, HUGO HENDRIK, scientific researcher; b. Antwerpen, Belgium, Apr. 12, 1955; s. Alfons Jozef and Godelieve Maria (Van Heysbroeck) D.; m. Rejane Bezerra Chaves, Aug. 4, 1994; 1 child, Veerle. MSc, U. Antwerp, 1978, PhD, 1988. Scientific researcher in biochemistry & teaching U. Antwerp, Antwerp, Belgium, 1981-88, 97-99; researcher in biochemistry U. Leuven, Leuven, Belgium, 1988-89; head control lab. svc., environ. Belgoprocess, Dessel, Belgium, 1989-95; tchr. chemistry and biology Antwerp, Belgium, 1996-97, 99-00. Contbr. articles to profl. jours. With Med. unit Belgian mil. svc., 1980-81, Germany. Mem. Belgian Biochemistry Soc., Vlaamse Milieu Deskundigen, Flanders Computer Club. Avocations: languages, science, jogging, squash, dancing. Home: Thibautstraat 116, Antwerp 2100, Belgium

DE PETRO, THOMAS GERARD, librarian, educator; b. Omaha, Oct. 16, 1954; s. Alfred Salvatore and LaVaughn (Jewell) D.P. BA, U. Colo., 1978; MLS, U. Tex., 1985. Libr. I Jefferson County Pub. Libr., Lakewood, Colo., 1979-84; teaching asst. U. Tex., Austin, 1985; libr. II Houston Pub. Libr., 1985-88; libr. NASA Johnson Space Ctr., Houston, 1988-89; engring. libr. Wichita State U., 1990-98, Tex. A&M, 1999—. Mem. Am. Soc. for Engring. Edn., ALA, Spl. Librs. Assn. Avocations: swimming, running, short-wave radio, foreign languages. Office: Tex A&m U College Station TX 77843-0001

DEPEYROT, MICHEL YVES-LOUIS, engineering company executive; b. Montauban, Tarn & Garonne, France, Aug. 19, 1940; s. Olivier Louis and Marthe (Favant) D.; m. Laura Chapman, June 22, 1967; children: Gilles, Thierry, Alexa, Joelle, Valerie. Degree in engring., Ecole Sup. d'Electricite, Paris, 1963; PhD, Stanford U., 1968; doctorate, U. Grenoble, France, 1976. Dir. research Centre Automatique Ensmp, Fontainebleau, France, 1968-70; product mgr. CII, Louveciennes, France, 1971-74; mgr. engring. DEC, Maynard, Mass., 1975-80; v.p. engring. Thomson-EFCIS, Grenoble, France, 1981-85; chmn., pres. Dolphin Integration S.A., Meylan, France, 1985—; mgr. Dolphin Delegation, Meylan, France, 1996—, Dolphin Integration GmbH, Duisburg, Germany, 1997—; research dir. INRIA, Rocouencourt, France, 1971-76. Author: Automata and Control Science, 1974. Served as capt. with French Navy, 1963-65. Roman Catholic. Clubs: Horseback Riding, CHA (Grenoble). Home: Fontclaire, 22 Rte de Chartreuse, 38700 Corenc-le-Haut La Tronche, France Office: Dolphin Integration SA, Zirst/8 Chemin Des Clos, Meylan France 38242

DE PFYFFER, ANDRE, lawyer; b. Lucerne, Switzerland, Nov. 3, 1928; s. Leodegar and Anna (Carvalho) de P.; children by previous marriage: Corinne, Francois; m. Francoise Garnier del Campo, 1983. Baccalaureat, U. Berne, 1947; postgrad. U. Geneva, 1947-50, 54. Admitted to Geneva Lawyers Assn., 1952, since practiced in Geneva; sr. ptnr. firm de Pfyffer & Assocs.; dir. Volvo Suisse S.A., Banque Paribas (Suisse) S.A.; vice chmn. Pargesa Holding, S.A.; past consul gen. of Sweden in Geneva. Decorated Commdr. Royal Order of the Polar Star (Sweden). Mem. Internat. Law Assn., Circle de la Terrasse. Home: 6 Rue Eynard, Geneva Switzerland Office: 6 Rue Bellot, Geneva Switzerland

DEPONDT, JOËL PIERRE DENIS, surgeon, educator; b. Paris, May 8, 1956; s. Claude Depondt and Christiane Pieyre; m. Martine Gadet, Sept. 14, 1985; 1 child, Claire. MD, Unité d'Enseignement et de Recherche X Bichat, Paris, 1987; MPhil in Biology, U. Paris VII, 1992, PhD, 2000. Intern Assistance Publique-Hosp., Paris, 1980-87; asst. prof. Bichat Hosp., Paris, 1987-90, assoc. prof., 1990—. Contbr. articles to profl. jours. Mem. French Soc. Head and Neck Plastic Surgery, French Soc. ENT-Head Neck Surgery, French Soc. Head Neck Oncology. Roman Catholic. Avocations: aviation, judo, scuba diving. Home: 55 Rue Gannerron, 75018 Paris France Office: Bichat Hosp-Head/Neck Surg, 46 Rue H Huchard, 75018 Paris France

DE PONTBRIAND, GAEL JEAN, international consultant; b. Deauville, Calvados, France, June 30, 1947; s. Romuald and Ghislaine (de Montmagner) du Breil de Pontbriand; m. Evelyne Bazin de Jessey, May 19, 1973; children: Isaure, Gersende, Romuald, Aymeric. BA, MA in Econ., M in Bus. Law, U. Paris, 1970, 72, 73; M in Polit. Sci., Inst D'Etudes Politiques Paris, 1971; MBA, U. Pa., 1974; Doctoral degree, U. Paris, Dauphine, 1975. Dep. gen. mgr. Continental Ill. Nat. Bank and Trust Co. of Chgo., Frankfurt, Fed. Republic Germany, 1982-84; gen. mgr. Continental Ill. Nat. Bank and Trust Co. of Chgo., Frankfurt, 1984-85; gen. mgr. for France Continental Ill. Nat. Bank and Trust Co. of Chgo., Paris, 1985-88; ptnr. Coopers & Lybrand Corp. Fin. SA, Paris, 1988—, also bd. dirs.; bd. dirs. Pricewaterhouse Coopers Corp. Fin. S.A., Branics S.A., Grouse SNEF S.A. Mem. Assn. of Fgn. Banks in Germany (founding mem., v.p. 1983-85), French Assn. Bank Controllers, French Assn. Bank Gen. Mgrs., Assn. Fin. Profls., Soc. of Econ., Assn. de la Nobelesse Francaise (Paris), Olympus Club (rep.), Vieilles Maisons Francaises Assn. (Paris). Home: Domaine du Closel, 49170 Savennieres France Office: PricewaterhouseCoopers, 15 rue Beaujon, 75008 Paris France

DE POORTER, PIERRE-EMMANUEL, technology executive; b. Roeselare, Belgium, Dec. 21, 1919. Engr., ECAM, Lyon, France, 1942. Engring. tech. dir. Damman-Croes Roeselare, Belgium, 1942-56, gen. mgr., 1956—; cons. engr. in field. Advisor to Minister of Fgn. Bus., Brussels, 1978-81, 81-84, 84-87, 87-90, 90-93, 93-96, 96-99. Mem. JAOC, Lions. Roman Catholic. Home: 16 ave F Verbiest, 2650 Antwerp-Edegem Belgium Office: Damon Croes SA, Spanjestreet 51, 8800 Roeselare Belgium also: Damman-Cades St, T6 Ave F Verbiest, 2650 Edegem-Antwerp Belgium

DE POURTALÈS, CHRISTIAN HUBERT, banker; b. Paris, Oct. 18, 1928; s. Max Arthur and Andy Elsy (de Luze) de P.; m. Caroline Sophie Hottinguer, July 1, 1957 (div. May 1986); children: Laure, Max Paul; m. Karin Ehrenfeuchter, Dec. 18, 1993; 1 child, Frédéric. BA in Philosophie, U. Paris, 1946. CPA, France. With Bank NSM, Paris, 1949—, ptnr., 1958—, v.p., 1968-80, ins. gen., 1980—; bd. dirs. NSMART, Placement Capitalisation, Paris, Placement Ct. Terme Premiere, Gestion Mobilière, von der Heydt & Co., Germany, Delbrück & Co., Germany. Served to capt. French Mil., 1948. Huguenot. Avocations: parks and gardens. Home: 34 bd Maillot, 92200 Neuilly-sur-Seine France also: Chateau de Martinvast, Martinvast 50690, France Office: NSM, 3 Ave Hoche, 75410 Paris Cedex 08, France

DE POUZILHAC, ALAIN DUPLESSIS, advertising executive; b. Sete, Herault, France, June 11, 1945; s. Pierre and Jeanine (Caffarel) de P.; m. Carole de Pouzilhac, Sept. 6, 1969; children: Edouard, Cedric, Philippine. Asst. advt. mgr. Publicis, Paris, 1968; advt mgr. DDB, Paris, 1968-75; exec. v.p. Havas Conseil, Neuilly, France, 1976-82, chmn., CEO, 1982-87; chmn., CEO HDM, Neuilly and Puteaux, France, 1987-89; chmn., CEO Eurocom, Neuilly, 1989—, CEO, 1989—; chmn., CEO EURO RSCG, Neuilly, 1991—, Havas Advt., 1996—. Avocations: soccer, rugby. Home: 21 rue de Miromesnil, 75008 Paris France Office: Havas Advt, 84 rue de Villiers, 92683 Levallois-Perret France

DEPPE, HANS-ULRICH, medical sociology educator, researcher; b. Frankfurt am Main, Germany, 1939. Author: Kranheit ist ohne Politik nicht heilbar, 1987, Soziale Verantwortung and Transformation von Gesundheitssystemen, 1996, Zur zozialen Anatomie des Gesundheitssystems, 2000; editor: Vernachlässigte Gesundheit, 1980. Mem. Internat. Assn. Health Policy (pres. 1992-94). Office: Universitätsklinikum, 7 Theodor-Stern-Kai, D-60590 Frankfurt a M Germany

DEPPISCH, PAUL VINCENT, data communications executive; b. Madison, Wis., Dec. 15, 1950; s. Vincent Francis and Evelyn Catherine (Eichmeier) D. Cable splicing foreman GTE Calif., Santa Monica, 1968-73; gen. foreman DataCom Inc., Santa Monica, 1973-78; sr. project mgr. A.I.D.C.O., North Hollywood, Calif., 1978-84; cons. Systex Group Ltd., Phoenix, 1984-90; pres. Ambient Data Tech. Inc., Upland, Calif., 1990—; founder, dir. Boogere Prodns. Internat., Santa Monica, 1973—; bd. dirs. Systex Group Ltd. Min. Universal Life Ch., Modesto, Calif. Mem. Bldg. Industry Cons. Svc., Inc., C. of C., L.A. World Affairs Coun. Avocations: hunting, fishing, community service. Home: PO Box 1712 Santa Monica CA 90406-1712 Office: Ambient Data Tech Inc 517 N Mountain Ave # 101 Upland CA 91786-5016

DE PRET, LODE JEAN-CLAUDE, engineering association executive, diplomat; b. Antwerp, Belgium, July 3, 1944; s. Roger H.G. and Laurentine J.C. (Cools) de P.; m. Viviane W.J. Lambregts, Mar. 6, 1974. Lic. pilot, Sotramat Aviation Acad., Belgium, 1964; student, Fgn. and Commonwealth Office, London, 1980. Lic. pilot FAA, 1969, Govt. of Nigeria, 1970. Airline capt. Cogeair, Kinshasa, Zaire, 1971-72; pilot sales mgr. ASPE SA, Gosselies, Belgium, 1973-75; head avionics divsn. SAI Electronics, Antwerp, Belgium, 1975-78; diplomatic officer Brit. Diplomatic Mission, Brussels, 1979-91, Luxembourg, 1989-91; v.p. Flemish Engrs. Assn. VIK, Hasselt,

Belgium, 1982—; mem. coun. Brit. Govt. Electronic Components Task Force, London, 1989-91; dir. external rels. Svc. Group for Offsets, Hasselt, 1992-97; amb., plenipotentiary head diplomatic representation Seborga to European Instns., 2000. Author market reports to books for Dept. of Trade, London, 1981, 89, 90, evaluation study for Belgian aeronautical industry fedn., 1996; contb. articles to profl. publs. Fellow white paper com. on offsets Vlerick Sch., U. Ghent, Belgium, 1992-93, Armed Forces Comms. and Electronics Assn., 1987-91. Office: VIK, Kunstlaan 16, 3500 Hasselt Belgium also: Rep de Seborga, 23 Val Des Seigneurs Bte 10, B-1150 Brussels Belgium

DEPREZ, GENE EDWARD, management consultant; b. Rochester, N.Y., Jan. 31, 1940; s. Jean Victor and Eleanor (Winnek) DeP.; m. Patricia Louise Donahue, June 23, 1962; children: Michel Jean, Therèsé Marie. BFA in Communications, Rochester Inst. Tech., 1962, MFA in Communications, 1968; postgrad. in community devel., pub. policy formation, Syracuse U., 1972-74. Head instl. resources Rochester (N.Y.) Inst. Tech., 1962-65, dir. communications, 1971-78; producer/dir., asst. to gen. mgr. Eastman Kodak Co. Market Edn. Ctr., Rochester, 1965-70; dir. communications Rochester Mus. and Sci. Ctr., 1970-71; pres., chief exec. officer Urbanarium, Inc., Rochester, 1978-82; mng. ptnr. Concept Ventures, Rochester, 1982-84; pres., chief exec. officer Partnerships Data Net, Inc., Washington, 1984-87; v.p. PHH Fantus Corp., N.Y.C., 1987-90, v.p., prin., mem. exec. com., 1990-94; founding ptnrr. Location Adv. Svcs., Inc., Morristown, N.J., 1993-94; prin. Fluor Daniel Consulting Global Location Strategies, Florham Park, N.J., 1995-97; nat. dir. Global Location Strategies Pricewaterhouse Coopers LLP, N.Y.C., 1997—; chmn. strategic planning HMO, 1981-82; vis. lectr. grad. comm. program Rochester Ins. Tech., 1983-84; mem. cmty. and pub. issues coun. Conf. Bd. Co-host Real to Reel TV News mag., 1981-82. Mem. exec. com. Arts for Greater Rochester, 1980-84; chmn., dir. Rochester Internat. Film Festival, 1972; chmn. exec. com. Rochester City Charter Commn., 1974-77; bd. dirs., sec. Genesee Hosp. Health Svc., Rochester, 1975-80; bd. govs. Park Avenue Found. and Club, Florham Park, 1993—. Recipient gold award N.Y.C. Internat. Film and TV Festival. Mem. Nat. Coun. for Urban Econ. Devel. (bd. dirs. 1996—, com.), Am. Soc. Assn. Execs., Pub. Rels. Soc. Am. (exec. com. Rochester 1980-84), Rochester-Monroe County Bar Assn. (chmn. long-range planning retreat 1982-83), Urban Land Ins., Nat. Civic League (all-Am. city selection com.), Internat. Assn. Mgmt. Cons., Internat. Strategic Leadership Forum, Internat. Assn. Corp. Real Estate Execs. (chpt. officer 1997—), Lake Mohawk (N.J.) Country Club (trustee 1990—, pres. 1997—), Rotary (bd. dirs. Rochester 1978-80). Democrat. Roman Catholic. Avocations: travel, photography, bicycling, cross country skiing. Home: 14 Oakwood Trl Sparta NJ 07871-1502 Office: Pricewaterhouse Coopers LLP 1177 Avenue of Americas New York NY 10036

DEPRIEST, C(HARLES) DAVID, engineering executive, retired air force officer; b. Mount Pleasant, Pa., Oct. 18, 1938; s. Charles Leonard and Elizabeth Carolyn (Hoover) DeP.; m. Blanca Reinoso Rivas, July 1, 1960 (div.); children: Lisa Lynn, Diane Krystie, David Eric. BSEE with distinction, Air Force Inst. Tech., 1974, MS in Electro-Optics, 1975. Cert. profl. logistician. Enlisted USAF, 1959, advanced through grades to col., 1984; squadron navigator USAF, Beale AFB, Calif., 1964-68; squadron radar navigator, wing flight examiner USAF, Wright-Patterson AFB, Ohio, 1968-72; chief missile guidance br. USAF armament lab., Eglin AFB, Fla., 1975-79; program element monitor, dep. chief, avionics & armament divsn. air staff HQ USAF, Washington, 1979-83; chief engring. material mgmt. directorate Warner-Robins ALC, Ga., 1984-86; dir. intercommand electronic warfare aero. systems divsn. Wright-Patterson AFB, 1986-88; dir. plans and ops. AF electronic combat office USAF, Wright-Patterson AFB, 1988-91; ret., 1991; mgr. Warner Robins applications dept. The Analytic Scis. Corp., Inc., Warner Robins, Ga., 1992-97; pres. DePriest Assocs., Inc., Warner Robins, 1997—. Decorated DFC, Legion of Merit, Air medal with silver oak leaf cluster, Meritorious Svc. medal with two bronze oak leaf clusters. Mem. IEEE (sr.), Air Force Assn., Assn. Old Crows, Rotary, Mensa, Tau Beta Pi. Office: DePriest Assocs Inc 805 Park Dr Warner Robins GA 31088-5174

DEPRIMO, GAETANO MANFRED, math educator; b. Weiden, Germany, July 19, 1948; s. Joseph Gaetano and Erna DeP. AB in Math., U. Calif., Berkeley, 1969; MA in Math., U. Calif., 1971. Instr. in math. Medgar Evers Coll./CUNY, Bklyn., 1971-76; lectr. in math. Montgomery Coll., Rockville, Md., 1976-78; instr. in math. Kankakee (Ill.) C.C., 1978-81; instr. in math. City Coll. of San Francisco, 1982-89, dept. chair, math., 1989-92, instr. in math., 1992—; apptd. mem. Calif. Math. Project, 1987-93, elected to Calif. Math. Project exec. com., 1989-93; cons. Southwestern Coll. Maths. Acad., Chula Vista, Calif., 1989-93. Chair steering com. Alliance for C.C. Ednl. Leadership, San Francisco, 1982; co-dir. math. achievement through systemic support grant program funded by Calif. Postsecondary Edn. Com., Dwight D. Eisenhower Profl. Devel. Program, San Francisco, 1995-99. Mem. Am. Math. Assn. of Two-Yr. Colls., Am. Math. Soc., Am. Fedn. Tchrs., Calif. Math. Coun., Calif. Math. Coun. C.C. (treas. 1987-90, Disting. Svc. award), Nat. Coun. Tchrs. of Math., Math. Assn. Am., Consortium for Math. and its Applications. Avocations: reading, music. Office: City Coll of San Francisco 50 Phelan Ave San Francisco CA 94112-1821

DE PUGET, ALBERT BORG OLIVIER, magistrate; b. Valletta, Malta, Apr. 15, 1932; s. Joseph and Helen Lowell. Diploma of Legal Procurator, Royal U. Malta, Valletta, 1954, LLD, 1958. M.P. Ho. of Reps., Malta, 1966-81; mem. Parliamentary Assembly Coun. Europe, Strasbourg, France, 1966-75; magistrate Cts. of Justice, Malta, 1983-87; amb. to France, Spain, Portugal, Switzerland and UNESCO, 1987-91, U.S., Washington, 1991-97; high commr. to Can., 1992-97; amb. designate to Mex., 1996; amb.-in-residence Ctr. for Global Edn., George Mason U., 1997—; lectr. multicultural diplomacy Elliott Sch. Internat. Affairs, George Mason U., 1998; law practice, 1958-83; vice chmn., sr. ptnr. Washington World Group Ltd., 1998; bd. dirs. Zammit Dimech and Basuttil, Advs., Malta. Editor: Studenti; mem. edit. bds. (newspapers) Patria, Il-Poplu, Malta Taghna, Encounter, In-Nazzjon Taghna; contbr. articles to profl. jours. V.p. Christian Dem. Group; mem. Bur. of the European Union of Christian Dems.; hon. v.p. Malta Coun. European Movement; internat. sec. Nationalist Party, Malta, 1975-77. Mem. La Valette Phil. Soc., The Casino (1852), Cercle de L'Union Interalliée, Internat. Club, Univ. Club. Roman Catholic. Avocations: reading, music, walking. Home and Office: 1673 Columbia Rd NW Apt 309 Washington DC 20009-3604

DE PUIG, LLUIS MARIA, international organization executive; b. Bascara, July 29, 1945; married, 2 children. History degree, Autonomous U. Barcelona; postgrad., Sorbonne, Paris. Historian, prof. contemporary history Autonomous U. Barcelona; mem. Spanish del. Assembly of Western European Union, 1990—; pres. Assembly of Western European Union, Paris, 1997—; rep. for Spain Coun. Europe Parlimentary Assembly; mem. Coun. Europe Assembly, 1983—, vice-chmn. com. on culture and edn., chmn. sub-com. on European social charter, 1984-89, v.p., 1993-96. Author history books; contbr. articles to profl. jours. Mem. Catalonian Socialist Party Bur., 1986—; pres. Gerona Fedn. of Socialist Party, 1993—. Office: Juli Garreta 4 2o 2, 17006 Girona Spain*

DE PURY, DAVID, financial company executive. Diplomat Govt. Switzerland, The Hague, Brussels and Washington, 1970-91; amb. plenipotentiary, del. for trade agreements Govt. of Switzerland, 1986-91; co-chmn. bd. ABB Asea Brown Boveri Group, Zurich, Switzerland, 1992-96; chmn. bd. Brown Boveri, Baden, Switzerland, 1992-96, de Pury Pictet Turrettini & Co. Ltd., Zurich, 1996—; chmn. Le Temps, French Swiss daily newspaper, 1998—; chmn. A A EIC Electricity Investment Co., 1997—; bd. dirs. Zurich Fin. Svcs. Group, Nestlé, Groupe Schneider Electric, Paris, Jaakko Pöyry Group, Helsinki, Electrowatt Engring.; mem. European adv. bd. Schroder Salomon Smith Barney, 2000—, Air Products, 2000—; mem. European adv. European Roundtable Industrialists, 1994-96; chmn. OECD Trade Com., chief negotiator GATT, 1989-91; gov. Switzerland Inter-Am. Devel. Bank, 1987-88; chmn. bd. Electricity Investment Co., 1997—; mem. Coun. World Econ. Forum. Mem. exec. com. Grad. Inst. Internat. Studies, Geneva, 1993—; vice chmn. Internat. Festival Music Lucerne. Office: de Pury Pictet Turrettini, de Pury Pictet Turrettini, Binzmuhlestrasse 14 PO Box 8242, CH 8050 Zurich Switzerland

DEPUYDT, XAVIER CHRISTOPHE LAURENT, film director; b. Ghent, Belgium, Oct. 1, 1971; s. Eli Joan Alfons Depuydt and Jacqueline Françoise Simone Campens. Diploma, RITS, Brussels, 1993. Asst. dir. RSL Prodn., Paris, 1995; dir. Vlaamse Radio TV, Brussels, 1995—. Author: (screenplay) Adam, 1997; contbr. articles to profl. jours. Mem. SABAM. Avocations: fitness, drawing, painting, photography, reading.

DE QUÉNETAIN, BERTRAND, publisher, editor, writer; b. Mayenne, France, Apr. 16, 1944; s. Pierre and Elizabeth (Regnault) de Q.; children: Marine, Erwan. Degree in math., Ecole Superieure des Travaux, Paris, 1966; degree in engring., Ecole Superieure du Bois, Paris, 1969. Engr. Deck House, Acton, Mass., 1970; exec. mgr. Tradinorm, Paris, 1970-78; mgr. gen. store Chausey Island, France, 1980-82; pub., editor L'Ancre de Marine, St. Malo, France, 1982—. Contbr. numerous articles to mags.; participant numerous TV and radio programs. Treas. St. Malo Spectacle, 1994-97. Mem. Brittany Pubs. Assn. (pres. 1997—), Yacht Club de France, Cercle de la Mer, Propeller Club of U.S.-St. Malo. Avocations: yachting, books. Office: L'Ancre de Marine, 4 Rue Porcon de la Barbinais, 35400 Saint-Malo France

DERA, JERZY, physics educator; b. Mosina, Poznan, Poland, Apr. 9, 1933; s. Jan and Cecylia (Zgola) D.; m. Stefania Teresa Dera; 1 child, Malgorzata; m. Maria Renata Preibisz, Apr. 20, 1991. MS in Physics, U. Poznan, 1956; D in Math.-Phys. Sci., Wroclaw (Poland) U., 1964, D in Habilitation Exptl. Physics, 1970. Cert. ordinary prof. Polish Acad. Scis., 1984. Jr. and sr. rsch. asst. Tech. U. Gdansk, Poland, 1956-64; rsch. scientist Polish Acad. Scis.-Inst. Geophysics, Warsaw and Sopot, Poland, 1965-70; asst. prof. Polish Acad. Scis.-Inst. Geophysics, Warsaw and Sopot, 1970-76; extraordinary prof. Polish Acad. Scis.-Inst. Oceanology, Sopot, 1976-84, ordinary prof., 1984—, dep. dir. sci. matter, 1976-89, dir. Inst., 1990—; part-time asst. and ordinary prof. Gdansk (Poland) U., 1976-98; mem. Nat. Commn. for the Sci. Titles and Degrees Nomination, Prime Min. of the Govt., Warsaw, 1994-99; mem. European Marine and Polar Sci. Bds., European Sci. Found., Strasbourg, 1995—. Author: Marine Physics, 1983, English edit., 1992 (award Gen. of the Polish Acad. Scis. 1984); co-author: The Southern Baltic, 1987 (II deg. of the Min. of Nat. Edn. 1989); contbr. articles to profl. jours. Active in devel. marine sci. and edn. in Poland, Gdansk divsn. Polish Acad. Scis., Sci. Soc. Gdansk, Nat. Groups of Experts and Nat. Coms., 1960—. Recipient Merit of the Gdansk Province, The Gdansk Province Coun., 1976, Golden Cross of Merit, Coun. of State, Warsaw, 1978; named Knight Polonia Restituta Order, Coun. of State, Warsaw, 1988. Mem. Polish Acad. Scis. (corr., mem. Polish nat. com. on oceanic rsch., chmn. 1981-90, editor-in-chief Jour. Oceanologia 1983—). Roman Catholic. Avocation: classical music. Office: Inst Oceanology PAS, Powstancow Warszawy 55, 81-712 Sopot Gdansk, Poland

DE RANTER, CAMIEL JOSEPH, chemist, educator; b. Hoboken, Antwerp, Belgium, Aug. 27, 1937; s. Antoon August and Clementine Leonie (Santens) DeR.; m. Monique Anna Blaton, Apr. 9, 1965; children: Carl, Johan. Lic. Chem. Scis., cert. in nuclear scis., Cath., Leuven, Belgium, 1960; DSc, Cath. U., Leuven, Belgium, 1964. Fellow So. Ill. U., Carbondale, 1969; docent in analytical chemistry Cath . U., Leuven, Belgium, 1970-74, prof., 1974-76, ordinary prof., 1976—; dean Inst. Pharm. Scis., Cath. U. Leuven, 1983-92, vice-dean, 1992-98. Editor, author: X-Ray Crystallography and Drug Action, 1984. Mem. Belgian Pharm. Soc., Belgian Biophys. Soc., Am. Crystallographic Assn., Koninklyke Nederlandse Chemische Vereniging, Koninklyke Vlaamse Chemische Vereniging, Quantitative Structure Activity Relationships Soc. (intern), Molecular Graphics Soc. Office: Lab Analytical Chemistry, Van Evenstraat 4, 3000 Leuven Belgium

DERCHIN, DARY BRET INGHAM, writer; b. Camden, N.J., Sept. 15, 1941; d. Charles and Dorothy Roberta (Ingham) Lambiase; m. Michael Wayne Derchin, Dec. 29, 1970; children: Taylor-Leigh, Danielle Ashlin Lacey. BA, Montclair State Coll., 1962; postgrad., NYU, 1965, New Sch., 1966. Tchr. Randolph, N.J., 1962-64; rsch. asst. NYU, N.Y.C., 1965-67, Bolivian Peace Corps Project, N.Y.C., 1966; co-head rsch. Derchin Enterprises, N.Y.C., 1970-75. Author: Real Talk, 1992; playwright Blue No More; contbr. articles to the N.Y. Times, Harper's and book the Big Picture, others; talk show host: The Better Sex with Danna Day, Sta. WALE, 1999—, KFNY, WEVD; spkr., guest talk shows. Mem. Drama League, Lincoln Ctr. Film Soc., Am. Film Inst., Friends of Poets and Writers, Univ. Club, Nat. Art Club (lit. com., film com., Joseph Kesselring Playwright award com.). Home: Laurel Cove PO Box 200 Fair Haven NJ 07704-0200

DERDENGER, PATRICK, lawyer; b. L.A., June 29, 1946; s. Charles Patrick and Drucilla Marguerite (Lange) D.; m. Jo Lynn Dickins, Aug. 24, 1968; children: Kristin Lynn, Bryan Patrick, Timothy Patrick. BA, Loyola U., L.A., 1968; MBA, U. So. Calif., 1971, JD, 1974; LLM in Taxation, George Washington U., 1977. Bar: Calif. 1974, U.S. Ct. Claims 1975, Ariz. 1979, U.S. Ct. Appeals (9th cir.) 1979, U.S. Dist. Ct. Ariz. 1979, U.S. Tax Ct. 1979, U.S. Supreme Ct. 1979; cert. specialist in tax law. Trial atty. honors program U.S. Dept. Justice, Washington, 1974-78; ptnr. Lewis and Roca, Phoenix, 1978—; adj. prof. taxation Golden Gate U., Phoenix, 1983-87; mem. Ariz. State Tax Ct. Legis. Study Commn., Tax Law Specialist Commn., Ariz. Property Tax Oversight Commn.; appt. Ariz. Property Tax Oversight Commn., 1997—. Author: Arizona State and Local Taxation, Cases and Materials, 1983, Arizona Sales and Use Tax Guide, 1990, Advanced Arizona Sales and Use Tax, 1987-96, Arizona State and Local Taxation, 1989, 93, 96, Arizona Sales and Use Tax, 1988-96. Arizona Property Taxation, 1993-96, ABA Sales and Use Tax Deskbook, Property Tax Deskbook. Past pres., bd. dirs. North Scottsdale Little League; apptd. Ariz. Property Tax Oversight Commn. Served to capt. USAF, 1968-71. Recipient U.S. Law Week award Bur. Nat. Affairs, 1974. Mem. ABA (taxation sect., various coms.), Ariz. Bar Assn. (taxation sect., former chair sect. taxation, former treas., chmn. state and local tax com., chmn. continuing legal edn. com., tax adv. com., others, mem. tax law specialist commn.), Maricopa County Bar Assn., Inst. Sales Taxation, Nat. Tax Assn., Inst. Property Taxation Met. C. of C., Ariz. C. of C. (chair tax com.), U. So. Calif. Alumni Club (past pres., bd. dirs.), Phi Delta Phi. Home: 10040 E Happy Valley Rd Scottsdale AZ 85255-2395 Office: Lewis and Roca 2 Renaissance Plz 40 N Central Ave Ste 1900 Phoenix AZ 85004-4429

DERE, WILLARD HONGLEN, internist, educator; b. Sacramento, Jan. 8, 1954; s. William Janson and Bessie Lon (Joe) D.; m. Julia Mei Lum, June 18, 1978; children: Melissa Ellen, Kathryn Elizabeth. AB, U. Calif., Davis, 1975, MD, 1980. Intern Health Sci. Ctr., U. Utah, Salt Lake City, 1980-81, resident, 1981-83; instr. internal medicine, geriatrics U. Utah, Salt Lake City, 1985-87, asst. prof., 1987-89; rsch. fellow U. Calif., San Francisco, 1983-85; asst. prof. Ind. U. Sch Medicine, Indpls., 1989-98; clin. assoc. prof. Ind. U. Sch. Medicine, Indpls., 1998—; clin. rsch. physician Lilly Rsch. Labs., Indpls., 1989-91, dir. European regulatory affairs, 1991, dir. endocrine rsch., 1994-98, exec. dir. clin. rsch., 1998—; dir. emergency rm. VA Med. Ctr., Salt Lake City, 1985-86; cons. U. Utah Student Health Svc., Salt Lake City, 1985-89, acting dir., 1987-88. Editor: (book) Practical Care of the Ambulatory Patient, 1989; Contbr. articles to profl. jours. Hon. assoc. investigator VA, San Francisco, 1984. Mem. ACP, AAAS, Am. Geriatrics Soc., Am. Soc. Bone and Mineral Rsch., Assn. Osteobiology. Presbyn. Achievements include research in adrenocortical function in AIDS, oncogene regulation in thyroid cells; multi-center antibiotic trials, drug safety; health economics; and SERMs (selective estrogen receptor modulators). Office: Lilly Corp Ctr Lilly Rsch Labs Ctr Indianapolis IN 46285-0001

DERERA, NICHOLAS FREDERICK, agricultural research scientist; b. Budapest, Hungary, Jan. 5, 1919; arrived in Australia, 1957; s. Jozsef and Lilly (Lendvai) D.; m. Roza Eva Gyarfas, Jan. 12, 1946; 1 child, Nicholas Joseph. Diploma in agrl. sci., Tech. U., Budapest, 1942, diploma in plant breeding, 1943. Cert. plant breeder Dept. Primary Industries, Australia. Plant breeder Hungarian Seed Culture Co. Ltd., Budapest, 1942-44; plant breeder, officer-in-charge Mauthner O. Co. Ltd., Szentes, Hungary, 1945-48; prin. rsch. officer Hungarian Ministry of Agr., Budapest, 1949-56; rsch. agronomist NSW Dept. Agr., Narrabri, Australia, 1958-61; plant breeder, officer-in-charge N.W. Wheat Rsch. Inst., Narrabri, 1961-73; dir. wheat breeding U. Sydney, Narrabri, 1973-81; project leader paprika rsch., mng. dir. Agrl. Sci. Adv. Svc., Ltd., Sydney, 1997—; cons. Hunter Valley Herb Farm, 1996-99; mng. cons. Burns, Philp & Co. Ltd., Sydney, 1983-84; sr. cons. A.J. Newport & Son, Winmalee, Australia, 1985—; hon. assoc. U. Sydney, 1994-99, adj. prof. U. Sydney, 1999—; co-convenor Reform of Edn. in Agr. Com., Sydney, 1993—. Author, editor: Preharvest Field Sprouting in Cereals, 1989; contbr. to book: Soft Wheat, 1981; contbr. over 80 articles to profl. publs. Recipient Meml. medal Farrer Trust, 1981, cert. of appreciation Returned Svcs. League, NSW br., 1979; named to Order of Australia by Queen of Australia, 1994. Fellow Australian Inst. Agrl. Sci. (emeritus, past pres.); mem. Accredited Agrl. Cons. (emeritus), N.Y. Acad. Scis., Masons, Rotary (pres. Baulkham Hills chpt. 1985-86, chmn. vocat. excellence award com. 1994-97). Achievements include development of breeds of climbing bean, tomatoes, caspicum, turf grasses, wheat, chamelaucium, poinsettia cultivars; development of research methodology of mechanical mass selection system and verification of limited section system; development of screening techniques for drought resistance, flag smut resistance, micro quality tests, sprouting damage resistance. Avocations: wine collecting, gardening. Fax: 61296390345. Office: Agrl Svc Adv Svc, 5 Lister St, Winston Hills NSW 2153, Australia

DERGUNOV, ALEXANDER DMITRIEVICH, biophysicist, researcher; b. Poltavsky Region, USSR, Jan. 25, 1953; s. Dmitryi Ivanovich and Anna Timofeevna Nagnyi; m. Ludmila Vasil'evna Yuzhakova, July 22, 1975; children: Alexander, Igor. BSc, Russian State Med. U., 1976; PhD, Inst. Biochemistry, Moscow, 1982. Rschr. Inst. Applied Microbiology, Moscow, 1980-83, USSR Cardiology Rsch. Ctr., Moscow, 1983-88; sr. rschr. Centre for Preventive Medicine, Moscow, 1988—. Contbr. articles to profl. jours. including Biochemistry (Russia), FEBS Letters, Biol. Chem. Hoppe-Seyler, and Biochim. Biphys. Acta. Fellow European Soc. Cardiology, 1992; recipient MAC '97 bursary in memory of Norberto Montalbetti, 1997. Mem. AAAS, Internat. Atherosclerosis Soc., N.Y. Acad. Scis. Avocation: computer hardware and software. Office: Ctr for Preventive Medicine, Petroverigsky St 10, 101953 Moscow Russia

DERGUNOV, YUZIY IVANOVICH, chemist, educator; b. Nizhny, Novgorod, Russia, Apr. 18, 1935; s. Ivan Vasilyevich and Yekaterina Stepanovna (Poverennova) D.; . Lyubov Vasilyevna, Oct. 3, 1964. Chemist, Rschr., Gorky (Russia) State U., 1957, Candidate Chemistry, 1963, D Chemistry, 1979. Rsch. worker Rsch. Inst. Chemistry, Gorky State U., 1957-60; dep. dir. rsch. work Rsch. Inst. Dzerzhinsk, Russia, 1963-96; prof., chair organic chemistry N.N. State Tech. U., Nizhny Novgorad, Russia, 1997; prof., chair bldg. materials N.N. State Architect U., Nizhny Novgorad, 1997—; tech. dir. Concern Sarov, Nizhny Novgorad, 1998—. Contbr. over 250 articles to profl. jours.; over 150 patents in field. Named Hon. Chemist, U. Chem. Industry, Russia, 1984. Mem. Acad. Engring. Scis., N.Y. Acad. Sci., Internat. Engring. Acad. (corr.). Orthodox Christian. Avocation: gardening. Home: pr Pobedy 3-39, 606000 Dzerzhinsk Russia Office: Concern Sarov, pt Oktyabrya 23-15, Nizhny Novgorad Russia

DE RIDDER, JACQUES HENRI, internist; b. Ghent, Belgium, Nov. 13, 1943; s. Robert and Juliette (Godtler) De R. MD, Catholic U. Louvain, 1967. Diplomate Am. Bd. Internal. Medicine. Cons. internist Clinique de la Basilique, Brussels, Belgium, 1975-82, Hillbrow Hosp., Johannesburg, South Africa, 1983-85, Clinique Saint Etienne, Brussels, 1985-91, Tawam Hosp., Al Ain, United Arab Emirates, 1991-94, Armed Forces Hosp., Dhahran, Saudi Arabia, 1995-96; chief of medicine Royal Commn. Med. Ctr., Yanbu, Saudi Arabia, 1996-98; with Centre Hospitalier de Laon, France, 1999-2000; cons. internist King Faisal Specialist Hosp. and Rsch. Ctr., Jeddah, Saudi Arabia, 2000—. Fellow ACP; mem. Belgian Soc. Cardiology. Avocations: skiing, windsurfing, scuba diving. Home: Hasseltbergstraat 1, B-1860 Meise Brabant, Belgium

DE RIJK, JOHANNES ADRIANUS, retired mathematics and physics educator, writer; b. Rotterdam, The Netherlands, Feb. 19, 1926; m. Magdalena Agterberg, May 24, 1977; children: Mechtilde, Hadewych. Diploma in tchg., Pedagogical Acad., Ondenbosch, The Netherlands, 1945. H.s. tchr. Utrecht, The Netherlands, 1952-86; founder 1st pub. obs. in The Netherlands. Author 250 books on math. and astronomy and on the Dutch artist M.C. Escher; founder several periodicals. Recipient Silver Carnation Prince Bernhard of The Netherlands, 1966. Mrm. Ars & Maths. (sec. 1986-97), The Sundial Circle (sec. 1982-97). Avocations: photography, miniature books, bookbinding, drawing. Home: Stationsstreet 114, 3511 EJ Utrecht The Netherlands

DERILO, ROSALIO OSIP, airport ground equipment mechanic; b. Looc, Salay, Philippines, June 11, 1945; s. Trifon Duarte and Corazon Cabasa (Osip) D.; m. Jesusa Sanches Ordoño, July 15, 1967; children: Reo, Rex, Jerome, Roy Anthony, Jerose, Ron Francis, Rod Mark. Student, Mindanao Sch. Arts & Trades, 1958-61, Xavier U., Cagayan de Oro City, Philippines, 1965. Mechanic Tan Taxi, Cebu City, Philippines, 1963-64, Mindanao Motors Corp., Cagayan de Oro City, Philippines, 1964-66; chief mechanic Sweet Ride Lines, Don Carlos, Philippines, 1967; supr. Dole Philippines, Gen Santos City, 1968-74, Paper Industry Corp. of the Philippines, Bislig, Surigao del Sur, 1974-81; supt. Almihdar Devel. Co. Ltd., Jeddah, Saudi Arabia, 1981-85; instr., org. mechanic, O.J.T. instr. Siyanco/Somc/Socp, Taif, Saudi Arabia, 1987-92; ground svcs. mechanic, tech. assessment coord. Saudia Air Lines, Jeddah, 1992—; automotive instr. Jose Valencia Acad., Polomoc, South Cotabato, Philippines, 1972; mechanics instr. Dole Philippines Inc., Polo Moloc, 1972-73. Author: New Astronomical Theory of Motion, 1989. Pres. Ch. Pastoral Coun., Forest Drive Village, 1986; v.p. Diocese Pastoral Coun., Bislig, 1987; mem. Cath. Faith Defenders of the Philippines, Cebu City, 1981. Mem. ASME, Knights of Columbus Internat. Roman Catholic. Avocations: repairing vehicles, reading science books and difference religious doctrine and philosophy of Catholic, Protestant and Islam, hunting, driving, swimming. Home: 1792 Forest Drive Village, San Roque Bislig 8311 Surigao del Sur, The Philippines Office: Saudi Arabian Airlines, PO Box 167 CC-813, Jeddah 21231, Saudi Arabia

DERIN, IVANOVA, biologist, researcher; b. Sofia, Bulgaria, June 3, 1956; d. Metodi Zarkov and Nevena (Boteva) I.; m. André Derin, Feb. 21, 1998; 1 child, Tzigantchev Atanas. MSc, U. Sofia, 1982; PhD, U. Paris VII, 1998. Rsch. specialist Acad. Scis., Sofia, 1982-85, rsch. assoc., 1985-86; rschr. Hosp. Saint Louis, Paris, 1992-98; vis. scientist, France and Belgium, 1991-92. Contbr. more than 30 articles to profl. jours. E-mail: derin@cyber-cable.fr.

DERKOWSKA, JAGODA, physician, ophthalmologist; b. Wroclaw, Poland, Feb. 2, 1966; d. Tomasz Cieszynski and Maria (Garbacz) Cieszynska; m. Wojciech Derkowski, Oct. 7, 1989; children: Pawel, Piotr, Barbara. B in Medicine, Med. Acad., Wroclaw, 1991. Asst., specialist ophthalmolgical outpatient dept. Kluczbork, Poland, 1997—; intern Internal Ward, Kluczbork, Poland, 1991-93; mem. ophthal. dept. Internal Ward, Kluczbork, 1993-97; cons. dist. Gen. Hosp., Kluczbork, 1997—. Mem. Polish Ophthalmol. Soc. Roman Catholic. Avocation: painting. Office: SP ZOZ Kluczbork Poradnia, Wolnosci 3, 46-200 Kluczbork Poland

DEROM, ERIC YVES, pulmonologist, educator, researcher; b. Ghent, Belgium, June 28, 1957; s. Fritz Derom and Anny Mattelaer. MD, State U. Ghent, 1982, PhD, 1991. Cert. in pneumonology and respiratory rehab. Tng. in internal medicine Univ. Hosp., Ghent, 1982-88, resident in pneumonology, 1990-92; fellow Cath. U. Louvain, Belgium, 1990-92; prof. medicine State U. Ghent, 1992—. Contbr. articles to med. jours. Mem. Am. Thoracic Soc., European Respiratory Soc., Belgian Soc. Pneumology. Roman Catholic. Home: James Ensorlaan 18, B-9051 Ghent Belgium Office: Univ Hosp Dept Resp Disease, De Pintelaan 185, B-9000 Ghent Belgium

DEROO, SALLY ANN, biology, geology and environmental science educator. BS, Eastern Mich. U., 1958; postgrad., 1958-63; MA, U. Mich., 1961, postgrad., 1963-92; postgrad., Wayne State U., 1964-68, Ohio State U., 1995—. Cert. elem. tchr., middle level, all subjects K-8; cert. high sch. level environ. scis., social studies, English, econs. 9-12; cert. tchr. mentally handicapped and emotionally impaired K-12; cert. Master Gardener, Mich. State U., 1997. Asst. prof. sci. Ea. Mich. U., Ypsilanti, 1958-63, asst. prof. biology and geology, 1968—, cons., 1958-89, tchr. spl. edn., cons., 1989—; tchr. sci. and geology Plymouth-Canton Cmty. Schs., 1963-95; curriculum specialist Ctrl. Mich. U., 1989-90; instr. dept. tchr. edn. Mich. State U., 1994-95; instr. sci. edn. Madonna U., asst. prof., mem. staff student tchr. edn. Dept. Edn., 1992—; asst. prof., mem. staff student tchr. edn. Dept. Edn. Madonna U.; advisor Salem H.S., 1990-95, Wayne State U., Detroit, 1995—,

Pitts. State U., Kans. at Greenbush, 1995-97, Oakland U. Sci. Edn., 1997—; ednl. cons. Scholastic, Inc., 1996-2000; sci./ednl. cons. DTE Energy, Detroit, 1998-2000; cons. Carolina Biol., 2000—; mem. satellite conf. Tchrs. Making a Difference, 1990; mem. support team Sci. Teaching Edn. STEP adv. bd. Madonna U., Livonia, Mich.; mem. math. and sci. challenge grant design com. Wayne County, 1991; adv. bd. SEMSplus Mich. Envirothon, steering com. Nat. Envirothon, 1996—; mem. adv. com., issues author sci. curriculum support guides Mich. Dept. Edn., 1989-90; mem. adv. coun. Mich. Dept. Edn.; mem. Mich. curriculum frameworks joint steering com., 1992—, mem. writing com. h.s. proficiency exam., 1993, 94, 95—, mem. adv. com. h.s. sci. proficiency test, 1993, 94, 95-96; dist. commr. Wayne County Soil Dist. USDA, 1996-2000; mem. citizens adv. com. Stockbridge Township, Mich., 2000—; project chair Project Cattail, Tchrs. and Students Making an Environ. Difference, 1992—; project dir. Gt. Lakes-Thunderbay Gt. Lakes Basin Work Shop, Alpena, Mich., 1990-93; cons. Detroit Edison (DTE) Solar Currents curricula, 1997—; Carolina biol. STC cons., Burlington, N.C.; sci. cons. Houghton Mifflin, Geneva, Ill., 1999—, cons. Houghton Mifflin, Co., 2000—; mem. ednl. planning com. Detroit Zool. Inst., 2000; facilitator numerous workshops; presenter in field. Author: (newsletter) Fledgeling, 1990—, (teaching manuals) Exploring Our Environment; contbg. writer Detroit Free Press sci. page; contbr. articles to sci. mags.; writer, dir. 26-week sci. TV series Explore with Me; sci. editor Ann Arbor Pubs., 1968-86; elem. publ. editor Mich. Sci. Tchrs.; adv. (tv waste mgmt. series) Neuton's Apple. Active Rouge River Restoration, 1988—, Friends of Mattaei Bot. Gardens Ann. Flower Show; established Model Adopt-a-Stream Project "River Watch" for Rough River Water Shed, 1994; planning asst. Cobo Ctr. 1st Annual Detroit Bloomfest, 1999—. Recipient Outstanding Educator award Mich. Jaycees, 1963, Best of West Edn. award, 1984, Outstanding Svc. Recognition award Mich. Assn. Mid. Sch. Educators, 1989, 90, gov.'s citation State of Mich., 1990, 91, Tchr. of Yr. Program award IBM, 1990, Can Doers award Mich. Tech. Coun., 1993, Recognition of Support and Dedication dept. natural resources Builder's Assn. Southeastern Mich., 1990, 91, 92; named Outstanding Sci. Educator, Metro Detroit Sci. Tchrs. Assn., 1994; listed in Guinness Book of Records 1990-95 for snail racing. Mem. NEA, Nat. Sci. Tchrs. Assn. (presenter, local leader, chair publicity regional conf. 1999), Mich. Sci. Tchrs. Assn. (dir.-at-large, chair outreach conf., Outstanding Svc. award 1997, Disting. Svc. award 1998), Nat. Mid. Level Sci. Tchrs. Assn. (treas.), N t. Resource Def. Coun., Mich. Sci. Leaders Assn. (bd. dirs.), Mich. Dept. Edn., Sci. Curriculum Devel. Assn. (mid. sch. goal-based curriculum), Wayne County Task Force (intermediate sch. dist. writing team 1989, bd. dirs.), Mich. Alliance for Outdoor Edn., Detroit Zool. Inst., Internat. Joint Commn. (Gt. Lakes), Mich. Reading Assn. (sci. conf. chairperson 1992—), Citizens Adv. Com., Phi Delta Kappa (editor newsletter U. Mich. chpt.). Address: Wayne State U Dept Edn, Gullen Ct Detroit MI 48202

DE ROSA, MICHELE, endocrinologist; b. Naples, Italy, Jan. 16, 1949; s. Colino and Renata (Palumbo) D.R.; m. Elisabetta Garofalo, Sept. 27, 1982; children: Renata Carla, Nicoletta, Mariano. MD, 2d Sch. Medicine, Naples, 1975, postgrad. in endocrinology, 1978, postgrad. in physiopathology of human reproduction, 1981, postgrad. in internal medicine, 1986. With U. Naples, 1975-87, rschr., 1980—; cons. MD Nat. Health Svc., Naples, 1976-85. Contbr. articles to profl. jours. Lt. Italian Army, 1977-78. Mem. Rotary. Roman Catholic. Home: Belsito 19, 80123 Naples Italy Office: U Federico II Dept Endocrinology, Pansini 5, 80131 Naples Italy

DE ROSA, MIRIO, marketing professional, consultant; b. Rome, June 7, 1961; arrived in Switzerland, 1995; s. Nicola and Luciana (Rossini) de R.; m. Barbara Selz, Feb. 2, 1995; 1 child, Lucas. Diploma in Acctg., C. Cattaneo, Rome, 1980; BBA, J. Cabot, Rome, 1988; Mktg. Mgmt. Specialization, E. Cogno & Assocs., Rome, 1987. Mktg. rschr. ASM, Rome, 1987-90; gen. mgr. MAP Mgmt. 360, Rome, 1990-95; mktg. rsch. mgr. Roche Pharma (Schweiz), Reinach, Switzerland, 1996-99; internat. mktg. rsch. mgr. F. Hoffmann-La Roche Ltd., Basel, Switzerland, 1999—. Co-author: (software) Marketing Manager for Excel, 1999, various software for mktg.; author 4 books Collana Fare Marketing, 1995. Mem. Am. Mktg. Assn., Assn. Shareware Profls. Avocations: scuba-diving, pool. E-Mail: mdr@datacomm.ch. Home: IM Goldbrunnen 39, 4104 Oberwil Basel, Switzerland Office: F Hoffman La Roche Ltd, Grenzacherstrasse Bldg 74, 4070 Basel Switzerland

DEROSE, PAUL CHRISTIAN, research chemist; b. Teaneck, N.J., Sept. 26, 1966; s. Thomas Charles and Joan (Simister) DeR. BA in Chemistry, Rutgers Coll., 1990; PhD in Chemistry, U. Pa., Phila., 1996. NRC/Nat. Inst. Stds. & Tech. postdoctoral assoc. Nat. Inst. Stds. & Tech., Gaithersburg, Md., 1996-98, analytical rsch. chemist, 1998—. Contbr. articles to profl. jours., including Chem. Physics, Molecular Physics, others. Mem. Am. Chem. Soc., Sigma Xi. Avocations: trumpet, wine, roller blading. Office: NIST 165 Stop 8394 Bldg 227 Rm A Gaithersburg MD 20899-0001

DE ROSE, VIRGINIA, chest physician, educator; b. Cosenza, Italy, Jan. 2, 1953; d. Gaetano and Ersilia (Mascherpa) De R. MD with honors, U. Florence, Italy, 1977; postgrad. with honors, U. Florence, 1980, postgrad. in internal medicine, 1988; PhD, U. Pavia, Italy, 1990. Cert. in respiratory diseases and internal medicine. Resident in internal medicine U. Florence, 1978-81; rsch. fellow in respiratory diseases U. Pavia, 1981-87; asst. prof. respiratory diseases U. Turin, Italy, 1988-92; assoc. prof. respiratory diseases U. Turin, 1992—; vis. scientist U. Nebr. Med. Ctr., Omaha, 1990-91, INSERM, U. Montpellier, France, 1997-98; mem. sci. com. nat. and internat. meetings. Contbr. articles to profl. jours. Recipient Nat. award for rsch. on lung cancer, 1985; grantee NIH, Nat. Heart, Lung and Blood Inst., 1991, Nat. Rsch. Coun., 1997. Mem. European Respiratory Soc. (assembly long range planning com. 1997-99, chmn. sci. group 1995-97, assembly sec. 1997-99, sec. sci. group 1993-95). Roman Catholic. Avocations: reading, swimming. Home: Via San Tommaso 24, 10121 Turin Italy Office: U Turin, Osp S Luigi Gonzaga 10, 10043 Orbassano Turin, Italy

DEROSSI, ARNAUD, medical services company administrator, physician; b. Neuilly Sur Seine, France, Oct. 8, 1959; s. Gerard and Anne (Dernoncourt) D. MD, Paris U., 1988; Degree in Disaster Medicine, Creteil U., 1986, Degree in Emergency Medicine, 1988; Degree in Aerospace Medicine, Tours U., 1992. Jr. med. doctor Samu/Necker Hosp. Paris, 1985-88, asst. prof., 1988—; sr. med. coord. Europ Assistance, Paris, 1990-92; chmn. Medic'Air Internat., Paris, 1991—, med. dir., 1991—; aeromed. cons. Medic'Air Internat., France, 1993—. Co-author: (book) Les Materiels et Techniques De R. Prehospitaliere, 1993, Protocoles, 1996; contbr. articles to profl. jours. Capt. Unite De Securite Civile No7, 1987-88. Fellow Am. Coll. Emergency Physicians; mem. Syndicat National De L'Aide Medicale Urgente, Assn. des Medecins Urgentiste Hospitaliers de France (bd. dirs. 1997—). Avocation: old sports cars. Home: 10 Rue Dulac, 75015 Paris France Office: Medic'Air Internat, 35 Rue Jules Ferry, 93170 Bagnolet Paris, France

DE ROTHSCHILD, ERIC ALAIN ROBERT DAVID, banker; b. N.Y.C., Oct. 3, 1940; s. Alain and Mary (Chauvin du Treuil) De R.; m. Maria-Beatrice Caracciolo di Forino, Dec. 21, 1983; children: James, Anna-Saskia, Pietro. Degree, Poly. Sch., Zürich, 1963. Gerant Château Lafite Rothschild, Paris, 1974—, Rothschild & Cie Banque, Paris, 1987—. Pres. Rothschild Found., Paris, Nat. Found. Graphic and Plastic Arts, Paris, Comite Action Social Israelite de Paris; mem. adminstrv. coun. Smithsonian Institution, D.C., 1996. Office: Rothschild & Cie Banque, 17 Ave Matignon, 75008 Paris France

DE ROUX, PATRICK, development and communication specialist; b. St. Jean de Luz, France, Mar. 20, 1946; s. Philippe de Roux and Suzanne d'Amade; m. Evelyne de Bouisfleury; 4 children. Mktg. mgr. Rank Xerox, Paris, 1971-76; sales dir. Richard le Droff, Paris, 1976-81; mktg. and sales internat. dir. VINCO, Paris, 1981-84; gen. mgr. Europcar France, Paris, 1984-91, ELIANCE, Paris, 1992-93; pres. Vedior Interim, Paris, 1994-97; dir. devel. and comm., mem. exec. com. VediorBis, Paris, 1998—. bd. dirs. SOPRATE, Paris, Tech. and Performance, Paris; pres. UNITECH, Paris, 1998—. Mem. Bd. Temping Profls. Union, French-Dutch C. of C. Office: VediorBis, 26-28 rue de Madrid, 75008 Paris France

DE ROY, LUC JOSEPH, cardiologist; b. Wemmel, Belgium, Oct. 29, 1944; s. Joseph Albert T. and Virginie (Vaessen) De R.; m. Michèle Caers, July 5, 1969; children: Joëlle, Gaëtan, Magali. MD, Cath. U. Louvain, 1970, postgrad., 1976; postgrad., U. Geneva, 1976. Intern, resident in internal medicine, cardiology U. Louvain, 1971-74; resident in cardiology U. Geneva, Switzerland, 1974-76; head of dept. internal medicine Mil. Hosp., Köln, Germany, 1976-80; head arrhythmia unit U. Clinic Louvain, Mont-Godinne, Belgium, 1977—; head divsn. cardiology Mil. Hosp., Brussels, 1990-91, head dept. internal medicine, 1991-97; cons. in cardiology arrhythmiology U. Louvain, 1977—, prof., 1997—; nat. del. European Working Group on Cardiac Pacing, 1991—; pres. Belgian Working Group of Cardiac Pacing and Electophysiology, 1995-99. Author: Les Troubles du Rythme Cardiaque, 1994, 3d edit., 2000; contbr. articles to profl. jours. Col. Med. Svc., Belgian Army, 1993. Mem. Sci. Soc. Mil. Medicine (v.p. 1991-97), Belgian Soc. Cardiology, N.Am. Soc. Pacing and Electrophysiology, European Soc. Cardiology (European working group on arrhythmias, European working group on cardiac pacing). Avocations: scientific readings, tennis. Home: 12 Ave Seigneurie de Spontin, B-1300 Wavre Belgium Office: Cliniques Univs Louvain UCL, Ave Therasse, B-5530 Yvoir Belgium

DE ROY, WALTER LODEWIJK VINCENT, engineering executive; b. Ekeren, Antwerp, Belgium, July 10, 1950; s. Willem and Maria (Van Damme) D.; m. Elisabeth Indigne, Jan. 5, 1977; children: Frederik, Sigrid, Gerwin. Civil Engr., Architect, K.U. Leuven, Belgium, 1977; postgrad., I.P.O. Inst., Antwerp, Belgium, 1990, I.P.O. Inst., Antwerp, Belgium, 1997. Site mgr. EGTA, Belgium, 1977-78; project mgr. Besix, Zaire/Brundi, 1979-85; exec. mgr. Sotraf, Zaire, 1985-88; gen. mgr. Zaireplate, Zaire, 1988-90, Kimin, Zaire, 1990-95; interim exec. mgr. E & Y Exec. Temporary Mgmt., Brussels, 1996—; sr. adviser in field. Dir. Social/Cultural Zaire, 1985-95. Mem. Koninklijke Vlaamse Ingenieursvereniging, Vlaamse Mgmt. Associatie. Avocations: reading, history, foreign civilizations, skiing. Home: Korte Lozanastraat 5/9, 2018 Antwerp Belgium

DERR, KENNETH T., retired oil company executive; b. 1936; m. Donna Mettler, Sept. 12, 1959; 3 children. BME, Cornell U., 1959, MBA, 1960. With Chevron Corp. (formerly Standard Oil Co. of Calif.), San Francisco, 1960—, v.p., 1972-85; pres. Chevron U.S.A., Inc. subs. Chevron Corp., San Francisco, 1978-84; head merger program Chevron Corp. and Gulf Oil Corp., San Francisco, 1984-85; vice-chmn. Chevron Corp., San Francisco, 1985-88, chmn., CEO, 1989-99; ret., 1999; bd. dirs. AT&T, Am. Productivity & Quality Ctr., Citigroup, Potlatch Corp. Trustee emeritus Cornell U. Mem. The Bus. Coun., San Francisco Golf Club, Orinda Country Clb, Pacific Union Club. Office: Chevron Corp PO Box 7643 575 Market St San Francisco CA 94105-2856

DERRICK, WILLIAM DENNIS, retired physical plant administrator, consultant; b. San Diego, Feb. 7, 1946; s. Charles Woodrow and Catherine Elizabeth (McCormick) D.; m. Lynda Ray Adams, June 15, 1964 (div. 1971); children: Tod Sean, Shannon Kay, Nicole Dione, Johnathon Robert; m. Frances C. Bouck, Nov. 19, 1979; children: Kaila June Warner, Bryan Charles. Student, U. Nebr., 1971-72, 73-74, U. Mont., 1974-77, 98-99, Internat. Corr., 1966-67, 81, Battelle Meml. Inst., 1985, Project Mgmt. Inst., 1986-95, 98—. Elec. draftsman City of Lincoln (Nebr.) Light Dept., 1964-65; asst. engr. to adjutant gen. Nebr. N.G. State of Nebr., Lincoln, 1965-66; owner, mgr., archtl. draftsman Lumberman's Plan Svc., Inc., Lincoln, 1966-70; owner, mgr. Lenny's Lounge, Missoula, Mo., 1978-80; engring. technician, constrn. insp., adminstr. USDA/Helena (Mont.) Nat. Forest, 1980-83; facilities project mgr. pub. office bldgs. div. City and County of Denver, 1984-86; supt. bldgs. and grounds Denver Pub. Libr., 1986-91; dir. phys. plant Red Rocks C.C., Lakewood, Colo., 1991-94; CEO Derrick, Inc., Stevensville, Mont. Mem. Local Govt. Study Commn., Stevensville, Mont., 1974; bd. dirs. Lewis and Clark County Fair Bd., Helena, Mont., 1979-83; candidate U.S. Ho. of Reps., 1999—. Mem. Project Mgmt. Inst. (cert. project mgr. profl. #619, v.p. programs Denver chpt. 1986-89, pres. 1990-91, v.p. pub. rels. 1992-93, bd. dirs., ex-officio). Avocations: computer technology, videography, photo journalism, intl. entrepenuerism, golf. E-mail: wder181822@aol.com. Home: 4400 S Jones Blvd Apt 2034 Las Vegas NV 89103-3343

DERRINGTON, SARAH CATHERINE, barrister; b. Townsville, Australia, May 10, 1968; d. David and Jennifer Anne (Kohler) Johnstone; m. Roger Marc Derrington, Jan. 13, 1990; children: Nicholas James, Stephanie Catherine, Emilie Sarah. BA, U. Queensland, Brisbane, Australia, 1988, LLB with honors, 1990, LLM, 1996, PhD, 1999. Barrister, solicitor Freehill Hollingdale & Page, Canberra, Australia, 1990-91; judges assoc. Supreme Ct. Queensland, Brisbane, Australia, 1991-92; solicitor Minter Ellison, Brisbane, Australia, 1992-93; sr. lectr. Queensland U. Tech., Brisbane, Australia, 1995—; lectr. U. Queensland, Brisbane, Australia, 1994-99, dir. ctr. for maritime law, 1999—; barrister pvt. practice, Brisbane, Australia, 1993—. Contbr. articles to profl. jours. Dir. Canteen-Australia Teenage Cancer Patients Assn., Sydney, 1990, sec., 1991. Mem. Maritime Law Assn. Australia & New Zealand (com. mem. 1996-97, sec. 1997—), Bar Assn. Queensland. Avocations: music, theatre, cooking, languages. Office: 16/95 Quay Ctrl, Brisbane 4000, Australia

DERSH, RHODA E., management consultant, business executive; b. Phila., Sept. 10, 1934; civ; d. Maurice S. and Kay (Wiener) Eisman; m. Jerome Dersh, Dec. 23, 1956; children: Debra Lori, Jeffrey Jonathan. BA, U. Pa., 1955; MA, Tufts U., 1956; MBA, Manhattan Coll., 1980. Interpreter Consul of Chile, 1954-57; various teaching and staff positions Albright Coll., Mt. Holyoke Coll., Amherst Coll., Marple Newtown Sch., 1957-58; pres., chief exec. officer Profl. Practice Mgmt. Assocs., Reading, 1976—, Pace Inst., Reading, 1981—, Pace Mgmt. Inc., 1983—; 1984-90; mem. regional adv. bd. First Union Bank, 1998—. Author: The School Budget is Your Business, 1976, Business Management for Professional Offices, 1977, The School Budget: It's Your Money, It's Your Business, 1979, Improving Public School Management Practices, 1979, Part-Time Professional and Managerial Personnel: The Employers View, 1979; contbr. articles to profl. jours. Bd. dirs. Pa. State Bd. Pvt. Lic. Schs., 1987-93; cons. dir. pub. sch. budget study project City of Reading, 1967-78, chmn. comprehensive community plan task force, 1973-75; chmn. pub. svc. cons. project 1980-90; panel chmn. budget allocations United Way, 1974-76; del. White House Conf. on Children Youth, 1970; co-founder World Affairs Coun., Reading and Berks County, 1963-65; chmn. Berks County Com. for Children Youth, 1968-72; commr. Trial Ct. Nominating Commn. of Berks County (Pa.), 1982-84; bd. dirs. United Way of Berks County, 1984-89; chmn. programs Leadership Berks, 1986-87; bd. dirs. Reading Ctr. City Devel. Corp., Berks Bus.-Edn. Coalition Corp., 1991—; mem. Greater Berks Devel. Bd., 1998—. Recipient Trendsetter award YWCA, 1985. Mem. AAUW (ednl. found. grant.), LWV, Pa. Assn. Pvt. Sch. Bus. Adminstrs. (bd. dirs. 1985-89), Berks County C. of C. (bd. dirs. 1983-86, chmn. edn. com. 1983-85), Am. Acad. Ind. Cons. (pres. 1978-80), Reading and Berks C. of C (Entrepreneur of Yr. 1985), Rotary (bd. dirs. Reading, Pa., chpt. 1989-90). Office: 606 Court St Reading PA 19601-3542

DERSTADT, RONALD THEODORE, health care administrator; b. Detroit, June 9, 1950; s. Theodore Edward and Dorothy J. (Semko) D.; m. J. Gail Adamson, June 9, 1990. BA, U. Detroit, 1971; M of Hosp. Healthcare Adminstn., Xavier U., 1975. Mgr. shared svcs. Bethesda Hosp. North, Cin., 1975-76; asst. adminstr. McCullough-Hyde Meml. Hosp., Oxford, Ohio, 1977-79; pres. Hospice of Cin., Inc., 1979-82; dir. strategic planning St. Francis-St. George Hosp., Cin., 1982-84; v.p. Mgmt. Dynamics, Inc., Cin., 1984-85; sr. v.p. St. Francis-St. George Mgmt. Co., Cin., 1986-88; v.p. Franciscan Health System of Cin., 1988-91; dir. hosp. affairs ChoiceCare, Cin., 1991-95; CEO Medquest, Owensboro, Ky., 1995-98; COO Ctr. for Chem. Addictions Treatment, Cin., 1998—; vice-chmn., bd. dirs. Franciscan Health Network, Cin., Franciscan Health Ventures, Cin. Treas., bd. dirs. Ohio Easter Seals Soc., Columbus, 1987-93; bd. dirs. S.W. Ohio Easter Seal Soc., Cin., 1986-92; adv. bd. Dater Jr. H.S., Cin., 1984-88. Fellow Am. Coll. Healthcare Execs.; mem. Healthcare Fin. Mgmt. Assn., Am. Hosp. Assn., Ohio Hosp. Assn. Avocations: boating, golf, radio control model building. Home: 4718 Zion Rd Cleves OH 45002-9686 Office: 830 Ezzard Charles Dr Cincinnati OH 45214-2525

DERUDDER, VINCENT J., insurance broker; b. Clichy, France, Feb. 23, 1948; s. Jean E. Derudder and Sylvette G. Maire; m. Pilar Balthazar-Ramirez (div. 1986). Grad., SUNY, U. Paris, Inst. Chaillot. Asst. dir. Société Bancaire Paris, Continental Airlines, Paris; dir. United Arab Leasing, Bahrain; pres. MCI-Iberica, Madrid, Spain; vice chmn. Amalinvest (Holdings), Luxembourg; mng. dir. European Bus. Network, Luxembourg. Mem. Inst. Dirs. Home: 3 Rue JP Sauvage, L-2514 Luxembourg Luxembourg Office: European Bus Network, 218 Rte de Longwy, L-1940 Luxembourg Luxembourg

DE RUITER, CORINE, clinical psychologist, researcher; b. Wisch, The Netherlands, Aug. 17, 1960; d. Peter de Ruiter and Betsy Alie Duitshof; m. Joseph Rogers Wiggins, May 27, 1992 (div. July 1997); 1 child, Julian Alexander Isaäc Wiggins. Doctorandus, Utrecht U., The Netherlands, 1986; PhD, U. Amsterdam, The Netherlands, 1989. Lic. clin. psychologist, behavior therapist. Rsch. clin. psychologist Utrecht U., 1986-90; sr. rschr. Leiden U., The Netherlands, 1990-92, U. Amsterdam, 1992-95; head dept. rsch. Dr. Henri van der Hoeven Clinic, Utrecht, 1995-99; prof. forensic psychology U. Amsterdam, 1999—. Editl. bd. Dutch Jour. Psychotherapy, 1990—, Dutch Jour. Behavior Therapy, 1992-95; contbr. articles to profl. jours., book chpt. Mem. Dutch Assn. Behavior Therapy (bd. dirs. 1992-94), Dutch Rorschach Found. (exec. sec. 1991—), Soc. Personality Assessment, Internat. Rorschach Soc. (chair sci. program com. 16th Congress). Avocations: jogging, reading. E-Mail: ruiter@psy.uva.nl. Office: U Amsterdam Dept Psychol, Roetersstraat 15, 1018 WB Amsterdam The Netherlands

DE RUSSY, CANDACE UTER, education reformer; b. Seattle, June 12, 1943; d. Lawrence Aloysius Uter and Sybil Ory Uter Morris; m. Cortes Eugene de Russy, Sept. 7, 1968; children: Gabrielle Voelkel, André Ory. BA cum laude, St. Mary's Dominican Coll., 1964; MA in French, Middlebury Coll., 1965; PhD in French, Tulane U., 1971. Instr. St. John Fisher Coll., Rochester, N.Y., 1971-73; asst. prof. Dominican Coll. of Blauvelt, Orangeburg, N.Y., 1972-78; exec. officer Am. Found. for Resistance Internat., N.Y.C., 1986-88; adj. prof. New Sch. for Social Rsch., N.Y.C., 1991-93; contbg. editor Crisis Mag., Washington, 1995—; appeared on numerous TV and radio commentary programs, including 60 Minutes, 1998. Contbr. numerous articles to profl. jours. Trustee SUNY, Albany, 1995—, Westchester C.C., Valhalla, N.Y., 1993-95; mem. adv. bd. Am. Coun. Trustees and Alumni, Ind. Women's Forum, Washington, 1992—, Found. for Ind. Rights in Edn., 1999—; mem. exec. com. Nat. Com. on Am. Fgn. Policy, N.Y.C., 1984-96. Recipient Frederick D. Wilhelmsen-L. Brent Bozell, Jr. award Cath. Social Action, 1998; NDEA grantee, 1966-71. Mem. Nat. Assn. Scholars, Soc. Cath. Social Scientists, Manhattan Inst. Republican. Roman Catholic. Avocations: study of ideas, iconography, current events, interior decorating, walking.

DE RUYVER, DIRK ANDRE, business development manager; b. Opbrakel, Belgium, Mar. 20, 1964; arrived in Japan, 1990; s. Roger De Ruyver and Jeannine Beetens; m. Ping Xu. Lic. of Econ. Scis., Cath. U. Leuven, Belgium, 1986, Lic. Japanology, 1990. Rep. for Japan Domo Group, Belgium, 1992-97; bus. devel mgr. for Japan Flanders Fgn. Investment Office, 1997—. Author: (geneal. study) From De Ruvere to De Ruyver, 1985, (Internet site) South-East-Flanders, 1999, (local history) History of the Centre of Recruitment of the Belgian Army, 1986. Monbusho scholar Japanese Ministry of Edn., 1990. Avocations: genealogy, Internet, classical music, local history of Flanders and Japan. Fax: 045 682 55 67. E-mail: ffio@gol.com. Office: Flanders Fgn Invest Office, Minatomirai 2-3-1 Nishi-ku, Yokohama Kanagawa-ken 220-6012, Japan

DERVARTANIAN, DANIEL VARTAN, biochemistry educator; b. Boston, July 16, 1933; s. Donabed and Nevart (Ouzounian) DerV.; m. Marie Elizabeth Ypma, May 15, 1964; children: Merle, Adrienne. AA, Boston U., 1953, BA, 1956; MS, Northeastern U., 1959; ScD, U. Amsterdam, The Netherlands, 1965. Wetenschappelijke medewerker U. Amsterdam, 1961-65; rsch. assoc. U. Wis., Madison, 1965-68; asst. prof. U. Ga., Athens, 1968-73, assoc. prof., 1973-78, prof. biochemistry, 1978—, assoc. dir. Sch. Chem. Scis., 1985-91, chmn. divsn. biol. scis., 1991—. Contbr. numerous articles to profl. jours.; editl. bd. Jour. Bioenergetics and Biomembranes, Boston, 1976-85, Jour. Bacteriology, Washington, 1980-82, Biochimica Et Biophysica Acta, Amsterdam, 1988-95; patentee in field. With U.S. Army, 1959-60. Recipient Rsch. Career award NIH, Bethesda, 1971-76; Rsch. grantee NSF, Washington, 1969-72, 84-87, 90-93, NIH, Bethesda, 1971-81, 85-95. Mem. Am. Soc. Microbiology, Am. Soc. Biochemistry and Molecular Biology. Armenian Gregorian (apostolic). Avocations: ancient European and American history, photography. Office: Univ Ga Divsn Biol Scis Biol Scis Bldg Rm 400 Athens GA 30602

DERVIEUX, FREDERIC, food products executive; b. Paris, Oct. 4, 1964; s. Fabien and Claudine (Michel) D.; m. Sigrid Eckhard, Apr. 24, 1992. Engring. Degree, ENSIA, Massy, France, 1990; grad., Tech. U. Muenchen, Munich, 1991. Cert. engring., Logistic supr. Nestle, Weiding, Germany, 1991-93; prodn. mgr. asst. Nestle, Madrid, 1993-94; prodn. mgr. Nestle, São Paulo, Brazil, 1994-95; dep. gen. mgr. Nestle, Qingdao, China, 1995-97; factory mgr. Nestle, Shanghai, China, 1997—; owner software co. Caim, Augsburg, Germany, 1991-93; cons. SGGC, Shanghai, 1999—. Sgt. German Air Force, 1988-89. Avocations: computer science, sociology, sport, travel, languages. Home: No 16 Rose Garden, 165 Guipin Lu, Shanghai 200233, China Office: Nestle, 355 Yun Qiao Rd, Pudong Shanghai 201206, China

DERWICH, MAREK, historian; b. Legnica, Silesia, Poland, July 3, 1956; s. Edmund and Renata (Reiff-Orłowska) D.; m. Elzbieta Dymitrowicz, June 24, 1978 (div. 1996); m. Maria Kurzydlo, July 11, 1998; 1 child, Agnieszka. Mgr., U. Wrocław, Poland, 1979, Doctorate, 1989, Dr. Habil., 1998. Dir. Lab. Rsch. sur l'Histoire Congregations et Ordres Religieux, Wroclaw, 1994—, also bd. dirs.; adj. prof. U. Wroclaw, 1989-97, prof., 1998—; vis. prof. Ecole des Hautes Etudes en Scis. Sociales, Paris, 1994, 96, U. Paris I, 1998, Ecole Pretique des Hautes Etudes; mem. coord. com. cultural exchs. in Europe XIV-XVIII, European Sci. Found., 1997—. Author: Benedictine Abbey of Łysiec, 1992, Benedictine Monasticism, 1998, Armours, Legends, Miths, 1987, 89; editor: La vie quotidien des moines, 1995, Quaestiones Maedii Aevi Novae, 1996—, Fonctions sociales et politiques du culte des saintes, 1999. Mem. Ctr. European des Recherches Congrégations Aodres Religiéux, Ctr. Archéologié Migtoire Médiéioles Établissements Religiéux, Commn. Internat. Histoire Ecclésiastique Comparée. E-mail: larhcor@uni.wroc.pl. Home: Horbaczewskiego 71/28, PL 54130 Wrocław Silesia, Poland Office: U Wroclaw LARHCOR Inst Hist, Szewska 49, 50-139 Wrocław Silesia, Poland

DERZAI, MATTHEW, retired telecommunications company executive; b. Heerlerheide, Limburg, The Netherlands, Sept. 2, 1928; s. Matt Derzai and Angela Ocepek; m. Karen Adele Stokes, June 14, 1958 (div. 1988); children: Melinda Anne, Cynthia Kim, Wendy Cheryl; m. Yolande M. Derzai, Apr. 1989. B of Applied Sci., U. Toronto, Can., 1955. Registered profl. engr. Engr. Bell Can., Montreal, 1954-64, staff engr., 1967-75; engr. AT&T, N.Y.C., 1964-67; head dept. tech. services Internat. Telecommunications Union, Geneva, 1975-79; computer services engr. Canadian Telecommunications Carriers Assn., Ottawa, Ont., Can., 1979-83; gen. mgr., sec.-treas. Frequency Coordination System Assn., Ottawa, 1983-94. Contbr. articles to profl. jours. Mem. IEEE, Assn. Profl. Engrs. Ontario. Avocations: skiing, boating.

DERZHKO, OLEG VOLODYMYROVYCH, physicist, educator; b. Lviv, Ukraine, Aug. 19, 1960; s. Volodymyr Vasylovych and Yaroslava Mykolaivna (Kotsovska) D.; m. Olesya Volodymyrivna Salo; children: Volodymyr, Iryna. Degree, Lviv State U., 1982; PhD, Odessa (Ukraine) State U., 1988. Sr. rschr. Inst. for Condensed Matter Physics, Lviv, 1982—; docent dept. theoretical physics Lviv Nat. U., 1991—. Contbr. articles to profl. jours. Recipient S. Hzhitskyi award West Sci. Ctr. Ukrainian Acad. Sci., 1994. Home: Rodyny Krushelnytskykh 22/8, 79017 Lviv Ukraine Office: Inst for Condensed Matter, Physics/Svientsitskii 1, 79011 Lviv Ukraine

DE SAEGER, SARAH MARIA DIANA GUIDO, pharmacist; b. Dendermonde, Belgium, Sept. 10, 1971; d. Jan and Georgette (De Ridder) De S.; m. Alex Boulonne, Aug. 10, 1996; 1 child: Jules Boulonne. Grad., U. Ghent, Belgium, 1994, PhD, 1999. Scientific rschr. U. Ghent, Belgium, 1994—. Inventor, patentee in field. Office: U Ghent Lab Food Analysis, Harelbekestraat 72, 9000 Ghent Belgium

DE SÁ E SILVA, ELIZABETH ANNE, secondary school educator; b. Edmonds, Wash., Mar. 17, 1931; d. Sven Yngve and Anna Laura Elizabeth (Dahlin) Erlandson; m. Claudio de Sá e Silva, Sept. 12, 1955 (div. July 1977); children: Lydia, Marco, Nelson. BA, U. Oreg., 1953; postgrad., Columbia U., 1954-56, Calif. State U., Fresno, 1990, U. No. Iowa, 1993; MEd, Mont. State U., 1978. Cert. tchr., Oreg., Mont. Med. sec., 1947-49; sec. Merced (Calif.) Sch. Dist., 1950-51; sec., asst. Simon and Schuster, Inc., N.Y.C., 1954-56; tchr. Casa Roosevelt-União Cultural, São Paulo, Brazil, 1957-59, Coquille (Oreg.) Sch. Dist., 1978-96; music tchr. Cartwheels Presch., North Bend, Oreg., 1997-99; tchr. piano, 1967-78; instr. Spanish, Southwestern Oreg. C.C., Coos Bay, 1991-94; pianist/organist Faith Luth. Ch., North Bend, Oreg., 1995—, vocal soloist, 1996—, voice tchr., 1997—. Chmn. publicity Music in Our Schs. Month, Oreg. Dist. VII, 1980-85; sec. Newcomer's Club, Bozeman, Mont., 1971. Quincentennial fellow U. Minn. and Found. José Ortega y Gasset, Madrid, 1991. Mem. AAUW (sec., scholarship chmn., co-pres., pres., treas., editor newsletter), Nat. Trust Hist. Preservation, Am. Coun. on Tchg. Fgn. Langs., Am. Assn. Tchrs. Spanish and Portuguese, Nat. Coun. Tchrs. English, Music Educators Nat. Conf., Oreg. Music Educators Assn., Oreg. Coun. Tchrs. English, Confedn. Oreg. Fgn. Lang. Tchrs., VoiceCare Network. Republican. Avocations: swimming, walking, travel, drama. Home: 3486 Spruce St North Bend OR 97459-1130

DE SAHB, MARQUIS ABDALLAH LEON, economics consultant; b. Aleppo, Syria, June 20, 1921; s. Leon and Guitta (Shelhot) de S.; LL.M., U. Beirut (Lebanon), 1945, Pharmacist, 1967; M.S., U. Sorbonne (Paris), 1950; Chem. Engr., E.N.S.C., Paris, 1950; Ph.D., U. Paris, 1969; Electronics Engr., ESIEE, Paris, 1981; m. Odile Samman, June 18, 1955; children—Dalal-Guitta, Mathilda, Leon, Rima-Ghislaine, Nahla-Helen, Namir-Nicolas. Dir. gen. No. Syria, Wheat Collection Scheme Govt. Syria, 1946-47; founder, chief exec. Marquis Leon de Sahb & Sons, Aleppo, 1951-61, Nat. Foundries & Mech. Workshops, Aleppo, 1952-66, Syrian Swedish Trading Co., Aleppo, Damascus, Syria, 1953-62, Transcontinental Econ. & Devel. Corp., Beirut, 1961-66, United Pharm. & Chem. Corp., Beirut, 1967-76, Al-Omrane Cons., Beirut, 1968—, Establissements A. de Sahb, internat. econ. cons., Beirut, 1970—; vis. prof. Dauphine U., Paris, 1978—; cons., expert Chamber Commerce and Industry, Paris, 1979—; lectr., cons. in field. Mem. Ministerial Com. Syrian 5-Yr. Plan, Damascus, 1960-61. Decorated Knight Holy Sepulchre, Cross Sci. Merit Paris, Grand Officer Order Constantine the Gt., Order Cedar Pres. Lebanon. Mem. Assn. Anciens Eleves de l'Ecole Nat. Superieure de Chimie, Paris, Nat. Order Pharmacists Lebanon, N.Y. Acad. Scis. Club: Vision (Paris). Author: Developpement et Questions d'Orient, 1972; Iran: A Front Page Candidate for Industrialization, 1974, Saudi Arabia: Pressing for Oil to Change into Lifeblood, 1974, From Petrodollars to Arab Steel, 1976, Egypt's Industrial Vocation, 1976, Saudi Arabia in the 1980's, 1978, Development of Expert Systems and the Resources of the Mind, 1988, Pétropuissance et Ordre Américain: La Nouvelle Question d'Orient, 1992. Home: 97 Blvd Murat, 75016 Paris France

DESAI, AASHISH Y., lawyer; b. Chgo., Oct. 7, 1968; s. Yadvendra and Shradhha Desei. BA in Econs., U. Tex., 1991; JD, U. Houston, 1996. Bar: Calif. 1996, U.S. Dist. Ct. (ctrl. dist.) Calif. 1996, U.S. Dist. Ct. Colo. 1998. Tchg. asst. U. Houston Law Ctr., 1994-95; summer assoc. Thompson & Knight, Dallas, 1994-95; jud. clk. Hon. Judge Maloney U.S. Ct. Appeals (5th cir.), Dallas, 1994-95; assoc. Law Offices of Alan Rubinstein, L.A., 1996-97, Mower, Koeller, Nebeker, Carlson & Haluck, Irvine, Calif., 1997—. Mem. ABA, Orange County Bar Assn. Avocations: golf, jazz, blues guitar, tennis, family. Home: 9 Darlington Irvine CA 92620-0221 Office: Mower Koeller Nebeker Carlson & Haluck 108 Pacifica PO Box 19799 Irvine CA 92623-9799

DESAI, HIREN D., software engineer; b. Amravati, India, Oct. 24, 1959; came to U.S., 1982; s. Deovrat R. and Nilly D. Desai; m. Ketki H. Desai, Dec. 9, 1990; children: Rahul, Meera, Priya. BTech in Electronics Engring., Varanasi (India) Inst. Tech., 1982; MS in Computer Sci., U. Ctrl. Fla., 1985; MBA, Emory U., 1995. Systems mgr. Ultra Pink, N.Y.C., 1985-86; systems cons. Granada Systems Design, N.Y.C., 1987-90; sr. software engr. Estek Products-Kodak, Charlotte, N.C., 1990-92; project mgr., sr. mem. tech. staff Bellsouth Telecom., Atlanta, 1992-98; mng. prin. cons. Oracle Cons. Svcs., Atlanta, 1998—. Recipient Mktg. Faculty Honor award and Decision & Info. Analysis award Emory U., Atlanta, 1996. Mem. IEEE, IEEE Computer Soc., Telephone Pioneers Am., Beta Gamma Sigma. Avocation: chess. Home and Office: 11650 Dunhill Place Dr Alpharetta GA 30005-6716

DESAI, JIGNASA, lawyer; b. India, Dec. 12, 1969; came to U.S., 1971; d. Dinker and Bharti Desai. BA, Rutgers Coll., 1991; JD, Rutgers U., Camden, N.J., 1994; student, U. Exeter, Eng., 1989. Bar: N.J. 1994, U.S. Dist. Ct. N.J. 1995. Jud. clk. to two judges New Brunswick, N.J., 1994-95; assoc. Lomurro, Davison, Eastman & Munoz, P.A., Freehold, N.J., 1995-98, sr. assoc., 1998-99; gen. counsel Dept. Def./Comms.-Electronics Command, Ft. Monmouth, N.J., 1999—; mcpl. prosecutor Twp. of Millstone, N.J., 1997-99; asst. twp. atty. Twp. of Manalapan, N.J., 1996-99. Trustee Legal Aid Soc., Monmouth County, 1996—. Mem. N.J. State Bar Assn. (minorities sect.), Women Lawyers in Monmouth, Rutgers Law Alumni Assn. (bd. dirs. 1994—). Office: Office of the Chief Counsel Dept of Def US Army Hdqrs CECOM AMSEL-LG-A Fort Monmouth NJ 07703-5000

DESAI, MAHESH DAHYABHAI, geotechnologist, consultant; b. Navasari, Gujarat, India, Apr. 30, 1936; s. Dahyabhai and Puspaben D. (Pathak) D.; m. Bhadraben M. Pathak, Dec. 20, 1941; children: Jagruti, Prakruti, Trupti. BE in Civil Engring., Maharaja Sayaji U., Baroda, India, 1958; PhD in Civil Engring., South Gujarat (India) U., 1973. Site engr. State Pub. Works Dept., Bombay, 1958-61; rsch. officer ctrl. water power commn. Govt. of India, Delhi, 1961-63; dep. dir. Ctrl. Soil and Materials Rsch. Sta., New Delhi, 1963-69; prof. S.V. Regional Coll. of Engring. and Tech., Surat, India, 1969-93; prof. PG Ctr. South Gujarat U., Surat, 1979-89; with environ. hazards pub. awareness Earth Work Found. Ground Engring., Surat, India, 1990, cons., 1993-97. Author: Sub-Surface Exploration by Penetrometers, 1970, Experimental Geotechnical Engineering, 1974, 2nd edit., 1994; editor: proceedings Internat. Conf. Constrn. Practices and Instrumentation, 1982, proceedings Nat. Conf. Geotech. Analysis Practices and Performance, 1991. mem. citizen coun. pub. awareness against flood projection, Surat, India, 1975; researcher on engring. aspects of plauge Ctr. for Social Studies, Surat, 1995. Recipient 1969-70 Import Substitution award Ministry of Industry Govt. of India, 1970; named Tech. Collobration Tng. Devel. visitor Brit. Coun., 1990. Fellow Indian Geotech. Soc. (exec. mem., Rabio Hazarat award for best paper 1970); mem. Instn. Engrs. Hindu. Avocations: travel, reading, social service. Home: Blh Sarjan Soc, B004 Heritage App, 395007 Surat Gujarat, India Office: Earthwork Found & Ground En, B/H Sarjan Soc B004 Heritage APP, 395007 Surat Gujarat, India

DESAI, NITIN DAYALJI, federal official; b. Bombay, July 5, 1941; s. Dayalji M. and Shantaben Desai; m. Aditi Gupta, Apr. 28, 1979; children: Kartikeya, Nandan. BA with honors, U. Bombay, 1962; MSc in Econs., London Sch. Econs., 1965. Econs. lectr. Liverpool (Eng.) U., 1965-67, Southampton (Eng.) U., 1967-70; cons. Tata (India) Econ. Consultancy Svcs., 1970-73; cons., adviser Planning Commn. Govt. of India, 1973-85, sr. adviser Brundtland Commn., 1985-87, spl. sec. Planning Commn., 1987-88, sec., chief econs. adviser Min. of Fin., 1988-90; dep. sec. gen. UNCED UN, Geneva, 1990-92; undersec. gen. for Pehuj coordination and sustainable devel. UN, N.Y.C., 1993-97, undersec. gen. for econ. and social affairs, 1997—. Office: UN DC2-2320 New York NY 10017

DESAI, PRAGNA DILIP, microbiology educator; b. Surat, Gujarat, India, June 10, 1943; d. Jayantilal Amritlal and Kumud Jayantilal (Sitwala) Patel; m. Dilip Mokshmadan Desai, Oct. 7, 1967; 1 child. BSc, Bhavan's Coll., Bombay, 1964; diploma in bacteriology, U. Toronto, Ont., Can., 1965, MSc, 1967; PhD, M.E.S. Abasaheb Garware Coll., Poona, India, 1982; diploma in edn. mgmt., S.N.D.T. U., Mumbai, 1998. Demonstrator Sch. Hygiene U. Toronto, 1965-70; demonstrator Faculty Dentistry, Toronto, 1968-70; lectr. K.J. Somaiya Coll., Mumbai, 1973-77, M.E.S. Abasaheb Garware Coll., Poona, 1977-80; lectr. Bhavan's Coll., Mumbai, 1980-91, head of dept. microbiology, 1991—; spkr. in field. Contbr. rsch. articles to profl. jours. Program coord. Nat. Environment Awareness Campaign, Mumbai, 1995-96, 96-97, 98-99; career guide Bhavan's Coll., Mumbai, 1991—; academician Excel Industries, Mumbai, 1998-99. Grantee P.E.O. Internat. Peace Scholarship, U. Toronto, 1966, Nat. Rsch. Coun. Can., U. Toronto, 1968-70, Univ. Grants Commn., 1978-79, 90-92. Mem. Am. Soc. Microbiologists, Assn. Food Sci. and Tech. India (life), Assn. Microbiologists India (life), Bharatiya Vidya Bhavan (life), Bhavan's Assn. Microbiologists (chmn. 1991—). Avocations: cooking nutritional food, studying traditions and cultures of people, visiting scientific exhibitions, touring historical places and monuments, vacationing at beach resorts. Home: D 12, Indrasukh Soc 4 Bungalow Rd, Mumbai 400053, India Office: Bhavan's Coll, Dept Microbiol Andheri W, Mumbai 400058, India

DESAI, RUPIN WALTER, English literature educator; b. Rangoon, Burma, Feb. 11, 1934; arrived in India, 1950; s. Walter Sadgun D. and Victoria Mukherjee; m. Evelyn Sarah Desai, Feb. 26, 1960; 1 child, Antipas. BA, Delhi (India) U., 1954, MA, 1956; PhD, Northwestern U., 1968. Lectr. Hindu Coll., Delhi, 1956-69; reader Delhi U., 1970-80, prof. English lit., 1980—. Author: Yeats's Shakespeare, 1971, (novel) Frailty, Thy Name Is O man, 1993; editor (jour.) Hamlet Studies, 1979. Fulbright scholar U.S. Ednl. Found., Washington, 1964; recipient grants Rockefeller Found., N.Y.C., 1965, Newberry Libr., Chgo., 1981. Mem. Thoreau Soc. (life). Office: U Delhi Dept English, Arts Faculty, Delhi 110 007, India

DESAI, SUNIL CHANDRAKANT, civil engineer, consultant; b. Baroda, Gujarat, India, Jan. 18, 1964; came to U.S., 1993; s. Chandrakant Chunibhai and Kantaben Chandrakant Desai; m. Rupam Sunil, Nov. 4, 1993; children: Katha, Charmi. BS, Sadar Patel U., Vvnagar, India, 1984, MS, 1991; diploma in bus. adminstrn., Sadar Patel U., 1990. Registered profl. engr., N.Y., Del. Asst. prof. Birla Vishvakarma Mahavidyalaya (Engring. Coll.), Vvnagar, Gujarat, India, 1984-94; mgr., civil engr. Jersey Tech. Labs. Inc., Newark, 1994-99; asst. civil engr. N.J. Dept. Transp., Ewing, 1999-2000; civil engr. N.Y.C. Dept. Transp., 2000—; cons. geotech. engr. Richard S. Kessler, Little Falls, N.J., 1994-99; cons. surveyor Gujarat Energy Devel. Agy., India, 1986-92. Contbr. articles to profl. jours. Hindu. Avocation: travel. E-mail: kathadesai@aol.com. Home: 706 Columbia Ave North Bergen NJ 07047-1625 Office: NYU Cept Transp 2 Rector St New York NY 10006-1819

DESAI, TUSHAR NANDLAL, pathologist, health facility administrator; b. Mahuva, Gujarat, India, Apr. 21, 1962; s. Nandlal M. and Kundanben N. Desai; m. Priti Tushar Shah, Feb. 11, 1987; q child, Ruchi T. BSc in Microbiology, Bombay U., 1983, diploma in med. lab. tech., 1984. Pathologist Lokmanya Tilak Mcpl. Gen. Hosp., Bombay, 1985-87; med. dir. Clinotek Pathology Lab., Bombay, 1987-88; chairperson, exec. med. dir. Aashirwad Pathology Lab., Bombay, 1988—. Exec. dir. med. camp, Bomay, 1990, 93, Param Keshave Bang, India, 1992. Mem. Assn. Clin. Biochemist India (life), Chembur (life). Avocations: tennis, cricket, table tennis, chess, swimming. Fax: 022-5128724. Home: Plot 73, Block 4, Nirmal, Garodia Nagar, Ghatkopar, Mumbai 400 077, India Office: Aashirwad Path Lab, 32/938 Pant Nagar, Bombay 400 075, India

DESAILLY, MARCEL, professional soccer player; b. Accra, Ghana, Sept. 7, 1968; arrived in France; Defender Nantes Football Club, France; winner French League title, 1992, Champions League, 1993; defender Olympique Marseille Football Club, France, 1992, AC Milan, Italy, 1993-97; winner European Champions Cup, European Supercup, Italian Championships; midfielder Chelsea, London. Voted best player Euro2000 Tournament. Achievements include being the first player to win the European Champions Cup in two successive seasons with different clubs. Office: Milan Assn Calcio SpA, Via Turati 3, 20121 Milan Italy also: Stamford Bridge, CFC Fulham Rd, London SW6 1HS, England*

DE SAINT PHALLE, THERESE, author; b. N.Y.C., Mar. 7, 1930; d. Alexandre and Helen Georgia (Harper) de St. Phalle; m. Baron Jehan de Drouas, Dec. 30, 1950; 1 son, Henri. Grad. high sch. Works include: (novels) La Mendigote, 1966, La Chandelle, 1967, Le Tournesol, 1968, Le Souverain, 1970, La Clairiere, 1974 (pub. as The Clearing in U.S. 1978), Le Metronome, 1980, Le Programme, 1985, L'Odeur de la Poudre, 1988; also TV films, motion picture scripts, short stories, articles; editor Flammarion, 1971-84. V.p., gen. mgr. Stock Pubs., 1984-91; pub. Plon, 1992—; mem. French com. United World Colls. Mem. PEN, Cavalier King Charles Spaniel Club, Les Gens du Livre (pres.), Islam et Occident, La Fraternitè d'Abraham (adminstr.). Roman Catholic. Home: 46 Blvd, Emile Augier, 75116 Paris France Office: 76 rue Bonaparte, 75006 Paris France

DE SAINT SEINE, GUILLAUME BENIGNE, financial executive; b. Neuilly, France, Nov. 29, 1961; s. Philippe Bengine De S. and Micheline Ledntine De Ferrand. Grad., IEP Paris, 1983, Paris IX, 1984. Asst. v.p. BNP, France, 1986-87; v.p. Banque Stern, France, 1987-89; co. sec. Elysees, France, 1990-92; sr. c.p. Banque Indosuez, France, 1992-96; dir. Schroders, England, 1996-99; head French corp. fin. Schroder France, England, 1999—. Lt. French Air Force, 1984-85. Mem. Saint-Lloud Country Club, Jockey Club. Avocations: golf, racing. Home: 137 Rue de Saussure, 75017 Paris France Office: Schroder France, 137 Fbg Saint-Honore, 75008 Paris France

DE SAIVE, MICHEL JRMS, commercial engineer; b. Neuchateau, Belgium, May 30, 1957; s. Pierre and Ghislaine Spits; m. Marinette Magdalena Falste; children: Mikael, Maxime. Comml. engr., Solvay Bus. Sch., Brussels, 1983. Auditor KPMG, Brussels, 1983-88, audit mgr., 1988-95, ptnr., 1995—; prof. in charge MBA-Inst. Cooremans, Brussels, 1992-93; asst. acctg. planning and control ULB-Free U. Brussels, 1986—; bd. mem. Provisional Auditor's Chamber, Bucharest, Romania, 1999; bd. v.p. Fgn. Investors Coun., Bucharest, 1999. Mem. Inst. des Reviseurs d'Entreprises du Royaume de Belgique (reviseur d'entreprises), Romania Corpul Expertilor Contabili si Contabililor Autorizati (fin. auditor 1999). E-mail: mdesaive@kpmg.ro. Fax: 40 1 401 336 1177. Office: KPMG 133, Calea Serbau Voda Sector 4, Bucharest Romania

DE SANCTIS, NANDO, pediatric surgeon; b. Rome, Oct. 5, 1934; s. Ennio de Sanctis and Hendrika Te-Kaeth; m. Fabiola Visocchi, July 12, 1964; children: Francesca, Enrica, Valentina, Ennio. MD, U. Naples, Fla., 1959. Resident in gen. surgery U. Naples, 1959-61, 64-65, resident in orthopedics, 1965-67; asst. Cardarelli Hosp., Naples, 1963-64; chief dept. orthopedics Children's Hosp. Santobono, Naples, 1974—; prof. U. Naples; hon. prof. Fed. U. Sao Paulo, Brazil, 1994. Author: Paediatric Orthopaedics, 1996; contbr. scientific papers in field; mem. editl. bd. Jour. Pediatric Orthopaedics B, 1991—; co-dir. Italian Rev. Traumatology and Pediatric Orthopaedics, 1994-96; contbr. over 129 papers to profl. publs. Lt. Italian Health Office, 1961-62. Recipient Honor medal Deutschland Lang. Paediatric Ortopaedic Soc. Mem. SITOP (pres. 1994-96), EPOS (editor EPOS News 1991—, v.p. 1997-98, pres. 1999—), IFPOS (chmn. 1996-98), OTODI (pres. 1991-93, hon.), SAOTI (hon.), ASAMI (hon.), SDOT (hon.), N.Y. Acad. Sci., CANEO (hon.), Venezuelan Surgery Soc. (hon.), Am. Acad. Sic., N.Y. Acad. Sci., AAOT (corr. mem.), SBOT (corr. mem.). Homeee: Via Tito Livio 9, 80122 Naples Italy Office: Hosp Children Santobono, Via Mario Fiore 6 Ortho 2, 80129 Naples Italy

DE SANCTIS, NICOLA, environmental services company executive; b. Ferrara, Italy, Apr. 24, 1961; s. Giuseppe De Sanctis and Valeria Francini; m. Raffaella Boglione, Apr. 29, 1989; children: Matteo, Filippo, Elena. Diploma in nuc. engring., U. Pisa, Italy, 1986; MBA, INSEAD, Fontainebleu, France, 1988. Indsl. divsn. mgr. Baxter Healthcare, Rome, 1988-89; strategic planning mgr. Agusta Spa, Milan, 1989-91, asst. to the pres., 1991-93; Sardinia divsn. mgr. Waste Mgmt. Italy, Cagliari, 1993-95; dir. acquisitions Waste Mgmt. Italy, Como, 1995-96, comml. and recycling divsn. dir., 1996-98, mcpl. divsn. dir., 1998-99; dir. distbn. Edison SpA, 2000—; advisor FISE Assn., Rome, 1995-99. Co-founder Social Coop., Cagliari, Aid Cmty., Genoa, Italy, 1979. Scholar Inpdai, 1974-80. Mem. INSEAD Alumni Assn. Roman Catholic. Avocations: sailing, reading, chess. Fax: 0-31892990. E-Mail: ndesanctis@libero-it. Home: Corso Sempione 1, 20145 Milan Italy Office: Waste Mgmt Italia spa, Via XXV Aprile 59, 22070 Como Italy

DE SANTO, DONALD JAMES, psychologist, educational administrator; b. Bklyn., July 5, 1942; s. Vincent James and Rose Ann (Dowd) DeS.; m. Loretta DePippo, Aug. 25, 1962; children: Dolores, Jennifer, Marisa. BA cum laude, St. Francis Coll., N.Y., 1964; MA in Clin./Child Psychology, St. John's U., 1966; profl. diploma, 1976; hon. degree, Oglala Lakota Coll., 1999. Asst. law libr. rsch. asst. Dewey, Ballantine, Bushby, Palmer & Wood, N.Y.C., 1960-64; rsch. asst. St. John's U., N.Y.C., 1964-65, tchg. fellow, 1965-66; project dir. 2 federally funded grants, 1975-76; dir. The Rugby Sch., Freehold, N.J., 1977—. Contbg. editor Channels jour. spl. educators, 1986-90, 96—. Mem. Nat. Trust Historic Preservation; mem. Youth Guidance; mem. Youth Guidance Com., Freehold, 1983—, chmn. econ. devel. com., 1984-86; mem. Econ. Devel. Com., Freehold, 1983-87; mem. Zoning Bd Adjustment, Freehold, 1985-86; commr. Lake Topanemus Commn., 1990-94; Rep. campaign chmn., Freehold, 1990, 91; bd. dirs. Monmouth County Transp. Assn., 1990, 91-92; mem. U.S. Selective Svc. Bd., 1991—; apptd. Selective Svc. Commn., 1992; v.p. Freehold Rep. Club, 1991-92; mem. adv. bd. Congl. Awards Com., 1994-98; mcpl. chmn. Freehold Borough Rep. Party, 1995; appt. Rep. Nat. Com., 1995; participant, amb. People to People, Beijing, 1995; trustee Monmouth County Mental Health Assn. Recipient Fire Prevention medal, N.Y.C., 1954, citation for outstanding contbn. to arts in edn. N.J. Commr. Edn., 1981, Pres. award Assn. Schs. and Agys. for the Handicapped, 1995-96, N.J. Very Spl. Arts award, 1996, N.J. Gov's. Arts in Edn. award, 1996; Title VIb Fed. grantee, 1972-78. Mem. NRA (life), APA (pub. rels. com. div. 16), Nat. Assn. Pvt. Schs. Exceptional Children, Coun. Exceptional Children, N.J. Assn. Schs. and Agys. for handicapped (sec., conf. chmn. 1983-84, pub. rels. chmn. 1984-86, Pres. award 1995-96), nat. Soc. Psychologists in Mgmt., Assn. for Help Retarded Children, Monmouth County Hist. Assn., N.J. Assn. Children With Learning Disabilities, Nat. Assn. Pvt. Schs. Exceptional Children, Optimists, Monmouth County Mental Health Assn. (bd. dirs.), Elks, Nat. Assn. of Sch. Psychologists, Psi Chi, Phi Delta Kappa. Roman Catholic. E-mail: Poppled@aol.com. Home: 222 Park Ave Freehold NJ 07728-2006 Office: care Rugby Sch at Woodfield PO Box 1403 Belmar NJ 07719-1403

DE SARNEZ, MARIELLE, foreign diplomat; b. Paris, Mar. 27, 1957. Mem. European Parliament, 1999—, mem. com. on women's rights and equal opportunities, mem. com. on environment, pub. health and consumer policy, substitute com. on constnl. affairs; mem. of bur. Group of the European People's Party (Christian Democrats) and European Democrats; mem. delegation for relations with the Maghreb countries and the Arab Maghreb Union. Mem. Union for French Democracy. Office: Parlement européen, Rue Wiertz ASP 13E246, B-1047 Brussels Belgium*

DESAULNIERS, MARCEL ANDRE, food service executive; b. Woonsocket, R.I., Aug. 2, 1945; s. Eugene Paul and Victoire Irene (Vermette) D.; m. Ann Lyn Nix, Oct. 21, 1968 (div. May 1976); children: Danielle, Marc; m. Constance Warren, July 9, 1977. Student, Culinary Inst. Am., 1963-65, A in Occupational Studies, 1975. Mgr. food prodn., quality control Colonial Williamsburg (Va.) Found., Va., 1970-74; exec. v.p., co-owner Williamsburg Food Brokers, Inc., 1974-80; exec. chef, co-owner Trellis Restaurant, Williamsburg, 1980—. Author: The Trellis Cookbook, 1988, Death by chocolate, 1992, The Burger Meisters, 1994, Dessert to Die for, 1995, An Alphabet of Sweets, 1996; host (TV series) Death by Chocolate. Mem. alumni adv. com. Culiniary Inst. Am., 1987—, trustee, 1988—. Sgt. USMC, 1966-68, Vietnam. Recipient Honor Roll Am. Chefs award Food and Wine Mag., 1983, Ivy award Restaurants and Instns. Mag., 1989, Silver Plate award Internat. Food Svc. Mfrs. Assn., 1994. Mem. Internat. Assn. Culinary Profls., Chaindes Rotisseurs, Am. Culinary Fedn. Avocation: long distance running. Home: 131 Ridings Cv Williamsburg VA 23185-3903 Office: Trellis Restaurant 403 Duke Of Gloucester St Williamsburg VA 23185

DESBRIERES, JACQUES, chemistry educator, researcher; b. Bron, France, Aug. 3, 1956; s. Bernard and Jeanne (DeMartini) D. Engr., Nat. Sch. Chemistry, Paris, 1978; DEng, U. Grenoble, France, 1980, Habilitation, 1991. Project leader Dowell Schlumberger, St. Etienne, France, 1981-88; prof. math. St. Louis Sch., St. Etienne, 1988-90; prof. chemistry U. Grenoble, 1990—. Inventor polymers for petroleum industry, cosmetic applications and polysaccharide derivatives. With French Air Force, 1980-81. Office: U Grenoble CERMAV/CNRS, BP 53, 38041 Grenoble Cedex 9, France

DESCAMPS, MICHEL MARCEL, animal biology educator; b. Lille, France, Dec. 17, 1944; s. Marcel Andre and Marie-Therese (Rassel) D.; m. Brigitte Marie-Therese Clarret, June 13, 1970; children: Catherine, Stephane. BS, U. Lille I, 1965, PhD, 1969, DSc, 1976. Asst. U. Lille I, 1966-70, asst. lectr., 1971-84, lectr., 1985-94, prof., 1994—; dir. ecophysiology of soil invertebrates U. Lille I, 1992-98. Co-author: Arthropod Brain, 1987, Endocrinology of Selected..., 1988, Morphogenetic Hormones of..., Vol. 2, 1990, Vol. 3, 1991, Reproduction Invertebres, 1997; contbr. articles to profl. jours. Fellow Societe Zoologique de France (Prix Strand). Avocations: photography, walking, cycling, trips, reading. Office: U Lille I, Lab Animal Biology, 59655 Villeneuve D'Ascq France

DE SCHAMPHELAERE, LUCIEN, engineer; b. Gyzenzele, Belgium, Apr. 3, 1931; m. Renee De Moor; children: Lieven, Mia, Wim, Steven. Student, Rykshogere Nyverheidsschool, 1952. With instrument devel. Agfa-Gevaert NV, Mortsel, Belgium, 1952-88, mgr. instrument dept., 1961-78, dir. electronic imaging dept., 1979-86, mng. dir. AGIF, 1987-88; with Xeikon nv, Mortsel, 1988-99, chmn., CEO, 1989-97, chmn., 1997-99; chmn., CEO Triakon nv., Mortsel, 1999—; bd. mem. IMECvzw, Option Internat. nv, Melexis nv., Xemex nv., Materialize nv., Hydro Sys. nv., ISEP nv. Patentee in field. Recipient Cary award Rochester Inst. Tech. Mem. Belgium Instrument Automation Control (hon. resident, bd. dirs.), Soc. Image Sci. and Tech. (hon.). Home: Hovestraat 151, 2650 Edegem Belgium Office: Triakon nv, Hendrik Kuyperstraat 51, 2140 Mortsel Belgium

DESCHAMPS, FREDERIC JACQUES, occupational medicine physician; b. Soissons, Aisne, France, Sept. 24, 1959. MD, Lille U., France, 1990, D Toxicology, 1993; tchr. occupational diseases & health, Med. U. Reims, France, 1995. Intern U. Hosp. Lille, 1986-90; resident U. Hosp. Reims, France, 1992-95; physician Dept. Occupational Diseases Hosp. Maison Blanche, Reims, 1995—; rschr. occupational cancers and occupational allergy. Mem. French Soc. Occupational Health, Internat. Assn. Occupational Health. Home: 82 Rue Libergier, 51100 Reims France Office: Hosp Maison Blanche, 45 Rue Cognacq-Jay, 51092 Reims France

DE SCHOUTHEETE DE TERVARENT, PHILIPPE, ambassador; b. Berlin, May 21, 1932; s. Guy and Jeanne (Darcy) De S.; m. Bernadette Joos, June 9, 1956; children: Marc-Antoine, Aimery. LLD, Lic. in Polit. Sci., U. Cath. de Louvain, 1953. Diplomatic postings Paris/Cairo/Madrid/Bonn, 1956-76; chief of cabinet to Fgn. Min., 1980-81, ambassador to Madrid, 1981-85; dir. gen. polit. affairs Fgn. Min., 1985-87; permanent rep. to European Union Brussels, Belgium, 1987-97; guest prof. U. Louvain la Neuve, Belgium, 1990—; ofcl. rep. of Order of Malta to European Union, 2000—. Author: La Cooperation Politique Européenne (2nd edit.), 1986, Une Europe pour Tous, 1997 (Adolphe Bentinck prize), The Case for Europe, 2000. Mem. Academie Royale de Belgique. Office: Inst d'Etudes Europeennes, 1 Place des Doyens, B 1348 Louvain-la-Neuve Belgium

DE SCHRYVER, ANTOON AUGUSTA, epidemiologist; b. Gent, Belgium, Mar. 9, 1955; s. Pierre Antoine and Hilda Maria (Bernard) D.; m. Rita Maria Stevens, Sept. 20, 1980; 1 child, Sofie. MD, Gent U., Belgium, 1980, Doctorate in Biomed. Scis., 1990. Cert. Occupational medicine, Gent U., Tropical medicine, Inst. for Tropical Medicine. Med. officer Kasongo-Lunda, Zaire, 1980-82; lectr. U. Gent, 1982-88; med. officer World Health Orgn., Geneva, Switzerland, 1988-91; occupl. physician IKMO, Bruge, Belgium, 1991-97; sr. lectr. U. Gent, Belgium, 1996—; occupl. physician Idewe, Gent, 1997—; tchr. Gent Nurse Sch., Belgium, 1986-88. Contbr. articles to profl. jours. Recipient rsch. fellowship, U. Gent., 1990-95, Health and Enterprise award, European Club for Health Care, Paris, 1996, Well-Being in Hosps. award, Ministry of Labour, Brussels, 1996. Mem. Belgian Assn. Pub. Health (sec.), Belgian Asssn. Occupational Physicians, Archives of Pub. Health (editl. bd.). Office: Idewe, Laurentplein 9, B9000 Gent Belgium

DE SCHUTTER, KRISHNA SERGE, organization administrator; b. Brussels, Mar. 29, 1971; s. Andre and Valentine (deCrombrugghe) De S. Degree in elec. civil engring., U. Cath. de Louvain, Belgium, 1994. Automation engr. Extraction De Smet, Antwerp, Belgium, 1994-95; adminstr. Handicap Internat., Kinshasa, Zaire, 1995-96; dir. Handicap Internat., Kinshasa and

Brazzaville, Congo, 1996-98; adminstr. Handicap Internat., Brussels, 1999—; engr. Electrabel, Brussels, 1998—. Mem. IEEE.

DESCORNET, MARC, information professional; b. Brussels, Jan. 28, 1970; s. Guy and Annick (Marechal) D. Radio realisator Action 106.9 FM, Brussels, 1995—, info. mgr., 1996—; radiio realisator Action 104.9 FM Canal 44, Braine-l'Alleud, 1998—; libr., documentalist Assn. Nat. d'Aide aux Handicapés Mentaux, 1997—. Home: General Gratry St 84A9, 1030 Brussels Belgium Office: Pluvierlaan 24, 1933 Sterrebeek Belgium

DESCOTES, GÉRARD LOUIS, organic chemistry educator; b. Lyon, Rhône, France, May 6, 1933; s. Claudius and Germaine (Guillot) D.; m. Colette Blanche Peccaud, Dec. 26, 1956; children: Sophie, Jean-Luc. Engr., U. Lyon, France, 1954, PhD in Chemistry, 1958. Registered chem. engr. Rschr. CNRS, France, 1954-62; prof. organic chemistry U. Lyon 1, 1962—; dir. Lab. Organic Chemistry, Lyon, 1962—, Assoc. Unit CNRS, 1992, Sci. Group Sucrochemistry, 1989. Editor: Carboyhdrates as Organic Raw Materials II, 1992; contbr. articles to profl. jours.; patentee in field. With French art., 1958-60. Mem. Am. Chem. Soc., French Chem. Soc., French Group Carbohydrates. Home: 60 Rue W Rousseau, 69006 Lyon France Office: U Lyon, 43 Bld 11-11-1918, 69622 Villeurbanne France

DE SERRES, MARK, research scientist; b. New Haven, June 1, 1955; s. Frederick Joeseph and Christine Marie de Serres; m. Suzan Council, May 30, 1976; children: Amanda, Lauren. BA in Zoology, U. N.C., 1980, MS in Pathology, 1987. Rsch. scientist II Burroughs Wellcome Inc., Research Triangle Park, N.C., 1993; rsch. scientist III Burroughs Wellcome Inc., Research Triangle Park, 1993-95; sr. rsch. scientist Glaxo Wellcome Inc., Research Triangle Park, 1995-96, rsch. investigator I, 1996-98, rsch. investigator II, 1998—. Contbr. articles to profl. jours. Sponsorship chmn. Tar Heel Sertoma Club, Chapel Hill, N.C., 1999. Named Sertoman of the Yr., Tar Heel Sertoma Club, Chapel Hill, 1999. Mem. AAAS, Am. Assn. Pharm. Scientists. Avocations: gardening, boating. E-mail: MD43304@glaxowellcome.com. Fax: 919-315-6003. Office: Glaxo Wellcome Inc 5 Moore Dr Research Triangle Park NC 27701

DE SEZE, AMAURY-DANIEL, bank executive; b. Paris, May 7, 1946; s. Arnaud and Jacqueline (Darcy) de S.; m. Elisabeth d'Estutt d'Assay, Dec. 14, 1974; children: Ghislain, François-Xavier. Student, U. Paris, 1980, Inst. Hautes Etudes Def. Nat., Paris, 1982, Stanford U., 1985. With Bull GE, 1968-72, Carnation - Gloria, 1972-73, Towers, Perrin, Forster and Crosby, Inc., 1973-75, Videocolor (Thomson), 1975-78; mem. exec. com., sr. v.p. AB Volvo, 1978-93; mem. mgmt. bd. Compagnie Financière de Paribas et Banque Paribas, Paris, 1993—; bd. dirs. Cobepa, Eiffage, Fives Lille, Groupe Bruxelles Lambert, Internat. Metal Svc., La Poste, Schneider, Sema Group PLC. Former judge Comml. Ct. of Dist. les Hauts de Seine, Nanterre, France. Chevalier dans l'Ordre Nat. du Mérite, 1991. Mem. Jockey Club. Home: 51 Blvd Beauséjour, 75016 Paris France Office: Compagnie Fin de Paribas, 3 Rue d'Antin BP 141, 75078 Paris Cedex 02, France

DESHAZER, RUTH SHOMLER, health facility administrator; b. Glendale, Calif., July 17, 1954; d. Russell Paul and Pauline April (Lathrop) Shomler; 1 child, Michael Jr. BA magna cum laude, San Diego State U., 1982; AS, San Diego Mesa Coll., 1993. Accredited records technician; cert. profl. of healthcare quality. Med. records technician, coder Scripps Healthcare, La Jolla, Calif., 1993-94; cont. quality improvement coord. Adventist Health Systems, National City, Calif., 1994-96; applications specialist MED Data Systems Inc., San Diego, 1996-97; health info. mgmt. cons. Pyramid Healthcare Cons., L.A., 1997; health info. mgmt. sr. cons. Elacor Resources Group, L.A., 1997-98; health info. mgmt. dir. Brea (Calif.) Cmty. Hosp., Pacifica Hosp. of the Valley, Burbank, Calif., 1998-99; ind. cons. in healthcare quality, info. mgmt. and survey preparation, L.A. and Orange County, Calif., 1999—; med. staff coord. MemorialCare Health Systems, Orange County, Calif., 1999—; med. staff coord. MemorialCare Health Sys., Orange County, Calif., 1999—. Contbr. articles to profl. jours. Mem. Calif. Assn. Quality Profls., San Diego Health Info. Assn. (various offices 1994-97), Greater Orange Counth Health Info. Assn. (pres.-elect 1998-99, pres. 1999-2000), Calif. Health Info. Assn. (nominating com. 1995-96, legis. com. 1996-97, convention com. 1997-98, chair convention com. 1998-99, membership com. 1998-99), Am. Health Info. Assn., Phi Beta Kappa, Phi Kappa Phi. Avocations: landscaping, floral design, swimming, travel. E-mail: cooknruth@aol.com.

DESHMUKH, KISHOR MADHUKAR, electronics and telecommunications engineer; b. Pune, Mahar., India, Oct. 27, 1955; s. Madhukar Laxman and Vijaya Madhukar (Ambike) D.; m. Seema Sharad Godbole, May 11, 1980; 1 child, Dhanashree. Diploma in Electronics/Telecom. Engring., Govt. Poly., Pune, 1976. Engr. Tecmark, Pune, 1976; technician DCM Data Products, Pune, 1976-77; tech. asst. Overseas Comm. Svc., Pune, 1977-80; dep. mgr. Meltron, Pune, 1980—. Mem. Inst. of Stds. Engrs., Indian Assn. for Quality and Reliability, Soc. EMC Engrs. India, Metrology Soc. India. Avocations: reading, technical literature collecting. Home: Paud Rd, 48-II/4 Ex-Servicemens Soc, Pune 411038, India Office: Meltron Agri Coll Campus, Shivajinagar, Pune 411005, India

DESHMUKH, PRAKASH RAMCHANDRA, scientist; b. Indore, India, Jan. 21, 1945; s. R. D. and M. R. (Limaye) D.; m. Pratibha P. Tare, July 12, 1953; children: Hanumant, Sudarshan. BS, Indore U., 1965, MS, 1967; MS Tech., Birla Inst. Tech. and Sci., Pilani, India, 1969; PhD, Banaras Hindu U., Varanasi, India, 1994. Scientist A Cen. Electronics Engring. Rsch. Inst., Pilani, 1975-78, scientist B, 1978-83, scientist C, 1983-88, scientist E1, 1988-93, scientist EII, 1993—; rsch. scholar U. Cambridge, Eng., 1978, U. Calif., Berkeley, 1984. Contbr. articles to sci. jours. Avocation: vocalist (Indian classical music). Office: Cen Elec Engring Rsch Inst, 333031 Pilani India

DESHPANDE, AJAY NARAYAN, process engineer, engineering executive; b. Pune, Maharashtra, India, Jan. 2, 1958; s. Narayan Raghunath and Usha Narayan (Bhatt) D.; m. Nivedita Soman, Feb. 18, 1991; children: Rahul, Meghana. BTech., Laxminarayan Inst. Tech., Nagpur, 1979; MTech., Indian Inst. Tech., Delhi, 1986. Engring. Mgr. process Engrs. India Ltd., New Delhi, 1980-94, project mgr., 1995—; lead engr. polymer Tabriz (Iran) Petrochem. Co. deputation Engrs. India Ltd., 1992; supt. officer Petronas Gas SDN BHD deputation Engrs. India Ltd., Kerteh, Malaysia, 1994-95; process engr. utility Technip deputation Engrs. India Ltd., Paris, 1995; mem. tech. nat. trial inspection for chem. weapons conv. Govt. India, New Delhi, 1994-95, process tech. audit com. petrochem. plant, Mumbai, India, 1989-90; project mgr. 300 Ktpa ethylene plant IPCL, 1996-99. King Edward Meml. Scholarship Nagpur U., 1977-78, J.N. Tata Endowment Scholarship J.N. Tata Edn. Trust, Mumbai, 1979-80; recipient Nagpur Elec. Light and Power Co. Ltd., Gold medal Nagpur U., 1978-79. Mem. Indian Inst. Tech. Alumni Assn., Rotaract Club (sec. Nagpur 1977-78, dir., 1978-79), Indian Inst. Chem. Engrs. Avocations: Indian classical music, athletic sports, literature, social communications, voluntary community service. Home: E-53, IFS Apts Mayr Vihar-I, Delhi 110 091, India Office: Engrs India Ltd EI House, 4th Fl Bhikaji Cama Place, New Delhi 110 066, India

DESHPANDE, RAJENDRA V., research scientist. BS, Abasaheb Garware Coll., Pune, India, 1984; MS, B. J. Med. Coll., Pune, 1987; PhD, Med. U. S.C., 1992. Postdoctoral rsch. fellow Meml. Sloan-Kettering Cancer Ctr., N.Y.C., 1992-95; postdoctoral rsch. scientist Pharmacia & Upjohn, Inc., Kalamazoo, Mich., 1995-97; rsch. scientist Amgen, Inc., Thousand Oaks, Calif., 1997—. Fax: 805-449-7464.

DÉSI, ILLÉS, physician; b. Budapest, Nov. 12, 1931; s. Imre and Anne (Adler) D.; m. Aniko Gergely, Aug. 5, 1962; children: John Imre, Andreas George. MD, U. Med. Sch., Budapest, 1956; MSc in Environ. Engring., U. Chem. Sch., Veszprém, Hungary, 1976; PhD in Medicine, Acad. Sci. Hungary, 1965, DSc in Medicine, 1979. Cert. specialist in lab. medicine, indsl., medicine, electroencephalography, pathophysiology and toxicology. Asst. prof. U. Med. Sch., Budapest, 1956-69; prof. dept. pub. health U. Med. Sch., Szeged, Hungary, 1984—; head divsn. of hygienic-toxicology Nat. Inst. of Health, Budapest, 1969-84. Editor-in-chief Geographia Medica, 1972-95; mem. editl. bd. Internat. Jour. Environ. Health Rsch., 1990—, Health and Place, 1995—, Jour. of Social Scis. & Medicines, 1995—, Central European Jour. of Occupational & Environ. Health, 1996—; contbr. numerous articles to profl. jours. Pres. Csongrad County Soc. of Environ. Protection, 1990—. Recipient award Hungarian Red Cross, 1960, Hungarian Acad. Sci., 1976, 83, Hungarian Hygiene Soc., 1986. Mem. Hungary-Medico Geographical Soc. (pres. 1972—), IUPAC (assoc.), Internat. Com. Occupational Health, Hungarian Hygiene Soc. (Szeged br.), Hungarian Acad. Sci. (pres. com. environ. health Szeged br. 1987—), Collegium of Hygiene, Collegium of Occupl. Health. Avocations: modern history, photography, excursion. Home: Lagymanyosi 13, H1111 Budapest Hungary Office: U Med Sch Dept Pub Health, Dom ter 10, H 6720 Szeged Hungary

DESIDERI, JEAN-ANTOINE, research scientist, aeronautical engineer; b. Nice, France, Aug. 3, 1951; s. Barthelemy and Henriette (Giry) D. Aero. Engr., Ecole Aeronautiqcue et Espace, Toulouse, France, 1974; MS, Iowa State U., 1976, PhD in Aerospace Engring., 1978; Habil., U. Nice, France, 1993. NRC assoc. NASA Ames Rsch. Ctr., Moffett Field, Calif., 1980-81; rsch. scientist Nat. Rsch. Inst. for Computer Sci. and Control, Sophia-Antipolis, France, 1983—. Co-recipient 1st prize Seymour Cray, 1991. Home: 2 Ave du Monastère, 06000 Nice France Office: INRIA BP 93, 2004 Route des Lucioles, 06902 Sophia Antipolis France

DE SILVA, EUGENE LAKSHMAN, academic administrator, educator; b. Colombo, Sri Lanka, Jan. 6, 1964; s. Angelo Lakshman and Latha (Nissanka) de S.; m. Cheryl Lowe, May 21, 1994; children: Catherine, James, Eugenie. Grad., Royal Soc. Chemistry, London, 1989; MSc, Manchester (Eng.) Met. U., 1997; PhD in Chemistry, U. Herts/Knioghtsbridge U., Denmark, 1997; PhD in Surface Engring., Manchester Met. U., 1998. Cert. chemistry, engring., mgmt., mfg. mgmt. systems. Prodn. supr. Exchemie Ltd., Sri Lanka, 1982-83; tech. rep. Chemanex Ltd., Sri Lanka, 1983-85; plant mgr. Ceylon Pencil Co., Sri Lanka, 1985-86; stringer journalist The Island/Sunday Times, Sri Lanka, 1986-89; mktg. dir. HE Sequence Suppliers, Sri Lanka, 1986-89; pres., founder Soc. Martial Arts, Manchester, Eng., 1994—; quality mgr. H. Marcel Guest Ltd., Manchester, Eng., 1997-99; prin. Coll. Higher Edn. of Martial Arts, U.K., 2000—; lectr. Leeds Coll. Tech., 2000—; cons. He Sequence Suppliers, Sri Lanka, 1989—. Author: Lecture Notes on Chemistry, 1998, In Recognition of Wisdom-A Degree in Martial Arms, 1998; organizer, editor Procs. Internat. Conf. Martial Arts and Internat. Jour. Martial Arts, 1998; patentee in field. Fellow Bus. and Tech. Inst., 1989, inst. Mfg., 1989, Inst. Mgmt. Systems, 1989, Soc. Martial Arts, 1994; inducted into Internat. Hall of Fame of Martial Arts, 2000. Mem. Soc. Martial Arts (pres. 1994—, editor jour. 1998—). Avocations: martial arts, reading, journalism, cinema. Achievements include being the first to design a university degree in martial arts, 1994. Home: 2 Bradney Close, Higher Blackley M9 8WN, England Office: Soc. Martial Arts, PO Box 34, Manchester M9 8DN, England

DE SILVA, G. P. S., judge. Chief justice Supreme Ct. of Sri Lanka, Colombo. Office: Supreme Ct, Superior Cts Complex, Colombo Sri Lanka*

DE SILVA, HANDUNNETTI SAKUNTALA V., physicist; b. Colombo, Sri Lanka, Oct. 11, 1960; s. Handunnetti Roland De S. and Phillippenge Tecla A. Jayasingha. BSc in Physics, U. Colombo, 1986; MS in Physics, U. Mo., Rolla, 1995. Demonstrator in physics U. Colombo, 1987-88, asst. lectr. in physics, 1989-92; tchg. asst. Northeastern U., Boston, 1992-93, U. Mo., Rolla, 1993-95, U. Nebr., Lincoln, 1996—. Mem. Am. Phys. Soc. Buddhist. Avocation: reading. Home: 1429 N 34th St Apt 2 Lincoln NE 68503-2001 Office: U Nebr-Lincoln 116 Brace Lab PO Box 880111 Lincoln NE 68588-0111

DE SILVA, KURUNERUGE TULEY DAYANAND, chemist, educator; b. Dar-Es-Salaam, Tanzania, May 28, 1936; s. Kuruneruge William and Grace (Jayasuriya) De S.; m. Neelanganie, Sept. 14, 1962; children: Jeevanie, Asika, Inosha. BSc with honors, U. Ceylon, Sri Lanka, 1960; BPharm, U. London, 1965; MSc, U. Manchester, Eng., 1969, PhD, 1971; DSc (hon.), U. Sri Jayewardenepura, 1996. Chartered chemist, pharmacist. Prof. chemistry U. Sri Jayewardenepura, 1976-89, dean applied sci. faculty, 1974-77, 85-88; sr. rsch. fellow U. Md., College Park, 1989-91; spl. tech. advisor UNIDO, Vienna, 1991-98; vis. prof. U. Md., College Park, 1979-80, U. Sri Jayemardenepura, 2000—; pres. Vidyodaya campus U. Sri Lanka, 1977-78; dir. Ayurveda Rsch. Inst., Colombo, Sri Lanka, 1975-78; cons. UNIDO, Vietnam, 1984, 88, 89; nat. cons. WHO/UNDP, Sri Lanka, 1984; cons. Open U., Sri Lanka, 1985—; advisor Curriculum Devel. Ctr., Sri Lanka, 1984-89; guest prof. Shenyang Pharm. U., China, 1994; mem. tech. adv. com. on drugs Min. Health, 1999—; cons. Nat. Commn. for Sci. and Tech., 2000. Editor: Manual on the Essential Oil Industry, 1996; co-author: (booklet) Vegetable Tanning, 1982; co-editor Vidyodaya Jour. Arts, Sci. and Letters, 1982-88, Vidya, 1964-89. Asst. sec. Orgn. of Profl. Assns. of Sri Lanka, 1986-88; mem. governing bd. Alcohol and Drug Info. Ctr., Sri Lanka, 1987-89; bd. trustees Dharmavijaya Found., Sri Lanka, 1985-89; chmn. adv. bd. All Ceylon Buddhist Students Fedn., Sri Lanka, 1977-88; v.p. exec. coun. Sarvodaya Sangamaya, Sri Lanka, 1988-90. Recipient Merit award Polymer Sci. Edn. Rubber and Plastic Inst., 1987; Commonweal Univ. Assn. U.K. Travelling fellow, 1986. Fellow Royal Soc. Chemistry U.K., Acad. Scis. Sri Lanka, Inst. Chemistry; mem. N.Y. Acad. Scis., Bur. of Internat. Coun. of Medicinal and Aromatic Plants, Pharm. Soc. Sri Lanka (pres. 1999—), Inst. Chemistry Ceylon (v.p. 1999—). Avocations: writing, scrabble, sports, music. Office: Dept Chemistry, U Sri Jayewarderepura, A1400 Nugegoda Sri Lanka

DESIMONE, LIVIO DIEGO, diversified manufacturing company executive; b. Montreal, Que., Can., July 16, 1936; s. Joseph D. and Maria E. (Bergamin) De S.; m. Lise Marguerite Wong, 1957, children: Daniel J., Livia D., Mark A., Cynthia A. B.Chem. Engring., McGill U., Montreal, 1957. Process engr. 3M Can., 1957-61; With 3M Co., St. Paul, 1961—; exec. v.p. life scis. sector 3M Can., St. Paul, 1981, exec. v.p. indsl. and consumer sector, 1984-86, exec. v.p. indsl. and consumer sector and pvt. svcs., 1986-89, exec. v.p. indsl. and electronic sector and corp. svcs., 1989-91, exec. v.p. info., imaging and electronic sector & pvt. svcs., 1991, exec. v.p., 1991; chmn. bd., CEO 3M Co., 1991—; bd. dirs. Cray Rsch. Inc., Dayton Hudson Corp., Gen. Mills Inc., Vulcan Materials Co. Bd. dirs. Jr. Achievement Inc. (nat.), Minn. Bus. Partnership, 3M Found.; trustee U. Minn. Found. Mem. Bus. Roundtable. Office: Minn Mining & Mfg Co 3 M Ctr Bldg 22014w05 Saint Paul MN 55144-0001

DÉSIR, HARLEM, foreign diplomat; b. Paris, Nov. 25, 1959. Mem. European Parliament, 1999—, mem. com. on industry, external trade, rsch. and energy, substitute com. on employment and social affairs; mem. Group of the Party of European Socialists; mem. delegation for relations with South Africa. Socialist Party. Office: Parlement européen, Rue Wiertz ASP 14G165, B-1047 Brussels Belgium*

DESJARDINS, BENOIT PIERRE, mining engineer, consultant; b. Caen, Calvados, France, Dec. 2, 1970; s. Jean-Marie Alfred and Bernadette Marie (Laura) D. Engr., Ecole Poly., France, 1993; Corps des Mines, Ecole de Mines, Paris, 1996. Engr. Pont à Mousson SA, 1993-94, French Minisry Industry, 1993-99; rschr. Daephine U., 1994-98; engr. Atomic Energy Commn., 1999—, French Minisry Industry, 1993-99; cons. SGGI, Paris, 1999—. Author: Anistopy and Diffusion in Rotating Fluids, 1999. Lt. French mil., 1990-93. Recipient prix Marie Louise Arconati-Visconti, Chancellerie des U. Paris, 1998. Mem. Amicale du Corps des Mines. Roman Catholic. Avocations: philately, running, tennis, squash, reading. Office: CEA/DAM/DCSA/SSA BP 12, Ctr de Bruyeres le Chatel, 91680 Bruyeres le Chatel France

DESJEUX, JEHAN-FRANÇOIS, pediatrician; b. Garches, France, Feb. 5, 1940; s. J. and Françoise (Candlot) D.; m. Marie France Lefort, Mar. 25, 1965; children: Olivier, Isabelle, Sphie, Virginie. MD, U. Paris Sch. Medicine, 1971. Resident Hopital d'enfants, Tunis, Tunisia, 1967-68, Hopital Sainte Justine, Montreal, 1968-69, hopitaux de Paris, 1969-72; rsch. assoc. Yale U., New Haven, 1972-74; chief pediat. clinic Hopitaux de Paris, 1974-78; rsch. dir. INSERM, Paris, 1982-97; prof., chair biology Nat. Conservatory Arts & Mètiers, Paris, 1990; scientific advisor Nestlè Found., Lausanne, Switzerland, 1996—; pres. scientific com. Action Contre la Faim, Paris, 1999—; dir. Scientific Inst. Tehcnology & Nutrition, Paris, 1990-95; cons. WHO, 1979-88.0. Co-author: Food, Genetics and Health in Children, 1994, La communication Scientifique; co-editor: Human Nutrition, 1996; editor Jour. Pediat. Gastroenterology & Nutrition, 2000—. Mem. French Acad. Medicine, Am. Gastroenterology Assn., French Assn. Nutrition (pres. 1980—). Roman Catholic. Avocations: hunting, fishing. Office: CNAM Chair of Biology, 2 rue Conte, 75003 Paris France

DESKUR, ANDRZEJ MARIA, archbishop; b. Sancygniow, Kielce, Poland, Feb. 29, 1924. Ordained priest Roman Cath. Ch., 1950. Consecrated bishop Titular See of Thenae, Roman Catholic Ch., 1974, archbishop, 1980; created cardinal Roman Catholic Ch., 1985; pres.-emeritus Pontifical Coun. for Social Communications; pres. Pontifical Acad. Immaculate Conception. Office: Palazzo S Carlo, Citta del Vaticano, 00120 Rome Vatican City*

DESMAREST, M. THIERRY, gas and oil executive. Ceo TotalFina, Paris; chmn., CEO Elf Aquitaine. Office: Elf Aquitaine, 2 place de la Coupole, 92400 Courbevoie France*

DESMET, STEPHANE JOSEPH, sales company executive; b. Brussels, Jan. 5, 1961; s. François and Jeannine (Mertens) D.; m. Pascale Franck, June 19, 1993; children: Alexia, Sarane. Degree in comml. engring., U. Mons, Belgium, 1984. Sr. auditor Arthur Andersen, Brussels, 1984-87; contr. Groupe Dupuis, Charleroi, Belgium, 1987-92, fin. mgr., 1992-99, sales mgr., 1999—. Office: Group Dupuis, Group Dupuis, 52 Rue Jules Destree, 6001 Mercinelle Belgium

DESMITH, DAVID W., writer; b. Rochester, N.Y., June 12, 1958; s. Robert Humphrey and Beverly (Wheeler) DeS.; m. Susan M. Hammerland, Oct. 24, 1987; children: Red Ernesto, Marcel Odie. BA, Johns Hopkins U., 1980; MA, U. Colo., 1982. Creative supr. Campbell-Mithun, Mpls., 1985-88; creative dir. Young & Rubicam, N.Y.C., 1989-91, Mezzina/Brown, N.Y.C., 1991-96; pres. DWD Creative Svcs. Inc., Yarmouth, Maine, 1996—. Author: A Camel Named Joe, 1998, The 100% Colombian Coffee Book, 1999; contbr. articles to mags. Mem. Golf Writers Assn. Am. E-mail: dwd612@aol.com. Home: 141 Wharf Rd Yarmouth ME 04096-5331

DESMOND, PAULA A., psychology educator; b. Birmingham, Eng., Oct. 28, 1971; d. Jerry and Maureen Desmond. BSc in Psycholgoy, Aston U., Eng., 1993; PhD in Psychology, Dundee (Scotland) U., 1997. Postdoctoral scholar U. Minn., Mpls., 1997-98; asst. prof. Tex. Tech. U., Lubbock, 1998—; mem. rsch. com. Tex. Dept. Transp., Austin, 1999—; presenter in field. Contbr. articles to profl. jours. Rsch. grantee Minn. Dept. Transp., 1997, Tex. Dept. Transp., 1999; Northcote scholar U. London, 1996. Mem. Human Factors and Ergonomics Soc. Avocations: piano playing, squash, tennis. E-mail: pdesmond@ttu.edu. Office: Tex Tech Univ Dept Psychology PO Box 42051 Lubbock TX 79409-2051

DESMOULIERE, ALEXIS, research scientist; b. Bordeaux, France, Oct. 2, 1957; s. André and Cécile (Deprecq) D.; m. Christine Latour, Aug. 13, 1983; children: Cécile, Isabelle, Hélène, Jeanne. D in Pharmacy, Bordeaux II U., 1982; PhD in Sci., Bordeaux I U., 1987, Internat. Cert. Human Ecology, 1988. Rsch. fellow Inst. Nat. de la Sante et de la Rsch. Med., Bordeaux, 1984-87; mgr. R&D Bio-Prodns. S.A., Périgueux, France, 1987-88; asst. prof. U. Medicine, Geneva, 1988-93; 1st class rschr. Nat. Ctr. Sci. Rsch., Lyon, France, 1993-98, Bordeaux, 1998—. Author: Smooth Muscle Cells: Molecular and Cell Biology, 1995, The Molecular and Cell Biology of Wound Repair, 1996. Capt. Navy, Health Svc., 1982-83. Mem. Am. Soc. Cell Biology, European Cytoskeletal Forum, European Vascular Biology Soc., European Tissue Repair Soc. (bd. dirs.). Fax: 05 56 51 40 77. E-mail: alexis.desmouliere@gref.u-bordeaux2.fr. Office: U Victor Segalen Bordeaux 2, 146 Rue Leo-Saignat, 33076 Bordeaux cedex France

DESMURS, JEAN ROGER, chemist, researcher; b. Saint-Remy, France, June 7, 1950; s. Marcel and Therese (Sylvestre) D.; m. Marie Louise Gruner, May 3, 1975; 1 child, Alexandre Nicolas. D of Chemistry, Ecole Nat Superior Chimie, Strasbourg, France, 1974. Cert. engr., chemist. Rschr. Rhone-Poulenc Rsch., Saint Fons, France, 1974-82, sr. rschr. analytical dept., 1982-83; rschr. Louvain-la-Neuve U., Belgium, 1982-83; sr. rschr. organic dept. Rhone-Poulenc Rsch., Saint Fons, France, 1987-91, head analytical dept., 1991-94, head organic dept., 1994-99; dir. rsch. pharm. ingredients, diphenols and aroma Rhodia Organique, Venissieux, France, 1999—; assoc. rschr. Rhone-Poulenc, Saint Fons, France, 1986-91, assoc. dir., 1992. Editor: Advances in Organobromine Chemistry 1, 1991, Advances in Organobromine Chemistry II, 1995, The Roots of Organic Development, 1996. Recipient Rsch. prize Rhone-Poulenc, 1989, 95. Mem. European Chem. Soc., French Chem. Soc. (Organic Divsn. prize 1990). Home: 38 Route de Ternay, F-69360 Communay France Office: Rhodia Organique, 6 Rue Georges Marrane BP 55, 69632 Venissieux Cedex, France

DESNÉ, ROLAND, classicist, educator; b. Issy Les Moulineaux, France, Apr. 24, 1931; s. Pierre and Antoinette (Caron) D.; m. François Guiheneuf, Oct. 16, 1954; 1 child, Marianne; m. Paulette Aubert, Dec. 31, 1987; children: François, Julie. CAPES and Agrégation Lettres Modernes, Ecole Normale Superieure Saint-Cloud, France, 1960; grad. in French Lit., U. Paris-Sorbonne, 1977. Prof. French Lycée Langues Étrangères, Lovetch, Bulgaria, 1954-55, Ecole Normale Instituteurs, Rouen, France, 1960-61, Lycée Paul Eluard, Saint-Denis, France, 1961-62; attaché recherche CNRS, Paris, 1962-66; asst. Faculte Lettres, U. Reims, France, 1966-67; prof. Faculte Lettres, U. Reims, 1967-97, prof. emeritus, 1997—; vis. prof. U. Budapest, Hungary, 1967, Wesleyan (Conn.) Coll., 1969, Austin (Tex.) U., 1971. Author: Les Materialistes Français 1750-1800, 1965; editor: Oeuvres Completes de Jean Meslier, 1970-72, 1972, Severl Diderot's Works in Oeuvres Completes de Diderot, 1974, Dix-Huitieme Siecle, 1969—. Mem. jury Fest. Internat. Theatre Univs., Nancy, France, 1967-70. Lt. French Air Force, 1955-57. Decorated chevalier Palmes Academiques; recipient Medaille Argent Ville Paris, 1989, Prix Union Rationaliste, 1973. Mem. French Soc. for 18th Century Studies (asst. sec. 1972-98), Internat. Soc. for History of French as a Fgn. Lang. (treas. 1987-89). Avocations: detective novels. Home: 23 Quai Grenèlle, 75015 Paris France

DE SOFI, OLIVER JULIUS, data processing executive; b. Havana, Cuba, Dec. 26, 1929; came to U.S., 1956; naturalized, 1961; s. Julius A. and Edith H. (Zsuffa) DeS. B.S. in Math. and Physics, Ernst Lehman Coll., 1950; postgrad. in agronomy U. Havana, 1952, B.S. in Aero. Engring., 1956; m. Phyllis H. Dumich, Feb. 14, 1971; children: Richard D., Stephen R., Kerri L. Dir. EDP tech. svcs. and planning Am. Airlines, N.Y.C., 1968-70; dir. Sabre II, Tulsa, 1970-72; v.p. data processing and communications Nat. Bank of N. Am., Huntington Station, N.Y., 1972-76, sr. v.p. data processing and communications, 1976-78, sr. v.p. systems and ops., 1978-79, sr. v.p. adminstrn., N.Y.C., 1979-80, exec. v.p. adminstrn. group, 1980-83; exec. v.p. data processing methodologies and architecture Anacomp, Inc., Ft. Lee, N.J. and Sarasota, Fla., 1983-84; v.p. corp. devel. Computer Horizons Corp., N.Y.C., 1984-86; pres., CEO Coast to Coast Computers Inc., Sarasota, 1986—, CEO, 1993-94; chief data processing cons. Arab Nat. Bank, Riyadh, Kingdom of Saudi Arabia, 1991-92; CEO, ; bd. dirs. The Bentley Group, San Francisco, Innovative Mgmt. Systems, Inc., Sarasota, Doks Enterprises, Inc., Carson City, C.C. Lawn Care, Inc., Sarasota; lectr. program for women Adelphi Coll. Mem. Data Processing Mgmt. Assn., Computer Exec. Round Table, Am. Mgmt. Assn., Sales Execs. Club, Bank Adminstrn. Inst., AAAS, Internat. Platform Assn., Nat. Rifle Assn. Republican. Club: Masons (Havana).

DESOIZE, BERNARD, biochemistry and molecular biology educator; b. Damery, France, June 25, 1946; s. Serge and Paule (Mineur) D.; m. Geneviève Lasserre, Sept. 9, 1972; 1 child, Aurélie. Degree in pharmacy, Faculty of Pharmacy, Reims, France, 1970; PhD, U. Reims, 1976. Rsch. fellow Columbia U., N.Y.C., 1974-75; asst. Faculty of Pharmacy, Reims, 1976-77; maître-asst. Faculty of Pharmacy, 1977-81, prof., 1981—; dir. pharmacology lab. anticancer ctr., Reims, 1986-96, biologist, 1977-86. Contbr. over 100 articles to rsch. and sci. jours. Mem. city coun. Reims, 1995—. Mem. European Orgn. Rsch. and Treatment of Cancer. Office: Faculté de Pharmacie, 51 rue Cognacy-Jay, 51000 Reims France

DE SONNEVILLE, LEO MARINUS JOHANNES, neuropsychologist, educator; b. Beverwijk, N Holland, The Netherlands, Feb. 3, 1947; s. Jan H. and Toni (Starmans) De S.; m. Marja Tiebout, Feb. 26, 1979; children: Jan, Daphne. MSc in Civil Engring., Delft U. Tech., The Netherlands, 1972; MSc in Psychology, Mcpl. U. Amsterdam, 1981; PhD, Free U. Amsterdam,

The Netherlands, 1988. Tchr. maths. Amsterdams Lyceum, 1973-74; tchr. asst. Mcpl. U. Amsterdam, 1977-81; rsch. neuropsychologist Free U., Amsterdam, 1981—; researcher, co-investigator Inst. Devel. Neurology, State U. Groningen, 1988-92; tchr. European Grad. Sch. Child Neuropsychology, Amsterdam, 1992—; co-investigator Child Clinic, U. Heidelberg, Germany, 1986-90, U. Hosp., Vienna, Austria, 1990—; co-investigator, cons. U. Hosp., Heidelberg, 1987-94, Children's Hosp./Harvard Med. Sch., Boston, 1991—. Author: Aspects of Information Processing, 1988; author computer programs; contbr. articles to profl. jours. Mem. Internat. Neuropsychol. Soc., Intrnat. Acad. Rsch. Learning Disability, Dutch Soc. Neuropsychology (bd. dirs. 1996—), N.Y. Acad. Scis., Soc. Neurosci. Avocations: sailing, road running, rowing. Home: Amsterdamseweg 483, 1181 BR Amstelveen The Netherlands Office: Free U Dept Pediat Neurology, PO Box 7057, 1007 MB Amsterdam The Netherlands

DE SOTO, ALVARO, diplomat; b. Argentina, Mar. 16, 1943; 2 children. Student, Internat. Sch., Geneva, Switzerland, Cath. U., Lima, San Marcos U., Lima, Diplomatic Acad. Lima; Degree (hon.), Inst. Internat. Studies, Geneva, 1992, St. Joseph's U., Phila., 1992. Acting dir. maritime sovereignty divsn. Ministry Fgn.; spl. asst. to sec.-gen. UN, 1982-86, asst. sec.-gen., exec. asst. to sec.-gen., 1987-91, personal rep. sec.-gen. Office Rsch. and Collection Info., 1991, rep. sec.-gen. in El Salvador peace negotiations, 1990-91, sr. polit. adviser to sec.-gen., 1992-94, asst. sec.-gen. for polit. affairs, 1995-99, under sec.-gen., spl. advisor to sec.-gen. on Cyprus, 1999—. E-mail: deSoto@un.org. Office: UN Rm S-3527 A New York NY 10017

DE SOUSA, ANTONIO REBELO, bank executive. Gov. Banco de Portugal, Lisbon. Office: Banco de Portugal, Rua do Comercio 148, 1100 Lisbon Portugal*

DE SOUZA, JOSÉ MARIA, physician; b. Belém, Brazil, May 11, 1932; s. José Santos Lucas and Irene De Souza; m. Fernanda Martins, Dec. 8, 1958; children: José Maria, Maria Tereza, Fernanda Maria. MD, U. Pará, Belém, 1958, D Pharmacy, 1963; PhD in Pharmacology, U. Sao Paulo, Ribelrão Preto, Brazil, 1972. Pub. health physician SESP, Abaetetuba, Brazil, 1959; physician Petrobras, Amazonia States, Brazil, 1960-61; legist Medico Legal Inst., Belém, 1961-76; prof. Fed. U., Belém, 1968-95; prin. investigator Health Ministry/WHO, Belém, 1979-85; coord. Malaria Program/Inst. Evandro Chagas, Belém, 1992—; temp. advisor WHO/Pan Am. Health Orgn.; advisor Brazil Health Ministry, 1979—; prin. investigator Mefloquine Project, Belém, 1979-85. Contbr. chpts. to books in field; editor bull. O Plasmodio, 1994. Town councillor, Abaetetuba, 1960. Recipient Navy's Friend medal Brazilian Navy, 1986, 5th Pediatrics Infectology Congress diploma Brazilian Pediat. Soc., 1996. Mem. Brazilian Soc. Tropical Medicine (regional pres.), Brazilian Soc. Pharmacology and Exptl. Therapeutic Medicine, Rotary Internat. (Service Above Self medal 1995-96). Roman Catholic. Avocations: walking, dancing, music, photography, videography. Home: 14 de Abril 1815, 66063140 Belém Pará, Brazil Office: Inst Evandro Chagas, Av Alimrante Barroso 492, 66090000 Belém Pará, Brazil

DE SOUZA, WILLIAM JEREMY, solicitor; b. London, Feb. 26, 1945; s. Guilherme Chambers and Vera Constance (Hayter) de S.; m. Caroline Lilian Elsie Adams, Jan. 30, 1988; 1 child, Amelia Cara Vera. MA in Jurisprudence, Oxford (Eng.) U., 1966. Articled clk. Farrer & Co., London, 1967-69, asst. solicitor, 1970-73, assoc., 1974-76, ptnr., 1976-96, cons., 1996-99; cons. White & Bowker, Winchester, Eng., 1999—. Co-author: The Property Investor & Vat, 1990, The Conveyancer's Tax Primer, 1999; editor: (loose leaf series) Land Taxation, 1991—; contbr. articles to profl. jours. including The Brit. Tax Rev., Pvt. Client Bus., Taxation, The Tax Jour., The Estates Gazette, Environ. Law Rev. Mem. The Law Soc. (corp. tax subcom. 1989-92), Holborn Law Soc. (revenue com. 1984—, chmn. 1995—), Royal Inst. Internat. Affairs, Brooks. Conservative. Anglican. Office: White & Bowker, 19 St Peter St, Winchester SO23 8DD, England

DE SOZA, PIERRE, surgeon; b. Saigon, Socialist Republic Vietnam, May 11, 1936; s. Albert and Marie (Le Thi Nham) De S.; m. Brioude Gisèle (div. 1982); children: Corinne, Celine; m. Elisabeth Spangen Berger, Aug. 29, 1987; 1 child, Arnaud. Degree in sci., Bordeaux U., 1955, degree in medicine, 1962, MD, 1968. Extern Hospices de Bordeaux, 1956-61; intern Centre Regionale Hospitalier, Bordeaux, 1961-67, head clinic, 1967-69; pvt. practice surgery Pessac, 1969-83; chief svc. Clinique Mutualiste, Pessac, 1983—; v.p. Com. Med. Cons., 1983; pres. Com. Hygiene, 1988. Lt. French Army, 1963-65. Mem. Soc. Carcinologie Privé. Roman Catholic. Avocation: golf. Home: 20 Alleée des Averans, 33610 Gazinet France Office: Clinique Mutualiste, 46 Ave Albert Schweitzer, 33600 Pessac France

DESPREZ, CHRISTOPHE, investment bank administrator; b. Lille, France, Nov. 13, 1959; s. Michel and Jacqueline (Phalempin) D.; m. Isabelle Prévost, Oct. 10, 1980; children: Julie, François-Xavier, Jean-Baptiste. Grad., Ecole Poly., 1978, Ecole Nat. des Ponts Chaussees, 1982; dipoma in Econ. Policy, Inst. d'Etudes Politiques, Paris, 1984; grad., Ecole Super. Scis. Ecr. et, 1984. Asst. exec. engring. dept. fin. and industry PARIBAS, Paris, 1982-83; head indsl. devel. divsn. French Ministry Industry, Donai, 1984-88; mgr. treasury dept. French Ministry Economy, Fin. and Budget, Paris, 1988-90, advisor to Min. Budget., 1990-91; chief of staff French Min. Rsch. and Tech., Paris, 1991-93; dir. Rothschild & Cie, Paris, 1993-95, mng. dir., 1996-98, gen. ptnr., 1999—; lectr. econs. and indsl. polity U. Paris XIII, 1988-91. Lt. French Army, 1978-79. Avocations: golf, fencing, half-marathon. E-mail: desprez.c@rothschild-cie.fr.

DESPREZ, MARTIN RÉMY, publishing company executive; b. Paris, May 26, 1939; s. Henry and Jeanne (Mailfert) D.; m. Veronique De Lestapis, June 27, 1964; children: Constance, Eric, Regis, Angelique. Degree, Hautes Etudes Commerciales, 1962. Product mgr. then mktg. mgr. Lesieur, Paris, 1964-73; dep. gen. mgr. Young Rubicam, Paris, 1973-74; exec. chmn. Havas Coun., Paris, 1975-80; gen. mgr. Amaury Group, Paris, 1981-90; owner, CEO, Cervam, Paris, 1991-93; chmn., CEO, Editions Du Juris-Classeur, Paris, 1994—; dir. Courrier De L'Ouest, Angers, France, 1982—, Editions Amaury, Paris, 1982—, Documentation Organique, Strasbourg, France, 1996—, Litec, Paris, 1994—. Lt. cavalry French Armed Forces, 1962—. Home: 50 Avenue Des Tilleuls, 75016 Paris France Office: Editions Du Juris-Classeur, 141 Rue de Javel, 75747 Paris Cedex 15, France

DESROCHERS, ALAN ALFRED, electrical engineer; b. Northampton, Mass., June 1, 1950; s. Alfred George and Helen Mary (Punska) D. BSEE, U. Mass., Lowell, 1972; MSEE, Purdue U., 1973, PhD, 1977. Assoc. engr. Lockheed Missiles & Space Co., Sunnyvale, Calif., 1974-75; asst. prof. Boston U., 1977-80; asst. prof. elec., computer and systems engring. Rensselaer Poly. Inst., Troy, N.Y., 1980-86; assoc. prof. Rensselaer Poly. Inst., Troy, 1986-90, prof., 1990—; summer faculty fellow USAF, Eglin AFB, Fla., 1978; cons. IBM, Cambridge, Mass., 1978-79, Alcoa, Pitts., 1983-85, Barron Assocs., Inc., Annandale, Va., 1985, Systolic Systems, Inc., San Jose, Calif., 1987, Kaiser Aluminum Co., Pleasanton, Calif., 1987, Law Offices of Frances E. Lehner, 1992—; vis. scientist Lab. for Info. and Decision Systems, MIT, 1987. Contbr. articles to profl. jours. Recipient V.L. Magoon Tchg. award Purdue U., 1977, LEAD award Soc. Mfg. Engrs., 1987; rsch. grantee NASA, Air Force Office Sci. Rsch., U.S. Army, IBM, Digital Equipment Corp., Alcoa, 1978-94. Fellow IEEE (edl. chmn. 1984-89); mem. Robotics and Automation Soc. of IEEE (elected officer 1989-95, editor Transactions on Robotics and Automation 1990-96), AAAS, N.Y. Acad. Scis., Sigma Xi, Eta Kappa Nu. Avocations: bicycling, sailing. Office: Rensselaer Poly Inst Elec Comp Sys Engring Dept 110 8th St Rm 7020 Troy NY 12180-3522

DESROCHERS, GERARD CAMILLE, surgeon; b. Marlboro, Mass., June 8, 1922; s. Emery Hector and Eliane (Lemire) DesR.; m. Ellen Franklin, Sept. 27, 1958; children: Gerard, Emery, Lewis, Anthony. AB, Coll. of Holy Cross, 1944; MD, Tufts Coll., 1947. Diplomate Nat. Bd. Med. Examiners. Gen. rotating intern St. Mary's Hosp., Waterbury, Conn., 1947-48; teaching fellow in pathology Tufts Med. Sch., 1948-49; straight surg. intern Boston City Hosp., 1949-50, asst. resident surgeon, 1950-51; resident in surgery New Eng. Med. Center, Boston, 1955-57; practice medicine specializing in surgery, Manchester, N.H.; gen. surgeon staff Cath. Med. Center, Manchester; med. dir. Sea Supply Corp., Bangkok, Thailand, 1953-54; asst. chief surgery VA Hosp., Manchester, 1971-78. Contbr. articles to profl. jours. Incorporator Cath. Med. Ctr., Thomas More Found., Merrimack, N.H.; adv. bd. Lincoln Inst.; mem. N.H. Right to Life Com.; mem. bd. of policy Liberty Lobby. Served as 1st lt. M.C., U.S. Army, 1970. Named Disting. Physician Am., 1989. Mem. AAAS, Manchester Med. Soc., Hillsboro County Med. Soc., Am. Coll. Occupational and Environ. Medicine. Home: 402 Sagamore St Manchester NH 03104-3937 Office: 648 Belmont St Manchester NH 03104-5137

DESSAUER, CARIN, journalist; b. Pottstown, Pa., Dec. 31, 1963; d. Ralph and Margot (Abrams) D.; m. Marc Richard Engel, May 29, 1988. BA cum laude, Bucknell U., 1985; postgrad., George Washington U., 1987. Reporter The Polit. Report, Washington, 1986-87; off-air reporter ABC News Polit. Unit, Washington, 1988; assoc. editor Congl. Quarterly's Politics in Am., Washington, 1989; contbg. editor Campaigns and Elections mag., Washington, 1989-91; head Washington polit. unit Cable News Network, 1990-91; assoc. polit. dir. CNN, Washington, 1991-95, dep. pol. dir., 1995-98, election dir., 1998—. Co-author: (monograph) Running to Win, 1988. Co-chair UJA Women's Bus. and Profl. Divsn., D.C. chpt., bd. dirs., cabinet, 1997—, exec. com., 1994-97; active Make A Wish Found., New Endeavors by Women. Mem. Phi Beta Kappa. Avocations: design, fitness, art, theatre, photography, travel. Office: CNN 820 1st St NE Washington DC 20002-4243

DESSAUX, YVES, microbiologist; b. Bois-Colombes, France, Nov. 10, 1956; s. Pierre and Madeline (Girardi) D.; m. Catherine Ramonede, Feb. 11, 1959; children: Elise, Jean-Baptiste. M of Biochem., U. Paris, 1976, D, 1982. Rsch. assoc. CNRS, France, 1982-87, CNRS and U. Ill., 1988, CNRS and U. Calif., 1989; rsch. assoc. CNRS, France, 1990-96, rsch. dir., 1996—. Author: Molecular Signals in Plant Microbe Communication, 1993; contbr. articles to profl. jours. With French Army, 1978-79. Rsch. fellow DGRST, Paris, 1980-82, CNRS-NSF, Paris and Washington, 1988, NATO, Paris, 1989. Mem. Internat. Soc. Molecular Microbe Interaction, Soc. French Microbiology, Soc. French Phytopathology. Office: ISV-CNRS, Ave de la Terrasse, F-91198 Gif-sur-Yvette France

DESSLER, ALEXANDER JACK, space physics and astronomy educator, scientist; b. San Francisco, Oct. 21, 1928; s. David Alexander and Julia (Shapiro) D.; m. Lorraine Hudek, Apr. 18, 1952; children: Pauline Karen, David Alexander, Valerie Jan, Andrew Emory. B.S., Calif. Inst. Tech., 1952; Ph.D., Duke, 1956. Sect. head Lockheed Missiles & Space Co., 1956-62; prof. Grad. Research Center, Dallas, 1962-63, prof. space physics and astronomy, 1963-82, 86-93; chmn. dept. Rice U., Houston, 1963-69, 79-82, 87-92, campus bus. mgr., 1974-76; dir. space sci. lab. MSFC NASA, Huntsville, Ala., 1982-86; sr. rsch. scientist Lunar and Planetary Lab. U. Ariz., Tucson, 1993—; sci. adviser Nat Aeros. and Space Council, 1969-70; pres. Univs. Space Research Assn., 1975-81. Editor Jour. Geophys. Research, 1965-69, Revs. of Geophysics, 1969-74, The John Wiley Space Science Text Series, 1968-76, Geophys. Research Letters, 1986-89, Atmospheric and Space Science Series, 1986—; adv. bd.: Planetary and Space Sci., 1963-92; assoc. editor Space Solar Power Rev., 1980-85. Served with USN, 1946-48. Recipient Outstanding Young Scientist award Tex. Wing Air Force Assn., 1964, medal for contbns. to internat. geophysics Soviet Geophys. Com., 1984, Stellar award for acad. devel., Rotary Nat., 1988. Fellow AAAS, Am. Geophys. Union (Macelwane award 1963, John Adam Fleming medal 1993); mem. Am. Astron. Soc., Internat. Assn. Geomagnetism and Aeronomy (v.p. 1979-83), Royal Swedish Acad. Scis. (fgn. mem.). Home: 1434 E Seneca St Tucson AZ 85719-3645 Office: U Ariz Lunar Planetary Lab 901 Gould-Simpson Bldg Tucson AZ 85721-0001

DESTANDAU, JEAN, neurosurgeon; b. Talence, Gironde, France, Aug. 23, 1953; s. Jacques and Monique (Jeanneney) D.; m. Agnes Coyne, July 15, 1977; children: Marie, Antoine. BSc, Orthez, France, 1970; MD, U. Bordeaux, France, 1983; Degree in Anatomy, U. Montpellier, France, 1985. Intern U. Bordeaux, 1979-83; asst. Pellegrin Hosp., Bordeaux, 1983-86; pvt. practice Bordeaux, 1987—; mem. staff Bagatelle Hosp., Bordeaux. Author: Movements of Carpal Bones, 1983, Radicular Avulsion, 1985; inventor in field of disc herniation. Mem. French Neurosurg. Soc., Rotary. Avocation: golf. Office: 145 Rue de la Pelouse de Douet, 33000 Bordeaux France

DESTATTE, PHILIPPE, historian, research institute administrator; b. Charleroi, Belgium, Oct. 28, 1954; s. Yves and Denise (Tygeman) D.; m. Marie-Anne Delahaut, July 7, 1979; children: Nicolas, Julien, Franklin, Virginie. Lic. in history, U. State, Liege, Belgium, 1979, Agregation, 1980. Prof. State Secondary Schs., Wallonia, Belgium, 1980-87; dir. Inst. Jules Destree, Charleroi, Belgium, 1987—; founder History Ctr. Wallonia, Namur, 1987—, René Levesque Ctr., Charleroi, 1988—; adminstr. Fondation Jules and Marie Destree, Fondation Maurice Bologne, Fondation Elie Boussart. Editor: Ecrits politiques wallons, 1986-88, Nos Artistes, 1986-88, L'Identité Walonne, Essai sur l'affirmation politique de la Wallonie, 1997, Le fédéralisme dans les Etats-Nations, 1999, Encyclopédie du Mouvement Waloon, 2000; contbr. articles on nationalism and Walloon movement to profl. jours. With Belgian Signal Corps, 1979-80. Mem. Socialist Party. Home: 34 sur les Roches, B-5563 Mour Belgium Office: Inst Jules Destree, Inst Jules Destree, 3 rue du Chateau, B-6100 Charleroi-Wallonis Belgium

DESTLER, I. M(AC), political scientist, foreign policy writer; b. Statesboro, Ga., Aug. 21, 1939; s. Chester McArthur and Katharine (Hardesty) D.; m. Harriett Kirkham Parsons, July 27, 1968; children: Mark Dodson, Katharine Elizabeth. B.A. magna cum laude, Harvard U., 1961; M.P.A., Princeton U., 1965, Ph.D., 1971. Peace Corps vol. U. Nigeria, Nsukka, 1961-63; asst. Senator Walter Mondale Washington, 1965-67; staff assoc. Pres.'s Task Force on Govt. Orgn., Washington, 1967; analyst, acting coordinator for Asia, Internat. Agrl. Devel. Service, U.S. Dept. Agr., Washington, 1967-69; Internat. Affairs fellow Council on Fgn. Relations, Washington, 1969-70; vis. lectr. Woodrow Wilson Sch., Princeton U., (N.J.), 1971-72; research assoc. Brookings Inst., Washington, 1972-76, sr. fellow, 1976-77; sr. assoc. Carnegie Endowment for Internat. Peace, Washington, 1977-83; sr. fellow Inst. Internat. Econs., Washington, 1983-87; prof. Sch. Pub. Affairs U. Md., College Park, 1987—; acting dean, 1994-95; dir. Md. seminar in U.S. fgn. policymaking, 1987-95; dir. Ctr. Internat. and Security Studies U. Md., 1991-99; cons. U.S. Office Mgmt. and Budget, 1977, 79, U.S. Dept. State, 1976, 93, U.S. Agy. for Internat. Devel., Ctrl. Asia, 1999-2000; vis. prof. Internat. U. Japan (Urasa), spring, 1986; vis. fellow Inst. Internat. Econs., 1987—. Author: Presidents, Bureaucrats and Foreign Policy - The Politics of Organizational Reform, 1972, 74, (with others) Managing an Alliance - The Politics of U.S.-Japanese Relations, 1976, (with Fukui and Sato) The Textile Wrangle - Conflict in Japanese-American Relations, 1969-71, 1979, Making Foreign Economic Policy, 1980, (with Gelb and Lake) Our Own Worst Enemy: The Unmaking of American Foreign Policy, 1984, American Trade Politics, 1986 (Gladys M. Kammerer award Am. Polit. Sci. Assn. 1987), 3d edit., 1995, (with Odell) Anti-Protection: Changing Forces in U.S. Trade Politics, 1987, (with Henning) Dollar Politics: Exchange Rate Policy Making in the United States, 1989, The National Economic Council: A Work in Progress, 1996, Renewing Fast-Track Legislation, 1997, (with Kull) Misreading the Public: The Myth of a New Isolationism, 1999, (with Balint) The New Politics of American Trade, 1999; co-editor: Coping with U.S.-Japanese Economic Conflicts, 1982, Beyond the Beltway: Engaging the Public in U.S. Foreign Policy, 1994. Recipient Disting. Internat. Svc. award U. Md., 1998. Mem. Council Fgn. Relations, Am. Polit. Sci. Assn., Nat. Acad. Pub. Adminstrn. Democrat. Presbyterian. Home: 701 River Bend Rd Great Falls VA 22066-2712 Office: U Md Sch Pub Affairs College Park MD 20742-0001

DESUTTER, MANU, senator; b. Heist, Flanders, Belgium, Nov. 28, 1938; s. Max and Anna (De Jonghe) D.; children: Frederic, Patrick, An, James, Virginie. Degree in Philosophy and Lit., Notre Dame de la Paix, Namur, 1959. City counselor City of Knokke-Heist, Belgium, 1965, alderman, 1967-73, mayor, 1973-79, dep., 1977-94, senator, 1991-95; pres. sect. fishering Ctrl. Econ. Coun. Decorated Officer in the Order of Leopold, 1991, Civic Medal 1st Class, 1989. Mem. C. of C. Brugge (v.p.). Christian Democrat. Roman Catholic. Home: Natienlaan 94, 8301 Knokke-Heist Belgium

DESVIGNES, JEAN-CLAUDE, virologist; b. Tours, France, July 10, 1936; s. René and Françoise (Verley) D.; m. Marlene Mesnard, Sept. 18, 1964; children: Christophe, Eric, Thierry, Maylis, Caroline. Agronomist engr., Alger, France, 1961. Virologist Tech. Ctr. Fruits and Vegetables, La Force, France, 1963—. Author: Virus Diseases of Fruit Trees, 1999; contbr. articles to profl. jours. Lt. Engr. Corps., 1961-63. Recipient Mérite Agricole Sec. of Agrl., 1994, Médaille Dor Acad. of Agrl., 1999. Roman Catholic. Avocations: singing, music. Home: Sabatie, F-24130 Prigonrieux Dordogne, France

DE SWART, JOHANNES HERMANUS, library director; b. Beverwijk, The Netherlands, Feb. 15, 1938; s. Jacobus Johannes Bernardus and Helena Petronella Maria (Smit) D.; m. Maria Josephina van Doornewaard, Aug. 7, 1938; children: Helena J.F.C., Jacobus J.B. Drs Psychology, Vrije U., Amsterdam, 1965, PhD, 1972. Orgn. cons. Raadgevers Bur. Berenschot, Amsterdam, The Netherlands, 1965-67; rschr., asst.prof. Vrije U., Amsterdam, 1967-83, dep. libr., 1983-87, libr. dir., 1987—; sec. UKB Assn. U. Libraries, Royal Library, Library Royal Netherlands Acad. Scis., 1991—; chmn. steering com. G.O. Tng. Inst. Library Personnel. Mem. steering com. Ons Tweede Thuis Aalsmeer, 1967-91; mem. steering bd. Stiching Zorgcentra De Lange Brug, 1993—; chmn. Fedn. Orgns. for Libr., Info. Documentation, 1998—. Mem. Found. Fedn. Dutch Libr. for the Blind. Avocations: tennis, hockey, bridge. Home: Sluisvaart 120, 1191 HG Ouderkerk The Netherlands Office: Vrije Univ Amsterdam Bibliotheek, De Boelelaan 1103, 1081 HV Amsterdam The Netherlands

DE SWART, RIK LUDOLF, biologist, researcher; b. Doetinchem, The Netherlands, Jan. 22, 1966; s. Leendert and Trineke (Folkerts) de S.; m. Hetty Joustra, June 8, 1995; children: Wieske Katharina, Jobbe Klaas. Student, Utrecht (The Netherlands) U., 1990; PhD, Erasmus U., Rotterdam, The Netherlands, 1995. Postdoc. Erasmus U., Rotterdam, 1996—. Avocations: sports, camping, computers. Home: Dr Kuyperlaan 40, 3445 CL Woerden The Netherlands Office: Erasmus U Dept Virology, PO Box 1738, 3000 DR Rotterdam The Netherlands

DESWARTE, YVES ANDRÉ, research director; b. Roubaix, France, Sept. 24, 1949; s. Louis A. and Simone M. (Delcroix) D.; m. Christine M. Dehoux, Mar. 1, 1975 (dec. Dec. 1975). MS in Engring., ISEN, Lille, France, 1972, ENSAE, Toulouse, France, 1973. R&D engr. Internat. Co. for Info., Velizy, France, 1973-76, Co. Info. Militaire, Spatiale et Aeronautique, Velizy, 1977-79; rsch. dir. Inst. Nat. Rsch. in Info. and Automatique, Toulouse, 1979—. Editor: ESORICS 92 Proceedings, 1992, 98 Proceedings, 1998. Served with French military, 1973-74. Mem. IEEE Computer Soc. (affiliate, rep. IFIP tc/11), Assn. for Computing Machinery, French Soc. Electricity and Electronics (sr. mem.). Achievements include patent for "système perfectionné de détection et essai de correction d'erreurs dans les équipements informatiques." Home: 2 Rue Garcia Lorca, Ramonville 31520, France Office: LAAS-CNRS, 7 Avenue du Colonel Roche, Toulouse 31077, France

DE SZY, GÉRARD CHARLES, economist, educator; b. Debrecen, Hungary, Oct. 11, 1939; arrived in Switzerland, 1958; s. Géza Árpád and Katalin Rózsa (Kurucz) de S.; children: Julie, François, Endre. MA in Sci. Comm., U. Geneva, 1960; MA in Econ. and Comm., U. Genoa, 1963, MA in Law, 1986; MA in Psychology, U. Lubiana, 1996; PhD, U. La Jolla, 1987. Cons. Royal Dutch Shell Italiana, Genoa, 1964-65, Commn. of European Union, Brussels, 1965-69, Battelle Rsch. Inst., Geneva, 1969-73, Sifida, Geneva, 1973-75, European Assn. Devel., Brussels, 1975-81, various other orgns., 1981—; rector Centro Interuniversitario Ticinese, Lugano, 1991; pres. Internat. Ctr. for Univ. Studies, Lugano, 1992; v.p. Internat. Ctr. for Applied Psychology, Bologna, Italy, 1995; vis. prof. numerous univs., 1986—. Author: Development and Underdevelopment, 1987, Micro-economics, 1988, Contemporary Economic Theories, 1991, Narcissism, 1996. Fellow Libero Patrocinature Lawyers' Assn.; mem. APA, Slovenian Psychologists Assn., Assn. Fiduciari Ticino (chartered economist), European Assn. for Internat. Edn. (Amsterdam), Lion's Club Budapest (Hungary). Democrat. Roman Catholic. Avocations: tennis, music, travel, literature, politics. Office: Internat Ctr Univ Studies, Via Besso 59, Lugano-Messagno Ticino 6903, Switzerland

DETERING, HEINRICH, literary critic; b. Neumuenster, Holstein, Germany, Nov. 1, 1959; s. Heinrich F.W. and Elisabeth (Wolff) D.; m. Christine Trinter, June 30, 1984; children: Jakob, Luise, Henrik. PhD, U. Goettingen, Germany, 1988, Habil., 1993. Mem. professorial staff Goettingen U., 1993-94; assoc. prof. U. Calif., Irvine, 1991, U. Munich, 1994-95; prof. U. Kiel, Germany, 1995—; vis. prof. U. Aarhus, Denmark, 1996, Bergen, Norway, 1999. Author: (books) Theodizee und Erzahlverfahren, 1990, Das offene Geheimnis, 1994; editor: (books) C.W. Dohm, Schriften, 1988, H. Wergeland, Sujets, 1995, H.C. Andersen, Maerchen, 1996, Grundzuege der Literaturwissenschaft, 1996, 3d edit., 1999, Grenzgaenge, 1997, Kulturelle Identitäten im der deutschen Literatur, 1998, (yearbook) Jahrlich der Raabe-Gesellschaft, 1994—. Recipient Akademiepreis, Akad. der Wissenschaften, Goettingen, 1990, Kuenstlerstipendium, Wiepersdorf-Jury, 1993. Mem. Deutsche Akademie fur Sprache und Dichtung, Kleist Soc. (bd. dirs. 1996-2000), Raabe Soc. (bd. dirs. 1990-2000, Raabe-Foerderpreis award 1989), Storm Soc. (bd. dirs. 1996—), Thomas Mann Soc. Home: Klinkerwisch 20, D-24107 Kiel Germany Office: Inst Literaturwissenschaft, Leibnizstrasse 8, D-24118 Kiel Germany

DETERT, MIRIAM ANNE, chemical analyst; b. San Diego, Calif., Sept. 16, 1925; d. George Bernard and Margaret Theresa Zita (Lohre) D. BS, Dominican Coll., San Rafael, Calif., 1947. Chem. analyst Shell Devel. Co., Emeryville, Calif., 1947-72, Houston, 1972-86. Photo participant Wax Rsch.: Quest, 1981; contbr. poetry to books including The International Library of Poetry - Best Poems of the 90's, Spirit of the Age, The Nightfall of Diamonds, The Long and Winding Road, Through Oceans of Time. Vol. Falkirk Cultural Ctr., San Rafael, 1987-91, M.D. Anderson Tumor Inst., Houston, 1978-86, Rep. Party, San Rafael, 1990, 94; mem. Jewish Comm. Ctr. Recipient Disting. Alumni award Dominican Coll., 1994. Mem. Marin Geneal. Soc. Republican. Roman Catholic. Avocations: etching, oil painting, geneal. rsch. on Detert name, swimming (Sr. Olympic Swimming award 1991).

DETREKÖI, ÁKOS, engineering educator, university administrator; b. Budapest, Hungary, Nov. 27, 1939; s. Géza and Ilona (Oláh) D.; m. Györgyi Kugler; children: László, Zsuzsa. Degree in civil engring., Tech. U. Budapest, 1963, D of Tech., 1967; PhD, Hungarian Acad. Scis., 1971, DSc, 1977. Asst. Tech. U., Budapest, 1963-68, sr. asst. faculty civil engring., 1968-72, docent, assoc. prof., 1972-80, prof., head dept. photogrammetry, 1980—; dean faculty engring. Tech. U. Budapest, 1986-90, rector, 1997—; chmn. com. geodesy Hungarian Acad. Sci., 1990—; chmn. nat. com. Internatl. Soc. Photogrammetry and Remote Sensing, 1986—; pres. Hungarian Humboldt Soc., 1994—. Co-author: Deformationsmessungen, 1981, Deformation Measurements, 1983, others; contbr. articles to profl. jours. Recipient Fashing Antal medal Minstry of Agrl., 1988, Lazar Deak medal Hungarian Soc. of Surveying, Mapping and Remote Sensing, 1993. Mem. Hungarian Soc. Surveying, Remote Sensing and Cartography (pres. 1994—), Internat. Assn. Surveyors (chmn. com. 6 1984-87, cert. appreciation 1990). Avocations: theater, swimming. Home: Nagybányai u 43/B, Budapest Hungary Office: Budapest Univ Tech Econ, Müegyetem rkp 3, H-1521 Budapest Hungary

DETSCHEL, FREDERICK WILLIAM, management consultant; b. Bklyn., Nov. 23, 1935; s. William Frederick and Johnann (Tighe) D.; m. Margaret Willette, (div. Nov. 1982); children: William, Kathy, Diana; m. Kathryn Ellen Rautio, Nov. 20, 1982. BS in Physics, CUNY, 1967; MS in Computer Info. Sci., Syracuse U., 1978. Tech. illustrator Volt Tech. Svcs., N.Y.C., 1959-63; devel. mgr. IBM Corp., Bethesda, Md., 1963-87; mgr. sys. programming Prodigy Svcs. Co., White Plains, N.Y., 1987-95; sr. cons., pres. FWD Enterprises Inc., Mashpee, Mass., 1995—; adj. prof. Haskell Indian Jr. Coll., Lawrence, Kans., 1977-78, Dutchess County C.C., Poukeepsie, N.Y., 1981-82; sr. cons. IBM Global Svcs. Network, 1996-99, Purdue Pharma L.P., 2000—; cons. FWD Enterprises Inc., Cape Cod, Mass., 1995—; bd. dirs. Independence House, Hyannis, Mass., 2000—. Author, designer Nagano Olympic Web Site Architecture, 1998. Deacon, elder Hopewell Ref. Ch. Am., Hopewell Junction, N.Y., 1992-96; pres. Barclay Hts. Homeowners Civic Assn., Saugerties, N.Y., 1979-81, Holland Mill Estates Homeowners Assn., Mashpee, 2000—. Sgt. USAF, 1954-58. Recipient Casey Jones scholar Acad. Aeronautics, Astoria, N.Y., 1953; cert. appreciation contbns. to 1996 IBM Atlanta Olympic Web Site, 1996. Libr. Congress (assoc. mem.), mem. Appalachian Mountain Club (S.E. Mass. chpt.). Republican. Mem. United Ch. Christ. Avocations: woodworking, bicycling, gardening, racquetball, travel. E-mail: FWDinc@yahoo. com. Office: FWD Enterprises Inc PMB281 39 Nathan Ellis Hwy Mashpee MA 02649-3267

DETTINGER-KLEMM, MARTIN, retired academic administrator, legal practitioner; b. Besigheim, Germany, May 15, 1927; s. Alfred and Lina (Lauffer) Klemm; m. Mechthild Elisabeth Walz, Aug. 1, 1934; children: Ilse Gabriele Villafuerte, Angela, Eckehard, Andreas, Johenna, Adelheid. Referendar Rr., U. Stuttgart, Germany, 1951, assessor, 1954; Dr of Law, U. Tübingen, Germany, 1956. Cert. lawyer, adminstr. Asst. Regional Bank, Heilbronn, Germany, 1957-58; assessor Landrastamt Goeppingen, 1958-59; referentlat Landkreistag Baden Wuerttenberg, 1959-61; vice head, dept. planning Ministry of Edn., Stuttgart, 1961-67, head, dept. planning, 1968-78; head, dept. univs. and colls. Ministry of Scis. and Arts, Stuttgart, 1978-92; ret., 1992; corr. mem. Acad. Raumforschung und Landesplanung, Germany, 1976—. Contbr. articles to profl. jours. Dir. Buegerverein Stuttgart-Vaihinger, 1997. Recipient Bundesverdienstkreuz, Govt. Fed. Rep. Germany, 1987, several awards from univs. and colls., 1985-91. Mem. Inst. Fgn. Rels., Bach Acad. Lutheran. Avocations: philosophy, music, history, hiking.

DETTMAN, IAN CHRISTOPHER, pharmaceutical manufacturing director; b. Melbourne, Victoria, Australia, Oct. 30, 1946; s. Glen Charles and Nancy Louisa (McMorran) D.; m. Mary Heather Fraser, Jan. 20, 1973 (div. 1996); children: Natasha Yeong Ae; m. Carol Anne Benson. BSc with honors, Monash U., Melbourne, 1973, PhD in Biochemistry, 1978. Lic. mfr. human sterile injectables and oral products. Mgr. Oakleigh Pathology Svc., Melbourne, 1979-89; natural therapist Melbourne, 1981-99; mng. dir. Biol. Therapies, Melbourne, 1989—; gov. Southern Sch. of Natural Therapies, Melbourne, com. mem., bd. dirs.; presenter, demonstrator med. confs., 1989-99. Co-author: Vitamin C Natures Miraculous Healing Missle, 1992; contbr. articles to profl. jours.; patentee in field. Cons. Drug Users and Parents Assn., Melbourne, 1980-83. Grantee Linus Pauling Inst., 1986. Fellow Australasian Coll. of Biomed. Scientists, Australian Natural Therapists Assn.; mem. Royal Australian Chem. Inst., Australian Soc. of Microbiology, Australian Inst. of Med. Lab. Scientists. Avocations: pianist, philatenist, astronomy, golf. Fax: 61-3-9587-1720. E-mail: biol@biol.com.au. Home: 10 20-30 Malcolm Rd, Braeside VIC, Australia Office: Biol Therapies, 20-30 Malcolm Rd, Braeside VIC 3195, Australia

DEURA, SHIGEYUKI, anatomy educator, researcher; b. Yokohama, Japan, May 30, 1926; s. Toshichika and Umeko Deura; m. Nobuko Shimonishi, May 5, 1974; 1 child, Tomoyuki. MD, Keio U., 1949, PhD, 1956. Asst. dept. physiology Keio U. Sch. Medicine, Tokyo, 1950-53; asst. dept. physiology Kobe (Japan) Med. Coll., 1953-55, lectr., 1955-57; asst. dept. anatomy Kyoto (Japan) U., 1957-63, lectr., 1963-64, asst. prof., 1964-71; prof. dept. anatomy Kawasaki Med. Coll., Kurashiki, Okayama, Japan, 1971-74; prof. Gifu (Japan) U. Sch. Medicine, 1974-90; prof. emeritus, 1990; prof. Fujita Health U. Sch. Medicine, Toyoake, Aichi, Japan, 1990-96; head rsch. staff, dir. sanitary inst. aged people Kawamura Hosp., Akutami, Gifu, Japan, 1996—; vis. prof. U. Santo Tomas, Manila, 1984—, Perpetual Help Coll. Medicine, Binãn, Laguna, The Philippines, 1994—. Author: Morphol. Biochem. Correlates of Neural Activity, 1964. Rsch. grantee NIH, 1965, Japanese Med. Assn., 1975, Kato Meml. Rsch. Fund, 1977. Mem. Japan Assn. Anatomists, Physiol. Soc. Japan, Japan Assn. Physiol. Scis., Internat. Brain Rsch. Orgn. Avocations: classical music, photography. Home: 15 Higashi Komazume-cho, Gifu 500-8168, Japan Office: Kawamura Hosp Neurol Rsch, 1-84 Dai-han-nya, Akutami Gifu 501-3144, Japan

DEUSCHL, GUENTHER, neurologist, educator, researcher; b. Lahr, Germany, Aug. 4, 1950. MD, U. Munich, 1980. Specialist in movement disorders, clin. neurology, clin. neurophysiology. Fellow dept. physiology U. Munich, 1978-80; resident Tech. U. Munich, 1980-82; resident in neurology U. Freiburg, Germany, 1982-86, asst. prof., 1986-95; prof. dept. neurology Christian Albrechts U. Kiel, Germany, 1995—, head dept. neurology, 1995—; vis. scientist NIH, Bethesda, Md., 1990-91. Contbr. articles to profl. jours. Recipient Parkinson's Disease award German Neurologic Soc. Mem. Movement Disorder Soc. (exec. com. 1994-98), German Soc. Clin. Neurophysiology (Kornmüller award 1986, exec. com. 1984-97), Internat. Fedn. Clin. Neurophysiology (exec. com. 1997—). Fax: 49-431-597-2712. E-mail: g.deuschl@neurologie.uni-kiel.de. Office: Christian Albrechts U Kiel, Dept Neurol Niemannsweg 147, 24105 Kiel Germany

DEUSCHLE, CONSTANCE JOAN, counselor, educational consultant; b. Indpls., July 16, 1945; d. Delmar Sanford and Mildred Cynthia (Kreis) Gray; m. John Hanlan Deuschle, Nov. 12, 1966; children: Peter John, Thomas Scott, Matthew James. ASN, Southwestern Mich. U., 1976; BS, Ind. U., 1989, MS, 1991, EdD, 1999. Counselor Concord Cmty. Schs., Elkhart, Ind., 1986-92; cons. Ind. Dept. Edn., Indpls., 1992—; counselor Elkhart, 1992—; cons. C.J. Cons., Goshen, Ind., 1992—; asst. prof. Ind. U., South Bend, 2000—. Co-author: Handbook for School Counselors: Stop the Bus, 2000; contbr. articles to profl. book. Educator drug & Alcohol awareness Concord Schs., 1983-92. Mem. Nat. Student Assistance Assn. (sec. 1995—), Ind. Assn. Student Assistance Programs (bd. dirs. 1994—). Roman Catholic. Avocations: writing, poetry, walking, travel. Home and Office: 58112 Orchard Ln Goshen IN 46528-9078

DEUTCH, RICHARD MICHAEL, writer, poet; b. St. Louis, Sept. 25, 1944; s. Emmanuel Meyer and Adele (Munie) D.; m. Maria Athina Trefely, Mar. 19, 1985; 1 child, David Joseph. BA with honors, Bard Coll., 1967. Lectr. in humanities U. Kans., Lawrence, 1968-71; Latin master St. Anthony's Prep. Sch., London, 1974-76; film critic Sun. Telegraph, Sydney, Australia, 1979-86; lit. agt. self-employed Sydney, Australia, 1989—. Author: (poetry) The Dime, 1970, Prayers, 1970, Letters Home from Nowhere, 1979, (anthology) Bedside Blue, 1989, (book) From Barbecue to Bouillabaisse, 1989, Your Book of Magic Secrets, 1991, The Australian Magician's Handbook, 1993, Heart, with Piano Wire (poetry), 2001; contbr. numerous articles to profl. publs. Recipient Lockwood awards Creative Writing, Bard Coll., 1967, Billy Blue Creative Writing awards, 1983-84. Mem. The Author's Guild, The Journalists Agy. Democrat. Avocation: metaphysics.

DEUTSCH, ALEXANDER AARON, surgeon; b. Hampton Court, Surrey, Eng., Mar. 6, 1941; arrived in Israel, 1973; s. Herman and Ida (Roth) D.; m. Gloria Shieldhouse, July 27, 1966; children: Anna, Rachel Paula, Zvi, David Zev. B Medicine B Surgery, Med. Sch., Liverpool, Eng., 1966. House surgeon Liverpool Royal Infirmary, 1966-69; surg. registrar United Liverpool Hosp., 1969-71; unit head surgery Beilinson Hosp., Petach Tiqua, Israel, 1980—, chief colorectal unit, 1990—; chief of surgery Bene-Beraq (Israel) Hosp., 1995—; asst. lectr. in anatomy Liverpool U., 1967-68; rsch. fellow Children's Hosp., Boston, 1972-73; vis. prof. Med. Sch., Toronto, Ont., Can., 1988-89; assoc. prof. Tel Aviv Med. Sch., 1990—. Contbr. over 100 articles to profl. jours. Travel scholar Israel Cancer Soc., 1982; Physicians Svcs. Inc. Found. grantee, 1984. Fellow Royal Coll. Surgeons Eng., Royal Coll. Surgeons Edinburgh; mem. Am. Soc. Colon and Rectal Surgery, Collegium Internat. Chirurgia Digestive. Jewish. Avocations: swimming, tennis. Home: 16 Hatechiya St, Kfar Sava 44250, Israel Office: Meyenai Hayehoshua Hosp, 17 Sharet St, Bene-Berar 51544, Israel

DEUTSCH, ANDRE, physician; b. Antwerp, Belgium, May 29, 1949; s. Jozua and Frieda (Baum) D.; m. Eliane Ruth Krengel, May 6, 1988; children: Olivier, Katia, Kevin. MD, Vrye U. Brussels, 1976. Intern then resident Middelheim Hosp., Antwerp, 1973, 75-76, inst. Bordet, 1973, 75, St. Peter's Hosp., Brussels, 1974, 76; pvt. practice family physician Antwerp, 1976—. Home: Rucaplein 15, 2610 Wilryk Antwerp Belgium Office: Belgielei 73, 2018 Antwerp Belgium

DEUTSCH, CLAUDE DAVID, physicist, educator; b. Paris, July 20, 1936; s. David and Caroline (Petrover) D.; m. Nimet Elabed, July 9, 1962; children: Alain, Eric. Degree in chem. engring., Ecole Nat. Supérieure, Paris, 1959; M in Theoretical Physics, U. Paris XI, Orsay, 1961; DSc, U. Paris VI, 1969. Mem. staff CNRS, Orsay, 1959-60, Inst. H. Poincaré, Paris, 1960-63; engr. CEA-EURATOM Nuclear Energy Ctr., Fontenay-aux-Roses, France, 1965-71; chief rsch. Nat. Ctr. Sci. Rsch. (CNRS), Orsay, 1973-80; dir. Plasma Physics Lab., Orsay, 1980-85, 94-99; vis. scientist U. Montreal, Can., 1973, U. Gainesville, Fla., 1974, MIT, Cambridge, 1976-78, ICTP, Trieste, Italy, 1981, Stanford U., Palo Alto, Calif., 1980, 83; vis. prof. Okayama (Japan) U., 1978-86, 89, Weizmann Inst., Rehovot, Israel, 1983, GSI, Darmstadt, Germany, 1987, Osaka (Japan) U., 1995, Tokyo Inst. Tech., 1999-2000; found. chmn. Internat. Workshop Atomic Physics Ion Driven Fusion, 1983; dir. Paris-Sud Info., Orsay, 1985-93, Ion-Plasma Interaction Rsch. Gathering, CNRS, Orléans, Orsay, 1989-96; mem. Nat. Com. on Plasma Sci., 1983; sci. dir. Les Houches (France) Winter Sch., 1995; chmn. Strongly Coupled Coulomb Systems 99, Saint Malo, 1999. Editor proc. for internat. confs. in field; mem. editl. bd. Jour. Physique, 1985-88; contbr. articles to profl. jours. With French Mil. Forces, 1963-64. Fellow Japan Soc. Promotion of Sci., 1978, 86, 89, NATO, 1980. Recipient bronze and silver C.N.R.S. medals. Fellow Am. Phys. Soc., French Phys. Soc. (prizes com. 1979-83, mem. coun. 1979-83); mem. European Com. Heavy Ion Fusion, 1993. Office: Plasma Physics Lab, Bat 212, 91405 Orsay France

DEUTSCH, DIDIER (DELAUNOY DEUTSCH), music producer, writer; b. Arcachon, France, Dec. 8, 1937; came to U.S., 1962; parents Ladislas Leopold and Simonne (Gruot) D. Baccalaureat, Michel Montaigne, Bordeaux, France, 1957. Dir. publicity CTI Records, 1973-77; publicity writer RCA Records, 1978-81; staff writer WEA Internat., 1983-86; record prodr. Columbia Records, N.Y.C., 1986—, Arista Records, 1997—, Rhino Records, 1995—, RCA Records, 1994-97, Time-Life Music, 1994-97; drama critic musicals. Contbr. articles to Stereo Review, The New York Times, After Dark, Pulse! and other mags. and newspapers. Served with French Navy, 1957-60. Recipient nomination Grammy award for Frank Sinatra: The Columbia Years, 1995, Sony Music: Soundtrack for a Century, 2000. Mem. Nat. Acad. Rec. Arts and Scis., Am. Theatre Critics Assn.

DEUTSCH, HERBERT ARNOLD, music educator; b. Baldwin, N.Y., Feb. 9, 1932; s. Barnet Baruch and Miriam (Meyersburg) D.; m. Margaret Ann Carbray, Oct. 10, 1955 (dec.); children: Lisbeth Ann, Edmund Barnet; m. Nancy DiNapoli Blau, Sept. 14, 1997. BS in Edn., Hofstra U., 1956; MusM, Manhattan Sch. Music, 1961; postgrad., NYU, 1973-75. Music faculty East Meadow (N.Y.) Pub. Schs., 1959-60; freelance musician N.Y.C. area, 1960-61; lectr. music Hofstra Univ., Hempstead, N.Y., 1961-63, instr., 1964-68, asst. prof., 1969-73, assoc. prof., 1974-79, prof., 1983—, dept. chair, 1995—; dir. mktg. Moog Music div. Norlin Corp., Buffalo, 1980-81, dir. sales/mktg., 1981-83; cons. Pulse Concepts, L.I., N.Y., 1971—, Jim Henson's Muppets, N.Y.C., 1983-86, Norlin Corp., Chgo., 1976-79; edn. cons. Music and Computer Educator, 1989-91. Author: Synthesis, 1975, 2d rev. edit., 1984, Electroacoustic Music: Its First Century, 1993; composer numerous mus. works; contbr. articles to profl. jours., 1972—, Am. Record Guide, 1987-93. Mem. Huntington (N.Y.) Spl. Edn. PTA, 1976-88; bd. dirs. Huntington Symphony, 1973-75, Suffolk County (N.Y.) Family Services, 1975-77. Served with U.S. Army, 1956-58. Recipient grad. assistantship Manhattan Sch. Music, 1961; Meet the Composer grantee, 1976, 86, 87, 88, 90, 91, 92, 93, 94, 95, 96, 97, 98, Estabrook Disting. Alumni award Hofstra U., 1996. Mem. ASCAP (award 1992, 93, 94, 96, 97, 98, 99, 2000), AAUP, L.I. Composers Alliance (founder, bd. dirs. 1972-91, v.p. 1991-95, pres. 1998-2000, archivist 2000—), Am. Fedn. Musicians, Music and Entertainment Industry Edn. Assn.

DEUTSCH, NINA, pianist; b. San Antonio, Mar. 15; d. Irvin and Freda (Smukler) D. BS, Juilliard Sch. Music, 1964; MMA, Yale U., 1973. Concert pianist internat. and U.S. tours, 1965-82; entertainer, solo pianist Holland Am. Cruise Lines, 1987, 89-90; freelance pianist, lectr. on music, 1990—; exec. v.p. Internat. Symphony, N.Y.C., 1978-82. Pianist: (records) Charles Ives, 1976, Vox Records; author: (plays) Portrait of Liberace, 1995, Portrait of Clara Schumann, 1987; contbr. to mags. and newspapers. Bd. dirs. Metzner Found. for Overseas Relief; Ft. Lee coord. Channel 13, 1974. Tanglewood fellow Wulsin Fellowship, 1966; grantee Phillips Petroleum Found., 1982; recipient award for Am. music Nat. Fedn. Music Clubs, 1975; Oberlin Coll. scholar. Mem. Yale Alumni Assn. Bergen County. Avocations: swimming, hiking, baking. Home: PO Box 405 Leonia NJ 07605-0405

DEUTSCH, TIBOR IVAN, chemist, researcher; b. Budapest, Hungary, Aug. 6, 1946; s. Erno and Llvia (Steiner) D.; m. Ida Juhasz, June 13, 1976; children: Tamas, Nora. Diploma in Chemistry, Eotvos Lorand U., Budapest, 1969, PhD in Physical Chemistry, 1974; student, Acad. Scis., Budapest, 1990. Rsch. fellow Rsch. Inst. Tungsram Ltd., Budapest, 1969-74; dept. head Chinoin Pharm. Works Ltd., Budapest, 1974-82; asst. prof. Eotvos U. Scis., Budapest, 1982-86; chief rsch. fellow Semmelweis U. Medicine, Budapest, 1986—; adv. 1st Clinic of Internal Medicine Semmelweis U. Medicine, Budapest, 1987-96. Author: (with others) Planning Drug Dosage, 1984, Clinical Pgarmacokinetics, 1990, Dealing with Medical Knowledge, 1994; co-author: AIDA: An Educational Simulator for Insulin Dosage Adjustment, 1997. Avocations: psychology, humour, tennis. E-mail: deutib@inf.sote.hu. Fax: 36-1-2100 328. Home: Karolyi Mihaly utca 11, 1053 Budapest Hungary Office: Semmelweis U Med Ctr Inform, Kalvaria ter 5, 1089 Budapest Hungary

DEV, VAS, biologist, researcher; b. Purkhali, Panjab, India, Mar. 15, 1954; s. Ram Sarup and Kala Wati (Bansal) Bindal; m. Pinki Rani Mangal, June 8, 1986; 2 children. BSc with honors, Panjab U., Chandigarh, India, 1975, MSc with honors, 1977; PhD, U. Notre Dame, 1983. Tchg. asst. U. Notre Dame, Ind., 1982-83; rsch. assoc. USDA/ARS, Fargo, N.D., 1983-85; sr. rsch. officer Indian Coun. Med. Rsch., 1986-88, Malaria Rsch. Ctr., Delhi, India, 1988—; officer-in-charge Malaria Rsch. Ctr., Sonapur, Assam, 1988—; cons. WHO, Delhi, 1991, Barkatullah U., Bhopal, India, 1992. Mem. editl. bd. Annals of Med. Entomology, 1994; contbr. numerous articles to profl. jours.; contbr., reviewer Current Sci. Assn., Bangalore, India, 1988. Mem. mgmt. com. Ctrl. Sch. Digaru, Assam, 1988. Merit scholar Chandigarh Union Territory, 1972-75, Govt. of India, 1978-82; grantee Ind. Acad. Sci., 1982; recipient prize for biomed. rsch. Indian Coun. Med. Rsch., 1995. Fellow Indian Soc. for Malaria and Communicable Disease; mem. Entomol. Soc. Am., Indian Soc. for Malaria and Other Communicable Diseases, Indian Soc. for Parasitology, Nat. Acad. Scis., N.Y. Acad. Scis., Sigma Xi. Hindu. Achievements include research in mosquito cytogenetics; produced a photomap of polytene chromosomes of the malaria vector species; description of the polytene chromosomes of the screw-worm fly; study of the cytogenetics of Aedes albopictus and Aedes aegypti; evaluation of insecticide impregnated bednets to control/reduce malaria incidence. Avocations: sightseeing, music, reading, astrology. Home: Village and PO Purkhali, Dist Ropar, Panjab 140108, India Office: Malaria Rsch Ctr, 22 Sham Nath Marg, Delhi 110054, India

DE VABRES, FRANÇOIS DONNEDIEU, banker; b. Neuilly-S-Seine, France, May 3, 1948; s. Jacques D. and Jacqueline D. (Bos) De V.; m. Sylvie M. Des Garets, Oct. 29, 1977; children: Antoine, Guillaume, Alexia. MBA, E.D.H.E.C., Lille, France, 1972; M. in Econs., U. Paris X, 1973. Comml. attache French Embassy, Brussels, Belgium, 1973-74; asst. v.p. BNP, Paris, 1975-77; U.S. rep. BNP, N.Y.C., 1978-80; inspector BNP, Paris, 1981-82; dep. gen. mgr. BNP, N.Y.C., 1983-86; v.p. Banqui Nat. Paris Direction Risques & Etudes Indsl., Paris, 1987-92; sr. v.p. BNP-DREI, Paris, 1993-99, sr. v.p. group risk mgmt., 2000—; sr. exec. Natio Cons., Paris, 1992—. Mem. Polit. and Econ. Soc., French-Am. C. of C. (councelor 1978-86). Avocations: reading, golf, skiing, tennis. Home: 3 Rue de Rouvray, 92200 Neuilly France Office: BNP PARIBAS DCR, 1 bd Haussmann, 75009 Paris France

DE VALERA, SILE, Irish government official. Minister arts, culture and the Gaeltacht Govt. of Ireland, DUblin, 1997—. Mem. Fianna Fail Party. Office: Dept Arts Culture Gaeltacht, 42-49 Hespil Rd, Dublin Ireland*

DE VALK, HAROLD WESSEL, internist; b. Bilthoven, Utrecht, The Netherlands, Oct. 25, 1959; s. Willem and Hilda Agatha (Gröllers) De V. B Pharmacy, U. Amsterdam, The Netherlands, 1978; MD, Erasmus U., Rotterdam, The Netherlands, 1985; PhD, Utrecht U., 1997. Resident in tng. Elizabeth Hosp., Amersfoort, The Netherlands, 1985-87, Utrecht U. Hosp., 1988-90; internist dept. internal med. Univ. Med. Ctr. Utrecht, 1991, sci. dir., mgr. diabetes project, 1991, internist-endocrinologist in inborn errors of metabolism, 1991, internist-endocrinologist, 1994; reviewer for sci. jours.; mem. ednl. bd. Univ. Med. Ctr. Utrecht. Contbr. articles to profl. publs. Mem. Am. Diabetes Assn., Am. Endocrine Soc., N.Y. Acad. Scis., Soc. for Study of Inborn Errors of Metabolism, European Assn. for Study of Diabetes, Internat. Diabetes Fedn., Dutch Soc. for Diabetes Rsch., Dutch Soc. for Endocrinology, Dutch Internist Soc. Office: Utrecht U Hosp, F02-124 Heidelbergslaan 100, 3584 CX Utrecht The Netherlands

DE VALK, MAURICE MICHEL ARMAND, occupational medicine physician, consultant; b. Roermond, The Netherlands, Oct. 3, 1955; s. Johan Henri and Thérèse (Hülshoff) De V.; m. Sylvia Hedwig Maria Bruins De Valk, Sept. 24, 1992; 1 child, Victor. BS in Architecture, Tech. U., Delft, The Netherlands, 1976; MD, State U., Leiden, The Netherlands, 1987; postgrad., Med. Corps Royal Navy, 1997—. Rschr., trainer, educator silicosis External Faculty Medicine and Pharmacy Hosp. Dupuytrain de Limoges, France, 1979; occupational physician KLM, 1987-90, Dutch Railways, 1990-93; head of occupational health Nationale Nederlanden, 1993-94; trainer Postgrad. Occupational Medicine, 1995—; pres. Intermedic Cons., 1995—; pres. Internat. Forum of Orgnl. Health, 1996—; designer course orgnl. health cons. Benelux U. Ctr., 1998—; chair 31st ann. conf. IFOH.; lectr. Royal Soc. Med., London, 1995, House of Lords, London, 1998, Dutch Mgmt. Assn., 1999; guest educator Neyenrode U., 1998—; regional auditor Intermedic Cons. Inc., 1998; interviewed by newspaper, radio and television; guest lectr. Royal Soc. of Medicine, London, 1995, House of Lords, London, 1998; lectr. NCW-VNO, 1998; postgrad. lectr. Neyenrode U., 1998; regional lead auditor Det Norske Veritas, 1998. Editl. dir. Arts & Bedryf, 1997—, Gezond Ondernemen, 1998—; editor: Organizational Health Vademecum, 1999; contbr. articles to profl. jours. Recipient Green Health Orgn. award The Hague, 1998. Fellow The Dickens Soc.; mem. The Dutch Soc. Occupl. Medicine, Ctrl. Com. Postgrad. Tng., Brit. Soc. Occupl. Medicine Internat. Stress Mgmt. Assn. (bd. dirs. 1995—), State U Leiden Soc. Medicine (educator). Roman Catholic. Avocations: golf, squash, skiing, painting. Home: Weissenbruchstraat 223, 2596GG The Hague The Netherlands Office: Intermedic Consultants, Lange Voorhout 12, 2514ED The Hague The Netherlands

DEVANARAYANAN, SANKARANARAYANAN, physics educator; b. Thiruvananthapuram, Kerala, India, Nov. 11, 1940; s. Sankaranarayana Narayana Iyer and Parvathy Ponnammal Subramoni; m. Chitra Seetha Subramani, June 2, 1976; children: Ajith Shankar D., Aparna Gayathri D. BS, U. Coll., Thiruvananthapuram, India, 1961; MS, U. Coll., 1963; PhD, Indian Inst. Sci., Bangalore, 1969; Diploma, U. Uppsala (Sweden), 1971; DSc, Internatl. U., California, 1999. Sr. rsch. asst. Indian Inst. Sci., Bangalore, 1969-70; SIDA fellow Inst. Physics, Uppsala, Sweden, 1970-71; lectr. U. Kerala, Thiruvananthapuram, India, 1971-75; reader U. Kerala, Thiruvananthapuram, 1975-84, prof., 1984—, head dept. physics, 1993—, chmn. bd. studies in physics, mem. faculty scis., 1993—, mem. acad. coun., 1993—; chmn. Departmental Doctoral Comm. in Physics, 1993—; mem. bd. studies in optoelectronics U. Kerala, Thiruvananthapuram, 1996—, mem. senate, 1998—; prof. U. P.R., Rio Piedras, 1989-91; delegation mem. Citizen Amb. Programme, Washington, 1996; mem. adv. bd. Asian Jour. Physics, 1996—; prin. investigator Rsch. Project, Kerala, India, 1985—; vis. prof. U. P.R., Rio Piedras, 1989-91; mem. bd. studies in physics U. Kerala, Thiruvananthapuram, 1979—; govt. apptd. Commn. of Enquiry U. Kerala, 2000. Author monograph in physics 1979, supervisor guide to several PhD theses and M. Phil. Dissertations; contbr. about 100 articles to profl. jours. in physics. Fellow Swedish Internat. Devel. Agy., 1970; merit scholar U. Kerala, 1961-63. Fellow Indian Cryogenic Coun., United Writers Assn.; mem. (life) Am. Phys. Soc., Indian Physics Assn., Indian Sci. Congress Assn., Indian Assn. Physics Tchrs., N.Y. Acad. Scis., Kerala Philatelic and Numismatic Assn., Religious Stamp Exch. Club. Avocations: philately, numismatics, Hindu philosophy, consulting, astrology-medical. Home: TC 40/239 (G-9) PRS Enclave, E V Rd, 695014 Thiruvanantapuram Kerala, India Office: U Kerala, Dept Physics, 695581 Kariavattom Thiruvananthapuram, India

DEVANE, PETER ANDREW, orthopaedic surgeon, educator; b. Taihape, New Zealand, Mar. 2, 1960; s. Maurice Patrick and Jean Mary (Lourie) D.; m. Judith Lynne Wildfong, May 29, 1993; 1 child, Patrick Andrew. MB, BChir, Otago U., Dunedin, New Zealand, 1983; MSc, U. Western Ont., London, Can., 1993. Intern Palmerston N. Hosp., New Zealand, 1984-86; resident Wellington (New Zealand) Hosp., 1987-90; locum orthopaedic surgeon Whakatane Hosp., New Zealand, 1991; orthopaedic fellow Univ. Hosp., London, Can., 1992-94; sr. lectr. orthopaedic surgery Wellington (New Zealand) Sch. Medicine, 1994—; orthopaedic cons. Wellington (New Zealand) Hosp., 1994—; vis. orthopaedic surgeon Wakefield Hosp., New Zealand, 1994—; dir. Wakefield Joint Replacement Inst., Wellington, 1994—. Contbr. articles to profl. jours. Recipient Parke-Davis award Palmerston North Hosp., New Zealand, 1984, Frank Stinchfield award Hip Soc., U.S.A., 1994, founders medal Can. Orthopedic Rsch. Soc., 1994. Fellow Royal Australasian Coll. Surgeons, New Zealand Orthopaedic Assn. Avocations: squash, golf, tennis. Office: Wellington Sch Medicine, PO Box 7343, Wellington South, New Zealand

DEVANEY, CAROL SUSAN, management consultant; b. Panama City, Panama, May 8, 1954; d. James Henry DeVaney and Andrea Wong Mahoney; m. C. Eldon Taylor, July 30, 1978; 1 child, Taryne Jade Taylor; 1 stepchild, Deborah A. Taylor (dec. 1997). BA, Cath. U., 1974, MSW, 1975. Nat. Acad. cert. social worker; lic. clin. social worker, Va. Cmty. educator Prince George Health Dept., Cheverly, Md., 1975-76; coord. social svcs. Detox Ctr., Cocoa, Fla., 1976-77; psychiat. social worker Brevard County Mental Health, Melbourne, Fla., 1977-79; sr. clin. social worker Chesterfield (Va.) Mental Health, 1979-81; coord. bus. programs Chesterfield County, Chesterfield, 1981-86; adminstr. orgnl. devel. and tng. Henrico County, Henrico, Va., 1986-90; owner, pres. DeVaney-Wong Internat., Potomac, Md., 1990—; instr. Rollins Coll., Patrick AFB, Fla., 1977-79; cons. Coun. on Aging, Chesterfield, 1981-86; instr., vol. U. Richmond Women's Program, 1981-92; adv. bd. Bermuda Run, Chesterfield, 1983-86. Contbg. author: Prevention in Community M.H. Practice, 1992; author: (profl. manual) Stress Management, 1983; co-author: (book, manual, video) Let's Talk Diversity, 1992, Managing Diversity. Cons., vol. 1708 Gallery, Richmond, 1989-90; mem. adv. bd. Georgetown Hill Child Care, Potomac, 1994-95; mem. Brind (Europe) Register Customer Recommended Cons., 1993-2000. Recipient program awards Nat. Assn. Counties, 1989-91. Mem. ASTD (v.p. comm. 1987-88, Richmond chpt. pres. 1989-90, founder/liaison nat. Ibero-Am. network 1990-97, D.C. met. v.p. programs 1997, v.p. programs Ft. Lauderdale chpt. 1998, internat. program adv. com. 2000—, Nat. Torch award 1999), NASW, Am. Bus. Women's Assn., Soc. for Human Resource Mgmt. (program com. Broward chpt.), World Future Soc., Brind Register Women's C. of C. Avocations: swimming, travel, ethnic cooking, languages, world philosophy.

DE VANSSAY, CALAIS PAUL, information systems manager; b. Paris, July 11, 1935; s. Henry and Madeleine (d'Artigues) de V.; m. Chantal de Gigord; children Bénedicte, Anne, Charles-Henri, Gauthier, Arnaud. Officer, Ecole Superior Mil. InterArmes, France, 1959; PhD, Paris U., 1966. Engr., computer mgr. Peugeot, Paris, 1964-70; sr. eng. Control Data Co., Paris, 1970-75; dir. Micado, Grenoble, France, 1975-77; chmn. Calais, Grenoble, 1977-81; CAD mgr. Creusot Loire, Paris, 1981-86; project dir. Technip, Paris, 1986, Alcoa, Perth, Australia, 1986-96; cons. Coun. Devel. & Valorisation, Paris, 1996. Author computer applications. Capt. French Cavalry, 1959-64. Mem. French Engrs. & Scientists Assn. Avocations: bridge. Office: CDV Conseil, 89 Ave Mozart, 75016 Paris France

DEVARAJAN, G., library and information science educator; b. Thazhava, India, Mar. 8, 1947; s. S. Janardhanan and V. Lekshmy; m. S. Sugathakumary, Feb. 8, 1977; children: Vishnu D. Pavoor, Bhagya. BSc, U. Kerala, India, 1970; MA, U. Kerala, 1978, PhD, 1992; M of Libr. Info. Sci., U. Madras, India, 1980. Libr. asst. Kerala U. Libr., 1973-74; asst. libr. Ctr. for Devel. Studies, India, 1975-82; lectr. dept. libr. sci. U. Kerala, 1983-95, reader dept. libr. sci., 1996—, dean faculty arts, 1998—, senate mem., 1999—; chmn. bd. studies in libr. sci. U. Kerala, 1985—, mem. faculty of arts, 1985—, mem. acad. coun., 1990—; sec. Ctr for Info. and Tech. Studies, 1992—. Author: User's Approach to Information in Libraries, 1989, Resource Allocation in University Libraries, 1993, Library Science Education and Manpower, 1995, Reading: Pain or Pleasure?, 1995, Library Information User and Use Studies, 1995, Progress in Information Technology, 1996, Bibliometrics, 1997, Fifty Years of Indian Librarianship, 1998, Information Technology in Libraries, 1999. Mem. Indian Assn. Spl. Librs. & Info. Ctrs., Indian Libr. Assn. (life), Kenala Libr. Assn. (pres. 1993). Avocations: reading, creative writing. Home: Devashee ulloor, Medical College PO, Trivandrum 695011, India Office: Dept Libr & Info Sci, U Kerala, Trivandrum 695034, India

DE VAUBUZIN, BARON See PIERRE-BENOIST, JEAN

DEVAULT, JOHN LEE, oil company executive, geophysicist; b. Kansas City, Mo., Aug. 4, 1937; s. Isaac Henderson and Evelyn Margaret (Rowell) DeV.; m. Janet Ann Miller, Sept. 11, 1968; children: Bryan Charles, Chris Lee. B Chem. Engring., Case Inst. Tech., Cleve., 1959; BS, MacMurray Coll., Jacksonville, Ill., 1961; MS, U. Houston, 1975. Lic. geophysicist, Calif., Am. Assn. Petroleum Geologists, Am. Inst. Profl. Geologists, Soc. Ind. Profl. Earth Scientists. Geophysicist United Geophys., Europe, Africa, Middle East, Australia-Asia, Alaska and Houston, 1961-74; pres. Sercel Inc., Houston, 1974-88; chmn. Jade Corp., Houston, 1988—. Contbr. articles to Oil and Gas Jour. Dir. Jaycees, Springfield, Ill., 1960; downstate v.p. Young Rep. Club, Springfield, 1960; bd. dirs. Honors Coll., U. Houston, 1990—, MacMurray Coll.; trustee Culver Legion-Culver Academies. Mem. Geophys. Soc. Houston (hon. life, pres. 1987), Soc. Exploration Geophysics (1st v.p. 1993), Am. Inst. Profl. Geologists (pres. Tex. sect.), Culver Club of Greater Houston (pres.). Mem. Disciples of Christ Ch. Home: 703 Queensmill Ct Houston TX 77079-2411 Office: Jade Corp PO Box 218567 Houston TX 77218-8567

DE VECCHIS, MICHEL PIERRE, marketing professional; b. Clermont Ferrand, France, May 23, 1946; s. Eurisio and Gabrielle (Ecourtemer) De V.; m. Martine Dubayle, Dec. 23, 1972; children: Christine, Pascal. Diploma in engring., Ecole Nat. Superieure Telecomm, 1969. Engr. LTT, Conflans, France, 1971-83, tech. dir., 1983-86; dir. internat. mktg. Alcatel Cable, Clichy, France, 1986-93, dir. telecomm. mktg., 1993-96, dir. standards, 1996—; chmn. component com. Cenelec Electronic, 1988—; sec. Internat. Electrotech. Commn., 1989—; chmn. tech. com. Eurotel Cab, 1991—. Patentee in field; contbr. articles to profl. jours. Office: Alcatel Cable, 54 Rue La Boetie, 75411 Paris Cedex 08 France

DE VEIRMAN, GEORGES H. G. E., sales and marketing executive; b. Wetteren, Belgium, Mar. 21, 1946; m. Marie-Ghislaine de Rijck, Apr. 20, 1974; children: Emmanuel, Sofie. Lic. in econs. and social scis., U. Leuven, Belgium, 1970; MBA, European INSEAD, France, 1977; postgrad., Oxford (Eng.) U., U. Geneva, Warsaw. Mgr. recruitment and placement Ford Motor Co., Genk, Belgium, 1971-73; sales mgr. home delivery and merchandising Alken Breweries, Belgium, 1973-75; asst. dir. mktg. and sales Lacsoons-Beatrice Foods, Louvain, 1975-76; mktg. mgr., dir. Antwerp, devel. mgr., 1977—; mktg. mgr., devel. mgr., dir. gen. IBM, Europe and Belgium, 1977-91; prin. Heidrick & Struegge, 1991-94; pres., CEO AECA Belgium and Europe, 1995—. Office: Av de Messidor 208, B-1180 Brussels Belgium

DEVENDORF, LOUISE MARIE, promoter, writer; b. LeRoy, Mich., Apr. 5, 1939; d. Louis George and Lucille Mariam (Dean) Hinkley; m. Richard George Devendorf, Aug. 10, 1974; 1 child, Laurie Anne Hinkley Walker. Grad. high sch., 1957. Underwriter asst. Mich. Mut. Liability, Grand Rapids, 1957-63; dance instr. Arthur Murray Studio, Grand Rapids, 1959-61; insp. Wolverine Worldwide, Big Rapids, Mich., 1965-85; office mgr. Advt. Assocs., Grand Rapids, 1985-89; free-lance writer and promoter Reed City, Mich., 1989—. Author: Some Nostalgia Pertaining to Pearls, 1995, (poetry) War in Haiti, 1996. Mem. City Coun., Reed City, 1988—; mem. ex officio Libr. Bd., Reed City, 1992—; bd. dirs. Osceola Cares, Osceola County, 1993—, pres.; active Phone Tree, Reed City, 1995—; musician Furniture City Orch., 1957-59; pres. Sr. Adult Ministries Ch. of the Nazarene, 1999—. Recipient award Internat. Soc. Poets, 1996; elected to Internat. Poetry Hall of Fame, 1997. Avocations: reading, playing music, helping people. Home: 311 W Franklin PO Box 91 Reed City MI 49677-0091

DE VENECIA, JOSE PEREZ, III, telecommunications industry executive; b. Manila, Aug. 10, 1963; s. Jose Claveria De Venecia, Jr. and Victoria Salazar Perez; m. (div.); 1 child, Jose Jaime G. IV. BSBA, The Am. U., Washington, 1989; MBA, Fordham U., 1994. Auditor Arthur Andersen & Co., Washington, 1989-91; sr. auditor Sycip, Gorres, Velayo & Co., Makati, The Philippines, 1991-92; sr. cons. Corp. Fin., Makati, The Philippines, 1992-93; pres./CEO Multimedia Telephony, Inc., Makati, The Philippines, 1995—. Mem. Rotary. Avocations: reading, scuba diving, golf. Office: Multimedia Telephony Inc, 105 HV dela Costa St FL 17, 1200 Makati The Philippines

DEVENNY, LILLIAN NICKELL, trophy company executive; b. Chesapeake, Ohio; d. Hayes Basil and Alice Irene (Noble) Nickell; m. John Paul DeVenny Jr., Dec. 31, 1955; children: Carrie DeVenny Paganini (dec.), John Hayes. Student, Covington Bus. Sch., 1954-55, Norfolk Coll., 1980-81. Office mgr., bookkeeper Nickell Electric Co., Covington, Va., 1950-55, exec., 1960-62; sec. 5th Naval Dist. Hdqtrs., Norfolk, Va., 1955-58, Profl. Realty, Virginia Beach, 1971; pub. rels. corp. sec. Hobby Industries, Virginia Beach, 1973-74; owner, sec.-treas. Deste Corp. t/a Hobby Assoc., Virginia Beach, 1974—; singer, actress Tidewater Dinner Theater, Norfolk, 1971-75; mem. numerous continuing edn. units. Writer column on Va. travel, 1978-79; editor newsletter, 1972-73. Founding mem., chair bd. dirs. Va. Opposing Drunk Driving, 1981—, state v.p., 1981-86, state pres., 1986—; adv. bd. Va. Commn. on Alcohol Safety, 1987-91: participant Va. Assembly on Future of Va.'s Cts., U. Va., Commn. Pub. Svc., 1989; mem. spl. White House briefing on ways to combat tragedy of drunk driving, 1989; active Va. Civilian-Mil. Comty. Safety Com., 1988, Va. Alcohol Safety Action Program Commn., 1991—; co-chair Va. Coalition Against Drunk Driving, 1989—; contbr. passage Omnibus Alcohol Safety Act, Va. Gen. Assembly, 1994; legis. liaison for CCATS Transp. Safety Coalition, 1998—; bd. dirs. Drive Smart Hampton Roads. Recipient Cmty. Svc. award J.C. Penney Co., 1985, Hometown Hero, Sta. WVEC-TV, 1986, Gov.'s Transp. Safety award, 2000. Mem. Internat. Ceramists Assn., Modern Woodmen Am. (regional sec. 1954). Episcopalian. Avocations: singing, costume design, reading, theatre, herb gardening. Office: Deste Corp t/a Hobby Assocs 5815 Hargrove St Norfolk VA 23502-4636

DEVERA, GERTRUDE QUENANO, education educator; b. Malasiqui, Pangasinan, Philippines, Dec. 15, 1924; came to U.S., 1950; d. Paulino Castro and Filomena (del Rosario) Magsanoc; m. Perfecto Tamondong DeVera, June 23, 1946 (dec. Sept. 1976). BA, San Francisco State U., 1952; postgrad., U. Calif., Berkeley, 11952-54; MA in English Lit., San Francisco State U., 1956. Calif. tchrs. cert. and life diploma. Tchr. San Francisco Unified Sch. Dist., 1956-88, demonstration tchr., 1958-59; mem. aux. bd. trustees Don Adriano Geslani Montessori Sch., Malasiqui, Luzon, The Philippines, 1997—; tchr. participant Project Read Behavioral Rsch. Labs., Palo Alto, Calif., 1967-68; cert. demonstrator Astra's Magic Math-Alphaphonics, 1987-88; rschr. in preventive medicine, San Francisco, 1975—. Editing chmn.: Guidelines for Use of the Eudcational Facilities Planning model, 1968 (NDEA award 1968). Summer Inst. grantee NDEA, U. Wash., Seattle, 1968; recipient Hon. Svc. awards Calif. Congress Parents and Tchrs. Inc., Sacramento, 1975, San Francisco 2nd Dist., 1980. Mem. AAUW (legis. interview com. 1970's), Internat. Platform Assn., World Affairs Coun. No. Calif., Libr. of Congress. Democrat. Roman Catholic. Avocations: reading, creative writing, public speaking, attending lectures, various cultural pursuits.

DEVERALL, BRIAN JAMES, plant pathology educator; b. Birkenhead, Cheshire, U.K., Jan. 3, 1935; s. William James and Marion (Brook) D.; m. Flora Josephine Lloyd, Aug. 20, 1960; children: Lloyd James, Sarah Monica, David Michael. BSc, U. Edinburgh, Scotland, 1957; D.I.C., Imperial Coll., London, 1960; PhD, U. London, 1960. Harkness fellow Commonwealth Fund, N.Y.C., 1960-62; lectr. U. London, 1962-70; prin. sci. officer Wye Coll., London, 1970-73; prof. plant pathology U. Sydney, Australia, 1973—, head dept. plant pathology, 1973-92, pro-dean faculty of agr., 1983-85, chair com. for grad. studies, 1987-91, head dept. crop scis., 1995-96; chair CSIRO Plant Pathology Rev., Australia, 1982-83. Author: Fungal Parasitism, 1969, 2d edit., 1981, Defence Mechanisms of Plants, 1977; co-editor: Dynamics of Host Defence, 1983, 2 others; contbr. over 90 articles to profl. publs. Fellow Am. Phytopathol. Soc.; mem. Internat. Soc. Plant Pathology (editor newsletter 1994—, v.p. 1988-93), Australasian Plant Pathology Soc. (pres. 1987-89), Brit. Soc. Plant Pathology, Bickley Park Cricket Club (hon. life v.p. 1970—). Avocations: cricket, gardening, sports, environmental issues. Home: 18 Bonnefin Rd, Hunters Hill NSW 2110, Australia Office: U Sydney, Faculty Agr, Sydney NSW 2006, Australia

DEVEREUX, ALAN ROBERT, industrialist; b. Frinton-on-Sea, England, Apr. 18, 1933; s. Donald Charles and Doris Louie (Durant) D.; m. Gloria Alma Hair, Sept. 5, 1959 (dec. 1985); 1 child, Iain Jeremy; m. Elizabeth Tormey Docherty, May 11, 1987. Group sales mgr. Sanitas Trust, London, 1958-67; dir. Norcros Plc, France, 1967-70; mng. dir. Scotcros Plc, Scotland, 1970-80; chmn. Scottish Tourist Bd., 1980-90; founder, chmn. Quality Scotland Found., 1990-95; chmn. Scottish Ambulance Svc., 1995-98; bd. dirs. Scottish Mut. Assurance, Gleneagles Hotel Plc, Scotland, Abbey Nat. Life Pk; chmn. CBI Scotland, 1977-79; founder Scottish Devel. Agy., 1977-83. Chmn. Glasgow City Mission, Scotland, 1994-99; bd. dirs. Children's Hospice Assn. for Scotland, 1994—. Recipient Scottish Free Enterprise award, 1978; named Comdr. British Empire, 1980, Dep. Lord Lt. of Renfrewshire, 1985. Mem. Br. Inst. Mgmt., Inst. Elec. Engrs. Mem. Ch. of Scotland. Avocations: mission work, charities, antique clock restoration. Home: South Fell, 24 Kirkhouse Rd Blanefield, Stirlingshire G63 9BX, Scotland

DEVERS, GAIL, track and field athlete; b. Seattle, Nov. 19, 1966. BA in Sociology, UCLA, 1988. Gold medalist, 100m Track and Field Barcelona Olympic Games, 1992; Gold medalist 100m, 100m Hurdles World Track and Field Championships, Stuttgart, Germany, 1993; Gold medalist, 100m Track and Field Atlanta Olympic Games, 1996, Gold medalist 4x100m relay, 1996; Gold medalist 4x100m relay World Championships, 1997. Nat. champion 100M hurdles, 1991, 92, 93, 95, 96; nat. indoor champion 60M, 1993; world indoor champion 60M, 1993; world champion 100M, 1993, 95; world champion 100M hurdles, 1993; Women's Sports Found. Athlete of Yr., 1997. Office: Elite Internat Sports and Mgmt 1034 S Brentwood Blvd Ste 1530 Saint Louis MO 63117-1215

DE VEYRAC, CHRISTINE, foreign diplomat; b. Toulouse, France, Nov. 6, 1959. Mem. European Parliament, 1999—, mem. com. on culture, youth, edn., the media and sport, substitute com. on environment, pub. health, consumer policy; mem. Group of the European People's Party (Christian Democrats) and European Democrats. Office: Parlement européen, Rue Wiertz ASP 13E210, B-1047 Brussels France*

DEVIATKIN, EVGENY ALEKSANDROVICH, physicist, researcher; b. Kolomna, Russia, Mar. 13, 1955; s. Aleksandr Mikhailovich and Tatyana Ivanovna (Bolmashov) D.; m. Elena Victorovna Victorovich, Dec. 9, 1983. MS, Moscow Inst. Physics Tech., 1979; PhD, Russian Acad. Sci., Moscow, 1995. Probationer-rschr. Inst. of Problems in Mech. Russian Acad. Sci., Moscow, 1979-82, jr. rschr., 1982-91, rschr., 1991—; hon. prof. Albert Schweitzer Internat. U. Contbr. articles to profl. jours. Grantee Aircraft Design Office, 1991, Internat. Sci. Found., 1993, INTAS, 1998. Mem. N.Y. Acad. Sci., European Soc. Applied Superconductivity. Avocations: pets, travelling, rowing, jogging. E-mail: deviat@ipmnet.ru. Home: Michurinsky Prospekt 10-1-17, 117192 Moscow Russia Office: Inst Problems Mechanics RAS, Vernadskogo 101, 117526 Moscow Russia

DEVICHENSKII, VYACHESLAV MIKHAILOVICH, physician, biochemist; b. Moscow, Nov. 11, 1938; s. Mikhail Pavlovich Devishenskii and Olga Ivanovna Trusakova; m. Elena Nikolaevna Dyachkova, Sept. 17, 1959 (div. 1976); 1 child, Olga; m. Valentina Alexandrovna Nikolaeva, June 14, 1984. Degree in medicine, Moscow Med. U., 1966, degree in tchg., 1980; D in Biology, Inst. Applied Molecular Biolog, Moscow, 1990. Cert. medical prof. Asst. dept. biochemistry Moscow Med. U., 1965-80; biochemistry lab. head Inst. Applied Molecular Biology, Moscow, 1980-90; dept. head clin. and lab. diagnostic Improvement of Qualification Inst., Moscow, 1990—; dep. dir. for sci. Inst. Biol. Medicine, Moscow, 1998—. Contbr. articles to profl. jours. Mem. Russian Orthodox Ch. Avocations: travel, photography, sports, fishing. Home: Bolshaya Akademicheskaya, UL 73/4, 26 Moscow Russia Office: Improvement Qualif Inst, Volokolamskoe Shosse 30, 123182 Moscow Russia

DE VILLENFAGNE DE VO, BARON JEAN, investment company executive; b. Zolder, Limburg, Belgium, July 7, 1949; s. Henri and Louise-Marie (de Lichtervelde) de V. de V.; m. Bénédicte Dumont de Chassart, Sept. 17, 1981; children: Savina, Maxime. Lic. and MA in Econ. and Social Scis., Facultes Universitaires Notre Dame de la Paix, Namur, Belgium, 1974. Sr. auditor Ernst & Whinney, Brussels, 1975-80; contbr. Bank Auditor, Brussels, 1976-80; portfolio mgr. Pvt. Mut. Fund, Brussels, 1980-91; mng. dir. Optinvest S.A., Brussels, 1983—; stock exchange adviser Internat. Portfolio Mgmt., Brussels, 1983-87; dir. Bullish Investment Fund, Luxembourg, 1984-89, Waterlozen N.V., Zolder, Belgium, Le Foyer Schaerbeekois, Brussels. Author software on adminstrv. mgmt. of portfolio. V.p. local sect. Christian Dem. Party, Schaerbeek, Brussels, 1989. Named hon. citizen City of Kankakee (Ill.), 1971. Mem. Inst. Profl. Comptables et Fiscalistes agrees (cert. 1994), European Fedn. Fin. Analysts Socs. (cer. fin. analyst) 1998), Cercle du Parc, Brussels Bus. Mediation Ctr. Avocations: tennis, skiing, shooting, bridge, graphology. Home and Office: Optinvest SA, Ave des Capucines 5, B-1030 Brussels Belgium

DE VILLIERS, FRANÇOIS PIERRE-ROUSSEAU, pediatrician, educator, researcher; b. Swakopmund, S.W.A., South Africa, May 10, 1950; s. Charl Johannes and Elena Susanna (Gardiner) De V.; m. Gai Talbot, Dec. 1, 1979; children: Gillian Katinka, Tertius Gregoire. MB, B of Surgery, U. Stellenbosch, South Africa, 1974; BA in Philos. Logic, U. South Africa, 1982; M of Medicine in Pediat., U. Witwatersrand, South Africa, 1987, PhD, 1990. Cert physician, specialist in paediats. and endocrinology South African Med. and Dental Coun. Intern/med. officer Edendale Hosp., Pietermaritzburg, South Africa, 1974-77; med. officer/sr. med. officer George Stegmann Hosp., Moruleng, South Africa, 1978-82; resident in pediat. Baragwanath Hosp., Johannesburg, South Africa, 1983-87; specialist in pediat. Johannesburg Hosp., 1987-90, sr. cons. in pediat., 1990-94; prof., chair pediat. and child health Med. U. So. Africa, Pretoria, 1995—; deputy dean (rsch.) faculty of medicine Med. U. South Africa, 1997—; mem. Technical Task Team, Integrated Management of Childhood Illness, Dept. of Health, Pretoria, 1997—, dir. MSc course U. Witwatersrand, 1991-94; med. assessor Regional Ct., Pretoria, 1994-98; mem. ethics com. Med. U. So. Africa, 1995—; mem. rheumatic fever policy com. Dept. Health, Pretoria, 1995—; examiner South Africa Coll. Medicine, 1994-98. Editor: Practical Management of Paediatric Emergencies, 1989, 3d edit., 1999; contbr. over 55 articles to profl. jours. Recipient Silver medal for family practice rsch. Noristan, Pretoria, 1983, Rsch. Excellence award Med. U. of South Africa, 1998. Fellow Am. Coll. Physicians; mem. Internat. Soc. Pediat. and Adolescent Diabetes, N.Y. Acad. Scis., Soc. for Endocrinology, Metabolism and Diabetes of South Africa, Am. Coll. Physicians. Methodist. Office: Med Univ So Africa, PO Box 221 Dept Pediat, Medunsa 0204, South Africa

DE VILLIERS, INGRID BARBARA, lawyer; b. Nigel, Gauteng, South Africa, Aug. 19, 1948; d. Ralph Kalman and Stella Joyce (Goldman) Lewin; m. Gavin Morikel Stewart, Dec. 5, 1970 (div. Mar. 1995); m. Richard Reginald de Villiers, Dec. 14, 1985; children: Katharine, Megan, Richard. BA, U. Witwatersrand, Johannesburg, South Africa, 1973; LLB, U. Natal, Durban, South Africa, 1985. Journalist South Africa Associated Newspapers, Johannesburg, 1968-75, Argus Newspapers, Durban, 1977-81; candidate atty. Shepstone & Wylie, Durban, 1985-86; fellow, atty. Legal Resources Ctr., Johannesburg, 1986-87; supervising atty. Campus Law Clinic, Johannesburg, 1989-93; pvt. practice Johannesburg, 1994-96; convening sr. commr. commn. for Conciliation, Mediation and Arbitration, Johannesburg, 1996-98; arbitrator, mediator Ind. Mediation Svc. of South Africa, 1990—; acting judge Labor Ct., South Africa, 1999; arbitrator, mediator Public Svc. Bargaining Coun. South Africa, 1999—, South African Airways Bargaining Forum, 1999—. Editor: Collective Bargaining, Deregulation and Democracy, 1991, Trends in South African Labor Law, 1992, IMSSA Arbitration Digest, 1994-96; mng. editor, contbr. jour. Employment Law, 1992-94. Father of the chapel South African Soc. Journalists, Durban, 1982; mem. com. Free Mandela Campaign, Durban, 1979-82; chmn. Detainees Support Com., Durban, 1983-84. Recipient Stellenbosch Farmers' Wineries award for enterprising journalism, 1976. Mem. Transvaal Law Soc., Assn. Univ. Legal Aid Clinics (v.p. 1989-90), South African Soc. Labor Lawyers (v.p. 1999). Avocations: piano, walking, bird watching, safaris, golf. Office: PO Box 651831 Benmore, Sandton Gauteng 2010, South Africa

DE VILLIERS, PIETER GIDEON, theologian, educator; b. Venterstad, South Africa, Apr. 20, 1947; s. Pieter and Judith (De Ridder) De V.; m. Susanna De Villiers, June 18, 1970; three children. BA, U. Stellenbosch, 1969, B in Theology, 1969; D in Theology, U. Kampen, 1973, U. Stellenbosch, 1976. Sr. lectr. U. Stellenbosch, South Africa, 1971-84; prof. U. South Africa, Pretoria, 1984-88, Rhodes U., Grahamstown, South Africa, 1989—. Avocations: squash, tennis, investment, reading. Office: Rhodes U, 6140 Grahamstown South Africa

DEVINE, ANTOINE MAURICE, lawyer; b. Milw., Apr. 19, 1957; s. John and Marietta Elizabeth D. BS in Fin., Jackson State U., 1979; JD, U. Tex., 1991. Bar: Calif. 1993. Asst. auditor Trustmark Bank, Jackson, Miss., 1979-81; sr. compliance examiner NASD Regulation, Inc., Dallas, 1981-84; adminstr., pres. Hall Securities Corp./Funding Capital, Inc., Dallas, 1985-86; pres. Devine Fin. Svcs., Bedford, Tex., 1987-88; assoc. Dennis & Coscia, San Diego, 1993-95; staff atty. San Diego Gas & Elec., 1995; corp. counsel Global Resource Investments, Ltd., Carlsbad, Calif., 1997-98; ptnr. Evers & Hendrickson, San Francisco, 1998-2000; pres. U.S. Pub. Shells, L.L.C., 1999—; spl. counsel Foley and Lardner, 2000—. Basketball coach Jackie Robinson YMCA, San Diego, 1994-97. Democrat. Avocations: golf, tennis, softball, jazz. Home: 266 Lenox Ave Apt 301 Oakland CA 94610-4605 Office: Evers & Hendrickson LLP 155 Montgomery St Fl 12 San Francisco CA 94104-4105

DEVINE, EUGENE PETER, lawyer; b. Albany, N.Y., Oct. 14, 1948; s. Eugene Peter and Phyllis Jean (Albanese) D.; m. Debra Ann Ziamandanis, Apr. 11, 1992; children: Kimberly, Tracy, Adrianne, Madeline. JD, Union U., 1975. Bar: N.Y. 1975, U.S. Dist. Ct. (no. dist.) N.Y. 1975, U.S. Supreme Ct. 1980. Asst. N.Y. Pub. Defender, Albany County, 1976-85; ptnr. Cooper, Erving & Savage, Albany, 1975-85, Devine, Piedment & Rutnik, 1985-91; chief pub. defender Albany County, 1994—; of counsel Carter Conboy, 1995—; chief atty. Albany County Dept. Social Svcs., 1985-88. Bd. dirs. Ronald McDonald House, Albany, 1980—, founding mem.; committeman Albany County Dem. Com., 1979—; treas. com. to elect Jim Tully N.Y. State Compt. N.Y. State Compt., 1980, vice chmn. Albany Med. Ctr. Found., 1994—. Mem. Woolferts Roost Country Club, Steuben Athletic Club, Albany Sons of St. Patrick (pres. 1984). Office: Carter Conboy Case Blackmore Napierski & Maloney 20 Corporate Woods Blvd Ste 8 Albany NY 12211-2362

DEVINEY, MARVIN LEE, JR., research institute scientist, program manager; b. Kingsville, Tex., Dec. 5, 1929; s. Marvin Lee and Esther Lee (Gambrell) D.; m. Marie Carole Massey, June 7, 1975; children: Marvin Lee III, John H., Ann-Marie K. Deviney Bowen. BS in Chemistry and Math., S.W. Tex. State U., San Marcos, 1949; MA in Phys. Chemistry, U. Tex., Austin, 1952, PhD in Phys. Chemistry, 1956. Cert. profl. chemist. Devel. chemist Celanese Chem. Co., Bishop, Tex., 1956-58; rsch. chemist Shell Chem. Co., Deer Park, Tex., 1958-66; sr. scientist, head group phys. and radio-chemistry Ashland Chem. Co., Houston, 1966-68, mgr. sect. phys. and analytical chemistry, 1968-71; mgr. sect. phys. chemistry div. rsch. and devel. Ashland Chem. Co., Columbus, Ohio, 1971-78; rsch. assoc., supr. applied surface chemistry Ashland Ventures Rsch. and Devel., Columbus, 1978-84, supr. electron microscopy, advanced aerospace composites, govt. contracts, 1984-90; inst. scientist, mem. internal R & D com. SW Rsch. Inst., San Antonio, Tex., 1990-97; pres. MLD Polymers/Composites, Inc., 1997—; R&D dir. Nuresco Polymers, 1998—; cons. polymer divsn. Southwest Tex. State U., 1998—; adj. prof. U. Tex., San Antonio, 1973-75, Ohio State U., 1990-91; mem. sci. adv. bd. Am. Petroleum Inst. Rsch. Project 60, 1968-74. Contbr. numerous articles to profl. jours.; patentee in field. Mem. ednl. adv. com. Columbus Tech. Inst., 1974-84, Cen. Ohio Tech. Coll., 1975-82, Hocking Tech. Coll., 1989-91. Lt. col., USAR, retired. Humble Oil Rsch. fellow, 1954. Fellow Am. Inst. Chemists (pres. Ohio Inst. 1978-82); mem. Tex. Acad. Sci., Am. Def. Preparedness Assn., Electron Microscopy Soc. Am., Materials Rsch. Soc., SAMPE Composite Soc., N.Am. Catalysis Soc., Am. Soc. Composites, Soc. Plastics Engrs., Soc. Automotive Engrs., Am. Chem. Soc. (chmn. chpt. exec. bd. 1969, bus. mgr. nat. div. Petroleum Chemistry, 1986-90, Best Paper award rubber div. 1967, 70, Hon. Mention awards 1968, 69, 73, symposia co-chmn., co-editor books on catalysis-surface chemistry 1985, carbon-graphite chemistry 1975), Engr.'s Coun. Houston (sr. councilor 1970-71), Sigma Xi, Phi Lambda Upsilon, Alpha Chi, Sigma Pi Sigma. Methodist.

DEVINS, ROBERT SYLVESTER, retired lawyer; b. N.Y.C., Mar. 19, 1949; s. Arthur Sylvester and Judith Delores (Whelan) D. BA, Tulane U., 1971; JD, Emory U., 1978. Bar: Ga. 1978, Fla. 1981, U.S. Dist. Ct. (no. dist.) Ga. 1978, U.S. Tax Ct. 1978, U.S. Ct. Appeals (5th cir.) 1978, U.S. Supreme Ct. 1982, U.S. Dist. Ct. (mid. dist.) Ga. 1994. Pvt. practice Atlanta, 1978-99; ret., 1999. Lt. USN, 1971-75. Mem. ABA, Internat. Bar Assn. (vice chmn. criminal law sect. 1985-87, chmn. 1987-89. rep. UN Conf. 1987, 89), Inter Am. Bar Assn., Nat. Assn. Criminal Def. Lawyers, Ga. Assn. Criminal Def. Lawyers, Assn. Trial Lawyers Am., Ga. Trial Lawyers Assn., Union International des Avocats. Avocation: reading. Home: Casa Ventosear 2335 S Ocean Blvd Palm Beach FL 33480-5368

DEVÍNSKY, FERDINAND, chemist, educator; b. Bratislava, Czechoslovakia, Aug. 17, 1947; s. Ferdinand and Edita (Lux) D.; m. Sylvia Poláková, July 3, 1970; children: Henry, Peter. MS, Slovak Poly. U., Bratislava, 1970; PhD, Comenius U., Bratislava, 1981, DSc, 1993. Rsch. fellow Rsch. Inst. of Drugs, Bratislava, 1970-72; from asst. lectr. to prof. Comenius U., Bratislava, 1972-92, prof. medicinal chemistry, 1992—; rsch. project dir. Faculty of Pharmacy, Bratislava, 1985—, dept. head, 1990—; vis. prof. Chelsea Dept. Pharmacy, London, 1986-87; vicerector Comenius U., Bratislava, 1991—, dir. toxicological ctr., 1995—, rector, 1997—. Author: Practice in Organic Chemistry, 1976, 5th edit., 1995, Organic Chemistry, 1979, 3d edit., 1993; editl. bd. Polish Jour. Environ. Sci., Drug Metabolism Drug Interactions, 1988, 92; patentee in field. Avocations: tennis, downhill skiing, driving. Office: Comenius U Pharmacy Faculty, Kalinčiakova 8, 832 32 Bratislava Slovakia

DE VISSCHER, FRANCOIS MARIE, investment banker; b. Louvain, Belgium, Sept. 24, 1953; s. Michel and Jacqueline (Velge) de V.; m. Maura Michaela Nicholson, Oct. 4, 1980; children: Patrick-Michel, Luke-Michel. BA in Applied Econs., U. Louvain, 1975; MBA, Rutgers U., 1977. CPA, N.Y. Staff asst. Coopers & Lybrand, Brussels, 1975-76; staff acct. Coopers & Lybrand, N.Y.C., 1977-79, sr. acct., 1979-80, supr. audit, 1980; assoc. Smith Barney, Harris Upham & Co., Inc., N.Y.C., 1981-82, 2nd v.p., 1983-84, v.p., 1985-88, mng. dir., 1988-90; pres. de Visscher & Co., Greenwich, Conn., 1990-98; ptnr. de Visscher, Olson & Allen LLC, Greenwich, 1998—; bd. dirs. Bekaert Corp. Pres. Family Firm Inst., Brookline, Mass.; trustee Whitby Sch., Greenwich, Conn. Mem. AICPA, Nat. Assn. Securities Dealers (registered rep.), N.Y. Soc. CPAs, Belgium Am. C. of C. (bd. dirs.), Bekaert N.V. Belgium (bd. dirs.), Larchmont (N.Y.) Yacht Club, Westchester Country Club (Rye, N.Y.), Pawling (N.Y.) Mt. Club. Avocations: sailing, shooting, fishing, golf. Office: de Visscher & Co 104 Field Point Rd Greenwich CT 06830-6481

DEVITA, MARIE N., physician; b. Weehawken, N.J., Feb. 27, 1928; d. Dominick and Maria (Medici) Nicoletti; m. Michael R. DeVita, Sept. 18, 1954 (div. 1972); children: Michael, Stephen, Maria, Robert, Thomas, Joseph, John. BS, Coll. St. Elizabeth, 1949; MD, Georgetown U., 1954. Intern St. Michael's Hosp., Newark, 1954-55; pvt. practice family medicine, Paramus, N.J., 1960—; med. dir. Transitional Care Ctr. Pascack Valley Hosp., Paramus, N.J., 1998—; chief med. examiner Paramus (N.J.) Pub. Schs., 1972—; dir. family practice divsn. Pascack Valley Hosp., 1985-91; pres. med. staff Bergen Pines County Hosp., 1990-93, 95-99. Mem. N.J. Med. Womens Assn. (pres. 1985-87). Office: 645 Cambridge Rd Paramus NJ 07652-4203

DEVITA, VINCENT THEODORE, JR., oncologist; b. Bronx, N.Y., Mar. 7, 1935; s. Vincent Theodore and Isabel DeV.; m. Mary Kay Bush, Aug. 3, 1957; children: Teddy (dec.), Elizabeth. BS, Coll. William and Mary, 1957; MD, George Washington U., 1961; DSc (hon.), N.Y. Med. Coll., 1987, Georgetown U., 1989. Diplomate: Nat. Bd. Med. Examiners, Am. Bd. Internal Medicine (subspecialty hematology, med. oncology). Intern U. Mich. Med. Center, Ann Arbor, 1961-62; resident in medicine George Washington U. Med. Service D.C. Gen. Hosp., 1962-63; clin. assoc. Lab. Chem. Pharmacology, Nat. Cancer Inst. NIH, Bethesda, Md., 1963-65; sr. resident in medicine Yale New Haven Med. Center, 1965-66; sr. investigator solid tumor service, medicine br. Nat. Cancer Inst. NIH, 1966-68, head solid tumor service, medicine br., 1968-71, chief med. br., 1971-74, dir. div. cancer treatment, 1974-80, clin. dir. inst., 1975-80; dir. Nat. Cancer Inst., Nat. Cancer Program, NIH, 1980-88; physician-in-chief Meml. Sloan-Kettering

Cancer Ctr., N.Y.C., 1988-91, attending physician, mem., 1988-93, Benno C. Schmidt chair clin. oncology, 1988-93; prof. medicine Cornell U. Med. Coll., 1989-93; dir. Yale Cancer Ctr., New Haven, 1993—; prof. medicine Yale U. Sch. Medicine, New Haven, 1993—; attending physician Yale-New Haven Hosp., 1993—; prof. epidemiology and pub. health, dir. of Yale Cancer Ctr. Yale U. Sch. Medicine, New Haven, 1994—; assoc. prof. medicine George Washington U. Med. Sch., 1971-75, prof. medicine, 1975-89; vis. physician Rockefeller U. Hosp., 1989-93; mem. expert advisory panel WHO, 1976-93; mem. Lasker Award Jury, 1974—; chmn. Com. French-Am. Agreement on Cancer Treatment Research, 1976; vis. prof. Stanford U. Med. Sch., 1972; 1st ann. Clowes lectr. Roswell Park Meml. Inst. Buffalo, 1973; mem. sci. com. 4th Internat. Congress on Anti-Cancer Chemotherapy, 1991-92, 5th Internat. Congress on Anti-Cancer Chemotherapy, also mem. internat. adv. bd., 1993—; mem. sci. adv. bd. Tobacco-Related Disease Rsch. Program State of Calif., 1991—, Hollings Cancer Ctr., 1991—; mem. adv. bd. Stop Cancer, 1991—; mem. sci. com. Italian-Am. Found. For Cancer Rsch., 1991—; mem. clin. adv. bd. Hybridon, Inc., 1993—; bd. dirs Imclone Systems Inc., Oncotech Inc., Oncos Inc. Mem. editl. bd. Cancer Rsch., 1981-91, Gynecologic Oncology, 1981-91, Hematol. Oncology, 1981-87; Physicians' Drug Alert, 1982—, Jour. Clin. Oncology, 1983—; assoc. editor Online Jour. Current Clin. Trials, 1991—, Cancer Investigation, 1983-87, Am. Jour. Medicine, 1983-88; mem. extramural bd. assoc. editors Physicians Desk Query (PDQ), Nat. Cancer Inst., 1989—; mem. editl. bd. or adv. editor numerous other med. jours.; contbr. numerous articles to med. jours. Mem. awards assembly Gen. Motors Cancer Research Found., 1981-85, adv. council, 1984—; mem. Armand Hammer Cancer Award Com., 1983—. Served with USMCR, 1955-61. Tobacco Rsch. Industry fellow, 1959; decorated Oren del Sol en el Grando de Official, Govt. of Peru, 1970; recipient Albert and Mary Lasker Med. Rsch. award, 1972; Superior Svc. award HEW, 1975; Esther Langer Found. award, 1976; Alumni medallion Coll. William and Mary, 1976; Jeffrey Gottlieb award, 1976; Bronze medal Am. Soc. Therapeutic Radiology, 1978, Karnofsky prize and lecture, 1979, Griffuel prize Assn. for Devel. Rsch. on Cancer, 1980, James Ewing award Soc. Surg. Oncology, 1982; Meml. Sloan-Kettering Cancer award, 1972; Disting. Svc. medal USPHS, 1983; Meyer and Anna Prentiss award, 1984; Second Emmanuel Cancer Found. award, 1984; Pierluigi Nervi award, Rome, 1985; Medal of Honor, Am. Cancer Soc., 1985; Barbara Bohen Pfeifer award Am.-Italian Found. Cancer Rsch., 1985; Stratton lectr. Am. Soc. Hematology, 1985, Leukemia Rsch. Fund lectr., London, 1985; Tenth Richard and Hilda Rosenthal Found. award, Am. Assn. Cancer Rsch., Inc., 1986; Stanley G. Kay Meml. award, D.C. Am. Cancer Soc., 1986, Sci. award Brady Cancer Rsch. Inst., 1987, Prix Cino del Duca, Paris, 1988, Pezcoller award Eur. Sch. Oncology, Trento, Italy, 1988, Surgeon Gen.'s Exemplary Svc. medal, 1988, Armand Hammer Cancer prize, 1990, Outstanding Achievement in Clin. Rsch. award Assn. Cmty. Cancer Ctrs., 1992; elected Conn. Acad. Sci. and Engring., 1994; recipient City of Medicine award, 1995. Fellow ACP, N.Y. Acad. Medicine; mem. AMA, Am. Soc. Clin. Oncology (chmn. program com. 1972, dir. 1973-76, pres. 1977-78), Am. Cancer Soc., Am. Soc. Hematology, Am. Assn. Cancer Rsch. (dir. 1976-79), Am. Fedn. Clin. Rsch., Am. Soc. Clin. Investigation, Assn. Am. Physicians, Soc. Surg. Oncology, Smith-Reed-Russel Med. Soc., Internat. Coun. for Coordinating Cancer Rsch. (pres. Am. bd. 1989-92), Alpha Omega Alpha.

DE VITO, JOSEPH, psychologist; b. Bklyn., Dec. 19, 1945; s. Salvatore and Rose De Vito; m. Gail Ann Cryan, July 29, 1972; children: Jill, Becky, Gary. BS, Manhattan Coll., 1967; MA, Columbia U., 1973; PhD, Ga. State U., 1978. Cert. psychologist. Conn. Psychologist Wyo. State Hosp., Evanston, 1978-80; dir. Washakie Mental Health Svcs., Worland, Wyo., 1980-82. Inst. for Motivational Devel., Edina, Minn., 1982-83, Morrow-Wheeler-Gilliam Mental Health, Heppner, Oreg., 1984-85; psychologist Washburn Child Guidance Ctr., Mpls., 1985-87, Luth. Social Svcs., International Falls, Minn., 1987-88; psychologist, assoc. Breyer and Cohen, Vernon, Conn., 1988-90; pvt. practice Middletown, Conn., 1990—; profl. mem. State Conn. Bd. Psychologist Examiners, Hartford, 1996—. With U.S. Army, 1969-70, Korea. Mem. Nat. Assn. Scholars, Conn. Psychol. Assn. Republican. Roman Catholic. E-mail: joseph.devito@snet.net. Office: 148 East St Middletown CT 06457-1907

DEVIVO, ANGE, former small business owner; b. Bay Shore, N.Y., Oct. 20, 1925; d. Romeo Zanetti and Karolina (Hodapp) King; m. John Michael DeVivo, Dec. 30, 1950; 1 child, Michael. Student, Washington Sch. for Secs., N.Y.C., 1945-46. Sec. Am. Airlines, N.Y.C., 1946-51; exec. sec. W.C. Holzhauer, N.Y.C., 1951-52; dist. sales mgr. Emmons Jewelers, Inc., Bound Brook, N.J., 1952-53; exec. sec. N.J. Rep. State Com., 1960-64; adminstrv. sec. Mercy Hosp., Charlotte, N.C., 1973-81; pres. Secs., Convs., Plus, Charlotte, 1983-91; prin. Ange DeVivo & Assocs., Inc., Charlotte, 1991-92. Editor: The North Carolina Republican Woman, 2d edit., 1994, 3d edit., 1995. Active in local politics in N.J., 1956-64, in Conn., 1964-68, in N.C., 1968-96; mem. Human Svcs. Coun., Charlotte, 1984-88; mem. Emergency Med. Svc. Adv. Coun., Charlotte, 1981-92, chmn., 1988-90; mem. Charlotte Women's Polit. Caucus, 1972-96, Mecklenburg Evening Rep. Women's Club, Charlotte, 1970—, pres., 1973-74, 1993-94, Women's Roundtable, 1994, 95; mem. citizens adv. com. Conv. and Visitors Bur., 1986-90; coord. Women's Equality Day celebration Mecklenburg County Women's Commn., 1990, coord., fin. chair, 1991-92, co-chmn., fin. chair, 1993-96, mem. adv. bd. 1993-96, vice chair bd., 1995; fundraiser March of Dimes and Leukemia, Ala., 1999. Recipient Order of Long Leaf Pine award Gov. of N.C., 1974, Entrepreneur of Yr. award Women Bus. Owners, 1987, Spl. Recognition award for devotion, dedication and untiring efforts Mecklenburg County Women's Commn., 1996; honoree N.C. Fedn. Rep. Women, 1987; nominee for Cmty. Svc. award, 1994. Mem. Rep. Women Today Ala. Roman Catholic. Avocations: politics, community volunteer work. First woman elected chairperson Mecklenburg County Republican Party, 1976.

DEVLETOGLU, JAN GUY, journalist; b. Istanbul, Turkey, Dec. 28, 1945; s. Kimes and Anna (Akian) D.; m. Angela Economopoulou, 1975 (div. 1988); children: Anne-Maral, Zoe. BA in Psychology, U. Istanbul, 1970, BA in History of Art, 1972; grad. with honors, The London Film Sch., 1975. Photo-reporter Near East Press Agy., Istanbul, 1964-66; Turkish News Agy., Rapport, SF (Sweden), Istanbul, 1966-71; London corr. Turkish News Agy., Istanbul, 1974-85, GUNES (Turkish Daily), Istanbul, 1985-90; London bur. chief Sabah Group, Istanbul, 1990—. Photographer (exhbn./book) Varto, 1964 (1st prize 1964-65), (book/jour. with Carl Elof Swenning) Turkey, 1968); dir. (documentary): Legs/Kirkpinar, 1969 (Hisar Film Festival 3d prize). Named Journalist of the Yr. Nat. Union Turkish Journalists, 1996; Armenian Benevolent Fund, Brussels Individuell Manniskohjolps, Sweden scholar, 1970-72. Mem. Fgn. Press Assn. London, Nat. Union Journalists London. Avocations: photography, film-making. Home: Flat 8, 20 Lower Sloane St, London SWIW 8BG, England Office: Sabah/Atv, 32 Sloane St 1st Fl, London SW1X 9NR, England

DEVLIN, JOHN GERARD, lawyer, author; b. Phila., Apr. 26, 1955; s. John and Catherine (Flannery) D.; m. Maureen Borneman, June 17, 1978; children: Caitlin, Colin, Courtenay, Conor. BA, Temple U., 1977, JD, 1980, LLM, 1996. Bar: Pa. 1980, N.J. 1992. Assoc. Spencer, Sherr & Moses, Norristown, Pa., 1980-82, Deasey, Scanlan & Bender, Phila., 1982-84; mng. atty. Devlin Assocs., P.A., Phila., 1984—. Author: Tort Liability for Bad Faith Claims, 1995. Mem. Union League Club, Phi Beta Kappa. Office: 1515 Market St Ste 2010 Philadelphia PA 19102-1920

DEVLIN, WENDE DOROTHY, writer, artist; b. Buffalo, Apr. 27, 1918; d. Bernhard Phillip Wende and Elizabeth May Buffington; m. Harry Devlin, Aug. 30, 1941; children: Harry, Wende, Jeffrey, Alexandra, Brian, Nicholas, David. BFA, Syracuse U., 1940. Author: (children's books) Old Black Witch, 1963, Old Witch and the Polkadot Ribbon, 1963, The Knobby Boys to the Rescue, 1965, Aunt Agatha, There is a Lion Under the Couch, 1968, How Fletcher was Hatched, 1970, (N.J. English Tchrs. award) A Kiss for a Warthog, 1970, Cranberry Thanksgiving, 1971, Old Witch Rescues Halloween, 1973 (Chgo. Book Fair award for excellence 1974) Cranberry Christmas, 1973, Cranberry Mystery, 1979, Hang on Hester, 1980, Cranberry Summer, 1991, Cranberry Valentine, 1986, Cranberry Autumn, 1994, The Trouble with Henriette, 1995; artist, painter comic strip Ragg Mopp, 1969-72; contbr. of many poems to Good Housekeeping mag.; one person show at Schering Plough, N.J.; represented in permanent collections at Midlantic Bank of N.J.. Nat. Westminster Bank of N.J., also many private collections. Mem. Rutgers Adv. Coun. on Children's Lit., 1980—. Recipient Arents award Syracuse U., 1977; named to N.J. Literary Hall of

Fame, 1989. Congregationalist. Home and Office: 443 Hillside Ave Westfield NJ 07090-2902 Office: Simon & Schuster 866 3rd Ave New York NY 10022-6221

DE VLUGT, WILLEM, packaging industry executive; b. Amsterdam, The Netherlands, July 20, 1942; s. Leendert B. and Margaretha (Stanek) De V.; m. Karin J. Menke, Aug. 12, 1968; children: Caroline, Willem, Evelyn. LLM, Free U., Amsterdam, 1968; cert. in advanced mgmt. pub. rels., Harvard Bus. Coll., Boston, 1985. Employee Van Leer, N.Y., Paris, Argentina, 1969-77; gen. mgr. Akzo, Argentina, The Netherlands, 1977-83; mng. dir. Van leer South Am., Sao Paolo, 1983=86; pres., chief exec. officer Van Leer Containers, U.S., 1986-89; mem. exec. bd. Van leer, Amstelveen, The Netherlands, 1989—, dept. chmn. chief exec. officer, 1991—, chmn. bd., CEO; now mem. bd. dirs Crovadis Group, Amersfoort, The Netherlands, 2000S. Office: Crovadis, Algolweg 9/15, 3821 BG Amersfoort The Netherlands*

DEVOL, GEORGE CHARLES, JR., manufacturing executive; b. Feb. 20, 1912; s. George C. and Elsa (Vance) D.; m. Evelyn R. Jahelka, Dec. 31, 1938; children: Christine, George C. III, Robert, Vance, Suzanne. PhD in Sci., U. Bridgeport, 1985. Pres. United Cinephone Corp., N.Y., 1933-39; project engr. Sperry Gyroscope Co., Garden City, N.Y., 1939-41; gen. mgr. Gen. Electronic Industries, Greenwich, Conn., 1941-45; pres. Devol Rsch. Co., Ft. Lauderdale, Fla., 1947—, Automatic Mfg. Sys., Inc., Ft. Lauderdale, 1984—. Patentee in field of indsl. robots (40 patents). Mem. Soc. Mfg. Engrs. (life), Ocean Reef Club, Key Largo Club, Lago Mar Club. Home and Office: 7460 NW 1st Pl Plantation FL 33317-2265

DE VOS, DIRK, medical director; b. Leiden, The Netherlands, July 7, 1947. BS, State U. Leiden, 1969, MS, 1971, PhD, 1975. Rsch. asst. State U. Leiden (The Netherlands), 1970-72, lectr., 1972-76; lectr. Acad. Hosp. Leiden, 1977-80; product specialist Bristol-Myers, The Netherlands, 1980-81; registrar in pharmacology State U. Leiden, 1982; med. dir. Pharm. BV, Haarlem, The Netherlands, 1981-98, v.p. med. affairs, 1998, sr. scientist, 1998—. With The Netherlands Med. Troops, 1976-77. Office: Pharmachemie BV Med Dept, Swensweg 5 POB 552, 2003 RN Haarlem The Netherlands

DE VOS, GEORGE ALPHONSE, psychologist, anthropologist; b. Detroit, July 25, 1922; s. Medard Joseph and Marina Marie (Tack) De V.; m. Suzanne Lake, Nov. 18, 1974; children: Laurie, Susan, Eric, Michael. BA in Sociology, U. Chgo., 1946, MA in Anthropology, 1948, PhD in Psychology, 1951. Chief psychologist, dir. psychol. tng. Elgin (Ill.) State Hosp., 1951-53; asst. prof. psychology U. Mich., Ann Arbor, 1955-57; assoc. prof. social welfare U. Calif., Berkeley, 1957-63, prof. anthropology, 1963-91, prof. emeritus, 1991—. Author: Oasis and Casbah, 1960, Japan's Invisible Race, 1966, Socialization for Achievement, 1973, Ethnic Identity, 1975, 3d edit., 1995, Responses to Change, 1976, Koreans in Japan, 1981, Heritage of Endurance, 1984, Religion and the Family, 1986, Culture and Self, 1985, The Rorschach Cross Culturally, 1989, Status Inequality, 1990, Social Cohesion and Alienation, 1992, Confucianism and The Family, 1998, Narrative Analysis Cross-Culturally, 2000. Fulbright fellow, Nagoya, Japan, 1953-55; NIMH fellow French Min. Justice, 1963; NSF fellow UN Social Def. Rsch. Inst., Rome, 1972-73; Fulbright Sr. Rsch. Sch. Cath. U. Rio Grande do Sul, Brazil, 1992. Mem. APA (pres. Soc. for Psychol. Anthropology 1984-85), Assn. Asian Studies, Am. Anthropology Assn. Home: 2835 Morley Dr Oakland CA 94611-2547

DEVOS, JEAN-MARIE, general secretary, lawyer; b. Costermansville, Belgian Congo, Nov. 23, 1951; s. Raymond and Denise Devos; m. Anne Schreiber, Oct. 19, 1974; 4 daus. Degrees in law, U. Brussels, 1974, spl. degree in internat. law, 1979. Auditor The Hague Acad. Internat. Law, 1975; ofcl. Ministry of Justice, Belgium, 1976-79; legal counsel European Chem. Industry Coun., Brussels, 1979-90; gen. sec. CEFIC, Brussels, 1990—; asst. faculty law U. Brussels, 1977-78. Contbr. articles to profl. publs. and conf. procs. Comdr. Belgian Air Force Res., 1975-76. Mem. Res. Officers Club, various profl. assns. Avocations: sailing, bicycling, jogging, classical music. Office: CEFIC, Ave E Van Nieusenhuyse 4, 1160 Brussels Belgium

DE VOS, LUC LEO, educator, writer; b. Ostend, Belgium, Dec. 6, 1946; s. Albert and Yolande (Swaenepoel) De V.; m. Williane Emilienne Schotsaert, May 8, 1969; children: Barbara, Willem. Lic. in Social and Mil. Scis., Royal Mil. Acad., Brussels, 1969; Lic. in Modern History, Cath. U. Leuven, Belgium, 1976; Cert. Superior Officer, Royal Higher Inst. Def., Brussels, 1981; Grad. in Profound Knowledge French, Royal Mil. Acad., 1976; PhD in History (hon.), Cath. U. Leuven, 1984. Commd. 2d lt. Belgian Armed Forces, 1967, advanced through grades to maj., 1984; asst. chair history Royal Mil. Acad., 1975-80; intelligence and ops. officer Belgian Armed Forces, Leuven, 1981-83; assoc. prof., chair history Royal Mil. Acad., 1983-90, prof., head dept. mil. art, 1990—; part time asst. Cath. U. Leuven, 1981-83, part time prof., 1995—; lectr. in field. Author: Effective Strength of the Belgian Armed Forces and Conscription Laws 1830-1914, 1986, Liberation From Normandy to the Battle of the Bulge, 1994, Battles In The Low Countries, 1995, The First World War, 2d edit., 1996. Recipient Prix J. de Saint-Genois, Royal Acad. Scis., Belgium, 1991, Marcel Minnaert prize Unie Nederland Vlaanderen, 1996. Mem. Nat. Com. van de Vlaamse Universiteitsprofessoren, Atlantic Assn. (bd. dirs 1993—), Royal Army Mus. (chmn. sci. coun. 1993). Avocations: travelling, skiing, walking. Home: Korbeek-Lostraat 80, 3360 Bierbeek Belgium Office: Royal Mil Acad, Ave de la Renaissance 30, 1000 Brussels Belgium

DEVOSS, EVELYN IDA, retired elementary education educator; b. Coles County, Ill.; d. Martin Glen and Jeannett Carrie (Bridges) Smith; m. Donovan Worth DeVoss, Aug. 19, 1944; children: Dianna Kay DeVoss Aigner, Joseph Don. BS, Ball State U., 1941, MS, 1963. Life lic. elem. edn. Tchr. one rm. sch. DeKalb County, Auburn, Ind., 1936-41; tchr. grade 2 Randolph County, Winchester, Ind., 1941-43; with Magnavox Materials Control Dept., Ft. Wayne, Ind., 1943-44; tchr. grades 5 and 6 Perry Twp. Delaware County, Muncie, Ind., 1944-45; tchr. Parker Monroe Ctrl. Bldg. Sch. Sys., Parker City, Ind., 1958-78; ret., 1978. Chairperson missions Farmland (Ind.) United Meth. Ch., 1978-90; book reviewer Farmland Book Club, 1981-99. Recipient award Randolph Achievement Com., Winchester, 1962. Mem. Nat. Ret. Tchrs. Assn., Ind. Ret. Tchrs. Assn., Randolph County Ret. Tchrs. Assn. (treas. 1980-85), Randolph County Hist. Soc., United Meth. Women-Farmland Meth. (v.p 1980-85), Purdue U. Ext. Club. Avocation: post card collecting. Home: 11228 W 700 N Farmland IN 47340-9365

DEVOUGE, CATHERINE, advertising executive; b. Paris, May 11, 1947; d. Pierre and Claude (Marcus) D. Diploma, Inst. d'Etudes Politiques, Paris, 1967; lic. de droit, U. Paris, 1970; MBA, Northwestern U., Evanston, Ill., 1983. Dir. accounts Publicis, Paris, 1970-77; bd. dirs Lintas Paris, 1977-86; coordinator internat. accounts Lintas Internat., London and Paris, 1987—. Avocations: sailing, skiing. Home: 40 Rue Trebois, 92300 Levallois France Office: Lowe Lintas Paris, 22 Quai La Megisserie, 75001 Paris France

DEVREESE, JOZEF THEOFIEL, physicist, researcher. Licentiaat, Katholieke U., Leuven, Belgium, 1960, PhD in Physics, 1964; Dr. (hon.), State U. Moldova, Kishinev, Rep. of Moldova, 1996. Theoretical physicist Nuclear Energy Ctr., Mol, Belgium, 1961-66; lectr. U. Antwerpen, Belgium, 1966-69, prof., 1969—; founder Lab. Theoretical Solid State Physics, Antwerpen, Belgium; sci. dir. more than 15 internat. confs.; lectr. in field. Editor: Polarons in Ionic Crystals and Polar Semiconductors, 1972; editor: (with F. Peeters) Polarons and Excitons in Polar Semiconductors and Ionic Crystals, 1984; author of over 15 book volumes; contbr. over 300 articles to profl. jours. Recipient laureate U. Leuven, 1971. Fellow Am. Phys. Soc., Inst. of Physics; mem. Internat. Acad. Creative Endeavor, Phys. Soc. (European, Am., German, Netherlands, Belgium chpts.), N.Y. Acad. Scis., Inst. Materials Sci. (chmn.). Avocations: organ music, chess. Office: Dep Naturkunde U Antwerpen, Universiteitsplein 1, B-2610 Antwerpen-Wilrijk Belgium

DEVRIES, DONALD LAWSON, JR., lawyer; b. Phila., May 1, 1947; s. Donald Lawson and Jeanne (Coleman) DeV.; m. Nancy Shafer, Aug. 10, 1977; children: Donald Lawson III, Emily Shafer; stepdaughter: Alison

Brady Beale. BA with honors, Dartmouth Coll., 1969; JD with honors, U. Md., 1973. Bar: Md. 1973, U.S. Dist. Ct. Md. 1973, U.S. Ct. Appeals (4th cir.) 1976, U.S. Ct. Appeals (D.C. cir.) 1989, U.S. Dist. Ct. D.C. 1991. Assoc. Semmes, Bowen & Semmes, Balt., 1973-80, ptnr., chmn. med. malpractice dept., 1980-88; founding and mng. ptnr. Goodell, DeVries, Leech & Gray, Balt., 1988—; chmn. dept. med. malpractice Semmes, Bowen & Semmes, 1980-88; mem. faculty Md. Inst. Continuing Profl. Edn. for Lawyers, 1984-95; gov.'s task force on Med. Malpractice Ins., 1985; master Am. Inns of Court, 1986-90. Contbr. Md. Law Rev., 1973. Trustee Roland Pk. Country Sch., 1987-94, Woodbourne Ctr., 1981-88; trustee, exec. com. South Balt. Gen. Hosp., 1983-88; mem. Canons and Other Bus. Coms. of Episcopal Diocese Md., 1984-95; vestryman St. David's Ch., 1982-85; bd. dirs. Md. affiliate Am. Heart Assn., 1986-90, co-chmn. Heart Ball, 1986, 87, 88, chmn. solicitation com. Shock Trauma Gala, 1988, 89, co-chmn., 1990, 91, bd. visitors Shock Trauma, 1989-93, chmn. 1990-93; chmn. Emergency Med. Svcs. Bd., Md., 1992—; mem. joint exec./legis. task force on med. malpractice ins., Md., 1985; mem. com. on uninsured persons Gov.'s Commn. on Health Care Policy and Financing, 1988-90. Fellow Am. Coll. Trial Lawyers; mem. ABA (spkr. ann. meeting 1984, moderator, program planner ann. meeting medicine and law com. 1986, 88, vice chmn. medicine and law com. torts and ins. practice sect. 1982-89, med. adv. panel medicine and law com. 1986-87, forum com. health law 1984—, faculty nat. inst. on med. malpractice 1987, 88, 89, 90, chmn. medicine and law com., torts and ins. practice sect. 1988-89), Internat. Assn. Ins. Counsel, Internat. Assn. Def. Counsel (faculty trial acad. 1991, moderator, program planner 1992, vice chmn. med. malpractice com. for newsletters 1989-90, program chmn. 1990-92, chmn. med. malpractice com. 1992-94, chmn. def. counsel com. 1997-99, exec. com. 1999—, George W. Yancey Meml. award 1998), Internat. Soc. Barristers, Assn. Def. Trial Attys., Am. Bd. Trial Advocates (pres. Md. chpt. 1993-95, nat. bd. dirs 1993—), Md. State Bar Assn. (spl. com. on health claims arbitration 1983), Md. Trial Lawyers Assn. (faculty 1983, 85), Md. Assn. Def. Trial Counsel, Def. Rsch. Inst., Wednesday Law Club, Maryland Club, Chesapeake Bay Yacht Club, Center Club. Republican. Office: Goodell DeVries Leech & Gray LLP 1 South St Ste 200 Baltimore MD 21202-7314

DE VRIES, DOUWE, oil company executive; b. Bussum, Netherlands, Oct. 25, 1922; came to U.S., 1952; naturalized, 1959; s. Pieter and Hiske (Hoekstra) DeV.; m. Robbie Ray Parsons, Apr. 2, 1953; children: Jessica, Peter. MSME, Delft (The Netherlands) U., 1952. Registered profl. engr., Netherlands, La. Drilling & prodn. engr. Shell Oil Co., Tex. N.Mex, 1954-58; spl. projects engr. Shell Devel. Co., Houston, 1958-60; project mgr. Shell Oil Co., La., 1960-68; pres., owner Project Engring., Inc., New Orleans, 1968-70; dir. engring. Stewart & Stevenson oilfield div., Houston, 1970-78; v.p. subsea prodn. NL Industries, Houston, 1978-81; pres., owner Oilfield Systems, Inc., Houston, 1981—; cons. Shell Oil Co., 1983-85, Fluor, 1986-87, Dailey Directional, 1988-89, Kvaerner Verft, Stavanger, Norway, 1990-92, Amoco Orient/CONHE, Houston, 1993-95, Brit. Borneo/McDermott, Houston, 1996-98, Chevron Quito Project, 1999; mentor Subsea Svcs., 1998—; expert witness product liability and patent infringement. Patentee: 14 patents including floating drilling and subsea completions, U.S., Brit., Internat., 1958-83. Elder Presbyn. Ch., New Orleans, 1960-69; sponsor U. Houston, Med. Ctr., Tex. A&M at Galveston, Houston Symphony, Mus. of Fine Arts; active in Rep. Orgn., Washington, 1980—; chmn. Houston-Baku Sister City Assn., 1970-80. Mem. ASME (hon. mem., com. mem., Holley medal 1979), Am. Petroleum Inst. (com. mem.), Marine Tech. Soc., Am. Coun. Master Mariners (hon.), Nat. Soc. Profl. Engrs., Tex. Soc. Profl. Engrs. (mem. Offshore Energy Ctr. Hall of Fame). Avocations: tennis, golf, fishing, yardwork, reading. Office: Oilfield Systems Inc 9219 Katy Fwy Ste 288 Houston TX 77024-1514

DE VRIES, KLASS, government official; b. Hoensbroel, The Netherlands, Apr. 28, 1943. Student, Hamline U.; grad., U. Utrecht, 1968. Mem. Delft Mcpl. Coun., 1970-72, Lower House, 1973; chmn. Parliamentary Defense Com., Parliamentary Select Com. Bldg. Subsidies, 1986-88; head Union Dutch Local Authorities, 1988; min. Ministry Social Affairs and Employment, The Hague, The Netherlands, 1998—; lectr. Erasmus U., 1971-73. Office: Ministry Social Affairs, Van Hannoverstraat 4 PO Box 90801, 2509 LV The Hague The Netherlands*

DE WAART, EDO, conductor; b. Amsterdam, Netherlands, June 1, 1941. Grad. with honors for oboe, Amsterdam Conservatoire, 1962. Chief condr., artistic dir. Sydney Symphony Orch., 1993—; artistic dir. Netherlands Radio Philharm. Orch., 1989—; chief conductor elect Netherlands Opera, 1999—. Oboist, Concertgebouw Orch., Amsterdam, 1963-64, asst. condr., 1966-67; asst. to Leonard Bernstein, N.Y. Philharm., 1965-66; condr. Rotterdam (Netherlands) Philharm., 1967-79, also prin. condr., music dir.; condr. Netherlands Wind Ensemble, 1967-71; condr., music dir., San Francisco Symphony Orch., 1977-85; music dir. Minn. Orch., 1986-95; artistic dir. Netherlands Radio Philharm. Orch., 1989—; chief condr., artistic dir. Sydney (Australia) Symphony Orch., 1993—; guest condr. Amsterdam Concertgebouw, Berlin Philharm., Boston Symphony, Chgo. Symphony, San Francisco Symphony, London Symphony, Cleve. Orch., N.Y. Philharm., Phila. Orch.; condr.: new prodn. Lohengrin, Bayreuth Festival, summer 1979; new prodn. Wagner's Ring, San Francisco Opera, 1985, Mozart's Figaro, Salzburg Festival, 1996, Strauss Der Rosenkavalier Bastille, Paris, 1997, Mozart's Magic Flute, Met. Opera, N.Y.C., 1998, Mozart's Figaro, Met. Opera, N.Y.C., 1999; rec. artist, Philips Records, Virgin Classics, BMG, EMI. Recipient 1st prize Metropoulos Competition, N.Y.C., 1964. Office: RFO NOB-Muziekcentrum van de Omroep Postbus 10, 1200 JB Hilversum The Netherlands Address: 52 Williams St Level 5, Sydney NSW 2011, Australia also: Harrison Parrott Ltd, 12 Penzance Place, London W11 4PA, England*

DE WACHTER, RUPERT, biochemical scientist; b. Antwerp, Belgium, Aug. 28, 1937. Licentiate in Scis., State U. Ghent, Belgium, 1959, DSc, 1967, Aggregate of Higher Edn., 1972. Rsch. asst. Lab. for Dietary Studies, U. Ghent, 1959-63, rsch. asst. Lab. for Phys. Biochemistry, 1963-64, rsch. asst., sr. asst. Lab. Physiol. Chemistry, 1964-72; prof. molecular biology, dept. biochemistry U. Antwerp, 1972—. Mem. editl. bd. Systematic and Applied Microbiology, Jour. Molecular Evolution; jour. referee in field. Mem. Belgian Soc. for Biochemistry and Molecular Biology (past bd. dirs.), Internat. Soc. for Molecular Evolution. Office: U Antwerp Dept Biochemistry, Universiteitsplein 1, B-2610 Antwerp Belgium

DEWAHL, DUNCAN COMRIE, stockbroker; b. North Tarrytown, N.Y., Oct. 31, 1958; s. David Allen and Lois (Dann) DeW.; m. Lael Elizabeth Wilcox, Sept. 23, 1989; children: Alexander Macmillan, John Comrie. BA, Franklin and Marshall Coll., 1980; MBA, Northeastern U., 1987. Mgmt. trainee The Bank of N.Y., N.Y.C., 1980-83; sys. analyst U.S. Trust Co., N.Y.C., 1983-85; treasury mgr. Analog Devices, Boston, 1987-90; br. mgr. Securities Rsch., Orlando, Fla., 1990-93; regional mgr. Securities Rsch., Orlando, 1993—; mem. pension fund selection com. Burgess Chambers & Assocs., Winter Park, Fla., 1992—. Bd. mem. lakes adv. com. City of Maitland, Fla., 1997. Mem. Winter Park Raquet Club. Republican. Presbyterian. Avocations: golf, wake boarding. Home: 541 Dommerich Dr Maitland FL 32751-4502 Office: Securities Rsch 200 W Welbourne Ave Winter Park FL 32789-4278

DEWALD, WILLIAM GUENTHNER, economist; b. Sioux City, Iowa, Nov. 9, 1928; s. William Frederick and Leah (Guenthner) D.; m. Ann Peterson, Mar. 6, 1952 (div. 1981); children: Jane Dewald Smirniotopolous, Ruth Dewald Baginski, Charlotte Dewald O'Brien, Robin Dewald Yarinsky; m. Aileen Lee, Mar. 9, 1984. BS, Northwestern U., Evanston, Ill., 1950; PhD, U. Minn., 1963. Assoc. economist Fed. Res. Bank, Mpls., 1957-60; assoc. prof. St. Olaf Coll., Northfield, Minn., 1960-62; asst. prof. U. Chgo., 1962-64; prof. Ohio State U. Columbus, 1964-85; sr. economist, dep. dir. planning and econ. analysis staff U.S. Dept. of State, Washington, 1985-92; sr. v.p., dir. rsch. Fed. Res. Bank of St. Louis, Mo., 1992-98; ret.; vis. scholar Res. Bank Australia, Sydney, NSW, 1966-67, Fed. Res. Bank, San Francisco, 1981; dir. fgn. econ. rsch. U.S. Labor Dept., Washington, 1973-74; cons. IMF, 1984-85; mem. adv. bd. Jour. Money, Credit and Banking, 1984—; Editor Jour. Money, Credit and Banking, 1975-83; contbr. articles to profl. jours. With U.S. Army, 1951-53. Recipient faculty fellowship Ford Found., 1969-70, Jour. Money, Credit and Banking grant NSF, 1983-84.

DEWAN, KUM KUM, mathematics educator, researcher; b. New Delhi, July 4, 1950; d. Pritam and Shakuntla (Sangar) Rai; m. Sikander Mohan, Dec. 4, 1973; 1 child, Puja. BA with honors, U. Delhi, 1969, MA, 1971; PhD, Indian Inst. Tech., Delhi, 1980. Rsch. scholar U. Delhi, 1971-72; math. lectr. Jamia Millia Islamia U., New Delhi, 1972-85, reader in math., 1985-93, prof. math., 1993—, mem. math. bd. studies, 1972-97, convener math. bd. studies, 1990-94, chmn. dept. math. admissions com., 1994-96, mem. faculty natural scis., 1995—, advisor student's union, 1997-98, fgn. students advisor, 1998—; postdoctoral fellow Indian Inst. Tech., New Delhi, 1991-92; vis. asst. prof. Concordia U., Montreal, Can., 1987. Contbr. more than 30 articles to profl. jours. including Jour. Math. Analysis & Applications, Jour. Approximation Theory, Bull. of Australian Mathematica Soc., Glasnik Mathematicki, Internat. Jour. Math. and Math. Statistics, Jour. Math. Student, India Jour. Pure & Applied Math., among others; adv., editor Jour. Discrete Math. Scis. & Cryptography, 1998—; presenter rsch. papers in various nat. and internat. confs. Fellow Indian Inst. Tech., 1971, U.G.C., 1971, C.S.I.R., 1972, U. Grants Commn., 1977; recipient Best Citizen of India award Internat. Pub. House, 1999, Secular India Harmony award, United Children's Movement, 1999. Mem. Forum for Interdisciplinary Math. (life, treas. 1995—, asst., sec. 1994), N.Y. Acad. Scis., Indian Math. Soc. (life), Indian Soc. Indsl. and Applied Math. (life), Internat. Ctr. for Theoretical Physics (life), Assn. Women in Math., Acad. Forum (life). Hindu. Avocations: social work, listening to music, visiting different places. Home: Asian Games Village, B-812 Nikka Singh Block, New Delhi 110049, India Office: Jamia Millia Islamia U, Dept Math, New Delhi 110025, India

DEWAR, JAMES MCEWEN, marketing, aerospace and defense executive, developing nations consultant; b. Williamsport, Pa., Aug. 4, 1943; s. James Livingston and Margaret Ann (McEwen) D.; m. Margaret Cawley, Feb. 27, 1982; children: Alec, Porter, Leah. BS in Internat. Affairs, Trinity U., 1965, postgrad., 1965-66. Mgr. Dash brand Procter & Gamble Corp., Cin., 1969-71; CEO, DeLair & Dewar, Inc., Tucson and Washington, 1972—; chmn. bd. Cabot South Asia Inc. subs. Cabot Corp., 1982-87; pres., dir.-gen. ASI, Inc. subs. Boeing Co., 1987-97; CEO, J. Dewar Indochine, Ltd., Hanoi, Vietnam, 1993—; pres., interim cons. CEO, N.Am. Automotive Project, Southfield, Mich., 1993-98; bd. dirs. Metz Constrn. Co., Marine Environ. Rsch. Corp., Computational Analysis Corp.; mem. Aerospace, Def. and Automotive Industry Devel. Commn., Detroit, 1994; developing nations cons., advisor to the govt. of U.S., Exec. Br., 1998—. Contbr. numerous articles to profl. publs. Bd. dirs. Casa de Los Ninos, Tucson, 1974-99, Safari Club Internat., Tucson, 1974-2000, Internat. Marine Fisheries Corp.; founding mem. Dist. Atty.'s Victim/Witness Adv. Program; mem. White House Talent Pool, 1975-76, White House Nat. Cambodia Crisis Com., 1979-80, U.S. Aerospace Indsl. Reps. in Europe; adj. Mil. Order World Wars, Tucson, 1977-80, perpetual mem.; chmn. internat. bd. advs. Ariz.-Sonora Desert Mus.; bd. advs. guardian ad litem program Superior Ct. Ariz. Capt. USAF, 1966-70, Vietnam. Recipient Key to City of Seoul, 1973, citation Pres. of Korea, 1973, award for work with Mother Teresa, Cabot Found., 1982-87. Mem. Am. Soc. Agrl. Cons., Dirs. Guild Am., Assn. Old Crows, Australian/Asian Order Old Bastards (Sydney), John Carroll Soc., Mountain Oyster Club, Automobile Club France, Maxim's Bus. Club (Paris), St. James Club, Chambers Club (New Delhi), Univ. Club (Washington), Hanoi Club. Republican. Roman Catholic. Office: 8201 Greensboro Rd Ste 100 McLean VA 22102

DEWAR, ROBERT LEITH, research physicist, educator; b. Melbourne, Victoria, Australia, Mar. 1, 1944; s. Robert Alfred and Elizabeth Ruth (Lord) D.; m. Margot Ellis Taylor; 1 child, Sophie. BSc, Melbourne (Australia) U., 1965, MSc, 1967; PhD, Princeton U., 1970. CTP postdoctoral fellow U. Md., College Park, 1970-71; rsch. assoc. Plasma Physics Lab. Princeton U., 1971-74, rsch. staff, prin. rsch. physicist, 1977-82; rsch. fellow Australian Nat. U., Canberra, 1974-77, sr. fellow, 1982-92, prof. phys. sci. and engring., 1992—. Contbr. articles to profl. jours. Fellow Am. Phys. Soc., Australian Inst. Physics, Australian Acad. Sci. Avocations: reading, bushwalking, Macintosh software development. Home: 49 Banambila St, Aranda ACT 2614, Australia Office: Australian Nat U, Rsch Sch Phys Sci & Engring, Canberra ACT 0200, Australia

DEWEES, DONALD CHARLES, securities company executive; b. Phila., Sept. 7, 1931; s. John Coleman and Elva (Burke) DeW.; m. Martha V. Folk, July 31, 1954; children: Donald C., Suzanne C., Gretchen F. BS in Commerce and Finance, Bucknell U., 1953; MBA, U. Pa., 1954. Data processing rep. Nat. Cash Register Co., Wilmington, Del., 1954-62; account rep. Francis I. duPont Co., Investments, Wilmington, 1962-67; br. mgr. Francis I. duPont Co., Investments, Balt., 1968; br. mgr. Butcher & Singer, Wilmington, 1969-71, v.p., 1971-76, 1st v.p., 1977, sr. v.p., 1978—, resident mgr., 1969-76, ltd. ptnr., 1976-87, exec. v.p., 1987, sr. exec. v.p., 1988—, mng. dir., 1988—, also bd. dirs.; mng. dir. Butcher & Singer, 1986-98, Wheat Securities, 1998-2000; dir. Mgmt. Scis. Inc., 1978-92, Bus. Trends Inc., 1977-91, Computer Terminals and Tapes Ltd., 1970-98, Wheat Securities, mng. dir. Wheat Securities Butcher & Singer, 1986-2000, Lloyds of London, 1985-2000, First Union Bank, 1998-2000; underwriting mem. Lloyds of London, 1985—; cons. in field. Author sales tng. publs. Active Wilmington YMCA; bd. dirs. Delawre Ctr. of Contemporary Arts, 1992-94, Ingleside Nursing Home, 1989—, Ch. Home Found., 1986-92, Episcopal Hom of Del., 1983-90, Del. Symphony, 1995—, Del. Art Mus., 1996—; bd. dirs. Del Marva Boy Scouts of Am., 1989—, chmn. endowment com., 1993—; vice chmn. Nat. Assn. Christians and Jews, 1991-98; mem. allocation com. United Way, 1994; bd. dirs. Am. Cancer Soc., 1994—, Leukemia Soc., 1995—; chmn. Edgar A. Thronson Charitable Found., 1995—. Served with AUS, 1952-53, 58-59, Korea. Mem. Fin. Analysts Soc., Am. Philatelic Soc., Phi Kappa Psi, Univ. Club (Wilmington), Collectors Club (N.Y.), Rodney Square Club, Masons, Shriners, Greenville Country Club, Bonita Bay Country Club. Home: 4200 Pyles Ford Rd Wilmington DE 19807-1734 also: 25 Kelly Ln Bethany Beach DE 19930-9549 Office: Wheat Securities 3801 Kennett Pike Greenville DE 19807-2321

DEWEESE, ELDONNA ROSE, librarian, editor; b. Mo., Nov. 7, 1940; d. Osborne Kuhn and Helena Elizabeth DeWeese. BA, Southwest Mo. State, 1984; MLS, Emporia State U., 1969; BS in Edn., Southwest Mo. State U., 1962; MA, Southwest Mo. State, 1984. Tchr. English, speech, libr. Pierce City (Mo.) H.S., 1962-68; ref. libr. Southwest Bapt. Coll., Bolivar, Mo., 1969-72, adminstrv. libr., 1972-82; grad. asst./ref. libr. Southwest Mo. State U., Springfield, 1982-85; computer software distbr. Micro Magic Systems, Bolivar, 1985-88; collection devel. libr. Southwest Bapt. U., Bolivar, 1991—. Editor/prodn. mgr. So. Bapt. Periodical Index, 1987—. Mem. ALA, Am. Soc. Indexers, Mo. State Poetry Soc., Mo. Libr. Assn., So. Bapt. Libr. Assn. Baptist. Avocations: reading, poetry, writing, church choir. E-mail: edeweese@sbuniv.edu. Office: Southwest Bapt Univ Libr 1600 University Ave Bolivar MO 65613-2578

DE WET, JACOBUS ANTHONY, civil engineer, physicist; b. Grahamstown, South Africa, July 27, 1929; s. Jacobus and Ina (Symonds) de W.; m. Eleanora Anne Charlewood, Jan. 6, 1960 (div. 1976); children: Jacobus, Andrew, Joanne, Guy; m. Priscilla Anne Saurma-Jeltsch, Mar. 19, 1976. BSc, London U., 1950; MSc, MIT, 1952, U. South Africa, 1965; PhD, U. South Africa, 1970. Rsch. officer CSIR, Pretoria, South Africa, 1956-62; cons. in field, 1962-70; from engr. to prin. rsch. officer Water Affairs, Pretoria, 1970-77; cons. in field, 1977-89. Mem. N.Y. Acad. Scis., S. African Inst. of Physics. Achievements include contbns. to nuclear field theory. Home: Box 514, 6600 Plettenberg Bay South Africa

DEWEY, ANNE ELIZABETH MARIE, lawyer; b. Balt., Mar. 16, 1951; d. George Daniel and Elizabeth Patricia (Mohan) D.; children: Brendan M., Andrew P., Meghan E. BA, Mich. State U., 1972; JD, U. Chgo., 1975; grad., Stonier Grad. Sch. Banking, East Brunswick, N.J., 1983. Bar: D.C. 1976. Legal clk. and atty. FTC, Washington, 1975-78; atty. and sr. atty. Comptr. of Currency, Dallas and Washington, 1978-86; assoc. gen. counsel, gen. counsel, spl. counsel Farm Credit Adminstrn., McLean, Va., 1986-92; counsel, closed bank litig. and policy sect. FDIC, Washington, 1993-94; gen. counsel, spl. advisor to dep. dir. Office of Fed. Housing Enterprise Oversight, HUD, Washington, 1994—. Mem. D.C. study devel. coun. Mich. State U., 1999—. Mem. ABA (bus. law sect., mem. banking law com., co-chair banking & fin. sevcs. com., adminstrv. law & regulatory practice sect. 1997—), FBA (bd. dirs. D.C. chpt. 1988-91, banking law com. exec. coun. 1995—), Women in Housing and Fin. (bd. dirs. 1982-83, gen counsel 1991-93), D.C. Bar Assn., Exchequer Club. Roman Catholic. Office: Office Fed Housing Enterprise Oversight 1700 G St NW Fl 4 Washington DC 20552-0003

DEWEY, JOHN F., geologist, educator; b. London, May 22, 1937; married; 2 children. BSc, London U., 1958, PhD, 1960, DIC, 1960; MA, Cambridge, 1965; ScD, U. Cambridge, 1987; MA, Oxford U., 1986, DSc, 1988; DSc (hon.), Meml. U. New Foundland, 1995; LLD (hon.), Nat. U. Ireland, 1998. Lectr. U. Manchester, Eng., 1960-64; Univ. lectr. Cambridge U., Eng., 1964-70; prof. SUNY, Albany, 1970-80, disting. prof., 1980-82; prof. geology U. Durham, Eng., 1982-86; prof. geology, dept. earth scis. U. Oxford, Eng., 1986—; prof. geology U. Calif., Davis, 2000—. Recipient Lyell medal Geol. Soc. London, 1983, Academia Europaea, 1990, Arthur Holmes medal, 1993, Wollaston medal Geol. Soc. London, 1999. Fellow Geol. Soc. Am. (Penrose medal 1992), Royal Soc., Am. Geophys. Union, U.S. Nat. Acad. Scis. (fgn. assoc.). Office: U Oxford Dept Earth Scis, University College, Oxford OX1 4BH, England

DEWHURST, RICHARD JAMES, instrumentation educator; b. Blackburn, Lancashire, Eng., Dec. 18, 1946; s. William James G. and Edna Elizabeth (Haydock) D.; m. Janet Margaret Allen, Aug. 1, 1970; 1 child, Rebecca Jane. BSc in Physics, Leeds (Eng.) U., 1968; PhD in Applied Physics, U. Hull, Eng., 1972; DSc, U. Manchester, Eng., 1994. Chartered physics, engring. Rsch. fellow U. Hull, 1972-75, lectr., 1978-87, dir. indsl. aid unit, 1983-86; lectr. U. Strathclyde, Glasgow, Scotland, 1975-78; sr. lectr. U. Manchester Inst. Sci. and Tech., 1987-95, prof. instrumentation, 1995—, head instrumentation and analytical sci., 1999—. Mem. editl. bd. Jour. Measurement Sci. & Tech., 1993—, Ultrasonics Jour., 1995—; patentee in field; contbr. articles to profl. jours. Recipient various rsch. awards and grants. Fellow Inst. Physics (chmn. materials and characterization group); mem. Inst. Non-Destructive Testing. Avocations: tennis, squash, hiking, gardening. Office: DIAS, UMIST, PO Box 88, Manchester M6O 1QD, England

DE WISPELEIR-LELY, ROGER ALOIS ADELIN, government agency administrator; b. Dendermonde, Belgium, June 5, 1943; s. Pierre Alois De Wispeleir and Odile Adeline Siccard; m. Mariette Georgette Lely, Aug. 5, 1968; 1 children: Barbara Georgette. M Applied Scis., Poly. Royal Mil. Acad., Brussels, 1968; MS in Radiobiology, Free U., Brussels, 1973; MS in Mil. Adminstrn., Royal Mil. Adminstr. Sch., Brussels, 1980. Cert. engr., architect, internat. auditor. Commd. Belgian Mil., 1960, advanced through grades to col.; prof. nuclear physics Royal Mil. Acad., Brussels, 1971-75; technician, adminstr., constrn. mgr. Belgian Ministry of Def., 1975-83, 87-93, software mgr. info. sys., 1983-87, br. mgr. fin. control, 1992-98; advisor Belgian Ministry of Def., Brussels, 1998—; lead assessor Belcert, Belgium, 1991—; dep. dir. reassurance firm Syban, Belgium, 1991-92. Author: Insitu Dimentioning of Military Bridges, 1968, Management Control of Non Profit Organizations, 1980; contbr. articles to profl. jours. Named Comdr. Order of the Crown, 1999. Mem. Assn. Polytechnicians, Royal Flemish Engrs. Orgn., Royal Flemish Automobile Club.. Roman Catholic. Avocations: drawing, oil painting, writing, fishing, classical music. Home: Keesdal 18, B-1730 Asse Belgium

DE WIT, MIEKE, research scientist; b. Amsterdam, The Netherlands, Aug. 25, 1958. M, ISS, 1982, Erasmus U., 1985. Rsch. coord. Erasmus U., Rotterdam, The Netherlands, 1986-91; dir. Bur. Boven, Rotterdam, 1992-97, de Wit Rsch. and Consultancy, Rotterdam, 1998—; cons. Emancipation Adv. Bd., Amsterdam, 1994-97, Women's Coun. City of Rotterdam, 1987-90. Author: De toekomst van Migrantenmeiden, 1998, Van inspraak naar samenspraak, 1994, De gedeelde Werkelykheid, 1993; editor: Politieke Vernieuwing en sekse, 1994, De hand boven het kind, 2000, Dagelijkse besognes, 2000. Chmn. Sonor, 1995—. Avocations: acting, photography. Fax: 010-476 4115. E-mail: mewit@xs4all.nl. Office: Rsch and Consultancy, Graaf Florisstraat 50, 3021 CJ Rotterdam The Netherlands

DE WITH, GIJSBERTUS, materials science educator; b. Leerdam, The Netherlands, May 19, 1950; s. Cornelis F.B. and Catharina H. (Pellicaan) De W.; m. Ada S. Van Proosdij, Oct. 11, 1978; 1 child, Martijn. MSc in Chemistry, U. Utrecht, 1974; PhD, Twente U., Enschede, The Netherlands, 1978. Rsch. Philips Rsch., Eindhoven, The Netherlands, 1978-95; prof. Eindhoven U., 1985-95, full chair, 1996—; bd. dirs. NKV, Destees, The Netherlands, 1985-89; advisor Philips Rsch., Eindhoven, 1996—; sci. dir. Materials Tech. Ctr., 1998—. Editor: Proceedings Solid State Reaction of Inorganic Solids, 1985, Euro-Ceramics I, 1989; mem. editl. bd.: Jour. Eur. Ceramic Soc.; contbr. chpt. to book. Home: Valkenierstraat 152, 5555 JE Valkenswaard The Netherlands Office: Eindhoven U of Tech, PO Box 513, 5600 MB Eindhoven The Netherlands

DEWITT, SALLIE LEE, realtor; b. Ft. Smith, Ark., Oct. 11, 1923; d. Lee and Claudia Cordelia Victoria (Vest) DeWitt. BS, U. Tex., 1944; student, U. Houston, 1971; postgrad. in Computers, Del Mar Coll., 1989. Real estate broker, Tex.; cert. profl. sec. Layout artist, copywriter Corpus Christi (Tex.) Caller-Times, 1945-56; exec. sec. to chief geologist Exxon Co., Houston, 1956-73; adminstrv. asst. to gen. mgr. Valley Telephone Coop., Inc., Raymondville, Tex., 1976-89; owner, mgr. Sallie Lee DeWitt Real Estate, Raymondville, Tex., 1980-89; broker assoc. Alfred Edge Realtors, Corpus Christi, 1990-95; broker, owner Sallie Lee DeWitt Real Estate, 1996—; property tax cons., Corpus Christi, 1992-94. Mem. Nueces County Hist. Soc., Corpus Christi, 1990—. Mem. AAUW, Women's Coun. Realtors, Corpus Christi Bd. Realtors, C.C. Town Hall, C.C. Bus. and Profl. Women, Civitan Internat., Tropical Trails Investment Club/Harlingen, Tex., Internat. Soc. Poets, Internta. soc. Photographers. Republican. Baptist. Avocations: poetry, piano, art, photography, genealogy.

DEWITT-ROGERS, JOHARI MARILYN, community college administrator; b. Montgomery, Ala., Jan. 28, 1950; d. Rufus Birchard and Mary Lease (Borders) DeWitt; m. Paul Sabu Rogers, Dec. 21, 1976; children: Malachi Omari, Kofi Ayinde. BS, Howard U., Washington, 1971, MEd, 1973; postgrad., U. So. Calif., 1980-83. Abstractor APA, Washington, 1971-72; media technician San Diego Unified Schs., 1974-75; media coord. L.A. Regional Family Planning, 1975-79; asst. producer KABC TV News, 1979-80; dir. audio visual svcs. U. So. Calif. Dental Sch., 1979-81; dir. media Pasadena (Calif.) City Coll., 1987—; cons. City of Pasadena, 1991-92. Author: (play) All That Glitters, 1989. Sec. Linda Vista PTA, 1991, v.p., 1992; pres. Sch. Site Coun., 1992, 93, 94. Recipient Paragon award Nat. Coun. Mktg. and Pub. Rels., New Orleans, 1990, Pro award Calif. Assn. C.C., 1990. Mem. Am. Assn. Women in Colls. and Jr. Colls. (chpt. pres. 1992-93), Assn. Calif. Community Coll. Adminstrs. (mentor program 1992), Dirs. Ednl. Tech. in Calif. Higher Edn., Delta Sigma Theta. African Methodist Episcopal. Avocations: reading, theatre, travel, crafts, crossword puzzles. Office: Pasadena City Coll 1570 E Colorado Blvd Pasadena CA 91106-2003

DEWLEN, ALTON LEROY (AL DEWLEN), writer; b. Memphis, Tex., Nov. 30, 1921; s. Aaron and Edna Louella (Sloan) D.; m. Jean Lamb, Sept. 9, 1942 (dec. 1990); 1 child, Michael Lee (2d lt. USMC killed in action Vietnam 1968); m. Nella Faye Wood Watson, Jan. 24, 1991. Student, Hillsboro (Tex.) Coll., 1939-41, Baylor U., 1941-42, U. Okla., 1952-55. Reporter Amarillo (Tex.) Globe-News, 1946-47; city editor Amarillo Times, 1947-51; staffer/night editor UP, Dallas, Okla. City, 1951-54; free-lance mag. writer, 1954-56, novelist, 1956—; polit., economic rschr. South Africa, 1972-75, Rhodesia, Namibia, South Africa, 1978-80, Kenya, 1982-86. Author: (novels) Night of the Tiger, 1956, The Bone Pickers, 1958, Twilight of Honor, 1961 (McGraw Hill Fiction award, 1962), Servants of Corruption, 1971, Next of Kin, 1977, The Session, 1981; editor: (Joe Wanjui) From Where I Sit, 1986; lectr. in fiction techniques. T/Sgt. USMC, 1942-45, PTO. Recipient Okla. Award for Literary Excellence U. Okla., 1970, Freedom Found. George Washington Medal for mag./newspaper article "Report to a Sleeping Son", 1969. Mem. (life) NRA; mem. Baylor Bear Found. Mem. Christian Ch. (Disciples of Christ). Avocations: woodcraft, shooting sports, football recruiting. Home: 3024 Maple Hill Cir Waco TX 76708-1557

DEWOLFE, MARTHA, singer, songwriter, publisher, producer; b. Arlington, Tex., Nov. 30, 1959; d. Homer C. and Grace R. DeWolfe. Student, N. Tex. State U., 1978-79, Larimer County Vocat.-Tech., Ft. Collins, Colo., 1983; cert. peace officer, Tarrant County Jr. Coll., Euless, Tex., 1984; student, North Ctrl. Tex. Coun. Govts., 1984-94, Southwestern Law Enforcement Sch. of Police Supervision. Police officer Grand Prairie (Tex.) Police Dept., 1984-94, sgt., 1989-94, supr. crime prevention unit, 1991-92; mem. Police Employee Rels. Bd., 1990-91; BMI assoc.; established Maui Records, 1992, Midnight Tiger Music, BMI, 1994. Albums include That Flame Keeps Burning, 1992, Take Good Care of My Heart, 1995, Mama Look, 1997; songs include Adrianna, Worse Than Being Lonely, All the Blue, Patsy Come Home, River of Tears, Take Good Care of My Heart, Once a Year, The Drought; acting credits include Paramount's "Denton County Massacre", 1993, and commercials; lead singer Wildcat Canyon Band, 1997—. Sec. Grand Prairie Police Assn., 1985-86. Recipient 1st place Tex. Comml. Art Skill Speed Competition, 1977-78. Mem. Fraternal Order Police, Grand Prairie Police Assn., Tex. Assn. Vet. Police Officers, Country Music Assn., Broadcast Music Internat., Nashville Songwriter's Assn. Internat., No. Calif. Songwriters Assn., Mensa. Avocations: pvt. pilot, cats, photography. Home: PO Box 266 Martinez CA 94553-0026

DE WREE, EUGENE ERNEST, manufacturing company executive; b. Fairbanks, Alaska, June 26, 1930; s. Henry Joseph and Bertha Agnes DeWree; m. Shirley May Russo, Apr. 16, 1955 (dec. Sept. 1990); children: Angela Kathryn, Mary Rebecca, Thomas Albert, Babette Gabrielle, Jane Elizabeth; m. Jean Stanley Mack, Sept. 4, 1993; children: John Currie, Brigget Currie. BSME, Cogswell Engring. Coll., 1955; MBA, Stanford U., 1979. Project engr. Heat and Control Co., San Francisco, 1955-59; chief appliations engr., then market mgr. Wesix Electric Heater Co., San Francisco, 1959-65; account mgr. Fisher Controls, San Francisco, 1965-76; market and sales mgr. TRW Mission, Houston, 1976-80; v.p. mktg.-sales Houston Heat Exch., 1980-82; mktg. mgr. Anderson, Greenwood & Co., 1982—; sr. ptnr. Affiliated Products, Inc.; pres. DeWree Enterprises, DeWree Rental Properties; ptnr., dir. Constrn. Info. Svcs., Cismap, TVMP; sr. v.p. Indsl. Market Rsch.; sr. v.p. strategic planning Industriminfo.com; dir. Creative Capers, San Francisco and Houston; ptnr. Indsl. Info. Resource; sr. v.p. strategic planning industrialinfo.com., 1984—. Mem. Belmont (Calif.) Pers. Bd., 1965; com. chmn. Boy Scouts Am., 1970; elected to bd. dirs. Cypress Forest Pub. Utility Dist. Harris County, Tex., 1981, 83, 85, 86-90, 92-96, Harris County Regional Water Supply; pres. Water Bd. Capt. arty. U.S. Army, 1951-53, Korea. Named Outstanding Jaycee of Yr., 1966. Mem. Am. Mgmt. Assn., Am. Nuc. Soc., Valve Mfg. Assn., Instrument Soc. Am. (sr.), Assn. Water Bd. Dirs., Water Pollution Control Fedn., Sales and Mktg. Execs., Houston Engring. and Sci. Soc., KC (3d degree, dep. Grand Knight, 4th degree trustee), Inner Circle, Pine Forest Country Club, Plaza Club, Engrs. Club (San Francisco). Republican. Roman Catholic. E-mail: API77069@aol.com. Home and Office: 5625 Fm 1960 Rd W Ste 610 Houston TX 77069-4213

DEWULF, LODE W.A., healthcare industry executive; b. Leuven, Belgium, Dec. 12, 1963; s. André and Maria (Nelissen) D.; m. Sabine K.J. Thijs, Oct. 23, 1992; 1 child, Benjamin. CandMedScis, Cath. U. Leuven, 1985, MD, 1989; DipPharmMed, Free U., Leiden, Netherlands, 1992. Cert. pharm. physician. Med. adviser Duphar, Brussels, Belgium, 1987-91; med. advisor Solvay Pharma, Brussels, 1991-94; internat. med. mktg. mgr. Solvay Pharms., Hannover, Germany, 1994-97; med. dir. Procter & Gamble Pharms., Staines, Eng., 1997-99; v.p. med. affairs Planet Medica, Brussels, Belgium, 1999—; chief med. officer, v.p. med. affairs Planet Media.com, Brussels, Belgium, 1999—; cons. bd. examiners Acad. of Osteopathy, Belgium, 1991—. Contbr. articles to profl. jours. Lt. Belgian Army, 1989-90. Fellow Royal Acad. Medicine, London; mem. Belgian Assn. Pharm. Physicians (sec. 1990-94); faculty, bd. mem. Pharm. Med. London, N.Y. Acad. Scis.; mem. British Assn. Pharm. Physicians (bd. mem. 1997—). Avocations: cooking, oenology, classical music, family life. Home: Eygenstraat 31, 3040 Neerijse Brabant, Belgium

DEXEUS, SANTIAGO, obstetrician-gynecologist; b. Barcelona, Spain, July 22, 1935; s. Santiago Dexeus and Montserrat Trias De Bes; m. Victoria Miras, May 18, 1983; children: Damian, Thaïs. Diploma in medicine, Barcelona U., 1959; MD, Madrid U., 1968, D with distinction (hon.), 1968; DHC, U. Coimbra, Portugal, 1996. Resident in ob-gyn. Barcelona U., 1959-61; tng. in cervical pathology St. Mary's Hosp., Manchester, U.K., 1961-62; training in early diagnosis of cancer Maternité de l'Hopital Cantonale de Geneva, 1962-63, Lab. d'Histopathologie, Paris, 1963; tng. on colposcopy Hosp. Creteil, Paris, 1963; tng. in laparoscopy Hosp. Broca, Paris, 1963; tng. in pelvic surgery Policlinico Careggi, Firenze Sch. Medicine, Italy, 1964; specialist in ob-gyn. Clinica Mater, 1964-74; head ob-gyn. Inst. Universitari Dexeus, Barcelona, 1974—; chair ob-gyn. rsch. Autonomous U. Barcelona; pres. Nat. Commn. Ob-Gyn., 1992—; mem. adv. coun. Min. of Health, 1995—, mem. study com.; pres. Internat. Fedn. Clin. Pathology and Colposcopy, 1999. Co-dir. jour. Progresos de Obstetricia y Ginecología; author/co-author numerous books in field. Named Hon. Pres. European Soc. Gynecol. Oncology; grantee Found. Juan March, 1961-63, 65. Fellow ACS (hon.), Am. Coll. Ob-Gyn. (hon.); mem. Internat. Fedn. Cervical Pathology and Colposcopy (pres. 1999—), Spanish Soc. Gynecology and Obstetrics. Avocations: golf, sailing. Office: Inst Universitari Dexeus, Paseo Bonanova 67, 08017 Barcelona Spain

DEXTER, DEIRDRE O'NEIL ELIZABETH, lawyer; b. Stillwater, Okla., Apr. 15, 1956; d. Robert N. and Paula E. (Robinson) Maddox; m. Terry E. Dexter, May 14, 1977; children: Daniel M. II, David Maddox. Student, Okla. State U., 1974-77; BS cum laude, Phillips U., 1981; JD with highest honors, U. Okla., 1984. Bar: Okla. 1984, U.S. Dist. Ct. (no. and ea. dists.) Okla. 1985, U.S. Dist. Ct. (we. dist.) Okla. 1987, U.S. Ct. Appeals (10th cir.) 1987; grad. Nat. Inst. Trial Advocacy Advanced Trial seminar. Jud. intern Supreme Ct. Okla., Oklahoma City, summer 1983; assoc. Conner & Winters, Tulsa, 1984-90, ptnr., 1991, shareholder, 1991-2000; assoc. dist. judge Tulsa County Dist. Ct., 2000—. Article editor Okla. L. Law Rev., 1982-84. U. Okla. scholar, 1983. Mem. ABA, Okla. Bar Assn. (advising atty. state champion H.S. mock trial team competition 1992), Tulsa County Bar Assn., Order of Barristers, Order of Coif, Am. Inns of Ct. (barrister), Delta Theta Phi. Republican. Baptist. E-mail: ddexter@cwlaw.com. Office: Conner & Winters 3700 First Place Tower 15 E 5th St Ste 3700 Tulsa OK 74103-4391

DEXTER, JAMES RILEY, internist, critical care specialist; b. Loma Linda, Calif., Feb. 22, 1948; s. Robert Allison and Moira Mae Dexter; m. Kathryn Louise Hutchinson, Dec. 18, 1972; children: Kymberly, Scott. BA in Modern Langs., Loma Linda U., 1971, MD, 1974. Lic. physician, Calif.; diplomate Nat. Bd. Med. Examiners, Am. Bd. Internal Medicine, Am. Bd. Pulmonary Diseases, Am. Bd. Critical Care Medicine. Intern in internal medicine Loma Linda U. Med. Ctr., 1974-75, resident in gen. surgery, 1975-76, resident in internal medicine, 1976-78, fellow in thoracic diseases, 1978-80, instr. internal medicine, 1978-80, asst. prof., 1980-87, assoc. prof., 1987-89, assoc. clin. prof., 1989—; adj. mem. faculty Sch. Allied Health Professions Dept. Respiratory Therapy, Loma Linda U., 1984—; asst. chief pulmonary sect. Jerry L. Pettis VA Hosp., Loma Linda, 1980-82, med. dir. pulmonary function lab., 1980-82, med. dir. respiratory care, 1980-89, med. dir. sleep lab., 1981-83, other adminstrv. and com. positions; program chmn. med. chest conf., Loma Linda U., 1980-82; med. dir. Calif. Soc. for Respiratory Care,, 1988-90; reviewer Calif. State Med. Rev. Orgn., 1990-94; med. dir. respiratory care dept. Redlands Cmty. Hops., 1991—, home health dept., 1994—; mem. active staff Loma Linda Univ. Med. Ctr., 1978—, Jerry L. Pettis VA Hosp., 1980-89; cons. staff Redlands Cmty. Hosp., 1980-89, San Gorgonio Meml. Hosp., Banning, Calif., 1993—. Contbr. articles to profl. jours. Fellow ACCP (RCA steering com. 1989-93), ACP; mem. AMA, Am. Thoracic Soc., Calif. Med. Assn., Calif. Thoracic Soc. (pres. 1995-96, chmn. clin. practice assembly 1990-92), Soc. Critical Medicine, San Bernardino County Med. Soc., Trudeau Soc. L.A. Office: Beaver Med Group 2 W Fern Ave Redlands CA 92373-5916

DEXTER, THOMAS MICHAEL, biomedical researcher; b. Eng., May 15, 1945; s. Thomas Richard and Agnes Gertrude (Deplege) D.; m. Frances Ann Sutton, 1966 (div. 1978); 2 children; m. Elaine Spooner; 2 children. BSc in Biology with honors, U. Salford, 1970, DSc, 1982; PhD in Medicine, U. Manchester, Eng., 1973; D (hon.), U. Salford, 1998, UMIST, Manchester, 1998, Mahidol U., Bangkok, Thailand, 1999. Rsch. technician Paterson Labs., Christie Hosp., Manchester, 1963-67, sci. staff mem., 1973—, head dept. exptl. hematology, 1998—; dir. Wellcome Trust, London, 1998—; vis. rsch. fellow Sloan Kettering Inst., N.Y., 1976-77; fellow Cancer Rsch. Campaign, U.I., 1978, Gibb rsch. fellow, 1990; prof. hematology, pers. chair

U. Manchester, 1983; dir. rsch. Paterson Inst. Cancer Rsch., Christie Hosp. NHS Trust, 1993, dir. rsch., 1997-98; lectr., presenter in field; mem. sci. adv. bd. Therexsys, Keele, U.K., 1992-98, Quadrant, Cambridge, Eng., 1994-97, Cangene, Toronto, Ont., Can., 1992-95; mem. Com. on Med. Aspects of Radiation in the Environ., 1993-98; mem. steering com. Effects of Extremely Low Frequency Elec. Magnetic Fields on Biol. Sys., 1989-97; mem. animal grants bd. Agr. and Food Rsch. Coun., 1992-94; mem. grants com. Cancer Rsch. Campaign, 1989-93; mem. sci. adv. panel Leukemia Rsch. Fund., 1986-88; mem. 17 editl. bd. for jours. in field; grant reviewer, site visitor various orgns. Editor: Stem Cells, 1988, Colony Stimulating Factors, 1989, Haemopoietic Growth Factors: Their Role in the Treatment of Cancer, 1990, Growth Factors in Differentation and Development, 1990, Growth Factors in Haemopoiesis, 1992, Filgrustim (r-met Hu G-CSF) in Clinical Practice, 1993, Tumor Biology; Regulation of Cell Growth, Differentiation and Genetics in Cancer, 1996; contbr. over 350 articles to profl. jours. Lady Tata Meml. scholar Paterson Labs., 1970-73; EMBO fellow Weizmann Inst., Israel, 1980. Fellow Royal Soc. (postdoctoral fellowship awards panel 1997—, mem. coun. 1995-97), Acad. Med. Scis., Royal Coll. Physicians (hon.), Royal Coll. Pathologists, Hungarian Hematology Soc. (hon.), Leukemia Care Soc. (v.p. 1996), Internat. Soc. for Exptl. Hematology (pres. 1988). Office: The Wellcome Trust, 183 Euston Rd, London NW1 2BE, England

DEY, KAMALENDU, chemistry educator; b. Madaripur, Bangladesh, May 31, 1940; arrived in India, 1961, naturalized, 1962; s. Gopal Chandra and Fulkumari Dey; m. Papri Chandra, Dec. 1, 1968; 1 child, Tania. BSc in Chemistry with honors, Dacca (Bangladesh) U., 1959, MSc in Inorganic Chemistry, 1960; PhD, Jadavpur U., Calcutta, India, 1965, Sussex (Eng.) U., 1968. Chartered chemist Royal Soc. Chemistry, London. Lectr. chemistry City Coll., Calcutta, 1961-66; hon. rsch. fellow Indian Assn. for Cultivation of Sci., Calcutta, 1962-66, Commonwealth Coun. for Sci. and Indsl. Rsch. pool officer, 1968-69; asst. prof. Indian Inst. Tech., Kharagpur, 1973; lectr. U. Kalyani, India, 1969-73, 1973-76, reader, 1977-84, prof., 1984—, head dept. chemistry, 1996-98. Contbr. over 135 rsch. articles and revs. to sci. jours. Sr. Humboldt Found. fellow U. Wurzburg, Germany, 1976; postdoctoral fellow Strathclyde U., Glasgow, Scotland, 1978. Fellow Royal Soc. Chemistry, West Bengal Acad. Sci. and Tech.; mem. NAS (life), Indian Chem. Soc. (life), Indian Sci. Congress Assn. (life), Indian Coun. Chemists (life), Indian Assn. for Cultivation of Sci. (life). Avocations: reading. Home: B-6/275 Kalyani, Nadia, W Bengal Kalyani 741235, India Office: Univ Kalyani, Dept Chemistry, W Bengal Kelyani 741235, India

DEY, NIBARAN CHANDRA, chemist; b. Dibrugarh, India, Oct. 1, 1949; s. Nityananda and Mokhyoda (Dutta) D.; m. Manjulika, Oct. 13, 1976; 1 child, Nikhilesh. BSc with honors, D.H.S.K. Coll., Diburgarh, India, 1969; MSc, Dibrugarh U., 1971, PhD, 1982. Lectr. Duliajan Coll., India, 1971-72; jr. sci. asst. C.E.C.R.I., Karaikudi, India, 1972-75; sr. sci. asst. R.R.L., Jorhat, India, 1975-79, scientist B, 1979-84, scientist C, 1984-89, scientist E, 1989-94, scientist E-II, 1994—. Contbr. articles to profl. jours. Mem. Soc. Advancement Electrochem. Sci. & Tech. (life), Assam Sci. Soc. Avocations: reading, literature, poetry, tennis. Office: Regional Rsch Lab, Jorhat 785006, India

DEY, RADHESHYAM CHANDRA, cytologist; b. Calcutta, India, Jan. 30, 1950; came to U.S., 1978; s. Bhairab and Satyabala D.; m. Indrani Roy Chowdhury, July 5, 1981; children: Smita, Anita, Ishan. BSc, Bangabasi Coll., Calcutta, 1970; MSc, U. Calcutta, 1972, cert. in life sci., 1974; CT, Brooke Army Med. Ctr., San Antonio, 1983; cert. leaderhsip mgmt., ednl. devel., quality improvement and equal opportunity, Walter Reed Army Med. Ctr., 1989; postgrad., Laval U., Quebec City, Can., 1995, Albert Einstein Sch. Medicine, N.Y.C., 1997. Registered cytotechnologist, Am. Soc. Clin. Pathologists, Internat. Acad. Cytology, Calif., Md. Rsch. fellow U. Calcutta, 1975-77; with Anthropol. Survey of India, Indian Mus. Calcutta, 1977-78; biol. science asst. Army Inst. Rsch., Washington, 1980-83; cytology specialist U.S. Army Hosp., Ft. Campbell, Ky., 1983-85, SHAPE Med. Ctr., SHAPE/Mons, Belgium, 1985-87; cytotechnologist Nat. Health Lab., Vienna, Va., 1988; supervisory cytologist Walter Reed Army Med. Ctr., Washington, 1988—; attended Indian Sci. Congress, U. New Delhi, Calcutta, Waltair, Gujarat, 1972-77, Internat. Congress of Cytology, Brussels, Belgium, 1987, Internat. Cytology Tutorials, Vienna, Austria, 1986, Tokyo, Japan, 1991, Harvard Med. Sch. Advances in Cytology, Boston, 1990, Coll. Am. Pathologists, Las Vegas, 1992, World Congress on Anthropol. & Ethnol. Scis., Mexico City, 1993, Williamsburg, Va., 1998, Am. Soc. Clin. Pathologists and Cytopathology, Seattle, Risk Mgmt., ASCP, Hunt Valley, Md., 2000, Advanced Techniques in Human Identification-Armed Forces Inst. Pathology, Washington, 1994, Palaeopathology, 1993, Forensic Anthropology, 1995, symposium USAF, Lackland AFB, Wilford Hall, Tex., 1999; participant Cytopathology Symposium, Washington Met. Assn. Cytology, 1999, 2000, New Directions for Leaders Focus 2000, Ft. Belvoir, Va., 1994, Immunol. Markers in Histopathology and Cytology, Inst. of Pathology, Ghent U. Hosp., Belgium, 1987, numerous seminars; mem. symposium for suprs. and team bldg. dynamics for mgrs. U.S. Army Walter Reed Med. Ctr., Washngton, 1995, 96; attended CAP/ASCP seminar L.A., 1998, Balt., 2000, symposium on cytopathology Met. Washington Assn. Cytology, 1999, Fine Needle Aspiration Cytology Meeting, Balt., 2000, risk mgmt. Am. Soc. Clin. Pathologists, Balt., 2000; vis. Indian Statis. Inst., Calcutta, 1999. Contbr. articles to profl. jours. Decorated U.S. Army Commendation medal, 1985, Achievement medal, 1984, Good Conduct medals, 1982, 85; recipient Decree of Merit for outstanding contbn. to medicine and health care, 1995, Excellence in Tchg. award Nat. Capital Region Consortium Pathology Residency, 1997, Comdr.'s award for civilian svc. U.S. Army Walter Reed Med. Ctr., 1997. Mem. AAAS, Internat. Acad. Cytology, Am. Anthropol. Assn., Am. Soc. Cytopathology, Am. Soc. Clin. Pathologists (mem. leadership and mgmt. workshop 2000), Am. Soc. for Cytotech., N.Y. Acad. Scis., Soc. of Armed Forces Med. Lab. Scientists, Belge de Cytologie Clinique (del. visit to People's Republic China 1987, 91, internat. team cytologists exch. sci. knowledge with USSR 1990), Md. Assn. Cytopathology, Ind. Sci. Congress, Indian Anthropol. Soc., Washington Met. Assn. of Cytology, Md. Assn. Cytopathology. Avocations: soccer, swimming, running, traveling, theater. Home: 2313 Snowflake Dr Odenton MD 21113-2237 Office: Walter Reed Army Med Ctr Dept Pathology Cytology Lab Washington DC 20307-0001

DEY, SUBHASISH, hydraulics educator; b. Jalpaiguri, India, Jan. 8, 1958; s. Bimalendu and Kana (Guha) D.; m. Swastika Talukder, Feb. 4, 1987; children: Sibasish, Sagarika. BCE, U. North Bengal, Jalpaiguri, 1981; M in Tech., Indian Inst. Tech., Kharagpur, 1984, PhD, 1992. Lectr. Regional Engrng. Coll., Durgapur, India, 1984-90, sr. lectr., 1990-98; asst. prof. Indian Inst. Tech., Kharagpur, India, 1998—; vis. prof. U. Stuttgart, Germany, summer 2000. Contbr. articles to sci. jours. Mem. Indian Soc. Hydraulics, Instn. Engrs., Internat. Assn. for Hydraulic Rsch. (The Netherlands), Nat. Geog. Soc. (hon.). Avocation: cricket. Home: Sarala Kutir, Race Course, W Bengal Jalpaiguri 735101, India Office: Indian Inst Tech, Dept Civil Engring, W Bengal Kharagpur 721302, India

DEY, SUHRIT K., mathematician, researcher; b. Calcutta, May 15, 1939; arrived in U.S., 1966; s. Gokul Das and Manimala D.; m. Sabita Kumar, Feb. 9, 1963 (wid. Oct. 1989); children: Sujata, Charlie; m. Roma Pratima Nath, Jan. 1, 1990. BA in Math with honors, Calcutta U., 1958, MA in Applied Math., 1960; PhD in Aerospace Engrng., Miss. State U., 1970. Lectr. in math. B.K.C. Coll., Calcutta, 1961-66; rsch. asst. aerospace engring. Miss. State U., 1966-70; asst. prof. math. Ea. Ill. U., Charleston, 1970-77; prof. math. Ea. Ill. U., 1979—; sr. rsch. assoc. NASA/Ames Rsch. Ctr., Moffett Field, Calif., 1980-83; vis. prof. von Karman Inst. of Fluid Dynamics, Brussels, 1978, Boston U., Ramstein AFB, Germany, 1985-86, U. Seidlec, Poland, 1986; vis. scientist Indian Stats. Inst., 1991, Naval Underwater Warfare Ctr., New London, Conn., 1992, Colo. Sch. Mines, 1992, Tech. U. Denmark, Lyngby, 1993, Indian Inst. Tech., Delhi, 1996, S.N. Bose Ctr. Basic Scis., 1994, 96, U. Rome, 1997, U. Alicante, 1998, Eafit U., Medellin, Colombia, 1998, U. Vilnius, Lithuania, 1999, Inst. of Math & Informatics; vis. scientist Stanford U., 1980, Miss. State U. ERC, 1990, Wright Patterson AFB, 1991. Inventor in field (Hinemann Found. award, Germany 1978), (NRC fellowship 1981); editor jours. in field. Recipient Rsch. Associateship NRC, Washington, 1981-82, others; NRC fellow, 1982. Mem. Indian Acad. Math. (life), Inst. Applied Sci. and Computations, Phi Kappa Phi. Achievements include inventing perturbed functional iterations, a numerical method to solve nonlinear models accurately; D-matrices to analyze nonlinear stability of difference equations; D-Mappings for norm ind. contraction in a function space; massive parallel computations to solve large-scale nonlinear models with a fast speed of convergence in computers with a large number of parallel processors; accurate computations for stiff equations in chem. kinetics; scientific analysis of consciousness in nature, mathematical analysis of omnipresence of consciousness. Home: 1106 Timberlane Dr Charleston IL 61920-1767

DE YBARRA Y CHURRUCA, EMILIO, bank executive; b. San Sebastian, Nov. 9, 1936; m. Mari Aznar Ibarra; 4 children. Dep. mgr. Banco de Bilbao, 1965, mgr. orgn. & pers. svc., 1967, dep. gen. mgr., 1970, bd. dirs., 1971, mng. dir., 1976, v.p., mng. dir., 1985; pres. Banco Bilbao Vizcaya, 1990—. Contbr. articles to profl. jours. Decorated Grand Cross of Civil Merit, Order of Isabel la Catolica. Avocations: tennis, sailing. Office: Banco Bilbao Vizcaya, S.A. Gran Via #1, 48001 Bilbao Spain*

DE YEREGUI, CARLOS GILBERTO, engineering executive; b. Montevideo, Uruguay, Apr. 12, 1946; s. Carlos Arturo and Elena Adriana (Montero) de Y.; m. Cecilia Guillem, Dec. 17, 1970; children: Juan Carlos, Francisco Javier, Santiago Andres. Degree in engring., U. Catolica del Ecuador, Quito, 1972. cert. engr. Constrn. engr. Degremont Ecuador, Quito, 1971-75; tech. mgr. Degremont Colombia, Bogota, 1976-80, gen. mgr., 1981-87; regional del. Degremont S.A. (France), Bogota, Mex. City, 1988-94; comml. dir. Lyonnaise des Eaux Am. Latina, Buenos Aires, 1995—; mem. bd. dirs. Aguas del Illimani, La Paz, Bolivia, 1997, Assn. de Ingenieria Sanitaria y Ciencias del Medio Ambiente, Buenos Aires, 1997. Recipient Golden award Ministry Pub. Works, Ecuador, 1972. Roman Cath. Avocation: tennis. Fax: 54-11-43131345. E-mail: cadey@leal.com.ar. Home: Av Libertador 2201 Piso 3, C1425AAI Buenos Aires Argentina Office: Lyonnaise Eaux Am Latina, Reconquista 823 Piso 11, C1003ABQ Buenos Aires Argentina

DEYOUNG, DAVID JEFFREY, state official; b. Hollywood, Calif., Sept. 30, 1954; s. David Henry and Lorraine DeY.; m. Susan Anne DeYoung, May 29, 1988 (dec. Oct. 1993); m. Kimberly Ann DeYoung, Sept. 5, 1999. BA in Psychology, U. Calif., Irvine, 1977, MA in Social Ecology, 1980. Rsch. analyst Orange County Probation, Orange, Calif., 1985-88; rsch. program specialist Calif. Dept. Motor vehicles, Sacramento, 1988—. Editl. bd. Jour. of Safety rsch., 1999—; contbr. articles to profl. jours. Pres. Davis (Calif.) Aquatic Masters, 2000—. Mem. Am. Evaluation Assn., Am. Statis. Assn., Sacramento Statis. Assn. (v.p. 1995, pres. 1996). Avocations: running, hiking, skiing, travel, swimming. Office: California Dept Motor Vehicles 2415 1st Ave Sacramento CA 95818-2698

DEYSHER, PAUL EVANS, training consultant; b. Reading, Pa., Oct. 16, 1923; s. Paul Stauffer and Ida Estelle (Evans) D.; m. Myrtle Constance Stover, June 17, 1950; children: David Paul, Mark Edward. BS, Albright Coll., 1945; M in Ednl. Adminstrn., Temple U., 1949. Math. and sci. tchr. Lebanon City (Pa.) Sch. Dist., 1950-56; asst. high sch. prin. Ocean City Sch. (N.J.) Dist., 1956-57; high sch. prin. Yeadon Sch. (Pa.), Dist., 1957-60; mgr. pers. adminstrn. Philco Corp., Phila., 1960-66; tng. specialist AMP, Inc., Harrisburg, Pa., 1966-80, supr. mgmt. tng., 1980-85, mgr. mgmt. tng. and devel., 1986; cons. and lectr. in field. Author: (poems) Anthologies of International Library of Poetry, 1999, 00; co-author: Transistor Fundamentals, 1962; contbr. chpts. to books and articles to profl. jours. Pres. Albright Coll., Lebanon County Alumni chpt., 1979—; trustee Albright Coll., Reading, Pa., 1985-89. Mem. NEA (life), Am. Soc. Pers. Adminstrn. (cert., sr. prof. in human resources), ASTD (past pres.), Phi Delta Kappa. Republican. Lutheran. Home: 39 S Mill St Lebanon PA 17042-3124

DEZA, RICARDO JUAN, research and development company executive; b. Buenos Aires, Feb. 4, 1942; s. Armando Deza and Lilia Fabiana Decia; m. Virginia Glassmann, Mar. 29, 1967; children: Marcelo, Gaston. Degree in acctg., U. Buenos Aires, 1966, lic. in acctg., 1969. Cert. acct. Mgr. fin. Cristaleria Formosa, San Justo, Argentina, 1965-67; cons. Latinoconsult SA, Buenos Aires, 1967-77; adminstr. Centro Atomico Bariloche, Argentina, 1977-94; mng. adminstr., fin. commr. Nacional de Energia Atómica, 1995-97; coord. adminstrn. C.T. Pilcaniyeu, 1998—. V.p. Tribunal de Cuentas, Bariloche, 1985-87. Avocations: mountain trekking, skiing. Office: Commn Nacional de Energia Atomica, Av del Libertador 8250, 1429 Buenos Aires Argentina

DE ZEEUW, PIETER TIMOTHEUS, astronomer; b. Sleen, Drenthe, The Netherlands, May 12, 1956; s. Gerardus and Antje (Gorter) deZ.; m. Ewine Fleur van Dishoeck, July 26, 1984. BS in Math. cum laude, Leiden U., 1976, BS in Astronomy cum laude, 1977, MSc in Astronomy cum laude, 1980, PhD in Astronomy cum laude, 1984. Tchg. asst. Leiden U., 1977-80, rsch. asst., 1980-84; long-term mem. Inst. for Advanced Study, 1984-88; sr. rsch. fellow Caltech, 1988-90; prof. astronomy Leiden U., 1990—; dir. Netherlands Rsch. Sch. for Astronomy, NOVA, 1993—; mem. Space Telescope Inst. Coun., Balt., 1996—; chmn. Bd. of Isaac Newton Group of Telescopes, La Palma, Spain, 1999—. Editor: (book) Structure and Dynamics of Elliptical Galaxies, 1987; contbr. numerous articles to profl. jours. and publs. Named one of the Top 100 Young Scientists in U.S., Sci. Digest, 1984; grantee NWO, Netherlands, 1996-2001; selected as NOVA Top Nat. Rsch. Combination in Netherlands, Dutch Govt., 1998. Mem. Am. Astron. Soc., Royal Astron. Soc., Internat. Astron. Union. Office: Leiden Observatory, Niels Bohrweg 2, 2333 CA Leiden The Netherlands

DEZELL, JAMES EDWARD, finance company executive; b. Cleve., Feb. 13, 1961; s. John Francis and Eileen (Sullivan) D.; m. Keri O'Brien, Oct. 2,1 993; 2 children. BS, Boston U., 1987; MBA, Boston Coll., 1995. Sr. acct. mgr. Fidelity & Deposit Co., Balt., 1988-99; regional v.p. NCM Group, Amsterdam, 1999—; guest lectr. Boston Coll., Chestnut Hill, Mass., 1995—. Republican. Avocations: photography, carpentry. Office: NCM Group 28 Commons Ln Hanson MA 02341-1174

DEZHU, WU, chemist; b. Xian, Shanxi, China, May 22, 1942; m. Wang Xiaoying, Dec. 27, 1968; children Yongqiang, Chunxia. Diploma, Xian (China) Polytechnic, 1965. Rschr. dept. radiochemistry Beijing, 1965-80; rschr. dept. isotope CIAE, Beijing, 1980-89, 91-99; vis. scholar dept. chemistry Sudbury, Canada, 1989-91. Avocations: music, swimming, opera. Home: Yuanxinjie Fangshan, Beijing 102413, China

DEZHURNY, IGOR IVANOVICH, radiocommunication engineer; b. Vorozhba, Sumskaya, Ukraine, Sept. 29, 1937; arrived in Russia, 1959; s. Ivan Gerasimovich Dezhurny and Olga Alexandrovna Blinova; m. Tamila Petrovna Kulick, July 9, 1960; children: Sergei, Leonid. Degree radiocomm. engr., Odessa Electrotech. Inst. Comm, 1959; postgrad., Voronezh Scientific-Rsch. Inst, 1968, candidate tech. sci., 1970. Engr. to sr. engr. p/b 121, Voronezh, USSR, 1959-64, head of lab., 1964-66; head of scientific tech. dept. Voronezh Scientific-Rsch. Inst. of Comm., 1989-92, head scientific tech. dept., dep. chief engr., 1992—; chief designer of land mobile radiocomm. systems Voronezh Scientific-Rsch. Inst. of Comm., 1966—, USSR Ministry of Comm. Means Industry, Moscow, 1981-91; gen. designer of land mobile radiocomm. systems Coun. for Mutual Econ. Aid, 1985-90; dep. chief designer Joint Soviet-Bulgarian Konstruktorat, Voronezh, USSR, Sophia, Bulgaria, 1973-90; chmn. Soviet (Russian) sect. subcom. 12F Internat. Electrotech. Commn., Voronezh, Russia, 1981—; cons. Cellurar Comm. of Chernozemie, Voronezh, 1998—; chief designer over 20 radiostations, equipment complexes and mobile radiocomms. systems. Contbr. numerous articles, books and reports to profl. publs.; patentee in field. Recipient 3 gold, 2 silver, 1 bronze medal USSR Nat. Econ. Achievement, 1967-85, Badge Outstanding Specialist of USSR Ministry of Radioindustry, 1968, Order Labour Red Banner Govt. of the USSR, 1974, Badge USSR State Com. for Stds., 1976, State Premium, Govt. USSR, 1983, Honorary Radio Operator of the USSR, USSR Ministry of Comm. Means Industry, 1983, Badge Outstanding Specialist, Ministry of Industry and Electronic of the People's Republic of Bulgaria, 1983, Medal Veteran of Labor Govt. of USSR, 1990. Mem. Popov's Scientific Tech. Soc. Avocations: collecting books, journals and newspapers, motor-touring. Home: F Engels Str 24A Flat 48, 394000 Voronezh Russia

DE ZILWA, MARY ELIZABETH, finance company executive; b. Colombo, Sri Lanka, Dec. 12, 1946; d. Devasagayam William and Mercy (Peraji) Rajial; m. Sept. 20, 1988 (dec.); m. Randolph De Zilwa, Jan. 22, 1992. Pvt. Sec. Dipl., Westminster Coll., London, 1971, Bus. Adminstrn. Dipl., 1972. Sec. Shaw Wallace & Hedges, Colombo, 1964-65, Am. Embassy, Colombo, 1964, Inland Revenue, London, 1965-67; with Nashua Copycat, London, 1967-69; adminstrv. mgr. Nashua Europe, London, 1969-73; internat. adminstrv. mgr. Nashua Internat., London, 1974-76, world accounts rep., 1976-78, product mgr., 1978-84, regional mgr., 1984-89, world accounts dir., 1990—. Chmn. Brith. Kidney Patients Assn., Berkshire, 1989. Mem. Bd. of Hope Internat. Charity for Children. Mem. Pvt. Secs. Assn. (pres.). Office: NRG Internat Anex House, London Rd, Bracknell Berkshire RG12 2XH, United Kingdom

DE ZORZI, SEBASTIANO, publisher, journalist; b. Udine, Italy, Aug. 20, 1926; s. Giorgio and Concetta (Tomasi) De Z.; m. Adriana Dell'Oste, Dec. 7, 1958; children: Maria Grazia, Cristina. Editor: Stralignano, 1956; editor, dir. Bibione Vacanze, 1968, Turismo Gradese, 1976. Home: Via Vendoglio 18, 33100 Udine Italy Office: Pubblistudio De Zorzi SAS, Via Marinoni 53, 33100 Udine Italy

DEZURKO, EDWARD ROBERT, retired art educator; b. N.Y.C., Mar. 25, 1913; s. Edward and Hattie (Lehman) DeZ.; m. Madith Smith, July 30, 1938 (div. 1962); children: Robin Klein, Sandra Krchnak; m. Grace Crump, Sept. 5, 1964. BS in Edn., U. Ill., 1939, BS in Arch., 1940; MS in Arch., Columbia U., 1942; PhD, NYU, 1954. former registered arch. Tchr. Champaign (Ill.) H.S., 1941; tchr. arch. Kans. State Coll., Manhattan, 1942-47, Rice U., Houston, 1947-62; head dept. art Austin Coll., Sherman, Tex., 1962-66; prof. art U. Ga., Athens, 1966-79, emeritus prof. art, 1979—; draftsman, illustrator U.S. Naval Ordnance Lab., Washington, 1943-44. Author: Early Kansas Churches, 1949, Origins of Functionalist Theory, 1957, Vistas and Mazes, 1997, Through Cracks in the Wall, 2000; contbr. articles to profl. jours. Recipient Ga. Poet of Yr. award Nat. League Am. Pen Women, 1997, Internat. Order of Merit award. Mem. AIA, Ga. Poetry Soc., Author's Club Athens, Pi Delta Phi, Zeta Zeta. Avocations: poetry, gardening, travel. Home: 220 Meadowview Rd Athens GA 30606-4226 Office: Lamar Dodd Sch Art U Ga Athens GA 30602

D'HAENENS, J., judge. First pres. Belgian Supreme Ct. of Justice, Brussels; pres. Belgian Supreme Ct. Justice, Brussels. Office: Supreme Ct of Justice, Palais de Justiceloo, 1600 Brussels Belgium*

DHALIWAL, RAJINDER SINGH, surgeon, educator; b. Barnala, Punjab, India, Oct. 18, 1948; s. Joginder Singh and Gurnam Kaur (Chahal) D.; m. Lakhbir Kaur Virk, Sept. 1976; children: Yadvinder, Bhalinder. MB BChir, Govt. Med. Coll., Patiala, India, 1971; MS in Surgery, Postgrad. Ins. Med. Edn./Rsch., Chandigarh, India, 1974, MCh in Cardiovasc. & Thoracic Surgery, 1978. Cert. in cardiovasc. and thoracic surgery. From lectr. cardiovasc. and thoracic surgery to asst. prof. Postgrad. Inst. Med. Edn. and Rsch., Chandigarh, 1978-85, assoc. prof. cardiovasc. and thoracic surgery, 1986-89, additional prof. cardiovasc. and thoracic surgery, 1989-99, prof. cardiovasc. and thoracic surgery, 1999—, head dept. cardiovasc. and thoracic surgery, 1998—. Contbr. numerous chpts. to med. books, articles to med. jours. Fellow WHO, 1997. Fellow ACS, Am. Coll. Chest Physicians, Rotary (coord. 1999—); mem. Nat. Acad. Med. Scis. Avocations: reading, photography, computers, traveling, music. Home: # 58 Sector 24A, 160023 Chandigarh India Office: Postgrad Inst Med Edn/Rsch, Sector 12, 160012 Chandigarh India

DHALL, DHARAM PAL, retired surgeon, consultant; b. Meru, Kenya, Dec. 8, 1937; s. Surjan Dass and Ram Pyari (Puri) D.; m. Tehseen Zehra Muzaffar, Dec. 28, 1973; children: Amar, Shammah. MB, Chb, U. Manchester, England, 1961; PhD, U. Aberdeen, Scotland, 1968, MD with commendations, 1969. Lectr. in surgery U. Aberdeen, 1966-67; clin. tutor in surgery Aberdeen U., 1967-70; sr. registrar Aberdeen Royal Infirmary, 1970-72; prof. surgery U. Nairobi, Kenya, 1972-74; dir. vascular and thrombosis rsch. Canberra, Australia, 1975-98; sr. cons. surgeon Canberra Hosp., 1975-98; ret., 1998; vis. fellow John Curtin Sch. Med. Rsch., Canberra, 1975-98; referee Nat. Heart Found., Australia, 1978—, various European and N.Am. scientific jours.; dir. Gadal Holdings Pty. Ltd., 1985-99, Nelseen Holdings Pty. Ltd., 1987-99, Satpal Holdings Pty. Ltd., 1996—, Saishah Pty. Ltd., 1999—; examiner in surgery Australian Med. Entry Cert. Fgn. Grads. Author: Sri Sathya Sai Human Values Programme: Lesson Plans Group 3, 1991, Sai Awareness Programme Vol. I, 1992; (with M. Bhuller) Sai Awareness Programme Vol. II, 1993; Divinity and Love - The Essence of Human Values, 1993, Sai Vision Vol. I, 1994, Sai Vision Vol. II, 1995, Sai Vision Vol. III, 1995, ACT and NSW Teacher's Workshop - Focus on Syllabus and Lesson Plans, 1996, Dynamic Dharma for Integrated Living, 1997, Stepping Stones to Peace, 1998, My Work is My Blessing, 1999, (with T.Z. Dhall) Dynamic Parenting, 1999, (with T.Z. Dhall) Workshops on Dynamic Parenting, 1999; contbr. articles to profl. jours.; editor: East African Med. Jour., 1973-74, Fibrinolysis, 1996; compiling editor Proceedings of 1st Convention of Overseas Chairpersons of Sri Sathya Sai Ctrs. Organizer Oriental Rug Soc. Canberra, 1981, Interfaith Forum, Canberra, 1993, (with T.Z. Dhall) 1st Sri Sathya Sai Symposium on Values Parenting, Putta, Pasthi, India, 1999; Australian nat. spiritual coord., Australian nat. Sai edn. coord. Sri Sathya Sai Orgn., 1992-95, Australian nat. edn. coord. in human values, 1994-98; dir. Inst. Sathya Sai Edn. Australia, Canberra, mem. faculty, Thailand; pres. Australian Soc. Advancement of Ea. and Western Music, Canberra, 1996; developer Edn. in Human Values for Parents program. Recipient Hallett award Royal Coll. Surgeons, London, 1963; grantee Nat. Heart Found., Australia, Nat. Health and Med. Rsch. Coun., Australia, Inst. de Recherches Internat. Servier, France, Pharmacia AB, Uppsala, Sweden. Fellow Royal Coll. Surgeons (Edinburgh), Royal Australasian Coll. Surgeons. Avocations: music, antique textiles, chess, golf. Home: PO Box 697, Queanbeyan NSW 2620, Australia

DHAMELINCOURT, PAUL ANDRE, chemistry educator, researcher; b. Noyelles/Selle, France, May 15, 1944; s. Benoit Clement and Marie Louise (Briau) D.; m. Marie-Claire Janine Deneufeglise, Mar. 23, 1974; 1 child, Benoit. B in Math., Tech., Lille (France) I U., 1965, PhD, 1979. Asst. prof. Lille I U., 1969-84, prof., 1985-89, full prof., 1990—; cons. Rhone-Poulenc, Paris, 1985. Author: Raman Microscopy, 1996; contbr. articles to profl. jours. Sgt. French Air Force, 1968-69. Recipient Silver medal Nat. Ctr. Sci. Rsch., Paris, 1983. Mem. French Phys. Chem. Assn., Nat. Assn. for Rsch. and Tech. Roman Catholic. Avocations: classical music, swimming. Office: Lab Spectrochem, IR and Raman Bat C5, 59655 Villeneuve d'Ascq France

DHANABALAN, SUPPIAH, organization executive, business executive; b. Singapore, Aug. 8, 1937; m. Tan Khoon Hiap, 1963; 2 children. BA with honors in Econs., U. Malaya, Singapore, 1960. Asst. sec. Ministry of Fin., Singapore, 1960-61; sr. indsl. economist, diep. dir. ops. and fin. Econ. Devel. Bd., Singapore, 1961-68; v.p., exec. v.p. Devel. Bank Singapore, Singapore, 1968-78; sr. minister of state Ministry of Nat. Devel., Singapore, 1978-79; sr. minister of state Ministry of Fgn. Affairs, Singapore, 1979-80, minister, 1980-88; minister Ministry of Culture, Singapore, 1981-84, Ministry of Community Devel., Singapore, 1984-86, Ministry of Nat. Devel., Singapore, 1987-92, Ministry of Trade and Industry, 1992-93; with Singapore Indian C. of C., 1992—; chair Parameswara Holdings, 1994—; sr. adviser Nuri Holdings Pte. Ltd., 1994—; chmn. DBS Group Holdings Ltd., Singapore; mem. parliament People's Action Party, Kallang Constituency, 1976-91. Avocations: golf, reading, squash. Fax: 323 0931. Office: care Singapore Fed C of C, 47 Hill St 03-01 Commerce Bldg, Singapore 0617, Singapore also: DBS Group Holdings Ltd, Tw 1 DBS Bldg 6 Shenton Way, Shing Kwan House Singapore 068809, Singapore*

DHANAPALA, JAYANTHA, diplomat. BA with honors, U. Peradeniya, Sri Lanka, 1961; MA, Am. U., Washington, 1976. Perm. rep. UN, Geneva, 1984-87; former dir. UN Inst. Disarmament Rsch., Geneva, 1987-92; Sri Lanka amb. to U.S., Sri Lanka Embassy, Washington, 1995-97; under-sec.-gen. disarmament affairs UN, N.Y.C., 1998—. Fax: 212-963-4066. E-mail: dhanapala@un.org. Office: care UN United Nations Plz New York NY 10017

DHANDE, PRAKASH LAXMAN, anatomy educator; b. Sangvi, India, Apr. 18, 1959; p. Laxman Omkar and Suman Laxman (Chaudary) D.; m. Vasudha Prakash Chaudary, June 22, 1986; 1 child, Ujwala. B in Vet. Sci. and Animal Husbandry, Bombay Vet. Coll., 1982, M in Vet. Sci., 1984,

PhD, 1998. Asst. prof. Bombay Vet. Coll., 1984-94, assoc. prof., 1994-96, prof., 1996—, chmn. dept. anatomy, 1995—; hostel monitor Bombay Vet. Coll., 1984—. Contbr. articles to profl. jours. Recipient Best Tchr. award Apang Maitry, Bombay, 1998. Mem. IAVA (exec. mem. 1992—, joint sect. to XII conv. 1997), ISNTAS (life), Bombay Vet. Coll. Alumni Assn. (joint editor jour. 1995—), Amateur Riders' Club (officer incharge 1997—).

DHANKHAR, J. N., business executive; b. Rohtak, India, Apr. 16, 1946; s. Tarif and Shryan (Devi) Rohtak; m. Jantree Devi, May 25, 1969; children: Seema, Ajay. LLB, Punjab U., Chandigarh, India, 1974; MCom, Himachal Pradesh U., Shimla, India, 1977; DPMIR, Punjabi U., Patiala, India, 1978; PhD, Rajasthan U., Jaipur, India, 1993. Cert. fin. cons. Lectr. Maharshi Dayanand U., Rohtak, 1977-81; mem. faculty Newe Bank of India, Chandigarh, 1981-86; co. sec. Indsl. Cables (India) Ltd., Rohtak, 1986-87; gen. mgr. Delhi Stock Exch., 1987-89; exec. dir. Jaipur Stock Exch., 1989—; mem. bd. studies Indian Inst. Rural Mgmt., Jaipur, 1998—. Author: Merchant Banking and Financing, 1995, Capital Issues and Listing, 1997, Indian Stock Market in Operation, 1996, Pricing of Securities in the Indian Stock Market, 1994, Mechanics of Stock Index Futures and Internet Trading, 2000. V.p. Block Welfare Soc., Muktanand Nagar, Jaipur, 1998-99. Recipient award for best acad. work on capital market Rajasthan Dev Soc., 1997. Fellow Inst. of Co. Secs. of India; mem. Inst. Mgmt. Execs. Bombay, Inst. Fin. Cons. Avocations: gardening, volleyball, reading, writing books. Home: H No 163 Muktanand Nagar, 302 018 Jaipur India Office: Jaipur Stock Exch Ltd, J Nehru Marg, Malviynaga, 302 017 Jaipur INdia

DHAON, DAYA KRISHAN, mining company executive; b. Lucknow, U.P., India, Aug. 2, 1934; s. Bijoy Krishan and Chanda (Khanna) D.; m. Veena Nanda, Feb. 11, 1961; children: Nikhil, Kanchan. BA, Lucknow (India) U., 1953, MA, 1955; MA, Cambridge (Eng.) U.; cert. mgmt., Harvard U., 1982. Sr. mgmt. exec. Bird & Co. Pvt. Ltd., Calcutta, India, 1959-70; chief exec. Hindustan Copper Ltd., Calcutta, 1970-78, Newspin Ltd., Lagos, Nigeria, 1978-80, Minerals & Metals Trading Corp., Delhi, 1980-83; sr. v.p. Hinduja Group Cos., London, 1983-86; mng. dir. Delhi Consulting Group Pvt. Ltd., New Delhi, 1987—; bd. govs. Indian Inst. Mgmt., Calcutta, 1982-83; dir. Timex Watches Ltd., India. Mem. Indian Internat. Ctr., The Saturday Club, The Internat. Ctr., Oxford and Cambridge Soc. India, Harvard Club Delhi. Home: C-512 Defence Colony, New Delhi 110 024, India Office: Delhi Consulting Group Ltd, B-72 phase 1 Sheikh Sarai, New Delhi 110 017, India

DHAR, GAURANGA CHANDRA, tropical medicine physician; b. Dhaka, Bangladesh, Oct. 2, 1957; s. Manoranjan and Fulrani D.; m. Dipanjali Aich, May 15, 1980; 1 child: Anton. MD, Rostov State Med. Inst., Rostov-on-Don, Russia, 1983; DTM&H, Mahidol U., Bangkok, 1992; MRSH (hon.), Royal Soc. of Health, London, 1996. Asst. surgeon Mymensingh Med. Coll. Hosp., Bangladesh, 1983-84; cons., pvt. practice Dhaka, 1985—. Fellow Royal Soc. of Tropical Medicine and Hygiene; mem. Bangladesh Pvt. Medical Practitioners Assn. (life), Bangladesh Acad. of Family Physicians (founding), Royal Overseas League, British Coun. (Dhaka), British Diabetic Assn., Australasian Coll. Tropical Medicine, Am. Soc. of Tropical Medicine and Hygiene, Tropical Medicine Alumni Assn. Thailand, Internat. Airline Passenger's Assn., Exec. Club Internat., Telegraph Global Network, Sovereign Soc., Oxford Club. Avocations: travel, music, television, reading journals and newspapers. E-mail: gaur@bangla.net. Home: Rd No 6/A Dhanmondi, Villa Rose House No 43, 1209 Dhaka Bangladesh

DHAR, JANAK DULARI, reproductive biologist; b. Srinagar, Kashmir, India, Mar. 14, 1942; d. Maheshwar Nath and Kamla (Raina) Fotedar; m. Tej Krishen Dhar, June 6, 1966; 1 child, Nitin. MSc, J&K U., Srinagar, 1963; PhD, Kashmir U., Srinagar, 1970. Postdoctoral fellow Ctrl. Drug Rsch. Inst., Lucknow, India, 1972-74, scientist, 1974-81, 1981-86, sr. scientist, 1986-89, asst. dir., 1989-94, sr. asst. dir., 1994—; sr. asst. dir. R&D, C.D.R.I., 1989—; vis. scientist Coun. Sci. Indsl. Rsch.-CNRS, Paris, 1989. Contbr. articles to profl. jours. Inventor in field. Recipient Cert. Commendation Dir. Gen. Coun. Sci. Idsl. Rsch., India, 1993; USSR Acad. Sci. postdoctoral fellow, 1980. Mem. Indian Soc. Study Reproduction & Fertility (life), Uttar Pradesh Assn. Advisor Sci. (life), Soc. Biol. Chemists (life), Internat. Soc. Applied Biology, N.Y. Acad. Scis., Nat. Acad. Scis. India, India Sci. Cong. Assn. Avocations: music, poetry, singing, horseback riding, reading. Home and Office: Ctrl Drug Rsch Inst, Chattar Manzil Palace, 226001 Lucknow India

DHAR, SANDIPAN, dermatologist, consultant; b. Howrah, W.Bengal, India, Sept. 2, 1963; s. Ramani Mohan and Anjali (Shee) D.; m. Subhra Dhar, Dec. 13, 1994. M.B.B.S., Calcutta Nat. Med. Coll., 1986; MD (Dermatology), Postgrad. Inst. Med. Edn. Rsch., Chandigarh, India, 1991. Diplomate Nat. Bd. Edn. Rotating houseman Calcutta Nat. Med. Coll. and Hosp., Calcutta, 1986-87, sr. house physician, 1988-89; jr. resident Postgrad. Inst. Med. Edn. and Rsch., Chandigarh, India, 1989-91, sr. resident, 1992-94; asst. prof. Govt. Med. Coll., Kota, India, 1995-97; cons. dermatologist Advanced Medicare and Rsch. Inst., Calcutta, 1997—. Contbr. over 162 articles to profl. jours., chpts. to books. Recipient Kataria Meml. Gold medal PGI, 1992, B.B. Gokhale Gold medal IAVDL, 1992. Mem. N.Y. Acad. Sci., Indian Jour. Dermatology Venereology and Leprology (editl. bd. 1998—), Assn. of Resident Drs. of Postgrad. Inst. Med. Edn. and Rsch. (joint sec. 1990-91), Indian Acad. Cutaneous Surgeons (gen. sec. 1997-98), Indian Med. Assn., Indian Assn. Dermatologists, Venereologists and Laprologists (joint sec. 1997-98). Avocations: reading, writing, music, singing, recitation. Home: S P D Block Baghajatin, 700 086 Calcutta India Office: N G Medicare, 123A Rash Behari Ave, 700 029 Calcutta India

DHAR, UPPEANDRA, scientist; b. Srinagar, India, Apr. 12, 1948; s. Ganesh and Rupa D.; m. Neelam Hanjura, Oct. 15, 1978; children: Upshi, Akshay. BS, U. Kashmir, India, 1968, MS, 1972, PhD, 1978. Rsch. officer CCRUM, U. Kashmir, Srinagar, India, 1979-90; scientist C G B Plant Inst. Himalayan Environment & Devel., Almora, India, 1990-93, scientist D, 1993-98, scientist E, 1998—. Author: Flora of Ladakh, 1977, Alpine Flora of Kashmir Himalaya, 1983, Medicinal Plants of Indian Himalaya, 1998; editor: Himalayan Biodiversity Conservation Strategies, 1993, Himalayan Biodiversity - Action Plan, 1997; contbr. articles to profl. jours. Sr. rsch. fellow Dept. Botany, Srinagar, 1976-78. Mem. Indian Inst. Pub. Adminstrn. (life), Indian Soc. Ecol. Econs. (life), Indian Soc. Naturalists (life). Avocations: reading, writing. Home: Karam Bhawan NTD Almora, Almora 263 601, India Office: GB Plant Inst Himalaya, Kosi-Katarmal, Almora 263 643, India

DHARA, VENKATA RAMANA, physician, educator; b. Gudivada, India, Nov. 14, 1953; came to U.S., 1985; s. Venkateswarlu and Sarojini Devi D.; m. Rosaline James Dodda, Feb. 16, 1979; children: Rahul, Vishal. MBBS, Pune (India) U., 1976; MD, Armed Forces Med. Coll., 1976; MPH, U. Medicine Dentistry N.J., 1987. Diplomate Am. Bd. Preventive Medicine. Intern Sion Hosp., Bombay, India, 1976-77; resident Robert Wood Johnson Med. Sch., Piscataway, N.J., 1985-87; med. dir. People's Clinic, Hyderabad, India, 1979-85; fellow in occupl. medicine Robert Wood Johnson Med. Sch., Piscataway, N.J., 1985-89; fellow Environ./Occpl. Health Scis. Inst., Piscataway, 1987-89; cons. Envirotech Cons., New Delhi, 1990-92; med. officer Agy. Toxic Substances Disease Registry, Atlanta, 1992-96; dir. occupl. medicine Choice Care, Atlanta, 1997-2000; clin. asst. prof. Morehouse Sch. Medicine, Atlanta, 1998—; med. dir. Emory Eastside Med. Ctr., Snellville, Ga., 2000—; cons. World Environment Ctr., N.Y.C., 1992-96, Internat. Labor Office, Geneva, 1992—; mem. Internat. Med. Commn. Bhopal, Toronto, Can., 1994—. Contbr. articles to profl. jours. Active Forum Protection Environment, Hyderabad, 1982-85. Recipient Disting. Svc. award Meridian Med. Group, 1997; grantee Nat. Inst. Environ. Health Scis., 1998—. Mem. Am. Coll. Occpl. Environ. Medicine. Avocations: writing, reading, snorkeling, yoga. E-mail:rdhara@aol.com. Office: Emory Eastside Occupl Health Ctr 1700 Medical Way Snellville GA 30078-2195

DHARIWAL, H.C., mechanical engineering educator, researcher; b. Jodhpur, India, Feb. 21, 1940; s. D.C. and Ugam Kanwar (Bhandari) D.; m. Nirmala H. Singhvi, Jan. 17, 1966; children: Kirti, Rishi. BS in Mech. Engring., Jodhpur U., Rajasthan, 1963; MTech in Internal Combustion Engines, Indian Inst. Tech., Bombay, 1966; PhD in Internal Combustion Engines, Azerbaizan Poly. Inst., 1978. Lectr. dept. mech. engring. Indian Inst. Tech., Bombay, 1966-78, asst. prof., 1978-90, assoc. prof., 1990—; cons. Inst. Armament Tech., Pune, India, 1988-96, Maharashtra State Rd. Transport Corp., Pune. Contbr. articles to sci. jours. Mem. Think Tank Sci. Understanding of Religions-Internat. Soc. Krishna Consciousness, Bombay, 1995; participator God Exist Internet mailing list, U.S., 1998—, Errancy Internet Mailing List, U.S., 1997. Fellow Instn. Mech. Engrs. (mem. coun. 1993-94); mem. Soc. Automotive Engrs., Combustion Inst. Mem. Friend's Eternal Universal Religion. Avocations: religious scriptures, understanding religion and creation. E-mail: hcd@me.iitb.ernet.in. Fax: 91-22-5783480. Office: Indian Inst Tech Bombay, Dept Mech Engring, Maharash Bombay 400076, India

DHARMAPRAKASH, SAMPYADY MEDAPPA, physics educator; b. Hosahalli, India, Apr. 20, 1960; s. Sampyady Medappa and Sampyady Susheela Gowda; m. Geetha Adkar; children: Nikhil Prakash, Nihar Prakash. BSc, Mysore (India) U., 1980; MSc, Mangalore (India) U., 1982, PhD, 1987. Lectr. Mangalore U., 1982—, rsch. guide, 1989—, reader, 1997—. Recipient Boyscast award Govt. of India, 1991. Avocations: watching TV, music. Office: Mangalore U, Mangalagangotri, Mangalore 574199, India

DHARMASAKTI, PRAMOND, scientist; b. Bangkok, Oct. 16, 1923; s. Chanai and Thomya D.; m. Panit Tosanont, May 1, 1951; children: Virasak, Kiattisak, Nittayasak. Breeding project mgr. Nong Nooch Tropical Garden, Chonburi, Thailand, 1994—. 2d lt. Thai Army, 1951-53. Muslim. Office: Nong Nooch Tropical Garden, Sukhumvit Hwy KM 163, Sattahip Chonburi 20250, Thailand

DHASMANA, RAJENDRA PRASAD, media person, consultant, film-maker, dramatist; b. Bagyali, India, June 10, 1937; s. Chandi Prasad and Kalpeshwari Devi (Nailwal) D.; m. Basanti Devi Lakhera, Dec. 11, 1962; children: Paridhi, Kendraj, Indivjal. BA, Saraswati Vidyalaya, Hapur, India, 1959; Postgrad. Diploma in Journalism, Postgrad. Diploma in Pub. Rels. Trainee journalist The Hindustan Times, New Delhi, India, 1960-64; freelance journalist, 1964-66; asst. editor Publs. divsn. The Collected Works of Mahatma Gandhi, New Delhi, 1966-79; news editor All India Radio, New Delhi, 1979-84, Doordarshan, New Delhi, 1984-93; chief editor publs. divsn. The Collected Works of Mahatma Gandhi, New Delhi, 1993-95; freelance journalist New Delhi, 1995—; chair Uttarasth, Garhwal Kumaon New Delhi; cons. Ico-Softek, New Delhi, 1998-99; dir. G-Media, New Delhi; vis. prof., papersetter, examiner in journalism Hemwati Nandan Bahuguna Garhwal U., Srinagar, India, 1990-98; spkr. in field. Author: Parvalaya, Gandhi Chayanika I and II, 1973; editor: Shailonmukh, Garhwal Gaurav, Shikhraj, Uttarayani, others; playwright. Mem. Indian Coun. for World Affairs (life), Uttarakhand Patrakar Parishad (pres. 1997-99, 2000—), Garhwal Hiteshini Sabha (pres. 1984-87), Uttarayani (life; cultural sec. 1996-97). Avocations: theatre, still photography, making of documentary films, social service. Home: 24 I P Extn Patparganj, G-7 Akash Bharati Apts, 110 092 Delhi India

D'HAUTERIVES, ARNAUD LOUIS ALAIN, painter; b. Braine, Aisne, France, Feb. 26, 1933; s. Louis and Germaine (Hincelin) d'H.; m. Renée Delhaye, June 1, 1959; children: Arielle Wright, Régis, Louis. Diploma, Art Sch., Reims, France, 1955, Nat. Superior Art Sch., Paris, 1957. Ofcl. painter Nat. Navy, Paris, 1981; pres. Fine Art Acad., Paris, 1987, 91-95, perpetual sec., 1996; curator Marmottan Mus., Paris, 1988-96, dir., 1997; dir. Marmottan Libr., Boulogne, France, 1997; v.p. Inst. France, Paris, 1987, 91-95; pres. Fine Arts Com., Paris, 1996, Chantilly Com., Paris, 1996. Lt. of Staff Lt. Gov. La.; academician Acad. Royale des Beaux-Arts de San Fernando, Spain. Decorated Officer Legion of Honour, Officer Nat. Order of Merit, Officer Arts and Lit. Chevalier Svcs. to Edn., Order Soleil Levant (Japan); recipient 1st prize, 1957, prize Case Velasquez, 1964, Critical prize, 1967, Orangerie prize Versailles Château, 1981. Mem. Acad. Overseas Scis., Artistic Coun. Nat. Mus., Russia Acad. Fine Arts, European Acad., Assn. Acad. Scis. Marseille, Acad. Arts Uzbekistan (fgn. mem.), Cir. de la Mer (hon.). Avocations: ethnography, gliding, travelling, books, history. Office: Acad Beaux Arts, 23, Quai de Conti, 75006 Paris France

D'HEURLE, FRANCOIS MAX, research scientist; b. Bois-Colombes, France, Nov. 23, 1925; s. Albert and Olette (Valentini) d'H.; m. Adma Jeha, May 6, 1950; children: Amal, David, Alain. BSc, Arts et Metiers, Paris, 1946; MSc, Mich. Tech. Univ., 1948; PhD, Ill. Inst. Tech., 1958; PhD honoris causa, Royal Inst. Tech., Stockholm, 1995. Rsch. asst. Univ. Chgo., 1948-55; rsch. assoc. Ill. Inst. Tech., Chgo., 1955-58; scientist IBM Rsch. Ctr., Yorktown Heights, N.Y., 1958—; adj. prof. Royal Inst. Tech., Stockholm, 1985—; staff mem. IBM T.J. Watson, Yorktown Heights, 1993—; workshop dir. Internat. Sch. on Solid State Physics, 1999. Contbr. 250 articles to profl. jours.; patentee in field. Recipient Indsl. Appl. of Physics award Am. Inst. Physics, 1991. Fellow IEEE (Cledo Brunetti award 1989), Am. Vacuum Soc. (Gaede Langmuir award 1990); mem. Mining, Metals Material Soc. (Reduction to Practice award 1998), Materials Rsch. Soc. Avocations: reading, history, music, fine arts, peace. E-mail: dheurle @ watson.ibm.com. Home: Spring Valley Rd Ossining NY 10562 Office: IBM Rsch Ctr PO Box 218 Yorktown Heights NY 10598-0218

DHILLON, KUNDAN SINGH, veterinary pharmacology educator; b. Punjab, India, June 20, 1934; s. Kehar Singh and Iser Kaur (Sandhu) D.; m. Varinder Kaur Sra, Feb. 19, 1985; children: Karamvir Singh, Rajvir Kaur, Manvir Kaur. BVSc, Punjab Coll. Vet. Sci., Hissar, India, 1956; MS, Ohio State U., 1961; PhD, Vet. Coll., Ludhiana, India, 1970. Vet. asst. surgeon Animal Husbandry Dept., Punjab, 1956-60; demonstrator Coll. Vet. Medicine, 1962, asst. rsch. officer, 1962-64, asst. prof. vet. pharmacology, 1964-71, assoc. prof., 1971-74; asst. prof. pharmacology U. Manitoba Med. Coll., Winnipeg, Can., 1976-77, rsch. assoc., 1977-80; dir. vet. clinics Punjab Agrl. U., Ludhiana, India, 1980-82, head dept. vet. pharmacology, 1987-91, prof., 1991-94, ret., 1994; pool officer Govt. India, Delhi, 1983-84; apptd. mem. Task Force on Deg Nala Disease in cattle and buffaloes Indian Coun. Agrl. Rsch., New Delhi, 1981. Contbr. chpts. to books and articles to profl. jours. Mem. Soc. Physiologists & Pharmacologists India (life), Alumnia Assn. Vet. Sci. (life), Punjab Vet. Coun. (life), N.Y. Acad. Scis., Sikh Rev. Achievements include discovery of aetiology and treatment of phosphorus deficieny Haemoglobinuria, Mastitis, Degnala Disease and Leucoderma in buffaloes & cows. Home: House No BXX 137 Prem Nagar, Ludhiana 141001, India Office: Dept Pharm Toxicology, Punjab Agrl Univ Vt Med, Ludhiana Punjab, India

DHILLON, VARINDERPAL SINGH, science educator; b. Hoshiarpur, Punjab, India, July 5, 1963; s. Surinder Singh and Devinder Kaur (Sahota) D.; m. Ipninder Kaur Sandhu, Mar. 19, 1991; 1 child, Harustatpreet Kaur. BSc, Dayanand Anglo Vedic Coll., Jalandhar, India, 1984; MSc, Guru Nanak Dev U., Amritsar, India, 1986, MPhil, 1988; PhD, Jamia Milia Islania, New Delhi, 1999. Cert. in human cytology. Asst. cytogeneticist Ctr. for Genetic Disorders Guru Nanak Dev U., Amritsar, 1991-94, lectr. dept. human genetics, 1994-95; cytogeneticist Loomba Med. Ctr., New Delhi, 1995-96; lectr. dept. zoology Govt. Coll. for Women, Amritsar, 1996—; in charge cytogenetics sect. Bhandari Hosp., Amritsar, 1992-95; cons. fertility clinic Randhawa Hosp., Amritsar, 1995—. Contbr. rsch. articles to med. and sci. jours. Mem. Indian Soc. Human Genetics. Shromani Akali Dal Sikh. Avocations: science lectures, raising awareness about AIDS. Home: 462 Basant Ave, 143 001 Amritsar Punjab, India

DHIMAN, B. S., management consultant; b. Punjab, India, Apr. 19, 1935; s. Gurcharan Singh and Joginder Kaur; m. Harjinder Kaur; children: Jaspreet Kaur, Kamal Preet Wasir. B in Tech. with honors, Indian Inst. Tech., Khargpur, 1957; MS in Structural Engring., MS in Mgmt. Mng. dir. Span Consultants Ltd., New Delhi, 1977—. Mem. FIIBE, FIWWA, MIABSE, MFIP, MIASS, MASCE, MPCI, MACI, MIGS, MIRC. Office: Span Consultants, 3-5 IInd Fl LSC J Blk, Saket New Delhi 110017, India

DHIMAN, SHAMBNOU DUTTA, agronomist, researcher; b. Meerut, UP, India, June 6, 1943; s. Ratan Lal Dhiman and Prem Vati; m. Raj Bala; 3 children. BS in Agr., Agra U., 1962; MS in Agr., Meerut U., 1973, MPhil, 1974, PhD of Agronomy, 1976. Asst. agronomist HAU, Hisar, India, 1976-83; agronomy scientist HAU Rsch. Sta., Gurgaon, India, 1984-89; rice agronomist HAU Rice Rsch. Sta., Kaul, India, 1989-91; sr. rice agronomist HAU Rice Rsch. Sta., Kaul, 1992-95, 98—; cons. Brit. Guayana, Georgetown, 1996-97. Author: Paddy, 1998. Mem. ISA, HSA. Hindu. Avocations: writing, gardening, naturopathy TV watching. Home: 11/14 HAU Campus, Haryana Kaul 136 021, India Office: HAU, Rice Rsch Station, Haryana Kaul 136 021, India

DHINDSA, KASHMIR SINGH, economics educator; b. Jalandhar, Punjab, India, Dec. 17, 1952; s. Karnail Singh and Charan Kaur Dhindsa; m. Manjit Kaur Pawar, Nov. 1979; children: Sukhpreet, Jasleen. BA, Punjab U., Chandigarh, India; postgrad. diploma, Glasgow (Scotland) U., 1971; MA in Econs., Leeds U., 1972; PhD in Econs., U. London, 1975, postgrad., 1989-91. Rsch. officer dept. econs. Punjabi U., Patiala, India, 1978-79; lectr. econs. G.N.D. U., Amritsar, Punjab, 1979-82, reader, assoc. prof. in econs., 1982-89, prof. econs. Punjab Sch. Econs., 1989—, prof., head dept., 1994-96, dean faculty econs. and bus., 1992-93; vis. fellow Sch. Oriental and African Studiess, U. London, 1989-91. Editor PSE Econ. Analyst, 1994-96, Indian Jour. Quantitative Econs., 1994-96; author: India's Export Performance: Some Policy Implications, 1981, Indian Immigrants in United Kingdom - A socio-economic Analysis, 1998; contbr. articles to profl. jours. Mem. Zymkhana Club. Avocations: reading books on positive mental attitude, biographies, travel, music, table tennis, lawn tennis. Home: House No 104, Vijay Nagar, Batala Rd, Amritsar, Punjab 143 005, India Office: Punjab Sch Econs, Guru Nanak Dev U, Amritsar, Punjab 143005, India

DHIR, VIJAY K., mechanical engineering educator; b. Giddarbaha, Panjab, India, Apr. 14, 1943; came to U.S., 1969; s. Harnand Lal and Parsinni Devi (Sofat) D.; m. Komal Lata Khanna, Aug. 31, 1973; children: Vinita, Vashita. BScME, Punjab Engring. Coll., India, 1965; MTechME, Indian Inst. Tech., 1969; PhD in Mech. Engring., U. Ky., 1972. Asst. devel. engr. Jyoti Pumps, Ltd., Baroda, India, 1968-69; postgrad. engr. Engring. Rsch. Ctr. Tata Engring. & Locomotive Co., Poona, India, 1969; rsch. asst. U. Ky., Lexington, 1969-72, rsch. assoc., 1972-74; asst. prof. chem., nuclear & thermal engring. dept. UCLA, 1974-78, assoc. prof., 1978-82, prof. mech., aerospace & nuclear engring. dept., 1982—, vice chmn. mech., aerospace & nuclear engring. dept., 1988-91, chmn. dept., 1994—; cons. Nuclear Regulatory Commn., Seabulk Corp., Ft. Lauderdale, Fla., Argonne (Ill.) Nat. Lab., Pickard, Lowe & Garrick, Inc., Irvine, Calif., Rockwell Internat., Canoga Park, Calif., GE Corp., San Jose, Calif., Battelle N.W. Lab., Richland, Wash., Phys. Rsch., Inc., Torrance, Calif., Nat. Bur. Stds., Gaithersburg, Md., Los Alamos (N.Mex.) Nat. Lab., Sci. Applications Inc., El Segundo, Calif., Brookhaven Nat. Lab., Upton, N.Y.; chmn. numerous conf. sessions. Contbr. over 100 articles to profl. jours., over 100 papers to procs./conf. & symposia records; assoc. editor Applied Mechs. Rev., 1985-88, Jour. Heat Transfer, Transactions ASME, 1993-96, ASME Symposium Vol., 1978; referee numerous jours. Fellow ASME (Heat Transfer Meml. Award Sci. Category 1992), Am. Nuclear Soc. Office: Sch of Engring & Applied Sc U Calif 46-147 K Engineering IV Los Angeles CA 90024

DHOBLE, NIRUPAMA SANJAY, science educator, researcher; b. Nagpur, India, Mar. 25, 1966; d. Gopal Maroti and Nilimi (Gopal) Joshi; m. Sanjay Janrao Dhoble, May 13, 1994; 1 child, Ketki Sanjay. BSc, Nagpur U., 1986, MSc, 1988, PhD, 1993. Lectr. Sevadal Women's Coll., Nagpur, 1994—. Author: Physical Chemistry, 1999, Inorganic Chemistry, 1999; contbr. some 30 articles to profl. jours. Mem. Sawali Sci. and Social Inst. Mem. Indian Assn. Nuclear Chemistry and Allied Scis., Marathi Vidhyan Parishad. Avocation: painting. Office: Sevadal Women's Coll, Umrer Rd, 400009 Nagpur, Sakkardara India

DHOBLE, SANJAY JANRAOJI, physics educator; b. Mohagaon, M. Pradesh, India, Dec. 26, 1967; s. Janraoji Dhondbaji and Kalavati Janraoji (Wanode) D.; m. Nirupama Sanjay Joshi, May 13, 1994; 1 child, Ketki. BSc, D.D. Coll., Chhindwara, India, 1986; MS in Physics, Jabalpur U., India, 1988; PhD in Physics, U. Nagpur, India, 1992. Jr. rsch. fellow UGC, Nagpur, 1988-90, sr. rsch. fellow, 1990-91; lectr. Kamla Nehru Coll., Nagpur, 1991—; tchr. dept. physics Nagpur, 1991—; coord. computer course Kamla Nehru Coll., Nagpur, 1994—; pres. Sawali Sci. Soc. Inst., Nagpur, 1996—. Author: Textbook of Physics, (BSC.I), 1997, Textbook of Physics (BSC.Final), 1997, Practical Physics (BSC.I), 1997; contbr. articles to profl. jours. Pres. Scientific and Social Inst., Nagpur, 1996—. Mem. Indian Laser Assn., Vidarbha Environ. Soc., Environ. Security Orgn., Indian Physics Tchrs.'s Assn. Avocations: swimming, creative writing. Office: Kamla Nehru Coll, Sakkardara Square, 440 009 Nagpur/Maharashtra India

DHONDT, GUIDO DOMINIQUE, civil engineering researcher; b. Brugge, Belgium, Feb. 10, 1961; s. Cyrille Dhondt and Yvonne Lievens; m. Barbara Elisabeth Euler, July 16, 1990; children: Jakob, Lea. Civil engr., Cath. U. Louvain, Belgium, 1983; MA in Civil Engring., Princeton U., 1985, PhD in Civil Engring., 1987. Fracture mechanics expert MTU (Motoren-und Turbinen-Union, Daimler-Benz Aerospace), Munich, 1987—; ptnr. Theoretical Rsch. Assocs., Groebenzell, Germany, 1993-96. Contbr. articles to profl. jours. Recipient Young Engring. prize Flemish Engring. Orgn. (KVIV), 1984. Mem. Abaqus German Fracture Mechanics Group (chmn.), Deutscher Verband für Materialforschung (mem. mixed-mode fracture group 1997—), Assn. Princeton Grad. Alumni, German Assn. Computational Mechanics, Internat. Assn. Computational Mechanics. Avocation: mountain hiking in the Alps. Home: Enzianstrasse 14, D-82194 Grobenzell Germany Office: MTU Motoren- Turbinen-Union, PO 50 06 40, D-80976 Munich Germany

D'HONDT, JEAN-LOUP LUCIEN, scientist, researcher; b. Pau, France, July 27, 1943; s. Jean-Marie Clément and Lucienne (Dupret) d'H.; m. Marie-José Antonowiez, Sept. 4, 1972. Lic. Scis., U. Bordeaux, 1965, DEA in Scis., 1966, PhD in Scis., 1967; DSc, U. Paris 6, 1976. Stagiaire of rsch. Nat. Ctr. of Sci. Rsch., Paris, 1968, attaché of rsch., 1969-77, chargé of rsch., 1977-91, dir. rsch., 1991—; assoc. prof. U. Oran, Algeria, 1970-71; mem. com. sci. and com. on hist. and sci. works, sect. scis. and history of scis. French Ministry Edn. Co-author: Metamorphoses Animales, 1995, Biologie du developpment, 1999; author Les Invertebres Marins meconnus, 1999; co-editor: Bryozoa Living and Fossil, 1991, others; contbr. over 250 articles to profl. jours. Recipient Scientific prize Conseil Gen. of Gironde, Bordeaux, 1968. Mem. French Soc. of Systematics (founding), Internat. Bryozoology Assn. (officer, conf. host), Zool. Soc. France (gen. sec., editor 1989—), Soc. History of Sci. Vie (founding, coun. mem. 1995-2000). Avocations: marine biology, history of sciences, protection of environment. Office: Nat Mus Natural History Lab Biology of Marine Invertebrates, 57 Rue Cuvier, 75005 Paris France

DHONG, HUN JONG, otolaryngologist; b. Seoul, Aug. 18, 1958; parents Young Song and Chun Ja Choi; m. Hi Jean Kim, Sept. 30, 1986; children: Hyun Jae, Hyun June. BS, Seoul Nat. U., 1983, MS, 1987, PhD, 1996. Clin. fellow Seoul Nat. U. Hosp., 1990-91; staff physician Seoul City Boramae Hosp., 1991-92; rsch. fellow U. Pa. Hosp., Phila., 1992-94; staff physician Samsung Med. Ctr., Seoul, 1994-96; assoc. prof. Sungkunkkwan U. Sch. Medicine, Seoul, 1997—. Mem. Korean Soc. Otolaryngology, Korean Rhinol. Soc., Internat. Rhinol. Soc. Office: Samsung Med Ctr, 50 Ilwondong Kangnam-gu, Seoul 135-710, Korea

DHONT, MARC, gynecologist; b. Oudenaarde, Belgium, Feb. 22, 1943; s. Omer and Augusta (Heyse) D.; m. Linda Van Caeneghem, Nov. 28, 1968; children: Karel, Nathalie, Stefanie. MD, U. Gent, 1968, PhD, 1987. Registrar dept. gynecology Ghent U., Belgium, 1974-79, cons. dept. gynecology, 1979-87, assoc. prof., 1987-91, prof. ob-gyn., 1991—, head dept. ob-gyn., 1991—. Author book chpts.; contbr. numerous articles to profl. jours. Mem. Am. Fertility Soc., European Soc. of Human Reproduction and Embryology, Internat. Menopause Soc. Office: Dept Ob-Gyn, De Pintelaan 185, B-9000 Ghent Belgium

DHULEY, JAYANT NILKANTH, pharmacologist; b. Pune, India, Sept. 17, 1961; s. Nilkanth Bapuji and Sanjeevani Nilkanth D. HSSC, Hislop Coll., Nagpur, India, 1976; BS, Nagpur U., Nagpur, India, 1981, MS in Biochemistry, 1983; MBA, IBMR, Chinchwad, Pune, India, 1991; PhD, Pune U., 2000. Rsch. fellow Hindustan Antibiotics, Ltd., Pune, 1984-86, rsch. asst., 1986-93; scientific exec. Hindustan Antibiotics, Ltd., Pune, India, 1993—. Contbr. articles to profl. jours. Mem. N.Y. Acad. Scis., Indian Pharmacol. Soc., Microbiol. Assn. India. Avocations: interior decoration, gardening, cooking, travel. Home: 22/21 Anandnagar Park, Kothrud Paud Rd, 411029 Pune India Office: Hindustan Antibiotics Ltd, Rsch & Devel Divsn, Pimpri Pune 411 018, India

DIAB, HASSAN BAHAEDDINE, electrical and computer engineering educator; b. Beirut, June 1, 1959; s. Bahaeddine Ali and Refca Abdallah (Taji) D.; m. Nuwar Radwan Mawlawi; children: Razan, Rami, Radwan. BSc with honors, Leeds (Eng.) Met. U., 1981; MSc in Sys. Engring., U. Surrey, Guildford, Eng., 1982; PhD in Computer Engring., U. Bath, Eng., 1985. Chartered engr., U.K.; charter profl. engr., Australia. Trainee engr. IBM, Winchester, Eng., 1979-80; sys. engr. IBM, Portsmouth, Eng., 1982; asst. prof. Am. U. Beirut, 1985-91, assoc. prof., 1991-97, prof., 1997—, chmn. dept. elec. and computer engring., 1998—; sys. analyst, cons. Hariri Found., Beirut, 1986-90; vis. prof. Sanaa (Yemen) U., 1989. Author: Design and Implementation of a Flight Simulation System, 1992; contbr. more than 80 articles to profl. jours. and internat. confs. Recipient Arab Scientists Shuman prize Shuman Found., 1992; Fulbright fellow USIA Coun. for Internat. Exch., U. Ill., Champaign-Urbana, 1988; DAAD rsch. scholar, U. Koblenz, Germany, 1999. Fellow Inst. Engrs. Australia (coord. in the Middle East 1991—); mem. IEEE (sr.), Instn. Elec. Engrs. (chartered engr.). Avocations: tennis, football, badminton. E-mail: diab@aub.edu.lb. Office: Am Univ Beirut, FEA Bliss St PO Box 11-0236, Beirut Lebanon

DIAB, KAMEL TAWFIK, agricultural products company executive; b. Kenna, Egypt, Apr. 25, 1921; s. Tawfik M. Diab; m. Neamat Mohamed el Tohamy, May 1951; children: Nagwa, Gihan, Alaa. BSc in Agriculture, Cairo U., 1942; BA in Law, Alexandria U., 1965; MA in Mgmt., Am. U. Cairo, 1971; PhD in Bus. Adminstrn., Am. World U., 1992. Tchr. Faculty Agriculture Cairo U., 1943; fruit farmer, 1944-58; gen. dir. Internat. Trading Co., 1959-61, Arab Fgn. Trade Co., 1961-66; chmn. El Wadi Co., 1967-74, Projects & Investments Consulting Co., Cairo, 1975—; Chmn., Diab, Kamel Tawfik, PICO Grp. & Modern Agrl. Co. Mem. Egyptian Bus. Assn., Egyptian Lebanese Businessmen Friendship Assn., Automobile Club. Office: PICO Group & Modern Agriculture Co, 3 Shagaret el Dor St, Cairo Egypt

DIAKITÉ, MADUBUKO ARTHUR R., association administrator, consultant; b. N.Y.C., Dec. 17, 1940; 1 child, Jason. Student, Hunter Coll., 1963-66; LLB, LaSalle Extension U., 1967; BA, Stockholm U., 1970, M Degree, 1972; LLM, Lund (Sweden) U., 1993. Postgrad. researcher Stockholm U., 1975-83; course adminstr., lectr. internat. fgn. studen program Internat. Swedish U., Folkuniversitet, Lund, Sweden, 1981-96; human rights project dir., CEO The English Internat. Assn., Lund, 1987—; founder, publ., mng. editor The Lundian Internat. Mag. The English Internat. Assn., 1987—; pub. rels. asst. Immigration Svc. Bur., Lund, Sweden, 1989-90; guest lectr. seminars dept. sociology Lund U., 1996-97, study group supr., 1990—; rschr. Raoul Wallenberg Inst. Author: Film, Culture and the Black Filmmaker: Functional Relationships/Parallel Development, 1980, Not Even in Your Dreams, 1992, A Piece of Glory, 1992, State Compliance with International Treaties Prohibiting Racial Discrimination in Employment, 1994; prodr., dir., writer, editor, cameraman: (film) For Personal Reasons (hon. mention 1972 Grenoble Festival of Short Films); editor: Resource Book on African Organisations in Sweden, 1997; internat. editor: The Nigerian Times Internat., 1995-96; contbr. book review to profl. jour. Mem. Am. Coun. of the UN Sys., Africana Network, UN Assn. Lund, Swedish Tchr.'s Union. Office: English Internat Assn, PO Box 722, 200 07 Lund Sweden

DIAKOMANOLIS, YVONNE HELEN CLAIRE, endocrinologist; b. Westminster, England, Aug. 5, 1947; arrived in Greece, 1974; d. Berthold Baruch and Erica Magdalena (Elzner) Apelbaum; m. Emmanuel S. Diakomanolis, July 27, 1974; children: Alexander, Louisa, Philip, Andreas. MA in Animal Physiology, St. Hilda's Coll., Oxford, Eng., 1969, BM, BCh, 1972; specialization as physician, Athens (Greece) U., 1982, MD, 1985. Surg. house officer vascular surgery Ctrl. Middlesex Hosp., London, 1973, med. house officer cardiology, 1973-74; tng. post in medicine Alexandra Therapeutic Clinic, Athens, 1977-78, 81-82; med. registrar endocrinology dept. Red Cross Hosp., Athens, 1986—; dir. Whitton & Co. Ins. Brothers, London, 1969-79. Active Amnesty Internat., Oxford, 1966-70, Friends of Children Soc., Athens, 1985—; co-orgn. Red Cross Diabetes Clinic, Athens, 1990—. Mem. European Assn. for the Study of Diabetes, Greek Diabetes Soc., Greek Endocrinology Soc., Greek Osteoporosis Soc., N.Y. Acad. Scis. Anglican. Avocations: show jumping, painting, traveling. Home: I Metaxa 54, 15237 Filothei Attika, Greece

DIAL, ELEANORE MAXWELL, foreign language educator; b. Norwich, Conn., Feb. 21, 1929; d. Joseph Walter and Irene (Beetham) Maxwell; m. John E. Dial, Aug. 27, 1959. BA, U. Bridgeport, Conn., 1951; MA in Spanish, Mexico City Coll., 1955; PhD, U. Mo., 1968. Mem. faculty U. Wis.-Milw., 1968-75, Ind. State U., Terre Haute, 1975-78, Bowling Green (Ohio) State U., 1978-79; asst. prof. dept. fgn. langs. and lit. Iowa State U., Ames, 1979-85, assoc. prof., 1985-96, emerita assoc. prof., 1996—; cons. pub. cos.; participant workshops; del. 1st World Congress Women Journalists and Writers, Mex., 1975, also mem. edn. commn. Contbr. articles, anthologies and revs. to scholarly jours. Active Gov.'s Commn. on Fgn. Langs. and Internat. Studies, 1988-95. NDEA grantee, 1967, Ctr. Latin Am. grantee, 1972, NEH summer seminar UCLA, 1981, U. Calif.-Santa Barbara, 1984. Mem. MLA, Am. Assn. Tchrs. Spanish and Portuguese, Midwest MLA, N. Ctrl. Coun. Latin Americanists, Midwest Assn. Latin Am. Studies, Clermont County Geneal. Soc., Ohio Geneal. Soc., Story County (Iowa) Geneal. Soc., Caribbean Studies Assn., Phi Beta Delta, Phi Sigma Iota, Sigma Delta Pi. Home: 119 9th St Ames IA 50010-6343 Office: Iowa State U Ames IA 50011-0001

DIAL, N(ATHANIEL) VICTOR, industrialist; b. Long Beach, Calif., June 21, 1938; s. N. Minter Dial and Elisabeth (Porter) Hinks; m. Alix Montgomery, Oct. 10, 1962 (div. 1979); children: N. Minter, Elisabeth Montgomery; m. Helene Grinda, Oct. 2, 1981; 1 child, William Henry. BA, Yale U., 1959. Trainee Ford Motor Co., Dearborn, Mich., 1961-62; asst. to car and truck mktg. mgr. Ford Internat., Brussels, 1963-67; area mgr., Africa Ford France, Paris, 1967-70; bus. devel. mgr. Ford of Europe, London, 1970-73; chmn., gen. mgr. Ford France, S.A., Paris, 1973-81; v.p. sales and mktg. Automobiles Peugeot, Paris, 1981-90; pres., CEO, bd. govs. Am. Hosp. Paris, 1978-92; bd. dirs. Arlington Capital Investors, HCI (Holdings) Ltd., Prestige Veneers, Ltd., Amper S.A.; chmn. Morgane Technology, PLC. Awarded Legion of Honor, govt. of France, 1988. Mem. Am. C. of C. in France (v.p. 1974-78, hon. dir. 1978-90, bd. dirs.), Polo de Paris, Queen's Club, White's London. Republican. Episcopalian. Avocations: squash, tennis, aviation, shooting. Office: 47 Rue Spontini, 75116 Paris France also: 40 St James's Pl, London SW1A 1NS, England

DIAMANDESCU, LUCIAN CONSTANTIN, physicist, researcher; b. Beceni, Buzau, Romania, May 10, 1947; s. Nicolae and Elena (Rapeanu) D.; m. Teodota Cristina Negulescu, May 5, 1973; 1 child, Dragos. Postgrad., Faculty Physics, Bucharest, Romania, 1965-70. Physics diplomate. Physicist Inst. Atomic Physics, Bucharest, 1970-75, rschr., 1975-77; prin. rschr. III Inst. Atomic Physics/Inst. for Physics and Tech. Materials, Bucharest, 1977-93; prin. rschr. II Inst. Atomic Physics/Nat. Inst. Materials Physics, Bucharest, 1993-96, prin. rschr. I, 1996—; mem. program com. Internat. Conf. on the Applications of Mossbauer Effect, Budapest, 1989; v.p. sci. coun. IFA/Inst. for Physics and Tech. of Materials, Bucharest, 1990-94; dep. dir. Solid State Magnetism Lab., Nat. Inst. Materials Physics, 1990-97, dir., 1997-99; dir. Structure and Dynamics Condensed Matter Lab., 1999—. Contbr. articles to profl. jours.; patentee in field. Vice lt. Romanian Mil., 1972. Recipient Rep. prize for rsch. Ministry Rsch. and Tech., Bucharest, 1984; postdoctoral fellow U. Venice, Italy, 1993, 2000. Mem. Romanian Phys. Soc., Romanian Soc. on Magnetic Materials, European Phys. Soc. Avocations: music, tennis, stamp. E-mail: DIAMAND@ALPHA1.INFIM.RO. Fax: 0040 1 493 0267. Home: Drumul Taberei 89 BL R1, SC A AP 23 ET V, R-77442 Bucharest Romania Office: IFA/Nat Inst Materials Phys, PO Box MG-7, R-76900 Bucharest Romania

DIAMANDIDIS, MICHAEL LEONIDAS, computer scientist, researcher; b. Thessaloniki, Greece, July 4, 1967; s. Leonidas Michael and Symeli John (Karypidou) D. BSc in computer sci., City Coll., Thessaloniki, Greece, 1994. Singular computer applications Thessaloniki, 1991-92; prof. computing 4th Dimension Sch., Langadas, 1992—; dir. info. sys. Municipality of Langadas, Greece, 1995; project leader Connection Biochem. Analyzer with Microbiology Software, 1995—; programming leader in cardiology, othalmology, otology, microbiology, orthopaedics, anesthesia projects, 1992—. Lt., 1986-89. Home: Ast Oinonomov 34, 57200 Langadas Greece Office: Vision Computer Applications, Dimotini Agora Fl 1 Office 2, 57200 Langadas Greece

DIAMANDOUROS, P. NIKIFOROS, political scientist, educator; b. Athens, Greece, June 25, 1942; s. John P. and Helen J. (Ghionis) D.; m. Magda Andrikidis, Sept. 4, 1971; children: John, Constantine. BA, Ind. U., Bloomington, 1963; MA, Columbia U., 1965, MPhil, 1969, PhD, 1972. Dir. devel. office Athens Coll., 1978-83; program dir. Social Sci. Rsch. Coun., N.Y., 1983-88; assoc. prof. U. Athens, 1988-93, prof. polit. Sci., 1993—; chmn. bd. dirs., CEO Nat. Ctr. for Social Rsch., Athens, 1995-98; nat. ombudsman of Greece, 1998—. Author: Cultural Dualism and Political Change in Postauthoritarian Greece, 2000; co-editor: The Politics of Democratic Consolidation, 1995; gen. series editor: The New Southern Europe, 1995—; contbr. numerous articles to profl. jours. Sec. Paremvassi Citizens' Assn., Athens, 1995-98. NEH grantee, 1977, Sr. Fulbright-Hayes grantee, 1977-78. Mem. Greek Polit. Sci. Assn. (pres. 1992-98), Modern Greek Studies Assn. (pres. 1985-88). Office: Dept Polit Sci U Athens, 19 Omirou St, GR-10672 Athens Greece

DIAMENT, ARON JUDKA, pediatric neurologist; b. Piaski, Poland, July 19, 1931; s. Moszek and Rywka (Zamel) D.; m. Regina Liberman, Mar. 10, 1956; children: Decio, Luis Henrique, Deborah Ester. Student, Coll. Estadual Canadá, São Paulo, Brazil, 1947, Coll. Bandeirantes, São Paulo, Brazil, 1948, 49; MD, U. São Paulo, 1955, PhD, 1971. Lic. pediatric neurologist. Chief of svc. of child neurology U. São Paulo, 1981—, assoc. prof. faculty medicine, 1984—. Author, editor: Child Neurology, 1980 (Jaboti award 1981), 2d edit., 1989, 3rd edit., 1996. Office: Rva Capote Valente 432, Cj 131-13 CEP, 05409 São Paulo Brazil

DIAMOND, GARY WARREN, physician, pediatrician; b. Newark, Oct. 6, 1953; came to Israel, 1989; s. Edward Diamond and Joan (Chase) Kessler; m. Ofra Heyd, Aug. 27, 1975; children: Noa, Tamir, Yael. BA, Hebrew U., Jerusalem, 1975; BS, Columbia U., 1978; MD, Sackler Sch. of Medicine, 1982. Diplomate Am. Bd. Pediatrics. Fellow child devel. unit Albert Einstein Coll. of Medicine, Bronx, N.Y., 1985-87; dir. pediatric HIV unit Rose F. Kennedy Ctr. Albert Einstein Coll. of Medicine, Bronx, 1987—, asst. prof., 1987—; pediatric svcs. dir. Gen. HMO, Ramat Gan, Israel, 1989—; instr. dept. pediatrics Sackler Sch. of Medicine, Tel Aviv, 1996—; dir. high risk infant and child unit Child Devel. Ctr., Schneider Childrens Med. Ctr. Israel, Petah Tikva, Israel, 1994—; attending physician Morrisania Health Ctr., Bronx, 1987-89; med. dir. devel. evaluation unit Ministry of Social Welfare, Rishonle Zion, Israel, 1992-95; med. dir. Aleh Handicapped Children's Assn., Bene Beraq, Israel, 1991-95; med. dir., fgn. adoption svcs. Humanikat, Herzelia, 1998—. Author: (with others) HIV Infection and Developmental Disabilities, 1992; contbr. articles to profl. jours. Cons. Am. Student's Well Being Assn. Tel Aviv U. Sch. Medicine, 1991—. Maj. Israel Army Med. Corps, 1992—. Recipient Ambulatory Pediatric Rsch. award Strauss Dairies, 1999. Fellow Am. Acad. Pediatrics, Am. Acad. of Devel. Medicine and Child Neurology, Israel Pediatric Assn. Avocation: photography. Home: 37 Moshe Dayan St, Kefar Sava 44539, Isreal Office: Schneider Childrens Med, Ctr of Israel 14 Kaplan St, Petah Tikua Israel

DIAMOND, HARVEY JEROME, machinery manufacturing company executive; b. Charlotte, N.C., Dec. 7, 1928; s. Harry B. and Jeanette (Davis) D.; m. Betty L. Ball, May 22, 1953 (dec. Nov. 1988); children: Michael, Beth, David Abby; m. Miriam Letey, 1989. BS, U. N.C., 1952. Sales mgr. Dixie Neon Supply House, Charlotte, 1950-61; pres., gen. mgr., chmn. bd., CEO Plasti-Vac, Inc., Charlotte, 1961—; pres., gen. mgr. Diamond Supply, Inc., 1971-84, chmn. bd. dirs., 1984—; pres. Plastic Prodn., Inc., 1973—, PVI Internat. Corp., 1980—; mem. dist. export coun. Dept. Commerce, 1979-93; del. White House Conf. on small Bus., 1980; bd. dirs. Maccabi USA/Sports for Israel. Author: (manual) Introduction to Vacuum Forming, 1976; patentee inverted clamping frame system for vacuum forming machines, process of vacuum forming plastics with vertical oven. Chmn. Mecklenburg Dem. Party, 1974-75, treas., 1972-74; del. Dem. Nat. Conv., 1972; bd. advisors Pfeiffer Coll., Misenheimer, N.C., 1977-89; participant White House conf. on Small Bus., 1978, White House Conf. on Anti-Inflation Initiatives, 1978; bd. dirs. U.S. Com. for Sports in Israel, 1995—. Recipient award for Activity in U.S. Trade Mission to S.Am., Dept. Commerce, 1967, March of Dimes award, 1966, Excellence in Exporting award N.C. Trade Club, 1981. Mem. Soc. Plastics Engrs., Soc. Plastics Industries, So. States Sign Assn. (bd. dirs. 1983-87), Southeastern States Sign Assn. (bd. dirs. 1991), Nat. Electric Sign Assn., Metrolina World Trade Assn. (v.p. 1982-83), Metrolina World Trade Club (pres. 1983-84), N.C. World Trade Assn. (bd. dirs. 1983-86, gen. chmn. ann. conv. 1984), US Comm. Sports in Isreal (bd. dirs. 1996—), Masons, Shriners. Jewish. Home: 3102 Oak Brook Dr Waxhaw NC 28173-7589 Office: PO Box 5543 Charlotte NC 28299-5543

DIAMOND, MICHAEL SHAWN, science and math educator, computer consultant; b. St. Louis, Jan. 26, 1960; s. Robert Dale Diamond and Jean Marie (Reutner) White; m. Jennifer Atkins Albrighton, Jan. 1, 1999. BSChemE, U. Mo., 1982; MEd, Hyles-Anderson Coll., 1989. Cert. engr.-in-tng.; lic., ordained to ministry Baptist Ch., 1989; endorsed advanced placement calculus and stats. tchr., S.C., reader for advanced placement math. Nuclear engr. Charleston (S.C.) Naval Shipyard, Nuclear Engring. Dept., 1983-88, asst. shift test engr., 1983-85, asst. shift refueling engr., 1985-88; systems mgr. and sci. tchr. Faith Bapt. Ch. and Schs., Canoga Park, Calif., 1989-90, sci. tchr., 1989-92; programming asst., cons. Peterson Rsch., Costa Mesa, Calif., 1989-92; sci. dept. chmn. Gethsemane Bapt. Christian Sch., Long Beach, Calif., 1990-92; math. computer tchr. Pinewood Prep. Sch., Summerville, S.C., 1993-97, computer and tech. chair, 1994-97, 99; tng. splst. Software Tng. Ctr., North Charleston, S.C., 1997-98; quality assurance analyst in product devel. Blackbaud, Inc., Charleston, S.C., 1998; math. tchr. Ft. Dorchester H.S., 1999—; adj. instr. transfer chemistry, math. and engring. Trident Tech. Coll., North Charleston, S.C., 1993—; contract computer instr. Tng. Alliance, Charleston, 1993. Sunday sch. tchr. Gethsemane Bapt. Ch., Long Beach, 1990-92, Summerville (S.C.) Bapt. Ch., 1996—; mem. choir Trident Bapt. Ch., Charleston, S.C., 1993-96; singles Sun. sch. tchr. Summerville (S.C.) Bapt. Ch., 1996-99. Mem. NSPE, Am. Nuclear Soc., Nat. Sci. Tchrs. Assn., S.C. Sci. Coun., Nat. Coun. Tchrs. Math., S.C. Math. Tchrs. Assn., Low Country Math. Tchrs. Assn., S.C. Assn. Adv. Placement Math Tchrs., U.S. Judo Assn. (Winner's Cir. award 1987, 88, 89), Internat. Soc. of Tech. Educators, Pi Kappa Alpha. Republican. Avocations: reading, softball, personal computers, church work. Home: 107 Sawtooth Ln Summerville SC 29485-5807

DIAMOND, PAUL STEVEN, lawyer; b. Bklyn., Jan. 2, 1953; s. George and Anna (Jaeger) D.; m. Robin Nilon. BA magna cum laude, Columbia U., 1974; JD, U. Pa., 1977. Bar: Pa. 1977, U.S. Dist. Ct. (ea. dist.) Pa, 1979, U.S. Ct. Appeals (3d cir.) 1979, U.S. Supreme Ct. 1983. Asst. dist. atty. Phila. Dist. Atty. Office, 1977-83; law clk. Supreme Ct. Pa., Phila., 1980; assoc. Dilworth, Paxson, Kalish & Kauffman, Phila., 1983-85, ptnr., 1986-91; ptnr. Obermayer, Rebmann, Maxwell & Hippel, Phila., 1992—; lectr. Temple U. Sch. Law, Phila., 1990-92; mem. civil prodecural rules com. Supreme Ct. Pa., 1995—, fed. judicial nominating commn., 1995—; treas. Pa. lawyers fund for client security bd. Supreme Ct. Pa., 1999. Author: Federal Grand Jury Practice and Procedure, 1990, rev. 2nd edit., 1993; vice-chmn. Amicus Curiae Briefs Comm., 1995—. Mem. ABA (criminal justice sect., Amicus Curiae briefs subcom. 1983—, grand jury subcom. 1991—), Am. Law Inst., Pa. Bar Assn., Phila. Bar Assn. Republican. Jewish. Office: Obermayer Rebmann Maxwell & Hippel One Penn Ctr 1617 John F Kennedy Blvd Philadelphia PA 19103

DIAMOND, RICHARD S., lawyer; b. Newark, June 26, 1960. BA in Econs./Bus. Adminstrn., Rutgers U., 1981; JD, Seton Hall U., 1985. Bar: N.J. 1985, Fla. 1991, U.S. Dist. Ct. N.J. 1991; cert. matrimonial trial specialist, cert. divorce mediator. Law sec. to Hon. Burton J. Ironson State of N.J., Union County, N.J., 1985-86; assoc. Law Firm of Robert Diamond, Springfield, N.J.; ptnr. Diamond Hodes & Diamond, Springfield, Gourvitz, Diamond, Hodes, Braun & Diamond, Springfield, Diamond & Diamond P.A., Millburn, N.J.; spkr., guest lectr. TV and radio broadcasts. Contbr. articles to profl. jours. Mem. Union County Bar Assn.), Essex County Bar (matrimonial practice), N.J. Bar Assn. (lectr., speaker). Avocations: racquetball, tennis, running. Fax: 973-379-9210. E-mail: njdivorcelawyer@aol.com. Office: Diamond & Diamond PA 225 Millburn Ave Ste 208 Millburn NJ 07041-1712

DIANZANI, MARIO UMBERTO, pathology educator; b. Grosseto, Italy, June 13, 1925; s. Edgardo and Irma (Bocelli) D.; m. Maria Assunta Mor, Aug. 18, 1956; children: Irma, Chiara, Umberto, Paola. Degree in medicine, U. Siena, Italy, 1948, degree in pharmacy, 1950; hon. doctorate, Brunel U., London, 1978; hon. doctorate in chemistry, U. Genoa, Italy, 1995; hon. doctorate, U. Buenos Aires, 1996. Asst. in gen. pathology U. Siena, 1948-50, prof. gen. pathology, 1964-65; asst. in gen. pathology U. Genoa, Italy, 1950-58; prof. gen. pathology U. Cagliari, Italy, 1958-64, U. Turin, Italy, 1965—; dean Faculty Medicine and Surgery, 1971-84; rector magnificus U. Turin, 1984-96. Author textbook of gen. pathology, 1970. Recipient Premio Feltrinelli, Accademia del Lincei, Rome, 1979, Trevor Slater award Internat. Free Radical Soc., 1994, Invernizzi prize, 1996. Roman Catholic. Avocations: archeology, fishing. Home: Corso D'Azeglio 118, 10126 Turin Italy Office: U Torino, Corso Raffaello 30, 10125 Turin Italy

DIAO, DONGFENG, engineering educator, consultant; b. Jilin, China, Dec. 24, 1961; m. Shumei Ma, Nov. 6, 1960; children: Xu, Meng. Master, Chinese Acad. Scis., 1986; PhD, Tohuku U., Sendai, Japan, 1992. Rsch. assoc. Tohoku U., Sendai, Japan, 1993-94; asst. prof. Shizuoka U., Hamamatsu, Japan, 1994-95, assoc. prof., 1995—; vis. prof. The Ohio State U., Columbus, 1996; guest prof. Shenzhen U., China, 1999—; cons. Fuji Indsl. Rsch. Inst. of Shizuoka Prefecture, Fiji City, Japan, 1998—. Mem. JSME, JSLE. Home: Hirosawa 1-22-6-5-12, Hamamatsu 432 8561, Japan Office: Shizuoka U, Johuku 3-5-1, Hamamatsu 432 8561, Japan

DIAS, SERGIO ANTONIO C. C. DA PENA, company financial executive; b. Lisbon, Portugal, Aug. 27, 1964; s. Liosario da Pena and Maria Helena Carvalho (Cardoso) D.; m. Ana Paula da Fonseca Marques, Apr. 15, 1989; 1 child, Joao Miguel Fonseca Marques da Pena Dias. Student, Cath. U. Portugal, Lison, 1981. Cert. economist. Account mgr. Banco Português Atlantico, Lisbon, 1986-89; asst. contr. Data Gen., Lisbon, 1989-91; fin. dir. Oracle Portugal, Lisbon, 1991—. Mem. Order of Economists. Roman Catholic. Avocations: reading, movies, strategic games.

DIAS-AGUDO, FERNANDO ROLDÃO, mathematician, educator; b. Mouriscas, Ribatejo, Portugal, Nov. 25, 1925; s. Leonel and Maria de Matos (Roldão) Dias-A.; m. Elia Farinha Raposo, Sept. 2, 1953, children: Maria Isabel, Maria Helena. BA in Math., U. Lisbon, 1947, PhD of Math., 1955; BA in Civil Engring., Tech. U. Lisbon, 1951. Tchg. asst. Tech. U. Lisbon, Portugal, 1948-49; tchg. asst. U. Lisbon, 1951-55, from asst. prof. to assoc. prof., 1955-68; prof. New U. Lisbon, 1975-82; prof. U. Lisbon, 1968-75, 82-95, prof. emeritus, 1995—. Author: Linear Algebra and Analytical Geometry, 1960, 2d edit., 1964, 3d edit., 1968, 4th edit., 1989, Differential and Integral Calculus, 1969, vol. 2, 1973, Real Analysis, vol. 1, 1989, vol. 2, 1990, vol. 3, 1992, 2d edit., 1994; contbr. articles to profl. jours. Mem. Acad. Scientiarun et Artium Europaea, Acad. Sci. Lisbon (treas. 1979—), N.Y. Acad. Sci., Sigma Xi. Home: Av Salvador Allende 35, P2780163 Oeiras Portugal Office: Acad das Ciencias de Lisboa, R Academia das Ciencias 19, P1249122 Lisbon Portugal

DIASIO, ILSE WOLFARTSBERGER, volunteer; b. Linz, Austria, Nov. 12, 1946; came to U.S., 1967; d. D.I. Gottfried and Elfriede (Stuchlik) Wolfartsberger; m. Robert B. Diasio, July 4, 1970; children: Christoph, Thomas, Michael. Grad. in phys. therapy, U. Vienna, 1965-67. Phys. therapist Yale-New Haven Hosp., 1968-71, Vis. Nurse Assn., Rochester, N.Y., 1971-72; symposium coord. dept. pharmacology U. Ala., 1988; vol. tchr. German, Pemberton Elem. Sch., Richmond, Va., 1980-84, Vestavia Hills Elem. and H.S., 1985-93; organizer student exch. program between Vestavia Hills H.S. and Seebacher Gymnasium, Graz, Austria, 1990, 91, 94. Bd. dirs. Pemberton (Va.) Elem. Sch. PTA, 1979-84, pres., 1982-84; bd. dirs. Va. Commonwealth U. Faculty Woman's Club, 1978-84; pres. Childrens Svc. League, 1992-93, treas. 1991-92, asst. treas. 1990-91, 2nd v.p., rec. sec., 1998-99; vol. Our Lady Queen of the Universe and Sacred Heart of Jesus Cath. Chs., 1988-90; St. Peter's rep. Alab. Arise, diocesan rep., rec. sec., 1988-94; mem. Peace and Justice Commn. of the Cath. Diocese of Birmingham, 1989-95, chair of commn., 1994-95; bd. dirs. Be an Apostle of Christ, 1988—; chair human concerns com. St. Peter's, 1988—; mem. Direct Svc. Network, 1989—; mem. Greater Birmingham Ministries program, 1989—; treas. Greater Birmingham UNA-USA chpt., 1992—; mem. COMPEER Bd., Birmingham, Ala., 1990-99; bd. dirs. Greater Birmingham Ministries, 1998—, chmn. direct svcs. work group, 1999—; mem. WOC, Call to Action, Bread for the World, CALC, Pax Christi, Amnesty Internat., Nat. Conf. of Cmty. and Justice, Smithsonian Inst., UNICEF, Coalition Against Hate Crimes, 1997—, Birmingham Com. on Fgn. Rels., 1998—; bd. dirs. Ala. chpt. Fulbright Assn., 1999—; organizer Christmas gift drive for needy families Angel Tree project St. Peter's Cath. Ch., 1988—; bd. dirs. LWV Greater Birmingham, 1999-2000. Recipient resolution City of Birmingham, 1999. Mem. AAUW, Nat. Mus. of Women in the Arts, U.S. Holocost Mus., Vereinigung Ehemaliger Körnerschülerinnen, LWV (bd. dirs. Greater Birmingham 1999-2000). Roman Catholic. Avocations: reading, music, skiing, cooking, travelling. Home: 1225 Branchwater Ln Birmingham AL 35216-2001

DIASIO, RICHARD LEONARD, power transmission executive, sports facility executive; b. Bridgeport, Conn., Nov. 25, 1937; s. Daniel Joseph and Rose Sarah (Agasi) D.; m. Julia Ann Krhla, Oct. 14, 1961; children: Richard J., Laura L., Christopher S. AS in Mech. Engring., Bridgeport Engring. Inst., 1965. Engr. U.S. Elec. Motors, Milford, Conn., 1962-64; sales profl. Reliance Electric, Hamden, Conn., 1964-66; sales mgr. Dynamatic div. Eaton Corp., Fairfield, N.J., 1966-72; mgr. regional sales Harnischfeger Corp., Woodbridge, N.J., 1972-74; mgr. nat. sales Kanematsu-Gosho, South Plainfield, N.J., 1974-77; dir. mktg. Ind. Gear Works, Indpls., 1977-78, gen. mgr., 1978-80; pres. Ind. Power Transmission Systems, Inc., Indpls, 1980—; pres. Putnam Park Corp., Putnam County, Ind., 1990—, Diasio Car Co., 1999—. With USAF, 1955-59. Mem. Soc. Mfg. Engrs. (sr.), Dramatists Guild, Authors League Am. Republican. Roman Catholic. Avocations: auto sports, writing. Office: Ind Power Transmission Sys 470 Northfield Dr Brownsburg IN 46112-2113

DIATLOFF-ZITO, CATHERINE, geneticist; b. Issy les Moulineaux, France, May 8, 1945; d. Alexis and Jacqueline (Caffin) Diatloff; m. Zito, Apr. 22, 1978; 1 child, Laetitia. DSc, U. Paris XI, Orsay, 1980. Scientist acad. rsch. CNRS, Paris, 1978—. Mem. French Soc. Genetics, N.Y. Acad. Scis.

DIATTA, JOSEPH, Nigerian diplomat; b. Fadama, Niger, May 15, 1948; s. Emmanuel and Saha (Sani) D.; m. Haoua Oumarou, Dec. 28, 1975; children—Sylvia, Amadou, Myriam, Linda. Licence en Droit, U. Abidjan, Ivory Coast, 1970; diplome, Institut International d'Adminstration Publique, Paris, 1971. Permanent sec. Ministry Fgn. Affairs, Niamey, Niger, 1975-79; amb. to Ethiopia, Niger Embassy, Addis-Abeba, 1979-82; amb. to U.S., Niger Embassy, Washington, 1982—; permanent rep. to UN, Permanent Mission of Niger, N.Y.C., from 1997. Office: Embassy of Niger Chancery 2204 R St NW Washington DC 20008*

DIAZ, ANDE N., academic administrator, educator, consultant; b. Rochester, N Y., July 1, 1962. Degree, Yale U., 1984, Harvard U., 1994. Account exec. Altman & Manley, Boston, 1986-87; project coord. Joseph Wetzel & Assocs., Boston, 1988-89; prodn. project mgr. Clifford Selbert Design, Cambridge, Mass., 1989; asst. dir. career svcs. Harvard U., Cambridge, Mass., 1990-97; asst. dean of student life Princeton (N.J.) U., 1997—; cons. in field. Author: Harvard College Guide to Careers in Public Service, 2000; contbr. articles to profl. jours. Mem. adv. bd. Cambridge Cmty. Svcs., 1995-97, Shackleton Schs. Inc., Ashby, Mass., 1996—. Mem. Yale Club Princeton (cmty. svc. fellowship coord.). Avocations: arts education, house renovation, jazz. E-mail: andediaz@princeton.edu. Office: Dean of Student Life Princeton Univ 313 W Coll Princeton NJ 08544-0001

DIAZ, CAMERON, actress; b. Long Beach, Calif., Aug. 30, 1972. Grad. high sch., Long Beach, Calif. Appeared in (films) The Mask, 1994, Feeling Minnesota, 1996, She's the One, 1996, The Last Supper, 1996, Keys to Tulsa, 1996, Head Above Water, 1996, My Best Friend's Wedding, 1997 (Blockbuster Entertainment award), a Life Less Ordinary, 1997, (television) Space Ghost Coast to Coast, 1994, Very Bad Things, 1998, Fear and Loathing in Las Vegas, 1998, There's Something About Mary, 1998 (N.Y. Film Critics Cir. award, MTV Movie award, Am. Comedy award), Invisible

Circus, 1999, Being John Malkovich, 1999, Any Given Sunday, 1999, Charlie's Angels: The Movie, 2000, Things You Can Tell Just by Looking at Her, 2000, Gangs of New York, 2000. Named Female Star of Tomorrow, Nat. Theatre Owners Assn., 1996.

DÍAZ, CÉSAR RODOLFO, public health services officer; b. Santiago del Estero City, Argentina, Feb. 1, 1934; s. César de Jesús Díaz and María Anselma Cordero de Díaz; Beatriz Inés Miranda; children: Héctor Pablo, María Isabel, Ana Inés. Diploma, Sch. Polit. Conduction, 1957. Cert. pub. health expert, Argentina; cert. Grad. Sch. Nat. Def., 1986. V.p. Cath. Action Moron Diocese, 1952-57; counselor Nat. Cath. Students Youth, 1957-59; under-procurer Mcpl. Inst. Social Security, Buenos Aires, 1961-69; cabinet officer Sec. Labor Rels. Ministry Labor, Argentina, 1969-72; gen. sec. Govt. Civil Pers. Union of Buenos Aires Province, 1970-73; 2d nat. sec. Govt. Civil Pers. Union of Argentine Republic, 1971-73; joint gen. sec. Labor Gen. Confederacy of Argentine Republic, San Martin, 1972-74; head Nat. Svc. Patrimony Nat. Inst. Mental Health, 1972-82, head adminstrn., 1983-90; diocesan pres. Christianity Courses Secretariate of San Justo, 1980-84; nat. and provincial rep. Justicialist Party, 1983-87; sr. advisor to presidency of Justicialist Party Honorable Ho. of Reps. of Argentine Republic, 1983-87; asst. dir. Ctr. Ablation and Transplantations Ministry of Health, Argentina, 1987-89; cabinet officer State Sec. Health, Argentina, 1987-89; nat. dir. Mental Health Argentine Rep., 1990-94; nat. pres. Agrupación Juan Facundo Quiroga Nat. Justicialist Movement, 1988—; v.p., honor relator V Internat. Forum Health, Buenos Aires, 1988; pres. Found. Salud Sin Fronteras, 1998—. Recipient Great medal Latin Am. Confederacy of State Agents, 1971, Gold Lion of Valencia award Assn. Española Bioengring. Hospitalaria and Internat. Fedn. Hosp. Security, 1989. Mem. Assn. Cath. Action Profls., Opus Dei (founding mem.). Office: Ave Amancio Alcorta 1602, 1283 Buenos Aires Argentina

DIAZ, FERNANDO, internist; b. Eibar, Spain, Mar. 22, 1964; s. Francisco and Isabel (Alcazar) D.; m. Africa Gonzalez, June 14, 1992; one child. MD, U. Pais Vasco, 1988, PhD, 1996. Resident Hosp. Galdakao, Galdacano, Spain, 1990-94, attending physician, 1995—. Home: Arragueta #7 2 A, 20600 Eibar Spain

DIAZ, GERARDO, second language educator, translator; b. Mexico City, June 23, 1957; s. Ventura Ochoa and Enriqueta Diaz; m. Georgina Coate, Feb. 22, 1986; children: Valeria, Victoria, Diliana. Diploma in TESOL, U. London, 1993, MA in Edn., 1995. Music instr. U. Autonomous Aguascalientos, Mex., 1976-80, English instr., 1978-00, French instr., 1983-84, 2d lang. instr., 1999-00, head lang. dept., 1987-93; freelance translator, Aguascalientes, 1993-98. Editor MEXTESOL Jour., 1995—. Avocations: music, reading, tennis, jogging, swimming. Office: U Autonoma Aguascaleintes, Avenida Universidad 940, 20100 Aguascalientes Mexico

DIAZ, LOURDES MAGDAYAO, human resource professional; b. Sibalom, Philippines, Dec. 6, 1939; d. Eulogio and Presentacion (Magdayao) D. Cert. in elem. tchg., Centro Escolar U., 1964, BS in Edn., 1964; BS in Elem. Edn., 1968; MA in Edn., De La Salle U., 1973; PhD, Centro Escolar U., 1994. Prof. English, reading Centro Escolar Univ., Manila, Philippines, 1965—; head human resource dept. Centro Escolar Univ., 1989—; elem. tchr. Centro Escola Univ., 1964-70, media liaison officer, 1987-89, sec. to pres., 1972-79, head reading dept., 1979-89, head pers. dept., 1989—, retirement bd. trustees, 1989—, sec. consumers cooperative 1989-93, vice-chair for pers. consumers cooperative 1994; rec. sec. Mendiola Consortium, 1974-79; speed reading specialist SPEECHPOER, 1977—. Author: Developmental Reading: A Text for Teachers and Students of Reading Edn., 1986, Speed Reading and Comprehension Level Two, 1981, Speed Reading and Comprehension Level Three, 1979. Mem. dept. lab. and employment nat. capital region Tripartite Indsl. Peace Coun., 1998—, chair mgmt. group Manila, 2000—; bd. mem. Michael Rigs Svc. Coop.; asst. treas. Michael Riggs U. Belt Coop.; mem. quality assurance coun. Internat. Std. Orgn., Ctr. Escolar U. Mem. Internat. Reading Assn., Nat. Capital Region Union Cooperatives (bd. dirs., com. on leadership and unification, com. on bus. devel. and consultancy, mem. editl. bd. 1999—), Philippine Assn. Personnel Mgmt. in Pvt. Schs. (pres. 1997—), Reading Assn. Philippines (sec. 1986-90), Philippine Assn. Univ. Women (CEU chpt. sec. 1982-87), CEU Consumers Coop. (pres. 1997—). Roman Catholic. Home: 2024 Estanislao St, Parkview Homes Sunvalley, Paranaque Manila Philippines

DIAZ, LUIS CRUZ, management corporation president; b. Manilla, The Philippines, Aug. 25, 1922. B in Acctg., Far Ea. U., Manila, 1945; MS in Econs., Columbia U., N.Y.C., 1953; PhD in Fiscal Studies, Lyceum of the Philippines, Manila, 1998. CPA, the Philippines. Cons. Dept. Fin., Manila, The Philippines, 1995-96; servant leader Divine Mercy Cath. Charismatic Cmty., Manila, The Philippines, 1994—; pres. JDM Mgmt. and Consultancy Corp., Quezon City, The Philippines; chmn. emeritus Diaz Murillo Dalupan CPA's, Makati City, The Philippines; charter pres., founder Nat. Assn. Accts. (Philippines), 1972-73; internat. dir. Nat. Assn. Accts., 1974-76, chmn., First Asia Pacific Basin Zonal Conf., 1975; pres. Assn. CPAs in Pub. Practice, 1978; chmn. Auditing Standards and Practices Coun., Mandaluyong City, 1986-92. Mem. Philippine Inst. CPAs (hon. life), Philippine Assn. Mgmt. Accts. (non. life, pres. 1972-73), The Riviera Golf and Country Club. Roman Catholic. Avocation: painting. E-mail: luisdiaz@tri-isys.com. Home and Office: JDM Mgmt and Cons Corp, 5 Mabuhay St Ctrl Dist 1101, Quezon City The Philippines

DIAZ-BARRIOS, ANTONIO, researcher; b. Buenavista, Tenerife, Spain, June 30, 1947; s. Antonio Diaz and Fermina Barrios; m. Marisela Bravo; children: Marian, Juan, Patricia, Javier. Degree in chemistry, Univ. de Oriente, Cumaná, Venezuela, 1971; MSc in Polymer Sci., Inst. Venezolano de Investigacione Cientificas, Caracas, Venezuela, 1975; PhD, U.M.I.S.T., Manchester, Eng., 1979; cert. in broadcasting, Univ. Ctrl. Venezuela, Caracas, 1996. Tchr. U.D.O., Cumaná, 1971; assoc. rschr. IVIC, Caracas, 1979-84; tchr. U. Simon Bolivar, Caracas, 1980-84; postgrad. tchr. IVIC, Caracas, 1979-84, chem. specialist, 1983, sr. rschr., 1983—; polymer sect. head Intevep, 1989-94, sr. specialist, 1994—. Contbr. articles to profl. jours.; patentee in field. Grantee Anzoatebui State, 1960-65, U.D.O., 1967-70, Foninves, 1975-79, IVIC, 1972-75. Avocations: tennis, scuba diving, cycling, broadcasting, travel. E-mail: diazakk@pdvsa.com. Office: Intevep SA Dept Products, PO Box 76343, 1070-A Caracas Venezuela

DIAZ-FRANCO, CARLOS, surgeon, anatomist, anesthesiologist; b. Valparaiso, Chile, Nov. 9, 1956; came to U.S., 1985; s. Ismael Segundo and Aida Rosa (Franco-Huerta) Diaz-Labarca; m. Jennifer Ann Leepard, Mar. 31, 1989 (div. May 1993). MD, U. Valparaiso, Chile, 1981. Instr. anatomy Sch. of Medicine Univ. Valparaiso, Chile, 1982; surgery resident U. Valparaiso, Chile, 1982-85; asst. prof. anatomy, surgery Univ. Valparaiso, Chile, 1983-89; vis. prof. anatomy Med. Coll. of Ohio, Toledo, 1985-86, 88-89; surgeon, pvt. practice Valparaiso U. Hosp., Chile, 1986-89; surgery resident Sinai Hosp., Detroit, 1990-91, anesthesiology resident, 1991-94; with dept. anesthesia Cook County Hosp., Chgo., 1994—; asst. prof. anesthesiology Rush Med. Coll., Chgo. Contbr. articles to profl. jours. Grantee WHO, 1985-86, Ednl. Commn. for Foreign Med. Grads., 1988-89. Fellow AMA, Am. Soc. Anesthesiologists, Latin Am. Soc. Regional Anesthesia. Roman Catholic. Avocations: reading, writing, traveling, tennis, ice skating. Home: 419 W Grand Ave # J Chicago IL 60610-4265 Office: Cook Co Hosp Dept Anesthesia 1835 W Harrison St Dept Chicago IL 60612-3785

DIAZ-LLANOS, ANTONIO EZEQUIEL, central government agency; b. Tenerife, Spain, Sept. 1, 1940; s. Salvador Gonzalez and Carmen Diaz-Llanos; m. Marie Bernardine Schutte, Oct. 7, 1967; children: Camilo, Friso; m. Maria Victoria Longares, June 10, 1983; 1 child, Almudena. Bachelor's, San Ildefonso, Tenerife, 1956; grad., U. La Laguna, Spain, 1961, Brugges (Belgium) U., 1966; LLD, U. Madrid, Spain, 1969. Prof. U. Madrid, 1966-82; govt. ofcl. Spain, 1969—; attaché Denmark Embassy, Copenhagen, 1974-77, Swedish Embassy, Stockholm, 1982-86. Author: Portugal Crossroad, 1973; contbr. articles to profl. jours. Lt. Spanish Army, 1963-64. Recipient Danish Royal Ridder, Denmark, 1975. Avocations: traveling, documentary film. Home: Menorca 33, 28009 Madrid Spain Office: Embajadores 106, 28045 Madrid 5, Spain

DIAZ-VERSON, SALVADOR, JR., investment advisor; b. Havana, Cuba, Dec. 31, 1951; s. Salvador and Metodia Diaz-V.; m. Patricia Dianne Floyd, Apr. 24, 1976; children: Salvador III, Patricia Elizabeth. BA in Fin., Fla. State U., Tallahassee, 1973. Chief investment officer Am. Family Life Assurance, Columbus, Ga., 1977-79; exec. v.p. Am. Family Corp., Columbus, 1980-83, pres., 1983-91, also dir.; pres. Diaz-Verson Capital Investment, 1991—; bd. dirs. Regions Bank, Ga.; pres., CEO Diaz-Verson Capital Investment Inc., 1992. Trsutee St. Francis Hosp., Fund Am. Studies; bd. dirs. United Way, Columbus, 1983—. Mem. Columbus C. of C. (bd. dirs. 1983—, chair 1989), Green Island Country Club, Country Club of Columbus. Roman Catholic. Office: Diaz-Verson Capital Investment 260 Brookstone Centre Pkwy Columbus GA 31904-2974

DIAZ-ZUBIETA, AGUSTIN, nuclear engineer, engingeering executive; b. Madrid, Spain, Mar. 24, 1936; came to U.S., 1953; s. Emilio Diaz Cabeza and Maria Teresa Zubieta Atucha; m. Beth Lee Fortune, Sept. 6, 1958; children: Walter Agustin, Michael Joel, Anthony John. B, U. Madrid, 1953; BSc in Physics, U. Tenn., 1958; MSc in Mech. Engring., Duke U., 1960; PhD in Nuclear Engring., U. Md., 1981. Nuclear engr. Combustion Engring., Tenn., 1954-58; instr. engring. Duke U., Durham, N.C., 1958-60; nuclear physicist Allis Chalmers Co., Washington, 1960-64; country mgr. South Africa Allis Chalmers Co., 1964-66; mgr. internat. power generation projects GE, N.Y.C., 1966-69, mgr. Europe and Middle East strategic planning, 1969-71; dir. internat. constrn. planning GE, Westport, Conn., 1971-75, dir. constrn., 1975-83; CEO GE Affiliate, Westport, 1983-87; v.p. internat. sales, devel. Internat. Tech. Corp., L.A., 1987-94; mng. dir. IT Italia S.P.A., IT Spain, S.A. Author: Measurement of Subcriticality of Nuclear Reactors by Stocastic Processes, 1981. Pres. Fairfield (Conn.) Assn. Condo Owners, 1983-87. Named Astronomer of Yr. Barnard Astronomical Soc., Chattanooga, 1957; fgn. exchange scholar U.S. Govt., 1953-58; grantee, NSF, 1958-60, U.S. Office of Ordinance Rsch. U.S. Army, 1958-60. Mem. Am. Nuclear Soc., Am. Soc. Mech. Engrs., Am. Soc. Profl. Engrs., Sigma Xi. Republican. Roman Catholic. Avocations: golf, tennis, swimming, sailing, music. Home: 47 Country Meadow Rd Rllng Hls Est CA 90274-5774

DIB, ALBERT JAMES, lawyer; b. Detroit, Oct. 14, 1955; s. James Benjamin and Salma (Nacoud) D. BA, U. Mich., 1977; JD, Wayne State U., 1980; cert., U. Exeter, England, 1980. Bar: Mich. 1981, U.S. Dist. Ct. (ea. dist.) Mich. 1981, U.S. Ct. Appeals (6th cir.). Assoc. Lopatin, Miller, Detroit, 1981-87; ptnr. Dib and Fagan P.C., Detroit, 1987—; mediator Macomb County; moot ct. judge Detroit Coll. Law, 1984, U-D Gallagher, 1998, 99; instr. Cen. Mich. U., 1988. Vestryman Christ Episcopal Ch., Detroit, 1974-77. Recipient Cert. Achievement Mich. High Sch. Mock Trial Tournament, 1984. Mem. ABA, ATLA (cert. trial adovcacy 1984, instr. trial advocacy 1987 birth trauma litig. gp.), Mich. Trial Lawyers Assn. (sustaining, past exec. bd.), Detroit Bar Assn. (speakers bur. com. 1986, Negligence law com. 1986), Detroit Trial Lawyers Assn., Macomb Bar Assn. (spkr. 1984), Wayne County Mediator (med. malpractice panel), Anthony Wayne Soc., Wayne State U. Law Sch. Alumni Assn. (exec. com.). Office: Dib and Fagan PC 25892 Woodward Ave Royal Oak MI 48067-0910

DIBB, CAROLINE SALLY, management educator, consultant; b. Kidsgrove, Eng., June 10, 1963; d. Henry Ashton Russell Jones and Patricia Anne Taylor-Jones; m. Lyndon Pendlebury Simkin, Aug. 16, 1991; children: Miranda Mae, Abigail Cally, Rebecca Sarah, James Ashton. BSc in Mgmt. Sci., U. Manchester Inst. Sci & Tec., Eng., 1984, MSc in Rsch., 1985; PhD in Mktg., U. Warwick, Coventry, Eng., 1989. Lectr. mktg. U. Warwick, 1988-96, sr. lectr., 1996-99, reader, 1999—, assoc. dean undergrad. programs, 2000—; presenter in field; reviewer; cons.; sr. examiner Chartered Inst. Mktg., Eng., 1993-95; external examiner U. Kent, Eng., 1996—; program com. mem. EMAC, Belgium, 1995, 96, 97, 98. Author: Marketing Concepts and Strategies, 1991, 3d edit., 1997, The Marketing Casebook: Cases and Concepts, 1994, 2d edit., 2000, The Marketing Planning Workbook, 1996, The Market Segmentation Workbook, 1996; contbr. articles to profl. jours. Fellow Acad. Mktg. Sci.; mem. European Mktg. Acad., Acad. Mktg. Group. Avocations: travel, music, entertaining, art, swimming. Office: U Warwick, Warwick Bus Sch, Coventry CV4 7AL, England

DIBBLE, SUZANNE LOUISE, nurse, researcher; b. Pittsburg, Calif., June 3, 1947; d. Charles Stanley and Evelyn Virginia (Hansen) D.; m. Myron Bottsford Palmer III, June 12, 1971 (div. July 1974); life ptnr. Jeanne Flyntz DeJoseph, 1984. BSN, U. Del., 1969; MSN, U. Calif., San Francisco, 1971, D Nursing Sci., 1986. RN, Del., Calif. Staff nurse emergency room Stanford (Calif.) U. Hosp., 1969-71, rschr. dept. nursing rsch., 1986-88; instr. med. and surg. nursing Stanford U., 1971-72, renal transplant nurse coord., 1972-73, nurse rschr. dept. diagnostic radiology, 1987-88; staff, charge, head nurse, then supr. Children's Hosp.-Stanford U., 1973-86; mem. faculty stats. dept. U. Phoenix, San Jose, Calif., 1985-92; pres. Data Mgmt. Assocs., San Carlos, Calif., 1985—; investigator, project dir. U. Calif., 1988—; rsch. grant cons. NIH, Oakland, Calif., 1992-94, Loma Linda (Calif.) U., 1995—; co-dir. Ctr. for Lesbian Health, U. Calif. San Francisco; manuscript reviewer Oncology Nursing Forum, Pitts., 1993-96, Med.-Surg. Nursing, Pittmn, N.J., 1994—, Jour. of Gay & Lesbian Med. Assn. Editor: Culture and Nursing Care, 1996; contbr. articles to nursing jours. Chmn. task force, mem. NOW, Palo Alto, Calif., 1978—; mem., chmn. Maternal, Child and Adolescent Health Bd., San Mateo County, Calif., 1987-90; mem. strategic planning com. San Mateo County Health Bd., 1989-90. Rsch. grantee Nat. Cancer Inst., 1992-97, Nat. Inst. for Nursing Rsch., 1994-99. Mem. ANA, Assn. for Care Children's Health (numerous offices), Oncology Nursing Soc. (numerous offices), Am. Statis. Assn., Sigma Theta Tau (pres. Alpha Eta chpt.). Democrat. Office: U Calif Box 0646 Inst Health & Aging San Francisco CA 94143-0646

DIBENEDETTO, ROBERT LAWRENCE, obstetrician, gynecologist, insurance company executive; b. New Orleans, Apr. 14, 1928; s. Salvador and Eunice Madeline (Frisch) DiB.; m. Mary Nathalie Roeling, June 20, 1951; children: Madeline E., Robert R., Lawrence W. Student, Tulane U., 1945-47; BS, La. State U., 1948, MD, 1952. Diplomate Am. Bd. Ob-Gyn. Intern Mercy Hosp., New Orleans, 1952-53; resident in pathology La. State U. Med. Sch., 1955-56, assoc. clin. prof. ob-gyn., 1963; resident ob-gyn. Charity Hosp., New Orleans, 1956-59; practice medicine specializing in ob-gyn. Baton Rouge, 1959—, pres., CEO, 1994—; ret.; v.p. investment and audit La. Med. Mut. Ins. Co., New Orleans, 1981-97; founding chmn. Mid-La. Health Systems Agy., 1976-77; chmn. bd. dirs., med. dir. Woman's Hosp., Baton Rouge; pres. Capitol Area Health Planning, 1975-76; mem. Perinatal Commn. of La., Bd. Health, Edn. Authority of La., State Health Coordinating Council. Served with USPHS, 1953-55. Mem. AMA (past del.), ACOG (past chmn. La. sect.), South Ctrl. Ob-Gyn. Soc., La. Med. Soc. (co-chmn. polit. action com., past pres.), East Baton Rouge Parish Med. Soc. (past pres.), City Club (Baton Rouge), So. Yacht Club (New Orleans), Baton Rouge Country Club. Republican. Roman Catholic. Home: 6666 Pikes Ln Baton Rouge LA 70808-4272

DI BERARDINO, ANGELO, religious organization administrator; b. Furci, Italy, Oct. 10, 1936. ThD, Facoltà San Luigi, Naples, Italy; PhD, U. La Sapienza. Ordained Roman Catholic priest, 1962. Pres. Internat. Assn. Patristic Studies; dean of faculty Istituto Augustinian, Rome. Mem. German Acad. Scis. Fax: 06-68006298. Office: Istituto Augustinian, Via Paolo VI 25, 00193 Rome Italy

DIBIAGGIO, JOHN A., university president; b. San Antonio, Sept. 11, 1932; s. Ciro and Acidalia DiBiaggio; children from previous marriage: David John, Dana Elizabeth, Deirdre Joan; m. Nancy Cronemiller, May 27, 1989. AB, Eastern Mich. U., 1954, D of Edn. (hon.), 1985; DDS, U. Detroit, 1958, LHD (hon.), 1985; MA, U. Mich., 1967; DSci. (hon.), Fairleigh Dickinson U., 1981; LLD (hon.), Sacred Heart U., Bridgeport, Conn., 1984, U. Md., 1985; DHL (hon.), U. New Eng., 1987, Tokyo U. Agr., 1991; LLD (hon.), U. Nigeria, Nsukka, 1992; LHD (hon.), Fitchburg State Coll., 1994, Amer. Coll. of Greece, 1998. Gen. practice dentistry New Baltimore, Mich., 1958-65; asst. prof., asst. to dean, dept. chmn. sch. dentistry U. Detroit, 1965-67; asst. dean student affairs U. Ky., Lexington, 1967-70; prof., dean sch. dentistry Va. Commonwealth U., Richmond, 1970-76; v.p. for health affairs, exec. dir. health ctr. U. Conn., Farmington, 1976-79; pres. U. Conn., Storrs, 1979-85, Mich. State U., East Lansing, 1985-92, Tufts U., Medford, Mass., 1992—; bd. dirs. Kaman Corp.; mem. Knight Found. Commn. on Intercollegiate Athletics, 1990—, PEW Health Professions Commn., 1990-93;. Author: (with others) Applied Practice Management: A Strategy for Stress Control, 1979; cons. jour. ADA, 1967—; contbr. articles to profl. jours. Chmn. adv. com. dental scholars R.W. Johnson Found.; mem. Pres. Com. for Argonne Nat. Lab. 6, 1986—; trustee U. Detroit, 1979-86, Am. Film Inst., 1988—, Forsyth Dental Ctr., 1993—; trustee Am. Cancer Soc. Found., 1993—, pres. 1999; trustee Oral Health Am., 1995-97; mem. bd. nominators Am. Inst. Pub. Svc., 1989-92; mem. coun. pres. Univs. Rsch. Assn., 1989-92; bd. dirs. Coun. for Aid to Edn., 1994-96, Mass. Nat. and Comty. Svc. Commn., 1994-97, Am. Coun. on Edn., 1995—, vice chmn., 1998, chmn., 1999, bd. dirs. Black Child and Family Inst., 1990, Mass. Campus Compact Exec. Com., 1995—, mem., exec. dir. search com., 1996, chair devel. com., 1996—, mem. governance com., 1996-98, chmn., 1998; mem. bd. assocs. Whitehead Inst. for Biomed. Rsch., 1995—, chmn., 1998; mem. Bus. Higher Edn. Forum, 1996—, WGBH Ednl. Found., 1992—, chmn. governance com., 1997—. Decorated Order of Merit, Italy; recipient Leadership award Sacred Heart U., Disting. Profl. of Yr. award Mich. Assn. Profls., 1985, Disting. Alumni award Eastern Mich. U., 1986; named Man of Yr., City of Detroit, 1985, Pierre Fauchard Gold Medal award, 1989. Fellow Am. Coll. Dentist, Internat. Coll. Dentists; mem. ADA (cons. jour.), APHA, Am. Assn. Dental Schs., Internat. Assn. Dental Rsch., Nat. Assn. State Univs. and Land Grant Colls. (chmn. 1986-87), NCAA Found. (bd. dirs. 1988—, mem. divsn. III pres.'s coun. 1997—), Am. Automobile Assn. (bd. dirs. 1994—), Am. Film Inst., Mass. Automobile Assn. (bd. dirs. 1992—), Nat. Italian Am. Found. (bd. dirs. 1988-94), Golden Key, Phi Kappa Phi, Omicron Kappa Upsilon, Beta Gamma Sigma, Alpha Omega Alpha (Achievement award 1993), Alpha Sigma Chi, Alpha Lambda Delta. Avocations: tennis, skiing, Packards. Office: Tufts U Office of Pres Medford MA 02155*

DIBLASI, DIANNE CLARK, editor; b. Bklyn., May 3, 1960; d. Arthur J. and Constance C. (Clark) Mandick; m. Paul J. DiBlasi; 1 child, Bryan Gene. BA in Journalism, NYU, 1982. Asst. editor Random House/Fodor's Travel Guides, N.Y.C., 1983-85; writer, editor Constrn. Products Rev. Mag., Boston, 1986-88; prodn. editor Prentice Hall, Englewood Cliffs, N.J., 1988-91; owner, cons. D. DiBlasi Editl. Svcs., Hillsdale, N.J., 1991—. Copy editor: Take My Word For It, 1986; prodn. editor: Creativities! Elementary Curriculum Art Activities, 1991, Parenting Toward Solutions, 1997; editor, writer Constrn. Products Rev., 1986-88. Mem. Hillsdale Playground Assn., 1994-96, Hillsdale Centennial Com., 1996; mem., chair com. Meadowbrook Faculty and Family Assn., Hillsdale, 1996—; host Fresh Air Fund, 1997—; docent Wildlife Conservation Soc., Bronx Zoo. Mem. Editl. Freelancer Assn. Avocations: cooking contests, fundraising. Home and Office: 189 Everdell Ave Hillsdale NJ 07642-1922

DIBLEY, KATHLEEN, journalist, public relations consultant; b. Surrey, Eng., Jan. 26, 1930; d. George Edward and Stella Winifred Agnes (Dwyer) D. Journalist Feature Svcs., London, 1953-57; promotor Wedgwood, London, 1957-60; dir. pub. rels. William Whitely, London, 1960-65; pub. rels. dir. Osborne, London, 1965-70, Sanderson, London, 1970-75; owner Editl. & Pub. Rels., 1976—. Contbr. articles to profl. jours.; editor Polio Bul. Trustee New Horizions Trust, London, 1986—, Abraham & Sarah Found., London, 1989—. Fellow Chartered Inst. Journalists; mem. Inst. Pub. Rels., Soc. Industrial Designers. Anglican. Avocations: music, art, painting, theatre. Home and Office: 126 Radnor Ave, Kent Bexleyheath DA162B4, England

DIBO, GABOR, chemist; b. Budapest, Jan. 8, 1953; s. Ferenc and Erzsebet (Krizmanits) D.; m. Maria Laton, June 21, 1977; children: Szilvia, Eszter. BS, Eotvos U., 1975, MS, 1977, PhD, 1982; candidate chem. sci., Hungarian Acad. Scis., 1993. Rsch. fellow Eotvos U., Budapest, 1977-80, instr., 1987-89, asst. prof., 1990-98, assoc. prof., 1998—; rsch. assoc. Hungarian Acad. Scis., Budapest, 1980-85; vis. scientist City of Hope Nat. Med. Ctr., Duarte, Calif., 1989-90; postdoctoral Osaka U., Japan, 1985-87, vis. prof., 1996. Contbr. articles to profl. jours. Sec. Hungarian-Japanese Friendship Soc., Budapest, 1988-93. Mem. Protein Soc., European Peptide Soc., Am. Peptide Soc., Japanese Peptide Soc. Avocations: soccer, tennis, gardening, music, travel. Office: Eotvos U Dept Organic Chemistry, PO Box 32, H-1518 Budapest Hungary

DIBUNDA KABUINJI, CRISPIN-MEDARD, presidents commissioner; b. Dibaya, Kasai, Aug. 9, 1937; s. Joseph Mulowa Bataillon and Helene Kamuanya D.; m. Antoinette Ntuba Bitupa, Oct. 10, 1962; children: Mulowa, Kabebi, Tshiebwe, Kamuanya, Mutombo, Kabasu Kayembe. Baccalaureat philo et leppres, U. Lovanium, 1963, lic. droit, 1966, diploma d'Etudes Specials de Droit Prive, 1969. Magistrat titre provisoire ETAT, Kinshasa, Congo, 1968; substitute procureur republique Parquet Dist., Kinshasa, 1970; conseiller Cour D'appel, Kisangani, 1970-73; pres. Cour D'appel, Lubumbashi, 1973-76; counseiller Cour Supreme de Justice, Kinshasha, 1976-96, pres., 1996-98, pres. emeritus, 1998—. Author: Langage et Technique de La Cour Supreme Be Justice en Cassation, 1979, Repertoire General de Jurisprudence De la Cour Supreme de Justice, 1990, Procedure devant la Section Adminstrative de la Cour Supreme de Justice, 1989; contbr. articles to profl. jours. Prof. Enseignement Kimbanguiste/Svc. Civique Oligatore, 1966-67, Centre de Formation Person. Jud., 1968-89, Ecole Nat. de Finances, 1980-84. Mem. Soc. Etudes Juridiques de Congo (pres. 1974—), Assn. Nat. d'Aide à la Lutte contre l'Exode Rural, 1980 (sec. gen.), l'Ordre National du Léopard (officer 1978). Roman Catholic. Avocation: football. Home: Rue Limete I no 1, Kinshasa Masina Republic Dem Congo Office: Editions Connaissance et, Pratique du Droit Congolais, Bp 5502 Kinshasa Gombe Republic of Congo

DI CASTRI, FRANCESCO, research scientist, educator; b. Noale, Venice, Italy, Aug. 4, 1930; s. Luigi and Irma (Liviero) di C.; m. Valeria Vitali, July 23, 1960; children: Alberto Paolo, Roberta Claudia. BA, Monza U., Italy, 1947; Master in Animal Prodn., U. Santiago, Chile, 1957, DVM, 1958; PhD (hon.), U. Kuopio, Finland, 1982. Prof. U. Chile, Santiago, 1961-69; dir. Austral U., Valdivia, Chile, 1969-71; dir. divsn. UNESCO, Paris, 1971-84; dir. Inst. Nat. Ctr. Sci. Rsch., Montpellier, France, 1984-90; asst. dir. gen. UNESCO, 1990-92, dir. rsch., 1993—; dir. rsch. CNRS; pres. Sci. Com. on Problems of Environment, Paris, 1988-92, Internat. Union of Biol. Scis., Paris, 1991-94, French Inst. of Environment, Paris, 1992-94, Internat. Soc. Mediterranean Ecologists, Montpellier, 1987-91. Author: Mediterranean-type Ecosystems, 1973, Bioclimatologia de Chile, 1976, Mediterranean-type Shrublands, 1981, Ecology in Practice, 1984, Time Scale and Water Stress, 1988, Biological Invasions: a Global Perspective, 1989, Biological Invasions in Europe, 1990, Biogeography of Mediterranean Invasions, 1991, Landscape Boundaries, 1992, Global Land Use Change, 1995, Time Scales of Biological Responses, 1995, Biodiversity: Science and Development, 1996, Environment in a Global Information Society, 1998; contbr. more than 700 articles to sci. jours. Recipient Academician award Acad. Agr., Paris, 1982, Acad. Scis., Moscow, 1994, Acad. Scis., Rome, 1996; decorated commander of Italian Republic, 1998. Avocations: cinematography, photography, history of Italy and Chile. Home: 49 Allee du Pic St Loup, 34980 Saint Clement de Riviere France Office: CEFE CNRS, 1919 Route de Mende BP 5051, 34033 Montpellier France*

DI CATALDO, ANDREA, pediatric oncologist, researcher; b. Catania, Sicily, Italy, Mar. 12, 1965; s. Filippo and Rosa (Magnano San Lio) DiC.; m. Daniela Pittala, Oct. 1, 1994; 1 child, Francesco. MD, U. Catania, Italy, 1989, postgrad. in pediatrics, 1993. Tng Gustave Roussy Inst., Paris, 1988-89; asst. divsn. pediatric hematology/oncology U. Catania, 1989-97, 2d dir. divsn. pediatric hematology/oncology, 1997—; asst. Gaslini Inst., Genoa, Italy, 1993. Contbr. articles to profl. jours. Mem. Internat. Soc. Pediatric Oncology. Roman Catholic. Avocations: soccer, music, reading, puzzles. Home: Via Passo Gravina 201, 95125 Catania Sicily Italy Office: Divsn Pediatric Hemat/Oncol, Via Santa Sofia 78, 95125 Catania Sicily Italy

DI CHIERA, DAVID, performing arts company executive; b. McKeesport, Pa., Apr. 8, 1935; s. Cosimo and Maria (Pezzaniti) DiC.; m. Karen VanderKloot, July 20, 1965 (div. 1992); children: Lisa Maria, Cristina Maria. BA in Music summa cum laude, UCLA, 1956, MA in Composition (scholar), 1958, PhD in Musicology, 1962; certificate in composition and piano (Fulbright Research grantee), Naples Conservatory of Music, 1959; D (hon.), U. Mich., 1998. Instr. music U. Calif., Los Angeles, 1960-61; asst. prof. music, asst. dean Oakland U., Rochester, Mich., 1962-65; chmn. music dept. Oakland U., 1966-73; founding gen. dir. Mich. Opera Theatre, Detroit, 1971—; founding dir. Music Hall Center for the Performing Arts, Detroit, 1973—, Opera Pacific, Calif., 1986-96; artistic dir. Dayton Opera Assn.,

1981-92; founding gen. dir. Opera Pacific, Costa Mesa, Calif., 1985-97; trustee Nat. Opera Inst.; adj. prof. Oakland U., Wayne State U. Producer, dir.: Overture to Opera series for, Detroit Grand Opera series, 1963-71; Composer various works for piano, violin, orch., voice; author articles on Italian opera for various encyclopedias; contbr. revs. and articles to music jours. Mem. Arts Com. New Detroit, Inc.; trustee, mem. exec. com. Music Center for Performing Arts; mem. Arts Task Force City of Detroit. Recipient Atwater Kent award U. Calif., Los Angeles, 1961; Certificate of Appreciation City of Detroit, 1970; citation Mich. Legislature, 1976; Michaelangelo award Boys' Town of Italy, 1980; award Arts Found. of Mich., 1981; President's Cabinet award U. Detroit, 1982; George Gershwin fellow, 1958; named A Michiganian of Yr., 1980; cavaliere della Repubblica Italiana. Mem. Am. Arts Alliance (exec. com.), Nat. Opera Assn., Internat. Assn. Lyric Theatre (v.p.), Am. Symphony League, Am. Musicol. Soc., OPERA Am. (pres. 1979-83), AAUP, Phi Beta Kappa, Phi Mu Alpha Sinfonia. Club: Detroit Athletic. Office: Mich Opera Theatre 1526 Broadway St Detroit MI 48226-2115

DICK, HANS BURKHARD, ophthalmologist; b. Brake, Germany, Sept. 21, 1963; s. Herwarth and Nora (Feus) D. MD, Justus-Liebig U., Giessen, Germany, 1993. Doctor dept. ophthalmology Justus-Liebig U., Giessen, 1991-93, clin. rschr., 1993-96; ophthalmologist Johannes-Gutenberg U., Mainz, Germany, 1996—, clin. prof., 1999. Author: Viscoelastic Substances in Ophthalmic Surgery, 1998. With Germany Army , 1983-85. Mem. European Soc. Cataract and Refractive Surgery, Am. Soc. Cataract and Refractive Surgery, Assn. Rsch. in Vision and Ophthalmology. : Wilhelm-Holzamer Str 9, 55129 Mainz Germany Office: Johannes Gutenberg U, Langenbeckstr Dept Ophthal, 55131 Mainz Germany

DICK, NEIL ALAN, architecture executive; b. Cleve., June 15, 1941; s. Harvey L. and Rose (Flom) D.; BArch, Ohio State U., 1965; MB, Cleve. State U., 1966: m. Bonnie M. Natarus, Sept. 3, 1967; 1 child, Rory D. Exec. v.p. J.R. Hyde & Assos., Pitts., 1967-70; dir. tech. and market devel. Stirling Homex Corp., Avon, N.Y., 1970-72; sr. housing coord. Nat. Housing Corp., Cleve., 1972-74; fin. and estate analyst Conn. Gen. Corp., Cleve., 1974-76; sr. v.p., dir. mktg. Cannon Design Inc., Grand Island, N.Y., 1976-82, also dir.; exec. v.p. Greiner, Inc. (formerly Daverman, Inc.), subs. Greiner Engring. Inc., Grand Rapids, Mich., 1983-88; v.p., group gen. mgr. Foth & Van Dyke, divsn. G.M., Green Bay, Wis., 1988-91; v.p., dir archtl. and engring. ops. URS Cons., Inc., Cleve., 1991-93; dir. devel. Cuhza, Inc., Princeton, N.J., 1993-97; prin. DickGroup Cons., Cleve., 1997—; bd. dirs. U. Wis., Green Bay, West Mich. Telecommunications Found., AIDS Found. Kent County; bd. dirs., trustee Celve. Sight Ctr., Grand Rapids C. of C. Found., Amherst (N.Y.) Dem. Com.; trustee Kendall Coll. Art & Design, Grand Rapids Art Mus., Neville Pub. Mus.; zone chmn., county fin. chmn., mem. exec. com. Erie County Dem. Com.; mem. Mich. Dem. State Com.; treas. Mich. 5th Congl. Dist. Dem. Com. Recipient Svc. award Erie County Dem. Com., 1979. Mem. Am. Soc. Healthcare Engrs., Soc. Am. Military Engrs., Soc. Mktg. Profl. Svcs. (regional coord.), Buffalo Area C. of C., Green Bay C. of C. (chair planning taskforce), Am. Hosp. Assn., Nat. Trust Hist. Preservation, Ohio State U. Alumni Assn., Mich. C. of C., Buffalo Mus. Sci., Albright Knox Art Gallery, Rotary, Alpha Rho Chi. Jewish. Clubs: Economic, Peninsular, Cascade Hills. Office: DickGroup 2928 Kingsley Rd Shaker Heights OH 44122

DICK, WOLFGANG RUDOLF, scientist; b. Greiz, Germany, Feb. 5, 1959; s. Rudolf and Christine (Vorwieger) D.; m. Galina Solodovchenko, Aug. 26, 1978; 1 child, Anton. Diploma in Physics, Kharkov (Ukraine) State U., 1982; D in Natural Scis., Acad. Scis. of GDR, Berlin, 1989. Scientist Zentralinstitut fuer Astrophysik, Potsdam, Germany, 1982-91, Sternwarte der Universitaet Bonn, Bonn, Germany, 1991-92, Bundesamt fur Kartographie u. Geodaesie, Potsdam, Germany, 1992—. editor: Mitteilungen zur Astronomiegeschichte, 1992—, Electronic Newsletter for the History of Astronomy, 1994—; co-editor: Acta Historica Astronomiae, 1998—. Sec. Working Group for the History of Astronomy in the Astronomische Gesellschaft, 1992—; mem. organizing com. Internat. Astron. Union, Commn. 41, 1997—. E-mail: wdi@potsdam.ifag.de. Home: Otterkiez 14, 14478 Potsdam Germany

DICKENS, E(NOCH) DANA, III, insurance company executive, mayor; b. Oct. 29, 1946; s. Enoch Dana and Mary Edwards Dickens; m. Linda Kay Rankin, Apr. 19, 1972. BA in History, N.C. Weslyan Coll., 1969. Tchr., coach Portsmouth (Va.) Pub. Schs., 1969-71; salary adminstr., emplyee benefist adminstr. Norland Co., Newport News, Va., 1971-73; employee benefist adminstr. Norfolk (Va.) Redevelopment & Housing Authority, 1973-74; v.p. G.F. Walls Agy., Isle of Wight, Va., 1974-85; pres. 1st Svc. Ins., Inc., Suffolk, Va., 1985—. Mayor City of Suffolk; mem. City Coun.; vice chmn., chmn. ordinance com. Planning Commn.; mem. Ins. Adv. Commn., Va.; bd. dirs. ARC. Mem. Rotary (pres., v.p., sec., treas.), Crittenden, Eclipse & Hobson Ruritan Club (pres., v.p., sec.). Methodist. Home: 9212 Wigneil St Suffolk VA 23433-1529 Office: 1st Svc Ins 2973 Bridge Rd Suffolk VA 23435-1713

DICKERMAN, ROBERT N., energy company executive; b. Boston, Sept. 29, 1955; s. Kenneth Lawrence and Lola (Glazerman) D.; m. Maira Esther Gutierrez, Jan. 1, 1959; children: David, Andres, Samuel, Sarah. BA in math., Union Coll., 1978; MBA, Univ. Chgo., 1980. Oil products trader Arco Products, L.A., 1980-84; wholesale mkt. mgr. Apex Oil Co., Balt., 1984-91; sales mgr. Louis Dreyfus Energy, Atlanta, 1991-92; pres. Dickerman Energy Cons., Atlanta, 1992-95; dir. commodity risk mgmt. Price Waterhouse, Houston, 1995-97; prin. Metzler & Assocs., Chgo., 1997; sr. v.p. Edison Source, L.A., 1997—. Recipient scholar award British-Am. Ednl. Found., London, 1973. Mem. Western Power Trading Forum, Western Systems Coord. Coun. Republican. Home: 101 Sutter Crk Monrovia CA 91016-1661 Office: Edison Source 955 Overland Ct San Dimas CA 91773-1718

DICKERSIN, KAY, researcher, educator; b. Phila., Nov. 10, 1951; d. George Richard and Barbara (Bray) D.; m. Robert Alan Van Wesep, June 30, 1973; children: Isaac, Edward. BA in Zoology, U. Calif., Berkeley, 1974, MA in Zoology, 1975; PhD in Epidemiology, Johns Hopkins U., 1989. Lectr. dept. epidemiology, faculty Ctr. for Clinical Trials, Johns Hopkins U., Balt., 1991—; asst. prof. U. Md. Sch. Medicine, Balt., 1989-96, assoc. prof., 1996-98, adj. assoc. prof., 1998—; assoc. prof. Brown U. Sch. Medicine, Providence, 1998—; dir. Balt. Cochrane Ctr., 1993-98; co-dir. New Eng. Cochrane Ctr., Providence, 1998—; bd. dirs. Nat. Cancer Adv. Bd. Recipient Ellen Barnett Meml. award Susan B. Komen Found. Race for the Cure, 1995; named to Women's Hall of Fame, Balt. City Commn. for Women, 1996; named one of Md.'s Top 100 Women, Md. Daily, 1998. Mem. Am. Epidemiol. Soc., Soc. for Clinical Trials. E-mail: kay dickersin@brown.edu. Fax: 401-863-9944. Home: 625 Angell St Providence RI 02906-5553 Office: New Eng Cochrane Brown Univ PO Box Gs2 Providence RI 02912-0001

DICKES, ROBERT, psychiatrist; b. N.Y.C., Apr. 15, 1912; s. Benjamin and Anna (Adler) D.; m. Bernice Livingston, June 12, 1938; children: Richard A., Susan R. Dickes Hubbard. B.S., CCNY, 1933; M.S., Emory U., 1934, M.D., 1938. Diplomate: Am. Bd. Internal Medicine, Am. Bd. Psychiatry and Neurology. Intern L.I. Coll. Hosp., Bklyn., 1938-39; asst. resident in internal medicine L.I. Coll. Hosp., 1938-39, resident in medicine, 1939-41, dir. med. clinics, 1946-50; asso. in medicine L.I. Coll. Medicine, 1946, asst. prof. psychiatry, 1949; fellow in medicine Western Res. U.-Lakeside Hosp., 1941-42; fellow in psychiatry Kings County Hosp. Center-SUNY Bklyn., 1950-52, mem. staff, 1952—, pres. med. br., 1977-78; clin. assoc. prof. psychiatry Downstate Med. Center SUNY, Bklyn., 1950-54, assoc. prof., 1954-56, clin. assoc. prof., 1956-61, assoc. prof., 1961-63, prof., 1963, 78-82, prof. emeritus, 1982—, tng. and supervising analyst, 1965—, acting chmn. dept. psychiatry, 1965-66, 71-72, dir. infant behavior study lab., 1973, dir. center human sexuality, 1973—, chmn. dept. psychiatry, 1975-78; clin. prof. psychiatry NYU Coll. Medicine, 1982—; cons. VA hosps., Bklyn., Northport, N.Y.; v.p. Am. Bd. Sexology, 1989—. Contbr. articles to profl. publs. Bd. govs., mem. acquisitions com. Bklyn. Museum. Maj. M.C. U.S. Army, 1942-46. Commonwealth fellow, 1941-42, 48-49. Fellow A.C.P., Am. Psychiat. Assn., Am. Coll. Psychiatry; mem. Am. Psychoanalytic Assn., Psychoanalytic Assn. N.Y. (treas. 1962-64), Bklyn. Psychiat. Soc. (pres. 1967), Kings County Med. Soc., Kings County Psychiat. Soc. (pres. 1967-68), Soc. Sex Therapy and Research (pres. 1979-81), Am. Bd. Sexology (v.p. 1989—).

DICKEY, JOHN SLOAN, JR., science association director; b. Washington, Jan. 24, 1941; s. John Sloan Sr. and Christina Margaret (Gillespie) D.; m. Joan Elizabeth Cass, Dec. 28, 1963 (div. 1977); 1 child, Nathaniel Hudson; m. Lynn McMath, June 6, 1978. BA, Dartmouth Coll., 1963; MS, Otago U., Dunedin, N.Z., 1966; PhD, Princeton (N.J.) U., 1969. Field geologist Brit. Newfoundland Exploration, Springdale, 1963; rsch. assoc. Smithsonian Astrophys. Obs., Cambridge, Mass., 1969-70; rsch. assoc. coll. obs. Harvard U., Cambridge, Mass., 1969-70, Carnegie Inst. of Washington, 1970-72; asst. prof. MIT, Cambridge, 1972-76, assoc. prof., 1976-79; program dir. geochemistry dept. NSF, Washington, 1979-81; prof. geology, head geology dept. Syracuse (N.Y.) U., 1981-88; dean sci., math. and engring. depts. Trinity U., San Antonio, 1988-98; dir. outreach and rsch. support Am. Geophys. Union, Washington, 1998—; pres. Centaur Geol. Svcs. Inc., Boston, 1978-82. Author: (textbook) Lectures in Earth and Planetary Science, 1987, On the Rocks, 1996. Fulbright fellow N.Z., 1964-65. Fellow Mineral. Soc. Am.; mem. AAAS, Geochem. Soc. (treas. 1987-93), Am. Geophys. Union, Geol. Soc. Washington, Internat. Assn. Cosmology and Geochemistry, Lawrence Durrell Soc. Home: 1401 33d St NW Washington DC 20007 Office: Am Geophys Union 2000 Florida Ave NW Washington DC 20009-1231

DICKEY, JOSEPH WILLIAM, utility executive, engineer; b. Decatur, Ill., Sept. 20, 1944; s. Lawrence Wayne and Helen Marie (Van Horn) D. BS in Chem. Engring., MIT, 1966, MS in Civil Engring., 1967; postgrad., U. Va., 1978. Registered profl. engr., Tenn., Fla. Plant mgr. Fla. Power & Light Co., Miami, 1973-76, mgmt. positions in nuclear energy and power resources, 1976-85, v.p. nuclear energy and nuclear ops., 1985-88, v.p. power resources, 1988-91; sr. v.p. fossil and hydro power TVA, Chattanooga, 1991-94; chief operating officer TVA, Knoxville, 1994-98; pres., CEO FGS & Assocs. LLC, 1999—; mem. subcom., chmn., officer EEI Prime Movers Com., Washington, 1980-85; mem. subcom., officer S.E. Electric Exch., Atlanta, 1988-91; speaker in field. Contbr. numerous articles to jours. and trade mags. Chmn. for Broward County MIT Ednl. Coun., 1978-91; bd. govs. Dept. Energy Robotics Program, 1987-88; mem. industry adv. coun. U. Fla. Coll. Engring., Gainesville, 1987-91; trustee, chmn. FPL Polit. Action Com., 1981-85, 83-84. Recipient Ishikawa medal Am. Soc. Quality Control, 1996. Fellow Fla. Engring. Soc.; mem. NSPE, ASCE (br. pres. 1974-75).

DICKEY, WILLIAM, gasteroenterologist; b. Ballymena, Northern Ireland, Apr. 2, 1959. BSc with honors, Queen's U., Belfast, 1980, MB, BCh, BAO, 1983, MD, 1990; European diploma of Gastroenterology, 1997. Intern, resident Royal Victoria Hosp., Belfast, 1983-86, rsch. fellow in cardiology, 1987-88; sr. registrar, tutor Queen's U., 1991-94; fellow in advanced endoscopy Acad. Med. Ctr., Amsterdam, 1994; pvt. practice Altnagelvin Hosp., Londonderry, No. Ireland, 1995—; hon. clin. lectr. Queen's U., Belfast, 2000—. Contbr. articles and revs. to profl. jours. on celiac disease and endoscopy. Fellow Royal Coll. Physicians Edinburgh, Royal Coll. Physicians London, Am. Coll. Gastroenterology; mem. Brit. Soc. Gastroenterology, Irish Soc. Gastroenterology, Am. Soc. Gastrointestinal Endoscopy. Office: Altnagelvin Hosp, Londonderry BT47 6SB, Northern Ireland

DICKINSON, ANTHONY RUSSELL, science educator; b. Bournemouth, Eng., Feb. 22, 1960; s. Leonard Stanley and Eileen Mary (Garrod) D.; m. W.Y. Dickinson, Dec. 9, 1994; 1 child, Emily Sarah Louise. BSc with honors, U. Sussex, Eng., 1987; DipNeurosci, U. Edinburgh, Scotland, 1988, PhD, 1996. Elec. test engr. Kentucky Organs, Dorset, Eng., 1977-79, Plessey & Co., Dorset, 1979-80; rsch. asst. Paraphysical Labs., Downton Wilts, Eng., 1980-85; ednl. cons. Brighton Aquarium, Eng., 1985-87; demonstrator U. Edinburgh, Scotland, 1988-91, lectr., 1992-99; vis. rsch. fellow Washington U., St. Louis, 1999—. Contbr. articles to profl. jours. Ho. warden Edinburgh U. Halls, 1990-99; residential advisor U. Sussex, 1985-87. Hon. rsch. fellow Edinburgh Vet. Sch., 1987-89. Mem. AAAS, British Psychol. Soc., British Planetary Soc., British Primatological Soc., Royal Zool. Soc. Scotland, Internat. Soc. Primatologists, N.Y. Acad. Scis. Achievements include development and characterization of intelligent systems both real and artificial; developer and inventor of 4 way implantable brain cannulae for surgical use. Home: Pollock Halls, 18 Holyrood Pk Rd, Edinburgh EH18 5AZ, Scotland

DICKINSON, GAIL KREPPS, educator; b. Lewistown, Pa., June 10, 1956; d. Harold and Esther (Bourdess) Krepps; m. Willis H. Dickinson, Dec. 22, 1979 (div. 1998); children: Margaret Lee, Elizabeth Ann. BS, Millersville U. Pa., 1977; MSLS, U. N.C., 1987; postgrad., U. Va., 1996—. Libr. Cape Charles (Va.) Pub. Sch., 1977-81, Broadwater Acad., Exmore, Va., 1981-85; instrnl. supervisor Union-Endicott Sch. Dist., Endicott, N.Y., 1987-96; asst. prof. U. N.C., Greensboro, 2000—; adj. prof. James Madison U., Harrisonburg, Va., 1997—. Mem. AAUW, ASCD, Am. Ednl. Rsch. Assn., Am. Assn. Sch. Librs. (bd. dirs. 1994-97), N.Y. Libr. Assn. (pres. sch. libr. media sect. 1994), Phi Delta Kappa. Avocations: reading, word and video games.

DICKINSON, JANE W., social services administrator; b. Sept. 27, 1919; d. Charles Herman and Rachel (Whaler) Wagner; m. E. F. Sherwood Dickinson, Oct. 23, 1943; children: Diane Jane Gray Clem, Carolyn Dickinson Vane. BA, Duke U., 1941; MEd, Goucher Coll., 1965. Exec. sec. Petroleum Industry Com., Balt., 1941-43, Sherwood Feed Mills Inc., Balt., 1943-79. Mem. exec. com. Children's Aid Md., 1960-61; mem. bd. women's aux. Balt. Symphony Orch., 1958-60; dist. chmn. Balt. Cancer Drive, 1957; co-chmn. Balt. United Appeal, 1968; bd. mgrs. Pickersgill Retirement Home. Mem. Three Arts Club (Balt., sec. 1958-60, bd. govs. 1960-64, 67-70, pres. 1970-72), Women's Club of Roland Park (bd. govs. 1960-64, 86-88, 92-94), Cliff Dwellers Garden Club, Alpha Delta Phi. Home: Apt 609 1055 W Joppa Rd Baltimore MD 21204-3748

DICKINSON, JOHN PHILIP, academic manager; b. Morecambe, England, Apr. 29, 1945; s. George Snowden and Evelyn (Stobbart) D.; m. Christine Houghton, Feb. 17, 1968; children: Rachel Louise, Vanessa Sarah, Anthony Jonathon. BA, U. Cambridge, 1967, MA, 1971; MSc, U. Leeds, 1968, PhD, 1971. Lectr. U. Leeds, U.K., 1968-71, U. Lancaster, U.K., 1971-75; sr. lectr. U. Western Australia, 1975-80, U. Dundee, U.K., 1980-81; prof. U. Stirling, 1981-85, U. Glasgow, Scotland, 1985-92; prin., chief exec. King Alfred's Coll., Winchester, U.K., 1992-2000; dir. Glasgow Bus. Sch., 1987-89, Ravan Publ. Co. Ltd., Australia, 1976-80, Urban Learning Found., London, 1992—, Brit. Coun. Ednl. Counselling Svc., KAC Enterprises Ltd., Winchester Bus. Sch. Ltd. Author: Statistics for Business Finance and Accounting, 1976, Management Accounting: An Introduction, 1988, Statistical Analysis for Accounting and Finance, 1990, Portfolio Analysis and Capital Markets, 1976; contbr. articles to profl. jours. Dist. organizer Christian Aid, Glasgow, 1989-92. Fellow Australian Soc. Accts., Royal Soc. Arts, Inst. Chartered Secs., Inst. Mgmt.; mem. Br. Acct. Assn. (chmn. 1994-95). Anglican. Avocations: photography, travel, languages, poetry. Home: Holm Lodge, 22 St James Ln, Winchester SO22 4NY, England Office: King Alfred's Coll, Winchester S022 4NR, England

DICKINSON, PETER, composer; b. Lytham St. Annes, Lancashire, England, Nov. 15, 1934; s. Frank and Muriel (Porter) D.; m. Bridget Jane Tomkinson, July 29, 1964; children: Jasper Edward Peck, Francis Charles Porter. BA, Cambridge (Eng.) U., 1956, MA, 1960; DMus, U. London, 1992; MusD (hon.), U. Keele, 1999; fellow Rotary Found., Juilliard Sch. Music, 1958-59. Freelance composer, writer, performer N.Y.C., 1959-61; lectr. Coll. St. Mark and St. John, London, 1962-66, Birmingham U., Eng., 1966-70; free-lance composer, writer, performer London, 1970-74; prof. music Keele U., Staffordshire, Eng., 1974-84, emeritus prof., 1984; free-lance composer London, 1984—; prof. Goldsmiths U. London, 1991-97, emeritus prof., 1997; head music Inst. United States Studies U. London, 1997—; pres. London Concert Choir, 1987-97; bd. dirs. Trinity Coll. Music, London, 1985-98, Inst. U.S. Studies, London U., 1994—. Composer orchestra, chamber, choral, keyboard and vocal music; numerous recs.; recorder as pianist; author: The Music of Lennox Berkeley, 1989, Marigold: The Music of Billy Mayerl, 1999; editor: 20 British Composers, 1975; contbr. book chpts.; contbr. articles to profl. jours. John Stewart of Rannoch scholar, 1955. Fellow Royal Soc. Arts (hon.), Royal Coll. Organists, Trinity Coll. Music (hon.); mem. Royal Coll. Music (assoc.), Royal Acad. Music (licentiate), Assn. Profl. Composers (founder), Sonneck Soc., Royal Music Assn., Royal Soc. Musicians. Avocation: book collecting. Address: Novello 257 Park Ave South New York NY 10010*

DICKMAN, MICHAEL DAVID, ecologist, limnologist, educator; b. Pitts., June 30, 1940; s. Avrom I. and Harriet T. (Trasin) D.; m. Daryl Ann Dubpernell, Aug. 11, 1962 (div. Oct. 1999); children: Sven D., Timothy A. BA, U. Calif., 1962; MS, U. Oreg., 1965; PhD, U. B.C., 1968. Thord-Gray postdoctoral fellow U. Uppsala, Sweden, 1968-69; asst. prof. biol. scis. Brock U., St. Catharines, Ont., 1974-93; prof., chair botany U. Hong Kong, 1993-95, chair, prof. ecotoxicology, 1995—, mem. senate, 1993—; dir. pollution abatement program Ottawa-Carleton Municipality, 1972-74; fellow Swire Inst. Marine Scis., Hong Kong, 1994—. Pub. av. com. Niagara River Remedial Action Plan, 1989-93; bd. dirs. Gt. Lakes United. Recipient Rawson Acad. Lectureship award, 1986, vice chancellor's award for collaborative rsch. with Nanjing, China, 1995. Mem. Soc. Can. Limnologists, Internat. Assn. Gr. Lakes Rsch. (tech. adv. com. 1985-89, apptd. Ont. environ. appeal bd. 1990-94). Office: U Hong Kong Dept Ecol and Biodiv, Pokfulam Rd, Hong Kong China

DICKS, PATRICIA DELORES, counselor, educator; b. Bridgeport, Conn., Oct. 28, 1948; d. James Sr. and Mary Mae Dicks. BS, Ctrl. Conn. State U., 1974; MS, U. Bridgeport, 1977; postgrad., U. Conn. Lic. profl. counselor. Counselor Housatonic Cmty. Coll., Bridgeport, 1981-82, instr. part-time, 1984-92, acad. counselor, 1982-83, counselor, 1983-85, dir. student activities, counselor, 1985-92, head counselor, 1992—; faculty advisor, Housatonic Comty. Coll., 1985-92. Cmty. worker Greater Bridgeport Interfaith Action, 1995. Mem. Conn. Coll. and univ. Counselors Assn. (sec. 1998—, Appreciation award 1999). Avocations: reading, college basketball, singing.

DICKSON, GREGORY JOHN, lawyer; b. Sydney, Australia, Dec. 8, 1958; s. Alexander and Margaret Dawn (Jennings) D.; m. Sharon Harcourt Jones, Apr. 26, 1990. BJuris, U. NSW, 1981; LLB, U. NSW, Australia, 1982, LLM, 1996. Accredited specialist in family law, Law Soc. of NSW; Appointed solictor Cmty. Panel for Young Offenders, NSW. Solicitor J.J. Cullen & Assoc., NSW, 1982-83, Warren & Co., NSW, 1983-84; ptnr. Warren, McKeon Dickson, NSW, 1984—, Waters Solicitors, NSW, 1996—, J.J. Francis & Co., NSW, 1994—, Shannon, Danieletto, Adler, NSW, 1995—, W.J. Barclay & Co., NSW, 1997—, Phillip Wood & Co., NSW, 1997—, Peter Saxton & Co., NSW, 1997—, Ian M. Genge & Co., 1996—, J.W. Orrell & Assoc., 1994—, Graeme V. Collins & Assocs., 1998—. Chmn. North Cronulla Precinct Com., 1992-95; pres., capt. U. NSW Australian Football Club, 1980-84. Mem. Law Soc. NSW, Royal Automobile Club Australia. Avocations: Australian football, sailing, military history, travel, reading and collecting books. Office: Warren McKeon Dickson, 20-24 Gibbs St/Miranda, 2228 Sydney Australia

DICKSON, MARKHAM ALLEN, wholesale company executive; b. Shreveport, La., June 10, 1922; s. Claudius Markham and Marjorie (Fields) D.; m. Margaret Shaffer, Sept. 4, 1943 (div. Mar. 1981); m. June Baldwin Dickson, Apr. 19, 1981; children: Louise Dickson Cravens, Claudius Markham, Markham Allen, Paul Meade. BS, MIT, 1947; MS, Calif. Inst. Tech., 1952, DD, Cranmer Theol. House Sem., 1996. Registered profl. engr., La.; ordained priest Episcopal Ch., 1973. Prodn. engr. Brewster Co., Shreveport, 1948-51; pres. Shreveport Druggists, 1951-52, Morris & Dickson Co. Ltd., Shreveport, 1952-95, also chmn. 1995—. Trustee Cranmer Theol. House Sem. Served to capt. USAAF, 1941-46. Recipient Conservationist of Yr. award DAR. Mem. Nat. Wholesale Druggists Assn. (Tech. award 1991). La Wholesale Drug Distbrs. (pres. 1981-90), La. Bd. Wholesale Drug Distbrs. (chmn. bd. 1988-92), Kappa Alpha, Shreveport Club, Masons (32nd degree, shrine). Office: Morris & Dickson Co Ltd 410 Kay Ln Shreveport LA 71115-3611

DICKSON, ROBERT BRENT, biomedical scientist, educator; b. Washington, June 13, 1952; s. Robert Russell and Marie (Altsheler) D. BS, Coll. William and Mary, 1974; PhD, Yale U., 1980. Postdoctoral fellow molecular biol. lab. Nat. Cancer Inst., NIH, Bethesda, Md., 1980-83, sr. staff fellow medicine br., 1983-88; assoc. prof. anatomy, cell biology, pharmacology Georgetown U., Washington, 1988-93, prof. cell biology and pharmacology, assoc. dir. basic sci. Lombardi Cancer Ctr., 1993—, dir. tumor biology PhD program, 1993—, prof., vice chmn. oncology Lombardi Cancer Ctr., 1999—. Author: Breast Cancer: Cellular and Molecular Biology (5 volume set), 1988-96, Drug and Hormonal Resistance in Breast Cancer, 1996, Hormones and Growth Factors in Development and Neoplasia, 1998. Office: Lombardi Cancer Ctr The Rsch Bldg 3970 Reservoir Rd NW Washington DC 20007-2126

DICKSTEIN, HARVEY LEONARD, pharmaceutical company executive; b. Springfield, Mass., Jan. 19, 1936; s. David and Ruth (Stein) D.; m. Judith Marie Barton, Mar. 26, 1966; children: Jason Adam, Debra Ann. BA in Biology, Am. Internat. Coll., 1957; MD, Tufts U., 1961. Diplomate Nat. Bd. Med. Examiners. Intern then resident Bronx Mcpl. Hosp. Ctr., 1961-63; surg. resident Springfield (Mass.) Hosp., 1963-64; surg. resident, then chief resident Boston U. Med. Ctr., 1964-66; med. monitor Baxter Labs., Morton Grove, Ill., 1968-69; assoc. dir. hosp. products div. Abbott Labs., North Chgo., Ill., 1969-72, assoc. dir. exptl. therapy, 1972-73; dir. clin. rsch. Johnson & Johnson, New Brunswick, N.J., 1973-83; group leader surg. anesthetic and dental products FDA, Rockville, Md., 1983-85; dir. regulatory med. affairs E.R. Squibb, New Brunswick, 1985-87; v.p. regulatory affairs Parke-Davis Div. of Warner-Lambert, Morris Plains, N.J., 1987-89, v.p. med. rsch., 1989-91; Intern then resident Bronx Mcpl. Hosp. Ctr., 1961-63; v.p. med. affairs Parke-Davis Div. of Warner-Lambert, Morris Plains, N.J., 1992-93, v.p. med. and regulatory affairs, consumer products R&D, 1993-96; v.p., med. dir. Metawork, Inc., Boston, 1996-97; v.p. clin. rsch. Transcend Therapeutics, Inc., Cambridge, Mass., 1997-98; pharm. cons., Cohasset, Mass., 1999—. Lt. comdr. USPHS, 1966-68. New England Arthritis and Rheumatism Found. summer scholar, 1959. Avocations: weight lifting, skiing, jogging. Home: 393 Beechwood St Cohasset MA 02025-1521

DICLAUDIO, JANET ALBERTA, health information administrator; b. Monroeville, Pa., June 17, 1940; d. Frank and Pearl Alberta (Wolfgang) DiC. Cert. in Med. Rsch. Libr. Sci., Luth Med. Ctr., 1962; BA, Thiel Coll., 1975; MS, SUNY, Buffalo, 1978. Registered record adminstr. Dir. med. records Bashline Hosp., Grove City, Pa., 1962, St. Clair Meml. Hosp., Pitts., 1963-73; asst. prof. Ill. State U., Normal, 1976-81; corp. dir. med. records Buffalo Gen. Hosp., 1981-85; dir. med. records Candler Hosp., Savannah, Ga., 1985-94, med. records analyst, 1994-98; pres. prn Assocs., Savannah, Ga., 1998—; med. record cons. White Cliff Nursing Home, Greenville, Pa., 1973-75; mgmt. cons. Gifford W. Lorenz MD, Savannah, 1992-94; Medicare compliance officer and coder Health Claims, Inc., Savannah, 1999—. Contbr. articles to periodicals. Bd. dirs. Mid-Ill. Areawide Health Planning Corp., Normal, 1979-81. Mem. Am. Health Info. Mgmt. Assn., Ga. Health Info. Mgmt. Assn., S.E. Ga. Health Info. Mgmt. Assn. Avocations: painting, story telling, dancing, reading. Office: 5105 Paulsen St Ste 225D Savannah GA 31405-4621

DICOCCO, MARC, career officer, flight test engineer; b. Lackland AFB, Tex., Aug. 17, 1962; s. Severino and Anne Marie (Bopp) DiC. BS in Aerospace Engring., Va. Poly. Inst., 1985; MS in Aerospace Engring., U. Dayton, 1990. Cert. acquisition officer in program mgmt., test and evaluation and systems engring. Commd. 2d lt. USAF, 1985; advanced through ranks to maj., 1997; technician Prophet 21 Systems Inc., Yardley, Pa., 1984-85; advance concepts design engr. USAF Aeronautical Systems Divsn., Wright-Patterson AFB, Ohio, 1985-88, acquisition officer in tng., 1985-88, test project mgr., 1988-90; F-15E flight test engr. USAF Weapons and Tactics Ctr., Nellis AFB, Nev., 1990-94; chief upper stages divsn. Titan 4 Launch Vehicle Program, Space and Missile Ctr., L.A. AFB, 1994-98; dep. dir. Advanced Fighters evaluation Air Forc Ops. Test and Evaluation Ctr., Kirtland AFB, N.Mex., 1998—. Decorated Air Force Commendation medal (2), Air Force Achievement medal (4), Air Force Meritorious Svc. medal. Mem. AIAA, Aircraft Owners & Pilots Assn., Air Force Assn. (life). Avocations: flying, physical fitness, fine arts, travel, writing.

DICONTI, MICHAEL ANDREW, trade organization executive; b. Glendale, Calif., Aug. 19, 1958; s. Andrew Raphael Jr. and Diane Rose

(Carlotti) DiC.; m. Veronica Donahue, Aug. 6, 1988; 1 child, Nolan James. AB in Psychology magna cum laude, Occidental Coll., 1980; MBA in Acctg./Fin., UCLA, 1983; MA in Polit. Sci., Johns Hopkins U., 1987, PhD in Polit. Sci., 1990. Tax advisor Arthur Young, L.A., 1983-85; instr. C.C. of Balt., 1985-90, Johns Hopkins U., Balt., 1987-90; exec. asst. to pres. The Bus. Roundtable, Washington, 1990-93, dir. adminstrn., 1993—. Author: Entrepreneurship in Training, 1992. Asst. treas. Edn. Excellence Partnership, Washington, 1993—. Fellow Inst. for Study of World Politics, Washington, 1987-88. Mem. Phi Beta Kappa, Psi Chi (pres. Occidental Coll. chpt. 1979-80). Avocation: running. Home: 11621 Ayreshire Rd Oakton VA 22124-1207 Office: The Bus Roundtable 1615 L St NW Ste 1100 Washington DC 20036-5624

DI COSOLA, LOIS BOCK, artist, educator; b. Bklyn., Jan. 23, 1935; d. Morris Bock and Lena Filangeri; m. Leonard Di Cosola, June 4, 1955; 1 child, Leonard. Student, Mus. Modern Art Sch., N.Y.C., 1951-52, Pratt Graphics Ctr., N.Y.C., 1973-75; B in Profl. Studies, SUNY Empire State Coll., Old Westbury, 1985. Graphic artist Seventeen Mag., 1953-54, Children's TV Workshop, Sesame St., 1969-70, Time Life Books, N.Y.C., 1973; writer, editor Sunstorm Arts Pub., 1980—; adj. prof. art Hofstra U., Hempstead, N.Y., 1990-91. Exhbns. include Carnegie Inst. Fine Arts, 1953, N.Y. World's Fair, Flushing Meadows, 1964, First Feminist Art Exhbn., N.Y.C., 1970. Recipient Printmaking award Carnegie Fine Art Inst., 1953, Augustus Saint Gaudens medal for fine draftsmanship, 1953, Art Dir.'s Club award, 1954, Curators award Mus. Modern Art, 1963, Harold Rosenberg James Brooks award, 1963-64, Guild Hall, 1963, 64, Curators award Whitney Mus., 1964, Curators award Guggenheim Mus., 1964; grantee Mus. Modern Art, 1951. Mem. Nat. Drawing Assn. (co-chair 1989-92), Profl. Artists Guild (v.p. 1967-68), Nat. Mus. Women in Arts (charter). E-mail: solabear99@cs.com.

DIDIĆ, ENES, political scientist, researcher; b. Zagreb, Croatia, Mar. 7, 1973; s. Midhat and Nada Obrovac D.; m. Nathalie Micheline Grenier, Nov. 23, 1996. M of Civil Engring., Faculty of Civil Engring., 1991; MA in Polit. Scis., Faculty of Polit. Scis., 1999. Leader working programs Semgrad, Zagreb, Croatia, 1992-93; staff mem. YHA, Canterbury, Eng., 1993; mem. adminstrn. YHA, Greater Yarnolith, Eng., 1994; mgr., translator Nekgrad, Zagreb, Croatia, 1999—; prof. politics and egnomy Birot Dinika, Zagreb, 1998—. Contbr. articles to profl. jours. Pres. Young Croatian Liberals-Zagreb br., Galoiveva, Zagreb, 1999, internat. sec., 1999. Mem. Croatian Army, 1991-94. Recipient Double Medallion and Acknowledgment Mare Nostrum Croaticum and Terra Nostra Croatica, 1999. Mem. Croatian Assn. for Internat. Rels. Studies, Internat. Assn. of Communicologists-Croatian Bd. of Communicology Assn., Croatian Assn. for Civil Engring. Mgr.s, Croatia-Japan Friendship Soc. (pres. sport and culture sect. 1997), Croatian Assn. for Vets. of War. Mem. Croatian Social Liberal Party. Avocations: boxing, languages, computers, traveling, art. Home: Varšavska 13/I, 10000 Zagreb Croatia

DIDION, JOAN, writer; b. Sacramento, Calif., Dec. 5, 1934; d. Frank Reese and Eduene (Jerrett) D.; m. John Gregory Dunne, Jan. 30, 1964; 1 child, Quintana Roo. BA, U. Calif., Berkeley, 1956. Assoc. feature editor Vogue mag., 1956-63; former columnist Saturday Evening Post, Life, Esquire; now contbr. The N.Y. Rev. of Books, The New Yorker. Novels include Run River, 1963, Play It As It Lays, 1970, A Book of Common Prayer, 1977, Democracy, 1984, The Last Thing He Wanted, 1996; books of essays: Slouching Towards Bethlehem, 1968, The White Album, 1979, After Henry, 1992; nonfiction Salvador, 1983, Miami, 1987; co-author: (with John Gregory Dunne) Screenplays for films The Panic in Needle Park, 1971, Play It As It Lays, 1972, A Star Is Born, 1976, True Confessions, 1981, Hills Like White Elephants, 1991, Broken Trust, 1995, Up Close and Personal, 1996. Recipient 1st prize Vogue's Prix de Paris, 1956, Morton Dauwen Zabel prize AAAL, 1978, The Edward MacDowell medal, 1996. Mem. Am. Acad. Arts and Letters, Am. Acad. Arts and Scis., Coun. Fgn. Rels. Office: care Janklow & Nesbit 445 Park Ave New York NY 10022-2606

DIDISHEIM, COUNT MICHEL GEORGE, foundation executive; b. Wimbledon, Eng., Apr. 18, 1930; s. René Baron Didisheim and Claire Maigret de Priches; m. Monika Countess Trauttmansdorff, Feb. 7, 1956; children: Christophe, Frédéric, François, Nathalie, Florence. Lic. in polit. scis., U. Brussels, 1951, lic. in colonial scis., 1951. Cabinet chief Ministry of Trade, Govt. of Belgium, Brussels, 1960-66, His Royal Highness Prince Albert, Crown Prince of Belgium, 1966-86; mng. dir. King Baudouin Found., Brussels, 1976-95, chmn., 1993-99; non-exec. dir. UCB, Brussels, 1995-2000; extraordinary prof. U. Louvain, Louvain-La-Neuve, 1973-81. Bd. govs. European Cultural Found., Amsterdam, 1995-2000, Coll. of Europe, 2000—; co-founder, bd. dirs. Ctr. European Policy Studies, Brussels, 1981-93. With Belgian Army, 1952-54, Korea. Decorated Grand Cross, Order of the Crown, Belgian Govt., 1995. Roman Catholic. Home: Dreve du Senechal 25, B-1180 Brussels Belgium Office: Fondation Roi Baudouin, Rue Brederode 21, B-1000 Brussels Belgium

DIDUKH, LEONID DMYTROVYCH, physicist, educator; b. Zhytomyr, Ukraine, Feb. 9, 1940; s. Dmytro Stepanovych and Mariya Vasylivna Didukh; m. Lyudmyla Pylypivna Kupcevych, Aug. 12, 1962; 1 child, Oksana. Diploma, Lviv (USSR) State U., 1962, PhD, 1969. Asst. Ternopil (USSR) State Tech. U., 1965-66, sr. lectr., 1966-70, docent, 1970-75, 84-94, head physics dept., 1975-84, prof., head physics dept., 1995—, dean mech. faculty, 1977-85, head Sunday Phys. & Math. Sch., 1995—; mem. acad. bd. Lviv State U., 1995—. Author: Correlation Effects in Materials with Narrow Energy Bands, 1978, Ordered States in Materials with Narrow Energy Bands, 1980; mem. editl. bd. Jour. Phys. Studies, 1996—. Exec. dir. Ternopil Region br. Ukrainian Fund Support Sci., 1999—. Mem. Ukrainian Phys. Soc. Avocation: collection of aphorisms. Fax: 380-352-254983. Home: 92/174 Bandery ave., 46011 Ternopil Ukraine Office: Ternopil State Tech U, 56 Rus'ka Str., 46001 Ternopil Ukraine

DIE, ANN MARIE HAYES, college president, psychology educator; b. Baytown, Tex., Aug. 15, 1944; d. Robert L. and Dorothy Ann (Cooke) Hayes; m. Jerome Glynn Die, June 5, 1971; 1 child, Meredith Anne. BS with highest honors, Lamar U., 1966; MEd, U. Houston, 1969; PhD, Tex. A&M U., 1977. Lic. psychologist. Asst. prof. dept. psychology Lamar U., Beaumont, Tex., 1977-82, assoc. prof., dir. Psychol. Clinic, 1982-86, dir. grad. programs in psychology, 1981-86, Regents prof. psychology, 1986, pres. faculty senate, 1985-86; pvt. practice clin. psychology Beaumont, 1979-87; prof. Tulane U., New Orleans, 1988-92, dean Newcomb Coll., 1988-92, assoc. provost, 1991-92; pres., prof. psychology Hendrix Coll., Conway, Ark., 1992—; adminstr. adolescent residential unit Mental Health/Mental Retardation S.E. Tex., 1979-80, mem. cmty. adv. com., 1981-87; cons. in field; coordinating bd. Tex. Coll. and Univ. Sys. Internship, 1986, chair, bd. dirs. Ednl. and Instl. Ins. Adminstrs., 2000—; bd. dirs. Nat. Merit Scholarship Corp., Acxiom Corp., Found. for Ind. Higher Edn., Air U., USAF. Contbr. articles to profl. jours. Mem. cmty. adv. com. Beaumont State Ctr. Human Devel., 1981-88; chair So. Collegiate Athletic Conf., 1996-97; participant Nat. Identification Program for Women, Am. Coun. on Edn., 1985, mem. govt. rels. commn., 1993-96, chmn., 1994-96, chmn. coun. of fellow, 1995-96, bd. dirs., 1997-2000; bd. dirs. Beaumont Civic Opera, Lamar U. Wesley Found., Tulane U. Wesley Found.; bd. govs. Isidore Newman Sch., 1991-92; trustee Robert Morris Coll., 1990-98, chmn. edn. com., 1990-94, chmn. pers. com., 1994-98; mem. univ. senate United Meth. Ch., 1993—, chair commn. on instnl. rev., 1997—; 1st v.p. Nat. Assn. Schs. & Colls. United Meth. Ch., 1996, pres. 1997-98; bd. dirs. Ouachita coun. Girl Scouts U.S., 1996-2000; mem. bd. visitors Air U., 1999—; mem. Internat. Women's Forum, 1995—, Ark. Women's Leadership Forum, 1995—, pres. 2000; mem. Ark. Commn. to Streamline State Govt., 1996—; mem. pres. commn. NCAA, 1997—, chmn. 1999-2000, mem. exec. com. 1999—; chair Assoc. Coll. of the South, 1997-99; bd. dirs. Ark. Repertory Theatre, 2000—, United Way of Faulkner County, 2000—. Am. Coun. Edn. fellow Coll. William and Mary, 1986-87; recipient Regents Merit award, 1979, Coll. Health and Behavioral Sci. Merit award, 1982, Lamar U.; named one of Top 100 Women in Ark., Ark. Bus., 1995-99. Mem. APA, Southwestern Psychol. Assn., Family Svcs. Assn. (bd. dirs. 1988-89), Tex. Psychol. Assn. (dir. divsn. acad. psychologists 1986), S.E. Tex. Psychol. Assn. (treas. 1978-80, pres. 1983), Mental Health Assn. Jefferson County, Nat. Register Health Svc. Providers in Psychology, Nat. Assn. Ind. Colls. and Univs. (bd. dirs., vice chmn. 1995, chair 1996). Home: 1256 Winfield St Conway AR 72032-2741 Office: Hendrix Coll 1600 Washington Ave Conway AR 72032-4115

DIEBEL, GARY R., architect; b. St. Paul. B in Architecture, U. Minn., 1983; M in Architecture, Cranbook Acad. Art, Bloomfield Hills, Mich., 1987. Architect DSPB, Inc., Virginia, Minn., 1983-85, Kodet Archl. Group, Ltd., Mpls., 1987-90, Diebel & Co., Burlingame, Calif., 1990—. Mem. AIA. Office: Diebel & Co PO Box 1044 Burlingame CA 94011-1044

DIEBEL, NELSON, Olympic athlete, swimmer. Olympic swimmer Barcelona, Spain, 1992. Recipient 100m Breaststroke Gold medal Olympics, Barcelona, 1992, 4x100 Medley Relay Gold medal Olympics, Barcelona, 1992.

DIEBOLD, FRANCIS X., economist, educator; b. Nov. 12, 1959; m. Susan S. Diebold; 3 children. BS in Fin. and Econs., U. Pa., 1981, PhD in Econs., 1986. Rsch. economist, mem. bd. govs. FRS, 1986-89; asst. prof. econs., J.M. Cohen term chair U. Pa., 1989-92, assoc. prof., 1992-96, prof., 1996-99, prof. stats. Wharton Sch., 1996-2000, dir. Inst. Econ. Rsch., Lawrence R. Klein prof. econs., 1999—; faculty rsch. fellow Nat. Bur. Econ. Rsch., 1993-99, rsch. assoc., 1999—; charter mem. Oliver Wyman Inst., 1996—; vis. prof. fin., econ., stats. Stern Sch. Bus., NYU, 1998-2000; vis. prof. Cambridge U., 1998, Princeton U., 1997, Johns Hopkins U., 1995, U. Chgo., 1993, London Sch. Econs., 1992, U. Minn., 1990; Benedum lectr. W.Va. U., 1992; mem. organizing com. Computational Fin., 1999—; mem. econs. panel NSF, 1998-2000, chmn. forecasting seminar, 1995—. Author: (with G. Rudebusch) Business Cycles: Durations, Dynamics and Forecasting, 1999, Elements of Forecasting, 1998, Empirical Modeling of Exchange Rate Dynamics, 1988; assoc. editor Rev. Econs. and Stats., 1993—, Jour. Bus. and Econ. Stats., 1993—, Jour. Forecasting, 1994—, Stata Tech. Bull., 1994—, Econometrica, 1994-97, Jour. Applied Econometrics, 1991-97, Jour. Empirical Fin., 1992-95, Econometric Revs., 1989-92; mem. adv. bd. Econ. Policy Rev., Fed. Res. Bank N.Y., 1997—, Macroecon. Dynamics, 1996—; co-editor Internat. Econ. Rev., 1993-99, Jour. Forecasting, 1990-94; contbr. articles to econ. and bus. jours.; spkr. at many profl. meetings and confs. Mem. bd. sr. scholars Nat. Ctr. for Ednl. Quality of Workforce, 1993-95. Fellow Wharton Fin. Instns. Ctr., 1997—; Alfred P. Sloan Found. rsch. fellow, 1992-94; grantee NSF, 1989-92, 92-94, 95-98, 98—, Pew Found., 1995-96, NSF and Cornell Super Computer Ctr., 1992-92. Fellow Econometric Soc. (program com. N.Am. winter mtg. 1999, program com. time-series econometrics 1993); mem. Am. Statis. Assn. (mem. editl. selection com. Jour. B sec., Econ. Stats., 1994, 2000, Zellner award selection com. 1995, sec./treas. bus. and econ. stats. sect. 1994, program chair 1991), Am. Econ. Assn., Am. Fin. Assn. E-mail: fdiebold@stern.nyu.edu. Address: NYU Dept Fin 44 W 4th St Ste 9-190 New York NY 10012-1106

DIECK, E. LEOPOLD, business owner, engineer, educator; b. Eisenach, Germany, July 24, 1940; s. E. Leopold and Ilse (Grasshoff) D. Diploma in Physics, U. Aachen, Germany, 1966, D. Engring., 1968. Mgr. Bertelsmann AG, Gütersloh, Germany, 1973-74, Barcelona, Spain, 1973-74; mgr. Dornier GmbH, Friedrichshafen, Germany, 1975-76; mng. dir. Pelikan Informationstechnik, Hamburg, Germany, 1981-82; owner, pres. Dr. E. Leopold Dieck Industriebeteiligungs KG, Paderborn, Germany, 1977—; gen. mgr. AEG-Telefunken, Konstanz, Germany, 1983-87; chmn., chief exec. officer AEG Olympia AG, Frankfurt, Germany, 1987-89; pres. AEG Electrocom GmbH, Konstanz, 1989-92; pres., chief exec. officer W. Schlafhorst A.G. & Co., Moenchengladbach, Germany, 1992-94; chief exec. officer Schleicher & Co., Internat. A.G., Markdorf, Germany, 1996—; chmn. bd. Pfeiffer Vaccum Tech. A.G., Asslar, Germany, 1996—; bd. dirs. Marina Punat (Croatia) AG, Aktiv Bau A.G.; chmn. Sun Lit Water Proof Engring. Co. Ltd., Beijing; prof. China Textile U., Shanghai. Inventor, patentee in nuclear field. Home and Office: Marktstrasse 40, 88212 Ravensburg Germany

DIECKERT, JÜRGEN, sports scientist; b. Gumbinnen, Germany, June 10, 1935; s. Kurt and Christel (Tiedemann) D.; m. Barbara Zigan, 1957; children: Jochen, Ulrich, Kurt Georg, Susanne. Diploma, U. Göttingen, Fed. Republic Germany, 1960; post diploma, U. Saarbrücken, Fed. Republic Germany, 1962, PhD in Sports Sci., 1968. Asst. prof. U. Saarbrücken, 1960-68; prof. sports sci. U. Oldenburg (Fed. Republic Germany), 1968—; vis. prof. U. Santa Maria (Brazil), 1980-83; mem. rsch. commn. Brazilian Ministry Edn., 1981-84;. Author, co-author 22 books on history, pedagogics, methods, and architecture of phys. edn. (3 transl. into Portuguese, 1 in Spanish, 1 in Japanese); editor 20 books in Brazil; author 6 TV films about Brazilian Indians. Pres. German Gymnastics Fedn., 1990-2000, pres. youth, 1962-66, pres. sport for all, 1970-74. Recipient award of merit Fed. U. Santa Maria, 1982. Home: Kaspersweg 107a, D-26131 Oldenburg Federal Republic of Germany Office: U Oldenburg, U Oldenburg, Ammerländer Heerstrasse, D-26129 Oldenburg Federal Republic of Germany

DIECKMANN, KLAUS PETER, urologist, educator; b. Bremen, Germany, June 12, 1950; s. Johann Heinrich and Hermine (Unrecht) D.; m. Monika Nowack, May 21, 1987; children: Thomas, Andreas, Oliver. MD, U. Göttingen, Germany, 1977. Diplomate in urology, Germany. Resident in surgery Krankenhaus Weende, Göttingen, 1977-80; vol. dr. German Vol. Svc., Tunduru, Tanzania, 1981-82; resident in urology Free U., Berlin, 1983-87, staff urologist Klinikum Steglitz, 1987-91, dep. head dept. Klinikum Steglitz, 1992-93; head dept. Albertinen-Krankenhaus, Hamburg, Germany, 1993—. Contbr. over 100 articles to profl. jours. Sgt. German Army, 1970-71. Mem. German Urol. Soc., Assn. German Urologists, Assn. Urol. Oncology. Avocations: sports, stamp collecting, collecting old urologic books. Office: Albertinen-Krankenhaus, Süntelstr 11, D-22457 Hamburg Germany

DIEDERICH, JOACHIM, computer technology educator, researcher; b. Rheine, Germany, Apr. 10, 1958; arrived in Australia, 1993; s. Josef Georg and Leopoldine Maria (Weinlich) D.; children: Holthaus, Leonie, Sophie, Andrea. Diploma, U. Muenster, Federal Republic of Germany, 1983; PhD, U. Bielefeld, 1985; Habilitation, U. Hamburg, Germany, 1995. Rsch. assoc. U. Muenster, 1983-85; head of project German Nat. Rsch. Ctr. Info. Tech., St. Augustin, Federal Republic of Germany, 1985-87, 91-93; post doctoral fellow Internat. Computer Sci. Inst., Berkeley, Calif., 1987-90; rsch. fellow U. Calif., Davis, 1990-91; prof. Queensland U. Tech., Brisbane, Australia, 1993—; bd. dirs. QUT-MLRC, Brisbane, Australia; pres., founder Internat. Knowledge Discovery Inst., 1999—. Author: Kognitive Parallelverbeitung, 1986, KI-Workstations, 1988, Simulation schizophrener Sprache, 1988, Artificial Neural Networks: Concept Learning, 1990. Grantee Australian Rsch. Coun., 1996-2000, Australian Telecomms. and Electronic Rsch. Bd., 1994-95. Mem. AAAS, Info. Soc. (Germany). Avocations: triathlon, duathlon, cycling, running. Office: Queensland Univ Tech, 2 George St, Brisbane 4000, Australia

DIEHL, ELKE, editor, journalist, lawyer; b. Mainz, Germany, July 2, 1954; d. Hermann and Ilse (Raidt) Diehl; m. Bernhard Peter Hartung, May 14, 1993. Law Degree, Johannes-Gutenberg U., Mainz, 1979, 2d Law Degree, 1982. Freelance journalist various newspapers, Wiesbaden, Germany, 1982-84; freelance TV journalist Mainz, 1985-88; editor All German Inst., Bonn, 1989-91, Fed. Agy. for Civic Edn., Bonn, 1992—; mem. jury Civic Edn. Sch. Contest, Fed. Agy. for Civic Edn., Bonn., 1991, 92, data protection commr., 1996—. Author essays and articles. Chair local com. Humanistic Union, Mainz, 1988-89; mem. Humanistic Union, München, 1987—. Mem. Soc. for German Lang., German Juvenile Ct. Assn., Journalistinnenbund, Terre des Femmes. Home: Quellenstr 12, D-53177 Bonn Germany Office: Fed Agy for Civic Edn, Berliner Freiheit 7, D-53111 Bonn Germany

DIEHL, KARL FRIEDRICH, urologist; b. Vienna, Austria, Feb. 10, 1960; s. Karl Heinz and Ingeborg (Kluegel) D.; m. Karin Zeigenhofer, April 14, 1958; children: Elisabeth, Lukas, Florian. MD, Univ. Vienna, 1983. Diplomate European Bd. Urology. Asst. physician in tng. Gen. Hosp., Melk, Austria, 1983-84, Sophienspital, Vienna, 1985-86; urologist in tng. Gen. Hosp., Korneuburg, Austria, 1987-91; head physician Tulln, Austria, 1991—; cons. urologist, Neurological Hosp., 1991—, Pvt. Hosp., Vienna, 1994—. Contbr. articles to profl. jours. Mem. Austrian Urological Soc. Mem. Old Catholic Ch. Avocations: motorbikes, fine wines, Disney collection. Office: Jahnstrasse 1-3, A 3430 Tulln Austria

DIEHL, PAUL FRANCIS, political science educator; b. Buffalo, N.Y., Apr. 4, 1958; s. John Henry Diehl and Ruth Marie Druar; m. Martha Griffen, Nov. 24, 1992; 1 child, Robert John. BA, Canisius Coll., 1980; MA, U. Mich., 1982, PhD, 1983. Vis. asst. prof. SUNY, Albany, 1984; asst. prof. U. Ga., Athens, 1984-89; assoc. prof. U. Ill., Urbana, 1989-94, prof., 1994—. Author: Territorial Changes adn International Conflict, 1992, International Peacekeeping, 1994, War and Peace in International Rivalry, 2000. Recipient Karl Deutsch award Internat. Studies Assn., 1998; Alan M. Hallene Univ. scholar U. Ill., 1993. E-mail: p-diehl@uiuc.edu. Office: Univ Ill 702 S Wright St Urbana IL 61801-3631

DIEKSTRA, FRANS NICOLAAS, English and literature educator; b. Groningen, The Netherlands, Apr. 16, 1937; s. Augustinus Hessephius and Petronella (Anraad) D.; m. Lieke Johanna Roefs, Aug. 10, 1965 (div. Sept. 1974); children: Froukje, Jasper; m. Joke Wilhelmina Hoefnagel, July 4, 1983; children: Frank, Meta. Grad. in English, U. Nymegen, The Netherlands, 1961, Doctor, 1968, grad. in Middle English Lang. and Lit., 1974. Lectr. Old and Middle English U. Nymegen, 1961-74, prof. Middle English lang. and lit., 1974—. Author, editor: A Dialogue Between Reason and Adversity, 1968, The Weye of Paradys and Voie De Paradis, 1991, Book for a Simple and Devout Woman, 1999; contbr. articles to profl. jours. Avocations: drawing, painting. Home: Straalmanstraat 34, 6521 JM Nymegen Gelderland The Netherlands Office: Univ Nymegen Dept English, Erasmusplein 1, 6500HD Nymegen Gelderland Netherlands

DIEL, MARK A.C., barrister; b. Hamilton, Bermuda, Sept. 27, 1959; s. Coles Raymond and Dianna Patricia (Greene) D.; m. Karen Louise Sidley, Sept. 27, 1986; children: Michael Coles, Meghan Elizabeth. BA, Queens U., Can., 1982; LLB with hons., Buckingham U., Eng., 1984. Bar: Eng., Wales, Bermuda. Assoc. Smith, Barnard & Diel, Hamilton, Bermuda, 1985-90, ptnr., 1990-98; sr. ptnr. Diel & Myers, Hamilton, 1998—; mem. fees complaints com. Bermuda Bar Coun., 1992-95; acting magistrate Bermuda, 1993—. Notary pub.; justice of the peace. Mem. Mid-Ocean Golf Club (dir. 1993-98), Bermuda C. of C. (chmn. e-bus. divsn. 2000—). Avocations: golf, gardening, skiing, scuba diving. Office: Diel & Myers, Chancery Hall 52 Reid St, HM12 Hamilton Bermuda

DIEMER, ARTHUR WILLIAM, real estate executive; b. Queens County, N.Y., Nov. 5, 1925; s. John and Elizabeth (Bernhard) D.; m. Opal Louise Droddy, Mar. 25, 1950; children: Paul A., Liddia E. Student, CCNY, 1943, St. Lawrence Univ., Canton, N.Y., 1944; BS, Dartmouth Coll., 1947; MS, Thayer Sch. of Engring., Hanover, N.H., 1948. Civil engr. Union Carbide, S. Charleston, W.Va., 1948-56; bldg. mgr. Union Carbide Realty Div., N.Y.C., 1960-67; v.p., pres. Cabot & Forbes Property Mgmt. Co., Boston, 1967-75; pres. Renaissance Ctr. Mgmt. Co., Detroit, 1975-77; co-founder, v.p. Renaissance Properties, Inc., Charlotte, N.C., 1977-84; pres. The Realty Evaluation Group, Inc., Charlotte, N.C., 1985—; Founder, pres. Discovery Assocs., Charlotte 1985—; mem. adv. commn. Ctr. for Bldg. Tech., U.S. Commerce Dept. Washington 1975-76, ad hoc com. U.S. Dept. Energy, Washington, 1974. Author articles in profl. jours. Incorporated Village of Bellerose, N.Y. commr. of parks, commr. of pub. works, elected trustee; bd. dirs. Lutheran Social Svcs., Detroit, 1976-77, Family Housing Svcs., Charlotte 1979-81. Mem. Internat. Grapho Analysis Soc., Dartmouth Club of Charlotte (pres. 1993-94). Republican. Lutheran. Home and Office: 4337 Silo Ln Charlotte NC 28226-5504

DIEMER, JEAN CLAUDE, textile company executive; b. Besancon, France, Nov. 2, 1929; s. Jacques Paul and Genevieve (Zuber) D.; m. Micheline Martin, May 25, 1957; children: Philippe, Eric, Isabelle. HEC, Hautes Etudes Commerciales, Paris, 1952. Cons. Groupe Vidal, Paris, 1958-64, Cofror, Paris, 1964-69; area mgr. Hachette S.A., Paris, 1969-80; pres. Regents Pub. Co., N.Y.C., 1979; controller Dollfus Mieg et Cie, Paris, 1980-87; dir. internal audit Dollfus Mieg et Cie, 1989; textile expert for the French govt. bus. cons., 1992. Home and Office: 54 Rue des Pres Hauts, Chatenay-Malabry France 92290

DIENER, THEODOR OTTO, plant pathologist; b. Zurich, Switzerland, Feb. 28, 1921; came to U.S., 1949, naturalized, 1955; s. Theodor Emanuel and Hedwig Rosa (Baumann) D.; m. Sybil Mary Fox, May 11, 1968; children by previous marriage: Theodor W., Robert A., Michael S. Diploma, Swiss Fed. Inst. Tech., 1946; DSc, Nat. Swiss Fed. Inst. Tech., 1948. Asst. Swiss Fed. Inst. Tech., Zurich, 1946-48; plant pathologist Swiss Fed. Exptl. Sta., Waedenswil, 1949-50; asst. prof. plant pathology R.I. State U., Kingston, 1950; asst. plant pathologist Wash. State U., Prosser, 1950-55; assoc. plant pathologist Wash. State U., 1955-59; rsch. plant pathologist agr. rsch. svc. USDA, Beltsville, Md., 1959-88, collaborator agr. rsch. svc., 1988-97; prof. botany, sr. staff sci. ctr. agr. biotech./dept. Botany U. Md., College Park, 1988—, acting dir. Ctr. Agr. Biotech., 1991-92, Disting. Univ. prof., 1994—; Disting. prof. U. Md. Biotech. Inst., 1998—, Disting. univ. prof. emeritus, 1999—, 1999—; lectr. univs. and rsch. instr.; Regent's lectr. U. Calif., Riverside, 1970; A.W. Dimock lectr. Cornell U., 1975, Andrew D. White prof.-at-large, 1979-81, James Law disting. lectr. N.Y. State Coll. Vet. Medicine, 1981; disting. lectr. Boyce Thomson Inst. for Plant Rsch., 1987, Hong Kong U. Sci. and Tech., 1992; Ernest Everett Just Meml. lectr. Howard U., Washington, 1990; disting. prof. U. Md., Coll. Park, 1994—, Biotech Inst., 1998; guest lectr. Israel Soc. for Microbiology, Rehovot, 1994, Royal Swedish Acad. of Scis., Stockholm, 1997, Swedish Agrl. U., Uppsala, 1997, Royal Netherlands Acad. Arts and Scis., Amsterdam, 1998, Alexander von Humboldt Assn., Washington, 1999. Author: Viroids and Viroid Diseases, 1979; editor: The Viroids, 1987; assoc. editor: Virology, 1964-66, 74-76; editor: Jour., 1967-71; mem. editorial com.: Ann. Rev. Phytopathology, 1970-74, Annales de Virologie, 1980-88; contbr. articles to profl. jours.; discoverer novel class of pathogens (viroids), 1971. Recipient Campbell award Am. Inst. Biol. Scis., 1968; Superior Svc. award USDA, 1969, Disting. Svc. award, 1975; Alexander von Humboldt award, 1975, Wolf prize in Agr., 1987, U.S. Nat. medal of Sci., 1987, Gov.'s citation, State of Md., 1988, E.C. Stakman award U. Minn., 1988; inducted into USDA Sci. Hall of Fame, 1989. Fellow Am. Phytopath. Soc. (Ruth Allen award 1976), N.Y. Acad. Scis., Am. Acad. Arts and Scis.; mem. NAS, AAAS, Leopoldina, German Acad. Natural Scientists. Home: 11711 Battersea Dr PO Box 272 Beltsville MD 20704-0272 Office: U Md Ctr For Agrl Biotech College Park MD 20742-0001

DIENSTBIER, JIŘÍ, diplomat, political scientist, journalist, writer; b. Kladno, Bohemia, Czechoslovakia, Apr. 20, 1937; s. Jirí and Anna (Hajek) D.; m. Jirina; children: Monika, Irena, Jirí, Kristina. MA, Charles U., Prague, Czechoslovakia, 1960; D (hon.), U. Burgundy. Journalist, commentator, corr. Far East, U.S.A. burs. Radio Prague, 1958-69; documentarist Design Inst., Prague, 1970-79; imprisoned for human rights activities Prague, 1979-82, night watchman, 1982-83, stoker, 1983-89; min. Ministry of Fgn. Affairs, Prague, 1989-92; dep. premier Prague, 1990-92; chmn. Civic Movement, 1992—; vis. prof. Claremont U., Calif., 1997-98, U. N.C., Chapel Hill, 1999; spl. rapporteur of UN Human Rights Commn. for Yugoslavia, Croatia and Bosnia-Herzegovina, 1995—; personal rep. of Czechoslovakian pres. Havel for Multilateralism and reform of UN. Author: The Night Started at 3 O'Clock, 1967, Dreaming of Europe, 1985, Radio Against the Tanks, 1988, From Dreams to Reality, 1999; contbr. more than 1,000 articles, essays to various newspapers, mags., profl. jours. Spokesman Charter 77, Czechoslovakia, 1979, 85; spokesman Civic Forum, Czechoslovakia, 1989. Mem. Internat. Press Inst., N.Y. Acad. Scis., Commn. on Global Governance. E-mail: j@dienstbier.cz. Home: Apolinářská 6, 12800 Prague Czech Republic

DIENSTBIER, ZDENĚK JOSEF, physician; b. Chrudim, Czech Republic, May 30, 1926; s. Josef and Anna (Fenclová) D.; m. Vera Volková, Oct. 17, 1950; children: Jan, Helena. MD, Charle's U., Prague, Czech Republic, 1950, PhD, 1954, DSc, 1964; MD (hon.), Humboldt U., Berlin, 1987. Physician 1st Med. Clinic, 1st Med. Facility Charles U., Prague, 1950-57, head Inst. Biophysics and Nuclear Medicine, 1957-91, vice dean 1st Med. Facility, 1960-64, vice rector, 1964-69; ret., 1991; pres. European Soc. Radiol. Biology, 1968-69; v.p. European Nuclear Med. Soc., 1973-74; pres. League Against Cancer, Czech Republic, 1990—. Contbr. articles to books and profl. jours. E-mail: lpr@lpr.cz. Home: Kladenská 28, 160 00 Prague Czech Republic Office: League Against Cancer, Na Slupi 6, 128 42 Prague Czech Republic

DIENY, BERNARD, physicist; b. Paris, Aug. 6, 1960; s. Jean and Aline (Beigbeder) D.; m. Marie-Pierre Boullez, Mar. 19, 1983; children: Thomas, Tiphaine, Manon, Gauthier, Clemence. BA in Physics, U. Orsay, France, 1980; PhD, U. Grenoble, France, 1985. Postdoctoral fellow Cen. Nat. Rsch. Sci., France, 1985-87, rschr. lab. Louis Néel, 1988-90; rsch. engr. Ctr. for Nuclear Studies of Grenoble, France, 1992-95, 97—; head rsch. group nanostructure and magnetism Ctr. for Nuclear Studies of Grenoble; vis. sci. IBM Almaden, 1990-91, U. Calif., San Diego, 1995-96. Inventor spin-valve structures; 15 patents in field; contbr. over 150 articles to sci. publs. Avocations: mountain climbing, rock climbing, sailing, clarinette. Office: CENG, DRFMC/SP2M/NM, 38054 Grenoble France

DIERAUER, JULIE DAWN, sculptor, secondary education educator; b. Menomonie, Wis., June 2, 1956; d. David Walter and Elaine Adeline Dierauer. BS in Art Edn., U. Wis., Stout, 1978; MA in Sculpture, U. Wis., Milw., 1980; MFA in Visual Art, Clayton U., 1986. Cert. art tchr. K-12, Minn. Dir. Faith Child Care Ctr., Mpls., 1981-86; child care tchr. (days) YWCA, Mpls., 1986-94; child devel. instr. (evenings) Mpls. Tech. Coll., 1987-94; art specialist Ind. Sch. Dist. 197, West St. Paul, Minn., 1994-98; art instr. St. Croix Luth. H.S., West St. Paul, Minn., 1998—; theatre drama tchr. Stepping Stone Theatre, St. Paul, 1994-98; curriculum writer, elem. art, Ind. Sch. Dist. 197, 1994-96, early childhood, Mrs. Green's, Anoka, Minn., 1986; founder cyclopsbabylon ceramic arts, Mpls., 1999. One-woman shows include Bethany Luth. Coll., 1999; commns. include U. West Marshfield, 1995. Recipient 1st place award Edina (Minn.) Art Ctr., 1987; Vt. Studio Ctr. fellow, 1991; named Roster Artist, Wis. Arts Bd., Madison, 1981-82. Mem. Minn. Crafts Coun. Socialist Workers. Evangelican Lutheran Synod. Avocation: landscape painting, still life drawing. E-mail: cyclopsbabylon@hotmail.com. Office: cyclopsbabylon ceramic arts 5444 Bryant Ave S Minneapolis MN 55419-1738

DIERCKS, FREDERICK OTTO, government official; b. Rainy River, Ont., Can., Sept. 8, 1912; s. Otto Herman and Lucy (Plunkett) D.; m. Kathryn Frances Transue, Sept. 1, 1937; children: Frederick William, Lucy Helena. B.S., U.S. Mil. Acad., 1937; M.S. in Civil Engring., MIT, 1939; M.S. in Photogrammetry, Syracuse U., 1950. Registered profl. engr., D.C. Commd. 2d lt. U.S. Army Corps Engrs., 1937; advanced through grades to col. U.S. Army, 1952; comdg. officer 656th Engr. Topographic Battalion, France and Germany, 1944-45, 29th Engr. Topographic Btn., The Philippines, 1947-48, U.S. Army Map Service, Washington, 1957-61; asst. dir. mapping, charting, and geodesy Def. Intelligence Agy., 1961-63; dep. engr. 8th U.S. Army, Korea, 1963-64; dir. U.S. Army Coastal Engring. Research Ctr., 1964-67; ret., 1967; assoc. dir. U.S. Coast and Geodetic Survey, Rockville, Md., 1967-74; U.S. mem. commn. on cartography Pan Am. Inst. Geography and History, OAS, 1961-67, alt. U.S. mem. directing council, 1970-74, exec. sec. U.S. sect., 1975-87. Decorated Legion of Merit (U.S.), Grand Cross Order of King George II (Greece), Comdr. Most Exalted Order of White Elephant (Thailand), Bronze medal U.S. Dept. Commerce. Fellow ASCE, Soc. Am. Mil. Engrs. (Colbert medal); mem. Am. Soc. Photogrammetry (hon. mem., pres. 1970-71, Luis Struck award), Am. Congress on Surveying and Mapping, N.Y. Acad. Scis., Army-Navy Club, Cosmos Club (Washington), Masons (32 degree), Sigma Xi. Republican. Presbyterian. Home: 9120 Belvoir Woods Pkwy Apt 216 Fort Belvoir VA 22060-2724

DIERKES, WILMA KAROLA, chemical engineer; b. Werlte, Germany, Dec. 24, 1964; arrived in Belgium, 1995; d. Johann and Margaretha (Büter) D. MSc, Tech. U., Hannover, Germany, 1990; M in Environ. Scis., Fondation U. Luxembourgeoise, Luxembourg, 1993; grad., SORK (Stichting Opleiding Rubber en Kunststoffen, Utrecht, The Netherlands, 1996. With Degussa, Brussels, 1991, Vredestein, Maastricht, The Netherlands, 1992-93; mgr. product application devel. Vredestein, Maastricht, 1993-99; with Robert Bosch Produktie NV, Tienen, Belgium, 1999—. Contbr. articles to profl. jours. Avocations: languages, sports, ecology. Office: Robert Bosch Produktie NV, Hamelendreef 80, 3300 Tienen Belgium

DIERKS, CHRISTIAN, attorney, physician, consultant; b. Johannesburg, South Africa, 1960; came to Germany 1962; m. Antje Rudolf, 1992; children: Julius, Harriet. Dr.med., U. Hamburg, 1987; Dr.iur., LMU, Munich, 1992; PD (asst. prof.), HU Berlin, 1999. Intern UKE, Hamburg, 1986-87; gen. practice medicine Munich, 1990-94; lectr. LMU, Munich, 1990—; atty. Haarmann, Hemmelrath & Ptnrs., Berlin, 1994-97; sr. ptnr. Dierks & Bohle, Berlin, 1997—; asst. prof. Inst. for Health System Rsch., Berlin; cons. in field. Sci. adv. bd. editor Pharmarecht; author: Medical Disclosure and Data Protection, 1992, Managed Care in Germany, 1994, Pharmaceutical Therapy and Law, 1995, Telemedicine and Statutory Health Insurance, 1999; editor: Therapeutic Refusal in Minors, 1995, Development of Medical Litigation, 1997, Legal Problems in Allocating Donor Organs, 1999, Legal Aspects of Telemedicine, 2000; contbr. articles to profl. jours., chpts. to books. Mem. adv. bd. Acad. for Manual Medicine, Muenster; mem. sci. coun. Kaiserin-Friedrich Stift., Berlin. Recipient German Pharm. Law prize, 2000. Mem. German Soc. for Medicine and Law (v.p. 1996—), German-South African Lawyers Assn. (chmn. 1992-98, hon. chmn. 1998—), Am. Soc. of Law, Medicine and Ethics, Health Professions Coun. of S. Africa. Office: Kurfuerstendamm 57, D-10707 Berlin Germany

DIESING, PAUL ROBERT, retired political scientist; b. Elgin, Ill., 1922; s. Arthur E. and Eleanor M. (Doederlein) D.; m. Eleanor Zuckman, Sept. 29, 1948; children: Richard, Molly, Sarah, Max. MA, U. Chgo., 1948, PhD, 1952. Lectr. U. Chgo., 1950-52; asst. prof. U. Ill., Urbana, 1952-62; vis. lectr. U. Colo., Boulder, 1962-63; prof. SUNY, Buffalo, 1963-92; ret., 1992; pres. Buffalo chpt. United Univ. Profs., Amherst, N.Y., 1985-87. Author: Reason in Society, 1962, Patterns of Discovery in Social Science, 1971, Science and Ideology, 1982, How Does Social Science Work?, 1991, Hegel's Dialectical Political Economy, a Contemporary Application, 1999; co-author: (with G. Snyder) Conflict Among Nations, 1977. Pres. musicians' bd. Amherst Symphony, N.Y., 1980-83. Served as pfc U.S. Army, 1943-46. Mem. Union Radical Polit. Economists. Avocations: chamber music, hiking.

DIESVELD, RENE JOHANNES, publishing executive; b. Amsterdam, Feb. 20, 1945; s. Hendrik and Dini (Kraneveldt) D.; m. Anne Godschalk, May 28, 1971; 2 children. M of Econs., U. Amsterdam, 1972. Fin. mgr. IBB-Kondor, Leiden, Holland, 1972-75; mng. dir. Keesing Pubs., Amsterdam, 1975—. Office: Keesing Internat Pub BV, Hogehilweg 13, 1101 CA Amsterdam Holland

DIETER, ROBERT SEAN, physician; b. Winfield, Ill., June 17, 1970; s. Raymond Andrew Jr. and Bette Renee (Myers) D.; m. Erin Leigh Dew, Dec. 6, 1997. BS, Ill. Wesleyan U., 1991; MD, U. Ill., 1996. Lic. physician, Ill. Intern in surgery U. Tenn. Hosp., Knoxville, 1996; resident in internal medicine U. Ill. Hosp., 1997-99; fellow in cardiology U. Wis., Madison, 1999—. Tutor U. Ill. Coll. Medicine, Chgo., 1992-96, Urban Health Program, Chgo., 1993-95. Dunning scholar U. Ill. Coll. Medicine, 1993. Mem. AMA, ACP, Am. Coll. Cardiology, Am. Coll. Chest Physicians, Internat. Coll. Surgeons, Wis. Med. Soc., Ill. State Med. Soc., Ill. State Acad. Sci., Chgo. Med. Soc. (adv. pub. health policy com. 1997-99, continuing med. edn. com. 1998-99), Alpha Omega Alpha. Lutheran. Avocations: hiking, fishing, hunting, reading and writing, travelling.

DIETERICH, KLAUS DIETER, molecular biologist, educator, writer; b. Kaiserslautern, Germany, Sept. 19, 1960; s. Herbert and Pauline (Gehm) D. MSc in Biology, U. Kaiserslautern, Germany, 1987; PhD, U. Heidelberg, Germany, 1990. Rsch. assoc. U. Fla., Gainesville, Fla., 1991; clin. monitor Abott, Wiesbaden, Germany, 1992-93; postdoctoral rsch. assoc. U. Calif., San Diego, 1993-96; asst. prof. U. Hosp., Magdeburg, Germany, 1996—; head of molecular biology lab. Inst. for Med. Tech., Magdeburg, Germany, 1998—; tchr. Studienkreis, Schwenningen, Germany, 1992, Handwerkskammer, Kaiserslautern, Germany, 1997—. Author: (books) Das Ende des Tunnels, 1990, Growth Factors, Differentiation Factors and Cytokines, 1990, Transmembrane signalling, intracellular messengers and implications for drug development, 1990, German Love Poetry, 1992, IGdA-Almanach 1992, 1992, Lyrik für die Westentasche, 1992, Das Gedicht, 1992, Nacht lichter ais der Tag, 1992, Autorenwerkstatt 34, 1992, Gedanken unserer Zeit, 1992, Angstschutzgebiet, 1992, Lesezeichen-Anthologie 4, 1993, Gaukes Jahrbuch, 1993, Klare Gedanken über sehr unklare Verhältnissë, 1993, Treasured Poems of America, 1995 (Distinguished Poet award 1995); contbr. articles to profl. jours. With German Alpine Corps, 1981-82. Grantee NIH, 1992, German Rsch. Found., 1993. Mem. German Authors' Assn., German Endocrinology Assn. Avocations: pilot, classical music, reading. Home: Bodestrasse 4, 39118 Magdeburg S Anhalt, Germany Office: Magdeburg U Hosp, Leipzigerstr 44, 39120 Magdeburg S Anhalt, Germany

DIETRICH, KLAUS, physicist, educator; b. Germany, 1946. Dipl. in physics, U. Würzburg, 1971, PhD, 1974. Semiconductor rsch. Dept. Physics U. Würzburg, Germany, 1971-78; applied rsch. Siemens, Munich, 1978-80; mem. R&D staff Messerschmitt Bölkow Blohm, Munich, 1980-87; prof. Fachhochschule, Schweinfurt, Germany, 1987—. Inventor and patentee in field. Mem. Soc. Photo Optical Engrs. Office: Fachhochschule, Ignaz Schon Str 11, D 97421 Schweinfurt Germany

DIETRICH, MELINDA, visual arts administrator; b. Bklyn., July 2, 1943; d. Charles Porter and Ethel Dietrich; children: Charles, Daniel, Vinton. Cert., Parsons Sch. Design, 1964; BFA, U. Hartford, 1968; MBA, Boston Coll., 1986. Art and graphics asst. JBW Graphics, N.Y.C., 1968-69; art dir. Chiquita Brands Inc., Boston, 1970-75; designer James Perry Contractor, Lexington, Mass., 1977-83; cons. Small Bus. Devel. Ctr., Boston, 1986-87; co-founder, designer John Vinton Arch., Lexington, 1988-91; exec. dir. Arts Lexington, 1992-94, Munroe Ctr. Arts, Lexington, 1994—; Request for Proposal cons. Lexington Friends Arts, 1994; prof. devel. Mass. Cultural Coun., Lexington, 1993. Exhibited in numerous exhbns., 1960—. Pub. rels. advisor Lexington Pub. Schs., 1988-91; steward Lexington Conservation Com., 1996—. Recipient numerous awards and grants. Mem. Lexington C. of C., Art Ctrs. Collaborative, Appalachian Mountain Club. Avocations: writing, poetry, bookmaking, gardening, painting. Office: Munroe Ctr Arts 1403 Mass Ave Lexington MA 02420-3804

DIETSCHI, DIDIER, dentist, researcher; b. Geneva, June 21, 1959; s. Jean and Jeanine (Vidonne) D. DMD, U. Geneva, 1984. Clin. asst. U. Geneva, 1984-89, sr. lectr. dept. operative dentistry, 1989-96, interim co-dir., 1996-98; pvt. practice, Bernex/Geneva, 1987—. Contbr. articles to profl. jours.; author: Metal Free Restorations, 1997. Recipient Prix E.Metral, U. geneva, 1989. Mem. Internat. Assn. for Dental Rsch., European Acad. Aesthetic Dentistry, Swiss Soc. Periodontology. Avocations: snow skiing, windsurfing. Office: Rue de Bernex 292B, 1233 Bernex Geneva Switzerland

DIETZ, ARTHUR TOWNSEND, investment counseling company executive; b. Mt. Vernon, N.Y., Oct. 30, 1923; s. William Arthur and Adele Townsend (Dods) D.; m. Mary Archer, June 29, 1947 (dec. 1980); children: Adele Archer Dietz, Laura Townsend Stamm, Amelia Edmunds Williams; m. Mary Laura Peavy, Sept. 16, 1982 (dec. 1992); m. Margie Nell Lee Baghose, Oct. 4, 1992. AB, Wesleyan U., Middletown, Conn., 1946; MA, Princeton U., 1948, PhD, 1953. Instr. Princeton U., 1948-49; asst. prof. Wesleyan U., 1949-54; Mills Bee Lane prof. fin. and banking, dir. MBA program Emory U., Atlanta, 1959-88; dir. Alpha Fund, Atlanta, 1972-85, Enterprise Funds, Atlanta, 1985—, Enterprise Accumulation Trust, 1995—; pres. ATD Adv. Corp., 1996—, Strategic Portfolio Mgmt., 1988-95; bd. trustees Emory U. Resolution in Honor, 1983; vis. prof. IMEDE, 1965-66; Robert Morris prof., Va., 1984-85. Author books; contbr. articles to profl. jours. Pres. Fernbank PTA, DeKalb County, Ga., 1959-60; mem. DeKalb County Devel. Authority, 1980-84; Retirement Facility for Elderly Authority, DeKalb County, 1982-84. Sgt. AUS, 1942-45, ETO. Named one of Outstanding Educators of Am., 1972; recipient Emory Williams Disting. Teaching award Emory U., 1983; Woodrow Wilson fellow, 1946. Fellow Fin. Analysts Soc.; mem. Phi Beta Kappa (pres. Gamma chpt. 1964-65). Methodist. Avocations: tennis, bridge. Office: ATD Adv 1917 Chamdun Way Atlanta GA 30341-1770

DIETZ, DAVID WILLIAM, structural engineer; b. Rochester, N.Y., Sept. 4, 1968; s. Francis H. and Linda (Haacke) D.; m. Jennifer Montgomery. BSME, Northwestern U., Evanston, Ill., 1990. Registered profl. engr., Ohio. Structural engr. Stark Truss, Inc., Edgerton, Ohio, 1991—. Mem. ASME, AIAA, NSPE. Avocations: theatrical performance, reading, biking. Home: PO Box 9512 Wichita KS 67277-0512 Office: Stark Truss Co 400 Component Dr Edgerton OH 43517

DIETZFELBINGER, HERMANN, hematologist, oncologist; b. Munich, Feb. 5, 1943; s. Hermann and Hedwig (Stählin) D.; m. Pia Hüttmann, Sept. 1980 (div. 1987); children: Nicola, Simon. MD, U. Erlangen, 1963, U. Munich, 1965, U. Vienna, 1965, U. Lausanne, 1966, U. Munich, 1968. Intern U. Hosp., Berlin, 1968-70, Städtisches Krankenhaus, Munich, 1968-70; resident Hosp. Munich-Schwabing, 1970-83, Ctrl. Pathology Inst., Tansania, 1972-74; oberarzt Stadtkrankenhaus Fürth, Germany, 1983-88, Tech. U., Munich, 1988-97; pvt. practice Herrsching, Germany, 1997—; doctorship U. Munich, 1968; cons. hematology and oncology; lectr in nursery schs., med. students. Author chpts. to textbooks; contbr. articles to profl. jours. Stabsarzt der Reserve, 1970. Mem. European Iron Club, European Soc. of Med. Oncology, Am. Assn. of Cancer Rsch., Am. Soc. of Hematology, Deutsche Krebsgesellschaft-Arbeitsgemeinschaft für Internistische Onkologie, Deutsche Gesellschaft für Hämatologie and Onkologie, Bund deutscher Internisten. Avocations: music (playing cello), programming in computer, Greek and graphic art, belletrist. Fax: 49 8152-29-389. Home: Baldurstrasse 9/11, D-80637 Munich Germany Office: Seestr 43, D-82211 Herrsching/Ammersee Germany

DIEZ, JOHN C., state legislator, business owner; b. Aug. 18, 1944; m. Janie Ficklin; children: Tami, John, Todd. Grad. h.s., Dutchtown, La. Owner Diez Office Supply, Gonzalez, La.; mem. La. Ho. of Reps., 1976—; chmn. Hwy., Trans., and Pub. Works com. La. Ho. of Reps., 1995—. Past pres., past v.p. Jambalaya Festival Assn. Mem. Am. Legion (past vice comdr.), East Ascension Sportsman's League, Ducks Unltd. Roman Catholic. Office: PO Box 608 Gonzales LA 70707-0608

DIEZ, JOSE, philosophy educator; b. Barcelona, Spain, June 28, 1961; s. Eduardo Diez and Pilar Calzada. Degree, U. Barcelona, 1984, PhD, 1993. Asst. prof. U. Barcelona, 1985-93; prof. U. Tarragona, Spain, 1993—. Author: Fundamentos de Filosofia de la Ciencia, 1997. Mem. Philosophy of Sci. Soc., European Soc. for Analytic Philosophy, Sci. & Arts Soc. Home: Rogerde Flor 141 6 1, 08013 Barcelona Spain Office: U Rovira i Virgili, Plz Imperial Tarraco 1, 43005 Tarragona Spain

DIEZ, JUAN JOSE BADIOLA, academic administrator. Rector U. Zaragoza, Spain. Office: U Zaragoza, C/Pedro Cerbuna 12, 50009 Zaragoza Spain

DIEZ DE VELASCO, MANUEL, barrister, educator; b. Santander, Spain, May 22, 1926; s. Faustino Manuel and Mercedes (Vallejo) D.; m. Josefina-Tomasa Abellan y Vota, 1959. Student, Valladolid U., U. Madrid, U. Rome, Internat. Law Acad., The Hague. Prof. internat. law U. Granada, Spain, 1959-61, U. Barcelona, Spain, 1961-71, U. Autónoma de Madrid, 1971-74, Complutense U. Madrid, 1974-91; judge Constl. Ct., 1980-86, EC Ct. Justice, 1988-94; prof. emeritus U. Cantabria, Santander, 1996—; mem. Inst. Droit Internat. Author: La Protection diplomatique des sociétés et des actionnaires, 1974, El Tribunal de justicia de las Comunidades Europeas, 1984, Instituciones de Derecho Internacional, 12th edit., 1999, Las Organizaciones Internacionales, 11th edit., 1999; author numerous papers. Mem. Consejo de Estado, 1995—. Mem. Spanish Assn. Profs. Internat. Law and Internat. Rels. (emeritus).

DIEZ GONZÁLEZ, ROSA M., foreign diplomat; b. Sodupe, Spain, May 27, 1952. Mem. European Parliament, 1999—, com. fgn. affairs/human rights/common security/def. policy, substitue com. on devel. and coop.; mem. Group of the Party of European Socialists; mem. delegation for relations with the countries of Ctrl. Am. and Mex. Mem. Spanish Socialist Workers' Party. *

DIGERONIMO, DIANE MARY, nursing educator, psychotherapist; b. Montclair, N.J., Aug. 31, 1945; d. Daniel Sebastian and Carmela Marion (Arminio) DiG. RN, St. Mary's Hosp., Passaic, N.J., 1968; BA, Jersey City State Coll., 1969, MA in Spl. Edn., 1979; MSW, Rutgers U., 1981. Cert. sch. nurse.; cert. health educator; cert. clin. hypnosis; cert. diabetic educator; CCRN; lic. clin. social worker. Nurse ICU Moutainside Hosp., Montclair, 1968-70, instr. nursing, 1970-74; nursing educator State Bds. Nursing Rev. Course LPN/RN, Montclair, 1974—; pres. Nursing Profl. Resources, Montclair, 1981—; vis. lectr. 1985—; pvt. practice psychotherapy, Montclair, 1981—; regional dir. N.J. Nurses Action Coalition, Essex County, 1976-81; vis. prof. various locations; nurse cons. and spkr. in field. Author: My Side of the Street, 1970, From Here To There, 1980, Care of the Critically Ill, 1994, Diabetic Screenings and Education, 1996; co-author: Machinary in Medicine, 1976; author poems (Golden Poet awad 1984); contbr. articles to profl. jours. Mem. ANA, NASW, N.J. Nurses Assn., N.J. Assn. Social Workers, Am. Legion Aux. Roman Catholic. Avocations: writing poetry, traveling, swimming, volunteer work. Home: 23 Stanford Pl Montclair NJ 07042-5009

DI GESU, GIUSEPPE, surgery educator; b. Trabia, Italy, Jan. 14, 1942; s. Salvatore and Carmela (Guzzardi) Di G.; m. Assunta Luisa Arnone, Sept. 4, 1969; children: Simona, Salvatore, Giuliana. Grad., Med. Chirurgia, 1968. Asst. gen. surgery Univ. Palermo (Italy), 1968-69; researcher gen. surgery Ministry of Pub. Edn. Italy, 1970-78; asst. prof. Univ. Palermo, 1978-80, assoc. prof., 1980-92, prof., 1992—; prof. postgrad. sch. gen. surgery U. Palermo, 1976, postgrad. sch. urgent surgery, 1983, postgrad. sch. digestive surgery, 1983, postgrad. sch. surg. oncology, 1983. Author of about 300 books; editor: Atti Accademia Scienze Mediche di Palermo; contbr. articles to profl. jours. Officer HEalt Regional Govt., Palermo, 1994. Mem. Lions (pres. 1990-91, Melvin Jones fellow 1992-93). Avocations: stamp collecting, music. Home: Magg Pietro Toselli N159, 90143 Palermo Italy Office: Policlinico Univ, Via Liborio Guiffre N5, 90127 Palermo Italy

DIGIESI, VINCENZO, internist, educator; b. Bari, Puglia, Italy, Oct. 18, 1934; s. Domenico Digiesi and Giuseppina D'Erchia; m. Bianca Maria Perroud, Sept. 4, 1961; children: Lilia, Cristina, Gemma. Degree in medicine and surgery, U. Florence (Italy), 1959. Vol. asst. Inst. Med. Pathology U. Florence, 1961-67; asst. prof. med. clinic. therapy U. Sassari (Italy), 1967-71; asst. prof. internal medicine U. Florence, 1971-83, assoc. prof. med. therapy and med. hydrology, 1993-95, assoc. prof. internal medicine, 1995—. Contbr. over 160 articles to profl. jours. Mem. Italian Soc. Internal Medicine, Italian Soc. Hypertension, Internat. Soc. Med. Climatology and Hydrology (hon.). Roman Catholic. Avocations: travel, antique-collection. Home: Via Cairoli 18, 50131 Florence Toscana, Italy Office: U Florence, piazza S Marco 4, 50121 Florence Toscana, Italy

DIGNAN, THOMAS GREGORY, JR., lawyer; b. Worcester, Mass., May 23, 1940; s. Thomas Gregory and Hester Clare (Sharkey) D.; m. Mary Anne Connor, Sept. 16, 1978; children: Kellyanne E., Maryclare E. BA, Yale U., 1961; JD, U. Mich., 1964. Bar: Mass. 1964, U.S. Supreme Ct. 1968. Assoc. firm Ropes & Gray, Boston, 1964-74; ptnr. firm Ropes & Gray, 1974—; spl. asst. atty. gen. State of Mass., 1974-76; trustee NSTAR. Asst. editor: Mich. Law Rev., 1963-64; contbr. articles to profl. jours. Bd. dirs. Family Counseling and Guidance Ctrs., Inc., 1967-76, 78-94, v.p., 1983-87, pres., 1987-89; trustee Cath. Charitable Bur. of Boston, Inc., 1994-97, Dana Hall Sch., 1994—; bd. dirs. Gov.'s Mgmt. Task Force, 1979-81, Mass. Moderator's assn., 1994—; mem. fin. com. Town of Sudbury, 1982-85, moderator, 1985—; bd. advisors Environ. Law Ctr., Vt. Law Sch., 1981—; mem. vis. com. U. Mich. Law Sch.; corporator Emerson Hosp., 1989—. Mem. Mass. Bar Assn., Boston Bar Assn., Am. Nuclear Soc., Am. Law Inst., Downtown Club, Nashawtuc Country Club, Order of the Coif, Phi Delta Phi. Republican. Roman Catholic. Home: 8 Saddle Ridge Rd Sudbury MA 01776-2772 Office: Ropes & Gray One International Pl Boston MA 02110

DIGNANI, MARIA CECILIA, physician; b. Buenos Aires, Argentina, July 2, 1963; d. Alberto and Ida Haydee Brandi D. MD, U. Nacional de Buenos Aires, Argentina, 1986; Specialist in Internal Medicine, Ministerio de Salud y Acciou Social, Argentina, 1997; Specialist in Infectious Diseases, Acad. Nacional de Medicina, Argentina, 1998. Resident in internal medicine Ctr. de Estudios Medicos e Investigaciones Clinicas "Norberto Qurruo", Buenos Aires, Argentina, 1987-90; fellow in infectious diseases Ctr. de Estudios Medicos e Investigaciones Clinicas-Fundacion de Lucha contra la Leucemia, Buenos Aires, Argentina, 1990-91, U. Tex. M.D. Anderson Cancer Ctr., Houston, 1991-94; head infectious diseases Fundaleu, Buenos Aires, Argentina, 1994—. Contbr. articles to profl. pubs. Mem. Am. Soc. Microbiology, Internat. Immunocompromised Host Soc., Sociedad Argentina de Infectologia, Internat. Soc. Human and Animal Mycology. Roman Catholic. Avocations: tango dancing, playing piano, movies, books, music. Home: Juncal 4540 6H, 1425 Buenos Aires Argentina Office: Fundaleu, Uriburu 1450, 1114 Buenos Aires Argentina

DI GUARDO, GIOVANNI, veterinary pathologist; b. Turin, Piedmont, Italy, July 4, 1958; s. Giuseppe and Giovanna (Marino) Di G.; m. Letizia Curini, July 12, 1987. DVM, U. Bologna, Italy, 1982. Diplomate European Coll. Vet. Pathologists, 1995. Tng. pathologist Faculty Vet. Medicine, U. Bologna, 1982-85; state veterinarian Health Ministry, Rome, 1985-87; vis. prof. dept. vet. clin. scis. Iowa State U., Ames, 1987-88; asst. vet. pathologist Istiuto Zoofilattice Experimentale delle Regioni, Toscana, 1987-93, chief vet. pathologist, 1993—. Contbr. articles to profl. jours. Cpl. Maj. Italian Army, 1983-84. Fulbright scholar, 1987-88, Coun. for Internat. Exch. Scholars. Mem. European Soc. Vet. Pathology, European Coll. Vet. Pathologists, N.Y. Acad. Scis., Fulbright Alumni Assn. Avocations: art, music, tennis, skiing, flying. Home: Viale Oceano Indiano, 100 00144 Rome Italy Office: Istituto Zoofrofilattice, Via Appia Nuova 1411, 00178 Rome Italy

DIHLE, ALBRECHT GOTTFRIED FERDINAND, classics educator; b. Kassel, Germany, Mar. 28, 1923; s. Hermann and Frieda (von Reden) D.; m. Marlene S.L. Meier, Oct. 1, 1949; children: Franziska, Stefanie, Andreas, Barbara, Katharina. PhD, U. Göttingen, Germany, 1946; ThD (hon.), U. Bern, Switzerland, 1982; DPhil (hon.), U. Athens, Greece, 1988; DLitt, Macquarie U., Australia, 1993. Lectr. U. Göttingen, 1950-58; prof. classics U. Cologne, Germany, 1958-74, U. Heidelberg, Germany, 1974-89; pres. Heidelberger Akademie der Wissenschaften, Heidelberg, Germany, 1990-94; vis. prof. Cambridge (Eng.) U., 1963, Harvard U., Cambridge, Mass., 1965-66, 89-90, Stanford (Calif.) U., 1968, U. Calif., Berkeley, 1973-74, Princeton U., 1983, Durban U., 1984, Perugia U., 1988, Macquarie U., Australia, 1993. With German Army, 1940-42. Decorated Order of Pour le Mérite, Oester. Ehrenzeichen. Fellow Brit. Acad.; mem. Am. Acad. Arts and Sci., Düsseldorf Acad. Sci., Heidelberg Acad. Sci., Göttingen Acad. Sci., Acad. Europaea, Acad. Inscriptions (corr.), Rotary (pres. 1980-81). Office: U Heidelberg, Marstallhof 4, D-69117 Heidelberg Germany

DI JESO, DUKE DON FERNANDO, biochemistry educator; b. Cosenza, Italy, Oct. 29, 1931; s. Pasquale and Adelaide (Scopa) di J. BA, Vittorio Emanuele II, Naples, Italy, 1949; MD, Univ. Med. Sch., Naples, 1955; PhD, U. Perugia (Italy), 1959; DSc, U. Paris, 1965. Lic. capt. of pleasure vessel. Rschr. Biochem. Inst., U. Med. Sch., Naples, 1952-54; rschr. biochem. dept. Cancer Inst., Naples, 1954-56; assoc. prof. phys. chemistry dept. U. Padua (Italy), 1956-57; rschr. biochem. dept. Cancer Inst., Naples, 1957-60; prof. libero docente Biochemistry Inst., U. Med. Sch., Naples, 1961; assoc. prof. biochemistry dept. Coll. de France, Paris, 1961-63; assoc. prof. Biochemistry Inst., U. Med. Sch., Pavia, Italy, 1963-67; assoc. prof. biochemistry and molecular biology dept. Cornell U., Ithaca, N.Y., 1967-69; prof. biochemistry Biochemistry Inst., U. Med. Sch., Pavia, 1969—; bd. dirs. Postdoctoral Med. Sch. Neurophysiopathology, U. Pavia, 1990-93; dir. Cardiovasc. Biochemistry Ctr., 1990-96; pres. ethics com. Interuniv. Ctr. for Adaptative Disorder and Headache, 1993-99; sci. and artistic advisor Internet Uniform Resources Locator Kronosnet.com, 1995—. Editor, author: Membrane-Bound Enzymes, 1971, Advances in Experimental Medicine and Biology, vol. 14; editor, pub. Medicina Democratica, 1976—, Glenans, 1985—, Aggiornamenti of the Italian Study Group on Radioimmunological Surgery and Immuno-Scintigraphy, 1993—, Sud-Mag., 1994-1996; internet editor, author. Pres. Cooperativa Editoriale Pavese, Pavia, 1969-75, Laureati Cattolici, Pavia, 1970, CISL-Universita, Pavia, 1975-79, Medicina Democratica, Italy, 1976-90, Lega Navale Italiana, Pavia, 1990—. Decorated ufficiale della Repubblica (Italy); Abroad Rsch. grantee NATO, Tr. An Italian Com. of Nat. Rsch. Coun., 1961-63, Italian Nat. Rsch. Coun., 1967-69; recipient Concorso Nazionale di Poesia Amisani, Mede Municipality and Amisani Assn., Mede, Italy, 1988, Premio Letterario Casentino, Casentino Prize Com., Stia, Italy, 1981, 88-93, Internat. D'Arte Moderna, Rome, 1992, Ungaretti, Sorrento, 1992, Naples, 1995, Luci di Poesia, Milan, 1993, Coppa Eduardo at Il Delfino d'Argento, 1993, Omaggio a Pirandello, Rome, 1994, Golfo di Napoli, Naples, 1994, Cascate di Stelle, Milan, 1995; Delfino

d'Argento, Anzio, 1997; Duke of St. John of Acre; Count Palatine by Emperor Leopold edict. Mem. Italian Soc. Biochemistry, Am. Chem. Soc., French Soc. Biology, Internat. Brain Rsch. Orgn., Italian Fulbright Assn. (mem. exec. bd., award 1967), Assn. Professionale Univ., Italian Soc. Cardioneurology, Italian Soc. Pharmacology, Italian Soc. Neurosci., Royal Soc. Medicine, Nobilis Academia Sanctae Theodorae Imperatricis, Senator Micenei Internat. Acad., Mr. Multi-Hulls of Glénans Internat. Assn., The Hist. file. Avocation: sailing. Office: Prima Cattedra Chim Biologi, U Pavia/CP 372, 27100 Pavia Italy

DIJKMANS, ROGER, environmental researcher; b. Hamont, Limburg, Belgium, Sept. 1, 1959; s. Albert Dijkmans and Eliza Cuppens; m. Mariette Konings, Sept. 10, 1982; children: Toon, Jan, Pieter, Seppe. Degree in engring. and chemistry, Cath. U., Leuven, Belgium, 1982, D in Agronomy, 1987. Rsch. asst. Rega Inst., Leuven, 1982-87, rsch. assoc., 1987-90; rsch. assoc. Nuclear Rsch. Ctr., Mol, Belgium, 1990-91; project leader Flemish Inst. Tech. Rsch., Mol, 1991—. Contbr. articles to profl. jours.; editor 15 books in field. With Belgian Army, 1985. Recipient Schamelhout-Koettlitz prize Belgian Royal Acad. Medicine, 1991. Home: Lage Weg 35D, 2470 Retie Belgium Office: Vito, Boeretang 200, 2400 Mol Antwerp Belgium

DIJKSTAL, HENRY FRANS (HANS DIJKSTAL), Dutch government official; b. Port Said, Egypt, Feb. 28, 1943. Grad., Mcpl. U. Amsterdam. Ind. fin. cons., lectr. mgmt. tng. Inst. Social Studies, The Hague, The Netherlands, 1970-78; dep. chmn. Assn. for Facilities for Disabled; mem. steering com. Haya van Someren Found.; supervisory dir. BV Restoplan; bd. mem. Appel and Hollandsche Comedie theatre cos.; People's Party for Freedom and Democracy mem. Mcpl. Coun., Wassenaar, 1974-86; alderman, 1978-83; mem. Parliament Lower House, 1982-94; min. home affairs, vice prime min. Govt. of Netherlands, 1994-98, floor leader VVD party, 1998—. With Dutch Air Force, 1965-67. Office: The Lower House, PO Box 20018, 2500 EA The Hague The Netherlands*

DIK, KHALED, health facility administrator, consultant; b. Haifa, Israel, Nov. 11, 1943; arrived in Australia, 1989; s. Loutfi Mosbah D. and Said Aga Sobhieh; m. Tatiana Dik Blagova, Feb. 8, 1970 (div. Feb. 1997); children: Walid, Maxim; m. Olga V. Rogotneva, Oct. 17, 1997. Physician, Petersburg Sch. Medicine, USSR, 1974, MA in Surgery, 1976; PhD in Orthopedics and Traumatology, Ctrl. Inst. Traumatology and, USSR, 1981. Surgeon Hyegia Hosp., Greece, 1988-89; counsellor Health Edn. Office, Australia, 1992-95; sr. cons. WHO, Afghanistan, 1995, UN Relief and Work Agy., Gaza, Palestine, 1997; med. dir. European Gaza Hosp., UNRWA field health program, 1997—; orthopedic cons. Lebanon, 1984-87; chief orthopedic svcs. Moh Setif, Algeria, 1981-83; gen. surg. Arab Emergency Hosp., Beirut, 1976-77. Contbr. articles to profl. jours. Boy scout Farouk, Lebanon, 1965. Mem. UN Club. Avocations: postal history. Home: PO Box 156, Surry Hills 2010 NSW, Australia

DIKAREV, BORIS NIKOLAEVICH, physicist, educator; b. Leningrad, USSR, Mar. 29, 1947; s. Nikolay Alekseevich and Anna Georgievna (Nechaeva) D.; m. Svetlana Evgenievna Krupina, July 4, 1969; children: Natalya Tarasevich, Konstantin. Hon. Diploma of Radiophysics, Dnepropetrovsk State U., Ukraine, 1970, Diploma Candidate of Sci. in Physics, 1978; Cert. Asst. Prof., State Acad. Civil Engring., 1980, Cert. Prof., 1995. Asst. State Acad. Civil Engring. and Architecture, Dnepropetrovsk, 1973-76, 76-78, asst. prof., 1978-81, head dept., 1985—, vice-rector, 1992—, prof., 1995—; asst. prof. U. Annaba (Algeria), 1981-85; mem. specialized coun. State U. Dnepropetrovsk, 1998; mem. Regional Commn. for Fgn. Students Affairs Adminstrn., Dnepropetrovsk, 1996; invited prof. U. Poitiers (France), 1994—, Nat. Inst. Applied Scis., Lyon, France, 1997—; mem. adv. com. Internat. Conf. Dielectric Liquids. Author: Problems of Physics, 1995; contbr. more than 100 articles to profl. jours. including Jour. Electrostatics. Grantee European Commn., 1996, grantee Inteant. Conf. on Electrostatics, 1997, 13 Internat. CDL, 1999. Mem. IEEE, French Soc. Electrostatics, Internat. Acad. Engrs. (academic adviser). Avocations: reading, collecting books, football, tennis. Office: Acad Civil Engring & Arch, 24-A Chernyshevsky St, 49092, Ukraine

DIKE, MARGARET HOPCRAFT, retired education administrator; b. Prescott, Ariz., July 15, 1921; d. Walter Irving and Margaret Jennie (Lindsay) Hopcraft; m. Sheldon Holland Dike, Nov. 28, 1941 (div. 1971); children: Lawrence, Walter, Robert, Martin, Martha. BA, U. N.Mex., 1941, MA, 1975. Draftsman U. Calif., Los Alamos, N.Mex., 1943-45; coord. Albuquerque Pub. Schs., 1972-85; ret., 1985; chair pub. adv. com. U. N.Mex., Albuquerque, 1973-74, chair search com. regional v.p., 1975. Co-editor: Bicentennial '76 - Albuquerque, 1977; editor booklet New Mexico Arts Resources Survey, 1957. Trustee Albuquerque Mus., 1969-81; chmn. Albuquerque R.R. Centennial, 1979-80, Keep Albuquerque Beautiful Edn., 1984—; pres. Albuquerque Sister Cities Found., 1985-87; Albuquerque Hist. Soc., 1971-78; N.Mex. Assn. for Cmty. Edn. Devel., 1980-82; chair Albuquerque Sister Cities Bd., 1988-91, 96—; life mem. N.Mex. PTA, pres., 1977-79, 92-95; sec. Edn. Forum N.Mex., 1988-89; chair, Ednl. Success Alliance, 1996-97. Recipient Lobo award U. N.Mex., 1968, Gov.'s award for outstanding N.Mex. women, Commn. on Status of Women, 1986, 90, N. Mex. Disting. Svc. award, 1996; named Woman on the Move for cmty. svc. YWCA, 1995, to Sr. Hall of Fame, 1995, Zia award U. N. Mex. Alumni Assn., 1999. Mem. AAUW (pres. N.Mex. 1989-93, pres. Albuquerque br. 1968-70, 2000—), Exec. Women Internat. (treas. 1983-85), Mortar Bd. (pres. alumni chpt. 1988-90, 96—, Nat. Cmty. Svc. award 1993), Albuquerque Assn. Ednl. Retirees (pres. 1998, 99), La Luz Am. Bus. Womens Assn., Phi Delta Kappa, Phi Kappa Phi, Phi Alpha Theta. Methodist. Avocations: travel, reading, camping, sewing.

DIKE, RAD (EDWARD CONRAD DIKE), artist; b. Maywood, Nebr., June 9, 1945; s. Raymond Hadyn and Mary Dorothy (Popp) D.; m. Laurel Ellen Rathbun, 1970 (div. 1971); m. Ann Doherty Langenbach, Feb. 14, 1985. think tank dir. Henry Dreyfuss Assn., N.Y.C., 1970-72; vis. prof. Pratt Inst. Sch. of Architecture, N.Y.C., 1970-72, adj. prof., 1972-77; organizer Nat Indsl. Design Conf., Pa., 1971; mentor prof. PhD leadership program NYU, 1974-77; guest lectr. CCNY, Cooper Union, N.Y. Sch. Interior Design, 1975-77; vis. prof. Parsons Sch. Design, 1976-77; spkr. Harvard Grad. Sch. Design, 1983. Exhibited in shows at Pratt Inst., N.Y.C., 1968, 69, U.S. Embassy, Stockholm, 1970, Smithsonian Air & Space Mus., Washington, 1971, Gotham Book Mart Gallery, N.Y.C., 1973, Field Taos, N.Mex., 1976, Nat. Peace Garden Travelling Show, 1989-92, Boston Athenaeum, 1992, 94, 96, Nat. Arts Club (Pres. award), 1995, Flickinger Arts Ctr., 1995, HGTV Arts Video, 1995, Virtuosity Art Internat. 3D CD ROM Mus., 1996; author: Architectural Common Sense, 1983; represented in permanent collections; inventor Mr. McCogitator robot, balcony-autogyro/boat/car balcony, 1969, naturally refined architecture, gesso/metal dusts paint tech.; prin. archtl. works include N.Y.C. Dept. Gen. Svc. Gardens, 1981, Hell's Kitchen Seedling Greenhouse, 1983, Whole Tree Cottage, 1988, Trussed Arched Tree Branches (Vt. Gov.'s Spl. Merit award), 1989, Arch Keystone Tree, 1990, Suspension Tree Facade, 1991, Chez Ploix, France, 1994—, others.. Cons., organizer First Earth Day, N.Y.C., 1970; laborer Green Guerillas, 1976-82; regional planning commr. So. Windsor (Vt.) County, 1989-90; bd. dirs. Hist. Windsor, 1991-93, trustee, 1994-95; founder Conservation Commn., West Windsor, 1990; commr. Vt. Road & Bridges Agy., 1990, Vt. Assn. Planners & Developers Agys., 1990; bd. advisors Preservation Inst. Bldg. Crafts, 1994—; bd. dirs. Am Inst. Wine & Food New England, 1993-95. Batchelder grantee, 1964-70, Ford Motor grantee, 1967-70, Travel grantee U.S. Dept. Commerce, Pratt Inst., 1969; recipient Armco Steel prize, 1969, Merit award NEA, 1984, Outstanding Electronics award USAF, 1959, Poetry award Quill & Scroll USA, 1960. Mem. Nat. Arts Club, Vt. Land Trust (life). Achievements include scientific research and demonstration on Squared Circle of da Vinci's Man, Disproof of Le Corbusier's Modular Man, Human Golden Trinity, Skyscraper as Garden-Engine, Heat chimney Skyscraper Cooling, Laws of Branches, Natural Refinement. Home: Dike Outlook Reading VT 05062

DIKKEN, JACOB JAN, manufacturing company executive; b. Ubbergen, The Netherlands, June 29, 1952; s. Hendrik Dikken and Klaaske DeBoer; m. Jeronima Elizabeth Koens, Mar. 18, 1l975; children: Fenneke, Noortje, Leona. Degree in engring., Tech. Coll., The Netherlands, 1974; AMP, Insead, Fontainbleau, France, 1997. Supt. Adriaan Volker, Abu Dhabi, United Arab Emirates, 1975-79; ops. mgr. Volker-Stevin, Norway, 1979-80; v.p. Volker-Stevin Can., Calgary, 1980-85; dir. oil and gas Volker-Stevin Can., Rotterdam, The Netherlands, 1985-92; area dir. Offshore Ham Dredging, Rotterdam, 1992-98; mng. dir. VDS Cable, Haren, The Netherlands, 1992—; mem. supervisory bd. Seateam Den Helder Netherlands, 1995-97, Seateam Tech., Oslo, 1997-98; chmn., bd. dirs. JJD Mgmt., Heeg, The Netherlands; ptnr. New Venture Ptnrs.; owner, dir. JJD Mgmt., JJD Beheer, Stoetery Seven. Co-inventor flow dredging; contbr. articles to profl. jours. Mem. Netherlands Engring. Assn., Internat. Pipelines and Offshore Contractors Assn. (bd. dirs. 1999—), Insead Advanced Mgmt. Program. Avocations: sailing, skiing, diving, golf, horses. Home: Lytshuzen 12, 8621 XG Heeg The Netherlands Office: VanderStoel Cable br, Nieuwe Stationsweg 9, 9750 AE Haren The Netherlands

DIKOVSKI, VLADLEN, physicist, researcher; b. Jitomirska, USSR, Dec. 12, 1929; s. Isaak Abrahamovich and Frida Isaevna (Farzer) Dikovski; m. Liliana Leonidovna Vinogradova, Oct. 15, 1965; 1 child, Dmitri Vladlenovich, July 19, 1966. Student, Mech. Inst., Moscow, 1947-48, U. Phys. Tech., Moscow, 1948-51, U. Phys., Leningrad, Russia, 1951-52; Candidat of Sci., Inst. Microapparatus, Moscow, 1968; DSc, Inst. Semiconductors, Moscow, 1990. Mid. sch. tchr. math. and physics, 1952-57; engr. Inst. Semiconductors, Moscow, 1956-57, maj. engr., 1957-59, sr. engr., 1959-65, dir. lab., 1965-66, 76—, dir. dept., 1966-76; mem. sci. coun. Inst. Semiconductors. Contbr. articles to profl. jours.; patentee in field. Avocations: yachting, mountain skiing. Fax: 7-095-366 5583. Home: 9 E-D-dorozhnii proezd corp, 1 apt 129, 113535 Moscow Russia Office: 27 E-D Okruzhnoy proezd, 105187 Moscow Russia

DIKSHIT, SURYA PRASAD, journalism and literature educator; b. Raebarely, India, July 6, 1938; s. Bhagawati Prasad and Shiva Dulari Dikshit; m. Manjula Tiwari, May 30, 1963; children: Swasti, Maneesha, Abhinav. BA, Lucknow (India) U., 1958, MA, 1960, PhD, 1965; DLitt, Magadh U., Bodhgaya, India, 1973. Lectr. Jodhpur (India) U., 1963-76; reader Lucknow U., 1976-86, prof. HOD Hindi, 1986-99, prof. HOD journalism, 1992-99; dir. Trikal Informatics, Lucknow, 1996—; v.p. Ayodhya Shodh Sansthan, Faizabad, India, 1997—; pres. Bhartiya Hindi Parishad, Allahabad, 1997—, Pub. Rels. Soc. India, Lucknow, 1998—. Author, editor 62 books, 1965-99; editor 5 mags.; contbr. articles to profl. jours. Pres. Sarwahit Vidyadham, Lucknow, 1998—. Recipient Sahitya Bhooshan award U.P. Govt., Lucknow, 1998. Mem. Hindi Sahitya Samelan Allahabad (Sahity Vachaspati award), K.K. Birla Found. (pres. 1998—), Ram Mohan Ray Found. Avocation: collecting manuscripts. Home: Sahityki D-54, Nirala Nagar 226020, India Office: Sanchar Bhawan, Lucknow Univ, Lucknow 226020, India

DI LAURO, CARLO, physical chemistry educator, researcher; b. Naples, Italy, Jan. 4, 1940; s. Felice and Angelina (Padula) di L; m. Franca Lattanzi, Feb. 14, 1981; children: Francesca, Giuliana. D in Indsl. Chemistry, U. Naples, 1963. Rsch. assoc. Reading, U.K., 1965; asst. prof. U. Naples, 1965-73; assoc. prof. U. Calabria, Italy, 1973-80; prof. U. Palermo, Italy, 1980-83; prof. phys. chemistry U. Naples, 1983—; rsch. assoc. Vanderbilt U., Nashville, 1968-69, U. We. Ont., London, Can., 1968-69; rsch. dir. CNRS, Orsay, France, 1986-87; vis. rsch. officer NRC, Ottawa, Ont., 1991-92; invited scientist CSIC, Madrid, 1995-96. Contbr. articles to profl. jours. Decorated chevalier des Palmes Academiques (France). Achievements include research in theory and application of vibro-rotational, ro-vibronic, and vibro-roto-contorsional molecular spectroscopy. Home: Via Bonito 27/C, I-80129 Naples Italy Office: Dept Pharm Chemistry, Via D Montesano 49, I-80131 Naples Italy

DI LELLO FINUOLI, GIUSEPPE, member European Parliament; b. Villa S. Maria, Italy, Nov. 24, 1940. Mem. European Parliament, Brussels, 1999—; mem. com. on citizens' freedoms and rights, justice and home affairs, com. on petitions, substitute mem. com. on agr. and rural devel., mem. del. for rels. with countries S.Am. and MERCCOSUR. Mem. Confed. Group of European United Left/Nordic Green Left. *

DILIBERTO, OLIVIERO, federal official, educator; b. Cagliari, Italy, Oct. 13, 1956. Law Degree. Dep., group leader Rifondazione Comunista Parliament, 1994-96; dep. Progressisti Parliament, 1996-98; mem. Transport, Postal and Telecom. Svcs. Commn., Party of Italian Communists, 1998; min. of justice D'Alema's govt., 1998-2000; gen. sec. Party of Italian Communists, 2000—; min. justice Italy, 1999; leader Italian Communist Party, Reformed; prof. Roman law U. Cagliari. Office: Chamber of Deputies, Piazza Montecitorio 1, I-00186 Rome Italy*

DILL, C. JEROME, deputy premier of Bermuda, barrister; b. Pembroke, Bermuda, Apr. 6, 1960; s. Charles Milton and Shirley Edwina (Emery) D. BA in Econs., Dalhouse U., N.S., Can., 1981; LLB with honors, London Sch. Econs., 1984; LLM, U. Coll., London, 1985. Bar: Coun. Legal Edn. Eng. 1985. Ptnr. Appleby, Spurling & Kempe, Bermuda, 1991—; min. human affairs and info. Bermuda Govt., 1993-95, min. edn. and human affairs, 1995—, senator, 1992-93, mem. Parliament for Pembroke West Ctrl., 1993—; dep. premier of Bermuda, 1995—; parliamentary sec. health, social svcs., and housing and edn. Chmn. edn. com. Human Rights Commn., Bermuda, 1990-92, chmn. investigations com., 1991; chmn. advt. com. Rd. Saftey Coun., Bermuda, 1990-92; mem. nat. com. Bermuda Operation Raleigh, 1990—; dep. chmn. United Bermuda Party, 1991-92; chmn. Bermuda Civic Ballet, 1994—; regional chair com. "O" IBA. Mem. Hon. Soc. of Inner Temple, Regional chair IBA com. "O", Bermuda C. of C. (exec. profl. svcs. divsn., mem. task force on labour legis.). Home: 12 Fairyland Ln, Pembroke HM 05, Bermuda Office: Appleby Spurling & Kempe, 41 Cedar Ave Cedar House, HM 12 Hamilton Bermuda*

DILLABER, PHILIP ARTHUR, budget and resource analyst, economist, consultant; b. Springfield, Mass., Aug. 24, 1922; s. Ralph E. and Grace (Holman) D.; m. Jacqueline M. Bertin, July 16, 1946; children: Anne Erline (Mrs. Donald Youngblood), Katherine Marie, John Philip, Patricia Elizabeth (Mrs. Joseph Mickley). BA with honors, Am. Internat. Coll., 1949; MBA, Ind. U., 1950; postgrad., U. Mich., Ind. U., 1950-54; PhD, Pacific Western U., 1985. Cert. govt. fin. mgr. Clk. rsch. and devel. div. Springfield Armory, 1946-47; rsch. asst. dept. econs. Ind. U., 1951, lectr. econs., 1955-57; orgn. and methods examiner USAF, Gulfport, Miss., 1952-53; mgmt. analyst 5th U.S. Army, Chgo., 1954-61; program progress and resources mgmt. analyst Continental Army Command, Ft. Monroe, Va., 1962-66; adminstrv. officer U.S. Army NIKE-X System Office, Alexandria, Va., 1967; program analyst Office Asst. Chief Staff Force Devel. Dept. Army, Washington, 1967-71, budget analyst Office Dep. Chief Staff Logistics, 1971-74; budget analyst Office Dep. Chief Staff Rsch., Devel. and Acquisition, Washington, 1974-80; sr. analyst Info. Spectrum, Inc., Arlington, Va., 1980-87; mem. Nat. Def. Exec. Reserve, Washington, 1985-97; cons. Profl. Group, Inc., 1992-99; del. Citizen Amb. Program Pub. Budgeting and Fin. Mgmt., People's Republic of China, 1995; mem. Nat. Exec. Svc. Corp., N.Y.C., 1997; guest lectr. econs. Purdue U., 1959-61. Decorated Commendation medal Regional Coun., Normandy, France, 1994, Wall of Liberty Meml. Mus., Caen, France, 1994; mem. Exceptional WWII Fin. Unit displayed U.S. Army Fin. Corps Mus., Ft. Jackson, S.C. Mem. Am. Econ. Assn., Nat. Contract Mgmt. Assn., Nat. Def. Indsl. Assn., Am. Assn. Budget Program Analysis, Project Mgmt. Inst., Assn. Govt. Accts. (cert. govt. fin. mgr.), Am. Soc. Pub. Adminstrn., Sons. of Am. Revolution, Assn. Def. and Emergency Resources, Beta Gamma Sigma. Home: 3003 Arkendale St Woodbridge VA 22193-1223

DILLARD, DEAN INNES, English language educator, college official; b. Melvern, Kans., Aug. 13, 1947; s. Alva Everett and Dorothy Marie (Whitney) D. BS in Edn., Emporia (Kans.) State U., 1969, MA, 1975, postgrad., 1977; postgrad., Ft. Hays State U., Hays, Kans., 1980. Tchr. English, Unified Sch. Dist. 379, Clay Center, Kans., 1969-70; tchr. English and social studies Unified Sch. Dist. 208, WaKeeney, Kans., 1972-84; instr. English, Neosho County C.C., Chanute, Kans., 1984—, chair divsn. liberal arts, 1996-99, interim v.p. acad. and student affairs, 1997-98, 99-00; fine arts task force Neosho County C.C., Chanute, 1990-91. With U.S. Army, 1970-71. Mem. MLA, Nat. Coun. Tchrs. English, The Assn. Lit. Scholars and Critics, Assembly on Lit. for Adolescents (life), Midwest Modern Lang. Assn., Kans. Assn. Tchrs. English (exec. bd. 1981-84), Neosho County C.C. Educators Assn., Am. Legion, VFW, Chanute Lions Club (zone chmn. 1988-90), Kappa Delta Pi. Republican. Home: 732 S Washington Ave Chanute KS 66720-2713 Office: Neosho County C C 800 W 14th St Chanute KS 66720-2639

DILLARD, JOHN ROBERT, lawyer; b. Sylva, N.C., Mar. 14, 1955; s. George Washington and Ethel Thomasine (Freeman) D.; m. Olga Malei, Feb. 3, 1998. BSBA cum laude, Western Carolina U., 1977; JD, Samford U., 1980; postgrad., Western Carolina U., 1986-88; PhD in Bus. Adminstr. with honors, S.W. U., 1989. Bar: N.C. 1980, U.S. Dist. Ct. (we. dist.) N.C. 1981. Sole practice Cashiers, N.C., 1980-81; ptnr. Alley, Killian, Kersten & Dillard, Waynesville, N.C., 1981-85; sr. v.p., atty. Commonwealth Land Title Co., Asheville, N.C., 1985-93; pres., state mgr. Stewart Title of N.C., Asheville, 1993—; legal counsel Woodmen of World Ins., Waynesville, 1982-85, bd. dirs.; sec. Beta-Zeta Ltd., Waynesville, 1982-84, bd. dirs.; cons. Nereus Inc., Greenville, Tenn., 1986-88; adj. faculty Asheville-Buncome Tech. Coll., 1990-93, Mars Hill Coll., 1992; instr. Nat. Bus. Inst., 1996. Legal counsel, bd. dirs. Lambda Chi Alpha, Cullowhee, N.C., 1983-85; adv. Jr. Achievement, Clyde, N.C., 1984. Recipient Unsung Brother award, Lambda Chi Alpha, 1974. Mem. ABA (cert. arbitrator), ATLA, N.C. Acad. Trial Lawyers, N.C. State Bar (mem. constl. law com. 1996—), N.C. Coll. Advocacy, Am. Land Title Assn., N.C. Real Property Assn., Masons, Woodmen (trustee 1982-99). Democrat. Episcopalian. Home: 4 Wagner Branch Dr Asheville NC 28804-1000 Office: 9 S Pack Sq Ste 301 Asheville NC 28801-3522

DILLARD, ROBERT PERKINS, pediatrician, educator; b. Ft. Benjamin Harrison, Ind., June 7, 1941; s. Harry Knight and Anna Frances (Perkins) D.; children: Robert Perkins, Ann Michele, Christopher Stevens, Catherine Colleen; m. Roberta L. Schaffner, Oct. 20, 1991; 1 child, Preston Fielding. AB, Transylvania U., 1963; MD, U. Ky., Lexington, 1967. Diplomate Am. Bd. Pediat., Am. Bd. Pediat. Gastroenterology; lic. physician, Ky., Fla., N.C. Intern U. Okla. Med. Ctr., Oklahoma City, 1967-68; resident in pediat. Children's Meml. Hosp., U. Okla. Med. Ctr., Oklahoma City, 1968-71; fellow pediat. gastroenterology and nutrition Children's Hosp. Med. Ctr., Cin., 1989-90; clin. asst. prof. pediat. U. South Fla. Coll. Medicine, Tampa, 1975-77; asst. prof. pediat. medicine, assoc. dir. ambulatory pediat. East Carolina U., Greenville, N.C., 1977-83, dir. pediat. nutrition support svcs., 1981-83; assoc. prof. pediatrics U. Ky. Coll. Medicine, Lexington, 1983, dir. level I nursery, asst. dir. gen. pediatrics, 1983-89, assoc. prof., dir. pediatric gastroenterology and nutrition, 1990-94, assoc. prof. multidisciplinary PhD program, 1993-94; dir. pediatric gastroenterology and nutrition Sacred Heart Children's Hosp., 1994-97, Nemours Children's Clinic, 1997—; sr. aviation med. examiner FAA, Lexington, 1983-94, Pensacola, 1994—. Author various handbooks, pamplets, manuals, and video; contbr. articles to profl. jours., chpts. to books. With USN, 1971-73, capt. Res. Recipient various grants. Fellow Am. Acad. Pediat., N.Am. Soc. Pediat. Gastroenterology and Nutrition; mem. NRA, Sons Confederate Vets., Am. Gastroenterology Assn., Aerospace Med. Assn., Soc. USN Flight Surgeons, U. Ky. Coll. Medicine Alumni Assn., So. Pediat. Gut Club. Republican. Avocations: flying, shooting, sailing, scuba diving, drawing. Office: Nemours Childrens Clin WC Payne Bldg 5149 N 9th Ave Ste 308 Pensacola FL 32504-8778

DILLE, JOHN ROBERT, physician; b. Waynesburg, Pa., Sept. 2, 1931; s. Charles Emanuel and Ruth Emma (South) D.; m. Joan Marie Sirtosky, Dec. 17, 1955 (wid. Mar. 1996); children: Paul Andrew, John Alan. BS, Waynesburg Coll., 1952; MD, U. Pitts., 1956; M in Indsl. Health, Harvard U., 1960. Diplomate Am. Bd. Preventive Medicine; cert. correctional health profl. Intern Akron City Hosp., 1956-57; resident in aerospace medicine USAF Sch. Aerospace Medicine, San Antonio, 1960-62; program adv. officer FAA Civil Aeromed. Rsch. Inst., Oklahoma City, 1961-64; western region flight surgeon FAA, L.A., 1965; chief FAA Civil Aeromed. Inst., U.S. Dept. Transp., Oklahoma City, 1966-87, ret., 1987; med. dir. Okla. Dept. Corrections, Oklahoma City, 1990-93; assoc. prof. U. Okla., 1961-98, dir. tng. residency in aerospace medicine, 1967-72; state surgeon Okla. Army N.G., 1990-91; surveyor Nat. Commn. on Correctional Health Care. Assoc. editor: Ag Pilot Internat. mag., 1980-98, Conservation Aeronautics mag., 1989-92, Above All mag., 1992; mem. editorial bd. Aviation, Space and Environ. Medicine, 1987-94; contbr. articles to profl. jours. With USAF, 1957-59; col. M.C., U.S. Army N.G., 1976-91. Recipient Meritorious award William A. Jump Found., 1968; named Army N.G. Flight Surgeon of Yr. 1987, Master Flight Surgeon, 1987. Fellow Aerospace Med. Assn. (mem. exec. coun. 1978-81, 93-98, chmn. history and archives com. 1982-90, chmn. sci. program com. 1985, 1st v.p., 1990-91, pres. 1992-93, Theodore C. Lyster award 1978, Harry G. Moseley award 1987, Armstrong lectr. 1997, chmn. nominating com. 1997-98), Am. Coll. Preventive Medicine (regent 1974-77); mem. Internat. Acad. Aviation and Space Medicine, Soc. U.S. Army Flight Surgeons (bd. govs. 1990-92, Order Aeromed. Merit), Mil. and Hospitaller Order St. Lazarus of Jerusalem, Am. Air Mail Soc. (bd. dirs. 1990-92), Res. Officers Assn., Soc. Correctional Physicians, Sigma Xi, Nu Sigma Nu. Presbyterian. Home and Office: 335 Merkle Dr Norman OK 73069-6429

DILLER, ANTHONY VAN NOSTRAND, Thai language educator, researcher; b. Oakland, Calif., Nov. 16, 1940; arrived in Australia, 1978; s. Elliot Van Nostrand and Berta Marie (Ill) D. BA, Williams Coll., 1962; MA in Edn., Johns Hopkins U., 1963; PhD, Cornell U., 1976. Coord. tng. Peace Corps, Hilo, Hawaii, 1968; rsch. supr. Cornell U., Ithaca, N.Y., 1972-73; lectr. Australian Nat U., Canberra, Australia, 1978-90; reader Australian Nat U., Canberra, 1990—, dep. dean, acting dean Faculty of Asian Studies, 1995—; keynote speaker Pan-Asiatic Linguistics Confs., Bangkok, 1988, 96, 99; dir. Nat. Thai Studies Ctr. Found., Canberra, Australia, 1991—. Contbr. Internat. Encyclopedia Linguistics, 1992; (anthology) The World's Writing Systems, 1996; co-author (CD ROM) Learning Thai Script, 1997; also contbr. over 50 articles to other pubs. in field. Vol. U.S. Peace Corps, Thailand, 1963-67; active in Australian lang. policy affairs. Fellow Australian Acad. of the Humanities; mem. Linguistic Soc. Am., Australian Linguistic Soc., Siam Soc. (Bangkok, life). Avocations: hiking, boating. Office: Australian Nat U, Faculty Asian Studies, Canberra ACT 0200, Australia

DILLIARD, MAXINE K., school psychologist; b. Mpls., June 11, 1935; d. Gilbert Thomas and Florence Ingrid (Jensen) Kirst; m. Herman V. Dilliard, Aug. 4, 1955 (dec. June 1968); children: Alan Frederick, Charles David. BA, U. Minn., 1965, MA, 1967, EdS, 1968. Lic. psychologist, Minn., sch. psychologist, Minn., Calif. Sr. acct. clk. U. Minn., Mpls., 1956-61, rsch. asst., 1965-67; prin. survey interviewer U. Minn. Hosp., Mpls., 1961-65; sch. psychologist Robbinsdale (Minn.) Sch. Dist., 1967-86, Victor Elem. Sch. Dist., Victorville, Calif., 1989—; self-employed human svcs. cons. Mpls., 1986-89. Mem. APA, Nat. Reading Assn., Assn. for Childhood Edn. Internat., Nat. Assn. Sch. Psychologists, Calif. Assn. Sch. Psychologists, Desert/Mountain Assn. Sch. Psychologists, Minn. Psychol. Assn., Phi Beta Kappa. Avocations: reading, travel, grandchildren. Home: 15252 Seneca Rd Spc 226 Victorville CA 92392-2271 Office: Victor Elem Sch Dist 15579 8th St Victorville CA 92392-3360

DILLING, KIRKPATRICK WALLWICK, lawyer; b. Evanston, Ill., Apr. 11, 1920; s. Albert W. and Elizabeth (Kirkpatrick) D.; m. Betty Ellen Bronson, June, 1942 (div. July 1944); m. Elizabeth Ely Tilden, Dec. 11, 1948; children: Diana Jean, Eloise Tilden, Victoria Walgreen, Albert Kirkpatrick. Student, Cornell U., 1939-40; BS in Law, Northwestern U., 1942; postgrad., DePaul U., 1946-47, L'Ecole Vaubier, Montreux, Switzerland; Degré Normal, Sorbonne U., Paris. Bar: Ill. 1947, U.S. Dist. Ct. (no. dist.) Ill., Ind., Mich., Md., La., Tex., Okla., Wis., Idaho, U.S. Ct. Appeals (2nd, 3rd, 5th, 7th, 8th, 9th, 10th, 11th, fed. and D.C. cirs.), U.S. Supreme Ct. Ptnr. Dilling and Dilling, 1948—; counsel Cancer Control Soc., Nat. Coun. for Improved Health; bd. dirs. Nutradelle Labs., Ltd., V.E. Irons, Inc.; v.p. Midwest Medic-Aide, Inc.; spl. counsel Herbalife (U.K.) Ltd., Herbalife Australasia Pty., Ltd.; lectr. on pub. health law. Contbr. articles to pub. health publs. Bd. dirs. Adelle Davis Found., Liberty Lobby. 1st lt. AUS, 1943-46. Recipient Humanitarian award Nat. Health Fedn. Mem. ABA, Ill. Bar Assn., Chgo. Bar Assn., Assn. Trial Lawyers Am., Cornell Soc. Engrs., Am. Legion, Air Force Assn., Pharm. Advt. Club, Rolls Royce Owners' Club, Tower Club, Cornell U., Chicago Club, Delta Upsilon. Republican. Episcopalian. Home: 1120 Lee Rd Northbrook IL 60062-3816

DILLINGER, STEPHAN ALEXANDER, structural dynamics engineer; b. Munich, Apr. 11, 1958; s. Anton and Leonore (Larisch) D.; m. Rosa Maria Zimlich, Oct. 14, 1988; 1 child, Alexander. Diploma, Tech. U., Munich,

1984. Test engr. IABG, Munich, 1985-88, test mgr., 1989-95, project mgr., 1995—. Lance-corporal Mountain Pioneers, 1977-78, Brannenburg, Germany. Recipient Excellent Diploma award, Verein Deutscher Ingenieure, Munich, 1985. Avocations: mountain hiking, sports, photography. Office: IABG, Einsteinstr 20, 85521 Ottobrunn Germany

DILLON, JOSEPH FRANCIS, lawyer; b. Bklyn., Oct. 15, 1938; s. Joseph and Elizabeth (Sullivan) D.; m. Pamela Margaret Higbee, May 15, 1966 (div. Feb. 1972); children: Elizabeth Margaret, J. Alexander; m. Diane L. Long, Mar. 17, 1978. BBA, St. John's U., 1960; LLB, U. Va., 1963. Bar: Va. 1963, N.Y. 1964, U.S. Tax Ct. 1965, Mich. 1968, Ohio 1975, Fla. 1983. Tax trial atty. IRS, Washington and Detroit, 1963-68; mem. Raymond & Dillon, P.C., Detroit, 1969-93, Dykema Gossett PLC, Detroit, 1993-97, Cox, Hodgman & Giarmarco, P.C., Detroit, 1997—; adj. prof. taxation U. Detroit Law Sch., 1977-87; spkr., planning chmn. Inst. CLE Programs; mem. magistrates merit selection panel and profl. assistance com. U.S. Dist. Ct. for Ea. Dist. Mich.; mem. U.S. Ct. Internat. Trade. Bd. dirs., mem. exec. com. Met. Ctr. for High Tech., Detroit, 1993-96. Cpl. USAR, 1958-64. Fellow Mich. State Bar Found.; mem. ABA (taxation and internat. sects. 1963—), FBA (officer, pres. Detroit chpt. 1978-82), Mich. Bar Assn. 1988—, (taxation counsel 1979-82, internat. sec. 1990—), Detroit Bar Assn. (taxation com. 1973—), Va. Bar Assn., N.Y. State Bar Assn., Ohio Bar Assn., Fla. Bar Assn., Am. Judicature Soc., Am. C. of C. in Japan, London Ct. of Internat. Arbitration, Inter-Pacific Bar Assn., Internat. Bar Assn., Greater Detroit-Windsor Japan Am. Soc. (bd. dirs. 1992—, exec. com. 1999—), Japanese Bus. Soc. Detroit Found. (v.p. 1992—), Greater Detroit C. of C. (nominating com. for dirs.), French-Am. C. of C. of Detroit (bd. dirs. 1997—), Detroit Athletic Club, Lochmoor Club, Vineyards Country Club, World Trade Club, Econ. Club (Detroit). Republican. Roman Catholic. Avocations: golf, squash, skiing. Fax: (248) 528-2773. E-mail: JDillon@CHGLAW.COM. Office: Cox Hodgman & Giarmarco PC 5th Fl Columbia Ctr 201 W Big Beaver Rd Troy MI 48084-4152

DILLON, ROBERT MORTON, retired association executive, retired educator, architectural consultant; b. Seattle, Oct. 27, 1923; s. James Richard and Lucille (Morton) D.; m. Mary Charlotte Beeson, Jan. 6, 1943; children: Robert Thomas, Colleen Marie Dillon Brown, Patrick Morton. Student, U. Ill., 1946-47; BArch., U. Wash., 1949; MA in Architecture, U. Fla., 1954. Registered architect, Fla. Designer-draftsman Williams and Longstreet (Architects), Greenville, S.C., 1949-50, William G. Lyles, Bissett, Carlisle & Wolff (Architects), Columbia, S.C., 1949-50, Robert M. Dillon and Wm. B. Eaton (Architects), Gainesville, Fla., 1952-55; staff architect Bldg. Rsch. Adv. Bd., Nat. Acad. Scis.-NRC, Washington, 1955-56, project dir., 1956-58, exec. dir., 1958-77; exec. sec. U.S. nat. com. for Conseil Internat. du Batiment, 1962-74; Sec. U.S. Planning Com. 2d Internat. Conf. on Permafrost, Yakutsk, USSR, 1972-74; exec. asst. to pres. Nat. Inst. Bldg. Scis., Washington, 1978-81, v.p., 1982-84, acting contr., 1983-84; exec. v.p. Am. Coun. Constrn. Edn., Washington, 1984-89, cons., 1989—; asst. prof. arch. Clemson Coll., 1949-50; instr., asst. prof. arch. U. Fla., 1950-55; lectr. structural theory and design Cath. U. Am., 1956-62; guest lectr. Air Force Inst. Tech., Wright-Patterson AFB, 1964-65; disting. faculty Acad. Code Adminstrn. and Enforcement U. Ill., 1972, professorial lectr. George Washington U., 1973-77, 81-82; vis. prof. Coll. Environ. Design U. Okla., 1984, adj. assoc. prof. bldg. sci., 1985-89, grad. sch. arch. Univ. Utah, 1978. Author: (with S.W. Crawley) Steel Buildings: Analysis and Design, 1970, 4th edit., 1993 (also 3d edit. pub. in Spanish 1992); contbg. author: Funk and Wagnall's New Ency., 1972, Ency. of Architecture, 1989; editor-in-chief: Guide to the Use of NEHRP Provisions in Earthquake Resistant Design of Buildings, 1987, Building Seismic Safety Coun., Nat. Inst. Bldg. Scis. Cons. Ednl. Facilities Labs., N.Y.C., 1958-71; mem. adv. com. low-income housing demonstration program HUD, Washington, 1964-67; mem. working groups U.S.-USSR Agreement on Housing and Other Constrn., 1975-85; mem. subpanel housing White House Panel on Civilian Tech., Washington, 1961-62; mem. advs. to F. Stuart Fitzpatrick Meml. Award Trustee, 1969-84, chmn., 1974-78; mem. adv. panel Basic Homes Program OEO and HUD, 1972-77; mem. Nat. Adv. Coun. Rsch. Energy Conservation, 1975-78; mem. adv. com. Coun. Am. Bldg. Ofcls., 1976-86; mem. tech. coun. on bldg. codes and stds.; sec. Home and Land Owners Assn., Angel Fire, N.Mex., 1991-95; co-chmn., sec. initial bd. dirs. Assn. Angel Fire Property Owners, 1995-96; mem. master plan task force Angel Fire Planning and Zoning Commn., 1997. Mem. AIA (com. rsch. for architecture 1962-67, chmn. 1969, chmn. com. archtl. barriers 1967-68, nat. housing com. 1970-72, 84-85, mem. emeritus 1990—), ASCE (life, task com. cold regions 1977-79, tech. coun. cold regions engring., exec. com. 1976-84, chmn. 1981, stds. com. 1987-94,), DAV (life), Nat. Acad. Code Adminstrn. (life, trustee 1976-80, exec. com. 1978-82, new bd. dirs. 1980-82, 83-84, sec.-treas. 1982-82), Am. Inst. Steel Constrn., Am. Inst. Constructors, Am. Coun. Constrn. Edn. (trustee 1990-96), Nat. Inst. Bldg. Scis. (cons. coun. 1984-93, honor award 1997). Home and Office: PO Box 232 Gold Beach OR 97444-0232 *Died Aug. 8, 2000.*

DILLY, MARIAN JEANETTE, humanities educator; b. Vining, Minn., Nov. 7, 1921; d. John Fredolph and Mabel Josephine (Haagenson) Linder; m. Robert Lee Dily, June 22, 1946 (dec. Oct. 1987); children: Ronald Lee, Patricia Jeanette Dilly Vero. Studetn, U. Minn., 1944-45; grad., John R. Powers Finishing Sch., N.Y.C., 1957, Zell McC. Fashion Career Sch., Mpls., 1957, Estelle Compton Models Inst., Mpls., 1966, Nancy Taylor Charm Sch., N.Y.C., 1967, Patricia Stevens Career Sch., Mpls., 1968; BS in English cum laude, Black Hills State U., Spearfish, S.D., 1975. Instr. Nat. Am. U., Rapid City, S.D., 1966-68; instr., dir. Nancy Taylor Charm Sch., 1966-68; hostess TV shows, 1966-74; lectr. in personality devel., dir., prodr. beauty and talent pageants, freelance coord. in fashion shows, judge beauty and talent pageants of local, state and nat. levels, 1966—. Actress bit parts Nauman Films Inc., 1970. Active ARC; dir., 1st v.p. Black Hills Girl Scout Coun., 1967-72; chmn. bd. dirs., pres. Luth. Social Svc. Aux., Western S.D. and Eastern Wyo., 1960-65; chmn. women's events Dakota Days and Nat. Premiere, 1968; bd. dirs. YMCA, 1976-81; mem. Dallas Symphony Orch. League, 1987-90, Dallas Mus. of Art League, 1987-90, Women's Club. Dallas County, Tex., Inc., 1987-90. Recipient award Rapid City C. of C., 1968, Fashion awards March of Dimes, 1967-72, Svc. award Black Hills Girl Scout Coun., award of appreciation Yellowstone Internat. Toastmistress Club. Mem. AAUW (sec., mem. exec.b d. 1988-90), Nu Tau Sigma (past advisor), Delta Tau Kappa, Singing Tribe of Wahoo. Avocations: golf, bridge, music, skiing. Address: 1607 Woodward St Erie CO 80516-7529

DILORENZO, SHARON HIESTAND, architect, real estate professional; b. Jennings, La., Oct. 11, 1946; d. Garland and Annabelle (Carter) H.; m. Frank Clifford DiLorenzo, Feb. 5, 1965; children: Anthony Garland, Michael Russell. B Design Arch., U. Hartford, 1968; MFA in Design and Arch., Sch. Art Inst. Chgo., 1972; PhD in Indsl. Psychology, U. Conn., 1980; CFP, Roosevelt U., 1990. Real estate investment planning profl. Prof. interior architecture Sch. of Art Inst. Chgo., 1971-76; prof. archtl. history Barat Coll., Lake Forest, Ill., 1979-80; constrn. mgr. Taubman Devel., Bloomfield Hills, Mich., 1980-84; constrn. mgr. Pritzger Sch. Medicine U. Chgo. Hosps. Ill. Capital Constrn. and Real Estate Mgmt., 1984-92; capital constrn. planning, real estate and mgmt. Ameritech, Barrington, Ill., 1992-94, Ehurd-Technics Ltd., Barrington, 1968—; downtown rehab. specialist Yale Grad. Sch. Arch., New Haven, New Haven Investments, 1968-70; multi-family investment planning specialist Handy-Help Svcs., Barrington, 1990-2000, Construction Market Data Group, 1991-2000. Arch./lithographer Hartford Atheneum, 1968, Prudential Ins., Metropolis. Recipient Supermarket of Yr., Enviro-Technics Ltd., Cert. Grocers Midwest, 1969, Frank Lloyd Wright Home and Studio Found. award, 1972, Indsl. Redevel. award AIA. Mem. AAUW, LWV, Barrington C. of C., Nat. Trust for Hist. Preservation, Architecture Soc. of Art Inst. Chgo., Graham Found. for Advanced Studies in Fine Arts. Roman Catholic. Avocations: model making, kite flying, swimming, boating, family camping. Studio: 3170 W Monroe St Apt 311 Waukegan IL 60085-3066 Office: PO Box 8172 Waukegan IL 60079-8172

DILS, RAYMOND RONALD, biochemistry educator; b. Birmingham, Eng., Mar. 16, 1932; s. François Gommaire and Minnie (Thomes) D.; m. Joan Agnes Crompton, Oct. 29, 1966; children: Ruth, Rachael. BSc in Chemistry with honors, U. Birmingham, 1954, PhD in Biochemistry, 1958, DSc, 1972. Chartered chemist, chartered biologist. Rsch. fellow dept. med. biochemistry U. Birmingham, 1958-61, lectr. dept. med. biochemistry, 1961-69; sr. lectr., acting head dept. biochemistry U. Nottingham, Eng., 1969-72, reader in biochemistry, 1972-76; prof. biochemistry and physiology U. Reading, Eng., 1976-97, prof. emeritus, 1997—; v.p. Thames Valley br. Workers Edn. Assn., 1978—; external examiner for degrees at various univs., 1970—. Mem. editorial bd. Biochem. Jour., London, 1973-79; chmn. editorial bd. Biologist, Jour. of Inst. of Biology, 1992-97; contbr. over 160 articles to profl. jours. Rsch. grantee Med. Rsch. Coun., Agrl. and Food Rsch. Coun., Brit. Nutrition Found., Cancer Rsch. Campaign. Fellow Royal Inst. Chemistry, Inst. Biology; mem. Biochem. Soc., Soc. for Endocrinology. Brit. Soc. for Cell Biology, Nutrition Soc., Assn. Univ. Tchrs. London (coun. 1991-95). Avocations: theatre, travel, reading. Office: U Reading Sch Animal and Microbial Scis, Whiteknights, PO Box 228, Reading Berks RG6 6AJ, England

DILTS, JON PAUL, law educator; b. Monterey, Ind., Sept. 7, 1945; s. Charles Albert and Janet Cecilia (Keitzer) D.; m. Anne Williams Avirett, Aug. 21, 1971; children: Christopher, Andrew. BA, Saint Meinrad Coll., 1967; MA, Ind. U., 1974; JD, Valparaiso U., 1981. Bar: Ind. 1981, U.S. Dist. Ct. (so. dist.) Ind. 1981. Reporter Peru (Ind.) Daily Tribune, 1972-73, wire editor, 1973-76, city editor, 1976-78; law clk. Ind. Ct. Appeals, Indpls., 1981-82; asst. prof. Ind. U., Bloomington, 1982-88, assoc. prof., 1988—, assoc. dean, 1985—. Author: The Magnificent 92 Indiana Courthouses, 1992; co-author: Media Law, 1994, 97; mem. editl. bd. Comms. Law & Policy, 1998—. Trustee Saint Meinrad Coll., Sch. Theology, 1996-98; mem. exec. bd. dirs. Hoosier Trails Coun., Boy Scouts Am., Bloomington, 1992-93. With U.S. Army, 1968-71. Mem. Assn. for Edn. in Journalism and Mass Comm. (head law divsn. 1987-88), Soc. Profl. Journalists, AP Mng. Editors Assn., Rotary. Democrat. Roman Catholic. Avocations: skiing, hiking, backpacking, canoeing, sailing. Office: Ind U Sch Journalism 940 E 7th St Bloomington IN 47405-7108

DILWORTH, CRAIG WILLIAM JAMES, environmental executive, educator, consultant; b. Ottawa, Ont., Can., Aug. 24, 1949; arrived in Sweden, 1975; s. William James and Lena (Schmidtke) D.; m. Karin Brita Maria Linnér, June 18, 1983; children: Erika, Cecilia. BA, Carleton U., Ottawa, Can., 1970, BA with hons., 1973, MA, 1977; PhD, Uppsala (Sweden) U., 1981. Lectr. Umeå (Sweden) U., 1984-86, U. Stockholm, 1989-98; environ. rsch. leader Gotland (Sweden) Coll., 1993-95; assoc. prof. philosophy Åbo (Finland) Acad., 1986—, Uppsala U., 1989—; mng. dir. Ecol. Futures Sweden, Stockholm, 1996—; mem. adv. com. Revista Peruana de Filosofia Aplicada, 1996—, Facta Philosophica, 1997—, Epistemologiques, 1999—, Epsitemologia, 2000—. Author: (books) Scientific Progress 3d edit., 1994, The Metaphysics of Sci., 1996, Sustainable Development and Decision Making, 1997; editor: (book) Idealization IV: Intelligibility in Science, 1992. Chairperson Kristineberg's Village Bd., Stockholm, 1994-95; founder and vice chairperson Kristineberg's Ecological Comty. Assn., 1995-98. Recipient Swiss U. scholarship, Govt. Switzerland, 1980-82; grantee Uppsala U., Sweden, 1978-79. Mem. Linacre Coll., Oxford, Eng. (vis. sr. mem.), Internat. Acad. Philosopy of Sci. (corr.). Avocation: squash.

DIMAANO, ROWENDA DUMLAO, pediatrician, consultant; b. Lianga, The Philippines, July 19, 1961; d. Florante Fedalizo and Fe (Litang) Dumlao; m. Angelo de Leon Dimaano, Mar. 24, 1983; children: Dean Angelo, Miguel Angelo, Rafael Angelo. BS in Biology, U. of the Philippines, 1981; MD, Far Ea. U., 1985. Med. diplomate. Intership Far Eastern Univ., 1986; residency in pediatrics Davao Med. Ctr., Davao City, The Philippines, 1987-91; cons. Andres Soriano Meml. Hosp., Bislig, The Philippines, 1992—. Active Picop Staff Ladies Assn., Bislig, 1992—, Daus. Mary Immaculate, Bislig, 1993—, Regional Emergency Assistance Comm. Team, Bislig, 1993—, Oasis of Love, Bislig, 1998—. Recipient Plaque of Merit, Philippine Pediat. Soc., Davao City, 1988, Cert. of Appreciation, Philippine Med. Assn., General Santos City, 1988, Cert. of Appreciation, Integrated Midwives Assn., Bislig, The Philippines, 1999. Mem. Cmty. Pediat. Soc. (v.p. 1998-99), Philippine Med. Assn. (sec. 1992-98), Rotary Spouses (pres. 1999-2000). Roman Catholic. Avocations: dancing, cooking, reading, gardening. Home: La Salle Dr, John Bosco Dist, Mangagos Bislig The Philippines Office: Dimaano Med Clinic, Espiritu St Mangagoy, Bislig Surigao del Sur The Philippines

DIMANCESCU, MIHAI D., neurosurgeon, researcher, educator; b. Maidenhead, Berkshire, Eng., Mar. 27, 1940; came to U.S., 1956, naturalized, 1963; s. Dimitri D. and Alexandra Irina (Radulescu) D.; m. Joan E. Brenner, Mar. 17, 1966; children: Stefan, Marc-Mihai. BA, Yale U., 1962; MD, U. Toulouse, France, 1968. Diplomate Am. Bd. Neurol. Surgery. Rotating intern Purpan Hosp., Toulouse, 1968-69; jr. resident in gen. surgery Hartford (Conn.) Hosp., 1969-70; jr. resident in neurosurgy Albert Einstein-Montefiore Hosp., Bronx, N.Y., 1970-72; rsch. fellow in spasticity and movement disorders U. Miami (Fla.)-VA Hosp., 1972-74; sr. resident in neurosurgery U. Miami, 1972-76, asst. instr. in neurol. surgery, 1975-76; pvt. practice in medicine specializing in neurosurgery Freeport and Garden City, N.Y., 1976—; dir. Internat. Coma Recovery Inst., Garden City, 1977—; mem. faculty, dir. brain studies Internat. Sch. of Evan Thomas Inst., Phila., 1980—; mem. staff, assoc. dir. dept. neurosurgery Franklin Gen. Hosp., Valley Stream, N.Y.; mem. staff, pres. med. bd. South Nassau Cmtys. Hosp., Oceanside, N.Y.; chief divsn. neurosurgery Mercy Med. Ctr., Rockville Ctr., N.Y., St. Francis Hosp., Roslyn, N.Y., Winthrop U. Hosp., Mineola, N.Y., North Shore U. Hosp., Manhasset, N.Y.; continuing med. edn. lectr., 1977—; cons. neurosurgery Inst. for Achievement of Human Potential, Phila., 1977—; mem. surg. core faculty Health Sci. Ctr., Sch. Medicine, SUNY-Stony Brook, 1980—; bd. dirs. South Nassau Cmty. Hosp.; mem. med. coun. L.I. Health Network. Contbr. articles to profl. jours. Bd. dirs. Inst. Achievement Human Potential, 1990—; bd. dirs. Princess Margarita Romania Found., chmn., 1998—. Recipient Golden medal World Orgn. Human Potential, 1978; VA grantee, 1972-74. Fellow ACS, Royal Soc. Arts; mem. AMA, Am. Assn. Neurol. Surgeons, Congress Neurol. Surgeons (Sci. Exhibit award 1974), Coma Recovery Assn. (chmn. bd. dirs. Garden City chpt. 1983), N.Y. State Neurosurg. Soc. (bd. dirs. 1983-88, pres.-elect 1986-87, pres. 1988), Med. Soc. State of N.Y. (neurosurg. del. interspltly. com. 1983-88), N.Y. State Head Injury Providers' Coun. (rotating chmn. 1986-87), World Med. Assn., Nassau County Med. Soc., Nassau Physicians' Rev. Orgn. Office: Neurol Surgery PC 88 S Bergen Pl Freeport NY 11520-3510 also: Neurol Surgery PC 950 Franklin Ave Garden City NY 11530-2906

DIMARA, EFTHALIA, statistics and information scientist, educator; b. Ioannina, Epirus, Greece, June 6, 1959; d. Evangelos and Marigo (Theodorou) D. Diploma in Math., U. Athens, Greece, 1982; Diplome D'Etudes Approfondies, U. Paris VI, 1985, Doctorat de 3e Cycle en Statistique, 1988. Tutor U. Paris I, Pantheon-Sorbonne, 1986-87; tchg. fellow U. Patras, Greece, 1988-93; lctr. U. Patras, 1993-97, asst. prof., 1997—; rschr. U. Patras, Patras, 1993—, chmn. info. tech. com., 1996; cons. Prefecture of Achaia, Patras, 1999—. Author: Tobacco Growth in Greece, 1997, Greek Agriculture in a Changing Intern. Environment, 1998. Mem. Greek Univs. Network, Greek Statis. Inst. Avocations: Greek traditional musical instruments, contemporary Greek poetry. Office: U Patras, PO Box 1391, 26500 Patras Greece

DIMARCO, FRANK PAUL, marine biologist; b. N.Y., Nov. 23, 1953; s. Frank John and Alice (Bezgemluk) Di.; m. Judith Ann Hagen, Nov. 26, 1983; children: Frank Benjamin, Luke Hagen. BS in biology, Norwich Univ., 1975; MPA in environ. planning, Long Island Univ., 1979, MS in marine biology, 1981. Instr. Marist Coll., Poughkeepsie, N.Y., 1983-86; rsch. assoc. Univ. Tex. Medical Branch, Galveston, Tex., 1986-95, sr. rsch. assoc., 1995—; environ. cons. City of Galveston, 1998-99. Contbr. articles to profl. jours. Coach Galveston Youth Soccer Club, 1994—, Houston Clear Lake High Sch. lacrosse, 1999—. Mem. World Aquaculture Soc., Pi Alpha Alpha, Sigma Xi. Avocations: long distance running, lacrosse, pvt. pilot. Fax number: 409 772 6993 E-mail: padimarc@utmb.edu. Home: 4608 Avenue O Galveston TX 77551-4930 Office: Univ Tex Medical Br League Hall Galveston TX 77550

DI MARTINO, JOSEPH, computer science educator; b. Tunis, Tunisia, Aug. 16, 1957; s. Nonce and Gilda (Falcone) Di M. Diploma in engring., Ecole Nat. Superieure Elec., Nancy, France, 1981; Diplome d'Etude Approfondie, U. Nancy I, 1981, D Engring., 1984. Sr. lectr. Crin, Nancy, 1985—. Contbr. articles to profl. jours; inventor in field. Avocations: draughts, chess, cinema, walking, reading. Office: U Henri Poincare Loria Lab, Nancy I Fac Sci Dept Info BP 239, 54506 Vandoeuvre France

DIMARTINO-NARDI, JOAN, pediatric endocrinologist, educator; b. Bronx, N.Y., Jan. 25, 1954. BS, Fordham U., 1976; MD, SUNY, Downstate, 1980. Intern Bronx (N.Y.) Mcpl. Med. Ctr., Albert Einstein Coll. Medicine; assoc. prof. Montefiore Med. Ctr., Bronx, 1986—. Contbr. articles to profl. jours. Mem. Soc. for Pediat. Rsch., Lawson Wilkins Pediat. Endocrine Soc., Endocrine Soc. Office: Montefiore Med Ctr 111 E 210th St Bronx NY 10467-2401

DI MASCIO, JOHN PHILIP, lawyer; b. Bklyn., Feb. 4, 1944; s. Eugenio and Stella (Scheuermann) Di M.; m. Angela Piccininni, Apr. 2, 1967 (div. 1980); children: John Philip, Jr., Christine, Thomas; m. Linda Nick, Oct. 19, 1997. BA, C.W. Post Coll., 1975; MA, L.I. U., 1976; postgrad., NYU, 1976-79; JD, St. John's U., 1983. Bar: N.Y. 1984, U.S. Dist. Ct. (ea. and so. dists.) N.Y. 1984, U.S. Ct. Appeals (2d cir.) 1984, U.S. Supreme Ct. 1997, U.S. Ct. Appeals for Armed Forces 1997, U.S. Ct. of Fed. Claims, 1997, U.S. Ct. Appeals (fed. cir.) 1997. Sr. ct. officer N.Y. State Supreme Ct., Mineola, 1970-82; assoc. Joel R. Brandes, PC, Garden City, N.Y., 1984; pvt. practice N.Y., 1984-87; ptnr. Di Mascio, Meisner & Koopersmith, Carle Place, 1987-93; pvt. practice Garden City, 1993—. Contbg. author Ann. Survey. With USN, 1962-69. Recipient acad. awards. Mem. ABA (bus. law, health law and family law sects.), N.Y. State Bar Assn. (family law com. 1982), Nassau County Bar Assn. (vice-chmn. matrimonial com. ethics com., family ct. com. 1984, editor Recent Decisions), Am. Inns of Ct. (N.Y. family law chpt.). Avocations: photography, boating. Office: 300 Garden City Plz Garden City NY 11530-3302

DIMASHKIEH, MOHIDDIN RIDA, dentist, educator, researcher; b. Damascus, Syria, Dec. 20, 1943; s. Rida Saad Al Dean and Mukarram Muhammad (Radi) D.; m. Nariman Jamil Ahmad, Nov. 16, 1977; children: Hala, Rida, Amir. DDS, Damascus U., 1968; MSc, London U., 1974; Clin. Cert., Eastman Dental Hosp., London, 1976. Dentist Pvt. Clinic, Damascus, 1968-70; rsch. fellow Eastman Dental Hosp., London, 1974-76; asst. prof. Coll. Dentistry, Damascus, 1976-81, assoc. prof., 1981-88, prof., 1988; prof. Coll. Dentistry, Riyadh, Saudi Arabia, 1988—; vice dean Coll. Dentistry, Damascus, 1981-88; chmn. dept. Coll. Dentistry, Riyadh, 1989-94, head divsn. fixed prosthodontics, 1989-98; mem. acad. coun. King Saud U., Riyadh, 1990-94. Author: Crowns and Bridges, 1985; contbr. articles to profl. jours.; patentee in field. Recipient Plaque of appreciation King Saud U. Coll. Dentistry, 1994. Mem. Syrian Dental Assn., Brit. Endodontic Soc., Saudi Dental Soc. (Plaque of appreciation 1994). Muslim. Avocations: close up photography, engineer design. Home: Omar Al Muktar St, Al Rawdah 2 PO box 285, Damascus Syria Office: King Saud U Coll Dentistry, PO Box 60169, Riyadh 11545, Saudi Arabia

DIMASI, LINDA GRACE, epidemiologist; b. Trenton, N.J., Feb. 7, 1949; d. Nick and Pearl LaVerne (White) D. BS in Biology, Alderson-Broaddus Coll., 1970; MPA, Rutgers U., 1992. Cert. pub. mgr. Field rep. N.J. State Dept. of Health, Trenton, 1971-85, epidemiologist, 1985—. Contbr. articles to profl. jours. Mem. ASPA, APHA, Phi Alpha Alpha. Avocations: flying, auto racing, traveling. Home: 35 Jennifer Ln Burlington NJ 08016-1144 Office: NJ State Dept of Health Divsn AIDS Prevention and Control CN 363 Trenton NJ 08625-0363

DIMBLEBY, ROBERT DAVID, publisher, translator; b. Matlock, Eng., Dec. 14, 1960; s. Raymone David and Elizabeth Ellen (Eaton) D.; m. Gabriela Fuhrmann, Aug. 29, 1997; 1 stepchild, Mona Fuhrmann. BA in Natural Scis. with honors, Cambridge (Eng.) U., 1982. Editl. asst. Physiol. Soc., Cambridge, 1983-84; prodn. editor Acad. Press, London, 1985-86; med. editor Springer-Verlag, Heidelberg, Germany, 1986-92; editor Hogrefe & Huber Pubs., Göttingen, Germany, 1993—. Home: Jheringstrasse 44, D-37081 Göttingen Germany

DI MELCHIORRE, SILVIO, investor, airline consultant, political scientist; b. Buenos Aires, May 23, 1972; s. Mario and Lidia Lucia (Galleguillo) Di M. Asst. in Jornadas Nietzsche, Buenos Aires, 1994, 98; grad. polit. science with specialty in internat. rels., U. Buenos Aires, 1997; grad. IATA-UFTAA basic course, Internat. Air Transport Assn. Learning Ctr., Geneva, 1998; student Quinto Programa Simulacion Bursatil, U. Buenos Aires, 1999. Pub. Tain Mag., Buenos Aires, 1987-88, Boletin Inf. Internacional, Buenos Aires, 1989-90; mng. dir. B.I.I. Worldwide, Buenos Aires, 1991-92; pres. SDM Internacional, Buenos Aires, 1993-95; founder, dir. Biblioteca Silvio Di Melchiorre, Buenos Aires, 1996-97; airline cons. Buenos Aires, 1996, airways policy adviser, 1997-2000; pvt. investor, 2000—; cons. in field, Buenos Aires, 1993-96; banking mediator, Buenos Aires, 1995-96; contbr. info. svc. Fundacion Poder Ciudadano, Buenos Aires, 1994. Author: (info. svc.) Io Club, 1992; (TV novel) Ramses II, 1995; (political expression) Airways Policy, 1998; (banking publication) La Banque, 1998. Donor publs. to libr. Univ. Del Salvador, Buenos Aires, 1996-97, Inst. del Servicio Exterior de la Nacion, Buenos Aires, 1997-98, Bolsa de Comercio de Buenos Aires, 1997—. Fax: 54-11-4372-5295. Home and Office: Bartolome Mitre 1676, Piso 3 Dpto 11 Cuerpo 2, C1037ABF Buenos Aires Argentina

DIMENTBERG, MIKHAIL FYODOROVICH, mechanical engineering educator; b. Odessa, Ukraine, Jan. 1, 1935; came to the U.S., 1991; m. Irina Akimovna Gyurdzhan, July 22, 1960; 1 child, Ol'ga Mikhailovna Gyurdzhan. Degree in Mech. Engring., Moscow Inst. Power Engring., 1958, Candidate Sci. in Engring., 1963; DSc in Engring., USSR Acad. Scis., Moscow, 1971. Engr. Aircraft Design Firm, Moscow, 1958-60; jr. scientist Inst. for Problems in Mechanics, Russian Acad. Sci., Moscow, 1960-68, sr. then leading scientist, 1968-91; Charles E. Schmidt disting. vis. prof. Fla. Atlantic U., Boca Raton, 1991; vis. prof. Worcester (Mass.) Poly. Inst., 1992-93, prof., 1993—. Author: Statistical Dynamics of Nonlinear and Time Varying Systems, 1988, Nonlinear Stochastic Problems of Mechanical Vibrations, 1980, Random Processes in Dynamic Systems with Variable Parameters, 1989; co-author: Vibroacoustical Diagnostics of Machines and Structures, 1991. Rsch. grantee Office Naval Rsch., 1993-96, NSF, 1997-2000. Avocation: chess. Office: Worcester Poly Inst Mech Engring Dept 100 Institute Rd Worcester MA 01609-2247

DIMEO, SANDRA B., occupational therapist; b. Utica, N.Y., Nov. 29, 1953; d. Frank and Palma Buttigliere; m. Steven Dimeo, Jan. 10, 1976; children: Jeffrey, Matthew. BS in Occupl. Therapy, Syracuse U., 1975; MS in Edn., SUNY, Cortland, 1994. Occupl. therapist Rehab. Svcs., Inc., Binghamton, N.Y., 1975-77; sr. occupl. therapist St. Peter's Hosp., Albany, N.Y., 1977-79; mgr. occupl. therapy dept. Newton (N.J.) Hosp., 1979-87; asst. prof. Herkiner County C.C., Herkiner, N.Y., 1988-92; assoc. prof. Syracuse U., 1992—. V.p. Oriskany (N.Y.) Ctrl. Sch. Bd. Edn., 1997-99, pres., 1999-2000. Mem. N.Y. State Occupl. Therapy Assn. (co-chair spl. interest sect. edn. 1997—), Am. Occupl. Therapy Assn. Avocations: cooking, baking. Office: Utica Coll Syracuse U 1600 Burrstone Rd Utica NY 13502-4857

DIMILIA, LEE, psychologist, consultant; b. Wollongong, Australia, Apr. 6, 1960; s. Rocco S. and Antonia (Caponegro) DiM. Diploma in tchg., Wollongong Inst. Edn., 1982; BA with honors, U. Wollongong, 1989, PhD, 1998; M of Edn. Studies, U. South Australia, Adelaide, 1997. Reg. psychologist New South Wales Health Bd. Cons. BHP, Wollongong, 1986—. Contbr. articles to profl. jours. including Internat. Jour. Indsl. Ergonomics, Asia Pacific Jour. Human Resources, others. Mem. Australian Psychol. Soc., Coll. Organizational Psychologists. Office: BHP, PO Box 1854, Wollongong NSW 2500, Australia

DIMITRAKOPOULOS, GIORGOS, member European Parliament; b. Athens, Greece, Sept. 18, 1952. Mem. European Parliament, Brussels; mem. com. on constl. affairs, com. on fgn. affairs, human rights, common security and def. policy, vice chmn. substitute del. for rels. with Mashreq countries and the Gulf. Mem. Bur., Group of European People's Party (Christian Dems.) and European Dems. Mem. New Democracy Party. *

DIMITRIENKO, IRINA DONATOVNA, mechanical engineer, applied mathematician; b. Berezniki, Russia, Apr. 20, 1962; d. Donat Pavlovich and Nina Andreevna (Zevakova) Baybakov; m. Yuriy Ivanovich Dimitrienko, Sept. 10, 1983; children: Olga, Alexander. MSc, Moscow Lomonosov State U., 1984, PhD in Physics and Math., 1990. Jr. rschr. Moscow Lomonosov State U., 1984-92, rschr., 1992-98, sr. scientist, 1998—; cons., chair gas and wave dynamics, Moscow Lomonosov State U., 1990—, dir. heterogeneous combustion program, Lab. Wave Processes, 1996—. Translator: (from Russian to English) Thermomechanics of Composites under High Temperatures,

1998; contbr. articles to profl. jours. Dir. Women's Coun., Mechanics and Math. Dept., Moscow Lomonosov State U., 1989-94. Grantee Internat. Sci. Found., 1994, Russian Acad. Scis., 1994-96, Russian Basic Rsch. Found., 1995-97. Mem. SIAM. Avocations: travel, modern music. Office: Moscow Lomonosov State U, Fac Mechanics and Math, 119899 Moscow Russia

DIMITRIJEVIC, MOMCILO DUSAN, agriculture educator, researcher; b. Belgrade, Yugoslavia, Aug. 1, 1963; Arrived in Greece, 1990; s. Dusan Peter Dimitrijevic and Nadezda Bozidar Gmizovic. BSc in Agrl. Engring., U. Belgrade, 1989, MSc in Biotech. Sci., 1997, PhD in Biotech. Sci., 1999; MSc in Hort. Prodn., Internat. Ctr. Advanced Mediterranean Agron. Studies, Chania, Greece, 1993. Asst. rschr. MAIChania, 1991-93, rschr., 1993-95, lectr., 1995-97; trainee European Dept. Divsn. Agr., Fishery, Forestry & Rural Devel., Luxembourg, 1995-96; rschr. Greek Rsch. Orgn., Chania, 1995—; advisor Omega-sys NM, Chania, 1998—. Co-author: The Design of a Prototype Greenhouse, 1995; contbr. articles to profl. jours. Scholar Internat. Ctr. Advanced Mediterranean Agronomic Studies, 1990-91, European Cmty., 1991-93, Greek State, 1994-96, European Parliament, 1995-96. Mem. Internat. Soc. Hort. Scientists. Avocations: reading, weightlifting, basketball. Fax: 30-821-81154. Home: Jase Ignjatovica 14, 11000 Belgrade Yugoslavia

DIMITRIOU, CONSTANTINE, insurance executive, consultant; b. Karditsa, Greece, Feb. 18, 1955; s. Athanasios and Asimo (Giena) D.; m. Brigitte Susanne Heinzle, Sept. 28, 1984; children: Irini, Alexander. Bachelor, Athens Bus. Sch., Greece, 1977; PhD in Mgmt., St. Gall U., Switzerland, 1983. Cert. bus. economist Econ. Chpt. Greece. Sales promotion mgr. Danemann, Switzerland, 1982; sci. cons. Nat. Ctr. of Planning and Rsch., Greece, 1986-87; tng. exec. Agrotiki Life, Greece, 1987-97, head internat. cooperation dept., 1997—; cons. and trainer, Greece, 1986—; assessor European Quality Award, 1999—. Author: Work-Unit Size and Organizational Effectiveness, 1983, Methods and Techniques for Motivating Employees, 2d edit., 1992, Human Resources Management, 1994; cons. editor Total Quality Mgmt., 2d edit., 1994. Lt. inf. Greek Army, 1983-85. Mem. Hellenic Mgmt. Assn., HSG Hochschulverein, European Found. for Quality Mgmt. (rep.), Assn. Grads. of German-speaking Univs. (pres.). Greek Orthodox. Office: Agrotiki Life Ins Co, 4-6 Syngrou Ave, 11742 Athens Attika, Greece

DIMITRIOU, PETROS PANAGIOTIS, seismologist; b. Bucharest, Nov. 13, 1958; s. Panagiotis Petros and Miroslava Iosif (Gatker) D. Diploma in physics, Dept. of Physics, Bucharest, 1979, MSc in Physics with honors, 1980; MSc in Engring. Seismology, U. Skopje, 1983; PhD in Civil Engring., U. Tokyo, 1986. Scientific collaborator U. Thessaloniki, Greece, 1987-95, assoc. prof., 1993-94; rschr. Inst. Engring. Seismology & Earthquake Engring., Thessaloniki, 1995—; vis. rschr. Geophys. Inst., Karlsruhe, Germany, 1987, Nat. Geophys. Inst., Rome, 1992, 93. Contbr. articles to profl. jours. Scholarship Ministry of Edn., Romania, 1975-80, Yugoslavia, 1980-83, Japan, 1983-86; grantee British Coun., 1990. Mem. AGU, EGS, Greek Physicists Union, Seismol. Soc. Am. Avocations: cycling, mountaineering, music, art. Home: Ipsilandi 74, GR-57001 Thessaloniki Greece Office: ITSAK, Georgikis Scholis 46, GR-55102 Thessaloniki Greece

DIMITRIOU, STAVROS GEORGE, electronics educator; b. Ermoupolis, Cyclades, Greece, Aug. 4, 1952; s. George S. and Catherine N. (Bournias) D.; m. Georgia K. Adamopoulou, July 24, 1988; children: George, Costas. BA, Sivitanidios Sch. Electronics, Athens, Greece, 1974; postgrad., Capital Radio Engring. Inst., Washington, 1975; MSc, U. Manchester, Eng., 1979. Lab. instr. Sivitanidios Sch. Electronics, 1975-76; design engr. Sovereign-E Co., 1975-78; lab. instr. Tech. Edn. Instn., Athens, 1978-86; lectr. electronics TEI, Athens, 1986—; tech. cons. Elektor mag., Athens, 1982—; researcher electronic generation of propulsion. Inventor audio multisplitter, endless ellipsoid cassette, wideband car antenna; contbr. articles on audio circuitry to profl. publs. Mem. IEEE. Christian Orthodox. E-mail: dimsta@ee.teiath.gr. Office: TEI, AG Spiridonos 0, Egaleo, 12243 Athens Greece

DIMITRIU, GABRIEL, mathematics educator; b. Iasi, Romania, Nov. 8, 1955; s. Ioan Gabriel and Tasia (Antoci) D.; m. Rodica Ioana Butureanu, July 30, 1983; 1 child, Valeriu Gabriel. BS, Al.I. Cuza U., Iasi, Romania, 1979, PhD in Math., 1999. Programmer Heavy Equipment Plant, Iasi, Romania, 1979-87; rschr. Inst. Rsch. Constrns., Iasi, Romania, 1987-94; analyst, programmer Computer Ctr. U., Iasi, Romania, 1985-86; asst. prof. dept. math. & info. U. Medicine & Pharmacy, Iasi, Romania, 1994—; head dept. U. Medicine & Pharmacy, Faculty Pharmacy, Dept. Math. & Info., Iasi, 1994—. Predoctoral fellow Inst. Math., Graz, Austria, 1992-93, SUNY Dept. Math., Binghamton, N.Y., 1995-96. Mem. Am. Math. Soc. European Math. Soc. Avocations: chess, travel. Office: U Medicine & Pharmacy, Univ Str 16, 6600 Iasi Romania

DIMITROV, PHILIP, ambassador; b. Sofia, Bulgaria, Mar. 31, 1955; s. Dimitar Vassilev and Katherine Philipov D.; m. Elena Valentinova Gueorgieva-Dimitrova, Aug. 18, 1988. Ed., English Lang. Sch., Sofia; atty. at law, Faculty of Law, Sofia U., 1977. Atty. at law Sofia, 1979-90; v.p. Union Dem. Forces for Fgn. Rels., Sofia, 1990, pres., 1990-94; prime min. Republic of Bulgaria, 1991-92; mem. Nat. Assembly of Bulgaria, 1991-92; mem. nat. exec. coun. Union of Dem. Forces, Sofia, 1996; vice chmn. Bulgaria Jt. Parliamentary Com. European Union, 1995-97; permanent Bulgarian amb. UN, N.Y.C., 1997-98; U.S. amb. Republic of Bulgaria, Washington, 1998—. Author: For They Lived, Lord, 1991; contbr. various articles on psychotherapy. v.p. Conservative Ecological Party, 1989; active Com for the Protection of Religious Rights, 1989; pro bono psychotherapist, Med. Acad. Sofia, 1978-85. Mem. Union of Democratic Forces Party. Christian Orthodox. Office: Embassy of Bulgaria 1621 22d St NW Washington DC 20008

DIMITRY, JOHN RANDOLPH, academic administrator; b. Detroit, Feb. 15, 1929; s. Dracos Alexander and Elizabeth Stanton (Bisland) D.; m. Audrey Oktavec, Aug. 20, 1952; children: Mark, Jane, Kate. Student, Spring Hill Coll., 1948-49; B.A., Wayne State U., 1952, M.S., 1954, Ed.D., 1966. Tchr., Highland Park (Mich.) Jr. Coll., 1954-61; asst. to pres. Macomb County C.C., Warren, Mich., 1963-65; dean center campus Macomb County Community Coll., 1966-67, pres., 1967-75; pres. Northern Essex Community Coll., Haverhill, Mass., 1975—; mem. Gov.'s Commn. on Higher Edn., 1973-75; pres. Mich. C.C. Assn., 1972-73; mem. Mass. Gov.'s State Job Tng. Coordinating Coun., 1983-91; mem. Mass. Commn. for Occupational Edn., 1982-88; chmn. NE Consortium of Colls. and Univs. in Mass., 1985-86, Mass. C.C. Pres. Assn., 1986-87, New England Regional Student Exch. Program ADv. Coun., 1992—. Bd. dirs. Lawrence Boys Club, Lawrence Yough Commn. Lt. U.S. Army, 1947-48, 52-53. Kellogg Found. fellow Community Coll. Adminstrn., 1961-63; recipient Leadership award Prudential Ins. Co. Am., 1992. Mem. Greater Haverhill C. of C. (pres. 1985-86). Home: Old Wharf Rd West Newbury MA 01985 Office: No Essex Community Coll Office of the Pres Elliott Way Haverhill MA 01830-2399

DIMITRY, SAID, chemical engineer, researcher; b. Cairo, Nov. 20, 1947; s. Alfonse Dimitry; m. Amira Youshia. BASc in Applied Chemistry, Cairo U., 1970; MASc in Chem. Engring., U. Tor., Can., 1981; BMS cert., Conestoga Coll., Waterloo, Can., 1991; MS, Case Western Reserve U., 1995. Cert. chem. engr. Quality control chemist Custom Pharms. Ltd., Fort Erie, Ont., Can., 1978-80; teaching asst. U. Toronto, 1980-82; rsch. engr. McMaster U., Hamilton, Ont., Can., 1982-84; mgr. R & D Relmech Mfg. Ltd., Ontario, Can., 1984-91; Specrete IP Inc., Cleve., 1991-94; grad. asst. Case Western Reserve U., Cleve., 1994-95; sr. project engr. SEALY, Inc., Trinity, N.C., 1996—. Patentee in field; contbr. articles to profl. jours. Office of Naval Rsch. scholar, 1994. Mem. NSPE, AIChE, Assn. Chem. Profession Ont. Avocations: reading, swimming, watching movies. Home: 4201 Auburn Hills Dr Greensboro NC 27407-7875

DIMOGLO, ANATOLY SERAFIMOVICH, chemistry researcher; b. Tomay, Moldova, Sept. 2, 1949; s. Serafim Ivanovich and Nina Grigorievna (Khlupina) D.; m. Nathaly Feodorovna Paukova, Aug. 22, 1971 (div. 1980); children: Stanislav, Eugene; m. Nathaly Mikhailovna Shvets, June 23, 1982. M, Kishinev (Moldova) State U., 1971, PhD, 1976; DSc, Rostov-Don (Russia) U., 1987. Sci. rschr. Inst. Chemistry Acad. Sci., Kishinev, 1975-79, sr. rschr. Inst. Chemistry, 1979-82, leading rschr. Inst. Chemistry, 1982-87, major rschr. Inst. Chemistry, 1987-91, chief of group computational chemistry Inst. Chemistry, 1991—; vis. prof. Erciyes U., Kayseri, Turkey, 1993-96, GYTE, Gebze, Turkey, 1997—; dep. dir. Inst. Chemistry, Acad. Sci., 1987-91; mem. staff Quantum-Net, Odessa, Ukraine, 1995—. Grantee Soros Found., N.Y.C., 1993, INTAS, Brussels, 1994, Ukraine, 1996. Mem. N.Y. Acad. Scis. Home: Blvd Traian 19/1 Apt 141, 277060 Kishinev Moldova Office: Inst Advanced Tech Gebze, PK 141, 41400 Gebze Kocaeli, Turkey

DIMOTAKIS, PAUL NICHOLAS, chemistry educator, researcher; b. Athens, Greece, Feb. 19, 1928; s. Nicholas Paul and Aikaterini Nicholas (Chiladaki) D.; m. Maria Paul Kalivretaki, May 23, 1969; 1 child, Nicholas. Diploma, U. Athens, 1953; PhD, Cambridge (Eng.) U., 1964. Rschr. Wine Inst., Athens, 1954-56; rschr. Democritos Nuclear Rsch. Ctr., Athens, 1956-69, sci. dir., 1967; dir. Min. Sci. and Culture, Athens, 1969-73; assoc. prof. U. Patras, 1973-75, full prof., 1975-84, emeritus prof., 1985—; vis. rschr. Jour. Rsch. Ctr. European Union, Ispra, Italy, 1984-85. Author: How to Prospect for Uranium, 1956, Radiochemistry, 1980, Chemistry Radiation, 1980, Wave Mechanical Theory of Atoms & Molecules, 1980, Advanced Inorganic Chemistry, 1984, Chaos Theory and the Greeks, 1996, Chaos & Harmony of Democracy of the Greeks, 1999; editor Chem. Rsch., 1954-56, Chemica Chronica, 1972, 86, 90. Pres. Mus. Nat. Sci. Friends, Athens, 1996. Mem. Greek Chemists Assn. (ssec. gen. 1990), Profs. Assn. Phys. Sci. (pres. 1980), Am. Nuclear Soc., AAAS. Avocations: piano, violin, painting, sailing. Home: 73 Marathonodromon, 15124 Maroussi Athens, Greece

DIMOVA, SILVIA LUBOMIROVA, engineer, researcher; b. Gorna Oriachovitza, Bulgaria, Apr. 13, 1958; d. Lubomir Borisov and Rusana Petkova (Vladeva) D.; m. Orlin Botchev, Aug. 2, 1978; 1 child, Iskra Orlinova. Engr., Poly. U., St. Petersburg, Russia, 1983; PhD, Bulgarian Acad. Scis., Sofia, 1987. Designer Energoproject, Sofia, 1983-84; assoc. prof. Ctrl. Lab. for Seismic Mechanics and Earthquake Engring., Sofia, 1987—. Contbr. articles to profl. jours. Alexander von Humboldt Found. fellow, 1992-93, STA fellow, Japan, 1998, NATO, Greece, 2000. Mem. Nat. Com. for Earthquake Engring. Avocations: cats, flowers. Office: Bulgarian Acad Scis Ctl Lab, PO Box 27, 1582 Sofia Bulgaria

DIMRI, JAGDISH PRASAD, language educator; b. Dimmar, India, Jan. 1, 1946; s. Hari Prasad and parvati Devi Dimri; m. Kalpeswari Dimri; 1 child, Mayank Prasad. MA, Sanskrit U., Varanasi, India, 1968; PhD, Moscow U., 1973. Lectr. Sanskrit U., 1967-73; lectr. Ctr. Inst. English and Fgn. Langs., Hyderabad, India, 1973-79, reader, 1979-82, prof., 1982—, head dept. Russian, 1980-84, 86-87, 91-93, dean fgn. langs., 1987-89, 93-95. Author: Russian 100, 1997; editor: Readings in Second Language Pedagogy, 1999. Avocations: reading, walking. Office: Ctrl Inst English/Fgn Langs, Hyderabad AP 500007, India

DIMSDALE, JOEL EDWARD, psychiatry educator; b. Sioux City, Iowa, Apr. 16, 1947; s. Lewis J. and Phyllis (Green) D.; m. Nancy Kleinman, Sept. 17, 1978; 1 child, Jonathan Jared. BA in Biology, Carleton Coll., 1968; MA in Sociology, Stanford U., 1970, MD, 1973. Diplomate Am. Bd. Psychiatry. Resident in psychiatry Mass. Gen. Hosp., Boston, 1973-76; instr. psychiatry Harvard U. Sch. Medicine, Boston, 1976-80, asst. prof., 1980-84, assoc. prof., 1984-85; assoc. prof., now prof. psychiatry U. Calif., San Diego, 1985—; cons. to Pres.'s Commn. on Mental Health, Washington, 1977-78, NIH, Washington, 1980—. Editor: Survivors, Victims and Perpetrators, 1980, Quality of Life in Behavior Medicine Rsch., 1995; editor-in-chief Psychosomatic Medicine, 1992—; mem. editorial bd. Internat. Jour. Behavioral Medicine, 1993—, Applied Biobehavioral Rsch., 1994—, Am. Jour. Human Biology, 1994—, Psychosomatics, 1996—, Archives of Indian Psychiatry, 1996—; contbr. articles to profl. jours. Fellow Am. Psychopathol. Assn., Am. Psychiat. Assn., Acad. Behavioral Med. Rsch. (coun. 1988-91, pres. 1991-92), Soc. of Behavioral Medicine (pres. 2000); mem. Am. Psychosomatic Soc. (coun. 1982-85, pres. 1999), Sigma Xi. Home: 1684 Lugano Ln Del Mar CA 92014-4126 Office: U Calif San Diego U Calif San Diego 9500 Gilman Dr La Jolla CA 92093-5004

DINAN, PIERRE DÉSIRÉ, economist, consultant; b. Vacoas, Mauritius, Mar. 12, 1937; s. Pierre Eugene and Irene Rita (Chasle) D.; m. Monique Marie Rivet, June 12, 1969; children: Claire, Agnes, Pascale, Anne, Marie-Aimée. BS in Econs., London Sch. Econs., 1961. Investment officer Devel. Bank Mauritius, 1964-67; sr. economist Mauritius Chamber of Agr., 1967-74; fin. contr. West East Ltd., Mauritius, 1974-84; sr. ptnr. De Chazal Du Mee, Mauritius, 1985—; dir. Food Canners Ltd., Mauritius, 1985—; pres. Mauritius Employers Fedn., 1998—; dir. various offshore funds inc. in Mauritius, 1992—. Pres. Justice and Peace Commn., Mauritius, 1971-80; chmn. Trust Fund for Treatment and Rehab. of Drug Addicts, Mauritius, 1986-88. Fellow Inst. Chartered Accts. Eng. and Wales; mem. Internat. Tax Profls. Assn. Roman Catholic. Avocations: reading, travel. Office: De Chazal Du Mee PO Box 799, 10 Rue Frere Felix Valois, Port Louis Mauritius

DINARIEV, OLEG JURIEVICH, physicist; b. Copenhagen, Denmark, May 30, 1955; s. Yurij Vladimirovich and Galina Pavlona (Labutina) D. BS, Moscow State U., 1977. Aspirant Moscow State U., 1977-81; scientific worker Math. Inst., Moscow, 1981-83; sr. scientific worker All Union Inst. Natural Gases, Moscow, 1983-89, Inst. Physics of the Earth, Moscow, 1989—; cons. Sys. & Info., Ltd., Moscow, 1996—. Mem. Soc. Petroleum Engrs. Avocation: power lifting. Office: IFZAN, B Gruzinskaja 10, 123810 Moscow Russia

DINCA, PETRUTA LUMINITA, physician, researcher; b. Bucharest, Romania, June 23, 1957; arrived in Spain, 1992; d. Nicolae and Maria (Ciobanu) Avarvarei; m. Gabriel Dinca, July 2, 1979; 1 child, Daniel. PhD, Inst. Pharmacy and Medicine, Bucharest, 1991, MD. Resident in medicine Filantropia Hosp., Bucharest, 1982-84; resident in immunology Cantacuzino Inst., Bucharest, 1984-88, specialist in immunology, 1988-91; Fogarty internat. fellow in immunology Mt. Sinai Hosp., N.Y.C., 1991-92; asst. prof. allergy Inst. Medicine and Pharmacy, Bucharest, 1991-94; resident in clin. neurophysiology Macarena Hosp., Seville, Spain, 1996-2000. Contbr. articles to profl. jours. Mem. Communist Party Bucharest, 1980-89. Recipient Young Scientists award Romanian Soc. Immunology, 1990. Mem. N.Y. Acad. Scis. Avocations: classical music, step aerobics. Office: Macarena Hosp, C/Fedriani 3, Seville Spain

DINE, THOMAS ALAN, foreign policy expert; b. Cin., Feb. 29, 1940; s. Stanley and Eunice (Cohen) D.; m. Joan Corbett, Mar. 19, 1967; children: Amy Eleana, Laura Rachel. BA, Colgate U., 1962; MA, UCLA, 1966. Vol. U.S. Peace Corps, Philippines, 1962-64; congl. liaison U.S. Peace Corps, Washington, 1966-67; personal asst. to Am. ambassador Am. Embassy, New Delhi, India, 1967-69; legis. asst. to U.S. Senator Frank Church, Washington, 1970-74; sr. analyst U.S. Senate Budget Com., Washington, 1975-78; fgn. policy advisor to U.S. Senator Edward Kennedy, Washington, 1979-80; exec. dir. Am. Israel Pub. Affairs Com., Washington, 1980-93; asst. adminstr. Europe and New Ind. States U.S. Agy. Internat. Devel., Washington, 1993-97; pres. Radio Free Europe/Radio Liberty, Prague, Czech Republic, 1997—. Contbr. articles to profl. jours. Harvard U. fellow, 1974-75, Brookings Instn. sr. fellow, 1979. Mem. Council on Fgn. Relations, Am. Hist. Assn., Soc. Historians of Am. Fgn. Policy, Cosmos Club. Jewish. Office: RFE/RL Inc, Vinohradska 1, 110 00 Prague 1, Czech Republic

DINELLI, GIOVANNI, biologist, researcher; b. Bologna, Italy, Nov. 19, 1964; s. Giancarlo and Maria Luisa (Rimondi) D.; m. Liliana Tamburello. Degree in Biology, U. Bologna, 1988, PhD, 1995. Rschr. in agronomy U. Bologna, 1989—. Contbr. articles to profl. jours. Mem. Internat. Humic Substances Soc. Avocations: guitar playing, basketball. Office: Univ Bologna Dept Agronomy, via Filippo RE 6/8, 40126 Bologna Italy

DINER, PATRICK ANTOINE, plastic surgeon; b. Paris, Oct. 31, 1953; s. Olivier and Helene (Servioz) D.; m. Sylvie Nedey, May 7, 1981; children: Alban-Louis, Constance-Marie. Resident Med. Sch. of Paris, 1979-84, chief resident, 1984-86; fellow Foch Hosp., Paris, 1986-89; asst. Trousseau Children's Hosp., Paris, 1989-91, adjoint chief, 1991—; plastic surgeon Red Cross Hosp., Paris, 1991—, Institut Arthur Vernes, Paris, 1994—. Author: Maxillocacial Plastic Dermatological; inventor endobuccal distractor. Mem. Club 89, Paris, 1982. Mem. Health Orgn. Medecin du Monde, Internat. Soc. of Craniofacial Surgery, Internat. Soc. Vascular Anomalies, French Plastic Reconstructive Aesthetic Surgery Soc., Stade Francais-Club, Kinkeliba. Roman Catholic. Office: Maison des Soeurs Augustine, 29 Rue de la Sante, 75013 Paris France

DINERSTEIN, ROBERT CHARLES, lawyer, bank executive; b. Bklyn., Aug. 4, 1942; s. Benjamin and Frances Dinerstein; m. Martha Lay. BA cum laude, Harvard U., 1963; JD, U. Mich., 1966. Asst. to corp. counsel law dept. City of N.Y., 1966-70; litig. assoc. Debevoise, Plimpton, Lyons & Gates, N.Y.C., 1970-73; corp. sec., assoc. gen. counsel Am. Airlines, Inc., N.Y.C., 1973-79; gen. counsel Citicorp, N.Y.C., 1982-87; exec. v.p., gen. counsel Shearson Lehman Bros., Inc., N.Y.C., 1987-90; mng. dir., gen. counsel Union Bank Switzerland AG, N.Y.C., 1991—. Trustee ARC Greater N.Y., N.Y.C., 1996—, Phipps Houses, N.Y.C., 1997—, Jewish Mus., N.Y.C., 1999—, Stamford (Conn.) Symphony Orch., 1999—. Mem. Securities Industries Assn. (mem. fed. regulation com. 1997, chmn. holding co. regulatory com. 1999—), Coun. Fgn. Rels., Coun. Sr. Internat. Legal Officers (mem. conf. bd.), Swiss-Am. C. of C. Fax: 212-821-5804. Home: 5 Riverside Dr New York NY 10023-2534 Office: UBS AG 299 Park Ave Fl 34 New York NY 10171-0002

DINESEN, LARS LUNDGARD, environmental consultant; b. Copenhagen, Mar. 16, 1965; s. Jørn and Annelise (Christensen) D. Candidate of Sci., U. Copenhagen, 1993. Rsch. fellow Zool. Mus., Copenhagen, 1993-95; dir. Regulus Consult, Copenhagen, 1995—; advisor Copenhagen Airports, 1995-99; advisor meadow mgmt. Roskilde Region, Denmark, 1990—; advisor joint forest mgmt. Tanzania to Danida, 1999—; nature conservationist Zool. Mus., Copenhagen, 1991-95, Danish Ornithological Soc., Vietnam, 1993, Thailand, 1996, 97, Tanzania, 1991-92, 94, 95, 97, 98, vice-chmn. internat. dept., BirdLife Denmark, 1994—; wetland mgmt. specialist Regulus Consult, Latvia, 1997; advisor WWF Internat. Freshwater Programme, 1998-99, Internal WWF Rev., East Kalimantan, Borneo, 1998. Editor Pica, 1989-93. Del. Ramsar Cop 7, Costa Rica, 1999, CBD Cop 4 Bratislova, 1998, Cop 5 Nairobi, 2000. Recipient Rsch. awards Aage V. Jensens Found., Tanzania, 1991-94, Nature Conservation award Beckett Found., Vietnam, 1993, Wetland Conservation award Fridmoth Found., Tanzania, 1995. Mem. Worldwide Fund for Nature, African Bird Club (country coord.), BirdLife Denmark. E-mail: regulus@inet.uni2.dk. Office: Regulus Consult, Valdemarsgade 19 2, 1665 Copenhagen Denmark

DINEVA-VLADIKOVA, PETIA SIMEONOVA, physicist, researcher; b. Vidin, Bulgaria, Jan. 4, 1951; d. Simeon Georgiev and Lubka Nikolova (Boiadjieva) D.; m. Jasen Borisov Vladikov, Dec. 13, 1975; children: Lachezar, Lubomir. MS in Physics, U. St. Kl. Ohridski, Sofia, Bulgaria, 1974; PhD, Bulgarian Acad. Scis., Sofia, 1986. Rsch. fellow Inst. Mechanics Bulgarian Acad. Scis., Sofia, 1975-86; asst. prof. Inst. Mechanics Bulgarian Acad. Scis., 1986-95, assoc. prof. Inst. Mechanics, 1995—; lectr. U. St. Kl. Ohridski, 1976-80, S.W. U., Sofia, Bulgaria, 1991-95. Contbr. articles to profl. jours. Avocations: tourism, reading, art. Office: Inst Mechanics, Acad G Bonchev Str Block 4, 1113 Sofia Bulgaria

DING, CHEN, computer scientist; b. Biejing, Oct. 13, 1970; s. Shengyao and Ruizhe (Liu) D.; m. Linlin Chen, July 2, 1994. BS, Beijing U., 1994; MS, Mich. Technol. U., 1996; PhD, Rice U., 2000. Rsch. asst. Mich. Technol. U., Houghton, 1994-96; rsch. asst. Rice U., Houston, 1996-99, rsch. assoc., 2000—; cons. Baylor Coll. of Medicine, Houston, 1996-97, Compaq Cambridge Rsch. Lab., Mass., 1999-2000. Contbg. author: (book) Springer-Verlag Lecture Notes in Computer Sci. Series, 1997, 99. Vice-chmn. Mich. Tech. Residence Coun., Houghton, 1995-96. Mem. IEEE (student), Assn. Computing Machinery (student). Avocations: jogging, basketball. E-mail: cding@rice.edu. Office: Rice Univ 132 Mississippi St Houston TX 77029-4531

DING, CUNSHENG, computer scientist, educator; b. Qian, China, Jan. 16, 1962; s. Changming and Caixian (Duan) D.; m. Weijuan Shan, July 8, 1988; 1 child. MSc, Xidian U., 1988; PhD, U. Turku, 1997. Engr. Xian Fgn. Lang. Inst., China, 1981-85; lectr. Xidian U., Xian, 1988-92; vis. scholar U. Karlsruhe, Germany, 1992-94; rschr. Turku Ctr. Computer Sci., Finland, 1997; lectr. Nat. U. Singapore, 1997—. Author: Chinese Remainder Theorem: Applications, 1996; contbr. articles to profl. jours. Home: 109 Clementi Rd #07-06, Singapore 129791, Singapore

DING, DAJUN, physicist, educator; b. Jilin, China, May 8, 1956; s. Peide and Shuduan (Xiao) D.; m. Limin Qian; 1 child, Ding. BS, Jilin U., Changchun, China, 1980, MS, 1983, PhD, 1987. Jr. rsch. asst. Laser Materials Factory, Jilin, 1974-76; lectr. Jilin U., 1984-87, assoc. prof., 1988-93, prof. physics, 1994—, dir. Inst. Atomic and Molecular Physics, 1997—; vis. scientist Oak Ridge (Tenn.) Nat. Lab., 1990-93; guest scientist Uppsala (Sweden) U., 1994; mem. acad. com. State Key Lab. of Superhard Materials, Changchun, 1995—. Recipient Sci. and Tech. Progress award State Edn. Commn. of China, 1994. Mem. Chinese Soc. Optics, Chinese Soc. Physics, European Materials Rsch. Soc. Avocations: photography, drawing, travel. Office: Jilin Univ Inst At & Mol Ph, Jiefang Rd 119, Changchun 130023, China

DING, HUEISCH-JY, radiologist, researcher; b. Tainan, Taiwan, June 5, 1958; d. Hia-Cang and Sung-Ching (Chung) D.; m. Ke-Hsiang Lin. BS in Edn., Nat. Changhua U., Chuanghua, Taiwan, 1981; MS, Nat. Tsiung Hua U., Hsinchu, Taiwan, 1983, PhD, 1992. Cert. Nat. Bd. Radiation Protection. Asst. prof. Kaohsiung Med. U., Taiwan, 1983-93, assoc. prof., 1993—, dir. dept. isotope rsch., 1995—; radiologist Hosp. Kaohsiung Med. U., Taiwan, 1983—; mem. exam com., test com., Ministry of Examination, 1995—, special issue com. of medicine and nurse, 1997—. Commr. manage com. dist. Kaohsiung, 1997-98. Mem. Soc. Nuclear Medicine, Soc. Chemistry, Soc. Nuclear Energy. Avocations: music, computer, movies, writing.

DING, JACK JIE, mechanical and structural engineer, lecturer; b. Dongtai, Jiangsu, China, Oct. 5, 1960; s. Xianguang and Cuiying (Wu) D.; m. Li Dong, May 28, 1988; children, Alexander, Philip. BE, Nanjing Inst. Tech., Yanch, China, 1982; ME, Xidian U., Xian, China, 1985; PhD, U. Melbourne, 1993. Design engr. Xian Electronics Rsch. Ltd., 1985-89; rsch. asst. U. Melbourne, 1989-92; lectr. Auckland (New Zealand) U., 1993, UNITEC Inst. Tech., Auckland, 1993—; vis. engr. Contraves A.G., Zurich, 1989; vis. fellow U. B.C., Vancouver, 1995. Author: Excel 5.0--Fundamentals and Application, 1995; referee Jour. Sound and Vibration; contbr. articles to profl. jours. MUPS scholar U. Melbourne, 1989. Mem. ASME. Achievements include design of surveillance radar, 1989. Office: UNITEC Inst Tech Mt Albert, Pvt Bag 92025, Auckland New Zealand

DING, NING, art theory educator; b. Ningbo, Zhejiang, China, Apr. 29, 1960; s. Xiuye and Meili (Fan) D.; m. Lei Chen, Mar. 26, 1986; 1 child, Yilin. BA, Ningbo Normal Coll., 1981; MA, Hangzhou (China) U., 1986; PhD, Beijing Normal U., 1988. Tchr. Xiaoshi H.S., Ningbo, 1982-83; tchg. asst. Chinese Acad. Art, Hangzhou, 1989-91, lectr., 1991-92, assoc. prof., 1992-96, prof. art theory, 1996—, asst. chmn., 1992-96, chmn. art history, 1996-99; with Peking U.; postdoctoral fellow Essex U., Colchester, Eng., 1993-94. Author: Dimensions of Reception, 1990, Psychology of Visual Arts, 1994 (Silver prize 1996), Dimensions of Duration, 1997, Depth of Art, 1999; editor: Modern Psychoaesthetics, 1993; internat. editor Lang. of Design, 1996—. Named Good Tchr. of Zhejiang Province, Zhejiang Com. of Edn., 1996; recipient First Prize for Rsch. in Humanities, State Commn. of Edn., China, 1996; fellow Harvard U., 1998. Avocations: cello, electronics, movies. E-mail: dingning@telekbird.com.cn. Home: Rm 310 Bldg 50 (#2), Beida Zhongguanyuan, Beijing 100871, China Office: Dept Art Studies, Peking Univ, Beijing 100871, China

DING, WEN, speech professional; b. Sichuan, China, May 2, 1966; p. Fen-Yuan Ding and Xian-Jin Li; m. Qing-Yan Guan, Dec. 26, 1994; children: Billy-Xu, Ding. BS, Fudan U., China, 1988, MS, 1991; PhD, Utsunomiya U., Japan, 1996. Invited rschr. ATR-ITU, Japan, 1996-98; speech synthesis engr. Entropic Inc., Washington, 1998-2000; software design engr. Microsoft Corp., Redmond, Wash., 2000—. Mem. IEEE. Office: Entropic Inc 1 Microsoft Way Redmond WA 98052-8300

DINGEMANS, JAN JOHAN, lawyer; b. Kerkwyk, The Netherlands, Feb. 14, 1964; s. Gysbert Dirk-Jan and Thea Aleida (DeLeeuw) D.; m. Marjolein Helena Kuperus, May 13, 1995. LLD, U. Leiden, 1988. Intern KLM, N.Y.C., 1988, Condon & Forsyth, N.Y.C., 1988; atty. Banning Van Kemenade & Holland, Hertogenbosch, The Netherlands, 1989-94; ptnr. Van Riet & Assocs., Utrecht, The Netherlands, 1994—. Mem. VIA, Kiwanis, Insolad. Avocations: skiing, golf, tennis, cars. Home: Dennenlaan 26, 5263 NR Vught The Netherlands Office: Van Riet & Assocs, Einsteindreef 111, 3562 GB Utrecht The Netherlands

DINGEMANS, PETER GEORGE VALENTIN, retired rear admiral, benefits administrator; b. Hove, Sussex, England, July 31, 1935; s. George Albert and Marjorie Irene (Spong) D.; m. Faith Viven Bristow, Mar. 25, 1961; children: Timothy, James, Piers. Student, Brighton Coll., Royal Naval Coll. Dartmouth, Royal Coll. Def. Studies, 1979. Served HM Ships Vanguard, Superb, Ark Royal, 1953-57; qualified Torpedo Anti Submarine specialist, 1961; comdr. HMS Maxton, 1967; student of RAF Staff Course, 1968, Directorate of Naval Plans, 1971-73; comdr. HMS Berwick, HMS Lowestoft, 1973-74; staff asst., chief of def. staff, 1974-76; capt. Fishery Protection, 1977-79; comdr. HMS Intrepid, 1980-83; commodore Amphibious Warfare, 1983-85; flag officer Gibraltar, 1985-87; COS to C-in-C Fleet, 1987-90, ret. dir., 1990; adminstr. Argosy Asset Mgmt. PLC, Ivory and Sime, 1990-91, 91-92; head payroll, benefits and ins. Slaughter and May, 1992—; gov. Brighton Coll., 1998-2000, mem. bd., 2000—; mem. coun. Sussex U., 1999—. Decorated companion Disting. Svc. Order, companion Order of Bath (Eng.). Mem. City Livery Club, Assn. of Old Brightonians (pres. 1994-97), Royal Naval Assn. (pres. Horsham), Brit. Legion (pres. Cowfold), Royal Naval Club of 1765 and 1785 (chmn. of trustees). Avocations: family, shooting, tennis. Office: Slaughter and May, 35 Basinghall St, London EC2V 5DB, England

DINGHUA GUAN, researcher, educational association administrator; b. Beijing, Peoples Republic China, Oct. 25, 1927; s. Zhuguang Guan and Gongwei Ye; m. Huiqun Huang, Jan. 06, 1956; children: Youfei Guan, Yougeng Guan. BA, Qinghua U., Beijing, 1950, Inst. Russian Lang., Beijing, 1953; PhD, USSR Acad. Scis., Moscow, 1960. Engr. Radio Beijing, 1953-57; lab. head Inst. Radiobroadcasting, Beijing, 1960-61; rschr. Inst. Electronics Academia Sinica, Beijing, 1961-64; rschr. Inst. Acoustics Academia Sinica, Beijing, 1964—, dep. dir., 1981-84, dir., 1984-93; chmn. Beijing Assn. Sensor Tech., 1986—, West Pacific Regional Comm. on Acoustics, 1994-97, WG96 Sci. Com. on Ocean Rsch. (SCOR), 1991-94. Author: Sound and Ocean, 1982; contbr. to profl. jours. Recipient Advanced Sci. Worker award Academia Sinica, 1964, Academia Sinica prize, 1980, Nat. Natural Sci. award Beijing State Com. Sci. and Tech., 1982, Sci. Worker with Outstanding Contribution award State Com. Sci. and Tech., 1984, Nat. Outstanding Sci. and Tech. Worker award, 1997. Mem. Acoustical Soc. China (v.p., sec. gen. 1982, pres. 1989-94), Chinese Soc. Oceanography (sec. gen. 1984, v.p. 1990-94, cons. 1999—), Soc. Lab. Instrument (pres. 1984—), Soc. Transducers Tech. (v.p. 1984, pres. 1990), Am. Soc. Acoustics, Soc. Sci. Instruments (mem. standing com. 1991—). Avocations: music, swimming, Chinese opera, Chinese history. Home: Bldg 812 Apt 1304, Huangzhuang, Beijing 100080, China Office: Inst Acoustics Academia Sinica, 17 Zhongguancun St, Beijing 100080, China

DINGU-KYRKLUND, ELENA, international migrations and ethnic relations researcher; b. Bucharest, Romania, June 24, 1959; arrived in Sweden, 1994; d. Ion and Ana (Lacatusu) Dingu; m. Linus Pavel Kyrklund, Sept. 9, 1993; 1 child, Johanna Marie-Christina. MA in Philology, U. Bucharest, 1991; MA in Internat. Rels., Nat. Sch. Polit. Studies, Bucharest, 1992; LLM in European and Comparative Law, U. Limburg, Maastricht, The Netherlands, 1993; MA in Social Anthopology, Stockholm U., 1998. Tchr. fng. langs. and cultures Office Serving the Diplomatic Corps., Bucharest, 1984-91; asst. prof. English Nat.. Sch. for Polit. Studies and Pub. Adminstrn., 1990-92; from lectr. to assoc. prof. English Acad. Econ. Studies, Bucharest, 1991-94; rsch. asst. task force for East Europe European Inst. for Pub. Adminstrn., Maastricht, 1992-93; rschr. Ctr. for Rsch. in Internat. Migrations-Ethnic Rels. Stockholm U., 1995—; tchr. English, Internat. Assn. European Culture, Bucharest, 1990-91; interpreter, translator Publicom, Romanian Agy. of C. of C. and Industry, Bucharest, 1985, 94; translator acad. articles and rsch. materials Romanian Inst. Info. and Documentation, Bucharest, 1986-88; translator acad. articles for Romanian Assn. for Internat. Law and Internat. Rels., Bucharest, 1991-92; panel mem. European documentation seminar Ctr. for European Studies, Maastricht, 1993; presenter in field. Author: (with Charles Westin) Reducing Immigration Reviewing Integration, 1996, Widening Gaps-Problems of Unemployment and Integration, 1997; co-author: Multiculturalism, Integration and Other Words/Conepts, 1999. Grantee Romanian Parliament, 1990-91, Romanian Ministry Fgn. Affairs, 1991-92, European Commn., Brussels, 1992-93. Mem. Internat. Migration and Ethnic Relations Rsch. Assn., Swedish Assn. for Problems of Devel., The Jurists Social Scientists and Economists Profl. Trade Union, U. Limburg Magister Juris Communis Alumni Assn. (founding). Avocations: classical and jazz music, travel, swimming, rowing, fine arts. E-mail: elena.dingu-kyrklund@ceifo.su.se. Home: Tunnlandsvägen 3, 168 36 Bromma Sweden Office: Stockholm U CEIFO, Rm B633, Universitetsvägen 10B, 106 91 Stockholm Sweden

DINGWALL, DAVID C., Canadian government official; b. South Bar, N.S., Canada, June 29, 1952; s. George R. and Isabell I. (Schaump) D.; children: Jay David, Leigh Anne, Jennifer Rae. BComm; LLB, Dalhousie U., N.S., 1974. Spl. asst. office of the min. of pub. health, atty. gen. govt. N.S., min. resp. N.S. human rights com. and task force status of women Canada, 1974-76; pvt. law practice, 1979-80; parliamentary sec. to min. energy, mines and resources House of Commons, Canada, 1982-84, M.P. from Cape Breton-East Richmond, 1980-93; vice-chmn. standing com. natural resources and pub. works House of Commons; chair liberal caucus Parliament Can., 1985-86, nat. exec., 1986-87; chief opposition whip House of Commons, 1990-93, opposition leader, 1990-91; min. Atlantic Can. Opportunities Agy., Pub. Works and Gov. Svcs. Canada, 1993-96; mem. Privy Coun., 1993-97; min. of health Canada, 1996-97; founder, lobbyist Wallding Internat., Ottawa, 1997—. Office: Wallding Internat, 350 Sparks St Ste 1208, Ottawa, ON Canada K1R F58*

DINGWELL, DONALD BRUCE, geoscientist, educator; b. Corner Brook, Can., June 29, 1958; s. Donald Charles Bruce and Ena Phyllis (Stratton) D.; m. Anke Hofmann, July 16, 1994. BS in Geology/Geophysics with honors, Meml. U. Nfld., St. John's, Can., 1980; PhD in Geology, U. Alta., Edmonton, Can., 1984; Dr.rer.nat.habil., U. Bayreuth, Germany, 1992. Asst. prof. U. Toronto, Can., 1986-87; sci. officer Bayerisches Geoinstitut, Bayreuth, Germany, 1987-2000; chair mineralogy and petrology Ludwig Maximiliano U., München, Germany, 2000—. Contbr. articles to profl. jours. Recipient Viktor Goldschmidt prize, 1991, Gerhard-Hess prize, 1993; Carnegie Inst. Washington fellow, 1984-86. Fellow Mineral. Soc. Am. (award); mem. AGU (sec. volcanology geochemistry and petrology sect.), Geochem. Soc. (dir.). Avocation: history. Office: IMPG/LMU, Theresienstr 41/III, D-80333 München Germany

DINH, DUNG, mathematician, researcher; b. Nong Cong, Vietnam, Oct. 30, 1951; s. Liem Nho Dinh and Luong Thi Le; m. Kim Phuong Do, Apr. 7, 1978; children: Duong Thuy, Dung Thuy. BSc, Moscow State U., 1973, MSc, 1975, PhD, 1979, DSc, 1985. Lectr. Hanoi (Vietnam) Poly U., 1979-80; rschr. Moscow State U., 1981-85; sr. rschr. Hanoi Inst. Info. Tech., 1985-90, prof., 1990—; dir. divsn. Inst. Info. Tech., 1993—. Dep. editor-in-chief Vietnam Jour. Math., 1989—; mem. editl. bd. East Jour. on Approximations, 1995—, S.E. Asian Bull. Math., 1996—; inventor in field. Mem. Vietnamese Math. Soc. (dep. gen. soc. 1994—), S.E. Asian Math. Soc., Am. Math. Soc. Office: Inst Info Tech, Nghia Do Cau Giay, Hanoi Vietnam

DINH, TUNG VAN, obstetrician, gynecologist, pathologist, educator; b. Hoi-An, Vietnam, Aug. 7, 1930; came to U.S., 1975; s. Vinh Van Dinh and Lan Thi Thai; m. Gia D. To, Sept. 1, 1957; children: Tuan, Tue, Tri, Tho. MD, Saigon Med. Sch., Vietnam, 1958. Diplomate Am. Bd. Ob-Gyn., Am. Bd. Pathology. Fellow in ob-gyn. pathology Johns Hopkins Hosp., Balt., 1960-61; resident in ob-gyn. and pathology U. Tex., Galveston, 1976-81; chief of surgery Duy Tan Mil. Hosp., Danang, Vietnam, 1958-60; dir. Danang Gen. Hosp., 1966-75; asst. prof. ob-gyn. Hué (Vietnam) Sch. Medicine, 1970-75; prof. ob-gyn. and pathology U. Tex. Med. Br., Galveston, 1988—; examiner Am. Bd. Ob-Gyn., Chgo., 1987, 88. Author: Syllabus of Gynecologic Pathology, 1990, 2000, Clinical Gynecologic Oncology Review, 1993, 98, 2000. Pres. Vietnamese Am. Assn., Danang, 1970. Recipient medal of Health Svcs., Edn. and Social Svcs., Govt. of South Vietnam, 1973, Golden Apple award U. Tex., Galveston, 1984, 87. Fellow Am. Coll. Ob-Gyn., Am. Soc. Clin. Pathologists, Internat. Soc. Vulvar Diseases; mem. Assn. Profs. Ob-Gyn., Internat. Soc. Gynecol. Pathologists. Avocations: fishing, gardening, travel, reading. Office: U Tex Med Br Dept Ob-Gyn 301 University Blvd Dept Ob Galveston TX 77555-5302

DINI, LAMBERTO, Italian government official; b. Florence, Italy, Mar. 1, 1931; married; 1 child. Degree in Econs., Florence U., 1955; postgrad., U. Minn., U. Mich. Economist, 1959-75; exec. dir. for Spain, Italy, Greece, Portugal and Malta IMF, Washington; dep. gov. Bank of Italy, 1979-93; min. of the treasury Govt. of Italy, 1994-96; prime min. Govt. of Italy, Rome, 1995-96, min. fgn. affairs, 1996—. Stringher scholar, Bank of Italy, Fulbright scholar, Govt. of U.S.A. Office: Office of Fgn Min, Palazzo le Farnesina I, 00194 Rome Italy

DI NICOLINI, CONTE DI THEODOR W. CONTE, fine arts and antiques dealer; b. Crystal City, Tex., Oct. 14, 1944; s. Theodor A. and Doris M. Nicolini; m. Linda Contessa A. Nicolini, Jan. 25, 1948. BA in Lit., U. Hamburg, Germany, 1969. Mng. dir. I&IDC, N.Y.C., 1971-73; art conservator Met. Mus., N.Y.C., 1975-81; art and antiques dealer, owner Akanthus, Oklawaha, Fla., 1984—; lectr. fine arts Mus. für Kunst & Gewerbe, Hamburg; lectr. workshop on Am. furniture 1680-1810, 1985; advising dir. Norman Sheperd Arts, Watermill, N.Y., 1981-84. Capt. U.S. Spl. Forces, 1969-70. Avocations: art history, sailing, car racing. E-mail: akanthus@prodigy.net. Home and Office: 15129 SE 103d RD Place Rd Ocklawaha FL 32179

DINIZ, PEDRO, race car driver; b. São Paulo, May 22, 1970. Race car driver Team Sauber Formel 1, Switzerland, 1989-90; profl. race car driver Alfa Reynard, South America, 1990-91, Red Bull Sauber Petronas Forumla One. Champion São Paulo karting, 1988. Office: Red Bull Sauber Petronas, Wildbachstrasse 9, 8340 Hinwil Oxfordshire OX8 5PE, Switzerland*

DINKEL, ROLF, economist; b. Dinkelsbuhl, Germany, Jan. 18, 1940; s. Kurt and Paula (Schmidt) D.; m. Berti Schomig, Nov. 18, 1972. MBA in Econs., U. Wurzburg, 1965, PhD in Econs., 1971. Assoc. prof. U. Wurzburg, Germany, 1965-69; dir. AKZO, Ltd., Obernburg, Germany, 1969-72; mgmt. cons. Prognos Ltd., Basel, Switzerland, 1972-81; mem. mgmt.com. HealthEcon Ltd., Basel, Switzerland, 1981-92, mng. dir., 1992—. Author: International Price Comparisons of Pharmaceuticals, 1977, Cost-Effectiveness-Analysis of Leukemia Therapies, 1982, Guidelines for Pharmaeconomic Analysis, 1988, Economic Analysis of Malaria Prophylaxis, 1990. Mem. Royal Soc. Medicine, Internat. Soc. Health Econs. Office: HealthEcon Ltd, Steinentorstrasse 19, 4001 Basel Switzerland

DINKELSPIEL, ULF ADOLF ROGER, ambassador; b. Stockholm, July 4, 1939; s. Max and Brita (Björnstjerna) D.; m. Louise Ramel, June 7, 1969; children: Charlotte, Peder, Jan. BBA, Stockholm Sch. Econs., 1960. Attaché Ministry for Fgn. Affairs, Stockholm, 1962; 1st sec. Swedish Embassy, Tokyo, 1963-65, Swedish Del. to the OECD, Paris, 1965-67, Ministry for Fgn. Affairs, Stockholm, 1967-75; econ. counselor Swedish Embassy, Washington, 1975-79; undersec. of state Ministry of Commerce, Stockholm, 1979-81; dep. permanent sec. gen. Ministry for Fgn. Affairs, Stockholm, 1981-82, amb., 1982-91; min. fgn. trade and European affairs Stockholm, 1991-94; pres. Swedish Trade Coun., 1995—.

DINKOVA-KOSTOVA, ALBENA TODOROVA, biochemist; b. Razgad, Bulgaria, Oct. 11, 1967; came to U.S., 1991; d. Todor Dinkov and Stoyanka Gencheva Krastev; m. Roumen Vesselinov Kostov, Aug. 11, 1991; 1 child, Stephan. MS, Sofia (Bulgaria) U., 1991; PhD, Wash. State U., 1996. Rsch. asst. Wash. State U., Pullman, 1991-96; rsch. scientist Johns Hopkins U., Balt., 1996—. Contbr. articles to med. jours.; internat. patentee. Loyal H. Davis grad. fellow Wash. State U., 1993-94; Cancer Found. Am. fellow, 1997-99; recipient 1st pl. award Natural and Phys. Scis. Rsch. Expn., 1995. Mem. Am. Chem. Soc., AAAS, Phytochem. Soc. N.Am. (Best Paper award 1993). Home: 2846 N Calvert St Baltimore MD 21218-4454 Office: Johns Hopkins Sch Medicine 725 N Wolfe St WBS 406 Baltimore MD 21205

DINSMOOR, ROBERT DAVIDSON, judge; b. El Paso, Tex., May 19, 1955; s. William Bell Jr. and Mary (Higgins) D. BA in Polit. Sci., Brigham Young U., 1979, JD, 1982. Bar: Tex. 1983, U.S. Dist. Ct. (we. dist.) Tex. 1985, U.S. Ct. Appeals (5th cir.) 1986, U.S. Supreme Ct. 1987. Rsch. assoc. J. Reuben Clark Law Sch., Brigham Young U., Provo, Utah, 1981-82; asst. dist. atty. El Paso (Tex.) Dist. Atty., 1983-90; dist. ct. judge State of Tex., El Paso, 1991—; spkr. Tex. County Judges Assn., 1992, 1992 Ann. Mex. Am. Bar Assn. of Tex. Conf., 1992, 97, St. Mary's U. Law Sch. Ethics Seminar, 1999, El Paso Bar Assn. Ethics Seminar, 1997-00, also various h.s. and mid. schs., El Paso, 1988—; co-founder El Paso Criminal Law Study Group. Contbr. articles to profl. jours. Bd. dirs. S.W. Repertory Orgn., El Paso, 1994-95; Sunday Sch. pres. Latter Day Saints Ch., 5th ward, El Paso, 1993-95; exec. sec. to bishop, 1995—. Recipient Outstanding Achievement award El Paso Young Lawyers Assn., 1990, Outstanding Jurist award, 1999. Mem. State Bar Tex. (mem. indigent representation com. 1994-98, 99—, victim/witness com. 1992-95, 97-98, 99—, chmn. 1999-00), El Paso Bar Assn. (mem. legal bar com., libr. com., criminal law com., others 1986—, bd. dirs. 1993-96, sec. 1996-97, treas. 1997-98, v.p. 1998-99, pres.-elect 1999-00, pres. 2000-01). Democrat. Avocations: playing piano, writing music, bicycle riding, basketball, accordion playing. Office: 120th Dist Ct County Bldg Rm 605 500 E San Antonio Ave El Paso TX 79901-2419

DINSMORE, WILBERT WALLACE, physician, consultant; b. Ballymoney, Northern Ireland, Mar. 15, 1954; s. William and Margaret (Wallace) D.; m. Margaret Ann Lamont, July 5, 1978; 1 child, Andrew. MB BCh BAO, Queen's U., Belfast, Northern Ireland, 1978, MD, 1984. Jr. hosp. posts Northern Ireland, 1978-87; cons. physician Royal Victoria Hosp., Belfast, 1987—; advisor in field. Mem. editorial bd. European Acad. Dermato-Venereology; editor Internat. Jour. STD and AIDS; founding editor Sexual Dysfunction; contbr. articles to profl. jours. Fellow Royal Coll. of Physicians of Ireland/Dublin, Royal Coll. of Physicians in Edinburgh; rsch. grantee Dept. Health and social Svcs., Belfast, 1983-84. Fellow Royal Coll. Physicians;. Achievements include research in erectile dysfunction; contributions to the development of the clinical trials of sildenafil. Avocations: golf, reading, dining. Home: 1 Brackenwood Ln, Belfast BT17 9JJ, Northern Ireland Office: Ryl Vict Hosp Dept Genito Urin Med, Grosvenor Rd, Belfast BT12 6BA, Northern Ireland

DINTCHEVA, NADKA TZANKOVA, physicist, engineer, researcher; b. Panaguriche, Plovdivska, Bulgaria, May 30, 1973; d. Tzanko Borisov Dintchev and Stoianka Georghieva Dintcheva Romankova. Grad. in engring. and physics, U. Plovdiv, Bulgaria, 1996. Collaborator U. Plovdiv, 1996-97; rschr. DICPM, U. Palermo, Italy, 1997—. Contbr. articles to sci. jours., including Polymer Degrad. Stability, Polymer Advanced Tech. Mem. Bird Life, Bulgaria, 1995. Recipient honors E. Hauda, Rotary Club, Florence, Italy, 1997; Tempus scholar U. Palermo, 1996, Fgn. Ministry scholar, 1998. Mem. Italian Assn. Macromolecules, N.Y. Acad. Scis. Orthodox. Avocations: drawing, reading, skiing. Office: U Palermo DICPM, Viale delle Scienze, 90128 Palermo Italy

DI NUNZIO, DOMINICK, educational administrator; b. Bristol, Pa., Mar. 7, 1931; s. Anthony and Mary (Minni) Di N.; m. Helen Mae Appleton, Dec. 29, 1953; children: Dominick, Mark, Douglas, Celeste. BS, Millersville (Pa.) U., 1953; MEd, Rutgers U., 1960, postgrad., 1960-63; postgrad., U. Pa., 1965-68, Temple U., 1969-71, Lehigh U., 1983; PhD, Walden U., 1972. Tchr., basketball coach Bristol H.S., 1955-61; vice prin. Pemberton Twp. (N.J.) H.S., 1961-65, prin., 1965-73; prin. Pemberton Twp. H.S. No. 2, 1973-76, Pemberton Twp. Elem. Schs., 1976-84; prin. Mid. Schs., 1984-91, asst. supt., 1991—; mem. acad. policy bd. Walden U., 1978-83. With U.S. Army, 1953-55. Recipient Legion of Honor, Chapel of Four Chaplains, 1982, Disting. Alumnus award Walden U., 1982; named Secondary Educator of Am., 1973. Mem. ASCD, NEA, N.J. Edn. Assn., Nat. Assn. Secondary Sch. Prins., N.J. Assn. Secondary Sch. Prins., Am. Assn. Sch. Adminstrs., Nat. Doctorate Assn., N.J. Schoolmasters Club, South Jersey Schoolmens Club, Coun. for Basic Edn., Nat. Soc. for Study Edn., Millersville U. Alumni Assn. (exec. com. 1972—, v.p. 1978-80, pres. 1980-82, Disting. Svc. award 1987), Walden U. Alumni Assn. (pres. 1978-84), Walden U. Mid. States Regional Assn. (pres. 1983-85), Order Sons of Italy in Am., Pemberton Rotary (pres. 1976-77, Paul Harris fellow 1996), Masons (worshipful master 1987, dist. G chmn. Masonic edn. 1988-91, facilitator dist. C Hiram Leadership program 1990—, chmn. dist. C membership devel. and retention 1992—), Phi Delta Kappa. Presbyterian. Home: 37 Underwood Rd Levittown PA 19056-2601 Office: PO Box 98 Browns Mills NJ 08015-0098

DIODOROS, I (DAMIANOS GEORGE KARIVALIS), patriarch of Jerusalem; b. Chios, Greece, Aug. 14, 1923; arrived in Israel, 1938; Degree in theology, U. Athens, Greece, 1957; PhD (hon.), Theol. Acad., Leningrad, USSR, 1981. Ordained priest Patriarchate of Jerusalem, 1947. Deacon Ch. of the Nativity, Bethlehem, 1944; superior Ch. of the Praetorium, Jerusalem, 1947-52; tchr., libr., archivist High Sch. of Patriarchate; pres. Eccles. Ct. Patriarchate Patriarchate of Jerusalem, 1958, draguman, 1959-62; consecrated titular archbishop of Hierapolis, 1962; apptd. patriarchal vicar Ammam, Jordan, 1962; elected patriarch of Jerusalem, 1981. Office: Greek Orthodox Patriachate St, PO Box 19632-633, Old City Jerusalem Israel*

DIODOSIO, CHARLES JOSEPH, lawyer; b. Pueblo, Colo., Apr. 27, 1951; s. Warren Joseph and Lucille Julia Diodosio. BSChemE, U. Colo., 1973; JD, Northwestern U., 1976. Assoc. McDermott, Will & Emery, Chgo., 1976-80; internat. counsel Beatrice Co., Chgo., 1980-84, v.p. Asia devel., 1984-88; chmn. TMGC Ltd., Chgo., 1988—, Meadow Gold Investment Holding Co., Beijing, 1993—. Mem. ABA, Ill. Bar. Fax: 760-327-1200. Home: 1387 Calle de Maria Palm Springs CA 92264-8503

DIOMIN, YURY VASILIEVICH, engineering educator, researcher; b. Gorlovka, Donetsk, USSR, Sept. 26, 1941; s. Vasily Eliseevich and Nina Stepanovna (Pogorelova) D.; 1 child, Rostislav. Engr., Railway Engrs. Inst., Dnipropetrovsk, Ukraine, USSR, 1966, PhD, 1972; DSc, Railway Engrs. Inst., Moscow, 1986. Engr. Railway Engrs. Inst., Dnipropetrovsk, Ukraine, USSR, 1966-69; researcher Inst. Tech. Mechanics, Dnipropetrovsk, 1969-79, chief dept., 1979-97; prof. State Tech. U. Railway Transport, Dnipropetrovsk, Ukraine, 1997-98, Inst. Rwy. Transp., Kiev, Ukraine, 1998—. Co-author: Self-Excited Vibrations and Stability of Motion of Railway Vehicles, 1984, Dynamics of Machine-Building and Transport Constructions, 1995; contbr. articles to profl. jours. Fellow Transport Acad. Ukraine. Office: Inst Rwy Transp, 19 Lukashevich St, 03049 Kiev Ukraine

DION, CELINE, musician; b. Charlemagne, Quebec, Can., Mar. 30, 1970. Albums include: Unison, 1990 (album of the year 1990), Celine Dion, 1992, Colour of My Love, 1993 (multi-platinum 1994), Premieres Anees, 1994, Dion Chante Plamondon, 1994, Des Mots Qui Sonnent, 1995, Power of Love, 1995, French Album, 1995, Live A Paris, 1996, Falling Into You (Grammy award 1997), C'est Pour Vivre, 1997, The Collection 1982-1988, 1997, Let's Talk About Love, 1997 (Best Album by a Female Artist Billboard Music award), S'il suffisait d'aimer, 1998, These are Special Times, 1998 (Grammy & Juno awds. 1999), All The Way, 1999; apperances include Real Love, 1979, Beauty & the Beast, 1991 (Grammy award 1992, best selling single 1992, Acad. award 1992), Sleepless in Seattle, 1993, Through the Fire, 1994, My Heart Will Go On (Record of Yr., Best Female Pop Vocal Performance Grammy awards), Titanic, 1999 (Best Soundtrack Single Billboard Music award). Recipient Favorite Female Pop/Rock Artist award Am. Music Awards, 1999, Favorite Adult Contemporary Artist award Am. Music Awards, 1999, Album of Yr. for Titanic Billboard Music awards, 1999, Album Artist Billboard Music award, 1999, Adult Contemporary Artist Billboard Music award, 1999. Office: Sony Music 550 Madison Ave New York NY 10022-3211*

DIONNE, GERALD FRANCIS, research physicist, educator, consultant; b. Montreal, Feb. 5, 1935; came to U.S., 1964, naturalized, 1980; s. Louis Philip and Clare Isabel (Flood) D.; m. Claudette Leblanc, June 29, 1963; 1 child, Stephen. BS summa cum laude, Loyola Coll., U. Montreal, 1956; B of Engring. magna cum laude, McGill U., Montreal, 1958, PhD in Physics, 1964; MS, Carnegie-Mellon U., 1959. Jr. engr. IBM Corp., Poughkeepsie, N.Y., 1959-60; sr. engr. Sylvania Electric Products, Woburn, Mass., 1960-61; rsch. asst., lectr. McGill U., 1964; sr. rsch. assoc. Pratt & Whitney Aircraft, North Haven, Conn., 1964-66; mem. rsch. staff Lincoln Lab., MIT, Lexington, Mass., 1966-96; expert svcs. pers. Lincoln Lab., MIT, Lexington, 1996—; grad student rsch. advisor, sci. and tech. advisor to industry and govt. Contbr. articles to sci. jours.; rschr. in magnetism, magnetoelastic and magneto-optic phenomena, superconductivity theory and devices, microwave, submillimeter-wave, optical and surface physics; holder patents for microwave, superconducting, and magnetic devices. NRC of Can. fellow. Fellow IEEE; mem. Am. Phys. Soc., Corp. Profl. Engrs. Que., Sigma Xi. Home: 182 High St Winchester MA 01890-3366 Office: 244 Wood St Lexington MA 02421-6426

DIONYSIOU, DEMETRIOS, mathematics educator and researcher; b. Athens, Sept. 11, 1939; s. Dionysius Demetrios and Demeter Dion (Kateva) D.; children: Dennis, Demeter, Evita. BSc in Math., U. Athens, 1963; BSc Spl. in Math., U. London, 1969, PhD in Math., 1973. Math. tchr. secondary schs. Greece, 1964-70; lectr. math. U. Athens, 1970-80; prof. Hellenic Air Force Acad., Attica, Greece, 1980—; head math. dept. Hellenic Air Force Acad., Attica, 1980—. Author numerous researches math., physics and books; referee, editorial bd. dirs. jour. Astrophysics and Space Science. 2d lt. Greek army, 1963-64. Mem. Math. Assn. Am., Math. Assn. Greece, Internat. Astron. Union, Royal Astron. Soc., Joint Assn. for Geophysics, Convocation of the U. London, Air Acad. of Greece. Home: 18 Amassias, 11634 Athens Greece Office: Hellenic Air Force Acad Dekelia, TGA 1010, 14565 Dekelia Greece

DIORIO, EILEEN PATRICIA, retired medical technologist, philosophy educator; b. Pitts., Mar. 17, 1938; d. Charles Frederick and Elizabeth (Maturkanich) Kozlowski; m. David Robert Kaslewicz, June 21, 1958 (div. May 1965); m. Alfred Frank Diorio, June 11, 1983; children: Suzanne C. Kaslewicz Ickes, Fredric C. Kaslewicz, Warren G. Kaslewicz, Jennifer Kaslewicz Dalessandro. Student, Duquesne U., 1956-58. Reg. Med. Technologist, Pa. Microbiology technician Presbyn. U. Hosp., Pitts., 1967-70; supr. virology/immunology lab. Allegheny Gen. Hosp., Pitts., 1970-90; co-dir. Himalayan Inst. Yoga Science & Philosophy of Pitts., 1977-96. Vol. med. lab. mgr. Himalayan Inst. Hosp., India, 1992-96. Avocations: playing violin, cooking, tchg. meditation and relaxation.

DIÓSI, LAJOS, physicist; b. Gyula, Hungary, June 16, 1950; s. Imre and Magdolna (Fodor) D. MS, Roland Eötvös U., Budapest, Hungary, 1973, PhD, 1976. Postgrad. Ctrl. Rsch. Inst. Physics, Budapest, 1973-76, rsch. assoc., 1976-88; sr. rsch. assoc. Rsch. Inst. Particle and Nuclear Physics, Budapest, 1988—. Editor: Stochastic Evolution of Quantum States in Open Systems, 1994; contbr. articles to profl. jours. Home: Rákóczi út 36, 1072 Budapest Hungary Office: Rsch Inst Particle and Nuclear Physics, PO Box 49 XII Konkoly Thege, 1525 Budapest 114, Hungary

DIOUF, JACQUES, intergovernmental organization administrator; b. Saint-Louis, Senegal, Aug. 1, 1938. BS in Agr., Ecole Nat. d'Agr., Grignon-Paris; MS in Tropical Agronomy, Ecole Nat. D'Application d'Agronomy, Nogent-Paris; PhD in Social Scis. of the Rural Sector, U. Sorbonne, Paris. Dir. European Office and Agrl. Programme of Mktg. Bd., Paris and Dakar, 1963-64; exec. sec. African Groundnut Coun., Lagos, Nigeria, 1965-71, West Africa Rice Devel. Assn., Liberia, 1971-77; sec. of state for sci. and tech. Senegal, 1978-83; mem., chmn. fgn. rels. com., sec. Parliament of Senegambian Confedn., Senegal, 1983-84, chmn. Friendship Parliamentary Group, Senegal-U.K., 1983-84; adviser to pres. and regional dir. internat. devel. Rsch. Ctr., Ottawa, Can., 1984-85; sec.-gen. Ctrl. Bank for West African States, Dakar, Senegal, 1985-90, spl. adviser to gov., 1990-91; amb. Senegal permanent mission UN, N.Y.C., 1991-93; dir.-gen. UNFAO, Rome, 1994—. Contbr. articles to profl. jours. Decoration Grand Commdr. in the Order of the Star of Africa (Liberia), Svcs. to Edn., Ministry of Edn. (France), Legion of Honour (France). Office: care FAO, Viale delle Terme di Caracalla, 00100 Rome Italy*

DI PAOLA, GUILLERMO ROGELIO, gynecologist; b. Buenos Aires, Oct. 7, 1930; s. Guillermo di Paola and Matilde Peter-Lucero; m. Irene del Cerro, May 4, 1956; children: Guillermo A., Federico, Maria Irene, Eugenia, Carolina. BS, Nat. Coll. Buenos Aires, 1948; MD, U. Buenos Aires, 1955, PhD, 1961. Intern Johns Hopkins U., Balt., 1956-57; adscripto U. Buenos Aires, 1958-61, docente autorizado, 1962-70, adj. prof., 1970-84, full prof., 1st chair gynecology, 1985-96; prof. emeritus U. Buenos Aires, Argentina, 1997; chmn. dept. ob-gyn. Univ. Hosp. José de San Martin, Cordoba, Argentina, 1995-2000; fellow in gynocologic oncology U. Florence, Italy, 1963. Mem. editl. bd. Gynecologic Oncology: Internat. Jour., 1988-91, Cervix and Lower Genital Tract, 1991, Jour. Internat. Gynecol. Cancer Soc., European Jour. Gynecol. Oncology, 1979—, Clin. and Exptl. Ob-Gyn., 1979—. Recipient Knight Great Cross of the Sovereign and Mil. Order of Malta, 1995, Commdr. of the Order of Merit of Italy, 1997, Comdr. with silver plaque Ecuestrian Order of St. Silvester, 1999; named Magister of Argentinian Medicine, 1997. Fellow Argentine Assn. Gynecologic Oncology (founder, pres. 1991-93), Internat. Soc. for Study Vulvovaginal Disease (founder, pres. 1970-73); mem. Internat. Fedn. Gynecology and Obstetrics (cancer com. 1990-98), Soc. Gynecologic Oncologists (assoc.), Internat. Gynecologic Cancer Soc. (councillor 1994-97, pres. 8th biennial meeting), European Gynecologic Oncology Soc., Italian Gynecologic Oncology Soc. (assoc.), Internat. Fedn. Cervical Pathology and Colposcopy (chmn. edn. com. 1990-96, chmn. internat. sci. com. 7th World Congress 1999), Italian Soc. Ob-Gyn. (hon.), Brazilian Gyn Soc. (hon.), Chilean Gyn Soc. (hon.), Johns Hopkins Surg. and Med. Soc., Howard Kelly Gynecol. Soc., Jockey Club Buenos Aires. Roman Catholic. Avocations: music, golf. Home: Once de Septiembre 1471, 1426 Buenos Aires Argentina Office: Centro Medico de la Mujer, Larrea 874, 1117 Buenos Aires Argentina

DI PIETRO, ANTONIO, Italian government official; m. Isabella Ferrara; 1 child, Cristiano; m. Susanna Mazzoleni. JD, U. Milan, 1978; postgrad., U. Pavia, 1979. Artisan Germany, 1970; with Aero. Constrns. Hdqs. Min. Def., 1973; mcpl. sec. Province of Como, 1979; police commr. Milan, 1980; jud. apprentice Superior Coun. Judiciary, Rome, 1981; pub. prosecutor Office of Atty. Gen., Bergamo, Milan, 1985—; computer cons. Ministry Grace and Justice, 1989; min. pub. works Govt. of Italy, Rome, 1996—; mem. European Parliament, Brussels, Belgium. Avocation: repairing furniture. Office: Via Milano 14, I-21052 Busto Arsizio Italy

DIPIETRO, MARK JOSEPH, lawyer; b. Memphis, Aug. 25, 1947; s. Joseph Mark and Anne E. (Dorsey) DiP.; m. Kathleen Ann (Rafferty), June 22, 1968; children: Mark, Lora, Matthew. BA in Chemistry, So. Ill. U., 1969; JD, John Marshall Law Sch., 1976. Bar: Ill. 1976, Minn. 1983. Chemist Univ. Conn. Med. Sch., Hartford, 1969-70, VA Hosp., Indpls., 1970-71, U.S. Steel Corp., Gary, Ind., 1971-76; atty. Standard Oil of Ind. (now BP-Amoco), Chgo., 1976-81; from assoc. to ptnr. Merchant and Gould PA, Mpls., 1981-91; sr. v.p., sec. Merchant & Gould PA, St. Paul, 1992—. Mem. Met. Airport Sound Abatement Com., Mpls., 1984. Mem. ABA, AAAS, Internat. Bar Assn., Am. Intellectual Property Assn., Minn. Intellectual Property Assn., Ramsey County Bar Assn. Roman Catholic. Avocations: reading, bicycling, aerobics, piano. Fax: 612 371-5323. Home: 815 Fairview Ave S Saint Paul MN 55116-2161 Office: Merchant & Gould 3100 Norwest Ctr 80 S 8th St Ste 3200 Minneapolis MN 55402-2215

DI PINTO, ALEX MARC LAURENT, management consultant; b. Marseilles, France, Sept. 14, 1965; s. Noël Gérard and Nicole (Merlino) Di P. MSc in Gen. Engring., Ecole Nationale Supérieure des Arts et Metiers, Paris, 1988. With CGI Informatique (IBM Global Svcs.), Paris, London, Amsterdam, The Netherlands, 1989-95, Bossard Consultants, Paris, 1995-96, SAP, Paris, 1996-97, PriceWaterhouseCoopers, Paris, Tokyo, 1997—. E-mail: a-di-pinto@hotmail.com.

DIRENZO, GORDON JAMES, sociologist, psychologist, educator; b. North Attleboro, Mass., July 19, 1934; s. Santo and Giulia (Petti) DiR.; m. Mary Kathleen Ryan, July 6, 1968; children: Maria Giulia, Chiara Veronica, Marco Santo. BA, U. Notre Dame, 1956, MA, 1957, PhD, 1963; postgrad., Harvard U., 1959, Columbia U., 1963-65, U. Colo., 1964. Lic. psychologist, Del.; cert. social psychologist. Instr. Coll. of St. Rose, Albany, N.Y., 1957-59; Instr. U. Portland, Oreg., 1961-62; asst. prof. Fairfield (Conn.) U., 1962-66; asso. prof. Ind. U., South Bend, 1966-70; prof. sociology U. Del., Newark, 1970—; mem. faculty Siena Coll., Albany (N.Y.) Med. Center, 1958-59, U. Notre Dame, 1960-61, Coll. White Plains, 1963-65, Bklyn. Coll., 1965, Western Conn. State U., 1964; mem. faculty SUNY, Stony Brook, 1980, Cortland, 1966; affiliate mem. med. and dental staff Med. Center Del., Wilmington, 1976-80, St. Francis Hosp., Wilmington, 1980—, Northeastern Hosp., Phila., 1982-85, Rockford Ctr., Wilmington, 1995—; pres. Behavior Cons., Newark, Del., 1975—; dir. Sociol. Cons. Group, North Attleboro, Mass., 1963-75; Fulbright-Hays prof. U. Rome, 1968-69, U. Bologna, Italy, 1980-81; mem., exec. sec., bd. examiners psychologists State of Del., 1991-99. Author: Personality, Power and Politics, 1967, Concepts, Theory and Explanation in the Behavioral Sciences, 1966, Personality and Politics, 1974, We, the People: American Character and Social Change, 1977, Sociological Perspectives, 1987, Human Social Behavior, 1990, The Social Individual, 1996, Personality and Society, 1998; contbr. articles to profl. jours. Recipient Disting. Svc. award Am. Assn. Family Practice, 1980, 82, 84, Excellence in Teaching award U. Del., 1991; fellow U. Notre Dame, 1959-60, Italian Ministry Edn., 1960, NSF, 1964; grantee Ford Found., 1960, NEH, 1975, Del. Inst. Med. Edn. and Rsch., 1975. Fellow Am. Sociol. Assn. (diplomate); mem. APA, AAUP, AAAS, Assn. Behavioral Scis. in Med. Edn., Soc. Personality and Social Psychology, Soc. for Advancement Social Psychology (bd. dirs. 1988-94), Am.-Italian Hist. Assn. (nat. exec. council 1977-80), Fulbright Alumni Assn., Internat. Sociol. Assn., Clin. Sociology Assn., Internat. Soc. Polit. Psychology (charter), Soc. Psychologists in Medicine, Internat. Polit. Sci. Assn., Soc. for Study Social Problems, Soc. Psychol. Study Social Issues, Eastern Sociol. Soc., Am. Sociol. Assn., Nat. Assn. Scholars, Alpha Kappa Delta. Home: 28 Deer Run Little Baltimore Farms Newark DE 19711 Office: U Del Dept Sociology Newark DE 19716

DIRESKE, PETER HANS, communications executive; b. Walsrode, Germany, Aug. 15, 1950; s. Gustav Adolf and Anna Erika (Rehle) D.; m. Beate Neubauer, Feb. 26, 1990; 1 child, Verena. Assoc. elec. engring., Tech. Sch. Braunschweig, 1983. CEO hpd-electronic, Schoeningen, Germany, 1980—. With German Armed Forces, 1971-83. Avocations: astronomy, geology. Office: hpd-electronic, PO Box 1321, D-38358 Schoeningen Germany

DIRKS, KENNETH RAY, pathologist, medical educator, army officer; b. Newton, Kans., Feb. 11, 1925; s. Jacob Kenneth and Ruth Viola (Penner) D.; m. Betty Jean Worsham, June 9, 1946; children: Susan Jan, Jeffrey Mark, Deborah Anne, Timothy David, Melissa Jane. M.D., Washington U., St. Louis, 1947. Diplomate: Am. Bd. Pathology. Rotating intern St. Louis City Hosp., 1948, asst. resident in gen. surgery, 1948-49; resident in pathology VA Hosp., Jefferson Barracks, Mo., 1951-53; resident in pathology, asst. chief lab. service VA Hosp., Indpls., 1953-54; resident in pathology Letterman Army Hosp., San Francisco, 1956-57; fellow in tropical medicine and parasitology La. State U., Central Am., 1958; asst. in pathology Washington U. Sch. Medicine, 1952-53; asst. chief lab. service VA Hosp., Jefferson Barracks, 1953; instr. pathology U. Ind. Med. Center, Indpls., 1953-54; commd. capt. M.C. U.S. Army, 1954, advanced through grades to maj. gen., 1976; dir. research Med. Research and Devel. Command, Washington, 1968-69; dep. comdr. Med. Research and Devel. Command, 1969-71, comdr., 1973-76; asst. surgeon gen., research and devel. U.S. Army, 1973-76; dep. comdr., comdr. Med. Research Inst. Infectious Diseases, Ft. Detrick, Frederick, Md., 1972-73; comdr. Fitzsimons Army Med. Center, Denver, 1976-77; supt. Acad. Health Scis., Ft. Sam Houston, Tex., 1977-80; assoc. prof. to prof. pathology and lab. medicine Coll. Med. Tex. A&M U., College Station, 1980-95; interim head dept. Coll. Medicine, Tex. A&M U., College Station, 1990-91; prof. emeritus pathology, 1995—; asst. dean coll. Coll. Medicine, Tex. A&M U., College Station, 1985-88; dir. dept. student health svcs. and A.P. Beutel Health Ctr. Tex. A&M U., College Station, 1989-95; dir. student health svcs. emeritus, 1995—. Contbr. articles to med. jours. Decorated D.S.M., Legion of Merit with oak leaf cluster, Meritorious Service medal, Army Commendation medal with oak leaf cluster. Fellow Coll. Am. Pathologists, Internat. Acad. Pathology. Address: 2513 Oak Cir Bryan TX 77802-2009

DIRZO, RODOLFO, ecology educator, researcher; b. Cuernavaca, Mex., June 26, 1951; s. Felix and Antonia (Minjarez) D.; m. Bertha Guillermina Gomez, Dec. 18, 1986; 1 child, Arturo. BSc in Biology, U. Morelos, Cuernavaca, 1974; MSc in Ecology, U. Wales, Bangor, U.K., 1977, PhD in Ecology, 1980. Rsch. asst. Nat. U. Mex., Mexico City, 1974-80, assoc. prof. ecology, 1980-83, prof. ecology, 1983-85; dir. Tropical Rsch. Sta., Veracruz, Mex., 1985-87; dep. chair Inst. Ecology, Nat. U. Mex., 1994-97, full prof. ecology, 1990—; prof., instr. Orgn. Tropical Studies, Costa Rica and U.S., 1982—; cons. Nat. Geographic Soc., Washington, 1995. Author, editor: Perspectives on Plant Population Ecology, 1984, Mexico Faces the Biodiversity Crisis, 1992, Tropical Forests: Biodiversity, 1996; mem. editl. bd. Trends in Ecology and Evolution, 1993—. Conservation & environment scholar Pew Charitable Trust, U.S., 1993; nat. rschr. Mex. Coun. Sci., Mexico City, 1990—. Mem. Mex. Acad. Sci. (chair biology 1996-97), Ecol. Soc. Am. (mem. pub. affairs com. 1996-98, governing bd. 1999—), Internat. Geosphere-Biosphere Program (mem. scientific com. 1997—), Assn. Tropical Biology (pres. 1993-94). Avocations: children's education, hiking, soccer, music, movies. Home: Olivarito 64 A-1, 01780 Mexico City Mexico Office: Nat Autonomous U Mex, Inst Ecology, 04510 Mexico City Mexico

DISALLE, MICHAEL DANNY, secondary education educator; b. Denver, May 16, 1945; s. Michael and Agnes Marie (Kulik) DiS.; m. Marikaye Lucas, June 22, 1968; children: Katharine Marie, Kristin Jean, Michael Charles, Matthew Gregory. BA, Regis Coll., 1967; MEd, Lesley Coll., 1992. Cert. tchr., Colo. Tchr. Assumption Sch., Welby, Colo., 1968-74, Cherry Creek High Sch., Englewood, Colo., 1974-95; poet, writer, 1995—. Author: (computer program/tchr.'s guide) Adventures of Tom Sawyer, 1983, One Day in the Life of Ivan Denisovich, 1984. Asst. den leader Boy Scouts Am., Aurora, Colo., 1988-89. Mem. ASCD, Nat. Coun. Tchrs. of English, Nat. Scholastic Press Assn., Journalism Edn. Assn., Colo. Lang. Arts Soc., Colo. State High Sch. Press Assn., Columbia Scholastic Press Assn. Avocations: fly fishing, gardening, cooking, fly tying.

DI SAMBUY, VITTORIO BALBO BERTONE, retired electronics company executive; b. Rome, Apr. 27, 1920; s. Federico Balbo Bertone and Sita (Halenke) Di S.; m. Alda Radaelli, 1963 (div.); 1 child, Yula; m. Giorgia Zeni, 1992. M Engring., Poly. Inst., Italy, 1945. Tech. mgr. Microfusione, Turin, Italy, 1948-58; mgr. bus. devel. Ledoga, Milan, 1958-67; gen. mgr. Borletti, Milan, 1967-76; cons. Motorola, Scottsdale, Ariz., 1976-85; chmn. Carlo Gavazzi, Milan, 1985-92; ret., 1992. cons. Rolm, Calif., 1980-85. Lt. Italian Navy, 1940-43, comdr. res. Mem. Centro Velico Caprera (bd. dirs. 1966-86), Ski Club 18 (pres. 1960-64), Rotary (Milan). Avocations: yachting, military and geopolitical studies. Home: Leopardi 27, 20123 Milan Italy

DISBERGER, DENNIS JAY, manufacturing executive; b. Syracuse, Kans., Sept. 9, 1958; s. Jay M. and Vina E. Disberger; m. Martha Ann Kater, June 6, 1981; children: Joel, Kara, Monica. BSME, Kans. State U., 1981, MBA, 1984. Cert. engr. Mgr. Disberger Harvesting, Hutchinson, Kans., 1976-81; quality supr. Caterpillar Tractor Co., Peoria, Ill., 1982, devel. engr., 1984-86; svc. mgr. Caterpillar Tractor Co., Hartford, Conn., 1986-90; quality mgr. Caterpillar Inc., Aurora, Ill., 1991-93, mktg. cons., 1993-95; program mgr. combines, new product introduction mgr. Caterpillar Claas Am., Omaha, 1996—. Asst. editor Farming on Track, 1996—. Mem. Am. Soc. Agrl. Engrs., Rotary, Optimist Club. Republican. Roman Catholic. Avocations: travel, horticulture. Home: 22775 Harrison St Gretna NE 68028-4144 Office: Caterpillar Claas Am 8951 S 126th St Omaha NE 68138-4001

DISERIO, FRANK JOSEPH, pharmaceutical company executive, consultant; b. N.Y.C., Oct. 3, 1931; s. Anthony and Catherine (Solimando) DiS.; m. Lauretta Brunck, 1954 (div. May 1984); children: Anthony Mark, Francis Joseph, Paul James; m. Marjatta Niemioja, Oct. 19, 1985). BS, NYU, 1963; MBA, Fairleigh Dickinson U., 1970; PhD, Union Inst., 1979. Ptnr. Foam Age Lounge, Inc. and Dawn W.W. Co., N.Y.C., 1956-59; from sales rep. to clin. rsch. dir. Sandoz Pharmaceuticals, Inc., East Hanover, N.J., 1959-80; dir. CNS Med Rsch., 1985-90; exec. dir. CNS clin. rsch., head OTC/analgesia clin. rsch. dept. Sandoz Rsch. Inst., East Hanover, 1988-95; pharm. devel. cons. Morristown, N.J., 1995—; assoc. prof. dept. family practice U. Medicine & Dentistry N.J. Sch. Osteo. Medicine, Stafford, 1998—. Contbr. articles to profl. jours. Capt. USAF, 1952-56. Mem. Internat. Headache Soc., Am. Headache Soc., Am. Acad. Neurology (non-clin. assoc.), Am. Soc. Clin. Pharmacology and Therapeutics, Nat. Bd. for Cert. in Headache Mgmt., N.Y. Acad. Scis., Rock Spring Club. Republican. Roman Catholic. Avocations: golf, travel, arts. Home: 24 Pippins Way Morristown NJ 07960-6971

DISHONG, DIANE ELIZABETH, medical/surgical nurse, rehabilitation nurse; b. Massillon, Ohio, Aug. 8, 1958; d. Theodore William and Judith Anne (Hoisington) Weiand; m. Morris William Dishong, Sept. 11, 1984; 1 child, Jeffrey William. Lic. practical nurse summa cum laude, Canton Practical Nursing Sch., 1984. Cert. in CPR, first aid. LPN, office nurse Canton, Ohio; LPN Timken Mercy Med. Ctr.; staff LPN Akron (Ohio) Gen. Med. Ctr.; LPN in chem. rehab. Massillon Cmty. Hosp.; staff nurse Stark County Eye Care Clinic; owner, CEO Bill's Beer Barn Beverage Drive Thru, Inc., Canton. Recipient hwy. safety award Nat. Hwy. Council. Mem. MADD, LPN Assn. Ohio.

DISLE, MICHEL, graphic designer; b. Neuilly-sur-Seine, France, Oct. 26, 1934; s. André and Lucie (Davesne) D.; m. Brigitte Aymeric, 1990; children from previous marriage: Caroline, Olivier; 1 child, Marie. Grad., Ecole Nat. Supérieure des Arts Appliqués, Paris, 1956, Cours Supérieur d'Esthétique Indsl., Paris, 1957. Jr. art dir. Publicis, Paris, 1960-65; art dir. McCann-Erickson, Paris, 1965-69; sr. art dir. Ted Bates, Paris, 1969-72; co-founder, creative dir., gen. mgr. Carré Noir, Paris, 1973-99; creative dir. DCC, 2000—. Creator personal emblem for former French pres. Francois Mitterrand, 1982. Roman Catholic. Avocation: heraldic artist. Home and Office: 52 Rue Borghèse, 92200 Neuilly-sur-Seine France

DISMUKES, VALENA GRACE BROUSSARD, photographer, former physical education educator; b. St. Louis, Feb. 22, 1938; d. Clobert Bernard and Mary Henrietta (Jones) Broussard; m. Martin Ramon Dismukes, June 26, 1965; 1 child, Michael Ramon. AA in Edn., Harris Tchrs. Coll., 1956; BS in Phys. Edn., Washington U., St. Louis, 1958; MA in Phys. Edn., Calif. State U., L.A., 1972; BA in TV and Film, Calif. State U., Northridge, 1981. Cert. phys. edn. tchr., standard svcs. supr. Phys. edn. tchr., coach St. Louis Pub. Schs., 1958-60; phys. edn. tchr., coach L.A. Unified Sch. Dist., 1960-84, health and sci. tchr., mentor tchr., 1984-93; coord. gifted and talented program 32d St./U.So. Calif. Magnet Sch., 1993-95, magnet coord., 1995; adminstrv. asst. Ednl. Consortium of Ctrl. L.A., Calif., 1993-95; free-lance photographer, 1970—; owner, bus. cons. Grace Enterprises, 1994-95; owner World Class Images, 1997—; coord. Chpt. I, 1989-93; mem. sch. based mgmt. team, 1990-93. Author: (photography book) As Seen, 1995; editor parent newsletter, 1975-80; photographs exhibited in solo shows include The Olympic Spirit, 1984, L.A.-The Ethnic Place, 1986, Impressions, 1999, Native Americans: Red Black Connection, 1999, Tibet-Photos from the Roof of the World, 2000, Chocolate Women, 2000; contbr. articles to profl. jours. Mem. adv. com. Visual Comm., L.A., 1980; bd. dirs. NACHES Found., Inc., L.A., 1985-86; mem. Cmty. Consortium, L.A., 1986-87; mem. adv. com. L.A. Edn. Partnership, 1986-87; mem. adv. bd. Expo Sports Club, L.A., 1994; co-founder Alliance of Native Am. of Southern Calif., 1999, v.p. 1999-00. Marine Educators fellow, 1992; photography grantee L.A. Olympic Organizing Com., 1984, Teaching grantee L.A. Edn. Partnership, 1987-89; recipient Honor award L.A.-Calif. Assn. Health, Phys. Edn. and Recreation, 1971. Mem. ACLU, NAACP, Urban League, Sierra. Avocations: travel, collecting dolls and baskets, ethnic art. Home: 3800 Stocker St Apt 1 Los Angeles CA 90008-5119

DISOGRA, CARLOS ESTEBAN, psychologist; b. Córdoba, Argentina, Feb. 3, 1964; s. Esteban and Maria Esther (Senestrari) D. BA, U. Córdoba, 1995. Pvt. practice Córdoba, 1995—; prof. Sch. Psychology, Nat. U. Córdoba, 1996—. Mem. APA (internat. affiliate), Córdoba State Coun. of Psychologists. Avocation: photography. Home and Office: Av Colón 1880 piso 2, dept 12, 5000 Cordoba Argentina

DI SPIGNO, GUY JOSEPH, international management consultant, industrial psychologist; b. Bklyn., Mar. 6, 1948; s. Joseph Vincent and Jeanne Nina (Renna) DiS.; m. Gisela Riba, May 23, 1979; children: Michael Paul, Abie Francis. BS, Carroll Coll., 1969; MA (fellow), No. Ill. U., 1972; MEd, Loyola U., 1974; PhD, Northwestern U., 1977. Instr. No. Ill. U., DeKalb, 1969-70; chmn. humanities dept. Quincy (Ill.) Boys' High Sch., 1970-71; dir. religious edn. St. Mary's Ch., DeKalb, 1971-72; dir. edn. Immaculate Conception Parish, Highland Park, Ill., 1972-77; dir. human resources Am. Valuation Cons., Des Plaines, Ill., 1977-79; psychologist Hay Assocs., Chgo., 1979-80; v.p. mktg. Exec. Assets Corp., Chgo., 1980-82; dir. mgmt. devel. and personnel svcs. Borg-Warner Corp., Chgo., 1982-84; ptnr., cons. psychologist Medina & Thompson, Chgo., 1984-91; pres. Exec. Synergies, Inc., Northbrook, Ill., 1991—. Contbr. articles to profl. jours. Mem. Highland Park Human Relations Commn., 1975-77, Home Owners and Businessmen's Assn., Highland Park, 1976-77; mem. legis. com. Vernon Hills (Ill.) Sch. Bd., alumni coun. Carroll Coll., 1981-83; soccer coach, Am. Youth Soccer Orgn., Glenview, Ill.; chmn.'s cabinet Ill. Dem. Party, 1988-92; benefactor Jesuit Partnership, Chgo. province, 1995—. Clifford B. Scott scholar, 1967; named to Order Ky. Cols. Mem. APA, Community Religious Edn. Dirs. (nat. vice chmn. 1971-73), Ill. Psychol. Assn., Nat. Registry Health Svc. Providers in Psychology, Am. Personnel and Guidance Assn., Soc. Indsl. and Orgnl. Psychology, Carroll Coll. Alumni Counsel, Phi Alpha Theta, Sigma Phi Epsilon. Home: 2330 Greenview Rd Northbrook IL 60062-6633 Office: 555 Skokie Blvd Ste 260 Northbrook IL 60062-2889

DISSEN, ERIK, immunologist, physician; b. Oslo, June 7, 1963; s. Bjarne Sigmund and Ingrid Anna (Ulvang) D.; m. Ragnhild Elise Oerstavik, Aug. 21, 1993; children: Haakon, Ingrid Anna. MD, U. Oslo, 1991, PhD, 1997. Rsch. fellow The Norwegian Cancer Soc., 1991-999; asst. prof. dept. anatomy U. Oslo; intern Molde Hosp., Norway, 1994-95. Contbr. articles to profl. jours. Lt. The Norwegian Royal Guard, 1996-97. Office: Univ Oslo Dept Anatomy, PO Box 1105 Blindern, 0317 Oslo Norway

DISSEN, JAMES HARDIMAN, lawyer; b. Pitts., Jan. 26, 1942; s. William Paul and Kathryn Grace (Reilly) D.; m. Shirley Ann Stark, Dec. 17, 1976; children: Elizabeth Ann, William Stark, Anna Kathryn. BS, Wheeling (W.Va.) Jesuit U., 1963; MBA, Xavier U., Cin., 1966; JD, Duquesne U., Pitts., 1972. Bar: Pa. 1972, U.S. Dist. Ct. (we. dist.) Pa. 1972, W.Va. 1973, U.S. Dist. Ct. (so. dist.) W.Va. 1973, U.S. Supreme Ct. 1976. Spl. agent Counter Intelligence U.S. Army Intelligence Corps, 1963-66; personnel mgr. Columbia Gas of Pa., Inc., Uniontown, 1969-73; dir. labor rels. Columbia Gas Transmission Corp., Charleston, W.Va., 1973-84, dir. personnel and labor rels., 1984-87, dir. employee rels., 1987-96; v.p. Columbia Nat. Resources, Charleston, W.Va., 1996—; bd. dirs. Fourth Venture Investment Group, Inc.; adj. prof. W.Va. Grad. Coll., 1996-97, Wheeling Jesuit U., 1997, U. Charleston, 1998; chmn., exec. com., bd. dirs. Star U.S.A. Fed. Credit Union. v.p., bd. trustees Highland Hosp., 1991—; bd. dirs. Inroads/W.Va., 1995—, Christmas in April, 2000—. Mem. ABA, W.Va. State Bar, Soc. Human Resource Mgmt., W.Va. C. of C. (chmn. human resource com.), St. Thomas Moore Soc., Charleston Tennis Club. Republican. Roman Catholic. Avocation: golf. Home: 1501 Brentwood Rd Charleston WV 25314-2307 Office: Columbia Natural Resources 900 Pennsylvania Ave Charleston WV 25302-3548

DISTLER, WOLFGANG, obstetrician-gynecologist; b. Köln, Germany, Dec. 16, 1945. MD, U. Düsseldorf, Germany, 1972. Rsch. fellow U. So. Calif., L.A., 1974-75; resident in ob-gyn. U. Düsseldorf, 1976-82, asst. prof. ob-gyn., 1982-85, assoc. prof. ob-gyn., 1985-94; prof., chmn. dept. ob-gyn. Tech. U. Dresden, Germany, 1994—. Office: Tech U Dresden Dept Ob-Gyn, Fetscherstrasse 74, D-01307 Dresden Germany

DITCH, SUSAN ANN, psychotherapist; b. Belleville, Ill., Mar. 29, 1962; d. George John and Margaret Ann (Doiron) Wahlig; m. Kevin Michael Olsen, Sept. 26, 1981 (div. Mar. 1986); 1 child, Sarah; m. Robert Jerry Ditch, Nov. 7, 1992; children: Joseph, Sarah, Kelly, Sean. BS in Social Work cum laude, St. Louis U., 1991, MSW, 1993. Lic. clin. social worker. Child and adult sexual assault counselor Call For Help, Edgemont, Ill., 1991-93; youth care worker Call for Help Luebben Ctr., Edgemont, 1992; individual and family therapist Luth. Child and Family Svcs., Sparta, Ill., 1993-98; dir. social svcs. Sparta Cmty. Hosp., 1998—; WRAP facilitator LAN # 5, 1997. Adult moderator Cath. Youth Orgn., New Athens, Ill., 1989-93; rape crisis advocate Sexual Assault Victims Care Unit, Edgemont, 1988-89. Mem. NASW, Cursillo in Christianity (Leaders Sch.). Roman Catholic. Avocations: baking, fishing, watching children's sporting events, camping, walking. Home: 101 N Jackson St New Athens IL 62264-1209 Office: Sparta Cmty Hosp 818 E Broadway St Sparta IL 62286-1820

DI TELLA, TORCUATO SALVADOR, sociology educator; b. Buenos Aires, Dec. 29, 1929; s. Torcuato Ciro and Maria Angela (Robiola) Di T.; m. Kamala Apparao (div. 1975); children: Victor, Andrés; m. Tamara Chichilnisky, May 25, 1979; children: Sebastián, Carolina. Grad. in engring., U. Buenos Aires, 1951; MA in Sociology, Columbia U., 1953; postgrad., London Sch. Econs., 1955-57. Rsch. prof. U. Chile, Santiago, 1957-58; vis. prof. polit. sci. U. Calif., Berkeley, 1967; vis. prof. Inst. Latin Am. Studies, U. London, 1969-71; expert UNESCO Rsch. Ctr., Rio de Janeiro, 1968; prof. Latin Am. Faculty Social Scis., Buenos Aires, 1972-83; prof. sociology U. Buenos Aires, 1959-66, 84—; vis. prof. St. Antony's Coll., Oxford (Eng.) U., 1970-71. Co-author: Sindicato y Comunidad, 1969; author: Clases sociales y estructuras políticas, 1973, La rebelión de esclavos en Haití, 1984, Latin American Politics, 1990, National Popular Politics in Early Independent Mexico, 1996; dir. Desarrollo Económico y Social, 1975-80. Mem. adminstrv. coun. Inst. di Tella, Buenos Aires, 1959—. Recipient Premio Konex, Konex Co., 1986. Mem. Inst. Desarrollo Económico y Social (bd. dirs. 1975—, pres. 1985—), Latin Am. Studies Assn., Club U. Buenos Aires, Club Belgrano. Avocation: gardening. Office: U Buenos Aires, Ciudad U Pabellon dos, 1425 Buenos Aires Argentina

DITLEVSEN, PETER DALAGER, educator; b. Copenhagen, Jan. 2, 1961; s. Ove Dalager and Aase (Rasmussen) D.; m. Anne-Sophie Hjort, June 5, 1987; children: Lea, Sara, Amalie. MS, U. Copenhagen, 1988; PhD, Tech. U. Denmark, Copenhagen, 1991. Asst. tchr. Inst. Math. U. Copenhagen, 1983-86; tchr. math. U. Engring, Copenhagen, 1986-88; rschr. Danish Meteorological Inst., Copenhagen, 1992-93; assoc. prof. Niels Inst., U. Copenhagen, 1994—. Editor: Modern Dynamical Meteorology, 1995; contbr. articles to sci. jours., popular sci. mags. and textbooks. Postdoctoral fellow Lawrence Berkeley Lab., U. Calif., Berkeley, 1991-92. Avocations: beekeeping, painting, theater. Home: Andedammen 2, 3460 Birkerod Denmark Office: Niels Bohr Inst Geophys Dep, Juliane Maries Vej 30, 2100 Copenhagen Denmark

DITRÓI-PUSKÁS, ZUÁRD, geologist, educator; b. Cegléd, Pest, Hungary, Sept. 15, 1948; s. Zuard and Magdolna (Zana) D.; m. Katalin Pancsovay, Sept. 29, 1973; 1 child, Gergely. MS in Geology, Eötvös U., Budapest, 1973, PhD in Geology, 1980. Asst. prof. dept. petrology/geochemistry Eötvös U., Budapest, 1973-81, sr. lectr., 1981-83, assoc. prof., 1986-95, head dept. petrology/geochemistry, 1995—; head dept. non-metallics Nat. Geol. Inst., Maputo, Mozambique, 1983-85; head gem lab. Gemas & Pedras Lapidadas, Maputo, Mozambique, 1985-86; cons., head gem lab. UN/DTCD, Maputo, 1985-86. Author: Gemmology (in Portuguese), 1986; co-author: (in Hungarian) Optical Mineralogy, 1993; contbr. articles to profl. jours. Mem. Hungarian Geol. Soc., Hungarian Acad. Scis. (pub. body 1996—). Roman Catholic. Avocations: nature conservation, touring. Office: Dept Petrology and Geochemistry, Muzeum krt 4/A, 1088 Budapest Hungary

DITTBERNER, GERALD JOHN, meteorologist, space scientist, engineer; b. St. Paul, Minn., Oct. 24, 1941; s. Norbert R. and Emily B. (Tarr) D.; m. Mary K. Doerning, Sept. 11, 1965; children: Colleen M., Matthew J., Brigitte C. BEE, U. Minn., 1964; MS in Meteorology, Space Sci. & Engring., U. Wis., 1969, PhD in Meteorology, 1977. Bd. cert. cons. meteorologist. Commd. 2d lt. USAF, 1964, advanced through grades to lt. col.; weather forecaster 12th squadron USAF, Thule AB, Greenland, 1969-70; chief satellite data processing air force global weather cen. USAF, Offutt AFB, Nebr., 1970-74; vice comdr. environ. tech. applications ctr. USAF, Scott AFB, Nebr., 1977-81; chief aerospace scis. div. 2d weather wing USAF, Ramstein AB, Fed. Republic of Germany, 1981-84; program mgr. office sci. research USAF, Bolling AFB, D.C., 1984-85; sr. prin. engr. Harris Corp., Alexandria, Va., 1985-88; sr. scientist Kaman Scis. Corp., Alexandria, Va., 1988-93; scientist Mentor Techs., Inc., Lanham, Md., 1993-95; program mgr., Nat.

Oceanic and Atmospheric Adminstrn. Nat. Environ. Satellite Data and Info. Svc., Washington, 1995—; scientist, field experimentor World Meteorol. Orgn., Barbados, West Indies, 1969; adj. prof. St. Louis U., 1976. Contbr. articles to profl. jours. Fellow AIAA (assoc., chmn. space ops. and support tech. com. 1993-94), Royal Meteorol. Soc.; mem. Am. Meteorol. Soc., Nat. Weather Assn. (v.p. 1979-80), Wis. Acad. Scis., Arts, and Letters, N.Y. Acad. Scis., Sigma Xi, Theta Tau. Roman Catholic. Avocations: camping, skiing, Porsche racing, travel. Office: Nat Environ Satelite Date and Info Svc Fb4 3301A Washington DC 20233-0001

DITTMER, LINDA JEAN, photographer, computer artist, retired photojournalist; b. Detroit, 1950; d. Max Gene Witherow and Julienne Heldegarde Sikorski; m. Dennis Robert, July 11, 1970 (div. Feb. 1987); 1 child, Jesse Michael. Student, Coll. Art and Design, Detroit, 1988-90; AAS, Oakland Coll., 1993; student, Wayne State U., 1994—. Prodr. Greater Media, Detroit, 1985-87; broadcaster Wismer Broadcasting, Port Huron, Mich., 1987-89; sports writer UPI, Detroit, 1992-93; freelance photojournalist AP, Detroit News, Detroit Free Press, 1989—; pvt. practice computer cons., Detroit, 1996—. Recipient Recognition award Children's Hosp. Detroit, 1986, Cert. Appreciation, Easter Seal Soc., Detroit, 1986, Presdl. Phys. Fitness Instr. award, 1990, Disting. Svc. award Arthritis Found., Detroit, 1992. Mem. Nat. Press Photographers Assn., Soc. Profl. Journalists, Internat. Massage Assn., Golden Key. Avocations: snowshoeing, hiking, skiing, music, theatre.

DITTRICH, VALERIE MONICA, investment consultant; b. Riverside, N.J., June 11, 1955; d. Francis George and Anne (Rohaly) D. BS in Commerce, Rider Coll., 1977; MBA, Drexel U., 1994. Registered investment advisor; lic. ins. agt., N.J., Pa. Investment adminstr. N.J. Nat. Bank, Trenton, 1977-80; instnl. sales asst. Merrill Lynch Govt. Securities, Phila., 1980-81; account exec. Paine Webber Inc., Phila., 1981-85, Smith Barney Harris & Upham, Phila., 1985-92; sales assoc. Prudential Securities, Inc., Jenkintown, Pa., 1992-94; investment cons. Samuel A. Ramirez & Co., Inc., N.Y.C., 1995; registered acct. adminstr. Wheat First Union, Phila., 1996-99; registered client svc. rep. Legg Mason Wood Walker, Inc., Marlton, N.J., 1999—. Mem. NAFE, Assn. MBA Execs., Omicron Delta Kappa (alumna chpt.). Republican. Roman Catholic. Avocation: heraldry. Home: 195 Greenwood Ave Riverside NJ 08075-4223

DITTRICHOVÁ, JAROSLAVA, psychologist, researcher; b. Prague, Czech Rep., June 19, 1929; d. Jaroslav and Vlastimila (Huptychová) Macháček; m. František Dittrich, July 21, 1953; children: Tomáš, Eva. PhD, Charles U., Prague, 1953, CSc, 1963. Rsch. asst. Inst. Pedagogy, Prague, 1953-54; rsch. asst. Inst. Care Mother and Child, Prague, 1954-63, rschr., 1963-72, chief Lab. Study Higher Nervous Functions,, 1972-92, rschr. (after retirement), 1992—; cons. U. Groningen, Holland, 1964, Max-Planck Inst. Psychiatry, Munich, 1969, INSERM, Paris, 1980; spkr. in field of infant behavior. Author: Sleep in Infancy, 1974; co-author: The Development of Preterm Infants Until the Age of 3 Years, 1964, Child Clinical Psychology, 1991, Advances in Pediatrics, 1985; mem. editl. bd. Jour. Sleep Rsch., Early Devel. Parenting, 1992. Recipient J.E. Purkyne medal Czech Med. Soc. Mem. European Sleep Rsch. Soc., Internat. Soc. Study Behavioral Devel., various Czech orgns. Unitarian. Avocation: literature. Home: Pod namestim 8, 182 00 Prague 8, Czech Republic Office: Inst Care of Mother & Child, Podolske nabrezi, 147 10 Prague 4, Czech Republic

DIUGUID, LEWIS WALTER, editor, columnist; b. St. Louis, July 17, 1955; s. Lincoln Isaiah and Nancy Ruth (Greenlee) D.; m. Valerie Gale Words, Oct. 25, 1977; children: Adrianne, Leslie Ellen. BJ, U. Mo., 1977. Reporter, photographer, copy and automotive editor Kansas City Times, Mo., 1977-85; asst. minority recruiting coord. Kansas City Times and Star, 1985—; asst. bur. chief Johnson County office The Kansas City Star, 1985-87, bur. chief Southland bur., 1987-92, columnist, 1987—, asst. city editor Southland bur., 1992-94, diversity trainer, 1993—, assoc. editor, met. columnist, 1994-99; v.p. cmty. resources, editl. bd. mem., columnist, diversity co-chair The Star Co., 1995—. Recipient Media award Ark of Friends of Greater Kansas City, 1990, 91, 92, 93, 94, 95, Black Achievers award, 1997, Mental Health award, 1991, Rsch. Mental Health Media award, 1992, Difference Maker award Urban League Greater Kansas City, 1992, Mo. C.C. Assn. Media award, 1993, Mental Health Awareness award Mental Health Kansas City, 1993, Pub. Affairs/Social Issues Unity award, 1993, 1st Place Kansas City Press Club award, 1993, Comprehensive Mental Media award State Mo., 1995, Project HEART award Swinney and Red Bridge Schs., 1995, Evelyn Wasserstrom award So. Christian Leadership Conf., 1996, Black Achievers award, 1997, James K. Batten Knight Ridder Excellence award for Cmty. Svc., 1998, Mo. Honor medal for disting. svc. in journalism U. Mo.-Columbia Sch. Journalism, 2000, Millennium award NAACP Br. 4071, 2000; named one of 100 Most Influential African Ams. in Greater Kansas City, 1992, 93, 94, 95, 96, 97; Inst. for Journalism Edn. fellow U. Ariz., Tucson, 1984. Mem. Nat. Assn. Black Journalists, Kansas City Assn. Black Journalists (pres. 1986, sec. 1987, v.p. 1993, treas. 1994-96). Roman Catholic. Avocations: jogging, weight lifting, bike riding, woodworking. Home: 12825 Oakmont Dr Kansas City MO 64145-1142 Office: Kansas City Times 1729 Grand Ave Kansas City MO 64108-1413

DIVAKAR, SOUNDAR, food scientist, researcher; b. Madras, Tamilnadu, India, Sept. 12, 1953; s. Bokkadurai Soundar and Adilakshmi (Perumal) S.; m. Sasikala Kothandapani, Nov. 9, 1987; 1 child, Vikram. BSc in Chemistry, U. Madras, 1974, MSc in Chemistry, 1976; PhD in Chemistry, Australian Nat. U., Canberra, 1982. R & D chemist M/S Reichhold Chems. Ltd., Madras, 1976-78; rsch. fellow Australian Nat. U., 1978-82; pool officer Coun. Scientific and Indsl. Rsch., Bangalore, India, 1983-87; scientist "c" Ctrl. Food Technol. Rsch. Inst., Mysore, India, 1987-92, scientist "e", 1992—; presenter numerous seminars and symposia in field. Contbr. numerous articles to profl. jours.; inventor and patentee in field. Mem. Nat. Magnetic Resonance Soc. India, Soc. Biol. Chemists, Assn. Microbiologists of India, Soc. Bioorganic Chemists. Avocations: astrology, reading, books, astronomy. Home: 643 M Block II State, Kuvempu Nagar, Mysore 570023, India Office: Ctrl Food Tech Rsch Inst, Dept Fermentation Tech, 570013 Mysore India

DIVAKARLA, SHAILAJA, ecological architect, researcher; b. Tanuku, India, Sept. 26, 1965; arrived in Australia, 1988; d. Moorthy Linga and Shanta (Vedula) Vajjhala; m. Raju Divakarla, Aug. 18, 1988; children: Kamini S., Pavani S. BArch, Jawaharlal Nehru Tech. U., Hyderabad, India, 1988; M Qual, U. Queensland, Brisbane, Australia, 1989; postgrad., U. Melbourne, Australia, 1991—. Architect Misra Tomey Architects, Hyderabad, 1987-88, Prangley Crofts & Ptnrs., Architects, Brisbane, 1988-89, Blythe Yeung & Menzies, Architects, Hobart, Australia, 1989, Johnson & Assocs. Architects, Hobart, 1990—; tutor in architecture U. Melbourne, 1991; cons. Bhadrachalam (India) Paper Ltd., 1988, Australian News Print Mills, Boyer, 1990, Advanced Enviro Safe, Sydney, 1996-98. Prin. works include design and constrn. of temple, 1987; contbr. articles to profl. jours.; musical performer TV, radio, 1984-89. Vol. Neighborhood Watch Scheme, Sydney, 1998, Sydney Sai Sansthan, 1998. Recipient Australian Postgrad. Rsch. award Commonwealth Govt. of Australia, 1991. Mem. Royal Australian Inst. Architects, Ecol. Architects Assn., Constructive Women Inc. Hindu. Avocations: painting, sketching, music, gardening, social work. Office: Advanced EnviroSafe, 7A Day Rd, Cheltenham Sydney NSW 2119, Australia

DIVALL, PAUL WILLIAM, psychiatrist, consultant; b. London, May 15, 1952; s. David William and Ida Christine (Chapman) D.; former wife Sally Cooper, Jan. 1, 1977; children: Rachel, Gracie. BA, U. Cambridge, Eng., 1974, MB, 1977, B Chir, 1977, MA, 1978. Sno/registrar Fulbourn Hosp., Cambridge, Eng., 1978-82; rsch. fellow Marriage Rsch. Ctr., London, 1982-84; sr. registrar in psychiatry Hosp., Bristol, Eng., 1984-87; cons. in old age psychiatry Bath (Eng.) Mental Care Trust, 1987—; psychiatric advisor Ctr. for Mental Health Svcs. Devel., Kings Coll. U. London, Eng., 1977—; hon. cons. psychiatrist St. Luke's Hosp. for Clergy, LOndon, 1993—. Editor and Contributor (book) Mental Health, Illness a Handicap in Marriage, 1986. Psychiatric advisor Samaritans, Bath, 1991—. Avocation: puzzle solving. Office: St Martin's Hosp, Midford Rd, Bath BA2 5RP, England

DIVAN, GAUTAM RAMANLAL, accountant; b. Mumbai, India, July 22, 1940; s. Ramanlal Chandulal and Babli Ramanlal Divan; m. Bapsy Gautam Bilimoria; children: Rahul G., Sharon G. B of Commerce, U. Bombay, Mumbai, 1959. Ptnr. Chandabhoy & Jassoobhoy, Mumbai, 1964—; bd. dirs. Bell Ceramics Ltd., India, Pesticides Industry Ltd., Baltic Consultancy and Svcs. Pvt. Ltd., Serendib Investments Pvt. Ltd. Author: Doing Business in India, 1984, rev. edit., 1999, Business Operations in India, 1989, rev. edit., 1998, Trusts and Trustees Rev. of India, Indian sect. Tolley's International Tax Planning, 3rd edit. Former chmn. Midsnell Internat., Indo-South African Bus. Com., Indo-Swiss Bus. Com.; rep. Swaythling Club Internat., Royal Overseas League; trusee Madgavkar Trust Vile Parle Kelavani Mandal. Recipient Arjuna award Maharashtra Gaurav Puraskar, 1964. Fellow Inst. Chartered Accts. of India (chartered acct.); mem. Internat. Fiscal Assn., Internat. Tax Payers Assn., All India Mgmt. Assn., Malaysian Inst. Charterd Accts., Royal Bombay Yacht Club, Bombay Gymkhana, Oriental Club, Oxford U. Yacht Club (hon.), Royal Overseas League (London)(hon.), Grand lodge India (master). Avocations: reading, music, traveling, food, computer. Office: Chandabhoy & Jassoobhoy, 134 Mittal Tower C Wing, 400 021 Mumbai India

DIVATIA, PARIKSHIT JAYENDRABHAI, consultant; b. Ahmedabad, India, Jan. 20, 1930; s. Jayendrabhai Vajubhai and Chandramati (Jayendrabhai) D.; m. Nandini Mahendra Desai, Feb. 9, 1957. BSc, Bombay U., 1951; MA, U. Columbia, 1953. Deputy dir bur. econ. & stat. Govt. of Bombay, 1955-62; chief market rsch. bur. ICICI Ltd., India, 1962-72; mng. dir. Pranava Indsl. Svcs., Ltd., India, 1972—; hon. chmn. Rural Devel. & Mgmt. Inst., India, 1996—; mem. Covering Coun., C.D.C., 1997—. Editor of numerous books. Pres. S.V.R.R., India; life mem. Bhartiya Vidhya Bhavan, India, 1970—. Fellow Econ. Devel. Inst., World Bank, 1967. Mem. Soc. Vocat. Rehab. of Retarded (pres.). Avocations: farming, social activities. Home and Office: 18 Sagar Tarang, Bhulabhai Desai Rd, Mumbai 400 036, India

DIVERRÈS, CATHERINE, choreographer; b. Bordeaux, France, Oct. 15, 1959. Dir. Ctr. Choregraphique de Rennes et de Bretagne, 1994—. Choreographer: Tauride, 1992, Ces Poussieres, 1993, Sky's Shadow, 1995, Fruits, 1996, Stances, 1997, Corpus, 1999, Le Double de la Bataille, 1999, (little song) 4 1, 2000. Fax: 02 99 36 48 59. Office: Ctr Choreography Nat Rennes, 38 r Saint-Melaine BP 6023, 35 060 Rennes Cedex 3, France

DIVIN, YURI Y., physicist; b. Chernyachovsk, USSR, Aug. 12, 1948; s. Yacob N. Divin and Ekaterina A. Evsev'eva; m. Galina V. Zholdak, Apr. 27, 1974; children: Margarita, Nicolai. Diploma in physics, Moscow Phys. Tech. Inst., 1972; PhD in Electronics, Acad. Scis., Moscow, 1979. Engr. Inst. Radio Engring., Moscow, 1972-76, rschr., 1976-86, sr. rschr., 1986—; vis. prof. Tech. U., Denmark, 1983, 84, 91, 92; vis. rschr. Rsch. Ctr. Juelich (Germany), 1994—. Patentee in field; contbr. numerous articles to profl. jours. German Acad. Exchange Svc. grantee, 1992; recipient Internat. Sci. Found. award, 1993. Mem. IEEE. Avocations: downhill skiing, water skiing. Office: IFF-IMF Rsch Ctr Jüelich, D-52425 Jüelich Germany

DIVINSKY, MICHAEL L., statistician; b. Romny, Ukraine, Jan. 26, 1947; arrived in Israel, 1991; s. Leonid M. and Liza I. D.; m. Dinah A. Iosevitch, Feb. 6, 1950; 1 child, Elizabeth. MSc, State U., Kiev, Ukraine, 1972; PhD, Rsch. Inst. Eng. Survey, Moscow, 1981. Sr. engr. Ukrgiintiz, Kiev, 1972-76; group leader, chief specialist Project Rsch. inst., Moscow, 1980-90; rsch. scientist Inst. Tech., Haifa, Israel, 1992-93; chief expert in stat. applications Pub. Works Dept., Tel Aviv, 1993—. Contbr. articles to profl. jours. Mem. Profl. Engrs. State Israel, Design and Rsch. Ctr. Avocations: astronomy, astrophysics. Office: Pub Works Dept Matls & Rsch, 55 Ben Zvi Rd, 61940 Tel Aviv Israel

DI VIRGILIO, NICHOLAS, voice music educator; b. North Tonawanda, N.Y.. BM, Eastman Sch. Music, 1958. Prof. voice, opera U. Ill. Sch. Music, Urbana, 1975—; leading tenor, Met. Opera, N.Y.C., 1970-73, N.Y.C Opera, 1966-74. With U.S. Army, 1952-54. Home: 2906 Sierra Dr Champaign IL 61822-5736 Office: U Ill Sch Music 1114 W Nevada St Urbana IL 61801-3859

DI VITA, ANTONINO, archaeology educator; b. Chiaramonte Gulfi, Ragusa, Italy, Oct. 19, 1926; s. Benedetto and Maria (Gafà) Di V.; m. Ginette Evrard, Aug. 11, 1962 (div.); children: Gianmarco, Sergio. Degree in Classical Studies, U Catania, Italy, 1947; postgrad. in Classical Archeology, Athens, 1950, Nat. Sch. Archeology, Rome, 1948-51. Asst. U. Palermo, Italy, 1951-55; curator Superintendence Antiquities, Siracusa, Italy, 1955; dir. Superinendence Antiquities Villa Giulia, Rome, 1959-62; adv. antiquities Tripolitania Lybian Govt., 1962-64; dir. Superintendence Antiquities, Firenze, Italy, 1965; prof. U. Perugia, Italy, 1959-68; prof. archaeology U. Macerata, Italy, 1968—, dean faculty classical studies and philosophy, 1969-74, rector, 1974-77; dir. Italian Sch. Archaeology, Athens, Greece, 1977—; cons. in field. Contbr. 300 articles to profl. jours. Recipient Medaglia Oro Ben. Cult., Italy, 1987; decorated Knight Great Cross Italian Republic, Archaiologiki Etaireia, Athina, 1987, Accademia dei Lincei, Rome, 1992. Roman Catholic. Avocation: research. Home: Via Guerrazzi 19, 00152 Rome Italy Office: Italian Sch Archaeology, Via Di S Michele 22, 00153 Rome Italy also: Hodós Parthenonos 14-16, 11742 Athens Greece

DIVJAK, TATJANA TANJA, marketing executive; b. Zagreb, Croatia, Apr. 30, 1963; d. Dusko and Zora (Sintic) Rascanin; m. Tihomir Divjak, Mar. 26, 1983 (div. 1991); 1 child, Loredana. BSc, U. Zagreb, 1986. Import mgr. INA, Zagreb, Croatia, 1985-92; dept. mgr. Kemikalija, Zagreb, 1993-94; dir. CTC, Zagreb, 1994-95; mktg. dir. Magma, Zagreb, 1995; dir. Total Mktg., Zagreb, 1995-98; mng. dir. Ogilvy & Mather, Zagreb, 1998—; cons. Integra, Brussels, 1992. Roman Catholic. Avocations: cycling, music. Home: Predovecka 17, 10000 Zagreb Croatia Office: Ogilvy & Mather, Kneza Mislava 14, 10000 Zagreb Croatia

DIWAKAR, DEEPTI, architect, dancer; b. Bangalore, Karnataka, India, Oct. 31, 1958; came to the U.S., 1995; d. Anant Ranganath and Shanta (Acharya) D. BArch, U. Coll. Engring., Bangalore, 1984; MA in Broadcast and Electronic Comm., San Francisco State U., 2000. Pvt. practice performer, tchr., choreographer various locations, 1991-96; TV and radio announcer All India Radio and All India TV, Bangalore, 1986-91; prin. arch. Adithya Archs., Bangalore, 1990-91. Author: The Tree of Verse, 2000; author of science fiction stories and poems. Jt. sec. exec. com. Soc. for Prevention of Cruelty to Animals, Bangalore, 1983-86; exec. com. mem. World Conf. on Religions for Peace, New Delhi, 1984-87; active Gandhi Peace Found., Bangalore, 1995—. Recipient The Great Diamond of Indian Classical Dance, World Devel. Parliament, West Bengal, India, 1989, Pres.' award for Literary Excellence, Iliad Press, Mich., 1995, 97; named Miss India for Miss World, Femina Mag., Bombay, 1981. Hindu. Avocations: painting, traveling, social work, reading, yoga. Home: 143 Lake St San Francisco CA 94118-1424 also: 233/1 Palace Upper Orchards, 560080 Bangalore India

DIX, GARY ERROL, engineering executive; b. Bieber, Calif., Jan. 10, 1942; s. Errol Alvin and Evelyn Nadine (Miller) D.; m. Lanaya Diane Easley, Jan. 4, 1964. BS in Mech. Engring., U. Calif., Berkeley, 1963, MS in Mech. Engring., 1965, PhD in Mech. Engring., 1971. Engr. Gen. Electric Nuclear, San Jose, Calif., 1965-71; mgr. thermal devel. Gen. Electric Nuclear, San Jose, 1971-75, mgr. safety and hydraulics, 1975-82, mgr. core methods, 1982-85, mgr. automation sys., 1985-89, mgr. quality assurance and automation, 1989-94, mgr. devel. programs, 1994-97; code rev. group cons. Nuclear Regulatory Commn., Washington, 1976-85; cons. in field, 1997—. Contbr. articles to profl. jours.; patentee in field. Fellow Am. Nuclear Soc. (exec. com. Thermal Hydraulics divsn. 1981-91, chmn. 1986-87); mem. ASME. Avocations: computers, wine, motorcycles, basketball, movies. Office: PO Box 2394 Saratoga CA 95070-0394

DIX, SAMUEL MORMAN, industrial engineer, physical economist, appraiser; b. Grand Rapids, Mich., Nov. 20, 1916; s. Horace Philip and Helen (Morman) D., m. Dorothy Swanson, Jan. 1951 (dec. 1981); children: Stephen, Peter, Pamela. BA, Dartmouth, 1939, MCS, 1940; postgrad., Univ. Calif., 1941-42. Plant industrial engr. Am. Box Board Co., Buffalo, N.Y., 1940-41; staff engr. Albert Ramond & Assocs., 1946-48; asst. to chief industrial engr. Gen. Foods Corp., N.Y., Can., 1948-52; ceo S.M. Dix & Assocs., Grand Rapids, 1952-86; farmer, mfg. and mktg. cons., Belmont, Mich., 1988—. Author: Energy: A Critical Decision for the United State Economy, 1977, The Cost of Future Freedom, 1982. Energy adv. to Pres. Ford, 1974-76, Congress Subcom. Energy and Power, 1976-78. With USNR, 1941-46. Mem. N.Y. Acad. Scis., Nat. Assn. Accts. (officer 1954-56), Am. Mktg. Assn., Am. Soc. Appraisers, Indsl. Mgmt. Soc. (founder West Mich. chpt.), World Future Soc. (contbr.). Avocations: tennis, golf, camping, music, farming.

DIXIT, PRAKASH MAHADEO, mechanical engineering educator; b. Kaledhon, India, May 28, 1951; s. Mahadeo Vishnupant and Parvati Mahadeo (Potdar) D.; m. Rekha Baraskar, May 8, 1980; 1 child, Rashmi. B in Tech. in Aero. Engring., Indian Inst. Tech., Kharagpur, 1974; PhD in Mechanics, U. Minn., 1979. Lectr. aero. engring. Indian Inst. Tech., Kharagpur, 1980-84; asst. prof. mech. engring. Indian Inst. Tech., Kanpur, 1984-91, assoc. prof., 1991-95, prof., 1995—; rschr., cons. orgns. including Aero. Devel. Agy., Bangalore, India, Hindustan Aeronautics Ltd., Lucknow, India, Naval Sci. and Tech. Lab., Visakhapatanam, India, Dept. Sci. and Tech., Govt. of India, Ministry of Non-Conventional Energy Sources, Govt. of India, Tata Iron and Steel Co., Jamshedpur, India. Contbr. articles to sci. jours. Avocations: reading philosophy, listening to classical music, badminton, chess. Office: Indian Inst Tech, Dept Mech Engring, Uttar Pr Kanpur 208016, India

DIXIT, UDAYAN MADHUKAR, ophthalmic surgeon; b. Pune, India, July 22, 1958; s. Madhukar Shrikrishna and Mohini Madhukar (Gokhale) D.; m. Naina Udayan Gore, Oct. 24, 1983. MB, BChir, B.J. Med. Coll., India, 1980, MS, 1985. Diplomate Nat. Bd. Examiners. Resident in ophthalmology Sassoon Hosp., India, 1982-83; sr. house officer ophthalmology Bolton Royal Infirmary, Eng., 1984, Hull Royal Infirmary, Eng., 1984; cons. Nayanjyut Eye Clinic, Pune, 1985—. Mem. Am. Acad. Ophthalmology, All India Ophthalmology Soc. (life), Maharashtra Ophthalmology Soc. Avocations: acting, tennis. Home: 12 Pallavi Hsgsoc S B Rd, 411016 Pune India Office: Nayanjyot Eye Clinic, Shreeman Apts Bhandarkar Rd, 411004 Pune India

DIXIT, VIJAY K., plastic surgeon; b. New Delhi, India, July 24, 1949; s. Shiv D. and Shanti D.; m. Deepa. MBBS, Maulana Azad Med., 1970; MD, Wayne State U., 1979. Diplomate Am. Bd. Plastic Surgery. Asst. clin. instr. Wayne State U., Detroit, 1980-86; attending surgeon St. John Macomb Hosp., Warren, Mich., 1980—, St. Joseph Mercy Hosp., Mich., 1980—, Mt. Clemersben (Mich.) Hosp., 1998—; surgical dir. Cosmetics and Plastic Surgery Clinic, Clinton, Mich., 1980—; lectr. in field. Sculptor in wood, glass and copper nuggets. Fellow ACS, Royal Coll. Surgeons; mem. Am. Soc. Plastic Surgeons, Mich. State Med. Soc., Macomb County Med. Soc., Am. Assn. Wood Carvers. Avocations: sculpturing, turning, photography. Office: Cosmetic and Plastic Surgery Clinic 37300 Garfield Rd Clinton Township MI 48036-2051

DIXON, CHARLES HARWOOD, retired secondary education educator, clergyman; b. Crieff, Perthshire, Scotland, Jan. 15, 1926; arrived in South Africa, 1953; s. Frank Metcalfe and Annie Mackie (Anderson) D.; m. Ann Rosemary Murton Chinn, July 8, 1957; children: Mary Louise, Susan Janet Brits, Kathleen Laura Seegers, Isobel Margaret Van Niekerk, Lucy Frances. BSc with honors, U. St. Andrews, Scotland, 1947, BD, 1953; BEd, Rhodes U., South Africa, 1981, MEd, 1990; DipEd, Edinburgh U., 1959; postgrad., U. Stellenbosch, 1998. Ordained to ministry Ch. of Eng., 1949. Chaplain St. Paul's Cathedral, Dundee, Scotland, 1949-53; missionary priest Diocese of St. John's, South Africa, 1953-67; dean St. John's Cathedral, Umtata, South Africa, 1967-72; tchr. Union H.S., Graaff-Reinet, South Africa, 1973-84; headmaster Nqweba H.S., Graaff-Reinet, 1985-88; sr. lectr. Transkei Tchrs. In-Svc. Coll., Umtata, 1989-93; tchr. Butterworth (South Africa) H.S., 1994-97; ret., 1997; rsch. officer Diocese of St. Johns, 1966-67; acting warden St. John's Coll., Umtata, 1954, 56, 59; chief examiner Transkei Edn. Dept., Republic of Transkei, 1980-86, moderator physics, 1990-95; curate-in-charge St. John's Ch., Maclear, 1989-99; vis. curate St.Matthew's Fellowship, East London, 1995-99; min. Graaff-Reinet Ch. England Fellowship. Author series of newspaper articles, series of mag. articles, rsch. reports. Mayor's chaplain Municipality of Graaff-Reinet, 1980. With Royal Observer Corps, Dundee, 1943-53. Recipient Dux medal Morrison's Acad., Crieff, 1942. Mem. South African Tchrs. Assn., South African Inst. Physics, N.Y. Acad. Scis., South African Assn. Tchrs. Phys. Sci. Avocations: music (piano, organ, choral singing), chess, astronomy.

DIXON, DENISE, psychologist; b. Rockville Center, N.Y., Aug. 14, 1964; d. Stephen c. and Aileen B. Dixon. AB, Smith Coll., 1986; MA, Yeshiva U., 1995, PhD, 1997. Rsch. cons. asst. Stanton Peele, PhD, Morristown, N.J., 1990-91; rsch. asst. Albert Einstein Coll. Medicine, Yeshiva U., Bronx, N.Y., 1993; study coord. Albert Einstein Coll. Medicine, Yeshiva U., Bronx, 1993-95, rsch. analyst, 1995-96; psychology intern Jackson Meml. Hosp., U. Miami (Fla.) Sch. Medicine, 1996-97; postdoctoral assoc. U. Miami, 1997-98; sr. rsch. assoc. U. Miami Behavioral Medicine Rsch. Ctr., 1998—; scientist mentor Sci.-By-Mail, Boston, 1999; presenter in field. Recipient Nat. Rsch. Svc. award NIMH, 1997-98; Acad. scholar Smith Coll., Northampton, Mass., 1982-86, Yeshiva U., Bronx, 1992-94, Rukin scholar Yeshiva U., Bronx, 1994-95. Mem. AAAS, APA, Psychoneuroimmunology Rsch. Soc. (Trainee award 1998), Soc. Pediat. Psychology, Soc. Health Psychology, Soc. Internat. Psychology. Avocations: tennis, running, photography, nature sports. E-mail: ddxn@yahoo.com and ddixon@mednet.med.edu.

DIXON, DOUGAL, writer; b. Dumfries, Scotland, Mar. 1, 1947; s. Thomas Bell and Margaret Ann (Hurst) D.; m. Jean Mary Young, Apr. 3, 1971; children: Gavin Thomas, Lindsay Kathleen. BSc with honors, U. St. Andrews, Scotland, 1970, MSc, 1972. Rschr./editor Mitchell-Beazley Ltd., London, 1973-78; editor Blandford Press, Poole, Dorset, 1978-80; touring lectr. Boyds Mills Press, various locations, 1993—; cinema proprietor/ptnr. Rex (Wareham) Ltd. Author: After Man, A Zoology of the Future, 1982, Time Exposure, 1984, Dougal Dixon's Dinosaurs, 1993 (Children's Book Coun. award 1994, Helen Roney Sattler award 1994, Ednl. Press award 1994), also approx. 50 others. Chmn. Sandford Mid. Sch. PTA, Wareham, 1985-87; gov. Sandford First Sch., Wareham, 1985-89; civilian instr. Air Tng. Corps, Wareham, 1981-90. Mem. Bournemouth Sci. Fiction and Fantasy Group (sec. 1979—), Soc. of Authors, Dinosaur Soc. U.K. (trustee 1996—). Avocations: film making, amateur drama, scuba diving. Address: 55 Mill Ln, Wareham Dorset, England BH2O 4QY

DIXON, E. A., JR., lawyer; b. Bryn Mawr, Pa., Dec. 12, 1939; m. Margaret Kennedy Cortright; children: Thomas W.W., Abigail C., Marion W., Meghan. AB, Princeton U., 1962; JD with honors, George Washington U., 1967. Bar: Pa. 1968, U.S. Dist. Ct. (ea. dist.) 1968. Assoc. Montgomery, McCracken, Walker & Rhoads, Phila., 1967-69; assoc. resident counsel Industrial Valley Bank, Phila., 1970-73; ptnr. Hepburn, Ross, Wilcox & Putnam, Phila., 1974-78; owner wholesale nursery business, 1979-85; atty. Monumental Title Corp., Severna Park, Md., 1985-86; mgr. comml. divsn. The Sentinel Title Corp., Balt., 1987-89; regional underwriting counsel Nations Title Ins. (formerly Nat. Attys and TRW Title), Trevose, Pa., 1989-96; sr. title counsel Lawyers Title Ins. Corp., Phila., 1996; N.J. area counsel Lawyers Title Ins. Corp., Iselin, 1997; counsel Stewart Title Guaranty Co., Wayne, Pa., 1998—; seminar spkr. Nat. Bus. Inst., N.J., 1995-96, Title Acad. N.J., 1995—. Contbr. articles to co. publs., 1990—. Mem. Quaker City Farmers. 2d lt. USAF, 1963-64. Mem. Pa. Land Title Assn. (exec. com. 1993-96), Pa. Bar Assn., The Phila. Club, Princeton Club (Phila.), St. Andrew's Soc. (Phila.), Montrose Club. Libertarian. Episcopalian. Avocations: horticulture, sailing, fly fishing, tennis. Office: 900 W Valley Rd Wayne PA 19087-1830

DIXON, GILES CLIFFORD, solicitor; b. Esher, Eng., Oct. 15, 1942; s. George Ian and Betty Llewellin (Notley) D.; m. Angela Hegarty, Dec. 9, 1972; children: Sarah, Andrew. BA in Jurisprudence with honors, Oxford (Eng.) U., 1963, MA, 1972. Solicitor of the Supreme Ct. of Eng. and Wales; accredited Ctr. for Dispute Resolution (CEDR) Mediator. Ptnr. Ellis Peirs & Young Jackson, London, 1970-77; legal advisor D.G. Jones & Ptnrs., Nicosia, Cyprus, 1977-81, ADGAS, Abu Dhabi, 1981-85; mng. ptnr. Fox & Gibbons, Dubai, United Arab Emirates, 1985-89; ptnr. Turner Kenneth Brown, London, 1989-95, Nabarro Nathanson, London, 1995—; Law Soc. and Bar Coun. del. to China, 1994, lecturing on constrn. law in Beijing; mem. legal sect. City-Kuwait Group, London, 1991-92; dir. Brit. Consultants

Bur., 1997—, Ctr. for Dispute Resolution, 1998—. Contbr.: Engineering & Constrn. Contract (NEC), 2d edit., 1995; coord. author: Specialist Engineering and Construction Contract (SEACC), 1992; author: CEDR Adjudication Rules, 1997-98; co-author (CD-ROM) Bliss-Plus, 1995-98; contbr. chpt. to book and articles to profl. jours. Founding mem. steering group to form Ctr. for Dispute Resolution in U.K., 1990-91; founding mem. Brit. Bus. Group in Dubai, 1988-89; dir. Middle East Assn., London, 1991-97, chmn., 1995-96. Mem. Internat. Bar Assn., Law Soc. Eng. Avocations: travel, gardening, cultural pursuits. Home: 65 Kew Green, Richmond TW9 3AH, England Office: Lacon House, The Obalds Rd, London WC1X 8RW, England

DIXON, JOHN SPENCER, international executive; b. London, Apr. 23, 1957; s. Richard Kennedy and Elizabeth Ann (Flaxman) D.; m. Karen Beth Swanson, Aug. 18, 1984; children: Katherine Elizabeth, John Spencer Jr. BA with honors, Oxford U., 1979, MA, 1985; MBA, Harvard U., 1982. Supply exec. Hi-Tec Sports Ltd., Essex, England, 1982-86; pres. Hi-Tec Internat. Ltd., Taichung, Taiwan, 1983-84; founder, ptnr. Transatlantic Mktg. Co., Essex, England, 1985—; exec. v.p. Decipher, Inc., Norfolk, Va., 1988-90; pres. Waller Whittemore & Co., Virginia Beach, Va., 1992—, PH Internat., Virginia Beach, Va., 1997—. Mem. Brit. Toy and Hobby Mfrs. Assn. Presbyterian. Avocations: music, sports. Home: 4829 Berrywood Rd Virginia Beach VA 23464-5874 Office: 1060 Laskin Rd Ste 22B Virginia Beach VA 23451-6381

DIXON, MICHAEL WAYNE, designer, writer, researcher; b. Honolulu, Hawaii, May 3, 1942; s. Gordon Alvin and Terry (Mendes) D.; m. Janis Marie Travis, Jan. 4, 1963 (div. 1977); children: Kimberlee Ann, Gregory Page, Morgan Ashley; m. Harlene Miller, Dec. 15, 1997. Tech. illustrator Rockwell Internat., Anaheim, Calif., 1962-66, Western Gear Corp., Lynwood, Calif., 1966-69; ind. biochem. rschr., 1968—; owner Unisex Clothing Store, Norwalk, Calif., 1969-71; mgr. Am. Health Industries, Downey, Calif., 1971-72; police officer Vernon Police Dept., L.A. Police Dept., 1972-81; designer, pres. Dornaus and Dixon Enterprises, Inc., Huntington Beach, Calif., 1979-88; freelance writer Huntington Beach, 1986—; founder, pres., CEO Maxcelint Labs., Inc., 2000—; founder, CEO Gusty Winds Corp., 1991—, Maxcelint Health Inc., 2000; founder, CEO Maxcelint Labs., Inc., 1999;. Author: pMg and Heart Wellness, 2000; inventor firearm safety devices, 10mm auto cartridge, Just'n Case police holster, MAWB cutter police bullet, BodyHugger holsters and ammunition holders, piper nigrum and acetic acid lachrymator, nutritional supplement formula that prevents atherosclerosis, potentiated magnesium (patentee); author: Bren Ten Owner's Manual, 1982, BodyShaping, 1985, BodyQuest, 1993, BodySense, 1993, BodyLanguage, 1993, Courtroom Rapport, 1993, Naked Truth, 1995, There is a Magic Bullet After All, 1996, Cardiovascular Disease, Potentiated Magnesium and the True Fountain of Youth, 1999, pMg and Heart Wellness, 2000; patent for first double ligand compounded coordination complex. Founder, dir. Street Smart Pepper Spray Hdqs. of Calif., 1994—. With USN, 1959-62. Mem. N.Y. Acad. Scis., Am. Film Inst., Rsch. Coun. Scripps Clinic and Rsch. Found., Smithsonian Instn., L.A. County Mus. Art, Linus Pauling Inst. Sci. and Medicine.

DIXON, PETER BISHOP, economist, educator; b. Melbourne, Australia, July 23, 1946; s. Herbert Bishop and Margaret Vera (Laybourne-Smith) D.; m. Orani Limpaamara, July 20, 1968; children: Janine Margaret, Barbara Bishop. B in Econs., Monash U., Melbourne, 1968; AM, Harvard U., 1970, PhD, 1972. Economist IMF, Washington, 1972-74, Res. Bank Australia, Sydney, 1974-75; sr. lectr. Monash U., 1975-78; assoc. dir. Impact Econ. Research, Melbourne, 1975-78; prof. econs. Latrobe U., Melbourne, 1978-83; vis. prof. Harvard U., Cambridge, Mass., 1983; prof., dir. U. Melbourne Inst. Applied Econs. and Research, 1984-91; prof. Faculty of Bus. and Econ., Monash U., Clayton, 1991—, dir. Ctr. of Policy Studies/IMPACT project, —; chmn. editorial bd. Australian Econ. Rev., Melbourne, 1984-90. Author: ORANI: A Multisectoral Model of the Australian Economy, 1982, others; contbr. over 100 articles to profl. publs. Co-recipient Research medal Royal Soc. Victoria, Melbourne, 1983. Fellow Australian Acad. Soc. Scis.; mem. Econ. Soc. Australia. Avocations: reading, gardening. Office: Monash U, Ctr Policy Studies/IMPACT, Clayton VIC 3800, Australia

DIXON, PHILIP MICHAEL, statistician, educator; b. Liverpool, Cheshire, Eng., Oct. 8, 1957; came to U.S., 1965; s. Peter Stanley and Kathleen Mary D.; m. Janet Alice Bentley, June 23, 1984; children: Peter, Michael. AB, U. Calif., Berkeley, 1978; MS, Cornell U., 1984, PhD, 1986. Biostatistician Savannah River Ecology Lab., Aiken, S.C., 1987-98; assoc. prof. Iowa State U., Ames, 1998—; statis. cons. Philip Dixon and Assocs., Ames. Recipient Disting. Achievement award Am. Statis. Assn., 1996. Office: Iowa State U 125 Snedecor Hl Ames IA 50011-0001

DIXON, PHILLIP GEORGE, electrical engineer, consultant; b. Windsor, Berkshire, Eng., Nov. 9, 1953; s. George Watkin and Dinah Jane (Jackson) D.; m. Yvonne Elizabeth Hartley, Sept. 1, 1973 (div.); children: Craig, James; m. Rosemary Julia Botterill, Nov. 22, 1986; children: Matthew, Simon. BSc in Electronics with honors, Knightsbridge U., Eng., 1992, PhD in Electronics, 1994. Registered engr. Engring. Coun. Free-lance engr. Multisolution Digital Designs, U.K., 1978-83; chief engr. AVS Broadcast, U.K., 1983-92; EMC cons. Maddox Broadcast, U.K., 1994-95, Philips Med. Systems, U.K., 1995-96, Cubic Transp. Sys. Ltd., U.K., 1996-99, Haefely Trench, Letchworth, Eng., 1999-2000, ERA Tech., Leatherhead, Eng., 2000—; cons. Haefely Trench EMC, 1997—, Varian Oncology Systems, 1994—, Inst. Gas Engrs., 1997—; EMC cons. ERA Tech. U.K., 2000—. Contbr. articles to profl. jours. Recipient City & Guilds of London Inst. Silver medal, 1978. Fellow IEEE. Avocation: ballroom dancing. Office: ERA Tech, Cleeve Rd, Leatherhead KT22 7SA, England

DIXON, ROBERT CLYDE, systems engineer, consultant; b. Greensboro, N.C., Jan. 8, 1932; s. Earnest Patrick and Alma Leona (Moore) D.; m. Nancy Tom Zurborg, July 9, 1955; children: David Thomas, Theresa Anne, Robert Weldon. BSEE, Pacific States U., 1961; MS in Sys. Engring., West Coast U., 1968. Registered profl. engr., Calif.; cert. bus. for tech. pers. UCLA, 1971, profl. designation in bus. UCLA, 1972. Sr. engr. Magnavox Rsch. Labs., Torrance, Calif., 1959-68; staff engr. TRW, Redondo Beach, Calif., 1968-71; sr. rsch. engr. Northrop Corp., Palos Verdes, Calif., 1971-74; sr. tech. staff asst. Hughes Aircraft Co., Fullerton, Calif., 1974-75; chief scientist Hughes Aircraft Co., Irvine, Calif., 1982-84; pres. Spectrack Sys. Inc., Cypress, Calif., 1975-82; cons. R.C. Dixon & Assocs., Cypress, 1975-85, Palmer Lake, Colo., 1985—; chief scientist Spread Spectrum Scis., Palmer Lake, 1981-89, Omnipoint Data Co. Inc., 1989-91, Omnipoint Corp., 1991-96; lectr. UCLA, Westwood, 1975-95, George Washington U., 1976—; chmn. bd. Ditrans Corp., 1999—; adv. com. Pinpoint Corp., 1997—; bd. dirs. Sunwest Corp. Author: Spread Spectrum Systems, 1976, 84, 96; editor: Spread Spectrum Techniques, 1976, Spread Spectrum Signals and Systems, 1985, Radio Receiver Design, 1998; contbr. articles to profl. jours. Elder's pres. Ch. of Jesus Christ of Latter Day Saints, Cypress, 1975, mem. High Coun., 1977-83; bd. dirs., trustee Colo. Emergency Med. Svcs. Found, 1997—, Robert and Nancy Dixon scholarship, 1994—. With USN, 1951-55. Fellow IEEE (co-editor spl. issue comms. transactions 1978, mem. procs. editl. bd.). Mormon. Office: RC Dixon & Assoc PO Box 100 Palmer Lake CO 80133-0100

DIXON, ROBERT F., telecommunications executive; b. Newport, R.I., July 5, 1948; s. Robert and Helen (Dowd) D. BFA, R.I. Sch. Design, 1970, BArch, 1971. Intern architect State of Conn., Hartford, 1971-72, engring. asst., 1972-73, mgmt. analyst I, 1973-75, mgmt. analyst II, 1975-78, mgmt. analyst assoc., 1978-80; prin. analyst telecommunications Office of the Comptroller, Hartford, 1980-83, dir. telecommunications div., 1983-89; dir. telecommunications Office of Info. and Tech., Hartford, 1989-96; dir. planning and architecture dept. info. tech. State of Conn., 1997—. Trustee R.I. Sch. Design, Providence, 1989—; pres. Rope Ferry Commons, a part of the Jordan Village Historic Dist., Waterford, 1987—. Mem. R.I. Sch. Design Alumni Assn. (pres. 1989-91), Coun. of State Govts. (strategic planning com. 1991—), Nat. Assn. State Telecommunications Dirs. (pres. 1991-93), Conn. Telecommunications Assn. (pres. 1985-86). Avocation: whitewater paddle-rafting. Office: State of Conn Dept of Info Tech 340 Capitol Ave Rm 405 Hartford CT 06106-1411

DIXON, SHIRLEY LEE, emergency physician; b. N.Y.C., Dec. 10, 1947; d. Henry Ester and Ethel Mae (Samuels) D. BS in Biology, CCNY, 1969; MD, Howard U., 1976; MPH, Columbia U., 1983. Diplomate Am. Bd. Forensic Examiners (mem., fellow), Am. Bd. Disability Analysts (sr. analyst). Intern Harlem Hosp. Ctr., N.Y.C., 1976-77, resident in internal medicine, 1979-81, attending physician dept. ambulatory care, 1981-83; attending physician La Guardia Med. Group PC, 1983-85; emergency rm. attending Interfaith Med. Ctr., 1985-87; med. dir. Triboro Divsn. U.S. Postal Svc., Flushing, N.Y., 1986-93; med. officer U.S. Postal Svc., 1993-96; attending emergency room VA Hosp., Bronx, 1993-96; mem. cmty. adv. bd. Harlem Hosp., 1981-83; attending physician night screening clinic Lincoln Hosp., 1989-91. Active People to People Citizen Amb. Program, Spokane, Wash., 1991. Served with USPHS, 1977-79. Health Professions scholar, USHPS scholar; Nat. Med. fellow. Mem. Am. Profl. Practice Assn. (life), Am. Acad. Experts in Traumatic Stress, N.Y. Acad. Scis., Assn. Clinicians for Underserved (charter). Home: 752 West End Ave New York NY 10025-6230

DIXON-NIELSEN, JUDY E(ARLENE), loan officer; b. Sweetwater, Tex., July 19, 1950; d. Robert E. Stewart and Verna May (Brown) Kirkpatrick; children: Tammy Taylor-Roubik, Tara R. Taylor; m. Kenneth L. Nielsen. Cert., U. Houston, 1986; BA in Mktg. and Mgmt. with honors, Ctr. Degree Study, Pa., 1992. Joined 3d Order Franciscan FODC/ECLISA. Ops. mgr. Retail Investment Group, Odessa, Tex., 1981-82; sales cons. Rupert Advt., Odessa, Tex., 1982-83; dir. training Paisano Girl Scout Coun., Corpus Christi, Tex., 1979; owner Gingerbread Bakery, Odessa, 1981-83; exec. dir. Nat. Multiple Sclerosis Soc., Midland, Tex., 1983-86; mktg. dir. Melvin, Simin & Assocs., Midland, Tex., 1986-87; exec. dir. West Tex. Rural Health Edn. Ctr., Odessa, 1987-91; owner Creative Svcs., Odessa, 1991—; loan officer M.L. Mortgage; cons. small bus. mktg., 1984—; mem. ministry to recovering women alcoholics and their families. Editor, pub. West Tex. Health Prospective mag., 1989-90; contbr. articles to profl. jours. Recipient Writing grant Ector County Ind. Sch. Dist., 1990-91, Nat. Vice Chmn.'s award Nat. Multiple Sclerosis Soc., Cmty. Involvement award N.W. Civic League, 1979, Silver Appreciation award United Way, 1977. Republican. Avocations: writing poetry, photography, charcoal drawing, image. Home and Office: 3827 Zion Ct NE Albuquerque NM 87111-4140

DIXSON, JEAN, social worker; b. Orchard, Nebr., July 23, 1941; d. Melvin Ursuvius and Bertha Violet (Barr) D.; m. Larry M. Pavlik, 1959 (div. 1980); children: Robin, Jacqueline, Richard (dec.), Daniel, Marc. BA in Social Work and English, Briar Cliff Coll., Sioux City, Ia., 1984. Outreach social worker Cmty. Ctr., South Sioux City, Nebr., 1983-84; specialist II Child Protective Svcs., Jacksonville, Tex., 1984-88; family social worker Child Protective Svcs., Louisville, 1989; clinician Child Protective Svcs., Shepherdsville, Ky., 1989; case mgr. Ministries United of South Central Louisville, 1990-97, South Louisville Cmty. Ministries, 1997—. Avocations: camping, collecting antique engines, music. E-mail: employment@cmky.org. Office: S Louisville Cmty Ministrs 204 Seneca Trl Louisville KY 40214-2815

DIYASHEV, RASIM NAGIMOVICH, science administrator, researcher; b. Almetyevsk, Tatarstan, Russia, June 27, 1935; s. Nagimulla Fakhrullovich Khusnullin and Bustan Fattakhovna Tasieva; m. Lilia Abdrakhmanovna Zagidullina, Aug. 1966; children: Ildar, Iskander. Student, Petroleum Inst., Ufa, Russia, 1956-61; D of Tech. Scis., All-Union Petroleum Scientific-Rsch. Inst., Moscow, 1983. Asst. workshop chief JSC Tatneft, Tatarstan, Russia, 1961-66; head of lab. TatNIP Ineft Inst., Bugulma, Russia, 1966-74; chief engr. of contract SONATRACH, Algeria, 1974-77; head of dept. TatNIP Ineft Inst., Bugulma, Russia, 1978-83, dep. dir., 1983—; mem. Tech.-Econ. Coun. JSC Tatneft, Almetyevsk, Russia, 1983—; mem. dissertation coun. Petroleum Tech. U., Ufa, Bashkortostan, 1990—, State Tech. U. Bugulma, Tatarstan, 1999—. Contbr. articles to profl. pubs. Recipient Gupkin award, 1982; named Honored Man of Sci. and Engring. of Tatarstan Republic, 1989, Honored Man of Sci. and Engring. of Russian Fed., 1993. Academician, mem. Russian Acad. Natural Scis., 1994 (Kapitsa medal 1996); mem. SPE, AAPG, EAGE. Home: Gogol St 66-12, 423200 Bugulma Tatarstan, Russia Office: TatNIP Ineft Inst, Jalil St 32, 423200 Bugulma Tatarstan, Russia

DJABIR, AHMED, diplomat. Rep. to UN Govt. of Comoros, 1997—. Office: Permanent Mission Republic Comoros 420 E 50th St New York NY 10022*

DJABOUROV, MADELEINE DARIA, physicist educator; b. Bucarest, Rumania, Jan. 20, 1949; arrived in France, 1963; d. Stefan and Laura (Stambolian) D. BA in Physics, U. Paris VI, 1971, DEA, 1972, D, 1976, D of Physics, 1986. Asst. prof., assoc. prof. Ecole de Physique et Chimie, Paris, 1973-93, prof., 1993—; cons. ELF, France, 1990-91, Kodak Pathé, 1995—. Editl. bd. mem. Polymer Gels and Networks, 1993-98; contbr. articles to profl. jours. Grantee NATO, 1986; recipient Jean Langlois prize, 1987, Chevalier de la Legion d'Honneur, 1999. Mem. Groupe Francais de Rheologie (sec. 1989, internat. del. 1995-98), Brit. Soc. Rheology. Home: 28 Ave Rene Coty, 75014 Paris France Office: Ecole de Physique et Chimie, 10 rue Vauquelin, 75231 Paris France

DJAKOVIC-SEKULIC, TATJANA LJUBOMIR, chemistry educator; b. Vojvodina, Novi Sad, Yugoslavia, July 23, 1965; s. Ljubomir Milan and Eva Franja (Kavečan) D.; m. Zoran Dušan Sekulič, Aug. 5, 1995. Grad. in engring., U. Novi Sad, 1989, MA, 1993, PhD in Sci., 1998. Asst. faculty of sci. U. Novi Sad, 1990-94, asst. prof. chemistry, 1994—. contbr. articles to profl. jours. Mem. N.Y. Acad. Scis., Matica Srpska, Serbian Chem. Soc. Avocations: recreational activities, aerobics. Office: Faculty of Scis, Trg Dositeja Obradovica 3, 21000 Novi Sad Vojvodina Yugoslavia

DJAPARDY, STEFEN SUTEDJO, gynecologist, oncologist; b. Medan, Indonesia, Oct. 25, 1936; s. Abdullah and Caecilia (Lierawati) D.; m. Mary Ratnawati, Jan. 21, 1968; children: Imelda, Rudy Michael, Veronica, Elisabeth. MD, U. North Sumatra, Medan, 1965, degree in ob-gyn., 1969; degree in gynecologic oncology, The Netherlands, 1989. Intern Dr. Pirngadi Hosp. U. North Sumatra Med. Sch., Medan, 1963-65, resident, 1965-69; cons. ob-gyn. onclology Pvt. Hosp., Medan, 1973—; lectr. U. North Sumatra, Medan, 1965-87, U. Meth., Medan, 1984-87; head sub-dept. gyn. oncology U. North Sumatra, 1973-87; prin. investigator trophoblastic diseases Internat. Devel. Rsch. Ctr. (Canada), Medan, 1982-87; vice-dir. Wahidin Gen. Hosp., Medan, 1968-72; physician ANGSA PURA Social Orgn., Medan, 1994—; lectr. in field. Contbr. articles to profl. jours. Recipient Med. Svc. honor Santa Elisabeth Hosp., Medan, 1980. Mem. Internat. Gyn. Cancer Soc., Internat. Cervical Pathology & Colposcopy, Netherlands Soc. Gynecol. Oncology, Netherlands Soc. Ob-Gyn., European Soc. Gynecol. Oncology (internat. adv. com. 1997). Roman Catholic. Avocations: tennis, swimming, singing. Home: Jl Cut Nyak Dien 30/24, 20152 Medan Indonesia Office: Jl Asia 86/132, 20214 Medan Indonesia

DJAVADI-OHANIANCE, LISA, biochemist, researcher; b. Tehran, Iran, Mar. 20, 1936; arrived in France, 1979; d. Hratchik and Hasmough (Khatchikian) Ohaniance; m. Fereydoun Djavadi, July 20, 1967; children: Kamran, Kambiz. Lic. in scis., U. Paris, 1959, D 3d cycle, 1962, D Etat, 1967. Assoc. prof. Tehran U., 1971-76, mem. rsch. coun., 1972-79; co-founder Inst. Biochemistry and Biophysics, 1971-79; head dept. Inst. Biochemistry and Biophysics Tehran U., 1976-79, prof., 1976-79; attaché rschr. Nat. Ctr. Sci. Rsch., Paris, 1962-69, chargée rschr., 1969-71, 82-86, dir. rsch., 1986—; permanent assoc. rschr. Scripps Clinic and Rsch. Found., La Jolla, Calif., 1976—; mem. sci. coun. dept. biochemistry and molecular genetics Inst. Pasteur, Paris, 1993—. Contbg. author: Protein Structure: A Practical Approach, 1989, The Immunochemistry of Solid-phase Immunoassay, 1991, Antibody Engineering: A Practical Approach, 1996, Epitope Mapping Protocols; Methods in Molecular Biology, 1996, Encyclopedia of Immunology, 2d edit., 1998; co-editor: The Structural Basis of Membrane Function, 1976; contbr. articles to sci. jours. Mem. French Soc. Biochemistry and Molecular Biology, N.Y. Acad. Scis., The Protein Soc. Avocations: classical and modern music, New Orleans jazz, painting, reading, decorating. Office: Inst Pasteur Cell Biochem, 28 rue du Dr Roux, 75015 Paris France

DJAWAD, SAID TAYEB See JAWAD, SAID TAYEB

DJAZMATI, SAMEH MOHAMED, engineering educator; b. Aleppo, Syria, Feb. 26, 1934; s. Mohamed Ata and Badia (Daas) D.; m. Rabaa Zarka, July 30, 1971; children: Basel, Nathalie. BSCE, Syrian U., Aleppo, 1956; BSc in Surveying, Ecole Poly. Fed., Lausanne, Switzerland, 1964, PhD, 1966; BSc in Photogrammetry, Internat. Inst. Aerial Survey and Earth Scis., Delft, The Netherlands, 1970. Cert. cons. engr. Resident engr. Segtraco, Aleppo, 1956-60; asst. prof. U. Aleppo, 1967-79, prof., 1979—, chief geodetic and surveying dept., 1986-89, dean faculty civil engring., 1989-95, chief geodetic and surveying dept., 1997—; vis. prof. Ecole Poly. Fed., Lausanne, 1974-76; rsch. fellow Internat. Inst. for Aerial Survey and Earth Scis., Enschede, The Netherlands, 1981-82; cons. Gen. Co. Engring. and Consulting, Aleppo, 1984—; rschr. Supreme Coun. Scis., Damascus, 1993—; chief of syndicate Syrian Syndicate of Engrs. in Aleppo, 1980; mem. Syrian Congress of Engrs.-Syndicate of Engrs., aleppo, 1989-95; mem. Supreme Coun. Scis., Damascus, 1993; Senator Syrian Parliament, 1999. Author 20 books in fields of surveying, math., geodesy, photogrammetry, programming; contbr. rsch. articles to profl. jours. Avocations: music, reading, chess. Home: Cairo St Mouhafaza Hamod Bd, Aleppo Syria Office: U of Aleppo, Faculty Civil Engring, Aleppo Syria

DJEREJIAN, EDWARD PETER, institute administrator, former diplomat; b. N.Y.C., Mar. 6, 1939; s. Peter Minas and Mary (Yazudjian) D.; m. Francoise Andrée Haelters, July 31, 1971; children: Gregory, Francesca. BS in Fgn. Svc., Georgetown U., 1960, hon. doctorate, 1992. Staff asst. to sec. of state U.S. Dept. of State, 1963-64; Political officer Am. Embassy, Beirut, Lebanon, 1965-69; political/labor officer Am. Consulate Gen., Casablanca, Morocco, 1969-72; spl. asst. Under Sec. of State, Washington, 1973-75; prin. officer Am. Consulate Gen., Bordeaux, France, 1975-77; political counselor Am. Embassy, Moscow, USSR, 1979-81; dep. chief of mission Am. Embassy, Amman, Jordan, 1981-84; dep. spokesman & dep. asst. sec. Dept. of State, Washington, 1984-85; spl. asst. to the pres., dep. press sec. The White House, 1985-86; prin. dep. asst. sec. for Near East/South Asia, 1987-88; Am. ambassador Am. Embassy, Damascus, Syria, 1988-91; asst. sec. Near Eastern and South Asian Affairs bur. Dept. State, Washington, 1991-93; amb. to Israel Tel Aviv, 1993-94; dir. James A. Baker III Inst. for Pub. Policy Rice U., Houston, 1994—; bd. dirs. Occidental Petroleum Corp., Global Industries, Ltd., GLG Universal Investments. 1st Lt. U.S. Army, 1961-62 (Korea). Recipient Presdl. award, Presdl. Meritorious Svc. award, 1988, Superior Honor award Dept. State, 1984, Disting. Honor award, 1993, Presdl. Disting. Svc. award, 1994, Ellis Island medal of honor, Moral Statesman award ADL, 1994. Mem. Coun. on Fgn. Rels. Armenian Apostolic. Avocations: writing, skiing. Office: Baker Inst Pub Policy Rice Univ 6100 Main St Houston TX 77005-1827

DJONDJOROV, PETER APOSTOLOV, mathematician; b. Velingrad, Bulgaria, Apr. 10, 1957; s. Apostol Petrov and Nadejda Nikolova (Postalova) D.; m. Ivanka Dimitrova Rakadjieva, Oct. 11, 1980; children: Apostol, Dimitar. M in Mechanics, U. St. Kliment Ohridski, Sofia, Bulgaria, 1982, PhD, 1992. Rsch. fellow Inst. Mechanics, Bulgarian Acad. Scis., Sofia, 1987—. Avocation: fishing. Office: Inst Mechanics, Acad G Bontchev Str Block 4, 1113 Sofia Bulgaria

DJORDJEVICH, MIROSLAV-MICHAEL, bank executive; b. Belgrade, Yugoslavia, 1936; came to the U.S., 1956; s. Dragoslav and Ruzica Georgevich; m. Marie Louise Hohman, 1963; children: Marie, Alexander, Michelle. BS, U. Calif., Berkeley, 1960; MBA, San Francisco State U., 1963; cert. advanced fin., U. Stanford. Fin. analyst Fireman's Fund Ins. Co., San Francisco, 1962-68, asst. v.p. investments, 1972-76, v.p. investments, 1976-78, v.p., treas., 1978-84; pres., CEO U.S. Fidelity and Guaranty Fin. Co., San Francisco, 1985-86; chmn., pres., CEO Capital Guaranty Ins. Co., San Francisco, 1986-94; pres., CEO Monad Fin., San Rafael, Calif., 1994-97, Bank S.E. Europe Internat., San Juan, P.R., 1997—. Author: About Happy Living, 1985. State pres. Calif. Young Reps., 1965-66; commr. Statue of Liberty Ellis Island Centennial Commn., 1986; pres. Serbian Unity Congress, 1990-93, Coun. for Dem. Changes, 1998—. Pvt. U.S. Army, 1961-63. Recipient Excellence award Am. Security Coun., 1967, Americanism medal Nat. Soc. DAR, 1969. Mem. First Serbian Benevolent Soc. (treas. 1978-82). Avocations: reading, tennis, politics. Office: Bank SE Europe Internat 1299 4th St Ste 307 San Rafael CA 94901-3029

DJORDJIS, FARID, physician; b. Leningrad, USSR, July 3, 1955; s. Louis and Yadviga (Novitskaia) D.; m. Anne Maurer, Mar. 7, 1993; children: Sophie, Nicolas. MD, U. Marseille, France, 1986, cert. in gastroenterology, 1988. Intern Hosp. St. Joseph, Marseilles, France; gastroenterologist U. Marseilles Hosp., 1986-92; physician Centre Maladits Appareil Digestif, Tarbes, France, 1992-98; gastroenterologist Clinique Pyrenees, Tarbes, France, 1998—. Contbr. articles to profl. jours. Mem. N.Y. Acad. Scis., European Endoscopic Ultrasound Soc., Echoendoscopic Club, Endoscopic and Proctologic French Soc. Avocations: karate, tennis, surfing. Home: Route de Tarbes, 65310 Tarbes France Office: Clinique Pyrenees, 28 Bd Du 8 Mai, 65000 Tarbes France

DJUKAN, PETAR, civil engineer; b. Capljina, Bih, Croatia, Dec. 11, 1940; s. Ivo and Marija Djukan; m. Zlata Bebic', Jan. 24, 1942; children: Ela Dokonal, Saša. BCE, U. Zagreb, Croatia, 1963, MS, 1981, PhD, 1989. Registered profl. engr. Designer P. K. Neretva, Metkovic, Croatia, 1963-70; project mgr. Industrogradna, Zagreb, 1970-74, tech. mgr., 1974-80; project mgr. Industrogradna, Iraq, 1980-82; tech. mgr. Civil Engring. Inst., Zagreb, 1983-90; faculty prof. U. Zagreb, 1985-93; gen. dir. Civil Engring. Inst. Croatia, Zagreb, 1990—. Author: Standardna Kalkulacija, 1988, Strojevi u Gradjevinarstvu, 1989; contbr. articles to profl. jours. Senate mem. Sabor R.H., Zagreb, 1992-98. Mem. Croatian Fidic Assn., Croatian Assn. Civil Engrs. Orgn. (pres.), Croatian Assn. Civil Engrs. (pres.), Croation Tech. Acad. Office: Civil Engring Inst Croatia, Rakusina 1, Zagreb 41000, Croatia

DJURASEK, STJEPAN, oil company executive, consultant; b. Varaždin, Croatia, Aug. 15, 1930; s. Djuro and Marija (Šafarić) D.; m. Jelena Starčević, 1955 (div. 1977); children: Davor, Alan; m. Neda Prpić, June 18, 1977. Grad. surveying engr., U. Zagreb, Croatia, 1955; geophys. expert, GSI, Croydon, Eng., 1968, Geophys. Trust, Krasnodar, Russia, 1972. Surveying engr. State Surveying Authority, Zagreb, 1954-59; chief geophysicist Geofizika, Zagreb, 1959-67, INA, Zagreb, 1967-86; exploration mgr. Nafta Lendava, Slovenia, 1986-91; editor-in-chief Nafta Jour., Zagreb, 1992—; geophys. expert Consulta, Zagreb, 1988-95; oil exploration expert Nafta Lendava, 1991-93. Inventor in field. Recipient Silver Working medal Govt., 1975. Mem. EAPG, Croatian Acad., Soc. Croatian Engrs. Avocations: amateur radio, amateur photography, fishing. Home: Švarcova 7, 10 000 Zagreb Croatia Office: Nafta Jour, Savska Cesta 64/IV, 10 000 Zagreb Croatia

DLAMINI, BARNABAS SIBUSISO, prime minister. Chartered acct., economist. Senator, mem. parliament Govt. Swaziland; prime minister Govt Swaziland, 1996—; exec. dir. IMF, Washington, 1992-96. Office: Office of Prime Minister, PO Box 395, Mbabane Swaziland*

DLAMINI-ZUMA, NKOSAZANA, South African government official; b. Jan. 27, 1949; married; five children. BSc in Zoology and Botany; MB, BChir, U. Bristol, Eng.; diploma tropical child health, U. Liverpool, Eng. Surgeon, pediatrician, rsch. scientist Med. Rsch. Coun., Durban, South Africa, 1991-94; min. of health Pretoria, South Africa, from 1994, now min. fgn. affairs; various ANC regional posts, 1988-94. Mem. African Nat. Congress. Office: Min Fgn Affairs Union Bldgs, E Wing, Govt Ave PB X152, Pretoria 0001, South Africa*

D'LOWER, DEL, manufacturing executive; b. Sept. 21, 1912; s. Max and Estere (Gerlatky) D.; m. Helen Fuchs, June 5, 1937 (dec. Mar. 1980); 1 child, Esther Ann. Student, U. Tulsa, 1942-44, New Sch., N.Y.C., 1960-63. Cosmetologist Seligman & Latz, N.Y.C., 1936-41, Del's, Tulsa, 1941-46; owner Delby beauty salon, N.Y.C., 1946-76; greeting card mfr., 1972; diversified bus. exec., pres., CEO Delby Sys., N.Y.C., 1975—; personal care products mfr., 1976. Author: Ginny the Pretty White Doe, 1973; composer: High Cheek bones, 1960, Only the Ashes Remain, The Wedding Waltz, Good Bye Diane, 1990, m' Dina Dinosaurian Coquette, 1993; patentee in field. Fellow ASCAP, 1992. Jewish. Avocations: creative writing, composing, poems, plays. Office: Delby System 1261 Broadway Ste 818 New York NY 10001-3506

DLUHY, DEBORAH HAIGH, college dean; b. Summit, N.J., Mar. 4, 1940; d. Richard Hartman Haigh and Elin Frederika Anderson Neumann; m. Robert George Dluhy, June 11, 1962; 1 child, Leonore Alexandra. BA, Wheaton Coll., 1962; postgrad., Boston U., 1962-63, U. Heidelberg, Germany, 1963-65; PhD, Harvard U., 1976. Instr. fine arts Wheaton Coll., Norton, Mass., 1975-76, Radcliffe Coll., Cambridge, Mass., 1977, Boston Coll., Newton, Mass., 1976-77, 78; devel. officer Mus. Fine Arts, Boston, 1978-84, asst. dir. devel., 1984-86; assoc. dean adminstrn. Sch. Mus. Fine Arts, Boston, 1986-87, dean acad. programs and adminstrn., 1987-93, dean, 1993—; dep. dir. edn. Mus. Fine Arts, Boston, 1999—. Trustee Wheaton Coll., Norton, Mass., 1988—, pres. Alumni Assn., 1994-2000; trustee Cultural Edn. Collaborative Boston, 1987-90; visitor Walnut Hill Sch., Natick, Mass., 1996—; pres. Pro Arts Consortium, 1999-2000. Woodrow Wilson fellow, 1963. Mem. Nat. Assn. Schs. Art and Design (evaluator 1996—, rsch. com. 1990-96, bd. dirs. 1996—), Copley Soc. Boston (hon. trustee 1997—), Assn. Ind. Coll. Art and Design (bd. dirs., mem. exec. com., chair, program com.). Home: 104 Fletcher Rd Belmont MA 02478-2018 Office: Sch Mus of Fine Arts 230 Fenway Boston MA 02115-5534

DLUZEWSKI, PAWEL, mechanical engineer; b. Warsaw, July 9, 1956; s. Henryk and Helena (Legawiec) D.; m. Elzbieta Teresa Szanek, June 25, 1983; children: Anna, Marta. MSc in Mech. Engring., Warsaw U. Tech., 1981; PhD, Inst. Fundamental Tech. Rsch., Warsaw, 1985, DSc. From asst. to assoc. prof. Inst. Fundamental Technol. Rsch., 1983—. Avocation: aquarium keeping. Home: Ciszewskiego 5m46, 02-777 Warsaw Poland Office: Inst Fundamental Technol Rsch, Inst Fundamental Tech Rsch, Swietokrzyska 21, 00-049 Warsaw Poland

DMITRICH, MIKE, state senator; b. Murray, Utah, Oct. 23, 1936; m. Bo Dmitrich; 3 children. Student, Coll. Eastern Utah, Utah State U. Formerly with Cyprus AMAX Minerals Corp.; mem. Utah Ho. of Reps., 1968-92, asst. minority whip, minority leader; mem. Utah State Senate, 1992—, mem. judiciary com., revenue and taxation com., mem. exec. appropriations com., senate minority whip, 1993-94. Democrat. Home: 566 N Dover Cir Price UT 84501-2206

DMITRIEV, ARTUR, ice skater. Recipient (all with Natalya Mishkutienok) 1st Pl. pairs figure skating World Figure Skating Championships, 1991, 92, Gold medal pairs figure skating Olympic Games, 1992, Silver medal pairs figure skating Olympic Games, 1994;Recipient (all with Oksana Kazakova) Silver medal pairs figure skating Goodwill Games, 1998, Gold at Challenge of Champions, 1998, Gold at the World Professional Championships, 1998, Gold medal pairs figures skating Winter Goodwill Games, 2000, won the Japan Open, 2000. *

DMITRIEV, IGOR SERGEEVICH, science history educator, chemist, researcher; b. Leningrad, Russia, Dec. 18, 1948; s. Sergei Grigorievich Klastornyi and Ludmila Vasilievna Dmitrieva; m. Natalia Yurievna Pavlova, Aug. 19, 1976; 1 child, Anna Igorovna Pavlova. BS, St. Petersburg State U., 1971, CSc, 1976, DSc, 1990. Rsch. scientist Chem. Rsch. Inst. St. Petersburg State U., 1971-84, sr. rsch. scientist, 1984-90, dir. D.I. Mendeleev Mus. Archives, 1990—, head dept. history and methodology of chemistry, 1990—; prof. continuing edn. Acad. Pedagogical Excellence, 1991—; prof., program developer Grants Russian Found. Humanitarian Studies, 1997-99. Author: Unknown Newton, 1999; co-author: Quantum Chemistry: Its Past and Present, 1980, Additional Types of Periodicity, 1988 (award 1989), History of Classic Organic Chemistry, 1992. Recipient Disting. Work award Ministry Higher Edn. Russia, 1999; grantee Russian Found. Humanitarian Studies, 1997, 98, 99. Mem. Russian Chemistry Soc. (head sect. history St. Petersburg chpt. 1990—, presidium mem. 1990—), History Sci. Soc. Avocations: classical music, piano, comedy. Home: Gorokhovaya 4 kv 11, 191186 Saint Petersburg Russia Office: Mendeleev Mus Archives, Mendeleevskaya 2, 199031 Saint Petersburg Russia

DMITRIEV, SERGEY, physicist; b. Novosokolniky, USSR, Mar. 21, 1948; s. Georgiy and Valentina (Lopaeva) D.; m. Ludmila Pechkina, May 29, 1976; children: Sergey, Natalya. M (hons.), Physical Tech. Inst., Moscow, 1972; PhD, Landau Inst. Theoretical Physi, Chernogolovka, USSR, 1975; D physics, math., sci., Inst. Radio Engring & Elec., Moscow, 1989. Jr. researcher Inst. Radio Engring & Elect., Fryazino, USSR, 1975-84, sr. researcher, 1984-91, leading researcher, 1991-93, head of lab., 1993—. Contbr. articles to profl. jours. Recipient grant Min. of Sci., Moscow, 1995, Gov. Stipend award, 1997. Mem. Inst. Radio Engring. & Elec. Avocations: football, fishing, history. E-mail address: kis177@ire216.msk.su. Office: Russian Acad Sci Inst, Vvedensky 1, Fryazino 141120, Russia

DMITRIEVA, NATALIA VLADIMIROVNA, physician, researcher; b. Moscow, Dec. 18, 1954; d. Vladimir Alexeevich and Serafima Vasilievna (Bougokhina) Koulakhova; m. Igor Evgenievich Dmitriev, Feb. 22, 1986 (div. 1995); 1 child, Anna. MD, Med. Acad., Moscow, 1978; PhD, NN Blokhin Cancer Rsch. Ctr. of Russia, Moscow, 1985; MD, NN Blokhin Cancer Rsch. Ctr., Moscow, 1995. Cert. oncology, infectious diseases, clinical microbiology. Intern N.N. Blokhin Cancer Rsch. Ctr. of Russia, Moscow, 1978-80, rschr., 1980-88, sr. rschr., 1988-96, head lab microbiologic diagnosis/treatment infections in oncology, 1996—. Co-author: Antibioprophylaxis in Medical Practice (in Russian) 1999; contbr. articles to profl. publs. Mem. ASM, Scientific Soc. for Clin. Microbiology, Scientific Soc. for Oncology. Orthodox. Avocations: Dachshund's kennel. Home: 3-d Khoroshevsky, Proezd 10-8, 123007 Moscow Russia Office: NN Blokhin Cancer Rsch Ctr, Kashirskoe shosse 24, 115478 Moscow Russia

DMOCHOWSKI, JAN RAFAL, surgeon, researcher; b. Warsaw, Poland, Aug. 27, 1927; came to U.S., 1968; s. Antoni and Teresa (Choloniewska) D.; m. Aleksandra Zylewicz, Dec. 31, 1953; 1 child, Maciej. MD, Med. Acad., Lodz, Poland, 1952, PhD, 1962. Assoc., sr. assoc., adj. prof. Med. Acad., Lodz, Poland, 1950-68, docent, 1967-68; res. fellow in surg. Harvard Med. Sch., Boston, 1963-65, 68-70, instr. surgery, 1970-76; dir. blood transfusion svc. Peter Bent Brigham Hosp., Boston, 1973-77; attending surgeon transplant svc. Peter Bent Brigham Hosp., 1975-76; assoc. surgery Peter Bent Brigham Hosp., Boston, 1975-77, dir. blood transfusion svc., 1973-77; surg. coord. St. Vincent's Hosp., Worcester, Mass., 1977-87, dir. surg. ICU, 1984-87; assoc. prof. surgery U. Mass Med. Sch., Worcester, 1977-81; sr. surgeon Lahey Clin. Med. Ctr., Burlington, Mass., 1987-92, cons. breast svc., 1987-92, ret. Contbr. numerous articles to profl. jours. Capt. M.C., Polish Resistance, Home Army. Fellow ACS. Avocations: photography, sailing, travel.

DMOWSKI, W. PAUL, obstetrician, gynecologist, endocrinologist, researcher; b. Lodz, Poland, May 17, 1937; came to U.S., 1964; naturalized 1988; s. Thaddeus and Mirona (Jakubowska) D.; m. May 20, 1967 (div. 1975); 1 child Andrzej T. MD, The Warsaw (Poland) Med. Acad., 1962; PhD in Endocrinology, Med. Coll. Ga., 1971. Diplomate Am. Bd. Ob. and Gyn., Reproductive Endocrinology/Infertility. Intern Warsaw U. Hosps., 1961-62; resident dept. ob-gyn Ottawa (Can.) Gen. Hosp., 1962-64, Beth Israel Med. Ctr., N.Y.C., 1964-67; Population Coun. rsch. fellow in gynecologic endocrinology Med. Coll. Ga., Augusta, 1967-69; asst. prof. dept. ob-gyn Pritzker Sch. Medicine, U. Chgo., 1971-74, assoc. prof. dept. ob-gyn Pritzker Sch. Medicine, 1974-79; prof. U. Ark. for Med. Scis., Little Rock, 1979-81, Rush Med. Coll., Chgo., 1981—; assoc. attending physician dept. ob-gyn Michael Reese Hosp. and Med. Ctr., Chgo., 1971-76, attending physician, 1976-79; attending physician U. Ark. for Med. Scis., 1979-81; sr. attending physician Rush-Presbyn.-St. Lukes Med. Ctr., Chgo., 1981—; attending physician Grant Hosp., Chgo., 1982—; mem. cons. staff dept. ob-gyn. Christ Hosp., Oak Lawn, Ill., 1982—; mem. courtesy staff MacNeal Hosp., Berwyn, Ill., 1989—; cons. staff dept. ob/gyn Elmhurst (Ill.) Hosp., 1994—; assoc. dept. ob-gyn. Good Samaritan Hosp., Downers Grove, Ill., 1999—; founder, dir. fertility unit Michael Reese Med. Ctr., 1973-79, co-dir. sect. reproductive endocrinology and infertility, 1976-79; dir. div. reproductive endocrinology and infertility U. Ark. for Med. Scis., 1979-81; founder, dir. fellowship tng. program in reproductive endocrinology and infertility Rush Med. Coll., 1982-88, dir. sect. reproductive endocrinology and infertility, 1981-88; founder, dir. in vitro fertilization and embryo transfer program Rush-Presbyn. St. Luke's Med. Ctr., 1983-88; founder, dir. family fertility ctr. Grant Hosp., 1988-95, Inst. for Study and Treatment Endometriosis, 1988—; presenter sci. exhibits in endometriosis and immunology to over 175 profl. meetings. Contbr. over 125 articles to profl. jours., 40 chapts. to books; numerous invited articles, letters to editor in field. Recipient Cert. Appreciation ACS, 1979; grantee, clin. investigator Winthrop Rsch. Inst., 1967—, Ill. Inst. Tech., 1971-72Program Applied Rsch. on Fertility Regulation, 1973-75, Nat. Ist. Child Health and Human Devel., 1973-75, Carnrick Labs., 1975-79, Organon Internat., 1979-82, Abbott Labs., 1984—, Hoechst-Roussel Pharm., 1985-90, ICI Pharm., 1988-92, Syntex Labs., 1992-94, Ostex Internat., 1993-95, Serono Labs., 1998—, Praecis Pharms., 1998—. Fellow Am. Coll. Ob-Gyn. (Prize award 1975, 76, Coll. award 1977); mem. AMA (Cert. Merit 1969, 76, 78), Am. Assn. Gynecologic Laparoscopists, Am. Assn. Tissue Banks, Am. Soc. Reproductive Medicine (Cert. award 1977, Ortho Symposium Award 1980, Poster award 1992), Am. Soc. for Immunology of Reprodn., Ark. Med. Soc., Assn. Profs. Gynecology and Obstetrics, Chgo. Assn. Reproductive Endocrinologists, Chgo. Gynecol. Soc., Chgo. Med. Soc., Endocrine Soc., Ill. State Med. Soc., Little Rock Gynecol. Soc., N.Y. Acad. Scis., Soc. for Advancement Contraception, Soc. for Gynecologic Investigation, Soc. Reproductive Endocrinologists, Soc. Reproductive Surgeons, Soc. for Study Reprodn., Soc. for Assisted Reproductive Tech. Office: 2425 W 22nd St Ste 102 Oak Brook IL 60523-4643

DMYTRYSHYN, BASIL, historian, educator; b. Poland, Jan. 14, 1925; came to U.S., 1947, naturalized, 1951; s. Frank and Euphrosinia (Senchak) Dmytryshyn; m. Virginia Roehl, July 16, 1949; children: Sonia, Tania. BA, U. Ark., 1950; MA, U. Ark, 1951; PhD, U. Calif.-Berkeley, 1955; hon. diploma, U. Kiev-Mohyla Acad., 1993. Asst. prof. history Portland State U., Oreg., 1956-59; assoc. prof. Portland State U., 1959-64, prof., 1964-89, prof. emeritus, 1989—, assoc. dir. Internat. Trade and Commerce Inst., 1984-89; vis. prof. U. Ill., 1964-65, Harvard U., 1971, U. Hawaii, 1976, Hokkaido U., Sapporo, Japan, 1978-79; adviser U. Kiev-Mohyla Acad., 1993. Author books including: Moscow and the Ukraine, 1918-1953, 1956, Medieval Russia, 900-1700, 3d edit., 1990, Imperial Russia, 1700-1917, 3d edit., 1990, Modernization of Russia Under Peter I and Catherine II, 1974, Colonial Russian America 1817-1832, 1976, A History of Russia, 1977, U.S.S.R.: A Concise History, 4th edit., 1984, The End of Russian America, 1979, Civil and Savage Encounters, 1983, Russian Statecraft, 1985, Russian Conquest of Siberia 1558-1700, 1985, Russian Penetration of the North Pacific Archipelago, 1700-1799, 1987, The Soviet Union and the Middle East, 1917-1985, 1987, Russia's Colonies in North America, 1799-1867, 1988, The Soviet Union and the Arab World of the Fertile Crescent, 1918-1985, 1994, Imperial Russia, 1700-1917, 1999, Medieval Russia, 850-1700, 2000; contbr. articles to profl. jours. U.S., Can., Yugoslavia, Italy, South Korea, Fed. Republic Germany, France, Eng., Japan, Russia, Ukraine. State bd. dirs. PTA, Oreg., 1963-64; mem. World Affairs Council, 1965-92. Named Hon. Rsch. Prof. Emeritus, Kyungnam U., 1989—; Fulbright-Hays fellow W. Germany, 1967-68; fellow Kennan Inst. Advanced Russian Studies, Washington, 1978; recipient John Mosser award Oreg. State Bd. Higher Edn., 1966, 67; Branford P. Millar award for faculty excellence Portland State U., 1985, Outstanding Retired Faculty award, 1994; Hillard scholar in the humanities U. Nev., Reno, 1992. Mem. Am. Assn. Advancement Slavic Studies (dir. 1972-75), Am. Hist. Assn., Western Slavic Assn. (pres. 1990-92), Can. Assn. Slavists, Oreg. Hist. Soc., Nat. Geog. Soc., Conf. Slavic and East European History (nat. sec. 1972-75), Am. Assn. for Ukrainian Studies (pres. 1991-93), Ctr. Study of Russian Am. (hon.), Assn. Study Nationalities (bd. mem.-at-large USSR & Ea. Europe 1993—), Czechoslovak Soc. Arts and Scis., Soc. Jewish-Ukraine Contacts, Assn. Home: 2745 S Via Del Bac Green Valley AZ 85614-1071

DNESTROVSKIJ, YURIJ NICOLAEVICH, physicist, scientist, educator; b. Moscow, Jan. 23, 1928; s. m. Tatiana Anatol'evna Germogenova; children: Natalia, Alexej. Scientist in physics, Moscow State U., 1952, PhD, 1955, DSc, 1968. Asst. Moscow State U., 1955-61, lectr., 1961-70, prof., 1970-74, 74—; head of lab. Kurchatov Inst., Moscow, 1974—. Contbr. articles to profl. jours. Mem. scientific coun. Moscow State U. Phys. Faculty, 1974—. Home: Berzarina St 19-1-124, 123585 Moscow Russia

DO, GIU DANG, physicist, researcher; b. Son Tay, North, Vietnam, Jan. 16, 1937; s. Tuan Ke and Thao thi (Nguyen) Do.; m. Hoang Yen Trinh Minh, July 28, 1970; children: Nhu Anh, Dang Son, Dang Liem. BS, U. Toulouse, France, 1958; MS, U. Paris, 1961, DSc, 1965. Asst. rsch. Nat. Ctr. Sci. Rsch., 1960-62, attache rsch., 1962, head rsch., 1964-71, master rsch., 1971-82, dir. rsch., 1982—; rsch. asst. U. Pa., 1962-64, rsch. assoc., 1966-67. Contbr. more than 100 articles to profl. jours. Avocations: humanitarian and social activities, sports, gardening. Office: U Paris Lab de Physique, Bat 211, 91405 Orsay France

DO, KIM-ANH, statistician educator; b. Saigon, Vietnam, Apr. 15, 1960; arrived in Australia, 1978; d. Duom Van and Duong Thi (Bui) D.; m. Bradley McIntosh Broom, July 14, 1990; 1 child, Alexander Do McIntosh. BSc, U. Queensland, 1983; MS, Stanford U., 1985, PhD, 1990. Rsch. statistician Bowman Gray Sch. Medicine, Winston-Salem, N.C., 1988-90; postdoctoral fellow Australian Nat. U., Canberra, 1990-92; sr. lectr. stats. U. Canberra, 1992-94; sr. lectr. Med. Stats. U. Queensland Med. Sch., Brisbane, Australia, 1995-99; assoc. prof. biostats. M.D. Anderson Cancer Ctr., Houston, 1999—; cons. Australian Bur. Agr. and Resource Econs., Canberra, 1990-94. Contbr. articles to profl. jours. Grantee Australian Rsch. Coun., 1990-94, Australian Acad. Sci., 1994, NIH, 2000. Mem. Internat. Biometrics Soc., Am. Statis. Assn., Inst. Math. Stats., Statis. Soc. Australia (coun. Canberra chpt., treas. Queensland chpt. 1994—). Home: 4526 Waynesboro Dr Houston TX 77035-3644 Office: MD Anderson Cancer Ctr Dept Biostats 1515 Holcombe Blvd Houston TX 77030-4009

DO, LUU VAN, mathematician, researcher, educator; b. Hai Hung, Vietnam, Mar. 6, 1944; s. Vang Van and Bay Thi (Tran) D.; m. Nhuan Thi Pham, Oct. 10, 1971; children: Chung Kim, Quang Ngoc. Grad., Hanoi (Vietnam) State U., 1968; PhD, Inst. Math., Hanoi, 1980. Rschr. Inst. Math., Hanoi, 1969-90, dep. dir., sr. rschr., 1990—, head dept. functional analysis, 1991-95, assoc. prof., sr. rschr., 1991—; co-organizer Internat. Conf. Applied Analysis, Hanoi, 1993; chmn. organizing com. Internat. Conf. on Applied Analysis and Optimization, Hanoi, 1997, Intenrat. Conf. on Probability and Stats. and Their Applications, Hanoi, 1999; tchr. math. under students, master and post-grad. students Vietnam and Australia, 1980-96; vis. prof. Inst. Math., Academia Sinica, Taiwan, 2000. Reviewer Jour. Math. Reviews, 1988—; contbr. articles to profl. jours. and books. Recipient fellowship Deutscher Akademischer Austauschdienst, Germany, 1992; vis. rsch. fellow U. Melbourne, Australia, 1993, 96. Mem. Math. Soc. Vietnam, Math. Soc. Hanoi, Am. Math. Soc. Avocations: research and teaching of mathematics, sports, music. Home: A3/5 208D Doi Can St, 10002 Hanoi Vietnam Office: Inst Math, PO Box 631 Bo Ho, 10000 Hanoi Vietnam

DO, THANH XUAN, pharmacist educator; b. Saigon, Vietnam, Jan. 19, 1938; s. Tuong Thanh and Thi Huong (Duong) D.; m. Thi Tuyet Pham, Sept. 29, 1946; children: Bernard, Louis Albert. MBA, Vietnam, 1974; Master's Degree, Paris V U., 1984; PhD, U. Nantes, France, 1988, DSc, 1990. Asst. Faculty of Pharmacy, Vietnam, 1965-66; lt., pharmacist ARVN, Vietnam, 1966-68, capt., pharmacist, 1968-70; asst. prof. Faculty of Pharmacy, Angers, France, 1980-88, assoc. prof., 1989—; cons. MLC/ARVN, Saigon, South Vietnam, 1966-70; bur. directorships MLC/MOH, Saigon, 1971-75. Contbr. articles to profl. jours. Mem. European Soc. Chronobiology, Physiol. Soc., PhDs Assn. Roman Catholic. Avocations: karate-do, judo. Office: Faculty of Pharmacy, Blvd Daviers, F-49100 Angers France

DO AMARAL, DIOGO FREITAS, Portuguese politician, educator; b. Povoa de Varzim, Portugal, July 21, 1941; s. Duarte F.A. and Maria Filomena (Campos) Trocado; m. Maria Jose Salgado Sarmento de Matos, 1965; 4 children. Prof. adminstrv. law Lisbon U., 1968-96, Portuguese Cath. U., 1978-96; mem. Council of State, Portugal, 1974-75, mem. Parliament, 1975, 1976-82, 1992-94, dep. Prime Minister and Minister Fgn. Affairs, 1980-81, dep. Prime Minister and Minister of Def., 1981-83; pres. Centre Democrat Party, 1974-82, 88-91; pres. European Union of Christian Democrats, 1981-82; presidential candidate, 1986; pres. 50th gen. assembly U.N., 1995-96; founder, chmn. Sch. Law U. Nova Lisbon, 1996—. Author: A Utilização do Dominio Publico Pelos Particulares, 1965, A Execuçao das Sentenças dos Tribunais Administrativos, 1967, Conceito e natureza do recurso hierarquico, 1981, Curso de Direito Administrativo, vol. 1, 2nd edit., 1994, O Antigo Regime E A Revolução (memorias politicas), 1995, Historia das Ideias Politicas, vol. I, 1998, D. Aqonso Heurigues, 2000. Home: Quinta da Marinha, Casa 50, 2750 Cascais Portugal Office: Av Fontes P Melo 35 13A, 1050 Lisbon Portugal

DOANE, HAROLD EVERETT, recording executive; b. N.Y.C., Oct. 17, 1904; s. Thomas J. and Mary S. (Blaisdell) D.; m. Mary G. Gardner, Dec. 20, 1936 (div. 1941); m. Faith S. Tracy, Oct. 17, 1943 (div. 1966); children: Priscilla Clare Tello, Richard Henry Tracy; m. Vivian Dillon Dunn, May 3, 1966. Asst. cameraman D.W. Griffith Orienta Point Studios, Mamaroneck, N.Y., 1921-22; radio announcer Sta. WGBU, Fulford, Fla., 1925-26, Sta. WBNY, N.Y.C., 1926-27, Sta. WMCA, N.Y.C., 1927, Sta. WKBQ, N.Y.C., 1927-28; owner Sta. WCOH, Mt. Vernon, N.Y., 1928-29; rsch. engr. N.Y.C., 1929-35; dir. Gramercy Pictures Corp., N.Y.C., 1935-37; prodr. Spotlight Prodns., Inc., 1940-41; tech. ops. dir. war fin. com. N.Y. State divsn. U.S. Treasury Dept., 1941-44; gen. mgr. Art Records, Miami, Fla., 1945-59, pres., 1959—; pres. Artrec Pubs., Miami, Fla., 1950—; mem. nat. adv. bd. Am. Security Coun.; rep. Pres. Task Force. Mem. Nat. Acad. Rec. Arts and Scis., Fla. Motion Picture and TV Assn., N.Y. Advt. Club. Republican. Home and Office: 2210 NE 120th St Miami FL 33181-2946

DOARTERO, CARLOS MARIA, ophthalmologist; b. Laprida, Buenos Aires, Argentina, Oct. 11, 1959; s. Carlos Mario and Elba Norma (De Luca) D. B, Colegio Nacional, Laprida, 1977; MD, Buenos Aires U., Buenos Aires, 1986. Resident Hosp. Pedro Lagleyze, Buenos Aires, 1987-89, chief of residents, 1990-91, staff, 1992—. With Army, 1978-79. Recipient Young Profl. award Rotary Club, 1990, Exchange Student award, 1976-77. Roman Catholic. Avocations: treaking, bicycling, travelling. Home: Misiones 369 6 D, Buenos Aires 1083 Argentina Office: Lagleyze Hosp, Clinica de Ojos, Santamarina 744, Tandil 7000, Argentina

DOBAY, SUSAN VILMA, artist; b. Budapest, Hungary, May 12, 1937; came to U.S., 1957; d. Otto and Lenke Stiasny Heltai; m. Endre Imre Dobay, Oct. 16, 1954; children: Vivian, Andrew. Diploma, Famous Artists Sch., Westport, Conn., 1963. Featured artist in exhbns. at Vasarely Mus., Budapest, 1993, Joslyn Arts Ctr., Torrance, Calif., 1994, Allied Arts Ctr., Richland, Wash., 1995, Deri Mus., Hungary, 1999; exhibited in group shows at Calif. Mus. Sci. and Industry, L.A., 1967, 75, UN Woman Conf., Nairobi, Kenya, 1985, Jillian Coldirow Fine Art, South Pasadena, Calif., 1993—, Hungarian Consulate, N.Y.C., 1996, Kortars Galleria, Budapest, 1996, Mus. Downtown L.A., 1998; illustrator Lloyd's Advt., L.A., 1963-64; fashion illustrator Pasadena Star News, 1965. Mem. World Fedn. Hungarian Artists, N.Y. Artists Equity, L.A. Artists Equity. Avocations: reading, travel, theater, movies, classical music. Home: 125 W Scenic Dr Monrovia CA 91016-1610

DOBBELMANN, REINIER PETRUS HUBERTUS MARIA, windsurf design company executive, naval architect; b. Nijmegen, Gelderland, The Netherlands, Dec. 4, 1948; arrived in France, 1976; s. Reinier Antonius Hubertus Maria and Annetje (Leeuwenberg) D.; m. Danielle Pesquie, Dec. 15, 1979; 1 dau., Laure-Anne. H.B.S.-B., Canisius Coll., 1967; Licentiatus Rerum Politicarum, U. Basel, Switzerland, 1973; Doctor Sciences Economiques, Sorbonne, Paris, 1983. Yacht designer Bur. d'etudes Langevin, Paris, 1975-77; owner Dobbelman, Paris, Vence, Cagnes, France, 1977-86; mng. dir. Dobbelman Ltd., Cagnes, 1986—; gen. mgr. Gaastra Sails France, 1987; mng. dir. ALKOS, 1990—. Patentee in field. Bd. mem. Toulouse Olympique Aerospatiale Club, 1995-98; mem. STADE TOULOUSAIN Natation, 1999—. Named Champion of Switzerland, Swiss Swimming Assn., 1969, 70, 71, Champion of Holland, Dutch Swimming Fedn., 1974; sailboard Dobbelmann DB2 named World Champion, 1983, 84, European Champion, 1983, Sailboard Dobbelmann World Champion, 1985, Master Swim Champion of France, 1995, 96, 97, 98, 99, World Master Swim Champion, Sheffield, Great Britain, 1996. Roman Catholic. Home: 26 Rue St Honest, 31000 Toulouse France

DOBBS, GEORGE ALBERT, funeral director, embalmer; b. Atlanta, Oct. 16, 1943; s. Albert F. and Ruby Lee (Haynes) D. Student Fla. Bapt. Theol. Coll., 1963-67; BA, Cornell U., 1974; AA in Mortuary Sci. and Adminstrn., John A. Gupton Coll., 1990. Cert. funeral svc. practitioner. Retail store mgr. Alterman Foods, Atlanta, 1962-74; ind. mng. agt. George A. Dobbs & Assocs., Decatur, Ga., 1974-78, motivational spkr., Hermitage, Tenn., 1992—; retail mgr. K-Mart Corp., Decatur, 1978-91; funeral dir., embalmer, SCI Nashville Group, , 1991-97; svc. ctr. coord. Nashville Family Funeral Homes, SCI Nashville Group, 1997—. Named Small Bus. Mgr. of Year, Dekalb Businessman's Assn., 1974, 76. Mem. Ga. Lodge of Rsch., Scottish Rite Rsch. Soc., Mo. Lodge of Rsch., Capital City Club, Mason (past master Ga. and Tenn.), Grotto, Knights of Mecca, Shriner (Ky. col. 1996—), Hon. Order of Ky. Cols. Baptist. Republican. Office: Woodlawn Funeral Home 660 Thompson Ln Nashville TN 37204-3608 Address: PO Box 290275 Nashville TN 37229-0275

DOBBS, HERBERT HOTALING, automotive executive, consultant, engineer, scientist, retired army officer; b. Mpls., July 5, 1931; s. Willis Clark and Mary Evalyn (Hotaling) D.; m. Joyce Belle Roberts, Mar. 20, 1954; children: Herbert H., Jr., Douglas Edwin, Graeme Clark. BSME, U. Minn., 1954; MSME, U. Mich., 1961, PhD in Mech. Engring., 1972; grad., U.S. Army Command and Gen., 1972, U.S. Army War Coll., 1977. Registered profl. engr., Mich. Commd. 2d. lt. U.S. Army, 1954, advanced through grades to col., 1977; assigned to Italy, 1955-57, Vietnam, 1966-67, Taiwan, 1975-76; ret., Ala., 1983; tech. dir. U.S. Army Tank-Automotive Command, 1983-85; chmn. Torvec, Inc., Pittsford, N.Y., 1986—; design engr. Aerojet Gen. Corp., Sacramento, 1957; mem indsl. adv. bd. mech. engring. dept. Wayne State U., 1986—, Oakland U.; cons. Dobbs Assocs., Rochester Hills, Minn., 1986—; mem. rsch. adv. com. USN, 1997; mem. or cons. U.S. Army Sci. Bd., 1994—; various govt. adv. bds., 1995-99; presenter in field; mem. adv. bd. Nat. Jr. Sci. and Humanities Symposium, 1995—. Contbr. articles to profl. jours.; patentee for turbulent flow research work and military research and development work. Advisor jr. sci. and humanities seminar U.S. Army, Navy, and Air Force, 1979-99; state chmn. MSPE Mathcounts, 1986—. Mem. AIAA, ASME, AAAS, NSPE, Mich. Soc. Profl. Engrs., Soc. Automotive Engrs., Soc. Mfg. Engrs., Assn. Unmanned Vehicle Systems Internat., Res. Officers Assn., Assn. U.S. Army, Detroit chpt., exec. bd. 1985-99, chmn. sr. sci. and humanities seminar 1988—), Armor Assn., NDIA. Avocations: reading, mathematics, woodworking, opera. E-mail: dobbs@oakland.edu. Home: 448 Maryknoll Rd Rochester Hills MI 48309 Office: Torvec Inc 11 Pondview Dr Pittsford NY 14534-9501

DOBES, RICHARD, consulting company executive; b. Prague, Czech Republic, Dec. 29, 1964; s. Josef and Jarmila (Stratilova) D.; m. Veronika Tvrznikova, Sept. 27, 1991. Engring. degree, Prague Sch. Econs., 1988; grad., Leadership Acad., Kobe, Japan, 1992. Cert. mgmt. cons. Export specialist Strojexport, Prague, 1988-90; sales mgr. Inventa, Prague, 1990-91; mng. ptnr. InterQuality, Prague, 1991-93; mng. dir. Czech Republic and Slovakia, ptnr. DYNARGIE, Prague, 1993—. Author: (handbooks) Quality Management in Automotive Industry, 1993, Total Quality Management, 1993; contbr. articles to profl. jours. V.p. Jr. Chamber Internat., Prague, 1991, country pres., 1992. 2d lt. Czechoslovak Army, 1988-89. Mem. ASTD, Soc. for Strategic Mgmt., Innovation and Entrepreneurship (bd. dirs. 1991-93), Czech Soc. for Human Resources, Am. C. of C. Avocations: squash, cycling, painting, skiing. Office: DYNARGIE Praha sro, Nam Miru 9, 120 53 Prague Czech Republic

DOBES, WILLIAM LAMAR, JR., dermatologist; b. Atlanta, Apr. 16, 1943; s. William Lamar and Sara (Wilson) D.; m. Martha Husmann, June 16, 1966; children: Margaret Alison, William Shane. BA, Emory U., 1965, MD, 1969. Diplomate Am. Bd. Dermatology. Intern Grady Meml. Hosp., Atlanta, 1969-70; fellow in dermatology Mayo Clinic, 1970-71; fellow U. Miami, 1971-73; clin. instr. Emory U. Sch. Medicine, Atlanta, 1973-77, asst. prof. dermatology, 1977-83, assoc. prof., 1983—; dir. immunofluorescense lab., 1978-85; mem. staff Crawford Long, Grady Meml., Piedmont hosps., Atlanta; dir. Skin Cancer Project, Emory U., 1981-89; chmn. profl. edn. unit Atlanta chpt. Am. Cancer Soc., 1980-86, also bd. dirs., pres., 1986-87, chmn. bd. dirs., 1987-88; pres. Carter's Atlanta, project chmn. Physicians Com., 1992-95. Contbr. articles to profl. jours. and texts. Chmn. Ga. med. bd. Lupus Found., 1988, bd. dirs. Whitney Rsch. Lab., 1998—. Dermatology Found. Rsch. award, 1979. Fellow Am. Dermatol. Assn.; mem. AMA, ACP, Soc. Investigative Dermatology, Am. Acad. Dermatology (chmn. com.

quality assurance 1982-84, adv. coun. 1985-95, ad coun. exec. com. 1991-95, com. on stds. of care 1987-91, chmn. CLIA task force 1993-97), So. Med. Assn. (vice chmn. 1983), Pan Am. Med. Assn., Am. Soc. Dermatologic Surgery, Ga. Dermatol. Assn. (pres. 1986-87), Atlanta Dermatol. Assn. (pres. 1979), N.Am. Clin. Dermatologic Soc., Soc. Tropical Dermatology, Med. Assn. Atlanta (bd. dirs. 1985-92, chmn. comm. com. 1985-90, sec. 1988-89, pres.-elect 1989-90, pres. 1990-91), Med. Assn. Ga. (Intersplty. Coun. 1984-97, com. on cancer 1988-93, pub. rels. com. 1988-94, del. to Ga. Med. Assn. 1985—, Outstanding Svc. award 1993), Atlanta Clin. Soc., Atlanta Olympic Med. Com. (chmn. dermatology sect. 1996), Emory U. Med. Alumni Assn. (pres. 1980, 86, exec. com. 1992-97), Phi Delta Theta (past pres.), Phi Chi (past pres.), Cherokee Town & Country Club (Atlanta). Home: 2807 Osbon Dr Atlanta GA 30319 Office: 2045 Peachtree St NE Atlanta GA 30309-1414 also: Emory U Sch Medicine Dept Dermatology Atlanta GA 30308

DOBESCH, GERHARD, ancient history educator; b. Vienna, Austria, Sept. 15, 1939; s. Carl and Gustave D. Dr.Phil, U. Vienna, 1962. Ord. prof. ancient history U. Graz, Austria, 1973-76; ord. prof. Roman history U. Vienna, 1976—. Author: Caesars Apotheose U. Könitgum, 1966; Isocrates, "Philippos", 1968; Kelten in Österreich, 1980, Vom äuBeren Proletariat zum Kulturtrager, 1994, Das europäische "Barbaricum" u.d. Zone d. Mediterrankultur, 1995. Mem. Austrian Acad. Scis. Roman Catholic. Office: Inst f Alte Geschichte, Dr Karl Lueger-Ring 1, A-1010, Vienna,, Austria

DOBIE, JEANNE H., artist; b. Phila., June 1, 1930; d. Aubin Joseph Dobie and Helen F. Kelleher; m. Theodore Andrew Klaus, Dec. 26, 1951; children: Jeanine Marie, Cherie Louise, Michelle Rene, Theodore Andrew, Monique Suzanne. Student, Phila. Mus. Sch. of Art, 1948-51. Faculty Rangemark Masterclass Program, Birch Harbor, Maine, 1973-77, Moore Coll. of Art, Phila., 1979-81; instr. watercolor seminars throughout U.S., Can., Europe; juror of selection Am. Watercolor Soc., N.Y.C., 1986, juror of awards, 1995; juror selection/awards Frye Mus., Seattle, 1990; artist adv. bd. Winsor & Newton Art Materials, Piscataway, N.J., 1973-75; juror for nat., regional and state watercolor socs., 1977—. Author/artist: (book) Making Color Sing, 1986; contbr. articles to profl. jours. Named to Pa. Honor Roll of Women, State of Pa., Capitol, Harrisburg, 1996, Achievement in the Arts award Phila. Water Color Club, 1996. Mem. Am. Watercolor Soc., Nat. Watercolor Soc. (High Winds medal 1980, Mary S. Litt medal 1985, juror of selection, L.A. 1997, Arches award 1981, Daler-Rowney award 1999), Midwest Watercolor Soc. (Am. Acad. of Art award 1985, Dupage Art award 1987, Edgar A. Whitney award 1989, Door County Art award 1992), Phila. Water Color Soc. (pres. Charles Taylor award 1976, Best of Show 1988, Grumbacher Gold medallions 1992, 95), Pa. Watercolor Soc. (Watson-Guptill award). Avocations: travel, designing houses. Home: 160 Hunt Valley Cir Berwyn PA 19312-2302

DOBLER, BRUNO, transportation executive; b. Switzerland, Nov. 18, 1952. MBA, U. St. Gall, Switzerland, 1989. Chmn. Horizon Swiss Flight Acad., Switzerland, 1979—; chief pilot Crossair, Switzerland, 1984-86; mng. dir. Classic Air, Switzerland, 1985—; V.p. Aerosuisse, 1994—. Office: Horizon Swiss Flight Acad Ltd, Ackerstr 4, 8180 Bulach Switzerland

DOBOSI, EMILIA JOSEPHINE, statistician, mathematician, researcher; b. Budapest, Pest, Hungary, Jan. 4, 1944; d. Alec and Emilia Maria (Valicsek) D. Tchr.'s Diploma in Math., Physics, Lorand Eotvos Sci. U., Budapest, Hungary, 1967, PhD, 1978. Theme leader Mathematical Rsch. Inst. Hungarian Scientific Acad., Budapest, 1991-94. Tchr. Antal Szerb H.S., Budapest, Hungary, 1967-71; mathematician Inst. of one of indsl. govt. offices, Budapest, Hungary, 1971-73, Office Machine Technics Enterprise, Budapest, Hungary, 1973-75; sect. head Hungarian Ctrl. Statistical Office, Budapest, Hungary, 1979-88; applied researcher Nat. Scientific Rsch. Found., Budapest, Hungary, 1991—. Contbr. articles to profl. jours. Recipient Diplomas Photo-Club, Budapest, 1979. Mem. Gesellschaft Klassifikation, John Von Neumann Computer Soc. (expert), JÁnos Bolyai Math. Soc. Avocations: photography.

DOBRESCU, MIRCEA VIRGIL, veterinary dentist, scientist, owner, consultant; b. Turnu-Magurele, Romania, Oct. 27, 1952; arrived in Germany, 1983; s. Mircea Florin and Virginia (Praporgescu-Gheorghiu) D. DVM, U. Bucharest, Romania, 1976, PhD in Vet. Medicine, 1993; M in Vet. Dentistry Sci., U. Munich, Germany, 1992. Asst. prof. pathology, diagnostics and clinics State Vet. Inst., Beit-Dagan, Israel, 1978, U. Tel Aviv Weizman Inst., Israel, 1978; specialist in microbiology, virusology, pathology, leukaemia Ctrl. Labs. for Diagnosis, Ministry of Agr., Bucharest, Romania, 1978-82; specialist in vet. dentistry and periodontology pvt. practice, Augsburg, Germany, 1989—; owner, sr. lectr. Sch. Joint Dentistry/Periodontology, 1992—; presenter at numerous animal sci. and vet. confs., seminars and workshops. Author: (book) Even the Horse Would Grin 1996; also 36 articles in profl. jours. and courses in Vet. Dentistry Sci., and Periodontology, 1991—. Mem. AAAS, N.Y. Acad. Scis., Romanian Oncol. Socs., Fedn. European Microbiol Socs., Internat. Union Microbiol. Socs. Home: Kazböckstr 23, 86157 Augsburg Bayern, Germany Office: Vet Dentistry Sci, Stettenstr 28, 86150 Augsburg Bayern, Germany

DOBRIAN, ANCA DANA E., biochemist, researcher; b. Bucharest, Romania, May 26, 1965; d. Eugen-Valeriu I. and Maria M. (Abraham) Jeledintan; m. Florin G. Dobrian, July 18, 1987. Lic. in biochemistry, Poly. Inst., Bucharest, 1988; PhD in Cell and Molecular Biology, Inst. Cell Biology-Pathology, Bucharest, 1997; postgrad, Eastern Va Med. Sch., Norfolk, 1998—. Biochemist Heavy Water Plant, Turnu Severin, Romania, 1988-90; rsch. inst. Inst. Cell Biology and Pathology, 1990-92, rsch. investigator, 1992-97. Contbr. articles to sci. jours., including Atherosclerosis, Recent Progress in Atherosclerosis Rsch., Biochimica Biophysica Acta, Jour. Clin. Investigation, Am. Jour. Physiol. Grantee UNESCO, 1995, grantee for med. scis. Romanian Acad., 1995-97. Mem. Romanian Soc. for Cell Biology (C. Velican award 1995), Romanian Soc. for Biochemistry. Mem. Christian Democrat Party. Orthodox. Avocations: photography, German literature, dogs, travel, Spanish painting. Home: Hristo Botev No 24 Apt 5, Bucharest Romania Office: Inst Cell Biology and Path, 8 BP Hasdeu St, RO-70646 Bucharest Romania also: Eastern Va Med Sch Dept Physiology 700 W Olney Rd Norfolk VA 23507-1607 also: 1005 Buckingham Ave Apt 237 Norfolk VA 23508-1523

DOBRIN, SHELDON L., architect; b. Chgo., June 2, 1945; s. Max and Sophie (Schuman) D.; m. Marlene K. Smith, Jan. 26, 1969; children: Stefanie, Jonathan. BArch, Ill. Inst. Tech., 1969, BS, 1970. Registered architect, Ill., Ind., Mich., Wis., Mo. Architect Form Assocs., Chgo., 1969; tchr. Chgo. Bd. Edn., 1969-72; architect Robert L. Friedman & Assocs., Ltd., Chgo., 1972-78; v.p. Robert L. Friedman, Chgo., 1978-90; prin. Friedman, Dobrin and Assocs., Northbrook, Ill., 1984-90; pres. Dobrin Assocs., Ltd., Lincolnshire, Ill., 1991—. Contbr. articles to profl. jours. Docent Chgo. Archtl. Found., 1971-78; mem. caucus bd. Highland Park Sch. Dist., 1988; mem. Highland Park Historic Preservation Commn., 1988-96; mem. Highland Park Design Rev. Com., 1999—. Recipient Spl. Recognition for Archtl. Design awards, 1985, 88, 89. Mem. AIA (Chgo. chpt. voting del. convs. 1985, 88, 89, com. chair 1993 conv.), Bldg. Ofcls. and Code Adminstrs. Internat., Nat. Coun. Archtl. Registration Bds. (cert.), Art Inst. Chgo., Alpha Epsilon Pi. Avocations: bicycling, travel. Office: Dobrin Assocs Ltd Ste 140 75 Tri-State Internat Lincolnshire IL 60069

DOBRINSKII, NIKOLAY L'VOVICH, ecologist, researcher; b. Salekhard, Tyumen', Russia, Nov. 19, 1958; s. Lev Nikolaevich and Lidiya Alekseevna (Hlebnikova) D.; m. Irene Petrovna Antropova, Mar. 7, 1987; 1 child, Maria. BS in Biology, Ural State U., Russia, 1981. Probationer rschr. Inst. Biol. Problems of the North, Magadan, Russia, 1981-82; post-grad. student Inst. Plant and Animal Ecology, Russian Acad. Sci., Ekaterinburg, Russia, 1983-86; engr. Inst. Plant and Animal Ecology, Russian Acad. Sci., Ekaterinburg, 1986-90; candidate scis., jr. rsch. worker Inst. Plant and Animal Ecology, Russian Acad. Sci., Ekaterinburg, Russia, 1990-93; rsch. worker Inst. Plant and Animal Ecology, Russian Acad. Sci., Ekaterinburg, 1993—. Author: (books) The Nature of Jamal, 1995, The Red Book, Jamalo-Nenetzkogo Okruga, 1997, Monitoring of the Biota of the Jamal Peninsula in Relation to the Development of Facilities for Gas Extraction and Transportation, 1997, Ekaterinburg: The URC AeroCosmoEcology, 1997. Grantee Russian Fedn., 1992-97, Soros, 1993-94. Mem. Russian Theriological Soc. Avocations: hunting, fishing. Home: Amundsena St Hse 61 Flt 477, 620146 Ekaterinburg Russia Office: Inst Plant & Animal Ecology, 8 March St 202, 620219 Ekaterinburg Russia

DOBRINSKY, JOSEPH, humanities educator; b. Vilna, Poland, Oct. 2, 1928; arrived in France, 1932; s. Isaac and Vera (Kremer) D.; m. Huguette Marcelle Moiseau (dec. Dec. 1985). Lic., Sorbonne, 1948, DES, 1949, agregation, 1951, LHD, 1974. French asst. King's Coll., London, 1951-52; schoolmaster Lycee, Chartres, France, 1952-53, St. Cloud, France, 1954-60; asst. agrege U. Tunis, 1960-61, U. Montpellier, France, 1961-65; maitre-asst. U. Montpellier, 1968-69, maitre de conferences, 1969-77, prof., 1977-87, prof. 1st class, 1987-88, prof. emeritus, 1988—; Author: La Jeunesse de Somerset Maugham 1874-1903, 1976, The Artist in Conrad's Fiction, 1989, several translations of English novels, 1981-93. Editor Lord Jim, Figures Mythiques, 1998. Lt. French Air Force, 1953-54. Mem. French Soc. Victorian and Edwardian Studies, Soc. Anglicistes de l'Enseignement Supérieur, Internat. Assn. U. Profs. English, Joseph Conrad Soc. Home: 290 Chemin de la Tramontane, 34980 Montferrier-sur-Lez France

DOBRITSA, SVETLANA VASILYEVNA, microbiologist; b. Altynaisky, Russia, Feb. 24, 1947; d. Vasily and Olga (Pil'nikova) Khor'kova; m. Anatoly Pavlovich Dobritsa, Oct. 28, 1971; 1 child, Anna. MS, Moscow U., 1971, PhD, 1976. Jr. rsch. scientist Inst. Applied Microbiology, Obolensk, Russia, 1976-80; from jr. rsch. scientist to sr. rsch. scientist Inst. Biochem. Physiol. Microorganisms Russian Acad. Scis., Pushchino, 1980-98; vis. scholar Agrl. U., Wageningen, The Netherlands, 1991, PanLabs, Inc., Bothell, Wash., 1993-94, U. Tenn., Knoxville, 1994-98; sr. rsch. scientist dept. environ. horticulture U. Calif., Davis, Calif., 1998-2000; sr. scientist New Chem. Entities, Inc., Bothell, Wash., 2000—. Grantee Interbioazot-2000, 1990, 93, Internat. Sci. Found., 1993, NAS, 1993, 95. Mem. Russian Microbiol. Soc. Home: 10317 NE 189th St Apt 61 Bothell WA 98011-3869 Office: New Chem Entities Inc 18804 N Creek Pkwy Bothell WA 98011-8012

DOBRJAKOVA, OLGA BORISOVNA, plastic surgeon; b. Kuibyshev, Novosibirsk, USSR, Mar. 15, 1964; d. Boris Semenovich and Sofia Sokolowa Dobrjakov; m. Andrey Nicolaevich Grebenkov, Aug. 31, 1982 (div. May 1994); m. Valery Semenovich Gulev, Sept. 20, 1994.; d. Boris Semenovich Dobrjakov and Sofia Sokolowa D.; m. Andrey Nicolaevich Grebenkov, Aug. 31, 1982 (div. May 1994); m. Valery Semenovich Gulev, Sept. 20, 1994. Med. diplomate, Med. Inst., Novosibirsk, USSR, 1987; Candidate of Sci., Omsk, Russia, 1993; MD, Moscow, 1997. Surgeon Railway-Klinic, Novosibirsk, USSR, 1987-89, Hosp. N12, Novosibirsk, 1990-91, Entropy, Novosibirsk, 1992-93, Siberian Inst. of Beauty, Novosibirsk, 1993—; dir. Siberian Inst. Beauty, 1993—. Author: Contour Mammaplastic, 1994; patentee method of preventive and treatment of capsulare contraction. 1st lt. MC, Russian Army Res. Mem. Soc. Plastic, Reconstructive and Aesthetic Surgeons. Office: Siberian Inst Beauty, Omskaya 89 10, 630132 Novosibirsk Russia

DOBROCKY, IVAN, radiologist; b. Safarikovo, Slovakia, June 5, 1961; arrived in Austria, 1996; s. Pavel and Viola (Nyari) D.; m. Marta Laukova, Sept. 29, 1984; children: Tomas, Petra. MD, Komenius U., Martin, Slovakia, 1985; Dr. Med., U. Vienna, Austria, 1998; PhD, Masaryk U., Brno, Czech Republic, 1998. Fellow F.D. Roosevelt Hosp., Banska Bystrica, 1985-96; mem. staff Imaging Ctr. Meidling, Vienna, 1996-98; fellow dept. radiology Privatklinik Döbling, Vienna, 1998—; rep. Jr. Radiologist Forum, Slovakia, 1996. Contbr. articles to profl. jours. Mem. European Congress Radiology, European Soc. Magnetic Resonance in Medicine and Biology. Avocations: amateur radio, digital communication, computers. Home: Hadelskai 94-96/2A/33, 1200 Vienna Austria Office: Privatklinik Dobling, Heilingenstadterstr 57-63, 1190 Vienna Austria

DOBROLYUBOV, ANATOLI IVANOVICH, engineering research facility administrator; b. Minsk, Belarus, June 30, 1930; s. Ivan Ivanovich and Anna Alexandrovna (Rymashevskaya) D.; m. Luisa Vladimirovna Kochanovskaya, Oct. 25, 1953; children: Victor, Tatyana, Ivan. Degree in engring., Poly. Inst., Minsk, 1953; PhD, Machine Sci. Inst., Minsk, 1962; DSc, Blagonravov Inst., Moscow, 1988. Machinery plant engr. Minsk, 1953-58; sci. researcher Machine Sci. Inst., Minsk, 1958-62, Mathem. Inst. Acad. of Sci., Minsk, 1962-65; head of sci. lab. Inst. of Engring., Cybernetics Acad. of Sci., Minsk, 1965—. Author: Travelling Deformatin Waves, 1991, Sliding, Rolling, and Waves, 1991, State Power as a Technical System, 1995, Wave Transfer of Matter, 1996, INSITU English Dictionary, 1998, 99. Grantee Am. Physics Soc., 1993, Soros Internat. Sci. Found., 1994. Avocations: touring, fishing. Home: Skorini Prosp 12 Apt 54, 220050 Minsk Belarus Office: Inst of Engring Cybernetics, Surganov St 6, 220012 Minsk Belarus

DÖBRÖNTE, ZOLTÁN, gastroenterologist; b. Celldömölk, Hungary, July 6, 1944; s. József and Ilona (Varga) D.; m. Katalin Kajdócsy, Jan. 15, 1972; children: Katalin, Zoltán. MD, Szeged (Hungary) U., 1968, PhD, 1985; habilitation, Szent-Györgyi Med. U., Szeged, 1996. Resident 2d dept. medicine Szeged U. Med. Sch., 1968-73, asst. prof. 1st dept. medicine, 1973-80, assoc. prof. 1st dept. medicine, 1980-85; head dept. endoscopy dept. Markusovsky Tchg. Hosp., Szombathely, 1985-88; head dept. 2nd medicine gastroenterology dept. Markusovsky Tchg. Hosp., 1988—; fellow Med. Klinik U. Erlangen (Germany), 1976-77; docent Szent-Györgyi Med. U., Szeged, 1987; cons. State Rlwy. Polyclinic, Szombathely, 1989—; prof. Pécs (Hungary) U. Med. Sch., 1998; councillor Mgmt. Markusovszky Tchg. Hosp., Szombathely, 1998—. Author: Investigation of Human Gastric Blood Flow, 1985; assoc. editor Endoscopia, 1998—; contbr. chpts. to books. Recipient Vas County medallion Cmty. of Vas County, Szombathely, Hungary, 1998; grantee Sci. Coun. Health, Budapest, Hungary, 1994, 97. Mem. Hungarian Soc. Gastroenterology (mem. governing bd. 1986—, pres. endoscopy sect. 1996—), Hungarian Soc. Internal Medicine (mem. governing bd. 1998—), Internat. Duodenum Club, Internat. Gastro-Surg. Club. Avocations: history, tourism. Office: Markusovszky Tchg Hosp, Markusovszky u 3, H-9700 Szombathely Hungary

DOBROTA, VIRGIL MIRCEA, telecommunications educator; b. Cluj-Napoca, Romania, Oct. 16, 1962; s. Toma and Cornelia (Popescu) D. Diploma in engring., Tech. U. Cluj-Napoca, 1987, PhD, 1995. Svc. engr. I.I.R.U.C., Cluj-Napoca, 1987-90; from asst. to assoc. prof. Tech. U. Cluj-Napoca, 1990—, head com. dept., 1997—. Mem. IEEE, Assn. Computing Machinery Special Interest Group Data Comm. Home: Uzinei Electrice 15/26, 3400 Cluj-Napoca Romania

DOBROVOL'SKIJ, DMITRIJ OLEGOVIČ, linguist; b. Moscow, May 10, 1953; s. Oleg Nikolaevič and Natalija Vladimirovna (Petrova) D.; m. Elena Borisovna Lopovok, July 26, 1975; children: Oleg, Boris. PhD, U. Leipzig, 1978; Dr.habil., Linguistic Univ., 1990. Lectr. German linguistics Linguistic U., Moscow, 1978-91; rsch. in field of Russian and gen. linguistics Russian Acad. Scis., Moscow, 1991—; prof. German linguistics Moscow State U., 1996—; ctr. dir. Inst. of European Studies, Chgo., 1994-97. Author: Phraseology and Linguistic Universals, 1988, Cognitive Aspects of Idiom Semantics, 1995, Idioms in the Mental Lexicon, 1997, (with E. Piirainen) Symbols in Language and Culture, 1997. Humboldt fellow AvH-Found., 1992. Mem. Soc. Linguisticae Europaeae. Avocations: sports, classical music, theatre. Home: 1st Baltijskij Per 3/25-32, 125315 Moscow Russia Office: Russian Acad Scis Inst Russian Lang, Volkhonka 18/2, 121019 Moscow Russia

DOBROWOLSKA, EWA, surgeon, pediatrician; b. Kolno, Poland, Jan. 25, 1953; d. Tadeusz and Karolina (Zaprawa) Brzozowski; m. Marek Dobrowolski, Sept. 28, 1974; children: Wojtek, Piotr. MD, Med. Acad. Białystok, Poland, 1977; pediatric surgeon I, Med. Acad. Lodz, Poland, 1981; pediatric surgeon II, Med. Acad. Cracow, 1988; gen. surgery I, Jagiellonian U., Cracow, 1998. Resident Coal Mining Hosp., Joistrsbie, Poland, 1977-78, City Hosp. Zyravdow, Poland, 1979-83; pediatric surgeon Dist. Hosp. Nony, Poland, 1984-94; fellowship Polish-Am. Pediatric Inst., Cracow, 1986-88; pediatric surgeon Hosp. Zliten, Lybya, 1989-90; fellowship U. Hosp., Augusta, Ga., 1986; mgr. pediatric ward, Żyrondoó, 1981-83. Mem. Solidarity movement, 1981—. Fellow Polish Med. Assn., Polish Assn. Pediatric Surgery, Pediatric Trauma Soc. Avocations: music, theatre, skiing, bicycling, reading. Home: Jasminowa 17, 33-300 Nowy-Sacz Poland

DOBRUSIN, MICHAEL, physician; b. Moscow, Sept. 19, 1947; arrived in Israel, 1990; s. Semion and Sofia (goldfeld) D.; m. Ramona Karagoz, Feb. 27, 1977; childrne: Vadim, Jane. MD, Crimean Med. Inst., Ukraine, 1979. Psychiatrist Mental Health Hosp., Simpheropol, Ukraine, 1979-85; med. dir. Mental Health Hosp., Cahchisarai, Ukraine, 1985-90; lectr. Crimean Med. Inst., Simpheropol, 1983-90; resident Hadassa Hosp., Jerusalem, Israel, 1991-92, Tel-Aviv U., Israel, 1993-94; resident Ben Gurion U., Beer Sheba, Israel, 1995, mem. med. faculty, 1996—; head dept. mental health ctr., 1998—. Mem. Israeli Med. Assn., Israeli Soc. Biol. Psychiatry, N.Y. Acad. Scis. Avocations: travel, climbing, diving, skiing. Home: Aushalom St 1, 84511 Beer Shebe Israel Office: Mental Health Ctr, Zadrik M Jerusalem 2, Beer Sheba Israel

DOBRY, ALIKI CALIRROE, artist; b. Alexandria, Egypt, Sept. 11, 1929; came to U.S., 1953; d. Apostolos and Irene (Papassinessiou) Zafiriadis; m. Edward Adams Dobry, July 2, 1954 (dec. July 1985); children: Mary M., Dorothy Ann., Alice Elizabeth. BA in Arts, U. Alexandria, Egypt, 1950; M in Arts, U. Ga., 1953; BA in Fine Arts, St. Mary's Coll., St. Mary's City, Md., 1992. Mgr. mail dept. Ford Motor Co., Alexandria, Egypt, 1952; English tchr. Great Mills H.S., Md., 1954-55; mgr., co-owner St. Mary's Vet. Hosp., Lexington Park, Md., 1955-87. One-woman shows include Gallery N. Psychico, Athens, Greece, 1995, Loffler Ctr., Gt. Mills, Md., 1997; exhibited in group shows at Internat. Bienale, Paris, 1993, Chapelle de la Sorbonne, Paris, 1994, Mattawoman Creek Art Ctr., Md., 1994 (supr. artist award 1994), Paris, 1994 (grand prix de Paris award 1994), Michael Stone Gallery, Washington, 1994, Gallery N. Psychico, 1995, Agora Gallery, N.Y.C., 1996, State of Art Gallery, Ithaca, N.Y., 1996, Nat. Soc. Artists, League City, Tex., 1997, Musée des Beaux Arts D'Unet of France, Mus. D'Art Moderne d'Hokkaido, Sapporo, Japan, 1997, So. Md. Higher Edn. Ctr., California, 1998, Gov.'s Mansion, Annapolis, 1998. Brownie leader Greek Girl Scouts, Alexandria, Egypt, 1949-50, hon. mem., 1990—; vol. March of Dimes, Leukemia Soc., Cancer Soc., Calif., Md., 1993—. Recipient scholarship Rotary Club Knights Templar, 1953; 2d prize Aurora Artists, 1995. Mem. Md. Fedn. Arts, Arts Alliance, Mattawoman Art Creek. Home: 23187 Falling Leaf Ln California MD 20619-6104

DOBRYDNJOV, IGOR LEONTI, anesthesiologist; b. Jelgava, Latvia, May 25, 1963; arrived in Estonia, 1980; arrived in Sweden, 1999; s. Leonti and Galina (Ivanova) D.; m. Jelena Varkki, Sept. 19, 1982; children: Alex, Olga; m. Olga Tsygankova, Jan. 8, 1995. MD, U. Tartu (Estonia), 1986. Nurse Children's Hosp., Tartu, 1983-86; anaesthesiologist Clin. Hosp., Tartu, 1986-87; anesthesiologist Emergency Hosp., Kohtla-Jarve, Estonia, 1987-99; cons. anaesthesiologist Orebro Ctr. Hosp., Sweden, 1999—. Contbr. articles to profl. jours. Mem. Estonian Med. Soc. (rep. 1985—), Estonian Soc. Anaesthesiologists, European Soc. Anaesthesiologists, Estonian Pain Soc., European Soc. Regional Anaesthesia, Internat. Soc. Study of Pain. Avocations: personal computer, travel. E-mail: igordobrydnjov@orebroll.se. Home: Wadkopingsvagen 27, 702 14 Orebro Sweden Office: Emergency Hosp, Dept Anesethesiology ICU, Orebro Ctr Hosp, 701 85 Orebro Sweden

DOBRZAŃSKI, LECH JAN, electronics executive; b. Starachowice, Poland, Mar. 31, 1951; s. Jan and Irena (Wiotr) D.; m. Iwona Gniadek, 1977; children: Grzegorz, Agnieszka. MS, Warsaw U. Tech., Poland, 1974; PhD, Inst. Elec. Materials Tech., Poland, 1994. Staff rsch. & devel. CEMI, Poland, 1977-76, leader rsch. & devel., 1976-88; head dept. rsch. & devel. ITME, Poland, 1988—. Contbr. articles to profl. jours. Mem. IEEE. Office: Inst Elec Materials Tech, Wolczynska 133, 01-919 Warsaw Poland

DOBRZYNSKA, MALGORZATA MARIA, research scientist, radiobiologist; b. Warsaw, Poland, Oct. 8, 1960; d. Władysław Wiktor and Stefania Teresa (Nowak) D. Student in Biology, Warsaw U., Poland, 1979-85; MSc, U. Warsaw, Poland, 1985; PhD, Nat. Inst. Hygiene, Warsaw, Poland, 1992. Rschr. Nat. Inst. Hygiene, Warsaw, Poland, 1986—; vis. scientist Bibra Internat., Carshalton, England, 1995-96, U. Padova, Italy, 1996-97. Royal Soc. fellow London, 1995. Mem. European Environ. Mutagen Soc., Polish Radiation Rsch. Soc. (award 1992). Roman Catholic. Office: Nat Inst Hygiene Dept Radia, 24 Chocimska St, 00-791 Warsaw Poland

DOBRZYNSKI, LEONARD, physics researcher; b. Lodz, Poland, Oct. 12, 1941; s. Leonard Franciszek and Berthe (Kuk) D.; m. Marie-Francoise Brisoux, May 27, 1971; children: Laetitia, Marie-Laure, Francois, Coralie. Diploma d' Etudes Physics, U. Paris, 1966; Diploma Engring., Inst. Superieur d'Electronique, Lille, France, 1968; Doctorate, U. Paris, 1968, U. Paris, 1969. Charge-de recherche Ctr. Nat. Rsch. Sci./U. Calif., Irvine, 1970-72, CNRS, Grenoble and Lille, France, 1972-76; dir. rsch. CNRS, Lille, 1976-85, Madrid, 1985-86; dir. rsch., 2nd class CNRS, Villeneuve d'Ascq, 1986-90, dir. rsch., 1st class, 1991—; maitre de confs. FUPL, Lille, 1969-84; prof. physics Fedn. U. and Polytechnique de Lille, 1984—. Editor: (book series) Handbook of Surfaces and Interfaces, Vol. 1 and 2, 1978, Vol. 3, 1980, (conf. proceedings) Dynamics of Interfaces, 1984; co-editor: Surface Sci. Reports jour., 1981—; author: Surface Phonons and Polaritons, 1980.. Recipient Prix Spl., Soc. des Scis., Lille, 1981. Mem. Soc. Francaise Physique, Soc. Europeenne de Physique, Am. Phys. Soc. Office: CNRS-USTL, UFR de Physique, F-59655 Villeneuve d'Ascq France

DOBRZYŃSKI, LUDWIK ROMAN, physicist; b. Asino, USSR, Jan. 27, 1941; arrived in Poland, 1946; s. Jerzy and Teofila Joanna (Preger) D.; m. Krystyna Woźniak, 1934 (div. 1976); 1 child, Luiza; m. Maria Janina Sołtan, July 4, 1985; 1 child, Dorota. MSc, U. Warsaw, Poland, 1963; PhD, Inst. Nuclear Rsch., Poland, 1968, DSc, 1975. From asst. to asst prof. Inst. Nuclear Rsch., Poland, 1963-82; from assoc. prof. to prof. U. Warsaw, 1983-97; prof. Soltan Inst. for Nuclear Studies, Poland, 1996—, U. Bialystok, Poland, 1997—; dir. lab. II, newsletter organizer, editor Inst. Nuclear Rsch., Poland, 1980-81; dean U. Warsaw, 1990-93, dept. head, 1983—; dept. dir. Soltan Inst. for Nuclear Studies, Poland, 1996; presenter in field. Author: Neutrons and Solid State Physics, 1994. Recipient Min. of Nat. Edn. award, Poland, 1994. Mem. Polish Phys. Soc., Polish Synchrotron Radiation Soc., Polish Neutron Seattering Soc. Avocations: music, dance, theater. Office: U Bialystok Inst Exptl Physics, Lipowa 41, 15-424 Bialystok Poland also: The Soltan Inst for, Nuclear Studies, 05-400 Otwock-Swierk Poland

DOBSON, BRIDGET MCCOLL HURSLEY, television executive and writer; b. Milw., Sept. 1, 1938; d. Franklin McColl and Doris (Berger) Hursley; m. Jerome John Dobson, June 16, 1961; children: Mary McColl, Andrew Carmichael. BA, Stanford U., 1960, MA, 1964; CBA, Harvard U., 1961. Assoc. writer General Hospital ABC-TV, 1965-73, head writer General Hospital, 1973-75; producer Friendly Road Sta. KIXE-TV, Redding, Calif., 1972; head writer Guiding Light CBS-TV, 1975-80, head writer As the World Turns, 1980-83; creator, co-owner Santa Barbara NBC-TV, 1983—, head writer Santa Barbara, 1983-86, 91, exec. producer Santa Barbara, 1986-87, 91, creative prodn. exec. Santa Barbara, 1990-91; pres. Dobson Global Entertainment, L.A., 1994—; bd. dirs. Emory U. Carlos Mus.; bd. advisors Atlanta Internat. Sch., 1997—. Author, co-lyricist: Slings and Eros, 1993; prodr. Confessions of a Nightingale, 1994; exhibited in gallery show acrylic paintings Swan Coach House, Atlanta, 1997, exhibited oil paintings Raymond Lawrence Gallery, Atlanta, 1999, Fay Gold Gallery, Atlanta, 1999. Bd. dirs. Carlos Mus., 1998—. Recipient Emmy award, 1988. Mem. Nat. Acad. TV Arts and Scis. (com. on substance abuse 1986-88), Writers Guild Am. (award for Guiding Light 1977, for Santa Barbara 1991), Am. Film Inst. (mem. TV com. 1986-88). Office: PO Box 52813 Atlanta GA 30355-0813

DOBSON, JOHN FRANCIS, physics educator, researcher; b. Melbourne, Victoria, Australia, June 29, 1946; s. Thomas Pye and Andrée Marie (Bouillon) D.; m. Astrid Baptistina Fernandes, Sept. 20, 1986; children: William, Sarah. BSc, Melbourne U., Australia, 1967, MSc, 1969; PhD, U. Calif., San Diego, 1974. Postdoctoral rsch. assoc. Cornell U., N.Y., 1975-76; lectr. Griffith U., Brisbane, 1977-84, sr. lectr., 1984-94, assoc. prof., 1994—; cons. Bell Telephone Labs., 1973; workshop organizer Griffith U. and Australian Dept. Edn. Employment and Tng., NSF, 1996, Brisbane, 1996. Editor: Density Functional Theory: Recent Process and New Directions, 1998; contbr. articles to profl. jours. Grantee Australian Rsch. Coun., 1996-99, 2000—, NSF, 1996. Fellow Australian Inst. Physics; mem. Am. Phys. Soc. Avocations: playing piano, jazz, pipe organ. Office: Griffith U Sch Sci, Nathan, Brisbane 4111 QLD, Australia

DOBSON, WENDY KATHLEEN, economics educator. BSN, U. B.C., 1963; MPA, Harvard U., 1971, MS, 1972; PhD in Econs., Princeton U., 1979. Pres. C.D. Howe Inst., Toronto, 1981-87; assoc. dep. minister Dept. Fin., Govt. of Can., Ottawa, Ont., 1987-89; prof., dir. Inst. for Internat. Bus. Rotman Sch. Mgmt., U. Toronto, 1999—; dir. Toronto-Dominion Bank, TransCan. Pipelines, MDS, Inc., IBM Can. Inc., DuPont Can. Inc., TD Waterhouse Nat. Bank; steering com. Pacific Trade Devel. Network; adv. com. Inst. Internat. Econs., Washington. Author: Japan in East Asia: Trade and Investment Strategies, 1993, Multinationals and East Asian Integration, 1997 (Ohira prize 1998), Financial Services Liberalization in the WTO, 1998, (chpts.) Bretton Woods: Looking to the Future, 1994, A Part of the Peace, 1994, Trade Technology and Economics: Essays in Honour of Richard G. Lipsey, 1997, Fifty Years After Bretton Woods: The Future of the IMF and the World Bank, 1995, The Growing Importance of the Asia Pacific Region in the World Economy: Implications for Canada, 1997, Trade Technology and Economics, 1997, Whither APEC?, 1997, Fiscal Frameworks in East Asia, 1998, Prisoners of the Past: Canada's Policy Framework for the Financial Services Sector, 1999; co-editor: Shaping Comparative Advantage, 1987, East Asian Capitalism: Diversity and Dynamism, 1996, Managing U.S. Japanese Trade Disputes, 1996; contbr. articles to profl. jours. Office: Rotman Sch Mgmt U Toronto, 105 St George St, Toronto, ON Canada

DO CARMO, ISABEL, physician; b. Barreiro, Estremadur, Portugal, Sept. 12, 1940; d. Joao and Felicidade Cortes Carmo; m. Ernesto Sousa (div.); m. Carlos Antunes (div.); m. Orlando Ramos (div.); children: Isabel Ramos, Sergio Antunes. PhD, MD, Lisbon Med. Sch., Portugal, 1965. Medical diplomate. Cons., rschr. eating disorders Lisbon, 1988—; med. tchr. Med. Sch., Lisbon, Portugal, 1970—; specialist in endocrinology Lisbon, 1971—; bd. dirs. Portuguese Soc. for Study of Obesity, Eating Disorders Soc. Author: Puta de Prisao, 1982, Saude em Tempo De Risco, 1993, Vida, Virus e Vicios, 1994, Anorexia Nervosa, 1994, Magros, Gordinhos & Assim-Assim, 1997. Bd. dirs. Brigadas Revoluciona, Portugal, 1970-74, Partido Revolucionario do Proletariad, Portugal, 1970-82, Forum Ecologista and Alternativo, Portugal, 1990—, Orderm dos Medicos, Lisbon, 1966-74. Office: Hosp Santa Maria, Ave Egas Moniz, 1600 Lisboa Portugal

DOCAVO ALBERTI, IGNACIO, zoology educator; b. Madrid, June 19, 1922; s. Ignacio and Maria (Alberti Merello) Docavo Nuñez; m. Amparo Ferran Rosario, May 5, 1952 (div. 1988); children: Amparo, Mercedes, Ignacio; m. Joaquina Vela Nuñez, May 4, 1988. Bachelor, Luis Vives Inst., Valencia, Spain, 1940; BS, U. Complutense, Madrid, 1948, PhD in Biol. Sci., 1956. Adj. prof. U. Valencia, Spain, 1949-59, prof. biology, 1959-78, prof. anthrop. & zoology, 1978-87, prof. emeritus, 1987-98, dean Faculty Biol. Sci., 1975; dir. Botanical Gardens, Valencia, Spain, 1962-87; dir. Inst. Applied Biology Inst. Alfonso Magnánimo Diputación, Valencia, Spain, 1962—; v.p. Inst. Alfonso El Magnánimo, Valencia, 1955-84; patron-sec. Torres Sala Entomology Found., Valencia, 1978-2000; dir. dept. zoology Faculty Biol. Sci., 1978-87. Author: Estudies of the Braconides General of Spain, 1960, A Contribution to Knowledge of Braconides of Spain, 1964, My Entomology Life, 1967, Insect Fauna of the Albufera and Surrounding, 1973, The Albufera of Valencia, it's birds and fish, 1979, Insect Fauna of Portacoeli Mountains, 1987. Pres. Diputación, Valencia, 1971-75, v.p., 1974-79; counsellor I Consell Pais Valenciá, Valencia, 1978-79; pres. Union Iberica de Zoos., 1980-88; Hon. dir. Bot. Gardens, Valencia, 1987. Recipient Premio Leonardo Torres Quevedo award Consejo Superior Investigaciones Científicas, Madrid, 1958, Premio Francisco Cerdá Reig. Inst. Alfonso El Magnánimo, Valencia, 1964, Golden medal Inst. Alfonso El Magnánimo. Mem. Assn. Española de Zoos and Acuarios (coord. Scin.), Real Soc. Española Historia Natural (pres. sect. Valenciana 1959-67). Roman Catholic. Avocations: entomology, swimming, outdoors activities, poetry, writing. Home: Inst Obrero de Valencia 35, 46013 Valencia Spain

DOCEKALOVA, DANIELA, investment company executive; b. Jihlava, Czech Republic, Sept. 11, 1975; d. Vladimir and Alice Docekal. Grad. h.s., Carbondale, Kans. Program and tng. asst. U.S. Peace Corps, Prague, Czech Republic, 1994-96; project mgr. CzechInvest, Prague, 1996-99; dir. German ops. CzechInvest, Dusseldorf, Germany, 1999—. Fax: 49 211 8307 366. E-mail: czechin@t-online.de. Office: CzechInvest, Heinrich Heine Allee 53, 40213 Dusseldorf Germany

DOCHERTY, ANNE, association executive; b. Kirkcaldy, Fife, Scotland, Oct. 5, 1936; d. James and Christina Inglis (Pollock) Auchterlonie; m. David James Guthrie Docherty, May 11, 1975 (div. 1986). MA, U. St. Andrews, Scotland, 1956, diploma in Edn., 1957; diploma in Adult Edn., U. Edinburgh, Scotland, 1969. Tchr. secondary schs. Scotland, 1957-67; adviser studies pvt. coll., Edinburgh, 1967-69; lectr. edn. colls., Scotland, 1969-80; asst. dir. Adult Edn. Inst., Scotland, 1980-87; dir. Soc. Companion Animal Studies, Glasgow, Scotland, 1987—; cons., rschr. Scottish Edn. Dept., 1987, 92. Editor Soc. Companion Animal Studies jour., 1989—, Nat. Assn. Ednl. Guidance for Adults jour. and occasional publs.; editor: (manual) When a Pet Dies, 1996; co-author: (manual) The Adult Guidance Pack, 1989. Hon. Mem. Nat. Assn. Ednl. Guidance for Adults (chair 1986-89, gen. sec. 1990-97), Internat. Assn. Human Animal Interaction Orgns. (v.p. 1995—). Avocations: gardening, walking, animals, literature, current affairs. Home and Office: 10B Leny Rd, Callander FK17 8BA, Scotland

DOCHERTY, ROBERT KELLIEHAN, II, minister; b. Newton, Mass., May 27, 1935; s. Alexander Harper and Mary (Campbell) D; m. Eileen Joyce Rockefeller, June 14, 1958; children: Robert K. III, Scott Rockefeller, Stacy Jean. BA, Sterling Coll., 1961, Moody Bible Inst., 1970; MS, Pittsburg (Kans.) State U., 1972; PhD, Kans. State U., 1981. Ordained to ministry Presbyn. Ch. (U.S.A.), 1977. Min. 1st Bapt. Ch., Frederick, Kans., 1959-63, Russell, Kans., 1964-67; campus min. Pittsburg State U., 1967-72; mem. State Staff Kans. Bapt. Conv., Topeka, 1972-77; min. United Presbyn. Ch., Pittsburg, 1977-85; co-pastor The Presbyn. Ch., Pittsburg, 1985-87; organizing pastor John Knox Presbyn. Ch., Wichita, Kans., 1988, pastor, 1988-95; pastor St. Andrew Presbyn. Ch., Kimberling City, Mo., 1995—; moderator Synod Ministries Divsn., Overland Park, Kans., 1990-96, Church Related Colls. Com., Overland Park; moderator com. on ministry Presbytery of John Calvin, 1996—. Author: Community Education with School Superintendents, 1980. Founder Help NOW Inc., Pittsburg, 1972; bd. dirs. Elm Acres Youth Home, Girard, Kans., 1973-79; chmn. United Way, Pittsburg, 1974, co-chmn., 1983; treas. Mt. Carmel Hosp. Found., Pittsburg, 1984-87; chaplain CAP, Wichita, 1988—; trustee Presbyn. Manors of Mid-Am., Wichita, Kans., Presbyn. Children's Svcs., St. Louis; pres. bd. Christian Assocs. of Tablerock Lake, Inc. Nat. Coun. Chs. Christ fellow, 1976; C.S. Mott Found. fellow Kans. State U., 1978. Mem. Kiwanis (gov. Kans. 1972-73). Office: St Andrew Presbyn Ch 30 James River Rd Kimberling City MO 65686-9702

DOCHERTY, THOMAS, English educator, cultural critic; b. Glasgow, Scotland, July 23, 1955; s. John Joseph Docherty and Agnes Brock (Downie Docherty) Collum; m. Bridie May Sullivan, Apr. 16, 1993; 1 child, Hamish John Sullivan Docherty. MA with honors 1st class, U. Glasgow, 1978; DPhil, U. Oxford, Eng., 1982. Rsch. lectr. Christ Church, Oxford, 1981-85; lectr. Corpus Christi Coll., Oxford, 1985-86, U. Coll. Dublin, Ireland, 1986-91; prof. English Trinity Coll., Dublin, 1991-94, U. Kent, Eng., 1994—. Author: Reading (Absent) Character, 1983, John Donne, Undone, 1986, On Modern Authority, 1987, After Theory, 1990, Postmodernism, 1993, Alterities, 1996, After Theory, 2d edit., 1996, Criticism and Modernity, 1999. Labour Party. Avocation: music. Office: U Kent, Sch English, Canterbury CT2 7NX, England

DOCHERTY, WILLIAM THOMAS, accountant; b. Lanark, Scotland, July 10, 1951; s. Edward and Molly (McGeoghan) D.; m. Carol O'Hare, Apr. 1, 1995. BA with honors, Strathclyde U., Glasgow, 1973. Chartered acct., 1986. Inspector of taxes Inland Revenue, 1973-81, dist. inspector of taxes, 1981-83; tax mgr. Arthur Andersen, 1983-89; ptnr., head of tax investigations practice Arthur Andersen, Manchester, Eng., 1996—; mng. tax cons. Price Waterhouse, 1989-92; tax ptnr., head of nat. tax investigations Robson Rhodes, 1992-96. Author: Tax Investigations, 1997; contbr. articles to profl. jours. Bd. dirs. Manchester YMCA, 1992—; hon. sec. Portico Libr., Manchester, 1992-97, chmn., 1997—. Mem. Brit. Inst. Mgmt., Manchester Literary and Philos. Soc. Roman Catholic. Avocations: walking, playing violin, opera, reading, music. Home: 1 Linden Rd Didsbury, M20 2QJ Manchester England Office: Arthur Andersen, Bank House 9 Charlotte St, M1 4EU Manchester England

DOCKHORN, ROBERT JOHN, physician, educator; b. Goodland, Kans., Oct. 9, 1934; s. Charles George and Dorotha Mae (Horton) D.; m. Beverly Ann Wilke, June 15, 1957; children: David, Douglas, Deborah. AB, U. Kans., 1956, MD, 1960. Diplomate Am. Bd. Pediat. Intern Naval Hosp., San Diego, 1960-61; resident in pediat. Naval Hosp., Oakland, Calif., 1963-65; resident in pediat. allergy and immunology U. Kans. Med. Ctr., 1967-69, adj. asst. prof. pediat., 1969—; resident in pediat. allergy and immunology Children's Mercy Hosp., Kansas City, Mo., 1967-69, chief divsn., 1969-83; practice medicine specializing in allergy and immunology Children's Mercy Hosp., Prairie Village, Kans., 1969-94, U. Mo. Med. Sch., Prairie Village, Kans., 1969-94; pres. Internat. Med. Tech. Cons., Inc., Kansas City, 1979—; with D&B Med. Consulting, LLC, Overland Park, Kans., 1999—; pres. I.M.T.C.I. (Internat. Med. Tech. Cons., Inc.), Kansas City, 1979-99; founder, CEO Internat. Med. Tech. Cons., Inc., Lenexa, Kans., subs. Immuno-Allergy Tech. Cons., Inc., Clin. Rsch. Cons., Inc. Contbr. articles to med. jours.; co-editor: Allergy and Immunology in Children, 1973. Fellow Am. Acad. Pediatrics, Am. Coll. Allergists (bd. regents 1976—, v.p. 1978-79, pres. 1981-82), Am. Assn. Cert. Allergists (pres. 1991—), Am. Acad. Allergy; mem. AMA, Kans. Med. Soc., Johnson County Med. Soc., Kans. Allergy Soc. (pres. 1976-77), Mo. Allergy Soc. (sec. 1975-76), Joint Coun. Socio-Econs. of Allergy (bd. dirs. 1976—, pres. 1978-79). Fax: 913-649-0464. Home: 8510 Delmar Ln Shawnee Mission KS 66207-1926 Office: D&B Med Consulting LLC 8220 Travis St Ste 117 Overland Park KS 66204-3963

DOCKRELL, JOHN HENRY, lawyer; b. Dublin, Aug. 23, 1943; s. Henry Percy and Dorothy Wadsworth (Brooks) D.; m. Janet Edith Caroline Millard; children: Samantha, Jonathan. BA, Dublin U., 1966. Solicitor, Ireland, 1966; barrister, Can., 1969. Lawyer Goodman & Carr, Toronto, Can., 1970-72; ptnr. William Fry, Dublin, 1972-77, Dockrell, Farrell, Dublin, 1977—; dir. Convertec Ltd., Ireland, Gaines Europe Ltd., Ireland; mem. ACL Internat./Internat. Assn. of Corp. Lawyers. Contbr. articles to profl. jours. and publs. County councillor Dublin County Coun., Dublin, 1985; chmn. Dun Laoghaire Rathdown County Coun., Dublin, 1994. Mem. Kildare St. Club and Carrickmines Lawn Tennis and Croquet Club. Mem. European People's Party. Anglican. Avocations: travel, reading, walking, tennis.

DOCKRILL, CHRISTOPHER FREDERICK, secondary education educator; b. Sydney, NSW, Australia, Mar. 28, 1952; s. Frederick and Thelma (Quirk) D.; m. Lynette Margaret Andrews, July 10, 1976; children: Mikaela Lynette, Luke Christopher, Matthew Ryan. BA in Eng.ish, History & Politics, Macquarie U., Sydney, 1976, diploma in edn., 1976. Cert. tchr. Articled clk. Williams Dibbs & Co. Solicitors, Sydney, 1970-72; English tchr. Kuring Gai H.S., Sydney, 1977-86; English head tchr. Kempsey (Australia) H.S., 1987—. Author: Power Plays, 1985, Modern Moralities, 1988, Dynamic Dramatics, 1991, Frankenstein-A Born Again Legend, 1992, Super Scripts, 1995. Avocations: fishing, surfing, writing. Home: PO Box 12, Crescent Head 2440, Australia

DOCKTERMAN, MICHAEL, lawyer; b. Davenport, Iowa, Dec. 14, 1954; s. Jerome and Elaine (Epstein) D.; m. Laura Di Giantonio, Sept. 25, 1983; 1 child, Eliana. BA, Yale U., 1975; JD, Duke U., 1978. Bar: Ill. 1978, U.S. Dist. Ct. (no. dist.) Ill. 1978, U.S. Dist. Ct. (ea. dist.) Mich. 1986, U.S. Dist. Ct. (ctrl. dist.) Ill. 1988, U.S. Dist. Ct. (so. dist.) Ill. 1991, U.S. Dist Ct. (we. dist.) Mich. 1995, U.S. Dist. Ct. (ea. dist.) Mo. 1996, U.S. Ct. Appeals (7th cir.) 1978, U.S. Ct. Appeals (4th, 6th and fed. cirs.) 1990, U.S. Ct. Appeals (2d cir.) 1993, U.S. Supreme Ct. 1992. Ptnr. Wildman, Harrold, Allen and Dixon, Chgo., 1978—. Co-author: IICLE Class Actions, 1986, 92, 2000; contbg. author: ABA Criminal Antitrust Litigation Manual; contbr. articles on corp. governance and compliance to profl. jours. Active Chgo. Vol. Legal Svcs., 1983—; adult bd. dirs. Greater Midwest region B'nai B'rith Youth Orgn., 1985—; bd. dirs. KAM Isaiah Israel Congregation, 1993-96, Duke Law Alumni Assn., pres.; trustee Max and Gretel Janowski Fund, Chgo., 1992-99; mem. The Chgo. Com., Chgo. Coun. on Fgn. Rels., Am. Refugee Com. Recipient Award for Advocacy Internat. Acad. Trial Lawyers, Leadership Devel. award B'nai B'rith Youth Orgn. Fellow Pvt. Adjudication Found.; mem. ABA (chair corp. governance subcom. Corp. Counsel com. Bus. Law Sect.), Chgo. Bar Assn., Legal Club Chgo., B'nai B'rith Justice Lodge. Office: Wildman Harrold Allen Dixon 225 W Wacker Dr Chicago IL 60606-1224

DOCZI, TAMAS PETER, neurosurgery educator; b. Szeged, Hungary, Aug. 25, 1949; s. Andras and Eva Katalin (Santa) D.; m. Eva Maria Prehoffer, May 16, 1950; children: Reka, Tamas. MD, U. Med. Sch., 1972. Resident U. Hosp., Szeged, Hungary, 1973-81, asst. prof., 1981-89; cons. U. Hosp., Zurich, 1985-91; prof. U. Hosp., Pecs, Hungary, 1992—. Contbr. articles to profl. jours. Recipient Upjohn prize Eans, 1984. Avocations: sports, music, gardening. Office: Univ Hosp, Ret v 2, H-7623 Pecs Hungary

DODARO, ROBERT JOHN, priest, theology educator; b. Pitts., Jan. 26; arrived in Italy, 1992; s. William Peter Dodaro and Margaret Durkot. BA with honors, Villanova U., 1977; lic. in theology and patristic studies, Inst. Patristicum Augustinianum, Rome, 1985; PhD in Theology, Oxford (Eng.) U., 1993. Ordained priest Roman Cath. Ch., 1982. Prof. Institutum Patristicum Augustinianum, Rome, 1992—, v.p., 1992—. Editor: Augustine and his Critics, 2000, Augustine: Political Writings, 2000; assoc. editor Augustinus-Lexikon, 2000—. Recipient Overseas Rsch. Student award Com. of Vice-Chancellors and Prins., U.K., 1988-90. Avocations: reading, tennis. E-mail: rdodaro@aug.org. Fax: 3906-68006298.

DODD, CHRISTOPHER JOHN, editor, writer; b. Bristol, England, Feb. 14, 1942. BA, Nottingham U., 1964. Journalist The Guardian, England, 1965-94; cons. River and Rowing Mus. Found., England, 1994—; editor Regatta Mag., England, 1987—; chmn. press World Rowing Champs, Nottingham, 1986, chief press officer, Indpls., 1994; rowing info. mgr. 1996 Olympic Games, Atlanta. Author: Henley Royal Regatta, 1981, Oxford and Cambridge Boat Race, 1983, The Story of World Rowing, 1992. žem. Internat. Rowing Fedn. (commn. media 1990—), Mus. Assn., Br. Soc. Sports History, Leander Club. Office: c/o Amateur Rowing Assn, 6 Lower Mall Hammersmith, London W6 9DJ, England

DODD, DANA EUGENE, energy industry financial manager; b. Oklahoma City; s. Eugene Arthur and Doris Virginia (Morgan) D.; m. Sandra Arlene Todd, Feb. 14, 1975; children: Eugene, Brandon, Tiffany. BS in Acctg., U. Cen. Okla., 1978. Cert. mgmt. acct., cert. fin. mgr. Inst. Mgmt. Accts. Acct. Conoco, Inc., Ponca City, Okla., 1978-79; mktg. analyst Conoco Chems. Co., Houston, 1979-80, coord. mktg. sys., 1980-84; acctg. analyst ANG Coal Gasification Co., Beulah, N.D., 1984-85, bus. planner, 1985-86, supr. budgeting and fin. analysis, 1986-88; mgr. budget svcs. Basin Electric Power Coop., Bismarck, N.D., 1988-97, mgr. bus. planning and analysis, 1997-99; mgr. info. svcs. and tech. Basin Electric Power Coop., Bismarck, 1999—. Mem. Bismarck Kiwanis Club (Circle K advisor 1994—). E-mail: ddodd@bepc.com. Office: Basin Electric Power Coop 1717 E Interstate Ave Bismarck ND 58503-0564

DODD, HIRAM, JR., lawyer; b. Birmingham, Ala., Aug. 13, 1946; s. Hiram and Mary (Martin) D.; m. Annie Mayhall, Dec. 17, 1970; children: Hiram III, Brian Alan, Amie Michelle. BA, Samford U., 1968, JD, 1971. Pvt. practice law Birmingham. Mem. Ala. Bar Assn., Ala. Criminal Def. Lawyers Assn. Republican. Episcopalian. Office: 2107 5th Ave N Ste 100 Birmingham AL 35203-3325

DODD, MORGAN CARY, fundraising executive; b. Bay Shore, N.Y., May 14, 1951; s. Daniel Cary Dodd and Jeanne (Bowlan) Zimmerman; m. Jurate Maria Grazina Victoria Koncius, Sept. 3, 1983; 1 child, Nicholas Koncius. BS in Fgn. Svc., Georgetown U., 1974. Cert. fund raising exec. Assoc. dir. alumni fund Georgetown Alumni Assn., Washington, 1976-83; ann. fund dir. Wolf Trap Found. for Performing Arts, Vienna, Va., 1985-86, Corcoran Gallery of Art, Washington, 1986-92; dir. ann. support Nature Conservancy, Arlington, Va., 1992-99; dir. donor rels. Nat. Pks. Conservation Assn., Washington, 1999—. Bd. dirs. Francis Scott Key Park Found., Washington, 1983-95. Mem. Nat. Soc. Fund Raising Execs. (bd. dirs. Greater Washington D.C. area chpt. 1990, ann. meeting. com. 1987-89, co-chmn. 1990, chmn. 1991), Planned Giving Study Group Washington. Avocations: sailing, antiques, travel, classical music. Home: 3155 Jocelyn St NW Washington DC 20015-1311 Office: Nat Pks Conservation Assn 1300 19th St NW Ste 300 Washington DC 20036-1628

DODD, ROBERT HUGH, medicinal chemistry researcher; b. Grand'Mére, Quebec, Can., Mar. 1, 1952; s. Paul Arthur and Gertrude Flore (Berthiaume) D. BSc (hons.), McGill Univ., Montreal, 1974; PhD in chem., Univ. British Columbia, Vancouver, Can., 1979. Postdoctoral fellow Univ. Geneva, Geneva, 1979-80; postdoctoral fellow Centre Nat. de la Recherche Scientifique, Gif-sur-Yvette, France, 1981-84, rsch. assoc., 1984-88, rsch. dir., 1989—. Contbr. over 70 articles to profl. jours. Recipient Young Scientist award French Medical Chem. Soc., 1989, fellowship Ogilvie Co., 1978. Mem. Soc. for Neuroscience, Soc. de Chimie Therapeutique. Avocations: skiing, squash, cycling, theatre, classical music. Office: Inst de Chimie des Substances Naturelles, CNRS, 91198 Gif-sur-Yvette France

DODDS, DALE IRVIN, chemicals executive; b. Los Angeles, May 3, 1915; s. Nathan Thomas and Mary Amanda (Latham) D.; m. Phyllis Doreen Kirchmayer, Dec. 20, 1941; children: Nathan E., Allan I., Dale I. Jr., Charles A. AB in Chemistry, Stanford U., 1937. Chem. engr. trainee The Texas Co., Long Beach, Calif., 1937-39; chemist Standard Oil of Calif., Richmond, 1939-41; chief chemist Scriver and Quinn Interchem., L.A., 1941-46; salesman E.B. Taylor and Co. Mfg. Rep., L.A., 1947-53, Burbank (Calif.) Chem. Co., 1953-57, Chem. Mfg. Co./ICI, L.A., 1957-68; pres., CEO J.J. Mauget Co., L.A., 1969-97; CEO J.J. Mauget Co., Arcadia, Calif., 1998—. Inventor: Systemic Fungicide, 1976; patentee in field; contributed to devel. Microinjection for Trees. Fellow Am. Inst. Chemists; mem. Am. Chem. Soc., L.A. Athletic Club, Sigma Alpha Epsilon Alumni (pres. Pasadena, Calif. chpt. 1973, 90). Republican. Christian Scientist. Office: JJ Mauget Co 5435 Peck Rd Arcadia CA 91006-5847

DODGE, ARTHUR BYRON, JR., business executive, marketing professional; b. Lancaster, Pa., June 13, 1923; s. Arthur Byron and Marion Frances (Cochran) D.; m. Margaretha Gerbert, Dec. 28, 1954; children: Arthur B., Andrew Nikolaus. Student, Williams Coll., 1942; BS in Econs., Franklin and Marshall Coll., 1947. With Dodge Cork Co., 1947-89, product mgr., 1947-50, factory mgr., 1952-57, mgr. fgn. divsn., 1958-61, v.p., sec., 1961-81, pres., 1981-90; bd. dirs. Dodge-Regupol, Inc., 1989—, chmn., 1990—; bd. dirs., sec. Gerbert, Ltd., Lancaster, 1979—, Intertrade, Inc., Lancaster, 1979-91. Trustee Episcopal Ch. Sch. Found., 1958-85, Lancaster Theol. Sem., 1998—; pres. Friends of SOS Children's Villages, 1979-85, bd. dirs., 1979-93; bd. dirs., treas. SOS Children's Villages USA, 1993-98; bd. dirs. 88th Inf. Divsn. Assn., 1988—, pres., 1996-97; bd. dirs. Meml. Trust, 1992—. Capt. AUS, 1942-45, 50-52. Decorated Bronze Star with cluster, Purple Heart with cluster, Meritorious Svc. award; battlefield commn. Italy, 1944. Mem. ASTM, Cork Inst. Am. (treas. 1980—), Newcomen Soc., Pa. Soc., Pa. Commn. Employment of Handicapped, Delta Upsilon, Hamilton Club, Lancaster Country Club. Republican. Office: 715 Fountain Ave Lancaster PA 17601-4547

DODGE, CLIFFORD HOWLE, geologist; b. Lancaster, Pa., Aug. 20, 1950; s. Richard Keller and Nancy Howle D.; m. Christine Miles, Apr. 4, 1981 (div. Aug. 1995). BA, Lehigh U., Bethlehem, Pa., 1972; MS, Northwestern U., Evanston, Ill., 1976. Registered profl. geologist, Pa.; cert. profl. geologist Am. Inst. Profl. Geologists. Hydrologist/geologist U.S. Geol. Survey/Water Resources Divsn., Harrisburg and Meadville, Pa., 1976-79; geologist Pa. Geol. Survey/Dept. Conservation and Natural Resources, Harrisburg, 1979—; expert witness Pa. Dept. Environ. Resources, Harrisburg, 1991, The Carbon/Graphite Group, Inc., Saint Marys, Pa., 1991. Contbr. numerous articles to profl. jours. and publs. Mem. Friends of the Lancaster Cemetery. Mem. Geol. Soc. Am., SEPM Soc. for Sedimentary Geology, History of Earth Sci. Soc., Harrisburg Area Geol. Soc., Demuth Found., Nat. Geog. Soc., Pa. Soc. Sons of the Revolution, Lancaster County Hist. Soc., Elk County Hist. Soc., Beverly Hist. Soc., Friends of the R.R. Mus. Pa., Sigma Xi, Theta Chi. Episcopalian. Home: 145 Primrose Dr Hershey PA 17033-2638 Office: Pa Geol Survey/DCNR PO Box 8453 Harrisburg PA 17105-8453

DODGE, HARRY LEON, retired secondary educator; b. Delte, Iowa, Sept. 17, 1914; s. George Russell and Frances Ida (Jones) D.; m. Lois Joy Cook, June 18, 1951; children: Steven Russell, David Clark. AB, U. Cinn., 1937; MDiv, Oberlin Coll. Sch. Theology, 1943; BE, U. Alta. (Can.), 1958; MA, U. Akron, 1971. Cert. secondary tchr., Ohio. Pastor Ch. of God, Conewango Valley, N.Y., 1943-46; tchr. Dayton (Ky.) City Schs., 1946-48, Bellevue (Ky.) City Schs., 1948-53; dean, prin. Alta. (Can.) Bible Inst., Camrose, 1953-57; tchr. McKinley H.S. Canton (Ohio) City Schs., 1957-81; substitute tchr. McKinley H.S. Stark County Schs., 1981—; treas. Kenyon D. Love Law Firm, Canton, 1989-99. Mem. Phi Delta Kappa (Kappan of Yr. 1999-2000). Republican. Mem. Ch. of God. Avocation: poetry. Home: 1369 Ivydale Ave SW Canton OH 44710-2237

DODIK, MILORAD, prime minister of Serb Republic. Elected to Rep. Assembly, 1990; founder, chmn. Party Ind. Social Dems., 1997; prime min. Republic of Serbia, 1998—. Mem. Party of Ind. Social Dems. Office: Office of Prime Min, Banja Luka Republic of Serbia*

DODONOV, VICTOR VASILIEVICH, physicist, educator; b. Kokchetav, USSR, Nov. 26, 1948; s. Vasiliy Pavlovich and Alexandra (Melnikova) D.; m. Lioubov Vladimirovna Belova, Mar. 6, 1979; children: Evgueni, Alexandre, Pavel. MA, Moscow Inst. Physics and Tech., 1972, PhD in Physics, 1976. Asst. prof. physics Moscow Inst Physics and Tech., 1972-77, assoc. prof. physics, 1977-96, vice-chmn. neutrino physics dept., 1985-93; sr. rschr., head of rsch. group Lebedev Physics Inst. Russian Acad. Scis., Moscow, 1991-96; vis. prof. Nat. Autonomous U. Mex., Cuernavaca, 1994-95, Fed. U. São Carlos, Brazil, 1993, 96—; affiliated rschr. Lebedev Physics Inst. Acad. Scis. USSR, Moscow, 1972-90. Co-author: Invariants and the Evolution on Nonstationary Quantum Systems, 1987; co-editor: Proceedings of the Third International Seminar Group Theoretical Methods in Physics, 1986, Proceedings of the XVIII Internat. Colloquium, Goup Theoretical Methods in Physics, 1991; vice-editor: Jour. of Group Theory in Physics, 1991-95; contbr. over 100 articles to profl. jours. Mem. Brazilian Phys. Soc., N.Y. Acad. Scis.

D'ODORICO, JOSE CANDIDO, magazine editor; b. Santa Fe, Argentina, Feb. 26, 1927; s. Angel and Rose (Mazzon) D'O.; m. Irene Reynalda D'Errico, Mar. 8, 1952; children: Edward, Monica, Alain. Grad., Air War Coll., Paris, 1963, Air War Sch., Buenos Aires, 1968; diploma, Inter-Am. Def. Coll., Washington, 1970. Commd. officer Argentine Air Force, 1949, advanced through grades to air commodore, transport pilot, 1949-61; prof. Air War Sch., 1963-68, 70—, dir., 1974, editor Air War Sch. mag. RESGA, 1992—; ret. Argentine Air Force, 1975. Editor Aeroespacio, 1975-92; corr. Armed Forces Jour. Internat., Revista Aérea. Home: Amenábar 640, 1426 Buenos Aires Argentina Office: Argentine Air Force Hdqs, P Zanni 250, 1104 Buenos Aires Argentina

DODSON, DARYL THEODORE, ballet administrator, arts consultant; b. Warrensburg, Mo., Oct. 9, 1934; s. Theodore and Ada Marie (Ayres) D. BS, Cen. Mo. State U., 1956. mem. Gov. S.C.'s Coun. of the Arts, 1974; mem. adv. panel Vt. Coun. on Arts, 1978; mgr. Am. tour 1st cultural exch., People's Republic of China and U.S., 1978, Nat. Ballet Cuba, 1979, Royal Ballet Eng., 1981; pres. Pine Cone Enterprises, Ltd., 1977-81; propr. Pine Cone Inn, Haverhill, N.H., 1978-81; mgr. Opera House, John F. Kennedy Ctr., Washington, 1981; mgr. U.S. and Can. tour Sweeney Todd, 1982; mgr. U.S. tours Amadeus, 1982-83, The Wiz, 1983-84, Les Miserables, 1988-92, Phantom of the Opera, 1992-00; mgr. N.Y. engagement The Golden Land, 1985; mgr. Porgy and Bess, 1986-87, La Cage Aux Folles, 1987, N.Y. and U.S. tour Paris Opera Ballet, 1988; gen. mgr. John Curry Skating Co., 1984. Asst. dir. The Mikado, N.Y.C. Opera, 1959; regisseur Chgo. Opera Ballet, 1960, asst. stage mgr. Am. Ballet Theatre, N.Y.C., 1960, stage mgr., 1961, prodn. stage mgr., 1961, prodn. mgr., 1963, gen. mgr., 1968-77. Served with U.S. Army, 1957-59. Mem. Theta Chi, Theta Alpha Phi. Episcopalian. Home: On The Commons Haverhill NH 03765 Office: 1650 Broadway Ste 800 New York NY 10019-6833

DODSON, MICHAEL IVAN GEORGE, international seminar company executive, photo journalist; b. Beckenham, Kent, Eng., Dec. 22, 1948; s. Michael and Ena (LLoyd); 1 child, Klara-Michelle. Cert. lectr. Med. underwriter Sun Life Can., London, 1969-88; dir., lectr. La Methode Silva, internat. mental devel. seminars, Paris, 1988—; overseas amb. Hungarian Lang. Sch., 2000—; syndicated photo journalist. Co-author: Silva Passport, 1982. Avocations: drawing, psychology, classic automobiles. Office: Concept Promotions Ltd, 24A Market Pl, Norfolk NR19 1AX, England

DOE, HIDEKAZU, chemistry educator; b. Kitakatsuragi-gun, Nara, Japan, Aug. 26, 1952; s. Shozo and Yoshie (Tsuchie) D.; m. Kazuyo Kawamoto, Nov. 27, 1982; 3 children. DSc, Kyoto (Japan) U., 1980. Rsch. assoc. Osaka (Japan) City U., 1980-93, lectr. in chemistry, 1993-98, assoc. prof. in chemistry, 1998—. Contbr. articles to Jour. Electroanalytical Chemistry, Inorganic Chemistry, Jour. Phys. Chemistry, others. Grantee Japan Ministry Edn., 1994, 95, 96. Mem. Am. Chem. Soc., Chem. Soc. Japan, Analytical Chem. Soc. Japan. Avocations: audio, tennis, camping. Office: Osaka City U Fac Sci, 3-3-138 Sugimoto, Sumiyoshi-ku Osaka 558-8585, Japan

DOEBBELING, BRADLEY N., physician, epidemiologist; b. Columbia, Mo., Jan. 26, 1959; m. Edward M. and Mary Olive Doebbeling; m. Caroline Carney, June 12, 1994; 1 child, Cormac. BS with honors, Colo. State U., 1981; MD with honors, U. Colo., 1985; MSc, U. Iowa, 1990. Diplomate Am. Bd. Internal Medicine, Am. Bd. Infectious Disease. Resident in internal medicine U. Iowa Hosps. and Clinics, Iowa City, 1985-88, fellow in gen. medicine and clin. epidemiology, 1988-89, fellow in infectious diseases and clin. epidemiology, 1989-91, chief resident in internal medicine, 1990-91, asst. prof. internal medicine, 1991-96, assoc. prof. internal medicine Colls. Medicine & Pub. Health, 1996—; epidemiologist Iowa City VAMC, Iowa City, 1996—; staff physician, cons. U. Iowa Health Care, Iowa City, 1991—; mem. grant rev. panel health svcs. R&D, Dept. Vets. Affairs, Washington, 1998—; mem. rev. panel Am. Inst. Biol. Scis., Washington, 1988—. Editor: Maxcy-Rosenau-Last Public Health and Preventive Medicine, 1998; contbr. articles to profl. jours. including New Eng. Jour. Medicine. Mem. disease reporting task force Iowa Dept. Pub. Health, Des Moines, 1999—; mem. implementation and edn. work group adv. coun. for adoption, devel., and implementation clin. practice guidelines Dept. Vets. Affairs, Washington, 1999—, mem. tech. planning com. Ann. Fed. Investigators Meeting on Gulf War Illness, 1997—; mem. faculty senate U. Iowa, Iowa City, 1998-2000. Grantee Dept. Vets Affairs, 1999—, Dept. Def., 1997—, Nat. Inst. Occupl. Safety and Health, 1993-96, 95—. Fellow ACP, Infectious Diseases Soc. Am.; mem. Am. Soc. for Microbiology (chair nosocomial infections sect. 1998-99), Soc. for Healthcare Epidemiology Am. (fin. com. 1998-2000). Avocations: reading, cinema, finance. Fax: (319) 356-3086. Office: U Iowa Coll Medicine Dept Internal Medicine 200 Hawkins Dr Iowa City IA 52242-1009

DOEBBELING, UDO MAX GEORG, research scientist; b. Neuenbûrg, Germany, May 30, 1958; s. Hans-Joachim Wolfgang and Dora Johanna Senta (Krüger) D. MSc, U. Karlsruhe, Germany, 1984, PhD, 1988. Postdoctoral fellow Inst. Molecular Biology U. Zurich, Switzerland, 1988-90, scientist Inst. Vet. Biochemistry, 1991-93; sr. scientist dermatology dept. Univ. Hosp. Zurich, 1994—. Reviewer Swiss Nat. Sci. Found., 1998—, various jours.; contbr. articles to profl. jours. With German Army, 1977-78. Doctoral fellow Forschungszentrum Karlsruhe, 1985-88; Postdoctral fellow German Acad. Exch. Svc., 1989-90; grantee Swiss Nat. Sci. Found., others. em. AAAS, Soc. Christian Dem. Grads. (cash auditor 1990-94), Union Swiss Socs. Exptl. Biology, Swiss Cancer League, Swiss Soc. Oncology, N.Y. Acad. Scis. Avocations: stamp and coin collecting. Office: Univ Hosp Zurich, Gloriastrasse 31, CH-8091 Zurich Switzerland

DOEHN, CHRISTIAN, urologist, researcher; b. Hamburg, Dec. 12, 1964; s. Carl Jensen and Helga I. Doehn. D. U. Hamburg, Germany, 1992; degree in urology, U. Lubeck, Germany, 1999. House officer U. Lubeck, 1992-93, registrar, 1994-95, 1995-99; registrar Royal Vict. Infirmary, Newcastle, United Kingdom, 1995; cons. urologist U. Lebeck, 1999. Author: Recent advances in Endourology, 1999; contbr. articles to profl. jours. Recipient Best Presentation award No. German Urol. Assn., 1997, Most Innovative Urology Video award World Congress Videourology, 1997, New Tech. award World Congress Videourology, 1998, Rudolf Schindler award, 2000. Mem. AAAS, German Assn. Urologists, Soc. Minimally Invasive Therapy, European Urol. Assn., Soc. Internat. d'Urologie, Endourol. Soc., Marienthal Tennis Hockey Club. Avocations: hockey. Office: Dept Urology Med Univ, Ratzeburger Allee 160, 23538 Lubeck Germany

DOEHRING, EKKEHARD, medical association administrator, pediatrician; b. Braunschweig, Lower Saxony, Germany, Oct. 30, 1954; s. Ekkehard and Rose Marie (Guertler) D.; m. Martina Schriever, Aug. 16, 1994; children: Lani Marie, Jakob. Approbation, Med. Sch. Hanover, Germany, 1981, D in Medicine, 1982. MD, Pediatrician, Allergologist, Parasitologist. Registrar Med. Hochschule, Hanover, Germany, 1981-90; cons. U. Bonn, Germany, 1991-94; vis. prof. Makerere U., Kampala, Uganda, 1992-98; med. dir. Interdisciplinary Therapy Ctr., Feldberg, Germany, 1995-97; dep. Gesundheitsamt (Germany) Neuruppin, 1998—; adv. WHO, Cairo, 1990, Niamey, Niger, 1996, DANIDA, Chiredzi, Zimbabwe, 1992; prof. Med. Sch. Hanover, Germany, 1995, Kampala, Uganda, 1991-92, 94, 96; pvt. dozent Med. Sch. Hanover, 1988. Editor: Book on Total Quality Management in Pediatrics. Grantee Multi-ctr. study TDR-WHO, Africa, 1991-95, Oncho study, Ghana, 1992-94, European Cmty. study, Senegal, Uganda, 1994-97. Mem. Ultrasound Soc. Germany, Am. Soc. Tropical Med. Hyg., German Soc. Tropical Medicine; bd. dirs. Working Group Tropical Pediatrics, German Soc. Pediat. Infectious Diseases. Avocations: scuba diving, stamp collecting, reading, chess. E-mail: edoehring@t-online.de. Home: Rosa Luxemburg Str 3, 16816 Neuruppin Neustadt, Germany Office: Gesundheitsamt Neuruppin, Neustädter Str 44, 16816 Neuruppin Germany

DOELLE, HORST WERNER, biotechnologist; b. Muehlhausen, Germany, Sept. 1, 1932; arrived in Australia, 1960; s. Heinrich E. and Ruth D. (Zander) D.; m. Gabriele D. Hesse, Mar. 15, 1958; children: Petra, Monica. Dr.rer.nat., U Gottingen, 1957; DSc, U. Queensland, 1976, PhD, 1966; DSc (hon.), U. New Eng., 1998. Microbiologist Scientific Brewing Inst., Munich, Germany, 1959; exptl. officer CSIRO, Griffith, Australia, 1960-63; sr. lectr. U. Queensland, Brisbane, Australia, 1964-76, assoc. prof., 1976-92; cons., dir. Microbiotech. P/L, Brisbane, Australia, 1992—; dir. MIRCEN-Biotech., Brisbane, 1987—; cons., tchr. UNESCO Tng. Courses, 1975—; reader (hon.) dept. microbilogy, dept. chem. engring. U. Queensland. Author: Bacterial Metabolism, 1975, Microbial Process Development, 1994; editor: Solid State Fermentation, 1992. Postdoctoral fellow Wine Rsch. Inst., Neustadt, 1957-59, A.V. Humboldt fellow, Bonn, Germany, 1970, UNIDO Wien fellow, Hanoi, Vietnam, 1991, UNESCO Prof. Biotechnology, Hanoi, Vietnam, 1993. Fellow Australian Soc. Microbiology; mem. Internat. Orgn. Biotech. & Bioengring. (chmn.). Lutheran. Achievements include patent on ethanol production using bacteria. Home and Office: 21 Belsize, Kenmore-Brisbane 4069, Australia

DOEPPER, RONALD FRIDRICH, chemical engineer; b. Dieburg, Hessen, Germany, Mar. 3, 1964; s. Helmut and Maria (Franz) D. Grad. in engring. of chemistry tech., Engenier Sch., Darmstadt, Germany, 1989. Analyst Infracor, Hanau-Wolfgang, Germany, 1989—; analytical and praparatio HPLC. Office: Infracor, Postfach 1345, 63403 Hanau Germany

DOERELL, PETER ERNST, publisher, editor, consultant; b. Aussig/Elbe, Austria, Mar. 4, 1918; s. Ernst Gustav and Lore (Watzlik) D.; m. Edith Roggenbuck, 1954 (div. 1959); 1 child, Claudia; m. Brigitte Röver, May 18, 1961; children: Michael, Oliver. JD, U. Hamburg, Germany, 1948. Asst. mgr. Verein Deutscher Düngerfabrikanten, Hamburg, 1947-49; mgr. Verband des Niedersächsischen Brennstoffhandels, Hannover, Germany, 1950-61; dir. European Coal Info. Agy., Brussels, 1962-78, Soc. Europeenne de Tankage et Pipeline S.A., Brussels, 1968-78; news editor Miller Freeman Publs., San Francisco, 1979-83; pub., editor Internat. Coal Letter, Brussels, 1983—; cons. GKW Consult, Mannheim, Germany, IPP Consult, Hildesheim, Germany. Coal News editor Internat. Mining, London, Engring. & Mining Jour., Chgo.; contbg. editor Sieg Tech, Bonn. Founding mem. Club Internat. Château St-Anne, Brussels; mem. Belgian nat. com. World Energy Coun. Mem. European Acad. Environ. Affairs. Liberal. Avocations: tennis, bridge, golf. Home: Zonienboslan 16, B-3090 Overijise Belgium Office: Rue Capouillet 19-21, B-1060 Brussels Belgium

DOERPER, JOHN ERWIN, journal editor, publishing executive; b. Wuerzburg, Germany, Sept. 17, 1943; came to U.S., 1963, naturalized resident, 1973; s. Werner and Theresia (Wolf) D.; m. Victoria McCulloch, Dec. 2, 1970. BA, Calif. State U., Fullerton, 1968; MA/ABD, U. Calif., Davis, 1972. Writer/author Seattle, 1984—; food columnist Washington, Seattle, 1985-88, Seattle Times, 1985-88; food editor Wash.-The Evergreen State Mag., Seattle, 1989-94, Pacific Northwest mag., 1989-94, Seattle Home and Garden, 1989-91; pub., editor, founder Pacific Epicure, Quarterly Jour. Gastronomy, Bellingham, Wash., 1988—; dir. Annual N.W. Invitational Chef's Symposium. Author: Eating Well: A Guide to Foods of the Pacific Northwest, 1984, The Eating Well Cookbook, 1984, Shellfish Cookery: Absolutely Delicious Recipes from the West Coast, 1985; author, illustrator: The Blue Carp, 1994, Wine Country: California's Napa and Sonoma Valleys, 1996, Pacific Northwest, 1997, Coastal California, 1998 (Lowell Thomas Travel Journalism Competition Gold medal 1999); contbr. articles to profl. jours., intro. and chpts. to books; co-author: Washington: A Compass Guide, 1995, Fodor's Pacific Northwest, 2000, Fodor's Seattle, 2000. Recipient Silver medal, White award for city and regional mags. William Allen White Sch. Journalism, U. Kans. Mem. Oxford Symposium Food and Cookery (speaker 26th Ann. Pacific N.W. Writer's Conf. 1982, 92). Avocations: food, wine, travel, painting, printmaking. Home: 610 Donovan Ave Bellingham WA 98225-7315

DOERR, HANS WILHELM, virologist; b. Arnstadt, Germany, Jan. 15, 1945; s. Wilhelm and Eva (Neuroth) D.; m. Silvia Middeldorf, June 13, 1975; children: Andrea, Simon. MD, U. Munich, 1971. From asst. to prof. U. Freiburg, U. Heidelberg, U. Frankfurt, Germany, 1972—; dir. Inst. Med. Virology, Frankfurt. Author: Contributions to Epidemiology of Infectious Diseases, 1978; co-author: Virological Safety of Biotechnologic Drugs, 1990, 97, Clinical Laboratory Diagnostics, 1998, Antiinfective Chemotherapy, 1996; editor: Monographs in Virology, 1997. Mem. German Assn. Against Virus Diseases (pres. 1995—). Avocation: history. E-mail: H.W.Doerr@em.uni-frankfurt.de. Fax: 49 69 6301 6477. Office: Inst Med Virol U Frankfurt, Paul-Ehsliich Ste 40, 60528 Frankfurt/Main Germany

DOERR, PATRICIA MARIAN, elementary and special education educator; b. Rochford, Essex, Eng., Mar. 14, 1947; came to U.S., 1976; d. Edward Earnest and Winifred May (Daniels) Earl; m. Hans Joachim Doerr, Dec. 17, 1983; children: Daniel, Nicholas, Carla. Cert. of Edn., Sussex U., 1968; Diploma in Edn. of Handicapped, London U., 1974; MS, Calif. Luth. U., 1986. Tchr. Long Road Jr. Sch., Canvey Island, Eng., 1968-70; tchr. scale 1 Belvedere (Kent, Eng.) Jr. Sch., 1970-71; tchr. scale 2 Bostal (Kent, Eng.) Manor Jr. Sch., 1971-73; tchr. scale 3, head remedial Warren Wood Boys Comprehensive Sch., Rochester, Kent, 1974-76; ednl. therapist Westvalley Ctr. for Ednl. Therapy, Canoga Park, Calif., 1977-79; tchr. K-2 Sundance Sch., Simi Valley, Calif., 1977-78; spl. tchr. Conejo Valley Unified Sch. Dist., Thousand Oaks, Calif., 1979-94; elem. tchr. Meadows Elem. Sch., Thousand Oaks, Calif., 1994—; ednl. cons. Scwrip & Independent, Ventura County, Calif., 1988—; mem. London Panel of Art Tutors, ILEA Evening Inst., 1969-73; mentor spl. edn. and lang. arts Conejo Valley Unified Sch. Dist., 1988-95. Recipient Award of Tchr. Excellence, AMGEN, 1996; Scwrip fellow Santa Barbara U., 1988. Mem. Calif. Assn. Mediated Learning (bd. dirs. 1991-95). Episcopalian. Home: 1933 Tamarack St Westlake Village CA 91361-1841

DOERRE, WERNER HEINZ, physicist; b. Prague, Nov. 7, 1935; s. Rudolf and Josefa D.; m. Sonnhild Haupt, Dec. 16, 1991; children: Peter, Katy-Anne. Diploma, Humboldt U., 1961, DSc, 1975. Rschr. Funkwerk Kupenick, Berlin, 1962-63; scientific asst. med. faculty Humboldt U., Berlin, 1964-65, project leader, 1965—. Mem. N.Y. Acad. Scis., Internat. Soc. Exposure Analysis. Office: Inst Microbiology/Hygiene, Schumannstr 20/1, D-10117 Berlin Germany

DOERRIES, CHANTAL-AIMÉE, barrister; b. Frankfurt, Germany, Aug. 26, 1968; d. Reinhard R. and Elaine (Sulli) D. BA with honors, U. Cambridge, Eng., 1990, degree in law, 1991, MA, 1994. Bar: Eng., Wales. Pupil barrister Chambers of Michael Beloff QC and Elizabeth Appleby QC, Grays Inn, Eng., 1992-93; barrister Chambers of John Blackburn QC, Grays Inn, 1994—. Editor Building Law Reports, 1999—. Recipient The Getrude de Gallaix Achievement award Fedn. Am. Womens Clubs Overseas, 1990; Diplock scholar The Honourable Soc. Mid. Temple, 1990. Mem. Tech. and Constrn. Bar Assn. (com. mem. 1996—, sec. 1997—), The Bar Pro Bono Unit, The Comml. and Common Law Bar Assn., Soc. Constrn. Lawyers, Bar European Group, The Hon. Soc. Mid. Temple, Cambridge Union Soc. (pres. 1989), New Hall Soc. (com. mem. 1997—), Gen. Coun. of Bar of Eng. and Wales (internat. rels. com.). Office: Atkin Chambers, 1 Atkin Bldg Gray's Inn, London WC1R 5AT, England

DOERSAM, CHARLES HENRY, JR., engineer; b. N.Y.C., Nov. 1, 1921; s. Charles Henry, Sr. and Mary Emily (Davenport) D.; m. Cynthia Ann Wick, Dec. 7, 1954 (div. dec. 1980); children: Charles Henry III, Donna Davenport, Dean Robert. BS in Engr., Columbia U., 1942, MSME, 1944; post grad., MIT, U. Mich., N.Y.U. Registered profl. engr., N.Y. Indsl. engr. Pratt & Whitney, East Hartford, Conn., 1941-42; tech. staff Bell Telephone Labs, N.Y.C., 1942-44; sr. project engr Specl. Devices Ctr., Sands Pt., N.Y., 1946-53; project mgr. Sperry Gyroscope Co., Lake Success, N.Y., 1953-60; new product planning mgr. Potter Instrument Co., Plainview, N.Y., 1960-62; dir. mktg. chief engr. Instruments for Industry, Hicksville, N.Y., 1962-64; prof. Polytech. Instit. of Bklyn., 1964-69; pres. Com Comp Inc, Hauppauge, N.Y., 1969-71; chmn., CEO Fiber Optic Sensors, Inc., Old Lyme, Conn., 1983—; pres. DOERCO Cons., CUB Computer Co., NUTEK Corp., Princeton Automated Labs., Pedagogy Rsch. Inst.; nat. chmn. IRE Profl. Group on Space Electronics, 1950. Pantentee in field; contbr. articles to profl. jours. Bd. Advisors Waldorf Sch., Garden City, N.Y., 1964-68, Portledge Sch., Locust Valley, N.Y., 1977. Mem. North Shore Yacht Club (commn. 1968-69), Point O'Woods Club. Republican. Congregationalist. Avocations: tennis, sailing, woodworking, gardening, constrn. Home and Office: 67 Shore Rd PO Box 927 Old Lyme CT 06371-0927

DOERSHUK, CARL FREDERICK, physician, pediatrics educator; b. Warren, Ohio, Dec. 24, 1930; s. Carl Frederick and Eula Blanche (Mahan) D.; m. Emma Lou Plummer, Aug. 21, 1954; children: Rebecca Lee, John Frederick, David Plummer. BA, Oberlin Coll., 1952; MD, Case Western Res. U., 1956. Intern U.S. Naval Hosp., Camp Pendleton, Ohio, 1956-57; resident in pediat. Cleve. Met. Gen. Hosp. and Babies and Children's Hosp., Cleve., 1959-61; postdoctoral pulmonary fellow Babies and Children's Hosp. USPHS, Cleve., 1961-63; sr. instr. to prof. pediatrics specializing in academic pediatric pulmonary medicine Case Western Res. U., Cleve., 1963-98, emeritus prof., 1998—. Co-editor Pediatric Respiratory Therapy, 1974, 3d edit., 1986; contbr. articles to profl. jours. Chmn. med. adv. coun. Cystic Fibrosis Found., Washington, 1966-72, bd. trustees, 1969-81, exec. com., 1969-74, v.p. med. affairs Cleve. chpt., 1965-90. Lt. M.C., USN, 1957-59. Named Young Man Yr. Cystic Fibrosis Found., 1970; recipient Richard C. Talamo Clinician Scientist award Cystic Fibrosis Found., 1997. Mem. Am. Pediatric Soc., Soc. Pediatric Research, Am. Acad. Pediatrics (exec. com. chest sect.), Am. Thoracic Soc. (chmn. pediatric pulmonary sect. 1971), No. Ohio Pediatric Soc., Acad. Medicine. Avocations: sailing, raising dahlias. Office: Rainbow Babies and Childrens Hosp 2101 Adelbert Rd Cleveland OH 44106-2624

DOERY, JAMES CLIFFORD GOWAR, pathologist, researcher; b. Melbourne, Australia, June 21, 1944; s. Stanley Gordon and Kathleen Gowar (Ritchie) D.; m. Rose Soo Cheng Lee Doery, Oct. 1, 1977; children: Mei Ling, Kee Ming, Mei Ping, Mei Ching. BS, U. Melbourne, Australia, 1966; MS, 1970; MD, McMaster U., Can., 1975. Cert. Nat. Bd. Exams., Australian Med. Examining Coun. Rsch. fellow Canadian Heart Found., Hamilton, 1967-69; med. registrar McMaster U. Med. Ctr., Hamilton, Can., 1976-78; Austin Hosp., Melbourne, Australia, 1979, St. Vincent's Hosp., Melbourne, Australia, 1980; chem. pathology registrar, 1981-84; prin. specialist in Chem. Pathology Monash Med. Ctr., Melbourne, Australia, 1985—; clin. tchr. Faculty of Medicine Monash U., Melbourne, Australia, 1987-92; hon. lectr. Dept. Pathology and Immunology Monash U., Melbourne, Australia, 1993-94; adminstr. Rsch. Ethics Com. Monash Med. Ctr., Melbourne, Australia, 1993—; hon. sr. lectr. dept. pathology-immunology Monash U., Melbourne, Australia, 1995—; dir. pathology, Moreland Hall, 1994—. Contbr. articles and book chpts. to profl. jours. Assessor Nat. Assn. Testing Authorities, Melbourne, Australia, 1988—, RACGP Lab. Accreditation , Melbourne, Australia, 1988—; mem. Pathology Consutative Com. to State Minister of Health, Victoria, Australia, 1986-88; cons. Indo-Chinese Ethnic Chinese Assn. Victoria, 1993-96' bd. mem., sec., pub. officer Anglican Chinese Mission Inc., 1986—. Recipient Undergraduate scholarship Commonwealth of Australia, 1963-66, Rsch. fwllowship Canadian Heart Found., Ottawa, 1971-72, med. scientist fellowship Canadian Heart Found., Ottowa, 1973-75, Travel award Internat. Soc. Hematology, 1972. Fellow Royal Coll. Pathologists of Australasia, 1984—; mem. Australian Assn. Clin. Biochemists, Australian Med. Assn., Australian Diabetes Soc., Am. Assn. Clin. Biochemists, Chinese Assn. Victoria, Chinese Health Found., Mus. Chinese Australian History. Avocation: Chinese Australian history. E-Mail: james.doery@med.monash.edu.au. Home: 304 Union Rd, Balwyn 3103, Australia Office: Monash Medical Ctr, 246 Clayton Rd, Clayton 3168, Australia

DOERZBACHER, RALPH ELMER, JR., career officer; s. Ralph Elmer Sr. and Pearl Anna Ethyl D.; m. Ruth Marie (dec. 1992), Aug. 25, 1956; children: Ralph Edward, Kimberly Ann, Dawn Marie, Eric Sprague. Degree in Physics, U. Pitts., 1957; degree in Applied Math., N.C. State U., 1970. Commd. 2d lt. USAF, 1960, advanced through grades to major; elec. warfare officer Fairchild AFB, Washington, 1960-65, Chambley AB, France, 1965-66, Tahkli AB, Udorn AB, Thailand, 1966-67; avionics integration engr. Wright Patterson AFB, Ohio, 1970-73, avionics test engr., 1977-80, flight test dir., 1981-83; elec. warfare officer Wurtsmith AFB, Mich., 1973-77. Pres. Cedar Bog Assn., Champaign County, Ohio, 1989—; trustee Champaign Land Trust, 1997—; Dist. Leader Boy Scouts Am., Champaign, 1980—. Recipient 4 Air medals. Mem. VFW, NRA, Am. Legion, Nature Conservatory, Rep. Club. Avocations: speleology, hiking, camping, ecology, marksmanship. E-mail: ericd@main-net.com. Home: 3133 Kiser Lake Rd Saint Paris OH 43072-9336

DOESCHER, WILLIAM FREDERICK, communications executive; b. Utica, N.Y., Dec. 9, 1937; s. Frederick William and Katherine Ann (Kipp) D.; m. Linda Blair, Nov. 25, 1977; children: Michelle Blair, Douglas C., Marc H. Blair, Cinda L. BA in Econs., Colgate U., 1959; MS in Journalism, Syracuse (N.Y.) U., 1961; postgrad. in advanced mgmt., Columbia U., 1973. Pub. rels. assoc., editor Chase Manhattan News Chase Manhattan Bank, N.Y.C., 1961-65; mgr. press rels. Inmont Corp., 1965-66; asst. corp. rels. mgr. U.S. Plywood Corp., 1966-67; pub. affairs mgr. ea. region Champion Internat. Corp., 1967-69, mgr. advt. svcs., then dir. corp. advt., 1969-71; v.p. pub. rels. and advt. Drexel Heritage Furnishings, Inc., 1971-78; v.p. comms. Dun & Bradstreet, Inc., 1978-83, v.p. pub. rels. and advt., 1983-96, sr. v.p. global comm., 1992—; sr. v.p., chief comm. officer Dun & Bradstreet Corp., 1996—; also pub. D&B Reports mag., N.Y.C., 1978-94. Author numerous articles in mags., periodicals. Bd. dirs. Direct Mktg. Assn., Jackie Robinson Found., BBBonline, PRSA Found.; mem., adv. com. S.I. Newhouse Sch. Pub. Comm. and its Distant Learning Program at Syracuse U.; bd. govs. Scarsdale (N.Y.) Golf Club; bd. dirs. N.Y.C. divsn. N.Y. Easter Seal Soc.; past pres. Nat. Combined Health Appeal; past pres. Scarsdale, N.Y. Civic Club; past bd. dirs. Colgate Alumni Corp., Nat. Easter Seal Soc., N.Y. Easter Seal Soc., N.Y.C. divsn. Am. Cancer Soc. With USAR, 1959-65. Mem. Pub. Rels. Seminar, Arthur Page Soc., Pub. Rels. Soc. Am., Wisemen. Office: 1 Diamond Hill Rd Murray Hill NJ 07974-1200

DOETSCH, MARKUS, communications/electrical engineer; b. Koblenz, Germany, Oct. 11, 1966; s. Manfred and Christine (Dahl) D. MSc, U. Kaiserslautern, Germany, 1996. Rschr. U. Kaiserslautern, 1996-98; project mgr. universal mobile telecomm. sys. Infineon Techs., Munich, 1998-2000; product mgr. Siemens Swiss Ltd., Bern, Switzerland, 2000—. Author: (book chpt.) CDMA Techniques for 3d Generation Mobile Systems, 1998; patentee in field. With PSY OP, 1986-88. Mem. IEEE, Verein Deutscher Elektrotechniker, Verein Deutscher Ingenieure. Avocation: skiing. Home: Sendnicher Weg 62, 56072 Koblenz Germany

DOETSCH, VIRGINIA LAMB, former advertising executive, writer; b. N.Y.C., Oct. 12, 1920; d. Andrew Thomas and Cameola Weeden (Burns) Lamb; m. Gunter H. Doetsch, Oct. 12, 1953 (div. Feb. 1972); 1 child, Hugo. BS, Northwestern U., 1941; postgrad., Columbia U., 1943-44, 46-47. Writer, dir. pub. rels. J. Walter Thompson, Frankfurt, Germany, 1953-56; v.p., creative group head Tatham-Laird & Kudner (now Euro RSCG Tatham), Chgo., 1959-76, Needham Harper & Steers (now DDB Chgo.), Chgo., 1976-83; free-lance advt. writer and prodr. Chgo., 1983—; writer, rschr. OmniTech Cons. Group now Diamond Tech. Ptnrs., Chgo., 1992-99. Bd. dirs. Better Bus. Bur., Chgo., 1973-76, Jr. Achievement, Chgo., 1973-76; fundraiser Chgo. Symphony Orch., 1990—, Women's Assn., 1990—. With ARC, China, Burma, India, 1944-46 (Bronze star). Named Woman of Yr., Am. Advt. Fedn., 1973. Mem. Women's Advt. Club Chgo. (Woman of Yr. award 1973), Chgo. Advt. Club (bd. dirs. 1973-76). Avocations: arts, swimming, walking, work. Home: 400 E Randolph St Apt 828 Chicago IL 60601-7309

DOGANCI, LEVENT, physician, career officer; b. Erzincan, Turkey, Mar. 21, 1957; s. Ihsan and Sitare Doganci; m. Pefyka Tumay Dinc, Oct. 12, 1981; children: Yigit, Yasemin. MD, Ankara U., 1981. Capt. Turkish Navy, 1981—; intern Turkish Navy, Ankara, 1981-82; physician Turkish Navy, Golcuk, 1982-84; resident Turkish Navy, Ankara, 1984-88; acting comdr. Naval H.Q. Clinic, Ankara, 1988-89; emergency medicine physician SHAPE, Mons, Belgium, 1989-92; chief internal medicine and infectious diseases Naval Hosp.-Iskenderun, Antakya, Turkey, 1992-94; assoc. prof., capt. Gulhane Mil. Med. Acad., Ankara, 1994—, cons. bone marrow transplantation unit, 1995—. Avocations: travel, music, gardening. E-mail: levdog@gata.edu.tr. Office: GATA, Mik.kl.mik AD, Etilk Ankara 06018, Turkey

DOGO, MELA YILA, economist, bank executive; b. Sansani, Gombe, Nigeria, Aug. 1, 1958; s. Yila Dogo Kwalli and Dijah Dogo Kwabit; m. Laraba Mela, July 28, 1984; children: Dorcas Mela, David Mela, Daniel Mela. BSc in Econs. with honors, U. Jos, Plateau, Nigeria, 1982, MSc in Econs., 1984; postgrad. in econs., U. Zaria, Nigeria. Asst. registrar Ministry Rural Devel., Bauchi, Nigeria, 1983; lectr. econs. Bauchi State Poly., 1983-90; part time lectr. Ahmadu Bello U., Zaria, 1987-94; economist Ctrl. Bank Nigeria, Abuja, 1990—. Mem. Nigerian Econ. Soc. (life), Royal Econ. Soc. Avocation: writing. Home: CBN Quarters, C25 Flat 150 WUSE 11, POB 5163 Garki Abuja FCT, Nigeria Office: Gov's Office CBN, 5 Obasanjo Way PMB, 0187 Garki-Abuja FCT, Nigeria

DOGRA, JAIDEEP, physician; b. Jodhpur, Rajasthan, India, Dec. 13, 1958; s. Yogender Pal and Chandan Prabha Dogra; m. Neelam Aneja, Nov. 17, 1987; children: Luvdeep, Pearl. M.B.B.S., S.P. Med. Coll., Rajasthan, 1982, MD, 1986. Med. officer S.P. Med. Coll., Rajasthan, 1986-87; med. officer Ctrl. Govt. Health Scheme, Jaipur, 1987-91, sr. med. officer, 1991-96, chief med. officer, 1996—. Reviewer DRUGS (Internat.). Contbr. articles to profl. jours. Recipient Young Scientist award Indian Coun. Med. Rsch., New Delhi, 1991, Young Investigator award Internat. Soc. Chemotherapy, Sweden, 1993; WHO Tropical Disease Rsch. grantee, 1988; Internat. League Dermatol. Socs. scholar, 1992, Outstanding Young Indian Awd., Indian Jr. Chamber. Fellow Royal Soc. Tropical Medicine and Hygiene (Pres.'s Fund 1995); mem. Assn. Physicians of India (life), European Soc. for Dermatological Rsch.; The Soc. for Investigative Dermatology Inc., Rotary. Avocations: antique collecting, meditation. Home: JDA Malviya Nagar, Shiva-Shakti C11, Jaipur 302017, India Office: Ctrl Govt Health Scheme, AG Colony, Jaipur 302015, India

DOGRAMATZIS, DIMITRIS, pharmaceutical company executive; b. City of Drama, Greece, Feb. 21, 1962; s. Vasilios and Maria (Mitrouli) D.; m. Maria Pepona, Sept. 26, 1998. BS in Pharmacy, U. Patras, Greece, 1984; Doctorate in Pharmacology/Toxicology, U. Tex. Med. Br., Galveston, 1988. Postdoctoral fellow in pharmacology U. Tex. Med. Br., 1989; rsch. assoc. M.D. Anderson Cancer Ctr., Houston, 1989-91; med. sales rep. Roche Hellas S.A., Athens, 1992-93, med. mgr., 1993-95; product mgr. Lundbeck Hellas S.A., Athens, 1995-97; country mgr. Greece, Serono Pharma Internat., Athens, 1997-98; mng. dir. Serono Hellas S.A., Athens, 1998—;

freelance translator SPECTRUM Comms., Galveston, 1987-88; freelance med. writer. Contbr. articles to profl. jours. Pvt. Greek Army M.C., 1991-92. Recipient Jane Welsh award for excellence in cardiovascular rsch. U. Tex. Med. Br., 1988, Travel award NATO, 1989. Mem. Greek Assn. CEOs, Greek Pharm. Mktg. Assn., Greek Pharmacists Assn. Avocations: sky diving, flying. Office: 3-5 Konitsis St, Marousi Athens 15125, Greece

DOHERTY, BARBARA WHITEHURST, chemical purchasing manager; b. Charlotte, Jan. 18, 1935; d. Frank Joseph and Geneva Kathryn (Pease) Whitehurst; m. Martin William Doherty, Sr., June 23, 1956 (div. June, 1975); children: Martin William, Jr., Frank Whitehurst. BA in Religion magna cum laude, Duke U., 1956. Cert. notary pub., 1982-97. Rsch. asst., dept. sociology Duke U., Durham, N.C., 1953-56; sec. Pelham (N.Y.) Visiting Nurse & Family Svc., 1958-59; adminstrv. asst. Mecklenburg Times, Charlotte, N.C., 1972-73; bookkeeper Carolina Waterbed Co., Charlotte, N.C., 1972-74; mgr., purchasing and inventory control Reagents, Inc., Charlotte, N.C., 1974-97. Author: poems appear in: Southern Poetry Review, 1992, 1993, 1995, Charlotte Observer, 1993, Sparrowgrass Poetry Forum, 1997. Treas. Charlotte (N.C.) Fair Housing, 1968-70; mem. Charlotte-Mecklenburg Schs. Emergency Sch. Assistance Adv. Com., 1972; Co-chair Paul Leonard for City Council Campaign, Charlotte, 1970; friend of the ct. Swann vs. Bd. Edn., Charlotte, 1972; vol. Marylyn Huff for Sch. Bd., Charlotte, 1970, 74; founder ACLU, Charlotte, 1980 (sec., 1980-82, treas., 1982-84); vol. Harvey Gantt for Mayor campaign, Charlotte, 1983, 85; co-founder, treas. Parents and Friends of Lesbians and Gays, Charlotte, 1988-90; bd. mem. Metrolina Cmty. Svc. Project, Charlotte, 1990-93 (treas., 1992-93). Mem. Phi Beta Kappa, Sigma Delta Pi. Democrat. Avocations: politics, African travel. Home: 1419 Ferncliff Rd Charlotte NC 28211-2220

DOHERTY, EILEEN PATRICIA, economics and finance educator, college dean, educational and media consultant, lawyer, lobbyist; b. Astoria, N.Y., Aug. 21, 1952; d. Joseph John and Joan Ellen (Conway) D.; m. Robert A. Ungar, June 11, 1988 (div. Apr. 1999). BA, St. John's U., 1974, MBA, 1978, JD, 1991; MA, Columbia U., 1976, EdM, 1985. Asst. to dean admissions St. John's U., Jamaica, N.Y., 1974-75, asst. to dir. instnl. rsch., 1975-76, asst. dean evening and weekend coll., 1976-80; asst. dean evening and weekend coll. St. John's U., Jamaica, 1976-80; assoc. dean, dir. evening and weekend coll. St. Vincent's Coll., 1981-88, prof. econs. and fin., 1988-90; prof. econs. and fin. Marymount Coll., Tarrytown, N.Y., 1992—; pres. Towland Ross Assocs. Inc., 1988—, Conway Cons., 1991—; law office mgr., legal asst. Ungar, Gerstman & Pomerance, Garden City, N.Y., 1991-92; of counsel Robert A. Ungar, P.C., Garden City, 1992-95, assoc. atty. Isserlis and Sullivan, Bethpage, N.Y., 1996; assoc. devel. counsel, acting exec. asst. to pres. Battery Park City Authority, N.Y., 1997-98; acting dir. city rels. CUNY, 1998-99; atty. Eileen P. Doherty, P.C., Whitestone, N.Y., 1998—. Assoc. editor The Forum, 1987-89, mng. editor, 1989-90. Hosp. vol. ARC, N.Y.C., 1967; rep. of city comptr. Ctrl. Astoria (N.Y.) Local Devel. Corp., 1982-90; mem. Queens Cmty. Planning Bd., 1980-83; actor, media rels. dir. Douglaston Manor Players, 1998-99, New Theatre Players, 2000. Mem. ABA (law student divsn. rep.), NAFE, N.Y. State Bar Assn., Queens County Bar Assn., Nassau County Bar Assn., Assn. Trial Lawyers Am., N.Y. State Trial Lawyers Assn., Am. Assn. Higher Edn., Am. Fin. Assn., Pres. Soc. Alumni Assn. (rec. sec. 1983-90), Whitestone Boosters Civic Assn., St. John's Alumni Assn. (silver anniversary class chair 1999), Mater Christi Diocesan H.S. Alumni Assn. (30th anniversary class chair), Phi Delta Kappa, Psi Chi, Kappa Delta Pi, Phi Delta Phi. Roman Catholic. Home: 15016 17th Ave Whitestone NY 11357-3121 Office: 150-16 17th Ave Whitestone NY 11357-3121

DOHERTY, GLEN PATRICK, lawyer; b. Toledo, Ohio, Jan. 3, 1963; s. Daniel Owen and Elaine (May) D.; m. Rhonda Jo Hugick, Nov. 14, 1998. BS, Cornell U., 1986; D in Law, Cornell Law Sch., 1989. Bar: Bar: N.Y. 1990, U.S. Dist. Ct. (no. dist.) N.Y. 1990, U.S. Dist. Ct. (so. and ea. dists.) N.Y., 1991. Assoc. Bond, Schoeneck & King, Syracuse, N.Y., 1989-91; assoc. Degraff, Foy, Holt-Harris & Kunz, LLP, Albany, 1991-96, ptnr., 1996—. Co-editor N.Y. Employment Law, 1997—; contbr. articles to profl. jours. Committeeman N.Y. State Reps., Colonie, 1991; designer Albany County Flag, 1979; bd. dirs. Albany Symphony Orch., 1999—. Mem. Lake George Club, Cornell Club of N.Y., Fort Orange Club, Phi Kappa Phi. Republican. Roman Catholic. Avocations: sailing, squash. Fax: 518-436-0210. E-mail: GPD@Degraff-Foy.com. Office: Degraff Foy Holt-Harris & Kunz LLP 90 State St Ste 1100 Albany NY 12207-1780

DOHERTY, LESLIE EDWARD, electronic engineer, research scientist; b. New London, Conn., Oct. 21, 1934; arrived in Australia, 1967; s. Henry Laurence and Mary Lettie (Bradshaw) D.; m. Sheila Ellen Edginton, Oct. 22, 1970 (dec. 1989); children: John, Philip; m. Alfia Alena Mustaeva, Aug. 22, 1996; children: Alexander, Katya. BS in Math. Sci., Adelaide U., 1978; M in Electronic Engring., U. South Australia, 1993, PhD, 1997. Electronic tech. British Aircraft Corp., Bristol, England, 1966-67, Spacetrack, Woomera, South Australia, 1967-68, Adelaide (South Australia) U., 1968-70; design engr. British Aerospace, Salisbury, South Australia, 1970-78; tech. systems officer Western Mining Corp., Parkside, South Australia, 1978-80; systems analyst Thorn EMI, Salisbury, 1980-84; tech. dir. Tracker Communications, Adelaide, 1984-85; chief engr. Suburban Group, Adelaide, 1985-90; rsch. scientist Def. Sci. & Tech. Orgn., Salisbury, 1991-99; cons., CEO Spectral Dynamics, 1999—; bd. dirs. Spectral Dynamics, Adelaide; supr. U. South Australia, 1990; cons. Cabads, Adelaide, 1989; adj. rsch. fellow U. South Australia, 1998. Patentee improvements in monitoring counters, frequency analyzer, reflex correlator, taximeter controlled display system; author: Minimum Requirements for Electronic Speech Production, 1992, Systems Reverse Engineering, 1997. Recipient commendation for sci. leadership and innovative rsch. Australian Sec. Def., 1997. Mem. Electronics Industry Assn., IEEE, Internat. Test and Evaluation Assn. Avocations: painting, music composition. E-mail: les.doherty@ieee.org. Home: 4/64 Shakespeare Ave, Magill SA 5072, Australia

DOHERTY, PETER CHARLES, immunologist; b. Brisbane, Australia, Oct. 15, 1940; came to U.S., 1988; s. Eric C. and Linda Doherty; m. Penelope Stephens, 1965; children: James, Michael. B.V.Sc (hons), U. Queensland, Australia, 1962, MVSc, 1966; PhD, U. Edinburgh, Scotland, 1970; DVs (hon.), U. Queensland; DSc (hon), Australian Nat. U. Vet. officer Animal Rsch. Inst., Brisbane, Australia, 1963-67; sci. officer Moredun Rsch. Inst., Edinburgh, 1967-71; postdoctoral fellow John Curtin Sch. Med. Rsch., Canberra, Australia, 1972-75, prof., head dept. exptl. pathology, 1982-88; from assoc. prof. to prof. The Wistar Inst., Phila., 1975-82; mem., chmn. dept. immunology St. Jude Children's Rsch. Hosp., Memphis, 1988—; Bd. dirs. Internat. Lab. Animal Diseases, Nairobi, 1986-92; mem. NIH exptl. virology study sect., 1982-83, 1990—. Contbr. chpts. to books, articles to profl. jours. Recipient Paul Ehrlich prize Fed. Republic Germany, 1983, Gairdner Internat. award for med. sci. Can., 1986, Lasker award for Basic Med. Rsch., 1995; Co-recipient Nobel Prize for medicine, 1996; Royal Soc. London fellow, 1987. Fellow Australian Acad. Sci. Avocations: walking, reading, skiing. Office: Saint Jude Children's Rsch Hosp 332 N Lauderdale St Memphis TN 38105-2794

DOHERTY, ROBERT FRANCIS, JR., aerospace industry professional; b. North Quincy, Mass., Aug. 7, 1954; s. Robert Francis and Rose Virginia (Wheeler) D. BS in Mgmt., U. Mass., Dartmouth, 1977. Sales mgr. Jordan Marsh Co., Boston, 1977-78; ops. mgr. Cramer Electronics, Newton, Mass., 1978-79; from d/e supr. to sect. mgr. nat. accts. Data Gen. Corp., Westboro, Mass., 1979-84; sales ops. mgr. Printronix, Inc., Malden, Mass., 1984-87; sales/contracts adminstrn. mgr. M/A-Com, Inc., Burlington, Mass., 1987-89; mktg. mgr. M/A-Com, Inc., Chelmsford, Mass., 1989-92; mgr. customer satisfaction M/A Com Inc., Lowell, Mass., 1992-94, internal cons. sys. applications products, 1994-95; program mgr. M/A-COM, Inc., Lowell, Mass., 1995-99; dir. program mgmt. M/A-COM divsn. Tyco Internat., Lowell, Mass., 1999—; newspaper corr., chair various restructuring coms.; cons. internal reengring. Active human rights groups, health founds. Mem. Nat. Contract Mgmt. Assn., Assn. of Old Crows, M/A-Com Mgmt. Club, Nat. Def. Indsl. Assn., Air Force Assn. Roman Catholic. Avocations: jogging, swimming, skiing, antiques, travel. Home: 84 Berkeley St Apt 1 Boston MA 02116-6262

DOHERTY, THOMAS JOSEPH, financial services industry consultant; b. Cambridge, Mass., Oct. 20, 1933; s. Thomas Joseph and Margaret Cecelia (O'Connell) D.; m. Carol Anne Conroy, Jan. 5, 1957; children: William, John, Robert, Susan. AB cum laude, Suffolk U., Boston, 1961. With Merrill Lynch & Co., Inc., N.Y.C., 1958-90; v.p. Merrill Lynch, Pierce, Fenner & Smith Inc., 1978-90; mng. dir. Merrill Lynch White Weld Capital Markets Group, 1979-83, Merrill Lynch Capital Markets, 1989-90; pres., chief exec. officer Merrill Lynch Specialists, Inc., 1985-90; trustee Cin. Stock Exch., 1979-83; past mem. Am. Stock Exch., N.Y. Stock Exch.; bd. govs Pacific Stock Exch., 1984-90. Served with AUS, 1953-55. Mem. Security Traders Assn. N.Y., Nat. Security Traders Assn. (chmn. exchange liaison com. 1986-87), Gen. Alumni Assn. Suffolk U. (bd. dirs. 1976-77). Republican. Roman Catholic.

DOHMEN, KAZUFUMI, physician, educator; b. Chikujo-gun, Fukuoka, Japan, June 3, 1959; s. Yoshiaki and Asano (Ono) D.; m. Kiyoko Yoshimaru, Jan. 15, 1986; 1 child, Saki. DMS, Kyushu U., Fukuoka, 1994. Resident Kyushu U., 1984-86, rsch. fellow, 1986-88; sr. resident Kyushu Koseinenkin Hosp., Hamanomachi Hosp., Fukuoka, 1988-94; rsch. fellow Mt. Sinai Sch. Medicine, CUNY, N.Y.C., 1994-96; physician-in-chief Saga (Japan) Prefectural Hosp., 1996—; clin. assoc. prof. Saga Med. Sch., 1998—. Fellow ACP, Japan Soc. Hepatology, Japanese Soc. Internal Medicine, Japanese Soc. Gastroenterology, Am. Soc. Internal Medicine. Avocations: reading, traveling, listening to music. Office: Saga Prefectural Hosp, 1-12-9 Mizugae, Saga 840 8571, Japan

DOHNANYI, CHRISTOPH VON, musician, conductor; b. Berlin, Sept. 8, 1929; s. Hans and Christina (Bonhoeffer) von D. Student, U. Munich, Hochschule fuer Musik, Munich, Fla. State U., Berkshire Music Ctr.; doctorate (hon.), Oberlin Coll., Cleve. Inst. Music, Case Western Res. U., Eastman Sch. Music, 1998. Coach, condr. Frankfurt (Germany) Opera, 1952-57, gen. music dir., artistic dir., 1968-77; gen. music dir. Lubeck, Germany, 1957-63, Kassel, Germany, 1963-66; dir. West German Radio Symphony, Cologne, 1964-70; artistic dir., chief condr., intendant Hamburg (Germany) State Opera, 1977-84; music dir. designate Cleve. Orch., 1982-84, music dir., 1984—; prin. condr. Philharmonia Orch., London, 1997—; guest condr. in U.S. and Europe, including Salzburg Festival, Chatelet Paris, Zurich Opera House, Israel Philharmonic, Orchestre de Paris, Vienna Philharmonic; prin. guest condr. Philharmonia Orch., London, 1994—. Recordings with Vienna Philharmonia include opera: Wozzeck, Lulu, Fidelio, Flying Dutchman, Salome, 5 Mendelssohn symphonies, works by Stravinsky, Tschaikovsky, Glass, Schnittke; recordings with Cleve. orch. include symphonies of Beethoven, Brahms, Schumann, Bruckner, Dvorak, Mahler, Mozart, Schubert; orchestral works by Bartók, Lutoslawski, R. Strauss, Webern, Ives, Ruggles, Birtwistle; opera Rheingold, Walkure. Recipient Scopus award Am. Friends of Hebrew U. in Jerusalem, 1996, Scroll of Remembrance for Von Dohnányi and Bonhoeffer Families in German resistance U.S. Holocaust Mus., Washington, 1995, Condr. of Yr. award Musical Am., 1992, Comdr.'s Cross Republic of Austria, 1992, Comdr. de L'Ordre des Arts et des Lettres, France, Cross Order of Merit, Germany, Bartok prize, Hungary, 1982, Goethe medal City of Frankfurt, 1979, Richard Straus prize Munich, 1951. Office: Cleve Orch 11001 Euclid Ave Cleveland OH 44106-1713 Address: Colbert Artists Mgmt 111 W 57th St Ste 1416 New York NY 10019-2211

DOHNO, SATOSHI, psychology educator, educational administrator; b. Miyoshi, Hiroshima, Japan, June 15, 1943; s. Misato and Shimayo (Fujikawa) D.; m. Keiko Kawashima, Aug. 21, 1977; children: Mai, Ami. BA, Hiroshima U., 1966, MA, 1971, PhD, 1995. Cert. clin. psychologist, ednl. psychologist, Japan; lic. tchr., Japan. Lectr. Hiroshima Bunkyo U., 1971-77, assoc. prof., 1977-86, prof., 1986-91, dir. Counseling Office, 1977-91; prof. psychology, dir. Counseling Office, Yamaguchi (Japan) U., 1991—, prin. handicapped children's sch., 1991—; vis. prof. U. Md., Balt., 1975-76. Author: Psychological Stress and Adjustment in Modern Society, 1999; editor: Modern Educational Psychology, 1985, Love and Loneliness in Modern People, 1994, Education from a Viewpoint of Psychology, 1994. Commr. Yamaguchi Edn. Office, 1992—, Yamaguchi Police Office, 1995—. Mem. APA, Japanese Psychol. Assn., Assn. for Japanese Clin. Psychologists. Home: 1-5-15 Bishamondai-Higashi, Hiroshim Asa-minami 731-0151, Japan Office: Yamaguchi U, 1677-1 Yoshida, Yamaguchi 753-8513, Japan

DOHRN, RALF, chemical engineer; b. Itzehoe, Germany, Feb. 23, 1958; s. Hans-Peter and Regina (Miehlke) D.; m. Anke Sievers-Paulsen, Aug. 26, 1983; children: Maike, Stefanie, Oliver. Diploma in Indsl. Engring., U. Hamburg, Germany, 1983; Dr. Tech. U., Hamburg, 1986, habilitation, 1994. Rschr. Tech. U. Hamburg, 1983-88, U. Calif., Berkeley, 1988-90; Oberingenieur Tech. U. Hamburg, 1990-96; sr. rschr. Bayer AG, Leverkusen, Germany, 1995—; lectr. Tech. U. Hamburg, 1994—. Author: Phasengleichgenichte in Mehrkomponentensystemen, 1986, Berechnung von Phasengleichgewichten, 1994; contbr. over 40 articles to profl. jours. Mem. local com. CDU, 1990-94, Junge Union, 1976-93. With Germany Army, 1977-78. Recipient Metal Industry award, 1987, Gerhard Hess Prize Deutsche Forschungsgemeinschaft, 1991, fellowship Konrad Adenauer Found., 1979-83, 83-84. Mem. VDI/GVC, Dechema, Deutscher Hochschulverband. Avocations: running, bike riding, family. Office: Bayer AG, Fluid Process Tech Gebaude B310, 51368 Leverkusen Germany

DOHY, JÁNOS, agricultural studies educator; b. Debrecen, Hajdu, Hungary, Mar. 5, 1934; s. János (Göllner) Dohy and Lujza Székely; m. Márta Pogány, July 10, 1960 (div. 1969); 1 child, János; m. Judith Marcsinyi, Sept. 6, 1969; children: Gábor, Péter. Cert. agrl. engring., U. Agrl. Sci., Gödöllö, Hungary, 1957, DAgr in Agrl. Engring & Animal Husbandry, 1963; CSc, PhD in Animal Breeding, Hungarian Acad. Scis., 1968, DSc in Animal Breeding, 1984; D (hon.), Pannon U., Keszthely, Hungary, 1994, U. Agrl. Sci., Debrecen, 1997. Rsch. assoc. Rsch. Inst. Animal Breeding, Budapest, Hungary, 1957-63; asst. prof. U. Vet. Medicine, Budapest, 1964-74; dep. dir. gen. rsch. Inst. Animal Breeding, Herceghalom, Hungary, 1974-75; sr. rsch. worker, dep. dir. gen. Agrl. Coll., Kaposvár, Hungary, 1976-80; prof., head dept. U. Vet. Medicine, Budapest, 1980-84; prof., head dept. U. Agrl. Sci., Gödöllö, 1984-99, dean, 1993-96; coun. mem. European Assn. Animal Production, Rome, 1982-88; mem. adv. bd. Livestock Production Sci., Wageningen, The Netherlands, 1988-98; mem. Sci. Qualifying Com., Budapest, 1988-95; mem. R&D com. Ministry Agr., Budapest, 1990—; chmn. sub-com. Jud. Agrl. Expert Commn., Budapest-Gödöllö, 1990-95; pres. Animal Breeding Soc., Budapest, 1990-95. Editor, co-author: Actual Questions of Applied Animal Genetics, 1978, Beef Cattle Breeding, 1985; co-editor, co-author: Handbook for Cattle Breeders, 1979 (prize of Ministry 1980); author: Genetics in Animal Production, 1979 (prize of Ministry 1980), Genetic Basis in Animal Breeding, 1989, Genetics for Animal Breeders, 1999; mem. adv. bd. Egyptian Jour. Animal Sci. Named Hon. Citizen of Nebr., Gov. Nebr., 1984; recipient Széchenyi prize Pres. of Hungary, Budapest, 1996. Mem. Acad. Scis. (corr. 1993, full 1998), Hungarian Acad. Sci. (pres. dept. agr. 1999—, Acad. prize 1976), Agrl. Biotech. Rsch. Ctr. (sci. coun. 1990—), Com. of Coun. for Accreditation, Hungarian Genetics Assn. (mem. presidium 1987—), Deutsche Gesellschaft für Züchtungskunde (hon.). Avocations: traveling, gardening, music, literature. E-mail: dohy@balin.office.mta.hu. Home: Bogár u 24b, H-1022 Budapest Hungary

DOI, KENJI, theologian, educator; b. Kyoto, Japan, Feb. 9, 1962; s. Junichiro and Yasuko (Ikeda) D.; m. Kaoru Saito, Apr. 16, 1989; 1 child. ThM, Kwanseigakuin U., Nishinomiya-shi, Japan, 1987; MA, Kyoto U., 1990, PhD, 1995. JSPS fellow, faculty of letters Kyoto U., 1995-98; asst. prof. Tamagawa U. faculty of letters, Tokyo, 1998—; vis. prof. Kobe Shoin Women's U., 1993-98, Kwanseigakuin U., 1996-98, Meiji Gakuin U., 1999—; guest rschr. Kobe Shouin Women's U. Inst. Rsch. of Christian Culture, 1996-98. Author: The Knowledge of God and Epektasis, (in Japanese, with English summary) 1998 (Hajime Nakamura prize, Hohshaku Inst. Comparative Religion and Culture 1999); co-author (with Y. Miyatani and others): The Meaning of Sex from the Point of View of Christianity, (in Japanese) 1999; co-author: (with S. Ashina, M. Tsuji) Challenge and Dialogue: Christianity in the Modern World (in Japanese), 2000. Rsch. grantee Niwano Peace Found., 1999, Japan Soc. Promotion Sci., 1995-97, 99-2000. Mem. N.Am. Patristic Soc. E-mail: PXL03303@nifty.ne.jp.

DOI, NORIHISA, computer science educataor and researcher; b. Nishinomiya, Hyogo, Japan, July 11, 1939; m. Harue Doi, Mar. 15, 1969; children: Eiichi, Miki. BE, Keio U., Yokohama, Japan, 1964, ME, 1966, PhD, 1975. Lectr. Inst. Info. Sci., Keio U., 1972-79, asst. prof., 1979-86, prof., 1986-89, prof. Sch. Sci. and Tech., 1989—, dir. Inst. Computer Edn., 1991—; mem. vis. faculty Carnegie-Mellon U., Pitts., 1975-76; vis. prof. U. Waterloo, Ont., Can., 1976; mem. Sci. Coun. Japan, Tokyo, 1994—. Author: Introduction to PASCAL, 1985, 2d edit., 1994, How To Program, 1987, Functions and Organization of Operating Systems, 1987, Introduction to the Language C, 1991. Mem. IEEE, Assn. for Computing Machinery, Japan Soc. for Software Sci. and Tech. Fax: 81-45-560-1262. Office: Keio U, Keio University, 3-14-1 Hiyoshi, Kohoku-ku, Yokohama 223-8522, Japan

DOI, SHOGO, economics educator; b. Fukuyama, Japan, Feb. 7, 1948; s. Kiyotada and Ayako (Kubota) D.; m. Keiko Fujii, Oct. 28, 1973; 2 children. M of Econ., Kwansei Gakuin U., Nishinomiya, Japan, 1972. Asst. prof. Shikuku Gakuin U., Zentsuji, Japan, 1976-77, assoc. prof., 1977-89, prof., 1989—. Author: Postal Savings in Shikoku Area in Japan, 1992, Introduction to Economics, 1996. Office: Shikoku Gakuin U, 3-2-1 Bunkyo-chou, Kagawa, Zentsuji 765-0013, Japan

DOI, TOSHIO, nephrologist; b. Osaka, Japan, Apr. 13, 1952; s. Shoichi and Nobuko (Doi) Morikawa; m. Izumi Iida, May 13, 1981; children: Kei, Akiko. MD, Kobe (Japan) U., 1977; PhD, Kyoto U., 1985. Clin. fellow Amagasaki Hosp., Hyogo, Japan, 1977-79, physician, 1979-84, assoc. chief divsn. internal medicine, 1984-85; instr. dept. pathology Kyoto U., 1985-89; vis. scientist metabolic disease br. NIDDK, NIH, Bethesda, Md., 1987-92; asst. prof. dept. geriatrics Kyoto Univ. Hosp., 1992-95, assoc. dir. divsn. artificial kidneys, 1995-99; cons. prof., chmn. dept. lab. medicine U. Tokushima, Sch. Medicine, Japan, 1995—. Mem. Am. Soc. Nephrology, Internat. Soc. Nephrology, Am. Soc. Investigative Pathology. Avocations: music, sports. Office: U Tokushima Sch Medicine, 3-18-15 Kuramoto-cho, Tokushima 770-8503, Japan

DOI, YUTAKA, electrical engineer; b. Osaka, Japan, Nov. 26, 1936; came to U.S., 1967; s. Hiroshi and Hiroko (Tsuyama) D.; m. Michiko Doi, Nov. 26, 1972; children: Masao, Mary. BA in Econs., Keio U., Tokyo, 1960; BS in Physics, Osaka U., 1967; MS in Physics, San Francisco State U., 1970; PhD in Mech. Engring., U. Miami, 1988. Registered profl. engr., Fla., Ariz. Banker Mitsui Bank, Osaka, 1960-62; tchg. asst. San Francisco State U., 1967-68, U. Calif., Berkeley, 1969-71; elec. engr. Yokogawa Hewlett Packard, Tokyo, 1972-74; rsch. asst. U. Miami, Coral Gables, Fla., 1974-79; prin. staff engr. Motorola, Tempe, Ariz., 1979-98; elec. engr. Johnson Matthey, St. Louis Park, Minn., 1998—; chmn. elec. simulation divsn. Internat. Electronic Mfg. Tech., Tokyo, 1991-92. Contbr. articles to profl. jours. Coun. mem. Keio U. Athletic Club, Tokyo, 1960. Mem. NSPE. Achievements include computer simulation of nuclear energy using nuclear optical model; flowmetry using nuclear magnetic resonance; three dimensional electric and magnetic fields simulation using finite element. Avocations: tennis, painting, piano. Home: 13111 Greenwood Rd Minnetonka MN 55343-8693 Office: Johnson Matthey 3965 Meadowbrook Saint Louis MO 55343

DOIG, STEPHEN GRANT, orthopedist; b. London, Feb. 15, 1954; arrived in Australia, 1956; s. William Grant and Doris Lydia (Berry) D.; m. Susan Jane Venables, Sept. 1980; children: Lachlan Andrew, Katya Gwendolen. MBBS, Melbourne (Australia) U., 1979. Trainee orthopaedics Australian Orthopaedic Assn., Melbourne, 1985-88; registrar orthopaedics Odstock Hosp., Salisbury, Eng., 1989-91; vis. orthopaedic surgeon Repatriation Hosp., Melbourne, 1991—; vis. orthopaedic surgeon Alfred Hosp., Melbourne, 1991—. Am. Field Svc. scholar, 1971, Queen's Scout, 1970. Fellow Royal Australasian Coll. Surgeons in Orthopaedics, Australian Orthopaedic Assn.; mem. Australian Med. Assn. Avocations: cricket, reading, travel, surfing. Office: 9 Erin St, Victoria Richmond 3121, Australia

DOIPHODE, VIJAY VISHWANATH, dean; b. Mahabaleshwar, Maharashba, India, Mar. 23, 1945; s. Vishwanath Waman and Malati (Vaidya) D.; m. Sandhya Vijay Kanade Sajivani, Jan. 26, 1969; children: Miland, Mandar. B.A.M.&S., Tilak Ayurved Mahavidyalay U., Pune, India, 1968, MASc, 1983, PhD, 1987. Jr. lectr. Tilak Ayurveda Mahavidyalaya U., Pune, 1971-80, asst. prof., 1980-90, assoc. prof., 1990-95, prof., 1995—, prin., 1990—; dean Ayurved faculty Pune U., 1995—; mem. of the del. Italy, 1996; lectr. Australian Acad. Natural Medicine, 1997; lectr. in field. Author: Kayachikitsa, 1999; chief editor Ayurvidya, 1989. Organizer health camps, eye camps NIMA, Pune. Recipient Gold medal for PhD, Inst. of Indian Medicine, 1988, 1st prize for PhD thesis Nat. Inst. Rsch. in Sharia, 1993. Mem. Rotary (dir. cmty. and internat. sect.). Home: Chintamani Apt 1025, B Sadashiv Peth, 411 030 Pune India Office: Tilak Ayurved Mahavidyalay, 483/2 Rasta Peth, 411 011 Pune India

DOJAHN, JULIE GOODMAN, chemist, educator; b. Beech Grove, Ind., May 9, 1956; d. Earl Luke and Patricia (Williamson) Goodman; m. William Herbert Dojahn, July 21, 1984. BA in Chemistry, Ind. State U., 1977; MEd in Secondary Edn., U. Houston, 1986, MS in Chemistry, 1994, PhD in Chemistry, 1999. Undergrad. teaching/rsch. asst. Ind. State U., Terre Haute, 1974-77; lab. technician Pillsbury Co., Inc., Seelyville, Ind., 1977-78; sr. lab. technician Pillsbury Co., Inc., Seelyville, 1978-79; quality assurance supr. Chgo. area Foremost-McKesson, Inc., San Francisco, 1979-81; divsn. quality control mgr. Hunt-Wesson, Inc., Valparaiso, Ind., 1981-82; quality assurance supr. Houston Riviana Foods, Inc., Houston, 1982-84; chemistry chair Alvin (Tex.) H.S., 1988-96; instr. chemistry U. Houston, 1997-99; R&D chemist Dow Chem. Co., Freeport, Tex., 1999—; cons. Amoco Chem. Co., Alvin, 1989-94; adj., rsch. assoc. U. Houston, Clear Lake, 1995-97. Author: (textbook) Fundamentals of Chemistry, 1990, 2d edit., 1991. Active Partnerships Between Bus. and Edn., Alvin, 1989-94; mem. Cmty. Adv. Panel, 1996-97. Recipient Honors scholarship Ind. State U., Terre Haute, 1974, Zeon fellowship U. Houston, Tex., 1993, 94, U. Houston fellow, 1997-98, Robert A. Welch fellow, 1998-99. Mem. AAUW, Am. Chem. Soc., Phi Kappa Phi, Alpha Lambda Delta, Sigma Delta Epsilon. Lutheran. Office: Dow Chem Co B-2009 2301 Brazosport Blvd Freeport TX 77541-3257

DOJE CERING, Chinese government official; b. Xiahe County, Gansu, China, 1939. Magistrate Gyaca County, China, 1962-66; various political offices China, 1966-82; vice chmn. Tibet Regional People's Congress, China, 1982-83; vice chmn. Tibet Regional People's Govt., China, 1983-86, chmn., 1986-90; vice min. civil affairs Beijing People's Govt., 1990-93, min. civil affairs, 1993—. Sec. Communist Youth League, Tibet Regional Com., Party Sec., Red Flag People's Commune, Nagqu County, 1970s; standing com. mem. Communist Party of China Tibet Regional Com., 1977, mem. Ctrl. Com. commn. for discipline inspection, 1978-82; mem. 14th Chinese Communist Party Ctrl. Com. Office: Gen Nen Jie, 9 Xi Huang Cheng, West Dist Beijing 100032, China*

DOJLIDO, JAN RYSZARD, hydrochemist, educator; b. Inowroclaw, Poland, June 14, 1930; s. Józef and Stanisława (Sudnik) D.; m. Jadwiga Szych, Feb. 14, 1953; children: Ewa, Marzena. MS, Tech. U., Warsaw, Poland, 1956, PhD, 1967, Dr. Habilis, 1977. Asst. Tech. U., Warsaw, 1954-55; head of dept. Inst. Water Mgmt., Warsaw, 1958-72; prof. Inst. Meteorology and Water Mgmt., Warsaw, 1972-85, 88—, Tech. U., Radom, Poland, 1993—; lectr. Brack (Libya) U., 1985-88. Author: Instrumental Methods of Water Analysis, 1980, Chemistry of Water and Water Pollution, 1993, Chemistry of Surface Waters, 1995. Mem. Polish Acad. Sci. (com. water mgmt. 1990—, com. analytical chemistry 1988-97). Home: Poli Gojawiczynskiej 15m15, 01-773 Warsaw Poland Office: Tech U Radom, Chrobrego 27, 26-600 Radom Poland

DÖKMECI, FULYA, obstetrician-gynecologist, educator; b. Ankara, Turkey, Feb. 22, 1962; d. Ali and Nurten (Özgen) Çeken; m. Abdülkadir Dökmeci; 1 child, Papatya Nur. MD, Ankara U., 1985, speciality in ob-gyn., 1991. MD Family Planning Ctr. Zekai Tahir Burak Hosp., Ankara, 1985-86; resident dept. ob-gyn. Ege U. Sch. Medicine, Izmir, Turkey, 1986-88; rschr. dept. ob-gyn. Chiba (Japan) U. Sch. Medicine, 1987-88; resident dept. ob-gyn. Ankara U. Sch. Medicine, 1988-91, specialist ob-gyn., 1991-96, assoc. prof., 1996—, dir. tng. med. instrs., 1998-99; cons. Johns Hopkins Project for Internat. Edn. of Gynecology and Obstetrics, Ankara, 1996. Fgn. affairs mem. Turkish Ice Sports Fedn., Ankara, 1997—. Mem. Accreditation Coun. for Gynecologic Endoscopy. Avocations: tennis, skiing, playing guitar, watching figure skating. Office: Ankara U Fac Medicine, Turna Cikmazi B 21/2, 06100 Cebeci Turkey

DOKMECI, VEDIA, architect, educator; b. Istanbul, Turkey, Sept. 10, 1939; d. Remzi and Aliye (Saydamel) Arpaci; m. Cengiz Mustafa Dokmeci, Feb. 15, 1965; children: Mehmet, Remzi. Dipl. engring., Istanbul Tech. U., 1962; MArch, Columbia U., 1969, PhD, 1972. Architect Archtl. Bur., Lausanne, Switzerland, 1962-64; asst. prof. Istanbul Tech. U., 1965-67, 77-88; sr. planner Health and Hosp. Gov., Chgo., 1972-74; assoc. prof. Istanbul Tech. U., 1977-88, prof., 1988—. Co-author: (with H. Ciraci) Beyoglu, 1990, (with Y. Dulger, L. Berkoz) Transformation of Istanbul's CBD, 1993, (with H. Yurekli, F. Erkok) Istanbul's Residential Doors, 1996. Recipient First prize Beyazit Plaza Competition, City Govt., Istanbul, 1988, Sci. prize Turkish Acad. Scis., 1999. Home: Ciragan C Bogazici #73-2, 80700 Istanbul Turkey Office: Faculty Architecture, Istanbul Tech Univ, 80191 Istanbul Turkey

DOKOUTCHAEV, VLADIMIR ANATOLIEVICH, communications company executive; b. Moscow, Nov. 1, 1958; s. Anatoliy Timofeevich Dokoutchaev and Anna Petrovna (Savina) Dokoutchaeva. Grad. engr. of comm., Moscow Telecomms. Inst., 1981, Tech. Candidate Scis., 1990, DSc, 1999. Engr. Moscow Telecomm. Inst., 1981-88, sr. sci. rschr., 1988-92, head sci. comm. lab., 1992-94; assoc. prof. Moscow Tech. U. Comm. and Informatics, 1994-99, prof., 1999—; gen. dir. Telesoft Ltd., Moscow, 1992—; qualified approved applications engr. MITEL Semiconductor, Canada, 1997. Author: Research and Development of Automatic Methods for Urban Digital Networks Design and Management, 1999; editor: Telecommunications Systems and Equipment Terms and Definitions, 1998; contbr. articles to profl. jours. Recipient Govt. medal 850th Anniversary of Moscow, 1997. Mem. Asn. for Producing Orgns. in Comm. (exec. dir. 1997—), N.Y. Acad. Scis., Russian Popov Sci. Soc. (diplom 1995). Avocations: books, swimming, tennis. E-mail: dva@tlsoft.msk.ru. Home: PO Box 47, 115563 Moscow Russia Office: Telesoft Ltd, Aviamotornay st 8a, 111024 Moscow Russia

DOKTOROV, ALEXANDER BORISOVICH, physicist, researcher, educator; b. Omsk, Russia, Feb. 23, 1947; s. Boris Dmitrievich and Nina Orestovna (Skolskaya) D.; m. Lyudmila Borisovna Efremova, July 3, 1991. Grad., Novosibirsk (Russia) State U., 1969, PhD in Physics, 1973. Union rschr. Inst. Chem. Kinetics and Combustion, Novosibirsk, 1973-80, sr. rschr., 1980-87, leader rschr., 1987-93, head dept., 1993—; asst. prof. Novosibirsk State U., 1974-85, assoc. prof., 1986-93, prof., 1994—. Contbr. articles to profl. jours. Recipient award Siberian br. Russian Acad. Scis., 1989, hon. award Russian Acad. Scis., 1999. Mem. Mendeleev Chem. Soc./Russian Acad. Scis. Avocations: reading, technology, travel. E-mail: doktorov@ns.kinetics.nsc.ru. Office: Inst Chem Kinetics/Combust, SB RAS, Institutskaya 3, 630090 Novosibirsk Russia

DOKU, EMMANUEL VICTOR, crop scientist, educator; b. Ada, Ghana, May 21, 1931; s. Christian and Augusta Buerkuor (Puplampu) D.; m. Mabel Vanderpuije, Aug. 26, 1961; children: Victor, Molly, Vera, Evelyn, Rudolf. BS in Agriculture, U. Coll. Gold Coast, Accra, 1956; diploma in agrl. sci., Sch. Agriculture, Cambridge, England, 1960; PhD, U. New England, 1976. Agrl. officer Ministry of Agriculture, Ghana, 1956-60; rsch. officer Coun. for Scientific and Indsl. Rsch., Ghana, 1960-64; lectr. U. Ghana, 1964-73, sr. lectr., 1973-77, prof., 1977-2000, emeritus prof., 2000, dean of faculty, 1981-86; cons. FAO/UN, Sri Lanka, 1984, Ethiopia, 1986-88, chief tech. adviser, Western Samoa, 1988-92; bd. chmn. Crops Rsch. Inst., Ghana, 1994-99. Author: Cassava in Ghana, 1969; editor: Grain Legumes in Ghana, 1976, Crop Improvement in Ghana, 1978. Recipient Disting. Svc. award Internat. Soc. for Tropical Root Crops, 1989. Fellow Ghana Acad. Arts and Scis. (hon. sec. 1993-96), Ghana Inst. Horticulture. Methodist. Achievements include research in areas of root crops and food legumes, mainly Vigna subterranea. Avocations: gardening, singing, walking. Home: PO Box 1455, Dansoman Accra Ghana Office: U Ghana, Crop Science Dept, Legon Accra Ghana

DOKUCHAEV, VLADIMIR PLATONOVICH, physicist, educator; b. Semenov, Russia, Aug. 19, 1932; s. Platon Ivanovich and Eugenia Ivanovna (Volskaya) D.; m. Ariadna Victorovna Tolmacheva, oct. 4, 1966; children: Juri, Lionid. Student, U. Gorkii, 1951-56, DSc, 1959. Rschr. Radio Inst., Gorkii, Russia, 1959-80; prof. U. Gorkii, 1980—; chmn., head dept. Gorkii State U., 1983-88; prof. Internat. Soros Sci. Edn. Program, 1998, 2000. Contbr. articles to profl. jours. Dep. dist. coun., City of Gorkii, 1968-72. Mem. Radio Soc. Russia. Avocations: swimming, gardening. Home: 142A Gorkii St Apt #41, 603000 Nizhny Novgorod Russia Office: Nizhny Novgorod State U, 23 Gagarin prospect, 603600 Nizhny Novgorod Russia

DOKURNO, ANTHONY DAVID, lawyer; b. Gardner, Mass., Mar. 14, 1957; s. Anthony Chester and Damey Anteena (Aleson) D. BA, Holy Cross Coll., 1979; JD, Vt. Law Sch., 1982; postgrad., Johns Hopkins U., 1993-94. Bar: Mass. 1982, U.S. Ct. Appeals for the Armed Forces 1986, U.S. Supreme Ct. 1987. Pvt. practice law Fitchburg, Mass., 1982-86; appellate counsel Navy-Marine Corps Appellate Rev. Activity, Washington, 1986-88; atty. admiralty div. JAG, Washington, 1988-90, atty. ops. and mgmt., 1991-93. Assoc. counsel, bd. vets. appeals Dept. Vets. Affairs, 1994-96; analyst Dept. of Def., 1996—. Comdr. USNR, 1998—. Mem. Maritime Law Assn., Navy League, Nat. Cryptologic History Found., Am. Legion, Naval Res. Assn., Mensa, Phi Beta Kappa. Home: 200 N Pickett St Apt 1504 Alexandria VA 22304-2127

DOLACK, MONTE A., artist; b. Great Falls, Mont., May 23, 1950; s. Michael George and Mary (Miller) D.; m. Linda LaFond, May 10, 1970 (div. 1972); m. Mary Beth Percival, May 11, 1984. Student, Mont. State U., 1969-70, U. Mont., 1970-74. Pvt. practice Missoula, Mont., 1974—; bd. dirs. Mont. Arts Coun., Missoula, U. of Mont. Fine Art Adv. Bd., Missoula; delegate Japan Economic Trade Org., Tokyo, 1995. Represented in numerous collections nationally; designed over 125 posters for state and nat. events. Adv. bd. Big Hole River Found., Mont., 1999; bd. mem. Mont. Trout Unlimited, 1995—. Named in 100 Montanans of the 20th Century Missolian Newspaper, 1999, Best of Show L.A. Soc. Illustrators, 1991. Mem. Japan Club (founding). Democrat. Avocations: fly-fishing, cultural travel, river floating, hiking, bird watching. E-mail: refuge@bigsky.net. Office: Monte Dolack Gallery 139 W Front St Missoula MT 59802-4303

DOLAN, ANDREW KEVIN, lawyer; b. Chgo., Dec. 7, 1945; s. Andrew O. and Elsie (Grafner) D.; children: Andrew, Francesca, Melinda. BA, U. Ill., Chgo., 1967; JD, Columbia U., 1970, MPH, 1976, DPH, 1980. Bar: Wash. 1980. Asst. prof. law Rutgers-Camden Law Sch., N.J., 1970-72; assoc. prof. law U. So. Calif., L.A., 1972-75; assoc. prof. pub. health U. Wash., Seattle, 1977-81; ptnr. Bogle & Gates, Seattle, 1988-93; pvt. practice law, 1993—. Commr. Civil Svc. Commn., Lake Forest Park, Wash., 1981; mcpl. judge City of Lake Forest Park, 1982-98. Russell Sage fellow, 1975. Mem. Order of Coif, Washington Athletic Club. Avocation: book collecting. Office: 5800 Columbia Ctr 701 5th Ave Seattle WA 98104-7097

DOLAN, DERMOT VINCENT, pharmaceutical company executive; b. Dublin, Ireland, Apr. 4, 1921; s. Dominick and Sarah (Nolan) D.; m. Susan Theresa Dolan, June 28, 1948; 1 child, Mary. Grad., Castleknock Coll., Dublin, 1938. Exec. Dominick A. Dolan & Co. Ltd., Dublin, 1938-55; mng. dir. Hedleys Labs. Ltd., Dublin, 1955-82, Ward Blenkinsop (Vet.) Ltd., London, 1982-88, Delta Pharms. Ltd., dublin, 1988—; bd. dirs. French Cosmetic Distbn. Ltd., Dublin, Ben Kat (Ireland) Ltd., Dublin, Internat. Alkaloids Ltd., Dublin. Mem. Hibernian United Svc. Club, Elm Park Golf Club. Roman Catholic. Avocations: swimming, theatre, horse racing. Office: Delta Pharms Ltd, 26 Airfield Ct, Dublin 4, Ireland

DOLAN, JAMES PATRICK, surgeon; b. Manorhamilton, Ireland, May 17, 1966; s. Patrick and Mary Rose D.; married. AA, DeAnza Coll., 1997; BS, San Diego State U., 1991; MD, Stanford U., 1995. Lic. physician. Contbg. author textbooks in field; contbr. articles to profl. jours. Capt. USAF, 1991—. Recipient Burchmit Meml. scholarship DeAnza Coll., 1997, rsch. award AHA, 1990, univ. scholar award SDSU, 1990, others. Mem. AMA, AAAS, Golden Key, Phi Beta Kappa.

DOLAN, LOUISE ANN, physicist; b. Wilmington, Del., Apr. 5, 1950. BA, Wellesley Coll., 1971; PhD in Physics, MIT, 1976. Jr. fellow in physics Harvard U., 1976-79; asst. prof. physics Rockefeller U., N.Y.C., 1979-82, assoc. prof., 1983-90, lab. head, 1990; prof. physics U. N.C., Chapel Hill, 1990—; program dir. for theoretical physics NSF, 1995. John Simon Guggenheim fellow, 1988. Fellow Am. Phys. Soc. (Maria Goeppert-Mayer award 1987). Office: U NC Dept Physics Chapel Hill NC 27599-0001

DOLAN, PETER J., corporate financial consultant; b. N.Y.C., July 22, 1927; s. Peter Dolan and Mary Fitzpatrick; m. Ruth E. Bachop, Aug. 26, 1950; children: Robert, Kevin, Paul, James, William, Eileen, Elizabeth, Mary. MS, Columbia U., 1954; BBA, Manhattan Coll., 1949. CPA, N.Y. Ptnr., nat. dir. Ernst & Young, N.Y.C., 1954-83; vice-chmn., dir. Universal Matchbox Ltd., Hong Kong, 1985-89; prin. P. J. Dolan Assocs., Algonquin Assocs., Fla., 1985—; dir. Springer-Verlag USA, N.Y., 1983-88, Hodder Assocs. LLC, N.Y., 1998—. Chmn. fin. com., dir. Marymount Manhattan Coll., 1988-92; mem. fin. com., dir. Calvary Hosp., N.Y., 1985-94; dir., pres. S.E. Yonkers Comty. Assn., N.Y., 1968-70; dir. Armonk (N.Y.) Pub. Schs., 1971-75. Recipient Ann. Outstanding award Campfire Girls, N.Y., 1970-72.

DOLAN, REGINA, security firm executive. CFO, sr. v.p. Paine Webber Group Inc., N.Y.C., sr. v.p., CAO, 2000—. Office: Paine Webber Group Inc Ste 302 1285 Avenue Of The Americas Fl Sconc New York NY 10019-6096*

DOLAN, THOMAS CHRISTOPHER, professional society administrator; b. Chgo., Dec. 31, 1947; s. Thomas Christopher and Bernice Mary (Doyle) D.; m. Georgia Ann Siebke, Feb. 14, 1983; children: William, Barbara, Lauren. BBA, Loyola U., Chgo., 1969; PhD, U. Iowa, 1977. Instr. U. Iowa, Iowa City, 1971-72; vis. fellow U. Wash., Seattle, 1973-74; asst. prof. U. Mo., Columbia, 1974-79; assoc. prof., dir. St. Louis U., 1979-86; v.p. Am. Coll. Healthcare Execs., Chgo., 1986-87, exec. v.p., 1987-91, pres., 1991—; mem. Accrediting Commn. on Edn. for Health Svcs. Adminstrn., Washington, 1985-86; chmn. Assn. Univ. Programs in Health Adminstrn., Washington, 1983-84; cons. HEW, Kansas City, Mo., 1974-79, State of Mo., Jefferson City, 1974-79. Author: Systems for Health Care Administration: A Model for the Education of Health Manpower, 1975; contbr. articles to profl. jours. Pres. Mental Health Assn. Boone County, Columbia, Mo., 1977-78, Mental Health Assn. Mo., Jefferson City, 1980-82; bd. dirs. Nat. Mental Health Assn., Washington, 1982-83, Alexian Bros. Hosp., St. Louis, 1980-86, Inst. for Diversity in Health Mgmt., 1994—; chair Assn. Forum, 1999—; chair-elect Am. Soc. Assn. Execs. Found., Washington, 1999—. Fellow Am. Coll. Healthcare Execs., Am. Soc. Assn. Execs. (cert. assn. exec.); mem. APHA. Roman Catholic. Avocations: golf, motorcycling, reading. Office: Am Coll Healthcare Execs 1 N Franklin St Ste 1700 Chicago IL 60606-3421

DOLAN, TOM, Olympic athlete; b. Sept. 15, 1975. Grad., U. Mich., 1998. Swimmer; gold medalist 400m individual medley Olympic Summer Games, 1994, 98; 14-time U.S. nat. champion; sponsor Carl-Burke Swim Club; 4 nat. titles, 1994, 98; gold medalist 400m Individual Medley Olympic Summer Games, Sydney, 2000. Spokesperson Am. Lung Assn. Achievements include the World record-holder 400m individual medley, Am. record-holder 500y, 1650 freestyle and 400y individual medley. Office: c/o USA Swimming 1 Olympic Plz Colorado Springs CO 80909-5746

DOLAND, JUDY ANN, administrative assistant, retired financial rating company associate; b. Duluth, Minn., June 29, 1940; d. Burnham Oscar and Mary Katherine (Sederholm) D. Student, Mt. San Antonio Jr. Coll., Walnut, Calif., 1960. Subs. ledger acct. Pacific Intermountain Express, L.A., 1963-64; various positions Dun & Bradstreet, L.A., 1958-63, 64-80, state sales guide rep., 1980-83; payroll cashier Dun & Bradstreet, Monterey Park, Calif., 1983-85; exec. sec. Dun & Bradstreet, Long Beach, Calif., 1985-90; exec. sec. L.A. zone Dun & Bradstreet, Van Nuys, Calif., 1990-92; exec. sec. Woodland Hills dist. Dun & Bradstreet, Woodland Hills, Calif., 1992-93, ret., 1993; adminstrv. asst., office mgr. Sharpe Heating & Ventilating, Alhambra, Calif., 1995-96; office mgr. Air Blast Inc., Alhambra, 1996—. Avocations: environmental protection, science, art, music, tennis.

DOLANSKY, VACLAV, marketing educator; b. Prague, Czech Republic, Sept. 2, 1937; s. Vaclav and Ludmila D.; m. Vera Pitelkova (div.); 1 child, Jana; m. Bozena Rosbergova, Apr. 14, 1989; children: Marketa, Vit. Diploma in Engring., Czech Tech. U., Prague, 1962, PhD, 1977, Assoc. Prof., 1980. Designer Motor-Cycle Co., Prague, 1956-57; asst. Czech Tech. U., 1962-80, assoc. prof., 1980—; owner Dolansky-Consulting, Prague, 1990—; head Czech-Swiss Inst., Prague, 1994-96; designer machine Motor-Cycle Co., Prague, 1956-57; seminar presenter Czech Tech. U., 1962-80, lessons presenter, 1980—. Translator: (books) Kotler: Marketing Management, 1992, 98 (Best Book of Yr. PROFIT 1993), Koontz, Weihrich: Management, Wisniewski: Quantitative Methods for Decision Makers, 1996, Donnelly, Gibson, Ivancevich: Management, 1997, Cooper, Lane: Practical Marketing Planning, 1999, Palmer, Weaver: Information Management, 1999; author: Project Management 1996. Avocations: playing violin, jogging. Office: Faculty of Machinery, Horska 3, 12800 Prague 2, Czech Republic

DOLBY, RAY MILTON, engineering company executive, electrical engineer; b. Portland, Oreg., Jan. 18, 1933; s. Earl Milton and Esther Eufemia (Strand) D.; m. Dagmar Baumert, Aug. 19, 1966; children—Thomas Eric, David Earl. Student, San Jose State Coll., 1951-52, 55, Washington U., St. Louis, 1953-54; BSEE, Stanford U., 1957; Ph.D. in Physics (Marshall scholar 1957-60, Draper's studentship 1959-61, NSF fellow 1960-61), Cambridge (Eng.) U., 1961, ScD (hon.), 1997. Comml. pilot instrument rating FAA. Electronic technician/jr. engr. Ampex Corp., Redwood City, Calif., 1949-53; engr. Ampex Corp., 1955-57, sr. engr., 1957; PhD research student in physics Cavendish Lab., Cambridge U., 1957-61, research in long wavelength x-rays, 1957-63; fellow Pembroke Coll., 1961-63; cons. U.K. Atomic Energy Authority, 1962-63; UNESCO adviser Central Sci. Instruments Orgn., Chandigarh, Punjab, India, 1963-65; owner, chmn., CEO Dolby Labs. Inc., San Francisco and Wootton Bassett, U.K., 1965—. Trustee Univ. High Sch., San Francisco, 1978-84; bd. dirs. San Francisco Opera; bd. govs. San Francisco Symphony; mem. Marshall Scholarship selection com., 1979-85. Served with U.S. Army, 1953-54. Decorated officer Most Excellent Order of Brit. Empire; recipient Beech-Thompson award Stanford U., 1956, Emmy award, 1957, 89, Trendsetter award Billboard, 1971, Top 200 Execs. Bi-Centennial award, 1976, Lyre award Inst. High Fidelity, 1972, Emile Berliner Maker of the Microphone award Emile Berliner Assn., 1972, Sci. and Engring. award Acad. Motion Picture Arts and Scis., 1979, Oscar award, 1989, Pioneer award Internat. Teleprodn. Soc., 1988, Edward Rhein Ring award Edward Rhein Found., 1988, Life Achievement award Cinema Audio Soc., 1989, Grammy award NARAS, 1995, Nat. Medal Tech., U.S. Dept. Commerce, 1997, Medal of Achievement, Am. Electronics Assn., 1997; named Man of Yr. Internat. Tape Assn., 1987; hon. fellow Pembroke Coll., Cambridge U., 1983. Fellow Audio Engring. Soc. (bd. govs. 1972-74, 79-84 Silver Medal award 1971, Gold medal award 1992, pres. 1980-81), Brit. Kinematograph, Sound and TV Soc. (outstanding tech. and sci. award 1995), Soc. Motion Picture and TV Engrs. (Samuel L. Warner award 1979, Alexander M. Poniatoff Gold Medal 1982, Progress award 1983, hon. mem. 1992), Inst. Broadcast Sound; mem. IEEE (Ibuka award 1997), St. Francis Yacht Club, Pacific Union Club, Tau Beta Pi. Achievements include inventions, research, publs. in video tape recording, x-ray microanalysis, noise reduction and quality improvements in audio and video systems; holder 50 U.S. patents. Office: Dolby Labs 100 Potrero Ave San Francisco CA 94103-4886

DOLCE, MAURO, structural engineer, educator; b. Rome, July 19, 1953; s. Lorenzo and Elda (Silvestri) D.; m. M. Cristina Zappelli, Sept. 1, 1983; children: Olimpia, Arianna. Degree in civil engring., U. La Sapienza, 1978. Ofcl. FS Railway Co., Rome, 1979-84; rsch. assoc. U. L'Aquila, Italy, 1984-88; from assoc. prof. to prof. U. Basilicata, Potenza, Italy, 1988—; dir. dept. structures, dep. fac. engrg. 1999—, U. Basilicata, 1995—; cons. Italian Seismic Survey, Rome, 1991—, Union Internat. des Chemins de Fer, 1995. Mem. Italian Assn. for Earthquake Engring. (steering com. 1995—). Office: U Basilicata, C da Macchia Romana, 85100 Potenza Italy

DOLE, ELIZABETH HANFORD, former charitable organization administrator, former secretary of labor, former secretary of transportation; b. Salisbury, N.C., July 29, 1936; d. John Van and Mary Ella (Cathey) Hanford; m. Robert Joseph Dole (former U.S. Senator from Kans.), Dec. 6, 1975. BA with honors in Polit. Sci., Duke U., 1958; postgrad., Oxford (Eng.) U., summer 1959; MA in Edn. and Govt., Harvard U., 1960, JD, 1965. Bar: D.C. 1966. Staff asst. to asst. sec. for edn. HEW, Washington, 1966-67; practiced law Washington, 1967-68; assoc. dir. legis. affairs, then exec. dir. Pres.'s Com. for Consumer Interests, Washington, 1968-71; dep. asst. to Pres. The White House, Washington, 1971-73; commr. FTC, Washington, 1973-79; chmn. Voters for Reagan-Bush, 1980; dir. Human Services Group, Office of Exec. Br. Mgmt., Office of Pres.-Elect, 1980; asst. to Pres. for pub. liaison, 1981-83; sec. U.S. Dept. Transp., 1983-87; with Robert Dole Presdl. Campaign, 1987-88; participant 1988 Presdl. and Congl. campaigns; sec. U.S. Dept. Labor, 1989-90; pres. ARC, 1991-99; mem. nominating com. Am. Stock Exch., 1972, N.C. Consumer Coun., 1972. Trustee Duke U., 1974-88; mem. coun. Harvard Law Sch. Assocs., mem. vis. com. Harvard Sch. Pub. Health, 1992-95; mem. bd. overseers Harvard U., 1989-95. Recipient Arthur S. Flemming award U.S. Govt., 1972, Humanitarian award Nat. Commn. Against Drunk Driving, 1988, Disting. Alumni award Duke U., 1988, N.C. award, 1991, Lifetime Achievement award (Breaking The Glass Ceiling) Women Execs. in State Govt., 1993, North Carolinian of the Yr. award N.C. Press Assn., 1993, Radcliffe medal, 1993, Leadership award LWV, 1994, Maxwell Finland award Nat. Found. Infectious Diseases, 1994, Disting. Svc. award Nat. Safety Coun., 1989, Raoul Wallenberg award for Humanitarian Svc., 1995, Christian Woman of Yr. award, 1996; named one of Am.'s 200 Young Leaders, Time mag., 1974, one of World's 10 Most Admired Women, Gallup Poll, 1988, one of 10 most fascinating people 1996 Barbara Walter's Spl., most inspiring polit. figure 1996 MSNBC, 3d most admired woman in Am. Good Housekeeping, 1996, 98; selected for Safety and Health Hall of Fame Internat., 1993; inducted into Nat. Women's Hall of Fame, 1995. Mem. Phi Beta Kappa, Pi Lambda Theta, Pi Sigma Alpha. Office: PO Box 58247 Washington DC 20037-8247

DOLE, ROBERT J., lawyer, former senator; b. Russell, Kans., July 22, 1923; s. Doran R. and Bina Dole; m. Elizabeth Hanford, Dec. 1975. Student, U. Kans., 1941-43, U. Ariz.; A.B., Washburn Mcpl. U., Topeka, 1952, LL.B., 1952; LL.D. (hon.), Washburn U., Topeka, 1969. Bar: Kans. 1952. Mem. Kans. Ho. of Reps., 1951-53; sole practice Russell, Kans., 1953-61; Russell County atty., 1953-61; mem. 87th Congress from 6th Dist., Kans., 88th-90th congresses from 1st Dist., Kans., U.S. Senate from Kans., 1969-96; chmn. Rep. Nat. Com., 1971-73; Senate majority leader U.S. Senate from Kans., 1985-86, Senate Rep. leader, 1987-96; of counsel Verner, Liipfert, Bernhard, McPherson & Hand, 1999—; Rep. vice-presdl. candidate, 1976; Rep. presdl. candidate, 1996. Chmn. Dole Found. Served with AUS, 1943-48, World War II. Decorated Purple Heart (2), Bronze Star with 2 clusters. Recipient Horatio Alger award Horatio Alger Assn. Disting. Ams., 1988, Presdl. medal Freedom. Mem. Am. Legion, VFW, DAV, 4-H Fair Assn., Masons, Shriners, Elks, Kiwanis, Kappa Sigma. Methodist. Office: Verner Liipfert Bernhard McPherson & Hand 901 15th St NW Ste 4 Washington DC 20005-2327

DOLE, TRUX, high technology marketing executive; b. Sharon, Conn., Sept. 6, 1964; s. C. Minot and Istar Haupt (Mudge) D.; m. Lauren Munro, July 12, 1997. BA in Polit. Sci., Duke U., 1987; MBA, U. Oreg., 1999. Asst. account exec. North Castle Ptnrs. Advt., Stamford, Conn., 1989-90; project dir. Americares Found., Inc., New Canaan, Conn., 1990-97, dir. program devel., 1991-97; competititive analysis intern In-Focus Sys., Wilsonville, Oreg., 1998; product mktg. mgr. Tektronix, Inc., Wilsonville, 1999-00, Xerox Corp., Wilsonville, 2000—. Prodr., dir. ednl. video Travel—The 3d Option, 1988. Mem. adj. bd. 10th Mountain Divsn. Found. Mem. Beta Gamma Sigma. Avocations: skiing, snowboarding, fly fishing, camping, hunting. E-mail: trux.dole@tek.com. Home: 1 Jefferson Pkwy Apt 229 Lake Oswego OR 97035-8816

DOLEAC, CHARLES BARTHOLOMEW, lawyer; b. New Orleans, Sept. 20, 1947; s. Cyril Bartholomew and Emma Elizabeth (St. Clair) D.; m. Denise Kilfoyle, Feb. 2, 1972; children: Keith Gabriel, Jessa Lee. BS cum laude, U. N.H., 1968; JD, NYU, 1971. Bar: Mass. 1972, N.H. 1972, Maine 1973. Law clk. to Justice Grimes N.H. Supreme Ct., Concord, 1972-73; assoc. Boynton, Waldron, Dill & Aeschliman, Portsmouth, N.H., 1973-76; ptnr. Boynton, Waldron, Doleac, Woodman & Scott, Portsmouth, 1977—; appointed mediator N.H. Superior Ct., 1992—; del. to tour Chinese legal system Chinese Ministry Justice, 1982; del. to People's Republic of China/U.S. joint session on trade investments and econ. law Chinese Ministry Justice/U.S. Dept. Justice, Beijing, 1987; propr. Portsmouth Athenaeum; moderator seminars on ethics for Leaders & Comparative Cultures and Values/East & West and Exec. Seminar Aspen Inst., 1990-95; mediator exec. sem. Aspen Inst., 1997-2000; mem. faculty Southwestern Legal Found. Internat. & Comparative Law Ctr., 1997—; official guest Fgn. Ministry Japan, Tokyo, 1998; spkr. ethics Ann. Nat. Conf. Appellate Ct. Clks., 1999-2000. Contbr. articles to profl. jours. Mem. citizens adv. coun. Portsmouth Cmty. Devel. Program, 1976-77; incorporator N.H. Charitable Found.; pres., bd. dirs. Seacoast United Way; chmn. Portsmouth Bd. Bldg. Appeals, 1976-77; chmn. stewardship com. Soc. Preservation New Eng. Antiquities, 1980-84, also trustee; pres. bd. trustees Strawbery Banke Mus., 1985-88; founder Daniel Webster Inn of Ct., 1993, Charles C. Doe Inn of Ct., 1994, Portsmouth Peace Treaty Forum, 1994; founder, pres. Japan-Am. Soc. N.H., 1988. NEH fellow, Aspen Inst.; named Citizen of Yr. Portsmouth, N.H., 1991. Fellow N.H. Bar Found; mem. ATLA, Mass. Bar Assn., Maine Bar Assn., N.H. Bar Assn., N.H. Trial Lawyers Assn., Maine Trial Lawyers Assn. Avocations: masters swimming. Home: Little Harbor Rd Portsmouth NH 03801 Office: Boynton Waldron Doleac Woodman & Scott PA 82 Court St Portsmouth NH 03801-4414

DOLECEK, QUENTIN EDWARD, electronics engineer; b. Sioux Falls, S.D., May 27, 1940; s. Richard Leroy and Avis Elaine (Preusch) D.; m. Patricia Naomi Naymick, Aug. 3, 1963; children: Koralleen, Kathryn. BSEE, U. Md., 1964; BSME, Cath. U., 1970, DSc, 1980. Electronic engr. Naval Ship R&D Ctr., Washington, 1958-63, head systems support, 1973-80; sr. staff JHU Applied Physics Lab., Laurel, Md., 1980-84, prin. staff, 1984-88, head algorithm devel. sect., 1989-93, chief engr., 1993—; cons. Dept. of Def., Washington, 1984-88, Interstate Electronics, L.A., 1986-90. Contbr. articles to profl. jours. Instr. ARC, Washington, 1980-83; troop leader Girl Scouts Am., 1980's. With USN, 1964-68. Named One of Top Ten Technology Talents Washington Technology, 1989; recipient Letter of Commendation, Dep. Undersec. of Def., 1984, 85, 90. Mem. IEEE, Wash. Soc. of Engrs. (Lifetime Achievement), Sigma Xi. Achievements include multiple patents in parallel processing; built first high-speed digital recorder/computer for U.S. sonars. Home: 13832 Dayton Meadows Ct Dayton MD 21036-1000 Office: JHU Applied Physics Lab John Hopkins Rd Laurel MD 20723

DOLEJS, VACLAV, chemical engineering educator; b. Prague, Aug. 29, 1941; s. Vaclav and Marie (Kadlecova) D.; m. Ivana Pulpanova, Sept. 22, 1972 (div. 1980); 1 child, Jane; m. Vera Kralickova, Mar. 2, 1991. MS, U. Chem. Tech., Prague, 1963; PhD, U. Chem. Tech., Pardubice, Czech Republic, 1973. Lectr. U. Chem. Tech., Pardubice, Czech Republic, 1964-66; sr. lectr. U. Pardubice, 1966—. Avocation: chess. Home: Kosmonautu 249, 530 09 Pardubice Czech Republic Office: U Pardubice, nam Cs legii 565, 532 10 Pardubice Czech Republic

DOLENKO, GEORGE NIKOLAEVICH, physicist; b. Novosibirsk, Russia, Aug. 8, 1946; s. Nicholas Petrovich and Julia Gaevna (Kiseleva) D.; m. Tatjana Nikolaevna Marchenko, May 19, 1977 (div. Feb. 1985); children: Julia, Inna; m. Elena Jur'evna Astashova, Jan. 6, 1999. Degree in physics, State U. Novosibirsk, Russia, 1968; PhD in Inorganic Chemistry, Russian Acad. Scis., Novosibirsk, 1974; D of Chemistry, Mendeleev Inst., Moscow, 1988. Jr. rschr. Inst. Inorganic Chemistry Russian Acad. Scis., Novosibirsk, 1972-84; sr. rschr. Inst. Organic Chemistry, Irkutsk, Russia, 1984-95; prof. organic chemistry Russian Ministry Internal Affairs, Irkutsk, 1995-99; prof. organic chemistry, sr. rschr. U. Consumer Coops., Novosibirsk, 1999—. Mem. Russian Acad. Ecology, N.Y. Acad. Scis., Internat. Coun. on Main Group Chemistry. Office: Siberian U of Consumer Coop, K Marax pr 26, 630087 Novosibirsk Russia

DOLEV, SHLOMI, computer science researcher, educator; b. Rehovot, Israel, Dec. 5, 1958; s. Haim and Rachel Dolev; m. Gali Naor, Oct. 5, 1983; children: Noa, Yorai, Hagar, Eden. BSc, Technion, Israel, 1984, BA, 1985, MSc, 1990, DSc, 1992. Rschr., lectr. Tex. A&M U., College Station, 1992-95; assoc. prof. dept. computer sci. Ben Gurion U., Beer-Sheva, Israel, 1995—; head dept. computer sci. Ben Gurion U., Beer-Sheva, 1998—. Author: Self-Stabilization, 2000; editor spl. issue Chgo. Jour. Theoretical

Computer Sci.; contbr. articles to profl. jours., including Distributed Computing, SIAM Jour. Computing, IEEE Trans. on Parallel and Distributed Sys. Capt. Israel Def. Forces, 1977-80. Mem. Assn. for Computing Machinery. Office: Ben Gurion U, Dept Computer Sci, Beer-Sheva Israel

DOLEZAL, JAROSLAV, research and development manager; b. Prague, Czech Republic, Dec. 31, 1946; s. Jaroslav and Frantiska (Cerna) D.; m. Jaroslava Nadenikova, July 20, 1972; children: Jakub, Barbora. MS, Czech Tech. U., 1970; PhD, Czech Acad. Sci., 1974. Rsch. scientist Czech Acad. Sci., Prague, 1974-79, sr. rsch. scientist, 1979-85, sr. prin. rsch. scientist, 1985-95; mgr. Honeywell Tech. Ctr., Prague, 1995—. Editor: Optimization-Based Computer-Aided Modelling and Design, 1994, 95, System Modelling and Optimization, 1996; contbr. articles to profl. jours. Recipient Acad. prize Czech Acad. Sci., 1989. Mem. IFIP (tech. rep. 1985, gen. assembly 1994—, Silver Core 1995), IEEE (Control Syss. Soc. 1996). Avocations: recreational sports, ballroom dancing, computers, mathematical immunology.

DOLEZAL, LADISLAV, biophysicist; b. Velke Losiny, Czech Republic, Aug. 6, 1947; s. Ladislav and Vera (Ossendorf) D.; m. Alena Kubickova, July 11, 1975; children: Ondrej, Radka, Stepan. Grad., Tech. U. Brno, Czech Republic, 1972. Manual worker Moravian Steel Factory, Olomouc, Czech Republic, 1962-67; design mgr. Rsch. Inst., Prague, 1973-75; rsch. engr. Med. Sch. U., Olomouc, 1975-96, prof. asst., 1996—. Inventor in field. Mem. IEEE (assoc.), Czech Soc. Ultrasound in Biology & Medicine. Roman Catholic. Avocations: amateur radio, biking, travel. Home: Jiraskova No 11, 77200 Olomouc Czech Republic Office: Palacky U Med Sch, Hnevotinska 3, 77515 Olomouc Czech Republic

DOLEZAL, VLADIMIR, neurobiologist; b. Prague, Czech Republic, June 12, 1952; s. Vladimir and Olga (Hujerova) D. MD, Charles U., Prague, Czech Republic, 1976; PhD, Czech Acad. Scis., Prague, Czech Republic, 1984. Rschr. Czech Acad. Scis., Prague, 1984—. Contbr. articles to profl. jours. Postdoctoral scholar Czech Acad. Scis., 1977-80, 81-84, Charles U. Faculty Phys. Edn. and Sports, 1980-81. Mem. ESN, ISN, IBRO. Avocation: sports. E-mail: dolezal@biomed.cas.cz. Home: Na valech 16, 160 00 Prague Czech Republic Office: Inst Physiology Czech Acad Scis, Videnska 1083, 142 20 Prague Czech Republic

DOLGIN, KEVIN JOHN, strategy consultant; b. Queens, N.Y., June 15, 1964; s. Michael Dolgin and Catherine Elisa Dolgin Denaro; m. Diane Giocanti, Apr. 11, 1987; children: Nicolas Paul, Marc Tristan. BA in Econs. summa cum laude, Fordham U., 1986; MBA, INSEAD, Fontainebleau, France, 1990. Fgn. exch. analyst Fed. Res. Bank of N.Y., N.Y.C., 1987-89; sr. mgr. Am. Express, Paris, 1990-93; cons. Strat*X, Paris, 1993-98; ptnr. Areks, Paris, 1999—. Internat. Study scholar Rotary Found., 1984. Mem. Phi Beta Kappa. Avocations: guitar, private pilot, writing fiction. Home: 68 rue Vauvenargues, 75018 Paris France Office: 39 Pierre Premier Serbie, 75008 Paris France

DOLGOBORODOV, ALEXANDER YURIEVICH, chemical physicist, research scientist; b. Kaliningrad, Moscow, Russia, Feb. 9, 1956; s. Yuriy Ivanovich and Nadezhda Ivanovna (Kharlamova) D.; m. Svetlana Mikhailovna Kazakova, Sept. 9, 1977; children: Irina, Michael. Degree in engrng. physics, Moscow Engrng. Phys. Inst., 1979; DSc, Russian Acad. Scis., 1985. Sr. scientist Inst. Chem. Physics Russian Acad. Scis., Moscow. Contbr. articles to profl. jours. including Tech. Physics, Soviet Jour. Chem. Physics, Chem. Physics Reports; patentee explosive tube accelerator. E-mail: aldol@chph.ras.ru. Office: Russian Acad Scis/Inst Chem, 4 Kosygin St, 117977 Moscow Russia

DOLHANCYK, DIANA See PAMIN, DIANA DOLHANCYK

DOLICE, JOSEPH LEO, multimedia art publisher, exhibition director; b. Newark, Oct. 12, 1941; s. Leon Louis and Mary Sabina (Lewandowski) D. BA, Iona Coll., 1963; MA, Hunter Coll., 1978. Dir., stage designer F. Richard Love Theatrical Prodns., White Plains, N.Y., 1969; stage designer various theater companies, N.Y., 1969-73; exhbn. dir. New Rochelle (N.Y.) Coun. on the Arts, 1977—; art dir. Stan Rose Assocs., N.Y.C., 1980-90; exhbn. dir. Fulton Gallery, N.Y.C., 1980-92; theater mgr. Village Gate, N.Y.C., 1987-92; art dir. Dezer Enterprises, N.Y.C., 1987-89; exhbn. dir. Janapa Gallery, N.Y.C., 1990; prodn. dir. Ruff Theatrical, Bklyn., 1991-95; publisher Dolice Graphics, N.Y.C., 1980—; a/v corporate and events tech. mgmt., various companies in N.Y.C. and Calif., 1994—. Author: Old New York Remembered, 1982; author, pub. Demo Directory, 1994-95, Free Computer Media, 1996, Vintage New York, 1998; exec. editor N.Y. Downtown News, 1987-89; contbr. articles to various pubs. Publicity dir. Putnam County Bicentennial Commn., Carmel, N.Y., 1976; exhbn. dir. Danbury (Conn.) State Arts & Crafts Fair, 1979-83; dir. Putnam Arts Coun. annual profl. art exhibit, 1976; advt. dir. TheARTgallery Mag., 1974-76; exhbn. dir. New Rochelle Coun. on Arts. With U.S. Army, 1964-66, U.S., Korea. Mem. Internat. Assn. Fine Art Digital Printmakers, Entertainment Svcs. and Tech. Assn., Mus. Store Assn. Affiliate, Montauk Artists Assn., Ctr. Book Arts N.Y.C., Internat. Assn. of Fine Art Digital Printmakers. Avocations: writing, theatrical and performance work. E-mail address: techman@erols.com. Fax: 212-260-9217. Office: Dolice Graphics 163 3d Ave Ste 321 New York NY 10003-2523

DOLIN, LONNY H., lawyer; b. Youngstown, Ohio, Jan. 24, 1954; d. Lawrence Joseph and Sonya (Sacks) Heselov ; m. Gordon S. Black, Aug. 20, 1988; children: Nathaniel, Brooke, Aaron, Benjamin, Lindsay. AB, Georgetown U., 1976; JD, Cath. U., 1979. Bar: Vt. 1980, N.Y. State Bar 1984, U.S. Dist. Ct. (we. dist.) N.Y. 1984. Assoc. Downs, Rachlin & Martin, Burlington, Vt., 1979-81; pvt. practice Burlington, 1981-84; assoc., then ptnr. Harris, Beach, Wilcox, Rubin & Levey, Rochester, N.Y., 1984-90; ptnr. Harris, Beach & Wilcox, Rochester, N.Y., 1990-93; former of counsel to U.S. Congressman Fred J. Eckert, N.Y.; ptnr. Lonny H. Dolin and Assocs., Rochester, 1993—; bd. dirs. Monroe County Legal Services Corp. Mem. Pittsford Town and County Com., N.Y., 1983—, Town of Pittsford Bd. of Zoning Appeals, N.Y., 1984—, vice chair 1990; chmn. Monroe County Comparable Worth Task Force, Rochester, 1985—, Fred J. Eckert Women's Adv. Council, Rochester, 1985—; del. The Jud. Dist. N.Y., Rochester, 1985—, chair 1990; bd. dirs. Nat. Council Jewish Women. Recipient Corpus Juris Secundum award West Pub. co., 1979. Mem. ABA, Vt. Bar Assn., N.Y. Bar Assn., Monroe County Bar Assn. (mem. practice and perf. com.), Greater Rochester Women's Bar Assn. (treas. 1986), Assn. Trial Lawyers Am., N.Y. State Trial Lawyers Assn., Genesee Valley Trial Lawyers Assn. (treas. 1990). Republican. Avocations: golf, skiing, tennis. Home: 9 Hidden Springs Dr Pittsford NY 14534-2897 Office: Ste 130 135 Corporate Wood St Rochester NY 14623•

DOLINNAYA, NINA GERMANOVNA, molecular biologist, researcher; b. Moscow, Mar. 8, 1948; d. German Efimovich and Galina Konstantinovna (Kiseleva) Luzshnova; m. Anatoly Ivanovich Dolinny, Jan. 22, 1970; 1 child, Juliya. MSc in Chemistry, Lomonosov Moscow State U., 1971, PhD in Biochemistry, 1978, DrSc in Biochemistry, 1993. Rsch. scientist Dept. chemistry, Lomonosov Moscow State U., 1971-85, sr. rsch. scientist, 1985-90, leading rsch. scientist, 1996—; rsch. staff Dept. Molecular Biology, Princeton (N.J.) U., 1991-92, 94-95. Patentee in field. Recipient Awards in Bio-organic Chemistry, Min. High Edn., 1978, 86; FEBS fellow, 1983; State Russian grantee for scientists, 1997; CNRS (France) fellow, 1999. Mem. Orthodoxal Ch. Avocations: dancing, books. Home: 4/6-A Kuusinena St #111, 123308 Moscow Russia Office: Princeton U Dept Molecular Biology Princeton NJ 08544-0001

DOLK, ARTHUR JOHAN, advocate, solicitor; b. Amsterdam, The Netherlands, Sept. 7, 1953. Degree in Law, U. Leiden, The Netherlands, 1979. Advocate/solicitor in maritime and ins. law Dolk-Verburg-Diamand, Amsterdam, 1979—. Mem. Dutch Bar Assn., Dutch Assn. for Transport Law, Assn. of Amsterdam Ins. Bourse. Fax: 31-20-6445482. E-mail: a.j.dolk@dolk-verburg-diamand.nl. Office: Dolk-Verburg-Diamand, Cronenburg 75, 1081 GM Amsterdam The Netherlands

DOLL, JACQUES LOUIS, physician; b. Colmar, France, May 3, 1949; s. Jean Henri and Marie-Antionette (Dirry) D.; m. Annic Jeanne Jaros, Sept. 9, 1976; children: Delphine, Antoine. MD, U. Paris XII, Creteil, France, 1978; postgrad., U. Paris XI, 1984. Resident in hepato-gastroenterology Paris, 1973-78; asst. Versailles (France) Hosp., 1978-96, head dept., 1996—; med. cons. Searle, paris, 1986-88, Torrent Healthworld, Paris, 1989—, Ministry of Justice, Paris, 1995-96. Recipient Prix Servir, Rotary, 1996. Mem. Info-Soins (pres. 1988-98), Ressy-Remisy (v.p. 1994—), VHCO (v.p. 1998—). Office: Ctr Hosp Versailles, 177 rue de Versailles, 78157 Le Chesnay France

DOLLERUP, CAY, philologist; b. Buenos Aires, Nov. 12, 1939; arrived in Denmark, 1946; s. Jens Peter and Margot Marie (Krebs) D.; m. Aase Poulsen, June 9, 1972 (div. 1976); 1 child, Carsten; m. Susanne Jorgensen, June 20, 1981; children: Karen Marie, Niels Peter. Cand. mag., U. Copenhagen, 1970. Jr. rsch. asst. dept. English U. Copenhagen, 1970-73, sr. rsch. fellow, 1973-76, sr. lectr., 1976—; sr. lectr. Ctr. Translation Studies, 1989—; founder rsch. unit exptl. studies in reader response, 1984; cons. linguistics svcs. EC, Brussels, 1974, 75; mem. exec. bd. acad. string Humanities Faculty, 1986-89; NATO referee, 1990—; co-founder European Soc. Translation Studies, 1993; lectr. tours China, 1993, 97, Hungary, Slovenia, 1995, Poland, 1996, Russia, 1998, Lithuania, 1999, South Africa, 2000, Romania, 2000; organizer First Lang. Internat. Conf., 1991, Second Lang. Internat. Conf., Elsinore, Denmark, 1993, Eleventh Internat. Conf. in Lit. and Psychoanalysis, 1994, Third Lang. Internat. Conf., 1995; Danish coord. Tempus (European Union) programme with Slovenia, 1994-97, with Poland, 1995-98, EU Leonardus-programme on the Delta-Concept, 1998—; Tempus contractor Tempus programme with Uzbekistan, 1994-95, VET Tacis, 1997-98. Author: Denmark, Hamlet and Shakespeare, 1975, Omkring Sproglig Transmission, 1978, Basic Dictionary of Danish, 1994, A Corpus of Consecutive Interpreting, 1996, Tales and Translation, 1999; editor: Vølve: Scandinavian Views on Science Fiction, 1978, Teaching Translation and Interpreting, vol. 1, 1992, vol. 2, 1994, vol. 3, 1996, Issues in Translation, 1998; contbr. 150 articles to profl. jours.; editor-in-chief Perspectives: Studies in Translatology, 1993—; Danish editor Lang. Internat., Interpreting, Psyart., and Studies in Tranls. Chmn. nat. com. univ. affairs Dansk Magisterforening, Copenhagen, 1977-80. With Danish Army, 1958-59. Mem. Internat. Reading Assn. MLA, World Assn. Applied Linguistics, Assn. Univ. Tchrs. (exec. bd. 1986-87), Det Filologisk Historiske Samfund. Home: Engtoftevej 4 2tv, DK-1816 Frederiksberg Denmark Office: U Copenhagen Dept English, Njalsgade 80, DK-2300 Copenhagen Denmark

DOLLET, MICHEL, virologist, plant pathologist; b. Rivoli, Algiers, Oct. 21, 1949; s. Roland and Genevieve Dollet; m. Lydia Esteban, 1974; children: Magalie, Olivier. Student, U. Louis Pasteur, Strasbourg, France, 1978, U. Montpellier, France, 1985. Researcher French Inst. Sci. Rsch. for Devel. and Coop., Abidjan, Ivory Coast, 1975-76, Nat. Inst. Agrl. Rsch.-Nat. Ctr. Sci. Rsch., St. Christol-Les-Ales, France, 1976-78; head common rsch. unit for virology Centre de Coopération internationale en recherche agronomique pour le développement (CIRAD), Montpellier, 1979—; promoter Lab. de Phytovirologie des Regions Chaudes CIRAD-ORSTOM, Montpellier, France, 1984, Internat. Phytomonas Workshop, Cayenne, Guiana, 1987, Santa Marta, Colombia, 1992, Montpellier, 1995; sabbatical dept. microbiology, immunology, and molecular genetics UCLA, 1998-99; mem. consultative group virus diseases of groundnut in Africa; cons. on plant pathology various cos. Senegal, Burkina, Cameroon, India, Vanuatu, Peru, Ecuador, Colombia, others, 1975-93. Chmn. Internat. Coun. on Lethal Yellowing, 1979-81. Mem. Internat. Orgn. Mycoplasmologists, Soc. Applied Biologists, Soc. Protozoologists, French Phyopathol. Soc. Am. Phytopathol. Soc. Avocations: bicycling, tennis, cinema, photography, music. Office: CIRAD, TA 30/G Campus Internat, 34398 Montpellier Cedex 5, France

DOLLFUS, AUDOUIN CHARLES, astronomer; b. Paris, Nov. 12, 1924; s. Charles Dollfus and Suzanne Soubeyran; m. Catherine Browne, June 19, 1959; children: Fanny, Corinne, Jean Tycho, Ariane. DSc in Math., U. Paris, 1955. Astron. aide Paris Observatory, 1956-57, adj. astronomer, 1957-65, head astronomer, 1965—. Contbr. over 350 sci. papers to profl. jours. Decorated officier Palmes Academiques (France), Médaille de Aéronautique; recipient prize Encouragement and Personal Initiative, 1958, Galabert prize Internat. Astronautics, 1973, diploma Tissandier Internat. Fedn. Aeronautics, 1991, Grand prize Acad. Scis. Paris, 1988; holder 3 ofcl. records for ballooning. Mem. Soc. Astron. France (pres. 1979-81, Janssen award 1994), Assn. Création et Diffusion Sci. (hon. pres. 1988—), Assn. Française Avancement Sci. (pres. 1993-95), Internat. Acad. Astronautics (trustee 1975-81), Russian Soc. Astronomy and Geophysics, Royal Astron. Soc. London (assoc.), Royal Astron. Soc. Can. (fgn.), Soc. French Explorers, Aero Club France (life, trustee), Explorers Club N.Y., Société Philomatique Paris. Avocations: aerostation, ballooning. Home: 77 Rue Albert Perdreaux, 92370 Chaville France

DOLMATOV, VALERIY KONSTANTINOVICH, physicist, researcher; b. Tashkent, Uzbekistan, Aug. 18, 1955; s. Konstantin Ivanovich and Antonina Petrovna Dolmatov; m. Lyudmila L'vovna Magdeychuk, May 31, 1975; children: Elena, Svetlana. MSc in Physics, Tashkent State U., 1977, PhD in Theoretical and Math. Physics, 1985. Engr. S.V. Starodubtsev Phys.-Tech. Inst., Tashkent, 1977, sr. engr., 1977-78, jr. scientist, 1978-86, scientist, 1986-88, sr. scientist, 1989-91, leading scientist, 1997—; sr. scientist Inst. Materials Sci., Tashkent, 1991-97; assoc. prof. Inst. Ry. Transport Engrs., Tashkent, 1988-89; contracted referee Internat. Assn., Brussels, 1998—; external referee PhD theses Supreme Attestation Com. on PhD Theses, Cabinet Mins. of Uzbekistan, Tashkent, 1995—. Contbr. articles to profl. jours. Alexander von Humboldt rsch. fellow, 1991-93, vis. scientist fellow Royal Soc. London, 1996; NSF Internat. Supplementary grantee, 1997-98, NATO Collaborative Linkage grantee, 1999. Mem. Am. Phys. Soc., European Phys. Soc. Avocations: soccer, table tennis, hiking, swimming. Fax: 998 (712) 35-42-91. E-mail: phyvkd@manson.phy-astr.gsu.edu. Home: Lokomotivnaya St 24-11, Tashkent 700167, Uzbekistan Office: SV Starodubtsev Phys-Tech, 2b G Mavlyanova Str, Tashkent 700084, Uzbekistan

DOLOCAN, VOICU DRAGOMIR, physics educator, researcher; b. Crimpoia, Olt, Romania, Sept. 18, 1939; s. Dragomir Gheorghe and Nicula Ion (Badoi) D.; m. Elena Dumitru Popescu, Oct. 16, 1976; children: Andrei, Voicu-Octavian. Physics diploma, U. Bucharest, Romania, 1963, PhD, 1970. Asst. prof. U. Bucharest, 1963-70, lectr., 1970-90, prof., 1990—. Author: Physics of Solid State Devices, 1978, Tunneling Phenomena, 1989, Superconductivity, 1997, Semiconductor Quantum Structures, 1997; contbr. articles to profl. jours. Recipient diploma Romanian Acad., 1975. Mem. N.Y. Acad. Sci. Orthodox. Achievements include research on recombination in semiconductors; a new method for magnetic and dielectric susceptibilities measurements based on reflection pulse technique. Avocation: poetry. Home: Bd Tineretului 1 Bl 5 Sc A, Bucharest Romania Office: U Bucharest Faculty Physics, Bucharest-Magurele POB MG11, Bucharest Romania

DOLUI, SWAPAN KUMAR, education educator; b. Kharagpur, India, Oct. 6, 1959; s. Bhabendu Sekhar and Anima Rani (Shaw) D.; m. Sutapa Bera, Mar. 7, 1988; 1 child, Swapnil. MSc, Calcutta U., 1983; PhD, IIT, Kuaragpur, India, 1987. Rsch. fellow IIT Kharagpur, 1983-86; rsch. exec. VAM Organic, India, 1986-89; scientist CBRI (CSIR), India, 1986-89; mgr. R&D VAM Organic, India, 1995-97; prof. Tezpur U., India, 1997—; lectr. in field. Inventor in field; contbr. articles to profl. publs. Recipient Cunninghum Meml. award Presidency Coll., Calcutta, 1983, Best Paper Presentation award MRSC, Hyderabad, 1994. Mem. MRSI (life), Indian Chem. Soc. (life), India Sci. Conf. (life). Bharat Sevashram Sang. Avocations: history of sci., travel, reading life history. Office: Dept Chem Sci, Tezpur Univ Napaam, 784028 Assam India

DOMA, EUGÈNE, engineering executive; b. Budapest, Hungary, June 9, 1956; arrived in Australia, 1967; s. Eugene Doma and Klara Kiss. B of Engrng., U. Newcastle, NSW, Australia, 1978. Registered profl. engr. Engr. Electricity Commn. NSW, Sydney, 1975-81; sys. engr. GE, Sydney, 1981-83; software devel. mgr. Toshiba (Australia), Sydney, 1983-84; mng. dir. Digisearch, Pty Ltd., Sydney, 1984—; bus. and info. tech. cons. to various orgns. including state and fed. govt. agys., Top 500 cos., and multi-nat. corps.; presenter ednl. material to execs., sales pers. and info. tech. profls.; tech. dir. Comml. Dynamics, Pty. Ltd., Sydney, 1979-81, Precise Bus. Sys., Pty. Ltd., Hunters Hill, NSW, 1984-85; gen. mgr. Paradyne Australia Ltd., North Sydney, 1985-88; bus. cons. Phoenix Contracting, Pty. Ltd., North Sydney, 1993-97; member of organizing committee for 1996 Focus Producers' Festival, co-creator and presenter of "Career Strategy workshops. Donor Art Gallery Soc. NSW, 1991—. Mem. IEEE, Inst. Engrs. Australia, Assn. Computing Machinery, N.Y. Acad. Scis. Office: Digisearch Pty Ltd, GPO Box 4748, Sydney NSW 1044, Australia

DOMANIN, ANDREI ALEXANDROVICH, pathologist; b. Tver, Russia, Aug. 27, 1960; s. Alexandr Pavlovich and Alexandra Pheodorovna (Vishniakova) D.; m. Irina Borisovna Davidova, July 12, 1991 (div. 1993). Physician, Med. Acad., Tver, 1983, postgrad., 1986, DMS, 1992. Cert. med. pathologist. Asst. Med. Acad., Tver, 1986-91, lectr., 1992—; chief of dept. Rlwy. St. Hosp., Tver, 1983-00. Author: (books) Villous Tumors of Large Bowels, 1987, Signet-ring Cells Cancer of Large Bowels, 2000; contbr. articles to profl. jours. Mem. Internat. Acad. Pathology, Russian Assn. Pathologists, N.Y. Acad. Scis. Avocation: boxing. Home: 56-203 Mogaiskogo St, 170043 Tver Russia Office: Tver State Med Acad, 4 Sovetskaia St, 170000 Tver Russia

DOMAŃSKI, CEZARY WOJCIECH, psychologist, educator; b. Dolice, Poland, Sept. 19, 1962; s. Michal and Wiktoria Maria (Dobrowolska) D.; m. Lucja Lena Spiewla, Sept. 3, 1992; 1 child, Aleksander Krzysztof. BS, Coll. Study of Food Industry, Lublin, Poland, 1984; MA, Maria Curie-Sklodowska U., Lublin, Poland, 1989; PhD, Polish Acad. Scis., 1996. U. asst. Maria Curie-Sklodowska U., Lublin, Poland, 1989-97; tutor Maria Curie-Sklodowska U., Lublin, 1997—. Contbr. articles to profl. jours. Recipient Rector's award, Rector of Maria Curie-Sklodowska U., 1993. Mem. Czech Entomol. Soc., Polish Botanical Soc. Avocations: genealogy, archival rsch. E-mail: cwdoman@sokrates.umcs.lublin.pl. Office: Maria Curie-Sklodowska U, Pl Litewski 5, 20-080 Lublin Poland

DOMARKAS, VLADISLAVAS, public relations administrator; b. Kartena, Lithuania, Aug. 17, 1939; s. Jonas and Barbora (Maciulskyte) D.; m. Stanislava Sakalauskaite Domarkiene, June 20, 1964; children: Andrius, Evelina. Student, Kaunas Poly. Inst., Lithuania, 1961; PhD Tech. Scis., 1967, 1977. Rschr., asst. prof., prof. Dept. Radioelectronics Kaunas Poly. Inst., Lithuania, 1961-93; rsch. scholar Calif. U. Santa Barbara, Stanford U., 1977-78; prorector, rector Kaunas Poly Inst., Lithuania, 1980-92; deputy minister Ministry of Fgn. Affairs of Rep. of Lithuania, 1993-94; min. Min. of Edn. and Sci. of Rep. of Lithuania, 1994-96; prof. Dept. Pub. Adminstrn. Kaunas U. Tech., 1997—; assoc. mem. The Lithuanian Acad. Scis., Vilnius, 1985—. Author (with R. Kazys) Piezoelectric Transducers for Measuring Devices, 1975, (with E. Pileckas) Ultrasonic Echoscopy, 1988, (with J. Matakas and others) Modern State, 1999; editor: Ultragarsas, 1986-95; contbr. over 100 papers in scientific periodicals and over 50 inventions in field. Deputy Lithuanian Supreme Coun., Vilnius, 1985-90. Recipient National awards Govt. and Acad. of Scis. of Lithuania, Vilnius, 1976-87. Avocations: travel, housebuilding. Home: Perkuno al 74, 3000 Kaunas Lithuania Office: Dept Public Adminstration, Donelaicio 20, 3000 Kaunas Lithuania

DOMBRET, ANDREAS RAYMOND, bank executive; b. Des Moines, Jan. 16, 1960; s. Max Raymond and Charlotte Maria (Genschow) D. Dipl., U. Muenster, Germany, 1987; postgrad., NYU, 1988. Asst. v.p. Deutsche Bank, Frankfurt, Germany, 1987-91; v.p. J.P. Morgan, London, N.Y.C., Frankfurt, 1992—. Author: Securitization Strategies, 1987, 2d edit., 1988.

DOMBROVSKII, VLADIMIR VALENTINOVICH, mathematician, educator, researcher; b. Kharkov, Ukraine, June 26, 1951; s. Valentin Ivanovich and Nina Pheodorovna (Kozlova) D.; m. Tatjana Vladimirovna Yaroslavceva, Nov. 12, 1972; 1 child, Katherine; m. Nadeghda Tikhonovna Chernenko, July 8, 1982; 1 child, Dmitrii. Candidate of Sci., Tomsk (Russia) State U., 1984, DSc, 1992. Cert. in math. Rschr. Siberian Physics Tech. Inst., Tomsk, 1975-87; from assoc. prof. to prof. Tomsk State U., 1987-95, head of dept. of math. methods in econs., 1995—. Author: (book) Order Reduction of Estimation and Control Systems, 1994, Quantitative Methods of Analysis of Financial Operations, 1998; contbr. articles to profl. jours. E-mail: dombrovs@ef.tsu.ru. Office: Tomsk State U, Lenina 36, Tomsk 634050, Russia

DOMBROVSKY, LEONID ALEXANDROVICH, mechanical engineer, researcher; b. Moscow, Aug. 10, 1948; s. Galina Victorovna Nikiforova, Feb. 24, 1987; children: Kirill, Konstantin. Grad. in Engrng., Moscow Inst. Physics and Tech., 1971, PhD, 1974; DS, Inst. Thermal Processes, Moscow, 1989. Sr. rschr. Inst. Thermal Processes, 1975-85, chief rschr., 1985-96; chief rschr. Inst. High Temperatures, Moscow, 1996—; cons. Siemens, Erlangen, Germany, 1997-98. Author: Radiation Heat Transfer in Disperse Systems, 1996; contbr. articles to profl. jours. Recipient grant Internat. Sci. Found., 1993. Mem. Nat. Com. on Heat and Mass Transfer, Sci. Coun. on Thermophysics and Thermal Engrng., N.Y. Acad. Scis. Avocations: window gardening, photography, gathering mushrooms. Office: Inst High Temperatures, Krasnokazarmennaya 17A, 111250 Moscow Russia

DOMBROWSKI, BOB, artist, publisher; b. Buffalo, Feb. 16, 1944; s. Edward A. and Mary Ann Dombrowski. BS, SUNY, Buffalo, 1965; postgrad., Cornish Inst., Seattle, 1975-76. Artist, N.Y.C., 1976—; owner, mgr. GB Art Co., N.Y.C., 1994—; cons. Cementex Corp., N.Y.C., 1989—. Creator, prodr. Ode to Birth of Shiva, 1987, Elegy for the Republic, 1991, Hwy. 17, 1993, On Thinking Thoughts, 1997; exhibited in group shows at Albright-Knox Art Mus., Buffalo, 1980, Ashford Hollow (N.Y.) Found., 1980, Storefront for Art and Architecture, N.Y.C., 1985, Franklin Furnace, N.Y.C., 1986, Nelson-Atkins Mus., Kansas City, 1989, Shedhalle (Rote Fabrik), Zurich, 1989, Barking Legs Dance Theater, Chattanooga, 1995 (Daimler-Chrysler Spirit of the Word award 1999); represented in permanent collections including N.Y.C. Cmty. Bd. #3, Nico Smith Gallery, N.Y.C., Mus. Modern Art Libr., N.Y.C., Bettina Riedel Ltd., Phila., Pernod Corp., N.Y.C., La Perla Garden, N.Y.C., Francis Pratt Usui, Nicholson, Pa., Cleve. Art Inst. Mem. Internat. Sculpture Ctr., N.Y. Artists Equity (bd. dirs. 1989-90). Avocations: photography, walking. Home and Office: 805 6th Ave New York NY 10001-6301

DOMENICO, VIOREL ION, journalist; b. Breaza, Romania, Mar. 20, 1947; s. Ion and Victoria (Dinescu) D.; m. Alexandra Leca. Grad. mil. coll., Breaza, 1965, 68. Comdr. Min. Def., Romania, 1968-74; reporter Jour. Army, Romania, 1974-78; pub. rels. officer Romanian Army, 1978-81, cinema worker film studio, 1981-90; from rev. editor to editor in chief Viata Armatei, Romania, 1990-99; dir. Army Cinema Film Studio, 2000—. Author: To Walk, 1982, Military Film's Instructive Values, 1986, After Execution Was Snowing, 1991, The Secret History of Romania Film, 1996. Mem. Union Profl. Journalists Romania, Union Romanian Cinema Workers. Home: Calea 13 Sept nr 93 Bl 83, et V Apt 13 Gl Cristescu 5, Bucharest 5 Romania

DOMENICONI, RETO, business executive; b. Zurich, Switzerland, Oct. 7, 1936. Diploma in mech. engrng., Fed. Inst. Tech., Zurich, Doctorate in Tech. Scis. With Arthur D. Little, Inc., 1964-68, Heberlein Group, Wattwil, Switzerland, 1968-75, Züllig Group, Rapperswil, Switzerland, 1976-82; with fin., control and administrn. Nestlé, S.A., Vevey, Switzerland, 1983—, exec. v.p.; pres. adminstrv. bd. Coutts & Co., Zürich, 1991—; bd. dirs. Nestlé, S.A., Switzerland, Sulzer Medica, Bobst Group; supervisory bd. mem. Suez Lyonnaise. Office: BOBST SA, Route des Flumeaux 50, 1008 Prilly Switzerland•

DÖMÉNY, JÁNOS, ambassador; b. Pécs, Hungary, June 5, 1934; s. János Dömény and Emerencia Farsang; m. Zsuzsanna Puskás, June 29, 1963; 1 child, Péter. LLD, U. Law, Budapest, Hungary, 1967; postgrad., Acad. Social Sci., Budapest, 1978-79. Sec. archives Hungarian Embassy, Polonia, Mongolia, 1957-59, attaché, 1959-61; sec. Hungarian Embassy, Cuba, 1963-67; coun., head of affairs Hungarian Embassy, Uruguay, 1971-75; dir. dept. Hungarian Embassy, Hungary, 1976-81; amb. Hungarian Embassy, La Florida, Venezuela, 1981-86, 90-95; dir. dept. Min. Fgn. Trade, Hungary, 1986-90; pres. Latin Am. Assn. Hungary, 1997—.

DOMHOFF, GEORGE WILLIAM, psychology and sociology educator; b. Youngstown, Ohio, Aug. 6, 1936; s. George William and Helen Susanne (Cornett) D.; m. Judith Clare Boman, Aug. 20, 1961 (div. July 1975); children: Lynne Starr, Lori Susanne, William Packard, Joel James. BA, Duke U., 1958; MA, Kent State U., 1959; PhD, U. Miami, 1962. Asst. prof. psychology L.A. State U., 1962-65; from asst. prof. to prof. psychology and sociology U. Calif., Santa Cruz, 1965—. Author: Who Rules America?,

1967, The Higher Circles, 1970, Fat Cats and Democrats, 1972, The Bohemian Grove and Other Retreats, 1974, Who Really Rules in New Haven?, 1978, The Powers That Be, 1979, Who Rules America Now?, 1983, The Mystique of Dreams, 1985, The Power Elite and the State, 1990, State Autonomy or Class Dominance, 1996, Finding Meaning in Dreams: A Quantitative Approach, 1996; co-author: Jews in the Protestant Establishment, 1982, Blacks in the White Establishment, 1991, Diversity in the Power Elite, 1998. Harbor commr. Santa Cruz Port Dist., 1977-78. Avocations: reading, sports. Office: U Calif Dept Psychology Santa Cruz CA 95064

DOMIANO, JOSEPH CHARLES, lawyer; b. Cleve., Oct. 21, 1928; s. Charles Joseph and Mary Grace (Santora) D.; m. Julie Ann Birinyi, Sept. 9, 1950; children: Joseph, Jr., Laura, John. BBA, Case We. Res. U., 1951; LLD, Cleve. State U., 1956. Bar: Ohio 1957. Ptnr. Mandanici & Domiano, Cleve., 1957-84, Sindell, Rubenstein, Cleve., 1984-87, Friedman, Domiano & Smith, Cleve., 1987—; prosecutor City of Maple Heights (Ohio), 1963-65; solicitor Village of Bentleyville (Ohio), 1974-94; law dir. City of Olmsted Falls (Ohio), 1992-93; mem. (life) 8th Dist. Jud. Law Conf., Cleve., 1994—. Contbr. articles to law jours.;m presenter in field. Bd. dirs. Maple Heights Little Theatre, 1962-65, Transitional Housing, Cleve., 1994—; mem. parish coun. Ch. of Resurrection, Solon, Ohio, 1992-94, mem. fin. coun., 1996—. Mem. ATLA, Ohio State Bar Assn., Ohio Acad. Trial Lawyers, Cleve. Bar Assn., Cleve. Acad. Trial Lawyers, Cuyahoga County Bar Assn. (pres. 1993-94), KC (mem. exec. com. 1985-86). Avocations: snow skiing, water skiing, sailing, golf, scuba diving. Office: Friedman Domiano & Smith 1370 Ontario St Fl 6 Cleveland OH 44113-1701

DOMINGO, CHRISTIAN, physician, researcher; b. Barcelona, Spain, June 27, 1960; s. Enric Domnigo and Mercè Ribas; m. Rosa Maria Mirapeix; 1 child, Alex. MD, UAB, Barcelona, 1984, PhD, 1991. Resident, fellow pulmonary medicine Barcelona, 1986-89, mem. staff ICU, 1989-92; mem. staff pulmonary medicine C.S. Parc Tauli, Barcelona, 1992—; vis. H. Croix Rousse, Lyon, France, 1987, Meth. Hosp., Houston, 1988. Rsch. grantee Fiss, Socap-Beca Oscar Rava. Mem. SEPAR, SOCAP, ACCP. Office: CS Parc Tauli, Parc Tauli S/N, 08208 Sabadell Spain

DOMINGO, FAUSTINO TEOPACO, neurosurgeon; b. Manila, May 17, 1930; s. Faustino M. Domingo and Valeriana M. Teopaco; m. Maria Rosario A. De Castro, Mar. 10, 1956 (dec. June 1993); children: Rene, Carlo Gino, Manolo Miguel, Nanette, Heidi. AA, U. Philippines, 1949, MD, 1954. Diplomate Philippine Bd. Neurol. Surgery. Resident in neurosurgery U. Philippines Med. Ctr., 1954-59; resident in neurology Univ. Hosps. U. Wis., Madison, 1959-60; fellow in neurosurgery Lahey Clinic, Boston, 1960-61; instr. U. of The Philippines Coll. Medicine, Manila, 1961-66, asst. prof. neurosurgery, 1966-74, assoc. prof. neurosurgery, 1974-91, prof. neurosurgery, 1991-95; chief divsn. neurosurgery U. of The Philippines/ Philippine Gen. Hosp., 1980-92, asst. chmn. dept. surgery, 1984-88; chmn. dept. surgery Manila Doctors Hosp., 1988—; cons. in neurosurgery Clark Air Base Hosp., 1963-67; fellow in neuropsychology Hosp. de la Salpetriere, Paris, 1975; Dr. Jose Abuel professorial chair in neurosurgery U. of The Philippines Coll. Medicine, 1987-92; examiner, past chmn. Philippine Bd. Neurol. Surgery; lectr. Sch. Allied Med. Professions, U. Philippines, Manila, Coll. of Nursing, U. Philippines, Coll. of Nursing, St. Paul Coll., La Concordia Coll. Author: Treatment Protocol for Tumors of The Central Nervous System, 1984; contbg. author: Cancer Brochure, 1984; contbr. articles to profl. jours. Neuropsychology scholar Govt. of France, 1974-75. Fellow ACS, Philippine Coll. Surgeons (pres. 1988), Philippine Soc. Neurol. Surgeons (pres. 1972-74, award of merit 1988), Philippine Med. Assn., Asian-Australasian Soc. Neurol. Surgeons (nat. del. exec. com. 1988-90), Asian Surg. Assn., Manila Med. Soc. Diplomate Philippine Bd. Neurol. Surgery. Office: Manila Doctors Hosp, 667 United Nations Ave, Ermita Manila 1000, The Phillipines

DOMINGO, PLACIDO, tenor; b. Madrid, Spain, Jan. 21, 1941; s. Placido and Pepita (Embil) D.; m. Marta Ornelas; children: Jose, Placido, Alvaro Maurizio. Student, Conservatory in Mexico City; hon. degree, Royal Coll. Music, 1982, Complutense de Madrid, 1989. Crwistic dir. Washington Opera, 1994—; artistic dir. L.A. Opera, 2000—. Made operatic debut in La Traviata, 1961; debut, Met. Opera, 1968; star tenor with opera cos. including, La Scala, Covent Garden, Hamburg State Opera, Vienna State Opera, N.Y.C. Opera, San Francisco Opera, Nat. Hebrew Opera in Tel-Aviv; leading roles: 116 operas including Don Rodrigo, Tosca, Andrea Chenier, Don Carlo, Carmen, La Boheme, Errani, Parsifal, Idomeneo; appeared in films: Traviata, 1983, Carmen, 1984, Otello, 1986; made more than 100 recs., including 93 full-length operas, for BMG (formerly RCA), DGG, Sony, Decca/London, Philips, Time Warner, EMI (Angel); made more than 50 videos; performed in concert, PBS TV spl. (with José Carreras & Luciano Pavorotti) The Three Tenors, L.A., 1994; condr. numerous performances at major opera houses, including Met. Opera, London's Covent Garden, Vienna State Opera; music dir. Seville World's Fair; active Operalia internat. vocal competition. Performed concerts to benefit victims of 1985 Mexican earthquake. Recipient 8 Grammy awards. Address: care Vincent & Farrell Assocs 157 W 57th St Ste 502 New York NY 10019-2210

DOMINGO MENDEZ, JOSE, supreme court president. Pres. Supreme Court, El Salvador. Office: Centro de Gobierno, José Simeón Cañas, San Salvador El Salvador*

DOMINGOS, JOAQUIM MARIA, physics educator, researcher, retired; b. Coimbra, Portugal, Nov. 15, 1929; s. Joaquim Maria Domingos and Maria Conceição Santos; m. Susan Mary Harrison, Aug. 19, 1970; 1 child, Richard. Degree in physics, U. Coimbra, 1959; PhD in Physics, Oxford (Eng.) U., 1971. Rsch. asst. U. Coimbra, 1960-70, aux. prof., 1971-81, prof. catedrático, 1982-99, ret., 1999. Contbr. articles to scientific jours., including Nuc. Physics, Phys. Rev., Internat. Jour. Theoretical Physics, Founds. of Physics, Nuovo Cimento, Progress of Theoretical Physics, Physica Scripta, and European Jour. Physics. Recipient grants Calouste Gulbenkian Found. 1966-71, 1981. Home: Rua do Brasil 450, 3030 Coimbra Portugal Office: Univ Coimbra, Dept de Fisica, Coimbra Portugal

DOMINGO SOLANS, EUGENIO, economics educator; b. Barcelona, Nov. 26, 1945. BS in Econs., U. Barcelona, 1968; PhD in Econs., Autonomous U. of Madrid, 1975. Prof. pub. finance, Faculty of Econs. U. Barcelona, 1968-70; prof. pub. finance Autonomous U. of Madrid, 1970—; prof. monetary policy and Spanish Tax Sys. Univ. Coll. of Fin. Studies, Complutense U. of Madrid, 1996—; vis. prof. York (U.K.) U., 1969; economist Banco Atlántico, 1970, 73-77, 78-79; economist Rsch. Group of Econ. and Social Devel. Plan Dept, Presidency of Spanish Govt., 1970-73; econ. advisor to Secretariat of State for Econ. Coordination and Planning of the Ministry of Economy, 1977-78; mgr. rsch. dept., Inst. of Econ. Studies, 1979-86; asst. pres. Banco Zaragozano, 1986-94; mem. governing coun., Exec. Commn. of Banco de España, 1994-98; mem. exec. bd. European Ctrl. Bank, 1998—. Contbr. numerous articles to profl. jours. Recipient Internat. Economy prize Qualification Commn. King Juan Carlos, 1981, 83. Office: U Complutense de Madrid, Ciudad Universitaria, Madrid Spain 28040*

DOMINGUEZ, CESÁREO AUGUSTO, physicist, educator; b. Buenos Aires, Oct. 1, 1942; s. Cesáreo Augusto and Estela (Baldrich) D.; m. Maria Laura Gentile, Feb. 29, 1968 (div. Mar. 1993); children: Florencia, Ximena; m. Sylva Lisette Schwager, May 19, 1993. MSc in Physics, U. Buenos Aires, 1968, D Physics, 1971. Rschr. Stanford (Calif.) Linear Accelerator Ctr., 1971-72; prof. physics Ctr. for Rsch. and Advanced Studies, Mexico City, 1972-78; vis. assoc. prof. Tex. A&M U., College Station, 1978-82; prof. physics U. F. Santa Maria, Valparaiso, Chile, 1983-85; vis. scientist Internat. Centre for theoretical Physics, Trieste, Italy, 1985-86; rschr. Deutsches Elektronen Synchrotron, Hamburg, Fed. Republic Germany, 1986-88; prof. theoretical physics U. Capetown, South Africa, 1988—, dir. Inst. Theoretical Physics and Astrophysics, 1990—; vis. staff Los Alamos (N.Mex.) Nat. Lab., 1979-82; mem. adv. com. program for devel. UN, Chile, 1984-85. Contbr. articles to sci. jours. Fellow Mex. Acad. Scis., 1977, John Simon Guggenheim Meml. Found., 1994, rsch. fellow Alexander Von Humboldt Found., 1986, Royal Soc. South Africa, 1996. Fellow Royal Soc. South Africa; Mem. Chilean Phys. Soc. (v.p. 1985). Avocations: wine tasting, sailing, tennis. E-mail: cad@physci.uct.ac.za. Office: U Cape Town, Dept Physics, Rondebosch Cape 7700, South Africa

DOMINGUEZ, DAVID ALAN, army reserve medical officer; b. Tachikawa AFB, Japan, Mar. 17, 1962; s. Raymond and Ethel Marie McCorkle D. BS, Calif. State Univ., 1993; physician asst., Univ. S. Calif. Sch. Medicine, 1993. Bd. cert. physician asst. Sgt. US Army, Fort Brag, N.C., 1980-83; battalion medical officer US Army Reserves/Nat. Guard, Calif., 1983—; physician asst. Talbert Medical Group FHP, Lawndale, Calif., 1994-96, High Deser Primary Care, Hesperia, Calif., 1996—. Decorated Army Commendation medal US Army, 1998; recipient Reserve Officer's award Excellence US Army Res., 1984, Commander's award Acad. Health Sci., 1988. Fellow Calif. Assn. PHysician Assts., Am. Acad. Physicans Assts.; mem. Flying Samaritans. Avocations: flying, fishing, skiing, SCUBA diving. Fax number: 760 241 7575. E-mail: david1pac@aol.com. Home: 20011 Us Highway 18 # Vil-114 Apple Valley CA 92307-2645 Office: High Deser Primary Care Hesperia Rd Victorville CA 92392

DOMINGUEZ BELLO, MARIA GLORIA, microbiologist, researcher; b. Caracas, Venezuela, Dec. 3, 1959; d. Francisco and Sira (Bello) D.; m. Luis Raul Pericchi; 1 child, Adriana Pericchi Dominguez. BSc, U. Simon Bolivar, Caracas, 1984; MSc, U. Aberdeen, Scotland, 1986, PhD, 1989. Postdoctoral fellow Venezuelan Inst. Sci. Rsch., Caracas, 1990-92, assoc. rschr., 1993-99, vice coord. grad. studies in physiology, 1994-98, rschr. assoc.-titular, 1999—; vis. scientist INRA, Theix, France, 1990, Purdue U. Ill., 1991, Cornell U., N.Y., 1996, CBM, U. Autónoma Madrid, 1997; postdoctoral fellow Rowett Inst., Aberdeen, 1993, INRA, 1993; bd. referees Internat. Found. Scis., Stockholm, 1994—; mem. internat. adv. com. Internat. Congress Nutrition of Herbivores, 1999—. Author articles in physiology and microbiology. Recipient Roi Baudouin award Internat. Found. Sci., Stockholm, 1993. Avocations: tennis, music, literature. Office: Venezuelan Inst Sci Rsch-CBB, KM 11 Panam Apostal 21827, 1020A Caracas Venezuela

DOMÍNGUEZ MENDOZA, BORIS, search and rescue technician, educator; b. Caracas, Venezuela, Feb. 4, 1959; s. Luciano Antonio and Guillermina (Mendoza) Domínguez; children: Amaloa Lourdes, Adhara Del Valle. Histologist, Vargas Hosp., Caracas, 1984; BEd, U. Cath. Andrés Bello, Caracas, 1997; human resources specialist, U. Simón Rodriguez, Caracas, 1999. Operative mem. Humboldt Rescue Team, Caracas, 1982; search and rescue officer Directorate Civil Aeronautic, Caracas, 1985—; jungle survival instr. Venezuelan Air Force, Caracas, 1983, search and rescue instr., 1987; rescuer Humboldt Rescue Team, Armero, Colombia, 1985; advisor Grupo de Rescate Gui-May, Caracas, 1987; tng. coord. Humboldt Rescue Team, Caracas, 1987-88; search and rescue specialist Civil Aviation Tng. Ctr., Maiquetía, Venezuela, 1997-98; instr. Civil Protection Inst., Caracas, 1997, 98, 99, La Guaira (Venezuela) Harbour Firemen Dept., 1997; safety expositor Maiquetia Internat. Airport, 1997; edn. expert Venezuelan Mil. Acad., Caracas, 1999. Tech. advisor: History of Venezuelan Air Accidents, 1986. Recipient plaque USCG, La Guaira, Venezuela, 1988, Gui-May Rescue Team, Caracas, 1999, diploma Chacao Mayoralty, Caracas, 1999. Mem. Venezuelan Educators Assn. Avocations: air plastic modeller, trekking, astronomical observer. Fax: 2 7620329. Home: Av Baralt Esquina Llaguno, Centro Residencial Apt 143, Llaguno Caracas 1010, Venezuela Office: PO Box 17652, 1015-A Caracas Venezuela

DOMINGUEZ ORTEGA, LUIS, medical educator, health facility administrator; b. Barcelona, Spain, Oct. 4, 1941; s. Jose Dominguez and Dolores Ortega (Araujo) Dominguez; m. Mercedes Sanchez Tamayo, Jan. 2, 1969; children: Elena, Jose Luis. Cert., Ramiro Maeztu Inst., Madrid, Spain, 1962; MD, Complutense U., Madrid, 1969, diploma in internal medicine, 1975; PhD, Complutense Univ., 1999. Cert. gen. practitioner. Postgrad. Clinico Hosp., Madrid, 1969-73; asst. physician emergency svc. Dept. of Internal Medicine, 12 de Octubre Hosp., Madrid, 1974-77, asst. physician, 1977—, asst. prof., 1977-86, assoc. prof., 1986—; dir., coord. sleep disorders unit 12 de Octubre Hosp., Madrid, 1990—; dir., founder sleep unit Ruber Clinic, Madrid, 1988-89, 91—; mem. faculty bd. 12 de Octubre Hosp., 1984-88; mem. hosp. bd. Med. Coll., Madrid, 1984-88, candidate to pres. hosp. bd., 1986; organizer, chmn. internat. meeting Advances in Sleep Disorders, Madrid, 1992; mem. project evaluation com. of Nat. Agy. for Evaluation and Prospective in Interministerial Bd. of Sci. and Tech.; dir. univ. course on sleep medicine Complutense U., Madrid, 1996-99; mem. reading com. Vigilia-Sueño Rev.; mem. evaluation-selection com. Anales de Medicina interna Rev. Member Club Liberal, Madrid, 1980-89; founder, v.p. Asociacion Nacional Medicos Empresarios, Spain, 1991—. FISS grantee, 1980-90, 92. Mem. Am. Sleep Disorders Assn., Nat. Assn. Internal Medicine, N.Y. Acad. Scis., Internat. Assn. Internal Medicine, European Sleep Rsch. Soc., European Assn. Internal Medicine, Spanish Assn. of Hypnosis, Am. Soc. Clin. Hypnosis, Iberian Assn. of Sleep Pathology. Roman Catholic. Avocations: music, literature, tennis, hunting. Office: Clinica Ruber, Juan Bravo no 49, 28006 Madrid Spain

DOMINICZAK, ANNA F., medical educator; b. Gdansk, Poland, Aug. 26, 1954; came to Scotland, 1982; d. Jacob and Joanna (Muszkowska) Penson; m. Marek Henryk Dominiczak, Dec. 26, 1976; 1 child, Peter. MD, Med. Sch. Gdansk, 1978, U. Glasgow, 1989. Registrar MRC Blood Pressure Unit, Glasgow, 1986-89, sr. registrar, 1989-91; from lectr. in medicine to sr. lectr. U. Glasgow, 1991-96, reader in medicine, 1996-97, Brit. Heart Found. prof. cardiovasc. medicine, 1997—. Editor: (book) Genetics of Hypertension, 1999; rapid comms. editor: Clinical Science, 1998—. Project grantee Brit. Heart Found., 1998, The Wellcome Trust, 1999, coop. group grantee Med. Rsch. Coun., 1999. Fellow Royal Coll. Physicians, Am. Heart Assn.; mem. Internat. Soc. Hypertension. Avocations: reading, modern literature. Office: U Glasgow, 44 Church St, Glasgow G11 GNT, Scotland

DOMMERMUTH, WILLIAM PETER, marketing consultant, educator; b. Chgo.; s. Peter R. and Gertrude Dommermuth; m. H. Joan Hasty, June 6, 1959; children: Karin, Margaret, Jean. BA, U. Iowa; PhD, Northwestern U., 1964. Advt. copywriter Sears, Roebuck & Co., Chgo.; sales promotion mgr. Sears, Roebuck & Co.; asst., then asso. prof. mktg. U. Tex., Austin, 1961-67; asso. prof. U. Iowa, Iowa City, 1967-68; prof. So. Ill. U., Carbondale, 1968-86, U. Mo., St. Louis, 1986—; CEO Optiphonics, Inc.; Cons. bus. firms. Author (with Kernan and Sommers): Promotion: An Introductory Analysis, 1970, (with Andersen) Distribution Systems, 1972, (with Marcus and others) Modern Marketing, 1975, Modern Marketing Management, 1980, Promotion: Analysis, Creativity and Strategy, 1984, 2d edit., 1989; contbr. articles to profl. jours. Mem. Am. Mktg. Assn., Am. Psychol. Assn., So. Mktg. Assn., Midwest Mktg. Assn., Phi Beta Kappa, Beta Gamma Sigma, Theta Xi, Delta Sigma Pi. Home: 11 Paris Ct Lake Saint Louis MO 63367-1506

DOMONKOS, JENŐ, biochemist, researcher; b. Szeged, Hungary, Nov. 30, 1921. PhD, Sci. U., Szeged, Hungary, 1946; Dr habilitation, Med. U., Szeged, 1965. Chief neurol. rsch. lab. Szeged, 1979-91; prof. emeritus Med. U., Szeged, 1991—. Contbr. articles to profl. jours.; co-author (with others) (books) Recent Developments in Neurobiology in Hungary, Vol. 1, 1967, Handbook of Neurochemistry Vol. 7, 1972. Mem. Biochem. Soc. Hungary, Physiol. Soc. Hungary. Office: Med U Rsch Lab PO Box 397, 6701 Szeged Hungary

DÖMÖSI, PÁL BÉLA, mathematician, computer scientist, educator; b. Munkács, Hungary, Oct. 29, 1943; s. Pál Dömösi and Erzsébet Balázs; m. Éva Rápolti, Mar. 12, 1977; children: Enikő, Réka, Boglárka. Diploma in teaching, U. A. József, Szeged, Hungary, 1966, diploma in math., 1969; D of Univ., U. L. Kossuth, Debrecen, Hungary, 1983; DSc, Hungarian Acad. Sci., Budapest, 1994. Asst. mathematician Hungarian Cable Work, Szeged, 1966-67; computer operator U. A. József, Szeged, 1967-68; mathematician Bldg. Co. So. Hungary, Szeged, 1968-79; aspirant Hungarian Acad. Sci., Budapest, 1979-82; sci. advisor U. L. Kossuth, Debrecen, Hungary, 1982-89; prof. algebra, number theory U. L. Kossuth, Debrecen, 1994-99; prof. computer sci. U. Debrecen, 1999—; lectr. Karl Marx U. Econs., Budapest, 1982-89; docent algebra and number theory U. L. Kossuth, 1989-94, prof. algebra and number theory, 1994-99; invited prof. U. Aizu, Japan, 1997-98. Mem. editl. bd. Publ. Math., Math. Japan, Sci. Math; contbr. articles to profl. jours.; mem. reviewer Math. Revs., R.I., 1976—. DAAD Rsch. fellow U. Hamburg, 1994, 99, Soros Rsch. fellow Kyoto Sangyo U., 1994-95, Tempus Individual fellow U. Twente, 1996, Invited Rsch. fellow U. Turku, 1999, Széchény Disting. Prof. fellow U. Debrecen, 2000—. Mem. Janos Bolyai Math. Soc., J. Neumann Computer Sci. Soc., Am. Math. Soc., Am. Biog. Inst. (hon. rsch. bd. advisors). Avocations: travel, computer programming, math. jokes, history of computer sci. Home: Thuri András u 10/B, H-4034 Debrecen Hungary Office: U L Kossuth, Egyetem ter 1, H-4032 Debrecen Hungary

DOMPKE, NORBERT FRANK, retired photography studio executive; b. Chgo., Oct. 16, 1920; s. Frank and Mary (Manley) D.; m. Marjorie Gies, Dec. 12, 1964; children: Scott, Pamela. Grad. Wright Jr. Coll., 1939-40; student Northwestern U., 1946-49. Cost comptroller, budget dir. Scott Radio Corp., 1947; pres. TV Forecast, Inc., 1948-52, editor Chgo. edit. TV Guide, 1953, mgr. Wis. edit., 1954; pres. Root Photographers, Inc., Chgo., 1955-91, also chmn. bd. dirs; bd. dirs. Root Studio, Inc., 1991-96, ret., 1996. Adv. com. photography & audiovisual tech., So. Ill. U., 1980-81; adv. bd. Gordon Tech. High Sch., 1979-86. Co-founder TV Guide, 1947. With USAAC, 1943-47. CPA, Ill. Mem. NEA, Nat. Sch. Press Assn., Nat. Collegiate Sch. Press Assn., United Photographers Orgn. (pres. 1970-71), Profl. Photographers Am., Profl. Sch. Photographers Am. (v.p. 1966-67, 87-88, sec.-treas. 1967-69, pres. 1969-70, dir. 1971-78, treas. 1985-86, sec. 1986-87, pres. 1988-89), Photo Mktg. Assn. (recipient disting. svc. award 1992), Photographic Art & Sci. Found. (hall of fame elector 1969-96), Ill. Small Bus. Men's Assn. (dir. 1970-73), Chgo. Assn. Commerce and Industry (edn. com. 1966-94), Ill. High Sch. Press Assn., North Cen. Assn. (visitation com. 1986), Chgo. Bible Soc. (bd. advisors), Ill. C. of C., Internat. Club. Home: 175 N Harbor Dr Apt 2602 Chicago IL 60601-7345

DOMSCHKE, ALFRED GUNTHER, mechanical and electrical engineering consultant; b. São Salvador, Bahia, Brazil, Apr. 4, 1926; s. Alfred Conrad and Gertrud (Lemcke) D.; m. Lydia Meneghini, Apr. 11, 1957; children: Lélia Virginia, Vera Lucia, Luciana Ines, Gisela Marina. Grad., Col. Alfredo Pucca, São Paulo, Brazil, 1949; degree in mech. and elec. engring., U. São Paulo, 1954. Cert. engr., Brazil. Aircraft maintenance mgr. Real S/A Transportes Aéros, São Paulo, 1953-61; prof. combustion engines Esc. Politec., U. São Paulo, 1959-66; supr. engine lab. Internat. Harvester Máquinas S/A, São Paulo, 1961-64; quality control mgr. Metal Leve S/A, São Paulo, 1964-66; mgr. product design Motores Perkins S/A, São Paulo, 1966-71; prodn. mgr. Mercedes Benz Brazil S/A, São Paulo, 1972-91, ret., 1991; cons. Inst. Mauá Tech., São Paulo, 1979—, part-time prof. combustion engines, 1980—; co-author, presenter profl. symposia, 1980, 82. Home: 2036, Rua Comendador Elias Zarzur, 04736003 São Paulo Brazil

DOMZELLA, JANET, retired library director; b. Marquette, Mich., Mar. 22, 1935; d. Jack Carl and Alice Margaret (Blom) Messenger; m. Theodore S. Wodzinski (div. 1974); children: Christopher, Joseph, Daniel; m. Perry Landon Domzella, July 15, 1977; stepchildren: Perry, Pamela. BS, No. Mich. U., 1973; MLS, U. Buffalo, 1979. Sch. libr. media specialist Niagara Falls (N.Y.) Bd. Edn., 1974-75, Iroquois Ctrl. Sch., Elma, N.Y., 1975-77; dir. Lewiston (N.Y.) Pub. Libr., 1977-2000; ret., 2000. Co-author: Lewiston: Self Guided Tour, 1986. Vol. firefighter Upper Mountain Vol. Fire Co., Lewiston, 1980-90, treas., 1984-90; mem. Town of Lewiston Bur. Fire Prevention, 1988-90; mem. adv. bd. Documentary Heritage Program, 1991-93; mem. pub. libr. program Coll. of Charleston (S.C.) Conf., 1998. Mem. ALA, N.Y. Libr. Assn. Democrat. Roman Catholic. Avocations: rosemaling, watercolor.

DONADO, JAIME ENRIQUE, dentist, researcher; b. Barranquilla, Atlantico, Colombia, Jan. 5, 1956; s. Dilio Cesar Donado and Gladys Manotas; m. María Angeles Diez; children: Juan Pablo, Carlos Felipe, Daniel Enrique. Degree in Dentistry, U. Javeriana, Bogotá, Colombia, 1977, Degree in Endodontics, 1980, MSc, 1997. Dir. dept. endodontics U. Javeriana, 1994—; mem. sci. com. Fed. Odontologica Colombiana, Bogotá, 1992—. Contbr. articles to profl. jours. Recipient Rsch. in Dentistry award Fed. Odontologica Colombiana, 1992, Rsch. awards Assn. Colombiana de Facultades de Odontologia, 1995, 98. Mem. Soc. de Endodoncia de Bogotá (sec. 1985-87), Soc. Colombiana de Endodoncia (pres. 1993—), Assoc. Iberolatinoamericana de Endodoncia (pres. 1998—). E-mail: jaimedonado@andinet.com. Office: Diag 109A # 17-23 of 101, Santa Fe de Bogotá DC, Colombia

DONAHOO, LEONARD E., retired engineer; b. Feb. 4, 1954. BS, USMA, 1976. Water treatment sales Nalco Chem., Cleve., 1981-84; auto coating sales BASF Corp., Atlanta, Ga., 1981-89. Pres. Ballard Assn. Choral Harmonics, 1999—. Home: 5615 Wolf Pen Trce Prospect KY 40059-9630

DONAHUE, THOMAS MICHAEL, physics educator; b. Healdton, Okla., May 23, 1921; s. Robert Emmett and Mary (Lyndon) D.; m. Esther Marie McPherson, Jan. 1, 1950; children: Brian M., Kevin E., Neil M. A.B., Rockhurst Coll., 1942, D.Sc. (hon.), 1981; Ph.D., Johns Hopkins U., 1947. Rsch. assoc., asst. prof. Johns Hopkins U., 1947-51; asst. prof. U. Pitts., 1951-53, assoc. prof., 1953-57, prof., 1957-74, dir. Lab. Atmospheric and Space Sci., 1966-74, dir. Space Rsch. Coordination Ctr., 1966-74; chmn. dept. atmospheric and oceanic sci. and Space Physics Rsch. Lab., U. Mich., Ann Arbor, 1974-81, prof., 1981-87, Edward H. White II disting. univ. prof. planetary sci. dept. atmospheric oceanic and space scis., dept. physics, 1987-94; disting. univ. prof. emeritus, 1994—; dir. ctr. for integrated study global change U. Mich., 1990-93; mem. phys. scis. com. NASA, 1972-77, adv. coun., 1982-88, solar system exploration com., 1981-82; mem. Arecibo adv. bd. Cornell U., 1971-76, 86-89, chmn. 1989; mem. Space Telescope Sci. Inst. Adv. Com., 1986-89, chmn., 1987-89; chmn. solar terrestrial rels. com. NAS, mem. atmospheric scis. com., mem. geophysics rsch. bd., mem. climate bd., chmn. space sci. bd. 1982-88, mem. nominating com., 1987-88; chmn. space sci. in the 21st Century study NAS, 1984-87, com. for U.S.-USSR workshop on planetary scis., 1988-91, com. on planetary and lunar exploration, 1992-93; chmn. sci. steering groups Pioneer Venus multi-probe and orbital missions to Venus, 1974-93, pub. affairs com. Am. Geog. Union; trustee-at-large Upper Atmosphere Rsch. Corp., 1975-87; vice-chmn. exec. com., trustee Univ. Corp. for Atmospheric Rsch., 1978-85; chmn. bd. trustees Univs. Space Rsch. Assn., 1978-82; mem. vis. com. Max Planck Gesellschaft fur Aeronomie, 1989-96; mem. nat. tech. adv. com. Nat. Inst. for Global Environ. Change, 1992; Marcel Nicolet lectr. Am. Geophys. Union, 1993. Editor: Space Research X, 1969; assoc. editor numerous publs., particularly specializing in atomic physics and properties of planetary atmospheres; editor: Venus, 1983; assoc. editor: Planetary and Space Sci. Served with AUS, 1944-46. Guggenheim fellow, Paris, 1960; recipient Public Svc. award NASA, 1977, 88, 8, achievement awards Disting. Public Svc. medal, 1980, Wellock Disting. Rsch. Accomplishments award U. Mich., 1981, Stephen S. Attwood award Excellence in Engring., U. Mich., 1994; Arctowski medal Nat. Acad. Sci., 1981, Fleming medal Am. Geophys. Union, 1981; Rsch. Excellence award Coll. Engring., 1981; Henry Russel lectr. U. Mich., 1987; Space Sci. award AIAA, 1988; 1st Space Sci. medalist Nat. Space Club, 1989. Fellow AAAS, Am. Phys. Soc., Am. Geophys. Union (pres. solar-planetary rels. 1972-75, v.p. 1969-72, chmn. pub. policies com. 1990-93, Marcel Nicolet lectr. 1993), Mich. Soc. Fellows; mem. NAS, Internat. Acad. Astronautics. Achievements include participation in Voyager mission to outer planets, Galileo mission to Jupiter, Cassini Mission to Saturn, Planet B Mission to Mars, Spacelab 1, Apollo 17, Apollo-Soyuz, chmn. sci. steering group Pioneer Venus multiprobe/orbiter missions. Home: 1781 Arlington Blvd Ann Arbor MI 48104-4105

DONALD, ATHENE MARGARET, physicist educator; b. London, May 15, 1953; d. Walter and Annette Marian (Tylor) Griffith; m. Matthew James Donald, July 3, 1976; children: James George, Margaret Frances. BA, Cambridge U., 1974, MA, 1977, PhD, 1977. Postdoctoral Cornell U., Ithaca, N.Y., 1977-81; rsch. fellow Cambridge (U.K.) U., 1981-85, lectr., 1985-95, reader, 1995-98, prof., 1998—; cons. DSM, Holland, 1993—. Co-author: Liquid Crystalline Polymers, 1992; contbr. articles to profl. jours. Recipient Locker award U. Birmingham, 1989. Fellow Am. Phys. Soc., Inst. Physics (CV Boys prize 1989), Royal Soc., Inst. Materials (Rosenhaim prize 1995). Avocations: music, walking, ornithology. Office: Cavendish Lab, Madingley Rd, Cambridge CB3 0HE, England

DONALDSON, DAVID, pathologist; b. Birmingham, Eng., Feb. 13, 1936; s. Henry and Esther D. MB, ChB, U. Birmingham Med. Sch., 1959. House physician Selly Oak Hosp., Birmingham, 1959-60; house surgeon Children's Hosp., Birmingham, 1960; sr. house officer in clin. pathology Queen Elizabeth Hosp., Birmingham, 1960-61; asst. resident med. officer, registrar in gen. medicine Gen. Infirmary, Leeds, Eng., 1961-62; registrar in gen. medicine Victoria Hosp., Keighley, 1963-64; lectr., hon. sr. registrar in chem. pathology Inst. Neurology (Nat. Hosps. for Nervous Diseases), London,

1964-70; cons. in chemical pathology East Surrey Hosp., Redhill, Eng., 1970—, Crawley (Eng.) Hosp., 1970—; vice chmn. med. sub-com. Marie Curie Meml. Found., London, 1978-83; clin. dir. pathology dept. East Surrey Hosp., 1991-94; chmn. East Surrey divsn. Brit. Med. Assn., 1992-93; chmn. South West Thames Chem. Pathology Adv. Group South Thames Regional Health Authority, London, 1995—. Author: Psychiatric Disorders with a Biochemical Basis, 1998; co-author: Diagnostic Function Tests in Chemical Pathology, 1989, Essential Diagnostic Tests in Biochemistry and Haematology, 1971; dep. hon. editor, mem. editl. bd. Jour. Royal Soc. Health, 1997—; contbr. over 100 chpts. to books and articles to profl. jours. Fellow Royal Coll. Pathologists, Royal Coll. Physicians, Royal Soc. Medicine, Royal Soc. Health, Royal Geog. Soc. (life), Internat. Coll. Nutrition (life, Zhu Shoumin award 2000), Med. Soc. London; mem. AAAS, Assn. Clin. Biochemists, Assn. Clin. Pathologists, European Atherosclerosis Soc., Brit. Hyperlipidaemia Assn., Brit. Assn. Advancement Sci., Med. Soc. London, N.Y. Acad. Scis., Worshipful Soc. of Apothecaries of London (faculty of history and philosophy of medicine and pharmacy), Harveian Soc. London. Avocations: piano, music, history of medicine, reading scientific literature. Home: 5 Woodfield Way, Redhill Surrey RH1 2DP, England Office: Chem Pathology Dept, East Surrey Hosp, Redhill Surrey RH1 5RH, England

DONALDSON, GEORGE BURNEY, environmental consultant; b. Oakland, Calif., Mar. 16, 1945; s. George T. and L. M. (Burney) D.; m. Jennifer L. Bishop, Feb. 16, 1974; children: Dawn Marie, Matthew George. AS in Criminology, Porterville Coll., 1972. Registered environ. assessor, Calif.; cert. transp. specialist. Police officer City of Lindsay, Calif., 1966-67; distbn. mgr. Ortho divsn. Chevron Chem. Co., Lindsay, 1967-73; safety specialist Wilbur-Ellis Co., Fresno, Calif., 1973-77, safety dir., 1977-79, dir. corp. regulatory affairs, 1979-97; sr. environ. cons. Geomatrix Cons., Inc., Fresno, 1997—; industry rep. to White House Inter-Govtl. Sci. Engring. and Tech. Adv. Panel, Task Force on Transp. of Non-Nuclear Hazardous Materials, 1980; industry rep. Transp. Rsch. Bd.'s Nat. Strategies Conf. on Transp. of Hazardous Materials and Wastes in the 1980s, NAS, 1981, Hazardous Materials Transp. Conf., Nat. Conf. of State Legislatures, 1982; spkr. and moderator in field; dir. Western Fertilizer and Pesticide Safety seminar, Sacramento, 1979; spkr. Southeastern Agrl. Chem. Safety seminar, Winston-Salem, N.C., 1986. Chmn. industry/govt. task force for unique on-site hazardous waste recycling, devel. task force for computerized regulatory software and data base sys., devel. task force modifying high expansion foam tech. for fire suppression; hazardous materials adviser, motor carrier rating com. Calif. Hwy. Patrol, 1978-79; bd. dirs., mem. exec. com. Californians for Food & Shelter. With U.S. Army, 1962-65. Mem. VFW, Western Agrl. Chems. Assn. (past chmn. transp., distbn. and safety com., outstanding mem. of yr. 1981, govtl. affairs com., regulatory affairs com., trustee polit. action com.), Nat. Agrl. Chems. Assn. (past chmn. transp. and distbn. com., occupl. safety and health com., environ. mgmt. com., state affairs com., moderator spring conf. 1989), U.S. Inter-Regional Coordinating Coun. (trans. and distbn. com.), Am. Soc. Safety Engrs., Calif. Fertilizer Assn. (transp. and distbn. com., environ. com.), Fresno Agrl. Round Table, Fresno City and County C. of C. (agrl. steering com., govt. affairs com.), Calif. C. of C. (environ. policy com.), Am. Legion, Elks. Office: Geomatrix Cons Inc 2444 Main St Ste 215 Fresno CA 93721-2734

DONALDSON, IAIN MALCOLM LANE, physiologist, educator, researcher; b. Bathgate, W Lothian, Scotland, Oct. 22, 1937; s. Archibald T. and Milly (Bailey) D.; m. J. Patricia Maule, July 18, 1961; 1 child, David. BSc, U. Edinburgh, Scotland, 1959, MB, ChB, 1962; MA by spl. resolution, Oxford U., Eng., 1973. Hon. lectr. U. Edinburgh, Scotland, 1966-69; Anglo-French rsch. scholar U. Paris, 1969; rsch. officer U. Oxford, Oxford, Eng., 1970-79; fellow and tutor in medicine St. Edmund Hall U. Oxford, 1973-79; prof. zoology U. of Hull, Eng., 1979-87; prof. neurophysiology U. Edinburgh, Scotland, 1987—; emeritus fellow St. Edmund Hall, U. Oxford, Eng., 1979—; mem. Dist. Health Authority Scarborough, Eng., 1981. Contbr. numerous articles on physiology of nervous system (with special reference to vision and eye movement). Fellow Royal Coll. Physicians Edinburgh; mem. Physiological Soc. Avocations: classical music, history of sci. and medicine, European lit. of middle ages. Office: U Edinburgh, Dept Neurosci, Edinburgh EH8 9LE, Scotland

DONALDSON, JAMES NEILL, banker; b. Washington County, Pa., Mar. 25, 1940; s. James Reed and Mary Alice (Neill) D. BA in Polit. Sci., Westminster Coll., 1962; MEd, U. Pitts., 1965, postgrad. in law, 1962-64. cert. trust and fin. advisor; accredited estate planner. Trust adminstr. Bankers Trust Co., N.Y.C., 1967-70, asst. trust officer, 1970-73; trust officer Bankers Trust Co., White Plains, N.Y., 1973-76, officer-in-charge Trust Adminstrv. Unit, 1976, v.p., 1976-78, head trust office, 1978-82, with Trust Adminstrn. Unit, 1982-83; head new bus. devel., trust and estates group Chem. Bank, N.Y.C., 1983-88, head trust and estates adminstrn. mgmt., 1989-90; sect. head mgr. trust and estates adminstrn. Chase Manhattan Bank, N.Y.C., 1990-96, personal trust sales Global Trust and Fiduciary Unit, 1996—; Chase rep. to Corp. Fiduciaries Assn. of N.Y.C.; editl. mini-adv. bd. Trusts & Estates Mag., 1997—; lectr. Bank Mktg. Assn. Conf., 1995, 99; mem. Estate Planning Coun. Westchester County (N.Y.), 1975—, bd. dirs., 1980-85, treas. 1986-87, v.p., 1988-89, pres. 1989; mem. Estate Planning Coun. Rockland County (N.Y.), 1973—, pres., 1984-85; mem. Estate Planning Coun. N.Y.C., 1983—, bd. dirs., 1988-91, 97—; lectr. estate adminstrn. Trust Div., N.Y. State Bankers Assn., 1975, 90, 93, 96, mem. estate planning com., 1980-83, mem. mktg. com., 1984—, chmn. 1989-94. Contbr. articles to profl. publs. Mem. Planned Giving Com., U. Pitts.; mem. planned giving com. N.Y. chpt. Arthritis Found. Mem. Phi Kappa Tau. Office: Chase Manhattan Pvt Bank 1211 Avenue Of The Americas New York NY 10036-8701

DONALDSON, JOHN CECIL, JR., consumer products company executive; b. Bklyn., Dec. 8, 1933; s. John Cecil and Josephine (Greason) D.; m. Marilyn J. Smith, Aug. 29, 1959; children: Susan, John III. AB, Brown U., 1956; MBA, U. Pa., 1959; postgrad., Bentley Sch. Acctg., 1957, LaSalle Law Sch., 1959. Various positions Gen. Motors Corp., Flint, Mich., 1960-71; zone mgr. Gen. Motors Corp., Buffalo, 1971-76; zone mgr. Gen. Motors Corp., Newark, 1976-77, mgr. forward product planning, 1977-78; from dir. sales and mktg. to v.p. Corbin Ltd., 1979-85; exec. v.p. and gen. mgr. TMG Corp., N.Y.C., 1986—; pres. Gen. Motors Exec. Club, Newark, N.J., 1977-78. Mem. Am. Mktg. Assn. Republican. Avocations: ice skating, tennis, golf. Home: 36 Nottingham Way Millington NJ 07946-1917 Office: TMG Corp 1290 Avenue Of The Americas New York NY 10104-0101

DONALDSON, PENNY LEEANNE, library director; b. Dodge City, Kans., Feb. 9, 1944; d. Harley Philip and Eunice Maxine Gover; m. Ervin George Donaldson, June 12, 1965; children: Pamela Johnston, Bruce, Jyrel, Arlee. BS, U. Kans., 1967; MLS, Emporia State U., 1993. Mem. interlibr. loan staff U. Kans. Librs., Lawrence, 1986-94, interlibr. loan libr., 1994-96; dir. Atchison (Kans.) Libr., 1996—. Bd. dirs. Kans. Interlibr. Loan Coun., 1994-96. Mem. DAR, AAUW (pres. 1999-2000), Kans. Libr. Assn., Magna Charta Dames, Rotary (newsletter editor 1996—), Atchison C. of C. (quality coun. 1996—, amb. 1996—), Atchison County Ext. Coun. (mem. exec. bd. 1999—). Republican. Presbyterian. Avocations: knitting, crocheting, sewing. Home: 622 N 4th St Atchison KS 66002-1938 Office: Atchison Libr 401 Kansas Ave Atchison KS 66002-2495

DONALDSON, SARAH SUSAN, radiologist; b. Portland, Oreg., Apr. 20, 1939. BS, RN, U. Oreg., 1961; MD, Harvard U., 1968. Intern U. Wash., 1968-69; resident in radiol. therapy Stanford (Calif.) Med. Ctr., 1969-72; fellow in pediatric oncology Inst. Gustave-Roussy, 1972-73; prof. radiol. oncology Stanford U. Sch. Medicine., 1973—. Office: Stanford U Med Ctr Dept Radio/Oncology 300 Pasteur Dr Palo Alto CA 94304-2203

DONALDSON, WILLIAM HENRY, financial executive, insurance company executive; b. Buffalo, June 2, 1931; s. Eames and Guida (Marx) D.; m. Sept. 17, 1960; children: Adam, Kimberly, Matthew. BA, Yale U., 1953, MA (hon.), 1970; MBA with distinction, Harvard U., 1958; LLD (hon.), Webster U., 1992; DPhil (hon.), St. Lawrence U., 1995; DHL (hon.), Alfred U., 1995. Chmn., chief exec. Donaldson, Lufkin & Jenrette, Inc., N.Y.C., 1959-73; undersec. of state U.S. Dept. State, Washington, 1973-74; spl. cons. to v.p. of U.S. Washington, 1974; dean, Beinecke prof. mgmt. Yale Grad. Mgmt. Sch., New Haven, 1975-80; chmn., CEO Donaldson Enterprises, Inc., N.Y.C., 1980-90; chmn., chief exec. N.Y. Stock Exch., N.Y.C., 1990-95; founder, sr. advisor Donaldson, Lufkin and Jenrette, Inc., 1996-2000; chair., pres., CEO Aetna Inc., Hartford, 2000—; bd. dirs. Aetna Life & Casualty, Bright Horizons Family Solutions, Inc., Mail.com Inc. Trustee, chmn. fin. com. Ford Found., N.Y.C., 1968-80; trustee Yale U., New Haven, 1970-75; ptnr. N.Y.C. Partnership; bd. dirs. Bus. Coun. of State of N.Y., 1990-96, Lincoln Ctr. for Performing Arts, N.Y.C.; trustee N.Y. Police Found., Marine Corps Univ. Found., Aspen Inst.; gov. Fgn. Policy Assn.; chmn. Carnegie Endowment for Internat. Peace, 1999—. 1st lt. USMC, 1953-55. Recipient Pres.'s Disting. Svc. award SUNY, 1976; named Businessman of Yr., AP, 1969. Mem. Inst. CFAs, Yale Mgmt. Sch. (chmn. bd. advisors 1995—), Coun. on Fgn. Rels. Office: 277 Park Ave New York NY 10172-0003 Address: Aetna Inc 151 Farmington Ave Hartford CT 06156-0001

DONALDSON, WILLIS LYLE, research institute administrator; b. Cleburne, Tex., May 1, 1915; s. Charles Lyle and Anna (Bell) D.; m. Frances Virginia Donnell, Aug. 20, 1938; children: Sarah Donaldson Seaberg, Susan Donaldson Pollock, Sylvia Donaldson Nelson, Anthony Lyle. B.S., Tex. Tech. U., 1938. Registered profl. engr., Pa., Tex. Distbn. engr. Tex. Electric Service Co., 1938-42, supervisory engr., 1945-46; asst. prof. elec. engring. Lehigh U., 1946-51, assoc. prof., 1953-54; with S.W. Research Inst., San Antonio, 1954—; v.p. S.W. Research Inst., 1964-72, v.p. planning and program devel., 1972-74, sr. v.p. planning and program devel., 1974-85, sr. cons., 1985—. Bd. dirs. San Antonio Chamber Music Soc., pres., 1962-72, 87-93, mem., 1954—. Capt. USNR, 1942-45, 51-53. Named Disting. Engr. Tex. Tech. U., 1969. Fellow IEEE, Am. Soc. Nondestructive Testing; mem. Armed Forces Communications and Electronics Assn. (disting. life), Sigma Xi, Tau Beta Pi, Eta Kappa Nu, Alpha Chi. Home: 104 Pontiac Ln San Antonio TX 78232-3507 Office: 6220 Culebra Rd San Antonio TX 78238-5166

DONALSON, MALCOLM DREW, classics educator; b. Albany, Ga., July 24, 1951; s. William Levon Donalson and Julia Janet King; m. Deborah Ellen Hoffman, June 25, 1988; children: Christopher Damian, Sabina Anuradha, Zoë Simone. BA in Latin and History, Fla. State U., 1974, MA in Classics, 1985, PhD in Humanities, 1991. Cert. tchr. latin and history, Fla. Tchr. Latin, Greek, and history Marianna (Fla.) H.S., 1974-84; tchg. asst. dept. classics Fla. State U., Tallahassee, 1984-89; tchr. Latin, Episcopal H.S., Baton Rouge, 1989-90, McKinley Mid. Magnet Sch., Baton Rouge, 1990-91, Istrouma Med. Magnet Sch., Baton Rouge, 1990-91; asst. prof. fgn. langs. Ala. Sch. Math. and Sci., Mobile, 1991—. Author: St. Jerome's Chronicon, 1996, The Domestic Cat in Roman Civilization, 1999; contbr. articles to profl. publs., including The Classical Outlook, The Classical Jour. Grantee Am. Hellenic Ednl. Assn., 2000. Mem. Am. Classical League, Classical Assn. Midwest and South, Classical Assn. Ala. Hindu. Avocation: classical coinage. Office: Ala Sch Math & Sci 1255 Dauphin St Mobile AL 36604-2519

DO NASCIMENTO, ALEXANDRE, archbishop; b. Malanje, Angola, Mar. 1, 1925. ordained priest Roman Catholic Ch., 1952. Prof. dogmatic theology in maj. sem. of Luanda (Angola); editor Cath. newspaper O Apostolada; in exile, Lisbon, Portugal, 1961-71, returned to Angola, 1971; then prof. Pius XII Inst. Social Scis.; consecrated bishop of Malanje, 1975; nominated archbishop of Lubango and apostolic adminstr. of Onjiva, 1977, archbishop of Luanda, 1986—; held hostage by Angolan guerrillas in 1982; elevated to Sacred Coll. of Cardinals, 1983; titular see, St. Mark in Agro Laurentino. Mem. Congregation for Evangelization of Peoples, Caritas Internationalis (pres. 1983-91), Congregation for Cath. Edn. Address: Archbishop, CP 87, 1230c Luanda Angola

DONATH, THERESE, artist, author; b. Hammond, Ind.; student Monticello Coll., 1946-47; BFA, St. Joseph's Coll., 1975; additional study Oxbow Summer Sch. Painting, Immaculate Heart Coll., Hollywood, Calif., Penland, N.C., Haystack, Maine; radio/TV personality, 1978-92. Interviewer, producer Viewpoint, Sta. WLNR-FM, Lansing, Ill., 1963-64; reporter, columnist N.W. Ind. Sentinel, 1965; freelance writer Monterey Peninsula Herald, 1981-85; contbg. author Monterey Life mag. 1981-85; asst. dir. Michael Karolyi Meml. Found., Vence, France, 1979; one-woman shows include: Ill. Inst. Tech., Chgo., 1971; group shows include: Palos Verdes (Calif.) Mus., 1974, L.A. Inst. Contemporary Art, 1978, Mus. Contemporary Art, Chgo., 1975, Calif. State U., Fullerton, 1973, No. Ill. U., DeKalb, 1971, Bellevue (Wash.) Mus. Art, 1986-87; represented in permanent collections including Kennedy Gallery, N.Y.C., also pvt. collections; creative cons. Aslan Tours and Travel, 1983-85; instr., lectr. Penland, N.C., 1970, Haystack Mountain Sch., Deer Isle, Maine, 1974, Sheffield Poly., Eng., 1978. Bd. dirs., sec. Mental Health Soc. Greater Chgo., 1963-64; exec. dir. Lansing (Ill.) Mental Health Soc., 1963-64. Recipient awards No. Ind. Art Mus., 1966, 70, 71, 73; grantee Ragdale Found., Lake Forest, Ill., 1982. Represented in The Mirror Book, 1978; author: Screams and Laughter, 1992; author, illustrator: Before I Die, A Creative Legacy, 1989; contbr. articles to profl. jours., newspapers; illustrator: Run Computer Run, 1983.

DONATH, TIBOR, anatomist; b. Budapest, Nov. 13, 1926; s. Arpad and Margit (Fleischmann) D.; m. Agnes Czimmermann, July 9, 1955; 1 child, Judit. MD, Semmelweis U., 1950; cand. med. sci., Hungarian Acad. Sci., 1964; degree in psychology, Eotvos Lorand U., 1969. Asst. dept. anatomy med. sch. Semmelweis U., Budapest, 1947-50, asst. prof., 1950-57, assoc. prof., 1957-69, prof., 1969-96, prof. emeritus, 1996—; dep. dean dental faculty Semmelweis U., 1969-72. Author: Structure of the Human Body, 5 edits., 1967-90, Anatomical Atlas, 7 edits., 1985-99, Explanatory Anatomical Dictionary, 1969; chief editl. bd. Orvosegyetem, 1989—. Recipient Verdienst Medaillon Mi. of Health, Germany 1969, Markusovszky award Hungarian Med. Jour., 1985, 88, Motesz award, 1995, Huzella award, 1995. Fellow Internat. Acad. Cytology; mem. Internat. Fedn. Assn. Anatomists (councillor 1991-97), Hungarian Anat. Soc. (pres. 1991-97), Soc. for Movement-Biology (pres. 1990—), Soc. for Med. Artists (v.p. 1992—). Avocations: arts, music, swimming, gardening. Home: Hattyu St 16, 1015 Budapest Hungary Office: Semmelweis U Dept Anatomy, Tuzolto St 58, 1094 Budapest Hungary

DONATI, ROBERT MARIO, physician, educational administrator; b. Richmond Heights, Mo., Feb. 28, 1934; s. Leo S. and Rose Marie (Gualdoni) D. BS in Biology, St. Louis U., 1955, MD, 1959. Diplomate Am. Bd. Nuclear Medicine. Intern St. Louis City Hosp., 1959-60; asst. resident John Cochran Hosp., St. Louis, 1960-62; fellow in nuclear medicine St. Louis U., 1962-63; pvt. practice specializing in nuclear medicine St. Louis, 1963-93; mem. staff St. Louis VA Med. Ctr., 1963-83, chief nuclear medicine svc., 1968-79, chief of staff, 1979-83; mem. staff St. Louis U. Hosps., 1963-93, interim chief exec. officer, 1987-88; mem. staff St. Mary's Health Ctr., 1984-93; mem. faculty Sch. Medicine St. Louis U., 1963—, asst. prof. internal medicine, 1965-68, assoc. prof., 1968-74, prof., 1974-93, prof. emeritus internal medicine, 1993—, prof. radiology, 1979-93, prof. emeritus radiology, 1993—, dir. div. nuclear medicine Sch. Medicine, 1968-87, sr. assoc. dean Sch. Medicine, 1983-93; exec. assoc. v.p. Med. Ctr., 1985-93, acting v.p., 1986; adj. prof. medicine Washington U. Sch. Medicine, 1979-83; rschr. in clin. investigative nuclear medicine and humoral control of cellular proliferation; fin. com. del. Am. Bd. Med. Spltys., 1984-90. Editor: (with W.T. Newton) Radioassay in Clinical Medicine, 1973, (with J. Edwards) Current Medical Practice, 1992; contbr. articles to profl. jours. Mem. Presdl. Adv. Commn. on VA, 1972, Inst. Medicine com. to estimate VA physician needs, 1988-90; bd. dirs. Alliance for Cmty. Health, Inc., 1986-96, Ind. Colls. and Univs. of Mo., 1985, Affiliated Med. Transport, Inc., 1985-89, Healthline Mgmt. Svcs., Inc., 1986-94, chmn., 1988-93, Healthline Corp. Health Metro St. Louis, 1992-94, Ctrl. Med. Ctr., Inc., 1988-89, Healthlink, Inc., 1987-93, Abbott Ambulance Co., Inc., 1989-94, chmn., 1992-94; mem. HEW Task Force on Health Effects Ionizing Radiation, 1978-79; mem. desegregation monitoring and adv. com. U.S. Dist. Ct., 1980. Decorated Army Commendation medal; recipient VA Disting. Service award, 1983, alumni Merit award St. Louis U., 1996. Mem. AMA (residency rev. com. for nuclear medicine 1978-80, coun. on med. schs. 1984-94), AAUP, Am. Bd. Nuclear Medicine (life, bd. dirs. 1980—, vice chmn. 1984-85, chmn. 1985-86), St. Louis Med. Soc., Am. Fedn. for Clin. Rsch. (councilor 1967-70), Ctrl. Soc. Clin. Rsch., N.Y. Acad. Scis., Soc. Nuclear Medicine (acad. coun. 1970—, trustee 1977-81, 90-92, assoc. chmn. sci. program 1978, mem. publs. com. 1979-83, chmn. 1982-83, mem. bus. advisors com. 1989-93, chmn. 1990-92), Am. Coll. Nuclear Physicians, Internat. Socs. Hematology, Soc. Med. Cons. to Armed Forces, Cosmos Club, Phi Beta Kappa, Sigma Xi, Alpha Omega Alpha. Roman Catholic. Home: 5335 Botanical Ave Saint Louis MO 63110-3123 Office: St Louis U Sch Medicine 1402 S Grand Blvd Saint Louis MO 63104-1004

DONATO, ROSARIO FRANCESCO, neurologist, educator; b. Castrovillari, Cosenza, Italy, Dec. 1, 1947; s. Antonio and Isabella (Ceravolo) D.; m. Ileana Giambanco, June 8, 1976; children: Valerio, Giulio. MD, Cath. U. Sacred Heart, Rome, 1973, specialization in neurology, 1977. Asst. prof. Cath. U. Sacred Heart, 1973-79; charged prof. U. Perugia, Italy, 1979-83, assoc. prof., 1983-86, prof., 1986—; dir. dept. exptl. medicine and biochem. sci. U. Perugia, 1993—; pres. Anatomical Surgical Acad. of Perugia, Italy, 1998—. Co-author: Anatomia Umana, 1990; contbr. articles to sci. jours. Recipient Federico Nitti award Italian Acad. Scis., Rome, 1978. Mem. Am. Soc. for Cell Biology, European Calcium Soc. (v.p. 1997-2000, pres. 2000—), Internat. Soc. for Neurochemistry. Avocations: antiques, music, reading, travel. Office: U Perugia Dep Exptl Med Biochem Sci, Via del Giochetto, 06122 Perugia Italy

DONATOS, GEORGE SPYRIDON, statistics and econometrics educator, consultant; b. Corfu, Greece, Feb. 23, 1944; s. Spyridon George and Anna Athanasios (Morfopoulou) D.; m. Maria Efstathios Dessinioti, Feb. 2, 1949; 1 child, Anna. BS in Math., U. Athens, Greece, 1967; BS, Nat. Tech. U., Athens, 1973; PhD in Econ., U. Athens, 1980; MS in Stats., Concordia U., Montreal, Can., 1983; Readership in Econ. (hon.), U. Athens, 1984. Registered profl. engr. Civil engr., cons. Athens, 1973-80; lectr. stats. and econometrics U. Athens, 1980-83, reader, 1984-85, prof., 1985—; rschr. Concordia U., 1981-83; cons. pub. orgns., Athens, 1985—; dir. Nat. Sch. Pub. Adminstrn., Athens, 1990-94; head sect. quantitative methods U. Athens, 1990—. Author: Methods of Programming, 1981, Properties of Econometric Estimators for Small Samples, 1984, Statistical Methods, 1988; contbr. articles to profl. jours. With Greek Army, 1967-70. Mem. Tech. Chamber Greece, Greek Statis. Inst., Greek Econ. Soc. Avocation: swimming. Home: Michalopoulou 3, 152 36 Penteli Athens Greece Office: Univ Athens Dept Econ, 8 Pesmazoglou Str, GR-10559 Athens Greece

DONAUER, ERICH, neurosurgeon; b. Steinwenden, Germany, Oct. 10, 1953; s. Pirmin and Maria Anna (Dietrich) D.; m. Gabriele Wevers, Oct. 15, 1983 (div. 1992); children: Johannes, Katharina; m. Silke Denda, Dec. 10, 1993; children: Franziska, Kristina, Bernadette. MD, U. Saarbrucken, 1979. Resident in neurosurgery U. Homburg, Germany, 1981-84; from resident stereotactic dept. to cons. neurosurgery Saarland U., Germany, 1984-95; chief neurosurgical clinic Ctr. Neurosurgery, Plau, Germany, 1995—; examination com. U. Saarbrucken, 1990-95. Served in German armed forces, 1979-81. Mem. AAAS, German Soc. Neurosurgeons. Avocations: painting, classical music, hunting, fishing, hiking. Home: Klinikum, Plau Am See Gerichtsbg, 19395 Plau Am See Gerichtsberg, Germany Office: Neurosurgical Clinic, 19395 Plau Germany

DONDO, ELIAKIM ARACKHA, water purification director, consultant; b. Kisumu, Kenya, Jan. 5, 1951; s. Joseph and Yunia (Auma) D.; m. Margaret Nabwire Arackha, Feb. 15, 1970. MBA, U. Eng., Oxford, 1985. Asst. sec. Insurance Co., Mombasa, Kenya, 1968-70; head statistics, mktg. Insurance Co., Nairobi, Kenya, 1970-77; acct. dir. Advertising, mktg., Nairobi, Kenya, 1977-84; mng. dir. Rothchild Engring., Nairobi, Kenya, 1985—; chmn., mng. dir. Water Pure Ltd., Nairobi, Kenya, 1997—. Chmn. USIGU Welfare Assn., Kenya, 1985-92. Seventh Day Adventist. Avocations: volleyball, football, dancing, choir, movies. Phone: 350528. Office: Water Pure Ltd, PO Box 54331, Nairobi Kenya

DONDUKOV, ALEKSANDR NIKOLAYERICH, Russian government official; b. 1954. Grad., Moscow Inst. of Aviation, 1977. Min. Sci. and Tech. Govt. of Russia, Moscow, 2000—. Office: Ministry of Sci & Tech, Tverskaya 11, 103905 Moscow Russia*

DONECHE, BERNARD JEAN, enology educator; b. Bordeaux, France, Mar. 1, 1950; s. Andre and Madeleine (Couget) D.; m. Françoise Weinzorn, Sept. 7, 1985; children: Marie, Anne-Sophie, Louis. MS, U. Bordeaux, 1972, PhD in Chemistry, 1976, DSc, 1987. Asst. Inst. of Enology, Bordeaux, 1974-79, sr. lectr., 1980-88, prof., 1988—; expert Internat. Vine and Wine Office, Paris, 1988—; tech. mgr. Internat. Wine Tasting Show, Bordeaux; relation press Inst. of Enology, 1980—. Editor: New Progress in Wine Microbiology, 1992, New Progress in Wine Chromatography, 1993, New Progress in Physical Treatments of Wine, 1994; contbr. chpts. to books and articles to profl. jours. Sec. HQ Infantry Divsn., 1977-78. Roman Catholic. Avocations: history, wines of the world. Home: 40 Rue Docteur A Barraud, 33000 Bordeaux France Office: Faculty of Enology, 351 Cours de la Liberation, 33405 Talence Cedex France

DONEGAN, CHARLES EDWARD, lawyer, educator; b. Chgo., Apr. 10, 1933; s. Arthur C. and Odessa (Arnold) D.; m. Patty Lou Harris, June 15, 1963; 1 son, Carter Edward. B.S.C., Roosevelt U., 1954; M.S., Loyola U., 1959; J.D., Howard U., 1967; LL.M., Columbia, 1970. Bar: N.Y. 1968, D.C. 1968, Ill. 1979. Pub. sch. tchr. Chgo., 1956-59; with Office Internal Revenue, Chgo., 1959-62; labor economist U.S. Dept. Labor, Washington, 1962-65; legal intern U.S. Commn. Civil Rights, Washington, summer 1966; asst. counsel NAACP Legal Def. Fund, N.Y.C., 1967-69; lectr. law Baruch Coll., N.Y.C., 1969-70; asst. prof. law State U. N.Y. at Buffalo, 1970-73; assoc. prof. law Howard U., 1973-77; vis. assoc. prof. Ohio State U., Columbus, 1977-78; asst. regional counsel U.S. EPA, 1978-80; prof. law So. U., Baton Rouge, 1980—; sole practice law Chgo. and Washington, 1984—; arbitrator steel industry, 1972, U.S. Postal Svc., New Orleans, D.C. Superior Ct., 1987—, Fed. Mediation and Conciliation Svc., 1985—, N.Y. Stock Exch.; vis. prof. law La. State U., summer 1981, N.C. Cen. U., Durham, 1988—, So. U., Baton Rouge, spring 1992; real estate broker; mem. bd. consumer claims Dist. D.C., 1988—; mem. Mayor's Transition Task Force, Washington, 1995; moot ct. judge Georgetown U. Law Sch., Washington, 1987—, Howard U. Law Sch., Washington, 1987—, Balsa, 1987—; spkr., participant nat. confs. on law, edn. and labor rels. Author: Discrimination in Public Employment, 1975; Contbr. articles to profl. jours., to Dictionary Am. Negro Biography. Active Ams. for Dem. Action; me. adv. com. D.C. Bd. of Edn. Named one of Top 42 Lawyers in Washington Area, Washington Afro-Am. Newspaper, 1993, 94, 95, 96' Ford Found. scholar, 1965-67. Columbia U., 1972-73, NEH Postdoctoral fellow in Afro-Am. studies Yale U., 1972-73. Mem. ABA (vice chmn. edn. and curriculum com. local govt. law sect. 1972-80, pub. edn. com. sect. local govt. 1974-84, chmn. liaison com. AALS, 1984, chair arbitration sect.), Nat. Bar Assn. (labor and employment law sect., steering com.), D.C. Bar Assn., Washington Bar Assn. (chmn. legal edn. com.), Chgo. Bar Assn., Fed. Bar Assn., Cook County Bar Assn., Am. Arbitration Assn. (arbitrator), D.C. Fee Arbitration Bd. (bd. govs. 1990—), Nat. Conf. Black Lawyers (bd. organizers), Nat. Futures Assn. (arbitrator), Nat. Assn. Securities Dealers (arbitrator), Assn. Henri Capitant, Roosevelt U. Alumni Assn. (rep. at George Washington U. 175th anniversary charter day convocation 1996), Loyola U. Alumni Assn. (v.p. Washington), Howard U. Alumni Assn. (rep. at Hunter Coll. Centennial 1970), Columbia U. Alumni Assn. (v.p. law Washington), Alpha Phi Alpha, Phi Alpha Kappa, Phi Alpha Delta. Home: 4315 Argyle Ter NW Washington DC 20011-4243 Office: 601 Pennsylvania Ave NW Ste 900 Washington DC 20004-3615 also: 311 S Wacker Dr Ste 4550 Chicago IL 60606-6622

DONELAN, PETER ANDREW, dermatologist; b. Memphis, Nov. 13, 1953; s. Richard T. and Irene M. (Jacobson) D. BA in Chemistry, Wake Forest U., 1975; MD, U. South Fla., 1978. Diplomate, Am. Bd. Dermatology. Intern U. South Fla., Tampa, Fla., 1978-79; resident in internal medicine U. South Fla., Tampa, 1979-80, resident in dermatology, 1980-83, assoc. clin. prof. medicine, 1984—; instr. dermatologic surgery VA Hosp., 1993—; pvt. practice, Tampa, 1983—; chief dermatology Tampa Gen. Hosp., 1987-88, U. Com. Hosp., 1993—. Mem. editorial bd. Bull. Hillsboro County Med. Soc., 1987—. Named to Best Doctors in Am., 1996-97. Fellow Am. Acad. Dermatology, Am. Soc. Dermatol. Surgery; mem. Fla. Dermatol. Soc., Leaders Soc. of Dermatology Found., Fla. Med. Soc., Green Jacket Club, Pres.'s Coun. Avocations: golf, skiing. Office: 3000 E Fletcher Ave Ste 200 Tampa FL 33613-4644

DONELY, GEORGE ANTHONY THOMAS, III, economist, consultant; b. New Orleans, Aug. 14, 1934; s. George A.T. and Valerie Clare (Burmaster) D.; m. Lisa Suzanne Young, June 30, 1963; 1 child, Valerie Jennie Young. AB in Econs. cum laude, Williams Coll., 1956; MA in Econs., Columbia U., 1958; PhD, U. Mashad, Iran, 1967. Economist Lionel D. Edie & Co., N.Y.C., 1959-60; instr. La. State U., New Orleans, 1960-61; joined Fgn. Service, Dept. State, 1961-69; economist IMF, Washington, 1969-91; mng. dir. sr. vol. program St. Mary's County, Md.; ret.; cons. Miss Lisa's Sugarless Foods, Inc., Washington, 1985-92. Contbr. articles to profl. jours. Mem. steering com. Friends of Music at Smithsonian, Washington, 1972—; vol. Md. Hist. Trust, Annapolis, 1982-85; bd. dirs., treas. Chamber Orch. So. Md., 1998-2000; mem. restoration adv. bd. Patuxent River NAS. Ford Found. fellow Columbia U., 1958. Mem. Am. Econ. Assn., Econ. History Assn., Round Table, St. Mary's River Yacht Club, Met. Club, Williams Club, Rotary (Paul Harris fellow). Home: St Richard's Manor 22880 Old Manor Ln Lexington Park MD 20653-2146

DONEV, VASSIL STEFANOV, finance company executive, financial consultant; b. Varna, Bulgaria, Mar. 22, 1955; s. Stefan Vassilev and Paraskeva Georgieva (Nikolova) D. MSc in Electronic Engrng., Tech. U., Varna, 1980; PhD in Electronic Engrng., Shirshov Inst., Moscow, 1988; MSc in Banking and Bank Mgmt., U. Econs., Varna, 1995. Cert. fin. and bus. cons. R&D engr. Naval Acad., Varna, 1980-81, labs. mgr., 1981-82; R&D engr. Inst. Oceanology, Varna, 1982-91; divsn. dir. T-Coor Consulting, Pretoria, South Africa, 1991-92; analyst Std. Bank, Pretoria, 1992-93; mng. dir. ABC Invest, Ltd., Varna, Bulgaria, 1994—; regional dir. Nat. Employment Agy., 1999—; cons. Trade Unions, Sofia, Bulgaria, 1994—; bd. dirs. Capital Co., Sofia. Patentee in field. Recipient Cert. of Recognition, USAID, Washington, 1996; named Bus. Cons. of the Yr., South African Assn. Bus. Cons., Pretoria, 1993, Broker of Yr., Nat. Stock Exch., Sofia, 1995. Mem. Assn. for Bus. Partnership (bd. mem. 1996), Union Stock Brokers (v.p. 1995—), Nat. Stock Exch., Am. Mgmt. Assn. Christian Orthodox. Avocations: skiing, gardening. E-mail: vass@abeis.bg. Fax: 359 52 601351. Office: Investco PLC 3A Tzar Simeon, PO Box 77, 9000 Varna Bulgaria

DONEVSKI, BOZIN, mechanical engineering educator, researcher; b. Gari-Debar, Macedonia, Jan. 5, 1946; s. Jordan and Petra (Dimovska) D.; m. Maria Wiesława Kuźnik, Dec. 31, 1980; 1 child, Stefan. Dipl.Ing. in Mech. Engrng., U. Sts. Cyril and Methodious, Skopje, Macedonia, 1970; postgrad., Lodz (Poland) Tech. U., 1975-79; PhD in Mech. Engrng., Warsaw (Poland) U. Tech., 1979; postgrad., U. B.C., Vancouver, Can., 1983-84. Rsch. engr. Breaking Equipment Factory, Metal Workers Co., Skopje, 1970-71; lectr. High Tech. Sch., Skopje, 1971-74; asst. prof. mech. engring. U. St. Clement Ohridski Faculty Tech. Scis., Bitola, Macedonia, 1981-85, assoc. prof., 1985-90, prof., 1990—; adviser Govt. Com. for Energy Devel., Skopje, 1980-81; vis. rsch. fellow McMaster U., Hamilton, Ont., Can., 1984-85, vis. prof. dept. mech. engring., 1988-89; vis. prof. Inst. Indsl. Scis., U. Tokyo, 1991-92, Inst. Energy Tech., Tech. U. Berlin, 1994. Editor: Engineering Education in Balkan Countries, 1966; contbr. articles to sci. jours., including Archives Thermodynamics and Combustion, Internat. Jour. Heat and Tech., Jour. Visualization Soc. Japan, Transactions Inst. Fluid Flow Machinery. Pres. Macedonian-Polish Assn. Friendship and Cooperation, Skopje, 1993—. Recipient internat. sci. award Natural Scis. and Engring. Rsch. Coun., 1991; World U. Svc. Can., Govt. Can. postdoctoral fellow U. B.C., 1983-84, rsch. fellow U. Tokyo, 1991-92, German Acad. Exch. Svc., Tech. U. Berlin, 1994; Trans-European Mobility Scheme for Univ. Studies individual mobility grantee, European Communities Office, 1991-92. Mem. ASME. Avocations: photography, jogging. Home: Blvd Jane Sandanski 93-2-1, 91000 Skopje Macedonia Office: U St Clement Ohridski, Fac Tech Scis, PO Box 99, 97000 Bitola Macedonia

DONG, JIN-KEUN, education educator; b. Korea, Jan. 30, 1950; s. Hyun and Geum-Seom (Youm); m. Kyung-Mee Kim, May 23, 1980; children: Jong-Hwa, Sung-Hwa. DDS, Kyunghee U., Seoul, 1974, MSD, 1981, PhD, 1986. Asst. prof. Wonkwang U., Iksan, Korea, 1982-85, assoc. prof., 1986-90; prof. Wonkwang U., 1991—; rsch. worker Nihon U. Sch. Dentistry, Tokyo, 1985-86; vis. prof. Zurich U., 1990-91; dir. Dental Hosp., Wonkwang U. Capt. Korean Army, 1974-77. Office: Wonkwang Univ, 344-2 Shinyong-Dong, Iksan/Chunbuk 570-749, South Korea

DONG, MAOQING, biochemist; b. Shandong, China, May 5, 1964. MD, Harbin Med. U., 1986; MS, Peking Union Med. Coll., 1989, PhD, 1992. Rsch. assoc. Nat. Ctr. Basic Scientific Rsch., Toulouse, France, 1992-94, Lyon, France, 1994-96; sr. rsch. fellow Mayo Clinic, Rochester, Minn., 1996—. Mem. AAAS, Am. Gastroenterol. Assn., N.Y. Acad. Scis., Am. Soc. Biochemistry & Molecular Biology. Home: 845 2d St SW Rochester MN 55902 Office: Mayo Clinic 200 1st St SW Rochester MN 55905-0001

DONG, YU-CHING, broadcast executive, association executive; b. Taipei, Taiwan, Oct. 27, 1956; s. Chi-chang and Shu-fang (Chao) D.; m. Lian Ping; children: Hsiang-kai, Hsiang-chung. B in English Lit., Soochow U., Taipei, 1979; M in Mass Comm., Morehead (Ky.) U., 1983. Editor China Post, Taipei, 1979; mng. editor Free China Jour., Taipei, 1983-85; dep. chief fgn. langs. Voice of Free China, 1986-87; writer China News, Taipei, 1990-91; chief of listeners' svc. Voice of Free China, Taipei, 1987-92, dep. dir., 1992-98; mgr. dept. programming Nat. Ctrl. Broadcasting Sys., 1998—; liaison officer Lian-Shaw Presdl. Campaign Office, 2000. Translator: Constitution and Rules (Internat. Archery Fedn.), 1997, "The Shape of Things to Come", 1999, Producers' Guidelines-The BBC's Values and Stds., 2000; mng. editor and author English-lang. newspaper Free China Jour., 1983-85; contbr. to Radio Monthly. Dep. dir. internat. affairs Chinese Taipei Amateur Baseball Assn., 19887-93; dir. internat. affairs Chinese Taipei Archery Assn., 1993-97; dir. gen. affairs Taipei Journalists Assn., 1994-95; liason officer Lian-Shaw Presdl. Campaign Office, 2000. Served with Taiwan Army, 1979-81. Mem. Nat. Assn. Broadcasters Republic of China (bd. dirs. 1999—). Mem. Kuomintang Party. Avocations: golf, table tennis, tennis, mountain climbing. Office: No 55 Pei-An Rd, Taipei Taiwan

DONHOFFER, DIETER KARL, physicist; b. Vienna, Austria, Aug. 5, 1939; s. Karl and Elfriede (Marek) D.; m. Astrid Birkner; children: Ewald, Erhard. PhD, U. Vienna, 1964. Sr. physicist Atomic Energy of Can., Ltd., Ottawa, Ont., 1967-68; project mgr. Gen. Nucleonics div. Tyco, Pomona, Calif., 1969; dir. rsch. EIC Electronic Instruments and Controls, Vienna, 1969-74; dept. head Austrian Rsch. Centre, Seibersdorf, Austria, 1974-93, head bus. devel. info. tech. dept., 1999—; cons. expert Internat. Atomic Energy Agy., Vienna, 1981, 83. Contbr. numerous articles to profl. jours. Roman Catholic. Avocations: classical music, skiing, mountain hiking. Office: Austrian Rsch Centre, A-2444 Seibersdorf Austria

DONIN, VALERY IL'YCH, physicist, researcher; b. Nerchinsk, Russia, Mar. 11, 1941; s. Il'ya Abramovich and Anna Africanovna (Lanskaya) D.; m. Tamara Edwardovna Kurtz, Oct. 23, 1962; 1 child, Julia. MSc, Tomsk (Russia) State U., 1963; PhD in Physics and Math., Acad. Scis., Novosibirsk, Russia, 1972; D in Physics and Math. Sci., Acad. Scis., Russia, 1989. Engr. Inst. Radiophysics and Electronics, USSR Acad. Scis., Novosibirsk, 1963-64; jr. rsch. scientist Inst. Semiconductor Physics, USSR Acad. Scis., Novosibirsk, 1964-75, sr. rsch. scientist, 1975-79; sr. rsch. scientist Inst. Automation and Electrometry, USSR Acad. Scis., Novosibirsk, 1979-90, head lab., 1990—. Author: High-Power Gas Ion Lasers, 1991; contbr. articles to profl. jours. Recipient first degree diploma Siberian Br. USSR Acad. Scis., 1973, hon. diploma USSR Acad. Scis., 1974, medal Exhbn. Nat. Econ. Achievements USSR, Moscow, 1979; hon. prof. Albert Schweitzer Internat. U. (Geneva), 2000. Mem. Rozhdestvensky Russian Optical Soc., N.Y. Acad. Scis. Avocation: mountain skiing. E-mail: donin@iae.nsk.su. Fax: (383-2) 333863. Office: Inst Automation/Electro RAS, Acad Koptyuga Pr 1, 630090 Novosibirsk Russia

DONINI, ANTONIO OSCAR, sociology educator; b. Córdoba, Argentina, Mar. 8, 1921; s. Adrian S. Donini and Natividad Lambert; m. Ana Maria Cambours, Mar. 6, 1938; children: Gabriela Maria, Adriana Maria. B of Lit., Inst. Classic Humanities, Córdoba, 1941; MPh, St. Michael Coll., Buenos Aires, 1946; MSc, Inst. Social Scis., Rome, 1957, PhD, 1960. Prof. sociology Cath. U., Buenos Aires, 1961-65, Calif. State U., Stanislaus-Turlock, 1966-82, U. Buenos Aires Law Sch., 1982-89, Nat. U. San Martin, Argentina, 1993—, Sch. Nat. Def., Buenos Aires, 1995—; chmn. sociology-anthropology dept. Calif. State U., Turlock, 1967-69; chmn. social scis. dept. U. Buenos Aires Law Sch., 1985-87; acad. dean dept. grad. studies U. Belgrano, Argentina, 1989; chmn. Sch. Grad. Studies, Nat. U. San Martin, 1993-96. Author: (books) Theory and Techniques of Sociology, 1968, The Agony of U.S.A., 1976, Religion and Society, 1985; co-editor: (book) Origins and Growth of Sociological Theory, 1982. Mem. Internat. Ctr. for Heritage Preservation, 1995—; mem. ethics com. Cancer Rsch. and Prevention Found., 1996-97; pres. Italian Cath. Fedn., Modesto, Calif., 1975-77. Fellow Internat. Inst. Sociology, Am. Sociol. Assn.; mem. Latin Am. Sociol. Assn. (sec. gen. 1964-67). Home: Av Santa Fe 1829 6o, 1123 Buenos Aires Argentina

DONISA, IOAN GHEORGHE, geographer, educator; b. Bivolari, Romania, Sept. 10, 1929; d. Gheorghe Iancu and Profira Constantin (Zaharia) D.; m. Angelica Stefan Verdes, Dec. 29, 1953; 1 child, Valentin Ioan. Licentiate, Iasi (Romania) U., 1954; D of Geography, Babes-Bolyai U., Cluj, Romania, 1966. Preparator Al I Cuza U., Iasi, 1955-58, asst., 1958-60, lectr., 1960-67, asst. prof., 1967-72, prof. geography, 1972—; vice-dean biology-geography-geology dept. Al I Iasi U., 1977-81, dean, 1981-89. Contbr., editor numerous articles to profl. jours. Geographic Soc. Romania (v.p. 1990-98). Home: Bd Dimitrie Cantemir Nr 2, Sc B Ap 14, 6600 Iasi Romania Office: U Al I Cuza, Bd Copou Nr 11, 6600 Iasi Romania

DONIZETTI, MARIO, painter; b. Bergami, Italy, Jan. 23, 1932; s. Guiseppe and Luigie (Animelli) D.; m. Constanza Andreucci, Jan. 16, 1958. Founder Ctr. Rsch. & Divulgatin of the Techs. of the Arts. Author: Why Figurative: Aesthetic Arguments, 1992; exhibited in one-man shows Ransini Gallery, Milan, 1955, La Bussola Gallery, Turin, 1959, Rotta Gallery, Genova, 1961, Leitheimer-Schloss Gallery, Donauworth, 1972, Bauer Gallery, London, 1961, Nat. Gallery, London, Quardiennale di'Roma-premio Suzzara, Museo d'Arte Moderne, Mus. :inacoteca Ambrosiana, Milan, 1983-84, Civico Mus. del Patriarcato, Aquileia, others; represented in permanent pvt. pub. collections Italy, Germany, Grance, Switazerland, USSA, U.S., U.K. most notably Mus. Treasury, St. Peter's Basilica, Vatican City, Museo Teatrale all Scala, Milan; commd. protraits include Edwige Feuille re, Jean-Louis Barrault, Marta Abba, Rudolf Nureyev, Marcel Marceau, Gianandrea Gavazzeni, Bittorio Gassman, Valentina Cortese, Carla Fracci, Ladu Diana Spencer (Time mag. cover Apr. 20, 1981), Indira Gandhi (Time mag. cover Nov 1984), Pope John paul II (Time mag. cover Feb. 1985; frescoes hist. Basilica Pintida, 1958; contbr. articles and philos. essays on art to jours. and revs.; disciverer the glazed and varnished egg yolk tempere and a new patel techique which is no longer secondary to fresco painting. Home: 13 via rocca, Bergamo Italy Office: 11 via Colleoni, Bergamo Italy

DONLEY, DENNIS LEE, school librarian; b. Port Hueneme, Calif., July 19, 1950; s. Mickey Holt and Joan Elizabeth (Smith) D.; m. Ruth Ann Shank, June 10, 1972; children: Eric Holt, Evan Scott. AA, Ventura Coll., 1970; BA with honors, U. Calif., Santa Barbara, 1973; MLS, San Jose State U., 1976. Cert. secondary tchr., Calif. Libr. media tchr. San Diego Unified Sch. Dist., 1975—; lectr. Calif. State U., L.A., 1987-89; libr. cons. San Diego C.C. Dist., 1990; chmn. sch. adv. com. Point Loma H.S., San Diego, 1986-87; coop. book rev. bd. San Diego County, 1984-86; creator adult sch. curriculum, 1984-86; contbr. Deadbase X, Deadbase 94, The Deadhead's Taping Compendium, Vols. 1-3. Mem. ALA, Calif. Libr. Media Educators Assn. Avocations: reading, music, fitness. Office: Hoover HS 4474 El Cajon Blvd San Diego CA 92115-4312

DONLON, CRAIG JAMES, oceanographer, researcher; b. Newcastle u Lyme, England, Nov. 8, 1966; s. James Patrick and Margaret Emily (Nixon) D.; m. Ruth Jaqueline Stevens, June 20, 1996; children: Aaron Joseph, Zaphyr Sage. BSc (hons), Lancaster U., England, 1989; PhD, Southampton U., England, 1994. Rsch. scientist U. Southampton, England, 1994-96; assoc. rsch. fellow Colo. Ctr. for Astrodynamics Rsch., Boulder, 1996-98; rsch. fellow European Commn. Joint Rsch. Ctr., Ispra, Italy, 1998—. Contbr. articles to profl. jours. Mem. Am. Geophysical Union. Avocations: mountaineering, sailing, skiing, walking. Home: 22 Via Cascina Pedroni, I-21023 Besozzo Italy Office: European Commn Jt Rsch Ctr, Space Applications Inst, I-21020 Ispra Italy

DONLON, JOSEPHINE A., diagnostic and evaluation counseling therapist, educator; b. N.Y.C., Apr. 3, 1921; d. Henry R. and Josephine V. (Klarer) Janssen; m. William James Donlon; children: William James, Gregory A., Michele L., DruAnn. R.N., Englewood (N.J.) Hosp., 1941; BA in Psychology, Colo. Coll., Colorado Springs, 1945; MEd, Nat. Coll. Edn., Evanston, Ill., 1975. Cert. in nrusing, spl. edn., Ill., Colo.; specialist in social maladjusted, learning disabled, educable mentally handicapped. Pediatric psychiat. nurse N.Y. State Psychiat. Inst., N.Y.C., 1941-42; supr. psychiat. nursing Colo. U. Psychiat. Inst., 1945-47; pub. health nurse Denver Sch., 1947-48; diagnostic educator Schaumburg (Ill.) Sch. Dist. 54, 1969-78; pvt. practice diagnostic evaluation and counseling Brookeville, Md., 1979-87, Pineland, Fla., 1987—. Leader Girl Scouts U.S.A., 1958-62; previously active PTAs in Colo. and Ill. Mem. Council Exceptional Children, Council for Children with Behavioral Disorders, Council for Ednl. Diagnostic Services. Research in genetic endocrine diseases of pancreas and thyroid and relation to learning and behavior. Home: PO Box 2212 Pineland FL 33945-2212

DONLON, PATRICIA ANNE, researcher; b. Dublin, Ireland, Jan. 28, 1943; d. Patrick Joseph McCarthy and Marcella Garr; m. Phelim Donlon, Sept. 30, 1965; children: Lorna, Sinead. BA with honors, Univ. Coll., Dublin, 1964, PhD, 1974; DLitt, Nat. U. Ireland, Galway, 1997; diploma libr. and info. studies, Univ. Coll., Dublin, 1979. Curator Chester Beatty Libr., Dublin, 1981-89; dir. Nat. Libr. Ireland, Dublin, 1989-97, chief herald of Ireland Geneal. Office, 1995-97; sr. rsch. fellow Inst. Irish Studies Queen's U., Belfast, No. Ireland, 1997-98; Sandars bibliography reader U. Cambridge, Eng., 1998-99; rsch. fellow Dublin Inst. Tech., 1999—; Burns libr. chair in Irish studies Boston Coll., 2000—; gov. U. Limerick, Ireland, 1997-02; exams. commr. Dept. Edn., Dublin, 1997—; chair judging panel Irish Times Lit. Prize, Dublin, 1999, Press/Photographers of Ireland Awards, Dublin, 1998-99. Author: (reference works) Twentieth Century Children's Writers, 1991, 94, 97, New Dictionary of Biography, 1999; editor: (books) Moon Cradle: Lullabies and Dandling Songs, 1992, Lucky Bag: Classic Irish Stories for Children, 1996. Recipient A.K. Henry medal Royal Coll. Surgeons of Ireland, 1994, Children's Books Ireland award for disting. svc. to children's lit., 1997. Mem. European Cultural Found. (mem. exec. com. 1994—), Libr. Assn. Ireland (coun. mem. 1982-85), Irish Mus. Assn. (chairperson 1991-93), Heritage Coun. Avocations: book collecting, music, theater and film, cookery. Fax: 353 1 2895605. E-mail: pdonlon@dit.ie. Office: Dublin Inst Tech, Rathmines Rd, Dublin Ireland

DONNACHIE, IAN, historian, educator; b. Lanark, Scotland, June 18, 1944. MA, U. Glasgow, 1966; MLitt, U. Strathclyde, 1969, PhD, 1976. Rsch. asst. U. Strathclyde, Glasgow, Scotland, 1967-68; lectr. in social studies Napier U., Edinburgh, Scotland, 1968-70; sr. tutor in history Open U., Edinburgh, 1970—, sr. lectr., dir. Ctr. Scottish Studies, 1985; lectr. Deakin U., Victoria, Australia, 1982; vis. fellow U. Sydney, N.S.W., Australia, 1985; hon. lectr. modern history U. Dundee, 1998. Author: A History of the Brewing Industry in Scotland, 1979, 2nd edit., Studying Scottish History, 1996; co-author: Industrial Archaeology in the British Isles, 1979, A Companion to Scottish History From the Reformation to the Present, 1989, The Manufacture of Scottish History, 1992, Historic New Lanark: The Dale and Owen Industrial Community Since 1785, 1993, 2nd edit., 1998; co-editor: Forward! Labour Politics in Scotland 1888-1988, 1989, A Companion to Scottish History, 1989, Modern Scottish History, 5 vols., 1998, Robert Owen: Owen of New Lamark and New Harmony, 2000, others. Fellow Royal Hist. Soc., Soc. Antiquaries Scotland; mem. Assn. Univ. Tchrs., Econ. and Social History Soc. Scotland, Scottish Brewing Archive Trust. Office: The Open U, Drumsheugh Gardens, Edinburgh EH3 7QJ, Scotland

DONNALLY, PATRICIA BRODERICK, online magazine editor; b. Cheverly, Md., Mar. 11, 1955; d. James Duane and Olga Frances (Duenas) Broderick; m. Robert Andrew Donnally, Dec. 30, 1977; 1 child, Danielle Christine. BS, U. Md., 1977. Fashion editor The Washington Times, 1983-85, The San Francisco Chronicle, 1985-2000; sr. fashion and beauty editor eLuxury.com, 2000. Recipient Atrium award, 1984, 87-89, 90, 94-98, 99, Lulu award, 1985, 87, award Am. Cancer Soc., 1991, Aldo award, 1994, George A. Hough III award, 1999, Atrium and George A. Hough III awards U. Ga. Avocation: travel. E-mail: donnallyt@hotmail.com.

DONNALLY, ROBERT ANDREW, lawyer, real estate broker; b. Washington, July 10, 1953; s. Reaumur Stearnes and Katherine Ann (Sutliff) D.; m. Patricia Kane Broderick, Dec. 30, 1977; 1 child, Danielle Christine. BA in Psychology, U. Md., 1976; JD, U. Balt., 1980; cert. in bus., Stanford U., 1996. Bar: Md. 1980, Calif. 1986. Pvt. practice Oxen Hill, Md., 1980-81; rsch. contract staff officer Dept. Def., Ft. Meade, Md., 1981-85; with legal and contractual ops. ARGOSystems, Inc., Sunnyvale, Calif., 1985-90; asst. dir. Inst. Def. Analyses, San Diego, 1990-91; dep. chief counsel ARGOSystems, Inc., 1991-93, chief counsel, corp. sec., 1993-98; chief counsel comms. and infomanagement divsn. Boeing Co., 1997-98; gen. counsel, mng. ptnr. BT Comml. Real Estate, Palo Alto, Calif., 1998-99; assoc. gen. counsel Inhale Therapeutic Sys. Inc., San Carlos, Calif., 1999—. Editor-in-chief The Forum, 1979-80. Active The Pillars Soc./United Way, 1991—. Waxter Legal scholar U. Baltimore, 1978. Mem. Am. Corp. Counsel, Nat. Contract Mgmt. Assn., Md. Bar Assn., Calif. Bar Assn., Assn. of Silicon Valley Brokers, Tae Kwon Do Assn. (Black Belt), Black Belt, Kukkiwon World Tae Kwon Do Assn. Avocations: martial arts, marathons, hiking, travel, reading. Office: BT Comml Real Estate 2445 Faber Pl Ste 250 Palo Alto CA 94303-3316 also Address: 150 Industrial Rd San Carlos CA 94070-6256

DONNAN, GEOFFREY ALAN, neurology educator, researcher; b. Sydney, Australia, Apr. 13, 1948; s. Victor Tennyson and Shirley Isobel (May) D.; m. Elizabeth Patricia Ayton, Nov. 6, 1976; children: Clare, Julia. MB BS, Melbourne U., Australia, 1972, MD, 1980. Staff neurologist Austin Hosp., Melbourne, 1983-93; prof. neurology Melbourne U., 1993—; dir. rsch. Nat. Stroke Rsch. Inst., Melbourne, 1995—; dir. neuroscis. Austin & Repatriation Med. Ctr., Melbourne, 1996—. Author: Lacunar and Other Subcortical Infarctions, 1995; co-author: Interventional Therapy in Acute Stroke, 1997. Rsch. grantee Nat. Health & Med. Rsch., 1986—. Fellow Royal Australian Coll. Physicians; mem. Australian Assn. Neurologists. Office: Dept Neurology, Burgundy St, Heidelberg 3084, Australia

DONNE, SIR GAVEN (JOHN), chief justice; b. Christ Church, New Zealand, May 8, 1914; s. Jack Alfred and Mary Elizabeth (Farrell) D.; m. Isabel Fenwick Hall, Jan. 3, 1946; 4 children. LLB, U. New Zealand, 1937. Barrister, soliciter, New Zealand, 1938. Stipendiary magistrate Auckland, 1958; puisne judge Supreme Ct. Western Samoa, 1970-71, chief justice, 1972-73; mem. Ct. of Appeal Western Samoa, 1975-82; chief justice Niue; chief justice Cook Islands, 1975-82, rep. of Queen Elizabeth, 1975-84; chief justice Nauru, Tuvalu, 1985—; mem. Ct. Appeal of Kiribati, 1986—. Mem. Takapuna Borough Coun., Auckland, 1957-58; mem. Auckland Regional Planning Coun., 1957-58. With Mid. Eastern and Italian Army, 1941-45. Decorated Knight of the Brit. Empire, 1979, Order of Merit (2d class) of the Fed. Republic of West Germany, 1978. Avocations: golfing, fishing, walking. Home: Meneng Nauru, Rd 4, Rotorua New Zealand Office: care Ministry of Justice, Yaren, Funafuti Tuvalu*

DONNELLEY, STRACHAN, philosopher; b. Chgo., Mar. 22, 1942; s. Gaylord and Dorothy Ranney Donnelley; m. Vivian Hilst, Aug. 24, 1968; children: Inanna, Naomi, Aidan, Ceara, Tegan. BA, Yale U., 1964; MA, New Sch. for Social Rsch., 1972, PhD, 1977. Mem. faculty Valparaiso (Ind.) U., 1967-69, Seminar Coll., New Sch., N.Y.C., 1978-85; dir. edn. Hastings Ctr., Garrison, N.Y., 1986-96, assoc. environ. ethics, 1989-96, pres., 1996-99, dir. humans and nature program, 1999—; mem. animal care and use com. Cornell Med. Sch., 1990-96; advisor Ctr. for Biodiversity, Am. Mus. Natural History, N.Y.C., 1995—. Editor spl. supplements Hastings Ctr. Report, 1990-98; contbr. articles to profl. jours. Trustee Nat. Humanities Ctr., Raleigh, N.C., 1993-99, Union Inst., Cin., 1980-92, U. Chgo., 1993—, New Sch. U., 1994—, Hotchkiss Sch., Lakeville, Conn., 1988-98; chmn. Gaylord and Dorothy Donnelley Found., Chgo., 1992—. Recipient Pres.' award Union Inst., 1999. Mem. Am. Philos. Assn., World Conservation Union. Democrat. Avocations: fly fishing, music, skiing, collecting. Office: Hastings Ctr 9D Garrison NY 10524

DONNELLY, AUGUSTINE STANISLAUS, financial executive; b. Pt. Douglas, Queensland, Australia, June 1, 1923; s. Augustine S. and Anne Brigid Donnelly; m. Sheila Bernadette O'Hagan, Feb. 15, 1947; children: Sharon, Melda, Peter. B of Commerce, U. Queensland, 1968. Chartered acct. A. W. Fadden, Queensland, 1938-42; stockbroker Corrie & Co., Queensland, 1954-57, T. M. Landy, Queensland, 1957-58; Queensland mgr. Devel. Fin. Corp. Group, 1958-69; mng. dir. Capital Svcs., Queensland, 1969-83, Donnelly Money Mgmt. Pty Ltd., Queensland, 1983-94, Trenta Pty. Ltd., Brisbane, 1994—. Author 49 books on investing, finance, bus. mgmt., acctg.; contbr. articles to profl. jours. Pres. Queensland Com. Overseas Students, 1987-90. Navigator Royal Australian Air Force, 1942-47. Mem. Securities Inst. Australia (Queensland bd. dirs. 1970-72), Australian Soc. Accts. (Queensland divsn. 1955-70, chmn. rsch. com. 1963-70, state pres. 1960-62), Brisbane Club, Tattersalls Club, Royal Auto Club Victoria, Queensland Cricketers Club. Avocations: golf, reading, video photography. Home: 31 King Arthur Tce, Tennyson Brisbane 4105, Australia Office: Trenta Pty Ltd, PO Box 5 Graceville E, Brisbane 4075, Australia

DONNELLY, BARBARA, artist, educator; b. Somerville, Mass.; d. Russell Winfield and Pearl Marie (Cameron) Chick; m. Robert Boag Donnelly, May 29, 1954; children: Kathleen, Sharon, Robert Jr., Patricia, Michael, Brian. AA, Boston U., 1954. Tchr. oil painting, watercolors Beverly (Mass.) Adult Edn., 1969-80, 83-90, tchr. basic drawing, 1970-90; tchr. Lakes Region Outdoor Painting, N.H., 1977-85; tchr. pen, ink No. Essex C. C., Newburyport, Mass., 1986-88; court rm. artist Channel 56, Boston, 1987—; tchr. watercolor Gloucester, Mass., 1993—; presenter Holiday Hill Painting Workshops, N.H., 1998-99. Illustrator: The Little Book Shop, 1989; cover artist: Palette Talk, 1990; one-woman shows include French Embassy, Washington, 1998; contbr. articles to profl. jours. Asst. chmn. Beverly Bicentennial Arts Festival, 1975, chmn. 1976. Named Internat. Artist-in-Residence, Dinan, France, "Les Amis de La Grande Vigne" Mus., 1996. Mem. Am. Artists Profl. League, Acad. Artists Assn., North Shore Arts Assn., Rockport Art Assn., New England Watercolor Soc. (Paul Strisik Meml. award 1998), Guild of Beverly Artists, Copley Soc. of Boston. Roman Catholic. Avocations: photography, computer art, architecture. Office: Barbara Donnelly Art Gallery 19 Harbor Loop Gloucester MA 01930-5003

DONNELLY, JAMES CORCORAN, JR., lawyer; b. Newton, Mass., June 10, 1946; s. James C. Sr. and Margery J. (MacNeil) D.; m. Carol R. Burns, June 28, 1968; children: James C. IV, Sarah Y. BA, Dartmouth Coll., 1968; JD, Boston Coll., 1973. Bar: Mass. 1973, U.S. Dist. Ct. Mass. 1974, U.S. Ct. Appeals (7th cir.) 1979, U.S. Ct. Appeals (1st cir.) 1983, U.S. Tax Ct. 1988, U.S. Dist. Ct. (no. dist.) Ohio 1991, U.S. Ct. Appeals (2d cir) 1994, U.S. Ct. Appeals (3d cir) 1999. From assoc. to ptnr. Hale & Dorr, Boston, 1973-84; sr. ptnr. Mirick, O'Connell, DeMallie & Lougee, Worcester, Mass., 1985—, chmn. litigation dept., 1993-97; bd. dirs. C.P. Bourg, Inc., New Bedford, Mass. Editor-in-chief 1972 Annual Survey of Mass. Law. Corporator Greater Worcester Cmty. Found., 1986—, mem. monitoring and evaluation com., 1997—; trustee Higgins Armory Mus., Worcester, 1985—, pres. 1994-97; corporator Worcester Art Mus., 1986—, pres., mem. coun., 1987-88; councilor Am. Antiquarian Soc., 1996—, treas., 1997—. Lt. U.S. Army, 1968-70. Decorated Army Commendation medal for meritorious svc., 1970. Fellow Mass. Bar Found., 1994; mem. ABA, Mass. Bar Assn., Worcester County Bar Assn. (co-chmn. fed. ct. com. 1995-98), Dartmouth Lawyers Assn., Worcester Club (bd. dirs. 1995-98), Dartmouth Club Ctrl. Mass. (exec. com. 1996—, pres. 1997—), Dartmouth Coll. Club (officers exec. com. 1997—, pres. 1999—). Avocations: sailing, bicycling, hiking, history. Home: 285 Salisbury St Worcester MA 01609-1661 Office: Mirick O'Connell 100 Front St Worcester MA 01608-1425

DONNELLY, MARTIN EUGENE, civil servant, lecturer; b. Newbury, Eng.; s. Eugene Donnelly; m. Carol Jean Heald, Mar. 30, 1985 (dec. May 1996); children: Anne, Francesca, Rosemary; m. Susan Jane Catchpole, Oct. 24, 1998. MA, Oxford (Eng.) U., 1979; diploma, Coll. of Europe, Bruges, 1980, Ecole Nat. Adminstrn., Paris, 1984. Pvt. sec. Her Majesty Treasury, London, 1982-83, prin., 1984-88; councillor Cabinet of Sir Leon Brittan, European Commn., Brussels, 1989-92; head divsn. Her Majesty Treasury, London, 1993-95; chargé de mission Tresor Francais, Paris, 1995-96; Econ.

and Monetary Union team leader Her Majesty Treasury, London, 1996-97; dep. head European Secretariat, Cabinet Office, London, 1997—; mem. coun. Fed. Trust, London, 1988-93; founding pres. U.K. Former Students of Ecole Nat. D'Adminstrn., 1986-88; cons. European Commn., London, 1993—; vis. lectr. European Bus. Summer Sch., 1991—. Roman Catholic. Avocations: family, reading, music, hill walking. Office: Cabinet Office, Whitehall, London SW1, England

DONNELLY, RUSSELL JAMES, physicist, educator; b. Hamilton, Ont., Can., Apr. 16, 1930; s. Clifford Ernest and Bessie (Harrison) D.; m. Marian Card, Jan. 21, 1956; 1 son, James. BSc, McMaster U., 1951, MSc, 1952, LLD, 1999; MS, Yale U., 1953, PhD, 1956. Faculty U. Chgo., 1956-66, prof. physics, 1965-66; prof. physics U. Oreg., Eugene, 1966—; chmn. dept. U. Oreg., 1966-72, 82-83; vis. prof. Niels Bohr Inst., Copenhagen, Denmark, 1972; co-founder Pine Mountain Obs., 1967; cons. GM Co. Rsch. Labs., 1958-68, NSF, 1968-76, 79-84, mem. adv. panel for physics, 1970-73, chmn., 1971-72; mem. adv. coms. on matls. rsch., 1979-84; mem. Task Force on Fundamental Physics and Chemistry in Space, Space Sci. Bd., NRC; cons. Jet Propulsion Lab., Calif. Inst. Tech., Pasadena, 1973-82; chmn. Sci. Adv. Com. for Low Temp. Facilities in Space, 1990-91; mem. fluid dynamics discipline working group, NASA, 1992-95; gen. chmn. 20th Internat. Conf. on Low Temp. Physics, 1993. Author: (with Parks, Glaberson) Experimental Superfluidity, 1967, (with Francis) Cryogenic Science and Technology: Contributions of Leo Dana, 1985, Quantized Vortices in Helium II, 1991; editor: (with Herman, Prigogine) Non-Equilibrium Thermodynamics Variational Techniques and Stability, 1966, High Reynolds Number Flows Using Liquid and Gaseous Helium, 1991, Procs. 20th Internat. Conf. Low Temperature Physics, Physica B, 1994; editor: (with Sreenivasan) Flow at Ultra-High Reynolds and Rayleigh Numbers; mem. editorial bd. Physics of Fluids, 1966-68, Phys. Rev. E, 1978-84, assoc. editor, 1987-93; mem. editorial bd. Jour. Phys. and Chem. Ref. Data, 1989-92, Handbook of Chemistry and Physics, 1989-98; contbr. articles to profl. jours. Bd. dirs. U. Oreg. Found., 1970-72, 88-91, investment com., 1990-91; bd. dirs. Oreg. Mus. Park Commn., 1975-87, chmn., 1975-82; bd. dirs. Oreg. Bach Festival, 1975-87, Oreg. Mozart Players, 1990-93. Alfred P. Sloan fellow, 1959-63; sr. vis. fellow Sci. Rsch. Coun., U.K., 1978; recipient Disting. Alumnus award McMaster U., 1992, Lars Onsager medal Norwegian U. Sci. and Tech., 1996; 1995 Chia-Shun Yih lectr. U. Mich., 1996 Fritz London Meml. lectr. Duke U, Howard Vollum award Reed Coll., 1997. Fellow AAAS, Am. Phys. Soc. (exec. com. div. fluid dynamics 1966-72, 80-84, 88-91, sec.-treas. 1967-70, 88-91, chmn. 1971-72, 82-83, APS Otto Laporte award 1974), Inst. of Physics (London); mem. Nat. Trust for Scotland, Soc. Archtl. Historians, Cosmos Club. Episcopalian. Achievements include research on physics fluids, especially hydrodynamic stability, turbulence and superfluidity. Home: 2175 Olive St Eugene OR 97405-2837 Office: Univ Oreg Dept Physics Eugene OR 97403-1274

DONNEM, SARAH LUND, financial analyst, non-profit and political organization consultant; b. St. Louis, Apr. 10, 1936; d. Joel Y. and Erle Hall (Harsh) Lund; m. Roland W. Donnem, Feb. 18, 1961; children: Elizabeth Prince Donnem Sigety, Sarah Madison. BA, Vassar Coll., 1958. Tech. aide, computer programmer Bell Labs, Whippany, N.J., 1959-60; chmn. placement vol. opportunities N.Y. Jr. League, 1972-73, asst. treas., 1974-75, chmn. urban problems relating to mental health, 1967-69, mem. project rsch. com., 1967-70, chmn., 1973-74, mem. bd. mgrs., 1973-74. chmn. cmty. rsch. Washington Jr. League, 1970-71, mem. bd. mgrs., 1970-71; mem. Stratford Hall (N.Y.) Com., 1970—; bd. dirs. East Side Settlement House, Bronx, N.Y., 1972—, v.p., 1975-76, chmn. Nat. Horse Show Benefit, 1976, winter antiques show com., 1994—, co-chmn. adv. com., 1991-94, mem. nominating com., 1990—, mem. investment com., 1993—; bd. dirs. Stanley M. Isaacs Neighborhood Ctr., N.Y.C., 1973-76, v.p., 1975-76; bd. dirs. Presbyn. Home for Aged Women, N.Y.C., 1974-76, v.p., 1976; mem. exec. bd. N.Y. Aux. of Blue Ridge Sch., 1971-75, sec. 1965-67, pres., 1973-75; budget and benevolence com. Brick Presbyn. Ch., N.Y.c., 1973-76, mem. social svc. com., 1973-74, chmn. fgn. students com., 1963-64; bd. dirs. Search and Care, N.Y.c., 1973--76, Project LEARN, cleve., 1990-96, 2000—; chmn. Literacy Fund, 1991-95, mem., 1995—; mem. Friends of Project LEARN, 1986—, mem. Fedn. Cmty. Planning, Cleve., coun. on Older Persons, 1978-82, mem. future Planning task Force, 1980-81, commn. on social concerns, 1982-84; trustee Golden Age Ctrs. Greatr cleve., 1979-92, investment com., 1993, 1st v.p., 1980-81, pres. 1981-85, chmn. Western Res. Antiques show, 1979, 80; chmn. cleve. antiques Show Silver Anniv., 2000; mem. women's adv. coun. Westrn Res. Hist. Soc., 1977—, coord. sec., 1978; mem. women's com. Cleve. Orch., 1979-85, Vassar Coll. cleve. sec. 1980-82, v.p., 1983, pres. 1984-86; mem. AAVC Club Liaison com., 1986-89, chmn. regional program com., 1987-89; bd. dirs. Cleve. Ballet, 1980—, exec. com. 1981, fin. com. 1982-88, 95-98, nominating com., 1988-90, 95—, co-chmn. 1997—; co-chmn. Yale Ball, 1983; bd. advisors Ret. Sr. Vol. Program, 1982, trustee, 1983-90, chmn. long range planning comm., 1986, sec. 1987-89; mem. Family Friends Adv. Coun., 1987-89; trustee Fairmount Presbyn. Ch., 1985-88; mem. long range planning com. United Way, Cleve., 1985-87; coord. Friends of Voinovich, 1987-89; womens adv. com. Voinovich for Governor, 1990, Voinovich for Senate, 1997-98, chmn. Voinovich Task Force on Aging, 1990-91, Ohio Adv. Coun. on Aging, 1991—legis. com., 1994—, chmn., Cuyahoga County Republican Policy Com., Fin. Com., 1999—, Plain Dealer adv. counsel for elderly coverage, 1991-93; chmn. Johns Hopkins Parents Fund, 1986-88, Project LEARN 15th Anniversary celebration (with Barbara Bush, hon. chmn.), 1989-90; coord. Decorative Arts Trust Cleve. Symposium, 1996; mem. Leadership Cleve. Class 1992; del. White House Conf. on Aging, 1995. Named Vol. of Yr. N.Y. Jr. League, 1975; recipient Sustainer Svc. award Jr. League Cleve., 1990. Mem. Nat. Inst. Social Scis. (membership com. 1972-92, trustee 1984-96), Nat. Soc. Colonial Dames, Colony Club (N.Y.C.), Chevy Chase Club (Washington), Intown club, Vassar Club, Kirtland Club (Cleve.). Address: 2945 Fontenay Rd Shaker Hts OH 44120-1726

DONNER, JÖRN JOHAN, film director, writer, legislator, diplomat; b. Feb. 5, 1933; s. Kai Reinhold and Greta (von Bonsdorff) D.; m. Inga-Britt W., 1954 (div. 1962); children: Johan, Jakob; m. Jeanette Bonnier, 1974 (div. 1988); children: Susanna, Otto; m. Bitte Westerlund, 1995; children: Daniel, Rudolf. BA in Polit. Sci. and Lit., Helsinki U., 1958. Film critic various jours., 1951-62; lit. critic various jours. Sweden, Finland, 1951-60; film critic Dagens Nyheter, Stockholm, Sweden, 1961-63; columnist various mags. Finland, Sweden, 1961-78, Hufvudstadsbladet, Helsinki, Finland, Sweden, 1961-92, 97-99, Blue Wings, Helsinki, Finland, Sweden, 1986-99; founder Finnish Film Archive, 1957; dir. Swedish Film Prodn. Cos., including Europa Film and Sandrews, 1963-66; founder, dir. Jörn Donner Prodns., 1966—; mem. bd. Marimekko Textile Co., several hotel cos.; CEO Swedish Film Inst., 1978-82. Author: Report from Berlin, 1958, Report from Berlin, 1961, Report from Danube, 1962, The Personal Vision of Ingmar Bergman, 1963, 44 others; writer, dir. 15 films including A Sunday in September, 1963, To Love, 1964, Adventure Starts Here, 1965, Rooftree, 1967, Black on White, 1968, Sixtynine, 1969, Portraits of Women, 1970, Anna, 1971, The World of Ingmar Bergman, 1975, Men Can't Be Raped, 1978, Dirty Story, 1984, Ingmar Bergman: On Life and Work, 1998, others; prodr. 60 films including Fanny and Alexander, 1982 (4 Acad. awards 1984), After the Rehearsal. Mem. Helsinki City Coun., 1968-72, 85-92; mem. Finnish Parliament, 1987-95, fgn. affairs com. 1987-95, vice chmn. banking supervision, 1991-95; am. Counsul-Gen. Finland, L.A., 1995-96; mem. European Parliament, 1996-99. Recipient Finnish State prizes Premio Opera Prima. Venice Film Festival, 1963; Vittorio de Sica prize, Sorrento, 1978.

DONNET, JEAN BAPTISTE, physical chemist, educator, consultant; b. Pontgibaud, France, Sept. 28, 1923; s. Antoine and Marie (Berouhard) D.; m. Suzanne Rittiman, Dec. 21, 1968; children by previous marriage: Anne-Michele, Pierre-Antoine, Marie-Christine. PhD in Physical Chemistry, U. Strasbourg, France, 1953; D Hon.c., U. Lodz, Poland, U. Neuchatel, Switzerland, 1993; Prof. Hon. Causa, U. Jiau Tung Shai Hai, China. With Ctr. Nat. de Recherche Scientifique, 1946-53; successively stagiere, attaché, chargé de recherche; prof., pres. U. Haute-Alsace, 1977-82; fundator, head Rsch. Ctr. Physico-Chemistry of Solid Surfaces, 1967-86; head Lab. Phys. Chemistry Inst. Chemistry for Surfaces and Interfaces ENSCMu. Author: Elastomeres, 1958, Les Noirs de Carbone, 1965, Carbon Black, 1976, 2d edit., 1993, Carbon Fiber, 1984, 3d edit., 1998, Active Carbon, 1988; contbr. over 400 articles to profl. jours.; patentee (18) in field. Maj. French Air Force. Decorated officer de la Legion d'Honneur, commdr. de l'Ordre du Merité, commdr. Acad. Palmes; recipient Gold medal Société pour l'Encouragement de l'Industrie Nat., 1976, Silver medal French Assn. Advancement Sci., 1979, George Skakel Meml. award Am. Carbon Soc., 1981, George Colwin medal Plastic award Rubber Inst., Eng., 1988. Fellow Plastic and Rubber Inst. (London indsl. bd.), Royal Soc. Chemistry, Am. Carbon Soc., Am. Carbon Soc., Am. Chem. Soc. (Rubber div., George Stafford Whitby medal 1989, Goodyear Gold medal 1998); mem. AAAS, N.Y. Acad. Sci., Soc. Française de Chimie (Lavoisier medal 1998), Soc. Plastic Engrs., French Assn. Rubber and Plastic Engrs., Deutsche Kautschuk Gesselshaft (Karl Harris medal 1985), Acad. d'Alsace (Hon. medal 1997), Indian Carbon Soc., Rotary. Office: ENSCM, 3 Rue A Werner, 68200 Mulhouse France*

DONNICI, PETER JOSEPH, lawyer, law educator, consultant; b. Kansas City, Mo., Sept. 5, 1939; s. Albert H. and Jennie (Danubio) D.; m. Diane DuPlantier, July 27, 1985; children: JuliaAnn Donnici Clifford, Joseph A., Joann Donnici Powers. BA, U. Mo., Kansas City, 1959, JD, 1962; LLM, Yale U., 1963. Bar: Mo. 1963, U.S. Supreme Ct. 1966, Calif. 1969. Asst. prof. law U. San Francisco, 1963-65, assoc. prof., 1965-68, prof., 1968-91, prof. emeritus, 1992—; assoc. Law Offices Joseph L. Alioto, San Francisco, 1967-72; sole practice San Francisco, 1974—; ptnr. Donnici & LuPo, San Francisco, 1982-92, Donnici, Kerwin, Phillips & Donnici, San Francisco, 1993—; chmn. L.L. Hillblom Found. & Charitable Trust, 1995—; asst. prosecutor Jackson County Prosecutor's Office, Mo., 1963; cons. to Office of Mayor of San Francisco, 1968-72; No. Calif. bd. dirs. Coun. on Legal Ednl. Opportunity, San Francisco, 1969-70; conciliator for housing discrimination cases HUD, San Francisco, 1976; cons. Calif. Consumer Affairs' Task Force on Electronic Funds Transfer, Sacramento, 1978-79; bd. dirs. Air Micronesia, Inc., DHL Internat., Ltd., Bermuda, Continental Micronesia; spl. counsel and del. to internat. confs. Commonwealth of No. Mariana Islands, 1983-84; faculty adviser U. San Francisco Law Rev., 1966-91; bd. counselors U. San Francisco, 1993—. Editor-in-Chief: U. Mo., Kansas City Law Rev., 1961-62; contbr. articles to profl. jours., 1964—. Lawyers' com. for Urban Affairs, San Francisco, 1965-68. Wilson scholar U. Mo.-Kansas City, 1956-62; Sterling fellow Law Sch., Yale U., 1962-63. Mem. Bench and Robe, Phi Delta Phi. Democrat. Roman Catholic. Home: 190 Cresta Vista Dr San Francisco CA 94127-1635 Office: One Post St Ste 2450 San Francisco CA 94104

DONNINI, JOSEPH R., JR., retail executive, lawyer; b. Wilkes-Barre, Pa., May 19, 1970; s. Joseph R. Sr. and Ann Marie Donnini. BA, Drew U., 1992; JD, Whittier Coll., 1995. Bar: Calif. 1996. Cons. Camden Group, El Segundo, Calif., 1995-96; prin. cons. Global Health Group, El Segundo, 1996-98; pres. CopaCatana & Juice Cabana, El Segundo, 1998—; part-time atty., El Segundo, 1996—. tchr. Am. Martyrs Sch. Bd., Manhattan Beach, Calif., 1995—, bd. dirs., 1998—. Mem. State Bar Calif. Republican. Roman Catholic. Avocations: fitness, tennis, skiing. Office: 222 N Sepulveda Blvd Ste 2000 El Segundo CA 90245-5614

DONNITHORNE, AUDREY GLADYS, research scholar; b. Sichuan, China, Nov. 27, 1922; arrived n Hong Kong, 1985; d. Vyvyan Henry and Gladys (Ingram) D. BA, Oxford (Eng.) U., 1948, MA, 1952. Rsch. asst. U. Coll. London, 1948-51, lectr., 1951-66; reader U. London, 1966-68; found. head Contemporary China Ctr., 1970-76; professorial fellow Australian Nat. U., 1969-85; hon. rsch. fellow Ctr. for Asian Studies U. Hong Kong, 1985—. Author: China's Economic System, 1966, British Rubber Manufacturing, 1958; co-author: Western Enterprise in Eastern Economic Development, 1954, Western Enterprise in Indonesia and Malaysia, 1957; founder, mng. dir. Shengning Yiyi Publs. Vol. liaison Cath. dioceses in S.E. China. Recipient Pro Ecclesia et Pro Pontifice medal Holy See, 1994. Roman Catholic. Home: Flat A3 18th Fl, 73 Bonham Rd, Hong Kong Hong Kong

D'ONOFRIO, DOMINICK ANTHONY, police officer, acting police chief; b. Passaic, N.J., July 18, 1944; s. Anthony and Filomena (Manicone) D'O.; m. Jill D'Onofrio; children: Tara, Emily. Cert., Lincoln Tech. Inst., Newark, 1968; grad., Bergen County Policy Acad., Mahwah, N.J., 1968; student, St. Alphonsus Coll., Woodcliff Lake, N.J. Cert. police instr. N.J. Police Tng. Commn. Police officer Lodi (N.J.) Police Dept., 1968—, lt., coord. Police Dept. Terminal Agy., tour comdr., 1992-94, ACT/comdr. Ctrl. Svc. Divsn., 1994-99, acting police chief, 1999—; owner D&D Oil Burner Svc. Co., 1975—; computer instr. Bergen County Police Acad. Fireman Lodi Vol. Fire Dept, 1978—, past pres. 1982-84, sgt. at arms 1987—. With U.S. Army, 1962-65. Decorated Nat. Def. medal U.S. Army, Army Commednation medal for Heroisim in Europe. Mem. NRA (cert. pistol, rifle and shotgun instr. N.J.), Internat. Assn. Identification, Internat. Assn. of Chiefs of Police, Internat. Narcotic Enforcement Officers Assn., N.J. State Honor Legion, N.J. Police Benevolent Assn., N.J. Detective Crime Clinic, N.J. Exempt Fireman's Assn., N.J. Mut. Aid Fire Assn., Bergen County Mut. Aid Soc., N.J. Vehicle Theft Investigators Assn., Internat. Auto Theft Assn. Investigators, N.J. Identification Officers Assn., Kodak Pro Passport Profl. Network, VFW. Roman Catholic. Avocations: photography, fishing, hunting, gun collecting, music. Home: 46 Mitchell St 106 Central Ave Lodi NJ 07644-3016

DONOGHUE, JOHN CHARLES, software management consultant; b. Oswego, N.Y., Sept. 19, 1950; s. James Charles and Marion Louise (Farrell) D.; m. Ann Marie Perry, Dec. 20, 1969; children: John Charles II, Kelly Anne. BS in Electronic Tech., Chapman Coll., 1981; student, U. Calif., Irvine, 1981-82; MA, U. Redlands, 1987; postgrad., Western State U. Coll., 1988-89, Azusa Pacific U., 1991-93. Enlisted USAF, 1969, advanced through grades to staff sgt., 1977, resigned, 1979; mgr. Lockheed Aircraft, Ontario, Calif., 1979-85; project engr. Northrop Corp., Pico Rivera, Calif., 1985-99; sr. prin. software engr. Raytheon Missile Syss., Tucson, 1999—; cons., Fontana, Calif., 1981—; mem. software coun. Northrop Corp., Hawthorne, Calif., 1987-97, software improvement network U. Calif., Irvine, 1988—, capability maturity model corr. group Software Engring. Inst., Pitts., 1993—, L.A. software improvement network U. So. Calif., 1994—; charter mem. Software Inspection and Rev. Orgn., Sunnyvale, Calif., 1981—. Vol. cons. S.W. Anthropol. Assn. Calif. State U., L.A., 1996-97, Resource Conservation Dist., Rancho Cucamonga, Calif., 1996-99, Southwest Mus., L.A., 1997—. Mem. IEEE, N.Y. Acad. Scis., Nat. Space Soc. Avocations: motorcycling, snorkeling. Office: Northrop Gruman Corp Mil Aircraft Sys Divsn 8900 Washington Blvd Pico Rivera CA 90660-3765

DONOGHUE, JOHN FRANCIS, archbishop; b. Washington, Aug. 9, 1928. Student, St. Mary's Sem., Cath. U. Ordained priest Cath. Ch., 1955. Chancellor and vicar gen. Washington Archdiocese, 1973-84; bishop Charlotte, N.C., 1984-93; archbishop archdiocese of Atlanta, 1993—. Home: 136 W Wesley Rd NW Atlanta GA 30305-3523 Office: Archdiocese of Atlanta Chancery Office 680 W Peachtree St NW Atlanta GA 30308-1931

DONOHO, TIM MARK, charity executive, entrepreneur; b. St. Louis, Sept. 25, 1955; s. James O. and Jean (Dace) D.; m. Deborah Ann Peeples, Feb. 27, 1981; children: Drew Morgan, Jourdan Alexis. BABA, Columbia Coll., 1979. Editor U.S. Army, Okinawa, Japan, 1973-77; sales mgr. Unival Investments, Okinawa, 1975-77; nat. dir. mktg. Pyramid Life Ins. Co., Springfield, Mo., 1978-82; chmn., owner Ins. Mktg. Group, Springfield, 1982-90; pres., owner Am. Dental Program, Inc., Ft. Lauderdale, Fla., 1984-97, Donoho Gruppe Cos., Ft. Lauderdale, 1985—; owner Advantage Dental Health Plans, Ft. Lauderdale, Fla., 1984-97; pub., editor, owner Prime Years News Mag., Ft. Lauderdale, 1985-92; chmn., owner Bus. Healthcare Coalition Inc., 1995-98; chmn. Express Bakery, 1998—. Bd. dirs. So. Fla. chpt. Nat. Multiple Sclerosis Soc., 1996-97; founder, chmn. bd. dirs. Pastors Closet, 1989—, Film the Bible, Inc., 1996—; bd. govs. Graves Archael. Mus., 1998—. With U.S. Army, 1973-77. Mem. Nat. Assn. Dental Plans (chmn. bd. dirs. 1996-97). Republican. Baptist. Avocations: tennis, golf, loudspeaker design. Home: 1075 Hillsboro Mile Hillsboro Beach FL 33062

DONOHUGH, DONALD LEE, physician; b. Los Angeles, Apr. 12, 1924; s. William Noble and Florence Virginia (Shelton) D.; m. Virginia Eskew McGregor, Sept. 12, 1950 (div. 1971); children: Ruth, Laurel, Marilee, Carol, Greg; m. Beatrice Ivany Redick, Dec. 3, 1976; stepchildren: Leslie Ann, Andrea Jean. BS, U.S. Naval Acad., 1946; MD, U. Calif., San Francisco, 1956; MPH and Tropical Medicine, Tulane U., 1961. Diplomate AM. Bd. Internal Medicine. Intern U. Hosp., San Diego, 1956-57; resident Monterey County Hosp., 1957-58; dir. of med. svcs. U.S. Depart. Interior, Am. Samoa, 1958-60; instr. Tulane U. Med. Sch., New Orleans, 1960-63; resident Tulane Svcs. V.A. and Charity Hosp., New Orleans, 1961-63; cons. Internat. Ctr. for Rsch and Tng., Costa Rica, 1961-63; asst. prof. medicine & preventive medicine La. State U. Sch. Medicine, 1962-63; assoc. prof., 1963-65; vis. prof. U. Costa Rica, 1963-65; faculty advisor, head of Agy. Internat. Devel. program U. Costa Rica Med. Sch., 1965-67; dir. med. svcs. Med. Ctr. U. Calif. (formerly Orange County Hosp.), Irvine, 1967-69; assoc. clin. prof. U. Calif., Irvine, 1967-79, clin. prof., 1980-85; pvt. practice Tustin, Calif., 1970-80; with Joint Commn. on Accreditation of Hosps., 1981; cons. Kauai, Hawaii, 1981—. Author: The Middle Years, 1981, Practice Management, 1986, Kauai, 1988, 4th edit., 1992, Our Ancestors, 1995, The Story of Koloa, 2000; co-translator; Rashomon (Ryonosuke Akutagawa), 1950; also numerous articles. Lt. USN, 1946-52, capt. USNR, 1966-84. Fellow Am. Coll. Physicians (life); mem. Delta Omega. Republican. Episcopalian. Home: 4890 Lawai Beach Rd Koloa HI 96756-9675

DONOVAN, ANNE, nursing educator; b. Innisfail, Queensland, Australia, Sept. 5, 1956; d. William John and Ellen (Lever) D. Diploma in applied sci., Queensland U. Tech., 1987; B in Nursing, Flinders U., Adelaide, Australia, 1993; MPhil, Griffith U., Brisbane, Australia, 1998. RN; reg. midwife, child health nurse. Nurse Cmty. Aid Abroad, Sudan, 1985-86, Aboriginal Cmty. Health Svc. Inc., Brisbane, 1987-88, Expo '88, Brisbane, 1988, Mater Pub. Hosps., Brisbane, 1988-90; lectr. Queensland U. Tech., Brisbane, 1990-93, Griffith U., Brisbane, 1993—; cons. educator Save Children Fund, Kathmandu, Nepal, 1990, Mt. Lavinia, Sri Lanka, 1992, Australian Bd. Missions, Yangon, Myanmar, 1994, 95, 96, 97, 99. State com. mem. Cmty. Aid Abroad, Brisbane, 1986-93, pub. spkr., 1986-2000. Mem. Internat. Women's Devel. Agy., Australian Problem Based Lng. Network, Med. Lobby Appropriate Mktg. Avocations: travel, reading, music, cultural diversity, swimming. Home: 4 Nitawill St Everton Pk, Brisbane 4053, Australia

DONOVAN, CHRISTOPHER FERRIER, physician; b. Glasgow, Scotland, Aug. 5, 1929; s. Rickard and Margaret Edith (Mackay) D.; m. Phyllis Muriel Thornton, July 23, 1955; children: Kevin, Caroline, Peter. MA, New Coll., Oxford, Eng., 1954; MB, BChir, Lond U., 1960. House surgeon, house physician, obstetric house surgeon Whittington Hosp., London; gen. practitioner trainee NHS, Barstaple Devon, Eng., 1962-63; gen. practitioner prin. NHS, North London, 1963-93; trainer NHS, 1971-91; med. adviser Thomas Coram Found., London, 1993—; chmn. Trust for Study of Adolescents, Brent Adolescent Ctr., 1993—; chmn., gen. practitioner tchrs. Royal Free Hosp., 1975-90; course organizer London U. and NHS, 1989-96; trustee Young Minds. Co-author: The Health of Adolescents in Primary Care, 1996; contbr. articles to profl. jours. Chmn. Omega Found., London, 1984—; chmn. local fundraising com. North London Hospice, 1994—. Mem. Royal Coll. Gen. Practitioners (chmn. working party on adolescents 1992—), Royal Soc. Medicine, Brit. Med. Assn. Anglican. Avocations: human behavior, cultural beliefs, travel, reading, sports. Home: 25 Middleway, London NW11 6SH, England

DONOVAN, FRANCIS PATRICK, retired diplomat; b. Ingham, Queensland, Australia, Feb. 1, 1922; s. John Francis and Mabel (Pryor) D.; m. Maria Kozslik; children: Patrick, Daisy. LLB, Law Sch., Queensland, 1946; MA, Jurisprudence Sch., Oxford, Eng., 1948, BCL, 1949; LLM (hon.), Law Sch., Adelaide, Australia, 1951; LLM, Law Sch., Melbourne, Australia, 1953. Barrister Supreme Cts. Queensland, Victoria. Prof. comml. law U. Melbourne, Australia, 1952-61; minister, comml. Geneva Dept. Fgn. Trade, Australia, 1964-66; spl. comml. advisor High Commn. of London, Australia, 1968-73; dep. head of mission EEC, Australia, 1974-76; amb. to OECD/Paris, Australia, 1977-80; amb. Spl. Trade del. to UNO, Geneva, 1980-82; v.p. Internat. Ct. of Arbitration LCC, Paris, 1994—; vis. prof. Columbia U., N.Y., 1957-58. Co-author: (books) Cases and Materials on Contract, 1961, Signed, Sealed, and Delivered, 1963. Lt. Australian Mil. Forces, 1941-46. Decorated Order of Australia, 1974, Knight Sovereign, Order of Malta, 1982, Chevalier Legion d'Honneur (France), 1998. Mem. Travellers' Club/London. Home: 25 Avenue Bosquet, 75007 Paris France

DONOVAN, ROBERT F., senior safety specialist, construction consultant; b. Darby, Pa., Dec. 11, 1936; s. Edward Reynolds and Janet Lillian (Burk) D.; m. Myrna Rosalie Poore-Gable, Nov. 23, 1968; children: Debora D. Bukey, Valerie J. Donovan, Patrick R. Donovan, Colleen D. Lawless; stepchildren: John J. Gable, Del R. Gable. Cert. project mgmt., Pa. State U., Malvern, 1993; BA, Eastern Coll., 1994. Cert. occupl. safety & health ACT instr.; cert. profl. environ. auditor. Chief warrant officer USMCR, 1954-76; field supr. Phila. Elec. Co., 1976-80, staff asst., 1980-88; tng. supr. Phila. Elec. Co., Berwyn, Pa., 1988-92; methods supr. PECO Energy Co., Plymouth Meeting, Pa., 1992-94; cons. RFD & Assocs., Frazer, Pa., 1994-96, ECS Risk Control, Inc., Exton, Pa., 1996—; Ark. field safety rep., 2000—. Contbr. article to profl. jour. Asst. emergency mgmt. coord. E. Whiteland Twp., Chester County, Pa., 1990—; radiological officer Pa. Emergency Mgmt. Agy., Pa., 1992—, Tex. Loss Control Rep., 1996—. Mem. ASTD, Am. Soc. Safety Engrs., Marine Corps Reserve Officer's Assn., Res. Officers Assn., Delta Mu Delta. Avocations: hiking, cross country skiing, orienteering, travelling in motor home or by train. Home: 409 Conestoga Rd Frazer PA 19355-1009 Office: 600 Eagleview Blvd Exton PA 19341-1121

DONOVAN, WILLIAM ALAN, retired librarian; b. Rochester, N.Y., Jan. 29, 1937; s. Joseph Leo and Wilhelmina (Fawcett) D. BA, St. John Fisher Coll., Rochester, 1958; MA, U. South Fla., 1981. Libr. Chgo. Pub. Libr., 1961-93. Cartoon gagwriter; contbr. articles and book revs. to profl. jours. With U.S. Army, 1958-61. Mem. ALA, Phi Kappa Phi, Beta Phi Mu. Roman Catholic. Home: 2233 Ednor St Port Charlotte FL 33952-4314

DONTH, ERNST-JOACHIM, physicist, educator; b. Dresden, Saxony, Germany, Dec. 12, 1936; s. Erich and Margarete (Hempel) D.; m. Jutta Elisabet Goldammer, Aug. 3, 1963; children: Stefan, Christine. Diploma in Physics, Tech. U. Dresden, 1960; PhD, U. Halle, Germany, 1969; DSc, Tech. U. Merseburg, Germany, 1973. Rsch. scientist Leuna-Werke, Germany, 1963-74; lectr. physics Tech. U. Merseburg, 1976-92; prof. physics U. Halle, 1993—. Author: Glasübergang, 1981, Relaxation and Thermodynamics in Polymers: Glass Transition, 1992; contbr. articles to profl. jours. Home: Wachbergstrasse 3, D-01326 Dresden Saxony, Germany Office: U Halle FB Physik, D-06099 Halle Germany

DONY, BIANCA MARIA, journalist-photographer; b. The Hague, The Netherlands, Nov. 8, 1935; d. Frans Lucien Marie and Maria Eduarda (Van Lanschot) D. Degree in social scis., U. Leiden, The Netherlands, 1969; M in Theology, Katholieke Theologische U., Amsterdam, 1977. Journalist Vry Nederland, Amsterdam, 1960-62; freelance lectr. The Netherlands, 1960-70, freelance journalist, 1962—; pub. Marco Polo Publicity, 1995—. Co-author: Nieuwe Hoop Voor Sicilie, 1967; author: Wy Zyn Rebellen, 1966, Onze Vader, 1985, Top Tien, 1996; pub. Un Monsieur de Venise Raconte, 1997. Blood donor, The Hague, 1983—. Mem. Nederlandse Journalisten Federatie. Roman Catholic. Avocations: drawing, Zen meditation, reading, walking, antiques. Home: Warmoezierstraat 36-38, 2512 VJ The Hague The Netherlands Office: Marco Polo Publicity, Warmoezierstraat 36/38, 2512 VJ The Hague The Netherlands

DONYA, ALEXANDER, polymer chemist, educator; b. Mariupol, Ukraine, Nov. 13, 1935; m. Lyudmila Ivchenko, Apr. 28, 1960; two children. Diploma, Kishinev U., 1958, MSc, 1968; DSc, Kiev U., 1989. Chief rschr. Mining Rsch. Inst., Makeyevka, Ukraine, 1958-63; jr. rschr. Inst. Chemistry Acad. Scis., Kishinev, Moldova, 1966-69; head chemistry dept. Civil Engring. Inst., Makeyevka, 1969-96; dean faculty of econs. Inst. Econs and Arts, Makeyevka, 1996—. Co-author: Nitrogencontaining Vinilarens, 1985, Nitrogencontaining Polyvinilarens, 1987; contbr. articles to profl. jours. Mem. Acad. Sci. Higher Edn. Ukraine. Office: Inst Econs & Arts, Ul Ostrovskogo 16, 86100 Makeyevka Donetsk, Ukraine

DOODY, JAMES ROBERT, educator, information technology consultant; b. Dublin, Ireland, Jan. 20, 1965. BSc, Dublin City U., 1990, MSc, 1991; PhD, Trinity Coll., Dublin. cons. Emn S.A., Lexembourg, Ireland, 1998. Bus. sys. cons. Digital Equipment Corp., 1988—; lectr. Dublin City U., 1990-91; lectr. St. Patrick's Coll., Maynorth, 1991-93, T Tallaght, Ireland, 1993—. Office: Dept Computer Sci, Tallaght, Dublin 24, Ireland

DOODY, LOUIS CLARENCE, JR., accountant; b. New Orleans, Feb. 5, 1940; s. Louis Clarence and Elsie Clair (Connors) D.; BCS, Tulane U., 1963; m. Barbara Virginia Pettett, Oct. 9, 1982; children by previous marriage:

Dana Lori, Mary Lyn, Kathleen Louise. Accountant, Louis C. Doody, C.P.A., 1963-68, partner Doody and Doody, C.P.A.'s, 1969—. C.P.A., La., Tex., Miss. Mem. AICPA, La. Soc. C.P.A.'s. Home: 36 Cypress Rd Covington LA 70433-4306 Office: 3838 N Causeway Blvd Ste 2525 Metairie LA 70002-8317

DOOGE, JAMES CLEMENT IGNATIUS, civil engineer, hydrologist, former senator; b. Birkenhead, Eng., July 30, 1922; s. Denis Patrick and Veronica Catherine (Carroll) D.; m. Roni O'Doherty, Nov. 25, 1946 (dec. Nov. 1991); children: Colm, Diarmuid, Cliona, Dara, Meliosa (dec. Feb. 2000). CBS, Dun Laoghaire; BE, BSc., Univ. Coll., Dublin, 1942, ME, 1952; MS, U. Iowa, 1956; DrAgrSci (hon.), U. Wageningen, 1978, DrTech (hon.), 1980; DSc (hon.), U. Birmingham, Eng., 1985, U. Dublin, 1988; D Engring. (hon.), Heriot-Watt U., 2000; Dr. (hon.), Cracow Tech. U., 2000. Jr. civil engr. Irish Office Pub. Works, 1943-46; design engr. E.S.B., 1946-58; prof. civil engring. Univ. Coll., Cork, Ireland, 1958-70, Dublin, 1970-81, 82-84; minister for fgn. affairs Ireland, 1981-82; leader Irish Senate, 1983-87; mem. Coun. of State, 1973-77. Recipient Horton award Am. Geophys. Union, 1959, Bowie medal, 1986, Ven Te Chow award ASCE, 1993, John Dalton medal European Geophys. Soc., 1998, Internat. Meteorology prize WMO, 1999. Mem. Instn. Civil Engrs. Ireland (pres. 1968-69, Kettle Premium and Plaque awards 1948, Mullins medal 1951, 62), Royal Irish Acad., Russian Acad. Scis. (fgn., pres. 1987-90), Spanish Acad. Sci. (fgn.), Internat. Assn. Hydrological Scis. (pres. 1975-79), Internat. Coun. Sci. Unions (pres. 1993-96), Royal Acad. Engring. (fgn.), Polish Acad. Sci. (fgn.). Roman Catholic. Home: 2 Belgrave Rd, Monkstown County Dublin, Ireland Office: U Coll, Earlsfort Terr, Dublin 2, Ireland

DOOLEY, ANTHONY HAYNES, mathematician; b. Melbourne, Australia, Feb. 8, 1951; s. James and Nanette (Norris-Smith) D.; m. Elizabeth Catherine Ives, Mar. 30, 1973; children: Christopher James, Jonathon Mark, Robert Anthony. BSc, Australian Nat. U., 1973, PhD, 1977. Tchg. fellow Sydney U., Australia, 1973; rsch. fellow Flinders U., Adelaide, Australia, 1977-80; rsch. fellow U. New South Wales, Sydney, 1980-83, from lectr. to prof., 1983—, head dept. pure math., 1993-99. Mem. Australian Math. Soc. Avocations: music, reading. Office: U New South Wales, Sch Maths, Sydney 2052, Australia

DOOLEY, CRAIG IRWIN, entrepreneur; b. Dallas, July 10, 1951; s. Clyde Edward and Dorothy Louise Dooley; m. Linda Susan Bowman, Aug. 9, 1975; children: Ryan, Erin, Megan, Shannon. BBA, Sam Houston State U., Huntsville, Tex., 1977. Sales and mktg. staff IBM, 1977; project mgr. Gen. Homes, 1980; pres. Dooley Homes, 1985; stockbroker Merrill Lynch, 1986; area pres. Royce Homes, Inc., Houston, 1987-89; pres., CEO, Polybutylene Specialists, Inc., Spring, Tex., 1989-98; COO, Safe Home, Inc., Conroe, Tex., 1998—. Scoutmaster, founder troop 136 Boy Scouts Am., Spring, 1988-98; life mem. Houston Livestock Show and Rodeo, 1991—; bd. dirs. Brisket Cases, Houston, 1992—; com. chmn. Houston Golf Assn., The Woodlands, Tex., 1996—. Named One of Top 25 Entrepreneurs of Yr., Ernst & Young, Houston, 1997; recipient Inc. 500 1997 award Inc. mag., 1997, Houston 100 award Houston Bus. Jour., 1997, Remodeler 100 award Remodeler mag., Houston, 1999. Mem. Sigma Phi Epsilon. Republican. Roman Catholic. Avocations: golf, tennis, travel, participating in his children's activities. Fax: 281-251-0909. E-mail: cidooley@hotmail.com. Home: 5502 Linden Ct Spring TX 77379-8864 Office: Safe Home Inc 27326 Robinson Rd Ste 206 Conroe TX 77385-8961

DOOLEY, MARK PATRICK, philosopher, humanities educator; b. Dublin, Leinster, Ireland, Jan. 12, 1970. BA, Nat. U. Ireland, Dublin, 1991, MA, 1993, PhD, 1997. Lectr. U. Coll. Dublin, 1993—, John Henry Newman scholar of theology, 1999—. Author: An Ethics of Responsibility, 1997, Questioning Ethics, 1998. Hong and Hong Rsch. scholar St. Olaf Coll., Minn., 1995, Internat. scholar Nat. U. Ireland, 1995; Faculty of Arts fellow U. Coll. Dublin, 1995. Mem. Irish Philos. Soc. (treas. 1996-97), Hegel Soc. Ireland (sec. 1993-94). Office: U Coll Dublin, Belfield 4, Dublin Leinster, Ireland

DOOLEY, MICHAEL LEIGH, medical equipment company executive; b. Liverpool, Eng., Mar. 9, 1967; s. Allan Keith and Avril Elizabeth (Thompson) D.; m. Ruth Lewis, Jan. 26, 1991 (separated 1996). BA in zoology (hons.), Oxford U., U.K., 1988; MBA, City Univ., London, 1990; Dip M, CIM, U.K., 1993. Fund raising coord. Oxford U. Appeal, Oxford, U.K., 1988; quality tech. Oxford Exhausts Ltd., Oxford, U.K., 1988-89; sales exec. HHW, Cheltenham, 1991-92, Ohmeda, U.K., 1992-94; product mgr. Ohmeda, Hatfield, U.K., 1994-96; internt. product mgr. BOC Ohmeda AB, Sweden, 1996-98; product mgr.-Europe Becton Dickinson Infusion Therapy Systems AB, Sweden, 1998-99, worldwide bus. leader, 1999-2000, marketing mgr., 2000—. Com. mem. Sports and Social Club, Hatfield, 1994; leader Dive Club, Helsingborg, 1998, 99. Mem. AMBA, CIM. Avocations: sailing, scuba diving. Office: Becton Dickinson Infusion Therapy Syss AB, PO Box 631, S-251 06 Helsingborg Sweden

DOONG, RUEY-AN, research chemist; b. Tainan, Taiwan, Aug. 19, 1964; s. Shang-Shi Doong and Su-ying Lin; m. Hsiang-Lin Peng, June 30, 1991; children: Chun-Wei (Kevin), Kuan-Wei (Alan). BS, Nat. Chung-Hsing U., Taichung, Taiwan, 1987; PhD in Environ. Engring., Nat. Taiwan U., Taipei, 1992. Asst. prof. chemistry Nat. Tsing Hua U., Hsinchu, Taiwan, 1994-98, assoc. prof. chemistry, 1998—; cons. Taipei City Govt., 1997—, Keelung (Taiwan) City Govt., 1999—. Contbr. articles to profl. jours. Lt., Taiwan Army, 1992-94, Chung-li. Mem. Am. Chem. Soc., Am. Soc. Microbiology, IAWQ. Avocations: reading, sports, stamps. Home: 7F-4 50 Ta-Hsueh Rd, Hsinchu 300, Taiwan Office: Nat Tsing Hua U Dept Nuc Sc, 101 sect 2 Kuang-Fu Rd, Hsinchu 300, Taiwan

DOORLEY, THOMAS LAWRENCE, III, management consulting firm executive; b. Sewickley, Pa., Aug. 15, 1944; s. Thomas Lawrence and Emma Lou (Sage) D.; m. Gail Lynn Schwartz, Feb. 3, 1968; children: Christopher Sage, Scott Frederick. BSChemE, Pa. State U., BA in Arts and Sci., 1967; MBA in Mktg., Columbia U., 1969. Cons. Westvaco, N.Y.C., 1968-69; sr. cons. A D Little, Cambridge, Mass., 1969-74, bus. unit mgr., 1974-76; founder, exec. v.p. Braxton Assocs., Boston, 1977-84; sr. ptnr. Deloitte Consulting, 1984-99, Deloitte Consulting Braxton Assocs., Boston, 1996—. Author: Teaming up for the 90's, 1991, Value-Creating Growth, 1999; contbr. articles to profl. jours. Chmn., bd. dirs. The Soccer Network, Boston, 1987—; mem. leadership club United Way Mass., Boston, 1986-90; coach Wellesley (Mass.) United Soccer Club, 1977-90; deacon Wellesley Congregational Ch., 1970's, sr. high youth advisor, 1970's. Woodrow Wilson fellow Columbia U., 1969. Mem. Columbia Bus. Sch. Club, Wellesley Country Club, Alliance Analyst and World Econ. Found. (advisory bd.). Avocations: running, fitness, reading, children. Home: 34 Arnold Rd Wellesley MA 02481-2841 Office: Deloitte Consulting Braxton Assocs 200 Clarendon St Ste 2000 Boston MA 02116-5021

DOPF, GLENN WILLIAM, lawyer; b. N.Y.C., June 6, 1953; s. William Bernard and Doris Virginia (Roxby) D. BS cum laude, Fordham Coll., 1975; JD, Fordham U., 1979; LLM, NYU, 1983. Bar: N.J. 1979, U.S. Dist. Ct. N.J. 1979, N.Y. 1980, U.S. Dist. Ct. (so. and ea. dists.) N.Y. 1980, U.S. Ct. Appeals (2d cir.) 1980, U.S. Ct. Internat. Trade 1981, U.S. Supreme Ct. 1983. Assoc. Martin, Clearwater & Bell, N.Y.C., 1980-81; ptnr. Kopff, Nardelli & Dopf, N.Y.C., 1982—. Mem. ABA, Assn. Bar City N.Y. Office: Kopff Nardelli & Dopf 440 9th Ave Fl 15 New York NY 10001-1688

DOPPALAPUDI, SAMBA MURTHY, surgeon, educator; b. Andhra Pradesh, India, Aug. 15, 1944; s. Ankamma Choudhary and Veeramma Doppalapudi; m. Madhavamma Yarlagadda, May 20, 1967; 1 child, Pavan Kumar. MB BChir, Rangaraya Med. Coll., Kakinada, 1969; M of Surgery, King George Hosp., Visakhapatnam, 1972. Cert. in medicine. Surgeon State Govt. of Andhra Pradesh Primary Health Ctr., 1976-80; surgeon State Govt. of Andhra Pradesh, Bapatla, 1980-84, Tenali, 1984-92; asst. prof. gen. surgery Guntur Med. Coll., 1992—. Recipient Kakumanu Vullaki award for health, 1990. Hindu. Avocations: reading news magazines, reading Hindu epics. Home: Veerannapalem Parchuru, Prakasam, Andhra Pradesh 523169, India Office: Govt Gen Hosp-Guntur, S-2 Unit, Guntur India

DOPPELFELD, VOLKER, automotive company executive. Chief fin. officer Bayerische Motoren Werke A.B., Munich, Germany; chmn. supervisory bd. Bayerische Motoren Werke AG; bd. dirs. BMW AG, Munich. Office: BMW AG BMW Haus, Petuelring 130, Munich 80788, Germany*

DOR, CHRISTIAN, automotive company executive. Chief fin. officer Renault, Boulogne-Billancourt, France. Office: 13-15 Quai Le Gallo, 92100 Boulogne-Billancourt France*

DOR, XAVIER MARIE, medical researcher; b. Marseille, France, Jan. 30, 1929; s. Georges Marie and Therese Marie (Favre) D.; m. Francoise de Bernonville, Dec. 23, 1950; four children. D in Medicine, cert. pediat., U. Paris, 1962; PhD in Sci., U. Nantes, France, 1976. Intern Pasteur Hosp., Paris, 1956-57, various hosps., Paris, 1957-62; head pediat. dept. Abidjan Hosp., 1962-68; practitioner Hosp. Pitié-Salpetrière, Paris, 1975-95; asst. prof. Pitié U., Paris, 1975-95; rschr. anatomy and organogenesis Pitié Hosp., 1975—; supr. MSc and Doctorate students Pitié U., 1982-94; spkr. in field. Author: Defending Anti-Abortion Views, 1998, 2nd edit., 1999; co-author: Cardiac Embriology, 1981, 2nd edit., 1992. Founder Sos Tout-Petits, Paris, 1986—. Recipient 1st prize Festival Sci. Film, San Sebastian, Spain, 1982; named Officer, Order for Merite Ivoirien, Abidjan, 1968. Mem. Soc. Francaise de Teratologie. Roman Catholic. Avocations: charity work, gardening.

DORATO, PETER, electrical and computer engineering educator; b. N.Y.C., Dec. 17, 1932; s. Fioretto and Rosina (Lachello) D.; m. Marie Madeleine Turlan, June 2, 1956; children: Christopher, Alexander, Sylvia, Veronica. BEE, CCNY, 1955; MSEE, Columbia U., 1956; DEE, Poly. Inst. N.Y., 1961. Registered profl. engr., Colo. Lectr. elec. engring. dept. CCNY, 1956-57; instr. elec. engring. Poly. Inst. N.Y., Bklyn., 1957-61, prof., 1961-72; prof. elec. engring., dir. Resource System Analysis U. Colo., Colorado Springs, 1972-76; prof. elec. and computer engring. U. N.Mex., Albuquerque, 1984—, chmn. dept., 1976-84; hon. chaired prof. Nanjing Aero. Inst., 1989; vis. prof. Politecnico di Torino, Italy, 1991-92. Author: Analytic Feedback Systems Design, 2000; co-author Linear Quadratic Control, 1995, Robust Control for Unstructured Perturbations, 1992, Robust Control-System Design, 1996; editor: Robust Control, Recent Results in Robust Control and Advances in Adaptive Control, reprint vols., 1987, 90, 91, IEEE Press Reprint Vol. Series, 1989-90; assoc. editor Automatica Jour., 1969-83, 89-92, editor rapid publs., 1994—; assoc. editor IEEE Trans on Edn., 1989-91; contbr. articles on control systems theory to profl. jours. Recipient John R. Ragazzini edn. award Am. Automatic Control Coun., 1998. Fellow IEEE (3rd Millenium medal); mem. IEEE Control Systems Soc. (Disting. Mem. award). Democrat. Home: 1514 Roma Ave NE Albuquerque NM 87106-4513 Office: U NMex Dept Elec Computer Eng Albuquerque NM 87131-0001

D'ORBÁN, PAUL THEODORE, psychiatrist; b. London, May 26, 1930; s. Charles and Constance Emily (Hill) D'O.; m. Jocelyn Laura Ho-a-Shu, Oct. 15, 1955; children: Charles Mark, Andrea Nora. MB ChB, Aberdeen U., 1956; diploma psychol. medicine, Royal Coll. Physicians, 1961, Royal Coll. Surgeons Eng., 1961. Med. officer Georgetown, Guyana, 1956-59; registrar Friern Hosp., London, 1960-62; cons. psychiatrist Kingston, Jamaica, 1962-65; med. officer Home Office, London, 1966-73; cons. psychiatrist St. George's Hosp., London, 1974-77; hon. sr. lectr. U. London, 1974-77; cons. forensic psychiatrist Home Office and Royal Free Hosp., 1977-87; hon. sr. lectr. U. London-Royal Free Hosp. Sch. Medicine, 1977-90; cons. forensic psychiatrist Royal Free Hosp., 1987-90; mem. working party on evaluation of treatment of drug dependence Med. Rsch. Coun., 1968-70; mem. panel of examiners Gen. Med. Coun. London, 1982-90; hon. cons. WHO, Iran, 1974, Egypt, 1978, Iraq, 1979. Author: (with others) Principles and Practice of Forensic Psychiatry, 1990, International Handbook of Addiction Behaviour, 1991, Forensic Psychiatry, 1993; contbr. numerous articles to profl. jours. Fellow Royal Coll. of Psychiatrists, Royal Soc. Medicine; mem. Brit. Acad. of Forensic Scis. Avocations: bridge, chess, fine arts. Home: 5555 Kiowa Rd RRN7, Victoria, BC Canada

DORCUS, MARK KEVIN, insurance company investment executive; b. Cranston, R.I., Feb. 17, 1959; s. Frederick Andrew and Elizabeth Jane Dorcus; m. Julie Anna White, May 19, 1985; children: Lindsey, Leslie. BS in Fin., U. R.I., 1981. CFA. Asst. analyst Standard & Poors Corp., N.Y.C., 1982-83, analyst, 1983-84, industry analyst, 1984-85, rating specialist, 1985-86; investment specialist Nat. Grange Mut. Ins. Co., Keene, N.H., 1986-89, portfolio mgr., 1989-98, v.p. investment ops., 1998—; pres. Nat. Grange Mut. Ins. Co. Employees Fed. Credit Union, Keene, 1989—; pres. investment mgmt. svcs. Main St. Am. Capital Corp., Keene, 1999—. Mem. fin. bd. United Ch. of Christ, Keene, 1996-2000, mem. investment com., 1998—. Mem. Assn. for Investment Mgmt. and Rsch., Boston Security Analyst Soc., Mass. Audubon Soc. Republican. Avocations: scuba diving, hiking, boating, skiing, cooking. E-mail: dorcusm@msagroup.com. Home: 58 S Lincoln St Keene NH 03431-3828 Office: Nat Grange Mut Ins Co 55 West St Keene NH 03431-3374

DORDA, ABUZEID OMAR, Libyan government official. Tchr., 1965-70; gov. of Misurata Govt. of Libya, 1970-72, min. inro. and culture, 1972-74; under-sec. Ministry Fgn. Affairs, 1974-76; sec. municipalities Gen. People's Com. Govt. of Libya, 1976-79, sec. for economy, 1979-82, sec. for agr., 1982-86, sec. gen. Gen. People's Com., 1990-94; sec. for gen. People's Congress N.Y.C., 1994-95, now Libyan permanent rep. to UN, 1997—. Office: Permanent Mission of Libya to UN 309 E 48th St New York NY 10017-1746

DORE, BONNY ELLEN, film and television production company executive; b. Cleve., Aug. 16, 1947; d. Reber Hutson and Ellen Elizabeth (McNamara) Barnes; m. Sanford Astor, May 22, 1987. BA, U. Mich., 1969, MA, 1975. Cert. tchr., Mich. Dir., tchr. Plymouth (Mich.) Community Schs., 1969-72; gen. mgr. Sta. WSDP-FM, Plymouth, 1970-72; prodn. supr. pub. TV N.Y. State Dept. Edn., 1972-74; producer TV series Hot Fudge Sta. WXYZ-TV, Detroit, 1974-75; mgr. children's programs ABC TV Network, L.A., 1975, dir. children's programs, 1975-76, dir. prime time variety programs, 1976-77; dir. devel. Hanna-Barbera, L.A., 1977; v.p. devel. and prodn. Krofft Entertainment, L.A., 1977-81, Centerpoint Prodn., L.A., 1981-82; pres., owner in assn. with Orion TV The Greif-Dore Co., L.A., 1983-87, Bonny Dore Prodns. Inc., L.A., 1988—; mem. Caucus of Writers, Producers and Dirs., 1989—; Marsh speaker Pres. Fund for Pres. Weekend U. Mich., 1989. Producer TV series The Krofft Superstar Hour, ABC, 1978 (2 Emmy awards 1979), comedy series The 1/2 Hour Comedy Hour (starring Arsenio Hall and Victoria Jackson), ABC, 1983-84, mini-series Sins (starring Joan Collins), CBS, 1986, comedy series First Impressions, CBS, 1987-88, mini-series Glory! Glory! (starring Ellen Greene, Richard Thomas and James Whitmore; 2 Ace cable awards), HBO, 1988-89, Lifetime Network, 1993-96, A&E Network, 1997, NBC movie Reason for Living, The Jill Ireland Story, 1990-91, ABC movie Captive!, 1991, The Sinking of the Rainbow Warrior, 1993-94, numerous others. Mem. fundraising com. U. Mich., 1990—; assoc. mem. Nat. Trust for Hist. Preservation, 1988—. Named Outstanding Young Tchr. of Yr., Cen. States Speech Assn., 1973; Cert. of Appreciation, Gov. of Mich., 1985, City of Beverly Hills, Calif., 1985, Coun. on Social Work Edn., 1990; recipient Action for Children's TV award, 1975, Gold medal Best TV Mini-series, Best TV Screenplay Silver medal Houston Internat. Film Festival, 1990, Best. TV Actress award, 1990, Best TV Supporting Actor, 1990, Best Music, 1990, Winner Best Mini Series Houston Film Festival, 1990. Mem. NATAS (caucus of writers, prodrs., dir. 1991—, co-chair, 1994-97, Disting. Svc. award 1996), Am. Film Inst. (corr. sec.), Women in Film (v.p. 1978-81, pres. 1980-81, life achievement award, 1998), Women in Film Found. (trustee 1981, chair 1994-96, exec. prodr. The Signature Series, co-chair 1994—), Nat. Cable TV Assn., Beverly Hills C. of C. (cons. 1985), Exec. Roundtable L.A. (trustee 1987—, disting. achievement award 2000), Hollywood Radio and TV Soc. Office: Bonny Dore Prodns Inc 9454 Wilshire Blvd Ph Beverly Hills CA 90212-2937

DORE, JAGDISH VISWANATH, management executive; b. Madras, India, July 23, 1950; s. Viswanath and Sarala (Krishnaswamy) D.; m. Gita Bhaskaran, Sept. 10, 1981; two children. B in Technology, Indian Inst. Technology, Madras, 1971; MBA, Xavier Inst., 1973. From mktg. svcs. mgr. to v.p. Sandoz India Ltd., Bombay, 1979-96; mng. dir. Novartis Enterprises, Bombay, 1996—. Mem. Bombay Mgmt. Assn. Office: Novartis Enterprises Ltd, "A" Block 6th Fl Shivsagar Estate, Worli Bombay 400018, India

DOREMUS, OGDEN, lawyer; b. Atlanta, Apr. 23, 1921; s. C. Estes and Mary (McAdory) D.; m. Carolyn Wooten Greene, Aug. 30, 1947 (dec. Aug. 1989); children: Celia Jane, Frank O., Dale Marie Doremus; m. Linda Parker, Dec. 4, 1992. BA, Emory U., 1946, JD, 1949. Bar: Ga. 1947; cert. U.S. postal mediator, 1999. Asst. solicitor gen. Atlanta, 1947-49; ptnr. firm Smith Field Doremus & Ringel, Atlanta, 1949-60, Falligant, Doremus and Karsman, Savannah, Ga., 1960-72, Doremus, Jones & Smith, P.C., Metter, Ga., 1972-94; of counsel Karsman, Brooks & Callaway, 1994—; prof. Woodrow Wilson Sch. Law, Atlanta, 1948-50; judge State Ct. Candler County, Ga., 1985—, chair uniform rules com. Coun. State Cts., 1990—; pres. Ga. Coun. State Ct. Judges, 1990-91, chair legis. com., 1997-99; mem. Jud. Coun. State of Ga., 1989-91, Unified Trial Ct. Commn., 1997; mem. ct. futures com. State Bar Ga., 1996—; bd. dirs. Ctr. for Law in the Pub. Interest, 1996—; judge Mcpl. Ct., Metter, Ga., 1997—; mem. commn. on judiciary Supreme Ct. Ga., 1999—. Mem. editorial adv. bd. Environ. Law, Reporter, 1969-80. Scoutmaster Boy Scouts Am., Atlanta, 1951-60, commn., 1961-70; chmn. Ga. Day and Savannah Arts Festival, 1968-72; mem. Atlanta City Coun., 1950-53; mem. Savannah Govtl. Reorgn. Commn., 1960-61, Ga. Ct. Futures Commn., 1991-93, 97—; adv. com. Nat. Coastal Zone Mgmt. Coun., 1978-86; trustee Ga. Conservancy; bd. dirs. Legal Environ. Assistance Found., 1983-86, Ga. Hazardous Waste Authority, 1989—, Chatham Environ. Forum, 1990-93; mem. strategic planning com. Coun. State Cts. Ga., 1996—; bd. dirs. Coastal Environ. Orgn. Ga., 1998—. Served with USAAC, 1942-46, ETO. Named Young Man of Yr. Atlanta, 1951; recipient Thomas H. gigniliat award Cultural Progress of Savannah, 1969, Tradition of Excellence award Ga. State Bar, 1988, 1st Ann. Coun. of State Cts. award named Ogden Doremus in his honor, 1993. Mem. ABA (chmn. environ. law com., gen. practice 1976-77), State Bar Ga. (chmn. ins. law sect. 1963-67, 77-83, cert. mediator Ga. commn. on dispute resolution, mediator for U.S. Postal Svc. 1999—), Savannah Bar Assn., Ga. Inst. Trial Advocacy (chmn. 1984-89), Izaak Walton league (founder Ga. chpt. 1950), Sierra Club (exec. com. Chattahoochee chpt. 1965-75, chair legal com. Ga. chpt. 1997—, Lifetime Achievement Ga. environ. coun. Citizenship award 1997, 99, Conservation Leadership award Ga. chpt. 1999), Common Cause, Sierra Club, Chatham Club, Chatham Tennis Club, Willow Lake Country Club, Atlanta Soc. Home: RR 2 Box 188A Metter GA 30439-9570 Office: Doremus and Assocs Courthouse Sq PO Box 702 Metter GA 30439-0702

DOREN, HENRY J.T., artist, painter; b. N.Y.C., May 20, 1929; s, Thaddeus Karol and Rozalia (Myslicki) Dutkiewicz; m. Anna Tanska (div. 1959); 1 child, Charles Henry (dec.); m. Eleanor Joyce Carlson, Nov. 24, 1962. BS, N.Y.U., 1948; MA, Ottawa U., Can., 1959; postgrad., Art Students League N.Y., 1959-62, Frank Reilly Sch. Art, 1962-64; MFA, Instituto Allende San Miguel de Allende, Mex., 1965. Freelance artist Labow Advt. Svcs., East Orange, N.J., 1965-69; asst. prof. Trenton (N.J.) State Coll., 1963-64; part-time art instr. Fairleigh Dickinson U., Madison, N.J., 1966-68; part time art instr. Seton Hall U., South Orange, N.J., 1967-72; assoc. prof. art County Coll. of Morris, Randolph, N.J., 1969-83; artist pvt. studio, Madison, N.J., 1983-96, Tucson, Ariz., 1996—; lectr. art assn. librs., N.J., 1970—; judge art orgns., N.J., 1975—; pub. NJ ARTform mag., 1979-83; organizer The Statler Art Inst.; part-time instr. Pima C.C., Tucson, 1998—. Author: (slides and booklet) Survey of Polish Art, 1976; (monographs) Drawing: Guide to Structural Concepts, Color Theory: Review of Color Principles and Applications, 1996, The Artists Atalier Guide to Principles in Drawing and Color Theory, 2000; editor art newsletter County Coll. Morris, 1976-83; pub. N.J. ARTform (art mag.), 1979-83; contbr. articles to profl. jours.; exhbns. one-man and group shows N.J. and N.Y., 1970, including Collection of Gov. Byrne and U.S. Sen. Bradley, N.J., 1981, Mother and Child Hosp., Lodz, Poland, 1987, Environment and 20th Century, Dom Polonii Mus., Pultusk, Poland, 1989, Consulate of the Polish Republic, N.Y.C., 1991. Exch. scholar, Polish Acad. Sci., Warsaw, 1974-75. Mem. Art Students League N.Y. (life). Avocations: music, film, photography. Home & Studio: 4822 E Water St Tucson AZ 85712-5716

D'OREYE DE LANTREMANGE, NICOLAS FREDERIC, physicist, researcher; b. Ixelles, Brussels, July 12, 1967; arrived in Luxembourg, 1994; s. Arnold and Bernadette (le Sergent d'Hendecourt) d'Oreye de Lantremange; m. Astrid Marie della Faille de Leverghem, Mar. 19, 1994; children: Sandrine, Adrien, Anouchka, Pierre. Sci. Degree in Physics, Cath. U. Louvain, Louvain-la-Neuve, Belgium, 1989; M in Instrumentation and Measurement, Cath. U. Louvain, 1991. Tchr. physics, biology and chemistry St. Michel H.S., Brussels, 1990; rschr. Royal Obs. Belgium, Brussels, 1990-94, European Ctr. for Geodynamics and Seismology, Walferdange, Luxembourg, 1994—; mem. organizing com. Workshops of the European Ctr. for Geodynamics and Seismology, 1991—; sci. collaborator Nat. Mus. Natural History of Luxembourg, 1994—; in charge Underground Lab. for Geodynamics, Walferdange, 1994—; sci. sec. Journées Luxembourgeoises de Géodynamique, 1996—. Co-editor: Cahiers du Centre Européen de Géodynamique de Séismologie, vol. 4, 1991. Cpl. Belgian Army Force, 1992. Mem. Internat. Union of Geodesy and Geophysics (sec. nat. com. 1999—), Internat. Assn. Volcanoe and Chem. of the Earth (nat. corr. 1999—). Roman Catholic. Office: European Ctr Geodyn & Seis, 19 rue Josy Welter, L-7256 Walferdange Luxembourg

DORF, GUY SAMY, physician, educator, consultant; b. Paris, Mar. 2, 1935; s. Joseph and Lea (Leon) D. MD, Paris U., 1967. Intern Paris Hosps., 1963-67; sr. resident Paris U., 1967-77; sr. lectr. Paris VII Med. Sch., 1977—; med. cons. Paris Hosps., 1977—; med. advisor Logais/Chiesi, Paris, 1970—. Contbr. over 100 articles to profl. jours. Lt. French Army, 1962-63. Recipient 40th Career Achievement award French Ministry Labour, 1997. Mem. Am. Soc. Parenteral and Enteral Nutrition, European Soc. Parenteral and Enteral Nutrition, French Soc. Study of Diabetes, European Soc. Study of Diabetes. Avocations: classical and contemporary music, cinema and theatre fan. FAX: 00 33 1 39 89 81 82. Office: 19 Rue De L'Arrivee, 95880 Enghien-Les-Bains France

DÖRFLER, WILLIBALD, mathematician, educator; b. St. Polten, Austria, June 20, 1944; s. Rudolf and Anna (Gischelbauer) D.; m. Maria Auinger, Feb. 28, 1969; children: Stefan, Monika, Martin. PhD, U. Vienna, Austria, 1967, Mag.rer.nat., 1968; habilitation, Tech. U. Vienna, Austria, 1973. Asst. prof. Tech. U. Vienna, Austria, 1968-74; prof. ednl. scis. U. Klagenfurt, Austria, 1974—, prorektor, 1990-93, rektor, 1993-99; vis. prof. Vanderbilt U., Nashville, 1979, U. Kassel, Germany, 1983. Author: Graphentheorie fur Informatiker, 1977, Mathematik fur Informatiker I, II, 1977, Einf id Mathematik fur Informatiker, 1988, contbr. numerous articles to profl. jours. Soviet Govt. fellow, Moscow, 1969. Mem. Am. Math. Soc., Austrian Math. Soc. (mem. bd.), Gesellschaft Didaktik der Mathematik (mem. bd.). Avocations: music, skiing, tennis. Home: Pamperlallee 9, 9201 Krumpendorf Austria Office: Universität Klagenfurt, Universitätsstrasse 65, 9022 Klagenfurt Austria

DORFMAN, ROBERT, economics educator; b. N.Y.C., Oct. 27, 1916; s. Samuel M. and Mina Ruth (Gordon) D.; m. Nancy Schelling, Nov. 6, 1949; children: Peter J., Ann E. BA, Columbia U., 1936, MA, 1937; PhD, U. Calif., Berkeley, 1950. Asst. statistician Bur. Labor Stats., Dept. Labor, Washington, 1939-41; statistician OPA, Washington, 1941-43; ops. analyst U.S. Air Force, S.W. Pacific and Washington, 1943-50; assoc. prof. econs U. Calif., Berkeley, 1950-55; prof. econs. Harvard U., Cambridge, Mass., 1955-87; prof. emeritus Harvard U., Cambridge, 1987—; mem. clean air sci. adv. com. EPA, 1978-84; mem. environ. studies bd. NRC, 1974-77; mem. Presdl. Commn. on Waterlogging and Salinity in West Pakistan, 1961-63, Presdl. Commn. on Employment and Unemployment Stats., 1962-63. Author: Prices and Markets, 1967, Economic Theory and Public Decisions, 1997; co-author: Linear Programming and Economic Analysis, 1958; co-editor: Economics of the Environment: Selected Readings, 1972, 3d edit. 1993; editor Quar. Jour. Econs., 1976-84. Guggenheim fellow, 1970-71. Fellow Am. Acad. Arts and Scis., Econometric Soc. (coun. 1962-64); mem. Am. Econs. Assn. (v.p. 1982, Disting. fellow 1993), Inst. Mgmt. Sci. (pres. 1965-66), Assn. Resource and Environ. Economists (v.p. 1981). Home: 81 Kilburn Rd Belmont MA 02478-2464 Office: Harvard U Dept Econs Littauer Ctr 234 Cambridge MA 02138

DORFMANN, HENRI, physician; b. Paris, Feb. 2, 1937; s. Max and Raja (Leikind) D.; m. Nicole Francine Nathusius, Sept. 4, 1974; childre: Bettina, Annabelle (dec.), Maxime. MD, Paris U., 1968. Resident Paris Hosp., 1964-68; asst. prof. U. Paris, 1968-75; chief dept. rheumatology France, 1977; assoc. prof. medicine Coll. Paris Hosp., 1987; Contbr. articles to profl. jours. Lt. French Army, 1963-64. Mem. Achievements include pioneering rsch. in arthscopy. Avocations: skiing, tennis, cycling. Office: Hosp R Ballanger, 93602 Aulnays Sous Bois France

DORION, ROBERT CHARLES, entrepreneur, investor; b. N.Y.C., Dec. 28, 1926; s. William J. and Adelaide (Bacardi) D.; m. Ana Maria Ferber, Nov. 26, 1954; children: Robert Patrick, Marianne Michelle, Nicholas Christian, Kristel Alexia. Student, Columbia U., 1943-44; B of Naval Scis., Dartmouth Coll., 1946. Buyer Balfour, Guthrie and Co. Ltd., 1948-49; capt. M/V Assault Shark Industries div. Borden & Co., 1950-51; pres. Dorion, Rubio and Cia, 1952-57; mgr., ins., mining and chem. dept. Grace & Co., 1954-59; sales mgr. Gen. Tires, Guatemala, 1960-61; chmn. El Salto, S.A., 1962-78; pres. Tecnicos En Seguros, S.A., 1979—, Marcas Mundiales, S.A., 1978-99; dir. emeritus Bacardi Ltd., Bermuda, pres. Marcas Mundiales S.A., dir. Industrias Rio Dulce S.A. Contbr. articles to profl. jours. Friend Am. Mus. of Nat. History, N.Y.C.; field assoc. Fla. Mus., Gainesville, Mote Marine Lab., Sarasota, Fla., Interamer. Scout Found. Fellow Internat. Oceanographic Found. (life); mem. Rotary (Paul Harris fellow), World Scout Orgn. (Baden-Powell fellow), Interam. Scout Found. (dir.), U.S. Navy Meml. Found. (dir.), U.S. Naval Inst. (life), Audubon Soc. (life), Internat. Wildlife Soc., Order of The Bronze Wolf. Avocations: Pre-Columbian archaeology, cryptozoolical studies, shark research, deep sea fishing. Office: care Bacardi Martini Ltd 2100 Biscayne Blvd Miami FL 33137-5014 also: Kristel SA Apt 195A, Guatemala City Guatemala

DORKEY, CHARLES EDWARD, III, lawyer; b. Phila., June 23, 1948; s. Charles Edward and Peggy O'Neal D.; children: Charles Edward IV, John Hilliard, Marjorie Lyddon. AB cum laude, Dartmouth Coll., 1970; JD, Univ. Pa., 1973. Bar: Pa. 1974, N.Y. 1975, D.C. 1977. Law clk. to hon. Samuel J. Roberts Supreme Ct. of Pa., 1973-74; assoc. Sullivan & Cromwell, N.Y.C., 1975-81; ptnr. Reboul, MacMurray, Hewitt, Maynard & Kristol, N.Y.C., 1981-84, Richards & O'Neil, N.Y.C., 1984-91, Haythe & Curley, N.Y.C., 1992-99, Torys, N.Y.C., 1999—; bd. dirs. Empire State Devel. Corp., N.Y.C. Water Fin. Auth., N.Y. State Job Devel. Auth., Harlem Cmty. Devel. Corp., 42d St. Devel. Project, N.Y. State Mortgage Loan Enforcement and Adminstrn. Corp., N.Y. Parks and Conservation Assn.; trustee Citizens Budget Commn., 1993-98; trustee N.Y. Hist. Soc., 1998—; mem. First Dept. Jud. Screening Com.; mem. State Ct. of Claims Jud. Screening Com.; mem. Departmental Disciplinary Com. of the First Jud. Dept.; mem. alumni coun. Dartmouth Coll., 1990-93, pres. class 1970, 1991-95; approved mediator U.S. Dist. Ct. (so. dist.); mediator N.Y. Panel Disting. Neutrals for Ctr. for Pub. Resources, Supreme Ct., N.Y. County, Judicial Hearing Office, State of N.Y., Banking Dept.; trustee N.Y. Interest Lawyer Acct. Fund. Overseer U. Pa. Law Sch., 1993-99; nat. chmn. Law Annual Giving, 1991-93. Mem. ABA, N.Y. State Bar Assn. (exec. com. comml. and fed. litigation sect. 1986—, fed. judiciary com. 1989—, internat. law and practice sect., com. internat. dispute resolution 1987—) Assn. of Bar of City of N.Y. (products liability com. 1983-86. fed. legis. com. 1990-93, state cts. of superior jurisdiction 1993-96, coun. jud. adminstrn. 1996-99, fed. judiciary 2000—), N.Y. Athletic Club. Republican. Congregationalist. Home: 205 E 69th St Apt 6C New York NY 10021-5431 also: 74 Pascal Ave Rockport ME 04856-5919 Office: Torys 237 Park Ave Fl 19 New York NY 10017-3161

DORLAND, ELIZABETH M., chemistry educator; b. Humboldt, Nebr., Nov. 17, 1948; d. Warren Bruce Dorland and Ruth Ann Lange; m. Robert E. Blankenship, June 26, 1971; children: Larissa Blankenship, Sam Blankenship. BS, Kans. State U., Manhattan, 1970; MS, U. Calif., Berkeley, 1971. Educator Diablo Valley Coll., Pleasant Hill, Calif., 1972-75, Seattle Cen. C.C., 1975-76, Shoreline C.C., Seattle, 1976-79, Am. Internat. Coll., Springfield, Mass., 1979-85, Glendale (Ariz.) C.C., 1985-94, Mesa (Ariz.) C.C., 1994—. Mem. Am. Chem. Soc. (mem. com. on computers in chem. edn. divsn. chem. edn. 2000-03). Democrat. Avocations: travel, hiking, reading, cooking, tennis. E-mail: liz.dorland@mcmail.maricopa.edu. Office: Mesa C C 1833 W Southern Ave Mesa AZ 85202-4822

DORMAN, FINCK, insurance agent; b. Louisville, Jan. 7, 1901; s. John Fred and Ina (Knoblock) D.; m. Beulah D. Morgan, Aug. 9, 1924 (dec. Apr. 1981); 1 child, Jane Dorman Chancellor (dec.); m. Ruth Walker McClurg, Aug. 4, 1982; stepchildren: Don McClurg, Jr., Sharon Ruth McClurg Berry. BSC, U. Louisville, 1923; postgrad. in factory mgmt., Purdue U., 1925; degree in life underwriting, U. Pa., 1938. CLU. Inspector Eli Lilly Co., Indpls., 1923-27; dept. head Swan Myers Co., Indpls., 1927-31; with Indpls. Life Ins. Co., 1931-90; gen. agy. Indpls. Life Ins. Co., Houston, 1944-67, lic. agt., 1967-90; retired, 1990; instr. U. Houston, 1950; counsel/lectr. upon request, 1992-98. Pres. Houston chpt. CLU, 1948-49; vol. Shrine Crippled Children Hosp., 1946-67, Am. Heart Assn., Houston, United Fund, Houston; past pres. Piney Point Estates Civic Club, Houston; lay reader Tex. Diocese Episc. Ch., Houston, 1955-84. With USCGR, 1944-45. Recipient Cross Crutch award for 15 Yrs. Svc. Shrine Hosp.; recipient Nat. Quality award 30 Yrs. Nat. Assn. Life Underwriters. Mem. Houston Bus. and Estate Planning Coun. (charter mem.), Masons (mem. choir 1922—), Shriners (chanters 1945-68). Avocations: golf, swimming, bridge. Home: 9464 Briar Forest Dr Houston TX 77063-1003 Office: Dorman-Martin Agy 8433 Katy Fwy Houston TX 77024-1923

DORMANN, JURGEN, chemical company executive; b. 1940. Student, U. Heidelberg, Fed. Republic Germany. Chmn., chief exec. officer, dir. Hoechst Celanese Corp., N.Y.C., until 1987; chmn. Hoechst Corp., Frankfurt, Germany, 1987—; chmn. mgmt. bd. Aventis, Strasbourg, France. Office: Aventis, Espace Europeende Enterprise, 67300 Schiltigheim Strasbourg, France*

DORMEYER, DETLEV ROBERT, religious studies educator; b. Leoben, Steiermark, Austria, Dec. 5, 1942; s. Robert and Marga (Fuhlrott) D.; m. Hildegard Wiemers, 1972; children: Julia, Sophia. Lic. Cath. theology, U. Münster, Germany, 1968; ThD, U. Münster, 1972. From asst. prof. to prof. Hochschule U., Münster, 1970-80, prof., 1980-97; prof. religious studies U. Dortmund, Germany, 1997—; vis. prof. U. Stellenbosch, South Africa, 1988, Theol. Inst. Cedara, South Africa, 1992, Furman U., Greenville, S.C., 1998. Author: The Passion of Jesus as a Behavioural Pattern. A Theological Analysis of the Tradition-Redaction-History of the Passion Narrative of Mark , 1974, The Bible Answers. An Introduction to the Interactional Analysis, 1978, The Gospel as Literary and Theological Genre, 1989, The New Testament among the Writings of Antiquity, 1993, English 1998, The Gospel of Mark as Ideal-Biography of Jesus Christ of Nazareth, 1999. Roman Catholic. Home: Bahnhofstr 56 b, 48308 Senden Germany Office: U Dortmund Fach Cath Theol, Emil Figge Str 50, D-44227 Dortmund Germany

DORMEYER, LAVON, school counselor; b. Salt Lake City, Sept. 17, 1949; d. George William and Adelia Pippy; m. Michael J. Dormeyer, July 31, 1971; children: Michael George, Piers Ian. BA, U. Utah, 1971; MA, Murray State U., 1986. Cert. tchr., Fla., guidance counselor. Tchr. Pre-discharge Edn. Program, Bad Kissingen, Germany, 1972-75, U.S. Army Edn. Ctr., West Berlin, Germany, 1976-79, St. Theresa Sch., Parkville, Mo., 1982-84; guidance counselor Cypress Elem. Sch., New Port Richey, Fla., 1987—; mem. Guidance Adv. Coun., Pasco Dist. Schs., Land O'Lakes, Fla., 1992-93, 93-94; mem. athletic adv. bd., Gaither H.S., 1990-91. Author: How I Weathered the Storm of Divorce, 1998; contbr. Classroom Guidance Activities Sourcebook for Elementary Counselors, 1997. Docent Lowry Park Zoo, Tampa, 1989-95; lectr., rehabilitator Fla. Bat Ctr., Punta Gorda, Fla., 1994—. Named Tchr. of Yr., Dist. Sch. Bd. Pasco County, 1995, 96. Mem. Pasco Counseling Assn. (Counselor of Yr. 1994-95), Tampa Rep. Women Federated (publicity chairperson 1997-98). Roman Catholic. Avocations: wildlife education and conservation, gardening, floral work, writing, reading. E-mail: batlady@juno.com. Office: Cypress Elem Sch 10055 Sweet Bay Ct New Port Richey FL 34654-5799

DORN, EDWARD HARVEY, design engineer, writer, illustrator; b. Youngstown, Ohio, May 20, 1952; s. James D. and Muriel S. (Hooper) D.; children: Timothy Edward Beaulieu-Dorn; m. Rebecca Harriman; 1 child, Hayley catherine Herriman-Dorn; m. Laura Beth Burnett Hall; 1 child, Emily Diana Anagqus. BFA, Roger Williams Coll., 1979; BA in Psychology, 1980, AS in Engring. Tech., 1980; postgrad., Southeastern Mass. U. Cert. clin. hypnotist. Design engr. Dorn Designs, Fall River, Mass., 1977—, Behaviour Rsch. Inst., Providence, R.I., 1981-82; dir. rsch. and devel. Boardman Stress & Rsch. Ctr., 1984-85; design cons. Equiptect Inc., Canfield, Ohio, 1985; pres. Wil Co., Westport, Mass., 1986—; owner, operator Organics, Ltd., Taunton, Mass.; mem. environ. planning com. Richamar Group, Albuquerque; pvt. clin. hypnotist, 1984—; adj. prof. Roger Williams U., 1979-80; art therapist Crystal Springs Sch., Assonet, Mass., 1980-81; cons. UNICEF, Air. N.G., others; lectr. U. Mass., Dartmouth, 1988. Author: The Eighth Decade, 1980, Visions Twisted Twice, 1989, Signposts, 1989, Environmental Apologue, 1990, numerous poems, essays, short stories; editor Nemesis Art Mag., 1977-81; contbr. over 40 articles to profl. publs.; inventor solar desalinator, 1977, reel-lock alarm, tunnel constrn. supports, cosmic trigger game, solar furnace and tracking system, underwater deciphering units, high tension wire ice remover, superconduction glideway, gas powered air gun, others. Mem. adv. com. disabled R. I. State Coun. Arts, 1983-84; spl. constable Fall River Police, 1983-86; band chief Native Lands, Salem, Ohio. Served with USN, 1971-73, Vietnam; R.I. Air N.G., R.I. Army N.G. Recipient numerous art-related awards. Mem. Alternative Med. Assn., August Derleth Soc., Vols. in Tech. Assistance, Roger Williams Coll. Honor Soc. (alumni rep. 1979—), Talia White Cloud Soc.

DORN, GORDON JOSEPH, artist, art educator; b. Sheboygan, Wis., Dec. 5, 1943; s. Frank and Olive G. (Rollman) D. BA in Edn., Wis. State U., 1966; MFA in Painting, U. Wis., 1969. Prof. art No. Ill. U., Dekalb, 1969—; state v.p. AAUP of Ill., 1990-92, state pres., 1992-96. One-man shows include Roy Boyd Gallery, Chgo., 1977, 79, 82, 85, 88, 91, 95, 97, 98, 2000; group exhbns. include Art Inst. Chgo., 1977, 79, Chgo. Internat. Art Exposition, 1997, 98, 99; patentee in field. Recipient prize Art Inst. Chgo., 1977; exhbns. reviewed in Chgo. Tribune, 1991, 95, 98, Chgo. Sun Times, 1982, 84. Avocations: writing education materials, inventing. Home: 9-B Regency Tower 5838 Collins Ave Miami FL 33140-2226 Office: Sch Art No Ill Univ Dekalb IL 60115

DORN, NORMAN PHILIP, management consulting firm executive; b. Ithaca, N.Y., Jan. 29, 1945; s. Saul James and Pearl Dorn; m. Evelyn Mary Samonas, July 3, 1966; children: Paul, Ian, Nathan, Mark. BS, Carnegie-Mellon U., 1966; MS, U. Pitts., 1969. Engr. Westinghouse Electric, Pitts., 1969-78; sr. engr. GPU Svc. Corp., Forked River, N.J., 1978-79; mng. dir. Accountable Systems Co. Internat. Inc., Toms River, N.J., 1979—. Mem. Telephone Pioneers, Masons, Toastmasters. Achievements include inventions, quality improvements, requirements process engineering, process controls development instruction, system stability analysis procedures, telecommunications technology, systems (applications) architecture and manufacturing management. Office: 1358 Hooper Ave # 137 Toms River NJ 08753-2882 Mailing: PO Box 3019 Lynchburg VA 24503-0019

DORNBUSH, K. TERRY, former ambassador, consulting company executive, educator; b. Atlanta, Oct. 31, 1933; m. Marilyn Pierce; 3 children. BA magna cum laude, Vanderbilt U.; postgrad., Emory U., N.Y. Inst. Fin. Former CEO, Hipolex Corp.; former pres. DOAG USA Inc.; former vice chmn. Am. Western Corp.; former ptnr. Courts & Co. & Investment Bankers; amb. to The Netherlands, Am. Embassy, The Hague, 1994-98; CEO, Nalim Holdings BV, cons., Amsterdam, The Netherlands, 1998—; mem. adv. bd. Rand Europe, Leiden, The Netherlands; prof. Nijenrode U., The Netherlands. Office: Rand Europe, Nwetonweg 1, 2333 CP Leiden The Netherlands

DORNELLES, FRANCISCO OSWALDO NEVES, Brazilian government official; b. Belo Horizante, Brazil, Jan. 7, 1935; 2 children. B od Law, Fed. U. Rio de Janeiro, M of Fin. Law, D of Fin. Law. Mem. coun. Adminstrn. Getulio Vargas Found.; spl. sec. Pres. Coun. ministers, 1961-62; mem. adminstrv. coun. Bank of Brazil, 1977-79; pres. fin. commn. Chamber of Deputies, 1989-93; min. Ministry Industry, Commerce & Tourism, Brasilia, Brazil, from 1996; now min. labor and employment Ministry Labor, Brasilia; prof. fin. law Fed. U. Rio de Janeiro. Office: Bloco F, 5 Andar, 70036900 Brasilia Brazil*

DORNEMANN, MICHAEL, book publishing executive. With Internat. Business Machines, Germany, 1970-76, BMW, Munich, Germany, 1977-78, The Boston Consulting Gourp Inc., Boston, 1978-82; chmn., ceo Bertelsmann Music Group, N.Y.C., 1987—. Office: BMG Entertainment 1540 Broadway 44th Fl New York NY 10036-4039

DÖRNER, DIETRICH, psychology educator; b. Berlin, Sept. 28, 1938; s. Claus Silvester and Hilde (Gothe) D.; m. Sigrid Hirsemann, Oct. 31, 1969; children: Stephanie, Jessica. Diploma in psychology, U. Kiel, Germany, 1965, PhD, 1969, PhD Habilitation, 1973. Prof. U. Düsseldorf, 1973-74, U. Giessen, 1974-75, U. Bamberg, 1975-89, 91—; dir. Max-Planck Soc., Berlin, 1990-91. Author: (books) Cognitive Organization of Problem Solving, 1974, Problem Solving as Information Processing, 1976, The Logic of Failure, 1985, Blueprint for a Soul, 1999; author, editor: (book) Lohhausen-How to Cope With Uncertainty and Complexity, 1983. Lt. German Parachuters, 1958-61. Recipient Leibniz award Deutsche Forschungsgemeinschaft, 1986. Mem. Rotary. Home: Am Ziedergraben 1, D-56103 Hallstadt Germany Office: Inst Theoretische Psychol, Markusplatz 3, D-96045 Bamberg Germany

DÖRNER, GERD GÜNTER, medical educator, researcher; b. Hindenburg, Silesia, Germany, July 13, 1929; s. Ludwig and Erna (Schweda) D.; m. Hildegard Pesalla, Dec. 6, 1958. MD, Humboldt U., Berlin, 1953. Intern Med. Clinic Charité, Berlin, 1953; resident Ob/gyn. dept., Fürstenberg/Oder, Germany, 1954-56, Inst. Pathology, Berlin-Buch, 1956-57, Inst. Exptl. Endocrinology Charité, Berlin, 1957-60; docent for Endocrinology Inst. Exptl. Endocrinology Charité, 1960-64, prof. for Endocrinology, 1964—. Author: Endocrinology of Sex, 1974, Hormones and Brain Differentiation, 1976, Systemic Hormones, Neurotransmitters and Brain Development, 1986; editor-in-chief: Exptl. and Clin. Endocrinology, 1975-92; contbr. about 400 articles to profl. jours., 50 writings to textbooks and handbooks. Recipient Nat. prize GDR, Goethe prize Berlin. Mem. Leopoldina, Internat. Acad. Sex Rsch., Internat. Soc. Neuroendocrinology, Internat. Soc. Psychoneuroendocrinology and Developmental Neurosciences, World Assn. Sexology, German Soc. Endocrinology (hon.), Hungarian Soc. Endocrinology (hon.). Roman Catholic. Avocations: sports, music. Fax: 0049-30-2802 3045. Home: Kavalierstrasse 19c, 13187 Berlin Germany Office: Inst Exptl Endocrinology, Schumannstrasse 20/21, 10098 Berlin Germany

DORNFELD, SYLVIA, radiologist; b. Dresden, Sachsen, Germany, Nov. 28, 1967; d. Stefan and Brigitte (Scheiblich) D. Student, Med. Coll., Dresden, 1993. Physician Tech. U., Dresden, 1993-99, radiation therapist, 1999—. Co-author: Controversies in Neuro-Oncology, 1999, Controversies in Neuro-Oncology, 1999; contbr. articles to profl. jours. Mem. DEGRO, ESTRO. Avocations: parrots, literatre, photography. Office: Tech Univ Med Faculty, Clinic for Strahlen Therape, 01307 Dresden Germany

DORNFEST, BURTON SAUL, anatomy educator; b. N.Y.C., Oct. 31, 1930; s. Irving and Yetta (Rosengarten) D.; m. Eveline Drucker, June 13, 1954; children; Michael Barry. BA, NYU, 1952, MS, 1954, PhD, 1960. Rsch. asst. dept. biostats. Sloan-Kettering Inst. and Meml. Hosp., N.Y.C., 1952-53; rsch. asst. dept. biology NYU, 1953-54, 56-58, instr. gen. sci., 1958-63; instr. anatomy N.Y. Med. Coll., 1963-64; instr. anatomy SUNY Health Sci. Ctr., Bklyn., 1964-67, asst. prof., 1967-73, assoc. prof., 1973-91; cons. study sect. Nat. Heart and Lung Inst., 1975; adj. prof. Med. Sch. CUNY, 1974-97; adj. prof. hematology sch. health scis. Hunter Coll., 1978-82, 90-91; adj. prof. anatomy Inst. Continuing Biomed. Edn., 1979-86, N.Y. Med. Coll., 1982-85, 91-96, Touro Coll. Ctr. Biomed. Edn., 1983-88, Einstein Coll. Medicine, 1991-99. Contbr. articles to profl. jours. Served with U.S. Army, 1954-56. NIH fellow, 1958-60, 61-63; Leukemia Soc., 1960-61; Nat. Inst. Arthritis and Metabolic Diseases grantee, 1964-71; Nat. Cancer Inst. grantee, 1973-75; Mildred Werner League for Cancer Research grantee, 1976-77; coprin. investigator NIH Heart, Blood and Lung Inst., 1982-85. Mem. AAAS, N.Y. Acad. Scis., Am. Soc. Hematology, Am. Assn. Clin. Anatomists, Internat. Soc. Exptl. Hematology, Am. Assn. Anatomists, Sigma Xi. Jewish. Home and Office: 96 Everett Rd Demarest NJ 07627-1225

DORNIER, PHILIPPE-PIERRE, consulting company executive, educator; b. Neuilly-sur-Seine, Hauts-de-Seine, France, Mar. 31, 1960; s. Pierre and Simone (Dupont) D.; Valerie Tertrais; children: Marguerite, Hermance, Virgile. Engring. degree, Ecole des Mines, Nancy, France, 1983; MBA, ESSEC, Paris, 1985; Auditeur, Inst. Hautes Etudes Def. Nat., Paris, 1996; PhD, Ecole des Mines, Paris, 1997. Prof. bus. ESSEC, Paris, 1986—; assoc. dean post-grad. program ESSEC, 1992-95, assoc. dean execs. program, 1996-99; CEO Newton Vaureal & Co., Paris, 1999—; cons. Eurequip, Paris, 1989-92. Co-author: Encyclopédia de Gestion, 1990, Global Operations and logistics, 1998; author: Plein flux sur l'entreprine, 1991. Mem. Comité logistique Civilo-Miltaire. Home: 21 rue de Général Foy, 75008 Paris France Office: Newton Vaureal & Co, 51 rue de Miromesnil, 75008 Paris France

DOROCKA-BOBKOWSKA, BARBARA, dentistry researcher; b. Poznań, Poland, Aug. 10, 1962; d. Waldemar Bobkowski, June 27, 1987; 1 child, Bobkowski Wojciech. MD, U. Med. Scis., Poznan, 1988, Dentistry Doctor, 1990, PhD, DDS, 1996. Med. diplomate, dentistry diplomate. Mem. student's scientific soc. U. Med. Scis., Poznan, 1984-90, asst. in dept. prosthetic dentistry, 1991-97, asst. lectr., 1997—; sec. Poznan Br. of Polish Stomatol. Soc., 1997—. Contbr. numerous articles to profl. jours. Mem. Polish Stomatol. Soc. (sec. Poznan br. 1997—, award for Scientific Rschs. 1995), Internat. Assn. for Dental Rsch. Avocations: Polish and Am. lit., psychology. Home: Zorza 7/9, 60-369 Poznań Poland Office: Dept Prosthetic Dentistry, U Med Scis/Swiecickiego 4, 60-781 Poznań Poland

DOROGAN, DUMITRU ANATOLIE, marine technologist; b. Sibiu, Romania, Oct. 28, 1947; s. Anatolie Ion and Elisabeta (Coseru) D.; m. Liliana Grigore, Jan. 14, 1977; children: Madalina, Alexandru. M, Polytech Inst., Iassy, Romania, 1970; PhD, U. Tex., 1973. Engr. Romanian Marine Rsch. Inst., Constanta, 1970-73, rschr., 1974-92, sr. rschr., 1992—, lab. head., 1992-95. Author: On Board Fish Processing Technology Handbook, 1985; inventor in field. Mem. NGO Oceanic Club. Avocations: travel, photography, diving, art and design. E-mail: dorogan@alpha.rmri.ro. Home: Aleea Capidava #1 Bloc V2, 8700 Constanta Romania Office: Romanian Marine Rsch Inst, BD Mamaia #300, 8700 Constanta Romania

DORON, TAMAR, pharmaceutical company executive; b. Novotarg, Poland, June 24, 1938; arrived in Israel, 1950; d. Samuel and Fella (Bergman) Blau; m. Ezekiel Jack Doron, Aug. 20, 1957; children: Bilhat Azar, Bosmat Sahar. BA, Hebrew U., Jerusalem, 1960. Mem. managerial team Taro Industries Ltd., Haifa, Israel, 1965-82; mng. dir., owner Pharma Medis Ltd., Holon, Israel, 1982—. Named Entrepreneur Woman of Yr. in field of medicine Israel Fedn. Women in Mgmt., 1992. Mem. Fedn. of Israel C. of C., Chamber of Commerce and Industry Israel-Am., Indsl. and Comml. Club. Avocations: medicine, art, astrology, classical literature. Home: Faierberg 4, IL-58294 Holon Israel Office: Pharma Medis Ltd, PO Box 2820, IL58128 Holon Israel

DO ROSARIO, ANTONIO GUALBERTO, Cape Verdean government official. Now dep. prime min. Govt. of Cape Verde, São Tiago. Office: Ministry of Econ Coordn, 170 Avda Amilcar Cabral, CP30 Praia Sao Tiago, Cape Verde*

DOROSHENKO, TATYANA FYODOROVNA, chemistr, researcher; b. Donetsk, Ukraine, Nov. 4, 1961; d. Fyodor Alekseevich and Villya Ustimovna (Titarenko) D.; m. Andrey Andreevich Lavrinenko, Nov. 11, 1989; 1 child, Anna Andreevna. Magistrate of hemistry with honors, Donetsk State U., 1985; D Chemistry, Nat. Ukrainian Acad. Scis., Donetsk, 1990. Chemical engr. rschr. Litvinenko Inst. Phys.-Organic and Coal Chemistry Nat. Ukrainian Acad. Scis., 1996—. Contbr. articles to sci. jours., chpt. to book. Avocation: dancing. Home: Karl Marx St 1/40, 83037 Donetsk Ukraine Office: Inst Phys-Org and Coal Chem, R Luxemburg St 70, 83114 Donetks Ukraine

DOROZHKIN, SERGEY VENIAMINOVICH, chemistry researcher; b. Moscow, USSR, June 24, 1961; s. Veniamin Ivanovich and Tamara Sergeevna (Egorova) D.; m. Elena Ivanovna Baeva, Dec. 16, 1988; 1 child, Denis. MS in Chem. Tech., Moscow Inst. Chem. Tech., 1984; PhD in Chemistry, Rsch. Inst. Fertilizers, Moscow, 1992. Engr. Rsch. Inst. Fertilizers, Moscow, 1984-87, jr. rschr., 1987-92, rschr., 1993-94; rschr. Italian-Russian Joint Venture Sovagrital, Moscow, 1992-93; microbiologist Swiss-Russian Joint Venture DIAplus, Moscow, 1994-96; postdoctoral fellow INSERM U 424 Louis Pasteur U., Strasbourg, France, 1996-97; postdoctoral fellow Biomaterials Ctr. Dental Faculty Nantes U., France, 1997-98; salesperson RITA Co., Moscow, 1998-99; insdl. engr. Trak Co., Moscow, 1999; postdoctral fellow bioceramics dept. ceramics Glas Engring. Aveiro U., Portugal, 1999-2000. Local leader All-Union Communistic Union of Young People, 1978-84. Grantee Nantes U., 1997, NATO, 1996, Internat. Sci. Found., 1993, Aveiro U., 1999. Russian Orthodox. Avocations: science, travel. Home: Kudrinskaja Sq 1-155, 123242 Moscow D-242, Russia

DORRAH, HASSEN TAHER, engineering executive, educator; b. Damietta, Egypt, Mar. 3, 1948; arrived in Can., 1970; s. Taher Hassen Dorrah and Fatma El-Tabie Mosbah; m. Azza Abdel Halim Elnaggar; children: Ahmed, Ayman, Dalia. BSEE, Cairo U., 1968; MSEE, U. Calgary, Can., 1972; PhD in Elec. Engring., U. Calgary, 1975. Registered profl. engr., N.B., Ont.; registered consulting engr., Egypt. Prof. elec. engring. Cairo U., Giza, Egypt, 1986—; pres. SDA Engring. Can. Inc., Toronto, Ont., 1990—; chmn. SDA Engring. Egypt, Cairo, 1991—; cons. SDA Engring., Can., Toronto, 1979-86, CAP Saudi Arabia, Riyadh, 1991—, Taqi and Sadiq Albahrna, Manama, Bahrain, 1994—, Ben Hareb Co., Abu Dhabi, United Arab Emirates, 1992-95, A. T. Kearney, Berlin, 1996—. Author 3 books; contbr. over 80 articles to profl. jours. Fellow U. Calgary, 1970-75; postdoctoral fellow U. N.B., Can., 1976; Best Indsl. Project fellow Cairo U., 1996. Mem. IEEE, Can. Businessmen Assn. of Riyadh. Avocation: photography. Home: 43 El-Hossean St, Giza Egypt Office: SDA Engring Consultants, 98 El-Tarir St, Dokki Sq Giza Egypt

DORRELL, JULIET LOUISE, business consultant, writer; b. Tonbridge, Kent, Eng., Aug. 6, 1942; d. Reginald James and Amy Vivien (Ward) Maitland; m. Ronald Springhall, July 21, 1961 (div. May 1968); children: Kathryn Vivien, Jonothan Karl; m. John Dorrell, Dec. 5, 1970; children: Kevin Jonathan, Paul Roderick, Claire Harriet, Guy Lawrence;. Student, London Coll. of Secretaries, 1960. Personal asst. Martlet Prodn., West London, 1978-79; dir. Travel Focus, Sussex, Eng., 1981; personal asst. Stanley Hall Perfumes, Sussex, 1982-83; temporary sec. various locations, London, 1983-85; project coord. Forward Trust Group, London, 1986-88; prin. JLD Assocs., Tonbridge, Eng., 1988-97; regional mgr. London & S.E. Inst. Supervision and Mgmt., 1997—. Author: Resource-Based Learning, 1993; contbr. articles to profl. jours. Mem. Inst. Supervision and Mgmt., Inst. Pers. and Devel. Mem. Ch. of Eng. Avocations: reading, walking, travel, gardening.

DORRELL, STEPHEN JAMES, British government official; b. Mar. 25, 1952; s. Philip Dorrell; m. Penelope Anne Wears Taylor; 4 children. BA, Brasenose Coll., Oxford, Eng., 1973. Pers. asst. to Right Hon. Peter Walker M.P., 1974; M.P. House of Commons, Eng., 1979—, PPS to sec. of state for energy, 1983-87, asst. govt. whip, 1987-88, lord comdr. of Her Majesty's Treasury, govt. whip, 1988-90, parliamentary under-sec. of state, 1990-92, fin. sec. to Her Majesty's Treasury, 1992-94, sec. of state for nat. heritage, 1994-95; sec. Estate for Health, 1995-97. Avocations: aviation, reading. Address: House of Commons, London SW1A 0AA, England

DORRIS, JOE MILLER, electronics company executive; b. Goodlettsville, Tenn., July 3, 1943; s. Reynold Bridgewater and Olva Allen Dorris; m. Claire Kendall, Aug. 15, 1964; children: Margaret, Mary. BSEE, Vanderbilt U., 1965; MBA, U. Memphis, 1970. Engr. McDonnell Aircraft, St. Louis, 1965-67, RCA, Memphis, 1967-70, Union Carbide, Cleve., 1970-78; sales rep. RO Whitesell, Huntsville, Ala., 1978-80; pres., CEO Trans Tron Ltd., Inc., Huntsville, 1995—; pres. Futaba Corp. Am., Schaumburg, Ill., 1980—. Avocations: genealogy, golf, tennis. E-mail: dorris@ix.netcom.com. Home:

2225 Governors Bend Rd SE Huntsville AL 35801-1306 Office: Futaba Corp of Am 1605 N Penny Ln Schaumburg IL 60173-4555

DORSCH, NICHOLAS WILLIAM CASPAR, neurosurgeon, educator, researcher; b. Sydney, Australia, Nov. 20, 1941; s. Ernst Georg and Patricia Ellen (Graham) D.; m. Barbara Lynette Harrison, Apr. 27, 1965; children: Simone Lise, Penelope Jane, Kristen Louise. MB, BS, U. Sydney, 1965. Accredited neurosurgeon, Australia. Resident, registrar Prince Henry Hosp., Sydney, 1965-67; surg. registrar Epsom (Eng.) Dist. Hosp., 1968-69; resident med. officer Nat. Hosp. for Nervous Diseases, London, 1970-71, neurosurg. sr. registrar, 1972-74; vis. med. officer St. George Hosp., Sydney, 1975-80, Royal Prince Alfred Hosp., Sydney, 1975-91; vis. med. officer Westmead Hosp., Sydney, 1979-86, staff neurosurgeon, 1986—, chmn. dept. neurosurgery, 1996—; clin. assoc. prof. U. Sydney, 1993—; cons. Bayer, Roche, Winthrop, Upjohn, Sydney, 1985—; guest prof. 10th Japanese Vasospasm Symposium, Kyoto, 1994; bd. dirs. NSW br., Australian Brain Found., 1990—. Contbr. numerous articles to med. jours., chpts. to books. Rsch. grantee Nat. Health and Med. Rsch. Coun., Australia, 1990, 93, Australian Brain Found., 1992, 95. Fellow Royal Australasian Coll. Surgeons, Royal Coll. Surgeons; mem. Neurosurg. Soc. Australasia, Soc. Brit. Neurol. Surgeons, Am. Assn. Neurol. Surgeons, Congress Neurol. Surgeons, World Fedn. Neurosurg. Socs. (tchg. faculty 1998—). Anglican. Avocations: classical music, tennis, computers, farming. Office: Westmead Hosp, Hawkesbury Rd, Westmead NSW 2145, Australia

DORSCH, WALTER JANOS M., allergologist, pediatrician, researcher; b. Weilheim, Bavaria, Germany, Jan. 11, 1949; s. Walter F.M. and Elizabeth (Szilágyi) D.; m. Barbara Guber; children: Katharina, Sebastian, Matthias, Sophia, Cordula, Raphael, Johannes. MD, U. Munich, Germany, 1974, PhD in Medicine, 1987; prof. in Pediatrics, U. Mainz, Germany, 1989. Fellow internal medicine, surgery, dermatology, pediatrics various med. instns., Germany, 1974-79; founder Allergy Ambulatory Children's Hosp., Munich, 1979-89; head of allergy and pneumology Children's Hosp., Mainz, 1989-93; pvt. practice allergy and pediat. ambulatory Children's Hosp., Munich, 1994—. Author, editor: Handbook on Late Phase Allergic Reactions, 1980; inventor anti-inflammatory treatment with onions, internat. patents, 1983, anti-inflammatory and antiasthmatic treatments with acetophenomes and galphimia glauca, internat. patents, 1988, antiinflammatory activity in human skin, patent 1992. Recipient hon. mention for sci. program Pharmacia, 1987. Mem. Coll. Internat. Allergology, German Soc. Allergology (mem. sci. bd. 1993, Förder prize 1995), German Soc. Phytotherapy (mem. sci. bd. 1993, Erich Fritz Weiss prize 1991). Avocations: photography, trekking. Office: Pediatric Ambulatory, Aidenbach Strasse 118, D-81379 Munich Germany also: Allgäu Clinic, Bad Wörishofen, Hindelang Germany

DORSETT, MARY ALICE, business and tax consultant; b. Dade City, Fla., Feb. 4, 1926; d. James Dorsett and Nannie Mae Johnson; m. W. Ray Hill, Jan. 29, 1962; children: Dwayne Oswald Hill, Countess Charisse Clarke. Student, Paine Coll., 1945-46; diploma, Nat. Trade & Profl. Sch., 1950. Owner Dorsett's Tax Svc., Tampa, Fla., 1951—, Dorsett's Bail Bonds, Tampa, 1952-73, Dorsett's Gen. Employment Agy., Tampa, 1955-73. Author: Wings, 1990. Founder Faith Mission, Tampa, 1962-73; charter mem. Cmty. Health Clinic, Tampa, 1977—. Recipient award Carr's Corner mag., 1959, Unsung Hero award TOBA, 1983, Trailblazer and Pioneer award Links, Sigma Delta kappa, 1986, 90, Ambassador of Goodwill award Johnson's Performing Arts, 1988, Woman of Firsts award, St. Petersburg Times newspaper, 1987, Woman on a Mission award Tampa Tribune newspaper, 1995, Drum Major plaque Dr. Martin Luther King Com., 1998, plaque Hillsborough County Sheriff's Dept. Mem. Health and Edn. Assn. (founder), Tampa Urban League (award 1987), Coun. Negro Women, Grand Union Pallbearer Soc. Baptist. Avocations: travel, music, drama, public speaking, television.

DORSEY, JEREMIAH EDMUND, pharmaceutical company executive; b. Worcester, Mass., Oct. 15, 1944; s. Jeremiah Edmund and Mary Theresa D.; m. Nadia S. Vidach, Dec. 6, 1970; children: Todd Edmud, Jaime Erin, Megan Elizabeth, Kelly Ann. AB, Assumption Coll., 1966; MBA, Farleigh Dickinson U., 1978. With Johnson & Johnson, New Brunswick, N.J., 1969-88; nat. indsl. engring. mgr. Johnson & Johnson, New Brunswick, 1975-76, supt. ops. and maintenance, 1976-88, dir. ops. mem. mgmt. bd., 1976-88; v.p. mktg., ops., gen. mgr. sales Johnson & Johnson Dental Products Co., New Brunswick, 1976-88; exec. v.p. The Kaelin Group, Bridgeton, N.J., 1988; pres. Towle Housewares Co., Newburyport, Mass., 1988-90; pres., CEO Foster Med. Supply, Inc., Dedham, Mass., 1990-92; group pres. Carvel Hall Corp., Crisfield, Md., 1990—; pres., COO West Pharm. Svcs. Inc., Lionville, Pa., 1992—; corp. officer J.E. Dorsey Co., Carvel Hall Corp., Crisfield, Md.; bd. dirs. West Co. de Mex., Daikyo Seiko, Tokyo, Schubert Seals, Horsens, Denmark, DanBioSyst, Nottingham, Eng., Geschaftsfuherer West Co., Europe. Editor: Spl. Forces Assn. News. Active N.J. Commn. for Discharge Upgrade, Appalachian Trail Conf.; mem. alumni bd. dirs. Assumption Coll., adv. com. U. P.R. Sch. of Pharmacy; mem. mil. acad. selection com. U.S. Senate; vice chmn. N.J. Vietnam Vets Leadership Program; mem.Mercer County Pvt. Industry Coun. (N.J.), N.J. SR-92 Coalition. With U.S. Army, 1966-69, Vietnam. Decorated Silver Star, Bronze Star, 2 oak leaf clusters, Purple Heart, 4 oak leaf clusters, Army Commendation medal, Air medal with oak leaf cluster, Medal of Honor., Gallantry Cross, Vietnam; recipient Corp. Affirmative Action award 1981. Mem. DAV, KC, Sierra Club, Spl. Forces Assn., Smithsonian Assocs., Soc. First Divsn., Tiger Karate Soc., (Black Belt), Johnson & Johnson Mgmt. Club, Delta Epsilon Sigma. Roman Catholic. Home: 30 Fox Ridge Dr Malvern PA 19355-2876 Office: 101 Gordon Dr Exton PA 19341-1320

DORSEY, JOHN HENRY, marine biologist; b. Long Beach, Calif., Oct. 7, 1949; s. John Ward and Mildred Barbara Dorsey; m. Deborah Ann Dorsey, Jan. 12, 1974; 1 child, Kristen Barbara. BS in Marine Biology, Calif. State U., Long Beach, 1972, MA in Biology, 1975; PhD in Zoology, U. Melbourne, Australia, 1982. Marine technician Marine Biol. Cons., Inc., Costa Mesa, Calif., 1970-73, marine biologist, 1974-76; rsch. asst. Calif. State U., Long Beach, 1973-75; cons. Caldwell-Connell Cons. Engrs.. Pty. Ltd., Australia, 1979; oceanographer ocean scis. dept. Interstate Electronics Corp., Anaheim, Calif., 1980-82; cons. Bur. of Land Mgmt., 1982-83; water biologist I Environ. Monitoring divsn. City of L.A., 1983-84, water biologist II, 1984-88, lab. mgr. I, 1988-92, lab. mgr. II, 1992-97; lab. mgr. II Stormwater Mgmt. divsn. City of L.A., 1997—; part-time lectr. Loyola-Marymount U., L.A., 1985—. Contbr. articles to profl. jours. Chair tech. adv. com. Santa Monica Bay Restoration Project, L.A., 1996—, mem. standard methods com., 1992—. U. Melbourne Rsch. grantee, 1976-80; recipient citations City of L.A. Bd. Pub. Works, 1987, 98. Mem. AAAS. Avocations: surfing, Tang Soo Do karate (1st Dan black belt). Office: City of Los Angeles Stormwater Mgmt Divsn 650 S Spring St Fl 7 Los Angeles CA 90014-1907

DORSEY-MURPHREE, BETTY JO, sociology educator, consultant; b. Brownsville, Pa., Jan. 15, 1932; arrived in Zimbabwe, 1955; d. Forrest Lee and Mary Virginia (Snodgrass) Dorsey; m. Marshall Warne, Sept. 22, 1951; children: Wendy, Stephen, Debra, Nyasha, Michael. BA, Asbury Coll., Wilmore, Ky., 1953; Postgrad. Cert. in Edn., U. London, 1963, Diploma in Edn., 1968, PhD, 1974. Prof. U. Zimbabwe, Harare, 1967—, chmn. dept., 1982-85; rsch. assoc. St. Antony's Coll., Oxford, Eng., 1977-79, sr. assoc. mem., 1981, 93; vis. prof. Stanford U., Palo Alto, Calif., 1989-90; cons. World Bank, Malawi, 1991, Can. Inst. Devel. Agy., Zimbabwe, 1991, Universalia, Montreal, Can., 1993-95, UNESCO, 1995-96. Author: Education, Race and Employment in Rhodesia, 1975, World Yearbook of Education, 1981, International Handbook on Educational Reform, 1992, International Perspectives on Education and Society, 1993, Gender Inequalities in Education in the Southern Africa Region: an Analysis of Intervention Strategies, 1996; contbr. articles to profl. jours. Treas. Budiriro Ednl. Trust, Eng. and Zimbabwe, 1982—; bd. trustees Nat. Mus. and Monuments, Harare, 1992—. Named hon. prof. grad. studies U. Belgrade, Yugoslavia, 1988. Mem. Internat. Sociol. Assn., History and Comparative Edn. Soc. So. Africa, Comparative and Internat. Edn. Soc. Methodist. Avocations: theater, music, reading, outdoor camping, art appreciation. Home: 46 Aberdeen Rd, Avondale Harare Zimbabwe Office: U Zimbabwe, PO Box 167 Mt Pleasant, Harare Zimbabwe

DORST, FRIEDHELM, educator; b. Castrop-Rauxel, Germany, Dec. 8, 1947; s. Friedrich-Wilhelm and Paula (Kilian) D. Staats examen, U. Muenster, Germany, 1973; studienrat, Hardenstein Gymn., Witten, Germany, 1981. Tchr. math., physics Ruhr-Gymnasium, Witten, 1981—. Fellow Brit. Interplanetary Soc.; mem. New Millennium Com. Planetary Soc., Vereinigung der Sternfreunde. Avocations: biking, solar eclipse expeditions, daylight observations of stars, observations of moon and planets.

DORST, JEAN PIERRE, zoologist; b. Mulhouse, France, Aug. 7, 1924; s. Victor J. and Gabrielle M. (Rusch) D.; m. Emmanuelle Munier, Feb. 15, 1985. Licence scis., U. Paris, 1945; Diplome, Office Rsch. Sci. & Tech., 1946; DrSci, U. Paris, 1949. Asst. Mus. Nat. d'Histoire Naturelle, Paris, 1947-49, sous-dir. of lab., 1949-64, prof. and chief curator lab. zoology, 1964-85, asst. dir. mus., 1970-75, dir. gen., 1975-85; expert UNESCO, FAO, IUCN, Paris, Rome, Geneva; expert and dir./chmn. Ministry of Environ., France; mem. various couns. and commns. Ministry of Edn., Paris. Author: Les Migrations des Oiseaux, 1962, Les animaux voyageurs, 1964, Before Nature Dies, 1965, South and Central America, 1967, others; contbr. over 700 articles to profl. jours. Officer Legion d'honneur, Golden Art, The Netherlands; cmdr. Nat. Merit. Mem. Inst. de France, Acad. of Scis., Acad. des sciences d'outre-mer, many others. Calvinist. Avocations: music, horse riding, philately. Home: 14 quai d'Orleans, F75004 Paris France Office: Mus, 55 rue de Buffon, F-75005 Paris France

DORTA-CONTRERAS, ALBERTO JUAN, neuroimmunologist; b. Habana, Cuba, Sept. 19, 1950; s. Ildefonso Dorta-Cabrera and Maria Isabel Contreras-Mejias. Licenciate in biochemistry, Havana (Cuba) U., 1975; postgrad., Internat. Immunology Tng. & Rsch. Ctr., Amsterdam, The Netherlands, 1979. Rechr. Inst. Gastroenterology, Habana, 1975-82; specialist clin. lab. Hosp. Pediatrico San Miguel, Habana, 1982-2000; prof. Facultad de Ciencias Medicas "Dr. Miguel Enriquez", Habana, 2000—; prof. Inst. Superior de Ciencias Medicas, Habana, 1976—; adj. prof. biology Habana U., 1982—; prof. U. Autonoma Guerrerro, Chipancingo, Mex., 1988-89, 91-92, 93—; mem. sci. com. Internat. Quincke Symposium, Göttingen, Germany, 1991; pres. organizing com. Roundtable on Devel. Neuroscis. in The Caribbean, Havana, 1993; bd. dirs. Neurosci. Caribbean Sch., 1993—. Author: Inmunoglobulinas Mayores en el Liquido Cefalorraquideo, 1989, Proteinas de Fase Aguda y Otras Proteinas en eL Liquido Cefalorraquideo, 1990; (with others) CNS Barriers and Modern CSF Diagnostics, 1993; patentee in field. Recipient Nat. Labor Hero, Cuba, 1978; Forjadores del Futuro medal Cuba, 1975, 78, 79, 80, 81, 84, 85, 86. Mem. Internat. Brain Rsch. Orgn., Caribbean Brain Rsch. Orgn. (gov. coun. 1993—), Am. Acad. Allergy Asthma and Immunology, Cuban Soc. Physiol. Scis. (sec. 1997), World Fedn. Neurology (CSF Rsch. Group 1996). Roman Catholic. Avocations: philatelist, reading. Office: Facultad de Ciencias Medicas Dr Miguel Enriquez, Apartado 10049, 11000 Ciudad Habana Cuba

DORTON, TRUDA LOU, medical, surgical and geriatrics nurse; b. Elkhorn Creek, Ky., Aug. 26, 1949; d. Earl D. and Joyce (Kidd) Marshall; m. Eugene Anderson, Nov. 26, 1966 (dec. Apr. 1971); children: Gena Lynn, Richard Eugene; m. Leon Dorton, Dec. 15, 1972; children: Leondra Michelle, Jerald Thomas, Jonathan Layne. AS, Pikeville Coll., 1993, student, 1993. RN, Ky.; cert. ACLS, PALS. Instr. computer usage Lookout (Ky.) Elem. Sch., 1983; water/sewage technician McCoy & McCoy Environ. Cons., Pikeville, Ky., 1984; owner Signs of the Times, Elkhorn City, Ky., 1979-89; sec.'s asst. humanities and social scis. divsns. Pikeville Coll., 1989-92; nurse aide Mud Creek Clinic, Grethel, Ky., 1992-93; charge nurse Jenkins (Ky.) Cmty. Hosp., 1993-94; case mix coord. Parkview Manor Nursing Home, 1994-95, minimum data set and nursing care plan coord., 1995; acute care nurse Harrison Meml. Hosp., Cynthiana, Ky., 1996—; vol. nurse aide Mud Creek Clinic, Grethel, 1989-92. Founder free blood pressure clinic H.E.L.P.S. Community Action Program, Hellier, Ky., 1983; co-founder H.E.L.P.S. Community Action Group, Hellier, 1983; mem. Ellis Island Centennial Commn., N.Y., 1986. Appalachian Honors scholar Pikeville Coll., 1989-92. Mem. Nat. Geog. Soc., Ky. Nursing Assn., Order Ky. Cols. (Honorable Ky. Col. 1989), Smithsonian Inst., Pikeville Coll. Alumni Assn. Democrat. Mem. Worldwide Ch. of God. Avocations: creating Indian jewelry and wall hangings, classical music. Home: RR 1 Box 80 Mount Olivet KY 41064 Office: Harrison Meml Hosp Acute Care 250 Millersburg Pike Cynthiana KY 41031-1603

DORTUNC, BETÜL ARAN, pharmaceutical technology educator, pharmacist; b. Istanbul, Marmara, Turkey, Jan. 9, 1949; d. Halil Ibrahim and Nahide (Celik) A.; m. Taner Dortunc, Sept. 7, 1981. BS, Istanbul U., 1972, PhD, 1978. Cert. pharmacist. Asst. faculty pharmacy Istanbul U., 1972-82; guest rschr. Albert Ludwigs U., Freiburg, Germany, 1981-82; tchg. staff faculty pharmacy Marmara U., Istanbul, 1982-83, asst. prof., 1983-85, assoc. prof., 1985-92, prof., 1992—, acting head pharms. divsn., 1983-88, mem. exec. com., 1988-91, 98—, head pharm. tech. dept., 1992—; rep. assts. faculty pharmacy Istanbul U., 1972-82. Co-author: Controlled Release Drug Delivery Systems, 1989, Pharmaceutical Technology Practices I, 1992, Pharmaceutical Technology Practices II, 1992, Bioavailability and Bioequivalancy, 1995. Recipient DAAD scholarships Deutscher Akademischer Austauschdienst, 1981-82, 96. Mem. Assn. U. Profs., Internat. Microencapsulation Soc., Turkish Pharmacists Assn. Social Democrat. Muslim. Avocations: music, painting (textile), sports, reading. Office: Marmara U Faculty Pharmacy, Dept Pharm Tech Tibbiye cad, 81010 Istanbul Turkey

DORWARD, DAVID CRAIG, African studies educator; b. Poughkeepsie, N.Y., Feb. 6, 1941; s. David William and Ella Francis (Bubeck) D.; married; children: Jennifer Elaine, Elizabeth Anne. BA, Union Coll., 1962; MA, N.Mex. State U., 1966; PhD, U. London, 1971. Fulbright lectr. Fourah Bay Coll., Freetown, Sierra Leone, 1969-72; rsch. fellow Ctr. of West African Studies, U. Birmingham, Eng., 1972-76; lectr. LaTrobe Univ., Melbourne, 1977-79, sr. lectr., 1980-99, assoc. prof., 2000—, dir. African Rsch. Inst., 1985—; cons. Mus. of Victoria, Melbourne, 1989—, Australian Coun. for Overseas Aid, 1989-99, ACFOA African Working Group, 1998—; dir. African Consultancy Svcs., Melbourne, 1993—; vis. fellow Humanities Rsch. Centre, Canberra, 1995; editl. cons. Microform Acad. Publs., Wakefield, Eng. Author: Namibia: International Dimensions to it's Decolonization, 1989; editor: Directory of Africanist in Australia, 1991, Yoruba: Art in Life An Thought, 1988. Exec. com. South African Legal Svcs. Pty. Ltd., Melbourne, 1991-92, Third World Forum, Australia, 1989-90; steering mem. African-Australian Edn. and Sport-Found., Victoria, 1989-90; cons. Australian Coun. for Overseas Aid, Canberra, 1990—. Grantee Social Sci. Rsch. Coun., 1976, Australian Coun., 1991, Australia Coun., 1987-88, 91, Myer Found., 1987-88. Mem. Royal African Soc., African Studies Assn. of Australasia and Pacific (sec./treas. 1978-82, 87-88, pres. 1989-91, 97-99), Royal Commonwealth Soc., Soc. for Internat. Devel., Australia-Mozambique Support Group, Australia-Namibia Solidarity Assn.. Home: 254 Old Eltham Rd, Lower Plenty 3093, Australia Office: African Rsch Inst, LaTrobe Univ, Bondoora 3083, Australia

DORWARD, NEIL LAWRENCE, neurosurgeon, educator; b. Farnborough, Kent, Eng., Sept. 4, 1965; s. Gordon Wallace and Barbara Frances (Meadows) D. BSc, U. London, 1985, MBBS, 1989, MS, 1999, FRCS, 1999. FRCS. Neurosurgery sr. house officer Western Gen., Edinburgh, Scotland, 1991-92, Nat. Hosp., London, 1992-93; neurosurgery registrar Royal Free Hosp., London, 1993-94, Charing Cross Hosp., London, 1994-95, Royal Free Hosp., London, 1995; clin. lectr. Inst. Neurology, London, 1996-97; cons., neurosurgeon, hon. sr. lectr. Royal Free Hosp. & Med. Sch., London, 1999—; hon. sr. lectr. Univ. Coll. Med. Coll., London, 1999—, pituitary, vascular and spinal surgery specialist, 2000—; hon. clin. lectr. Nat. Hosp., London, 1996-97. Author: (book chpts.) Operative Neurosurgery, 1997, Advanced Neurosurgical Navigation, 1997. European Applications for Surg. Interventions project grantee European Union, 1996-97. Fellow Royal Coll. Surgeons Eng.; mem. Soc. Brit. Neurol. Surgeons, Brain Rsch. Assn. Avocations: distance running, eventing, classical music.E-mail: neil.dorward@rfh.nthames.nhs.uk. Office: Royal Free Hosp Dept Neuro, Pond St, London NW32QG, England

DOS ANJOS, MARIO NEGREIROS, endocrinologist; b. Manaus, Brazil, Apr. 20, 1927; s. Francisco B. and Francisca N. (Negreiros) Dos A.; m. Cláudia Prado), Feb. 23, 1957; children: Mario Augusto, Paulo Alexandre, Silvia Regina. MD, U. Fed. Fluminense, Rio de Janeiro, 1956, PhD in Endocrinology, 1971; M in Endocrinology and Metabolism, Pontificia Univ. Catolica, Rio de Janeiro, 1959. Intern, resident Hosp. dos Servidores, 1960-64; attending physician Hosp. dos Servidores do Estado, Rio De Janeiro, 1960-64; dept. chief Hosp. Antonio Pedro, Rio De Janeiro, 1964-84; prof. endocrinology U. Fed. Fluminense, Rio De Janeiro, 1971—; rschr. Conselho Nacional de Pesquisa, Rio de Janeiro, 1974-84; sci. cons. Fundacão de Amparo À Pesquisa RJ, Rio de Janeiro, 1995; chmn. sci. dept. Acad. fluminense de Medicina, 1994-96. Author: A Criança Diabética, 1971 (Gold medal 1971), Obesidade, 1984, Diabete Mellitus, 1988, Os Males da Medicina, 1994; contbr. articles to profl. jours. Recipient Commendation award Niterói Mayor, 1987; named Estate Citizen from Rio de Janeiro, Rio de Janeiro Mayor, 1984. Mem. AAAS, Am. Diabetes Assn., N.Y. Acad. Sci., Assn. Latino Am. Diabetes, Brazilian Diabetes Assn. (founding mem., gen. sec.), Brazilian Assn. for the Study of Obesity, Lit. Acad. in Niteroi, Rotary (internat. rels. chmn. 1992-96). Roman Catholic. Avocations: amateur radio, photography, music, computers, art. Office: Icaraí, Rua Miguel de Frias 51/202, 24220000 Niterói Brazil

DOSAYLA, ALBERTO DEQUITO, construction company sales executive, consultant; b. Cadiz, The Philippines, June 7, 1941; s. Francisco Dolor and Adoracion (Dequito) D.; m. Ruth Billones, Sept. 4, 1965 (dec. 1993); children: Rubert, Adora Lisa, Rebecca, Ruth Grace, Ailene Joy, Alberto, Jr. BSME cum laude, Ctrl. Philippine U., Iloilo City, 1962. Registered profl. mech. engr., The Philippines. Instr. Coll. Engring. Ctrl. Philippine U., 1962-63; project supr. PIECO, 1963-64; ter. supt. trans./maintenance supt. FILOIL Mktg. Corp., 1964-74; head mktg. tech. svcs. Petrophil (Petron) Corp., The Philippines, 1974-81; mgr. engr. svcs. Philippine Nat. Co. Co., 1981-87; gen. mgr. Fed. Petroleum Corp., The Philippines, 1987-88; v.p. for engring. CPM Indsl. Fabrication, Manila, 1988-90; v.p. for corp. projects Connell Bros. Co., Manila, 1990-94; tech. sales dir. RJS Indsl. Constrn. and Devel. Corp., Quezon City, The Philippines, 1995—; prin. cons. A.D. Dosayla & Assocs., 1972—; project cons. Coml. Wheels Plating, 1994; vice chmn. com. on mech. engring. tech. panel on engring. and architecture and maritime edn. Commn. on Higher Edn., 1996—; cons. on tribology UN Indsl. Devel. Orgn., 1988; cons. on mech. engring. Leyte project Philippine Nat. Oil Co., 1996-97; commr./bd. mem. Philippine Energy Regulatory Bd., 1998—. Adviser Las Piñas (The Philippines) Village Assn., 1985—; vol. Philippine Cancer Soc., 1993, Philippine Tb Soc., 1993. Maj. Res. Armed Forces The Philippines, 1985-86. Recipient achievement award Ctrl. Philippine U., 1972, plaque of appreciation, 1980, letter of commendation and appreciation Ayala Found., 1992, svc. award and cert. of appreciation Philippine Cancer Soc., 1993; scholar Ctrl. Philippine U., Negros Occidental provincial scholar; named Outstanding Profl. in the Field of Mech. Engring., Profl. Regulation Commn. award, 1998; recipient Disting. Centralian award Ctrl. Philippine U., 1999. Fellow Philippine Soc. Mech. Engrs. (life, nat. pres. 1992, Presdl. award in leadership 1985, 90, 95, Presdl. award in achievement 1986, 91, Presdl. award in svc. 1987-90, 93-94, plaques of appreciation various chpts. 1992); mem. ASME. Roman Catholic. Avocations: lawn and table tennis, bowling, basketball, country tours and travel. Fax: (632)-872-7080; (632) 631-5871. E-mail: adosayla@mail.erb.gw.ph. Home: Pamplona, Las Pinas, 14 1st St, Las Pinas Vlg, Metro Manila The Philippines Office: Energy Reg Bd/Pacific Ctr, San Miguel Ave/Ortigas Ctr, Pasig City The Philippines

DOSE, MATTHIAS, medical director; b. Goeppingen, Germany, May 17, 1949; s. Paul and Ingrid (Stahl) D.; m. Agnes Maria Grossmann, Dec. 24, 1955; children: Johanna, Max. MD, Tech. U., Munich, 1981. Resident St. Mary's Hosp., Cologne, Germany, 1978-79, U. Mannheim, Germany, 1979-80; sr. rschr. Max Planck Inst. Psychiatry, Munich, 1984-89; vice dir. Psychiat. Dist. Hosp., Ansbach, Germany, 1989-93; dir. Psychiat. Dist. Hosp., Taufkirchen, Germany, 1993—; prof. Tech. U., Munich, 1999; vice chmn. dept. psychopharmacology Max Planck Inst. Psychiatry, 1985-89. Author: Spektrum Neuroleptika, 1991. Rsch. fellow Max Planck Inst. Psychiatry, 1980-84. Mem. German Assn. Psychiatry, European Coll. Neuropsychopharmacology, World Fedn. Neurologists. Avocations: reading, jazz, mountaineering. Office: Bezirkskrankenhaus Taufkirchen, Braeuhausstr 5, D-84416 Taufkirchen Germany

DOSHI, VIUL PRAFUL, pharmaceutical executive; b. Vadodara, Gujarat, India, June 20, 1963; s. Praful Keshav and Manjula Praful (Mehta Manjula) D.; m. Sangeeta Vipul Shah, Nov. 26, 1986; children: Dhwani, Mrugal. Diploma in interior decoration, Nat. Inst. Design, 1982; BSc in Microbiology, Gujarat Coll., India, 1983; MSc in Microbiology, Sch. Sci., India, 1985, diploma in industry and mgmt., 1987. From sterile are incharge to head tech. svcs. MJ Pharma Ltd., India, 1985-92; from mgr. to dep. gen. mgr. quality assurance Sunpharm. Ltd., Vadodara, India, 1992-96, gen. mgr. quality assurance, 1996—. Recipient Acad. award Glenzaids GMP Acad., 1999. Mem. ISPE, Indian Pharm. Assn. Avocations: interior decorating, reading, travel, mind reading. Home: 1/B Vidhyadhar Soc, 390015 Vadodara India Office: Sun Pharm Ltd, Sailja Complex Akota, 390020 Vadodara India

DOSIOS, THEODOSIOS, thoracic surgeon; b. Aliakmon Kozanis, Macedonia, Greece, May 21, 1939; s. Ioannis and Chrysoula (Devliotou) D.; m. Glykeria Athanasiadou, Dec. 12, 1970; children: Chrysoula, Theologia, Ioannis, Raphael. MD, U. Aristoteleion, Thessaloniki, Greece, 1963. Cert. thoracic and cardiovascular surgeon. Resident in gen. surgery Athens (Greece) U., 1967-71; resident in thoracic and cardiovascular surgery Allegheny Gen. Hosp., Pitts., 1972-75; cons. thoracic surgeon Air Force Gen. Hosp., Athens, 1975-89; assoc. prof. thoracic and cardiovascular surgery Athens U., 1991—. Brig. Gen. Greek Air Forces, 1963-89. Office: 2 Chatzigianni Mexi Str, 11528 Athens Greece

DOSS, FRANK ALLEN, electronic technician; b. Bryn Mawr, Pa., Feb. 19, 1958; s. Willard M. and Jane (Pendergrast) D.; m. Delia G. Maier, Feb. 2, 1995. Tech. diploma, Sparten Sch. Aeronautics, Tulsa, 1982; ABA, Nat. Bus. Coll., 1985. Shipping clk. LPB, Frazer, Pa., 1985-89, with electronic assembly dept., 1989-90; with comm. dept. Metromedia/ITT, Frazer, Pa., 1990-91; alarm tech. Design Security, Myrtle Beach, S.C., 1991-92; gas attendant Paradise Petroleum, Big Pine Key, Fla., 1992-94. Author: Island in Paradise, 1995. Sgt. USAF, 1978-82. Avocations: sculpture, painting, music, writing, cycling.

DOSS, HALIM SHAFIK, mathematician, educator; b. Alexandria, Egypt, May 4, 1950; arrived in France, 1968; s. Shafik Halim and Leila Henry (Ayrout) D.; m. Catherine Gabrielle Bachelet, Apr. 12, 1986; children: Claire, Elise, Marie. Lic in Math., U. Paris 6, 1971, MS in Math., 1972, Doctorat, 1975, D es Scis., 1980. Asst. prof. math. U. Paris 6, 1974-88; prof. math. U. Haute Normandie, Rouen, France, 1988-93, U. Paris 9 (Dauphine), 1993—; maitre de confs. Ecole Polytechnique, Palaiseau, France, 1984. Contbr. articles to profl. jours. Coptic Catholic. Avocations: music, literature. Office: U Paris 9 (Dauphine), Place du Marechal de Lattre de Tassigny, 75775 Paris Cedex 16, France

DOSS, MIRKO, cardiac surgeon; b. Arnstadt, Germany, May 12, 1967; s. Gideon and Marianne (Truebenbach) Dlingea; m. Silke Kerstin Doss, Dec. 6, 1996; 1 child, Constantin. Grad., Ernst-Moritz-Arndt U., 1993. Intern in surgery Berlin Heart Inst., 1992; intern in postoperative intensive care Calif. Pacific Med. Ctr., San Francisco, 1993; house officer in surgery Queen Elizabeth Hosp., London, 1994, house officer in cardiology, 1995-96; sr. house officer cardiothoracic surgery Guy's and St. Thomas Hosp., London, 1995-96; specialist registrar in cardiac surgery U. Ulm, Germany, 1996—; specialist registrar cardiothoracic surgery U. Frankfurt, Germany, 1999—. Mem. AAAS, German Soc. Thoracic & Cardiovasc. Surgery. Avocations: swimming, scuba diving. Home: Sachsenhauser-Landwehrweg 68b, 60599 Frankfurt am Main Germany

DOS SANTOS, CARLOS, ambassador. Rep. to UN Republic of Mozambique. Office: Permanent Mission Republic Mozambique 420 E 50th St New York NY 10022-8002

DOS SANTOS, CARLOS ALBERTO, physics educator; b. Areia Branca, RN, Brazil, Oct. 7, 1947; s. Clodomiro Alves and Albertina Ferreira dos S.; m. Liana Longo, June 21, 1975; 1 child, Clarisse Longo dos Santos. BSc, Cath. Pontifica U., Rio de Janeiro, 1973; MSc, Fed. U. Rio Grande South, Porto Alegre, Brazil, 1978, PhD in Physics, 1984. Prof. physics Fed. U. Rio Grande North, Natal, Brazil, 1974-92, Fed. U. Rio Grande South, 1992—;

referee Inst. Physics, Bistrol, 1997—; cons. Nat. Coun. Sci. and Tech., Brazil, 1985—. Co-author: Multi-dimensional Scaling and Hierarchical Analysis, 1991; contbr. articles to sci. jours., including Nuc. Instruments and Methods, Phys. Rev. B., others. Mem. Brazilian Soc. Physics. Office: Inst Fisica UFRGS, Campus do Vale CP 15051, 91501970 Porto Alegre RS, Brazil

DOS SANTOS, JOSE EDUARDO, president of Angola; b. Aug. 28, 1942; s. Eduardo Avelino and Jacinta Jose Paulino. Grad., Patrice Lumumba U., Moscow, 1969; petroleum engring., Baku Inst. Petroleum and Gas, 1969. Joined Movimiento Popular de Libertação de Angola (MPLA), 1961; pres. Republic of Angola, Luanda, 1979—; went into exile, 1961; founder, v.p. MPLA Youth, Leopoldville, Congo (now Kinshasa, Zaire); returned to Angola and participated in war against Portuguese, 1970-73; mem. MPLA Ctrl. Com. 2nd Polit. Bur., 1974—, then chmn.; coord. MPLA Fgn. Relations Dept., 1975-79; sec. Ctrl. Com. for Edn., Culture and Sport; then sec. Nat. Reconstruction; sec. Econ. Devel. and Planning, 1977-79; minister of planning, pres. Nat. Planning Commn., 1978-80; mem. polit. bur. Popular Movement for the Liberation of Angola. Office: Office of Pres Palacio Povo, PBx R 17 Setembro, Luanda Angola*

DOS SANTOS FERREIRA, RODOLPHE, economics educator, researcher; b. Lisbon, Portugal, Jan. 20, 1941; s. Antonio and Maria Isabel Hattenberger Rosa dos Santos Ferreira; m. Marie-Claire Mathilde Erhart, Dec. 29, 1969; 1 child, David. Grad. in econs., U. Strasbourg, France, 1965, M in Econs., 1966; Doctorat d'Etat in Econs., U. Louis Pasteur, Strasbourg, 1974. Lectr. U. Strasbourg, 1966-75; prof. U. Louis Pasteur, Strasbourg, 1976—; chmn. Faculty of Econs., Strasbourg, 1977-80; co-dir. Bur. d'Economie Théorique et Appliqué, Strasbourg, 1979-92; sr. mem. Inst. U. de France, 1996. Contbr. articles to profl. jours. Mem. Nat. Com. for Sci. Rsch., Paris, 1991-00. Named Officier des Palmes Academiques, Ministry of Edn., 1999. Mem. French Econ. Assn. (2d v.p. 1999-00, mem. directorial com. 1988-96, 98—), Assn. Charles Gide (mem. adminstrn. coun. 1989-99). Avocation: hiking. Fax: (33)3 90 41 40 50. E-mail: rdsf@cournot.u-strasbg.fr. Office: U Louis Pasteur, 61 ave de la Forêt Noire, 67085 Strasbourg France

DOS SANTOS N., MIGUEL VALLE, chemical company executive, consultant; b. Niteroi, Rio de Jan, Brazil, Jan. 12, 1964; s. Jacyr Valle and Ruthe (Pedroza Valle) Dos Santos; m. Claudia Santiago Rangel, Dec. 31, 1993; children: Lilian Rangel de Oliveira, Livia Rangel Valle Dos Santos. B.Chem.Engring., UFRJ, Rio de Janeiro, 1990. Registered chem. engr., Brazil. Probationer Petroquisa, Rio de Janeiro, 1989-90; exec. R.N.S., Cabo Frio, Brazil, 1991-95, C.N.A., Arraial do Cabo, Brazil, 1995—. Avocations: numismatics, chess. Home: Rua 7 Casa 75 Vila Indust, 28930000 Arraial do Cabo Brazil Office: Companhia Nacional Alcalis, Rua Gal Alfredo Bruno Mart, 28930000 Arraial do Cabo Brazil

DOST, MARK W., lawyer; b. Attleboro, Mass., May 22, 1955; s. Raymond and A. Louise (Fraser) D.; m. Karen M. Sullivan, Aug. 1976; children: Christopher, Stephen, Gregory, Isaac. AB summa cum laude, U. Mass., 1978; JD cum laude, Boston Coll., 1981. Bar: Conn. 1981, U.S. Dist. Ct. Conn. 1986, U.S. Tax Ct. 1985. Atty. Gager & Henry, Waterbury, Conn., 1981-95; ptnr. Tinley, Nastri, Renehan & Dost, Waterbury, 1995—. Author: (with John V. Galiette) Planning for Retirement Benefit Distributions, 1995, 2d revised edit., 1999. Fellow Am. Coll. Trust and Estate Counsel; mem. ABA, Conn. Bar Assn. (exec. com., elder law sect. 1991—, exec. com., estates and probate sect. 1991—, chair elder law sect. 1994-96, chair publs. com. 1997-2000), Nat. Acad. Elder Law Attys. Office: Tinley Nastri Renehan Dost 60 N Main St Waterbury CT 06702-1403

DOSTÁL, JAN, hotel, tourist and gaming industry executive; b. Prague, Czech Republic, Dec. 28, 1950; s. Ladislav and Věra (Sulková) D.; m. Marcela Nohejlová (div. 1985); children: Jan, Klára. Degree in engring., U. Econ. Faculty of Commerce, Prague, 1976. Various positions ČEDOK Hotel and Travel Corp., Prague, 1976-80; mgr. ČEDOK Hotel and Travel Corp., Rome, Italy, 1981; divsn. head ČEDOK Hotel and Travel Corp., Prague, 1982-85, asst. to gen. dir., 1985-89; gen. dir. Casinos Czechoslovakia, Prague, 1989-92, Belvedere Hotel, Prague, 1992—; CEO VIP Club Casino, Prague, 1993—; bd. dirs. Travel Agy. H & Hotels, 1992. Mem. Czech Hotel Assn. Prague, Czech Gaming Bd. Prague. Avocations: tennis, skiing, golf, fishing. Home: Pod Hybsmankou 12, 150 00 Prague 5, Czech Republic Office: VIP Club as, Vaclavske namesti 7, 110 00 Prague 1, Czech Republic

DOSTAL, ZDENEK, mathematics educator, researcher; b. Olomouc, Moravia, Czech Republic, May 20, 1946; s. Zdenek and Eva (Parizkova) D.; m. Marie Simeckova; children: Matej, Michal. MSc, Palacky U., Olomouc, 1970, Rerum Naturarum Doctor, 1971; PhD, Math. Inst. Czechoslovak Acad. Scis., Prague, 1979. Analyst Pozemni Stavby N.C., Olomouc, 1970-75; lectr. U. Mining and Metallurgy-Tech. U., Ostrava, 1975-79; rschr. Mining Inst. Czechoslovak Acad. Scis., Ostrava, 1979-92; assoc. prof. U. Zambia, Lusaka, 1987-88; prof. head U. Mining and Metallurgy-Tech. U., Ostrava, 1992—. Contbr. articles to profl. jours. including Internat. Jour. Numerical Methods Engring. and Internat. Jour. Computer Maths. Mem. Am. Math. Soc., Soc. for Indsl. and Applied Math., Union Czech Math. and Physicists. Avocations: literature, sports. Office: VSB Tech U Ostrava, 17 Listopadu, CZ 70833 Ostrava Moravia, Czech Republic

DOSTI, ROSE, newspaper columnist, author; b. N.Y.C., Feb. 6, 1931. Student, Hunter Coll., 1949-51, Ithaca Coll., 1952-53. Staff writer L.A. Times, 1964-92, columnist, 1992—. Author: (cookbooks) Light Style, 1979, rev., 1991, New California Cuisine, 1986, Mid East Mediterranean, 1982, rev., 1993, Dear SOS, 1994, Dear SOS Desserts, 1996. Avocations: art, sculpture, piano, singing, exercise.

DOSWALD-BECK, LOUISE, lawyer, international association executive; b. Birmingham, Eng., July 7, 1952; d. Paul Randolf and Helene (Fotiadis) Beck; m. Josef Georg Doswald, June 3, 1977; children: Nathalie Doswald, Alistair Doswald. LLB, Bristol (Eng.) U., 1973; LLM, Univ. Coll., London, 1974. Barrister; internat. lawyer. Lectr. Law Faculty, Exeter (Eng.) U., 1975-77; rschr./cons. Faculty of Law, Bern (Switzerland) U., 1978-79; lectr. Univ. Coll., London, 1982-86; lawyer, legal adviser Internat. Com. of the Red Cross, Switzerland, 1987-94, sr. legal advisor, 1995, dep. head of legal divsn., 1996-98; head legal divsn. Internat. Com. of the Red Cross, 1998—; adviser, drafting coord. Internat. Inst. of Humanitarian Law, San Remo, Italy, 1988-95. Author numerous articles on internat. human rights law; author articles monographs and book chpts. on use of force and internat. humanitarian law; editor manual on law and naval warfare; editor, organizer meetings of experts on battlefield laser weapons, other meetings. Swiss Nat. Fund grantee, Bern, 1980-81. Mem. Am. Soc. Internat. Law, Internat. Law Assn., Soc. Mil. Law and the Law of War. Avocations: reading, modern ballet, aerobics. Office: Internat Com of the Red Cross, 19 Ave de la Paix, 1202 Geneva Switzerland

DOTAN, ARON, linguistics educator; b. Stuttgart, Germany, Jan. 12, 1928; arrived in Israel, 1933; s. Nisan Arie and Haya Taube (Spindel) Deutscher; m. Ruth Ventura, Nov. 21, 1923; children: Zevi, Haya, Tamar. MA, Hebrew U., Jerusalem, 1952, PhD, 1963. Acad. sec. Acad. Hebrew Lang., Jerusalem, 1951-64; prof. Tel Aviv U. and Bar Ilan U., 1964-96; vice-dean humanities Tel Aviv U., 1966-67, chmn. dept. Hebrew lang., 1967-74, dean Rosenberg Sch. Jewish Studies, 1975-77, incumbent Schreiber chair in history of Hebrew lang., 1990-99, prof. emeritus, ombudsman, 1996—; vis. prof. Sorbonne, Paris, 1967-68, Yale U., New Haven, 1973-74, Queens Coll., CUNY, N.Y., 1980; dir. rsch. Nat. Ctr. Sci. Rsch., Lyon, France, 1990; head Cymbalista Jewish Heritage Ctr., 1998—. Author: Diqduqe Ha-Teamim by Aaron Ben-Asher, 1967, Thesaurus of the Tiberian Masora, 1977, Ben Asher's Creed—The History of the Controversy, 1977, The Dawn of Hebrew Linguistics, 1997; editor: The Holy Scriptures (The Biblical Hebrew Text), 1974; editor numerous books and series; contbr. articles to profl. jours. Mem. Acad. Hebrew Lang., 1966—; pres. Internat. Orgn. for Masoretic Studies, 1992—, v.p., 1990-91; coun. mem. World Union Jewish Studies, 1993—; mem. coun. Wolf Found., Israel, 1983—; mem. Israel Broadcasting Authority, 1980-88. Fellow Inst. for Advanced Studies, Jerusalem, 1983-84, Annenberg Rsch. Inst. for Judaic Studies, Phila., 1988-89, 91. Home: 89 University St, 69345 Tel Aviv Israel Office: Tel Aviv U, Dept Hebrew and Semitic Lgs, 69978 Tel Aviv Israel

DOTO, PAUL JEROME, accountant; b. Newark, July 22, 1917; s. Anthony and Edith Margaret (Mascellaro) D. BS, NYU, 1947. CPA, N.J., N.Y.; registered mcpl. acct., N.J.; registered pub. sch. acct., N.J. Acct. John Hewitt Foundry Co., East Newark, N.J., 1941-43; acct. S.D. Leidesdorf & Co., N.Y.C., 1947-56; CPA Peat Marwick Mitchell & Co., N.Y.C., 1956-64; asst. controller Lincoln Ctr. for the Performing Arts Inc., N.Y.C. 1964-69; controller Seton Hall U., South Orange, N.J., 1969-74, Belart Products, Applied Coatings, Maddock, Inc., N.J., 1974-80, Internat. Trading Sales, Inc., Pan Atlantic Paper Co., N.Y.C., 1980; cons. Controller's Office, City N.Y., 1966. Bd. dirs. Parkway, Ltd., 1973-78. Served with AUS, 1943-46. Mem. Nat. Police Hall of Fame. Mem. N.Y. State Soc. CPA's (chmn. govtl. accounting com. 1963-64, chmn. internal control quest on aid of municipalities N.Y. State), AICPA (40 yr. mem.), Cath. Accts. Guild (bd. govs. 1961-64), N.J. Soc. CPA's, Fin. Exec. Inst., Am. Acctg. Assn., N.Y. Assn. Profs., Smithsonian Assocs. (charter), Nat. Wildlife Fedn., Am. Legion, Am. Mus. Natural Hist. N.Y.C. (assoc.). Address: PO Box 13 Claymont DE 19703-0013

DOTTARELLI, SERGIO, accountant; b. Viterbo, Italy, Aug. 24, 1940; s. Ameglio and Eleonora (Cerocchi) D.; m. Gabriella Ambrosetti, Dec. 28, 1968; children: Giorgio, Guido. Diploma in acctg., U. Leonardo da Vinci, 1958. Clk. Banco di Roma, Milan, 1959-61, Rome, 1961-72; from officer to mgr. Figeroma, Rome, 1973-85; gen. mgr. Sogepo, Rome, 1986-95; mng. dir. Euramerica Gestioni and Euramerica Fiduciaria, Rome, 1995, 97; cons. Consulta Nazionale Per Lo Sviluppo Dei Fondi Pensione. Contbr. numerous articles on fiscal questions in fund mgmt. and quasi-banking to daily press and profl. jours. Lt. Italian army, 1964-65. Mem. Rotary. Avocations: skiing, hiking. Home: Via Baleari 228, 00121 Roma Italy

DOTY, PHILIP EDWARD, accountant; b. Red Oak, Iowa, Dec. 9, 1943; s. Wade Bryan and Vera Mae (Dodd) D.; m. Della Corrine Mack, Dec. 23, 1967; children: Sarah, Anne. BSBA, Drake U., 1967. CPA, Colo. Ptnr. Arthur Andersen LLP, Denver, 1967-2000, dir. oil and gas practice and tng., 1987-2000; ret. Treas. Mile High United Way, Denver, 1984-88, 2000—, bd. dirs., 1998—; treas. Mile High br. Girl Scouts U.S.A., 1987-92; bd. dirs. Leadership Denver Assn., 1987-89, Artreach, Inc., Denver, 1986-89, Colo. Ballet, 1992-98; mem. exec. bd. Denver Area coun. Boy Scouts Am., 1998—. With USAR, 1967-73. Mem. AICPA (nat. coun. 1994-97), Am. Petroleum Inst., Petroleum Accts. Soc. (pres. 1989), Ind. Petroleum Assn. Mountain States (bd. dirs. 1987-97, treas. 1991-92), Colo. Soc. CPA's (pres. 1994), Denver Petroleum Club (sec.-treas. 1988-91, Man of Yr. award 1993, bd. dirs. 1997-99), Columbine Country Club, Classic Car Club Am. (dir. Colo. region 1996-98, treas. 1999—), Beta Gamma Sigma. Republican. Baptist. Avocations: classic cars, skiing, hunting.

DOTY, SHAYNE TAYLOR, organist; b. Memphis, Aug. 19, 1961; s. Robert Allen and Janice Moffet Doty. BA, Duke U., 1983; diploma, Conservatoire Nat. Superieur Musique Lyon, 1986; MM, So. Meth. U., 1991. Rsch. assoc. Capital Campaign for Arts and Scis., Duke U., 1983-84; organist, choirmaster St. Paul's Episcopal Ch., Washington, 1991-98; organist Am. Cath., Paris, 1995-96; asst. dir. corp. and found. rels. U. Md., College Park, 1997-98; sr. major gift officer Met. Opera Assn., N.Y.C., 1998—. Organ recitalist including St. Denis, Paris, St. Paul's, Toronto, Nat. Cathedral, Washington; ensembles Les Arts Florissants, Washington Bach Consort, N.C. Symphony and Winston-Salem Symphony. Mary Duke Biddle scholarship Duke U., 1979-83; Frank Huntington Beebe fellow, 1984-86. Mem. Assn. of Anglican Musicians, Am. Guild of Organists. Episcopalian. Office: Met Opera Assn Lincoln Ctr New York NY 10023

DOU, HENRI JEAN-MARIE, engineering educator; b. Marseille, Provence, France, May 14, 1939; s. Henry Ulrich and Yvonng (Tagliavento) D.; m. Mireille Vic, Aug. 15, 1942; children: Jean-Marie Jerôme, Carine Isabelle. Degree in engring., IPSOI, France, 1962; DSc, U. Marseilles, 1966. Attaché Ctr. Nat. Rsch. Sci., Marseilles, 1964-60, chargé, 1969-72, dir., 1972-90; prof. U. Marseilles, 1990—; expert cons. d'Apel d'Aix en Provence, 1980; mem. Interministerial Commn. of Elaborated Info., France, 1994. Author: La Veille Technologique, 1992, Veille Technologique et Competitivite, 1995, Les bonnes pratiques de la Veille Technologique, 1999; editor: Advanced Institute Strategies and Advanced Studies on Marine Pollution, 1980; contbr. chpt. to book. Pres. Ste. Française de Bibliometrie, Paris, 1992-2000; mem. Coun. Adminstrn. Centre Regional de Documetation Pedagogique, Marseilles, 1997—; session admin. Inst. des Hautes Etudes de la Défense Nationale, Marseilles, 1980. Recipient Palmes Academiques, Academie Aix Marseilles, 1989. Mem. Inst. de Petroleochimie et de synthese organique industrelle Alumni Assn. (pres. 1989—). Avocations: tennis, mountain climbing, water sports. E-mail: dou@crrm.u-3mrs.fr. Home: 160 Ave du Prado, 13008 Marseilles France Office: U Marseilles 3, CRRM, 13397 Marseilles Cedex 20, France

DOU, HUA-SHU, mechanical engineering educator; b. Shandong, China, Aug. 24, 1958; s. Ji-Yuan and Yu-Ying (Cai) D.; m. Ying-Ying Chen, Sept. 25, 1985; 1 child, Zhao-Le. BS, Northeast U., Shenyang, China, 1982, MS, 1984; PhD, Beijing U. of Aero. and Astro., 1991. Tchr. Gaoqing High Sch., Shandong, China, 1975-78; asst. Northeast U., 1985-87, lectr., 1987-88; assoc. prof. Tsinghua U., Beijing, 1993-94; vis. rsch. fellow Tohoku U., Sendai, Japan, 1994-95; vis. prof. Hosei U., Tokyo, 1995-96; rsch. scientist U. Sydney, Australia, 1996—. Contbr. articles to profl. jours. Postdoctoral fellow Tsinghua U., 1991-93. Mem. AIAA, ASME. Avocations: music, literature, basketball, watching television. Office: Dept of Mechanical Engineering, Univ of Sydney, Sydney NSW 2006, Australia

DOU, KAI, physicist; b. Changchun, China, Mar. 19, 1958; came to U.S., 1996; s. Qingchun and Shuzhen (Wu) D.; m. Xia Wu, May 20, 1986; 1 child, Sibo. BS, Jilin U., Changchun, 1982; MS, Chinese Acad. Scis., Changchun, 1986, PhD, 1992. Rsch. asst. to rsch. assoc. Changchun Inst. of Physics, Chinese Acad. Scis., 1983-92, assoc. prof., 1993-95, prof., 1995—; vis. sci. Lab. Aime Cotton, Orsay, France, 1992-93, Okla. State U., Stillwater, 1996—. Contbr. articles to profl. jours. Recipient Outstanding Young Sci. award Jilin Soc. Sci. and Tech., 1994. Mem. Optical Soc. Am., Materials Rsch. Soc., Internat. Soc. Optical Engring., Physical Soc. China, Luminescience Soc. China. Avocations: music, travel, tennis. E-mail: dou@okstate.edu. Office: Okla State Univ 205 Psi Chemisty Dept Stillwater OK 74078-0001

DOU, WENBIN, millimeter wave researcher, educator; b. Kun Ming, Yun Nan, China, July 8, 1954; s. Ru Hong Dou and Feng Zhen Tang; m. Rui Kun Huang, Jan. 26, 1982; 1 child. BA, U. Sci. and Tech. China, Hefei, 1978; MS, U. Electronics, Sci. & Tech., Chengdu, China, 1983, PhD, 1987; postgrad., S.E. U., Nanjing, China, 1989. Assoc. prof. S.E. U., Nanjing, 1989-94, prof. millimeter wave technology, 1994—. Author: Millimeter Wave Ferrite Devices-Theory and Technology, 1996; contbr. articles to profl. jours. Recipient 2nd grade prize of progress in sci. and tech. Ministry of Machinery and Electronics of China, Beijing, 1989, 91, 2nd grade prize of progress in sci. and tech. State Edn. Com., Beijing, 1992. Mem. China Inst. Electronics (sr.). Achievements include research in millimeter wave for communication, optical and engineering applications. Avocations: swimming, traveling, music, television. Office: Southeast Univ, 2 Sipailou, Nanjing 210096, China

DOUBELL, R.D., investment banking executive; b. Melbourne, Victoria, Australia, Feb. 11, 1945; s. Douglas Clayton and Amy Beryl (Stanley) D.; m. Jennifer Christine Walker, Aug. 19, 1972; children: Anna, Andrew, James. BS, Melbourne U., 1965; MBA, Harvard U., 1974. Mktg. officer Shell Co. of Australia, Melbourne, 1965-72; v.p. Citibank, N.A., London, 1974-86, Goldman Sachs & Co., Sydney, Australia, 1986-94; dir. Deutsche Bank AG, Sydney, 1995-99; exec. chmn. Australian Derivatives Exch. Ltd., 1999—; pres. Athletics NSW Ltd., Sydney, 1996; dir. Stadium Australian Ltd., 1998. Recipient Olympic Gold medal for 800 meter track and field, 1968. Home: 36 Cranbrook Rd, Rose Bay NSW 2029, Australia

DOUBINSKIY, MICHAEL ILLICH, lawyer; b. Kiev, Ukraine, July 31, 1961; s. Ely B. and Svetlana M. Doubinskiy; 1 child, Svetlana; m. Ann N. Menchynskaya, Feb. 23, 1995. Engr. with honor, Poly. Inst., Kiev, 1989; Patent Atty., Poly. Inst., Kharkiv, 1995. Cert. atty-at-law State, 2000. Mng. ptnr. Intels Agy., Kiev, 1993—; atty. Interregional Acad. Personnel Mgmt., 1998—. Mem. Ukrainian Assn. Patent Attys. (mem. bd. 1997), Ukrainian Group of Internat. Assn. for Protection of Indsl. Property (mem. bd.), Internat. Trademaker Assn. (mem. external affairs com. 1999), Internat. Bar Assn. Office: Intels Agy Ste 41, 14-A Borschagovskaya St, 03055 Kiev Ukraine

DOUBLEDAY, CHARLES WILLIAM, dermatologist, educator; b. Houston, Oct. 1, 1954; s. Leonard Charles and Margaret (Walker) D.; m. Verlinde Van den Berge Hill, June 22, 1985; children: George Marchant, Julia Van den Berge, Walker Hill. BA with honors, U. Tex., Austin, 1976; MD, U. Tex., Houston, 1981. Diplomate Am. Bd. Dermatology, 1987. Rotating intern John Peter Smith Hosp., Ft. Worth, 1981-82; resident in dermatology U. Tex. Med. Sch., 1982-83, 85-87, fellow in dermatology, 1985, clin. asst. prof. dermatology, 1988—; pvt. practice, Houston, 1987—. Contbr. articles to med. jours. Recipient high sci. quality award Soc. for Investigative Dermatology, 1986; rsch. fellow Dermatology Found., 1985. Fellow Am. Acad. Dermatology; mem. Tex. Med. Assn., Harris County Med. Soc., Tex. Dermatol. Soc., Houston Dermatol. Soc., U. Tex. Houston Health Sci. Ctr. (devel. coun., 1994-96), bd. dirs. Republic Nat. Bank, The Park People, mem. Houston Country Club. Republican. Episcopalian. Avocations: tennis. golf. Office: 515 Post Oak Blvd Ste 535 Houston TX 77027-9494

DOUBRAVOVA, JARMILA, humanities researcher; b. Chrudim, Czech Republic, June 23, 1940; d. Jaroslav and Jarmila (Vonaskova) D.; m. Jan Smolik, July 1961 (div. 1964); m. Bohumir Dubec, Sept. 1976 (div. 1983); 1 child, Michal. PhD in Aesthetics/Musicology, Charles U., Prague, Czechoslovakia, 1962, PhDr, 1965. Specialist in semiotics. Asst. Acad. of Scis., Prague, 1966-70, rsch. fellow, 1970-89, prin. rsch. fellow, 1990—; asst. prof. Inst. Art History, Charles' U., Prague, 1997—. Author: Music and Visual Arts, 1982, (scriptum) Semiotics and Musical Semiotics, 1991, Semantic Gesture, Dialogue and Imagination, 1997; co-editor, author: Czech and Slovak Semiotics, 1992. Recipient grant for Semiotics and Musicotherapy, 1991-93, grant for Semiotics of Contemporary Arts, 1994-96. Mem. Internat. Assn. for Semiotic Studies (chair Czech group 1996), Deutsche Gesellschaft für Semiotik, World Union of Jewish Studies, N.Y. Acad. Scis., Masaryk's Sociol. Soc., Czech Cybernetic Soc., Aesthetic Soc., Umelecka Beseda Arts Club. Avocations: swimming, gymnastics, gardening. Office: Charles U Dept Aesthetics, Celetna 20, 11000 Prague Czech Republic

DOUCAKIS, NICOLAS P., production engineer and executive; b. Athens, July 17, 1949; arrived in Switzerland, 1972; m. Costas and Litsa (Douzeni) D.; divorced; children: Alexis, Nicolas P., Marc. MA in Prodn. Engring., St. Catherine's Coll., Cambridge, Eng., 1970; postgrad., Harvard U., 1972. Engr. Caterpillar Overseas, Geneva, 1972-73, sales mgr., 1975-79; dir. European ops. FND Industries (Overseas), Geneva, 1979-83, v.p., 1983-85; CEO Fibermesh (Suisse) S.A., Geneva, 1985—; mktg. advisor Hood Sales (Europe) S.A., Geneva, 1983. Author: Ball Bearings in the Automotive Industry, 1969. Fellow Liberal Party, Geneva, 1980, sec., 1980-82; fellow Greek Cmty. of Geneva, 1990-93. Mem. Am. Club of Geneva, Nautic Club of Geneva, Tennis Club of Geneva. Orthodox. Avocations: golf, tennis, water skiing. Fax: 022-34779 52. Office: Fibrocem Corp, PO Box 104, 1211 Geneva 25, Switzerland

DOUCETTE, DAVID ROBERT, computer systems company executive; b. Pitts., Feb. 2, 1946; s. Adrian Robert and Mary Alyce (Newland) D. BSEE cum laude, Poly. Inst. Bklyn., 1968, MSEE, 1970, PhD, 1974. Asst. prof. electrical engring. Poly. Inst. N.Y. (now Poly. U.), 1973-74, assoc. prof. computer sci., 1975-82, prof., 1982—, dir., 1994—, assoc. dean, 1997—; sr. staff specialist advanced planning Gruman Data Sys. Corp., Bethpage, N.Y., 1979-80, program mgr., 1979-80, mgr. graphics sys., 1980-84, from asst. dir. to dir. interactive sys. support, 1984-86; dir. interactive sys. Gruman Data Sys., Corp., Bethpage, N.Y., 1986-94; pres., CEO D3Software Corp., 1994—. Active Nassau County Hist. Soc., Garden City Hist. Soc. Recipient Achievement award Engrs. Joint Coun. L.I., 1999. Mem. IEEE (past sect. chmn., Centennial medal, Third Millennium medal), Assn. Computing Machinery (past chpt. chmn.), Nat. Space Soc., Planetary Soc., Nat. Eagle Scout Assn., Sigma Xi, Tau Beta Pi, Eta Kappa Nu, L.I. Early Fliers Club. Office: Poly U Dept Computer/Info Sci 901 Route 110 Farmingdale NY 11735-3906

DOUCHKESS, GEORGE, lawyer; b. N.Y.C., Apr. 19, 1911; s. Frank A. and Dorothy (Grunberg) D.; m. Sonia Sloshay; children: Donald, Barbara. BBA in Acctg., CCNY, 1936; JD, Bklyn. Law Sch., 1939. Bar: N.Y. 1940, U.S. Dist. Ct. (ea. and so. dists.) N.Y. 1951, U.S. Supreme Ct. 1991. Claim supr. Aetna Casualty and Surety Co., N.Y.C., 1940-44; compensation hearing atty. Liberty Mut. Ins. Co., N.Y.C., 1944-47; compensation atty. Preferred Accident and Ins. Co., N.Y.C., 1947-51; U.S. supt. divsn. compensation claims, compensation atty. Gen. Fire and Casualty Co., N.Y.C., 1951-65; compensation atty. Zurich Am. Ins. Co., N.Y.C., 1965-96. Mem. Torch and Scroll. Republican. Home: 715 Park Ave New York NY 10021-5047

DOUGAN, SERAFIN SERICHE, prime minister of Equatorial Guinea. Prime min. Govt. of Equatorial Guinea, Malabo, 1996—. Office: Office of Prime Min, Malabo Equatorial Guinea*

DOUGHERTY, FLOYD WALLACE, design engineer; b. Birmingham, Ala., Oct. 25, 1942; s. Floyd Patrick and Mary Josephine (Wallace) D.; m. Dana Dean Lesley, Sept. 2; 1 child, Lesley Dean. BS, Auburn U., 1966; BSCE, U. Ala., 1970. Registered prof. engr., Ala., Miss., Ga. Design engr. Paul B. Krebs & Assocs., Birmingham, Ala., 1967-87; pres., owner F.W. Dougherty Engring. & Assocs., Birmingham, Ala., 1987—. Dir. Dean & Co. Variety TV Show, Birmingham, 19805. Sgt. U.S. Army Corp Engrs. Mem. ASCE, Am. Water Works Assn., Ala. Water & Pollution Control Assn., Water Environment Fedn. (George W. White award 1996), Ctrl. Ala. Am. Concrete Inst. (Outstanding Achievement award 1999). Republican. Baptist. Avocations: fishing, skiing.

DOUGHERTY, GEOFFREY, health science educator, researcher; b. Londonderry, No. Ireland, Aug. 7, 1950; s. Henry and Maud (Lowry) D.; m. Hajidah Abdul Samad; children: Daniel, Aisha, Nadia. BSc with honors, Manchester (Eng.) U., 1971; PGCE, Leeds (Eng.) U., 1974; PhD, Keele U., Stoke, Eng., 1979. Rsch. fellow Swiss Fed. Inst. Tech., 1979-80; lectr. Sci. U. Malaysia, 1980-83; sr. rsch. fellow Monash U., Melbourne, Australia, 1983-84; sr. lectr. U. of the South Pacific, Fiji, 1984-86; prin. lectr. Oxford (Eng.) Brookes U., Oxford, Eng., 1986-91; prof., chmn. radiologic scis. Kuwait U., 1992—; sr. cons. Oxconsult, Oxford, 1988-92; course tutor Open U., Milton Keynes, Eng., 1989-92; rsch. prof. Swarthmore (Pa.) Coll., 1990. Author: Introduction to Semiconductors, 1980, Electronics, 1981; contbr. over 50 articles to profl. jours. including Health Physics, Jour. Inorganic Biochemistry; 3 patents in field. Recipient Hans Sloane medal Brit. Mus., 1968. Fellow IEE, Australian Inst. Physics; mem. IEEE (sr. mem.). Avocations: photography, music. Office: Kuwait U, PO Box 31470, 90805 Sulaibikhat Kuwait

DOUGHERTY, JAMES, orthopedic surgeon, educator, author; b. Lawrence, Mass., July 31, 1926; s. James A. and Maude D. (Dillard) D.; m. Marilyn Hays (dec.); m. Rita Buchman; children: James (dec.), Charles, Janice, Jonathan, Christopher. BS, Trinity Coll., Hartford, Conn., 1950; MD, Albany Med. Coll., N.Y., 1951. Diplomate, examiner and monitor Am. Bd. Orthopaedic Surgery, 1965-82; diplomate Am. Bd. Forensic Examiners, Am. Bd. Forensic Medicine. Intern U. Chgo. Clinics, 1951-52, resident, 1951-56, instr., 1955-56; chmn. divsn. orthop. surgery SUNY, Syracuse, 1958-60; prof. clin. surgery Albany Med. Coll., 1960-96, attending surgeon, 1961-94, chief of staff, 1987-89, prof. emeritus, 1996—; trustee Albany Med. Ctr., 1993-95; cons. Subacute Care Alternative Project, Washington. Author: Ponies In The Window, 1998, (hymns) Life's Narrow Pathways, A Babe Was Born; mem. editl. bd. Techniques in Orthops.; contbr. articles to profl. jours. Mem. Bd. Edn. Ravena-Coeymans-Selkirk Ctrl. Schs., Ravena, N.Y., 1960-75; med. dir. N.Y. Sr. Games, 1986-89; trustee Schaeffer Meml. Libr., 1990-92, Albany Med. Ctr., 1993-95; bd. dirs. Inst. for Study of Aging, 1990-99. Served with U.S. Army, 1944-46. Recipient Alumni medal Albany Med. Coll., 1951. Fellow Am. Acad. Orthopaedic Surgeons; mem. Crawford Campbell Soc. (founder, pres. 1978-88), U. Chgo. Surg. Soc., Northeastern Regional Assn. Sports Medicine

(chmn. 1984-89), Albany Med. Coll. Alumni Assn. (trustee 1990-99, pres. 1994-96, Mer itorious Svc. award 1996), Internat. Platform Assn., Sr. and Ret. Physicians' Assn. of Lee County Fla. (founder, pres. 1997-98), Alpha Omega Alpha, Sigma Psi, Sigma Nu. Presbyterian. Home: 3510 Pine Fern Ln Bonita Springs FL 34134-1918 Office: 1444 Western Ave Albany NY 12203-3495

DOUGHTY, DAVID WILLIAM, marketing executive; b. Leeds, Eng., July 14, 1954; s. Raymond William and Irene Tillotson (Schumacher) D.; m. Bryony Margaret Smith, Sept. 28, 1978 (div. June 1992); children: Olivia, John; m. Pamela Sherratt Hodgson, July 30, 1992; 1 child, Alexander. BSc in Applied Sci. Physics, Hull U., Eng., 1976; MSc in Opto-Electronics, Essex U., Eng., 1977; MA in Co. Dir., Leeds Bus. Sch., 1998. Mgr. BICC Power Cables, Erith, Eng., 1977-80, Marconi Comm. Sys., Hackbridge, Eng., 1980-83; cons. DTI Mapcon, Harpenden, Eng., 1983-86; mng. dir. RDA, Stevenage, Eng., 1986-89; sales engr. Feedback Inc., Berkeley Heights, 1989-90; sr. cons. SGI, London, 1990-91, WSTI, London, 1991-93; tech. and mktg. dir. Feedback Instruments, Crowborough, Eng., 1993-97; mng. dir. Mgmt. Sys. Solutions, Heathfield, Eng., 1994—, Aquarius Bus. Computer Solutions, Abingdon, Eng., 1998—; dir. Inteco, Cracow, Poland, Pinnacle Info. Svs., Winchester, Eng. Contbr. article to profl. jour. Fellow Inst. Dirs. (diploma in co. direction 1995); mem. IEEE, IEE (chartered), Inst. Physics (chartered), British Computer Soc. (chartered). Avocations: music, squash, motorcycling.

DOUGHTY, MARK ANTHONY, lawyer; b. Pasadena, Calif., Aug. 18, 1951; s. Lawrence Richard and Bertha Lou D.; children: Matthew James, Luke Anthony. BA in Bus. Law, Calif. State U., Chico, 1976; JD, U. Pacific, Sacramento, Calif., 1979. Bar: Calif. 1979, U.S. Dist. Ct. (ea. dist.) Calif. 1979; lic. real estate broker. Law clk. Calif. Ct. Appeals (5th cir.), Fresno, Calif., 1979-80; assoc. Ashby and Guth, Yuba City, Calif., 1980-82; ptnr. Ashby, Guth and Doughty, Yuba City, 1982-86, Ashby & Doughty, Yuba City, 1986-92; prin. Law Offices of Mark A. Doughty, Yuba City, 1992—. Pres. Russian Radio Bible Inst. Mem. Network Profls. Yuba City, Consumer Attys. of Calif. (bd. govs. 19th dist.), Fellowship of Christian Businessmen, Yuba Sutter Bar Assn. (pres. 2001), Consumer Attys. Gold Country (pres. 1999—). Republican. Avocations: fathering, golf, private pilot, hunting, boating. Fax: 530-674-1180. E-mail: mark@golaw.com. Office: Law Offices of Mark A Doughty PO Box 3420 Yuba City CA 95992-3420

DOUGHTY, MICHAEL LEE, financial advisor; b. Corpus Christi, Tex., July 11, 1950; s. C.E. "Gene" and Peggy Ruth Doughty; m. Barbara Kyes, Sept. 4, 1971; children: Matthew James, Allison Machelle. BA, U. Nev., 1972. CFP. V.p. sales Sahara Luggage Co., San Jose, 1979-82; territory mgr. Airway Luggage Co., San Jose, 1982-87; fin. advisor, master planner Am. Express Fin. Advisors, Sacramento, 1987—, dist. mgr., 1998-99. Mem. Internat. Assn. Fin. Planners, Sacramento Capital Club. Office: American Express Fin Advisors Bldg A-sou 2710 Gateway Oaks Dr Sacramento CA 95833-3505

DOUGHTY, ROBERT NEIL, cardiologist; b. Hassocks, England, Apr. 11, 1964; s. Dennis and Patricia (Sadler) D.; m. Lesley Joan Hogg, July 24, 1992. MBBS, U. London, 1987. Cardiologist U. Auckland, New Zealand. Fellow Royal Australasian Coll. Physicians; mem. Royal Coll. Physicians U.K. Home: 149a Riddell Rd, Glendowie Auckland, New Zealand

DOUGINSKY, MICHAEL ILLICH, lawyer; b. Kiev, July 31, 1961; s. Illya Bencionovich and Svetlana (Moyseevna) D.; m. Elena Nikolaevna Zaharova, May 3, 1986 (div.); 1 child, Svetlana; m. Anna Nikolaevna Menchynskaya, Feb. 23, 1995. Degree in engring. with honors, Polytech. Inst., Kiev, 1989; JD, Polytech. Inst., Kharkiv, 1995. Mng. ptnr. INTELS Agy., Kiev, Ukraine, 1993—. Contbr. articles to profl. jours. Mem. Ukrainian Assn. of Patenty Attys. (bd. dirs. 1997), Ukrainian Group Internat. Assn. for Protection of Indsl. Property (bd. dirs. 1998), Internat. Trademark Assn. (external affairs com. 1999), Internat. Bar Assn. Office: INTELS Agy, 14-A Borschagovskaya Str 41, 03055 Kiev Ukraine

DOUGLAS, CINDY HOLLOWAY, mortgage company executive; b. Queens, N.Y., Aug. 8, 1960; d. Richard Stephen and Beverly Bunny (Harris) Tannenbaum; m. David Milton Holloway (div. Mar. 1986); 1 child, Benjamin Jerome; m. Michael William Douglas, Mar. 21, 1998. BA, Calif. State U., Fullerton, 1981. Lic. real estate broker. Waitress Bob's Big Boy, San Bernardino, Calif., 1984-85; receptionist RNG Mortgage Co., San Bernardino, 1985; loan processor Quality Mortgage Co., Colton, Calif., 1985-88, loan officer, 1988-91; loan officer RNG Mortgage, 1991-92; v.p., br. mgr. Mountain West Fin., 1992-97; prodn. and mktg. mgr. South Pacific Fin., 1997-97; real estate loan mgr. Arrowhead Credit Union, 1998-2000; cons. mortgage banking, brokerages and credit unions, 2000—. Mem. San Bernardino Bd. Realtors (spl. events com. 1988—, comm. com. 1990—), Nat. Trust for Hist. Preservation, San Bernardino Execs. Assn., Assn. Profl. Mortgage Women (bd. dirs. 1989-90, v.p. 1992-93, Affiliate of Yr. award 1990), San Bernardino Execs. Group (bd. dirs. 1994—). Home: PO Box 3187 Crestline CA 92325-3187

DOUGLAS, DENZIL, prime minister of Saint Kitts and Nevis; b. Jan. 14, 1953. BSc, B in Medicine, B in Surgery, U. West Indies. Polit. leader Labour Party, St. Christopher and Nevis, dep. chmn.; pub. rels. officer St. Paul's Cmty. Coun., St. Christopher and Nevis; prime min., min. nat. security, fgn. affairs, fin., planning and info. Govt. St. Kitts and Nevis. Office: Office of the Prime Minister, Church St PO Box 186 Govt Hdqs, Basseterre Saint Kitts and Nevis*

DOUGLAS, IAN, physical geography educator; b. Wembley, Middlesex, Eng., Dec. 12, 1936; s. Ronald Walter and Edna Maud (Cadle) D.; m. Maureen Ann Bowler, Nov. 16, 1963; children: David Lindsay (dec.), Aidan Andrew, Fiona Katherine. BA, Oxford (Eng.) U., 1961, B.Litt., 1963; PhD, Australian Nat. U., Canberra, Australia, 1967. Lectr. U. Hull, Eng., 1966-71; prof. U. New Eng., Armidale, Australia, 1971-78; prof. U. Manchester, Eng., 1979-97, emeritus prof., 1997—; vis. lectr. U. Malaya, Kuala Lumpur, Malaysia, 1966, 69-70; invited prof. U. Paris I Panthéon-Sorbonne, 1991, 97-98; bd. dirs. Salford and Trafford Groundwork Trust; chmn. bd. govs. Commonwealth Human Ecology Coun., 1999—; sci. coord. lowland catchment rsch. thematic programm Nat. Environment Resh. Coun., 2000—; chmn. working party, UK SCOPE, 2000—. Author: Rates of Denudation in Selected Small Catchments, 1973, Humid Landforms, 1977, The Urban Environment, 1983; co-editor: Environmental Change and Tropical Geomorphology, 1985. Mem. New Eng. Regional Adv. Coun., Armidale, 1974-78, Armidale Dist. Devel. Com., Armidale, 1974-78, NSW Land Conservation Group, Sydney, Australia, 1977-78, Tech. Adv. Com., State Pollution Control Commn., Sydney, 1977-78. With Royal Artillery, Brit. mil., 1956-58. Fellow Royal Geog. Soc. (coun. mem. 1991-92); mem. Instn. Water and Environ. Mgmt., Inst. Australians Geographers (pres. 1978), Inst. Brit. Geographers (coun. mem. 1984-87), Brit. Geomorphological Rsch. Group (pres. 1981-82), Brit. Hydrological Soc., British Assn. Advancement Sci. (pres. sec. E georgraphy 1993). Office: U Manchester Sch Geography, Oxford Rd, Manchester M13 9PL, England

DOUGLAS, JAMES FREDERICK, nephrologist; b. Portadown, Ireland, Sept. 22, 1938; s. James and Annie Hildegarde (Harte) D.; m. Giselle Sook An Lim, Apr. 27, 1973; children: Jeremy, Timothy, Andrew. BA in Jurisprudence, Oxford U., 1959, B in Civl Law, 1960, MA, 1965, BmBCh, 1969; MBBCh, QUB Belfast, U.K., 1969. Barrister-at-law Middle Temple, London, 1964; FRCP/U.K., 1986. Lectr. Coll. of Law, London, 1962-64; house officer Royal Victoria Hosp., Belfast, 1969-70; tutor/sr. house officer Queens U., Belfast, 1970-71; eye casualty officer Radcliffe Infirmary, Oxford U., 1971-72; registrar nephrology Belfast City Hosp., 1972-74; No. Ireland Kidney Rsch. Fellow Belfast, 1974-75; cons. nephrologist Belfast City and Royal Victoria Hosps., 1975—, dir. nephrology, 1988-96; mem. Transplant Regulatory Authority, U.K., 1996—, UK Transplant Support Authority, U.K., 1995—. Contbr. articles to profl. jours. Mem. Renal Assn., European Dialysis and Transplant Soc., Brit. Transplant Soc., Transplantation Soc., Internat. Soc. of Nephrology, British Transplant Games Com. (chmn. Belfast Games 1998). Mem. Ch. of Ireland. Office: Belfast City Hosp Dept Nephrology, Lisburn Rd, BT 97AB Belfast Northern Ireland

DOUGLAS, JUDITH ANN, secondary educator; b. Goomeri, Queensland, Australia, Feb. 26, 1929; d. Robert Pride and Doreen Cicely (Ryan) Stumm; m. W.H.B. Douglas, Dec. 27, 1950 (div. 1970); children: Simon, Rachel, Ian. BA, Queensland U., 1949; postgrad., U. NSW, Australia, 1980-86. Cert. tchr. Mistress in charge English/French Presbyn. Girls Sch., Warwick, Queensland, 1950; vol. tchr., worker mental hosps., hosp., schs., U.K., 1955-59; secondary tchr. Abbotsleigh, Wahroonga, NSW, 1968, 69; secondary sr. tchr., remedial tchr. NSW Dept. Edn., Sydney, 1970-91; vis. tchr. to handicapped schs. and hosp. schs., 1980-90; adv. to bd. Citizen Advocacy, Bondi Junction, NSW, 1992. Mem. com. for various orgns. for handicapped, Sydney, 1960—; inaugural founder Inala, Rudolf Steiner Sch. for Handicapped, Sydney, 1960-75; active Aboriginal edn., Goomeri, 1946-54. Mem. Australian Fedn. Univ. Women (exec. mem., N.C.W. rep., pres. No. Dist. 1997-99), New Eng. Girls Sch. Old Girls Union (mem. com. 1983-95), Nat. Coun. Women (exec. mem. 1986-96, editor 1987-2000), Epilepsy Assn. NSW, NSW Coun. for Intellecual Disabilities, N.Y. Acad. Sci. Avocations: reading, gardening, classical music, theater, swimming.

DOUGLAS, KATHLEEN MARY HARRIGAN, psychotherapist, educator; b. Boston, Apr. 24, 1950; d. John Joseph and Kathleen Margaret (Connolly) Harrigan; m. Dr. Robert E. Douglas, Feb. 24, 1977; children: David, Pamela, Elizabeth. Student, Uxbridge, England; BA in Psychology, Sophia U., Tokyo, 1972; MA in Counseling Psychology, Chapman U., Orange, Calif., 1983; PhD in Counselor Edn., U. Fla., 1990. Elem tchr. Marymount Prep Sch., Palos Verdes, Calif., 1973-99; pvt. practice Orlando, Fla., 1985-95; psychology prof. Valencia C.C., Orlando, Fla., 1989-93; prof. Fla. Inst. Tech., 1990-94; asst. prof., grad. acad. advisors, clin. internship supr. Troy State U., Orlando, Fla., 1993-97; software developer of clinically oriented software, 1994—; assoc. prof. Barry U., Orlando, 1999—; drug/alcohol counselor Ft. Belvoir, Va., 1981-82; counselor Orange County Mental Health Ctr., Winter Park, Fla., 1982-83; child abuse therapist Thee Door, Orlando, 1983-84; presenter in field. Author: The Therapeutic Superhighway, 1995. Counselor Winter Park Towers Nursing Home, 1985; vol. group counselor Hillcrest Halfway House, Orlando, 1985. 1st Lt. U.S. Army, 1976-80. Recipient Marion medal Cath. Ch., Boston, 1966, Civic award Spouse Abuse, Inc., Orlando, 1984. Mem. Am. Assn. for Counseling and Devel., Kappa Delta Phi, Pi Lambda Theta, Chi Sigma Iota. Roman Catholic. Home: 1781 Lake Berry Dr Winter Park FL 32789-5911

DOUGLAS, KENNETH JAY, food products executive; b. Harbor Beach, Mich., Sept. 4, 1922; s. Harry Douglas and Xenia (Williamson) D.; m. Elizabeth Ann Schweizer, Aug. 17, 1946; children: Connie Ann, Andrew Jay. Student, U. Ill., 1940-41, 46-47; J.D., Chgo. Kent Coll. Law, 1950; grad., Advanced Mgmt. Program, Harvard, 1962. Bar: Ill. 1950, Ind. 1952. Spl. agt. FBI, 1950-54; dir. indsl. relations Dean Foods Co., Franklin Park, Ill., 1954-64, v.p. fin. and adminstrn., 1964-70, chmn. bd., chief exec. officer, 1970-87, chmn. bd., 1987-89, vice-chmn., 1989-92; bd. dirs. Andrew Corp. Mem. Chgo. Com. With USNR, 1944-46. Mem. Chgo. Club, Econ. Club, Execs. Club, Comml. Club (Chgo.), Oak Park Country Club, River Forest Tennis Club, Old Baldy Country Club (Wyo.). Republican. Office: 1440 W North Ave Ste 207 Melrose Park IL 60160-1425

DOUGLAS, P.C., producer, director, reporter, editor; b. Houston; s. Hilda Florence Carrithers. BA in Broadcast Journalism, Tex. Tech. U., 1994. Reporter/photographer KCBD-TV, Lubbock, Tex., 1992-93; copy editor La Ventana, Tex. Tech. U., Lubbock, 1993-94; reporter The Independent, Gallup, N.Mex., 1994; radio announcer KDLK/KLKE, Del Rio, Tex., 1994; reporter Del Rio News-Herald, 1994; reporter/photographer KOSA-TV, Odessa, Tex., 1994-96; radio announcer KQRX-FM, Odessa, 1995-96; flight attendant Southwest Airlines, Dallas, 1996-97; polit./govtl. reporter Houston News Today, 1997-98; media coord. Motivators, Inc., Houston, 1998-99; prodr., dir., reporter, editor, anchorperson Houston Internat. Bus. Ch., 1999—; video editor KTRK-TV ABC, Houston, 2000—. Co-prodr.: (TV documentary) Lubbock Hispanic Women Leaders, 1993 (1st place award 1993). Media vol. Make-A-Wish Found. West Tex., Odessa, 1994-96. Recipient 1st place award Soc. Profl. Journalists, 1993. Avocations: Hawaiian culture and history research, travel, stamp collecting. Home: 1205 Banks St Houston TX 77006-6007 Office: Houston Internat Bus Ch 3013 Fountain View Dr #100 KTRK-TV 3310 Bissonnet Houston TX 77005

DOUGLAS, ROBERT MATHESON, medical educator, program director; b. Hamley Bridge, Australia, Dec. 8, 1936; s. John and Ruth Violet (Hitchcox) D.; m. Rosemary Lillian Duguid, May 14, 1960; children: John Matheson, Charles Duguid, Kirsty Ann. MB BS, U. Adelaide, Australia, 1960, MD, 1974; MA, U. Pa., 1972. Physician specialist New Guinea Dept. Pub. Health, Papua, 1967-70; asst. prof. rsch. medicine U. Pa., Phila., 1970-73; sr. lectr. and reader in epidemiology U. Adelaide, 1975-83, reader and chair dept. cmty. medicine, 1983-87, dean faculty of medicine, 1988; dir., prof. Nat. Ctr. for Epidemiology and Population Health Australian Nat. U., Canberra, 1989—; chair tech. adv. group on accute respiratory infection World Health Orgn., Geneva, 1983-87; chair rev. group on accute respiratory infection Cochrane Collaborator, Oxford, Eng., 1994—; adj. prof. U. Sydney, Canberra, 1994—. Editor: Accute Respiratory Infection in Childhood, 1985; editor (internat. newsletter) Accute Respiratory Infection, 1985-89. Pres. Australia and New Zealand Soc. for Epidemology and Rsch. in Cmty. Health, 1978-80; found. sec. Moresby Cmty. Devel. Group, 1969-70; mem. Australian Capital Ter. Bd. of Health, 1990-93; mem. Nat. Health and Med. Rsch. Coun. for Australia, 1990-91. Named Officer Order of Aus., 2000. Fellow Royal Australian Coll. Medicine, Royal Australian Coll. Gen. Practitioners, Royal Australian Coll. Physicians (faculty pub. health medicine), Australian Epidemiological Assn. (pres. 1987-91). Mem. United Ch. of Australia. Avocations: jogging, golf, tennis, bushwalking, music. Home: 34 Nungara Pl, Aranda ACT 2614, Australia Office: Australian Nat U, Nat Ctr Epidemology & Popul, Canberra ANN 0200, Australia

DOUGLASS, DONALD ROBERT, banker; b. Evanston, Ill., Oct. 7, 1934; s. Robert William and Dorothy (Gibson) D.; m. Susan Douglass. BBA, U. N.Mex., 1959, MBA, 1966. With Security Pacific Nat. Bank, L.A., 1961—, mgmt. trainee, 1962-63; asst. mgr. Security Pacific Nat. Bank, Vernon, Calif., 1963-64; asst. mgr. Security Pacific Nat. Bank, Whittier, Calif., 1964, asst. v.p., 1965; asst. v.p., credit officer regional adminstrn. Security Pacific Nat. Bank, L.A., 1966-69; v.p. Security Pacific Nat. Bank, San Francisco, 1969-74; mgr. corp. accts. credit adminstrn. No. Calif. Corp. Banking, 1974-77; group v.p. Annco Properties, Burlingame, Calif., 1977-79; v.p., sr. loan officer Borel Bank and Trust Co., San Mateo, Calif., 1979-83, sr. v.p., 1983-84; exec. v.p. mortgage banking divsn. comml. property sales Borel Bank and Trust Co., Los Altos, Calif., 1984-87; ptnr. Key Equities, Inc., San Mateo, 1987—; ptnr., broker Centre Fin. Group, Inc., San Mateo, 1987—, Centre Fin. Group South Inc., Menlo Park, 1987—; pres. ServiCtr. Mortgage, Inc., 1996—, Sage Fin., Inc., 1999—; instr. Am. Inst. Banking, 1963, Coll. San Mateo, 1982—; nat. adv. bd. Anderson Schs. Mgmt. U. N.Mex. With AUS, 1954-56. Mem. U. N.Mex. Alumni Assn., Sigma Alpha Epsilon, Delta Sigma Phi. Republican. Presbyterian. Home: 745 Celestial Ln San Mateo CA 94404-2771

DOUGLASS, ENID HART, educational program director; b. L.A., Oct. 23, 1926; d. Frank Roland and Enid Yandell (Lewis) Hart; m. Malcolm P. Douglass, Aug. 28, 1948; children: Malcolm Paul Jr., John Aubrey, Susan Enid. BA, Pomona Coll., 1948, MA, Claremont (Calif.) Grad. Sch., 1959. Research asst. World Book Ency., Palo Alto, Calif., 1953-54; exec. sec., asst. dir. oral history program Claremont Grad. U., 1963-71, dir. oral history program, 1971—, lectr. history, 1977—; mem. Calif. Heritage Preservation Commn., 1977-85, chmn. 1983-85. Contbr. articles to hist. jours. Mayor pro tem City of Claremont, 1980-82, mayor, 1982-86; mem. planning and rsch. adv. coun. State of Calif.; mem. city coun. City of Claremont, 1978-86; founder Claremont Heritage, Inc., 1977-80; bd. dirs., 1986-95; bd. dirs. Pilgrim Pla., Claremont; founder, steering com., founding bd. Claremont Cmty. Found., 1989-95, pres., 1990-94. Mem. Oral History Assn. (pres. 1979-80), Southwest Oral History Assn. (founding steering com. 1981, J.V. Mink award 1984), Nat. Coun. Pub. History (founding com. 1980), LWV (bd. dirs. 1957-59, Outstanding Svc. to Cmty. award 1986). Democrat. Avocation: tennis. Home: 1195 N Berkeley Ave Claremont CA 91711-3842 Office: Claremont Grad U Oral History Program 710 N College Ave Claremont CA 91711-3921

DOUGLASS, JOHN ANGUS, financial adviser; b. Kirkby Stephen, Cumbria, Eng., Feb. 26, 1938; s. Philip and Lilian (Fletham) D.; m. Barbara Winn, Aug. 20, 1960; children: Jacqueline, Odette. Ed., Allen Tech. Coll., 1953-56. Mng. dir. Sedbergh (Eng.) Motor Co. Ltd., 1960-86; with Allied Dunbar, Sedbergh, 1986-92; ptnr. J. Rothschild Partnership, Sedbergh, 1992-98; ind. fin. advisor, 1998—; officer in charge Cumbria Fire Svc., Sedbergh, 1963-86. Councilor Sedbergh Rural Dist. Coun., 1969-74, Parish Coun., Sedbergh, 1974-77. With Royal Air force, 1958-60. Mem. Life Assurance Assn. (by diploma). Avocations: flying, photography. Fax: 015396 20536. E-mail: john.douglass@ifa.net. Home and Office: Uplands, Winfield Rd, Sedbergh LA10 5AZ, England

DOUILLET-BREUIL, ANNE-CÉLINE, biochemistry researcher; b. Dijon, France, May 25, 1970; d. André and Marie-Thérèse (Jolivot) Douillet; m. Patrick Breuil, Aug. 19, 1995 (div.). Lic. and Maitrise in Biochemistry, U. Burgundy, Dijon, 1995, postgrad., 1999—. Rschr. in phytopathology U. Burgundy, 1999—. Contbr. articles to profl. jours. Avocations: skiing, wine tasting, nature. Home: 20 Rempart de la Comèdie, 21200 Beaure France Office: Inst Jules Guyot, BP 27877, 21078 Dijon Cedex France

DOULAI, PARVIZ, engineering educator; b. Tehran, Iran, Feb. 6, 1953; arrived in Australia, 1986; s. Nemat-olah and Khadijeh (Hatefi-Darestani) D; m. Mahrokh Hosseini-Hashemi, Jan. 6, 1983; children: Amin, Negin, Negar. B Engring., U. Tabriz, Iran, 1972; MSc, U. Bradford, Eng., 1981; PhD, U. Queensland, Brisbane, Australia, 1991. Lectr. Isfahan (Iran) U. Tech., 1981-84; rsch. scientist Mobarakeh Steel Complex, Isfahan, 1984-86; rschr. U. Queensland, Brisbane, 1986-90; rsch. engr. U. Auckland, New Zealand, 1990-92; sr. lectr. U. Wollongong, Australia, 1992—, rep. Asia-Pacific Rsch. Links, 1993-95, internat. rep., 1994-95; dir. energy systems Mobarakeh Steel Complex, Isfahan, 1985-86; cons., baluchistan U. Seestan, Zahedan, Iran, 1982-83. Editor Electric Power Quality, 1995, World Wide Web Archive for Electric Power Engring. Edn. Mem. IEEE, Inst. Engrs. Australia, Australasian Assn. Engring. Edn. Moslem. Avocations: computer programming, squash, music. Home: 3 Harkness Ave, Keiraville NSW 2500, Australia Office: U Wollongong, Dept Elec & Computer Engr, Wollongong NSW 2522, Australia

DOULL, ADRIAN MONTEITH, executive; b. Durban, South Africa, June 29, 1944; s. Alexander and Rebecca Monteith (Black) D.; m. June Rhoda Kemsley, June 6, 1969 (div. 1983); children: Matthew, Dominic; m. Susan London Kirchheimer Davies, May 7, 1983; 1 child, Harry Alexander. V.p. Anglo Am. Corp., Toronto, Can., 1973-76; sr. v.p. fin. Hudson Bay Mining, Toronto, Can., 1976-81; v.p. fin. Minorco, Luxembourg, 1981-83; sr. v.p. Inspiration Resources Corp., N.Y.C., 1983-86, exec. v.p. and COO, 1986-87; pres. Settler Svcs. Internat., Doullens, France, 1987-98; dir. Europe, Africa, Mid. East Cambridge Energy Rsch. Assocs., 1998—; trustee Arcata Trust, N.Y.C., 1985-90; pres. Danville Corp., N.Y.C., 1985-87, dir. Europe, Africa and Middle East, Cambridge Energy Rsch. Assocs. Home: Chateau de Remaisnil, 80600 Doullens France Office: 21 Blvd de la Madelaine, 75001 Paris France

DOUMANIS, ORESTIS KONSTANTINOS, publisher, architectural critic; b. Thessaloniki, Macedonia, Greece, Oct. 23, 1929; s. Vassilios and Christina (Michailidou) D.; m. Mariella Christea, June 5, 1972. Diploma, Nat. Tech. U., Athens, Greece, 1952. Editor-in-chief Architektoniki, Athens, Greece, 1963-64; contbg. editor World Architecture, London, 1963-67; editor-in-chief Technika Cronika, Athens, 1964-67; contbg. editor Contemporary Architecture, Lausanne, Switzerland, 1981-91; pub., editor Architecture in Greece, Athens, 1967—, Design & Art in Greece, Athens, 1970—; lectr. Nat. Tech. U., Athens, 1958-61; press and publ. dir. Tech. Chamber of Greece, Athens, 1964-67; mem. experts com. Mies van der Rohe Architectural Award, Barcelona, Spain, 1988-92, Carlsberg Archtl. Award, Copenhagen, 1991-97. Co-editor: Shelter in Greece, 1974; author: Takis Ch. Zenetos, A Biography, 1978, Guide to Post-War Greek Architecture, 1984; columnist on architecture Zygos, 1961-63. Mem. bd. dirs. Friends of the Mus. of Modern Art, Athens, 1990—; cons. on visual arts Ministry of Culture, Athens, 1994-95; v.p. Hellenic Inst. of Architecture, Athens, 1995—. Ensign Greek Navy, 1953-55, Athens. Recipient Bronze medal Internat. Biennale of Architecture, 1985. Mem. Greek Assn. Engrs. (sec. gen. 1964-67), European Cmty. of Journalists, Tech. Chamber of Greece. Greek Orthodox. Avocations: travel, classical music, art collecting, photography. Home: 7 Iridos St, 152 37 Philothei-Athens Greece Office: Architecture in Greece Press, 5 Kleomenous St, 106-75 Athens Greece

DOUMAS, ATHANASIOS APOSTOLOS, plastic surgeon; b. Trikala, Thessaly, Greece, July 7, 1955; s. Apostolos Athanasios and Kassiani Apostolos (Koukourli) D. Grad., Aristoteles Med. Sch., Salonico, Greece, 1980; postgrad. urology, G. Hosp., Trikala, Greece, 1982. Resident gen. surgery St. Paul Gen. Hosp., Salonico, Greece, 1985-89; resident microsurgery Servidores Estad Gen. Hosp., Rio, Brazil, 1990-91; fellow plastic surgery U. Buenos Aires, 1991; resident pediat. plastic surgery Polimed Gen. Hosp., San Catarina, Brazil, 1991-92; resident plastic surgery Santa Casa Gen. Hosp., Rio, 1993-96; resident prof. pitanguy U. Pontificia Unic. Catolica-Inst. Carlos Chagas, Rio, 1993-95; resident Inca Gen. Hosp., Rio, 1996; pvt. practice Mother Hosp., Athens, Greece, 1997—; mem. Trikala Med. Assn., 1981-84, Salonico Med. Assn., 1985; gen. surgeon Greek Social Security Svc., Salonico, 1989-90; lectr. Inca Gen. Hosp., Rio, 1996. Contbr. articles to profl. jours. Med. officer Greek Army Forces, 1982-84. Fellow Internat. Coll. Surgeons, Hellenic Soc. Plastic Surgery; mem. Alunos Ex Ivo Pitanguy Assn., Brazilian Soc. Plastic Surgery, Hellenic Surg. Soc., Athens Med. Assn. Avocations: squash, basketball, reading literature. Home and office: Ctr Plastica, 49 Vas Sofias Ave, 106 76 Athens Kolonaki, Greece

DOUMENGE, FRANÇOIS ANDRÉ, museum director; b. Viane, France, Oct. 9, 1926; s. Jean Hippolyte and Marie-Antoinette Victoria (Viguier) D.; m. Lydie Francine Sicart, Oct. 21, 1946 (div. 1980); children: Jean-Pierre, Yves, Charles, Luc; m. Kiyoko Kanno, Apr. 15, 1981. Degree, Faculte des Lettres, 1947, PhD, 1966. Prof. Jr. Coll., Paulhan, France, 1948-53; sr. prof. Lyceum, Montpellier, France, 1953-57; lectr. U. Paul Valéry, Montpellier, 1957-61, asst. prof., 1961-67, prof., 1968-76; prof. U. Abidjian, Ivory Coast, 1967-68; rector, chancellor Acad. and Univ., French West Indies, 1976-79; prof. Natural History Nal Mus., Paris, 1979-88; dir. Oceanographic Mus., Monaco, 1989—; dir. Tropical Rsch. Inst., Abidjian, 1967-70; project mgr. South Pacific Island Fisheries Devel. Agy., 1971-73; sec. gen. Internat. Com. Scientific Exploration Mediterranean, Monaco, 1988—; commr. Internat. Whaling Commn., Cambridge, U.K., 1993—. Author: L'Homme dans le Pacifique Sud, 1966, Japanese Fisheries and Aquaculture, 1960-79; editor: Annales de Geographie, 1980—, Bull. Inst. Oceanographie, 1989—. Dep. mayor Town Coun., Montpellier, 1959-77; councillor French Nat. Rch. Coun., Paris, 1972-84. Decorated officer Legion of Honor, officer Ordre St.-Charles, officer Marine Merit, officer Acad. Palms. Mem. Overseas Scientific and Tech. Rsch. Office (pres. coun. adminstrn. 1987-88), Internat. Union for Conservation of Nature (pres. commn. of ecology 1990-94). Mem. Gaullist Party. Roman Catholic. Avocation: stamp collecting, swimming. Office: Oceanographic Museum, Ave Saint-Martin, Monaco Ville 98000, Monaco

DOUMLELE, RUTH HAILEY, communications company executive, broadcast accounting consultant; b. Nov. 6, 1925; d. Clarrie Robert Hailey and Virginia Susan Ferguson; m. John Antony Doumlele, May 8, 1943; children: John Antony, Jr., Suzanne Denise Doumlele Owen. Cert. in commerce, U. Richmond, 1968; BA, Mary Baldwin Coll., 1982. Sta. acct. Sta. WLEE-Radio, Richmond, Va., 1965-67, bus. mgr., 1967-73; area bus. mgr. Nationwide Cmms. Inc., Richmond, 1973-75; corp. bus. mgr. Neighborhood Comms. Corp., Inc., Richmond, 1978-86, asst. v.p., 1981-86; owner Broadcast Acctg. cons., Midlothian, Va., 1986-95; treas., dir. Guests of Honor, Ltd., Richmond, 1984-89; sec. Inner Light, Inc., 1984-96; docent Va.'s Gov.'s Mansion, 1997—. Contbr. articles to profl. jours., hist. and astrol. publs.; mem. editl. rev. bd. The Woman C.P.A., 1980—. Pres. Powhatan County Hist. Soc., 1999—. Mem. DAR, Am. Soc. Women Accts. (chpt. pres. 1974-76, contbg. editor The Coord. 1990, Chgo., Woman of Achievement award 1991), Broadcast Fin. Mgmt. Assn., Nat. League Am. Pen Women (br. pres. 1984-86), Am. Fedn. Astrologers, Va. Assn. Amateur Athletic Union (records chmn. 1959-62), Women's Club of Powhatan, Selective Svc. Sys. Local Bd., Powhatan Hist. Soc. (pres. 1999—). Episcopalian. Avocations: salt water fishing, Civil War history, travel, astrology. Home and Office: 2510 Chastain Ln Midlothian VA 23113-9400

DOURMISHEV, ASSEN LYUBENOV, dermatologist, researcher; b. Mokresh, Bulgaria, Feb. 10, 1938; s. Lyuben Arssenov and Galabina Todorova (Toudjarova) D.; m. Nora Dimitrova Tafradjiiska, Sept. 12, 1965; 1 child, Lyubomir. MD, Sofia (Bulgaria) Med. Sch., 1965; PhD, Sofia Med. Acad., 1976, DSc, 1988. Physician Montana (Bulgaria) Hosp., 1965-67, Alexander's Univ. Hosp., Sofia, 1967-69; rsch. worker Sofia Med. Acad. Dept. Dermatology, 1969-72, asst., 1972-74, sr. asst., 1974-82, chmn., 1991-95, head of clinic, 1991—; assoc. prof. Inst. of Dermatology, Sofia, 1982-88, head of clinic, 1984-89, dir., 1989-91; prof. Med. Acad. Sofia, 1990—; nat. expert dermatology, Bulgarian Ministry of Health, 1990-97; pres. Bulgarian Forum Herpes Infections, Sofia, 1996—. Author: Disorders of Melanin Pigmentation, 1986, Functional Diagnosis in Dermatology, Applied Venereology, 2000; editor-in-chief Dermatology and Venereology, 1992—. Sgt. Bulgarian Army, 1957-59. Fellow Am. Acad. Dermatology; mem. Bulgarian Soc. Dermatology, European Soc. Dermatol. Rsch., European Acad. Dermatology and Venereology. Avocations: classical music, driving, chess, volleyball, football. Home: Complex Mladost Bl 46 Vh 7, 1784 Sofia Bulgaria Office: Dept Dermatology Venereolog, 1 St G Sofiisky Blvd, 1431 Sofia Bulgaria

DOUROUX, LUCIEN, retired credit executive. Mng. dir. Credit Agricole, Paris, CEO, -99. Office: Credit Agricole, 91-93 Blvd Pasteur, Paris 75015, France*

DOUTY, ROBERT WATSON, minister, educator; b. Phila., June 20, 1943; m. MarshaLee Wood, Apr. 22, 1972. BA in Psychology, Calif. State U., Long Beach, 1969; MS in Edn., U. Bridgeport, 1974; MDiv, Alliance Theol. Sem., Nyack, N.Y., 1993. Ordained to ministry Am. Bapt. Chs., 1990; teaching cert., N.Y. Tchr. Garrison (N.Y.) Sch., 1980—; chmn. bd. deacons 1st Bapt. Ch., Ossining, N.Y., 1980-82, dir. Christian edn., 1985-91; assoc. pastor 1st Bapt. Ch., Ossining, 1990-96; dir. Christian edn. St. Philip's Episc. Ch., Garrison, N.Y., 1996-98; pastor Cold Spring (N.Y.) Bapt. Ch., 1998—; deacon 1st Bapt. Ch., 1973-82, chmn. missions, 1990-95; chaplain Phelps Hosp., Tarrytown, N.Y., 1988—. Author: Star City: A Classroom Management System, 1989; author: (with others) In the Footsteps of Birdy Edwards, 1980; contbr. articles to mags. Victory 94 team leader to elect Gov. George Pataki, 1994. With U.S. Navy, 1962-65. Mem. Am. Assn. Christian Counselors, Baker St. Irregulars (The Priory Sch.). Home: 138 Lindsey Ave Buchanan NY 10511-1610

DOUZENIS, ATHANASSIOS, psychiatrist; b. Athens, Dec. 28, 1959; s. John and Ismene (Varkaraki) D.; m. Sharon Rose Steedman, July 31, 1993; children: Phoebe-Christina, Joanna Ismene. M Med Sci., U. Ioannina Med. Sch., Greece, 1989; PhD, Med. Sch., Athens, 1995. SHO Riverside Mental Health Trust-Roth H.A., London, 1988-90; registrar Riverside Mental Health Trust, London, 1990-92, sr. registrar, 1992-94, cons. psychiatrist, 1994; cons. psychiatrist Croydon Health Authority, London, 1994; dir. methadone programs Athens, 1996—; sr. lectr. in forensic psychiatry U. Athens Med. Sch., 2000—. Author: Criminality and Mental Illness in Greece, 1995. Home: 3 Akamantos St, 118-51 Athens Greece Office: Okana, 40 Eressou, Athens Greece

DOVER, SIR KENNETH JAMES, retired Greek scholar; b. Croydon, Eng., Mar. 11, 1920; s. Percy Henry and Dorothy Valerie (Healey) D.; student Balliol Coll., Oxford (Eng.) U., 1938-40, 45-47, MA, 1946, DLitt, 1974, student Merton Coll., 1948, hon. fellow; LLD, Birmingham U., St. Andrews U.; DLitt, U. Bristol; U. Liverpool, U. London, St. Andrews U., U. Durham; DHL, Oglethorpe U.; m. Audrey Ruth Latimer, Mar. 17, 1947; children: Alan Hugh, Catherine Ruth. Fellow, tutor Balliol Coll., Oxford (Eng.) U., 1948-55, hon. fellow, pres. Corpus Christi Coll., 1976-86, hon. fellow; prof. of Greek, St. Andrews U., 1955-76; chancellor St. Andrews U., 1981—; prof.-at-large Cornell U., 1983-89; vis. lectr. Harvard U., 1960; Sather vis. prof. U. Calif., 1967; prof. Stanford U., winter quarter, 1987-92. Served with artillery Brit. Army, 1940-45; mentioned in dispatches. Created Knight, 1977. Fellow Brit. Acad. (pres., 1978-81, Kenyon medal 1993); mem. Hellenic Soc. (pres., 1971-74), Classical Assn. (pres., 1975), Am. Acad. Arts and Scis., Netherlands Acad. Arts and Scis. Author: Greek Word Order, 1960; Lysias and the Corpus Lysiacum, 1968; Aristophanic Comedy, 1972; Greek Popular Morality in the Time of Plato and Aristotle, 1974; Greek Homosexuality, 1978; The Greeks, 1980; Greek and the Greeks (Collected Papers I), 1987; The Greeks and Their Legacy (Collected Papers II), 1988, Marginal Comment (memoirs), 1994, The Evolution of Greek Prose Style, 1997; contbr. to other books and articles; editor: Aristophanes' Clouds, 1968; Theocritus, 1971; Plato, Symposium, 1980, Perceptions of the Ancient Greeks, 1992, Aristophanes' Frogs, 1993. Home: 49 Hepburn Gardens, Saint Andrews KY16 9LS, Scotland

DOW, JOHN DAVIS, physicist; b. Paterson, N.J., Nov. 6, 1941; s. Robert Frederick and Dorothy (Davis) D.; m. Carole Schulte; children: Sharon, Cynthia, Diana. BS, U. Notre Dame, 1963; PhD, U. Rochester, 1967. Faculty of physics Princeton (N.J.) U., 1967-72, U. Ill., Urbana, 1972-83, U. Notre Dame, Ind., 1983-91, Ariz. State U., Tempe, 1990—; mem. com. NRC, Washington, 1981-88; guest prof. Tsinghua U., Beijing, 1989—. Editor-in-chief Superlattives and Microstructures jour., 1984-96; contbr. over 400 articles to profl. jours. Recipient Mercury X-plan Sable car award Ford Motor Co., 1987, Gov.'s Citation, State of Ind., 1987. Fellow Am. Phys. Soc. E-mail: cats@dancris.com. Home: 6031 E Cholla Ln Scottsdale AZ 85253-6971 Office: Ariz State Univ Dept Physics Tempe AZ 85253

DOWD, DAVID JOSEPH, banker, builder; b. Long Island City, N.Y., June 6, 1924; s. David Joseph and Elsie (Schaeffler) B.; children—Laury, David, Patrick, Carol. BS in Bus. Adminstrn, NYU, 1949. Asst. v.p. Irving Trust Co., N.Y.C., 1952-64; v.p. Franklin Nat. Bank, N.Y.C., 1964-66; sr. v.p. Security Nat. Bank, Huntington, N.Y., 1966-72; pres. Nassau Trust Co., Glen Cove, N.Y., 1972-75, Bankers Service Co., 1975—; pub. Long Island Financial Newsletter, 1976-82; pres. Victorian Homes, Inc., 1980-97. Pres. Suffolk County council Boy Scouts Am., 1969-70; chmn. Suffolk Community Devel. Corp., 1973-74; Trustee Stony Brook Found., State U. N.Y., 1972. Served with USMCR, 1942-45, 51-52. Mem. N.Y. State Bankers Assn. (chmn. group VII 1972-75), L.I. Bankers Assn. (dir. 1969-74), Suffolk County Bankers Assn. (pres. 1971-72), Empire State C. of C. (dir. 1969-75). Address: PO Box 1057 Shelter Island NY 11964-1057

DOWD, MICHAEL BURKE, architect; b. Alexandria, Va., Dec. 1, 1958; s. Thomas John and Catherine Jean (Burke) D.; m. Hilary Mackenzie, Aug. 16, 1986; 1 child, Iris Burke. BA, U. Wash., 1980, MArch, 1983, postgrad. Registered architect Nat. Coun. Archtl. Registration Bds., Wash., Oreg. Designer Charles Bergmann, Architect, Seattle, 1983, Ibsen Nelsen & Associates, Seattle, 1983-84, GBD Architects, Portland, Oreg., 1984-93; pvt. practice Portland, 1993-95; designer Mackenzie & Down Architecture & Planning, Inc., Portland, 1995—; mgr. Graham St. Holdings, LLC, 1998—. Corr. ARCADE Jour., 1983— (Blue ribbon 1985); contbr. archtl. drawing to mags. and profl. jours. Recipient U.S. Masters Swimming NW Zone medal, 1999. Mem. AIA (exhbn. Portland Oreg. chpt. 1988, chmn. design com. 1989-90, lecture com. 1991). Avocation: competitive swimming. Home: 2722 SW Rutland Ter Portland OR 97201-1854

DOWDEN, JOHN MICHAEL, mathematician, educator; b. Whitchurch, U.K., Nov. 28, 1940; s. Harry Clifford and Marjorie Ada Emily (Frame) D.; m. Antoinette Willetts; children: Susan Mary, Frances Elizabeth. BA, Cambridge (Eng.) U., 1963; PhD, Essex U., U.K., 1967. Chartered mathematician and physicist. From asst. lectr. to sr. lectr. U. Essex, 1965-92, reader, 1992-98, prof., 1998—; external examiner in field. Patent welding of coated metals; contbr. articles to profl. jours. Rsch. grantee European Union, 1990, 92, U.K. Rsch. Coun., 1985, 91, 93. Fellow Inst. Math. and its Applications; mem. AIAA, Inst. Physics, Laser Inst. Am., European Inst. for Joining Materials. Anglican. Avocations: playing church organ, travel, choral music. Office: Univ Essex, Dept Math, Colchester C04 3SQ, United Kingdom

DOWDESWELL, JULIAN ANDREW, glaciologist; b. Farnham Common, U.K., Nov. 18, 1957; s. Robert and Joan M. (Longshaw) D.; m. Evelyn K. Lind, Aug. 20, 1983; children: Victoria, Adam. BA, U. Cambridge (Eng.), 1980, PhD, 1985; MA, U. Colo., 1982. Sr. asst. rschr. Scott Polar Rsch Inst.-U. Cambridge, 1989-92, asst. dir. rsch., 1992-94; lectr. U. Wales, Aberysywyth, 1986-89, prof., dir. Ctr. Glaciology,, 1994-98, dir. Inst. Geography and Earth Scis., 1997-98; prof. Sch. Geog. Scis., U. Bristol, Eng., 1998—; mem. earth sci. and tech. bd. U.K. Natural Environment Rsch. Coun., 1997-00, polar sci. and tech. bd., 1995-97, polar sci. expert group, 1997-99, earth scis. peer rev. group, 1996-00. Co-editor: Glacimarine Environments: Processes and Sediments, 1990, The Arctic and Environmental Change, 1996, Glacial and Oceanic History of the Polar North Atlantic Margins, 1998. Gov. Plascrug Sch., Aberysywyth, 1996-98. Recipient The Polar medal Her Majesty Queen Elizabeth II, 1995; scholar Jesus Coll., Cambridge, 1980. Mem. Royal Geog. Soc. (Gill Meml. award 1998), Internat. Glaciological Soc. (mem. coun. 1993-96, chair publs. com. 1995—). Avocations: hill walking, skiing. Office: Sch Geog Scis, U Bristol, Bristol BS8 1SS, England

DOWDY, HOMER EARL, writer, retired philanthropic foundation executive; b. Flint, Mich., July 16, 1922; s. Homer G. and Gladys A. (Russell) D.; m. Nancy Elizabeth Showalter, June 14, 1947; children: Peggy Dowdy Denning, Rebecca Dowdy Johnson, Barbara Dowdy Wills, David, Jennifer Dowdy Rasmussen, Susan Dowdy Dix. BA, Wheaton Coll., 1947; DPS (hon.), U. Md., 1982. Reporter, editor The Milepost, Ames, Iowa, 1947-48, The Flint Jour., 1948-62; project dir., sr. v.p. C.S. Mott Found., Flint, 1963-82; exec. v.p. Food for the Hungry Internat., Geneva, 1982-87; chmn. exec. com. Nat. Recreation and Parks Assn., Washington, 1974-75. Author: (biography) Christ's Witchdoctor, 1963, (fiction) Loving Luddy, 1997. Founder Genesee County (Mich.) Park Sys., 1966; mem. Genessee County Parks and Recreation Commn., Flint, 1966-81, also pres.; founding mem. Flint Inst. Music, 1966; founding mem. Genesee Cmty. Devel. Conf., 1963; ch. officer, Flint, 1950-82. Master sgt. U.S. Army, 1943-46, PTO. Named Young Man of Yr., Flint Jaycees, 1957. Republican. Avocations: gardening, jogging. Home: 908 Boom Way Annapolis MD 21401-6889

DOWEIDAR, HAMDY DOWEIDAR, physics educator, researcher; b. Mansoura, Dakahlya, Egypt, July 15, 1941; s. Doweidar Taki-El Din Doweidar and Nazla El-Motwalli Dawoud; m. Ehetedal Mohye-El Din El-Kasaby, Nov. 17, 1968; children: Hanan, Mohammed, Wael, Mai. BSc in Physics and Chemistry, U. Assuit, Egypt, 1964; MSc in Phys. Chemistry, U. Cairo, 1969; PhD in Applied Physics, High Sch. Architecture and Bldg., Weimar, Germany, 1974. Asst. Nat. Rsch. Ctr., Cairo, 1965-74, rschr., 1974-75; from lectr. to assoc. profl. Faculty of Sci., Mansoura (Egypt) U., 1975-86, prof., 1992—, founder, supr. Galss Rsch. Lab., 1977—; vis. assoc. prof. Ecole Normal Superier, Algeria, 1980-84; vis. prof. Faculty of Sci., U. Sanâa, Yemen, 1990-94. Contbr. over 50 articles to sci. publs., including Jour. Physics, Solid State Ionics, Phys. Chem. Glassas, Jour. Non-Cryst. Solids. Recipient Egyptian State Prize in Physics, 1999. Mem. Egyptian Soc. Solid State Physics, Egyptian Soc. Crystallography. Muslim. Avocations: classical music, nature, travel. E-mail: sinfac@mum.mans.eum.eg. Office: Faculty Sci Dept Physics, Mansoura U, Mansoura 35516, Egypt

DOWELL, ANTHONY JAMES, SR., ballet dancer; b. London, Feb. 16, 1943; s. Arthur Henry and Catherine Ethel D. Studied with, June Hampshire; student, Royal Ballet Sch. Dancer Covent Garden Opera Ballet, 1960; dancer Royal Ballet, 1961-78, prin. dancer, 1966—, asst. to dir., 1984-85, assoc. dir., 1985-86, artistic dir., 1986—; producer Swan Lake for Royal Ballet, 1987; guest artist Am. Ballet Theatre, N.Y.C., 1977-79. Created: dance roles in ballets The Dream, 1964, Monotones, 1965, Jazz Calendar, 1968, Shadowplay, 1967, Enigma Variations, 1968, Meditation, 1971, Anastasia, 1971, Triad, 1972, Pavane, 1973, Manon, 1974, Four Schumann Pieces, 1975, A Month in the Country, 1976, Contre Dances, 1979, Winter Dreams, 1991; appeared in: film Valentino; guest artist: Nat. Ballet Can., 1979, 81. Knight comdr., 1995, Order Brit. Empire, 1973; Recipient award Dance mag., 1972. Office: Royal Ballet Royal Opera House, Covent Garden, London WC2E 9DD, England

DOWER GOLD, CATHERINE ANNE, music history educator; b. South Hadley, Mass., May 19, 1924; d. Lawrence Frederick Dower and Marie (Barbieri) Barber; m. Arthur Gold, Mar. 24, 1994 (dec. Oct. 1998); children: Carolyn D. Gold, Judith G. Enteen. AB, Hamline U., 1945; MA, Smith Coll., 1948; PhD, The Cath. U. Am., 1968. New England rep. Gregorian Inst. Am., Toledo, 1948-49; tchr. music, organist St. Rose Sch., Meriden, Conn., 1949-53; supr. music Holyoke (Mass.) Pub. Schs., 1953-55; instr. music U. Mass., Amherst, 1955-56; prof. music Westfield (Mass.) State Coll., 1956-90, prof. emerita, 1991--; columnist and freelance writer Holyoke Transcript Telegram, 1991-93; organist St. Theresa's Ch., South Hadley, 1937-41, St. Michael's Ch., N.Y., 1945-46; concert series presenter Westfield State Coll., 1987-91, rschr. tchr.; vis. scholar U. So. Calif., 1969; vis. assoc. prof. music Herbert Lehman Coll. CUNY, 1970-71. Author: Puerto Rican Music Following the Spanish American War, 1898-1910, 1983; (monograph) Yella Pessl, 1986, Alfred Einstein on Music, 1991, Yella Pessl: First Lady of the Harpsichord, 1993; presenter Irish Concert Springfield Symphony Orch., 1981 (plaque 1982). Pres. Coun. for Human Understanding Holyoke, 1981-83, Friends of Holyoke Pub. Libr., 1990-91; bd. dirs., chmn. nominating com. Holyoke Pub. Libr., 1987-89; bd. dirs. Holyoke Pub. Libr. Corp., 1991-94, Women's Symphony League, The Symphony Orch., 1992-94; bd. dirs., sec. Life Long Learning Soc. of Fla. Atlantic U., 1994-97; presiding officer inauguration Dr. Irving Buchman pres. of Westfield State Coll.; mem. ethics com. Holyoke Hosp., 1988-94; sec. Haiti Mission, 1982-94; bd. overseers Mullen U., 1993; hon. mem. bd. Coun. Human Understanding, 1994; hon. mem. WSC Found., 1994; co-chair United Jewish Appeal/Jewish Fedn. Boca Lago Women's Divsn., South Palm Beach County, 1996-97; 1st. v.p. fin. and adminstrn. Temple Beth El Women in Reformed Judaism, Boca Raton, 1997-99. Recipient citation Academia InterAmericana de P.R., 1978, Holyoke Pub. Libr., 1983, plaque Mass. Tchrs. Assn., Boston, 1984, medal Equestrian Order Holy Sepulchre of Jerusalem, Papal Knighthood Soc., Boston, 1984, Performance award Gov. Dukakis, Mass., 1988, award for Puerto Rican Jour. Al. Margens, 1992, Human Rels. award Coun. for Human Understanding, Holyoke, 1994; named Lady Comdr., Equestrian Order of the Holy Sepulche of Jerusalem, 1987, with star, 1990, Career Woman of Yr., Quota Internat. Holyoke, Mass., 1988; Westfield State U. concert series named Catherine A. Dower Performing Arts Series in her honor, 1991; recipient 1st prize in Raddock Eminent Scholar Chair Essay Contest, Fla. Atlantic U., 1996. Mem. Nat. Soc. Arts and Letters, Am. Musicol. Soc., The Coll. Mus. Soc., Ch. Music Assn. Am. (journalist), Acad. Arts and Scis. of P.R. (medal 1977), Internat. Platform Assn., Friends of the Holyoke Pub. Libr. (pres. 1990-91), Irish Am. Cultural Inst. (chmn. bd. 1981-89), Holyoke Quota (v.p. 1976-79, pres. 1979-81, 90-92, chmn. speech and hearing com. 1987-94), B'nai B'rith of Boca Lago (sec. bd. dirs. 1994-1999, newsletter editor 1999—), Lifelong Learning Soc. Fla. Atlantic U. (sec. 1994-97), Phi Beta Kappa. Democrat. Home: 8559 Casa Del Lago Boca Raton FL 33433-2107

DOWIYOGO, BERNARD, Nauruan government official; b. Feb. 14, 1946. Student, Australian Nat. U. Mem. parliament Govt. of Nauru, 1973—, pres., 1976-78, 89-95, min. justice, 1983-89, min. health and edn., 1989, min. civil aviation, 1992-95, min. island devel. and industry, 1992-95, min. external affairs, 1992-95, min. public svc., 1992-95; chmn. Bank of Nauru, 1985—. Sec. Nauru Gen. Hosp.; gen. mgr. Nauru Coop. Soc. Office: Govs Office, Yaren Nauru also: Bank Nauru, Civic Ctr, Nauru Nauru*

DOWLING, DORIS ANDERSON, business owner, educator, consultant; b. Clover Valley, Minn., Sept. 24, 1917; d. Gustaf Axel and Amanda Sophia (Karlsson) Anderson; m. John Joseph Dowling, Jan. 8, 1943 (dec. Feb. 1953); 1 child, Mary Kathryn. Home econs. degree, U. Minn., Virginia, 1937. Fashion coord., lectr. Fair Store/Montgomery Ward, Chgo., 1939-65, Marshall Field's, Chgo., 1967-82; founder, owner Doris Anderson Sewing Schs., 1948—; cons. colls., textile industry, retail stores, 1948—; lectr. retail stores, 1954-94. Author: Simplified Systems of Sewing and Styling, 1948. Career counselor, trainer, Chgo., 1948-82. Recipient Future Farmers Am. award Duluth C. of C. Coun. Agr., 1934. Mem. Nat. Needlework Assn., Fashion Group Internat. Inc., Assn. Crafts & Creative Industries, Chgo. Apparel Ctr., Merchandise Mart. Avocations: designing, gardening, writing, research. Home and Office: Doris Anderson Sewing Schs 222 E Pearson St Apt 1108 Chicago IL 60611-7356

DOWLING, JOHN CLARKSON, language educator; b. Strawn, Tex., Nov. 14, 1920; s. Albert Clarkson and Georgia Anna (Turrill) D.; m. Constance Guinevere Ford, Dec. 26, 1949; 1 child, Robert Clarkson. BA, U. Colo., 1941; MA, U. Wis., 1942, PhD, 1950. Instr. Spanish U. Wis., Madison, 1951-53; prof., head fgn. langs. Tex. Tech. U., Lubbock, 1953-63; prof., chmn. Spanish & Portuguese Ind. U., Bloomington, 1963-72; prof., head romance langs. U. Ga., Athens, 1973-79, dean grad. sch., 1979-89, prof. alumni found., 1980-91, prof. emeritus alumni found., 1992—; vis. prof. romance langs. U. Tex., Austin, 1957; vis. prof. Spanish U. Iowa, Iowa City, 1993; interim dean arts & humanities Fla. Atlantic U., Boca Raton, 1995. Author: Saavedra Fajardo, 1957, 2d edit., 1977, Moratin, 1971, Jose Melchor Guomis, 1974; contbr. articles to profl. jours. Mem. exec. com. grad. deans African-Am. Inst., N.Y.C., 1985-92. Lt. (j.g.) USNR, 1942-46; lt. comdr. USNR, 1946-66. Rsch. grantee Am. Philos. Soc., 1971, 74; A.C. Markham Travel fellow, U. Wis., 1950-51, J.S. Guggenheim fellow, 1959-60. Mem. Am. Assn. Tchrs. Spanish & Portuguese, Hispanic Soc. Am. (corr.), Critica Hispanica Dieciocho. Episcopalian. Home: 145 Hancock Ln Athens GA 30605-4747

DOWLING, VINCENT JOHN, lawyer; b. N.Y.C., Dec. 20, 1927; s. Victor Hurlin and Joan Agnes (Reardon) D.; m. Jane Cooney, Apr. 16, 1958; children: Vincent John Jr., Douglas J., S. Colin, Joseph G. BS, Lehigh U., 1949; JD, U. Conn., 1957. Bar: Conn. 1957, Mass. 1985, Fla. 1986, U.S. Dist. Ct. Conn. 1958, U.S. Ct. Appeals (2d cir.) 1960, U.S. Ct. Claims 1986. Chief mfg. engr. Veeder-Root, Inc., Hartford, Conn., 1949-58; ptnr. Dowling & Dowling, Hartford, Conn., 1958-65, Cooney, Scully & Dowling, Hartford, Conn., 1965—; lectr. constrn. law. Capt. U.S. Army, 1951-53. Mem. ASME, ABA, Conn. Bar assn. (liaison com. with ctrs., constrn. law com., alt. dispute resolution com., chmn. specialization com.), Am. Arbitration Assn., Nat. Panel Constrn. Arbitrators and Mediators, Nat. Arbitration and Mediation (panel), Fed. Bar Assn., Mass. Bar Assn., Fla. Bar Assn., Internat. Bar Assn., Diocesan Attys. Assn., Hartford Golf Club, Hartford Club, John's Island Club (Vero Beach, Fla.), Kappa Alpha Soc. Roman Catholic. Address: 10 Columbus Blvd Hartford CT 06106-1976

DOWN, DAVID KYRLE, editor; b. Melbourne, Australia, Apr. 9, 1918; s. Leslie Kyrle and Mabel Taylor (Ker) D.; m. Goldie Malvern Scarr, Sept. 8, 1946; children: Kendall, Glenda, Michelle, Selina, Ted, Richley. Editor (monthly mag.) Diggings, (bi-monthly mag.) Archaeological Diggings. Adventist. Avocations: tennis, archaeological excavating. Home: 2 Neridah Ave, Mt Colah 2079, Australia Office: PO Box 341, Hornsby 2077, Australia

DOWN, ROSS WILLIAM, secondary school educator; b. Mildura, Victoria, Australia, June 17, 1953; s. Geoffrey William and Roma Lorraine (Geerckens) D.; m. Elizabeth May Brooksbank, Mar. 26, 1988; children: Jennifer, Sophie. BA, Monash U., Melbourne, Australia, 1980; grad. diploma in ednl. adminstrn., Melbourne U., 1986. Leading tchr. level 3 Sandringham Secondary Coll., Melbourne, 1989—; state chairperson for psychology Victoria Bd. of Studies, Melbourne, 1992—. Author: Psychology: VCE Units 3 & 4, 1996, 2d edit., 1999, VCE Psychology Student Workbook, 1996; writer, presenter (video) Victorian Board of Studies Advice for Psychology Teachers; presenter TV series. Coord. of student blood donation program Red Cross Blood Bank, Melbourne, 1993—. Internat. tchg. fellowship Victoria Dept. of Edn., 1987. Mem. Am. Psychol. Assn. Mem. Ch. of Eng. Office: Sandrigham Secondary Coll, Holloway Rd, Sandringham VIC 3191, Australia

DOWN, WILLIAM JOHN DENBIGH, bishop; b. July 15, 1934; s. William Leonard Frederick and Beryl Mary (Collett) D.; m. Sylvia Mary Aves, 1960; 4 children. BA, St. John's Coll., Cambridge, 1957, MA, 1961; student, Ridley Hall, Cambridge. Deacon, 1959, ordained priest, 1960. Asst. curate St. Paul's Ch., Salisbury, 1959-63; chaplain Missions to Seamen, South Shields, 1963-65, Hull, 1965-71, Fremantle, Western Australia, 1971-74; dep. gen. sec. Missions to Seamen, 1975, gen. sec., 1976-90; chaplain St. Michael Paternoster Royal, 1976-90; bishop of Bermuda, 1990-95; asst. bishop of Leicester Eng., 1995—; priest-in-charge St. Mary's Ch., Leicester, Eng., 1995—; chaplain RANR, 1972-74; hon. asst. curate St. Johns', Stanmore, 1975-90; hon. chaplain Worshipful Co. Carmen, 1977-90, hon. chaplain emeritus, 1990; hon. chaplain of Farriers, 1983-90, hon. chaplain emeritus, 1990; hon. chaplain of Innholders, 1983-90; hon. canon of Gibraltar, 1985-90; hon. canon of Kobe, 1987—. Author: On Course Together, 1989; contbg. author: Chaplaincy, 1999. Freeman City of London, 1981. Fellow Nautical Inst.; mem. Commonwealth Trust Club, Marylebone Cricket Club (assoc.). Avocations: sports, ships, sea, travel, walking. Office: St Mary's Vicarage, 56 Vicarage Ln, Humberstone Leicester LE5 1EE, England

DOWNEN, ROBERT LYNN, international affairs analyst and consultant, editor, writer; b. Wichita, Kans., Apr. 18, 1951; s. Lyndall Roy and Ruth Ann (Branstetter) D.; m. Holly Hutchens, Sept. 1, 1980; children: Heather Anna Christine, Lindsey Rose Lynn. BA cum laude, Washington U., St. Louis, 1973; MA, George Washington U., Washington, 1975. Legis. asst. to Bob Dole, U.S. Senate, Washington, 1973-79; dir. Pacific stds. Ctr. for Strategic and Internat. Studies/Georgetown U., Washington, 1979-84; dir., spl. projects U.S. State Dept./Asia, Washington, 1984-89; v.p. Neill and Co., Washington, 1989-94; sr. v.p. Jefferson Waterman Internat., Washington, 1994-98; pres. Downen Consulting, 1998—. Author: The Taiwan Pawn, 1979, To Bridge the China Strait, 1984; editor: Multi-System Nations and International Law, 1982, The Emerging Pacific Community, 1984. Mem. adv. group Dole for Pres., Washington, 1996, Reagan for Pres., Washington, 1980. Named Kans. DeMolay of Yr., Order of DeMolay, 1969, DeMolay Legion of Honor award, 1983; recipient Wolcott Scholar award Internat. High Twelve Clubs, Mo., 1974, Hon. Mem. award Sojourners Lodge AF & AM, Panama Canal Zone, 1978. Mem. Masons, Phi Beta Kappa, Sigma Nu. Republican. Baptist. Avocations: photography, genealogy, study of American history and government, travel. Home: 4009 Terrace Dr Annandale VA 22003-1856

DOWNER, ALEXANDER JOHN GOSSE, Australian government official; b. Sept. 9, 1951; s. Sir Alexander Downer; m. Nicola Robinson, 1978; 4 children. Grad., Radley Coll.; BA, U. Newcastle-upon-Tyne, U.K. Mem. Australian Diplomatic Svc., 1976-81; sr. fgn. affairs rep. South Australia, 1981; polit. advisor to prime min., 1982-83; dir. Australian C. of C., 1983-84; liberal mem. Ho. Reps. for Mayo, South Australia, 1984—; shadow min. for arts, heritage and environment, 1987, shadow min. for housing, small bus. and customs, 1988-89, shadow min. for trade and trade negotiations, 1990-92, shadow min. for def., 1992-93, fed. shadow treas., 1993-94, shadow min. for fgn. affairs, 1995-96, min. fgn. affairs, 1996—; mission to European communities, embassy to Belgium and Luxembourg, 1977-80; leader Liberal Party, 1994-95. Avocations: reading, music, tennis. Office: Dept Fgn Affairs and Trade, Ste M1-47 Parliament House, Canberra ACT 2600, Australia

DOWNER, ROBERT NELSON, lawyer; b. Newton, Iowa, July 15, 1939; s. Lowell William and Mabel Mary (Hannon) D.; m. Jane Alice Glafka, May 29, 1971; children: Elise Michele, Andrew Nelson. BA, U. Iowa, 1961, JD, 1963. Bar: Iowa 1963, U.S. Dist. Ct. (so. dist.) Iowa 1963, U.S. Dist. Ct. (no. dist.) Iowa 1964, U.S. Supreme Ct. 1995. Assoc. Meardon Law Office, Iowa City, 1963-68; mem. Meardon, Sueppel & Downer PLC and predecessor firms, Iowa City, 1969—; dir., sec. KZIA, Inc., Cedar Rapids, Iowa, 1975—, Iowa City Tennis & Fitness Ctr., 1987-93; trustee The Oaknoll Found., Iowa City, 1990-98, Herbert Hoover Presdl. Libr. Assn., West Branch, Iowa, 2000—; dir. Christian Retirement Svcs., Inc., Iowa City, 1967-82, Iowa State Bar Found., 1996—. Pres. Greater Iowa City Area C. of C., 1979; bd. trustees Iowa City Pub. Libr., 1971-75, chair, 1973-74; chair adminstrv. bd. First United Meth. Ch., Iowa City, 1985-87; del. Rep. Nat. Conv., New Orleans, 1988; mem. Iowa Supreme Ct. Commn. on Continuing Legal Edn., 1975-83, Task Force on Domestic Abuse, 1993-94; bd. dirs. Iowa City Area Devel. Group, 1993—, chmn., 1996-97, co-chair, 2000—; mem. Cmty. Found. Johnson County, Iowa, 2000—. Recipient Excellence in Svc. award Legal Svcs. Corp. Iowa, 1996. Fellow Am. Coll. Trust & Estate Counsel (state chair 2000—), Am. Bar Found., Iowa State Bar Found.; mem. ABA, Iowa State Bar Assn. (chair probate, property and trust law com. 1988-90, chair probate sect. 1990-93, v.p. 1993-94, pres.-elect 1994-95, pres. 1995-96), Johnson County Bar Assn. (pres. 1976), Rotary Club Iowa City (pres. 1988-89). Republican. Methodist. Home: 2029 Rochester Ct Iowa City IA 52245-3246 Office: Meardon Sueppel & Downer PLC 122 S Linn St Iowa City IA 52240-1830

DOWNES, TONI IRENE, educator; b. Sydney, Australia, Nov. 4, 1953; d. Keith and Kathleen May (Wallace) Hilder; m. James Michael Downes, Jan. 19, 1974; children: Greg, Christine, Jenni. BEd, U. Sydney, Australia, 1975;

MEd, U. Toronto, 1981; PhD, U. Western Sydney, 1998. Tchr. NSW Dept Edn., Australia, 1975-80; ednl. adv. Cath. Edn. Office, Sydney, Australia, 1983-86; lectr. U. Western Sydney, Australia, 1987-90, sr. lectr., 1990-95, assoc. dean faculty edn., 1995—; assoc. prof. U. Western Sydney, 1998—. Co-author: In Control: Young Children Learning with Computers, 1994, Learning in an Electronic World, 1995; contbr. articles to profl. jours. Fellow Australian Coun. Computers; mem. Australian Coll. Edn., Internat. Fedn. Info. Processing. Roman Catholic. Avocations: computing, reading, squash. Home: 6 Seaview St, Cronulla 2230, Australia Office: U Western Sydney, PO Box 555, Campbelltown 2560, Australia

DOWNEY, BRIAN PATRICK, lawyer; b. Pitts., Sept. 1, 1964; s. Edmond John and Mary Elizabeth (Wallace) D.; m. Linda Alice McKay, Oct. 9, 1993. BA, Dartmouth Coll., 1987; JD, Dickinson Sch. of Law, 1990. Bar: Pa. 1990, U.S. Dist. Ct. (we. dist.) Pa. 1991, U.S. Dist. Ct. (ea. and mid. dists.) Pa. 1994, U.S. Ct. Appeals (3rd cir.) 1994. Assoc. counsel Eckert Seamans Cherin & Mellott, Pitts., 1990-92; asst. counsel Pa. Dept. of Labor, Harrisburg, 1992-94; ptnr. Pepper Hamilton, LLP, Harrisburg, 1994—. Mem. Friends of Tom Foley Com., Harrisburg, 1994. Mem. ABA, Pa. Bar Assn., Dauphin County Bar Assn. Democrat. Roman Catholic. Avocations: creative writing, golf, reading fiction. Office: Pepper Hamilton LLP 200 One Keystone Plz Harrisburg PA 17108

DOWNEY, GARY NEIL, marine corps officer; b. Rochester, N.Y., Nov. 3, 1957; s. Arnold Blaine and Barbara Ann (Quiggle) D. Assoc., Va. Coastal Cmty., Woodbridge, Va., 1978. Commd. USMC, advanced through grades to cwo-5, 1998—; security guard USMC, Casablanca, Morocco, 1980-86; pers. officer USMC, Camp Lejeune, N.C., 1986-89, Hqrs. USMC, Washington, 1989-94; course developer Marine Corps Inst., Washington, 1994-97; pers. officer Basic Sch., Quantico, Va., 1997-99; adjutant Marforlant, Norfolk, Va., 1999—. Author: (corr. courses) Supply Chiefs Guidebooks, 1994, Basic Pay Entitlements, 1995, Sassy Computer Classes, 1996. Scoutmaster Boy Scouts Am., 1978-94. Decorated Purple Heart, Meritorious Svc. medal. Mem. Internat. Soc. Performance Instrs. Democrat. Roman Catholic. Avocation: computers. Home: 1900 Dulles Ct Virginia Beach VA 23464-8709 Office: Basic Sch 1348 Ingrahm St Norfolk VA 23551-0001

DOWNEY, JAMES CECIL, retired music and humanities educator; b. Grand Bay, Ala.; s. James Fred and Thelma Hamilton Downey; m. Phyllis Barber, Jan. 23, 1952; children: James Vance, Joy Lyndell, Jennifer Anne, Robert Joel. BA, William Carey Coll., 1963; MMus, U. So. Miss., 1965; PhD, Tulane U., 1968. Prof. music William Carey Coll., Hattiesburg, Miss., 1966-96; prof. humanities William Carey Coll., Hattiesburg, 1989-96; dean Gulfport (Miss.) campus William Carey Coll., 1982-85, coord. continuing edn., 1985-86; state officer Am. Musicological Soc., 1966-96. Contbr. articles to profl. jours. Founder, dir. Gulf Coast Cmty. Chorus, Biloxi, Miss., 1982. With U.S. Army, 1954-56. Recipient Jaap Kunst award Soc. for Ethnomusicology, 1964. Democrat. Baptist. Avocation: gentleman farmer. Home: 530 Knight Rd Sumrall MS 39482-3826

DOWNIE, LEONARD, JR., newspaper editor, author; b. Cleve., May 1, 1942; s. Leonard and Pearl Martha (Evenheimer) D.; m. Barbara Lindsey, July 15, 1960 (div. 1971); children: David Leonard, Scott Leonard; m. Geraldine Rebach, Aug. 15, 1971 (div. 1997); children: Joshua Mark, Sarah Elizabeth; m. Janice Galin, Sept. 12. 1997. B.A., Ohio State U., 1964, M.A., 1965, LLD (hon.), 1993. Reporter, editor Washington Post, 1964-74, met. editor, 1974-79, London corr., 1979-82, nat. editor, 1982-84, mng. editor, 1984-91, exec. editor, 1991—; bd. dirs. L.A. Times-Washington Post News Svc., Internat. Herald Tribune. Author: Justice Denied, 1971, Mortgage on America, 1974, The New Muckrackers, 1976. Trustee Georgetown Day Sch., 1988-93. Recipient Gavel award ABA, 1967, Front Page 1st pl. award for newswriting Washington-Balt. Newspaper Guild, 1967, 68, award John Hancock Ins. Co., 1969; Alicia Patterson Found. fellow, 1971-72. Mem. Am. Soc. Newspaper Editors. Office: Washington Post Co 1150 15th St NW Washington DC 20071-0002

DOWNING, CYNTHIA HURST, therapist, addiction and abuse specialist; b. Fort Wayne, Ind., Sept. 10, 1942; d. James Dickson Hurst and Bernadette (Dygert) Lawyer; m. James S. Downing, Sept. 9, 1961 (div. 1979); children: David, Elizabeth, Jeffrey. BA in Psychology, Ursuline Coll., 1980; MA in Human Svcs., John Carroll U., 1982; PhD, Saybrook Inst., 1991. Lic. profl. counselor, Ohio; cert. chm. dependency counselor III-E, Ohio; nat. cert. addiction counselor II, master addiction counselor. Counselor United Meth. Alcohol and Chem. Counseling, Berea, Ohio, 1980-82; clin. dir. Earthrise Recovery Svcs., Inc., Chagrin Falls, Ohio, 1982—; clin. dir. chem. dependency Brentwood Hosp., Cleve., 1985; program coord. for recovery svcs. U. Hosp. & Health Sys.: Laurelwood Hosp. & Counseling Ctrs., 1998—; coord. case study, instr. Ctr. Applied Scis. Corp. Nat. Relapse Prevention Cert. Sch., Chgo., 1988-98. Author: Triad: The Evolution of Treatment for Chemical Dependency, 1989; mem. editorial adv. bd. Behavioral Health Mgmt. mag., 1991—; contbr. articles to profl. jours. Mem. Nat. Assn. Alcoholism and Drug Abuse Counselors, Nat. Assn. Relapse Prevention Specialists (charter), Assn. Humanistic Psychology, Internat. Soc. for the Study of Dissociation. Office: Earthrise Recovery Svcs Inc 25 W Summit St Chagrin Falls OH 44022-2724

DOWNING, DARRELL W., aviation educator, department chair; b. Ottumwa, Iowa, July 9, 1944; s. Lowell B. Downing. BS, Truman State U., 1967, MA, 1971. Cert. airplane pilot with FAA ratings of comml., instrument, seaplane, multi FAA airframe and powerplant, FAA inspection authorization, FAA designated mechanic examiner. Pres., CEO Indepent Aviation, Granite City, Ill., 1980-89; prof. St. Louis U., 1989-99; chmn. aviation dept. Indian Hills C.C., Ottumwa, Iowa, 1999—; com. chmn. Univ. Aviation Assn., Auburn, Ala., 1992-99; chief pilot Ainad Shrine Hosp. Flight Unit, 1996-99; cons. Great Lakes Composite Consortium, St. Louis, 1997-99; instr. FAA, St. Louis, 1998-99. Recipient Diamond award of tng. FAA, 1995; named Instr. of Yr., Aviation Tech. Edn. Coun., 1993, Instr. of Yr., Flight Safety Internat., 1994. Mem. Soc. Automotive Engrs., Coun. on Aviation Accreditation, Univ. Aviation Assn. (mem. misc. com. chairs 1989, com. chmn. 1992-99), Phi Delta Kappa. Achievements include inventor of composite work station. Avocation: building airplanes. Office: Indian Hills CC Aviation Dept 525 Grandview Ave Ottumwa IA 52501-1359

DOWNING, GEORGE DOWELL, psychology educator, researcher; b. Schenectady, N.Y., June 3, 1940; s. George Dowell Jr. and Elizabeth Jean (Aikens) D.; m. Carole Gammer, Sept. 15, 1976. BA, Williams Coll., 1962; MA, Yale U., 1964, PhD, 1966. Instr. Williams Coll., Williamstown, Mass., 1966-68; prof. psychology Calif. Sch. Profl. Psychology, San Rafael, 1972-74; trainer, supr. Family Therapy Inst. Mann, San Rafael, 1974-78; pvt. practice, cons. to psychiat. instnl. staffs Neuilly-sur-Seine, France, 1979—; prof. Klagenfurt (Austria) U., 1991-99; chief psychologist infant psychiatry unit, Salpêtrière Hosp., Paris, 1994—; cons. numerous psychiat. hosps. and treatment ctrs. in Germany, Switzerland, France, Sweden, Italy, 1979—. Author: Körger und Wort in der Psychotherapie, 1996; contbr. numerous articles to profl. jours.

DOWNING, ROBERT JAMES, artist; b. Hamilton, Ont., Can., Aug. 1, 1935; s. Albert James and Dora Florence (Figgins) D.; m. Miriana Kaludjerovic, Sept. 27, 1980; children by previous marriage: Sara Lynn, Michael John. Police constable City of Hamilton, 1957-60; lectr. U. Toronto, 1967-68; part-time lectr. Fanshawe Coll. Art and Tech., 1969-71, Ont. Coll. Art and Design, 1971-73, 81-82, Banff Ctr. Sch. Fine Art, 1974, Calif. State U., Long Beach, 1974-78, La Salle, Singapore, 1987-88; vis. lectr. Sheridan Coll., Art's Sake, Ont. Coll. Art and Design, Toronto, 1979-80; art program dir. Appleby Coll., Oakville, 1973; prepared, implemented visual and tactile awareness program for secondary sch. art and design tchrs. Molepolole Coll. Edn., Botswana, 1985-86; artist-in-residence Dynamics Graphics Project, U. Toronto, 1997-99. One-man shows include Dunkelman Gallery, Toronto, Can., 1963, Galerie Agnes Lefort, Montreal, Can., 1968, Whitechapel Art Gallery, London, 1969, York U. Art Gallery, Toronto, 1970, Gallery House Sol, Georgetown, 1971, Robert McLaughlin Gallery, Oshawa, 1972, U. Alta., Can., 1973, Cultural Resources Ctr., Huntington Beach, Calif., 1978, Coll. Pk., Toronto, 1981, A Room in the Artist's Home, Toronto, 1985, Art Gallery Hamilton, 1992, The Japan Found., Toronto, 1997; group exhbns. include Mil. Hdqrs. Bldg., Ottawa, 1956, John Pace Gallery, Laguna Beach, Calif., 1964, Ont. Arts Coun., 1967, Nat. Gallery Can., 1967, Rothmans Art Gallery, 1968, Montreal Mus. Fine Arts, 1968, Richard DeMarco Gallery, Scotland, 1969, middelheim Pk., Belgium, 1971, Arts Coun. Gt. Brit., 1971, Ont. Soc. Artists, 1972, Winnipeg Art Gallery, 1972, Burnaby Art Gallery, B.C., 1973, Centennial Gallery and Libr., Oakville, Ont., 1973, Long Beach Mus. Art, 1976, Smithsonian Inst., 1978, Pollock Gallery, Toronto, 1978, David Mirvish Gallery, Toronto, 1979, Koffler Ctr., Toronto, 1981, Nat. Gallery Botswana, 1986, Singapore Sci. Ctr., 1988; commns. include Jan Wallace Archtl. Offices, Laguna Beach, Calif., 1964, U. Toronto Med. Scis. Bldg., 1967, Mohawk Coll. Art and Tech., Hamilton, 1968, U. Waterloo Student Svds. Bldg., 1971, Sheraton Conv. Ctr., Toronto, 1972, Valley Bank Nev., Las Vegas, 1975, United Gas Pipe Line Co., Houston, 1976, Jefferson Shopping Mall, Louisville, 1978, Westinghouse Can. Ltd., Toronto, 1981, Esso Singapore Pte. Ltd., 1987, Singapore Sci. Ctr., 1988; completed CD Rom of life's work, 1999; represented in pub. collections. Nat. Gallery Can., Art Gallery Ont., U. Western Ont., Agnes Etherington Art Ctr., Ont. Sci. Ctr., Govt. of Ont., Singapore Nat. Theatre Trust, Can. Confedn. Ctr. Cultural rep. Texaco Can., Inc., 1980-81. Photographer with Royal Can. Navy, 1952-57. Recipient Ont. Arts Coun. award, 1967, 78, 79, Can. Coun. award, 1967-71, 79, 85. Mem. Can. Artists Rep. (founder 1967), Sculpture Soc. Can., Ont. Soc. Artists (exec. coun. 1979-80), Royal Can. Acad. Arts. E-mail: rdowning@idirect.com. Address: Ste 1602, 78 Holly St, Toronto, ON Canada M4S 3C9

DOWNING, WILLIAM H., life insurance agency executive; b. Kenosha, Wis., Nov. 13, 1919; s. Virgil Leonard and Charlotte Olivia Downing; m. Lois Elizabeth Downing, June 9, 1950 (dec. May 1997); children: Scott William, Mark Bradley. Student, Marquette U., 1937-38; BA, U. Ky., 1942; LLB, Mpls. Coll. Law, 1952. Owner, mgr. Bill Downing, advt., Bakersfield, Calif., 1951-57, Bill Downing & Assocs., Bakersfield, 1957—. Office: PO Box 1148 Bakersfield CA 93302-1148

DOWNS, HARTLEY H., III, chemist; b. Ridgewood, N.J., Oct. 21, 1949; s. Hartley Harrison and Jennie Mae (Smith) D.; m. Cindy Marie Millen, June 19, 1976; children: Kathryn Marie, Jennifer Anne, Susanna Jayne. BS, Grove City Coll., 1971; MS, Indiana U. of Pa., 1973; PhD, W. Va. U., 1978; postgrad., U. Colo., 1976-77. Postdoctoral rsch. assoc. chemistry dept. U. So. Calif., L.A., 1977-78; staff chemist corp. rsch. labs. Exxon Rsch. and Engring. Co., Linden, N.J., 1978-81, Houston, 1981-83, Annandale, N.J., 1983-86; rsch. scientist, surface chemistry and corrosion sci. group supr. Baker Performance Chems., Houston, 1986-91, rsch. mgr., 1991-92, tech. dir., 1992-97; tech. dir. Baker Petrolite, Houston, 1997—. Contbr. articles to profl. jours., chpt. to book; patentee in field. Recipient Award for Grad. Rsch., Sigma Xi, 1973, Union Carbide award W.Va. U., 1975, Stan Gillman award U. Colo., 1977, Tech. Merit award Baker-Hughes, 1989, 91, 93. Mem. Am. Chem. Soc., Soc. Petroleum Engrs., Offshore Operators Com. (task force on environ. sci.), NACE Internat. (chmn. task force on oil industry biocides 1996—, symposium chmn. mineral scale deposit control in oilfield ops. 1994, 98, chmn. corrosion/94 and corrosion/98 symposia, vice-chmn. microbiol. control in oil industry ops. corrosion/2000 symposium), Phi Lambda Upsilon. Presbyterian. Office: Baker Petrolite PO Box 27714 Houston TX 77227-7714

DOWNS, JAMES FRANCIS, anthropologist, journalist, educator; b. Pasadena, Calif., Dec. 20, 1926; s. James Griffith and Martha (Switzer) D.; m. Gay Sterling, 1961 (div. 1970); children: Christian James, Martha Joy Wedgeworth, Mark C.; m. Shizuko Watabe, Nov. 25, 1992; stepchildren: Maki Watabe, Ai Watabe. BA, U. Calif., Berkeley, 1958, MA, 1960, PhD, 1961. Asst. prof. U. Rochester, N.Y., 1961-63; assoc. prof. Calif. State U., L.A., 1962-63, U. Ariz., Tucson, 1963-69; prof. U. Hawaii, Hilo, 1969-80; sr. instructional technologist, program mgr. Univ. Rsch. Corp., Md., 1986-90; dir. Thunderbird Japan Ctr. Thunderbird Am. Grad. Sch. Internat. Mgmt., Ariz., 1992-99; chmn. Ctr. for Cross-Cultural Edn. Tng. Rsch., U. Hawaii, 1970-74; co-prin. investigator Tibetan Rsch., NSF, 1966-68; prin. investigator Navajo Rsch., NIMH, 1961-62; cons. cross-cultural bus. orgns., 1982—; vis. scholar Tokyo U. Fgn. Studies, 1986-87. Author: Two Worlds of the Washo, 1963, The Navajo, 1974, Human Variation, 1965, Human Nature, 1967, Tibetan Pilgrimage, 1987. Warrant officer USN/USNR, 1944-47, 50-51, 74-75, 78-81. Decorated Navy Commendation medal; named Ky. Col. Mem. Am. Anthropol. Assn. (bd. dirs. 1978), Soc. Internat. Cultural Tng. and Rsch. (bd. dirs. 1977), Nat. Assn. for Practice Anthropology (pres. 1978), Nat. Turfwriters Assn. (assoc.), Fgn. Corrs. Club, Japan. Democrat. Buddhist. Avocation: horseback riding. Office: Thunderbird Japan Ctr, STEC Bldg 3, Nishishinkuku Tokyo 160-0023, Japan

DOWNS, JON FRANKLIN, drama educator, director, writer; b. Bartow, Fla., Sept. 15, 1938; s. Clarence Curtis and Frankie (Morgan) D. Student, Ga. State Coll., 1956-58; BFA, U. Ga., 1960, MFA, 1969. Drama dir. Ga. Perimeter Coll. (formerly DeKalb Coll.), Clarkston, 1969-99. Dir., author The Beastly Purple Forest (marionettes) U. Ga., 1968, Dracula: A Horrible Musical, DeKalb Coll., 1971; dir. A Streetcar Named Desire, DeKalb, 1974, Brigadoon, DeKalb, 1981, West Side Story, 1983, Amadeus, 1984, Noises Off, 1986, The Three Musketeers, 1988, A Midsummer Night's Dream, 1990, A Little Night Music, 1991, Hamlet, 1993, over 200 others; actor Wedding in Japan, N.Y.C., 1960, Dark at the Top of the Stairs, N.Y.C. and on tour, 1961, A Life in the Theatre, DeKalb Coll., 1981, numerous others; designer Sweeney Todd, DeKalb Coll., 1970, Romulus, 1971, Grass Harp, 1972, many others; writer, dir. plays Tokalitta, Gold!, The Vigil; on tour of Ga. summers 1973-76; author: The Illusionist, 1979, Rapunzel, 1997; film reviewer So. Flair mag., 1994—, arts editor, 2000—. Grantee arts sect. Ga Dept. Planning and Budget, 1973, 74, State Bicentennial Commn., 1975, Nat. Bicentennial Commn., 1975. Mem. Southeastern Theater Conf. (state rep. 1971-73), Ga. Theater Conf. (exec. bd. 1970-73, 79-82). Home: 1124 Forrest Blvd Decatur GA 30030-4736

DOWSE, GARY KENNETH, medical epidemiologist; b. Perth, Australia, June 7, 1958; s. Kenneth Frederick and Lorna Kathleen (Williams) D.; m. Tamara Joan Copestake. BMedSc (hons), U. Western Australia, Perth, Australia, 1981, MB BS, 1983; MSc in Epidemiology, U. London, 1986. Med. officer SCG Hosp., Perth, Australia, 1983-84, PM Hosp., Perth, Australia, 1985; sr. epidemiologist Internat. Diabetes Inst., Melbourne, Australia, 1986-95; pub. health physician Midwest Pub. Health Unit, Geraldton, Australia, 1995-97; med. epidemiologist Pub. Health Divsn. Disease Control, Perth, 1997—; short-term cons. WHO, Papua New Guinea, Western Samoa, China, 1989-95, Ministry of Health Govt. Mauritius, 1993, Ministry of Health, Singapore, 1992. Contbr. over 120 articles to refereed profl. jours. and book chpts. to books. Recipient PF Sobotka Undergrad scholarship U. Western Australia, 1980, PF Sobotka Postgrad. scholarship, 1985. Fellow Australasian Faculty of Pub. Health Medicine, Australasian Epidemiol. Assn., Pub. Health Assn. Australia. Office: Disease Control Svc Health Dept Western Australia, Stirling St, PO Box 8172, Perth 6849, Australia

DOWSON, JONATHAN HUDSON, psychiatrist, educator; b. Leeds, Eng., Mar. 19, 1942; s. John Heaton and Margaret Blanche (Hudson) D.; m. Lynn Susan Dothie, Dec. 29, 1965; children: Emma, James, Jonathan. BA, Cambridge U., 1967, MA, 1967, MD, 1985; PhD, Edinburgh U., 1974. Lectr. anatomy Edinburgh U., U.K., 1969-72; lectr. psychiatry Edinburgh U., 1973-75; cons. Wessex Health Authority, U.K., 1975-77; lectr. psychiatry, cons. Cambridge U., U.K., 1977—; fellow commoner, dir. studies in clin. medicine Queens' Coll. Cambridge, Eng., 1985—. Author: Personality Disorders: Recognition and Clinical Management, 1995; author, editor: Treatment and Management in Adult Psychiatry, 1983. Fellow Royal Coll. Psychiatrists (cert.). Office: Cambridge U Dept Psychiatry, E4 Addenbrooke's Hosp, Cambridge CB2 2QQ, England

DOWTON, S. BRUCE, academic dean. BS with hons., U. Sydney, 1980, MD. Pediatric intern, resident Children's Hosp. Med. Ctr., Boston, fellow Divsn. of Cell Biology; fellow Divsn. of Cell Biology Harvard Med. Sch., Boston; with Sch. of Medicine Washington U., St. Louis, 1986-93, assoc. dean for med. edn., 1993-96, assoc. vice-chancellor, 1996-98; prof., dean faculty of medicine U. NSW, Sydney, 1998—. Office: Faculty of Medicine, Univ of New South Wales, Sydney NSW 2052, Australia*

DOX, IDA, medical illustrator, writer; b. Honduras, Central America, July 8, 1927; came to U.S. 1947; d. John and Catherine (Headman) D.; m. B. John Melloni; children: H. Paul, June L., Peter J., Roy G. BFA, Newcomb Coll., New Orleans, 1950; MS, Johns Hopkins U., 1954; PhD, U. Md., 1990. Med. illustrator Georgetown U. Med. Ctr., Washington, 1954-69; med. illustrator select com. on assassinations of J.F. Kennedy and Martin Luther King, Jr. of U.S. Ho. of Reps, Washington, 1978-79; med. illustrator/author Bethesda, Md., 1969—. Author: Melloni's Illustrated Medical Dictionary, 1979 (Best Med. Book award 1979), Diccionario Medico Illustrado de Melloni, 1983, The Harper Collins Illustrated Medical Dictionary, 1993, Melloni's Illustrated Review of Human Anatomy, 1988 (award of excellence 1989), Attorney's Illustrated Medical Dictionary, 1995, Melloni's Student Atlas of Human Anatomy, 1997, Melloni's Illustrated Dictionary of Obstetrics and Gynecology, 1999; contbr. articles to profl. jours. Recipient L.S. Neill prize, Newcomb Coll., 1949; E. Woodward Meml. prize, 1950, Indsl. Graphics Internat. award, 1977. Address: 9308 Renshaw Dr Bethesda MD 20817-2228

DOYÉ, PETER KARL, linguistics educator; b. Berlin, May 28, 1927; s. Alfred and Margarethe (Pankau) D.; m. Gisela Brigitte Brée, Feb. 13, 1954; children: Frank, Lutz. Tchr.'s cert., U. Berlin, 1951. Tchr. schs. Berlin, 1951-60; asst. Pädagogische Hochschule, Berlin, 1960-62, lectr., 1962-66; prof. Tech. U., Braunschweig, Fed. Republic Germany, 1966—. Author: Systematische Wortschatzvermittlung, 1971, Typologie der Testaufgaben Daf, 1988, The Intercultural Dimension, 1999, others. Mem. Deutsche Gesellschaft für Fremdsprachenforschung. Home: Blumenstr 23, 38162 Cremlingen Germany Office: Tech U, Bültenweg 74/75, 38106 Braunschweig Germany

DOYLE, ANTHONY JAMES, radiologist; b. London, Apr. 26, 1955; s. John Patrick and Ruth Lilian (Ison) D. BSc, U. Auckland, New Zealand, 1975; MB, ChB, U. Otago, New Zealand, 1981. Intern Otago Health, 1982, Canterbury (New Zealand) Health, 1983; resident in radiology Auckland Hosp., 1984-87; instr. radiology Med. U S.C., 1988; asst. prof. radiology U. Utah, 1989-94; joint clin. head radiology dept. Middlemore Hosp., Auckland, 1995—; dir. Manukau Radiology, Auckland, 1995-97; advisor Health Funding Authority, New Zealand. Contbr. chpts. to books, articles to profl. jours. Scholarship Bd. New Zealand jr. scholar 1973. Royal Australian and New Zealand Coll. Radiology, Am. Roentgen Ray Soc., Radiol. Soc. N.Am., Assn. Univ. Radiologists. Avocations: music, sailing, skiing. E-mail: adoyle@middlemore.co.nz. Office: Middlemore Hosp Dept Radiol, Hospital Rd, Auckland 6, New Zealand

DOYLE, ANTHONY PETER, lawyer; b. Washington, July 13, 1953; s. Francis X. and Anna (Klekotka) D.; m. Maria H. Duda, Aug. 13, 1977; children: Jeffrey Anthony, Joseph Edward, Natalie Maria, Andrew Michael. AA, Berkshire Community Coll., Pittsfield, Mass., 1972-75; BS magna cum laude, Worcester State Coll., 1977; JD, Western New Eng. Coll., 1980. Bar: Mass. 1980; U.S. Dist. Ct. Mass. 1981; U.S. Ct. Appeals (1st cir.) 1981, U.S. Supreme Ct. 1999. Pvt. practice Pittsfield, 1980-84; ptnr. Doyle & Cormier, Pittsfield, 1985-88, Barry, Doyle & Cormier, Pittsfield, 1989, Barry & Doyle, Pittsfield, 1989—. Pres. Hospice of Cen. Berkshire, Pittsfield, 1988-90; v.p. HospiceCare of the Berkshires, Pittsfield, 1990-92, pres. 1992—; bd. dirs. Dalton (Mass.) Youth Ctr., 1986-89, Community Recreation Assn., Dalton, 1989-95; exec. com. Appalachian Trails Dist. Boy Scouts Am., Dalton, 1989-96; mem. Zoning Bd. Appeals, Dalton, 1995—, chmn., 1997—, Dalton Coun. Aging, 1997—. Recipient commendation Western Mass. Pro Bono Referral Svc., 1983-87. Mem. Mass. Bar Assn., Berkshire Bar Assn. (exec. com. 1989-91, v.p. 1997—, pres. 1999—). Roman Catholic. Avocations: skiing, tennis. Home: 108 Barton Hill Rd Dalton MA 01226-2005 Office: Barry & Doyle 8 Bank Row Ste 2 Pittsfield MA 01201-6224

DOYLE, DAVID ANTHONY, barrister, solicitor; b. Melbourne, Victoria, Australia, June 13, 1947; s. Anthony James and Margaret (O'Reilly) D.; m. Ann Godfrey Stewart, Dec. 18, 1976 (div. Mar. 1985); children: Ben, Adele, Peter. BA honors, Melbourne U., 1968, LLB, 1970; PhD, Oxford U., 1978. Bar: Australia. Lectr. La Trobe U., Australia, 1980-90; gen. editor Doyles Dispute Resolution Practice (CCH). Fellow Inst. Arbitrators and Mediators Australia. Roman Catholic. Avocations: sailing, sculpture, photography. Office: The Builders Lawyer, 4 Goulburn Street, Sydney 2000, Australia

DOYLE, DAVID PATRICK, marketing and cost management specialist, educator, writer; b. Dublin, Ireland, June 2, 1952; s. Patrick and Kathleen (O'Connor) D.; m. Pascale Ovart, Oct. 5, 1984; children: Marie-Astrid, Constance. Higher diploma in Mktg., Dublin Inst. Tech., 1974; diploma in Stats., Trinity Coll. U., Dublin, 1975; MBA, Mktg. Inst. Ireland, 1975. Trade advisor Irish Trade Bd., Paris, 1975-77; account exec. Ted Bates S.A., Paris, 1978-79; dep. fin. contr. Orgn. Econ. Cooperation and Devel., Paris, 1980-84, budget officer, 1985-90, adminstr., coun. sec., 1991-96; adj. prof. Am. U. Paris, 1985-89; spkr./lectr. Mgmt. Ctr. Europe, Brussels, 1981-98; vis. prof. Hautes Études Commerciales (HEC) Bus. Sch., Paris, 1989—; spkr. Chartered Inst. Mgmt. Accts. (CIMA), London, 1992; vis. prof. Essec Sch. Mgmt., Paris, 1996—. Author: Strategic Management/Le Management Strategique, 1990, Cost Control: A Strategic Guide, 1994, Adding Value to Marketing, 1999. Mem. Mktg. Inst. Ireland (grad.). Avocation: golf. Home: Villa Mayfair, 28 Rue Pasteur, 92210 Saint Cloud France

DOYLE, EL MARQUES DECLAN, tourism professional; b. Wexford, Ireland, July 10, 1954; s. Martin Doyle and Eileen Finery; m. Condesa Eugenia Villalobos. Diploma in Econs., U.C.D., Dublin, 1976; Diploma in Mktg., Harvard U., 1977; Diploma, BGT, Madrid, 1989. Ptnr. EGM & G, Dublin, 1978-81; owner Matton, Ltd., Dublin, 1980-85, CIVL, Spain, 1984-97, Mammon S.A., Spain, 1989-97; dir. Expo Ager S.A., Spain, 1993—; dir./del. FAI, Paris, 1984—. Patentee in field. Mayor of Town Coun., Ager, 1994. Office: c/ La Fent S/N, C Marques Ager, 25691 2 Lieida Spain

DOYLE, GERARD FRANCIS, lawyer; b. Needham, Mass., Oct. 25, 1942; s. John Patrick and Catherine Mary (Lawler) D.; m. Paula Marie Dervay, may 14, 1983; children: Laura Dervay, Meredith Lawler, Philip John. BS in Indsl. Adminstrn., Yale U., 1966; JD, Georgetown U., 1972. Bar: D.C. 1973, U.S. Dist. Ct. D.C. 1973, U.S. Ct. Fed. Claims 1976, U.S. Ct. Appeals (fed. cir.) 1982, U.S. Supreme Ct. 1982, Va. 2000. Group head for operating submarine reactors and reactor tech Div. Naval Reactors AEC, Washington, 1970-72; atty. Morgan, Lewis & Bockius, Washington, 1972-76; legal counsel Am. Nuclear Energy Coun., Washington, 1975-76; ptnr. Cotten, Day & Doyle, Washington, 1976-87; ptnr. Doyle & Savit, Doyle, Simmons & Bachman, Doyle & Bachman, Washington, 1987-99, Arlington, Va., 1999—; legal counsel Assn. Fed. Data Peripheral Suppliers, Washington, 1979; dir. M Internat., Inc.; author and lectr. in field; columnist Federal Computer Week, 1989. Served in USN, 1966-71. Recipient outstanding young man of yr. award, 1976. Mem. ABA (coun. publ. contract law sect. 1989-92), D.C. Bar Assn., Fed. Bar Assn., Am. Arbitration Assn. (panel arbitrators), Nat. Contract Mgmt. Assn., Met. Club (Washington), Yale Club (Washington), Washington Golf & Country Club. Republican. Roman Catholic. Home: 901 Whann Ave Mc Lean VA 22101-1570 Office: Doyle & Bachman 4245 Fairfax Dr Arlington VA 22203-1637

DOYLE, MICHAEL WILLIAM, political science educator; b. Honolulu, Sept. 14, 1948; s. William Francis and Marie (Kornely) D.; m. Amy Gutmann; 1 child, Abigail. BA, Harvard U., 1970, PhD, 1977. Lectr. U. Warwick (Eng.), 1976-77; asst. prof. Princeton (N.J.) U., 1977-84, prof., 1987—, Sanford prof. politics and internat. affairs, 1999—; dir. Ctr. Internat. Studies, 1997—; from asst. to assoc. prof. Johns Hopkins U., Balt., 1984-87; Welling prof. George Washington U., Washington, 1999-2000; Benjamin Meaker prof. U. Bristol (Eng.), 1999; bd. trustees Princeton U. Press, 1999—. Author: Empires, 1986, UN Peacekeeping in Cambodia, 1995, Ways of War and Peace, 1997; chmn. editl. bd. World Politics, 1997—. V.p. Internat. Peace Acad., N.Y.C., 1993-94. Mem. Coun. Fgn. Rels. Office: Princeton U Ctr Internat Studies Bendheim Hl Princeton NJ 08544-0001

DOYLE, PATRICK JAMES, pharmacologist; b. Salisbury, Eng., Dec. 10, 1964; s. Michael Patrick and Maureen Doris (White) D.; m. Sophie Athena Gwenael Nortier-Desfaveries, July 9, 1993; children: Victor James, Sebastian Michael Patrick. BSc in Pharmacology, Sunderland Polytech., 1986; PhD of Pharmacology, Sunderland U., 1990. Postdoctoral rschr. U. Geneva, 1990; investigator, instr. Geneva Dept. Pub. Instrn., 1993-96; cons. Nat. Cons. Referals, Inc., San Diego, 1994. Contbr. articles to profl. jours. Mem. Irish Assn., Berne, Geneva, 1993—. Grantee Swiss NSF, 1994-96. Mem. Internat. Brain Rsch. Orgn., Internat. Diabetes Fedn. (life), European

Neurosci. Assn., N.Y. Acad. Scis., Human Brain Map Project, Am. Physiol. Soc. Avocations: rugby, squash. Home: Freie Strasse 11, 4001 Basel Switzerland Office: F Hoffman La-Roche, PRBM, Basel Switzerland

DOYLE, WILL LEE, writer, editor; b. Bklyn., Apr. 27, 1919; s. John Joseph and Mary Elizabeth (Farley) D.; m. Adele Virginia Puricelli, Mar. 21, 1947; children: Grace, Rosemary, Barbara, Joan. Student, NYU, 1946. Copywriter Geyer, Newell & Ganger Agy., N.Y.C., 1946-52; copy supr., client liaison N.W. Ayer & Son, Inc., N.Y.C., Phila., 1953-59, Lambert & Feasley, Albert Frank Guenther Law, Levitt & Sons, N.Y.C., 1960-69; editor The Canarsie Courier, Bklyn., 1969-73; editor bldg. code, elec. code, city charter The Ofcl. Directory of the City of N.Y., N.Y.C., 1973-84; ret., 1984; guest judge poetry The Lyric Mag., Blacksburg, Va., 1993. Author: (plays) The Fubliks' Pickle, 1985, David the King, 1987, Rising Star, 1988, Storms at Evening, 1992, (books) The Limerick Odyssey, 1993, A Mem-War, 1994, The Hammers of Homer, 1995. With 755th Tank Battalion, 1941-45. Recipient Cert. of Recognition, Am. TV Commls. Festival, N.Y.C., 1962; other various certs. and citations. Avocations: gardening, billiards. Home: 168 Wittenberg Rd Bearsville NY 12409

DOYLE, WILLIAM, historian, educator; b. Burton Agnes, Yorkshire, Eng., Mar. 4, 1942; s. Stanley Joseph and Mary Alice (Bielby) D.; m. Christine Thomas, Aug. 2, 1968. BA, Oriel Coll., Oxford, 1964, MA, 1968, DPhil, 1968. Lectr. U. York, Eng., 1967-81; prof. modern history U. Nottingham, Eng., 1981-85; prof. history U. Bristol, Eng., 1986—; vis. prof. U. S.C., Columbia, 1969-70, U. Bordeaux, France, 1976, EHESS, Paris, 1988, All Souls Coll., Oxford, 1991-92. Author: The Parlement of Bordeaux, 1974, Old European Order, 1978, Origins of French Revolution, 1980, Oxford History of the French Revolution, 1989, Officers Nobles & Revolutionaries, 1995, Venality, The Sale of Offices in the Eighteenth Century France, 1996, Jansenism, 1999, La Vénalité, 2000; contbr. articles to profl. jours. Fellow British Acad., Royal Hist. Soc.; mem. Academie de Bordeaux, Academie de Besancon, United Oxford Cambridge Club, Athenaeum Club. Avocations: books, traveling. Office: U Bristol Dept Hist Studies, 13 Woodland Rd, Bristol BS8 1TB, England

DOYLE-MARINO, HELEN, special education educator; b. Belleville, N.J., Oct. 26, 1970; d. James Martin and Theresa Ann Doyle; m. Christopher Michael Marino, June 30, 1996. BA in Spl. Edn., William Paterson Coll., Wayne, N.J., 1995; MA in Spl. Edn., N.J. City U., Jersey City, 1999, MA in Urban Edn. and Adminstrn., 2000. Cert. supr., N.J. Asst. tchr. Deron Sch., South Orange, N.J., 1988-90; tchr. of handicapped Kearny (N.J.) Bd. Edn., 1996-97; dir. for adults with disabilities, program dir. Mal Condon Canteen, Belleville, 1994—; support provider Easter Seals of N.J., Belvidere, 1997—; tchr. of handicapped for learning disabled Montclair (N.J.) Bd. Edn., 1997-99; tchr. of handicapped for mild cognitively impaired Nutley (N.J.) Bd. Edn., 1999—. Office: Nutley Bd Edn 301 Harrison St Nutley NJ 07110-2614

DOZ, ANDRÉ, philosopher, educator; b. Issy Les Moulineaux, France, Aug. 13, 1928; s. Barthélemy Doz and Hélène Batardon; m. Claire Schiff, Aug. 24, 1953; children: Catherine, Sylvie, Francois. Degree, Sorbonne U., 1950, PhD, 1969; Doctorat d'Etat, U. Poitiers, 1986. Rschr. Ctr. Nat. Rsch. Sci., Paris, 1957-62; tchr. Ecole Normale D'Instituteurs, Orleans, Le Bourget, France, 1962-69; asst., lectr. U. Amiens, France, 1969-88; prof. U. Dijon, France, 1988-94; prof. emeritus U. Dijon, 1994—. Transl., commentor Hegel, La Théorie de la Mesure, 1970, 2d edit., 1994; author: La Logique de Hegel et les Problèmes Traditionnels de L'Ontologie, 1987; editl. staff mem. Paroisse U., 1996—; contbr. articles to profl. jours. Roman Catholic. Home: 12 Square Desaix, 75015 Paris France

DOZ, YVES LUCIEN, researcher; b. Paris, Sept. 8, 1947; m. Nicole Lesk Doz; children: Marianne, Gabriel. MBA, HEC, Jouy, France, 1970; DBA, Harvard U., 1976. Mgr. SNIAS, Marignane, France, 1970-71; lectr. CESA, Jouy, 1971-73; rschr. Harvard U., Boston, 1974-76; asst. prof. Harvard U., 1976-80; assoc. prof. INSEAD, Fontainebleu, 1981-86, prof., 1986—; faculty dir. MTI, INSEAD, 1987-94; John H. Loudon prof. internat. mgmt. INSEAD, 1990-94, Timken prof. of global tech. and innovation, 1994—. Author: Alliance Advantage, 1998, The Multinational Mission, 1987, Strategic Management in Multinational, 1986, Government Control and Multinational Management, 1979. Fellow Acad. of Internat. Bus.; Acad. of Mgmt., Strategic Mgmt. Soc. Office: INSEAD, Bld de Constance, 77305 Fontainebleu Cedex France

DOZIER, WILLIAM EVERETT, JR., newspaper editor and publisher; b. Delhi, La., June 12, 1922; s. William Everett and Harriet E. (Miles) D.; m. Eleanor Ruth Roye, Sept. 1, 1944; children: Martha Carolyn Dozier Hunnicutt (dec. July 1995), Sarah Rebecca. BA in Journalism, La. Tech. U., 1943. Assoc. editor Delhi Dispatch, 1936-39; reporter, state editor New Orleans Times-Picayune, 1946-50; editor Courier-Times-Telegraph, Tyler, Tex., 1952-65; pres., editor, pub. Kerrville (Tex.) Daily Times, 1965-88; pres. Hills o'Texas Publs., Inc., 1982-92; gen. ptnr. Frio-Nueces Publs. Ltd., 1976—. V.P. Kerrville Music Found. and Performing Arts Soc., 1978-84, also bd. dirs.; bd.d irs. Adm. Nimitz Ctr. Found., Fredericksburg, Tex., 1976—; chmn. United Fund campaign, Kerrville, 1967; mem. adv. bd. Salvation Army, 1967—; v.p. Tex. State Arts & Crafts Fair Assn., 1980-90, also bd. dirs., 1972-92; lay leader First United Meth. Ch., Kerrville, 1984-86, past chmn. bd. trustees, chmn. adminstrv. bd.; trustee Schreiner Coll., 1987-96, 97—, Sid Peterson Meml. Hosp., 1989—. Served with USN, 1943-46, 50-52, ret. comdr., 1973. Mem. Am. Soc. Newspaper Editors, Am. Newspaper Pubs. Assn., Nat. Newspaper Assn., Tex. AP Mng. Editors Assn. (pres. 1964-65), Tex. Press Assn. (pres. 1979-80), Tex. Daily Newspaper Assn. (dir. 1984-87), Tex. Press Found. (pres. 1982-92), So. Newspaper Pubs. Assn. (chmn. smaller newspaper com. 1983-84, dir. 1984-87), Kerr County C. of C. (pres. 1973-74), W. Tex. C. of C. (regional v.p. 1981-84, pres. 1985-86), Tex. C. of C. (founding dir. 1987-90), Masons (Tyler), Kiwanis (lt. gov. divsn. 5 Tex.-Okla. dist. 1974, pres. Kerrville 1973, Disting. Club Pres. 1973, Disting. Lt. Gov. 1974), Sigma Delta Chi. Home: 2428 Rock Creek Dr Kerrville TX 78028-6504 Office: 815 Jefferson St Ste A Kerrville TX 78028-4581

DRABANT, BERNHARD, mathematical physicist, researcher; b. Karlsruhe, Germany, June 5, 1963; s. Joachim and Anneliese (Ruckgaber) D. PhD in Math. Physics, U. Munich, 1993. Postgrad. rsch. fellow Max-Planck Inst. for Physics, Munich, 1991-93; guest scientist Max-Planck Inst., Munich, 1993-94; German Sci. Found. rsch. fellow dept. math. U. Amsterdam, The Netherlands, 1994-95; assoc. rschr. dept. math. U. Leuven, Belgium, 1996-97; vis. investigator dept. theoretical physics U. Valencia, Spain, 1997—; rsch. assoc. dept. applied math. theoretical physics U. Cambridge, Eng., 1998—. Contbr. articles to profl. jours. Fgn. Investigator grantee Spanish Ministry of Edn. and Sci., 1996, associated sci. grantee Rsch. Coun., U. Leuven, 1995, Marie-Curie grantee European Union, 1997, rsch. grantee German Sci. Found., 1994, Royal Soc. Visitor grant, 1999; Bye fellow Robinson Coll., U. Cambridge, Eng., 1999. Fellow Cambridge Philos. Soc. Office: Dept Applied Math and Theoretical Physics, U Cambridge/Silver St, Cambridge CB3 9EW, England

DRABBLE, MARGARET, writer; b. Sheffield, England, June 5, 1939; d. John Frederick and Kathleen Marie (Bloor) D.; m. Clive Swift, June 27, 1960 (div. 1975); children: Adam, Rebecca, Joseph; m. Michael Holroyd, 1982. BA with honors, Newnham Coll., Cambridge, 1960; DLitt (hon.), U. Sheffield, 1976, U. Manchester, 1987, U. Keele, 1988, U. Bradford, 1988, U. East Anglia, 1994, U. York, 1995. Author: (novels) A Summer Bird-Cage, 1963, The Garrick Year, 1964, The Millstone, 1965 (John Llewelyn Rhys Meml. award 1966), Jerusalem the Golden, 1967 (James Tait Black Meml. book prize 1968), The Waterfall, 1969, The Needle's Eye, 1972 (Yorkshire Post Book of Yr. award 1972), The Realms of Gold, 1975, The Ice Age, 1977, The Middle Ground, 1980 (ALA notable book citation 1981), The Radiant Way, 1987, A Natural Curiosity, 1989, Gates of Ivory, 1991, The Witch of Exmoor, 1996, Angus Wilson: A Biography, 1995; (short stories) Hassan's Tower, 1966, The Reunion, 1968, The Gifts of War, 1970; (non-fiction) Arnold Bennett, A Biography, 1974, For Queen and Country: Britain in the Victorian Age, 1978, A Writer's Britain, 1979; (play) Bird of Paradise, 1969; (screenplays) Laura, 1964, Isadora, 1968, Thank You All Very Much, 1969; (criticism) Wordsworth, 1966; editor: Jane Austen, Lady Susan, The Watsons, and Sanditon, 1975, The Genius of Thomas Hardy, 1976, Oxford Companion to English Literature, 1985, 6th edit., 2000, The Concise Oxford Companion to English Literature, 1987, Angus Wilson a Biography, 1995. Recipient E.M. Forster award Natl. Inst. and Am. Acad. of Arts and Letters, 1973. Office: care Peters Fraser & Dunlop, Drury House 34-43 Russell St, London WC2B 5HA, England

DRABEK, ANNA MARIA, historian; b. Vienna, Austria, Apr. 23, 1936; d. Josef and Ludmila (Pecina) D. PhD, U. Vienna, 1964. Asst. U. Vienna, 1964-71; rschr., adminstrv. asst. Österreichische Acad. Wissenschaften, Vienna, 1971-97; lectr. U. Wien, Inst. for Geschichte, Inst. for Slawistik, Vienna, 1980—. Author: Reisen and Reisezeremoniell der Römischdeutschen Herrscher im Spätmittelalter, 1964, Die Verträge der Fränkisch-deutschen Herrscher, 1976; co-author: Die Juden in den Böhmischen Ländern, 1983, Die Böhmischen Länder Zwischen Ost and West. Festschhrift f. Karl Bosl, hrsg. v. Karl Seibt, 1983, Prag-Czernowitz-Jerusalem Der Österreichische Staat and die Juden vom Zeitalter des Absolutismus bis zum Ende der Monarchie, 1984, Volk, Land and Staat. LandesbewuBtsein, Staatidee and Nationale Frage in der Geschichte Österreichs, 1984, Vereinswesen and Geschichtspflege in den Böhmischen Ländern, 1986, T.G. Masaryk (1850-1937), vol. 2, 1989, Vaterlandsliebe and Gesamtstaatsidee im Österreichischen 18, Jahrhundert, 1989, Standefreiheit und Staatsgestaltung in Ostmitteleuropa, 1996; co-author, co-editor: RuBland and Österreich zur Zeit der Napoleonischen Kriege, 1989; co-editor: Veröffentlichungen der Kommission for die Geschichte Österreichs, 1997, Zentraleuropa-Studien, 1997; contbr. articles to profl. jours. Mem. Inst. for Österreichische Geschichtsforschung, Historische Kommission der Österreichischen Acad. Wissenschaften, Inst. for Geschichte der Juden in Österreich (adv. bd. 1987—), Österreichische Gesellschaft für Geschichte des 18 Jahrhunderts Internat. Commn. for the History of Rep. and Parliamentary Instns., Historische Commn. der Böhmischen Länder (bd. dirs.), Collegium Carolinum. Avocations: music, literature, philosophy, theology. Home: Starkfriedg 16/1, Vienna A-1190, Austria

DRÁBEK, PAVEL, mathematician, educator; b. Pardubice, Czech Republic, July 29, 1953; s. Oldřich and Zdeňka (Chocholoušová) D.; m. Danuše Hlavsová, Mar. 26, 1977; children: Danuše, Pavel. MS, Charles U., Prague, Czech Republic, 1977; Cand. Sci., Acad. Scis., Prague, 1981, ScD, 1990. Rsch. fellow Math. Inst. of Acad. Sci., Prague, 1977-78; lector Tech. U., Plzeň, Czech Republic, 1978-79, asst. prof., 1979-87, assoc. prof., 1987-91; prof. math. U. West Bohemia, Plzeň, 1991—, chmn. dept. math., 1990-99. Author: Solvability and Bifurcation of Nonlinear Equations, 1992, Integrálni Rovnice, 1991; co-author: Integralgleichungen, 1996, Quasilinear Degenerated and Singular Equations of Elliptic Type, 1997. Mem. Am. Math. Soc., European Math. Soc., Union Czech Mathematicians and Physicists. Avocations: tennis, soccer, tourism. Office: Univ of West Bohemia, Univerzitni 22, 30614 Plzen Czech Republic

DRABIK, PIOTR, molecular biologist, chemist, educator; b. Zamosc, Poland, May 14, 1972; s. Jozef and Zofia (Tokarczyk) D. M Athletic Tng., U. Sch. Phys. Edn., Gdansk, Poland, 1995, D Athletic Tng., 1998; M Molecular Biology, U. Gdansk, 1997. Asst. U. Sch. Physical Edn., 1995-97, tutor, 1997—. Co-author: Physical Activity, 1996; contbr. articles to profl. jours. Recipient 9th pl. European Championship Taekwondo, 1996. Avocations: taekwondo, astronomy, philosophy. Home: Gdanca St 10B/34, 80-321 Gdańsk Poland Office: U Gdańsk Fac Chemistry, Stowackiego 18, 80-952 Gdańsk Poland

DRABKOVA, VALENTINA GAVRILOVNA, microbiologist, researcher; b. Bologoe, Tver, USSR, Dec. 7, 1936; d. Gavriil Efimovir and Anna Andreevna (Abramova) D. MSc, Leningrad State U., 1961; PhD, Fishery Inst., St. Petersburg, 1967; DSc, Moscow State U., 1985. Rsch. asst. Inst. Limnology Russian Acad. Scis., Leningrad, 1961-67, jr. rsch. scientist, 1967-71, sr. rsch. scientist, 1971-83, chief lab., 1983-89; dep. dir. Inst. Limnology Russian Acad. Scis., St. Petersburg, 1989—, mem. sci. coun., 1970—, vice chmn. spl. sci. coun. for acad. degrees, 1991—; Author: Intensity of Microbiological Processes in Lakes, 1981; contbr. more than 150 articles to profl. jours. Recipient Medal of Order of Merit to Fatherland Pres. of Russia. Mem. Club of Scientists. Avocation: historical literature. Home: Kondratievski pr 61-25, 195197 Saint Petersburg Russia Office: Russian Acad Scis Inst Limn, Sevastyanova 9, 196105 Saint Petersburg Russia

DRACHNIK, CATHERINE MELDYN, art therapist, artist, counselor; b. Kansas City, Mo., June 7, 1924; d. Gerald Willis and Edith (Gray) Weston; m. Joseph Brennan Drachnik, Oct. 6, 1946; children: Denise Elaine, Kenneth John. BS, U. Md., 1945; MA, Calif. State U., Sacramento, 1975. Lic. family and child counselor; registered art therapist. Art therapist Vincent Hall Retirement Home, McLean, Va., Fairfax Mental Health Day Treatment Ctr., McLean, Arlington (Va.) Mental Health Day Treatment Ctr., 1971-72, Hope for Retarded, San Jose, Calif., Sequoia Hosp., Redwood City, Calif., 1972-73; supervising tchr. adult edn. Sacramento Soc. Blind, 1975-77; ptnr. Sacramento Divsn. Mediation Svcs., 1981-82; instr. Calif. State U., Sacramento, 1975-82, 92-93, 1999; instr. Coll. Notre Dame, Belmont, Calif., 1975-96; art therapist, mental health counselor Psych West Counseling Ctr. (formerly Eskaton Am. River Mental Health Clinic), Carmichael, Calif., 1975-93; instr. Sacramento City Coll., 1997—; instr. U. Utah, Salt Lake City, 1988-92; lectr. in field. uthor: Interpreting Metaphors in Children's Drawings, 1995; one-woman shows include Vacaville (Calif.) Art Gallery, 1995, Dublier Gallery, Sacramento, 1997, Thistle Dew Gallery, Sacramento, 1998, Jeffery Bldg. Gallery, Sacramento; exhibited in group shows Art of Calif. Mag., 1993, Calif. State Fair, Sacramento, 1995, 97, 98, 2000, Haggin Art Mus., Stockton, Calif. 1994, 95, 96, 97, 98, 99, 2000, Watercolor West, Brea, Calif., 1998, West Valley Art Mus., Phoenix, Rocky Mountain Nat. Watercolor, Golden, Colo., 1999, Elliot Fouts Art Gallery, Granite Bay, Calif., 1999, Am. Watercolor Soc., N.Y., 2000. Active charitable orgns. Mem. Am. Art Therapy Assn. (hon. life, pres. 1987-89), No. Calif. Art Therapy Assn. (hon. life), No. Calif. Arts, Inc., Nat. Art Edn. Assn., Am. Assn. Marriage and Family Therapists, Kappa Kappa Gamma Alumnae Assn. (pres. Sacramento Valley chpt. 1991-92), Alpha Psi Omega, Omicron Nu. Republican. Avocations: swimming, golf, theater. Home and Office: 4124 American River Dr Sacramento CA 95864-6025

DRACKER, ROBERT ALBERT, physician; b. Queens, N.Y., July 28, 1956; s. Albert Donald and Lee (Patruno) D.; m. Maria Elizabeth DiRubbo Dracker; children: Maria Lynn, Robert, Michael. BA in Biology, N.Y.U., 1978; MD, SUNY Health Sci. Ctr., 1982; MS in Health Svcs. Mgmt., New Sch. for Social Rsch., N.Y.C., 1995. Intern dept. pediat. SUNY Health Sci. Ctr., Syracuse, 1982-83, resident dept. pediat., 1983-85, fellow in pediatric hematology and oncology, 1985-87, fellow in blood banking and transfusion medicine, 1987-88, rsch. asst. prof. dept. pathology, 1988-89, dir. transfusion medicine dept. pathology, 1989-93; attending physician ARC, 1994-98; pvt. practice, North Syracuse, N.Y., 1988—; med. dir. and founder Infusacare Med. Svcs., P.C., N. Area Pediat., P.C.; rsch. scientist I Masonic Med. Rsch. Lab., Utica, N.Y., 1989—; med. dir. MetraHealth Ctrl. N.Y., 1995-97; assoc. med. dir. POMCO, Syracuse, 1994-97; med. dir. Viacord Inc., Boston, 1998—; med. advisor, reviewer Ctrl. N.Y. Blue Cross/Blue Shield, Health Svcs. Adminstrn.; chmn. Ctr. N.Y. Divsn. Review Island Peer Review Orgn., 1988-90; physician reviewer N.Y. State Office of Med. Misconduct; physician reviewer for dispute resolution, Empire State Med. Scientific and Edn. Found.; consulting physician Jowonio Sch., 1983-85, Devillo Sloan Sch. for Handicapped, 1983-85, Walsh Med. Facility, N.Y. State Dept. Corrections, 1991-97; Neonatal Transport Physician, 1983-86; med. dir. MRDS, Syracuse, 1999—. Contbr. numerous abstracts, letters, presentations, articles to profl. jours. Recipient AMA Physicians' Recognition award 1989-92, 92-95, 95-98, 99—, N.Y.U. Alumni award, The Dr. Charipper award, Pediatric Resident Teaching award; grantee Nat. Heart, Lung and Blood Inst, 1984-89, 88-90, Cutter Divsn.of Miles Labs., 1988-89, 90- 91, Pathology Med. Svc. Group SUNY Health Sci. Ctr., 1991-92, Hendricks Fund SUNY Health Sci. Ctr. at Syracuse, 1992. Mem. ARC, AMA, Ctrl. N.Y. AIDS Profl. Group, Vis. Nurse Assn. Ctrl. N.Y., N.Y. State Dept. Health, Ctrl. N.Y. Hosp. Assn., Just For Babies, St. Joseph's Hosp. and Health Ctr., Cmty. Gen. Hosp., Crouse Irving Meml. Hosp., Patients' Choice, Am. Assn. Blood Banks, Am. Acad. Pediatrics, Blood Bank Assn. N.Y. State, Am. Soc. for Apheresis, Med. Soc. N.Y. State, Onodaga County Med. Soc., Onondaga County Pediatric Soc., Internat. Soc. of Hematotherapy and Graft Engring., Am. Soc. for Blood and Marrow Transplantation, Am. Acad. Pediatrics, Phi Beta Kappa, Alpha Omega Alpha. Roman Catholic. Avocations: reading, woodworking, research and development, coaching baseball, photography.

DRAEGER, KENNETH W., retired high technology company executive; b. Wyandotte, Mich., July 30, 1940; s. Wilfred Draeger and Marjorie (Rapp) Draeger Fair; m. Carol Ann Ahola, Sept. 7, 1963; children: Kimberley, Tracey. BS, Western Mich. U., 1962; MBA, Wayne State U., 1967. Analyst fin. staff Fort Motor Co., Dearborn, Mich., 1964-69; exec. v.p. Cyphernetics Corp., Ann Arbor, Mich., 1969-76; pres. ADP Network Svc. Div., Ann Arbor, Mich., 1976-81; group v.p. Informatics Gen. Corp., Franklin Lakes, N.J., 1981-84; chmn., chief exec. officer, pres. Compute Corp. of Am., Cambridge, Mass., 1984-86; chief exec. officer, pres. Autographix, Waltham, Mass., 1986-88; pres. Agfa Compugraphic, Wilmington, Mass., 1988-92; chmn., CEO, bd. dirs. DecisionOne Corp., Frazer, Pa., 1992-98, chmn., 1992-98; ret. DecisionOne Corp., Frazer, 1998; bd. dirs. Galileo Electro-Optics Corp., Sturbridge, Mass. Home: 41238 N 109th Pl Scottsdale AZ 85262-3223

DRAGAN, JOSIF CONSTANTIN, gas industry executive; b. Lugoj, Romania, June 20, 1917; arrived in Italy, 1941; s. Stefan and Cornelia Livia (Murariu) D.; m. Teresa Maria Morighoni Guglielmi, May 9, 1959 (Mar. 1986); m. Daniela Veronica Gusa, Nov. 16, 1995. LLM, U. Bucharest, Romania, 1938; LLD, U. Rome, 1940, M in Polit. Econ. Scis., 1961; Dr. h.c., U. Craiova, Romania, 1995. Pres., mng. dir. Butan Gas, Rome, Italy, 1948—, Romania; pres., mng. dir. Petrogaz, Athens, Greece, Propangas, Wien, Austria, Drachen Gas, Frankfurt, Germany, Dragon Gas, Tanger, Morocco; pres., founder European Dragan Found., Italy, Spain, Romania, 1967—, Superior Ctr. Adv. Bus. Mgmt., Bucharest, Dragan European U., Lugoj; pres. Italian Romanian C. of C., Milan, Bucharest, 1973—. Founder, editor Bull. Européen, Rome, 1950—; author: From Dracula's Country, 1973, We, The Thracians, 2 vols., 1976, Geoclimate and History, 1989, The True History of Romanians, 1996. Pres. UNESCO Ctr., Milan; pres., founder Golden Age U., Milan; Gt. Referendary Archont, Ecumenical Orthodox Ch., Constantinople. Recipient Gold medal for cultural merits Italian Ministry Instrn.; named Cavaliere Gran Croce al Merito, Pres. of Italian Rep., Rome, Commander of Order of King Constantine of Greece; recipient Gold medal of European Worth, Luxembourg. Mem. Soc. del Giardino Milan, Giuridic Studies Inst. Rome, Rotary, Romania Assn. European Unity (pres. 1949), Roma. Mem. Gt. Conservative Party London. Mem. Romanian Cath. United Ch. Avocations: yachting, diving. Office: Butan Gas SpA, Via Larga 9/11, 20122 Milan Lombardy, Italy

DRAGANOVA, NADEJDA IVANOVA, physician, educator; b. Byal Briag, Shumen, Bulgaria, Sept. 27, 1938; d. Ivan and Ivanka Ivanova (Markova) D.; m. Ditcho Pentchev Dimov, Dec. 10, 1961; children: Ivailo, Nevena. MD, Higher Med. U., Sofia, Bulgaria, 1962; PhD, Med. Acad., Sofia, 1977. Lic. physician occupational health. Pvt. practice City Hosp., Sevlievo, Bulgaria, 1962-68; rsch. scientist Nat. Inst. Occupational Health, Sofia, 1968-74, Med. Acad., Sofia, 1974-88; assoc. prof. Nat. Ctr. Hygiene, Sofia, 1988—; expert occupl. health Ministry Health, Sofia, 1995—; cons. occupl. hygiene Ministry Health, Sofia, 1996—. Co-author: Ergonomics in Industry, 1969; inventor hand-dynamometer, 1977; contbr. articles to profl. jours. Fellow Union Scientist in Bulgaria; mem. Bulgarian Med. Assn. Avocations: tourism, classical music, jazz, gardening. Home: Midjur Str 29, 1421 Sofia Bulgaria Office: Nat Ctr Hygiene, 1431 Sofia Bulgaria

DRAGILA, STACY, track and field athlete; b. Auburn, Calif., Mar. 25, 1971. Major meets include placing 1st in pole vaulting USA, 1996, USA Indoor, 1996, 2nd USA, 1995. Office: 1 Rca Dome Indianapolis IN 46225-1023

DRAGO, JOSEPH ROSARIO, urologist, educator; b. Jersey City, N.J., Oct. 28, 1947; m. Diane Lavacca; children: Andrea, Daniella, Denise. BS, U. Ill., 1968, MD, 1972. Diplomate Nat. Bd. Med. Examiners, Am. Bd. Urology; cert. Yag Laser, laparoscopic surgery. Intern Pa. State U. Milton S. Hershey Med. Ctr., 1972-73, resident in urology, 1973-77, instr. urology, 1976-77; asst. prof. urology, dir. urology oncology U. Calif., Davis, 1977-79; asst. prof. urology, dir. urology oncology Milton S. Hershey (Pa.) Med. Ctr., 1979-80, assoc. prof. to prof. of surgery, dir. urologic oncology, 1980-85; assoc. staff Children's Hosp., Columbus, Ohio, 1985—; interim chief of staff elect, prof., dir. urologic oncology Ohio State U. Arthur G. James Cancer Hosp., Columbus, Ohio, 1990-92; with Easton (Pa.) Warren Urology, Easton, Pa., 1992-95; pvt. practice Washington, N.J., 1995—; Mem. editl. bd. In Vivo Jour.; advisor Internat. Urologic Svcs., Inc., 1987; cons. in field; visiting prof. over 30 univs. and hosps. Author 12 book chpts.; reviewer various profl. jours., 1979—; contbr. articles to profl. jours. Recipient various rsch. grants, 1978-81. Fellow Internat. Coll. Surgeons in Urology; mem. AMA, Am. Coll. Surgeons, Am. Fertility Soc., Am. Inst. Ultrasound in Medicine, Am. Soc. Andrology, Am. Urologic Assn., Assn. Academic Surgery, Assn. Surgical Edn., Hershey Surgical Soc. (sec.-treas. 1983-85), Pa. Med. Soc., Phila. Urologic Soc., others. Home: 3295 Beaufort Dr Bethlehem PA 18017-1955 Office: 224 Roseberry St Phillipsburg NJ 08865-1632

DRAGOLJUB, KOCIĆ ALEKSANDAR, physician, administrator; b. Niš, Serbia, Sept. 2, 1930; s. Aleksandar and Ljubica (Savic) Kocić; m. Sonja Dunkic, Mar. 11, 1931; children: Alen, Aleksandra. MA, Sch. Medicine, Zagreb, Croatia, 1957; postgrad., Sch. Pub. Health, Zagreb, 1962; MSc, Sch. A. Stampar, Zagreb, 1967; diploma in internal medicine, U. Hosp. Clinic, Zagreb, 1968. Physician Med. Ctr., Požega, Croatia, 1959-72; head dept. internal medicine Gen. Hosp. Med. Ctr., Nova Gradiška, Croatia, 1972—; head allergy dept. Gen. Hosp., 1972—. Mem. Croatian Med. Assn., Hrvatski Lije cnicki Zbor (diplomate). Avocations: sculpture, radioamaterism, philatelia. Home: Çvjetni Trg 12 D/I, RH35400 Nova Gradiska Croatia Office: Gen Hosp, Štrosmajerova 17, RH35400 Nova Gradiska Croatia

DRAGOUN, OTOKAR, physicist, researcher; b. Sedlec, Czech Republic, Mar. 15, 1937; s. Otakar and Pavlína (Štréblová) D.; m. Naděžda Novotná, July 5, 1961; children: Ivana, Alena. Diploma in engring., Czech Tech. U., Prague, 1962; PhD, Czech. Acad. Sci., Prague, 1967; DSc, Charles U., Prague, 1985. Rschr. Nuclear Physics Inst. Czech Acad. Sci., Prague, 1962-67; postdoctoral fellow Max-Planck-Inst. for Nuclear Physics, Heidelberg, Germany, 1966-69; head of rsch. group Nuclear Physics Inst. Czech Acad. Scis., Prague, 1971—; sr. scientist Nuclear Physics Inst. Czech Acad. Sci., Prague, 1985—; vis. prof. faculty physics Tech. U., Munich, summer 1992, spring 1994; vice-chmn. com. for def. of PhD thesis Acad. Sci., Prague, 1985-91; mem. com. for def. of DSc thesis, Charles U., Prague, 1986—, mem. sci. coun., faculty math. and physics, 1993-96, external lectr., 1986—. Contbr. revs. and sci. papers to profl. publs.; patentee in field. Mem. Union Czech Math. and Physicists (Medal Sci. Achievement 1988). Office: Acad Sci Czech Republic, Nuclear Physics Inst, CZ-25068 Rez Czech Republic

DRAGSETH, JOYCE LYNN, county official; b. Colman, S.D., Dec. 24, 1950; d. George Edward and Gladys Lucille (Almquist) Amert; m. John Albert Dragseth, Sept. 27, 1969; children: Gregory, Bradley, Amy. Cert. appraiser/assessor, S.D. Computer coord. Chuck's Jack and Jill, Madison, S.D.; dep. dir. equalization Lake County Govt., Madison, dir. equalization. Pres. Ch. Women of Life, Nunda, S.D., 1995, sec., 2000; fin. officer Town of Nunda, 1985—. Mem. S.D. Assn. of Assessing Officers (dist. chair, edn. com., audit com., class instr., nominating com., legis. com.), N. Ctrl. Region of Assn. of Assessing Officers. Democrat. Lutheran. Avocations: quilting, gardening, reading. Home: PO Box 125 210 Church Dr Nunda SD 57050 Office: Lake County Govt 200 E Center St Madison SD 57042-2956

DRAGULIN, DAN, engineering educator; b. Bucharest, Romania, Oct. 23, 1967; s. Mircea and Adina Michaela (Tomescu) D.; m. Elisabeta Mihaela Antonescu, July 1, 1987 (div. Jan. 1996); 1 child, Mircea. Degree in Engring., U. Bucharest, Romania, 1992, Doctor Degree, 1998; LSM, Tech. U. Darmstadt, GErmany, 2000. Rsch. engr. Nat. Inst. Heat Techs., Bucharest, Romania, 1992-95; vis. asst. U. Bucharest, 1992-95, asst., 1995—; vis. asst. U. Bucharest, 1992-95; rschr. in field. Mem. Am. Soc. Materials, Deutsche Akademische Austauschdienst. Avocations: philately, skiing, ice hockey, tennis. Home: Aleea Stanila Nr 3 Bl H9, Sc 3 Ap 45 sector 3, 74609 Bucharest Romania Office: U Bucharest, Dept Phys Metlalurgy, Bucharest Romania

DRAKE, C. CHRISTOPHER, literature educator; b. Pleasant Hill, Tenn., Mar. 12, 1947; s. Charles H. and Marjorie (Rush) D.; m. Youngshik Kim, June 9, 1976. BA, Wesleyan U., Middletown, Conn., 1969, MA, 1970; PhD,

Harvard U., 1987. Cert. acupuncturist, Japan. Asst. prof. Atomi Coll., Niiza, Saitama, Japan, 1978-81, assoc. prof., 1981-89, prof., 1989—, v.p., 1992-94. Editor, translator: Dead Languages: Selected Poems of Tamura Ryuichi, 1984; contbr. articles to profl. jours. Translation grantee Nat. Endowment for Arts, 1990. Mem. Linked Verse Soc. Japan, Edo Period Lit. Soc., N.Am. Kant Soc. Avocations: writing poetry, writing Japanese linked verse, film making. E-mail: ccdrake@atomi.ac.jp. Office: Atomi Coll, Nakano 1-9-6, Niiza Saitama-ken 352-8501, Japan

DRAKE, E. MAYLON, academic administrator; b. Nampa, Idaho, Feb. 8, 1920; s. Austin Henry and Daisy Naomi (Smith) D.; m. Lois Elloise Noble, Oct. 12, 1940; children: E. Christopher, Cameron Lee. BS, U. So. Calif., Los Angeles, 1951, MS, 1954, EdD, 1963. Mgr. Frederick Post Co., San Francisco, 1943-47; asst. supt. Baldwin Park (Calif.) Schs., 1947-51; supt. Duarte (Calif.) Schs., 1951-64, Alhambra (Calif.) City Schs., 1964-70; dep. supt. Los Angeles County Schs., 1970-78; dir. Acad. Ednl. Mgmt., Los Angeles, 1978-80; pres. L.A. Coll. Chiropractic, Whittier, 1980-90, chancellor, 1990-93, chancellor emeritus, 1993—; adj. prof. U. So. Calif., 1964-90, bd. councilors, 1991—. Author Attaining Accountability in Schools, 1972; contbr. articles to profl. jours. Pres. Industry-Ednl. Council So. Calif., 1978; dir. United Way 1970; dir. Greater Los Angeles Zoo Bd., 1970; dir. Planned Parenthood of Pasadena, Calif., 1996; trustee L.A. Coll. Chiropractic Whittier, Calif., 1996. Recipient Am. Educator's medal Freedom Found.; named Educator of Yr. Los Angeles Chiropratic Soc., 1981. Mem. Coun. on Chiropractic Edn. (pres. 1988-90), Rotary (pres. Duarte 1954-56, bd. dirs. Alhambra 1964-70). Republican. Presbyterian. Avocation: performing arts. Home: Casa de Ville 206 445 S Los Robles Ave Pasadena CA 91101-3273 Office: LA Coll Chiropractic PO Box 1166 Whittier CA 90609-1166

DRAKE, JAMES RICHARD, insurance agent; b. Det., Dec. 3, 1941; s. Heber Holbrook and Lena Elizabeth D.; m. Cocoa Titus; children: Sage Christian, Danika Detrich. BA, U. Det., 1964; MA, U. Wis., 1965; postgrad., Cornell U., 1965-67, 68-69. Cert. ins. Ins. broker various organizations, San Francisco. Danforth fellow Danforth Found., 1964-69. Mem. Am. Acad. Poets. E-mail: jamesdrake@earthlink.net.com.

DRAKE, LAURA, theater director, performer; b. Eureka, Calif., Mar. 1, 1949; d. Stephen Drake and Laura Anne (Filingerie) Morel. BA in Interdisciplinary Creative Arts, San Francisco State U., 1973; MFA in Dramatic Prodn., U. Tex., 1985. Dir., coord. Austin (Tex.) Theatre Artists' Collective, 1984-85; artistic dir. Creatrix Prodns., New Orleans, 1985-89; asst. prof. theatre U. Southwestern La., Lafayette, 1987-91; appt. artist, spare/changes artistic resident Atlantic Ctr. for Arts, 1990; artistic dir. Gabriella Rosetti Prodns., N.Y.C., 1992—; founder, gen. ptnr. Designer's Edge Studio, N.Y.C., 1993—; adj. asst. prof. performing arts, guest dir. CUNY, 1993—. Writer, performer (performance art): Duck/Blind, 1990, Stages: Aphro-Diaspora, 1990 (NEA Inter-Arts award 1990); dir./producer Interdisciplinary Performance Festival, 1988-91 (Lafayette, La.). Morton Brown Rsch. fellow U. Tex., Austin, 1981, 82; recipient Partnership award Acadiana Arts Coun., 1988-91, Inter-Arts award Nat. Endowment for the Arts, 1990, New Performance award La. Div. of the Arts, 1990. Mem. Artists' Alliance (Lafayette, program com. 1989-91, bd. dirs.), Festival International de Louisiane (bd. dirs. 1989-91), Phi Kappa Phi, Alpha Psi Omega. E-mail: ldrake@hejira.hunter.cuny.edu. Home and Studio: 1691 3d Ave Apt 3A New York NY 10128-2113

DRAKE, RICHARD PAUL, physicist, educator; b. Washington, Oct. 25, 1954; s. Hugh Hess and Florence Jean (Steele) D.; m. Joyce Elaine Penner, Aug. 30, 1980; children: Katherine Anne, David Alexander. BA in Philosophy and Physics magna cum laude, Vanderbilt U., 1975; PhD in Physics, Johns Hopkins U., 1979. Physicist Lawrence Livermore (Calif.) Lab., 1979-89; assoc. prof. dept. applied sci. U. Calif., Davis, 1989-91, prof., 1991-93; dir. Plasma Physics Rsch. Inst. Lawrence Livermore Nat. Lab., 1990-96; vis. prof. U. Mich., Ann Arbor, 1996-98, prof. space sci., dir. Space Physics Rsch. Lab., 1998—; ski instr. Squaw Valley (Calif.) USA, 1985-92; chair Anomalous Absorption Conf., Tahoe City, Calif., 1987; referee NSF, Nature, Phys. Rev. Letters, other jours. Contbr. over 130 articles to sci. publs. Mem. Fellow Am. Phys. Soc.; mem. AAAS, Am. Geophys. Union, Am. Astron. Soc., Am. Vacuum Soc., Optical Sci. Am., Phi Beta Kappa. Achievements include fundamental experiments and theory on waves, instabilities, and turbulence in plasmas; laboratory astrophysics; time-dependent systems. Home: 3204 W Dobson Pl Ann Arbor MI 48105-2580 Office: U Mich Campus 2455 Hayward St Ann Arbor MI 48109-2143

DRAKE, STANLEY JOSEPH, association executive; b. New Britain, Conn., Mar. 8, 1916; s. Joseph Nicholas and Alice (Tokarzewska) E.; m. Virginia Allen, Oct. 6, 1940 (dec. Apr. 1993); children: Alice Drake Berg, Janet Drake Gardner, Jane Drake Dover. BS in Bus. Edn., Bryant Coll., Smithfield, R.I., 1937; MS, Temple Bar Coll., Mpls., 1944; PhD, McKinley Roosevelt Inst, Chgo., 1948; D. Pedagogy (hon.), Bryant Coll., 1963; DBA (hon.), Ind. No. U., 1966; Dr.Bus.Adminstrn., Cleary Coll., 1967; LHD, Internat. Fine Arts Coll., 1968; EdD, Ft. Lauderdale U., 1973. Instr. Mt. Vernon (Ohio) Coll., 1945-48, Broward Coll., Ft. Lauderdale, Fla., 1948-56; pres. Ft. Lauderdale Coll., 1956-76; adj. prof. Tampa (Fla.) Coll., 1977-78, Orlando Coll., 1978-81, Gaston Coll., Dallas, N.C., 1981-94. Author: Thoughts from the Bible, 1991, The Essentials of Esperanto, 1993. Mem. Am. Assn. of Pres. of Ind. Colls. and Univs. (pres. 1967-68, sec. 1969-70), Am. Assn. Specialized Colls. (pres. 1965-67), UN Assn. of U.S.A., Internat. Soc. Friendsihp and Good Will (pres. 1982—, sec. gen. 1978-82). Republican. Avocations: music, travel. Home and Office: Ste 434 8592 Roswell Rd Atlanta GA 30350-1870

DRAKES, DAVID HEDLEY FOSTER, marketing consultant; b. Kilwinning, Scotland, UK, Sept. 20, 1943; s. Donald Frank and Kathleen (Caldecott) D.; m. Tricia Margaret Mary Henshall, Sept. 12, 1975. MA, St. Catharine's Coll., Cambridge, England, 1966. Acct. supervisor Doyle Dane Bernbach Ltd., London, 1966-70; dir. Aalders Marchant Weinreich, London, 1970-72; founder, dir. Intellect Games, London, 1973-76; mng. dir. Mktg. Solutions, Ltd., London, 1977-82; mng. ptnr. The Mktg. Partnership, Ltd., London, 1983—. Trustee London Opera Festival, 1990—. Mem. Mktg. Soc., Market Rsch. Soc., Inst. Sales Promotion (chmn. 1986-88), Sales Promotion Cons. Assn. (chmn. 1989-93). Avocations: opera, ballet, theatre, squash. Home: 6 Park Village E, NW1 7PX Regents Park London England Office: The Mktg Partnership Ltd, 69 Hatton Garden, London EC1 N8JT, England

DRANCHAK, LAWRENCE JOHN, retired mechanical engineer; b. Scranton, Pa., Sept. 1, 1929; s. John J. and Rose (Barron) D.; m. Leota Mae Zimmerman, Aug. 14, 1954 (dec. Aug. 1999); children: Diana Rose, John Lawrence. BSME, Ind. Inst. Tech., 1956, DME (hon.), 1994. Ohio master gardener. Quality control technician Wright Aero. Corp., Woodridge, N.J., 1945; weaver L&M Weaving Corp., Scranton, 1947-50; automotive engr. Ford Motor Co., Dearborn, Mich., 1956-94; ret., 1994. Inventor automobile door magnetic weatherstrip. Cub scout advisor Boy Scouts Am., Taylor, Mich., 1963-68; adult advisor CAP, Dearborn, 1970-79; advisor Jr. Achievement, 1975-76. With U.S. Army, 1950-52, N.G., 1947-50. Mem. Soc. Automotive Engrs., Am. Legion, VFW. Republican. Roman Catholic. Avocations: gardening, feline husbandry, radio control model aircraft, computers, old automobile and truck rebuilding. Home: PO Box 165 Continental OH 45831-0165

DRANGER, JAN, industrial designer; b. Stockholm, Sept. 29, 1941; s. Stig Dranger and Margareta Torndahl; m. Lena Rubin, 1966 (div. 1975); children: Jon, Joanna; m. Lou R. Ekwall, Mar. 4, 1977. Grad., Royal Coll. Art and Design, Stockholm, 1968. Registered architect, indsl. designer. Founder, owner and mng. dir. Innovator Design AP, Stockholm, 1968-78, Innovator Consult AB, Stockholm, 1968-78, Dranger Design AB, Stockholm, 1978—; news design DFE AB, 1995—. Patentee furniture designs, 1972, 82, 93; designs represented at Nat. Mus. Sweden, Victoria and Albert Mus., London. Recipient first prize Scandinavian competition Svensk Form Swedish Design Assn., Stockholm, 1964, Chair-of-the-Yr. award German Nat. Design Assn., Stuttgardt, 1972, Ecology and Product Design awards IF Düsseldorf, Germany, 1999, Rote Punkt Design award, Essen, Germany, 1999, Hon. awards Switzerland, Valencia, Spain, Stockholm, 1999, Good Design award Chicago Athenaeum, 1999. Mem. Swedish Indsl. Designers, Swedish Inventors Assn. Avocation: sailing. Office: Dranger Design AB, Stora Skuggans V 11, Stockholm 11542, Sweden

DRAPALIK, BETTY R., civic worker, artist; b. Cicero, Ill., July 4, 1932; d. Henry William and Jennie Margaret (Robbins) Degen; m. Joseph James Drapalik, Oct. 30, 1951; children: Betty Jennifer Drapalik Coryell, Joseph Henry. Grad. high sch., Cicero. Sec., clk. Gt. Lakes (Ill.) Naval Base, until 1982; sect. to asst. dir. Arden Shore Boys' Home, Lake Bluff, Ill., 1984-87. Group exhbns. include Anderson Art Ctr., Kenosha, Wis., 1994-99, Dellora A. Norris Cultural Arts Ctr., St. Charles, Ill., 1998, 99, 2000, Women's Works, Old Courthouse Art Ctr., Woodstock, Ill., 1994, 95, 2000, Cmty. Gallery of Art, Coll. of Lake County, Grayslake, Ill., 1993, 94, 96, 97, 98, 99, David Adler Cultural Ctr., Libertyville, Ill., 1994, 97, 98, 99, 2000, Lake County Mus. Wauconda, Ill., 1996, 97, 98, 99, 2000, Green Belt Cultural Ctr., North Chgo., Ill., 2000, Wauconda Pub. Libr., 99, Kenosha Pub. Mus., 1998 (award of excellence 1998), Layson Gallery, Waukegan, Ill., 1993, Spotlight Gallery, Kenosha, Wis., 1998, 99, Monne's Gallery, Kenosha, 1998, Clausen Art Shop, Wilmette, IL, 1999, Gull Lake Gall., Richland, MI, 1999, 2000, Nippersink Gallery, Richmond, Ill., 1999, Hardy Gall., Ephraim, Wis., 1996, 97, 98, 99, 2000 (purchase awd. 1998), Deer Path Gallery, Lake Forest, Ill., 1999, Waukegan Visual Arts Ctr., 1998, Hawthorne Hollow Art Festival, Kenosha, Wis., 1997, 98, Deer Path Art League Festival, Lake Forest, Ill., 1997, 99, Lake County Art League (1st pl. watercolor Fine Arts Festival at North Point Marina, Winthrop Harbor, Ill., 1996, 2nd pl. watercolor 1997, 98, 1st pl. watercolor, 1999, pub. rels. chair 1997, 98, 99, Best of Show Fall Membership Show 1996, 97, Award of Merit watercolor 1998, award of Excellence Spring Membership Show, 1999), Truman State U., Kirksville, Mo., 1997, Red River Watercolor Soc. juried show Moorhead (Minn.) State U., 1997, Kenosha Art Assn. and Lake County Art League Combined Art Event, 1997 (Best of Show 1997) (3rd Place 2000), Zion (Ill.) Zion Chamber Orch. Concert and Art Contest, 1998 (Best of Show, 1st Pl.), N.W. N.Mex. Arts Coun., Farmington, 1997, Gull Lake Gallery, Richland, Mich., 1999, 2000, Nippersink Gallery, Richmond, Ill., 1999, 2000; two-person shows include Jack Benny Ctr. for the Arts, Waukegan, 1996, 98; one-woman shows include Jack Benny Ctr. for the Arts, 1995, Wauconda Area Pub. Libr., 1999. Former leader and mem. pub. rels. com. Girl Scouts U.S.; visual arts cons. Green Belt Cultural Ctr. Lake County Forest Preserve District, Lake County, Ill. Recipient purchase award Coll. of Lake County, Grayslake, Ill., 1994, numerous other courtesy awards; featured in Art Mag., 1997. Mem. Lake County Art League (resource person, pres., various bd. positions, liaison rep. between Green Belt Cultural Ctr. of Lake County Forest Preserve Dist. and Lake County Art Groups and Artists), Lakes Region Watercolor Guild (rec. sec., co-program chair, exhibit chair), Midwest Watercolor Soc., Deerpath Art League, Red River Watercolor Soc., Kenosha Art Assn., N.W. Area Arts Coun., Bloomin' Artists, Internat. Starcraft Camper Club (Ill. chpt. sec./treas. 1975), Nat. Mus. Women in the Arts (charter). Evangelical. Avocations: watercolor, photography, camping, gardening, hiking. Home and Studio: 2018 W Grove Ave Waukegan IL 60085-1607

DRAPALOVA, IVA, journalist; b. Svepravice, Czech Republic, Apr. 4, 1925; d. Antonin and Lucie (Urbankova) Vaclavik; m. Bohdan Jelinek, June 21, 1947 (div. 1952); m. Lubor Frantisek Karel Drapal, Jan. 30, 1953; children: Dan, Ales. Sociologist, Edinburgh U., 1945; PhD, Masaryk U., 1948. Tchr. Ministry of Edn., Zlate Hory, Czech Republic, 1952-53; free lance translator, 1953-68; translator AP, Prague, Czech Republic, 1968-69; bur. chief AP, Prague, 1972-88; stringer L.A. Times, 1988—. Contbr. articles to profl. jours.; translator. Mem. Czech Coun. Fgn. Rels., Prague, 1994—, Czech Soc. UN, Prague, 1995—. Mem. Assn. Fgn. Journalists. Avocations: gardening, collecting egg cups. Home and Office: Mezi Lysinami 9, 14700 Prague Czech Republic

DRAPER, GERALD LINDEN, lawyer; b. Oberlin, Ohio, July 14, 1941; s. Earl Linden and Mary Antoinette (Colotto) D.; m. Barbara Jean Winter, Aug. 26, 1960; children: Melissa Leigh Price, Stephen Edward Draper. BA, Muskingum Coll., 1963; JD, Northwestern U., 1966. Bar: Ohio, 1966, U.S. Dist. Ct. (so. dist.) Ohio, 1966, U.S. Ct. Appeals (6th cir.), 1975, U.S. Supreme Ct., 1980. Ptnr. Bricker & Eckler, Columbus, Ohio, 1966-88, Thompson, Hine & Flory, Columbus, 1989-95, Draper, Hollenbaugh, Briscoe, Yashko & Carmany, Columbus, 1996-99, Roetzel & Andress, Columbus, 1999—. Trustee, past pres. Wesley Glen Retirement Ctr., Columbus, 1979-95; trustee Meth. Elder Care Svcs., Inc., 1995—, Muskingum Coll., New Concord, Ohio, 1988-92, 93—, vice chair, 1994—; trustee, pres. Wesley Ridge Retirement Ctr., 1995-2000. Fellow Am. Coll. Trial Lawyers, Am. Bd. Trial Advocates; mem. ABA (Ho. of Dels.), Ohio State Bar Assn. (pres. 1990-91), Ohio State Bar Found. (trustee 1992-97), Columbus Bar Assn. (pres. 1982-83, Bar Svc. medal 1998), Columbus Bar Found. (pres. 1984-86), Nat. Conf. of Bar Found. (trustee 1987-90, 91-94), Ohio Continuing Legal Edn. Inst. (trustee 1992-98, chair 1997-98), Ohio Assn. Hosp. Attys., Def. Rsch. Inst. Avocations: travel, golf, photography. Office: Roetzel & Andress 155 E Broad St Columbus OH 43215-3609

DRAPER, ROBERT WILLIAM, social worker; b. Harbel, Margibi, Liberia, Apr. 3, 1943; s. Daniel Seguel Pyne Draper and Emma Garmai (Clinton) Walker; m. Musu Doris Draper, Aug. 22, 1958; 1 child, Taylor. Diploma in Sociology, U. Liberia, 1973. Cert. social worker, trauma counselor, curriculum devel. profl. Nat. gen. sec. YMCA, Liberia, 1981-87; exec. dir. Monrovia YMCA, 1980-85; devel. sec. Nat. Coun. of YMCA, 1986-88; dep. nat. coord. Readjustment Commn., Liberia, 1991-96; assoc. exec. Africa Alliance of YMCAs, Kenya, 1977-98; CEO Dramus Multi Bus., Monrovia, Liberia, 1998-99; adminstrv. mgr. Meridian Bao Bank Mon, Liberia; sec. gen. Liberia Nat. Youth Coun., Liberia; pres. Social Workers Assn., 1975-80; v.p. Rsch. Fellows of Liberia, 1981-84. Public affairs officer Free Democratic Party, Monrovia, 1996; pres. Y5 Mon Club, Liberia, 1985, sr. sen. U.L. Student Assn., Monrovia, 1971. Mem. Family Planning Assn. (regional rep. 1976-81), Meth. Men's Fellowship (Father of Yr. award 1986, Protocol Officer 1983), Lions (sec. 1982-84). Free Democratic Party of Liberia. Methodist. Avocations: jogging, singing, camping. Home: Cabnal Housing Estate Old, PO Box 537, Monrovia Liberia Office: Dramus Multi/Bus Enterprise, Sinkor Monrovia/Box 537, Monrovin Liberia

DRATCU, LUIZ, psychiatrist, psychopharmacologist, consultant, educator; b. São Paulo, Brazil, Mar. 30, 1957; arrived in Eng., 1986; s. Nicolau and Marina (Portnoi) D.; m. Tania Wasserstein, July 4, 1997. MD, Escola Paulista de Medicina, São Paulo, 1981, MPhil, 1986; MRCPsych, Royal Coll. of Psychiatrists, London, 1988; PhD, U. London, 1996. Resident in psychiatry Hosp. Servidor Publico Estadual, São Paulo, 1982-84; postgrad. in psychopharmacology Escola Paulista de Medicina, São Paulo, 1984-86; registrar in psychiatry Maudsley Hosp., London, 1986-89; hon. sr. registrar, clin. rschr. Inst. Psychiatry U. London, 1989-93; sr. registrar in psychiatry Guy's & St. Thomas Hosp./United Med. & Dental Sch.-U. London, 1993-95; cons. psychiatrist, sr. lectr. Guys & St. Thomas Hosp. Sch. of Medicine, 1995—; med. adviser Brazilian Consulate Gen., London, 1991—; tutor and examiner MSc in mental health scis. United Med. and Dental Sch., London, 1993—; vis. prof. Hosp. Servidor Publico Estadual, São Paulo, 1996—; cons. in perinatal psychiatry Guy's Hosp., London, 1996—; guest lectr. various univs. and med. schs., Brazil and U.K. Author: Patient Management Problems in Psychiatry, 1991; editor: Manual de Psiquiatria, 1995; contbr. articles to profl. jours. Recipient Brit. Coun. Tech. Cooperation award Brit. Ministry of Fgn. and Commonwealth Affairs, 1986-89; grantee Nat. Coun. for Sci. Devel., Brazilian Ministry of Edn., 1984-86, Med. Rsch. Coun., U.K., 1989-93. Mem. Royal Coll. Psychiatrists, Brit. Assn. for Psychopharmacology, Collegium Internat. Neuro-Psychopharmacologicum, Assn. European Psychiatrists. Achievements include development of a dopaminergic model for panic disorder; research on panic patients demonstrating electroencephalophic abnormalities which indicate cerebral hypoxia and cognitive distortions that may induce chronic anxiety. Office: Thomas Guy House Guy's Hosp, 47 Weston St, London SE1 3RR, England

DRAUGHON, FRANCES ANN, microbiology educator; b. Tazewell, Va., Apr. 30, 1952; d. Raymond Jefferson Moore and Helen Frances (Johnson) Fox; m. Kenneth Earl Draughon, Dec. 15, 1973 (dec. Mar. 1988); children: William Bradford, Andrew Kenneth. BS in Microbiology, U. Tenn., 1973, MS in Food Sci., 1976; PhD in Food Sci., U. Ga., 1979. Asst. prof. microbiology U. Tenn., Knoxville, 1979-83, Roddy Rsch. assoc. prof., 1983-89, prof., 1989—; dir. food safety initiatives, 1998—; USDA-SBIR panel mgr., 2000; dir. UTIA Food Safety Initiative, 1998—; co-dir. Tenn. Food Safety Initiative. Chairperson Inst. Agr. Adv. Coun., U. Tenn., 1988-90. Recipient Nealand Tacie Peacock U. Tchg. award, 1999, Gamma Sigma Delta Rsch. award, 1999. Mem. So. Assn. Agrl. Scientists (chairperson food sci. sect. 1988, Devel. Scientist award 1978, Grad. Scientist award 1979, Profl. Scientists award 1993), Inst. Food Technologists (mem. program com. 1990-93), Am. Soc. Microbiology, Internat. Assn. Milk Food and Environ. Sanitarians (v.p. 1993-94, program chair 1993, pres. 1995-96), Tenn. Assn. Milk and Food Protection (pres. 1994) Sigma Xi (sec. 1981-84), Phi Kappa Phi (sec. 1981-84), Phi Tau Sigma (pres. 1983-84). Democrat. Presbyterian. Avocations recreational vehicle camping, racquetball, wilderness hiking. Office: U Tenn Food Tech and Sci PO Box 1071 Knoxville TN 37901-1071

DRAUR, RONALD ALVIN, retired cardiologist; b. Toledo, May 21, 1940; s. Albin and Ann Caroline Draur; m. Georgina Anderson, 1988; children: Geri, Diana, Ronald, Thomas, Danel, Cherish. BS in Biology, Loyola U., Chgo., 1961, MD cum laude, 1965. Diplomate Am. Bd. Internal Medicine, Bd. Cardiovasc. Disease. Intern Mercy Hosp. and Med. Ctr., Chgo., 1965-66, resident in internal medicine, 1966-67; resident in internal medicine Edward G. Hines VA Hosp., Hines, Ill., 1967-68; cardiovasc. fellow Edward G. Hines VA Hosp., Hines, 1968-70; attending physician Nebr. Meth. Hosp., Omaha, 1972-96, dir. cardiovasc. svcs., 1974-95; ret.; chmn. various med. staff coms. Meth. Hosp., Omaha, 1974-96; pres.-elect, pres. Nebr. Meth. Hosp., Omaha, 1991-95. Contbr. articles to profl. jours. Maj. USAF, 1970-72. Fellow Am. Coll. Cardiology (emeritus), Am. Heart Assn., Soc. for Cardiac Angiography and Interventions (emeritus); mem. Phi Sigma Tau, Alpha Sigma Nu. Republican. Roman Catholic. Avocations: photography, music, shooting, horseback riding, computers. E-mail: rdpicard@wavecom.net.

DRAWIN, HANS-WERNER, physicist; b. Hamburg, Germany, Jan. 21, 1930; s. Werner Franz and Gerda (Millahn) D.; m. Marianne Kunow, Dec. 27, 1957; children: Thomas, Angela, Stefan. Diploma in physics, U. Kiel, Germany, 1954, PhD, 1956. Lab. chief Atlas-Werke Aktien Gesellschaft, Bremen, Germany, 1956-60; rschr. Euratom-Commissariat à l'Energie Atomique, Fontenay-aux-Roses, France, 1960-86, Euratom-CEA, Cadarache, France, 1986-94; lectr. U. Paris-Orsay, France, 1968-86, U. Rennes, France, 1971-73; prof. U. Orleans, France, 1973-75; guest prof. U. Nagoya, Japan, 1988; cons. Ctr. Nat. de la Rsch. Sci., Paris, 1968-94, Internat. Atomic Energy Agy., Vienna, Austria, 1978-95. Author: (with P. Felenbok) Data for Plasmas in Local Thermodynamic Equilibrium, 1965, Phénomènes de Vibration et de Propagation, 1975; editor: (with K. Katsonis) Atomic and Molecuar Data for Fusion, 1981, (with R.K. Janev) Atomic and Plasma-Material Interaction Processes in Controlled Thermonuclear Fusion, 1993; contbr. articles to profl. jours. Mem. German Phys. Soc., Gundelfingen Assn. of Arts (chmn. 1996-2000).

DRAZNIN, JULES NATHAN, educator; b. Chgo., May 14, 1923; s. Charles G. and Goldie (Malach) D.; m. Shirley Bernstein, Apr. 9, 1950; children: Dean, Jody, Michael. Student, Wright City Coll., Chgo., 1941; BA in Journalism, Calif. State U., Northridge, 1978, MA in Higher Edn., 1984. Various journalism positions City News Bur., Chgo. Am., Chgo., 1941; promotions and publicity Balaban & Katz Theaters, Chgo., 1942-43; asst. dir pub. rels. Combined Jewish Appeal, Chgo., 1944; prin. J.N. Draznin Assocs., Chgo., 1945-50; account supr. Olian & Bronner Advt. Agy., Chgo., 1951-53; dir. advt. Chgo. Defender, Robert S. Abbott Pub. Co., 1953-55; freelance cons. Chgo., 1955-60; v.p. pub. rels. Harshe-Rotman, Chgo., 1956; pub. rels. dir. Abel and Lamensdorf Properties, Chgo., 1960-62; editor-in-chief, assoc. pub. Indsl. News Bender Publs., Calif., 1962-64; labor editor, spl. features writer Valley News and Green Sheet, Calif., 1964; ind. ins. agt. Calif., 1965-74; lectr. pub. rels. UCLA and Calif. State U., L.A.; prof. journalism and pub. rels. L.A. Trade Tech. Coll., 1975-95, chmn. lang. arts dept., 1984-90, ret., 1995; prof. journalism and pub. rels. L.A. City Coll., L.A. Pierce Coll., L.A. Southwest Coll., East L.A. Coll., L.A. Mission Coll.; guest lectr. Calif. State U., Northridge. Coord. Mass Media AARP/Vote Vols., 1996—, apptd. state legis. com. AARP, 1998—, also spokesperson on social security and medicare. Mem. Assn. for Edn. in Journalism and Mass Comm., Soc. Profl. Journalists. Avocations: golf, classical music, travel.

DRCHAL, VACLAV, physicist, researcher; b. Prague, Czechoslovakia, May 21, 1945; s. Vaclav and Vlasta (Langerova) D.; m. Jaroslava Glozova, Feb. 12, 1970; children: Vaclav, Jan. Grad., Charles U., Prague, 1968, RNDr, 1974; CSc, Czechoslovak Acad. Scis., Prague, 1974. Rsch. scientist Inst. Solid State Physics, Czechoslovak Acad. Sci., Prague, 1974-78; rsch. scientist Inst. Physics, Czechoslovak Acad. Sci., Prague, 1979-84, sr. scientist, 1985-92; sr. scientist Inst. of Physics, Acad. Sci. of the Czech Republic, Prague, 1993—. Co-author monograph and jour. articles. Recipient State prize Czechoslovak Govt., 1982, prize Czechoslovak Acad. Scis., 1989, Czech Acad. Scis., 1998. Mem. Union of Czech Mathematicians and Physicists, Am. Phys. Soc. Office: Acad Sci Czech Republic Inst Physics, Na Slovance 2, CZ-18221 Prague 8, Czech Republic

DRDÁCKY, MILOŠ FERDINAND, civil engineer, researcher; b. Havlickuv Brod, Czech Republic, Dec. 12, 1945; s. Miloš František and Božena Barbora (Noaková) D.; m. Jitka Semrádová, June 25, 1970 (div. Aug. 1994); children: Tomáš, Jana. Diploma engr., Czech Tech. U. Prague, 1968; PhD, Acad. Scis. Czech Republic, 1978. Head Ctrl. Lab Exptl. Mechanics, Prague, Czech Republic, 1986-93, Assn. Rsch. Ctr. Hist. Structures and Sites, Prague, Telc, 1995-98; vice dir. Inst. Theoretical and Applied Mechanics, Prague, 1988-90, sci. sec., 1990-93, dir., 1998—; rsch. fellow Acad. Scis. Czech Republic, Prague, 1968—; reader U. Indsl. Arts, Prague, 1984-90, Tech. U. Liberec, Czech Republic, 1995—, Czech. Tech. U., Prague, 1996—; head Town Architect Office Municipality of Telč, Czech Republic, 1993-98. Co-author, co-editor: Contact Loading and Local Effects in Thin Walled Plated and Shell Structures, 1992, Experimental Model Research and Testing of Thin Walled Structures, 1997; editor, co-author: (series) Lessons from Structural Failures, 1991—; co-author: Industrial Construction of Dwelling Houses, 1971. Vol. trainer Sokol, Prague-Troja, 1973—. Grantee Czech Grant Agy., 1994—, Ministry of Culture, 1996—. Mem. Internat. Assn. Bridges and Structural Engrng., Internat. Soc. Tech., Law and Ins., Internat. Assn. Shell Structures. Roman Catholic. Avocations: sports, history of civil engineering and architecture. Home: nam Zachariase z Hradce 34, 588 56 Telc Czech Republic Office: Inst Theor and Applied Mech, Prosecká 76, 190 00 Prague Czech Republic

DREBUSHCHAK, VALERI ANATOLIEVICH, physicist, researcher; b. Rudnoe, Kazakhstan, May 23, 1958; s. Anatoli E. and Valentina T. (Farafonova) D.; m. Tatyana N. Khutornaya Drebushchak, Oct. 19, 1982; children: Irina, Marina. Student, Novosibirsk State U., Russia, 1980; D in Chemistry, United Inst. Geology, Novosibirsk, Russia, 1993. Engr. United Inst. Geology, Geophysics and Mineralogy, Novosibirsk, Russia, 1980—, sr. rschr., 1993—. Co-author: New Approaches to Investigation of Physical and Chemical Properties of Zeolites, 1989; contbr. papers in field. Named Young Scientists for Applied Rschrs., Siberian Branch Russian Acad. Scis., 1987, 88. Mem. Internat. Confedn. for Thermal Analysis and Calorimetry. Office: Inst Mineralogy and Petro, Prospect Ak Koptyuga 3, 630090 Novosibirsk Russia

DRECHSLER, HEIKE, Olympic athlete; b. Gera, Germany, Dec. 16, 1964. Winner Gold medal long jump World Championships, 1983, 93; winner Bronze medals 100 and 200 meters Seoul, 1988, winner Silver medal long jump, 1988; winner 4th consecutive IAAF World Cup European long jump, 1998; winner Gold medal Sydney, 2000. Set world jr.record heptathlon, 1981; set world jr. record in long jump, 1983; set world long jump record, 1995. Office: European Athletic Assn, Postfach 710316, Frankfurt 60493, Germany*

DRECHSLER, WOLFGANG DIETER, research scientist, educator; b. Hagen, Westfalia, Germany, Feb. 26, 1934; s. Alfred and Hildegard (Trenkpohl) D.; m. Karin Meyer, Apr. 19, 1962; 1 child, Rodion. Diploma in physics, U. Bonn, Germany, 1961; Dr.rer.nat., U. Heidelberg, Germany, 1963. Visitor European Orgn. Nuc. Rsch., Geneva, 1965, rsch. assoc., 1966-68; visitor Inst. Math. Sci., Madras, India, 1968-69, Internat. Ctr. Theoretical Physics, Trieste, Italy, 1969; rsch. assoc. Stanford Linear Accelerator Ctr., Stanford, 1969-70; staff mem. M-Planck-Inst. for Physics, Munich, 1970—; prof. Ludwig-Maximilians-Univ., Munich, 1981—. Co-author: Fiber Bundle Techniques in Gauge Theories, 1977; contbr. articles to profl. jours. Mem. Nat. Geog. Soc., German Phys. Soc., N.Y. Acad. Scis. Avocations: mountaineering, tennis. Office: Max-Planck-Inst Physics, Foehringer Ring 6, 80805 Munich Germany

DREES, WILLEM BERNARD, philosophy, theology educator; b. The Hague, Apr. 20, 1954; s. Willem Drees and Anna Erica Gescher; m. Zwanet Roeters, June 2, 1983; children: Johannes M., Annelot C.M., Esther E.E. Diploma in Theoretical Physics, Utrecht U., The Netherlands, 1977; DTh cum laude, U. Groningen, The Netherlands, 1989; PhD, Vrye U., Amsterdam, 1994. Tchr. math. and physics various high schs., The Netherlands, 1977-85; rsch. fellow U. Groningen, 1986-89; resident mem. Ctr. of Theol. Inquiry, Princeton, N.J., 1993; acad. fellow Vrye U., Amsterdam, 1989—; prof. in philosophy of nature and of technology U. Twente, Enschede, The Netherlands, 1995—; vis. fellow dept. philosophy Princeton U., 1993; Idreos lectr., Oxford, 1998; Samuel Ferguson lectr. U. Manchester, U.K., 1999; lectr. in field; assoc. Zygon Ctr. for Religion and Sci. Author: (books) Religion, Science and Naturalism, 1996, Beyond the Big Bang: Quantum Cosmologies and God, 1990, others; editor: The Human: More than Matter? Religion and Reductionism, 1997. Fulbright grantee, 1987, 93; recipient awards Templeton Found., 1994-96, Legatum Stolpianum, 1995. Mem. European Soc. for Study of Sci. and Theology (mem. coun., newsletter editor 1990—). E-mail: willemb@drees.nl. Home: Hertog Hendriklaan 11, 3743 DL Baarn The Netherlands Office: Bezinningscentrum Vrye Univ, De Boelelaan 1105, 1081 HV Amsterdam The Netherlands

DREHER, RICHARD CARL, telecommunications executive, educator; b. LaFayette, Ind., Sept. 22, 1958; s. Carl Edward and Joanne (Crowe) D.; m. Darcy Lynn Vail, July 4, 1981; children: Aubrey Joan, Austin Carl. AS, Arapahoe C.C., Littleton, Colo., 1981; BSEE, U. Colo., 1983. Registered profl. engr, Tex.; cert. automotive svc. excellence credintial. Entrepeneur Automotive Technician, Denver, 1978-83; lab. dir. U. Colo., Denver, 1981-83; lead elec. engr. Tex. Instr., Dallas, 1983-84; mem. tech. staff Adv. Bus. Comms., Dallas, 1984-87; Instr. Brookhaven Coll. of Automotive Tech., 1985-95; sr. sales support engr. DSC Comms., Plano, Tex., 1987-90; U.S. mgr., tech. sales support Ericsson Telecom., Richardson, Tex., 1990-95; dir. adv. tech. Pocket Comms., Washington, 1995-97, Evolving Sys. Inc., Englewood, Colo., 1997-99; gen. mgr. e-Teleconsultants LLC, Denver, 1999—; coord. telecom. Collin County C.C., Plano, Tex., 1992-95; staff mem., instr. Brookhaven Coll. Automotive Tech., 1985-97; instr. cont. edn. Ms. Automechanics various schs., 1984—. Contbr. articles to profl. jours. and public magazines on telecommunications, newspapers; inventor integrated circuit fault simulator, 1984; contr. textbook: Cellular and Personal Communications Services, 1996; co-author: (textbook) The Comprehensive Guide to Wireless Technology, 1998. Mem. com. Citizens to Keep Murphy (Tex.) Elem. Student Together, 1994-95. Recipient Outstanding Young Men of Am., 1988, IEEE Comm. Soc., Outstanding Svc., 1984, 89, 91. Mem. IEEE (sr., chmn. Comm. Soc., adv. and past pres. Dallas sect.), Soc. Automotive Engrs., Toastmasters Internat. (pres. 1983-95). Home and Office: 7528 Indian Wells Ln LoneTree CO 80124

DREIFKE, GERALD EDMOND, electrical engineering educator; b. St. Louis, June 21, 1918; s. Herman A. and Anna Margaret (Hollenbeck) D.; m. Lorraine Ann Feldhaus, June 9, 1951; children: Mark A., Matthew G., Laura Maria, Anne Marie. B.S., Washington U., 1948, M.S., 1948, D.Sc. (NSF fellow), 1961. Registered profl. engr., Mo. Layout man Curtiss-Wright Co., St. Louis, 1936-39; design engr. Curtiss-Wright Co., 1939-44; layout man Douglas Aircraft Co., 1939; instr. engring. St. Louis U., 1948-50, asst. prof., 1950-54, assoc. prof. elec. engring., dir. grad. program elec. engring., 1954-61, prof. elec. engring., 1961-71; mgr. research and devel. Union Electric Co., 1971-77; cons., 1977—; vis. prof. physics U. Mo.-St. Louis, 1979-94; cons. Emerson Electric Co., 1951-71, Monsanto Co., 1961-71; mem. tech. staff Bell Telephone Labs. N.J., summer 1963. Editor-in-chief: ISA Transactions, 1966-89; contbr. articles profl. jours. Mem. St. Louis County Bd. Elec. Examiners, Gov.'s Sci. Adv. Com. Mo. Served with USNR, 1944-45. Recipient certificate of merit WPB, 1942; research grants NSF, 1964; research grants NASA, 1965; research grants Monsanto Co., 1965-69; Nancy McNair-Ring Outstanding Faculty award St. Louis U. chpt. Gamma Pi Epsilon, 1965-66. Fellow ISA; mem. Am. Soc. Engring. Edn. (past sec., com. chmn.), IEEE (past chmn. St. Louis sect.), Mo. Soc. Profl. Engrs. (past pres. St. Louis chpt., Engr. of Yr. St. Louis chpt. 1977), St. Louis Elec. Bd. Trade, Sigma Xi, Tau Beta Pi, Eta Kappa Nu, Pi Mu Epsilon, Phi Eta Sigma. Home: 6 Westmoreland Pl Saint Louis MO 63108-1228

DREIFUSS, RUTH, Swiss government official; b. St. Gallen, Jan. 9, 1940. Degree in econs., U. Geneva, 1970. Journalist, asst. prof. econs. and social scis. U. Geneva, 1970-72; mem. SPS, 1965—; sec. Swiss Fedn. Trade Unions, 1981-89; mem. Mpls. Assembly, Bern, Switzerland, 1989-92; fed. councillor, head Fed. Dept. Interior Swiss Govt., Bern, 1993—; v.p. Swiss Govt., until 1998, pres., from 1998; chief Fed. Dept Home Affairs, Bern. Mem. Social Democratic Party. Address: Bundeshaus, Inselgasse, CH-3003 Bern Switzerland*

DREIKE, BEATE MONIKA, German and linguistics educator, researcher; b. Halle/S., Germany, Mar. 23, 1940; arrived in Ireland, 1975; d. Bernhard Heinrich and Amanda Augusta (Kary) D. MA, U. Bonn, Germany, 1967, Dr phil, 1971. Asst. and rsch. fellow U. Bonn, 1968-71; postdoctoral fellow U. Edinburgh, Scotland, 1971-73; sr. rsch. fellow Linguistisch-Maschinelle Sprachbearbeitung, Bonn, 1973-75; lectr. German and linguistics Univ. Coll. Cork, Ireland, 1975-94, sr. lectr., 1994—; external examiner Inst. Tech. Tallaght, Dublin, 1996, Dundalk, Ireland, 1996, Nat. Coll. Indsl. Rels., Dublin, 1996. Author: Herders Naturauffassung in ihrer Beeinflussung durch Leibniz' Philosophie, 1973; contbr. numerous articles to profl. jours., including Folia Linguistica, Studia Linguistica, Wirkendes Wort, Studia Germanica Gandensia and Germanist books. Confidential contact person with Germany and interpreter for So. Health Bd., Ireland, 1979. Mem. Internat. Union for Germanic Speech and Lit. Sci., European Linguistics Soc., Linguistic Assn. Gt. Britain. Avocations: Italian art, classical music, sailing.

DREINHÖFER, KARSTEN EBERHARD, orthopedic surgeon, educator, researcher, health economist; b. Osnabruck, Germany, Dec. 23, 1961; s. Hanns Eberhard and Lore (Quaas) D. Student, Tufts U., Harvard U., 1988; grad., Med. Hochschule Hannover, 2000, European Bus. Sch. Resident in trauma surgery U. Hannover, 1989-91; fellow musculoskeletal tumor ctr. dept. orthopaedics Univ. Hosp., Lund, 1991-92; resident in orthopedics U. Ulm, 1992-96, attending physician, 1996—; European dir. profl. edn. Johnson & Johnson Orthopaedics, 1997-99; dir. devel. Decade of Bone and Joint Disease, 1999—. Author: Traumatic Dislocation of the Hip, 1992; contbr. articles to profl. jours. German Acad. Exch. Svc. scholar, 1986, German Rsch. Soc. scholar, 1992. Mem. AAAS, Am. Acad. Orthopaedic Surgeons, German Orthopedic Soc., N.Y. Acad. Scis., Scandinavian Sarcoma Group, European Orthopaedic Rsch. Soc. Avocations: sports, international exchanges, traveling. Office: Dept Orthopedic Surgery, Oberer Eselsberg 45, 89081 Ulm Germany

DREISBACH, JOHN GUSTAVE, investment banker; b. Paterson, N.J., Apr. 24, 1939; s. Gustave John and Rose Catherine (Koehler) D.; m. Janice Lynn Petitjean; children: John Gustave Jr., Christopher Erik. BA, NYU, 1963. With Dreyfus & Co., 1959-62, Shields & Co., Inc., 1965-68, Model, Roland & Co., Inc., N.Y.C., 1968-72, F. Eberstadt & Co., Inc., N.Y.C., 1972-74; v.p. Bessemer Trust Co., 1974-78; pres. Cmty. Housing Capital, Inc., 1978-80; chmn., pres. John G. Dreisbach, Inc., Santa Fe, 1980—, JDG Housing Corp., 1982—, JGD Mgmt. Corp., 1996—; gen. ptnr. numerous real estate ltd. partnerships; bd. dirs., pres. The Santa Fe Investment Conf., 1986—; assoc. Sta. KNME-TV. Mem. Santa Fe Cmty. Devel. Commn.; bd. dirs. Friends of Berry Pomeroy Ch. With USAFR, 1964. Mem. Internat. Assn. for Fin. Planning, Nat. Assn. Securities Dealers, Inc., NYU Alumni Assn., N.Mex. First, Friends of Vieilles Maisons Francaises Inc., Mensa, Santa Fe C. of C., Augustan Soc., St. Bartholomew's Cmty. Club, Essex Club, Hartford Club, Amigos del Alcalde Club. Republican. Mem. Ch. of Eng. Avocations: travel, art, arch-design appreciation, classical music, Shotokan karate (1st Dan). Fax: 505-989-7381. Home: 11 Castle Ct, Totnes Devon TQ9 5PD, England Office: 369 Montezuma Ave Santa Fe NM 87501-2626

DREISBACH, MARY ELIZABETH, manufacturing engineer; b. New Haven, Nov. 27, 1966; d. Raymond Allen and Dorothy Louise (Seal) Dreisbach. BSME and Materials Sci., U. Conn., 1989; MS in Materials Engring., Rensselaer Poly. Inst.; AS in Plastics Engring., Quinebaug Valley Cmty. Tech. Lic. profl. engr., Conn. Mfg. engr. United Technologies Corp., Pratt & Whitney, East Hartford, Conn., 1988-93; sr. mfg. engr. Haydon Switch and Instrument Inc., Waterbury, Conn., 1993-97, sr. project engr., 1997-98, mfg. engring. mgr., 1998-2000, mgr. mfg., 2000—. Bd. dirs. Airpax Fed. Credit Union, 1996-98, supervisory com., 1993-96, chmn., 1996-98, pres., 1998—. Mem. Am. Soc. Materials, Materials Rsch. Soc., Soc. Mfg. Engrs. (cert. mfg. engr.). Home: 492 Prospect St Willimantic CT 06226-2028 Office: Haydon Switch & Instrument 1500 Meriden Rd Waterbury CT 06705-3981

DREISCHUH, ALEXANDER ALEXANDROV, physics educator, researcher; b. Sofia, Bulgaria, Aug. 7, 1961; s. Alexander Alexandrov and Leonora Dimitrova (Tzenova) D.; m. Tanja Nikolova Andreeva, Apr. 14, 1985; 1 child, Alexander. MS in Physics, Sofia (Bulgaria) U., 1987, PhD in Physics, 1991. Engring. physics; narrow field; quantum electronics and laser tech. Engr. Inst. Indsl. Cybernetics and Robotics Bulgarian Acad. Scis., Sofia, 1987; asst. prof. Sofia U., 1991-98, assoc. prof., 1998—; postdoct. fellow Max-Planck-Inst. Quantum Physics, Garching, Munich, Germany, 1997-2000. Contbr. more than 50 articles to sci. jours.; translator (in Bulgarian) Laser-Spektroskopie (W. Demtröder). Fellow Alexander Von Humboldt Found., Bonn, Germany, 1997—. Grantee Austrian Office Acad. Exch., Ministry Sci. Rsch. and Arts, 1996; Max Planck fellow, 1999-2000. Mem. Bulgarian Phys. Union, SPIE. Avocations: skiing, swimming. Office: Sofia U Dept Physics, 5 J Bourchier Blvd, BG-1164 Sofia Bulgaria

DRENHAUS, ULRICH KARL GUSTAV, anatomist, researcher; b. Witten, Germany, June 29, 1946; s. Gustav and Gisela Drenhaus; m. Noboku Omori, Sept. 24, 1976; children: Julia, Mark, Michael, Hanni. D in Natural Scis., Christian-Albrechts U., Kiel, Germany, 1975. Collaborator U. Kiel, 1972-77, U. Bochum, 1977-86; collaborator, lectr. U. Fribourg, Switzerland, 1987—. Contbr. over 60 publs. related to paleodemography, human biology, anatomy and neuroscience. Recipient 1st prize im microphotography German Assn. Biologists, 1999, spl. prize in microphotography, 1997, 98, 99. Mem. Swiss Soc. for Anatomy, Histology, and Embryology (sec., treas. 1998—), European Fedn. Exptl. Morphology (del. 1998—), Am. Assn. Anatomists, N.Y. Acad. Scis., Anatom. Soc., European Anthropol. Assn. Avocation: genealogy. E-mail: ulrich.drenhaus@bluewin.ch. Office: Inst Anatomy & Spl Embryol, Rue A Gockel 1, CH-1700 Fribourg Switzerland

DRENTH, PIETER JOHAN DIEDERIK, psychology educator, consultant; b. Appelscha, Friesland, The Netherlands, Mar. 8, 1935; s. Gerrit and Froukje (Wouda) D.; m. Maria Annetta E. De Boer, 1959; children: Gerard D., Johannes Ch., Martin P. Candidate in psychology, Free U., Amsterdam, The Netherlands, 1955, doctoral in psychology, 1958, PhD in Psychology, 1960; D (hon.), State U. Ghent, 1981; U. Paris, 1996. Selection dept. Royal Dutch Navy, 1955-60; rsch. fellow Standard Oil Co. N.J., N.Y.C., 1960-61; sr. lectr. Free U., Amsterdam, 1962-67, prof. psychology, 1967-98, head dept. work and orgnl. psychology, 1967, vice chancellor, 1983-87, dean faculty psychology and edn., 1998—; vis. prof. Washington U., St. Louis, 1966, U. Wash., Seattle, 1977; cons. Unilever, Rabo-Bank, Mandev, The Netherlands, 1975—; pres. 1st European Conf. Psychology, Amsterdam, 1989; mem. sci. com. adv. panel NATO, Brussels, 1969-83, chmn., 1980-83; mem. supervisory bd. Shell Nederland B.V., 1991—; mem. European Sci. and Tech. Assembly EC Brussels, chmn. Social Sci. Rsch. Coun., The Netherlands, 1995—. Author 5 books; co-author 14 books; co-editor 12 books; contbr. numerous articles to profl. jours., also tests and manuals. Bd. dirs. Netherlands-Am. Com. for Ednl. Exchange, 1986—, Found. Praemium Erasmianum, Amsterdam, 1989—. 1st lt. Royal Dutch Navy, 1958-60. Knighted Order of the Lion of the Netherlands, 1991; decorated comdr. Order of Oranje Nassau, 1996. Mem. APA (fgn. affiliate), Royal Netherlands Acad. Arts and Sci. (gen. sec. 1987-90, pres. 1990-96), Academia Europaea, Netherlands Inst. Psychologists (Heymans award 1986), European Network Profs. in Indsl.-Orgnl. Psychology, Netherlands Orgn. for Advancement Pure Rsch. (coun. 1975-85), Internat. Assn. Applied Psychology (pres. divsn. orgnl. psychology 1982-86), European Assn. Acads. Sci. (pres. 2000—), N.Y. Acad. Scis., Rotary. Home: Pekkendam 6, 1081 HR Amsterdam The Netherlands

DREPAUL, LORIS OMESH, internist, infectious diseases physician; b. Georgetown, Guyana, Feb. 6, 1960; naturalized U.S. citizen; s. Frank Eric and Iris Ismay Etwaria (Masih-Das) D. BA (honors in philosophy)/BS, Bklyn. Coll., CUNY, 1985; MD, NYU, 1989. Diplomate Am. Bd. Internal Medicine. Intern St. Luke's Hosp.-Columbia U. Coll. Physicians and Surgeons, N.Y.C., 1989-90, resident in internal medicine, 1990-91; resident in internal medicine Booth Meml. Med. Ctr.-NYU Sch. Medicine, Queens, 1991-92; fellow in infectious diseases Bronx (N.Y.) VA Med. Ctr.-Mt. Sinai Sch. Medicine, 1992-94; attending in infectious diseases Mary Immaculate Hosp, Queens, Cath. Med. Ctr.-Albert Einstein Coll. Medicine, Bronx, 1995-96; mem. faculty, attending in infectious diseases Highland Hosp., Rochester, N.Y., 1997-98; pvt. practice, Rochester, 1997-98; founder HIV/AIDS Bilingual Primary Care Outreach Program, Bridge Plaza Rehab. Clinic, Queens, N.Y., 1995-96; med. dir. Cmty. Health Network, Inc., Rochester, 1997-98. Mem. AMA, ACP, Med. Soc. State N.Y., Phi Beta Kappa. Avocations: music, bridge, chess, soccer, computers. E-mail: drepaul@pol.net.

DRESCHER, JUDITH ALTMAN, library director; b. Greensburg, Pa., July 6, 1946; d. Joseph Grier and Sarah Margaret (Hewitt) Altman; m. Robert A. Drescher, Aug. 10, 1968 (div. 1980); m. David G. Lindstrom, Jan. 10, 1981. AB, Grove City Coll., 1968; MLS, U. Pitts., 1971. Tchr. Hempfield Sch. Dist., Greensburg, 1968-71; children's libr. Cin. Pub. Libr., 1971-72; br. mgr. Cin. Pub. LIbrary, 1972-74; dir. Rolling Meadows (Ill.) Pub. Libr., 1974-79, Champaign (Ill.) Pub. Libr., 1979-85, Memphis/Shelby County Pub. Libr. and Info. Ctr., 1985—; cons. Providence Assocs., Dallas, 1986-94; Tenn. del. White House Conf. on Librs. and Info. Svcs. Task Force, 1991-92; mem. Tenn. Sec. of State's Commn. on Tech. and Resource Sharing, 1991, 93, steering com. Tenn. Info. and Infrastructure, 1994-97, nat. adv. panel for assessment of role of sch. and pub. librs. U.S. Dept. Edn., 1995-98. Mem. Rhodes Coll. Commn. on 21st Century, Memphis, 1986-88, presdl. adv. com. Rhodes Coll., 1992—; mem. Leadership Memphis, 1987—, selection com., 1992-96; mem. Memphis Arts Coun., 1989-94; bd. dirs. Literacy Coun., 1986-91, Memphis NCCJ, 1989-93, Memphis Grants Info. Ctr., 1992-97, sec., 1993-95; bd. dirs. Memphis Literacy Found., 1988-92, v.p., 1989-90; bd. dirs. Goals for Memphis, 1988-93, chair edn. com., 1989-91, chair nominating com., 1992, leadership acad., 1999—; bd. dirs. U. Memphis Soc., 1998—; mem. exec. adv. bd. Children's Mus., 1988-94, exec. adv. coun. U. Memphis, 1989-99; mem. allocations subcom. United Way, 1989-91, allocations com. Memphis Arts Coun., 100 for the Arts, 1989-91, Libr. Self-study Com. U. Memphis; pres. adv. coun. Lemoyne Coll.; mem. search com. for dean of librs. U. Memphis, 1999—, Leadership Acad., 1999—. Recipient Govt. Leader award U. Ill. YWCA, 1981; Communicator of Yr. award Pub. Rels. Soc. of Am., 1992. Mem. ALA (chmn. intellectual freedom com. 1986-87, coun. 1992-99), Tenn. Libr. Assn., Memphis Libr. Coun., Pub. Libr. Assn. (v.p., pres. 1994-95), Rotary (bd. dirs. 1992-94, sec. 1993-94, chair mem. devel. com. 1994-95), Beta Phi Mu. Home: 1505 Vance Ave Memphis TN 38104-3810 Office: Memphis Shelby County Pub Libr & Info Ctr 1850 Peabody Ave Memphis TN 38104-4021

DRESCHER, KURT WALTER, physicist, educator; b. Wittgendorf, Germany, Dec. 22, 1930; s. August Hermann and Ida (Hörnig) D.; m. Annelore Eva Kunze, Aug. 23, 1958 (dec. Nov. 1994); 1 child, Wolfram Kurt; m. Renate Gertrud Agnes Finke, Mar. 22, 1996. Diploma in physics, Tech. U., Dresden, 1956, Dr.rer.nat., 1962, Dr. Engring. Habil, 1981. Head dept. Microelectronic Rsch. Ctr., Dresden, 1962-73; prof. Tech. U., Chemnitz, Germany, 1973-81; head microelectronic labs. Tech. U., Chemnitz, 1975-82; prof. Tech. U., Dresden, 1981-98, head microelectronic labs., 1990-98; ret., 1998—; pres. Saxonian Inst. Microelectronics, Dresden, 1995-2000. Contbr. over 90 articles to profl. publs.; holder 37 German patents, 56 fgn. patents. Mem. ISHM, Electrochem. Soc. Home: Taubenheimer Str 3, D-01324 Dresden Germany Office: U Tech, Mommsenstr 13, D-01062 Dresden Germany

DRESSEL, HENRY FRANCIS, retired lawyer; b. Bklyn., Apr. 11, 1914; s. Henry Philip and Ernestine (Delmar) D.; m. Rose Marie Valentine, Nov. 24, 1937; 1 child, Diana (Mrs. Anthony P. Fradella). AB, Washington Square Coll., NYU, 1943, JD, 1949. Bar: N.Y. 1949. Clk. corp. law firm Chadbourne, Stanchfield & Levy (and its successors), N.Y.C., 1933-43; pvt. practice law N.Y.C., 1950-86; ptnr. Dressel & Altman, P.C.; of counsel Berger & Steingut, 1986-2000. Lt. USNR, 1943-46. Named hon. col. Okla., 1958, Okie, 1969. Mem. N.Y. State Bar Assn., Assn. Bar City of N.Y., Am. Judicature Soc., Justinian Soc., Internat. Footprint Assn., Phi Delta Phi. Democrat. Episcopalian. Home: 42 Clubhouse Ln Marlboro NJ 07746-1712 Office: Dressel & Hatab PC 18 E 50th St New York NY 10022-6817

DRESSEL, MARGARET JANE, artist, art educator; b. Brookline, Mass., Aug. 25, 1949; d. Chauncey Lovett Megargle and Esther Laura Field; m. Richard Dressel; children: Bethany, Keith. Student, Moore Coll. Art, 1967-68, Nat. Acad. Art, 1985-86; Assoc. in Occupl. Studies, Pratt Inst., 1985. Owner, artist Peggy Dressel Studio, Oakland, N.J., 1990—; graphic designer Intra Design Inc., Ramsey, N.J., 1990-94; illustrator, asst. Jacqui Morgan Studio, N.Y.C., 1986-90; painting instr. Ramsey Adult Sch., 1996—, Glen Rock (N.J.) Cmty. Sch., 1997—, Art Ctr. No. N.J., New Milford, 1999—; founder Pastel Plus, N.J., pres., 1997—; mem. Blackwell St. Ctr. Arts; chmn. CAA Nat. Juried Exhbns., Ridgewood, N.J., 1993, 94, 95. One-woman shows include St. Peter's Ch., N.Y.C., 1992, Blackwell St. Gallery, Dover, N.J., 1994, Lena DiGangi Gallery, West Paterson, N.J., 1994, Ringwood Manor W. Wing Gallery, N.J. State Pk., 1994, ADP, Inc. Gallery, Roseland, N.J., 1995, Dow Jones & Co., S. Brunswick, N.J., 1994, 96; N.Y. Theol. Sem., N.Y.C., 1998, The Interch. Ctr., N.Y.C., 1998; represented in numerous juried exhbns. and pvt. collections; illustrator mags., books, brochures, ads, posters; featured artist poster and calendar N.J. Fine Artist Collection, 1998. Recording sec. Oakland Libr. Bd., 1979-80, pres., 1980-82. Recipient Purchase award Degas Pastel Soc., 1992, Merit award Degas Pastel Soc., 1992, Cynthia Googdal Meml., Ridgewood Art Inst., Nat. Bergen Mus., 1997, others; named Best in Show, Inserria Corp., 1992. Mem. Cmty. Arts Assn. (pres. 1994-96), Southea. Pastel Soc. (signature mem.), Oreg. Pastel Soc. (signature mem.), Am. Artist Profl. League. Democrat. Methodist. Avocations: art, music, traveling, gardening. Office: Peggy Dressel Studio 11 Rockaway Ave Oakland NJ 07436-2122

DRESSEN, FREDDY SIMEON, lawyer; b. Courbevoie, France, Oct. 12, 1946; s. Simeon and France (Durrleman) D.; m. Christiane Colle, Sept. 12, 1970; children: Anne, Arnaud. JD, Paris U., 1970, Adv. Legal Deg., 1971; LLM, Cornell U., Ithaca, N.Y., 1972. Practicing atty.-at-law, France. Ptnr. Lussan Brouilaud, Paris, 2000—; vol. French Peace Corps, Tunis, Tunisia, 1972-73; clk. European Communities Commn., Brussels, 1974; assoc. Cahill Gordon & Reindel, Paris, 1974-80; European counsel Cahill Gordon & Reindel, 1980-2000. Mem. Assn. Française des Avocats Conseils d'Entreprises, Am. Club Paris, Cornell U. Coun., Cornell Club of France. Home: 80 rue Bonaparte, Paris France 75006 Office: Cahill Gordon & Reindel, Lussan Brouillaud, 250 bis Blvd St-Germain, Paris France 75007

DREVET, JOEL R., biology educator; b. Bayonne, France, Dec. 28, 1960. PhD, Claude Bernard U., Lyon, France, 1989. Rsch. asst. U. Can., Calgary, 1990-91, rsch. assoc., 1991-93; asst. prof. Blaise Pascal U., Aubiere, France, 1993-94, assoc. prof., 1994-98, prof. cell biology, 1998—. Office: CNRS UMR 6547, 24 Ave de Landais, 63177 Aubiere Cedex, France

DRÉVILLON, JEAN YVES, retired psychology educator; b. Brest, Brittany, France, Sept. 4, 1927; s. Emile and Jeanne (Lavanant) D.; m. Josette Le Pouësard, Sept. 8, 1950; children: Marie-Pierre, Marc, Philippe. License in Psychology and Philosophy, Caen U., Paris, 1959, MA, 1960, PhD in Psychology, 1961; State Doctorate, Paris-Sorbonne U., France, 1975. State diploma of vocat. guidance counselor, Paris, 1950; cert. orgn. and methods of work counselor, Paris, 1957. Vocat. guidance counselor COP, Saint Lo/Cherbourg, France, 1950-58; dir. counselling svc. Cherbourg, 1958-64; head Counsellors Edn. Inst. U. Caen, 1964-80, asst. lectr. psychology, 1968-75, prof. psychology, 1975-92, emeritus prof., 1992—, dean scis. of life unit, 1975-78, 86-89, head dept. psychology, 1978-89, head Sch. Psychologists Edn. Ctr., 1978-82; expert UNESCO, Paris, 1976, European Cmty., Bruxelles, 1977, cons., 1982-84; founder. Pres. of Sch. for Parents, Caen, 1978-96. Author of 17 books including L'Orientation Scolaire et Professionnelle, 1966 (2 edits., 6 translations), Pratiques Educatives et Developpement Operatoire, 1980 (2 translations), Fonctionnement Cognitif et Individualite, 1986; author, editor: Les Aides Cognitives, 1992; contbr. articles to profl. jours. Sgt. French Mil., 1947-48. Named comdr. Acad. Palms Order, 1982. Mem. Nat. Fedr. Schs. for Parents and Educators (adminstr. 1992-2000), Internat. Assn. Applied Linguistics (pres. 2000—), N.Y. Acad. Scis., Acad. Scis., Art and Letters. Avocations: painting, sculpture, sailing, shooting, judo. Home: 17 Rue Gustave Flaubert, 14300 Caen Normandy, France Office: U Caen Normandy, Esplanade de la Paix, 14032 Cedex Caen Normandy, France

DREW, JEANETTE HELEN, medical scientist researcher; b. Melbourne, Victoria, Australia, Mar. 13, 1965; d. Leslie and Georgia (Salli) D.; m. Kevin Michael Tomlinson, Dec. 22, 1996. B in Applied Sci., Royal Melbourne Inst. Tech., Australia, 1990; grad. diploma edn., U. Melbourne, Australia, 1992; M in Health Scis., La Trobe U., Melbourne, 1997. Rsch. asst. Rsch. Ctr. for Cancer & Transplantation U. Melbourne, Australia, 1982-87; med. scientist Peter MacCallum Cancer Inst., Melbourne, Australia, 1987-92; sr. scientist Alfred Group of Hosps., Melbourne, Australia, 1992-94; cytometry applications cons. BioFlow, Melbourne, Australia, 1994-95; pre-doctoral student U. Western Australia, Perth, 1995—; hon. rsch. fellow Women & Infants Rsch. Found., Perth, 1996—; convenor Western Australian Cytometry Users Group, Pert, 1996—. Editor Benchpress, 1990-93. Student rep. Student Rights Coun., Royal Melbourne Inst. Tech., 1988-90; metro-political student rep. Melbourne City Coun., 1990-91; student rep. Applied Sci. Faculty, Royal Melbourne Inst. Tech., 1989-91; scientist rep. Australian Hosp. Assn., 1993. Fellow Royal Microscopical Soc., U.K., 1994, E.H. Flack Rsch. award Alfred Group Hosps., E.H. Flack Rsch. Trust, Victoria, Australia, 1993. Mem. Australian Inst. Med. Scientists (hon. sec. 1990-93, publicity coord. 1992-93, continuing edn. convenor 1996—, Postgrad. Rsch. Excellence Scholarship 1993), Internat. Soc. Analytical Cytology, European Soc. for Analytical Cytometry. Avocations: snow skiing, water skiing, softball, roller blading, sailing. E-mail: jdrew@absgyn.uwa.edu.au. Office: Women & Infants Rsch Found, 374 Bagot Rd, Subiaco 6008, Australia

DREWES, ASBJØRN MOHR, internist, gastroenterologist; b. Århus, Denmark, July 23, 1956; s. Vagn Mohr and Vibeke (Schmidt) D.; m. Karen MØlgaard Jensen, Sept. 7, 1956; children: Julie, Line, Anne. MD, Arhus U., 1983. Intern dept. internal medicine Skive and Nyk Mors Hosp., 1983-84; resident dept. internal medicine Nyk Mors Hosp., 1984-88; resident dept. rheumatology Viborg Hosp., 1988-91; resident dept. internal medicine Aalborg Hosp., 1991-94; internist Aalborg U., 1989—; sr. registrar depts. internal medicine Aalborg Hosp., 1991—; assoc. prof. Aalborg U. and Aarhus U., 1997-99; head of rsch./dept. med. gastroenterology Aalborg (Denmark) Hosp., 1999—. Contbr. articles to profl. jours. Mem. European Sleep Rsch. Soc., Danish Soc. Gastroenterology, Internat. Assn. for the Study of Pain. Avocations: riding, driving with horses. Fax: 45 99322503. E-mail: drewes@smi.auc.dk. Home: Himmelbjergvej 1, DK-8600 Silkeborg Denmark Office: Aalborg Hospital, Dept Med Gastroenterology, DK-9000 Ålborg Denmark

DREWRY, DON NEAL, safety engineer; b. Chgo., Oct. 6, 1949; s. Ruben Neal and Vlasta A. (Waleck) D.; m. Patricia Ann English, Mar. 8, 1975; children: Neal Thomas, Michelle Lynn. BA, Govs. State U., 1978; BS in Engring., U. Hartford, 1984; MS in Fire Protection Engring., Worcester Polytech. Inst., 1986. Mfg. engring./NC programmer Bloomer-Fisk, Chgo., 1974-75; inspector, supr. Hartford Steam Boiler, Chgo., 1975-78; asst. mgr. quality assurance svc. Hartford Steam Boiler Inspection and Ins. Co., 1978-80, project engr., 1980-81, rsch. engr., 1982-84, fire protection cons., 1984-87; regional mgmt. property engr. Hartford Steam Boiler Inspection and Ins.

Co., Basking Ridge, N.J., 1987-92, regional manage ins. engr., 1992-94; br. mgr., property program mgr. power generation HSB Profl. Loss Control, Basking Ridge, 1994-97, v.p. industry svcs., 1997-99, v.p. loss control svcs., 1999—; com. fire protection task force Edison Elec. Inst., Washington, 1995. With USN, 1970-74. Mem. ASME, Soc. Fire Protection Engrs., Nat. Fire Protection Assn. (com. NFPA-850 1985—), Nat. Bd. of Boiler and Pressure Vessel Inspectors. Home: 1401 Sycamore Ave Easton PA 18040-8106 Office: HSB Profl Loss Control 188 Mount Airy Rd Basking Ridge NJ 07920-2021

DREWS, RUDEIGER, military officer; b. Rastenburg, Poland, Feb. 12, 1942; m. Barbara Briesemann; children: Carolin, Robin. Commd. lt. German Army Forces Command, 1964, advanced through grades to lt. gen., 1998; co. comdr. 3d co. tank battalion 54 German Army Forces Command, Wolfhagen, 1971-73; gen. staff tng. officer Bundeswehr Command and Staff Coll., Hamburg, 1973-75; officer studies Northag, Mönchengladbach, 1976-79; officer Armored Brigade 34, Kassel, 1979-81; comdr. tank battalion Armored Brigade 34, Neumünster, 1981-83; asst. br. chief Armed Forces Staff, Bonn, 1983-84, spokesman for press, 1984-86; chief of staff 6th Armored Inf. Divsn., Neumünster, 1986-88; liaison officer Office of Fed. Pres., Bonn, 1988-90; comdr. 8th Armored Brigade, Lüneburg, 1990-91, Combat Arms Sch. 2/Armor Sch., Munster, 1991-94, Mil. Dist. Roman Five, 10th Armored Divsn., Sigmaringen, 1994, German Army Forces Command, Koblenz, 1998—. Office: German Army Forces Command, Von-Kuhl-Strasse 50, 56070 Koblenz Germany

DREXLER, HEINRICH JURGEN, food product executive; b. Freiburg, Breisgau, Germany, July 8, 1939; s. Hermann Gottlieb and Anna Elisabeth (Hahndorf) D.; m. Ulrike Anneliese Neugebauer, July 6, 1966; children: Claudia Karin, Cornelia Birgit. Dipl. engr., Tech. U. Berlin, 1966; dr. rer. nat., U. Hohenheim, 1971. Cons. F.E.S. Germany, Pindorama, Brazil, 1973-74; scientist, rschr. Inst. Food Tech., Stuttgart, Germany, 1974-76; mgr. R&D Spreda/Eckes, Burgdorf, Switzerland, 1976-83; mgr. food flavors Firmenich S.A., Geneva, Switzerland, 1986-88; mgr. R&D Kambly S.A., Trubschachen, Switzerland, 1988-93; food industry expert E.C. Phare Project, Bucharest, Romania, 1996; quality mgmt. cons. Qualicon, Kirchberg, Switzerland, 1994-96, quality sys. auditor SQS, Zollikofen, Switzerland, T.U.V., Thun, Switzerland, 1994-98; programming analyst CUEPE, Geneva, 1988-2000; software developer U. Siegen, Germany, 1994-01; industry expert G.T.Z./A.F.C. Project, Sofia, Bulgaria, 1997; quality sys. expert European Cmty. Phare Project, Sarajevo, Bosnia and Skopje, Macedonia, 1997-98; quality mgr. Miracle Holding AG, Langenthal, Switzerland, 2000—. Translator: Technology of Fruit Juice Processing, 1973; contbr. articles to profl. jours. Mem. Swiss Soc. Food Sci. and Tech. Avocations: mountain hiking, sailing, skiing. Home: Gyrisberg 140, CH-3400 Burgdorf Bern, Switzerland Office: Quaso Gmbh, 3422 Kirchberg BE, Switzerland

DREXLER, JOANNE LEE, art appraiser; b. Washington, Mar. 21, 1944; d. Elias J. and Beatrice Charlotte (Goldberg) D.; m. James R. Cohen, May 31, 1965; children: Terri I., Brett F. Student, Louvre, Paris, 1963-64; BA, Tufts U., 1965; Diamond and Pearl Cert., GIA, N.Y.C., 1974. Tchr. of French Stuyvesant H.S., N.Y.C., 1965-66; decorator, art cons. Joanne Cohen Interiors, Mamaroneck, N.Y., 1967-69; assoc. prof. Hofstra U., L.I., N.Y., 1979-80; pres. Esquire Appraisals, N.Y.C. and Larchmont, N.Y., 1969—; TV appearances include CNN, Sept. 1991; cons., lectr. in field; art judge various contests, art dealer. Organizer, curator N.C. in N.Y. art show Nat. Arts Club, 1993, African Am. art show Nat. Arts Club, 1994; weekly columnist Gannett chain newspapers, 1980-86. Mem. Am. Soc. Appraisers (sr.; v.p. Hudson Valley White Plains chpt. 1989, bd. dirs. 1997, pres. White Plains chpt. 1993-94, 97-98), Appraisers' Assn. Am. (cert.), Nat. Arts Club N.Y. (exhbn. com.). Avocations: travel, swimming, horseback riding. Home: 23 Trudy Ln Bedford NY 10506-1337 Office: Esquire Appraisals Inc 630 1st Ave New York NY 10016-3700

DREYFUS, FRANÇOIS-GEORGES, history educator; b. Paris, Sept. 13, 1928; s. Robert and Hélène (Bloch) D.; m. Nicole Fourment, Sept. 8, 1953. MA, U. Paris, 1950, Agrégé d'Histoire, 1952, PhD, 1968. Tchr. high sch., Strasbourg, France, 1953-58; asst. CNRS, Mainz, Germany, 1958-61; asst. prof. U. Strasbourg, 1961-68, prof., 1968-91, dir. Inst. Polit. Studies, 1969-80; prof. history Sorbonne, U. Paris, 1991-99; dir. rsch. in social scis. Ministry of Univ., Paris, 1979-81; dir. Inst. for European Studies, Strasbourg, 1980-92. Author: Histoire de Vichy, 1990, L'Allemagne contemporaine, 1991, Histoire de la Résistance, 1995; editor: France and EC, 1993, Le IIIo Reich, 1998, Passions Republicaines, 2000. Vice chmn. Club 89, Paris, 1991—. Decorated officer Legion of Honor, comdr. Palmes Academiques (France), Bundesverdienstkreuz 1st class (Germany). Mem. Rotary (pres. Strasbourg 1974-75). Mem. Gaullist Party. Lutheran. Office: 18 rue ND de Lorette, 75009 Paris France

DREYFUS, GÉRARD, electronics engineering educator; b. Alger, Algeria, May 10, 1948; s. Jacques and Colette (Narboni) D.; m. Catherine Gans, July 10, 1971; children: Nicolas, Rémi. Degree in engring., Sch. Physics and Indsl. Chem., Paris, 1971; D in Scis., U. Paris, 1976. Rschr. Nat. Ctr. Sci. Rsch. (CNRS), Paris, 1971-74; asst. prof. electronics Sch. Physics and Indsl. Chemistry (ESPCI), Paris, 1974-82, prof., 1982—; sci. advisor NETRAL, Paris, 1994—; cons. XRS, Orsay, France, 1993, Michelin, Clermont-Ferrand, France, 1998. Author: La Méthode du Recuit Simulé, 1988; editor: Neural Networks from Models to Applications, 1988. Pres. Sci. et Musique, Orsay, 1995—. Recipient Coupe du Président de la République, 1980. Mem. IEEE (sr.). Office: ESPCI Lab d'Electronique, 10 rue Vauquelin, F-75005 Paris France

DREYFUS, LEE SHERMAN, international speaker; b. Milw., June 20, 1926; s. Woods Orlow and Clare (Bluett) D.; m. Joyce Mae Unke, Apr. 5, 1947; children: Susan Dreyfus Fosdick, Lee S. Jr. BA, U. Wis., 1949, MA, 1952, PhD, 1957; LLD (hon.), Lakeland Coll., Wis., 1978; LHD (hon.), Blackbourne Coll., Ill., 1984; LCD (hon.), Marian Coll., Wis., 1985; LLD (hon.), Hangyang U., Seoul, Korea, 1982. Assoc. prof., gen. mgr. Radio WDET Wayne State U., Detroit, 1952-62; prof., gen. mgr. WHA-TV U. Wis., Madison, 1962-67; chancellor U. Wis., Stevens Point, 1967-79; gov. State of Wis., Madison, 1979-83; pres., COO Sentry Ins. Corp., Stevens Point, 1983-84; pres. L.S.D. Inc., Waukesha, Wis., 1985—; internat. spkr. Washington Spkrs. Bur., Alexandria, Va., 1988—; chief of mission U.S. AID, Vietnam, 1967-74; bd. dirs. Am.-Can. Great Lakes Commn., Washington, 1979-83, Marcus Corp., Assoc. Bank Corp., Nat. Telemedia, Inc.; del. Am. Assn. State Coll. and Univ., China, Taiwan, Poland, 1973-76. Radio child actor regular weekly drama broadcasts Sta. WISN Milw., 1933-44; creator world's 1st intercontinental video classroom, U.S. to France, 1965. Regent U. Wis., Madison, 1990-96; trustee Emerson Coll., Boston, 1988-91; co-chmn. Wis. Sesquicentennial, Madison, 1996—; presdl. del. to Benin, Africa, 1991; spl. del. State Dept. Acad. Mission to Cyprus, 1983; chmn. Wis. Cable TV Commn., Madison, 1972; mem. Wis. Land Stewardship Commn., 1998, Wis. Humanities Commn., 1998. With USNR, 1944-46; comdr.-in-chief Wis. N.G., 1979-83. Recipient Dist. Pub. Svc. medal Dept. Def., 1982, Pres.'s Gold medal U.S. Army, 1984; named Man of the Yr., Kappa Sigma, 1980; named to Hall of Fame, DeMolay Internat., 1991. Mem. Nat. Inst. Former Govs. (sec. 1990-94), Am. Legion (life), VFW (life), Masons (33 deg.), Shriner. Republican. Episcopalian. Avocations: charitable fund raising, reading, civic projects, politics. Home: 3159 Madison St Waukesha WI 53188-4409 Office: PO Box 1776 Waukesha WI 53187-1776

DREYFUS, SUSAN KAHN, elementary education educator; b. Atlanta, Dec. 8, 1946; d. Truman Frederick and Gloria Charlotte (Shefsky) Kahn; children: Diane, Wendy, David. BS, U. Memphis, 1970; M in Adminstrn., Trevecca Nazarene Coll., 1991. Tchr. Montrose (Ark.) Acad., 1976-77, Memphis City Schs., 1986—; founder Circuit Playhouse, Inc., Memphis, 1969; leader The Creative Cir., Overland Park, Kans., 1982-84. V.p. Dem. Women of Memphis, 1993-94, exec. com., 1991-93; vol. Hadassah, Memphis, 1981—, Memphis Polit. Caucus, 1991—; treas. Memphis Women's Leadership Forum, 1998—; vol. Memphis Race for the Cure. Mem. NEA, Tenn. Edn. Assn., Memphis Edn. Assn., ASCD, Tchrs. English, Memphis Assn. Tchrs. Maths., Nat. Reading Assn. Jewish. Avocations: stamp collecting, fitness training, reading, travel. Home: 860 Creekside Dr Memphis TN 38117-5004

DREYFUSS, PATRICIA, chemist, researcher; b. Reading, Pa., Apr. 28, 1932; d. Edmund T. and Anna J. (Oberc) Gajewski; m. M. Peter Dreyfuss, Jan. 30, 1954; children: David Daniel, Simeon Karl. BS Chemistry, U. Rochester, 1954; PhD, U. Akron, 1964. Postdoctoral fellow U. Liverpool (Eng.), 1963-65; rsch. chemist B.F. Goodrich, Brecksville, Ohio, 1965-71; rsch. assoc. Case Western Res. U., Cleve., 1971-73, sr. rsch. assoc., 1973-74; rsch. assoc. Inst. Polymers Sci., U. Akron, Ohio, 1974-84; sr. rsch. scientist, rsch. prof. Mich. Molecular Inst., Midland, 1984-90; vis. rsch. fellow U. Bristol, 1972; cons. in field, 1974—; vis. prof. Polish Acad. Scis., Poland, 1974; adj. prof. Cen. Mich. U., Mt. Pleasant, Mich. Tech U., Houghton, 1986-92, Mich. Molecular Inst., Midland, 1990-92. Author: Poly (Tetrahydrofuran), 1982; contbr. numerous articles to profl. jours.; co-author books. Flutist West Suburban Philharm. Orch., Lakewood, Ohio, 1969-75, Midland (Mich.) Cmty. Orch., 1990-97; Explorer advisor Explorer post 2069 Boy Scouts Am., Akron, 1975-81; sec., bd. dirs. Adhesion Soc., 1976-88; treas. LWV, 1959-60; mem. ensemble Blessed Sacrament Ch., Midland; occasional flute soloist. Centennial scholar U. Rochester, 1950-54; Sohio fellow U. Akron, 1960, NSF Coop. Grad. fellow, 1961-63, Internat. fellow AAUW, 1964-65, NIH Spl. fellow, 1972-73; recipient Vol. awrd Odyssey of the Mind, Region V, 1999-2000. Mem. Am. Chem. Soc. (cen. region mtg. chmn. 1984-90, loc. sec. chmn., vice chmn., sec. and bd. dirs. Akron chpt. 1974-84, bd. dirs. Midland chpt. 1985-89, Outstanding Leadership Performance award 1981, Disting. Svc. award Akron chpt. 1985), AAUW (bd. dirs. Akron chpt.). Achievements include 4 patents in field. Home: 3980 N Old Pine Trl Midland MI 48642-8891

DREZE, XAVIER ETIENNE URIEL MARIE, marketing educator; b. Louvain, Belgium, Dec. 8, 1964; s. Jacques H. D. and Monique Mayence. Ingenieur comml. et de Gestion, Univ. Cath. de Louvain, Louvain-la-Neuve, Belgium, 1985; MBA, U. Chgo., 1992, PhD, 1995. Asst. prof. mktg. U. So. Calif., L.A., 1995—. Bd. dirs. Found. Jules et Jose Dreze, Belgium, 1995—. Mem. Alpha Kappa Psi. Avocation: sailing. Office: U So Calif Marshall Sch Bus Los Angeles CA 90089-0001

DRIEL, BAS VAN, laboratory manager; b. Rotterdam, The Netherlands, Aug. 3, 1961; s. Nicolaas Van and Alida Van (Van Rumpt) D.; m. Conny Van Nieuwendijk, Dec. 3, 1963; children: Alies, Jelske. HBO in Microbiology, Vant Hoff, Rotterdam, 1981, HBO in Clin. Chemistry, 1983, HBO in Med. Biol., 1983. Microbiol. lab. technician SSDZ, Delft, The Netherlands, 1985-90; head dept. immunology/serology SSDZ, Delft, 1990-98; lab. mgr. dept. microbiology Alcontrol Biochem. Food, Hertogenbosch, The Netherlands, 1998—. Soldier Med. Dept., 1984-85. Mem. Nederlanse Vereniging voor Microbiologie. Avocation: running marathons. Office: Alcontrol Biochem Food BV, Koenendelseweg 11, 5222BG Hertogenbosch The Netherlands

DRIESSEN, BART, lawyer; b. Rotterdam, The Netherlands, June 3, 1967; arrived in Belgium, 1994.; s. Alousius Karel Driessen and Mimy Kosse. LLM, Cath. U. Nijmegen, The Netherlands, 1989; MA in Internat. Rels., U. Kent at Canterbury, Eng., 1991; Dr. univ. summa cum laude, Eötvös Loránd Tudomány Egyetem, Budapest, Hungary, 1993. Mem. Brussels Bar 1994. Spl. asst. Mr. Gijs M. de Vries, Mem. European Parliament, Brussels, 1993; legal rschr. Unrepresented Nations and Peoples Orgn., The Hague, The Netherlands, 1993-94; assoc. Akin Gump Strauss Hauer Feld & Dassesse, Brussels, 1994-96; sr. assoc. Vermulst & Waer Advocaten, Brussels, 1996-99; auxiliair European Commn. (DG Trade), 1999-2000; sr. assoc. Vermulst Waer & Verhaeghe, Brussels, 2000—. Author: (book) A Concept of Nation in International Law, 1992, (study) Anti-dumping and Safeguards in the Euro-Mediterranean Association, 1998; contbr. articles to profl. jours. Fax: 32 2 534 5888. E-mail: bartdriessen@hotmail.com. Office: Vermulst Waer & Verhaeghe, Rue Blanche 33, Brussels Belgium

DRIJVERS, HENDRIK WILLEM, Semitic languages/cultures of Near East educator; b. Winschoten, Groningen, Netherlands, Sept. 25, 1934; s. Jan and Sara Hendrika (Poppen) D.; m. Antonia Johanna Schutte, Mar. 23, 1953; children: Jan Willem, Nelleke, Gerhart, Hendrik Jan, Margreet. D in Semitic Langs., U. Groningen, 1965, PhD in Semitic Langs., 1966, DDiv, 1969. Ordained to ministry Dutch Reformed Ch., 1957. Assoc. prof. Semitic langs. U. Groningen, 1970-76, ordinary prof., 1976—, dean faculty of arts, 1981-84; vis. prof. Inst. for Advanced Studies, Princeton, 1977-78; chmn. sect. arts Dutch Acad. Coun., 1981-87; mem. governing bd. U. Groningen, 1972-74. Author: The Book of the Law of Countries, 1965, Bardaisan of Edessa, 1966, Baal Shamin, Lord of Heaven, 1971, Old Syriac Inscriptions, 1972, The Religion of Palmyra, 1976, Cults and Beliefs at Edessa, 1980, East of Antioch, 1984, History and Religion in Late Antique Syria, 1994, The Finding of the True Cross, 1997, The Old Syriac Insciptions of Edessa, 1999; editor: Religion, Culture and Methodology, 1973, IV Symposium Syriacum, 1987. Mem. Dutch Acad. Avocation: collecting art and studio glass. Home: TWS Mansholtstraat 50, 9728 MB Groningen Netherlands Office: Faculty of Arts U Groningen, PO Box 716, 9700 AS Groningen Netherlands

DRIKAKIS, DIMITRIOS, mechanical engineer, educator; b. Athens, Greece, Mar. 30, 1965; Arrived in Eng. 1995; s. Theoklis and Maria (Chasapi) D.; m. Stavroula Alevizakou, Sept. 5, 1992. BSc, MSc in Mech. Engring., Nat. Tech. U. Athens, 1987, PhD, 1991. Rsch. and tchg. asst. Nat. Tech. U. Athens, 1988-91; rsch. assoc. U. Erlangen (Germany) - Nurenberg, 1992-93, head rsch. group, project leader, 1993-95; lectr., coord. European project U. Manchester (Eng.) Inst. of Sci. and Tech., 1995-99; reader in computational fluid dynamics Queen Mary and Westfield Coll., U. London, 1999—; coord. U.K.-North pilot ctr. of European Rsch. Cmty. on Flow Turbulence and Combustion, 1995-99. Contbr. articles to profl. jours. Rsch. grantee Engring. and Phys. Scis. Rsch. Coun., 1996, 97, 98—, Commn. European Cmtys., 1995, 96—. Achievements include development of advanced computational fluid dynamics methods, currently used by industrial and university research groups. E-mail: d.drikakis@qmw.ac.uk. Home: 262 Buckhurst Way, Hazel Grove Buckhurst Hill Essex IG9 6JG, England Office: Queen Mary & Westfield Coll, U London Dept Engring, London E1 4NS, England

DRINAN, ROBERT FREDERICK, priest, law educator; b. Boston, Nov. 15, 1920; s. James and Ann (Flanagan) D. BA, Boston Coll., Newton, 1942, MA, 1947; LLB, Georgetown U., Washington, 1949, LLM, 1950. D.C. Bar, 1950, Mass. Bar, 1956, U.S. Supreme Ct. 1955. Dean, prof. Boston Coll. Law Sch., Newton, Mass., 1956-70; mem. congress House of Reps., Newton, 1971-81; prof. law Georgetown U., Washington, 1981—; mem. Nat. Exec. Com., Am. Judicature Soc., 1962-64, Assn. Am. Law Schs., 1967-69, Harvard U. Divinity Sch., 1975-78, House of Delegates of Am. Bar Assn., 1994-97; chmn. Boston Bar Assn., 1964, Am. Bar Assn., 1966-67, Mass. Bar Assn., 1962-69, U.S. Commn. on Civil Rights, 1962-70, Am. Bar Assn., 1982-86. Fellow ABA, AACS; mem. Lawyrs Com. for Human Rights, Common Cause. E-mail: drinan@law.georgetown.edu. Office: Georgetown U Law Ctr 600 New Jersey Ave NW Washington DC 20001-2075

DRINKO, JOHN DEAVER, lawyer; b. St. Marys, W.Va., June 17, 1921; s. Emery J. and Hazel (White) D.; m. Elizabeth Gibson, May 14, 1946; children: Elizabeth Lee Sullivan, Diana Lynn Martin, John Randall, Jay Deaver. AB, Marshall U., 1942; JD, Ohio State U., 1944; postgrad., U. Tex. Sch. Law, 1944; LLD (hon.), Marshall U., 1980, Ohio State U., 1986, John Carroll U., 1987, Capital U., 1988, Cleve. State U., 1990; DHL (hon.), David N. Myers Coll., 1990, U. N.H., 1992, Baldwin-Wallace Coll., 1993, Ursuline Coll., 1994, Notre Dame Coll., 1997, U. Rio Grande, 1999. Bar: Ohio 1945, D.C 1946, U.S. Dist. Ct. (no. dist.) Ohio 1958. Assoc. Baker & Hostetler, Cleve., 1945-55, ptnr., 1955-69, mng. ptnr., from 1969, sr. adviser to mng. com.; chmn. bd. Cleve. Inst. Electronics Inc., Double D Ranch Inc., Ohio; bd. dirs. Cloyes Gear and Products Inc., McGean-Rohco Worldwide Inc., Orvis Co. Inc., Preformed Line Products Inc. Trustee Elizabeth G. and John D. Drinko Charitable Found., Orvis-Perkins Found., Thomas F. Peterson Found., Mellen Found., The Cloyes-Myers Found., Marshall U. Found.; founder Consortium of Multiple Sclerosis Ctrs., Mellen Conf. on Acute and Critical Care Nursing, Case Western Res. U. Disting. fellow Cleve. Clinc Found., 1991; Ohio State Law Sch. Bldg. named in his honor, 1995, libr. at Marshall U. named in his honor, 1997; inducted into Bus. Hall of Fame, Marshall Univ., 1996. Mem. ABA, Am. Jud. Assn., Bar Assn. Greater Cleve., Greater Cleve. Growth Assn., Ohio State Bar Assn., Jud. Conf. 8th Jud. Dist. (life), Soc. Benchers, Case Western Res. U. Law Sch. Assn., Cleve. Play House, Cleve. Civil War Round-table, Mayfield Country Club, Union Club, The Club at Soc. Ctr., O'Donnell Golf Club, Order of Coif, 33o Scottish Rite Mason, Knight Templar, York Rite, Euclid Blue Lodge No. 599 (Jesters, Shrine, Grotto). Republican. Presbyterian. Home: 4891 Middledale Rd Cleveland OH 44124-2522 also: 1245 Otono Dr Palm Springs CA 92264-8445 Office: Baker & Hostetler LLP 1900 E 9th St Ste 3200 Cleveland OH 44114-3475

DRINNON, JANIS BOLTON, artist, poet, author, volunteer; b. Pineville, Ky., July 28, 1922; d. Clyde Herman and Violet Ethiele (Hendrickson) Bolton; m. Kenneth Cleveland Drinnon, June 13, 1948; 1 child, Dena Daryl. Grad. high sch., Middlesboro, Ky., 1943; student, Lincoln Meml. U., Harrogate, Tenn., 1947-48; commercial art cert., Art Instrn. Sch., Mpls., 1968; student, Newspaper Inst. Am. Author: In HIS Care: A Book of Inspirational Poetry, 1998. Organizer, prodr., dir. religious plays drama dept. Alice Bell Bapt. Ch., Knoxville, Tenn.; mem. New Hopewell Baptist Ch., Knoxville. Recepient Editors Choice award The Nat. Libr. of Poetry; Named to the Internat. Poetry Hall of Fame in 1996. Mem. Internat. Soc. Poets (disting. mem., nom. poet of the year 1995, 96, 97, 99, 2000). Republican. Avocations: arts, crafts, oil painting, composing poetry. Home: 7434 Hodges Ferry Rd Knoxville TN 37920-8136

DRISCOLL, DAVID LEE, chiropractor; b. Storm Lake, Iowa, Aug. 3, 1954; s. Glenn Francis and Jeannine Ann (Layer) D.; m. Joan Marie Valle, Sept. 8, 1973; children: Jennifer Marie, Matthew Bryan. D Chiropractic, Logan Coll. Chiropractic, Chesterfield, Mo., 1978. Pvt. practice Colorado Springs, 1978—. Fellow Internat. Biocranial Acad. (assoc. instr., ednl. dir.), Internat. Acad. Clin. Acupuncture; mem. Am. Chiropractic Assn., Colo. Chiropractic Assn., El Paso County Chiropractic Assn., Internat. Biocranial Acad. (ednl. dir.). Republican. Roman Catholic. Avocations: volleyball, golf, reading. Home: 813 Crown Ridge Dr Colorado Springs CO 80904-1731 Office: Driscoll Chiropractic 1819 W Colorado Ave Colorado Springs CO 80904-3836

DRISCOLL, DIANA SANDERSON, optometrist, consultant; b. Anderson, Ind., July 12, 1957. BA in Psychology, U. Tex., 1980; OD, U. Houston, 1985. Lic. optometrist, Tex. Ptnr. Vision Ctrs., Austin, Cedar Park,, Tex., 1988-91; pvt. practice San Antonio, 1988-95; ptnr. Total Eye Care, Colleyville, Tex.; pres. Priority Cons., Inc., 1999—; pres., founder Practice Dynamics, Inc., San Antonio, 1988-92; ptnr. Profl. Cons., Lubbock, Tex., 1988-91; ptnr., founder Opticians Rev., Austin, 1988-92, Profl. Money Mgmt., Inc., 1992-94; guest radio and TV programs. Exec. program dir. Prevent Blindness, Austin, 1985, vol., 1988—; vol. Big Bros.-Big Sisters, San Antonio, 1991-93. Recipient Hydrocurve Contact Lens award Barnes-Hind, 1985, Found. of Excellence award Tex. Assn. Optometrists, 1983. Mem. Am. Optometrists Assn., Tex. Assn. Optometrists (Found. of Excellence award 1983), Tarrant County Optometric Soc., Soc. for Therapeutic Optometrists. Republican. Avocations: kids, finance, running, music, skiing. Office: Total Eye Care 5005 Colleyville Blvd Colleyville TX 76034-5866

DRISCOLL, RICHARD STARK, retired land evaluation and land use planner; b. Denver, Sept. 16, 1928; s. Myron William and Edith Helene (Stark) D.; m. Joyce Lynn Yarbrough, Jan. 9, 1954; children: Vicki Lynn Driscoll Kiefe, Kelly Sue. BS, Colo. A&M, 1951; MS, Colo. State U., 1957; PhD, Oreg. State U., 1962. Range scientist USDA Forest Svc., Portland, Oreg., 1952-56; rsch. project leader USDA Forest Svc., Portland, 1956-62, Washington, 1962-65, Ft. Collins, Colo., 1965-77; R & D program mgr. USDA Forest Svc., Ft. Collins, 1977-83; cons. FMA Internat., Inc., Gardnerville, Nev., 1983-91; land-use expert UN-FAO, Rome, 1983-89; land use cons. Fust (Föderung von Umweltstudien), Achenkirch/Tyrol, Austria, 1993. Author, editor: Photo Interpretation for Ranges and Range Management, 1997; contbg. author Range Resources: Inventory, Evaluation, Monitoring, 1975; contbr. articles to profl. jours. Dist. chmn. Bend (Oreg.) area Boy Scouts Am., 1969, com. chair troop 26, Ft. Collins, Colo., 1989; mem., chair various coms. Westminster Presbyn. Ch. and Timnath Presbyn. Ch., Ft. Collins, 1972—; mem. and moderator com. on ministry Plains and Peaks Presbytery Presbyn. Ch. U.S.A., 1991-99, mem. com. lay pastor group, 1999—. Recipient presdl. citation for meritorious svc. Am. Soc. Photogrammetry and Remote Sensing, 1978, 86. Mem. Am. Inst. Biol. Scis., Soc. Range Mgmt. (chair, com. mem., Outstanding Achievement award 1983), Nat. Assn. Ret. Fed. Employees (chpt. pres. 1993-95, mem. and chair various cms. 1988-2000, fed. v.p. for dist. IV), Xi Sigma Pi, Beta Beta Beta, Sigma Xi. Achievements include research on use of remote sensing technology for rangeland inventory and classification, range management planning and management, ecological land classification for land use planning in the U.S., and land evaluation, planning and management in the tropics and central Europe. Home and Office: 2217 Sheffield Dr Fort Collins CO 80526-1640

DRISKELL, CLAUDE EVANS, college director, educator, dentist; b. Chgo., Jan. 13, 1926; s. James Ernest and Helen Elizabeth (Perry) D., Sr.; B.S., Roosevelt U., 1950; B.S. in Dentistry, U. Ill., 1952, D.D.S., 1954; m. Naomi Roberts, Sept. 30, 1953; 1 dau., Yvette Michele; stepchildren—Isaiah, Ruth, Reginald, Elaine. Practice dentistry, Chgo., 1954—. Adj. prof. Chgo. State U., 1971—; dean's aide, adviser black students Coll. Dentistry U. Ill., 1972—; dental cons., supervising dentist, dental hygienists supportive health services Bd. Edn., Chgo., 1974. Vice pres. bd. dirs. Jackson Park Highlands Assn., 1971-73. Served with AUS, 1944-46; ETO. Fellow Internat. Biog. Assn., Royal Soc. Health (Gt. Britain), Acad. Gen. Dentistry; mem. Lincoln Dental Soc. (editor), Chgo. Dental Soc., ADA, Nat. Dental Assn., (editor pres.'s newsletter; dir. pub. relations, publicity; recipient pres.'s spl. achievement award 1969) dental assns., Am. Assn. Dental Editors, Acad. Gen. Dentistry, Soc. Med. Writers, Soc. Advancement Anesthesia in Dentistry, Omega Psi Phi. Author: The Influence of the Halogen Elements upon the Hydrocarbon, and their Effect on General Anesthesia, 1962; History of Chicago's Black Dental Professionals, 1850-1983; author, editor and publisher: Original Forty Club's 75th Anniversary Book (1920-1995), author, editor and archivist Forty Club, 1920-95; asst. editor Nat. Dental Assn. Quar. Jour., 1977—; contbr. articles to profl. jours. Home: 6727 S Bennett Ave Chicago IL 60649-1031 Office: 11139 S Halsted St Chicago IL 60628-3910

DRIVER, MARTHA WESTCOTT, English language educator, writer, researcher; b. N.Y.C., Oct. 24; d. Albert Westcott and Martha Louise (Miller) D. BA, Vassar Coll., 1974; MA, U. Pa., 1975, PhD, 1980. Lectr. English Vassar Coll., N.Y.C., 1980-81; from asst. prof. to assoc. prof. Pace U., N.Y.C., 1981-95, prof. English, 1995—, dir. honors program, 1998—; cons. N.Y. Pub. Libr., 1984; seminar participant Folger Inst., Folger Shakespeare Libr., 1994. Editor Jour. of The Early Book Society, 1998-2000; guest editor Film & History: The Middle Ages, 1998-99, Literary and Linguistic Computing, 1999; contbr. articles to profl. jours. Vestry mem. Ch. of the Incarnation, N.Y.C., 1995-99; mem., lectr. St. John the Divine, N.Y.C., 1995. Rsch. tools grantee NEH, 1995, travel grantee Am. Coun. Learned Socs., 1995; fellow Houghton Libr. Harvard U., 1996-97. Mem. Early Book Soc. (chair 1988—), Coll. Art Assn., Medieval Acad. Am., Modern Humanities Rsch. Assn. (U.K.), Medieval Club of N.Y. (conf. coord. 1989-94. pres. 1987-89), Internat. Ctr. Medieval Art, Internat. Arthurian Soc., Medieval Feminist Art History Project, New Chaucer Soc. Episcopalian. Avocations: dancing, museums, theater, concerts. Office: Pace U English Dept 41 Park Row New York NY 10038-1508

DROB, SANFORD L., psychologist; b. Bronx, N.Y., June 17, 1952; s. Frank E. and Sylvia Rapaport Drob; m. Liliana Rusansky, Sept. 8, 1996; children: Elliot, Robin, Amarilla, Martin. BA in Religious Studies, SUNY, Stony Brook, 1973; PhD in Philosophy, Boston U., 1981; MA, L.I. U., 1981, PhD in Clin. Psychology, 1987. Lic. psychologist, N.Y. Faculty, clin. asst. prof. NYU Med. Sch., N.Y.C., 1982—; psychologist NYU-Bellevue Forensic Psychiatry Svc., N.Y.C., 1984—; pvt. practice clin. and forensic psychologist N.Y.C., L.I., 1987—; dir., psychol. assessment Bellevue Hosp., N.Y.C., 1995—; forensic psychol. cons. Capital Defenders Office, Legal Aid Soc., Bronx Nassau Dist. Atty., U.S. Atty., N.Y. State 18B Panel, 1990—; faculty John Jay Coll. Criminal Justice, N.Y.C., 1991—. Editor-in-chief N.Y. Jewish Rev., 1987-90; contbr. articles to profl. jours. Mem. APA. Jewish. E-mail: forensicdx@aol.com. Office: Bellevue Hosp 19 West Forensics 1st Ave and 27th St New York NY 10016

DROBNÍK, JAROSLAV, biology educator; b. Prague, Czech Republic, Dec. 20, 1929; s. Bretislav and Anna (Walterová) D.; m. Věra Kozderková, Aug. 22, 1959; children: Zuzana, Jana. BS in Biology, Charles U., Prague, Czech Republic, 1953, PhD in Biology, 1956. Asst. prof. Faculty of Sci. Charles U., Prague, Czech Republic, 1956-62; vis. prof. Mich. State U., Lansing, 1962-65; assoc. prof. Faculty of Sci. Charles U., Prague, 1965-70; rschr. Inst. of Macromolecular Chemistry, Prague, 1971-77; head of lab. Inst. of Macromolecular Chemistry, Prague, 1977-89; full prof. Faculty of Sci. Charles U., Prague, 1989—; head of biophysics dept. Charles U., Prague, 1961-70, dir. of Inst. of Biotech., 1989—; head of Polymer Biochem. Lab., Inst. Macromolecular Chemistry, 1977-89. Team mem. in the invention of platinum cytostatics, 1963-69; devel. of Pt-cytostatic prodn. in Czech Republic, 1979-83. Mem. European Assn. for Cancer Rsch., Czechoslovak Biotech. Soc., Czech Biochem. Soc. Home: Vondroušova 1207, 163 00 Prague 6, Czech Republic Office: Inst of Biotechnology of the Charles Univ, Viničná 5, 128 44 Prague 2, Czech Republic

DROBYSHEV, ANATOLY IVANOVICH, chemist, educator; b. Leningrad, USSR, May 7, 1946; s. Ivan Maximovich (Drobyshev) and Nina Mikhailovna (Spiridonova)D.; m. Anna Evgenevna Aladyshkina, Dec. 12, 1945; children: Alexei, Alexandra. MSc in Physics, Leningrad State U., 1970, Candidate of Chemistry, 1977, D of Phys. and Math. Sci., 1989. Engr. Chem. Sci. Rsch. Inst. Leningrad State U., 1970-77, scientist, 1977-79, sr. scientist, 1979-90, chief scientist, 1990-96; assoc. prof. chemistry St. Petersburg (Russia) State U., 1996-97, prof. chemistry, 1997—; mem. sci. coun. chem. faculty St. Petersburg State U., 1990—, mem. specialized coun. doctor degrees, 1991—; mem. gas analysis com. sci. bd. analytical chemistry Russian Acad. Scis., 1998—. Author: Spectral Analysis of Pure Substances, 1994, Background of Atomic Spectral Analysis, 1997, Technology of Atomic Emission Spectrographic Analysis, 1999; patentee in field. Avocations: philosophy, environmental issues. Home: Apt 7, Bolshaya Posadskaya 7a, 197046 Saint Petersburg Russia Office: St Petersburg U Dept Chem, Universitetskii pr 2, 198904 Saint Petersburg Russia

DROCHNER, WINFRIED HANS-GEORG, veterinarian, educator; b. Königsberg, Eastern Prussia, Feb. 22, 1943; s. Walter and Ella (Laschinski) D.; m. Marion Elfriede Dickler, June 21, 1972; children: Matthias, Rainer, Ulrich. Diploma in agr., U. Giessen, Germany, 1967, D of Agr., 1969, vet., 1972; D Med. Vet., Vet. Sch. Hanover, Germany, 1974; Dr. honoris causa, Agrl. U. Kaunas, Lithuania, 1997. Cert. fachtierart for animal nutrition. Acad. asst. U. Cologne, Germany, 1972-74, Vet. Sch., Hanover, 1974-79; asst. Min. Agr., Bonn, Germany, 1980-81; pvt. docent Vet. Sch., Hanover, 1982-83; prof. Vet. Sch., 1984-91; dir. Inst. Animal Nutrition Hohenheim U., Germany, 1991—; rsch. coord. Rsch. Farm, Hanover, 1975-79; coord. tng. program Aufbanstudium, Hanover, 1983-86; leader sect. animal protection German Vet. Soc., 1983-99; leader, spkr. Rsch. Group Fusario Toxins, Hohenheim, 1995-99. Author: (textbook) Animal Nutrition, 1999; contbr. sci. monographs to profl. publs. Recipient Henneberg/Lehmanna award U. Göttingen, 1984. Mem. German-Lithuanian Soc. Avocations: chess, history, languages. Home: Dresden Str 23, 70794 Stuttgart Germany Office: U Hohenheim, Emil-Wolff Str 8-10, 70543 Stuttgart Germany

DROEGE, PETER F., designer, planner, educator; b. Würzburg, Bavaria, Germany, Apr. 6, 1952; s. Friedrich and Elfriede (Doellein) D. Diplom-Ingenieur, Tech. U. Munich, 1976; MArch in Advanced Studies, MIT, 1978. Assoc. prof. urban devel. engring. U. Tokyo Rsch. Ctr. for Advanced Sci. and Tech., 1992-93; prof., dir. postgrad. urban design program U. Sydney (Australia) Faculty Architecture, 1993—; task organizer SHC Solar City program Internat. Energy Agy., 1999—; project mgr., sr. designer Carr, Lynch Assocs., 1979-82; pres. Porter and Droege, Inc., 1983-86; prin. arch. Commonwealth of Mass., 1985-87; leader missions UN Devel. Program, 1986-88; advisor Andersen Cons./Kinhill Pty. Ltd., Sydney, 1988-89; dir., mem. core team Initiative 2050, Nat. Capital Planning Commn./MIT, 1988-90; advisor on urban devel. and design City of Amsterdam, The Netherlands, 1991-92, City of Dordrecht, The Netherlands, 1993; various exec. consultancies and adv. assignments, Australia, 1993—; chmn. NSW Urban Design Adv. Com. on Ultimo-Pyrmont, 1994-98; advisor Nat. Urban and Regional Devel. Rev., 1993-94; adviser, mem. urban planning com. Property Coun. Australia, 1995—; mem. Sydney Harbour Foreshores Design Panel, 1998—; mem. Melbourne Docklands Urban Design Amenity and Integration Panel, 1997—; conf. dir. and presenter in field; gen. mgr. urban devel. Internat. Strategic Analysis Team, Sydney, 1996—. Contbr. articles to profl. jours.; travelling group exhibit Harvard U. across Europe and U.S., 1985-88. Co-recipient 2D award nat. urban design competition Boston Visions, 1988, grand prize Internat. Concept Design Competion for Advanced Info. City, Japan, 1987, grand prize Sagami Bay coastal zone concept competition, Japan, 1990; scholar German Acad. Exch. Svc., 1976-77; travel grantee Graham Found., 1977-78; fellow MIT Ctr. for Advanced Visual Studies, 1981-82.

DROESE, SIEGFRIED OTTO, engineering educator, researcher; b. Stettin, Germany, Sept. 24, 1943; m. Margarete Kalous, Oct. 22, 1971; children: Sylvia, Rainer. BS, Tech. Coll., Lübeck, Germany, 1968; MS, Tech. U., Braunschweig, Germany, 1973, D in Engring., 1984. Project engr. contracting firm, Hamburg, Germany, 1968-69; sr. project mgr. contracting firm, Braunschweig, Germany, 1973-79; sr. lectr. Tech. U., Braunschweig, 1979—; registered cons. engr., Braunschweig, Germany, 1991—; expert Highway Authority, Hannover, 1992—, German Railroad Authority, Bonn, 1997—. Author: Protection Against Corrosion of Slipformed Structures, 1984, Experiments to Establish Formwork Pressure and Formwork Friction in Slipforming, 1990; contbr. articles to profl. jours. Chief of staff Civil Def., Braunschweig, 1960-88. Fellow Engrs. Chamber (Hannover, Germany). Avocations: collecting historic radio sets. Office: TU Braunschweig Massivbau, Pockelsstr 3, D-38106 Braunschweig Germany

DRÖGEMÜLLER, HANS-PETER, academic administrator; b. Hamburg, Germany, Mar. 10, 1932; s. Hans and Charlotte (Westerkamp) D.; m. Margret Ehrhardt, July 4, 1960 (div. Feb. 1979); 1 child, Susanne; m. Jutta Bodendieck, Dec. 29, 1980 (dec. Jan. 1985). DPhil, U. Hamburg, Germany, 1956. Scientific contbr. Thesaurus Linguae Graecae, Hamburg, Germany, 1955-57; asst. prof. German Grammar Sch., Athens, Greece, 1957-58; prof. Grammar Schs., Hamburg, 1958-68; dir. Tchrs. Tng. Coll., Hamburg, 1969-74; scientific corr. Athens, 1975-82, Tehran, Iran, 1975-82, Neapolis Lakonias, Greece, 1983—. Author: Short German Grammar for Greeks, 1962, 68, Syracuse, Topography and History of a Greek Town, 1969, Latin Language in Modern Education, 1972, Handbook for Teachers Training, 1977, Iranian Diary, 1983, The Liberty of the Greeks and the Poet Dionysios Solomos, 1999. Chmn. German Youth Movement, 1954-58; mem. Villagers Assn., Kambos Voion, Greece, 1978-97. Mem. Initiative Group Greek Culture, Classical Assn. Home: Hermannstal 70, D 22119 Hamburg Germany

DROLSHAGEN, LEO FRANCIS, III, radiologist, physician; b. Detroit, June 9, 1956; s. Leo Francis Jr. and Janet Marie (Phillppart) D.; m. Barbara Sharon Ritchie, June 29, 1979; children: Leo VI, Colin, Eric, Helena. BA English magna cum laude, U. Detroit, 1977; MD, Wayne State U., 1981; postgrad., Armed Forces Inst. of Pathology, Washington, 1985. Diplomate Am. Bd. Radiology, Nat. Bd. Med. Examiners. Resident in radiology Henry Ford Hosp., Detroit, 1981-85; fellow Vanderbilt U. Hosp. Sch. of Medicine, Nashville, Tenn., 1985-86; radiologist Radiologist P.A., Ft Smith, Ark., 1986—; med. dir., magnetic resonance imaging St. Edward Mercy Med. Ctr., Ft Smith, 1986-90; chief, dept. radiology St. Edward Mercy Med. Ctr., 1988-91, vice chief of med. staff elect, 1991-92; v.p. Radiologist P.A., Ft. Smith, 1991-97, pres., 1997—; chief of staff St. Edward Mercy Med. Ctr., 1992—; clinical asst. prof. of Magnetic Resonance Imaging U. Ark., St. Edward Mercy Med. Ctr. Author: (with others) Magnetic Resonance Imaging of the Normal and Abnormal Female Pelvis, 1986, The Pelvis, 1986, Critical Diagnostic Pathways in Radiology, 1987; contbr. articles to profl. jours. Recipient Tchr. of the Year in Sonography award Vanderbilt U. Med. Ctr., 1985-86, Howard Walsh Meml. award U. Detroit, 1977. Mem. AMA, Am. Coll. Radiology, Radiologic Soc. N.Am., Am. Inst. Ultrasound in Medicine, Am. Coll. Radiology, Soc. Magnetic Resonance Imaging in Medicine, Sebastian County Med. Soc., Mensa, Ft. Smith C. of C., Ducks Unlimited, Bonsai Club. Avocations: volleyball, racquetball, piano, swimming. Home: 8223 Cleburne Ct Fort Smith AR 72903-4362 Office: Radiologist PA PO Box 3887 1501 S Waldron Rd Ste 109 Fort Smith AR 72903-2568 also: St Edward Mercy Med Hosp Dept Radiology Fort Smith AR 72903

DRONAMRAJU, KRISHNA RAO, geneticist; b. Pithapuram, India, Jan. 14, 1937; came to U.S., 1963; s. Bapiraju and Rajeswaramma (Vankayalapati) D.; m. Sheila Marion McHarg, Mar. 31, 1962 (div. 1978); 1 child, Raj Gopal. MSc, Agra (India) U., 1957; PhD, Indian Statis. Inst., Calcutta, 1966. Rsch. fellow U. Alberta, Edmonton, Can., 1966-68; asst. prof. U. Saskatchewan, Saskatoon, Can., 1968-69; chief geneticist Lancaster (Pa.) Cleft Palate Clinic, 1969-73; writer, lectr. Balt., 1973-77; pers. cons. City of Balt., 1978-79, job devel. advisor, 1979-81; sr. fellow U. Tex., Houston, 1982-85; pres., dir. Found. for Genetic Rsch., Houston, 1985—; vis. prof. Hershey (Pa.) Med. Ctr., 1969-73, Osmania U., Indian, 1995; mem. reconbimant DNA adv. com. NIH, Bethesda, Md., 1992—; hon. rsch. fellow U. London, 1994; vis. prof. U. Paris, 1994, Jawaharlal Nehru U., New Delhi, 1994; hon. prof. Albert Schweitzer Internat. U., Geneva. Author: Cleft Lip and Palate: Aspects of Reproductive Biology, 1986, The Foundations of Human Genetics, 1989, If I am To Be Remembered, The Life and Work of Julian Huxley with Selected Correspondence, 1993; editor: Haldane and Modern Biology, 1968, Haldane, The Life and Work of J.B.S. Haldane with special reference to India, 1985, The History and Development of Human Genetics: Progress in Different Countries, 1992, Haldane's Daedalus Revisited, 1995, Haldane in India, 1997, Science and Society, 1998, Biological and Social Issues in Biotechnology, 1998; contbr. articles to profl. jours. Mem. bd. dirs. Sickle Cell Assn., Houston, 1992—. Recipient merit award History of Sci. Soc., 1989, Yellapragada Subbarow award for med. rsch., 1997, Y. Nayudamma award for sci. and tech., India, 1997. Mem. AAAS, Am. Soc. Human Genetics. Avocations: travel, nature walks. Fax: (713) 667-5881; email: kdronamraj@aol.com. Office: Found for Genetic Rsch PO Box 27701 Houston TX 77227-7701

DROUIN, EMMANUEL, medical physiologist; b. Pleurtuit, France, Sept. 9, 1965; s. Yves and Therese (Legrand) D.; m. Marie Masson, May 11, 1961; children: Guillaume, Anne-Sophie. BA, U. Tours, 1988, MA, 1989; PhD, U. Nantes, 1994. Clin. rsch. engr. dept. neonatology Hosp. Mothers and Children, Nantes, France, 1994—; clin. rsch. engr. dept. neonatology Grad. Sch. Mgmt., Nantes, 1997, asst. prof. physiology, 1998—; clinic mgr. Notre Dame de Grâces, Nantes, 1998—. Office: 22 rue Morand, 44000 Nantes France

DROULERS, STEPHANE NICOLAS, investment banker; b. Neuilly sur Seine, France, Nov. 9, 1952; s. Jean Gaston and Sibylle Helene (De Lander) D.; m. Constance Genevieve Chastenet de Castaing, Sept. 8, 1979; children: Eleonore, Oriane. Diploma, Inst. Superieur de Gestion, Paris, 1976. Analyst Lazard Freres, Paris, 1977-81, fonde de pouvoir, 1982-84, sous directeur, 1985, directeur adjoint, 1986, directeur, 1987-89, gerant, 1990-94, gen. ptnr., 1995—; mng. dir. Chateau de Carles, Bordeaux. Cadet French Marines, 1976-77. Mem. Golf de Morfontaine, Travellers Club. Avocations: contemporary art, music, golf, wine, archeology. Home: 5 Rue Dufrenoy, 75116 Paris France Office: Lazard Freres & Cie, 121 Boulevard Haussmann, 75008 Paris France

DROUSSIOTIS-BURNS-COWAN, SARAH A., transportation company executive; b. Limassol, Cyprus, Jan. 1, 1937; d. William David and Despina (Michael Tornaritis) Burns-Cowan; m. Anthony Peter Droussiotis; children: Peter A., Annabel A. Grad. in Advt., Speech, TV Scriptwriting, Internat. Corr. Sch., Eng., 1974; grad. in Mktg., CPC, Cyprus, 1976; grad. in Bus. Adminstrn., Inst. Mgmt., Cyprus, 1978. Adv.'s clk. P.L. Cacoyiammis & Co. Legal Firm, Limassol, 1953-62; sales mgr. Petros S. Droussiotis Merchants, Limassol, 1962-75; export mgr. K&S Droussiotis Trading Exporters, Limassol, 1975-79; exec. asst. Francoudi & Stephanou Shipping Travel and Tourism, Limassol, 1979—. Mem. Com. UN Assn., Limassol, 1996—, Cyprus Red Cross Soc., Limassol, 1961—, Cyprus Anticancer Assn., Limassol, 1966; treas., exec. com. mem. Cyprus Girl Guides Assn., Limassol, 1962-70; commr. of Limmasol, 1970-75; mem. Assn. for Welfare of Blind, Limassol, 1978—. Recipient Silver medal for humanitarian svc. Girl Guides Assn. Greece, 1974, Silver medal for bravery Cyprus Girl Guides Assn., 1980. Avocations: photography, reading, music, philosophy study, sports. Home: PO Box 50237, 91 St Andrew St, Limassol 3602, Cyprus

DROVGOS, ATHANASSIOS EFSTATHIOS, journalist; b. Athens, Greece, Aug. 5, 1960; s. Efstathios Athanassios and Eleni Kostantine (Kovtroupi) D. BA, Patras (Greece) U., 1982; diploma, Nat. War Sch., Athens, 1983; MA, Webster U., St. Louis, 1985; PhD, State U. Amsterdam, The Netherlands, 1989. Cert. in arms control, def. analyses, mil. sci.; NATO expert. Sr. analyst MoD, Athens, 1991-93; newspaper columnist Afternoon News, Athens, 1993-97; columnist, mil. analyst Vradini, Athens, 1997—; newspaper def. diplomatic analyst Akropolis, Athens, 1998—; rsch. fellow, sr. def. analyst MoD, Athens, 1999—; with Alpha News TV, Athens, 1999—; sr. Author: (book) Air Forces in the 21st Century, 1999; editor Bull. Strategic Analysis, 1993-95, Polit. Affairs jour., 1996-97. Polit. analyst Battle for Athens, 1994—; sr. advisor Alexandros, Papagoy-Athens, 1996—; editor regional newspaper Apihisi, 1999—; mayor Athens Dimitrios Avramopoulos. Gen. staff mil. svc., 1990-91. Fellow Israeli Govt., 1993, Greek Govt., 1994, Dangreek Fedn. Ret. Mil. Officers, 1998. Fellow MoD (mil. analyst 1999—), Greek Com. Atlantic Affairs (mil. analyst 1997—), Hellenic Com. Strategic Studies (advisor 1995—). Avocations: basketball, football, hockey, golf. Fax: 30-1-6518273. Home: Konstantinpoleos 27, 15562 Athens Holargos, Greece

D'ROZARIO, MICHAEL ATUL, bishop; b. Dhaka, Bangladesh, Nov. 23, 1925; s. Vincent and Dominga (Gomes) D'R. MA, U. Notre Dame, 1954; DD, 1970. ordained priest, 1953, bishop, 1970;. Parish priest cathedral Archdiocese of Dhaka, 1960-70, supt. Cath. schs., 1960-70; lectr. logic Notre Dame Coll., Dhaka, 1960-70; bishop of Khulna, pres. Caritas Bangladesh, 1990—. Mem. Cath. Bishops Conf. Bangladesh (v.p.). Avocations: literature, music. Office: Bishop's House, Main Rd Sonadanga, Khulna 9000, Bangladesh

DROZDA, JEFFERY ALLEN, government affairs administrator; b. Canton, Ohio, Aug. 30, 1967; s. Richard Allen and Linda Maye Drozda; m. Cheryl Lynn Drozda, Oct. 2, 1993; children: Elizabeth Kimberly, Nicholas Jeffery. BA, U. Notre Dame, 1989. Legis. asst. Congl. Affairs, GSA, Washington, 1989-91; legis. asst. to house leadership Ohio Ho. of Reps., Columbus, 1991-93; exec. asst. to commr. Pub. Utilities Commn. Ohio, Columbus, 1993-96; mgr. Fed. Regulatory Affairs, Am. Electric Power, Washington, 1996-97; mgr. govt. affairs Am. Electric Power, Indpls., 1997—; commr. Ind. Film Commn., Indpls., 1999—. Chmn. Notre Dame Students for Bush, U. Notre Dame, Ind., 1989; bd. dirs. Notre Dame Club Washington, 1990; mem. platform com. Ind. Rep. State Conv., Indpls., 2000; mem. state com. Bush for Pres., Indpls., 2000. Named one of Outstanding Young Men of Am., 1989. Mem. Notre Dame Club Indpls., Hawthorns Golf and Country Club (com. 1999—), Indpls. Athletic Club. Roman Catholic. Avocations: golf, religious history, political history. E-mail: jadpax3@aol.com. FAX: 317-636-7681. Home: 533 Worth Ct Carmel IN 46032-4402 Office: Am Electric Power 101 W Ohio St Indianapolis IN 46204-1906

DROZDECK, STEVEN RICHARD, management consultant; b. N.Y.C., Apr. 23, 1951; s. Frank S. and Jane (Dzingelewski) D. Student, Poly. Inst. Bklyn., 1960-70; BS in Fin. cum laude, N.Y. Inst. Tech., 1973. Cert. master practitioner, 1985, trainer of neuro linguistic programming, 1987. Pres. Unltd. Leadership Potential, S.I., N.Y., 1973-74; account exec. Merrill Lynch, Pierce, Fenner & Smith, Bklyn., 1974-78, S.I., 1978-80; sr. sales trainer Merrill Lynch, Pierce, Fenner & Smith, N.Y.C., 1980—, adminstrv. mgr. tng. sch., 1983—, asst. v.p., 1984—; pres. Drozdeck & Assocs., 2000—; affiliate Ea. Neuro Linguistic Programming Inst., 1984—, market and sales cons., 1986, mgr. of fin. cons. profl. devel., 1987, mem. devel. team The Art of Friendly Persuasion, 1984-89; affiliate Comm. Tech., 1989—; affiliate of Lingues-Tech., 1990—; founder, pres. Tng. Groups, Inc., 1990-91, exec. v.p. Fin. Forum, mng.dir. Drozdeck & Gretz Assocs.; pres. SD Mktg. Groups; co-dir. Drozdeck & Gretz Assocs., 1997. Co-author: Empowering Innovative People, 1991, Consultative Selling Techniques for Financial Professionals, 1990, The Effective Manager, 1991, What They Don't Teach You in Sales 101, 1991, The Broker's Edge, 1994, Professional Selling: A Consultative Approach, 1995, Managing Your Business for Success, 1998, The Money Managers Universe, 1998, The P.R.O.G.R.E.S.S. Model, 2000; columnist for Sr. Cons. mag., Bank Securities Jour., Registered Investment Advisor, 1998—. Mem. Internat. Assn. Fin. Planners, Nat. Soc. Registered Reps. (chartered), N.Y. Stockbrokers Club, N.Y. Stock Exch. Qualifications Com. for Gen. Securities Exam., Nat. Assn. Securities Dealers Qualifications Com. Home and office: 494 River Heights Blvd Logan UT 84321-5664

DROZDOV, IGOR ALEXEEVICH, metallurgical engineering educator, researcher; b. Murom, USSR, Nov. 19, 1931; s. Alexey Ivanovich and Mria Sergeevna (Katkova) D.; m. Galina Alexandrovna Bistina, July 17, 1959; children: Elena Igorevna, Alexey Igorevich. Grad. in metall. engring., Poly. Inst., Gorky, Russia, 1954; postgrad., Aviation Inst., Kuibyshev (now Samara), Russia, 1962; PhD, Poly. Inst., Minsk, Belarus, 1964. Cert. USSR Dept. Superior Edn. Engr. aircraft factory, Saratov, Russia, 1954-56, radio factory, Gorky, 1956-58; rsch. worker Powder Metallurgy Lab., Aerospace U. (formerly Aviation Inst.), Samara, 1959-62, sr. rsch. worker, 1964-83, chief rschr., 1983—, engr., rschr., 1962-64, asst. prof. metall. engring., 1964-69, assoc. prof., 1969-99, full prof., 1999—, leader trade union metall. dept., 1964-90. Editor works on powder metallurgy, 1983, 86, 90; contbr. articles to sci. jours., including Powder Metallurgy, Physics Metals and Metal Knowledge, Metal Knowledge and Heat Working of Metals; patentee in field. Recipient Vet. of Labor medal, Russia, 1991. Mem. N.Y. Acad. Scis. Avocations: chess, volleyball, skiing, farming, hunting mushrooms. Home: 193-3 Samarskaya, 443001 Samara Russia Office: Samara State Aerospace U, 34 Moskoyskoye Shosse, 443086 Samara Russia

DROZDOWSKI, HELEN ELAINE CSWAYKUS, retired educator; b. Lackawanna, N.Y., May 13, 1926; d. John and Anna (Manko) Cswaykus; m. Norbert Drozdowski, Nov. 5, 1955 (dec. Feb. 1996); 1 child, Barry. Diploma in nursing, Meyer Meml. Hosp., 1948; BSN, SUNY, Buffalo, 1967, MS in Edn., 1972. RN, N.Y. Asst. head nurse Meyer Meml. Hosp., Buffalo, 1948-49, head nurse, 1949-54, supr., 1954-56; tchr. Bd. Ednl. Svcs., Buffalo, 1954-56; dir. health occupations Buffalo Bd. Edn., 1980-83; pres. Lackawanna Retired Tchrs., 1992—. Vol. Hopevale for Toubled Adolescents, 1995—; coord. Sr. Citizen Ctr., 1991; vol. reading instr. Correctional Facility N.Y. State, 1992—; emergency pantry com. Buffalo Food Bank, 1992—, mem. adv. bd., 1994—; bd. dirs. Cath. Guild for the Blind, Buffalo, 1983—. With USN, 1945-48. Named Outstanding Female Educator SUNY, Buffalo, 1975, Woman of Yr. Am. Bus. Women, 1976-77, Citizen of Yr., Lackawanna C. of C., 1991; recipient Student Alumni award Bd. Coop. Edn. Svc., 1974, Erie County Achievement award, 1991, Western Zone Citation award, 1993, Svc. award Lackawanna Mayor Staniszewski, 1997. Mem. N.Y. State Ret. Tchrs. (bd. dirs. 1992—, pres. 1992—, friendly svc. chair 1990), Alpha Lambda (v.p., sec. 1972-74, award 1974). Avocations: coins, photography, spectator sports. Home: 93 Cleveland Ave Lackawanna NY 14218-3521

DROZDZIEL, MARION JOHN, aeronautical engineer; b. Dunkirk, N.Y., Dec. 21, 1924; s. Steven and Veronica (Wilk) D.; m. Rita L. Korwek, Aug. 30, 1952; 1 child, Eric A. BS in Aero. Engring., Tri State U., 1947, BSME, 1948; postgrad., Ohio State U., 1948, Niagara U., 1949-51, U. Buffalo, 1951-52. Stress analyst Curtiss Wright Corp., Columbus, Ohio, 1948; project engr. weight analysis Bell Aerospace Textron, Buffalo, 1949-52, stress analyst, 1952-60, asst. supr. stress analysis, 1960-64, chief stress analysis propulsion, 1964-79, chief engr. stress and weights, 1979-84, staff scientist, 1984-85, cons. structures and fractures mechanics, 1985—; mem. Am. Aerospace Materials Del. to USSR, 1989, Am. Aerospace Industries Del. to People's Republic China, 1991, Am. Aerospace Materials Del. to Czechoslovakia and Commonwealth Ind. States, 1992. Del. Internat. Citizens Ambassador Prog.; active Buffalo Fine Arts Acad., N.Y. Acad. Scis., Disabled Am. Vets.; mem. tech. socs. coun. Niagara Frontier. With U.S. Army, 1944-47. Recipient cert. of achievement NASA-Apollo, 1972, Wisdom award of honor Wisdom Soc. for Advancement of Knowledge, Learning and Rsch. in Edn., 2000; cert. commendation U.K. NATO program, 1982; named to Wisdom Hall of Fame, Wisdom Soc. for Advancement of Knowledge, Learning and Rsch. in Edn., 2000. Mem. AAAS, AIAA (Mem. Chmn.'s award 1988-90, 92-93), Soc. Reliability Engrs. (bd. dirs. 1998, 99, 2000), U.S. Naval Inst., Am. Space Found., Nat. Conservancy, Nat. Audubon Soc., Sierra Club, Am. Acad. Polit. and Social Sci., Acad. Polit. Sci., Union Concerned Scientists, Air Force Assn., Nat. Space Soc., Soc. Allied Weight Engrs., Planetary Soc., Am. Mgmt. Assn., Bibl. Archeology Soc., Archeol. Inst. Am., Cousteau Soc., Smithsonian Assocs., Buffalo Audubon Soc., Bell Mgmt. Club, Natural History Mus., Internat. Hypersonic Rsch., Disabled Am. Vets, Kosciuszko Found., Polish Arts Club Buffalo, Exch. Club of Tonawandas (sec. 1996-98, bd. dirs. 1999-2000), Nat. Exch. Club (Disting. Sec. award 1996, 97, 98, 99). Republican. Roman Catholic. Achievements include development of criteria and methods of structural analysis extending analyses into the plastic and creep ranges for titanium and columbium rocket nozzle extensions; of criteria and methods of structural analysis for extendable rocket nozzle extensions, including rapid nozzle deployment involving plasticity; of methods of structural analysis for low strength, high ductility steels, aluminums, and teflons as positive expulsion devices for zero gravity application in propellant tanks including bellows, reversing heads, rolling diaphragms devices and collapsing or folding concepts; structural analysis on "X" series of aircraft, on Mercury, Gemini, and Apollo spacecraft reaction control and propulsion systems; structural and weight analysis of programs involving rocket engines, propulsion systems, aircraft, air cushion vehicles, surface-effect ships, laser systems avionics, airborne and ground antennae, Army tanks and fighting vehicles. Home and Office: 152 Linwood Ave Tonawanda NY 14150-4020

DROZE, J. TOM, market researcher; b. Mesa, Ariz., Dec. 9, 1959; s. William F. Droze. BS in Bus. Adminstrn., U. Phoenix, 1992, MA in Orgnl. Mgmt., 1996, mktg. cert.; tchg. cert., Ariz. C.C. Site selection cert. NACORE Internat. Sr. market analyst U-Haul Internat., Phoenix, 1987-89, program mgr., 1989-93, field support mgr., 1993-94; real estate market analyst CSK Auto, Inc., Phoenix, 1994-96, sr. mgr. market rsch., 1996—. Republican. Avocation: vintage motorcycles. E-mail: JTD0588@aol.com and TDroze@cskauto.com. Fax: 602-234-1361. Office: CSK Auto Inc 645 E Missouri Ave Phoenix AZ 85012-1369

DRU, JEAN-MARIE PAUL, communications executive; b. Boulogne-Billancourt, France, Jan. 24, 1947; s. René Dru; m. Marie-Virginie Corre; children: Pierre-Marie, François-Marie, Noemie, Clemence, Matthieu. HEC, Bus. Sch., France, 1969. Acct. exec. Dupuy-Compton, Paris, 1970-72, exec. creative dir., 1972-77; mng. dir. Young & Rubicam, Paris, 1977-81, CEO, 1981-83; co-founder BDDP, Boulogne-Billancourt, France, 1984-98; pres. Internat. TBWA Worldwide, Boulogne-Billancourt, 1998—. Author: The Creative Leap, 1984, Disruption (Overturning Conventions and Shaking Up the Marketplace, 1996. Pres. Cannes Advt. Film Festival Jury, 1983, 98, Outdoor Advt. Grand Prix, 1987, 88. Mem. EAAA. Office: TBWA Worldwide, 162-164 rue de Billancourt, 92100 Boulogne France

DRUCK, MARK, theater director, producer, writer; b. Carbondale, Pa., Oct. 28; s. Jack L. and Mabelle (Breschel) D.; 1 child Lisa Druck Dodenhoff. BA, Pa. State U.; student, N.Y. Dramatic Workshop, 1948-51. Freelance newspaper/pub. relations N.Y.C., 1948-55; owner, producer Mark Druck Prodns., N.Y.C., 1969; tchr. prodn. and acting New Sch. for Social Rsch., N.Y.C., 1975-82; prof. Fashion Inst. Tech., N.Y.C., 1988-91, 98-99; mem. New Dramatists alumni exec. com.; mem. fin. com. Badische Trade Consortium, 1998—. Writer, dir.: (plays) All-American, 1951 (off-Broadway award 1952), Showcase: Crisis at Quiet Rest, 1950, Half a Loaf, 1951, The Most Decorated Man in Town, 1952, There's a Man in the Boathouse, 1958, Chairman of the Board, 1985, 97, Garden, 1988, 98, Love in Acheron, 1994, 2B4U, 1995, Soho Boxes, 1995, Keylight, 1999, Nick's Wife, 1998, The Woman from 29, 2000, also numerous TV commls. and indsl. films; author: (screenplays) The Sinner, 1955, Terrifying Silence, 1990, Tatha, 1993, The Empty Office, 1994, (novels) Bix and Bones, 1997, Instant Dead, 1979, The Final Mission, 1978. Past pres. Skyline Found., N.Y.C. Maj. USAF, 1942-46, USAFR, 1946-70. Mem. Nat. Acad. TV Arts and Scis. (chmn. spl. events com., bd. govs.), Dramatists Guild (life), Res. Officer's Assn. Home and Office: 300 E 40th St New York NY 10016-2188

DRUCKER, ALISON R., lawyer; b. Chgo., June 24, 1948; d. Clarence Drucker and Evelyn Weiss; m. Thomas Ludwig Holzman, May 29, 1977; children: Aaron Drucker Holzman, Beth Drucker Holzman. BA, U. Chgo., 1968, MA, 1970; postgrad., U. Wis., 1971-75; JD, Georgetown U., 1984.

Bar: Md. 1985. Human rels. rep. Pa. Human Rels. Commn., Phila., 1976-78; equal opportunity specialist Edn. Dept. Office Civil Rights, Washington, 1978-81; trial atty. U.S. Dept. Justice, Washington, 1984-95, sr. litig. counsel, 1995—. Topics editor Georgetown Law Jour., 1983-84. Campus coord. nat. bd. NOW, 1967-68; mem. Montgomery County Child Care Commn., Rockville, Md., 1990-91. Avocations: theater, foreign films, reading mysteries, gardening, photography. Home: 7020 Wilson Ln Bethesda MD 20817-4950

DRUCKER, PETER FERDINAND, writer, consultant, educator; b. Vienna, Austria, Nov. 19, 1909; came to U.S., 1937, naturalized, 1943; s. Adolph Bertram and Caroline D.; m. Doris Schmitz, Jan. 16, 1937; children: Kathleen Romola, J. Vincent, Cecily Anne, Joan Agatha. Grad., Gymnasium, Vienna, 1927; LLD, U. Frankfurt, 1931; 25 hon. doctorates. Economist London Banking House, 1933-37; Am. adviser for Brit. banks, Am. corr. Brit. newspapers, 1937-42; cons. maj. bus. corps. U.S., 1940—; prof. philosophy, politics Bennington Coll., 1942-49; prof. mgmt. NYU, 1950-72, chmn. mgmt. area, 1957-62; Clarke prof. social sci. Claremont Grad. Sch. (Calif.), 1971—; prof. dept. art Pomona Coll., Calif., 1979-85. Author: The End of Economic Man, 1939, new edit. 1995, The Future of Industrial Man, 1941, new edit. 1995, Concept of the Corporation, 1946, new edit., 1993, The New Society, 1950, new edit., 1993, Practice of Management, 1954, new edit., 1993, America's Next Twenty Years, 1957, The Landmarks of Tomorrow, 1959, new edit., 1996, Managing for Results, 1964, new edit., 1993, The Effective Executive, 1966, new edit., 1993, The Age of Discontinuity, 1969, new edit., 1996, Technology; Management and Society, 1970, Men, Ideas and Politics, 1971, Management: Tasks, Responsibilities, Practices, 1974, new edit., 1993, The Unseen Revolution: How Pension Fund Socialism Came to America, 1976, new edit. (new title: The Pension Fund Revolution, 1996), People and Performance, 1977, Management, An Overview, 1978, Adventures of a Bystander, 1979, new. edit., 1998, Managing in Turbulent Times, 1980, new edit., 1993, Toward the Next Economics and Other Essays, 1981, (essays) The Changing World of the Executive, 1982, Innovation and Entrepreneurship, 1985, new edit., 1993, (essays) The Frontiers of Management, 1986, 8th edit., 2000, The New Realities, 1989, Managing the Non-Profit Organization, 1994, (essays) Managing for the Future, 1992, 7th edit., 2000, (essays) The Ecological Vision, 1992, Post Capitalist Society, 1993, (essays) Managing in a Time of Great Change, 1995, Drucker on Asia: A Dialogue With Isao Nagauchi, 1997, (essays) Drucker on the Profession of Management, 1998, Management Challenges for the 21st Century, 1999, (anthology) The Essential Drucker, 2000; (fiction) The Last of All Possible Worlds, 1982, The Temptation to Do Good, 1984; co-author: The Song of the Brush: Japanese painting, 1979; producer: movie series The Effective Executive, 1969, Managing Discontinuity, 1971, The Manager and the Organization, 1977, Managing for Tomorrow, 1981, The Future of Manufacturing, 2000; producer 25 audiocassette series The Non-Profit Drucker, 1988. Recipient gold medal Internat. U. Social Studies, Rome, 1957; Wallace Clark Internat. Mgmt. medal, 1963; Taylor Key Soc. for Advancement Mgmt., 1967; Presdl. citation NYU, 1969; CIOS Internat. Mgmt. gold medal, 1972; Chancellor's medal Internat. Acad. Mgmt., 1987. Fellow AAAS (council), Internat., Am., Irish Acads. Mgmt., Brit. Inst. Mgmt. (hon.), Am. Acad. Arts and Scis.; mem. Soc. for History Tech. (pres. 1965-66), Nat. Acad. Pub. Adminstrn. (hon.), Peter F. Drucker Found. Non Profit Mgmt. (hon. chmn).

DRUHE BRANDT, IRIS CLAIRE, retired elementary school educator; b. New Orleans, Oct. 28, 1935; d. Olivia Catherine Clair and Frederick George Druhe; m. Eugene Maximillian Brandt, June 11, 1960; children: Fred, Brenda, Philip. BA, So. La. U., 1956. Tchr. 2d and 3d grades New Orleans, 1956-59; tchr. 2d grade Pensacola, Fla., 1961; pre-sch. tchr. Escondido, Calif., 1984-89. Vol. sec. Indian Wells Youth Football League; active Brownie's and Cub Scouts Am.; mem. Episcopal Women St. Marks; vol. nutritional advisor, counselor Wellness Clinic, Morena Valley, Calif., 1998—. Mem. AAUW (chair ways and means com.), Officers Wives Assn. (hospitality chmn., v.p., pres.), Navy Relief Soc. (chmn. Lafayette chpt. 1961), Women's Assn. Commn. Officer's Mess, San Diego North County Diabetes Support Group, Humane Soc. of U.S. Home: 4527 Coronado Dr Oceanside CA 92057-4252

DRUKER, ALEXANDRU-ERMINIU, physicist, researcher; b. Bucharest, Romania, Dec. 23, 1945; s. Otto and Gherghina (Dragan) D.; m. Vasilica Grigore, Aug. 16, 1975; 1 child, Rucsandra-Loreley. BS, U. Bucharest, Romania, 1971. From physicist to specialist scientific rschr. Nat. Inst. Metrology, Bucharest, 1971—; head metrology ionizing radiations lab. Nat. Inst. Metrology, 1985—. Recipient Romanian Acad. prize in Physics, 1974. Home: Bldg TD2, Apt 42, Sector 6, Aleea Topoloveni 5, Bucharest 77462, Romania Office: Nat Inst Metrology, Vitan-Birzesti nr 11, Sector 4 Bucharest Romania

DRULINER, MARCIA MARIE, education educator; b. Dec. 18, 1946. M in Secondary Edn., U. Nebr., 1974; PhD, Marquette U., 1992. Assoc. prof. edn. Concordia Coll., Bronxville, N.Y., 1993-95; asst. prof. edn. Northwestern Coll., Orange City, Iowa, 1998—. Home: 2308 Mcconnell Ave Auburn NE 68305-3043

DRUMMER, DOROTHY JEAN, executive search consultant, lawyer; b. Racine, Wis., Apr. 13, 1949; d. Paul Alan and Ruth Ellen (Fanning) D.; children: Michelle Morton, Brad Morton and Ben Morton. AB, Smith Coll., 1970; JD, Rutgers U., 1975. Bar: N.Y. 1976, Tex. 1986. V.p., counsel to the chmn. Am. Stock Exchange, N.Y.C., 1976-82; v.p. Am. Bus. Conf., Washington, 1980-85, exec. v.p., 1985-87, cons., 1987-89; dir. Spencer Stuart, Houston, 1987-91; prin. Dorothy Drummer & Assocs., Austin, Tex., 1992—. Exec. dir. Pres.' Task Force on Pvt. Sector Initiatives, Washington, 1981-82. Office: 400 W 15th St Ste 600 Austin TX 78701-1673

DRUMMER, OLAF HEINO, forensic pharmacologist, toxicologist, educator; b. Unterot, Germany, Sept. 16, 1952; arrived in Australia, 1955; s. Heino Oskar and Edelgard (Becher) D.; m. Christine Mary Theresa Ryan, Apr. 16, 1977; children: Haydn Olaf, Annalisa Elizabeth. B in Applied Sci., Royal Melbourne (Australia) Inst. Tech., 1974; PhD in Medicine, U. Melbourne, Australia, 1981. Tech. officer Royal Melbourne Inst. Tech., 1974; rsch. asst. Melbourne U., 1975-76; sr. rsch. officer Nat. Health and Med. Rsch. Coun., Melbourne, 1977-80, rsch. fellow, 1988-89; asst. dir. Victorian Inst. Forensic Pathology, Melbourne, 1989—, assoc. prof. forensic medicine, 1993—; cons. toxicologist Monash U., 1989—; mem. Australian Drug Evaluation Com., Canberra, 1988-95. Contbr. numerous articles to med. and legal jours. Mem. Australian Acad. Forensic Sci., Australian Soc. Clin. and Exptl. Pharmacology and Toxicology, Royal Australian Chem. Inst., Internat. Assn. Forensic Toxicologists (treas., exec. officer). Lutheran. Avocations: gardening, philately. Office: Victorian Inst Forensic Path Med, 57-83 Kavanagh St, Southbank 3006 VIC, Australia

DRUMMOND, FRANCES, psychotherapist, author; b. Scarisbrick, Lancs., Eng., Aug. 10, 1924; d. William and Theresa (Gleeson) D. BA, U. Liverpool, Eng., 1945; BA in Psychology with honors, Sheffield (Eng.) U., 1959. Cert. clin. psychologist. Tchr. Latin The Girls' Sch., Barrow-in-Furness, Eng., 1948-56; clin. psychologist S.W. Met. Reg. Hosp. Bd., London, 1962-67, State of N.J., Ancora, 1967-72, State of Western Australia, Perth, 1972-87; pvt. practice Perth, 1987-94, Preston, Eng., 1994—. Author: The Boundaries That Freud Ignored. Recipient Dame Evelyn Fox award Meml. Fund, U.K., 1960. Mem. APA (fgn. affiliate), Brit. Psychol. Soc. (chartered), Brit. Soc. Projective Psychology. Avocations: travel, theatre, crosswords, doll collecting. Home: Flat 22 Moorlands, 103 Garstang Rd, Preston PR1 1NN, England

DRUMMOND, JON, Olympic athlete. Sprinter U.S.A. Track and Field Team, Atlanta, 1996; co-winner Gold Medal 4X100 meter relay Sydney, 2000; co-winner Silver Medal 4X100 relay U.S. Championships, 1997. Office: USA Track and Field Team One RCA Dome Ste 140 Indianapolis IN 46225*

DRUNG, DIETMAR, electronics engineer, researcher; b. Mühlacker, Germany, Oct. 14, 1958; s. Dieter and Gertrud (Roller) D.; m. Claudia Hogh, Apr. 25, 1980; children: Tabea, Benjamin. Diploma in engring., U. Karlsruhe, 1982, PhD, 1988. Rschr. U. Karlsruhe, 1983-88, Phys.-Tech. Bundesanstalt, Berlin, 1988—. Author: (with others) SQUID Sensors: Fundamentals, Fabrication and Applications, 1996; contbr. articles to profl. jours. including IEEE. Evangelic. Avocation: reading. Office: Phys-Tech Bundesanstalt, Abbestrasse 2-12, D-10587 Berlin Germany

DRURY, JAMES JOSEPH, III, management consultant; b. Chgo., Mar. 10, 1942; s. James Joseph Drury and Helen Sophie Wagner; m. Peggy Diane Snyder, June 10, 1984; 1 child, James. BS in Aero. Engring., U. Notre Dame, 1964; MBA in Mktg. and Fin., U. Chgo., 1966. Mgr. strategic planning Boeing Co., Seattle, 1966-69; v.p. Donald R. Booz & Assoc., Chgo., 1969-74; prin. Ernst & Young, Chgo., 1974-79; ptnr. Nordeman Grimm, Chgo., 1979-84; vice chmn. Spencer Stuart, Chgo., 1984—; bd. dirs. Spencer Stuart. Bd. dirs. Chilmark Fund II, U. Chgo. Grad. Bus. Sch. Adv. Coun.; bd. trustees Music of the Baroque; chmn. U. Chgo./Spencer Stuart Dirs. Coll. Mem. U.S. Polo Assn., Chgo. Club, Univ. Club Chgo., Barrington Polo Club. Avocations: polo, fishing.

DRUSINI, ANDREA GIOVANNI, anthropology educator; b. Valdagno, Veneto, Italy, July 13, 1947; s. Giuseppe and Maddalena (Frigo) D. MD, Med. Sch., Padova, Italy, 1972, diploma in radiology, 1975; diploma in philosophy, U. Padova, 1981, diploma in history of medicine, 1986, internat. diploma in human ecology, 1991. Med. diplomate. Intern Inst. Radiology, Med. Sch. U. Padova, 1973-777, rsch. investigator dept. biology Med. Sch., 1980-91, assoc. prof. anthropology, 1992—; phys. anthropologist Italian Archaeol. Mission, Nasca, Peru, 1986—, Easter Island, 1992-96, Centro Studi e Richerche Ligabue, Venice, Turkmenistan, 1993, Physicians for Human Rights, 1999; participant Excelsa Project E.C. Author: Osteologia Umana, 1992, Biologia Umana, 1994, Paleontologia Umana, 1996; contbr. articles to profl. jours. Fellow Human Biology Assn.; mem. AAAS, European Anthropol. Assn., Am. Anthropol. Assn., Am. Assn. Phys. Anthropology, Acad. Olimpica Vicenza, Rotary (pres. 1997-98). Roman Catholic. Avocations: classic guitar and lute playing, baroque music singing. Home: Riviera Tiso da, Camposampiero 29, 35100 Padua Veneto, Italy Office: U Padua Dept Biology, Via Trieste 75, 35121 Padua Veneto, Italy

DRUTCHAS, GERRICK GILBERT (BARON KHABAROVSKY), investigator; b. Detroit, Sept. 23, 1953; s. Gilbert Henry and Elaine Marie (Rutkowski) D.; 1 child, Gilbert Henry II. BA, Mich. State U., 1975; postgrad., U. Redlands, 1983-85. Pres. Argentum Publs., L.A., 1986—; dir. Le Baron Investigations, Pasadena. Dir. Childrens Welfare Found. Sgt. USAR, 1981-85. Named Baron, Royal House of Alabona-Ostrogojsk, 1992. Mem. Order of the Swan (chevalier), Order of St. Angilbert (chevalier), K. of P. (past chancellor 1983, 84), Delta Sigma Phi. Unitarian. Avocations: chess, coin collecting, writing fiction and non-fiction. Home: 601 E California Blvd Pasadena CA 91106-3852 Office: Le Baron Investigations Pasadena CA 91106

DRUZHININ, VLADIMIR NICKOLAEVICH, psychologist, researcher, consultant; b. Dunilovo, Yaroslavl, Russia, Aug. 12, 1955; s. Nickolay Konstantinovich and Kapitolina Nickolaevna (Borisova) D.; m. Natalia Valentinovna Artemieva, July 28, 1979; children: Dmitriy, Svetlana. PhD in Psychology, Inst. Psychology, Moscow, 1982. Rschr. Inst. Psychology, Russian Acad. Sci., Moscow, 1978-86, head of lab., 1986-92, dep. dir., 1992—; prof. Moscow State U., 1988—; dir. Inst. Psychol. Edn., Moscow, 1995—. Author: Experimental Psychology, 1996, Psychology of General Abilities, 1995, Psychology of Family, 1996, Structure and Logic of Psychological Research, 1994. Recipient Rubinstein award Russian Acad. Sci., 1996. Mem. Acad. Humanitarian Scis. Avocations: poetry, sports. Home: Letnaya 32 1 150, 141021 Moscow Russia Office: Inst Psychology/RAS, Yaroslavskaya str 13, 129366 Moscow Russia

DRYANSKY, GERALD Y., writer, editor, film producer, screenwriter; b. N.Y.C., Jan. 14, 1938; m. Joanne Axelrod; children: André, Larisa. AB, Princeton U., 1959; AM, Harvard U., 1960; MS, Columbia U., N.Y.C., 1961. European dir. Fairchild Pubs., Paris, 1965-75; dir. external affairs Bidermann Group, Paris, 1975-77; Paris editor German Vogue, Paris, 1979-81; writer, comms. cons. Paris, 1981-84; editor-at-large European Travel and Life, Paris, 1984-87; European editor Conde Nast Traveler, Paris, 1987—; v.p. Andara Films, Paris, 1995—. Author: Other People, 1972, The Heirs, 1978; contbr. Vogue, Town & Country, Architectural Digest, Esquire, Elle. Bd. dirs. Friends of Florence, Italy, 1998—; chmn. Princeton Alumni schs. Com., Paris, 1983. Mem. Anglo Am. Press Assn., Harvard Club N.Y.C. Office: Andara Films, 96 Ave Kléber, 75116 Paris France

DRYER, RICHARD, mechanical design engineer; b. Annapolis, Md., Oct. 20, 1950; s. Harold Milton and Beatrice (Sachs) D.; m. Barbara Ellen Horonzy, Mar. 8, 1980; children: Joshua Aaron, Danielle Nicole. BSE, Old Dominion U., 1974. Engr. mech. design GE Ordnance Systems Products Dept., Pittsfield, Mass., 1973-79; sr. design engr. GE Aerospace Instruments and Electrical Systems Dept., Wilmington, Mass., 1979-80; prin. engr. AAI Corp., Hunt Valley, Md., 1980-99; sr. prin. mech. engr. Raytheon Missle Sys., Tuscon, Ariz., 1999—; pres. Syngergy Reisterstown, Md., 1987—. Contbr. articles to profl. jours. Mem. Am. Def. Preparedness Assn., Internat. Soc. Terrain Vehicle Systems. Avocations: target shooting, trap, skeet, sporting clays. Home: 12792 N Lantern Way Oro Valley AZ 85737-8999 Office: Raytheon Missle Sys PO Box 11337 Tucson AZ 85734-1337

DRYGA, ALEXANDER IOSIFOVITSCH, physicist; b. Kegichovka, Ukraine, Feb. 27, 1928; s. Iosif Afanasievitsch and Uljana Ilinichna (Ivanova) D.; m. Valentina Sofina, Feb. 22, 1953; children: Victory, Inna. PhD, Moscow Tech. U., 1973. Engr. Novokramatorsky Mashinostroitelny zavod, Kramatorsk, 1950-54; asst. prof. Donetsk Tech. U., 1954-60; rsch. dir. Kramatorsk Rsch. Inst. Engring., 1960-68; from assoc. prof. to rsch. dir. lib. vibrotechnology Donetsk State Engring. Acad., Kramatorsk, 1968—. Author: Ferroconcrete Machinery, 1967, The Ferroconcrete in Engrineering, 1967; contbr. articles to profl. jours.; patentee in field. Mem. N.Y. Acad. Scis. Home: Marata St 6/64, Kramatorsk Donetsk, Ukraine 84301 Office: Donetsk State Engring Acad, Shkadinova st 72, Kramatorsk Donetsk, Ukraine 84313

DRYJSKI, MACIEJ LUKASZ, vascular surgeon, educator; b. Warsaw, Poland, Jan. 3, 1951; arrived in Sweden, 1974, came to U.S., 1985; s. Jozef Dryjski and Aniela (Grochowska) Dryjska; m. Hanna Iwona Bielawska, June 4, 1977; children: Dominika, Olivia, Sebastian. MD, Med. Acad., Warsaw, 1974; PhD, Karolinska Inst., Stockholm, 1984. Resident in gen. surgery Karolinska Inst. and Hosp., 1978-83, attending surgeon, instr. surgery, 1983-85; rsch. assoc. in clin. pharm. Duke U., Durham, N.C., 1985-86; asst. prof. medicine and surgery Jefferson U., Phila., 1986-88, resident in gen. surgery, 1988-89; resident in vascular surgery U. South Fla., Tampa, 1989-91; assoc. prof. surgery Karolinska Inst. and Hosp., 1991-94, SUNY, Buffalo, 1994—; dir. cardiavascular rsch., dir. vascular lab. Kaleida Health, Buffalo, 1994—. Editl. bd. Polish Jour. Surgery; contbr. articles to profl. jours., chpts. to boks; jour. referee. Senator SUNY, Buffalo, 1999—. Recipient Swedish Med. Rsch. Coun. award for rsch. in U.S., 1985-87. Fellow ACS, N.Y. Acad. Scis.; mem. Eastern Vascular Soc., Western N.Y. Vascular Soc., Buffalo Surg. Soc., Internat. Soc. Cardiovasc. Surgery, Internat. Soc. Thrombosis and Haemost, Swedish Med. Soc., Internat. Soc. Applied Cardiovasc. Biolog., Insternat. Soc. Endovasc. Surgery, Soc. Clin. Vascular Surgery. Roman Catholic. Avocations: tennis, skiing, sailing, golf. Home: 280 Quail Hollow Ln East Amherst NY 14051-1634 Office: SUNY Millard Fillmore Hosp 3 Gates Cir Buffalo NY 14209-1120

DRYZEK, JERZY, physicist, researcher; b. Wojcieszow, Poland, Dec. 5, 1956; s. Stanislaw and Anna (Padula) D.; m. Ewa; 1 child, Mateusz. PhD, Acad. Mining and Metallurgy, Cracow, 1986. Lectr. Pedagogical U., Cracow, 1991-92; tutor Inst. Nuclear Physics, Cracow, 1987—. Contbr. articles to profl. jours. Roman Catholic. Avocations: tinkering, astronomy, politics. Home: ul J Lea 162/5, 31-133 Cracow Poland Office: Inst Nuclear Physics, ul Radzikowskiego 152, 31-342 Cracow Poland

DRZEZGA, ALEXANDER EDUARD, nuclear medicine physician; b. Munich, May 12, 1971; s. Wolfgang and Monika (Paul) D. Med. license, Tech. U. Munich, 1996, MD, 1998. Intern dept. nuclear medicine Tech. U. Munich, 1997-98, resident dept. nuclear medicine, 1998-99, coord. nuclear neuroimaging rsch. group, 1999—; reviewer Jour. Nuclear Medicine, 1999—, Biol. Cybernetics, 1999—. Contbr. articles to profl. jours. Mem. Soc. Nuclear Medicine, Deutsche Gesellschaft für Nuklearmedizin. Avocations: playing piano, sailing, skiing. Office: Nuklearmedizinische Klinik, Ismaninger Str 22, 81675 Munich Germany

D'SOUZA, ALAN S., tax consultant, real estate agent, pianist, writer; b. Calcutta, India, Jan. 11, 1954; came to U.S., 1967; s. Anthony C. and Irene E. (Azavedo) D'S.; m. Mary Ann Conanan, Aug. 6, 1985; children: Angela Bernadette, Anna Maria. BS in Physics, N.E. Mo. State U., 1974; postgrad. in Bus. Adminstrn., U. New Orleans, 1985; diploma in Real Estate, Bob Brooks Sch. of Real Estate, Baton Rouge, 1996. Bus. and estate cons. Hinsdale-Oakbrook (Ill.) Assoc., 1979-82; pianist Marriott Hotels, Lake of the Ozarks and Canal St., New Orleans, 1982-84; revenue officer IRS, Baton Rouge, 1985-89; tax cons., pianist, writer Baton Rouge, 1989—; vol. income tax assistance IRS, Baton Rouge, 1985—. Author: (series) Latin Jazz, 1995-96; author customer svc. manual Beckley Cardy Co., 1974-79; author: (with others) DSK Favorites: Our Best Home Cooking, 1996; featured performer, pianist (Smithsonian event) Beyond Category: The Musical Genius of Duke Ellington, 1996; contbr. articles to profl. jours. Mem. Soc. Profl. Journalists, Acad. Polit. Sci., Jazz Soc. Baton Rouge (founding bd. dirs. 1990—, author newsletter 1992-96, editl. advisor newsletter 1995—), Baton Rouge C. of C. (founding mem. internat. trade coun. 1990—), Smithsonian Instn., Libr. of Congress Assocs. (assoc.). Democrat. Roman Catholic. Avocations: reading, music, writing, soccer, tennis, travel. Home: 15728 Council Ave Baton Rouge LA 70817-5503 Office: Coldwell Banker MacKey Co 4111 S Sherwood Forest Blvd Baton Rouge LA 70816-4369

D'SOUZA, GREGORY, priest, educator; b. Mangalore, Karnataka, India, Nov. 17, 1940; s. Marian and Paschalya D'Souza. BTh, St. Joseph's Theol. U., Alwaye, India, 1970; MA in Philosophy, Karnataka U., 1974; PhD, Mysore (India) U., 1978; ThM, Teresianum, Rome, 1982, ThD, 1984. Ordained priest Roman Cath. Ch., 1970. Rector St. Joseph's Monastery, Mangalore, 1972-75; prior Carmelite Monastery, Margao, India, 1975-78; del. provincial Mangalore, 1979-81; provincial Karnataka Provinciace, 1990-93; dean Coll. Philosophy, Mysore, 1984-87; chair dept. christianity U. Mysore, 1990—; chmn. bd. studies, bd. exam. and selection bd. postgrad. dept. Christianity, U. Mysore; vocation dir. Manjummel Province, Cochin, India, 1970-80, counselor, 1978-71; dir. Vocation Home, coord. African Mission, Mangalore, 1970-75, Dhyanavana, Mysore, 1994—; senato Diocese of Mangalore, 1972-75; founder, dir. Dhyanavana, Internat. Inst. Spirituality, Mysore. Author: Teresian Mysticism and Yoga, 1981, The New Man in St. John of the Cross, 1985, Transforming Flame, 1989; co-author: Discernment in Prayer, 2000; translator, editor: Spiritual Doctrine of St. John of the Cross, 1981; editor: Interculturality of Philosophy and Religion, 1997. Mem. Discalced Carmelite Order, Indian Christian Philosophers' Assn. (exec. mem. 1984-90), India Theol. Assn. (exec. mem. 1990-94), Religious Conf. India in Mysore (pres. 1994—). Avocations: stamp collecting, music, working in slums, gardening. Home: Dhyanavaha, 570007 Mysore Karnataka India Office: Univ Mysore, Dept Christianity, 57006 Mysore Karnataka India

D'SOUZA, LEO SWIBERT, biotechnologist; b. Mangalore, India, Mar. 1, 1932; s. Cyprian and Theresa (Pinto) D'S. MSc, St. Joseph's Coll., Tiruchirapalli, India, 1961; Licentiate in Theology, Sankt Georgen, Frankfurt, Germany, 1966; PhD, Max-Planck Inst., Cologne, Germany, 1970. Rsch. scientist Max Planck Inst., Cologne, 1966-70, rsch. assoc., 1970-72; prof. St. Joseph's Coll., Bangalore, 1973-90; prin. St. Aloysius Coll., Mangalore, India, 1980-90, rector, 1992-98; dir. rsch. St. Joseph's Coll., 1973-80, Lab. of Applied Biology, Mangalore, 1980—. Contbr. (book) Biotechnology in Agriculture Forestry, 1995; contbr. articles to profl. jours. V.p. Parisara Vokkuta, 1993-95. Mem. N.Y. Acad. Scis., Internat. Assn. Plant Tissue Culture, Plantation Crop Soc. Jesuit. Office: Lab Applied Biology, St Aloysius Coll, Mangalore 575003, India

DU, BAI-PING, science educator; b. Xi'an, Shaanxi, China, May 23, 1939; s. Chun-Shan Du and Xian-po Hu; m. Yu-Dong Wang; children: Jian-gang, Jian-xuan. B, Xi'an Jiaotong (China) U., 1962. Asst. researcher China N. Vehicle Rsch. Inst., 1962-70; tech. Xian Railway Signal Plant, 1970-72; from asst. prof. to prof. Xian Jiaotong U., 1973—. Key rschr. Bull. Scientific and Technol. Achievement, 1989, 91, 92. Recipient: Scientific and Technol. award State Edn. Commn., 1988, Mech. and Elec. Industry Ministry, 1992, Honour award Mech. and Elec. Industry Ministry, 1991. Fellow Chinese Heave Cast and Forging Assn.; mem. Chinese Scienfific and Technology Assn., N.Y. Acad. Scis. Office: Xian Jiaotong U, Rsch Inst Strength Material, 710049 Xian Shaanxi, China

DU, TENGDA, researcher, engineer, physicist; b. Ningbo, Zhejiang, China, Sept. 16, 1964; s. Zhongyu and Xine (Zhu) D.; m. Liheng Wang, Jan. 16, 1990; children: Weining, Angela. BS, Zhejiang U., Hangzhou, China, 1984, MS, 1987; PhD, U. Ctr. Fla., Orlando, 2000. Rsch. scientist Shanghai (China) Inst. Metallurgy, 1987-93; calibration technologist Raytheon, Midland, Ont., Can., 1997-98; rsch. assoc. U. Ctrl. Fla., 1998-2000; engr. New Forus Inc., Santa Clara, Calif., 2000—. Contbr. articles to Phys. Rev. Letters, Applied Physics Letters, Jour. Applied Physics. Recipient 2d prize for advanced sci. and tech. Chinese Acad. Scis., Beijing, 1991, 1st prize, 1992. Mem. AAAS, Am. Phys. Soc. E-mail: tengda.du@yahoo.com. Office: New Focus Inc 2630 Walsh Ave Santa Clara CA 95051-0905

DU, XIAOGUANG, mechanical engineer, engineering executive; b. Shanghai, Nov. 9, 1957; s. Baoguang Du and Guanglan Han. BS, Shanghai JiaoTong U., 1982; M in Mfg., Tong Ji U., Shanghai, 1987; M in Sci. and Tech., Okla. State U., 1994. Mech. engr. Shanghai Crane and Convey Co., 1982-84; lectr. Tong Ji U., Shanghai, 1984-91; finite element analysis specialist Quality Metalcraft Inc., Livonia, Mich., 1996—; v.p. ND Machinery Inc., Southfield, Mich., 1996—. V.p. Chinese Friendship Assn., Okla. State U., Stillwater, 1993. Avocations: swimming, boxing, reading. Office: Quality Metalcraft Inc 33355 Glendale St Livonia MI 48150-1615

DU, XIAO-MING, pharmaceutical scientist; b. Inner Mongolia, China, Sept. 17, 1956; s. Cheng-Wu Du and Feng-Xiang Wang; m. Ming-Yi Sun. BS, Shenyang (China) Pharm. U., 1982. Pharmacist Inst. Pharm. Scis., Dalian, China, 1982-86, lectr., 1987-91, assoc. prof., 1992-93; vis. rschr. Setsunan U., Osaka, Japan, 1993-95, Seiwa Pharm. Ltd., Tokyo, 1995-98, Kyushu U., Fukuoka, Japan, 1998—. Contbr. articles to profl. jours. (1st pl. award for med. sci. Dailan City 1988, 1st pl. award for sci. and tech. young rschr. Liaoning Province 1991). Fellow Pharm. Soc. China, Pharm. Soc. Japan, Japanese Soc. Pharmacognosy. Avocations: painting, calligraphy. Fax: 81-293-433058. E-mail: Du-07@kita.mektron.co.jp. Office: Kyushu U, 3-1-1 Maidashi, Higashi-ku, Fukuoka 812-8582, Japan

DU, YANQING, electrical engineer; b. Hangzhou, China, Apr. 23, 1971; came to U.S., 1994; d. Zhonghai and Liane (Ye) Du. BS in Elec. Engring., Northwestern Poly. U., China, 1993; MS in Elec. Engring., Northwestern Poly. U., 1994, MIT, 1999; PhD in Elec. Engring., MIT, 1999. Elec. Engr. MIT, 1999. Tchr. Northwestern Poly. U., Xi'an, China, 1992-93; engr. Exponent Failure Analysis Assocs., Menlo Pk., Calif., 1999—. Contbr. articles profl. jours.; presenter in field. Recipient Am. Pub. Power Assn. scholarship, 1995, 1996, 1998, An Wang grad. fellowship MIT, 1998, Wang Tiwu fellowship. 1994, 2d prize Contest for Exptl. Skills and Sci. Invention, Xi'an, 1992. Mem. IEEE, Dielectrics and Elec. Insulation Soc., Power Engring. Soc., Sigma Xi. Avocations: hiking, ping pong, soft rock, swimming. E-mail: ydu@exponent.com. Office: Exponent Failure Analysis Assocs 149 Commonwealth Dr Menlo Park CA 94025-1133

DU, ZHEN-PING, software engineer, research fellow; b. Nanjing, China, June 2, 1962; arrived in New Zealand, 1991; s. Pei-Dian Du and Gui-Ying Chen; m. Jian-Jian Zhao, June 2, 1987; children: Charley Jia Cheng Du, William Jia Ming Du. BE in Automatic Control, S.E. U., Nanjing, 1984, ME in Automatic Control, 1987, PhD in Automatic Control, 1990; ME with Distinction (hon.), U. Canterbury, Christchurch, New Zealand, 1994. Lectr. Hohai U., Nanjing, 1990-91; postdoctoral fellow in transp. U. Canterbury, Christchurch, New Zealand, 1991-93, postdoctoral fellow in power sys., 1995-96, acad. supr., 1995-96; Asia area mgr. CHART Instruments, Ltd., Christchurch, New Zealand, 1996-98; sr. software engr. Forum 8 (NZ) Ltd., Christchurch, New Zealand, 1998-2000, Genie Sys. Ltd., Auckland, New Zealand, 2000—; cons. Power Quality Consultants, Christchurch, 1996-97; dir.-gen. Sys. and Control Soc. Eastern China Youth, 1990-91; referee IEE Proceedings-Generation, Transmission, and Distbn., Eng., 1996—. Contbr.

articles to profl. jours. including Transp. Rsch., IEE Proceedings. Mem. Internat. Fedn. Automatic Control. Avocations: painting, photography, video recording. Home: 21 Harbour Lights Close, West Harbour West Harbor Auckland New Zealand

DUA, MULAKH RAJ, journalism educator, author, columnist; b. Sargodha, Punjab, Pakistan, July 1, 1934; s. Krishanlal and Rambai (Ahuja) D.; m. Ravi K. Arora, Oct. 7, 1962 (dec. 1990); children: Ramneik Dua-Braroo, Puneit Dua-Pankaj, Sumeit Dua-Aggarwal. Bachelor's degree, Delhi U., 1955; MA in Econs., Panjab U., 1957, diploma in journalism, 1958; MA in English Lit., Agra (India) U., 1962; MA in Mass Comm., Calif. State U., Northridge, 1978. Copy editor The Indian Express, New Delhi, 1959-63; sr. lectr. journalism dept. Panjab U., Chandigarh, India, 1963-68; editor University News, New Delhi, 1968-71; dep. dir. Ministry of Labor Govt. of India, 1971-77; asst. prof. Calif. State U., 1977; assoc. prof., head mass comm. dept. Calicut U., Kerala, India, 1978-79; prof., head, faculty adviser Indian Inst. Mass Comm., New Delhi, 1979-98; ret., 1998. Author: Programming Potential of Indian Television, 1980, Themes in Indian Communication, 1981; co-editor: Media and Development, 1995, Culture of Communication, 1997, Press as Leader of Society, 1998. Recipient 2d prize Population Edn. Soc., 1996; grantee Calif. State U., 1977, honors World Assn. Press Couns., Istanbul, Turkey, 1998. Mem. Commonwealth Assn. Educators in Journalism and Comm., Asian Mass Comm. Rsch. and Info. Ctr. Singapore, Indian Inst. Mass Comm. (governing body 1980-82, 92-94, Indian Adult Edn. Assn. (life), Panjab U. Journalists Soc. (mem. governing bd. 1980-92, pres. 1992—). Avocations: popular writing on media, media research and criticism, higher education, cultural issues. Fax: 011-0124-61353147. E-mail: murad038@hotmail.com. Home and Office: 38 Nat Media Ctr Complex, Haryana Gurgaon 122002, India also: care Dr Ramneik Dua-Braroo 173 Hawthorne Ave Apt 172 Central Islip NY 11722-1322

DUAN, SHAOBO, geographer, researcher; b. Yingshan, Sichuan, China, Oct. 24, 1923; s. Zhiping Duan and Shude He; m. Endo Zhu, Jan. 1, 1965; children: Hui, Li. BA, Fudan U., Shanghai, China, 1949. Tchr. Jingguan Chang Primary Sch., Chongqing, 1943-44; tchr. geography Qixiu Girl's Middle Sch., Shanghai, 1949-53; tchr. geography Shanghai Tchrs.' Coll., 1954-78, lectr. in geography, 1979-85, assoc. prof., 1986-94; prof. Zhejiang Coll. Edn., Hangzhou, China, 1995—. Author: (with others) A Physical Geography of Oceania, 1987, Geographical Name Dictionary of Shanghai, 1989, The Theory and Practice of Urban Ecological Economy, 1988 (Works of Excellence award 1992), World Geography--A Textbook for College Students, 2d edit., 1989. Recipient Natural Environment of Shanghai award, 1990, others. Mem. Shanghai Popular Sci. and Tech. Assn., Shanghai Geog. Soc., Shanghai Environ. Sci. Soc., Shanghai Ecol. Economy Soc. (dir.). Avocations: swimming, taijiquan, Qigong, walking, jogging. Home: Dorm No 22-54-37, Lane 70 Guilin Rd, 200234 Shanghai Peoples Republic of China Office: Shanghai Tchrs U Dept Geog, 100 Guilin Rd, 200234 Shanghai Peoples Republic of China

DUAN, TAIZHONG, petroleum geologist, educator; b. Tianmen, Hubei, China, Aug. 12, 1961; m. Siaojie Wang, Mar. 10, 1987; children: Xiaolong, Xiaowei. BSc, Jianghan Petroleum Inst., Jingzhou, China, 1982; MSc, Chengdu (China) Coll. Geology, 1988; PhD in Engring., U. Trondheim, Norway, 1996. Asst. lectr. Jiangham Petroleum Inst., Jingzhou, 1982-87, lectr., 1987-92, asst. prof., 1992-95; rsch. fellow Rsch. Coun. Norway/U. Trondheim, 1992-95, U. Adelaide, Australia, 1995-97; postdoctoral fellow Colo. Sch. Mines, Golden, 1997-98, rsch. asst. prof., 1998—. Contbr. articles to profl. jours. Recipient 3d Youth Geosci. award Geol. Soc. China, 1992. Mem. Am. Assn. Petroleum Geologists. Fax: 303-273-3859. E-mail: tduan@mines.edu. Office: Colo Sch Mines Dept Geology/Geol Engring. 1500 Illinois St Golden CO 80401-1843

DUARTE, PATRICIA M., real estate and insurance broker; b. Truro, Mass., Feb. 23, 1938; d. Antone Jr. and Marjorie (Beckley) Duarte. Grad. H.S., Provincetown, Mass. Lic. ins. and real estate broker; constrn. supt. Sec. various ins. agys., Amherst, Mass., 1957-60; ins. and real estate agt. Duarte Ins. & Real Estate, Truro, 1960-66, owner, prin. agt., 1966-78; ins. risk mgr. J.L. Marshall & Sons, Inc., Pawtucket, R.I., 1979-92; owner, mgr. Patricia-Duarte Real Estate, Rockport, Maine, 1988-97; restorer antique homes New Eng., Mass., 1979—. Mem., sec. Truro Planning Bd., 1965-72, chmn., 1974-78; mem. exec. com. Cape Cod Planning and Econ. Devel. Com., 1971-76; mem. Reelect Brawn for Senate Com., Camden, Maine, 1988; mem. Rockport Planning Bd., 1991-94, Rockport Comprehensive Plan Implementation Com., 1991-94; co-chmn. Rockport Capital Improvement Com., 1991-96; bd. dirs. Cape Cod chpt. Am. Heart Assn., 1963-70; mem. Opera House Commn., 1992-94. Mem. Penobscot Bay Bd. Realtors, Profl. Ins. Agts. New Eng. (bd. dirs. 1974-76), Gen. Fedn. Women's Clubs (2d v.p. Camden chpt. 1989), Hist. Preservation Assn. St. Thomas (arts coun. 1998-99, bd. dirs. 1998). Republican. Roman Catholic. Avocations: gourmet cooking, travel, photography, architectural and interior design. Address: PO Box 294 Port Clyde ME 04855-0294

DUATTI, ADRIANO, chemist, radiochemist; b. Ostellato, Ferrara, Italy, May 17, 1952; s. Alvaro and Liliana (Ricci) D.; m. Maria Grazia Ghisini, Oct. 30, 1976; children: Francesca, Federica. PhD, U. Ferrara, 1976. Rsch. asst. U. Ferrara, 1978-81, sr. rsch. fellow, 1981-86, invited prof., 1990; assoc. prof. U. Bologna, Italy, 1986-98; prof. U. Ferrara, Italy, 1998—. Contbr. articles to profl. jours.; patentee in field. Sgt. Italian Mil., 1976-77. Nat. Rsch. Coun. rsch. grantee, 1984. Mem. Soc. Nuclear Medicine, Italian Assn. Nuclear Medicine, N.Y. Acad. Scis., European Radiopharmacy Com. Avocations: painting, running, tennis, quantum mechanics. Office: U Ferrara Dept Clin & Exptl Med, Via L Borsari 46, 44100 Ferrara Italy

DUBAR, CLAUDE ROGER, sociologist; b. Lille, Nord, France, Dec. 11, 1945; s. Gaston Dubar and Marie-Louise Hubo; s. Elisabeth Marie Charlon, Sept. 9, 1967; (div. 1990); children: Emmanuel, Francois. PhD, Paris-Vincennes, 1970; Doctorate, Paris-Sorbonne, France, 1984. Asst. Faculty of Arts, Lille, 1967-71; prof. Sch. of Letters, Beyrouth, 1971-73; rschr. CNRS, Paris, 1973-77; prof. U. Lille, 1977-90; dept. mgr. CEREQ, Paris, 1990-93; prof. U. Versailles, 1993; cons. Edn. Ministry, Paris, 1989-93; vice-chmn. U. Lille, 1981-84; director Lab., Lille, 1984-90, Lab. St. Quentin en Yvelines, 1995. Author: La Socialisation, 1991 (Reed award 1995, 2000), La Formation Professionnelle Continue, 1984 (Reedition award 1990, 96, 2000), Sociologie des Professions, 1998, editor: Genèse et dynamique des Groupes professionnels, 1994, Cheminements Professionnels et Mobilité Sociale, 1992, La Crise des identité, 2000. Mem. French Soc. Sociology (pres. 1999). Office: Printemps, 47 Blvd Vauban, 78047 Guyancourt France

DUBÉ, LAWRENCE EDWARD, JR., lawyer; b. Chgo., Sept. 25, 1948; s. Lawrence Edward and Rosemary Nora (Cooney) D.; m. Paula Ann Goodgal, Jan. 10, 1982; 1 child, Charles Bernard. BA in Polit. Sci. cum laude, Knox Coll., 1970; JD with distinction, U. Iowa, 1973. Bar: Ill. 1973, Md. 1982, Pa. 1982, D.C. 1983, U.S. Supreme Ct., 1987. Field atty. NLRB, Chgo., 1973-80, supr. atty., 1980-81; sole practice Balt., 1981-85; assoc. Grove, Jaskiewicz, Gilliam & Cobert, Washington, 1985-87; ptnr. Dubé & Goodgal, P.C., Balt., 1987—. Author: Management on Trial-The Law of Wrongful Discharge, 1987, New Employment Issues: How to Shield your Business from Costly Lawsuits, 1988, Employment References and the Law, 1989; co-author: The Maryland Employer's Guide to Labor and Employment Law, 1984. Mem. Am. Arbitration Assn. (arbitrator), Nat. Assn. Securities Dealers (arbitrator). Home: 622 W University Pky Baltimore MD 21210-2908 Office: Dubé & Goodgal PC 2400 Boston St Ste 407 Baltimore MD 21224-4787

DUBE, RAJESH, financial consultant; b. Kanpur, UP, India, June 30, 1965; s. Hari Shanker and Vimla (Tewari) D.; m. Rashmi Trivedi, Nov. 23, 1991; children: Rupali, Rangoli. Advt. and sales promotion, BITS, 1995. Jr. cons. Rad Multi Sys., Lucknow, India, 1986-87; from sr. asst. to sr. officer Housing Devel. Fin. Corp. Ltd., Lucknow, 1987-96; resident mgr., cons. Housing Devel. Fin. Corp. Ltd., Kanpur, 1996-99; mgr. Housing Devel. Fin. Corp. Ltd., Ludhiana, 1999—. Mem. Ganges Club. Avocations: reading, social service, playing shuttle badminton. Home: HIG 85 Preetam Nagar, UP Allahabad 211 001, India Office: Housing Devel Fin Corp Ltd, SCO 19 Feroz Gandhi Market, Ludhiana 141001, India

DUBE'-ODELL, DORICE SUZANNE, career officer; b. L.A., Sept. 2, 1958; d. Howard Ernest and Sylvia Diane (Kohler) Dube'; m. Mark Wesley Odell, Apr. 23, 1983. AS in Bus., L.A. C.C., 1981; BSBA, U. Phoenix, 1988; MS in Aeronautics and Engring., Columbia State U., 1999, postgrad., 1999—. Claims processor Blue Cross Blue Shield, Colton, Calif., 1982-84; mortgage ins. and tax specialist Shearson Lehmen Am. Express Mortgage Corp., San Bernardino, Calif., 1982-84; o-ring tech. writer Bourns Aerospace, Riverside, Calif., 1984-85; C-141 B Starlifter loadmaster (aircrew mem.) 728th Mil. Airlift Squadron, Norton AFB, Calif., 1985-89; MX rail Garrison missile project/rail & track identification Earth Tech., San Bernardino, Calif., 1987-88; aeromed. ops. evacuation officer 68th Aeromed. Evacuation Squadron, Norton AFB, 1989-94; ops. officer 452 Aeromed. Evacuation Squadron, March Air Res. Base, 1991-94; ops. group exec. officer HQ 452 Ops. Group, March Air Res. Base, Calif., 1994—. Sports planner Spl. Olympics, Calif. and Frankfurt, Germany, 1977—; charter mem. San Diego Zool. Soc., 1994—. With U.S. Army, 1976-85, capt. USAFR, 1985—. Decorated Army Commendation medal Dept. of the Army, Seoul, Korea, 1980; recipient Air Force Meritorious Svc. medal, Air Force Commendation medal, Air Force Achievement medal, Air Force and Army Commendation medal. Mem. Women in Mil. Svc. Assn. (charter mem.), The Bus. Press (Bus. Press Woman of Yr. nominee, 1998). Democrat. Roman Catholic. Avocations: sports, aeronautic history, folk art, researching various topics. E-mail: DOdell9313@aol.com. Home: 19339 Lambeth Ct Riverside CA 92508-6217 Office: HQ 452 Ops Group 1250 Graeber St Ste 16 March AFB CA 92518-1706

DUBERNARD, JEAN-MICHEL, surgeon, educator; b. Lyon, Rhone, France, May 17, 1941; s. Maurice and Marie-Louise (Boissel) D.; m. Catherine Feuillade, 1967; children: Carole, Gil, Estelle. Student, Lyon Med. Sch., 1959-65, Harvard Med. Sch., Boston, 1965-67; MD, U. Lyon, 1967, PhD. Prof. urol. surgery U. Lyon, 1977—; chief dept. urology and transplant surgery Hosp. Herriot, Lyon, 1979—. Contbr. numerous articles and books in the field of transplantation and urology. Dep. du Rhone, French Nat. Assembly, 1986—, v.p. social affairs com.; dep. mayor of Lyon in charge of finances and programming, 1983—. Decorated Chevalier, Ordre National du Merite, 1982, Ordre des Palmes Academique, 1983. Mem. Gaullist Party. Home: 1 Bd des Belges, 69006 Lyon France Office: Service d'Urologie/Chirurgi, Hospital E Herriot, 69473 Lyon France

DUBEY, CHANDRA VARTY, technical consultant; b. Bhadari, Bihar, India, Feb. 1, 1931; s. Kuldeep Dubey and S. Upadhyay; m. Kunti Pandey; children: C. Vijay, Chandra Vikas, Chandra Vinay, Vatsala. BSc, Banaras (India) Hindu U., 1952; BSc in Engring., Glasgow (Scotland) U., 1956. Dep. gen. mgr. Bharat Heavy Electricals, Bhopal, India, 1963-77; cons. Preece Cardew & Rider, Brighton, Eng., 1977-83, Ewbank Preece Ltd., Brighton, 1973-94, Mott MacDonald Ltd., Brighton, 1994—, Fuji Electric Co. Ltd., Kawasaki, Japan, 1989—; mng. dir. Dubey Cons. & Engrs. Pvt. Ltd., Bhopal, 1994-99, also bd. dirs. Fellow Instn. Engrs. India (chmn. M.P. state ctr. 1974-75); mem. IEEE. Avocations: reading books and periodicals, gardening, music. Home: H-416/E-7 Arera Colony, Bhopal MP 462016, India Office: Dubey Cons & Engrs Pvt Ltd, H-416 Chandralok E-7 Arera, Bhopal MP 462016, India

DUBEY, KUMUDINI, high school principal; b. Gram Kunda Dish, Chhindwara, India, Apr. 9, 1940; d. Brij Bhooshal Lal and Rajkumari Sharma; m. Ramkrishan Dubey, May 30, 1955; children: Alok, Asheesh. BA, Yobadpur U., India, 1960; MA, Bikram U., India, 1964; BEd, Sagar U., India, 1966. Prin. Govt. HS Gandhi Chok, India. Author: Sudhi Aai, 1970, Aprapya Bhatkan, 1973, Shakuntala, 1984, Noor Yahan, 1989, Didi, 1990, Surbhi KeAshas, 1993, Saransh, 1994, Swar Matri, 1997, Veer Badhooti, 1998. Avocations: writing, reading. Homew: Ganesh Pura, Ganj Basoda, Dish Vidisha MP 464221, India Office: Prin Govt HS, Ghandi Chok, Ganj Basoda 464221, India

DUBIEF, JEAN, climatologist; b. Rennes, France, Oct. 28, 1903; s. Henry Georges Adolphe and Berthe (Biver) D.; m. Marguerite Tenthorey, Feb. 19, 1954 (dec. Aug. 1996); 1 child, Yves. Ingenieur, Ecole Nat. Sup. Agronomique, Algeria, 1920; ScD, U. Alger, 1953. Mem. Faculty of Scis., mem. staff Inst. Meteorology and Earth Physics Algeria, 1924-62; chief Obs. Phys. de Globe, Tamanrasset, Algeria, 1931-42; adj. physician Inst. Earth Physics, Paris, 1962-68; rschr. climatology Cameroon, 1965-70; chmn., CEO Tenthorey, 1969-83. Author: Essai sur L'Hydrologie Superficielle du Sahara, 1953, Le Climat du Sahara, Vol. 1, 1959, Vol. 2, 1963, Daie Sahara, eine Klima-Wuste, 1971, L'Ajjer. Sahara central, 1999; contbr. articles to profl. jours. Served with French Army, 1939-40, 42-54. Decorated chevalier Legion of Honor, chevalier du Merite Saharien, chevalier du Merite Agricole, officer Palmes Academiques. Mem. Union Geodesic et Geophysique Internat., Geographie Soc. Paris, Assn. French Geographers, La Rahla Club, Explorers Club (N.Y.C.). Roman Catholic. Address: 150 Rue de l'Universite, 75007 Paris France

DUBIN, MARTIN STEVEN, principal; b. Queens, N.Y., July 1, 1950; s. Herman and Fay Dubin; m. Ellen Marlene Kohn, Aug. 18, 1973; children: Rachel Fay, David Isaac. BA, Hofstra U., 1972, MS in Edn. with univ. honors, 1974; D of Edn., Vanderbilt U., 1981. Cert. nursery, kindergarten, grades 1-6, social studies 7-9, spl. classes for emotionally disturbed K-12, Va.; kindergarten, elem. 107, spl. edn. for emotional disturbance and learning disabilities, elem. prin., secondary prin. Tchr. emotionally disturbed Mt. Vernon Ctr., Alexandria, Va., 1974-76; head tchr. emotionally disturbed Riverside Elem., Alexandria, 1976-77; resource tchr. emotionally disturbed Franconia Ctr., Alexandria, 1977-81; dept. chmn. learning disabled Robinson Secondary, Fairfax, Va., 1981-83; prin. Armstrong Ctr., Reston, Va., 1988-90, Franconia Ctr., Alexandria, 1990-97, Crestwood Elem., Springfield, Va., 1997-98; adminstrv. prin. Hayfield Secondary, Alexandria, 1998—; adj. prof. George Mason U., Fairfax, 1988-93; learning disabilities/mild mental retardation specialist Area IV Adminstrv. Office, Fairfax, 1983-88; grant evaluator U.S. Office of Edn., Washington, spring 1991, 93, 95. Pres. Adat Reyim, Springfield, Va., 1997-99; mem. Springfield Coalition, 1997-98. U.S. Office of Edn. rsch. grantee, 1979. Mem. CEC, Nat. Assn. Elem. Sch. Prins., Phi Delta Kappa. Achievements include study in how attitudes of non-disabled students influence the integration and mainstreaming of emotionally disabled students. Avocations: photography, coin collecting, traveling, gardening. Office: Hayfield Secondary Sch 7630 Telegraph Rd Alexandria VA 22315-3898

DUBINSKY, ANATOLY, mechanical engineering researcher; b. Moscow, June 22, 1948; arrived in Israel, 1994; s. Valentin and Geola Dubinsky; m. Alla Tikhonova, Mar. 14, 1974 (div.); 1 child, Julia. From engr. to head of rsch. lab. Rsch. Inst. of Gas Industry, Moscow, 1971-94; rschr. Lomonosov State U., Moscow, 1973-94; sr. rschr. Ben-Gurion U. of the Negev, Beer-Sheva, Israel, 1994—. Author: Computer Monitoring of Gas Pipelines, 1988, Mathematical Modeling of Gas Pipeline Units, 1988, Mathematical Models and Methods of Localized Interaction Theory, 1995; contbr. over 100 articles to profl. jours. Recipient medals Exhbn. of Nat. Economy Achievements, Russia, 1978, 85. Fellow Am. Math. Soc., Israel Math. Soc. E-mail: dubin@menix.bgu.ac.il. Home: PO Box 10030, 84102 Beer Sheva Israel Office: Ben-Gurion U of the Negev, PO Box 653, 84105 Beer Sheva Israel

DUBOCHET, JACQUES, biophysics educator; b. Aigle, Vaud, Switzerland, June 8, 1942; s. Jean Emmanuel and Liliane (Baenziger) D.; m. Christine Wiemken, Apr. 21, 1978; children: Gilles, Lucy. Grad. in physics, Fed. U., Lausanne, Switzerland, 1967; PhD in Biophysics, Bioctr., Basel, Switzerland, 1972, postgrad., 1972-78. Head lab. for applied electron microscopy European Molecular Biology Lab., Heidelberg, Germany, 1978-87; prof. biophysics, head dept. ultrastructural analysis U. Lausanne, 1987—, head sect. biology, 1998—. Contbr. articles to sci. jours., including DNA Observation, Cryo-electron Microscopy. 1st lt. Swiss Army. Mem. Soc. Cryobiology, Swiss Soc. Biomed. Ethics. Avocations: politics, mountain climbing, environmental protection. Office: U Lausanne, Batiment Biologie-Niveau 1, 1015 Lausanne Switzerland

DUBOEUF, FRANCOIS PAUL, bone mineral researcher, consultant; b. Grenoble, Isére, France, Mar. 10, 1959; s. Jules Marie and Marie-Thérese (Charvet) D. BSc, U. Lyon (France) I, 1983, MSc, 1984, PhD in Human Biology, 1990. Technician in dual energy x-ray absoptiometry Nat. Inst. Med. Health and Rsch., Lyon, 1985-93, engr., 1993—; cons. Sopha Med., France, 1989-92, LC Med., France, 1995—, Kontrom Instrument France, Hologic France. Contbr. articles to Clin. Rheumatology, Osteoporosis Internat., Brit. Jour. Radiology, Jour. Bone and Muscle Rsch. Recipient young investigator award Internat. Conf. on Calcium Regulating Hormones, Florence, Italy, 1992. Mem. Info. Group on Osteoporosis. Roman Catholic. Avocations: travel, jogging, swimming, reading. Office: INSERM Edouard Herriot Hosp, 5 Pl d'Arsonval, 69437 Lyon Cedex 03, France

DUBOIS, JACQUES-EMILE, chemistry and information science educator, researcher; b. Lille, France, Apr. 13, 1920; s. Paul and Marie Emilienne (Chevrier) D.; m. Bernice Claire Shaaker, May 24, 1952; children: Rhoda Nicole, Alain. PhD in Phys. Sci., U. Grenoble, 1947; Dr. hon. causa, U. Regensburg. Dir. chem. inst., dean sci. faculty Univ. Saar, 1949-57; prof. chem. informatics U. Paris VII, 1957-90; adv. sci., higher edn. Minister of Edn., Paris, 1962-63, dep. dir. higher edn., 1963-65; dir. R&D Ministry Def., Paris, 1965-77; founder, pres. Ardic, Paris, 1971—; co-dir. inst. Curie, Paris, 1977-80; sci. dir. Gen. Electric Co., Paris, 1979-82; mem. liberation com. ISERE, 1944-45; v.p. Codata Internat., Paris, 1980-84, pres., 1994-98; v.p. Ctr. for Scientific Def. Studies, U. Marne-la-Vallée, 1994—, chmn. Iupac Interdiv. Com. on Machine Documentation, 1969-77. Co-editor: (3 books) Data and Knowledge in a Changing World, 1996; bd. consulting editors Tetrahedron, 1983-90; author numerous chpts. in books and encys.; inventor DARC Topological Sys. for on-line info. sys. and for computer assisted design in chemistry; patentee in field; contbr. numerous articles to profl. jours. Named Comdr. Legion of Honor French Govt., 1989; recipient Jecker prize, Berthelot medal French Acad. Sci., 1965, Stas medal Belgian Chem. Soc., 1950, Grand Prix de la Technique City of Paris, 1975, Resistance medal French Govt., 1946, CAOC medal, 1991; named comdr. Acad. Palms French Govt., 1962, comdr. de l'Ordre du Mèrite France, comdr. de l'Ordre du Mèrite de l'Allemagne, 1975; Fulbright Smith-Mund grantee U. Columbia, 1956. Mem. French Phys. Chmistry Soc. (pres. 1974-76), French Chem. Soc. (coun. 1965-68), Faraday Soc., Am. Chem. Soc. (Skolnik award 1992). Home: 100 rue de Rennes, 75006 Paris France Office: ITODYS Univ Paris VII, 1 Rue Guy de la Brosse, 75005 Paris France

DUBOIS, MARIE-ASTRID, accountant; b. Tullins, France, May 21, 1961; d. Philippe and Claude (Silvy) D. BA, U. Lausanne, 1983; MBA, U. Barcelona, 1986. Auditor Arthur Andersen, Lyons, France, 1986-88; mgmt. devel. staff The Dexter Corp., Windsor Locks, Conn., Switzerland, 1988-90; cash mgmt. internat. The Dexter Corp., Windsor Locks, Belgium, 1991-92; European treasury mgr. The Dexter Corp., 1992-94, asst. treas., 1994-96; dir. fin. The Dexter Corp., Grüningen, Switzerland, 1996-97; asst. treas. A.C. Nielsen, Wavre, Belgium, 1997—. Avocations: golf, skiing, tennis, bridge. Office: AC Nielsen Waterloo Office Park, AC Nielsen, Einstein 6 Bldg F, B 1300 Wavre Belgium

DUBOIS, PAUL MARTIN JOSEPH, non-profit organization executive; b. N.Y.C., Oct. 14, 1945; s. Donald A. and Nancy J. (Grennel) DuB.; children: Kara, Charlene, John, Cynthia, Nate, Joshua, Caleb, Aaron, Rangell, Willie. BA, New Sch. Social Rsch., 1965; PhD, Cornell U., 1975; DHL, Anna Maria Coll., Mass., 1996, Goddard Coll., Vt. Trustee emeritus, hon. pub. Ctr. Living Democracy, Brattleboro, Vt.; exec. Inst. for Cmty. and Race Rels., Rutland, Mass. Author: The Hospice Way of Death, 1977, Modern Administrative Practices, 1980, Handbook of Interracial Dialogue; co-author: The Quickening of America, 1994. Avocation: writing. Home and Office: Inst for Cmty and Race Rels 12 Millbrook St Rutland MA 01543-1452

DU BOISE, KIM REES, artist, photographer, art educator; b. Hattiesburg, Miss., Apr. 7, 1953; d. Samernie and Margaret J. (Mitchell) R.; divorced; children: Timothy L., M. Ashley (dec.). BA, U. So. Miss., 1986, M of Art Edn., 1988; postgrad., U. Ala., 1994-95. Art tchr. grades 7-12 Columbia (Miss.) Acad., 1975-76; with prodn./ad design Columbian-Progress/Sunday Mirror (News), Columbia, 1980-81; with advt. design/prodn. Washington Parish ERA-Leader (newspaper), Franklinton, La., 1981; art tchr. grades kindergarten-12 Hattiesburg Prep. Sch., 1984-85; instr. art Pearl River C.C., Poplarville, Miss., 1987-94; artist/photographer Dogwood Studios, 1988-97, Photo Arts Studio, 1997—; adj. instr. U. So. Miss., 1996-97, 98—; festival coord. Very Spl. Arts Festival, SE Dist., Poplarville, Miss., 1989-94; art show juror Lamar County Home Extension Art Show, Lumberton, Miss., 1988; fine art juror Pearl River County Fair Competition, Poplarville, 1989; juror Picayune PTA Competition and Annual Art Competition-Picayune Meml. High Sch., 1990; participant regional round-Table on discipline based art edn. Getty Ctr. for Edn. in Arts, Tulsa, 1988. Participant Ann. Bi-State Competition, 1986, 96; group exhbn. MSC/JCAIA Art Exhbn., 1991, Miss. Cmty. Jr. Coll. Art, 1991-92, Art by Art Tchrs. MAEA, 1992, mixed media/photography Ann. Juried Art Student League Exhibit, 1995, photography Black Warrior 10 Exhibit, U. N.Mex., 1995, So. Miss. Art Assn. Annual Juried Competitions, 1996, 97, 98, USM Faculty Art Exhibit, 1998, 2000, USM Art Alumni Exhbn., 1996. Chmn. troop 21 Dixie Com. Boy Scouts Am., Hattiesburg, 1989-93; mem. Miss. Jaycettes/Marion County Jaycettes, Columbia, 1976-84, U.S. Jaycee Women, 1976-84. Named one of Outstanding Young Women of Am., 1981-84, First Lady #83 (Life Mem.) Miss. Jaycettes, 1982, Winner Speak-Up Competition, Miss. Jaycettes, 1981. Mem. Miss. Art Edn. Assn., Nat. Art Edn. Assn., New Orleans Mus. of Art (assoc.), So. Miss. Art Assn., Nat. Mus. of Women in the Arts (charter), Am. Crafts Coun., Nature Conservancy, U. So. Miss. Alumni Assn., Walter Anderson Mus. Art, Kappa Delta Pi. Episcopalian. Avocations: camping, fishing, reading.

DU BOIS-REYMOND, ALARD, foundation administrator; b. Zurich, Switzerland, Feb. 2, 1961; s. Prosper and Heidi (Oesch) du B.; m. Victoire Sathoud, Feb. 2, 1992. M in Econs., U. Zurich, 1986. Asst. Swiss Bank Coop., Zurich, 1986-88, Gesellschaft fur technische Zusammenarbeit, Brazzaville, Congo, 1988-89; office head Internat. Com. of the Red Cross, Borama, Somalia, 1989-91; head ops. Internat. Com. of the Red Cross, Addis Ababa, Ethiopia, 1991-92; dept. head Internat. Com. of the Red Cross, Zagreb, Croatia, 1993-94; head desk Internat. Com. of the Red Cross, Geneva, Switzerland, 1994-96; sec. gen. Pro Infirmis, Zurich, 1996—. Home: Weinplatz 3, 8001 Zurich Switzerland Office: Pro Infirmis, Feldeggstrasse 71, 8032 Zurich Switzerland

DUBOST, THIERRY HUGHES, English language educator; b. Cherbourg, France, June 4, 1958; s. Jacques Léon and Thérèse Berthe (Pruvost) D.; m. Eliane Jacqueline Fontaine, Aug. 26, 1983; children: Clarissa, Valentin. Lic., U. Caen, France, 1981, MA, 1982, DEA, 1984; PhD, U. Paris IV Sorbonne, 1993. Prof. Lycée Chartier, Bayeux, France, 1988-91, Coll. des Dorits, Falaise, France, 1991-92; asst. prof. U. Caen, 1993-94, assoc. prof., 1994—; head of English studies Open U., Caen, 1994-98; dean Distance Learning Ctr. U. Caen. Author: (book) Struggle, Defeat or Rebirth: Eugene O'Neill's Vision of Humanity, 1997; co-editor: (books) La Femme Noire américaine, aspects d'une crise d' identité, 1997, George Bernard Shaw, un dramaturge engagé, 1998, Du Dire à l'Etre-Tensions identitaires dans la littérature nord-américaine, 2000; translator: (play) Death and the King's Horseman, 1986. Home: 14 rue des Champs St George, 14700 Falaise France

DUBOVSKI, BORIS GRIGORIJ, nuclear physicist; b. Kharkov, Ukraine, Feb. 17, 1919; s. Grigori B. and Maria S. Mazo D.; m. Klaudia Ivanovna Mysyak, Oct. 17, 1948; children: Leonid, Vadim, Pavel. Prof., Highest Attestation Com., USSR, 1972; DSc, Inst. Physics/Power Engring., 1966; MS in Physics, Kharkov State U., 1940. Sci. dir. of nuclear reactors Mayak, Ozersk, 1948-53; head of nuclear safety dept. IPPE, Obninsk, Russia, 1953-77, sr. rschr., 1978-91; cons. State Duma of Russia, 1992-97; prof. Cen. Inst., Obninsk, 1968-74. Author: (monographs) Critical Masses, 1966, Devices of Direct Charing, 1971, co-author: Influence of Radiation to Materials, 1950. Maj. Russian mil., WWII, 1941-44. Named Disting. Inventor of Russia, Supreme Soviet, Moscow, 1969; recipient Stalin Premium, Govt. USSR, 1949, 51, others. Mem. Nuclear Soc. of Russia (bd. dirs. 1993-99). Office: IPPE, Bondarenko Sq 1, 249020 Obninsk Russia

DUBOVSKI, PAVEL, mathematician, educator; b. Obninsk, Kaluga, Russia, Dec. 12, 1961; s. Boris and Klaudia (Mysyak) D.; m. Irina Goldman, July 3, 1999; 1 child, Vladimir. BSc, Moscow Engring. Physics Inst., 1981; MSc, Moscow State U., 1984, PhD, 1989. Rschr. Moscow Engring.-Physics Inst., Obninsk, 1984-85; asst. prof. Inst. Nuclear Power Engring., Obninsk, 1985-90, assoc. prof., 1990-95; sr. rschr. Russian Acad. Scis., Moscow, 1995—; vis. rschr. Seoul Nat. U., 1993-94; sci. chief Sci. Tech. Park,

Obninsk, 1994-96. Author: Mathematical Theory of Coagulation, 1994; contbr. articles to profl. jours. Recipient All Union Student Rschr. award USSR Acad. Scis., 1981. Mem. N.Y. Acad. Scis., Am. Math. Soc. Avocations: tourism, stamp collecting. Home: 4 Pushkin St Apt 7, 249020 Obninsk Kaluga, Russia Office: Russian Acad Scis Inst Numerical Math, 8 Gubkin St, 117333 Moscow Russia

DUBRAY, BERNARD MAURICE, radiation oncologist; b. Boulogne-Billancourt, France, Apr. 8, 1957. MD, Paris V, 1989; PhD, Paris VII, 1996. Cert. Radiology Option Radiation Oncology, Paris XI, 1991. Resident AP-HP, Paris, 1982-89; vis. scientist MD Anderson Cancer Ctr., Houston, 1989-90; instr. Inst. G. Roussy, Villejuif, France, 1990-92; staff mem. Inst. Curie, Paris, 1992-99; prof. dept. radiation oncology Centre Henri Becquerel, Rouen, France, 1999—. Civil svc. Ctr. Hosp., 1983-84, Fort de France. Mem. Am. Soc. Clin. Oncology, Am. Soc. Therapeutic Radiology and Oncology, European Soc. Therapeutic Radiology and Oncology, Radiation Rsch. Soc. Office: Centre Henri Becquerel, Rue d'Amiens, 76038 Rouen France

DUBROVSKY, JOSEPH G., biologist; b. Moscow, Nov. 4, 1957; s. Gregory I. and Lelia G. (Jankovskaya) D.; previous marriage: Marina O. Lubich; 1 child, Anna; m. Natalia B. Doktor, Nov. 26, 1994. MS in Biology, Moscow State Pedagog. Inst., 1980; PhD, Acad. of Scis. of USSR, Moscow, 1987. Assoc. rschr. Inst. Gen. Inorganic Chemistry/USSR Acad. of Scis., Moscow, 1980-83; rschr. Inst. Agrl. Biotech./USSR Acad. of Agrl. Scis., Moscow, 1987-90; sr. rschr. Timiryazev Acad. of Agr., Moscow, 1990-91, Ctr. for Biol. Rsch., La Paz, Mexico, 1991—. Contbr. articles to profl. jours. Recipient Personal prize USSR D.I. Mendeleev's Chem. Soc., 1986, Nat. Rschr. of Mexico prize Level 1, 1993—. Mem. Internat. Soc. Root Rsch., Bot. Soc. Am., Am. Soc. Plant Physiologists. Achievements include rsch. in plant growth, devel. and morphogenesis at physiol. and structural level. Avocations: languages (English, Russian, Spanish, Polish), photography. Office: Ctr Biol Rsch (CIBNOR), AP 128, La Paz 23000, Mexico

DUBRULE, PAUL JEAN-MARIE, hotel and restaurant company executive, wine producer; b. Tourcoing, France, July 6, 1934; s. Paul and Suzanne (Mamet) D.; children: Laurel, Elenore, Maxence (dec.), Ambre, David. Diploma, Institut Hautes Etudes, Geneva, 1958. Asst. to Bernardo Trujillo, Dayton, Ohio, 1962-63; co-chmn. ACCOR, France, 1967—; wine prodr. Domaine Cavale, Luberon, France. Mayor of Fontainebleau, France, 1992, 95, senator, 1999—; co-founder World Travel and Tourism Coun., Brussels. Decorated Chevalier de l'Ordre Nat. du Merite and officer de la Legion d'Honneur (France). Home: 121 rue Saint Merry, 77300 Fontainebleau France Office: ACCOR, 2 rue de la Mare Neuve, 91021 Evry Cedex, France also: Winery La Cavale, 84160 Cucuron France

DUBUCS, JACQUES PAUL, research scientist; b. Bayonne, France, Mar. 16, 1953; s. Jacques and Marguerite (Charnet) D.; m. Monique Bouvet Dit Marechal, Feb. 28, 1976; children: Julie, Hadrien, Lucie. Aggregation in philosophy, Ecole Nat Superieure St. Cloud, Paris, 1976; D Logique, U. Paris I, 1978, Doctorat d'Etat, 1984. Tchr. philosophy Lycee Voltaire, Paris, 1978-90; lectr. U. Paris I, 1979-80; maitre asst. math. E.N.S., Rabat, Morocco, 1980-85; chargé rsch. CNRS, Paris, 1985-93, dir. rsch., 1993; sci. rschr. CNRS, 1985—. Author: Logic and Its History, 1995; editor: Philosophy of Probability, 1993; co-editor: Logical Methods for Cognitive Science, 1995; mem. editl. com. Jour. Theory and Decision, 1995—. Office: IHPST, 13 Rue du Four, 75006 Paris France

DUBUISSON, BERNARD LOUIS, science educator, administrator; b. Brive, France, Oct. 12, 1945; s. René Dubuisson and Ginette (Dessus) Come; m. Francine Filleul, July 8, 1967; children: Marie-Pierre, Sophie, Severine. Engr., Nat. Inst. Applied Scis., Lyon, France, 1966; 3rd cycle degree, U. Lyon, France, 1968, Dr. Scis., 1971. Asst. prof. Nat. Inst. Applied Scis., 1969-73; prof. U. Compiegne, France, 1973-91, prof. classe exceptionnelle, 1991—; dep. dir. Nat. Ctr. Sci. Rsch., Paris, 1992—; head Heuristique et Diagnostic des Systemes Complexes (Heudiasye) Lab. U. Compiegne, 1980-94; cons. Ministry of Edn., Paris, 1983-85. Author: Systems Diagnosis Using Pattern Recognition, 1990; editor European Jour. Automated Systems, 1991; contbr. over 50 articles to profl. jours. Designated Chevalier des Palmes Acad., Ministry of Edn., Chevalier ordre du Merite. Mem. IEEE (sr.), Soc. Electriciens et Electroniciens (pres. 1998—), bd. dirs., Cetim and Ensta. Avocations: history, reading. Home: 33 Rue Saint Hubert, 60610 La Croix Saint Ouen France Office: U Compiegne UMR CNRS, Heudiasyc BP 20529, 60205 Compiegne Cedex, France

DUBURS, GUNARS, chemist; b. Riga, Latvia, June 12, 1934; s. Janis and Elfrida (Treibere) D.; m. Renate Ozolina, July 22, 1967; 1 child, Daina. PhD, Latvian Acad. Scis., 1961; Dr. chem. habil., Inst. Organic Synthesis, Riga, 1979, prof. chemistry, 1988. Rsch. fellow Latvian Inst. Organic Synthesis, Riga, 1957-64, head lab., 1964—, dep. dir., 1980—; head br. dept. organic chemistry U. Latvia, Riga, 1986—; dep. chmn. divsn. chem. and biol. scis. Latvian Acad. Scis., Riga, 1994—. Editor: Biomembranes: Structure, Functions, Methods of Investigation, 1977, Biomembranes: Structure, Function, Medical Aspects, 1981. Recipient awards Latvian Acad. Scis., 1970, 71, 72, 80, 84, G. Vanag's medal, 1984, D.H. Grindel's award Grindex, 1996, award Latvian Chamber Mins., 1999. Mem. Latvian Chem. Soc., Latvian Biochem. Soc., Latvian Soc. Medicinal Chemistry, Internat. Soc. Heterocyclic Chemistry, Internat. Soc. Biometeorology. Home: Ieriku 43-2, Riga LV 1084, Latvia Office: Latvian Inst Organic Synthe, Aizkraukles 21, Riga LV 1006, Latvia

DU BUSKE, LAWRENCE M., immunologist, allergist, rheumotologist; b. Jersey City, Oct. 16, 1954. BS, Northwestern U., 1976, MD, 1978. Diplomate Am. Bd. Allergy and Immunology, Am. Bd. Internal Medicine, Am. Bd. Rheumatology. Dir. Allergy and Arthritis Family Treatment Ctr., Gardner, Mass., 1984—, Immunology Rsch. Inst. New England, Fitchburg, Mass., 1990—; clin. instr. Harvard Med. Sch., Boston, 1984—; cons. Brigham and Women's Hosp., Boston, 1984—, co-dir. allergy fellow training program , 1994-98; cons. Schering Plough, Kenilworth, N.J., 1994-2000, Hoechst Marion Roussel Pharms., Kansas City, Kans, 1995-97, Upjohn Pharms., Mich., 1997; adv. bd. Hycor Biomedical, Garden Grove, Calif., 1985-97, cons., 1995-97. Contbg. Editor Asthma & Allergy Proceedings, 1994—, Jour. Allergy & Clin. Immunology Supplement, 1996-97, Internal Jour. Immune Rehab., 1998—; contbg. author Exercise Induced Allergy Syndromes. Fellow ACP, ACR, ACAAI, Am. Acad. Asthma, Allergy and Immunology (chmn. practice and therapeutics com. 1996—, chmn. practice stds. coun. 1999—). Avocations: tennis, piano, jazz. Office: Immunology Rsch Inst New Eng 358 Elm St Gardner MA 01440-3926

DUCANTO, JOSEPH NUNZIO, lawyer, educator; b. Utica, N.Y., Mar. 18, 1927; s. Joseph and Martha (Purchine) D'Acunto; m. Connie Davis (div. May 1990); children: Anthony D. DuCanto, James C. DuCanto; m. Patricia Naegle; children: 1 child, William P. Heiman. BA, Antioch Coll., 1952; JD, U. Chgo., 1955. Bar: Ill. 1955, U.S. Tax Ct. 1960, U.S. Ct. Mil. Appeals 1960, U.S. Supreme Ct. 1960. Rsch. asst. Law and Behavioral Sci. Rsch. Project U. Chgo., 1954-55; assoc. Cotton, Fruchtman & Watt, Chgo., 1955-62; ptnr. Bentley, Campbell, DuCanto & Silvestri, Chgo., 1962-80; prin. Schiller, DuCanto & Fleck, Ltd., Chgo., 1981-2000; chmn., CEO Securatex, 1982—; adj. prof. family law Loyola U., Chgo., 1968-92; frequent lectr. on family law, taxation, fin. planning and estate planning in connection with divorce. Author: Tax Aspects of Litigation, 1979; contbr. articles, essays on family law and fed. taxation, trusts and estates to profl. publs.; editor, pub. Tax, Fin. and Estate Planning Devels. in Connection with Divorce and Family Law, 1970-85; mem. editorial bd. Fair Share, 1981—, Equitable Distbn. Reporter, 1981—, Matrimonial Lawyer Strategist, 1982—. Served with USMCR, 1944-47, PTO, Guam, Iwo Jima, China. Fellow Am. Acad. Matrimonial Lawyers (nat. pres. 1977-79, chmn.-dir. Inst. Matrimonial Law 1976-85), Am. Coll. Probate Counsel; mem. Ill. State Bar Assn. (bd. govs. 1983-89), Scribes, Tavern Club, Cliff Dwellers Club, Union League Club. Republican. Unitarian. Office: 200 N LaSalle 27th Floor Chicago IL 60601-1089

DUCASSOU, DOMINIQUE, medical educator, nuclear medicine physician; b. Bayonne, France, May 13, 1943; s. Pierre and Jeanne (Deslous) D.; m. Colette Maisterrena, Aug. 30, 1966 (div. 1981); m. Genevieve Royer, Nov. 11, 1983; 1 child, Stephane. Pharmacien, U. Bordeaux, France, 1965, prof. medicine, 1970; Medecin, U. Bordeaux II, 1976. Doyen Faculty of Medicine-U. Bordeaux, 1977-87; dir. Rsch. Unit, 1986-93; pres. U. Bordeaux II, 1987-92; mem. superior rsch. counsel U. Bordeaux, 1995—; chief nuc. medicine svc. Cmty. Hosp. U. Bordeaux, 1976—. Contbr. articles to sci. publs. Regional counselor d'Aquitaine, Bordeaux, 1993—; adj. mayor City of Bordeaux, 1995—. Capt. M.C., French Mil., 1965-70. Decorated chevalier Legion of Honor (France), officer Palmes Academiques (France), officer Ordre du Mérite (France). Mem. RPR Party. Roman Catholic. Avocations: sports, music. Office: CHU Bordeaux, Ave de Magellan, 33600 Pessac AQTN, France

DU CASTEL, VIVIANE SABINE, political analyst, economics educator; b. Luxembourg, Mar. 21, 1965; d. André François and Monique Jeanine (Ruinat de Gournier) Du C.; m. Jean-Marc Suel, Nov. 3, 1993. Lic. in Germanic Studies, German Studies Ctr., Strasbourg, France, 1989; grad. in Diplomacy and Internat. Orgns. Adminstrn., U. Paris, 1992; grad. in def. and strategy, Higher Sch. Internat. Studies, Paris, 1990; D of Polit. Sci., U. Nice, France, 1995. Stage in analyst EEC, CCE, DGIII, E4, Brussels, 1990-91, SGDN, Paris, 1991-92; polit. analyst Paris, 1992—; tchr. econs. Cours Descartes, Paris, 1992—. Author: From Königsberg to Kaliningrad: Europe in Front of a New Russian Overlands, 1996, Bielorussia, a drift out to sea independence, 1999; contbr. articles to profl. jours. Mem. Inst. Francaise des Relations Internat., les Fontaines, Groupe Rencontre. Roman Catholic. Home: Rue de Mezieres 15, 75006 Paris France

DUCHÁČEK, VRATISLAV, chemistry educator; b. Hradec Králové, Bohemia, Czechoslovakia, Feb. 16, 1941; s. Otto Ducháček and Věra (Tejnská) Ducháčková; m. Marie Lebedová, Mar. 26, 1960; children: Vratislav, Marie. MSc, Inst. Chem. Tech., Prague, Czechoslovakia, 1963, PhD, 1968, DSc, 1991. Researcher Inst. Chem. Tech., Prague, 1967-68, scientist, 1968-79, sr. scientist, 1979-80, assoc. prof., 1980-93, prof., 1993—; cons. Econ. Commn. for Europe, UN, Geneva, 1984-86; mem. rsch. bd. advisors Am. Biog. Inst., Raleigh, 1994—; hon. mem. adv. coun. Internat. Biog. Assn., Cambridge, 1997—. Author over 200 publs. including Polymers as Materials for Packaging, 1987, Elastomers and Rubber Compounding Materials, 1989, Advances in Polymer Blends and Alloys Technology, Vol. 5, 1994, Structure-Physical Properties Relationships of Block Copolymers and Polymer Blends, 1997; mem. editl. bd. Jour. Polymer Engring., 1993—. Fellow Am. Biog. Inst. (Internat. Cultural Diploma of Honor 1994, Twentieth Century Achievement award 1995, 2000 Millenium Medal of Honor, 1998); mem. N.Y. Acad. Scis., Czech Soc. Indsl. Chemistry (chmn. rubber divsn. 1993—, diploma of honor 1974, 77, 79), Internat. Rubber Conf. Orgn. (com. mem. 1993—), Polymer Networks Group, Soc. Plastics Engrs. Avocations: medicine, linguistics, dramatic art, history, tourism. Office: Inst Chem Tech Polymer Dept, Technicka 5/1905, 166 28 Prague Czech Republic

DUCH MARTORELL, CÉSAR, economist; b. Barcelona, Spain, Oct. 3, 1950; s. César Duch Plana and Pilar Martorell Paris; m. Maria Parera Torns, July 25, 1976; children: Salvi, Cesar, Ivette. Degree in Econs., Cen. U., Barcelona, 1974, Degree in Law, 1980; PhD in Econs., U. Barcelona, 1994. Rschr. Macrometrica, Barcelona, 1973-75, rsch. mgr., 1975-76, mktg. mgr., 1976-77; study and adminstrn. mgr. Inpacsa, Barcelona, 1977-80, div. mgr., 1980-84, export mgr., 1984-89; comml. dir. European Paper Packaging Investment Corp., 1989—, Papelera Barral Sa. and Papelera Navarra, 1990; dir. Group de Bissy España, SA, Barcelona, 1991—; mng. dir. ESMA U., Barcelona, 1993—; CEO Consell de Cent 92, 1994—, Columnea S.L., 1999—, Check Mgmt. Inst., Prague, Prague, 1994—; lectr. advt. and mktg. research Univ. Bus. Coll., Sabadell, Spain, 1982—; lectr. mktg. Russian mgrs. C.E.I., 1992; lectr. European Strategic Mktg. Assn., Paris, 1992; lectr. ESMA Prague, 1994-2000; coordinator internat. mgmt. Esmai, Barcelona, 1984—; lectr. ESCE Paris, 1988, 89, 90, 91, 92, 93, 94, 95, 96; lectr. Exports Club, Montpellier, France, 1990; lectr. Marseille C. of C., Dunquerque C. of C., Perpignan C. of C., 1990; conf. spkr. U. Orebro, Sweden, 1995, 96, C. of C. in Marseilles, 1996, Amsterdam Sch. of Bus., 1995, 96, Sch. of Commerce in Marseilles, 1996, U. Leonard De Vinci, Paris, 1996, C. of C. in Paris, 1996. Author: Trading Companies, 1988, Advertising Media, 1986, International Marketing, 1988, ESMAI, Techniques of Market Research, 1987, Marketing Cases, 1989. Mem. European Mktg. Assn., Barcelona Advt. Assn., Barcelona Mktg. Club (sec. bd. dirs. 1986, merit award 1986, adv. Spanish Fedn. of Mktg. 1988), Coll. Pub. Rels. (v.p. 1990), Markerama Mktg. Club (pres. jour. mktg. 1990), Mktg. Club Barcelona (pres. 1994-99, mem. senate com. 2000—). Avocations: tennis, swimming. E-mail: esma@nexus.es. Home: Carlos III, 62 60 4a, 08028 Barcelona Spain Office: ESMA, Consell de Cemt 42, 08014 Barcelona Spain

DUCHON, BEDRICH MILAN, engineering and economics educator, researcher; b. Prague, Czech Republic, Oct. 27, 1937; s. Helena Duchonova. M in Engring., Czech Tech. U., Prague, 1962, PhD in Econs., 1977. Scientific rschr. Power Engring. Rsch. Inst., Prague, 1962-68; chief specialist State Statis. Bur., Prague, 1968-69; project analyst Energo-Project, Prague, 1970-71; scientific rschr. Sch. Econs., Prague, 1971-78, prof. econs., 1978-81; prof. econs. Czech Tech. U., 1981-94, head dept. econs., 1994—; mem. Acad. Coun. Prague, 1993-95, Scientific Coun. Prague, 1993—. Author: Economics and Management, 1994, Management of Small Business, 1995; contbr. articles to profl. jours. Mem. Soc. Friends of USA, Prague, 1990-92, Soc. Friends of Italy, Prague, 1991—. Recipient rsch. grants Stockholm Tech. Inst., 1988, INSEAD, Fontainebleau, France, 1993, Universita Politecnica, Madrid, 1994. Mem. Energie, Assn. for Advancement of Modelling and Simulation Techniques in Enterprises, World Assn. for Case Method Rsch. & Case Method Application—Europe, N.Y. Acad. Scis. Avocations: music, history, travel, tennis, cars.

DUCKETT, STEPHEN JOHN, university dean, economist; b. Sydney, Australia, Feb. 18, 1950; s. Alan Edward and Ruth Eason (Wilson); m. Terri Jurgens Jackson. B in Econs., Australian Nat. U., 1971; M in Health Adminstrn., U. NSW, Australia, 1973; PhD, UNSW, Australia, 1981. Lectr. U. NSW, Australia, 1974-80, sr. lectr., 1980-83; dep. dir. rsch. Health Dept. Victoria, Australia, 1983-85, dep. regional dir., 1985-88, regional dir., 1988-91, dir. policy, 1991-92; dir. acute health Health & Community Svcs., Victoria, 1992-93; dean health scis. La Trobe U., Victoria, 1996—; sec. (head) Commonwealth Dept. Human Svcs. and Health, Canberra, Australia, 1994-96; chmn. bd. dirs. Bayside Health. Bd. dirs. Brotherhood St. Laurence, Melbourne. Fellow Australian Coll. Health Svc. Execs. Anglican. Home: 10 Ravenswood Ave, Ivanhoe 3079, Australia Office: La Trobe U, Faculty Health Scis, Bundoora 3083, Australia

DUCLOHIER, HERVÉ PIERRE, biophysicist; b. St. Malo de Phily, France, June 15, 1948; s. Pierre and Janine (Betin) D.; m. Sharon Cooper, Oct. 2, 1982 (div. Aug. 1988); m. Béatrice Duclos; 1 child, Alicia. B Math., Lyceum Châteaubriand, France, 1967; D Engring., U. Bordeaux, France, 1977, DSc in Physics, 1982; PhD in History of Sci., U. Paris, 1991. Cert. engr. in agrl. and food industry ENSIAA. Attaché rsch. CNRS, Bordeaux, 1976-82; postdoctoral fellow physiol. lab. Cambridge (Eng.) U., 1982; attaché rsch. 1st class CNRS/U. Paris Sud, 1983-85; attaché rsch. CNRS/U. Rouen, France, 1986-91, dir. rsch., 1991-99; dir. rsch. CNRS/U. Rennes, France, 1999—; project leader numerous rsch. projects; rschr. Marine Biol. Lab., Woods Hole, Mass., 1995. Contbr. articles to profl. jours., chpt. to book. With French Army, 1973-74. Grantee Brit. Coun., 1978, Royal Soc./U. Cambridge, 1982; Dr. Lee vis. scholar Christ Church Coll., 1997. Mem. Biophys. Soc., Soc. Neurosci., Physiol. Soc. Avocations: tennis, golf, history of science. Office: U Rennes I UPRES-A 6026, Lab Interactions Cell/Molec, 35042 Rennes France

DUCREUX, CHRISTIAN PIERRE, neuroscientist, educator; b. Toulon, France, Nov. 26, 1943; s. Gaston and Marcelle (Espagne) D.; m. Mireille Martin, 1972 (div. 1986); m. Thérèe Faure-Gignoux, 1992. BSc, U. Aix-Marseille, France, 1967, MSc, 1968, PhD, 1982. Maitre conf. U. II Marseille, France, 1971—. Mem. Neurosci. Soc., Physiol. Soc., Excursion Soc. (pres. 1995). Avocations: photography. Office: CNRS LNB 1, 31 Chemin J Aiguier, 13402 Marseille France

DUCZYNSKI, MARGARET SCHILT (MARGARET SCHILT AUSTIN), lawyer; b. Buffalo, June 5, 1950; d. Earl Alfred and Mary Margaret (Belk) Schilt; children: Emily Jean, Nathan Earl, John Robert, Michael PEter. BA, U. Mich., 1972, JD, 1979; MA, Northwestern U., 1973. Bar: Mich. 1979, Ill. 1991. Ptnr. Dobson, Griffin, Austin and Berman, Ann Arbor, Mich., 1979-88. Mem. ALA, Am. Assn. Law Librs., Mich. Bar Assn., Ill. Bar Assn. Home: 340 W Diversey Pkwy Apt 1520 Chicago IL 60657-6224

DUDA, RICHARD FRANK, architect, engineering executive; b. New York, Sept. 23, 1923; s. Frank and Emma Louise Duda; m. Wynema Jane Bond, May 3, 1945; children: Wynema Jane, Richard Frank, Lesley June, Desiree Joan. Cert. in Meteorology, NYU, 1944; BS in Chem. Engring., Rensselaer Poly. Inst., 1948. Registered profl. engr., N.Y. Project engr. Kellex-Vitro Engring. Co., N.Y.C., 1948-54; project mgr. Vitro Engring. Co., N.Y.C., 1954-62, chief process engr., mgr. chem. programs, 1962-67; project mgr. Parsons-Jurden, N.Y.C., 1967-68; project dir. Nuclear Materials and Equipment Co., Apollo, Pa., 1968-70; mgr. facilities design and constrn. nuclear fuel divsn. Westinghouse Power Sys., Monroeville, Pa., 1970-73; engring. mgr. nuclear fuel divsn. Westinghouse Power Sys., Monroeville, 1973-79, mgr. fuel cycle planning advanced energy sys. divsn., 1980-84; cons. Fuel Cycle Svcs. Inc., Greensburg, Pa., 1984-85; project mgr. Ralph M. Parsons Co., Pasadena, Calif., 1985-90; v.p. Ralph M. Parsons Co., Pasadena, 1990-94; cons. Westinghouse-Savannah River, Aiken, S.C., 1994-99, SC&A Inc., McLean, Va., 1994-99; ret., 1999; liaison chmn. industry interface State Dept. and Arms Control Agy., 1983-84; nuclear industry expert U.S. Internat. Nuclear Fuel Cycle Evaln. Asst. scoutmaster Boy Scouts Am., Paramus, N.J., 1960-62, cubmaster, 1960. 1st lt. USAF, 1943-46. Republican. Presbyterian. Avocations: gardening, reading. Home: 23151 Cannon Ridge Ln Middleburg VA 20117-2952

DUDA, SEWERYN JOZEF, geophysicist, educator; b. Chorzow, Poland, Apr. 20, 1933; s. Josef Wilhelm and Hedwig Angela (Hammerling) D.; m. Theresia Maria Dorothea Mrziglod, Dec. 24, 1955 (dec. June 1979); children: Chrysanth-Caesar, Laurent-Claudius, Marcel-Titus. MS, U. Warsaw, Poland, 1955; PhD, Royal U. Uppsala, Sweden, 1961, DrSc, 1967. Asst. U. Warsaw, 1955-58; scientist Seismos GmbH, Hannover, Germany, 1958-60; project scientist Royal U. Uppsala, 1962-65; from asst. to full prof. St. Louis U., 1967-74, adj. prof., 1974—; prof. geophysics U. Hamburg, Germany, 1974-98, prof. emeritus, 1998—; UNESCO expert in seismology, Tokyo, 1970; vis. prof. St. Louis U., 1966, U. Roorkee, India, 1979—, U. Opole, Poland, 1997. Contbr. articles to profl. jours. Fellow Assn. Exploration Geophysicists India (hon.); mem. Deutsche Geophysikalische Gesellschafdt, Deutsche Gesellschaft für Polarforschung, Am. Geophys. Union, Seismol. Soc. Am., Soc. Exploration Geophysicists, European Assn. Exploration Geophysicists. Home: Mozartstrasse 19, 31157 Sarstedt Germany Office: Hamburg U Inst Geophysics, Bundesstrasse 55, 20146 Hamburg Germany

DUDCZAK, ROBERT WILHELM, internist; b. Vienna, Austria, Jan. 1, 1944; s. Vladislav and Barbara (Lutz) D.; m. Heidelinde Auguste Steinmann, Sept. 8, 1973; 1 child, Julia Ruth. MD, U. Vienna, 1970. Dir. divsn. nuclear medicine U. Vienna Clinic, Austria, 1984-92; head dept. nuclear medicine Lainz City Hosp., Vienna, 1992-98, AKH-Vienna, U. Vienna, 1998—; prof nuclear medicine U. Vienna, 1998—; lectr. U. Vienna, 1984-91, prof. 1991—; cons. Ministry of Health, Vienna, 1990—, Austrian Nuclear Medicine Soc., Vienna, 1985—. Reviewer med. jours.; contbr. articles to profl. jours. Chmn. ethics com. Soc. Clin. Pharmacology, Vienna, 1988-94, advisor ethics com. Pastoral Inst., Vienna, 1990—. With Austrian Med. Corp., 1975. Recipient Nuclear Medicine award Byk Mallinkeodt, 1982, Rheumatology Medicine award Ministry of Health, 1981, Internal Medicine award Hoechst Austria, 1984, Billroth award Austrian Med. Chamber, 1988. Mem. European Nuclear Medicine Soc., Austrian Nuclear Medicine Soc. (adv. bd. 1985), Austrian Diabetes Soc. (adv. bd.), Austrian Soc. Internal Medicine, Austrian Atherosci. Soc., Am. Soc. Nuclear Medicine, Am. Soc. Clin. Chemistry. Roman Catholic. Avocations: reading, gardening. Office: Lainz Hosp Dept Nuclear Med, U Vienna Dept Nuclear Med, Wahringergurtel 18-20, 1090 Vienna Austria

DUDDECK, FABIAN EMANUEL MARO, engineering educator; b. Duesseldorf, Germany, Apr. 26, 1965; s. Heinz and Marianne D.; children: Johann, Benno, Elias. D in engring, Tech. U. of Munich, 1997. Asst. prof. tech. U. Munich, 1990-98; rschr. Ecole Poly., Palaiseau, France, 1998, Tech. U., Munich, 1999—. Avocations: philosophy of scis. and tech., painting, history of art and architecture. Email address: fabian@baume.bauwesen.tu-muenchen.de. Home: Reichenbachstrasse 2, Munich 80469, Germany Office: Tech U of Munich, Arcisstrasse 21, Munich 80333, Germany

DUDDEN, ARTHUR POWER, historian, educator; b. Cleve., Oct. 26, 1921; s. Arthur Clifford and Kathleen (Bray) D.; m. Adrianne Churchill Onderdonk, June 5, 1965; 1 child, Alexis Dudden; children by previous marriage: Kathleen Dudden Rowlands, Candace L. Dudden (Schweitzer). A.B., Wayne State U., 1942; A.M., U. Mich., 1947, Ph.D., 1950. Faculty Bryn Mawr Coll., 1950—, prof. history, 1965-92, Fairbank prof. humanities, 1989-92, Katharine E. McBride prof. history, 1992-95, 98-99; instr. CCNY, summer 1950; vis. asst. prof. Am. civilization U. Pa., 1953-54, ednl. coord. spl. program Am. civilization, 1956, mem. faculty Inst. Humanistic Studies for Execs., 1953-59, vis. assoc. prof. history, summers, 1958, 62-65, vis. prof. history, 1965-68; vis. assoc. prof. Princeton (N.J.) U., 1958-59, Haverford Coll., 1962-63; vis. prof. Trinity Coll., summer 1965; cons. Peace Corps, 1962-66; mem. Bicentennial Com. on Internat. Confs. of Americanists, 1973-76; pres. Fulbright Assn. of Alumni, 1976-80, exec. dir., 1980-84; cons. Nat. Archives, 1993-95; adj. prof. history Lehigh U., 1993-95. Author: Teachers Manual to the American Republic, vols. I and II, 1959, 60, 70, Understanding the American Republic, vols. I and II, 1961, 70, Objective Tests, The American Republic, 1962, The Assault of Laughter, 1962, The United States of America: A Syllabus of American Studies, 2 vols, 1963, The Instructor's Guide to the United States, 3d edit, 1972, The Student's Guide to the United States, 2d edit, 1967, Joseph Fels and the Single Tax Movement, 1971, Pardon Us, Mr. President!, 1975, The Fulbright Experience, 1946-1986, 1987, American Humor, 1987, The American Pacific, 1992, paperback edit., 1993; editor: Woodrow Wilson and the World of Today, 1957, The Logbook of the Captain's Clerk, 1995; compiler: International Directory of Specialists in American Studies, 1975; contbr. Ency. Am. Social History, 1993, Ency. U.S. Fgn. Rels., 1997. Served with USNR, 1942-45. Sr. Fulbright scholar Denmark, 1959-60 and West Europe, 1992. Mem. Fellows Am. Studies (sec.-treas. 1957-59, pres. 1960-61), Am. Studies Assn. (treas. 1968, 72, exec. sec. 1969-72, Bode-Pearson prize 1991), Am. Hist. Assn., Orgn. Am. Historians (local arrangements chmn. Phila. 1969), Hist. Soc. of Pa. (bd. trustees 1993-99). Home: 829 Old Gulph Rd Bryn Mawr PA 19010-2910

DUDEK, JAROMIR, pharmacist, consultant; b. Sobesice, Czech Republic, June 4, 1929; s. Jaroslav and Marie (Zdenkova) D.; m. Ladislava Trejbalova, Jul. 22, 1959; 1 child, Hana. PhMr, Masaryk U., Czech Republic, 1952; RNDr, Komensky U., Bratislava, Slovak Republic, 1968. Pharmacist Tachov, Czech Republic, 1952-54, Direction of Pharmacy, Plzen, Czech Republic, 1954-89, Faculty Hosp., Plzen, Czech Republic, 1989-92; health ins. Plzen, Czech Republic, 1993-2000; examiner for social and clinical pharmacy IPVZ, Praha, Czech Republic, 1954-2000; chmn. com. pharmaceutical info. MZd, Praha, Czech Republic, 1981-91; spokesman of clinical pharmacy Praha, 1981-90; rsch. clinical pharmacy, Praha, 1989-90; adv. bd. Faculty of Social and Clinical Pharmacy, 1996-2000; com. mem. info. system in Czech Republic, Praha, 1991-92. Author: Free Open Drugs, 1992 (Dona award 1992), Lexicon for Health, 1994, Latin-Czech-German-Slovak-English Dictionary of Medicinal Plants, 1999; co-author: Informations for Rational and Secure Medical Treatment I, 1986, Informations for Rational and Secure Medical Treatment II, 1990. Mem. Pharmaceutical Soc. (chmn. 1968-73 in Dist. West Bohemia). Protestant. Avocations: hobbies, dance, highmountain touring. Home: Blatenska 22, 307 02 Plzen Czech Republic Office: General Health Ins, Havlickova 3, 305 88 Plzen Czech Republic

DUDEK, STANISLAV, publisher, editor; b. Ceske Budejovice, Czech Republic, Jan. 31, 1956; s. Stanislav and Vera (Horejsova) D.; m. Dagmar Sucha, Jan. 31, 1991; children: Daniela, Marketa, Dita, Kamila. Grad., Tech. H.S., Ceska Budejovice, 1975. Price mgr. Strojimport Fgn. Trade Ltd., Prague, Czech Republic, 1977-90; editor-in-chief Computerworld CZ, Prague, 1990-93; pub., cons. DDAir Agy., Prague, 1990—; author, translator English and German books, 1990—. Editor bull. Czechoslovak Aviation His. Soc., 1989-98; editor, translator various computer and aviation oriented

articles and books; contbr. articles to profl. publs. Mem. Am. Aviation Hist. Soc., Czech Avhistorical Soc., Navy League, Austrian Avhistorical Soc., Internat. Orgn. Journalists, Hewlett & Packard Press Club. Avocations: writing, photography, scale modelling, cooking. Home: Livornská 428, CZ 10900 Prague 10, Czech Republic

DUDERSTADT, JAMES JOHNSON, academic administrator, engineering educator; b. Ft. Madison, Iowa, Dec. 5, 1942; s. Mack Henry and Katharine Sydney (Johnson) D.; m. Anne Marie, June 24, 1964; children: Susan Kay, Katharine Anne. B in Engring. with highest honors, Yale U., 1964; MS in Engring. Sci. Calif. Inst. Tech., 1965, PhD in Engring. Sci. and Physics, 1967. Asst. prof. nuclear engring. U. Mich., 1969-72, assoc. prof., 1972-76, prof., 1976-81; dean U. Mich. (Coll. Engring.), 1981-86; provost, v.p. acad. affairs U. Mich., 1986-88, pres. univ., 1988-96, pres. emeritus, prof. sci. engring., 1996—; dir. Millennium Project, 1996—. AEC fellow, 1964-68; recipient E. O. Lawrence award U.S. Dept. Energy, 1986, Nat. medal of Tech., 1991; named Nat. Engr. of Yr., NSPE, 1991. Fellow Am. Nuclear Soc. (Mark Mills award 1968, Arthur Holly Compton award 1985); mem. NAE (coun.), Am. Phys. Soc., Nat. Sci. Bd. (chair 1991-94), Am. Acad. Arts & Scis., Sigma Xi, Tau Beta Pi, Phi Beta Kappa. Office: Millennium Project 2001 Media Union Ann Arbor MI 48109

DUDKOWIAK, ALINA, physicist, researcher, educator; b. Smigiel, Poland, Feb. 13, 1964; d. Jerzy and Krystyna (Cichoszewska) D. MSc, U. Poznan, Poland, 1987, PhD in Phys. Scis., 1992. Rsch. and tchg. asst. U. Poznan, 1988-93, adj. asst. prof., 1993—. Contbr. more than 29 articles to Jour. Photochemistry and Photobiology, Photosynthesis Rsch., Spectrochim. Acta, others. Recipient Teams award Rector of Poznan U. Tech., 1996, 97. Roman Catholic. Avocations: travel, mountain tourism. Home: Dmowskiego 16/3, PL60-221 Poznan Poland Office: Poznan U Tech, Piotrowo 3, PL60-965 Poznan Poland

DUDLEY, GEORGE ELLSWORTH, lawyer; b. Earlington, Ky., July 14, 1922; s. Ralph Emerson and Camille (Lackey) D.; m. Barbara J. Muir, June 28, 1950 (dec. Feb. 1995); children: Bruce K., Camille Dudley McNutt, Nancy S., Elizabeth Dudley Stephens. BS in Commerce, U. Ky., 1947; JD, U. Mich., 1950. Bar: Ky. 1950, D.C. 1951, U.S. Dist. Ct. (we. dist.) Ky. 1962, U.S. Ct. Appeals (6th cir.) 1987. Assoc. Gordon, Gordon & Moore, Madisonville, Ky., 1950-51; pvt. practice law Louisville, 1952-59; ptnr. Brown, Ardery, Todd & Dudley, Louisville, 1959-72; ptnr. Brown, Todd & Heyburn, Louisville, 1972-92, of counsel, 1992—, mem. mgmt. com., 1972-90, chmn., 1989-90. Pres. Ky. Easter Seal Soc., Louisville, 1971-72; treas. Ky. Dem. Party, Frankfort, 1971-74; bd. dirs. Alliant Adult Health Svcs., Louisville, 1976—; 1st v.p. Nat. Easter Seal Soc., Chgo., 1981. Capt. inf. U.S. Army, 1943-46, ETO; capt. JAGC, U.S. Army, 1951-52. Mem. ABA, Ky. Bar Assn., Louisville Bar Assn., U.S. 6th Cir. Jud. Conf. (life), Harmony Landing Country Club (pres. 1978-79), Tavern Club, Barristers Soc., Omicron Delta Kappa. Presbyterian. Avocations: golf, tennis, travel, sports spectator. Home: 1905 Crossgate Ln Louisville KY 40222-6405 Office: Brown Todd & Heyburn 3200 Providian Louisville KY 40202

DUDLEY, SAMUEL CALVERT, physician; b. Norfolk, Va., July 21, 1964; s. Samuel Calvet and Elizabeth C. D.; m. Victoria Atwill, Oct. 14, 1999; 1 child, Nicholas D. BA with highest distinction, U. Va., 1985; MD, Med. Coll. of Va., 1989, PhD in Physiology, 1991. Med. resident U. Chgo., 1991-93, cardiology fellow, 1993-97; med. faculty Emory U., Atlanta, 1997—. Contbr. articles to profl. jours.; contbg. author books in field. Recipient Scientist Devel. award AHA, 1999, Beginning Grant-in-Aid, S.E. affil., 1998, others. Mem. Sigma Xi, Phi Kappa Phi, Alpha Omega Alpha, Phi Beta Kappa. E-mail: sdudley@emory.edu. Office: Emory Univ 1639 Pierce Dr Atlanta GA 30322-0001

DUDLEY-ROBEY, EDWARD GILES, public health physician, television host; b. L.A., Jan. 19, 1974; s. Francis Dudley and Eddy Robey. PhD in Pub. Health, Columbia State U., Metairie, La., 1997; M in Sports Sci., Internat. Sports Sci. Assn., Santa Barbara, Calif., 2000. Medic U.S. Army, 1991-93; med. dir. The Salvation Army, San Fernando Valley, 1994—; disaster health svcs. nurse ARC, San Fernando Valley, Calif., 1995—; pres. The Robey Group, Sherman Oaks, Calif., 1996—; host Issues in Pub. Health, Sherman Oaks, 2000—. Inventor healthcare computer sys., 1995; clin. reviewer ICU Quick Reference Guide, 1997. Mem. Am. Coll. Healthcare Adminstrs. (faculty), Jewish War Vets. (JAG officer 1998), Am. Legion. Jewish. Avocations: weightlifting, basketball, shooting, community service. Office: The Robey Group 14413 Weddington St Apt 6 Sherman Oaks CA 91401-5626

DUDNIKOV, VADIM G., physicist, researcher; b. Gunda, Buryat, Russia, Sept. 15, 1943; came to U.S., 1995; s. Georgy V. and Klavdiya P. (Bambakova) D.; m. Galinai Sapozhnikova; children: Andrei, Irina. M degree, Novosibirsk State U., 1965; PhD, Inst. Nuclear Physics, Novosibirsk, 1967. Sr. scientist Inst. Physics, Novosibirsk, 1967-78, head lab., 1978-92; prof. Novosibirsk State U., 1986-89, head gen. physics, 1989-92, prof., 1993-95; vis. scientist Oak Ridge (Tenn.) Nat. Lab., 1993, Brookhaven Nat. Lab., Upton, N.Y., 1992-93, U. Md., College Park, 1995; chief scientist Superior Design, Inc., Peabody, Mass., 1995-98; pres. Sci. Tech. Cons., Beverly, Mass., 1998; scientist Fermi Nat. Accelerator Lab., Batavia, Ill., 1999—. Inventor charge exch. injection, method negative ion prodn., and surface-plasma sources. Mem. Am. Phys. Soc. Avocation: history. Home and Office: 1660 Brookdale Rd Naperville IL 60563-2177

DUDZIŃSKI, PIOTR, mathematician, researcher; b. Słupsk, Poland, Feb. 8, 1966; s. Henryk and Krystyna Dudzińska; m. Renata Olempijuk, Dec. 26, 1989. MSc, U. Gdańsk, Poland, 1990; PhD, U Gdansk, Poland, 1998. Asst. Inst. Math., U. Gdansk, 1990—. Recipient award Gdańsk Sci. Soc., 1994; grantee KBN, 1996. Office: Inst Math U Gdańsk, Wita Stwosza 57, 80-925 Gdańsk Poland

DUDZIŃSKI, PIOTR ANTONI, mechanical engineering educator, consultant; b. Środa Śl—ska, Poland, Nov. 14, 1949; s. Stanisław and Erika (Michalska) D.; m. Jolanta Anna Wasiela, July 28, 1951; 1 child, Dominika. MSc, Wrocław U. Tech., 1973, D in Tech. Sci., 1977; Doctor Habilitatus, Tech. U. Dresden, Germany, 1991. Cert. of fluency in German, Goethe Inst., Berlin; cert. expert off-highway vehicles Soc. Polish Mech. Engrs. Lectr. Wrocław U. Tech., 1977-85, 87-88, 1991-95, prof., 1995—; Alexander von Humboldt fellow Fridericana U. Karlsruhe, Germany, 1985-87, U. Berlin, Germany, 1993; staff Tech. U. Dresden, Germany, 1989-91; cons. Intertractor, Gevelsberg, Germany, 1995—, Bldg. Mechanization and Mineral Mining Rsch. Inst., Warsaw, 1995—. Contbr. articles to profl. jours.; inventor in field. Recipient Polish Ministry of Edn. award Min. of Edn., Warsaw, 1978, 89; Alexander von Humboldt fellow Alexander von Humboldt Found., Bonn, Germany, 1985, 93. Fellow Polish Acad. Sci. (sect. sec. 1994); mem. Internat. Soc. for Terrain Vehicle Sys. (sec. Ctrl. and Ea. Europe 1996—), Internat. Assn. for Automation and Robotics in Constrn., Societas Humboldtiana Polonorum, N.Y. Acad. Sci. Roman Catholic. Avocations: swimming, trekking, skiing, windsurfing, history of politics. Office: Wrocław U Tech I-16, Wybrzeze Wyspianskiego 27, 50 370 Wrocław Poland

DUE, OLE, judge, educator; b. Korsör, Sealand, Denmark, Feb. 10, 1931; s. Henrik Peter and Jenny Christine (Jensen) D.; m. Alice Maud Halkier Nielsen; children: Poul Henrik, Pernille, Peter, Torben. LLB, Copenhagen U., 1955; JD (hon.), Stockholm U., 1991. Civil servant Ministry of Justice, Copenhagen, 1955, head divsn., 1970, head dept., 1975, appeal ct. judge a.i., 1978; judge Ct. of Justice of the European Communities, Luxembourg, 1979, pres., 1988-94; hon. prof. Copenhagen U., 1994—; mem. Danish del. Hague Conf. on Pvt. Internat. Law, Netherlands, 1964-76. Contbr. articles to profl. jours., chpts. to books. Decorated grand cross Order of Dannebrog (Denmark), Ordre de la Couronne (Belgium), Ordre de la Couronne de Chene (Luxembourg); named hon. bencher Gray's Inn, London, 1988, King's Inns, Dublin, 1989. Mem. Danish Inst. Internat. Affairs (chmn. bd. dirs. 1995—). Home: 116 Mördrupvej, DK-3060 Espergärde Sealand, Denmark Office: U Copenhagen, Retsvidenskabeligt Inst A, DK-1455 Copenhagen Denmark

DUELFER, EBERHARD J.C., business educator; b. Wuppertal, Rhineland, Germany, Mar. 14, 1924; s. Paul G. and Louise J. (Brinkmann) D.; m. Helga R. Grimm, June 8, 1957 (wid. July 1993); children: Christian Michael, Bernd Ullrich. Diplomvolkswirt, U. Marburg, Germany, 1953; D Rer.Pol., U. Marburg, 1956, Dr.Habil., 1961. Mgr. Inst. f. Cooper.Studies, Marburg, 1953-61; ILO-expert Ouagadougou, Upper Volta, 1961-62; sr. lectr. U. Marburg, 1962-63; prof., Inst. dir. Tech. U., Darmstadt, Germany, 1964-67; prof., Inst. dir. Inst. for Cooperation in Developing Countries, 1967-92, prof. emeritus, 1992—; cons. OECD, Paris for Andalucia, Spain, 1965-68; rsch. cons. FAO/UN numerous African and Asian countries, Rome, 1968-81; cons. Ministry f. Econ. Cooperation, Bonn, Germany, 1975-77; vis. prof. U. ITESM, Mexico City, 1977, Tech. U., Chemmitz, Germany, 1993-95; chmn. numerous scientific commns. in field.; cons. bd. Roth Industrie GmbH & Co., Buchenau; mem. bd. Inst. of Cooperative Sci., Marburg U. Author: (textbook) Internationales management in unterschiedlichen Kulturbereichen, 5 edits. 1991-97, bilingual version, 1999; contbg. editor/author: International Handbook of Cooperative Organizations, 1994; contbr. numerous articles to profl. jours., books and publs. Mem. br. coun. Deutsche Stiftung, Berlin, 1986-95; chmn. supr. bd. Marburger Bank, Germany, 1976-94, others. Officer German Navy, 1940s. Recipient of Golden medal of merits Nat. Assn. Cooperatives, 1984. Mem. Acad. Scientiarum et Artium Europaea, N.Y. Acad. Scis. Office: Univ Fachbereich Wirtsch, Wiss/Am Plan 2, Hessen Marburg 35037, Germany

DUENAS, LAURENT FLORES, health and nursing consultant; b. Yigo, Guam, Jan. 9, 1947; d. Joaquin Garcia and Maria Acosta (Calvo) Flores; m. Jimmy J. Duenas, Jan. 9, 1971; children: James Richard, Sherry Marie, Kenneth Ray. ADN, U. Guam, 1968; BSN, Mont. State U., 1969; MPH, U. Hawaii at Manoa, 1984. RN, Guam, Mont. Staff nurse nursing sect. Dept. Pub. Health and Social Svcs., Guam, 1969-70, nurse supr. I, 1970-71, nurse supr II, 1972-78, asst. adminstr. Bur. Community Health and Nursing Svcs., 1978-89, detailed adminstr., 1986-88, adminstr., 1989-95; ret. Dept. Pub. Health and Social Svcs., 1995; health and nursing cons. Guam Legislature and U. Guam, 1996—; bd. dirs., chair Pacific Basin Maternal Child Health Resource Ctr., Mangilao, Guam, 1984-96, Pacific Basin MCH coord., Honolulu, 1984-95; mem. State and Territorial Dirs. Nursing, 1987—; mem. Interagy. Leadership Consortium for Individual's with Spl. Needs, 1990—; mem. Maternal Child Health Task Force, 1996—, Gov.'s Vision 2000 Health Task Force, 1996—; chair Nurse Leaders Com., 1995-98, mem., 1998—; preceptor nursing students U.Guam, 1995—; presenter in field. Author: Caring for Young Children, modified version, 1998. Recipient Centennial award Nat. League of Nursing, 1994, Gov.'s Chief Gadao Disting. award, 1995. Mem. ANA (cert. nurse adminstr. 1991-95, 95—), APHA, Y'netnon Famaloan-Dem. Women Leaders, Am. Pacific Nursing Leaders Conf. Assn. (treas., 1986-92, vice mem. 1986—), Commn. on Licensure, Guam Bd. Nurses Examiners (bd. dirs., chair 1981-90), Guam Nurses Assn. (bd. dirs. 1992—, Leadership award 1988, Nursing Excellence award 1990, Guam Nurse of Yr. 1993, Pub. Health Unit award 1994, Guam Legis. Resolution 1995, 98). Democrat. Roman Catholic. Avocations: crocheting, collecting recipes, baking, campaigning strategies, visiting sick. Home: 3 NC Yigo GU 96929 Office: PO Box 11142 Yigo GU 96929-0142

DUERR, DIANNE MARIE, educator, sports medicine consultant; b. Buffalo, July 14, 1945; d. Robert John and Aileen Louise D. BS in Health and Phys. Edn., SUNY, Brockport, 1967; cert., SUNY, Oswego, 1982; postgrad., Canisius Coll., 1970-71. Cert. tchr., N.Y. Tchr. North Syracuse (N.Y.) Sch. Dist., 1967—; tchr. dept. orthopedic surgery SUNY Upstate Med. U., Syracuse, 1982—; creator Inst. for Sports Medicine and Human Performance SUNY Health Sci. Ctr., Syracuse, 1988; coord. scholastic sports injury reporting system project SUNY, 1985-98; mem. com. on scholastic sports-related injuries NIH Inst. Arthritis, Musculoskeletal and Skin Diseases, 1993-96. Author: SSIRS Pilot Study Report, 1987, SSIRS Fall Study Report, 1988, SHASIRS Report, 1991; creator Scholastic Sports Injury Reporting System, 1985, Scholastic Head and Spine Injury Reporting System, 1989. Co-chmn. sports medicine USA Amateur Athletic Union, Nat. Jr. Olympic Games, Syracuse, 1987; vol. sports medicine N.Y. State Sr. Games, 1990-95, sports medicine coord., 1990-95, U.S. Roller Skating Nat. Championships, 1995, N.Y. State Womens Lacrosse Championships, 1995; mem. com. sports injury surveillance Ctrs. for Disease Control, 1995; cons. N.Y. Sci., Tech. and Soc. Edn. Project, 1995; sports medicine coord. for U.S. Nat. Precision Ice Skating Championships, 1997, Youth Basketball of Am., Northeast Regional Tournament, 1999. Mem. AAUW, N.Y. State AAHPERD (pres. exercise sci. and sports medicine sect., 1994-98), Am. Coll. Sports Medicine, United Univ. Profs., Women's Sports Fedn., Am. Fedn. Tchrs., N.Y. United Tchrs., North Syracuse Tchrs. Assn., Phi Kappa Phi. Avocations: swimming, cycling, ice skating, reading, photography. Home: 418 Buffington Rd Syracuse NY 13224-2208 Office: SUNY 4400 University Hosp 750 E Adams St Syracuse NY 13210-1834

DUFF, ANDREW NICHOLAS, government official; b. Birkenhead, Eng., Dec. 25, 1950; s. Norman Bruce and Diana (Wilcoxson) D. MA, U. Cambridge, 1972, MLitt, 1979. Rsch. officer Hansard Soc., London, 1974-76; fellow Joseph Rowntree Reform, London, 1989-92; dir. Fed. Trust, London, 1993-99; liberal dem. mem. European Parliament, 1999—. Author: Electoral Reform of the European Parliament, 1996, Reforming the European Union, 1997, Understanding the Euro, 1998; editor: The Treaty of Amsterdam: Text and Commentary, 1997, (with J. Pinder and R. Pryce) Maastricht and Beyond: Building the European Union, 1994. Councillor, City of Cambridge, Eng., 1982-90; v.p. Liberal Dems., 1994-97. Recipient OBE award, 1997. Office: Orwell House, Cowley Rd, Cambridge CB4 0PP, England

DUFF, GRANT WILLIAM, accountant; b. Cape Town, South Africa, Mar. 5, 1962; s. Roy Lintott and Joan Barbara (Hoffmeyer-Hedley) D.; m. Yvonne Redfern, Nov. 23, 1985; children: Gareth, Kristen. B of Commerce, Rhodes U., Grahamstown, South Africa, 1982; B Compt. with honors, UNISA, Pretoria, South Africa, 1985; CA (SA), SACA, Johannesburg, South Africa, 1987. Exec. mgr. Denel Ltd., Pretoria, 1987-97; gen. mgr. SA Bankers Svcs. Ltd., Johannesburg, 1997—; dir. AST Ltd., Pretoria, 1997, Sybase SA (Pty) Ltd., Johannesburg, 1997. Dir. Cornwall Hill Coll., Irene, South Africa, 1999-2000; bd. dirs. Cebacwas, Pretoria, 1996-2000. NCO Chief of Staff, 1985-86. Baptist. Avocation: fly fishing. Home: PO Box 1672, 0027 Groenkloof South Africa

DUFF, JAMES MICHAEL, conductor, musical director; b. West Palm Beach, Fla., Apr. 5, 1954; s. Dillard H. and Fern E. (Duff) D.; m. Priscilla Sue Wood, July 7, 1978; children: Jennifer Sue, Christine Michelle, Kimberly Erin. MusB, U. Fla., 1976. Mus. dir. Dinner Theatres, Inc., Dallas, 1980, Golden Gate Mus. Theatre, Naples, Fla., 1980; asst. mus. dir. Coachlight Dinner Theatre, Nanuet, N.Y., 1981; conductor, mus. supr. Walls Co., Hollywood, Calif., 1983; asst. mus. dir. Melody Top Theatre, Milw., 1981, 84, 86; keyboardist The News Onstage, N.Y.C., 1985; mus. supr. Burt Reynolds Inst. for Theatre Tng., Jupiter, Fla., 1981-88; conductor, mus. dir. Burt Reynolds Jupiter Theatre, 1981-88, Am. Theatre Prodns., N.Y.C., 1986-89; resident musical dir. Marriott's Lincolnshire (Ill.) Theatre, 1991-96. Musical dir. (nat. co.) Nunsense, 1988-89, (3d nat. co.) Les Misérables, 1989-91; composer Phantom of the Country Opera, 1994, Ms. Cinderella, 1996, Female Problems, An Unhelpful Guide, 1998, At Wit's End, 2000. Recipient Outstanding Alumnus award U. Fla., 1997.

DUFF, MICHAEL JAMES, physicist; b. Manchester, Jan. 28, 1949; s. Edward and Elizabeth (Kaylor) D.; m. Lesley Yearling, 1984; children: Jessica, Matthew. BS, Queen Mary Coll., U. London, 1969; PhD, Imperial Coll., U. London, 1972. Postdoctoral fellow in theoretical physics Internat. Ctr. Theoretical Physics, Trieste, Italy, Oxford (Eng.) U., U. London, Brandeis U., Waltham, Mass., 1972-79; faculty mem. Imperial Coll., 1979-88; sr. physicist CERN, Geneva, 1984-87; prof. physics Tex. A&M U., College Station, 1988-92, Disting. prof. physics, 1992-99; Oskar Klein prof. physics U. Mich., Ann Arbor, 1999—. Contbr. articles to profl. jours. Fellow Am. Phys. Soc. Avocations: water colors, golfing. Home: 846 Arboretum Dr Saline MI 48176-1354 Office: U Mich Dept Physics 3425 Randall Lab Ann Arbor MI 48109-1120

DUFFIELD, DAVID, computer company executive. BS in Elec. Engring., Cornell U., MBA. Mktg. rep., sys. engr. IBM; co-founder Info. Assocs.; chmn., pres., chief product arch. Integral Sys., Calif.; pres., CEO, chmn. PeopleSoft, Pleasanton, Calif. Home: 4460 Hacienda Dr Pleasanton CA 94588 Office: PeopleSoft Inc 4411 Peoplesoft Pkwy Pleasanton CA 94588-3358*

DUFFIN, ANTHONY CECIL, podiatrist, researcher; b. Sydney, Australia, July 20, 1954; s. Raymond Cecil and Dorothy (Bullen) D.; m. Denise Ann Dawe, Jan. 14, 1978; children: James Anthony, Lyndal Ann. A. diploma in podiatry, Inst. Tech., Sydney, 1981; BSc with honors, Brighton U., 1996; postgrad., U. Western Sydney, 1997—. Registered podiatrist. Pvt. practice Beecroft, Australia, 1982—; hon. cons. podiatrist Royal Alexandra Hosp. Children, Sydney, 1985—; lectr. U. Western Sydney, Macarther, Australia, 1997—; clin. tutor Inst. Tech., Sydney, 1984-85; mem. expert panel diabetes problems NSW Health Dept., North Sydney, 1995-96. Contbr. articles to profl. jours. Mem. Australian Podiatry Assn. (continuing edn. award 1997, 99), Podiatric Biomechanics Australia, Diabetes/Podiatry Group (pres. 2000—). Avocations: skiing, outdoor activities. Office: Beefcroft Podiatry Clinic, 29/6-8 Hannah St, Sydney NSW 2119, Australia

DUFFY, IRENE KAREN, artist; b. Chgo., Mar. 10, 1942; d. Andrew Earl and Irene Margaret Kane (Barthley) James; m. James Ora Duffy, Jan. 24, 1963 (div. Oct. 20, 1993); children: Dawn Ann, James Sean, Maureen Marie. BA, Wash. State U., 1985, MFA, 1989. Juried invitational exhbns. include Gallery X "Out of the Box", Art Inst. Chgo., 1995, Wash. State U./U. Ill., 1994, Virginia Inn, Seattle, 1993, Chase Gallery, Spokane, 1992, Union Gallery, Pullman, 1991, Acad. Arts, Riga, Latvia, 1990, Galeria 5, Caracas, Venezuela, 1989; collections include Johanna Bur. for the Handicapped, Chgo., Gordon Gilkey Collection, Portland Art Mus., Modern Art Gallery, Leningrad, Russia, Neill Pub. Libr., Vetreria 2001, S.R.L., Murano, Italy. Bd. dirs. Pullman/Moscow Regional Airport, 1981-84; mem. Global Vols. Project, Ostuni, Italy, 1998, Passport in Time Forest Svc., 2000. Recipient Civic Appreciation award City of Pullman (Mayor Pete Butkus), 1984. Mem. Palouse Folklore Soc., Lions Club Internat. Avocations: folk dancing, flying, travel, gardening. Home: PO Box 215 Palouse WA 99161-0215 Studio: Artspace 114 E 525 Church PO Box 247 Palouse WA 99161-0247

DUFFY, JOHN LEWIS, retired Latin, English and reading educator; b. Whittemore, Iowa, Oct. 6, 1934; s. Lewis A. and Dorothy (Bestenlehner) D.; m. Anne O'Brien, July 19, 1958; children: Jane, Paul, Sarah, Steven. BA, Loras Coll., Dubuque, Iowa, 1956; MS Ed, Creighton U., 1961; student, U. Minn., summer 1967. Jr. and sr. H.S. tchr., coach Presentation Acad., Whittemore, Iowa, 1957-58; H.S. tchr. Clear Lake (Iowa) Cmty. Schs., 1958-61; teaching asst. U. Iowa, Iowa City, 1961-62; tchr. Latin Larkin H.S., Elgin, Ill., 1962-96; students' coun. advisor Larkin H.S., Elgin, 1965-71; chmn. English and fgn. langs. Larkin H.S., Elgin, Ill., 1969-77; chmn. English and reading divsn. Larkin H.S., Elgin, 1977-96; tchr. prep. courses for ACT, PSAT and SAT Elgin YWCA and Larkin H.S., Elgin, 1977-96. Summer chef's asst. The Frugal Gourmet, WTTW-TV, Chgo., 1983. Bd. trustees Elgin C.C., 1975—, chmn., 1980-81, 85-87, 97—, vice-chmn., 1981-84, 94-95; bd. dirs. Elgin Area Cath. Social Svcs., 1981-90, pres., 1986-88; mem. St. Laurence Parish Bd., 1974-79, Edn. Commn., 1972-79, chmn. Edn. Commn., 1974-79; state advisor Iowa Jr. Classical League, 1960-61. Named Kane County Disting. Educator of Yr., 1982, Outstanding Young Men in Am., 1970; recipient Outstanding Young Educator award Elgin Jaycees, 1969. Mem. Assn. C.C. Trustees (chmn. ctrl. region nominating com. 1981-82, sgt.-at-arms ann. conv. 1982, mem. com. on internat. rels. 1983-84, chmn. future directions com. 1984-86, chmn. ctrl. region 1987-88, fed. rels. commn. 1985-93, vice-chmn. fed. rels. commn. 1987-88, chmn. fed. rels. commn. 1988-89, chmn. ctrl. region nominating com. 1992-93, Ctrl. Region Trustee of Yr. award 1991, bd. dirs. 1983-89), Am. Assn. C.C. (bd. dirs. 1990-93), Ill. C.C. Trustees Assn. (chmn. fed. rels. com. 1982-87, bd. rep. 1986-95, 97—, exec. com. 1981-84, 98-2000, chmn. west suburban region 1981-84, 98-2000), Ill. Edn. Assn. (chmn. ad hoc com. on tchr. tenure 1972-73, state legis. chmn. 1972-73, legis., chmn. northeastern divsn. 1968-71), Elgin Tchrs. Assn. (welfare chmn. and chief negotiator 1963-65, pres. 1966-67), Elgin Assn. Sch. Adminstrs., Am. Classical League, Ill. Classical League, Nat. Coun. Tchrs. English, Ill. Coun. Tchrs. English, Am. Assn. Cmty. and Jr. Colls. Fax: 847-429-0408. Home: 192 Kathleen Dr Elgin IL 60123-5914 also: 4840 Heron Run Cir Leesburg FL 34748-7819

DUFFY, JOSEPH AUGUSTINE, Roman Catholic bishop; b. Dublin, Ireland, Feb. 3, 1934; s. Edward and Brigid (MacEntee) D. BA with honors, Maynooth Coll., Ireland, 1954, BD with honors, 1957, MA with honors, 1960. Bishop of Clogher Roman Cath. Ch., Monaghan, Ireland, 1979—. Editor (local history) Clogher Record, 1963-75; author (guide) Lough Derg Today, 1969, Patrick in His Own Words, 1972, 2d edit., 2000, Monaghan Cathedral, 1988. Avocations: Irish history, travelling, walking. Home and Office: Tigh an Easpaig, Monaghan Ireland

DUFFY, LOUANN C., career counselor; b. Holdredge, Nebr., Mar. 7, 1947; d. Guy F. and Martha M. Fuller; m. Mitch G. Myers, July 23, 1970 (dec. 1984); children: Louis P. Myers, Cary David Myers; m. Robert G. Duffy, Apr. 24, 1986. BS in Elem. Edn., U. Colo., 1970; MA in Orgnl. Mgmt., U. Phoenix, Denver, 1994. Registered career cons., Internat. Assn. Career Counseling Firms. Project office coord. U.S. West Internat., Englewood, Colo., 1989-96; human resources cons. Coopers & Lybrand, Denver, 1997; career counselor Dunn & Nelson, Denver, 1997—; mng. cons., bd. mem. Dendrite Design L.L.C., Aurora, Colo., 1997—. Presenting team mem. Worldwide Marriage Encounter. Roman Catholic.

DUFFY, MARY KATHLEEN, neonatal nurse; b. Oak Park, Ill., Aug. 10, 1949; d. William F. and Mary F. (Lang) D. ADN, Triton Coll., River Grove, Ill., 1976; BSN with honors, Ill. Benedictine Coll., Lisle, 1986. Staff nurse gen. med./surg. unit MacNeal Hosp., Berwyn, Ill., 1976-80, staff nurse, level II nursery, 1980-86; staff nurse, neonatal intermediate intensive care nursery DeKalb Gen. Hosp., Decatur, Ga., 1986-87; staff nurse level II nursery MacNeal Hosp., Berwyn, 1987-88; staff nurse level III neonatal intensive care unit Good Samaritan Hosp., Downers Grove, Ill., 1988—. Mem. Nat. Assn. Neonatal Nurses, Sigma Theta Tau.

DUFFY, ROBERT EDWARD, fluid dynamics engineer, consultant; b. Scranton, Pa., May 27, 1930; s. Walter Anthony Duffy and Irene Naomi Gaffney; m. Ann Louise D., Nov. 26, 1953; children: R. Brian, Patricia Ann, Suzanne. BS in Aero. Engring., Rensselaer Poly. Inst., 1951, MS in Aero. Engring., 1955, PhD, 1965. Aero. engr. USAF, Dayton, Ohio, 1951-52; asst. prof. aero. engring. Rensselaer Poly. Inst., Troy, N.Y., 1956-65; rsch. engr., cons. Grumman Aircraft Co., Bethpage, N.Y., 1957-63; assoc. prof. aero. engring. Rensselaer Poly. Inst., 1966-90; ret., 1990; pres., owner R.E.D. Assocs., Wynantskill, N.Y., 1988—; cons., U.S. Govt., N.Y. State Govt., various corps., 1955—. Contbr. over 60 articles and papers to profl. jours. and conf. procs. Treas. North Greenbush (N.Y.) Pub. Libr., 1968-73; chmn. North Greenbush Planning Bd., 1971-88. Fellow AIAA (assoc.; assoc. editor Jour. Aircraft 1981—); mem. ASME, Kiwanis, Burden Lake Country Club (treas. and owner 1968-74). Roman Catholic. Avocations: golf, fishing, log home building. Home and Office: R E D Assocs 3 Zelenke Dr Wynantskill NY 12198-8628

DUFFY-KING, JAN, journalist, multimedia consultant; b. Edinburgh, Scotland, July 21, 1965; came to U.S., 1991; s. John and Annie Elizabeth (Devine) Wallace; 1 child, Shelley (dec.). BA with honors, U. Oxford, Eng., 1987. Journalist Mirror Group Newspapers, London, 1987-90; editor Mirror Group Newspapers, Amsterdam, 1990-91; author JWE Internat., N.Y.C., 1991-93; Internet cons. eurotrash.com., N.Y.C., 1993—; bd. dirs. Johnboy Records, London. Author: Zuid-Amerikaanse Reis Gids, 1993. Lt. Dutch Army, 1983-87. Named Journalist of Yr., Nat. Union of Journalists, 1990. Avocations: flying helicopters, free-fall parachuting, travel. Office: eurotrash.com 5 Penn Plz New York NY 10001-1810

DUFOUR, JACQUES JULIEN, mining engineer; b. Paris, Mar. 14, 1938; s. Julien Gustave and Marguerite Jeanne (Rodriguez) D.; m. Françoise Marie Bertein, July 25, 1960; children: Philippe, Christophe, Xavier. Degree in civil engring., Ecole Nat. Superieure Mines, Paris, 1961, diploma in geology, 1969. Plant mgr. Cie Raffinage Shell Berre, France, 1964-70; dept. head Soc. Petroles Shell, Pauillac, France, 1971-76, Paris, 1977-81; rschr. Koninlijk Shell Lab., Amsterdam, The Netherlands, 1982-85; mgr. Soc. Anonyme Shell Rsch., Grand 'Couronne, France, 1985-94; rsch. project mgr. Conservatoire Nat. Arts et Metiers, Paris, 1995—; bd. dirs. Soc. Mediteraneene d'Exploita-

tion Thermique, Aix en Provence, France, 1977-81. Contbr. articles to profl. jours.; patentee in field. Lt. arty. French Army, 1961-64. Avocations: running, painting. Home: 224 Ave du Maine, 75014 Paris France Office: CNAM Nuclear Sci Lab, 2 Rue Conte, 75003 Paris France

DUFOUR, THIERRY FRANÇOIS, neurosurgeon, consultant; b. Charenton le Pont, France, Mar. 9, 1960; s. Raphaël Dufour and Denise Carini; m. Dominique Rabattu, Oct. 31, 1992; children: Marine, Lena, Charlotte, Margot. MD, U. Rennes I, France, 1993. Resident U. Paris VII, 1985, Rennes, 1986-90, 91, Erlangen, Germany, 1990-91, Marseille, France, 1992; chef de clinique U. Rennes, 1993-97; praticien Hospitalier du Cen. Hospitalier Régional, Orleans, France, 1997—; mem. Syndicat Autonome des Internes, Rennes, 1986-92, pres., 1989-90; v.p. Inter Syndicat Nat. des Internes des Hopitaux, Paris, 1991-92, Inter Syndicat des Chefs de Clinique, Rennes, 1993; pres., founder Syndicat des Chirurgiens Hospitaliers, Paris, 1998—. Contbr. articles to profl. jours. Mem. French Soc. Neurosurgery, European Soc. Pediat. Neurosurgery, French Soc. Pediat. Neurosurgery (founder). E-mail: dufour.th@wanadoo.fr. Office: Ctr Hospitalier Regional, PO Box 6709, 45067 Orleans Cedex 2 France

DUGAEV, VITALII KONSTANTINOVICH, physicist, researcher; b. Krasnodar, Russia, Nov. 1, 1945; arrived in Ukraine, 1991; s. Konstantin Nikiforovich and Evgenija Mikhailovna (Zholokhova) D.; m. Tatyana Igorevna Sokolovskaya, June 10, 1967; children: Serguei, Mikhail. MSc in Engring., Lviv Polytechnic Inst., 1968; PhD in Physics, Chernivtsy State U., 1980. Jr. rschr. Inst. Materials Sci. Problems Chernivtsy State U., 1977-85, sr. rschr., 1985-97, lab. mgr., 1997—. Contbr. articles to profl. jours. including Soviet Phys. JETP, Phys. Rev. B, including others. Home: 12 Cheluskintsev Apt 2, 58000 Chernivtsi Ukraine Office: Chernivtsy State U Inst Mat, Sci Problems, 5 I Vilde St, 58001 Chernivtsi Ukraine

DUGAR, CHAND RATAN, textiles executive; b. Sardarshahr, India, Apr. 11, 1953; s. Bhairudan and Anachi Devi (Buchcha) D.; m. Kamala Patawari Dugar, Feb. 6, 1975; 1 child, Nil. B in Comms. (hon.), Calcutta (India) U., 1972. Cert. CPA, 1974. Audit, articled clk. M/s Singhi & Co., Calcutta, India, 1971-75; sr. asst., 1975-76; joint pres. M/s Eastern Spinning Mill, Calcutta, India, 1976-91; gen. mgr. P.T. Elegant Textile Industry, Indonesia, 1992-97, pres., dir., 1997—; advisor M/s Midnapors Cotton Mills, India, 1989-91, Indo Phil Textile Mills, Philippines, 1992, Indo-Thai Synthetics Co., Thailand, 1992; cons. Indonesian Consortium Indonesia Devel. Citra awards, 1998-99. Recipient Grid award Grid Orgn. Devel. Group, Malaysia, 1996, Sahwali award Indonesian Environ. Mgmt. & Info., 1996, Best Exec. award Asean Programme-Cons. Indonesian Consortium Indonesia Devel. Citra Awards, 1998-99. Home: Banidabas, Sardar Shahar 331403, India Office: PT Elegant Textile Industry, Desa Ubrug Jatiluhur, Purwakarta 41100, Indonesia

DUGDALE, JOHN SYDNEY, retired physics educator; b. Settle, England, Feb. 10, 1922; s. William Eddy and Harriet Gertrude (Harger) D.; m. Barbara Baird Henderson, Oct. 30, 1954; children: Elizabeth, John. BA, Oxford (Eng.) U., 1948, DPhil, 1951. Postdoctoral fellow Nat. Rsch. Coun., Ottawa, Ont., Can., 1951-53, rsch. worker, 1953-65; prof. physics U. Leeds, Eng., 1965-87; ret., 1987. Author: Entropy and Low Temperature Physics, 1966, Electrical Properties of Metals and Alloys, 1977; editor: Contemporary Physics, 1981-92, Electrical Properties of Disordered Metals, 1995, Entropy and its Physical Meaning, 1996; contbr. articles to physics jours. Lt. RAF, 1942-46, ETO. Fellow AAAS, Royal Soc. Can., Inst. Physics (London). Home: Greenside, Goose Green Gullane, LS165NS East Lothian EH312AU, Scotland Office: U Leeds, LS2 9JT Leeds England

DUGGAN, JOHN MALCOLM, gastroenterologist; b. Sydney, NSW, Australia, Sept. 30, 1927; s. Joseph Charles and Myrtle Agnes (Cobbin) D.; m. Mary Catherine Plasto, Jan. 10, 1953; children: Catherine, Christopher, Anne, Bernard, James, Michael. MB BS, Sydney U., 1951, MD, 1981. Assoc. prof. Newcastle U., Australia, 1975—; mem. Repatriation Med. Authority, Australia, 1994—. Editor: Jour. of Quality in Clin. Practice, 1991—. Fellow Royal Australasian Coll. of Physicians (Coll. Medal), Royal Australasian Coll. Med. Adminstrs. (hon.), Royal Coll. Physicians (London), Quality Soc. of Australia, Order of Australia. Home: 33 Hebburn St, Hamilton 2303, Australia

DUGGAN, JOSEPH PATRICK, public affairs executive; b. St. Louis, July 5, 1955; s. Martin Lawler and Mary Margaret (Mae) D.; m. Juanita Sheryl Donaghey, Oct. 29, 1983 (div. July 1996); children: James Joseph Lawler, Edward Scott Wilson. BA in Classics magna cum laude, U. Dallas, 1976. Editl. writer The Greensboro (N.C.) Record, 1977-79; asst. editor editl. page Richmond (Va.) Times-Dispatch, 1979-81; spl. asst. to ambassadors Jeane Kirkpatrick & Edward Rowny U.S. Dept. of State, Washington, 1981-85, 86-91; speechwriter to Pres. The White House, Washington, 1991-92; budget & econ. policy advisor Office of U.S. Rep. Christopher Cox, Washington, 1993-94; comm. & policy dir. U.S. Senate Commerce Com., Washington, 1994-95; v.p., dir. media rels. Powell Tate, Washington, 1995-98; sr. v.p. The DCS Group, Washington, 1998—; mem. bd. visitors Georgetown U. Inst. Polit. Journalism, Washington, 1985, Inst. Comparative Politics and Econs., 1983-84. Founder, chmn. Washington Cath. Forum, 1985; comm. advisor Rep. Nat. Conv., San Diego, 1996. Mem. U.S. Senat Press Secs. Assn., Cosmos Club. Roman Catholic. Home: 3632 Jenifer St NW Washington DC 20015-1752 Office: The DCS Group 410 1st St SE Washington DC 20003-1819

DUGIĆ, MIROLJUB MOMČILO, researcher, science educator; b. Kragujevac, Yugoslavia, June 18, 1961; s. Momčilo Vidoje and Stanica Dragutin (Ignjatović) D. Grad. Physicist, Faculty of Sci., Kragujevac, 1985, PhD in Physics, 1997; MS in Physics, Faculty of Physics, Beograd, Yugoslavia, 1993. Lectr. Faculty Sci., Kragujevac, 1986-98, asst. prof., 1998—. Contbr. articles to sci. jours. Avocation: recreational activities. Home: Nikole Pašića 37/8A, 34000 Kragujevac Yugoslavia Office: Radoja Domanovića 12, PO Box 60, 34000 Kragujevac Yugoslavia

DU GRANRUT, CLAUDE, diplomat; b. Versailles, France, Nov. 16, 1929; d. Robert and Germaine (Guyot-Sionnest) De Renty; m. Bernard De Granrut; five children. Diploma, Inst. Polit. Sci., Paris, 1950. Journalist Paris, 1955-57; staff attachee Agrl. Dept., Paris, 1957-58; head dept. Prof. Tng. Pub. Agy., Paris, 1968-71; min.'s staff Labor Ministry, Paris, 1971-73, Edn. Ministry, Paris, 1973-74; head dept. Women's Labor Com., Paris, 1973-77; dep. minister handicapped workers Labor Ministry, Paris, 1978-87; state high ct. magistrate Lyon Ct. Appeals, France, 1987-94; v.p. regional coun. of Picardy European Com., Amiens, France, 1994—; mem. com. of the Region of the European Union, 1994—. Author: Place Aux Femmes, 1973, Europe, Le Temps Des Regions, 1993, La Citoyennete Europeenne, 1997. Mem. L Forum Club, French Women in Pub. Office (pres. 1997). Home: 8 rue de la Montagne Aighan, 60300 Senlis France

DUGUA, PIERRE-YVES, journalist; b. Bône, Algeria, France, Nov. 10, 1960; came to U.S., 1982; s. Georges Jean and Denise Henriette (Harger) D.; m. Lisa Ann Utley, Jan. 11, 1986; children: Georges, Celia, Elise. Diploma, Inst. d'Etudes Politiques, Paris, 1981; MA, Johns Hopkins U., 1984. Dep. rep. Banque Paribas, Washington, 1984-89; U.S. corres. La Cote DesFosses-L'Agefi, Washington, 1990-96; U.S. bus. corres. Le Figaro, Washington, 1996—, Radio France, Washington, 1991—. Fundraiser Medicine for Autism Today, Washington, 1998—. Mem. Scis.-Po Alumni of Washington (pres., co-founder 1997-99). Home: 4208 Dresden St Kensington MD 20895-3816

DUGUID, JENNIFER KAREN MARY, hematologist; b. Hamburg, Germany, Aug. 26, 1947; arrived in Eng., 1948; d. John and Aileen Mary (Barry) D.; m. John David Creer, Mar. 29, 1947 (dec.) children: Thomas James, Simon John. MBChB, Liverpool (Eng.) U., 1970. Sr. registrar Mersey Health Authority, Liverpool, 1977-83; med. officer Liverpool Blood Transfusion Ctr., 1983-89, cons. hematologist, 1989-95; lead clinician Mersey & North Wales Nat. Blood Ctr., 1995-97; cons. haematologist, lead clinician for cancer Wrexham Maelor Hosp., Wales, 1997—; lectr. U. Liverpool, 1989—; examiner Royal Coll. Pathologists, London, 1995—; spkr. in field. Author: (chpt.) Developing Techniques in Blood Transfusion, 1990, Infection & Hematology, 1994, Hematology, 1997—; mem. editl. bd. Clin. Lab. Hematology, 1995—; contbr. articles to profl. jours. Wellcome Rsch. fellow U. Liverpool, 1975-77. Fellow Royal Coll. Pathologists; mem. British Soc. Hematology (sec. transfusion task force 1997—, sec. Brit. com. for stds. in hematology), British Blood Transfusion Soc. (founding, coun. 1993-96), Coun. Royal Coll. Pathologists. Avocations: tennis, skiing, reading, cooking. Office: Dept Haematology Wrexham, Haelor Hosp, Wrexham LL137TD, England

DUHAMEL, OLIVIER, foreign diplomat; b. Neuilly-sur-Seine, France, May 2, 1950. Mem. European Parliament, 1999—, mem. com. on citizens' freedoms/rights, justice/home affairs, substitute com. on constnl. affairs; mem. Group of the Party of European Socialists; mem. delegation for relations with the countries of S.Am. and Mercosur. Mem. Socialist Party. Office: Parlement européen, Rue Wiertz ASP 14G242, B-1047 Brussels Belgium*

DUHME, CAROL MCCARTHY, civic worker; b. St. Louis, Apr. 13, 1917; d. Eugene Ross and Louise (Roblee) McCarthy; m. Sheldon Ware, June 12, 1941 (dec. 1944); 1 child, David; m. H. Richard Duhme, Jr., Apr. 9, 1947; children: Benton (dec.), Ann, Warren (dec.). AB, Vassar Coll., 1939. Tchr. elem. sch., 1939-41, 42-44; moderator St. Louis Assn. Congl. Chs., 1952; dir. Christian edn. First Congl. Ch., St. Louis, 1959-62, trustee, 1964-66, mem. ch. coun., 1974-75, 84-85, 87-89, bd. deaconesses, 1978-81, bd. deacons, 1982-85, 92-95; chmn. bd. Christian Edn., 1987-88; former bd. dirs. Community Music Schs., St. Louis, Community Sch., Ch. Women United, John Burroughs Sch., St. Louis Bicentennial Women's Com., St. Louis Jr. League; pres. St. Louis Vassar Club; pres. bd. dirs. YWCA, St. Louis, 1973-76, chmn. ann. fund, 1989-90; bd. dirs. North Side Team Ministry, 1968-84, Chautauqua (N.Y.) Instn., 1971-79, mem. adv. coun. to bd., 1987—; adv. coun. Mo. Bapt. Hosp., 1973-89; exec. com. bd. dirs. Eden Theol. Sem., 1981-95, presdl. search com. 1986-87, 92-93, v.p. bd. dirs., 1991, chmn. 150th Anniversary com., 1996—; sec. bd. dirs. UN Assn., St. Louis, 1976-84, coun. of advisors, 1993—, nat. coun. 1995—; mem. nat. coun. UN-USA, 1995—; pres. bd. dirs. Family and Children's Svc. Greater St. Louis, 1977-79; mem. chancellor's long-range planning com. Washington U., 1980-81, mem. Nat. Coun., Sch. Social Work, 1987—; chmn. Benton Roblee Duhme Scholarship Fund; trustee Joseph H. and Florence A. Roblee Found., St. Louis, 1984—, pres., 1984-90, bd. dirs.; chmn. Chautaugua Bell Tower Scholarship Fund, 1961—; bd. dirs. Nat. Inland Waterways Libr., St. Louis Merc. Libr. Mem. corp. assembly Blue Cross Hosp. Svc. of Mo., 1978-86. Recipient Mary Alice Messerley award for volunteerism Health and Welfare Coun. St. Louis, 1971; Vol. of Yr. award, YWCA, 1976; Woman of Achievement award St. Louis Globe Democrat, 1980; Outstanding Lay Woman nomination Mo. United Ch. of Christ, 1991; Outstanding Alumna award John Burroughs Sch., 1992. Home: 8 Edgewood Rd Saint Louis MO 63124-1817

DÜHMKE, ECKHART, radiation oncology educator; b. Berlin, July 22, 1942; s. Martin Walter and Christa Anna Luise (Horrer) D.; m. Eva Leopoldine Herta Bagge, Dec. 31, 1970; children: Anna Katharina, Elisa Maria, Rudolf Martin, Victoria Christina. MD, U. Kiel, Germany, 1969, Habilitation in Med. Radiology, 1980. Resident dept. radiology U. Kiel, 1970-74, specialist in radiology, 1975-80, specialist in radiotherapy, lectr., 1980-85; prof. radiation oncology, chmn. dept. radiotherapy U. Göttingen, Germany, 1985-93, provisional chmn. dept. diagnostic radiology, 1985-87, provisional chmn. dept. radiation physics and biology, 1987-91, dir. div. radiology, 1989-93; chmn. dept. radiotherapy and radiation oncology U. Munich, 1993—; vis. prof. dept. radiation oncology and nuclear medicine Hahnemann U., Phila., 1984. Co-author: Handbook of Medical Radiology, 1974; author: Medicinal Radiography with Fast Neutrons, 1980; co-editor, editor: Function Preserving Therapy of Laryngeal Carcinoma Proc., 1990-91; also numerous articles on diagnostic and therapeutic radiology. Mem. German Roengten Soc., German Cancer Soc., Am. Soc. Therapeutic Radiology and Oncology, European Soc. Therapeutic Radiology and Oncology, Am. Soc. Clin. Oncology. Lutheran. Avocations: skiing, sailing. Office: Munich Dept Radiotherapy and Radiation Oncology, Marchioninistr 15, D-81377 Munich Germany

DUHOVNIK, JOŽE, mechanical engineer; b. Količevo, Slovenia, Mar. 23, 1948; s. Ivan and Ana (Zerovnik) D.; m. Majda Zavasnik, Oct. 11, 1973; children: Primož, Klemen, Luka. Grad., U. Ljubljana, Slovenia, 1971, M Mech. Engring., 1974, D Mech. Engring., 1980. Design leader Sava (Semperit), Kranj, Slovenia, 1971-72; asst. U. Ljubljana, 1972-77; head design dept. SCT Sloveniya, Lubljana, 1978-79; assoc. prof. U. Ljubljana, 1980-82; rschr. U. Tokyo, 1983; head Inst. for CAD, Lecad, 1983—; prof. mech. engring. U. Ljubljana, 1984-89, 97—; head design dept. SCT Sloveniya, Lubljana, 1978-79; rschr. U. Tokyo, 1983; pres. corp. Litostroj, Ljubljana, 1990-96; v.p. Slovene Rwy. Co., Ljubljana, 1991-96; mem. rehab. team Litostroj, 1990; head Inst. CAD, LECAD, 1983—. Author: Farmer's Machine, 1985, 87; editor: Expert Systeme/CAD, 1990; reviewer Jour. Mech. Engring. and CAD. With Slovenian army, 1974-75. Home: Zontarjeva 19, 1215 Medvode Slovenia Office: U Ljubljani, Askerceva 6, 1000 Ljubljana Slovenia

DÜHRKOP DÜHRKOP, BÁRBARA, foreign diplomat; b. Hannover, Germany, July 27, 1945. Mem. European Parliament, 1999—, vice-chair com. on budgets, substitute com. on environment, pub. health, consumer policy; mem. of bur. Group of the Party of European Socialists; mem. delegations to the parliamentary coop. coms. and delegations for relations with Ukraine, Belarus and Moldova; mem. Mem. Delegation to the European Econ. Area Joint Parliamentary Com. Mem. Spanish Socialist Workers Party. Office: Parlamento Europeo, Rue Wiertz ASP 11G342, B-1047 Brussels Belgium*

DUINSLAEGER, LUC ANDRÉ, surgeon; b. Ostend, Flanders, Belgium, July 31, 1959; s. Marcel Duinslaeger and Astrid De Vreese; m. Kathleen Ver Schoore; children: Giles, Cédric, Alec. MD, Free U. Brussels, 1984, Degree in Vascular Surgery, 1990, Degree in Intensive Care, 1997. Lect.r Paramedic Sch., 1980-87; resident ICU Acad. Hosp., Brussels, 1990-93; head clinic Burn Ctr., Brussels, 1990-99; head Tissue Bank, Brussels, 1996-99; cons. in field. Contbr. articles to profl. jours. Maj. Belgian Army. Home: De Ring 5, 9220 Hamme Flanders, Belgium Office: Mil Hosp Queen Astrid, 1120 Brussels Belgium

DUISENBERG, WILLEM FREDERIK, bank executive; b. Heerenveen, The Netherlands, July 9, 1935. D in Econs. cum laude, U. Groningen, The Netherlands, 1961, PhD, 1965; hon. doctorate, New U. Lisbon, Portugal. Tchg. asst. U. Groningen, 1961-65; mem. staff IMF, Washington, 1965-69; spl. advisor to governing bd. De Nederlandsche Bank, NV, Amsterdam, 1969-70, exec. dir., 1981-82, pres., 1982-97; prof. macroecons. U. Amsterdam, 1970-73; min. of fin. The Netherlands, 1973-77; M.P. Govt. of The Netherlands, 1977-78; mem., vice chmn. exec. bd. Rabobank Nederland, 1978-81; pres. European Monetary Inst., 1997-98, European Ctrl. Bank, Frankfurt, 1998—; pres. Bank for Internat. Settlements, 1988-90, chmn. bd., pres., 1994-97; chmn. com. govs. Ctrl. Banks of Mem. States of EEC, 1993; mem. coun. EMI, 1994-97, gov. IMF, Washington, 1992-97. Author: Economic Consequences of Disarmament, 1965, The IMF and the International Monetary System, 1966, The British Balance of Payments, 1969, Some Remarks on Imported Inflation, 1970. Decorated knight Order of the Netherlands Lion (The Netherlands), comdr. Order of Orange-Nassau (The Netherlands), comdr. Order of the Netherlands Lion (The Netherlands), grand cross Order of Merit (Luxembourg), knight grand cross Royal Order of the Star of the North (Sweden), grand cross Order of Merit (Senegal), grand cross Order of the Crown (Belgium); comdr. Legion d'Honneur, France. Mem. European Assn. for Banking History (mem. bd. patrons 1990—). Office: European Ctrl Bank, Kaiserstrasse 29, 60311 Frankfurt am Main, Germany

DUJELLA, ANDREJ, mathematician, researcher; b. Pula, Croatia, May 21, 1966; s. Josip and Zaga (Vukasovic) D.; m. Valentina Paladin, July 3, 1993; children: Marta, Dominik. Grad., U. Zagreb, Croatia, 1990, Master, 1993, PhD in Math., 1996. Postgrad. fellow dept. math. U. Zagreb, 1990-93, asst., 1993-97, asst. prof. math., 1997—. Co-author: Mathematical Competitions, 1996; author: Fibonacci Numbers, 2000. Mem. Croatian Math. Soc., Am. Math. Soc., Fibonacci Assn. Roman Catholic. Avocation: singing. Office: U Zagreb Dept Math, Bijenička Cesta 30, 10000 Zagreb Croatia

DU JIZENG, physiologist, neuroendocrinologist, educator, foundation administrator; b. Shanxi, China, Apr. 12, 1939; s. Qia and Peizhen (Li) Ji-Zeng; m. Qingfen Li, Apr. 1, 1967; children: Wei, Ye, Yu. PhD in Physiology, Beijing U., 1965. Lectr. biology N.W. Plateau Inst. Biol. Chinese Acad. Sci., Xining, China, before 1980; asst. prof. physiology N.W. Plateau Inst. Biol. Chinese Acad. Sci., Xining, 1980-85, assoc. prof., 1986-88, prof., dir., supr. for PhD students, 1989—; vis. asst. scientist U. Calif., Berkeley, 1983-84, San Francisco, 1984-85; vis. prof. U. Birmingham, U.K., 1991-92; prof., dir. for PhD students, Beijing Normal U., 1988—; dir. and prof. Physiol. Lab. of Hypoxia, Shanghai Inst. Physiology Chinese Acad. Scis., 1990—; dir. for PhD students Shanghai Inst. of Physiology, Chinese Acad. Scis., chair dir. acad. degree com. for MD, PhD, 1989, for postdoctoral, 1994—; mem. Polit. Consultative Conf., Qinghai Provence, 1992—; adv. com. Hypoxia Symposia, Chateau Lake Luise, Alta., Can., 1995—. Assoc. editor: Acta Plateau Biology Sinica, 1988—; editl. bd. Chinese Jour. Applied Physiology, 1993—, Acta Theriologica Sinica, 1987—, editorial bd. Chinese Jour. Neuroscience, 1998—; editor: Proceedings of 7th International Snow Leopard Symposium, 1994. Mem. com. Internat. Qinghai Culture Exch. Soc., Xining, 1993—. Recipient 2 Nat. awards for Achievement in Scis. and Tech., China, 1978, 3 awards Qinghai Province, 1979, 94. Mem. Chinese Assn. Physiol. Scis. (mem. coun. 1994—, v.p. comparative physiology 1995—, mem. standing com. digestion, endocrine, reprodn., metabolism 1995—), Chinese Pathophysiology Soc. (mem. com. hypoxia and respiratory com. 1993—), Chinese Theriological Soc. (mem. coun. 1987—), Chinese Zool. Soc. (mem. com. acad. and periodicals 1990—, coun. comparative endocrinology 1996—), mem. Internat. Union Physiol. Scis., Soc. for Endocrinology U.K., Chinese Med. Soc. (mem. standing com. 1995), Chinese High Altitude Med. Assn., Chinese Phamacologica Soc., Internat. Mountain Medicine Soc. Avocations: volleyball, basketball, national style dancing, instrument playing. Home: Beijing Normal Univ, 6-3-501 Lizhe Bldg, Beijing 100875, China Office: Zhejian Univ, Dept Biol Sci and Tech, Hangzhou Zhejian 310027, China

DUJON, DIANE MARIE, director, activist; b. Boston, Dec. 29, 1946; d. Alfred and Agnes C. (Hall) White; 1 child, Lisa M. Dujon. BA, U. Mass., 1983, MS, 1996. Asst. dir. assessment Coll. Pub. and Cmty. Svc. U. Mass., Boston, 1984-93, co-dir. assessment Coll. Pub. and Cmty. Svc., 1993-97, dir. independent learning Coll. Pub. and Cmty. Svc., 1997—. Co-editor: For Crying Out Loud: Women's Poverty in U.S., 1996 (Myers Ctr. for the Study of Human Rights in N.Am. Outstanding Book award 1997); prodr. (radio documentary) Workfare: Anatomy of a Policy, 1982 (Alice award 1982), Nat. Commn. on Working Women. V.p. Survivors, Inc., Boston, 1986—. Recipient Earl Douglas award City Mission Soc., 1987; named Unsung Heroine Rosie's Place, 1997. Mem. Nat. Welfare Rights Union, Mass. AFL-CIO (mem. exec. women's com. 1997), U. Mass. Profl. Staff Union (bd. mem. chpt. Svc. Employees Internat. Union, Local 509). Baptist. Office: U Mass/Boston 100 Morrissey Blvd Boston MA 02125-3300

DUKE, ANTHONY DREXEL, sociologist, educator, philanthropist; b. N.Y.C., July 28, 1918; s. Angier Buchanan and Cordelia (Biddle) D.; children by previous marriage: Anthony D. Jr., Nicholas R., Cordelia Duke Jung, Josephine Duke Brown, December Duke McSherry, John O., Douglas D.; m. Maria Luly de Lourdes Alcebo, Sept. 27, 1975; children: Lulita C., Washington A., James B. Student, Princeton U., 1941; DHL (hon.), Adelphi Coll., 1957, L.I. U., 1988, Drexel U., 1991. With Import Export Co., 1946-50; prin. A.D. Duke Realty, Inc., 1955-65; chmn. bd. dirs., pres., founder Boys Harbor Inc., 1937—. Trustee Big Brother Movement, 1951-63; past trustee Henry St. Settlement, N.Y.C.; del. Internat. Conf. Pvt. Sector Initiatives, 1986; hon. commr. Manhattan Borough Projects, 1954-57, Civic Affairs and Pub. Events, N.Y.C.; mem. N.Y.C. Youth Bd., 1955-58; rep. Internat. Rescue Com., Vietnam War, Meriel refugee crisis Cuba, 1983; active Save the Children, Pomfret Sch., Duke U., U.S. Naval Acad. Lt. comdr. USNR, 1941-46, PTO, ATO, ETO. Decorated Bronze Star. Recipient Town and Country Most Generous Am. award 1988, Save the Children award, 1977; Presdl. citation for pvt. sector commendation, 1986, Citation for Promotion of Human Welfare Commonwealth of Mass., 1987. Mem. Bodman and Achelis Found., Nat. Com. on Am. Fgn. Policy, Maidstone Club (former gov.), Piping Rock (former gov.), River Club, Racquet and Tennis Club, Beaver Dam Club. Home: PO Box 177 East Hampton NY 11937-0177 Office: Boys Harbor Inc 1 E 104th St New York NY 10029-4495

DUKE, ELLEN KAY, planned giving administrator; b. Indpls., June 7, 1952; d. Richard Thomas and Ruby Mae (Wright) D. Student, Chapman Coll., Orange, Calif., 1972; BS in Pub. Affairs, Ind. U., Bloomington, 1975; postgrad., Portland State U., 1980-81; MPA, Calif. State U., 1998. Cert. playground safety specialist/inspector; cert. Dale Carnegie Pub. Speaking instr., 1987-93. Newsreporter Salem Statesman, Corvallis, Oreg., 1976-78; com. adminstr. Oreg. State Legislature, Salem, 1979-80; pub. involvement coord. Met. Regional Svc. Dist., Portland, 1981-82; account mgr. Thunder & Visions, Portland, 1982-83; project asst. Amdahl Corp., Sunnyvale, CAlif., 1983-84; spl. project coord. Computerland Corp., Hayward, Calif., 1984-89; prodr., lead facilitator Sage, Inc., Walnut Creek, Calif., 1982—; loan broker Capital Trust Mortgage, Campbell, Calif., 1994—. Co-author (ednl. film) Communication Skills, 1975. Pub. rels. dir. local YMCA; chairperson Corvallis Budget Commn., Oreg., 1978; commr. Hayward Libr., 1985—, Alameda County Consumer Affairs, Oakland, 1985; rep. Nat. Dem. Conv., N.Y.C., 1982. Named Able Toastmaster, Toastmasters Internat., 1981; grad. Leadership Oakland, 1991. Mem. NAFE, ASTD, Pub. Rels. Soc. Am., Nat. Planned Giving Coun., Nat. Soc. for Fund Raising Execs. (planned giving coun.), Kansas City Coun. on Philanthropy, Sierra Club (San Francisco). Office: Assn Unity Churches 401 SW Oldham Pkwy Lees Summit MO 64081-2747

DUKE, GEORGE WESLEY, financial executive; b. Nashville, Dec. 27, 1953; s. Harold Wesley and Justine Hope (Perry) D.; m. Lucy Neale; children: Elizabeth, Margaret, Hope. BBA, Coll. William and Mary, 1976; M Taxation, Va. Commonwealth U., 1981; MBA, Darden Sch., 1983; MEd, Vanderbilt U., 1989; M of Liberal Arts, Johns Hopkins U., 1992. CPA, Va. Acct. KPMG Peat Marwick, Richmond, Va., 1976-81; v.p. Jacques-Miller, Nashville, 1983-86; sr. v.p. Alex Brown Kleinwort Benson, Balt., 1986-94; prin. LaSalle Ptnrs. (formerly Alex Brown Kleinwort Benson), Balt., 1994-99; mng. dir. LaSalle Investment Mgmt. (formerly LaSalle Ptnrs.), Balt., 1999—. Mem. AICPA, Pension Real Estate Assn., Ctr. Club, Darden Sch. Alumni Assn. (past pres. alumni bd.). Office: LaSalle Investment Mgmt 100 E Pratt St Baltimore MD 21202-1009

DUKE DE LEONEDES OF SPAIN SICILY GREECE, HIS ROYAL HIGHNESS See SANCHEZ, LEONEDES MONARRIZE WORTHINGTON

DUKKON, AGNES, humanities educator; b. Györszemere, Hungary, Nov. 11, 1949; d. Jozsef and Agnes (Horváth) D. Cert. Tchr., Eötvös Loránd U., Budapest, Hungary, 1973, MA, 1975, Russian and Hungarian Philology Diplomas, 1990; PhD, Acad. Scis., Budapest, 1990. Tchr. Sec. Sch., Szombathely, Hungary, 1973-74; asst. Tchr.'s Tng. Coll., Szeged, Hungary, 1974-77; lectr. Tchr.'s Tng. Coll., Budapest, Hungary, 1977-93; prof. Tchr.'s Tng. Coll. ELTE, Budapest, 1993—. Author: (book series) Russian Writers with Hungarian Eyes, 1983, 89, Dosztojevskij and Belinsky, 1992; author, editor: Tolstoj (two short stories), 1995, Crime and Punishment of Dostojevskij, 1997; co-author: History of Russian Literature from Beginning to 1940, 1997. Recipient Medal Eötvös Coll., Budapest, 1989. Fellow Acad. Sci. Hungary (mem. Renaissance, Barocco team). Mem. Calvinist Ch. Avocations: tourism, music, books. Office: ELTE TFK, Kazinczy U 23-27, 1075 Budapest Hungary

DULANEY, RICHARD ALVIN, lawyer; b. Charlottesville, Va., Oct. 18, 1948; s. Alvin Tandy and Susie Lloyd (Sims) D. B.A., Yale U., 1971; J.D., Coll. William and Mary, 1977. Bar: Va. 1977, U.S. Dist. Ct. (ea. dist.) Va. 1978. V.p. Christian Ctr., Charlottesville, Va., 1972-73; rsch. asst. Marshall-Wythe Sch. Law, Williamsburg, Va., 1975; assoc. Niles & Chapman, Remington, Va., 1977-79; gen. ptnr. Niles, Dulaney & Parker, Culpeper, Va., 1980-92; of counsel Chandler, Franklin, and O'Bryan, Culpeper, Va., 1988—; ptnr. Niles Dulaney Parker and Lauer LLP, Culpeper, 1992-98, Dulaney, Parker, Lauer & Thomas LLP, Culpeper, 1999—; bd. dirs. Rappahanock Legal Svcs., Fredericksburg, Va., 1981-83. Bd. dirs. Christian Ctr., Syria, Va., 1974-89, U. Sci. and Philosophy Swannanoa, Waynesboro, Va., 1985—,

The Quest Inst., Charlottesville, Va., 1986-87; mem. Bd. Zoning Appeals, Culpeper County, Culpeper, Va., 1983-90. Mem. Piedmont Bar Assn., Va. Bar Assn., Va. Trial Lawyers Assn., Am. Trial Lawyers Assn., Culpeper Bar Assn. (pres. 1985-86), New Haven chpt. Pierson Fellowship Club, Omicron Delta Kappa. Home: PO Box 511 Culpeper VA 22701-0511 Office: Dulaney Parker Lauer & Thomas LLP PO Box 190 Culpeper VA 22701-0190

DULBECCO, RENATO, biologist, educator; b. Catanzaro, Italy, Feb. 22, 1914; came to U.S., 1947, naturalized, 1953; s. Leonardo and Maria (Virdia) D.; m. Gulseppina Salvo, June 1, 1940 (div. 1963); children: Peter Leonard (dec.), Maria Vittoria; m. Maureen Rutherford Muir; 1 child, Fiona Linsey. M.D., U. Torino, Italy, 1936; D.Sc. (hon.), Yale U., 1968, Vrije Universiteit, Brussels, 1978; LL.D., U. Glasgow, Scotland, 1970. Asst. U. Torino, 1940-47; research asso. Ind. U., 1947-49; sr. research fellow Calif. Inst. Tech., 1949-52, asso. prof., then prof. biology, 1952-63; sr. fellow Salk Inst. Biol. Studies, San Diego, 1963-71; asst. dir. research Imperial Cancer Research Fund, London, 1971-74; dep. dir. research Imperial Cancer Research Fund, 1974-77; disting. research prof. Salk Inst., La Jolla, Calif., 1977—, pres., 1989-92; pres. emeritus Salk Inst., La Jolla, 1993—; prof. pathology and medicine U. Calif. at San Diego Med. Sch., La Jolla, 1977-81, mem. Cancer Ctr.; with Nat. Rsch. Coun. Milan; vis. prof. Royal Soc. G.B., 1963-64, Leeuwenhoek lectr., 1974; Clowes Meml. lectr. Atlantic City, 1961; Harvey lectr. Harvey Soc., 1967; Dunham lectr. Harvard U., 1972; 11th Marjory Stephenson Meml. lectr., London, 1973, Harden lectr., Wye, Eng., 1973, Am. Soc. for Microbiology lectr., L.A., 1979; mem. Calif. Cancr Adv. Coun., 1963-67; mem. vis. com. Case Western Res. Sch. Medicine; adv. bd. Roche Inst., 1968-71, Inst. Immunology, Basel, Switzerland, others; esperto Italian Nat. Rsch. Coun.; trustee Am.-Italian Fedn. for Cancer Rsch.; mem. bd. dirs. Scientific Counselors Dept. Etiology NCI; cons. Nat. Rsch. Coun. ESPERTO, 1994—. Trustee La Jolla Country Day Sch., Am.-Italian Fedn. for Cancer Rsch.; bd. mem. sci. counselors dept. etiology Nat. Cancer Inst. Recipient John Scott award City Phila., 1958, Kimball award Conf. Pub. Health Lab. Dirs., 1959, Albert and Mary Lasker Basic Med. Rsch. award, 1964, Howard Taylor Ricketts award, 1965, Paul Ehrlich-Ludwig Darmstaedter prize, 1967, Horwitz prize Columbia U., 1973, (with David Baltimore and Howard Martin Temin) Nobel prize in medicine, 1975, Targa d'oro Villa San Giovanni, 1978, Mandel Gold medal Czechoslovak Acad. Scis., 1982, Via de Condotti prize, 1990, Cavaliere di Gran Croce Italian Rep., 1991, Natale Di Roma prize, 1993, Columbus prize, 1993; named Man of Yr., London, 1975, Italian Am. of Yr., San Diego County, 1978; hon. citizen City of Imperia (Italy), 1983, City of Arezzo, City of Sommariva Perno, City of Catanzaro, City of Torino; Guggenheim and Fulbright fellow, 1957-58; decorated grand ufficiale Italian Republic, 1981; hon. founder Hebrew U., 1981. Mem. NAS (Selman A. Waksman award 1974, com. on human rights), Am. Assn. Cancer Rsch., Internat. Physicians for Prevention Nuclear War, Am. Philos. Assn., Academia Nazionale del Lincel (fgn.), Academia Ligure di Scienze e Lettre (hon.), Royal Soc. (fgn.), Fedn. Am. Scientists, Am. Acad. Arts and Scis., Comitato di Collaborazione Culturale (hon. mem.), Alpha Omega Alpha. Home: 7525 Hillside Dr La Jolla CA 92037-3941 Office: Ufficio di Milano, Via Calzecchi 10, 20133 Milan Italy also: Salk Inst PO Box 85800 San Diego CA 92186-5800

DULGUEROV, PAVEL, otolaryngologist-head and neck surgeon, educator; b. Sofia, Bulgaria, July 12, 1957; arrived in Switzerland, 1972; s. Athanas and Evdokia (Stambolieva) D.; m. Nicole B. Fournet, June 15, 1986 (div. 1991); m. Nancy E. Newsom, Mar. 14, 1991. Med. degree, U. Geneva, Switzerland, 1983. Lic. physician, Calif. Rsch. fellow U. Fla., Gainesville, 1984-85; rsch. fellow dept. otolarngology-head and neck surgery Johns Hopkins U., Balt., 1985-87; resident dept. surgery divsn. head and neck surgery UCLA, 1988-91, chief resident dept. surgery divsn. head and neck surgery, 1991-92; premier chef de clinique dept otolaryngology-head and neck surgery Geneva U. Hosp., 1992-99; chargé d'enseignement faculty of medicine U. Geneva, 1992-99; médecin-adjoint dept otolaryngology-head and neck surgery Geneva U. Hosp., 2000—; pvt. docent U. Geneva, 2000—; clin. supr. U. Geneva, 1992—, head tumor bd., 1993—, lectr. med. students, 1993, supr. operating room, 1992—. Contbr. book chpts.: Current Therapy in Otolaryngology - Head and Neck Surgery, 1993; contbr. articles and papers to med. jours. Mem. Am. Acad. Otolaryngology-Head Neck Surgery, Federatio Medicum Helveticorum, Swiss Soc. for Med. Informatics. Office: Geneva U Hosp, 24 rue Micheli-du-Crest, CH-1204 Geneva Switzerland

DULÍČEK, PETR, hematologist; b. Hradec Králové, Czech Republic, Oct. 16, 1963; s. Karel and Jana (Cejnarová) D. PhD, 1999. Resident 1st dept. internal medicine Univ. Hosp., Hradec Králové, 1988-91, fellow 1st dept. internal medicine, 1991-94, cons. dept. hematology, 1994—; vis. clinician Mayo Clinic, Rochester, Minn., 1997. Home: Jungmannova 1447, 500 02 Hradec Králové II, Czech Republic Office: Univ Hosp Dept Hematology, Sokolská 408, 500-35 Hradec Králové Czech Republic

DULICHENKO, ALEXANDER DMITRI, linguist, Slavist, researcher; b. Krasnodarski, Krai, Russia, Oct. 30, 1941; s. Dmitri Alexei and Eudokia Tikhon (Zmievskaya) D.; m. Ludmila Vassili Brynza, Apr. 8, 1975; children: Dmitri, Vassili. CandScis, Inst. of Slavistics, Moscow, 1974; DrHabilitatus, Inst. of Linguistics, Minsk, USSR, 1981. Philological diplomate. Tchr. secondary sch., Turkmenia, USSR, 1966-68, 70-76; asst. U. Samarkand, USSR, 1968-70; lectr. U. Tartu, USSR, 1976-81, docent, 1981-85; prof. U. Tartu, USSR, then Estonia, 1985—; chief Slavic philology dept. U. Tartu, Estonia, 1992—. Author: Slav'anskie Literaturnye Mikroyazyki, 1981, Mezdunarodnye Vspomogatel'nye Yazyki, 1990, Russkii Yazyk Konca XX Stoletia, 1994, Yugoslavo-Ruthenica, 1995, Etnosociolingvistika Perestrojki v SSSR, 1999, others. Recipient awards and grants. Mem. Estonian Com. Slavicists (pres. 1993—), Internat. Com. Slavicists, Internat. Acad. Scis., N.Y. Acad. Scis. Russian Orthodox. Avocations: books, music, travel, nature. Home: Box 31, 50002 Tartu Estonia Office: Ulikooli 18A, 50090 Tartu Estonia

DULLES, FREDERICK HENDRIK, lawyer; b. N.Y.C., Mar. 12, 1942; s. William Winslow and Joanna (deLeu) D.; m. Martine Pred'homme, Aug. 26, 1977; 1 child, Emilie Pred'homme. AB cum laude, Harvard U., 1964; JD, Columbia U., 1968, MBA, 1968. Bar: D.C. 1971, N.Y. 1972. Assoc. Shearman & Sterling, N.Y.C. and Paris, 1971-80; counsel Philip Morris Inc., N.Y.C., 1980; asst. gen. counsel, 1981-83; dir. regional counsel EFTA-Eastern Europe-Middle East-Africa region, Lausanne, Switzerland, 1983-92; counsel Pirenne Python Schifferli Peter & Ptnrs., Geneva, 1993-94; ptnr. McDermott, Will & Emery, Chgo., 1994-96, McFadden, Pilkington & Ward, London, 1997—; of counsel Jackson & Nash, LLP, N.Y.C., 2000—; internat. exec. Assn. Internat. des Etudiants en Sciences Economiques et Commerciales, 1961-66, U.S. gen. counsel, 1977-80. Lt. Security Group Command, USNR, 1968-71. Decorated Navy Achievement medal. Mem. Am. Bar Assn., Assn. Bar City N.Y., Swiss Arbitration Assn., Am. Mgmt. Assn., Internat. Bar Assn., Harvard Club (N.Y.C., Boston). Republican. E-mail: dulles@compuserve.com. Office: Jackson & Nash LLP 330 Madison Ave Fl 18 New York NY 10017-5095

DULLES, JOHN WATSON FOSTER, history educator; b. Auburn, N.Y., May 20, 1913; s. John Foster and Janet Pomeroy (Avery) D.; m. Eleanor Foster Ritter, June 15, 1940; children: Edith, John, Ellen, Avery. AB, Princeton U., 1935; MBA, Harvard U., 1937; BS in Metall. Engring., U. Ariz., 1943, Metall. Engr., 1951. Clk. The Bank of N.Y., N.Y.C., 1937-38; miner Callahan Zinc-Lead Co., Patagonia, Ariz., 1938-41; head ore dept., smelter operator Cia Minera de Peñoles, S.A., Monterrey, Mex., 1943-49, head comml. divsn., 1949-51, asst. gen. mgr., 1951-59, exec. v.p., 1959; v.p. Cia Minera de Peñoles, S.A., Belo Horizonte, Brazil, 1959-62; prof. history U. Ariz., Tucson, 1966-91; univ. prof. L.Am. studies U. Tex., Austin, 1962—; advisor to U.S. delegation to OAS Conf., Vina Del Mar, Chile, 1967; cons. U.S. Dept. State, Bur. Intelligence and Rsch., 1968-72. Author: Yesterday in Mexico, 1961, Vargas of Brazil, 1967, Unrest in Brazil, 1970, Anarchists and Communists in Brazil, 1973, Castello Branco: The Making of a Brazilian President, 1978, President Castello Branco, 1980, Brazilian Communism, 1935-1945, 1983, The São Paulo Law School, 1986, Carlos Lacerda: Brazilian crusader, Vol. 1, 1991, Vol. 2, 1996. Recipient Achievement medal U. Ariz., 1960, Ptnrs. of the Alliance Medal, Brazilian Govt., 1966. Fellow Calif. Inst. Internat. Studies; mem. The Am. Soc. of the Most Venerable Order of the Hosp. of St. John of Jeruslaem (knight), Am. Hist. Assn., Tex. Inst. of Letters, Theta Tau (Alumni Hall of Fame), Inst. History and Geography Brasil. Avocation: tennis. Office: Univ of Texas at Austin PO Box 7934 Austin TX 78713-7934

DULZON, ALFRED ANDREEVITCH, university executive; b. Saratov, USSR, July 31, 1937; s. Andrei Petrovitch and Victoria Iosifovna (Glock) D.; m. Olga Evgenjevna Maltseva; children: Vitali, Andrei. Engr., Poly. U., Tomsk, 1960, D of Engring., 1966, prof. D of Engring., 1993. Lectr. Poly. U., Tomsk, 1960-63, head of dept., 1966-74; dep. dir. High Voltage Rsch. Inst., Tomsk, 1974-82, dir., 1992-93; v.p. Poly. U., Tomsk, 1993—. Author: (books) Lightning Protection of Transmission Lines, 1965, Lightning Protection of Substations, 1970, Overvoltages in 6-35 kV Networks, 1989, Personal Management and Organizational Behavior, 2000; contbr. articles to profl. jours. Recipient Medal for Labor, Govt. USSR, 1970, Inventor of USSR badge USSR State Com. for Inventions and Discoveries, 1980, For Excellent Results badge Ministry of Higher Edn. of USSR, 1986, Order of Honor, Pres. of Russia, 1996, Honored Scientist of Russian Fedn., Pres. of Russia, 2000. Mem. (sr.) IEEE. Fax: 007-3822-415208. E-mail: vizepres@tpu.ru. Office: Tomsk Poly U, 30 Lenin Ave, Tomsk 634034, Russia

DUM, JANE ELIZABETH, psychologist; b. Boston, Mar. 17, 1948; d. James Allan and Roberta Jessey (Campbell) Cochran; m. Christian Thomas Dum, Sept. 9, 1972 (div. Oct. 1998); children: Betsy-Jane, Robert Christian. BS, U. Mass., 1971; MA, U. Chgo., 1974; Dr.rer.nat., Ludwig-Maximilian U., Munich, 1979. Rsch. scientist Max-Planck-Inst., Munich, 1973-80, Inst. for Clni. Psychology, Munich, 1992-93; therapist U.S. Mil., Munich, 1990-92; pvt. practice therapist Munich, 1997—. Mem. APA (internat. affiliate), Bund Deutscher Psychologen. Episcopalian. Office: Prälat-Zistl Str 4, D-80331 Munich Germany

DUMAN, HASAN, information scientist, researcher; b. Antalya, Adigüzel, Turkey, May 1, 1946; s. Mustafa and Havva (Ünsal) D.; m. Canan Aytaçoğlu, May 10, 1969; children: Korkut, Burcu; m. Hüsniye Sacide Öztürk, June 6, 1997. Degree, U. Ankara, Turkey, 1968. Dir. Beyazit State Libr., Istanbul, Turkey, 1977-85; gen. dir. librs. and publications Ministry of Culture, Ankara, Turkey, 1986-90, cons. of minister, 1990-95, pres. dept. pubs., 1997-98; counsellor cultural affairs Embassy of Rep. of Turkey, Cairo, 1996; lectr. U. Gazi, Ankara, Turkey, 1999-2000; v.p. Congress Muslim Librs. and Info. Scientists, Kuala Lumpur/Malesia, 1989-95. Author: Union Catalogue of the Periodicals in Arabic Script in the Libraries of Istanbul, 1986, Cultural Cooperation Between Turkey and Turkic Republics, 1992, International Information and Document Supply Centers, 1993, The Role of Turkey in the World of Manuscripts, 1997, A Bibliography and Union Catalogue of Ottoman Year-Books, 1999-2000, A Bibliography and Union Catalogue of Ottoman-Turkish Serials and Newspapers from the Beginning to the Introduction of the Modern Turkish Alphabet, 1828-1928. Founder, pres. Found. for Info. and Documentation Svcs., Ankara, 1990—. Mem. Turkish Librs. Assn. (branch pres. 1982-84, pres. 1994-95), Turkey Profl. Union of Scientific and Literary Work Owners. Avocations: reading, travel, jogging, gardening. Home: 7 Cad, Kültür Sitesi No 104, 06370 Batikent-Ankara Turkey Office: Found Info & Documentation, 7 Cad Kultur Sitesi No 104, 06370 Ankara Turkey

DUMAS, CHARLES, filmmaker, educator; b. Albany, Ga., Sept. 7, 1945; m. Josephine; children: Allison, Alexandra, Robert, Jonathan. BA, New Paltz Coll., 1975; JD, Yale U., 1978; MA, New Sch. Social Rsch., 1983; Hendler fellow, Am. Film Inst., 1992. Lawyer IBM, 1978-80; pres. Legal Svcs. of Hudson Valley, N.Y., 1979-81, Dumas Enterprise, N.Y.C., 1983-89; exec. dir. Loaves & Fish Traveling Repertory Co., Pa., 1986-89; assoc. prof. Pa. State U., 1995—. Dir., scriptwriter: Up From Slavery, 1990, The Garden, 1994, We are...not quite...Penn State, 1995, 491 St. Mark's Place, 1996, Brother's Keeper, 1997, Surfacing, 1999, TJ and Sally, 2000; actor (movies) Peacemaker, Deep Impact, Copland, Die Hard with a Vengance, Jumpin' Jack Flash; dir. (plays) Uncle Tom's Cabin, Raisin in the Sun. Dem. State Senate candidate, N.Y., 1980. Democrat. Roman Catholic. Office: Pa State Univ Sch Theatre Arts State College PA 16801

DUMAS, MICHAEL GODFREY JOSEPH, artist; b. Whitney, Ont., Can., Sept. 20, 1950; s. Alphyr Adrian and Caroline Anna (Cenzura) D.; m. Ellen Kocsis, July 19, 1975; 1 child, Shae Shannon-Mae. Student, Art Instrn. Sch., Mpls., 1968, Humber Coll., 1970; postgrad., Humber Coll., 1971, Cornell U., 1984. Apprentice to his. painter Lewis Parker Lazare & Parker Studios, 1971-72; adv. bd. mem. Art Impressions mag., 1993-97. Major exhibits include Nat. Mus. Nat. Sci., Ottawa, Ont., 1977, Theodore Roosevelt Inaugural Nat. Hist. Site, Buffalo, N.Y., 1977, McMichael Can. Coll., Kleinburg, Ont., 1981, Royal Botanical Gardens, Hamilton, 1985, R.O.M., 1987-88, Yamanaakako-Takamura Mus. Art, 1991-2000, Mitsukoshi Galleries, Tokyo, 1994-00, Algonquin Gallery, Algonquin Park, Ont., 1995-00, Suntory Mus. Art, Osaka, 1995, Suntory Mus. Art, Tokyo, 1996, Matsuya Gallery, Tokyo, 1997, Sogo Gallery, Osaka, 1997, Yumehodaka Mus., Nagano, 1997, Spanierman Gallery, N.Y., 1998, Mitsukoshi Gallery, Sendai, 1999-00, Cedar Ridge Creative Ctr., Scarborough, 1999; represented in permanent collections including Internat. Mus. Art Inspired By Nature, Gloucester, Eng., Yamanakako-Takamura Mus. Art, Japan; major conservation events include The Spirit of the Wild fundraiser and exhibit, 1982, Kenya Wild Elephant fundraiser, Toronto, 1987, 91, Bird Preservation fundraiser, Osaka, Japan, 1990, Save the Rhino Trust, Namibia, 1998; commd. to design four coins for Royal Can. Mint, 1994, commd. to design Can. commemorative postage stamps; author: Nature in Art, 1991; columnist Angler & Hunter, 1976-83; contbr. articles to mags. Recipient Waterfowl Art award Ducks Unltd., 1983-84, Carling-O'Keefe Profl. Conservation award, 1986, Wildlife Conservation award Ont. Min. Natural Resources, 1987, Bronze Teal Conservation award Ducks Unltd., 1989; named Artist of the Yr., Can. Collector's Clubs, 1987, first winner by competion Wildlife Habitat Can., 1990, Internat. Flyway Artist, Ducks Unltd., Inc., 1992, Artist of the Yr., Ont. Fedn. Anglers and Hunters, 1993-98, Outdoor Card Program award Ont. Ministry of Natural Resources, 1998, Twentieth Century Achievement award Am. Biog. Inst., 2000. Fellow Internat. Biog. Assn. (Eng., life); mem. Soc. Animal Artists, Soc. Wildlife Art of the Nations (charter). Avocations: travel, photography, camping. Address: PO Box 8314 RR 1, Peterborough, ON Canada K9J 6X2

DUMBLETON, DUANE DEAN, college president, educator; b. Shiocton, Wis., May 30, 1939; s. Reginald William and Marguerite Eva (Testin) D.; m. Nancy M. Cavins; children: Laura Layli, Mary Bahiyyih, Rama Ali Sequoyah, Nuriyyih Alexandra, Benjamin Idal. BS, U. Wis., 1962; MA, Syracuse (N.Y.) U., 1969; EdD, U. Ga., 1973. Tchr. geography Hillsborough County Pub. Schs., Tampa, Fla., 1962-63; tchr. English, Geneva (N.Y.) Pub. Schs., 1964-65; tchr. world culture Onondoga County Pub. Schs., Syracuse, 1965-70; tchr. English, Clarke County Pub. Schs., Athens, Ga., 1970-71; mem. faculty Fla. C.C., Jacksonville, 1973—, div. chmn. humanities dept., prof. Asian humanities, edn., 1978-83; campus pres. Fla. Community Coll., Jacksonville, 1988—. Author: Education for American Indians, 1973; contbr. articles to profl. jours. Mem. Jacksonville Cmty. Coun., Inc., 1986—; mem. com., bd. pres. Interfaith Coun., Jacksonville, 1989—; mem. com. Spiritual Assembly of Bahais, Jacksonville, 1974-2000, Pine Castle, Inc., 1994-99, Sister Cities Assn., Jacksonville, 1989-92, Urban Core Citizens Planning Adv. Com. Recipient Svc. award Jacksonville Jaycees, 1978, Jacksonville Bahai Community. Mem. Community Colls. for Internat. Devel. (bd. dirs., sec. 1988-92), Assn. Bahai's Studies, Fla. Assn. Community Colls., Leadership Jacksonville Alumni Assn., Urban League (bd. dirs.). Avocations: writing poetry and essays, public speaking. Home: 526 Los Palmas Dr Ornage Park FL 32003-8207 Office: Fla CC 3939 Roosevelt Blvd Jacksonville FL 32205-8945

DUMERER, LORRAINE JOANNE, social studies educator, clinician; b. Providence, July 10, 1946; d. John and Edith (Flippin) Florio; m. James Edward Dumerer, Nov. 23, 1966; children: James, Marc, Jennifer, Matthew, Paul. Student, Stetson Hill Coll., 1964-66, St. Louis U., 1966; AB, U. Ill., 1969, MAT, 1972; postgrad., Tex. Women's U., 1987-88, U. Tex., Dallas, 1993, So. Meth. U., 1999—. Cert. social studies tchr., Tex. Tchr. Dayton (Ohio) Pub. Schs., 1970-71, St. Benedicts Sch., San Antonio, 1979-80, Incarnate World High Sch., San Antonio, 1980-81, Diocese of Dallas, 1981-88, Dallas Ind. Sch. Dist., 1988-97; dean, chmn. social studies dept. Long Trail Sch., Dorset, Vt., 1997-98; tchr. Carrollton-Farmer's Branch Ind. Sch. Dist., 1998—; coach mock trial teams, 1996—; coach Fed Challenge econs. competition, 1998-2000, North Dallas H.S. CIS-site based team, 1996, 97; mem. R.L. Turner H.S. CIC-site based team, 1999—; clinician Acad. Clin. Svc., Dallas, 1985—; coord. nat. history day Diocese of Dalls, 1985-87; coord. Jane Goodall CHIMP project, 1991; chmn. dept. social studies, student coun. advisor North Dallas H.S., 1993-97; ednl. cons., presenter Specialty Limited English Proficient Integration, Tex. Coun. Social Studies, Advanced Placement Reading Strategies, Cross-grade Level Curriculum Integration; Creating an inclusive AP and Pre-AP Program; participant NEH Inst., 1995, Woodrow Wilson Inst., U. Tex., Dallas, 1993, 94, 1995, Woodrow Wilson Inst., U. Tex. Dallas, 1993, 94; Econs. for Leaders participant Found. for Tchg. Econs., So. Meth. U., 2000. Author: The Dilemma of Ethicial Citizenship for the Political Outsider in American History; author poetry; contbr. chpt., essay and poem Widening the Circle. Referee coord. N.E. Youth Soccer Assn., 1979-80, coach, 1979-80; coach, referee Mesquite Soccer Assn., 1981-86, referee liaison, 1981-82, sec., 1982-83, commr. of coaches, 1982-83. Mellon grantee, 1994; named Tchr. of Yr. Dallas Coun. for Social Studies, 1996. Mem. Nat. Coun. of Social Studies (presenter 1994-2000), Tex. Coun. for Social Studies (sec. Peter's Colony Coun. for social studies 1998-99, v.p. 2000), North Tex. Women's Soccer Assn. (capt. 1989-95), Ctr. for Applied Linguistics (cons. World Culture Project 1996). Avocations: writing, soccer. E-mail: dumererl@cfbisd.edu.; dumererl@earthlink.net. Home: 3535 Misty Meadow Dr Dallas TX 75287-6027

DU MESNIL DU BUISSON, LAURENT, book publisher, educator; b. Paris, Jan. 1, 1952; s. François and Marie Thérèse (de Courcy) du Mesnil du Buisson; m. Béatrice de Blocquel de Croix de Wismes, Jan. 8, 1975; children: Aymeric, Laure, Alexis, Arthur. Diploma, Inst. d'Etudes Politiques, Paris, 1972; Lic. in Law, Paris U., 1973, D in Law with distinction, 1974; MS in Journalism, Syracuse U., 1975. Publs. officer Ctr. African de Formation Rsch. Adminstrv. Devel., Tangier, Morocco, 1976-79; book pub. Dunod, Paris, 1979-82, sr. pub., 1982-85; mgr. Dunod Gauthier Villars, Paris, 1985-90; pres., CEO Maxima Laurent du Mesnil Editeur, Paris, 1990—; tchr. Law Sch. Paris, 1983-94; maitre de conf. Ecole des Hautes Etudes Comml., 1988—, charge de cours, 1985-88. Recipient Fulbright scholarship, 1975. Mem. Soc. du Manoir d'Argentelles Mus. (sec. gen. 1985—), Jockey Club (Paris). Avocation: history. Home: 22 rue de Bourgogne, 75007 Paris France Office: Maxima Laurent du Mesnil, 192 Blvd St Germain, 75007 Paris France

DUMIČIĆ, KSENIJA, statistics educator; b. Zaprešić, Croatia, Sept. 7, 1956; d. Radoslav and Vera (Cirkveni) Frankić; m. Srdan Dumičić, Oct. 6, 1979; children: Mirna, Dinka. BA in Econs., U. Zagreb, Croatia, 1979, MA in Econs., 1985, PhD in Econs., 1992. Market rschr. Josip Kraš, Zagreb, 1979-81; rsch. asst. faculty econs. U. Zagreb, 1981-96, asst. prof., 1996-2000, assoc. prof., 2000—; cons. Ctrl. Bur. Stats., Zagreb, 1991-97, PULS-Rsch. Agy., Split, Croatia, 1993—; expert in stats. UNESCO, 1996-98;. Co-author: Methodology of Scientific Research, 1999; contbr. articles to profl. jours. Mem. IASS, ESOMAR, Operational Rsch. Croatian Soc. Avocations: English, music, cooking, Silva method, network marketing. Office: Faculty Econs, Trg J F Kennedy 6, 10000 Zagreb Croatia

DUMITRESCU, CONSTANTIN P., internist; b. Ulmi, Dambovita, Romania, Sept. 2, 1929; s. Petre G. and Ana I. (Andreescu) D.; m. Viorica J. Tetu, Aug. 28, 1954; 1 child. MD, U. Medicine, Bucharest, Romania, 1954, PhD, 1968. Gen. practice medicine Bezdead, Romania, 1954-59; asst. U. Medicine, Bucharest, 1959-62, asst. prof., 1962-75, assoc. prof., 1975-91, prof. medicine, 1991—; cons. in internal medicine and diabetes, Bucharest, 1959-91; chief physician Diabetes Clinic, M. Malaxa Hosp., Bucharest, 1991—; vice dean Post Univ. Faculty of Medicine, Bucharest, 1970-72. Contbr. over 413 articles to profl. jours.; author 15 books including: How to Treat Excess and Shortness of Weight, 1974, Practical Basis of Prophylactic and Curative Dietetic Nutrition, 1987 (Victor Babes prize of Romanian Acad. 1990), Citoprotection and alimentation, 1991, Diabetes and Pregnancy, 1991. Capt. Romanian Mil. Mem. Romanian Assn. for Study of Obesity (1st pres. 1991-97), Romanian Assn. for Study of Diabetes, European Assn. for Study of Diabetes, European Assn. for Study of Obesity. Home: Paris St 59A, 71249 Bucharest Romania Office: Clinic Hosp N Malaxa, Sos Vergului 12, Bucharest II Romania

DUMITRESCU, MICHEL PAUL, aerospace researcher; b. Bucharest, Dec. 6, 1954; s. Lucien Z. and Lucia (Droc) D.; m. Cecile Brun, June 21, 1993; 1 child, Mélisande Hélène Mathilde. Diplomate engr., Polytech. Inst. Bucharest, 1981; PhD, U. Provence, 1994. Engr. Helicopter Plant, Brasov, Romania, 1981-82, TAROM, Bucharest, 1982; sr. engr. Aeronautical Inst., Bucharest, 1983-91; engr. Nat. Scientific Rsch. Ctr., Marseilles, France, 1995—; mem. adv. com. Shock Waves Symposia, 1996, scientific coms., 1996. Contbr. articles to profl. jours. Mem. AIAA (sr.), Soc. Automotive Engrs.-Aerospace. Home: 3 rue de l'Eglise, 83910 Pourrieres France Office: U Provence Ctr St Jerome, Escadrile Normandie Nieman, 13397 Marseille France

DUMITRU, RODICA STĂNESCU, chemist, researcher; b. Cîmpina, Prahova, Romania, July 22, 1949; d. Ion and Elena (Popa) D.; m. Constantin Stanescu; 1 child. Physicist-Chemist, U. Bucharest, Romania, 1972, PhD in Chemistry, 1995. Chemist Inst. Pub. Health, Bucharest, Romania, 1972-79, rschr., 1979—; cons. Inst. of Pub. Health, Bucharest, Romania, 1985-90. Author: (book); contbr. articles to profl. jours. Grantee: Colloquim Spectros Internat., York, Eng., 1993, 22d European Congress on Molecular Spectroscopy, Essen, Germany, 1994, Internat. Congress on Occupational Health, Stockholm, Sweden, 1996, WHO, Budapest, 1997. Mem. Ea. Orthodox Ch. Avocations: travel, reading. Home: Bl A4, Sc B, Apt 25, V Oltului Str No 6, 77422 Bucharest Romania Office: Inst Pub Health, 1-3 Dr Leonte Str, 76256 Bucharest Romania

DUMMETT, SIR MICHAEL ANTHONY EARDLEY, philosopher, educator; b. June 27, 1925; s. George Herbert and Iris (Eardley-Wilmot) D.; m. Ann Chesney, 1951; 5 children (2 dec.). Ed., Christ Ch., Oxford; PhD (hon.), U. Nijmegen, 1983; LittD, Oxford, 1989; LittD (hon.), U. Caen, 1993, U. Aberdeen, 1993. Asst. lectr. philosophy Birmingham U., 1950-51; Commonwealth Fund fellow U. Calif., Berkeley, 1955-56; reader in philosophy of math. U. Oxford, 1962-74; fellow All Souls Coll., Oxford, 1950-79, sr. rsch. fellow, 1974-79, sub-warden, 1974-76, emeritus fellow, 1980; Wykeham prof. logic U. Oxford, 1979-92; fellow New Coll., Oxford, 1979-92; hon. fellow New Coll., 1998; vis. lectr. U. Ghana, 1958; vis. prof. Stanford U., 1964, 66, U. Minn., 1968, Princeton U., 1970, Rockefeller U., 1973; William James lectr. in philosophy Harvard U., 1976; founder mem. Oxford Com. for Racial Integration, 1965, chmn., 1966; mem. exec. com. Campaign Against Racial Discrimination, 1966-67; mem. legal and civil affairs panel Nat. Com. for Commonwealth Immigrants, 1966-68; chmn. Joint Coun. for Welfare of Immigrants, 1970-71. Author: Frege: Philosophy of Language, 1973, 2d edit., 1981, The Justification of Deduction, 1973, Elements of Intuitionism, 1977, rev. edit., 2000, Truth and Other Enigmas, 1978, Immigration: Where the Debate Goes Wrong, 1978, Catholicism and the World Order, 1979, The Game of Tarot, 1980, Twelve Tarot Games, 1980, The Interpretation of Frege's Philosophy, 1981, Voting Procedures, 1984, The Visconti-Sforza Tarot Cards, 1986, Ursprünge der Analytischen Philosophie, 1987, rev. English edit., 1993, Frege and Other Philosophers, 1991, The Logical Basis of Metaphysics, 1991, Frege: Philosophy of Mathematics, 1991, Grammar and Style, 1993, The Seas of Language, 1993, Il Mondo e l'Angelo, 1993, I Tarocchi Siciliani, 1995, (with R. Decker and T. Depaulis) A Wicked Pack of Cards, 1996, Principles of Electoral Reform, 1996; contbr. articles to profl. jours. Knighted, 1999; recipient von Humboldt prize, 1982, Lakatos Philosophy of Sci. award London Sch. Econs., 1994, Rolf Shock Philosophy and Logic prize, 1995. Fellow Brit. Acad.; mem. Am. Acad. Arts and Scis. (hon. fgn.), Academia Europaea. Home: 54 Park Town, Oxford OX2 6SJ, England

DUMOND, ROBERT WILFRED, mental health consultant, lay pastoral worker; b. Lawrence, Mass., Nov. 1, 1952; s. Wilfred Albert and Claire Marie (Dumas) D.; m. Doris Ann Cocchiaro, May 1, 1976; children: Amy Marie, Matthew Christian, Claire Elizabeth. BA in Psychology, U. Mass., 1974; MA in Counseling Psychology, Assumption Coll., Worcester, Mass., 1982. Lic. cert. social worker, Mass.; lic. mental health counselor, Mass.; cert. rape investigator, Mass.; lic. clin. mental health counselor, N.H.; lic. marriage and family therapist, Mass.; lic. rehab. counselor, Mass.; cert. justice of peace, N.H., 1988—; nat. cert. counselor Am. Acad. Cert. Clin.

Mental Health Counselors; cert. trainer prison fellowship, 1998—. Child care counselor St. Anne's Home, Inc., Methuen, Mass., 1971-74; dir. region IV The Key Program, Inc. (formerly Cmty. Advancement Program), Lawrence, 1974-79; dir. victim/witness assistance program Commonwealth of Mass., Essex County Dist. Atty's Office, Lawrence, 1979-83, Haverhill, 1983-87; mem. continuing edn. faculty Franklin Pierce Coll., Salem, N.H., 1984—; prin. psychologist Commonwealth of Mass. Dept. Correction, Concord, 1987-91; mental health clinician EMSA Correctional Care, Inc., various cities, Mass., 1992-94; mental health adminstr. Correctional Med. Svcs., Inc., Gardner, Mass., 1994-95; vol. mental health cons., educator Roman Cath. Diocese of Manchester, N.H., 1997—, State of N.H., Concord, 1997—; pastoral/correctional liaison Roman Cath. Diocese of Manchester and State of N.H. Dept. of Corrections, 1997—; v.p., bd. dirs. C'ESTA, Inc., Manchester, 1995—; cons. Safer Soc. Program and Press, Orwell, Vt., 1992-94, Fed. Emergency Mgmt. Agy., Boston, 1991-92; mem., provider Dept. Mental Health, Cmty. Mental Health and Retardation Area Bd., Lawrence, 1981-83; cons., faculty mem. Nat. Coun. on Crime and Delinquency, Hackensack, N.J., 1980-82; cons. City of Hartford, Conn., 1976; gov.'s appointee N.H. State Rehab. Coun., Concord, 1998—; mem. N.H. HIV Prevention Cmty. Planning Group, Concord, 1998—; sr. lectr. divsn. Grad. and Profl. Studies Franklin Pierce Coll., N.H., 1998—. Contbr. articles to profl. jours. and tng. manuals; contbg. author manuals, resource handbooks, ednl. audiotapes. Pastoral care vol. St. Joseph's Hosp., Nashua, N.H., 1997—; bd. dirs. Lazarus Ho. Ministries, Inc., Lawrence, 1986-89, Family Svcs. Assn. Greater Lawrence, Inc., 1982-84, Mental Health and Retardation Svcs., Inc., Lawrence, 1981-83, N.H. Brain Injury Assn., 1997—; mem. human rights com. Area Agy. for Developmental Disability, Nashua, 1997—; disability rights advocate U. N.H. Inst. Disabilities, Concord, 1997—; mem. steering com. Citizens for Discipline in the Schs., Hudson, N.H., 1995-97; participant, panelist, profl. expert various confs., commns., and pub. hearings, in areas of juvenile justice, prison sexual assault, prison conditions, child abuse, and violent crime; mem. No. Essex (N.H.) Com. Against Sexual Assault, 1985-87, co-chair, 1986-87; pres. Mass. Dept. Social Svcs. Area Bd. #12, 1980-81; mem. Mass. Office for Children Statewide Adv. Coun., 1975-77; pres. Greater Lawrence Coun. for Children, 1975-76; vol. coord. prison ministries Roman Cath. Diocese Manchester, N.H., 1998—. Recipient Beyond Excellence Recognition award, Commr. Mass. Dept. Correction, Boston, 1990, Liberty Bell award for Outstanding Cmty. Svc., Lawrence Bar Assn., 1976. Mem. APA (assoc. mem., chair symposium 103rd conf. and session 98th conf. 1990 divsn. 18 criminal justice sect.), Nat. Assn. Cath. Chaplains (student mem.), Acad. Criminal Justice Scis. (roundtable convenor 1995, workshop panelist 1992), Am. Acad. Psychiatric Svcs. to Children (presenter 36th and 37th Ann. Confs., 1985, 86), Nat. Orgn. Victim Assistance (presenter Ann. Conf. 1981, nominated to U.S. Dept. Justice Symposium 1984), The Perspectives Network, Inc., New England Assn. Child Care (presenter 1975 spring and fall meetings), New Hampshire Brain Injury Assn., Knights of Columbus (coun. 5162, officer 1998—, dep. grand knight 1999—, 4th degree mem., youth dir. 1997—, Knight of Yr. 1997). Roman Catholic. Avocations: playing guitar, Biblical archeology, antiquarian books, on-line computing, writing. E-mail: rwdumond@aol.com. Home: 27 Baker St Hudson NH 03051-3606

DUMONT, BRUNO, film director; b. Lille, 1958. MPhil. Dir. La Vie De Jesus, 1996 (Spl. Mention for Camera d'Or, Prix Jean Vigo, Prix du Tournage at Avignon, FIPRESCI Internat. Critics prize Chgo., Palmera d'Oro at Valence, Internat. Critics award at Sao Paulo, Sutherland Trophy for Best Feature Film at London, Fassbinder award, Best First Film at Alexandria, Prix Arsenals at Riga, Discovery of the Yr. citation European Film Awards), L'Humanité, 1999. Office: Tadrart Films, 83 A rue Bobillot, 75013 Paris France

DUMONT, EDWARD ABDO, architect, interior designer; b. Bklyn., July 4, 1961. AA, Miami Dade Community Coll.; BArch, U. Fla., 1984. Designer Paul, Paul and Madrid Architects, Houston, 1984-87; project mgr. William Crosskey and Assocs. Architects, Hartford, Conn., 1987-89, Brand Allen Architects, Houston, 1989-98, Gensler-Houston, 1998-99; with Gotsdiner Archs., Houston, 1999—. Mem. Rice Design Alliance, Tex. Soc. Interior Designers, Mus. Fine Arts Houston, U. Fla. Nat. Alumni Assn. Avocations: art, photography, furniture design. Home: 4412 Effie St Bellaire TX 77401-5617 Office: Gotsdiner Archs 5712 Val Verde St Ste 200 Houston TX 77057-5829

DUMONT, IVY L., government official; b. Rose's, L.I., Bahamas, Oct. 2, 1930; married; 2 children. Tchrs. Cert., Bahamas Tchrs. Tng. Coll., 1954; EdB, U. Miami, Fla., 1970; MPA, Nova U., 1977, D in Pub. Adminstrn., 1978. Tchr., head tchr., then dep. dir. edn. Min. of Edn. and Culture, Nassau, 1948-75; dep. permanent sec. Min. of Works and Utilities, Nassau, 1975-78; mgr. Roy West Trust Corp., 1978-90; apptd. senator and min. health and environment Govt. Bahamas, 1992-95; min. edn. and tng. Govt. Bahamas, Nassau, 1995—. Mem. Free Nat. Movement. Office: Ministry of Edn, Shirley St PO B N-3913, Nassau Bahamas also: PO Box SS-5316, Farrington Rd, Nassau Bahamas*

DUMONTIER, CHRISTIAN ALAIN, physician, consultant; b. Pau, France, June 24, 1959; s. Paul and Nicole (Goureau) D.; m. Isabelle Cecile Perret Dumontier, May 22, 1987; children: Marine, Arthur, Jolann. MD, Necker, Paris, 1987. Med. student Faculté de Médecine, Paris, 1976-82; resident Orthopedic and Gen. Surgery Paris, 1982-87; fellow Plastic and Reconstructive Surgery, Nancy, France, 1987-88, Orthopedic Surgery, Paris, 1988-90; cons. Orthopedic Surgery Paris, 1992—, pvt. practice, 1990—; cons. Transplantation of Organs, France, 1999; peer reviewer, Revue de Chirurgie Orthopedique and La Main. Editor: Surgery of the Nail, 1999; contbr. articles to profl. jours. Gen. sec. Syndicate of Orthopedic Surgeons, 1997-99; pres. Syndicate of Hand Surgeons, 1997-99. Avocations: tennis, racquet squash, art, philosophy. Home phone: (331) 43 06 58 55. Home: 1 Rue de Stael, 75015 Paris France Office: Inst de la Main, 6 Square Jouvenet, 75016 Paris France

DUMONTIER, CLARISSA W., lawyer; b. Jefferson City, Mo., Apr. 13, 1957; d. James Albert and Ann Marguerite (Dyer) W.; m. Bruce John DuMontier, July 19, 1980; children: Benjamin John, Clark William. BS in Edn., U. Mo., 1977, JD, 1982. Bar: U.S. Dist. Ct. (we. dist.) Mo. 1982. Assoc. atty. Harlan, Harlan, and Still, Boonville, Columbia, Mo., 1982-84; asst. pros. atty. Cooper County, Mo., 1986-2000, Howard County, Fayette, Mo., 1994-2000, Randolph County, Moberly, Mo., 1994-2000, Chariton County, Keytesville, Mo., 1994-2000; mem. Child Support Adv. Com. Child Support Enforcement divsn., Jefferson City, 1991-94, Child Support Guidelines Com. Mo. Supreme Ct., Jefferson City, 1993, Pros. Atty's. Adv. Com. Child Support Enforcement divsn., Jefferson City, 1998-2000, Change Ctl. bd. Child Support Enforcement, Jefferson City, 1999-2000. Chmn. Mo. River Festival Arts, Boonville, 1993-94; pres. SS. Peter and Paul Home and Sch., Boonville, 1997-98. Mem. Mo. Child Support Enforcement Assn. (cert. appreciation), Cooper County Bar Assn. (treas. 1992, 98, v.p. 1998-2000, pres. 2000—). Republican. Roman Catholic. Avocations: piano, watercolor painting, writing, being a church organist. Office: Pros Atty Child Support Divsn 613 N Valley Dr Boonville MO 65233-1874

DUMORTIER, JACQUELINE BIBAUW, scientific publications administrator; b. Anvers, Belgium, Aug. 24, 1941; d. Robert and Suzanne (Sestier-Civet) Bibauw; m. Michel Dumortier; 1 child, Emmanuelle. MA in Philosophy and Lit., U. Brussels, 1963. Scientific rschr. Nat. Found. Scientific Rsch., Brussels, 1964-69; adminstrv. mgr., sub-mgr. books Soc. Latin Studies, Brussels, 1982—. Avocations: photography, frames, genealogy.

DUMORTIER, RENAUD, plastic surgeon; b. Tourcoing, Nord, France, Jan. 24, 1968. 1st Med. Degree, U. Lille, France, 1988, MD, 1999. Tng. in microsurgery, craniofacial surgery, esthetic surgery; mem. staff plastic surgery svc. Hosp. Roger Salengro, Lille, France, 2000—. Contbr. articles to med. jours., including European Jour. Plastic Surgery, Jour. Craniofacial Surgery. Home: 14 Sq du Ramponneau, 59800 Lille France Office: Hosp Roger Salengro, Pl Marechal Leclerq, 59037 Lille France

DUMOULIÉ, CAMILLE MARC, education educator; b. Nogaro, Gers, France, Oct. 29, 1955; s. Louis Dumoulié and Giselle Junca. State D, Sorbonne, Paris, 1989. Tchr. secondary schs., France, 1981-88; lectr. Dijon U., France, 1988-91; prof. Stasbourg U., France, 1991-96, Paris X-U., France, 1996—. Author: Nietzsche and Artaud, 1992, Don Juan or the Heroism of Desire, 1993, This Obscure Object of Desire, 1995, Antonin Artaud, 1996, The Desire, 1999. Home: 48 Rue Faubourg St Martin, Paris 75010 1, France Office: U Paris X 200, Ave de la Republique 92001, Nanterre Cedex 1, France

DUMOULIN, MICHEL MARCEL ÉTIENNE ÉMILE, history educator; b. Uccle, Brussels, Belgium, Oct. 2, 1950; s. Marcel Dumoulin and Hélène Schnorrenberg; m. Annie Leblanc, Sept. 28, 1974; children: François, Victoria. Student, Coll. St. Vincent, Soignies, Faculty Univ. St.-Louis, Brussels; PhD in History, U. Cath. de Louvain, Belgium, 1981. Rsch. asst. Belgian Hist. Inst., Rome, 1975-76; rsch. fellow Belgian Nat. Fund for Sci. Rsch., 1977-81; asst. Cath. U. Louvain, Belgium, 1981-87; first asst., lectr. Cath. U. Louvain, 1987-90, prof., 1991—; vis. prof. Inst. for European Studies, Strasbourg, France, 1986—. Author: Les Relations Italo-Belges, 1861-1914, 1991, Racines du Futur, vol. 4, 1993 (Eugène Lameere prize 1995), Paul van Zeeland (1893-1973), 1997, Spaak, 1999; editor Historians of Contemporary Europe, 1986—. Gen. sec. European Cmty. Liaison Com. Historians, Luxembourg, 1988—; pres. European Cmty. Studies Assn.-Belgium, Brussels, 1991—. Jean Monnet chair in history European Cmty., 1991; Jacques Delors grantee Fundacion de Yuste, Spain, 1996. Mem. Royal Acad. for Overseas History Hist. Commn., Inst. for European Studies (pres. 1994—). Home: Ave de l Observatoire 30, B-1180 Brussels Belgium Office: Inst d études Européennes, Place des Doyens 1, B-1348 Louvain-la-Neuve Belgium

DUNAIEF, LEAH S., newspaper editor, publisher, writer; b. N.Y.C., Aug. 21, 1940; d. Rudolph and Mollie Salmansohn; m. Ivan F. Dunaief, Feb. 24, 1963; children: Joshua, Daniel, David. BA, Barnard Coll., 1962; MBA, Columbia U., 1982. Writer, rschr. Time Inc., N.Y.C., 1963-67; founder, editor, pub. Village Times, Setauket, N.Y., 1976—, now pres., chmn. bd.; founder, editor, pub. North Shore Homes, 1978, Village Beacon, Rocky Point, N.Y., 1986—, St. James (N.Y.) Times, 1988—, Port Times, Port Jefferson, N.Y., 1989—, Times of Smithtown, N.Y., 1993—, Times of Nesconset, 1993, Port Jefferson Record, 1994—, North Shore Record, 1994, Prime Times, "For Those Who Weren't Born Yesterday", 1995, Parent Connection, 1998. Contbr. N.Y. Times, Time-Life Sci. Libr.; contbr., pub. Women's Bar News of State of N.Y. Active Spkr. Stanley Fink's Small Bus. Commn. for L.I., Congressman Mrazek's Women's Issues Com.; assoc. trustee Dowling Coll., Oakdale, N.Y.; edn. com. Mus. at Stony Brook; bd. dirs. Stony Brook Found. Realty, SUNY; adv. bd. W. Averill Harriman Coll. Policy Analysis and Pub. Mgmt. SUNY at Stony Brook; chmn. adv. com. Barnard Mag. Barnard Coll., Columbia U.; v.p. Three Village C. of C.; dir. Coun. Dedicated Mchts., Miller Pl. Recipient media awards for state and nat. press assns. including more than 300 awards for Journalistic Excellence N.Y. Press Assn., 1976, Proclamation of N.Y. State Senate, 2000; named Woman of Yr. in Comms., Town of Brookhaven, 1987, Honoree of Yr., Greater Port Jefferson Arts Coun., 1997, Miller Place-Mt. Sinai Hist. Soc., 2000, Proclamation of County of Suffolk, 2000. Mem. N.Y. Press Assn. (pres. 1984-85, 3rd pl. Best Column award 1994, 2nd pl. Best Column award 1995, ex-officio mem. bd. dirs.), Nat. Newspaper Assn. (state chmn. 1982—, 1st pl. award for investigative reporting 1985), L.I. Press Club (1st pl. award for best weekly column 1987). Office: Village Times Box 707 185 Route 25A Setauket NY 11733-2946

DUNAS, ETIENNE, space industry executive; b. Colombes, France, Jan. 18, 1957; d. Gerard and Madeleine (Guieau) D.; m. Ghislaine, 1983 (div. 1997); children: Florian, Vincent; m. Annick Le Garrec, May 22, 1999. M in Elec., U. Bordeaux, 1975, PhD, 1980. Tech. support mgr. Feutrier, Paris, 1982-84; software cons. Serita, Toulouse, France, 1984-87; from software devel. mgr. to tech. mgr. Alcatel Space Industries, Toulouse, 1987—.

DUNAWAY, BRIDGET, lawyer; b. London, Ky., Sept. 8, 1962; d. Daniel Keith and Jewell D. BA, Ea. Ky. U., 1984; JD, U. Ky., 1989. Bar: Ky. Ins. adjuster, 1984-89; assoc. Taylor, Kellery & Dunaway, London, Ky., 1989-91, ptnr., 1991—. Bd. dirs. Ky. Def. Counsel, 1995-99; mem. Cmty. Band and Orchestra, 1996—. Mem. Ky. Bar Assn. for Women (bd. dirs. 1994—). Avocations: music, softball, tennis. Office: Taylor Keller & Dunaway PLC 1306 W 5th St London KY 40741-1615

DUNBAR, MAURICE VICTOR, English language educator; b. Banner, Okla., May 24, 1928; s. Moyer Haywood and Louise Edna (Curry) D.; m. Carol Ann Cline, July 28, 1948 (div. 1963); children: Kurt, Karl, Karla, Karen, Kristen. AA, Compton Jr. Coll., 1948; BA, U. Calif., Berkeley, 1952; MA, Calif. State U., Sacramento, 1965. Tchr. elem. sch. Lone Tree Sch., Beale AFB, Calif., 1962-64; tchr. jr. high sch. Anna McKenney, Marysville, Calif., 1964-66; tchr. high sch. Yuba City (Calif.) High Sch., 1966-67; instr. jr. coll. Foothill Coll., Los Altos Hills, Calif., 1967-82; prof. English De Anza Coll., Cupertino, Calif., 1982-98; ret., 1998. Author: Fundamentals of Book Collecting, 1976, Books and Collectors, 1980, Collecting Steinbeck, 1983, Hooked on Books, 1997; contbr. articles to profl. jours. With U.S. Army, 1948-58, PTO. Mem. Masons, Shriners (orator, librarian San Jose Scottish Rite Temple, 1982—), K.C.C.H., Scottish Rite, B'nai B'rith. Avocations: book collecting, reading, travel, vis. univ. campuses.

DUNCAN, CHARLES HOWARD, business education educator; b. Tarentum, Pa., Jan. 11, 1924; s. James Boyd and A. Elizabeth (Wilson) D.; m. Mary Jane Ferrier, Nov. 23, 1954; children—Betsy Ann, Laurel Ann. B.S., Indiana (Pa.) U., 1950; M.Ed., U. Pitts., 1954, Ed.D., 1959; Litt.D. (hon.), Geneva Theol. Coll., 1979. Asst. dir. Franklin Comml. Coll., Connellsville, Pa., 1950-52; tchr. Butler (Pa.) Sr. High Sch., 1952-54; instr. U. Pitts., 1954-59; prof. Indiana (Pa.) U., 1959-65, Eastern Mich. U., Ypsilanti, 1965-85; prof. emeritus Eastern Mich. U., 1965, head dept. bus. edn., 1965-75. Author: College Typewriting, 1964, 13th edit., 1993; services editor typewriting: Business Education Forum, 1968-70. Vol. instr. Wayne County Econ. Opportunity Com.; lay chairperson 9th dist. Mich. Synod Lutheran Ch. in Am., 1977; trustee Geneva Theol. Coll., Maggie Valley, N.C., 1979-82. Served with USNR, 1943-47. Recipient certificate of appreciation Wayne County Econ. Opportunity Com., 1968. Mem. Nat. Bus. Edn. Assn., Eastern Bus. Edn. Assn., Tri-State Bus. Edn. Assn., Pa. Bus. Edn. Assn. (past treas.), Mich. Bus. Edn. Assn. (past publicity dir.), Delta Pi Epsilon. Home: 2245 Valley Dr Ypsilanti MI 48197-4355

DUNCAN, DORIS GOTTSCHALK, information systems educator; b. Seattle, Nov. 19, 1944; d. Raymond Robert and Marian (Onstad) D.; m. Robert George Gottschalk, Sept. 12, 1971 (div. Dec. 1983). BA, U. Wash., Seattle, 1967, MBA, 1968; PhD, Golden Gate U., 1978. Cert. data processor, systems profl., computer profl., data educator. Comm. cons. Pacific N.W. Bell Tel. Co., Seattle, 1968-71; mktg. supr. AT&T, San Francisco, 1971-73; sr. cons., project leader Quantum Sci. Corp., Palo Alto, Calif., 1973-75; dir. co. analysis program Input Inc., Palo Alto, 1975-76; lectr. acctg. and info. systems Calif. State U., Hayward, 1976-78, assoc. prof., 1978-85, prof., 1985—, coord. computer info. sys., 1994-97; dir. info. sci. dept. Golden Gate U., San Francisco, 1982-83, mem. info. systems adv. bd., 1983-85; cons. pvt. cos., 1975—; vis. prof. U. Wash., Seattle, 1997-98; spkr. profl. groups and confs. Author: Computers and Remote Computing Services, 1983; contbr. articles to profl. jours.; mem. editl. rev. bd. Jour. Info. Systems Edn., 1992-97. Loaned exec. United Good Neighbors, Seattle, 1969; nat. com. woman bd. dirs. Young Reps., Wash., 1970-71; advisor Jr. Achievement, San Francisco, 1971-72; mem. nat. bd. Inst. for Certification of Computer Profls. Edn. Found., 1990-93; bd. dirs. Computer Repair Svcs., 1992-94. Recipient Disting. Rsch. award Allied Acads., 1999; named Computer Educator of Yr., Internat. Assn. Computer Info. Systems, 1997. Mem. Data Processing Mgmt. Assn. (Meritorious Svc. award, Bronze award 1984, Silver award 1986, Gold award 1988, Emerald award 1992, Diamond award 1994, Double Diamond award 1999, Nat. grantee, 1984, dir. edn. chmn. San Francisco chpt. 1984-85, sec. and v.p. 1985, pres. 1986, assn. dir. 1987, bylaws chmn. 1987, chair awards com. 1992-95, nat. bd. dirs. spl. interest group in edn. 1985-87), Am. Inst. Decision Scis., Western Assn. Schs. and Colls. (accreditation evaluation team 1984-85), Assn. Computing Machinery, Jr. Club of Seattle (Beautiful Home award Foster City 1994, 95, winner Tournament of Christmas Lights 1996), Bus. Honor Soc., Beta Gamma Sigma. Achievements include subspecialties: Information systems (information science). Current work: curriculum development, professional certification, industry standards, computer literacy and user education, system analysis and design, design of databases and data banks, electronic commerce. Office: Calif State U Sch Bus & Econs Hayward CA 94542

DUNCAN, ELIZABETH CHARLOTTE, marriage and family therapist, educational therapist, educator; b. L.A., Mar. 10, 1919; d. Frederick John de St. Vrain and Nellie Mae (Goucher) Schwankovsky; m. William McConnell Duncan, Oct. 12, 1941 (div. 1949); 1 child, Susan Elizabeth Duncan St. Vrain. BA, Calif. State U., Long Beach, 1953; MA, UCLA, 1962; PhD, Internat. Coll., 1984. Cert. marriage and family therapist; cert. clin. psychopathologist, Wash. Dir. gifted program Palos Verdes (Calif.) Sch. Dist., 1958-64; TV tchr., participant ednl. films Los Angeles County, 1961-64; dir. U. So. Calif. Presch., L.A., 1965-69, Abraham Maslow rsch. assoc., 1962-69; pvt. practice family counseling Malibu, Ventura, Eastsound, Seattle, Calif., Wash., 1979—; pvt. practice psychotherapy West Seattle, 1994—; psychotherapist Children's Program North Sound Regional Support Network, 1992; resident psychologist for film series Something Personal, 1987—; mem. Rsch. Inst. of Scripps Cliic, La Jolla, Calif.; charter mem. Inst. Behavioral Medicine, Santa Barbara, Calif.; pub. spkr., lectr. comm.; cons. in field. TV performer in documentary The Other Side, 1985; creator: Persephone's Child, 1988. Active Chrysalis Ctr., L.A., 1984-86; mem. Ventura County Mental Health Adv. Bd., 1985-86, United Way, L.A., 1985-92; mem. Menninger Found. San Juan County, Wash., 1992; mem. adv. bd. North Sound Regional Support Network, 1992, Amb.'s People to People, San Juan County Network, 1998-00. Recipient Emmy award for best documentary Am. Acad. TV Arts and Scis., 1976; named Child Adv. of Yr., Calif. Mental Health Adv. Bd., 1987. Mem. AACD (Disting. Svc. award 1990), Transpersonal Psychol. Assn., Calif. State Orgn. Gifted Edn. (sec. 1962-64), Internat. Platform Assn., Am. Assn. for Marriage and Family Therapy (supr. licenses). Democrat. Avocations: swimming, plays, concerts, boating, political issues, especially women and child abuse.

DUNCAN, GEORGE, chemicals executive, accountant; b. Nov. 9, 1933; s. William D. and Catherine (Gray) Murray; m. Frauke Ulrike Schnuhr, 1965; 1 child. BS in Econs., London Sch. Econs.; MBA, U. Pa. Chartered acct. Ceo Truman Hanbury Buxton and Co. Ltd., 1967-71, Watney Mann Ltd., 1971-72; vice chmn. Internat. Distillers and Vintners Ltd., 1972; chmn. Lloyds Bowmaker Fin. Ltd. (formerly Lloyds and Scottish plc), 1976-86; dir. Lloyds Bank Plc, 1982-87; dir. Laporte plc, London, 1987—, chmn., 1995—; bd. dirs. City of London Trust PLC, Assoc. Brit. Ports PLC, Calor Group. Mem. European Advtsg. Bd., Freeman (City of London), Brook's. Avocations: opera, golf. Office: Nations House, 103 Wigmore St, London W1H 9AB, England*

DUNCAN, IAIN JEFFREY, physician; b. Dundee, Scotland, Aug. 30, 1960; arrived in Australia, 1970; s. William David and Jean Jeffrey (Anderson) D.; m. Fiona Rubin Neave, May 28, 1983; children: Kate, Emily, Nicholas. BM, Sydney U., 1983, BS, 1983. Resident Royal North Shore Hosp., Sydney, 1983-85; med. registrar Canberra Hosp., Australia, 1985-87; sr. registrar The Queen Elizabeth Hosp., Adelaide, Australia, 1988-89; rheumatologist The Canberra Hosp., Australia, 1990—, dir. rheumatology, 1995-99; cons. nuclear medicine & ultrasound Canberra Imaging Group, 1999—; dir. physician tng. Canberra Hosp., 1992-97. Contbr. articles to profl. jours. Westminster Sch. scholar, Adelaide, 1972. Mem. Royal Australian Coll. Physicians (chmn. 1994-96), Australasian Soc. Ultrasound Medicine (chmn. 1998—), Australian & New Zealand Soc. Nuclear Medicine, Australian Rheumatology Assn. (concillor 1995-99). Avocations: skiing, golf. Office: PO Box 79, Garran 2605, Australia

DUNCAN, ROBERT ALLAN, astronomer; b. Adelaide, Australia, June 11, 1929; s. Allan Petrie and Norma Elisabeth (McLean) D.; m. Rosslyn Marie Sorensen, Feb. 6, 1967; children: Emma Louise, Michael Robert. BSc with 1st class honors, U. Adelaide, 1953, DSc, 1965. Technician Inst. of Med. and Vet. Scis., Adelaide, 1945; rsch. officer upper atmosphere sect. CSIRO, Sydney, 1953-69; prin. rsch. scientist divsn. of math. and statis. CSIRO, Adelaide, 1970-73; prin. rsch. sci. Australia Telescope Nat. Facility, Sydney, 1973—; rsch. fellow Nat. Bus. of Stds., Boulder, Colo., 1961-62; vis. scientist High Altitude Observatory, Boulder, 1981-82. Contbr. articles to profl. jours. Mem. Willoughby Symphony choir and orch.; music libr., 1995-99. Fellow Australian Inst. of Physics, Astronomical Soc. Australia (newsletter editor 1986-98); mem. Internat. Astronomical Union. Avocations: backpacking, skiing, skating, choral singing. Office: Australia Telescope Nat, PO Box 76, Epping 2121, Australia

DUNCAN, ROBERT BANNERMAN, strategy and organizations educator; b. Milw., July 4, 1942; s. Robert Lynn and Irene (Hoenig) D.; m. Susan Jean Phillips, June 12, 1965; children: Stephanie Olcott, Christopher Robert. BA, Ind. U., 1964, MA, 1966; PhD, Yale U., 1971. Asst. prof. Northwestern U. Kellogg Grad. Sch. Mgmt., Evanston, Ill., 1970-73, assoc. prof. orgn. behavior, 1973-76, prof., 1976, Earl Dean Howard prof. orgn. behavior, 1980-83, J.L. Kellogg disting. prof. strategy and orgns., 1983-86, 92—, J. Allen disting. prof. strategy and orgns., 1986-89; Richard L. Thomas prof. leadership orgnl. change Northwestern U., Evanston, 1996—; assoc. dean acad. affairs Northwestern U. Kellogg Grad. Sch. Mgmt., Evanston, Ill., 1975-76, 80-82, 84-86; provost, chief acad. affairs Northwestern U., Evanston, 1987-92. Co-author: Innovations and Organizations, 1973, Strategies for Planned Change, 1977; also numerous articles in profl. jours. Fellow Acad. Mgmt. (chair nat. program 1980-81, pres. 1983-84). Avocation: sailing. Office: Northwestern U Grad Sch Mgmt Leverone Hl Evanston IL 60208-0001

DUNCAN, ROBERT MICHAEL, banker, lawyer, Republican national committeeman; b. Oneida, Tenn., Apr. 14, 1951; s. Robert C. and Barbara (Taylor) D.; m. Joanne Kirk, June 3, 1972; children: Robert Michael. BA, Cumberland Coll., 1971; JD, U. Ky., 1974; postgrad., U. Wis., 1977-80; LLD (hon.), Cumberland Coll., 1990; owner pres. mgmt. program, Harvard U., 1990. Cert. lener-bus. banking, 1994. V.p. Inez (Ky.) Deposit Bank, 1974-77, exec. v.p., 1977-81, chmn., 1981—; chmn. Community Holding Co., Inez, 1983—; with First Nat. Bank (now Inez Deposit Bank FSB), Louisa, Ky., 1984—; dir. Cin. Br. of Cleve. Fed. Res. Bank, 1987-90; chmn. Morehead State U., 1985-86; trustee, chmn. Alice Lloyd Coll., Pippa Passes, Ky., 1978—, acting pres., 1993-94; ptnr. Kirk Ins. Agy., 1978—; mem. class XX Pres.'s Commn. on Exec. Exchange assigned to White House Office Pub. Liaison as asst. dir.; dir. Christian Appalachian Project, 1995—. Del. Rep. Nat. Conv., 1972, 76, 92, 96, chair contest com. 2000 conv.; nat. committeeman for Ky., Rep. Nat. Com., vice chmn. so. region, 1992—, exec. com., 1996; chmn. Ky. Rep. Com., 1995; trustee Highlands Regional Med. Ctr., 1977—; active Govt. Rels. Coun., White House Conf. on Small Bus., 1995; chmn. Govs. Scholars, 1995—, bd. dirs. 1996—; chmn. East Ky. Corp., 1996, vice chmn. Ctr. Econ. Devel.; chmn. Bunning for U.S. Senate campaign, 1998; midwest regional chmn. Bush presdl. campaign, 1999. Named Cumberland Coll. Outstanding Alumnus, 1976, Outstanding Young Man, Ky. Jaycees, 1982; U. Ky. fellow, 1978, White House fellow finalist, 1989; recipient Cmty. Leadership award McConnell Scholars U. Louisville, Cmty. Leadership award, 1999. Mem. Am. Bankers Assn., Ky. Bankers Assn. (pres. 1985-86, dir.), ABA, Ky. Bar Assn., Ky. C. of C. (dir.), Kiwanis (lt. gov. 1983-84). Baptist. Home: PO Box 331 Inez KY 41224-0331 Office: PO Box 365 Inez KY 41224-0365

DUNCAN, SHEILA LONGMUIR BLACK, retired gynecologist; b. Glasgow, Scotland, Apr. 29, 1931; d. Thomas Black Duncan and Jessie Grant Cameron. MB, BChir, Glasgow U., 1955, MD, 1968. Clin. trainee various hosps., Glasgow, 1955-60; registrar Elizabeth Garrett Anderson Hosp., London, 1960-62; rsch. registrar Charing Cross Hosp., London, 1963-67; rsch. fellow Nuffield Inst., Oxford, Eng., 1967-69; sr. lectr., reader U. Sheffield, Eng., 1969-96; ret. Editor: Brit. Jour. Ob-Gyn., 1981-99; contbr. chpts. to books, articles to profl. jours. Traveling fellow Coun. Europe, 1976. Fellow Royal Coll. Obstetricians-Gynecologists London, Royal Soc. Medicine; mem. Brit. Med. Assn., Neonatal Soc., Blair-Bell Rsch. Soc. Presbyterian. Home: 54 Quarry Ln, Sheffield S11 9EB, England

DUNCAN, TYRONE EDWARD, mathematics educator; b. N.Y.C., July 16, 1941; s. Prince and Margaret Alice Duncan; m. Bozenna Janina Pasik, May 21, 1983; 1 child, Dominique. BEE, Rensselaer Poly. Inst., 1963; MS, Stanford U., 1964, PhD, 1967. Asst. prof. U. Mich., Ann Arbor, 1967-71; assoc. prof. SUNY, Stony Brook, 1971-74; prof. math. U. Kans., Lawrence, 1974—. Recipient Olin K. Petefish award in basic scis. Kans. Endowment

Assn., 1999. Fellow IEEE; mem. Am. Math. Soc., Math. Assn. Am., Soc. for Indsl. and Applied Math. E-mail: duncan@math.ukans.edu. Home: 1208 Schwarz Rd Lawrence KS 66049-2833 Office: U Kans Math Dept Lawrence KS 66045-0001

DUNDAROV, STEFAN GEORGIEV, virologist, researcher; b. Plovdiv, Bulgaria, Sept. 11, 1932; s. Georgy Iwanov and Nadejda Jordanova (Tabakova) D.; m. Elena Lambreva Tomova, Feb. 25, 1962 (div. Sept. 1964); children: Geo Stefanov; m. Daniela Lubenova Lepavzova, Jan. 15, 1969; 1 child, Georgy Stefanov. MD, Med. Inst., Plovdiv, Bulgaria, 1956; PhD, Nat. Ctr. Infectious and Parasitis Disease, Sofia, Bulgaria, 1969; DSc, Nat. Ctr. Inf. Paras. Disease, Sofia, Bulgaria, 1977. Chief labs. Hosp., Topolovgrad, Bulgaria, 1956-58; head physician Hosp., Topolovgrad, 1958-60; head lab. herpes viruses Nat. Ctr. Infectious and Parasitic Diseases, Sofia, 1960—, head dept. virology, 1987-93, prof., 1987—, dir., 1989-93; mem. Govt. Sci. Coun. Microbiology, Sofia, 1987—; head Govt. Com. Virology, Sofia, 1990—. Author, editor: Microbiology, 1993; vice head editor Jour. Infectology, 1990—; mem. internat. editl. bd. Jour. Acta Virilogica, 1981-90; contbr. articles to profl. jours.; patentee in field. Recipient Exhbns. awards Humboldt Found., Germany, 1971, 73, 79. Mem. Bulgarian Soc. Virology (pres. 1988—), N.Y. Acad. Sci. Home: 58 b Dunavstr, 1202 Sofia Bulgaria Office: NCIPD Dept Virology, 44a Stoletov Blvd, 1233 Sofia Bulgaria

DUNDAS, CHARLES CHRISTOPHER, educational administrator; b. July 19; s. Charles D. Dundas and Janet M. Shaw. MA with honors, U. Glasgow, 1999. Mem. bd. mgmt. Glasgow U. Union, 1997-99; v.p. Glasgow U. (GUSRC), 1998—. Author: A History of Debating in Glasgow, 1997, The Last Duel Fought in Europe, 1999. Br. pres. Glasgow Liberal Democrats, 1998-98. Avocations: reading, writing, history, politics, hillwalking. Office: c/o GUU, 32 University Ave, Glasgow G12 8LX, Scotland

DUNDAS, PHILIP BLAIR, JR., lawyer; b. Middletown, Conn., Apr. 29, 1948; s. Philip Blair and Madolyn Margaret Dundas; m. Elizabeth Anne Adorno, Aug. 9, 1969; children: Philip Blair III, Chapman P. BA, Wesleyan U., Conn., 1970; JD, Washington and Lee U., 1973. Bar: N.Y. 1974. Assoc. Shearman & Sterling, N.Y.C., 1973-81, ptnr., 1981—, ptnr. in charge of Abu Dhabi, United Arab Emirates Office, 1981—. Mem. ABA, Internat. Bar Assn., N.Y. State Bar Assn., Assn. Bar City N.Y., Union Internationale des Avocats, Clinton Country Club. Home: 288 Old Kelsey Point Rd Westbrook CT 06498-2132

DUNDERBERG, ISMO, theology educator, researcher; b. Helsinki, Finland, June 17, 1963; s. Joili Virolainen and Elma Dunderberg; m. Päivi Salmesvuori, 1985; children: Fanni, Linus, Olga. MTh, U. Helsinki, 1988, lic. Theology, 1993, ThD, 1994. Asst. bibl. studies U. Helsinki, 1992-93, rschr. bibl. studies, 1993-95, docent New Testament studies, 1994—. Author: Johannes und die Synoptiker: Studien zu Joh 1-9, 1994. Rsch. fellow Acad. Finland, 1995—. Mem. Soc. Bibl. Lit., Studiorum Novi Testamenti Soc., Finnish Exegetical Soc., Internat. Assn. for Coptic Studies. Avocations: cross-country skiing, mountain biking. Office: Univ Helsinki PO Box 33, Dept Bible Studies, 00014 Helsinki Finland

DUNÉR, KARIN GUNILLA, lawyer; b. Danderyd, Stockholm, Oct. 29, 1963; d. Kjell Gunnar and Ingrid Gunilla (Körner) Jonsson; m. Tor Anders Ulfsson Dunér, Dec. 5, 1987; children: Karl Hannes, Elin Hillevi. French studies, Stockholm U., 1984-85, ML, 1988. Jr. judge City Ct., Nacka, Stockholm, 1988-93; assoc. Lagerlöf & Leman, Stockholm, 1993-98; legal advisor Swedish Environ. Protection Agy., 1998—. Contbr. chpt. to book, articles to newsletters. Scholar The Tessin Found., 1984; recipient award The Cassel Found., 1987. Office: Swedish Environ Prot Agy, 10648 Stockholm Sweden

DUNGAN, JOHN RUSSELL, JR. (TITULAR VISCOUNT DUNGAN OF CLANE AND HEREDITARY PRINCE OF ARA), anesthesiologist; b. Boston, Dec. 12, 1953; s. John Russell and Nancy Pauline (Beaton) D.; m. Nancy Elizabeth Perkins, July 12, 1986 (div. 1997); children: Elizabeth Adelaide, Thayer Warren, Eleanor Grace Appleton. AB magna cum laude, Harvard U., 1977, EdM, 1978; DDS, Baylor U., 1984; MD cum laude, Creighton U., 1989. Diplomate Nat. Bd. Anesthesiology (dir. 1989-92, 97—, v.p. 1997—), Am. Acad. Pain Mgmt. Instr. anesthesiology Boston U. Sch. Medicine, 1986-89; attending staff anesthesiologist, residency instr. Boston City Hosp., 1986-89; anesthesiologist, chief Tobey Hosp., Wareham, Mass., 1989-91; chief of anesthesia Mary Lanning Hosp., Hastings, Nebr., 1991—; chief of surgery Mary Lanning Hosp., Hastings, 1995, 2001; pres. Hastings Anesthesiology Assocs., 1992—; chmn. pharmacy and therapeutics, 1993-94, 96—. Author: The Kings of the Picts and Dál Riads, 1976, The Beatons, 1976, Angus Macdonald, 1977; contbr. articles to profl. jours. Rschr. nat. trust Restoration of Celbridge Chapel and Cemetery, Kildare, Ireland, 1995. John Eliot scholar, 1967, Nat. Merit scholar, 1971; Internat. fellow English-Speaking Union, 1971-72; Harvard Coll. scholar, 1975-77, John Harvard scholar, 1976; head and comdr. Mil. Order Knights of Leinster; named to Honorable Order of Ky. Cols. Mem. Am. Soc. Anesthesiologists, English-Speaking Union U.S., Nebr. Soc. Anesthesiologists, N.Y. Biog. and Geneal. Soc., N.Y. Irish History Roundtable, N.Eng. Historic Geneal. Soc., United Empire Loyalists Assn. (Can.), Phi Beta Kappa, Cum Laude Soc. (Tabor chpt.), Hasty Pudding Inst. 1770, Harvard Club of Nebr., Old Tonbridgian Soc., The Wild Geese, Clan Dungan (acting chief and pres. 1998—). Republican. Episcopalian. Avocations: Medieval and Jacobean British history research, family history. Home: Heartwell Park 923 N Elm Ave Hastings NE 68901-4021 Office: Hastings Anesthesiology 608 W 6th St Hastings NE 68901-5124

DUNHAM, FRANK WILLARD, lawyer; b. Phila., Sept. 16, 1942; m. Elinor Rockwell, Dec. 25, 1965; children: Frank W. III, John Durgin. BS, Va. Tech. U., 1965; JD, Catholic U., Washington, 1970. Bar: Va. 1970, U.S. Dist. Ct. (ea. dist.) Va. 1970, D.C. 1970, U.S. Dist. Ct. D.C. 1970, U.S. Ct. Appeals (4th cir.) 1971, U.S. Ct. Appeals (3d cir.) 1975, U.S. Tax Ct. 1983, U.S. Supreme Ct. 1980. Naval architect Naval Sea Systems Command, Arlington, Va., 1965-71; law clk. U.S. Dist. Ct., Alexandria, Va., 1970-71; asst. U.S. atty. Justice Dept., Alexandria, 1971-76; 1st asst. U.S. atty. U.S. Dept. Justice, Alexandria, 1976-78; assoc. Leonard, Cohen, Gettings and Sher, Arlington, 1978-83; ptnr. Cohen, Gettings, Alper and Dunham, Arlington, 1983-90, Cohen, Gettings & Dunham, Arlington, 1991—. Contbr. article to profl. jour. Dir. Ft. Hunt Youth Athete Assn., Fairfax County, Va., 1980—; mem. 10th jud. dist. grievence com. Recipient Disting. Svc. award Waynewood Civic Assn., 1985. Mem. Fed. Bar Assn. (pres. No. Va. chpt. 1998-99), Alexandria Bar Assn., Va. Trial Lawyers Assn. (chmn. criminal law sect. 1991-92), Va. Assn. Def. Attys., Arlington County Bar Assn. Avocations: tennis, coaching baseball. Office: Cohen Gettings & Dunham 2200 Wilson Blvd Ste 800 Arlington VA 22201-3375

DUNHAM, JOAN ROBERTS, administrative assistant; b. Dayton, Ohio, Jan. 25, 1933; d. Harold Hathaway and Lydia Roberts Dunham. BA, U. Colo., 1954; postgrad., U. Pa., 1959-65, U. Chgo., 1971-72. Office clk. Daniels & Fisher Stores, Denver, 1954-56; clk., stenographer Dept. of State, Madras, India, 1957-59; clk., stenographer, analyst Dept. of State, Washington, 1966-69; clk. admissions office Temple Buell Coll., Denver, 1968-71; typist, adminstrv. clk. State of Colo., Denver, 1987-99; ret., 1999. Fgn. lang. fellow U.S. Dept. Health, Edn. and Welfare, U. Pa., 1961-62. Republican. Christian Scientist. Home: 1350 Josephine St Unit 210 Denver CO 80206-2243

DUNION, CELESTE MOGAB, consultant, township official; b. Atlantic City, Mar. 6, 1932; d. Cyril Joseph and Lavina Edna (Bolen) Mogab; m. John Joseph Dunion, May 8, 1954 (dec. Apr. 1978); children: Dana, John, Robert, Denise. Tech. degree, Am. Acad. Dramatic Arts, N.Y.C., 1951; grad. advanced govt. fin. inst., Georgetown U., 1986. Cert. govt. fin. mgr.; lic. notary pub., Pa. Asst. to bus. mgr. Rose Tree Media Sch. Dist., Media, Pa., 1969-78; dir. fin., tax collector, treas. Twp. of Middletown, Glen Riddle, Pa., 1978-98; profl. model, N.Y.C., Phila., Atlantic City; mem. Christy Modeling Agy., Phila. Models Guild, Atlantic City Models Guild, Atlantic City Press Bur.; cons. in fin. mgmt. peer-to-peer program Pa. Dept. Cmty. Affairs, Harrisburg, 1988-96; treas., bd. dirs. Pa. Mcpl. Investment Program, 1990-98. Past sec. Wyncroft Civic Assn.; former committeewoman Middletown Twp; treas. Middletown Republican Women, 1998—. Recipient Dedicated Pumper award Lenni Fire Co., 1983, President's award Lima Fire Co., 1985, Outstanding Leadership award Pa. East Govt. Fin. Officers Assn., 1986, Cmty. Svc. award Middletown Fire Co., 1996. Mem. Govt. Fin. Officers Assn. (Pa. rep., nat. cash mgmt. com., women's fin. network, Mid-Atlantic rep.), Assn. Govt. Accts., Pa. Govt. Fin. Officers Assn. (past pres., sec., Southeast bd.), MidAtlantic Govt. Fin. Officers Assn. (Pa. rep., mem. legis. com.), Women's Fin. Officers Network (chmn. membership), Delaware County Tax Collectors Assn. (v.p. 1984-85, pres. 1986), Pa. Tax Collectors Assn., Pa. Assn. Notaries. Republican. Roman Catholic. Avocations: silk flower arranging, tap dancing, country western dancing, writing poetry, cooking. E-mail: cmdcgfm1@aol.com. Office: CMD/CGFM Darlington Woods 153 Kingswood Ct Glen Mills PA 19342-2016 also: Darlington Woods 135 Kingswood Ct Glen Mills PA 19342-2016

DUNKLE, KEITH ALLEN, military officer; b. Waverly, Mo., Feb. 2, 1958; s. Elden Thomas Dunkle and Margaret Alice Petet; m. Brenda Ann Dulle, Oct. 8, 1994. BS, BA, Cen. Mo. State U., 1990. Commd. 2d lt. U.S. Army, 1990, advanced through grades to capt., 1999; security officer nuclear weapons detachment 558th U.S. Field Arty., Perivolaki, Greece, 1991-92; field arty. officer 41st Field Arty. Regiment, Ft. Stewart, Ga., 1992-95; spl. forces operational detachment "A" comdr. 7th Spl. Forces Group, Ft. Bragg, N.C., 1996-99; aide-de-camp U.S. Army South, P.R., 1999—. Avocations: chess, reading, outdoor sports. E-mail: kaddunk@worldnet.att.net. Home: PO Box 1030 Osage Beach MO 65065-1030

DUNLAP, DONALD KELDER, rental company executive; b. Johnson City, N.Y., Nov. 30, 1964; s. Leslie David and Eunice Krom Dunlap; m. Anna Elizabeth Beaty, Aug. 18, 1985; 1 child, Donald Kelder Jr. MusB, Mars Hill Coll., 1985; MBA, Winthrop U., 1994. Co-mgr. Winner's Corp., Asheville, N.C., 1985-87; supr. Meml. Mission Hosp., Asheville, 1987; asst. mgr. Rose's Stores, Inc., Hendersonville, N.C., 1988-89; sr. asst. mgr. Rose's Stores, Inc., Brevard, N.C., 1989-90; sta. mgr. The Hertz Corp., Charlotte, N.C., 1990-95; pool fleet mgr. The Hertz Corp., Atlanta, 1995-98, region yield mgr., 1998—. Organist Stockbridge Presbyn. Ch., 1998—. Mem. South Metro Concert Band (treas. 1996-97, chmn. 1997-99). Avocations: music, literature, computers. Home: 722 Monticello Ln McDonough GA 30253-7910 Office: The Hertz Corp SE Region 4751 Best Rd Ste 400 Atlanta GA 30337-5600

DUNLAP, RILEY EUGENE, sociologist; b. Wynne, Ark., Oct. 25, 1943; s. Riley W. Dunlap Jr. and F. Eugenia (Jones) Anderson; m. Lonnie Jean Brown, Aug. 20, 1966; children: Sara Jean, Christopher Eugene. MS, U. Oreg., 1969, PhD, 1973. From asst. prof. to prof. sociology Wash. State U., Pullman, 1972-85, 85-96, Boeing Disting. prof. environ. sociology, 1996—; mem. socioeconomic peer review panel Office of Exploratory Rsch., U.S. EPA, 1991; mem. panel on aesthetic attributes in water resources planning NRC/Nat. Acad. Scis., 1982; Gallup fellow in environment George H. Gallup Internat. Inst., 1992—. Editor, author: (jour. symposium) Am. Behavioral Scientist, 1980, Internat. Sociology, 1998; editor book: American Environmentalism: The U.S. Environmental Movement, 1970-90, 92, Pub. Reactions to Nuclear Waste, 1993. Gallup Orgn. scholar for environment, 1999—. Fellow AAAS (rural sociol. soc. rep. to sect. K 1986-89); mem. Internat. Sociol. Assn. (pres., rsch. com. on environ. and soc. 1994-98), Am. Sociol. Assn. (chmn. sect. on environ. sociology 1981-83, disting. contbn. award 1986), Rural Sociol. Soc. (chmn. natural resources rsch. group 1978-79, award of merit 1985), Soc. for Study of Social Problems (chmn. environ. problems divsn. 1973-75). Achievements include being credited as co-founder of field of environmental sociology. Fax: (509) 335-2125.. E-mail: dunlap@wsu.edu. Office: Washington State Univ Dept Sociology Pullman WA 99164-0001

DUNLAP-WILLIAMS, NANCY A., rehabilitation management company executive, nurse; b. Athens, Ohio, July 24, 1956; d. Thomas and Doris Williams; 1 child, Robert Mitchell Williams. Student, Bowling Green (Ohio) U., 1975-78; diploma, The Toledo Hosp. Sch. Nursing, 1983; postgrad., Portland (Oreg.) State U., 1987-88. RN, Ohio; cert. life care planner, U. Fla., Ocoee, 1998; cert. case mgr., disability examiner. Critical care trauma nurse The Oreg. Health Scis. U., Portland, 1983-89; nurse cons., legal intern Hendricks Law Offices, Portland, 1989-91; rehab. cons., edn. coord. Gen. Rehab. Svcs., Inc., Columbus, Ohio, 1989-94; pres., CEO, founder, owner Rehab. Mgmt. Svcs., Columbus, 1994—. Mem. editl. bd. Long-Term Care Interface. Vol. advisor Advocate Ct. Appointed Spl. Advocates of Franklin County. Mem. Nat. Assn. Rehab. Profls. Pvt. Sector, Am. Assn. Nurse Life Care Planners, Am. Assn. Occupl. Health Nurses, Internat. Assn. Life Care Planners, Internat. Acad. Life Care Planners, Ohio Nursing Assn., Ohio Bur. Workers Compensation (accredited). Office: Rehab Mgmt Svcs 5020 Reed Rd Ste D Columbus OH 43220-2581

DUNLAY, CATHERINE TELLES, lawyer; b. Cin., Apr. 5, 1958; d. Paul Albert and Donna Mae Telles; m. Thomas Vincent Dunlay, July 10, 1981; children: Christine Jennifer, Thomas Paul, Brian Patrick. Student, Ind. U., 1976-78; BA in English Lit. summa cum laude, U. Cin., 1981; JD summa cum laude, Ohio State U., 1984. Bar: Ohio 1984. Teaching asst., legal rsch. and writing Ohio State U. Coll. of Law, Columbus, 1982; law clk. Brownfield, Bowen & Bally, Columbus, 1983; assoc. Schottenstein, Zox & Dunn, LPA, Columbus, 1984-91, atty., principal, 1991—. Mng. editor Ohio State Law Jour., 1983-84; co-author Health Span, 1993, Akron Law Rev., Fall 1993; co-editor Health Law Jour. of Ohio, 1994-95. Grad. Columbus Leadership Program, 1991; mem. admissions/inclusiveness com. United Way of Franklin County, Columbus, 1991-94, 96. Recipient C. Simeral Bunch award for Acad. Excellence, Ohio State U., 1984, Law Jour. Past Editors award, 1984. Mem. ABA, Ohio State Bar Assn. (chair healthcare law com. 2000—), Columbus Bar Assn., Ohio Women's Bar Assn., Women Lawyers of Franklin County (trustee, treas. 1990-93, 91-92), Am. Health Lawyers Assn., Soc. of Ohio Hosp. Attys., Order of the Coif. Roman Catholic. Avocations: cooking, hiking, camping, reading. Office: Schottenstein Zox & Dunn 41 S High St Ste 2600 Columbus OH 43215-6109

DUNLOP, DAVID WALLACE, economist, educator; b. Placerville, Calif., July 6, 1942; s. William Wallace and Sarah Nevada (Ross) D. BS, U. Calif., Berkeley, 1965; MA, Mich. State U., 1969, PhD, 1973. Lectr. dept. agrl. econs. Mich. State U., East Lansing, 1971-72; asst. prof. econs. dept. Vanderbilt U., Nashville, 1972-79; asst. prof. Dept. Community Medicine Meharry Med. Sch., Nashville, 1972-79; economist, health economist U.S. Agy. for Internat. Devel., Washington, 1979-82; vis. prof. dept. community medicine Dartmouth Med. Sch., Hanover, N.H., 1979-82; vis. prof. dept. fin. and econs. and program in health mgmt. Boston U., 1983-86, assoc. rsch. fellow, 1984—; sr. economist ABT Assocs., Inc., Cambridge, Mass., 1986-88; health economist Econ. Devel. Inst World Bank, Washington, 1988-91, cons., task mgr. for health programs in Ethiopia and Eritren, 1991-97; mem. exec. com., bd. govs. Nat. Coun. Internat. Health, Washington, 1984-90; convenor Faculty Forum on Internat. Health, Assn. Univ. Programs in Health Adminstrn., Washington, 1984-88; adj. prof. Sch. of Pub. Health U. North Carolina, 1979-93; adj. prof. dept. community and family medicine, 1982—. Co-editor: Health: What is it Worth?, 1979, An International Assessment of Health Care Financing: Lessons for Developing Countries, 1995; editor Jour. Social Sci. and Medicine, 1977-82. Grantee Midwestern U. Consortium for Internat. Activities, 1970, U.S. Nat. Ctr. for Health Svcs. Rsch., 1975. Mem. Am Econs. Assn., Am. Pub. Health Assn. Avocations: running, hiking, travel. Office: Dartmouth Med Sch Dept Cmty & Family Medicine Strassenburgh Hall Hanover NH 03755

DUNLOP, FRANK, theater director; b. Leeds, Eng., Feb. 15, 1927; s. Charles Norman and Mary (Aarons) D. BA in English with honors, University Coll., London, 1978; Dhc (hon.), U. Edinburgh, U. Heriot-Watt; postgrad., Shakespeare Inst., Old Vic Sch, London. Dir. Piccolo Theatre, Manchester, Eng., 1954, Arts Coun. Midland Theatre Co., 1955; asst. dir. Bristol Old Vic, 1956; dir. Nottingham Playhouse, 1961-63; author, dir. of Les Freres Jacques Adelphi Theatre, London; founder, Young Vic Theatre, London, 1969, dir., 1969-78, 80-83. Assoc. dir. Nat. Theatre, London prodns. including Edward II, The White Devil, Macrune's Guevara, Home and Beauty, the Captain of Kopenick, also adminstrv. dir.; dir. plays at Vic Theatre: the Taming of the Shrew, The Comedy of Errors, The Maids and Deathwatch, The Alchemist, Bible One, French Without Tears, Joseph and the Amazing Technicolor Dreamcoat, Much Ado About Nothing, Macbeth, Antony and Cleopatra, King Lear; dir. plays Belgian Nat. Theatre, including Pantagleise, 1970, Antony and Cleopatra, 1971, Pericles, 1973; dir. Midsummer Night's Dream at Edinburgh (Scotland) Festival and Saville Theatre, London, 1967; dir. Joseph and the Amazing Technicolor Dreamcoat at Bklyn. Acad. Music, N.Y.C.; dir. BAM Theatre Co., plays include: The Three Sisters, The New York Idea, The Devil's Disciple, The Play's the Thing, Julius Caesar; Broadway prodns. include Sherlock Holmes, Scapino, Habeas Corpus, Camelot; dir. Edinburgh Internat. Festival, 1984-91, L'Elisir D'Amore Opera De Lyons and fmilm, 1992-97, My Fair Lady, Frankfurt and Hamburt, Germany, Vienna, Austria, 1993-94, Heathcliff, London, 1996, Carmen, London, 1997, School for Wives, Belgium, 1998, the Invisible Man, Cleve., 1998-99, Scapimo, Beit Lessin Theatre, Israel, 1999. Decorated comdr. Brit. Empire, Chevalier De L'ordre des Arts et Lettres, France. Office: Piccolo Theatre Co, 13 Choumert Sq, London SE15 4RE, England also: care Ernest Nives 157 W 57th St New York NY 10019-2210

DUNLOP, JAMES MONTGOMERY, physician, consultant; b. Greenock, Scotland, Aug. 25, 1930; s. Gabriel and Margarel Louise (Leiper) D.; m. Joyce Lilian Hill, Sept. 15, 1960; children: Jonathan William, Joanne Wendy, Douglas Graham. MB, BS, BAO, Trinity Coll., Dublin, Ireland, 1959, MA, 1962; DPH, Glasgow (Scotland) U., 1964. Port med. officer Grangemouth, Stirling, 1963-66; chief asst. county med. officer North Riding, Yorkshire, 1966-70; dep. med. officer of health Hull, 1970-74, dist. cmty. physician/dist. med. officer/dir. pub. health, 1974-95; med. referee Hull Crematorium, Humberside, 1970—; med. advisor U. Lincolnshire and Humberside, 1970-99, Kingston Comm., 1970—, Stagecoach Transport, 1970—, Humber Bridge Bd., 1970-99; gov. Epsom Coll., Surrey, Eng., 1992—, chmn. conjoint com., London, 1992-93. Author: Dr Dunlop's Mixture, 1998; contbr. articles to profl. jours. Dir. Housemartin Housing Assn., 1987—, Hull United Charities, 1994—. Recipient Smith award Royal Inst. Pub. Health and Hygiene, London, 1992. Fellow Faculty of Pub. Health Medicine London (treas. 1991-95), Royal Coll. Physicians London, Soc. Pub. Health (pres. 1993-94, treas. 1996-98, John Kershaw award 1990), Brit. Med. Assn. (chmn. charitable trusts 1990—), Royal Phil. Soc. Presbyterian. Avocations: stamp collecting, writing on medical history, lecturing. Home: 136 Westella Rd Kirkella, East Yorkshire HU10 7RR, England

DUNN, ANNE YVONNE, advocacy organization executive; b. Detroit, Feb. 15, 1948; d. Reginald King and Gwendolyn Leah (Reynolds) Hawkins; divorced; 1 child, James Jay Dunn II. BA, Calif. State Coll., L.A., 1985. Coun. dep. 1st Dist., L.A., 1980-85; mgr. Cmty. Devel. Dept. Pacoima Enterprise Zone, L.A., 1985-90; asst. exec. dir. Commn. on the Status of Women, L.A., 1990—. Singer Jubilee Singers, 1968—. Founding mem. L.A. County Women's Caucus, 1991, L.A. City Domestic Violence Task Force, 1995, Women Against Racism, L.A., 1995; mem., co-chair L.A. County Domestic Violence Coun., 1992-97. Recipient certs. of appreciation L.A. City Coun. and Mayor, 1981, 82, 90, 91, plaque L.A. City Coun., 1996, commendation U.S. Assembly State of Calif., 1990, L.A. County Bd. Suprs., 1995, 96. Mem. Women's Legis. Coaliation, Nat. Assn. Commns. on Women, Albert McNeil Jubilee Singers, William Grant Still Performing Arts Soc. (v.p. 1989—). Avocations: performing arts, creative arts, travel, reading, saltwater aquariums. Office: Commn on Status of Women 200 N Main St CHE 7th Fl Los Angeles CA 90012

DUNN, CRAIG ANDREW, entertainer, conductor, composer, educator; b. Point Pleasant, N.J., Nov. 11, 1947; s. Andrew Robert and Ruth Agnes (Schott) D.; m. Crystal Lynn Kesler, May 26, 1970. MusB, U. Cin., 1972; MusM, Ohio U., 1973; EdD, Nova Southeastern U., 1996. Cert. tchr., Fla. Dir. bands Greenville (S.C.) Sr. H.S., 1973-74, Bayonne (N.J.) H.S., 1974-75; studio instr. Buddy Rogers Music Studios, Inc., Cin., 1975-78; music specialist, music dir. Diocese of St. Petersburg, Fla., 1979-88; music specialist Sch. Dist. of Hillsborough County, Tampa, Fla., 1988—; performing artist, entertainer, 1972—, emtertainer, performer on luxury cruise ships, 2000—; mem. adv. bd. Am. Youth Symphony Band and Chorus, Pitts., 1980-85, artistic advisor, coach, 1980, 83, 85; dir. sch. dance and choral ensembles Fla. State Fair, 1992—. Pub. composer popular and religious music. Mem. Music Educators Nat. Conf., Fla. Music Educators Assn., Nat. Acad. Songwriters. Avocations: orchestrating, writing, reading. Home: 11800 4th St E Isle of Capri Treasure Island FL 33706

DUNN, DANA-LORI, counselor; b. Covina, Calif., Aug. 6, 1957; d. Lowell Roland Butterfield and Dorothy Jane Whay Butterfield; m. Mark Philip Dunn, Nov. 3, 1979; children: Ian Roland, Brittany Jane. Cert. Program land devel. cmty. planning, U. Calif., Irvine, 1991; PhD in Metaphysics, U. Metaphysics, Studio City, Calif., 1996. Ordained Metaphys. min. Internat. Metaphys. Ministry, 1995; bd. cert. pastoral counselor; cert. hypnotherapist Am. Bd. Hypnotherapy. Sec. Garrett Airesearch, Torrance, Calif., 1975-78; adminstrv. asst. Panel-Air Corp., Costa Mesa, Calif., 1979-81; exec. sec. Rockwell Internat., Newport Beach, Calif., 1984-86; adminstrv. asst. Las Flores Group, Inc., Dana Point, Calif., 1990-92, Cymbolic Scis. Internat., Aliso Viejo, Calif., 1992-93; acctg. asst. Quigley Ins. Svcs., Mission Viejo, Calif., 1993-95; pvt. practice Aliso Viejo, 1995—. Author: A Leap of Faith: Back to the Garden, 1998, The Power and the Glory of the RAYS, 1998. Active Nat. Campaign for Tolerance. Recipient Bus. award Bank of Am., 1975, Meritorious Achievement award IBC, 2000. Mem. Lucis Trust, Noetic Scis., Planetary Soc. Republican. Avocations: pianist, composer, hiking, skiing. Home: 23572 El Rio Aliso Viejo CA 92656-1110

DUNN, DORIS MARJORY, retired educator, volunteer; b. Chgo., Jan. 7, 1921; d. William Christian and Mary Esther (Hoffman) Rose; m. Jack Harold Wheeler Dunn, Sept. 19, 1945 (dec. June 1978); children: Randall L., Jon G., Bonham. BS in Edn., Ind. U., 1942; postgrad., Northwestern U., 1943-44; MS, Valparaiso U., 1973. Life lic. in teaching, Ind. Tchr. Crown Point (Ind.) High Sch., 1963-74, Lowell (Ind.) High Sch., 1942-45; sch. tchr., jr. coll. tchr., 1976-78; asst. to engring.libr. U. Tex., Austin, 1947-49. Pres. LWV, Crown Point, 1974; pres.-elect Good Samaritan Hosp. Aux., v.p., 1988-89, pres., 1989-90; buyer Good Samaritan Gift Shop, 1989—; chmn. ways and means Assistance League, 1988-89, regional coun. rep., 1990-91, mem. resource devel. nat. bd., 1991-98; pres. Luckiamute Water Bd., 1988—; mem. Republican Senatorial Inner Circle, State of Oreg., 1997-98. Mem. P.E.O. (pres. 1989-90), Corvallis Country Club. Ladies Orgn. (pres. 1989-90), Kappa Kappa Kappa (pres. 1975), Delta Kappa Gamma. Methodist. Avocations: wood carving, golf, flying, stained glass creation, travel. Home: 12260 Rolling Hills Rd Monmouth OR 97361-9758

DUNN, FLOYD EMRYL, psychiatrist, neurologist, consultant; b. Wilkes-Barre, Pa., Apr. 25, 1910; s. Adrian Anson and Frances Amanda (Culver) D.; m. Wilda Kathryn Lauer, Aug. 14, 1943; children: Kathryn Alice (dec.), Deborah Lee. Student, Temple U., 1929-32; DO, Phila. Coll. Osteo. Medicine, 1936. Diplomate Am. Osteo. Bd. Neurology and Psychiatry. Resident in neurology, psychiatry Still-Hildreth Hosp., 1941-45, staff psychiatrist, 1945-49; chmn. divsn. neurology, psychiatry Kirksville Coll. Osteo. Medicine, 1945-48, Kansas City Coll. Osteo. Medicine, U. Health Scis., Mo., 1949-68; mem. staff VA Hosp., Knoxville, Iowa, 1968-76, chief psychiatry svc., 1970-76; clin. prof. neurology, psychiatry Coll. Osteo. Medicine, Des Moines, 1970-74; mem. Nat. Bd. Examiners for Osteo. Physicians and Surgeons, 1965-74, Excellence award, 1974; cons. neurology, psychiatry, Chgo., 1974-96; cons., examiner sect. of disability determinations Mo. Dept. Elem. and Secondary Edn., Jefferson City, 1985-96. Author: (monograph) History of the American College of Neuropsychiatrists, 1984; contbr. articles to profl. jours. Mem. Iowa Adv. Coun. on Mental Health Ctrs., Des Moines, 1972-78, Cen. Regional Adv. Coun. for Comprehensive Psychiat. Svcs., Columbia, Mo., 1978-86. Fellow Am. Coll. Neuropsychia-

trists (life, sec.-treas. 1948-52, pres. 1954-55, 63-64, Disting. Svc. award 1967, Disting. Fellow award 1984, 1st Fellows' Lecture Honoree 1989), Am. Assn. on Mental Deficiency; mem. AMA (life), Am. Osteo. Assn. (life, editl. cons. publs. 1958-95, del. 1960-69, pres.'s adv. coun. 1973), Am. Coll. Neuropsychiatrists (life), Am. Osteopathic Assn. (life, cons. examiner of neurology and psychiatry residency tng. programs 1988-91), Mo. Assn. Osteo. Physicians and Surgeons (hon. life, del. 1958-69, v.p. 1969-70), Lions (pres. Gravois Mills, Mo. chpt. 1984-85, sec. 1985-88, del. to internat. conv. 1985, 86, 87), Masons (32d degree), Abou Ben Adhem Temple, Elks (life), Alpha Phi Omega, Phi Sigma Gamma (pres. grand coun. 1952-53, coun. sec.-treas. 1953-59, editor Speculum 1959-65, 95—, Meritorious Svc. award 1965, 87-91, exec. sec.-treas. grand coun. 1980-95). Republican. Methodist. Avocations: photography, travel, journalism. Home: 30171 Millcreek Loop Gravois Mills MO 65037-4118

DUNN, HERBERT IRVIN, lawyer; b. Balt., July 19, 1946; s. Albert M. and Hilda F. (Winakur) D.; m. Marsha Edith Greenfield, Apr. 1, 1979; children: Marla Phyllis, Jonathan Howard. BS with high honors, U. Md., 1969, JD, 1971. Bar: Md. 1971, D.C. 1971, U.S. Ct. Claims 1972, U.S. Tax Ct. 1972, U.S. Dist. Ct. D.C. 1971, U.S. Ct. Appeals (D.C. cir.) 1971, U.S. Supreme Ct. 1975. Atty.-adviser Office of Gen. Counsel U.S. Gen. Acctg. Office, Washington, 1971-83, sr. atty., 1983—. Served with USAR, 1968-74. Mem. FBA (treas. younger lawyers divsn. 1977-79, nat. coun. 1978-79, 91—, Capitol Hill chpt. exec. coun. 1975-83, v.p. 1990-91, pres.-elect 1991-92, pres. 1992-93, v.p. D.C. cir. 1994—, nat. exec. com. 1999—, v.p.s for the cirs. chmn. 1999—, found. advisor 1999—), Md. Bar Assn., Northwest Br. Citizens Assn. (sec. 1988-95, 1st v.p. 1995-99), Omicron Delta Epsilon. Office: 441 G St NW Washington DC 20548-0001

DUNN, HORTON, JR., organic chemist; b. Coleman, Tex., Sept. 3, 1929; s. Horton and Lora Dean (Bryant) D. BA summa cum laude, Hardin-Simmons U., 1951; MS, Case Western Res. U., 1975, PhD, 1979. Instr. chemistry Hardin-Simmons U., 1951; ONR fellow Ohio State U., Columbus, 1951-52; teaching fellow in chemistry Purdue U., Lafayette, Ind., 1952-53; rsch. chemist Lubrizol Corp., Cleve., 1953-70, dir. tech. info. ctr., 1970-79, supr. rsch. divsn., 1980-98, cons. in chemistry, 1998—; chmn. bd., bus. mgr. Isotopics, Cleve., 1964-67, editor, 1961-63, supr. rsch. divsn., 1989-97, cons. in chemistry, 1998—. Contbr. articles to profl. jours.; patentee in field. Treas. Cleve. Cir. Decorative Arts Trust, 1990-91, 93—, v.p., 1992-93; active Cleve. Art Assn., Cleve. Mus. of Art, Rock and Roll Hall of Fame, Mus. Founders Club.; mem., vol. Grest Lakes Sci. Ctr., Cleve. Mus. Natural History; mem. Cleve. Bot. Garden. Fellow Am. Inst. Chemists; mem. AAAS, SAR (life), Am. Chem. Soc. (treas. Cleve. chpt. 1968-70, chmn. 1987, bd. dirs. 1990—), Am. Soc. for Info. Sci. (chpt. pres. 1973-74), Royal Soc. Chemistry (life), Soc. Tribologists and Lubrication Engrs., Nat. Coun. Met. Opera, Royal Oak Soc. (life), Cleve. Tech. Soc. Coun. (treas. 1987), Cleve. Art Assn., Univ. Club, Cleve. Club, Cleve. Play House Club, Rock and Roll Hall of Fam Mus. Founders Club (charter). Fax: 216-541-6431. Home and Office: 1 Bratenahl Pl Apt 103 Bratenahl OH 44108-1152 Office: Lubrizol Corp 29400 Lakeland Blvd Wickliffe OH 44092-2298

DUNN, JAMES RANDOLPH, corporate executive; b. Newport News, Va., June 23, 1948; s. Joseph Thomas Jr. and Nancy C. (Hall) D.; m. Muriel Word, Mar. 17, 1978; children: Emily Muriel, Allison Margaret. BSBA in Acctg., Old Dominion U., 1970; postgrad., Fairleigh Dickinson U., 1973. CPA, Tex., Md. Operational auditing Exxon Co. U.S.A., Md., N.J. and Houston, 1970-82; v.p., CFO Modern Furniture Rentals, Houston, 1982-84; sr. v.p., CFO Tex. Pipe and Supply Co., Inc., Houston, 1984—; pub. acctg. James R. Dunn, CPA, Houston, 1980-82; spkr. in field. Mgr. Little League Baseball, Md. Sgt. USMCR, 1970-76. Recipient Life Flight Man of Yr. award Hermann Hosp., Houston, 1994. Mem. AICPA, Tex. Soc. CPA (Houston chpt.), Md. Assn. CPA, Alpha Kappa Psi (life, chaplain), Am. Legion. Republican. Episcopalian. Avocations: tennis, gardening, collecting, golf, speaking to students on perseverance and motivation. Home: 6921 Cutten Pkwy Houston TX 77069-1790 Office: Tex Pipe and Supply Co Inc 2330 Holmes Rd Houston TX 77051-1014

DUNN, JEFFREY EDWARD, neurologist; b. Shaker Heights, Ohio, Nov. 27, 1960; s. John Kenneth and Mary Margaret (O'Neill) D.; m. Sandra Lee Judy, Feb. 3, 1990; children: Caitlin Irene, Bronwyn Leigh, Colin John Donald. BA in French Lit., Haverford (Pa.) Coll., 1983; MD, Temple U., 1989. Diplomate Am. Bd. Psychiatry and Neurology. Molecular immunologist Fox Chase Cancer Ctr., Phila., 1984-85; intern Ea. Va. Grad. Sch., Norfolk, 1989-90; resident in neurology U. Wash., Seattle, 1990-93; attending physician Neurol. Assocs. of Wash., Bellevue, 1993—; clin. asst. prof. neurology U. Wash., Seattle, 1993—; founder, med. dir. Overlake Multiple Sclerosis Ctr., Bellevue, Wash., 1996—. Guest physician TV: MS Update, Denver, 1994, ALS Update, Seattle, 1995. Recipient Cert. of Excellence in MS Rx, Prodigy Online Com., 1995; named to Outstanding Young Men of Am., 1996. Fellow Royal Soc. Medicine; mem. Am. Acad. Neurology, Am. Neurol. Assn., World Congress Neurology, North Pacific Soc. of Psychiatry and Neurology. Avocations: golf, skiing, camping, outdoor recreation. Office: Neurol Assocs of Wash 13107 121st Way NE Kirkland WA 98034-3051

DUNN, JOHN CLINTON, writer, editor, organization executive; b. Little Rock, Mar. 12, 1942; s. Eugene William and Clara Ava (Samuel) D.; m. Wanda Padgett, Aug. 29, 1970; children: Jonathan Victor, Gene Stephen, Samuel Padgett. Student, U. Ala., 1961-64; BA in English, Columbus (Ga.) State U., 1974. Reporter, city editor, state editor The Columbus Enquirer, 1967-75; dir. pub. rels. LaGrange (Ga.) Coll., 1975-78; editor News/Daily of Clayton County, Jonesboro, Ga., 1978-80; asst. exec. dir. Ga. Tech. Alumni Assn., Atlanta, 1980—. Editor Ga. Tech. Alumni Mag., Tech. Topics alumni newspaper. With U.S. Army, 1964-67. Avocations: gardening, tennis, reading, travel. Home: 9450 Brown Rd Jonesboro GA 30238-5962 Office: Georgia Tech Alumni Assn 225 North Ave NW Atlanta GA 30332-0001

DUNN, RICHARD JOSEPH, retired investment counselor; b. Chgo., Apr. 5, 1924; s. Richard Joseph and Margaret Mary (Jennett) D.; s. Richard Joseph and Margaret Mary (Jennett) D.; m. Marygrace Calhoun, Oct. 13, 1951 (dec. May 2000); children: Richard, Marianne, Anythony, Gregory, Noelle. AB, Yale U., 1948; LLB, Harvard U., 1951; MBA, Stanford U., 1956. Bar: Tex. 1952. Mem. Carrington, Gowan, Johnson & Walker, Dallas, 1951-54; investment counselor Scudder, Stevens & Clark, San Francisco, 1956-84, v.p., 1965-77, sr. v.p., 1977-84, gen. ptnr., 1974-84, ret. Served with AUS, 1943-46. Decorated Combat Infantry Badge, Bronze Star, Purple Heart, Knight of the Sovereign Mil. Hospitalier Order of St. John of Jerusalem of Rhodes and of Malta, Western Assn., 1978, chancellor, 1987-93, pres. 1993-99, sovereign coun., 1999, knight of obedience, 1990, Grand Cross of Merit, 1999, Grand Cross The Sacred Mil. Constantinian Order of St. George, 1995, Knight of St. Gregory, 2000; recipient Assumpta award Archdiocese of San Francisco, 1996. Roman Catholic. Home: 530 Junipero Serra Blvd San Francisco CA 94127-2727

DUNN, ROBERT RIDDELL, air conditioning company executive; b. Brighton, Victoria, Australia, Apr. 12, 1929; s. Harold Mirams and Daisy (Riddell) D.; m. Shirley Faye Osborne, Aug. 9, 1952; children: Bambi Jo Ann, Bradley Robert. Degree in mech. engring., Footscray Inst. Tech., Melbourne, Victoria, 1948, degree in elec. engring., 1949. Chartered profl. engr. Cadet engr. State Electricity Com., Victoria, 1949; sales mgr. Hendy Heating Industries, Victoria; engr. Airtemp divsn. Chrysler Corp., Dayton, Ohio, 1956-58; mgr. Airtemp divsn. Chrysler Corp., Adelaide, Australia, 1958-60; mng. dir., CEO Dunn Air Conditioning, Melbourne, 1960-98; bd. dirs. Directflo P/L Melbourne, DAC Internat. PL Melbourne, Dunn Air Conditioning W.A. P/L, Perth, West Australia. Paul Harris fellow, 1985. Fellow Australian Inst. Co. Dirs.; mem. ASHRAE (life), Australian Inst. Refrigeration, Air Conditioning and Heating, Australian Refrigeration Equipment Mfg. Assn. (nat. pres. 1976-93), Inst. Engrs., Rotary Internat. (gov. 1993-94), Commonweatlh Golf Club (pres. 1994-97). Avocations: golf, tennis. Home and Office: 4 Brandon Rd, Brighton VIC 3186, Australia

DUNN, WILLIAM BRADLEY, lawyer; b. Newark, Dec. 2, 1939; s. Ernest William and Ruth Harriet (Bradley) D.; m. Judy Ann Shepherd, Aug. 2, 1988; children: John, Peter, Brian, Kelly. AB, Muskingum Coll., 1961; JD, U. Mich., 1964. Bar: Mich. 1964. Mem. Clark Hill PLC (formerly Clark, Klein & Beaumont), Detroit, 1964—; lectr. in field. Contbr. articles to legal jours. Mem. ABA (chair sect. real property, probate and trust law 1989-90, mem. ho. of dels. 1990-98, mem. standing com. on professionalism 1993-96, mem. standing com. on ethics and profl. responsibility 1998—), Am. Coll. Real Estate Lawyers (pres. 1983-84), Urban Land Inst., Internat. Assn. Attys. and Exec. Corporate Real Estate. Episcopalian. Home: 6398 Catalpa Ct Troy MI 48098-2231 Office: Clark Hill PLC 500 Woodward Ave Ste 3500 Detroit MI 48226-3435

DUNNE, JOHN WALTER, neurologist; b. Perth, Australia, Jan. 15, 1953; s. Robert John and Enid Valma (Pollock) D.; m. Sandra Lynne Kermode, Feb. 23, 1986; children: Patrick, Michael, Joseph, Mary. MBBS, U. Western Australia, Perth, 1977; diploma, Royal Coll. of Ob-gyn.'s, Perth, 1979. Resident Royal Perth Hosp., Perth, 1977-78, Princess Margaret Hosp. Children, King Edward Hosp. Women, Perth, 1979; registrar Royal Perth Hosp., 1980-85; fellow Mayo Clinic, Rochester, Minn., 1986-88; head neurophysiology labs., cons. neurologist Royal Perth Hosp., 1989—; chmn. Western Australian Comprehensive Epilepsy Svc., Perth, 1992—; clin. lectr. U. Western Australia, Perth, 1989—; med. advisor Nat. Epilepsy Assn. Australia, 1991—, Western Australian Spasmodic Sysphonia Group, 1991—; vis. epileptologist Sir Charles Gardner Hosp., Perth, 1993—. Reviewer Med. Rsch. Found. Western Australia, 1991—; contbr. numerous articles to profl. jours. Mayo clinic fellow, 1985, S.J. Billings overseas traveling fellow Royal Australian Coll. of Physicians, 1985, P.F. Sobotka postgrad. fellow U. Western Australia, 1985. Mem. Australian Assn. of Neurologists (clin. neurophysiology com.), Epilepsy Soc. of Australia (state rep.), Am. Assn. of Electrodiagnostic Medicine. Avocations: cycling, mountaineering, classical guitar. Office: Royal Perth Hosp, PO Box X2213 GPO, Perth 6001, Australia

DUNNE, REGIS MARY, bioethics professional; b. Toowoomba, Queensland, Australia, Nov. 9, 1926; d. Denis Stephan and Delia Emily (O'Brien) D. Diploma med. sci., Queensland U. of Tech., Brisbane, 1953; fellow med. lab. sci., Australian Inst. of Med. Scientists, 1963; postgrad., U. St. Louis, Loyola U., Chgo., 1980; D Univ., Queensland U. Tech., 1995. Joined Sisters of Mercy, Brisbane, Australia, 1946. Tchr. Sisters of Mercy, Brisbane, 1946-48; trainee med. lab. scientist Mater Hosp., Brisbane, 1949-53, microbiologist, 1953-74, sr. scientist microbiology cytogenetics, 1968-79; founder, dir. Queensland Provincial Bioethics Com., Brisbane, 1981-94; rsch. ethics cons. Mater Rsch. Ctr., Brisbane, 1995—; microbiologist, clin. diagnostic lectr. Queensland, 1953-74; pioneer cytogeneticist, cons., Queensland, 1968-79; cons. med. ethics, rsch. ethics, Australia, 1981-94; founder, dir. Bioethics Ctr., 1981-94; lectr. in field. Contbr. articles to profl. jours. Mem. Queensland Com. Enquiry into IVF and Related Matters, 1982-84, Australian Nat. Bioethics Consultative Com., 1988-91, Australian Nat. Health and Med. Rsch. Couns., 1991—, Australian Health Ethics Com., Med. Rsch. Com., Australian Human Gene Therapy Com., 1994—, Queensland Ethics Adv. Coun. Fellow Australian Inst. Med. Scientists; mem. Human Genetic Soc. Australia (life), Australian Soc. Microbiologists, Australian Soc. Bioethics, Am. Soc. Law and Medicine. Avocations: reading, sewing, patchwork. Home: Mater Hosp Convent, Raymond Tce, South Brisbane 4101, Australia Office: Mater Rsch Inst, Mater Hosps Complex Aubigny Pl, South Brisbane 4101, Australia

DUNNE, STEPHEN MICHAEL, dental surgeon; b. London, Jan. 17, 1954; s. Dennis Theobald and Shirley Ann (Buckley) D.; m. Lucinda Karen Hooker, Apr. 12, 1980; children: Rebecca Lucinda, Matthew James, Oliver William. B in Dental Surgery, U. London, 1976, PhD, 1989; Lic. in Dental Surgery, Royal Coll. Surgeons, Eng., 1977. House surgeon UCH Dental Sch., London, 1977, asst. lectr., 1978-79, lectr., 1980-88, sr. lectr., cons., 1989; sr. lectr., cons. The King's Dental Inst., London, 1989-99; dental surgeon GKT Dental Inst., London, 1999—; fellow in dental surgery Royal Coll. Surgeons, Eng., 1983; lectr. in field. Co-author: Silver Amalgam in Clinical Practice, 1993, Oral Diagnosis: the Clinician's Guide, 2000; contbr. articles to profl. jours. Fellow Royal Coll. Surgeons; mem. Brit. Soc. Restorative Dentistry, London Dental Fellowship, Internat. Assn. Dental Rsch., Assn. Tchrs. Conservative Dentistry, Cons. Restorative Dentistry. Office: GKT Dental Inst, Caldecot Rd, London SE5 9RW, England

DUNNETT, DENNIS GEORGE, state official; b. Auburn, Calif., Aug. 5, 1939; s. George DeHaven and Elizabeth Grace (Sullivan) D. AA in Elec. Engring., Sierra Coll., 1959; AB in Econs., Sacramento State Coll., 1966. Engring. technician State of Calif., Marysville, 1961-62; data processing technician State of Calif., Sacramento, 1962-67, EDP programmer and analyst, 1967-74, staff services mgr. and contract adminstr., 1974-76, hardware acquisition mgr., 1976-86, support services br. mgr., information security officer, 1986-90, chief Office Security and Operational Recovery, 1990-92, spl. projects mgr., 1992-93, customer support ctr. mgr., 1994, procurement mgr., 1994-97, chief bur. adminstrn., 1997—. Mem. AARP, IEEE Computer Soc., Assn. Info. Tech. Profls., Assn. Inst. Cert. of Computers Profls. (certs.), Calif. Assn. Mgrs. and Suprs., Fine Arts Mus. of San Francisco, Crocker Art Mus. Home: 729 Blackmer Cir Sacramento CA 95825-4704 Office: Teale Data Ctr 2005 Evergreen St Sacramento CA 95815-3831

DUNNETT, STEPHEN BRUCE, neurobiologist; b. Bromley, Kent, England, Jan. 28, 1950; s. Peter Sydney and Margaret Eileen (Johnson) D.; m. Sarah-Jane Richards. BA in Math., Cambridge (England) U., 1972, MA, 1976, PhD in Psychology, 1981; BSc in Psychology, Birkbeck Coll., 1978, DSc, 1999. Social worker London Borough of Southwark, 1972-78; vis. rsch. scientist U. Lund, Sweden, 1981-82; rsch. fellow U. Cambridge, 1982-83, demonstrator, 1983-87, lectr. in neurobiology, 1987-95, reader, 1995-99; profl. fellow Cardiff U., 2000—. Editor: Neural Transplantation, 1990, Neural Transplantation, A Practical Approach, 1992, Functional Neural Transplantation, 1994, Neural Repair, Transplantation and Rehabilitation, 1999, Neural Transplantation Methods, 2000, Functional Neural Transplantation II, 2000, Brain Damage, Brain Repair, 2000; editl. bd. Brain Rsch., Behavioural Brain Rsch., Exptl. Brain Rsch., Neuroreport, Neurosci., Advances in Neurosci., Posters in Neurosci., Restorative Neurology and Neurosci., Jour. Neural Transplantation; contbr. articles to profl. jours. Recipient Spearman medal Brit. Psychol. Soc., 1988, Alfred Mayer medal Brit. Neuropathol. Soc.; fellow Clare Coll., 1981. Mem. European Neurosci. Assn., Soc. for Neurosci., Brain Rsch. Orgn. E-mail: dunnett@cf.ac.uk. Office: Cardiff U Sch Biosciences, Museum Ave, Cardiff CF10305, United Kingdom

DUNNEWIJN-BUDE, MARIANNE HUBERTINA, dean; b. Beek, Limburg, The Netherlands, Sept. 23, 1945; d. Leonardus Hubertus Bude and Cornelia Maria (Herckhoffs) Nuyens; m. Johannes Petrus Peters, May 16, 1966 (div. Apr. 1969); m. Theodor Johannes Dunnewijk, Aug. 17, 1970; children: Boris, Feikve. Cmty. Worker, Profl. U. Social Work, Sittard, The Netherlands, 1967; Sociology, Cath. U. Brabant, Tilburg, The Netherlands, 1977. Cmty. worker, 1967-69; mentrix Ignatius Hosp., Breda, The Netherlands, 1969-70; asst. Cath. U. Brabant, Tilburg, 1974; reseracher IVA Rsch. Ctr., Tilburg, 1977-80; prof. U. Katholieke Leerwanken, Tilburg, 1981-87; dean Fontys Profl. U., Tilburg and Eindhoven, 1988—. Author: De Bijstandsmaatschappelisk Werner En Zhon Opleiding, 1978; editor: Urllwen of de Eerste R.J., 1992. Dir. Child Home, Tilburg, 1972-75, sch., Tilburg, 1976-79, cmty. svc., 1982-88, Coll. Sectoral Advice, The Netherlands, 1996—. Home: Wienwland str 30, 50385N Tilburg The Netherlands Office: Fontys Profl U, Postbus 347, 5600 Ah Eindhoven The Netherlands

DUNNILL, MICHAEL GILES SIMPSON, dermatologist; b. Oxford, U.K., July 9, 1964; s. Michael Simpson and Hilda (Eastman) D.; m. Kim Elaine Woods; 2 children, Oliver, Constance. MBBS, St. George's Hosp., 1987. Registrar St. George's Hosp., London, 1990-92; rsch. assoc. St. Thomas's Hosp., London, 1992-95; sr. registrar Royal Hosp. London, 1995-97; cons. Bristol (Eng.) Royal Infirmary, 1997—. Contbr. articles to profl. jours. Mem. British Assn. Dermatologists, Royal Coll. Physicians. Office: Bristol Royal Infirmary, Malborough St, Bristol BS1 3NU, England

DUNNILL, PETER, biochemical engineer; b. Harrow, Eng., May 20, 1938; s. Eric and Marjorie (Moseley) D.; m. Patricia Mary Lievesley, Aug. 11, 1962; 1 child, Paul. BSc, U. London, 1961, PhD, 1963, DSc, 1978. Rsch. staff Royal Instn., London, 1963-64; lectr. Univ. Coll. London, 1964-79, reader, 1979-84, prof., 1984—, dir. Advanced Ctr. for Biochem. Engring., 1991—; mem. Biotech. Directorate, 1982-88, U.K., Biotech. Joint Adv. Bd. Rsch. Coun., 1989-92; mem. coun. Biotech. Biol. Scis. Rsch. Coun., U.K., 1994-96. Recipient Heatley medal Biochem. Soc., 1997. Fellow Instn. Chem. Engrs. (Donald medal 1995), Royal Acad. of Engring., Royal Soc. Chemistry, Order Brit. Empire. Avocation: music. Home: 14 Cornwall Ave, London N3 1LD, England Office: Univ Coll London, Torrington Pl, London WCIE 7JE, England

DUNNING, HERBERT NEAL, government official, physical chemist; b. Hazard, Nebr., June 2, 1923; s. Herbert P. and Maude Lillian (Welsh) D.; m. Margaret Stovall (div. 1973); 1 child, Margaret Diane Aulik; m. Raquel Reichmann, Oct. 10, 1974; 1 child, Denise Raquel. BS, Kearney State Coll., 1944; MS, U. Nebr., 1948, PhD, 1950; postdoctoral studies, U. Minn., 1964-66. Dir. surface chemistry lab. Dept. Interior, Bartlesville, Okla., 1951-60; rsch. dir. Gen. Mills, Inc., Mpls., 1961-70, Delmark Foods and Pharm., Mpls., 1970-71; dir. divsn. foods rsch. FDA, Washington, 1972-74; dir. office mng. assistance FDA, Rockville, Md., 1979-90; pres. NDA, Inc., Rockville, 1991—; dir. divsn. oil and gas, U.S. ERDA, Washington, 1974-78; leader US-USSR exchange on natural gas tech., 1976-78; Donald E. Fox Meml. lectr. Kearney State Coll., 1983. Contbr. articles to profl. jours., publs. and books; patentee in field. Lt. USNR, 1944-46. Recipient Superior Performance award U.S. Bur. Mines, 1959, Meritorious Svc. award Dept. Interior, 1969, Merit award FDA, 1985, Outstanding Alumnus award Kearney State Coll., 1989, Disting. Svc. award Dental Mfrs. Am., 1993. Fellow AAAS; mem. Am. Chem. Soc., AIChE, Am. Soc. Quality Control (Svc. award 1985), Explorers Club. Avocations: oil painting, water skiing, golf. Home and Office: 8309 Bryant Dr Bethesda MD 20817-3136 also: 3480 Cedar Lake Ct Bonita Springs FL 34134-7998

DUNNING, JOHN HARRY, economics educator; b. Eng., June 26, 1927; s. John Murray and Anne Florence (Baker) D.; m. Christine Mary Brown, Aug. 4, 1975; 1 son by previous marriage, Philip. BSc in Econs., U. London, 1952; PhD, Southampton U., 1957; PhD (hon.), U. Uppsala, Sweden, 1975, U. Autonoma Madrid, 1991; U. Antwerp, 1997. Lectr. U. Southampton, 1952-64; mem. faculty U. Reading, Eng., 1964-92, found. prof. econs., 1964-74, Esmee Fairbairn prof. internat. investment and bus. studies, 1975-87, chmn. dept. econs., 1964-87, ICI rsch. prof. internat. bus., 1987-92, 94—; vis. prof. U. Western Ont., London, Can., 1968-69, U. Calif. Berkeley, 1976; vis. prof. internat. mgmt. U. Boston, 1976; prof. internat. bus. Rutgers U., N.J., 1989—; chmn. Economists Adv. Group Ltd.; mem. chems. econ. devel. com. Royal Econ. Soc., 1970-77; mem. S.E. Econ. Planning Coun., 1965-69; mem. coms. econ. and social rsch. coun. OECD, European Commn., UN; lectr. Ireland, 1993, Switzerland, 1994, China, 1995, Sweden, 1996, Hong Kong, 1997; hon. prof. U. Beijing, 1995. Explaining International Production, 1988, Multinational Enterprises, Technology and Competitiveness, 1988, The Multinational Enterprises and the Global Economy, 1993, The Globalization of Business, 1993, Alliance Capitalism and Global Business, 1997; editor: The Multinational Enterprise, 1971, International Investment, 1972, Economic Analysis and Multinational Enterprise, 1974, Structural Change in the World Economy, 1990, The Theory of Transnational Corporations, 1992, The New Globalism and Developing Countries, 1997, Governments, Globalization and International Business, 1997, Regions, Globalization and the Knowledge Based Economy, 2000, Globalization at Bay, 2000; contbr. articles to acad. and profl. jours. Home: Holly Dell Satwell Close, Rotherfield Greys, Henley-on-Thames Oxon RG 9 4QT, England Office: U Reading, Whiteknights Pk, Reading Berkshire, England

DUNOVSKY, JIŘÍ, pediatrician, educator; b. Prague, Czech Republic, Apr. 16, 1930; s. Frantisek and Jaromira (Vajsarova) D.; m. Eva Vackova, 1951 (div. 1964); children: Eva, Veduna; m. Eva Ruzickova; children: Jiri, Katerina. MD, U. Charles, Prague, 1955, candidate sci., 1971, DSc, PhD, 1985, prof. pediat., 1987. Resident pediat. Hosp. Tábor, Czech Republic, 1955-58, Hosp. Benešov, Czech Republic, 1958-61; chief pediatrician Hosp. Vlasim, Czech Republic, 1961-64; med. officer Ministry of Health, Prague, 1964-68; asst. prof. Postgrad. Inst. for Physicians, Prague, 1968-79, chief pediat. dept., 1979-91, chief od soc. pediat. dept., 1991-93, chief od Child Crisis Ctr., 1993-96; ret., 1997; tchr. social pediat. Healthsocial Faculty South Bohemian U., 1997—; faculty edn. Charles U., Prague, 1997—; sci. advisor Czech Family Planning Assn., Prague, 1997—; vice-dean health Soc. Faculty South Bohem U., Prague, 1997—; chmn. SOS Childrens' Villages, Prague, 1968-73, 89-94; expert WHO/EURO, Copenhagen, 1983, Unicef, Geneva, 1985; v.p. Czechoslovak Pediat. Soc., Prague, 1982-90; chmn. The Found. of Crisis Children Ctr., Prague, 1993. Author: Position of the Child in Society Concerning to Social Abandonment, 1970, Child and Disorders of Family, 1985; author, editor: Social and Juridical Problems in Paediatrics, 1980, Social Pediatrics, 1989, Child Abuse and Neglect, 1995, System of Preventive Pediatric Investigation, 1989, Social Paediatrics, 1999. Founder, chmn. Assn. SOS Childrens Villages in Czechoslovakia, Prague. Lt. Health Svcs., 1956-58; founder Children's Crisis Ctr., Prague, 1992—. Recipient medal J.A. Comenius, 1994, medal for excellent care of children. Fellow Am. Acad. Pediatrics (hon.), Soc. Pediatric Assn. Germany (hon.), Czech Assn. Soc. Pediatrics (hon. chmn.); mem. N.Y. Acad. Sci. Avocation: history. Home: Schnirchova 32, 170 00 Prague Czech Republic Office: Czech Family Planning Assn, Panská 1, Prague 1, Czech Republic

DUNPHY, DEXTER COLBOYD, management educator; b. Sydney, NSW, Australia; s. Myles Joseph and Margaret Tinsley (Peet) D.; m. Beverley Merrilyn Slade; children: Mark Roland, Kristen Gay, Roger Barrington. BA in Edn. with honors, U. Sydney, 1956, diploma of edn., 1957, MEd with honors, 1961; PhD, Harvard U., 1964. Tchr. NSW Dept. Edn., Sydney, 1957, 59-60; tchg. fellow Sydney U., 1958; lectr. Sydney Tchrs. Coll., 1961; rsch. asst., tchg. fellow Harvard U., Cambridge, Mass., 1961-64, lectr., asst. prof., 1964-67; sr. lectr. sociology U. NSW, Sydney, 1967-69, prof. bus. adminstrn., 1970-82, prof. mgmt., 1983-99; head dept. orgnl. behavior U. NSW, Sydney, 1970-82, dir. Ctr. for Corp. Change, 1991-97; disting. prof. U. Tech. Sydney, 2000—. Author: (books) The General Inquirer, 1966, The Primary Group, 1972, Organizational Change by Choice, 1981, Under New Management, 1990, Beyond the Boundaries, 1994, The Sustainable Corporation, 1998. Fulbright sr. scholar; recipient Mike Pontifex award for Outstanding Contbn. to human resources profession, Australian & New Zealand Acad. Mgmt. Disting. Mem. award. Mem. Australian Human Resources Inst. Home: 53 Mill Hill Rd Bondi Jnctn, 2022 Sydney NSW, Australia Office: U Technology Faculty of Bus, PO Box 123, 2052 Sydney NSW, Australia

DUNPHY, STEVEN, educator, real estate broker; b. Stamford, Conn.; s. John Joseph and Georgena Byers (Cuthbert) D. BA, Hampshire Coll., 1977; MBA, U. Pa., 1980; PhD, Ind. U., 1990. Licensed real estate broker, Ind. Asst. prof. U. Akron, Ohio, 1997—; owner Dunphy Properties, Bloomington, Ind., 1985—. Contbr. articles to profl. jours. Avocations: swimming, reading. Office: U Akron 259 S Broadway Akron OH 44325-0001

DUNSTAN, RICHARD HUGH, biological scientist, educator; b. London, Apr. 21, 1959; arrived in Australia, 1959; s. Richard English and Elspeth Anne (Bonython) D.; m. Margaret Macrae Macdonald, Sept. 10, 1983; children: Sarah Claire, Jennifer, Nicholas Andrew. BAgSc, Adelaide (Australia) U., 1981, BAgSci with honors, 1982; DPhil, Oxford U., U.K., 1986. Postdoctoral rsch. asst. Oxford (Eng.) U., 1986-88; Queen Elizabeth II nat. rsch. fellow Melbourne (Australia) U., 1988-90; lectr. Newcastle (Australia) U., 1990-94, sr. lectr., 1995—; environ. cell biology rschr. Newcastle U., 1990—, rschr. in chronic fatigue, 1992—; bd. dirs. Bioscreens Pty. Ltd., Newcastle. Contbr. articles to Biochem. and Molecular Medicine, Royal Soc. London, Biomed. and Archives Environ. Contamination and Toxicology, others. Gowrie scholar, 1982-85; Exhbn. of 1851 Brit. rsch. scholar, 1982-85. Mem. AAAS. Avocations: sports, reading. Office: U Newcastle Biol Sci Dept, Callaghan, 2308 Newcastle Australia

DUNTON, JAMES RAYNOR, publisher; b. Wilmington, Del., June 17, 1955; s. Guthrie Raynor III and Jane (Hill) D. BA, U. Va., 1977; MBA, Boston U., 1981. Editor Quorum Books, Westport, Conn., 1984-87; sr. editor Praeger Pubs., N.Y.C., 1987-91, editor-in-chief, 1991-94; pub. acad. and trade Greenwood Pub. Group, Westport, 1994-96; dir. publs. Ctr. for Strategic and Internat. Studies, Washington, 1996—. Mem. Va. Club of N.Y. Home: 1520 16th St NW Apt 704 Washington DC 20036-1448 Office: Ctr for Strategic and Internat Studies 1800 K St NW Washington DC 20006-2202

DUONG, DUY QUANG, mechanical engineer, research scientist; b. Hai Duong, Vietnam, Dec. 9, 1949; arrived in Australia, 1969; s. Huan Van and Xuyen Thi (Nguyen) D. BE in Mech. Engring., U. Tasmania, Hobart, Tasmania, Australia, 1974; M of Engring. Scis., U. New South Wales, Sydney, Australia, 1976, PhD in Gas Dynamics, 1982, M of Commerce in Econs. and Fin., 1986. Part time tutor U. New South Wales, Sydney, 1975-79, rsch. asst., 1975-76; tutor Hawkesbury Agrl. Coll., Richmond, NSW, Australia, 1979-80; mech. engr. Dept. Housing and Constrn., Sydney, 1982-86; rsch. engr. Nat. Bldg. Tech. Ctr., Ryde, NSW, Australia, 1986-88; rsch. scientist Commonwealth Sci. and Indsl. Rsch. Orgn., Ryde, 1988-91, sr. rsch. scientist, 1991-99; dir. Duong and Assocs., 2000—; fire safety cons. Sydney Internat. Airport, Darling Harbor Centennial Project, others, Sydney, 1987—; guest scientist Nat. Bur. Standards, Washington, 1988-89. Author: (poetry in Vietnamese) Tho Nguyen Tran Duong Quang, 1975, Ta Tinh, 1980, Y Xua, 1999; contbr. articles to profl. jours. Recipient Colombo Plan scholarship Australian Govt., Sydney, 1969-74. Mem. Internat. Assn. for Fire Safety Sci., N.Y. Acad. Scis. Buddhist. Avocations: table tennis, poetry, econs., novels, classical music. Home and Office: Hurlstone Park, 10/74 Floss St, NSW Sydney 2193, Australia

DUONG, PHAN TRIEU, science and technology company executive, researcher; b. Hanoi, Vietnam, May 11, 1959; s. Phan and Do Hong (Chinh) Anh; m. Nguyen Thi Bich Ha, Feb. 28, 1982; children: Phan Nhat Minh, Phan Nhat Nam. Diploma, Fgn. Trade Coll., Hanoi, 1981, U. Laws, Vietnam, 1986. Specialist Assn. Vietnam Lawyers, 1982-87, Fgn. Trade Rsch. Inst., Vietnam, 1987-91; gen. dir. Tourinco, Vietnam, 1991—; pres. Golden Villas Project, Vietnam, 1993—; mem. BOM, Saigon Village Project, Vietnam, 1993—; v.p. VE and JA Joint Venture, Vietnam, 1995—. Author: Some Legal Matters in Foreign Investment in Vietnam, 1989; editor, translator: Sample Contracts of Foreign Joint-Venture, 1976; rschr. aritmetic and formular of prime number. Mem. Assn. Vietnamese Lawyers, Vietnam-Japan Friendship Assn. Avocations: music, books, swimming.

DUPÂQUIER, JACQUES ANDRÉ, historian, demographer; b. Sainte-Adresse, France, Jan. 30, 1922; s. Robert and Thérèse (Roger) D.; m. Nicole Balloche, July 23, 1945 (div. 1983); children: Jean-François, Yves, Michel, Robert; m. Paulette Carvaillo, Mar. 26, 1983. SEC, Instn. Saint Joseph, France, 1940; SUP, Lycée Louis le Grand, Paris, 1942, Ecole Normale Supérieure, 1945. History tchr. Pontoise and Montmorency, 1946-62; master for search Nat. Sci. Rsch. Ctr., Paris, 1962-65; asst. prof. U. Sorbonne, Paris, 1965-68; assoc. prof. Ecole pratique des Hautes Etudes, Paris, 1968-70; prof., dir. studies Ecole des Hautes Etudes en Scis. Sociales, Paris, 1970-96. Co-author: Histoire de la Démographie, 1985, Histoire de la Population Française, 1983 (Spl. prize of Acad. 1990), Histoire des Populations de l'Europe, 1998, Histoire de la Populaton Mondiale au XX Siacle, 1999. Decorated chevalier de la Légion d'honneur, 1982 Ordre des Arts et Lettres, officer Ordre des Palmes Acad. (France); recipient Médaille d'Argent, Nat. Sci. Rsch. Ctr., 1981. Mem. Acad. Europaea, N.Y. Acad. Scis., Soc. Démographie Hist., Inst. de France, Acad. Sci. Morales et Politics. Home: 197 Rue Saint Jacques, 60240 Delincourt France

DU PELOUX, CYRILLE, communications engineer; b. St Etienne, France, Feb. 15, 1954; s. Jean and Christiane (Delattre) Du P.; m. Priscilla Desprairies, Dec. 13, 1980; children: Renaud, Lorraine, Alexis. Degree in engring., Poly. U. Paris, 1977, Ponts et Lhaussees, Paris, 1979. Chief dept. Min. Industry, Paris, 1979-84; chief of svc. Bouygues, Paris, 1985-87; from gen. sec. to gen. mgr. TF1, Paris, 1987-92; chmn., CEO Lyonnaise Comms., Paris, 1992-98; CEO TPS, 1996-99; COO Group Bull, Louveciennes, France, 1999—. Served in French air army, 1976-77. Recipient order of merit French state, 1996. Home: 40 Ave de Saxe, 75007 Paris France Office: BULL, 68 rte de Versailles, 78934 Louveciennes France

DU PLESSIS, JEAN JACQUES, law educator; b. Newcastle, Natal, South Africa, Sept. 4, 1959; arrived in Australia, 1999; s. Petrus Johannes and Orpa (Lubbe) Du P.; m. Tharien Van den Heever, Jan. 8, 1993; 1 child, Armand. BProc, Bloemfontein, South Africa, 1981; LLB, Bloemfontein, South Africa, 1983, LLM, 1986, LLD, 1991. Adv. Supreme Ct. South Africa. Sr. lectr. U. of the Free State, Bloemfartein, 1986-90, assoc. prof., 1991; prof. Rand Afrikaans U., Johannesburg, South Africa, 1992-98; assoc. prof. Deakin U., Geelong, Australia, 1999-2000, prof. law, head Sch. Law, 2000—. Alexander von Humboldt scholar Alexander von Humboldt Stiftung, Münster, 1995. Avocations: photography, traveling, cooking. Office: Deakin Univ, Waurn Ponds, Geelong VIC 3217, Australia

DUPLIJ, STEPAN ANATOLIEVICH, physicist, researcher; b. Chernyshevsk, Russia, Aug. 29, 1954; s. Anatolij Stepanovich and Lidia Andreevna (Putz) Duplij; m. Diana Rostislavovna Nadopta, Sept. 10, 1997. MSc, Kharkov (Ukraine) State U., 1978, PhD, 1982, Dr. Hab., 1999. Sr. staff rschr. Kharkov State U., 1983-94; Alexander von Humboldt fellow U. Kaiserslautern, Germany, 1994-97, sr. staff rschr., 1997—. Author (book of poetry) Page of The West, 1995, Alien, 1995, Angel, 1997, In Cry, 1999; author, composer (CD's) Motifs of Years, 1995, Blitz, 1996; contbr. articles to profl. jours. Mem. Am. Math. Soc., European Phys. Soc., Internat. Assn. Math. Physics. Avocations: poetry, guitar, Midi, computers, classical and symphonic rock music . E-mail: steven.a.duplij@univer.kharkov.ua. Home: Kirova 5 Apt 43, 61001 Kharkov Ukraine Office: Kharkov Nat U, Theory Group Nuclear Phys, Kharkov 61077, Ukraine

DUPONT, ERIC, laboratory administrator; b. Arvida, Que., Canada, May 3, 1965; s. Louis Dupont and Viviane Bouchard. BSc in Biochemistry, Laval U., Que., 1988, cert. in bus. adminstrn., 1991, PhD in Physiology and Endocrinology, 1992; postgrad. in neurondocrinology. Founder, pres., CEO Aeterna Labs., Que., 1991—, chmn. sci. adv. bd. Patentee in field. Recipient fellowship Med. Rsch. Coun. Canada, 1990-93, 20th Century award Achievement; laureate Fideide High Tech., 1994, laureate Fideide Co. Yr., 1997, laureate of Raymond Blass medal, 1996. Mem. AAAS, ACS, SPEQM (bd. dirs.), YPO, AACR, N.Y. Acad. Scis. Avocations: hunting, painting, boating. Office: Aeterna Labs, 1405 Boul du Parc Technolog, Quebec, PQ Canada G1P 4P5

DUPONT, WESLEY DAVID, lawyer; b. Putnam, Conn., Nov. 1, 1968; s. Thomas Edward Sr. and Patricia Fay Dupont. BA magna cum laude, Brown U., 1992; JD with honors, U. Conn., 1995. Bar: Conn. 1995, N.Y. 1995, U.S. Dist. Ct. Conn. 1995. Assoc. Kelley Drye & Warren LLP, Stamford, Conn., 1995—; sec. Fano Securities LLC, Greenwich, Conn., 1997—, Fano Holdings Corp., 1998—. Contbr. articles to profl. jours. Atty., Stamford Symphony, 1998—. Mem. ABA, Conn. Bar Assn., N.Y. State Bar Assn., The Corp. Bar, Phi Delta Phi. Avocations: fly-fishing, running, golf. Office: Kelley Drye & Warren LLP 281 Tresser Blvd Stamford CT 06901-3229

DUPOUY-CAMET, JEAN, parasitologist, educator; b. Caracas, Venezuela, May 15, 1953; s. Jacques and Christiane (Beauvais) Dupouy-C.; m. Claire Tournus, June 18, 1977; children: Loïse, Marie. MD, CHU St. Antoine, 1979; MSc, USTL, 1986; PhD, U. R. Descartes, 1993. Asst. CHU Cochin, Paris, 1981-88, maitre de conf., 1988-96, prof., 1996—; mem. Internat. Commn. Trichinellosis, 1996—. Author, editor: La Trichinellose une Zoonose en Evolution, 1991; contbr. articles to profl. jours. Recipient Silver medal Paris Med. U., 1979. Mem. Am. Soc. Microbiology, French Soc. Parasitology (bd. dirs.), French Soc. Med. Mycology. Home: 19 Residence Tournemire, 91940 Les Ulis France Office: Cochin Hosp U R Descartes, 27 Fbrg St Jacques, 75014 Paris France

DUPPS, JOHN AVERY, JR., machinery company executive; b. Middletown, Ohio, Sept. 1, 1942; s. John Avery and Mary (Norris) D.; m. Patricia Murphy, Oct. 5, 1968; children: Emily Kathleen, Julia Marie, Mary Katherine. BSChemE, U. Notre Dame, 1964. V.p. The Dupps Co., Germantown, Ohio, 1966-82, pres., 1982—; bd. dirs. First Nat. Bank, Germantown. Chmn. Mid Miami Healthcare Found., Middletown, 1994-99, C-J H.S. Devel. Adv. Coun., Dayton, Ohio, 1998—. Mem. Am. Oil Chemists Soc., Meat Industry Suppliers Assn. (pres. 1988-89), Process Equipment Mfrs. Assn. (pres. 1999—).

DUPRAT, PIERRE, safety and research director; b. Paris, Nov. 22, 1945; s. Marcel and Fernande (Vitran) D.; m. Nelly Françoise Madelaine, May 26, 1948; children: Marion, Christophe. D of Vet. Medicine, Paris/Alfort, 1970; PhD in Med. Econometry, Pantheon/Sorbonne, Paris, 1976; PhD in Toxicology, Pharmacy and Med. Sch., Lyon, France, 1986. Cert. in vet. medicine, vet. pathology European Coll. Vet. Pathologists. Rsch. pathology asst. Agr. Ministry, Paris/Alfort, 1970-72; head pathology and hematology Inst. Nat. Recherche et de Securité, Nancy, France, 1972-79; rsch. pathologist Merck, Riom, France, 1979-81, head of pathology, 1981-86, dir. pathology, 1986-96, sr. dir. Safety Assessment and Rsch. Ctr., 1996—; dir. vet. theses in pathology Riom Rsch. Ctr.; mem. sci. com. Pharmacy and Med. Sch. of Clermont-Ferrand. Contbr. numerous articles to profl. jours. and books. Mem. SOT, STP, SFAT, ISOT. Avocations: collecting antiques and antique cars and motorcycles. Home: Chateau de Jayet, 63260 Saint Genes du Retz Auvergne, France Office: MSD-Chibret, Rte de Marsat Riom, 63963 Clermont-Ferrand Cedex, France

DUPRÉ, JOHN A., philosophy educator; b. Pembury, Kent, Eng., July 3, 1952; s. Desmond John and Catherine Lane (Poole) D.; m. Lynda Laurel-Ann Oppenheim, Oct. 6, 1977 (div. 1981); m. Regenia Ann Gagnier, Sept. 13, 1989; children: Gabriel Gagnier, Julian Gagnier. BA, Oxford (Eng.) U., 1981; PhD, Cambridge (Eng.) U., 1981. Jr. rsch. fellow St. John's Coll., Oxford, 1980-82; asst. prof. Stanford (Calif.) U., 1982-89, assoc. prof., 1989-95, prof. philosophy, 1975-96; prof. London U., 1996—; sr. rsch. fellow U. Exeter, Eng., 1996—, prof. philosophy, 2000—. Author: The Disorder of Things: Metaphysical Foundations of the Disunity of Science, 1993; editor: The Latest on the Best: Essays on Evolution and Optimality, 1987; contbr. numerous articles to profl. jours. and anthologies. Recipient Rsch. Leave award Arts and Humanities Rsch. Bd. U.K., 1999—; Harkness fellow Commonwealth Fund of N.Y., 1978-80; Stanford Humanities Ctr. fellow, 1985-86. Mem. Am. Philos. Assn., Philosophy of Sic. Assn., Aristotelian Soc. Avocations: gardening, playing the viola da gamba, botany. Office: U Exeter Dept Sociology, Rennes Dr, Exeter Devon EX4 4RJ, England

DU PREEZ, ROSE, management consultant; b. Harare, Zimbabwe, Apr. 10, 1963; arrived in South Africa, 1979; d. Allan J. and Margaret J. (Anderson) Du P. B Commerce, U. South Africa, Pretoria, 1992; MBA, U. Witwatersrand, Johannesburg, South Africa, 1994. Sales mgr. Xerox Corp., Johannesburg, 1987-92; nat. sales mgr. Firechem, Midrand, South Africa, 1993; mng. dir. Service Monitor, Johannesburg, 1993—; chmn. Call Ctr. Networking Group, Johannesburg, 1997—. Avocations: travel, gourmet food, movies. Office: Service Monitor, PO Box 75128, Gardenview 2047, Republic of South Africa

DUPRIEST, DOUGLAS MILLHOLLEN, lawyer; b. Ft. Riley, Kans., Dec. 28, 1951; s. Robert White and Barbara Nadine (Millhollen) DuP. AB in Philosophy with high honors, Oberlin Coll., 1974; JD, U. Oreg., 1977. Bar: Oreg. 1977, U.S. Dist. Ct. Oreg. 1977, U.S. Ct. Appeals (9th cir.) 1977. Assoc. Coons & Anderson and predecessors, Eugene, Oreg., 1977-81, Hutchinson, Harrell et al, 1981; ptnr. Hutchinson, Cox, Coons & DuPriest and predecessors, 1982—; adj. prof. sch. law U. Oreg., 1986; mem. task forces Wetlands Mgmt., 1988-89, 92-93. Author: (with others) Land Use, 1982, Administrative Law, 1985; contbg. editor Real Estate & Land Use Digest, 1983-86; articles editor, mng. bd. mem. U. Oreg. Law Rev., 1976-77. Bd. dirs. Home Health Agy., Eugene, 1977-79, pres., 1978-79; bd. dirs. Oreg. Environ. Coun., Portland, 1979-84, pres., 1980-81; mem. Lane Econ. Com., 1989-91; chair voters pamphlet com. Eugene City Club, 1993. Recipient Disting. Svc. award Oreg. Environ. Coun., 1988. Mem. Oreg. Bar Assn. (exec. com. real estate and land use sect. 1978-81). Home: 225 Dartmoor Dr Eugene OR 97401-6620 Office: Hutchinson Cox Coons & DuPriest 777 High St Ste 200 Eugene OR 97401-2750

DUPUIS, OLIVIER, member European Parliament; b. Ath, Belgium, Feb. 25, 1958. Mem. European Parliament, Brussels, 1999—; mem. com. on constl. affairs, com. on petitions, substitute mem. com. on fgn. affairs, human rights, common security and def. policy, mem. dels. for rels. with countries South Asia and South Asia Assn. for Regional Cooperation, mem. dels. to parliamentary cooperation coms. and dels. for rels. with Transcaucasian republics of Armenia, Azerbaijan and Georgia, substitute mem. del. to European Union-Romania joint parliamentary com. Mem. Tech. Group Ind. Mems. Office: Via di Torre Argentina 76, I-00186 Rome Italy aslo: 10 rue des Riches Claires, B-1000 Brussels Belgium*

DUPUY, PATRICK FRANCIS, dermatologist; b. Vouziers, France, Mar. 3, 1954; s. François Alexis and Anne-Marie Josephine (Collin) D.; m. Catherine Jeanne Denize, Mar. 30, 1992; children: Paul, Laure. MS in Cellular and Molecular Biology, Pasteur's Inst., 1983; degree clin. rsch. methodology, Faculty of Medicine, Paris, 1984; MD, U. Caen, 1985. Bd. cert. dermatologist. Asst. prof. dept. dermatology McGill U., Montreal, 1985-87; rschr. lab. dermatology French Nat. Inst. of Health and Med. Rsch., Creteil, France, 1987-90; internat. clin. leader Roche Labs., Strasbourg, France, 1990-94; head clin. rsch. dept. dermatology and cosmetology Pierre-Fabre Rsch. Inst., Toulouse, France, 1994—. Reviewer several European jours.; contbr. articles to profl. publs. V.p. European Fedn. for Osteogenesis-Imperfecta, Eindhoven, The Netherlands, 1996. Recipient Laureate of the Dermatol. Rsch. prize French Soc. of Dermatology, 1989; rsch. grant Ligue Contre le Cancer and Assistance Publique, 1984, Pres. Gold medal Amiens U. Hosp., 1984. Mem. European Orgn. for Rare Disorders, European Soc. of Dermatol. Rsch., European Acad. of Dermatology and Venereology. Avocations: history, sports, swimming, golfing. Office: Pierre Fabre Rsch Inst, Allee Camille Soula BD74, 31322 Castanet Tolosan France Address: Inst De Recherche Pierre Fabre, 17 Avenue Jean-Moulin, 81106 Castres Cedex France

DUPUY, PEDRO, film company executive; b. Guantanamo, Cuba, Feb. 22, 1922; s. Facundo and Edicta (Dupuy) Ilisastigui. Degree, U. Sci. & Philosophy, Waynesboro, Va.; student, Conservatory of Art & Music, Florence, Italy. Performer various, U.S., Europe, Asia; choreographer/dancer Sta. KTLA-TV, Sta. KCOP-TV, Paramount, L.A.; prodr./dir./choreographer/star Dupuy Prodns., N.Y.C., L.A., Las Vegas; record, video prodr. Dupuy Records/Prodns./Pub., Inc., Studio City, Calif.; prin. Moro-Landis/Dupuy Ltd. Studios, Studio City; talent mgr., cons. Dupuy Mgmt., Glendale, Calif., 1992—; chmn., CEO F.H.S. Legacy Corp., Film Entertainment, L.A., 1998—; pres., mgr. Baxter Hugo Prodns., LLC, Glendale, 1999—; founder, pres. F.H.S. Legacy Corp.'s Actor-Writer Seminar, 1995—; contbg. dir./choreographer Variety Club Telethon, Easter Seals Telethon, Jerry Lewis MDA Telethon. Author: The Artist Unfolds Communication Through the Spirit, 1997, Mastery of Movement Through Dance, 1998; contbr. articles to profl. jours. Vol. prodr./dir. of stage plays Alemany Cath. Sch., L.A. Recipient Award of Commendation L.A. County Bd. Suprs., L.A. Mayor Tom Bradley. Mem. AFTRA, ASCAP, Am. Guild Variety Artists, Am. Fedn. Musicians, Nat. Assn. Recording Merchandisers, Conf. Personal Mgrs., Inc. E-mail: fhslegacy@aol.com. Office: F H S Legacy Corp PO Box 9271 Glendale CA 91226-0271

DUQUE, ALBERTO, physician, clinical pharmacologist; b. Onteniente, Valencia, Spain, May 7, 1958; s. Francisco Duaue and Matilde Oliart; children: Alba, Victor. Degree in biology, Barcelona U., 1980; MD, UAB, Barcelona, 1985; M in Pharmacoepidemiology, Hosp. S. Pau, Barcelona, 1990. Head drug safety CIBA-Geigy, Spain, 1991-96, GCP officer, 1992-94, sr. epidemiologist, 1994-98; head drug safety Novartis, Spain, 1996—. Editor: Nuevas Perspectivas de FV, 1998; contbr. articles to profl. publs. Lt. Cavalry, 1982-83. Mem. ISPE, ESOP. Avocations: history, philosophy of science, particle physics. Office: Navartis Farmaceutica, Gran Via 764, 08013 Barcelona Spain

DUQUE, RICARDO GERMAN, analytical chemist; b. Panama City, Panama, Nov. 14, 1970; came to U.S., 1988; s. Gabriel E. and Hilda Teresa (Soto) D. BS in Biochemistry, UCLA, 1993; MS in X-Ray Crystallography, Calif. State U., Northridge, 1998. Lab. asst. Inst. Geophysics and Planetary Physics, UCLA, 1991-94, Jerry Lewis Neuromuscular Rsch. Ctr., UCLA, 1993-94; tchg. asst. Calif. State U., Northridge, 1993-98; high sch. sci. tchr. Bridges Acad., L.A., 1996-97; analytical chemist Micropolis, L.A., 1996-97; sr. head media engr., head-disk interface, advanced tech. Maxtor Corp., Milpitas, Calif., 1998—. Mem. ACS, UCLA Assn. Chemists and Biochemists, UCLA Alumni Assn., Sigma Xi Sci. Rsch. Soc. (Donald Bianchi award 1996). Office: 510 Cottonwood Dr Milpitas CA 95035-7403

DUQUESNE, STEPHAN P., textiles executive, consultant; b. Rouen, France, May 24, 1967; came to U.S., 1993; m. Lizette M. Duquesne. M in Internat. Bus., U. Paris, 1991. Internat. liaison officer UN, Sarajevo, Bosnia, 1992-93; dir. internat. sales Thomaston (Ga.) Mills, 1994-98, Cone Mills, Greensboro, N.C., 1998-99; v.p. internat. sales Burlington Industries, Greensboro, 1999—. 1st lt. UN, 1992-93. Decorated Bronze Star, French Army, Bosnia, 1992, UN medal of honor, Bosnia, 1992. Avocations: flying, sky diving, cooking.

DUQUETTE, DONALD NORMAN, law educator; b. Manistique, Mich., Apr. 3, 1947; s. Donald Francis and Martha Adeline (Rice) D.; m. Kathy Jo Loudenbeck, June 17, 1967; 1 child, Gail Jean. BA, Mich. State U., 1969; JD, U. Mich., 1974. Bar: Mich. 1975. Children's caseworker Mich. Dept. Social Svcs., Muskegon, 1969-72; asst. prof. pediatrics and human devel. Mich. State U. Coll. Human Medicine, East Lansing, 1975-76; clin. prof., dir. child advocacy law clinic U. Mich., Ann Arbor, 1976—, co-dir. interdisciplinary project on child abuse and neglect, 1979-89, dir. permanency planning legal svcs., 1984—, dir. interdisciplinary grad. edn. in child abuse-neglect, 1986-92, dir. Kellogg child welfare law program, 1995-98; bd. visitors U. Ariz. Sch. of Law, 1995-99; legal cons. U.S. Children's Bur., Pres. Clinton's Initiative on Adoption and Foster Care, 1997-98; bd. dirs. Nat. Assn. Counsel for Children, 1999—. Author: Advocating for the Child, 1990, Michigan Child Welfare Law, 1990, rev. edit., 1994; mem. editl. bd. Child Abuse and Neglect Internat. Jour., 1985-90; conbr. articles to profl. jours. Commr. Washtenaw County Bd. Commrs., 1981-88; bd. dirs. Children's Trust Fund for Prevention of Child Abuse, 1983-85; mem. Permanency Planning Com. Mich. Supreme Ct., 1982-85, Probate Ct. Task Force, 1986-87, Govs. Task Force on Children's Justice, 1992—. Named Citizen of Yr. Huron Valley NASW, Ann Arbor, 1985; recipient Rsch. in Advocacy award Nat. Ct. Apptd. Spl. Advocate Assn., Seattle, 1985, Outstanding Legal Advocacy award Nat. Assn. of Counsel for Children, 1996, Hicks Child Welfare Leadership award Mich. Fedn. Children's Agys., 1998. Mem. Am. Profl. Soc. on Abuse of Children, Mich. State Bar (co-chair Children's Task Force 1993-95). Democrat. Unitarian. Avocations: piano, sailing. Home: 1510 Linwood Ave Ann Arbor MI 48103-3659 Office: U Mich Sch Law Child Advocacy Law Clinic 625 S State St Ann Arbor MI 48109-1215

DUQUOC, CHRISTIAN, educator; b. Nantes, France, Dec. 22, 1926; s. André and Andrieu Marie D. Student, Coll. St. Stanislas, Nantes, 1938-45, Chambery, Fribourg, Paris, 1947-54; D in Theology, U. Lyon, France, 1967; Docteur (hon.), U. Neuchatel, Geneva, Switzerland, 1985, 92. Prof. Univ., Lyon, 1957-92; supt. U. of Montreal, Can., 1965-71; prof. Univ., Geneva, 1978-90; supt. Neuchatel, Fubourg, Lausanne, Fribourg, Lausanne, 1980-90; dir. Assn. Concilium, Nimègue, The Netherlands, 1970—. Contbr. articles to profl. jours. Roman Catholic. Office: Assn Lumiere et Vie, 2 Place Gailleton, 69002 Lyon France

DUR, PHILIP FRANCIS, political scientist, educator, retired foreign service officer; b. St. Louis, June 30, 1914; s. Alphonse and Sarah (Ralston) D.; m. Elena Delgado, June 30, 1942; children: Elena (Mrs. Philip A. Morris), Philip, Stansbury, Carmen (Mrs. Norman B. Conley, Jr.), Jacqueline (Mrs. James Chase Sheppard), John. A.B., Harvard U., 1935, Ph.D., 1941; post-grad., Fgn. Service Inst., 1961. Consul, pub. affairs officer Lyon, France, 1948-51; chief Office Pub. Affairs, Office U.S. High Commr. for Germany, Bonn, 1951-52; consul, exec. officer Bremen, Germany, 1952-53; comml. controls officer Mil. Security Bd., Coblenz, Germany, 1953-54; consul Colon, Panama, 1954-55, Yokohama, Japan, 1955-58; pub. affairs adviser Dept. State, 1958-61; consul Nagoya, Japan, 1961-65; Jefferson Caffery prof. polit. sci. U. Southwestern La., Lafayette, 1965-84; prof. emeritus U. Southwestern La., 1984—, faculty senate, 1969-84; adviser Council for Devel. of French in La., 1968—; mem. U. Southwestern La. Found., 1969-71; pres. France-Amerique de la Louisiane Acadienne, 1970-72; resident dir. La. Consortium Colls. and Univs., Montpellier, France, 1976-77; organizer, exchange prof. La. Ctr. for Studies, U. Paul Valéry, Montpellier. Served to lt. comdr. USNR, 1942-46. Decorated Acad. Palms (France); recipient Nat. Medal of Honor, DAR, 1983, 1st prize French poetry Deep South Writers Conf., 1995. Mem. Am. Fgn. Service Assn., La. Historical Assn., Phi Beta Kappa. Home: 517 Woodvale Ave Lafayette LA 70503-3435

DURALI, SABAN TEOMAN, philosophy educator; b. Kozlu, Turkey, Feb. 7, 1947; s. Sabih and Hilda Durali; m. Piyeret Durali. Diploma, U. Istanbul, 1973, PhD, 1977, D in Habilitation, 1982. Lectr. U. Istanbul, 1975-81, asst. prof. philosophy, 1981-83, assoc. prof., 1983-88, prof., 1988—, head chmn. History of Philosophy sect. Dept. Philosophy, 1995—; vis. lectr. Pa. State U., 1985, Centro Estudios Filosoficos, Mexico City, 1991; vis. prof. Internat. Inst. Islamic Thought and Civilization, Malaysia, 1992-93, 95, Inst. fü Wissenschaftstheorie und Wissenschaftsforschung, U. Vienna, 1994. Author: An Introduction to the Problem of the Living Beings, 1982, 87, Philosophy of Biology, 1991, Aristotle's Study of Science and the Problem of the Living Beings, 1995, A New System of Philosophy-Science from the biological Standpoint, 1996, The Anglo-Judaic Contemporary Global Civilization, 1996, Introduction to Philosophy-Science, 1998; contbr. articles to profl. jours. Mem. Insternat. Soc. History, Philosophy and Social Studies of Biology, Centro Estudios Filosoficos, turkish Philosophical Assn. Moslem. Avocations: mountaineering, wandering, travel. Fax: 90 212 284 39 81. Home: 21/1 Bann Apt Sehithakkihan, 80600 2 Istanbul Turkey Office: U Istanbul Dept Philosophy, Bayazit, 34459 Istanbul Turkey

DURÁN, LORI JEAN, systems programmer; b. Spencer, Iowa, June 15, 1958; d. Ronald Edwin and Norma Lea (Jipson) Carlson; m. Juan Cruz Durán, Jan. 8, 1994; children: Gabrielle Renée, Lauren Elizabeth. BA, Iowa State U., 1983; MA, U. Tex., 1986. Systems programmer V Tex. Workforce Commn., Austin, 1986—. Republican. Baptist.

DURAN, MICHAEL CARL, bank executive; b. Colorado Springs, Colo., Aug. 27, 1953; s. Lawrence Herman and Jacqueline Carol (Ward) D. BS magna cum laude, Ariz. State U., 1980. With Valley Nat. Bank (name now Bank One, Ariz., N.A.), Phoenix, 1976—; corp. credit trainee Bank One Ariz. (formerly Valley Nat. Bank Ariz.), Phoenix, 1984-85; comml. loan officer Valley Nat. Bank Ariz. (name now Bank One Ariz.), Phoenix, 1985-86; br. mgr., asst. v.p. Valley Nat. Bank Ariz. (name now Bankone, Ariz.), Phoenix, 1986-90, comml. banking officer, asst. v.p., 1990-93, credit mgr., v.p., 1993-99, relationship mgr., v.p., 1999—; cons. various schs. and orgns., 1986—; incorporator Avondale Neighborhood Housing Svcs., 1988. Mem. Cen. Bus. Dist. Revitalization Com., Avondale, Ariz., 1987-88, Ad-Hoc Econ. Devel. Com., 1988; coord. Avondale Litter Lifters, 1987-88; vol. United Way, Phoenix, 1984; bd. dirs. Jr. Achievement, Yuma, Ariz., 1989-91, vol., Phoenix, 1993—; yokefellow 1st So. Bapt. Ch. of Yuma, 1990-91; treas. Desert View Bapt. Ch., Gilbert, Ariz., 1998—. Recipient Outstanding Community Svc. award City of Avondale, 1988. Mem. Robert Morris Assocs., Ariz. State U. Alumni Assn. (life), Toastmasters, Kiwanis (local bd. dirs. 1986-88), Beta Gamma Sigma, Phi Kappa Phi, Phi Theta Kappa, Sigma Iota Epsilon. Democrat. Baptist. Avocations: art, photography, hiking, jogging. Home: 925 N Quartz St Gilbert AZ 85234-3661

DURAND, LOURENS GERHARDUS, manufacturing executive; b. Pretoria, Transvaal, South Africa, Oct. 16, 1949; s. Lourens Gerhardus Jacobus and Jose Louise White Durand; m. Winnefred Van Der Merwe, Oct. 6, 1973; children: Donovan, Eileen. BSc in Indsl. Chemistry, Witwatersrand U., Johannesburg, South Africa, 1971; MSc, U. Natal, Durban, South Africa, 1981. Devel. chemist S.A. Oil Mills, Randfontein, South Africa, 1971-73; chief chemist Delmas Milling, Randfontein, 1973-76; sr. rsch. chemist Cerebos Food Corp., Durban, South Africa, 1976-81; tech. svcs. mgr. African Products, Johannesburg, 1981—. Contbr. articles to profl. jours. Mem. South African Assn. for Food Sci. and Tech., South African Chem. Inst., Inst. of Food Technologists. Avocations: drawing/painting, writing, Bonsai trees. Office: African Products Pty Ltd, 2 Dick Kemp St Meadowdale, Gauteng 1600, South Africa

DURAND, PIERRE-YVES, physician, nephrologist; b. Moyenmoutier, Vosges, France, Jan. 13, 1957; s. Jean D. and Marie-Therese Lasserre; m. Christiane Delacroix, May 29, 1985; children: Loïc, Salomé. MD, U. Nancy, France, 1986, Legal Medicine, 1987, Nephrology, 1989. Svc. chief Altir, Nancy, France, 1993—; cons. U. Hosp. Nancy, France, 1986—; dir. Peritoneal Dialysis Svc., Nancy, 1993—. Author book on automated peritoneal

dialysis; contbr. over 200 articles to profl. jours.; inventor intra-abdominal hydrostatic measuring method. Mem. Assn. Plants, Glenan Nautic Ctr. (capt. 1980), French Soc. Nephrology, Internat. Soc. Peritoneal Dialysis. Avocations: ship cruising.

DURAND, THOMAS HENRY, government intelligence officer; b. West Islip, N.Y., Nov. 5, 1965; s. Paul Frederick and Marianne (Kline) D.; m. Rosanne Eleanor, July 24, 1993; 1 child, Victoria. BA in History, SUNY, New Paltz, 1989. From immigration inspector to sr. intelligence officer U.S. Immigration & Naturalization Svc., McLean, Va., 1990—. Mem. Internat. Assn. Law Enforcement Intelligence Analysts, John Birch Soc. Avocations: history, music, foreign languages, literature. e-mail: Thomas.H.Durand@usdoj.gov. Officey: USINS Forensic Document Lab 8000 Westpark Dr Ste 325 Mc Lean VA 22102-3105

DURAND-DELGA, MICHEL, geologist, educator; b. Gaillac-sur-Tarn, France, May 18, 1923; s. Emile Durand-Delga and Marthe Cassan; m. Thérèse Wenger, Nov. 1947 (div. 1973); children: Bernard, Jacques, François, Arnaud; m. Claudie Guerrier, Oct. 10, 1973; 1 child, Juliette. DS, Sorbonne U., Paris, 1955; DHC, Cagliari U., Italy, 1993. Lectr. asst. Coll. de France, Paris, 1946-47, Inst. Nat. Agronomique, Paris, 1947-58; sr. lectr. Sorbonne U., 1958-63; prof. Paris VI U., 1963-72; prof. U. Toulouse (France) III, 1972-85, emeritus prof., 1986—; mem. Internat. Commn. on History of Geol. Scis. Author: Geology of the Numidic Chain, 1955; editor: Geological Development of the Mediterranean and Alpine Europe Areas, 1960-63; contbr. articles to profl. jours. Recipient Demolombe prize Acad. Scis., Paris, 1956, hon. medal St. Kliment Ohridski, Sofia U., 1994. Mem. Soc. Geologique France (Prestwich prize 1972), Geol. Socs. of Poland (hon.), Geol. Socs. of Bulgaria (hon.), Geol. Socs. of Italy, Geol. Soc. of Spain, Geol. Socs. of Switzerland, Polish Acad. Sci. (hon.), Acad. Romania (hon.), Real Acad. Scis. and Arts Barcelona (hon.), Hungarian Acad. Scis. (hon.), Acad Scis. Paris. Avocations: genealogy, history of geology, history of France. Home: 8 rue Charles-Lefebvre, F 77210 Avon France

DURANI NACK, CLAIRE JOYCE, artist, educator, author; b. N.Y.C., Dec. 2; d. Myron Pearlstein and Rae Rita Adele Feldman Nack; m. Naudeen Mahmoud Khan Durani (divorced). Student, NYU. Cert. tchr. N.Y. Freelance fashion artist Saks Fifth Ave, N.Y.C.; pres. Claire Durani Nack Corp., Rensselaer, N.Y.; prof., lectr. Hudson Valley C.C., Troy, N.Y., Fashion Inst. N.Y., N.Y.C. Author: Facts, Fools and Ghouls, Essays and Soloquies, The Cad with the Wad, Life's A Theatre, Plot, Counterplot, Plot, Conversations with Myself, the americans, Spiders Web Unspun, An Unfamiliar Place, The Adventures of Cora, Upward Bent, The Journals of Claire Durant, The Cat Book, The Scrapbook of Claire Duranni Nack, The Gold Book of Claire Durani Nack, the Silver Book of Claire Durani Nack, A Light's Work, Sports Children's Coloring Book, Fashions and Hats, Something Happened, (play) Liz Miller; one-woman shows include Vernisage Gallerie, Ligoa Duncan Gallerie, State Mus. N.Y., Shelnut Gallery, Troy; fasion drawings included in British Harpers Bazaar, L'Officiel mag., Paris. Recipient Cert. of Excellence Silver Poets Soc. Am. Mem. Millionaires Club. Avocations: collecting model aircraft, clothes, hats, art books, jewelry. Home: 416 East St Rensselaer NY 12144-2303

DURANT, BLONDELLE ANGELIA, dermatologist, educator; b. St. Johns, Antigua, Mar. 23, 1951; arrived in Barbados, 1979; d. Rawdon Stewart and Helen Keturah (Simon) Edwards; m. Dalton Henderson Durant, Dec. 22, 1973; children: Dean, Tracey. MBBS, U. W.I., 1975; postgrad., U. London, 1978-79, diploma in dermatology, 1979; MD with splty. in dermatology, Inst. Dermatology, Guy's and Thomas' Hosp., London, England. Intern Univ. Hosp., Kingston, Jamaica, 1975-76, staff physician, 1976-77; observer in dermatology Bristol (Eng.) Royal Infirmary, 1977-78; assoc. cons. Queen Elizabeth Hosp., Bridgetown, Barbados, 1979-85; assoc. lectr. U. W.I., St. Michael, Barbados, 1980—; pvt. practice dermatology St. Michael, 1979—. Fellow Am. Acad. Dermatology; mem. Internat. Soc. Dermatology, Caribbean Dermatology Assn. Methodist. Avocations: dancing, singing, gardening.

DURANT, PENNY LYNNE RAIFE, writer, speaker, educator; b. Albuquerque, May 22, 1951; d. John Carl and Patricia Fay (Bremermann) Raife; m. Omar Duane Durant, Jan. 2, 1971; children: Geoffrey Alan (dec.), Adam Omar. Student, Lawrence U., Appleton, Wis., 1969-70; BS, U. N.Mex., 1973, MA, 1980. Mem. adv. bd. Soc. Children's Book Writers and Illustrators/N.Mex., Albuquerque, 1996—. Author: Make a Splash!, 1991, Prizewinning Science Fair Projects, 1991, When Heroes Die, 1993 (Lambda Lit. award 1993, 1st prize juvenile novel Nat. League Am. Pen Women 1993, award of excellence N.Mex. Press Women 1993), Bubblemania!, 1995, Exploring the World of Plants, 1995, Exploring the World of Animals, 1995, More Prizewinning Science Fair Projects, 1998; works put to music, performed include We Are One, Aki's Story, Mayhem and Malarkey; conbr. articles to Parents Mag., Durango Mag., Working Parents, The Luth. Sec. bd. dirs. Albuquerque Children's Theatre, 1995-98. Mem. Nat. League Am. Pen Women (v.p. Albuquerque br. 1990, sec. 1996, state letters chair 1996), S.W. Writers Workshop, Soc. Children's Book Writers and Illustrators (mem. adv. bd. N.Mex. chpt. 1997-2000). Democrat. Lutheran. Home: 305 Quincy St NE Albuquerque NM 87108-1344

DURBANO, FEDERICO, psychiatrist, researcher; b. Genoa, Italy, June 19, 1963; s. Sergio and Annamaria (Zucchiatti) D.; m. Elena Galassini, May 21, 1994. MD, U. Milan, 1989. Med. diplomate; psychiatry diplomate forensic psychiatry. Fellow in psychiatry Ospedale Maggiore, Milan, 1984-92; med. asst. Ospedale Treviglio, 1992-95; med. asst. Cernusco, Milan, 1996, med. dir. psychiatry, 1997—; cons. Effetti Edit., Milan, 1992-97, Bollettino S.I.P., Milan, 1997, Psichiatria Oggi, Milan, 1997; classic guitar tchr. Mem. editl. bd. Bulletin Italian Neuropsychopharmacological Assn. Mem. Italian Assn. Behavioral Therapy, Italian Psychiat. Assn., Italian Alpinistic Assn. Avocations: music, theater, poetry, swimming, diving. Home: Via Bergognone 31, I-20144 Milan Italy Office: Psychiatric Unit, Via Serbelloni 1, I-20064 Gorgonzola Milan, Italy

DURBIN, MARGOT JANE, librarian; b. Memphis, July 15, 1958; d. Richard Louis and Carolyn (Bohrer) D.; children: Carolyn Eileen Morris, Robert Benson Morris. BA, Marshall U., 1992; MLIS, U. S.C., 1995. Literacy coord. Hamlin (W.Va.)-Lincoln County Pub. Libr., 1992-95; audiovisual supr. Cabell County Pub. Libr., Huntington, W.Va., 1995-97, popular svcs. coord., 1997-97; bd. dirs. Appalread, Logan, W.Va., 1999—, Barnett Child Care Ctr., Huntington, W.Va., 1999—. Editor Forum newsletter, 1996-99. Mem. ALA, W.Va. Libr. Assn. E-mail: mdurbin@cabell.lib.wv.us. Office: Cabell County Pub Libr 455 9th St Huntington WV 25701-1417

DURBIN, RICHARD JOSEPH, senator; b. East St. Louis, Ill., Nov. 21, 1944; s. William and Ann D.; m. Loretta Schaefer, June 24, 1967; children: Christine, Paul, Jennifer. B.S. in Econs., Georgetown U., 1966, J.D., 1969. Bar: Ill. 1969. Chief legal counsel Lt. Gov. Paul Simon of Ill., 1969; mem. staff minority leader Ill. Senate, 1972-77, parliamentarian, 1969-77; practice law, 1969—; assoc. prof. med. humanities So. Ill. U., 1978—; mem. 98th-104th Congresses from 20th Dist. Ill., 1983-97; U.S. senator from Ill., 1997—, mem. Judiciary com., govtl. affairs com., budget com.; mem. appropriations com., subcoms. on agriculture, rural devel. and related agys., def., legis. br., and D.C. (ranking mem.), 1999—; mem. budget com.; mem. govt. affairs com. subcom. on oversight of govt. mgmt., restructuring and the D.C., 1999—, and permanent subcom. on investigations, 1997—; mem. select com. on ethics, 1999—; asst. Dem. fl. leader. Campaign worker Sen. Paul Douglas of Ill., 1966; staff Office Ill. Dept. Bus. and Econ. Devel., Washington; candidate for Ill. Lt. Gov., 1978; staff alt. Pres.'s State Planning Council, 1980; advisor Am. Council Young Polit. Leaders, 1981; mem. YMCA Ann. Membership Roundup, YMCA Bldg. Drive, Pony World Series; bd. dirs. Cath. Charities, United Way of Springfield, Old Capitol Art Fair, Springfield Youth Soccer; mem. Sch. Dist. 186 Referendum Com., Springfield NAACP. Democrat. Roman Catholic. Office: US Senate 364 Russell Sen Office Bldg Washington DC 20510-0001

DURBIN, THOMAS D., physicist; b. Mar. 15, 1966. BS in Physics, U. Calif., Riverside, 1988, MS in Physics, 1989, PhD in Physics, 1994. Asst. rsch. engr. U. Calif Ctr. Environ. Rsch. & Tech., Riverside, 1994—.

DURCA, ERIC MARCEL, physician for addictions; b. Paris, Oct. 12, 1957; s. Ludovic and Nicole Aimée (Coullet) D.; m. Bettina Doris Begyn, Apr. 8, 1986. MD, U. Paris XIII, 1987; cert. de toxicomanies, U. Montréal, Que. Resident various hosps., Paris, 1984-87, sr. physician for alcoholic diseases, 1987-90; sr. physician, head Westfälische Klinik für Psychiatrie, Germany, 1990-92; sr. physician, med. supt. gerontology Med. Ctr. Belligneux, Hauteville, France, 1993-94; sr. physician for alcoholic diseases Centre Hospitalier, Lorrain, Martinique, 1994-96; with C.M.P., Orval, France, 1996—; sr. physician for addictions Hôpital Dept. de Felleries-Liessies, Solre-Le-Chateau, France; instr. nursing sch., Germany, 1991-92, France, 1993-94. Mem. N.Y. Acad. Scis., ASAM, Soc. Francaise Alcoologie. Roman Catholic. Avocations: hiking, skiing. Home and Office: Hosp Dept Felleries-Liessies, 59740 Solre Le Chateau France

DURDEVICH, MICHO, mathematician, researcher; b. Petrovac na Mlavi, Serbia, Yugoslavia, Sept. 8, 1966; arrived in Mex., 1993; s. Petar and Anka (Luchich) D. Grad. Physicist, Faculty of Physics, Belgrade, Yugoslavia, 1987, MS, 1989, Dr. Theoretical Physics, 1993. Asst. Belgrade U., 1987-89, prof., 1989-93; postdoctoral fellow Nat. Autonomous U. of Mex., Mexico City, 1993-95, prof. math., 1995—. Contbr. articles to profl. jours. Recipient Winning Place in Serbian Scholar Championship in Math., Serbian Math. Soc., 1983, Spl. Oct. Prize for Diploma Work Belgrade City Parliament, 1987; Serbian acad. Sci. grantee, 1986. Mem. Mex. Nat. Sys. of Rschrs. Avocations: computers, origami. Office: U Nat Auto Mex Inst Math, Area Invest Cientifica, 04510 Mexico City Mexico

DUREHED, LENNART NILS, photographer; b. Gothenburg, Sweden, Jan. 2, 1950; s. Nils Arnold and Majken Alfrida (Johansson) D.; m. Alison Joy Kerr, Nov. 20, 1976; children: Emma, Jessica. Student, Photography Sch., Gothenburg, Sweden, 1967-69. Photographer HT-bild-Picture Agy., Gothenburg, 1970-73; asst. Irving Penn Studio, N.Y.C., 1973-76; freelance photographer Stockholm, 1976-77; dir. Camera Obscura Gallery, Stockholm, 1977-83; photographer Stockholm, 1984—. Author (photography book) A Priori, 1996; photographer: (Japanese cookbook) Ryori, 1986, (Thai cookbook) Thai Taan, 1991, Royal Summer Garden Book, 1996. Bd. dirs. Friends of Photography Mus., Stockholm, 1980-82, XpoSeptember Photosymposium, Stockholm, 1998-99, F48 Photogallery, Stockholm, 1997-98. Grantee Swedish Culture Adv. Bd., Stockholm, 1984, Boris Kuno grantee Sollentuna (Sweden) Kommun, 1993. Studio: Luntmakargatan 52, SE113-58 Stockholm Sweden

DUREK, THOMAS ANDREW, computer company executive; b. Sharpsville, Pa., July 1, 1929; s. Joseph Adam and Helen Barbara (Ondish) D.; m. Phyllis H. Norris, Aug. 1, 1987. BA, Pa. State U., University Park, 1953; MA, Baylor U., 1957; MS, Stanford U., 1959. Mgmt. scientist USAF, Pentagon, Washington, 1959-65; project engr. North Am. Rockwell Corp., Washington, 1965-68; systems engr. TRW, Inc., Washington, 1968-81; facility mgr. TRW, Inc., Patuxant, Md., 1981-82; project mgr. TRW, Inc., Washington, 1982-86; project mgr., prin. mem. tech. staff Software Productivity Consortium, Herndon, Va., 1986-89; sr. tech. staff, software technologist Systems Integration Group TRW, Inc., Fairfax, Va., 1989-92; founder, prin. TAD Assocs., Bethesda, Md., 1992—; personal investment software developer; professorial lectr. George Washington U., 1960-66, George Mason U., 1991; chair software reusability conf. Nat. Inst. for Software Quality and Productivity, 1989-91, mem. adv. bd., 1991-96, chair info. systems engring. for downsizing conf., 1993; speaker in field of software reuse and productivity. Contbr. articles to profl. jours. Mem. parish coun. Church of St. Stephen Martyr, Washington, 1970-78, pres. 1975-78, liturgical min., 1973-87, mem. pastoral coun. Shrine Most Blessed Sacrament, Washington, mem. continuing edn. com., 1993-96; established religious edn. audio-cassette libr., 1995—; mem. Action in Montgomery, 2000—. Home and Office: 7915 Quarry Ridge Way Bethesda MD 20817-6956

DUREL, HENRI JEAN-MARC, English language educator; b. Grenoble, Isère, France, Sept. 3, 1949; s. Pierre Jean-Louis and Anne-Marie (Roche) D.; m. Anne-Catherine Lamielle, June 27, 1975; children: Helene, Carolina. MA in English, Oxford (Eng.) U., 1986; BA in Classics, U. Paris, 1970; Agrégation, French Ministry Edn., Paris, 1973; diploma, Inst. Polit. Scis., Paris, 1976. Rschr. Nat. Ctr. Sci. Rsch., Paris, 1974-75; jr. lectr. U. Nancy, France, 1975-80; lectr. English, U. Lyon, France, 1980—; mem. Ecole Normale Supérieure, Paris; mem. rsch. team, Lyon, St. Etienne, Clermont-Ferrand, France, 1993—. Author: (monograph) Francis Bacon: Des Bibles à la Science, 1992; also numerous articles. Besse scholar New Coll., Wadham Coll., Oxford U., 1970-72. Mem. AAAS, Soc. Anglicistes Enseignement Supérieur, Assn. René Cassin, Assn. U. pour Entente et Liberté, Oxford Union Soc., N.Y. Acad. Scis. Roman Catholic. Avocations: stamp collecting, skiing. Home: 29 Rue Cavenne, 69007 Lyon France Office: U Jean-Moulin Lyon 3, 1 Rue de l'Université, 69007 Lyon France

DUREY, PETER BURRELL, retired librarian; b. Sunderland, Eng., Aug. 24, 1932; arrived in New Zealand, 1970; s. Preston Burrell and Doris (Marshall) D.; m. Patricia Mary Antill, 1965 (div. 1984); children: Sarah, Kate. BA, U. Durham, Eng., 1953. Grad. asst. Newcastle upon Tyne (Eng.) Pub. Libr., 1956; sr. asst. libr. U. Reading, Eng., 1957-63; sub-libr. U. Sussex, Eng., 1963-66; dep. libr. U. Keele, Eng., 1966-70; univ. libr. U. Auckland, New Zealand, 1970-98—, univ. libr. emeritus, 1998—. Author: Staff Management in University and College Libraries, 1976; editor: The Purpose and Practice of Medicine, 1960; also numerous articles. Chmn. Meadowbank cmty. com. Auckland City Coun., 1987-89, mem. Ea. Bays cmty. bd., 1990-92, mem. Hobson cmty. bd., 1993-98, Remuera Cmty. Ct., 1998—. Sgt. Brit. Army, 1953-54. Fellow New Zealand Libr. Assn. (pres. 1981), Libr. Assn.; mem. Australian Libr. and Info. Assn. (assoc.), Amnesty Internat., Auckland Wine and Food Soc., Rotary. Avocations: theatre, cinema, toy theatres, painting, swimming. E-mail: peterdurey@clear.net.nz. Home: 711-D Remuera Rd, Remuera Auckland 1005, New Zealand

DURFEE, SHELLEY ANN, editor, writer; b. Washington, Jan. 16, 1969; d. Robert L. and Jean (Harrison) D. BA in English and Italian, U. N.H., 1991; MA in English Lit. and Theory, Tulane U., 1995. Cert. literacy tchr. Memphis Literacy Coun. Freelance writer New Orleans and Memphis, 1995—; sr. writer, dir. creative devel. Nat. TeleLearning Network, New Orleans, 1995-97; editor, writer The Downtowner Mag./Downtown Prodns., Inc., Memphis, 1997—; ptnr., publ. TAP Publishing Co., Crossville, Tenn., 1991—. Author, script editor: (ednl. video) In A Flash, 1997. Bd. dirs., sec. Memphis Performing Arts Conservatory, Memphis, 1998—; bd. dirs. Memphis Heritage, Inc., 1999—; judge youth talent contest Mid-South Fair, 1998—. Mem. AAUW, Ploughmans Internat. Writing Forum. Avocations: racquetball, tennis, collecting and riding vintage bicycles, learning new languages, travel. Home: 2069 Vinton Ave Memphis TN 38104-5348 Office: 431 S Main St Memphis TN 38103-4440

DURGIN, FRANK HERMAN, II, aeronautical engineer; b. Exeter, N.H., Aug. 24, 1926; s. John Frank and Eudora Bissette (Gallant) D.; m. Marianne Hamilton, June 15, 1953; children: John, Jane, Laura, Sally, Frank. SB, MIT, 1948, SM, 1954, cert. engr., 1957. Rsch. engr. Naval Supersonic Lab. MIT, Cambridge, Mass., 1948-61, sr. scientist Aeroelastic Lab., 1961-69, assoc. dir. Wright Bros. Wind Tunnel, 1969-91; pvt. cons., Belmont, Mass., 1991—. Contbr. articles to profl. publs. Mem. Town Meeting, 1963-96; mem. Ran Sch. Com., Belmont, 1966; active Waverly Congl. Ch., 1960-95. With U.S. Army, 1946-47. Mem. AIAA, NSPE, ASCE (chmn. manual of practice for wind tunnel testing of bldg. and structures 1981-86, chmn. manual update 1991-98). Achievements include research in solving major engineering problems at John Hancock Bldg., Boston, Sears Tower, Chgo., Coll. Life Ins. Co. Hdqrs., Indpls., pedestrian wind assessments for many buildings in Boston. Home: 19 Payson Rd Belmont MA 02478-2720

DURHAM, HARRY BLAINE, III, lawyer; b. Denver, Sept. 16, 1946; s. Harry Blaine and Mary Frances (Oliver) D.; m. Lynda L. Durham, Aug. 4, 1973; children: Christopher B., Laurel A. BA cum laude, Colo. Coll., 1969; JD, U. Colo., 1973. Bar: Wyo. 1973, U.S. Tax Ct. 1974, U.S. Ct. Appeals (10th cir.) 1976. Assoc. Brown, Drew, Apostolos, Massey & Sullivan, Casper, Wyo., 1973-77; ptnr. Brown & Drew, Casper, Wyo., 1977-98, Brown, Drew & Massey, LLP, 1998—. Articles editor U. Colo. Law Rev., 1972-73. Bd. dirs. Casper Symphony Assn. 1974-88, v.p. 1979-82, pres. 1983-87; bd. dirs. Natrona County United Way, 1974-76, pres., 1975-76; mem. City of Casper Parks and Recreation Commn., 1985-94, vice chmn., 1987-94; Rep. precinct committeeman, 1999—. Named Permanent Class Pres., Class of 1969, Colo. Coll., mem. Nat. alumni coun.; recipient State Heroes award Sporting Goods Mfg. Assn., 1997. Mem. ABA, Wyo. Bar Assn., Natrona County Bar Assn., Nat. Assn. Railroad Trial Counsel, Phi Beta Kappa, Casper Amateur Hockey Club (bd. dirs. 1970-77, sec. 1974-77), Wyo. Amateur Hockey Assn. (bd. dirs., sec. 1974-85, pres. 1985-88). Republican. Home: 3101 Hawthorne Ave Casper WY 82604-4975 Office: 159 N Wolcott St Ste 200 Casper WY 82601-7009

DURHAM, JAMES MICHAEL, SR., marketing consultant; b. Shreveport, La., May 27, 1937; s. Judson Burney and Edith Eloise (Whittington) D.; m. Constance Manuela Alvarez, June 4, 1960; children: Jennifer Paige Esperanza Kessler, James Michael Jr., Christopher Jon, David Bradley, Matthew Craig. BS in Math., Centenary Coll. of La., 1959; MSME, N.Mex. State U., 1963; MS in Sys. Mgmt., U. So. Calif., 1981; MBA, Mich. State U., 1988. Commd. 2d lt. U.S. Army, 1959, advanced through grades to col., 1979, mgmt. analyst Army Office Chief of Staff, 1972-74; command and staff positions 3d Infantry Div. U.S. Army, Wurzburg, Germany, 1974-77; student U.S. Army War Coll., Carlisle Barracks, Pa., 1977-78; product mgr. U.S. Army Tank-Automotive Materiel Readiness Command, Warren, Mich., 1978-80; commander Mainz Army Depot, Mainz, Germany, 1980-83; exec. officer to deputy commanding gen. U.S. Army Devel. and Readiness Command, Alexandria, Va., 1983; program mgr., tactical vehicles U.S. Army Tank-Automotive Command, Warren, Mich., 1984-86; ret. U.S. Army Tank Automotive Command, Warren, Mich., 1986; dir. tank automotive programs Cypress Internat., Troy, Mich., 1986-89; v.p. govt. business Cummins Engine Co., Inc., Columbus, Ind., 1989-92, v.p. govt. products, 1992-95, ret., 1995; pres. Cummins Mil. Sys. Co., Inc., Columbus, 1992-93, JD Interests Inc., Farnham, Va., 1995—; guest lectr. Wayne State U. Chmn. Bartholomew County Solid Waste Mgmt. Dist. Citizens Adv. Com., 1991-95, Bartholomew County Solid Waste Mgmt. Authority, 1993-95, Bartholomew County Landfill Site Selection Com., 1993; co-chmn. Project Water, Columbus, 1990-95; chmn. bd. dirs. Am. Youth Activities Assn., Mainz, Germany, 1980-83, pres. Am. Youth Activities Assn., Kitzingen, Germany, 1975-77; bd. dirs. Indpls. Mus. Art-Columbus Gallery, 1995; chmn. devel. com. Richmond County (Va.) Habitat for Humanity, 1996—, bd. dirs., 1997—, v.p., 1998, pres., 1999—; trustee No. Neck chpt. Assn. for the Preservation of Va. Antiquities, 1999, vice dir., 2000. Decorated Legion of Merit with oak leaf cluster, Bronze Star, Vietnam campaign medal with 60 device, Vietnamese Cross of Gallantry with palm. Mem. ASME, Nat. Def. Indsl. Assn. (exec. bd. tank and automotive sys. divsn. 1991—, steering com. combat vehicle sys. divsn. 1988—, chmn. 1991-95, steering com. tactical vehicle sys. sect. 1986-95), Assn. U.S. Army, Soc. Mfg. Engrs., Soc. Automotive Engrs., Ret. Officers Assn. (sec. Potomac chpt. 1997-98, dir. 1999—, mem. No. Neck chpt.), U.S. Army Ordnance Corps Assn., Hist. Soc. Northern Neck of Va. (bd. dirs. 1998—). Republican. Avocation: reading. Home: 2494 Simonson Rd Farnham VA 22460-2212

DURIAN, STEWART WILLIAM, design engineer; b. Milw., Sept. 7, 1962; s. Stephen and June (Fraser) D.; m. Victoria Wolf, 1996; 1 child, Sean Ryan. AS in Engring., U. Wis., Sheboygan, 1982; BS in Mech. Engring., U. Wis., Milw., 1984, MS in Mech. Engring., 1986. Rsch. engr. Babcock & Wilcox-Alliance Rsch. Ctr., 1987-89; design engr. Cooper Power Sys.-Transformer Products Divsn., 1989-93, project design engr., 1993-95, sr. engr., 1995—, supr. engring devel. lab., 1996—, supr. thermal design, 1998—. Achievements include research on natural convection thermohydraulics in both confined channels and in unconfined environments, forced directed and non-directed cooling of electrical apparatus, and general transformer performance; involved in advanced product design, development and testing resulting in several patents and patent applications. Home: 1534 Irving Pl Waukesha WI 53188-2236 Office: Transformer Product 1900 E North St Waukesha WI 53188-3844

DURIEUX, ERIC, environmentalist; b. Lyon, France, Dec. 9, 1961; s. Jacques and Michele (Viollet) D.; m. Sophie Paillard, Dec. 24, 1988; children: Alice, Gaspard, Elsa. PhD in Physics, U. Geneva, 1990; MBA, U. Chgo., 1996. Project mgr. CERN, Geneva, 1987-92; head shot per shot lidar group Fed. Poly. Sch., Lausanne, Switzerland, 1992-97; dir. health, safety and environ. Merial Ltd., Lyon, France, 1998-2000; cons. IBM, Switzerland, 2000—. Author: Instrument Development for Atmospheric Research and Monitoring, 1997; contbr. articles to profl. jours. Grantee Swiss Federal Office for Edn. and Sci., 1992, Swiss Commn. for Applied Rsch., 1996, Rank Prize Fund, 1994.

DURIEUX, SYLVAIN, materials science researcher, educator; b. Paris, Mar. 28, 1971; s. Hubert and Chantal (Boulin) D. Maitrise, Joseph Fourier, 1993; DEA, INSA, Lyon, 1994, PhD in Materials Sci., 1998. Rschr. Inst Nat. des Scis. Appliquees, Lyon, 1994-98, tchr., 1995-98. Recipient Champion des Alpes Federation Francaise de Rugby, 1996. Mem. Assn. des Anciens de Physique et Applications (v.p. 1996), Rugby Club Chartreuse Neron, Union Sportive de Saint Egreve. Avocation: rugby. E-Mail: durieuxs@club-internet.fr. Fax: 33 4 72 43 85 39. Home: 59 rue du Vercors, 38000 Grenoble France

DURKIN, DOROTHY ANGELA, university official; b. Glen Cove, N.Y., June 23, 1945; d. Frank Vincent and Rose Marie Durkin; 1 child, David Francis. BA, SUNY, Stony Brook, 1968; MA, NYU, 1974. Adminstrv. asst. SUNY, Stony Brook, 1965-67; prodn. editor Holt, Rhinehart & Winston, Inc., Stony Brook, 1967-69; editor Hill & Wang Pub., Inc., N.Y.C., 1969-70; asst. dir. pub. info. NYU Sch. Continuing Edn., 1970-72; assoc. dean pub. affairs and student svcs. Sch. Continuing and Profl. Studies NYU Sch. Continuing Edn. and Profl. Studies, 1983—; cons. N.Y.C. Ctr. for Lifelong Learning, 1974; producer TV series Continuum, Sta. WNYC, 1974. Editor: NSF student mag., 1961. Recipient Merit award Andy Advt., 1972, Art Dirs. Club, 1980, Soc. Illustrators, 1980, Big Apple award N.Y. Radio Broadcasters Assn., 1985, Admissions Mktg. Report awards, 1987-88, 98, 99, Catalog Age awards, 1988, 93. Mem. Univ. Continuing Edn. Assn. (chair info. svcs. 1980-81, nat. award chair, chair mktg. adv. com. 1989-98, group leader Learn From Success series 1989-90, bd. dirs. 1991-93, membership com. 1994-95, mktg. conf. planning com. 1993-00, presenter, Bronze, Silver and Gold awards 1978, 81-99, Internat. Leadership in Continuing Edn. award 1999), Am. Coll. Pub. Rels. Assn. (nat. award 1973), Coun. for Advancement and Support of Edn. (awards 1982-83, 85-87, 89-90, 92-94), Women in Comms. (job chair), Pub. Rels. Soc. Am. (Am. demographics adv. bd. 1989-90), Direct Mktg. Assn. (Echo Leadership award 1987, 88), Internat. Direct Mktg. Assn., SUNY Alumni Assn. (bd. dirs.), The College Bd. (speaker, cons.), Learning Resources Network. Office: NYU Sch Continuing Edn 7 E 12th St Fl 11 New York NY 10003-4475

DURLABHJI, YOGENDRA, gem and jewelry company executive; b. Jaipur, Rajasthan, India, Apr. 7, 1950; s. Khailshanker and Hemlata (Ajmera) D.; m. Nirmala Surana; children: Ruchi, Shikha. BA, St. Stephen's Coll., Delhi, India, 1970, MA, 1972; advanced diploma in ednl. studies, Cambridge (Eng.) Inst. Edn., 1979; associateship, U. London, 1980. V.p. games and sports St. Stephen's Coll., Delhi, 1971-72; mgn. ptnr. M/s K.S. Durlabhji, Jaipur, India, 1985, M/s K.S.D. Exports, Jaipur, 1995; chmn. Confedn. Indian Industry, Rajasthan State Coun., Jaipur, 1997; mng. trustee Santokba Durlabhji Trust, Jaipur, Durlabhji Trust for Devel., Jaipur, Durlabhji Environment Friendly Trust, Jaipur, Avedna Ashram Trust, Jaipur. Mem. Confedn. Indian Industry, Nat. Sports Com., Delhi, 1997, CII Nat. Com. on Edn. and Literacy, Delhi, 1997, CII Nat. Environ. Com., Delhi, 1997, CII Infrastructure Subcom., Delhi, 1997, CII Internat. Trade Subcom., Delhi, 1997, World Econ. Forum Global Growth Cos. Mem. Raj. Squash Rackets Assn. (pres.), Cricket Club India (life), Internat. Lawn Tennis Club of India (hon. sec.), Ashok Club (life), Jai Club (life), Jaipur Club (life), Raj. Polo Club (life), Oxford and Cambridge Soc. of India (life), Internat. Colored Stone Assn. (life), The Almost Wimbledon Club (founder mem.), Stephanians in Rajasthan (founder mem.), Oberoi Exec. Club, Belvedere Chambers. Avocations: sports, traveling, promotion of education and health care activities. Home: Emerald House D-31, Subhash Marg C-Scheme, 302001 Jaipur India Office: M/s K S Durlhabhji D-31, Emerald House Subhash Marg, 302001 Jaipur India

DURLACH, JEAN PIERRE, endocrinologist, researcher; b. Paris, Aug. 16, 1925; s. Henry and Louise (Schwoob) D.; m. Marie Therese Guiheneuf, May 25, 1955; children: Vincent, Anges, Cecile, Sylvie. MD, U. Paris, 1953,

degree in endocrinology, 1958; MD (hon.), Hohenheim-Stuttgart U., 1970. Cons. in endocrinology Paris U., 1953-77, dir. Ctr. Studies on Mg Metabolism, 1977-89. Recipient 7 awards French Nat. Academias of Medicine, 1951-85; named Officer, Order of Merit of Republic of Germany, 1984, Knight, Legion d'Honneur, Ministry of Health, 1994. Mem. Accademia Romana di Scienze Mediche Roma, Soc. Endocrinology (hon.), German Soc. Rsch., Polish Soc. Rsch., Hungarian Soc. Rsch., others. Avocations: collecting panda bears and watches. Fax: +33(0)1-40-88-36-13. Home: 64 rue de Longchamp, 92200 Neuilly/Seine France

DURLU, TAHSIN NURI, physics educator; b. Ayas, Ankara, Turkey, June 17, 1945; s. Hasan Tahsin and Nezahat (Parlak) D.; m. Fatma Zehra Cayköylü, Feb. 15, 1975; 1 child, Tugba. BSc, Ankara U., 1968, MSc, 1970; MSc, Oxford (England) U., 1971, PhD, 1974. Bd. dirs. Petroleum Office, Ankara, 1984-88; cons. Prime Minister's Office, Ankara, 1984-89; prof. physics Mid. East Tech. U., Ankara, 1985-88; bd. dirs. Turkish Petroleum Inc., Ankara, 1988-89; prof. physics Ankara U., 1988—; pres. Kirikkale (Turkey) U., 1997—. Author 7 books in physics; editor 5 books in physics; contbr. articles to profl. jours. Recipient scholarship British Coun., 1970, Turkish Govt., 1970-74, Turkish Tech. and Sci. Rsch. Coun., 1978, 89, 96. Mem. Inst. Physics, Turkish Soc. Physics. Avocations: collecting old handwritten books, collecting books, collecting old stamps. Home: Turgutreis Caddesi 49/6, 06570 Ankara Turkey Office: Ankara Univ Sci Faculty, Tandogan, 06100 Ankara Turkey

DURMUSOGLU, FATIH, obstetrician-gynecologist, educator; b. Ankara, Turkey, June 11, 1958; s. Ziya and Suheyla Durmusoglu; m. Lutfiye Mulazimoglu, Aug. 8, 1999. MD, Bursa (Turkey) Med. Sch., 1981. Resident in ob-gyn. Ankara Maternity, 1981-86; postdoctoral fellow Johns Hopkins U., Balt., 1987-89; asst. prof. Marmara U. Hosp., Istanbul, 1989-92, assoc. prof., 1992-99, prof. ob-gyn., 1999—, bd. dean's office, 1996-99, chief adminstr., 1999; coord. phase IV Sch. Medicine, Istanbul, 1990—. Contbr. articles to profl. jours. Recipient 2d place presentation award Schering-German, 1999. Mem. Am. Soc. Reproductive Medicine (assoc.), N.Am. Menopause Soc., Turkish Soc. Gynecologists. Avocations: biking, skiing, jogging, photography. Home: Dr Kazim Lakay Sok, 11/8 Ciftehavuzlar, 81030 Istanbul Turkey Office: Marmara U Hosp, Tophanelioglu Cad, 81190 Istanbul Turkey

DU ROCHER, JAMES HOWARD, lawyer; b. Racine, Wis., Aug. 4, 1945; s. Howard James and Frances Ann (Rasmussen) Du R.; m. Rosalyn Ann, Sept. 2, 1972; children: Jessica Lynn, James Howard, Emily Rosalyn. Student, U.S. Mil. Acad., 1963-65, Ripon Coll., 1965-66; JD, U. Wis., 1969. Bar: Wis. Assoc. Stewart, Peyton, Crawford & Josten, Racine, 1969-78; pres. Du Rocher, Murphy, Murphy & Schroeder, S.C., Racine, 1978-96, Du Rocher Law Offices, S.C., 1996—; bd. dirs., Careers Industries, Inc., pres., 1988-89. Bd. dirs. Racine Area United Way, 1973-79, v.p., 1977-79; chmn. Park Trails Dist. Boy Scouts Am., 1979-82; bd. dirs. Careers for Retarded Adults, Inc., 1982, pres., 1983, 90; bd. dirs. A-Center of Racine, Inc., 1978-85, pres., 1985; bd. dirs. Careers Industries Support Found., Inc., 1993-2000; deacon Atonement Luth. Ch., Racine, 1978-81; mem. adv. bd. Children's Svc. Soc. Wis. Capt. JAGC, U.S. Army, 1969-73. Decorated Bronze Star. Mem. State Bar Wis., Mason, Rotary (pres. Racine-West club 1998-99). Home: 5531 Whirlaway Ln Racine WI 53402-1865 Office: 827 Main St PO Box 1406 Racine WI 53401-1406

DUROSINMI, MUHEEZ ALANI, hematologist consultant; b. Abeokuta, Nigeria, Apr. 2, 1952; s. Bisiriyu Ayinla and Hamdalat Adunni (Egberongbe) D.; m. Lateefat Moyosore Williams, May 9, 1981; 1 child, Rafiat Oluwatosin. MB BS, Ibadan (Nigeria) Med. Sch., 1978. Fellowship of Med. Coll. Pathology; Fellowship West African Coll. Physicians. Resident hematologist U. Coll. Hosp., Ibadan, Nigeria, 1980-85; reader Obafemi Awolowo U., Ile-Ife, Nigeria, 1992—; cons. hematology OAUTHC, Ile-Ife, 1986—. Co-author: (book) Transfusion, 1985; contbr. articles to profl. jours. Named Commonwealth Med. fellow Royal Marsden Hosp., London, 1994-95. Mem. Nigerian Med. Assn., Assn. Pathologists of Nigeria, Internat. Soc. Hematologists (European and African Divsn.). Islam. Avocations: internat. politics, reading, travel. Office: Haematology Dept, Obafemi Awolowo U, Ife-Ife Nigeria

DUROUX, AXEL RENAUD, communications company executive, journalist; b. Lyon, Rhone, France, May 25, 1963; s. Paul-Emile Duroux and Myriam Buclin; m. Marina Dernis, Mar. 12, 1998; 1 child, Paul-Emile. PhD, Law Sch., Paris, 1986; grad., French Press Inst., 1997. Reporter SIPA Press, Paris, 1986-88; TV reporter LA Cinq, Paris, 1989-92; mgr. corp. comms. IBM, France, 1992-94; gen. mgr. 740 Radio, France, 1994-95; CEO RTL 2 Radio, France, 1995—, Fun Radio, France, 1997—. Author: La Jeanne, 1989. Office: 22 rue Bayard, 75008 Paris France

DUROVIC, LUBOMIR JAN, Slavonic languages educator; b. Vazec, Czechoslovakia, Feb. 9, 1925; arrived in Sweden, 1966; s. Jan and Olga Maria Anna (Palicova) D.; m. Ludmila Ruzekova, June 30, 1951; children: Vladimir, Natasa. PhDr., Comenius U., Bratislava, 1951; DSc, Czechoslovak Acad. Scis., Prague, 1966. Asst. Comenius U., Bratislava, Czechoslovakia, 1950-56, assoc. prof., 1956-66, prof., 1967-70, head dept. Russian, 1955-57; lectr. State U., Uppsala, Sweden, 1966-69, assoc. prof., 1969-72; prof. Royal U., Lund, Sweden, 1972-91, head dept. Slavic Langs., 1972-91, ret., 1991; vis. prof. U. Aarhus, Denmark, 1970, Yale U., 1974, U. Zürich, Switzerland, 1991-93, U. Bern, Switzerland, 1994, U. Prague, 1996. Author: Modalnost, 1956, Paradigmatics of Russian, 1964, 70; editor: Slavica Lundensia 1-13, 1973-91, Russian Linguistics Jour. 4-16, 1978-92, (series) Slavica Suecana 1992—; contbr. to numerous scholarly papers and textbooks. Mem. Czechoslovak Soc. Scis. & Arts (v.p. 1988-90), Royal Soc. Humanities, Scandinavian Assn. Slavicists (pres. 1987-90), Czechoslovak Linguistic Soc. (hon.), New Soc. Letters at Lund, Prague Linguistic Cir. (hon.). Lutheran. Home: Spexarevagen 5B, S-224 71 Lund Sweden Office: Dept Slavonic Langs, Finngatan 12, S-223 62 Lund Sweden

DÜRR, ERNST, economist, educator; b. Cologne, Rhineland, Germany, June 2, 1927; s. Ernst and Katharina (Velser) D.; m. Martha Peschl, Dec. 11, 1959. Diploma, Kaufmann U., Cologne, Germany, 1953; Dr. rer. pol., U. Cologne, Germany, 1955. Referee Ins. Co., Cologne, Germany, 1943-50; privatdozent U. Cologne, Germany, 1963-64; full prof. econs. U. Erlangen-Nuremberg, Germany, 1965-92, prof. emeritus, 1992—; assoc. prof. Univ. Austral de Chile, Valdivia, Chile, 1984; hon. prof. Nat. U. Asuncion, Paraguay, 1987. Author: Wirkungsanalyse d. monetären Konjunkturpolitik, 1968, Wachstumspolitik, 1977, Politica Economica, 3 Vols., 1995, 2d edit., 1997; editor: Soziale Marktwirtschaft in Entwicklungsländern, 1991. Mem. econ. adv. bd. Fed. Ministry of Econs., Bonn, 1975—. Mem. Verein Für Socialpolitik, Rotary Club Nürnberg. Home: Buchenstr 13, D-90537 Feucht Germany

DURR, LESLIE MARTINA, nurse, psychotherapist; b. Jamaica, N.Y., May 23, 1945; d. Leonard John Durr and Ida Martina Wissel; m. Floyd Hurt, Aug. 8, 1970 (div. 1990); children: Eric Marshall Hurt, Morgan Leslie Hurt. BSN, Syracuse U., 1967; MSN, Hunter Coll., 1973; PhD, Va. Commonwealth U., 1998. Cert. clin. nurse specialist, Am. Nurses' Credentialing Ctr. Clin. nurse specialist DeJarnette Ctr., Staunton, Va., 1992-96; mgr., clin. nurse specialist Martha Jefferson Home Care, Charlottesville, Va., 1996-98; adminstr. Lafayette Acad. & Treatment Ctr., Charlottesville, Va., 1998-99; pvt. practice psychotherapist Charlottesville, Va., 1988—; adj. faculty Va. Commonwealth Sch. Nursing, 1998; pvt. practice med.-legal nurse cons., Charlottesville, 1997—. Contbr. articles and revs. to profl. jours. Mem. bd. Monticello Area Cmty. Action Agy., Charlottesville, 1997—; vol. debriefer Thomas Jefferson Emergency Svcs. Coun., Charlottesville, 1985-93; vol. nat. depression screening, Charter Hosp., Charlottesville, 1997. Mem. Charlottesville-Albemarle Mental Health Assn. (bd. mem. 1987-90). Episcopalian. Home: 3074 Doctors Xing Charlottesville VA 22911-5733 Office: 918 9 1/2 St NE Charlottesville VA 22902-5311

DURRANT, JOHN, publishing executive; b. London, July 6, 1949; s. Edward Henry Samual Stokes and Phyllis (Howard-Spink) D.; m. Susan Clark, June 29, 1974; children: Oliver Jon, Thomas Edward, William Jack. Diploma in mgmt. studies, Brooks U., 1978. Promotions mgr. W.B. Saunders & Co., Ltd., London, 1968-73; mktg. dir. EBC - Clio, Oxford, Eng., 1973-75, mng. dir., 1975-78; mng. dir., chmn. Clio Press Ltd., Oxford, Eng., 1978-93; mng. dir., proprietor Isis Pub. Ltd., Oxford, 1993—, Soundings Ltd., Newcastle-upon Tyne, 1999—. Author microcomputer software guide, 1985. Avocations: classical and blues guitar, stained glass creations. Office: Isis Pub Ltd 7 Centremead, Osney Mead, Oxford OX2 OES, England

DURRANT, M. PATRICIA, diplomat. Perm. rep. of Jamaica to UN N.Y.C., 1995—. Office: Perm Mission of Jamaica to UN 767 3rd Ave Fl 9 New York NY 10017-2023*

DURRANT, STEVEN FREDERICK, physicist, chemist; b. London, Apr. 4, 1959; s. Frederick George and Elizabeth Doris (Patterson); m. Lucia Regina Jafelice, Dec. 6, 1989. BSc in Physics with honors, U. Birmingham, Eng., 1981; MS in Med. Physics, U. Surrey, Guildford, Eng., 1986, cert. in adult edn., 1987, PhD in Analytic Chemistry, 1989. Scientist atmospheric scis. divsn. Nat. Physics Rsch. Lab., Coun. Sci. and Indsl. Rsch., Pretoria, South Africa, 1982-85; rschr. lab. organic films dept. applied physics Inst. Physics Gleb Wataghin-Unicamp, Campinas SP, Brazil, 1990-91; vis. rschr. lab. plasma processes dept. applied physics Inst. Physics Gleb Wataghin-Unicamp, Campinas SP, 1994-96; asst. prof. CCE, U. Estadual Londrina, 1997; rschr. dept. semiconducts, instruments, photonics Faculty Elect. Engring. and Computation Unicamp, Campinas, SP, Brazil, 1998—; referee Royal Soc. Chemistry Jours., Eng., 1990—; rsch. assoc. dept. chemistry U. Mass., Amherst, 1992-93; presenter in field. Contbr. over 40 articles to profl. jours. including Analyst, Jour. Vacuum Sci. and Tech., Thin Solid Films, Jour. Applied Physics. BP Internat. grant U. Surrey, Eng., 1988, Birthright grant, Surrey, 1989, State U. Campinas grant, Rsch. Support Found. São Paulo State, 1990-91, Brazilian Fed. Rsch. Coun., 94-96. Mem. N.Y. Acad. Sci., Brazilian Vacuum Soc., Brazilian Phys. Soc. Avocations: reading, creative writing. Office: DSIF-FEEC-Unicamp, Ave Albert Einstein N 400, 13083970 Campinas SP, Brazil

DURRELL, LEE MCGEORGE, conservationist; b. Memphis, Sept. 7, 1949; arrived in Jersey, 1979; d. Harold Love and Harriet Elizabeth (Northcross) McGeorge; m. Gerald Malcolm Durrell, May 24, 1979 (dec. Jan., 1995). BA, Bryn Mawr Coll., 1971; PhD, Duke U., 1979. Hon. dir. Durrell Wildlife Conservation Trust, Jersey, 1995—; mem. coun. Fauna and Flora Internat., Cambridge, 1992—; chairperson Durrell Trust for Conservation Biology, Canterbury, 1991—; hon. bd. dirs. Wildlife Preservation Trust Can., Toronto, 1991—, Wildlife Preservation Trust Internat., Phila., 1995—. Co-author: (with Gerald Durrell) (book) The Amateur Naturalist, 1981; author: (book) The State of the Ark, 1986; co-presenter TV Documentaries, 1981-91; contbr. numerous articles on wildlife conservatin to popular and sci. publs., 1980—. Home and Office: Durrel Wildlife Conserv Tr, Trinity Jersey, Channel Islands JE3 5BP, England

DURRENBERGER, WILLIAM JOHN, retired army general, educator, investor; b. Wadena, Minn., Mar. 15, 1917; s. John George and Mary Angela (Weibeler) D.; m. Alma Mary Pagliai, Jan. 3, 1947; children: William John, Robert Scott, Philip Michael. Student, U. Minn., 1935-40, Brit. Coll. Mil. Sci., 1943; B.S., U. Md., 1951; M.B.A., Syracuse U., 1954; grad., Indsl. Coll. Armed Forces, 1960. Commd. 2d lt. U.S. Army, 1939, advanced through grades to maj. gen., 1968; chief logistics plan div. (UN Command), Korea, 1960-61; dep. comdr. Ordnance Weapons Command Illinois, 1962; comdg. officer Springfield (Mass.) Armory, 1963-65; comdg. gen. Army Tank Automotive Center Warren, Mich., 1965-66; comdg. gen. U.S. Army Weapons Command Rock Island, Ill., 1966-68; dep. chief of staff Logistics; acting chief staff U.S. Army, Pacific, 1968-70; ret., 1970; dir. Des Moines/Polk County (Iowa) Met. Criminal Justice Center, 1971-73; asst. v.p. ednl. services Drake U., 1971-81; profl. asso. Mitchell & Mitchell Economists, 1979-82. Author over 100 tech. intelligence reports on Brit. and German combat vehicles and weapons, 1943-46. Decorated D.S.M. with oak leaf cluster, Bronze Star, Army Commendation medal with oak leaf cluster. Mem. Assn. U.S. Army, Cath. League Religious and Civil Rights, Am. Legion, VFW (nat. aide-de-camp to comdr.-in-chief, 1986), KC, DAV, Ret. Officers Assn. Roman Catholic. Home: 2708 Lynner Dr Des Moines IA 50310-5835

DURRER, RUTH, theoretical physicist; b. Kerns, Switzerland, Jan. 22, 1958; d. Josef Gregor and Marie Antoinette (Dillier) D.; m. Martin Zimmermann, Aug. 5, 1988; children: Florian, Melchior, Anna. Diploma in Physics, U. Zurich, 1983, PhD in Theoretical Physics, 1988. Asst. U. Zurich, 1984-88; postdoctoral fellow Cambridge (Eng.) U., 1988-89; vis. lectr. Princeton (N.J.) U., 1989-91; asst. prof. theoretical physics U. Zurich, 1992-95; prof. theoretical physics U. Geneva, Switzerland, 1995—; mem. com. NUPECC, 1996—. Contbr. numerous articles to profl. jours. Mem. Swiss Phys. Soc. (sec. 1992-94), Am. Phys. Soc., Am. Astron. Soc. Office: Ecole de Physique, 24 quai E Ansermet, CH-1211 Geneva Switzerland

DURRIEU, ALAIN-JACQUES, diabetologist, nutritionist; b. Cazeres, France, July 22, 1943; s. Jean and Hortense (Duclos) D.; m. July 13, 1966; children: Gilles, Marie-Christine. MD, U. Toulouse, 1971. Registered physician, Conseil de l'Ordre des Médecins. Intern, resident Hosp. Hotel Dieu, Toulouse, France, 1966-67; resident Hosp. Gen., Tarbes, France, 1968-73; pvt. practice diabetes/nutrition Biarritz, France, 1973—; cons. in occupational medicine and hygiene Social Security, Bayonne, France, 1980—, chem. industry, Tarpos, France, 1973—, others; rschr. in multipurpose computer aided problem solving and nimble network. Contbr. articles to profl. jours. Bd. dirs. Group de recherches pedagogiques en diabétologie. Lt. French Air Force, 1970-71. Decorated Vermeil Cross, Paris, 1991, 92, Gold Cross, 1993. Mem. AAAAs, Rsch. Group in Diabetes Edn., French Nutrition Assn., Hygiene and Pub. Health Assn., Nat. Coun. French Engrs. and Scientists, Union des Ingenieurs et Scientifiques dubassin de l'Adour, Am. Diabetes Assn., Assn. de Langue Française pour l'étude du Diabete et des maladies métaboliques, Internat. Diabetes Fedn., Internat. Soc. for Sys. Scis., Human Factors Soc., Am. Soc. for Quality Control, N.Y. Acad. Scis., Am. Telemedicine Assn. Roman Catholic. Avocation: yachting. Home: Rue Madeleine Villa Argia, Bidart France 64210 Office: Résidence Tolédo, 1 Rue de la Poste, Biarritz France 64200

D'URSEL, BERNARD, tax specialist; b. Brussels, Aug. 15, 1961; s. Guy d'Ursel and J. de la Croix d'Ogimont. Lic. jur., Cath. U., Louvain-la-Neuve, Belgium, 1984; lic. tax sci., Ecole Superieure Scis Fiscales, Brussels, 1989. Tax adviser Fabrimetal, Brussels, 1989-91; lawyer Jones Day Reavis & Pogue, Brussels, 1991-93, Cruyplants Eloy Hupin & Ptnrs., Brussels, 1993-97; tax adviser tax dept. Fortis Bank, Brussels, 1997—. Author: Guide Pratique de Fiscalite, 1993-96. E-mail: bernard.d'rsel@fortisbank.com. Avocations: skiing, cycling, antiques. Home: Box 11, Ave de Broqueville 103, 1200 Brussels Belgium Office: Fortis Bank, Rue Montagne du Parc 3, 1000 Brussels Belgium

DURUP, JEAN, physical chemistry educator; b. Paris, July 8, 1932; s. Gustave Ernest and Emilia (Russman) D.; m. Marie Lucienne Le Judec Ferguson, Feb. 17, 1953 (div. 1978); children: Sylvie, Florence, Juliette Anne, Nolan Winfield; m. Nicole Mathez, Mar. 7, 1998. PhD, Sorbonne, Paris, 1959. Rsch. fellow CNRS, Paris, 1952-61, Orsay, France, 1961-68; prof. U. Paris-Sud, Orsay, 1968-85; prof. U. Paul Sabatier, Toulouse, France, 1985-97, prof. emeritus, 1997—; cons. Centre d'Etudes de Saclay, Gif-sur-Yvette, France, 1976-95, Sci. and Tec, St.-Aubin, France. Author: Les Reactions entre Ions Positifs et Molecules en Phase Gazeuse, 1960. Initiator Comite Audin, Paris, 1958. Mem. AAAS. Office: Irsamc, 118 Rte de Narbonne, Toulouse 31062, France

DURYEE, WILLIAM RANKIN, retired cell physiology educator, consultant; b. Saranac Lake, N.Y., Nov. 11, 1905; s. George Van Waganen and Margaret Van Nest (Smith) D.; m. June 30, 1931 (dec. Jan. 1983); 1 child, Sanford Huntington. BA in Biology, Yale U., 1927, PhD in Zoology and Anatomy, 1933. Instr. Northwestern U., Evanston, Ill., 1937-40; chief med. publs. Office Surgeon Gen., Washington, 1944-45; with NRC, Washington, 1945-46; sr. fellow Nat. Cancer Inst., NIH, Bethesda, Md., 1948-55; head cell physiology unit WCI, Bethesda, 1950-55; prof. cell physiology George Washington U., Washington, 1955-60, rsch. prof. pathology, 1960-70, prof. emeritus, 1971—; cons. biology rsch. Arlington, Va., 1979—; invited lectr. U. Pa. Bicentennial Conf., Phila., 1941; mem. sci. adv. coun. Damon Runyon Meml. Fund, N.Y.C., 1961-68; profl. assoc. com. on growth NRC, 1946-48; guest investigator U. Copenhagen, 1984-85, U. Munich, 1985. Mem. edit. bd. Jour. Nat. Cancer Inst.; contbr. articles to sci. jours., including Biol. Bull, Sci., Anat. Record, Annals N.Y. Acad. Sci.; made first films of living genes. Maj. Med. Adminstrv. Corps, U.S. Army, 1939-45. Fellow N.Y. Acad. Scis. (hon.); mem. AAAS (coun. 1958-64), Am. Inst. Biol. Scis. (co-founder, governing bd. 1953-57), Royal Soc. Medicine (affiliate, London), Am. Soc. Physiology, Biophysics Soc. (charter), Washington Acad. Medicine, Philos. Soc. Washington, Cosmos Club (chmn. libr. com.). Episcopalian. Achievements include performed first microdissection on the human egg, first isolation of living chromosomes from amphibian eggs, a first dissection of nucleoli, first radioautographs of single cells; discovered gene loops and circular DNA strands; made first films of living genes. Avocation: philately. Home: 3241 N Woodrow St Arlington VA 22207-4458

DUSANE, RAJIV ONKAR, materials science educator, researcher; b. Akola, India, Oct. 2, 1960; s. Onkar Namdeo and Suman Onkar (Nagarkar) D.; m. Suvarna Rajiv Babras, May 13, 1989; 1 child, Shriram. BSC, Nagpur U., Akola, 1982, MSc, 1984; PhD in Applied Physics, Poona (India) U., 1990. Lectr. Poona U., 1991-92; lectr. Indian Inst. Tech., Bombay, 1992-94, asst. prof., 1994-98, assoc. prof., 1998—; rsch. fellow Kaiserslautern U., Germany, 1995-96; bd. dirs. Shiva SC Inc.; cons. Surya Tech. Consultants Ltd., Pune, India, 1994—. Contbr. articles to profl. jours. Rsch. grantee Univ. Grants Commn., Poona, 1991, Coun. Sci. and Indsl. Rsch., Poona, 1992. Mem. Materials Rsch. Soc. of India. Avocations: sports, reading, gardening. Office: Metall Engrg/Materials Sci, Indian Inst Tech, Bombay 400076, India

DUSATKO, DRAHOMIR, geodesist, researcher; b. Kolin, Czech Republic, Sept. 3, 1934; s. Josef and Marie (Zemanova) D.; children: Helena, Zbynek. Degree in Geodesist Topography, Litomerice Topograph Sch., 1955; degree in Geodesy, Military Acad., Brno, 1962; Candidate of Sci. of Geodesy/Geology. Geodesist, topographer, instr. Military Topography Inst., Dobruska, Czech Republic, 1962-67, gravimetrist, 1967-76, chief of seism geodesist dept., 1977-85, chief of centrum of geodesy, 1985-90; with DoD Czech Army, Prague, 1990-94; researcher Military Geography Inst., Prague, 1995—. Author: Connection of the West European Networks to the Geodetic Datum, 1989, Extrapolation of Gravity Above the Surface of Earth From Terrestrial Gravity Anomalies, 1970-75, Transformation of the Home Geodesy Civil Datum to the Army Datum, 1990, History of Geodesy, 1994; contbr. articles to sci. jours. Mem. N.Y.U., 1994, Geod., Cartor. Soc., 1976—, Nat. Tech. Mus., 1993—. Col. Topographic Svc. of Czech Army. Mem. Greek Soc., History of Sci. Home: Dětská 2079/65, 100 00 Prague 10, Czech Republic Office: Military Geog Inst, Rooseveltova 23, 160 01 Prague Czech Republic

DUŠEK, KAREL, macromolecular chemist; b. Prague, May 6, 1930; s. Bedrich and Josefa (Vodňanská) D.; m. Dagmar Veselá, Sept. 17, 1957 (dec. Feb. 1987); 1 child, Jana Klimová; m. Miroslava Smrckova, Sept. 11, 1999. MS, Inst. Chem. Tech., Prague, 1953; PhD, Inst. Phys. Chem. Acad. Sci., Prague, 1958; DSc, Acad. Sci. Czech Republic, 1970. Rsch. fellow Rsch. Inst. Synthetic Resins, Pardubice, Czechoslovakia, 1956-65; from sr. scientist to prin. scientist Inst. Macromolecular Chemistry Acad. Sci., Prague, 1965—; prof. chemistry U. Pardubice, 1996—; assoc. prof. physics Charles U., Prague, 1995—; prof. Acad. Sci. Bordeaux, France, 1994, INSA, Lyon, 1994; dept. head Inst. Macromolecular Chemistry, 1975-92, projects coord., 1992—. Editor: Epoxy Resins and Composites, 1985-87, Responsive Gels, 1993; contbr. articles to profl. jours. Mem. Am. Chem. Soc., Polymer Networks Group (chmn. 1990-94, treas. 1994—), European Polymer Fedn. Avocations: swimming, skiing, hiking. Home: Zeyerova Alej 33, 162 00 Prague Czech Republic Office: Inst Macromolecular Chem, Heyrovskeho Nam 2, 162 06 Prague Czech Republic

DUŠEK, MILOSLAV, physicist, researcher; b. Prague, Czech Republic, July 6, 1964; s. Miroslav and Marta (Adamcová) D. Rerum Naturalium Doctor, Charles U., Prague, 1988, PhD, 1994. Cert. in optics. Rschr. Charles U., Prague, 1988-94, Palacky U., Olomouc, Czech Republic, 1994—. Translator: Fundamentals of Photonics, 1994; co-patentee in field; contbr. articles to profl. jours. Mem. Union Czech Mathematicians and Physicists. Avocations: music, hiking. Home: Vrbová 1476, cz-25001 Brandys n Lab Czech Republic Office: Palacky U Dept Optics, 17 listopadu 50, cz-77200 Olomouc Czech Republic

DUŠKOVÁ, MARKÉTA, plastic surgeon, consultant; b. Praha, Czechoslovakia, Sept. 19, 1950; d. Vilém Voldán and Anna (Maříková) Fadrhoncová; m. Josef Dušek, Aug. 31, 1984; children: Josef, Markéta. MD, Charles U., Prague, Czechoslovakia, 1974, PhD, 1985. Bd. cert. plastic surgeon. Jr. registrar dept. gen. surgery Charles U. Hosp., Praha, 1974-77, sr. registrar dept. gen. surgery, 1977-79, rschr. dept. plastic surgery, 1979-83, sr. registrar dept. plastic surgery, 1983-87, asst. prof. dept. plastic surgery, 1987—. Mem. Internat. Plastic and Reconstructive Surgery Assn., Czech Soc. Aesthetic Plastic Surgery (pres. 1996—). Avocations: scuba diving, gardening. Fax: 420-2-671 63241. Office: Dept Plastic Surgery, Charles U Srobarova 50, 100 34 Praha 10, Czech Republic

DUST, MARGARET CECILE, psychology educator; b. East Chicago, Ind., Aug. 1, 1947; d. Isidor Gerhardt and Nettie Zelenda (Klingspor) D. BA in Polit. Sci., Loyola U., Chgo., 1969; postgrad., John Marshal Law Sch., 1970-71; BA in Psychology, Purdue U. Calumet, 1977; MS in Indsl. Psychology, Ill. Inst. Tech., 1985; PhD in Ednl. Psychology and Stats., Andrews U., 1995. Lic. secondary sch. tchr., Ind. Field worker ARC, Vietnam, 1969-70; coord. of advising Purdue U. Calumet, Hammond, Ind., 1978-82; instr. psychology Purdue U. Calumet, Hammond, 1978-88, asst. prof. psychology, 1988-90; assoc. prof. psychology Chgo. State U., 1990—; assessment cons. Calumet Coll., Whiting, Ind., 1999-2000; presenter in field. Grantee for data analysis NSF, San Francisco, 1994; grantee for rsch. tng. and minority students Corp. for Tng. Minority Students, Chgo., 1998, 99. Mem. APA, Soc. for Computers in Tech., Ind. Coun. for the Humanities, Vietnam Vets. Am. (post traumatic stress disorder chair chpt. 285). Avocations: photography, gardening, world traveling. E-mail: bij6mcd@csu.edu. Home: 215 Greiving St Dyer IN 46311-1810 Office: Chgo State Univ 9501 S King Dr Chicago IL 60628-1501

DUSZA, RAYMOND KASPAR, county legislator; b. Buffalo, N.Y., Jan. 6, 1935; s. Joseph Peter Dusza and Stella Bertha Sucharski; m. Theresa Rita Skowron, Feb. 13, 1960; children: Susan Marie Dusza Barrett, Timothy Raymond. Student, U.S. Inst. Army Edn. Ctr., Cornell U. From sect. steward to pres. local 1581 Internat. Union Elec. Workers-Westinghouse, Cheektowaga; legislator Erie County 8th Dist., chmn. govt. affairs com., vice-chmn. pub. safety com.; del., bd. mem. Greater Buffalo AFL-CIO Coun.; vol. bd. dirs. Neighborhood Info. Ctr. With 82nd Airborne Divsn. Recipient Eagle Citizen of Yr. Labor award AM-POL, Coun. of Sr. Citizen's Clubs of Buffalo and Erie County Disting. Cmty. Svc. award, Pub. Svc. award People, Inc., Gen. Pulaski Assn. Labor award, Cheektowaga Southside Little League Appreciation award; named Hon. Firefighter Membership, annually 1989—. Mem. Fraternal Order Eagles, K.C., Polish Falcons Club, Am. Legion, Depew/Cheektowaga Taxpayers' Assn., AMVETS Buddy Knaus Post, Cath. War Vets.', Ushers Soc., St. Josaphat's Parish Holy Name Soc. Democrat. Roman Catholic. Avocations: home care and maintenance, flower gardening, long distance walking. Office: Erie County Legis 2956 Union Rd Buffalo NY 14227-1420

DUTCHER, JANICE JEAN PHILLIPS, oncologist; b. Bend, Oreg., Nov. 10, 1950; d. Charles Glen and MayBelle (Fluit) Phillips; m. John Dutcher, Sept. 8, 1971 (div. 1980). BA with honors, U. Utah, 1971; MD, U. Calif., Davis, 1975. Diplomate Am. Bd. Internal Medicine, Am. Bd. Med. Oncology. Intern Rush-Presbyn. St. Luke's Hosp., Chgo., 1975-76, resident, 1976-78; clin. assoc. Balt. Cancer Rsch., Nat. Cancer Inst., 1978-81, sr. investigator, 1981-82; asst. prof. U. Md., Balt., 1982; asst. prof. Albert Einstein Coll. Medicine, N.Y.C., 1983-86, assoc. prof., 1986-92, prof., 1992-98; course co-dir. Advances in Cancer Treatment Rsch. Albert Einstein Coll. Medicine, Manhattan, 1984-96; prof. medicine N.Y. Med. Coll., 1998—; assoc. dir. for clin. affairs Comprehensive Cancer Ctr., Our Lady of Mercy Med. Ctr., 1998—; chmn. biol. response mod. com. Ea. Coop. Oncology Group, Madison, Wis., 1989-95, mem. exec. com., 1995-97, chair renal subcom., 1998—; mem. data safety com. Nat. Heart Lung Blood Inst., Bethesda, Md., 1990-95; mem. biologic response modifier study sect. Nat. Cancer Inst., Bethesda, 1988, 90, 94, 96; mem. NIH Consensus Panel on Early Melanoma, 1992; mem. FDA Oncology Drug Adv. Bd., 1995-99, chair FDA-ODAC,

1996-99, NCI subcom. D for program project rev., 1995-98, mem. subsplty. med. oncology bd. Am. Bd. Internal Medicine, 1997—; mem. NCI subcom. A for Cancer Ctrs., 1998—. Editor: Handbook of Hematology/Oncology Emergencies, 1987, Modern Transfusion Therapy, 1990; sect. editor: Neoplastic Diseases of the Blood, 4th edit., 2000; mem. editl. bd. Jour. Immunotherapy, Med. Oncology, Jour. Clin. Oncology, Jour. Clin. Pharm., Ann. Intern. Med.; contbr. articles to Blood, Leukemia, Jour. Clin. Oncology, Jour. Immunotherapy, Clin. Cancer Rsch., Soc. Am. Cancer Jour. Recipient Beecham award in Hematology So. Blood Club, 1983, Henry C. Moses Clin. Rsch. award Montefiore Med. Ctr., 1989, Outstanding Alumnus award U. Calif., Davis, 1989; named Outstanding Young Investigator Ea. Coop. Oncology Group, 1993; recipient numerous grants. Fellow ACP; mem. Am. Soc. Clin. Oncology (program com. 1988, 97, grants award com. 1998—, chair awards com. 1999—), Am. Assn. Cancer Rsch. (faculty workshop clin. trials methodology 1996, 97, 98, 99, 2000, internat. trials workshop 1999, 2000), Am. Soc. Hematology, Soc. for Biol. Therapy, Am. Radium Soc. (chair Jane Way com. 1995-96, exec. com. 1997-99), Phi Beta Kappa (Presdl. scholar 1968), Alpha Lambda Delta, Phi Kappa Phi, Alpha Omega Alpha. Achievements include findings related to management of alloimmunization to platelet transfusions, intensive maintenance of patients with acute leukemia, studies of new biologic response modifiers as antitumor drugs, management of renal cell cancer and breast cancer, study and treatment with biologic antitumor agents. Address: Our Lady of Mercy Medical Cen Comprehensive Cancer Cen 600 E 233rd St Bronx NY 10466-2604

DU THOIT, PIERRE GERARD, financial company executive; b. Mouseron, Belgium, Aug. 21, 1938; s. Alfred Jean and Marie Cornelie (Vandenberghe) Du T.; m. Patricia Hilary Antoneich, Apr. 28, 1962; children: Marc, Monique, David. Grad., St. Aidans, South Africa, 1955. CFP. Draftsman Socoman, Pt. Elizabeth, South Africa, 1959-60, Pilkington Bros., Pt. Elizabeth, 1960-62; prodn. engr. Ford Motor Co., Pt. Elizabeth, 1962-65, Frystark, Cape Town, South Africa, 1965-67; gen. mgr. Afcol, Johannesburg, South Africa, 1967-73, Anglo Union, Johannesburg, 1973-75; agt. Legal & Gen., Johannesburg, 1975-80; sr. cons. So. Life, Johannesburg, 1980-84; sr. dir. Alexander Fores, Johannesburg, 1984—. Fellow Inst. Life and Pension Advisers; mem. CFP. Roman Catholic. Avocations: reading, bridge, chess. Office: Alexander Forbes, 61 Katherine St, 2146 Sandton Gauteng, South Africa

DUTKIEWICZ, TOMASZ, physician; b. Stettin, Pomerania, Poland, Sept. 2, 1954; s. Zdzislaw and Maria (Gorczyca) D.; m. Jolanta Gwiazdowska, July 2, 1977; children: Grzegorz, Anna. Physician, Acad. Medicine, Stettin, 1977, MD, 1982; Med. Diagnostician, Nat. Ctr. Post-Grad. Edn., Warsaw, Poland, 1983; M, Ecole Centrale, Paris, 1996. Registered physician; registered translator. Intern State Clin. Hosp., Stettin, 1977-78, resident, 1978-92; rsch. assoc. U. Chgo., 1987-88; head Ctrl. Hosp. Lab., Stettin, 1989-90; acad. tchr. Acad. Medicine, Stettin, 1978-92; physician/holistic Medilog, Stettin, 1989—; cons. Indsl. Health Care, Stettin, 1982-84, Pharmacia, Uppsala, Sweden, 1985-87; head corp. planning VOBIS Computer Poland. Coauthor: Laboratory Diagnostics, 1989; patentee in field. Recipient award Acad. Medicine, Stettin, 1977. Mem. Assn. Clin. Biochemists, Soc. Francaise de Biologie Clinique, Gesellschaft Toxicologische und Klinische Chemie. Avocations: music, poetry, biking. Home: Konopnickiej 53, 71-132 Szczecin Poland

DUTOIT, CHARLES, conductor; b. Lausanne, Switzerland, Oct. 7, 1936. Studied at, Conservatory of Lausanne, Acad. Music, Geneva, Academia Musicale Chigiana, Siena, Conservatory Benedetto Marcello, Venice, Italy; attended session in conducting, Berkshire Music Center, Tanglewood, Mass.; DMus (hon.), McGill U., Montreal U., Laval U. Prin. condr. NHK Symphony Orch., N.Y.C., 1996, Montreal Symphony Orch. Formerly violinist with Lausanne Chamber Orch.; debut as condr. with Bern Symphony Orch., Switzerland, 1963; condr. and asst. music dir., Bern Symphony Orch., 1964, later music dir.; condr. and artistic dir., Radio-Zurich Orch., Switzerland, 1967; also guest condr. Vienna Opera; mus. dir. Nat. Symphony Orch. of Mex., Orch. Nat. de France, 1991—; apptd. chief condr. Goteborg Orch., Sweden, 1975; music dir., condr., Montreal Symphony Orch., 1977—; prin. guest condr. Minn. Orch., 1982-85; prin. condr., artistic dir. Phila. Orch., 1990-91; artistic dir., prin. condr. summer festivals Phila. Orch., at Mann Ctr. for Performing Arts, Saratoga Performing Arts Ctr.; prin. condr. NHK Symphony Orch., Tokyo, 1996; guest condr. all major orchs., S.Am., Europe, Japan, Australia, U.S., Can. and Israel, rec., Deutsche Gramophon, Erato, CBS, Decca/London, Philips, EMI; with Bavarian Radio Symphony, Boston Symphony Orch., Montreal Symphony Orch., L.A. Philharm., many London orchs., others. Recipient Canadian Music Coun. medal, 1988. Office: KM Artits LTD 40 W 57th St New York NY 10019-4001 Office: Orch Symph de Montreal, 260 de Maisonneuve Blvd W, Montreal, PQ Canada H2X 1Y9*

DUTTA, ALOKE KUMAR, electrical engineering educator; b. Calcutta, India, Nov. 24, 1960; s. Ajit Kumar and Chaya (Bose) D.; m. Ruchira Ghosh, Jan. 23, 1989; 1 child, Anwesha. BEE, Jadavpur U., Calcutta, 1982; MS, La. State U., 1985, PhD, 1989. Mgmt. trainee E.I.L., Assam, India, 1982-83, jr. engr., 1983; tchg./rsch. asst. La. State U., Baton Rouge, 1984-89, instr., 1990; asst. prof. Indian Inst. Tech. Kanpur, 1990-97, assoc. prof. elec. engring., 1997—, chmn. SUGC, 1995-96, chmn. APEC, 1994-95, convenor DUGC, 1994-96; counselor IEEE up-sect. Indian Inst. Tech. Kanpur Student Br., 1992-94. Contbr. articles to profl. jours. Recipient 5 medals Edn. Coun., Calcutta, 1982, Kaiser fellowship La. State U., Baton Rouge, 1986-87, nat. fellowship Edn. Coun., Calcutta, 1976, 78. Mem. IEEE (sr., mem. exec. com. UP sect. 1992—, sec. UP sect. 1998—, vice chmn. 2000—), Phi Kappa Phi, Eta Kappa Nu. Avocations: long drives, sightseeing, cricket, music, movies. Home: 3034 IIT Kanpur, Kanpur 208016, India Office: Indian Inst Tech Kanpur, Dept Elec Engring, Kanpur 208016, India

DUTTA, ANAND SWAROOP, medicinal chemist, pharmaceutical researcher; b. Mathura, India, Dec. 22, 1940; arrived in U.K., 1970; s. Gyan Swaroop and Krishna Kumari (Chibber) D.; m. Rajyashree Loomba, Feb. 11, 1970; children: Mohit, Sapna. BS, Agra (India) U., 1958, MS, 1960, PhD, 1964. Scientist B Ctrl. Drug Rsch. Inst., Lucknow, India, 1963-67; with Cleve. Clinic, 1967-68, Ind. U. Med. Ctr., Indpls., 1968-70; tech. officer ICI Pharms., Macclesfield, U.K., 1970—; sr. scientist Zeneca Pharms., Macclesfield, 1989—, rsch. assoc., 1991—; rsch. assoc. Astrazeneca, Macclesfield, 1999—. Author: Small Peptides, Chemistry, Biology and Clinical Studies, 1993; contbr. articles to profl. jours. Recipient award for drug discovery Soc. Drug Rsch., 1991. Mem. European Peptide Soc. (program com. mem. 1997—, U.K. rep. 1998—), Am. Chem. Soc. (medicinal chemistry sect.). Hindu. Achievements include discovery of Zoladex (goserelin) used for the treatment of prostate cancer/breast cancer; 15 patents in field. Office: Astrazeneca, Alderley Pk Macclerfield, Cheshire SK10 4TG, United Kingdom

DUTTA, BIRENDRA NATH, former college principal; b. Chandernagore, India, Jan. 2, 1930; s. Bhupendra Krishna and Mrinalina Dutta; m. Manisha Dutta, Oct. 5, 1965; children: Anasua Roychowdhury, Anuradha Pakira. BA, Calcutta U., 1956, MA, 1959, PhD, 1973. Lectr. Shillong (India) Coll., 1963-70; prin. Khalisani Coll., Chandernagore, India, 1970-88; mem. W.B Coll. Svc. Commn., Calcutta, 1988-92; pres. governing body Women's Coll. Hooghly, Chinsurah, India, 1987-97, Khalisani Coll., 1997—. Author: Comparative Study of Sanskrit and Bengali Mahabharata; contbr. articles to profl. jours. Active in spreading edn. among rural people by establishing schs., colls. and libr.s. Avocation: social and cultural activities. Home: College Rd, PO Khalisani 7212138, Chandernagore India

DUTTA, DILIP KUMAR, economist; b. Calcutta, W. Bengal, India; arrived in Australia, 1986; m. Pompa Dutta. BA with hons., U. Calcutta, India, MA; PhD, U. Calif., Berkeley, 1985. Lectr. Indian Sch. of Mines, Dhanbad, Bihar, India, 1977-78; post doctoral fellow Australian Nat. U., Canberra, 1986-88; sr. lectr. U. Sydney, NSW, Australia, 1988—; dir. Ctr. for South Asian Studies. Fellow Indian Inst. Mgmt. Office: U Sydney, Dept Econs, Sydney NSW 2006, Australia

DUTTA, DIPAK, engineering consultant; b. Bhanga, India, Feb. 13, 1935; arrived in Germany, 1959; s. Rajkumar and Bijaliprova Dutta; m. Helma Graewin, June 9, 1967. BS, Calcutta (India) U., 1954; M Engring., Tech. U., Berlin, 1966. Tchr. Calcutta schs., 1955-56; trainee Verolme United Shipyard, Rotterdam, The Netherlands, 1957-58; product devel. engr. Mannesmann Tubular Works, Duesseldorf, Germany, 1966-74, dept. chief, 1975-94; cons. Tubular Structures, Ratingen, Germany, 1995—; mem. European Convention for Constrnl. Steelwork, Brussels, 1974—; sec. Internat. Inst. Welding, 1972-80; mem. Com. Internat. for Devel. and Study of Tubular Constrn., Geneva, 1972-83, chmn. tech. commn., 1984-94. Author: Handbuch Hohlprofile in Stahlkonstruktionen, 1988, Hohlprofilkonstruktionen, 1999; editor, author: (English, French, German and Spanish) Construction with Hollow Steel Sections, Series 1-7, 1991-98. Avocations: jogging, animal welfare, history, philosophy, religion. Home and Office: Marggrafstrasse 13, 40878 Ratingen Germany

DUTTA, GOUTAM, researcher; b. Jamshedpur, India, Apr. 4, 1957; s. Samir Kumar and Shephali D.; m. Gopa Roy, Apr. 20, 1999. B of Tech. (hons.), Indian Inst. of Tech., Kharagpur, India, 1979; MBA, Xaviers Labor Rels. Inst., Jamshedpur, India, 1988; PhD, Northwestern Univ., 1996. Asst. mgr. Tata Steel, India, 1980-85; deputy mgr. Tata Steel, Jamshedpur, India, 1985-89, mgr., 1989-91; rsch. asst. Northwestern Univ., Evanston, Ill., 1991-96; lectr. London Sch. Econs. and Political Sci., U.K., 1996-97; assoc. prof. Indian Inst. of Mgmt., Ahmedabad, India, 1997—; cons. Am. Rolling Mill Co., Ohio, 1995-96; chmn. Internat. Federation of Operational Rsch. Soc., OR for Devel. Prize Contest, London, Ont., Can., 1996—. Contbr. articles to profl. jours.; inventor in field. Recipient First Prize Franz Edelman award Inst. of Ops. Rsch. and Mgmt. Sci. & Coll. of Practice of Mgmt. Sci., 1994, IFORS OR for Devel. prize Internat. Fedn. of Operational Rsch. Soc., 1993, Honoured Best Citizens of India award Internat. Publ. House, 1999, Vikas Ratna award India Internat. Friendship Soc., 1999, Bharat Nirman Excellence award Front for Nat. Programs, New Delhi, 2000. Mem. Inst. of Engineers India, N.Y. Acad. Scis., Inst. of Operational Rsch. and Mgmt. Sci., Internat. Fedn. of Operational Rsch. Soc. Avocations: jogging, bicycling, table tennis. E-mail:goutam@iimahd.ernet.in. Home: Transit House, No 16 IIM Campus, Gujarat Ahmedabad 380 015, India Office: Indian Inst Mgmt, Ahmedabad Wing 3 PMQ Area, Gujarat 380 015, India

DUTTA, MANORANJAN, economics educator; m. Kanak; 1 child, Kavery Dutta Kaul. PhD, U. Pa., 1962. Prof. econs. Rutgers U., New Brunswick, N.J., 1962—; lectr. U. Calcutta, 1951-58; asst. prof. various colls. W. Bengal Edn. Svc., 1951-58; editor Jour. Asian Econs., 1990—; Rsch. in Econ. Studies, 1986—; cons. Mathematica, Princeton, N.J., 1969-70; adj. prof. Pace University, N.Y., 1975; dir., pres., bd. trustees Am. Com. Asian Econ. Studies; dir. Coun. for State Econ. Studies; chmn. Nat. Adv. Coun. for South Asian Affairs; speaker, presenter and vis. lectr. in field. Contbr. numerous articles to profl. jours. Fulbright-Smith-Mundt fellow, 1958, 59, Rutgers U. Faculty Rsch. fellow, 1967, 87, Nat. Sci. Found., 1973, 76; grantee U.S. Dept. Labor, 1978, Rutgers U. Rsch. Coun., 1979, N.J. State Dept. Industry and Labor, 1979, Ford Found., 1980, 81, Port Authority N.Y. and N.J., 1981, 85, Am. Tel. and Telegraph Co., 1981, John D. and Catherine T. MacArthur Found., 1988, USAID, 1994, U.N. Devel. Program, 1996, Asia Devel. Bank, 1998; recipient cert. of appreciation Bureau of the Census U.S. Dept. Commerce, 1982, Honor award Assn. Asian Indians in Am., 1985, Honored Am. award Congl. resolution signed by Pre. Reagan, 1985. Am. Econ. Assn., Am. Statis. Assn., Am. Assn. for Advancement of Sci., Am. Assn. for Asian Studies, Am. Assn. Univ. Profs. (chmn. bargaining team 1973-74, v.p. 1974-75), Asia Soc. N.Y., Assn. Indian Econ. Studies, Am. Com. on Asian Econ. Studies, Ea. Econ. Assn., Econometric Soc., N.Y. Acad. Scis., Calif. Inst. Internat. Studies, 1980 Census Adv. Com. for Asia-Pacific Ams. Fax: 732-932-1558. E-mail: mdutta@rci.rutgers.edu. Office: Rutgers U Faculty Arts and Scis 75 Hamilton St New Brunswick NJ 08901-1248

DUTTA, NABA KUMAR, polymer scientist, educator; b. Calcutta, India, Nov. 23, 1957; arrived in Australia, 1994; s. Sunil Krishna and Laxmi Rani (Bose) D.; m. Namita Roy Choudhury; 1 child, Ankit Kumar. Bsc with honors, U. Calcutta, 1978, B in Tech., 1982; PhD, Indian Inst. Tech., Kharagpur, 1991. Rubber technologist Nat. Engring. Industries (Rubber), Calcutta, 1982-86; postdoctoral rsch. scientist Ctr. Nat. de la Rsch. Sci., Mulhouse, France, 1991-93; rsch. fellow Monash U., Melbourne, Australia, 1994-97; sect. leader U. S. Australia, Adelaide, 1997—. Contbr. articles to profl. jours. Rsch. fellow Dept. Sci. and Tech., India, 1986. Mem. Am. Chem. Soc., Soc. Plastics Engrs., Royal Australian Chem. Inst., Soc. Rheology. Avocations: history, music, philosophy. Office: U S Australia, Mawson Lakes Blvd, Mawson Lakes 5095, Australia

DUTTA, NIRMA LENDU, mining engineer; b. Sylhet, Bangladesh, May 3, 1938; s. Narendra Nath and Parul (Choudhury) D.; m. Indrani Sangupta, Nov. 18, 1967; children: Joydeep, Valentina. BSc in Mining Engring., B.H.U., Varanasi, India, 1959; BL, Ranchi (India) U., 1970. Cert. 1st class colliery mgr. DGMS, India, ops. rsch. and computers cert. NITIE, India, mgmt. objective cert. IIM, India. Colliery mgr. NCDC Ltd., India, 1959-71; mine supt. Coal Mines Authority, India, 1971-75; gen. mgr., CEO Greaves Cotton & Co. Ltd., India, 1975-86; mng. dir. Indian Longwall Ltd., India, 1986-91, Gullick Equipment Ltd., India, 1991-96; dir., gen. mgr. Joy Mining Machinery, India, 1996—; chief exec. Greaves Midwest Ltd., Bangalore, India, 1984-86; cons. Joy Mining Machinery Ltd., U.K., 1997—. Pioneer work in underground mining (Bronze medal MGMI 1971). Recipient Nat. Mineral award Ministry of Mines, Govt. of India, 1969, Scroll of Honor for contbn. to mining industry BHU, 1985, Silver medal MGMI, 1981. Mem. Inst. Engrs., Mining, Geo. and Met. Inst. India (mem. coun., treas. 1987-99), Calcutta Club Ltd. Avocations: bridge, social service. Home: 423 G Block New Alipore, Calcutta 700 053, India Office: Joy Mining Machinery, 1A Janki Shah Rd Hastings, Calcutta 700 022, India

DUTTAMAJUMDER, SANJOY KUMAR, plant pathologist; b. Calcutta, India, Jan. 16, 1958; s. Santosh and Kamala (Ghosh) D.; m. Kankana Ghosh, July 26, 1991; 1 child, Saumya. BSc in Agriculture with honors, Bidhan Chandra Krishi Viswavidyalaya, Kalyani, 1980; MSc, Indian Agrl. Rsch. Inst., New Delhi, 1982, PhD, 1986. From scientist to sr. scientist Indian Coun. Agrl. Rsch., New Delhi, 1985—. Mem. The Indian Phytopathol. Soc., Indian Sci. Congress Assn., N.Y. Acad. Sci. Hindu. Avocations: photography, chess, palmistry. Office: Indian Inst Sugarcane Rsch, Rae Bareli Rd PO Dilkusha, Lucknow 226 002, India

DUTTON, ANDREA GUILLEN, science educator; b. Ontario, Calif., Mar. 2, 1952; d. Eliseo Zendejas and Mary Ann (Salgado) Guillen; m. Robert D. Dutton, Nov. 26, 1981; 1 child, Kara Ann. B in Vocat. Edn., Calif. State U., San Bernardino, 1994, MA in Edn., 2000. Diagnostic imaging technologist Nat. Med. Enterprise, 1972-92; clin. instr., radiographer Doctor's Hosp., Montclair, Calif., 1978-85; adj. faculty Chaffey C.C., Rancho Cucamonga, Calif., 1981-94; faculty mem., prof. radiology Chaffey C.C., Rancho Cucamonga, 1994—; adv. mem. Chaffey Coll. Radio Tech. Adv. Com., 1982—. Contbg. author: Basic Medical Techniques and Patient Care in Imaging Technology, 1995. Bd. mem. Chaffey Coll. Found., 1990-93, Heritage Rsch. and Support Found., 1999; mem. Specialized Svcs. Bur., San Bernardino, 1992—; nat. del. Rep. Nat. Party, San Diego, 1996. Mem. Am. Soc. Radiologic Technologists, Calif. Soc. Radiologic Technologists, Calif. Tchrs. Assn., Radiologic Technologists Educator's Calif. (sec. 1999-2000), Phi Kappa Phi. Avocations: snow skiing, baking, world travel. E-mail: radteddutton@yahoo.com. Office: Chaffey Cmty Coll 5885 Haven Ave Rancho Cucamonga CA 91737-3002

DUTTON, FRANK ELROY, data processing executive; b. Warren, Ohio, Nov. 16, 1946; s. Robert Wade and Ann Victoria (Sessions) D.; m. Nancy June Gephart, Nov. 6, 1965 (div. 1981); children: Cynthia, Frank, Robert; m. Margaret Elizabeth Sessions, Dec. 16, 1981 (div. Dec. 1987); m. Paula Kay Gately, Feb. 14, 1992 (div. Sept. 1994). With sales dept. Zylco Cutlery Rena Ware Distrs., Warren, 1964-68; advt. salesman Directory Dept. Ohio Bell Telephone Co., Cuyahoga Falls, 1968-69; pvt. practice residential constrn. Warren and Hammond (La.), 1970-74; technician J. Ray McDermott & Co., New Orleans, 1974-83, McDermott Internat., Antwerp, Belgium, 1975, McDermott SE Asia, Singapore, 1981-83; owner Computer Time, Inc., Hammond, 1983-85; mgr. tech. services Industry Programs, Inc., Houston, 1985-86; owner Affordable Automation, Houston, 1987-89; program, analyst The Phillips Group, Stafford, Tex., 1989-92; owner software and hardware integrator IHMS Software Support, Hemphill, Tex., 1992—; owner computer software, internet web site design hosting Fred Software, Hemphill, 1998—; cons. in computer communications Southmark Industries, Houston, 1986-87, Crown Broadcasting, Hammond, La., 1987-89, Bee-Line Delivery Svc., Houston, 1986-89. Author, designer various computer games, utility software programs, computer software for radio stas., computer software for retail furniture stores, Turbo Pascal Toolbox, 1988 (award of disting. tech. communication 1989, award of excellence Internat. Soc. Tech. Communication 1989), French transl., 1988, Portuguese trans., 1990, French trans., 1990; contbr. articles to profl. jours. Served with USAR, 1966-72. Recipient semi-finalist award Global Info. Infrastructure, 1999. Mem. Am. Mensa Soc. Avocation: astrology. Home and Office: HC 52 Box 842 Hemphill TX 75948-9625

DUTTON, LESLIE RUTH, music educator; b. Odessa, Tex., Dec. 1, 1968; d. Tommy Joe and Esther Ruth Dutton; m. Bryan Allen, June 11, 1988 (div. May 11, 1999). MusB, East Tex. State U., 1992, MusM, 1994. Voice instr. Panola Coll., Carthage, Tex., 1994-96; choir dir. Covenant Presbyn. Ch., Lubbock, Tex., 1996—; assoc. dir. orgnl. mgmt. Lubbock Christian U., 1996-99. Mem. Nat. Assn. Tchrs. Singing, Nat. Music Tchrs. Assn., Sigma Alpha Iota. Lutheran. Home: 53 Linwood Dr Marshall TX 75672-2383

DUUS, GORDON COCHRAN, lawyer; b. Ridley Park, Pa., Oct. 17, 1954; s. Frank Martin and Shirley (Cochran) D.; m. Mary Ellen Moses, Nov. 9, 1985; children: Alexander, Hannah, Julianne. BA magna cum laude, U. Pa., 1977; JD with honors, George Washington U., 1981. Bar: D.C. 1981, N.J. 1982, Calif. 1987, U.S. Dist. Ct. N.J. 1982, U.S. Supreme Ct. 1989. Assoc. Previti, Todd, Gemmel, Fitzgerald & Nugent, Linwood, N.J., 1982-87; ptnr., chmn. environ. law dept. Margolis, Chase, Kosicki, Aboyoun & Hartman, Verona, N.J., 1987-90, Cole, Schotz, Meisel, Forman & Leonard, Hackensack, N.J., 1990—; mem. faculty Cook Coll. of Rutgers U., New Brunswick, N.J., 1991—, Nat. Bus. Insts., Saddlebrook, N.J., 1992, Govt. Inst., Atlantic City, 1995; spkr. in field. Contbr. articles to profl. jours. Mem. ABA, N.J. Bar Assn., Bergen County Bar Assn. Office: Cole Schotz Meisel Forman & Leonard 25 Main St Hackensack NJ 07601-7015

DUVAL, DAVID ROBERT, professional golfer; b. Jacksonville, Fla., Nov. 9, 1971. Student, Ga. Tech. Profl. golfer PGA, 1993—; mem. Walker Cup team, 1991, Presidents Cup team, 1996, 98, Ryder Cup Team, 1999. Winner Nike Wichita Open, 1993, Nike Tour Championship, 1993, Michelob Championship at Kingsmill, 1997, Walt Disney World/Oldsmobile Classic, 1997, The Tour Championship, 1997, Tucson Chrysler Classic, 1998, Shell Houston Open, 1998, NEC World Series of Golf, 1998, Michelob Championship at Kingsmill, 1998, Mercedes Championship, 1999, Bob Hope Chrysler Classic, 1999, The Players Championship, 1999, Bell South Classic, 1999, Ryder Cup, 1999; recipient Dave Williams award, 1993, Jasper award, Jacksonville, 1996; named Collegiate Player of Yr., 1993. Avocations: reading, fly fishing, surfing, skiing, baseball. Office: PGA of Am Box 109601 100 Ave of Champions Palm Beach Gardens FL 33410

DUVAL, ELISABETH L.I.M., pediatric intensivist; b. Schoten, Belgium, Jan. 18, 1963; d. Franciscus Duval and Mariette Vanginkel; m. Geert Veeckman, Apr. 23, 1989 (div. July 1996); children: Maren, Ianthe, Ilke. MD summa cum laude, U. Antwerp, 1988. Pediatrician U. Hosp. Ghent, Belgium, 1988-92; fellow in intensive care Wilhelmina's Children's Hosp., Utrecht, The Netherlands, 1994-95, resident pediat. ICU, 1995-99; dir. pediat. ICU U. Antwerp, 1999—; cons., clin. expert Sensor Medics, Bilthoven, The Netherlands, 1997—; instr. advanced pediat. life support The Netherlands, 1998—. Contbr. articles to profl. jours. Mem. European Soc. Pediat. Intensive Care. Roman Catholic. Avocation: flute. Office: U Antwerp Univ Hosp, UZA Wilzykstraat 10, Edegem Belgium

DUVAL, JOSEPH MARIE LOUIS, archbishop; b. Chenx, Haute Savoie, France, Oct. 11, 1928; s. Albert and Jeanne (Benoit) D. Licenciate in law, U. Paris; licenciate in canon law, Gregorian U., Rome. Ordained priest, 1952. Parish vicar Saint-Maurice, Annecy, France, 1957-58; prof. canon law Grand Seminaire d'Annecy, 1958-63, prof. moral theology, 1963-67, head, 1967-71; Episcopal vicar Saint-Jorioz, 1971-79; aux. bishop to Cardinal Paul Gouyon; archbishop Rennes, France, 1974-78; asst. archbishop Rouen, France, 1978-81, archbishop, 1981—; v.p. Conf. Épiscopale Française, 1987-90, pres., 1990-97. Office: Archevêché, Rue Bonnetiers, 76000 Rouen France

DUVAL, MICHAEL RAOUL, investment banker; b. San Francisco, July 18, 1938; s. Richard and Sylvia Raoul-Duval. A.B., Georgetown U., 1961; J.D., U. Calif., San Francisco, 1967. Bar: Calif. 1967, U.S. Supreme Ct. 1971. Atty. U.S. Dept. Transp., Washington, 1967-70; staff asst. to Pres., asso. dir. Domestic Council, spl. counsel to Pres., Washington, 1970-77; various exec. positions Mead Corp., Dayton, Ohio, 1977-84; mng. dir. First Boston Corp., N.Y.C., 1984-90; ltd. ptnr. Anthem Ptnrs., L.P., N.Y.C., 1990-92; chmn. Michael Duval & Assocs., Ltd., Santa Fe, 1994—; bd. dirs. British Aerospace Holdings, Inc. Mem. Def. Policy Bd., 1989-94, SEC's Emerging Markets Adv. Com., 1989, Nat. Commn. on Fin. Instn. Reform, Recovery and Enforcement, Washington. Capt. USMC, 1960-64. Mem. N.Y. Council Fgn. Relations. Republican. Roman Catholic.

DUVALL, CHARLES PATTON, retired internist, oncologist; b. Evanston, Ill., June 16, 1936; s. Charles Fleming and Edith (Osgood) D.; m. Nancy Ash, June 21, 1958; children: Lawrence Charles, Stephen Rogers, Douglas Patton, Lauren Duvall Meacham. AB, Cornell U., 1958; MD, U. Rochester, N.Y., 1962. Diplomate Am. Bd. Internal Medicine, Am. Bd. Med. Oncology. Intern Yale New Haven Med. Ctr., 1962-63; resident in internal medicine U. Rochester, 1963-64; clin. assoc. Nat. Cancer Inst., NIH, Bethesda, Md., 1964-66; resident in medicine Georgetown U. Hosp., Washington, 1966-67, USPHS spl. fellow in hematology, 1967-68; physician Foxhall Internists, Washington, 1968-2000; ret., 2000; clin. prof. medicine Georgetown U. Hosp., Washington, 1968-2000; vice chmn. dept. medicine Sibley Hosp., Washington, 1987-90, chmn., 1990-91; mem. emeritus staff Washington Hosp. Ctr., 1988—. Contbr. articles to profl. jours. Elder Bradley Hills Presbyn. Ch., Bethesda, 1974-77; chmn. bd. Blue Cross Blue Shield Nat. Capital area, Washington, 1986-94, Group Hospitalization Med. Svcs., Inc., Washington, 1986-94; vice chmn., bd. trustees Vols. in Medicine Inst., Hilton Head, S.C. Lt. comdr. USPHS, 1964-66. Recipient 5 Yr. Svc. award Am. Cancer Soc., 1978. Fellow ACP (Outpatient Tchg. award 1998, Laureate award 2000); mem. Am. Soc. Internal Medicine (DC chpt. pres. 1977, pres. rsch. found. 1987-88, pres.-elect 1988-89, pres. 1989-90, speaker ho. of dels. 1991-95, chmn. federated coun. internal medicine 1989-90, Spl. Recognition award 1979-2000), AMA (del. 1988-93, coun. on legislation 1991-2000, coun. on legislation chmn. 1996-97), Spltys. and Svcs. Soc. (pres. 1990-91, sect. coun. IM), Coun. Internal Medicine (chmn. sect. 1987-88), Osler Soc. D.C. (pres. 1978-79), Clin. Pathologic Soc. (pres. 1995-96), Congl. Country Club, Country Club of Hilton Head (S.C.), Bear Creek Club, Alpha Omega Alpha, Sigma Chi. Republican. Presbyterian. Avocations: golf, skiing, photography, painting. Home: 316 Seabrook Dr Hilton Head Island SC 29926-1979

DUVALL, JACK, television executive, fund raiser, writer; b. San Diego, July 10, 1946; s. John William and Margaret (Clark) DuV. AB cum laude, Colgate U., 1968. Mgmt. cons. Ohio Bell, Cleve., 1969; spl. agt. Air Force Office of Spl. Investigations, 1969-72; compliance officer Price Commn. U.S., Washington, 1972-73; chief industry compliance br. Cost Living Council, Exec. Office Pres. U.S., Washington, 1973-74; dir. pub. affairs Nat. Soybean Processors Assn., Hearing Industries Assn., Nat. Assn. Child Devel. Edn., and Food Protein Council, Washington, 1975-80; dir. corp. relations U. Chgo., 1980-85; v.p. program resources WETA TV/Radio, Washington, 1985-89; prin. Mars Hill, Alexandria, Va., 1989—; cons. Albert Einstein Peace Prize Found., Chgo., 1983-84; advisor-cons. Mil. Reform Inst., Washington, 1984-87, Sta. KCET-TV, 1989-91, Sta. WTVS-TV, 1990-92, The Learning Channel, 1990-92, Vision Interfaith Satellite Network, 1990-95, Jefferson Energy Found., 1990-91, Nat. Found. for People with Disabilities, 1990-91, Compass Films, Ltd., 1990-91, NOVA Child Devel. Ctrs., 1989-90, Hr Prodns., 1991-92, Nat. Park Trust, 1992, Lifetime Med. TV, 1991-92, Boston Ballet, 1992-93, Maritime Heritage Prints Video, 1992-93, Mind Ext. U., 1992-93, Jefferson Ctr. New Dem. Processes, 1993, Brit. Consulate Gen. L.A., 1990-95, Sta. WLIW-TV, 1992-93, Sta. WBGU-TV, 1992-93, Com. on Constitutional Sys., 1990-94, Colonial Williamsburg Fd., 1993-94, Christian Sci. Monitor, 1994, Nat. Video Comms., 1994-95, TCI, Inc., 1995-96, Md. Pub. TV, 1995-96, Turner Broadcasting Sys., 1995-96, S.C. Ednl. TV, 1996-98, First Ch. of Christ Scientist, 1996-97, Hedrick Smith Prodns., 1995-98, Advanced Network & Svcs., Inc., 1997-98, White House Writers Group, 1998, Walker Prodns., 1998, Santa Monica Pictures, 1999—; coord. Working

Group on Ednl. Tech. and Programing, 1992-93. Author: (with others) Historical Working Papers of the Economic Stabilization Program, 1975; co-author: A Force More Powerful, 2000; exec. prodr. TV series Economic life, 1993, Learning About Democracy, 1993, A Force More Powerful, 2000; contbr. poems and articles to various publs. Speechwriter Sen. Adlai Stevenson Ill. gov. campaign, 1982; Ill. spokesman Sen. Gary Hart pres. campaign, 1983-84; mem. Nat. Dem. Platform Com., Washington, 1984, Social Services Adv. Bd., Alexandria, 1986-87, mem. bd. advisors Ctr. for A New Democracy, Washington, 1985-87; issues, speech advisor presdl. campaign Gov. Michael S. Dukakis, 1987-88; mem., bd. dirs. Arlington Inst., 1991—; pres. 5th Ch. of Christ Scientist, Washington, 1997-98. Capt. USAF, 1969-72. Mem. Delta Sigma Rho, Phi Beta Kappa, Phi Alpha Theta. Office: Mars Hill PO Box 707 Alexandria VA 22313-0707

DUVALL, LAWRENCE DELBERT, insurance company executive; b. Jacobsburg, Ohio, Mar. 5, 1942; s. Lawrence and Lillian Elizabeth (Brocklehurst) D.; m. Sandra Lee Parrish, May 16, 1970. BS in Indstl. Mgmt., Ohio State U., 1964; MBA, Columbia U., 1976; BS in Meterology, Northwestern U., 1966. Cert. constrn. engr., N.Y. Exec. mgmt. trainee Crum & Forster, N.Y.C., 1967-69; inland marine underwriter, mgr. Am. Home Assurance Co., Constrn. Div., N.Y.C., 1969-73; Southwestern regional property mgr. Am. Home Assurance Co., Dallas, 1973-76; mgr. Ins. Co. of the State Pa., Dallas, 1976-82; atty.-in-fact A. I. Lloyds Ins. Co., Dallas, 1976-82; southwestern regional property mgr. Nat. Union Fire Ins. Co., Dallas, 1973-76; v.p. A.I. G. Energy Inc., N.Y.C., 1982-86, Starr Tech. Risk Agy., Inc., N.Y.C., 1986-94; dir. Worldwide Utilities, 1994—; v.p. Am. Internat. Underwriters, 1994—. Fundraiser USMC Dependent Scholarship Fund, 1987—. With USMC, 1963-67, Vietnam. Decorated Silver Star, Purple Heart with gold star; Medal of Merit (Vietnam); named Constrn. Cons. of Yr., U. Wis., 1971. Mem. Soc. Petroleum Engrs., Conf. Spl. Risk Underwriters, Tex. Ins. Adv. Assn. Avocations: automobile racing, flying. Home: 171 Park Rd Parsippany NJ 07054-1731 Office: 70 Pine St New York NY 10270-0002

DUVALLET, GÉRARD, parasitologist; b. Lyon, France, Mar. 8, 1948; s. Roger and Gabrielle (Cheze) D.; m. Rolande Toussaint, Aug. 12, 1972. MSc, U. Paris, 1970, specialization diploma, 1971, Agregation, 1972. Med. entomologist Overseas Scientific Rsch. and Tech. Ctr., Burkina Faso, 1973-75; med. parasitologist French Ministry Cooperation, Burkina Faso, 1975-81; sr. scientist, Dept. Livestock Prodn. & Veterinary Medicine French Agrl. Rsch. Org. for the Tropics and Subtropics, Burkina Faso, 1981-94; head tng. French Agrl. Rsch. Org. for the Tropics and Subtropics, Montpellier, France, 1994-99; prof. biol. Univ. Montpellier, France, 1999—; dir. Rsch. Ctr. on Animal Trypanosomoses, Burkina Faso, 1986-87; mem. expert group FAO, Rome, 1988-92. Contbr. over 50 articles to sci. jours. Civil mil. svc. in cooperation with Burkina Faso, 1973-74. Recipient Merite Agricole award French Ministry Agr., 1996. Fellow French Soc. Systematics, French Soc. Parasitology. Avocations: golf, aviation, bird watching. Office: Univ Paul Valery, Montpellier 3 Rte De Mende, 34199 Montpellier Cedex 5, France

DUVENECK, GERT LUDWIG, physicist; b. Soest, Germany, Aug. 28, 1956; s. Gerda Duveneck Henke; m. Ulla Angelika Metz, Dec. 5, 1986; 1 child, Larissa-Sophie. Diploma, Georg August U., Gottingen, 1983, PhD, 1986. Rsch. scientist Max-Planck Inst. for Biophys. Chemistry, Gottingen, 1981-86; rsch. scientist/postdoctoral fellow Columbia U., N.Y.C., 1986-88; rsch. scientist Ciba-Geigy HG, Basle, Switzerland, 1988-90, rsch. project leader, 1990-95; head rsch. group leader Novartis Pharma AG, Basle, 1995-99; co-founder Zeptosens AG/Bioanalytical Solutions, Witterswil, Switzerland, 1999—; lectr. in field. Contbr. articles to profl. jours.; patentee in field. Achievements include specialization in optical planar waveguides and fluorescence spectroscopy. Fax: 41 61 726 8171. E-mail: gert.duveneck@zeptosens.com. Office: Zeptosens AG, Benkenstrasse 254, Ch-4108 Witterswill Switzerland

DUVERGER, PATRICK, executive. Grad., Ecole Polytech., 1958, Ecole Nat. Superieore Mines, Paris, 1961. Engr. Corps de Mines, 1964-69; tech. advisor various French cabinets, 1969-74; sales mgr. Societe Generale, Paris, 1975-82, deputy head divsn., 1982-86, head, 1986-87, exec. v.p., 1987-89, exec. v.p. capital markets divsn., 1989-95, deputy CEO, 1995-97, co-CEO, 1997-2000; ret., 2000. Office: Societe Generale, 29 Blvd Haussman, 75009 Paris France

DUVVUR, SATYANARAYANA RAO, engineering company executive; b. Nellore, Andhra Pra, India, Nov. 3, 1935; s. Narayanaiah and Ramanamma (Gudur) D.; m. Subhasri Pillarisetti, Jan. 30, 1964; 2 children. BEng, Coll. Engring., Kakinada, India, 1956. Mem. faculty Engring. Coll., 1956-57; design engr. Western Rlwy., 1957-60; asst. divisional engr. S.E. Rlwy. and S.C. Rlwy., 1961-74; dep. gen. mgr. S.C. Rlwy, 1975-77; rlwy. specialist RITES (India), Baghdad, Iraq, 1980-85; chief engr. constrn. N.E. Frontier Rlwy., Guwahati, India, 1985-87; divsn. rlwy. mgr. Indian Rlwys., Vijayawada, 1987-89; gen. mgr. Ircon Internat., Ltd., Dhaka, Bangladesh, 1989-91; dir. works Ircon Internat., Ltd., New Delhi, 1991-93; v.p. Tata Projects Ltd., Hyderabad, India, 1994-95, CEO, mng. dir., 1996-2000; track specialist Rites/Iraqi Rwy., Baghdad, 1980-85; exec. com. tata Cons. Engrs., Mumbai, India, 1996—. Chmn. Karunalayam Charitable Trust, Hydrabad, 1997. Capt. Indian Territorial Army, 1964-78. Fellow UNDP, 1977; recipient Rlwy. award South Eastern Rlwy., Calcutta, 1968. Avocations: photography, reading, music, travel. Home: 6-1-280/2a Padmarao Nagar, 500 025 Secunderabad AP, India Office: Tata Projects Ltd, Suryodaya 1-10-60/3, 500016 Hyderabad AP, India

DUYCK, KATHLEEN MARIE, poet, musician, retired social worker; b. Portland, Oreg., July 21, 1933; d. Anthony Joseph Dwyer and Edna Elisabeth Hayes; m. Robert Duyck, Feb. 3, 1962; children: Mary Kay Boeyen, Robert Patrick, Anthony Joseph. BS, Oreg. State U., 1954; MSW, U. Wash., 1956. Cert. NASW, Oreg. Adoption worker Cath. Svcs., Portland, 1956-61, Cath. Welfare, San Antonio, 1962; musician Tucson Symphony, 1963-65; prin. cellist Phoenix (Ariz.) Coll. Orch., 1968-78, Scottsdale (Ariz.) Symphony, 1974-80; poet, 1993—. Author: (poetry cassettes) Visions, 1993 (Contemporary Series Poet 1993), Visions II, 1996 (Contemporary Series Poet 1996); contbr. to 13 Nat. Libr. of Poetry Anthologies. Rep. worker Maricopa County Reps., Phoenix, 1974; mem. Scottsdale Cultural Coun.; NASW bd. Cath. Charities Rep., Portland, 1959-61. Recipient Golden Poet award World of Poetry, 1991, 92, Editor's Choice awards Nat. Libr. Poetry, 1993—, Sec. gift Phoenix Exec. Bd., 1976. Recognition award Archbishop Howard, 1961, 5-Yr. Kathleen Duyck award Cello Congress V, 1996. Mem. Internat. Poetry Hall Fame, Ariz. Cello Soc., Nat. Libr. Poetry, Internat. Soc. Poets, Phoenix Symphony Guild (exec. bd. 1970-80). Republican. Roman Catholic. Avocations: pianist, photography, poetry, artistic collections, attending concerts. Home: 4545 E Palomino Rd Phoenix AZ 85018-1719

DUYEN, VO HA, lawyer; b. Binh Duong, Vietnam, Apr. 10, 1969; d. Vo Van Linh and Ha Thi Cuc. BA, U. Pedagogy, Ho Chi Minh City, Vietnam, 1992; LLB, U. Ho Chi Minh City, 1995; LLM, Temple U., 2000. Diploma traditional medicine; cert. auditing and fin. control. Asst. to fin. contrl. Vietnam region Luks Internat. Ltd., Dong Nai, Vietnam, 1992-94; mng. dir. Song Loc Co. Ltd., Ho Chi Minh City, 1994-95; assoc. Russin & Vecchi, LLP, Ho Chi Minh City, 1995—; tchr. U. Pedagogy, Ho Chi Minh City, 1994-95; vis. atty. Ablondi, Foster, Sobin & Davidow, Washington, 2000. Author: British Accounting in Practice, 1993; contbr. articles to profl. jours., chpt. to book. Active Vietnam Youth Union, 1984-92. Fulbright scholar, 2000. Mem. Vietnam's Lawyers' Assn., Bar Vietnam, Assn. Fellows and Legal Scholars (hon.). Avocations: astrology and philosophy, reading, Zen meditation, music. Office: Russin & Vecchi, LLP, Nguyen Hue Blvd Dist 1, Ho Chi Minh City Vietnam

DUYSENS, LOUIS N.M., biophysicist; b. Heerlen, Netherlands, Mar. 15, 1921; s. Wilhelmina A. Kesler, 1952; children: Frank, Tom, Inge. M in Physics and Math., Utrecht (Netherlands) U., 1947, PhD in Biophysics, 1952. Sci. rschr. biophys. rsch. group U. Utrecht, 1947-56; fellow Carnegie Instn. of Wash., Stanford, Calif., 1952-53; rsch. assoc., photosynthesis project dept. botany U. Ill., Urbana, 1953-54; prof. dept. biophysics U. Leiden, Netherlands, 1956-86, organizer new lab. of biophysics, 1958. Contbr. articles to profl. jours. Recipient Kettering award for excellence in photosynthesis. Mem. Am. Soc. Plant Physiologists, Netherlands Biophys. Soc., Am. Biophys. Soc., Netherlands Biochem. Soc., Nat. Acad. Scis. U.S. (fgn. assoc.), Holland Soc. Scis., Royal Netherlands Acad. Scis. Achievements include establishment of the path and mechanism of transfer of electronic excitation toward reaction centers and of the kind and function of subsequent photosynthetic redox reactions. Home: C de Bourbonlaan 2, 2341-VD Oegstgeest The Netherlands

DÜZBASTILAR, MUSA KAZIM, micropaleontologist, marine scientist, researcher; b. Izmir, Turkey, Apr. 1, 1944; s. Faik and Kevser (Elmas) D.; m. Meltem Yurdun, Jan. 6, 1971; children: Ozan Faik, Özge. BSc, Ege U., Izmir, 1968, MSc, 1970, PhD in Geol. Engring., 1976. Asst. Ege U. Faculty of Sci., Izmir, 1968-76, asst. prof., 1976-80; assoc. prof. Dokuz Eylül U., Izmir, 1980-89, prof., 1989—, vice dir. Inst. Marine Sci., 1989-91, head of marine sci. Inst. Marine Sci., 1991—; Author: Introduction to Scubadiving, 1985; author/editor Bull. of Turkish Geologists, 1991-93, 97; contbr. articles to profl. jours. Mem. Chamber Turkish Geologists, Karsiyaka Sports Club. Avocations: scuba diving, football, sailing, tennis, table tennis. Home: 1771 Sokak No 35/4, 35540 Karsiyaka Izmir Turkey Office: Deu Deniz Bilimleri Enst, 1884/8 Sokak No 10, 35540 Inciralti Izmir Turkey

DVOEGLAZOV, VALERI VLADIMIROVICH, physicist, educator; b. Saratov, Russia, Nov. 18, 1961; s. Vladimir and Zinaida (Urzhumtseva) D. MSc, Saratov State U., 1983; PhD, Joint Inst. Nuclear Rsch., 1991. Engr. Saratov State U., Russia, 1986-88; from jr. rschr. to rschr. Scientific & Technol. Ctr., Saratov, 1991-92; from asst. to docent Saratov State U., 1992-93; postdoctoral fellow Inst. Physics Autonomous U. Mex., Mexico City, 1993-94; prof. Escuela de Fisica, Zacatecas, Mexico, 1994—. Mem. Am. Assn. Physics Tchrs., Am. Phys. Soc., N.Y. Acad. Scis. Office: UAZ Escuela de Fisica, Av Preparatoria #301, 98060 Zacatecas Mexico

DVOICHENKO-MARKOV, DEMETRIUS, history educator; b. Saloniki, Greece, July 10, 1921; came to the U.S., 1942, naturalized, 1943; s. Vladimir and Eufrosina M. (de Markov) Dvoichenko de Kovalevski; m. Inna Moore, July 18, 1952; (children: Vlad, Laria. Baccalaureate, German Ev. Lyceum, Rumania, 1941; cert., U. Basel, Switzerland, 1948, Wiedeman Bus. Acad., 1948; AB, UCLA, 1950; MA, Columai U., 1951. Libr. Spanish Legation Bucharest Kingdom Romania, 1940-41; translator, rsch. analyst U.S. Ward Dept., office chief coun. for war crimes, Nuremberg, Germany, 1946-47; rsch. analyst Dept. Def., Washington, 1952-53; asst. field dir. ARC, Alexandria, Va., 1954-56; tchr. German and Spanish Wakefield H.S., Arlington, Va., 1956-57; instr. Russian and social sci. Monmouth Coll., W. Long Branch, N.J., 1957-61; asst. prof. Monmouth Coll., W. Long Branch, 1961-81, assoc. prof., 1981-92, prof. emeritus, 1992—; instr. Russian lang., Western civilization I and II, geography S.W. Asia Ft. Monmouth, N.J., 1959-63, 83; lectr. history and geography Newark State Coll., 1964-69; lectr. history Trenton (N.J.) State Coll., 1985, War Crimes Then and Now; tchr. lectr. Brookdale C.C., Lincroft, N.J., 1994; instr. Sr. Citizens Activities Network, Eatontown, N.J., 1994-95; presenter in field. Published articles broadcast in Romanian transl. on radio voice Am.; contbr. articles and revs. to profl. jours. Mem. Gov.'s Commn. on Ea. European and Captive Nation history, State of N.J., 1985-89. Served with U.S. Army, 1942-45. Recipient Dimitrie Cantemir medal Rumanian Nat. Acad. Sci., 1975, Bronze Serban Canatacuzino medal Internat. Cultural Assn. romanian Ethnicity, Vienna, Austria, 1983, Faculty Assn. Donald C. Warnke award for disting. svc. Monmouth Coll., 1992; Am. Coun. Learned Socs. travel grantee, 1971. Mem. Am. hist. Assn., Assn. Am. Geographers, UCLA Alumni Assn., Am. Assn. Advancement Slavic Studies, Assn. Study of the Nationalities (USSR and Eastern Europe), Am. Assn. SE European Studies, AAUP, U.S. Commn. on Mil. History, N.J. Commn. on Eastern European and Captive Nation History, Am.-Romanian Acad. Arts and Scis., Acad. People of Sci. from Romania, N.J. Ednl. Assn., Soc. Romanian Studies, Knights Malta, Delta Tau Kappa, Phi Alpha Theta, Gamma Theta Upsilon. Mem. Eastern Orthodox Ch. Home: 359 Lowden Ct Apt 68 Long Branch NJ 07740-6310 Office: Monmouth U West Long Branch NJ 07764

DVORA, SUSAN (SUSAN BERNSTEIN), non-profit organization professional; b. Chgo., May 17, 1938; d. Herman and Frances Dobkin Powell; m. Phillip Bernstein, Sept. 4, 1957 (div. July 1995); children: Kenneth, Robert, Michael. BA in Human Svcs., Northeastern Ill. U., 1978, postgrad., 1978-80. Real estate salesperson Martin-Marbry, Skokie, Ill., 1971—; exec. dir. Land of Lakes region B'nai Brith Women Internat., Chgo., 1978-83; founder, pres. Nat. Forum of Women, Woodstock, Ill., 1980-83; dir. resource devel. Travelers & Immigrants Aid, Chgo., 1983-86; dir. Ctr. Ch.-State Studies, DePaul U. Sch. of Law, Chgo., 1986-90; cons. to non-profit orgns., Chgo., Md., Israel, and South Africa, 1986—; owner, mgr. Siza Gallery, Evanston, Ill., 1989-92. Dir., prodr. (documentary) Legacy of Charlotte Perkins Gilman, 1996. Dir. alumni rels. Agrl. Edn. Found., Templeton, Calif., 1995-97; active Ill. Women's Agenda, Chgo., 1978-82; mem. Gov.'s Commn. on Status of Women, 1981; asst. to sculptor Andries Botha human rights work, South Africa, 1999—; sec., treas. Create Africa South. Named Citizen of Yr., Lerner-Life Newspapers, Skokie, 1979-80. Democrat. Jewish. Avocations: swimming, reading, travel. E-mail: svedvora@aol.com. Address: PO Box 2311 Avila Beach CA 93424

DVORAK, BRUCE IRVIN, environmental engineer, educator; b. Hastings, Nebr., July 19, 1964; s. Verne Irvin and Helen Luree Dvorak; m. Karrie Louise Cole, July 5, 1997; 1 child, Katie. BS in Civil Engring., U. Nebr., 1987; MS in Environ. Health Engring., U. Tex., 1990, PhD in Environ. Engring., 1994. Engr.-in-tng., Nebr. Asst. prof. U. Nebr., Lincoln, 1994-2000, assoc. prof., 2000—. Contbr. articles to profl. jours. Grantee US EPA, 1998, U.S. Geol. Survey, 1999. Mem. Am. Water Works Assn. (student awards com. 1997—), Nebr. Water Environment Assn. (chair student activities com. 1994—). E-mail: bdvorak@unlinfo.unl.edu.

DVORAK, KATHLEEN S., business products company executive; married; 2 children. BS in Edn., No. Ill. U., 1978; MBA in Fin., DePaul U., 1988. Tchr. math. Conrady Jr. H.S., 1977-82; dir. investor rels./corp. comms. United Stationers Inc., Des Plaines, Ill., 1982-97, v.p. investor rels., 1997-2000; v.p. investor rels. and fin. adminstrn. United Stationers Inc., Des Plaines, 2000—. Recipient Howard Beasley Managerial Excellence award. Mem. Nat. Investor Rels. Inst. Home: 1032 Oakwood Dr Westmont IL 60559-1040 Office: United Stationers Inc 2200 E Golf Rd Des Plaines IL 60016-1257

DVORAK, VACLAV JOSEPH, computer science educator; b. Brno, Czech Republic, Oct. 8, 1941; s. Stanislav and Marie (Novackova) D.; m. Eva Karyova, June 29, 1968; children: Peter, Vaclav. MSc, Tech. U., Brno, 1963, PhD, 1968. Cert. elec. engr. Rschr. Rsch. Inst. Math. Machines, Prague, 1963-73; postdoctoral fellow, asst. prof. U. Alta., Edmonton, Can., 1968-70; rsch. scientist, assoc. prof. Tech. U., Brno, 1974-91, prof., dept. computer sci. and engring. head, 1991-97; assoc. prof., head Higher Inst. Electronics, Beni Walid, Libya, 1978-80; assoc. prof. Acadia U., Wolfville, Can., 1988-90; cons. AMF Electronics Lab., Sterling, Va., 1981-82; vis. prof. U. Waikato, Hamilton, New Zealand, 1998, U. Tasmania, Hobart, Australia, 1999. Author: Microprocessor-Based System Design, 1984 (Textbook of Yr. 1985), Processor Architecture, 1999. Lt. Czechoslovak Army, 1964. Rsch. grantee PECO, European Communities, Czech Republic and Poland, 1993, Grant Agy. Czech Republic, 1994, 95, Copernicus, EC Network, 1995. Mem. IEEE Computer Soc. Roman Catholic. Avocations: windsurfing, skiing, travel, mountain hiking. Home: Horska 39, 61600 Brno Czech Republic

DVORETSKY, ANATOLY IVANOVICH, science administrator, educator, researcher; b. Dmukhailovka Vlg., Ukraine, Jan. 1, 1937; s. Ivan Ivanovich and Maria Karpovna (Gupalo) D.; m. Ludmila Nikolaevna Prots, July 24, 1964 (dec. 1995); children: Vadim Anatolievich, Yury Anatolievich. Student, Veterinary Inst., Kharkov, Ukraine, 1954-59; postgrad., State U., Dniepropetrovsk, Ukraine, 1964-67, PhD, 1969; DSc in Biology, Kavetsky Inst. Exptl. Pathology and Oncology, Kiev, Ukraine, 1988. Physician, bacteriologist Biofactory, Dniepropetrovsk, Ukraine, 1959-61, chief biochem. lab., 1961-64; postgrad. asst. State U., Dniepropetrovsk, Ukraine, 1964-68, lectr. chair of biochem., 1968-74; vice-dir. State U. Rsch. Inst. Biology, Dniepropetrovsk, Ukraine, 1974-90, chief radiobiology lab., 1974—; head chair of hydrobiology, ecology, ichthyology State U. Biologic-Ecologic Dept., Dniepropetrovsk, Ukraine, 1990—; prof. State Com. on Pub. Edn., Moscow, 1989; Soros prof., Soros Found., 1994. Author: Transmembrane Ion Transport Under Ionizing Radiation action on an Organism, 1990 (Palladin Prize 1996); co-author Cell Membranes Under Radiation Influence, 1988; contbr. articles to profl. pubs. Recipient State prize State Com. Pub. Edn., Moscow, USSR, 1988; hon. rep. of sci. and technics Presdl. Adminstrn. Kiev, Ukraine, 1998. Fellow European Radioecological Soc.; mem. Ukrainian Radiobiological Soc. (v.p. 1991—), European Soc. Radiation Biology, Ukrainian Ecological Acad. Scis. Avocations: summer residence rest, fishing, seaside rest. Office: Rsch Inst Biology State Univ, 13 Nauchny Ln, 49625 Dniepropetrovsk Ukraine

DVORKIN, EDWARD, physician; b. Gomel, Belarus, June 12, 1937; arrived in Israel, 1974; s. Leib and Rachel (Murashkovsky) D.; m. Svetlana Krukov, Mar. 8, 1963; 1 child, Ilana. Grad., Pavlov Med. Inst., Leningrad, USSR, 1960, State Advanced Med. Tng. Inst., Leningrad, USSR, 1965. Med. diplomate in otorhinolaryngology and acupuncture. Physician City Hosp., Magadan, USSR, 1960-63, Lenin Hosp., Leningrad, 1963-65, Vsewolozsk Hosp., Leningrad, 1965-66, City Policlinic, Leningrad, 1966-74, Klalit Sick Found., Lod, Israel, 1975-78, Leamit Sick Found., Ramat-Gan, Israel, 1978—; dir. Lab. for Electromagnetic Ecology, Tel-Aviv, 1984. Author: Damned Places, 1994, Auricular Medicine, 1999; pub., editor-in-chief Coherence, 1998. Named hon. mem. German Med. Acupuncture Soc., 1991. Mem. Med. Soc. Acupuncture Israel Med. Assn. (chmn. 1984), Internat. Assn. for Auricular Medicine (bd. mem.). Home: Mahrozet St 32 Apt 29, PO Box 3167, 59131 Bat-Yam Israel

DVORNIK, ŠTEFICA, laboratory administrator, biochemistry educator; b. Osijek, Croatia, Jan. 12, 1958; d. Stjepan and Slavica (Sučić) Dušanek; m. Ivo Dvornik, Nov. 25, 1989; children: Ivana, Toni. Grad., U. Pharmacy and Biochemistry, Zagreb, Croatia, 1980; postgrad., Med. U., Zagreb, 1989; PhD, Med. U. Rijeka, 1997. Mem. staff Lab. Clin. Hosp., Rijeka, Croatia, 1982-92, headmaster, 1992—; tchr. U. Medicine, Rijeka, 1987—. Mem. Croatian Soc. Med. Biochemists, Chamber Med. Biochemistry Croatia, Croatian Soc. Pharmacology. Roman Catholic. Avocations: walking, books, music, swimming, bicycling. Home: Slavka Krautzeka 84, 51000 Rijeka Croatia Office: Clin Hosp Lab, Tome Strizicá 3, 51000 Rijeka Croatia

DVURECHENSKAYA, SERAFIMA YAKOVLEVNA, chemist; b. Volgograd, Russia, Aug. 14, 1946; d. Yakov Grigorievich and Faina Lvovna Barkan; m. Anatoly Vasiljevich Dvurechensky, Mar. 29, 1968; 1 child, Helen. PhD in Chemistry, Novosibirsk State U., 1969. Cert. rschr., chemist. Jr. rschr. Inst. Inorganic Chemistry, Novosibirsk, Russia, 1973-83, sr. rschr., 1987—; project mgr., sci. sec. Water and Environ. Problems; sci. sec. of sci. com. on environment Siberian br. Russian Acad. Scis., Novosibirsk, 1987-96. Contbr. articles to sci. jours. Home: Morskoy Prospect 52 Apt 24, 630090 Novosibirsk Russia Office: Inst Water and Environ Prob, Morskoy Prospect 2 Apt 417, 630090 Novosibirsk Russia

DVURECHENSKII, ANATOLY VASIL'EVICH, physicist; b. Barnaul, Russia, Apr. 10, 1945; s. Vasilii Arsent'evich and Efrosin'ya Grigor'evna (Gredasova) D.; m. Serafima Yakovlevna Barkan, Mar. 28, 1968; 1 child, Cheblakova. BSc, Novosibirsk (Russia) State U., 1968; PhD, Inst. Semiconductor Physics, Novosibirsk, 1974, D in Physics-Math. Sci., 1988, prof., 1993. Cert. semiconductor physics. Jr. rschr. Inst. Semiconductors Physics, Novosibirsk, 1970-81, sr. rschr., 1981-86, leading rschr., 1986-87, head lab. Siberian br. Russian Acad. Scis., 1987—; asst. prof. Novosibirsk State U., 1987-91, prof., 1991—. Author: Pulsed Annealing of Semiconductor Materials, 1982 (state prize USSR govt. 1988); contbr. articles to profl. jours. Sr. lt. Russian Mil., 1964-67. Fax: 3832-332771. E-mail: dvurech@isp.nsc.ru. Office: Inst Semiconductors Physics, Lavrent ev prospekt 13, 630090 Novosibirsk Russia

DWEIK, RAED A., physician, researcher; b. Hebron, Jordan, Aug. 20, 1964; came to U.S., 1990; s. Abdul-Rahim a. and Fikrat (Salhi) D.; m. Erin Makley, Sept. 23, 1995; children: Zayn, Sana. MB BS, U. Jordan, 1988. Diplomate Am. Bd. Internal Medicine, Am. Bd. Pulmonary Disease, Am. Bd. Critical Care Medicine. Resident Wright State U., Dayton, Ohio, 1990-93; fellow Cleve. Clinic Found., 1993-96; staff physician Cleve. Clinic, 1996—. Contbr. aticles to profl. jours. Fellow ACP, Am. Coll. Chest Physicians, Royal Coll. Physicians and Surgeons; mem. AMA, AAAS, Am. Thoracic Soc. Achievements include investigating regulation of nitric oxide production in the lungs by oxygen and the role of nitric oxide in lung physiology and pathology. Office: Cleve Clinic Found A-90 9500 Euclid Ave Cleveland OH 44195-0001

DWIGGINS, CLAUDIUS WILLIAM, JR., chemist; b. Amity, Ark., May 11, 1933; s. Claudius William and Lillian (Scott) D. BS, U. Ark., 1954, MS, 1956, PhD, 1958. With U.S. Dept. of Energy Bartlesville Tech. Ctr., Okla., 1958-83, chemist, 1958-60, project leader surface physics project, 1960-65, project leader petroleum composition rsch. project, 1965-80, supervisory rsch. chemist, thermodynamics divsn., 1980-83; sr. chemist Nat. Inst. Petroleum and Energy Rsch., 1983-84, cons., 1984—. Contbr. articles to profl. jours. Am. Oil Co. fellow, Coulter-Jones scholar. Mem. Am. Chem. Soc., N.Y. Acad. Scis., AAAS, Am. Crystallographic Assn., Am. Inst. Physics, Sigma Xi (sec. 1966-67), Alpha Chi Sigma, Delta Sigma Phi (treas. 1952). Home: 1211 S Keeler Ave Bartlesville OK 74003-4756

DWIGHT, REGINALD KENNETH **See JOHN, ELTON HERCULES**

DWINELL, ANN JONES, special education educator; b. Lowell, Mass., Oct. 28, 1934; d. George Hubert and Bridget Jones; m. Roland A. Dwinell, Dec. 23, 1956; children: Theresa, Joseph, Richard, John. BA, Framingham State Coll., 1972; MEd, Lesley Coll., 1974; PhD, Boston Coll., 1991. Cert. Eng. tchr., moderate spl. needs instr., Mass., adminstr., supt., spl. edn. adminstr., R.I. Spl. edn. tchr., adminstr. Marlborough (Mass.) Pub. Sch., 1972-78; core chairperson Malden (Mass.) Pub. Schs., 1978-80, spl. edn. specialist, 1980—. Contbr. articles to profl. jours. Mem. NEA, Mass. Tchrs. Assn. (rep. 1983-85, liaison 1987—), Phi Delta Kappa. Roman Catholic. Avocations: dancing, music, boating, reading.

DWINFOUR, KOFI ANTWI, marketing executive; b. Kumasi, Ghana, Aug. 4, 1961; arrived in Eng., 1968; s. Daniel K. and Agnes (Opoku) D.; m. Daphne A. Bolden, Ph.D. BSc, London Sch. of Economics and Pol. Sci., London, 1983; MBA, London Guildhall U., 1996. Sales mgr. Haymarket Press, London, 1983-85; divsnl. mgr. EMAP Plc, London, 1985-88; cons. Equinox, London, 1988-91; regional mktg. advisor BTEC, London, 1991-93; dir. mktg. London Guildhall U., 1993-96; sr. mktg. cons. Visual FX plc, 1997-98; head mktg. Bus. Link London City Partners Ltd., 1998-99; head mktg. & ops. Focus Group Ltd., London, 1999—; dir. Vocat. Edn. Pub. Ltd., C9 Group PLC. Mem. Chartered Inst. Mktg., Inst. Direct Mktg., exec. com., Ghana Union London, 1997—. Avocations: collecting music compact discs, health and fitness. Home: The White House 61 Central Hill, London SE19 1BS, England Office: Focus Ctrl London Group Ltd Ctr Point, 103 New Oxford St, London WC1A 1DR, England

DWIVEDI, DINESH CHANDRA, engineering executive; b. Surat, Gujrat, India, Sept. 20, 1951; arrived in Indonesia, 1990; s. Nand Lal and Kusum Lata Dubey; m. Shailja Mishra, Jan. 25, 1977 (dec. July 1992); children: Abhijeet, Shruti. BE with honors, Birla Inst. Tech. & Sci., Pilani, India, 1972. Engr. trainee J.K. Synthetics Ltd., Kota, India, 1972-73; mgmt. trainee J.K. Synthetics Ltd., 1973-74, asst. engr., 1974-78, supt. elec. engring., 1982-84, asst. mgr., 1984-87, mgr., 1987-90; engr., sr. engr. Africa Synthetic Fibres, Nairobi, Kenya, 1978-80, 80-82; project mgr. Jaykeytech, Gaziabad, India, 1990; sr. mgr. Indorama Synthetics, Purwakarta, Indonesia, 1990-95; asst. gen. mgr. Indorama Synthetics, 1995-97, dep. gen. mgr., 1997—; editor Beritarama (inhouse mag. of Indorama). Mgr. Indorama Cricket Club, 1997-99; gen. sec. Indorama Club, 1995-96, 97-2000. Mem. India Club, Rotary (chmn. Polio Plus com. 1989). Avocations: music, sports, reading. Home: Desa Kembang Kuning Ubrug, Jatiluhur PO Box 2, Purwakarta 41101, Indonesia Office: PT Indorama Synthetics, Desa Kembang Kuning Ubrug, Purwakarta 41101, Indonesia

DWIVEDI, SHAILENDRA KUMAR, veterinarian; b. Gorakhpur, India; s. Chandrika Prasad and Bageshwari Devi D.; m. Usha Pandey, June 19, 1970; 1 child. B in Vet. Sci., Agrl. U., Pantnagar, India, 1968, M in Vet Sci., PhD, Agrl. U., Hisar, India, 1975. Reg. vet. practitioner Vet. Coun. India.

Asst. prof. vet. medicine Agrl. U., Hisar, 1974-76; scientist Indian Vet. Rsch. Inst., Izatnagar, 1976-86, head exptl. med. surg., 1987-90, prin. scientist, 1990-94, head medicine, 1994—; vis. prof. U. Mosul, Iraq, 1980-82, 90; mem. subcon. Animal Welfare Bd., Delhi, 1993-94. Editor Indian Jour. Vet. Medicine, 1988-89, 92-96; patentee in field. Recipient Ram Lal Gold medal Indian Herbs, 1992, Hari Om Ashram Trust award Indian Coun. Agrl. Rsch., 1997. Fellow Nat. Acad. of Agrl. Sci., Nat. Acad. of Vet. Sci. (India), Indian Assn. Advancement Vet. Rsch., Indian Soc. Vet. Medicine (pres. 1996-98, P.L. Narayana Rao award 2000); mem. Lab. Animal Assn. India. Home: C 923 Rajendra Nagar, Izatnagar 243122, India Office: Divsn Medicine, Indian Vet Rsch Inst, Izatnagar 243122, India

DWIVEDI, UPENDRA NATH, biochemistry educator; b. Varanasi, India, Oct. 1, 1956; s. Rama Nath and Shivadasi (Upadhyay) D.; m. Namrata Shukla, Nov. 23, 1980; children: Ramya, Amlesh. BS, Banaras Hindu U., Varanasi, India, 1975, MSc, 1977, PhD, 1981. Cert. biochemist, molecular biologist, researcher and educator. Scientist Nat. Chem. Lab. Coun. Sci. and Indsl. Rsch., Pune, India, 1982-85; reader Lucknow (India) U., 1985-95, prof., 1995—; postdoctoral fellow Mich. Tech. U., Houghton, 1991-93. Author: Atharv-Ved Chikitsa, 1984. Recipient Biotech. Overseas award Dept. Biotech., 1991. Avocation: swimming. Home: B 12/120E 1 Bhelupura, Varanasi 221001, India Office: Lucknow Univ, Biochemistry Dept, Lucknow 226007, India

DWORIN, MICKI (MAXINE DWORIN), automobile dealership executive; widowed; children: Judy, Diane. V.p. Dworin Chevrolet, Inc., East Harford, Conn., 1955-83, Dworin Auto Leasing; pres. Eastern Auto Ins., Conn. Chevrolet Dealers Assn., Tarrytown Zone Dealer Coun., Atlantic Coast Region Dealer Coun., Boulevard, Inc. Sec. BBB, Hartford, Conn.; vol. coord. Vol. Broward, 1998-99, Children's Diagnostic and Treatment Ctr., 1996-98, Am. Cancer Soc., 1994-96, Kids in Distress, 1991-95; hon. trustee Hartford Coll. for Women; sec., bd. govs. Point of Am. Condominium; coord. Trinity Coll.; bd. dirs. Combined Health Appeals; chmn. King David Soc., 1995-96. Mem. Advt. Assn. Grtr. Hartford.

DWORKIN, MARTIN, microbiologist, educator; b. N.Y.C., Dec. 3, 1927; s. Hyman Bernard and Pauline (Herstein) D.; m. Nomi Rees Buda, Feb. 2, 1957; children—Jessica Sarah, Hanna Beth. B.A., Ind. U., 1951; Ph.D. (NSF predoctoral fellow), U. Tex., Austin, 1955. NIH research fellow U. Calif., Berkeley, 1955-57; vis. prof. U. Calif., summers 1958-60; asst. prof. microbiology Ind. U. Med. Sch., 1957-61; assoc. prof., 1961-62; assoc. prof. U. Minn., 1962-69, dir. MD/PhD tng. program, 1990-97, prof., 1969—; vis. prof. U. Wash., summer 1965, Stanford U., 1978-79; vis. scholar Oxford (Eng.) U., 1970-71; Found. for Microbiology lectr., 1973-74, 76-77, 81-82; Sackler scholar Tel Aviv U., 1992. Author: Developmental Biology of the Bacteria, 1985, Microbial Cell-Cell Interactions, 1991; contbr. numerous articles, revs. to profl. publs.; mem. editorial bd. Jour. Bacteriology, 1967-74, 86-88, Ann. Revs. Microbiology, 1975-79, The Prokaryotes, 2d edit., editor-in-chief 3d edit. Alt. del. Democratic Nat. Conv., 1968; mem. Minn. Dem. Farm Labor Central Com., 1969-70. Served with U.S. Army, 1946-48. Recipient Career Devel. award NIH, 1963-68, 68-73; John Simon Guggenheim fellow, 1978-79. Fellow Am. Acad. Arts and Scis.; mem. Am. Soc. Microbiology (vice chmn. div. gen. microbiology 1977-78, chmn. 1978-79, div. councillor 1980-82), Soc. Gen. Microbiology (Eng.). Home: 2123 Hoyt Ave W Saint Paul MN 55108-1314 Office: U Minn Dept Microbiology Minneapolis MN 55455

DWORKIN, MICHAEL LEONARD, lawyer; b. Bridgeport, Conn., Oct. 10, 1947; s. Samuel and Frances (Stein) D.; m. Christina Lyn Hildreth, Sept. 25, 1977; children: Jennifer Hildreth, Amanda Hildreth. BA in Govt. with honors, Clark U., 1969; JD with honors, George Washington U., 1973. Bar: D.C. 1973, Calif. 1975, U.S. Supreme Ct. 1978, U.S. Ct. Appeals (9th cir.) 1982, U.S. Claims Ct. 1983. Atty. FAA, Washington, L.A., 1973-77, United Airlines, San Francisco, 1977-81; pvt. practice San Francisco, 1981-95, San Mateo, Calif., 1995—; instr. Embry Riddle Aeronautical U., San Francisco, 1980-81; dir. Poplar Ctr., San Mateo, Calif., 1979-86. Benefactor Hiller No. Calif. Aviation Mus. Jonas Clark scholar Clark U., 1966-69. Mem. ABA, Lawyer Pilot's Bar Assn., Nat. Transp. Safety Bd. Bar Assn. (regional v.p. 1986-87, 90-99, chmn. rules com. 1985-99, pres. 2000—), Aircraft Owners and Pilots Assn., Conn. Aviation Hist. Assn., Benefactor-Hiller Aviation Mus., San Mateo County Bar Assn., Bar Assn. San Francisco, Internat. Soc. Air Safety Investigators (bd. dirs. San Francisco regional chpt. 1988-89), State Bar Calif., D.C. Bar Assn., Regional Airline Assn., Commonwealth Club of Calif., New England Air Mus. Jewish. E-mail: law@avialex.com. Office: 155 Bovet Rd Ste 455 San Mateo CA 94402-3112

DWORZANSKI, JACEK PAWEL, analytical biochemist, researcher; b. Wloclawek, Poland, Jan. 5, 1952; came to U.S., 1987; naturalized, 1999; s. Augustyn Franciszek and Cecylia (Piasecka) D.; m. Maria Teresa Siedlecka, June 12, 1987. MS, Med. U. of Silesia, Katowice, Poland, 1976; PhD, Jagiellonian U., Cracow, Poland, 1981, DSc, 1997. Instr., teaching fellow Med. U. of Silesia, Katowice, 1976-82, asst. prof., 1982-87; postdoctoral fellow U. Utah, Salt Lake City, 1987, Johns Hopkins U., Balt., 1987-88; rsch. assoc. U. Utah, Salt Lake City, 1989-93, asst. dir. micro analysis and reaction chemistry, 1995-99; assoc. prof. biochemistry Med. U. Silesia, Katowice, 1999—; vis. prof. U. Utah, 1993-99. Co-author: (with H.L.C. Meuzelaar) Modern Techniques for Rapid Microbiological Analysis, 1991; mem. editl. bd. Field Analytical Chemistry and Tech.; contbr. articles to profl. jours. Recipient Internat. Fogarty fellowship NIH, 1987. Mem. AAAS, Am. Soc. Mass Spectrometry, Am. Chem. Soc., Polish Inst. Arts and Scis. Am. Roman Catholic. Achievements include development of analytical methods based on pyrolytic derivatization for chromatographic and mass or ion mobility spectrometric analysis of complex organic and bioorganic materials, including whole bacterial cells, suitable for characterization and identification of polymers (melanins, sporopollenins), fossil resins, lipids as well as rapid detection and identification of microorganisms. Office: Med U of Silesa, Nareyzow 1, 41-206 Sosnowiec Poland

DWYER, GERALD PAUL, JR., economist, educator; b. Pittsfield, Mass., July 9, 1947; s. Gerald Paul and Mary Frances (Weir) D.; m. Katherine Marie Lepiane, Jan. 15, 1966; children: Tamara K., Gerald P. III, Angela M., Michael J.L., Terence F. BBA, U. Wash., 1969; MA in Econs., U. Tenn., 1973; PhD in Econs., U. Chgo., 1979. Economist Fed. Res. Bank, St. Louis, 1972-74, Chgo., 1976-77; asst. prof. Tex. A&M U., College Station, 1977-81; asst. prof. Emory U., Atlanta, 1981-84, sr. rsch. assoc. Law and Econ. Ctr., 1982-84; assoc. prof. U. Houston, 1984-89; prof. Clemson (S.C.) U., 1989-99, acting head dept. econ., 1992-93; asst. v.p. Fed. Res. Bank Atlanta, 1997-98, v.p., 1998—; vis. scholar Fed. Res. Bank, St. Louis, 1987-89, Atlanta, 1982-84, 94-97, Fed. Reserve Bank of Mpls., 1995; cons. FTC, Washington, 1983-84, Arthur Bros., Corpus Christi, Tex., 1980-81, Amerigas, Houston, 1985, Western Container Corp., 1987, Metrica, Inc., Bryan, Tex., 1989-93; vis. fin. economist Commodity Futures Trading Commn., Washington, 1990; vis. instr. U. Ga., 1999—. Contbr. articles to profl. jours. NSF trainee U. Tenn., 1970-72; Weaver fellow Intercollegiate Studies Inst., 1974-75, Earhart Found. fellow, 1975-77; rsch. grantee NSF, Earhart Found. Mem. Am. Econ. Assn., Am. Stats. Assn., Econometric Soc., Econ. Hist. Assn., We. Econ. Assn., So. Econ. Assn., Beta Gamma Sigma, Phi Kappa Phi. Avocation: computers.

DWYER, JERRY F., mathematics educator; b. Cork, Munster, Ireland, Oct. 2, 1959; s. Jerh and Kate D. BA, Nat. U. Ireland, Cork, 1980, MS, 1982, PhD, 1986. Lectr. Regional Coll., Cork, 1984-89; rsch. assoc. U. Manchester (Eng.), 1989; rsch. scientist MIT, Cambridge, 1990-91; instr. U. Colo., Boulder, 1991—; mem. K-12 math outreach U. Colo., Boulder, 1997-99. Contbr. 10 articles to profl. jours. Avocations: running, soccer, reading, radio. Office: U Colo Math Dept PO Box 395 Boulder CO 80309-0395

DWYER, JOHN M., mathematician, statistician, computer scientist; b. Ann Arbor, Mich., June 8, 1937; s. Paul Sumner and Florence Baylis (Brown) D.; children: Anne Louise, Laura Beth. BA, U. Mich., 1959, MS, 1965; PhD, Tex A&M U., 1971. Asst. prof. stats. U. Wyo., Laramie, 1962-66; asst. prof. math. U. Detroit, 1969-73, assoc. prof. math., 1974—, chair, 1974-77, interim chair, 1989-91; vis. assoc. prof. dept. mgmt. and mktg. Northern Mich. U., Marquette, 1983-84; dir. rsch. Detroit Inst. Abuse Rsch. and Tng., 1973-74; cons. Detroit Tax Assessor's Office, 1971; expert witness Focus: HOPE, Detroit, 1981-86; panelist "Ask the Professor" radio show U. Detroit, 1977-83. Mem. AAAS, Math. Assn. Am., Union of Concerned Scientists, Assn. for Computing Machinery, Computer Profls. for Social Responsibility (co-founder Mich. chpt. 1997, chair 1998). E-mail: dwyerjm@unmercy.edu. Office: U Detroit Mercy Dept Math and Computer Sci P O Box 19900 Detroit MI 48219-0900

DWYER, JOHN MICHAEL, medical educator, medical administrator; b. Melbourne, Victoria, Australia, Sept. 9, 1939; s. John Christopher and Rose Lanna (Greig) D.; m. Catherine Anne Thrower, Nov. 29, 1966; children: Justin, Gabrielle, Christopher. MB, BS, U. Sydney, 1964; PhD, U. Melbourne (Australia), 1971. Intern St. Vincent's Hosp., Sydney, 1964, resident med. officer, 1965-66, med. registrar, 1968-69; rsch. fellow Garvan Inst. Med. Rsch., Sydney, 1967, Walter & Eziza Hall Inst., Melbourne, Australia, 1969-71; postgrad. fellow Yale U., New Haven, Conn., 1971-72, mem. faculty Sch. Medicine, 1972-85; prof. medicine U. New S. Wales (Australia), 1985—; clin. dir. Prince of Wales Hosp., 1985—; cons. NASA, U.S.A., 1977-80, Glaxo Corp., U.S.A., 1978-85, Sandoz Pharm. Switzerland, 1978-89. Author: The Body at War, 1995; contbr. 180 articles to med. jours. Decorated Order of Australia Govt. of Australia, 1991. Fellow Royal Australasian Coll. Medicine. Avocations: classical music, tennis. Office: Prince of Wales Hosp, c/o div medicine High St, 2031 Sydney Randwick, Australia

DWYER, JOHN THOMAS, JR., educator, researcher; b. Memphis, June 4, 1953; s. John Thomas and Leona (DeMere) D.; children: John T. III, Caryn Desiree. AA, Shelby State C.C., 1975; diploma, Memphis Police Acad., 1975; BA, U. Memphis, 1983. Officer Memphis Police Dept., 1975-94, sr. rschr., 1986-91, divsn. coord., 1992-94; substitute tchr. Fayette County (Tenn.) Schs., 1996—; cons. S.Y. Wilson & Co., Arlington, Tenn., 1994-97; rschr. initiator crisis intervention unit. Organizer 1st gun buyback program, 1993. Recipient Lifesaving medal City of Memphis, 1983, Medal of Merit, City of Memphis, 1988, Patriotism medal Nat. Assn. Chiefs of Police, 1993. Mem. Gen. Soc. Colonial Wars, Children of the Confederacy, Memphis Police Assn. Democrat. Roman Catholic. Home: 3605 Ivy Rd Eads TN 38028-3223

DWYER, JUDITH MARGARET, health service administrator; b. Brisbane, Australia, Mar. 20, 1951; d. Patrick Francis and Joie Elwyn (Malone) D.; m. Charles Irving Meisner, Oct. 31, 1975 (div. 1982); 1 child, Rachel Sarah Meisner. BA, U. Queensland, 1973; diploma, Victoria Coll., 1981; MBA, U. Adelaide, 1989. Cert. health exec. Dir. Julia Farr Ctr., Adelaide, 1985-87; CEO Family Planning Assn., Adelaide, 1987-89; dir. health programs S.A. Health Commn., Adelaide, 1989-91; dep. CEO Women's Children's Hosp., Adelaide, 1991-95; CEO Flinders Med. Ctr., Adelaide, 1995-99, So. Health Care Network, Melbourne, 1999-2000; assoc. prof. health svcs. mgmt. La-Trobe U., 2000—; 9ir. Australian Inst. Health & Welfare, Canberra, 1995-98, Prince Henry's Inst. of Medical Rsch., Melbourne, 1999—; pres. Women's Hosp. Australia, 1994-95; assoc. prof. Flinders U., 1997-99, mem. resources com., 1996-99; adj. prof. Inst. Pub. Health, Monash U., 2000—; spkr. at numerous confs.; participant in various convs. Contbr. articles to profl. jours. Mem. AHA Nat. Learning Set, 1993—; justice of peace South Australia, 1986-99. Recipient Women's Health award Australian Med. Assn., 1998, MBA Soc. prize, 1989; numerous rsch. grants. Fellow Australian Coll. Health Svc. Execs. (assoc.); mem. Pub. Health Assn. Australia, Tandanya Nat. Aboriginal Cultural Ctr. (assoc.), Australian Inst. Co. Dirs. Avocations: food, wine, conversation, walking. Office: Sch Pub Health, LaTrobe U, Bundoora 3083, Australia

DWYER, RICHARD ANTHONY, retired English educator; b. Riverside, Calif., Nov. 24, 1934; s. Richard F. and Marian Irene (Imus) D.; m. Roxanne L. Huskey, Aug. 20, 1964; 1 child, Philip. BA, UCLA, 1956, MA, 1960, PhD, 1965. Instr., asst. prof. Purdue U., West Lafayette, Ind., 1964-66; asst. prof., assoc. prof. U. Fla., Gainesville, 1966-71; prof. Fla. Internat. U., Miami, 1971-90; ret. Fla. Internat. U., 1990; CEO Aranar Capital, Salt Lake City, 1990—. Bd. dirs. Fla. Endowment for the Humanities, 1971-76. Author: (book) Boethian Fictions, 1976; co-author: (books) Lying on the Eastern Slope, 1984, Sagebrush Trilogy, 1990. Judge Silver Knights Awards, Miami, 1977. Recipient Am. Philos. Soc. grant, 1969. Mem. Medieval Acad. Am. (chmn. Elliott Prize com. 1980), Western Literature Assn., Nat. General. Soc., Phi Beta Kappa. Avocation: games of chance. E-mail: rdwyer@networld.com. Home: 426 S 1000 E Apt 501 Salt Lake City UT 84102-3097

DWYER, RICHARD PETER, physician; b. Lidingo, Sweden; s. Peter John and Anne-Marie Vera (Sjöblom) D.; m. Elisabeth Ulla Tennerus, Aug. 31, 1991; children: Christopher, Oscar, Jacob, Vendela. MD, Karolinska Inst., Stockholm, 1987, fully qualified dr., 1989. Cert. specialist in infectious diseases. Intern Kullbergska Hosp., Katrineholm, Sweden, 1987-89, Roslagstulls U. Hosp. Infectious Diseases, Stockholm, 1989-92; intern Huddinge (Sweden) Univ. Hosp., 1992-95, ward physician, 1996-98, cons. physician, 1999—; Contbr. med. articles to profl. jours. Mem. Swedish Med. Assn., Swedish Assn. Infectious Diseases Specialists, Swedish Cons. Assn. Avocation: Shorinji Kempo. Fax: 46 8 616 25 15. E-mail: richard.dwyer@telia.com. Office: Huddinge Univ Hosp, Halsovagen, 141 86 Huddinge Sweden

DWYER, WILLIAM H., real estate company executive; b. Milw., Sept. 6, 1950; s. Thomas H. and Eileen M. Dwyer; m. Sue D., Sept. 6, 1980; 2 children. BS, U. We. Wis., 1973. Cert. property mgr.; accredited resident mgr. Real estate broker Dwyer/Klose Realtor; pres. Premier Real Estate Mgmt., LLC (formerly Calvin Akin), Brookfield, Wis.; v.p. Barthein & Co., Inc. Office: Premier Real Estate Mgmt LLC 12630 W North Ave Brookfield WI 53005-4626

DY, FRANCISCO JUSTINIANO, public health consultant; b. Manila, The Philippines, Sept. 17, 1912; s. T. C. and Epifania Marquez)Justiniano) D.; m. Fe Lakandola De la Fuente (dec. July 1986); children: Fe Josefina, Francisco Jr., Francisco III, Fay Jeanelle. MD, U. The Philippines, 1937; MPH, Johns Hopkins U., 1942. Prof. malariology U. of the Philippines, 1950-51; dep. chief malaria sect. WHO, Geneva, 1950-51; regional malaria advisor Western Pacific Region WHO, The Philippines, 1951-58, dir. health svcs. Western Pacific Region, 1958-66, regional dir., 1966-79, regional dir. emeritus, 1979—; prof. cmty. medicine U. of the Philippines, 1971-74, prof. internat. health, 1970-75. Lt. col. U.S. Army, 1942-45. Decorated Legion of Merit (with oak leaf cluster); recipient Disting. Svc. Star, Philippine Govt., 1945; named Most Disting. Alumnus U. of Philippines Alumni Assn., 1976; recipient 1st Class Health medal Republic of Vietnam, 1975, Ancient Order of Sikatuna, Philippine Govt., 1979, Disting. Order of Diplomatic Svc., Republic of Korea, 1979. Fellow Philippine Pub. Health Assn., Philippine Assn. for Advancement of Sci. (founder); mem. Philippine Nat. Sci. Soc., Delta Omega. Roman Catholic. Avocation: planting fruit trees. Home: 901 EDSA Philam Homes, 1104 Quezon City The Philippines Office: WHO, United Nations Ave, 1000 Manila The Philippines

DYACHENKO, PETER, physicist, researcher; b. Maloiaroslavets, Kaluga, Russia, Nov. 18, 1938; s. Peter Semen and Anastasia Tit (Riaba) D.; m. Ludmila Aleksander Krebs, Dec. 21, 1963; children: Monahova Anna, Aleksander. Grad., Moscow Engrng.-Phys. Inst., 1962; D Phys.-Math. Scis., Inst. Phys. & Power Engrng., Obninsk, Russia, 1993. Laboratorian Inst. Physics and Power Engrng., Obninsk, 1956-65, jr. rsch. scientist, 1965-70, rsch. scientist, 1970-71, sr. rsch. scientist, 1971-81, head lab., 1981-95, dir. dept., 1995—; academician Laser Acad. Scis. of Russia, Kaluga, 1997. recipient Vet. Truda medal Govt. of Russia, Moscw, 1991, medal II degree order Za Zaslugi Pered Otechestvom, Pres. Russia, Moscow, 1995. Fellow Nuclear Soc. Russia, Moscow Sci. Soc.; mem. Russian Acad. Natural Scis. (corr.). Avocations: car touring, yachting, fishing, walks in the woods, searching for mushrooms. Office: Inst Physics & Power Engrin, Bondarenko Sq 1, 249020 Obninsk Kaluga, Russia

DYACHENKO, VLADIMIR DANYLOVICH, chemistry educator; b. Brusovka, Lugansk, Ukraine, May 17, 1961; s. Daniel Fomich and Maria Nikolaevna (Telnaya) D.; m. Svetlana Vladimirovna Melnik, Sept. 13, 1986; children: Dyachenko Ivan, Dyachenko Iren. Diploma in Chemistry and Biology, Pedagog. Inst., Lugansk, Ukraine, 1983; Cand. of Chem. Scis., Aspiranture of Pedagog. Inst., Lugansk, Ukraine, 1990. Aspirant Pedagog. Inst., Lugansk, 1985-90, jrs. scientific fellow chem. dept., 1987-90, head of lab. or organic synthesis, 1990-93, chemistry educator, 1993—, head of chemistry dept., 1995—. Inventor in field. Lt. Ukrainian Mil. Sch., 1985. Office: Pedagog Inst, ul Oboronnaya 2, 348011 Lugansk Ukraine

DYADKIN, YURIY DMITRIEVICH, earth sciences educator; b. Urzum, Kirov, Russia, Nov. 26, 1929; s. Dmitriy Ivanovich and Alexandra Nikolaevna (Lopatina) D.; m. Irina YakovlevnaGamsulova, Oct. 26, 1954; 1 child, Tatiana. Mining engr., Leningrad (USSR) Mining Inst., 1952, candidate tech. scis., 1955, D of Tech. Scis., 1965. Asst., prof. Leningrad Mining Inst., 1956—, prorector on rsch., 1968-72, head dept. ore mining and mining thermophysics, 1968-91; head dept. ore mining St. Petersburg (Russia) Mining Inst., Tech. U., 1991-97. Author: Principles of Mining Thermophysics for the North, 1968, Mining of Geothermal Deposits, 1989; author (with others) Comprehensive Rock Engring., 1993; editor Jour. Phys. Processes in Mining, 1973—; mem. editl. bd. Internat. Jour. Rock Mechanics and Mining Scis., 1978—. Recipient The Badge of Honour, Supreme Coun. USSR, Moscow, 1963, grants of scholarship Fulbrights Program of Internat. Exchange, U. Minn., 1979, Stanford U., 1987; named Honored Scientist of Russia, Fedn., Moscow, 1980. Mem. Russian Geothermal Assn. (pres. 1991), Internat. Geothermal Assn. (bd. dirs. 1995), Internat. Bur. Mining Thermophysics (presidium mem. 1976), Acad. Natural Scis. of Russia (academician 1992), Internat. Acad. Ecology and Protective Sci. (academician 1996), Acad. of Discovery (academician 1997). Home: 30 Nalichnaya Apt 121, 199226 Saint Petersburg Russia Office: St Petersburg State Mining Inst, 2 21st Linia, 199026 Saint Petersburg Russia

DYAKONOV, LEV PETER, research scientist; b. Volkovitsy, USSR, May 16, 1928; s. Peter Alex and Praskovya Philip Siltchenkova D.; m. Helen Victor Vasilieva, Sept. 15, 1950; children: Yuri, Tatiana. MS, Vet. Acad., Moscow, 1952; postgrad., All-Union Inst. Exptl. Vet., Medicine, Moscow, 1955-58, PhD, 1960, Dr. Sci., 1973, Prof., 1977. Cert. vet. surgeon. Vet. North Caucuses Region, USSR, 1952-55; staff scientist All-Union Inst. Exptl. Vet. Medicine, Moscow, 1958-60, sr. scientist, 1960-74, head of tissue cultures and nutrient media lab, 1975-90, head of cell biotechnology and nutrient media tech. lab., 1990—; scientific sec. All-Union Protozoologists Soc., Moscow, 1968-76; mem. pharmacology coun., Moscow, 1972-92. Co-author: (book) Veterinary Parasitology, 1999, Agricultural Biology, 1985; patentee in field. Head trade union, VIEV, Moscow, 1963-64. Recipient state prize USSR Coun. Ministers, Moscow, 1990; honored scientist Russian Fedn., Moscow, 1989. Mem. Russian Cell Culture Assn., European Tissue Culture Soc., N.Y. Acad. Scis., Vet. Biology Br. (vice-chmn. 1990-96), Russian Agr. Acad., Russian Nature Scis. Acad. Avocations: reading, poetry, swimming.

DYAKONOV, VLADIMIR PAVLOVITH, higher education educator; b. Kiev, Ukraine, Feb. 7, 1940; s. Pavel Vasilievith Dyakonov and Anna Moiseevna Voydeslaver; m. Zoya Pavlovna Krivalova; 1 child, Vladimir Vladimirowith. Cand. Tech. Scis., U. Moscow, 1969, D Tech. Scis., 1981; postgrad., Internat. Acad. Pedagog. Edn., Moscow, 1998. Engr. Azi Nefteltim, Azerbajan, 1967-69; asst. prof. Smolensk br. Moscow Power Engring. Inst., 1970-73; head indsl. electronics, chair Smolensk br. Moscow Power Engring. Inst., 1974-96; prof. informatic Smolensk State Pedagog. U., 1996-97, head phys. and informatics electronics, 1998—. Author: Handbook on Calculation in Calculators, 1989, (with others) The Revolutionary Guide to QBasic, 1996, System Symbolic Mathematician: Mathematica 2 and Mathematica 3, 1998, Internet Handbook for Users, 1999, 30 others; holder 61 patents in electronics; contbr. over 400 articles to profl. jours. Dep. Smolensk City Senate, 1991-94. Grantee Russian Ministry of Edn., 1998, Wolfram Rsch. Inc.; Soros Prof. grantee, 1999. Avocations: music, writing books. E-mail: dyak@keytown.com. Home: October Revolution St 13 72, 214004 Smolensk Russia Office: Smolensk State Pedagog U, Prjevalsky St 4, 214000 Smolensk Russia

DYANKOV, ALEXANDER IVANOV, technical education educator, mechanical engineer; b. Sofia, Bulgaria, Mar. 15, 1929; arrived in France, 1969; s. Ivan Kanchev and Evdokia Alexandrova (Christova) D.; m. Elena Assenova Kambourova, June 25, 1951; 1 child, Manuella. MSc in Mech. Engring., Tech. Univ., Sofia, 1953; tchr. trainer, Postgrad. Inst., Sofia, 1958; MSc in Pedagogics, Sofia State U., 1964. Lectr. Tech. Coll., Sofia, 1954-60; sr. asst. prof. engring. Tech. Univ., Sofia, 1960-69; UNESCO expert UNESCO/Internat. Labour Orgn. (Internat. Bank Reconstruction and Devel.) Projects, Singapore, 1969-74; sr. UNESCO expert UNESCO/Internat. Labour Orgn. (Internat. Bank Reconstruction and Devel.) Projects, Babol, Iran, 1974-77; program specialist UNESCO Regional Office Asia & Pacific, Bangkok, Thailand, 1977-87; sr. UNESCO specialist UNESCO Hdqrs., Paris, 1987-93; cons. UNESCO Mauritius, 1991, Albania, 1993, Eritrea, 1994; cons. Asian Devel. Bank, Papua New Guinea, 1994-95, 96; cons. UNESCO, Bosnia-Herzogovina, 1996, UN Devel. Program, Botswana, 1997, Rep. Korea, 1999, Belgium, 1999, Pakistan, 1999. Author 3 textbooks and a teachers' guide, including Methodology, 1961-65, UNESCO Monograph, 1992; contbr. numerous articles to profl. jours.; author 10 ednl. TV programs, Media Ctr., Singapore, 1972; organizer numerous internat. seminars, meetings and workshops, 1977-87. Active supporter Movement Beyond War, U.S., 1990—. Recipient creative tchr. merit award Ministry Edn., Sofia, 1959, Specialist of Program Learning award ILO Internat. Ctr., Turin, Italy, 1971. Mem. Bulgarian Engrs. and Archs. Assn., Internat. Assn. Engring. Pedagogics, Union Bulgarian Scientists, Assn. UNESCO Ret. Personnel. Home: 10 rue Henri Regnault, F-92400 Paris France Office: UNESCO ED/SVE/TVE, 7 Place de Fontenoy, 75007 Paris France

DYAULI, DAVID PHILIPO, pediatrician; b. Iambi, Tanzania, Oct. 11, 1930; s. Philipo Mambala and Magdalena Muguli (Gyimbi) D.; m. Salome Petro, Oct. 30, 1956 (dec. Nov. 1957); 1 child; m. Eliwaza Ntulu Loti, Oct. 28, 1958; 7 children. BS, Gustavus Adolphus U., 1964; MB, BChir, U. East Africa, Daressalaam, Tanznia, 1969; diploma in child health, Royal Coll. Physician/Surgeon, Glasgow, Scotland, 1975. Med. registrar Ministry of Health, Kiomboi, Tanzania, 1970-71; med. officer in charge ELCT Ctrl. Diocese, Iambi, 1971-73, 75-91, pediatrician, 1975-91; med. sec. ELCT Ctrl. Diocese, Singida, Tanzania, 1976-91; pvt. practice Huduma Clinic, Singida, 1993—; exec. mem. Christian Med. Bd. Tanzania, 1980-91. Mem. Med. Assn. Tanzania (presenter Ngirwamungu Meml. lectr. 1988), Pediat. Assn. Tanzania, Med. Assn. Tanzania, Tanzania Christian Med. Assn. Lutheran. Avocations: soccer, gardening, music, hunting game, volleyball. Office: Huduma Clinic, PO Box 752, Singida Tanzania

DYBCZYNSKI, RAJMUND STANISLAW, chemistry educator; b. Warsaw, Poland, Nov. 8, 1933; s. Stefan Rajmund and Halina (Petrulewicz) D.; m. Izabella Boratynska; children: Anna Maria, Magdalena Barbara. MSc, Warsaw U., 1955; PhD, Inst. Nuclear Rsch., Warsaw, 1963, DSc, 1971; prof. chemistry, Inst. Nuclear Chemistry/Tech., Warsaw, 1987. Rsch. scientist Inst. Gen. Chemistry, Warsaw, 1955-57; rsch. scientist Inst. Nuclear Rsch., Warsaw, 1957-65, head lab., 1965-75, 80-83; first officer Internat. Atomic Energy Agy., Vienna, 1975-80; head lab. Inst. Nuclear Chemistry and Tech., Warsaw, 1983-95, head of dept., 1995—; mem. com. for analytical chemistry Polish Acad. Scis., Warsaw, 1981—; mem. several adv. and cons. groups Internat. Atomic Energy Agy., Vienna, 1981-96; mem. scientific coun. Inst. Nuclear Rsch., Warsaw, 1981-82, Inst. Nuclear Chem. and Tech., 1987—, Ctrl. Lab. for Radiol. Protection, Warsaw, 1990-91, 95-99, Rsch. Ctr. for Prodn. Isotopes, 1990-91, 95-99. Co-author: Separation and Preconcentration Methods in Inorganic Trace Analysis, 1982; assoc. editor: Jour. Radioanalytical and Nuclear Chemistry Letters, 1976-97; regional editor: Geostandards Newsletter, 1979-96, Jour. Chemia Analityczn, 1988-2000; editl. adv. bd. Jour. Radio & Nuclear Chemistry, 1977-2000; contbr. articles to profl. jours. Recipient individual award State Coun. Peaceful Uses of Atomic Energy, 1963, collective award Min. Sci. Higher Edn. and Technology, 1983. Roman Catholic. Office: Inst Nuclear Chemistry/Tech, Dorodna 16, 03-195 Warsaw Poland

DYBCZYNSKI, WLADYSLAW, electrical engineer, educator; b. Wilamowice, Poland, Dec. 4, 1935; s. Jan and Rozalia (Kuczmierczyk) D.; m. Wanda Wladyczuk, Aug. 20, 1960; children: Anna, Pawel. Diploma in engring., Warsaw U. Technology, 1959; DSc, Posnan U. Technology, 1979, Warsaw U. Technology, 1987. Lab. leader Film Tech. Rsch. Ctr., Warsaw, 1959-90; from asst. prof. to assoc. prof. Bialystock U. Technology, 1983—. Author: Film and TV Lighting Equipment, 1992, Design of Lighting Systems, 1997; contbr. articles to profl. jours. Mem. Polish Commn. on Il-

lumination. Home: Bonifraterska 10b-43, 00-213 Warsaw Poland Office: Bialystok U Technology, Wiejska 45C, 15-351 Bialystok Poland

DYCK, ANDREW ROY, philologist, educator; b. Chgo., May 24, 1947; s. Roy H. and Elizabeth (Beck) D.; m. Janis Mieko Fukuhara, Aug. 20, 1978. BA, U. Wisc., 1969; PhD, U. Chgo., 1975. Sessional lectr. U. Alta., Edmonton, Can., 1975-76; asst. prof. U. Minn., Mpls., 1977-78; vis. asst. prof. Classics UCLA, 1976-77, asst. prof., 1978-82, assoc. prof., 1982-87, prof., 1987—, chmn. dept. classics, 1988-91; mem. Inst. for Advanced Study, Princeton, 1991-92; vis. fellow All Souls Coll., Oxford, 1998, Clare Hall, Cambridge, 1999. Author: A Commentary on Cicero, De Officiis, 1996; editor: Epimerismi Homerici, 2 vols., 1983, 95, Essays on Euripides and George of Pisidia and on Helidorus and Achilles Tatius (Michael Psellus), 1986. Alexander von Humboldt-Stiftung fellow, Bonn, Fed. Republic of Germany, 1980-89; NEH fellow, 1991-92. Mem. Am. Philol. Assn., Calif. Classical Assn., U.S. Nat. Com. on Byzantine Studies. Office: UCLA Classics Dept 405 Hilgard Ave Los Angeles CA 90095-9000

DYCK, GEORGE, psychiatry educator; b. Hague, Sask., Can., July 25, 1937; came to U.S., 1965; s. John and Mary (Janzen) D.; m. Edna Margaret Krueger, June 27, 1959; children: Brian Edward, Janine Louise, Stanley George, Jonathan Jay. Student, U. Sask., 1955-56; B of Christian Edn., Can. Mennonite Bible Coll., 1959; MD, U. Man., 1964; postgrad., Menninger Sch. Psychiatry, 1965-68. Diplomte in psychiatry and geriatric psychiatry Am. Bd. Psychiatry and Neurology; cert. psychiatrist Royal Coll. Physicians and Surgeons, Can. Fellow cmty. psychiatry Prairie View Mental Health Center, Newton, Kans., 1968-70; clin. dir. tri-county svcs. Prairie View Mental Health Ctr., 1970-73; prof. dept. of psychiatry U. Kans.-Wichita, Wichita, 1973—; chmn. dept. of psychiatry U. Kans.-Wichita, 1973-80, 98-99; med. dir. Prairie View, Inc., 1980-89; dir. geriatric psychiatry U. Kans., 1993—; cons. Shenyang Psychiat. Hosp., People's Republic of China, 1990, Palestinian Mental Health Program, West Bank, 1990; mem. Kans. Hosp. Closure Commn., 1995; bd. dirs. Kidron Bethel Retirement Svcs., Newton, Kans., 1994—. Bd. dirs. Mennonite Mut. Aid, Goshen, Ind., 1973-85, Chmn., 1982-85; bd. dirs. Mid-Kans. Cmty. Action Program, 1970-73, Wichita Council Drug Abuse, 1974-76, Kauffman Mus. North Newton, 1995-98. Fellow Am. Psychiat. Assn. (pres. Kans. chpt. 1982-84, dep. rep. 1984-86, rep. 1986—, cert. in adminstrv. psychiatry 1984); mem. AMA, Kans. Med. Soc., Kans.-Paraguay Ptnrs. (treas. 1986-89). Mennonite. Home: 1505 Hillcrest Rd Newton KS 67114-1340 Office: U Kans Sch Medicine Wichita Dept Psychiatry 1010 N Kansas St Wichita KS 67214-3124

DYE, BRADFORD JOHNSON, JR., lawyer, former state official; b. Tallahatchie County, Miss., Dec. 20, 1933; married; 3 children. BBA, LLB, U. Miss. Bar: Miss. 1959. Practiced law Grenada, Miss., 1959-61; later in Jackson, Miss.; mem. Miss. Ho. of Reps., 1960-64, Miss. Senate, 1964-68; dir. Agrl. and Indsl. Bd., 1968-71; treas. State of Miss., 1972-76; lt. gov. State of Miss., 1980-92; ptnr. Pyle, Dreher, Mills & Dye PA, 1992—; bd. dirs. Fed. Home Loan Bank, Dallas; southeastern adv. bd. Alexander Proudfoot Productivity Mgmt. Co.; formerly served with U.S. Senate Judiciary Com. Staff; pres. Jackson Fed. Savs. Assn., 1976-79; charter pres. Bus. Sch. Alumni Assn. Univ. of Miss. Charter v.p. Grenada Jaycees; former mem. adv. bd. Miss. State U. Sch. Bus. and Industry; bd. dirs. Jr. Achievement; active state heart fund drive, ARC, United Way, Cancer Drive, YMCA Youth Sports; del. Dem. Nat. Conv., 1980, 84. Mem. U. Miss. Bus. Alumni Assn. (charter pres.), Masons, Shriners, Pi Kappa Alpha. Methodist. Office: Pyle Dreher Mills & Dye 779 Avery Blvd # 200 Ridgeland MS 39157-5218

DYE, JAMES LOUIS, chemistry educator; b. Soudan, Minn., July 18, 1927; s. Ray Ashley and Hildur Ameda Dye; m. Angeline Rosalie Medure, June 10, 1948; children: Roberta Rae, Thomas Anthony, Brenda Lee. AA, Virginia (Minn.) Jr. Coll., 1948; BA, Gustavus Adolphus Coll., 1949; PhD, Iowa State U., 1953; DSc (hon.), No. Mich. U., 1992. Rsch. assoc. Iowa State U., Ames, 1953; asst. prof. chemistry Mich. State U., East Lansing, 1953-60, assoc. prof., 1960-63, prof., 1963-94, chmn. dept. chemistry, 1986-90, prof. emeritus, 1994—; vis. scientist Ohio State U., Columbus, 1968-69; cons. AT&T Bell Labs., Murray Hill, N.J., 1982-83. Author: Thermodynamics and Equilibrium, 1978; contbr. over 200 articles to profl. jours. With U.S. Army, 1945-46. NSF fellow, 1961-62, Guggenheim fellow, 1975-76, 90-91, Fulbright scholar, 1975-76; recipient Disting. Alumni award Gustavus Adolphus Coll., 1969. Fellow AAAS; mem. NAS, Am. Acad. Arts and Scis., Am. Chem. Soc. (Inorganic Chemistry award 1997), Am. Inst. Chemists (Chem. Pioneer award 1990), Am. Phys. Soc., Materials Rsch. Soc., Phi Kappa Phi, Sigma Xi (rsch. awards 1968, 87), Golden Key (teaching award 1986). Lutheran. Avocations: fishing, golf. Home: 2698 Roseland Ave East Lansing MI 48823-3847 Office: Mich State Univ Dept Of Chemistry East Lansing MI 48824

DYE, O. DAVID, speech and theatre educator; b. Bruce, Miss., Apr. 28, 1943; s. O.L. and Celestine (Cain) D.; m. Judith Gray Ferrell, Aug. 8, 1965; children: Gwin Elizabeth, David Ferrell. BS, Miss. State U., 1965; MFA, Fla. State U., 1967, PhD, 1970. Prof. speech and theatre Troy (Ala.) State U., 1970—, chmn. dept., 1970-95, dean coll. comm. and fine arts, 1997—; chmn. Ala. festival Am. Coll. Theatre Festival, 1977-87. Dir. (stage plays) The Importance of Being Earnest, 1973 (reg. award Am. Coll. Theatre Festival), Master Harold...and the Boys, 1985 (nat. award Am. Coll. Theatre Festival, performed at Kennedy Ctr., Washington 1986), Brighton Beach Memoirs, 1990 (2d alt. nat. Am. Coll. Theatre Festival), The Memorandum, 1991 (regional award Am. Coll. Theatre Festival). Dir. Theatre for Youth Ensemble, 1970-99; bd. dirs. Troy-Pike Habitat for Humanity, 1995-97; mem. theatre adv. panel Ala. Coun. on Arts and Humanities, 1983-86, 88, 98, 99. Recipient Amoco Gold medallion Am. Coll. Theatre Festival, 1980, Dirs. Choice award, 1986, 90; tour grantee Ala. Coun. on Arts and Humanities, 1971-86, festival grantee, 1977-86. Mem. Ala. Conf. Theatre and Speech (assoc. pres. 1973, Marian Galloway award 1988, Hall of Fame award 1995), Phi Kappa Phi (regent and nat. bd. dirs. 1995—). Home: 417 Murphree St Troy AL 36081-2116 Office: Coll Comm and Fine Arts Troy State U Troy AL 36082-0001

DYE, ROBERT HARRIS, retired manufacturing company executive; b. N.Y.C., Feb. 22, 1918; s. Abatha Agusta and Julia (Harris) D.; m. Tereseua Vergine, May 13, 1950; 1 child, Leslie Julie. BSEE, Purdue U., 1942. Engr. Gen. Elec. Co., Schenectady, 1942-43, 46-47; field engr. Gen. Elec. Co., Key West, Fla., 1947-49; prog. mgr. Gen. Elec. Co., Schenectady, 1949-53; divsn. chief guidance and control Dept. of Navy, Newport, R.I., 1953-56; sect. mgr. Gen. Precision Co., Little Falls, N.J., 1956-60; prog. mgr. Gen. Precision Co./Singer, Little Falls, 1960-87; ret. Lt. USN, 1942-46. Mem. IEEE, Submarine Vet. WWII, NRA, Am. Legion. Republican. Achievements include development of procedures for mine field penetration by submarine. Avocation: woodworking.

DYER, ALAN, chemist, educator; b. Salford, Eng., Mar. 29, 1934; s. Colin Dyer and Florence Hunt/ m. Dilys Patricia Groves, Aug. 30, 1958; children: Andrew Simon, Fiona Elizabeth Ruth, Jennifer Frances, Christopher David. BSc with honors, U. Sheffield, Eng., 1954; PhD, Kings Coll., London, 1958; DSc, U. Salford, 1981. Chartered chemist, Eng. Tchr. Worsley Wardley Grammar Sch., Lancashire, Eng., 1957-59; lectr. Royal Tech. Coll., Salford, Eng., 1959-61; lectr., sr. lectr. Royal Coll. Advanced Tech., Salford, 1961-64; lectr. U. Salford, 1964-70, sr. lectr., 1970-85, reader, 1985-97, prof. chemistry, 1997—; tech. dir. Brit. Zeolite Co., Eng., 1994—; cons. to numerous chem. cos. including Laporte, ICI, BNFL, Duracell, Alcan Chems. Author: Liquid Scintillation Counting, 1971, Zeolite Molecular Sieves, 1988; contbr. over 200 articles to profl. jours. Fellow Royal Soc. Chemistry (Silver medal 1994); mem. English Lacrosse Assn. (copres. 1995—, Centurion award 1996), Radiochem. Methods Group (chmn. 1982-94). Avocations: Lacrosse administration, bridge, walking, geology. Office: U Salford, Salford M5 4WT, England

DYER, ARLENE THELMA, retail company owner; b. Chgo., Oct. 23, 1942; d. Samuel Leo Sr. and Thelma Arlene (Israel) Lewis; m. Don Engle Dyer, July 3, 1965 (div. 1970); 1 child, Artel Terren. Cert. in mgmt. effectiveness, U. So. Calif., 1987; cert. ryan Designated Subjects, U. So. Calif., L.A., 2000. Community resource rep. Calif. State Employment Devel. Dept., Los Angeles, 1975-76, spl. projects rep., 1976; employment services rep. Culver City, Calif., 1977; contract writer L.A., 1976-80, employment program rep., 1980—; pres. Yabba and Co., L.A., 1981-83; pres., designer, cons. Spiritual Ties Custom Neckwear, L.A., 1985—; pres. Dyer Custom Shirts, Blouses and Suits, Beverly Hills, Calif., 1988—; founder self-evaluation seminar; pres. MYSELF, Inc., 1998. Author: Who Are You and What Are You All About?, 1994, Escaping to the Workplace, 1996, I Got the Job!. . .Now What?, 1998, You Got the Job?...Now What?, 1999; exhibited in fashion shows, Calif., 1984—; radio personality, 1995. Vol. Big Sister Gwen Bolden Found., L.A., 1986, Juvenile Hall, 1996; mem. Operation PUSH, Chgo., 1983, Mahogany Cowgirls & Co.; program chair Black Advs. in State Svc., 1987—; leader Girl Scouts U.S., L.A., 1982, L.A. Urban League; spirit team leader Calif. Special Olympics; mem. Big Sisters of L.A. Recipient IRWIN award, 1998. Mem. NAACP (Beverly Hills-Hollywood chpt.), Nat. Alliance Homebased Businesswomen (v.p., program chair 1987), NAFE, Nat. Spkrs. Assn. (Grtr. L.A. chpt.), Calif. State Employees Assn., Greater L.A. C. of C., Kiwanis Club, U. So. Calif. Alumni Assn., L.A. Urban League, Black Women's Forum. Democrat. Club: 92d St Block. Avocations: traveling, reading, bicycling, roller skating.

DYER, CHARLES ARNOLD, lawyer; b. Blairstown, Mo., Aug. 29, 1940; s. Arnold and Mary Charlotte (West) D.; children: Kristine, Erin, Kathleen, Kerry. BJ, U. Mo., 1962; JD, U. Calif., 1970. Bar: Calif. 1971, U.S. Supreme Ct. 1976. Ptnr. Dyer & White, Menlo Park, Calif.; judge Pro Tem Mcpl. and SuperiorCt., San Mateo County, Calif.; judge Pro Tem Superior Ct., Santa Clara County, Calif., arbitrator, mediator; lectr. in field. Bd. dirs. Boys Club of San Mateo, 1971-83, pres., 1975; mem. exec. coun. Boys Clubs of Bay Area, 1977-83; mem. Dem. Nat. Fin. Com., 1978. Served to capt. USNR, 1963-93, ret. Mem. Calif. Bar Assn., San Mateo County Bar Assn., Santa Clara County Bar Assn., Palo Alto Bar Assn., Consumer Attys. Calif., Consumer Attys. San Mateo County, Assn. Atty. Mediators, Trial Lawyers Pub. Justice, Am. Bd. Trial Advs., Nat. Bd. Trial Advocacy, Am. Arbitration Assn. Roman Catholic. Office: Dyer & White 800 Oak Grove Ave Menlo Park CA 94025-4477

DYER, CROMWELL ADAIR, JR., lawyer, international organization official; b. St. Louis, Sept. 9, 1932; came to The Netherlands, 1973; s. Adair and Tompie Leora (Giles) D.; m. Margaret Copeland Peickert, June 12, 1958 (div. Aug. 1976); children: Gretchen, Jack, Julie, Stephen; m. Susan Aynesworth, Aug. 20, 1977; stepchildren: Carol Godso, Amanda McDonough, Donne Brown. BA, U. Tex., 1954; JD, 1961; LLM, Harvard U., 1971. Bar: Tex. 1961, U.S. Dist. Ct. (no dist.) Tex. 1965, U.S. Dist. Ct. (ea. dist.) Tex. 1966, U.S. Ct. Appeals (5th cir.) 1965, U.S. Ct. Appeals (11th cir.) 1982, U.S. Ct. Appeals (9th cir.) 1999. Law clk. FTC, Washington, 1960; assoc. Branscomb, Gary, Thomasson & Hall, Corpus Christi, Tex., 1961-62; staff atty. So. Union Gas Co., Dallas, 1962-64; assoc. Dedman & May, Dallas, 1964-65, White, McElroy & White, Dallas, 1965-67; sole practice, 1967-73; sec. Hague Conf. on Pvt. Internat. Law, The Hague, The Netherlands, 1973-78; 1st sec., 1978-93, dep. sec. gen., 1993-97, observer, cons. to intergovtl. orgns., 1976-97; lectr. Asser Coll. Europe, 1992-96, Davis Sch. Law U. Calif. Davis, 1996, Brigitte M. Bodenheimer Meml. Lecture on the Family, 1996; condr. seminars. Honoree of symposium: Globalization of Child Law The Role of the Hague Conventions, 1999; co-author: Report on Trusts and Analogous Institutions, 1982; contbr. articles to profl. jours. Mem. jury for award of Diploma in Internat. Law Hague Acad., 1980, 84, 85, 86, 87, 91, 94, 95, 96, dir. studies, 1985, course on Unfair Competition in Pvt. Internat. Law, 1988. Lt. (j.g.) USN, 1954-57. Mem. ABA (Leonard J. Theberge award for pvt. internat. law, sect. internat. law and practice 2000), ATLA, Am. Soc. Internat. Law, Am. Fgn. Law Assn., Inter-Pacific Bar Assn., Inter-Am. Bar Assn., Travis County Bar Assn., Dallas Bar Assn., Internat. Soc. Family Law, Assn. Louis Chatin pour la Def. des Droits de l'Enfant (Paris), Club du jeudi (pres. 1983-85, The Hague). Fax: 512 231-9498. E-mail: adyer@jump.net. Office: 9130 Jollyville Rd Ste 250 Austin TX 78759-7473

DYKE, JOHN GEOFFREY, mathematician, engineer; b. Liverpool, Eng., Feb. 23, 1948; s. George Charles and Ruth (Jones) D. BSc, J.M.U., Liverpool, 1970; MSc, Open U., 1992; PGCE, U. Wales, 1989. Rsch. fellow Brunel U., Uxbridge, Eng., 1974-76; sys. engr. Plessey Radar, Addlestone, Eng., 1976-78; cons. Checknorth Ltd., Cardiff, Wales, 1978-82, Racal SMS Ltd., Chessington, Eng., 1982-83; sr. lectr. U. Glamorgan, Pontypridd, Wales, 1983-93; tutor Open U., Cardiff, 1994—. Contbr. articles to profl. jours. Mem. Ch. of Wales. Avocations: walking, languages, music. Office: Open Univ in Wales, 24 Cathedral Rd, Cardiff CF11 9SA, Wales

DYKMAN, LEV ABRAMOVICH, microbiologist; b. Saratov, Russia, July 3, 1962; s. Abram Lvovich and Angelina Nikolaevna (Jakovleva) D.; m. Natalya Mikhailovna Barabasch, Jan. 16, 1988; 1 child, Roman Lvovich. Pediatrist, Med. Inst., Saratov, 1985. Paediatrist Hosp. Kochkurovo, Mordovija, 1985-88; rsch. worker Inst. Biochemistry and Physiology of Plants and Microorganisms Russian Acad. of Scis., Saratov, 1988—. Contbr. articles to profl. jours. Grantee Internat. Sci. Found., 1993. Avocations: lit., music, hunting. Office: IBPPM RAS, Prospect Entuziastov 13, RF410015 Saratov Russia

DYKSTRA, ANNEKE GESKE, economist, educator; b. Haarlem, The Netherlands, Apr. 18; d. Eeltje and Victoire (van Katwyk) D; two children. MA in Sociology, U. Groningen, 1981, MA in Econs., 1983, PhD, 1988. Asst. prof. U. Leiden, The Netherlands, 1982-83; rsch. asst. U. Groningen, The Netherlands, 1983-86; sr. rschr. Inst. Econ. Rsch. U. El Salvador, 1987-89; asst. prof. Open U., Heerlen, The Netherlands, 1990-91, U. Maastricht, The Netherlands, 1991-95; sr. lectr. Inst. Social Studies, The Hague, The Netherlands, 1995-2000; asst. prof. econs. program pub. adminstrn. Erasmus U., Rotterdam, The Netherlands, 2000—. Author: Industrialization in Sandinista Nicaragua, 1992; editor, author: Gender and Economics: A European Perspective, 1997.

DYKSTRA, DAVID CHARLES, management executive, consultant, accountant, author, educator; b. Des Moines, July 10, 1941; s. Orville Linden and Ermina (Dunn) D.; children: Suzanne, Karin, David S. BSChemE, U. Calif., Berkeley, 1963; MBA, Harvard U., 1966. CPA, Calif. Corp. controller Recreation Environs., Newport Beach, Calif., 1970-71, Hydro Conduit Corp., Newport Beach, 1971-78; v.p. fin. and adminstrn. Tree-Sweet Products, Santa Ana, Calif., 1978-80; pres., owner Dykstra Cons., Irvine, Calif., 1980-88, Marcer Island, Wash., 1998—; pres. Easy Data Corp., 1981-88; pub. Easy Data Computer Comparisons, 1982-87; sr. mgr. Deloitte & Touche, Costa Mesa, Calif., 1988-90; prof. mgmt. info. sys. Nat. U., Irvine, 1984-90; pub. Dykstra's Computer Digest, 1984-90; pres., owner Golden West Pers., Long Beach, Wash., 1992-93; exec. v.p. Tegris Corp., Bellevue, Wash., 1994-98. Author: Manager's Guide to Business Computer Terms, 1981, Computers for Profit, 1983; contbr. articles to profl. jours. Chmn. 40th Congl. Dist. Tax Reform Immediately, 1977-80; mem. nat. com. Rep. Com.; vice-chmn. Orange County Calif. Rep. Assembly, 1979-80; bd. dirs. Corona Del Mar Rep. Assembly, 1980-94, v.p., 1980-87, pres., 1987-89; mem. Mercer Island Presbyn. Ch., 1998—. Mem. AICPA, Am. Mgmt. Assn., Calif. Soc. CPAs, Data Processing Mgmt. Assn., Am. Prodn. and Inventory Control Soc., Ind. Computer Cons. Assn., Internat. Platform Assn., Data Processing Mgmt. Assn., Orange County C. of C., Newport Beach C. of C., Harvard U. Bus. Sch. Assn. Orange County (bd. dirs. 1984-90, v.p. 1984-86, 87-88, pres. 1986-87, 91-92, chmn. 1993-94), Harvard U. Bus. Sch. Assn. So. Calif. (bd. dirs. 1986-87, 91-92, v.p. 1992-93), Harvard U. Bus. Sch. Assn. Puget Sound, Town Hall, Mercer Island Presbyn. Ch., Mercer Island Country Club, John Wayne Tennis Club, S. Cowichan Lawn Tennis Club, Lido Sailing Club, Columbia Tower Club, Rotary (bd. dirs. 1984-86). Home and Office: 3465 W Mercer Way Mercer Island WA 98040-3355

DYKSTRA, WILLIAM DWIGHT, business executive, consultant; b. Grand Rapids, Mich., June 15, 1927; s. John Albert and Irene (Stable Kamp) D.; m. Ann McGuiness, Nov. 2, 1957 (dec. 1988); children: William Hugh, Mary Irene. AB, Hope Coll., 1949; MBA, Ind. U., 1951. Asst. mgr. Ply-Curves, Inc., 1950; originator magnesium metal furniture, 1951; pres. Dwight Corp., 1952-56, W.D. Dykstra Group, Grand Rapids, 1956—; pres. Burton L. Norton Co., 1990, Tie Life Care, Inc.; bd. dirs. Sheldon Co., Orchard Machine Co., Equine World, Inc. Author: Management and the 4th Estate, New Profits for Management. George F. Baker Scholar selector; elder Dutch Ref. Ch. Recipient Outstanding Furniture Merit award, 1955, Vehicle Color Design award, 1967, P.I.A. Graphic award, 1971, Am. Advt. Fedn. award, 1971, 73, 76, Disting. Entrepreneur Alumnus award Ind. U., 1983. Mem. Am. Econs. Assn., Am. Inst. Graphic Arts (Packaging award 1965, 67), Acad. Polit. Sci., Am. Mktg. Assn. (Mktg. Man of Yr. 1981), Engring. Soc. of Detroit, Soc. Packaging and Handling Engrs., Rotary, Phi Kappa Psi, Pi Kappa Delta. Republican. Home: 1145 Edison Ave NW Grand Rapids MI 49504-3919 Office: Old Tallmadge Grange Hall 1845 Leonard St NW Grand Rapids MI 49544-9510

DYLAN, BOB (ROBERT ALLEN ZIMMERMAN), singer, composer; b. Duluth, Minn., May 24, 1941. Student, U. Minn., 1960; self-taught on guitar, piano, autoharp, harmonica; Mus.D. (hon.), Princeton U., 1970. Performer numerous tours and concerts, 1960—. Albums include Bob Dylan, The Free Wheelin' Bob Dylan, The Times They Are a Changin', Another Side of Bob Dylan, Bringing It All Back Home, Highway 61 Revisited, Blonde on Blonde, John Wesley Harding, Nashville Skyline, Self Portrait, New Morning, Desire, Infidels, Empire Burlesque, Dylan, Planet Waves, (with The Band) Before the Flood, 1986, Hard Rain, Blood on the Tracks, (with The Band) The Basement Tapes, Street Legal, Slow Train Coming, Knocked Out Loaded, 1986, (5 record set) Biograph, 1960—, Down In The Groove, 1988, (with Traveling Wilburys) Traveling Wilburys, 1988, (with Grateful Dead) Dylan and the Dead, 1989, Oh Mercy, 1989, Under The Red Sky, 1990, (with Traveling Wilburys) Vol. 3, 1990 (Grammy award), The Bootleg Series, 1961, 1990, Good as I Been to You, 1992, World Gone Wrong, 1993, Unplugged, 1995, Time Out of Mind (Grammy award 1998); film appearances include Don't Look Back, Renaldo and Clara, Eat the Document, Pat Garrett and Billy the Kid, Concert for Bangla Desh, Hearts of Fire, 1987; composer numerous songs including Blowin' in the Wind, Like a Rolling Stone, Lay, Lady, Lay, Subterranean Homesick Blues, Forever Young, Gotta Serve Somebody, Don't Think Twice, It's Alright, A Hard Rain's A-Gonna Fall, The Times They are A-Changin', Just Like a Woman, I'll Be Your Baby Tonight, I Shall Be Released, Mr. Tambourine Man, Simple Twist of Fate, Paths of Victory, others; author numerous publs. including Tarantula, 1966, 71, Writings and Drawings by Bob Dylan, 1973, The Songs of Bob Dylan from 1966-1975, 1976, Lyrics, 1985, Drawn Blank, 1994; interactive CD-ROM: Highway 61 Revisited, 1995. Inducted into Rock and Roll Hall of Fame, 1988; Grammy nomination (Best Rock Duo or Group Performance, 1994) for "My Back Pages" (with Roger McGuinn, Tom Petty, Neil Young, Eric Clapton, and George Harrison). Achievements include devising and popularizing folk-rock. Office: Columbia Records 550 Madison Ave New York NY 10022-3211*

DYMICKY, MICHAEL, retired chemist; b. Synewidsko Wyzhne, Urkraine, Oct. 1, 1920; came to U.S., 1949; s. Mykola and Eva (Andrushkiw) D.; m. Olga Zhmurko, Jan. 22, 1943; children: Lida Dymicky Pakula, Oksana Dymicky Matla. Degree in chem. tech., Chem. Tech. Polytechnic, Lwiw, 1943; BS, U. Innsbruck, Austria, 1947, Doctorandum, 1949; PhD, Temple U., 1960. Chemist Am. Sugar Refining Co., Phila., 1949-52; rsch. chemist U. Pa. Med. Sch., Phila., 1952-53, Wyeth Inst. Med. Rsch., Radnor, Pa., 1953-56, 59-62; rsch. chemist Agr. Rsch. Svc. USDA, Phila., 1956-59, 66-89; assoc. prof. Kutztown (Pa.) U., 1962-65; gen. sec. Internat. Student Svcs., Innsbruck, 1947-49. Author: Servant of God Metropolitan Andrei Sheptyts'kyi, 1996; contbr. articles to profl. jours.; patentee in amino acid derivatives and anticlostridial agts. Mem. adv. bd. and chmn. pub. rels. com. Menor Jr. Coll. Jenkintown, Pa., 1976-82. Recipient Citation of Merit DAV, 1970, Chem. Abstract Svc., 1971, USDA, 1989; Inventor's award U.S. Dept. Commerce, 1987. Mem. Am. Chem. Soc. (student adviser 1963-65), Shevchenko Sci. Soc. (coun. 1968—). Avocations: swimming, volleyball, making perfumes. Home: 9653 Dungan Rd Philadelphia PA 19115-3221

DYMNIKOVA, IRINA, physicist; b. Khabarowsk, Russia, May 21, 1943; arrived in Poland, 1988; d. Gawriil and Paraskiewa (Marshuk) Timofiejew; m. Wladimir Dymnikov, Oct. 10, 1970 (div. 1986); children: Pawel, Maria. MSc with honors, U. Leningrad, Russia, 1966; PhD in Theoretical and Math. Physics, Inst. Physics, Tartu, 1978; Dr.Hab. in Theoretical Physics, U. Warsaw, 1992. Rschr. A.F. Ioffe Inst., Leningrad, 1966-88; adj. N. Copernicus Astron. Ctr., Warsaw, 1990-96; prof. physics U. Warmia and Mazury, Olsztyn, Poland, 1996—; lectr. Williams Coll., Williamstown, Mass., 1992. Contbr. articles to profl. jours. Recipient Gold medal Min. of Edn., 1960, Gravity Rsch. Found. award, 1991. Mem. Nat. Geog. Soc., N.Y. Acad. Scis., Internat. Soc. on Gen. Relativity and Gravitation, Planetary Soc. Avocations: psychology, playing piano, reading. Office: Inst Math Informatics & Physics, Zolnierska 14, 10-561 Olsztyn Poland

DYMOND, SIMON OLIVER, psychologist, educator, behavior analyst; b. Newport, Gwent, Wales, Feb. 15, 1973; s. Roger Douglas and Patricia Frances (Brace) D. BA in Psychology, U. Coll. Cork, Ireland, 1993, PhD, 1996. Tutor, demonstrator U. Coll. Cork, Ireland, 1993-96, lectr., 1995-96; rsch. officer U. Wales, Bangor, 1996-97, tchg. fellow, 1997-98; lectr. dept. psychology Anglia Poly. U., Cambridge, Eng., 1998—. Avocation: music. E-mail: s.dymond@anglia.ac.uk. Office: Anglia Poly Univ Psychology, East Rd, Cambridge CB1 1PT, England

DYNE, ALISON MARGARET, psychologist; b. Brisbane, Queensland, Australia, June 30, 1965; d. Kenneth Ian and Lynette Gail (Duffils) D. BA in Psychology, U. Queensland, 1985, BA in Psychology with honors, 1986, PhD in Psychology, 1992. Registered psychologist, Queensland. Tutorial asst., fellow U. Queensland, 1987-91, lectr., 1992, 95-96; sr. rsch. asst. QUT, Brisbane, 1992-93; asst. prof. Bond U., Gold Coast, Australia, 1993-94; sr. rev. and evaluation officer Queensland Police Svc., 1997—; cons. James Hardie Bldg. Sys., Brisbane, 1997. Author: Psyche: Experiments that Changed Psychology, 1997; contbr. articles to profl. jours. Mem. Whistleblowers Action Group, Queensland, 1994—. Recipient Australian Postgrad. Rsch. award DEET, 1987-91. Mem. APA. Office: Queensland Police Svc, 100 Roma St, Brisbane QLD 4000, Australia

DYNE, PETER GOLDING, import company executive; b. Wellington, New Zealand, Feb. 27, 1966; s. Leslie Golding and Fay Dianne (Pycroft) D.; m. Eleanor Margaret Taylor, Jan. 13, 1996; 1 child, William Golding Stewart. Branch mgr. Golding Handcrafts, Wellington, 1997-93, importation and distbr. mgr., 1994—. Singer: Nat. Youth Choir New Zealand, 1983-94, St. Paul's Cathedral, 1976-91, The Tudor Consort, 1987-98, Sacred Heart Cathedral, 1992—, Voices New Zealand, 1998—. Trustee, treas. The Wellington and Region Neonatal Unit Charitable Trust. Recipient numerous awards. Anglican. Avocations: singing, acting. E-mail: golding@paradise.net.nz. Office: Golding Handcrafts, Rostrevor House Marion St, Wellington New Zealand

DYOMIN, VICTOR VALENTINOVICH, optician, educator; b. Zolotoe, Russia, Sept. 8, 1958; s. Valentine G. and Zoya N. (Loseva) D.; m. Svetlana Yu Kugaevskaya, Apr. 16, 1982; children: Irene, Julia. Grad., Tomsk (Russia) State U., 1980, PhD, 1988. Asst. prof. Tomsk State U., 1981-83, sr. educator, 1986-91, assoc. prof., 1991—; rsch. scientist Siberian Phys.-Tech. Inst., Tomsk, 1981-88; sr. scientist Tomsk State U., 1988-97, Inst. Optical Monitoring, Tomsk, 1997—. Contbr. articles to profl. jours.; inventor in field. Names Soros assoc. prof. Internat. Soros Sci. Edn. Program, Russia, 1995, 97, 99; rsch. grantee Russian Found. Basic Rsch., 1994-95, travel grantee Nat. Sci. Found., Internat. Sci. Found., Internat. Commn. Optics, 1995, 96, 99, 2000. Mem. Optical Soc. Am. Home: PO Box 1873, 634049 Tomsk Russia Office: Tomsk State U, 36 Lenin Ave, 634050 Tomsk Russia

DYPVIK, HENNING, geologist, educator; b. Oslo, Norway, Sept. 11, 1950; s. Kare Albert Johan and Kirsten (Solum) K.; m. Bente Bue, Aug. 11, 1973; children: Andreas, Kjersti, Eivind. BS, U. Oslo, 1974, PhD, 1985. Sci. asst., asst. prof. U. Oslo, 1974-85, assoc. prof., 1985—. Editl. bd. mem. Africa Geoscience Rev., 1995—; contbr. articles to profl. jours. Mem. Soc. Sedimentary Geology, Norsk Geol. Forening. Avocations: skiing, carpentry, boating, music. Office: Dept Geology, Univ Oslo, N-0316 Blindern Oslo, Norway

DYR, WANDA STANISLAWA, biomedical researcher; b. Sadoleś, Poland, June 13, 1944; d. Zdzislaw and Marianna (Sobotka) Wycech; m. Janusz Stanislaw Dyr, Oct. 26, 1963 (dec. 1986); children: Jacek Maciej, Michal Adam. MS, Copernicus U., Torun, Poland, 1980; PhD, Med. Acad., Warsaw, Poland, 1989. Sr. specialist Inst. Psychiatry and Neurology, Warsaw, 1980-89; sr. lectr. Med. Acad., Warsaw, 1984-91; adj. Inst. Psychiatry and Neurology; vis. scientist Inst. Psychiat. Rsch., Indpls., 1991-92; head drug addiction lab., Inst. Psychiatry and Neurology, Warsaw, 1989—.

Contbr. articles to scientific jours. Mem. Solidarity Union, 1980—. Recipient postdoctoral grant Kosciuszko Found., N.Y., 1991. Mem. European Soc. Biomed. Rsch. Alcoholism (award for meeting Stuttgart, Germany 1995, award for meeting Stockholm 1997), Internat. Soc. Biomed. Rsch. Alcoholism, European Behavioral Pharmacol. Soc. (award for meeting Berlin 1994). Roman Catholic. Office: Inst Psychiatry & Neurology, Al Sobieskiego 1/9, 02-957 Warsaw Poland

DYSON, NORMAN ALLEN, physicist, educator; b. Huddersfield, Eng., May 15, 1929; s. Arthur Lewis and Annie (Howard) D.; m. Elizabeth Mary Bainbridge, Dec. 20, 1952; children: Jane Elizabeth, Helen Christina, Ruth Mary Anne. BA, Cambridge U., 1952, MA, 1956, PhD, 1956. Chartered physicist. Sci. staff Med. Rsch. Coun. U.K., 1955-59; lectr. physics U. Birmingham, Eng., 1959-74, sr. lectr. physics, 1974-94; ret. Author: X-Rays in Atomic and Nuclear Physics, 2d edit., 1990, Radiation Physics with Applications in Medicine and Biology, 2d edit., 1993; contbr. articles to profl. jours. Mem. Inst. Physics U.K., Soc. Radiol. Protection, Inst. Phys. and Engring. in Medicine. Home: Wendover, 32 Bromsgrove Rd, Romsley near Halesowen B62 0ET, England

DYSON, PETER LAWRENCE, physicist, educator; b. Coburg, Victoria, Australia, June 2, 1942; s. Horace James and Margaret Augusta (Stocks) D.; m. Diane Florence Clark, Mar. 26, 1966; children: Paul, Jane. BSc with honors, U. Melbourne, Australia, 1964, PhD, 1967. NAS-NRC resident rsch. assoc., sr. resident rsch. assoc. NASA Goddard Space Flight Ctr., Greenbelt, Md., 1967-69, 72; Queen Elizabeth II fellow La Trobe U., Bundoora, Victoria, Australia, 1969-71; lectr. in physics La Trobe U., Bundoora, 1971-72, sr. lectr., 1973-78, reader, 1978-92, head Sch. Physics, 1993-94, 97-99, prof., 1993—, assoc. dean for rsch. Faculty Sci. and Tech., 1996—; vis. scientist U. Tex., Dallas, 1973. Contbr. articles to profl. jours. Fellow Australian Inst. Physics (chmn. Victorian br. 1993-94), Instn. Engrs. Australia; mem. IEEE, Am. Geophys. Union, Am. Assn. Physics Tchrs. Achievements include experimental investigations of properties of ionospheric irregularities and the dynamics and thermodynamics of the thermosphere; applications of radio wave propagation theory to communications and radar. Avocations: walking, reading, theatre, football, cricket. Office: La Trobe Univ, Bundoora 3083, Australia

DYVIG, PETER P., ambassador; b. Nordborg, Denmark, Feb. 23, 1934; m. Karen Moller, 1959. LLM, U. Copenhagen, 1959; postgrad., Sch. Advanced Internat. Studies, 1963-64. 2d sec. Ministry Fgn. Affairs, Copenhagen, 1964; 1st sec. Danish Del. to NATO, Paris and Bruxelles, 1965-69; head of sect. Ministry Fgn. Affairs, Copenhagen, 1969-73, head div., 1973; minister councellor Danish Embassy, Washington, 1974; dep. under sec. polit. affairs Ministry Fgn. Affairs, Copenhagen, 1976, under sec. polit. affairs, 1980-83, state sec., 1983-86; amb. to U.K. Gt. Britain and No. Ireland, 1986-89, amb. to U.S., 1989-95, amb. to France, 1995-1999, chamberlain to Her Majesty Queen Margrethe II of Denmark, 1999—; chmn. exec. bd. European Ctr. Minority Issues, Flensburg, Germany, 1999—; chmn. bd. dirs. Naibou du Danemark, Paris, 2000—, Brit. Import Union, 2000—. Order of Dannebrog (Comdr. 1st class). Home and Office: Tryggehvile Allè 9, DK-2920 Charlottenlund Denmark

DZAKAH, MAWUNYO FRANCIS, prison officer; b. Keta, Volta, Ghana, Jan. 15, 1963; s. Humphrey Akpaluku and Kwashiinor (Fiaxo) D.; m. Faustina Atiatorme; children: Rita, Maltida, Dorothy, Rose and Rosaline (twins). Attended, Keta Bus. Coll., 1976-81. Account clk., prison officer Ghana Prisons Svc., Winneba, Ghana, 1983—. Sgt. Prisons, 1991-94. Roman Catholic. Office: Ghana Prisons Svc, PO Box VD 24, Yendi Northern Region, Ghana

DZAKPASU, CONOR CAESAR KOFI, political science educator; b. Dzodze, Volta, Ghana, Sept. 2, 1942; s. Kwaku Agbe and Sodamade (Kpogo) D.; m. Victoria Ami Seadey, Sept. 27, 1961; children: Hopeson, Rosalind, Senanu, Agbesi, Esther, Edem, Elikem. BA in Polit. Sci. with honors, U. Ghana, Legon-Accra, 1972, MA in Polit. Sci., 1976. Tchr. Ghana Edn. Svc., Hevi, 1965-69; tutor, asst. head G.E.S. Krachi Sec. Sch., Kete-Krachi, Ghana, 1972-73; tutor G.E.S. Ghanata Sec. Sch., Dodowa, Ghana, 1974-75; sr. supt. Ghana Edn. Svc. Our Lady of Apostles Sec. Sch., Ho, Ghana, 1975-77; resident tutor, lectr. U. Ghana, Legon, 1977-86, sr. resident tutor, sr. lectr., 1986—; prin. Kumasi (Ghana) Workers Coll., 1982-98; spl. advisor Ewe Chieftaincy Affairs, Kumasi, 1988-98; head tchg., rsch. Inst. Adult Edn., Legon, 1998—; dep. dir. Adult Edn., Legon, 1999—; spkr. in field. Contbr. articles to profl. jours. Dir. Mutual Help Group, Dzodze, 1996—. Recipient Cert. of Achievement, Govt. Ghana/U.S. Agy. Internat. Devel., 1979. Mem.Am. Ednl. Rsch. Assn. Avocations: animal husbandry, horticulture, writing, walking. Office: Inst Adult Edn U Ghana, PO Box 31, Legon Accra, Ghana

DZELME, JURIS, accreditations agency administrator, researcher; b. Talsi, Latvia, Aug. 1, 1945; s. Roberts and Zenta (Putelis) D.; m. Galina Umiskova, July 16, 1968. Grad., Leningrad (USSR) U., 1969; CandSci, Latvian Acad. Sci., Riga, 1979, Doctor Physics, 1991. Rschr. U. Latvia, Riga, 1972-79, sr. rschr., 1979-92; head divsn. Ministry of Edn., Riga, 1992-94; dir. Higher Edn. Quality Evaluation Centre, Riga, 1994—; lectr. U. Latvia, 1972-97, leading rschr., 1992-97. Co-author monograph, inventions; contbr. more than 40 articles to profl. jours. Mem. standing com. Ius Primi Viri, Rome, 1993—. Sr. lt. Soviet Army, 1969. Pharetempus Program project grantee, Brussels, 1996. Mem. Scientists Assn. Latvia (mem. coun. 1988-95), N.Y. Acad. Sci., Internat. Network of Quality Assurance Agys. (New Zealand). Mem. Social Dem. Labour Party of Latvia. Avocations: psychology, philosophy. Home: Ruses 28-170 PO Box 186, LV 1029 Riga Latvia Office: Higher Edn Quality Eval Ctr, Valnu 2, LV 1098 Riga Latvia

DZIDO, TADEUSZ HENRYK, chemist, educator; b. Ostrow Lubelski, Poland, Dec. 16, 1950; s. Zygmunt and Jadwiga (Klementewicz) D.; m. Boguslawa Niedziela, June 4, 1977; children: Tomasz Marcin, Przemyslaw Maciej. MS, M. Curie-Sklodowska U., 1973, PhD, 1980. Asst. Med. Acad., Lublin, Poland, 1973-80, sr. scientist, 1980—; bd. dirs. Chromdes, Lublin. Contbr. articles to profl. jours.; patentee in field. Scholar S.E.A. Found., 1981-82, A.v.H. Found., 1987-89; recipient award Polish Ministry of Health, 1979, 95. Mem. N.Y. Acad. Scis., Polish Chem. Soc., Polish Pharm. Soc., Soc. Humboldiana Polonorum. Roman Catholic. Avocations: fishing, chess, travel. Office: Med Acad Inorg Analyt Chem, Staszica 6, 20-081 Lublin Poland

DZIDONU, CLEMENT KWAKU, computer science educator, author; b. Accra, Ghana, Nov. 23, 1955; arrived in Zimbabwe, 1996; s. Gabriel Kwami Dzidonu and Dorothy Kofishi Amegbo; children: Winnie, Trina. Diploma with distinction in journalism, London Sch. Journalism, 1980; BSc with honors, U. Surrey, Guildford, Eng., 1983; PhD, Trinity Coll., Dublin, Ireland, 1988. Chartered statistician; cert. info. sys. practitioner, Eng. Lectr. Trinity Coll., Dublin, 1984-95, sr. rsch. fellow, 1995—; Info. Tech. expert Commonwealth Secretariat, London, 1996—; sr. lectr. Nat. U. Sci. and Tech., Zimbabwe, 1996—; prof. info. tech. Touro U. Internat., Los Amitos, 1999—; prof. computer sci. Valley View U., Accra, Ghana, 1999—; lectr. U. Galway, Ireland, 1989-91; vis. lectr. Makerere U., Uganda, 1990, 91, 92; IT cons. European Union, 1989-91, FAO, Rome, 1994-95; pres. Internat. Ctr. for Info. Tech., 1994—; bd. mem. Informatics Devel. Inst., Dublin, 1995—; founder Electronic Distance Edn. Consortium for Africa, 1995—; founder The African Network for Info. Tech. Experts and Profls., 1994; pres., CEO Internat. Inst. for Info. Tech., Accra, Ghana, 1998—. Author: The Computer Jargon Book, 1994, Demystifying The Computer, 1995, Intro To Computers and Computing, 1996, All You Need To Know About Computers, 1996, Simplified Illustrated Guide to Computer Hardware Jargon, 1994, Desktop Guide to Computer Software, Processing and Applications Jargon, 1994, Beginners and Expert's Guide to Computer Networks, 1994, Born to Win, Born to Succeed, 1996. Pres. Nat. Union Ghanaian Students, U.K., 1981-83; coord. African Networks for Info. Tech. Experts and Profls., 1994—, Electronic Distance Edn. Consortium for Africa, 1996—. Fellow Instn. Analysts and Programmers; mem. Brit. Computer Soc., Inst. Indsl. Engrs., European Inst. Indsl. Engrs., Irish Computer Soc., N.Y. Acad. Scis., Internet Soc., Assn. Profl. Computer Consultants (Eng.). Avocations: reading, volunteer work, walking, bicycling. Address: PO Box AN-19782, Accra-North GHANA

DZIEDUSZKO, JANUSZ WLADYSLAW, electrical engineer; b. Jaslo, Poland, Aug. 25, 1939; came to U.S., 1966; s. Wladyslaw and Waleria (Pankiewicz) D.; m. Lucyna Janina Ryba, Apr. 15, 1963; 1 child, Philip. MSEE, Acad. Mining and Metallurgy, Cracow, Poland, 1962. Sr. systems engr. Westinghouse Electric, Pitts., 1967-79, 86-90; mgr. hardware devel. BBC Brown Boveri, Pitts., 1979-84; mgr. power line comm. GE, Malvern, Pa., 1984-85; mgr. product devel. ABB Power Transmission & Distbn. Co., Coral Springs, Fla., 1990-97; exec. consulting R&D engineer ABB Electric Sys. Tech. Inst., Raleigh, N.C., 1997—. Contbr. papers to profl. confs. Mem. choir St. Michaels Roman Catholic Ch., Cary, N.C., 1989—. Mem. IEEE. Democrat. Achievements include 3 patents in digital data communication and data acquisition; significant contribution in data communication and microprocessor product design for electrical power industry. Avocations: classical music, bicycling, chess. Home: 5412 Pine Dr Raleigh NC 27606-9589 Office: Electric Sys Tech Inst 1021 Main Campus Dr Raleigh NC 27606-5202

DZIEGIEL, LESZEK, ethnologist; b. Mysłowice, Poland, Sept. 15, 1931; s. Władysław and Maria (Warszawska) D.; m. Elżbieta Kieniewicz, Oct. 9, 1960; 1 child, Maciej. MA in Ethnology, U. Cracow, 1955, PhD in Ethnology, 1972. Tchr. Secondary Sch., Katowice, Poland, 1960-67; rschr. U. of Agrl., Cracow, 1969-83; assoc. prof. Jagiellonian U., Cracow, 1983-93, full prof., 1993—; dir. Inst. of Ethnology Jagellonian U., 1983-99; freelance journalist. Editor Ethnological Studies, 1989—; author: Rural Community of Iraqi Kurdistan, 1981, Wezeł kurdyjski/Kurdish Knot, 1992, Swoboda na smyczy.Wspomnienia 1946—, 1996, Freedom on the leash, 1996, Paradise in a Concrete Cage, 1998. Scholarship Norwegian Fgn. Office, 1966, 86. Roman Catholic. Avocations: mountain hiking, tourism, making photos. E-mail: dziegiel@grodzki.phils.uj.edu.pl. Home: Słomiana 25/23, 30-316 Cracow Poland Office: Instytut Etnologii UJ, Grodzka 52, 31-044 Cracow Poland

DZIEMBALA, LEON JERZY, statistician, researcher, educator; b. Chorzow, Katowice, Poland, July 16, 1933; s. Jerzy Leon and Elzbieta Maria (Andrysek) D.; m. Renata Maria Czaplicka, Feb. 12, 1966; 1 child, Marek. MSc, Acad. Econs., Katowice, 1956, PhD, 1960. Asst. Hight Sch. Econs., Katowice, 1953-55, sr. asst., 1955-60; sr. lectr. Acad. Econs., Katowice, 1961-68, assoc. prof., 1968-92, prof., 1991—; prof. Silesian Mgmt. Hight Sch., Katowice, 1994—, Hight Sch. Banking, Poznan, 1997—; titular lectr. Acad. German Managerial Pers., Bad Harzburg, 1992; head affiliated cons. br. Acad. Econs., Katowice, 1966-70, dep. dir. Inst. Econometrics, 1982-84, 87-90, head dept. Demography Statistics of the Inst. Econometrics, 1990—. Co-author: Statistical Methods in Industrial Enterprise, 1962, Selected Problems of Statistics and Econometrics, 1965 (Min. of Higher Edn. award 1966), Statistical Quality Control, 1968, Application of the Mathematical Methods in the Economy of Industrial Enterprise, 1968, Fundamentals Statistics, 1982; author: Study of Live Hazard in a Region of Ecological Disaster, 1991 (Rector of Acad. Econs. award 1993), Selected Problems of Descriptive Statistics and Demography, 1997, contbr. articles to profl. jours. Recipient award Min. of Sci., Higher Edn. and Technics of Poland, 1978, 83, Student Tchr. and Sci. Achievements Gov. of Katowice Province, 1986, Tchr. Merit of the Polish Rep., State Coun. Poland, 1985, Rector of Acad. Econs., 1979, 84-96. Mem. Polish Statis. Assn., Polish Demographic Assn. Roman Catholic. Avocations: bridge, chess, collecting stamps, swimming. Home: Chrobrego 25/97, 40-881 Katowice Poland Office: Acad Econs, Bogucicka 14, 40-226 Katowice Poland

DZIEWANOWSKA, ZOFIA ELIZABETH, neuropsychiatrist, pharmaceutical executive, researcher, educator; b. Warsaw, Poland, Nov. 17, 1939; came to U.S., 1972; d. Stanislaw Kazimierz Dziewanowski and Zofia Danuta (Mieczkowska) Rudowska; m. Krzysztof A. Kunert, Sept. 1, 1961 (div. 1971); 1 child, Martin. MD, U. Warsaw, 1963; PhD, Polish Acad. Sci., 1970. MD recert. U.K., 1972, U.S., 1973. Asst. prof. of psychiatry U. Warsaw Med. Sch., 1969-71; sr. house officer St. George's Hosp., U. London, 1971-72; assoc. dir. Merck Sharp & Dohme, Rahway, N.J., 1972-76; vis. assoc. physician Rockefeller U. Hosp., N.Y.C., 1975-76; adj. asst. prof. of psychiatry Cornell U. Med. Ctr., N.Y.C., 1978—; v.p., global med. dir. Hoffmann-La Roche, Inc., Nutley, N.J., 1976-94; sr. v.p. and dir. global med. affairs Genta Inc., San Diego, 1994-97; sr. v.p. drug devel. and regulatory Cypros Pharms. Corp., Carlsbad, Calif., 1997-99; pres., med. dir. New Drug Assocs., La Jolla, Calif., 1999—; lectr. in field U.S. and internat. confs. Contbr. articles to profl. publs. Bd. dirs Royal Soc. Medicine Found.; mem. alumni coun. Cornell U. Med. Ctr. Recipient TWIN Honoree award for Outstanding Women in Mgmt., Ridgewood (N.J.) YWCA, 1984. Mem. AMA, AAAS, Am. Soc. Pharmacology and Therapeutics, Am. Coll. Neuropsychopharmacology, N.Y. Acad. Scis., PhRMA (vice chmn. steering com. med. sect., chmn. internat. med. affairs com., head biotech. working group), Royal Soc. Medicine (U.K.), Drug Info. Assn. (Woman of Yr. award 1994), Am. Assn. Pharm. Physicians. Roman Catholic. Achievements include original research on the role of the nervous system in the regulation of respiratory functions, research and development and therapeutic uses of many new drugs, pharmaceutical medicine and biotechnology; molecular biology derived as well as conventional products including antisense, interferon efficacy in cancer, virology and AIDS and drugs useful in cardiovascular, immunological, neuropsychiatric, infectious diseases, and others; impact of different cultures on medical practices and clinical research; drug evaluation and development management strategies of pharmaceutical industries; treatments against cardiac and brain ischemia, cytoprotection; speaker in field.

DZIOPAK, JÓZEF, civil engineering educator; b. Hyżne, Rzeszów, Poland, Aug. 24, 1947; s. Stanisław and Maria (Rybka) D.; m. Elena Neverova, Aug. 24, 1994; 1 child, Arina; children from a previous marriage: Slotwińska Dominika, Dziopak Julianna, Dziopak Maria. M in Tech., Civil Engring., Rzeszów, Poland, 1967; MSc in Engring., Cracow U. Tech., 1972, PhD in Engring., 1983; DSc in Engring., Wrocław (Poland) U. Tech., 1993. Cert. civil and sanitary engring. Vice dir. Inst. Sanitary Engring. and Environ. Protection, Cracow, 1984-88; head divsn. Sanitary Engring. and Tech. Infrastructure, Cracow, 1991—; head dept. Water Supply and Sewage Sys., Częstochowa, Poland, 1994-98; dir. Inst. Environ. Engring., Częstochowa, 1997; dean Faculty Environ. Engring. and Protection, Częstochowa, 1997-99; dir. Patent Tng. Courses, Poznań, Poland, 1979-81; cons. Project Offices Poland, Germany, Russia, Sweden and Finland, 1984—; dir. Tng. Courses, Cracow, 1986-88; expert Ministry Environ. Protection, Warsaw, 1993—. Author: Mathematical Model of Storm Water Retention Basin, 1984, Multichamber Storage Reservoirs in the Sewerage System, 1997; 17 patents in field, contbr. over 125 articles to profl. jours. Chief Young Scientists Com., Cracow, 1976-79; chmn. Local Solidarnost Com., Cracow, 1980-81. Recipient Testimonial award World Exhbn. Achievements, Plovdiv, 1985, Sci. Progress Ctr., Katowice, 1985, Collective award Impex XIII, Pitts., 1997, spl. merit award 2nd Messe Kansai, Osaka, 1997, award of excellence, Golden Key award, London Internat. Inventions Fair, London, 1997, Awd. for 1st Category of Internatl. Water Supply Symposium, Tokyo, 1998. Mem. Internat. Acad. Ecology and Life Protection Scis., Russia Internatl. Network of Engs. and Scientists for Global Resonsibility, Germany, Polish Geothermal Assn. Democrat. Roman Catholic. Achievements include 17 patents, 55 projects realizated, 51 expert opinions. Avocations: volleyball, dancing, traveling, photography, collecting pigs. Home: Juliusza Lea 244/8, 30-133 Cracow Poland Office: Tech U Kielce Al 1000-lecia, Panstwa Polskiego 7, 25-314 Kielce Poland

DZIUBA, ANDRZEJ FRANCISZEK, priest, religious studies educator; b. Pleszew, Poland, Oct. 10, 1950; s. Stanisław Dziuba and Ludwika Szlachciak. BA, Primatial Priests' Sem., Gniezno, Poland, 1968; MTh, Pontifical Theol. Faculty, Poznań, Poland, 1975; Lic.Th., Cath. U., Lublin, Poland, 1976, DD, 1979, PhD, 1989; postgrad., Inst. Cath., Paris. Ordained priest Roman Cath. Ch., 1975. Asst. parish priest Holy Trinity, Łobżenica, Poland, 1975-76; sec. Primate of Poland, 1981-98, dir. sec., 1984-98; asst. parish priest St. Martin's Ch., Warsaw, Poland, 1981-98, St. Barbara's Ch., Warsaw, 1998—; prof. Cath. U. Lublin, 1989—, Cath. U., Warsaw, 1995—, Primatial Priest's Sem., Gniezno, 1998—; theol. councillor Primate of Poland, 1998—. Author: Mikołaj z Mościsk, teolog moralista XVII, 1985, Informator Katolicki 89/90, 1990, Droga Krzyżowa, 1991, Różaniec święty, 1992, Kościół katolicki w Polsce Informator, 1993, Jezus nam przebacza. przygotowanie do sakramentu pojednania, 1994, Matka Boża z Guadalupe, 1995, Kościół katolicki w Polsce Informator, 1995, Orędzie moralne Jezusa Chrystusa, 1996, Dynamika wiary 1997, Kościół katolicki w Polsce. Informator, 1997, Droga krzyżowa, 1998, Biography of H.E. Cardinal Józef Glemp, 1998, Cardinal Stefan Wyszynski, Primate of Poland. A Life Sketch, 2000; contbr. articles to profl. jours. Recipient medal of Wacław Niżyński, 1992, medal of Fryderyk Chopin, 1992, Cross with Godl Star of Merit of Holy Sepulchre of Jerusalem, 1996; named hon. chaplain to His Holinnes Pope John Paul II, 1990, Prelate to His Holinnes Pope John Paul II, 1996, Kt. Comdr. of Equestrian Order of Holy Sepulcher od Jerusalem, 1996, Hon. Conventual Chaplain of Ordes of Malta, 1998, Canon Met. Chpt. Warsaw, 1998, Kt. Ecclesiastical Grace of Sacred Mil. Constantinian Order, 1999. Fax: 81 533-04-33, 22 635-87-45. Home: ul Nowogrodzka 49, 00-695 Warsaw Poland Office: Al Racławickie 14, 20-950 Lublin Poland Office: ul Miodowa 17, 00-246 Warsaw Poland

DZUBA, VLADIMIR ANDREYEVICH, physicist, researcher; b. Lesozavodsk, Primorsky, Russia, Nov. 28, 1952; s. Andrey Prokopevich and Maria Nikitichna (Khomichouk) D.; m. Elena Mikhaylovna Bazhanova, Sept. 25, 1975; children: Marina, Dmitri. MS, Novosibirsk State U., Russia, 1975; PhD, Inst. Nuclear Physics, 1984; DS, Inst. Spectroscopy, Moscow, 1990. Researcher Inst. Nuclear Physics, Novosibirsk, 1975-90, Inst. Semiconductor Physics, Novosibirsk, 1990-93, Sch. of Physics, UNSW, Sydney, Australia, 1993—. Contbr. articles to profl. jours. Office: Sch of Physics, Univ New South Wales, 2052 Sydney Australia

DZUL, PAUL J., physician, medical journal editor; b. Milno, Ukraine, Oct. 14, 1921; came to U.S., 1949; s. John M. and Maria H. Dzul; m. Irene Dzul; children: Andrew I., George O. Grad., Lviv (Ukraine) Med. Inst., 1944, Med. U., Graz, Austria, 1945; MD, Med. U., Innsbruck, Austria, 1948; degree honoris causa, Odessa (Ukraine) Med. U., 1996, Lviv Med. U., 1998. Instr. Wayne State U., Detroit, 1960-62, asst. prof., 1962-66, assoc. prof., 1966-90, prof. emeritus, 1990—; pres. Lakeshore Ear, Nose & Throat, St. Clair Shores, Mich., 1966-90. Editor in chief Jour. Ukrainian Med. Assns. N.Am., 1967—. Fellow ACS, Am. Acad. Otolrayngology-Head and Neck Surgery, World Fedn. Ukrainian Med. Assns. (pres. 1992—). Home: 21 Woodland Shores Dr Grosse Pointe MI 48236-2633 Office: World Fedn Ukrainian Med Assns PO Box 36305 Grosse Pointe MI 48236-0305

DZYAK, GEORGY VIKTOROVICH, internist, educator, university official; b. Dnipropetrovsk, Ukraine, Mar. 20, 1945; s. Viktor Nikolaevich and Lidiya Petrovna (Ivannikova) D.; m. Loudmila Antonovna Shvedchenko, Apr. 17, 1972; 1 child, Viktor. MD, Dnipropetrovsk State Med. Acad., 1980, Candidate Med. Scis., 1970, DMS, 1980. Asst. prof. internal medicine Dnipropetrovsk State Med. Acad., 1971-74, assoc. prof., 1974-79, prof., head dept., mayor med. mil. svcs., 1979—, vice rector, 1987-96, rector, 1996—; mem. coun. sci. and techs. Cabinet Ministries Ukraine, 1997—; expert Ukrainian Higher Accreditation Bd., 1991—. Author: (monographs) Clinical Reography, Atrial Fibrilation, 1979, Rheumatism and Acquire Heart Valvular Diseases, 1982, Arterial Hypertension, 1998. Decorated Order for Achievements III Degree (Ukraine). Mem. Acad. Med. Scis. Ukraine, Assn. Cardiologists Ukraine (dep. chmn. 1989—), Acad. Med. Scis. Poland, U.S. Acad. Scis. (corr.). Home: 1 Fuchik St Apt 21, 49027 Dnipropetrovsk Ukraine Office: Dnipropetrovsk State Med Ac, 9 Dzerzhinsky St, 49044 Dnipropetrovsk Ukraine

DZYALOSHINSKII, IGOR EKHIELIEVICH, physicist; b. Moscow, Feb. 1, 1931; s. Ekhiel Moiseevich and Maria Semionovna (Aseeva) D.; m. Elena Aronovna Lebedeva, Dec. 2, 1960; 1 child, Elena. MA in Physics, Moscow State U., 1953; PhD in Physics, Inst. for Phys. Problems, Moscow, 1957, DSc in Physics, 1962. Sr. rschr. Inst. for Phys. Problems, Moscow, 1957-65; head dept. magnetism Landau Inst. for Theoretical Physics, Moscow, 1965-91; prof. physics U. Calif., Irvine, 1992—. Author: Methods of Quantum Field, Theory in Statistical Physics (in Russian, English, Japanese and Chinese), 1962, 3d edit., 1975, 2d Russian edit., 1998. Decorated Order of Red Banner of Labour, Order of Honor, Medal of Vet. of Labour, Govt. of Russia; recipient State prize Govt. USSR, 1984. Fellow Am. Phys. Soc.; mem. Russian Acad. Scis. (Lomonosov prize 1962, Landau prize 1989), Am. Acad. Art and Scis. (hon. fgn. mem.). Achievements include research in theory of weak ferromagnetism; theory of van der Waals forces in condensed media; theory of one-dimensional metals. Avocation: history. Office: Univ Calif Dept Physics Irvine CA 92697-0001

DZYUBLIK, ALEXEY YAROSLAV, physicist, physics educator; b. Kiev, Ukraine, Mar. 4, 1946; s. Yaroslav Feofan and Nina Anton (Pilipenko) D.; m. Olga Yakov Ishkova, Aug. 22, 1975; children: Valentina, Nadezhda. Grad., U. Kiev, Ukraine, 1963-68; PhD, Inst. Theoretical Physics, Kiev, Ukraine, 1972, DSc (hon.), 1987. Jr. rschr. Inst. Nuclear Rsch., Kiev, Ukraine, 1972-79; sr. rschr. Inst. Nuclear Rsch., Kiev, 1979-88, leading rschr., 1988—; prof. U. Kiev, 1996-99. Contbr. articles to profl. jours. Home: Dreiser str3 Apt 23, 02217 Kiev Ukraine Office: Inst Nuclear Rsch, pr Nauki 47, 03028 Kiev Ukraine

E, JISHENG, engineer; b. Lanzhou, Gansu, People's Republic of China, Apr. 9, 1956; s. Lin E and Yuhua Yan; m. Aiyang Zhang; 1 child, Haibo. B Engring., Zhejiang U., Hangzhou, People's Republic of China, 1982; M Phil, Chinese Acad. Scis., Lanzhou, 1985; PhD, Brunel U., London, 1995. Team leader Lanzhou Inst. of Chem. Physics/Chinese Acad. Scis., Lanzhou, 1985-86; acad. chief asst. State Key Lab. of Solid Lubrication CAS, Lanzhou, 1986-89; rsch. fellow Brunel U., London, 1990-95; sr. engr. GKN Technology, Ltd., Wolverhampton, U.K., 1995—; vis. scholar Swansea Tribology Ctr., 1989-90; guest prof. Lanzhou Inst. of Chem. Physics Chinese Acad. Sci., 2000—. Patentee in field; inventor in field; contbr. articles to profl. jours. Grantee Nat. Rsch. award for Young Chinese Rschrs., 1986; recipient Nat. 3rd prize of Innovation in China, Chinese Govt., 1994, Nat. 3rd prize in Scis. and Tech., Chinese Govt., 1985. Mem. Inst. Mech. Engrs., Brit. Engring. Coun. (chartered engr.). Avocations: Chinese Qi-Gong, healing, reading, touring. Office: GKN Tech Ltd, Birmingham New Rd, WV4 6BW Wolverhampton WV4 6BW, England

EABY, CHRISTIAN EARL, lawyer, small business owner; b. Reading, Pa., June 16, 1945; s. David Russell and Pearl Haller (Root) E.; m. Dace Rekis, Jan. 4, 1986. BA in Univ. Studies, U. N.Mex., 1976, JD, 1980. Bar: N.Mex. 1980, Pa. 1990, U.S. Dist. Ct. (ea. dist.) Pa. 1992. Tchr. Albuquerque Pub. Schs., 1976; ednl. dir. N.Mex. Pub. Employees Coun., 1977; tutor Am. Indian Law Ctr. U. N.Mex., 1978-79; pvt. practice Albuquerque, 1980-90; owner Eby Clock Co., New Holland, Pa., 1990-95; pvt. practice New Holland, 1990—; past legal coun. N.Mex. Vietnam Vets. of Am. Contbr. articles to profl. jours. Bd. dirs. U. N.Mex. Cancer Ctr., 1984-92, Albuquerque United Artists Downtown Ctr. for Arts, Ea. Lancaster County Sch., 1990-93; pres. Coalition Albuquerque Neighborhoods, 1983-85, Nob Hill Neighborhood Assn., 1980-86; mem. task force Albuquerque Goals Com.; founding dir., sec. Nob Hill Main St., 1987; founding dir. Casa Esperanza Cancer Patients Homes, 1987. Mem. ABA, ATLA (product liability sect.), Am. Arbitration Assn., Am. Numismatic Assn., N.Mex. Bar Assn., N.Mex. Trial Lawyers Assn., Albuquerque Bar Assn., Pa. Bar Assn. (workers' compensation sect.), Lancaster Bar Assn., Pa. Trial Lawyers Assn., Nat. Assn. Watch and Clock Collectors, Nat. Trust Hist. Preservation, Hist. Preservation Trust of Lancaster County, Lancaster Mennonite Hist. Soc., Lancaster Hist. Soc., Hist. Soc. of Cocalico Valley, Eby Family Assn. (pres. 1992—). Avocations: geneology, numismatics, horology, restoring 1727 family home. Fax: 717-656-3434. E-mail: cee@eabylaw.com. Home: 405 Peters Rd New Holland PA 17557-9389 Office: 352 E Main St Ste 230 Leola PA 17540-1961

EAGAN, MARIE T. (RIA EAGAN), chiropractor; b. Rockville Ctr., N.Y., June 17, 1952; d. John F. and Mary (Ebner) E. BA, Goddard Coll., 1975; D in Chiropractic Medicine, N.Y. Chiropractic Coll., 1983. Pvt. practice chiropractic medicine N.Y.C., 1983—; chiropractic examiner N.Y. State Bd. Chiropractic, 1995. Bd. dirs. Chalice Found., L.A., 1986. Fellow N.Y. Chiropractic Assn., Am. Chiropractic Assn., Internat. Chiropractic Assn. Democrat. Office: 231 W 21st St Apt B New York NY 10011-3116

EAGAN, SHERMAN G., producer, communications executive; b. Peoria, Ill., Feb. 12, 1942; s. Joseph K. and Gracia (Sherman) E.; m. Paige Mannelly, Aug. 13, 1966; children: S. Joseph, Shannon Colleen. BA, U. N.Mex., 1967; postgrad., Northwestern U., 1967-68. Mgr. sales adminstrn. NBC-TV, Chgo., 1967-68; copywriter, producer D'Arcy Advt., St. Louis, 1968-69, Ad Com div. Quaker Oats, Chgo., 1969-71; writer CBS TV, Chgo., 1971-75; producer CBS News, N.Y.C., 1975-79; producer, dir. CBS Sports, N.Y.C.,

1979-84; pres. Conn. Yankee Internat., Darien, 1984—; cons. Tokyo Broadcasting Co., 1976-84. Producer, dir. U.S. Open Tennis, 1980-90, Daytona: Drama, Danger, Dedication, 1991; producer, dir. Daytona 500, 1992, producer, 1994; dir., writer Battle of the NASCAR Legends, CBS, 1991; dir. Internat. Emmy Presentation, 1989, supervising producer The Winners, 1991; exec. producer IBM TV, 1993, 94; producer NFL Sunday, Fox Sports, 1995-98; editor: Aerodynamic Trading, 1995. Recipient Emmy award NATAS, 1984, 86, Telly award, 1995, 96, 97, 98, Exec. Prodr. and Dir. Entrepreneur of Yr. awards CNBC, 1996, 97, field producer Fox Superbowl Sunday, 1997; 1st Classic Telly award for Best Bus. Video of Last 20 Yrs. Mem. Dirs. Guild Am. Office: Conn Yankee Internat Inc 9 Mott Ave Ste 107 Norwalk CT 06850-3359

EAGLES, HOWARD ALAN, agronomist; b. Sydney, N.S.W., Australia, Sept. 11, 1946; s. John Henry Alan and Gladys May (Rowling) E.; m. Deborah Anne Allen, Jan. 4, 1975; children: Peter Samuel, Ruth Allison, Miriam Irene. BSc in Agr., U. Sydney, 1968; PhD, Iowa State U., 1975. Rsch. agronomist N.S.W. Dept. Agr., Narrabri, 1968-70; grad. rsch. asst. Iowa State U., Ames, 1970-75; scientist Dept. Sci. and Indsl. Rsch., Palmerston North, New Zealand, 1975-89; prin. geneticist Dept. Agr., Horsham, Victoria, Australia, 1989-94, prin. scientist, 1994—; vis. fellow CIMMYT, El Batan, Mex., 1988; program leader tech. transfer CRC for Molecular Plant Breeding, 1997—. Editor: (monograph) Maize: Management to Market, 1985, (proceedings) Proceedings Agronomy Society of New Zealand, 1986-87, Application of New Technologies to Barley Improvement, 1991; contbr. over 50 articles to profl. jours. Pres. West End Sch. PTA, Palmerston North, 1986-87. Recipient C.P. Wilsie award Iowa State U., 1974. Achievements include demonstration that soybeans could be a viable commercial crop in northern New South Wales; devel. of procedures to study the genetics of growth of seedlings under low temperature conditions; demonstration that highland Mexican maize could improve maize for cool, temperate environments; devel. of inbred lines of maize from predominantly highland Mexican germ plasm. Home: 32 Tucker St, Horsham VIC 3400, Australia Office: Victorian Inst Dryland Agr, Pvt Bag 260, Horsham VIC 3401, Australia

EAGLETON, TERENCE (FRANCIS), English literature educator; b. Feb. 22, 1943; s. Francis Paul and Rosaleen (Riley) E. MA, Trinity Coll., Cambridge, PhD; DLitt (hon.), Salford, 1993, Nat. U. Ireland, 1996, Santiago di Compostela, 1999. Fellow in english Jesus Coll., Cambridge, 1964-69, Oxford U.; tutorial fellow Wadham Coll., 1969-89, lectr. in critical theory, 1989-92; fellow linacre Coll., 1989-92; Thomas Warton prof. English and lit., fellow St. Catherine's Coll. U. Oxford, 1992—. Author: Criticism and Ideology, 1976, Marxism and Literary Criticism, 1976, Literary Theory: An Introduction, 1983, The Function of Criticism, 1984, The Ideology of Aesthetic, 1990, Ideology: An Introduction, 1993, Heathcliff and the Great Hunger, 1995, The Illusions of Postmodernism, 1997, The Idea of Culture, 2000. Avocation: Irish music. Office: St Catherine's Coll, Oxford 0X1 3UJ, England

EAKER, DAVID LESLIE, biochemist, educator; b. Little Falls, N.Y., July 17, 1935; arrived in Sweden, 1962; s. Leslie Snell and Dorothy Mae (Tripp) E.; m. Birgit Katrin Agmalm, Apr. 17, 1965; children: Ingrid Molly, Sonja Teresa, Erik David. AB, Hamilton Coll., Clinton, N.Y., 1957; PhD, Rockefeller U., 1962. NIH postdoctoral fellow Uppsala (Sweden) U., 1962-64, Swedish Natural Sci. Rsch. fellow, 1965-72, docent in biochemistry, 1973—; chmn. dept. of biochemistry Uppsala (Sweden) U., 1984-98. Editor Symposium Proc. Natural Toxins, 1980; contbr. over 70 articles to profl. jours. Mem. N.Y. Acad. Scis., Sigma Xi, Phi Beta Kappa. Avocations: hiking in the mountains, gardening, building, cooking. Home: Långvägen 17, S-756 52 Uppsala Sweden Office: Uppsala Univ, Dept Biochemistry Box 576, S-751 23 Uppsala Sweden

EAKS, DUANE LEE, counseling psychologist; b. Montrose, Colo., Mar. 6, 1940; arrived in Australia, 1972; s. Ivan Wesley and Francis Helen (Willis) E. BA, No. Colo. U., 1963; MA, San Diego State U., 1967; EdD, U. Calif., Berkeley, 1972. Cert. counseling psychologist. Tchr. in high schs., Padroni, Colo., 1963-66; tchr., counselor Juvenile Hall, Riverside, Calif., 1967-68; univ. lectr. State Coll. of Victoria, Australia, 1972-75; sr. counseling psychologist Royal Melbourne Inst. Tech. U., Melbourne, Australia, 1975-96, head dept. counseling, 1996—; psychol. cons. Victorian Edn. Dept., 1980-90, Victorian AIDS Coun., 1986—; freelance photographer. Author 5 tng. manuals; contbr. articles to profl. jours. Ch. elder New Wave Christian Fellowship, Melbourne, 1986—; vol. trainer Victorian AIDS Coun., Australia, 1986—. No. Colo. U. scholar, 1959-63, San Diego State U. Nat. scholar, 1966-67. Fellow Fedn. Australian Astrologers (sec. 1982-86, v.p. 1996—); mem. Australian Psychol. Soc., Ivanhoe Photog. Soc. (v.p. 1996-97, pres. 1997—, Slide and Print Photographer of Yr. 1995, 98, 99). Avocations: art, public speaking, travel, physical fitness. E-mail: duane@conect.com. Home: PO Box 331, Heidelberg Victoria 3084, Australia

EAMES, ROBERT HENRY ALEXANDER, archbishop, primate; b. Belfast, Northern Ireland, Apr. 27, 1937; s. William Edward and Mary Eleanor (Alexander) E.; m. Ann Christine Daly, June 25, 1966; children: Niall William Adrian, Michael Harvey Alexander. LLB with honors, Queen's U., Belfast, 1960, PhD in Law, 1963, LLD (hon.), 1989. Ordained priest Ch. of Ireland, 1964. Priest Ch. of Ireland, 1964-75, bishop of Derry and Raphoe, 1975-80, bishop of Down and Dromore, 1980-86, archbishop of Armagh, primate of all Ireland, met., 1986—; chmn. priorities com. Ch. Ireland, 1977-79; select preacher U. Oxford, 1987; Irish rep. to Anglican Consultative Coun. and Standing Com.; chmn. commn. on communion and women in the episcopate Archbishop of Canterbury, 1988-90; select preacher U. Cambridge, 1988. Author: Form of Worship for Teenage Groups, 1965, The Quiet Revolution: The Disestablishment of the Church of Ireland, 1970, Through Suffering, 1973, Thinking Trough Lent, 1978, Chains to be Broken, 1990; contbr. articles to Irish Legal Quar., Northern Ireland Legal Quar., other jours. Chmn. bd. govs. Royal Sch., Armagh. Created life peer of Gt. Britain, 1995. Hon. fellow Guild Ch. Musicians. Office: The See House, Cathedral Close, Armagh BT61 7EE, Northern Ireland also: Church House, Abbey St, Armagh Northern Ireland

EARLAM, RICHARD JOHN, surgeon, consultant; b. Liverpool, Eng., Mar. 26, 1934; s. Francis and Elsie Noeline (Skippers) E.; m. Roswitha Teuber, Sept. 6, 1969; children: Melissa, Caroline. MB BChir, U. Cambridge, Eng., 1958, MA, 1963, MChir, 1970. House surgeon Royal Infirmary, Liverpool, 1958; surg. registrar Royal No. Hosp., 1964; rsch. asst. Mayo Clinic, Rochester, Minn., 1966-67; surg. asst. Univ. Klinik, München, Germany, 1968; sr. lectr. London Hosp., 1970-72; cons. gen. surgeon Royal London Hosp., 1972-98; chmn. N.E. Thames Regional Adv. Com. Gen. Surgery, 1986-91; chmn. Med. Rsch. Coun. Oesophageal Cancer, London, 1985-89; chmn., sec. Helicopter com., 1988-93; chmn. N.E. Met. Surg. Soc., London, 1986-91. Author: Clinical Tests of Oesophageal Function, 1976; editor: ABC of Major Trauma, 1991, 3rd edit., 2000, The Royal London Hospital/Daily Express Helicopter Emergency Medical Service, 1992, 2d edit., 1996; inventor in field. Capt. Royal Army M.C., 1960-62. Fulbright scholar, 1966; Alexander von Humboldt stipendiat, 1968. Fellow Royal Coll. Surgeons, Royal Soc. Medicine; mem. Collegium Internat. Chir. Digestivae, Soc. Polish Surgeons. Avocations: tennis, woodworking, beekeeping, mountains.

EARLE, PATRICIA NELSON, artist; b. West Point, N.Y., Dec. 18, 1942; d. Wilton Haynsworth and Patricia Ann (Nelson) Earle; m. James Edward Lipscomb III, 1970 (div. 1998); 1 child, Drayton Earle; stepchildren: James E. Lipscomb IV, Claude Benjamin Lipscomb. AA, Mt. Vernon Coll., 1963; BS, Furman U., 1986. Exhibited in solo shows at Furman U., Greenville, S.C., 1993, Barnes and Noble, Greenville, 1997, Cafo Ristretto, Greenville, 1997; group exhbns. include Taos (N.Mex.) Art Assocs., 1994, Carolina/Ga. Blood Ctr., Greenville, 1998, Art in the Park, Greenville, 1996, 97, others; represented in pub. collections including Liberty Life Corp., N.Y.C., Carolina First Bank, Greenville, Summit Nat. Bank, Greenville, Erskine (S.C.) Coll., numerous pvt. collections. Mem. Upstate Visual Arts, Jr. League of Greenville. Democrat. Episcopalian. Avocation: travel. E-mail: TEarleArt@aol.com. Home: 622 Mcdaniel Ave Greenville SC 29605-2830

EARLE, PAUL W., financial executive, consultant; b. Englewood, N.J., Feb. 1, 1940; s. David P. Jr. and Elizabeth T. (Ingraham) E.; m. Mary Evelyn Maxon, Aug. 8, 1968 (div. June 1990); children: Paul Jr., Charles Cottrell, Sarah Pettit, Noah Pettit; m. Ellen A. Rudnick, June 14, 1992. BA, Princeton U., 1961; MBA, U. Chgo., 1966. Fin. analyst Zenith Radio Corp., Chgo., 1966-68; assoc. dir. Am. Hosp. Assn., Chgo., 1968-79; exec. dir. The Vol. Effort, Chgo., 1979-82; chief fin. officer New Eng. Deaconess Hosp., Boston, 1982-88; sr. dir. Spencer Stuart, Chgo., 1988—. Mem. Shoreacres, 1989—. Home: 1316 Woodland Ln Riverwoods IL 60015 Office: Spencer Stuart 401 N Michigan Ave Ste 3400 Chicago IL 60611-4244

EARLE, VICTOR MONTAGNE, III, lawyer; b. N.Y.C., June 13, 1933; s. Victor Montagne and Marian Jeanette (Litonius) E.; m. Lois MacKennan, Dec. 28, 1955 (div. Jan. 1980); children: Jane Stewart, Susan Elizabeth, Anne McCallum; m. Karen Peterson Howard, Aug. 24, 1985. AB, Williams Coll., 1954; LLB, Columbia U., 1959. Bar: N.Y. 1960, U.S. Supreme Ct. 1963. Law clk. to Hon. Leonard Moore, U.S. Ct. Appeals (2nd cir.), 1959-60; assoc. Cravath, Swaine & Moore, N.Y.C., 1960-68; gen. counsel KPMG, N.Y.C., 1968-86, Peat, Marwick Internat., 1978-86; ptnr. Cahill, Gordon & Reindel, N.Y.C., 1986-89; sr. v.p., gen. counsel Minet, N.Y.C., 1989-93; gen. counsel KWELM Cos. and KWELM Holdings Ltd., N.Y.C., London, 1993-98, sr. counsel, 1998-2000; of counsel O'Melveny & Myers, N.Y.C., 2000—; lectr. constl. and corp. law issues, U.S. and abroad. Contbr. articles to profl. jours. and popular mags. With U.S. Army, 1954-56. Recipient Constitutional Law prize Columbia U. Mem. ABA, N.Y. State Bar Assn., Assn. of Bar of City of N.Y. (judiciary com. 1983-86), Am. Law Inst., Lawyers Com. Civil Rights under Law (trustee), Legal Aid Soc. (bd. dirs. 1980-86), Fund for Modern Cts. (bd. dirs.), Columbia U. Alumni Assn. (bd. dirs. 1982-87). Office: O'Melveny & Myers 153 E 53d St New York NY 10022-4611

EARLY, ALEXANDER RIEMAN, III, judge; b. Phila., Sept. 22, 1917; s. A.R. Jr. and Elizabeth Frances (Dence) E.; m. Mary Celeste Worland, Aug. 15, 1959; children: A.R. IV, Lucia C. Stroh, Elizabeth V., John Drennan V. BA, Cornell U., 1938; LLB, Harvard U., 1941. Bar: Calif. 1946. Pvt. law practice L.A., 1946-50; sr. atty. Divsn. of Hwys., State of Calif., 1950-55; asst. U.S. atty. Lands divsn. U.S. Dept. Justice, L.A., 1955-57; asst. county counsel Los Angeles County, Calif., 1957-72; judge Superior Ct., L.A., 1972-87; judge to Chief Justice Supreme Ct. U.S. Ct. Appeals (2nd appellate dist.) divsn. 7, 1985; ret., 1987; judge by assignment, 1987—; ret., 1987; judge to Chief Justice Supreme Ct. U.S. Ct. Appeals (4th appellate dist.) divsn. 2, 1988; adj. prof. Southwestern Law Sch., L.A., 1970-79. Contbr. articles to profl. jours. Mgr. internat. fedn. rels. boxing venue 1984 Olympics. Comdr. USNR, 1941-46. Served U.S. Navy in Destroyers, Pacific (earned nine battle stars); dir. sinking I.J.N. sub. RO-38, 1943. Decorated comdr. Order Polonia Restituta (Poland); knight grand cross Order of Holy Sepulchre (Vatican), Law Enforcement medal SAR, 1981. Mem. Am. Bd. Trial Advs., Nat. Conf. State Tax Judges, Calif. Soc. Sons of Revolution (pres., Disting. Svc. award), Soc. War of 1812 (vice pres. gen., Disting. Svc. award), Soc. Cincinnati, Md. Hist. Soc., U.S. Naval Inst., Aztec Club, Navy League, Rules Com. (chmn.), BAJI Com. Roman Catholic. Avocations: American history, genealogy, camellia seedlings. Home: 3017 Kirkham Dr Glendale CA 91206-1127

EARLY, AMES S., healthcare system executive; b. Allison, Iowa, Apr. 18, 1937; s. W.C. and F. Eva Early; m. Beryl J. Early; 1 child, Barbara. BA, Drake U., 1959; MHA, U. Iowa, 1961. Adminstrv. resident, adminstrv. asst. U. Minn. Hosp., Mpls., 1961-67; exec. dir. Mary Francis Skiff Meml. Hosp., Newton, Iowa, 1967-68; asst. adminstr. Mercy Hosp., Miami, Fla., 1968-76; pres. Scripps Meml. Hosp., La Jolla, Calif., 1976-91; exec. v.p., COO Scripps Instns. Medicine and Sci., ScrippsHealth, 1991-93; pres., CEO Scripps Health, San Diego, 1994-98, vice chmn., CEO, 1999, bd. dirs., 1999—. Pres. So. Fla. Hosp. Assn., 1974-75, bd. dirs., 1971-76; bd. dirs. Fla. Hosp. Assn., 1974-76, Comprehensive Health Planning of So. Fla., 1974-76, Nat. Coun. Cmty. Hosp., 1974—, Hosp. Coun. San Diego and Imperial Counties, 1978-86, Calif. Polit. Action Com., 1979-85, Calif. Health Decisions, 1994—, Catholic Healthcare West (bd. mem. 1996-99), San Diego Econ. Devel. (bd. mem. 1998-99), Blue Cross/Hosp. Adv. Com., 1982, Vol. Hosp. Am. West, 1986-91, San Diego Hospice (bd. mem. 1997—); mem. peer rev. panel Fla. Blue Cross Assn., 1975-76; trustee Calif. Assn. Hosp. and Health Sys., 1984-92, mem. exec. com., 1984-90, mem. legis. com., 1985, mem. hosp. med. staff bylaws com., 1985-86, treas., 1987, chmn., 1989; mem. Healthcare Forum. Recipient Headline of Yr. in Healthcare San Diego Press Club, 1987. Mem. Am. Coll. Healthcare Execs., Am. Hosp. Assn., Am. Assn. Hosp. Planning. Office: Scripps Health 4275 Campus Point Ct San Diego CA 92121-1513

EARLY, BERT HYLTON, lawyer; b. Kimball, W.Va., July 17, 1922; s. Robert Terry and Sue Keister (Hylton) E.; m. Elizabeth Henry, June 24, 1950; children—Bert Hylton, Robert Christian, Mark Randolph, Philip Henry, Peter St. Clair. Student, Marshall U., 1940-42; A.B., Duke U., 1946; J.D., Harvard U., 1949. Bar: W.Va. 1949, Ill. 1963, Fla. 1981. Assoc. Fitzpatrick, Marshall, Huddleston & Bolen, Huntington, W.Va., 1949-57; asst. counsel Island Creek Coal Co., Huntington, W.Va., 1957-60, assoc. gen. counsel, 1960-62; dep. exec. dir. ABA, Chgo., 1962-64, exec. dir., 1964-81; sr. v.p. Wells Internat., Chgo., 1981-83, pres., 1983-85; pres. Bert H. Early Assocs. Inc., Chgo., 1985-94, Early Cochran & Olson, Chgo., 1994-98; of counsel Early Cochran & Olson, 1999—; dir. Am. Bar Found., Chgo., 1993-95; instr. Marshall U., Huntington, W.Va., 1950-53; legal search cons. and lectr. in field. Bd. dirs. Morris Meml. Hosp. for Crippled Children, 1954-60, Huntington Pub. Libr., 1951-60, W.Va. Tax Inst., 1961-62, Huntington Mus. Art, 1961-62; mem. W.Va. Jud. Coun., 1960-62, Huntington City Coun., 1961-62; bd. dirs. Cmty. Renewal Soc., Chgo., 1965-76, United Charities Chgo., 1972-80, Hinsdale (Ill.) Hosp. Found., 1987-93, Internat. Bar Assn. Found., 1987-89; bd. dirs. Am. Bar Endowment, 1983-95, sec., 1987-89, treas., 1989-91, v.p., 1991-93, pres., 1993-95, dir. emeritus, 1995-2000; mem. vis. com. U. Chgo. Law Sch., 1975-78; trustee Davis and Elkins Coll., 1960-63; mem. Hinsdale Plan Commn., 1982-85. 1st Lt. AC, U.S. Army, 1943-45. Fellow Am. Bar Found., Ill. Bar Found. (charter); mem. ABA (ho. of dels. 1958-59, 84-93, chmn. young lawyers divsn. 1957-58, Disting. Svc. award young lawyers divsn. 1983), Am. Law Inst. (life), Internat. Bar Assn. (asst. sec. gen. 1967-82), Nat. Legal Aid and Defender Assn., Legal Aid Soc. Chgo., Am. Judicature Soc. (bd. dirs. 1981-84), Fla. Bar, W.Va. Bar Assn., Chgo. Bar Assn. Presbyterian. Office: Early Cochran & Olson Inc 401 N Michigan Ave Ste 515 Chicago IL 60611-4280

EARLY, JAMES H., JR., lawyer; b. Henderson, N.C., May 6, 1939; s. James Howard and Nettie Anna (Hicks) E.; children from previous marriage: James H. III, Anna Elizabeth, Mary Elizabeth. AA, Mars Hill Coll., 1960; BA, Wake Forest U., 1962, LLB, 1964, JD, 1970. Bar: N.C. 1964, U.S. Dist. Ct. (mid. dist.) N.C. 1970, U.S. Ct. Appeals (4th cir.) 1995; cert. mediator Superior Cts. of N.C., 1992. Pvt. practice Winston-Salem, 1964—; mediator Adminstrv. Office of the Cts. of N.C., 1992—; mediator Am. Arbitration Assn., 1992—. Contbr. articles to profl. jours. With U.S. Army, 1957. Chmn. fundraising Cub Scouts/Boy Scouts Am., Little League, Pop Warner, Indian Guides, March of Dimes, others. With U.S. Army. Mem. ABA, ATLA, N.C. Bar Assn. (chmn. continuing legal edn. subcom., mem. effectiveness and quality of life com., moderator skills course com.), , Forsyth County Bar Assn. (sec. 1970-71), N.C. Acad. Trial Lawyers, Phi Alpha Delta (alumni advisor 1969-84, Outstanding Alumnus award 1967), Kiwanis (pres. 1989-90, 91-92), Masons. Baptist. Avocations: hunting, fishing, walking horses, bird dogs, racing. Home: 144 Sterling Pt Ct Winston Salem NC 27104 Office: 1320 Westgate Center Dr Winston Salem NC 27103-2933

EARLY, PIANAPUE KEPT, pastor, writer; b. Monrovia, Liberia, Nov. 9, 1959; came to U.S., 1990; s. Joseph Cephas and Annie (Logan) E.; m. Michele Jacques Early, July 6, 1996; children: Darboanee, Troehndeh, Kawadah. MDiv, Interdenom. Theol. Ctr., Atlanta, 1993, D of Ministry, 1999; ThM, Emory U., 1996. Editor Info. Ministry, Monrovia, 1985-90; instr. Liberian Govt., Monrovia, 1986-90; pastor United Meth. Ch., Sawyerville, Ala., 1999—, St. Matthew United Meth. Ch., Akron, Ala., 1999—, Jackson Chapel United Meth. Ch., Sawyerville, 1999—. Vol. fire fighter Akron Fire Dept., 1999. Mem. Liberian Cmty. Ga. (com. chair 1993-95, youth coord. 1995-99), Coalition Concerned Africans (youth coord. 1997-99). Avocations: soccer, jogging, reading, writing. E-mail: keptpe@bellsouth.net. Home: PO Box 7 Sawyerville AL 36776-0007 Office: Jackson Chapel 68 Jackson Rd Sawyerville AL 36776-5040

EARLY, WILLIAM TRACY, journalist; b. Scurry County, Tex., Feb. 20, 1934; s. Willis Worley Jr. and Lillian Marian (Walton) E. BA, Baylor U., 1954; BDiv, Southeastern Bapt. Sem., 1958; ThD, Union Theol. Sem., 1963. Ordained minister So. Bapt. Conv, 1957. Pastor Urbanna (Va.) Bapt. Ch., 1964-68; editl. asst. World Coun. Chs., N.Y.C., 1968-69; freelance journalist N.Y.C., 1969—. Author: Simply Sharing, 1980. 1st lt., chaplain U.S. Army, 1957-59. Democrat. Home: 102 W 80th St Apt 31 New York NY 10024-6304

EARWOOD, BARBARA TIRRELL, artist; b. Quincy, Mass., July 18, 1920; d. Irving John and Vernice Estelle (Carraway) Tirrell; m. Armer Fred Earwood, May 30, 1942; children: Elsie E. Belk, Melinda Earwood Crain, Edward A. Student, Angelo State U., 1968-69; grad., Washington Sch. Art, 1974, North Light Art Sch., 1989; postgrad., Robert E. Wood Sch., 1978-80. 4th v.p. San Angelo (Tex.) Art Club, 1973-74; pres. Big Country Art Assn., Abilene, Tex.; pres. Region XVII Tex. Fine Arts Assn.; bd. dirs. West Tex. Art Guild, Sonora, 1992-95; tchr. Barbara Earwood Art Sch., Sonora, 1970-93; rancher family ranch; sec., treas. Am. Plains Artist, 1999, 2000. Permanent exhbts. include First Nat. Bank Sonora, Sutton County Libr.; artist Girl Scouts Am. pamphlet. Leader Girl Scouts Am., Sonora, 1952-53. Recipient State citation Tex. Fine Arts Assn., 1971, 72, 43, 74, 75, 76, Purchase prize, 1975, Best of Show award San Angelo Stock Show, 1973. Mem. Tex. Watercolor Soc. (signature mem., Purple Sage, Russell Rogers Purchase award for transparent watercolor 1974), Southwestern Watercolor Soc. (signature), San Antonio Watercolor Group (signature), Am. Plains Artists (signature). Episcopalian. Avocations: music, swimming, walking, stamp collecting. Home: PO Box 525 Del Rio TX 78841-0525

EASON, MARCIA JEAN, lawyer; b. Dallas, Aug. 31, 1953; d. John Keller and Sara Marguerite (Prindle) McCarron; m. S. Lee Meredith, Sept. 12, 1981 (div. Oct. 1989); m. David O. Eason, Aug. 21, 1993; stepchildren: Chelsea, Shannon, Valerie. BA magna cum laude, Trinity U., 1975; JD, U. Houston, 1979. Bar: Tex. 1978, U.S. Dist. Ct. (so. dist.) Tex. 1978, U.S. Ct. Appeals (5th cir.) 1979, Tenn. 1985, U.S. Dist. Ct. (ea. dist.) Tenn. 1985, U.S. Supreme Ct. 1985, U.S. Ct. Appeals (6th cir.) 1986, U.S. Ct. Appeals (4th cir.) 1994. Ptnr. Byrnes & Martin, Houston, 1984-85, Miller & Martin, Chattanooga, 1987—. Pres., bd. dirs. Chattanooga's Kids on the Block, 1987-94; bd. dirs., chair AIM Ctr, Chattanooga, 1993—; campaign chair, attys. divsn. United Way, Chattanooga, 1994, leadership campaign chair, 1998. Mem. ABA, Tenn. Bar Assn. (bd. govs.), Chattanooga Bar Assn. (com. chair 1985-86), Tenn. Supreme Ct. Commn. (mem. racial and ethnic and gender fairness, mem. enhancing pub. trust in ct. sys.), Tenn. Lawyers Assn. for Women (co-chair com. 1994, treas. 1995-97, pres. 1998). Home: 33 Rock Crest Dr Signal Mountain TN 37377-2326 Office: Miller & Martin 832 Georgia Ave Ste 1000 Chattanooga TN 37402-2289

EAST, BRENDA KATHLEEN, writer; b. Dartford, Kent, Eng., June 18, 1937; came to U.S., 1955; d. Charles Ernest and Kathleen Edith (Wilkinson) E.; m. Ronald Grant Bierer, Mar. 12, 1955 (div. 1983); children: Grant Keith B., Carolyn Joy Bierer-Carlisle, Ronda Lynn Bierer-Atwell, Heber Jay B., Janet Ray B., David East B. Student, Gravesend (Kent) Coll. Art, 1951-52; grad., Inst. Children's Lit., Conn., 1992. Contbr. articles to profl. jours. and mags. Home: 1423 Us Highway 93 N Victor MT 59875-9770

EAST, PATRICIA L., psychologist; b. Washington, Nov. 18, 1958; d. William J. and Joyce E. East; m. William r. Ganelin, Aug. 31, 1985; children: Kevin J., Steven S. BS, U. Denver, 1980; PhD, Pa. State U., 1986; postdoctoral work, U. Calif., Irvine, 1989. Asst. prof. U. Calif. San Diego Sch. of Medicine, 1990-95, assoc. rsch. scientist, 1996—; grant reviewer NSF, 1995-96, Dept. HHS, 1996-97, NIH, 1997-2001. Co-author: (book) Adolescent Pregnancy and Parenting, 1996; contbg. author: The Study of Temperament: Changes, Continuities, and Challenges, 1986, Biological-Psychosocial Interactions in Early Adolescence: A Life-Span Perspective, 1987, Promoting Human Wellness: Frontiers for Research, Policy, and Practice, 2000, others; contbr. articles to profl. jours.; mem. editl. bd. Internat. Jour. of Behavioral Devel., 1991-97, Devel. Psychology, 1994-97, Jour. of Rsch. on Adolescence, 1995—. Recipient Nat. Rsch. Svc. award NIH, 1987, First Ind. Rsch. Support and Transition award, 1992, Disting. Lectr. award Calif. Wellness Found., 1996; grantee NIH, 1987, 90, 92, HHS, 1989, 90, 97, 98, others. Mem. Internat. Soc. Behavioral Devel., Soc. for Rsch. in Child Devel., Soc. for Behavioral Pediatrics, Soc. for Adolescent Medicine, Nat. Coun. for Family Rels.

EASTBURN, MARTIN HOWARD, engineer; b. Winston-Salem, N.C., Oct. 28, 1947; s. Lee Marvin and Lola Louise (Livermore) E.; m. Barbara Jean Bell, Sept. 2, 1965; 1 child, Sean. BS, Tex. A&M U., 1969, MS, 1972. Sr. adj. prof. electronics Tarrant County Jr. Coll., Ft. Worth, 1970-80; applications engr. Schlumberger, Austin, Tex., 1980-81; sr. applications engr. Schlumberger, Austin, 1981-82, product specialist, 1982-85; product devel. specialist Schlumberger, Simi Valley, Calif., 1985-87; technologist Schlumberger, San Jose, Calif., 1987-95; sr. scientist Schlumberger, San Jose, 1995-98; DRAM applications engring. mgr. Mitsubishi, Sunnyvale, Calif., 1999-2000; applications mgr. Internat. Microcircuits, Inc., Milpitas, Calif., 2000—. Mem. NRA (life, second amendment task force, Legion of Honor 1998), Order of De Molay (sr. De Molay, chaplin). Republican. Methodist. Achievements include patent for pattern generator with extended register programming. Avocations: home shop machinist, remote control airplanes, photography. E-mail: oldtree@pacbell.net. Home: 145 View Rd Felton CA 95018-9611 Office: Internat Microcircuits Inc 525 Los Coches St Milpitas CA 95035-5423

EASTHAM, JOHN DEREK, comprehensive school principal, consultant; b. Bolton, Eng., Apr. 30, 1931; s. John Edward and Lily (Haslam) E.; m. Ann Georgina Taylor, Mar. 31, 1956; children: Zillah, Sara. Cert. edn., London U., 1953. Tchr. Royal Air Force Edn. Dept., E. Anglia, U.K., 1950-51; asst. tchr. Newmarket Secondary Sch., Suffolk, Eng., 1953-56, tchr., head sci. dept., 1956-72; founding head tchr. Scaltback Middle Sch., Newmarket, Eng., 1972-90; ret., 1990; part-time schs. industry liaison officer Suffolk C.C., Bury St. Edmunds, 1990-91, lectr. Newmarket Evening Inst., 1953-57; proprietor Edn. Cons., Suffolk, 1991-95. Councillor Mildenhall (Eng.) Parish Coun., 1961-74, chmn., 1972-74, trustee Parish Coun. Charities, 1969—; chmn. West Row (Eng.) Playing Field & Village Hall Assn., 1960-67. With Edn. Br. RAF, Nat. Svc. Conscription only, 1950-51. Mem. Soc. Edn. Consultants, U.K. Register Expert Witnesses. Mem. Church of England. Avocations: gardening, golf. Home: Scrogg's Cott Pamment's Ln, West Row, Mildenhall, Bury Saint Edmunds IP28 8NN, England

EASTHOPE, GARY, sociology educator; b. Liverpool, Eng., May 29, 1945; arrived in Australia, 1980; s. Charles Thomas and Helen (Hornby) E.; m. Christine Adams, Mar. 25, 1967; children: Michael, Hazel. BA, Leeds. U., 1966, MA, 1967; PhD, Exeter U., 1972. Tchr. secondary sch. Essex, England, 1967-68; rsch. officer Exeter U., Devon, England, 1968-71; lectr. edn. New Univ. Ulter, Coleraine, No. Ireland, 1971-73; lectr. sociology U. E. Anglia, Norwich, England, 1973-80; lectr. sociology U. Tasmania, Hobart, Australia, 1980-81, sr. lectr. sociology, 1981-92, assoc. prof., 1993—. Author: History of Social Research Methods, 1974, Community Hierarchy and Open Education, 1975, Healers and Alternative Medicine, 1986; co-author: The Practice of Teaching, 1986, 90; contbr. articles to profl. jours. Office: U Tasmania, Sandy Bay, Hobart Tasmania 7001, Australia

EASTLAND, S. STACY, lawyer; b. Houston, Oct. 27, 1948; s. Seaborn and Anne (Stacy) E.; m. Tara Gardner, Mar. 24, 1972; children: Tara Doran, Seaborn Gardner. BS, Washington & Lee U, 1971; JD, U. Tex., 1974. Assoc. Baker & Botts, Houston, 1974-81, ptnr., 1982—; bd. dirs. Houston Estate and Fin. Forum, Camp Mystic, Inc.; mem. Tex. Bd. Legal Specialization in Estate Planning and Probate Law. Bd. dirs. Oscar Neuhaus Found., St. John Meml. Endowment Fund, Houston chpt. Ortin Soc., DePelchin Children's Ctr., Inst. Child and Family Svcs.; trustee Kelsey-Seabold Found. Fellow Am. Coll. Probate Counsel; mem. ABA (com. 1990—, publs. coord. probate and trust divsn. 1992-93, bylaws and handbook com. 1992—, sec. adv. Revision Uniform Partnership Act 1987—, publs. com. 1992-93, budget and fin. com. 1991-92, chair divsn. coord. ann. meeting programs 1987-89), Am. Coll. Trust and Estate Counsel (bd. regents, chmn. transfer tax study com. 1988-93), Tex. State Bar Assn., Houston Bar Assn., Houston Country Club, Tex. Allegro Club. Episcopalian. Avocations: tennis, golf. Home: 3730 Piping Rock Ln Houston TX 77027-4032*

EASTMAN, DONNA KELLY, composer, music educator; b. Denver, Sept. 26, 1945; d. Donald Lewis and Frances Marie (Smith) Kelly; m. John Bernard Eastman, July 1, 1973; children: Jonathan Kelly, James Alan; stepchildren: Barbara Kathleen, Sally Toye. B Music Edn., U. Colo., 1967; MA, U. Md., 1973, D in Mus. Arts, 1992. Pvt. studio tchr., coach, 1960—; choral dir. Dept. Def. Overseas Schs., Okinawa, Japan, 1970-72; dir. Choraleers Choral Ensemble, Stuttgart, Germany, 1974-76, Bangkok (Thailand) Music Soc. Ensemble and Madrigal Singers, 1982-84; instr. in music No. Va. C.C., Alexandria, 1986-89; creator, pianist, vocalist Am. Music Programs for U.S. Mission, Thailand, 1981-84; vis. asst. prof. Ill. Wesleyan U., Bloomington, 1994; vis. composer Sweet Briar (Va.) Coll., 1998, Grinnell (Iowa) Coll., 1999. Composer choral, orchestral, opera, vocal/instrumental solo and chamber, and electronic works; recs. include Captsone Records-Soc. of Composers, Inc. Series CPS 8632, 1996, and New Music for Flute and Piano, CPS 8664, 1999; Living Artist Recs.-Music from the Setting Century Series, Vol. 2, 1996; New Ariel Recordings-Contemporary American Eclectic Music for the Piano Series, AE002, 1996; Columbine Chorale Recs.--European Tour, 1999; contbr. to jours. Fellow Charles Ives Ctr. for Am. Music, 1990, 93, Ragdale Found., 1991, Va. Ctr. for Creative Arts, 1991-99; recipient 6 Internat. Composition awards Composers' Guild, 1991—, Internat. Piano Composition award Roodeport Internat. Eisteddfod, South Africa, 1991, Glad-Robinson-Youse Composition award Nat. Fedn. Music Clubs, 1992, Internat. Choral Composition award Florilège Vocal de Tours, France, 1995, Keyboard award Delius Composition Competition, 1997, Margaret Fairbank Jory Copying Assistance award Am. Music Ctr., 1999, Nat. Music Composition Competition award Nat. League of Am. Pen Women, 2000. Mem. Soc. for Electro-Acoustic Music in the U.S., Internat. Alliance for Women in Music, Soc. of Composers, Inc. (life), Nat. Mus. Women in Arts (charter), Broadcast Music, Inc., Am. Composers Forum, Southeastern Composer's League, Friday Morning Music Club Washington, Phi Kappa Phi, Pi Kappa Lambda, Sigma Alpha Iota. Avocations: travel, handicrafts, photography. Home: 6812 Dina Leigh Ct Springfield VA 22153-1019

EASTMAN, FRANCESCA MARLENE, volunteer, art historian; b. Jamaica Plain, Mass., Jan. 26, 1952; d. Therald Carlton and Martha Jane (Welch) E.; m. Edward Charles Goodstein, Aug. 27, 1989. AB in Art History, Manhattanville Coll., 1972; MA in Art History, Clark Art Inst./Williams Coll., 1974; postgrad., Stanford U., 1976-80. Intern Mus. of Fine Arts, Boston, summers 1971-73; lectr. in art Regis Coll., Weston, Mass., 1974-76; sr. house assoc. Stanford (Calif.) U., 1977-80, tchg. fellow, 1978-79; student svcs. intern Menlo Coll., Atherton, Calif., 1980-81; now freelance editor. Bd. sec. Trinity Episcopal Sch., Menlo Park, Calif., 1992-96, bd. chair, 1996-98; adv. bd., chair Trinity Sch., 1998—; trustee David B. and Edward C. Goodstein Found., L.A., 1995—; vol. scholarship com. Peninsula Cmty. Found., San Mateo, Calif., 1995—; grad. Leadership Redwood City, Calif., 1995—; arts commr., chair Town of Atherton, Calif., 1996-2000, 75th ann. com. leadership coun., 1998, chair, 1999—; mem. steering com., chair edn. com., founding trustee Episcopal Sch. of the Peninsula, Foster City, Calif., 1996—. Mem. Cornell Club (N.Y.C.), Williams Club (N.Y.C.), Pacific Athletic Club. Democrat. Roman Catholic. Avocations: herb gardening, piano.

EASTMAN, JOHN ROBERT, educator; b. San Diego, June 30, 1945; s. John Henry and Theresa (Wimberger) E. BA, Va. Poly. Inst. and State U., 1968; PhD, Julius-Maximilians U., Wuerzburg, 1985. Cert. tchr., Va. Tchr. So. H.S., Harwood, Md., 1968-69; instr. for English Dolmetscher Inst., Wuerzburg, 1976-83; bilingual tourist guide Arbeitsamt, Wuerzburg, 1976-85; summer sch. tchr. Archbishop Spalding H.S., Severn, Md., 1992; substitute tchr. Ft. Meade High Sch., 1990, Old Mill H.S., 1992, Anne Arundel Co., Md., 1987-97; tchr. Peninsula Cath. H.S., Newport News, Va., 1997—. Author: Papal Abdication in Later Medieval Thought, 1990; editor: Aegidius Romanus, De Renunciatione Pape, 1992; contbr. Internat. Medieval Bibliography, 1995—; contbr. articles to profl. jours. Mem. Am. Hist. Assn., Southeastern Medieval Assn., Nat. Coalition Ind. Scholars, Capital Area Ind. Scholars (sec.-treas. 1992-94, newsletter editor 1994-96), Am. Philol. Assn. Home: 11311 Winston Pl Apt 8 Newport News VA 23601-2238

EASTMAN, JOSEPH RILUS, III, pathologist; b. Indpls., Nov. 20, 1954; s. Joseph Rilus Jr. and Ann Shelton Eastman; m. Celia Kay Eastman. AB, Ind. U., 1979, MD, 1984. Diplomate Am. Bd. Pathology. Pathologist U. Rochester, N.Y., 1998—. Fellow Am. Soc. Clin. Pathologists, Coll. Am. Pathologists. Address: 111 Elmerston Rd Rochester NY 14620-4537

EASTMAN, W. DEAN, secondary school educator; b. Lawrence, Mass., Feb. 22, 1948; s. Weston D. and Harriett R. Eastman. BS in Social Sci. Edn., Drake U., 1970; MS in Edn., Springfield (Mass.) Coll., 1976, cert. advanced grad. adminstrn. studies, 1977; M in Liberal Arts, Harvard U., 2000. Coach track and field Springfield Coll. and U. Mass., Lowell, 1970-81; tchr. social sci. Beverly (Mass.) H.S., 1970—; vis. prof. edn. Drake U., 1994-95. Contbr. articles to publs. including Scholastic Coach, Track Technique, Jour. Phys. Edn. and Recreation, Harvard Newsletter: Civil Perspective, Local History Mag.; featured in (book) I Am a Teacher, 1990, (mags.) Tchg. Tolerance, Boston Mag.; featured for work with homeless students Today Show, NBC-TV, 1991; host 10-part series on immigration Mass. Ednl. TV, 1992. Mem. ednl. steering com. Mass. Civil Liberties Union, Boston, 1990—. Christa McAuliffe fellow Mass. Dept. Edn., 1989; recipient Outstanding Tchr. award John F. Kennedy Presdl. Libr., 1989, Am. Tchr. award Disney Channel, 1991, Alumni Achievement award Drake U., 1991; named one of Outstanding Young Men of Am., 1982. Mem. Nat. Assn. Scholars. Avocations: surf casting, poetry, Harvard football games. Office: Beverly HS 100 Sohier Rd Beverly MA 01915-5533

EASTMOND, RAWLE C., Barbadian government official; b. Oct. 23, 1923; married; 2 children. BA, U. West Indies, Diploma in Edn.; LLB, London U.; postgrad., LEC Hugh Wooding Law Sch., Trinidad and Tobago. Tchr. Coop. H.S., Coleridge and Parry Sch., St. Leonard's Boys', U. W. Indies, Cave Hill; atty.; former min. agriculture and rural devel. Govt. of Barbados, Christ Church, now min. environment, energy & natural resources. Office: Govt HQ Bay St, Saint Michael Barbados*

EASTOE, JOHN ERIC, chemist; b. London, Nov. 3, 1926; s. Eric Wilfred and Winifred Mabel (Trundle) E.; m. Beryl Musson, Apr. 14, 1951; children: Sally Ann, Richard John. BSc, Imperial Coll. Sci. and Tech., 1947, PhD, 1950; DSc, Royal Coll. Surgeons Eng., 1965, fell in dental surgery, 1985. Rsch. officer Brit. Gelatine and Glue Rsch. Assn., London, 1950-57; sr. rsch. fellow dept. dental sci. Royal Coll. Surgeons Eng., London, 1957-80; prof. oral biology U. Newcastle upon Tyne, Eng., 1980-90, emeritus prof., 1990—; external examiner U. Hong Kong, Kuala Lumpur, Singapore, 1984-92; trustee Oral and Dental Rsch. Trust, London, 1992—. Author: Practical Analytical Methods for Connective Tissue Proteins, 1963, Practical Chromatographic Techniques, 1964, Biochemistry and Oral Biology, 1977, 88, The Galactic Track: A Compass for the Universe; contbr. articles to profl. jours. Recipient Prix ORCA European Orgn. for Rsch. on Fluorine and Dental Caries Prevention, 1965. Mem. Biochem. Soc. (editl. advisor 1985-90), Internat. Assn. for Dental Rsch. (pres. Brit. divsn. 1988-90, Colgate Prize for Dental Rsch. 1960, Basic Rsch. in Biol. Mineralization award 1969), Assn. Basic Sci. Tchrs. in Dentistry (chmn. 1981-90), Newcastle Astron. Soc., Newcastle upon Tyne Soc. Antiquaries. Achievements include discovering amelogenins, 1960. Avocations: walking, travel, music, photography, astronomy. Home and Office: 15 Campus Martius, Heddon on the Wall, Newcastle on Tyne NE15 OBP, England

EASTWOOD, CLINT, actor, film director, former mayor; b. San Francisco, May 31, 1930; m. Dina Ruiz. Student, Oakland Tech. High Sch.; attended, Los Angeles City Coll. Worked as lumberjack in Oreg. before being drafted into the Army; formed Malpaso Prodns., 1969; chmn. AT&T/Pebble Beach Pro Am. Golf Tournament; owner, pres. Malpaso Records Co., Mission Ranch Resort, Carmel, Calif.; owner, co-ptnr. Prime Golf/Tenama Clothing Co., owner/pres. Malpaso Records Co., owner Mission Ranch Resort, Carmel, Calif., owner/co-partner Prime Gold/Tenama Clothing Co. Starred in TV series Rawhide, 1959-1966. Motion pictures include: (actor) Revenge of the Creature, 1955, Francis in the Navy, 1955, Lady Godiva, 1955, Tarantula, 1955, Never Say Goodbye, 1956, The First Travelling Saleslady, 1956, Star in the Dust, 1956, Away All Boats, 1956, Escapade in Japan, 1957, Ambush at the Cimmaron Pass, 1958, Lafayette Escadrille, 1958, A Fistful of Dollars, 1964, For a Few Dollars More, 1965, The Good The Bad and The Ugly, 1966, The Witches, 1967, Hang 'Em High, 1968, Coogan's Bluff, 1968, Where Eagles Dare, 1969, Paint Your Wagon, 1969, Two Mules for Sister Sara, 1970, Kelly's Heroes, 1970, The Beguiled, 1971, Dirty Harry, 1972, Joe Kidd, 1972, Magnum Force, 1973, Thunderbolt and Lightfoot, 1974, The Enforcer, 1976, Every Which Way But Loose, 1978, Escape from Alcatraz, 1979, Any Which Way You Can, 1980, City Heat, 1984, (dir. Amazing Stories TV) Vanessa in the Garden, 1985, Pink Cadillac, 1989, In the Line of Fire, 1993; (dir.) Breezy, 1973, (dir., actor) Play Misty For Me, 1971, High Plains Drifter, 1973, The Eiger Sanction, 1975, The Outlaw Josey Wales, 1976, The Gauntlet, 1977, Bronco Billy, 1980, The Rookie, 1990, A Perfect World, 1994, Absolute Power, 1996; (actor, prod.) Tightrope, 1984, The Dead Pool, 1988; (dir., prod.) Bird, 1988, Midnight in the Garden of Good and Evil, 1997; (dir., actor, producer) Firefox, 1982, Honky Tonk Man, 1982, Sudden Impact, 1983, Pale Rider, 1985, Heartbreak Ridge, 1986, White Hunter, Black Heart, 1990, Unforgiven, 1992 (Academy Award Best Director, Best Picture), The Bridges of Madison County, 1995, Absolute Power, 1997, True Crime, 1998, Space Cowboys (dir./actor/prodr.), 2000; (exec. producer) Thelonious Monk-Straight, No Chaser, 1989, The Stars Fell on Henrietta, 1995; (cameo) Casper; singer (Midnight soundtrack album) Ac.cent.uate the Positive, 1997, (with Randy Travis) Smokin' the Hive; documentaries include Don't Pave Main St., 1994, Eastwood After Hours: A Night of Jazz. Mem. Nat. Coun. Arts, 1973; chmn. (Monterey) AT&T/Pebble Beach Pro-Am Golf Tournament. Office: c/o Leonard Hirshan Wm Morris Agy Inc 151 S El Camino Dr Beverly Hills CA 90212-2704

EATON, AMOS JORGE, management consultant; b. Asuncion, Paraguay, Feb. 19, 1944; s. Robert James and Dorothy Iris Veronica (Kent) E.; m. Susan Yvonne Deslauriers, May 29, 1966 (div.); children: Amos Joseph, Catherine Veronica. BA in Econs., U. Vt., 1966. Sr. programmer Aetna Life & Casualty Co., Hartford, Conn., 1969-71; gen. prin. Bus. Start-Up & Turn-Around Svcs., Stoneham, Mass., 1970—; sr. analyst Royal Typewriter Co. divsn. Litton Industries, Hartford, 1971-72; project mgr. Zayre Corp., Framingham, Mass., 1972-73; pres. Eaton-Turner, Inc., North Reading, Mass., 1974-83; exec. v.p., CFO Kerlar Comm., Inc., 1991-97; founding mem., bd. mem., 1st pres. Essex Aggie Found., 1993-94; chmn. Web Design Profls., 1999—, ProjectQuotes.com Corp., 1999—. Chmn. Stoneham Rep. Town Com., 1988-90; chmn. CURE for the Commonwealth Com., 1990-95, Woburn Rep. City Com., 1994—; auditor, bd. dirs. Mass. Action Coalition, 1992-93; mem. Atty. Gen.'s task force to abate waste, fraud and abuse in the workman compensation sys., 1993-95, Gov.'s adv. com. info. tech., 1994-98; founder, chmn. Changing Tide Com., 1996—; elected Rep. state committeeman 4th Middlesex Senatorial Dist., 2000. Served to 1st lt. U.S. Army, 1966-68. Mem. NRA (endowment), Internat. Platform Assn., Mass. Chief Police Assn., Phi Delta Theta. Office: PO Box 80576 Stoneham MA 02180-0006

EATON, BERNARD, magazine publisher, editor; b. Blackpool, England, Apr. 2, 1926; s. Frederick and Emily (Delguera) E.; m. Vera Maud Abbott, Nov. 19, 1949; children: Nigel, Michael, David. Reporter Acton Gazette, London, 1942-43; reporter, feature writer Sunday Chronicle, London, 1943-44, 47-54; feature writer People Newspaper, London, 1954-58; pub. rels. officer Granada TV, London, 1958-62; founder., mng. dir. Publicity Projects, London, 1962-70; publisher, editor Diver Mag., London, 1963—; editor-in-chief Diver Mag., 1999—. Founder, chmn. Nat. Underwater Conservation Yr., 1977, Nat. Underwater Conservation Soc., 1979, Marine Conservation Soc., 1985. Mem. Br. Sub Aqua Club. Avocations: diving, cruising, photography, literature. Office: Eaton Publs, 55 High St Teddington, Middlesex England TW118HA

EATON, CHARLES EDWARD, English language educator, author; b. Winston-Salem, N.C., June 25, 1916; s. Oscar Benjamin and Mary Gaston (Hough) E.; m. Isabel Patterson, Aug. 16, 1950. Student, Duke U., 1932-33; A.B., U. N.C., 1936; postgrad., Princeton, 1936-37; M.A., Harvard, 1940; DLitt (hon.), St. Andrews Coll., N.C., 1998. Instr. English U. Mo., 1940-42; prof. creative writing U. N.C., 1946-51; Am. vice-consul Rio de Janeiro, Brazil, 1942-46; fellow Bread Loaf Writers Conf., 1941, Boulder Writers Conf., 1942. Author: (poems) The Bright Plain, 1942, The Shadow of the Swimmer, 1951, The Greenhouse in the Garden, 1956, Countermoves, 1963, On the Edge of the Knife, 1970, The Man in the Green Chair, 1977, Colophon of the Rover, 1980, The Thing King, 1983, The Work of the Wrench, 1985, New and Selected Poems, 1942-87, 1987, A Guest on Mild Evenings, 1991, The Country of the Blue, 1994, The Fox and I, 1996, The Scout in Summer, 1999, The Jogger by the Sea, 2000; (art criticisms) Karl Knaths: Five Decades of Painting, 1973, Robert Broderson: Paintings and Graphics, 1975; (short stories) Write Me From Rio, 1959, The Girl from Ipanema, 1972, The Case of the Missing Photographs, 1978, New and Selected Stories: 1959-89, 1989; (novel) A Lady of Pleasure, 1993; contbr. (anthologies) Best American Short Stories, 1952, American Literature: Readings and Critiques, 1961, Epoch Anthology, 1968, Best Poems of the Year, 1955-65, 68-70, 74-75, O. Henry Prize Stories, 1972, New Southern Poets, 1974, The Poet in Washington, 1977, Contemporary Poetry of North Carolina, 1977, Contemporary Southern Poetry, 1979, Anthology of Magazine Verse, 1980, 81, 85, 1980 Arvon Poetry Competition Anthology, The Direction of Poetry, 1988, The Courage to Grow Old, 1989, The Rough Ride Home, 1992, N.C. Poetry Soc. Anthology, 1992, Contemporary Authors Autobiographical Series, 1994; Anthology of Magazine Verse, 1997, Voices from Home, 1997. The Zeppelin Reader, 1998, Word and Witness: 100 Years of North Carolina Poetry, 1999. Mem. vis. com. Ackland Mus., U. N.C., 1987-98. Recipient Ridgely Torrence Meml. award, 1951, Gertrude Boatwright Harris award, 1955, Ariz. Quar. award, 1955, 56, 82, Roanoke-Chowan Poetry Cup, 1970, Oscar Arnold Young Meml. award, 1971, Golden Rose award New Eng. Poetry Club, 1972, Alice Fay di Castagnola award Poetry Soc. Am., 1974, Ariz. Quar. award, 1977, 79, Arvon Found. award London, 1980, Brockman award N.C. Poetry Soc., 1984, 86, Hollins Critic award, 1984, Roanoke-Chowan Poetry award, 1987, 91, Fiction award Kans. Quar./Kans. Art Commn., 1987, N.C. award for lit., 1988, Fortner award, 1993. Mem. Am. Acad. Poets, Poetry Soc. Am., New Eng. Poetry Club, N.C. Poetry Soc., N.C. Art Soc., North Caroliniana Soc., Phi Beta Kappa, Sigma Nu. Clubs: Harvard U.; Chancellors U. N.C. Address: 808 Greenwood Rd Chapel Hill NC 27514-3908

EATON, GARY DAVID, physician; b. South Bend, Ind., Oct. 20, 1952; s. William Joseph and Virginia Lee (Dreibelbis) E; children: Lynn, Heather, Brooke. AA in Fire Sci. Technology, Red Rocks C.C., Golden, Colo., 1978; BS in Biology, L.A. Coll. Chiropractic, Whittier, Calif., 1985, D Chiropractic Medicine, 1985; DO, U. Osteo. Med. and Health Sci., Des Moines, 1992. Diplomate Am. Acad. Disability Evaluating Physicians; bd. cert., Am. Bd. Phys. Medicine and Rehab.; cert. chiropractic physician, Utah, physician/surgeon, Mo. Firefighter, paramedic City of Aurora, Colo., 1976-82; chiropractic physician Pinehurst, Idaho, 1985-88; resident physician U. Ky., Lexington, 1992-94; staff physician, pvt. practice Tyler, Tex., 1994-95; resident U. Mo., Columbia, 1995-97; clin. fellow musculo skeletal medicine Rusk Rehab. Ctr., Columbia, 1997-98. Mem. AMA, Internat. Spinal Injection Soc., Am. Acad. Phys. Medicine and Rehab. Republican. Avocations: photography, fly fishing, shotgun sports. Home: PO Box 30697 Columbia MO 65205-3697

EATON, GEORGE WESLEY, JR., petroleum engineer, oil company executive; b. Searcy, Ark., Aug. 3, 1924; s. George Wesley and Inez (Roberson) E.; m. Adriana Amin, Oct. 28, 1971; 1 child, Andrew. BS in Petroleum Engring., U. Okla., 1948. Registered profl. engr. Tex., N.Mex. Petroleum engr. Amoco, Longview, Ft. Worth, Tex., 1948-54; engring. supr. Amoco, Roswell, N.Mex., 1954-59; dist. engr. Amoco, Farmington, N.Mex., 1959-70; constrn. mgr. Amoco Egypt Oil Co., Cairo, 1970-81; ops. mgr. Amoco Norway Oil Co., Stavanger, 1981-84; petroleum cons. G.W. Eaton Cons., Albuquerque, 1984-94; adj. prof. San Juan Coll., Farmington, 1968-70. Bd. dirs. Paradise Hills Civic Assn., Albuquerque, 1986-89; elder Rio Grande Presbyn. Ch., Albuquerque, 1987-90; mem. Rep. Nat. Com., Washington, 1986-92. Mem. N.Mex. Soc. Profl. Engrs. (bd. dirs. 1967-70), Soc. Petroleum Engrs. (Legion of Honor), Egyptian Soc. Petroleum Engrs. (chmn. 1980-81). Home: 5116 Russell Dr NW Albuquerque NM 87114-4325

EATON, GORDON PRYOR, geologist; b. Dayton, Ohio, Mar. 9, 1929; s. Colman and Dorothy (Pryor) E.; m. Virginia Anne Gregory, June 12, 1951; children: Gretchen Maria, Gregory Mathieu. BA, Wesleyan U., 1951; MS, Calif. Inst. Tech., 1953, PhD, 1957. From instr. geology to asst. prof. Wesleyan U., Middletown, Conn., 1955-59; from asst. prof. to assoc. prof. U. Calif., Riverside, 1959-67, chmn. dept. geol. sci., 1965-67; with U.S. Geol. Survey, 1963-65, 67-81, 94-97; dep. chief Office Geochemistry and Geophysics, Washington, 1972-74; project chief geothermal geophysics Office Geochemistry Geophysics, Denver, 1974-76; scientist-in-charge Hawaiian Volcano Obs., 1976-78; assoc. chief geologist Reston, Va., 1978-81; dean Tex. A&M U. Coll. Geoscis., 1981-83; provost, v.p. acad. affairs Tex. A&M U., 1983-86; pres. Iowa State U., Ames, 1986-90; dir. Lamont-Doherty Earth Obs. Columbia U., Palisades, N.Y., 1990-94, U.S. Geol. Survey, Reston, Va., 1994-97; prin. Pac NW, SeaMountain Country, Colo., Tex., Wash., W.Va., 1997—; former mem. Commn. on Internat. Edn., Am. Coun. Edn.; mem. bd. earth scis. and resources; ocean studies bd., and com. on formation of nat. biol. survey NRC, also mem. geophysics study com.; bd. dirs. Midwest Resources, Inc., Bankers Trust; mem., chair adv. com. U.S. Army Command and Gen. Staff Coll.; adv. bd. Sandia Nat. Lab. Geoscis. & Environ. Ctr.; adv. bd. Ohio State U. Ctr. Mapping. Mem. editl. bd. Jour. Volcanology and Geothermal Rsch., 1976-78; contbr. articles to profl. jours. Trustee Wesleyan U., 1995-98; pres., bd. dirs. Iowa 4-H Found., 1986-90; mem. adv. bd. Sch. Earth Sci. Stanford (Calif.) U., 1995-2000; mem. U.S. del. sci. & tech. com. Gore-Chernomyrdin Commn., 1996-97; mem. vis. com. Colo. Sch. Mines. Standard Oil fellow Calif. Inst. Tech., 1953; NSF grantee, 1955-59. Fellow Geol. Soc. Am., AAAS. E-mail: geaton@whidbey.net. Home: 709 N Snowberry Ln Coupeville WA 98239-3110 Office: SeaMountain Country 705 N Snowberry Ln Ste O Coupeville WA 98239-3110

EATON, JOEL DOUGLAS, lawyer; b. Miami, Fla., Oct. 31, 1943; s. Joe Oscar and Patricia (MacVicar) E.; m. Mary Benson, June 24, 1967; children: Douglas, Darryl, David. BA, Yale U., 1965; JD, Harvard U., 1975. Bar: Fla. 1975, U.S. Dist. Ct. (so. dist.) Fla. 1976, U.S. Ct. Appeals (5th cir.) 1976, U.S. Supreme Ct. 1978, U.S. Ct. Appeals (11th cir.) 1981, U.S. Ct. Appeals (Fed. cir.) 1996. Ptnr. Podhurst, Orseck, Josefsberg, Eaton, Meadow, Olin & Perwin, P.A. and predecessors, Miami, 1975—. With USN, 1965-71. Decorated Air medal with Bronze Star and numeral 14, Navy Commendation medal with 2 gold stars, Cross of Gallantry (Viet Nam). Mem. ABA, ATLA, Am. Law Inst., Acad. Fla. Trial Lawyers, Fla. Bar Assn. (appellate rules com. 1981—, chmn. 1989-90, jud. evaluation com. 1995-98, Fla. std. jury instn. com. 1998—), Am. Acad. Appellate Lawyers. Democrat. Office: Podhurst Orseck Josefsberg Eaton Meadow Olin & Perwin PA 25 W Flagler St Ste 800 Miami FL 33130-1720

EATON, JOSEPH W., sociology educator; b. Nuremburg, Germany, Sept. 28, 1919; s. Jacob and Flora (Wechsler) E.; m. Helen Goodman, June 8, 1947; children: David, Seth, Debra, Jonathan. BS, Cornell U., 1940; PhD, Columbia U., 1948. Faculty Wayne State U., Detroit, 1947-56; lectr., then vis. prof. Sch. Social Welfare, U. Calif. at Los Angeles, 1956-60; prof. social work research U. Pitts., 1960-70, dir. advanced program, 1966-69, prof. sociology in pub. health and social work research, 1970-73; prof. sociology in pub. health and social work research Sch. Pub. and Internat. Affairs, 1974—, prof., later dir. program in econ. and social devel.; co-dir. U.S. Comparative Mgmt. Survey Title Ins., 1999—; Russell Sage Found. vis. prof. Western Res. U. (Med. Sch.), 1958-59; project dir. Conf. on Social Welfare Consequences of Migration and Residential Movement, 1969; dir. instn. bldg. program Interuniv. Rsch. Consortium, 1966-71; curriculum cons., later dir. social work and social adminstrn. program U. Haifa, Israel, 1970-74 USIA cons., lectr., Africa, 1979, Sweden, Fed. Republic Germany, 1982, 86, Romania, 1982, Abu Dhabi, Pakistan, Egypt, Sudan, Israel, 1986, Nepal, Pakistan, Egypt, Ethiopia, Iraq, 1988, Yugoslavia, USSR, 1989; Fulbright lectr. and cons., 1979, Nat. Acad. Scis. guest scholar in Poland and German Dem. Republic, 1980; co-dir. Jordan River Basin Water Resources Devel., U.S. Inst. Peace, 1992—; co-investigator search for inherited causes of schizophrenia in a genetically isolated cmty., 1997—; co-prin. investigator A Pub. Policy-Oriented Audit of Title Ins., 1999—. Author: (with Saul M. Katz) Research Guide on Cooperative Group Farming, 1942, Exploring Tomorrow's Agriculture, 1943, (with Albert Mayer) Man's Capacity to Reproduce, 1954, (with Robert J. Weil) Culture and Mental Disorders, 1955, (with Kenneth Polk) Measuring Delinquency, 1961, Stone Walls Not a Prison Make: The Anatomy of Planned Adminstrative Change, 1962, Prisons in Israel, 1964, (with Michael Chen) Influencing the Youth Culture: A Study of Youth Organization in Israel, 1970, The Rurban Village, 1980, Can Business Save South Africa, 1980, Card Carrying Americans: Security, Privacy and the National ID Card Controversy, 1986, (with Yuri Lvov) Capitalist Communism, 1991; also contbr. chpts. to books, articles to profl. jours.; editor: Institution Building and Development, 1972. Mem. cable svc. adv. com. City of Pitts. City Coun., 1994—, chmn. cable communications adv. com., 1996—. With AUS, 1941-46. Faculty Research fellow Social Sci. Research Council, 1962. Mem. Nat. Assn. Social Workers (chmn. research council 1968-71), Internat. Assn. Social Psychiatry (mem. council 1969-72), Am. Soc. for Pub. Adminstrn. Home: 5844 Beacon St Pittsburgh PA 15217-2004

EATON, KIMBERLY NAPOLI, medical scientist, academic administrator; b. Pitts., Apr. 28, 1952; d. Frederic Haywood and Nancy Jane (Hawk) Reynolds; m. Roy Michael Napoli, Aug. 17, 1987 (div. Oct. 1989); m. Steve Eric Eaton, June 1, 1991. BS, Pa. State U., 1974; PhD, U. Pitts., 1983. Rsch. asst. Montefiore Hosp., Pitts., 1974-76; med. technologist Children's Hosp., Pitts., 1978-83, U. Pitts., 1984-85; rsch. chemist NASA, Houston, 1985-86; asst. prof. U. Tex. Houston Med. Sch., 1986-94, assoc. prof., 1994—, asst. dean for admissions, 1997—; invited reviewer Clin. Chemistry, 1994—, Transplantation Internat., 1998—; participant orgn. biannual congress Internat. Assn. Therapeutic Drug Monitoring and clin. Toxicology, 1995-99. Mem. editl. bd. Therapeutic Drug Monitoring, 1998—. Vol. local recruiter Pa. State Alumni Assn., Houston, 1999—. Mem. Am. Soc. Clin. Pathologists, Am. Assn. for Clin. Chemistry (treas. 1987—), Internat. Assn. Therapeutic Drug Monitoring and Clin. Toxicology (sec. 1999—), Clin. Ligand Assay Soc., Tex. Assn. Advisors to Health Professions, Transplantation Soc., Phi Lambda Upsilon. Presbyterian. Avocations: charcoal and pencil artistry, reading, watching sunsets. Office: U Tex Houston Med Sch 6431 Fannin St Ste 6230 Houston TX 77030-1501

EATON, MARTIN DAVID, geographer, educator, researcher; b. Ilkeston, Derbyshire, Eng., Nov. 8, 1961; s. Leonard Martin and Sheila Ann (Binnington) E.; m. Siobhan Mary Grose, Jan. 5, 1996; children: Eaton, Ronan David. BA in Geography with honors, Staffordshire Poly., Stafford, Eng., 1983; PhD in Geography, U. Exeter, 1989. Demonstrator practical geography U. Exeter, 1984-87; lectr. geography Staffordshire Poly., Stoke-on-Trent, 1988-89; lectr. human geograph U. Ulster, Coleraine, No. Ireland, 1989-93, lectr. European regional devel., 1993—. Contbr. articles to profl. jours. Dept. Econ. Devel. Belfast Rsch. grantee, 1996; Linked studentship Econ. and Social Rsch. Coun. U.K., 1985-88; Portuguese Govt. scholar, 1986. Fellow Royal Geog. Soc.; mem. Assn. for Contemporary Iberian Studies, Anglo-Portuguese Soc. Avocations: playing soccer, philately, viniculture. Office: Univ Ulster Sch Environ Studies, Cromore Rd, Coleraine BT52 1SA, Northern Ireland

EATON, NANCY RUTH LINTON, librarian, university dean; b. Berkeley, Calif., May 2, 1943; d. Don Thomas and Lena Ruth (McClellan) Linton; m. Edward Arthur Eaton III, June 19, 1965 (div. 1980). AB, Stanford U., 1965; MLS, U. Tex., 1968, postgrad., 1969. From cataloger to asst. to dir. U. Tex. Libr., Austin, 1968-74; automation libr. SUNY, Stony Brook, 1974-76; head tech. svcs. Atlanta Pub. Libr., 1976-82; dir. libr. U. Vt., Burlington, 1982-89; dean libr. svcs. Iowa State U., Ames, 1989-97; dean univ. librs. Pa. State U., University Park, Pa., 1997—; bd. dirs. Ctr. for Rsch. Librs., 1988-92, chair, 1989-90; del. user's coun., mem. exec. com. Online Computer Libr. Ctr., Inc., Dublin, Ohio, 1980-82, 86-88, trustee, 1987—, chair bd. trustees 1992-96; mgr. Nat. Agrl. Text Digitalizing Project, 1986-92; bd. dirs. New Eng. Libr. Network, 1987-89. Co-author: Optical Information Systems: Implementation Issues for Libraries, 1988.; co-editor: A Cataloging Sampler, 1971, Book Selection Policies in American Libraries, 1972; contbr. articles to profl. jours. U.S. Office of Edn. post-master's fellow, 1969; Dept. Edn. Title II-C grantee, 1985, 87-88, Title II-D grantee, 1992-96. Mem. ALA, Libr. and Info. Tech. Assn. (pres. 1984-85, bd. dirs. 1980-86), Assn. Rsch. Librs. (bd. dirs. 1994-97). Democrat. Avocations: tennis, walking. Home: 441 Homan Ave State College PA 16801-6337 Office: Pa State Univ 510 Paterno Library University Park PA 16802-1812

EATON, RICHARD GILLETTE, surgeon, educator; b. Forty Fort, Pa., Dec. 3, 1929; s. Walter L. and Ruth (Shaw) E.; B.A., Franklin and Marshall Coll., 1951; M.D., U. Pa., 1955; m. Du Ree Hunter, June 13, 1954; children: Bradford (dec.), Holly, Hillary. Intern, U. Pa. Grad. Hosp., 1956; gen. surg. resident Peter Bent Brigham Hosp., Boston, 1957; orthopedic resident Children's Hosp. Med. Center, Mass. Gen. Hosp. and Peter Bent Brigham Hosp., Boston, 1959-62; hand surgery fellow J.W. Littler, Roosevelt Hosp., N.Y.C., 1962, now attending orthopedic surgery and reconstrn., chief hand surgery service; prof. clin. orthop. surgery Columbia Coll. Physicians and Surgeons, N.Y.C. Ruling elder Huguenot Presbyn. Ch., Pelham, N.Y. Capt., M.C., U.S. Army, 1957-59. NIH fellow, 1963-64. Diplomate Am. Bd. Orthopedic Surgeons. Mem. Am. Acad. Orthopedic Surgery, Am. Orthopaedic Assn., Am. Soc. Surgery of Hand, A.C.S., Interurban Orthopedic Club, N.Y. Acad. Medicine, J.W. Littler Soc., N.Y. Soc. Surgery of Hand. Author: Joint Injuries of the Hand, 1971; also articles. Home: 640 Ely Ave Pelham NY 10803-2402 Office: St Luke's-Roosevelt Hosp CV Starr Hand Ctr 1000 10th Ave New York NY 10019-1192

EBACHER, ROGER, archbishop; b. Amos, Que., Can., Oct. 6, 1936. Ordained priest Roman Cath. Ch., 1961; ordained bishop of Diocese of Baie-Comeau, Que., 1979; chevalier de Colombe de 4e degré, 1983; apptd. bishop Diocese of Gatineau-Hull, Que., 1988, archbishop, 1990—. Address: 180 Mont-Bleu, Hull, PQ Canada J8Z 3J5

EBBELS, BRUCE JEFFERY, physician, health facility administrator; b. N.Y.C., Dec. 26, 1924; s. Walter Jeffery and Mildred Christiana (Bruce) E.; m. Shirley Marie Cooley, July 3, 1950; children: Bruce Jeffery Jr., Cynthia, Stephanie, Leslie, David. Student, Colgate U., 1943-44; MD, N.Y. Med. Coll., 1948. Intern Hurley Med. Ctr., Flint, Mich., 1948-49; resident in internal medicine VA Hosp., Richmond, Va., 1951-54; pvt. practice gastroenterology and internal medicine Watertown, N.Y., 1954-90; med. dir. N.Y. Air Brake Co., Watertown, 1992-94; med. coord. VA Clinic, Watertown, N.Y., 1994-97; med. cons. Credo Cmty. Ctr. Addiction, Watertown, Carthage, N.Y., 1992—; staff Genesis Healthcare, Watertown, N.Y., 1998-99; chief medicine Mercy Hosp., Watertown, N.Y., 1975-78, House of the Good Samaritan Hosp., Watertown, 1978-83, pres. med. staff, 1978; cons. in internal medicine E.J. Noble Hosp., 1960-88, Lewis County Gen. Hosp., 1960-88, Carthage Area Hosp., 1966-88; cons. in field. Contbr. chpt. to book. Pres. Jefferson County Assn. for Mental Health, Watertown, 1969-70; bd. trustees Watertown (N.Y.) Savs. Bank, 1971—; bd. vestry Trinity Ch., Watertown, 1972-78. Capt. USNR, 1979—. Recipient John Philips Rice Svc. award Jefferson County Assn. for Mental Health, Watertown, 1970, Disting. Svc. award Jefferson County divsn. Am. Heart Assn. Fellow ACP (life), Am. Coll. Gastroenterology (sr.); mem. AMA (life), Med. Soc. State N.Y. (life), Med. Soc. Jefferson County (life; pres. 1979-80), Staplin Creek Soc. (past pres.). Republican. Episcopalian. Avocations: aquatic sports, scuba diving, writing, lecturing. Home: 283 Thompson Blvd Watertown NY 13601-4123

EBBERS, BERNARD J., communications executive. BA in Phys. Edn., Miss. Coll. Pres., CEO WorldCom, 1985-98; pres., CEO, chmn. MCI WorldCom, Jackson, Miss., 1998—. Office: care MCI WorldCom Inc 500 Clinton Center Dr Clinton MS 39056-5630

EBBESON, KAREN ANN, retired social worker; b. Wayne, Nebr., Mar. 19, 1937; d. Elwin Alva and Blanch Alene (Buchanan) Fels; m. Gordon Frank Wedel, Sept. 3, 1964 (div. 1978); children: Rodrick, Terry Lynn, Michelle Marie, Kimberly; m. James Otto Ebbeson, June 16, 1979; stepchildren: Christy, Frida, Erika, Jeffery. BS, U. Wis., 1960; postgrad., U. Wis., Milw. and Madison, 1970's. Cert. social worker, Wis. Social worker Dane County Dept. Social Svcs., Madison, Wis., 1960-61, Outagamie County Dept. Social Svcs., Appleton, Wis., 1961-64, Milwaukee County Dept. Social Svcs., Milw., 1964-66, Waukesha County Dept. Social Svcs., Waukesha, Wis., 1972-77, Door County Dept. Social Svcs., Sturgeon Bay, Wis., 1977-87, Door County Counseling Svcs., Sturgeon Bay, 1987-91, 1991-97; pvt. practice social worker Family Bridges-Social Work Svcs. for All Ages, Sturgeon Bay, 1994-97; mem. Teen Pregnancy Task Force, 1993-96; organizer Grief Support Task Force, Door County, Wis., 1995-97. Pres. Local Planned Parenthood Assn., 1989-97, Wis. Inter Profl. Com. on Div., 1988-97, chairperson, 1990-98; active Peninsula Chamber Choir, 1988—, Meth. Ch. Choir; bd. mem. Birch Creek Assn., Door County, 1990-92; chair family selection com. Habitat for Humanity, 1991-96; mem. allocation com. United Way, 1997-98; chairperson local Habitat for Humanity, 1999—; mem. pastor parish com. Meth. Ch. Coun., 1999. Mem. LWV (state bd. mem. 1980-92, bd. dirs. D.C. chapt. 1980-88, pres. 1986-88, com. chair children at risk study 1995-96, prodn. publ. 1998, v.p. 1999—). Democrat. Methodist. Avocations: art, skiing, sailing, singing, golf. Home: 3292 Lake Forest Park Rd Sturgeon Bay WI 54235-9148

EBEID, ATEF MOHAMMED, Egyptian government official; b. 1932; married; 2 children. PhD in Bus., U. Ill., 1962. Mgmt. cons. Ministry of Industry, Egypt, 1955-63, 67-84; min. cabinet affairs, min. state for adminstrv. devel. Egyptian Govt., 1984-93, min. state for pub. sector, adminstrv. devel. and environ., 1993—, min. bus. sector, 1993-99; prime min. Egyptian Govt., Cairo, 1999S; mgmt. cons. Ministry of Electricity, Egypt, 1965, Ministry of Housing, 1966, Ministry of Higher Edn., 1967, Ministry of Info., 1968; mgmt. cons. to UNDP, 1971, ILO, 1981; mgmt. cons., then pres. Internat. Mgmt. Ctr., 1973-84; prof. mgmt. Cairo U., 1982-84. Office: Office of the Prime Minister, Sharia Magles al-Shaab, Cairo Egypt*

EBEID, NADIA RIAD MAKRAM, government official; b. 1943. MA in Polit. Sci., Am. U., 1977. Min. Ministry Environ. Affairs, Cairo, 1997—; vis. prof., Nigeria, 1977-78. Office: Ministry Environ Affairs, Sharia Magles al-Shaab, Cairo Egypt*

EBEL, FRIEDRICH, law educator; b. Goettingen, Germany, July 18, 1944; s. Wilhelm and Elisabeth (Nix) E.; m. Helga Waffenschmidt, May 22, 1970 (div. 1989); children: Heike, Anne; m. Iris Born Scheel, June 28, 1991. JD (hon.), U. Tuebingen, Fed. Republic of Germany, 1973. Lectr. U. Tuebingen, 1977; prof. law U. Bielefeld, Fed. Republic of Germany, 1978-81; prof. Free U., Berlin, 1981—. Author: Über Legaldefinitionen, 1974, Berichtung, 1978, Magdeburger Recht I, II, 1983, 89, 95, Sachsenspiegel, 1993, 99, Römisches Rechtsleben, 1988, Rechtsgeschichte I, II, 1989/98, 93, Der Rechte Weg, 2000, also 13 others; contbr. numerous articles and revs. to profl. jours. E-mail: febel@zedat.fu-berlin.de. Office: Free U, Boltzmannstr 1, 14195 Berlin Germany

EBEL, KLAUS DIETRICH, pediatric radiologist; b. Berlin, Aug. 13, 1924; s. Werner and Dorothea (Fiedler) E.; m. Margret Schoener, Aug. 22, 1953; children: Martin, Susanne, Henrike. PhD, U. Cologne, Germany, 1971. Diplomate Pediatrics, Radiology, Pediatric Radiology. Dir. dept. radiology Children's Hosp., Cologne, 1962-89; vis. prof. Benin city, Nigeria, 1988, U. Nairobi, Kenya, 1991-96. Author: Roentgen Examinations in Children, 1968, 2d edit., 1979, Differential Diagnoses in Pediatric Radiology, 1999; editor Pediatric Radiology Jour., 1973-90. Mem. German Roentgen Soc., European Soc. Pediatric Urology, European Soc. Pediatric Radiology (hon.). Avocations: tennis, photography, video, literature. Home: Birkenweg 3, 50859 Cologne Germany

EBELL, C(ECIL) WALTER, lawyer; b. Baker, Oreg., June 26, 1947; s. Cecil John and Sylvia Jean (Malone) E.; m. Dianna Rae Gentry, June 2, 1980; children: Anne, Erik, Michael. BS, Oreg. State U., 1970; MS, U. No. Colo., 1973; JD, Lewis and Clark Coll., 1977. Bar: Oreg. 1977, Alaska 1978, U.S. Ct. Appeals (9th cir.) 1981, U.S. Supreme Ct. 1985, Wash. 1990. Pvt. practice Portland, Oreg., 1977-78; ptnr. Hartig, Rhodes, Norman & Mahoney, Anchorage, 1978-84, Jamin, Ebell, Bolger & Gentry, Kodiak, Alaska, 1984-90, Jamin, Ebell, Schmitt & Mason, Seattle, 1990—. Press sec., Clay Myers for Gov. campaign, Oreg., 1974. Capt. USMC, 1970-73. Mem. ABA, Assn. Trial Lawyers Am., Rotary. Democrat. Avocations: photography, fishing, skiing. Office: Jamin Ebell Schmitt Mason 300 Mutual Life Bldg 605 1st Ave Seattle WA 98104-2207

EBENBAUER, ALFRED, university administrator; b. Oct. 13, 1945. Prof. Willkommen am Institut für Germanistik U. of Vienna, Vienna. Office: Vienna Univ, Dr Karl Lueger-Ring 1, 1010 Vienna Austria*

EBENEZER, DURAISINGH DIAMOND, acoustical engineer; b. Madras, India, Dec. 12, 1960; s. G. Paul and Mabel Julia (Moses) D.; m. Indra Lily Azariah, Aug. 19, 1991; children: Christine Priscilla, Joshua Peter. B of Tech., Indian Inst. Tech., Madras, 1983; MS, U. R.I., 1986, PhD, 1990. Scientist Naval Phys. & Oceanographic Lab., Kochi, India, 1990—. Mem. Acoustical Soc. India. E-mail: tsonpol@vsnl.com. Home: Lily's Clinic, Thrikkakara, Kochi 682021, India Office: Naval Physics and Oceanographic Lab, Thirkkakara, Kochi 682021, India

EBENEZER, IVOR SHADRACK, neuropharmacology educator; b. Pietermaritzburg, South Africa, Dec. 22, 1953; s. Shadrack and Ivy (James) E. BSc (with hons.), U. Sunderland, Eng., 1978; PhD, U. Newcastle Upon Tyne, Eng., 1982. Rsch. asst. U. Newcastle Upon Tyne, Eng., 1983-86; vis. lectr. U. Sunderland, Eng., 1984; higher sci. officer Inst. Animal Physiology and Genetic Rsch., Cambridge, Eng., 1986-88; vis. scientist Mahidol U., Thailand, 1994—; sr. lectr. U. Portsmouth, Eng., 1989—; dir. neuropharmacology rsch. group U. Portsmouth, 1990—; vis. scientist Babraham Inst., Cambridge, Eng., 1990—. Contbr. over 100 sci. articles to profl. rsch. jours. Recipient UN fellowship, 1978-82, New Initiative fellowship Agrl. & Food Rsch. Coun., 1986-89, Guildford Methodology award, 1993. Mem. Brit. Pharmacological Soc., Brain Rsch. Assn., Internat. Brain Rsch. Orgn. Mem. Brit. Pharmacological Soc., Endocrinology Soc., British Neurosci. Assn., Internat. Brain Rsch. Orgn. Office: U Portsmouth Neuropharm Rsch Grp, Sch Pharmacy & Biomed Sci, Portsmouth PO1 2DT, England

EBERBACH, STEVEN JOHN, retired electronics company executive; b. Ann Arbor, Mich., Apr. 30, 1943; s. Robert Ottmar and Marie (Eichelberger) E.; m. Mary Jean Head, Oct. 15, 1983; children: Amy Elizabeth, Michael James, Amanda Claire, Kathryn Louise. BSEE, MIT, 1965; MBA, U. Mich., 1967. Engr. U. Mich. Space Physics Rsch. Lab., Ann Arbor, 1967-73; founder, owner, engr., pres. and chmn. DCM Corp., Ann Arbor, 1974-99; ret., 1999. Inventor loudspeaker design. Mem. IEEE, IEEE Consumer Elect. Soc., IEEE Signal Processing Soc., Audio Engring. Soc., Foresight Inst. (sr. assoc.). Avocations: sailing, photography, cross country skiing, computer sci. and programming. Home and Office: 4455 E Loch Alpine Dr Ann Arbor MI 48103-9422

EBERHARD, FRANZ VALENTIN, association executive; b. St. Johann, Carinthia, Austria, Feb. 1, 1947; s. Johann and Theresia (Krušic) E.; m. Irmgard Kothmaier, Aug. 4, 1968; children: Christoph, Stephan. LLD, U. Vienna, Austria, 1970; D Polit. Sci., U. Paris, 1973. Lectr. U. Vienna, 1970-82, U. Paris II, 1972-73; sec. Constl. Ct., Vienna, 1974-78; sec. gen. Austrian Rectors' Conf., 1978-82; dir. European Centre Higher Edn., UNESCO, Bucharest, Romania, 1982-86; sec. gen. Internat. Assn. Univs., Paris, 1987—; dir. Internat. Univs. Bur., UNESCO, Paris, 1987—. Editor in chief Higher Edn. in Europe, 1982-86; co-editor Adminstrv. Law and Adminstrv. Sci., 1976-82; pub. dir. Higher Edn. Policy, 1988—; contbr. articles on pub. law, polit. sci. and higher edn. to profl. jours. Office: Internat Assn Univs, 1 rue Miollis UNESCO House, 75015 Paris France

EBERHARD, GORAN U.O., psychiatry educator; b. Landskrona, Sweden, June 10, 1934; s. Egon G. and Elisabeth J. (Nilsson) B.; m. Marie-Louise E. Andrén, Mar. 24, 1956; children: Jonas, Malin, Marten, David, Jakob. MD, Univ. Lund, Lund, Sweden, 1960, PhD, 1968. Chief psychiatrist Lund, 1970-72, Linkoping, Sweden, 1973-74; chief psychiatrist Helsingborg, Sweden, 1975-83, Malmo, Sweden, 1984-87, Trelleborg, Sweden, 1992-95; pvt. practice Lund, 1995—. Author: Twin Studies; contbr. articles to profl. jours. With Swedish Airforce, 1974-80. Mem. Swedish Psychiatric Assn. (pres. 1981-83). Home and Office: O Vallgaten 29, 22361 Lund Sweden Office: Psy kelin, S:T Larsomradet PO Box 638, 22009 Lund Sweden

EBERHARDSTEINER, JOSEF MARKUS, civil engineer; b. Linz, Austria, Aug. 16, 1957; s. Josef and Lidwina (Gilhofer) E.; m. Margit Kloss, Dec. 3, 1983; children: Lukas, Lisa. Dipl. Ing., U. Tech. Vienna, Austria, 1983, D in Technology, 1989. Registered profl. engr., Vienna. Asst. U. Tech. Vienna, 1983-91, head exptl. dept., 1992—, asst. prof., 1995—. Fellow Austrian Soc. Exptl. Stress Analysis; mem. Gesellschaft für Angewandte Math. und Mechanik, Verein Deutscher Ingenieure. E-mail: Josef.Everhrd-steiner@tuwien.ac.at. Office: U Tech Vienna, Adolf-Blamauer-Gasse 1-3, A 1030 Vienna Austria

EBERL, KARL, research scientist; b. Landshut, Germany, Dec. 2, 1957; m. Elisabeth Gerlinde Fleissner, Sept. 28, 1979; 1 child, Philipp. Cert. electrician, Landshut, Germany, 1976; diploma in physics, Tech. U. Munich, 1986; PhD in PHysics, Walter-Schottky-Inst., Garching, Germany, 1990. Mem. rsch. staff Walter-Schottky Inst., 1986-90; guest scientist IBM T.J. Watson Rsch. Ctr., Yorktown Heights, N.Y., 1990-91; supr. rsch. group Max-Planck-Inst. for Solid State Rsch., Stuttgart, Germany, 1992—; mgr. MBE Komponenten GmbH, Weil der Stadt, Germany, 1989—; cons. in field; lectr. U. Hamburg, Germany, 1995; mem. adv. com. internat. sci. confs. Author, editor: Low Dimensional Structures, 1995; contbr. numerous articles to profl. jours.; patentee in field. Recipient advanced rsch. award NATO, 1994. Mem. Deutsche Physikalische Gesellschaft, Materials Rsch. Soc. Office: Max-Planck Inst Solid State, Heisenbergstr 1, 70569 Stuttgart Germany

EBERLIE, RICHARD FRERE, trade association director; b. Luton, Eng., May 28, 1932; s. William Felix and Winifred Maud (Spinks) E.; m. Joan Anne Noble, Oct. 28, 1966. MA, Cambridge U., 1956. Dist. officer Colonial Svc., Tanganyika, 1957-63; asst. sec. Tanganyika Tea Growers Assn., 1963-65; pvt. sec. to high commr. Aden, 1965-67; com. sec. Confederation of British Industry, London, 1967-72, dep. dir., 1975-89, dir., 1989-97; group mgr. British Stds. Instn., London, 1972-75; mem. Health and Safety Commn., London, 1980-89; del. Internat. Labor Conf., Geneva, 1983-86, UNICE, Brussels, 1989-97; mem. adv. com. Health and Safety, Luxembourg, 1982-89. Author: Harmonisation of Standardization in Europe, 1969; contbr. articles to profl. jours. Sec. Tanganyika Soc. for the Blind, 1959-64; mem. Tonbridge and Malling Borough Coun., Kent, 1984-89; chmn. govs. Ightam Sch., Kent, 1985-89. Lt. Dorset Regiment, 1950-53. Avocations: oil painting, Mozart, gardening.

EBERLING, GEORGE GIFFORD, federal agency administrator; b. Staten Island, N.Y., Dec. 9, 1961; s. Jerome George and Jessie Theresa (White) E. BSBA, The Citadel, 1985; MS in Forensic Sci., Nat. U., San Diego, 1990; MA in Internat. Rels., U. San Diego, 1999; diploma, U.S. Naval War Coll., 1996. Commd. officer USN, San Diego, 1985-89; sales rep. ADT Security, San Diego, 1989; post enumeration supervisor U.S. Dept. Commerce, San Diego, 1990; acct. analyst U.S. IRS, San Diego, 1991-92; investigative cons. JRM Cons., San Diego, 1992; from applications adjudicator to ctr. adjudications officer U.S. Immigration & Naturalization Scs., Laguna Niguel, Calif., 1992—. Mem. U.S. Naval Res. Assn. Republican. Roman Catholic. Avocations: reading, writing poetry, computers, theater, travel.

EBERT, JAMES DAVID, research biologist, educator; b. Bentleyville, Pa., Dec. 11, 1921; s. Alva Charles and Anna Frances (Brundege) E.; m. Alma Christine Goodwin, Apr. 19, 1946; children—Frances Diane, David Brian, Rebecca Susan. AB, Washington and Jefferson Coll., 1942, ScD, 1969; PhD, Johns Hopkins U., 1950; ScD (hon.), Yale, 1973, Ind. U., 1975, Duke U., 1992; LLD (hon.), Moravian Coll., 1979. Jr. instr. biology Johns Hopkins U., 1946-49, Adam T. Bruce fellow biology, 1949-50, hon. prof. biology, 1956-86, hon. prof. embryology Sch. Medicine, 1956-86; instr. biology Mass. Inst. Tech., 1950-51; asst. prof. zoology Ind. U., 1951-54, assoc. prof., 1954-56, Patten vis. prof., 1963; dir. dept. embryology Carnegie Instn. of Washington, 1956-76, pres., 1978-87, trustee, 1987—; prof. biology Johns Hopkins U., 1987—, dir. Chesapeake Bay Inst., 1987-92; vis. scientist med. dept. Brookhaven Nat. Lab., 1953-54; Philips vis. prof. Haverford Coll., 1961; instr. in charge embryology tng. program Marine Biol. Lab., summers 1962-66, trustee, 1964-98, hon. trustee, 1998—, pres., 1970-78, 91-98, dir., 1970-75, 77-78, dir. emeritus, 1999—; mem. Commn. on Undergrad. Edn. in Biol. Scis., 1963-66; vis. com. for biol. and phys. scis. Western Res. U., 1964-68; mem. panels on morphogenesis and biology of neoplasia of com. on growth NRC, 1954-56; adv. panel on genetic and developmental biology NSF, 1955-56, mem. divisional com. for biology and medicine, 1962-66, mem. univ. sci. devel. panel, 1965-70, adv. com. for instl. devel., 1970-72; mem. panel basic biol. rsch. in aging Am. Inst. Biol. Sci., 1957-60; mem. panel on cell biology NIH, USPHS, 1958-62, child health and human devel. tng. com., 1963-66; mem. bd. sci. counselors Nat. Cancer Inst., 1967-71, Nat. Inst. Child Health, 1973-77; mem. Com. on Scholarly Communication with People's Republic of China, 1978-81, chmn., 1989-95; chmn. Nat. Com. on Sci. Edn. Stds. & Assessment, 1992-93, Com. on Transportation and a Sustainable Environment, Transportation Rsch. Bd., 1995-97; vis. com. to dept. biology MIT, 1959-68, Harvard, 1969-75, Princeton, 1970-76; chmn. bd. sci. overseers Jackson Lab., 1976-80; mem. Inst. Medicine; bd. dirs. Baxter Internat., Transcend Therapeutics, Inc. (formerly Free Radical Sci., Inc.). Author: (with others) The Chick Embryo in Biological Research, 1952, Molecular Events in Differentiation Related to Specificity of Cell Type, 1955, Aspects of Synthesis and Order in Growth, 1955, Interacting Systems in Development, 2d edit., 1970, Biology, 1973, Mechanisms of Cell Change, 1979, This Our Golden Age, 1994; mem. editl. bd. (with others) Abstracts of Human Developmental Biology; editor: (with others) Oceanus; contbr. articles to profl. jours. Trustee Worcester Found. Lt. USNR, 1942-46. Decorated Purple Heart. Felow AAAS (v.p. med. scis. 1964), Am. Acad. Arts and Scis., Internat. Soc. Devel. Biology; mem. NAS (chmn. assembly life scis. 1973-77, v.p. 1981-93, chmn. Govt., Univ. and Industry Rsch. Roundtable 1987-92, chmn. on transp. and a sustainable environment 1994-97), Korean Acad. Sci. and Tech. (hon. fgn. mem.), Am. Philos. Soc., Am. Inst. Biol. Scis. (pres. 1964, President's medal 1972), Am. Soc. Naturalists, Am. Soc. Zoologists (pres. 1970), Soc. Study Growth and Devel. (pres. 1957-58), Phi Beta Kappa, Sigma Xi, Phi Sigma. Home: 4100 N Charles St Baltimore MD 21218-1065 Office: Marine Biol Lab Woods Hole MA 02543

EBERWEIN, JEFFREY ROBERT, military officer; b. Lancaster, Pa., Apr. 8, 1969; s. William Joseph and Linda Ellen Eberwein; m. Karin Elizabeth Love, Mar. 12, 1994. BA in English, Boston Coll., 1991; postgrad., Brown U., 1999—. Commd. 2d lt. USMC, 1991, advanced through grades to capt., 1995; 1st lt., bat. motor transport USMC, Camp LeJeune, N.C., 1993-94, platoon comdr., 1994-95, co. exec. officer, 1995, regimental motor transport, 1995-96; capt. logistics ops. USMC, New Orleans, 1996-99; platoon comdr. USMC, Providence, R.I., 1999—. Republican. Presbyterian. Avocations: reading, martial arts. Home: 70 Thomas Olney Cmn Providence RI 02904-2804

EBINER, ROBERT MAURICE, lawyer; b. L.A., Sept. 2, 1927; s. Maurice and Virginia (Grand) E.; m. Paula H. Van Sluyters, June 16, 1951; children: John, Lawrence, Marie, Michael, Therese, Kathleen, Eileen, Brian, Patricia, Elizabeth, Ann. JD, Loyola U., L.A., 1953. Bar: Calif. 1954, U.S. Dist. Ct. (cen. dist.) Calif. 1954. Pvt. practice West Covina, Calif., 1954—; judge pro tem L.A. Superior Ct., 1964-66, arbitrator, 1979—; judge pro tem Citrus Mcpl. Ct., 1966-70; mem. disciplinary hearing panel Calif. State Bar, 1968-75. Bd. dirs. West Covina United Fund, 1958-61, chmn. budget com., 1960-61; organizer Joint United Funds East San Gabriel Valley, 1962, bd. dirs., 1961-68; bd. dirs. San Gabriel Valley Cath. Social Svcs., 1969—, pres., 1969-72; bd. dirs. Region II Cath. Social Svc., 1970—, pres., 1970-74; trustee L.A. Cath. Welfare Bur. (now Cath. Charities), 1978—; charter bd. dirs. East San Gabriel Valley Hot Line, 1969-74, sec., 1969-72; charter bd. dirs. N.E. L.A. County unit Am. Cancer Soc., 1973-78, chmn. by-laws com., 1973-78; bd. dirs. Queen of the Valley Hosp. Found., 1983-89; organizer West Covina Hist. Soc., 1982—; active Calif. State Dem. Cen. Com., 1963-68; mng. meet dir. Greater La Puente Valley Spl. Olympics, 1985-88, Bishop Amat Relays, 1981-94; mem. MSAC Relays Com., 1978-94; campaign mgr. Congressman Ronald B. Cameron, 1964. With U.S. Army, 1945-47. Recipient L.A. County Human Rels. Commn. Disting. Svc. award, 1978, Thomas A. Kiefer Humanitarian award, 1993; named West Covina Citizen of Yr., 1986, San Gabriel Valley Daily Tribune's Father of Yr., 1986. Mem. ABA, Calif. Bar Assn., L.A. County Bar Assn. (arbitrator 1975—), Fed. Ct. So. Dist. Calif. Assn., L.A. Trial Lawyers Assn., Ea. Bar Assn. L.A. County (pres. Pomona Valley 1965-66), West Covina C. of C. (pres. 1960), Am. Arbitration Assn. (arbitrator 1965—), KC, Bishop Amat H.S. Booster Club (bd. dirs. 1973-96, pres. 1978-80), Kiwanis (charter West Covina, pres. 1976-77, lt. gov. divsn. 35 1980-81, Kiwanian of Yr. 1978, 82, Disting. Lt. Gov. 1980-81, bd. dirs. Cal-Nev-Ha Found. 1986-98, pres. 1994-96). Avocation: collector of historical Olympic and political memorabilia. Office: 100 N Citrus St Ste 520 West Covina CA 91791-1694

EBISU, TOSHIHIKO, neurosurgeon, neuroscientist; b. Hiroshima, Japan, July 11, 1957; s. Satoshi and Hiroko (Deguchi) E.; m. Fumiko Utsumi, Mar. 21, 1988; children: Shiori, Yuki James, Chisato. MD, Kyoto Prefectural U. Medicine, 1984, PhD, 1994. Vis. postdoctoral fellow U. Calif., San Francisco, 1992-94; staff dept. neurosurgery Matsushita Meml. Hosp., Osaka, Japan, 1994-95; asst. prof. dept. neurosurgery Meiji U. Oriental Medicine, Kyoto, 1995-97, assoc. prof., 1997—. Contbr. articles to profl. jours. Mem. Japanese Neurosurg. Soc., Internat. soc. for Magnetic Resonance in Medicine, Soc. Neurosci. Office: Meiji U Oriental Medicine, Hiyoshi-cho, Funai-gun Kyoto 629-0392, Japan

EBISUZAKI, YUKIKO, retired chemistry educator; b. Mission City, B.C., Can., July 25, 1930; came to U.S., 1957; d. Masuzo and Shige (Kusumoto) E. BS with honors, U. Western Ont., London, Can., 1956, MS, 1957; PhD, Ind. U., 1962. Postdoctoral U. Pa., Phila., 1962-63; faculty rsch. assoc. Ariz. State U., Tempe, 1963-67; acting asst. prof. UCLA, 1967-75; assoc. prof. N.C. State U., Raleigh, 1975-99, assoc. prof. emeritus, 1999—. Contbr. articles to profl. jours. Ont. Rsch. Found. fellow Ont. Rsch. Coun., 1957-60, Gerry fellow Sigma Delta Epsilon, 1977-78. Mem. Am. Chem. Soc., Sigma Xi.

EBNER, MICHL, member European Parliament; b. Bozen, Bolzano, Italy, Sept. 20, 1952. D in Law Studies, U. Bologna. Journalist Dolomiten, 1971-79; mem. bd. Athesia; mem. European Parliament, Brussels, 1994-99; mem. com. on agr. and rural devel., substitute mem. com. on constl. affairs and com. on environ., pub. health and consumer policy, chmn. del. to European Union-Slovenia joint parliamentary com. Mem. Bur., Group of European People's Party (Christian Dems.) ane European Dems. Mem. South Tyrol People's Party. Office: Verlagsanstalt Athesia, Lauben 41, I-39100 Bozen/Bolzano Italy

EBRÍ, BERNARDO TORNÉ, physician, researcher; b. Zaragoza, Spain, Oct. 26, 1949; s. Bernardo Ebri and Araceli Torne; m. Inmaculada Casas Verde, June 28, 1975; children: Bernardo, Inmaculada, Pablo, Daniel, Sandra. BSc, Maristas, Zaragoza, 1965; MD, U. Zaragoza, 1972, PhD, 1978. Specialist in internal medicine. Rsch. fellow Edn. and Sci. Ministry, Madrid, 1973-76; asst. prof. U. Zaragoza, 1973-86; med. resident Miguel Servet Hosp., Zaragoza, 1974-77, med. asst., 1977—; prof. applied music J.R. Santamaría Ctr., Zaragoza, 1986—; assoc. prof. Faculty of Medicine, Zaragoza, 1987—; cons. internal medicine Miguel Servet Hosp., 1974—, advisor med. residents, 1977—; med. homeopathic-naturist, Zaragoza, 1993—. Author, editor: Maduracion Osea Sobre Tarso y Carpo, 1988; author: Medicina y Musica, 1996, Etiopatogenia Y Fisiopatología de la Hipertension Arterial Esencial, 1997, La Otra Cara De La Medicina: Qué es el Hombre?, 1999, La Otra Cara De La Medicina: Hombre Ante el Color y la Muerte i Hay alfo desperes de erte Vida?, 2000; contbr. articles to profl. jours. Pres. Tng. of Christians, Zaragoza, 1986-90; mem. Life Protection Assn., Zaragoza, 1986—. Served in mil. hosp. Spanish Army, 1973-74. Recipient award for Best Acad. Record, Zaragoza City Coun., 1973. Mem. Acad. of Medicine Zaragoza, Spanish Soc. Internal Medicine, N.Y. Acad. Scis. Roman Catholic. Avocations: cycling, philately, tennis, walking. Home: Ermita 20 13-1D, 50009 Zaragoza Spain Office: Hosp Miguel Servet, Isabel La Catolica 1, 50009 Zaragoza Spain

EBY, LLOYD MARTIN, editor, writer, educator, filmmaker; b. Fayetteville, Pa., Feb. 9, 1943; s. Lloyd Arthur and Leona Ruth (Martin) E.; m. Susanna Mast, 1964 (div.); m. Anna Wasilewska, 1974 (div.); m. Pauline Pilote, Oct. 26, 1981; children: Jessica Anne, Christopher Lee, Stephanie Claire. AB, Washington U., St. Louis, 1967; MA, Fordham U., 1982, PhD, 1988. Lectr. in philosophy SUNY, Albany, 1969-70; mem. humanities faculty U. Md., U. Coll., College Park, 1990—; dir. of publics Internat. Cultural Found., N.Y.C., 1987-89; asst. sr. editor The World and I Mag., Washington, 1990—; adj. prof. philosophy U. D.C., 1990-92; adj. lectr. in philosophy Unification Theol. Sem., Barrytown, N.Y., 1979-90; cons. Internat. Cultural Found., N.Y.C., 1980-84, New Ecumenical Rsch. Assn., Barrytown, N.Y. and N.Y.C., 1978-84; pres. Afghanistan Documentary Film Project, N.Y., 1987-88. Author/editor: (book) Art and Technology, 1986;

author: Business and Professional Ethics, 1993, The World and I Mag., 1986—; contbr. articles to profl. jours. Dist. leader Unification Ch. of Washington, Cheverly, 1996-97; fundraiser Rep. Party of N.Y., 1980. Nominated for Stanley Drazek award in tchg. U. Md. Univ. Coll., 1994. Mem. Am. Philos. Assn., Prof. World Peace Assn., Chesapeake Rifle and Pistol Club, Morgan Hill Gun Club. Avocations: skeet and rifle shooting, photography, film and film studies, reading. E-mail: leby@worldandimag.com. Office: The World & I Mag 3600 New York Ave NE Washington DC 20002-1947

EBY, MAUREEN ANN, medical surgical nursing consultant; b. Sale, Great Britain, Aug. 4, 1948; d. Robert Turner and Eileen Patricia (Holmes) E. BA, U. Md., 1972; AASc magna cum laude, No. Va. C.C., 1981; postgrad., U. Birmingham, Eng., 1993—; PG diploma, South Bank U., Eng., 1992. RN, Va., DC., Calif. Staff nurse cardiac x-ray John Radcliffe Hosp., Oxford, England, 1984-86, staff nurse intensive care unit, 1986-91; nurse tchr. Sir Gordon Roberts Coll. Nursing, Northampton, England, 1991-92; lectr. medical surgical nursing Univ. Birmingham, Birmingham, Eng., 1992-94, sr. curriculum tutor, 1994-96; cons. Medical Surgical Nursing, Oxford, 1996-97; sr. lectr. Open U., Milton Keynes, Eng., 1997—. Co-author: Whistleblowing, 1994, Critical Practice, 2000; contbr. articles to profl. jours.; editor Nursing Ethics, 1993—. Dir., treas. Freedom to Care, Surrey, Eng., 1992-96; mem. exec. com. Voluntary Euthanasia Soc., 1994-97; nurse expert Action for Victims of Medical Accidents, London, 1990—; RCN rep. Nat. Coun. of Women, London, 1992-94, British Acad. of Experts, London, 1994—, No. Eng. rep. European Ctr. for Profl. Ethics, 1993—; mem. coun. Internat. Ctr. for Nursing Ethics, 1999—. Recipient Nursing scholarship award Am. Lung Assn., 1979-80, 80-81. Fellow Royal Soc. for the Encouragement of Art, Nightingdale Soc.; mem. Royal Coll. Nursing, Sociolegal Studies Assn., Assn. Univ. Tchrs. Avocations: textile art, modern jazz dancing. Home: Warren Lodge, Croughton, Brackley NN13 5LW, England Office: The Open Univ Health & Social Welfare, Walton Hall, MK7 6AA Milton Keynes England

EBY, MICHAEL JOHN, marketing research and technology consultant; b. South Bend, Ind., Aug. 3, 1949; s. Robert T. and Eileen Patricia (Holmes) E.; m. Judith Alyson Gaskell, May 17, 1980; children: Elizabeth, Katherine. Student, Harvey Mudd Coll., 1969-70; BS in Biochemistry with high honors, U. Md., 1972, MS in Chemistry, 1977; postgrad., IMEDE, Lausanne, Switzerland, 1984. Product mgr. LKB Instruments Inc., Rockville, Md., 1976-79; mktg. mgr. LKB-Produkter AB, Bromma, Sweden, 1979-87; strategic planning mgr. Pharmacia LKB Biotech. AB, Bromma, 1987-88; dir. mktg. Am. Bionetics, Hayward, Calif., 1988-89; pres. PhorTech Internat., San Carlos, Calif., 1989—. Author: The Electrophoresis Explosion, 1988, Electrophoresis in the Nineties, 1990, DNA Amplification, 1993, Blotting and Hybridization, 1993, Capillary Electrophoresis, 1993, Global Laboratory Product Usage, 1994, Densitometers and Image Analysis, 1995, Microplate Equipment, 1995, Synthetic Oligonucleotides, 1995, Electrophoretic Gel Media, 1995, Visualization Reagents, 1995, U.S. Laboratory Product Usage, 1996, Cell Biology Reagent Systems, 1996, Centrifugation, 1996, Molecular Biology Reagent Systems, 1997, DNA Diagnostics, 1997, DNA Amplification in Europe, 1998, Recombinant Protein Expression Systems, 1998, DNA Sequencing in Europe, 1998, Cytokines and Growth Factors, 1998, Molecular Biology Reagent Systems in the Far East, 1998, HPLC in the Life Sciences, 1998, Cytokines and Growth Factors, 1998, Cell and Tissue Culture, 1998, Monoclonal Antibodies, 1999, Microplate Instrumentation in Europe, 1999, DNA Sequencing, 1999, Worldwide Directory of Life Science Distributors, 2000; contbr. articles to profl. jours. Mem. AAAS, European Soc. Opinion and Mktg. Rsch., Am. Chem. Soc., Am. Soc. Cell Biology, The Electrophoresis Soc., Spirit of LKB Internat. Assn., U. Md. Alumni Assn., Am. Mensa Ltd., Calif. Separation Sci. Soc. Episcopalian. Avocations: astronomy, cheesemaking, photography, travel. Office: PhorTech Internat 238 Crestview Dr San Carlos CA 94070-1503

ECCLES, JOHN DAWSON, textiles executive; b. Apr. 20, 1931; s. 1st Viscount E.; m. Diana Catherine Sturge, 1955; 4 children. Student, Winchester Coll., Eng., 1944-45, Magdalen Coll., Eng.; BA, Oxford U., 1954; DS (hon.), Cranfield Inst. Tech., 1989. Mng. dir. Head Wrightson & Co. Ltd., 1968-77, chmn., 1976-77; dir. Glynwed Internat. plc, 1972-96, Courtalds Textiles plc, 1992—; chmn. Courtalds Textiles plc (now SaraLee), 1995-2000, Chamberlin and Hill plc; chmn. Acker Deboeck corp. psychologists. Mem. Indsl. Devel. Adv. Bd., 1989-93; chmn. bd. trustees Royal Botanic Gardens, Kew, Eng., 1983-91. Mem. Brook's. Avocations: gardening, theatre. Address: 6 Barton St, SW1P 3NG London England Office: Chamberlin and Hill plc, Chuckery Foundry Walsall, West Midlands WS1 2DU, United Kingdom*

ECE, MEHMET CEM, engineering educator, researcher; b. Luleburgaz, Turkey, Apr. 27, 1956; s. Kadir and Nazmiye (Dudukcu) E. BS in Mech. Engring., Tech. U. Istanbul, Turkey, 1979; MS in Mech. Engring., Lehigh U., Bethlehem, Pa., 1981; PhD in Mech. Engring., 1986. Rsch. asst. Lehigh U., Bethlehem, Pa., 1979-86; asst. prof. Trakya U., Edirne, Turkey, 1987-90, assoc. prof., 1990-96, prof., 1996—, dean Sch. Engring. and Arch., 1997—; head Mech. Engring. Dept. 1992-94, 1996—, head Thermo-Fluids Divsn., 1995—, mem.adminstrn. bd. sch. engring., 1992—, Trakya U., Edirne, Turkey. Contbr. articles to profl. jours. Recipient Internat. Scientific Pub. award, 1992, 94, 96, 2000. Avocation: photography. Office: Mechanical Engineering Dept, Trakya University, 22030 Edirne Turkey

ECEVIT, BULENT, b. Istanbul, Turkey, May 28, 1925; s. Fahri and Nazli E.; BA, Robert Coll., 1944; Faculty Linguistics, Ankara, 1944-46, Sch. Oriental and African Studies, London U., 1946-48; m. Rahsan Aral, Aug. 22, 1946. Mem. press and publicity dept. Turkish Govt., 1944-46; ofcl. Turkish Press Attache's Office, London, 1946-50; news editor Ulus, Ankara, 1950-53, polit. columnist, 1956-60; polit. columnist Halkci and Ulus, Ankara, 1954-56; M.P., 1957-60, 61-80, 91; prime minister, 1974, 78-79 (resigned); mem. Constitutent Assembly, 1960; minister labor, 1961-65; polit. columnist Milliyet, 1965; sec.-gen. Republican People's Party, 1965-71, chmn., 1972-80, prime minister, Ankara, Turkey, 1999—; detained after coup, Sept. 1980, released Oct. 1980; jailed 3 times for expressing polit. views, 1981-82; chmn. Dem. Left Party, 1987-88, 89—; guest writer Winston-Salem (N.C.) Jour., 1954-55. Served to lt. Turkish Army, 1951-52. Rockefeller Found. fellow Harvard U., 1958. Moslem. Author: Poems, 1976; poems pub. in W.Ger., USSR, Romania, Yugoslavia, and Denmark; (polit. works) Left of Center, 1966, The System Must Change, 1968, Ataturk and the Revolution, 1970, Conversations, 1974, Democratic Left, 1974, Foreign Policy, 1975, Workers and Peasants Together, 1976, Poems, 1976, New Developments in the Exploitative System, 1980, Independence and Freedom, 1984, The Changing World and Gurhey, 1990, Mithat Pasha and the Historical Process of the Turkish Economy, 1990, The Impact on Turkish Politics of the Social Culture, Anti-Memoirs, 1991; also translations. Home: Or-an Sitesi 69/5, Ankara Turkey Office: Office of the Prime Minister, Eski Basbakanlik Binasi, Ankara Turkey*

ECHALUSE, LUELLA HERMOSILLA, banker; b. Zambales, The Philippines, Feb. 10, 1976; d. Ludovico Ebuen and Linda (Hermosilla) E. AB in Sociology, U. Santo Tomas, Manila, 1997, MA in Pub. Adminstrn., 1999. Customer svc. asst. Philippines Comml. Internat. Bank, Manila, 1997-98, customer svc. support, 1998—. Mem. Tomasian Media Cir., U. Santo Tomas, 1997, Scarlet, 1997, Sociol. Soc., 1996. Roman Catholic. Avocations: playing tennis, cross-stitch, reading books, surfing the Internet. Home: B F Homes, 45 Ninang Virginia St, Caloocan City The Philippines Office: Phil Comml Internat Bank, 14-16 1420 J Abad Santos, 1012 Manila The Philippines

ECHAURREN, JUAN CARLOS, physics and electronics researcher; b. Santiago, Chile, July 21, 1966; s. Juan De Dios Echaurren and Ana Maria Valdés. Degree in instrumentation/automatization, U. Santiago de Chile, 1988; postgrad., Ctr. Profl. Devel. and Productiveness, Chuquicamata, Chile, 1991-92, Ramsey Tech., Mpls., 1993; postgrad. in civil engring., Mariscal Sucre U., Calama, Chile, 1994-96. Telecomm. specialist Sitelco Telecomm., Santiago, 1987-88; analytical equipments specialist Codelco Chile divsn. Chuquicamata (Chile), 1989-90, mass flow sensor equipment specialist, 1990—. Author: Radio Transmission and Its Application to the Automatic Control, 1988, Physics and Mathematical Fundaments for the Construction of a Strictly Analytical Matter Theory, 1994, Polynomial Structure for Mass Distributions in Horizontals, Inclined and Mixed States Interviewing Physics-Mathematical Model, 1997, Exact Solutions of Polynomial Order to the Schrodinger and Wheeler - Dewitt Equations According the Application of Methods in Laplace Transforms. Mem. Am. Assn. of Physics Tchrs., Am. Math. Soc., Mensa Internat. Avocations: fishing, painting, poetry, computers. E-mail: Juanechaurren@discoverymail.com. Home: Rupanco 7-H, Población Los Lagos, Chuquicamata Segunda Región, Chile Office: Codelco Chile, Divsn Chuquicamata, Chuquicamata Segunda Región, Chile

ECHAUZ, ROMEO R., finance company executive; b. Hinigaran, The Philippines; m. Lourdes Talag. AA, Manila Law Coll., 1946, LLB, 1948, LLD (hon.), 1975. Bar: The Philippines 1948. Chmn., pres. Std. Ins. Co., Inc., 1958; pres. Midland Ins. Corp., 1963-87, Cardinal Life Ins. Corp., 1965-77; chmn. Filipinas Mfrs. Bank, 1966-78; chmn. bd. dirs. Filipinas Retirement Paradise, Inc.; pres. Stanisco Towers Corp.; bd. dirs. Std. Ins. Co., Inc., LTE Devel. Corp. Chmn. bd. trustees Manila Law Coll. Found.; bd. trustees Santo Bambino Found., Inc.; pres. Surety Assn. The Philippines, 1958-59, Philippine Chamber Ins. & Surety, 1961-64; bd. dirs. C. of C. of The Philippines; econ. and fiscal asst. Ho. of Reps., 1960; bd. dirs., chmn., exec. com. Ateneo Alumni Assn., 1950. Named Surety Man of Yr., Bus. Writers Assn. The Philippines, 1958, Ins. and Surety Man of Yr., 1963. Fellow Internat. Bankers Assn.; mem. Philippine Constitution Assn., Philippine Bar Assn., Integrated Bar of the Philippines, Philippines-Japan Soc., Philippines-Japan Econ. Coop. Com., Manila Overseas Press Club, Baguio Country Club, Club Filipino, Casino Espanol de Manila, Lions. Home: 836 Torres St, Mandaluyong City The Philippines Office: Ste 1001 Std Ins Bldg, 999 Pedro Gil St, Ermita Manila Philippines

ECHEMPATI, RAGHU, mechanical engineering educator, consultant; b. Guntur, India, Oct. 6, 1948; came to U.S., 1979; s. Raja Gopal and Subhadra (Prativadi) E.; m. Pankaja Karri, June 1, 1978; children: Sharwari, Aparna. BEng, Andhra U., Waltair, India, 1970; MTech, Indian Inst. Tech., Kharagpur, 1972, PhD, 1978. Registered profl. engr., Miss. Postdoctoral assoc. U. Fla., Gainesville, 1979-81; asst. prof. Indian Inst. Tech., New Delhi, 1977-87, Wash. State U., Pullman, 1988-90, Mich. Tech. U., Houghton, 1990-94, U. Miss., University, 1994-97; asst. prof. Kettering U., Flint, Mich., 1997—, Bosch prof., 1997—; cons. Batesville (Miss.) Am., Indian Railways, Lucknow, India, 1978-82, Greneda (Miss.) Elem. Sch., 1995, CMI-Schneible, Holly, Mich., 1998; dir. Indus Industries, India, 1987-97. Reviewer: Mechanics of Materials, 1996; contbr. articles to profl. jours., book chpts. Recipient Young Scientist award Dept. Sci. & Tech., India, 1984. Fellow ASME (chmn. Saginaw (Mich.) Valley chpt.); mem. Soc. Mfg. Engrs., Assn. Machines & Mechanisms (life), Soc. Automobile Engrs., Am. Soc. Engring. Edn. Office: Kettering Univ Flint MI 48504

ECHENIQUE, PEDRO MIGUEL, physicist, educator; b. Isaba, Navarra, Spain, June 8, 1950; s. Pedro Echenique and Felisa Landiribar. BS, U. Navarre (Spain), 1972; PhD, U. Cambridge (Eng.), 1976, U. Autonoma Barcelona (Spain), 1977. Prof. physics U. Barcelona, 1978-80; min. edn. Basque Govt., Spain, 1980-83, min. edn. and culture, govt. spokesman, 1983-84; prof. physics U. Basque Country, San Sebastian, Spain, 1986—; vis. prof. U. Cambridge, 1984-86. Co-author: Solid State Physics Series, vol. 43, 1990; contbr. articles to profl. jours. Overseas fellow Churchill Coll., Cambridge, 1985; recipient Euskadi prize Basque Govt., 1996, Dupont Sci. prize, 1996, Sci. Coun. Found. of Bank of Bilbao Vizcaya and Coun. of Excellence Eusko Ikaskuntza, Munibe prize, 1996, Principe de Viana prize Govt. of Navarra, Principe de Asturies prize, 1998, Max Planck Physics prize, 1998, Basque of the Yr., 1998, Gold medal UPV/EHU, 1999, Gold Medal City of St. Sebastian; overseas fellow Churchill Coll., Cambridge. Fellow Am. Phys. Soc.; mem. Spanish Acad. Scis., Royal Acad. Sic. and Arts Barcelona. Avocations: skiing, squash, literature. Home: Po de Igueldo 3-28, 20008 San Sebastian Guipuzcoa, Spain Office: Facultad de Quimica, Po Manuel de Lardizabal 3, 20009 San Sebastian Guipuzcoa, Spain

ECHEVARRÍA, ENRIQUE, physiology educator, researcher; b. Bilbao, Spain, July 25, 1960; s. Enrique Echevarria and Julia María Orella; m. María del Mar. González de Garibay, Aug. 15, 1986; children: Luis Javier, Silvia. Grad. in medicine, UPV/EHU, Bilbao, Spain, 1983, PhD, 1991, Premio Extraordinario Doctorado (hon.), 1991. Diplomate in Occupl. Medicine, Ministerio de Sanidad Bilbao, 1987. Assoc. prof. U. Basque Country, Bilbao, 1988-93; titular prof. UPV/EHU, 1994—; sec. Academia de Ciencias Médicas, Vitoria, Spain, 1996-99. Contbr. articles to profl. jours. Recipient Premio de Investigación, Academia de Ciencias Médicas, Vitoria, Spain, 1998. Mem. European Neurosci. Assn., Soc. Española de Neuroscis., Soc. Vasca de Medicina del Trabajo. Roman Catholic. Avocations: trekking, science fiction, Basque sports, classical music. Office: U Basque Country Dept Phys, PO Box 450 Sch Pharmacy, 01080 Vitoria Spain

ECHEVERRIA, MARIA DE LAS MERCEDES, genetic researcher; b. Balcarce, Buenos Aires, Argentina, Dec. 9, 1965; d. Felix and Rosa Carmen (Carboniari) E. Lic. Biol. Sci., Nat. U. Mar Del Plata, Buenos Aires, 1990; postgrad., Nat. U. Mar Del Plata, Balcarce. Tchg. asst. Faculty Agrarian Sci., Nat. U. Mar del Plata, Balcarce, 1988-89, 91—, jr. rschr., 1991—. Nat. Coun. Sci. and Tech. Rsch. fellow, 1991-93, 93-95, Japan Internat. Cooperation Agy. fellow, 1994. Mem. Argentine Soc. Genetics. E-mail: mecheverria@balcarce.inta.gov.ar. Office: Faculty of Agrarian Sci, cc 276, Balcarce, Buenos Aires Argentina 7620

ECHEVEVERRIA, JOHN D., lawyer; b. Providence, Apr. 17, 1953; s. Durand and Patricia Smith Echeverria; m. Carin Fay Pratt, Sept. 19, 1988; children: Nicholas, Edward. BA, Yale U., 1976, M Forestry Sci., 1981, JD, 1981. Law clk. to Hon. Gerhard Gesell U.S. Dist. Ct., Washington, 1981-82; assoc. Hughes, Hubbard & Reed, Washington, 1982-87; gen. counsel, conservation dir. Am. Rivers, Washington, 1987-92; gen. counsel Nat. Audubon Soc., Washington, 1992-97; dir. Environ. Policy Project, Washington, 1997—. Co-author: Rivers at Risk, 1992; editor: Let the People Judge, 1995. Office: Environ Policy Project Georgetown U Law Ctr 600 New Jersey Ave NW Washington DC 20001-2022

ECHOLS, IVOR TATUM, retired educator, assistant dean; b. Oklahoma City, Dec. 28, 1919; d. Israel E. and Katie (Bingley) Tatum;. AB, U. Kans., 1942; postgrad., U. Nebr., 1945-46; MS in Social Work, Columbia U., 1952; postgrad., U. So. Calif., 1961-62, DSW, 1968. Tchr. social studies h.s. Holdenville, Okla., 1942-43, Geary, Okla., 1943-45; caseworker ARC, Chgo., 1946-47; resident group worker Dosoris House for Teen-Age Girls Cmty. Svcs. Soc., N.Y.C., 1950-51; supr. group work Walnut Grove Ctr. Neighborhood Clubs, Oklahoma City, 1948-51; program dir. Camp Lookout YWCA, Denver, 1951; dir. program svcs. Presbyn. Neighborhood Svcs., Detroit, summer 1960; supr. group work Merrill-Palmer Inst., Detroit, 1951-70; asst. dir. Merrill-Palmer Camp, Dryden, Mich., 1951-59; prof. Sch. Social Work U. Conn., West Hartford, 1970-89, also asst. dean, ret., 1989; del. Inter-Univ. Consortium of Social Devel., Nairobi, Kenya, 1974, Hong Kong, 1980; mem. Conn. adv. com. U.S. Commn. Civil Rights. Mem. ad hoc com. Citizens Concerned with Equal Ednl. Opportunity, Detroit, 1964—; cons. to NEA Conf. Family Camping Washington, 1959, ednl. film Scott Paper Co., Phila., 1963, 64; summer study skills project Presbyn. Ch. Bd. Nat. Missions, Knoxville, Tenn., 1965—; nat. sec. United Neighborhood Ctrs. Am., N.Y.C.; pres. Protestant Cmty. Svcs., Detroit, 1969-70; trustee Conn. Energy Found., 1987-92; commr. Conn. Hist. Commn., 1986-96, ret., 1996. ARC scholar; fellow Nat. Urban League, Porter R. Lee fellow, fellow NIMH; recipient Educator Human Rights award UN Assn., 1987, Sojourner Truth award Detroit chpt. Nat. Assn. Negro Bus. and Profl. Women, 1969, UN Assn. award for Edn. and Women's Rights, 1987, Maria R. Stewart Women's Rights award Conn. Women's Ednl. and Legal Found., 1991, Outstanding Women award U. Conn., 1991, Achievement award Assn. Advancement Soc. Groupwork, 1994, 1st Truth award Capitol C.C. Hartford, 1999; named Conn. Social Worker of Year NASW, 1979; Ivor J. Echols Endowment Fund named in her honor U. Conn. Found., 1990. Mem. Nat. Assn. Colored Women's Clubs (participant White House conf. on Children and Youth 1960), A.M.E. Ministers Wives, Acad. Certified Social Workers (hon.), Nat. Assn. Black Social Workers (honored as founding mem. 1968), Nat. Trust for Hist. Preservation, Delta Sigma Theta (Delta Dear recognition 1998). Mem. A.M.E. Ch. Home: 51 Chestnut Dr Windsor CT 06095-1113 Office: U Conn 1798 Asylum Ave Ste 1 West Hartford CT 06117-2603

ECHU, IBRAHIM, civil service professional; b. Alome, Kogi, Nigeria, Nov. 5, 1964; s. Echu Otubeje and Hajara Odoh Echu; m. Bilkis Ibrahim Sule, Mar. 30, 1997; 1 child, Rahmat Ibrahim. BA with honors, U. Jos, Nigeria, 1990, BSc, 1997. Cert. Nigerian Inst. Pub. Rels., Nigerian Inst. Tng. and Devel. Profl. Indsl. Tng. Fund, Jos, 1994-97, tng. devel. officer, 1997—; prin. cons. Prime Functions, Jos, 1997—. Author: Industrial Training Fund at 25, 1996; author of essays. Islam. Avocations: reading, table tennis, traveling, debating, sharing jokes. Home: OFU LGA, Alome Kogi, Nigeria

ECK, KENNETH FRANK, pharmacist; b. Alma, Kans., Feb. 4, 1917; s. Clarence Joseph and Rosa Barbara (Noller) E.; m. Ouida Susie Landon, July 2, 1938 (dec. Sept. 1986); children: Alan Grantland, Mark Warren, Dana Landon; m. Lorraine B. Wooster Rubottom, Apr. 14, 1989. BS in Pharmacy summa cum laude, Southwestern Okla. State U., 1950. Ptnr., mgr. Taylor Drug Store, Healdton, Okla., 1950-51, Taylor-Eck Drug Store, Healdton, 1951-59, Johnson-Eck Drug Store, Healdton, 1959-72; pres. Eck Drug Co., Inc., Healdton, 1972-87, cons., relief pharmacist, 1987—; cons., relief pharmacist Eck Drug and Gift, Waurika, Okla., 1987—; affiliate instr. pharmacy Southwestern Okla. State U., Weatherford, 1970-87, mem. dean's adv. com. Sch. of Pharmacy, early 1980's; bd. dirs. med. adv. bd. Dept. Human Svcs. Okla., Oklahoma City, 1990-91. Columnist Healdton Herald, 1996—. Rep. Silver Haired legis. (senator, 1986-88, elected Floor leader), 1982-86, past mem. governing bd. Healdton Mcpl. Hosp.; mem. Okla. Profl. Responsibilty Tribunal of Okla. Bar Assn., 1983-88, vice chief master, 1988; past mem. bd. dirs. Carter County chpt. ARC, Ardmore, Okla.; bd. dirs. Healdton Oil Mus., 1993—, treas., 1997-98; pres. bd. dirs. Okla. Pharmacy Heritage Found., 1994-95; mem. fin. com. Healdton br. Chickasaw Libr., 1993, past pres.; bd. dirs. Healdton Econ. Devel., 1993-95; former mem. Okla. Dept. Human Svcs. Mental Health Task Force; deacon Ch. of Christ, 1945—; mem. Healdton City Coun., 2000—; mem. focus com. So. Okla. Tech. Ctr. (Votech), 2000—; mem. ethics com. SODA-ELDERCARE Program, 2000; mem. program adv. com. 4H Youth Devel. Ctr., 2000. With USN, 1942-45, PTO. Recipient Achievement award Merck Sharp & Dohme, 1991, Bowl of Hygeia, 1985, outstanding svc. award Okla. Profl. Responsibility Tribunal of Okla. State Bar Assn., citation State of Okla. Ho. of Reps., 1996, 97; named to Hall of Fame, Okla. Pharmacy Heritage Found., 1996; named Outstanding Older Oklahoman, Soda Dist., 1997, Alumnus of Yr. Healdton H.S., 1988, Disting. Alumni S.W. Okla. State U., 1978, Pharmacy Preceptor of Yr., 1978. Mem. VFW (life, post comdr. Healdton 1974-78), Okla. Pharm. Assn. (pres. 1990-91, plaque 1991), Pharmacy Providers Okla. (bd. dirs. 1990-91), Healdton C. of C. (bd. dirs. 1975—, pres. 1984-85), So. Okla. Devel. Assn. (coun. area agy. on aging adv. bd. 1987—, 1st v.p. 1994-95, pres. 1995-96), Nat. Assn. Retail Druggists (profl. affairs com. 1990-91), Am. Legion (post comdr. Healdton 1985—), Lions (eye bank bd. 1993-95, coord. campaign Sight-First 1993-94, pres. Healdton 1994-95), Silvered Haired legis. Alumni (v.p., 1998). Democrat. Avocations: photography, travel, fishing, boating, reading. Home: 1033 E Texas Rd Healdton OK 73438-3017

ECK, MATTHIAS HEINRICH, lawyer; b. Bielefeld, Germany, July 10, 1959; s. Walter and Johanna (Seufert) E.; m. Regine Anna-Maria Hagen, Oct. 6, 1962. Rechtsreferendar, U. Tübingen, Germany, 1986; Rechtsassessor, U. State of Ba-Wü, Stuttgart, Germany, 1989; JD, U. Munich, Germany, 1992. Asst. lectr. U. Tübingen, Germany, 1989-92; lawyer CMS Hasche Sigle, Stuttgart, Germany, 1992—; mng. dir. Schönbuch (Germany) Collection, 1995-96; lectr. U. Chemnitz, German, 1994-95, Tech. Coll. Esslingen, 1999—; chmn. adv. bd. Schönbuch Collection, 1997—; chmn. bd. Bytesteps Ag. Author: (book) New Ways to Protect Design, 1992, Unfair Exploitation of Third Parties Property, 1997. Mem. Studienvereinigung Kartellrecht, Dt. Vereinigung für gewerbl. Rechtsschutz und Urhebrecht, Internat. Assn. for Protecting Indsl. Property. Avocations: skiing, sailing, furniture design. Office: 1 CMS Hasche Eschenlohr, Pelt Schöttlestr 8, 70597 Stuttgart Germany

ECKBO, EIVIND HIGFORD, lawyer, deputy member of parliament; b. Stockholm, Aug. 10, 1927; arrived in Norway, 1933; s. Eivind Jensen and Alice (Higford) E.; m. Berit Haga, May 29, 1950 (div. 1963); children: Ellen, Eivind, Rolf, Ragnhild; m. Liv Matheson, Oct. 22, 1965 (div. 1984); children: Anja, Katja; m. Margaret Thorgrimsen, Sept. 21, 1989; stepchildren: Elisabeth, Fredrik. Student in bus. sch., Treider U., Oslo, 1945; law student, U. Oslo, 1952. Lic. practical lawyer, 1954. Owner, adminstr. Borgja Farm, Telemark, Norway, 1950-84; dir. Oslo and Boe (law firm), Telemark, 1954—; bd. dirs. various property cos., Oslo, Copenhagen, 1946—; chmn. bd. dirs. Eckbo Found., Oslo, 1962-83; dir. Libertas (free enterprise orgn.), Oslo, 1962-65; founder, chmn. Red Cattle Orgn., Telemark, 1956-66; chmn. Vet. Org. Oslo, 1993-95, 97-99. Bd. dirs. Mcpl. Audit Oslo, 1992-99; bd. dirs. Norwegian State Audit Orgn., Oslo, 1990-94, 2d leader 1998—; chmn., 2d leader Norwegian Progressive Party, 1973-84; spokesman, mem. Telemark County "parliament", 1975-87; dep. Norwegian parliament 1985-97. Cavalry/heavy vehicles, 1946-47, Norway and Germany, leader Oslo Cmty. Com. Rental Control, 1995—, mem. Oslo appeal com. of tax-cases, 1995-99. Mem. Norwegian Ostrich Assn. (founder, chmn. 1993-96), Norwegian Jockey Club (mem. bd., chmn. 1977-80, 81-86), Swedish Jockey Club (hon.), Aedle Hesteavl Copenhagen (hon.). Mem. Norwegian Progressive Party. Norwegian State Church. Avocations: horseback riding, horse breeding, carpentry. Home: Kristianiasvingen 55, 0782 Oslo Norway Office: Borgja Bygg A/S, PO Box 99 Slemdal, 0710 Oslo Norway

ECKEL, JAMES J., flight test engineer; b. Newark, Oct. 26, 1949; s. John Joseph and Margaret Agnes (Ellison) E.; m. Barbara Ann Stout Keeley, June 7, 1954. BEEE, Stevens Inst. Tech., 1971; MA, U. No. Colo., 1980; postgrad., Greenwich U. Officer USAF, 1972-80; asst. supt. Reynolds Elec. & Engring. Co., Las Vegas, 1980-84; sr. project leader Northrop Grumman Corp., 1984—. Recipient nat. def. medal USAF, 1972, combat crew medal, 1979. Mem. AIAA, AOC, Soc. Flight Test Engrs. Republican. Roman Catholic. Avocations: racquetball, model railroading, soaring, bicycling, horseback riding. Home: 4514 Ripon Rd Crystal Lake IL 60012-2026 Office: Northrop Grumman Corp 600 Hicks Rd Rolling Meadows IL 60008-1015

ECKEL, KARL, education educator; b. Lindheim, Hesse, Germany, Apr. 21, 1929; s. Heinrich and Emma (Stroh) E.; m. Ruth Heister, July 23, 1952; children: Isis Wendt, Angela Eckel. Tchg. cert., U. Frankfurt (Germany), 1954; PhD, U. Tübingen (Germany), 1973. Tchr. math. and physics sr. h.s., Frankfurt, 1954-58, 60-73, Valencia, Spain, 1958-60; prof. edn. sci. U. Frankfurt, 1974-94; project dir. German Inst. for Internat. Ednl. Rsch., Frankfurt, 1960—. Author: Instruction by Computer, 1972, 73, 74, Didaktiksprache, 1989, Instruction Language, 1993, On the Stagnation in the Social Sciences and in Educational Research in Particular, 1994. Avocation: singing. Home: Am Pfarrain 14, 63674 Altenstadt Hesse, Germany Office: Inst Internat Edn Rsch, Schloss Strasse 29, 60486 Frankfurt Hesse, Germany

ECKELMAN, RICHARD JOEL, engineering specialist; b. Bklyn., Mar. 25, 1951; s. Leon and Muriel (Brietbart) E.; m. Janet Louise Fenton, Mar. 21, 1978; children: Christie, Melanie, Erin Leigh. Student, Ariz. State U., 1988—. Sr. engr., group leader nondestructive testing Engring. Fluor Corp., Irvine, Calif., 1979-83; sr. engr. nondestructive testing McDonnell Douglas Helicopter Co., Mesa, Ariz., 1983-91; engring. specialist Convair div. Gen. Dynamics, San Diego, 1991-94; sr. tech. specialist McDonnell Douglas Techs., Inc., San Diego, 1994-96; scientist, engr. The Boeing Co., Mesa, Ariz., 1996-99; sr. scientist, engr. The Boeing Co., Huntington Beach, Calif., 1999—. Mem. Am. Soc. Nondestructive Testing (nat. aerospace com. 1987—, sec. Ariz. chpt. 1987-88, treas. 1988—, sect. chmn. 1989—, sect. bd. dirs. 1990-91), Am. Soc. Quality Control, Soc. Mfg. Engrs., Lindbergh Yacht Club. Avocations: racquetball, sailing. Home: 2 Keel Ct Long Beach CA 90803-4307

ECKENHOFF, EDWARD ALVIN, health care administrator; b. Durham, N.C., Mar. 4, 1943; s. James Edward and Bonnie Lee E.; m. Judi G. Vicich, May 27, 1978. BA, Transylvania U., 1966; MA, U. Ky., 1968; MHA, Washington U., 1974. V.p., adminstr. Rehab. Inst. Chgo., 1976-82; pres., chief exec. officer Nat. Rehab. Hosp., Washington, 1982—; asst. prof. dept. community and family practice Med. Sch., Georgetown U., Washington, 1983-94; v.p. Medlantic Healthcare Group, 1987-99; v.p. Medlantic Healthcare Group, 1987-98; pres. Nat. Rehab. Services Corp., 1987-92; chmn. bd. NASCOTT, IBIS; instr. Med. Sch., Northwestern U., preceptor Grad. Sch.

Bus.; mem. Ill. Commn. on Health Assistance Programs; mem. Ill. adv. com., chmn. exec. com. Internat. Yr. of Disabled; surveyor Commn. on Accreditation of Rehab. Facilities, bd. dirs., 1980-82; bd. dirs. Nat. Assn. Rehab. Facilities, 1982-83; mem. com. on accreditation and edn. Am. Phys. Therapy Assn.; mem. Healthcare Rsch. Devel. Inst.; bd. dirs. Am. Med. Rehab. Provider Assn., chmn. bd. dirs. Contbr. articles to profl. jours. Bd. dirs. Am. Occupl. Therapy Found., Easter Seal Soc., Boy Scouts Am., Chgo. Area Coun., Nat. Area, 1987-87, Operation ABLE Chgo., Access Living of Met. Chgo., Am. Chamber Symphony, Chgo. Named Washingtonian of the Yr., Washingtonian Mag., 1989; recipient Citation for Disting. Svc., AMA, 1990. Fellow Inst. Medicine Chgo., Am. Coll. Hosp. Execs.; mem. Am. Hosp. Assn. (chmn. governing coun. for rehab. hosps. 1985, trustee 1991-93, chmn. policy com. 1993, mem. exec. com. 1993), Am. Congress Rehab. Medicine (chmn. policy and devel. com.), Chgo. Hosp. Coun. (chmn. com. rehab. 1978-82, exec. com. 1983), Healthcare Devel. and Rsch. Inst., Am. Med. Rehab. Providers Assn. (chmn. bd. dirs. 1999—), Nat. Orgn. on Disability (Medicacare coverage adv. com. 1999—). Episcopalian. Office: Nat Rehab Hosp 102 Irving St NW Washington DC 20010-2949

ECKERSLEY, NORMAN CHADWICK, bank executive; b. Glasgow, Scotland, June 18, 1924; came to U.S., 1969; s. James Norman and Beatrice (Chadwick) E.; m. Rosemary J. Peters, May 23, 1986; 1 child, Anne. D Laws, Strathclyde U., Scotland. With Chartered Bank, London and Manchester, 1947-48; acct. Bombay, 1948-52, Singapore, 1952-54, Sarawak, 1954-56, Pakistan, 1956-58, Calcutta, 1958-59, Hong Kong, 1959-60; asst. mgr. Hamburg, 1960-62; mgr. Calcutta and Thailand, 1962-67; pres. Chartered Bank London, San Francisco, 1964-74, chmn., CEO, 1974-79; chmn. Std. Chartered Bancorp, 1978-82; dep. chmn. Union Bank, San Francisco and L.A., 1979-82; chmn., CEO The Pacific Bank, San Francisco, 1982-93; chmn. emeritus, 1993; chmn. Diners Club (Asia), 1967-69, Devel. Bank Thailand, 1967-69, Scottish Am. Investment Com., U. Strathclyde Found.; chmn. Balmoral Fin. Corp., 1995-99; exec. Bank of the Orient, San Francisco, 1999—. With RAF, 1940-46. Decorated D.F.C., comdr. Order Brit. Empire. Mem. Overseas Banks Assn. Calif. (chmn. 1972-74), Calif. Coun. Internat. Trade, San Francisco C. of C., World Trade Assn., Hong Kong Assn. (San Francisco) (bd. dirs.), Royal and Ancient Club, St. Andrews (Scotland), Royal Troon Golf Club (Scotland), World Trade Club, San Francisco Golf Club, Pacific Union Club (San Francisco). Mem. Ch. of Scotland. Home: 11718 Saddle Rd Monterey CA 93940-6653 Office: Bank of the Orient 233 Sansome St Fl 12 San Francisco CA 94104-2305

ECKERSTEN, CHRISTER CURT, automotive company manager; b. Malmoe, Sweden, May 23, 1949; s. Curt and Elsie Eckersten; m. Karin Lindblad, July 6, 1977; 1 child, Christina. MS, Lund (Sweden) Tech. H.S., 1973. Engr. Philips Electronic Ind., Sweden, 1974-82; mgr. devel. Philips Electronic Ind., 1982-94; tech. mgr. CelsiusTech Electronics, Jarfalla, Sweden, 1994—. Contbr. papers to profl. jours.; inventor in field. Office: CelsiusTech Electronics, Nettov 6, 17588 Jarfalla Sweden

ECKERT, ANNE, neuroscientist, researcher; b. Saarbruecken, Germany, Mar. 1, 1964; d. Paul Joseph Nikolaus and Gertrud (Bourguignon) E. MS, U. Marburg (Germany), 1990; PhD, U. Heidelberg (Germany), 1994. Postdoct. assignment Ctrl. Inst. Mental Health, 1994-97; postdoct. faculty dept. pharmacology U. Frankfurt, 1997—. Rsch. fellow Boehringer Ingelheim Fond, 1995; grantee Alzheimer Forschung Internat. e.V., 1997; recipient Organon award German Soc. Biol. Psychiatry, 1994. Mem. Soc. Neuroscis. Home: Rheindammstr 21, D-68163 Mannheim Germany Office: U Frankfurt Dept Pharmacol, Bioctr Marie-Curie-Str 9, Frankfurt D-60439, Germany

ECKERT, ERNST R. G., mechanical engineering educator; b. Prague, Czech Republic, Sept. 13, 1904; came to U.S., 1945, naturalized, 1955; s. Georg and Margarete (Pfrogner) E.; m. Josefine Binder, Jan. 30, 1931; children: Rosemarie Christa Eckert Kohler, Elke, Karin Eckert Winter, Dieter. Diploma Ing., German Inst. Tech., Prague, 1927, Dr.Ing., 1931; Dr. habil., Inst. Technology, Danzig, 1938; Dozent, Inst. of Technol., Braunschweig, Germany, 1940; hon. doctorates, Inst. Tech., Munich, 1968, Purdue U., 1968, U. Manchester, Eng., 1968, U. Notre Dame, 1970, Poly. Inst. Romania, Jassy, 1973, U. Minn., 1995, Czech Republic, 1999. Chief engr., lectr. Inst. Technology, Danzig, 1934-38; sect. chief thermodynamics Aero. Research Inst., Braunschweig, 1938-45; prof., dir. Inst. Technology, Prague, 1943-45; cons. USAF, 1945-49, Lewis Flight Propulsion Lab., NASA, 1949-51; prof. mech. engring. dept. U. Minn., 1951-73, dir. thermodynamics and heat transfer and of heat transfer lab., 1955-73, Regents' prof. emeritus mech. engring., 1973—; former vis. prof. Purdue U.; former cons. Gen. Electric Co., Trane Co.; U.S. rep. aerodynamics panel Internat. Com. Flame Radiation. author: (with Drake) Introduction to the Transfer of Heat and Mass, 1950, 2d edit., 1959, Heat and Mass Transfer, (translated by J.F. Gross), 1963; others in German, Russian, and Chinese, (with Goldstein) Measurement Techniques in Heat Transfer, 1970, 2d edit., 1976, (with Drake) Analysis of Heat and Mass Transfer, 1972; Chmn. hon. editorial adv. bd. Internat. Jour. Heat and Mass Transfer; former editor: Thermal Scis. series, Wadsworth Pub. Co., Belmont, Cal.; editor: Thermo and Fluid Dynamics; co-chmn. adv. editorial bd.: Heat Transfer-Japanese Research; co-editor: Energy Developments in Japan; chmn. hon. editorial adv. bd.: Letters in Heat and Mass Transfer; editorial adv. bd.: Numerical Heat Transfer; contbr. articles to sci. mags. Mem. Nat. Commn. Fire Prevention and Control, 1970-73. Recipient Max Jacob Meml. award, 1961, Disting. Teaching award U. Minn., 1965, award Western Electric Fund, 1965, gold medal French Inst. Energy and Fuel, 1967, Vincent Bendix award, 1972, Alexander von Humboldt U.S. sr. scientist award, 1980, A.V. Luikov medal, 1979, Aircraft Gas Turbine Tech. award, 1994, gold medal Czech Acad. Sci., 1994, Founders award Nat. Acad. of Engring., 1995; rsch. fellow Japan Soc. Promotion Sci., 1982. Fellow N.Y. Acad. Scis., AIAA; mem. ASME (hon.), NAE (Gold medal and Founders award 1995), Wissenschaftliche Gesellschaft für Luft und Raumfahrt, Sigma Xi, Pi Tau Sigma, Tau Beta Pi. Home: 60 W Wentworth Ave W Saint Paul MN 55118-3881 Office: Mech Engring Dept U Minn Minneapolis MN 55455

ECKL, WILLIAM WRAY, lawyer; b. Florence, Ala., Dec. 2, 1936; s. Louis Arnold and Patricia Barclift (Dowd) E.; m. Mary Lynn McGough, June 29, 1963; children: Eric Dowd, Lynn Lacey. BA, U. Notre Dame, 1959; LLB, U. Va., 1962. Bar: Va. 1962, Ala. 1962, Ga. 1964. Law clk. Supreme Ct. of Ala., 1962; ptnr. Gambrell, Harlan, Russell & Moye, Atlanta, 1965-68, Swift, Currie, McGhee & Hiers, Atlanta, 1968-82, Drew, Eckl & Farnham, Atlanta, 1983—. Served to capt. JAGC, USAR, 1962-65. Mem. Am. Bd. Trial Advocates, Trial Attys. Am., Lawyers Club of Atlanta, Brookwood Hills Club. Roman Catholic. Home: 348 Camden Rd NE Atlanta GA 30309-1513 Office: Drew Eckl & Farnham 880 W Peachtree St PO Box 7600 Atlanta GA 30357-0600

ECKLIN, ROBERT LUTHER, materials company executive; b. Lancaster, Pa., Sept. 26, 1938; s. Luther Joseph and Ella Frances (Smith) E.; m. Loretta Rohrer Stoner, Sept. 3, 1960; children: Robert Luther, Jr., Suzanne Beth, Kristina Ann, Stephanie Ann. B in Archtl. Engring., Chgo. Tech. Coll., 1961; postgrad., Dartmouth U., 1983, cert., 1984. With Corning Inc., N.Y.C., 1961—; pres. Corning Engring. Corning (N.Y.) Glass Works, 1982-86, corp. v.p. bus. devel., chmn. Corning Engring., 1986-88, sr. v.p., 1988-99, exec. v.p., 1999—; chmn. Maklin Ltd., Stone-on-Trent, Eng., 1983-86; ptnr. Ecklin & Ecklin Investments, Lancaster, 1986—; bd. dirs. Corning, U.S. Precision Lens, Cin., Alfred Ul. Tech. Resources, Pitts.-Corning Corp.; chmn. bd. dirs. Cormetech Inc., Durham, N.C. Chmn. Com. of 50, Corning, 1985—; mem. rsch. adv. bd. N.Y. State U.; pres. Univ. Industry Pub. Partnership for Econ. Growth. Mem. Corning C. of C. Republican. Methodist. Home: 248 Cedar St Corning NY 14830-3128 Office: Corning Inc MP HQ EZ Riverfront Plz Corning NY 14831-0001

ECKLUND, PETER JOHNSON, musician; b. San Diego, Sept. 27, 1945; s. John Edwin and Mary (Sizer) E. BA, Yale U., 1967, MAT, 1969. Trumpet player David Bromberg Band, 1973—, Gregg Allman Band, Macon, Ga., 1974, Orphan Newsboys, 1988—, Woody Allen band, N.Y.C., 1988-92, Peter Ecklund Trio, N.Y.C., 1991—, Howard Fishman Quartet, N.Y.C., 1998—, Jay Ungar/Molly Mason Band, West Hurley, N.Y., 1994—; tchr./performer Augusta Festival/Davis & Elkins Coll., Elkins, W.Va., 1999, 2000, Ashokan Festival - Fiddle and Dance, Ashokan, N.Y., 1992—; lectr./performer N.Y. Brass Conf. for Scholarships, N.Y.C., 1991, 95, 98, Am. Music Soc., Toronto, Ont., 2000. Author: (book) Louis Armstrong - Great Trumpet Solos, 1995, Bix Beiderbecke - Great Cornet Solors, 1998; musician, composer, prodr. (CD): Strings Attached, 1996, Gigs, 1999; cornet soloist: Ken Burns film The Civil War, John Sayles film, 8 Men Out, (film) Fried Green Tomatoes, Bonnie Raitt album, Give It Up. Mem. Historic Brass Soc. (editl. bd. 1991—). Home and Office: 130 W 16th St New York NY 10011-6281

ECKMAN, CHARLES CLARKE, food company executive; b. Battle Creek, Mich., Sept. 18, 1958; s. Charles George and Lauretta May (Daniel) E.; m. Teresa Lee Chapralis, May 20, 1985; children: Charles John, Daniel Robert. Student, Hope Coll., 1979, Walt Disney U., 1981, Calif. State U., Fullerton, 1982, Harvard U., 1987. Supr. retail Walt Disney, Anaheim, Calif., 1977-82; field sales Gen. Foods, 1982-88; h/q planning, mktg. Gen. Foods, N.Y.C., 1988-91; sr. field sales mgr. Gen. Foods, various cities, 1991-94; gen. mgr. Kraft Foods, Richmond, Va., 1994-98; v.p. sales, strategy Kraft Foods, London, 1999—; mem. exec. bd. ECR Europe, Brussels, 1999—. Avocations: vintage cars. Home: 13 Lime Tree Walk, GU25 45W Virginia Water Surrey, England Office: Kraft Foods Internat, Bayshill Rd, GL50 3AE Cheltenham England

ECKOLT, KLAUS RUDOLF, physicist; b. Braunschweig, Germany, Mar. 9, 1941; s. Albert and Else (Meier) E.; m. Doris Elisabeth Bordan, Dec. 1, 1965; two children. Diploma in engring., Tech. U. Braunschweig, 1968; DSc, Tech. U. Hannover, 1983. Scientist PTB, Braunschweig, Germany, 1969—. Office: Phys Tech Bundesanstalt 4.11, Bundesallee 100, 38116 Braunschweig Germany

ECKSTEIN, KARL LUDWIG, anesthesiologist; b. Nuernberg, Bavaria, Germany, Dec. 2, 1940; s. Ludwig Gotthold and Hedwig (Bohn) E.; m. Araceli Vicente, Dec. 7, 1973; 1 child, Rose Yvonne. MD, U. Tuebingen, Germany, 1967. Diplomate Am. Bd. Anesthesiology. Intern Germany, 1967-68, Hosp., Englewood, N.J., 1968-69; resident BMCH, N.Y.C., 1970-72, U. Hosp., Ulm, Germany, 1973-75; chief anesthesia dept. Virngrund-Klinik, Ellwangen, Germany, 1975—; nursing sch. dir., Ellwangen, 1982-89, vice hosp. dir., 1978-94. Contbr. articles to profl. jours. pres. Red Cross, Ellwangen, 1991-94. Mem. Am. Soc. Anesthesiology, German Anesthesia Assn., ASRA. Avocations: travel, skiing. Home: Karl-Stirner Str 55, D-73479 Ellwangen Germany Office: Virngrund-Klinik, Dalkinger Str 8-12, 73479 Ellwangen Germany

ECOLE, JEAN JOSEPH, philosophy and metaphysics researcher; b. Craon, France, Mar. 2, 1920; s. Ernest and Marie (Goupil) E. Licence, U. Rennes, France, 1947, Doctorat, 1956. Prof. philosophy Coll. Mayenne, France, 1945-55; prof. metaphysics U. Angers, France, 1955-70; rschr. Centre Nat. de la Recherche Scientifique, Paris, 1950-85. Author: La Métaphysique de l'être dans la Philosophie de Lavelle, 1957, La Métaphysique de l'être dans la Philosophie de Blondel, 1959, Introduction à l'Opus Metaphysicum de Wolff, Index Auctorum ad quos Wolffius remittit, 1985, Etudes et documents photographiques sur Wolff, 1988, La Métaphysique de Christian Wolff, 1990, Métaphysique de l'être, doctrine de la connaissance et philosophie de la religion chez Louis Lavelle, 1994, Nouvelles études et nouveaux documents photographiques sur Wolff, 1997, Louis Lavelle et le renouveau de la métaphysique de l'ête ausiècle, 1997; editor: Ontologia-Cosmologia-Psychologia Empirica-Psychologia Rationalis-Theologia Naturalis-Logica-Horae subsecivae Marburgenses-Opuscula metaphysica of Christian Wolff, 1962-83, De l'existence of Louis Lavelle, 1984. Dir., founder Collection Europaea Memoria, 1997. Decorated comdr. Légion d'Honneur. Roman Catholic. Home: 58 Route Stratègique, Col des Quatre Chemins, 06300 Nice France

ECONOMIDES, ANASTASIOS A., computer science educator; b. Thessaloniki, Greece, Nov. 29, 1961; s. Achilleas and Maria (Iosifidou) E. Diploma in Electrical Engring., Aristotelion U., Thessaloniki, 1984; MS in Computer Engring., U. So. Calif., 1987, PhD in Computer Engring., 1990. Asst. prof. Tele-Informatics, Computer Networks U. Macedonia, Thessaloniki, 1993—. Contbr. articles to profl. jours. With Greek mil., 1991-92. Fulbright fellow, 1985, Greek State fellow, 1985-89; recipient 6 awards Greek Ministry Edn., 1973-79. Mem. IEEE, Assn. for Computing Machinery, Tech. Chamber of Greece, Greek Computer Soc. Avocations: trekking, rafting, swimming, yachting. Office: U Macedonia, Thessaloniki 54006, Greece

ECONOMOPOULOS, GEORGE CHRISTOS, cardiothoracic surgeon; b. Tananarive, Madagascar, Jan. 19, 1950; s. Christos and Sophie (Gonis) E.; m. Susan Marie Zoladz, May 2, 1981. MD, Athens (Greece) U., 1974. Diplomate Am. Bd. Surgery, Am. Bd. Thoracic Surgery. Intern surgery Misericordia-Lincoln Hosp., N.Y.C., 1978-79; resident surgery Syracuse (N.Y.) U., 1979-81, U. Conn., New Britain, 1981-83; fellow vascular surgery Tex. Heart Inst., Houston, 1983-84; resident cardiothoracic surgery Wayne State U., Detroit, 1984-87; physician Harper Hosp., St. John Hosp., Grace Hosp., Athens, 1987-89; surgeon Henry Ford Hosp., Detroit, 1989-90; physician Tucson Med. Ctr., 1990-91; surgeon Hygia Hosp., Athens, Greece, 1991-93; asst. dir. Onasis Cardiovascular Ctr., Athens, 1993—. Office: Onassis Cardiac Surgery Ctr, 356 Sygrou Ave, 17674 Athens Greece

ECONOMOU, ANASTASIOS, chemist, researcher; b. Athens, June 6, 1965; s. Spilios and Kleovouli (Kallinteraki) E. BSc in Chemistry, U. Athens, 1988; MSc in Analytical Sci., U. Manchester, Eng., 1989, PhD in Analytical Sci., 1993. Rsch. assoc. UMIST, Manchester, 1993-97, U. Athens, 1997-99; rsch. scientist in chemistry Wine Inst., Athens, 1999—; sci. referee RSC, 1993—; lectr. in field. Contbr. articles to profl. jours. Recipient Gordon Kirkbright award DIAS/UMIST, 1995, Award of Excellence, Benakion Instn., 1999; RSC grantee, 1998. Mem. Royal Soc. of Chemistry, Am. Chem. Soc., Nat. Geog. Soc., Philosophy of Sci. Assn. Home: 60 Neorion St, 18534 Piraeus Greece Office: Wine Inst, 1 S Venizelou St, 14123 Athens Greece

EDBERG, STEFAN, former professional tennis player; b. Vastervik, Sweden, Jan. 19, 1966. Mem. Sweden Davis Cup Championship team, 1994. Began playing tennis at age seven; won Australian Open, 1985, 87, Wimbledon, 1988, 90, U.S. Open, 1991, 92, numerous other tournaments around the world. Recipient Gold medal 1984 Olympics, L.A., Bronze medal 1988 Olympics, Seoul, South Korea. Ranked top tennis player in world, 1990, 91. Address: care ATP Tour 201 Atp Tour Blvd Ponte Vedra Beach FL 32082-3211*

EDDINGTON, ROD, air transportation company executive; b. Perth, Australia, 1950. DPhil, Oxford U. Exec. chmn. Ansett Holdings; dep. chmn. New Ltd.; chief exec. British Airways, 2000—; rsch. lectr. Pembroke Coll., Oxford, 1978-79. Mem. Victorian Bus. Round Table, Global Bus. Policy Coun.; adv. com. Victorian Govt. Asia. Rhodes scholar Western Australia, 1974. Mem. Asialink Bd., Asia Soc. AustralAsia Centre, Fremantle Football Club (bd. mgmt.). Avocations: cricket, Australian rules football, rugby, bridge. Office: British Airways, Waterside, Harmondsworth UB7 0GB, England*

EDDINS, JAMES WILLIAM, JR., marketing executive; b. Wadesboro, N.C., Dec. 22, 1944; s. James William and Mildred Ruth Eddins; m. Barbara Ann Nelson, Oct. 2, 1965 (div. 1986); 1 child, Christopher; m. Ann Manley McAdams, Sept. 25, 1988; 1 stepchild, Keith. AB, Pfeiffer Coll., 1966; M.Pub. Sch. Adminstrn., Appalachian State U., Boone, N.C., 1968; postgrad., U. N.C., 1969. Prin. Stanly County Bd. Edn., Albemarle, N.C., 1966-70; gen. sales mgr. ITT Continental Baking Co., Tampa, Fla., 1970-75; reg. sales mgr. Sunshine Biscuit Co., Tampa, 1975-81; nat. sales mgr. Beatrice Foods, Bakery div., Augusta, Ga., 1981-83; dir. sales/mktg. Bensons, Inc., Athens, Ga., 1983-86; reg. sales mgr. Sunshine Biscuit Co., Greenville, S.C., 1986-87; dir. sales, nat. accts. Christie-Brown and Co., Burlington, N.C., 1987—; dir., v.p. Atlas Mktg.-Food Broker, Charlotte, N.C., 1996—; cons. in field. Active in past various charitable orgns. Named Oustanding Prin., Stanly County Bd. Edn., 1970. Mem. Biscuit Cracker Distbrs. Assn., Nat. Food Distbrs. Assn. Republican. Methodist. Avocations: tennis, basketball, travel. Home: 3230 Ardmore St Burlington NC 27215-8109 Office: Christie-Brown & Co PO Box 994 Burlington NC 27216-0994

EDDISON, ELIZABETH BOLE, entrepreneur, information specialist; b. Bronxville, N.Y., June 3, 1928; d. Hamilton Biggar and Elizabeth Owsley (Boyle) Bole; m. John Corbin Eddison, Feb. 10, 1951 (dec. Jan. 1993); children: Jonathan B., Elizabeth O., Martha C. AB, Vassar Coll., 1948; MS, Simmons Coll., 1973. Pres., bd. dirs. Lahore (Pakistan)-Am. Sch., 1959-61; chmn. evaluation com. Karachi (Pakistan)-Am. Sch., 1961-63; treas. bd. dirs. La Paz Coop. Sch., Bolivia, 1963-65; v.p. Assn. Am. Fgn. Svc. Women; coord. social svcs. Urban Svc. Corps, Washington Pub. Schs., 1965-69; sec. bd. dirs. Colegio Nueva Granada, Bogota, Colombia, 1969-71; chmn., treas. Warner-Eddison Assocs., Inc., Cambridge, Mass., 1973-88, pres., 1981-88; chmn., v.p. Inmagic Inc., Woburn, Mass., 1984-98; chmn., emeritus v.p., 1998—; mem. steering com. State House Conf. on Small Bus., Mass., 1986-88; mem. bd. advisors Internat. Sch. Info. Mgmt., Irvine, Calif., 1984—; mem. adv. coun. Engring. Info., Inc., N.Y.C., 1989-93; computer applications com. Cary Meml. Libr., Lexington, Mass., 1986; mem. State Adv. Commn. on Librs., Boston, 1993-96. Compiler: Words that Mean Business, 1981; contbr. articles to profl. jours. Mem. adv. com. on internat. and tech. devel. U.S. Dept. State, 1980-83; mem. small bus. com. Mass. Gov.'s Bus. Adv. Coun., 1985-89; co-chmn. Lexington Dem. Town Com., 1990-92; active Mass. Bd. Libr. Commrs., 1990-91; mem. bd. corporators Symmes Hosp., Arlington, Mass., 1992-94; mem. Bd. Selectmen, Lexington, 1993—; mem. adv. bd. Babson Coll. Info. Tech. and Svcs. Divsn., 1996—. Recipient Alumni Achievement award Simmons Coll., 1986, Disclosure Achievement award Libr. Mgmt. Bus. and Fin. div. Spl. Librs. Assn., 1987. Mem. Am. Soc. Info. Scis., Info. Industry Assn. (chmn. emeriti com. 1983-88, small bus. forum 1986-89, entrepreneur award com. 1989-90, co-chmn. publs. com. 1984-87, Entrepreneur award 1989), Assoc. Info. Mgrs. (chmn. publs. com. 1984-86, bd. dirs. 1984-86, Knox award 1988), Spl. Librs. Assn. (chmn. program com. libr. mgmt. divsn. 1984-85, profl. devel. com. 1987-88, chmn.-elect 1988, chmn. 1989-90, bd. dirs. 1991-94, mem. consultation com. 1994-96, chmn. endowment fund program com. 1996-98, chair bylaws com. 1998-2000), Nat. Info. Stds. Orgn. (bd. dirs. 1994-97), Beta Phi Mu. Democrat. Office: Inmagic Inc 800 W Cummings Park Woburn MA 01801-6372

EDDISON, JOHN F. P., naval architect; b. Leeds, Eng., July 28, 1950; s. William A. and Maisie F. (Pembridge) E.; m. Jane E. Watts, May 24, 1980; children: Sarah, Simon. BSME, U. Coll., London, 1973, MSc in Naval Architecture, 1974. Chartered engr. Naval architect Ministry of Def., U.K., 1969—. Mem. Royal Instn. of Naval Architects.

EDDLEMAN, FLOYD EUGENE, retired English language educator; b. Mena, Ark., Dec. 3, 1930; s. Floyd Newton and Ruby Kate (Cannon) E. BSE, U. Cen. Ark., 1951; MA, U. Ark., 1955, PhD, 1961. Teaching asst. U. Ark., Fayetteville, 1953-55, 56-58; instr. U. Colo., Boulder, 1955-56; instr. English, Tex. Tech U., Lubbock, 1958-62, asst. prof., 1962-65, assoc. prof., 1965-75, prof., 1975-90, prof. emeritus, 1991—. Author: American Drama Criticism, 1976, 79, 84, 89, 92; co-editor: Almayer's Folly in the Cambridge Edit. of the Works of Joseph Conrad, 1994; contbr. articles to profl. jours. Sgt. U.S. Army, 1951-53. Democrat. Mem. Christian Ch. (Disciples of Christ). Avocations: travel, collecting bison art objects. Home: 2400 44th St Apt 228 Lubbock TX 79412-1547

EDDY, FRANK STERLING, human resources manager, teacher; b. Quenset Point, RI, Nov. 10, 1951; s. Robert Sterling and Emalyn (Crandall) E.; m. Jean Marie McVeigh, July 28, 1973: children: Shannon, Catelyn. BS in Edn., Ctrl. Conn. State U., 1973; MA, Rensselaer Polytech. Inst., Hartford, 1987. cert. tchr. Conn. Indsl. edn. instr. Meriden Bd. Edn., Meriden, Conn., 1973-74, Manchester Bd. Edn., Manchester, Conn., 1974-80; employment recruiter Hamilton-Sunstrand United Techs. Corp., Windsor Locks, Conn., 1980-81; col. relations adminstr. Hamilton-Standard United Techs. Corp., Windsor Locks, Conn., 1981-83, human resources rep., 1983-85, mgr. employee relations, 1985-87, labor relations rep., 1987-89; mgr. indsl. relations United Techs. Corp. Automotive, Dearborn, Mich., 1989-93; mgr. human resources Pratt & Whitney-United Technologies Corp., Middletown, Ct., 1993-98, East Hartford, 1998—; cons. Hamilton Sunstrand-United Technologies Corp., Windsor Locks, Conn., 1978-80; bd. dirs. Middlesex Cmty. Tech. Col., Middletown, Conn., 1996-97. Vol. World Special Olympics, New Haven, Conn., 1995. Republican. Roman Catholic. Avocations: judo, golf, painting. Home: 21 Brookview Cir Manchester CT 06040-6853 Address: 400 Main St East Hartford CT 06108-0968

EDE, FRED OKOTCHY, marketing educator; b. Nigeria, May 6, 1949; came to U.S., 1979; s. Philemon Okeke and Mabel Uzo (Okochi) E.; children: Fred Jr., Phillip, Chidi. BS in Mktg., U. Nigeria, 1977; MBA, U. Detroit, 1980; PhD, U. S.C., 1985. Asst. lectr. dept. mktg. Inst. Mgmt. and Tech., Enugu, Nigeria, 1978-79; grad. rsch. asst. U. S.C., 1980-85; asst. prof. dept. bus. adminstrn. Allen U., 1982-85; assoc. prof. S.C. State U., 1983-85; assoc. prof. dept. fin. and mktg. Norfolk State U., 1985-98; prof. bus. adminstrn. dept. bus. adminstrn. and econs. Benedict Coll., Columbia, S.C., 1998—; chmn. bus. fin. and investment session 28th Internat. Atlantic Econ. Conf., Montreal, 1989, chmn. mktg. session, 1989; reviewer mktg. communications track Acad. Bus. Adminstrn. Conf., 1991—. Contbr. articles to profl. jours. Fellow Acad. Mktg. Sci.; mem. Am. Mktg. Assn., Nigerian Inst. Mktg., Alpha Mu Alpha. Home: 3509 Lake Ave Apt 1119 Columbia SC 29206-5198

EDELBAUM, PHILIP R., lawyer; b. Bklyn., June 2, 1936; s. Maurice and Selma (Samuels) E.; m. Corinne Edelbaum, May 29, 1960 (div. Mar. 1974); children: Stacey K. Boretz, Evan Mark. BA, Adelphi U., 1957; LLB, NYU, 1960. Bar: N.Y. 1961, U.S. Dist. Cts. (so. and ea. dists.) N.Y. 1962, U.S. Ct. of Appeals (2d cirs.) 1964, (3d cir.) 1977, U.S. Supreme Ct. 1965. Atty. criminal div. Legal Aid Soc., N.Y.C., 1961-63; pvt. practice N.Y.C., 1963—; faculty Nat. Inst. Trial Advocacy-N.E. Region, Nat. Inst. Trial Advocacy-N.E. Master Advocates, Hempstead, N.Y., 1985—, Cardozo Law Sch. intensive trial advocacy program, 1993—, ABA/USTA Trademark Trial Advocacy Inst., 1993—, Widener U. Sch. Law intensive trial advocacy program, 1995—; faculty trial techniques program Hofstra U. Sch. of Law, Hempstead, 1985—. Chmn. pool feasibility com. Town of Eastchester, N.Y., 1971-72. Mem. Nat. Def. Lawyers Criminal Cases, N.Y. Criminal Bar Assn., Assn. Bar City N.Y. (com. on criminal cts. op. and budget 1988-92, chmn. com. on criminal advocacy 1995-98, mem. com. criminal justice 1992-98, com. to study alts. to incarceration and probation 1993-94, CLE com. 1998—, numerous sub-coms. on criminal justice 1988-98). Avocations: classical music, bird watching, N.Y. Mets, cooking. Home: 345 E 93d St New York NY 10128-5515 Office: 39 Broadway Rm 1440 New York NY 10006-3003

EDELMAN, BERNARD PAUL, lawyer, counselor. BA with high distinction, U. Mich., 1981; JD, Northwestern U., 1985. Bar: Ill. 1985, U.S Dist. Ct. (no. dist.) Ill. 1985. Assoc. Friedman & Koven, Chgo., 1985-86; ptnr. Rosenthal & Schanfield, Chgo., 1987-94, Arnstein & Lehr, Chgo., 1994-99; ptnr., chmn. transaction group Grotefeld & Denenberg, Chgo., 1999—; spl. asst. atty. gen. Ill. Atty. Gen.'s Office, Springfield, 1997—; spl. hearing officer Ill. Dept. Profl. Regulation, Chgo., 1996, Office Banks & Real Estate State Ill., Chgo., 1997—; chairperson Cook County Mandatory Ct. Annex Arbitration Program, Chgo., 1994—. Co-founder, pres., bd. dirs. The LaSalle St. Coun., Chgo., 1991—; bd. dirs. LaSalle St. Found., Chgo., 1994—; rep. City of Chgo., Dept. Cultural Affairs, North LaSalle St. Project, Project Adv. Panel, 1998—. Angell Scholar U. Mich., 1981; Crain's Chgo. Bus. honoree 40 Under 40, 1993. Mem. Econ. Club Chgo., Execs. Club Chgo., Mid Day Club (Chgo.), Pi Sigma Alpha. Avocations: golf, tennis, political history, photography. Fax: (312) 551-0264. E-mail: bpe@gd-llc.com. Office: Grotefeld & Denenberg 100 W Monroe St Ste 1800 Chicago IL 60603-1912

EDELMAN, DANIEL JOSEPH, public relations executive; b. N.Y.C., July 3, 1920; s. Selig and Selma (Pfeiffer) E.; m. Ruth Rozumoff, Sept. 3, 1953; children: Richard, Renee, John. Grad., Columbia U., 1940; MS, 1941. Reporter Poughkeepsie (N.Y.) newspapers, UPI, 1941-42; news writer CBS, 1946-47; staff mem. Edward Gottlieb & Assocs., 1947; pub. rels. dir. Toni Co., Chgo., 1948-52; founder, chmn. 42 offices Daniel J. Edelman, Inc. (Edelman Pub. Rels. Worldwide and P.R. 21), Chgo., 1952—. Mem. Ill. Lottery Control Bd., 1974; mem. comm. com. Boy Scouts Am., Chgo.; chmn. vis. com. U. Chgo. Libr., 1976; bd. dirs. Ill. Children's Home and Aid Soc., Chgo.; chmn. sustaining fellows individual campaign Chgo. Art Inst., 1982; bd. dirs. Lyric Opera Chgo.; dir. Comm. for Econ. Growth of Israel.

With U.S. Army, 1942-46. Recipient Disting. Alumnus award Columbia U., 1988, John Jay award Columbia U., 1990; named Pub. Rels. Profl. of Yr. Pub. Rels. News, 1993, Agy. of Yr. Inside PR Mag., 1993, Lifetime Achievement All-Star Inside PR mag. award, 1998, St. Bonaventure U. Tom Mosser award, 1998; named to Chgo. Bus. Hall of Fame, Jr. Achievement, 1998. Fellow Pub. Rels. Soc. Am. (past chmn. counselor sect., Gold Anvil award for outstanding contbns. to pub. rels. profession 1999, 32 Silver Anvil awards, Top Gun Career Achievement award 1998, award for outstanding contbn. to the pub. rels. profession 1999), Young Pres. Orgn. (chmn. Chgo. chpt. 1963), Chief Execs. Orgn., Arthur Page Soc. (Hall of Fame 1997), Pub. Rels. Seminar, Chgo. Club, Std. Club, Harmonie Club, Mid-Am. Club, Casino Club, Arts Club, Phi Beta Kappa. Jewish. Home: 1301 N Astor St Chicago IL 60610-2186 Office: Edelman Pub Rels Aon Ctr 200 E Randolph Dr Chicago IL 60601-6436

EDELMAN, GERALD MAURICE, biochemist, neuroscientist, educator; b. N.Y.C., N.Y., July 1, 1929; s. Edward and Anna (Freedman) E.; m. Maxine Morrison, June 11, 1950; children: Eric, David, Judith. B.S., Ursinus Coll., 1950, Sc.D., 1974; M.D., U. Pa., 1954, D.Sc., 1973; Ph.D., Rockefeller U., 1960; M.D. (hon.), U. Siena, Italy, 1974; DSc (hon.), Gustavus Adolphus Coll., 1975, Williams Coll., 1976; DSc Honoris Causa, U. Paris, 1989; LSc Honoris Causa, U. Cagliari, 1989; DSc, Georgetown U., 1989; DSc Honoris Causa, U. degli Studi di Napoli, 1990, Tulane U., 1991, U. Miami, 1995, Adelphi U., 1995, U. Bologna, 1998, U. Minn., 2000. Med. house officer Mass. Gen. Hosp., 1954-55; asst. physician hosp. of Rockefeller U., 1957-60, mem. faculty, 1960-92, assoc. dean grad. studies, 1963-66, prof., 1966-74, Vincent Astor disting. prof., 1974-92; mem. faculty and chmn. dept. neurobiology Scripps Rsch. Inst., La Jolla, Calif., 1992—; mem. biophysics and biophys. chemistry study sect. NIH, 1964-67; mem. Sci. Council, Ctr. for Theoretical Studies, 1970-72; assoc., sci. chmn. Neurosciences Research Program, 1980—, dir. Neurosci. Inst., 1981—; mem. adv. bd. Basel Inst. Immunology, 1970-77, chmn., 1975-77; non-resident fellow, trustee Salk Inst., 1973-85; bd. overseers Faculty Arts and Scis., U. Pa., 1976-83; trustee, mem. adv. com. Carnegie Inst., Washington, 1980-87; bd. govs. Weizman Inst. Sci., 1971-87, mem. emeritus; researcher structure of antibodies, molecular and devel. biology. Author: Neural Darwinism, 1987, Topobiology, 1988, The Remembered Present, 1989, Bright Air, Brilliant Fire, 1992, A Universe of Consciousness: How Matter Becomes Imagination, 2000. Trustee Rockefeller Bros. Fund., 1972-82. Served to capt. M.C. AUS, 1955-57. Recipient Spencer Morris award U. Pa., 1954, Ann. Alumni award Ursinus Coll., 1969, Nobel prize for physiology or medicine, 1972, Albert Einstein Commemorative award Yeshiva U., 1974, Buchman Meml. award Calif. Inst. Tech., 1975, Rabbi Shai Shacknai meml. prize Hebrew U.-Hadassah Med. Sch., Jerusalem, 1977, Regents medal Excellence, N.Y. State, 1984, Hans Neurath prize, U. Washington, 1986, Sesquicentennial Commemorative award Nat. Libr. Medicine, 1986, Cécile and Oskar Vogt award U. Dusseldorf, 1988, Disting. Grad. award U. Pa., 1990, Personnalité de l'année, Paris, 1990, Warren Triennial Prize award Mass. Gen. Hosp., 1992m C.V. Ariens-Kappers medal, 1999, medal of the Presidency of the Italian Republic, 1999. Fellow AAAS, N.Y. Acad. Scis., N.Y. Acad. Medicine; mem. Am. Philos. Soc., Am. Soc. Biol. Chemists, Am. Assn. Immunologists, Genetics Soc. Am., Harvey Soc. (pres. 1975-76, Am. Chem. Soc., Eli Lilly award biol. chemistry 1965), Am. Acad. Arts and Scis., Nat. Acad. Sci., Am. Soc. Cell Biology, Acad. Scis. of Inst. France (fgn.), Japanese Biochem. Soc. (hon.), Pharm. Soc. Japan (hon.), Soc. Developmental Biology, Coun. Fgn. Rels., Century Assn., Cosmos Club, Phi Beta Kappa, Sigma Xi, Alpha Omega Alpha. Office: Scripps Rsch Inst Dept Neurobiol SBR-14 10550 N Torrey Pines Rd La Jolla CA 92037-1000

EDELMAN, JANICE, artist, educator; b. Phila., Apr. 13, 1933; d. Samuel and Anna (Finkelstein) Fishman; 1 child, Susan Helfrich. Degree, Art Inst. Phila., 1956; studied with, Henry Hensche, Provincetown, Mass., 1957, Boris Blai, Phila., 1979-80. Cert. art tchr., Pa. Advt. illustrator John Wanamaker, Phila., 1954-66; advt. art dir. Strawbridge & Clothier, Phila., 1967-76; comml. art instr. Hussian Sch. of Art, Phila., 1976-77; head of art dept. Montgomery County Vocat. Sch., Upper Moreland, Pa., 1978-79; watercolor instr. Woodmere Art Mus., Phila., 1991—; docent Woodmere Art Mus., 1989-91; judge juror Glassboro State Coll., N.J., 1992, Norristown Art League, 1999; bd. dirs. Friends of Moore Coll. of Art, Phila., 1977; lectr. in field. Exhibited in group shows at Fashion Group of Phila., 1955, 57, (Fine Arts Gala award 1955, 1st prize 1957), Phila. Club Advt. Women 12 Ann., 1966, 67 (1st prize for layout 1966, for art-layout 1967), 13th Ann., 1974 (1st prize for art-layout 1974, 75), Artist Guild of Delaware Valley 25th Ann., 1975 (Bronze award 1975), Art Dirs. Club of Phila. 39th Ann., 1979 (2 awards for excellence, layout design 1979), Am. Coll., 1985, Phila. Water Color Club 67th Ann., 1985, 70th Ann., 1988, 71st Ann., 1989, 74th Ann., 1992, 75th Ann., 1993 (award of excellence 1988, show chmn. 1992), Watercolor Soc. Ala. 45th Ann., 1986, Oreland Art Ctr. Ann., 1986 (1st prize in watercolor 1986), Artilleries Gallery, 1987, Perkiomen Valley Retirement Cmty., 1987, Charlotte Watercolor Soc., 1987, Woodmere Art Mus. 47th Ann., 1987, 48th Ann., 1988, 49th Ann., 1989, 52nd Ann., 1992, 56th Ann., 1996, Abington Art Ctr. Ann., 1988, Pa. Watercolor Soc. 10th Ann., 1988, 11th Ann., 1989 (Grumbacher award 1988), 20th Ann., 1999, Salmagundi Club 11th Ann., N.Y., 1988, 16th Ann., 1993 (Merit award 1988), Yellow Spring Art Show, 1989, Art Inst. Phila., 1989, Phila. Art Show, 1989, 90, Balt. Watercolor Soc., 1990, Susquehanna Art Soc. 84th Biennial, 1990, Barn Studio Gallery, 1990, Greater Harrisburg (Pa.) Arts Coun., 1993, Springfield Art League 74th Nat., 1993, Artist Guild Nat., Scottbluff, Nebr., 1993, Batavia (N.Y.) Soc. Artists 9th Nat., 1993, Watercolor Art Soc., Houston, 1994, W.Va. Water Color Soc., 1994, Watercolor West XXVI Ann., Brea, Calif., 1994, Main Line Arts Festival, Haverford, Pa., 1994, Nat. Watercolor Soc., Calif., 1995, Pitts. Watercolor Soc. Ann., Pa., 1995, Bald Eagle Art League Nat., Pa., 1995, North West N.Mex. Arts Coun. (award), 1997; solo show Woodmere Art Mus., Phila., 1997, Phila. Water Color Club 98th juried exhibition, 1998, Pa. Watercolor Soc. Ann., 1999, Atlantic City (N.J.) Art Mus., 1999, Krasdale Gallery, N.Y., 1999. Mem. mus. com. Keneseth Israel Congregation; chair Art Study Group, exec. sec. Ret. Execs. and Profls., Cheltenham, Pa., 1999—; juror Norristown Art League, 1999, art lectr., 1999, 2000. Mem. Am. Watercolor Soc. (assoc.), Nat. Watercolor Soc. (assoc.), Pa. Watercolor Soc., Phila. Watercolor Soc., Art Dirs. Club Phila. (pres. 1978-80), Phila. Water Color Club (v.p. 1993-94). Jewish. Avocations: painting, traveling, reading, creative cooking. Home: 3500 Hale Rd Huntingdon Valley PA 19006-3230

EDELMAN, MURRAY JACOB, political science educator; b. Nanticoke, Pa., Nov. 5, 1919; s. Kalman and Sadie (Wiesenberg) E.; m. Bacia Stepner, June 15, 1952; children: Lauren Beatrice, Judith Sybil, Sarah Miriam. B.A., Bucknell U., 1941; M.A., U. Chgo., 1942; Ph.D., U. Ill., 1948. Mem. faculty U. Ill., 1948-66, prof. polit. sci., 1958-66, chmn. dept. polit. sci., 1965-66; prof. polit. sci. U. Wis., 1966—, George Herbert Mead prof., 1972—, WARF sr. disting. research prof., 1984-90, prof. emeritus, 1990—. Author: The Licensing of Radio Services in the United States, 1927-47, 1950, National Economic Planning by Collective Bargaining, 1954, The Politics of Wage-Price Decisions: A Four Country Analysis, 1965, (with R.W. Fleming) The Symbolic Uses of Politics, 1964, Politics as Symbolic Action: Mass Arousal and Quiescence, 1971, Political Language, 1977, Constructing the Political Spectacle, 1988. Served with USAAF, 1942-45. Guggenheim fellow, 1962-63, 83-84; Fulbright grantee Austria, 1952; Fulbright grantee Italy, 1956; NEH sr. fellow, 1974-75. Mem. Am. Polit. Sci. Assn. (v.p. 1988-89). Home: 1824 Vilas Ave Madison WI 53711-2232

EDELMANN, LAMBERT, cell biologist, researcher; b. Dortmund, Germany, May 19, 1961; s. Karl and Renate Edelmann. Diploma, U. Freiburg, Germany, 1989; PhD, Yale U. and U. Tübingen, 1995. Postdoctoral assoc. U. Basel, Switzerland, 1995-97, Harvard Med. Sch., 1998—. Yale Student fellow, 1991-94; Human Frontiers Sci. Orgn. fellow, 1995-97. Mem. Gesellschaft Biol. Chemie, Am. Soc. for Cell Biology, Am. Soc. for Neurosci. Office: MGH Cancer Ctr Bldg 149 13th St Charlestown MA 02129

EDELSTEIN, ROSEMARIE (HUBLOU), nurse educator, medical and legal consultant; b. Drake, N.D., Mar. 3, 1935; d. Frances Jerome and Myrtle Josephine (Merbach); m. Harry George Edelstein, June 22, 1957 (div.); children: Julie, Lori, Lynn, Toni Anne. BSN, St. Teresa of Avila Coll., Winona, Minn., 1956; MA in Edn., Holy Names Coll., Oakland, Calif., 1977; EdD, U. San Francisco, 1982, postgrad., 1987; postgrad. in pub. health, U. Ariz., 1985—; cert. pub. health nurse, U. Calif., Berkeley, 1972. Dir., clin. supr. San Francisco Sch. for Health Professions, 1971-74, Rancho Arroyo Sch. of Vocat. Nursing, Sacramento, 1974-75; intensive care nurse Kaiser-Permanente Hosp., San Rafael, Calif., 1976-77; dir. insvc. edn. Ross Hosp., Calif., 1977-78; assoc. dir. nursing St. Francis Meml. Hosp., San Francisco, 1978-85; med.-legal nursing cons., med.-surg. staff nurse met. hosps., San Francisco, 1985-90, St. Luke's Hosp., Duluth, Minn., 1990-91, St. Charles Hosp., New Orleans, 1992, U. Tex. Med. Br., Galveston, 1992-94; staff nurse family medicine faculty practice, 1995; med.-surg. nurse St. Anthony of Padua Hosp., Oklahoma City, 1994-95; nurse Northgate Conv. Hosp., San Rafael, 1995—; night charge nurse Creekside Conv. Hosp., Santa Rosa, Calif., 1996; charge nurse medications, treatment and Alzheimer's Unit, Fallon Conv. Ctr., Nev., 1996, charge nurse Medicare Unit, WHite Pine Conv. Ctr., Ely, Nev., 1997; emergency rm. and ICU nurse Battle Mt. Gen. Hosp., Nev., 1997; nurse supr. Medicare-Med. Seaview Care Ctr. Sun Corp., Eureka, Calif., 1997-98; mem. staff Walker Post Manor Oxford, NE Lantis Corp., 1998, The Lincoln Ambassador, 1999, Rapid City (S.D.) Care Ctr. Beverly Enterprises, 2000—; invited mem. People to People Nursing Edn. and Adminstrn., candidate to East Asia, Philosophy, 1985; postgrad. candidate U. Zurich, Switzerland, 1988. Author: The Influence of Motivator and Hygiene Factors in Job Changes by Graduate Registered Nurses, 1977; Effects of Two Educational Methods Upon Retention of Knowledge in Pharmacology, 1981; co-author: (with Jane F. Lee) Acupunture Atlas, 1974. Candidate U.S. Senate Inner Circle, 1988, 89. Lt. col. USAR Med. Res. Mem. Am. Heart Assn., Calif. Nurses Assn., Sigma Theta Tau. Roman Catholic.

EDEN, ALVIN NOAM, pediatrician, author; b. Bklyn., Mar. 21, 1926; s. Emanuel M. and Rae (Taran) Edelstein; m. Elaine R. Jaffe, Nov. 20, 1952; children: Robert, Elizabeth. BA, Columbia Coll., 1948; MD, Boston U., 1952. Intern Bellevue Hosp., N.Y.C., 1952-53; resident in pediat. Univ. Hosp., N.Y.C., 1953-55; pvt. practice specializing in pediat. Forest Hills, N.Y., 1955—; assoc. clin. prof. pediat. NYU Sch. Medicine, 1960-84; chmn., dir. dept. pediat. Wyckoff Heights Med. Ctr., Bklyn., 1959; lectr. SUNY-Downstate Med. Ctr., Bklyn., 1984-86, assoc. clin. prof. pediat., 1986-90; assoc. clin. prof. pediat. Cornell Med. Coll., 1990-99, clin. prof., 1999—. Author: Growing Up Thin, 1975, Handbook for New Parents, 1978, Positive Parenting, 1980, Dr. Eden's Healthy Kids, 1987; contbr. articles to profl. jours.; author text and reference materials. With USMC, 1944-46. Mem. N.Y. Pediatric Soc. (pres. 1980-81), Queens Pediatric Soc. (pres. 1972-73), N.Y. Acad. Medicine (chmn. pediatric sect. 1985-89), Am. Acad. Pediatrics (chmn. nutrition com. chpt. 2 1985-89). Avocation: tennis. Home: 710 Park Ave New York NY 10021-4944 Office: 10721 Queens Blvd Forest Hills NY 11375-4451

EDEN, F(LORENCE) BROWN, artist; b. Jericho Center, Vt., Oct. 10, 1916; d. Arthur Castle and Eva Merita (Lowrey) Brown; m. Edwin Winfield Eden, Sept. 4, 1937; children: Donna Jean, Sandra Elizabeth, Kathy Lynn. Student, U. Fla. Extension, 1955-59, U. Mich., 1963. Art instr. Ann Arbor (Mich.) City Club, 1962-63; tchr., oil painting, printmaking Jacksonville (Fla.) Art Mus., 1963-68. One-woman shows include The Fox Galleries, Atlanta, 1986, Harmon Galleries, Sarasota, 1987, 89-90, 92-93, Gallery Contemporanea St. Augustine, Jacksonville, Artist Assocs. Gallery, Atlanta, 1965-1990, The Hodgell Gallery, Sarasota, 1997-2000, The Center, Ponte Vedra, Fla., 1999, Kent Campus Gallery, Fla. C.C., Jacksonville, Fla., 1999; represented in permanent collections Fed. Res. Bank Atlanta, Bank Am., Coca-Cola Co., So. Bell, Sheraton Corp., AT&T, Trust Co. Ga., Shell Oil, Touche Ross, Cooper and Lybrand, Delta Airlines "Crown Rm.," 5th Dist. Ct. Appeals Bldg., Daytona Beach, Fla., Edwin and Ruth Kennedy Mus. Am. Art, U. Ohio, Athens; exhibited in group shows at Ala. Nat. Watercolors, Fla., Ga. Nat., Audubon Nat., Painters in Casein and Acrylics Nat., N.Y.C. Mem. Jacksonville Mus. Art (chmn. area VI Fla. artist group 1979-89). Recipient First award Fla. Artist Group, 1971, 79, Fla. Artists, 1969, The Painting award Major Fla. Artists, 1979, numerous other 1st place awards. Mem. Am. Women Artists, Nat. Mus. of Women in the Arts (charter mem.), So. Watercolor Soc., Fla. Watercolor Soc. (Signature artist), Ga. Watercolor Soc., Ala. Watercolor Soc., Jacksonville Coalition of Visual Artists, Fla. Artists Jacksonville, Fla. Crown Treasures. Avocation: playing organ. Home and Studio: 5375 Sanders Rd Jacksonville FL 32277-1333

EDEN, NATHAN E., lawyer; b. Key West, Fla., Mar. 24, 1944; s. Delmar M. and Lois (Archer) E.; m. Cindy Pike, Jan. 4, 1964 (div. Mar. 1984); 1 child, Jennifer S. BA, U. Fla., 1966; JD magna cum laude, Stetson U., 1969. Bar: Fla. 1969, U.S. Dist. Ct. (so. and mid. dists.) Fla. 1969, U.S. Ct. Appeals (5th cir.) 1969, U.S. Ct. Appeals (11th cir.) 1982. Assoc. Nelson, Stinnett, Surfus, et al, Sarasota, Fla., 1969; ptnr. Feldman & Eden & predecessors, Key West, 1970-84; sole practice Key West, 1984-99; of counsel Lazzara and Paul, P.A., Tampa, 1982—; ptnr. Browning, Eden, Sireci & Klitenick, 1999—; bd. atty. Utility Bd. of Key West, 1974—; asst. pub. defender State of Fla., Key West, 1970, county solicitor State of Fla., Key West, 1970-72; chief asst. state atty State of Fla., Key West, 1972-74; U.S. magistrate, U.S. Dist. Ct. (so. dist.) Fla., 1974-78. Mem. jud. nominating com. 16th Jud. Cir. State of Fla., 1995, bd. dirs. Hospice Monroe County. Mem. Acad. Trial Lawyers, Fla. Acad. Trial Lawyers, Nat. Assn. Criminal Def. Lawyers, Fla. Bar Assn. (bd. govs. 1976-80), North Am. Hunt Club, NRA. Democrat. Avocations: hunting, softball, jogging, basketball. Office: 402 Applerouth Ln Key West FL 33040-6535 also: Lazzara and Paul PA 606 E Madison St Ste 2001 Tampa FL 33602-4017

EDEN, OSBORN BRYAN, pediatric oncology educator; b. Birmingham, Eng., Apr. 2, 1947; s. Eric Victor and Gwendoline (Hambly) E.; m. Randi Forsgren, May 15, 1970; children: Ivar, Tonje. MB, BS, Univ. Coll. and Hosp., London, 1970. House physician Univ. Coll. and Hosp., 1970-71; sr. house officer, Isle of Wight, London, Edinburgh, Scotland, 1972-74; registrar Royal Hosp. for Sick Children, Edinburgh, 1974-76, cons. clin. hematologist, 1982-91; postdoctoral fellow Stanford (Calif.) U. Med. Sch., 1976-77; lectr. pediatric oncology U. Edinburgh, 1977-78; cons. Bristol (Eng.) Children's Hosp., 1979-81; prof. St. Bartholomew's Hosp., London, 1991-94; prof. pediat. oncology Christie Hosp., Manchester, Eng., 1994—; chmn. Med. Rsch. Coun., Leukemia Working Party, Eng., 1991-00. Contbr. 10 chpts. to books; contbr. over 200 articles on pediatric cancer to profl. publs. Trustee Sargent Cancer Care, London, 1984-98, med. advisor, 1998—; chmn. U.K. Children's Cancer Group, 1989-92, mem. com. on med. affects of radiation in the environment. Fellow Royal Coll. Physicians (Edinburgh), Royal Coll. Physicians (London), Royal Coll. Pathology, Royal Coll. Pediatrics and Child Health; mem. Internat. Soc. Pediatric oncology (sci. com. 1992-98, chmn. sci. com. 1996-98). Avocations: reading, music, theatre, photography, hiking. Home: 5 S Gillsland Rd, Edinburgh EH10 5DE, Scotland Office: Christie Hosp, Wilmslow Rd, Manchester M2O 4BX, England

EDENS, BETTY JOYCE, reading recovery educator; b. Hillsboro, Tex., Oct. 20, 1944; d. Edward Alton and Mary Alma (Pendley) Harbin; m. Eugene Cliett Edens, May 29, 1964; children: Michael Eugene, Anne-Marie DeWitt, Kristen Babovec. BEd, Ind. U., 1985; MS Tex. A&M of Commerce, 1995. Cert. elem. tchr., reading tchr., Tex. 1st grade tchr. Monday Primary, Kaufman, Tex., 1986-93; 1st grade tchr. Franklin Elem., Hillsboro, Tex., 1993-96, reading recovery tchr., 1994-98, 99-00, 2nd grade tchr., 1998-99; reading recovery tchr. Hillsboro Elem. Sch., 1999—. Mem. early literacy com. TSRA, 1998, Susan G. Komen Found. Mem. Reading Recovery Coun. of N.Am., Internat. Reading Assn., Tex. Reading Assn., Monday Rev. Club. Republican. Mem. Ch. of Christ. Avocations: recreational reading, walking, computers.

EDENS, FRED JOE, petroleum engineer; b. Guymon, Okla., Oct. 3, 1952; s. Bill H. and D. Jeanne (Clifford) E.; m. Becky A. Yost, Oct. 25, 1976; children: Jason, Jarrod. BCE, Okla. State U., 1974. Registered profl. engr., Tex. Civil engr. U.S. Army Corps Engrs., Tulsa, 1975-81; petroleum engr. Amoco Prodn. Co., Liberal, Kans., 1981-84; prodn. foreman Amoco Prodn. Co., Casper, Wyo., 1984-86, facilities engr., 1986-89; mech. engr. Amoco Prodn. Co., Denver, 1989-92; petroleum engr., field foreman Amoco Prodn. Co., Ratliff City, Okla., 1992-98; petroleum engr. BP Amoco Plc., Perryton, Tex., 1998—. Capt. USAF, 1974-85. Mem. Soc. Petroleum Engrs. Republican. Baptist. Home: 2506 Texas St Perryton TX 79070-5848 Office: BP Amoco PO Box 1005 Perryton TX 79070-1005

EDEOGA, HILARY ODO, biological sciences educator, researcher; b. Eha-Amufu, Enugu, Nigeria, Nov. 28, 1960; s. Ogenyi Eze and Idenyi Ebe (Nwaeze Ogbodo) E.; m. Georgina Ibizugbe Ukpebor, Mar. 5, 1990. BSc, U. Port Harcourt, Nigeria, 1984, MSc, 1989, PhD, 1991. Asst. lectr. Bendel State U., Ekpoma, Nigeria, 1988-91, coord. pre-degree sci. program botany unit, 1990-91, gen. duties officer dept. botany, 1991-92; lectr. II, Edo State U., Ekpoma, 1991-93, lectr. I, 1993-96, sr. lectr., 1996-99, gen. studies officer Faculty Natural Scis., 1991-95, coord. indsl. tng. dept. botany, 1990-92, 94-95; assoc. prof. dept. biol. scis. Fed. U. Agr., Umudike-Unuahia, Nigeria, 1999—; environ. cons. Tropical Rubber Nigeria Ltd., Sapele, 1989-99, DBEI, Nigeria Ltd.Benin, 1998—, Chamcent Ltd., Benin, 1999—; conf. presenter Nigerian Soc. Plant Protection. Co-author, co-editor: Foundations of Biology, 1993; co-author: History and Philosophy of Science and Technology, 1994; contbr. over 50 articles and abstracts to sci. jours., including Jour. Exptl. Applied Biology, Nigerian Annals Natural Sci., Jour. Econ. Taxonomy, Jour. Plant Anat. Morphology, Feddes Report, Jour. Applied Biology, Jour. Med. Lab. Sci., New Botany, Jour. Root Crops, Global Jour. Pure and Applied Sci. Mem. Genetics Soc. Nigeria (conf. presenter), Bot. Soc. Nigeria (conf. presenter), Sci. Soc. Nigeria (conf. presenter). Roman Catholic. Home: Dr HO Edeoga's Comp, Amede, PO Box 20, Eha-Amufu Enugu, Nigeria Office: Michael Okpara U Agr, Biol Scis, Umudike PMB 7267, Umuahia Abia St, Nigeria

EDER, REINHARD, food technologist; b. Klosterneuburg, Austria, Apr. 14, 1963; s. Reinhard and Leopoldine (Schwarzinger) E.; m. Maria Theresia Podsednik. PhD in Food Tech., U. Vienna, 1988. Tech. Agrl. Rsch. Inst., Leifers, Italy, 1979-83, Gosser Brewery, Leoben, Austria, 1983-84, Findus-Nestle, Bjuv, Sweden, 1984-85; engr. Vogelbusch-Bioengring., Vienna, 1985-87; chemist Verbandsmolkerei Bern, Switzerland, 1987, Hbla Wein-u. Obstbau, Klosterneuburg, 1988—; cert. winetaster Austrian Wine Control, Klosterneuburg, 1991—; head dept. chemistry Hbla Wein U. Obstbau, 1994—. Author: Food Pigments, 1994, Wildfruchte, 1993, Food Analysis by HPLC, Weinfehler. Mem. Austrian Oenologists (vice sec. 1992—), Assn. Austrian Food and Biotechnologists, Assn. Austrian Chemists, Groupe Polyphenols, Internat. Chemometrics Soc., East Malling Rsch. Assn., Deutscher Oenologenverband Inst. Food Technologists (expert and del at O.I.V.). Roman Catholic. Home: Hermannstrasse 2, A-3400 Klosterneuburg Austria Office: Hbla Wein u Obstbau, Wiener Strasse 74, A-3400 Klosterneuburg Austria

EDER-RIEDER, MARIA ANNA, law educator; b. Töshing, Carinthia, Austria, Dec. 16, 1950; d. Anton Ernst and Martha (Schuster) Rieder; m. Richard Georg Eder, Dec. 3, 1983; 1 child, Astrid Maria. Dr.iur., Mag.iur., U. Salzburg, Austria, 1975, Dr.phil., 1980. Asst. Inst. Penal Law U. Salzburg, 1975-84, lectr., 1984—. Author: Die Freiheitsentziehenden Vorbeugenden Massnahmen, 1985, Der Opferschutz, 1998.

EDET, ANIEKAN EFFIOM, geologist; b. Anua-Uyo, Akwa Ibom, Nigeria, Oct. 25, 1962; s. Effiom Ekpenyong and Alice Effiom E.; m. Grace Aniekan Ayakem, June 5, 1999. BS in Geology, U. Calabar, Nigeria, 1983; PhD in Geology, U. Calabar, 1993; MS in Geology, U. Ibadan, Nigeria, 1985; Cert., U. Tuebingen, Germany, 1989. Asst. lectr. U. Calabar, 1986-90, lectr. 2, 1990-93, lectr. 1, 1993-96, sr. lectr., 1996-99; sr. cons. Teks Geotech. Cons., Portharcourt, Nigeria, 1994—; spl. asst. Unical Consult, Calabar, 1996—. Mem. com. NMGS, Calabar, 1995, NAH, 1991. Grantee DAAD, Germany, 1988, 93, 99. Mem. Internat. Assn. Hydrogeologists, Nigerian Mining and Geoscis. Soc. Avocations: films, football, swimming, group discussion, outings. Office: Dept Geology/U Calabar, PO Box 3609, Calabar/Cross River Nigeria

EDFELDT, AKE WERNER, information specialist, educator; b. Stockholm, Feb. 24, 1926; s. Johan Verner and Emy Elisabet (Fagerlund) E.; m. Maj Bildt, Aug. 25, 1957 (div. 1965); children: Eric Johan Werner, Fredrik, Cattie, Ylva, Mikaela; m. Kerstin Anna Brita Joëlson, Jan. 3, 1979. MA, Stockholm U., 1953, PhD, 1954, EdD, 1960. Asst. prof. Stockholm U., 1960-65, assoc. prof., 1965-68, prof. edn., 1970-84, 84-90, prof. emeritus, 1991—; mng. dir. Informationskonsult Inc., 1965-85, chmn., 1986—; prof. edn. Turku Acad., Finland, 1968-70; inspector RMI Sch. Advt. and Mktg., Sweden, 1989-97. Contbr. articles to profl. jours. Mem. State Bd. Film Censors, Stockholm, 1967-76; chmn. Swedish Nat. Group Jazz History, 1998—; expert to several state coms. on comm. and violence towards children. Recipient Hon. Silver plaque Stockholm Cmty. Bd., 1990, The Bass Player Mark of Distinction, The Swedish Jazz Fedn., 2000. Mem. Internat. Assn. Reading and Learning Disabilities, Rotary (pres. 1983-84). Avocations: hunting, vintage car motoring, vintage jazz records collecting. E-mail: ake.w.edteldt@swipnet.se. Home: Gamla Tyresövägen 388, S-12134 Stockholm Enskede, Sweden Office: Informationskonsult AB, Hagtornsvägen 13, S-12134 Stockholm Enskede, Sweden

EDGAR, JIM, former governor; b. Vinita, Okla., July 22, 1946; m. Brenda Smith; children: Brad, Elizabeth. Grad., Eastern Ill. U., 1968; postgrad., U. Ill., Sangamon State U., 1971-74. Legis. intern pres. pro tem Ill. Senate, 1968; key asst. to speaker ho. Ill. Ho. of Reps., 1972-73; aide to pres. Ill. Senate, 1974, to Ho. minority leader, 1976; mem. Ill. Ho. of Reps., 1977-79; dir. legis. affairs Ill. Gov., 1979-80; sec. state State of Ill., 1981-91; gov. State of Ill., 1991-98; disting. fellow Inst. Govt. and Publs. U. Ill., Urbana, 1999—; co-lead gov. Nat. Gov.'s Assn. Transp. Com., 1995-96; chair Edn. Commn. of States, 1993-94; chair Nat. Gov.'s Assn. Com. on Econ. Devel. and Commerce, 1992-93; pres. Coun. State Govts., 1992-93; chair Gov.'s Ethanol Coalition, 1992-93; chair Nat. Gov.'s Assn. Com. on Econ. Devel. and Tech. Innovation, 1991-92. Precinct committeeman, treas. Coles County Rep. Com., 1974; dir. state svc. Nat. Conf. State Legislatures, 1975, 76; mem. campaign com. Ill. Ho. of Reps.; pres. Nat. Assn. Secs. of State, 1988; exec. com. Coun. State Govts., 1988, v.p. exec. com., 1991, pres., 1992-93; bd. dirs. Nat. Commn. Against Drunk Driving, 1989; chmn. Ill. Literacy Coun., 1989; chmn. Edn. Commn. of the States, 1993-94; chmn. Gov.'s Ethanol Coalition, 1992-93; pres. Bd. Coun. State Govts. Mem. Nat. Govs. Assn. (chmn. econ. devel. and commerce com. 1992-93, strategic planning rev. task force 1991—, past chmn. task force on edn., mem. edn. goals panel, chair com. econ. devel. and technol. innovation 1991-92, edn. commn. of states 1993-94, co-lead gov. transp. com. 1995-96), Coles County Hist. Soc. (pres. 1976-79). Baptist. Office: U Ill Inst Govt and Pub Affairs 1007 W Nevada St # MC-037 Urbana IL 61801-3812*

EDGAR, MICHAEL ALAN, orthopaedic and spinal surgeon; b. London, July 6, 1937; s. Alan Thomas and Mary (Robey) E.; m. Hilary Ann Warner, June 29, 1963; children: Alison, Jocelyn, Claire. MA, Cambridge, 1962, MB, 1963, MChir, 1977. Sr. orthopaedic registrar Royal Nat. Orthopaedic Hosp., 1971-73; spinal rsch. fellow UCLA, 1973; cons. orthopaedic surgeon The Middlesex, London, 1973-92; dir. of spinal deformity unit Inst. of Orthopaedic Univ., London, 1977-92; cons. UCLA Hosp., 1993—; orthopaedic cons. to Football Assn., 1983; civil adv. in orthopaedic Royal Air Force, 1985—, hon. sec. British Orthopaedic Assn., 1989-92; pres. British Scoliosis Soc., 1994-95. Contbr. articles to profl. jours.; mem. editl. bd. Jour. Bone and Joint Surgery, 1983-86. Mem. Royal Coll. Surgeons (coun. 1995—), Scoliosis Rsch. Soc. U.S.A. (coms. 1995—). Avocations: sailing, fell walking, antique collecting. Office: 149 Harley St, London WIN2DE, England

EDGE, DAVID OWEN, science educator; b. High Wycombe, Eng., Sept. 4, 1932; s. Stephen Rathbone Holden and Kathleen Edith (Haines) E.; m. Barbara Corsie, Feb. 21, 1959; children: Aran Kathleen, Alastair Clouston, Gordon. BA in Physics, Cambridge U., 1955, MA, 1959, PhD in Radio Astronomy, 1959. Producer Sci. Talks BBC, London, 1959-66; dir. Sci. Studies Unit Edinburgh (Scotland) U., 1966-89, reader Sci. Studies, reader emeritus, 1979—, mem. Univ. Ct., 1983-86; quality assurance auditor Higher Edn. Quality Coun./Quality Assurange Agy., 1992—; chair Sci. Policy Support Group, 1989-93. Co-author: Astronomy Transformed, 1976; co-editor: Science in Context, 1982; joint editor Social Studies Sci. 1971-82, editor, 1982—. Hdqrs. adviser Scout Assn., Scotland, 1967-85; cir. steward Meth. Ch., Edinburgh and Forth Cir., 1984-86. Soc. for Humanities fellow Cornell U., 1973. Fellow AAAS, Royal Astron. Soc., Royal Soc. Arts, Royal Soc. Edinburgh; mem. Soc. for Social Studies Sci. (council 1980-81, pres. 1985-87, Bernal prize 1993), N.Y. Acad. Scis., History of Sci. Soc., Brit. Soc. for History of Sci., Brit. Assn. for Advancement Sci., Scout and Guide Grad. Assn. (pres., former chmn.), European Assn. for Study of Sci. and Tech. Mem. Liberal Democrats. Avocations: music, travel, sports, editing footnotes. Home: 25 Gilmour Rd, Edinburgh EH16 5NS, Scotland

EDGE, WILLIAM E. BASIL, retired pediatrician; b. Witbank, Gauteng, South Africa, Sept. 25, 1923; s. Arthur Edwin and Gladys Nellie (Hind) E.; m. Suzanne Marie-Antoinette Dubayle, July 7, 1951; children: Francine, Marion, Phillip. B Medicine B Surgbery, U. Witwatersrand, Johannesburg, South Africa, 1947; BA summa cum laude, U. Natal, Durban, South Africa, 1998. Intern in medicine and surgery Johannesburg (South Africa) Gen. Hosp., 1948; resident ob-gyn. St. George's Hosp., London, 1949, West Middlesex Hosp., 1950; resident surgeon Am. Hosp. Paris, 1951; sr. lectr., pediatrician U. Natal, 1958-97, ret., 1997—. Co-author: Your Child, 1976; author: Encyclopaedia of Child Care, 1986. Cpl. South African Def. Forces, 1944-45. Fellow Royal Coll. Physicians; mem. South African Med. Assn. (br. pres. 1971). Democrat. Achievements include co-inventor first neonator respiratory alarm monitor. Avocations: wildlife, antique restoration. Home: 273 Chelmsford Rd, Durban Natal 4001, Republic of South Africa

EDGELL, HENRY STEWART, geologist, educator; b. Hobart, Tasmania, Australia, Sept. 23, 1927; s. Henry Colin and Joan Stewart (Fisher) E.; m. Golbahar Avazzadeh, July 28, 1957; children: Stewart Cameron, Henry Colin. BSc with 1st class honors, U. Sydney, 1950; diploma, Swiss Geol. Soc., 1953; PhD in Geology, Stanford U., 1954. Geologist Bur. of Mineral Resources, Canberra, Australia, 1949-52; geologist/stratigrapher Richfield Oil Corp., 1954-57; head dept. paleontology Consortium, Iran, 1957-61; lectr. in geology U. Canterbury, Christchurch, New Zealand, 1961-62; govt. paleontologist Geol. Survey of Western Australia, Perth, 1962-65; asst. prof. geology Am. U., Beirut, 1966-70; assoc. prof. geology Pahlavi U. (now Shiraz U.), Shiraz, Iran, 1971-73, prof. geology, 1974-79, chmn. geology dept., 1977-78; chief paleontologist Occidental Oil Co., Tripoli, Libya, 1974-76; prof. geology Garyounis U., Benghazi, Libya, 1979-81; chief geologist Bass Strait Oil and Gas, Melbourne, Australia, 1981; sr. geologist Australian Occidental Pty. Ltd., Brisbane, Australia, 1982-83; regional geologist ARAMCO, Dhahran, Saudi Arabia, 1983-84; prof. geology King Fahd U. of Petroleum and Minerals, Dhahran, 1984-93; cons. geologist Petro Consult, Canberra, Australia, 1993—; vis. prof. UN econ. geol. expert Ctr. Applied Geology, Jeddah, Saudi Arabia, 1971; guest lectr., vis. prof. Kuwait U., 1979; cons. geologist Stone & Assocs., Houston, Beirut, 1965-66; ind. cons., 1967—; project mgr. Karst and Groundwater Project, Saudi Arabia, 1985-93; co-prin. investigator Shuttle Imaging Rader-C (SIR-C) project, Saudi Arabia, 1987-93. Author: Groundwater Resources Evaluation of Saudi Arabia, 1987 (Prince Mohammad Bin Fahd award for sci. excellence 1990); contbr. articles to profl. jours. Mem. PC Users Group, Canberra, 1997—, Microsoft Communique, Sydney, 1991—. Robert H. Palmer scholar Stanford U., 1952-54; Shell grantee for fundamental rsch., Stanford U., 1952-53, Rockefeller grantee Am. U. Beirut, 1967-69. Fellow Geol. Soc. Am., Geol. Soc. (London); mem. Am. Assn. Petroleum Geologists (Cert. of Recognition 1979), Geol. Soc. Australia, Swiss Geol. Soc., Sydney U. Union (life), Stanford Alumni (life), Paleontol. Assn. (U.K.), S.E.P.M., Internat. Assn. of Hydrogeologists. Avocations: travel, research, writing. Home: 8 Barkly Crescent Forrest, Canberra ACT 2603, Australia Office: Petro Consult, 8 Barkly Crescent, Canberra ACT 2603, Australia

EDGELL, STEPHEN EDWARD, psychology educator, statistical consultant; b. Inglewood, Calif., June 20, 1947; s. Stephen F. and Evelyn L. (Humborg) E.; m. Donna M. Grassello, Aug. 17, 1974. AA in Math., El Camino Jr. Coll., Gardena, Calif., 1968; AB in Psychology, Calif. State U., Long Beach, 1970; PhD in Math. Psychology, Ind. U., 1974; MA in Math., U. Louisville, 1987. Tchg. and rsch. asst. Ind. U., Bloomington, 1971-72, rsch. asst., computer sys. programmer, 1972, fellow, 1972-73, assoc. instr., 1973-74; asst. prof. psychology U. Louisville, 1974-80, assoc. prof., 1980-85, prof., 1985—, dir. exptl. psychology program, 1983, 88-91; mgr. software devel. Shelton Metrology Lab., Paducah, Ky., summer 1979; cons. on statis. analysis and exptl. design, product design, customer profile analysis, discrimination, computer software sys.; presenter in field at confs. and profl. meetings. Contbr. articles to profl. jours. Fellow NIMH, 1970-71. Mem. Soc. for Judgment and Decision Making (sec.-treas. 1986-89, newsletter editor 2000—), Soc. for Math. Psychology, Am. Statis. Assn., Psychometric Soc., Psychonomic Soc., Cognitive Sci. Soc., Sigma Xi. Achievements include research on judgment, decision making and choice with emphasis on using mathematical models, artificial neural network models, artificial intelligence and computer simulation of decision making, including Bayesian methods, development of statistical techniques. Home: 10604 Grassy Ct Louisville KY 40241-2011 Office: U Louisville Dept Psychology Louisville KY 40292-0001

EDGERTON, DEBRA, artist, educator; b. Junction City, Kans., Mar. 15, 1958; d. Hughes and Tamie E.; m. Terry Baxter, Apr. 13, 1991; children: Noah Hunter, Jesse Dylan. Student, Am. Acad. Art, Chgo., 1979; BFA, U. Kans., 1980. Artist Hallmark Cards, Kansas City, Mo., 1981-86; freelance artist Flagstaff, Ariz., 1986—; instr.'s. asst in printmaking U. Kans., Lawrence, 1987, instr. painting Lawrence Art Ctr., 1991-93, Sr. Citizen Ctr., Lawrence, 1992, No. Ariz. U., Flagstaff, 1993—. Exhibited in group shows Tex. Watercolor Soc., Ann. Allied Artists of Am. 86th Ann. Exhbn., Midwest Watercolor Soc. Ann. Transparent Exhbn., Am. Watercolor Soc.'s Ann. Exhbn., Nat. Watercolor Soc.'s Ann. Exhbn. Mem. Round Table for Arts, Lawrence, 1991-92; mayoral appointee Lawrence Art Commn., 1992-93; pres. Lawrence Art Guild Assn., 1992. Recipient Excellence award Geary County Sch. Dist., 1991, Merit award Ariz. Aqueous, 1994; Profl. Devel. grantee Kans. Art Commn., 1992, Tech. Asst. grantee Lawrence Arts Commn., 1992. Mem. Am. Watercolor Soc., Nat. Watercolor Soc., Allied Artists Am., Midwest Watercolor Soc. (life). Office: No Ariz U PO Box 6020 Flagstaff AZ 86011-0001

EDGERTON, RICHARD, restaurant and hotel owner; b. Haverford, Pa., May 2, 1911; s. Charles and Ida (Bonner) E.; m. Marie Lytle Page, Oct. 24, 1936; children: Leila, Margaret, Carol. LLD (hon.), Berry Coll., Mt. Berry, Ga. Chmn. Lakeside Inn Properties, Inc., Mt. Dora, Fla., 1935-80; pres. emeritus Twoton Inc.; owner 35 Burger King restaurants, Pa., 1967—; gen. mgr., pres. Buck Hill Falls (Pa.) Co., 1961-65; pres., CEO Eustis Sand Co., Mt. Dora, Fla., 1961—; founding dir. Fla. Service Corp., Tampa; v.p., dir. 1st Nat. Bank, Mt. Dora. Mem. Gov.'s Little Cabinet, Fla. Hotel & Restaurant Commmr., 1955-61. Trustee emeritus Berry Coll.; bd. dirs. Mt. Dora Cmty. Trust Fund; past. mem. Lake County Fla. Indsl. Devel. Commn.; past trustee Lake Sumter Mental Health Ctr. Found.; trustee emeritus Lake Sumter C.C. Served to lt. USNR, 1944-46; ETO. Named to Mid-Fla. Bus. Hall of Fame, 1994. Mem. Am. (dir.), Fla. (hon., past pres.) hotel and motel assns., N.H. Hotel Assn. (past pres.), Newcomen Soc., Welcome Soc., Pa. Soc. Clubs: Mt. Dora Yacht (past commodore, present fleet capt.), Mt. Dora Golf. Lodge: Mt. Dora Kiwanis (past pres.). Home: PO Box 175 234 W 3d Ave Mount Dora FL 32757

EDGERTON, ROBERT BRECKENRIDGE, anthropologist, educator; b. Maywood, Ill., Nov. 28, 1931; s. Robert Alfred and Marjorie Adelaide (Close) E.; m. Karen Ito. PhD, UCLA, 1960. Faculty dept. psychiatry UCLA, 1962—, prof., 1996—. Author: The Cloak of Competence, 1967, Rules, Exceptions and Social Orderr, 1985, Sick Societies, 1992, Death or Glory, 1999. Sgt. USAF, 1951-54. Am. Assn. on Mental Deficiency Rsch. awardee, 1976; recipient Career Rsch. award Acad. Mental Retardation, 1995. Fellow AAAS, Am. Assn. Arts and Scis.; mem. Soc. for Med. Anthropology (pres. 1976-77), Soc. for Psychol. Anthropology (pres. 1985-86). Office: UCLA Dept Psychiatry Los Angeles CA 90024

EDGREN, GRETCHEN GRONDAHL, magazine editor; b. Portland, Oreg., Mar. 17, 1931; d. Jack W. and Alice Belle (Wells) Grondahl; m. James McNeese, Oct. 22, 1955 (div. Nov. 1974); children: Amy, Terence James; m. Alvin H. Edgren, Dec. 14, 1984. BJ, U. Oreg., 1952. Staff writer The Oregonian, Portland, 1952-61; editor Sunday mag. The San Juan (P.R.) Star, 1963-65; inventory and info. specialist USAF and U.S. Army Recruiting Command, San Antonio and Chgo., 1965-67; assoc. editor VIP mag. Playboy Clubs, Chgo., 1967-69, mng. editor, 1969-70; assoc. editor Playboy mag., Chgo., 1970-74, sr. editor, 1974-92, contbg. editor, 1992—. Author: The Playboy Book, 1994, The Playmate Book, 1996, Inside the Playboy Mansion, 1998; editor: New Credit Rights for Women, 1976; contbr. articles to mags. Adv. bd. Old Oreg. Alumni mag. U. Oreg., Eugene, 1988-96; bd. dirs. Civic Arts Coun., Oak Park, Ill., 1976-84, pres., 1979-80, Village Players, Oak Park-River Forest (Ill.) Symphony Assn., Oak Park Concert chorale, 1975-91; mem. Oak Park Cable TV Commn., 1984-86; active Anna Maria Island (Fla.) Cmty. Chorus, 1992—, Anna Maria Island Turtle Watch, 1992—. Mem. Confrerie des Vignerons de St. Vincent Mâcon (maitresse du chpt. 1988-92), Webfoot Soc. U. Oreg., Phi Beta Kappa, Delta Delta Delta. Episcopalian. Avocations: singing, sailing, travel, loggerhead turtle rescue, wines.

EDHOLM, STEN G., career officer; b. Lidingoe, Sweden, Dec. 24, 1948; s. Gunnar and Barbro (Hellman) E.; m. Monette Harwall, May 24, 1974; children: Michael, Madelaine. Officer Swedish Army, 1971-91; mktg. dir. Hagglunds Vehicle, 1991-93; dir. Swedish Army Aviation, 1993-97; head Armed Forces HQ Planning Dept., 1997-99, head Armed Forces HQ Internat. Ops., 1999—. Sec. Rotary, Lidingo, 1999—. Brig. Gen., Swedish Army, 1998—. Avocations: skiing, hunting, sailing, navigation, wine. Office: Joint Ops Command, S-10251 Stockholm Sweden

EDIN, ESAT RASIM, real estate developer; b. Istanbul, Turkey, Apr. 6, 1960; s. Seci Ahmet and Sirin Hatice (Durusoy) E.; m. Mehpare Taki, Oct. 2, 1993; children: Murat, Cem, Serra. BA, Yale U., 1981. Gen. mgr. Dena Shipping, Istanbul, 1981-83; comml. mgr. Isikurt Transit, Istanbul, 1983-85, Edin Holding, Istanbul, 1985—; CEO Kemer Yapi, Istanbul, 1986—; bd. dirs. Kemer Yapi, Omerli Yapi, Edsan Insaat, Edin Emlak, Edin Holding, Göktürk Yapi. Developer town of Kemer Country, 1994, 96. Mem. Turkish Businessmen's and Industrialists Assn., Young Pres. Orgn., Turkish Developers Assn. (vice chair), Kemer Golf and Country Club (founder, chmn.). Avocations: tennis, riding, golf, film. E-mail: esat-edin@kemercountry.com. Home: Kemer Country Gokturk Beldesi, Istanbul Turkey Office: Kemer Yapi ve Turizm AS Edin & Suner Plz, 14 Meydan Sok Akadlar, 80630 Istanbul Turkey

EDINBURGH, DUKE OF See PHILIP, PRINCE

EDIS, ANTHONY JOHN, surgeon; b. Melbourne, Victoria, Australia, Sept. 20, 1942; m. Lynne Bold, Jan. 21, 1965; children: Sean, Simon, Graeme, Jamie. MBBS with hons., U. Western Australia, 1966, MD, 1971. Cert. Am. Bd. Surgery; FACS, FRACS. Rsch. asst. Mayo Postgrad. Sch. Medicine, 1968-70, resident in surgery, 1970-78; fellow in endocrine surgery Boston U., 1973-74; asst. prof. U. Minn./Mayo Postgrad. Sch. Medicine, 1974-78; assoc. prof. Mayo Sch. Medicine, 1978-80, U. We. Australia, 1980-87. Co-author: (books) Surgical Disorders of the Adrenal Gland, 1975, Manual of Endocrine Surgery, 1975, 2d edit., 1984. Office: Ste 42, 146 Mounts Bay Rd, 6000 Perth Australia

EDIS, GLORIA TOBY, pediatrician; b. N.Y.C., Dec. 6, 1939; d. Murray Alvin and Anna G. (Goldstein) E.; m. Myron Royal Schoenfeld, June 14, 1959; children: Bradley, Glenn, Dawn, Melody. BA, Cornell U., 1960; MD, NYU, 1963. Intern Montefiore Hosp., N.Y.C., 1963-64; pediatric resident Columbia Presbyn. Med. Ctr., N.Y.C., 1966-68; pediatrician Scarsdale (N.Y.) Pediatric Assocs., 1977—; pediatric attending Albert Einstein Med. Coll., Bronx, 1968-70; pediatrician Barsky Med. Group, N.Y.C., 1970-80. Fellow Am. Acad. Pediatrics; mem. AMA, Westchester County Med. Soc., Cornell Alumni Assn. Avocations: hiking, cycling, reading, weight training, theater. Office: Scarsdale Pediatric Assn 2 Overhill Rd Scarsdale NY 10583-5323

EDLESON, MICHAEL EDWARD, economist, finance educator, consultant, writer; b. St. Louis, Apr. 25, 1958; s. Edward and Joan Edelson; m. Jan Katherine Taulman, Sept. 6, 1981; 1 child, Christopher. BS with distinction, U.S. Mil. Acad., 1979; MBA with highest honors, Suffolk U., 1986; MS, MIT, 1986, PhD, 1990. Commd. 2d lt. U.S. Army, 1979; with Army Corps Engrs., 1979-84; asst. prof. fin. econs. U.S. Mil. Acad., West Point, N.Y., 1986-90; asst. prof. fin. Harvard Bus. Sch., Boston, 1990-96; vis. assoc. prof. fin. Tuck Sch. Dartmouth Coll., 1995-96; dir. risk mgmt. Infinity fin. Tech., 1996-97; v.p. NASD, 1997-99; sr. v.p., chief economist NASD/Nasdaq, 1999—; bd. dir. Geodynamics Corp. Author: Value Averaging, 1991, 2d edit., 1993, Armed Forces Guide to Personal Financial Planning, 1991; columnist National Forum, 1994—; contbr. articles to profl. jours., chpts. to books; creator of the Value Averaging Investment Technique, 1988. Fellow, grantee, Army Rsch. Inst., 1988, 89, 90, Sci. Rsch. Lab., 1988, 89. Mem. Fin. Mgmt. Assn. (1996-2000), Internat. Assn. Fin. Engrs., Fin. Execs. Inst., Phi Kappa Phi.

EDLUND, ROBERT MAURITZ, electrical engineer; b. Malmoe, Skaane, Sweden, Nov. 25, 1967; s. Sture Ingmar and Rosita (Navarro) E.; m. Susanna Eva Ollen, Dec. 31, 1990; children: Jonathan, Henrietta. Degree in Engring., Pauli, Malmoe, 1987; MS in Elec. Engring., Lund (Sweden) Inst. Tech., 1994. Computer repairman Wayne Europe, Malmoe, 1988-89; devel. engr. AMUY Hadar, Malmoe, 1994-95; sus. engr. Kockums Naval Sys., Malmoe, 1995-97, dept. mgr., 1997—. Recipient Celsius High Potential award, 1998. Avocation: basketball. Home: Knutstorpsg 71, 21622 Malmoe Sweden Office: Kockums Naval Sys, 20555 Malmoe Sweden

EDMISTON, JOSEPH TASKER, state official; b. Monterey Park, Calif., Oct. 27, 1948; s. Tasker Lee and Beula Viola (Bates) E.; m. Pepper Salter Abrams, 1985; children: William Tasker, Charles Henry. AA, East L.A. Coll., 1968; AB, U. So. Calif., 1970. Mgr. of ct. process Roy Rottner & Associates, Hollywood, Calif., 1970-73; So. Calif Coastal coord. Sierra Club, L.A., 1973-76, energy coord., Sacramento, Calif., 1976-77; dir. State of Calif. Santa Monica Mountains Land Acquisition Program, 1979-80; exec. dir. Santa Monica Mountains Comprehensive Planning Commn., L.A., 1977-79; exec. dir. Santa Monica Mountains Conservancy, State of Calif., 1980—; regents lectr. Coll. Environ. Design U. Calif., Berkeley, 1995—. Pres. Associated Students, East L.A. Coll., 1968. Recipient Weldon Heald Conservation award Sierra Club, 1970; Hollywood Heritage, Inc. (bd. dirs.). Mem. Marine Tech. Soc. (dir. L.A. region sect. 1975-77), Coastal Soc., Am. Planning Assn. (vice dir. policy L.A. Sect. 1989-90), Phi Rho Pi, Delta Sigma Rho, Tau Kappa Alpha. Democrat. Office: 5810 Ramirez Canyon Rd Malibu CA 90265-4421

EDMONDS, VELMA MCINNIS, nursing educator; b. N.Y.C., Feb. 17, 1940; d. Walter Lee and Eva Doris (Grant) McInnis; children: Stephen Clay, Michelle Louise. Diploma, Charity Hosp. Sch. Nursing, New Orleans, 1961; BSN, Med. Coll. Ga., 1968; MSN, U. Ala., Birmingham, 1980; postgrad., La. State U. Med. Ctr., 1994—. Staff nurse Ochsner Found. Hosp., New Orleans, 1961-63, 1987—, clin. educator, 1987-89; staff nurse Suburban Hosp., Bethesda, Md., 1963-65; asst. DON svc., dir. staff devel. Providence Hosp., Mobile, Ala., 1967-70; staff nurse MICU U. So. Ala. Med. Ctr., Mobile, 1980-82, clin. nurse specialist, nutrition/metabolic support, 1982-84; instr., coord., BSN completion program Northwestern State U. Coll. Nursing, Pineville, La., 1984-86; head nurse So. Bapt. Hosp., New Orleans, 1986-87; instr. nursing La. State U. Health Sci. Ctr., New Orleans, 1989-91, asst. prof. nursing, 1991—; clin. coord. Transitional Hosp. Corp., 1994-95; gov.-apptd. mem. La. Bd. Examiners in Dietetics and Nutrition, 1990-98, sec.-treas., 1996-97; cons. on internat. health and nursing edn., 1992—; rschr. with recently immigrated Honduran women. Advisor Hispanic C. of C., New Orleans; mem. adv. bd. Cmty. Vietnamese Outreach Program, Meth. Hosp., New Orleans; chmn. Silent Auction, New Orleans Dollars for Scholars Found., 2000. Recipient Excellence in Nursing group award Ochsner Fedn. Hosp., New Orleans, 1987, cert. Merit Tuberculosis Assn. Greater New Orleans, 1961. Mem. ANA, Nat. Soc. Nutrition Edn., La. State Nurses' Assn. (dist. 7), Am. Soc. Parenteral and Enteral Nutrition, La. State Soc. Parenteral and Enteral Nutrition (program and edn. coms.), Mobile Area Nonvolitional Nutrition Support Assn. (past pres.), Transcultural Nursing Soc., Soc. Nutrition Edn., La. Hispanic C. of C., Sigma Theta Tau. Office: LSU Health Scis Ctr Sch of Nursing 1900 Grarier St New Orleans LA 70112

EDMONDS, WARREN S., patent agent; b. Paterson, N.J., July 19, 1960; s. James S. and Sadie B. Edmonds; m. Janet S. Edmonds, June 16, 1984; children: Shenise A., Stanley J., Jarren V. BS in Physics and Math., Del. State U., 1982. Registered to practice before U.S. Patent and Trademark Office. Patent examiner U.S. Patent and Trademark Office, Washington, 1982-95; patent agt. Litman Law Offices, Ltd., Arlington, Va., 1995-2000, Pillsbury, Madison and Sytro, LLC, Washington, 2000—. Assoc. minister Warner Bapt. Ch., Bailey's Crossroads, Va., 1990—; active Good News prison ministry Prince William Adult Detention Ctr., Manassas, Va., 1999—, KAIROS prison ministry, Woodbridge, Va., 1999—. Home: PO Box 4754 Arlington VA 22204-0754 Office: Litman Law Offices Ltd 3717 Columbia Pike Arlington VA 22204-4255

EDMONDSON, FRANK KELLEY, JR., lawyer, legal administrator; b. Newport, R.I., Aug. 27, 1936; s. Frank Kelley Sr. and Margaret (Russell) E.; m. Christiane Semirot, Mar. 5, 1959 (div. Sept. 1969); children: Mylene Anne, Yvonne Marie, Catherine May; m. Elaine Sueko Kaneshiro, Aug. 17, 1970 (div. June 1992); m. Karen Louise Bishop, Feb. 27, 1993 (div. Feb. 1996). BBA, Ind. U., 1958; MBA, So. Ill. U., 1978; JD, U. Puget Sound, 1982. Bar: Wash. 1982, U.S. Dist. Ct. (we. dist.) Wash. 1983. Commd. 2d lt. USAF, 1959, advanced through grades to maj., 1969, ret., 1979; contracts specialist Wash. State Lottery, Olympia, 1982-85, asst. contracts adminstr., 1985-87; contracts officer 1989 Washington Centennial Commn., 1987-90; fin. svc. officer Office of the Adminstr. for the Cts., 1990-92; contracts officer, office of adminstr. for the cts. State of Wash. Supreme Ct., Olympia, 1992-99; mem. Seattle U. Sch. Law, Law Alumni Soc. Nat. Coun., 1997—, scholarship com. Wash. State Employees Credit Union, 1995—. Bd. dirs. Friends of Chambers Creek, Tacoma, 1981-90; mem. pro bono panel Puget Sound Legal Assistance Found., Olympia, 1985-90; mock trial program com. Youth and Govt. YMCA, 1994-96. Mem. ABA, Wash. State Bar Assn. (spl. dist. counsel 1993-95), Thurston County Bar Assn., Govt. Lawyers Bar Assn. (sec. 1985-86, 1st v.p. 1986-87, pres. 1987-89, liaison to Wash. State Bar Assn. 1989-93), Beta Gamma Sigma, Coll. Club. Home: 6600 Miner Dr SW Tumwater WA 98512-7282

EDMONDSON, JOHN, publisher; b. Chester, U.K., Nov. 20, 1950; s. Kenneth Driver and Mary Edna (Macmaster) E. BA with honors, U. Warwick, U.K., 1973. Asst. editor The Metals Soc., London, 1974-76; various to pub. dir. Butterworth Heinemann, Guildford, U.K., 1976-89; mng. dir., owner I.P. Pub., London, 1990—. Author: Traveller's Literary Companion to France, 1997; editor Industry and Higher Edn. jour. 1990—; editor: James Boswell's "The Journal of a Tour to Corsica", 1996; editor/compiler: Dickens in France, 1996. Mem. The Dickens Fellowship, Inst. Contemporary Arts, Ind. Pubs. Guild, Soc. Acad. Pubs., Inst. Pubs. Avocations: writing, reading, film, theatre. Office: IP Pub Ltd Coleridge House, 4-5 Coleridge Gardens, London NW6 3QH, United Kingdom

EDMONDSON, STEPHEN JOHN, cardiothoracic surgeon, consultant; b. Scunthorpe, Eng., Aug. 21, 1950; s. George and Jean Mary (Stanton) E.; m. Barbara Bridget Duncan, July 17, 1976 (div. 1992); children: Adam, John; m. Yolande Monique Laret, Feb. 5, 1994; children: Augustus, Sienna. BS with class I honors, U. London, 1971, MB BChir, 1974; postgrad., North Middlesex Hosp. Cons. St. Bartholomew's Hosp., London, 1984—. Contbr. papers to med. jours. Fellow Royal Coll. Surgeons Eng., Royal Coll. Physicians U.K., Royal Coll. Physicians U.K.; mem. European Soc. Cardiothoracic Surgery, Soc. Cardiothoracic Surgeons Gt. Britain. Avocations: soccer, tennis, football. Office: 50 Wimpole St, London W1M 7DG, England

EDMUND, NORMAN WILSON, educational researcher; b. Feb. 27, 1916. Cert., U. Pa., 1939. Founder, pres. Edmund Sci. Co., Barrington, N.J., 1942-75; ednl. rschr. Ft. Lauderdale, Fla., 1989—. Author: The General Pattern of the Scientific Method, 1994, The Scientific Method Today, 2000. E-mail: nwe@scientificmethod.com. Office: 407 NE 3rd Ave Fort Lauderdale FL 33301-3233

EDREES, BURHAN MOHAMMED, pediatric nephrologist, consultant, researcher; b. Makkah, Saudi Arabia, Feb. 1, 1957; s. Mohammed Burhan Edrees and Saleha Salem Zaiter; m. Najeelah Mustafah Baz, Mar. 2, 1981; children: Yassir, Mohammed, Bayan, Mustafa, Heba. MB BS in Medicine and Surgery, King Saud U., Riyadh, Saudi Arabia, 1980; diploma in child health, Edinbrough U./Saudi Ministry Health, Riyadh, 1983. Med. diplomate. Resident in pediat. Al-Hada Mil. Hosp., Taif, Saudi Arabia, 1981-85; cons. in pediat. Al-Hada Mil. Hosp., Taif, 1990-93, pediat. nephrologist, 1996—; resident in pediat. Essen U., 1985-90; fellow in pediat. nephrology King Faisal Specialist Hosp., Riyadh, 1993-95, U. Va., Charlottesville, 1995-96; chief resident in pediat. Al-Hada Mil. Hosp., Taif, 1983-85, dir. pediat. nephrology, 1996—. Mem. Internat. Soc. Nephrology, Internat. Pediat. Nephrology Assn., Am. Soc. Nephrology, Nat. Kidney Found. Avocations: clinical science research, reading, swimming. Home and Office: Al-Hada Mil Hosp, PO Box 1347, Taif Saudi Arabia

EDSON, CHARLES LOUIS, lawyer, educator; b. St. Louis, Dec. 14, 1934; s. Harry G. and Mildred (Solomon) E.; m. Susan Kramer, Mar. 29, 1959; children: Richard, Nancy, Margaret. AB, Harvard U., 1956, LLB, 1959. Bar: Mo. 1959, U.S. Supreme Ct. 1966, D.C. 1967. Assoc. Lewis, Rice, Tucker, Allen & Chubb, St. Louis, 1959-65; chief ops. officer Legal Svcs. Program, OEO, Washington, 1966-67; gen. counsel Pres.'s Commn. on Postal Orgn., Washington, 1967-68; chief pub. housing sect. Officer of Gen. Counsel, HUD, Washington, 1968-70; ptnr. Lane and Edson, P.C., Washington, 1970-89, Kelley, Drye & Warren, Washington, 1989-93, Peabody & Brown, Washington, 1993-99, Nixon Peabody, Washington, 1999—; adj. prof. law Georgetown U. Law Sch., Washington, 1970-76; HUD coord. Pres. Carter's Transition Staff, 1976-77. Co-author: A Practical Guide to Low and Moderate Income Housing, 1972, A Leased Housing Primer, 1975, A Section 8 Deskbook, 1976, Guide to Federal Housing Programs, 1982, Secondary Mortgage Market Guide, 1985, HDR Affordable Seniors Housing Handbook, 2000. Councilman Town of Somerset, Md., 1976-78; trustee Md. Hist. Trust, 1995—. With USNR, 1953-61. Alt. White House fellow, 1965. Mem. ABA (chmn. forum com. on affordable housing and comm. devel. 1991-93, chmn. spl. housing and urban devel. 1987-90), Harvard U. Law Sch. Assn. D.C. (pres. 1972-73), Cosmos Club (Washington). Home: 5802 Surrey St Chevy Chase MD 20815-5419 Office: 401 9th St NW Ste 900 Washington DC 20004-2134

EDSON, HERBERT ROBBINS, retired foundation and hospital executive; b. Upper Darby, Pa., Dec. 26, 1931; s. Merritt Austin and Ethel Winifred (Robbins) E.; m. Constance Anne Lowell, May 20, 1961 (div. Nov. 8, 1967); m. Rose Anne McGowan, July 25, 1970; children: Patricia Anne, David William, Merritt Austin III, Herbert Robbins Jr. BA, Tufts U., 1955; MBA, U. Pa., 1972. Commd. 2d lt. USMC, 1955, advanced through grades to major, 1967, adminstr., mgr., supr. various orgns., 1955-72; controller III Marine Amphibious Force and 3d Marine Div. USMC, Camp Butler, Japan, 1972-73; dir. acctg. Marine Corps Supply Activity USMC, Phila., 1973-75; ret. USMC, 1975; cons. acctg. Ardmore, Pa., 1975-77; CFO Mercy Meml. Hosp. Corp., Monroe, Mich., 1977-92, Mercy Meml. Hosp. Found., Monroe, 1986-92, Monroe Health Ventures Inc., 1986-92, Monroe Community Health Svcs., 1989-92, Byerly Hosp., Hartsville, S.C., 1992-95, Byerly Found., Hartsville, S.C., 1995-97; ret., 1997; assoc. Quorum Health Resources, Inc., Brentwood, Tenn., 1992-95. Co-pres. Custer Elem. Sch. Parent Tchr. Orgn., Monroe, 1985-87; v.p., trustee Christ Evang. Luth. Ch., Monroe, 1981-86; dir. Monroe County C. of C., 1982-84; treas., chmn. Taylor Endowment Fund com. St. Paul's Evang. Luth. Ch., Ardmore, Pa., 1974-76, trustee, chmn. property com., 1976. Decorated Purple Heart, Navy Commendation medal, Combat Action ribbon. Mem. NRA (life), U.S. Naval Inst. (life), Marine Corps Assn. (life), 1st Marine Div. Assn. (life), Edson's Raiders Assn. (hon. life 1st Marine Raider Bn.), Ret. Officers Assn. (life), Am. Assn. Ret. Persons, Nat. Geog. Soc., Edson Geneal. Assn., Marines Meml. Club, Army and Navy Club. Republican. Lutheran. Home: PO Box 569 Ellenton FL 34222-0569

EDSTON, ERIK HAMPUS, medical examiner, consultant; b. Stockholm, Sweden, Apr. 25, 1948; s. Horace Walter and Ofelia Gunvor (Bengtsson) Edstone; m. Bi Edsgren, June 4, 1984; children: Hamlet and Hampus (twins). BA, U. Uppsala, Sweden, 1970; PhD, U. Linköping, Sweden, 1982. Diplomate in clin. anat. pathology, forensic medicine. Jr. med. examienr Linköping, 1975-82; jr. pathologist St. Göran's Hosp., Stockholm, 1985-88; sr. pathologist Sabbatsberg's Hosp., Stockholm, 1989; sr. med. examiner Stockholm, 1990-93; sr. pathologist County Hosp., Jönköping, Sweden, 1993-94; sr. med. examiner Linköping, 1995—; cons. med. examiner Ctr. for Torture Survivors, Stockholm, 1993—. Co-author: Yearbook, Centre for Torture Survivors, 1993, 97, Traumatized Refugees in Swedish Healthcare, 1994; columnist Runner's World Swedish edit. Mem. N.Y. Acad. Scis., European Acad. Allergology and Clin. Immunology, Swedish Soc. for Health and Human Rights. Avocations: hunting, dogs, ultra-distance running, writing fiction, acting. Home: Karl Dahlgrensgatan 5, 58228 Linköping

Sweden Office: Univ Hosp, Inst Forensic Medicine, S-58185 Linköping Sweden

EDUARD, SERBAN, physician, researcher; b. Vucana-Bai, Romania, Mar. 14, 1927; s. Stelian and Haritina (Savu) S.; m. Luchiana Cristea, Oct. 11, 1955; children: Carmen-Christiana, Corneliu-Eduard. MD, U. Medicine, Bucharest, Romania, 1953, PhD, 1970. Physician Pucioasa (Romania) Hosp., 1953-92, dir., 1955-74; rschr. Med. Ct. Apitherapy, Bucharest, 1970-99, coord., 1974-88. Co-author: Apitherapy Today, 1976. Major Romanian Army, 1953-54. Fellow Portuguese Soc. Reumathology; mem. Acad. Scis., Internat. Assn. Study Pain, N.Y. Acad. Scis. Romanian Orthodox. Avocations: lecturing, music. Home: 24 Str. Nifon Balasescu, Bucharest-2 Romania Office: 31 C. A. Rosetti Str., Bucharest Romania

EDWARD, PRINCE (ANTONY RICHARD LOUIS EDWARD), member of British royal family, television producer; b. Mar. 10, 1964; s. Prince Philip, Duke of Edinburgh and Queen Elizabeth II. Student, Cambridge U. Former house tutor, jr. master Wanganui Colligiate Sch., New Zealand; mem. prodn. team Andrew Lloyd Webber's Really Useful Theatre Co.; joint mng. dir. Ardent Prodns. Ltd., 1993—. 2d lt. Royal Marines, 1983. Office: Buckingham Palace, London SW1A 1AA, England*

EDWARD, DAVID ALEXANDER OGILVY, judge; b. Perth, Scotland, Nov. 14, 1934; s. John O.C. and Margaret I. (MacArthur) E.; m. Elizabeth Y. McSherry, Dec. 22, 1962; children: Anne, Giles, John, Katherine. MA, U. Coll., Oxford, 1959; LLB, U. Edinburgh, 1962, LLD (hon.), 1993; LLD (hon.), U. Aberdeen, 1997, Napier U., 1998. Queen's Counsel, Scotland, 1974. Pres. Coun. of E.C. Bars and Law Socs., 1978-80; prof. law U. Edinburgh, 1985-89; judge Ct. of 1st Instance EC, Luxembourg, 1989-92, Ct. of Justice, Luxembourg, 1992—. Office: European Ct of Justice, L-2925 Luxembourg Luxembourg

EDWARD, DAVID ANDREW, environmental engineer; b. Sierra Vista, Ariz., Nov. 24, 1962; s. Edmond Stricklan and Jeanne Clark (Herbert) E.; m. Paula Elizabeth Woods; children: Paul David, Stephen Seth, Elizabeth Rachelle, Luke Andrew, Peter Elijah. BS in Petroleum Engring., West Va. U., Morgantown, 1986; MBA, U. Louisville, 1991. Registered profl. engr., Ky., Ind., Va., Ill., Ga. Commd. 2nd. lt. U.S. Army, 1985; advanced through grades to capt., 1992; exec. officer A Co. 3/81st Armor Regiment, Ft. Knox, Ky., 1987-88; asst. adjutant 1st Armor Tng. Brigade, Ft. Knox, Ky., 1988-89; adj. 4/13th Armor Regiment, Ft. Knox, Ky., 1989-90; platoon leader, exec. officer A Troop 5/12 Cavalry Regiment, Ft. Knox, 1990; ops. mgr. Earth Sci. Techs., Inc., Louisville, 1990-92; project engr. Commonwealth Tech., Inc., Lexington, Ky., 1992-93; project mgr., 1993-97, The Evergreen Group, Inc., Crestwood, Ky., 1997-98; sr. project mgr. Advanced Techs. Intl. Inc., 1998-99; pres. PSE Engring., 1999—. Chmn. various coms. Alpha Phi Omega Svc. Fraternity, W.Va. U., Morgantown, 1981-86; post mgr. Army Emergency Relief Fund Drive, Ft. Knox, 1988; Sunday sch. tchr. Beulah Presbyn. Ch., Louisville, 1988, 92; com. mem. Goals for Greater Louisville, 1992; mem. citizens adv. com. Jefferson County (Ky.) Pub. Schs., 1992; mem. Bluegrass Tomorrow Regional Devel. Com., 1992; mem. adv. com. Ohio River Corridor Master Plan, 1994; mem. Jefferson County Comprehensive Land Use Adv. Com., 1994; mem. Ky. Profl. Engrs. Disaster Response Com., 1993, 94, chmn., 1996—; den leader Cub Scouts, Louisville, 1995—; youth soccer coach N.E. Louisville YMCA, 1995—. Named Ky. Col., State of Ky., 1989. Mem. ASCE, NSPE, Am. Acad. Environ. Engrs., Soc. Petroleum Engrs., Soc. Am. Mil. Engrs., Hazardous Materials Mgrs. (Ky. chpt.), Nat. Ground Water Assn., Am. Assn. Cost Engrs., Air and Waste Mgmt. Assn., Louisville C. of C. (chmn. water com. 1996-98), Kentuckiana Post-Soc. Am. Mil. Engrs. (membership chmn. 1997-98), U. Louisville Alumni Assn., Scottish-Am. Mil. Soc., W.Va. U. Alumni Assn., Nat. Eagle Scout Assn., Tau Beta Pi. Home: 4507 Deepwood Dr Louisville KY 40241-1006

EDWARDS, ANTHONY WILLIAM FAIRBANK, biometry educator; b. London, Oct. 4, 1935; s. Harold Clifford and Ida M.A. (Phillips) E.; m. Elsa H.C. Edlund, Aug. 9, 1958; children: Ann Ruth, David Thomas, Charlotte. BA, Cambridge (Eng.) U., 1957, MA, 1960, PhD, 1960, DSc, 1972. Sr. lectr. Aberdeen (Scotland) U., 1965-68; asst. dir. rsch. Cambridge U., 1968-78, reader in biometry, 1978—; chmn. Cambridge U. Libr., 1993-98. Author: Likelihood, 1972, Foundations of Mathematical Genetics, 1977, Pascal's Arithmetical Triangle, 1987, (with H.A. David) Annotated Readings in the History of Statistics, 2000. Fellow Royal Statis. Soc.; mem. Internat. Biometric Soc. (pres. Brit. region 1992-94). Avocation: gliding. Home: Nickersons, Barton Cambridge CB3 7BG, England Office: Gonville and Caius Coll, Cambridge CB2 1TA, England

EDWARDS, BENJAMIN FRANKLIN, III, investment banker; b. St. Louis, Oct. 26, 1931; s. Presley William and Virginia (Barker) E.; m. Joan Moberly, June 13, 1953; children: Scott P., Benjamin Franklin IV, Pamela M. Edwards Bunn, Susan B. B.A., Princeton U., 1953. With A.G. Edwards & Sons, Inc., St. Louis, 1956—; pres. A.G. Edwards & Sons, Inc., 1967—, chmn., 1983—, also CEO, 1983—; bd. dirs. Jefferson Bank and Trust Co., Psychol. Assocs., Helig-Meyers, Inc., N.Y. Stock Exch., Washington U., St. Louis Art Mus., Barnes Hosp. Mem. U. Mo., St. Louis, Civic Progress, Arts and Edn. Coun. With USNR, 1953-56. Mem. Investment Bankers Assn. (gov. 1968—), Securities Industry Assn. (gov. 1974-81, chmn. 1980—). Presbyterian. Clubs: Old Warson Country (St. Louis); Bogey. Office: A G Edwards & Sons Inc 1 N Jefferson Ave Saint Louis MO 63103-2205

EDWARDS, BERT TVEDT, accountant; b. Washington, Aug. 23, 1937; s. Archie Campbell and Geniana (Rasmussen) E.; m. Susan Elizabeth Dye, July 18, 1964; children: Christopher Andrew, Stacey Elizabeth. BA, Wesleyan U., 1959; MBA, Stanford U., 1961. CPA, D.C. With Arthur Andersen LLP, Washington, 1961-69, 70-94, mgr., 1965-69, 70-71, ptnr., 1971-94, ret. ptnr., cons., 1994-98; fin. v.p. Leisure Time Industries, Inc., 1969-70; CFO, asst. sec. U.S. Dept. State, 1998—; mem. U.S. Comptr. Gen. Auditing Stds. Adv. Coun., 1985-88, 2000—. Trustee Barker Found., 1968-78, 94-96, treas., 1968-71, 1st v.p., 1971-72, pres., 1972-75; trustee, treas. Population Reference Bur., Inc., 1975-98, vice chmn., 1993-94; bd. dirs. Jr. Achievement Met. Washington, Inc., 1973-87, treas., 1973-74, 2d v.p., 1974-75, 1st v.p., 1975-77, pres., 1977-78, chmn., 1978-80; bd. dirs., treas. Heritage Walk Homes Corp., 1975-80; mem. Spl. Adv. Commn. for Indsl. and Comml. Devel., D.C. City Coun., 1972-74; mem. D.C. Mayor's Commn. on Budget and Fiscal Priorities, 1989-91, 93-95, mem. D.C. Tax Rev. Commn., 1996-98; chmn. JA Nat. Bus. Leadership Conf., 1978; chmn. Metro Washington Boys and Girls Clubs Ann. Congl. Dinner, 1993, dinner com. mem. 1992-98, found. bd., 1995—; treas. Nat. Com. Pub. Employee Pension Syss., 1993-98; bd. dirs., treas. Bethany West Recreation Assn., 1994-98; bd. dirs. D.C. Appleseed Found. Ctr. for Law and Justice, 1995-98, treas., 1998; bd. dirs. Com. for Capital City, 1995-98; mem. cmty. rels. bd. Sta. WAMU, 1994-97, CFO coun., chmn. standards com., 1999—. Recipient Outstanding Achievement award Stanford U., 1982, Outstanding Publ. award Soc. Mil. Comptrollers, 1984, Bronze Leadership award Jr. Achievement, 1979, Silver Leadership award, 1981; Victor Royall fellow Stanford U., 1960-61. Mem. AICPA (govt. acctg. and auditing com. 1981-84, 1985-88, 89-92, fed. govt. audit subcom. 1981-84, ad hoc task force univ. audit 1985-87, task force on quality of govt. audits 1986-87, author, editor single audit course 1985-92, 94-96, task force on quality of fed. program audits 1991-94), Greater Washington Soc. CPAs (chmn. membership com. 1973-74, chmn. SEC com. 1974-75, chmn. govt. acctg. com. 1979-81, chmn. rels. with DC govt. com., 1995-98, Lifetime Pub. Svc. award 1997), Assn. Govt. Accts. Edn. and Rsch. Found. (chmn. bd. dirs. 1993-95), Va. Soc. CPAs, Inst. Mgmt. Accts., Am. Acctg. Assn. (vice chair govt. nonprofit sect. 1993-94), Assn. Sch. Bus. Ofcls., Govt. Fin. Officers Assn. (co-chmn. ann. conf. 1987), Orgn. Am. States (chmn. bd. external auditors 2000—), Md. Pub. Fin. Officers Assn. (bd. dirs. 1992-94), Assn. Govt. Accts. (Andy Barr Lifetime Achievement award 1993), Govt. Fin. Officers Assn. Met. Washington (co-founder, bd. dirs. 1984-91, outstanding svc. award 1993), Met. Washington Bd. Trade, Wesleyan U. Alumni Club Wash. (pres. 1969-71), Univ. Club (mem. bd. admissions 1976-82, chmn. 1980-82, bd. govs. 1982-85). Methodist. Home: 7805 Stable Way Potomac MD 20854-1790 Office: US Dept State 2201 C St NW Rm 7427 Washington DC 20520-7427

EDWARDS, C. KAREN, consultant company executive; b. Washington, Dec. 2, 1949; d. Charles Frederick and Christine (Oakley) Edwards; m. James Walker Pearce, Apr. 5, 1980; children: Ryan Christopher, Loren McKenzie. BA, U. Tenn., 1970; postgrad., George Washington U., 1971-72. Russian linguist Dept. of Def., Washington, 1971-74; pers. specialist AEC, Oak Ridge, Tenn., 1975-78; labor rels. specialist Dept. Energy, Oak Ridge, 1978-82, supervisory pers. mgr., 1982-91, directives/stds. mgr., 1991-96; pres. Pegasus Cons. Corp., Lenoir City, Tenn., 1996—; cons. Dept. Energy and Dept. Energy contractors, Oak Ridge and Washington, 1996—. Author: A Practical Guide to Work Smart Standards, 1997. Bd. dirs. Oak Ridge Civic Music Assn., 1976-80; pres. bd. dirs. Knox Arabian Horse Club, Knoxville, 1982-87; vol. Spanish tchr. Woodland Elem. Sch., Oak Ridge, 1996-97. Recipient Hammer award Vice Pres. Gore, Washington, 1996. Mem. Internat. Arabian Horse Assn., Arabian Horse Registry, Soc. Fed. Labor Rels. Profls., Beefmaster Breeders Universal, Phi Beta Kappa. Avocations: horses, farming, art, creative writing, reading. Office: Pegasus Consulting Corp 254 Babbs Rd Lenoir City TN 37771-3616

EDWARDS, CARL NORMAN, lawyer; b. Norwood, Mass., Jan. 22, 1943; s. Wilfred Carl and Cecile Marie-Anne (Pepin) E.; m. Mary Louise Buyse, Jan. 22, 1982. MEd, Suffolk U., 1969; postgrad., Harvard U.; JD, Boston Coll., 1998; PhD, U. So. Calif., 1997. Cons. dept. social rels. Harvard U., Cambridge, Mass., 1966-69; rsch. fellow Harvard U., Cambridge, 1969-71, lectr. social rels., 1971-72; cons. rsch. psychologist Cambridge Computer Assocs., Mass., 1966—; rsch. social psychologist Tufts-New Eng. Med. Ctr., 1969—; assoc. clin. prof. psychiatry Tufts U. Sch. Medicine, 1971—; dir. Four Oaks Research Inst., Norfolk, Mass., 1974—; sr. assoc. for policy planning and research Justice Resource Inst., 1971—; field faculty grad. program Goddard Coll., Plainfield, Vt., 1972-82; chmn. bd. dirs. MEDx Systems, Ltd., Dover, Mass., 1985—; chmn. bd. trustees Ctr. for Birth Defects Info. Services, Inc., Dover, 1984—; tchr. seminars; cons. to major corps., govt. agys. and pub. instns. in human dynamics and pub. policy; lectr., thesis adviser, program devel. cons. schs., colls., insts. Author: Drug Dependence: Social Regulation and Treatment Alternatives; contbr. articles to profl. jours., monographs, revs. Mem. USNG, 1963-64. Mem. Am. Psychol. Assn., Mass. Psychol. Assn., Soc. Psychol. Study Social Issues, Peace Rsch. Soc., Nat. Pilots Assn., Nat. Trust for Hitoric Preservation, Harvard Club, Appalachian Mt. Club, Norfolk Hunt Club, Blue Ridge Hunt Club. Home: Four Oaks PO Box 1776 Dover MA 02030-0279

EDWARDS, CARL RAY, II, lawyer; b. Detroit, July 14, 1947; s. Carl Ray Sr. and Alice Edwards; m. Alice B. Jennings; children: Patrick Phillips, Kwameena Edwards-Montgomery, Tonya, Ronald, Saraun, Carl Ray. BA, Mich. Luth. Coll., 1970; MA, U. Detroit, 1972; JD, Wayne State U., 1974. Bar: Mich., 1975. Prin. Philo, Atkinson, Darling, Steinberg & Edwards, Detroit, 1975-82; pres. Edwards & Jennings P.C., Detroit, 1982—. Recipient Presdl. citation Nat. Assn. for Equal Opportunity in Higher Edn., 1981. Mem. ATLA, Nat. Bar Assn., State Bar of Mich. (legal del. to USSR and People's Republic of China 1988), Mich. Trial Lawyers Assn. (treas. 1984-85, sec. 1985-86, v.p. 1986-87, pres. 1987-88); founder Peoples Law Sch., 1978. E-mail: creabj@yahoo.com. Office: Edwards & Jennings PC 407 E Fort St Ste 605 Detroit MI 48226-2972

EDWARDS, CAROLYN MULLENAX, public relations executive; b. French Camp, Calif., Dec. 3, 1943; d. Charles Harold and Jessie Jewel Mullenax; m. Helton Pressley (div.); m. Dennis D. Edwards, May 29, 1993. BFA, U. Tulsa, 1967; MEd, Ea. N.Mex. U., 1976. Artist Wessels Agy., Spokane, Wash., 1968-70; pub. rels. dir. Spokane (Wash.) Symphony Soc., 1970-72; advt. coord. Crescent Dept. Store, Spokane, 1972-73; art dir., copywriter Sta. KMTY Radio, Clovis, N.Mex., 1976; news editor Clovis News Jour., Clovis, 1976-77; promotion and art dir. Sta. KENW-TV, Portales, N.Mex., 1977-78; coord. alumni affairs and pubs. Ea. N.Mex. U., Portales, 1978-80; dir. pubs., TV and pub. info. Ea. N.Mex. U., Clovis, 1985-90; dir. mktg. & pub. info. Clovis Community Coll. (formerly Ea. N.Mex. U.-Clovis), 1990-98; producer pub. affairs program Sta. KMCC-TV, Clovis, 1981-84, 1981-84; devel. and pub. info. dir. Mental Health Resources Inc., Portales, N.Mex., 1980-85; asst. dir. alumni affairs Ea. N.Mex. U., Portales, 1998-00, dir. pubs., 2000—. Bd. dirs. N.Mex. Outdoor Drama Assn., San Jon, 1986-95, Univ. Symphony League, Clovis, 1984-88. Named N.Mex. Press Women Communicator of Acheivement, 1999. Mem. N.Mex. Press Women (scholarship chair 1994-99, comm. awards 1981-99, treas. 2000—), Nat. Fedn. Press Women (comm. awards 1984-97), Am. Women in Radio and TV, Clovis C. of C. (bd. dirs. 1984-89), Jr. League (Lubbock, Tex.), Coun. for Advancement and Support Edn. (sec.-editor dist. IV 1990-92, design award 1991, 99), Nat. Coun. for Mktg. and Pub. Rels. (dist. IV award 1989-91, 93-97, 99, nat. award 1993-98), Altrusa Club, Nat. Assn. of Vocational and Tech. Edn. (awards 1995-96), Delta Delta Delta (former dist. alumnae officer, chair Delta century fund, graphics cons.). Republican. Episcopalian. Avocations: reading, classical music, free lance art, volunteer work, dancing. Office: Ea NMex Univ Univ Rels Sta # 6 Portales NM 88130

EDWARDS, CHARLES MUNDY, III, financial consultant; b. N.Y.C., Jan. 30, 1935; s. Charles Mundy Jr. and Nancy Blow (Rawls) E.; m. Janice Elaine Petty, Oct. 22, 1966; children: Melanie LeMoyne, Meghan Elizabeth Adams. AB, Princeton U., 1957; postgrad., NYU, 1959-63. With Shearson Lehman Bros., Inc., N.Y.C., 1959-85, assoc., asst. v.p., v.p., sr. v.p.; prin. Grumman Hill Assocs., Inc., Westport, Conn., 1985—; cons. Lynch & Mayer, Inc., N.Y.C., 1994; bd. dirs. EOMG, Inc., Virginia Beach, Va. Treas. fund for Ednl. Advancement, Newark, 1985-87, pres., 1988-90, v.p., 1990-97, trustee, 1985—; trustee Family Svc. Assn. of Summit, 1987-91; pres., adminstrv. bd. United Meth. Ch., Summit, 1987-94, trustee, 1990-94; mem. City Planning Bd., Summit, 1989-91; mem. adminstrv. bd. Mt. Bethel United Meth. Ch., Marietta, Ga., 1995—, mem. fin. com., 1995—, chmn. endowment com., 1997—; bd. advisors Thurston Arthritis Rsch. Ctr., Chapel Hill, N.C., 1999—. 1st lt. USMCR, 1957-59. Mem. Princeton Quadrangle Club, Beacon Hill Club (pres. 1987-88, v.p. 1986-87, treas. 1985-86), Chattahoochee Plantation Tennis Club. Republican. Methodist. Home: 495 Atlanta Country Club Dr Marietta GA 30067-4684

EDWARDS, DARREL, psychologist; b. San Francisco, July 9, 1943; s. Darrus and Rose Pearl (Sannar) E.; children: Alexander Hugh, Peter David, James Royce. BS in Psychology and Philosophy, Brigham Young U., 1965, MS in Psychology and Philosophy, 1967, PhD in Clin. Psychology and Philosophy, 1968. Diplomate Am. Bd. Profl. Psychology. Postdoctoral fellow in psycholinguistics Pa. State U., 1969; commd. lt. (j.g.) USN, 1970, advanced through grades to lt. comdr., 1978; dir. psychologist Tri Community Svc. Systems, San Diego, 1973-78; prof. Calif. Sch. Profl. Psychology, San Diego, 1971-78; dir. Grid Rsch., San Diego, 1978-83; pres. The Edwards Assoc., San Diego, 1983—; pres. Strategic Vision, 1987—; cons. strategist for govt. and pvt. sector, U.S., Eng., France, Germany, Italy, Mex., Brazil, Argentina, Russia, Republic of China, Japan, Can., 1978—; established Inst. for Value-Centered Life, 1999. Co-inventor in field; contbr. articles to profl. jours. Cons., researcher U.S., U.K., France, Germany, Hungary, Japan, Brazil, Argentina, Mexico, Colombia, Kenya, Central America, India, Italy, Republic of China, Russia, numerous other countries, 1986—. Mem. Am. Psychol. Assn. Achievements include creation of Values Centered research and consulting procedures, The Inst. for Value Centered Life, Training Value Centered Vision of principles of excellence; total quality measures for the automotive industry; total customer experience measures for 30 product and service categories; Values in America bi-annual survey; four fold principles of motivation; ValueCentered theory, clinical interview, and intervention; quality research in medicine service delivery and outcomes; founder Inst. for a Value Centered Life for evaluating, reporting, and honoring Value Centered lives, products, and services. Office: The Edwards Assocs PO Box 420429 San Diego CA 92142-0429

EDWARDS, DORIS PORTER, computer specialist; b. Lambert, Miss., Jan. 18, 1962; d. Willie Morris and Carrie Mae (Tillman) E.; 1 child, Stacy Nicole. AA in Computer Sci., Draughons Coll., Memphis, 1981. Counselor French Riviera Spa, Memphis, 1989-90; pvt. practice, computer application developer Memphis, 1990—; owner, fin. cons., fund locator Developing Processing in Comm., Memphis, 1998—; bus. owner Developing Processing in Comms.; fin. cons., cream developer. Developer cosmetic cream. Jehovah's Witness. Avocations: mathematics, reading. Home and Office: 2638 Burns Ave Memphis TN 38114-4913

EDWARDS, ELWOOD GENE, mathematician, educator; b. New Bern, N.C., Jan. 5, 1944; s. Calvin and Blanche Ethel (Edwards) E.; m. Lucretia Walker; children: Ronnie, Glenn, Myrei Chrysti. BA, CCNY, 1966; MA, NYU, 1969; MS, Columbia Pacific U., 1982, PhD, 1982; DD (hon.), Am. Bapt. U., 1980. Cert. math. tchr., N.Y. Ins. cons. Met. Life Ins. Co., N.Y.C., 1966-68; tchr., math. specialist-tchr. trainer N.Y.C. Bd. Edn., 1968—; lectr., adj. prof. CUNY, 1969-78; tax preparer Bklyn., 1973—; tutor math., Spanish, English, Bklyn., 1969—. Contbr. articles to profl. jours. V.p. 89th St./Ave. B Block Assn., Bklyn., 1987-89. Mem. AAAS, Soc. for Indsl. and Applied Math., Am. Statis. Assn., The Planetarium Soc., Nat. Coun. Tchrs. Math., Math. Assn. Am., Am. Math. Soc., N.Y. Acad. Sci., Phi Theta Kappa. Democrat. Universalist. Avocations: reading, walking, bowling, golf, creating recreational math puzzles.

EDWARDS, F. (FREDERICK) GARY, architect, health facility planner; b. Melbourne, Australia, Aug. 3, 1943; s. Frederic Kingsley and Dorothy Vernon (Harrison) E.; m. Kathryn Margaret Winford, Nov. 3, 1979; children: Simon John Just, Ingrid Emily Just, Phillipa Claire Edwards. Diploma in architectural design, U. Melbourne, 1974; diploma in architecture, Royal Melbourne Inst. Tech., 1975. Registered architect Victoria (Australia), Archts. Accreditation Coun. Australia. Draftsman then architect Stephenson & Turner, Melbourne, 1961-83, assoc. and sr. health facility planner, 1983-91; co-founding prin. Health Facilities Cons. Architect, Melbourne, 1991—; v.p., life gov. Child and Family Care Network, Inc., Melbourne, 1983—; co-founding dir. Health Planners Australia, Melbourne, 1993-98, Newpolis P/L, Melbourne 1996-98, ArcHealth Pty Ltd., Melbourne, 2000—; examiner Architect's Registration Bd. Victoria; architect and health facility planner major health related bldg. devel. including acute hosps. and aged care facilities throughout Australia and internationally. Fellow Royal Australian Inst. of Architects (convenor complaints com., former councilor, practice bd. mem., Pres. award 1995); mem. Assn. Consulting Architects-Australia, Royal Inst. of British Architects, Inst. of Hosp. Engring. Australia, Australian Inst. of Company Dirs., Royal Melbourne Inst. of Tech. (assoc.). Clubs: Royal Automobile Victoria, Citroen Car Victoria, Lodge, Fine Arts, Melbourne and Old Scotch Football Clubs. Developer of health facility models for optimum functionality, quality care and cost effectiveness, including for day surgery/procedures, multi-purpose services and integrated care; adviser in preparation of many generic guidelines for health facilities for governments. Avocations: photography, boating, motoring, Citroen cars, politics, freemasonry. Fax: 61-3-98821402. E-mail: nfca@one.net.av. Home and Office: Health Facilities Cons Arch, 10 Cochran Ave, Camberwell VIC 3124, Australia

EDWARDS, GEORGE CHARLES, III, political science educator, writer; b. Rochester, N.Y., Jan. 3, 1947; s. George Charles Jr. and Mary Elizabeth (Laing) E.; m. Carmella Rose Pierce, May 22, 1981; 1 child, Jeffrey Allan. BA, Stetson U., 1969; MA, U. Wis., 1970, PhD, 1973. Asst. prof. polit. sci. Tulane U., New Orleans, 1973-78; assoc. prof. polit. sci. Tex. A&M U., College Station, 1978-81, prof., 1981-90, disting. prof., 1990—, Jordan prof. in liberal arts, 1991—, dir. Ctr. for Presdnl. Studies, 1991—; vis. asst. prof. U. Wis.-Madison, 1976; vis. prof. U.S. Mil. Acad., West Point, N.Y., 1985-88, Peking U., Beijing, 1993, Hebrew U., Jerusalem, 1997; pres. Presidency Rsch. Group, 1984-85; lectr. U.S. Info. Svc., Europe, 1985, 89, U.S., 1988, 92, Brazil, 1988; cons. NSF, Washington, 1977—, Internat. Rep. Inst., Moscow, 1994, Ctr. for Strategic and Internat. Studies, Washington, 1990-91, Nat. Acad. Pub. Adminstrn., Washington, 1987-88; bd. dirs. Roper Ctr. Pub. Opinion Rsch.; bd. advisors Stetson U., Transition to Governing Project; bd. acad. advisers Ctr. for Congl. and Presdl. Studies; exec. com. White House Interview Program. Author: Presidential Approval, 1990, At the Margins, 1989, Government in America, 1989, 91, 94, 96, 97, 98, 99, 2000, Presidential Leadership, 1985, 90, 94, 97, 99, The Public Presidency, 1983, Presidential Influence in Congress, 1980, Implementing Public Policy, 1980, The Policy Predicament, 1978; editor: Researching the Presidency, 1993, National Security and the U.S. Constitution, 1988, The Presidency and Public Policy Making, 1985, Studying the Presidency, 1983, Public Policy Implementation, 1984, Perspectives on Public Policy-Making, 1975, Reinventing the Presidency, 2000; editor Presdl. Studies Quarterly; mem. editl. bd. Am. Jour. Polit. Sci., 1985-87, 94—, Jour. Politics, 1997—, Am. Politics Quar., 1981-87, Presdl. Studies Quar., 1978—, Congress and the Presidency, 1981—, Policy Studies Jour., 1981-83, Am. Rev. Politics, 1994—; contbr. articles to profl. jours. Pres. Greenfield Plaza Condominium Assn., Bryan, Tex., 1980-81; mem. East Tex. 2000 Commn., 1980. Capt. USAR, 1971-79. Decorated for Disting. Civilian Svc. U.S. Army, 1960; Woodrow Wilson fellow, 1969-70, Ford fellow, 1970-73. Mem. Am. Polit. Sci. Assn. (sect. pres. 1984-85), Am. Assn. Pub. Opinion Rsch., So. Polit. Sci. Assn., Midwest Polit. Sci. Assn., Policy Studies Orgn., Ctr. Study of Presidency (bd. dirs. 1978—), Phi Beta Kappa, Pi Sigma Alpha, Phi Alpha Theta, Pi Alpha Alpha, Phi Kappa Phi. Avocations: collecting art, skiing, tennis, scuba diving, sailing. Home: 2910 Coronado Dr College Station TX 77845-7716 Office: Tex A&M U The Ctr For Presdl Studies College Station TX 77843-0001

EDWARDS, HARRY LAFOY, lawyer; b. Greenville, S.C., July 29, 1936; s. George Belton and Mary Olive (Jones) E.; m. Suzanne Copeland, June 16, 1956; 1 child, Margaret Peden. LLB, U. S.C., 1963, JD, 1970. Bar: S.C. 1963, U.S. dist. Ct. S.C. 1975, U.S. Ct. Apls. (4th cir.) 1974. Assoc. Edwards and Edmunds, Greenville, 1963; v.p., sec., dir. Edwards Co., Inc., Greenville, 1963-65; atty. investment legal dept. Liberty Life Ins. Co., Greenville, 1965-67, asst. sec., asst. v.p., head investment legal dept., 1967-70; asst. sec. Liberty Corp., 1970-75; asst. v.p. Liberty Life Ins. Co., 1970-75; sec. Bent Tree Corp., CEL, Inc., 1970-75; sec., dir. Westchester Mall, Inc., 1970-75; asst. sect. Libco, Inc., Liberty Properties, Inc., 1970-75; pvt. practice, Greenville, 1975—. Editor U. S.C. Law Rev., 1963. Com. mem. Hipp Fund Spl. Edn., Greenville County Sch. System; mem. Boyd C. Hipp II Scholarship Com., Wofford Coll. Spartanburg, S.C.; mem. scholarship com. Liberty Scholars, U. S.C., 1984, 86-2000. With USAFR, 1957-63. Mem. ABA, S.C. Bar Assn., Greenville County Bar Assn., Phi Delta Phi, Greenville Lawyers, Poinsett Club (Greenville). Baptist. Home: 106 Ridgeland Dr Greenville SC 29601-3017 Office: PO Box 10350 Greenville SC 29603-0350

EDWARDS, HUW, psychiatrist, consultant; b. Carmarthen, Dyfed, Wales, Dec. 22, 1938; s. Evan Dewi and Doris Maud (Evans) E.; m. Brenda Annie Burgess, June 22, 1963; children: Siwan Angharad, Catrin Sioned, Manon Heledd. M.B.B.S., U. London, 1962; DPM, Conjoint Bd., London, 1966. House surgeon Met. Hosp., London, 1962; house physician Prince of Wales Hosp., London, 1963; sr. house officer Whitchurch Hosp., Cardiff, Wales, 1963-65, registrar, 1965-66, sr. registrar, 1966-69; cons. psychiatrist St. David's Hosp. and West Wales Gen. Hosp., Carmarthen, 1969-99; vis. commr. Mental Health Act Commn., 1995-97; med. mem. Mental Health Rev. Tribunal for Wales, 1995—. Author: Facing Life, 1979, The Worm in the Apple, 1981, Full Circle, 1994. Magistrate, Carmarthen, 1985; med. advisor Carmarthen Mind, 1986—. Fellow Royal Coll. Psychiatrists London; mem. Welsh Med. Soc. (pres. 1997), Welsh Psychiat. Soc. (chmn. 1996). Mem. Plaid Cymru polit. party. Congregationalist. Avocations: book collecting, gardening, archaeology, natural history. Home: Garth Martin, Ffordd Henfwlch, Carmarthen SA33 5EG, Wales Office: Canolfany Prior, 132 Priory St, Carmarthen SA31 1DS, Wales

EDWARDS, JAMES ALFRED, lawyer; b. Orlando, Fla., Feb. 18, 1954. BA in Psychology with high honors, Auburn U., 1976; JD with high honors, U. Fla., 1979. Bar: Fla. 1979, U.S. Dist. Ct. (no. dist.) Fla. 1979, U.S. Dist. Ct. (mid. and so. dists.) Fla. 1981, U.S. Ct. Appeals (5th cir.) 1979, U.S. Ct. Appeals (11th cir.) 1982, U.S. Supreme Ct. 1984; bd. cert. civil trial lawyer Fla. Bar Assn. Ptnr. Rumberger, Kirk & Caldwell, Orlando, Fla., 1979-89, Roth, Edwards & Smith, P.A., Orlando, Fla., 1989-2000, Cabaniss, Conroy & McDonald, LLP, Orlando, 2000—; sustaining mem. Product Liability Adv. Coun., Detroit, 1989—. Mem. Fla. Bar Assn. (cert. civil trial lawyer, mem. trial lawyers, appellate practice sects., equal opportunity law sector), Orange County Bar Assn. (mem. professonalism com.). Avocations: fishing, water skiing, snow skiing. Fax: 407-246-1895. E-mail: jedwards@cabaniss.net. Office: Cabaniss, Conroy & McDonald LLP 390 N Orange Ave Ste 1600 Orlando FL 32801-1675

EDWARDS, JAMES BENJAMIN, accountant, educator; b. Atlanta, Apr. 27, 1935; s. James T. and Frances L. (McEachern) E.; m. Virginia Ann Reagin, Feb. 21, 1958; children: James Benjamin II, Chad Reagin, Calli

Ann, Judy Clair. BBA in Fin., U. Ga., 1958, MBA, 1962, PhD in Bus. Adminstrn., 1971. CPA Tenn., Ga., S.C.; cert. mgmt. acct.; cert. internal auditor; cert. in data processing; cert. cost analyst. Contr. Better Maid Dairy Products, Inc., Athens, Ga., 1958-62; staff acct. Max M. Cuba & Co., Atlanta, 1962-63; mng. ptnr. Wilson, Edwards and Swang, accts., Nashville, 1964-66; ptnr. Q.F. Lester & Co., Athens, 1967-68; v.p., chmn. bd. dirs. Gen. Data Svc. Inc., Athens, Ga., 1970-71; internal cons. J.W. Hunt and Co., CPAs, Columbia, 1983-84; v.p. Integrated Cost Mgmt. Systems Inc., Arlington, Tex., 1990-91; instr. David Lipscomb Coll., Nashville, 1963-66; instr. Nashville Ctr. U. Tenn., 1964-66; instr. acctg. U. Ga., Athens, 1966-71; asst. prof. U. S.C., Columbia, S.C., 1971-73, assoc. prof., 1973-77, prof., 1977—, fellow Bus. Partnership Found., 1977-90; William W. Bruner Disting. Faculty fellow U. S.C., Columbia, 1990—; instr. staff tng. program local C.P.A. firms, Nashville, 1963-66. Editor: (ann. publs. Warren, Gorham & Lamont, Inc.) Emerging Practices in Cost Management and, Activity-Based Mnagment, Handbook of Cost Management for Service Industries, 1997—; contbr. articles on mgmt. acctg. to profl. publs. Coach Little League Baseball, Columbia, 1972-76; bd. dirs. Atlanta Bible Camp, Inc.; bd. dirs. Ga. Christian Found., Inc., pres., 1968-69; bd. dirs. Spring Valley Edn. Found., 1983-93, v.p., 1983-85, treas., 1985-93. Recipient 8 nat. awards for contbns. to acctg. lit. Mem. Am. Acctg. Assn., Am. Inst. CPAs, Inst. Internal Auditors, Planning Execs. Isnt. (asst. editor nat. mag. 1971-77), Am. Inst. Decision Scis. (v.p. Southeastern sect. 1975-76), Inst. Mgmt. Accts. (pres. Columbia chpt. 1973-74, nat. rsch. com. 1974-75, nat. edn. com. 1977-80, 95—, nat. dir. 1975-77, pres. Carolinas coun. 1976, nat. v.p. 1980-81), S.C. Soc. CPAs, S.C. Assn. Acctg. Instrs. (founding pres. 1972-73), Omicron Delta Epsilon, Beta Alpha Psi, Delta Sigma Pi, Sigma Chi. Mem. Ch. of Christ. Clubs: Five Points Optimist of Athens, Spring Valley Band Boosters. Office: c/o U SC Sch Acctg Darla Moore Sch 1705 College St Columbia SC 29208-0001

EDWARDS, JANICE G., medical educator; b. Grand Rapids, Mich., Apr. 11, 1957; d. Edward Cecil and Grace Jane Thompson; m. Joseph L. Edwards, Sept. 4, 1982; children: Ben, Laura, Paul, Ellen. BA, Albion Coll., 1978; MS, Sarah Lawrence Coll., 1981. Genetic counselor Richland Meml. Hosp., Columbia, S.C., 1981-97, dir. genetic counseling, 1981-97; assoc. prof. ob-gyn U. S.C., Columbia, 1997—, co-dir. genetic counseling grad. program, 1999—. Mem. editl. bd. Jour. Genetic Counseling, 1990-95. Youth advisor Lake Murray Presbyn. Ch., Chapin, S.C., 1998—. Recipient Commendation for Excellence, S.C. Commn. on Higher Edn., 1991, 98. Mem. Am. Bd. Genetic Counseling (sec. 1998, accreditation chair 1998—), Nat. Soc. Genetic Counselor (chair profl. issues 1989-91, co-chair annual edn. conf. 1994), Assn. Genetic Counseling Program Dirs. Republican. Presbyterian. Avocation: needlepoint. E-mail: jedwards@richmed.medpark.sc.edu. Office: U SC Sch Medicine Two Medical Pk Columbia SC 29203

EDWARDS, JOHN MILTON, geneticist, educator; b. London, Mar. 26, 1928; s. Harold Clifford and Margaret Ida (Phillips) E.; m. Felicity Clare Toussaint. Internships in neurology, psychiatry, medicine and pathology, London, 1953-55. Ships surgeon Antarctic, 1952-53; lectr. U. Birmingham, Eng., 1956-58; rschr. Med. Rsch. Coun., Oxford, Eng., 1958-60; lectr., reader, prof. Birmingham U., 1960-75; prof. rsch. U. Oxford, 1975-95; geneticist Children's Hosp. Philadelphia, 1960—; vis. prof. Paediatrics New York Hosp., 1967. Fellow Royal Coll. Physicians, Royal Soc., Keble Coll. Avocations: skiing, walking. Home: 78 Old Rd. Oxford OX3 7XP, England Office: Oxford U Biochemistry Dept, South Parks Rd, Oxford OX1 3QU, England

EDWARDS, JONATHAN, Olympic athlete; b. London, May 10, 1966. Geneticist Royal Victoria Infirmary; winner Bronze medal triple jump World Championships, 1993, winner Silver medal triple jump World Championships, 1997, winner European title triple jump, 1998; winner Gold medal triple jump Sydney, 2000. Named European Athlete of Yr., 1999. Holder world record on successive jumps, only legal jump in history longer than 60 ft. Track and Field World Championships, Gothenburg, Sweden, 1995; record for 4th and 6th best jumps European Championships, 1998. Office: Brit Athletic Fedn, 225a Bristol Rd, Edghastan, Birmingham B5 7UB, England*

EDWARDS, KATHRYN INEZ, educational technology consultant; b. L.A., Aug. 26, 1947; d. Lloyd and Geraldine E. (Smith) Price; 1 child, Bryan. BA in English, Calif. State U., L.A., 1969, supervision credential, 1974, adminstrn. credential, 1975; MEd in Curriculum, UCLA, 1971; PhD, Claremont Grad. Sch., 1979. Tchr., L.A. Pub. Schs., 1969-78, adv. specially funded programs, 1978-80, advisor librs. and learning-resources program, 1980-81, instructional specialist, 1981-84; cons. instructional media L.A. County Office of Edn., Downey, Calif., 1984-90; coord. ednl. media and tech. Pomona (Calif.) Unified Sch. Dist., 1990-92; cons. edn. tech. Apple Computer, Inc., 1992-96; client mktg. rep. IBM; sales devel. mgr. SUN Microsys., 1999—; cons. Walt Disney Prodns., Alfred Higgins Prodns., others; mem. distance lng. think tank U.S. Office Edn., 1997. Author guides and curriculum kits. Appointed by assembly speaker Willie Brown to Calif. Ednl. Tech. Com., 1990-92, Calif. State Assembly Resolution from Gwen Moore, 1988, Edn. Coun. for Tech. in Learning, 1993-96; mem. spl. com. Cable Access Corp. Cowners, 1991-92. Recipient cert. commendation Senator Diane Watson, 1988; Mabel Wilson Richards scholar, 1968, Calif. Congress Parents and Tchrs. scholar, 1968; UCLA fellow, 1968; named Outstanding Woman of Yr. L.A. Sentinel, 1987. Mem. Nat. Assn. Minority Polit. Women, Internat. Reading Assn. (speaker nat. conv. 1988), L.A. Reading Assn. (pres.), Calif. Assn. Tchrs. of English (conf. del. 1982), Assn. Supervision and Curriculum Devel., Calif. Media and Libr. Educators Assn. (state conf. co-chair 1989, v.p. legal divsn. 1992—), Nat. Assn. Media Women (Media Woman of Yr. 1987), Alpha Kappa Alpha. Democrat. Roman Catholic. Avocations: reading, gardening, travel. Office: IBM Corp 355 S Grand Ave Los Angeles CA 90071-3161

EDWARDS, KENNETH NEIL, chemical engineer, consultant; b. Hollywood, Calif., June 8, 1932; s. Arthur Carl and Ann Vera (Gomez) E.; children: Neil James, Peter Graham, John Evan. BA in Chemistry, Occidental Coll., 1954; MS in Chem. and Metall. Engring., U. Mich., 1955. Prin. chemist Battelle Meml. Inst., Columbus, Ohio, 1955-58; dir. new products rsch. and devel. Dunn-Edwards Corp., L.A., 1958-72; sr. lectr. organic coatings and pigments dept. chem. engring. U. So. Calif., L.A., 1976-80; bd. dirs. Dunn-Edwards Corp., L.A.; cons. Coatings & Plastics Tech., L.A., 1972—. Contbr. articles to sci. jours. Recipient Judo Masters belt (6th dan), Korean Judo Assn., 2000. Mem. Am. Chem. Soc. (chmn. divisional activities 1988-89, exec. com. divsn. polymeric materials sci. and engring. 1963—, chair divsn. 1970, mem. devel. adv. com. 1996-99, Disting. Svc. award 1996, chair Disting. Svc. award selection 1997—, chair So. Calif. local sect. 1999), Korean Judo Assn. (Judo Masters belt 2000), Alpha Chi Sigma (chmn. L.A. prof. chpt. 1962, counselor Pacific dist. 1967-70, grand profl. alchemist nat. v.p. 1970-76, grand master alchemist nat. pres. 1976-78, nat. adv. com. 1978—). Achievements include patents for air-dried polyester coatings and application, for process and apparatus for dispensing liquid colorants into a paint can, fluidic fillers, and for mechanical mixers. Home: Bottle Bay Rd Sagle ID 83860 also: 2926 Graceland Way Glendale CA 91206-1331 Office: Dunn Edwards Corp 136 W Walnut Ave Monrovia CA 91016-3444

EDWARDS, LARRY DAVID, internist, educator; b. Macomb, Ill., June 20, 1937; s. Richard Marshall and Anna Louise (Hare) Edwards; m. Ann Leanor Will, Mar. 31, 1959; children: Elliott, Sharon, Beth. Pre-Med, U. Ill., 1961, MD, 1965. Diplomate Am. Bd. Internal Medicine, Am. Bd. Infectious Disease, Am. Bd. Geriatric Medicine, Nat. Bd. Med. Examiners, Am. Bd. Med. Mgmt., Am. Coll. Healthcare Execs; cert. physician exec., healthcare exec. Rotating intern USPHS Hosp., Staten Island, N.Y., 1965-66, resident in internal medicine, 1966-68; fellow in infectious diseases Rush-Presbyn.-St. Luke's Med. Ctr., Chgo., 1968-70; instr. dept. internal medicine U. Ill. Coll. Medicine, Chgo., 1968-70; asst. prof. depts. internal medicine, preventive medicine, microbiology Rush Med. Coll., Chgo., 1972-74; assoc. prof. internal medicine U. Ill. Coll. Medicine, Rockford, 1974-80, prof., 1980-81; prof. internal medicine Oral Roberts U. Sch. Medicine, Tulsa, 1981-90; dir. div. infectious diseases Rockford Sch. Medicine, 1974-81, dep. head dept. biomed. scis., 1980-81; prof. internal medicine U. Va., Charlottesville, 1991-92; chief of staff VA Med. Ctr., Salem, Va., 1990-92; assoc. dean for acad. affairs VA, U. Va., Charlottesville, 1991-92; adj. assoc. prof. epidemiology, U. Ill. Sch. Pub. Health, 1977-81; affiliate dept. medicine, Abraham Lincoln Sch. Medicine, U. Ill., Chgo., 1980-81; dir. div. infectious diseases Oral Roberts U., 1981-84; assoc. dean clin. affairs Oral Roberts Sch. Medicine, 1981, 84, vice chmn. dept. internal medicine, 1981-83, chmn., 1983-86, chmn. preventive and internat. medicine, 1987-88, dean, 1984-90, v.p. for health affairs, 1987-90 and chief operating officer City of Faith Med. & Rsch. Ctr., 1989-90; med. dir. Cen. Bapt. Home for Aged, Norridge, Ill., 1968-74, Columbia County Homes, Wyocena, Wis., 1974-80; asst. dir. infectious diseases, hosp. epidemiologist, dir. infectious disease research Rush-Presbyn.-St. Luke's Hosp., Chgo., 1972-74, asst. sci. dept. microbiology, 1970-74; asst. med. dir. Mcpl. Contagious Disease Hosp., Chgo., 1970-74; cons. infectious diseases numerous other hosps. and med. ctrs.; med. dir. City of Faith Hosp., Tulsa, 1984-87, chmn. bd., 1989-90; bd. dirs. City of Faith Clinic, Tulsa, 1985-87; pres. Infectious Diseases Cons. Svcs., Inc., Barnhart, Mo., 1993—. Contbr. numerous articles to med. jours. Advisor resource com. Sch. Health Coalition of N.W. Ill., 1979-81; mem. med. adv. com. State of Ill. Refugee Health Services Program, 1980-81; mem. Ill. health services task force State of Ill. Dept. Pub. Health, 1980-81; mem. infectious disease adv. com. Tulsa City-County Health Dept., 1981-88; mem. physician manpower adv. com. Okla. Bd. Regents, 1984-88; mem. Oral Roberts U. Titan Scholarship Bd., 1985-87; v.p. World-Wide Med. Missions, Oral Roberts Evangelistic Assn., 1986-88, pres. 1989-90; mem. Leadership Roanoke Valley, 1991-92. Served with U.S. Army, 1955-58, with USPHS, 1965-70, lt. col. USAR, 1985, col. 1990-97, ret., 1997. Recipient Smith, Kline and French fellowship for study in Ethiopia, 1964; named Outstanding Faculty Mem. of Yr. Oral Roberts U. Sch. Medicine, 1982-83. Fellow ACP, Infectious Diseases Soc. Am., Am. Coll. Physician Execs., Am. Coll. Healthcare Execs. Avocations: reading, writing.

EDWARDS, SIR LLEWELLYN ROY, company executive; b. Aug. 2, 1935; s. Roy Thomas and Agnes Dulcie Gwendoline Edwards; m. Leone Sylvia Burley, 1958 (dec.); 3 children; m. Jane Anne Brumfield, 1989. MB, BChir, U. Queensland, 1965, LLD (hon.), 1988. Qualified electrician; qualified med. practitioner. RMO, registrar surgery Ipswich Hosp., 1965-68; gen. practice Ipswich, 1968-74; MLA Ipswich Queensland Parliament, 1972-83; min. health Queensland, 1974-78, dep. premier, treas., 1978-83; dep. med. supt. Ispwich Hosp., 1984; exec. cons. Jones Lang Wootton, Brisbane, 1989—; chancellor U. Queensland, 1993—; mem. senate U. Queensland, 1984—; chmn. Multifunction Polis Corp.; chmn., CEO World Expo 88 Authority, 1984-89, Australian Coachline Holdings Ltd., 1992-96; bd. dirs. Westpac Banking Corp., James Hardie Industries Pty Ltd., T.N.Z. (Aust) Pty. Ltd.; chmn. Pacific Film and TV Corp. Fellow Royal Australian Coll. Med. Adminstrs., Australian Inst. Mgmt.; mem. Rugby Union. Avocations: tennis, walking, music. Office: U Queensland, 8 Ascot St, Brisbane Qld 4072, Australia

EDWARDS, LLOYD JEROME, biostatistician; b. Chattanooga, Tenn., Mar. 21, 1958; s. Haywood Columbus and Clara Mae (Hurt) E.; m. Lori Rochel Carter, June 17, 1995; 1 child, Kalimba. BA in Math., Morehouse Coll., 1980; MA in Math. Stats., U. Md., 1982; PhD in Biostats., U. N.C., 1990. Software engr., statistician TRW Defense Systems Group, McLean, Va., 1983-86; grad. rsch. asst. U. N.C., Chapel Hill, 1986-90, vis. asst. prof., 1990-91, asst. prof., 1991-98, assoc. prof., 1998; assoc. prof. Duke U. Med. Ctr., 1998—; stats cons. Rho, Inc., Chapel Hill, 1990—, pvt. practice, Chapel Hill, 1991—; prin. investigator Ctrs. for Disease Control and Prevention, Hyattsville, Md., 1993-98; investigator rsch. supplement NIH, Bethesda MD, 1991-95. Contbr. articles to profl jours. including New Eng. Jour. Medicine, Jour. Computation and Simulation, Physiology and Behavior. Tutor math., City of Washington, 1981, St. Joseph's AME Ch., Durham, N.C., 1997. Mem. Am. Stats. Assn., Pi Mu Epsilon (pres. 1979), Phi Beta Kappa. Home: 3819 Swarthmore Rd Durham NC 27707-5437 Office: Divsn of Biometry Duke Univ 249 Hanes House Durham NC 27710-0001

EDWARDS, MICHAEL AUBREY, writer, foundation executive; b. Liverpool, Eng., June 29, 1957; s. David Arthur and Millicent Elizabeth (Heathcote) E.; m. Cora Anne Castro. BA summa cum laude with honors, U. Oxford, U.K., 1978, MA, 1981; PhD, U. Coll. London, 1982. Rschr., tutor U. Coll. London, 1978-82; devel. officer Vol. Svc. Overseas, London, 1982-84; regional rep. OXFAM-UK, Zambia, Malawi, 1984-88; dir. Prasad Found., India, 1988-90; head rsch. Save the Children Fund, London, 1990-96; pres. Edwards Assocs., London, 1996-98; sr. adviser The World Bank, Washington, 1998-99; dir. Governance and Civil Soc., Ford Found., N.Y.C., 1999—; sr. cons. UNCHS, Nairobi, Kenya, 1989—; assoc. Inst. for Devel. Policy and Mgmt., Manchester, U.K., 1992—; advisor Commn. on Future of Vol. Sector, London, 1995-96; advisor to numerous charities in over 20 countries, 1995—. Author: Future Positive, 1999; contbr. over 40 articles to profl. jours.; co-editor: Making a Difference, 1992, Beyond the Magic Bullet, 1995, Too Close for Comfort, 1997, Global Citizen Action, 2000. Del. World Bank-Ngo Com., Washington, 1993-96; chair Internat. Childrens Rights Info. Network, Paris, 1995; mem. Nexus Network, U.K., 1996—. Recipient Rsch. fellowship Leverhulme Trust, London, 1995-96, Simon Indsl. and Profl. fellowship U. Manchester, 1996. Mem. Devel. Studies Assn. (sec. 1993-96). Mem. Brit. Labour Party. Avocations: reading, travel, soccer, meditation. Home: 211 W 56th St Apt 36H New York NY 10019-4326

EDWARDS, OTIS CARL, JR., theology educator; b. Bienville, La., June 15, 1928; s. Otis Carl and Margaret Lee (Hutchinson) E.; m. Jane Hanna Trufant, Feb. 19, 1957; children: Carl Lee, Samuel Adams Trufant, Louise Reynes. BA, Centenary Coll., 1949; postgrad., Duke U., 1949-51; STB, Gen. Theol. Sem., 1952; postgrad., Westcott House, Cambridge, Eng., 1952-53; STM, So. Meth. U., 1962; MA, U. Chgo., 1963, PhD, 1971; DD, Nashotah House, 1976. Ordained priest Episcopal Ch., 1954. Curate Episcopal Ch., Baton Rouge, 1953-54; vicar Episcopal Ch., Abbeville, La., 1954-57, Waxahachie, Tex., 1960-61; rector Episcopal Ch., Morgan City, La., 1957-60; priest in charge Episcopal Ch., Chgo., 1961-63; instr. Wabash Coll., 1963-64; asst. prof. Nashotah House, Wis., 1964-69; assoc. prof. Nashotah House, 1969-72, prof., 1972-74, sub-dean, 1973-74, acting dean, 1973-74; dean Seabury-Western Theol. Sem., Evanston, Ill., 1974-83; prof. Seabury-Western Theol. Sem., 1983-93, prof. emeritus, 1996; chaplain, scholar in residence Coll. Preachers; Chmn. Coun. for Devel. of Ministry, Episcopal Ch., Coun. Sem. Deans; mem. Bd. for Theol. Edn.; mem. Gen. Bd. Examining Chaplains; vis. prof. Notre Dame, 1986—, Duke U., 1996; rsch. assoc. The Newberry Libr.; interim priest Episcopal Ch., Asheville, N.C. Author: How It All Began, 1973, The Living and Active Word, 1975 (with Robert Bennett) The Bible for Today's Church, 1979, Luke's Story of Jesus, 1981, (with John Westerhoff) A Faithful Church: Issues in the History of Catechesis, 1981, Elements of Homiletic, 1982, How Holy Writ Was Written, 1989; book rev. editor Anglican Theol. Rev., 1971-76, v.p. of corp., 1975-85; contbr. articles and book revs. to various jours. and mags. Chmn. campus affairs com.; trustee Kendall Coll.; sec. Commn. on Faith and Order Nat. Coun. Chs.; bd. dirs. Native Am. Theol. Assn., Univ. North Carolina at Asheville Found.; v.p. bd. dirs. Coll. for Srs./U. N.C., Asheville; program com. Kanuga Confs., Inc., Friends of St. Benedict. Recipient Spl. award Mystery Writers Am., 1965; grantee The Conant Fund, Pew Foun., St. Paul's Ministry and Mission Found., Indpls. Mem. Soc. Bibl. Lit., Cath. Bibl. Assn., Am. Acad. Religion, Chgo. Soc. Bibl. Rsch., Acad. Homiletics, (pres.), Societas Homiletica (exec. coun., treas.), Coll. of Preachers (long-range planning com.), Mystery Writers of Am. Democrat. Home: 115 Murphy Hill Rd Weaverville NC 28787-8630

EDWARDS, PATRICK MICHAEL, sales consultant; b. Burbank, Calif., Sept. 20, 1947; s. Kenneth Charles and Thelma Kay (Allen) E. BS, Calif. Poly State U., 1975. Med. salesperson Burroughs Wellcome Co., Research Triangle Park, N.C., 1975-79; master cons. G.D. Searle & Co., Chgo., 1979—; bd. dirs. Calif. Poly. Alumni Assn., 1999—. Author photo essay in Ford Times mag., 1989. With USCG, 1968-72. Mem. Assn. of Pharm. Reps. (pres. 1986), Toastmasters Internat. Republican. Avocations: photography, hiking, biking, sailing, scuba diving. Home and Office: 344 N 16th St Grover Beach CA 93433-1850

EDWARDS, PAUL ARTHUR, quality assurance company executive; b. Dorking, Surrey, Eng., Feb. 27, 1944; s. Frank Joseph and Lillian Martha (Geeson) E.; m. Lea Marjatta Louhimies, July 9, 1989. Master mariner, Dept. Trade and Industry, London, 1970. Chief officer P & O Bulk Shipping, London, 1974-81; dock master Port of Bristol, Eng., 1981-82; master Pentmarine (1982) Ltd., Hong Kong, 1982-84; sr. insp. Saybolt U.K., London, 1984-86; mgr. Saybolt S.A., Limassol, Cyprus, 1987-90; exec. dir. Saybolt, Moscow, 1991-96, Saybolt Internat. Bv., Rotterdam, The Netherlands, 1996; team leader UN Oil Monitoring Teams, Iraq, 1996-98; team leader food monitoring teams EC Fund for Russia Project, 1999—. Mem. Inst. Petroleum (London). Avocations: fishing, gardening, skiing, running, computer studies, archery.

EDWARDS, PRISCILLA ANN, paralegal, business owner; b. Orlando, Fla., Sept. 28, 1947; d. William Granville and Bernice Royster; m. Charles R. King, Apr. 2, 1981. Paralegal cert., U. Calif., Berkeley, 1994. Paralegal Charles R. Garry Esquire, San Francisco, Calif., 1989-90, Marvin Cahn Esquire, San Francisco, 1990-91; owner, mgr. Fed. Legal Resources, San Francisco, 1991—; speaker Sonoma State U., Santa Rosa, Calif., 1993. Publisher: (book) Zero Weather, 1981. Recipient Wiley W. Manuel award for pro bono legal svcs. Bd. Govs. State Bar of Calif., 1994, 95, 96, 97, 98. Episcopalian. Avocations: horseback riding, mountain biking.

EDWARDS, RALPH M., librarian; b. Shelley, Idaho, Apr. 17, 1933; s. Edward William and Maude Estella (Munsee) E.; m. Winifred Wylie, Dec. 25, 1969; children: Dylan, Nathan, Stephen. B.A., U. Wash., 1957, M.Library, 1960; D.L.S., U. Calif.-Berkeley, 1971. Libr. N.Y. Pub. Libr., N.Y.C., 1960-61; catalog libr. U. Ill. Libr., Urbana, 1961-62; br. libr. Multnomah County Libr., Portland, Oreg., 1964-67; asst. prof. Western Mich. U., Kalamazoo, 1970-74; chief of the Central Libr. Dallas Pub. Libr., 1975-81; city librarian Phoenix Pub. Libr., 1981-95, ret., 1996—. Author: Role of the Beginning Librarian in University Libraries, 1975. U. Calif. doctoral fellow, 1967-70; library mgmt. internship Council on Library Resources, 1974-75. Mem. ALA, Pub. Library Assn. Democrat. Home: 2884 Spring Blvd Eugene OR 97403-1662

EDWARDS, ROSS ALEXANDER, aircraft systems engineer; b. Manchester, Lancashire, Eng., Sept. 23, 1955; s. John Thomas and Frances Everall (Thompson) E.; m. Jane Rebecca Andrews, Aug. 21, 1986; children: Jasmine Anne Catherine, Lawrence Thomas Robert, Poppy Jane Alexandra. BSc in Electronics with honors, U. Manchester, Eng., 1977. Sys. engr. Brit. Aerospace, Warton, Eng., 1977-84; tech. instr. Internat. Edn. Svcs., Tokyo, 1984-86; asst. dir. rsch. The Dove Project, Southampton, Eng., 1986-88; mgr. Canon Software U.K., Wallington, Eng., 1989-90; R&D mgr., tech. cons. sys. design and arch. Brit. Aerospace (now BAE SYS.), Warton, 1990—; chmn. arch. working group U.K. Avionic Sys. Standardization Com., 1997-99. Contbr. articles to profl. jours. Avocation: ninpo (Japanese martial art). Office: BAE Sys, W328J Warton Aerodrome, Preston Lancashire PR4 1AX, England

EDWARDS, SIR SAMUEL FREDERICK, physicist, educator; b. Swansea, Wales, Feb. 1, 1928; m. Merriell Bland, 1953; 4 children. Ed., Cambridge U., Harvard U.; DSc (hon.), U. Bath, U. Edinburgh, U. Loughborough, U. Salford, U. Birmingham, 1976, U. Strasbourg, 1986, U. Wales, 1987, U. Sheffield, 1989, U. Dublin, 1991, U. Leeds, U. Swansea, 1994, East Anglia, 1995. Mem. Inst. Advanced Study, Princeton, N.J.; rsch. fellow U. Birmingham; prof. U. Manchester; emeritus Cavendish prof. physics Cavendish Lab.; pro vice chancellor Cambridge U., 1992-95, vice chancellor, 1992-95; fellow, pres. Gonville and Caius Coll.; vis. prof. U. Calif., San Diego, 1980-81; dir. Lucas Industries, 1981-93; chmn. Sci. Rsch. Coun. U.K., 1973-77, Def. Sci. Adv. Coun., 1977-80; chief sci. advisor U.K. Dept. Energy, 1983-88; program dir. ITP U. Calif., Santa Barbara, 1997. Contbr. articles to profl. jours. Recipient Sci. pour l'Art prize Louis Vuitton Moet Hennessy, 1993, Boltzmann medal Internat. Union Pure and Applied Physics, 1995. Fellow Royal Soc. (Davy medal 1985), Inst. Physics (Maxwell medal, Guthrie medal), Royal Soc. Chemistry, Inst. Math. (Gold medal 1986), Am. Phys. Soc. (High Polymer Physics prize), Brit. Assn. Advancement of Sci. (chmn. 1977-82, pres. 1988-89), Brit. Soc. Rheology (Gold medal 1991), French Acad. Scis. (fgn. assoc.), NAS (fgn. assoc.), French Phys. Soc. (hon.), European Phys. Soc. (hon.); mem. Athenaeum Club. E-mail: sfe11@phys.cam.ac.uk. Home: 7 Penarth Pl, Cambridge CB3 9LU, England Office: Cavendish Lab, Cambridge CB3 OHE, England

EDWARDS, SAMUEL ROGER, internist; b. Santa Barbara, Calif., Aug. 11, 1937; s. Harold S. and Margaret (Spaulding) E.; m. Marcia Elizabeth Dutton, June 17, 1961; children: Harold S. II, Charles Dutton. BA, Harvard U., 1960; MD, U. So. Calif., 1964. Intern Presbyn. Hosp., Phila., 1964-65; resident in internal medicine U Calif., San Francisco, 1968-70; fellow in cardiology Pacific Presbyn. Med. Ctr., San Francisco, 1970; pvt. practice specializing in internal medicine Santa Paula, Calif., 1971-94; med. dir. Santa Paula Convalescent, Twin Pines Convalescent Hosps., 1974-95; pres. med. staff Ventura (Calif.) County Med. Ctr., 1979-80, med. dir., 1983-95, hosp. adminstr., 1995—; mem. clin. faculty UCLA Sch. Medicine, 1980-95; bd. dirs. Citizens State Bank of Santa Paula, 1975-97, chmn., 1994-97; bd. dirs. Limoneira Co., 1985—, Santa Barbara Bank and Trust, 1999—; chief dept. medicine Ventura County Gen. Hosp., 1975; chief med. staff Santa Paula Meml. Hosp., 1977. Lt. Comdr. USNR, 1966-68. Recipient Disting. Svc. award Ventura County Heart Assn., 1974. Fellow ACP; mem. AMA, Am. Coll. Hosp. Execs. Episcopalian. Home: 19789 E Telegraph Rd Santa Paula CA 93060-9693 Office: 243 March St Santa Paula CA 93060-2511

EDWARDS, SCOTT, human resource specialist; b. Chgo., Dec. 13, 1963; s. David Prober; m. Mitsuko Kaneko, July 16, 1995; children: Nicholas Masataka, Alexander Tomohiro. Asst. mgr. Sakura Bank, Tokyo, 1990-98; staff chief Kao Corp., Tokyo, 1998—. Sgt. USMC, Honolulu, 1981-86. Mem. Soc. Human Resources Mgmt., Am. C. of C. in Japan. Avocations: computer, woodworking. E-mail: 311285@kasatnet.kao.co.jp. Office: Kao Corp, 1-14-10 Nihonbashi Chou-ku, Tokyo Tokyo 103-8210, Japan

EDWARDS, SIAN, conductor. Grad., Royal No. Coll. Music; studied with, Sir Charles Groves, Norman Del Mar, Neeme Järvi; student, Lennigrad (USSR) Conservatory, 1983-85; studied with I. A. Musin. Worked with London Philharm., Royal Philharm., London Sinfonietta, Scottish Nat. Orch., City of Birmingham (Eng.) Symphony Orch., the Hallé, the BBC Philharm., BBC Scottish Symphony, Royal Liverpool Philharm.; music dir. English Nat. Opera, 1993-95. Condr. Scottish Opera, Glyndebourne Festival Opera, The Royal Opera, Covent Garden, Orchestre de Paris, Ensemble Modern, Hamburg Radio Orch., Shudwestfunk Orchester, Danish Radio Orch., L.A. Philharm. Orch., Phila. Orch., Minn. Orch., Nat. Symphony Orch., Pitts. Symphony Orch., Cleve. Orch.; recs. include Mozart Symphonies Nos. 40 & 41 London Philharm. Orch., Tchaikovsky with Royal Liverpool Philharm. Orch., John Adams with Ensemble Modern, Judith Weir's opera Blond Eckbert with English Nat. Orch. Office: Ingpen & Williams Ltd, 26 Wadham Rd, London SW15 2LR, England

EDWARDS, SYLVIA ANN, artist; b. Boston, Jan. 30, 1937; d. Junius Griffiths and Sylvia Emma (Mailloux) E.; m. Sadredin M. Golestaneh (div.); children: Shirin, Nader, Leila. Diploma, Mass. Coll. of Art, Boston, 1957, Boston Mus. of Fine Arts, 1958; postgrad., Modern Art Studies, London, 1980-81. Solo exhbns. include: CCA Gallery, Oxford, Eng., 1996, Sala Gallery, Provincetown, Mass., 1993, Munson Gallery, Chatham, N.J., 1992, Jaeshke Gallery, Braunschweig, Germany, 1991, Natalie Knight Gallery, Johannesburg, S. Africa, 1991, Bankamura, Tokyo, 1991, Gallery K. Hyazaki Perfecture, Tokyo, 1991, Mitsukoshi Mihonbashi Br., Tokyo, 1991, The Berkeley Square Gallery, London, 1991, Gallery Szent Gyorgi, Falmouth, Mass., 1998—; numerous others; group exhbns. include Cadogan Contemporary Art, London, 1996, Berkeley Square Gallery, Seoul, Korea Art Expo, 1996, N.Y. Art Expo, N.Y.C., 1994, Lond Internat. Contemporary Art Fair, 1989, The Bath Arts Festival, Bath, Eng., 1988, Paris Art Salon, 1986, 87, 88, numerous others; pub. collections include Nat. Mus. for Women in the Arts, Washington, Cape Mus. of Fine Arts, Dennis, Mass., Mus. of Fine Arts, Alexandria, Egypt, Governate of Alexandria, Mass. Gen. Hosp., Boston, London Lighthouse, U.K., Midwest Mus. of Am. Art, Elkhart, Ind., Tate Gallery, London; publs. include Valley of Sils, Lithograph, 1982, New Mexico Watch, lithograph, 1982, (covers) Arts Rev., 1982, 85, others; painter numerous UNICEF cards, Greenpeace publs., World Wildlife/U.K., book covers, reference and art books, others. Mem. U.K. UNICEF Com. Mem. London Royal Acad., World Watercolor Soc.,

Chelsea Arts Club/London. Avocations: writing, theatre, travel, swimming, reading. Studio: 14 Cadogan Square, London SW1X 0JU, England

EDWARDS, TEENA ANN, community health nurse, educator; b. Denver, Mar. 16, 1951; d. Clifford Milton Delzell and Gratia Iola (Countryman) Hoffman; m. Richard Allison Edwards, June 16, 1973; children: Matthew, Wayne, Sarah Beth. BS, U. No. Colo., 1973; MS, Tex. Woman's U., 1978; DrPH, Loma Linda U., 1998. RN, Tex. Asst. prof. Tex. Christian U., Ft. Worth, 1977; staff nurse Mont. Deaconess Med. Ctr., Great Falls, 1978-79, Tucson Med. ctr., 1982; instr. U. Ariz. Coll. Nursing, Tucson, 1982-84; clin. nurse specialist Penrose Community Hosp., Colorado Springs, Colo., 1984-85; pub. health nurse El Paso County Health Dept., Colorado Springs, 1986; nursing cons. SAFE/WITH Project, Honolulu, 1986; pub. health nurse SAFE Program, Honolulu, 1986; nursing supr. SAFE/WITH Program, Honolulu, 1987; dir. ASPECTS program Tripler Army Med. Ctr., Honolulu, 1988-92; program dir. March AFB, Calif., 1992-94; nurse specialist Travis AFB, Calif., 1994-96; asst. prof. Tex. Woman's U., Dallas, 1997—; mem. rsch. com. Tripler Army Med. Ctr., 1989-92; presenter at profl. confs.; outreach mgr. March AFB, 1992-95; nurse specialist David Grant Med. Ctr., Travis AFB, 1995-96. Active Girl Scouts U.S., 1988—. Recipient appreciation pin Hawaii coun. Girl Scouts U.S., 1992. Mem. NAACOG, NAFE, APHA, Am. Soc. Psychoprophylaxis in Obstetrics. Avocations: handicrafts, reading, gardening. Home: PO Box 338 Moffett Field CA 94035-0338

EDWARDS, TERESA, basketball player. Diploma, U. Ga., 1986. Profl. basketball player Vicenia, Magenta, Italy, 1987-88, Nagoya, Japan, 1989-93, Valencia, Spain, 1994, Tarbes, France, 1994. 1st Am. basketball player to compete in 4 Olympics; recipient bronze medal 1994 World Championship team, USA Olympic Team (co-capt.), 1992, Pan Am. Games, 1991, 2 gold medals World Championship and Goodwill Games, 1986, gold medal, 90, gold medal Olympics, 1984, 88, 96, bronze medal Olympics, 1992, Pan Am. Games, 1987, Jr. Pan Am. team, 1983; earned MVP honors Nat. Sports Festival; named USA Basketball's Female Athelete of Yr., 1987, 90, All-Am. Kodak Naismith Women's Basketball News Svc., Street & Smith's; selected All-SEC 1st team, 1984, 85, 86; one of only 3 Ga. women basketball players to have her number retired. Office: USA Basketball 5465 Mark Dabling Blvd Colorado Springs CO 80918-3842

EDWARDS, VICTOR HENRY, chemical engineer; b. Galveston, Tex., Oct. 17, 1940; s. Philip Lacey and Margaret Ruth (Hopkins) E.; m. Mary Margaret Litzmann, June 10, 1963; children: Henry L., Mary E. BA, Rice U., 1962; PhD in Chem. Engring., U. Calif., Berkeley, 1967. Registered profl. engr., Tex. Asst. prof. chem. engring. Cornell U., Ithaca, N.Y., 1967-73; mgr. adv. tech. U.S. Nat. Sci. Found., Washington, 1971-72; rsch. fellow Merck, Sharp, Dohme Rsch., Rahway, N.J., 1973-76; supr. rsch. engring. United Energy Resources, Houston, 1976-79; vis. prof. environ. engring. Rice U., Houston, 1979-80; sr. process engr. Fluor Engrs. and Constructors, Houston, 1980-82; southwest editor Plant Services mag., Chgo., 1982-85; project engr. Allstates/BE&K, Inc., Houston, 1984-90, lead process engr., 1990-93, process engring. mgr., 1993-94; prin. engr. process and environ. Allstates/BE&K, Inc., 1994-95; process dir. Kvaerner Engrs. and Constructors, Houston, 1995—; tech. adv. com. Mary Kay O'Connor Process Safety Ctr., Tex. A&M U., 1995—. Contbr. articles to profl. jours. Organizing com. Woodlands (Tex.) Harvest Festival, 1979-86; chmn. industry adv. coun. dept. chem. engring. Prairie View A&M U., 1991-94. Recipient Disting. Svc. award dept. chem. engring. Prairie View A&M U., 1992, 94, Shield of Irenee award for excellence in engring. design E.I. duPont de Nemours & Co., 1994, 98, Environ. Excellence award, 1994, Safety, Health, and Environ. Excellence award, 1996. Fellow AIChE (chmn. Process Plant Safety Symposium 1992, program co-chmn. 1994, exec. position 1 1993, chmn. 1995, South Tex. sect. chmn. 2d internat. plant ops. and design conf. 1997, Churchwell award South Tex. sect. 1981, Disting. Svc. award 1991); mem. AAAS, NSPE, Am. Chem. Soc. (chmn. Ithaca sect. 1969, councilor divsn. biochem. and microbial tech. 1970-77), Engrs. Coun. Houston (councilor 1987-92), N.Y. Acad. Scis. (life mem.), Rice U. Alumni Assn. (class of '62 reunion com. 1982, 87, 92, 97, co-chmn. fundraising drive 1998). Methodist. Avocations: reading, tennis, sailing, golf. Office: Kvaerner Engrs and Constructors 7909 Parkwood Circle Dr Houston TX 77036-6565

EDWARDS, WILLIAM BENNETT, firearms industry consultant, gun dealer; b. Auburn, N.Y., Nov. 10, 1927; s. John Bowen and Virginia Hampton (Bean) E.; m. Virginia Jane Davis, Jan. 12, 1954. Fed. firearms dealer, U.S.A. Pvt. practice Afton, Va., 1963—; prin., owner Benet Arms Co., various, 1947—; technical dir. Mars-Centennial Arms Co., Chgo., 1955-62; prin., owner Gold Rush Gun Shop, various, 1964—; artistic creator Pastimes LTD, Staunton, Va., 1985-92; cons. Saddam Hussein, 1990-91, Pres. Clinton, 1993. Author: The Story of Colt's Revolver, 1953, Civil War Guns, 1962; editor Conspiracy Press, 1994—; inventor. With USNG, 1949-51. Mem. NRA, Sons of Confederate Veterans, Va. Arms Collectors Assn. Republican. Unitarian. Avocations: observation of Jesuit plans. Home and Office: Conspiracy Press 6049 Howardsville Tpke Afton VA 22920-2509

EDWARDS, WILLIAM JAMES, broadcasting executive; b. Birmingham, Ala., Mar. 30, 1915; s. Perron Austin and Eugenia (Evans) E.; m. Julia M. Stacey, May 15, 1937; children: Julia Beverly, Linda J. Edwards Riley. Student, Birmingham-Southern Coll., 1935-37; LLD (hon.), Saginaw Valley State U., 1994, Northwood U., 1995. Announcer, Sta. WBRC, Birmingham, 1933-34; program dir. Sta. WMBR, Jacksonville, Fla., 1934; announcer Sta. WLW, Cin., 1938; comml. mgr. Storer Broadcasting, Fairmont, W.Va., 1939-42; news commentator Sta. KMTR (now KLAC), Hollywood, Calif., 1944-45; exec. Sta. WIBC, Indpls., 1942-44; founder, pres. Lake Huron Broadcasting Corp., Saginaw, Mich., 1947—; pres. G.C.C. Communications of Houston, Inc., Suncoast Stereo Corp., St. Petersburg, Fla.; (Stas. KRBE-FM & AM, Houston, WQYK, Tampa-St. Petersburg); dir. Design Craftsmen, Inc., Midland, Mich.; Co-chmn. Saginaw chpt. ARC, 1951, gen. fund chmn., 1952. Pres. Saginaw Symphony Orch. Assn., 1954; pres. United Fund Saginaw County, 1960-62, Saginaw Community Chest, 1960-62; chmn. YWCA Adv. com., 1955-68; mem. Saginaw Libr. Commn., 1952-70, Am. Coun. United Funds, 1965-66; bd. of fellows Saginaw Valley State U., 1968-75; trustee Alvin M. Bentley Found., Owosso, Mich., 1969—, Birmingham-So. Coll., Ala., 1989—; pres. Julia M. and William J. Edwards Found.; gen. ptnr. Edwards Family Partnership, chmn. bd. govs., 1994; chmn. bd. govs. Northwood U., West Palm Beach, Fla., 1991—, bd. trustees, Midland, Mich., 1993—. With Armed Forces Radio Svc., USN, 1945-46. Recipient Disting. Svc. award Jaycees, 1951, Outstanding Bus. Leaders award Northwood U., West Palm Beach, Fla., 1991; named Saginaw Man of Yr., 1950. Mem. Birchwood Golf and Country Club, USN League (chpt. dir.), Govs. Club of Palm Beaches, Ballen Isles Country Club, City Club of Palm Beaches, Palm Beach Round Table (bd. dirs. 1994), Masons, Shriners, Rotary (pres. Saginaw club 1959-60). Republican. Methodist. Home: 1275 S Ocean Blvd Palm Beach FL 33480-5008 Office: Birchwood Farms Estate 840 US Hwy 1 Ste 315 North Palm Beach FL 33408

EDWARDS-LEBOEUF, RENEE CAMILLE, public relations professional, logistics engineer; b. Falls Church, Va., Aug. 6, 1961; d. Walter Thomas and Elizabeth Ann Holt. BS, George Mason U., Fairfax, 1983; MS, Central Mich. U., Merrifield, 1988; grad. program mgmt. course, Def. Systems Mgmt. Coll., 1990. Cert. contracting officer's rep. Logistics analyst The BDM Corp., McLean, Va., 1983-85; deputy program mgr. COMARCO/IBS, Arlington, Va., 1985-88; logistics mgr., speaker, briefer SWL, Inc., Arlington, Va., 1988-89; mem. profl. staff Def. Systems Mgmt. Coll., Ft. Belvoir, Va., 1989-92; dir. computer-aided acquisition and logistics support tng. and edn. Office Asst. Sec. of Def. Prodn. and Logistics, Falls Church, Va., 1992-93; dir. pub. affairs U.S. Dept. Commerce, Nat. Tech. Info. Svc., Springfield, Va., 1993—; co-chmn. computer aided acquisition Logistics Systems Rsch. Group. Contbr. articles to profl. jours. Bd. dirs. Woodwalk Condominium, Burke, Va., 1987-96, mem. indsl. tech. adv. com., 1997-99. Named Best Speaker Toastmasters, McLean, 1985, Best Evaluator Toastmasters, McLean, 1985; recipient Excellence award Dept. Def., 1993, Outstanding Svc. award Dept. Commerce, 1996. Mem. Soc. of Logistics Engrs., Pub. Rels. Soc. Am. Republican. Avocations: racquetball, cycling, embroidery, guitar. Office: US Dept Commerce NTIS 5285 Port Royal Rd Springfield VA 22161-0001

EEBER, LUDMILLA, acquisition librarian; b. Volosovo, Russia, Apr. 7, 1941; d. Trofim and Lidia (Eber) Fyodorov. Diploma, Tartu (Estonia) State U., 1971, cert. in art, 1968. Tchr. English Rakvere (Estonia) Boarding Sch., 1968-69; tchr. Hellenurme (Estonia) Children's Home, 1970-71; sr. acquisition libr. Tartu (Estonia) U. Libr., 1971—. Lutheran. Avocations: hiking, gardening, politics, art. Home: Jaama 183-3, 50705 Tartu Estonia Office: Tartu Univ Library, W Struve 1, 50091 Tartu Estonia

EEG-HENRIKSEN, FRIDE, sociologist; b. Oslo, Sept. 6, 1950; d. Jan and Vibeke (Frimann-Dahl) E.; m. Lars Petter Grue; children: Jan, Kristin. BA, U. Oslo, 1971; Magister Artium, U. Oslo, 1976. Editor jour. Praxis Pax Pub Co., Norway, 1977-79; rschr. Inst. Studies Rsch. & Higher Edn., Oslo, 1979-85, dept. head, 1987; dir. Ctr. Women's Studies, U. Oslo, 1987-95, NIKK, Nordic Inst. Women's Studies & Gender Rsch., Oslo, 1995—. Contbr. articles to profl. jours. Home: Villaveien 38, 0371 Oslo Norway Office: NIKK, PO Box 1156 Blindern, 0317 Oslo Norway

EEKELAAR, JOHN MICHAEL, law educator; b. Johannesburg, South Africa, July 2, 1942; came to U.K., 1960; s. Jan frederick and Delphine (Stoughton) E.; m. Pia Nicole Lewis, Aug. 5, 1978; children: Louise, Catherine. LLB, King's Coll., London, 1963; BCL, Oxford U., 1965, MA, 1966. Barrister-at-law, U.K. Fellow and tutor in law Pembroke Coll., Oxford, 1965—; lectr.-in-law Oxford U., 1966-90, reader in family law, 1990—, chmn. Bd. of Faculty Law, 1989-92; rschr., cons. Ctr. for Socio-Legal Studies, Oxford, 1976-00. Author/editor numerous books, chpts., articles in family law; founding co-editor Internat. Jour. Law Policy, The Family, 1985—; gen. editor Oxford Jour. Legal Studies, 1993—. Chmn., sec. Oxford Girls Choir, 1990-00. Mem. Internat. Soc. Family Law (pres. 1985-88, exec. coun.). Liberal Democratic Party. Avocation: music. Office: Pembroke College, Univ of Oxford, Oxford OX1 1DW, England

EEKELS, JOHANNES, retired educator, consultant; b. Roermond, The Netherlands, Mar. 29, 1917; s. Johannes and Anna Catharina (Tevonderen) E.; m. Agatha Maria Wiegel, Jan. 2, 1947; children: Margriet, Hans, Frans, Leo, Thomas, Annelies. Chem. engr., Inst. Chem. Engring., London, 1950; MPhil cum laude, U. Utrecht, The Netherlands, 1968; Dr. Engring. Sci., U. Twente, Enschede, The Netherlands, 1973. Chartered engr., London. Rsch. asst. Shell Netherlands, Amsterdam, 1935-40; rschr. Utr. Asphalt Fabriek, Krimpen a/d Yssel, The Netherlands, 1941-43; plant mgr. Utr. Asphalt Fabriek, Krimpen a/d Yssel, 1943-47, site dir., 1947-57; dir. R&D Cindu Chem. Industry, Uithoorn, The Netherlands, 1958-80; full prof. Delft (The Netherlands) U. Tech., 1976-87; cons. Own Consulting Bur., Uithoorn, 1985-95; retired Own Consulting Bur., 1995; guest lectr. Holland, Belgium, Sweden, Denmark, Chechoslovakia, Switzerland, Great Britain, others, 1965—; cons. for various cos., The Netherlands, 1975—. Author:Industriele Doelontw., 1973; editor-in-chief: Ondernemen en Vernieuwen, 1985; co-editor: Evaluation and Deicison in Design, 1990; co-author: Product Design and Methodology, 1991, English edit., 1995, Industriele Produkt ontwikkeling, 3 parts, 1995-2000; contbr. articles to profl. jours. Mem. bldg. com. Roman Cath. Ch., Krimpen a/d Yssel, 1950-57. Cpl. Infantry, 1937-39, 40, The Netherlands. Decorated War Cross, Netherlands Govt., The Hague, 1945, Large Gold medal Netherland Soc. for Industry and Trade, Haarlem, 1966, Knight in the Order of the Dutch Lion, The Queen of the Netherlands, Soestdyk, 1988; recipient ICED award Internat. Soc. Sci. Engring. Design, Tampere, Finland, 1997. Fellow Inst. Chem. Engring. Great Britain; mem. Royal Inst. Engrs. (chmn. curatorium Klvl-chair, Delft U. Tech., Mem. of Merit 1999), Netherland Soc. for Philosophy (bd. mem. 1969—, hon. sec. 1969-75), Internat. Conf. Engring. Design (sect. chmn. 1985-93, chmn. many working groups), Lawn Tennis Club (pres. 1953-58, hon. pres. 1959-93). Roman Catholic. Avocations: music, art, nature, sports. Fax: 31(0)297-533123.

EELES, ROSALIND ANNE, oncology consultant; b. London, Oct. 4, 1959; d. Michael Breakspear and Kathleen Sylvia (Cameron) E.; m. Douglas Frederick Easton, Sept. 11, 1982. MA, Cambridge (England) U., 1984; MB BS, St. Thomas Hosp., London, 1984. Jr. lectr. Royal Marsden Hosp., Inst. Cancer Rsch., Sutton, England, 1985-86; sr. house officer medicine St. Peter'sHosp., Chertsey, England, 1986-87; registrar Royal Marsden Hosp., Inst. Cancer Rsch., 1987-90, sr. lectr., hon. cons. cancer genetics & clin. oncology, 1994—; vis. asst. prof. U. Utah, Salt Lake City, 1993-94; cons. in field. Author: PCR & It's Applications, 1993; editor: Genetic Predisposition to Cancer, 1996. Clin. rsch. fellow ICR, Sutton, 1990-93. E-mail: ros@icr.ac.uk. Office: Royal Marsden Hosp Inst Cancer Rsch, Downs Rd, Sutton SM2 5NG, England

EERKENS, JEFF W., nuclear scientist, laser engineer, educator; b. Djakarta, Indonesia, June 11, 1931; came to U.S., 1950; s. Josephus Wilhelmus and Elisabeth Maria (Zijderveld) E.; m. Martha Laura Stone, June 1, 1959 (div. May 1964); 1 child, Laura Elisabeth; m. Else Gertrude DeKock, Aug. 19, 1968; children: Jelmer Willem, Mieke Karen, Boukje Elisabeth. BS in Engring. Physics, U. Calif., Berkeley, 1954, MS in Nuclear Engring., 1957, PhD in Engring. Sci., 1960. Registered profl. engr., Calif. Nuclear engr. Aerojet-Gen.-Nucleonics, San Ramon, Calif., 1957-60; staff scientist Aerospace Corp., El Segundo, Calif., 1960-63; laser sys. br. chief Northrop Space Labs., Hawthorne, Calif., 1963-67; chief scientist Sci. and Tech. Assocs., West Los Angeles, Calif., 1967-71; program mgr. AiRsch. divsn. Garrett Corp., Torrance, Calif., 1971-77; pres. LISCHEM Corp., Lawndale, Calif., 1977-85; pres. Isotope Tech., Pacific Palisades, Calif., 1990-93, Columbia, Mo., 1993—; rsch. prof. nuclear engring. U. Mo., Columbia, 1993—. Author: Rocket Radiation Handbook, 3 vols., 1973, 74; editor, author: Laser Isotope Separation, 1995. Recipient Best New Product award Lasers and Applications, 1985. Mem. Am. Nuclear Soc., Optical Soc. Am., Internat. Isotope Soc., Am. Chem. Soc. Achievements include 11 patents in fields of molecular laser isotope separation, laser design, neutrino communication system, nuclear pumped lasers and grasers, fuel cells. Avocations: swimming, sport flying of gliders and private aircraft. Office: Isotope Techs PO Box 7162 Columbia MO 65205-7162

EFFERTH, THOMAS A., biologist, educator, researcher; b. Worms, R.-Pfalz, Germany, 1960; m. Monika M. Efferth. Diploma, Tech. U., Darmstadt, Germany, 1986; PhD in Theoretical Medicine, German Cancer Rsch. Ctr., Heidelberg, Germany, 1990; cert. univ. lectr., Tech. U., Aachen, Germany, 1997. Sci. fellow U. Aachen, Germany, 1992-98; asst. prof. U. Erlangen-Nuremberg, Germany, 1998—, rsch. mgr., 1998—; dir. Virtúal Campús U. Koblenz-Pfalz, Mainz, Germany, 2000—; lectr. and presenter in field. Contbr. over 60 articles to profl. jours.; ad hoc referee for jours. and grant applications. Served with German Mil., Diez, 1979-80. Mem. Am. Assn. Cancer Rsch., German Assn. Biochemistry and Molecular Biology, German Assn. Cell Biology, S.W. German Assn. Internal Medicine. Fax: 49 6131 3746089. E-mail: efferth@uni-koblenz-landau.de. Office: VCRP U Koblenz-Landau, Isaac-Fulda-Allee 3, 55124 Mainz Bavaria, Germany

EFFRON, SETH ALAN, editor, journalist; b. July 23, 1952; m. Nancy G. Thomas; children: Rebecca, Eve. BA in Polit. Sci. with honors, U. N.C., 1974. Asst. to editor Fayetteville (N.C.) Times (now Fayetteville Observer-Times), 1974-75, reporter, 1975-77; reporter Tallahassee Dem., 1977-80; reporter Wichita (Kans.) Eagle-Beacon (now Wichita Eagle), 1980-82, 83-85, coord. legis. coverage, 1982; stage govt. and polit. reporter Greensboro (N.C.) News & Record, 1985—; editor, founder the insider, N.C. State Govt. News Svc., Raleigh, 1993-96; exec. editor on-line content Nando Media, Nando Times, Raleigh, 1996-99; account exec. Capital Strategies, Raleigh, 2000—; NEH summer fellow Williams Coll., 1979; lectr. Freedom Forum Media Studies Ctr., Columbia U., N.Y.C., 1995, Annenberg Washington program Northwestern U., 1995, Ctr. for Pub. TV, U. N.C., N.C. Fellow, U. N.C., 1993, Press Assn., 1994, Inst. for Polit. Leadership, 1994, Salzburg (Austria) Seminar, 1994, Human Svcs. Automation Conf., 1994. Author: 100 Proof Pure Old Jess: Jesse Helms Quoted, 1993, Coachspeak: Triangle ACC Men's Basketball Coaches Quoted, 1995, North Carolina Almanac of Government and Politics 95-96, 1995; contbr. articles to popular publs., including Los Angeles Herald-Examiner, Des Moines Register, Christian Science Monitor. Mem. adv. panel Z. Smith Reynolds Found., 1988-91; mem. area edn. adv. bd. Broughton H.S., 1996—; v.p. Fred A. Olds Elem. Sch. PTA, 1994-95, pres., 1995-96; bd. dirs. Edenton St. United Meth. Ch. Child Devel. Ctr., 1986-88, 93-94. Nieman fellow Harvard U., 1991-92; recipient Cert. of Merit, Am. Acad. Trial Lawyers, 1975, Pub. Svc. award N.C. Press Assn., 1976, various reporting awards, most recently News Enterprise award William Allen White Found., 1985, 2nd pl. awards N.C. Press Assn., 1987, 89, 3rd pl. awards, 1990. Home: 308 Dixie Trl Raleigh NC 27607-7018 Office: Capital Strategies 615 Willard Pl Raleigh NC 27603-1705

EFIMOV, ALEXANDER VASILIEVICH, chemist; b. Lugovaya, Russia, May 12, 1954; s. Vasilii and Antonina (Khabarova) E.; m. Irina Viktorovna Komarova, Jan. 20, 1979; 1 child. BSc, Moscow State U., 1976; MSc, Inst. Protein Rsch. Russia, 1983; DSc, Moscow State U., 1995. From probationer to prin. rschr. Inst. Protein Rsch. Russia, Pushchino, 1976—. Mem. Inst. Protein Rsch. Office: Inst Protein Rsch, Russian Acad Scis, 142290 Pushchino Russia

EFIMOV, ANDREI MARKOVICH, spectroscopist, researcher; b. Leningrad, Russia, Sept. 12, 1937; s. Mark Vasil'evich and Vera (Voikina) E.; m. Kira Nikolaevna Ivanova, July 23, 1974. MS, Leningrad State U., 1960; PhD, Vavilov State Optical Inst., Leningrad, 1967, DSc, 1991. Engr. Vavilov State Optical Inst., 1961-63, jr. rschr., 1964-68, sr. rschr., 1969-89, leading rschr., 1989—; prof. Inst. Fine Mechanics and Optics, St. Petersburg, Russia, 1994—; guest prof. Friedrich-Schiller U., Jena, Germany, 1998; glass scientist, 1963—. Author: Optical Constants of Inorganic Glasses, 1995; contbr. over 70 articles to profl. publs.; mem. editl. bd. Glass Phys. Chemistry, 1985—. Recipient State prize of Soviet Union, Coun. of Mins. of Soviet Union, Moscow, 1980. Mem. D.S. Rozhdestvenskii Optical Soc. Avocations: underwater hunting, cross-country skiing, mountain skiing, photography. Home: 9 flat 31 ho Nauki Str, 195256 Saint Petersburg Russia Office: Vavilov State Optical Inst, 36-1 Babushkina St, 193171 Saint Petersburg Russia

EFKLIDES, ANASTASIA, psychology educator; b. Thessaloniki, Greece, Mar. 4, 1949; d. Ioannis and Kalliopi (Avraam) Kostaridou; m. Ioannis Efklides, Feb. 24, 1974; children: Ekaterini, Kalliopi, Nafsika. BA of Philosophy, Aristotle U., 1972, PhD in Psychology, 1983. Rsch. asst. Aristotle Univ., Thessaloniki, 1976-83, lectr., 1983-86, asst. prof., 1986-91, assoc. prof., 1991-94, prof., 1994—; tchg. staff In-Svc. Tng. of Tchrs., Thessaloniki, 1979—; expert in edn. and tng. Commn. of the European Union, Brussels, 1994—; Erasmus and Tempus coord. Aristotle U., 1992—, v.p. dept. philosophy, edn. and psychology, 1991-93; head sch. psychology, 1995-99. Author: (Greece) Cognitive Psychology, 1992, Psychology of Motivation, 1995, Psychology of Thinking, 1997, Issues in Geropsychology and Gerontology, 1999; editor: The Neo-Piagetian Theories of Cognitive Development, 1992, Mind, Intelligence and Reasoning, 1994; editor jour. Psychology, 1997—; contbr. articles to profl. jours. Recipient Award for Grad. Studies Hellenic Inst. of Awards, 1974-78. Mem. European Assn. for Rsch. on Learning and Instrn. (nat. corr. 1989—, SIG coor. 1992-97), Hellenic Psychol. Soc. (gen. sec. 1993-95, mem. exec. com. 1995-99), N.Y. Acad. Scis. Christian Orthodox. Home: 10 Mackenzie King Str, 54622 Thessaloniki Greece Office: Aristotle Univ, 54006 Thessaloniki Greece

EFLAND, SIMPSON LINDSAY, entrepreneur; b. Efland, N.C., May 5, 1913; s. Mack Paul Sr. and Mary Estelle (Forrest) E. AB in Edn., Univ. N.C., 1935; postgrad., U. Ala., 1940; BS in Engring., U. Tenn., 1942, profl. cert., 1942. Lic. real estate broker. TVA-safety/health engr. Tenn. Valley Authority, Knoxville, 1935-42; head coach boxing, track, wrestling, cross-country U. Tenn., Knoxville, 1939-42, asst. coach football, 1939-42; safety engr. Dupont Corp., St. Paul, 1942; owner, organizer, exec. Orange Hosiery Mills, Inc., Efland, 1946-94; engr., exec. Sinclair Refining, B. P., ARCO, Atlanta, 1971-76; cattleman, realtor, entrepreneur, corp. owner, lessor, 1976—; organizer, dir. N.C. Cattleman's Assn., Raleigh, 1946, N.C. Cattleman's Found., Inc., 1980; artificial inseminator, breeder Am. Breeder Svc., Wis., 1970. County commr. Orange County, Hillsborough, N.C., 1950-56; dir. N.C. Ednl. Found., Chapel Hill, 1950; various offices N.C. Dem. Party, Raleigh, 1946-80, Orange County Dem. Party, Hillsborough, 1946-80; organizer Efland Vets. Housing Assn., 1947, Efland Town Coun., Efland, 1941-47, Orange County Fire Dept., Hillsborough, 1952; chmn. Orange County Voiture 1266 40 & 8 Nursing Tng. Program, Chapel Hill, 1951—; organizer, dir., treas. Orange County Med. Found., Inc., Hillsborough, 1974—; organizer, dir Efland Check Multi-Purpose Ctr., 1965; mem. N.C. Country Squire, Raleigh, 1952, United Fund-Orange County Budget Com., Hillsborough, 1966; mem., officer YMCA, 1936-42, WILDLIFE, 1985—; life mem. Boy Scouts Am., 1925-35; pres., dir. Hillsborough Legion Meml. Hut, Inc., 1988—; mem. inter-frat. coun. U. Tenn., 1941-42. Lt. Comdr. USN, 1942-46. Recipient various campaign ribbons. Mem. NRA, Am. Assn. Ret. Persons, Am. Legion, Peter Tare, Inc. (organizer, dir.), N.C. Farm Bur., Gen. Francis Nash Vets, Legion Brigade (comdr.), U. N.C. Alumni Assn. (life), U. N.C. Living Legends (organizer), U. N.C. Monogram Club, PT Boats, Inc. (organizer, dir.), Sons of Confederacy, Century Club U. Tenn., Moose (charter, 1st gov., organizer), Delta Sigma Phi (pres. 1940-42), Omicron Delta Kappa. Democrat. Methodist. Achievements include invention and patent of a yarn tension and lubricating device to take dark rings out of full-fashioon nylon hosiery, 1946. Home: PO Box 66 3416 Southern Dr Efland NC 27243-8403

EFREMIDIS, ANNA PAPASTAVROU, oncologist, hematologist, educator; b. Ioannina, Epirus, Greece, Nov. 20, 1947; d. Ioannis and Ioulia P.; div. 1989; children: Christos, Maria. MD summa cum laude, Med. Sch., Thessaloniki, Greece, 1971. Resident in internal medicine Bklyn. Jewish Hosp., N.Y.C., 1974-77; fellow in hematology Montefiroe Hosp., Bronx, N.Y., 1977-79; fellow in oncology Mt. Sinai Sch. Medicine, N.Y.C., 1979-80; lectr. med. oncology Mt. Sinai Sch. Medicine, 1979-81, asst. prof. med. onocology, 1982-86, lectr., 1986—; attending physician Mt. Sinai Hosp., 1980-86; dir. med. oncology Elmhurst Hosp., Queens, N.Y., 1981-86; lectr. Mt. Sinai Sch. of Med., N.Y.C., 1986—; assoc. prof. hematology U. Crete, Greece, 1985—; dir. med. oncology St. Savas Oncology Hosp., Athens, 1986—; dir. BMT unit St. Savas Oncology Hosp., 1989—. Recipient N.Y.C. Hosp. Devel. grant, 1982, Fortl grant, Brussels, 1993, RPR grant, Paris, 1997. Fellow ACP. Avocations: reading books, gymnastics. E-mail: savoncolb@ath.forthnet.gr. Home: Zakynthinou 33, Papagou, 15669 Athens Greece Office: St Savas Oncology Hosp, 171 Alexandras Ave, 11522 Athens Greece

EFREMOV, ANATOLI VASILIEVICH, physicist; b. Kertch, Crimea, USSR, Dec. 26, 1933; s. Vasili Mikhailovich and Anastasiya Petrovna (Klimova) E.; m. Alla Vladimirovna Morozova, 1958; children: Vladimir, Vasili. Diploma, Inst. Phys. Engring., Moscow, 1958; PhD, Joint Inst. Nuclear Rsch., Dubna, Russia, 1962, DSc, 1971. Jr. sci. rschr. Joint Inst. Nuclear Rsch., 1958-62, sci. rschr., 1962-64, sr. sci. rschr., 1964-88, leader rsch. group, 1988—; prof., lectr. Inst. Electronics and Automation, Dubna, 1976—. Contbg. author, editor, cons. in theoretical elem. particles physics: Physical Enciclopedy Dictionary, 1984; contbr. more than 160 articles to profl. jours. Chmn. town orgn. Knowledge (orgn. for edn. of adults), Dubna, 1976-91. Grantee Internat. Sci. Found., 1992, Russian Found. for Basic Rsch., 1993, 96, Russian Govt., 1997; decorated Order Kiril and Methody 1st degree, 1982. Mem. Russian Physics Soc., N.Y. Acad. Scis. Avocations: sailing. Office: Joint Inst Nuclear Rsch, Lab Theoretical Physics, 141980 Dubna Russia

EFREMOV, ROMAN GERBERTOVICH, biophysicist, researcher; b. Reutov, Russia, May 2, 1960; s. Gerbert Alexandrovich and Irina Sergeevna (Kalinnikova) E.; m. Olga Mikhailovna Osetrova, Jan. 25, 1986; 1 child, Anastasia Romanovna. MS with honors, Moscow Engring. Physics Inst., 1983; PhD in Phys. and math. scis., M.V. Lomonosov State U., Moscow, 1986, DSc in Phys. and Math. Scis., 2000. Rschr. Shemyakin Inst. Bioorganic Chemistry, Russian Acad. Scis., Moscow, 1986-90, sr. rschr., 1990—; prof. Univ. Sci. and Tech. Lille, France, 1994-97; invited prof. fellowships of the U. Lille and U. Reims, France, 1992—. Author: Surface-enhanced Raman Spectroscopy of Biomolecules: Principles and Applications, 1989; contbr. articles to profl. jours. Rsch. grantee French Ministry Rsch., Paris, 1993; recipient Academia Europaeae Robert Koch Found., London, Moscow, 1993. Mem. Internat. Info. Acad. (assoc. academician). Office: U Sci & Tech Lille, Bat C8, 59655 Villeneuve d'Ascq France Office: Russian Acad Scis, Ul Miklukho-Maklaya 16/10, 117871 Moscow Russia

EFREMOVA, SLAVA VIKTOROVNA, geologist, petrologist, researcher; b. Ozero-Kureevo, Altayskii kray, USSR, Nov. 17, 1926; d. Viktor Fedorovich and Anisja Georgievna (Ishenina) Britviny; m. Anatolii Iva-

novich Efremov, Nov. 2, 1951 (dec. June 1994); children: Natalja, Galina. Geologist diploma with distinction, Voronehz State U., USSR, 1948; postgrad., aspirant, USSR Acad. Scis., Moscow, 1950-54. Engr., geologist Kazmetallgeologia, Alma-Ata, USSR, 1948-49; geologist Basaginskaja party Kazgeoldept., Alma-Ata, 1949-50; jr. scientific worker Inst. Geol. Scis. USSR Acad. Scis., Moscow, 1954-55; with Inst. Geology of ore deposits, mineralogy, petrography and geochemistry USSR Acad. Scis., 1955-71, sr. sci. worker Inst. Geology of ore deposits, mineralogy, petrography and geochemistry, 1971-81, 81—; scientific sec. Terminological Commn. Interdepartmental Petrographical Com., Moscow, 1965—; mem. subcommn. Systematic of Igneous Rocks IUGS Comm. Systematic on Petrology, 1972—, spl. coun. Moscow Geol.-Prospecting Acad., 1978—. Contbr. articles to profl. jours., chpts. to books. sec. geol. group scientific-tech. commn. Soviet Socs. Friendship and Culture Collaboration Between Peoples of USSR and Fgn. Countries, Moscow, 1965-87. Grantee Russian Found. Fundamental Investigation, 1996-97; recipient Honor Badge Union of Soviet Socs. Friendship and Culture Connection with Fgn. Countries, 1984. Mem. Moscow Soc. Investigations of Nature (mem. petrography sect. 1955—), All-Union Mineralogical Soc., N.Y. Acad. Scis. Avocations: theater, orchard. E-mail: slava@igem.msk.su. Home: Egerskaja 5 bldg 2 flat 16, 107014 Moscow Russia Office: IGEM RAS, Staromonetny 35, 109017 Moscow Russia

EFROS, VICTOR DANILOVICH, physicist researcher; b. Russia, June 11, 1942; s. Daniil A. and Naciezhda G. (Kreimer) E.; m. Ninel I. Pushkina, July 20, 1967; 1 child, Alexey. MSc, Moscow State U., 1966; PhD, Kurchatov Inst., Moscow, Russia, 1974, DSc, 1987. Jr. scientist Kurchatov Inst., Moscow, 1967-74, sr. scientist, 1974-89, head scientist, 1989-2000; prof. U. Trento, Italy, 2000—; vis. fellow The Niels Bohr Inst., Copenhagen, 1993, 94, 97, U. Surrey, Eng., 1994, 95, 96, Tech. U. Vienna, Austria, 1995, 96, European Ctr. for Theoretical Nuclear Physics, Italy, 1996, 97, U. Trento, Italy, 1994-99. Contbr. articles to profl. jours. Recipient Kurchatov prizes, 1973, 90, Internat. Sci. Found. and Russian Govt. award, 1995, Russian Found. for Basic Rsch. grant, 1993, 97-99. Home: Leningradskoe shosse, 125445 Moscow Russia Office: Kurchatov Inst, Kurchatov Sq 1, 123 182 Moscow Russia

EFSTATHIADIS, STILIANOS GEORGE, transportation engineer and planner; b. Athens, Greece, Aug. 31, 1966; s. George K. and Aikaterini (Haralampidou) E.; m. Maria Atmnatzidou; 1 child. Diploma in Civil Engring., Nat. Tech. U. Athens, 1990; MS in Engring., U. Tex., 1992. Grad. rsch. asst. U. Tex., Austin, 1990-92; sr. rsch. scientist Nat. Tech. U. Athens, 1993-94; spl. cons. Informer S.A., Athens, 1994; project engr. Impetus Cons., Ltd., Athens, 1994-96, project mgr., 1996-97, sr. assoc., 1997-99; founder, mng. dir. Impetus Engring., S.A., 1997-99, SGE & Assocs., Athens, 1999—. Sgt. Greek Army Engr. Corps, 1992-94. Winner 1st pl. in chess championship Greek Railways Assn., Athens, 1981. Mem. ASCE (assoc.), Inst. Transp. Engrs. (assoc.), Hellenic Inst. Transp. Engrs., Assn. Civil Engrs. of Greece (spl. sci. com. transp. projects 1996—), Tech. Chamber of Greece (registered profl. engr.). Mem. Greek Orthodox Ch. Avocations: golf, tennis, skiing, open sea sailing, chess. E-mail: efstathiadis@hotmail.com. Office: 104 Agiou Meletiou St, 11252 Athens Kallithea, Greece

EFTHIMIOU, JOHN, physician, researcher; b. London, Aug. 19, 1953; s. Andrew and Katherine (Koulia) E.; m. Karen Elizabeth Jackson; children: Natasha, Gariella, Max, Francesca, Amelia. BSc in Biochemistry with 1st class honor, Guy's Hosp. Med. Sch., London, 1974, B. in Medicine, B. in Surgery, 1977; MD, U. London, 1990. Ho. officer, sr. ho. officer Guy's Hosp., London, 1977-79; sr. ho. officer, registrar Brompton Hosp., London, 1980-81; registrar U. Coll. Hosp., London, 1981-83; lectr. U. Coll., London, 1983-85; sr. registrar Oxford, Eng., 1986-92; head clin. devel. Glaxo Wellcome R&D, London, 1992—. Contbr. chpts to books on respiratory muscles, myopathies, drug treatment of respiratory diseases and Behcet's syndrome and over 50 articles to profl. jours. N., E. Thames Regional Rsch. fellow U. London, 1983; Regional Rsch. fellow Oxford U., 1988. Fellow Royal Coll. Physicians. Avocations: gothic architecture, philosophy, tennis, boule. Office: Dept Resp Med, 3 Iron Bridge Rd, Uxbridge UD11 1BU, England

EFTHYMIOU, PETROS, member European Parliament; b. Larisa, Greece, Mar. 27, 1950. Mem. European Parliament, Brussels; mem. com. on fgn. affairs, human rights, common security and def. policy, com. on culture, youth edn., the media and sport, mem. substitute del. for rels. with U.S. Mem. group of Party of European Socialists. Mem. Panhellenic Social Movement. Office: European Parliament, Rue Wiertz ASP 13G157, B-1047 Brussels Belgium*

EFTHYMIOU-VERNADET, MARIE-LOUISE, occupational medicine physician; b. Cambrai, Nord, France, May 10, 1932; d. Charles and Lucie (Rouanet) Vernadet; m. Thomas Efthymiou, Mar. 5, 1962; children: Dimitri, Barbara. MD, Faculty of Medicine, Paris, 1972, Degree in cardiology, 1972, Degree in occupational medicine, 1973. Resident Faculty of Medicine, Paris, 1959-63, chief of clinics, 1963-68; prof. U. Paris VII, 1972—; dir. Poison Ctr., Paris, 1982—, Inter-Univs. Inst. Occupational Health, 1992—. Editor: (book) Intoxication of Children, 1991; contbr. over 400 articles to profl. jours. Avocation: photography. Home: 16 Rue Sainte Felicite, 75015 Paris France Office: Poison Ctr, 200 Rue Faubourg St Denis, 75010 Paris France

EFTIMIE, NICOLAE, chartering, brokerage, and import-export company executive; b. Bucharest, Nov. 19, 1953; s. Dumitru and Ana (Drânga) E.; m. Luminitza Marie-Jeanne Teodoru, July 12, 1976; children: Oana-Monica, Anda-Cristina. BE in Internat. Econ. Rels., Acad. for Econ. Studies, 1977, M in Fin. Mgmt.; B in Law, U. Bucharest Law Sch., 1988. Staff mem. Policolor Varnish and Paints Co., Bucharest, 1977-80; broker in shipping Navlomar Shipbroker-Shipagent, Bucharest, 1980-91; mgr. of customs dept. ARCIF-Land Reclamation, Hilla-Baghdad, 1984-85; P.D.G. Hathor Impex Ltd., Bucharest, 1992-98; CEO, mem. Stock Exch. Navlomar Co., Bucharest, 1999—. Mem. Navlomar (bd. dirs. 1994). Avocations: bridge, chess. Home: Apt 2 Sector 2, 25 Spatar Nicolae Milescu, Bucharest Romania Office: Navlomar SA, 6 Dumbrava Rosie St Sector 2, Bucharest Romania

EGAN, EDWARD M., archbishop; b. Oak Park, Ill., Apr. 2, 1932; s. Thomas J. and Genevieve (Costello) E. PhB, St. Mary of Lake, Mundelein, Ill., 1954; STL, Gregorian U., Rome, 1958; JCD, Gregorian U., 1963. Ordained priest Roman Catholic Ch., 1957. Sec. to Albert Cardinal Meyer Archdiocese of Chgo., 1958-60, sec. to John Cardinal Cody, 1966-68, co-chancellor, 1969-71; faculty Pontifical N.Am. Coll., Vatican City, 1960-65; judge Sacred Roman Rota, Vatican City, 1971-85; aux. bishop, vicar for edn. Archdiocese of N.Y., N.Y.C., 1985-88; bishop of Bridgeport Conn., 1988-2000; archbishop N.Y.C., 2000—; chmn. bd. trustees Sacred Heart U., Fairfield, Conn., 1988-2000, chmn. bd. Bishop Curtis Homes, Fairfield County, Conn.; mem. adminstrv. bd. U.S. Cath. Conf., 1991-94, 96-99; chmn. bd. govs. Pontifical N.Am. Coll., Vatican City, 1991-95; trustee Thomas More Coll., Merrimack, N.H., 1995—; chmn. bd. trustees St. Joseph Med. Ctr., Stamford, Conn., 1988-89; chmn. Inner-City Found. for Edn. and Charity, Fairfield County, Conn., 1992—. Office: 238 Jewett Ave Bridgeport CT 06606-2845

EGAN, WESLEY WILLIAM, JR., former ambassador; b. Madison, Wis., Jan. 21, 1946; s. Wesley William and Ruth (Skeuse) E.; m. Virginia Warren, Aug. 15, 1967; children: Wesley Matthew, Kimberly Katherine. B.A. with honors, U. N.C., 1968. Vice consul Am. Consulate Gen., Durban, South Africa, 1972-74; spl. asst. to sec. state Dept. State Washington, 1974-77; 1st sec. Am. embassy, Portugal, 1977-79; dep. chief mission Am. embassy, Republic Zambia, 1979-82; ambassador to Republic of Guinea-Bissau, 1983-85, Chief of Staff to Dep. Sec. of State, 1985-87; Dep. Chief of Mission Am. Embassy, Lisbon, Portugal, 1987-90, Cairo, Egypt, 1990-93; amb. Hashemite Kingdom of Jordan, 1994-98; dep. insp. gen. Dept. of State, Washington, 1998—. Mem. Am. Fgn. Service Assn.; life mem. U. N.C. Alumni Assn. Episcopalian. *

EGBERTS, MARVIN E., management consultant, psychologist; b. Naarden, The Netherlands, Dec. 2, 1942; s. Jacob V. and Doreen M. (Copyn) E.; m. Ellen Arnold, Apr. 19, 1968 (dec. Sept. 1995); children: Jeroen, Jolien. Master's degree, U. Utrecht, 1969. Cert. mgmt. cons., psychologist, The Netherlands. Project leader U. Amsterdam, 1967-74; sr. cons., ptnr. de Galan & Voigt, Amsterdam, 1974-77; ptnr. Assn. for OD, Bilthoven, The Netherlands, 1977-88; mgmt. cons., orgnl. psychologist Marvin Egberts BV, Bilthoven, 1989—. Author: The Manager as Coach, 1993; co-author: Change Management, 1996; contbr. articles to profl. jours. Bd. dirs. SiZaDorp Groep Arnhem, 1989—. Mem. Internat. OD Assn. (v.p. 1986-94, bd. dirs. 1995-99), Dutch Cons. Assn.

EGBON, MICHAEL IMARAUHI, communication educator; b. Benin City, Nigeria, Aug. 22, 1941; s. Egbon Samuel and Omonuwa Egbon (Idahosa) Amadasun; m. Isoken Egbon, May 22, 1970 (div. 1988); children: Esosa, Naimat, Owen, Amen, Nosa, Osato; m. Christiana Zaman, July 25, 1997; children: Adesuwa, Osarugue. Diploma in drama, U. Ibadan, Nigeria, 1968; BFA, Howard U., 1973; MA, U. Wis., 1975, PhD, 1977; diploma in comm. policy & planning, Inst. Social Studies, Nairobi, 1983. Programming asst. Radio Nigeria, Benin City, 1968-70; instr. English lang. & lit. City Grammar Sch., Benin City, 1970-72; tchg. asst. U. Wis., Madison, 1977-78; lectr. Bayero U., Kano, 1978-90, prof. mass comm., 1992—; media infocus cons. Nigerian TV Authority, 1997-98, discussant, 1980. Playwright: Ekuase, 1968, The Floating Clouds, 1970 (1st prize), Olokun, 1974; mem. editl. bd. Commonwealth Assn. for Edn. in Journalism and Comm.; contbr. articles to profl. jours. Vis. scholar Howard U., Washington, 1990-91, Fulbright scholar Am. Coun. Internat. Exch. of Scholars, 1990-91; Rsch. grant Commonwealth Assn. for Edn. in Journalism and Comm. Mem. IAMCR, Commonwealth Assn. Edn. in Journalism & Mass Comm. (founding v.p. 1986). Anglican. Avocations: table tennis, dancing, creative writing. Home: 10 Oho Ln Uselu Quarters, Benin City Nigeria Office: Bayero Univ, PO Box 3011, 3011 Kano Nigeria

EGE, YAVUZ, economist; b. Gemlik, Turkey, Feb. 25, 1947; s. Hüsamettin and Seniha (Çakmak) E.; m. Aylin Çelenkler, June 30, 1979; 1 child, Duygu. BA in Econs., Faculty Polit. Scis., Ankara, Turkey, 1968; MBA, Acad. Econs. and Comml. Scis., Ankara, 1974; MA in Econs., U. Kent, Eng., 1980; PhD in Econs., U. Kent, 1989. Sr. economist State Planning Orgn., Ankara, 1975-84, dept. head, 1984-88, dir. gen., 1988-90, dep. undersec., 1990-93, advisor, 1996—; advisor Prime Ministry, Ankara, 1993-96, undersec. fgn. trade, 1997—; pres. Güven Ins. Inc., Istanbul, Turkey, 1989-92. Active Higher Coun. Informatics, Ankara, 1989-93, Coun. Higher Edn., Ankara, 1996-97, Econ. and Social Coun., Ankara, 1996-97, mem. competition bd., 1997; pres. Nat. Policy Rsch. Found., Ankara, 1996—. Lt. Turkish mil., 1972-73. Brit. Tech. grant Brit. Govt., 1979-83. Mem. Turkish Assn. Econs., Informatics Assn. Turkey, Assn. Bus. Adminstrn. Turkey. Avocations: gardening, contract bridge. Office: Fgn Traded Undersec, Ebu Ziya Tevfik Sok 15/2, Emek Çankaya Ankara 06680, Turkey

EGELAND, EINAR SKARSTAD, organic chemist, researcher; b. Mandal, Norway, Dec. 10, 1966; s. Nikolai Hansen and Severine Regine (Skarstad) E. MSc, U. Trondheim, 1991; D in Analytical Organic Chemistry, Norwegian U. Sci. and Tech., 1997. Asst. U. Trondheim, 1991-94, asst. researcher, 1991-96, rschr., 1998—. Contbr. articles to profl. jours. With Norwegian Civil Svc., 1996-98. Mem. Phycol. Soc. Am., Internat. Phycol. Soc. Avocations: choirs, music, handicrafts, comics, reading. Home: Yggdrasilveien 1D, NO-7033 Trondheim Norway Office: NTNU Dept Chemistry, Glöshaugen, NO-7491 Trondheim Norway

EGELHOF, PETER, research scientist, physics educator; b. Mainz, Germany, Feb. 3, 1953; s. Rolf and Betty (Dengler) E.; m. Andrea Hofen, June 16, 1995. Diploma, U. Heidelberg, Germany, 1976; PhD, U. Heidelberg, 1978; habilitation, U. Mainz, 1993. Sci. asst. Max-Planck Inst. for Nuc. Physics, Heidelberg, 1976-78, sci. staff, 1978-81; sci. staff divsn. physics U. Basel, Switzerland, 1981-85; asst. prof. divsn. physics U. Mainz, 1985-87, lectr. divsn. physics, 1993-99; sci. staff, group leader Gesellschaft Schnerionen Forschung, Darmstadt, Germany, 1987—; prof. U. Mainz, 1999; chmn. 3rd Internat. Conf. on Nuc. Physics at Storage Rings, Bernkastel-Kuesl, Germany, 1996. Editor Nuc. Physics A626, 1997; referee Jour. Physik, 1993—; contbr. articles to profl. jours. Group leader local group World Wide Fund, Speyer, Germany, 1994—; com. mem. Tennis Club Weiss-Rot, Speyer, 1994-95. E-mail: egelhof@dipmza.physik.uni-mainz.de. Fax: 06131-39-23428. Office: U Mainz Inst Physics, Postfach 39 80, 55099 Mainz Germany

EGELUND, NIELS, diplomat; b. Copenhagen, July 4, 1946; m. Jette Albech Egelund. Commd. officer Royal Life Guards, Denmark, 1967-71; with Ministry of Fgn. Affairs Govt. of Denmark, 1972-76; 1st sec. of Embassy Danish Embassy, Washington, 1976-80; head divsn., Ministry of Fgn. Affairs Danish Embassy, 1980-85; counsellor, dep. chief of mission Danish Embassy, Bonn, Germany, 1985-87; head of dept., Ministry of Fgn. Affairs Danish Embassy, 1987-92; under-sec., polit. dir., amb., Ministry of Fgn. Affairs, 1992-94; amb., chief adviser fgn. and def. policy Office of Prime Minister, Denmark, 1994-99; perm rep. of Denmark to NATO Brussels, 1999—. Decorated Comdr. of Order of Dannebrog, Kingdom of Denmark. Office: NATO Hdqrs, Blvd Leopold III, 1110 Brussels Belgium*

EGER, THOMAS, periodontist, researcher; b. Speyer, Germany, June 6, 1962; s. Wolfgang Walter and Kaethi (Waldburger) E.; m. Martina Bitter, Aug. 1, 1987; children: Anika, Jens. D in Med. Dentistry, Ruprecht-Karls U., Heidelberg, Germany, 1987; postgrad., Westfaelische-Wilhelms U., Munster, Germany, 1993. Lt. col. German Armed Forces Ctrl. Hosp., Koblenz, Germany, 1981—; chief periodontist dept. periodontology German Armed Forces Ctrl. Hosp., Koblenz, 1993—; comdr., head Ctr. for Dental Spltys., dir. periodontology German Armed Forces Ctr. Hosp., Koblenz, 1998—. Author: Furkationsbehandlung, 1998; editor Neue Arbeitsgruppe Parodontologie-News, 1996—; contbr. articles to profl. jours. Mem. Internat. Assn. for Dental Rsch., Neue Arbeitsgruppe Parodontology (pres. 1996—), Deutsche Gesellschaft für Parodontologie, Am. Acad. Periodontology. Avocations: family activities, curling, long distance running, painting. Office: German Armed Forces Hosp, Ruebenacherstr 170, 56072 Koblenz Germany

EGERTON, CHARLES PICKFORD, anatomy and physiology educator; b. Toronto, Ont., Can., Mar. 17, 1939; (parents Am. citizens); s. Matthew Davis and Margaret Swain (Pickford) E.; m. Carol Anne Carlson, Dec. 16, 1976; children: Matthew, Andrew, Victoria. BA in Zoology, Duke U., 1962; BS in Medicine, U. Okla., Oklahoma City, 1978; MS in Sci. Edn., U. So. Miss., 1981, PhD in Sci. Edn., 1991, MPH in Health Edn., 1994. Cert. physician asst. Nat. Commn. on Cert. Physician Assts. Commd. 2d lt. USAF, 1962, advanced through grades to maj., 1980, ops. officer, 1962-76; primary care med. officer USAF, Keesler AFB, Miss., 1978-88; ret., 1988; instr. anatomy and physiology Miss. Gulf Coast C.C., Gautier, 1992—; mem. Miss. Health Adv. Coun., Jackson, 1990—; guest lectr. dept. physician asst. studies U. South Ala. Author: Student Study Guide for Anatomy and Physiology; editor: Physician Assistant Handbook, 1995, Principles of Anatomy and Physiology, 9th edit.; contbr. articles to profl. jours. Lectr. Miss. Inst. Drug-Free Sch., Hattiesburg, 1992; lectr. single parent-displaced spouse, Guatier, 1994-97; dir. smoking cessation Keesler AFB Med. Ctr., 1986-88; lay reader St. Luke's Anglican Ch., Gulfport, Miss., 1986-94. Mem. Am. Assn. Anatomists, Am. Acad. Physician Assts., Human Anatomy and Physiology Soc., Miss. Acad. Scis., Miss. Sci. Tchrs. Assn., Phi Delta Kappa, Eta Sigma Gamma. Democrat. Avocation: boating. Home: 6008 E Moreton Pl Ocean Springs MS 39564-2725 Office: Miss Gulf Coast CC PO Box 100 Gautier MS 39553-0100

EGERTSON, THILDA WENNES, retired librarian and secondary educator; b. Decorah, Iowa, Aug. 26, 1904; d. Ole Lewis Wennes and Caroline Larson; m. Hagbard O. Egertson (dec. 1985); children: Jordan Wennes (dec.), Margarethe Wennes, Paul Wennes, Sylvia Wennes. BA in Psychology, UCLA, 1950; MA in Spl. Edn., Calif. State U., L.A., 1955; postgrad., U. Minn., 1955-56. 5 tchg. credentials, Calif. Legal sec. Will/Nelson Law Firm, Decorah, 1924-27; tchr. spl. edn. L.A. City Schs., 1953-60; tchr. parochial Westchester and North Hollywood Elem., 1950-53; libr. L.A. City Schs., 1960-70, Luth. Bible Coll., L.A. and Anaheim, 1972-94. Contbr. articles to profl. publs. Vol. libr. Theological Coll., S. Africa, Ethiopia, 1963-64, Nigeria, 1966, New Guinea, 1966, Wycliffe Bible Translators, Mexico City, 1973, Union Theol. Sem. Librs., 1973, Am. Luth. Theol. Sem., St. Paul, 1993; tchr. Honolulu, 1967, Papogo Indians' Librs., Sells, Ariz., 1979, Fairbanks, Ala., 1981, Adelaide, Australia, 1994. Thilda Wennes Egertson Libr. named in her honor. Mem. Luth. Ch. Libr. Assn. (nat. pres. 1976, mem. adv. bd., award for orgn. of chpts. and tchg.). Republican. Lutheran. Avocations: writing, reading, knitting, tatting, traveling. Home: 118-K 1571 Golden Rain Rd Seal Beach CA 90740-4973

EGGERS, JAMES WESLEY, executive search consultant; b. Des Moines, Feb. 7, 1925; s. Paul William and Opal Imo (Cardiff) E.; m. Marjorie Mardell Freel, Aug. 2, 1947; children: James S., Barbara Bucher, Mark D. Grad., Knoxville High Sch., 1943. Farmer Knoxville, Iowa, 1948-55; sales rep. Iowa Power & Light Co., Des Moines, 1953-60, Cedar Rapids, Iowa, 1960-62; sales exec. Thomas D. Murphy Co., Red Oak, Iowa, 1962-67; pres., owner Eggers Cos., Omaha, 1967—; bd. dirs. Nebr. State Bank, Omaha; owner, mgr. Exec. Realty and Mgmt. Co., Omaha, 1979—. Bd. dirs. local Meth. Ch., Nebr. Meth. Hosp. Found.; chmn. local dist. George Bush for Pres. campaign, Nebr., 1988; chmn. State of Nebr. Merit Coun., Lincoln, 1979-83; mem. nat. adv. cabinet Guideposts, Pawling, N.Y.; chmn. and mem. various civic bds. Mem. Nebr. Assn. Pers. Cons. (pres. 1974-75), Nat. Assn. Pers. Cons. (mem. nat. com. 1979-83, cert.), Omaha C. of C. (bd. dirs. 1980-83), Rotary (bd. dirs. Omaha chpt. 1983—, sgt.-at-arms 1986-90), Masons, Shriners. Republican. Avocations: reading, travel, religious study, walking. Office: Eggers Cons Co Inc Eggers Plz 11272 Elm St Omaha NE 68144-4788

EGGERT, ROBERT JOHN, SR., economist; b. Little Rock, Dec. 11, 1913; s. John and Eleanora (Fritz) Lapp; m. Elizabeth Bauer, Nov. 28, 1935 (dec. Dec. 1991); children: Robert John, Richard F., James E.; m. Annamarie Hayes, Mar. 19, 1994. BS, U. Ill., 1935, MS, 1936; candidate in philosophy, U. Minn., 1938; LHD (hon.), Ariz. State U., 1988. Research analyst Bur. Agrl. Econs., U.S. Dept. Agr., Urbana, Ill., 1935; sec. War Meat Bd., Chgo., 1942-45, prin. marketing specialist, 1943; rsch. analyst U. Ill., 1935-36, U. Minn., 1936-38; asst. prof. econs. Kans. State Coll., 1938-41; asst. dir. mktg. Am. Meat Inst., Chgo., 1941-43; economist, assoc. dir. Am. Meat Inst., 1943-50; mgr. dept. mktg. rsch. Ford div. Ford Motor Co., Dearborn, Mich., 1951-53; mgr. program planning Ford div. Ford Motor Co., 1953-54, mgr. bus. rsch., 1954-57, mgr. mktg. rsch. mktg. staff, 1957-61, mgr. mktg. rsch., mem. div. op. com., 1961-64, mgr. internat. mktg. rsch. mktg. staff, 1964-65, mgr. overseas mktg. rsch. planning, 1965-66, mgr. mktg. rsch. Lincoln-Mercury div., 1966-67; dir. agribus. programs Mich. State U., 1967-68; staff v.p. econ. and mktg. rsch. RCA Corp., N.Y.C., 1968-76; pres., chief economist Eggert Econ. Enterprises, Inc., Sedona, Ariz., 1976—; lectr. mktg. U. Chgo., 1947-49; chmn. Fed. Statistics Users Conf., 1960-61; adj. prof. bus. forecasting No. Ariz., 1976-79; mem. econ. adv. bd. U.S. Dept. Commerce, 1969-71, mem. census adv. com., 1975-78; mem. panel econ. advisers Congl. Budget Office, 1975-76; interim dir. Econ. Outlook Ctr. Coll. Bus. Adminstrn. Ariz. State U., Tempe, 1985-86, cons., 1985—; mem. Econ. Estimates Commn. Ariz., 1979—; apptd. Ariz. Gov.'s Commn. Econ. Devel., 1991—, vice chmn. investment adv. coun. Ariz. State Retirement System, 1993-98; trustee Marcus J. Lawrence Med. Ctr. Found., 1992-96, Flagstaff Inst.; chmn. market rsch. com. Gov.'s Strategic Partnership for Econ. Devel.; co-chmn. Ariz. Sr. Industries Cluster, 1995-97. Contbr. articles to profl. lit.; founder, editor emeritus: monthly Blue Chip Econ. Indicators, 1976—; exec. editor Ariz. Blue Chip, 1984—, Western Blue Chip Econ. Forecast, 1986—, Blue Chip Job Growth Update, 1990—, Mexico Consensus Econ. Forecast, 1993—, National Consensus Forecast of Labor Employment, Sedona Sales Tax Collections, 1998—, Compensation and Productivity, 2000. Mem. long range planning com. Ch. of Red Rocks, 1998—. Recipient Econ. Forecast award Chgo. chpt. Am. Statis. Assn., 1950, 60, 68; Seer of Yr. award Harvard Bus. Sch. Indsl. Econs., 1973, Golden Gloves Boxing award, U. Ill., 1935. Fellow Am. Statis. Assn. (chmn. bus. and econ. stats sect. 1957—, pres. Chgo. chpt. 1948-49), Nat. Assn. Bus. Economists (coun. 1969-72); mem. Coun. Internat. Mktg. Rsch. and Planning Dirs. (chmn. 1965-66), Am. Mktg. Assn. (dir., v.p. mktg. mgmt. divsn. 1972-73, nat. pres. 1974-75), Fed. Stats. Users Conf. (chmn. trustees 1960-61), Conf. Bus. Economists (chmn. 1972-74), Am. Quarter Horse Assn. (dir. 1966-73), Ariz. Econ. Roundtable, Am. Econs. Assn., Phoenix Econ. Club (hon.), Ariz. C. of C. (bd. dirs. 1991-95), Alpha Zeta. Republican. E-mail: eee@sedona.net. Office: Eggert Econ Enterprises Inc PO Box 4313 West Sedona AZ 86340-4313

EGGERT, RUSSELL RAYMOND, lawyer; b. Chgo., July 28, 1948; s. Ralph A. and Alice M. (Nischwitz) E.; m. Patricia Anne Alegre, 1998. AB, U. Ill., 1970, JD, 1973; postgrad., Hague Acad. Internat. Law, The Netherlands, 1972. Bar: Ill. 1973, U.S. Supreme Ct. 1979. Assoc. U. Ill., Champaign, 1973-74; asst. atty. gen. State of Ill., Chgo., 1974-79; assoc. O'Conor, Karaganis & Gail, Chgo., 1979-83; legal counsel to Ill. atty. gen., Chgo., 1983-87; ptnr. Mayer, Brown & Platt, Chgo., 1987—. Contbr. various articles to profl. jours. Mem. ABA. Democrat. Office: Mayer Brown & Platt 190 S La Salle St Ste 3100 Chicago IL 60603-3441

EGGERT-KRUSE, WALTRAUD, physician; b. Emden, Germany; d. Horst and Catharina E.; 3 children. MD, U. Heidelberg, Germany, 1978. Prof. dept. gyn. endocrinology & reprodn. Women's U. Hosp., U. Heidelberg, Germany. Contbr. articles to profl. jours. Office: Voss Str 9, 69115 Heidelberg Germany

EGGINTON, EVERETT, educational administrator; b. N.Y.C., Apr. 6, 1943; s. Hersey Benner and Mary Florence (Twining) E.; m. Wynn Meagher, Sept. 27, 1986; 1 child from previous marriage, William Everett. BA in Econs., Colgate U., 1965, MA in Social Sci. Edn., 1968; MS in Comparative Edn., Syracuse U., 1971, PhD in Edn., 1974; EdD (hon.), U. Francisco Gavidia, San Salvador, El Salvador, 1990. Asst. prof. U. Louisville, 1974-78, acting dir. Internat. Ctr., 1978-79, assoc. prof., 1978-84, prof. edn., 1984—, dir. L.Am. Ctr., 1986—, chair ednl. founds., 1989—, dir. Internat. Ctr., 1996—; sr. policy analyst U.S. Dept. Health, Washington, 1980-81; pres. Consortium of Ctrl. Am. Univs., 1990-96, sec.-gen., 1991-98; cons. Ministries of Edn., El Salvador and Honduras, World Bank, U.S. AID, 1992—. Contbg. editor U.S. Libr. of Congress, Washington, 1980-88; contbr. revs., articles to profl. publs. and encys. Fulbright/Stanford fellow U. Santiago Compostela Espana, 1977, HEW fellow, 1979-80, Fulbright Rsch./Lectr. award El Salvador, 1999—. Home: 2600 Broadmeade Rd Louisville KY 40205-2208 Office: U Louisville Sch Edn Bldg 338 Louisville KY 40292-0001

EGGLESTON, CLAUD HUNT, III, company executive, venture capitalist; b. Buffalo, June 21, 1954; s. Claud Hunt Jr. and Arlene (Shank) E.; m. Ann Pendleton, Feb. 14, 1988; children: Brett Andrew, Blake Edward Hunt. BA, Union Coll., 1976; MS, Columbia U., 1979, MEd, 1979. Pres. Checo Electronics, Schenectady, N.Y., 1974-78; chief fin. officer, bus. mgr. performing arts div. Smithsonian Inst., Washington, 1978-79; staff mgr. long lines AT&T, Washington, 1980-81; dist. mgr. strategy and product devel. Morristown, N.J., 1981-82; mgr. venture devel. consumer products Morristown, 1982-84, corp. mgr. bus. devel., 1984-85; gen. mgr. Asia Internat., Morristown, 1985-87; dir. new ventures U.S. West Inc., Denver, 1987-88, exec. dir. mergers and acquisitions, 1988-90; v.p. bus. devel. and mktg. Corel/Ventura Software Inc., San Diego, 1990-92; mng. dir. Crest Tech. Ventures, Inc., Poway, Calif., 1992—; pres. Tech. Trends Technology Focus, Inc., San Diego, 1992-2000; CEO, pres. Fiberocity, San Diego, 2000—, Basic 4 Commn., 2000—. Editor: Financing Independent Education, 1978. Recipient Young Entrepeneur award Schenectady C. of C., 1975; Klingenstein fellow Columbia U., 1977-78. Mem. Am. Mgmt. Assn., Met. Club (Denver).

EGGLESTON, G(EORGE) DUDLEY, management consultant, publisher; b. Buffalo, June 11, 1936; s. George Staub and Betty (Ball) E.; m. Susan Michaels, June 4, 1960 (div. Sept. 1987); children: George Dudley Jr., Michele Blair; m. Linda Stephens, Mar. 31, 1990 (div. Sept. 1996). BE, Vanderbilt U., 1960; MBA, Ga. State U., 1979. Product mgr. Exxon Chem., N.Y.C., 1960-71; sales mgr. Exxon Chem. Sweden, Stockholm, 1968-69; real estate agt. Woodward & Assocs., Atlanta, 1971-74; v.p. JFK Land Co., Atlanta, 1974-75; pres. Dudley Eggleston Co., Atlanta, 1975—, Maids Unique, Atlanta, 1976-81, Eggleston Cons. Internat., Atlanta, 1981—; pub. revenue-producing Web site eggcon.com, compensation reports for sr. real estate execs. Pres. Fanwood-Scotch Plains, N.J., Jaycees, 1968. Capt. USMC, 1960-63. Mem. Urban Land Inst., Beta Gamma Sigma. Republican. Episcopalian. Avocations: boating, skiing, hiking.

EGGLESTON, GILLIAN, research chemist, scientist; b. Blackburn, Eng., Aug. 9, 1963; came to U.S., 1992; d. Geoffrey and Grace (Ross) E.; m. Gerald Myers, Aug. 9, 1992; 1 child, Grace Olivia Myers. BSc with honors,

Nottingham U., 1984; PhD, Cranfield U., 1989. Agrl. devel. vol. Student aid for Agrl. Devel., Guatemala, 1988-89; postdoctoral biochemist Internat. Inst. Tropical Agr., Ibadan, Nigeria, 1989-91; cons. World Bank in The Gambia, 1992; vis. scientist biochem. dept. U. Mo., Columbia, 1993; rsch. chemist So. Regional Rsch. Ctr.-USDA-ARS, New Orleans, 1994—, lead scientist, rsch. chemist, 1998—; grant appraiser AAUW Internat. Fellowship Grant Awards Panel, Washington, 1997—; assoc. referee Assoc. Ofcl. Analytical Chemists Internat., Gaithersburg, Md., 1998—. Contbr. papers, articles, and book chpts. to profl. pubs. and confs. Mem. altar guild Grace Meml. Episcopal Ch., 1996—. Recipient Outstanding Paper award Am. Assn. Sugarcane Techs., 1999, Early Career Scientist award USDA Mid South Area, 1999; Indsl. grantee Am. Sugarcane League, 1998. Mem. Am. Chem. Soc. (carbohydrate divsn.), Sugar Industry Technologists, Iota Sigma Pi. Avocations: archaeology, knitting, sewing, food preservation. Office: So Regional Rsch Ctr-USDA-ARS 1100 Robert E Lee Blvd New Orleans LA 70124-4305

EGGLETON, ARTHUR C., Canadian government official, member of Parliament; b. Toronto, Ont., Can., Sept. 29, 1943; 1 child, Stephanie. Acct., up to 1969; mem. Toronto City Coun., Met. Toronto Coun., 1969-91, city budget chief, 1973-80; mayor City of Toronto, 1980-91; mem. from York Centre in City of North York Parliament of Can., 1993—, pres. treasury bd., minister for infrastructure, 1993-96; min. international trade Can., 1996-97, min. nat. def., 1997—; mem. Bd. Fedn. Can. Mcpls.; chmn. Internat. Programs Com.; co-chmn. Nat. Action Com. Race Rels., apptd. Minister for Internatl. Trade, 1996, apptd. pres. of treas. bd. and Minister, Infrastructure, 1993, appointed Minister of Natl. Defense, 1997, vice chmn. of cabinet com. on Econ. Policy. Mem. Met. Toronto Police Commn., Bd. Can. Nat. Exhbn. Recipient Civic Award of Merit, City of Toronto, 1992. Mem. York Centre for City of Toronto. Office: M Gen Pearkes Bldg 13N, 101 Colonel By Dr, Ottawa, ON Canada K1A 0K2

EGHBAL, MORAD, geologist, lawyer; b. Tehran, Iran, June 7, 1952; s. Mohammad Ali and Fari Eghbal; m. Niloofar Sadjadi, July 17, 1983; children: Elaheh, Aria. BA, George Washington U., 1975, MA, 1977; JD, Howard U., 1989; LLM, U. of the Pacific, 1991. Asst. George Washington U., Washington, 1972; asst. to dir. Smithsonian Instn., Washington, 1972-75; spl. advisor to dir. Georgetown U., Washington, 1975; cons. Leo A Daly, Washington, 1975, Kodak, Rochester, N.Y., 1976; ofcl. del. 2d Circum-Pacific Energy and Mineral Resources conf., Honolulu, 1978; CEO, MERE Enterprises, Washington, 1976-87; fgn. assoc. Pestalozzi, Gmuer & Heiz, Zurich, 1989; law clk. to Hon. William B. Bryant, U.S. Dist. Ct. D.C., Washington, 1990-91; trustee, CFO Riess Inst., Washington, 1983—; dir., pres. The Grail Corp., 1983—; dir., v.p. exploration Gasco, Inc.; judge oral arguments and mels. regional and internat. semi-finals, finals Jessup Competition Internat. Law Students Assn., 1990-2000, past mem. bd. dirs.; adj. prof. legal and ethical studies U. Balt., 1994-95, adj. prof. law, 1995-99, prof. internat. mgmt., 1998-99, vis. asst. prof. law, internat. mgmt. and legal, ethical and hist. studies, 1999—; guest spkr. Tulane U., 1994, New Eng. Sch. Law, 1995, Mercer U. Sch. Law, 1997, U. Balt., 1999, Middle East Inst., 1999. Rschr. The Divining Hand (E.P. Dutton), 1973-79; keynote spkr. symposium Dickinson Sch. Law, Carlisle, Pa., 1991; author: 1995 Philip C. Jessup Internat. Law Moot Ct. Competition Problem, 1995. Recipient Cert. Achievement, Circum-Pacific Energy & Mineral Resources conf., 1978, Ga. U., 1980, 2d Place Nat. Roscoe Hogan Environ. Law Essay contest award ATLA, 1988, Outstanding Student Adv. award Met. Trial Lawyers Assn., 1989. Mem. ABA, Nat. Bar Assn., Internat. Law Assn., Am. Assn. Petroleum Geologists (founding mem. energy minerals divsn.), Geol. Soc. Am., Soc. Econ. Paleontologists and Mineralogists, Potomac Appalachian Trails Club, Nat. Capital Area Paralegal Assn., Nat. Bar Assn., Internat. Law Students Assn. (past mem. bd. dirs.), Nat. Lawyers Club, U.S. Japan Trade Coun., Am. Inns Ct. (Prettyman/Leventhal chpt.), Phi Delta Phi. E-mail: eghbal@riess.org. Office: Riess Inst 9555 Friendship Station Washington DC 20016-9555

EGI, NORIHIKO, computer software company executive; b. Odawara, Japan, Dec. 8, 1940; s. Fumihiko and Hiroko (Suzuki) E.; m. Itoko Kojima, Oct. 7, 1965; children: Masahide, Akiko, Tadasu. BSc, U. Tokyo, 1964, MSc, 1966. Engr. Chiyoda Corp., Yokohama, Japan, 1966-87, gen. mgr., 1987-97, assoc. dir., 1997-99; pres. IT Engring. inc., 1999—. Fellow Soc. Instrument and Control Engrs. (pres.). Avocations: golfing, reading. Home: 525-1-1-302 Shinano-cho, Totsuka-ku, Yokohama 244-0801, Japan Office: Chiyoda Corp, 2-12-1 Tsurumi-chuo, Tsurumi-ku, Yokohama 230-8601, Japan

EGITO, ERYVALDO SOCRATES TABOSA DO, pharmacist, consultant, researcher, educator; b. Timbauba, Brazil, Mar. 3, 1964; s. Elias Cavalcanti do and Suzana (Tabosa) E.; m. Lucila Carmem Monte, Nov. 16, 1990. Pharmacist, Fed. U. Pernambuco, Recife, Brazil, 1984, Indsl. Pharmacist, 1985; M, Paris XI U., 1992, PhD, 1994. In quality assurance control Searle Industry, Sao Paulo, Brazil, 1986-87; in drug control Dept. of Health, State of Rio Grande Norte, Natal, Brazil, 1987-88; injection sect. mgr. LAFEPE Industry, Recife, 1988-90; asst. prof. Fed. U. Pernambuco, Recife, 1995-97, Fed. U. Rio Grande do Norte, Natal, Brazil, 1997—; postdoctoral fellow U. Ga. Coll. Pharmacy, Athens, 2000—; cons. Brasilian Govt., Brasilia, 1994-96; tech. cons. LAFEPE, 1996-98, LABOGEM, Sao Paulo, 1996-97. Contbr. articles to profl. jours. Recipient Chibret Sc. award Merck Shart and Dohme, 1993. Mem. Brazilian Cosmetic Assn., Assn. Pharmacie Galenique Industriel. Roman Catholic. Avocations: music, tennis, biking. Home: Rua Praia Areia Branca 8948, 59094450 Natal Brazil Office: U Fed Rio Grande Norte, Rua Gal Gustavo C Farias, 59010180 Natal RN, Brazil

EGLETON, CLIVE (FREDERICK) (JOHN TARRANT), writer; b. Harrow, Eng., Nov. 25, 1927; s. Frederick and Rose (Wildman) E.; m. Joan Evelyn Lane, Apr. 9, 1949 (dec. 1996); children: Charles, Richard. Commd. Brit. Army, 1945, advanced through grades to lt. col., 1975, trooper in Royal Armoured Corps, 1945-46; lt. and rifle platoon comdr. Staffordshire Regiment Brit. Army, India, 1946-48; lt. and transp. officer Brit. Army, Japan, 1949-51; lt. and anti-tank platoon comdr. Brit. Army, Ireland and Germany, 1952; capt. Brit. Army, various countries, 1953-59, major, 1960-70; lt. col. Brit. Army, Nottingham, Eng., 1970-75; ret. Brit. Army, 1975; intelligence agt. Cyprus, 1955-56, the Persian Gulf, 1958-59, East Africa, 1964; civil servant Ministry of Def., 1981-89. Author: (non-fiction) The Stealing of Muriel McKay, 1978, The Baldau Touch, 1981; (novels) A Piece of Resistance, 1970, Last Post for a Partisan, 1971, The Judas Mandate, 1972, Seven Days to a Killing, 1973, The Bormann Brief, 1974, Skirmish, 1975, State Visit, 1976, The Mills Bomb, 1978, Backfire, 1979, The Eisenhower Deception, 1981, A Falcon for the Hawks, 1982, The Russian Enigma, 1982, A Conflict of Interests, 1983, Troika, 1984, A Different Drummer, 1985, Picture of the Year, 1987, Missing from the Record, 1988, Death of a Sahib, 1989, In the Red, 1990, Last Act, 1991, A Double Deception, 1992, Hostile Intent, 1993, A Killing in Moscow, 1994, Death Throes, 1994, A Lethal Involvement, 1996, Warning Shot, 1997, Blood Money, 1998, Dead Reckoning, 1999; (as Patrick Blake) Escape to Athena, 1979, Double Griffin, 1981; (as John Tarrant) The Rommel Plot, 1977, The Clauberт Trigger, 1978, China Gold, 1982. Mem. Crime Writers Assn., Soc. Authors. Mem. Ch. of Eng. Home and Office: Dolphin House, Beach House Ln, Bembridge Isle of Wight PO35 5TA, England

EGLOFF, JULIUS, III, geologist; b. Washington, Sept. 19, 1946; s. Julius and Cassandra Mary Sue (Adreon) E.; m. Cassie LeAnn Tumlin, Feb. 17, 1980 (div. June 1994); children: Cassandra Desiree, Julius Tristan, Heidi Sara Louise, Amalie LeAnn. BS in Geology, U. Miami, 1969; postgrad., Oreg. State U., 1972, La. State U., 1979-80, U. R.I., 1986-87. With Nautical Chart div. Cartographic Br. U.S. Naval Hydrographic Office, Suitland, Md., 1965; with Deep Ocean Surveys div. Geology and Geophysics Br. U.S. Naval Oceanographic Office, Washington, 1966, with Deep Ocean Vehicle Br., 1967, oceanographer Global Ocean Floor Analysis Research Project Code 038, 1968-76; geologist, oceanographer Seafloor Geoscis. div. Code 361 U.S. Naval Ocean Rsch. and Devel. Activity, Nat. Space Tech. Lab., Bay St. Louis, Miss., 1976-89; chief exec. officer Re-Evaluations Co., Pass Christian, Miss., 1980—; chief geologist, pres. Deep Ventures, Ltd. Oil and Gas Exploration, Inc., 1983-86; geologist U.s. Naval Ocean and Atmospheric Rsch. Lab., Stennis Space Ctr., Miss., 1989-91, U.S. Naval Rsch. Lab., 1992-94; petroleum exploration geologist Pearl River Petroleum Corp., Pass Christian, Miss., 1990-96; v.p./pres. Gulf Coast Writers Assoc., 1995-98; lectr. on geology, coastal sediments, plate tectonics and oil gas exploration; exch. student coord. Internat. Edn. Forum, 1995-98; substitute tchr. Bay-Waveland Sch. Sys., 1995-98. Illustrator: Atlantis, Bermuda Truangle, and Others; contbr. sci. and tech. papers to profl. jours., chpts. to books. Mem. Nat. Rep. Senatorial Com., Rep. Presdl. Task Force; sec. BSL Cmty. Assoc., 1997-98. Fellow Explorers Club; mem. Am. Assn. Petroleum Geologists, Baton Rouge Geol. Soc., New Orleans Geol. Soc., Miss. Geol. Soc., Am. Geophys. Union, Gulf Coast Writers Assn., Sigma Xi. Avocations: writing and researching historical charts, mapping techniques, shipwrecks, origins of religions, and archaeological subjects. Home: PO Box 802 Pass Christian MS 39571-0300

EGNER, BERTHOLD KARL, business executive; b. Karlsruhe, Germany, July 23, 1939; came to France, 1976; s. Karl Friedrich and Elisabeth Paula (Dörflinger) E.; m. Nicole Elisabeth Duprey, Sept. 3, 1965; children: Cyril, Christian, Benjamin. MA in Econs., U. Mainz, Fed. Republic Germany, 1965; MBA, INSEAD, Fontainbleau, France, 1970. Fin. contr. Villeroy and Boch, Fed. Republic Germany, 1965-69; mgr. mktg. Ideal Std. Europe, Brussels, 1970-76; dir. mktg. Kleber-colombes, Paris, 1976-81; dir. sales and mktg. Lafarge-Coppee, Paris, 1981-83; mng. dir. Gail Internat., Paris, 1983-84; dir. mktg. and sales Paulstra Hutchinson, Paris, 1984-85; mng. dir. VDO France, Paris, 1986—; mem. supervisory bd. Sachs, France. Avocations: theatre, literature, painting, golf. Home: 12 Rue Baratier, 95160 Montmorency Val D'oise, France Office: VDO France SA, 10-12 Ave S Allende, 93804 Epinay sur Seine France

EGOLF, PETER WILLIAM, physicist; b. Zurich, Switzerland, Aug. 26, 1953; s. Willi Arnold and Eileen Jean (Pickford) E.; m. Hildegard Klara Zett, Sept. 9, 1983; children: Seraina Patricia, Aaron Peter. Ing. Höhere Tech. Lehranstalt, Lucerne State Coll. Engring., Switzerland, 1977; diploma in Physics Eidgenössische Tech. Hochschule, Swiss Fed. Inst. Tech., Zurich, 1984, D Natural Scis., 1990. Cert. engr., physics. Apprentice Sulzer AG, Aarau, Switzerland, 1969-73, heating designer, 1973-74; rsch. fellow Sulzer AG, Winterthur, Switzerland, 1985-87; head lab. Hesco PG, Rüti, Switzerland, 1977-78; asst. Swiss Fed. Inst. Tech., Zurich, 1984-85, 87-90; rsch. fellow Swiss Fed. Labs. Materials Testing and Rsch., Dübendorf, Switzerland, 1990—. Inventor difference-quotient turbulence model, 1994, (with H. Manz) new melting/freezing model, 1994, (with H. Manz) translucent solar glass storage wall, 1992, new law of near-wall turbulence, 2000. With Swiss Army, 1973. Recipient Rsch. and Innovation Exhbn. award Swiss Fed. Inst. Tech., Zurich, 1988, Technologiestandort Schweiz, Solothurn, 1996, Spl. prize Swiss Bank Soc., Zurich, 1996. Mem. Internat. Inst. Refrigeration (leader working party on "ice slurries"), Swiss Phys. Soc., Swiss Soc. Refrigeration. Avocations: fistball, drawing and painting, philosophy and history of natural sciences, reading literature, travel. Home: Alte Wildegerstrasse 5, 5702 Niederlenz (Aargau), Switzerland Office: Swiss Fed Labs Materials Testing & Rsch, 8600 Dübendorf Zurich, Switzerland

EGOROV, VLADIMIR VALENTINOVICH, theoretical physicist, researcher; b. Moscow, USSR, June 11, 1949; s. Valentin Pavlovich and Vera Grigoryevna (Abroskina) E.;m. Ludmila Moiseevna Ostrovkina, Sept. 30, 1969; 1 child, Olga Vladimirovna. BSc in Physics and Math., USSR Acad. Pedagogical Scis., Moscow, 1966; MSc in Nuclear Physics, Moscow Phys. Engring. Inst., 1972; PhD in Physics and Math., USSR Acad. Sci., Moscow, 1981. Lab. asst. Nuclear lab. Inst. Theoretical and Exptl. Physics/USSR Acad. Sci., Moscow, 1971-72; rsch. engr. Lab. Prospective Investigations, Ctrl. Rsch. inst. Chemistry and Mechanics, Moscow, 1972-74; sr. rsch. engr., solid state physics dept. K.E. Tsiolkovskii Inst. Aviation Tech., Moscow, 1974-77; jr. rsch. scientist Optical Lab., P.N. Lebedev Phys. Inst., USSR Acad. Sci., Moscow, 1981-83; sr. rsch. engr., Inst. Chem. Physics USSR Acad. Sci., Moscow, 1983-89; rsch. scientist biophysics dept. Moscow Inst. Physics and Tech., Moscow, 1989; sr. rsch. scientist phytochemistry dept. Inst. Chem. Physics, Russian Acad. Sci., Moscow, 1989—; lectr. Inst. Aviation Tech., Moscow, 1974-77. Contbr. articles to profl. jours. Grantee Soros Found., 1993, 96, Swiss Nat. Sci. Found., 1997, Deutsche Forschungsgemeinschaft, Germany, 1997, Wilhelm and Else Heraeus Found., Germany, 1999. Mem. Internat. Union Pure and Applied Chemistry (affil.). Avocations: travel, swimming, music, literature, art. E-mail: vvegorov@redline.ru. Office: Photochem Dept/Chem Phys, Russian Acad Sci/4 Kosygina St, 117977 Moscow Russia

EGOROV, VLADISLAV VICTOROVITCH, chemist, researcher; b. Moscow, May 30, 1950; s. Victor Nazarovich and Valentina Ignatyevna (Maslovskaya) E.; m. Elena Mikhailovna Rasskazova, Aug. 29, 1993; 1 child, Alyona Vladislavovna. Degree, Lomonosov U., Russia, 1972, PhD in Chemistry, 1979, DSc in Chemistry, 1993. Rschr. Lomonosov U., 1972-93; chief, chair inorganic and analytical chemistry Scryabin Acad., Moscow, 1993—; chief lab. biochemistry Russian Acad. Natural Scis., 1997—. Contbr. over 200 articles to sci. jours.; 30 patents in field. Mem. Acad. Agrarian Edn., Acad. Natural Scis. Avocations: poetry, art. Home: Stavropolskaya Str 9/10, 109559 Moscow Russia Office: Mosciw State Acad Vet Med, Scryabin Str 23, 109472 Moscow Russia

EGOYAN, ATOM, film director; b. Cairo, July 19, 1960; arrived in Can., 1962; s. Joseph and Shushan (Devletian) E.; m. Arsinee Khanjian; 1 child, Arshile. BA in Internat. Rels. with honours, U. Toronto, Ont., Can., 1982; Phd (hon.), Trinity Coll., U. Toronto and U. Victoria. Dir. Ego Film Arts, Toronto, 1982—; films shown at internat. film festivals of Sydney, Birmingham, Melbourne, Valladolid, Picadilly, Cleve., Berlin, Hong Kong, Locarno, Melbourne, Jerusalem, London, L.A., Miami, Turin, Cairo, Antwerp, Montreal, Uppsala, Ghent, Chgo., Chgo., Sao Paulo, N.Y.C., Edinburgh, San Francisco, Rotterdam, also others. Writer, dir., prodr. (feature films) Next of Kin, 1984 (Gold Ducat award Mannheim Internat. Film Week 1984), Family Viewing, 1987 (Internat. Critics award 1988, Best Feature Film award Uppsala, Priz Alcan, Festival du Nouveau Cinema, Montreal), Speaking Parts, 1989 (best screenplay prize Vancouver Internat. Film Festival), The Adjuster, 1991 (spl. prize of jury Moscow Film Festival, Golden Spike award Valladolid Film Festival), Calendar, 1993 (prix Berlin Internat. Film Festival), Exotica, 1994 (Internat. Film Critics award Cannes Film Festival 1994, Prix de la Critique award for best foreign film 1994, Acad. award nominee), Salome Canadian Opera Co., 1996, Houston Grand Opera, 1997, The Sweet Hereafter, 1997 (Grand Prix, Internat. Critics prize Cannes Film Festival 1997, Acad. award nominee), Elsewhereless, 1998, Dr. Ox's Experiment, 1998, Felicia's Journey, 1999. Recipient Officer Order Can., other numerous awards and nominations for awards. Avocation: classical guitar. Office: Ego Film Arts, 80 Niagara St, Toronto, ON Canada M5V 1C5*

EGRI, BORISZ, animal health educator, veterinary surgeon; b. Budapest, Hungary, Jan. 15, 1954; s. Imre Kovacs and Margit Jokla; m. Jelena Mosolowa, May 31, 1978; children: Borisz, Diana. Vet. Surgeon, Skriabin Acad. Vet. Sci., Moscow, 1978; MSc, U. Vet. Sci., Budapest, 1985; PhD, Skriabin Acad. Vet. Sci., 1987; D of Habil. Agr., Pannon U. Agrl. Sci., Mosonmagyarovar, Hungary, 1995. Vet. surgeon State Farm, Hortobagy, Hungary, 1978-80; asst. prof. Faculty Animal Welfare, Hodmezövásárhely, Hungary, 1981-84; prof. Pannon U. Agrl. Sci., 1984—; guest lectr. U. Agrl. Sci., Gödöllö, Hungary, 1991-92, U. Vet. Sci., Budapest, 1991-96. Coauthor: (textbooks) Hunting Encyclopedia, 1994, Animal Health, 1995, Diseases of Wild Animals, 2000; contbr. articles to profl. jours. Master ensign Hungarian Army, 1981—. Mem. Am. Biog. Inst. (rsch. bd. advisors 1997—), World Assn. Advancement Vet. Parasitology, Internat. Biog. Ctr. (adv. coun. 1997), N.Y. Acad. Scis. Avocations: art, music, horses, nature, naturism. E-mail: egrib@.mtk.nyme.hu. Office: U West Hungary Faculty Agrl Scis, Var 4, H-9201 Mosonmagyarovar Hungary

EGRI, PETER, English and comparative literature educator; b. Budapest, Hungary, Jan. 27, 1932; s. György and Rózsi (Kornis) Deutsch; m. Erzsébet Abaffy, Aug. 19, 1958. BA, L. Eötvös U., Budapest, Hungary, 1954, MA, 1959; PhD, DSc, Hungarian Acad. Scis., Budapest, 1971. Asst. prof. dept. English U. Debrecen, Hungary, 1960-73; assoc. prof. comparative lit. U. Budapest, 1973-78, prof. dept. English studies, 1978—; corp. mem. Hungarian Acad., 1993—; mem. Nat. Com. of Accreditation, Budapest, 1992-96; lectr. U. London, 1965-66; IREX fellow Harvard U., Cambridge, Mass., 1970-71; ACLS fellow U. Calif., Berkeley, 1976-77; Brit. Coun. fellow U. Leeds, Eng., 1981-82. Author: Hemingway, 1967, James Joyce and Thomas Mann, 1967, Dream, Vision and Reality, 1969, The Reality of Poetry, 1975, Chekhov and O'Neill, 1986, The Birth of American Tragedy, 1988, Alienation and Dramatic Form, 1988, Value and Imagination: Shelley, Turner, Field and Chopin, 1994, Modern Games with Renaissance Forms: From Leonardo and Shakespeare to Warhol and Stoppard, 1996, others. Recipient award for scholarly activity in comparative lit. Hungarian Acad., 1992, Orszägh award, 1997, Eötvös medal, 1999. Mem. Modern Philol. Soc. (dep. chmn. 1988-95), James Joyce Soc., Eugene O'Neill Soc. Office: ELTE Sch English and Am Studies, Ajtosi Durer sor 19, 1146 Budapest Hungary

EGRY, IVAN TAMAS, physics educator; b. Budapest, Hungary, Aug. 20, 1947; s. Gyula and Magda (Varga) E.; m. Sabine Schroeder, Apr. 25, 1978. Diploma, U. Frankfurt, Main, Germany, 1972; MS, U. Oxford, Eng., 1974; Dr. rer. nat., U. Aachen, Germany, 1976, Habilitation, 1981. Rsch. asst. U. Aachen, Germany, 1973-85; sr. rsch. German Aerospace Ctr., Cologne, Germany, 1985—; project mgr. European Space Agy., 1985-88; project scientist German Space Agy., 1991—; dir. NATO Advanced Rsch. Workshop, 1993; organizer workshop on subsecond thermophysics, 1995; vis. prof. MIT, 1992. Recipient Borchers medal U. Aachen, 1976; named sr. scientist DLR, 1994. Fellow German Phys. Soc.

EHINGER, ALBERT LOUIS, JR., securities trader; b. Lansing, Mich., May 20, 1927; s. Albert Louis and Irene B. (Cavanaugh) E.; m. Anita Jean Gay, Feb. 9, 1963; 1 child, Andrew. BA, Mich. State U., 1950; MBA, U. Pa., 1954. Researcher Nat. Bur. Econ. Research, N.Y.C., 1954-55; bond portfolio mgr. Nat. City Bank, Cleve., 1955-57, Chem. Bank, N.Y.C., 1957-61; bond dept. mgr. Parabas Corp., N.Y.C., 1962-64; bond investment officer SwissRe Corp., N.Y.C., 1964-70; bond trader Wood, Struthers & Winthrop, Inc., N.Y.C., 1970-74; mng. ptnr. Albert Ehinger & Ptnrs., N.Y.C., 1974—; sr. ptnr. Fieldsend, Ehinger & Co., N.Y.C., 1986—. Pres. Albert and Anita Ehinger Found., N.Y.C., 1983—; trustee Robert R. Livingston Masonic Library, N.Y.C., 1987—. Served with USNR, 1945-46. Mem. Money Marketeers N.Y.U. (bd. dirs. 1987—), Soldiers, Sailors and Airmen's Club, Catherine Lorilard Wolfe Art Club (hon. male mem. 1986—), Union Club, St. George's Soc. N.Y., Masons. Episcopalian. Avocations: sailing, art collecting. Home: 444 E 82nd St New York NY 10028-5903 Office: One World Fin Ctr 200 Liberty St New York NY 10281-1003

EHINGER, BERNDT ERIK JOHANNES, ophthalmology educator; b. Boden, Sweden, Sept. 6, 1937; s. K. Gustav J. and Birgit E. (Leksell) E.; m. B. Marianne Andersson, Aug. 13, 1960; children: Mats O.J., Åsa K., Karin B., U. Magnus J. MD, U. Lund, Sweden, 1964, PhD, 1966. Tutor dept. histology U. Lund, 1956-66, asst. prof. dept. histology, 1967, jr. staff mem. dept. ophthalmology, 1967-72, sr. staff mem. dept. ophthalmology, 1972-75; prof. ophthalmology U. Lund, Malmö, 1975-78, Lund, 1978—; lectr. dept. ophthalmology Harvard Med. Sch., Boston, 1991—; hon. lectr. Acta Ophthalmologica, 2000. Contbr. over 300 articles to profl. jours. Recipient Hirsch's prize Karolinska Inst., Stockholm, 1981, Alcon award Alcon Rsch. Inst., 1984, 95, Paul Kayser Internat. award of merit in Retina Rsch., Retina Rsch. Found., 1990, Hilda och Alfred Eriksson's Awd. from the Royal Swedish Acad. of Scis. and the Hjalmar Schiotz Hon. Medal in 1998, Norwegian Opthalmological Soc., Acta Hon. Lectr., Nordic Ophthalmological Com., 2000. Office: Univ Lund Hosp, Dept Ophthalmology, S-221 85 Lund Sweden

EHINGER, ELISABETH (BICHE) W., editor-in-chief, journalist; b. Antwerp, Belgium, Dec. 31, 1941; d. Charles George E. and Marie Caroline Heilig; div., 1980; children: Hugo Lucke, Anne Lucke. Classic Humanities, Dames v/h Christelijk Onderwijs, Antwerp, Belgium, 1956; Modern Langs., St. Maria Inst., Antwerp, Belgium, 1959. Head telemarketing ICU Belgium, Brussels, 1975-80; head clients svc. CED Samsom, Brussels, Belgium, 1980-85; copy writing Verbeken, Zevergem, Belgium, 1983-85; journalist Wolters Kluwer België, Belgium, 1985—; editor-in-chief Kluwer Editl., 1995—; asst. to publ. Wolters Kluwer België, 1997—. Editor: Corrector Larousse Medische Ency., 1989, EC-Study Werkgelegenheid in Europa, 1990, Het Kamertje aan gene Zijde, 1994. Mem. VJPP/Press Assn. Avocations: reading, travel. Office: Kluwer Editl, Kouterveld 2, B-1831 Diegem Belgium

EHLERMANN, CLAUS-DIETER, law educator; b. Scheessel, Germany, June 15, 1931; s. Kurt and Hildegard (Justus) E.; m. Carola Dolores Grumbach, Feb. 4, 1959; children: Nicola, Barbara. Degree in law, U. Heidelberg, Germany, 1953; D, U. Heidelberg, 1955; degree in law, Land Baden-Württemberg, Germany, 1959. Rsch. asst. Fed. Constl. Ct., Karlsruhe, Germany, 1959-61; legal advisor European Cmty.-Commn., Brussels, 1961-73, dep. fin. contr., 1973-77, dir. gen. legal svc., 1977-87, spokesman, 1987-90, dir. gen. competition, 1990-95; prof. European Cmty. law European Univ. Inst., Florence, Italy, 1995—; mem. appellate body World Trade Orgn., Geneva, Switzerland, 1995—. Office: World Trade Orgn, Rue de Lausanne 154, CH 1211 Geneva Switzerland

EHLERS, ELEANOR MAY COLLIER (MRS. FREDERICK BURTON EHLERS), civic worker; b. Klamath Falls, Oreg., Apr. 23, 1920; d. Alfred Douglas and Ethel (Foster) Collier; BA, U. Oreg., 1941; secondary tchrs. credentials Stanford, 1942, master gardener cert. Oreg. State U., 1993; m. Frederick Burton Ehlers, June 26, 1943; children: Frederick Douglas, Charles Collier. Tchr., Salinas Union High Sch., 1942-43; piano tchr. pvt. lessons, Klamath Falls, 1958—. Mem. Child Guidance Adv. Coun., 1956-60; mem. adv. com. Boys and Girls Aid Soc., 1965-67; mem. Gov.'s Adv. Com. Arts and Humanities, 1966-67; bd. mem. PBS TV Sta. KSYS, 1988-92, Friends of Mus. U. Oreg., 1966-69, Arts in Oreg., 1966-68, Klamath County Colls. for Oreg.'s Future, 1968—; co-chmn. Friends of Collier Park, Collier Park Logging Mus., 1986-88, sec. 1988—; chpt. pres. Am. Field Svc., 1962-63; mem. Gov.'s Com. Governance of Community Colls., 1967; bd. dirs. Favell Mus. Western Art and Artifacts, 1971-80, Community Concert Assn., 1950—, pres., 1966-74; established Women's Guild at Merle West Med. Ctr., 1965, sec. bd. dirs, 1962-65, 76-90, bd. dirs., 1962—, mem. bldg. com. 1962-67, mem. planning com., chmn. edn. and rsch. com. hosp. bd., 1967—; pres., bd. dirs. Merle West Med. Ctr., 1990-92, vice chmn., 1992—. Named Woman of Month Klamath Herald News, 1965; named grant to Oreg. Endowed Fellowship Fund, AAUW, 1971; recipient greatest Svc. award Oreg. Tech. Inst., 1970-71, Internat. Woman of Achievement award Quota Club, 1981, U. Oreg. Pioneer award, 1981. Mem. AAUW (local pres. 1955-56), Oreg. Music Tchrs. Assn. (pres. Klamath Basin dist. 1979-81), P.E.O. (Oreg. dir. 1968-75, state pres. 1974-75, trustee internat. Continuing Edn. Fund 1977-83, chmn. 1981-83), Pi Beta Phi, Mu Phi Epsilon, Pi Lambda Theta. Presbyterian. Home: 1338 Pacific Ter Klamath Falls OR 97601-1833

EHLINGER, RALPH JEROME, lawyer; b. Oconto, Wis., Mar. 22, 1941; s. Jerome Nicholas and Margaret Ann (Otradovec) E.; m. Nancy L. McKinley, Dec. 26, 1966 (div. Oct. 1986); children: Nicholas Joseph, Martha Johanna; m. Mary Verstegen, Sept. 25, 1987; children: Autumn V., Andrea V., Jenna V., Jenna V. BA in Philosophy, St. Paul Sem., 1963; JD, Georgetown U., 1968. Bar: Wis. 1968, U.S. Dist. Ct. (ea. dist.) Wis. 1969, U.S. Dist. Ct. (we. dist.) Wis. 1977, U.S. Ct. Appeals (7th cir.) 1983, U.S. Supreme Ct. 1986, D.C. 1988, U.S. Ct. Appeals (4th cir.) 1988. Ptnr. Meissner, Tierney, Ehlinger & Whipp, Milw., 1968-86; pvt. practice Milw., 1986-87; counsel Casson, Harkins & LaPallo, Washington, 1987-88; pres. Ehlinger & Krill, SC, Milw., 1988-99, Ehlinger Law Office, Milw., 2000—; adj. prof. law Marquette U. Law Sch., 1999—; dir. Milw. Bar Assn., 1990-93. Articles editor: The Georgetown Law Jour., 1967-68 (Outstanding Editor 1968); editor-in-chief: The Milwaukee Lawyer, 1982-84. Trustee Wis. Sch. Profl. Psychology, Milw., 1990-93; bd. pres. Grand Ave Club, Milw., 1990-92, Mental Health Assn., Milw., 1992-93; dir. Centro Legal Por Derechos Humanos, 1996—. Mem. Am. Judicature Soc., Milw. Bar Assn. Found. (pres. 1994-97), Nordic Ski Club (life), Milw. Bar Assn. (Lawyer of Yr. award 1997). Democrat. Roman Catholic. Avocations: instrumental and vocal music, cross-country skiing, backpacking, canoeing, poetry. Office: Ehlinger Law Office W175 N 11117 Stonewood Dr Germantown WI 53022

EHLINGER, THIERRY, pharmaceutical company executive; b. Luxemburg, Jan. 7, 1965; s. Aloyse and Liette (Hertzig) E.; m. Lise Delcourt; children: Claire, Thibaut, Mathieu, Flora. Diploma, Hautes Etudes Comml., Paris, 1988. Auditor Cabinet Robert Mazars, Paris, 1988-89; fin. analyst Roussel UCLAF, Paris, 1990-92; CFO, Roussel Centro-Am., Guatemala City, 1993-94, Labs. S.A.R.S.A., Rio de Janeiro, 1994-95, Hoechst Marion Roussel, Sao Paulo, Brazil, 1996-98; head Subsidiaries Financing Hoechst AG, Frankfurt, Germany, 1999; head treasury planning & benefits fin.

Aventis SA, Strasbourg, France, 2000—. Mem. Group HEC Sante. Avocations: opera, classical music. Office: Aventis SA, Avenue de l'Europe, 67300 Schiltigheim France

EHMANN, ANTHONY VALENTINE, lawyer; b. Chgo., Sept. 5, 1935; s. Anthony E. and Frances (Verweil) E.; m. Alice A. Avina, Nov. 27, 1959; children: Ann, Thomas, Jerome, Gregory, Rose, Robert. BS, Ariz. State U., 1957; JD, U. Ariz., 1960. Bar: Ariz. 1960, U.S. Tax Ct. 1960, U.S. Supreme Ct. 1968; CPA, Ariz.; cert. tax specialist, trusts and estates specialist. Spl. asst. atty. gen., 1961-68; mem. Ehmann and Hiller, Phoenix, 1969—. Rep. dist. chmn. Ariz., 1964; pres. Grand Canyon coun. Boy Scouts Am., 1987-89, mem. exec. com., 1981—, v.p. western region, 1991-99; bd. dirs. Nat. Cath. Com. on Scouting, 1995—. Recipient Silver Beaver award Boy Scouts Am., 1982, Bronze Pelican award Cath. Com. on Scouting, 1981, Silver Antelope award Boy Scouts Am., 1994. Fellow Am. Coll. Trusts and Estate Counsel; mem. State Bar Ariz. (chmn. tax sect. 1968, 69), Ctrl. Ariz. Estate Planning Coun. (pres. 1968, 69), KC (grand knight Glendale, Ariz. 1964, 65), Serra Internat. (pres. Phoenix 1992-93, dist. gov. ariz. 1993-95), Knight of Holy Sepulchre, Knight of Malta, Legatus. Republican. Roman Catholic. Office: Ehmann & Hiller 2525 E Camelback Rd Ste 720 Phoenix AZ 85016-4229

EHNHOLM, PAUL CHRISTIAN, biochemistry educator; b. Tampere, Finland, Oct. 18, 1939; s. Gunnar and Ruth (Wickström) E.; m. Birgitta Rosengren; children: Sara, Sonja, Sam, Simon. MD, U. Helsinki, 1970, docent med. chemistry, 1974. Rsch. & teaching asst. U. Helsinki Dept. Serology & Bacteriology, 1965-71; head dept. forensic serology Ctrl. Pub. Health Lab., Helsinki, 1977-91; head dept. biochem. Nat. Pub. Health Inst., Helsinki, 1992—; vis. scientist Gladstone Found. Labs., San Francisco, 1982-83, Baker Med. Rsch. Inst., Melbourne, Australia, 1987-88; vis. prof. U. Adelaide, Australia, 1998-99. Contbr. articles to profl. jours. NIH rsch. fellow, Cornell U., 1971-72, U. Calif., San Diego, 1971-73, sr. rsch. fellow Finnish Med. Rsch. Coun., 1974-77. Mem. European Atherosclerosis Soc. (bd. dirs.), Minerva Found. Inst. Med. Rsch., Internat. Atherosclerosis Soc. Office: Nat Pub Health Inst, Mannerheimintie 166, FIN00300 Helsinki Finland

EHRENFREUND, PASCALE, astrochemist; b. Vienna, Austria, June 24, 1960; d. Heinz and Helgard (Bargell) E.; m. Bernard H. Foing, Aug. 20, 1988; children: Alexander, Victoria. M of Natural Scis., U. Vienna, 1988, PhD, 1990. Fellow European Space Agy., Leiden, The Netherlands, 1990-91, Ctr. Nat. détudes Spatiales, Paris, 1991-93; MCA European Cmty., Leiden, 1994-96; fellow Austrian Acad. Sci., Vienna, 1996-99; dozent U. Vienna, NOVA (Netherland's Sch. Astronomy), Leiden, 1999—. Editor: Laboratory Astrophysics and Space Research, 1999. Avocation: fencing. Office: R & B Sackler Lab Obs, PO Box 9513, 2300 RA Leiden The Netherlands

EHRENGRUBER, MARKUS ULRICH, neurobiologist; b. Munich, Dec. 23, 1965; Arrived in Switzerland, 1966; s. Hans Sebastian Ehrengruber and Elisabeth Maria Augustin; m. Franziska Andrea Schneider, Mar. 29, 1995. Tchg. lic., U. Berne, Switzerland, 1990, MS, 1990; PhD, U. Berne, 1994. Mem. Swiss med. unit UN, Namibia, 1989; grad. rsch. asst. Inst. Biochemistry U. Berne, 1990; rsch. fellow, mem. faculty Calif. Tech. U., Pasadena, 1994-97, sr. rsch. fellow, 1997-98; jr. group leader Brain Rsch. Inst. U. Zurich, Switzerland, 1998—; vis. scientist Children's Hosp. L.A., 1993-97; resident assoc. Calif. Tech. U., Pasadena, 1995-97. Contbr. papers to profl. jours.; patentee in field. Founder, leader Youth Group for Nature Conservation, Worblental, Switzerland, 1983-87; cofounder, coworker Com. for Nature Conservation, Bolligen, Switzerland, 1985-94; com. mem. Swiss Soc. for Ornithology, 1993-95, Bernese Soc. for Ornithology, Berne, 1985-00. Postdoctoral fellowship for future rschrs. Swiss Nat. Sci. Found., 1994, postdoctoral fellowship for experienced rschrs., 1995, Donald E. and Delia B. Baxter Found. Endowed Sr. Postdoctoral fellow, Calif. Tech. U., 1997; rsch. grantee Swiss Nat. Sci. Found., 1999. Mem. Swiss. Soc. for Neurosci., Swiss. Physiol. Soc., Soc. for Neurosci. (Washington). Roman Catholic. Avocations: traveling, ornithology, photography, nature conservation. Fax: (01141 1) 635 3303. E-mail: ehrengru@hifo.unizh.ch. Office: Brain Rsch Inst, Winterthurerstrasse 190, 8057 Zurich Switzerland

EHRENGUT, WOLFGANG FRANZ, pediatrician, immunologist; b. Munich, Germany, 1919; s. Leopold and Mathilde Ehrengut; m. Jutta Lange; children: Stephan, Thomas, Hubert, Christoph, Ursula, Johannes. D, U. Munich, 1949. With U. Pediat. Polyclinic, Munich, 1947-55, Bavarian Vaccination Inst., 1955-60; dir. Inst. Vaccinology and Virology, Hamburg, Germany, 1960-84; habilitation U. Hamburg, 1967; prof. vaccinology, Hamburg, 1974. Author books in field; contbr. articles to profl. jours. Served with German Army, 1939-45. Recipient prize German Pediat. Soc., 1960, Michael prize German Internat. League Against Epilepsy, 1974; fellow WHO, 1965, Chevalier de l'Ordre Nat. du Mali, 1980. Roman Catholic. Achievements include research in vaccine damages. Home: Am Kroog 6, 22147 Hamburg Germany

EHRENHALT, AMARANTH ROSLYN, artist, painter, print maker, sculptor; b. Jan. 15; d. Jack and Sylvia (Justman) E.; div.; 2 children. Student, Pa. Acad. Fine Arts, 1951; BFA, U. Pa.; postgrad., Barnes Found., Merion, Pa., 1949-51. Tchr. Otis Art Inst., L.A., Fleisher Art Meml., Phila. Represented in corp., pvt. and pub. collections. Recipient 1st Packard prize Pa. Acad. Fine Arts, Esther and Adolph Gottlieb grant, 1985. Mem. ARELIS, ADAGP, PAN, Artist's Rights Assn. (Paris). Avocations: languages (English, French, Italian and Spanish), travel. E-mail: amaranth@ehrenhalt.com. Home: 145 rue des Blains, 92220 Bagneux France Office: 61 via Stagio Stagi, 55045 Pietrasanta Italy

EHRENPREIS, ELI DANIEL, physician, educator, biomedical researcher; b. N.Y.C., Jan. 22, 1958; s. Seymour and Bella Ruth Ehrenpreis; m. Ana Esther Epelbaum, June 17, 1984; children: Benjamin, Jamie, Joseph. BS in Biology, Northeastern Ill. U., 1981; MD, Chgo. Med. Sch., 1985. Diplomate Am. Bd. Internal Medicine. Intern Univ. Ill., 1985-86, resident, 1986-88; fellow gastroenterology and clin. pharmacology Northwestern U., Chgo., 1988-91; staff physician Cleve. Clinic Fla., Ft. Lauderdale, 1991-96; asst. prof. clin. medicine U. Chgo., 1996—; tng. program dir. gastroenterology U. Chgo., 1997—. Author: A Clinicians Guide to Prescription Drugs, 2000. Grantee NIH, Washington, 2000. Mem. Am. Coll. Gastroenterology, Am. Gastroenterologic Assn. Jewish. Avocations: playing cello, gardening, outdoor activities. E-mail: eehrenpr@medicine.bsd.uchicago.edu. Office: Univ Chgo Gastroenterology Divsn 5841 S Maryland Ave # Mc4076 Chicago IL 60637-1463

EHRENSTORFER, SIEGMUND ALBERT, chemist, consultant; b. Regensburg, Germany, Feb. 14, 1931; s. Albert and Klara (Ring) E.; m. Rita Margarete Werling, Dec. 29, 1959 (dec.); 1 child, Eva-Maria. Diploma chemistry, U. Munich, Germany, 1958; D degree, U. Munich, 1961, food scientist, 1967. Sci. fellow Biol. Rsch. Sta., Munich, 1960-62; chemist Allgäuer Alpenmilch AG, Munich, 1962-65, Pub. Ins. Food Control, Augsburg, Germany, 1966-93; cons. chemist Augsburg, 1993—; cons. chemist in field. Contbr. articles to profl. jours. Mem. German Chem. Soc., German Soc. Natural Scis., Swiss Soc. Nutrition, Am. Chem. Soc., Assn. Ofcl. Analytical Chemists. Home: Schertlinstr 11/23, D-86159 Augsburg Germany Office: Bgm Schlosser Str 6 a, 86199 Augsburg Germany

EHRESMANN, ANDRÉE, mathematician, educator; b. Nice, France, Sept. 7, 1935; m. Charles Ehresmann (dec. 1979). D in Math., U. Paris, 1962. Researcher Ctr. Nat. de la Recherche Scientifique, France, 1957-63, Delegation Gen. a la Rsch. Sci. et Technique, France, 1963-66; prof. of math. U. Picardie a Amiens, France, 1967—; cons. Ponts et Chaussées, Paris, 1959-62. Editor-in-chief: Cahiers de Topologie et Geometrie Differentielle Categoriques, 1972; editor: Charles Ehresmann, Oeuvres Completes et Commentees, 1980-83; contbr. articles to profl. jours. Recipient Prix Lannelongue Acad. des Scis. de Paris, 1986, Prix Emergence et Téléologie Assn. Française des Scis. et Tech. de l'Info. et Sys., Paris, 1994. Mem. Soc. Math. de France, Assn. Francaise de Cybernetique Economique et Technique. E-mail: ehres@u-picardie.frurl. Office: Univ de Picardie Fac de Math, 33 Rue Saint Leu, F80039 Amiens France

EHRGOTT, MATTHIAS, mathematics educator, researcher; b. Pirmasens, Germany, Dec. 15, 1966; s. Hermann and Heide (Blaser) E. MSc, U. Kaiserslautern, Germany, 1992, PhD, 1997. Rschr. U. Kaiserslautern, 1991-97, asst. prof. math., 1997-2000; lectr. engrng. sci. U. Auckland, New Zealand, 2000—. Author: Multiple Criteria Optimization, 1997; editor: (with H.W. Hamacher) Education: Private or Public Affair?, 1997, Finanzierung ohne Zinsen: Utopie oder Wirklichkeit?, 1997, Decision Analysis Using Optimization Software; contbr. articles to European Jour. Operational Rsch., Jour. Optimizchion Theory and Applications, Discrete Applied Math., Optimization. Mem. Multiple Criteria Decision Making, Soc. for Ops. Rsch., Mensa. Avocations: Shakespeare, painting, hiking. Office: U Auckland Dept English, Pvt Bag 92019, 67653 Auckland New Zealand

EHRHART, JOSEPH EDWARD, retired television broadcast engineer; b. Monterey Park, Calif., Dec. 27, 1933; s. Theophile George and Catherine Louise (Spaulding) E.; m. Mary Frances Bos, Nov. 30, 1957; children: James Edward and Teresa Louise. AA in Electronics, Pasadena City Coll., 1954. 1st class lic. radiotelephone, FCC. Child actor MGM, RKO, United Artists, Republic, Warner Bros., 20th Century Fox, Universal, Hollywood, Calif., 1939-54; TV broadcast engr. Sta. KOAT-TV, Albuquerque, 1957, Sta. KOB-TV, Albuquerque, 1958, Sta. KHJ-TV, Hollywood, Calif., 1959, ABC, Hollywood, 1960-93; videotape supr. Sta. KABC-TV, Hollywood, 1987-93; ret. Sta. KABC-TV, 1993. Scoutmaster Boy Scouts of Am., Montrose, Calif., 1970-72; choir dir., Holy Redeemer Cath. Ch., Montrose, 1967-75, mem. Am. Assn. of Variable Star Observers, 1973-78. Served in USNR, 1954-56. Mem. Soc. Motion Picture and TV Engrs., Cath. Press Coun., Mensa, Pacific Pioneer Broadcasters, Soc. for Preservation and Encouragement of Barber Shop Quartet Singing in Am., L.A. Astron. Soc., Am. Legion. Lodges: KC, Order of the Alhambra. Avocations: church choir, instrumental music. Home: 1255 N Broadway Apt 348 Escondido CA 92026-2865

EHRIG, HARTMUT, computer science educator, mathematician; b. Angermünde, Germany, Dec. 6, 1944; s. Kurt and Gerda (Haufschild) E.; m. Gertraud Summerer; children: Karsten, Timo, Rita. PhD in Math., Tech. U. Berlin, 1971, Habilitation in Computer Sci., 1974. Asst. dept. math. Tech. U. Berlin, 1970-72, asst. prof. computer sci., 1972-76, assoc. prof., 1976-85, prof., 1985—, dir., vice dir. Inst. Software and Theoretical Computer Sci., 1978-95; dir. Inst. Comm. and Software Engrng., 1995—; vis. prof. IBM, Yorktown Heights, U. So. Calif., Tech. U. Catalunya, Spain, U. Pisa, Italy; Kloosterman prof. U. Leiden, 1993; lectr. in field. Author: Fundamentals of Algebraic Specifications, Vol. 1, 1985, Vol. 2, 1990, Algebraic Specification Techniques and Tools for Software Development, 1993, Mathematisch Strukturelle Grundlagen der Informatik, 1999; contbr. more than 400 articles to proceedings, profl. jours.; editor numerous jours. Grantee Deutsche Forschungsgemeinschaft, Germany, 1981—, European Rsch. Program ESPRIT 1 + 2, 1985-92, ESPRIT Basic Rsch., 1989—, BMFT Project Korso, 1992-95, German Ministry Rsch. and Tech. Project Espress and Konteng, 1999—, Tng. and Mobility of Rschr. Network GetGrats, 1996—, DFG Rsch. Group Petrinet-Tech., 1996—, DFG Priority Program Software Specification, 1998—; ESPRIT WG Appligraph, 1997—. Mem. IEEE, Soc. for Informatics, Assn. for Computing Machinery, Soc. Design and Process Sci., German Math. Soc., European Math. Soc., European Assn. for Theoretical Computer Sci. (v.p.), European Assn. Software Sci. and Tech. (v.p.). Avocation: rowing. Home: Ambossweg 9, 13437 Berlin Germany Office: Tech U Berlin, Franklinstrasse 28/29, 10578 Berlin Germany

EHRLACHER, ALAIN, engineering educator; b. Bone, Algeria, Nov. 11, 1952; s. Robert and Eliane (Grech) E.; m. Brigitte Faussurier, Sept. 19, 1981; children: Virginie, Charles. Dr. d'Etat, U. Paris 6, 1985; student, Ecole Poly., Paris, 1976, Ecole des Ponts, 1978. Ing. en chef des ponts et chausées. Adj. dir. rsch. Ecole Nat. Ponts et Chausées, Paris, 1982-85, prof., 1988—; dir. CERAM-Ecole Nat. Ponts et Chausées, Paris, 1985-98; maitre conf. Ecole Poly., Paris, 1990—. Contbr. articles to profl. jours. Home: 5 rue Basse des Carmes, 75005 Paris France Office: Ecole Nat Ponts et Chausees, 6/8 Av Blaise Pascal, 77455 Marne la Vallée Paris, France

EHRLICH, CHARLES DAVID, physicist; b. Miami, Fla., Sept. 10, 1951; s. Maurice Lee and Bena Zeva (Shechtman) E.; m. Susan Rae Morris, June 2, 1974; children: Rebecca, Gabriel. BS, U. Miami, 1973; PhD, U. Pa., 1979. Physicist R&D Varian Assocs. Extrion Div., Gloucester, Mass., 1979-83, mgr. batch process product devel., 1984; staff physicist Nat. Bureau of Standards, Gaithersburg, Md., 1984-87; group leader, pressure group Nat. Inst. Standards & Tech., Gaithersburg, Md., 1987-94, program analyst, 1994-95, sr. program analyst, 1995-96, dep. chief, tech. stds. activities program, 1996-99, nat. measurement and stds. needs assessment coord., 1999-2000, chief tech. stds. activities program, 2000—; U.S. rep. Internat. Orgn. Legal Metrology, 2000—; workshop organizer Nat. Inst. Stds. and Tech., 1987-89; instr. 1990-94; rep. to Internat. Sts. Orgn. Joint Tech. Adv. Group 4 on Metrology; invited conf. procs. author Proceedings of 4th Italy-U.S. Bilateral Seminar, 1992. Contbr. articles to profl. jours. Boy scout asst. patrol leader Boy Scouts Am., Gaithersburg, 1991-94, cub scout den leader Cub Scouts Am., Gaithersburg, 1989-91. Recipient Bronze Medal award U.S. Dept. Commerce, 1992, Best Paper award Nat. Conf. Standards Labs., 1997, Andrew J. Woodington award for Professionalism in Metrology Measurement Sci. Conf., 1999. Sem. Internat. Orgn. Legal Metrology (U.S. rep.), Am. Soc. Testing & Materials (vice chmn. 1986-90), Am. Vacuum Soc. (chmn. 1987-91), Internat. Bur. Weights and Measures (session chmn. Paris 1993, mem. high pressure working group of comité consultatif pour la masse et les grandeurs apparentées 1987-94), Nat. Conf. Stds. Labs. (chmn. 1989-98),Intrinsic Derived Sts. Com., Internat. Joint Com. Guides for Metrology, Am. Nat. Stds. Inst. Exec. Stds. Coun. Achievements include invited keynote speaker IMEKO World Congress, Turin, Italy, 1994; invited speaker Shanghai and Beijing, China, 1994, Bratislava, Slovakia, 1991 explained measured equilibration time constants in helium permeation leaks. Home: 103 Summit Hall Rd Gaithersburg MD 20877-1848 Office: Nat Inst Standards & Tech Gaithersburg MD 20899

EHRLICH, DAVID GORDON, film director, educator; b. Elizabeth, N.J., Oct. 14, 1941; s. Max and Jeannette (Gordon) E.; m. Marcela Josepha Rydlova, July 17, 1975. BA in Govt., Cornell U., 1963; sculpture cert., Madras Sch. Fine Arts, India, 1964; MA in Dramatic Art, U. Calif., Berkeley, 1966; MFA in Film, Columbia U., 1975. Artist-in-residence Vt. Coun. on Arts, Montpelier, Vt., 1978—, N.H. Coun. on Arts, Concord, N.H., 1986—; vis. prof. film studies Dartmouth Coll., Hanover, N.H., 1993—; Lectr. art U. Vt., 1977-82; adj. asst. prof. interdisciplinary arts SUNY, Purchase, 1971-75; instr. animation summer session U. Calif., Berkeley, yearly 1988-93, summer session U. Hawaii, Honolulu, yearly 1991-98, Mongolia Coll. Art, Ulan, Baatar, Mongolia, CAS Sch., Karachi, Pakistan, 1993; mem. adv. bd. ADA Animation Inst., Shanghai, 1988—; vis. prof. film MRDH Coll., Volda, Norway, 1990-91; art therapy cons. Manhattan State Hosp., 1975-76; presenter various internat. confs. and festivals. Author: The Bowel Book, 1981; dir., animator: (animated short films) Vermont Etude, 1977, Robot, 1977, Vermont Etude, No. 2, 1979, Robot Two, 1979, Precious Metal, 1980, Dissipative Dialogues, 1982, Precious Metal Variations, 1983, Point, 1984, Dissipative Fantasies, 1986, Pixel, 1987, Dryads, 1988, Academy Leader Variations, 1987, Animated Self-Portraits, 1989, A Child's Dream, 1990, Dance of Nature, 1991, Genghiz Khan, 1993, Etude, 1994, Interstitial Wavescapes, 1995, Robot Rerun, 1996, Asifa Variations, 1997, Radiant Flux, 1999; mem. editl. bd. Animation Jour., 1991—; contbr. articles to profl. jours.; films in collections at MOMA, Pacific Film Archive, Berlin ASIFA Animation Archive, Tokyo Internat. Animation Libr., Montreal Cinematheque Quebecoise, Moscow Film Archive; film retrospectives include Balt. Film Forum, Cinanima Animation Festival, Portugal, 1990, N.W. Film & Video Study Ctr., 1989, Pacific Film Archives, Shanghai Animation Festival, 1988, Mus. Modern Art, Varna World Animation Festival, Bulgaria, Belgrade Film Inst., Yugoslavia, 1987, Sinking Creek Film Celebration, Vienna Art Acad., 1986, Mus. Moving Image, 1985, Turin (Italy) City Hall, Cakovec Cultural Ctr., Yugoslavia, 1984, SUNY at Plattsburgh, Bradford Coll., 1982, Animators Gallery, N.Y.C., 1982, BVAU Gallery, Boston, Umwelt Galerie, Stuttgart, Germany, 1979. Recipient awards Cannes Film Festival, Chg. Film Festival, San Francisco Film Festival, Am. Film Festival, Krakow Film Festival, Cinanima Film Festival, Houston Film Festival, WorldFest, Charleston Film Festival, Roshd Film Festival, Iran, Murcia Film Festival, Spain; travel grantee Arts Internat., N.Y.C., 1992-93, Am. Film Inst. grantee, 1988, Holographic Film Found grantee, 1978, 83, 84; Fulbright fellow, 1963-64. Mem. Nat. Expressive Therapy Assn. (chair adv. bd. NETA Jour., cert. expressive therapist), Internat. Animation Assn. (exec. bd. 1988—, v.p. 1991—), Soc. Animation Studies (mem. steering com. 1999—), , Asian Cinema Studies Soc., Vt. Coun. on Arts (filmmaking grantee 1978, 79, 84, 86, 89, 90, 91), Mongolia Soc., Miagmar Animation Workshop (bd. dirs. 1992—). Avocations: composing music, painting, sculpture, dancing, travel. Office: Dartmouth Coll Film Studies Wilson Hall Hanover NH 03755

EHRLICH, FREDERICK, surgery consultant, orthopedist, rehabilitation specialist; b. Czernowitz, Bukowina, USSR, Mar. 23, 1932; came to Australia, 1947; s. Alexander and Klara (Schneider) E.; m. Shirley Rose Eastbourne, Sept. 26, 1959; children: Paul, Rachel, Simon, Adam, Miriam, Mark. MB, BS (hons.), Med. Faculty, U. Sydney, 1955; BA, Macquarie U., Sydney, 1970, PhD, 1979, MA, 1996; Dip.Phys. and Rehab. Medicine, Australian Postgrad. Fedn. in Medicine, Canberra, 1974. Intern Royal Newcastle Hosp., N.S.W., 1955, rotating resident, 1955-57; resident surg. officer Charing Cross and Fulham Hosp., Hammersmith, London, 1958-59; surg. registrar Royal Newcastle Hosp., 1959-63; dir. surg. svc. State Psychiat. Svc., Sydney, 1962-75; prin. advisor State Geriatric and Rehab. Svcs., N.S.W., 1975-77; pvt. practice cons. surgeon Sydney, Australia, 1979—; hon. cons. Sydney Hosp., 1977—; cons. geriatrics and rehab. Hornsby Hosp., Sydney, 1977—, St. George Hosp., Sydney, 1990—, orthopaedic surgery Spastic Ctr. New South Wales; vis. gen. and orthopaedic surgeon Marrickville Dist. Hosp., Sydney, 1977—; prof. rehabilitation, aged and extended care U. New South Wales, also chmn. med. bd., Chatswood Community Hosp., Sydney, 1978—, Concord Hosp., 1987—. Author: Chronic Illness in New South Wales, 1977 and more than 40 monographs, papers; editor: The Demography of Disability, 1969; New Thinking on Housing for the Aging, 1973; Aging in a Metropolis, 1974; Rehabilitation and Geriatric Services; Report of a Task Force, 1978. Cons. Subnormal Children's Welfare Assn., Multiple Sclerosis Soc., 1968-75. Fellow Royal Coll. Surgeons Eng., Royal Coll. Surgeons Edinburgh, Australian Coll. Rehab. Medicine (found. mem.), Royal Coll. Psychiatrists, Australasian Faculty of Rehab. Medicine, Total Care Found. (hon. life), Adv. Council on Visually Handicapped (hon. life), Australia Assn. Gerontology (pres. New South Wales div.), New South Wales Council on Aging (chmn.), Australasian Jewish Med. Fedn. (pres.). Jewish. Home: Box A2011, South Sydney NSW 1235, Australia

EHRLICH, MARGARET ISABELLA GORLEY, systems engineer, mathematics educator, consultant; b. Eatonton, Ga., Nov. 12, 1950; d. Frank Griffith and Edith Roy (Beall) Gorley; m. Jonathan Steven Ehrlich. BS in Math., U. Ga., 1972; MEd, Ga. State U., 1977, EdS, 1982, PhD, 1987; postgrad., Woodrow Wilson Coll. of Law, 1977-78. Cert. secondary tchr., Ga. Tchr. Dekalb County Bd. Edn., Decatur, Ga., 1972-83; chmn. dept. math. Columbia H.S., Decatur, Ga., 1978-83; with product development Chalkboard Co., Atlanta, 1983-84; math. instr. Ga. State U., Atlanta, 1983-92; pres. Testing and Tech. Svcs., Atlanta, 1983—; course specialist Ga. Pacific Co., Atlanta, 1984-86; sys. engr. Lotus Devel. Corp., 1986-89; rsch. assoc. SUNY-Stony Brook, 1976; modeling instr. Barbizon Modeling Sch., Atlanta, 1991; instr. Ga. State Coll. for Kids, 1984-85; test-taking cons., hon. mem. Comm. Workers of Am. Local 3204, Atlanta, 1985—. Author: (software user manual) Micro Maestro, 1983, Music Math, 1984; (test manual) The Telephone Company Test, 1991, AMI Pro Advanced Courseware, 1992, A Study Guide for the Sales and Service Representative Test, 1993, A Study Guidy for the Technical Services Test, 1995; (book) Philadelphia Methodist Church 1860-90: Members and History, 1998, Mrs. Beall's Mill, 1999; mem. editl. bd. CPA Computer Report, Atlanta, 1984-85. Tchr. St. Phillips Ch. Sch., Atlanta, 1981-88; vol. Joel Chandler Harris Assn., Atlanta, 1984-87; mem. Atlanta Preservation Soc., 1985, Planned Parenthood, St. Phillips welcome com., 1988-96, drug and alcohol counseling HOPE, 1988-96; sponsor Fair Test 1991—, Ctr. Fair and Open Testing, parish choir St. Phillips Ch., 1995-96; team leader guest svcs. Atlanta Com. Olympic Games, 1996. Named State Tchr. Achievement Recognition Tchr. DeKalb County Bd. Edn., 1979, 80, 81, Most Outstanding Tchr., Barbizon Sch. of Modeling, 1980, Colo. Outward Bound, 1985, Disting. Educator, Ga. State U., 1987; recipient Jefferson Davis Gold Medal, United Daughters of Confederacy, 1999. Mem. LWV, Math. Assn. Am., Nat. Coun. Tchrs. Math., Ga. Coun Tchrs. Math., Math. Assn. Am., Assn. Women in Math. (del. to China Sci. and Tech. Exch., 1989-90), Ga. Hist. Soc., First Families of Ga., DeKalb Personal Computer Instr. Assn. (pres. 1984), Hamilton Nat. Geneal. Soc. (treas. 1998-99), Aux. Med. Assn. Ga., Daus. of Confederacy, Atlanta Track Club, N.Y.C. Track Club. Democrat. Episcopalian. Avocations: piano, jogging, fashion modeling, skiing, harp. E-mail: DrMaggie@worldnet.att.net. Home: 240 Cliff Overlook Atlanta GA 30350-2601 Office: PO Box 500173 Atlanta GA 31150-0173

EHRLICH, THOMAS, law educator; b. Cambridge, Mass., Mar. 4, 1934; s. William and Evelyn (Seltzer) E.; m. Ellen Rome, June 18, 1957; children—David, Elizabeth, Paul. AB, Harvard U., 1956, LLB, 1959; LLD (hon.), Villanova U., 1979, Notre Dame U., 1980, U. Pa., 1987. Bar: Wis. bar 1959. Law clk. Judge Learned Hand U.S. Ct. Appeals 2d Circuit, 1959-60; spl. asst. to legal adviser Dept. State, 1962-64; spl. asst. to under-sec. U.S. Dept. State, 1964-65; assoc. prof. law Stanford (Calif.) U., 1965-68, prof., 1968-75, also dean, 1971-75, Richard E. Lang dean and prof., 1973-75; pres. Legal Services Corp., Washington, 1976-79; dir. Internat. Devel. Coop. Agy., Washington, 1979-81; provost, prof. law U. Pa., Phila., 1981-87; pres., prof. law Ind. U., Bloomington and Indpls., 1987-94; vis. prof. Duke U., Durham, 1994; Disting. Univ. scholar Calif. State U., San Francisco, 1995—; vis. prof. Stanford Law Sch., 1994-99; sr. scholar Carnegie Found. for Advancement of Tchg., 1997—. Author: (with Abram Chayes and Andreas F. Lowenfeld) The International Legal Process, 3 vols., 1968, (with Herbert L. Packer) New Directions in Legal Education, 1972, International Crises and the Role of Law, Cyprus, 1958-67, 1974; editor: (with Geoffrey C. Hazard Jr.) Going to Law School?, 1975, (with Mary Ellen O'Connell) International Law and the Use of Force, 1993, The Courage to Inquire, 1995, Philanthropy and the Nonprofit Sector in a Changing America, 1998, Civic Responsibility and Higher Education, 2000. Office: Carnegie Found Advancement of Tchg 555 Middlefield Rd Menlo Park CA 94025-3443

EHRNST, ANNEKA CECILIA, immunologist, virologist; b. Östersund, Sweden, Oct. 29, 1945; d. Fredrik Vilhelm and Gabriella Frida (Porshag) E.; m. Robert Gustav Grundin, Aug. 28,1971; children: Gustav Robert, Gabriel Ehrnst. MD, Karolinska Inst., Stockholm, 1972; PhD, Karolinska Inst., 1978. Assoc. prof. clin. immunology Karolinska Inst., 1980; lab. physician in clin. immunology Nat. Bacteriology Lab., Stockholm, 1973-82, dep. head polio vaccine devel., 1982-83; rsch. fellow, Fogarty intern scholar Harvard Med.Sch., Boston, 1981-82; sr. clin. virologist Stockholm County Microbiology Lab., 1983-93; sr. clin. virologist Huddinge Hosp., Stockholm, 1993—, dep. head clin. virology lab., 1993-95; sec., chair rsch. students Karolinska Inst., 1973-75, mem. recruitment group in med. microbiology, 1974-75; sci. sec. 5th internat. Conf. on Cytomegalovirus, Stockholm, 1995. Editor Suppl. Scandinavian Jour. Infectious Disease, 1995. Mem. Nat. Rsch. Student Group for Nat. Policies, 1975; mem. support group for editl. policy moderate conservative party, 1992. Swedish Med. Rsch. Coun. grantee. Mem. Scandinavian Soc. Immunology, European Soc. Clin. Virology, N.Y. Acad. Scis., Nat. Geographic Soc., Internat. Soc. Infectious Diseases. Avocations: writing essays, genealogy, classical music. Fax: 468-653 6227. Office: Karolinska Inst, Microbiol/Tumorbiology Ctr, SE-17177 Stockholm Sweden

EHSAN, NOUSHIN, architect; b. Tehran, May 25, 1944; d. Mashaallah and Zahra E. (div.); children: Babak, Bryan. BArch, Tehran U., 1969; MArch, UCLA, 1972. Lic. architect, N.Y. Pres. Accessible Architecture, N.Y.C., 1985—; mng. dir. Beb Cons., N.Y.C., London, Paris and, Tehran, 1974-85; asst. prof. Rensselaer Polytech. Inst., Troy, N.Y., 1972-74; assoc. prof. N.E. London Polytechnic, London, 1979-80; dir. of design Benham-Kite, L.A., 1969-72; keynote spkr. Internat. Symposiums, various cities, China, 1995—; adj. prof. Harvard U., Boston, 1973-74; cons. City Planning Dept., Albany, 1973-74; dir. of design Gruen/Farman Farmayan, Tehran, 1974-75; guest lectr. Xian U., China, 1995, 96, Chongqing U., China, 1997, China Inst. in Am., N.Y.C., 1998; keynote spkr. Internat. Conf. in Chongqing and Shanghai, 1997, 96; lectr. series: Sch. of Architectures, Thailand, Singapore, S. Africa, 1995-96. Contbr. articles to profl. jours. Recipient 1st prize winner Elderly Housing Design, Housing Authority, Sacramento, 1972. Mem. AIA (Design award 1984—), Peace Mus. (adv. bd. 1998—), Price and Internat. Orgn. for Habitation or Orphange (bd. dirs. 1997—), U.S. China Friendship Assn. (bd. dirs. 1998—), Friends of Upper Eastside Preservation (bd. dirs. 1998—), European Bahai Bus. Forum For Bus. Attic. Baha'i. E-mail: accessible@worldnet.att.com.

EICHEL, HANS, federal official; b. Kassel, Germany, Dec. 24, 1941; married; 2 children. Joined German Social Dem. Party, 1964, mem. exec. com., 1984—, chmn. in the Land of Hesse, 1989—; mem. Kassel City Coun., 1968-75; chief mayor of Kassel, 1975-91; min. pres. of Hesse, 1991-99; fed. minister of fin. German Govt., 1999—. Mem. Kassel City Coun., 1968-75, Nat. Exec. of the Young Socialists, 1969-72; chmn. SPD Group on the Kassel City Coun., 1970-75; chief mayor of Kassel, 1975-91; mem. SPD Nat. Exec., Bonn, 1984. Office: Fed Ministry Fin, Wilhelmstrasse 97, D-10117 Berlin Germany

EICHEL, RÜDIGER-ALBERT, physicist, researcher; b. Cologne, Germany, June 5, 1970; s. Hans and Brunhild (Götz) E. Diploma in physics, U. Cologne, 1998. Cert. rschr. in solid state physics. Rschr. Nat. Inst. Applied Sci., Toulouse, France, 1993-94, German Aerospace Ctr., Cologne, 1997-98, Swiss Inst. Tech., Zurich, Switzerland, 1998—. Inventor in field; contbr. articles to profl. jours. Mem. German Phys. Soc., European Electron Paramagnetic Resonance Soc. Avocations: playing trumpet, saxophone, piano, guitar, bass. Home: Am Zollhaus 7, D-51069 Cologne Germany Office: Swiss Inst Tech, Universitätstr 20, CH-8092 Zürich Switzerland

EICHELBAUM, SIR (JOHANN) THOMAS, retired chief justice of New Zealand; b. May 17, 1931; s. Walter and Frida E.; m. Vida Beryl Franz; 3 children. LLB, Victoria U. Coll. Bar: Queen's Counsel 1978. Ptnr. Chapman Tripp & Co., Wellington, New Zealand, 1958-78; judge High Ct. New Zealand, Wellington, 1982-89, chief justice, 1989-99; now head Royal Commn. on Genetic Modification; non-permanent judge Ct. Final Appeals, Hong Kong, 2000—. Editor-in-chief: Fundamentals of Trial Techniques, 1989. Decorated knight grand cross Order Brit. Empire; Privy Councillor, 1989. Mem. Wellington Club. Avocations: reading, music, walking. Address: Lowry Bay, Eastbourne New Zealand*

EICHENBAUM, JOSEPH WALTER, ophthalmologist; b. N.Y.C., Jan. 4, 1948; s. Irving and Renee (Cooperman) E.; m. Annette Tykocinski, Aug. 21, 1970; children: Gary, Kenneth. BA, AA, Yeshiva U., 1969; MD, Yale U., 1973; MPH, Columbia U., 1999. Diplomate Nat. Bd. Med. Examiners, Am. Bd. Ophthalmology. Asst. clin. prof. Mt. Sinai Hosp., N.Y.C., 1978—; cons. in ophthalmology Beth Israel North Hosp., N.Y.C., 1980—. Editor: Treatment of Retinopathy of Prematurity, 1989; contbr. articles to profl. jours. Named one of best doctors in Greater Metro N.Y. Area. Fellow ACS, N.Y. Acad. Medicine; mem. N.Y. County Med. Soc., N.Y. State Med. Soc. Avocations: playing accordion, tennis, swimming. Office: 1050 Park Ave New York NY 10028-1031

EICHHORN, GUNTHER LOUIS, chemist; b. Frankfurt am Main, Germany, Feb. 8, 1927; s. Fritz David and Else Regina (Weiss) E.; m. Lotti Neuhaus, June 25, 1964; children: David Mark, Sharon Julie. AB in Chemistry, U. Louisville, 1947; MS, U. Ill., 1948, PhD, 1950. From asst. prof. to assoc. prof. chemistry La. State U., 1950-57; commd. officer USPHS, 1954-57; assoc. prof. chemistry Georgetown U., 1957-58; guest scientist Naval Med. Rsch. Inst., 1957-58; chief sect. molecular biology Gerontology Rsch., NIH, Balt., 1958-78, chief lab. cellular and molecular biology and head sect. inorganic biochemistry, 1978-94; scientist emeritus NIH, 1994—; counsellor La. State U. Hillel Found., 1952-54; pres. Nat. Inst. Child Health and Human Devel. Assembly Scientists, 1972-73; mem. panel nickel NRC, 1974; disting. lectr. Mich. State U., 1972; lectr. Internat. Conf. on Biology and the Future of Mankind, Paris, 1974; Watkins vis. prof. Wichita State U., 1983; organizer symposium Internat. Conf. Bioinorganic Chemistry, The Netherlands, 1987; lectr. Internat. Conf. Molecular Mechanisms of Metal Toxicity and Carcinogenicity, Urbino, Italy, 1988, Bailar Symposium, Houston, 1992, G.L. Eichhorn Symposium on Metals, Nucleic Acids, Transcription and Aging, 1995; acting sci. dir. Nat. Inst. Aging, 1988; Henry Lardy lectr. S.D. U.; lectr. Metal Ion Nucleic Acid Interactions Conf., Amsterdam, The Netherlands, 1991; organizer, presenter and lectr. in field. Editor: Inorganic Biochemistry, 1973; co-editor: Advances in Inorganic Biochemistry, 1978—; mem. editl. bd. Mechanisms of Ageing and Development; contbr. articles to profl. jours. Gen. Aniline and Film Co. grantee, 1949; Ohio State U. fellow, summers 1951-52; recipient Woodcock medal U. Louisville, 1947, Md. Chemist award, 1978, NIH Dir.'s award, 1979, Sr. Exec. Svc. bonus award, 1982, 88. Fellow AAAS, Am. Inst. Chemists, Gerontol. Soc. (fin. com. 1980-82, research and edn. com. 1982-83); mem. Am. Chem. Soc., N.Y. Acad. Scis., Am. Inst. Biol. Chemists, Biophys. Soc. Achievements include reseach in metal-ion induced stabilization and destabilization of DNA double helix, mechanism of RNA degradation by metal ions, nucleic acid conformational changes induced by metal ions; structural basis by which RNA polymerase produces fidelity in transcription (of DNA to RNA), catalysis of double bond cleavage by metal ions, discovery of Schiff base tautomers in vitamin B6-metal complexes; molecular age changes involving metal ions, proteins and nucleic acids. Home: 10500 Rockville Pike Rockville MD 20852-3359 Office: NIH NIA Gerontology Rsch Ctr 5600 Nathan Shock Dr Baltimore MD 21224-6825

EICHLER, DAVID STEVEN, physics educator; b. N.Y.C., Feb. 7, 1951; s. Elliot and Florence (Perlo) E.; m. Aviva Weisel, Aug. 26, 1973; children: Maor, Raanan, Ari, Noam. BS, MS, MIT, 1972, PhD, 1976. Rsch. asst. MIT, Cambridge, 1972-76; rsch. assoc. U. Chgo., 1976-78; asst. prof. U. Md., College Park, 1978-83, assoc. prof., 1983-90; assoc. prof. Ben Gurion U., Beer Sheva, Israel, 1983-89, prof., 1989—, Arnow chair of astrophysics, 1994—. Contbr. articles to profl. jours. Postdoctoral fellow NSF, 1978, Sloan fellow Alfred Sloan Found., 1981; named Disting. Young Scientist, Md. Acad. Scis., 1985. Avocation: piano.

EICHLER, SYLVIA MARIA, auditor, international consultant; b. Miltenberg, Bavaria, Germany, Feb. 7, 1968; d. Kurt and Elfriede Katharina (Dietzel) E. MBA, U. Erlangen, Nürnberg, Germany, 1992. Cert. tax cons.; CPA. Sr. cons. PriceWaterhouseCoopers, Frankfurt, Germany, 1992—; assoc. expert UN Econ. Commn. for Europe, Geneva, 1990, UN Conf. Trade and Devel., Geneva, 1991. Avocations: languages, skiing, sailing, swimming, tennis, golf. Home: Fichtestrasse 22, 65189 Wiesbaden Germany

EICHMAN, CHARLES MELVIN, career assessment educator, school counselor; b. Ft. Hays, Kans., June 16, 1950; s. Melvin Joseph and Barbara Ann (Bennett) E. BA, U. No. Colo., 1972; MA, Fuller Theol. Sem., 1974; cert., U. Mo., 1989, 91. Cert. vocat. evaluator, vocat. guidance specialist, sch. counselor, job devel. specialist, rehab. counselor, job placement specialist, secondary sch. tchr. Youth activity coord. YMCA, Glendale, Calif., 1972-74; counselor U. Colo., Colorado Springs, 1975-76; resident hall advisor U. No. Colo., Greeley, 1976-77; secondary tchr., coach Jefferson County Dist. R-1, Lakewood, Colo., 1978-80; pres., owner Big Sky C.F.M. and Mgmt. Resources, Rock Springs, Wyo., 1980-85; secondary tchr. Boulder (Colo.) Valley Dist. RE-2, 1986-88; vocat. evaluator and dir. Platte County Dist. RE-111 Vocat. Evaluation Ctr., Platte City, Mo., 1988-92; pres., owner Career Assessment Svcs., Arvada, Colo., 1992-94; sch. counselor, head dist. elem. at-risk student program Albany Schs. Re-1, Laramie, Wyo., 1993-94; sch. counselor, dir. dist. model Kids at Risk program New Horizons Alt. H.S., Sch. Dist. 25, Pocatello, Idaho., 1994—, developer counseling program. Contbr. articles to profl. jours. Mem. ACA (one of 25 nat. legis. inst. participants 2000), Am. Vocat. Assn., NEA, Nat. Rehab. Assn., Nat. Assn. Vocat. Edn. Spl. Needs Pers. (region III com. chair 1989-90, cert. of recognition 1990), Nat. Assn. Vocat. Assessment in Edn., Am. Sch. Counselors Assn., Am. Assn. Marriage and Family Therapy, Vocat. Evaluation and Work Adjustment Assn. (Wyo. rep. 1993-94, conf. presenter 1991), Mo. Vocat. Spl. Needs Assn. (exec. v.p. 1990-92, conf. speaker 1989-92, Outstanding Achievement award 1990-91, certs. of appreciation 1988-91), Mo. State Tchrs. Assn., Mo. Sch. Counselors Assn. (conf. speaker 1989-91), Mo. Vocat. Assn. (conf. speaker 1992), Idaho Edn. Assn., Idaho Sch. Counseling Assn., Idaho Counseling Assn. (chair pub. policy and legislation com. 1999, 2000, conf. presentor, exec. bd. mem.), Idaho Assn. Marriage and Family Therapy, Idaho Vocat. Guidance Assn. (com. chair 1997), Idaho Vocat. Assn., Idaho Assn. Career Devel., Kiwanis. Avocations: handball, skiing, outdoor adventure trips, creative arts activities, swimming. Office: PO Box 4931 Pocatello ID 83205-4931

EICK, OLAF J., engineer, scientist; b. Berlin, Oct. 14, 1967; s. Detlef Eick and Heidrun (Bragulla) Lueckmann. MS, Tech. U., Berlin, 1993; PhD, U. Ulm, Germany, 1999. Trainee Medtronic, Duesseldorf, Germany, 1993-94, product specialist, 1994; dist. mgr. sales Medtronic, Duesseldorf, 1995-96; scientist Bakken Rsch. Ctr., Maastricht, The Netherlands, 1996—. Contbr. articles to profl. jours.; inventor in field. Avocation: tennis. Office: Bakken Rsch Ctr, Endepolsdomein 5, 6229 GW Maastricht The Netherlands

EICKELBERG, OLIVER, physician; b. Dortmund, Germany, May 3, 1968; came to U.S., 1998; s. Jurgen and Ilse E.; m. Christiane Eickelberg, Mar. 27, 1997; children: Paula Madita, Lucy Carlotta. MD, U. Basel, 1997. Medical diplomate Germany, 1997. Postdoctoral scientist Univ. Basel, Switzerland, 1997-98; postdoctoral fellow Yale U., New Haven, Conn., 1998—. Contbr. articles to profl. publs. Active Conn. Fund for the Environment, 1999—. Recipient Young Scientist award Internat. Union of Biochemistry and Molecular Biology, 1997, travel award Am. Soc. Cell Biology, 1996. Mem. Am. Soc. for Biochemistry and Molecular Biology, N.Y. Acad. Scis., European Respiratory Soc. (Cell and Molecular award 1997). Avocations: music, sports, photography. Office: Yale Univ Sch Med 310 Cedar St # Lb20 New Haven CT 06510-3218

EICKHOFF, EKKEHARD, retired German ambassador, historian; b. Berlin, June 8, 1927. BA, Juniata Coll., 1950; MA, Marquette U., 1951; PhD, Sarrbricken U., 1953; Dr.phil.habil., U. Stuttgart, 1976. With Fg. Svc., Germany, 1953-92; asst. to pres. Germany, 1974-80; amb. South Africa, 1980-83, Ireland, 1983-84; amb.-at-large Fed. Fgn. Office, Bonn, 1984-88; amb. Turkey, 1988-92; ret. Author: Seekring und Seepolitik Zwischen Islam und Abendland, 1966, Venedig, Wien und die Osmanen, 1970, Byzantinische Wietpolitik, 1981, Venezia, Vienna e i Turchi, 1991, Theophanu und der Konig, 1996, Kaiser Otto III, 1999, others. Decorated great cross Order of Merit (Germany), chevalier Legion of Honor (France), knight comdr. Royal Victorian Order (Gt. Brit.), others. Mem. German Archaeol. Inst., Turkish Hist. Inst. (corr.). Address: Hegelstr 15, D-53117 Bonn Germany

EID, ZEINA, physician, researcher; b. Beirut, Lebanon, May 8, 1966; d. Joseph and Siham (Yared) Eid; m. Hadi Antoun, June 10, 1995. BSc in Biology, Am. U. Beirut, 1987, MD, 1991; postgrad., U. Paris VII, 1995, U. Paris VI, 1996. Diplomate Am. Bd. Internal Medicine. Resident in medicine NYU Med. Ctr., N.Y.C., 1991-94; physician asst., clin. trial coord. Bichat Hosp., Paris, 1994—; clin. rsch. scientist virology Glaxo Wellcome, France. Mem. ACP, European AIDS Clin. Soc. Avocations: literature, classical music, swimming, skiing.

EID ANTOUN, ZEINA, research physician; b. Beirut, May 8, 1966; d. Joseph Eid and Siham Yared; m. Hadi Antoun, June 10, 1995; 1 child, Carla. BSc in Biology, Am. U., Beirut, 1987, MD, 1991; specialist in internal medicine, NYU, 1994. Physician Hosp. Bichat, Paris, 1994—; clin. rsch. physician Agence Nationale de Recherche sur le SIDA, France, 1995-98, GlaxoWellcome Pharm. Industry, Marly-le-roi, France, 1998—. Grantee Agence Nationale de Recherche sur le SIDA, Paris, 1995-98. Avocations: theatre, music, swimming. E-mail: za55499@glaxowellcome.co.uk. Fax: 33 1 39 17 84 82. Home: 110 rue de Longchamp, 75116 Paris France Office: GlaxoWellcome, 100 rte de Versailles, 78163 Marly-le-roi France

EIDELHOCH, LESTER PHILIP, physician, educator, surgeon; b. N.Y.C., Jan. 7, 1932; s. Abraham David Eidelhoch and Ella (Sarah) Lovinger; m. Cecily Ruth Rosenberg, Apr. 28, 1963; children: Alison Marc, Arthur Mark, Meredith Marc. BA, Columbia U., 1952; MD, NYU, 1956. Diplomate Am. Bd. Med. Examiners. Intern Strong Meml. Hosp., Rochester, N.Y.; resident Harvard Surg. div. Boston City Hosp., 1958-62; pvt. practice New Hartford, N.Y., 1965—; med. dir. Walsh Med. Ctr., Rome, N.Y., 1991—; mem. faculty SUNY. Bd. dirs. Jewish Fedn., Utica (N.Y.) Symphony, Charles T. Sitrin Home. Lt. comdr. USN, 1962-64. Recipient Lindner Surg. award NYU. Fellow ACS, Royal Coll. Medicine; mem. N.Y. Cen. Soc. Surgeons, Cen. N.Y. Acad. Medicine, Oneida County Med. Soc. Republican. Avocations: skiing, sailing. Home and Office: 6 Old Willow Rd New Hartford NY 13413-2419

EIDELMAN, ARTHUR ISAAC, pediatrician, neonatologist; b. N.Y.C., Mar. 10, 1939; arrived in Israel, 1978; s. Julius and Edith (Kalmanowitz) E.; m. Arleen Sandra Pilzer, June 16, 1960; children: Aura, Yael, Ronain, Emanuel. BA, Yeshiva U., 1959, BHL, 1959; MD, Einstein Med. Sch., N.Y.C., 1963. Diplomate Am. Bd. Pediat., Am. Bd. Neonatology. Intern, resident, fellowship Yale New Haven Hosp., N.Y.C., 1963-67; dir. newborn svcs. Einstein Hosp., N.Y.C., 1969-78, assoc. dir. pediat., 1972-78; dir. neonatology dept. Shaare Zedek Med. Ctr., Jerusalem, 1978—, med. dir., 1981-82; vis. rsch. scholar Yale U. Child Study Ctr., New Haven; assoc. prof. pediat. Hebrew U., Jerusalem; prof. pediat., Einstein Coll. Medicine. Internat. neonatology editor Jour. Perinatology; editl. bd. Jour. Human Lactation. Lt. comdr. USPHS, 1967-69, Washington. Fellow Am. Acad. Pediat.; mem. U.S. Soc. Pediatric Rsch., European Soc. Pediatric Rsch., Am. Pediatric Soc., Acad. Breastfeeding Medicine. Fax: 972-2-5620689. E-mail: eidel@cc.huji.ac.il. Home: Jabotinsky 42, 92182 Jerusalem Israel Office: Shaare Zedek Med Ctr, PO Box 3235, 91031 Jerusalem Israel

EIDERMAN, BORIS ALEXANDROVICH, scientist, researcher; b. Kharkov, Ukraine, USSR, Feb. 23, 1934; s. Alexandr Moiseevich Eiderman and Maria Borisovna Seigerov; m. Susanna Semenovna Nuger, Feb. 29, 1963; 1 child, Arye. MSc, Mining Inst., Kharkov, USSR, 1957; PhD, Acad. Inst., Moscow, 1968, DSc, 1986. Engr. Machine Bldg. Works, Kharkov, USSR, 1957-61; head mechanics sect. Inst. Kharkov, 1961-66; sr. scientist Acad. Inst., Moscow, 1967-86, leading scientist, 1986-91; scientist Coll. of Tech., Jerusalem, 1992-93; chief scientist SorTech Separation Techs. Ltd., Jerusalem, 1997—; sci. guidance Acad. Inst., Moscow, 1971-91, prof. 1989-91; prof. Mining Inst. for Spl. Skills, Moscow, 1989-91; with sci. guidance Coll. of Tech., Jerusalem, 1994-98. Author: Mechanisms for Formation of Traffic and Energy Expenditure of Conveyer, 1984, Scraper Conveyers, 1993, Parameters and Calculation Methods for Conveyers, 1987; patentee in field. Recipient Prize winner USSR Coun. of Ministers, 1983, Medal Exhbn. of Achievement of the USSR, 1982; grantee Ministry of Industry and Trade of Israel, 1992, 97. Mem. Forum for Bulk Solids Handling, N.Y. Acad. Scis. Avocations: history, ethnography, science, fiction, inventing. Home: Neve Yakov 509/11, 97350 Jerusalem Israel Office: SorTech Ltd, Ha Marpe 8, 91450 Jerusalem Israel

EIDSVOLD, GARY MASON, physician, public health officer, medical educator; b. Morris, Minn., Sept. 28, 1938; s. Lyman Woodrow and Julia Magdalene (Mason) E. BA, St. Olaf Coll., 1960; MD, U. Minn., 1964; MPH, Johns Hopkins U., 1966. Diplomate Am. Bd. Preventive Medicine. Rotating intern Long Island Coll. Hosp., Bklyn., 1964-65; resident in preventive medicine Johns Hopkins U. Sch. Pub. Health, Balt., 1965-68; asst. prof. Haile Selassie U., Gondar, Ethiopia, 1967-68; dir. Indian Health Svc. Hosp., Tuba City, Ariz., 1968-70; South Bronx Health Officer N.Y.C. Health Dept., 1970-73, North Bklyn. Health Officer, 1973-74, Bronx and Staten Island dir., 1974-78; N.Y.C. med. dir. N.Y. State Health Dept., 1978-97, amb. care program dir., 1978-85, home health and HMO program dir., 1978-85, Medicaid program dir., 1978-95, alternative delivery sys. program dir., 1995, managed care program dir., 1995-97, family helath managed care program dir., 1997—; clin. asst. prof. dept. preventive medicine N.Y. Med. Coll., N.Y.C.; clinical asst. prof. dept. preventive medicine N.Y. Med. Coll., N.Y.C., 1971-73; asst. prof. SUNY Health Sci. Ctr., Bklyn., 1973—; lectr. Columbia U. Sch. Pub. Health, N.Y.C., 1973-83; faculty New Sch. Soc. Rsch., N.Y.C., 1974-75. Contbr. articles to profl. jours. Coun. and com. chmn. Trinity Ch. in the City of N.Y., 1972-76, St. John's Evang. Luth. Ch., N.Y.C., 1988—. Surgeon, USPHS, 1968-70. Recipient outstanding leadership award, East N.Y. Health Coalition, Bklyn., 1973. Fellow Am. Coll. Preventive Medicine, Am. Tchrs. Preventive Medicine; mem. Am. Pub. Health Assn. (chmn. Health Adminstrn. Sect. 1979-81), Pub. Health Physicians Assn. N.Y.C. (pres. 1973-76), Pub. Health Assn. N.Y.C. (bd. dirs. 1975-81), Nat. Assn. County Health Officers (bd. dirs. 1975-78), Lutheran Soc. Svcs. Metro N.Y. (bd. dirs. 1991-94), Norwegian Am. Hist. Soc. (life). Democrat. Lutheran. Avocations: Norwegian language, genealogy, cooking, gym, music. Home: 71 Grand St New York NY 10013-2219 Office: NY State Health Dept Penn Plz Fl 2 New York NY 10001-1803

EIE, LEIF, retired air transportation executive; b. Flekkefjord, Norway, July 12, 1929; arrived in U.S., 1952, naturalized, 1954; s. Lars and Aagot Dagmar E.; m. Patricia MacKean; children: Lisa Britt, Christian. Student, U. Wash.; army leadership course with honors, 1953; bus. and English with distinction, Heilbronn Army Edn. Ctr., 1954. From ticket counter staff to sales mgr. Scandinavian Airline Sys., N.Y.C., 1952-64; dist. sales mgr. Scandinavian Airline Sys., Seattle, 1965-70; Northwestern area mgr. Scandinavian Airline Sys., 1970-91; ret., 1991. Hon. vice-consul Royal Norwegian Consulate, Wash., 1990; founder Nordic Heritage Mus., Seattle. Served with Norwegian Air Force. Decorated knight Order of Northern Star (Sweden), Honor medal, St. Olav medal, knight Royal Norwegian Order Merit; Leif Eie Scholarship named in his honor Norwegian Am. C. of C., Pacific Lutheren U., Tacoma, Leif Eie Oral History Project named in his honor Nordic Heritage Mus.; named Norwegian of the Yr. award His Majesty King Ovav V, 1988, Honored Citizen, City of Tacoma, Wash., 1988; Leif Eie Day proclaimed by Mayor of Seattle, 1988; recipient Boy Scouts Am. award, 1976, Ski for Light award, 1976, First Citizen of Seattle award, 1977, Disting. Svc. award Pacific Luth. U., 1977. Mem. Sons of Norway, Norwegian Seamen War Vets. Assn., Norwegian Singers Assn., Rebuild Nat. Park Soc., Finnish Am. C. of C., Norwegian Am. C. of C. (hon. bd. dirs., Man of Decade 1985), Swedish Am. C. of C. (bd. dirs.), Seattle C. of C., Norwegian Comml. Club, Swedish Club, Danish Club, Washington State Codfish Club. Avocations: playing guitar, painting, salmon fishing, composing music. Home: 11865 E Samson Pl Tucson AZ 85748-2064

EIFLER, CARL FREDERICK, retired psychologist; b. Los Angeles, June 27, 1906; s. Carl Frederick and Pauline (Engelbert) E.; m. Margaret Christine Aaberg, June 30, 1963; 1 son, Carl Henry; 1 adopted son, Byron Hisey. BD, Jackson Coll., 1956; Ph.D., Ill. Inst. Tech., 1962. Insp. U.S. Bur. Customs, 1928-35, chief insp., 1936-37, dep. collector, 1937-56; bus. mgr. Jackson Coll., Honolulu, 1954-56, instr., 1955-56; grad. asst. instr., research asst. Ill. Inst. Tech., Chgo., 1959-62; psychologist Monterey County Mental Health Services, Salinas, Calif., 1964-73; ret., 1973. Contbg. author Psychon. Sci., vol. 20, 1970; co-author: The Deadliest Colonel; author, pub.: Jesus Said. Served with U.S. Army, 1922-23, 40-47; col. ret. Decorated Combat Infantryman's Badge, Legion of Merit with 2 oak leaf clusters, Bronze Star medal, Air medal, Purple Heart; named to Military Intelligence Corps Hall of Fame, 1988; recipient Albert Gallatin award U.S. Treas. Dept., 1963, Gen. William J. Donovan award, 1993, Knowlton award Mil. Intelligence Corps, June 1997; Eifler Sports Plaza and Mus. named in his honor, Ft. Huachuca, Ariz., June 1997. Mem. AAUP, Am. Psychol. Assn., Western States Psychol. Assn., Calif. Psychol. Assn., Res. Officers Assn. (Hawaii pres. 1947), Assn. Former Intelligence Officers (bd. govs., Western coord.), Pearl Harbor Survivors, 101 Assn., Assn. U.S. Army Vets. of OSS (past bd. govs., Western coord., v.p.), Ret. Officers Assn., Masons, KT, Shriners, Elks, Nat. Sojourners, Psi Chi. Home: 22700 Picador Dr Salinas CA 93908-1116

EIGEL, JAMES ANTHONY, environmental engineer; b. St. Louis, Mar. 1, 1939; s. Edwin George and Catherine Margaret (Rohan) E.; m. Carolyn Margaret Sudheimer, June 10, 1972 (div. 1990); 1 child, Christine. BS, St. Louis U., 1961, postgrad. Ordained to ministry Episcopal Missionary Ch., 1998. Rsch. chemist Falstaff Brewing Corp., St. Louis, 1965-67; rsch. chemist water divsn. City of St. Louis, 1967-71; rsch. chemist Continental Telephone, Hickory, N.C., 1971-75; mgr. main analysis labs. Hoechst Celanese, Spartanburg, S.C., 1975-85; dir. pretreatment/lab. svcs. Macon-Bibb County (Ga.) Water Authority, 1985-89; mgr. tech. svcs. Pima County Wastewater Mgmt., Tucson, Ariz., 1989—. Contbr. articles to profl. jours. Mem. Am. Chem. Soc., Am. Water Works Assn., Water Environ. Fedn., Lions (pres. 1988-89). Mem. Am. Anglican Ch. Achievements include patent for electrical insulation protector. Office: Pima County Wastewater Mgmt 2600 W Sweetwater Dr Tucson AZ 85705-6915

EIGEN, MANFRED, physicist; b. Bochum, Germany, May 9, 1927; s. Ernst E. and Hedwig (Feld) E.; m. Elfriede Müller; 2 children. Studies in physics and chemistry, U. Gottingen, Germany; hon. degrees, U. Göttingen, U. Chgo., Washington U., St. Louis, Nottingham U., Bristol U., U.K., Hebrew U., Jerusalem, Cambridge U., U.K., Debrecen U., Techn. U., Munich, Bielefeld U., Utah State U. Sci. asst. Inst. Phys. Chemistry U. Göttingen, 1951-53; mem. staff, then chmn. Max Planck Inst. Phys. Chemistry, Göttingen. Author tech. papers. Co-recipient Nobel prize in chemistry, 1967, Max-Planck-Forschungs-Preis, Alexander von Humboldt-Stiftung, 1994, Paul Ehrlich award, 1996. Mem. Bunsen Soc. Phys. Chemistry (Bodenstein Preis 1956), Faraday Soc., NAS, Royal Soc. (fgn. mem., Paul Ehrlich award 1996). Achievements include studying evolution of biol. macromolecules; research on control of enzymes. Office: Max Planck Inst, 37077 Göttingen Germany

EIJK, WILLEM JACOBUS, religious studies educator, bishop; b. Duivendrecht, The Netherlands, June 22, 1953; s. Dirk and Johanna (Baden) E. MD, U. Amsterdam, Holland, 1978; PhD in Medicine, State U. Leiden, Holland, 1987; PhD in Philosophy, U. St. Thomas Aquinas, Rome, 1990; Sacrae Theologiae Licentiatus, Pontificia U. Lateranense, Rome, 1990. Ordained priest Roman Cath. Ch., 1985. Asst. physician U. Amsterdam, 1978-79; asst. parish priest Parish Ch. St. Anthony Padua, Blerick, Holland, 1985-87; prof. moral theology Major Sem. Diocese Roemond, Holland, 1990-99; bishop of Groningen, The Netherlands, 1999—; prefect of studies Maj. Sem. Diocese Roermond, 1991-97; mem. coun. advice Nederlands Artsen Verbond, 1991-2000; mem. directive com. Juristen Vereniging Pro Vita, Holland, 1992-98; pres. Found. Med. Ethics, Maastricht, Holland, 1993—, Medo Internat. Acad. Inst. Studies Marriage and Family, Kerkrade, Holland, 1994-96; prof. moral theology faculty of theology Lugano, Switzerland, 1997-99; mem. Internat. Theol. Commn., Rome, 1997—. Author: Self-Chosen Death Because of a Lethal and Incurable Disease, 1987, The Ethical Problems of Genetic Engineering of Human Beings, 1990; author, editor series publ. Found. Med. Ethics.; contbr. over 50 articles to profl. jours. Roman Catholic. Avocations: music, organ playing. Home and Office: Marktstraat 19, 9712 PB Groningen The Netherlands

EIKELBERG, MARKUS PETER, mathematician, data processing expert; b. Essen, Germany, Nov. 5, 1960; s. Helmuth Peter and Margarete (Poensgen) E.; m. Ulrike Thewes, June 28, 1984; children: Deborah Johanna, Dorothee Friederike. Degree in Math and Cath. Theology, Ruhr U., Bochum, Germany, 1985, D Natural Sci., 1990. Teaching and rsch. asst. Inst. for Math. Ruhr U., Bochum, 1985-91; system programmer Victoria Versicherung, Düsseldorf, Germany, 1991-93, leader computer ops. planning and implementation group, 1994-96; faculty for mechatronics & mech. engring. Fachhochschule, Bochum, 1996—, prof. math. & informatics, 1996—; lectr. math. Faculty Mech. Engring. Fachhochschule Bochum, 1990-91, 93-96. Author: Einführung in die Arbeit mit Maple V, 1998; contbr. articles to sci. and profl. jours. Mem. Deutsche Mathematiker Vereinigung, European Math. Soc., Gesellschaft für Informatik. Roman Catholic. Avocations: music, gardening. Home: Am Hagenbusch 8, 45259 Essen Germany Office: Fachhochschule Bochum, Lennershofstr 140, 44801 Bochum Germany

EIKELENBOOM, PIETER, psychiatrist, researcher; b. Leiden, The Netherlands, Mar. 13, 1946; s. Jacobus and Hendrika (Van Harten) E.; m. Sophia Johanna Margaretha Van Olst, Sept. 15, 1972; 1 child, Merijn. MD, Vrije U., Amsterdam, 1973, PhD, 1978, psychiatrist, 1983. Rsch. scientist Vrije U., Amsterdam, 1975-78, asst. psychiatrist, 1978-82, psychiatrist-lectr., 1982—, prof. gerontopsychiatry, 1991—. Contbr. articles to profl. jours. Grantee Preventiefonds, The Hague, 1990, Netherlands Med. Rsch. Coun., 1994, 95, 96. Mem. Dutch Soc. for Immunology, Dutch Assn. Psychiatry. Social Democrat. Home: Van Spaenstraat 33, 1181 DV Amstelveen The Netherlands Office: Vrije U Dept Psychiatry, Valeriusplein 9, 1075 BG Amsterdam The Netherlands

EIKENBERRY, ARTHUR RAYMOND, writer, service executive, researcher; b. Sebring, Fla., June 5, 1920; s. Leroy Albertus and Vernie Cordelia (Griffin) E.; m. Carol Jean Parrott, June 10, 1955; children: Robin Rene, Shari LaVon, Jan Rochelle, Karyn LaRae, Kelli Yvette. Student, Pasadena (Calif.) Jr. Coll., 1939, Kunming U., China, 1944-45. MSgt. Army Air Corps, 1941-45, re-enlisted in grade of TSgt., 1947; advanced through grades to SMSgt. USAF; ret., 1973, mgmt., pers., adminstrv. and security insp.; mgr. property control, real estate agent TR Devel. Co., Englewood, Colo., 1973-74; real estate agt. The Pinery, Parker, Colo., 1974-75; mgr., patient acctg. dept. Univ. Colo. Health Scis. Ctr., Denver, 1975-89; ret., 1989. Author: Investment Strategies for the Clever Investor, 1989, LOTTO GURU (Omni-Personal Selection Systems & Strategies), 1989. Charter mem. U.S. Congl. Adv. Bd. Fellow Internat. Biog. Ctr. (hon. life patron, dep. dir. gen.); mem. Am. Biog. Inst. (life, dep. gov., nat. adviser), World

Inst. of Achievement (disting.), Masons, Eastern Star, Royal Order of the Amaranth. Address: Apt 2085 9901 W Sahara Ave Las Vegas NV 89117-5903

EIN, DANIEL, allergist; b. Liege, Belgium, Nov. 26, 1938; came to U.S., 1941; s. Max Motel and Sabine (Toeman) E.; m. Marion Hess, June 25, 1961 (div. 1978); children: Mark David, Jon Spencer; m. Marina Wallach, Apr. 10, 1988; stepchildren: Jacqueline A. Newmyer, Tory Newmyer. AB, Columbia U., 1959; MD, Albert Einstein Coll. Medicine, 1964. Diplomate Am. Bd. Internal Medicine, Am. Bd. Allergy and Immunology. Intern Bronx Mcpl. Hosp., N.Y.C., 1964-65; staff assoc. Nat. Cancer Inst., Washington, 1965-67, clin. assoc., 1967-68; asst. resident Mass. Gen. Hosp., Boston, 1968-69; sr. investigator Nat. Cancer Inst., Washington, 1969-71; pvt. practice Washington, 1971—; clin. prof. medicine George Washington U., Washington, 1982—, Georgetown U., Washington, 1996—; founder, pres. Capital Physicians Network, 1994-99. Contbr. articles to profl. jours. and newspapers. Fellow ACP, Am. Acad. Allergy (AMA del. 1994), Am. Coll. Allergy (bd. dirs. 2000—); mem. Joint Coun. of Allergy (pres. 1998—), Med. Soc. of D.C. (pres. 1991), Greater Washington Allergy Soc. (pres. 1979), Cosmos Club. Jewish. Achievements include discovery of OZ factors on human immunoglobulin light chains. Home: 4636 Kenmore Dr NW Washington DC 20007-1924

EINAGA, YOSHIYUKI, chemist; b. Himeji, Hyogo, Japan, Jan. 28, 1945; s. Tetsuo and Tsuyako (Yamanaka) E.; m. Naoko Yagi, May 13, 1973; children: Hiroyuki, Yukiko, Michiko. BS, Kyoto U., 1967, MS, 1969, PhD, 1972. Instr. Osaka U., Toyonaka, Japan, 1973-88; assoc. prof. chemistry Kyoto U., 1988-99; prof. chemistry Nara Women's U., 1999—; sr. rsch. chemist Carnegie-Mellon U., Pitts., 1979-81. Contbr. articles to profl. jours. Mem. Am. Chem. Soc., N.Y. Acad. Scis., Soc. Polymer Sci. Japan, Soc. Rheology Japan. Avocation: gardening. Home: Nishikyoku, Ooenishishinbayashi 6-9-18, Kyoto 610-1141, Japan

EINARSSON, GISLI, physiatrist, educator; b. Reykjavik, Iceland, June 5, 1948; s. Einar Asgrimsson and Sigridur Asa Gisladottir; m. Sigrun Benediktsdottir, Dec. 26, 1970; children: Asa Bjork, Einar Orn. MD, U. Göteborg (Sweden), 1976, PhD in Medicine, 1990. Cons. surgeon Iceland, 1981, Sweden, 1982; chief physician NLFI Rehab. Hosp., Iceland, 1989-91; cons. specialist Reykjalundur Rehab. Ctr., Reykjavik, 1992-93; chief physician, head dept. phys. medicine and rehab. Nat. U. Hosp., Reykjavik, 1994—; lectr. U. Iceland, 1989—, bd. dirs. sch. phys. therapy, Nat. U. Hosp. Iceland, Reykjavik; chief cons. physician Ctrl. Govt. Iceland, Reykjavik, 1992—; team physician Nat. Paralympic Com., Iceland, attending, Atlanta, 1996; bd. dirs. Nat. Univ. Hosp. Author: Muscle Adaptation and Disability in Late Poliomyelitis, 1990 (Danish nat. Assn. Rschrs.' for Traffic and Poliovictims award 1991). Fellow Scandinavian Swedish and Icelandic Soc. Gen. Surgery, Scandinavian and Swedish Soc. Phys. Medicine and Rehab., Icelandic Soc. Phys. Medicine and Rehab. (chmn. 1995-97). Avocations: sailing (cert. Swedish capt.), private pilot. Home: Breidagerdi 6, 108 Reykjavik Iceland Office: Dept Phys Medicine Rehab, Nat U Hosp, 101 Reykjavik Iceland

EINARSSON, GUDFINNUR, seafood products company executive; b. Hnifsdal, Iceland, Oct. 17, 1922; s. Einar Gudfinnsson and Elisabet Hjaltadottir; m. Maria Kristin Haraldsdottir, Apr. 17, 1955; children: Einar Kristinn, Haraldur, Gudrun Kristin. Final degree, Comml. Coll., Iceland. Mng. dir. E. Gudfinnsson, Ltd., Bolungarvik, Iceland, 1940—; chmn. bd. Coldwater Seafood Co., U.S.A., 1979—. Home: Fjardargata 17, 220 Hafnarfjordur Iceland

EINARSSON, GUDMUNDUR VIKAR, urologist, educator; b. Reykjavík, Iceland, Feb. 8, 1949; s. Einar and Edda Vikar (Gudmundsdóttir) E.; m. Steinunn Gudmundsdóttir, Sept. 20, 1969; children: Edda, Thora. Matriculation exam., Reykjavik Jr. Coll., 1969; MD, BChir, U. Iceland, Reykjavík, 1977. Intern Akranes (Iceland) Hosp., 1976-77; resident in gen. surgery Nassau County Med. Ctr., East Meadow, N.Y., 1977-79; resident in urology Downstate Med. Ctr.-Kings County Hosp. SUNY, Bklyn., 1979-82; chief urology Landspitalinn-Univ. Hosp., Reykjavík, 1982—; assoc. prof., Med. Sch. U. Iceland, Reykjavík, 1987—. Contbr. chpt. to: Penis Reimplantation, 1993. Office: Univ Hosp, Landspitalinn, 101 Reykjavík Iceland

EINARSSON, STIG GÖSTA, veterinarian, educator; b. Kristianstad, Sweden, Dec. 8, 1940; s. Einar and Anna Karlsson; m. Laila Evy-Mari Rönnberg, June 22, 1969; children: Charlotte, Peter, Johan, Catharina. Matriculation, Läroverk, Kristianstad, 1959; veterinarian, Coll. Vet. Medicine, Stockholm, 1965, PhD in Vet. Medicine, docent, 1971; Dr.med.vet honoris causa, U. Oslo, 1996, U. Copenhagen, 1998. Asst. Coll. Vet. Medicine, Stockholm, 1965-66, lectr., 1966-71, assoc. prof., 1972-78; prof. Swedish U. Agrl. Sci., Uppsala, Sweden, 1979—; head of dept. ob-gyn. Swedish U. Agrl. Sci., Uppsala, 1980—; sec. gen. standing com. Internat. Congress Animal Reproduction, 1980-96. Mem. Internat. Soc. Andrology, Soc. for Study Fertility, Soc. for Study Reprodn., Nordic Assn. for Andrology, Nordic Vet. Soc. for Animal Reprodn. (sec.-gen. 1974-82), European Soc. Domestic Animal Reprodn. (v.p. 1996—), European Coll. Animal Reprodn. (pres. 1999—), Royal Swedish Acad. Agrl. and Forestry, Soc. Theriogenology. Office: Sweden U Agrl Scis, Dept Ob-Gyn PO Box 7039, 75007 Uppsala Sweden

EINARSSON, SVEINN, theatre director; b. Reykjavik, Iceland, Sept. 18, 1934; s. Einar Ol Sveinsson and Kristjana Thorsteinsdottir; m. Thora Kristjansdottir, Oct. 17, 1964; 1 child, Asta Kristjana. Fil. Kand., U. Stockholm, 1958, Fil. Lic., 1964. Artistic dir., gen. mgr. Reykjavik Theatre Co., 1963-72, Nat. Theatre Iceland, 1972-83; counselor Ministry Culture, Reykjavik, 1983—; radio producer, 1959-61; dir. RTCDrama Sch., 1964-69; mem. faculty U. Iceland, 1971-72, 76-77, 79-80, 86; drama critic, 1959-61; head program prodn. state TV, 1989-93; artistic dir. Reykjavik Arts Festival, 1998-2000; dir. 80 stage plays, radio plays, TV-film plays, adaptations, transl. Author: The Theatre by the Lake, 1972, Icelandic Theatre, Vol. I, II, 1991-96, The Electricity Man, 1998, Bandamannaja, 1992, The Annoldi Saja, 1996, Daughters of Jue Paet, 1998; (play) The Egg of Life, 1984; I am Gold and Diamonds, 1985; book on theatre My Nine Years Down There, 1984; (children's book) Gariella in Portugal, 1985 (Children's Book of Yr. 1985); also articles, radio and TV plays. Grantee French Govt., Sci. Fund Iceland. Mem. Nordic Theatre Com., Nordic Theatre Union (v.p. 1976-82, pres. Iceland div. 1972—), Internat. Theatre Inst. (exec. com. 1977-81, v.p. 1979-81). Club: Rotary. Home: 26 Tjarnargata, Reykjavik Iceland Office: Ministry of Culture, Reykjavik Iceland

EINAV, BEN-AMI, performing arts group administrator; b. Bucarest, Romania, May 6, 1947; arrived in Israel, 1960; s. Heinrich and Miriam (Kusman) Weiner; m. Hedva Avnon, Oct. 29, 1970; children: Dalit, Orly. BA, Hebrew U., Jerusalem, 1971, MA in Communication cum laude, 1974. Research dir. Israel Inst. Applied Social Research, Jerusalem, 1971-74; spokesman Technion-Israel Inst. Tech., Haifa, 1974-85; dir. gen. Haifa Symphony Orch., 1985-97; gen. mgr. Bat Sheva Dance Co., Tel Aviv, 1997-98; dir. divsn. culture Haifa Municipality, 1999—; lectr. Haifa U., 1976-82; pub. relations cons., No. Israel, 1980-85. Fellow Israel Painters and Sculptors Assn.; mem. Internat. Pub. Rels. Assn., Israel Pub. Rels. Assn., Israel Assn., Internat. Soc. Performing Arts Adminstrs., Am. Symphony Orch. League. Home: 21A Sea Rd, Haifa 34741, Israel Office: Dir Divsn Culture, 5 Baerwald St POB 4811, 31047 Haifa Israel

EINHORN, NINA, gynecologic oncologist; b. Lodz, Poland, Feb. 14, 1925; arrived in Sweden, 1946; d. Artur and Fanny (Wygodzki) Rajmic; m. Jerzy Einhorn, Oct. 1, 1949; children: Lena, Stefan. MB, U. Uppsala, Sweden, 1949; MD, Karolinska Hosp., Stockholm, 1954; PhD, Karolinska Inst., 1972. Physician South Maternity Hosp., Stockholm, 1954-61, Sabbatsberg Hosp., Stockholm, 1961-64; physician Radiumhemmet, Stockholm, 1964-71, associated prof., dep. dir., 1972-86, head dept. gynecol. oncology, 1986-91; pvt. practice Stockholm, 1992-99; chmn. Coop. Ovarian Cancer Study Group, 1978-91. Contbr. over 227 articles to profl. jours. Chmn. Swedish-Jewish Appeal, 1994-99; chmn. sci. bd. Stockholm Cancer Soc., 1997—. Fellow Am. Coll. Radiology; mem. Swedish Med. Soc. (Traffenfelts Order award 1976), European Soc. for Therapeutic Radiotherapy and Oncology, Soc. Gynecologic Oncology, Internat. Gynecologic Cancer Soc. (pres. 1989-91). Home: Kevingestrand 43, 183 31 Danderyd Sweden Office: Radiumhemmet Karolinska Hosp, Box 100, 171 76 Stockholm Sweden

EINODER, CAMILLE ELIZABETH, secondary education educator; b. Chgo., June 15, 1937; d. Isadore and Elizabeth T. (Czerwinski) Popowski; m. Joseph X. Einoder, Aug. 5, 1978; children: Carl Frank, Mark Frank, Vivian Einoder, Joe Einoder, Tim Einoder, Sheila Einoder, Jude Einoder. Student, Fox Bus. Coll., 1954; BEd in Biology, Chgo. Tchrs. Coll., 1964; MA in Analytical Chemistry, Gov.'s State U., 1977; MA in Adminstrn. and Supervision, Roosevelt U., 1986; postgrad, 1992—. Secretarial positions Chgo., 1955-64; tchr. biology Chgo. Bd. Edn., 1964—, tchr. biology and agr., 1975-81, tchr. biology, agr. and chemistry, 1981—; human rels. coord. Morgan Park High Sch., Chgo., 1980—, tchr. biology Internat. Studies Sch., 1983—, mem. adv. bd., 1989—; owner Einoder Masonry, 1997—, Einoder Antiques, 1996—; career devel. cons. for agr. related curriculum; internat. baccalaureate tchr., Chgo. pub. schs. consulting tchr., 1997; bd. dirs., edn. cons. Neighborhood Coun., 1974; rep. Chgo. Tchrs. Union, 1969; exec. bd. dir. The Lira Ensemble, 1996—; mem. Renaissance Circle, DePaul U.; mem. edn. com. Polish-Am. Initiative of Chgo. Cmty. Trust, 1999—. Bd. dirs., founding mem., author constn. Cmty. Coun., 1970—; bd. dirs., edn. cons. Neighborhood Coun., 1974; rep. Chgo. Tchrs. Union, 1969; exec. bd. dirs. The Lira Ensemble, 1996—. Mem. AAAS, NSTA, Polish Inst. for Arts and Sci., Am. Chem. Soc., Am. Biology Tchrs. Assn., Nat. Assn. Women Bus. Owners, Found. Women Contractors, Copernicus Found., Kosciuszko Soc., Polish Arts Club, Phi Delta Kappa, Iota Sigma Pi. Home: 10637 S Claremont Ave Chicago IL 60643-3101 Office: 1744 W Pryor Ave Chicago IL 60643-3497

EIS, SERGIO RAGI, orthopedic surgeon; b. Rio de Janeiro, Apr. 8, 1962; s. Ivo Ragi and Oriette (Ramos) E.; m. Irani Fim Francischetto, Sept. 5, 1988; children: Isabella, Marina. MD, U. Rio de Janeiro, 1987, PhD, 1990. Orthopedic surgeon Ctr. Army Hosp., Rio de Janeiro, 1988-91; tech. supervisor CSST Pvt. Hosp., Rio de Janeiro, 1989-91; orthopedic surgeon Children's Hosp., Rio de Janeiro, 1991-92; tech. supervisor Bone Densitometry Ctr. Espirito Santo, Brazil, 1991—. Mem. Brazilian Soc. Bone and Mineral Metabolism Rsch. (pres. 1993-95), Brazilian Soc. Bone Densitometry (pres. 1995-97, scientific dir. 1997-99), Espirito Santo Med. Assn. (sec. 1995-97), Spanish Soc. Bone and Mineral Metabolism Rsch., Latin Am. Soc. for Clin. Densitometer (pres.-elect). Avocation: personal computing. Office: CEDOES, Rua Joao Da Silva Abreu 78, 29055450 Vitoria ES, Brazil

EISELE, JOHN EUGENE, lawyer; b. Mpls., Apr. 22, 1938; s. James William and Fayloa Geneva E.; m. Patricia Anne Thornburg, Mar. 2, 1962 (div. Feb. 1981); children: John Michael, William Todd. BA, Ind. U., 1961, JD, 1968. Bar: Ind. 1968, U.S. Dist. Ct. Ind. 1968, U.S. Supreme Ct. 1990. Personnel, foreman GM, Anderson, Ind., 1964-68; hearing officer Ind. Pub. Svc. Commn., Indpls., 1968-70; deputy prosecutor Madison County, Anderson, 1970, pub. defender, 1971-76, atty., 1968—. Mem. Anderson Police Merit Commn., 1997—. 1st lt. U.S. Army, 1962-64. Mem. Ind. Bar Assn., Ind. Trial Lawyers Assn., Madison County Bar Assn. (pres. 1989), Am. Legion, Anderson Country Club (sec./bd. dirs. 1991-94), Exch. Club. Avocations: fishing, jogging, weightlifting. Home: 514 Ironwood Ln Anderson IN 46011-1650 Office: Eisele Lockwood & Eisele 200 E 11th St Ste 100 Anderson IN 46016-1779

EISELSBERG, OTTO H., diplomat; b. Vienna, Mar. 7, 1917; s. Anton and Agnes (von Pirquet) E.; m. Brigitta Haffner, Jan 23, 1973; 1 child, Anna-Margherita. Student, Consular Acad., Vienna, 1936-38, Wittenberg Coll., Springfield, Ohio, 1938-39; Dr. iurus, U. Vienna, 1939. Called to bar Austrian Fgn. Office, Vienna, 1948-49; sec. Austrian Embassy, London, 1950-51; permanent del. ECE, Geneva, 1952; chargé d'affaires e.p. Austrian Embassy, Canberra, Australia, 1953-55; councilor Austrian Embassy, Moscow, 1958-60, Paris, 1961-63; amb. to Japan Tokyo, 1967-71; amb. to France Paris, 1974-82. Author: Erlebte Geschichte, 1997. Recipient decorations from Austria, France, Germany, Hungary, Australia, Japan, South Korea. Mem. Rotary.

EISELT, MICHAEL, pathophysiologist, researcher; b. Gera, Thuringia, Germany, Mar. 9, 1956; s. Alfons and Ursula (Böhme) E.; m. Gabriele Bensch, Nov. 23, 1985; 1 child, Andreas. Med. diploma, Friedrich-Schiller U., Jena, Germany, 1984, MD, 1987. Cert. physician, EEG cert. Sci. asst. Friedrich-Schiller U., Jena, 1983-90, 92, Hosp. A. Béclère, Clamart, France, 1991. Contbr. articles to profl. jours. Grantee European Sci. Found.'s European Tng. Program in Brain and Behavior, 1991, European Sleep Rsch. Soc., 1992. Mem. German Soc. Pathol. and Clin. Physiology, German Soc. Clin. Neurophysiology, German Physiol. Soc. Office: Friedrich-Schiller U, Inst Pathophysiology, 07740 Jena Germany

EISEN, ERIC ANSHEL, lawyer; b. N.Y.C., Apr. 9, 1950; s. Morton and Victoria (Goldstein) E.; m. Claire L. Shapiro, Jan. 6, 1979; children: Rebecca, Jennifer, Melissa. AB, U. Mich., 1971, JD magna cum laude, 1975. Bar: Alaska 1976, D.C. 1977, Md. 1988. Law clk. to presiding justice Alaska Supreme Ct., Fairbanks, 1975-76; assoc. Covington & Burling, Washington, 1976-81; assoc. Birch, Horton, Bittner, Washington, 1981-85, ptnr., 1985-93; ptnr. Eisen Law Offices, Bethesda, Md., 1993—; speaker various seminars and colloquia on energy and bus. matters. Contbr. articles legal publs. Pres. Wildwood Hills Citizens Assn., Bethesda, Md., 1987—; sec. N. Bethesda Cong. Citizens Assns., 1989-90. Mem. ATLA, Fed. Energy Bar Assn. (antitrust com.), D.C. Bar Assn., Montgomery County Bar Assn. (intellectual property, bus. and litigation sects.), Toastmasters, Order of Coif. Avocation: woodworking. Office: Eisen Law Offices 10028 Woodhill Rd Bethesda MD 20817-1218 also: 1101 30th St NW Ste 500 Washington DC 20007-3708

EISENBERG, ADI, chemist; b. Wrocław (Breslau), formerly Germany, Feb. 18, 1935; emigrated to U.S., 1951; s. Oscar and Helene E.; m. Sandra M. Kloner, June 9, 1957 (div. 1985); 1 son, Elliot. BSc, Worcester Poly. Inst., 1957; MA, Princeton U., 1959, PhD, 1960. Postdoctoral fellow U. Basel, Switzerland, 1961-62; asst. prof. chemistry UCLA, 1962-67; assoc. prof. chemistry McGill U., Montreal, Que., Can., 1967-74; prof. McGill U., 1975—; dir. Polymer McGill, 1991-99, Otto Maass Prof. Chemistry, 1993—; cons. in field. Author 7 books in field; contbr. articles to profl. jours. NATO fellow, 1961-62; Killam Research fellow, 1987-88; recipient E.W.R. Steacie award, 1998. Fellow Am. Phys. Soc. (chmn. div. high polymer physics 1975-76), Chem. Inst. Can. (Macromolecular Sci. and Engring.-Dunlop award 1988, E.W.R. Steacie award 1998); mem. Am. Chem. Soc., Sigma Xi. Achievements include patents in field. Office: McGill University, 801 Sherbrooke St W, Montreal, PQ Canada H3A 2K6

EISENBERG, ELIYOHU, academic researcher and administrator; b. Haifa, Israel, Feb. 9, 1952; s. Jacob and Malka (Ludomirsky) E.; m. Batsheva Davidowitch, Oct. 24, 1973; children: Michal, Yaacov. BS in Edn. of Tech. & Sci., Israeli Inst. Tech., Haifa, 1979, MS in Edn. of Tech. & Sci., 1983, DS in Edn. of Tech. & Sci., 1987. Profl. tutor Everyman's U., Israel, 1986-87; planner, developer new tech. ctr. Open U., 1988-90; curriculum designer Ministry of Edn. & Culture Coms., Israel, 1991-92; founder, nat. exec. dir. ORT-STEP Inst., Johannesburg, South Africa, 1992-96; dep. dir. gen. for R&D ORT Israel, Tel Aviv, 1996—; rschr. in field; lectr. Israeli Inst. Tech., Haifa, 1990-92; presenter in field. Contbr. articles to profl. jours. Col. Israeli Defense Forces, 1970-74. Gutwirth fellow Israeli Inst. Tech., 1978, rsch. fellow, 1987-88, vis. rsch. fellow Open U., Milton Keynes, England, 1988-90; recipient Kennedy Leigh award Israeli Inst. Tech., 1987. Jewish. Avocations: piano, volleyball. Home: 32/12 Margalit, 34464 Haifa Israel Office: ORT Israel Head Office, 39 King David Blvd, Tel Aviv 61160, Israel

EISENBERG, JOSEPH MARTIN, psychologist; b. Bklyn., June 19, 1944; s. David and Dora (Levine) E.; m. Susan Joan Kahn, Aug. 16, 1980; children: Ian, Lara, Jason, Davida. BA in Psychology magna cum laude, C.W. Post Coll., 1966; M.A. in Psychology, U. Alta, 1969, PhD in Psychology, 1971. Cert., lic., Md.; cert. clin. hypnotherapist, Negotiation Inst. Psychol. diagnostician, counselor dept. psychology U. Alta, Can., 1969-70; field rschr. Dept. Youth Alta, 1969-70; assoc. dir. Toronto (Ont.) YMCA Ctr. for counseling and Human Rels., 1970-71; chief psychologist Salvation Army House of Concord, Toronto, 1971-72; dir. outpatient svc. St. Vincent Hosp. Cmty. Mental Health Ctr., Erie, Pa., 1972-73; dir. Erie County Ctr. for Learning Disabilities, 1973-74; pvt. practice psychology Erie and Balt., 1972—; v.p. in charge personnel and comm. Bridge Energy Corp., Balt., 1981—, Reason House, Balt., 1981-97; spl. cons. Md. Children and Family Svcs., Inc.; mem. profl. adv. bds. Balt. Assn. children with Learning Disabilities; cons. Mormac Ltd., 1979-97; forensic cons. Howard County/Balt. County/Carroll County, Office of Pub. Defendeers and Balt. City Solicitor's Office, 1977—. Co-author computer software; contbr. articles to profl. jours. Chmn. Carroll County Child Abuse Consultation Com., 1978-80; dir. Psychol. Svcs. for the Metabolic Nutrition Program, 1986-89; mem. profl. adv. bd. Catonsville Group Home, 1980-81. Recipient Richard P. Runyon award, 1966. Mem. Am. Psychol. Assn., Md. Psychol. Assn., Am. Bd. Profl. Disability Cons., Am. Bd. Cert. Managed Care Providers, Psi Chi, Phi Theta. Office: 1402 York Rd Ste 207 Lutherville MD 21093-6031

EISENBERG, NANCY HOPE, psychology educator, researcher; b. Cin., Mar. 12, 1950; d. Stanley C. and Marion (Rosenberg) E.; m. Jerry Douglas Harris, Mar. 11, 1983; 1 stepson: Michael Harris. BA, U. Mich., 1972; MA, U. Calif., Berkeley, 1975, PhD, 1976. Lectr. sch. social work U. Calif., Berkeley, 1975-76; asst. prof. psychology Ariz. State U., Tempe, 1976-80, assoc. prof., 1980-86, prof., 1986-91, regents prof., 1991—; mem. adj. faculty U. Oreg. 1994-95, Oreg. State U., 1993—; vis. prof. U. Otago, Dunedin, New Zealand, 1994, Inst. for Psychology Tech. U. Berlin, 1981 ; guest scientist Max Planck Inst., Berlin, 1981, 86, Tech. U., Berlin, 1986; cons. Disney Cable TV, 1988, MacArthur Found. and Dept. Justice, 1992, Childrne's TV Resource and Edn. Ctr., San Francisco, 1992, Hallmark Cards Philanthropic Fund, 1992-93, PETA, 1994, Nat. Inst. Healthcare Rsch., 1999, KCTS Seattle, 1996—, Brilliant Beginnings, 1999. Author: Roots of Caring, Sharing and Helping: The Development of Prosocial Behavior in Children, 1977, Altruistic Emotion, Cognition and Behavior, 1986, (with P. Mussen) The Roots of Prosocial Behavior in Children, 1991 (Japanese translation 1991), The Caring Child, 1992 (Japanese translation); editor The Development of Prosocial Behavior, 1982, Contemporary Topics in Development Psychology, 1987, (with J. Strayer) Empathy and its Development, 1987, (with E. Staub and J. Reykowski) Social and Moral Values: Individual and Societal Perspectives, 1990 (Polish translation 1990), New Directions in Child Development, 1989, Handbook of Child Psychology: Socialization, Personality and Social Development, 1998; contbr. chpts. to numerous psychology texts; contbr. articles to profl. jours.; editor Psychol. Bull., 1996—; cons. editor Devel. Psychology, 1979-95, Jour. Genetic Psychology, 1984—, Genetic Psychology Monographs, 1984—, Merrill-Palmer Quarterly, 1985-90, Contemporary Ednl. Psychology, 1990-94, Jour. Applied Devel. Psychology, 1990—, Jour. Personality and Social Psychology, 1994-95, Psychology of Women Quarterly, 1994-95; assoc. editor Jour. Early Adolescence, 1981—, Personality and Social Psychology Bulletin, 1987-90, Merrill Palmer Quarterly, 1991-95; mem. pub. bd. Soc. Rsch. Child Devel., 1991-93, 96-99. Mem. gov. coun. Soc. Rsch. Child Devel., 1993-98. Grantee NIH, 1985-86, NSF, 1985-89, 88-92, 89-91, 92-97, 94-95, Ariz. State U., 1976-77, 79, 82, 88, 89, 89-90, Canadian Social Sci. Rsch. Coun., 1989-91, Internat. Rsch. Exch. Bd., 1985-89, Nat. Inst. Child Health and Human Devel., 1984-86, NIMH, 1978-79, 80-81, 87—; scholar Child Devel. Found., 1982-83; recipient Rsch. Scientist Devel. award Nat. Inst. Child Health and Devel., Bethesda, Md., 1986-90, NIMH, Washington, 1991-96, 96—, Career Development award Nat. Inst. Child Health and Devel., 1986-90. Fellow APA (divsn. 7 and 8, mem. gov. coun. 1988-89, numerous coms.), Western Psychol. Assn. (pres. 1995-96); mem. Soc. Rsch. Child Devel. (pub. bd. 1991-93, 96-99, mem. gov. coun. 1993-98), Internat. Soc. Study Behavioral Devel. (chair pubs. com. 1994-99), Soc. Exptl. Social Psychology, Internat. Soc. Study Emotion, Soc. Psychophysiol. Rsch., Soc. Rsch. Adolescence (chair pubs. com. 1989-92), Phi Beta Kappa. Avocations: hiking, crafts. E-mail: nancy.eisenberg@asu.edu.

EISENMANN, OLIVIER DAPHNIS, concert organist; b. Zürich, Switzerland, June 7, 1940; s. Will E. and Eva (Westphal) E. D. U. Zürich, 1971; student Will E. Eisenmann and Sava Savoff, Conservatory Lucerne, 1945-49; Stiftsorganist, Lucerne, until 1976. First performed as pianist, 1948, pianist, accompanist, 1957—, organist, 1972—; artistic dir. several internat. concert series. Performed in concerts and tours in Europe, Asia, U.S., Australia, Mexico City, South America, Washington Cathedral, Riverside Ch., N.Y.C., Boston, Seattle, Singapore, Riga, Tallinn, St. Petersburg, Chelyabinsk, Kazan, Russia, the Ukraine, Notre Dame de Paris, Dijon, Lyon, Bruges, Bonn, Münsterbasilika, Aachen, Cologne, Berlin, Munich, Hamburg, St. Paul's Cathedral, London, York Minster, cathedrals in Lincoln, Chester, Worcester, Edinburgh, Dublin, Haarlem, Rotterdam, Oslo, Göteborg, Stockholm, Dresden, Turku, Helsinki, Copenhagen, Vienna, Salzburg, Graz, Bratislava, Budapest, Ljubljana, Slovenia, Madrid, Barcelona, Brussels; festivals in PL-Oliva, Bonn, Trier Cathedral, Rostock, Czechoslovakia, Verona, Turin, Naples, Rome Ragusa, Gent, Moscow, Ufa, Nischni Nowgorod, Yalta, São Paulo, Montevideo, Buenos Aires, Morelia, Guadalajara, Mex., Internat. Festival of Music, Lucerne, Internat. Hong Kong Arts Festival; soloist in orch. concerts with Southwestgerman Philharmony, German Bach-Orch., State Philharmony Kosice, Slovakia, Singapore Symphony Orch.; radio and TV programs in 9 countries, a dozen records, 6 CDs; editor LNN Lucerne, 1971-76; author: Friedrich der Grosse im Urteil seiner schweizerischen Mitwelt, 1971; contbr. articles to booklets and newspapers. Mem. Internat. Soc. Contemporary Music (mng. bd., ctrl. Swiss chpt.). Address: Chalet Brisenblick, 6353 Weggis, Lucerne Switzerland

EISENMANN-KLEIN, MARITA, plastic surgeon; b. Gars/Inn, Bavaria, Germany, Sept. 5, 1947; d. Johann B. and Therese (Thaler) Eisenmann; m. Helmfried Klein, Mar. 12, 1977; children: Julian, Silvan, Konstantin. MD, Ludwig-Maximilians U., Munich, Germany, 1974; diploma in quality mgmt. Bd. cert. gen. surgeon, plastic surgeon, hand surgeon. Surg. intern Hosp. Muenchen-Schwabing, Munich, 1974; med. and ob-gyn. intern Ludwig-Maximilians U. Hosp., Munich, 1975; combined intern, resident Maimonides Med. Ctr., N.Y.C., 1975-76; resident in surgery City Hosp., Muenchen-Schwabing, 1976-83; gen. surgeon City Hosp., Munich, 1983-84, resident in plastic surgery, 1984-87; plastic surgeon City Hosp., Muenchen-Bogenhausen, 1987-88; dir. surgery and plastic surgery Kreiskrankenhaus Nittenau, Germany, 1988-93; dir. dept. plastic surgery Caritas Krankenhaus St. Josef, Regensburg, Germany, 1994—; pres. European Com. on Quality Assurance and Med. Devices, 1992-99. Author: Qualitaetsmanagement in der Medizin, 1997, Qualitaetsmanagement im Gesundheitswesen, 1999, Breast Implants: the Past, the Present, the Future, European Plastic Surgery Rev., 1999. Bd. dirs. Red Cross Kreisverband, Regensburg, Germany, 1997—. Recipient Travel award Bavarian Assn. Surgeons, 1983. Mem. Assn. German Plastic Surgeons (bd. dirs. 1990-92), Internat. Confedn. Plastic, Reconstructive and Aesthetic Surgery (del. of mid. and so. Europe 1995—, bd. dirs., mem. aux. com., chmn. quality assurance com., bd. dirs of Found.), Internat. Soc. Aesthetic Plastic Surgery (mem. membership com.), European Soc. Mastology, Internat. Assn. Univ. Plastic Surgeons, Am. Soc. Plastic Surgery. Roman Catholic. Avocations: contemporary art, jazz dance, windsurfing, skiing, golf. Office: Caritas Krankenhs St Josef, Landshuter Str 65, 93053 Regensburg Germany

EISENSTADT, G. MICHAEL, diplomat, author, lecturer, research scholar; b. Free City of Danzig (now Gdansk, Poland), Nov. 16, 1928; s. Isidor and Edith (Lange) E.; 1 child, Judith Luzann. BA, Queens Coll., 1951; MS, U. Wis., 1952; postgrad., Russian Inst. Columbia U., 1954-56, Fgn. Svc. Inst., 1982-83. Instr. history Queens Coll., Flushing, N.Y., 1955-60; jr. officer Am. Embassy, Belgrade, Yugoslavia, 1960-61; cultural officer Am. Consulate Gen., Guayaquil, Ecuador, 1962-63; asst. cultural affairs officer Am. Embassy, Belgrade, Yugoslavia, 1963-67; cultural attaché Am. Embassy, Warsaw, Poland, 1968-71; br. pub. affairs officer Am. Embassy, Bonn, Fed. Republic of Germany, 1973-76; counselor for pub. affairs Am. Embassy, Budapest, Hungary, 1977-80; dep. counselor for pub. affairs Am. Embassy, Bonn, 1983-84; counselor for pub. affairs Am. Embassy, Belgrade, 1984-88; dep. policy officer Voice of Am., Washington, 1971-73; dir. Office Internat. Visitors USIA, Washington, 1980-82; mem. sr. seminar State Dept., Washington, 1982-83; dir. Office European Affairs USIA, Washington, 1988-89; diplomat-in-residence NYU, 1989-90; dir. N.Y. Reception Ctr. USIA, 1990-92; sr. rsch. scholar Inst. East Cen. Europe Columbia U., 1992-94; cons. on the Balkans, Ea. and Ctrl. Europe, countries of the former Soviet Union; chmn. coordinating com., chmn. drafting com. Conf. on Peace and Tolerance, Istanbul, 1994; chmn. coordinating com. Conflict Resolution Conf., Vienna, 1995; election observer OSCE in Serbia, 1997; coord. Peace and Tolerance Conf. on Kosove, Vienna, Austria, 1999; election observer Appeal of Conscience Found. in Russia, 1999. Sec. Appeal of Conscience Del. to Switzerland, 1997; dir. internat. programs Appeal Conscience Found. With

U.S. Army, 1952-54. Mem. Internat. Conf. and Seminar Assn. (pres.). Home: 880 5th Ave Apt Phe New York NY 10021-4951

EISENSTADT, SHMUEL NOAH, sociologist, educator; b. Warsaw, Poland, Sept. 10, 1923; arrived in Israel, 1935; s. Michael and Rosa (Baruchin) E.; m. Shulamith Yaroshevsky, Sept. 6, 1948; children: Michael, Irit Meir, Alexander. MA, Hebrew U. Jerusalem, 1944, PhD in Sociology, 1947; postdoctoral studies, London Sch. Econs., 1947-48; D in Polit. Sci. (hon.), U. Helsinki, 1986; LLD (hon.), Harvard U.; PhD (hon.), Tel Aviv U.; LLD (hon.), Hebrew Union Coll., 1992. With Hebrew U. Jerusalem, 1946—, chmn. dept. sociology, 1951-69, Rose Isaacs prof. sociology, 1959—, dean Faculty Social Scis., The Eliezer Kaplan Sch. Econs., 1966-68; fellow Ctr. for Advanced Studies in Behavioral Scis., Stanford, Calif., 1955-56; vis. mem. London Sch. Econs., 1958; vis. prof. U. Oslo, 1958, U. Chgo., 1960, 71, 89-95, MIT, 1962-63, Harvard U., 1968-69, 75-81, U. Mich., 1970, U. Zurich, 1975, Stanford U., 1984, 86, 87, 88, 89, U. Wash., 1986; disting. vis. prof. U. Alberta, 1989, others; Tanner lectr. on human values U. Calif., 1989; fellow Netherlands Inst. for Advanced Study, Wassenaar, 1973; Simon vis. prof. U. Manchester, 1978; vis. fellow Australian Nat. U., 1978; rsch. fellow Hoover Inst., 1986-89; Max Weber vis. prof. U. Heidelberg, 1997; vis. prof. Erfurt U., 1998, 99. Author: The Absorption of Immigrants, 1955, 2d edit., 1978, From Generation to Generation, 1956, 2d edit., 1970, Essays on Sociological Aspects of Political and Economic Development, 1961, The Political Systems of Empires, 1963, 69, Modernization, Protest and Change, 1966, Israeli Society, 1968, Political Sociology of Modernization (Japanese), 1968, Tradition, Change and Modernity, 1975, (with M. Curelaru) The Form of Sociology, 1976, Revolution and the Transformation of Societies, 1973, (with L. Roniger) Patrons, Clients and Friends, 198, (with A. Shachar) Culture, Society and Urbanization, 1987, Transformation of Israeli Society, 1985, European Civilization in a Comparative Perspective, 1987; editor: Comparative Social Problems, 1964, The Decline of Empires, 1967, Comparative Perspectives on Social Change, Post-Traditional Societies, 1973, Origins and Diversity of Axial Age Civilizations, 1986, (with L. Roniger and A. Seligman) Centre Formation, Protest Movements and Class Structure in Europe and the U.S., 1987, Patterns of Modernity, 1987, (with M. Abitol and N. Chazan) The Early State in African Perspective, 1988, (with I. Silber) Knowledge and Society: Studies in the Sociology of Culture, Past and Present, 1988, Power, Trust and Meaning, 1995, Japanese Civilization-A Comparative View, 1996, Die Antinomien der Moderne: Die Jakobinischen Grundzuge der Moderne und des Fundamentalismus, 1998, Fundamentalism, Secretarianism and Revolution, 1999, Paradoxes of Democracy: Fragility Continuity and Change, 2000, other books in the field; contbr. numerous articles to profl. jours.; med. editl. bd. Comparative Studies in Soc. and History, Econ. Devel. and Cultural Change, Comparative Politics, Am. Behavioral Scientist, Comparative Polit. Studies, Youth and Soc., Jour. Polit. and Mil. Sociology, Civilizations, other profl. jours. Recipient Kaplun prize in Social Scis., 1969, Rothschild prize in Social Scis., 1970, Israel prize in Social Scis., 1973, Internat. Balzan prize, 1988, Max Planck Rsch. award, 1994; hon. fellow London Sch. Econs., 1988. Fellow Israel Soc. Assn. (hon.), Israel Soc. Soc., Open Univ. of Israel; mem. AAAS, NAS (fgn. assoc.), Am. Sociol. Assn. (McIver award 1964), Internat. Sociol. Assn. (coms. on polit. sociology, social stratification), Am. Philos. Soc., Inst. Comparative Civilizations (Brussels), Soc. for the Study of Internat. Problems (trustee Switzerland), Israel Acad. Scis. and Humanities, Israel Coun. Cmty. Rels. (chmn. 1960-64), Israeli Sociol. Assn. (pres. 1969-71). Office: The Hebrew U, Dept Sociology, Jerusalem Israel

EISENSTEIN, BARRY IRA, pharmaceutical executive; b. Bklyn., Feb. 14, 1948; s. David and Dorothy (Marcus) E.; m. Joyce Helene Kass, Aug. 31, 1969; children: Julie Kay, Matthew Adam. AB in Chemistry, Kenyon Coll., 1968; MD, Columbia U., 1972. Diplomate Am. Bd. Internal Medicine, Am. Bd. Infectious Diseases, NBME. Asst. prof. medicine U. Tenn. Ctr. for the Health Scis., Memphis, 1977-80, assoc. prof. medicine, 1980-82, assoc. prof. microbiology, 1981-82; assoc. prof. medicine, microbiology U. Tex. Health Sci. Ctr., San Antonio, 1982-86, chief div. infectious diseases, medicine, 1985-86, dir. molecular pathology tng. program, 1984-86; dir. molecular pathogenesis tng. program U. Mich., Ann Arbor, 1986-92; prof., chmn. microbiology, immunology and internal medicine U. Mich. Med. Sch., Ann Arbor, 1986-92; v.p. Lilly Rsch. Labs., Eli Lilly, Inpls., 1992-97; prof. medicine U. Ind. Sch. Medicine, 1992-97; v.p. sci. and tech. Beth Israel Deaconess Med. Ctr., Boston, 1996—; prof. medicine Harvard Med. Sch., 1997—; mem. exec. com. U. Mich. Med. Sch., Ann Arbor, 1989-92; mem. sci. adv. coun. Abbott Labs., Inc., Abbott Park, Ill., 1989-91; examiner microbiology Nat. Bd. Med. Examiners, Phila., 1990-91. Contbr. articles to profl. jours. Rsch. grantee NIH, 1975-92; recipient Rsch. Career Devel. award NIH, 1982-87, Clin. Investigator award NIH, 1979-82. Fellow ACP, Infectious Diseases Soc. Am., Am. Acad. Microbiology; mem. Am. Soc. for Microbiology (chmn. div. B 1988-89, rep. GPI div. 1992—), Am. Fedn. for Clin. Rsch., Cen. Soc. for Clin. Rsch., So. Soc. for Clin. Investigation, Am. Soc. for Clin. Investigation, Assn. Am. Physicians, Phi Beta Kappa, Sigma Xi. Home: 754 Newton St Chestnut Hill MA 02467-2606 Office: Beth Israel Deaconess Med Ctr 330 Brookline Ave Boston MA 02215-5400

EISER, ARNOLD ROBERT, internist, bioethicist; b. Newark, N.Y., Jan. 2, 1949; s. Harold H. and Anne Eiser; m. Barbara Joyce Andrews, June 15, 1975; 1 child, Arielle Veronica. BA magna cum laude, U. Pa., 1970; MD, Northwestern U., 1974. Intern Pa. Hosp., 1974-75; resident Med. Coll. Pa., 1975-77; fellow Hahnemann U., 1977-79; nephrologist Elmhurst (N.Y.) Hosp. Ctr., 1979-95, assoc. chief nephrology, 1993-95, dir. ambulatory care, 1995-97, dir. med. residency program, 1996-97; chief sect. gen. internal medicine U. Ill., Chgo., 1997—; prof. medicine U. Ill., 1997—; assoc. prof. medicine Mt. Sinai Sch. Medicine, N.Y.C., 1986-97; adj. assoc. Hastings Ctr., Briarcliff Manor, N.Y., 1994-98. Contbg. author: The Kidney in Collagen Vascular Diseases, 1993, Violence Against Women: Philosophical Perspective, 1998; contbr. articles to profl. jours. Fellow ACP, Inst. Medicine Chgo.; mem. Coll. Physician Execs., Soc. Gen. Internal Medicine. Avocations: reading, writing, travel, jogging. Fax: 312-413-8283. E-mail: aeiser@uic.edu. Office: MC 787 840 S Wood St Chicago IL 60612-7317

EISERER, LEONARD ALBERT CARL, publishing executive; b. Polar, Wis., June 3, 1916; s. Herman Frederick and Anna Elizabeth (Schnieder) E.; m. Lorraine Elizabeth Hickey, June 28, 1941; children: Carol Jean, Elaine Roberta, Leonard Arnold, Beverly Arlene. B.A., Roosevelt U., Chgo., 1937; M.S. in Journalism, Northwestern U., 1939. Editor Am. Aviation Publs., Inc., Washington, 1939-51, v.p., gen. mgr., 1952-57, exec. v.p., sec., 1958-62; pres., pub. Sports Age, Inc., Washington, 1962-63; chmn., CEO Bus. Pubs., Inc., Silver Spring, Md., 1963—. Chmn. Carol Jean Cancer Found., Inc.; bd. dirs. U. N.C. at Greensboro Excellence Found.; pres., dir. Eiserer-Hickey Found., Inc.; dir. Univ. Club of Washington Found. Lt. USN, 1942-46. Named to Hall of Fame Newsletter Pubs. Found., 1994, Man of Yr. Univ. Club of Washington, 1995; inductee Hall of Achievement, Northwestern U. Medill Sch. Journalism, 1997. Mem. Air and Waste Mgmt. Assn., Water Environ. Fedn., Soc. Profl. Journalists, Nat. Press Club, Univ. Club, Newsletter Pubs. Assn. Home: 9101 Sligo Creek Pky Silver Spring MD 20901-3360 Office: Bus Pubs Inc 951 Pershing Dr Silver Spring MD 20910-4400

EISERMANN, WALTER FRIEDRICH, education educator; b. Hamburg, Germany, Apr. 5, 1922; s. August Emil and Auguste Helene (Nackenhorst) E.; m. Ortrud Witschko, Mar. 26, 1958, (div. 1987); children: Lorenz, Gundolf. PhD, U. Tuebingen, Fed. Republic Germany, 1958. Tchr. secondary pub. schs., Hamburg, 1958-60; docent Tchrs.' Coll., Stuttgart, Fed. Republic Germany, 1960-64; prof. of pedagogics Low Saxony Coll. Edn., Braunschweig, Fed. Republic Germany, 1964-78; prof. of pedagogics Tech. U., Braunschweig, Fed. Republic Germany, 1978-89, emeritus, 1989; vice-dean Coll. Edn., Braunschweig, 1965; cons. Ministry Edn., Low Saxony, 1967-70. Author: Ueber die Moeglichkeit einer Gewissenserziehung, 1958; editor: Eduard Spranger: Psychologie und Menschenbildung, 1974; co-editor Massstaebe-Perspektiven des Denkens von Eduard Spranger, Eduard Spranger: Gesammelte Schriften, 1969-80; contbr. articles to profl. jours. With German mil. 1941-45. Mem. Internat. Acad. Humanization of Edn., 1995, N.Y. Acad. Scis., 1996. Home: Tiergarten 95, D-38116 Braunschweig Federal Republic of Germany

EISHINKII, ALEXANDR MOISEEVICH, mathematician, researcher; b. Dnepropetrovsk, Ukraine, Oct. 1, 1936; s. Moisei Isaacovich and Elizaveta Aronovna (Ginzburg) E.; divorced. Student, Moscow State U., 1967, Poly. Inst., Krasnodar, Russia, 1969. Rschr. State U., Dnepropetrovsk, Ukraine, 1970-74; tchr. Ednl. Sch., Dnepropetrovsk, Ukraine, 1974-83; rschr. Nat. Mining U., Dnepropetrovsk, Ukraine, 1983-2000. Contbr. over 200 articles to profl. jours. Mem. Internat. Acad. Ecology and Life Protection Scis., N.Y. Acad. Scis. Avocations: poetry, theatre, classical music, classical literature, collecting books. Home: Serova 3 Str Apt 7, 49000 Dnepropetrovsk Ukraine

EISLER, DAVID LEE, provost; m. Patricia Johnson; children: Heather, Lindsay. BM high distinction, Univ. Mich., 1972; MM summa cum laude, Yale Univ., 1975; DMA high distinction, Univ. Mich., 1978. Mem. faculty Weber State Univ., Ogden, Utah, 1975-78; coord. instrumental music Troy State, 1978-90, exec. dir. southeast band clinic, 1979-90, dir., grad. studies, 1980-90, asst. dean. of fine arts, 1982-90; dean. coll. fine arts Eastern New Mex., 1990-96; provost Weber State Univ., Ogden, Utah, 1996—; faculty Troy State U., 1975-90; host Strike up the Band on NPR, 1979-90, clinician and cons., G. Leblanc Corp., 1984-96, concert soloist, recitalist; conductor Fla. Jr. H.S. All State Band, 1989; grants evaluator, panelist N.Mex. Arts Divsn.; cons. TLT Group, 1998—; steering com. Utah Edn. Network, 1998—. Contbr. articles to profl. jours. Judge Nat. Assn. Music Edn.; founding mem. High Plains Art Coun., exec.bd. Conquistador Coun., Boy Scouts Am. Named Vol. of Yr. Cmty. Svcs. Ctr., 1993-94, WSU Exemplary Collaboration Awd., 1999. Mem. Am. Assn. Higher Edn., Rotary Internatl., Pi Kappa Lambda, Kappa Kappa Psi, Phi Mu Alpha, Tau Beta Sigma, Phi Kappa Phi. Office: Weber State Univ 1004 University Cir Ogden UT 84408-1004

EISNER, MICHAEL DAMMANN, entertainment company executive; b. Mt. Kisco, N.Y., Mar. 7, 1942; s. Lester and Margaret (Dammann) E.; m. Jane Breckenridge; children: Breck, Eric, Anders. BA, Denison U., 1964. Began career in programming dept. CBS; asst. to nat. programming dir. ABC, 1966-68, mgr. spls. and talent, dir. program devel.-East Coast, 1968-71, dir. program devel. East Coast, 1968-71; dir. feature films and program devel. ABC, $D, $D, 1969; v.p. daytime programming ABC, 1971-75, v.p. program planning and devel., 1975-76, sr. v.p. prime time prodn. and devel., 1976; pres., chief operating officer Paramount Pictures, 1976-84; chmn., chief exec. officer Walt Disney Co., Burbank, Calif., 1984—; governor Mighty Ducks of Anaheim, 1993. Trustee Denison U., Calif. Inst. Arts; bd. dirs. Am. Hosp. of Paris Found., Conservation Internat., UCLA Exec. Bd. for Med. Sci. Office: Walt Disney Co 500 S Buena Vista St Burbank CA 91521-0006

EISTRUP, CARL, toxicologist, researcher; b. Copenhagen, Oct. 28, 1949; s. Frode H. and Ruth (Hansen) E.; m. Kirsten H. Soerensen, Jan. 21, 1979; children: Christian, Astrid. DVM, U. Copenhagen, 1979. Registered toxicologist, Eng. Pvt. practice vet. Slagelse, Denmark, 1979-80, 81-84; cons. Leo Pharms., Copenhagen, 1980-81; sr. toxicologist Novo Industries, Copenhagen, 1984-95; mgr., rsch. scientist Novo Nordisk, Copenhagen, 1995—. Contbr. articles to profl. jours. Lutheran. Avocations: hunting, dog training. Home: Rungstedvej 10, 2970 Hørsholm Denmark Office: Novo Nordisk, Novo Nordisk Park, 2760 Maaloev Denmark

EITAN, RAPHAEL, chemical company executive; b. Israel, Nov. 23, 1926; s. Noach Hantman; m. Miriam Lutzansky; children: Yael, Sharon, Yuval. BSC in Economics, U. London, 1958. With Israeli Intelligence Cmty., 1960's-70's; advisor to prime minister Prime Minister's Office, Israel, 1976-80; advisor to Minister of Defense, Israel, 1980-85; chmn. bd. dirs. ICL, Tel Aviv, 1986-93, GBM, Inc. U.K., Givataim, Israel, 1993—. Office: Reesimex Inc, 24 Habarzel St, 69710 Tel Aviv Israel

EIZENSTAT, STUART E., ambassador, lawyer; b. Chgo., Jan. 15, 1943; m. Fran Eizenstat; children: Jay, Brian. AB cum laude, U. N.C., 1964; LLB, Harvard U., 1967; LLD (hon.), Yeshiva U., 1998, Weizmann Inst. Sci., 1999, U. N.C., 2000, Jewish Theol. Sem., 2000, Hebrew Coll., 2000. Bar: Ga. 1967, D.C. 1981. Mem. White House staff, 1967-68; mem. nat. campaign staff Hubert H. Humphrey, 1968; law clk. U.S. Dist. Ct. No. Dist. Ga., 1968-70; ptnr. Powell, Goldstein, Frazer & Murphy, Washington, 1970-77, 81-93, vice chmn., 1991-93; asst. to Pres. U.S. for domestic affairs and policy, 77-81, dir. White House Domestic Policy Staff, 1977-81; amb. to European Union Brussels, 1993-96; spl. envoy Dept. State Property Claims in Ctrl. Europe, 1995—; undersec. for internat. trade Dept. Commerce, Washington, 1996-97; envoy Pres. of U.S. for Promotion of Democracy in Cuba, 1996-97; undersec. of state for econ., bus. and agrl. affairs Dept. Commerce, Washington, 1997-99; alt. gov. World Bank, 1998-99, Regional Devel. Banks, 1998-99; dep. sec. Dept. Treasury, 1999—; spl. rep. of Pres. and Sec. of State on Holocaust Issues, 1999—; adj. lectr. J.F. Kennedy Sch. Govt., Harvard U., 1981-92; guest scholar Brookings Inst., Washington, 1981; mem. Energy Coord. Coun., Econ. Policy Group, 1977-81, Pres. Bush task force on U.S. Internat. Broadcasting, 1991; head U.S. del. CSCE Econ. Forum, 1994; lectr. coll., bus. and civic groups. Co-author: Andrew Young: The Path to History, 1973;Environmental Auditing Handbook, 1984; co-editor: The American Agenda: Report to the 41st President of the United States, 1988, reprint, 1989; contbr. articles to profl. jours. and newspapers. Vice-pres. Jewish Publ. Soc., 1981-85; chmn. Inst. U.S. Jewish-Israeli Relations, 1982-86; bd. dirs. Woodrow Wilson Center for Internat. Scholars, 1978-87, Jerusalem Found., 1992-93, Eurasia Found., 1993; pres. Greater Washington Jewish Community Ctr., 1989-91; mem. exec. com. Ctr. for Dem. Policy, 1982-93; bd. visitors U. N.C., Chapel Hill, 1987-90; co-dir. The American Agenda (with Pres. Ford and Pres. Carter), 1991; trustee Jerusalem Inst. Mgmt., 1987-93; mem. coun. Harvard Law Sch. Assn., 1988-92, Gov.'s Commn. on Fed. Funding, Commonwealth of Va., 1986, Com. on Federalism and Nat. Purpose, 1984-85; chmn. Econ. and Budget Strategy Com., Montgomery County Coun., 1986; v.p., bd. dirs. Am. Assocs., Ben-Gurion U. of the Negev. N.Y.C., 1981-89; trustee Washington Inst. for Jewish Leadership and Values, 1988—, Brandeis U., 1991—; commr. Commn. on Jewish Edn. in N.Am., 1988-90; v.p. Atlanta Bur. Jewish Edn., 1973-76; mem. exec. com. Atlanta Jewish Community Center, 1970-76; mem. B'nai Brith Youth Commn., Washington, 1981-82; bd. dirs. United Synagogues Am., 1981-84.; internat. bd. dir. Weizmann Inst., 1989-93; active in Dem. party and political campaigns. Recipient Man of Yr. award Nat. Capital Assn., State Dept. award for Public Svs., 1996. B'nai B'rith Lodges, 1982, Outstanding Svc. to Summer Youth Program U.S. Dept. Labor, 1980, Outstanding Svc. award Hebrew Aid Immigration Soc., 1980, Outstanding Svc. award Opportunities Industrialization Ctrs., 1979, award Washington Internat. Bus. Coun., 1978, award Nat. Coalition Involved People, 1977, Young Man of Yr. award Am. Assn. Jewish Edn., 1973-74, Leadership award Acad. Jewish Religion, 1989, Tree of Life award Hadassah, Boston, 1989, Myrtle Wreath award Fla. Atlantic Region Hadassah, 1991, Benjamin Cardozo Professionalism award Atlanta Jewish Fedn., 1992, Export Finance award Coalition for Employment Through Exports, 1993, award for pub. svc. Sec. of State, 1996, Moral Statesman award Anti-Defamation League, 1997, Phillip Klutznick B'Nai B'Rith award for Outstanding Pub. Svc., 1996, award for transatlantic svc. European Inst., 1997, Myrtle Wreath award Hadassah, 1997, 98, Transatlantic Svc. award European Inst., 1997, award for courage and conscience Israeli Knesset, 1998, Leadership award Sec. of State, 1999. Fellow Nat. Acad. Pub. Adminstn., Ctr. for Excellence in Govt.; mem. ABA (spl. com. on lawyers in govt., mem. com. govt. standards 1992-93), Atlanta Bar Assn., D.C. Bar Assn., Ga. Bar Assn., U.S. C. of C. (Internat. Policy Com. 1982-89), Nat. Fgn. Trade Coun. (Internat. Trade Comm.), Washington Policy Coun. (Internat. Mgmt. and Devel. Inst.), Phi Beta Kappa, Phi Eta Sigma. Democrat. Jewish. Home: 9107 Brierly Rd Chevy Chase MD 20815-5654 Office: US Dept Treasury 15 Pennsylvania Ave NW Washington DC 20220-0001

EJERCITO, NAPOLEON CAMPOS, otolaryngologist; b. Manila, Oct. 30, 1921; s. Fortunato Monzon and Concepcion (Campos) E.; m. Felicitacion Paz Santos, Apr. 20, 1945 (dec.); children: Eleonora, Victor, Robert, Barbara. MD, U. of The Philippines, 1945. Diplomate Am. Bd. Otolaryngology-Head and Neck Surgery. Jr. malariologist USPHS, The Philippines, 1946-50; physician Dept. of Health, The Philippines, 1950-52; prof. Coll. Medicine U. of The Philippines, 1956-86; otolaryngologist Cancer Inst., 1957-86; pvt. practice otolaryngology-head and neck surgery, ret., 1986; otolaryngology cons. USAF Clark Field Air Base, The Philippines, 1961-67. Contbr. articles to med. jours. Named to Hall of Fame, Philippine Soc. Otolaryngology. Mem. Philippine Bd. Otolaryngology-Head and Neck Surgery (sr. advisor 1995—, founder, incorporator, 1st pres.), Philippine Soc. Otolaryngology-Head and Neck Surgery (founding mem., past pres.). Office: Marshfield Clinic 1000 N Oak Ave Marshfield WI 54449-5703

EJIRI, TAKASHI, lawyer; b. Ichikawa, Chiba, Japan, May 16, 1942; s. Heihachiro and Yaeko (Amemiya) E.; m. Ikuko Nakabe, Nov. 3, 1968; children: Masataka, Takeaki. LLB, Tokyo U., 1967; LLM, Harvard U., 1970. With Sonda & Takahashi, Tokyo, 1969, Dune, Morris & Heksher, Phila., 1970, Anderson & Martin, N.Y.C., 1971, Anderson, Mori % Rabinovitz, Tokyo, 1971-77; co-founder Masuda & Ejiri, Tokyo, 1977-93; prin. Asahi Law Offices, 1993—; mem. Trilateral Commn., 1998—. Mem. Japan Fedn. of Bar Assn. (vice chmn. internat. rels. com. 1986-94), Inter Pacific Bar Assn. (sec. gen. 1995-99), Tokyo Bar Assn. Avocation: fishing. Office: New ATT Bldg, 2-11-7, 107 Minato Tokyo, Japan

EJITUWU, NKPAROM CLAUDE, history educator, researcher; b. Ikuru Town, Andoni, Nigeria, Nov. 19, 1940; s. Campbell Claude and Evelyn Kalaruba (Odiari) E.; m. Eugeniah Nne Akpa, June 15, 1974; children: Ugbana, Campbell, Ataisi, Ejituwu Jr. BA, Yankton (S.D.) Coll., 1969; MA, U. Wis., 1971; PhD, U. Lagos, Nigeria, 1977. Clk. Civil Svc., Calabar, Nigeria, 1960-66; lectr. U. Lagos, Nigeria, 1973-79; commr. Civil Svc. Commn., Rivers State, Nigeria, 1979-81, chmn., 1982-84; head history dept. U. Port Harcourt, Nigeria, 1986-95, prof., 1994—; dir. Coll. of Continuing Edn., 1998—; mem. governing coun. Rivers State Coll Edn., 1988-92, U. Sci. and Tech., 1992-94. Author: (book) A History of Obolo (Andoni) in the Niger Delta, 1991, The Multi-Disciplinary Approach to aFrican History, 1998; contbr. chpt. in book, articles in profl. jours. Chmn. Andoni Chieftancy Com., 1978, Unification Com., Andoni, 1988, Andoni Progressive Union, 1989—; mem. Nigerian Field Soc., 1988—, Nat. Boundary Commn., 1992—. Named Patron Club 2-1 Nigeria, Port Harcourt, 1985, Honorary Vis. Scholar USIA, 1995. Mem. Hist. Soc. Nigeria (coun. 1988—, pres. Port Harcourt br. 1993—), Am. Studies Assn. Nigeria (asst. sec. 1989-95). Anglican. Avocations: bird watching, water-gazing, fishing, tennis, nature watching. Home: U Port Harcourt, 10 Ali Cape Verde, Rivers State Port Harcourt Nigeria Office: Dept History, U Port Harcourt, Rivers State Port Harcourt Nigeria

EJZENBERG, BERNARDO, pediatrician, educator, researcher; b. Curitiba, Parana, Brazil, Apr. 26, 1951; s. Israel Majer and Helena (Zugman) E.; m. Vania Tyschler, June 20, 1975; children: Dani, Priscila. Diploma in medicine, U. São Paulo, Brazil, 1974, M in Pediat., 1985, PhD in Pediat., 1990. Resident Clinicas Hosp. U. São Paulo, 1975-76, instr., preceptor dept. pediat., 1977, prof. dept. pediat., 1978—; supr. emergency svcs. Clinicas Hosp. U. São Paulo, 1980-89, med. chief pediat. ward, 1990-92, coord. rsch. and pub. Univ. Hosp., 1993—; program head, prof. pediat. pneumology postgrad. program Santa Casa Med. Sch., 1996—; vis. prof. dept. pediat. Itajuba Sch. Medicine, Minas Gerais, Brazil, 1976-85; consulting auditor, mem. fin. com., consulting mem. rsch. and ethics com. Children's Inst. São Paulo, 1990—; nat. cons. for antiinfective therapy Roche Labs., Brazil, 1993-98; directive mem. pediat. divsn. Univ. Hosp. U. São Paulo, 1993—; spkr., presenter in field. Contbr. articles to profl. jours.; mem. editl. bd. Pediatria Jour., 1996—, Rev. Paul. Pediatria. Vol. prof. and cons. for betterment of pub. hosps. in São Paulo mcpl. area, 1976—; advisor Pedro de Alcantara Found., 1980—; cons. St. Agustin Found. and Orgn., 1976-90; contbg. mem. Congregacao Israelita Paulista, Rabbi Morguenstein Synagogue, Peretz Sch. Mem. AAAS, Brazilian Med. Assn., Brazilian Pediat. Soc. (named hon. Pediat. Pulmonologist 1996), São Paulo Pediat. Soc. (mem. editl. bd.), N.Y. Acad. Scis. Jewish. Avocations: gardening, family outings, walking, participating in Jewish cultural events. Home: Ave Min Gabriel Resende Passos, 267 Apt 121, 04521-021 São Paulo Brazil Office: U São Paulo Hosp Univ, Av Linneu Prestes 2565, 05508-90 São Paulo Brazil

EKAMBARAM, RAJASEKARAN, chemist, researcher; b. Thanjavur, Tamilnadu, India, Nov. 5, 1966; s. Ekambaram and Muthulaxmi. BSc, A. Veeriya Vandayar Meml. Sri Pushpam Coll., Thanjavur, India, 1987; MSc, Nat. Coll., Trichy, India, 1989; PhD, Indian Inst. Tech., New Delhi, 1995. Rsch. fellow Bharathidasan U., Trichy, 1989-90, Indian Inst. Tech., 1991-95; postdoctoral fellow U. Nebr., Lincoln, 1996—. Inventor in field. Home: Umbalapadi-Post, Tamil Nadu Chennai 614203, India

EKANEM, ETOK OKON, food science educator; b. Nkim Itam, Itu Akwa Ibom, Nigeria, Dec. 1, 1959; s. Okon Akpan and Affiong Okon (Idiong) E.; m. Dorathy Etok Dickson, Sept. 15, 1990; children: Ime-Otobong, Akanubong, Enomfon. BSc in Agr., U. Maiduguri, Nigeria, 1984; MSc in Food Tech., U. Ibadan, Nigeria, 1990; PhD in Food Tech., U. Sci. & Tech., Port-Harcourt, Nigeria, 1998. Agrl. officer Agrl. Devel. Corp., Ilorin, Nigeria, 1984-85; tchg. asst. U. Cross River State, Uyo, Nigeria, 1986-90, asst. lectr., 1990-91; lectr. U. Uyo, Nigeria, 1992-96, sr. lectr., 1997—; resource person Agrl. Devel. Project, Uyo, 1996—; environ. cons. Shell Petroleum Co., Port-Harcourt, 1997-98, Mobil Producing Unlimited, Lagos, Nigeria, 1998, Akwa Ibom State Govt., Uyo, 1998. Contbr. articles to profl. jours. Treas. Nkim Itam Village Coun., Itu, Nigeria, 1994-97; sec. acad. staff union univs. U. Uyo, 1997—. Govt. scholar Nigeria, 1988-89. Mem. Nigerian Inst. Food Sci. & Tech. (chpt. sec. 1995-99), Nigerian Soc. Animal Prodn., N.Y. Acad. Sci., U. Ibadan Alumni Assn. (treas. 1991—). Mem. Peoples Dem. Party. Presbyterian. Avocations: travelling, hunting, fishing, dancing, music. Home: No. 9 Ibanga St, Uyo Nigeria Office: U Uyo, Faculty Agr, 1017 Uyo Nigeria

EKBLAD, ULF STAFFAN, physicist, researcher; b. Stockholm, Sweden, June 5, 1953; s. Ernst Lennart and Hanna Lena (Vennerberg) E. BS in Math. and Physics, U. Stockholm, 1977. Scientist Def. Rsch. Establishment, Linkoping, Sweden, 1985-88; sr. scientist Def. Rsch. Establishment, Linkoping, 1988—; expert to Ministry of Fgn. Affairs, Sweden, 1990-93; asst. attache Swedish Embassy, Paris, 1994; mem. Def. Satellite Comm. Panel, 1995—. Contbr. articles to profl. jours. French Ministry of Fgn. Rels. scholar, 1982. Mem. Swedish Napoleonic Soc. (sec. 1997—), Alliance Française (auditor 1996-2000, com. mem. 2000—). Avocations: languages, history, philosophy, genealogy. Office: Def Rsch Establishment, PO Box 1165, 581 11 Linköping Sweden

EKBLADH, DAVID KARL FRANCIS, historian, researcher; b. Chapel Hill, N.C., Oct. 5, 1972; s. Lamar Erik Valentin and Anita Burger Ekbladh. BA, Am. U., 1994; MA, Columbia U., 1997, MPhil, 1998. Program technician Nat. Archives, Washington, 1993-94; archivist Del. Pub. Archives, Dover, 1995; rsch. asst. Carnegie Commn. on Prevention Deadly Conflict, N.Y.C., 1996-99, rsch. assoc., 1999—; script advisor Fox TV Not Just News, Washington, 1994-95. Organizer Alternative Spring Break, N.Y.C., 1998-2000; advisor Cmty. Impact, Columbia U., N.Y.C., 1998-2000. Fellow East Asian Inst. Columbia U. (rsch. fellow); mem. Am. Hist. Assn., Orgn. Am. Historians, Assn. for Asian Studies, Phi Alpha Theta. Avocations: swimming, squash, skiing, reading, hiking. E-mail: dke2@columbia.edu.

EKBOM, KARL EDVARD, neurologist; b. Stockholm, Oct. 28, 1935; s. Karl-Axel and Hedvig Charlotta (Stalhane) E.; m. Christina Ingrid Bergnas, June 18, 1960; children: Karl-Johan, Anders, Tomas, Helena. MD, PhD, Karolinska Inst., Stockholm, 1970; MEd, Karolinska Inst., 1974. Resident in internal medicine Soder Hosp., Stockholm, 1962-65; resident in neurology Karolinska Hosp., Stockholm, 1965-71; asst. cons. neurology Soder Hosp., Stockholm, 1972-78; head dept. neurology Soder Hosp., 1978-96; cons. dept. neurology Huddinge (Sweden) U. Hosp., 1997—. Editor: Migraine in General Practice, 1993; contbr. articles to profl. jours. Mem. Swedish Med. Soc., Internat. Headache Soc. (bd. dirs. 1987-93), World Fedn. Neurology (bd. dirs. rsch. group 1972—), Swedish Migraine Soc. (sec. 1968-88, chmn. 1989-95), Swedish Neurol. Soc. (chmn. 1980-82), European Headache Fedn. (v.p. 1992-94). Avocations: music, literature, photography. Home: Martinvagen 9, S-16850 Bromma Sweden Office: Huddinge U Hosp, Dept Neurology, S-14186 Huddinge Sweden

EKDAHL, KARL GUSTAF, medical officer, educator; b. Lund, Sweden, June 26, 1959; m. Cecilia Cardell; children: Victor, Eric. MD, Lund U., 1986, PhD, 1995; diploma in tropical medicine and hygiene, Mahidol U., Bangkok, 1993. Cert. specialist of infectious diseases Swedish Bd. Health and Welfare. Physician Kristianstad Hosp., Sweden, 1986-89; registrar Lund U. Hosp., 1989-93, sr. registrar, 1993-96, cons. infectious diseases specialist, 1993-98; communicable diseases control officer Malmö (Sweden) U. Hosp., 1996-98; chief med. officer Swedish Inst. for Infectious Disease Control

Karolinska Inst., Stockholm, 1998—, program mgr. for infectious disease control in Baltic region, 1998—, assoc. prof., 1999; referee Scandinavian Jour. Infectious Diseases, 1996—. Author: Recurrent Pheumonia, 1993, Complement Analysis in Patients with Bacteremic Pneumococcal Infections, 1995, Hepatitis B Variants in Chronic Carriers, 1995, Penicillin-resistant pneumococci, 1998; editor Smittstydd, 1999—, EpiNorth, 1999—; mem. editl. bd. Microbial Drug Resistance, 1999—, Eurosurveillance, 1999—. Recipient award Swedish Soc. Infectious Diseases, 1991, South Swedish Soc. Infectious Diseases, 1992; grantee Royal Physiographic Soc., 1993. Fellow Swedish Soc. Medicine (award 1997); mem. Swedish Med. Assn., European Soc. Immunodeficiencies. E-mail: karl.ekdahl@mtc.ki.se. Office: Karolinska Inst, Swedish Inst Inf Dis Contrl, SE-17182 Solna Sweden

EKDAWI, NAGI, chemist, researcher; b. Giza, Cairo, Egypt, Aug. 6, 1960; s. Kamel and Marcelle (Abd El Malik) E.; m. Suzette Ekdawi, July 12, 1988; 1 child, Ann-Marie. BSc with honors, U. Sydney, Australia, 1984, MSc, 1985. arrived in Australia, 1970;. Chemistry tutor U. Sydney, 1982-84; R&D chemist Berger and Brit. Paints, Sydney, 1984-88; product devel. engr. MM Cables, Sydney, 1988-90; sr. materials engr. Alcatel, Sydney, 1990-92; sr. scientist G.E.C. Marconi, Sydney, 1992-94; scientist new product devel. C.S.R., Sydney, 1994—; referee Jour. Colloids and Surfaces, Sydney, 1986-87; bus. mgr. Pobanco Paints, Sydney, 1988-90; bus. dir. Colour Brite Coatings, Sydney, 1990-91. Contbr. articles to profl. jours. Justice of Peace, Atty. Gen.'s Dept., New S. Wales, 1989—; supr. for underprivileged children, Liverpool, 1989-93; advisor and com. mem, Tech. and further edn. system, Liverpool, 1989-92. Mem. Liberal party. Coptic Orthodox Christian. Avocations: riding horses, swimming, squash. Home: 19 Strawberry Rd, NSW Casula NSW 2170, Australia Office: CSR Rsch Ctr, 376 Victoria St, NSW Wetherill Park 2164, Australia

EKEL, PETR YAKOV, electrical engineer, educator; b. Kiev, Ukraine, Sept. 27, 1950; s. Yakov Petr Ekel and Tsilia Yakov Matusovskaya; m. Valentina Valentin Shlikhta, July 31, 1971; children: Anatoliy, Marianna. MSEE with honors, Kiev Poly. Inst., 1973, PhD, 1981; DSc, Coun. Mins. USSR, Moscow, 1990. Cert. sr. rschr. and full prof. Higher Certifying Commn., Coun. Mins. USSR, Moscow. Engr. Kiev Poly. Inst., 1973-74, jr. rschr., 1974-76, sr. rschr., 1976-86, assoc. prof., 1986-90, full prof. Nat. Tech. U. of the Ukraine, 1990—; head lab. for modeling and optimization electric power and engring. sys. Rsch. Inst. Automation and Energetics, Kiev, 1991-93; assoc. prof. Pontifical Cath. U. Minas Gerais, Belo Horizonte, Brazil, 1998-99, full prof., 1999—; vice head, acting head energy dept. Ukrainian Acad. Engring. Scis., Kiev, 1991-93; cons. Parana State Energy Co., Curitiba, Parana, Brazil, 1997—. Author: Models and Methods of Optimizing and Controlling Modes of Operation of Power Supply Systems, 1994; contbr. articles to profl. jours. Mem. organizing com. Ukrainian Jewish Congress, Kiev, 1992. Grantee Nat. Coun. for Sci. and Technol. Devel., Fed. U. Santa Maria/Rio Grande do Sul, Brazil, 1993-95, Minas Gerais Found. for Rsch. Support, Belo Horizonte, Pontifical Cath. U. Minas Gerais, 1997-98. Mem. Ukrainian Acad. Engring. Scis., N.Am. Fuzzy Info. Processing Soc. Achievements include patent for the mode of power consumption control of an enterprise. Avocations: philately, reading, swimming. E-mail: ekel@pucminas.br. Fax: 55 31 3194225. Home: Apt 302, Rua Carioca 675, 30730420 Belo Horizonte MG, Brazil Office: Pontifical Cath U MG, Ave Dom Jose Gaspar 500, 30535610 Belo Horizonte MG, Brazil

EKE-OKORO, SUNDAY THEOPHILUS, medical educator; b. Arochukwu, Abia, Nigeria, Nov. 11, 1945; came to U.S., 1996; s. Eke-Okoro and Lydia Nnennaya Agwu; m. Stella Mgbeke Okoroafor, Apr. 25, 1981; children: Chukwuemeka, Odinakachi, Onyekachi, Chizorom. BSc, U. Ibadan, Nigeria, 1975; MSc, Simon Fraser U., Burnaby, B.C., Can., 1979; D in Med. Sci., U. Linkoping, Sweden, 1985. Cert. Nigerian Bd. Rehab. and Therapists. Assoc. prof., chmn. dept. med. rehab. Coll. Medicine, U. Nigeria, Enugu, 1986-96; rsch. fellow Inst. for Disability Prevention and Wellness U. Medicine and Dentistry N.J., Stratford, 1996—. Contbr. articles to profl. jours. mem. AIDS Rsch. Com. South Jersey, Voorhees, 1997-99; sec. South Jersey Men's Bible Study Fellowship, Sicklerville, 1998-99; trustee Solomon Wesley United Meth. Ch., Blackwood, 1999. Mem. N.Y. Acad. Scis. Avocations: tennis, writing. E-mail: ekeokoro@bellatlantic.net and ekeokost@umdnj.edu. Fax: 856-566-6397. Home: #H-14 1501 Little Gloucester Rd Blackwood NJ 08102 Office: U Medicine & Dentistry NJ Laurel Rd Stratford NJ 08084

EKESBO, INGVAR ANDERS GUSTAF, science educator; b. Otterstad, Sweden, Dec. 3, 1928; s. Karl-Ivar and Stina (Johansson) Andersson; m. Irma I.M. Larsson, 1952; children: Karin, Hakan, Eva. DVM, Royal Vet. Coll., Sweden, 1955, PhD, 1966; Dr honoris causa, U. Zurich, 1987, U. Riga, 1998. Vet. Nat. Vet. Bd., Sweden, 1955-70; prof. Royal Vet. Coll., Sweden, 1970-77; prof. Swedish U. Agrl. Sci., 1977-93, prof. emeritus, 1993—; hon. assoc. Royal Coll. of Vet. Surgeons, London, 1999; dept. head Swedish U. Agrl. Sci., 1977-93. Contbr. 200 articles to profl. jours. Recipient Justusvon Leibig prize Kiel U., 1975. Mem. Internat. Soc. Applied Ethology (hon.), Internat. Soc. Animal Hygiene (hon.). Office: Swedish U Agrl Sci, Swedish U Agrl Sci, Veterinargatan, 53223 Skara Sweden

EKEUS, ROLF CARL, diplomat; b. Kristinehamn, Sweden, July 7, 1935; s. Axel Erik Eriksson and Margit Carolina Johansson; m. Christina Kerstin Oldfelt, 1970; children: Carolina, Cecilia, Helena, Oscar, Carl, Henrik. LLB, U. Stockholm, 1959; LLD, Calif. Luth. U., 1999. Asst. judge Karlstad Dist. Ct., Sweden, 1959-62; 2d sec./1st sec., counselor Swedish Fgn. Svc., various locations, 1962-83; ambassador Conf. on Disarmament, Geneva, 1983-89, Conf. Security and Cooperation in Europe, Vienna, Austria, 1989-93; exec. chmn. UN Spl. Commn. on Iraq, 1991-97; ambassador Swedish Embassy, Washington, 1997—; chmn. Stockholm Internat. Peace Rsch. Inst., 2000—; chmn. com. on chem. weapons Conf. Disarmament, Geneva, 1984, 87; mem. adv. bd. UN Sec. Gen. on Disarmament, N.Y.C., 1999—; mem. adv. bd. Ctr. on Non-Proliferation, Monterey (Calif.) Inst., 1997—, Ctr. on violence and Human Survival, John Jay Coll. Criminal Justice, N.Y., 1997—. Mem. Canberra (Australia) Commn. on Elimination of Nuclear Weapons, 1997—, Tokyo Forum on Non-Proliferation and Disarmament, 1998—, Eminent Persons Group on Curbing Illicit Trafficking in Small Guns, 1999—. Recipient Wateler Peace prize Carnegie Found., 1997, Pro Merito award Ordre Souverain et Militaire du Temple de Jerusalem, 1998, Disting. Pub. Svc. award Am. Jewish Com., 1998. Office: Embassy of Sweden 1501 M St NW Ste 900 Washington DC 20005-1701

EKHAISE, OSARO FREDERICK, microbiologist; b. Iguobazuwa, Edo State, Nigeria, Apr. 16, 1967; s. Udo Simeon and Asonmwonotiti Victoria (Oronsaye) E.; m. Ikponmwosa Bridget Imafidon, Oct. 3, 1995; 1 child. BS with honors, U. Benin, Benin City, Nigeria, 1990, MS, 1992; PhD, U. Bayreuth, Germany, 2000. Microbiologist Chiwendu Hosp., Nbansi, Nigeria, 1990-91; asst. lectr., microbiologist U. Benin, Benin City, 1994-95. Contbr. articles to profl. jours. With nat. svc. Nat. Youth Svc. Corps., Nigeria, 1989-90. German scholar German Acad. Austauschdienst, 1995; recipient award Nigerian Breweries, 1989. Mem. Nigerian Soc. Microbiology, Am. Soc. Microbiology. Avocations: sports, travel, reading. Home: Albrecth Dürer Str 18, Bayreuth Bavaria, Germany Office: U Bayreuth Lehrstul Microbi, Universitätstr 30, 95440 Bayreuth Bavaria, Germany

EKICI, SYNAN, physician; b. Kirsehir, Turkey, Nov. 10, 1970; s. Kenan and Gülüzar Ekici. MD, Hacettepe U., Ankara, Turkey, 1995. Intern Hacettepe U., Ankara, 1994, resident in urology, 1995, chief resident in urology, 1999, specialist in urology, 2000. E-mail: ekicisg@hotmail.com. Home: Dikmen Caddesi, Dikmen Yildizi Sokagi 26/6, 06450 Ankara Turkey Office: Hacettepe U, Sihhiye, 06100 Ankara Turkey

É KISS, KATALIN, linguist, researcher; b. Debrecen, Hungary, May 31, 1949; d. Sándor É Kiss and Juliánna Égerházi; m. Tamás Zétényi, Nov. 6, 1981; children: András, Tamás, Zsófia. MA, Kossuth L. U., Debrecen, 1973; PhD, Hungarian Acad. Scis., Budapest, 1979, D of Habilitation, 1987. Lectr. Kossuth L. U., 1972-79; sr. rschr. Linguistic Inst., Hungarian Acad. Scis., 1986-87, sci. counsellor Linguisic Inst.,, 1988—; assoc. prof. Eötvös L. U., Budapest, 1980-86; prof. Eötvös L. U., 1995—. Author: Configurationality in Hungarian, 1987; contbr. articles to profl. jours.; editor, co-author: The Syntactic Structure of Hungarian, 1994, Discourse-Configurational Languages, 1995. Recipient New Europe prize Ctrs. Advanced Studies, Princeton, N.J., 1994; fellow Ctr. Advanced Study Behavioral Scis., Stanford, Calif., 1992-93. Avocations: classical music, skiing. Office: Linguistic Inst H Acad Scis, Benczur utca 33 1399 pf 701/518, H 1250 Budapest Hungary

EKKUNDI, VADIRAJ SUBBANNA, chemist, researcher; b. Gadag, Karnatak, India, Dec. 25, 1957; s. Subbanna Ranganath and Indira (Kalamdani) E.; m. Veena Vadiraj Kulkarni, Jan. 25, 1988; children: Akshya Vadiraj, Warsha Vadiraj. BSc, Karnatak U., Dharwad, India, 1978, MSc, 1980; PhD, Indian Inst. Tech., Bombay, 1985. Rsch. asst. Hindustan Lever Ltd., Bombay, 1981-85; exec. R&D Wyeth Lab. Ltd., Bombay, 1985-86; asst. mgr. R&D Atul Products Ltd., Atul, India, 1991-93; mgr. R&D Hindustan Ciba-Geigy Ltd., Bombay, 1993-96, sr. mgr. R&D, 1996—; postdoctoral rsch. scientist Boston Coll., 1989-91; postdoctoral scientist Tech. U. Braunschweig, Germany, 1986-89. Patentee in field; contbr. chpt. to book. Fellow Alexander von Humboldt Found., 1986-89, Boston Coll., 1989-91. Mem. Am. Chem. Soc., Indian Assn. Bio-Organic Chemists (life). Avocations: travel, Indian classical music. Office: Ciba India Pvt Ltd, Off Aarey Rd, Goregaon East Bombay 400063, India

EKLUND, KLAS, economist; b. Ängelholm, Sweden, July 16, 1952; m. Pernilla Ström. Licentiate of econs., Stockholm Sch. of Econs., 1985. Dep. under sec. of state Ministry of France, 1982-87, 87-89; policy adviser Prime Minister's Office, 1987; chmn. govt. Productivity Commn., 1990-91; chief economist Sweden Post, 1992-94, Skandinaviska Enskilda Banken, 1994—. Author: Vår Ekonomi, 1st edit., 1987, 9th edit., 1999, How Dangerous is the Budget Deficit?, 1994, Chasing the Disappearing Tax Bases, 1998. Office: Skandinaviska Enskilda, Banken, 10640 Stockholm Sweden

EKLUND, PATRIK EIVIND, computer scientist, educator; b. Vasa, Finland, July 9, 1958; arrived in Sweden, 1994; s. Holger Verner and Fanny Alice (Söderback) E.; m. Soili-Maria Olli, Sept. 19, 1987. MS, Abo Akademi U., 1981, PhD, 1986. Asst. prof. Abo Akademi U., Turku, Finland, 1985-89, 1990; sr. rschr. Finnish Acad., Helsinki, 1991-94; prof. Umeå (Sweden) U., 1995—; scientific leader several nat. rsch. projects. Editor conf. procs.; contbr. articles to profl. jours. Mem. IEEE.$d. Avocations: classical guitar, golf. Office: Umeå U, Dept Computing Sci, S90187 Umeå Sweden

EKMAN, GUNNAR ERNST ÅKE, psychiatrist; b. Stockholm, Bromma, Sweden, Mar. 5, 1940; s. Ernst Leonard and Karin (Ekegren) E.; m. Else-Britt Kjellqvist; 1 child, Anna; m. Karin Malmgren, July 31, 1991; 1 child, Ludvig. MD, Karolinska Inst., Stockholm, 1969; BA, Stockholm U., 1981. Lic. psychiatrist. Resident Karolinska Hosp., Stockholm, 1969-75; cons. psychiatrist Nacka Project, Stockholm, 1976-77, Hässelby-Vällingby Project, Stockholm, 1978-84; from instr. to asst. prof. Karolinska Inst., Stockholm, 1984-94, pvt. practice, 1994—; cons. various institutions for people with infantile autism, 1989. Contbr. articles to profl. jours. Mem. Swedish Psychoanalytical Assn. (assoc.), Swedish Assn. Physicians. Home and Office: Styrmansgatan 25, S-114 54 Stockholm Sweden

EKMANN, BJOERN, foreign language educator; b. Copenhagen, Mar. 29, 1935; s. Hilmert and Gudrun Margrethe (Hansen) E.; m. Lis Birgit Clausen, June 15, 1956 (dec. July 1977); children: Ulrik, Susanne; m. Elin Kirstine Petersen Kristensen, Aug. 25, 1984. MA, PhD, U. Copenhagen, 1961. Lectr. U. Tuebingen, Germany, 1963-65; from lectr. to asst. prof. U. Copenhagen, 1965—, dir. studies, 1999—; lectr. Royal Danish Sch. Ednl. Studies, 1969-72; external examiner German, Danish Tchrs.' Academies, 1971-98; asst. prof. Tech. U. Denmark, 1990-96; vis. prof. pedagogical U. Bydgoszcz, Poland, 1994-96; lectr. in field. Author: Die sozialen und moralischen Anschauungen Bertolt Brechts, 1967, Tegn og Tydning. Tekstfortolkning på semiotisk grundlag I-III, 1979, editor, commentator: Novalis: Hymnen an die Nacht, 1983; editor Text & Kontext, 1987—; asst. editor Jahrbuch fuer Internat. Germanistik, 1985—; contbr. articles to profl. jours. Founder support group for polit. refugees from Bosnia, Lyngby, 1992—. Cpl. Royal Danish Army, 1961-63. Recipient Friendship prize Gazeta Wyborcza, Bydgoszcz, 1993. Mem. Danish-German Soc. Copenhagen (vice chmn.). Radical Liberal Party Denmark. Lutheran. Home: Benvedvaenget 17, DK 2830 Virum Denmark Office: U Copenhagen Inst German, Njalsgade 80, DK 2300 Copenhagen S, Denmark

EKOVICH, STEVEN RUDY, international relations educator; b. Jersey City, Sept. 17, 1948; s. Sam Rudy and Zora (Sarapa) E.; m. Francine Simon; children: Muriel, Nathaniel. BA, U. Calif., Irvine, 1975, MA, 1979, PhD, 1984; postgrad., Sch. Advanced Studies Social Scis., Paris, 1978-79, 81-82. Lectr. U. Calif., Irvine, 1975-82; assoc. prof. Ecole Polytechnique, Paris, 1984—; mem. faculty Hautes Etudes Commerciales, Paris, 1985-99; assoc. prof. Am. U. Paris, Paris, 1994—; asst. course leader Regent campus Paris programme Diplomatic Acad. London, U. Westminster, 1999—; asst. courle leader Regent campus Paris programme The Diplomatic Acad. London, U. Westminster, 1999—; lectr., cons., 1988-2000; Fulbright prof., Tunisia, 1990. With USAF, 1969-72, Vietnam. Fulbright scholar, 1990. Mem. Am. Hist. Assn., Soc. Historians Am. Fgn. Rels., Soc. Study N.Am. Home: 7 rue Leon Delhomme, 75015 Paris France Office: Am U Paris/Internat Affairs, 31 Ave Bosquet, 75007 Paris France

EKPO, BASSEY OFFIONG, environmental educator, researcher, consultant; b. Calabar, Nigeria, Aug. 16, 1964; s. Etim Ekpo and Ekanem Oqua Otop; m. Rose Ekeng Henshaw, Dec. 21, 1993; children: Lawrence B., Raphael B. BSc, U. Calabar, 1989, MSc, 1995, PhD, 2000. Grad. asst. U. Calabar, 1990-95, asst. lectr., 1995-98, lectr. II, 1998—; cons. Unicalcons, U. Calabar, 1998—; dir., cons. Bacom Cons., Calabar, 1996—; project coord. petroleum & environ. geog. rsch. group, U. Calabar, 1999—. Contbr. articles to sci. and profl. jours. Mem. European Assn. Organic Geochemists, Nigerian Assn. Petroleum Explorations (fin. sec. 2000), Nigerian Environ. Soc. Avocations: football, swimming, reading. Office: U Calabar Dept Pure Applied Chemist, PMB 1115, Calabar Nigeria

EKSPERIANDOVA, LJUDMILA PETROVNA, chemistry researcher; b. Kalinin (now Tver), USSR, Apr. 14, 1947; d. Peter Nikitovich Sukhomlinov and Yevdokija Petrovna Khavluk; m. Anatolii Valentinovich E., Aug. 9, 1970; children: Irina, Dmitrii. BSc in Chemistry, Kharkov State U., USSR, 1972, DSc in Chemistry (hon.), 1983. Lab. asst. Single Crystals Rsch. Inst., Kharkov, USSR, 1966-74; jr. rschr. Single Crystals Rsch. Inst., Kharkov, 1974-86, rschr., 1986-91; sr. rschr. Single Crystals Rsch. Inst., Kharkov, Ukraine, 1991—; lectr., asst. Single Crystals Rsch. Inst., Kharkov, Ukraine, 1997—. Contbr. numerous articles to profl. jours. Avocations: classical music, chorus singing, travel, poetry. Office: Inst Single Crystals, Lenin Ave 60, 310001 Kharkov Ukraine

EKUE, FOLI, marketing executive; b. Belfast, No. Ireland, May 9, 1962; s. Kofi and Oladoyin (Agoro) E. BS, Loughborough (Eng.) U., 1983; MS, Loughborough (Eng.(U., 1984; MBA, IESE U. Navarra, Barcelona, Spain, 1994. Field engr. Schlumberger, Ijmuiden, Holland, 1985-86; mng. dir. Wordmac Ltd., Loughborough, 1987; sr. field engr. Schlumberger, Bombay, 1988-90; gen. field. engr. Schlumberger, Aberdeen, Scotland, 1991; support programs mgr. Hewlett-Packard, Grenoble, France, 1994-95, product mgr., 1996-99; retail solutions mgr. Hewlett Packard, Barcelona, Spain, 1999—. Avocations: skiing, cycling, hiking.

EKUNNO, EMMANUEL PRINCEWILL, sales and marketing executive; b. Offa, Nigeria, Feb. 1, 1956; s. Josaih Ifeacho and Comfort Nwugo (Nweze) E.; m. Gloria Chimankpam Oguachuba. BPharm, U. Ife, Nigeria, 1979. Pharm. sales rep. Pfizer, Nigeria, 1981-86, mktg. rsch. mgr., 1986-87, product mgr., 1987-89, sr. product mgr., 1989-92, mktg. mgr., 1992-96, dir., 1996-97; v.p. Neimeth, Nigeria, 1997-99, sr. v.p., 1999—; dir. Loria-Manuels, Nigeria, 1995—; 2d v.p. Advan, Nigeria, 1995—. Pastor Livingproof Bible Ch., Lagos, 1996, ch. coord., 1997—. Recipient Amb. of Pharmacy award Healthcare Pub., Disting. Mktg. award U. Zik, Nigeria, 1997; named Most Disting. Bus. Pharmacist, U. Ife, 1998. Mem. Pharm. Soc. Nigeria, OAU Jaycees (patron). Avocations: golf, lawn tennis, religious books, jazz music, travelling. Home: 34 Adeleke St, Ikeja Lagos Nigeria Office: Neimeth Internat Pharms, No 1 Henry Carr St, Ikeja Lagos Nigeria

EKVALL, TOMAS INGEMAR, environmental scientist, consultant; b. Göteborg, Sweden, Aug. 31, 1963; s. Bert Ingemar and Anna-Britta Ekwall; m. Inger Margareta Berg, Aug. 10, 1991; children: Tove Karin Linnea, Sara Anna Margareta. BSc in Physics, U. Gothenburg, 1987; License Engring., U. Lund, Sweden, 1991; PhD in Environ. Sci., Chalmers U. Tech., Göteborg, 1999. Contract rschr. Chalmers Industriteknik, Göteborg, 1991-2000; acting prof. Chalmers U. Tech., Göteborg, 2000—. co-author: A Clean Future-Our Responsibility for the Environment, 1988, A Clean Future-Facts on Environmental Management, 1989 (Liber Great Non-Fiction award 1989), Nordic Guidelines on Life-Cycle Assessment, 1995; subject editor Jour. Cleaner Prodn., 1998—; contbr. articles to profl. jours. Mem. Soc. Environ. Toxicology and Chemistry (chmn. Europe working group on scenario devel. 1999—). Avocations: choral singing. E-mail: tomas.ekvall@entek.chalmers.se. Fax: 46-31-772 35 92. Home: Kommendörsgatan 25J, SE-41459 Göteborg Sweden Office: Energy Sys Tech, Chalmers U Tech, SE-41296 Göteborg Sweden

ELABD, MOHAMED YEHIA, metal products executive; b. Cairo, Dec. 3, 1950; s. Saad Eldin and Laila Mahmoud (Sabri) E.; m. Iman Ahmed Sarhan, Dec. 2, 1977; children: Hisham, Ghada. BSCE, U. Cairo, 1973, diploma in metall. engring., 1981. Operation mgr. Arab Contractor, Cairo, 1974-77; prodn. mgr. Modern Foundries, Cairo, 1978-84, gen. mgr., 1984-91, pres., 1991—; mng. dir. Elabd Internat. Trading, Cairo, 1993—; cons. Egyptian Co. for Metal Processing Ramadan, Egypt, 1989—, Abu Zaabal Engring., Cairo, 1994—. Recipient Internat. Godl Star for Quality, BID, Spain, 1992, Cert. of Excellence, Ministry of Industry, Egypt, 1994. Mem. Am. Mgmt. Assn., Am. Foundrymen's Soc., Heat Treatment Soc. of Am. Soc. Metals (founding), Egyptian Foundryman's Soc. (bd. dirs. 1998). Avocations: music, playing violin, theater, tennis, travel. Office: Modern Foundries Co, PO Box 167 Imbaba-Nile Rd T, Cairo 11214, Egypt

EL ABRIDI, OMAR, diplomat; b. Rabat, Morocco, Oct. 20, 1942; s. Mohamed El A. and Fadila Aghnaj; m. Amina Bellakhdar; children: Mounir, Sanaa, Mehdi. Defense attache Moroccon Embassy, Rome, 1997—. Vapt. Moroccon Navy, 1967-92. Avocations: reading, bridge, travel. Home: 128 via Luigi Chiala, 00139 Rome Italy Office: Moroccan Embassy, 08/10 Via Lazzaro Spallanza, 00161 Rome Italy

EL-ADAWI, MOHAMED ABDELHADY KAMEL BAUMY, physicist, educator; b. Giza, Egpyt, Oct. 17, 1939; s. Kamel Baumy El-Adawi; children: Eman, Hanan, Doaa, Ahmed. BS in Sci. and Edn., Faculty of Tchrs., Cairo, 1960, spl. diploma in edn., 1964; BS in Physics with 1st class honors, Cairo U., 1968; PhD in Physics and Tech., Moscow Engring. Power Inst., 1973. Tchr. physics Ministry of Edn., 1960-63; demonstrator physics Ain Shams U., Cairo, 1963-74, lectr., 1974-81, assoc. prof., 1981-86, prof. theoretical physics, 1986—, head dept. physics, 1993-97, vice-dean Faculty of Edn., 1997—. Contbr. articles to profl. jours.; author books; mem. editl. adv. bd. Surface Instrumentation & Vacuum Technology. Recipient Nat. award in Sci., Egyptian Acad. Scis., 1988; Nat. Distinction medal Pres. Mobarak, 1995. Mem. N.Y. Acad. Scis. Avocations: reading, writing, music. Fax: (202) 2581243. Office: Ain Shams U, Faculty of Education VDean, Cairo Egypt

ELAGÖZ, SEZAI, physicist; b. Sivas, Turkey, Mar. 7, 1963; s. Cahid and Kimya (Yuksek) E.; m. Hulya Ercan, 1985; 3 children. BS, Ankara (Turkey) U., 1984; MSc, U. Mich., 1990, PhD in Physics, 1993. Rsch. asst. Cumhurivet U., Sivas, Turkey, 1984-87, U. Mich., Ann Arbor, 1989-93; rschr. U. Cumhurivet, Sivas, 1993-95, assoc. prof. physics, 1995—. Contbr. articles to profl. jours. Muslim. Avocations: table tennis, reading, biking, soccer. Office: Cumhurivet U, Fizik Bolumu Fed Edebivat, 58140 Sivas Turkey

EL-AHL, MOHAMMAD HAMZA, pediatrician, educator; b. Mansoura, Egypt, June 25, 1936; s. Hamza Ibrahim Sayed El Ahl and Sabra Mohammad Amer; m. Sawasn Ahmed Ragha, Sept. 3, 1970; children: Ahmed, Yahya. B Medicine B Surgery, Alexandria (Egypt) U., 1960, diploma in child health, 1962, diploma of medicine, 1963. Resident Alexandria U. Hosp., 1961-70; registrar Great Ormond St. Hosp., London, 1971-72; cons. Maadi Mil. Hosp., Cairo, 1972-80, head dept., 1980-86; prof. Mil. Med. Acad., Cairo, 1980—; chmn. Tabarak Children's Hosp., Cairo, 1987—; cons. pediat. svcs. Egyptian Army hosps. Author: (in Arabic) Your Baby in His First Year, 1994, How to Care for Your Sick Child, 2000; co-author jour. Biomed. Optoelectronic Instrumentation, 1995. Gen. Egyptian armed forces, 1986-94. Recipient Egyptian Rep. award Ministry of Def., 1994. Fellow Royal Coll. Physicians (Glasgow); mem. Egyptian Pediat. Assn., Egyptian Neonatology Assn., Internat. Soc. Optical Engring., Royal Coll. Physicians (London). Democrat. Muslim. Avocations: music, meditation, swimming. Office: Tabarak Children's Hosp, Golf Land 3 Husain Zuhdi St, 11361 Cairo Egypt

EL ALFI, MOHAMED BAHAA EL DIN, engineering company executive; b. Cairo, Jan. 1, 1945; s. Abdul Hay Mahmoud El Alfi; m. Elham Ahmed Kamel, Sept. 17, 1979. BSc in Mech. Power Engring., U. Cairo, 1968; MA in Mgmt. Sci., Am. U., Cairo, 1977. Engr. Civil Aviation, Cairo, 1968-72; tech. studies and composing room mgr. Al Ahram, Cairo, 1972-77; ops. mgr. Johnson Wax, Cairo, 1980-86; gen. mgr. Domo Egypt, Alexandria, 1987-90; vice chmn. B.M.F. Group, Cairo, 1990-94; mng. dir. Arab Aluminum, Cairo, 1994—; cons. Cairo Internat. Mgmt. Ctr., 1977-80. Patentee in package design and natural atomizer. Mem. Egyptian Businessmen Assn. Cairo, Indsl. Investors Soc. Ismalia (chmn. 1995—), Egyptian Ops. Rsch. Soc., Heliopolis Sporting Club. Moslem. Home: 79 Abo Bakr El Sedik, Heliopolis, 11361 Cairo Egypt

ELAM, DIANE MICHELE, English literature educator; b. Riverside, Calif., Apr. 17, 1958; d. Douglas Bradly and Leslie J. (Parman) E.; m. William John Readings, Aug. 9, 1988 (dec. Oct. 1994). AB, Kenyon Coll., 1980; MA, Brown U., 1984, PhD, 1988. Asst. prof. Bryn Mawr (Pa.) Coll., 1988-91; asst. prof. Ind. U., Bloomington, 1991-94, assoc. prof., 1994-95; asst. prof. McGill U., Montreal, Que., Can., 1993-94, adj. prof., 1994-96; prof. U. Wales, Cardiff, 1995—. Author: Romancing the Postmodern, 1992, Feminism and Deconstruction: Ms en Abyme, 1994; editor: Feminism Beside Itself, 1995. Rsch. grantee Social Scis. and Rsch. Coun. of Can., 1993-94, Que. Fonds pour la Formation de Chercheurs et l'Aide à la Recherche, 1993-94. Mem. MLA. Office: U Wales Ctr Critical Theory, PO Box 94, Cardiff CF1 3XB, Wales

EL-AMAWI, AHMED, government official; b. 1932; married; 3 children. BA in Law, 1968. Elected head Gen. Trade Union Fedn., 1987, Syndicate Com., 1966; sec., then chmn. Gen. Syndicate Chems.; mem. founding com. NDP; min. Ministry Manpower & Immigration, Cairo, 1993—; chmn. IHO, 1997-98, ALO, 2000—. Office: Ministry Manpower, 3, Yussef Abbas St, Cairo Egypt

EL-AMRI, FATHI ALI, chemistry educator; b. Tripoli, Libya, Feb. 26, 1952; s. Ali Omar and Amna Mohamed (Egliwan) El-A.; m. Nuria Eshtawu Ebredan, June 29, 1978; children: Amna Fathi, Anis Fathi. BS, U. Tripoli, Libya, 1974; MS, U. Nebr., 1979, PhD, 1983. Demonstrator U. Tripoli, Libya, 1974-76, lectr., 1983-86, asst. prof., 1986-90, assoc. prof., 1990-94, prof., 1994—; sr. cons. Tajura Nuclear Rsch. Ctr., Tripoli, 1983—; sr. cons., dir. ctrl. lab environ. protection Tech. Ctr. Environ. Protection, Tripoli, 1990—. Inventor in field. Mem. Internat. Soc. Trace Element Rsch. in Humans. Office: U Al-Fateh Chemistry Dept, PO Box 13361, Tripoli Libya

ELANDER LINDBERG, NOOMI CHRISTIN, psychotherapist, psychologist; b. Alingsås, Sweden, May 16, 1937; d. Viktor Eugen and Elisabet Elin (Jonsson) Elander; m. Erik Lindberg, May 16, 1964. Grad., Nursing Sch., Gothenburg, Sweden, 1960, Midwife Edn. Instn., Stockholm, 1962; BA, U. Stockholm, 1975, grad. in psychology, 1978; MD, PhD in Psychosomatic Medicine, Karolinska Inst., Stockholm, 1997. RN, Sweden; cert. tchr. psychotherapy and supervision, 1999; registered psychologist, psychotherapist, midwife, Sweden. Oper. room nurse Sahlgrenska Hosp., Gothenburg, 1960-61, Södersjukhuset, Stockholm, 1962-64; nurse Strängnäs (Sweden) Rheuma Hosp., 1964-67, Sch. Health Svc., Täby and Danderyd, Sweden, 1969; midwife and oper. room nurse Gävle (Sweden) Hosp., 1967-68; midwife Maternity Hosp., Stockholm, 1968-69; pvt. practice psychotherapy, Stocksund, Sweden, 1978—; psychologist Nat. Bd. Occupl. Health and Safety, Stockholm, 1979-81. Contbg. author: Psychosomatic Medicine, 1991; contbr. articles to sci. jours., including Psychotherapy Psychosomatics, Am. Jour. Indsl. Medicine, Acta Odont Scand, Work and Stress, Zeitschrift Rheumatologie, also Swedish jours. Mem. Swedish

Psychol. Assn., Swedish Nat. Psychotherapy Ctr., Swedish Soc. Medicine, Assn. Psychosomatic Medicine, Assn. Psychosomatic Ob-Gyn. Mem. Swedish Nat. Ch. Avocations: gardening, literature, opera music, antiques. Fax: 46-8-6558430. Office: PsykoSoma Ltd, Egilsvägen 5, 182 78 Stocksund Sweden

ELARABY, NABIL A., Egyptian diplomat; b. Cairo, Mar. 15, 1935; m. Nadia Teymour; children: May, Marwan, Hisham. Licencie en Droit, Cairo U., Egypt; LLM in Internat. Law, NYU, U.S.A., JSD. Legal advisor to Egyptian del. UN Mid. East Peace Conf., Ministry of Fgn. Affairs, Geneva, 1973-75; counsellor to mission from Egypt UN, Geneva, 1974-76; amb., dep. permanent rep. of Egypt UN, N.Y.C., 1978-81, 91-99; amb. extraordinary and plenipotentiary, permanent rep. of Egypt UN, Geneva, 1987-91; permanent rep. UN, N.Y.C., 1991—; legal advisor, dir. legal and treaties dept. Ministry of Fgn. Affairs, Geneva, 1976-78, 83-87; Egyptian amb. India, 1981-83; arbitrator (Suez Canal dispute) ICC Internat. Ct. of Arbitration, Paris, 1989; judge Jud. Tribunal Orgn. Arb Petroleum, 1990; commr. U.N.C.C.; ptnr. Zaki Hashem & Ptnrs., Attys. at Law; represented Egypt in the following UN Orgns. The Gen. Assembly, Security Coun., Econ. and Social Coun., Human Rights Commn., 1966—; head Egyptian Del. UN Conf. on Disarmament, 1987-91; led Egyptian Delegation to Egyptian-Israeli Arbitration Tribunal Taba Talks, 1986-89; former chair numerous UN coms. and working groups; pres. Security Coun., 1996; lectr. The Hague Acad. of Internat. Law, Columbia U., NYU, Duke U., Yale U., The Egyptian Soc. Internat. Law, Am. Soc. Internat. Law, and many others. Contbr. to profl. jours. and internat. law publs. Adlai Stevenson fellow UN Inst. for Tgn. and Rsch., 1968, Spl. fellow, 1973. Mem. Egyptian Soc. Internat. Law (bd. dirs.), Am. Soc. Internat. Law, Internat. Law Assn. (am. br.), Inst. World Affairs (bd. dirs.). Address: 23 Kasr El Nil St, Cairo 11211, Egypt

EL AYOUBY, NADIA S., industrial hygienist; b. Alexandria, Egypt, May 16, 1946; d. Salah El-Din El Ayouby and Zenba A. Bayoumi; m. Hussein E. Ghazi, Aug. 31, 1973 (div. Feb. 1980); 1 child, Bahair H. Ghazi. MS, Alexandria U., 1973, W.Va. U., 1988, W.Va. U., 1990. Rsch. asst. Plant Tech. Inst. Egypt, Cairo, 1969-75; rsch. asst. W.Va. U., Morgantown, 1976-80, rsch. assoc., 1986-90; rsch. technologist Nat. Inst. Occupl. Safety and Health, Morgantown, 1982-86, rsch. indsl. hygienist, 1997—; indsl. hygienist Dept. Vets. Affairs, Parkersburg, W.Va., 1990-91, White River Junction, Vt., 1995-97; indsl. hygienist cons. Environ. Monitoring of Occupl. Health, Morgantown, 1991-95; cons., lectr. in field. Contbr. articles to profl. publs. W.Va. U. scholar, 1989-90. Mem. Am. Stds. Testing and Materials, Am. Indsl. Hygiene Assn. Fax: 304 285-6049. E-mail: nae7@cdc.gov. Home: 997 Vandalia Rd Morgantown WV 26501-6249 Office: NIOSH/DSR/PTB 1095 Willowdale Rd Morgantown WV 26505-2888

ELAZAR, DAHLIA SABINA, sociology educator; b. Mexico City, Apr. 11, 1956; arrived in Israel, 1961; d. Isaiah Austryjak and Aliza Rebecca Dunn; m. Amit Elazar, Mar. 6, 1981; 1 child, Anna Rebecca. BA, Tel Aviv U., 1984; MA, UCLA, 1987, PhD in Sociology, 1993. Lectr. Tel Aviv U., 1993—. Author: The Making of Fascism Class, State and Counter Revolution Italy 1919-1922. Recipient nat. scholarship Phi Beta Kappa, L.A., 1990-91. Mem. Am. Sociol. Assn., Israeli Sociol. Assn.

EL-BAHRAWI, MOHAMMED EL-SAYED, physics educator, researcher; b. El-Salheia, El-Sharkia, Egypt, May 1, 1944; s. El-Sayed Sadek El-Bahrawi and Khadra Aly Khalil; m. Hoda Mohammed Eissa, Mar. 1, 1973. BSc in Physics, Ain Shams U., Cairo, 1965, MSc in Physics, 1970; PhD in Physics, Stuttgart (Germany) U., 1979. From asst. rschr. to asst. lectr. Nat. Inst. for Stds., Giza, Egypt, 1965-73, from rschr. to asst. prof., 1979-94, prof., 1994—; head optical and mech. divsn. Nat. Inst. for Stds., Giza, 1994-95, chief exec. calibration bur., 1996-99, head mass dept., 1997-99. Contbr. sci. articles to profl. jours. Office: Nat Inst for Stds, Tersa St, 12211 Giza Egypt

EL BAHRI, LOTFI, pharmacologist, toxicologist, researcher; b. Tunis, Tunisia, July 25, 1945; s. Mohsen and Jalila Bahri; m. Bibia Gytta Chenoufi, Sept. 3, 1974; children: Abdessatar, Habib. DVM, U. Paul Sabatier (France), 1969; cert. microbiology and immunology, U. René Descartes, Paris, 1972; MSc, U. de Créteil, Alfort, France, 1977; PhD in Pharmacology and Toxicology, Alfort, France, 1981. Asst. Pasteur Ins., Tunis, 1969-75; maître asst. Vet. Sch., Sidi Thabet, Tunisia, 1977-80, agregé in pharmacology and toxicology, 1983-87; assoc. prof. pharmacology and toxicology Ecole InterEtats des Scis. et Medecine Vétérinaires Dakar (Senegal) Vet. Sch., 1985—; prof. pharmacology and toxicology Vet. Sch., Sidi Thabet, Tunisia, 1988—, head of dept. fundamental scis., 1997-2000; dean, Nat. Vet. Sch., 1984-87; gen. mgr. Found. Nat. d'Amelioration de la Race Chevaline, 1991-94; cons. Internat. Found. Sci., Stockholm, 1988—; expert in vet. drugs, Tunisia and France. Contbr. articles to profl. jours. Moslem. Avocations: travel, agriculture, soccer. Home: N2 Ave de l'Amphitheatre, 2016 Carthage Tunisia Office: Nat Sch Veterinary Medicine, Dept Toxicology/Pharm, 2020 Sidi Thabet Tunisia

EL BANNA, RAGAB MOURSI, publishing company executive, magazine editor; b. Damanhour, El Behira, Egypt, Sept. 17, 1936; s. Moursi El Banna; 2 children. BA in Philosophy, Alexandria (Egypt) U., 1960; diploma in journalism, Cairo U., 1971. Corr., writer Al Ahram, newspaper, Cairo, 1971-80, asst. editor-in-chief, 1980-87, vice editor-in-chief, 1987-94; editor-in-chief, writer October mag., Cairo, 1994—; chmn. Dar Al Maaref Pub. House, Cairo, 1994—; mem. Nat. Com. for Culture, Art and Lit., Cairo, Higher Coun. Islamic Afairs, Cairo.; prof. journalism Cairo U., 1974. Author: History Not For Sale, Looking for a Future, Religious Illiteracy and War Against Islam, (short stories) Little Smile, The West and Islam, History of Copts in Egypt; weekly columnist Al Ahram, 1970—. Mem. Egyptian Soc. Econs. and Polit. Sci. Office: Dar Al Maaref, 1119 Corniche El Nil St, Cairo Egypt

ELBAZ, JEAN SAUVEUR, plastic and aesthetic surgeon; b. Constantine, Algeria, July 28, 1933; s. Jonathan and Suzanne (Kalifa) E.; m. Beatrice Silvestre de Sacy, June 15, 1970; 1 child, Sophie. M.D., Med. Sch. Paris, 1963. Intern, Hosp. of Paris, 1956-60, resident, 1962-65; practice medicine, specializing in plastic and aesthetic surgery, Paris, 1963—; staff various hosps., Paris, 1963-78; asst. anatomy U. Paris, 1960-62; expert for Ct. of Paris, 1975—; prof. plastic and aesthetic surgery U. Paris, 1970. Author: Plastic Surgery of the Abdomen, 1979; Chirurgie Plastique de l'Abdomen, 1977; Mammary Prosthesis, 1982; Face Lifting, 1983, Lipo-succion and Plastic Surgery of the abdomen, 1989. Served to maj. French Army, 1960-62. Recipient Internat. Prize award Plastic and Aesthetic Suergery Soc. Mexico, 1977. Mem. French Soc. Plastic and Aesthetic Surgery (hon., pres. 1989), French Coll. Plastic and Aesthetic Surgery (hon. pres.), Internat. Confedn. Plastic and Reconstructive Surgery, Internat. Soc. Aesthetic Plastic Surgery. Jewish. Club: Club 33 av Foch. Home: 3 rue Leonard de Vinci, 75016 Paris France Office: 144 rue de Courcelles, 75017 Paris France

EL-BEBLAWI, HAZEM ABDEL AZIZ, international organization administrator; b. Cairo, Egypt, Oct. 17, 1936; married; children: Dina, Karim, Salma. LLB (hon.), Cairo U. Faculty of Law, 1957; grad. diploma in polit. economy, U. Grenoble, France, 1958; grad. diploma in pub. law, U. Cambridge Fitzwilliam Coll., England, 1959; PhD in Doctorat d'Etat et Scis. Economiques, U. Paris, 1964. Legal adviser State Coun., Egypt, 1957-60; from asst. prof. to full prof. econs. U. Alexandria Faculty of Law, 1965; adviser Ministry of Planning, Cairo, 1966-67; head econ. unit Ctr. Strategic and Polit. Studies, Al-ahram, Cairo, 1972-73; sr. economist The Arab Fund for Econ. and Social Devel., 1974-76; dir. rsch. dept. Ministry of Fin., Kuwait, 1980-83; chmn. Export Devel. Bank of Egypt, 1985-95; under sec. gen. UN Exec. Sec. & Social Commn. for Western Asia; vis. prof. Ecole Pratique des Hautes Etudes, La Sorbonne, Paris, 1968, U. Calif., L.A., 1979; teaching at U. Cairo, U. Ain Shams, U. Kuwait, Am. U. in Cairo, UCLA, 1981. Author numerous books in English, Arabic and French, 1975; contbr. articles to profl. jours. (in French and English); editl. bd. Jour. Arab Affairs, Calif., 1981; editor: Fin. & Industry Jour. Egyptian Govt. scholarship, 1960-65. Office: ESCWA, PO Box 11-8575, Beirut Lebanon

EL-BEDEIWY, ABD-EL-FATTAH AHMED, pathology educator, consultant; b. El Zarka, Egypt, Mar. 17, 1939; s. Ahmed El-Bedeiwy Negeid; m. Nadia Abd-El-Moneim Nada. MBCh, U. Cairo, 1963, diploma in pathology, 1967, diploma in gen. surgery, 1968, MD, 1971. Demonstrator dept. pathology Faculty of Medicine, Mansoura (Egypt) U., 1971-75, asst. prof., 1975-79, prof. pathology, 1979, prof., head dept. pathology, 1984-90, vice dean Student Affairs, 1991-94, prof. emeritus, 1999—; cons. Mansoura U., 1984; prof. dept. pathology, faculty of medicine, King Abdel-Aziz U., Jeddah, Saudi Arabia, 1979-84, 94-98; mem. sci. com. pathology Permanent U., Cairo. Author: Modern Pathology, 1989; editor Mansoura Med. Jour., 1980—; contbr. articles to sci. and profl. jours. Fellow WHO, London, 1974-75. Mem. Internat. Acad. Soc. Pathology (Arabic br.), Egyptian Med. Syndicate, Gezirat El-Ward Social Club, Soc. Social Devel. of El-Zarka Damietta. Democrat. Moslem. Avocations: reading, walking, table tennis, chess, fishing. Office: Mansoura U Fac of Medicne, El Gomhoria, Mansoura Egypt

EL-BEHAIRY, MOHAMED M., retired political science educator; b. Cairo, Oct. 30, 1931; s. Mohamed Elsayed and Ihsan Mustafa (El-Qadi) El-B.; m. Sharon Botkin, Mar. 24, 1959; children: Carrie Ihsan, Carima Carol, Joseph Mohamed, Jasmine Sharon. B in Commerce, Cairo U., 1953; MA, U. Minn., 1956; PhD, Ohio State U., 1961. Asst. prof. polit. sci. Defiance (Ohio) Coll., 1961-63; prof. polit. sci. SUNY, Buffalo, 1963-94, chmn. dept., 1967-69, 84-87; ret., 1994; vis. prof. Am. U., Cairo, 1969-70, King Saud U., Riyadh, Saudi Arabia, 1976-77, 79-80, 82-84; paper presenter at internat. and nat. confs.; TV amd radio appearances. Co-author: OPEC and National Development, 1977, Human Sexuality: An Encyclopedia, 1994; translator/analyst: Egypt & Libya from Inside, 1994. Mem. Assn. Egyptian-Am. Scholars, Assn. Egyptian Scholars (co-founder 1958), Arab Cultural Assn. (past pres.), Islamic Soc. N.Am., Islamic Soc. Niagara Frontier (co-founder 1974, past pres.). Home: 1430 E River Rd Grand Island NY 14072-2332 Office: SUNY 1300 Elmwood Ave Buffalo NY 14222-1004

ELBEIN, ALAN DAVID, medical science educator; b. Lynn, Mass., Mar. 20, 1933; s. Gersh and Golda (Stryer) E.; m. Elaine J. Brooks, June 21, 1953; children: Steven Conrad, Bradley Martin, Richard Craig. AB, Clark U., 1954; MS, U. Ariz., 1956; PhD, Purdue U., 1960. Rsch. assoc. in biochemistry Med. Sch. U. Mich., Ann Arbor, 1960-63; rsch. assoc. in biochemistry U. Calif., Berkeley, 1963-64; asst. prof., then assoc. prof. biology Rice U., Houston, 1964-69; prof. Health Sci. Ctr. U. Tex., San Antonio, 1969-90; prof., chmn. biochemistry dept. U. Ark. Med. Sci., Little Rock, 1991—; mem. study sect. NSF, 1972-75, NIH, 1983-87, 93-97; mem. editl. bd. Jour. Biol. Chemistry, Arch. Biochem. Biophysics, Plant Physiology, Glycobiology, Jour. Bacteriology, Eur. Jour. Biochem. Editor: Swainsonine; contbr. articles, revs. to profl. jours. Disting. Faculty scholar UAMS, 1996-97. Mem. Am. Chem. Soc., Am. Soc. Plant Physiology, Am. Soc. Biol. Chem. and Molecular Biology. Jewish. Achievements include numerous patents and publs. Home: 23 Fontenay Cir Little Rock AR 72223-9569 Office: U Ark Med Scis Dept Biochem & Mol Biology 4301 W Markham St Little Rock AR 72205-7101

EL-BENNA, JAMEL, research scientist; b. Djerba, Tunisia, Nov. 15, 1962; arrived in France, 1984; s. Salah and Hiza (Ben-Ouirane) El-B.; m. Sonia Ben-Brahim, Aug. 10, 1994; children: Meriam, Lamia. Brevet de Technicien Superier in Biology, Faculté Medicine, Tunis, Tunisia, 1985; MS, U. Paris XI, 1987, Diplome d'Etudes Approfondues, 1988, PhD in Biology, 1992. Postdoctoral staff The Scripps Rsch. Inst., LaJolla, Calif., 1992-95; rschr. Ctr. Nat. de la Recerche Scientifiique Inst. Nat. de la Sante Et de la Recherche Medicale, Paris, 1995—. Contbr. chpt. to book and articles to profl. jours. Recipient Arthritis Found. award, San Diego, 1994, Recherche et Partage award, Paris, 1996, Assn. Française de la Polyarthrite award, Paris, 1997. Office: INSERM-U479 Faculte XBichat, 16 rue Henri Huchard, 75018 Paris France

ELBER, RON, computer science educator; b. Rehovot, Israel, Mar. 28, 1957; s. Yair and Rachel Neter Elber; m. Victoria Buch, Aug. 1983 (div. Aug. 1996); 1 child, Dassi; m. Virginia Yip, 2000; 1 child, Nurit. BSc, Hebrew U., 1981, PhD in Chemistry and Physics, 1984. Postdoctoral Harvard U., Boston, 1984-87; asst. prof. chemistry U. Ill., Chgo., 1988-91, assoc. prof. chemistry, 1992-94; assoc. prof. chemistry and biology Hebrew U., Jerusalem, 1994-96, prof. chemistry and biology, 1996-98; prof. computer sci. Cornell U., Ithaca, N.Y., 1999—; cons. Tera Computers, Israel, 1996-98, Peptcor, Israel, 1996—; acting dir. NIH Resource for Parallel Computing, Ithaca, 1999—; organizer numerous scientific meetings. Editor: Recent Development in the Theoretical Studies of Proteins, 1996. Sgt. Israel Def. Forces, 1978-81. Scholar U. Ill., 1990-92; recipient Alon fellow State of Israel, 1992; recipient numerous grants. Mem. AAAS, N.Y. Acad. Sci., ACS, Israel Chem. Soc., Soc. Indsl. and Aplied Maths. Avocations: chess, hiking. Office: Cornell U 4130 Upson Hall Ithaca NY 14853-7501

ELBERS, ARMIN RUDOLF WILFRED, epidemiologist, educator; b. Amsterdam, The Netherlands, Jan. 27, 1961; s. Wil Aloysius and Joke Maria Catharina (Snoek) E.; m. Annemarie Dirkzwager, June 29, 1996; children: Laurens, Kari. MS in Agr., Wageningen U., The Netherlands, 1986; PhD, U. Utrecht, The Netherlands, 1991; MS in Population Medicine, Ont. Vet. Coll., Guelph, Can., 1992. Head dept. epidemiology Animal Health Svc. So. Netherlands, Boxtel, 1992-95; head dept. epidemiology and stats. Nat. Animal Health Svc. Netherlands, Boxtel, 1995-97, epidemiologist dept. pig health, 1997—; staff epidemiologist Classical Swine Fever Crisis Ctr., Uden, The Netherlands, 1997-98; mem. monitoring rsch. group Ministry of Agrl., The Netherlands, 1996-97. Contbr. articles to profl. publs. Mem. Dutch Soc. Vet. Epidemiology and Econ. (pres. bd. dirs.), Dutch Soc. Epidemiology (cert.). Avocations: mountain climbing, hiking, skiing, horseback riding, volleyball. Home: Roemer Visscherlaan 71, 3705 SE Zeist Utrecht, The Netherlands Office: Animal Health Svc, Molenwijkseweg 48, 5282 SC Boxtel NoordBrb, The Netherlands

ELBESHBISHI, AMAL NAGAH, economics educator, consultant, researcher; b. Mansoura, Dakahlia, Egypt, Sept. 14, 1965; d. Nagah Aly Elbeshbishi and Mervat Hassan Abed; 1 child, Mariam. BA in Econ. with distinction, Mansoura U., 1986, MA in Econ., 1992; MA in Econ., Fordham U., 1999, PhD in Econ., 2000. Instr. econ. Mansoura U., 1986-92, asst. lectr., 1992-96, asst. prof., 1999—; adj. prof. econ. Fordham U., fall 2000—. Moslem. Avocations: reading, writing, classical music, poetry, travel. Office: Mansoura U Dept Econ, Gomhoria St, Mansoura Dakahlia, Egypt

ELBOIM-DROR, RACHEL, education educator; b. Poland, July 28, 1931; arrived in Israel, 1936; d. Zvi and Bracha (Greenberg) Elboim; m. Yehezkel Dror; children: Asael, Otniel, Itiel. BA, Hebrew U., 1953; EdM, Harvard U., 1955, EdD, 1959. Secondary sch. tchr. diploma. Lectr. edn. Hebrew U., Jerusalem, 1965-74, sr. lectr. edn., 1974-80, assoc. prof. edn., 1980-89, full prof., 1989—, dir. divsn. edn. policy, planning and adminstrn., 1977-80; cons. Ministry Edn., Israel, 1965-67, 70-74; editor Elsevier Internat. Book Series in Edn. Policy, 1972-74; mem. adv. com. Israeli Govt. Author: Socio-Political History of Education in Palestine, 4 vols., 1986-90, Yesterday's Tomorrow-Zionist Utopias, 2 vols., 1993 (Witzniser prize for Best Book of Jewish History, 1993), A Night in Tel-Aviv, 1996, Clean Death, 1999; mem. editl. bd. profl. jours. Mem. directorate Tchr. Coll. Israel, 1992-95; mem. governing com. Ben-Zvi Rsch. Found., Jerusalem, 1996—; mem. pedagogic com. Kerem Coll., Jerusalem, 1998—; vol. worker with disadvantaged youth. Recipient Jerusalem Edn. prize Jerusalem Municipality, 1992. Office: Hebrew Univ Jerusalem, 91905 Jerusalem Israel

EL BUSHRA, HASSAN EL MAHDI, epidemiology, research scientist; b. Kadugli, Kordofan, Sudan, Mar. 24, 1953; Arrived in Saudi Arabia, 1992; s. El Mahdi El Bushra and Zeinab Mohammed Al-A'lim Ahmed; m. Amna Osman Abdulgadir, Aug. 9, 1984; children: Mohammed, Salah El-Din, Eymmanne, Osama. MB, BS, U. Khartoum, Sudan, 1977, M in Cmty. Medicine, 1982; MPH in Epidemiology, UCLA, 1986, PhD, 1990. Ho. physician Shaab and Khartoum Tchg. Hosps. and El Obeid Civil Hosp., 1977-78; med. officer El Obeid and Omdurman Civil Hosp. Students' Health Svcs., U. Khartoum, 1978-80; tchg. asst. dept. cmty. medicine faculty medicine U. Khartoum, 1980-82, lectr., asst. prof. dept. cmty. medicine, faculty medicine, 1982-92; clin. asst. prof. dept. family and cmty. medicine King Saud U., Riyadh, Saudi Arabia, 1992—; cons. med. epidemiologist Field Epidemiology Tng. Program, Riyadh, 1992-99; scientist rschr., med. epidemiologists dept. biostat. epidemiology and sci. computing King Faisal Specialist Hosp. and Rsch. Ctr., 1999—. Contbr. articles to profl. jours. Recipient award Japanese Internat. Corp. Agy., 1984, African Dissertation Internship award Rockefeller Found., 1988. Mem. Internat. Epidemiol. Assn., Sudanese Soc. Preventive and Social Medicine. Muslim. Avocations: drawing, fine arts. Home: PO Box 62281, Riyadh 11585, Saudi Arabia Office: King Faisal Specialist Hosp, PO Box 3354 MBC 03, Riyadh 11211, Saudi Arabia

ELDADA, LOUAY A., fiber optic engineer; b. Oct. 3, 1966; s. Chafic and Adela (Salam) E.; m. Katharina Hannelore Haegi, June 28, 1991; 1 child, Seraina Adela. BSEE, Columbia U., 1989, MSEE, 1991, MPhil in Elec. Engring., 1993, PhD in Elec. Engring., 1994. Staff engr. AlliedSignal, Inc., Morristown, N.J., 1994-97; sr. staff engr. AlliedSignal, Inc., Morristown, 1997-99, prin. engr., 1999-2000; mgr. device devel. Corning, Inc., 2000; chief tech. officer Telephotonics, Inc., Wilmington, Mass., 2000—. Author: Photonic Integrated Circuits, 1994, Future Trends in Microelectronics, 1998, WDM Components, 1999; contbr. articles to Jour. Lightwave Tech., Photonics Technol. Letters, Applied Optics. mem. IEEE, Internat. Soc. for Optical Engring., Optical Soc. Am., Lasers and Electro-Optics Soc., Communications Soc. Achievements include 9 patents in the area of fiber optics. Avocations: photography, painting, karate, skiing, biking. Office: 100 Fordham Rd Wilmington MA 01887-2154

EL DANAF, AHMED ABDEL-HADY, plastic surgeon; b. Cairo, July 29, 1951; s. Abdel-Hady Hassan and Islah Abass (Mohsen) El D.; m. Manal Abdel-Moniem Mohsen, Jan. 20, 1983; children: Heba, Mohamed. M in Gen. Surgery, Cairo U., 1981; diploma in Microsurgery, Lyon (France) U., 1981; diploma in oral & maxillofacial surgery, Nancy (France) U., 1983, 87, MD, PhD in Plastic Surgery, 1985; cert., French Coll. Plastic Surgery, Paris, 1982. Resident plastic surgery Ed Herriot Hosp., Lyon, 1980-81; attached specialist maxillofacial surgery Nancy Ctrl. Hosp., 1981-83; cons. plastic surgeon Armed Forces Hosp., Tabuk, Saudi Arabia, 1985-88; lectr. plastic surgery Mataria Teaching Hosp., Cairo, 1988-91; cons. plastic surgeon King Abdulaziz Hosp., Jeddah, Saudi Arabia, 1991-93; chief plastic surgery King Abdulaziz Hosp., Jeddah, 1993—; cons. and chief dept. plastic surgery Al Mataria Tchg. Hosp., 1994—. Contbr. articles on plastic surgery to profl. jours. With Egyptian mil., 1977-78. Mem. Egyptian Soc. Plastic Surgeons, French Soc. Plastic Surgeons, Internat. Soc. Burn Injuries and Microsurgery. Moslem. Office: 12311-Dokki, 139-A Tahrir St, Giza Egypt

ELDER, MARY LOUISE, librarian; b. Ann Arbor, Mich., Sept. 7, 1937; d. John Dyer and Elsie (Phelps) E. BA, St. Louis U., 1959; MA, U. Chgo., 1962; postgrad., U. Calif., Berkeley, 1965-69. Libr. U. Chgo., 1961-63; rare book cataloger U. Kans., Lawrence, 1963-65; rare books libr. St. Louis Pub. Libr., 1969-74; rare book cataloger Duke U., Durham, N.C., 1979-84, Smithsonian Inst., Washington, 1984-91, Libr. Congress, Washington, 1991—. Mem. ALA, Am. Printing History Assn., Bibliog. Soc., Bibliog. Soc. Am., Cath. Libr. Assn., Soc. History Authorship, Reading and Publishing, Alpha Sigma Nu. Office: Libr Congress Washington DC 20540-0001

ELDER, MURDOCH GEORGE, obstetrician, gynecologist, educator; b. Calcutta, India, Jan. 4, 1938; s. Archibald James and Lotta Annie (Craig) E.; m. Margaret Adelaide McVicker, Oct. 3, 1964; children: James Stuart, Andrew Murdoch. MB ChB, U. Edinburgh, 1961, MD, 1973; DSc, U. London, 1994. Lectr. U. Malta, 1969-71; sr. lectr., reader U. London, 1971-78; prof., head dept. ob-gyn. Royal Postgrad. Med. Sch. Inst. Ob-Gyn., London, 1978-98; chmn. divsn. pediatrics Royal Postgrad. Med. Sch. Inst. Ob-Gyn., 1996-98; Dir. Clin. research centre WHO, London, 1980-92; examiner univs. London, Liverpool, Leeds, Bristol, Glasgow, Oxford, Cambridge, Edinburgh, Singapore, Malaysia, Malta, Birmingham, Dundee, Rotterdam, Helsinki, Malaya, 1971—; mem. Hammersmith and Queen Charlottes Spl. Health Auth., 1982-84; mem. WHO scientific ethics rsch. group, 1997—. Co-author: Current Fertility Control, 1978; editor: Preterm Labor, 1982, 2d edit., 1997, Reproduction, 1986. WHO scholar, Royal Coll. Ob-Gyn scholar, 1976-77; recipient silver medal Hellenic Ob-Gyn. Soc., 1983, bronze medal Helsinki U., 1997; grantee U.K. Fellow Royal Coll. Surgeons Edinburgh, Royal Coll. Ob-Gyn London; mem. Assn. Profs. Ob-Gyn (sec. 1985). Address: Easter Calzeat, Broughton Biggar ML12 6HQ, Scotland

ELDER, RICHARD BRUCE, artist, writer; b. Hawkesbury, Ont., Can., June 12, 1947; s. David Murdoch and Edrie Maud (Campbell) E.; m. Kathryn LeRoy, Sept. 4, 1970. Student, McMaster U., 1969; MA, U. Toronto, 1970; B of Applied Arts in Media Studies, Ryerson Poly. Inst., 1976. curator film programs for Can. Coun., 1982, Can. Images, 1982, 83, Festival of Festivals, 1984, Art Gallery Ont., 1986, 89, Internat. Exptl. Film Congress, 1989. Prodr. (film) The Book of All the Dead, 1975-94; works exhibited at Mus. Modern Art, Millennium, N.Y.C., San Francisco Cinematheque, Hood Mus., Atlanta, Kino Arsenal, Berlin, Festival of Festivals, Ctr. Georges Pompidou, George Eastman House, Albright-Knox Gallery, Munich Stadtmuseum, Cineteca, Bologna, Italy; retrospectives of film work Art Gallery Ont., 1985, Cinémathèque Québecoise, 1986, Anthology Film Archives, 1988, 95, Senzatitolo, Treno, Italy, 1996, Images '97, Toronto, The Antechamber, Regina, Can., 2000; author: Image and Identity: Reflections on Canadian Film and Culture, 1989, The Body in Film, 1989, Stan Brakhage: A Retrospective, 1977-95, 1995, A Body of Vision, 1997; author: The Films of Stan Brakhage in the American Tradition of Ezra Pound, Gertrude Stein, and Charles Olson, 1998; contbr. articles to profl. jours. Recipient Can. Film award for best exptl. film, 1976, L.A. Film Critics Circle award for best ind. exptl. film, 1980, Auswortiges Amt. F.G.R. study tour, 1986; grantee Can. Coun., Ont. Arts Coun., Social Scis. and Humanities Rsch. Coun. Can.; Sarwan Sahoto Disting. scholar Ryerson Poly. U., 2000. Address: Unit 5, 692 St Clarens Ave, Toronto, ON Canada M6H 3X1

ELDIN, GÉRARD, banker; b. Cannes, France, Mar. 21, 1927; s. Charles and Elise Eldin; m. Marie-Cecile Bergerot, June 4, 1960; children: Jean-Marc, Elizabeth, Fréderique, Grégoire. MA, M in Law, U. Aix en Provence, France, 1950, Ecole Nat. d'Adminstrn., Paris, 1954; D in Commerce (hon.), Bethany Coll., W. Va., 1988. Inspector of fin. Min. Fin., Paris, 1954-58, with treas. dept., 1958-62, dep. dir., 1965-70; counsellor Pvt. Office of Min., Paris, 1962-65; dep. sec. gen. Orgn. for Econ. Cooperation and Devel., Paris, 1970-80; dep. gov. Credit Foncier de France, Paris, 1980-86; chmn., chief exec. officer Banque Cen. de Compensation, Paris, 1987-90; chmn. Foneier Ct. Terme, Paris, 1987-90; bd. dirs. Compagnie Fonciere de France, Paris, Soc. Immobiliere Paix-Daunou, Paris, Compagnie Francaise d'Epargne et de Credit, Paris, Soc. des Immeutles de France, 1994—; chmn., chief exec. officer Soc. d'Etudes Immobilieres et d'Expertises Foncières, 1990-95, chmn. CEO credit-logement, 1995-96. With French Resistance Movement, 1943-44. Decorated knight Ordre de la Legion d'Honneur, commdr. Ordre Nat. du Merite. Mem. French Reformed Ch. Home: 32 Rue des Archives, 75004 Paris France

ELDON, STEWART GRAHAM, diplomat; b. Accra, Ghana, Sept. 18, 1953; s. John Hodgson and Rose Helen Eldon; m. Christine Mary Eldon, Jan. 14, 1978; children: Laura Madeleine, Thomas Henry. BA, U. Cambridge, Eng., 1974, MSc, 1976, MA, 1977. Pvt. sec. to Min. of State Fgn. and Commonwealth Office, London, 1983-86; 1st sec. U.K. Mission to UN, N.Y.C., 1986-90; dep. crisis mgr. (Gulf War) Fgn. and Commonwealth Office, 1990-91; counselor Cabinet Office, London, 1991-93, U.K. Dels. to NATO and Western European Union, Brussels, 1994-97; dir. Fgn. and Commonwealth Office, 1997-98; amb. and dep. permanent rep. U.K. Mission to UN, 1998—; fellow Ctr. for Internat. Affairs, Harvard U., Cambridge, Mass., 1993-94. Named Officer of Order of Brit. Empire, 1991, Companion of Order of St. Michael and St. George, 1999. Mem. Instn. Elec. Engrs. London (assoc.), Harvard Club N.Y. Avocations: travel, computers, science fiction. Office: UK Mission to UN PO Box 5238 New York NY 10150-5238

ELDREDGE, CHARLES CHILD, III, art history educator; b. Boston, Apr. 12, 1944; s. Henry and Priscilla Marion (Bateson) E.; m. Jane Allen MacDougal, June 11, 1966; children: Henry Gifford, Janann Bateson. BA, Amherst Coll., 1966; PhD, U. Minn., 1971. Curator asst. Minn. Hist. Soc., St. Paul, 1966-68; mem. edn. dept. Mpls. Inst. Arts, 1967-69; teaching asst. art history U. Minn., 1968-70; asst. prof. art history, curator collections Spencer Mus. Art, U. Kans., Lawrence, 1970-71; dir. mus. Spencer Mus. Art, U. Kans., 1971-82, assoc. prof., 1974-80, prof., 1980-82; dir. Nat. Mus. Am. Art, Washington, 1982-88; Hall disting. prof. of Am. art U. Kans., Lawrence, 1988—; C.H. Hynson vis. prof. U. Tex., Austin, 1985; trustee Watkins Cmty. Mus., Lawrence, 1972-76, Assn. Art Mus. Dirs., 1982, 87, Reynolda House Mus. Am. Art, 1986-88, Amherst Coll., 1987-93; trustee

Georgia O'Keeffe Found., 1989-95; rsch. assoc. Smithsonian Instn., 1988—; founder Smithsonian Studies in Am. Art, 1987. Author: Marsden Hartley: Lithographs and Related Works, 1972, Ward Lockwood, 1894-1963, 1974, American Imagination and Symbolist Painting, 1979, Charles Walter Stetson, Color and Fantasy, 1982, Pacific Parallels: Artists and the Landscape in New Zealand, 1991, Georgia O'Keeffe, 1991, Georgia O'Keeffe: American and Modern, 1992, The College on the Hill, 1996, Reflections on Nature: Small Paintings by Arthur Dove, 1997; co-author: The Arcadian Landscape: 19th Century American Painters in Italy, 1972, Art in New Mexico, 1900-1945, 1986, American Originals: Selections from Reynolda House, Mus. of American Art, 1990, Life Cycles: The Charles E. Burchfield Collection, 1996, John Steuart Curry: Inventing the Middle West, 1997, The Regionalist Vision of William Dickerson, 1997; gen. editor The Register of Mus. Art, 1971-82; editl. bd. Am. Studies, 1974-77, Am. Art, 1996—. Smithsonian Instn. fellow Nat. Collection Fine Arts, 1979; Fulbright scholar N.Z., 1983; Found. Visitor fellow U. Auckland, 1993, Smithsonian fellowship Nat. Mus. of Am. Art, 1995; recipient Outstanding Alumnus award u. Minn., 1986. Mem. Coll. Art Assn. Am., Am. Studies Assn., Am. Assn. Mus., Assn. Art Mus. Dirs., Authors Guild. Office: U Kans Dept Art History 209 Spencer Mus Art Lawrence KS 66045-0001

ELDRIDGE, CHARLES RAY, military officer, military science educator; b. Dayton, Ohio; m. R. Darlene Eldridge. BS, The Citadel, 1979; MBA, Golden Gate U., 1989; MS, Syracuse U., 1999. Commd. 2d lt. U.S. Army, 1979, advanced through grades to lt. comdr., 1995; prof. mil. sci., dir. dept. mil. sci. Syracuse (N.Y.) U., 1996—. Address: 991 John Brown Rd Henderson TN 38340-1031

ELDRIDGE, DOUGLAS ALAN, lawyer; b. Boulder, Colo., Mar. 15, 1944; s. Douglas Hilton and Clara Effie (Young) E.; m. Benna June Germann, June 24, 1967; children: Heather Dana, Ethan Douglas, Hilary Beca. BA, Yale U., 1966; LLB, U. Pa., 1969; cert., Nat. Inst. Trial Advocacy, Boulder, 1973. Bar: N.Y. 1972, U.S. Dist. Ct. (no. dist.) N.Y. 1973, U.S. Supreme Ct. 1975. Staff atty. Onondaga Neighborhood Legal Svcs., Syracuse, N.Y., 1971-74, exec. dir., 1974-76; counsel N.Y. State Divsn. of Substance Abuse Svcs., Albany, 1976-79; dep. counsel N.Y. State Health Dept., Albany, 1979-80; dep. counsel N.Y. State Energy Office, Albany, 1980-82, asst. counsel, 1982-87; gen. counsel Commn. for Siting Low-Level Radioactive Waste Disposal Facilities, Troy, N.Y., 1987-95; sole practice, 1995—; govt. affairs counsel N.Y. Rehab. Assn., Inc. Contbr. articles to legal jours. Bd. dirs. Coun. Cmty. Svcs. United Way of Northeastern N.Y., Albany, 1980-90, pres., 1986-88; bd. dirs. United Way Ea. N.Y., 1986-88, Mohawk-Hudson Found., 1986-89. Recipient Reginald Heber Smity Cmty. Lawyer fellowship OEO, 1969-71. Mem. N.Y. State Bar Assn., Albany County Bar Assn. (chair legis. com. 1998-99), Onondaga County Bar Assn., Assn. of Bar of City of N.Y., Yale Alumni Schs. Com., Yale Alumni Assn. Northeastern N.Y., Assn. of Yale Alumni (rep. 1985-88, 94-97), University Club (bd. dirs. 1998—). Home: 9 Pinedale Ave Delmar NY 12054-3012

ELDRIDGE, RICHARD MARK, lawyer; b. Okmulgee, Okla., June 20, 1951; s. H.G. and Marcheta (Barnes) E.; m. Nellene Jane Mark, Aug. 20, 1971; children: Richard Mark Jr. (dec.), Christopher Bryan, Ryan Matthew, Michael Jonathan. BA, Okla. State U., 1973; JD, U. Tulsa, 1975. Bar: Okla. 1976; U.S. Dist. Ct. (no. dist.) Okla. 1976, U.S. Dist. Ct. (ea. dist.) Okla. 1989; U.S. Ct. Appeals (10th cir.) 1977, U.S. Dist. Ct. (we. dist.) Okla. 1991. Ptnr. Jacobus, Green & Eldridge, Tulsa, 1976-78; spl. judge Dist. Ct., Tulsa, 1979-81; ptnr. Rhodes, Hieronymus, Jones, Tucker & Gable, Tulsa, 1981—; adj. prof. Oral Roberts U., Tulsa, 1985. Tchr. Couples for Christ, Asbury United Meth. Ch., Tulsa, 1979—; pres., sec. Christian Businessmen's Com., Tulsa, 1981-93; chmn. Asbury Presch. Bd., Tulsa, 1985-95; trustee Metro Christian Acad., 1998—. Recipient Cert. of Achievement, Am. Acad. Jud. Edn., 1979. Mem. Okla. Bar Assn., Tulsa County Bar Assn. Democrat. Avocation: coaching baseball and basketball. Home: 2916 E 88th St Tulsa OK 74137-2507 Office: Rhodes Hieronymus et al 100 W 5th St Ste 400 Tulsa OK 74103-4287

ELDROUBI, ASMA ABDEL-AZIZ SALEH, business educator; b. Port Sudan, Sudan, Apr. 24, 1958; d. Abdel-Aziz Saleh and Aisha Mahmoud (Abdel-Bagi) E.; m. Idris Mohamed Malik, Dec. 26, 1979 (dec. Feb. 1983); 1 child, Amal; m. Abdel-Rahman Mohamed El Hassan, Nov. 12, 1992. Diploma, Khartoum Polytech., Khartoum, Sudan, 1980; postgrad. diploma in Bus. Adminstrn., U. Birmingham, U.K., 1988, MBA, 1989. Sec. Youneel for Trading Svcs., Khartoum, 1980-82; teaching asst. Sudan Univ. Sci. & Tech., Khartoum, 1982-88, lectr., 1990-93; lectr. Univ.Qatar, Doha, 1993—. Author: Audio Typing Textbook, 1984. Avocation: reading. Office: Univ Qatar, PO Box 120114, Doha State of Qatar

ELDRUP, EBBE, physician; b. Copenhagen, May 28, 1956; s. Erik Aage and Inga Christine (Jørgensen) E.; m. Lisbeth Marchen Krogh Hansen, Sept. 29, 1984; children: Julie, Andreas. MD, U. Copenhagen, 1981. Registrar Herlev (Denmark) U. Hosp., 1981-85, assoc. prof., 1985-89, sr. registrar, 1994—; sr. registrar Glostrup (Denmark) U. Hosp., 1990-94. Contbr. over 35 articles to profl. jours. Mem. Copenhagen Philatelist Club.

EL EBIARY, MUSTAFA, physician, researcher; b. Alexandria, Egypt, Aug. 15, 1959; s. Muhammad A. and Carmen (Alarcón) El E.; m. Isabel Loren, Jan. 14, 1995; 1 child, Daniel. BS, U. Alexandria, Egypt, 1977; MD, 1982; PhD, U. Barcelona, Spain, 1993. Internship U. Alexandria (Egypt) Hosp., 1983-84; resident Grek Hosp., Alexandria, Egypt, 1984-88; fellowship Hospital Clinic, Barcelona, Spain, 1988-90; rsch. dir., 1990—, sr. ICU physician, 1992—; prof. medicine U. Barcelona, Spain, 1992—; pulmonary/critical care cons., Barcelona, Spain, 1992—; inst. review bd. U. Barcelona, Spain, 1992—; rsch. dir. SEPAR, Spain, 1994—; guest researcher Winthrop Hosp., N.Y., 1996—. Author: Am. Jour. Respiratory Critical Care Medicine, 1992; contbr. articles to profl. jours. Recipient research grant CIRIT/Fundacion Clinic, Barcelona, Spain, 1996, FISss award Min. of Health, Spain, 1995. Mem. SPEAR, European Soc. Intensive Care Medicine, Am. Thoracic Soc., N.Y. Acad. Scis. Avocations: art, anthropology, music. Home: Av Barcelona 21 2o 2a, 08750 Molins de Rei Spain Office: Hosp Clinic Pneumology Svc, Villarroel 170, 08036 Barcelona Spain

ELEK, ANDREW LESLIE, economic policy consultant; b. Bekessaba, Hungary, Nov. 20, 1946; arrived in Australia, 1957; s. Paul and Maria (Pal) E.; m. Jane Alison Lyttle, June 17, 1972; children: Catriona, Sophia. BA in Econs. with honors, Australian Nat. U., 1969, PhD in Econs., 1976. 1st asst. sec. fin. Papua New Guinea, 1977-80; sr. economist World Bank, Washington, 1980-85; chief economist Econ. Planning Adv. Coun., Australia, 1985-87; 1st asst. sec. for fgn. affairs and trade, Australia, 1987-90; sr. rsch. fellow Australian Nat. U., Canberra, 1990-93; coord. Parent Advocacy, Canberra, Australia, 1994; rsch. assoc. Australian-Japan Rsch. Ctr., Canberra, Australia, 1995—; dir. Bellendena Ptnrs., Australia, 1995—. Contbr. articles to profl. jours. Mem. adv. panel Found. Devel. Coop., Australia,1991—; mem. Australian com. Pacific Econ. Coop., 1990-94; mem. editl. panel Asian Pacific Econ. Lit., 1991-94. Decorated Order of Australia; Rhodes scholar, 1969. Mem. Huntingfield Landcare Group (sec. 1995-99). Avocations: wine growing, horticulture, reading, bushwalking. Office: Bellendena Ptnrs, 240 Tinderbox Rd, Tinderbox 7054, Australia

EL-EMARY, NASR AHMED, adult education educator, researcher, consultant; b. Alexandria, Egypt, Jan. 25, 1942; s. Ahmed Mohamed El-Emary and Khalil Nema Abdou; m. Reiko Toshiaki Shibuya, Feb. 29, 1976 (div. Sept. 1982); children: Suzan, Amir; m. Tahani Hassan El-Faham, Jan. 25, 1983; children: Ahmed, Amany. B in Pharmacy and Pharmacy Chemistry, Alexandria U., 1965; M.Sc. Pharmacy Sci., Assiut U., Egypt, 1969; cert. Japanese Language Course, Osaka (Japan) U., 1972; Dr. Pharmacy, Pharmaceutical INst. Tohoku U., Sendai, Japan, 1976. Demonstrator Assiut U., 1965-69; rsch. student Tohoku U., 1972-76; asst. prof. of Phytochemistry, 1980-84, prof. phytochemistry, 1984—, vice dean for postgrad. studies and rsch., 1990-93; external examiner in pharmacognosy and phytochemistry various Egypt universities; cons. Allaqi Med. Plants Project Assiut U., 1989—; lectr. various univs.; supr. to three postgrad. rsch. students; advisor to Allaqi project in conservation of medicinal plants and phytochemical rsch. Editl. sec. Pharm. Bul., 1990-93. Rsch. grantee Ministry Edn., Japan, 1972-76. Mem. Brit. Iris Soc., Soc. Cultivation, Processing and Import Medicinal Plants, Assn. Producing, Processing and Export Medicinal Plants. Avocations: light music, calligraphy, ornamental plants cultivation, tennis, computer. Office: Assiut U, Faculty of Pharmacy, 71526 Assiut Egypt

ELEMES, YIANNIS EYAGGELOS, chemistry educator, researcher; b. Serres, Macedonia, Greece, Feb. 19, 1962; s. Eyaggelos Ioannis and Zinovia Constantinos (Toutouxis) E.; m. Katerina Periklis Kovanidou, July 18, 1987; 1 child, Zinovia. Bachelor's degree, U. Ioannina, Greece, 1985; PhD, U. Crete, Iraklion, 1990. Postdoctoral fellow UCLA, 1991-92, U. Uppsala, Sweden, 1993-95; lectr. U. Ioannina, 1994-99, asst. prof. chemistry, 1999—. Contbr. rsch. articles to profl. jours. With Greek Army, 1992-93. Recipient rsch. and tng. assistantship U. Crete, 1985; Human Capital and Mobility fellow European Union, 1993. Mem. Am. Chem. Soc., Greek Chemists Assn. Avocations: soccer, tennis, music, reading. Office: U Ioannina, Dept Chemistry, 45110 Ioannina Epiros, Greece

EL-ENANY, RASHEED, Arabic literature educator; b. Giza, Egypt, July 17, 1949. BA, Cairo U., 1970; PhD, Exeter (Eng.) U., 1984. Lectr. U. Exeter, 1978-94, reader, 1994-99, head dept., 1995-98, prof. modern Arabic lit., 1999—; subject assessor Higher Edn. Funding Coun. for Eng., 1996-98; lit. critic. Author: Naguib Mahfouz: The Pursuit of Meaning, 1993. E-mail: r.el-eneny@exeter.ac.uk. Office: Inst Arabic/Islamic Studies, Prince of Wales Rd, Exeter EX4 4JZ, England

ELENIUS, VALTER ANTON, retired ophthalmology educator; b. Helsinki, Finland, Sept. 7, 1923; s. Edvard and Elsa Helena (Kyander) E.; m. Irma Liisa Tammia; children: Marianne Kristina, Helena Ingrid, Klaus Peter. Candidate of medecine, U. Helsinki, 1947; licentiate of medicine, U. Turku, 1951, MD, 1951, PhD, 1958. Asst. dr. U. Turku Dept. Ophthalmology, Finland, 1953-56, asst. chief, 1961-69, assoc. prof., 1969-88, acting chief, 1985-87, ret., 1988; rsch. fellow Nobel Inst. for Neurophysiology Karolinska Inst., Stockholm, 1956-58, vis. scientist, Max-Planck Inst. Exptl. Eye Rsch., Bad-Nauheim, Germany, 1959, dept. ophthalmology U. Geneva, 1960; vis. physiol. optician U. Calif., Berkeley, 1963. Author articles in electrophysiology and psychophysiology of vision. Lt. Army of Finland, 1941-44. Decorated Finnish Mil. Cross of Freedom IV Order, knight I Order of White Rose of Finland. Mem. Ophthal. Soc. Finland (chmn. 1982-84). Avocations: visual arts, gardening, country life. Home: Janessaari 26, 20900 Turku Finland

ELEQUIN, CLETO, JR., retired physician; b. Antique, Philippines, Oct. 18, 1933; s. Cleto and Enriqueta (Tengonciang) E.; m. Nancy Johnson, May 14, 1958; children: Tracy, Thomas Kyle, Stuart Scott. M.D., Far Eastern U., Philippines, 1957. Rotating intern Good Samaritan Hosp., Lexington, Ky., 1957-58; gen. practice resident Central Bapt. Hosp., Lexington, 1958-59; psychiat. resident State Hosp., Danville, Pa., 1959-60, 61-62; psychiat. resident with child psychiatry State Hosp., New Castle, Del., 1962-63; staff physician Eastern State Hosp., Lexington, 1960-61, dir. Fayette County Project, dir. intensive treatment service, 1964-67, supt., 1969-71; dep. commr. Dept. Mental Health, State Ky., 1967-69; practice medicine, specializing in family practice Pecos, Tex., 1971-72, Austin, Tex., 1974-89; ret.; cons. psychiatrist Texas Youth Commn., Peyote, Tex., Permian Basin Cmty. Mental Health-Mental Retardation, Odessa, Tex., Prude Ranch for Emotionally Disturbed Children and Adolescents, Ft. Davis, Tex., Dept. Mental Health-Mental Retardation State of Tex.; vis. lectr. in medicine and psychiatry Am. U. of the Caribbean, Plymouth, Montserrat; asst. dep. commr. Tex. Dept. Mental Health and Mental Retardation, Austin, 1973-74, dep. commr. mental health, 1974; pvt. practice family practice and psychiatry, Austin, 1974-85; mem. attending staff Brackenridge Hosp., St. David Med. Ctr., Seton Med. Ctr., Shoal Creek Hosp.; med. dir. Mary Lee Sch. and Found., 1974-80, bd. trustees, 1980-85; attending psychiatrist U. Ky. Med. Ctr., 1964-71, Good Samaritan Hosp., 1969-71, Ctrl. Bapt. Hosp., 1966-71; cons. psychiatrist U. Ky. Student Health Svc., 1965-71, Peace Corps, 1966-68, Bur. Rehab. State Ky., 1965-71, Blue Grass Cmty. Care Ctr., 1967-71, Covington (Ky.) Cmty. Care Ctr., 1969-71, Hazard Cmty. Care Ctr., 1969-71, Danville (Ky.) Cmty. Ctr., 1969-71, Maysville (Ky.) Cmty. Care Ctr., 1969-71; clin. instr., asst. clin. prof. dept. psychiatry U. Ky. Med. Ctr., 1964-69, assoc. clin. prof., 1969-71; cons. psychiatrist Tex. Youth Commn. Tex. Dept. of MH-MR, State of Tex.; pvt. practice in psychiatry, Austin, 1974-85; mem. attending staff Brackenridge Hosp., St. David Med. Ctr., Seton Med. Ctr., Shoal Creek Hosp.; med. dir. Mary Lee Sch. and Found., 1974-80, mem. bd. trustees, 1980-85. Mem. Profl. Adv. Coun. Community Mental Health-Retardation Ctr., Lexington, 1967-71; mem. Lexington Hosp. Coun., 1969-71. Mem. AMA, Am. Psychiat. Assn., Am. Acad. Family Physicians (life), Assn. Med. Supts. Mental Hosps., Tex. Med. Assn., Travis County Med. Soc., Austin Psychiat. Soc. Home: 10101 Jupiter Hills Dr Austin TX 78747-1322

ELER, JOANIR PEREIRA, animal breeding educator, researcher, consultant; b. Conselherio Pena, Brazil, Mar. 15, 1951; s. Waldemar and Dalva (Eler) Pereira; m. Marcia Noelia, July 24, 1982; children: Nuria Cristina, Luciano Henrique. DVM, UFRRJ, Rio de Janeiro, 1974; MS, Nat. Vet. Sch., Toulouse, France, 1979; PhD, U Sao Paulo, Brazil, 1987. Veterinarian Dalla B. Farms, Colatina, Brazil, 1975; with ext. svc. EMATER, Castro, Brazil, 1976; rschr. EMBRAPA, Sao Carlos, Sao Paulo, Brazil, 1977-88; prof. animal breeding U. Sao Paulo, 1988—; vis. prof. U. Nebr., 1992-94; cons. genetic evaluation CFM Farms and Other Groups, Brazil, 1994—. Contbr. articles to profl. jours. Mem. Brazilian Soc. Animal Sci., Brazilian Soc. Animal Breeding, Am. Soc. Animal Sci. Presbyterian. Avocations: camping, fishing. E-mail: Joapeler@usp.br. Fax: 019-561-8606. Office: U Sao Paulo, Rua Duque de Caxias Nor 225, 13630970 Pirassununga SaoPaulo, Brazil

ELERAKY, MOHAMMED ALY, neurosurgeon; b. Tanta, Egypt, Mar. 1, 1965. MD with honors, Tanta U., Egypt, 1988; M in Gen. Surgery, 1993; PhD in Neurosurgery, U. Ariz., 1999. Diplomate Am. Bd. Neurosurgery. House officer Tanta U. Hosp., Egypt, 1989-90; resident El Maadi Armed Forces Hosp., Cairo, Egypt, 1990-91; resident Tanta U. Hosp., Egypt, 1991-94, asst. lectr. neurosurgery, 1994-96. Contbr. articles to profl. jours. Spine Surgery rsch. fellow Barrow Neurol. Inst., Phoenix, 1996-98. Mem. Am. Assn. Neurol. Surgery, Congress Neurol. Surgery, N.Am. Spine Soc. Home: 9 Anwer Basha St, Tanta Egypt

ELFERS, THOMAS EARL, lawyer, educator; b. Kenosha, Wis., Sept. 4, 1942; s. Earl and Marguerite Elfers; m. Cynthia Marie Johnson, Oct. 30, 1963 (div. Dec. 1981); children: Renee Lynn, Jacqueline Leigh, Michael Thomas, Kristen Kay; m. Therese Wenderski, July 21, 1984. BS, U. Wis., 1965; MEd, Wayne State U., 1972; PhD, U. Mich., 1981; JD, U. Detroit, 1988. Bar: Fla. 1989, Mich. 1989, U.S. Dist. Ct. (so. and middle dists.) Fla. 1990, DC 1991, U.S. Ct. Appeals (DC cir.) 1991, U.S. Ct. Appeals (11th cir.) 1999. Supr. labor rels. and pers. Ford Motor Co., Mt. Clemens, Mich., 1965-77; dir. employee rels. Macomb Intermediate Sch. Dist., Mt. Clemens, 1977-89; atty. Morgan, Lewis & Bockius, Miami, Fla., 1989-90; dir. labor rels. City of Warren, Mich., 1991; acting supervisory trial atty. Equal Employment Opportunity Commn., Miami, 1992-97; sr. assoc. counsel Palm Beach County Sch. Dist., West Palm Beach, Fla., 1997-99; ptnr. Bare & Elfers, P.A., Miami, 2000—; adj. prof. Nova South Ea. U., Ft. Lauderdale, Fla., 2000. Mem. Phi Kappa Phi, Alpha Sigma Nu. Home: 14036 SW 148th Ln Miami FL 33186-5730 Office: Bare & Elfers PA 6601 SW 80th St Miami FL 33143-4661

EL-FOULY, MOHAMED MOSTAFA, agricultural researcher, educator, consultant; b. Alexandria, Egypt, Mar. 25, 1939; s. Mostafa M.R. and Amna Hussein (El-Arnaoudy) El-Fouly; m. Gisela Helga Britten, Dec. 22, 1966; children: Tamer, Mariem. BSc in Agr., Alexandria U., 1959; DAgr., Tech. U. Munich, 1963. Cert. agrl. engr. Rsch. assoc. Inst. Plant Nutrition, Tech. U., Munich, 1961-63; rsch. fellow Saar U., Saarbruecken, Germany, 1963-65, BASF Ag, Limburgerh, Germany, 1965-66; rschr., assoc. prof. Nat. Rsch. Ctr., Cairo, 1966-77, rsch. prof. dept. botany, 1977—, head of botany dept., 1995-97, head agrl. and biol. rsch. divsn., bd. dirs., 1997-99; organizer/condr. workshops in field; mem. nat. coms. for Internat. Union Conservation of Nature, Internat. Union Physiol. Scis., UNESCO, program Man and Biosphere, SCOPE; mem. sci. promotion com. Profs. Higher Coun. for Sci. Rsch.; adv. bd. Egyptian Fertilizer Devel. Ctr.; mem. internat. adv. bd. Coun. for Promotion of Children's Sci. Pubs. in Africa, Nairobi, Kenya, African Acad. Scis., 1990—, mem. fellowship granting com., 1991-95. Author 8 books and booklets on goal-oriented project planning; contbr. over 200 articles to profl. jours.; author 7 popular sci. books; editor/co-editor 25 procs. of confs. and workshops. Bd. dirs. German Secondary Sch., Cairo, 1981-95. NUFFIC (Netherlands) fellow, 1961, DAAD (Germany) fellow, 1969, Alexander von Humboldt Found. fellow, 1975-76, 86, 94; Bavarian Ministry Higher Edn. scholar, 1961-63; recipient Disting. Achievement award NRC, 1981. Fellow African Acad. Scis.; mem. Assn. for Advancement of Agrl. scis. Africa (exec. com. 1975-78, 78-81, hon. sec. gen. 1981—, acting adminstrv. sec. gen. 1984—), Max Eyth Soc. Germany (corr.), Internat. Coun. for Plant Nutrition, Internat. Assn. for Optimizing Plant Nutrition (mem. permanent com. 1982—, v.p. 1997—, coord. internat. working group on foliar fertilization 1988—), Egyptian Soc. Plant Nutrition and Fertilization (pres.), Egyptian Soc. Environ. Scis. Microbiol. Soc., Egypt Bot. Soc., Egyptian Soc. Physiol. Scis., Egyptian Soc. Algae Rsch. (pres.). Avocations: photography, stamp collecting, travel. Office: Nat Rsch Ctr, El-Tahrir St Dokki, 12622 Cairo Egypt

EL GABALY, SHERIF-MOSTAFA, chemical company executive; b. Alexandria, Egypt, Feb. 15, 1949; s. Mostafa El Gabaly and Nabila (Hassan) Bassyouny; m. Nevine Abdel Moneim Seif, Sept. 1977; children: Mostafa, Naela, Mansour. BS in Chem. Engring., Cairo U., 1970; PhD in Chem. Engring., Higher Inst. of Chemical Tech., Sofia, Bulgaria, 1976. Research engr. Indsl. Orgn. of Arab League States, Cairo, 1976-77; petrochem. engr. Qatar Gen. Petroleum Corp., Doha, Qatar, 1977-80; gen. mgr. NE Africa dist. The Dow Chem. Co., Cairo, 1980-88; cons. The Dow Chem. Co., 1989—; mng. dir., bd. dirs. Internat. Fertilizer and Chem. Co., Egypt; chmn. Agrin Serve Co. (rep. Dow Agrochemicals), 1989—, Olitech-Egypt (rep. Olivetti Co. in Egypt), 1989—; mng. dir. Arabian Fats, Oils and Chems. Co., 1989, Advanced Chem. Engring. Systems, 1989—; mem. Industry and Energy Com., Egypt, 1989—; pres., main shareholder Ferchem; main shareholder CMB; owner Polyserve for Fertilizers and Chems.; chmn. bd. East Oweinat Devel. Co. Chmn. Egyptian Assn. Fertilizers, Traders and Distrbrs., 2000—. Mem. Am. C. of C. (bd. dirs. 1987), Egyptian Businessmen's Assn. (bd. dirs. Egypt/Japan and Egypt India, bd. mem. Egypt/Sudan bus. coun.). Home: 33 Mohamed Mazhar St, 3 Yemen St, Giza Arab Republic of Egypt Office: Agrin Serve, 22 Syria St, Mohandessin Giza Arab Republic of Egypt

EL GAMAL, YOUSRY SABER, engineering dean, computer consultant; b. Alexandria, Egypt, Sept. 25, 1947; s. Saber Hussein and Badria Ahmad (Taman) El G.; m. Moushira Hussein El Gamal, Nov. 29, 1981; children: Sarah, Samar. BSc, Alexandria U., 1968; MSc, Ain Shams U., Cairo, 1977; DSc, George Washington U., 1985. Radar engr. Air Defence, Egypt, 1968-71; rschr. Atomic Energy Authority, Cairo, 1971-74; lectr. Internat. Atomic Energy Agy., Turin, Italy, 1974-76, Arab Maritime Acad., Alexandria, 1976-87; chmn. Electronics and Computer Ops., Alexandria, 1987-90; dean Coll. Engring., Alexandria, 1990-97, v.p. edn. rsch., 1997—; cons. C. of C., Alexandria, 1993—. Editor Arab Maritime Transport Acad.; chief editor Personal Computer Club Mag. V.p. Friends of Music and Arts, Alexandria, 1986—; mem. Friends of Environ., Alexandria, 1991—. Recipient fellowships Internat. Atomic Energy Agy., Turin, Italy, 1974, Amideast, Washington, 1982, Richard Merwin award George Washington U., Washington, 1984. Mem. IEEE, Am. Soc. Engring. Edn., N.Y. Acad. Sci., Sci. Computer Soc. (pres. 1987—), Personal Computer Club (chmn. 1990—). Avocations: tennis, swimming, classical music, fine arts. Home: Montazah Bldg H Apt 92, Borg Misr Liltamir, Alexandria Egypt Office: Arab Acad for Sci and Tech, PO Box 1029, Alexandria Egypt

EL GAMMAL, HUSSEIN MOKHTAR, organization official, researcher, consultant; b. Cairo, Aug. 5, 1935; s. Ahmed Mokhtar and Nefissa Mohammed (El-Fawal) El-Gammal; m. Affaf Abdel-Hamid Hosni, June 22, 1961; children: Hala, Randa, Diena. BSME, Cairo U., 1956, diploma in advanced studies, 1961, MSc, PhD in Control Sys., 1968; postgrad., U. Toulouse, France, 1969-70. Dept. chief Egyptian Petroleum Corp., Cairo, 1957-61, Egyptian Aero. Establishment, Cairo, 1961-69; sr. lectr. U. Hertfordshire, Eng., 1970-80; devel. advisor Royal Commn. for Jubail and Yanbu, Saudi Arabia, 1980-84; sr. advisor Kuwait Inst. for Sci. Rsch., 1985-90; mng. dir. Social Fund for Devel., Cairo, 1991—; vis. prof. U. Hertfordshire, 1999; cons. Ferraris Engring. and Devel. Co. Ltd., Edmonton and London, 1971-84, FESTO Pneumatic Ctr., Berkein, Germany, 1977-87, Firemaster Internat., Alta., Can. 1991, Thomson CSF, France, 1981-83; vis. fellow Cranfield Inst. Tech., UK, 1987-92. Contbr. articles to profl. jours.; patentee for improvements in or relating to apparatus for use in measurement of flow rate of fluid flow, for suction type flowmeter (Brit.). Team mem. Olympic Games, Rome, Tokyo. Named to Mex. Order Law, Culture & Peace, Grade de Commendeur d'ordre Nat. du Merite; recipient 10th king Baudouin Internat. Devel. prize. Mem. Internat. Assn. Mgmt. Tech., World Assn. Small and Med. Enterprises, Coun. Eng. Com. on Mech. Engring., Brit. Inst. Measurement and Control, Am. Soc. Mech. Engrs., Egyptian Soc. Engring., Brit. Instn. Mech. Engring., Brit. Inst. Mgmt., Heliopolis Sporting Club, Gezira Sporting Club, Auto Club. Moslem. Avocations: swimming, water polo, squash, racquetball. Home: Heliopolis, 3 Halim Abou Sif St Apt 11, Cairo Egypt Office: Social Fund For Devel, Hussein Hegazi St Off El Eini St, Cairo Egypt

EL GANZORY, MOHAMED AHMED, quality control engineer, inspector; b. Cairo, Sept. 23, 1968; s. Ahmed Abd Elaziz and Nefesa Metwally (Mahmoud) El G. Quality control engr. Alexandria Madia, Egypt, 1991-93; QASQ control engr. Barge 11, Petroget, Egypt, 1993—. Mem. Egyptian Welding Soc. Home: Elasafra Bahary, Elsalam St Bldg Two, Alexandria Egypt

ELGAR, MARK ADRIAN, evolutionary biologist, educator; b. Stourpaine, Dorset, Eng., July 25, 1957; arrived in Australia, 1970; s. Ronald Elgar and Audrey Percy; m. Cathryn Cutler, Apr. 8, 2000. BSc with honors, Griffit U., Brisbane, Australia, 1980; PhD, Christ's Coll., U. Cambridge, Eng., 1985. SERC rsch. fellow U. Oxford, Eng., 1985-87; univ. rsch. fellow U. New South Wales, Sydney, Australia, 1987-89, Queen Elizabeth II rsch. fellow, 1989-91; asst. prof. U. Melbourne, Australia, 1991-94, assoc. prof., 1995-98, prof., 1999—; vis. rsch. fellow Christenson Rsch. Inst., Madang, Papau New Guinea, 1989, 93; cons. Australian Broadcasting Corp., Melbourne, 1992—; vis. prof. U. Pierre Marie Curie, Paris, 1998. Editor: Cannibalism: Ecology and Evolution Among Diverse Taxa, 1992; assoc. editor, book rev. editor Australian Jour. Ecology, 1996—; assoc. editor Behavioral Ecology & Sociobiology, 1994—; mem. editl. bd. Behavioral Ecology, 1993—, Australian Jour. Zoology. Grant reviewer NSF, 1990—, Australian Rsch. Coun., Canberra, Australia, 1988—. Rsch. grantee Australian Rsch. Coun., 1989—. Mem. Internat. Soc. Behavioral Ecology (councillor 1994-98), Internat. Coun. Ethologists (corr. sec. 1996-99), Australasian Evolution Soc. (pres. 1999—). Office: U Melbourne Dept Zoology, Victoria 3010, Australia

ELGAVISH, ADA, molecular and cellular biologist; b. Cluj, Romania, Jan. 23, 1946; came to U.S. 1979; d. David and Malca (Neuman) Simchas; m. Gabriel A. Elgavish, Dec. 28, 1968; children: Rotem, Eynav. BSc, Tel-Aviv U., 1969, MSc, 1972; PhD, Weizmann Inst. Sci., Rehovot, Israel, 1978. Postdoctoral vis. fellow NIH, Balt., 1979-81; instr. U. Ala. Sch. Medicine, Birmingham, 1981-82, rsch. assoc., 1982-84, rsch. asst. prof., 1984-89, asst. prof. comparative medicine, 1989-92, assoc. prof., 1992—; scientist Cell Adhesion and Matrix Rsch. Ctr., Birmingham, 1995—, Ctr. Metabolic Bone Disease, Ctr. for Aging, 1996; mem. Cancer Ctr.; founder Diacell, Inc., 1998. Grantee Cystic Fibrosis Found., 1986-90, Am. Lung Assn., 1987-92, NIH, 1989—, Interstitial Cystitis Assn., 1998, Am. Inst. Cancer Rsch., 2000, Pfizer, 2000. Mem. AAAS, Am. Physiol. Soc., Am. Urol. Assn., Soc. for Basic Urol. Rsch., Sigma Xi. Home: 1737 Valpar Dr Birmingham AL 35226-2343 Office: U Ala Sch Medicine Dept Comparative Medicine Birmingham AL 35294-0001

ELGAVISH, GABRIEL ANDREAS, physical biochemistry educator; b. Budapest, Hungary, July 29, 1942; arrived in Israel, 1957, came to U.S., 1979; s. László and Katalin Barbara (Szentmiklóssy) Schwarcz; m. Ada Stephanie Simcas, Dec. 28, 1967; children: Rotem László Abraham, Eynav Elgavish. BSc, Hebrew U., Jerusalem, 1967; MSc, Tel-Aviv U., 1972; PhD, Weizmann Inst. of Sci., 1978. Vis. fellow NIH, Balt., 1979-81; asst. prof. U. Ala., Birmingham, 1981-87, assoc. prof., 1987-95, prof., 1995—. Contbr. articles to profl. jours. 1st lt. Israeli Army, 1961-64. Mem. Am. Chem. Soc., Am. Soc. for Biochemistry and Molecular Biology, Am. Heart Assn./

Basic Sci., Soc. Magnetic Resonance in Medicine. Jewish. Achievements include patents on Contrast Agents for Nuclear Magnetic Resonance Imaging; research in biomedical nuclear magnetic resonance spectroscopy. Office: U Ala THT 336 1900 University Blvd Birmingham AL 35233-2008

EL GHARBAWI, MOHAMED AHMED, consulting surgeon, physician, educator, poet; b. Zagazig, Sharkya, Egypt, Apr. 16, 1952; s. Ahmed Mohamed El Gharbawi and Sabah Hamed Ibrahim; m. Nival Mosa Rizk, May 19, 1977 (div. Apr. 1988); 1 child, Hadeel; m. Effat Abdul Mohsen Mohamed, July 14, 1990; children: Merhan, Marwan, Mohannad, Shahd, Farah. MB, BChir, Zagazig (Egypt) U., 1975, MSc in Gen. Surgery, 1979, MD in Gen. Surgery, 1985; diploma in modern mgmt., Cambridge Tutorial Coll., Eng., 1993, diploma in bus. mgmt., 1995. Diplomate Am. Bd. Quality Assurance and Utilization Rev. Physicians. House officer Zagazig U. Hosps., 1976-77, resident in gen. surgery, 1977-80, asst. lectr., 1980-85, lectr. faculty of medicine, 1985-89, asst. prof., 1989; cons. in gen. surgery Samarec Med. Svcs., Khobar, Saudi Arabia, 1989-93; cons. surgeon, quality improvement physician Saudi Aramco, Dhahran, Saudi Arabia, 1994—; cons. in modern medicine, Nicosia, Cyprus, 1993. Author: Illness and Cure in the Songs of Poets, Abulkasim Al-Zahrawi and the Effect of Arabs on Surgical Science, 6 books of Arabic poems, 1987-93; contbr. over 30 sci. articles to med. jours.; author numerous poems. Mem. N.Y. Acad. Scis., Egyptian Surgeons Soc., Internat. Soc. Quality Health Care, Am. Coll. Physician Execs., Egyptian Soc. for Quality in Health Care, Egyptian Med. Syndicate, Arab African Soc. Gastroenterology and Endoscopy, Nat. Assn. for Healthcare Quality, Egyptian Philatelic Soc., Nat. Geog. Soc., Writers' Union, Al-Sharkya Sports Club. Democrat. Muslim. Avocations: writing poetry, stamp collecting, sports. E-mail: elgharma@aramco.com.sa. Home: PO Box 273, Zagazig Sharkya, Egypt Office: Saudi Aramco Med Svcs, PO Box 11204, Dhahran 31311, Saudi Arabia

ELGIN, DUANE, writer, activist; b. Nampa, Idaho, Feb. 7, 1943; s. Clifford Walter and Mary Earl Elgin; div. 1977; children: Clifford, Benjamin, Matthew. BA, Coll. Idaho, 1966; MBA, U. Pa., 1968, MA, 1969. Sr. profl. Nat. Commn. Population Growth and Am. Future, Washington, 1970—; sr. social scientist SRI Internat., Menlo Park, Calif., 1970—; writer, activist Calif., 1977—; cons. in field. Author: Voluntary Simplicity, 1981, 2d edit., 1993, Awakening Earth, 1993, Promise Ahead, 2000; co-author: Changing Images of Man, 1982. Bd. dirs. Choosing Our Future, Calif., 1981-89. E-mail: duane@awakeningearth.org.

ELGUINDY, MOHAMED SAYED, medical educator, cardiologist, consultant; b. Beni-Suef, Egypt, July 5, 1943; s. Sayed Khalil Elguindy and Alia Abdel Rahman Abu Teira; m. Shadia Mohamed Sarhan, Oct. 20, 1973; children: Radwa, Ahmed. MBBCh, Cairo (Egypt) U., 1965, MD, 1973. Sr. resident Cairo U., 1970-74, lectr. in cardiology, 1974-79, asst. prof., 1979-84, prof., 1984-99, chmn. dept. cardiology, 1999—; chief of cardiology Security Forces Hosp., Riyadh, Saudi Arabia, 1990-93; cons. Arab Contractor Hosp., Cairo, 1985-90, dir. cardiology, 1990—. Author: Essentials of Medicine, 2d edit., 1999, Essentials of Cardiology, 2d edit., 1999; mem. editl. bd. Cairo U. Med. Jour., 1990, Bull. Egyptial Soc. Cardiology. Fellow Am. Coll. Cardiology; mem. Royal Coll. Physicians London. Avocation: photography. Office: Manial Univ Hosp, ElManial Cairo Egypt

ELHADDAD, MERVET AHMED, mineralogy educator; b. Suez, Egypt, Oct. 26, 1950; d. Ahmed Moustafa Elhaddad and Souad Mohamed Koshk; m. Mohamed Mokhtar Sultan, June 15, 1992; 1 child, Amr Mohamed. BSc in Geology, Cairo U., 1972; PhD in Geology and Mineralogy, Mining Inst., Leningrad, USSR, 1978. Demonstrator dept. geology Cairo U., 1972-73; rsch. scientist Nuclear Scis. Ctr., U. Fla., Gainesville, 1982-83, Peace fellow, 1985-86; rsch. scientist U. Heidelberg, Germany, 1990-92; asst. prof. dept. geology Assiut (Egypt) U., 1979-82, 83-85, assoc. prof., 1986-90, 92-96, prof. mineralogy, 1996—. Contbr. articles to profl. jours. Mem. Geol. Soc. Am. (Cordillerian sect.), Brit. Mineral. Soc., Egyptian Mineral. Soc., Egyptian Geol. Soc. (presenter 1994), Am. Geophys. Union, German Mineral. Soc., Nat. Geog. Soc. Achievements include the first to discover and record platinum mineralization in Eqyptian rocks; research on lanthanides in 13 Egyptian phosphorite mines, marly carbontes of Elmansouri from diagenesis to amphibolite facies, hydrothermal formation of sulphides in Lab and their relation to natural environment, economic assessment of platinum in ultramafic rocks of Egypt, land use change assessment in relation to soil condition from 1967 to date. Office: Geology Dept Faculty Sci, Assiut Univ, Assiut Egypt

ELHAG, HAMID MOHAMED, agriculturist, plant biotechnologist, research scientist; b. Shendi, Sudan, Jan. 1, 1949; s. Mohamed Elhag Fadlalla and Algodaliya Salih Alshowaya; m. Samya Abdalla Abbas, Dec. 24, 1980; children: Ammar, Hiba, Hind, Azza. BSc, Khartoum (Sudan) U., 1974; MSc, U. Calif., Riverside, 1979; PhD, Purdue U., 1985. Rsch. asst., asst. dir. Food Rsch. Ctr., Khartoum, 1975-78; rsch. assoc. Purdue U., West Lafayette, Ind., 1985-86; rschr. King Saud U., Riyadh, 1986—. Mem. AAAS, Am. Soc. Horticultural Scis., Internat. Assn. Plant Tissue Culture, Saudi Biol. Soc. Democat. Muslim. Avocations: swimming, tennis, soccer, jogging. Office: King Saud U Dept Pharmacognosy, PO Box 2457, Riyadh 11451, Saudi Arabia

EL-HAKAMY, ABDULWAHAB A., English educator; b. Taif, Saudi Arabia, 1950; s. Ali M. and Z.A. (Sibyany) El-H.; m. Salwa T. Idressy, 1970; children: Areej, Arwa, Ali. BA, Coll. Edn., Makkah, 1969; MA, Mich. State U., 1973; PhD, U. Mich., 1979. Asst. prof. Umm AlQura U., 1980-88, assoc. prof., 1988—. address: PO Box 7087, Makkah Saudi Arabia

EL HASSAN, ELHASSAN SIDAHMED, consultant physician; b. Shendi, Sudan, Jan. 1, 1945; arrived in United Arab Emirates, 1976; s. Sidahmed El Hassan and Algisma Abdulla El Samani; m. Khadiga Fadul El Mulla Hussein, July 4, 1972; children: Osama, Rabab, Yahya, Eiman, Ahmed, Mona. MB, BChir, U. Khartoum, Sudan, 1969; diploma in anesthesia, U. Copenhagen, 1972. Sr. house officer K.C. Hosp., Khartoum, 1969-72; fellow Anesthesiology Ctr., Copenhagen, 1972-73; sr. house officer Tindal Hosp., U.K., 1973-75; specialist physician K.C. Hosp., 1975-76; specialist physician Rashid Hosp., Dubai, United Arab Emirates, 1976-80, cons. physician, 1980—; cons. gastroenterologist, Rashid Hosp., 1980—, chief digestive diseases unit, 1994—, chmn. sci. com. gastroenterology sect., 1995-96; sr. lectr. Dubai Med. Coll., 1988—. Sec. Sudanese Student Union, London, 1975-76. Fellow Royal Coll. Physicians Edinburgh; mem. Royal Coll. Physicians U.K., Sudanese Social Club (vice chmn. 1992-94). Avocations: swimming, fishing, camping, gardening.

EL-HAWARY, MOETAZ MAHER, civil engineering educator; b. Domiat, Egypt, Mar. 21, 1958; s. Maher Mahmoud El-Hawary; m. Iman Mohamed Abdulatif, July 14, 1991; children: Mohanad, Lina. BSc with honors, King Saud U., Saudi Arabia, 1980; MSc, U. Calif., Davis, 1982, PhD, 1987. Quantity engr. Arabco Establishment, Saudi Arabia, 1980; rsch. engr. U. Calif., Davis, 1987; asst. prof. civil engring. Cairo U., Fayoum, Egypt, 1988-92, concrete lab dir., 1991-92; prof. civil engring., 2000—; asst. prof. civil engring. Kuwait U., 1992-2000; cons. Cairo U., 1988-92, Kuwait U., 1992—; expert G.C.C. Comml. Arbitration Ctr., 1996—; speaker at internat. confs. Contbr. articles to profl. jours. Tchr. Ctr. for Cmty. Svc., Kuwait, 1995. Mem. ASCE, Egyptian Soc. Earthquake Engrs. Avocations: reading, music, swimming. Office: Kuwait Univ Dept Civil Eng, PO Box 5969, Safat 13060, Kuwait

EL-HELW, MAGED RAGHEB, law educator; b. Samanoud, Gharbia, Egypt, May 20, 1940; s. Ragheb Mohamed and Shouk Mohamed (Shehata) El-H.; m. Laila Mahmoud Kasem; children: Karim, Amr, Hadi. LLB, Faculty of Law, Alexandria, Egypt, 1963; Diploma in Pvt. Law, Faculty of Law, 1964, Diploma in Pub. Law, 1966, PhD, 1969. Lectr. Faculty of Law, 1969-75, assoc. prof., 1975-76, prof., 1981-88, prof., head pub. law dept., 1992—; assoc. prof., head pub. law Faculty of Law & Sharia, Kuwait, 1976-81, prof., head law dept. Faculty of Sharia & Law, Al-ein, United Arab Emirates; cons. Alexandria U., 1970-76, Wipco, Alexandria, 1985-88; lectr. and coord. O&M Orgn., Alexandria, 1969-88; atty. Supreme Ct., Cairo, Egypt, 1981—; presenter in field. Author: Principle of Kuwaiti Administrative Law, 1978, Administrative Law and Civil Service Law in Kuwait, 1980, Popular Referendum and Islamic Law, 1983, Administrative Law, 1987, Public Administration, 1987, Administrative Jurisdiction in Lebanon, 1988, Principles of Administrative Law in U.A.E., 1990, Governmental Systems and Emirates Constitution, 1991, Environmental Law, 1992, Administrative Jurisdiction, 1994, Constitutional Law, 1995, Political Systems, 1996, Administrative Contracts and Arbitration, 2000; contbr. articles to mags. Mem. Medicine & Law, Alexandria, 1972—, Environment Friends, Alexandria, 1995. Avocations: reading, painting, sports. Home: 9 Abdel Hamid El-deeb St, Tharwat Alexandria Egypt Office: Law Faculty, Mostafa Mosharafa St El-shatby, Alexandria Egypt

EL HEMALY, ABDEL KARIM MOHAMAD ALY AHMAD, obstetrician, gynecologist, educator; b. Khartoum, Sudan, June 6, 1940; s. Mohamad Aly Ahmad El Hemaly and Sania Abdel Whab El Far; m. Laila Abdel Samie Mousa, May 22, 1975; children: Mohamad, Moustafa. MB, BChir, Faculty of Medicine, Cairo, 1963, D of Ob-Gyn., D of Surgery, 1966. House officer Cairo U. Hosps., 1963-64, registrar in ob-gyn., 1965-67; registrar in ob-gyn. Irvine Maternity Hosp., Scotland, 1971-76; lectr. in ob-gyn. Faculty of Medicine, Cairo, 1976-82, asst. prof. ob-gyn., 1982-87, prof. ob-gyn., 1987—; cons. in ob-gyn. Nat. Health Ins., Cairo, 1977—. Contbr. articles to profl. jours. Fellow Royal Coll. Surgeons (Glasgow); mem. Royal Coll. Ob-Gyn. (London). Moslem. Avocations: sports, music, reading. Home: 3 Emad El Din Kamel St, Cairo 11371, Egypt Office: Faculty of Medicine, Al Azhar U, Cairo Egypt

ELIA, ANNIBALE, linguist, educator; b. Salerno, Italy, Dec. 4, 1949; s. Giovanni and Vittoria (Zito) E.; m. Maddalena della Volpe, July 27, 1989; children: Massimiliano, Alessandro. Grad., U. Naples (Italy), 1972, PhD, 1979. Rschr. U. Naples, 1973-75, Nat. Ctr. Sci. Rsch., Paris, 1975-77; assoc. prof. U. Salerno (Italy), 1978-86, prof. linguistics, 1986—; dir. linguistics inst. U. Salerno, 1980-96, pres. comm. faculty, 1991—, dir. comm. dept., 1996—; pres. sci. com. Lexicon SPA Co., Salerno, 1987—. Author: Per Saussure Contro Saussure, 1978, Le Verbe Italien, 1984, (software) Electronic Dictionary of Italian, 1995 (Eureka grant 1996); contbr. articles to Linguisticae Investigationes, 1980-90. Mem. Academia Europea, Italian Linguistics Soc., Italian Philosophy Lang. Soc. Avocations: painting, sculpture. Office: Comm Dept U Salerno, Via Ponte D Melillo, 84084 Fisciano Salerno, Italy

ELIA, MICHELE, mathematics educator; b. Berzano, Asti-Piemonte, Italy, Jan. 2, 1945; s. Luigi and Cristina (Fogliatti) E. Dr. engr., Politecnico di Torino, 1970. Researcher FIAT, Torino, Italy, 1970-71, Politecnico di Torino, 1971-77, assoc. prof. math., 1977-90, prof., 1990—. Author: (with others) The Information Theory Approach to Communications, 1977; Contbr. articles to profl. jours. Mem. IEEE (sr.), Unione Matematica Italiana, Am. Math. Soc., Math. Assn. Am., Soc. Indsl. and Applied Math., N.Y. Acad. Scis. Roman Catholic. Home: Via G Marconi 3, Castiglione Torinese, 10090 Turin Italy Office: Politecnico di Torino Dipartimento Elettronica, Corso Duca degli Abruzzi 24, 10129 Turin Italy

ELIAN, MARTA, neurologist, medical counsellor; b. Oradea, Romania; d. Laszlo Steiner and Magda Laszlo; m. Ezra Eilender Elian, Aug. 23, 1949 (dec. 1982); children: Amnon, Yoram. MD, Hebrew U., 1958; diploma in hypnotherapy/integral therapy, London, 1989; diploma in reality therapy, Dublin, 1993. Staff neurologist Children Med. Ctr., Boston, 1959-62; neurologist, sr. lectr. Tel Aviv Univ. Hosp., 1962-73; neurologist Hosp. for Epilepsy, Zurich, 1974-75; staff psychiatrist Psychiat. Hosp., Zurich, 1975-76; cons. neurophysiologist Nat. Health Svc., London, 1976-93, cons. neurologist, 1993-98; pvt. practice, expert witness. Contbr. 100 articles to profl. jours. Avocations: friends, travel, theater, music. Home: 32 A Queens Grove, London NW8 6HJ, England

ELIAS, AZIZEH ANN, research scientist; b. Sioux City, Iowa, Nov. 11, 1973; d. John and Nawall Elias. BS in Chemistry, U. North Fla., 1997. Asst. scientist Vistakon, Jacksonville, Fla., 1997—; lab. instr. U. North Fla., Jacksonville, 1998-99. Sunday sch. tchr. St. George Orthodox Ch., Jacksonville, 1992-96, youth group advisor, 1995—. Mem. Am. Chem. Soc. Avocations: reading, rollerblading, working out, foreign languages. E-mail: aelias@visus.jnj.com.

ELIASSEN, KJELL ARNOLD, political scientist, educator, researcher; b. Skien, Telemark, Norway, May 18, 1946; s. Willie Arnold and Esther Johanne (Kristiansen) E.; m. Ellen Agnes Ulltveit-Moe, June 26, 1970; children: Hanne, Tore. Degree, U. Bergen, 1971. Rsch. asst. U. Bergen, Norway, 1969-71, rschr., 1971-72; assoc. prof. U. Aarhus, Denmark, 1972-80; dep. dir. gen. Ministry of Planning, Oslo, 1980-81; rsch. dir. Norwegian Sch. Mgmt., Oslo, 1981-83, prof., 1983—; v.p. Norwegian Sch. Mgmt., 1985-89; dir. Centre for European and Asian Studies, 1988—; chmn. bd. Nat. Weather Forecasting Inst., Norway, 1986-94; prof. U. Libre Bruxelles, 1994—. Editor: Making Policy in Europe, 1993, 2nd edit., 2000, Managing Public Organizations, 1993, The European Union: How Democratic Is It?, 1996, European Union Foreign and Security Policy, 1998, European Telecommunications Liberalisation, 1999; author books, articles and book chpt. in field. Fellow Chr. Michelsens Found., 1970-72, Brit. Coun., 1976, Ford Found., 1977. Mem. Labour Party. Avocation: travel. Home: Holmenveien 53, N-0376 Oslo Norway Office: Norwegian Sch Mgmt, Elias Smithsvei 15, N-1301 Sandvika Norway

ELIASSEN, SVEIN LEONARD, engineer; b. Bergen, Norway, July 18, 1947; s. Reidar and Sigrid (Amundsen) E.; m. Sylvi Schjölberg, June 5, 1949; children: Ståle, Knut. BSc in Engring., Norwegian Inst. Tech., 1970, PhD in Engring., 1974. Postdoctoral fellow Norwegian Inst. Tech., 1972-74; sr. engr. Det. Noroke Veritas, 1974-77, prin. engr., 1977-83; prin. engr. Statoil, Stavanger, 1983-92, sr. advisor, 1992—. Avocations: athletics, orienteering. Home: Markveien 44, N-4030 Hinna Norway Office: Statoil, N-4035 Stavanger Norway

ELIASSON, INGEMAR E., Swedish government official; b. 1939; m. Carin M. Eliasson, 1966; 3 children. Diploma, Stockholm Sch. econs., 1971. H.S. econs. tchr. Hallstahammar, 1967-69; planning officer Local Authority, Hallstahammar, 1969-70; polit. asst. Liberal Parliamentary Group, 1970-76; under-sec. Swedish Ministry of Labor, 1976-79, under-sec. for coord., 1979-80, minister of labor, 1980, minister of labor and energy, 1981-82; mem. Swedish Parliament, 1982-90; chmn. standing com. for social affairs Swedish Parliament, 1982-85, mem. com. for fgn. affairs, 1985-90; parliamentary leader Liberal Party, 1985-90; vice chmn. Liberal Party, 1983-90; chmn. Stockholm Stock Exch., 1991-98; chmn. bd. dirs. Swedish Nat. Housing Fin. Corp., 1990—, Swedish News Agy., 1996-99; bd. dirs. SAS Sweden, 1991-99; chmn. Swedish-Norwegian Investment Fund, 1997—. Chmn. bd. dirs. Future Culture Found., 1995-98; gov. Värmland, 1990—. Address: Residenset, 652 25 Karlstad Sweden

ELIASSON, NILS, diplomat, international organization executive. Dir. Conf. on Security and Cooperation in Europe, Prague, Czech Republic, 1991-94; amb. for human rights Ministry of Fgn. Affairs, Sweden, 1994-96; amb. to Bosnia/Herzegovina, Sarajevo, 1997—. Office: Swedish Embassy, Ferhadija 20, Sarajevo Bosnia-Herzegovina

ELIBOL, ORHAN, ophthalmic surgeon; b. Ankara, Turkey, June 15, 1963; s. Nihat and Firdevs (Tabak) E.; m. Neriman Gedik, July 3, 1988; children: Burak, Alperen. MD, Gazi U., 1987. From resident to asst. prof. Cumhuriyet U., Sivas, Turkey, 1987-96; asst. prof. Kocaeli U., Turkey, 1996-97, assoc. prof., 1997-98; cons. ophthalmology Kocaeli SSK Hosp., 1998—. Home: Yahya Kaptan A/10 #11, 41050 Kocaeli Izmit, Turkey

ELIBOL, TARIK, gastroenterologist; b. Sept. 1, 1939; s. Ismail Cemal and Nuriye (Tutkun) E.; m. Eileen Elibol, Aug. 30, 1997; children: Kimberly, Lisa, David, Adam, John. MD, U. Istanbul, 1964. Resident in internal medicine E.J. Meyer Hosp. U. Buffalo, 1964-66; fellow in gastroenterology Cleve. Clinic, 1966-68; clin. asst. prof. medicine U. Buffalo, 1975—; practice medicine specializing in digestive diseases Buffalo, 1969—; former chief of staff DeGraff Meml. Hosp.; mem. staff Erie County Med. Center. Fellow ACP, Am. Coll. Gastroenterology; mem. Am. Soc. Internal Medicine, Am. Soc. Gastrointestinal Endoscopy, N.Y. State Med. Soc., Erie County Med. Soc., Western N.Y. Soc. Gastrointestinal Endoscopy (past pres.), Western N.Y. Gastrointestinal Liver Soc. (pres. 1980—), Western N.Y. Physician Found. (pres. 1980—). Home: 55 Leicester Rd Buffalo NY 14217-2111 Office: 2949 Elmwood Ave Kenmore NY 14217-1356

ELIDAN, JOSEF, otolaryngologist, educator; b. Jerusalem, July 17, 1945; s. Aahron and Bronia Elidan; m. Sara Frish, Apr. 12, 1967; children: Sharon, Gal, Orly. MD, Hebrew U., Jerusalem, 1970. Resident in otolaryngology Hadassah U. Hosp., Jerusalem, 1977-81, sr. physician, 1981-84, 86-90; head dept. otolaryngology Hadassah U. Hosp., 1991-2000, prof., 2000—; fellow UCLA, 1984-86; lectr. Med. Sch. Hebrew U., Jerusalem, 1981-86, sr. lectr., 1987-90, assoc. prof., 1991—. Inventor system for induction of vestibular evoked potentials, 1981, 89, balloon catheter for intraesophageal pressure measurements, 1991. Maj. Israeli Med. Corp, 1971-73. Recipient Outstanding Rsch. award Faculty of Medicine, 1982; grantee Ministry of Sci., 1987-89, Israel-U.S. Binat. Fund, 1991-93, 94-95, Ministry of Health, 1992-93. Mem. Israel Med. Assn., Am. Acad. Otolaryngology, Assn. for Rsch. in Otolaryngology, The Barany Soc., Collogium Otorhinolaryngologicum, Israeli Soc. Otolaryngology Head Neck Surgery (pres. 1997—). Avocation: playing violin. Home: 30 Hantke St, Jerusalem 96629, Israel Office: Hadassah U Hosp, Ein Kerem, 91120 Jerusalem Israel

ELIE, BERNARD MICHEL, software engineer; b. Caen, France, Aug. 15, 1945; m. Anne Marie Lemenager, Aug. 8, 1969; children: Sophie, Benedicte, Caroline. Degree electrical engring., ISEP, Paris, 1968; MS, Case Western Res. Univ., 1970. Software engr. Honeywell-Bull, France, 1971-74, release mgr., 1974-76, project mgr., 1976-80; EDP mgr. CEAC, France, 1980-82; chief engr. SOCOTEC, France, 1982-85; divsn. engr. BULL, France, 1985; mng. dir. Info. Builders, France, 1989—. Pres. H.S. bd., Versailles. Avocations: sailing, rowing. Home: 6 Ave de Villeneuve l'Etang, 78000 Versailles France Office: Information Builders, 2 rue Troyon, 92316 Sèvres Cedex, France

ELINOV, NIKOLAY PETROVICH, microbiologist, educator, researcher; b. Markino, Russia, Oct. 1, 1928; s. Petr Osipovich and Natalia Nikolayevna (Zotova) E.; m. Margarita Grigoryevna Zamarayeva, July 3, 1951; children: Helen, Natasha. MS in Pharmacy, Chem.-Pharm. Inst., St. Petersburg, Russia, 1950, PhD, 1953, D Biol. Scis., 1963; MD, Pediat. Med. Inst., St. Petersburg, 1966. Asst. Chem.-Pharm. Inst., 1953-55, asst. prof., 1955-64, prof., 1964-68, chief dept. microbiology, 1968-97, dean pharmacy and engring. microbiology faculties, 1953-56, dep. dir. tchg. and rsch. programs, 1960-65, dep. dir. rsch. programs, 1966-72, rector, 1972-86; dept. rschr. BAN Russian Acad. Scis., St. Petersburg, 1997-98; dep. dir. rsch. programs Med. Acad. for Postgrad. Edn., Kashkin Rsch. Inst. Med. Mycology, St. Petersburg, 1998—. Author: The Pathogenic Yeast-like Organisms, 1964, General Regularities of a Structure and Development of Microbes Producents of BAS, 1977, Chemistry of Microbial Polysaccharides, 1984, Chemical Microbiology, 1989, The Principles of Biotechnology, 1995, others. Fellow Presidium Microbiology Soc. (chmn. mycol. sect. 1967—; mem. Engring. Acad. St. Petersburg, N.Y. Acad. Scis., Internat. Union Microbiology Socs. (yeast commn. 1968—). Home: Sea-by Ave 25 Apt 6, 197183 Saint Petersburg Russia Office: Kashkin Rsch Inst Med Mycol, Santiago de Cuba Str 1/28, 194291 Saint Petersburg Russia

ELINSON, VERA MATVEEVNA, engineer; b. Moscow, Feb. 2, 1948; d. Matvei Jlyich and Bertha Josifovna (Kamenetskaya) E.; m. Boris Moiseevich Basok, Jul. 17, 1970; 1 child, Julia Borisovna. Cert., Moscow, 1966; diploma, Mendeleev Moscow State Chem. and Tech. Inst., 1972; D in sci., Moscow, 1981. Engr. Design Office, Moscow, 1972-77; engr. Inst. of Vacuum Tech., Moscow, 1977-81, jr. scientist, 1981-83, sr. scientist, 1983-85, leading scientist, 1985-91, head of lab., 1991-95; assoc. prof. Jsiolkovsky Moscow State Aviation Tech. U., 1995—. Contbr. numerous articles to profl. jours. Recipient Eureka award, Brussels, 1996. Mem. N.Y. Acad. Scis. Avocations: reading, tourism, cooking. Office: Moscow State Aviation Tech, 27 Petrovka St, 103767 Moscow Russia

ELISHAKOFF, ISAAC, engineering educator; b. Kutaisi, Georgia, USSR, Feb. 9, 1944; came to U.S., 1989; s. Bentzion and Margaret Leah (Taronishvili) E.; m. Esther Papismado, July 22, 1949; children: Bentzion, Orly. BA, Moscow Power Engring Inst. Tec, Moscow, 1966; MSc, Moscow Power Engring Inst. Tec, 1968, PhD, 1971. Lectr. Abhazian U., Sukhumi, USSR, 1971; from lectr. to prof. Technion U., Haifa, Israel, 1972-84; with Fla. Atlantic U., Boca Raton; lectr. Delft (The Netherlands) U. Tech., 1979-80, vis. prof., 1990, 92; ; vis. chair, prof. U. Notre Dame, South Bend, Ind., 1985-86; vis. prof. Naval Postgrad. Sch., Monterey, Calif., 1987; Castigliano Disting. prof. U. Palermo, Italy, 1992; pres. Inst. Uncertainty Modelling, Inc., Delray Beach, Fla.; disting. lectr. Am. Soc. Mech. Engrs. 1996—. Author: Probabilistic Methods in Structures, 1983, 2d edit., 1999; co-author: Convex Models of Uncertainty in Applied Mechanics, 1990, Random Vibrations and Reliability of Composite Structures, 1992, Probabilistic and Convex Modelling of Acoustically Excitted Structures, 1994, Non-Classical Problems in Buckling of Stuctures, 2000; editor: Random Vibration-Status of Recent Developments, 1986, Refined Dynamical Theories of Beams Plates and Shells, 1987, Buckling of Stuctures-Theory and Experiment, 1988, Stochastic Structural Dynamics-Progress in Theory and Applications, 1988, Vibration and Behavior of Composite Structures, 1989, Nonlinear Structural Systems Under Random Conditions, 1990, Impact and Buclking of Structures, 1990, Symbolic Computations and Their Impact on Mechanics, 1990, Stochastic Structural Dynamics-New Applications, 2 vols., 1991, Whys and Hows in Uncertainty Modeling, 1999; gen. adv. editor Elsevier Sci. Publishers, Amsterdam, The Netherlands. Recipient Bathseva De Rothschild prize, 1973, Medallion Tokyo U., 1992. Fellow Am. Acad. Mechanics, Japan Soc. Promotion Sci. Avocations: religion, reading, writing, theatre. E-mail: ielishak@me.fau.edu. Office: Fla Atlantic U 777 Glades Rd Boca Raton FL 33431-6424

ELISSA, RAJA ISSA, newspaper publishing executive; b. Jaffa, Israel, Oct. 14, 1922; s. Issa Daoud and Zahia (Malak) E.; m. Nadia Samuel Farajalla, Aug. 5, 1945. BA, Am. U., Beirut, Lebanon, 1942; journalism student, Columbia U., N.Y.C., 1960. Sub-editor Falastin Newspaper (Arabic), Jaffa, 1942-45, dep. editor, 1945-48; pub., editor Falastin Newspaper (Arabic), Jerusalem, 1950-67, Jerusalem Star (English), 1966-67; editor Palestine News (English), Jerusalem, 1967; chmn., vice chmn., bd. dirs. Jordan Press and Publ. Co., Amman, 1967-76; dep. dir. gen. Jordan Press Found., Pub. of Al Rai & Jordan Times (Arbic and English), Amman, 1977-88; chmn., gen. mgr. Jordan Distbn. Agy. Ltd., Amman, 1970—. Office: Jordan Distbg Agy Ltd PO Box 375, 11118 Sha'ban St 1st Cir-Jebel, Amman Jordan

ELIX, DOUGLAS THORNE, computer company executive; b. Adelaide, Australia, July 27, 1948; s. David Llewellyn and Margaret Thorne (Martin) E.; m. Robin Claire Wallace; children: Claire, Penelope, David, Sarah. Dir. banking region IBM Australia Ltd., 1987-89; dir. fin. industry IBM Asia Pacific, Tokyo, 1990-91; dir. of ops. IBM Australia Ltd., 1991-92, gen. mgr. fin. svcs., 1992-93, asst. mng. dir., CEO, 1993-96; dir. fin. industry IBM Asia Pacific, Tokyo, 1990-91; pres., CEO Integrated Sys. Solution Corp., Somers, N.Y., 1996; gen. mgr. IBM Global Svcs., N.A., 1997-99, IBM Global Svcs. Ams., 1999—; sr. v.p., group exec. IBM Global Svcs.; bd. dirs. Royal Bank of Can., IBM Global Svcs. Australia Ltd., Bus. Coun. Australia. Chmn. Roseville Coll. Found., Sydney, 1994—. Fellow Australian Inst. Mgmt. Office: IBM Global Svcs M/D 4305 Rt 100 Somers NY 10589

ELIZABETH, HER MAJESTY (ELIZABETH ANGELA MARGUERITE), The Queen Mother; b. Aug. 4, 1900; d. 14th Earl Strathmore; m. Duke of York (later His Majesty King George VI), 1923 (dec. 1952); children: Princess Elizabeth (later Her Majesty Queen Elizabeth II), Princess Margaret Rose. Reigned as Queen Consort, 1936-52. Lady Order of Garter, Lady Order of Thistle. Decorated Imperial Order Crown India, dame grand cross Royal Victorian Order. Address: Her Majesty Queen Elizabeth-The Queen Mother, Clarence House/St James's, London SW1A 1BA, England also: Castle of Mey, Caithness-shire Scotland also: Royal Lodge Windsor, Great Park, Berkshire England*

ELIZABETH, HER MAJESTY II (ELIZABETH ALEXANDRA MARY), Queen of United Kingdom of Great Britain and Northern Ireland, and her other Realms and Territories, head of the Commonwealth, Defender of the Faith; b. Apr. 21, 1926; d. King George VI (formerly Duke of York) and Queen Elizabeth (formerly Duchess of York); m. Prince Philip, Duke of Edinburgh, Nov. 20, 1947; children: Charles Philip Arthur George, Anne

Elizabeth Alice Louise, Andrew Albert Christian Edward, Edward Antony Richard Louis. Succeeded to throne following death of father, Feb. 6, 1952, crowned Queen, June 2, 1953. Address: Buckingham Palace, London SW1A 1AA, England

ELIZALDE, EMILIO, mathematical physicist; b. Balaguer, Lleida, Spain, Mar. 8, 1950; s. Hermenegildo and Maria (Rius) E.; m. Maria Carme Torrent; children: Sergi, Aleix. M in Physics, Barcelona U., 1972, M in Math., 1973, PhD in Physics, 1976. Assoc. prof. Tarrega Coll., Spain, 1978-80, Bellvitge Coll., Spain, 1980-82; assoc. prof. U. Barcelona, Spain, 1982-84, prof., 1984; vis. prof. U. Hamburg, Germany, Pa. State U., U. Trento, U. Berlin, U. Trondheim, Norway, U. Hiroshima, Japan, MIT, Cambridge; prin. rschr. CSIC, 1993. Author: Zeta Regularization Techniques with Applications, 1994, Ten Physical Applications of Spectral Zeta Functions, 1995; contbr. over 400 articles to profl. jours.; translator, referee in field. Fellowship Alexander von Humboldt, 1978, Spl. Exch. Program, Japan, 1994. Mem. Am. Math. Soc., European Math. Soc. Phys. Soc., Real Soc. Esp de Fis, Cat. Math. Soc., Nat. Geog. Soc., N.Y. Acad. Sci., European Phys. Soc. Office: CSIC/IEEC Dept ECM Fac Phys, U Barcelona, 64708028 Barcelona Spain

ELIZAROV, ALEXANDER IVANOVICH, physicist, researcher, educator; b. Svetlovodsk, Kirovograd, USSR, Sept. 9, 1941; s. Ivan Ivanovich Elizarov and Maria Andreyevna Koloskova; m. Olga Petrovna Nagnojnaja, May 6, 1966; children: Lyubov Alexandrovna, Mikhail Alexandrovich. Diploma in radiophysics, State U. Kiev, USSR, 1958; M in Physics-Math., Poly. Inst., Leningrad, USSR, 1975, D in Physics-Math., 1991, DSc (hon.), 1991. Cert. engr. Physicist, engr. Plant Pure Metal, Svetlovodsk, 1965-67, chief rsch. lab., 1975-85, chief ctrl. rsch. lab., 1985-91; sci. worker Inst. Semiconductors, Kiev, 1970-75; prof. physics, chair Poly. Inst., Kremenchug, Ukraine, 1991-98; prof. ecology Inst. Econs. and Advanced Techs., Kremenchug, 1998—. Contbr. articles to profl. jours. Mem. Acad. Scis. (corr.). Avocation: water tourism. Fax: 05366-3-11-44. Home: 24/37 Proletarska vul., 315300 Kremenchug Ukraine

EL KAMEL, ALI, chest physician, educator, researcher; b. Borgine, Sousse, Tunisia, Jan. 23, 1953; s. Laid and Fatma El Kamel; m. Saloua El Kamel, May 5, 1990; children: Zied, Mehdi. BS, Lycee Garcons, Sousse, 1971; MD, Medecine tunis, Tunisia, 1977. Internal trainee U. Medicine, Tunis, 1978-79; resident Pneumology Hosp., Ariana, Tunisia, 1980-83, asst., 1984-89; prof. U. Medicine, Monastir, Tunisia, 1990, head dept. respiratory disease, 1990—. Contbr. articles to profl. jours. Mem. Internat. Union Against Tuberculosis and Lung Disease, Société de Pneumologie de Langue Française, Groupe d'Oncologie thoracique de Langue Française. Home: Res SIDI Dhaher Khezama Est, Jasmin 4 #11, Sousse Tunisia Office: Univ Hosp Dept Resp Disease, Fattouma Bourguiba, 5000 Monastir Tunisia

EL KHATEEB, GABER KADRY, quality assurance executive; b. Fowa, Egypt, Oct. 18, 1939; s. Kadry Hussein El Khateeb and Amina Mohamed Ibrahim; m. Naima Abdel-Aziz El-Massry, Jan. 1, 1952; children: Dahlia, Marwa, Sherif. BSc in Pharm. and Pharm. Chemistry, Alexandria (Egypt) U., 1959; M Pharm. Industries, Cairo U., 1982; PhD, Pacific Western U., 1990. Commd. officer Egyptian Army, 1960, advanced through grades to maj. gen.; sr. officer field med. supplies Egyptian Army, Cairo, 1960-71, sr. officer ctrl. med. labs., 1971-74, prodn. and planning sr. sect. officer, 1974-82; chmn., comdr.-in-chief Egyptian Pharm. Plant, Guiza, 1982-90; CEO mktg., bd. dirs. Minapharm Pharm., Cairo, 1991-95; quality assurance dir. Amriya Pharm., Alexandria, 1995—; med. supplies cons. Health Ins., Egypt, 1985-89, planning cons., 1990-95. Contbr. numerous articles to profl. jours. Mem. supreme adv. com. Egyptian Nat. Party, Cairo, 1992—. Muslim. Home: 62 El-Hegaz St, Heliopolis Egypt Office: Amriya Pharm Ind Co, Km25 Alexandria-Cairo Deser, POB 111 Manshiya Alexandria 111, Egypt

EL-KHAWAS, ELAINE, college educator; b. 1943. BA, George Wash. Univ., 1965; MA, U. Chgo., 1968, PhD, 1984. V.p. Am. Council on Edn., Washington, 1973-96; prof. U. Calif., L.A., 1996-99, George Washington U., Washington, 1999—; cons. World Bank, OECD, UNESCO, 1995-99.

ELKIN, VLADIMIR IVANOVICH, mathematician, educator; b. Dolgoprudnyi, Moscow, Russia, Aug. 9, 1949; s. Ivan Arhipovich and Olga Ivanovna (Yuchanova) E.; m. Ludmila Anatolievna Chvanova, Dec. 6, 1975; 1 child, Olga. Cand. Sci., Moscow Phys. Tech. Inst., Dolgoprudnyi, 1979; DSc, Russian Acad. Scis., Moscow, 1992. Phy. math. diplomate. Jr. scientist Computing Ctr. Russian Acad. Scis., Moscow, 1978-86, sr. scientist Computing Ctr., 1986-93, chief scientist Computing Ctr., 1993—; lectr. Moscow Phys. Tech. Inst., Dolgoprudnyi, 1978—. Contbr. sci. articles to profl. jours. Recipient State Sci. Stipend award, 1994, 97, 2000; grantee Internat. Sci. Found., 1993, 95, Russian Fundamental Rsch. Found., 1993, 95, 99. Mem. Am. Math. Soc. Avocation: driving. Home: 3-Frunsenskaya ul 1 Apt 185, Moscow 119270, Russia Office: Russian Acad Scis Comp Ctr, ul Vavilova 40, Moscow 117967, Russia

ELKINGTON, STEVE, professional golfer; b. Inverell, Australia, Dec. 8, 1962; m. Lisa Elkington; children: Annie, Samuel. Grad., U. Houston, 1985. Winner Players Championship, 1991, Kmart Greater Greensboro Open, 1990, Infiniti Tournament Open, 1992, Buick Southern Open, 1994, Mercedes Championships, 1995, PGA Championships, 1995, Doral-Ryder Open, 1997, 99, Buick Challenge, 1998; mem. Pres. Cup Team, 1994. 3 time winner PGA Tour. Office: care PGA Tour 112 Tpc Blvd Ponte Vedra Beach FL 32082-3046 Office: PGA America PO Box 109601 100 Ave of The Champions Palm Beach Gardens FL 33410

ELKINS, ROBERT NEAL, lawyer; b. Tampa, Fla., Dec. 11, 1944. BA, Vanderbilt U., 1967; MBA, U. So. Miss., 1972; JD, U. Ga., 1976. Bar: Ga. 1976, Fla. 1976, U.S. Dist. Ct. (mid. and no. dists.) Ga. With Las Vegas City Attys. Office, 1976-77; asst. dist. atty. Office of Dist. Atty., Athens, Ga., 1978-83; ptnr. Fortson Bentley & Griffin, Athens, 1983—; mem. adv. com. Athens Tech. Paralegal Studies, 1983—. Bd. dirs. Athens Clark Libr., 1980-96, Clark County unit Am. Cancer Soc., 1980—; mem. Leadership Athens, 1983. Capt. USAF, 1968-73. Mem. Western Cir. Bar Assn. (sec.-treas. 1985-86, pres. 1999-2000), Athens Rotary Club (pres. 2000—). Avocations: flying, sailing, biking. Office: Fortson Bentley & Griffin PO Box 1744 Athens GA 30603-1744

ELKINS, STEVEN PAUL, architect; b. Ephrata, Wash., Feb. 18, 1949; s. Hugh Kyle Elkins and Fern Irene (Vining) Johnson; m. Linda Louise Harris, Aug. 6, 1977; children: Andrea Rouleau, Michael Rouleau, Jennifer. BArch, Wash. State U., 1972. Registered architect, Wash., Oreg. Designer, draftsman Eng & Wright Architects, Vancouver, B.C., Can., 1972-73, Harthorne-Hagen-Gross, Inc., Seattle, 1973-75, Leo A. Daly Co., Seattle, 1975-77; architect Lawrence Campbell & Assocs., Kent, Wash., 1977-81; prin. Steven P. Elkins Architects, Inc., Seattle, 1981—. Mem. community adv. com. Auburn (Wash.) Gen. Hosp., 1985—, mem. planning and bldg. com. Campus Way Covenant Ch., Federal Way, Wash., 1985—. Recipient Award of Excellence Wash. Precast Concrete Industry Assn., 1985, 86, Appreciation award Vocat. Indsl. Clubs Am., Wash., 1985, 86., Superintendant of Pub. Instrn., Auburn Sch. Dist., 1987. Mem. AIA (corp.), Nat. Trust for Hist. Preservation. Democrat. Protestant. Club: Washington Athletic. Avocations: skiing, river rafting, hiking, sailing. Home: 1326 183rd Ave NE Bellevue WA 98008-3440 Office: 2821 Northup Way Ste 225 Bellevue WA 98004-1439

ELKINS-ELLIOTT, KAY, law educator; b. Dallas, Nov. 21, 1938; d. William Hardin and Maxidine (Sadler) E.; m. Michael Gail Hodgson, July 7, 1960 (div. Dec. 1974); children: Michael Brett, Ashley Kim, Samantha; m. Frank Wallace Elliott, Aug. 15, 1983. AA with honors, Stephens Coll., 1958; JD, U. Okla., 1964; LLM, So. Meth. U., 1984; MA, U. Tex., Dallas, 1990. Bar: Okla. 1964, Tex. 1982, U.S. Dist. Ct. (no. dist.) Tex. 1982, U.S. Supreme Ct. 1984, U.S. Dist. Ct. (we. dist.) Okla. 1989. Assoc. Ben Hatcher and Assocs., Oklahoma City, Okla., 1964-65; dir., gen. counsel Take-A-Tour Swaziland, Mbabane, Swaziland, 1966-74; atty. Dept. Health and Human Svcs., Dallas, 1975-80; hearing officer EEOC, Dallas, 1980-84; atty. pvt. practice, Dallas, 1984-92; vis. assoc. prof. Tex. Wesleyan U. Sch. Law, Dallas, 1992-95; arbitrator State Farm Ins., Dallas, 1991-96; adj. prof. Wesleyan U. Sch. Law, 1995—, coach nat. ABA champion negotiation team, 1998; mediator pvt. practice, Dallas, 1991—; coord. cert. in conflict resolution program Tex. Woman's U., 1996—; cons. in field. Author: (with others) West Texas Practice, 1995. Mem. ABA (peer mediation and cmty. com. 1997—, alternative dispute resolution sect.), Tex. Bar Assn. (ADR sect. coun. mem. 1998—, chair publs. com.), Tex. Bar Found., Tex. Initiatives for Mediation in Edn. (founder, planning com. 1993-95), Soc. for Profls. in Dispute Resolution (pres. Dallas region 1995-97), Tex. Assn. Mediators, Assn. Atty. Mediators, Dallas Bar Assn. (coun. mem. 1993-94), Acad. Family Mediators, Toastmasters (v.p. 1993-94, pres. 1996-97), AIM for Peacepath. Avocations: singing, public speaking, peer mediation training. E-mail: k4mede8@flash.net. Home: 2120 N Rough Creek Ct Granbury TX 76048-2903 Office: 2401 Turtle Creek Blvd Dallas TX 75219-4712

ELKINSON, JEFFREY PHILIP, barrister; b. Dublin, Ireland, Nov. 29, 1955; arrived in Bermuda, 1988; s. Cecil and Bella (Kaitcer) E.; m. Fiona Michele Levenston, Aug. 28, 1988; children: Kilian, Damian. BA in Legal Sci., U. Dublin, 1978, LLB, 1978, MA, 1987; BL, Kings Inn, Dublin. Bar: Ireland 1978, Eng., Wales 1982, Hong Kong 1985, NSW (Australia) 1985, Bermuda 1989, N.Y. 1987, U.S. Ct. Internat. Trade, U.S. Ct. Appeals (D.C. cir.) 1998. Pvt. practice barrister Dublin, 1978-85; crown counsel Atty. Gen. Hong Kong, 1985-87; pvt. practice barrister Hong Kong, 1987-88; barrister, atty. Conyers, Dill & Pearman, Bermuda, 1988—. Author: International Council for Commercial Arbitration Handbook, 1995, Butterworths Offshore Cases and Materials, 1996, Spitz's Tax Havens of the World, 1996. Trooper Royal Hong Kong Regiment., 1985-87. Fellow Chartered Inst. Arbitrators (br. chmn. 1995—); mem. South Ea. Admiralty Law Inst. (charter arbitrator). Home: 2 Harbour Gardens, 2 Harbour Rd, Paget Bermuda Office: Conyers Dill & Pearman, 2 Church St, HM 11 Hamilton Bermuda

ELKOMOSS, SABRY GOBRAN, physicist; b. Elkoussia, Egypt, Apr. 2, 1925; immigrated to France, 1957, naturalized, 1959; s. Gobran Bishay and Rifka Morcos Elkomoss; B.Sc. in Math. with distinction, Alexandria U., 1949; M.Sc. in Physics, 1953; D.Scis. Physiques (French Govt. scholar 1951-52), U. Strasbourg (France), 1955; m. Arlette Meyer, Dec. 11, 1957; children—Anita, Alexander. Asst., Alexandria U., 1949-56; mem. staff Nat. Center Sci. Research, 1952-62; sr. research scientist, exec. adv. space and missile div. Douglas Corp., Santa Monica, Calif., 1963-64; sr. staff mem. space and missile div. Litton Industries, Beverly Hills, Calif., 1964-66; research scientist plasma div. McDonnell Corp., St. Louis, 1966-67; maitre recherches Nat. Center Sci. Research, Strasbourg, 1967—; lectr. U. Ein Shams, Cairo, also prof. physics Lycee Francais, Alexandria, 1956-57. Fulbright advanced scholar, 1959-61; postdoctoral asso. research U. Notre Dame, 1959-63. Mem. Am. Phys. Soc., New York Acad. of Sci. (sec. European study group solid state spectroscopy), Sigma Xi. Mem. Coptic Orthodox. Ch. Contbr. articles to profl. jours. Home: 4 rue de Stockholm, 67000 Strasbourg France

ELKONIN, LEV ALEKSANDROVICH, geneticist; b. Saratov, Russia, Aug. 11, 1957; s. Aleksandr Yakovlevich and Raisa Yakovlevna (Malkina) E.; m. Elena Il'inichna Avgustevich, July 24, 1981; 1 child, Aleksandra. M in Biology, State U., Leningrad, 1979; PhD in Genetics, N.I. Vavilov All-Union Inst. Plant Prodn., Leningrad, 1988; D in Biol. Sci., N.I. Vavilov All-Union Inst. Plant Prodn., St. Petersburg, 1999. Cert. biologist. Rsch. scientist Volga-Region Inst. Sorghum, Saratov, 1980-85; leader rsch. group Inst. Agr. South East Regions, Saratov, 1985-90; head lab. Volga-Region Inst. biotech., Saratov, 1990-97; leader rsch. worker Inst. Agr. South-East Region, Saratov, 1998—. Contbr. articles to profl. jours.; patentee in field. Mem. EUCARPIA, Nicolay Ivanovich Vavilov Geneticists and Breeders Soc.

ELLEDER, MILAN, pathologist, educator; b. Praha, Czech Republic, Dec. 5, 1938; s. Jaroslav and Věra (Horáková) E.; m. Dana Baladová, Mar. 22, 1966; children: David (dec. 1992), Daniel, Andrew. MD, Charles U., Prague, Czech Republic, 1964. Cert. Bd. Pathology. Resident in pathology Gen. Faculty Hosp., Prague, 1964-67; asst. prof. 1st Faculty Medicine, Charles U., Prague, 1967-89, assoc. prof., 1989—, vice-dean for rsch., 1991-96; head Inst. for Inherited Metabolic Disorders 1st Faculty Medicine, Charles U., Prague, 1994—. Contbr. monographs; contbr. articles to profl. jours. Recipient awards Czechoslovakia Soc. Pathology, 1974, 79, 90, Czechoslovakia Ministry of Health for Rsch. in Lysosomal Enzymopathies, 1986, Czech Neurol. Soc., 1995. Mem. European Study Group for Lysosom. Disease (com. mem. 1997—). Avocation: serious music. Home: Fr Křížka 14, 170 00 Praha 7, Czech Republic Office: Charles U Hosp, Ke Karlovu 2 Bldg D, 12808 Praha 2, Czech Republic

ELLEDGE, GLENNA ELLEN TUELL, journalist; b. Welch, W.Va., Aug. 2, 1931; d. William Jackson and Ellen Annabelle (Jackson) Tuell; div.; children: Carl Gene, Jerry Elwood, Ernest Everett. Certificate in comptometer, Capital City Coll., 1949; student, Wytheville (Va.) C.C., S.W. Va. C.C., Richlands, Va. Intermont Coll. Accounts clk. Household Fin. Corp., Charleston, W.Va., 1951-52; with incest divsn. FBI, Washington, 1953; asst. bookkeeper and acctg. clk. Ft. McNair Officers Open Mess, Washington, 1953-54; stat. analyst Office Strategic Intelligence, Washington, 1954-55; stock control 836th Supply Squadron, Langley AFB, Va., 1957-59; acct., office asst. Comml. Contracting, Troy, Mich., 1970-71; office svcs. asst. Southwestern State Hosp., Marion, Va., 1971-95; staff writer, photographer Saltville (Va.) Progress, 1977-81, Saltville News-Messenger, 1981-93, Family Cmty. Newspapers, Marion, 1993—; fire brigade Southwestern State Hosp., Marion, 1986-93, instr. CPR, 1986-89, adv. bd., 1986-93. Vol. Air Force Family Svcs., 1956-69, den mother Cub. Scouts Am., 1962-67; bd. dirs. Smyth County Crisis Ctr., Marion, 1971-81; sec., pres. Smyth Coun. Santa's Elves, Marion, 1974-78, Family Oriented Group Home parent Group Home Juveniles 28th Juvenile Domestic Rels. Ct., Abingdon, Va., 1978-81; EMT, instr. Am. Heart Assn., Smyth, Wise, Grayson Counties, 1986-89; mem. and former sunday sch. tchr., supr. Laural Springs United Meth. Ch.; chairperson Mayor's promotional com., Marion, 1994-95; mem. Surry County (N.C.) Hist. Soc., Grayson County (Va.) Hist. Soc. Mem. Nat. Fedn. Press Women (del. 1978, awards), Va. Press Women (del. 1978, awards), Va. Press Assn. (awards), Nat. Press Assn., Nat. Soc. DAR, Nat. Soc. Col. Dames XVII Century, Jamestowne Soc. Republican. Avocations: writing, reading, gardening, camping, traveling. E-mail: ellglen@hotmail.com; fax: (540) 783-9713. Office: PO Box 901 Marion VA 24354-0901

ELLEFSON, PAUL VERNON, forestry educator; b. St. Paul, May 21, 1939; s. Jewel Victor and Dagney Hazel Ellefson; m. Peggy A. Ellefson, Apr. 21, 1967; children: Jennifer, Bonnie. BS, U. Minn., 1961, MS, 1965; PhD, Mich. State U., 1971. Forester USDA Forest Svc., San Francisco, 1961-64; economist USDA Forest Svc., Phila., 1965-68; rschr. U. Minn., St. Paul, 1964-65, prof., 1976—; economist Dept. Natural Resources, Lansing, Mich., 1970-72; dir. policy programs Soc. Am. Foresters, Washington, 1972-75; cons. FAO UN, Rome, 1971-99; chair forest com. NAS, 1995-97; chair Minn. Govs. Forest Coun., St. Paul, 1995-99; vice-chair adv. com. on power plant siting and transmission line location Minn. Environ. Quality Bd. Author: Economic Research, 1988, Forest Policy, 1990; assoc. editor Jour. Evaluation Rev., 1985-99, Jour. Forest Econs. and Policy, 1995-99; contbr. articles to profl. jours. V.p. Ramsey-Washington Metro Watershed Dist.; bd. dirs. Seventh Am. Forest Congress; chair Minn. Statewide Forest Resource Policy and Program Implementation Roundtable. Recipient award for outstanding svc. to conservation Am. Forestry Assn., Resolution of Appreciation, Minn. State Senate, Norwegian Marshall Fund award. Fellow Soc. Am. Foresters (chair task force on fed. lands in Alaska, com. on accreditation, chair nat. com. on forest policy, chair policy com. 1980-92); mem. Sons of Norway, Nature Conservancy. E-mail: pellefso@forestry.umn.edu. Office: Univ Minn 1530 Cleveland Ave N Saint Paul MN 55108-1004

ELLEGARD, ALVAR, educator; b. Goteborg, Sweden, Nov. 12, 1919; s. Karl and Hulda (Torell) E.; m. Ulla Asklund, Feb. 2, 1946; children: Kajsa, Anders, Lars. PhD, U. Goteborg, 1953. Jr. lectr. U. Manchester, Eng., 1947-49; from assoc. prof. to prof. U. Goteborg, 1953-84, dean, 1981-84. Author: (books) Darwin and the General Reader, 1990, Jesus—A Hundred Years Before Christ, 1999; contbr. articles to profl. jours. Fellow Royal Acad. Letters, History, and Antiquities. Avocations: gardening, star gazing. Home: Rattgatan 2, S-42676 V Fröluna Sweden

ELLEGARD, ROY WHITNEY, appraiser; b. Hartford, Conn., Sept. 16, 1957; s. Roy Taylor and Jeanette (Whitney) E.; m. Bernadette O'Brien, May 22, 1999. BA in Econs., U. Richmond, 1980. Appraiser Stone & Webster, Inc., N.Y.C., 1980-82; cons. Arthur Andersen & Co., N.Y.C., 1983; sr. cons. Arthur D. Little, Inc., Metro Park, N.J., 1984-87; nat. dir. machinery and equipment valuation advisors Ernst & Young LLP, N.Y.C., 1987-98; mng. dir. corp. value consulting Pricewater House Coopers LLP, 1998—. Mem. Am. Soc. Appraisers (sr., pres. Princeton chpt. 1992-93, 98-99), Kappa Alpha Alumni Assn. (treas. Princeton chpt. 1990-92), Princeton Club N.Y. Republican. Episcopalian. Home: 175 E 96th St Apt 8K New York NY 10128-6204 Office: Pricewaterhouse Coopers 1177 Avenue Of The Americas New York NY 10036-2714

ELLENBOGEN, MARC S., entrepreneur, philanthropist; b. Heidelberg, Germany. AB in Polit. Sci. and German Lit., Syracuse U., 1985, MA in Devel. Econs. and Internat. Law, 1989. Cert. trained mediator for alternative dispute resolution. Project coord. N.Y. Pub. Interest Rsch. Group, N.Y.C. and Buffalo, N.Y., 1985-89; dir. United Svcs. Orgns., Rhein-Neckar region, Germany, 1990-93; cons. OPMAS-E Project, ITT Def., Mannheim, Germany, 1993-94; founder, mng. dir. M.S.E. Group, Ludwigshafen and Prague, Germany, Czech Republic, 1994—; adj. prof. U. Pardubice, Czech Republic, 1994—; sr. assoc. Global Affairs Inst. Maxwell Sch. Citizenship and Pub. Affairs, Syracuse U., 1997—; vis. fellow Magdalen Coll., Oxford U., 2000; prof. U. Windsor, Ont., Can., 1999—. Co-editor: Human Rights: An International and Comparative Law Bibliography, 1983; co-author: TQM im Krankenhaus, 1998; contbr. articles to mgmt. jours. Patron, Helsinki Com. of the Czech Republic, Prague, 1995—; trustee Anglo-Am. Coll., Prague, 1996—; sr. advisor to Chancellor Gerhard Schroeder, Campaign for German Chancellor, Germany, 1998; chair Soc. for Internat. Acad. Cooperation e.V., Mannheim, Germany, 1993—. N.Y. State Legislature grad. scholar, 1989-90; Inst. for Advanced Studies assoc. fellow U. Windsor, Ont., 1999—. Mem. Assn. U.S. Army, Deutsche Atlantische Gesellschaft, von Clausewitz-Gesellschafr, Univ. Club of Washington, Prague Soc. for Internat. Cooperation (pres. 1999), Corps Rheno-Nicaria zu Mannheim, Lambda Chi Alpha. E-mail: ellenbogen@mse-info.com. Home: Lisztstrasse 121, 67063 Ludwigshafen Germany Office: MSE Group, Media carre, Turmstrasse 8, 67059 Ludwigshafen Germany

ELLENTUCK, ELMER, journal editor; b. N.Y.C.; s. Max and Deena (Bregman) E.; m. Beatrice Reiner, Nov. 25, 1946 (dec. Feb. 1982); m. Tara Marcus, June 28, 1985; 1 child, Daniel. BBA, CCNY, 1939; LLB, St. John's U., N.Y.C., 1948. Bar: N.Y. Gen. asst. O.N. Heilbut, N.Y.C., 1948-49; pvt. practice law N.Y.C., 1949-60; editor Prentice Hall, Inc., N.J., 1960-64, Bus. Rsch. Pubs., 1964-96, Employee Rels., 1996—. Co-author: Business Management Handbook, 1968; author: Employee Discipline, 1968. Sgt. USAAF, 1945-46. Mem. N.Y. County Lawyers Assn., Nat. Press Club, Masons. Avocations: reading, fishing, walking. Home and Office: 750 Kappock St Apt 915 Riverdale NY 10463-4615

ELLER, WARREN BERNSON, retired insurance agency executive; b. Alpena, Mich., Apr. 8, 1931; s. William Carl and Rachel Bernson E.; student U. Mich., 1954-55, Wayne State U., 1955-56; m. Marilyn Walling, Oct. 30, 1954 (div. 1983); children: Marc William, Brian Theodore, Cynthia Marie; m. Dolton Rosilda Missick, Sept. 29, 1983; children; Dawson Romano, Anettra Tishura-Missick. Agt., Northwestern Mut. Life Ins. Co., 1957-59; asst. mgr. Occidental Life of Calif., 1959; founder, pres. Warren B. Eller Agy., Inc., Farmington, Mich., 1959-93, ret., 1993. With USAF, 1950-54; Korea. Mem. Nat. Assn. Life Underwriters, Detroit Assn. Life Underwriters (pres. 1967-68), Life Underwriter Polit. Action Com. (trustee 1970), Risk Appraisal Forum (founder). Lutheran. Office: PO Box 4101 Sarasota FL 34230-4101

ELLERBUSCH, FRED, environmental engineer; b. Germany, Mar. 5, 1951. BSCE in Environ. Engring., N.J. Inst. Tech., 1973, MS in Environ. Engring., 1980. Registered profl. engr., N.J.; diplomate Am. Acad. Environ. Engrs.; cert. hazardous materials mgr. Staff engr. Elson T. Killam Assocs., Inc., Millburn, N.J., 1973-74; staff environ. engr. Indsl. Environ. Rsch. Lab. U.S. EPA, Edison, N.J., 1974-77; environ. systems engr. METREK div. MITRE Corp., McLean, Va., 1977-78; regulatory conformance coord. Bristol-Myers Products div. Bristol-Myers Squibb Co., Bridgewater, N.J., 1978-83, mgr. regulatory compliance and govt. affairs, 1983-85, dir. safety, security and environ. affairs, 1985-89; dir. corp. environ. affairs Rhone-Poulenc Inc. affiliate Rhone-Poulenc SA, Monmouth Junction, N.J., 1989-95, dir. environ. affairs and remediation, 1995-96; dir. health, safety, environ. affairs Rhone-Poulenc Inc. affiliate Rhone-Poulenc SA, Monmouth Junction, 1996-98; pres. Systemsthink, Warren, N.J., 1998—; scientist in residence N.J. Inst. Tech., 1998—; v.p. Nat. Environ. Policy Inst., 1999; acting dir. Ctr. Policy Studies, 1999—; adj. prof. environ. engring. grad. div. N.J. Inst. Tech., Newark, 1980-83; seminar leader div. continuing edn. N.J. Inst. Tech., Newark, 1977-90; chair unified environ. statute sector Nat. Environ. Policy Inst., 1995-99. Co-author: Electrotechnology Applications in Manufacturing, Vol. 2, 1978, Industrial/Hazardous Waste Impoundment, 1979, Biomass Applications and Technology, 1980; co-editor: Carbon Adsorption Handbook, 1978, Guide for Industrial Noise Control, 1982; contbr. articles to profl. publs. Mem. nat. panel consumer arbitrators Better Bus. Bur. Mem. Acad. Hazard Control Mgmt., Acad. Hazardous Materials Mgmt. (bd. examiners 1984-85), Am. Indsl. Health Coun. (govt. affairs com. 1987, sci. policy com. 1988—, vice chmn. 1989,) Am. Sci. Affiliation, Chem. Mfrs. Assn. (mem. various coms.), N.Y. Acad. Scis., Soc. for Risk Analysis, N.J. Water Control Assn., N.J. Inst. Tech. (indsl. adv. bd. 1986—), Nat. Environ. Tng. Assn., N.J. Acad. Scis., Pharm. Mfrs. Assn. (environ. control resource com. 1985-89), others. Home: 73 Ferguson Rd Warren NJ 07059-5501 Office: SystemsThink LLC PO Box 4225 Warren NJ 07059-0225

ELLERO, ANTONIO SERGIO DUTRA, metallurgical engineer, planning executive; b. São Paulo, Brazil, July 19, 1960; s. José Valentim and Lygia (Dutra) E.; m. Sonia Carvalho, Mar. 8, 1986; children: Ivan, Caio. BS in Metallurg. Engring., Fac. de Engenharia Indsl., São Paulo, 1984; postgrad., Nijenrode U., Breukelen, The Netherlands, 1990, MBA, 1992. Product engr. Agos Villares S.A., São Paulo, 1984-88; process engr. Caterpillar S.A., São Paulo, 1988-94; planning exec. Mangels Indsl. S.A., São Paulo, 1994-98; asst. to dir. CSN, São Paulo, 1998—. Contbr. articles to profl. jours. Mem. Brazilian Tire and Rim Assn. (v.p. 1997-98). Avocations: reading, swimming, travel, playing the saxophone. Home: Casa 43, Av Portugal 1057, 04559002 São Paulo SP, Brazil Office: CSN Av Pres Juscelino Kubitscher, 1830 Torre I 13 Fl, 04543900 São Paulo Brazil

ELLESTAD, MYRVIN HAROLD, cardiologist; b. Santa Maria, Calif., Aug. 17, 1921; s. Melvin H. and Myrtle Ivy (Dunton) E.; m. Lera C. Ellestad; 8 children. AB, U. Calif., Berkeley, 1943; MD, U. Louisville, 1946. Diplomate Am. Bd. Internal Medicine with subspecialty in cardiology. Intern Jersey City Med. Ctr., 1946-47, resident, 1949-50; resident Seaside Meml. Hosp., Long Beach, Calif., 1950-51; fellow in pathology, USPHS cancer trainee San Francisco County Hosp., 1951-52; pvt. practice cardiology Long Beach, 1952—; med. dir. Meml. Heart Inst., Long Beach Meml. Med. Ctr., 1986-91, dir. rsch., 1991—, dir. cardiac care line, 1995—; dir. heart failure svc. Meml. Heart Inst., 1995—, dir. emergency chest pain ctr., 1989—; physician Children's Diagnostic Heart Clinic, Meml. Hosp., Long Beach, Calif., 1952-70; sr. attending physician Meml. Hosp., Long Beach, 1954—, chief dept. medicine, 1962-63, vice chief of staff med. ctr., 1976-77, chief of staff med. ctr., 1977-80, bd. trustees med. ctr., 1981—, dir. divsn. clin. physiology, 1957-80, chief divsn. cardiology med. ctr., 1962-88; attending physician, mem. cardiac catheterization team Harbor Gen. Hosp., Torrance, Calif., 1955-63, chief of staff, 1961; asst. clin. prof. UCLA Med. Sch., 1955-63, assoc. clin. prof., 1963-73; clin. prof. medicine U. Calif.-Irvine, 1973—; cardiology cons. U.S. Naval Hosp., Long Beach, 1966-88, Fed. Air Surgeon, FAA Bd. Appeals, 1971-86, 90—, NASA, Johnston Space Ctr., 1977-78, Nat. Inst. Biol. Scis., 1978-82. Editl. bd. Clin. Cardiology, Jour. Cardiac Rehab., Annals of Sports Medicine, Am. Jour. Cardiology, Am. Jour. Noninvasive Cardiology, Jour. Electrocardiology; author: Stress Testing, 1975-95 (4 edits.), The World and its Animals, 1998. Lt. (j.g.) USNR MCR, 1947-49. Recipient Outstanding Young Man of the Yr. award Long Beach Jr. C. of C., 1959, Nat. Honors Achievement award Angiology Rsch. Found., 1969. Fellow Am. Coll. Cardiology (gov. So. Calif. 1976-79, chpt. sec.-treas. 1990—), Am. Heart Assn. (coun. on clin. cardiology), Am. Coll. Chest Physicians, Royal Soc. Medicine; mem. Calif. Soc. Internal Medicine, Long Beach Soc. Internal Medicine (pres. 1954), Long Beach

Heart Assn. (pres. 1959), Am. Acad. Sports Physicians (bd. govs. 1980), Am. Coll. Sports Medicine, Am. Physiol. Soc., Coun. of Geriatric Cardiology (bd. dirs. 1997). Avocations: tennis, skiing. Office: Memorial Heart Inst 2801 Atlantic Ave Long Beach CA 90806-1737

ELLESTRÖM, LARS, comparative literature educator, critic; b. Ängelholm, Skåne, Sweden, Aug. 29, 1960; s. Agne and Berit (Fribrock) E.; m. Thérèse Stringer, Dec. 8, 1989 (div. Jan. 1996); children: Julia, Joakim. MA, Lund (Sweden) U., 1985, PhD, 1992. Asst. prof. Lund U., 1993-98; assoc. prof. Vaxjo U., 1998—. Author: Vårt Hjärtas Vilt Lysande Skrift: Om Karl Vennbergs Lyrik, 1992, Divine Madness: On Interpreting Literature, the Visual Arts and Music Ironically, 2000, Att analysera lyrik En Introduktion, 1999; editor: Samtida: Essäer om Svenska Författarskap, 1990, I Diktens Spegel: Nitton Essäer Tillägnade Bernt Olsson, 1994. Grantee Erik Philip-Sörensens Stiftelse, 1992-93, award Swedish Acad., 1993. Fellow New Soc. Letters; mem. Internat. Assn. Word and Image Studies, Internat. Assn. Word and Music Studies. Avocations: riding, poultry farming, environmental questions. Home: Ramnhult, 240 13 Genarp Sweden Office: Vaxjo U, Sch Humanities, 351 95 Vaxjo Sweden

ELLETT, JOHN SPEARS, II, retired taxation educator, accountant, lawyer; b. Richmond, Va., Sept. 17, 1923; s. Henry Guerrant and Elizabeth Firmstone (Maxwell) E.; m. Mary Ball Ruffin, Apr. 15, 1950; children: John, Mary Ball, Elizabeth, Martha, Henry. BA, U. Va., 1948, JD, 1957, MA, 1961; PhD, U. N.C., 1969; CPA, Va., La.; bar: Va. 1957. Lab. instr. U. Va., Charlottesville, 1953-58; instr. Washington and Lee U., 1958-60; asst. prof. U. Fla., 1967-71; assoc. prof. U. New Orleans, 1971-76, prof. taxation, 1976-94; prof. emeritus, 1994—; trainee Va. Carolina Hardware Co., Richmond, 1948-51; acct. Equitable Life Assurance Soc., Richmond, 1951-52; staff acct. Musselman & Drysdale, Charlottesville, 1952-54; staff acct. R.M. Musselman, Charlottesville, 1957-58; mem. U. New Orleans Oil and Gas Acctg. Conf., 1973-92; bd. dirs., publicity chmn. U. New Orleans Energy Acctg. and Tax Conf., 1993-94, bd. dirs. publicity com.; pres. Maxwelton Farm and Timber Corp., 1994—; treas. U. New Orleans Estate Planning Seminar, 1975-78, lectr. continuing edn.; CPCU instr. New Orleans Ins. Inst., 1975-78. Served with AUS, 1943-46. Mem. AICPA, Am. Acctg. Assn., Am. Assn. Atty.-CPAs (chmn. ptnrship. taxation continuing edn. com. 1989, ptnrship. taxation com. 1990, organized La. chpt., v.p. 1991-93), Va. Soc. CPAs, Soc. La. CPAs, Va. Bar Assn. Democrat. Episcopalian. Author books; contbr. articles to prof. jours. Home: 177 Maxwelton Rd Charlottesville VA 22903-7859

ELLICKSON, ROBERT CHESTER, law educator; b. Washington, Aug. 4, 1941; s. John Chester and Katherine Heilprin (Pollak) E.; m. Ellen Zachariasen, Dec. 19, 1971; children: Jenny, Owen. AB, Oberlin Coll., 1963; LLB, Yale U., 1966. Bar: D.C. 1967, Calif. 1971. Atty. adviser Pres.'s Com. on Urban Housing, Washington, 1967-68; mgr. urban affairs Levitt & Sons Inc., Lake Success, N.Y., 1968-70; prof. law U. So. Calif., L.A., 1970-81, Stanford U., Calif., 1981-85; Robert E. Paradise prof. natural resources law Stanford U., 1985-88; Walter E. Meyer prof. of property and urban law Yale U., New Haven, 1988—; dep. dean Yale U., 1991-92. Author: (with Tarlock) Land-Use Controls, 1981, Order Without Law, 1991 (Triennial award Order of the Coif), (with Rose & Ackerman) Perspectives on Property Law, 2d edit., 1995, (with Been) Land Use Controls, 2d edit., 2000. Mem. Am. Acad. Arts and Scis., Am. Law and Econs. Assn. (pres. 2000—), Am. Law Inst. Office: Yale U Law Sch PO Box 208215 New Haven CT 06520-8215

ELLIG, BRUCE ROBERT, personnel executive; b. Manitowoc, Wis., Oct. 15, 1936; s. Robert Louis and Lucille Marie (Westphal) E.; 1 child, Brett Robert; m. Janice Reals. BBA, U. Wis., 1959, MBA, 1960. With Pfizer, Inc., N.Y.C., 1960-96, mgr. compensation and pers. rsch., 1968-70, corp. dir. compensation and benefits, 1970-78, v.p. compensation and benefits, 1978-83, v.p. employee rels., 1983-85, v.p. pers., 1985-95, v.p. employee resources, 1995-96; ret., 1996; speaker in field; mem. Pfizer standing coms., 1985-96, corp. edn. Employee Compensation and Mgmt. Devel., Retirement Plan, Retirement Plan Assets, Savs. and Investment, Corp. Adv. Coun., 1996—; cons. Orgn. Resources Counselors Inc., 1996—; bd. dirs. Headway Corp. Resources Inc.; adv. panel Career Ctrl., wave adv. bd. Author: Compensation and Benefits: Analytical Strategies, 1978; Executive Compensation: A Total Pay Perspective, 1982; Compensation and Benefits: Design and Analysis, 1985, Future Focus: Human Resources in the 21st Century, 1998; contbg. author: Encyclopedia of Professional Management, 1978; Handbook of Business Administration, 1984, Tomorrow's Human Resources Management, 1997; cons. editor Compensation and Benefits Rev.; mem. adv. bd. Jour. Compensation and Benefits; adv. bd. Executive Compensation Reports, 1999—; contbr. articles to profl. jours. Mem. Mayor's Adv. Pay Commn., N.Y.C., 1977-78, chmn., 1980; mem. bus. sector staff Coun. on Wage and Price Stability, 1979-80; mem. Ctr. for Advanced Human Resource Studies Cornell U., 1985-95, Presdl. Quadrennial Pay Commn., 1976, U.S. Civil Svc. Commn. Merit Pay Task Force, 1979; adv. bd. Ky. Ednl. TV, 1987-90, Global Remuneration Orgn. Named Person of Yr., U. Wis. Alumni Club of N.Y., 1995, Human Resource Exec. of Yr., Human Resource Exec. Mag., 1995; recipient Am. Compensation's Keystone award, 1999; Aresty fellow Wharton Bus. Sch. Fellow Nat. Acad. Human Resources (life), Employer Benefits Rsch. Inst., Wharton's Aresty Inst.; mem. Am. Compensation Assn. (life, certification program developer 1996—), N.Y. Assn. Compensation Adminstrs. (charter pres.), Am. Mgmt. Assn., Wall of Fame, N.Y. C. of C. and Ind. (human resource com.), N.Y. Pers. Mgmt. Assn. (past pres.), N.E. Sr. Human Resources Exec. Mtg. Group, Bus. Roundtable, Conf. Bd. (adv. coun. human resource mgmt.), Human Resources Roundtable Group, Pers. Round Table (life), Soc. Human Resource Mgmt. (life mem., chmn. bd. dirs. 1996, faculty staff 1996—, Lifetime Achievement award 1999), Wharton/Spencer Stuart Dir. Inst., U. Ill. Ctr. Human Resource Mgmt. (past ptnr.), Sr. Execs. Forum, U. So. Calif. Ctr. for Effective Orgns. (adv. bd. emeritus), U. Wis. Bus. Sch. Alumni (bd. dirs. emeritus), Phi Beta Kappa, Beta Gamma Sigma, Phi Eta Sigma,, others. Republican. Roman Catholic. Office: 25 East End Ave New York NY 10028-7052

ELLIN, MARVIN, lawyer; b. Balt., Mar. 6, 1923; s. Morris and Goldie (Rosen) E.; m. Stella J. Granto, Aug. 2, 1948; children: Morris, Raymond, Elisa. JD, U. Balt., 1953. Bar: Md. 1953, U.S. Supreme Ct. 1978; diplomate Am. Bd. Forensic Examiners. Practice law Balt., 1953—; mem. firm Ellin & Baker, 1957—; specialist in med. malpractice law; cons. on med. and legal trial matters; lectr. ACS, U. Md. Law Sch., U. Balt. City, Yale U. Sch. Medicine, Johns Hopkins Hosp., U. Calif., San Francisco, U. N.J.; former mem. chmn.'s adv. coun. com. on judiciary U.S. Senate. mem. editl. adv. bd.: Ob/Gyn Malpractice Prevention; contbr. chpts. on med. malpractice to various profl. publs. including Radiation Therapy of Benign Diseases. Fellow Internat. Acad. Trial Lawyers; mem. ABA, Am. Soc. Law and Medicine. Home: 13414 Longnecker Rd Glyndon MD 21071-4805 Office: 1101 Saint Paul St Baltimore MD 21202-2662

ELLING, LOTHAR, biochemist, researcher; b. Aachen, Germany, July 21, 1959; s. Gerhard and Marianne (Gier) E.; m. Monika Heilkenbrinker, Oct. 27, 1987; children: Christina Sarah, Lukas Simon. Diploma in Biology, Tech. U., Aachen, 1984, PhD, 1988; Habilitation, U. Duesseldorf, 1997. Postdoctoral fellow Inst. Enzyme Tech., Juelich, Germany, 1988-90, group leader, 1990—. Inventor in field. Recipient postdoctoral fellowship Dechema, Frankfurt, 1988. Mem. Gesellschaft fuer Biochemie und Molekular Biologie, Dechema, Golche. Office: U Duesseldorf Inst Enzyme Tech, Inst Enzyme Tech, D-52426 Jülich Germany

ELLINGHAM, MARK, publishing executive; b. Salisbury, Eng., Apr. 8, 1959; s. Jeremy and Barbara (Somerset) E.; m. Natania Jansz, 1993; 1 child, Miles. BA in English, Bristol U., 1981. Publisher Rough Guides, Eng., 1982-99, Sort of Books. Avocations: music, travel, football. Office: 62-70 Shorts Gardens, London WC2H 9AB, England

ELLINGSON, MARY, secondary education educator, city councilman; b. Carroll, Iowa, Oct. 8, 1938; d. Raymond William and Mildred Ressa Leonard; m. William Arthur Ellingson, June 11, 1960; children: Mary, Anne. BS with honors, Iowa State U., 1961; MS, George Williams Coll., 1983. Tchr. various schs., 1967—; councilman City of Naperville, Ill., 1995—; rsch. cons. Naperville Schs., 1988-95. Co-author: The Baby Book: A Resource Manual of Services for Children Under 3 Years Old, 1990, YMCA Infant/Toddler Child Care, 1990; contbr. articles to profl. jours. Mem. Nat. Child Task Force YMCA, Chgo., 1980-83, rsch. assoc., 1983-88; mem. edn. adv. com. 13th Congl. Dist., 1990-97; co-chmn. Celebration 2000, Naperville, 1996—; bd. dirs. Citizen Appreciate Police, Naperville, 1998—, Naperville Cmty. Outreach, 1998—, Naper Settlement Mus., 1999—; co-chair tourist bur. Naperville Devel. Partnership, 1999—. Recipient Leadership award Celebration 2000, 1999, Disting. Svc. award Jaycees, 2000, Suburban Pk. & Recreation award Pk. Dist., 2000; named Citizen of the Yr. Am. Legion, 2000. Mem. Nat. Flute Assn., Naperville C. of C., Chgo. Flute Assn., Kappa Omicron Nu, Phi Kappa Phi. Avocations: gardening, walking. Office: 400 S Eagle St Naperville IL 60540-5279

ELLIOT, ELISA LOUISE, microbiologist; b. Mpls., Nov. 21, 1956; d. Arthur McAuley and Carol Ann (Brand) Elliot; children: Melissa Nhe, Monygeywa Duang John. Student, Tex. A&M U., 1974-76; BS in Microbiology, Tex. Tech U., 1977; PhD, U. Md., 1984. Med. technician, med. technologist Scott and White Clinic and Hosp., Temple, Tex., 1977-78; grad. teaching asst. U. Md., College Park, 1978-79, 82-84; asst. prof. seafood microbiology U. Alaska-Fishery Indsl. Tech. Ctr., Kodiak, 1984-87; rsch. microbiologist U.S. Dept. Agr. Food Safety and Inspection Svc., Beltsville, Md., 1987-89; adj. prof. Univ. Coll., U. Md., College Park, 1987-90; microbiologist FDA, Washington, 1989-92, 97—, sci. policy analyst, 1992-97. Contbr. chpts. to books, articles to profl. jours. Bd. dirs. Kodiak Women's Resource and Crisis Ctr., 1986-87; mem. Girl Scouts Am. NSF grantee, 1973; NSF grad fellow, 1979-82. Mem. Am. Soc. Microbiology (sec. Alaska br. 1985-87, councillor 1986-87), Nat. Shellfisheries Assn., Nature Conservancy, Alpha Lambda Delta, Phi Kappa Phi. Avocations: bicycling, folk and swing dancing, hiking, piano. Office: FDA HFS-615 Ctr for Food Safety & Applied Nutrition 200 C St SW Washington DC 20204-0001

ELLIOT, LIGIA GOMES, researcher, evaluator; b. Rio de Janeiro, Brazil, Mar. 30, 1944; d. Francisco Elliot-Filho and Elza Gomes Elliot. MA in Edn., Fed. U. Rio de Janeiro, 1976; MA in Latin Am. Studies, UCLA, 1979, PhD in Edn., 1980. Primary sch. tchr. Sec. of Edn., Rio de Janeiro, 1962-69, normal sch. tchr., 1970-76, asst., 1981-90; prof. U. Gama Filho, Rio de Janeiro, 1972-76; project cons., coord., dir. evaluation ctr. Cesgranrio Found., Rio de Janeiro, 1997—; rschr. Nat. Coun. Tech. Devel. and Rsch., 1981-85; vice-coord. Grad. Program in Edn., Fed. U. Rio de Janeiro, 1990-95, head of dept. Edn. Founds., 1992-93; cons. Ministry of Army, Brazil, 1996-97. Author: Children on the Streets of the Americas, 1999; co-editor: Em Aberto-Avaliacao Edn., 1995. Rsch. scholar grantee USIS, L.A., 1986; grantee AERA Com. on Internat. Rels., New Orleans, 1988, Fulbright Commn., Calif., 1993. Home: 114 Apt 803, Rua Gen Ribeiro da Costa, 22010050 Rio de Janeiro Brazil Office: Cesgranrio Found, Rua Cosme Velho 155, 22241090 Rio de Janeiro Brazil

ELLIOTT, BARRY JOHN, trust company executive; b. Haywards Heath, W. Sussex, Eng., May 8, 1952; s. Cecil Harry and Peggy Eileen (Thair) E.; m. Gillian Cuthbertson, July 21, 1973; children: Mark Andrew, Louise Michelle. BA in Econs., U. Durham (Eng.), 1973. Asst. sec. Chartered Inst. Pub. Fin. and Accountancy, London, 1982-83; dep. treas. Victoria Health Authority, London, 1983-85; unit gen. mgr. Westminster and St. Stephen Hosps., London, 1985-87; dep. dir. fin. N.W. Thames Regional Health Authority, London, 1987-89; dir. resources Riverside Health Authority, London, 1989-92; regional dir. fin. and info. S.E. Thames Regional Health Authority, S.E., 1992-94; dir. fin. Barts and The London NHS Trust, London, 1994—; treas. London Lighthouse, London, 1988-92. Mem. Healthcare Fin. Mgmt. Assn. (chmn. N.E. Thames br. 1996-97, chmn. 1999—). Avocations: golf, photography. Home: 20 Greenlands Close, RHI5 0AR Burgess Hill West Sussex, England Office: Barts and London NHS Trust, 1st Fl North Wing, EC1A 7BE London West Smithfield, England

ELLIOTT, BILLIE R., gallery owner, art educator; b. Dallas, Dec. 30, 1952; d. Ray Wood and Billie Ruth (Rawson) E. BFA, Stephen F. Austin State U., 1975, MA, 1977. Cert. tchr., Tex. Arts and crafts ctr. mgr. Stephen F. Austin State U., Tex., 1979-85; passenger svc. rep. Am. Airlines, Dallas, 1985—; prof. art, painting, and drawing Collixi County C.C., Plano, Tex., 1990—, gallery dir., 1995—. Home: 7631 Rambler Rd Apt 164 Dallas TX 75231-3705 Office: Collixi County C C 2800 Spring Creek Ave Plano TX 75074

ELLIOTT, CLIVE CHRISTOPHER HUGH, ornithologist, international civil servant; b. Aug. 8, 1945; s. Hugh Francis Ivo and Elizabeth (Phillipson) E.; m. Marie-Thérèse Rüttimann, Sept. 26, 1975; children: Ivo, Nicolas. Honours Zoology, Oxford (Eng.) U., 1967; PhD, Cape Town (South Africa) U., 1973. Rsch. officer U. Cape Town, 1968-74; ornithologist FAO UN, Ndjamena, Chad, 1975-78; project mgr. UN, Arusha, Tanzania, 1978-86, Nairobi, Kenya, 1986-89; country project officer, ops divsn. AGOE UN, Nairobi, 1989-95; sr. officer UN, Rome, 1995—. Author: Quelea Quelea Africa's Bird Pest, 1989, (with R.L. Bruggers) Migratory Pests, 1995—; contbr. articles to profl. jours. Mem. South African Ornitol. Soc. (coun. 1970-74), Brit. Ornithologists Union. Home: Di Caracalla, via Delle Terme, 00134 Rome Italy Office: FAO Box 30470, Nairobi Kenya

ELLIOTT, EDWIN DONALD, JR., law educator, federal administrator, environmental lawyer; b. Chgo., Apr. 4, 1948; s. Edwin Donald and Mary Jane (Bope) E.; m. Geraldine Gennet (div. 1980); m. Mary Ellen Savage, Nov. 22, 1980 (div. 1999); children: Eve Christina, Ian Donald; m. Gail Charnley. BA, Yale U., 1970, JD, 1974. Bar: D.C. 1975, U.S. Dist. Ct. D.C. 1975, U.S. Ct. Appeals (2d cir.) 1982. Law clk. to judge U.S. Dist. Ct. D.C., Washington, 1974-75, U.S. Ct. Appeals, Washington, 1975-76; assoc. Leva, Hawes et al, Washington, 1976-80; assoc. prof. law Yale U., New Haven, 1981-84, prof. law, 1984-89, 91-92; asst. adminstr., gen. counsel U.S. EPA, Washington, 1989-91; Julien & Virginia Cornell chair environ. law and litigation Yale U., New Haven, 1992-94, adj. prof. law, 1994—; cons. Fried, Frank, Harris, Shriver & Jacobson, N.Y.C., Washington, 1991-93; ptnr., head of DC Environ. Practice Fried, Frank, Harris, Shriver & Jacobson, Washington, 1993-96; ptnr. Paul, Hastings, Janofsky & Walker, Washington, 1996—, co-chair nat. environ. practice group; adj. prof. law Georgetown U., Washington, 1997—; advisor Fed. Cts. Study Com., UN Environment Programme, 1993; cons. Asian Devel. Bank, 1994, Carnegie Com. Sci., Tech. and Govt., 1989-93, chair Role of Sci. and Risk Assessment; with Nat. Environ. Policy Inst., 1994—, Overseas Pvt. Investment Corp., Washington, 1983-85, Adminstrv. Conf. U.S., 1987-89, Aetna Ins. Co., 1987-89, G.D. Searle Co., 1988-89; spl. litigation counsel GE Co., Fairfield, Conn., 1985-89; gen. series editor Prentice Hall Environ. Series. Co-author: Sustainable Environmental Law, 1993; bd. advisors Environment Law Reporter; mem. editl. bd. Jour. Indsl. Ecology. Resources for the Future fellow, 1989. Mem. ABA (vice chmn. com. on separation of powers 1985-89, jud. rev. 1992—, environ. values 1993—, chair govt. policy liaison), Environ. Law Inst., Gruter Inst. for Law and Behavioral Rsch. (adv. bd. 1986—), Nat. Environ. Policy Inst. (chair sci. and risk assessment), Yale Club N.Y.C., New Haven Lawn Club. Republican. Presbyterian. E-mail: edelliot@phjw.com. Home: 826 A St SE Washington DC 20003-1340 also: 56 Beach Ave Milford CT 06460-8156 Office: Paul Hastings Janofsky & Walker 1299 Pennsylvania Ave NW Washington DC 20004-2400 also: Yale Law Sch PO Box 208215 New Haven CT 06520-8215

ELLIOTT, GARY WAYNE, forest products company executive; b. Washington Court House, Ohio, July 5, 1949; s. Edwin Lee and Virginia Ellen (Schiller) E.; m. Martha Jane Garinger, Sept. 6, 1969 (div. 1980); 1 child, Candace Celeste; m. Lavada Hubbard, Nov. 27, 1982; stepchildren: Patricia Reneé, Michael Patrick. BA, Miami U., Oxford, Ohio, 1971, MBA, 1973. From labor pool to supr. sales svc. Champion Internat. Corp., Hamilton, Ohio, 1973-82; mktg. svcs. mgr., adminstrv. mgr. Nationwide Papers Div. Champion Internat. Corp., Elk Grove, Ill., 1982-87; mgr. Nationwide Papers Div. Champion Internat. Corp., Glendale Heights, Ill., 1987-91; dir. order svcs. Champion Internat. Corp., Hamilton, Ohio, 1991-94; v.p., divsn. mgr. Dairy Pak divsn. Champion Internat. Corp., Ft. Worth, 1994-99; v.p. ops. Blue Ridge Paper Products, Inc., DairyPak divsn., 1999—. Avocation: golf. Office: 1901 Windsor Pl Fort Worth TX 76110-1800

ELLIOTT, GEORGE ARMSTRONG, III, artist, journalist; b. Wilmington, Del., July 24, 1929; s. George Armstrong Elliott Jr. and Amy Lewis (Rupert) Thomas; m. Shirley Barbara Henin, Oct. 16, 1965. BA, Colgate U., 1951; cert. in journalism, Columbia U., N.Y.C., 1964. Reporter, copy editor, corr. local and nat. newspapers and news agys., 1950-66, Balt. Sun, 1955-62, N.Y. Herald Tribune, 1964, New York Daily News, 1965-66; adminstrv. asst./press sec. Spiro T. Agnew, Baltimore County Exec., Towson, Md., 1962-65; campaign press mgr. Spiro T. Agnew, Baltimore County Exec., 1962; campaign press sec., speechwriter Spiro T. Agnew, Gov. of Md., 1966; pub. affairs dir. Md. State Rds. Commn., Balt., 1967-69; legis. asst. U.S. Congresswoman from Mass. Margaret M. Heckler, Washington, 1969-71; spl. asst. U.S. Sec. of Commerce Peter G. Peterson, Washington, 1972; campaign writer John H. Chafee for U.S. Senator, Providence, 1972; speechwriter Chmn. of FTC Lewis Engman, Washington, 1973; dir. nat. campaign for 55 m.p.h. speed limit U.S. Dept. Transp., Washington, 1976-77; spl. asst., speechwriter U.S. Congressman from Minn. Albert H. Quie, Washington and Mpls.-St. Paul, 1978; press sec. Rep. Margaret M. Heckler, Washington, 1979-81; prin. writer Nat. Alcohol Fuels Commn., Washington, 1980; writer Nat. Commn. on Air Quality, Washington, 1980-81; internat. pub. rels. counsel A. F. Sabo Assocs., Washington, 1981; Washington and East Coast corr. Jet Cargo News, Washington, 1984-93; profl. Chinese brush painting artist, 1993—; writer former Md. Gov. Theodore R. McKeldin for Mayor, Balt., 1963; writer for numerous congrl. and local polit. campaigns, 1962-63. Exhibitions include M-Pac Fine Arts Shows, Sugarloaf Mt. Works Shows, Towson, Md., Invitational Art Exhibit, Waterford, Va., Art Mart and Garden tour, Wilmington, Brandywine Arts Festival, Washington, Sydney (NSW, Australia) Internat. Art Soc., 1996, Internat. Salon de Haute-Loire, Puy-en-Velay, France, 1997, 99, Lalit Kala Nat. Acad. Art, New Delhi, 1998, 99-2000, Overseas Chinese Culture and Art Festival, 2000, Internat. Cultural Union, Haifa, 2000—, Balt. City Hall Courtyard Galleries, Largo, Md., 2000, Marlboro Gallery, 2000. With U.S. Army, 1951-54. Ford Found. fellow in advanced internat. reporting Grad. Sch. Journalism, Columbia U., 1963-64. Mem. Nat. Assn. Govt. Communicators, Overseas Press Club Am., Washington Ind. Writers, Montgomery County Art Assn., Internat. Artists Support Group (pres. 1999—), Sumi-e Soc. Am. Home and Office: 5800 Aberdeen Rd Bethesda MD 20817-3804 Address: 5826 Bradley Blvd Bethesda MD 20814-1128

ELLIOTT, HAROLD MARSHALL, geography educator; b. Sebring, Fla., Jan. 4, 1943; s. Vernon G. and Elise Elliott; m. Anna J. Lang, Jan. 24, 1975; children: Dora Louise, Sarah Ariel; 1 child from previous marriage, Laura Diane. BA, San Francisco State U., 1964, MA, 1970; diploma, Infantry OCS, Ft. Benning, Ga., 1965; PhD, U. Okla., 1978. Ticket agt. United Airlines, San Francisco, Calif., 1961-64; instr. Coll. San Mateo, Lawton, Calif., 1969, Cameron U., Lawton, Okla., 1970-72; security agt. Pinkerton's, Inc., Santa Monica, Calif., 1976-77; instr. Fla. Internat. U., Miami, Utah, 1977-78; from asst. prof. to assoc. prof. Weber State U., Ogden, Utah, 1979-88, prof., 1988—, chmn. dept. geography, 1994—; chmn. Dept. Geography, 1994—; cartographer Thomas Bros. Maps, L.A., 1977; asst. planner Coral Gables (Fla.) City Planning Dept., 1978. Assoc. editor: The Scottish-American Patriot, 1999—; contbr. numerous articles to profl. jours. including Geog. Analysis, Econ. Geography, APCG Yearbook, Southeastern Geographer, Annals of Regional Sci., Urban Geography, Jour. Geography, Prof. Geographer, others. Del. Weber County Dem. Conv., 1980-83 (Geography Prof. of Yr. 1981, 82, Ogden Standard-Examiner "Apple for the Teacher" Teaching award 1992); pres. Utah Geog. Soc., 1993—; mem. Utah mil. and vets. affairs com. 1st lt. U.S. Army, 1964-67. Recipient Bronze Citizenship award SAR, 2000. Mem. ACLU, Assn. Am. Geographers, Assn. Pacific Coast Geographers, Am. Mensa, Am. Geog. Soc., Nat. Coun. for Geog. Edn., Fla. Soc. Geographers, Internat. Geog. Union, Scottish-Am. Mil. Soc. (post adj. 1999—), Res. Officers Assn., Vietnam Vets. Am., Mil. Order World Wars, Order Crown of Charlemagne, Sons Union Vets., Okla. Acad. Scis., Burlingame H.S. Alumni Assn., Toastmasters Internat., Nat. Eagle Scout Assn., Am. Planning Assn., Audit Bur. Circulations, Utah Scottish Assn., United Empire Loyalists' Assn. Can., Geneal. Assn. Nova Scotia, First Families Mass., First Families Ohio, Gamma Theta Upsilon, Alpha Phi Omega. Office: Weber State U Geography Dept Ogden UT 84408-0001

ELLIOTT, HOLLY HALL, retired occupational therapist; b. L.A., Jan. 20, 1920; d. Wilford Raymond and Adnee (Wright) Hall; m. James Wagner Elliott, May 7, 1944(dec. Dec. 1968); children: James Paul, Dennis Hall, Mark Andrew. BA in Music, U. Calif., L.A., 1941; MS in Counseling, Sacramento (Calif.) State U., 1970. Counselor, therapist U. Calif., San Francisco, 1970-80; instr. San Francisco State U., 1980-85; rsch., writing Laugley Porter Psychiat. Inst., San Francisco, 1985-92, retired, 1992; adv. com. Calif. State Dept. Rehab., Sacramento, 1980-84; cons. in field; lectr. in field. Author: Mental Health Assessment of Deaf Clients, 1987, Mental Health Assessment Special Conditions, 1989; contbr. articles to profl. jours. Pres. El Dorado County Bd. Edn., Placerville, Calif., 1962-68, Deaf Svcs. Network, San Francisco, 1978-85. Mem. Nat. Com. Devel. Deaf Ministries United Methodist Ch. (gen. coun.), United Methodist Congress of the Deaf (bd. dirs., pres. 1982-88), Assn. Late Deafened Adults (I. King Jordan award 1994), Deaf Svcs. North (pres. 1974-85, Bridge award 1984), Delta Kappa Gamma (hon.). Democrat. Avocations: research, writing, disability access for churches. Home: 1300 NE 16th Ave Apt 1408 Portland OR 97232-4405

ELLIOTT, JOHN DORMAN, business executive; b. Oct. 3, 1941; s. Frank Faithful and Anita Caroline Elliott; m. Lorraine Clare Golder, 1965; 3 children; m. Amanda Drummond Moray, 1987; 1 child. BCom (hons.), U. Melbourne, Australia, 1962, MBA, 1965. With BHP, Melbourne, 1963-65, McKinsey and Co., Melbourne & Chgo., 1966-72; mng. dir. Henry Jones (IXL), 1972; acquired Carlton and United Breweries Elders IXL (Henry Jones IXL merged with Elder Smith Goldsbrough Mort), 1983; chmn., chief exec. Elders IXL Ltd., 1985-90; dir. Haoma Mining NL, 1994; dir. CXA Comm., Melbourne, 1995, chmn., 1997—; dir. Water Wheel Holdings, Ltd. Fed. treas. Liberal Party Australia, 1985-87, fed. pres., 1987-90; pres. Carlton Football Club, 1983—. Clubs: Melbourne, Australian, Savage, Royal Melbourne Tennis. Avocations: football, tennis. Office: 411 Collins St 1st Fl, Melbourne 3000, Australia

ELLIOTT, MICHELLE CATHERINE, special education educator; b. Weisbaden, Germany, Oct. 15, 1975; d. Thomas Weber and Cassandra Marie McCune; m. Paul Mark Elliott, June 19, 1998. BA in Edn., Webster U., St. Louis, 1998. Cert. tchr., Mo., Alaska. Before and after sch. provider Youth Ctr., Scott AFB, Ill., 1994-98; tchr. Bernard Elem., St. Louis, 1998-99, Crawford Elem., Eielson AFB, Alaska, 1999—. Avocations: sports, reading, traveling, cooking. Fax: (907) 372-3306. E-mail: melliott@northstar.k12.ak.us. Office: Crawford Elem 504 Raven's Way Dr Eielson AFB AK 99702

ELLIOTT, RICHARD HOWARD, lawyer; b. Astoria, N.Y., Apr. 30, 1933; m. Judith A. Kessler, Dec. 26, 1956; children: Marc Evan, Jonathan Hugh, Eve; m. 2d, Diane S. Schaefer, Nov. 18, 1978; children: Alexis, Sara Jane, Benjamin, David. BS, Lehigh U., 1954; JD cum laude, U. Pa., 1962. Bar: U.S. Dist. Ct. (ea. dist.) Pa. 1962, Pa. Supreme Ct. 1962, U.S. Ct. Appeals (3d cir.) 1963, U.S. Dist. Ct. (mid. dist.) Pa. 1976. Assoc. Clark, Ladner, Fortenbaugh & Young, Phila., 1962-69, ptnr., 1970-75; ptnr. Elliott & Magee, Doylestown, Pa., 1976—; moderator Permanent Jud. Commn., Presbytery of Phila.; v.p., dir. Bucks County Soc. Prevention Cruelty to Animals; former pres., dir. Pa. Soc. for Prevention of Cruelty to Animals; gen. counsel, dir. Pa. Fedn. Humane Socs., adj. faculty Bucks County Cmty. Coll.; mem. Pa. Navigation Commn., 1977-80. Lt. USN, 1954-59. Mem. ABA, Pa. Bar Assn., Phila. Bar Assn., Bucks County Bar Assn. Democrat. Home: 1205 Victoria Rd Warminster PA 18974-3923 Office: Elliott & Magee 1795 S Easton Rd Doylestown PA 18901-2837

ELLIOTT, ROSALIND MAY, intensive care nurse; b. Port Vila, Vanuatu, July 26, 1969; d. Oswald Norman and Joyce (Rowe) E. BSc in Health Studies 1st class honors, U. Surrey, Eng., 1997. RN St. Bartholomews Hosp., London, 1991-92, Kings Coll. Hosp., London, 1993-98, Royal North Shore Hosp., Sydney, Australia, 1999—. Contbr. articles to nursing jours. Avocations: swimming, cycling, running, traveling, playing tennis.

ELLIOTT, THOMAS CLARK, JR., lawyer; b. Portland, Maine, July 10, 1955; s. Thomas Clark and Lucille Eda (Davis) E.; m. Kathleen J. Swan, Dec. 31, 1985; children: Devin Lundeen, Harrison Bradford. BA, DePauw U., 1977; JD, Ill. Inst. Tech., 1981. Bar: Ill. 1981, U.S. Dist. Ct. (no. dist.) Ill. 1981, U.S. Dist. Ct. (ea. dist.) Mich. 1984, U.S. Dist. Ct. (ea. dist.) Wis. 1988, U.S. Dist. Ct. (ctrl. dist.) Ill. 1995, U.S. Ct. Appeals (7th cir.) 1981,

U.S. Ct. Appeals (fed. cir.) 1983. Assoc. McDougall, Hersh & Scott, Chgo., 1981-87, Jones, Day, Reavis & Pogue, Chgo., 1987-88, Niro, Scavone, Haller, Niro & Rockey, Chgo., 1988-89; ptnr. Rockey, Rifkin & Ryther, Chgo., 1989-96; shareholder Rockey, Milnamow & Katz, Chgo., 1997—. Mem. ABA, Chgo. Bar Assn., Intellectual Property Law Assn. Chgo. Office: Rockey Milnamow & Katz 4700 Two Prudential Plz Chicago IL 60601

ELLIOTT, THOMAS MICHAEL, association executive, educator, consultant; b. Evansville, Ind., Aug. 4, 1942; s. Thomas Ira and Pauline (Dawson) E.; m. Susan M. Spiers, July 8, 1967 (div. Aug. 1975); 1 son, Christopher Michael; m. Loretta S. Glaze, Jan. 28, 1976. AB in Zoology, Ind. U., 1965, MS in Higher Edn., 1967, EdD, 1970. Asst. to pres. Purdue U., West Lafayette, Ind., 1972-73, asst. provost, 1973-74; exec. dir. Nat. Commn. United Methodist Higher Edn., Nashville, 1974-77; dep. commr. Mo. Dept. Higher Edn., Jefferson City, 1977-79; exec. dir. Ark. Dept. Higher Edn., Little Rock, 1979-82; exec. dir., CEO IEEE Computer Soc., Washington, 1982—; ptnr. Planning Mgmt. Services Group, Washington, 1976-82; cons. numerous colls. and univs. Author: Computer Simulation System, 1975; contbr. articles to profl. jours. Bd. dirs., mem. exec. com. So. Regional Edn. Bd., Atlanta, 1980-82; mem. Cabinet of Gov. Bill Clinton and Gov. Frank White, State of Ark., 1979-82. Mem. IEEE (sr.), IEEE Computer Soc., State Higher Edn. Exec. Officers Assn., Am. Soc. Assn. Execs., Am. Mgmt. Assn. Home: 1735 Q St NW Washington DC 20009-2407 Office: IEEE Computer Soc 1730 Massachusetts Ave NW Washington DC 20036-1903

ELLIOTT, VIRGIL IRL, JR., artist, writer; b. St. Louis, Aug. 30, 1944; s. Virgil Irl Elliott Sr. and Dollye Cleo McAlister; m. Lillian Rose Peiffer, 1963 (div. 1966); 1 child, Steven Christopher; m. Victoria Anne Lore, Sept. 3, 1988. Student, U. Mo., Kansas City, 1965, U. Mo., St. Louis, 1966, Washington U., 1967-68. Cert. Am. Portrait Soc. Freelance musician, 1969—, artist, 1966—; freelance comml. artist Sonoma County, 1976-82, art instr., 1985—; art instr., dir. Penngrove, Calif., 1993—; art instr. Coll. Marin, Ignacio, Calif., 1995-98; mem. artists adv. panel Calif. State Fair Art Show, Sacramento, 1987. Contbr. articles to profl. jours; art represented in pvt. and pub. collections. With U.S. Army, 1963-66. Mem. ASTM (com. artists' materials 1998—), Am. Soc. Portrait Artists (Signature award 1996), Am. Soc. Classical Realism. Avocation: music. Office: 111 Goodwin Ave Penngrove CA 94951-8660

ELLIOTT, VIRGINIA F. HARRISON, retired anatomist, kinesiologist and educator, investment advisor, publisher, philanthropist; b. St. Louis, Mar. 15, 1918; d. George Benjamin and Florence Gertrude (McManus) H.; m. William Hector Marsh, Dec. 1, 1963 (dec. Dec. 1986); m. George William Elliott, Oct. 27, 1991; stepchildren: Carolyn Frances Roberts, George William II, Robert Bonner (dec. Apr. 1995), Cathrine Susan Dimino. BS, U. Wis., 1940, PhD, 1959; MA, Columbia U., 1944. Lectr. Columbia U., N.Y.C., 1943-46; asst. prof. Mary Washington Coll. of U. Va., Fredericksburg, 1946-48; asst. prof. Oreg. State U., Corvallis, 1948-50, assoc. prof., 1950-59; instr. Army Med. Acad./Brooks Army Med. Ctr., San Antonio, 1959-60, assoc. prof., 1960-64; lectr. U. Tex. Med. Sch., Galveston, 1962-64, Hadassah Med. Sch., Hebrew U. of Jerusalem, 1965; lectr. grad. sch. U. Wis., Madison, 1964; pvt. practice stock market investment lectr. Washington, 1969-84, pub. stock market letter, 1969-84; ret., 1984; fashion model, 1936-47, with John Robert Powers Schs., Phila., Pitts., N.Y.C., 1943-47; cons. U. Tex. Med. Sch., 1962-64, U.S. Pentathlon Team, San Antonio, 1960-64, Dentists for Treatment of Pain from Muscular Tension, San Antonio, 1960-64; vis. prof. grad. sch. U. Wash., Seattle, 1961; lectr. in field. Contbr. articles to profl. jours. Mem. bd. visitors Sch. Edn., U. Wis., Madison, 1992-95, now emeritus; mem. Washington com. Nat. Coun. on Women's Giving. Recipient Civilian Meritorious Svc. award U.S. Civil Svc., 1965; Amy Morris Homans fellow, 1958; hon. fellow U. Wis., 1956, 58, 59. Fellow AAHPERD, Tex. Acad. Sci.; mem. Am. Alliance Health, Physical Edn., Recreation and Dance, Am. Assn. Anatomists divs. Fedn. Am. Socs. for Exptl. Biology (emeritus). Avocations: designing clothing, furniture, landscaping and boats, sculpting, painting. Home: 6333 Cavalier Corridor Falls Church VA 22044-1301

ELLIOTT, WALTER ALBERT, artist; b. Wembley, Middlesex, Eng., Oct. 24, 1926; s. Albert Edward and florence Elizabeth (Byrne) E.; m. Beryl Jean Clark, Mar. 11, 1951; children: Laura, Mark. Engring apprentice, deHavilland Engring. Coll., Edgware, Middlesex and Hatfield, Eng., 1944-47; student, Hammersmith Poly., London, 1955-60, Harrow Coll. Art, 1955-60. Design devel. engr. deHavilland Engine Co. Ltd., 1947-58; mng. dir. Pilton Archway Galleries, N. Devon. One man shows: Barnstaple Atheneum, 1970-81, Burton Gallery, Bideford, Devon, Ilfracombe (Devon, Eng.) C.C., Pilton Gallery, Devonshire, North Devon Coll., Barnstable Devon; group shows: Mall Galleries, London, 1970-95, Royal Inst. Galleries, 1965-70, Fedn. Brit. Artists, Exeter (London) U., 1977-78, Salon de Paris, 1984, others; represented in collections: N. Devon Atheneum, Barnstaple, 1970-81, also Can., Australia, U.S., Eng., Europe; major works include: The Ascent of Man, Refugees, The Eternal Artist, Human Symphony, others; permanent exhbn. Elliott Gallery, Braunton, N. Devon, 1985—; contbr. articles to profl. jours. Recipient Certificate awards, 1948, 1st prize deHavilland Art Soc., 1973-74, 1st prize Devon County Art Exhbn., 1981; named Academician of Italy gold medal, Accademia Italia, 1981, numerous others. Fellow Brit. Interplanetry Soc.; mem. Fedn. Brit. Artists, Internat. Assn. Art, United Soc. Artists, Pastel Soc., Ilfracombe Art Soc. (pres.), Soc. Graphic Fine Art. Office: Sollake Studio, 2 Warfield Villas, Ilfracombe North Devon EX34 9NZ, England

ELLIOTT, WARREN G., lawyer; b. Pueblo, Colo., Jan. 3, 1927; s. Wallace Ford and Hazel (Ellsworth) E.; m. Martha McCabe, June 20, 1953 (div. Sept. 1980); children: Mark, Winthrop, Carolyn, Byron. Student, U. Nebr., 1944-45, U. Colo., 1947-49; AB, U. Colo., 1973; LLB, U. Mich., 1952. Bar: Colo. 1952, Conn. 1976, D.C. bar 1978. Asst. city mgr., city atty. Pueblo, 1952-55; adminstrv. asst., legislative counsel U.S. Senator Gordon Allott, 1956-61; asst. gen. counsel Life Ins. Assn. Am., Washington, 1961-68; gen. counsel Aetna Life & Casualty Co., Hartford, Conn., 1968-78; mem. firm Hedrick & Lane, Washington, 1978-79; ptnr. Nossaman, Guthner, Knox & Elliott, Washington, 1979-85; of counsel Epstein, Becker & Green, P.C., Washington, 1986—. Bd. dirs. Friends of the Hopkins Ctr.; trustee Opera North. Served with USAAC, 1944-46. Mem. ABA, Fed. Bar Assn., Phi Gamma Delta, Phi Alpha Delta. Home: 1 Chambers Rd Hanover NH 03755-2308 also: 316 W De La Guerra St Apt B Santa Barbara CA 93101-3787

ELLIS, ALFRED WRIGHT (AL ELLIS), lawyer; b. Cleve., Aug. 26, 1943; s. Donald Porter and Louise (Wright) E.; m. Kay Genseke, June 1965 (div. 1976); 1 child, Joshua Kyle; m. Sandra Lee Fahey, Feb. 11, 1989. BA with honors, U. Tex., Arlington, 1965; JD, So. Meth. U., 1971. Bar: Tex., U.S. Dist. Ct. (no., so., ea. and we. dists.) Tex., U.S. Ct. Appeals (5th cir.), U.S. Supreme Ct.; cert. personal injury and civil trial lawyer. Atty. Woodruff, Kendall & Smith, Dallas, 1972; ptnr. Woodruff & Ellis, Dallas; pvt. practice Dallas, 1983-96; of counsel Howie & Sweeney, 1996—; instr. So. Meth. U. Law Sch. Trial Advocacy; past pres. Law Focused Edn., Inc. Past mem. City of Dallas Urban Rehab. Standards Bd., Dallas Assembly, Salesmanship Club, Dallas; bd. dirs. Dallas Habitat for Humanity, 1998—; trustee Hist. Preservation League, 1992-94; tournament dir. Dallas Regional Golden Gloves Tournament, 1976-96; pres., bd. dirs. Dallas Coun. on Alcoholism, 1980. Capt. U.S. Army, 1965-69. Fellow Roscoe Pound Found.; named one of Outstanding Young Mem of Am., 1977, named Boss of Yr. Dallas Assn. Legal Secs., 1978; recipient Certs. of Recognition (8) D.I.S.D., 1971-83, Wall St. Jour. award So. Meth. U. Law Sch., 1972, Hayward McMurray award Dallas Jaycees, 1975-76, Spl. Recognition award All Sports Assn., 1977, Cert. of Appreciation for Exceptional and Disting. Vol. Svc. Gov. Mark White, 1983, Community Spirit award Dallas Bus. Jour., 1993, Disting. Svc. award Dallas All Sports Assn., 1993,award Nancy Garms Meml. for outstanding Contr. to Law Focus Edn., 1996-Leon Jaworski award. Fellow Tex. Bar Found. (sustaining life), Dallas Bar Found. (trustee); mem. ATLA, Am. Bd. Trial Advocates (diplomate, sec.-treas. Dallas chpt. 1998, pres. 1999), Am. Coll. Legal Medicine (assoc.), Legal Svcs. of North Tex. (bd. dirs., Outstanding Svc. award 1990), State Bar Tex. (lectr. seminars, bd. dirs. 1991-94, 95, Excellence in Diversity award 1994, Outstanding 3d Yr. Dir. award, Judge Sam Williams Local Bar Leadership award), Dallas Bar Assn. (bd. dirs. 1978, chmn. bd. dirs. 1986, v.p. 1987-88, pres. 1990), Dallas Trial Lawyers Assn. (pres. 1977, Disting. Cmty. Svc. award 1990), Tex. Trial Lawyers Assn., Tex. Equal Access to Justice Found. (bd. dirs. 1994-96), Coll. State Bar of Tex. (bd. dirs. 1997-2000), Dallas All Sports Assn. (pres.-1980), Tex. Commn. for Lawyer Discipline, Tex. Ctr. for Legal Ethics and Professionalism (bd. dirs. 1999—), Tex. Legal Svcs. Ctr. (bd. dirs. 1999—). Avocations: tennis, skiing. Office: 2911 Turtle Creek Blvd Ste 1400 Dallas TX 75219-6258

ELLIS, ANDREW JOHN, airline pilot; b. Sydney, Australia, Feb. 13, 1969; s. John and Jenny (Wischer) E. BA, U. New South Wales, 1989. Pilot Royal Australian Air Force, 1987-97, Cathay Pacific Airways Ltd., Hong Kong, China, 1997—. Mem. Securities Inst. Australia.

ELLIS, ANNE ELIZABETH, fundraiser; b. Orngestad, Aruba, Aug. 21, 1945; d. Thomas Albert and Anne Elizabeth (Belis) Wolfe; m. Earl Edward Ellis, Feb. 14, 1970. BS, La. State U., 1967. Fashion coord. Baton Rouge, 1962-67; textile researcher La. State U., Baton Rouge, 1965-67; buyer I.H. Rubensteins., Baton Rouge, 1967-68; fashion distbr. J.C. Penney, Inc., Arlington, Tex., 1969-70; asst. buyer J.C. Penney, Inc., Dallas, 1970-73; exec. dir. Nassau County Mus. Fine Art Assn., Roslyn, N.Y., 1985-88; speaker C.W. Post U., Greenvale, N.Y., 1988—; cons. in field. Chmn., editor: (cookbook) Specialities of the House, 1981-83. Bd. dirs., com. chmn. Congregational Ch., Manhasset, N.Y., 1975-96; exec. v.p., bd. dirs., com. chmn. Jr. League Internat.; benefit gala chmn., com. chmn. Grenville Baker Boys & Girls Club, Locust Valley, N.Y., 1983-91; pres. bd., vice-chmn. cmty. outreach, benefit gala chmn. Tilles Performing Art Ctr. L.I. U., Greenvale, N.Y., 1985—; bd. dirs., benefit co-chmn. Nassau County Family Assn. Svcs., Hempstead, 1988-96; benefit vice-chmn. Glen Cove/North Shore Cmty. Hosp., 1989-93; mem. exec. bd., exec. v.p., trustee WLIW, L.I. Pub. TV, 1990—, chmn. bd. dirs., 1997-99; trustee Cmty. Found. of Oyster Bay, 1991-94; trustee Dowling Coll., Oakdale, N.Y., 1993-98, exec. bd., 1997-98; adv. bd. Westbury (N.Y.) Gardens, 1993-97; chmn. adv. bd. Long Island chpt. Save the Children, 1995—; trustee L.I. U., 1998—. Recipient Vol. of Yr. award Jr. League L.I., 1984, 85, Outstanding Vol. Svcs. and Commitment award County of Nassau, 1989, Juliette Low award Nassau County Girl Scouts, L.I., 1991, Disting. Leadership award, L.I., 1991, Outstanding Community Vol. award Jr. League of L.I., 1991-92, Disting. Svc. medal L.I. State Parks Found., 1999, Women of Achievement award Jr. League L.I., 2000. Mem. P.E.O. (pres. 1985-87), The Creek Inc., Meadowbrook Club Inc., Nat. Arts Club, Lost Tree Club, Forest Creek Club, Kappa Kappa Gamma (alumna pres. 1971-72). Republican. Congregationalist. Avocations: golf, gardening, needlepoint.

ELLIS, BRIAN WILLIAM, surgeon; b. Hove, Sussex, Eng., Nov. 28, 1947; s. Frank A.E. and Beryl Christine (Holdsworth) E.; m. Loveday Ann Pusey, July 10, 1976; children: Rebecca, David. MB, BChir, U. London, 1970. Cons. urol. surgeon, dir. surgery Ashford (Eng.) & St. Peter's Hosps. NHS Trust, 1983—; cons. surgery Brit. Airways, 1993—, Med. Sys. Ltd., 1984—, Med. Software Ltd., 1986—. Editor: Hamilton Bailey's Emergency Surgery, 12th edit., 1995, Jour. of Integrated Care, 1996. Hon. sr. clin. rsch. fellow St. Mary's Hosp., London, 1988—. Fellow Royal Coll. Surgeons of Eng.; mem. Brit. Assn. Urol. Surgeons (mem. coun. 1996), Urology Team of Yr. award 1998. Avocations: wine, roses, music. Home: Graylands, 124 Brox Rd, Surrey Ottershaw KT16 0LG, England Office: Ashford Hosp, Dept Urology, Middlsx Ashford TW15 3AA, England

ELLIS, DONALD LEE, lawyer; b. Dallas, Oct. 2, 1950; s. Truett T. and Rosemary (Tarrant) E.; children: Angela Nicole, Laura Elizabeth, Natalie Dawn, Donald Lee II. BS, U. Tulsa, 1973; JD, Oklahoma City U., 1976. Bar: Tex. 1979, Okla. 1977, U.S. Dist. Ct. (ea. dist.) Tex. 1978, U.S. Dist. Ct. (we. dist.) Okla. 1978, U.S. Ct. Appeals (5th cir.) 1984, U.S. Supreme Ct., 1984, U.S. Ct. Appeals (11th cir.). Spl. agt. FBI, Washington, 1976-78; asst. dist. atty. Smith County, Tyler, Tex., 1979-80; mem. firm Barron & Ellis, Tyler, 1980-84, Ellis & Woods law firm, 1984-85; sole practice, Tyler, 1985—. Bd. dirs. Mental Health Assn., Tyler, 1983-87. Mem. Assn. Trial Lawyers Am., Tex. Bar Assn., Okla. Bar Assn., Smith County Bar Assn., Soc. Former Spl. Agts. FBI, Tex. Trial Lawyers Assn., FBI Agents Assn., Lawyers-Pilot Bar Assn. Home: PO Box 131221 Tyler TX 75713-1221 Office: 217 W Houston St Tyler TX 75702-8137

ELLIS, ELDON EUGENE, surgeon; b. Washington, Ind., July 2, 1922; s. Osman Polson and Ina Lucretia (Cochran) E.; m. Irene Clay, June 26, 1948 (dec. 1968); m. Priscilla Dean Strong, Sept. 20, 1969 (dec. Feb. 1990); children: Paul Addison, Kathe Lynn, Jonathan Clay, Sharon Anne, Eldon Eugene, Rebecca Deborah; m. Virginia Michael Ellis, Aug. 22, 1992. BA, U. Rochester, 1946, MD, 1949. Intern in surgery Stanford U. Hosp., San Francisco, 1949-50, resident and fellow in surgery, 1950-52, 55; Schilling fellow in pathology San Francisco Gen. Hosp., 1955; ptnr. Redwood Med. Clinic, Redwood City, Calif., 1955-87; med. dir. Redwood Med. Clinic, Redwood City, 1984-87; semi-ret. physician, 1987—; med. dir. Peninsula Occupl. Health Assocs., San Carlos, Calif., 1991-94; physician Peninsula Occupl. Health Assocs., San Carlos, 1995-99, Sequoia Med. Clinic, Redwood City, Calif., 1999—; asst. clin. prof. surgery Stanford U., 1970-80; dir. Sequoia Hosp., Redwood City, 1974-82. Pres. Sequoia Hosp. Found., 1983-92, bd. dirs.; pres., chmn. bd. dirs. Bay Chamber Symphony Orch., San Mateo, Calif., 1988-91; mem. Nat. Bd. Benevolence Evang. Covenant Ch., Chgo., 1988-93; mem. mgmt. com. The Samarkand Retirement Cmty., Santa Barbara, Calif.; past pres. Project Hope Nat. Alumni Assn., 1992-94, bd. dirs., 1994—; med. advisor Project Hope, Russia Commonwealth Ind. States, 1992. With USNR, 1942-46, 50-52. Named Outstanding Citizen of Yr., Redwood City, 1987. Mem. AMA, Calif. Med. Assn., Am. Coll. Chest Physicians, Am. Heart Assn. (v.p. 1974-75), Calif. Heart Assn. (pres. 1965-66), San Mateo County Heart Assn. (pres. 1961-63), San Mateo Med. Soc. (pres. 1969-70), San Mateo County Comprehensive Health Planning Coun. (v.p. 1969-70), San Mateo Surg. Soc., Stanford Surg. Soc., San Mateo Individual Practice Assn. (treas. 1984-97), Cardiovasc. Coun., Calif. Thoracic Soc., Commonwealth Club. Republican. Mem. Peninsula Convenant Ch. Home: 2305 Wooster Ave Belmont CA 94002-1549 Office: Sequoia Med Clinic 633 Veterans Blvd Redwood City CA 94063-1408

ELLIS, EMORY LEON, retired biochemist; b. Grayville, Ill., Oct. 29, 1906; s. Walter Leon and Bertha May (Forman) W.; m. Marion Louise Faulkner, Sept. 17, 1930 (dec. Aug. 1994). BS, Calif. Inst. Tech., 1930, MS in Chemistry, 1932, PhD in Biochemistry, 1934. Registered profl. engr., Calif. Chemist U.S. FDA, L.A., 1934-35; rsch. assoc. CalTech, Pasadena, 1935-43; dept. head U.S. Navy Ordnance Test Sta., China Lake, Calif., 1943-54; dir. ordnance plan Rheem Ordnance Lab, Downey, Calif., 1954-57; project leader Inst. for Def. Analysis, Washington, 1957-63; cons. U.S. Navy Weapons Ctr., China Lake, 1966-68; ptnr. Devcom, La Habra, Calif., 1965-68. Contbr. chpt. in books and articles to profl. jours. Recipient Naval Ordnance Devel. award USN, 1945, Alumni Disting. Svc. award Calif. Inst. Tech., 1970; Paul Harris fellow Rotary Internat., 1993. Mem. AAAS, Am. Chem. Soc., Tau Beta Pi, Sigma Xi. Avocations: writing essays, travel. Home: 506 Pioneer Ct Santa Maria CA 93454-3442

ELLIS, FRANK, radiotherapeutic oncologist; b. Sheffield, Eng., Aug. 22, 1905; s. James Thomas and Beatrice May (Laming) E.; m. Mary Dorothy Parr, Sept. 3, 1932 (dec.); children: David J.P., Janet D., Anne R., John P., Francis M.L. BSc, Sheffield U., 1927, MSc, 1928, MB, ChB with honours, 1929, MD with distinction, 1944; DS (hon.), Ohio State U. Dir. radiotherapy dept. Sheffield, 1931-43, Royal London Hosp., 1943-50; dir. radiation oncology Churchill Hosp., Oxford, 1950-70; prof. physician U. So. Calif., L.A., 1970-71; prof. dir. radiotherapy dept. Med. Coll. Wis., Milw., 1971-74; physician radiotherapy Meml. Sloan Kettering, N.Y.C., 1974-76; prof. physician United Hosp. Newark, N.J., 1976-78; ret., 1978. Contbr. over 200 articles to profl. jours. Named to Order of Brit. Empire. Fellow Royal Coll. Physicians, Royal Coll. Radiology (Gold medallist), Inst. Physics & Engring. Medicine (hon.), Am. Coll. Radiology (hon.). Mem. Soc. of Friends. Home: 2 Wyndham House, Plantation Rd, Oxford OX2 6JJ, England

ELLIS, FRANK, economics educator; b. London, Dec. 2, 1947; s. John Ellis and Margaret Selby; m. Jane Ellis DeBoer, Dec. 30, 1972; children: Clare, Josephine. BSc in Agrl. Econs., U. Reading, Eng., 1970; MSc in Econs., London Sch. Econs., 1972; DPhil in Econs., U. Sussex, Eng., 1978. Rsch. fellow Inst. Devel. Studies Sussex U., 1973-80; econ. advisor Union of Banana Exporting Countries, Panama, 1975-77; sr. rsch. fellow econ. rsch. bur. U. Dar es Salaam, Tanzania, 1979-80; from lectr. to sr. lectr. to reader Sch. Devel. Studies, U. East Anglia, Norwich, Eng., 1981-97, prof., 1997—; agrl. econs. advisor Fiji Employment and Devel. Mission, Suva, Fiji, 1982-83; team leader integrated planning unit BULOG, Indonesia, Jakarta, 1987-89; chair Dudley Seers Prize Panel, London, 1994-99. Author: (acad. textbooks) Peasant Economics, 1988, 2d edit., 1993, Agricultural Policies in Developing Countries, 1992; editl. bd.: Jour. Devel. Studies, 1990—; contbr. articles to profl. jours. Rsch. grantee Natural Resources Inst., 1990-92, Econ. and Social Com. of Dept. for Internat. Devel., 1996-98, Rural Livelihoods and Diversity in Developing Countries, 2000, Policy Rsch. Program of Dept. for Internat. Devel., 2000-2003. Mem. Soc. for Internat. Devel., Agrl. Econs. Socs. U.K., Devel. Studies Assn. U.K. Avocations: hiking, swimming, film, music. Fax: 44 1603 464267. E-mail: f.ellis@uea.ac.uk. Office: U of East Anglia, Sch Devel Studies, Norwich NR4 7TJ, England

ELLIS, GEORGE EDWIN, JR., chemical engineer; b. Beaumont, Tex., Apr. 14, 1921; s. George Edwin and Julia (Ryan) E. BSChemE, U. Tex., 1948; MS, U. So. Calif., 1958, MBA, 1965, MS in Mech. Engring., 1968, MS in Mgmt. Sci., 1971, Engr. in Indsl. and Systems Engring., 1979. Rsch. chem. engr. Tex. Co., Port Arthur, 1948-51, Houston and Long Beach, Calif., 1952-53; rsch. chem. engr. Space and Info. Divsn., N.Am. Aviation Co., Downey, Calif., 1959-61, Magna Corp., Anaheim, Calif., 1961-62; chem. process engr. AiResearch Mfg. Co., L.A., 1953-57, 57-59; chem. engr. Petroleum Combustion & Engring. Co., Santa Monica, Calif., 1957, Jacobs Engring. Co., Pasadena, Calif., 1957, Sesler & Assocs., L.A., 1959; rsch. specialist Marquardt Corp., Van Nuys, Calif., 1962-67; sr. project engr. Conductron Corp., Northridge, Calif., 1967-68; info. systems asst. L.A. Dept. Water and Power, 1969-92; instr. thermodynamics U. So. Calif., L.A., 1957. With USAAF, 1943-45. Mem. ASTM, ASME, AIChE, Nat. Assn. Purchasing Mgmt., Nat. Contract Mgmt. Assn., Am. Inst. Profl. Bookkeepers, Am. Soc. Safety Engrs., Am. Chem. Soc., Am. Soc. Materials, Am. Electroplaters and Surface Finishers Soc., Nat. Assn. Corrosion Engrs., Inst. Indsl. Engrs., Am. Prodn. and Inventory Control Soc., Am. Soc. Quality, Am. Indsl. Hygenists Assn., Steel Structure Painting Coun., Soc. Plastics Engrs., Inst. Mgmt. Accts., Soc. Mfg. Engrs., L.A. Soc. Coating Tech., Assn. Finishing Processes, Chem. Coatings Assn. Internat., Nat. Fire Protection Assn., Soc. Tribologists and Lubrication Engrs., Pi Tau Sigma, Phi Lambda Upsilon, Alpha Pi Mu. Home: 1344 W 20th St San Pedro CA 90732-4408

ELLIS, GEORGE FRANCIS RAYNER, astronomy educator; b. Johannesburg, South Africa, Aug. 11, 1939; s. George Rayner and Gwendoline (MacRobert) E.; m. Sue Parkes (div.); children: Margaret, Andrew; m. Mary Roberts MacDonald. BSc, U. Cape Town, South Africa, 1961, B Comm., 1982; PhD, Cambridge (eng.) U., 1964; hon. degree, Haverford Coll., 1996, U. Natal, Durban. South Africa, 1998. Lectr. Cambridge U., 1968-73; prof. U. Cape Town, 1973-87, SISSA, Trieste, Italy, 1988-93, Cape Town U., 1990—; vis. prof. Hamburg, Fed. Republic of Germany, Chgo., Boston, Tex., London Univ. Author: (with S. Hawking) Large Scale Structure of Space Time, 1973, (with D. Dewar) Low Income Housing Policy, 1980, Before the Beginning, 1993, The Moral Nature of the Universe (with N. Murphy), 1996. Chmn. Friends of the Ciskei People, Cape Town, 1978-83; clk. S.A. Yearly Meeting of Quakers, Cape Town, 1982-86; chmn. Quaker Svc., Cape Town, 1978-86, South African Inst. Race Rels., Cape Town, 1986-88. Recipient South African Math. Soc. award, 1998, Star of Africa medal; Peterhouse fellow U. Cambridge, 1965-67, U. Cape Town fellow, 1978. Fellow Royal Soc. South Africa (v.p. 1990-92, pres. 1992-96, Herschel medal 1978), Royal Astron. Soc.; mem. Internat. Soc. Gen. Relativity and Gravitation (pres. 1987-91), Internat. Astron. Union. Home: 3 Marlow Rd Kenilworth, Cape Town 7700, South Africa Office: U Cape Town, Dept Math and Applied Math, Rondebosch 7700 Cape, South Africa

ELLIS, JAMES ALVIS, JR., lawyer; b. Lubbock, Tex., Mar. 19, 1943; s. James Alvis and Myrle Alice (Peden) E.; m. Sandra Gay Gillespie, June 18, 1966; children: Claire Ellis Gentry, James Alvis III. BA, Tex. Tech U., 1965; JD, U. Tex., 1968. Bar: Tex. 1968, U.S. Dist. Ct. (no., so., ea. and we. dists.) Tex. 1969, U.S. Ct. Appeals 1970, U.S. Supreme Ct. 1980; cert. in civil trial law Tex. Bd. Legal Specialization. Law clk. to presiding judge U.S. Dist. Ct. (we. dist.) Tex., 1968-69; assoc. Carrington, Coleman Sloman & Blumenthal, Dallas, 1970-74, ptnr., 1975—. Pres. Dallas Jr. Bar Assn., 1972. Fellow Tex. Bar Found., Dallas Bar Found.; mem. ABA, State Bar Tex., Dallas Bar Assn. Presbyterian. Club: Crescent. Office: Carrington Coleman Sloman & Blumenthal 200 Crescent Ct Ste 1500 Dallas TX 75201-1848

ELLIS, JAMES JOLLY, landscape resort official; b. Meadville, Pa., Mar. 3, 1937; s. Walter Harmon and Nerea Isabel (Farver) E. AA, Orlando Jr. Coll., 1959; BS in Bus. Adminstrn. and Econs., Rollins Coll., 1981. With Orlando (Fla.) Parks and Forestry Dept., 1961-70; supr. landscape dept. Walt Disney World, Fla., 1970-78, 81-82; supr. landscape dept. Walt Disney Village Comtys., Orlando, 1978-81, horticulture area mgr. over rd. maintenance/spl. projects, 1995-2000; owner, operator Chestnut Grove Nursery and Landscape Co., 1988—. Served with U.S. Army, 1959-60. Mem. Am. Mgmt. Assn., Fla. Turf Grass Assn. Republican. Lutheran. Home: 705 S Summerlin Ave Orlando FL 32801-4021 Office: 1410 Renee Ave Orlando FL 32825-5226

ELLIS, JOHN, small business owner; b. Amherst, Ohio, Sept. 15, 1929; s. Edward Pierson and Jean (Scott) E.; m. Carolyn Elizabeth Collier, Dec. 29, 1951; children: Linda Ellis Wieand, Jeanine Ellis Klausing, Jeanette Ellis Hale, John Edward. BS, Bowling Green State U., 1953; MA, Case Western Res. U., Cleve., 1958; EdD, Harvard U., 1964. Tchr. pub. schs., Lorain, Ohio, 1953-54, prin., 1957-61, asst. supt. schs., Massillon, Ohio, 1963-64, supt. schs., 1964-66, Lakewood, Ohio, 1966-71, Columbus, Ohio, 1971-77; adj. prof. ednl. adminstrn. Ohio State U., Columbus, 1971-77; exec. dep. commr. edn. U.S. Office Edn., Washington, 1977-80; supt. schs., Austin, Tex., 1980-90; commr. N.J. Dept. Edn., 1990-92; owner Ellis Broadcasting Corp., Wimberley, Tex., 1992-00;Elder local Presbyn. Ch. Served with USAF, 1947-49, 54-57. Recipient Massillon Young Man of Yr. award, 1965; named to Saturday Rev. Honor Roll, 1977. Mem. Phi Delta Kappa, Pi Kappa Alpha, Phi Alpha Theta, Kappa Delta Pi, Gamma Theta Upsilon. Lodge: Rotary; consultant, 2000S. Home: 500 Leath Hollow Dr Wimberley TX 78676-5207

ELLIS, JOHN HEYWOOD, materials testing specialist; b. Leeds, Eng., Apr. 10, 1955; s. Cedric Heywood and Betty (Bell) E.; m. Frances Margaret Wood, May 16, 1981 (div. Oct. 1985); 1 child, Thomas Edward; m. Kathleen Hampshire, Dec. 27, 1985; 1 child, Andrew Heywood. BS in Materials Sci., Sheffield (Eng.) U., 1976; diploma in mgmt. studies, Leeds Met. U., 1993. Chartered engr. Metallurgist Osborn Steels, Sheffield, 1976-77; metallurgist AETC Ltd., Leeds, 1977-92, mgr. process dept., 1992-95, non-destructive testing specialist, 1995—. Coach jr. rugby league. Level III grantee ASNT, 1996, Pratt & Whitney, 1996. Mem. Engring. Coun. (chartered engr.), Inst. Materials (profl. mem.), Leeds Materials Soc. (treas. 1987), Am. Soc. Non-Destructive Testing. Conservative. Anglican. Home: 25 Church Approach, Garforth Leeds LS25 1JD, England Office: AETC Ltd, Victoria Ave, LS19 7AY Yeadon Leeds, England

ELLIS, JOHN MUNN, III, insurance company financial executive; b. Morristown, N.J.; s. John M. and Mary Jane (Berg) E.; widowed; children: John Jaz M., Blair M. BA, Kans. Wesleyan U., 1975; BS, Kans. State U., 1978; postgrad., Harvard Bus Exec. Mgmt. Sch, 1985. CLU. Agt. N.Y. Life Ins. Co., Topeka, 1976-78, sales mgr., 1978-83, assoc. gen. mgr., 1983-85; exec. mgmt. cons. N.Y. Life Ins. Co., N.Y.C., 1985-88; gen. mgr. N.Y. Life Ins. Co., Fairfield, Conn., 1988-96; regional dir. tng. and devel. for ins. ops. in Middle East and Africa, agy. dir. for Oman, Qatar, Kuwait, Bahrain, United Arab Emirates, Pakistan Am. Life Ins. Co., Sharjah, United Arab Emirates, 1996-98; agy. dir., profit ctr. head v.p. AIG-AIA, China, 1998-2000, tech. adv. Indonesia and India, exec. mgmt. advisor, 2000—. Mem. Fairfield bldg. com. YMCA. Mem. Nat. Assn. Life Underwriters (cert. life underwriters tng. coun.), Fairfield C. of C. (past pres., v.p. fin. 1989-93, bldg. com. 1993), Gen. Agts. and Mgrs. Assn. (bd. dirs. 1989-95, pres. 1994-95, nat. membership com. 1995-2000), Am. Quarter Horse Assn. (life), Lions (pres. Auburn, Kans. 1989), Rotary, Optimists, Masons. E-mail: john.ellis@aig.com. Address: AIG Lippo Matahari Lippo Cyber Tower, Jl Bulevar Palem Raya # 7, Lippo Karawaci 1200 Tangerang 15811, Indonesia

ELLIS, JUNE B., human resource consultant; b. Portland, Ind., June 17; children: Kenneth G., Reyn K. BS, Mary Washington Coll., 1942; MSW, Tulane U., 1953; PhD, Internat. U., 1977. Asst. dir. social services East La. State Hosp., Jackson, 1960-62; instr. Tulane U. Sch. Social Work, New Orleans, 1962-63, asst. prof. dept. psyhiatry, Sch. Medicine, 1963-68; exec. dir. Family Service-Travelers Aid, Ft. Smith, Ark., 1967-71; pres. Child and Family Cons., Ft. Smith, 1971—; dir. Human Resource Devel. Ctr., Ft. Smith; mem. adv. bd. Suspect Child Abuse and Neglect; cons. Volvo Health Care, Goteborg, Sweden, 1974-92, Kontura Personal, 1974-92, Christian Counseling Ctr., Vellore, India, 1974—; mem. Tulane Alumni Bd., 1978-88; mem. continuing profl. edn. com. Tulane Univ. Sch. Social Work, 1996—. Author: TA Tally, 1974, TA Talk, terms and references in transaction, 1976, BEING, 1982. Mem. Ark. Gov.'s Commn. on Status of Women, 1970-73, Ark. Gov.'s Com. Drug Abuse Prevention; cons. Cuban Resettlement Program, Ft. Chaffee, Ark., 1980; del. leader to China, 1984; mem. adv. bd. Jr. League Am.; mem. scholarship selection com. Whirlpool Corp.; bd. mem. Ctr. for Long Life Learning, Tulane U.; coord. Western Ark. Health Advocacy Svc., 1995—; mem. adv. bd. Ctr. for Long Life Living, Tulane U., 1996; cons. gerontology, Tulane U., 1998—; judge Odyssey of the Mind, Tex. Sch. Sys., 1998—; appointee rehab. adv. coun. Presbyn. Hosp. of Dallas, 2000—. Named Outstanding Alumni, Tulane U., 1984. Mem. ASTD, AAUS, AAUW, Am. Acad. Psychotherapists, Am. Group Psychotherapy Assn., Am. Orthopsychiat. Assn., Acad. Cert. Social Workers, Western Ark. Mental Health Assn. (adv. bd.), Conf. for Advancement of Pvt. Practice in Social Work, Am. Assn. Ret. Persons, Am. Assn. of Individual Investors, Park Cities Club. Episcopalian. Office: 3437 Westminster Ave Dallas TX 75205-1336

ELLIS, RAYMOND CLINTON, JR., association executive; b. Chgo., May 11, 1921; s. Raymond Clinton and Frances Geraldine (Hersma) E. PhB, U. Chgo., 1950, MBA, 1953. Cert. hospitality tech. profl.; cert. lodging security dir.; cert. hospitality educator. Various positions Marshall Field & Co., Chgo., 1938-52, safety dir., 1953-55; staff rep., dir. small bus. program Nat. Safety Coun., Chgo., 1955-61; dir. mem. rels. Variety Stores Assocs., N.Y.C., 1961-64; fleet safety coord. Am. Ins. Assn., N.Y.C., 1964-67; group adminstr. Hotel Safety Group, N.Y.C., 1967-77; dir. risk mgmt. and ops. Am. Hotel and Motel Assn., N.Y.C., 1977-92; exec. v.p. Am. Hotel and Motel Assn. Gen. Agy., Inc., N.Y.C., 1977-92; sec., project dir. Am. Hotel and Motel Assn. Rsch. Found., N.Y.C., 1977-92; mem. bd. trustees, sec. Hotel Assn. Group Trust, 1977—; mem. occupational safety and health com. Bus. Rsch. Adv. Coun., Bur. Labor Stats., U.S. Dept. Labor, 1971—; mem. overseas security adv. coun. U.S. Dept. State, 1989—; security cons. to lodging industry, 1993-94; ops. cons. Am. Hotel and Motel Assn., 1993-94; apptd. adj. prof. hotel and restaurant mgmt. Conrad N. Hilton Coll. of Hotel and Restaurant Mgmt., U. Houston, 1994—, dir. tech. rsch. and edn. ctr., 1994-97, dir. loss prevention mgmt. inst., 1994—; mem. consumer adv. coun. Underwriters Labs., 1984—. Author: Security and Loss Prevention Management for the Lodging Industry, 1985, 2d edit., 1999; editor: Student Manual-Security Course, 1978, Security and Loss Prevention Management Manual, 1996, A Guide to Occupational Safety and Health Standards Compliance for the Lodging Industry, 1997; contbr. articles to profl. jours.; mem. tech. bd. Hotel & Motel Mgmt. Mag., 1988-97; editl. adv. bd. Hotel Security Report; mem. editl. bd. Hospitality Law; pub. monthly loss prevention bull. Am. Hotel and Motel Assn., 1995—, prevention sect. Lodging Law, 1998—. Elder N.Y. Ave. Presbyn. Ch., D.C. With USAAF, 1943-46, ATO. Named to Hospitality Tech. Hall of Fame, Hospitality Fin. and Tech. Profls., 1989, Lamp of Knowledge award for Outstanding Educator, Edn. Inst. Am. Hotel & Motel Assn., 1999. Mem. ASTM, Am. Soc. Safety Engrs., Vets. of Safety, Nat. Fire Protection Assn. (mem. exec. com. and dir. lodging sect.), Nat. Safety Coun. (Disting. Svc. to Safety award 1986, mem. and sec. exec. com. svcs., retail and logistics divsn.), Am. Soc. Indsl. Security (mem. lodging sect. 2000—, Ray Ellis Jr. Lodging Security ann. award named in his honor 2000). Republican. Avocations: bell collecting, travel. E-mail: rellis@uh.edu. Home: 4444 Cullen Blvd Apt 105 Houston TX 77004-2624 Office: Conrad Hilton Coll S4800 Calhoun Blvd Houston TX 77204-0001

ELLIS, ROBERT HARRY, music educator, parochial school educator; b. Fairmont, W.Va., Jan. 18, 1941; s. Robert Dale and Lemma Ann (Layman) E. BA in Edn., Fairmont State Coll., 1962; MMus, W.Va. U., 1963; postgrad., U. Cin., 1968-72. Cert. tchr. music, English. Music instr. Fairview and Farmington High Sch., W.Va., 1963-65; assoc. prof. music Glenville (W.Va.) State Coll., 1965-68; tchg. fellow in music theory Coll.-Conservatory Music U. Cin., 1968-72; music instr. Rygaards Internat. Sch., Copenhagen, 1972-73; owner, instr. Musitech Music Studio, Fairmont, W.Va., 1973—; music instr. Fairmont Cath. Grade Sch., 1973—; pastoral musician Parish St. Peter the Fisherman, Fairmont, 1973—; mem./composer Diocesan Music Commn., Diocese of Wheeling-Charleston, W.Va., 1978-90. Editor, typographer quarterly state newsletter WVMTA News, 19982000; contbr. articles to Clavier mag., Keyboard Companion; composer: composition for installation of bishop for choir, brass, bells, cantor, organ, congregation Te Deum, 1985. Recipient Music award Internat. Women's Clubs, 1973, Marion County Recognition award County Commn. Marion County, 1993, Disting. W. Virginian award Gov. W.Va., 1998—. Mem. W.Va. Music Tchrs. Assn. (dist. chair 1988-94), Nat. Pastoral Musicians (state pres. 1980-86). Episcopalian. Avocations: computer desktop publishing, book collecting, sound-system, 3-D stereo photography. Home: 1011 Speedway St Fairmont WV 26554-4447 Office: Musitech Music Studio 416A Madison St Fairmont WV 26554-2946

ELLIS, ROBERT JEFFRY, health facility executive; b. Augusta, Ga., Aug. 15, 1935; s. Herbert Monroe and Dorothy Louise (Doney) E.; m. Ann Marie Jarvis, July 19, 1969; 1 child, Tonya Dawn. BA in Mktg./Creative Writing, Columbia Pacific U., San Rafael, Calif., 1980, MA in Mktg./Creative Writing, 1981. Asst. mgr. Publix Employees Fed. Credit Union, Lakeland, Fla., 1970-75; mktg. rep. L.B. Sowell Corp., Tampa, Fla., 1977-82, Cooper Distbrs., Inc., Orlando, Fla., 1983-86; co-founder, exec. v.p. Nat. Labs., Inc., Winter Haven, Fla., 1987-96; co-founder, dir. EuroMed Ltd., Thetford, Eng., 1989-2000; pvt. practice Winter Haven, Fla., 2000—; film prodr. Focus Prodns., Hollywood, Calif., 1991; dir. Greystone Med. Group, Inc., Memphis, 1996-2000; CEO Med Stat Inc., Memphis, 1996-98, Nat. Labs., 1999-2000. Composer film soundtrack recording, 1973. Mem. Am. Radio League (pub. svc. awards 1970, 76). Avocation: amateur radio. Office: Nat Labs PO Box 7349 Winter Haven FL 33883-7349

ELLIS, STEPHEN, social sciences researcher; b. Nottingham, Eng., June 13, 1953; s. Derek Hugh John and Hilda Mary (Kingscote) E. BA, U. Oxford, Eng., 1975, PhD, 1981. Rschr. Amnesty Internat., London, 1982-86; editor Africa Confidential, London, 1986-91; dir. Afrika-Studiecentrum, Leiden, The Netherlands, 1991-94; sr. rschr. Afrika-Studiecentrum, Leiden, The Netherlands, 1994—. Editor: Africa Now, 1995, Enterprises et Entrepreneurs Africains, 1995; author: L'Affaire Rainandriamampandry, 1990, Comrades Against Apartheid, 1992. Office: Afrika-Studiecentrum, PO Box 9555, 2300 RB Leiden The Netherlands

ELLIS, STEPHEN GEOFFREY, medical educator, physician; b. Ross, Calif., Oct. 24, 1951; s. William Herbert and Katharine (Curtis) E.; m. Sandra Joan Dushman, June 3, 1984; children: Jessica, Gary. BS in Chemistry, Stanford U., 1973; MD, UCLA, 1978. Diplomate Am. Bd. Internal Medicine, Am. Bd. Cardiovascular Disease, Am. Bd. Interventional Cardiology. Intern Cedars-Sinai Med. Ctr., L.A., 1978-79, resident, 1979-81; asst. prof. medicine U. Mich., Ann Arbor, 1986-89, assoc. prof., 1989-91; prof. medicine Cleveland Clin., Ohio State U., Cleve., 1991—; mem. various adv. bds. Contbr. over 200 articles to med. jours. Softball coach Beachwood (Ohio) Recreation Ctr., 1996—. Fellow Am. Coll. Cardiology, Am. Acad. Scis. Office: Cleveland Clin Found 9500 Euclid Ave Cleveland OH 44195-0001

ELLISON, BETTY D., retired elementary educator; b. Meriwether County, Ga., Jan. 28, 1950; d. Haywood Sr. and Mary Susan (Green) Daniel; m. Darthus Ellison, Jr., June 25, 1972; children: Darthus III, Keith Brandon. BA, Morris Brown Coll., 1972; MA, Atlanta U., 1975. Cert. tchr. Tchr. Meriwether County Bd. Edn., Greenville, Ga.; reading specialist Talbot County Bd. Edn., Talbotton, Ga.; advisor Nat. Jr. Honor Soc. Ga. State Tchrs. scholar; named County Star Tchr., 1991. Mem. NEA, Ga. Assn. Educators, Assn. for Supervision and Curriculum Devel., Zeta Phi Beta, Pi Delta Phi. Home: 88 Johnson Ave Manchester GA 31816-1602

ELLISON, EARL OTTO, computer scientist; b. Elizabeth, N.J., Apr. 26, 1938; s. Thorleif and Reidun Ingeborg (Andersen) E.; m. Judith Roque Impoc, Feb. 2, 1997; 1 child, Reidun Impoc. BS, Am. U., Washington, 1964, postgrad., 1964-66. Head supplies and equipment at Pentagon C & P Telephone Co. (now Bell Atlantic), Arlington, Va., 1956-62; tax acct. Trust Dept. Nat. Bank of Washington, 1964-65; methods analyst Automation Industries, Consol. Am. Svcs. Mgmt. Cons. Subs., Washington, L.A., 1965; mgmt. instr. fed. supply svc. GSA, Washington, 1965-67, contract negotiator info. tech. svc., 1967-77, computer sys. contracting officer, 1977-97; pres. Teledesic Svcs., Inc., Washington, 1997—. Author: Revenue Code of 1962: Effects on the Multi-National Firm, 1965. Judge ballroom dancing U.S. Ballroom Dancing Assn., Eastern seaboard, 1986—; swimming and diving coach Pike Br. Swim and Tennis Club, Alexandria, Va., 1966—. With USNR, 1961-62. Mem. The Beethoven Soc. Am. (exec. bd. 1993—), Norwegian Soc., Sons of Norway (prin. bldg. fund 1985—, Washington chpt. pres. 1994—, counselor 1993—, investment adv. 1979—, internat. del. to conv. 1988). Presbyterian. Avocations: swimming, diving, ballroom dancing. Home: 6324 Telegraph Rd Alexandria VA 22310-2969 Office: 710 W Peachtree St NW Atlanta GA 30308-1139 also: Rosfjord, 4580 Lyngdal Norway

ELLISON, HENRY PHILLIPS, military officer; b. Columbia, S.C., Sept. 26, 1969; s. David Gaillard Ellison Jr. and Cornelia (Fleming) Mayer. BS in Geopolitics, U.S. Mil. Acad., West Point, N.Y., edu3. Commd. 2d lt. U.S. Army, Ft. Benning, Ga., 1994-97, advanced through grades to capt., 1997, capt. 51st Fighter Wing, 1997-98; capt. G3 I Corps U.S. Army, Ft. Lewis, Wash., 1998-2000; capt., BN intelligence officer 218 FA U.S. Army, Ft. Lewis, 2000—. Episcopalian. Avocations: college football, stamp collecting, music. Home: 3916 Kilbourne Rd Columbia SC 29205-1561 Office: US Army 2800 Limited Ln NW Apt J12 Olympia WA 98502-2747

ELLISON, ROBERT W., sculptor; b. Detroit, Dec. 13, 1946; s. Owen and Mary Ellison. BFA, Mich. State U., 1969, MFA, 1971. sculpture design instr. Mich. State U., Lansing, 1970-71, Kentfield, Calif., 1972-77. Steel sculptures include Untitled, 1969, Borbourygmi, 1979, Contest, 1990, Mr. Zebra and Friends, 1999. Recipient 1st pl. award 21st Annual All Calif. Juried Show. Mem. Cultural Arts Coun. Sonoma. Avocation: growing cactus and succulents. Home and Office: Ellison Studio 6480 Eagle Ridge Rd Penngrove CA 94951-9574

ELLISON, WILLIAM THEODORE, marine engineer; b. Wilmington, N.C., Nov. 30, 1941; s. Robert Jay and Marie Catherine (Robinson) E.; m. Annelise Manecky, Dec. 18, 1987; children: Britt Kirsten, Hans Salter, Katerina Astri-Marie. BS, U.S. Naval Acad., 1963; MSME, MIT, 1968, PhD, 1970. Retired cap. USNR, 1986; scientist, v.p. Cambridge (Mass.) Acoustical Assn., Inc., 1974-83; pres., CEO Marine Acoustics, Inc., Newport, R.I., 1983—. Contbr. articles to profl. jours. Fellow Explorers Club; mem. Acoustical Soc. Am., Tau Beta Pi, Sigma Xi. Achievements include designing passive acoustical whale tracking system for population assessment of endangered species in the Arctic; pioneering work in impact of underwater sound on marine resources.

ELLIS-VANT, KAREN MCGEE, elementary and special education educator, consultant; b. La Grande, Oreg., May 10, 1950; d. Ellis Eddington and Gladys Vera McGee; m. Lynn F. Ellis, June 14, 1975 (div. Sept. 1983); children: Megan Marie, Matthew David; m. Jack Scott Vant, Sept. 6, 1986; children: Kathleen Erin, Kelli Christine (dec.). BA in Elem. Edn., Boise State U., 1972, MA in Spl. Edn., 1979; postgrad. studies in curriculum/instrn., U. Minn., 1985-86. Tchr. learning disabilities resource rm. New Plymouth Joint Sch. Dist., 1972-73, Payette Joint Sch. Dist., 1973; diagnostician project SELECT, 1974-75; cons. tchr. in spl. edn. Boise Sch. Dist., 1975-90, tchr. 1-2 combination, 1990-91, team tchr. 1st grade, 1991-92, 95—, site based leadership team, 1997-99; chpt. 1 program cons., 1992-95, mem. Idaho Mgmt. Change Project, 1997-99, Learning for the 21st Century project, 1999—; mem. profl. Stds. Commn., 1983-86. Contbr. articles to profl. jours.; editor, author ednl. texts and comminique; conductor of workshops, leadership tng. coop. learning and frameworks. Bd. dirs. Hotline, Inc., 1979-82; mem. Idaho Coop. Manpower Commn., 1984-85; mem. First United Meth. Ch., childcare bd., 1998—. Recipient Disting. Young Woman of Yr. award Boise Jayceettes, 1982, Idaho Jayceettes, 1983; Coffman Alumni scholar U. Minn., 1985-86. Mem. NEA (mem. civil rights com. 1983-85, state contact for peace caucus 1981-85, del. assembly rep. 1981-85), NSTA, ASCD, Internat. Reading Assn. (v.p. Boise chpt. 1996-97), NCTE, Internat. Coop. Learning Assn., Idaho Edn. Assn. (bd. dirs. region VII 1981-85, pres. region VII 1981-82), Boise Edn. Assn. (v.p. 1981-82, 84-85, pres. 1982-83), Nat. Coun. Urban Edn. Assn., World Future Soc., Coun. for Exceptional Children (pres. chpt. 1978-79), Nat. Coun. Tchrs. English, Minn. Coun. for Social Studies, Calif. Assn. for Gifted, Assn. for Grad. Edn. Students, Phi Delta Kappa. Office: Highlands Elem 3434 Bogus Basin Rd Boise ID 83702-1507

ELLMANN, DOUGLAS STANLEY, lawyer; b. Detroit, July 15, 1956; s. William Marshall and Sheila Estelle (Frenkel) E.; m. Claudia Joan Roberts, Feb. 16, 1985; children: Ben Bosworth, Liam Roberts. AB, Occidental Coll., 1978; JD, U. Mich., 1982. Bar: Mich. 1982, U.S. Dist. Ct. (ea. dist.) Mich. 1982, U.S. Ct. Appeals (6th cir.) 1982. Assoc. Butzel, Keidan, Simon, Myers & Graham, Detroit, 1982-84; ptnr. Ellmann & Ellmann, Detroit, 1984-86; atty. Wise & Marsac, Detroit, 1987-89; U.S. panel trustee, 1989—; prin. Ellmann & Ellmann, P.C., Ann Arbor, Mich., 1989—; spl. asst. atty. gen., 1986; sec. bankruptcy trustees U.S. Bankruptcy Ct. (ea. dist.) Mich., 1993—, mem. bench bar com., 1994—. Author: Selected Issues in Asset Protection, 1994, My Advice: Next Time Go Solo, 1994, LWUSA; co-author: Winning Labor Arbitrations, 1987. Founder Amnesty Internat., Detroit, Lawyer's Support Network; mem. nat. com. U. Mich. Law Sch. Fund, 1986—. Mem. ABA (vice chair bankruptcy com. 1995—), Mich. Bar Assn. (rep. assembly 1983-89, 90-92, exec. counsel young lawyers sect. 1985-87, mem. client security fund com. 1987-95), State Bar Mich. (mem. manditory CLE com. 1989-96, chmn. 1995-96), Washtenaw County Bar Assn. (chmn. banking, bus., bankruptcy com. 1995—). Home: 4575 W Loch Alpine Dr Ann Arbor MI 48103-9081 Office: 308 W Huron St Ann Arbor MI 48103-4204

ELLMANN, SHEILA FRENKEL, investment company executive; b. Detroit, June 8, 1931; d. Joseph and Rose (Neback) Frenkel; m. William M. Ellmann, Nov. 1, 1953; children: Douglas Stanley, Carol Elizabeth, Robert Lawrence. BA in English, U. Mich., 1953. Dir. Advance Glove Mfg. Co., Detroit, 1954-78; v.p. Frome Investment Co., Detroit, 1980-96, pres., 1996—. Mem. U. Mich. Alumni Assn., Nat. Trust Hist. Preservation. Home: 28000 Weymouth Dr Farmingtn Hls MI 48334-3267

ELLMANN, WILLIAM MARSHALL, lawyer, mediator, arbitrator, researcher; b. Highland Park, Mich., Mar. 23, 1921; s. James I. and Jeannette (Barsook) E.; m. Sheila Estelle Frenkel, Nov. 1, 1953; children: Douglas S., Carol E., Robert L. Student, Occidental Coll., 1939-40; AB, U. Mich., 1946; LLB, Wayne State U., 1951. Bar: Mich. 1951. Pvt. practice law Detroit, 1951—; ptnr. Ellmann & Ellmann, 1970—; spl. com. atty. gen. Mich. to study use state troops in emergencies, 1964-65; mem. exec. Inst. Continuing Legal Edn., 1964-68; mem. Mich. Employment Rels. Commn., 1973—, chmn., 1983-86; commr. Mackinac Island State Park Commn., 1979-85, chmn., 1983-86; panel mem. numerous orgns. Author: Of Hemingway, Toscanni and Arbitration: Practical Considerations for Preparing Winning Cases, 1985, A Reply to the Ambassador on Russia, 1991, (with Douglas S. Ellmann) Winning Labor Arbitrations, 1987; contbr. articles to profl. jours. With USAAF, 1942-46. Fellow Am. Bar Found.; mem. ABA (ho. of dels. 1969-72), Am. Arbitration Assn. (mem. adv. council), Nat. Acad. Arbitrators, Detroit Bar Assn. (vice chmn. pub. relations com. 1959), State Bar Mich. (commr. 1959-69, pres. 1966-67, co-chmn. com. on qualification jud. candidates 1970-78, mem. Detroit News secret witness panel 1983), Practicing Law Inst. (adv. council 1969-70, spl. asst. atty. gen. 1970-78), Sigma Nu Phi. Home: 28000 Weymouth Ct Farmington Hills MI 48334-3267 Office: Ellmann & Ellmann 308 W Huron St Ann Arbor MI 48103-4204

ELLOIAN, PETER, artist, educator; b. Cleve., Apr. 20, 1936; s. Oscar Elloian and Haigouhi Minasian; m. Carolyn Ann Autry, May 27, 1966; 1 chld, Cybele Justine. BFA, Cleve. Inst. Art, 1962; MFA, U. Iowa, 1965. Instr. art Toledo Mus. Art Sch. Design, 1966-87; prof. art U. Toledo, 1987—; vis. artist, tchr. Lacoste (France) Sch. of Arts, fall 1984, summer and fall 1987. Exhibited in group shows Portsmouth (Va.) Arts Ctr., 1980, Rutgers U., 1981, Yugoslav Portrait Gallery, Bosnia, 1982, 86, Biella, Italy, 1982, 87, House of Humor and Satire, Bulgaria, 1995, 97, 99. With U.S. Army, 1957-59, West Germany. Recipient Gascar award Hunterdon Nat. Print Exhibn., N.J., 1992, Award, Bulgaria, 1995. Mem. Soc. Am. Graphic Artists, Boston Printmakers. Home: 26114 W River Rd Perrysburg OH 43551-9128

ELLWOOD, PETER BRIAN, bank executive; b. Manchester, Eng., May 15, 1943; s. Isaac and Edith Ellwood; m. Judy Ann Windsor, Sept. 14, 1968; children: Elizabeth, Rachel, Richard. LLD (hon.), Leicester U., 1994; D (hon.), U. Ctrl. Eng., 1995. Chief exec. Barclaycard, Northampton, U.K., 1985-89; chief exec. retail banking TSB Group PLC, London, 1989-91, chief exec. retail banking and ins., 1991-92, group chief exec., 1992-95; dep. group chief exec., chief exec. retail fin. svcs. Lloyds TSB Group Plc., London, 1995-97, CEO., 1997—; non-exec. dir. Royal Philharm. Orch., Ltd.; chmn. Visa Internat., San Francisco, 1994-99. Fellow Royal Soc. Arts; mem. Inst. Mgmt. (companion) Nene Coll. Ct., Royal Theatre Northampton (trustee). Office: Lloyds TSB Group PLC, 71 Lombard St, London EC3P 3BS, England

ELMA, BAYANI BORJA, physician; b. Manila, Philippines, Nov. 3, 1942; s. Medardo Romero and Hiwaga Rada Borja E.; m. Maria Mercado Chavez-Elma, July 4, 1971; children: Michael Anthony, Mary Anne. Degree in Preparatory Medicine, U. Philippines, 1963; MD, U. of the East, Quezon City, Philippines, 1968. Diplomate Am. Bd. Quality Assurance, Utilization Review Physicians. Vice-chief of staff Md. Gen. Hosp., Balt., 1985-90, dir., trustee, 1988-95, chmn., prof. affairs com., 1992-95; mem. panel editl. advisers Internal Medicine for the Specialist, Livingston, N.J., 1990—; editl. bd. Md. Med. Jour., Balt., 1993-96; pres. Assn. of Philippine Physicians in Md., 1997-99. Pres. U. East Med. Alumni Assn., 1992-94; dir., trustee U. East Med. Alumni Found., 1994—; vice-chmn. Govs. Commn. on Asian-Pacific Am. Affairs, Balt., 1992—; alt. del. House Del. Balt. City Med. Soc., 1997-99; vice-chmn. bd. trustees U. East Med. Alumni Found., 1998—. Named One of the Twenty Outstanding Filipino Am. U.S. and Can. Filipino Image mag., 1998-99. Mem. Am. Coll. Physician Execs. Republican. Roman Catholic. Avocations: reading, writing, traveling. Home: 10907 Tony Dr Lutherville MD 21093-3618 Office: 3023 Eastern Ave Baltimore MD 21224-3902

EL-MAHALLAWY, NAHED ABDEL-HAMID, mechanical engineering educator, researcher; b. Cairo, Egypt, Jan. 10, 1947; s. Abdel-Hamid El-M.; m. Mohamed Ahmed Taha; children: Iman, Omneya. BSc, Ain Shams U., Cairo, 1969, MSc, 1972, PhD, 1976. Demonstrator Ain Shams U., 1969-73, asst. lectr., 1973-76, asst. prof. mech. engring., 1977-83, assoc. prof., 1983-88, prof. mech. engring., 1988—; vis. prof. Am. U., Cairo, 1990-91, 95-99. Editor: Advances in Continuous Casting, 1992, Advances in MMC, 1993; contbr. over 100 articles to internat. jours. and confs. Recipient State prize in engring. scis. Acad. Rsch. and Tech., 1982, Nat. Egyptian Sci. and Art medal, 1982, award German Acad. Exch., 1984, Fulbright sr. award, 1988. Home: 24 Abu Gaafar El Nahas, Ard-El-Golf, Heliopolis, Cairo Egypt Office: Ain Shams U Faculty of Engring, PO Box 8022, Massaken Nasr Cairo Egypt

ELMALEH, JOSEPH, private investor; b. Beirut, Aug. 28, 1938; s. Elie Rene and Suzanne (Farhi) E. BSChemE, Israel Inst. Tech., Haifa, 1962; PhD, DIC Imperial Coll., London U., 1968. Rep. Israeli Ministry Indsl. Devel. in Europe, 1962-68; lectr. ops. rsch. Grad. Sch. Mgmt. Sci., Imperial Coll., 1968-73; mgmt. cons. Finind S.A., 1971-74; CEO Jerusalem Oil Exploration Ltd., 1982-95, East Mediterranean Oil and Gas Ltd., 1980—, Isramco, Inc., 1983-95, Pass-port Ltd., 1992-95; bd. dirs. Alexandria Real Estate Equities Inc., UrbanAmerica LP. Bd. dirs. Acad. of St. Martin-in-the Fields Orch., 1991-94. With Israeli Army, 1956-59. Leo Baeck rsch. fellow, 1962-65. Mem. RAC Club (London), Harmonie Club (N.Y.C.), Met. Club (N.Y.C.). Office: Upper Grays, 38 Aldwick Ave, Aldwick PO21 3AQ, England

EL MALIK, EL FADIL MOHAMED ALI, physician, surgeon, educator, consultant; b. Argo, Sudan, Mar. 29, 1948; s. Mohamed Ali Taha and Maymouna Elzubeir El Malik; m. Batoul Ibrahim Osman, Dec. 22, 1977 (dec. Dec. 1988); 1 child, El Fatih; m. Hind Hamad El Malik, Jan. 31, 1993; children: Atheel, Mohamed. MB BS, U. Khartoum, Sudan, 1973. Physician-in-tng. Ministry of Health, Khartoum, 1973-77, Royal Coll. Surgeons in Ireland, Dublin, 1977-79; specialist gen. surgeon Ministry of Health, Khartoum, 1979-80; rsch. fellow renal transplant Royal Free Hosp., London, 1980-82; sr. registrar Royal Postgrad. Med. Sch., London, 1983-84; cons. urologist Ministry of Health, Khartoum, 1984-91; assoc. prof. King Khalid U., Abha, Saudi Arabia, 1991—; chief urology Asir Ctrl. Hosp., Abha, 1997—. Contbr. more than 15 articles to profl. jours. including Kidney Internat., Transplantation, Jour. Hepatology, Gastroenterology, and Infectious Diseases, Brit. Jour. Urology, Annals of Saudi Medicine, Jour. Andrology, East African Med. Jours., among others. Ronald Gerard rsch. fellow Royal Free Hosp. (London), 1981; recipient scholarship Japanese Internat. Coop. Agy., 1990, Rsch. fund award Nat. Kidney Rsch. Fund, 1983. Fellow Royal Coll. Surgeons (Ireland), ACS, Internat. Coll. Surgeons; mem. N.Y. Acad. Scis., Arab Soc. Nephrology and Renal Transplantation, African Assn. Nephrology and Renal Transplantation. Avocations: reading, photography, sports. Home: No 250 Bin Mahfonz Compound, Sir Thapta Abha, Saudi Arabia Office: King Khalid U Coll Medicine, Prince Sultan St/PO Box 641, Abha Saudi Arabia

ELMANAMA, ABDELRAOUF ALI, laboratory administrator, medical educator; b. Gaza, Gaza Strip, Palestine, Jan. 16, 1967; s. Ali Mohammad and Amna Mohammad Abdel-latif; m. Sarah A. Dimapuro, Aug. 15, 1987; children: Mohammad, Islam. BS in Med. Tech., Southwestern U., Cebu, Philippines, 1990; MS in Microbiology, U. Santo Tomas, Manila, Philippines, 1993. Specialized med. technologist Ministry of Health; cert. food microbiology trainer, hazard analysis and critical control point assessment trainer. Rsch. asst. Islamic U. Gaza, Palestine, 1993-94, lectr., 1994—; head asst. med. tech.; med. lab. dir. Gaza Diagnostic Ctr., 1998—; mem. Food Safety Com., Gaza; cons. Palestinian Stds.; founder Medicalicrobiology Lab. dar Asslam Hosp., 1997. Dir. 1st Scientific Day, 1995. Fellow Brit. Coun., 1999. Muslim. Avocations: reading, basketball. Office: Islamic U, Al-Thalathini St, Gaza Palestine

EL MASRI, YOUSSEF M.I., nuclear physicist; b. Beirut, Sept. 25, 1944; s. Mamoud Ismail and Zomorod (Khalifa) El M.; m. Josine J.J. Elsen, Dec. 23, 1970; children: Naji, Sami, Jihad. BS, U. Louvain, Belgium, 1968; MS in Physics, U. Louvain, 1969, PhD in Nuclear Physics, 1974, Postgrad. Degree in Radioprotection, 1979. Rsch. fellow, univ. asst. Cath. U. Louvain, 1969-74, rsch. assoc. in nuclear physics, 1975-78, rsch. group leader, 1988—, prof., 1993—, dir. Inst. Nuclear Physics, 1999—; invited scientist Julich Nuclear Rsch. Ctr., Germany, 1975-76; exch. vis. Lawrence Berkeley Lab., Calif., 1976-77; rsch. group sr. tenur staff mem. Nat. Found. Belgian Sci. Rsch., Brussels, 1979—; mem. exec. com., bd. trustees Belgian Phys. Soc., 1983-86; invited scientist Inst. Nuclear Physics of Grenoble, France, 1985; mem. adv. com. for vis. profs. U. Louvain, 1986-90, bd. dirs. LLN Cyclotron, 1988—; promoter and coord. sci. agreement U. Louvain and Tex. A&M U., 1988—; permanent mem. sci. coun. French "Joliot-Curie Internat. Sch. in Nuclear Physics", France, 1990—. Contbr. over 200 articles to profl. jours. Decorated comdr. Order of the Crown (Belgium); Exch. vis. Cyclotron Inst./Tex. A&M U., 1998. Mem. Inst. Nuclear Physics UCL (dir. 1999), Belgian Phys. Soc., European Phys. Soc. Avocations: history, travel in Asia and Middle East. Office: Inst Nuclear Phys/U Louvain, Chem du Cyclotron 2, B-1348 Louvain-la-Neuve Belgium

EL MATRI, MOHAMED AZIZ, medical educator; b. Tunis, Tunisia, Sept. 19, 1943; s. Mahmoud and Kmar (Ben Cheikh Ahmed) El M.; m. Leila Tritar, Aug. 1, 1975; children: Omar, Ali, Mohamed, Khaled. MD, Faculty of Medicine, Tunis, 1971; degree in Nephrology, Faculty of Medicine, Paris, 1973. Resident Coll. Medicine Paris, 1972-73; asst. prof. med. faculty Faculty of Medicine, Tunis, 1973, prof., 1983; cons. Hosp. Charles Nicolle, Tunis, 1973-78, chief unit, 1978-96; chmn. Tunis Dialysis Ctr., 1996—; temporary advisor WHO, Geneva, 1990—. Contbr. chpt. to: Ambulatory Peritoneal Dialysis, 1990, (2 chpts.) Organ Transplantation, 1991; guest editor Transplantation Procs., 1993, 97, Arab African Nephrology and Renal

Transplantation Proceedings, 1996. Recipient Medal of Health, Republic of Tunisia, 1995. Mem. European Renal Assn. (London, keyman 1991-95), Mid. East Soc. for Organ Transplantation (Ankara, Turkey, pres. 1994-96), African Assn. Nephrology (Cairo, pres. 1995-97), Arab Soc. Nephrology and Renal Transplantation (Cairo, pres. 1999—), Arab Med. Union (sec. gen. 1991), Tunisian Soc. Intensive Care (pres. 1995), Conseil Ordre des Medecins Tunisia (v.p. 1994-98), Arab Assn. Telemedicine (pres. 1999), N.Y. Acad. Scis., Tunisian Soc. Telemedicine (pres. 1999), Tunisian Soc. Nephrology (pres. 2000). Avocations: tennis, sailing. Home: Cité El Mahrajène, PO Box 290, 1082 Tunis Tunisia

EL-MELEIGI, MOHAMED ABDEL-SATTAR, plant pathology educator; b. Kafr El-Shekh, Egypt, May 13, 1947; s. Abdel-Sattar and Banat Mohamed (Saleh) El M.; m. Zakia Mahmoud Hassan, Mar. 29, 1975. BSin Plant Pathology, U. Alexandria, Egypt, 1969, MS, 1972; PhD, N.D. State U., 1978. Teaching asst. U. Alexandria, Egypt, 1969-74, N.D. State U., Fargo, 1974-78; rsch. assoc. U. Ky., Lexington, 1978-79; rsch. assoc. Kans. State U., Manhattan, 1979-82; asst. prof., 1982-83, 83-85; asst. prof. King Saud U., Burydah, Saudi Arabia, 1985-89, assoc. prof., 1985-89, prof., 1989—; plant protection dept. head King Saud U., 1983-96, wheat project dir., 1986-98; vis. prof. Colo. State U., 1992, Okla. State U., 1997. Author: Wheat Diseases, 1992; contbr. articles to profl. jours. Mem. Am. Phytopathological Soc., Arab Plant Protection Soc., Saudi Biol. Soc., Egyptian Soc. Plant Protection, Saudi Agrl. Soc., HDRA Organic Farming Inst. Avocations: painting, writing. E-mail: meleigi@sahara.com.sa. Office: Coll Agrl Plant Protection, PO Box 1482, Buraydah Saudi Arabia

ELMENDORP, JACOB J., engineering educator; b. Vlaardingen, The Netherlands, Aug. 19, 1958; s. Hendrik Elmendorp and Jannetje Scheepmaker; m. Maria De Graaff, Aug. 15, 1980; children: Margriet, Rik. MSc, Delft (The Netherlands) U., 1981, PhD, 1986. Rsch. physicist Shell Rsch., Amsterdam, The Netherlands, 1986-93; dir. R & D Avery-Dennison, Leiden, The Netherlands, 1994-97; v.p. R & D Avery-Dennison, Painesville, Ohio, 1997-99; prof. polymer engrng. U. Delft, 2000—. Contbr. articles to profl. jours. Avocations: sailing, guitar building. Home: Lovenholm 3, 2133 JN Hoofddorp The Netherlands Office: U Delft, Julianalaan 136, Delft The Netherlands

ELMER, MICHAEL BENDIK, legal administrator; b. Feb. 26, 1949; m. Lise Skovby, 1993. Cand. jur., U. Copenhagen, 1973. Civil servant Min. of Justice, 1973-76, 77-82, head of divsn., 1982-87, 88-91; dep. judge Hillerød, 1976-77; high ct. judge Eastern High Ct., Copenhagen, 1987-88; v.p. a.i. Maritime and Comml. Ct., Copenhagen, 1988; dep. permanent sec. for justice, head of cmty. law and human rights dept., 1991-94; advocate gen. EC Ct. of Justice, Luxembourg, 1994-97; v.p. Maritime & Comml. Ct., Copenhagen, 1998—; assoc. prof. U. Copenhagen, 1975-85; asst. pub. prosecutor, 1980-81; part time judge Ct. of Ballerup, 1981-82; external examiner Danish law schs., 1985—. Author of several books and articles, especially on property law, cmty. law and penal law. Office: Maritime & Comml Ct, Bredgade 70, DK-1260 Copenhagen Denmark

EL-METENAWY, TAREK MOHAMMED, veterinarian; b. Badrachine, Giza, Egypt, Feb. 14, 1957; s. Mohammed Ahmed El-M.; m. Eman Mohammed Hamzawy, Aug. 10, 1989; children: Tasnem, Omar, Abd-Al-Rhman. B Vet. Sci., Faculty Vet. Medicine, Egypt, 1980, M Vet. Sci., 1985, PhD, 1988. Veterinarian Nat. Rsch. Ctr., Egypt, 1981-83, sr. veterinarian, 1983-85, asst. rschr., 1985-88, rschr., 1988-93, asst. prof., 1993—. Contbr. articles to profl. jours.; patentee in field. Avocation: reading. Fax: 00202-3370931. Address: Nat Rsch Ctr Parasit Dept, Al Tarrer St, Giza Egypt also: PO Box 1353, Bureidah Al-Qassam Saudi Arabia

EL MHAMEDI, ABDERRAHMAN, engineering educator, researcher; b. Ait Braim, Tiznit, Morroco; s. Bihi El Mhamedi and Fadma Ouchahma; m. Mina El Farissi, Aug. 10, 1992; children: Inas, Yassin. Dectorat Thesis in Automatic Control, Inst. Nat. Poly. Grenoble, France, 1990; habilitation, Louis Pasteur U., Strasbourg, 1998. Cert. engrng. Rschr. Automatic Control Lab., Grenoble, 1986-91; asst. prof. Ecole Nat. Supirieure des Arts et Indistries de Strasbourg, 1991—; cons. LAG, Grenoble, 1986-91; dir. ACNOS-Project, Strasbourg, 1994-98. Author: Enterprise Engineering and Integration, 1997; contbr. articles to profl. jours. Mem. Groupement de Rsch. en Productique. E-mail: ElMhamedi@ensais.u-strasbg.fr. Fax: 00 388 241 490. Home: 1 rue de l argile, 67800 Hoenheim France Office: ENSAIS, 24 Blvd de la Victoire, 67084 Strasbourg France

EL-MIDANY, TAWFIK, engineering educator; b. Tanta, Gharbia, Egypt, Mar. 2, 1940. BS in Prodn. Engrng., Higher Tech. Inst., Helwan, Egypt, 1966; diploma, Manchester (Eng.) U., 1976, MSc, 1977, PhD, 1979. Grad. asst., prodn. engr. HTI and Mil. Factories Orgn., Helwan, 1966-73; head planning divsn. Metal Casting Foundry, Helwan, 1973; instr. engring. graphics U. Petroleum and Minerals, Dhahran, Saudi Arabia, 1973-75; spl. rsch. asst. Inst. Sci. and Tech. Manchester U., 1977-79; from asst. to assoc. prof. prodn. engring. King Abdulaziz U., Jeddah, Saudi Arabia, 1980-87; from assoc. prof. to prof. prodn. engring. Mansoura (Egypt) U., 1987-94, prof., chmn. indsl. prodn. engring., 1994—; cons. pvt. indsl. engring., 1988—. Author: Dictionary of Production Engineering Terminology, 1989, Forming Processes and Equipment, 1988, Jigs and Fixtures Design, 1995, Computer Automated Manufacturing and Flexible Technologies, 1994, Introduction to Numerical Control of Machine Tools, 1994, Principles of Metal Casting, 1999. Recipient State Prize award in Engring. Sci., 1997, Disting. award in Engring. Sci. U. Mansoura, 1998; scholar German Govt., 1968-69; grantee Manchester U., 1976-77, 77-79. Fellow Inst. Mfg. (Eng.), Inst. Mgmt. Specialists (Eng.), Inst. Bus. and Tech. Mgmt. (founder) (Eng.); mem. ASME, Egyptian Engring. Syndicate, Brit. Numerical Engring. Soc., Al Zuhor Sport Club. Avocations: music, reading, table tennis, social activities, traveling. Office: Mansoura U Faculty Engring, PO Box No 2, Mansoura 35516, Egypt

EL MIEDANY, YASSER MAHROUS, rheumatologist, consultant; b. Alexandria, Egypt, June 30, 1961; s. Mahrous Abdulhalim and El Bagoury Mohammed (Mounira) El Miedamy. MBChB, U. Cairo, 1984, MSc, 1987, MD, 1994. Resident Ain Shams U. Hosp., Cairo, 1987-90, asst. lectr., 1990-94, lectr. rheumatology, 1994—. Author: Basic Rheumatology for Postgraduate, 1995. Mem. Am. Coll. Rheumatology, Brit. Soc. Rheumatology. Avocations: tennis, table tennis, football, swimming. Fax: 202 247 44 72. E-mail: miedanyrd@usa.net. Home: 2 Italian Hospital St, Abbassia, Cairo 11381, Egypt Office: Ctr Rheumatic Diseases, Dr Hussain Kamel St, Cairo 11351, Egypt

EL MOLAHEZ, HEGAZI HUSSEIN, plastic surgeon, consultant; b. Cairo, Egypt, Oct. 16, 1938; s. Hussein Mohamed and Haeima Mahmoud (El Sweffy) El M.; m. Maggy Kamal El Din El Sourogy, June 2, 1967; children: May, Mohamed, Maged. B, Cairo U., 1963, MB, 1963, DS, 1969. Cert. surgery Eqyptian Ministry Health. Gen. surgeon Hilmia Mil. Hosp., Cairo, 1963-73; plastic surgery Bangor Hosp., Scotland, 1974-75; registrar Royal Infirmary Hosp., Edinburgh, U.K., 1975-76; cons. Helmia Mil. Armed Forces, Cairo, 1976-80; sr. cons., head, dir. plastic and burn ctr. Burn Ctr. Armed Forces, Cairo, 1981-88; sr. cons. Nasser Inst. Ministry of Health, Cairo, 1989-90; sr. cons., head plastic and reconstructive surgery King Fahed Gen. Hosp., Gezan, Saudi Arabia, 1998—; hon. cons. Coll. Fracais de Chirrurge, Paris, 980-81; prof. Mil. Med. Acad., Armed Forces, Cairo. Gen. Armed Forces Egypt, 1963-91. Fellow Royal Coll. Surgeons; mem. Internat. Soc. Aesthetic Plastic Surgery, Mediteranean Burn Club, Internat. Soc. Burn Injuries, Soc. de Chirruge Plastic. Avocations: paratroops, reading, music, sight seeing. E-mail: elmolahez@yahoo.com. Office: King Fahad Gen Hosp, Gezan Saudi Arabia

ELMQVIST, THOMAS KNUT LENNART, plant ecologist; b. Björkö, Sweden, Sept. 20, 1955; m. Eva M. Pontén, Sept. 23, 1987; children: Emeli, Jonathan, Moa, Sebastian. PhD, U. Umeå, Sweden, 1987. Asst. prof. Natural Sci. Rsch. Coun., Umeå, Sweden, 1990-94; assoc. prof. U. Umeå, Sweden, 1994-96; sci. rsch. dir. Swedish Biodiversity Ctr., Uppsala, Sweden, 1996—; adv. bd. Swedish Soc. for Nature Conservation, Stockholm, 1989-91; reference group Swedish Nature Sci. Rsch. Coun., Stockholm, 1993-95. Author: (book) The Rain Forest and the Flying Foxes, 1993; contbr. articles to profl. ecol. jours. Mem. N.Y. Acad. Sci., Tropica Biology Assn. (coun.). Achievements include assistance in the creation of four rainforest preserves in Western Samoa, South Pacific, in conjunction with research on endangered flying fox species. Home: Dobelnsgatan 32H, 75237 Uppsala Sweden

ELMS, DAVID GEORGE, civil engineering educator, consultant; b. London, June 3, 1934; s. George and Winifred J. (Williams) E.; m. D. Josephine Vernon Lord (div. 1977); children: Simon George Whiteley, Timothy Frederick, Nicholas David; m. Margaret M. Norris, July 2, 1977; 1 child, Jennifer Mary Norris. BA, Cambridge (Eng.) U., 1957; MSE, Princeton U., 1961, PhD, 1964. Engr. De Havilland Aircraft Co., Hatfield, Eng., 1957-60; tchr. U. Canterbury, Christchurch, New Zealand, 1964-2000, prof. civil engring., 1978-2000; dir. Optimx Ltd., Wellington, 2000—; mem. spl. com. on nuclear propulsion Prime Min. Office, New Zealand, 1992. Author: Linear Elastic Analysis, 1970; co-author: The Safety of Nuclear Powered Ships, 1992; editor: Owning the Future, 1998; contbr. more than 100 articles to profl. jours. Recipient Disting. Contbn. to Engring. Edn. medal Australasian Assn. for Engring. Edn., 1993. Fellow Royal Soc. New Zealand (coun. mem. 1998—), Inst. Profl. Engrs. New Zealand; mem. ASCE, Assn. for Engring. Edn. for S.E. Asia and the Pacific (pres. 1991-94). Mem. Soc. of Friends. Avocations: music, reading, walking. Home and Office: 61A Kidson Ter, Christchurch 2, New Zealand

EL-NADI, FATHI ALI, management consultant, management educator; b. Mansura, Dakahlia, Egypt, July 4, 1940; s. Mitwalli A. El-Nadi and Nagia M. Badr; m. Amal A. El-Tonnamly, Dec. 26, 1965; children: Sahar, Mohamed. BSc, High Comml. Inst., Mansura, Egypt, 1962; BA, Cairo U., 1967, MA, 1973; PhD, Pacific Western U., L.A., 1988. Quality edn. sys. cert. instr. Philip Crosby Assn. Inc. Adminstrn. mgr. Airways Engring., Jeddah, Saudi Arabia, 1973-74; regional dir. Skidmore, Owings & Merrill, Jeddah, 1974-83; mgr. human resources Johnson Wax Egypt, Cairo, 1983-85; dir. human resources and indsl. rels. GM Egypt, 1985-90; dir. human resources and quality productivity Bristol-Myers Squib, Cairo, 1990-91; mng. cons. Vision Consulting, Cairo, 1991—; profl. program advisor Am. U. in Cairo, 1985-88; prof. mgmt. and human resources Arab Acad. for Scis. and Tech., Alexandria, Egypt, 1996; prof. mktg. Ecole Superieure Libre des Scis. Commerciales Appliquees; acad. advisor Nova Southeastern U., Ft. Lauderdale, Fla., 1998; human resource cons. Chemonics Int. Corp., Washington, 1997—. Author: (books) Management Portraits, 1997, Memories of a Travelling Manager, 1998; editor: (mag.) NASR Automotive Magazine, 1969; contbr. to Bus. Monthly. Chmn. Nerco Dev Soc., Cairo, 1996. Maj. Egyptian M.C./Naval Res., 1962-64. Mem. Am. Mgmt. Assn., Soc. for Human Resource Mgmt., Am. C. of C. Muslim. Avocations: tennis, traveling, reading. Fax: 202-754-6000. E-mail: visioncn@usa.net. Office: Vision Consulting, 25a Naguib Mahfouz St, Nerco City, Degla, Maadi Cairo Egypt

EL-NAGGAR, MOSTAFA MOHAMMED, anatomy educator, researcher, clinician; b. Mehalla El-Kobra, Egypt, Feb. 6, 1949; arrived in Saudi Arabia, 1982; s. Mohammad El-Sayed El-Naggar and Rosa Abdulhamid El-Sayed; m. Azza Mokhtar Bahr, June 24, 1985; children: Dina, Dalia. MBBCh, Mansoura (Egypt) U., 1972, MSc, 1976, PhD in Human Anatomy, 1980. House officer Mansoura U. Hosp., 1973-74; demonstrator Mansoura U., 1974-77, asst. lectr., 1977-80, lectr., 1980-82; asst. prof. anatomy King Abdulaziz U., Jeddah, Saudi Arabia, 1982-88, assoc. prof. anatomy, 1988—; prin. investigator, King Abdulaziz U., 1989-91, mem. exam. control, 1988—. Co-editor English edit. of Islamic additions of book The Developing Human—Clinically Oriented Embryology, 1983; contbr. articles to biomed. jours. Mem. Unit of Islamic Medicine, King Abdulaziz U., 1983-86. With Egyptian Army, 1974-75. Recipient rsch. grants King Abdulaziz U., 1983, 86, 89, 97, 99. Mem. Soc. Endocrinology, Am. Assn. Anatomists, Egyptian Anat. Soc., Anat. Soc. Great Britain. Moslem. Avocations: tennis, squash, jogging, chess, reading. Home: PO Box 19, Mehalla El-Kobra Egypt Office: King Abdulaziz U Coll Med, PO Box 9029, 21413 Jeddah Saudi Arabia

EL NAHAS, ABDEL MEGUID, nephrology; b. Cairo, Egypt, Dec. 1, 1949; s. Hassan and Fatma (El Hegazy) El N.; m. Penelope Anne Hanan, Apr. 30, 1983; children: Gemma, Holly. MBChB, Med. U. Geneva, 1974; PhD, Royal Med. Postgrad. Sch., London, 1984. Sr. resident Mass. Gen. Hosp., Boston, 1978-79; registrar Royal Free Hosp., London, 1982-84; lectr. U. Wales Coll. Medicine, Cardiff, 1984-86; cons. Sheffield Kidney Inst., U.K., 1986—; prof. nephrology U. Sheffield, 1996—. Fellow Royal Coll. Physicians. Muslim. Avocations: reading, history, mysticism, walking, swimming. Office: Sheffield Kidney Inst, Herries Rd, Sheffield S5 7AU, England

ELNASHAI, AMR SALAH, civil engineer; b. Giza, Egypt, May 8, 1954; arrived in U.K., 1978; s. Salah Eldin and Eitedal (Rizk) E.; m. Neveen Elnashai; children: Shadie, Adham. BSc, U. Cairo, 1977; MSc, Imperial Coll., 1979, PhD, 1984. Asst. lectr. Cairo U., 1977-79; rsch. asst. Imperial Coll., London, 1980-84, lectr., 1985-89, reader, 1989-94, prof. earthquake engring., 1994—, head of sect., 1994—; sr. engr. Wimpey Offshore, London, 1985; prin. cons. EQE Internat., 1996—; nat. tech. contact Brit. Stds. Inst., London, 1991—; tech. coord. Euroocode 8, Dept. Environ., London, 1991—; vis. prof. U. So. Calif., L.A., 1990-95, Inst. Indsl. Sci., Tokyo U., 1990, 92, 95; prin. cons. EQE Internat., 1996. Author: (with others) Structures Subjected to Dynamic Loads, 1990; series editor: Innovation in Structures and Construction, 1993; founder, gen. editor: Jour. Earthquake Engring.; contbr. numerous articles to profl. jours. U.K. del. European and Internat. Assn. Earthquake Engring., 1992. Fellow Royal Acad. Engineering, Am. Soc. Civil Engineers, Inst. Structural Engineers; mem. Soc. Earthquake and Civil Engring. Dynamics (vice chmn. 1990-92, chmn. 1992-94), European Assn. Earthquake Engring. (U.K. nat. del.), Japan-UK Seismic Risk Forum (founder 1995). Achievements include rsch. on earthquake design, testing and analysis, field investigation of eleven major earthquakes in USA, Japan, Middle East, Greece, Turkey, Egypt and Algeria. Home: Cedar Cottage Sts Heath, West End Woking GU24 9RB, England Office: Imperial Coll, Civil Engring Dept, Imperial Coll Rd, London SW7 2B4, England

ELODI, PÁL, biochemist, educator; b. Budapest, Hungary, Feb. 10, 1927; s. Bèla and Bèlàné (Weinberger) Erzsébet; m. Zsuzsanna Berkovits, Aug. 21, 1952; children: András, Anna. MS, Eötvös Loránd U., Budapest, 1950; PhD in Biochemistry, Hungarian Acad. of Sci., Budapest, 1957; DSc, Hungarian Acad. of Scis., Budapest, 1965. Asst. tchr. biology Eötvös Loránd U., 1950-51; sr. rsch. cons. Inst. Biochemistry, Hungarian Acad. Sci., 1951-73; chmn. dept. biochemistry U. Med. Sch. of Debrecen, Hungary, 1973-93, prof. biochemistry, 1993—; sci. advisor State Coun. of Rsch. and Higher Edn., Budapest, 1965-66; chmn. biochem. com. Hungarian Acad. Scis., 1971-85. Author: (textbook) Biochemistry, 1980, 4th edit., 1989 (award for high quality 1983), 3 handbooks on protein structure; editor Acta Biochimica et Biophysica Hungarica. Recipient Rsch. award Hungarian Acad. Sci., 1966, Silver medal Govt. of Hungary, 1964, 87. Mem. Hungarian Biochem. Soc. (sec. in chief 1989-90). Home: Árpád fejedelem u 63, H-1036 Budapest Hungary Office: Univ Med Sch Debrecen, PO Box 6, H-4012 Debrecen Hungary

ELOR, TAMAR FREIMAN, anthropologist; b. Tel-Aviv, Israel, Aug. 5, 1955; d. David and Yona (Opatovski) Freiman; m. Yair Elor, June 23, 1975; children: Uri, Shaul. BA, Tel-Aviv U., 1979, MA, 1984; PhD, Bar-Ilan U., 1990. Rsch. and tchg. asst. Tel-Aviv U., 1980-90; lectr. anthropology Hebrew U., Jerusalem, 1992—. Author: Educated and Ignorant: on Ultna Orthodox Women and Their World, 1994, Next Spring: Women and Literacy in Modern Orthodoxy, 1998-99. St. Israel def. force, 1973-75. Fulbright Found. scholar, 1995. Office: Hebrew Univ, Mount Scopns, 91905 Jerusalem Israel

ELPERIN, LOUIS SOLOMON, physician; b. L.A., June 8, 1958; s. Harry and Dina (Budgor) E.; m. Beth Ann Cyrlin, June 27, 1982; children: Dina Tiffany and Jason Michael. BA in Biology magna cum laude, UCLA, 1980; MD, Loma Linda U., 1986. Diplomate Am. Bd. Internal Medicine. Intern Loma Linda (Calif.) U. Med. Ctr., 1986-87, resident, 1987-89; attending physician Kaiser Permanante, Woodland Hills, Calif., 1989—; mem. pharmacy and therapeutics com. Kaiser Permanete, Woodland Hills, 19905, med. records com., 19915, internal medicine compensation com. 19925, internal medicine residency program coord., 19935; chmn. peer rev. com., clin. instr. medicine UCLA. Contbr. articles to profl. jours. Mem. Temple Aliyah, Mulwood Homeowners' Assn., Woodland Hills, 1995. Mem. ACP, Phi Eta Sigma, Alpah Omega Alpha. Democrat. Jewish. Avocations: bicycling, photography. Office: Kaiser Permanente 5601 De Soto Ave Woodland Hills CA 91367-6798

ELPHICK, HENRY RICHARD FRANCIS, investment banker; b. Oxford, Eng., Sept. 22, 1970; s. Richard Michael and Mary Frances (Owen) E. MA in Jurisprudence, Oxford (Eng.) U., 1993. Solicitor Linklaters & Paines, London and N.Y., 1994-97; asst. mgr. N.M. Rothschild & Sons, Ltd., London, 1997-99; assoc. dir. UBS-Warburg Dillon Read, London, 1999—. Anglican. Avocations: wine, travel, science fiction. E-mail: henry.elphick@wdr.com. Office: Warburg Dillon Rd, 2 Finsbury Ave, London EC2M 2PP, England

EL-RAGHY, TAMER, research educator; b. Cairo, Aug. 19, 1970; came to US, 1994; s. Saad M. El-Raghy and Fatma Ahmed; m. Naala M. El Tantawy, Sept. 6, 1993; children: Nour, Yousef. BS, Cairo U., 1992, MS, 1994; PhD, Drexel U., 1997. Instr. Cairo U., 1992-94; rsch. prof. Drexel U., Phila., 1997—; cons. Kanthal AB, Hallastaamar, Sweden, 1999. Patentee in field. Mem. ASM (chmn. scholarship com. 1999), TMS, Am. Ceramic Soc. Avocations: biking, reading, judo (black belt). E-mail: tamer.elraghy@drexel.com. Home: 2101 Chestnut St Apt 1817 Philadelphia PA 19103-3133 Office: Drexel U 32d and Chestnut Philadelphia PA 19104

EL RIDI, RASHIKA AHMED FATHI, immunology educator, researcher; b. Ismailieh, El Kanal, Egypt, June 23, 1943; d. Ahmed Fathi M. Fahmy El Ridi and Aida H. Kamel El Arnaouti; m. Abdel-Moneim M. Ibrahim Tallima, Dec. 20, 1977 (div. June 1986); 1 child, Hatem Abdel-Moneim. BS, Cairo U., 1964, MSc, 1969; PhD in Immunology, Czechoslovak Acad. Scis., 1975. Rsch. asst. Cairo U. Faculty Sci., 1964-75, lectr. immunology, 1975-80, assoc. prof., 1981-86, prof., 1986—, dir. reptilian immunology rsch., 1976-88; dir. immunity against schistosomiasis rsch., Egyptian Orgn. for Sera and Vaccines, 1988-95. Contbr. articles to sci. jours., including Jour. Exptl. Zoology, Jour. Parasitology, Ency. Immunology; developer potential vaccine against human schistosomiasis. Rsch. grantee Sandox Found. for Gerontol. Rsch., 1987, 89; Fulbright fellow, 1994. Mem. Egyptian Soc. for Immunology, Egyptian Soc. for Zoology. Avocations: reading, sports, gardening. Home: 11 El Tobgy St, Cairo 12311, Egypt Office: Cairo U Faculty Sci, Zoology Dept, Giza Cairo 12613, Egypt

ELROD, EUGENE RICHARD, lawyer; b. Roanoke, Ala., May 14, 1949; s. James Woodrow and Selma Fromer (Steinbach) E. AB, Dartmouth Coll., 1971; JD, Emory U., 1974. Bar: Ga. 1974, D.C. 1976, U.S. Ct. Appeals (D.C. cir.) 1985, U.S. Ct. Appeals (5th cir.) 1987, U.S. Dist. Ct. D.C. 1987, U.S. Ct. Appeals (11th cir.) 1987, U.S. Supreme Ct. 1987, U.S. Ct. Appeals (10th cir.) 1997. Trial atty. Fed. Power Com., Washington, 1974-76; atty.-advisor Fed. Energy Adminstrn., Washington, 1977; assoc. Sidley & Austin, Washington, 1977-80, ptnr., 1981—; mem. adv. bd. The Keplinger Cos., Houston. Mem. selection com. for Woodruff scholars Emory U. Law Sch., Dartmouth '71 Exec. Com. Mem. ABA, D.C. Bar Assn., Ga. Bar Assn., Energy Bar Assn. (chmn. oil pipeline com. 1982-83, tax com. 1980-81, 92-95, liaison with adminstrv. law judges 1986-87, ethics com. 1997—, bd. dirs. 2000—), Dartmouth Club (exec. com. class of 1971), Book Club of Calif. Avocations: running, book collecting, gardening. Home: 4300 Hawthorne St NW Washington DC 20016-3571 Office: Sidley & Austin 1722 I St NW Fl 7 Washington DC 20006-3705

EL-RUFAIE, OMER EL-FAROUK AHMED, psychiatry educator, consultant; b. Nuri, Sudan, Mar. 9, 1941; s. Ahmed Al-Rufaie Abdul-Hadi and Zeinab Mohmed Kheir Shannan; m. Aysha Said Ahmed El-Hassan, Aug. 23, 1956; children: Hind, El-Harith, Sofyan, Habab. MB, BS, Khartoum (Sudan) U., 1966; Diploma in Psychol. Medicine, U. London, 1974. Intern Khartoum Teaching Hosp., 1966-67, registrar in psychiatry, 1971-72; sr. house officer Port-Sudan (Sudan) Civil Hosp., 1967-71; clin. asst. Maudsley Hosp. and Inst. Psychiatry, U. London, 1972-75; cons. psychiatrist Sudan Ministry Health, Khartoum, 1975, Abu Dhabi (United Arab Emirates) Ctrl. Hosp., 1975-82; asst. prof., then assoc. prof. King Faisal U., Dammam, Saudi Arabia, 1982-90; assoc. prof. United Arab Emirates U., Al Ain, 1990-98, prof., chmn. dept. psychiatry faculty medicine, 1998—. Contbr. articles to med. jours. Fellow Royal Coll. of Psychiatrists (London); mem. Arab Psychiat. Assn., United Arab Emirates Med. Assn., also others. Home and Office: UAE U Faculty Medicine, UAE U Faculty Medicine, PO Box 17666, Al-Ain United Arab Emirates

ELS, THEODORE ERNEST, professional golfer; b. Kempton Park, South Africa, Oct. 17, 1969; s. Cornelius and Hester E. Diploma, Jan de Klerk Tech. Coll. mem. nat. teams Dunhill Cup, 1992, 93, 94, 95, 96, 97, 98, 99, World Cup, 1992, 93, 96, 97, Pres.'s Cup, 1996, 98. Winner numerous matches, including U.S. Open 1994, World Match Play Championship, 1994-96, Buick Classic, 1996-97, U.S. Open, 1997; named PGA European Player of Yr., 1994; South African Sportsman of the Yr., 1994, winner Bay Hill Invitational, 1998, Nissan Open, 1999, Alfred Dunhill PGA Championship, 1999. Mem. Kempton Park Golf. Avocations: squash, movies. Address: c/o PGA European Tour, Wentworth Dr Virginia Water, Surrey GU25 4LX, England

EL-SAIED, HOUSSNI ALI MOHAMED, chemist, educator, researcher; b. Alexandria, Egypt, Mar. 21, 1943; s. El-Said M. Ali Gabril and Bahia El-Saied El-Bagoury; m. Laila Mohi-El din Farag, July 16, 1972; children: Ola, Amr. BSc, Alexandria U., 1964; MSc, Cairo U., 1969, PhD, 1973. Asst. rschr. Nat. Rsch. Ctr., Cairo, 1966, rsch. asst., 1966-73, rschr., 1973-78, assoc. rsch. prof., 1978-84, rsch. prof., 1984—, head chem. industries divsn., 1995-99, head cellulose and paper dept., 2000—; cons. Ho. Egypt, 1986—, Egyptian Ctrl. Bank, Cairo, 1988—; mem. rsch. projects and devel. office Nat. Rsch. Ctr., Cairo, 1988—; mem. gen. assembly Egyptian Wooden Co., Cairo, 1993—. Mem. Agrl. Rsch. Leaders, Egypt, 1988—, Soc. Nat. Rsch. Ctr. Housing, 1994—. Recipinet Nat. Rsch. Ctr. of Egypt prize in chemistry, 1996; grantee Alexander von Humboldt, 1976, AIDS, 1980. Fellow Egyptian Soc., Syndicate Sci. Professions Egypt, Egyptian Soc. Polymer Sci. and Tech.; mem. Am. Chem. Soc., Oil & Colour Chemists Assn., Egyptian Soc. Solid State and Applications. Avocations: reading, plantation, sports. Office: Nat Rsch Ctr, El-Tahrir St, 12622 Cairo Egypt

EL-SAKHAWY, MOHAMED MOHAMED AHMED, chemist, researcher; b. Shebin El-Kom, Egypt, Jan. 15, 1963; s. Mohamed Ahmed El-Sakhawy and Amal Abdel Kader El-Khwaga; m. Amany Twfik El-Shabory, Nov. 7, 1996. BSc in Chemistry with hons., Faculty of Sci., Menoufia, Egypt, 1984, MSc in Organic Chemistry, 1991; PhD in Organic Chemistry, Faculty of Sci., Cairo, 1996. Rsch. asst. Nat. Rsch. Ctr., Cairo, 1989-91, asst. rschr., 1991-96, rschr., 1996—. Contbr. articles to profl. jours. Mem. Egyptian Syndicate Scientific Professions, Egyptian Soc. Polymer Sci. Tech. Avocations: reading, coin collecting, stamp collecting. Office: Nat Rsch Ctr Paper Dept, El-Tahrir St, Cairo 12622, Egypt

EL-SAKKOUT, HAMDI SAYYID AHMED, arabic literature educator; b. Tanta, Egypt, Mar. 23, 1930; parents Sayyid Ahmad El-Sakkout and Amina Hasan Wahdan; m. Elizabeth Sartain; chidlren: Hani, Ihah. BA, Cairo U., 1955; diploma in edn., Ain Shaims U., 1956; PhD, Cambridge U., 1965. Lectr. Daral'Umm Cairo U., 1965-67; prof. Am. U. in Cairo, 1967—; dir. 20th Century Egyptian Writing Project Am. U. in Cairo, 1986-87; vis. cons. Sultan Qabus U., Oman, 1985-87; judge fiction prize Egyptian Coun. Culture, 1981-83. Author: The Egyptian Novel and Its Main Trends from 1913-1952, 1971, Egyptian One-Act Plays, 1973, (series) Leaders of Contemporary Arabic Literature in Egypt, 1975—, Bibliography to the Arabic Novel, 1998. Mem. Nat. Supreme Coun. Culture, Cairo, 1991—. Recipient King Faisal Internat. Prize for Lit., 1995. Office: Am U in Cairo, 113 Kasr El Anin, Cairo 11511, Egypt

EL-SAMRAGY, YEHIA, diary scientist, educator, researcher, consultant; b. Cairo, Egypt, Nov. 7, 1950. PhD in Dairy Sci. and Tech., Ain Shams U., Cairo, 1981. Instr. Ain Shams U., Cairo, 1981-86, assoc. prof., 1987-91; postdoctoral fellow Cornell U., Ithaca, N.Y., 1986; vis. rschr. prof. Utah State U., Logan, 1991-96; asst. dir. AgLing Program, US-AID funded project, 1997-98; R&D cons. Nat. Agrl. Devel. Co., Riyadh, Saudi Arabia, 1999—. Mem. Egyptian Nat. Com. Milk and Dairy Products. Grantee Fulbright Found, 1991, 92, 94, 95; Peace fellowship, 1986. Mem. Am. Dairy Sci. Assn., Inst. Food Tech., Internat. Assn. Food Prot., Egypt Soc. Dairy

Sci., Egypt Soc. Food Sci. and Tech., Egypt Soc. Applied Micro. Office: PO Box 5823, Heliopolis West, 11771 Cairo Egypt

EL SANAFAWY, MOHAMED AHMED, civil engineer; b. Kafr El-Shiekh, Egypt, Dec. 1, 1948; s. Ahmed Mohamed El Sanafawy and Mamdaha Taha Rizk; m. Fatma Nassen Ali, July 7, 1978; children: Ahemd, Mustafa, Heba, Eman. BSCE, Alexandria (Egypt) U., 1975; higher diploma in soil mechanics, Cairo U., 1984. Civil engr. Arab Contractor, Seuz, Egypt, 1975-80; sr. engr. Arab Contractor, Cairo, 1980-85, constrn. mgr., 1985-90, project mgr., 1994-98, asst. gen. mgr., 1998—; project mgr. Saline Water Corp., Ryadh, Saudia Arabia, 1994, Al Hemaki Corp., El Kharj, Saudia Arabia, 1990-94. Author: Egyptians Tunnells, 1989. Mem. Egyptian Engring. Soc., Egyptian Engring. Syndicate, Egyptian Tunnelling Soc. Avocations: tennis, swimming, reading. Home: 6 Lus Ebn Saad, Helioplis 11351, Cairo Office: Arab Contractor, 34 Adly, Cairo Egypt

EL-SAYED, EMAD, chemistry educator; b. Alexandria, Egypt, Mar. 17, 1967; s. Mohamed and Spyridoula (Sycamnias) El-S. BS in Chemistry, Alexandria U., 1989; MS in Chemistry, U. Mass. and Alexandria U., 1994; PhD, U. Geneva, 1999. Tchg. asst. Alexandria U., 1990-94, asst. lectr. chemistry, 1994-99; postdoctoral assoc. Swiss Fed. Inst. of Tech., Zurich, 1999—; exch. visitor U. Mass., Amherst, 1993; asst. U. Geneva, 1994-98; lectr. chemistry, 1994-98. Mem. AAAS, Am. Chem. Soc., New Swiss Chem. Soc. Avocations: travel, classical music, astrophysics, learning languages, astrophysics. Office: Lab Orgn Chemistry ETH, 16 Universitatstrasse, CH-8092 Zurich Switzerland

ELSAYED, KHALED, educator; b. Cairo, Egypt, Feb. 9, 1965; s. Mohamed Fuad Elsayed and Fawkkia Mohamed (Said) E. BScEE (hons.), Cairo Univ., 1987, MSc in Engring. Math.; 1990; PhD in Computer Sci., North Carolina State Univ., 1995. Asst. lectr. Cairo Univ., 1987-90; rsch. and teaching asst. N.C. State Univ., Raleigh, 1991-94; software scientist Alphatronix Inc., N.C., 1993-95; modeling cons. Broadband Tech., 1994; sr. mem. scientific staff Northern Telecom, Dallas, 1995-97; asst. prof. Cairo Univ., 1996—; adj. asst. prof. The Am. Univ. Cairo, 1996—; cons. Nat. Telecommunications Inst., Cairo, Egypt Telecom, Cairo. Contbr. articles to profl. jours.; patentee in field. Pres. Egyptian Student Assn. N.C. State Univ., 1993. Recipient scholarship Univ. Alberta, Can., 1990, fellowship Internat. Ctr. for Pure and Applied Math., 1988, Cairo Univ.,1 982-90, Presedential medal of Excellence Gov. Egypt, 1982. Mem. IEEE, Egyptian Syndicate of Engrs. Avocations: travel, photography, racquetball. Office: Cairo Univ, Dept Elec & Communications, Giza 12613, Egypt

EL-SAYED, KHALIL MOHAMAD, aerospace engineer; b. Zahleh, Lebanon, July 9, 1950; came to U.S., 1976; s. Mohamad Hassan and Hadia Yussef (Ali Ahmed) E.; m. Wilma Beatriz Ramirez, Oct. 11, 1976; children: Mohamad Omar, Marie Joumana, Ramzi Khalil, Sami Omar. BS in Engring. Tech., Northrop U., 1983; BSBA, U. Phoenix, 1983, MBA, 1986; BT2, Ecole des arts et métiers, Beirut, 1972. Aircraft A&P mechanic Middle East Airlines, Beirut, 1972-76; aircraft mechanic Steward Davis Inc., Long Beach, Calif., 1976-77; airframe and power plant mechanic Aircraft Tank Service, Burbank, Calif., 1977-78; leadman, devel. mechanic Northrop Corp., Hawthorne, Calif., 1978-81, mfg. engr., 1981-83, sr. mfg. engr., 1983-88, sr. structural design engr., 1988-90, project engr., 1990—; gen. mgr. El-Sayed Pubs., Hawthorne, Calif., 1990-97; airbus programs team leader Honeywell Aerospace, Torrance, Calif., 1997-98; ECS rep. in Europe Honeywell Aerospace, Torrance, 1998—. Author, pub.: Arabic As Spoken in Lebanon, 1983, 2d edit., 1990, The Visitor's Guide to the Americas, 1990, Arabic As Spoken in Saudi Arabia and Kuwait, 1991. Active L.A. County Youth Motivation Task Force, 1986-97. Mem. Soc. Mfg. Engrs., Robotics Internat., Aircraft Owners and Pilots Assn., AIAA, Young Astronauts Program (chpt. establisher, advisor 1986). Republican. Muslim. Avocations: flying, reading, camping, biking, ping pong. E-mail: kal.el-sayed@honewell.com. Home: 11403 Jenkins St Artesia CA 90701-2610 Office: Honeywell Aerospace, 1 Avenue Didier Daurat, 31700 Blagnac France

EL SEBAE, ABDEL KHALEK HAMED, toxicology educator; b. Santa, Gharbieh, Egypt, July 20, 1927; s. Hamed El-Sebae Amer and Nafisa Amin Shaheen; m. Kamelia Aly Kadry, Oct. 8, 1953; children: Aly, Ashraf, Suzy. BS, Agr. Pesticide Chem., Alexandria, Egypt, 1948; MS, Pesticide Chem. and Toxicology, Alexandria, Egypt, 1953, PhD, 1961. Tchr. and rsch. asst. Faculty of Agr. Alexandria U., 1948-61, lectr. pesticide, chem., and toxicology, 1961-65, assoc. prof. pesticide, chem., and toxicology, 1965-71, prof. pesticide, chem., and toxicology, 1971-72, head of the plant prodn. dept., 1972-78, UNARC assoc. dir., 1979-83, chmn. Pesticide/Chem. Divsn., 1983-87, prof. environ. chemistry and toxicology, 1987—. Mem. Egyptian Soc. for Pest Control and Environmental Protection (pres.). Office: Faculty of Agri, Aflatoon St, Alexandria Univ, Chatby, Alexandria Egypt

EL-SEBAIE, HISHAM ISMAIL, surgeon; b. Giza, Egypt, May 12, 1959; s. Ismail Taha El-S. and Zeinab Hamed El-Sobky. MBBcH, Cairo U., 1984, MS, 1994, MD, 1999. Intern Kasr el-Aini, Cairo, 1997-98; resident NCI, Cairo, 1994-98, rschr., 1994-99, cons. microsurgery, 1999—; author: Clinico Path Study of Gastric Cancer, 1990, Conservative Breast Surgery, 1998. Mem. Egyptian Soc. Blood Doners, Guizira Sporting Club, Shooting Club. Avocations: weitht lifting, shooting, hunting, swimming, diving. Home: 49 Charles De Caulle St, Cairo Egypt Office: 174 El Tahreer St, Cairo Egypt

ELSELL, DOROTHEE, portfolio management executive; b. Darmstadt, Germany. Diploma in math. and econs., Tech. U., Darmstadt, Germany, 1989; DVFA/CEFA, DVFA, Frankfurt, Germany. Cons. Commerzbank, Frankfurt, 1989-90; portfolio strategist CICM, Frankfurt, 1991-94, portfolio mgr., 1994—. Recipient 3d pl. award Micropal, 1998, Lipper, 1998. Avocation: trekking. Office: CICM, Plate der Einheit, 60327 Frankfurt Germany

ELSEN, SHELDON HOWARD, lawyer; b. Pitts., May 12, 1928; m. Gerri Sharfman, 1952; children: Susan Rachel, Jonathan Charles. AB, Princeton U., 1950; AM, Harvard U., 1952, JD, 1958. Bar: N.Y. 1959, U.S. Supreme Ct. 1971. Ptnr. Orans, Elsen & Lupert, N.Y.C., 1965—; adj. prof. law Columbia U. Law Sch., 1969—; chief counsel N.Y. Moreland Act Commn. on UDC, 1975-76; asst. U.S. atty. So. Dist. N.Y., 1960-64; cons. Pres.'s Commn. Law Enforcement Adminstrn. Justice, 1967; mem. faculty Nat. Inst. Trial Advocacy, 1973; panel chair 1st dept. disciplinary com. N.Y., 1990-96. Contbr. articles to profl. jours. Fellow Am. Coll. Trial Lawyers; mem. Assn. of Bar of City of N.Y. (v.p. 1988-89, chmn. com. on fed. legislation 1969-72, chmn. com. on fed. cts. 1983-86, chmn. nominating com. 1986-87, chmn. com. amenities in land use process for N.Y.C. 1987-88), Am. Law Inst. (adviser Transnat. Rules of Civil Procedure 1999—), Phi Beta Kappa. Home: 50 Fenimore Rd Scarsdale NY 10583-2251 Office: 1 Rockefeller Plz New York NY 10020-2102

ELSENER, G. DALE, lawyer; b. Frederick, Okla., Mar. 26, 1951; s. Gordon Lee and Anita Lois (Vaughan) E.; m. Janet Lynn Scism, June 21, 1980; children: Kelli Jan, Hayley Lynn, Garrett Dale. BS, Okla. State U., 1973; JD, Okla. U., 1976. Bar: Okla. 1976, U.S. Dist. Ct. (ea. and we. dists.) Okla. 1984. Assoc. Richard S. Roberts, Wewoka, Okla., 1976-78; ptnr. roberts & Elsener, Wewoka, 1979-86; sole practice, 1986-90; city atty. City of Wewoka, 1986—. Chmn. bd. trustees Seminole County Law Libr., 1986; chmn. Seminole County Econ. Devel. Adv. Com., 1986; bd. dirs. Rural Water Dist. 3, Cromwell, Okla., 1982-90; mem. Mandatory Continuing Legal Edn. Commn., 1991-97; mem. Seminole Econ. Devel. Coun., 1997-2000. Mem. Okla. Bar Assn. (real property and mineral law sects.), Seminole County Bar Assn., Seminole C. of C. (pres. 1998). Office: Elsener & Cadenhead PO Box 2067 Seminole OK 74818-2067

ELSER, DANNY R., financial planner; b. Butte, Mont., June 22, 1953; s. Duane Donald and Edith N.H. (Tam) E.; m. Janet L. Bottom, Dec. 1, 1974; children: Sara E., Katie V., Andrew J., Patrick M. BS, Colo. St. U., 1976. CLU. Mgr. Coll. Life, Bloomington, Ind., 1976-82, Prin. Fin. Group, Bloomington, 1982-86; prin. Fin. Strategies Corp., Bloomington, 1986-88; mgr. No. Colo. Prin. Fin. Group, 1988-89, Prin. Fin. Group, Billings, Mont., 1989—. Bd. dirs. Cmty. Svc. Coun., Bloomington, 1982-85; mem. Young Reps., Bloomington, 1982-86; mission chmn. Evang. Cmty. Ch., Bloomington, 1985-86, missions com. Faith Evang. Ch., Ft. Collins, Colo., 1987-88, 91—, mem. ch. coun., 1991—; ch. lay leader, coun. mem., missions com. Faith Evang. Ch., Billings; bd. dirs. working com. Mont. Found. Consumer Ins. Edn. Bd.; bd. dirs., coach Little Guy Football, 1993—; coach Little League, 1991—, Amateur Athletics Wrestling, 1990—; Fellowship of Christian Athletes state dir., 1995—. Mem. Nat. Assn. Life Underwriters (Nat. Quality and Sales Achievement award 1980-88, Outstanding Young Man of Am., 1983-85), Ind. State Assn. Life Underwriters (Bloomington chpt. bd. dirs. 1980-84, state bd. dirs. 1985-86), S.E. Mont. Assn. Life Underwriters (sec., prog. chmn., v.p. 1989-92, pres. 1992-93), Internat. Assn. Fin. Planning, Nat. Assn. Security Dealers (registered rep.), So. Ind. Estate Planning Forum, Million Dollar Round Table, Bloomington C. of C. (chmn. leadership Bloomington 1982-86), Ft. Collins C. of C. (bus. excellence com.), No. Rocky Mountain Chpt. CLU (sec., treas. 1988, bd. dirs. chartered fin. cons. 1988), Mont. Gen. Agts.-Mgrs. Assn. (bd. dirs. 1989—, Nat. Mgmt. award 1989, 90, 91, 92, 93, 94, 95, pres. 1992-94, past pres. 1991-92), Mont. Soc. CLU and Chartered Fin. Cons., Bloomington Jaycees (pres. 1982-86), ECC Club (mission chmn. 1985-86). Republican. Office: Prin Fin Group 401 N 31st St Ste 950 Billings MT 59101-8101

EL SERAFY, SALAH ELDIN, economist, consultant; b. Damietta, Egypt, Apr. 18, 1927; came to U.S., 1972; s. Taha El Serafy and Aziza Asmar; m. Susan Mary deBargue Hubert, Dec. 27, 1957; children: Joseph E., Sam. BCom with honors, Alexandria (Egypt) U., 1947; BSc in Econs. with honors, U. London, 1952; DPhil in Econs., Oxford (Eng.) U., 1957. Prof. econs. Alexandria U., 1958-64; rsch. fellow econs. Harvard U., Cambridge, Mass., 1962-63, Ctr. Mid. Ea. Studies, Cambridge, Mass., 1963-64; project dir. The Economist Intelligence Unit Ltd., London, 1964-72; sr. econ. advisor World Bank, Washington, 1972-92; ind. econ. cons. Arlington, Va., 1993—. Author, joint editor: Environmental Accounting for Sustainable Development, 1989; author: Economics of National Income, (in Arabic) 1961; contbr. articles to profl. jours.; inventor El Serafy method for estimating income from depletable resources; mem. editl. bd. Ecol. Econs., 1996-99, Environ. Taxation and Acctg., 1996—. Mem. Royal Econ. Soc. (life), Internat. Soc. Ecol. Econs. Avocations: reading, writing, music, hiking. Home and Office: 3118 17th St N Arlington VA 22201-5202

ELSESSER, BRIAN D., historian, educator; b. Norfolk, Va., Oct. 10, 1968; s. James R. and Lionelle H. Elsesser; m. Christine G. Elsesser, May 29, 1999. BA, Boston U., 1991; MA, U. Mo., Columbia, 1993; PhD, St. Louis U., 2000. Instr. history St. Louis Cmty. Coll., 1995—; bd. mem. Edn. Outreach, West-End Outreach, St. Louis, 1999—; gen. coord. Loisirs Culturel a L'Etranger, Paris, 1996—. Contbg. author: America Lives, 2000. Treas. Md. House Assn., St. Louis, 1997—; mem. 28th Ward Dem. Party, St. Louis, 1997—. Scholar St. Louis Post Dispatch, 1987. Mem. Metropolis St. Louis, Ctrl. West End Assn., Am. Historians Assn., Mo. Hist. Soc., Crossroads Alumni Assn. (bd. mem. 1999), Mo. Hist. Soc. Avocations: tropical fish, collecting modern art. E-Mail: elsesser1@aol.com.

EL SHAKANKIRY, HANAN MOSTAFA, pediatrics educator, consultant; b. Giza, Giza, Egypt, June 12, 1961; d. Mostafa Abd El Hady El Shakankiry and Afaf Abd El Haleem El Shamy; m. Ahmed Fawzy El Shakankiry, Sept. 16, 1978; children: Sarah, Mohamed. MBBCh, Ain Shams U., Cairo, 1984, MSc in Pediat., 1989, PhD in Pediat., 1993, MS in Neuropsychiatry, 1999. Resident dept. pediat. Ain Shams Hosps., 1986-89, asst. lectr. pediat., 1990-94, lectr., 1994-99, asst. prof., 1999—. Recipient Dedication award Egyptian Med. Syndicate, 1998. Mem. Am. Epilepsy Soc., Egyptian Perinatal Soc., Egyptian Pediat. Soc., N.Y. Acad. Scis. Avocations: swimming, music, sailing, travel, anthropology. Home: 35 El Andalos St, Heliopolis Cairo Egypt Office: Fac Medicine Dept Pediat, Ain Shams U Abbasia, Cairo Egypt

EL SHAKER, MOHAMMED MOHAMMED AMIN, physician, orthopedic surgeon; b. Deir Ezzor, Syria, May 25, 1955; s. Mohammad Amin and Jawida Jaber (Allouni) El S.; m. Iman Orfan Al Abari; children: Ammar, Sara, Faisal, Abdulrahman. B in Medicine and Surgery, Al-Azhar U., Cairo, 1980. House officer Al Azhar U. Hosp., Cairo, 1981-82; jr. resident in surgery King Faisal Specialist Hosp. and Rsch. Ctr., Riyadi, Saudi Arabia, 1982; sr. resident in orthopedics King Faisal Specialist Hosp. and Rsch. Ctr., Riyadh, Saudi Arabia, 1984-86, chief resident in orthopedics, 1986-87, orthopedic surgeon, 1987—, coord. postgrad. activities dept. family medicine, 1995—, coord. mortality and morbidity com., 1993—, mem. pediat. rehab. subcom., 1996—, mem. rehab. com., 1996—, chmn. West Compound residential com., 1991—; tng. resident in orthopedics U. B.C., Vancouver, Can., 1992; spkr. numerous symposiums. Author: (booklet) Fractures, Osteoporosis, Use Spray Anesthesia in Sport Injuries; contbr. articles to profl. jours. including Saudi Med. Jour., Surg. Neurology, Jour. Bone and Joint Surgery, Spine, Anti-Microbial Agts. and Chemotherapy. Mem. Am. Acad. Orthopaedic Surgeons, Soc. Internat. de Chirurgie Orthopedic (Belgium), Saudi Sports Medicine Assn. (Saudi Arabia), Saudi Osteoporosis Group. Avocations: swimming, tennis, soccer. Office: King Faisal Sp Hosp & Rsch, MBC-62 PO Box 3354, Riyadh 11211, Saudi Arabia

EL-SHANTI, HATEM ISAM, pediatric geneticist; b. Tripoli, Libya, Jan. 1, 1960; s. Isam and Samiha (Adili) El-S.; m. Sohair Abul-Haija, Sept. 22, 1994; 1 child, Jawa. MD, Cairo U., 1983; MSc, Ind. U., 1989. Diplomate Am. Bd. Pediatrics, Am. Bd. Med. Genetics in Clin. Genetics & Cytogenetics. House officer, gen. practitioner Cairo Univ. Hosps., 1984-85; tchg. asst. Jordan U. Sci. & Tech., Irbid, 1985-87; resident, fellow U. Iowa, Iowa City, 1989-93; asst. prof. Jordan Univ. Sci. and Tech., 1993-98, assoc. prof., 1998—; dir. cytogenetics lab., 1993—. Fellow Am. Acad. Pediatrics, Am. Coll. Med. Genetics; mem. European Soc. Human Genetics. Avocations: reading, sports, history of science and medicine. Home: PO Box 3211, 21110 Irbid Jordan Office: Jordan U Sci & Tech, Sch Medicine/Pediatrics, Irbid Jordan

ELSHARKAWY, ADEL MOHAMED, engineering educator; b. Egypt, Sept. 26, 1955; s. Mohamed Elsharkawy and Sadia Tawfak Loutfy; m. Nagwa Nabeh Abdelhalim, Jan. 1, 1986; children: Moh-Nabih, Leena. PhD, Colo. Sch. Mines, 1991. Asst. prof. Suez Canal U., Egypt, 1991-92; asst. prof. Kuwait U., 1992-98, assoc. prof., 1998—. Mem. Soc. Petroleum Engr., Soc. Core Analysis, Am. Chem. Soc. Avocations: table tennis, football. Home: PO Box 5969, Safat 13060 Kuwait

EL-SHARKAWY, MABROUK ABDUL-SALAM, agronomist, researcher, consultant; b. Shobratana, Gharbiah, Egypt, Apr. 7, 1937; arrived in Colombia, 1980; s. Abdul-Salam Ahmed and Farah Ali (Ghorab) Sharkawy; m. Stella Navarro, Jan. 17, 1989; 1 child, Farah. BS with honors, Faculty of Agr., Alexandria, 1958; MS, La. State U., 1961; PhD, U. Ariz., 1965. Rsch. asst. Nat. Rsch. Ctr., Cairo, 1958-60; assoc. physiologist U. Calif., Davis, 1965-66; physiologist Ministry of Agr., Cairo, 1966-68; prof. U. Libya, Tripoli, 1968-78, head dept. plant prodn., 1970-72, head agron. divsn., 1972-75, head tech. follow-up dept., 1975-76, co-founder, cons. agrl. studies office, 1975-80; head plant prodn. dept. Arab Orgn. Agr. Devel., Arab League, Tripoli, 1978-80; physiologist Cen. Internat. Agr. Tropical, 1980-97, project mgr. Cassava integrated prodn. sys., 1988-96; cons. agrl. rsch. & devel., 1998—. Author, editor (bull.) Crop Rsch. Kufra Oasis, 1975; editor: Libyan Jour. Agr., 1974-78, Plant & Soil, The Netherlands, 1980-90; contbr. over 130 articles to profl. jours., procs., chpts. to books. Student senator U. Ariz. Senate, Tucson, 1964-65, pres. Internat. Student Club, 1964-65. U. Alexandria fellow, 1955-58, U. Calif. fellow, 1965-66; Egyptian Govt. scholar, 1959-65; recipient Citation Classic award, Classic Inst. Sci. Info., 1986, over 600 citations in lit. Mem. AAAS, Am. Inst. Biol. Scis., Am. Soc. Agronomy and Crop Sci., N.Y. Acad. Scis., Sigma Xi. Achievements include discovery of C3/C4 syndrome in plant photosynthesis, desert farming system of North Africa, physiological characteristics of Cassava productivity in the tropics; selection of cassava cultivars resistant to drought and poor soils, integrated cassava production systmes in hillside and marginal lands, selection of wheat and barley cultivars for desert conditions, characterization of cotton germ plasm for leaf photosynthesis, characterization of cassava germ plasm for leaf photosynthesis in relation to crop productivity in humid, seasonally dry and semiarid environments, discover of leaf "Kranz" anatomy and photorespiration reassimilation in C4 photosynthesis species including maize, tropical grasses and amaranthus species. E-mail: elsharkawy@telesat.com.co. Home and Office: AA 26360, Cali Valle, Colombia

EL-SHAZLY, AMR ESSAM, otolaryngologist, researcher; b. Cairo, Egypt, Apr. 20, 1966; s. Essam and Afaf (Faheem) El-S.; m. Noha Nasser, Aug. 2, 1991; children: Suzanne, Sherief. B of Medicine and Surgery, King Saud U. Sch. of Medicine, 1990; D in Otolaryngology, Kumamoto U., 1997. Intern King Khaled U. Hosp. and Affiliated Hosps., Riyadh, Saudi Arabia, 1990-91; otolaryngologist Security Forces Hosp., Riyadh, Saudi Arabia, 1991-92, Riyadh Med. Complex, 1992-93; otolaryngologist, rsch. fellow Kumamoto U. Sch. of Medicine, 1993-98; otolaryngologist Whiston Hosp., Maseyside, U.K., 1998-99, St. George's Hosp., London U., 1999-2000, Frimley Park Hosp., Surrey, Eng., 2000—. Contbr. articles to profl. jours. Mem. AAAS, Japanese Soc. of Allergology, Egyptian Med. Syndicate, Brit. Otolaryngology Rsch. Soc. Avocations: sports, travelling, listenting to music. Office: Frimley Pk Hosp Dept ENT, Portsmouth Rd, Frimley Camberley Surrey GU165UJ, England

EL-SHEMY, HANY ABDEL-AZIZ, science educator, researcher; b. Komhamada, Behera, Egypt, Apr. 16, 1966; parents Abdel-Aziz El-Shemy and Khairiea Ibrahim El-Faramawy. BSc, Cairo U., Giza, Egypt, 1988, MSc, 1992, PhD, 1996. From demonstrator to asst. lectr. Cairo U., Giza, 1990-96, lectr., 1996—; postdoctoral rschr. Hiroshima (Japan) U., 1999—. Contbr. articles to profl. jours. Recipient Pirze award; study grantee, Italy, 1992, tng. grantee, U.S., 1998. Muslim. Avocations: travel, scientific promotion, new discoveries. Fax: 0081-0824-0791. E-mail: helshemy@hotmail.com. Home: 464 Al-Haram Apt 8 2 Fl, Giza Egypt Office: Hiroshima U, 1-4-4 Kagamiyama, Higashihiroshima 739-8528, Japan

EL-SHENNAWY, KHAMIES MOHAMMED, physical science educator; b. Alexandria, Egypt, Mar. 10, 1945; s. Mohammed Ali and Fahima Hafiz (Hamam) El-S.; m. Sammia Abdel-Fatah Nassar, Sept. 14, 1973; children: Lamiaa, Ahmed, Wallaa. BS, Alexandria U., 1968, diploma, 1976, MS, 1980, PhD, 1987. diploma of High Studies, Communication of English, 1973. Svc. mgr. Ford Aerospace, Egypt, 1984-85; svc. mgr. Olympia Inc., Egypt, 1985-86, Emerson Inc., Egypt, 1985-87; educator Benghazi U., Libya, 1987-88; prof. Arab Acad. for Sci. & Tech., Alexandria, Egypt, 2000—. Author: (book) Comm. Engring., 1992; contbr. articles to profl. jours.; patentee in field. Col. Egyptian Signal Navy Dept., 1968-84. Sr. mem. IEEE; mem. Engring. Syndicate 1968—, Vets./War Victims. Moslem. Avocations: music, reading. Home: 8 Pharaana St Flat 5, Alexandria Egypt Office: Arab Acad for Sci & Tech, PO Box 1029, Alexandria Egypt

EL-SHERIF, MAHMOUD A., electrical engineering educator; b. Cairo, July 7, 1942; came to U.S., 1981; s. Abd-El-Rahman E. and Hakmat Kaleb (El-Saied) E.; m. Jeylan Talaat El-Mansoury, Mar. 15, 1950; children: Dina, Dalia, Mohamed. BSc in Comm. Engring., Cairo U., 1966; Diploma in Electronic Engring., Alexadria (Egypt) U., 1977, MSc in Electro-Physics, 1980; MSEE, U. Pa., 1983; PhD in Elec. Engring., Drexel U., 1987. Engr. The Egyptian Telecom. Orgn., Cairo, 1966-67; radar instr. Air Def. Inst., Alexandria, 1967-77, radar dept. chmn., 1977-81; dean engring. edn. Air Def. Coll., Alexandria, 1987-89; rsch. prof. Drexel U., Phila., 1989-94, dir., founder Fiber Optics and Photonics Lab., 1994—, dir., founder Fiber Optics and Photonics Mfg. Engring. Ctr., 1997—; prin. investigator NASA Lewis Rsch. Ctr., 1991-95, Dept. Def., 1990—; pres. Photonics, Inc., Wilmington, Del. and Phila., 1990—; cons. David Sarnoff Rsch. Ctr., Princeton, 1996—. Mem. laser tech. delegation U.S. Citizen Ambassador Program, Spokane, Wash., 1996—. Recipient 1st Class Medal of Disting. Performance, Pres. of Egypt, 1971, Medal and cert. of Appreciation, Egyptian Engring. assn., 1987. Fellow Optical Soc. Am.; mem. IEEE, Am. Ceramic Soc., Internat. Soc. Optical Engrs., Soc. for Advancement of Material and Processing Engrs. Achievements include research on optical fibers as active devices; inventor first fiber-optic modulator, coupler, switch and multiplexers; inventor novel structure of Bragg optical fibers; novel process for manufacturing of sapphire optical fibers (core, clad, jacket) for IR transmission and application up to 1700 degrees centegrade; leadership in design/development of intelligent and smart structures with fiber optic systems embedded in materials for in-situ real-time characterization and health monitoring of stuctures; development of smart soldier's uniform with embedded fiber optic biological sensors for automatic detection of battle field biological threats. Avocations: chess, travel, history, movies, classical music. Home: 1117 Hillcrest Rd Narberth PA 19072-1223 Office: Drexel Univ Dept Material Engring 32d and Chestnut Sts Philadelphia PA 19104

ELSINGER, JULIE ANNE, registered nurse, medical transcriptionist; b. Sheboygan, Wis., Apr. 20, 1946; d. Robert Louis and Marie Martha (Henning) Reichert; m. Julian Harvey Wassink, Aug. 14, 1965 (div. 1970); m. Anthony LaSalle Elsinger, Nov. 13, 1985. Med. asst. diploma, Lakeshore Tech. Sch., Sheboygan, Wis., 1965; RN, Milw. Area Tech. Coll., 1981; student, U. Wis. Med. asst. Plymouth (Wis.) Clinic, 1965-70; med. sec. St. Mary's Hosp.-Milw. County Gen.; exec. sec. to chief of staff Deaconess Hosp., Wauwatosa, Wis., 1972-74; RN transplant unit Froedtert Meml. Luth. Hosp., Wauwatosa, Wis.; med. transcriptionist, RN telephone triage St. Joseph Hosp., West Bend, Wis., 1999—, RN telephone triage, 1999—. Chairperson Germantown (Wis.) Shoreland Wetland Com. Mem. Nat. Wildlife Fedn., People for the Ethical Treatment of Animals, Sierra Club. Lutheran. Avocations: reading, animal activism, scuba diving, nature. Home: W156n11580 Pilgrim Rd Germantown WI 53022-3432 Office: St Joseph Hosp 551 S Silverbrook Dr West Bend WI 53095-3898

ELSNESS, JOHAN, English language educator; b. Fredrikstad, Norway, Feb. 27, 1947; s. Sverre and Ellen Marie (Maastad) E.; m. Turid Fosby Elsness, Jan 2. 1971; children: Frode, Eir Marie. PhD, U. Oslo, 1992. Tchr. Sarpsborg Sr. H.S., Norway, 1974-75; asst. prof. U. Oslo, Norway, 1975-82, assoc. prof., 1983-93, prof., 1993—; rsch. fellow Norway Rsch. Coun. for Sci. and Humanities, 1984-87; radio announcer Norway Nat. Radio, 1972-74; vis. prof. Brown U., Providence, R.I., 1986, 88, 92, 94, St. Olaf Coll., Minn., 1997. Author: The Perfect and the Preterite in Contemporary and Earlier English, 1997. Deputy mem. Norway Parliament, 1989-93. Cpl. Norwegian Army, 1970. Roman Catholic. Office: Univ Oslo, PO Box 1003, Blindern Oslo N-0315, Norway

EL SODA, MORSI ABOU EL SEOUD, agricultural studies educator; b. Guizeh, Egypt, Nov. 28, 1948; s. Abou El Seoud El Morsi and Fatma (El Gammal) El S.; m. Fafette Mohamed Bahgat Sammakia, July 2, 1970; children: Ahmed, Mohamed. BSc in Agr., Alexandria (Egypt) U., 1970, MSc in Agr., 1973; postgrad., Nat. Inst. Agron. Rsch., Jouy en Josas, France, 1974-76; PhD, U. Caen, France, 1976; DSc, Paris VII, 1980. Cert. prof. dairy tech. Asst. lectr. Faculty of Agr., Alexandria, 1971-74, from asst. prof. to assoc. prof., 1976-86, prof., 1986—, vice dean cmty. devel. and environ. affairs, 2000—; adj. prof. U. Laval, Que., Can., 1995; invited spkr. several sci. meetings; cons. in dairy field. Author: (book chpts.) Developments in Food Science, Food Flavor: Generation, Analysis and Process Influence, 1994, Liposomes and the Agro Food Industry in Liposomes: New Systems and New Trends in Their Application, 1995, Microbiology and Biochemistry of Cheese and Fermented Milk, 1997; contbr. revs. to profl. jours. Decorated Chevalier dans l'ordre des palmes academiques French Ministry of Edn., 1991, promoted to Officier, 1996. Mem. Internat. Dairy Fedn. (gen. sec. 1988), Egyptian Soc. for Dairy Tech., Am. Dairy Sci. Assn. (Marschall/Rhodia Internat. Dairy Sci. award 1998, U. Alexandria award sci. distinction, 2000), French Agy. for Tech., Indsl. and Econ. Coop. Avocations: playing squash, tennis, and soccer; reading, music, horseback riding. E-mail: morsi elsoda@hotmail.com. Home: 87-Abd-El-Salam Aref St, Alexandria Glym, Egypt Office: Alexandria U, Dept Dairy Microbiology, Alexandria Egypt

ELSON, CHARLES MYER, law educator; b. Atlanta, Nov. 12, 1959; s. Edward Elliott and Suzanne (Goodman) E.; m. Aimee F. Kemker, Dec. 18, 1993; 1 child, Caroline Kemker. AB magna cum laude, Harvard U., 1981, postgrad., 1981-82; JD, U. Va., 1985. Bar: N.Y. 1987, D.C. 1988, U.S. Dist. Ct. (so. and ea. dists.) N.Y. 1987, U.S. Ct. Appeals (11th cir.) 1987. Law clk. to judge U.S. Ct. Appeals (11th cir.), Atlanta, 1985-86; assoc. Sullivan & Cromwell, N.Y.C., 1986-90; asst. prof. Stetson U. Coll. Law, St. Petersburg, Fla., 1990-93, assoc. prof., 1993-96, prof., 1996—; Edgar S. Woolard Jr. prof. corp. governance U. Del., 2000—, dir. Ctr. for Corp. Governance, 2000—; vis. prof. law U. Ill., Champaign-Urbana, 1995, Cornell U. Law Sch., Ithaca, N.Y., 1996, U. Md. Law Sch., Balt., 1998; cons. Holland & Knight, 1995—, Towers, Perrin, 1998; bd. dirs. Auto Zone, Inc., Nuevo Energy Co., Sunbeam Corp., Investor Responsiblity Rsch. Ctr., Gulfcoast Legal Svcs. Corp., 1991-99. Bd. dirs. Big Apple Circus, Ltd., N.Y.C., 1987-93, Circon Corp., 1997-99; trustee Talladega Coll., 1994—, Tampa Bay Performing Arts Ctr., 2000—, Tampa Mus. Art, 1993-99. Salvatori fellow Heritage Found., 1993-

94. Mem. ABA, Am. Law Inst., Assn. Bar City N.Y., Chevaliers du Tastevin, Down Town Assn., Nat. Assn. Corp. Dirs. (adv. coun. 1997—, commn. dir. compensation 1995, commn. dir. professionalism 1996, com. on securities litig. reform and fraud detection 1997, com. on succession planning 1998, com. on audit coms. 1999, com. on the role of the bd. in strategic planning 2000), Harvard Club N.Y.C., Univ. Club N.Y.C. Home: 3315 W Mullen Ave Tampa FL 33609-4657 Office: Law Coll 1401 61st St S Saint Petersburg FL 33707-3246

ELSOROUGI, MOHAMED KAMAL ELDINE, medical educator, pneumologist, physiologist; b. Cairo, Oct. 26, 1938; s. Kamal Eldine Mohamed and Zeinab Mohamed (Gombolat) E.; m. Bassama Abd El Aziz Nasef, Apr. 21, 1964; children: Mohamed Mohamed, Waleed Mohamed. M.B.B.Ch., Cairo U., 1962, diploma of Chest Diseases and Tb, 1965, diploma of Gen. Medicine, 1968, MD in Chest Diseases and Tb, 1973. House officer Cairo U. Hosps., 1962-63, resident chest diseases, 1963-65; clin. demonstrator faculty of medicine Cairo U., 1966-68, asst. lectr. faculty of medicine, 1968-73, lectr. chest diseases faculty of medicine, 1973-78, asst. prof. chest diseases faculty of medicine, 1978-83, prof. chest diseases faculty of medicine, 1983—, chmn. chest diseases dept., 1996—; cons. pneumologist Arab Contractors Med. Ctr., Cairo, 1982—, Mil. Hosps., Cairo, 1982—, Al-Salam Internat. Hosp., Cairo, 1982-86, Nile Badrawy Hosp., 1982—, El Fayrouz Hosp., Dokki, 1986—; sr. pulmonary physiologist Al Azhar U., Cairo, 1980—, Assiut (Egypt) U., 1980—, Benha (Egypt) U., 1980—, Cairo U., 1980—; external prof., examiner univs. Author: Chest Diseases, 1982; mem. editl. bd. Egyptian Jour. of Chest Diseases and Tb, 1980—; contbr. articles to profl. jours. With Egyptian Armed Forces, 1965-66. Recipient Med. Svc. medal Egyptian Med. Sendicate, 1994, med. Armed Forces Med. Svcs., 1995, Profl. Hassan Hamdy award for best physiol. rsch., 1995. Fellow Am. Coll. Chest Physicians, Royal Soc. Medicine, Internat. Acad. Chest Physicians and Surgeons; mem. AAAS, Egyptian Med. Assn., Egyptian Soc. Chest Diseases and Tb (bd. dirs. 1965—), Internat. Union Against Tb and Lung Diseases, N.Y. Acad. Scis., European Respiratory Soc., Pan Arab Assn. Chest Medicine and Surgery (bd. dirs. 1993—), World Assn. Bronchology, Am. Assn. Bronchology, Am. Thoracic Soc. Avocations: photography, touristic travelling, sports, swimming, tennis. Home: 27 Omar Bakeer St, 11361 Heliopolis Cairo, Egypt Office: Cairo Univ, Chest Dept Faculty Medicine, Manial Cairo Egypt

EL-SOWYGH, HAMAD Z., education and science educator; b. Durma, Riyadh, Saudi Arabia, June 15, 1944; s. Zaid Ibrahim and Haya Hamad (Authman) El-S.; m. Hussah Abdulrahman Kuroni, June 12, 1951 (dec. 1973); children: Zeyad, Gahadi, Tagreed, Yazeed, Abdulrahman. BS, U. Riyadh, 1971; MA, U. So. Calif., 1977; PhD in Physics and Geology Edn., U. N.Mex., 1981. Cert. profl. in biophysics/dowzing. Tchr. physics KAMA, Riyadh, 1971-74, lab. instr., 1971-74, physics and math. tchr., 1982—, chair sci. dept., 1982-90, 96-99, chair civil studies dept., 1991-94; math. tchr. P.A.I., Riyadh, 1982-86; sec. and tech. cons. T.V. Est., Riyadh, 1986-89; rschr. K.A.S.T., Riyadh, 1988-99; sci. and tech. edn. cons. Ministry of Def., Riyadh, 1997—; rschr. in physics and geology edn. Author: Basic Mechanics, 1998, (with others) Attitude Toward Science Lab., 1998; author, translator in field. Mem. Am. Assn. Dowzing, Phys. and Ednl. Assn. Office: PO Box 20854, Riyadh 11465, Saudi Arabia

ELSTE, GUENTHER HEINO ERICH, astrophysicist; b. Jauer, Germany, Apr. 21, 1923; came to the U.S., 1962; s. Arno Heino Erich and Charlotte Marie Anna (Kramer) E.; m. Annelie Luise Puhl, June 3, 1950; children: Volker, Brigitte Wallis. BS, Georgia Augusta U., Göttingen, Germany, 1952, PhD, 1954. From rsch. asst. dept. astronomy to rsch. assoc. U. Mich., Ann Arbor, 1954-56, asst. prof., 1962-68, assoc. prof., 1968-91, assoc. prof. emeritus, 1992—; Wissenschaftlicher asst. U. Sternwarte, Göttingen, 1957-62; cons. Environ. Rsch. Inst. Mich., Ann Arbor, 1994-95; guest investigator Orbiting Solar Obs., Boulder, Colo., 1976; mem. working group Radiative Inputs of Sun to Earth rsch. project, Boulder, 1990. Contbr. articles to profl. jours. Bd. dirs. Washtenaw Ski Touring Club, Ann Arbor, 1974-83; instr. Washtenaw County Ski Clinics, Ann Arbor, 1974-80. Mem. Astronomische Gesellschaft, Am. Astron. Soc., Internat. Astron. Union, Sci. Rsch. Club (pres. 1974-75). Avocations: track and field, cross country skiing, swimming, Deutsches Sportabz. Gold 10. Office: U Mich Dept Astronomy 1045 Dennison Bldg Ann Arbor MI 48109-1090

ELSTER, TOBY, oil company executive; b. Calipatria, Calif., Feb. 15, 1923; s. Jack and Pauline (Gelles) E.; m. Mary M. Benest, 1949 (div. 1975); children: Marc, Louis, Paulette; m. T. Alayne Corbell, Jan. 28, 1979. BSBA, Wichita State U., 1948, BA in Geology, 1950. Staff geologist Nat. Coop. Refining Assn., Wichita, 1953-55, Petroleum, Inc., Wichita, 1955-56; cons. Wichita, 1956-68, 70—; sr. v.p. exploration Acme Oil Corp., Wichita, 1968-70; bd. dirs. Am. Consolidated Holding Corp. Author: (autobiography) The Clouds, The Sky, and I, (under Stan T. Stanley) novels, numerous short stories; contbr. articles to profl. jours. Wing comdr. CAP, Wichita, 1968-70, mem. CAP, 1965—. Capt. USAFR, 1942-83. Mem. Soc. Ind. Profl. Earth Scientists (Svc. award 1970, 72, chmn. Wichita chpt. 1970, nat. dir. 1971-72, chmn. environ. com. Wichita chpt.), Am. Assn. Petroleum Geologists, Kans. Geol. Soc., Soc. Exploration Geophysicists, Soc. Econ. Paleontologists and Mineralogists, Rocky Mountain Geol. Soc., Am. Arbitration Assn., Wichita State U. Alumni Assn. (adv. counsel to bd. dirs. 1988, life), VFW (life), Petroleum Club, Cosmopolitan Club, Embassy Club (bd. dirs. 1988, 89, 90, Wichita Downtown Lions Club, Moose, Elks. Office: Pan-Western Petroleum Inc Board of Trade Ctr Board Of Trade Ctr Ste 501 Wichita KS 67202

ELSTON, ANDREW STEPHEN, publishing executive; b. Elmira, N.Y., Sept. 17, 1951; s. Stuart Bowen and Marie Ann (Bauer) E.; m. Kathleen Anne Collins, Dec. 21, 1951; children: Megan Kathleen, Kate Alexandra. BA in English, SUNY, Buffalo, 1974; MA in English, U. Wash., 1979. Sr. editor The Book Pub. Co., Inc., Seattle, 1975-79; entertainment editor Hawaii Press Newspapers, Inc., Honolulu, 1979-81; dir. Bishop Mus. Press, Honolulu, 1981-83; mng. editor Info. for Industry, Inc., Phila., 1983-85; v.p. pubr. svcs. NewsNet, Inc., Bryn Mawr, Pa., 1985-86, exec. v.p., 1987—; pres. NewsNet, Inc., Bryn Mawr, 1991-97; dir., pub. Alliances Qpass, Inc., Seattle, 1998—. Mem. Info. Industry Assn. (exec. com. electronic svcs. div. 1988—, pub. policy and govt. rels. coun., 1989-91), Spl. Librs. Assn., Am. Soc. Info. Sci.

ELSUNNI, MOHAMED ELTAYEB, electrical engineer, consultant; b. Wadmedani, Sudan, Apr. 15, 1950; s. Eltayeb Ahmed and Nafesa Alhadi (Alshafi) E.; m. Hanan Alfadil Alnour Shamseldin. MS, Belyorussian U., Minsk, USSR, 1978, Strathclyde U., Glasgow, Scotland, 1982. Chartered engr. Asst. engr. Ministry Irrigation, Wadmedani, 1978-80, engr., 1980-83, chief engr., 1983-85, rsch. engr., 1985-89; sr. engr., ctrl. region Saudi Consol. Electric Co., Alkarj, Saudi Arabia, 1989—. Sec. gen. Engring. Sendicate, Wadmedani, 1982-86, pres., 1987-89; sec. gen. Dem. Allies, Wadmedani, 1985-89. Fellow IEE, IE Australia; mem. IEEE (sr.), Inst. Engring. Australia, Inst. Elec. Engrs. UK, N.Y. Acad. Scis. Avocations: squash, travel, reading. Office: SCECO, Ctrl Region, PO Box 75, Alkharj 11942, Saudi Arabia

EL-TAJI, MOHAMED SAMI MAHMOUD NADIM, engineering executive, consultant; b. Cairo (Palestinian), Jan. 7, 1947; s. Mahmoud Nadim Abdel Rahman and Mahila Ishak (Budeiri) El-T.; m. Nadia Salim Kotob, Sept. 9, 1963; children: Nadim, Omar. BSc in Chem. Engring., Cairo U., 1971; MSc in Sys. Engring., U. London, 1976. Chartered engr., Eng. Instrument engr. Amoco/Gupco, Gulf Suez, Egypt, 1972-74; instrument engr. A Fluor Ltd., London, 1976-78, sr. control sys. engr., 1978-80, prin. control sys. engr., 1980-84; supervisory control sys. engr. Fluor Daniel Ltd., London, 1984-90; tech. mgr. control sys. engr. Fluor Daniel Ltd., Camberley, Eng., 1990-97; process control mgr., tech. cons. advanced control dynamic simulation Fluor Daniel Ltd., Camberley, 1997—. Chmn. Internat. Judo and Karate Acad. Fellow Inst. Measurement & Control; mem. Fedn. European Assns. Nat. Engrs., Instrument Soc. Am. (sr.). Islamic. Avocations: judo (2d dan black belt, all Egypt champion 1965-70), karate (1st dan black belt). E-mail: sami.el-taji@fluorDaniel.com. Home: 16 Ashbrook Rd Old Windsor, Windsor SL42LS, England Office: Fluor Daniel Ltd, Watchmoor Pk River Sideway, Camberley Surrey GU15 3AQ, England

EL-TATAWY, HESHAM IBRAHIM, civil engineer; b. Cairo, Apr. 5, 1960; s. Ibrahim Fahmi El-T. BS in Engring., Al-Azhar U., Cairo, 1984; Specialization Cert. Constrn. Engring., Am. U., Cairo, 1992. Inspector civil engr. Ministry of Defense, Cairo, 1984-87; onsite civil engr. 1st Class Constrn. Co., Cairo, 1987-88; inspector civil engr. Cons. Engring. Office, Kuwait, 1988-90, 92-95; quality control inspector engr. Shell J.V. with E.G.P.C., Egypt, 1990-92; sr. inspector civil engr. Cons. Engring. Office, Cairo, 1996—; geotech. engr. Cons. Engring. Office, Cairo, 1985-88, repair adv. engr., Kuwait, 1992-95. With Mil. Works Dept., 1984-87. Mem. Egyptian Soc. Engrs., Am. Soc. Engrs., Bahrain Soc. Engrs., Am. Soc. Quality Control, Fedn. Arab Engrs. (comm. com. 1996), Kuwait Soc. Engrs., Nat. Sporting Club, Rotary Internat. (dist. gov. No. 2450 Giza North). Home: 35 El-Dourry St, Agouza, Cairo 12411, Egypt

EL-TAWIL, MAGDY ABDUL-ATY, mathematician; b. Cairo, Jan. 8, 1955; s. Abdul-Aty Ibrahiem El-Tawil and Fatema Mohammed Hegazy; m. Maryam Afify Saleh, May 13, 1983; children: Marwa, May, Manar, Fatema, Reem. BSEE, Cairo U., 1978, MSc in Engring. Math., 1984, PhD in Engring. Math., 1989; BSc in Math., Ain Shams U., Cairo, 1981. Demonstrator Cairo U., 1978-83, rsch. asst., 1984-88, asst. prof. engring. math., 1989-93, assoc. prof., 1994-99, prof., 1999—. Co-author: Introduction to Alegbra and Analytical Geometry (in Arabic); contbr. articles to profl. jours. including Jour. Med. and Biol. Engring. and Simulation Study, Applied Math. Modelling, Jour. Math. Analysis and Applications, Matrices (in Arabic), Probabilities (in Arabic), Introduction to Numerical Analysis (in Arabic), Specialized in Stochastic Analysis of Engring. Sys., Jour. Chaos, Solitons and Fractals. Grantee Internat. Ctr. Theoretical Physics, Trieste, 1982, 87. Avocation: football. E-mail: meltawil@alpha1-eng.cairo.eun.eg. Office: Cairo U Faculty Engring, Engring Math Dept, Cairo Egypt

EL-TAWIL, SAMIR ZAKY, metallurgist, educator, researcher; b. Imbaba, Giza, Egypt, Apr. 18, 1938; s. Zaky Abdel-Wahid E.; children: Osama, Ayman, Rasha, Ayah. BSc, Cairo U., 1960, MSc, 1964, PhD in Inorganic Chemistry, 1969. Asst. rschr. NRC, Egypt, 1960-64; asst. lectr. NRC, 1964-70; rschr. Ctrl. Metallurg. Rsch. Devel. Inst., Helwan, Egypt, 1970-75; asst. prof. Ctrl. Metallurg. Rsch. Devel. Inst., Helwan, 1975-82; prof. Ctrl. Metallurg. Rsch. Devel. Inst., 1982—, head pyro-metallurgy divsn., 1970-93, head extractive met. dept., 1993—. Contbr. articles to Erzmetall, Nat. Metall. Lab. Tech. Jour., Indian Jour. Technol., Egypt Jour. Chemistry, Jour. Inst. Fuel, Jour. Applied Chem. Biotechnol., Bulletin Nat. Rsch. Ctr., Jour. Ceramic Soc. Japan, Jour. Mines, Metals, Fuels, Industries Minerale Les Techniques, Thermo Chemica Acta, Iron Steel Internat., Neu Hütt, Chem. Engring. Jour., Au Fbereitungs Technik, Jour. Metals, High Temerature Tech., Anti-Corrosion Methods Materials, AMSE Transactions, Transactions Indian Inst. Metallurgy, Modelling Simulation Control, Internat. Jour. Refractory Metals Hard Materials, Can. Matallurg. Quar. Mem. N.Y. Acad. Sci., Acad. Sci. Tech., Scientists Sindicate. Achievements include patents in field. Fax: 5010639. E-mail: rucmrdi@rusys.eg.net. Home: 16 Abdel-Rahman El-Sharkawy, 12411 Sahafien Egypt Office: Ctrl Metallurg Rsch Inst, PO Box 87, Helwan Egypt

ELTAYEB, SALAH ELZEIN, deputy director general, publisher, consultant; b. Elobeid, Kordofan, Sudan, Aug. 24, 1942; s. Elzeim Eltayeb Yousif and Fatima Ardalla Idrees; m. Salwa Mukhtar Ali, Aug. 22, 1949; children: Elzein, Mukhtar, Israa, Mohammed. BSc in Econs., U. Khartoum, 1970; MSc in Sociology, Reading U., England, 1974, PhD in Politics, 1978; diploma in French, U. Sorbonne, Paris, 1976. Asst. prof. U. Khartouna, Sudan, 1979-84, Kind Saud U., Riyadh, Sudan, 1984-90; dir. econ. studies Alrashid Co., Riyadh, Sudan, 1990-91; dep. dir. gen. E.W.P.D., Riyadh, Sudan, 1992—; dean U. Khartoum, Sudan, 1980-84; staff head King Saud U., Riyadh, 1986-90; dir. Econ. studies Alrashid Co., Riyadh, 1990-91. Author: The Students Movement in the Sudan (1940-1970), 1971, Transition in Algeria, 1989, Formation of the FLN, 1989; exec. supr. Global Arabic Encyclopedia. Scholar Ul. Khartoum, 1972-74, 76-79. Mem. British Soc. Middle Eastern Studies, Sudan Studies Soc. (England and Am. chpts.). Islamic. Avocations: tennis, swimming, squash. Office: EWPD, PO Box 17582, Riyadh 11494, Saudi Arabia

ELTE, JAN WILLEM FREDERIK, internist; b. Amsterdam, The Netherlands, July 25, 1946; s. Philip and Johanna Mathilda Louise (Schulein) E.; m. Elisabeth Alice Pool, Mar. 24, 1973; children: Josine, Derk Jan, Maurits. MD, U. Leiden, The Netherlands, 1972, Internal Medicine, 1978, Endocrinology Diploma, 1991. Staff mem. U. Hosp., Leiden, 1978-83; cons. phys. St. Jozef Ziekenhuis Gouda, The Netherlands, 1983-86, St. Franciscus Gasthuis, Rotterdam, The Netherlands, 1987—; hon. staff mem. U. Hosp., Rotterdam, 1987—; mem. European Bd. Endocrinology; del. European Fed. Internal Medicine, 1996—. Founding dep. editor: European Jour. of Internal Medicine, 1989-99; editl. bd. Postgrad. Med. Jour., 1987—; co-editor/author: (book) Differentiele diagnostiek in de interne geneeskunde, 1994; author: (book) Diabetes Mellitus, 1992. Lt. med. svcs., 1972-73, The Netherlands. Fellow Royal Soc. Medicine; mem. European Assn. Study Diabetes. Avocations: internat. tie collecting, tennis, skiing, reading. Office: Saint Franciscus Gasthuis, Kleiweg 500, NL3045PM Rotterdam The Netherlands

ELTGEN, JEAN-JACQUES PIERRE, digital printers manufacturing executive; b. Audincourt, Doubs, France, Oct. 31, 1942; s. Pierre Victor and Jeanne (Receveur) E.; m. Danielle Michelle Maillard, Sept. 4, 1965; children: Bruno, Didier, Sophie. MS, French Aerospace Sch., Paris, 1967. Design engr. Bull GE, St. Ouen, France, 1969; electronic design mgr. Bull GE, Belfort, France, 1969-73; product planning staff Honeywell-Bull, Belfort, 1973-76; R & D mgr. Cii-Honeywell Bull, Belfort, 1976-89; dir. cooperation Groupe Bull, Belfort, 1989-91; dir. sci. and tech. Nipson Printing Sys., Belfort, 1992-98; v.p. rsch. Nipson, 1998—. Contbr. numerous articles to profl. jours.; patentee in field. Lt. French Air Force, 1967-68. Mem. Soc. for Imaging Sci. and Tech. (Europe program chmn. congress 1994, adv. com. 1995-96), NIP Tech. Coun., Local Hist. Soc. Avocations: downhill skiing, computers, genealogy, golf. Office: Nipson Printing Systems, 28 Rue Thierry Mieg, 90005 Belfort France

ELTGROTH, GEORGE VINCENT, lawyer; b. Columbus, Ohio, July 22; s. George Matthias and Berkina Estelle (Bunce) E.; m. Bernardine Rita Farrell, Oct. 30, 1939 (dec.); children: Peter, Mary Ellen, Hugh, Mark, Stefan, Lucia Eve; m. Jacqueline Bernard D'Arty, Mar. 8, 1971. BSEE, Johns Hopkins U., 1944; JD, U. Md., Balt., 1947. Bar: D.C. Patent atty. Electronics Lab., GE, Syracuse, N.Y., 1953-59; divsn. patent counsel info. processing GE, N.Y.C., 1959-65, group patent counsel info. handling, 1965-71; patent counsel for Far East, GE, N.Y.C. and Tokyo, 1971-75; patent counsel for Eruope, Africa and Mid. East, GE, N.Y.C., London, Paris, 1975-79; counsel for internat. treaties and patents GE, N.Y.C., 1979-81; ret., 1981; cons. on intellectual property law, Stanford, Conn., from 1981, Las Vegas, Nev. Mem. ABA, IEEE (sr.). Home: 3601 Cambridge St Apt 265 Las Vegas NV 89109-4047

ELTOHAMI, OMER AHMED, engineering educator; b. Khartoum, Sudan, Aug. 26, 1953; s. Ahmed Eltomhami and Fatima Abdul Raheem (Mohammed) Elrayah; m. Amal Mohammed Elhassan, Feb. 25, 1984; children: Mohammed, Mussab. BSc in Engring., Khartoum U., 1977; MSc, Cranfield U., Bedford, U.K., 1983, PhD, 1997. Chartered engr., U.K. Rsch. asst. Ind. Rsch. & Cons. Ctr., Khartoum, 1977-83, rschr., 1983-87, asst. prof. rsch., 1987-88, head engring. dept., 1988; asst. prof. Jeddah (Saudi Arabia) Coll. Tech., 1988—; mem. Rehab. Program (food ind.), Khartoum, 1986-87; sec. Engring. Ind. Com., Khartoum, 1988; mem. Master Plan for Engring. Ind., UNDP, Khartoum, 1987-88. Contbr. articles to profl. jours. Mem. ASME, Inst. Elec. Engrs., Sudanese Engring. Soc. (cons.). Avocations: reading, technical writing, stamp collecting, drawing. Home: Flat 504 Makkah Rd, 21541 Jeddah Saudi Arabia Office: Jeddah Coll Tech, PO Box 17608, 21494 Jeddah Saudi Arabia

EL-TURK, SAID NEJAM, contracting and trading company executive; b. Amman, Jordan, May 16, 1946; s. Nejam and Suad El-T.; m. Abir Taher, Sept. 7, 1979; children: Suad, Zeid, Abdullah, Yasmin. Student, Terrae Sanctae, Amman, 1965; BS, Hammersmith Coll., London, 1970; MS, U. Nebr., 1975; PhD, Kennedy Western U., 1991. Cert. C. Eng; F.I. Struct. E.; Masce; Mse; Aci. Design engr. Sir Frederick Snow & Ptnrs., London, 1970-72, Leo Daly, Omaha, 1972-74; pres. El-Turk Contracting & Trading Co., Amman, 1974—; chmn. New English Sch., Amman, 1988—; rep. Gate Avionics Ltd., U.K. Author: A Page Of The Red Days (Arabic), 1988. Fellow Instn. of Structural Engrs.; mem. Am. Soc. Engrs., U.S. Instn. of Structural Engrs., US/Arab C. of C., Soc. of Engrs. Avocations: swimming, theatre, reading. Home and Office: El-Turk Contracting & Trading Co, PO Box 5476, Amman Jordan

ELUF-NETO, JOSÉ, physician, researcher; b. Sao Paulo, Brazil, Feb. 21, 1951; s. Emilio and Norma (Hossne) Eluf; m. Oliveira Marcia Benedita; 1 child, Ana Carolina O.; m. Valeria Buccheri. MD, U. Sao Paulo, 1974, MSc, 1985; PhD, London Sch. Hygiene/Trop. Med., 1993. Med. diplomate. Lectr. Faculty of Medicine, U. Sao Paulo, 1983-93, sr. lectr., 1993-99, reader, 1999—; cons. Ministry of Health, Brazil, 1995—, Brazilian Rsch. Coun., 1996—, Nat. Cancer Inst., Brazil, 1998—. Contbr. articles to profl. jours. Grantee Internat. Agy. for Rsch. on Cancer, Lyon, 1990, Ministry of Health, Brazil, 1995, EEC, 1998. Mem. Soc. for Epidemiol. Rsch., Soc. Postgrad. Pub. Health, Internat. Epidemiol. Assn. Home: R Barao de Capanema, 443 ap 7, 01411 Sao Paulo Brazil Office: Dept Prev Med-FMUSP, Ave Dr Arnaldo 455, 01246 Sao Paulo Brazil

ELVIN, MARK, historian, educator, translator; b. Cambridge, Eng., Aug. 18, 1938; arrived in Australia, 1990; s. Herbert Lionel and Mona Bedortha (Dutton) E.; m. Anne Katherine Stevenson, Nov. 3, 1962 (div. 1979); children: John Gawain, Charles Lionel; m. Dian Montgomerie, June 3, 1989; step-children: Catherine, Julian Peter. BA with distinction, Cambridge (Eng.) U., 1959, PhD, 1968. Asst. lectr. Cambridge U., 1964-68; rsch. fellow Clare Hall, Cambridge, 1967-68; lectr. Glasgow (Scotland) U., 1968-72, Oxford (Eng.) U., 1973-89; ofcl. fellow St. Antony's Coll., Oxford, 1973-89; emeritus fellow, 1990—; rsch. prof. Australian Nat. U., 1990—; vis. prof. École Normale Supérieure, Paris, 1993. Author: The Pattern of the Chinese Past, 1973, Another History: Essays on China From a European Perspective, 1996, Changing Stories in the Chinese World, 1997; co-author: Cultural Atlas of China, 1983; co-editor: Sediments of Time. Environment and Society in Chinese History, 1998. Del. Nat. Tertiary Edn. Industry Union; vice-chmn. Oxford City Liberal Party, 1975-79. Fellow Acad. Humanities Australia; mem. Ind. Scholars Australian Assn. (nat. coun. mem. 1998—). Avocations: chess, writing poetry and children's stories (as John Dutton), photography. E-mail: john.dutton@bigpond.com. Office: Pacific & Asian History, RSPAS Australian Nat U 9, Canberra ACT 0200, Australia

ELWAKIL, AHMED ELSAYED, electronic engineer, researcher; b. Cairo, June 4, 1972; s. Elsayed Elwakil. BSc in Electronic Engring., Cairo U., 1995, MSc in Electronic Engring., 1997; postgrad., Nat. U. Ireland, Dublin, 1997—. Asst. lectr. Nuclear Rsch. Ctr., Cairo, 1995-97; Newman rsch. scholar Nat. U. Ireland, 1997—; course dir. Internat. Ctr. for Theoretical Physics, Trieste, Italy, 1998, 99. Contbr. articles to sci. jours., including Internat. Jour. Electronics, Internat. Jour. Circuit Theory and Application, Internat. Jour. Bifurcation and Chaos, Chaos, Solitons and Fractals. Rsch. grantee Egyptian Acad. Sci., Enterprise Ireland, 1998, 99. Mem. IEEE, IEE. Avocations: reading, music. Office: Nat U Ireland Univ Coll, Dept Electronic-Elec Eng, Dublin 4, Ireland

ELWIN, JAMES WILLIAM, JR., lawyer; b. Everett, Wash., June 28, 1950; s. James William Elwin and Jeannette Georgette (Zichy-Litscheff) Sherman; m. Regina K. McCabe, Oct. 25, 1986. BA, U. Denver, 1971, MA, 1972; JD, Northwestern U., 1975. Bar: Ill. 1975, U.S. Dist. Ct. (no. dist.) Ill. 1975, U.S. Ct. Appeals (7th cir.) 1977, U.S. Supreme Ct. 1980, U.S. Ct. Fed. Claims 1989. Trial atty. antitrust divsn. U.S. Dept. Justice, Chgo., 1975-77; asst. dean Sch. Law Northwestern U., Chgo., 1977-82, assoc. dean, 1982-2000; dir. profl. devel. and tng. Shearman & Sterling, N.Y.C., 2000—; exec. dir. Corp. Counsel Ctr., 1984-2000; planning dir. Corp. Counsel Inst., Garrett Corp. and Securities Law Inst., Chgo., 1983-2000; dir. Short Course for Pros. Attys., 1981-2000, Short Course for Def. Lawyers in Criminal Cases, Chgo., 1979-2000. Bd. dirs. Legal Assistance Found. of Chgo., 1985-97; vice chmn. Gov.'s Adv. Coun. on Criminal Justice Legis., 1986-91. Fellow German Acad. Exch. Svc., 1986; Fulbright scholar, Germany, 1990. Mem. Chgo. Coun. Fgn. Rels. (mem. Chgo. com.), Chgo. Bar Assn. (bd. mgrs. 1983-85), Chgo. Bar Found. (bd. dirs. 1985-93, pres. 1989-91), Ill. Inst. Continuing Legal Edn. (bd. dirs. 1978-90, chmn. 1987-88), Am. Law Inst., Legal Club (pres. 1991-92), Univ. Club, Law Club City of Chgo., Phi Beta Kappa, Pi Gamma Mu. Office: Shearman & Sterling 599 Lexington Ave Ste N721 New York NY 10022-6030

ELWOOD, J. MARK, epidemiologist, researcher. MD, Queen's U., Belfast, No. Ireland, 1976, DSc, 1981. Specialist in epidemiology and pub. health U.K., Can., Australia, New Zealand. Prof. epidemiology U. Nottingham, Eng., 1981-89, U. Otago, New Zealand, 1989-99. Author: Epidemiology and Control of Neural Tube Defects, 1992, Causal Relationships in Medicine, 1988, Critical Appraisal of Epidemiological Studies and Chinese Trials, 1998. E-mail: mark.elwood@ncci.org.au. Office: Nat Cancer Ctrl Initiative, 1 Rathdowne St, Carlton VIC 3053, Australia

ELY, SCOTT ADAMS, heamtopathologist, researcher; b. Caracus, Venezuela, Dec. 5, 1964; came to U.S., 1967; s. Eugene Wesley and Diana (Lowe) E.; m. Susan Fitzgerald. MD, Tulane U., 1991, MPH, 1991. Attending hematopathologist N.Y. Presbyn. Hosp., N.Y.C., 1998—; asst. prof. dept. pathology Weill Med. Sch., Cornell U., 1998—. Contbr. articles to med. jours. Mem. Soc. Hematopathology, U.S. Acad. Pathology, Can. Acad. Pathology. Avocations: cycling, tennis. E-mail: s12564@pol.net. Office: Cornell U NY Presbyn Hosp 100 E 77th St New York NY 10021-1850

EL-ZAHHAR, NABIL EID, psychologist; b. Dumiate, Egypt, Jan. 21, 1945; s. Eid Ragab and Zeinab Ahmad (Kaud) El-Z.; m. Yousria Hassan Awad, Jul. 21, 1950; children: Hisham, Khaled, Mohamad. MA in edn., Azahar Univ., Cairo, 1974; MSc, Helwan Univ., Cairo, 1976; PhD, Univ. S. Calif., 1982. Asst. prof. Coll. Commerce Cuez Canal Univ., Egypt, 1982-85, asst. prof. Coll. Edn., 1985-87, assoc. prof., 1987-92; chair dept. Edn. psychology Cuez Canal Univ., 1988-90, vice dean Coll. Edn., 1990-92, dean Coll. of Edn., 1992—; cons. Military Recruitment & Selection, Egypt, 1993-96, Egyptian Olympic Com., 1993-95, World Scout Orgn., Geneva, 1990-93, Illiterates & Adult Edn., Ismailia, Egypt, 1993-97. Author: Social Psychology, 1987, General Psychology, 1990, Mental & Emotional Structe of Personality, 1987, Anxiety & Arousability Inventory, 1986. Pres. Child Mental Retardation Assn., 1994, Gulf Sport Club, 1993-96. With Res. Officer, 1967-73. Recipient scholarship Egyptian Gov., 1976, Fulbright Sr. grant Fulbright Commn., 1987, Medal of Honor Egyptian Scout Fedn., 1992. Mem. Stress and Anxiety Rsch., Internat. Coun. of Psychologist, Am. Psychological Assn., World Fedn. of Adolescentology (founder). Avocations: walking, scouting, travelling. Home: 9 Asma Fahmi St Third Quart, Heliopolis Cairo 11341, Egypt Office: Coll Edn Suez Canal Univ, 41522 Ismailia Egypt

EL-ZANFALY, HELMY TAWFIK, microbiologist, educator; b. Zifta, Egypt, Sept. 15, 1942; s. Tawfik El-Azab El-Zanfaly and Nafisa (Aly) Ghonim. BSc, Cairo U., 1964, MSc, 1969, PhD, 1974; Diploma Environ. Scis. and Technology, Delft (The Netherlands) U., 1976. Rschr. asst. Nat. Rsch. Ctr., Cairo, 1965-74, rschr., 1974-80, asst. prof., 1980-85, prof. water and sewage microbiology, 1985—; cons. Greater Cairo Water Authority, 1980—. Contbr. articles to profl. publs. Rsch. fellow Deutscher Akademischer Austauschdienst, Germany, 1989, 94-95, 98-99, 2000, Fulbright Commn., 1990. Mem. Health Related Water Microbiology. Avocations: travel, stamps, coins. E-mail: zanfaly@usa.net. Office: Nat Rsch Ctr, Tahrir St, Dokki Egypt

EL ZEIN, HASSAN LABIB, publisher; b. Tyre, Lebanon, 1927; arrived in Egypt, 1975; s. Labib Ali and Fatimah El Zein; m. Taghrid Ibrahim, July 9, 1949; 9 children. MA, Am. U. Beirut, 1946; PhD, Cambridge U., 1978. Owner, pres. Dar Al-Kitab Allubnani, Beirut, Dar Al-Kitab Al-Masri, Cairo, Dar Al-Kitab-Malaysia Kualalumpur, Dar Al-Kitab Al-Islami, Jakarta, Indonesia, Dar Al-Kitab Casablanca, Maroc. Author 5,000 books, Encyclopedia of Al-Akkad, 26 vols., 1964, Encyclopedia of Dr. Taha Hussein, 20 vols., 1970, Encyclopedia of Ibn Khaldoun, 14 vols., 1956, Encyclopedia of Al. Andalous, 18 vols., 1988, Encyclopedia of Dr. Abdulhalim Mahmoud Sheikh Al-Azhar, 17 vols., 1986, Twenty First Century Encyclopedia, 10 vols., 1998, others. Mem. various C. of C.'s. Avoca-

tions: sports. Fax: 202-3924657. Office: Dar Al-Kitab Al-Masri, 33 Kasr Elnil St, PO Box 156 Ataba Cairo 11511, Egypt

EMAN, HENNY JAN (J. H. A. EMAN), prime minister of Aruba, lawyer. Leader Arubaanse Volkspartij; mem. Coun. of Ministers, 1986—; prime min., min. gen. affairs Oranjestad, Aruba, 1986-89; prime min. Govt. of Aruba, Oranjestad. Office: Office of Prime Minister, LG Smith Blvd 76, Oranjestad Aruba*

EMANDI, ANA, chemist; b. Neamt, Podoleni, Romania, June 11, 1953; d. Ioan and Iulia (Parlea) Bordea; m. July 30, 1983; children: Ioan, Teodor. Student, Petru Rares Coll., Neamt, 1972; Masters in Chemistry, Bucharest U.; PhD in chemistry, Polytech. Inst., Iasi, 1976; student, Petru Rares Coll., Neamt, 1990-94. Chemist, rschr., prof. U. Bucharest, Romania; chemist Chem. Plant Dudesti ICECHIM, Bucuresti, 1979; head chemist for devices Rsch. and Prodn. Semiconductor Stuffs Plant, 1981; prof's. asst.faculty chemistry and chem. tech. inorganic chemistry dept. Nat. Inst. Chemistry-Polytech. Inst., Bucharest, 1990; PhD prof. faculty chemistry inorganic chemistry dept. Bucharest U., 1994—; tchr., presenter at various seminars in field. Contbr. articles to profl. sci. jours. Rsch. 2nd prize award Nat. Students' Session, 1977. Mem. Chem. Soc. Achievements include assisting at the piloting and in chemical industry problemssuch as new technologies in obtaining complex metal dye material used in cosmetics, obtaining the dye material Indawiren, synthesis and characterization ofthe complex metal dye material used in biology, study of the relation structure property by means of modern spectroscopics techniques of the complex metal dye material for genuine and synthetic leather. Avocations: music, old monuments, photography. Office: Univ Bucharest, Dumbrava Rosie St 23, Dist 2 Bucharest Romania

EMANUELSSON, HAKAN U., cardiologist, researcher; b. Kinna, Sweden, Feb. 28, 1947; s. Knut E. and Barbro A-B (Ekwall) E.; m. Anna-Karin E. Karlsson, Sept. 25, 1971; children: Ylva, Johan, Klara. MD, U. Goteborg, Sweden, 1972, PhD, 1983. Diplomate in medicine. Postdoctoral fellow County Hosp., Halmstad, Sweden, 1973-77; postdoctoral fellow Univ. Hosp., Goteborg, 1978-79, sr. cons., 1980-96, assoc. prof., 1983-96, dir. cardiology, 1991-96; staff Orebro (Sweden) Med. Ctr., 1997; vis. prof. Thorax Ctr., Rotterdam, Netherlands, 1992; cons. Swedish Bd. Health, 1995—. Contbr. articles to profl. jours.; rschr. in field. Mem. Swedish Soc. Cardiology (pres.-elect 1995-97). Christian. Home: Krokslatts Parkgata 60, S-43168 MÖlndal Sweden Office: Örebro Med Ctr Hosp, S-70185 Örebro Sweden

EMBABI, NABIL SAYED, geography educator, researcher; b. Tanta, Gharbiya, Egypt, Oct. 29, 1936; s. Sayed Embabi Abdel-Razekc; m. Faiza Mohamed Salem; children: Sherif, Doa'a. BA with honors, Ain Shams U., Cairo, Egypt, 1958, diploma, 1959; PhD, Bristol (Eng.) U., 1967. Lectr. Ain Shams U., Cairo, 1968-73, asst. prof., 1973-79, prof., 1983-88, 92—, head geography dept., 1983-88, 94-97; prof. Qatar U., Doha, 1979-83; prof. United Arab Emirates, Al-Ain, 1988-92, head field and tng. dept. Remote Sensing Ctr., 1989-92. Author: (with M.M. Ashour) Sand Dunes of Qatar Peninsula, Vol. 1, 1983, Vol. 2, 1985, (with A.A. Ali) The Depressions of Qatar Peninsula, 1990; chief editor: The Nat. Atlas of the United Arab Emirates, 1992; contbr. articles to profl. jours. Mem. Egyptian Geog. Soc., Inst. Egypt, N.Y. Acad. Scis. Home: 20 IBN Qotaiba St, 7th Dist, Cairo Nasr City Egypt Office: Ain Shams U Dept Geog, Faculty of Arts, Abbasiya Cairo, Egypt

EMBLETON, TOM WILLIAM, horticultural science educator; b. Guthrie, Okla., Jan. 3, 1918; s. Harry and Katherine (Smith) E.; m. Lorraine Marie Davidson, Jan. 22, 1943; children: Harry Raymond (dec.), Gary Thomas, Wayne Allen, Terry Scott, Paul Henry. BS, U. Ariz., 1941; PhD, Cornell U., 1949; Diploma de Honor al Ingeniero Agronomo, Coll. Engring. Agronomy, Santiago, Chile, 1991. Jr. sci. aide Bureau Plant Industry USDA, Indio, Calif., 1942, horticulturist Bureau Plant Industry, 1942, 1946; asst. horticulturist Wash. State Coll., Prosser, 1949-50; asst. horticulturist to prof. hort. sci. U. Calif., Riverside, 1950-86, prof. hort. sci. emeritus, 1987—; cons. in field, 1973—. Contbr. numerous articles to profl. jours. Scoutmaster, coun. committeeman, pack com. Riverside Boy Scouts of Am., 1952-74. Recipient Citrograph rsch. award Citrograph mag., 1965, Chancellor's Founders' award U. Calif., 1990, Salter award Calif. Citrus Contol Coun., 1999, Celebration of Citrus, Past, Present, and Future award U. Calif.-Riverside, 2000. Fellow AAAS, Am. Soc. Hort. Sci. (Wilson Popenoe award 1985, chmn. western region 1958-59); mem. Internat. Soc. Horticultural Sci., Internat. Soc. Citriculture (hon., exec. bd. 1984-96), Am. Soc. Agronomy (honor award 1993), Soil Sci. Soc. Am., Western Soc. Soil Sci., Calif. Avocado Soc. (life, honor award 1987), Coun. Soil Testing and Plant Analysis, Coun. Agrl. Sci. and Tech., Lemon Men's Club (Honor award 1987, life), U. Calif. Riverside Faculty Club (pres. 1958), Sigma Xi (pres. Riverside chpt. 1981-82), others. Achievements include research on use of leaf analysis as guide for citrus and avocado fertilization; on providing a means of substantially reducing nitrate pollution of ground-waters from citrus fertilization. Home: 796 Spruce St Riverside CA 92507-3039 Office: U Calif Dept Botany Plant Scis Riverside CA 92521-0001

EMBLIDGE, DAVID MURRAY, editor, writer; b. Buffalo, Sept. 27, 1945; s. Ralph Joseph and Jeane Anne (Johnston) E. BA, St. Lawrence U., 1967; MA in English, U. Va., 1968; PhD in Am. Studies, U. Minn., 1973. Prof., dir. am. studies Simon's Rock Early Coll., Great Barrington, Mass., 1973-79; dir. devel. Shakespeare & Co., Lenox, Mass., 1980; freelance writer Stockbridge, Mass., 1981-82; acquisitions editor Cambridge U. Press, N.Y.C., 1983-87; exec. editor Continuum Pub., N.Y.C., 1988; pub., co-owner Berkshire House Pubs., Stockbridge, Mass., 1989-92; dir., owner David Emblidge-Book Prodrs., Great Barrington, Mass., 1993—; cons. The Nature Conservancy, Arlington, Va., 1994, Mass. Found. for Humanities and Pub. Policy, 1982. Author: Hikes in Southern New England, 1998; co-author: Writer's Resource, 1997; editor: The Appalachian Trail Reader, 1996. Com. mem. Mass. Audubon-Berkshire Sanctuaries, Lenox, Mass., 1994—; bd. dirs. Berkshire County Hist. Soc., Pittsfield, Mass., 1993-96. Fellow Fulbright Commn., France, 1976-77, rsch. fellow NEH, Yale U., 1979. Mem. Am. Book Prodrs. Assn., Williams Club. Avocations: sailing, hiking, writing. E-mail: demblidge@aol.com. Office: David Emblidge Book Prodr PO Box 915 Great Barrington MA 01230-0915

EMBODY, DANIEL ROBERT, biometrician; b. Ithaca, N.Y., July 10, 1914; s. George Charles and Mary Madeline (Riceman) E.; m. Margaret Constance Gran, Mar. 21, 1946 (dec. Mar. 1961); children: James Michael, Daniel Robert, David Richard. BS, Cornell U., 1938, M.S., 1939, postgrad., 1939-42; postgrad., N.C. State Coll., summer 1940. Instr. limnology Cornell U., Ithaca, N.Y., 1940-42; sr. math. analyst Arnold Bernard & Co., N.Y.C., 1947-48; statistician Wash. Water Power Co., Spokane, 1949-53; head statistics sect. E.R. Squibb & Sons-Olin, New Brunswick, N.J., 1953-57, mgr. electronic data processing svc. ctr., 1958-63, coord. sci. computations, 1964-65; math. statistician Bur. Ships, Navy Dept., Washington, 1965-67; biometrician Dept. Agr., Beltsville, Md., 1967-72; staff biometrician animal and plant health inspection svc. Dept. Agr., Hyattsville, Md., 1972-87; sr. ptnr. EIC Assocs., Hyattsville, 1981—; cons. Idaho Fish and Game Dept., 1950-60, U.S. Geol. Survey, 1953-58, N.J. Dept. Fish and Game, 1953-60. Contbr. articles to profl. jours. Lt. comdr. USNR, 1942-46, ETO. Mem. IEEE, NRA, Am. Statis. Assn., Biometric Soc., Entomol. Soc. Am. (cert.; emeritus), N.Y. Acad. Scis., Assn. Computing Machinery, Am. Legion, Am. Fisheries Soc., Sigma Xi, Gamma Alpha. Home & Office: 7414 Jefferson St Hyattsville MD 20784-1758

EMBRECHTS, JEAN JACQUES, research engineer, educator; b. Namur, Wallonia, Belgium, Feb. 12, 1958. Degree in Civil Engring., U. Liege, Belgium, 1981; PhD in Applied Sci., U. Liege, 1987, Agrégé de L'Enseignement Supérieur, 1994. Rsch. asst. U. Liege, 1982-87, sr. rsch. asst., 1987-89, rsch. assoc., 1989-94, sr. rsch. assoc., 1994-99, prof., 1999—; Belgian del. Commn. Internat. Eclairage, 1994—; head of conf. U. Liege, 1993-99. Contbr. articles to profl. jours. Recipient Walsh-Weston bronze medal award Chartered Inst. Bldg. Svs. Eng., London, 1984, Prize du Comité Nat. Belge de l'Eclairage and Assn. Belge de l'Eclairage, Belgian Nat. Com. on Illumination, Brussels, 1989, Student Prize Assn. Engrs. Montefiore, Liege, 1981, Poster prize Lux Europa Congress, 1993. Mem. IEEE, Belgian Acoustical Soc., Audio Engring. Soc. Office: University of Liege, Sart-Tilman B28 Montefiore, B-4000 Liege 1, Belgium

EMBREE, ROBERT ARTHUR, retired psychologist, minister; b. Anselmo, Nebr., Sept. 11, 1927; s. Ernest N. and Elmina F. (Cantrell) E.; m. Valda J. Franz, Aug. 23, 1950; children: Marlowe C., Rodney C. BA, York (Nebr.) Coll., 1951; MDiv, United Theol. Sem., Dayton, Ohio, 1954; MA, U. Omaha, 1957; PhD, U. Denver, 1964. Ordained to ministry, United Meth. Ch.; emeritus diplomate Am. Bd. Sexology. Minister Evang. United Brethren Ch., Omaha, 1954-57, Presbyn. Ch., Waterloo, Nebr., 1957-58; instr. psychology Teikyo Westmar U. (formerly Westmar Coll.), LeMars, Iowa, 1958-93, prof. emeritus, 1993—; former bd. dirs. Found. for Sci. Study of Sex. Contbg. editor: The American Board of Sexology: An Outline of Sexology, 1993 (study guide); contbr. articles to books and profl. jours. Trustee, Westmar Coll. Endowment Trust, LeMars, 1990-96; charter bd. dirs. Plains Area Mental Health Ctr., LeMars. With U.S. Army, 1946. Fellow Soc. for Sci. Study of Religion; mem. APA, Soc. for Sci. Study of Sex (bd. rep. 1985-88, pres. Mid-continent region 1990-91), Am. Assn. of Sex Educators, Counselors and Therapists, Iowa Psychol. Assn. Achievements include development of personal beliefs scale. Avocations: genealogy, guitar and keyboard playing. Home: 926 3rd Ave SE Le Mars IA 51031-2650

EMBRY, RONALD LEE, physician, diagnostic radiologist; b. Louisville, May 19, 1947; s. Rodney Y. Sr. and Velma F. (Davis) E.; m. Cynthia Jane Chung Ai, Oct. 15, 1988. B of Gen. Studies, U. Ky., 1974, MS in Pharmacology, MD, 1978; MPA in Health Svcs., U. San Francisco, 1997. Diplomate Am. Bd. Radiology with subspecialty in vascular and interventional radiology. Intern in categorical diagnostic radiology Tripler Army Med. Ctr., 1978-79, resident in diagnostic radiology, 1979-82; diagnostic radiologist Hilo Radiologic Assocs., Ltd., 1985-90; diagnostic radiologist, dept. radiology Tripler Army Med. Ctr., Honolulu, 1990-91; primary interventionalist St. Mary's Med. Ctr., San Francisco, 1991—; assoc. clin. prof. diagnostic radiology U. Hawaii, Honolulu, 1985—; vol. clin. prof. Stanford U. Hosp., 1994-96. Contbr. articles to profl. jours. Instr.-trainer BCLS, Hawaii Heart Assn., Honolulu, 1979-84. Maj. U.S. Army, 1978-85. Mem. AMA, Honolulu County Med. Soc. (bd. govs. 1990-91), Am. Cancer Soc. (bd. dirs. Hawaii Pacific div. 1989-91), Hawaii Med. Assn. (chmn. com. legis. issues, mem. com. health econs., mem. com. med., moral, ethical, and legal issues), Hawaii Radiol. Soc. (sec./treas. 1991-92), Am. Coll. Radiology, Radiol. Soc. North Am., San Francisco Med. Soc., Calif. Med. Assn., San Francisco Radiol. Soc., Calif. Radiol. Soc., Phi Beta Kappa. Republican. Avocations: dog shows, golf, woodworking, stained glass, travel. Office: Dept Radiology 450 Stanyan St San Francisco CA 94117-1079

EMBRY, STEPHEN CRESTON, lawyer; b. Key West, Fla., Feb. 13, 1949; s. Jewell Creston and Julia Martine (Taylor) E.; m. Priscilla Mary Brown, Aug. 21, 1971; children: Nathaniel, Julia, Jessamyn. BA, Am. U., 1971; JD, U. Conn., 1976. Bar: Conn. 1976, U.S. Dist. Ct. Conn. 1976, U.S. Ct. Appeals (2d, 5th and 9th cirs.). Staff aide to Pres. The White House, Washington, 1969-72; assoc. Turner & Hensley, Great Bend, Kans., 1976, O'Brien, Shafner, Bartinik, & Stuart, Groton, Conn., 1976-85, Embry and Neusner, Groton, Conn., 1985—. Editor: Longshore and Harborworkers Textbook; mem. editl. bd. Matthew Bender, BRB Reporter; contbr. articles to profl. publs. Mem. Groton Rep. com., 1976-83, North Stonington Rep. com., 1984-88; chmn. Groton Housing Authority, 1979-80. Mem. ATLA (chair workers compensation sect. 1984-85, bd. dirs. workplace injury litigation group, sec. 1999-2000), Maritime Claimants Attys. Assn. (bd. dirs. 1980—), Conn. Trial Lawyers, Conn. Bar Assn. (exec. bd.), Thames Club, Grange. Democrat.

EMEK, SHARON HELENE, risk management consultant; b. Bklyn., Oct. 23, 1945; d. Hyman Sampson and Cynthia Gertrude (Roth) Rabinowitz; children: Aleeza Judith, Joshua Michael, Elana Yael. BA, CCNY, 1967; MA, Bklyn. Coll., 1970; EdD, Rutgers U., 1977. Cert. ins. counselor. Dir. preliminary program for small coll. Bklyn. Coll., 1969-71, 73-74; dir. Am. Ctr. Reading Skills, Tel Aviv, 1972; asst. prof. Brookdale C.C., Lincroft, N.J., 1975-77, Rutgers U., New Brunswick, N.J., 1977-82; pres. The Emek Group, Inc., N.Y.C., 1980-98, CEO Metro Ptnrs., Inc., N.Y.C., 1998—; spkr. profl. meetings. Author: Answers for Managers, 1986, Dealing Successfully with Key Management Issues, 1986; contbr. articles to profl. jours. Apptd. to Mayor's Small Bus. Adv. Bd., N.Y.C., 1998—; mem. Small Bus. Rsch. and Tech. Adv. Coun. IBM, 1998—; founding bd. dirs. Nat. Mus. Women's History, 1997—; bd. dirs. Family Bus. Coun. Greater N.Y., 1997-98; bd. dirs. econ. devel. com. sect. N.Y. Womens Agenda; bd. dirs. Inst. for Student Achievement, N.Y.C., 1999—, Women's Econ. Devel. Task Force, N.Y.C., 1999—. Recipient Promising Rsch. award Nat. Coun. Tchrs. English, 1978, Woman of Power and Influence award NOW, N.Y.C., 1999,. Mem. Profl. Ins. Agts. Assn., Nat. Assn. Women Bus. Owners (bd. dirs., pres. 1997-98, Mem. of Yr. 1997), Ind. Ins. Agts. Assn., Ins. Fedn. N.Y., Ins. Brokers Assn. N.Y., Coun. Ins. Brokers Greater N.Y., Nat. Assn. Ins. Women (Helen Garvin Outstanding Achiever in Ins. Industry award 1999), Assn. Profl. Ins. Women, Women's Pres. Orgn., Women, Inc., Women's Leadership Forum, Emily's Life (majority coun.), Coun. Ins. Brokers Greater N.Y. Avocations: writing, reading, jogging, tennis, travel. Office: MetroPartners Inc Wall St Plz Fl 20 New York NY 10005

EMELCHENKO, GENNADI ANATOL'EVICH, physicist, researcher; b. Orenburg Dist., USSR, Jan. 2, 1947; s. Anatolli Vasil'evich Antonov and Eudokia Ivanovna Emelchenko; m. Larisa Petrovna Kotomina, July 11, 1969; children: Alexander, Vladimir. Diploma in physics, Ural Poly. Inst., Swerdlowsk, USSR, 1971; PhD, Russian Acad. Sci., Moscow, 1974; DSc, Russian Acad. Sci., Chernogolovka, 1992; D (hon.), Ural Tech. U., Ekaterinburg, 1999. Jr. rsch. assoc. Inst. Solid State Physics Russian Acad. Sci., Chernogolovka, 1975-80; sr. rsch. assoc. Inst. Solid State Physics Rissian Acad. Sci., Chernogolovka, 1980-92; head lab. Inst. Solid State Physics Russian Acad. Sci., Chernogolovka, 1992—. Grantee Internat. Sci. Found., 1995, Am. Phys. Soc., 1995, INTAS, 1997-00. Fax: (096) 576-4111. Office: Inst Solid State Physics, Institue prosp. 15, 142432 Chernogolovka Russia

EMELY, MARY ANN, association executive; b. Bridgeport, Conn., Aug. 10, 1947; d. John and Stefanie Maria (Hutta) Horvath; m. Timothy Vellrath, Sept. 7, 1968 (div. Mar. 1975); 1 child, Wendy Amethyst Vellrath Delbrook; m. Charles H. Emely, Sept. 1, 1979. BA, U. Conn., 1969; postgrad., U. Bridgeport, 1975-76, Ohio U., 1982-83. Adminstrv. asst. ARC, Bridgeport, 1973-78; dir. mem. svcs. Comprehensive Assn. Cons., Ft. Washington, Pa., 1978-81; exec. dir. Muskingum County Respiratory Disease, Zanesville, Ohio, 1981-83; assoc. exec. dir. The Vol. Ctr., Syracuse, N.Y., 1984-86; dir. mem. programs NEA, Rockville, Md., 1986-91; dir. mem., mktg. Am. Geophys. Union, Washington, 1991-93; sr. dir. membership Coun. for Exceptional Children, Reston, Va., 1993-94; dep. exec. dir. Spl. Librs. Assn., Washington, 1994-95; exec. dir. Fedn. Govt. Info. Processing Couns., Fairfax, Va., 1995-99; mng. dir. Nat. Assn. Profl. Employer Orgns., Alexandria, Va., 2000—; cons. Comprehensive Assn. Cons., Garrisonville, Va., 1991—; mng. dir. Nat. Assn. Profl. Employer Orgns., 2000—. Editor Husky P.A.W. Print, 1995-96, Fedn. Facts, 1995-99; columnist Female Exec., 1994-95. Bd. dirs. Pub. Employees Roundtable, Washington, 1995-99; mem. Nat. Rep. Coalition for Choice, Washington, 1993—, Jr. League of Washington, 1986—. Mem. NAFE, Am. Soc. Assn. Execs. (cert., mentor diversity programs 1994-95), Am. Radio Relay League, Greater Washington Soc. Assn. Execs., Found. for Internat. Meetings, Mercedes Benz Club of Am., U. Conn. Alumni Assn. (Washington chpt., pres. 1996-99), Kappa Alpha Theta. Methodist. Avocations: gardening, flower arranging, reading, travel. Home: PO Box 96 Garrisonville VA 22463-0096 Office: 901 N Pitt St Ste 150 Alexandria VA 22314

EMELYANOV, ALEXANDER ALEXANDROVITCH, physicist, researcher; b. Lipetsk, USSR, July 2, 1948; s. Alexander Fedorovitch and Klavdiya Petrovna (Tikhonova) E.; m. Nina Pavlovna Belova, Jan. 21, 1983; children: Ekaterina, Konstantin. Physicist, State U., Tomsk, USSR, 1971; PhD, Poly. Inst., Tomsk, 1979; postgrad., Power Inst., Alma-Ata, USSR, 1986; DSc, Power Sci. Rsch. Inst. of Kazakhstan, 1998. Sr. rsch. assoc. High Voltage Rsch. Inst., Tomsk, 1974-80; dean Engring. Faculty, asst. prof. Power Inst., Alma-Ata, 1980-87; head dept. Kazakh Nat. Tech. U., Ust-Kamenogorsk, Kazakhstan, 1987-96, sr. rsch. asst., 1996-98; dir. East Kazakhstan br. Inst. Power Engring. and Telecomm., Almaty, 1997-98; head dept. East Kazakhstan Tech. U., 1998—. Author: Pulsed Electrical Conditioning Electrodes in Vacuum, 1999; contbr. articles to profl. jours.; author procs. Avocations: volleyball, chess, swimming, skiing, Russian baths. Home: Ul Lugovaya 29 Apt 31, 492010 Ust-Kamenogorsk Kazakhstan Office: East Kazakhstan Tech U, Ul Lugovaya 19, 406286 Ust-Kamenogorsk Kazakhstan

EMELYANOV, VIKTOR VLADIMIROVICH, information science educator; b. Leningrad, Russia, Jan. 27, 1949; s. Vladimir Ivanovich and Klavdiya Ivanovna (Chernova) E.; m. Irina Dmitrievna Kossakovskaya, Jan. 18, 1974 (dec. Sept. 1990); children: Marina, Tatiyana; m. Mazina Klavdievna Ksenofontova, Mar. 11, 1998; 1 child, Vera. Phd, Bauman Moscow State Tech. U., 1981, DSc, 1995. Lic. engr. Engr. Inst. Machine Bldg. Problems, Moscow, 1973-80, head lab., 1980-88; asst. prof. Bauman Moscow State Tech. U., 1988-96, prof., 1996—; dir. Youngest Rscht. Ctr., Moscow, 1997—. Author: Management in Flexible Manufacturing Systems, 1990, Introduction to Intelligent Simulation: The RAO Language, 1998, Online Control of the Material Cutting on the Sawmill, 1999; mem. editl. bd. Jour. Softwre and Systems. Grantee Russian Found. Basic Rsch., 1996-98, 99—; recipient hon. award Russian Acad. Scis., 1997—. Mem. Russian Assoc. Artificial Intelligence (coun. mem.). Avocations: submarine sport, theatre, music. Home: Ap 421 Bl 4 H 59, St Festivalnaya, 125502 Moscow Russi Office: Bauman Moscow State Tech U, N 5 St 2nd Baumanskaya, 102005 Moscow Russia

EMERIT, INGRID META, research director; b. Mainz, Germany, Apr. 22, 1931; d. Karl and Meta (Paulus) Kleinkauf; divorced; children: Astrid, Marc, Beatrice, Sibylle. MD, U. Heidelberg, Germany, 1956; spl. pediats., Univ. Hosp., Heidelberg, 1961. Asst. pediat. clinic U. Heidelberg, 1956-61; tng. pediat. cardiology Paris, 1961-62; attachee de recherches Nat. Ctr. Sci. Rsch., Paris, 1963, chargée de recherches, 1966, dir. rsch., 1972—; vis. prof. Columbia U., Vancouver, Can., 1986-87; head of dept. U. Paris VI, 1972—; cons. WHO, 1993, 94; mem. organizing com. Gordon Conf., Santa Barbara, Calif., 1986. Editor, author: Antioxidants in Therapy and Disease Prevention, 1990; co-editor: (with Britton Chance) Free Radicals and Aging, 1992. Pres. SOS Chernobyl Assn., Paris, 1991—. Mem. Soc. for Free Radical Rsch. (pres. 1991-92), Soc. Française de Recherches sur les Radicaux Libres, Ukranian Assn. Physicians of Chernobyl. Avocations: music, art, travel, tennis, gardening. Home: 132 rue Leon Maurice Nordmann, 75013 Paris France Office: U Paris VI Inst Biomedical, 15 rue de l'Ecole de Med, 75006 Paris France

EMERSON, CHERRY LOGAN, retired chemist; b. Charlotte, N.C., Sept. 30, 1916; s. Cherry Logan and Sina Harris (White) E.; m. Mary Kimball Lewis, Sept. 12, 1942; children: Mary, Katharine, Laura, William, Warren, Edwin. AB, MA, Emory U., 1939; MS, MIT, 1941; DSc (hon.), Emory U., 1994. Registered profl. engr., Mass., Ga. Chemist Monsanto Chem. Co., 1940-47; founder, CEO Emerson & Cuming, Inc., Canton, Mass., 1947-78; CEO Emerson & Cuming, Inc. div. W.R. Grace & Co., 1978-80; ret., 1980; mem. adv. bd. Liberty Mut. Ins. Co., Boston, 1959-79; mem. rsch. review com. Shepherd Spinal Ctr.; established seminar series presented nationally and internationally. Patentee in field. Mem. vis. com. Music and Theater Arts MIT; supporter Friends of Music at Emory; founder Emerson Ctr. Computational Sci. at Emory. Fellow Am. Inst. Chemists; mem. NSPE, AIChE, Am. Chem. Soc. Republican. Mem. United Ch. of Christ. Achievements include development of equipment for processing human blood, a picker stick for textile looms, an adhesive system for shoes, the air roasting system for edible nuts, a flooring material for anechoic chambers. Avocations: wood working, golfing, reading, music. Office: CL Emerson PO Box 53127 Atlanta GA 30355-1127

EMERSON, DIANE MARIE, marketing executive; b. Superior, Wis., Oct. 6, 1953; d. Robert Leroy and Imogene Augusta (Sayers) E. BS, U. Minn., 1981, MBA, 1983. Dir. The Kingman Cons. Group, St. Paul, 1983-84; mgr. corp. mktg. rsch. H.B. Fuller Co., St. Paul, 1984-88, mgr. corp. market devel., 1989-92, dir. mktg., 1992-94; project mgr. customer mgmt. sys., 1994-96; principal cons. Philadelphia Consulting Group, Auckland, New Zealand, 1998; pres. Diane EmersonConsulting, 1999—. Mem. planning group Minn. Women's Press, St. Paul, 1984-87; mem. adv. bd., 1987-96; mem. planning adv. com. Como Conservatory, 1985-96, cons., mem. fundraising steering com., 1986; chmn. landscaping task force Hubert Humphrey Job Corps, St. Paul, 1986-88. Mem. planning adv. com. Como Conservatory, 1985-89, Como cons., fundraising steering com. 1986; chair person landscaping task force Hubert Humphrey Job Corps, St. Paul, 1986-88. Mem. Minn. Hort. Soc. (bd. dirs. 1985-92, 2d v.p. 1987, pres.-elect 1988, pres. 1989-90), World Future Soc., Auckland C. of C., New Zealand Women in Mgmt. Network (exec. com. 1999—). Mem. Dem. Farm Labor Party. Avocations: landscaping, photography, world travel. E-mail: diane emerson@hotmail.com.

EMERSON, H. GARFIELD, investment banker, lawyer; b. Leamington, Ont., Can., Jan. 20, 1941; s. Donald Garfield and Eleanor Irene (Morris) E.; m. Melissa Jane, May 30, 1964; children: Melissa Ann, Taylor Garfield. BA in history with hons., U. Toronto, 1963, LLB, 1966. Apptd. Queen's Coun., 1980; bar: Can. Ptnr. Davies, Ward & Beck, Toronto, 1970-90; pres., CEO N.M. Rothschild & Sons, Can., Toronto, 1990—; chmn. Rogers Comms., Inc., Toronto, 1993—; dir. CAE, Inc., Toronto, Can. Deposit Ins. Corp., Ottawa, N.M. Rothschild Corp. Fin., London, Rogers Cantel, Toronto, Rothschild N.Am. Inc., N.Y. Editor: Canadian Corporation Precedents, 1970-90, Canadian Securities Law Precedents, 1985-90. Mem. bus. bd., pres. investment com. U. Toronto, 1995—; chmn. Victoria U. Campaign, 1996—. Mem. York Club, Can. Club (bd. dirs. 1998—), Toronto Club, Nat. Club (bd. dirs. 1991-93), Can. Pyschiat. Found. (bd. dirs. 1993-97), Can. Coun. of Christians and Jews (bd. dirs. 1993—), Sigma Chi (Significant Sig award 1996). Avocations: golf, tennis, skiing. Office: NM Rothschild & Sons Can, Box 77/1 First Canadian Pl, Toronto, ON Canada

EMERSON, PETER ALBERT, physician, consultant; b. London, Feb. 7, 1923; s. Albert Richard and Gwendoline Doris (Davy) E.; m. Ceris Hood Price, Nov. 22, 1947; 2 children. BA in Natural Sci., U. Cambridge (Eng.), 1944, MA in Natural Sci., 1949; MBBChir, St. Georges Med. Sch., London, 1946; MD, U. London, 1952. Med. registrar St. George's Hosp., London, 1952-55; chief asst. Royal Brompton Hosp., London, 1955-58; asst. prof. medicine SUNY, Brooklyn, 1958-59; cons. physician Westminster Hosp., London, 1959-88; clin. cons. Chelsea and Westminster Hosp., 1988—; dean Westminster Med. Sch. U. London, 1981-84; civilian cons. Royal Navy, Eng., 1970-89; mem., rep. UK splsts. Coun. Union European Med. Splsts. Editor, co-author: (textbook) Thoracic Medicine, 1981; contbr. articles to profl. jours., chpts. to books. Trustee Westminster Med. Sch. Rsch. Trust, Garfield Weston Trust Rsch. into Cardiac Surgery, Virgin Healthcare Trust. Squadron leader med. br. Royal Air Force, 1947-52. Fellow Royal Coll. Physicians (examiner 1964-85, v.p. 1985-86, chief examiner 1985-86), ACP (hon.); mem. Brit. Thoracic Soc., Am. Informatics Assn., Assn. Physicians. Avocation: tennis. Home: 3 Halkin St, SW1X 7DJ London SW1X 7DJ, England Office: Chelsea & Westminster Hosp, Dept Info Sys 396 Fulham Rd, SW1O 9NH London England

EMERSON, SUSAN, oil company executive; b. Bryan, Tex., Nov. 2, 1947; d. Joseph Nathanial and Lorraine Parks; m. John S. Emerson, June 5, 1970 (div. 1984); children: John H., Christopher P.; m. Gerald W. Parker, May 4, 1985. Owner Emerson Ins. Agy., San Antonio, 1970-84, Emerson Oil Co., San Antonio, 1970—; bd. dirs. Washington Hosp. Ctr. Mem. Washington Hosp. Ctr. Women's Aux., 1988—; mem. D.C. Rep. Com., 1991—, alt. del. Rep. Nat. Conv., Washington, 1992, 4th ward committeewoman, 1992; commr. Adv. Neighborhood Commn., Washington, 1990—; 2d v.p. 4D Commn., Washington, 1990—; founder Boarder Baby Project, 1991—; Rep. candidate for D.C. del. to Congress, 1992; vice chmn. Cheshire County Rep. Com., Cheshire County Rep. Womens Club; chmn. Rindge Rep. Com.; Justice of the Peace, Notary Pub. Recipient Sr. Adv. Silver Fox award Wash. Hosp. Women's Aux., 1989, Vol. award, 1990. Mem. LWV, DAR, D.C. Hosp. Assn. (trustee 1989), Am. Hosp. Assn. (D.C. del. 1990-92), Vis. Nurses Assn. (bioethic com. 1991—), Rindge Hist. Soc. (life), Tex. Breakfast Club, Rindge Womens Club, Rindge Garden Club. Lutheran. Avocations: travel, gourmet cooking, gardening, needlepoint. Home: 571 Route 119 Rindge NH 03461-3704

EMERY, FRANK EUGENE, publishing executive; b. Wichita, Kans., May 14, 1934; s. Frank A.C. and Nellie Mae (Bloss) E.; m. Sara Manette Marble, Nov. 3, 1956 (div. 1983); children: Frank, Mark W., Timothy T., Todd A.; m. Sandra Kay Adamson, June 28, 1988. BA, U. Kans., 1955, MD, 1959. Diplomate Am. Bd. Orthopedic Surgery, Nat. Bd. Med. Ex-

aminers. Intern U. Kans. Med. Ctr., Kansas City, 1959-60, resident radiology, 1960-61, resident gen. surgery, 1961-62; resident orthopedic surgery U. Tex. Med. Br., Galveston, 1968; fellow Orthopedic Rsch. and Edn. Found. U. Edinburgh, Scotland, 1968; pvt. practice specializing in orthopedic surgery Springfield, Mo., 1969-73; asst. prof. surgery, orthopedics U. Tex. Med. Br., Galveston, 1973-77, assoc. prof. surgery, orthopedics, 1977-78, dir. Arthritis Minimal Care Unit, 1975-76; pub. Ft. Scott (Kans.) Tribune, 1980—; pres. Tribune Monitor Co., Ft. Scott, 1982—; bd. dirs. Tribune Monitor Co., Ft. Scott, Gateway Comm., Wichita; gen. ptnr. Hotel Ptnrs., I, II, III, IV, Wichita. Contbr. articles to med. publs. V.p. Mo. and Ark. River Basins Assn., 1984-86; co-chmn. Gov.'s Task Force Pub. Sector Funding, Kans., Main St. Program, Topeka, 1985-86; chmn. basin adv. com. Kans. Water Authority, Topeka, 1986-90; bd. dirs. Kans. C. of C. and Industry, Topeka, 1990-91; councilman S.E. Kans. Econ. Alliance, 1998—. Lt. comdr., surgeon USPHS, 1991-93. Pediatric psychiatry fellow NIH, 1957; fellow United Cerebral Palsy Found., 1967-68. Fellow Am. Acad. Orthopedic Surgeons; mem. Kans. Press Assn., Inland Press Assn., Am. Soc. for Surgery of the Hand, Sigma Xi, Nu Sigma Nu, Delta Upsilon. Avocations: boating, swimming, hiking, mountain climbing. Home: 4559 E Creeksbend Ln Springfield MO 65809-3395 Office: Fort Scott Tribune 6 E Wall St Fort Scott KS 66701-1423

EMERY, HENRY ALFRED, engineer; b. Northfield, N.H., Feb. 9, 1926; s. Henry A. and Ruth (Trask) E.; children: Trask, Timothy, Ptarmigan. BA, U. Maine, 1950; Petroleum Engr., Colo. Sch. Mines, 1956; MBA, U. Denver, 1966. Registered profl. engr., Colo. With Mobil Pipeline Co., 1950-53, Portland Montreal Pipeline Co., 1956-59; maintenance design engr., planning supr., engring. supt., project mgr. Pub. Svc. Co., Colo., 1959-72; pres. Computer Graphics Co., Denver, 1972-78; divsn. mgr. Kellogg Corp., Littleton, Colo., 1978-82; chmn., CEO Emery DataGraphic Inc., Englewood, Colo., 1982-86; pres. Emery DataGraphic divsn. Harris-McBurney Co., 1987-93, Emery & Assoc., Inc., Greenwood Village, 1993—. Mem. Automated Mapping/Facilities Mgmt. Internat., Urban Regional Info. Sys. Assn., Am. Water Works Assn., Tau Beta Pi. Democrat. Home and Office: 7462 E Princeton Ave Denver CO 80237-2300

EMHARDT, CHARLES DAVID, lawyer; b. Indpls., Feb. 13, 1931; s. John William and Martha Jack (Macdougall) E.; m. Ann Devaney, Nov. 12, 1954; children—John D., Carol A., Frederick D., Martha A., Lucy E. B.S. in Engring. Mechanics, Purdue U., 1952, A.S. in Elec. Engring. Tech., 1966; LL.B., Harvard U., 1955. Bar: D.C. 1955, Ind. 1958, U.S. Patent Office 1955. Patent atty. Western Electric Co., Washington, Balt., 1955-57; assoc. Harold B. Hood, Indpls., 1957-59, Lockwood, Woodard, Smith & Weikart, Indpls., 1959-64; ptnr. Woodard, Emhardt, Naughton, Moriarty & McNett and previous firm Woodard, Weikart, Emhardt & Naughton, Indpls., 1964—. Republican precinct committeeman, 1965-70. Served with Army NG, 1955-66. Mem. ABA, Ind. State Bar Assn. (chmn. pat. sect. 1967-68), Indpls. Bar Assn. (bd. 1979-81, chmn. ethics com. 1982-83). Presbyterian. Clubs: Woodstock, Indpls. Athletic, Masons, Shriners. Home: 4801 Fauna Ln Indianapolis IN 46234-9531 Office: Woodard Emhardt Naughton Moriarty & McNett 3700 Bank One Ctr 111 Monument Cir Indianapolis IN 46204-5100

EMI, TOSHIHIKO, materials engineering educator, consultant; b. Nishinomiya, Japan, Feb. 23, 1935; s. Yoshio and Jyuko (Tsumura) E. B in Engring., Osaka (Japan) U., 1958; DSc, Hokkaido U., Sapporo, Japan, 1967; hon. prof., U. Sci. and Tech., Beijing, 1994. Rschr., steelmaking lab., Iron & Steel Rsch. Labs. Kawasaki Steel Corp., Chiba, Japan, 1958-80, gen. mgr., dept. process metallurgy rsch. divsn. tech. rsch., 1980-85, dep. dir., tech. rsch. divsn., 1985-89; pres. Rheotecnology Ltd., Tokyo, 1989-93; bd. mem. Kawasaki Steel Corp., Tokyo, 1989-92; prof., head Base Metal Rsch. Sta. Tohoku U. Inst. Advanced Materials Processing, Sendai, Japan, 1993-98; Jernkontoret prof. dept. metallurgy Royal Inst. Tech., Sweden, 1998-99; bd. dirs. Japan Inst. Metals Sendai, Japan; adj. prof. CISR, MSE-Dept. Carnegie Mellon U., Pitts., 2000—; Miegunyah disting. vis. prof. U. Melbourne, 1999. Editor (jour.) Materials Transactions, Japan Inst. Metals, 1994-96; assoc. editor (jour.) Steel Rsch., Verein Deutscher Eisenhüttenleute, Düsseldorf, Germany, 1988—; internat. patentee in field (Tawara award 1981, Disting. Invention, 1981, Ichimura prize, 1985. Named Howe Meml. lectr., Iron and Steel Soc.-AIME, Warrendale, Ohio, 1989; recipient Tawara award 1981, Treatise award, 1983, Tanigawa-Harris prize Japan Inst. Metals, 1990. Mem. Japan Inst. Metals, Iron & Steel Soc.-AIME (disting. mem., J. Chipman award 1999), Engring. Acad. Japan, Iron & Steel Inst. Japan (bd. dirs., Nishiyama prize 1985, Sci. Achievement Meritorious prize 1997), Verein Deutscher Eisenhüttenleute (Germany). Avocations: classical music, painting, skiing, scuba diving. Home: Oomaki 1149-163, Urawa-shi Saitama 336-0922, Japan Office: Emu Tech, Omoaki 1449-163 Urawa-Shi, Saitoma 336-0922, Japan

EMIG, CHRISTIAN CHARLES, biologist, researcher; b. Colmar, Alsace, France, Dec. 10, 1941; s. Charles and Cornélie (Wohlhüter) E.; m. Anne Bouisson, Sept. 5, 1965; 3 children. D Oceanography, U. Marseille, France, 1965, DS, 1972. Monitor in microbiology and zoology U. Marseille, 1962-64; rschr. Ctr. Nat. Rsch. Sci., Marseille, 1965-85, assoc. dir., 1978-82, program dir., 1983-88, rschr. dir., 1985-2000; rsch. prof. U. Madrid, 1990; head oceanographic cruises, 1975-90; cons. in field. Author 13 books; editor 9 books; contbr. over 200 articles to profl. jours.; editor sci. film on oceanographic methods, 1987. Race judge French Sail Fedn., 1995—. Mem. Inst. des Hautes-Etudes de la Def. Nat., 1985; pres. Sail Club Nautique Provencal de la Recherche Sci., Marseille, 1970-77. Calvinist. Avocations: sailing, swimming, travel. Home: 20 Rue Chaix, 13007 Marseille France Office: Ctr Oceanology, Rue de Batterie-des-Lions, 13007 Marseille France

EMILSEN, WILLIAM WAYNE, church historian, minister; b. Leeton, NSW, Australia, Oct. 7, 1948; s. Ronald Malcolm Nunn-Pattrick and Laurel Edna (Campbell) Lesniak; m. Susan Elizabeth Grinsell, May 4, 1974; children: Elizabeth, Adrian. BSc with honors, U. NSW, 1971; BD with honors, U. Sydney, Australia, 1981, MA, 1986, PhD, 1993. Ordained to ministry Uniting Ch. in Australia, 1980. Chaplain U. Sydney, 1978-82; min. Uniting Ch. Synod, Sydney, 1983—; ch. historian United Theol. Coll., North Parramatta, Australia, 1993—; mem. Anglican/Uniting Ch. Dialogue, 1994-96. Author: Winter Harvest, 1987, Violence and Atonement, 1994; editor: Remodelling God, 1982, The India of My Dreams, 1995, Cannibal Jack. The New Zealand Journal of William Diaper 1846-1847, 1996, The Goldfields Journal of William Diaper, 1999, Mapping the Landscape: Essays in Australian and New Zealand Christianity, 2000; editor Uniting Ch. Studies, 1994—. Avocations: swimming, bush walking. Office: United Theol Coll, 16 Masons Dr, North Parramatta NSW 2151, Australia

EMLEN, JOHN M., ecologist; b. Sacramento, Jan. 15, 1938; s. John T. and Virginia M. Emlen; m. Ellen K. Pikitch, Dec. 17, 1978 (div. 1995); 1 chld, Scott M.; m. Ursula K. Faust, June 16, 1996. BA, U. Wis., 1961; PhD in Zoology/Ecology, U. Wash., 1966. Asst. prof. U. Colo., Boulder, 1966-68, SUNY, Stony Brook, 1968-71; assoc. prof. Ind. U., Bloomington, 1971-83; sr. scientist U.S. EPA, Corvallis, Oreg., 1984-87; rsch. ecologist USFWS, Nat. Biol. Svcs., U.S. Geol. Survey, Seattle, 1987—. Author: Ecology: An Evolutionary Approach, 1963, Population Biology, 1974; contbr. numerous articles to profl. jours. Trustee Environ. Def. Fund, Stony Brook, 1969-72. Mem. Ecol. Soc. Am. Avocations: writing ficiton, piano, hiking, bird watching. E0mail: john emlen@usgs.gov. Office: USGS Biol Resources 6505 NE 65th St Seattle WA 98115-5016

EMMANOUEL, ANDREW JOHN, barrister; b. Athens, May 25, 1943; s. John Andrew and Adamantia Apostolos (Spanoudi) E.; Evangelia Aristogiton Voulgaraki, Nov. 14, 1973 (div.); children: Maranda, Joanna, Ava; m. Kathrine George Timi, May 5, 1988. B of Law, Nat. U., 1966, B of Polit. Sci., 1976, B of Econs., 1976; PhD, Pacific North Western U., 1979. Barrister Bar Assn., Piraeus, Greece, 1968—; dir. legal dept. Victoria Ins. Co. S.A., Athens, 1970-84, Merchant Marine Vesta, Piraeus, 1979-81; legal advisor SGS Hellas SA, Athens, 1984-87, Hellenic Astronautical Soc., Athens, 1985-98, Internat. Assn. Cosmos and Philosophy, Athens, 1989—; asst. prof. law Faculty Nat. U., Athens, 1969-75; prof. philosophy of law Parsel Inst., Chgo., 1989-99; co-proprietor Transsci. Rev.; pres. Emmanuel Environ. Rsch. Inst., Chgo., 1997. Author/editor: The Indefinitesnees of Inheritance Affidavit, 1975, The Philosophy of Social and Labour Laws, 1979, Space Policy, 1986; contbr. articles to profl. jours. Ensign Greece Navy, 1966-68. Mem. Hellenic Astro. Soc. (v.p. 1986-98), Assn. of Sci. Problematism (pres. 1989—), Internat. Assn. Cosmos and Philosophy (bd. dirs.), Assn. Aristotelian Studies (bd. dirs. 1994-98), Bar Assn. of Piraeus, The Planetary Soc., Bulgarian Astro. Soc. (hon. mem.), Acad. Humanities (elected corr. mem. 1996), Greek Karate Fedn. (pres. judiciary com. 1992). Social-Democrat. Avocations: classic music, playing piano, painting, fishing. Home: Pindaros Str 17, 18010 Kipseli Village Greece Office: Law Firm A J Emmanuouel, 56 Alexandras Ave, 11473 Athens Greece

EMMANUEL, ARGHIRI, educational consultant; b. Patras, Greece, June 22, 1911; s. Charalambos and Katina (Menounou) E.; m. Nicole Bingen, Jan. 27, 1961 (dec. Jan. 1990); 1 child, Catherine. MA in Econs., Comml. Scis, U. Athens, 1932; postgrad., Faculté de Droit, U. Athens, 1932-34; postgrad. in art history, Ecole du Louvre, Paris, 1957-60; PhD, Sorbonne, Paris, 1968. Chief exec. officer Castado-Vimaco Ltd., Bunia, Zaire, 1937-42, Comituri Ltd. (merger Castado-Vimaco Ltd.), Bunia, 1946-56; ret., 1981; supr. students' theses French univs., 1981—; dir. studies econ. dept. Paris VII U., 1969-71; dir. studies in option no. 8 internat. econ. relations Inst. Econ. & Social Studies, IEDES, Paris I U., 1971-81. Author: L'Echange Inégal, 1969, 2nd edit., 1972, 3rd edit., 1975, 4th edit., 1978, Le Profit et les Crises, 1975, Salari, Sottosviluppo, Imperialismo, 1973, Technologie Appropriée ou Technologie Sous-Developpée, 1981, La Dynamique des Inégalités, 1985; co-author: Les Problémes de la Planification Socialiste, 1968, Um Proletariado Explorador, 1971, Interrogations Récentes sur la Théorie du Commerce International, 1974, Marxismo e Democrazia Nei Paesi della Europa Occidentale, 1978, Le Nouvel Ordre Intérieur, 1980, Introduction to the Sociology of Developing Societies, 1982; contbr. articles to profl. jours. Vol. Greek Liberation Forces, Middle East, 1942-45. Home: 53 Rue de l' Amiral Mouchez, 75013 Paris France

EMMANUEL, BOSCO, chemistry researcher; b. Tirunelveli, Tamil Nadu, India, Sept. 24, 1954; s. Emmanuel and Theresa (Perez) Rodriguez; m. Alice Fernandez, 1987; children: Infant Gabriel, Marie Gerard Marcian. BSc, Scott Christian Coll., Nagercoil, India, 1975; MSc, Madurai (India) U., 1977; PhD, Indian Inst. Sci., Bangalore, 1982. Postdoctoral fellow Indian Inst. Sci., Bangalore, India, 1983, Carleton U., Ottawa, Can., 1984-85; assoc. rschr. State U., Utrecht, The Netherlands, 1986; CSIR fellow Regional Rsch. Lab., Trivandrum, India, 1987-90; vis. scientist Inst. Math. Scis., Madras, India, 1990-91; scientist Ctrl. Electrochem. Rsch. Inst., Karaikudi, India, 1991—. Contbr. articles to Jour. Chem. Physics, Jour. Electroanalytical Chemistry, Phys. Rev. E. Grantee Dept. Sci. and Tech., Govt. of India, 1996, Oil and Natural Gas Commn., Govt. of India, 1995. Fellow Soc. for Advancement Electrochem. Sci. and Tech. Roman Catholic. Home and Office: Ctrl Electrochem Rsch Inst, Rsch Dept, Tamil-Na Karaikudi 630 006, India

EMMANUEL-REBUFFAT, DENISE SOLANGE PAULINE, archaeologist, educator; b. Paris; d. Georges and Ida (Deheurles) Emmanuel; m. René Rebuffat. Lic. and maîtrise, Sorbonne, Paris, 1954; agrégation Lettres, Sorbonne, 1955, D. Lettres, 1971. Maître confs. Faculté des Lettres, Rabat, Morocco, 1961-63, Aix-en-Provence, France, 1963-67; prof. U. Nantes, France, 1967-79, U. Paris X, 1979—. Author: Miroir Étrusque, 1973, Corpus Speculorum, Louvre, Corpus Speculorum France, Provinces, 1988, 91, Monuments Académie, Mon. Corsica, 1976, 80. Recipient prize Acad. Inscriptions Belles-Lettres, 1986, 98. Mem. Soc. Etudes Latines, Soc. French Archaeology, Soc. Nat. Antiquaries, Com. Internat. Corpus Speculorum Italy, Inst. Studies Etruscan and Italian. Office: Univ Paris X, 200 Av de la République, 92001 Nanterre France

EMME, STEFAN PETER, dermatologist; b. Kaufbeuren, Bavaria, Germany, June 5, 1962; s. Wolfgang Heinrich and Martha Katharina (v. Abele) E.; m. Elisabeth Maria Eva Vass zu Bihar, Sept. 2000. MBBCh, Technische U., Munich, 1991, MD, 1992. Intern Dermatologische Klinik und Poliklinik Technischen, U. Munich, 1991-93, resident dermatology, 1993-97; pvt. practice Erding, Germany, 1998—; cons. dermatologist, allergologist, 1997—. Author: Intramuscular injections, 1995. Mem. Corps Curonia, Munich, 1985, Rotaract Club, Munich, 1987-91. Decorated Mil. and Hospitaler Order St. Lazarus of Jerusalem, Sovereign Mil. Order of Malta, knight of Mayishal Grace. Avocation: golf. Home: Lange Zeile 15 a, 85435 Erding Germany

EMMELUTH, BRUCE PALMER, investment company executive, venture capitalist; b. L.A., Nov. 30, 1940; s. William J. and Elizabeth L. (Palmer) E.; children: William J. II (dec.), Bruce Palmer Jr., Carrie E.; m. Canda E. Samuels, Mar. 29, 1987. Sr. investment analyst corp. fin. dept. Prudential Ins. Co. Am., L.A., 1965-70; with Seidler Amdec Securities, Inc., 1970-90, sr. v.p., mgr. corp. fin. dept., 1974-90, also bd. dirs.; ptnr. VK Ventures, VK Capital, 1982-2000; exec. vice pres., mng. dir. corp. fin., mgr. corp. fin. dept., mem. exec. com., mem. mgmt. com. First Securities Van Kasper, L.A., 1990—, also bd. dirs.; ptnr. VK Ventures, VK Capital, L.A., 1992-2000; pres., bd. dirs. SAS Capital Corp., venture capital subs. Seidler Amdec Securities, 1977-90, First Security Van Kasper; bd. advisors Entreprenurial Studies Program, Anderson Grad. Sch. Mgmt. UCLA, 1985—, past. bd. dirs. Active Calvary Ch., Pacific Palisades, Calif. With U.S. Army N.G., 1965-71. Home: 2038 Palisades Dr Pacific Palisades CA 90272-1921 Office: First Securities Van Kasper 10877 Wilshire Blvd Ste 1700 Los Angeles CA 90024-4372

EMMERICH, KLAUS RUDOLF, journalist; b. Frankfurt, Germany, June 6, 1928; s. Albert Emmerich and Hilde (Kübel) E.; m. Irmgard Haber, 1953; children: Wolfgang E., Beatrice C. Student, U. Bonn, Fed. Republic Germany, 1953-56. Reporter Wirtschaftsverlag, Vienna, 1947-48; econ. reporter Vereinigte Wirtschaftsd., Frankfurt, 1949-52, Deutsche Zeitung, Stuttgart, 1952-56, Hamburg Abendblatt, 1957-63; bur. chief Deutsche Welle Broadcasting, Bonn, 1963-64; chief econ. dept. Westdeutscher Rundfunk, Bonn, 1964-69; fgn. corr. Die Presse, Vienna, 1955-69, Austrian Radio and TV, Fed. Republic Germany, 1969-79; editor in chief Austrian TV, 1979-80; fgn. corr. Austrian Radio and TV, Vienna, 1980-92; freelance writer Vienna, 1992—. Author: New South Politics, 1973, (with others) The American Century/Das Amerikanische Jahrhundert, 1988, Anders als die anderen, 1992, EG pro und contra, 1993, Future, 1999, The Germans, 2000. Decorated Golden Sign of Honor, pres. Austria, 1968; named hon. prof. Austrian Ministry Sci. and Rsch. U. Vienna, 1990.

EMMERSON, BRYAN THOMAS, physician, educator; b. Townsville, Queensland, Australia, Sept. 5, 1929; s. Leonard Joseph and Thelma Ann (Thomas) E.; m. Elva Brett, Apr. 28, 1955; children: William Brett, Stephen Bryan. MBBS, U. Queensland, 1952, MD, 1962, PhD, 1973. Sr. lectr. in therapeutics U. Queensland, Brisbane, 1960-62, reader in medicine, 1963-73, prof. medicine, 1974-94, prof. emeritus, 1994—, chmn. dept. medicine, 1984-94; councillor Queensland Inst. Med. Research, 1978-94, Royal Australasian Coll. Physicians, 1979-86, Queensland Conservatorium of Music, 1981-96; chmn. divsn. medicine Princess Alexandra Hosp., 1981-84, 95-96; cons. emeritus Princess Alexandra Hosp. Author: Hyperuricaemia and Gout in Clinical Practice, 1983, Getting Rid of Gout, 1996; mem. editorial bd. Nephron, Clin. and Exptl. Rheumatology; contbr. 160 articles to profl. jours. Bd. dirs. Australian Kidney Found., 1970—, chmn. med. and sci. adv. com., 1978-84; bd. dirs., v.p. Arthritis Found. Queensland, 1985—. Recipient Weinholt prize U. Queensland, 1950, Masonic Bursary, 1950, Parr prize Australian Rheumatology Assn., 1966, Susman prize Royal Australasian Coll. Physicians, 1978; named Officer Order of Australia, 1997; USPHS fellow, 1967; hon. fellow St. John's Coll. Mem. Australasian Soc. Nephrology (life, pres. 1972-74), Australian Med. Assn., Australian Rheumatology Assn. (v.p. 1978-91, pres. 1992-93), Assn. Univ. Clin. Profs. Australia (chmn. 1978-81), Spina Bifida Assn. of Queensland (hon. life). Anglican. Clubs: Queensland, University. Office: Princess Alexandra Hosp, Ipswich Rd, Brisbane Queensland 4102, Australia

EMMERSON, SIMON THOMAS, musician, educator, composer; b. Wolverhampton, Eng., Sept. 15, 1950; s. Thomas and Dorothy (Tipper) E. BA, Cambridge (Eng.) U., 1972; PhD, City U., London, 1982. Lectr. in music City U., London, 1978-87, sr. lectr., 1987-93, reader in music, 1993—; dir., mem. com. Sonic Arts Network, London, 1979—. Editor, contbr.: The Language of Electroacoustic Music, 1986, Timbre Composition in Electroacoustic Music, 1994; contbr. articles to profl. jours.; composer CD music recordings including Dreams, Memories and Landscapes, 1993. Recipient Bourges (France) Electroacoustic award, 1985. Home: 106 Trinity Rise, London SW2 2QT, England Office: City U Dept Music, Northampton Sq, London EC1V OHB, England

EMMERT, MARK ALLEN, academic administrator, educator; b. Tacoma, Dec. 16, 1952; s. Chester Eugene and Naomi Abigale E.; m. DeLaine Sharon Smith, June 24, 1977; children: Stephen Kenneth, Jennifer Ashley. BA in Polit. Sci., U. Wash., 1975; MPA, Syracuse U., 1976, PhD, 1983. Asst. prof. Northern Ill. U., DeKalb, 1983-85; prof., adminstr. U. Colo., Denver, 1985-91; provost, prof. Mont. State U., Bozeman, 1991-94; chancellor, prof. U. Conn., Storrs, 1994-99, La. State U., Baton Rouge, 1999—. Contbr. articles to profl. jours. Bd. dirs. Boy Scouts Am., Baton Rouge, 1999—, La. Rsch. Park, 1999—, LUMCON, 1999—; coun. chmn. Nat. Assn. State Univ. and Land Grant Coll., 1998-99. Am. Coun. on Edn. fellow U. Colo., 1988, Fulbright fellow, Germany, 1990-91. Mem. Rotary, Phi Kappa Phi, Golden Key Honor Soc., Alpha Lambda Delta. Avocations: reading, golf, scuba diving, fly fishing. Office: La State Univ 156 Thomas Boyd Hl Baton Rouge LA 70803-0001

EMMETT, MICHAEL, physician; b. Linz, Austria, Oct. 29, 1945; came to U.S., 1949.; s. Issac and Pearl (Gladstone) E.; m. Rachel Kozuch, Aug. 2, 1969; children: Mira, Daniel, Joshua. BS, Pa. State U., 1967; MD, Temple U., 1971. Diplomate Am. Bd. Internal Medicine, Am. Bd. Internal Medicine, Nephrology. Intern, then resident Yale U. Med. Ctr., New Haven, 1971-74; nephrology fellow Hosp. U. of Pa., Phila., 1974-76; clin. asst. prof. medicine U. Tex. Southwestern Med. Sch., Dallas, 1976-80, clin. assoc. prof. medicine, 1980-85, clin. prof. medicine, 1985—; Ralph Tompsett prof. medicine Baylor U. Med. Ctr., Dallas, 1986—, dir., nephrology/metabolism, 1986-96, dir. nephrology endocrinology labs, 1986—, chief of medicine, 1996—; cons. physician Parkland Hosp., Dallas, 1976—, Presbyn. Hosp., Dallas, 1976—. Contbr. articles to profl. jours. Fellow ACP; mem. Am. Fedn. Clin. Rsch., Dallas County Med. Soc., Tex. Med. Assn., So. Med. Soc., Am. Soc. Nephrology, Internat. Soc. Nephrology. Avocations: tennis, skiing. Office: Baylor U Med Ctr 3500 Gaston Ave Dallas TX 75246-2096

EMMETT, PETER CHARLES, air force officer; b. Liverpool, Merseyside, Eng., June 2, 1951; s. Robert William and May (Robinson) E.; m. Nadia Karen Neale, Mar. 2, 1974; children: Helen, Fiona, Ruth, Robert. BSc with honors in Physics, Liverpool, 1975; PhD in Physics, Edinburgh (Scotland) U., 1980; MSc in Electronic Warfare, Cranfield U., Shrivenham, Eng., 1998. Chartered comm./electronics engr. Rsch. scientist Inst. of Occupl. Medicine, Edinburgh, 1975-85; commd. flight lt. Royal Air Force, 1985, advanced through grades to squadron leader, 1993—; Eurofighter lead software analyst RAF, Boscombe Down, Eng., 1993-94; sr. mil. advisor info. warfare defense Evaluation and Rsch. Agy., Malvern, Eng., 1994-97; specialist intelligence duties Ministry of Def., London, England, 1998—, Ministry of Defense, London, England, 1998—; squadron leader Royal Air Force. Contbr. articles to profl. jours. Mem. Instn. of Elec. Engrs., Armed Forces Comms.-Electronics Assn., Royal United Svcs. Inst. Ch. of Eng. Avocations: writing, foreign languages, restoration of French farmhouse. Office: Min of Def Rm 350, Old War Office Whitehall, London SW1A 2EU, England

EMÖDY, LEVENTE ANDRÁS, microbiologist, researcher; b. Hosszuhetény, Baranya, Hungary, June 14, 1944; s. Zoltán Ödön and Teodora Ilona (Prohászka) E.; m. Agnes Maria Bedekovits, Sept. 20, 1969; children: Balázs, Barnabás, Teodora. MD, Univ. Med. Sch., Pécs, Hungary, 1969, Specialist in Lab. Medicine, 1972, PhD, 1984, DSc, 1992. Med. diplomate in lab. medicine. Rsch. fellow Univ. Med. Sch., Pécs, 1969-70, asst. lectr., 1970-84, lectr., 1985-93, prof. microbiology, 1993—, head dept. microbiology, 1993—; cons. microbiologist Univ. Med. Sch., Pécs, 1985-93. Contbr. articles to The Lancet, Jour. Biol. Chemistry, Jour. Bacteriology, Molecular Microbiology. Res. lt. Hungarian Army, 1970-73. Named Prof. of Profs., Hungarian Med. Student Assn., Debrecen, 1994, Tutor of Yr. in Univ. Med. Sch., Ministry of Edn., 1995; Copernicus grantee European Cmty., 1995. Mem. Microbiology Profl. Bd., Microbiology Soc. (exec. bd.), Internat. Union Microbiol. Socs. (Hungarian rep. 1994—). Roman Catholic. Achievements include description of the pathogenetic role of Proteus/Morganella hemolysin; description of a new class of fimbriae on Salmonella enteritidis; description of matrix protein binding for Yersinia, Helicobacter and Aeromonas. Home: Bajcsy Zs 33, 7622 Pécs Hungary Office: Univ Med Sch, Szigeti ut 12, 7643 Pécs Hungary

EMONS, HANS-HEINZ, chemist; b. Herford, Germany, June 1, 1930; s. Hans and Melanie Ursula Magda (Müller) E.; m. Maria Margarete Schwind, June 4, 1955; children: Hendrik, Beatrice. Dipl.chem., Tech. U., 1954, Dr.rer.nat., 1957, Dr.sc. (hon.), 1975; Dr.rer.nat. (hon.), Tech. Hochschule, 1984; Dr.mont.Eh, Montanuniversity, 1988. Asst. and asst. prof. Tech. U., Dresden, Germany, 1954-58; asst. prof. to assoc. prof. Tech. Hochschule, Merseburg, Germany, 1959-65, prof., 1965-75, rector, 1968-75; prof. Bergakademie, Freiberg, Germany, 1975-88, rector, 1982-88; head dept., scientist Ctrl. Inst. of Inorganic Chemistry, Berlin, 1988-92; v.p. Acad. of Scis. of German Dem. Republic, 1988-89; guest prof. U. Oslo, Norway, 1982, sr. rsch. fellow, 1988; vis. prof. Rensselaer Polytech. Inst., Troy, N.Y., 1983, State U. of Ohio, Cin., 1992; guest prof. Tech. U., Bratislava, Slowakia, 1992, Tech. U., Burgas, Bulgaria, 1993; sr. scientific adviser Tech. U., Trondheim, Norway, 1994, 95, 98; sr. expert Chem. Plant, Zoucheng, China, 1995, Turfan, China, 1998, Urumgi-Liaocheng, China, 2000. Author, co-author: Technical Inorganic Chemistry, 4th edit., 1990, Chemical Microscopy, 1973, Mit dem Salz durch die Jahrtausende, 2d edit., 1986, Problems of Air, 1990, other books; contbr. articles to profl. jours.; patentee in field. Min. of edn. Gov. of German Dem. Republic, Berlin, 1989-90. Recipient Emil Votecek medal Tech. U., 1973, Clemens Winkler medal Chem. Soc. of GDR, 1981, Kurnakow medal Acad. of Scis. of USSR, 1982. Mem. Gesellschaft Deutscher Chemiker, DECHEMA, Internat. Soc. of Electrochemistry, Leibniz-Soc., Norwegian Acad. of Scis. and Letters (fgn. mem.), Royal Norwegian Acad. of Scis. and Letters (fgn. mem.), Saxonian Acad. of Scis. Avocations: history, theatre, music. Home: Max-Ernst-Weg 25, D-38642 Goslar Germany

EMRICH, HINDERK MEINERS, neurologist, psychiatrist, educator; b. Witzenhausen, Germany, July 2, 1943; s. Wilhelm and Lina Helene (Hinderks) E.; m. Marita Maria Pleyer, Jan. 22, 1993; 1 child, Lydia-Maria. Med. statesexam, Free U. Berlin, 1968; MD, U. Bern, Switzerland, 1968; psychiatrist, Max-Planck-Inst., Munchen, Germany, 1978; prof. psychiatry, U. Munich, 1978, MD habilitation, 1987. Chair dept. clin. pharmacology Max-Planck-Inst., Munich, 1984-85, chair dept. adult psychiatry, 1986-91; chair dept. adult psychiatry Med. Sch. Hannover, Hannover, Germany, 1992—; guest prof. C.G. Jung Inst. Psychoanalysis, Munich, 1992—, Media Art Sch., Cologne, Germany, 1995—, Ben-Gurion-U., Beer-Sheva, Israel, 1996-97. Author: Psychiatrische Anthropologie, 1990; author, editor: Integrative Biological Psychiatry, 1992, Vom Nutzen des Vergessens, 1996; patentee in field. Recipient Alfred-Hauptmann award Epilepsy-Liga, Cologne, 1994, Lise-Meitner-Alexander von. Humboldt award State of Israel, Jerusalem, 1996. Mem. Internat. Soc. Deep Psychology (chair 1996). Roman Catholic. Avocations: psychology, philosophy, film making, psychoanalysis. Office: Med Sch Hannover, Carl-Neuberg St 1, D-30625 Hannover Germany

EMTSEV, VADIM VALENTINOVICH, physicist, researcher; b. Kotelnich, Russia, Apr. 16, 1941; Valentin Andreevich Emtsev and Sophia Kuzminichna Ovchinnikova; m. Larissa Borisovna Drabkina, 1968 (div. Feb. 1970); m. Nina Mikhailovna Katkova, July 31, 1970; children: Valentin, Constantin. MD, Kalinin Polytech., Leningrad, Russia, 1964; PhD, Physicotech. Inst., Leningrad, Russia, 1974. Engr. optoelec. State Inst. Applied Physics, Kazan, Russia, 1965-68; sr. rsch. fellow Ioffe Physicotech. Inst., St. Petersburg, Russia, 1984—; assoc. prof. St. Petersburg U., 1988—. Co-author: (with T.V. Mashovets) Impurities and Defects in Semiconductors, 1981; assoc. editor Semiconductors jour., 1993—; contbr. articles to profl. jours. Jr. rsch. fellow Ioffe Physicotech. Inst., 1971-84. Mem. Am. Phys. Soc. Russian Orthodox. Avocations: classical music, jazz music, ballet, ancient history. Office: Ioffe Physicotech Inst, Politekhnicheskaya 26, 194021 Saint Petersburg Russia

EMVALOMENOS, DIMITRIS, lawyer; b. Athens, Greece, Aug. 7, 1962; s. George and Evangelia Emvalomenos. LLB, U. Athens, 1987; LLM, U. London, 1988. Assoc. Baltazanis & Ptnrs., Piraeus, 1983-87, Morland

Navigation Co., London, 1988-89, Zepos & Zepos, Athens, 1989-90; ptnr. Bahas, Gramatidis & Assocs., Athens, 1990—. Author: Product Liability in Europe, 1993, International Mergers & Acquisitions Law, 1991; contbr. articles to profl. jours. Office: Bahas Gramatidis & Assocs, 9 Navarhou Nikodimou St, 105-58 Athens Greece

ENACHE, EDUARD, network engineer; b. Bacau, Romania, Apr. 8, 1969; s. Alecsandru and Maria Enache; m. Ecaterina Moraru, June 31, 1993. Diploma in automatics engring., Computer & Automatics Faculty, Iasi, Romania, 1993. Software engr. SIS, Bucarest, Romania, 1993-94; alarm sys. engr. SIS, Bucarest, 1994-97; automatics engr. Bucovina Mineral Water S.A., Vatra Dornei, Romania, 1997-99; network engr. Dorna Apemin S.A., Vatra Dornei, 1999—. Lt. Romanian Infantry, 1987-88. Avocations: electronics, automotives. E-mail: eedi@hotmail.com and itapemin@warpnet.ro. Fax: 30-375335. Home: Ap 10, Azurului 4 Bl 27, 5975 Vatra Dornei Suceava, Romania Office: Dorna Apemin SA, M Eminescu 49, 5975 Vatra Dornei Suceava, Romania

ENANY, AMR HASSAN, multinational business executive, entrepreneur; b. Cairo, Aug. 5, 1967; s. Hassan Mohamed Enany and Hoda Abbas Helmi; m. Honayda Saleh Seirafi, Dec. 15, 1994. BSBA, U. So. Calif., 1989; MS in Polit. Sci., Stanford U., 1992, MBA, 1993. Chmn. Mid. East Digital Satellite TV Co., Mid. East Internet By Satellite Co. Enany Group Cos. Holding; vice-chmn. 1st Arabian Mktg. Co., 1st Arabian Svcs. Co., 1st Arabian Co. for Computer Sys., 1st Arabian Real Estate Devel. Co. Ltd., Al Enany Machinery Co. Ltd., Enany Constrn. & Trading, Al Manara Constrn. Co. Ltd., Mall of Egypt, Co., Al Majaz Trading & Contracting Co. Ltd.; vice chmn., mng. dir. Al Riyadh Co. for Maintenance & Operation; pres., CEO ALAMRIA Trading & Indsl. Investments Co. Ltd., Jeddah, Saudi Arabia; bd. dirs. 1st Arabian Mgmt. Co. Ltd., 1st Arabian Indsl. Co, Dubai, United Arab Emirates, Al Rihab Investments & Devel. Co., Cairo, Saudi-Egyptian Real Estate Devel. Co., Cairo. Mem. World Econ. Forum (Global Leader of Tomorrow 1997), Stanford Alumni Assn., Grad. Sch. Bus. Alumni Assn., Young Pres.' Orgn. (chpt. chmn. Saudi chpt. 1999-2000). Avocations: tennis, water skiing, golf, horseback riding, reading. Home: PO Box 52225, 21563 Jeddah Saudi Arabia Office: ALAMIRA Trading/Indsl Inv, Al Malek Rd, 21563 Jeddah Saudi Arabia

ENARSON, DONALD ARTHUR, internist, educator; b. Camrose, Alta., Can., Dec. 9, 1946; s. John Emanuel and Amy Eleanor (Backstrom) E.; m. Penelope Marjorie Stevens, Dec. 1, 1975. BSc, U. Alta., Edmonton, 1969, MD, 1970. Diplomate Am. Bd. Internal Medicine. Cons. Mangyan Devel. Program, Calapan, The Philippines, 1978-80; asst. prof. U. B.C., Vancouver, 1980-85, assoc. prof., 1985-87; prof. U. Alta., Edmonton, 1987-93, adj. prof., 1993—; dir. sci. activities Internat. Union Against Tb and Lung Disease, Paris, 1991—; supr. Africa Com. for Rehab. of So. Sudan, Juba, 1974-75. Author 16 books; contbr. over 30 chpts. to books, over 120 articles to sci. publs. Fellow Royal Coll. Physicians (Can.), Royal Coll. Physicians (Edinburgh). Anglican. Office: Int Union Ag Tb and Lng Dis, 68 Blvd Saint-Michel, 75006 Paris France

ENCE, MATTHEW DUANE, lawyer; b. Lynnwood, Calif., Apr. 12, 1968; s. Mac Delbert and Linda Louise Ence; m. Sherri LaVerne Ence, May 27, 1994; children: Shelby LaVerne, Sarah Pearl, Sydney Rose. AS, Dixie Coll., 1990; BA, Calif. State U., Bakersfield, 1992; JD, U. Pacific, Sacto., 1995. Eligibility worker Kern County Dept. Human Svcs., Bakersfield, Calif., 1991-92; assoc. Kurth & Assocs., Las Vegas, Nev., 1995, Potter Law Offices, Las Vegas, Nev., 1996—; panel mem. med./dental screening bd., So. Nev., 1999—. Asst. scoutmaster Boy Scouts Am., 1996-99. Gary V. Schaber Meml. scholar, McGeoge Sch. Law, U. of the Pacific, 1993-94. Mem. ABA (lt. gov. law sch. divsn. 1994-95), ATLA, State Bar Assn. of Nev., Clark County Bar Assn., Nev. Trial Lawyers Assn., Consumer Attys. of L.A. Mem. Ch. Jesus Christ of Latter Day Sts. Avocations: family history, camping, hiking. Office: Potter Law Offices 1125 Shadow Ln Las Vegas NV 89102-2314

ENCEL, SOLOMON, education educator, consultant; b. Warsaw, Poland, Mar. 3, 1925; arrived in Australia, 1929; s. Gustav and Ethel (Kutner) E.; m. Diana Helen, June 23, 1949; children: Vivien, Deborah, Daniel, Sarah. BA, U. Melbourne, 1949, MA, 1952, PhD, 1960. Lectr. U. Melbourne, Victoria, Australia, 1952-55; reader Australian Nat. U., Canberra, 1956-66; prof. U. New South Wales, Sydney, Australia, 1966-90; emeritus prof. U. New South Wales, 1990—; commr. Edn. Commn. New South Wales, 1980-83; mem. Higher Edn. Bd. New South Wales, 1981-83; mem. Australian Sci. and Tech. Council, 1975; mem. Nat. Health and Med. Rsch. Coun., 1991-94; mem. com. on aging N.S.W., 1993-97. Author: Equality and Authority, 1970, Women and Society, 1974, Cabinet Government in Australia, 1974, The Japanese Connection, 1989, Ageing and Social Policy in Australia, 1997. With Australian Air Force, 1944-45. Fellow Australian Acad. Social Scis., Sociol. Assn. Australia (pres. 1969-71). Mem. Australian Labor party. Jewish. Club: U. New South Wales. Avocations: walking, music, wine. Office: Univ New South Wales, Sydney NSW 2052, Australia

ENCHEV, VENTZESLAV GEORGIEV, pathologist, cytologist, researcher; b. Svishtov, Bulgaria, Apr. 30, 1953; s. Anna Protassieva (Pampulova) Encheva; divorced. MD, Med. Acad., Sofia, Bulgaria, 1977, PhD, 1985. Med. diplomate. Pathologist, cytologist Third City Hosp., Sofia, 1995-98, Nat. Ctr. for Financing of Healthcare, 1999—. Contbr. articles to profl. jours. Fellow Alexander von Humboldt Found., 1988-90. Mem. European Soc. Analytical Cellular Pathology, European Soc. on Telepathology and Telemedicine, Internat. Soc. on Diagnostic Quantitative Pathology, N.Y. Acad. Scis. Eastern Orthodox. Avocations: classical opera, symphonic concerts, tennis, swimming, art. Home: 6 Vishneva St, 1164 Sofia Bulgaria

ENCINAS SAN MARTIN, JUAN PABLO, microbiologist, research; b. Madrid, Mar. 14, 1958; s. Pablo Encinas and Juana San Martin; m. Carmen Araceli Alonso Pelegrin, May 6, 1989; children: Pablo, Maria. Grad. in pharmacy, U. Madrid, 1981; specialist in microbiology, U. Oviedo, Spain, 1984; PhD in Vet. Medicine, U. Leon, Spain, 1993. Cert. specialist in indsl. and food microbiology; cert. rschr. in food hygiene and food tech. Intern microbiology dept. Pharmacy Sch., Madrid, 1977-80; rschr. biochemistry dept. Consejo Superior de Investigaciones, Madrid, 1980-81; internal resident Hosp., Oviedo, 1982-85; microbiologist Antibioticos Sociedad Anonima, Leon, 1985—; with Pharmacist Coll., Oviedo, 1982-83; vis. prof. clin. analysis, Madrid, 1984; rschr. Food Hygiene Dept., Leon, 1987—; cons. Mine Sch., Leon, 1989—; participant Conferencia Consenso: Listeria, León, 1992; dir. Summer Course, Leon, 1997—. Author: Circulating Glucose Insulin and..., 1983, Microbiological Hazards and PPC, 1993; co-author: GMPs and QC/QA, 1992. Ofcl. Spanish Army, 1981. Mem. Am. Soc. for Microbiology, Sociedad Española de Microbiologia, N.Y. Acad. Sci. Avocations: cycling, mushrooms, mountains, skiing. Home: Urbanizacion Monteleon 179, 24196 León Spain Office: Antibiotics SA, Av Antibiotics 59-61, 24080 Leon Spain

END, HENRY, interior and industrial designer; b. Salford, Eng., Nov. 3, 1915; came to U.S. 1946; s. Maximillian and Adela (Blain) E.; m. Jessica Marion Claas, July 5, 1947; 1 child, Lindsay. Student architecture and art, St. Martin's Sch. Art, London, 1930; A.R.C.A., Royal Coll. Art, London, 1934. Founder, pres. Henry End Assoc, Miami, Fla., 1950—; founder Internat. Design Ctr. Los Angeles and Miami, 1960; designer sets 20th Century Fox, Warner Bros., Universal, Selznick. Interior designer hotels and restaurants, condominiums, office bldgs., including Cocoanut Grove, Los Angeles, Carlton Tower and Heathrow Hotel, London, Mayflower, Washington, Hotel Quito, Ecuador, El Conquistador, P.R., Carlton Beach, Bermuda, Lucayan Beach Hotel, Grand Bahama Island, Nassau Beach Hotel, Penta Hotels, London and Munich, Fed. Republic Germany, Ritz Carlton, Montreal, Que., Can., Seacoast Towers West, Seacoast Towers V, 733 Park Ave. Bldg., N.Y.C., The Whitehall, Chgo., Marriott chain motor hotels, tourist hotels for Govt. Tunisia, Hilton,Munich, Sheraton Brussels, Sheraton Buenos Aires, Rio de Janeiro, Hyatt Internat., Brussels, Montreal, Iran and Jamaica, Esso Hotel, Antwerp, Belgium, UN Hotel N.Y.C., S.S. Norway, Pavillion Hotel, Miami, Ledra Marriott, Athens, Lakeside Regent, Palm Beach, Fla.; designer feature exhibits Room of Tomorrow, Designs for Dining, Internat. Hotel Expn., N.Y.C., Chgo., Los Angeles, Internat. Restaurant Expn., Chgo., U.S. Rubber Pavilion, Coliseum, N.Y.C.; author: Interiors Book of Hotels and Motor Hotels, 1963, Interiors 2nd Book of Hotels, 1976, Hyatt Regency, Miami, Plaza Hotel, N.Y.C. Served with RAF, 1940-46. Recipient spl. citation AIA, awards Art Dirs. Club, Design Derby citation Société Culinaire Philanthropique, 13 design awards Instns. Mag.; named to Hall of Fame, Interior Design Mag., 1985. Fellow Royal Soc. Arts; mem. Am. Soc. Interior Designers (citation of merit, 2 design awards).

ENDACOTT, JOHN BRENDAN, chemist; b. Frankston, Australia, Nov. 23, 1935; s. Arthur John and Margaret (Keane) E.; m. Lourdes Mendoza, Dec. 12, 1969 (dec. Jan. 1976); children: John Vincent, Marcia Margaret, Damien Arthur, Nicole Marie; m. Gabrielle Mary McHugh, May 6, 1977. Diploma in med. lab. technology, Royal Melbourne Inst. Tech., Australia, 1962, diploma in applied chemistry, 1966. Lab. asst. U. Melbourne, 1954-55; trainee med. lab. technologist Repatriation Gen. Hosp., Heidelberg, Australia, 1956-61, sr. med. lab. technologist, 1961-62; chief blood bank technologist St. Vincent's Hosp., Melbourne, 1962-64; blood bank technologist Royal Children's Hosp., Melbourne, 1964-68; lab. mgr. applied chemistry Swinburne U. Technology, Hawthorn, Australia, 1968-98; ret. Fellow Royal Australian Chem. Inst. (chair chem. edn. group Victorian br. 1978-79). Roman Catholic. Avocations: language studies, classical music, reading, mystery fiction. Home: 30 Hawthorn Glen, 3122 Hawthorn VIC 3122, Australia

ENDALE, TAMRAT, geophysicist, educator; b. Addis Ababa, Ethiopia, Aug. 13, 1966; child of Michael Endale and Bogaleche Gemeche; m. Misrak Fisseha Michael, Nov. 11, 1991. BSc, Addis Ababa U., 1987; MSc, U. Aix-Marseille (France) I, 1992, PhD, 1997. Metrologist Ethiopian Std. Inst., Addis Ababa, 1987-91; asst. lectr. U. Aix-Marseille II, 1992-93, U. Aix-Marseille III, 1993-97; asst. prof. U. Sao Paulo, Brazil, 1997—. Contbr. articles to profl. jours. Master degree fellow French Govt., 1991; PhD fellow French Govt., 1993; postdoctoral fellow Found. for Sci. Rsch. State of Sao Paulo, 1997. Mem. Am. Geophysical Union, European Geophysical Soc., French. Assn. in the Search of Human Origin, African Regional Std. Orgn. Avocations: philatelist, hiking, swimming, reading. Fax: 5511-8185034. Office: IGN U Sao Paulo, Rua do Natao 1226, 05508 Sao Paulo Brazil

ENDERS, ELIZABETH MCGUIRE, artist; b. New London, Conn., Feb. 18, 1939; d. Francis Foran and Helen Cuseck (Connolly) McGuire; m. Anthony Talcott Enders, June 9, 1962; children: Charles Talcott, Alexandra Eustis, Camilla, Ostrom II. BA, Conn. Coll., 1962; MA, NYU, 1987. Trustee Artists Space, N.Y.C., 1986-95, Conn. Coll., New London, 1988-93; assoc. dept. prints and illustrated books Mus. Modern Art, 1993—, Lyman Allyn Art Mus., 1994—. One-woman shows include Paul Schuster Gallery, Cambridge, Mass., 1966, Ulysses Gallery, N.Y.C., 1992, 94, Lyman Allyn Art Mus., New London, Conn., 1994, Charles Cowles Gallery, N.Y.C., 1995, Norbert Considine Gallery, Princeton, N.J., 1997; exhibited in group shows at Boston Symphony Orch., 1982, NYU, 1983, Conn. Conn., 1988, Bronx Coun. on Arts, 1990-91, Addison Gallery Am. Art, 1993, Angel Art, L.A., 1993, Lyman Allyn Art Mus., New London, Conn., 1994-95, So. Alleghenies Mus. Art, Loretto, Pa., 1994, Artists Space Multiple, 1995, New Mus. Contemporary Art, N.Y.C., 1995, Denise Bibro Fine Art, N.Y.C., 1995, N.Y. Studio Sch., N.Y.C., 1995, Divine Design '95, L.A., Spring Benefit Raffle, Sculpture Ctr., N.Y.C., 1996, 97, 98, 2000, Charles Cowles Gallery, N.Y.C., 1996, Fax Art Week, Copenhagen, Assn. Danish Graphic Artists, 1996, Open Studio, Downtown Arts Festival, N.Y.C., 1997, 98, Dieu Donne Papermill, 1997, 99, Charles Cowles Gallery, N.Y.C., 1998, 2000, Denise Bibro Fine Art, 1998, Lyman Allyn Art Mus., 1998, Lyman Allyn Art Mus., 1999, Robert Brown Gallery, Wash. D.C., 1999, New York Acad. of Art Benefit Auction, 1999, Cooley Gallery, Old Lyme, Conn., 1999, (Benefit for the Nature Conservancy); traveling group show Artists Space, 1992, 94, Southeastern Ctr. Contemporary Art, Winston-Salem, N.C., 1993, Allentown (Pa.) Art Mus., 1994, Cleve. Ctr. Contemporary Art, 1994, Salt Lake Art Ctr., Salt Lake City, 1995, Kemper Ctr. Contemporary Art and Design, Kansas City, Mo., 1996, Bass Mus. of Art, Miami Beach, Fla., 1997, Flint (Mich.) Inst. Arts, 1998, Blaffer Gallery, U. Houston, TX, 1998, Contemporary Art Ctr., Va. Beach, 1998, Tampa Mus. of Art, 1998-99, Art Mus. of Southeast Tex., 1999, Fresno Metropolitan Mus., Calif., 2000; represented in permanent collections at Addison Gallery of Am. Art, Andover, Mass., Graham Gund, Cambridge, Daimler Benz North Am. Corp., Lyman Allyn Art Mus., Conn. Coll., New London. Mem. nat. fin. coun. Dem. Nat. Com., Washington, 1988—. Recipient Citation of Appreciation, Conn. Coll., 1990, medal, 1993. Fellow Frick Collection (N.Y.C.); mem. The Drawing Soc., The Bklyn. Mus., Williams Coll. Mus. of Art, Mus. Modern Art, Williams Club. Democrat. Roman Catholic. Home: 530 E 86th St New York NY 10028-7535

ENDO, NORIO, physician, educator; b. Tokyo, Japan, Feb. 19, 1941; s. Toshio and Kiyo (Hatakeyama) E.; m. Makiko Shishito; children: Noriaki, Miki. MD, Keio U., Tokyo, 1966. Diplomate Am. Bd. Pediatrics, Japanese Bd. Internal Medicine, Japanese Bd. General Physicians. Intern U.S. Air Force Hosp., Tachikawa, Japan, 1966-67; intern and resident U. Mich. Hosp., 1967-71; assoc. prof. Kitasato U., Kanagawaken, Japan, 1971-98; pres. Endo Clinic, Tokyo, Japan, 1974—; examining physician U.N., N.Y.C., 1980—; med. cons. KLM Royal Dutch Airline, Amsterdam, The Netherlands, 1982—. Author: Pediatric Clinic, 1972. Avocation: travel. Office: Endo Clinic, 2-24-13-305 Kamioosaki, 141-0021 Shinagawaku Tokyo, Japan

ENDO, TAMIO, engineering physicist, educator; b. Sakai, Osaka, Japan, Apr. 5, 1949; s. Nobuyuki Endo and Eiko (Kitamura) E.; m. Harumi Oda, Feb. 11, 1983; 1 child, Yukino. B Engring. in Indsl. Chemistry, Gifu (Japan) U., 1973, B Engring. in Elec. Engring., 1976, M Engring., 1978; D Engring., Kyoto (Japan) U., 1987. Asst. prof. Mie U., Tsu, Japan, 1978-87, assoc. prof., 1987—; vis. rschr. Japanese Ministry Edn., U. Calif., San Diego, 1995; invited spkr. various schs. and labs. Author: Studies of High Temperature Superconductors, 1995, Solid State Physics 33, Vol. 14, 1998, Crystal Growth Methods and Processes, 2000. Tennis coach Anoh City (Japan) Coun., 1992—. Winner, Mie Nat. Ofcls. Tennis Match, Ministry Gen. Affairs, Japanese Govt., 1993, Mie Sch. Ofcls. Tennis Match, Mie Prefectural Tennis Assn., 1982. Mem. Japan Soc. Applied Physics, Phys. Soc. Japan, Inst. Electronics, Info. and Comm., Materials Rsch. Soc. Am., Materials Rsch. Soc. Japan. Avocations: tennis, swimming. Home: Tabata Ueno, Anoh 514-2325, Japan Office: Mie U Faculty Engring, Kamihama, Tsu 514-8507, Japan

ENDOH, MASAHIKO, microbiologist, educator; b. Niigata, Japan, Feb. 19, 1952; m. Mayumi Endoh. BS, Kitasato U., Tokyo, 1974; MS, Kitasato U., 1976, PhD, 1987. Rsch. assoc. Kitasato U., Tokyo, 1976-87, asst. prof., 1987-91, assoc. prof., 1991-95; assoc. prof. Daiichi Coll. Pharm. Sci., Fukuoka, 1995-97, prof., 1997—. Author: Pathogenesis and Immunity in Pertussis, 1988; contbr. articles to profl. jours. Mem. Internat. Assn. Biol. Stds., Japan Soc. Microbiology, Am. Soc. Microbiology. Avocations: observing animal behavior, tennis, skiing, swimming. Home: 2-37-10-105 Ijiri Minamiku, Fukuoka 811-1302, Japan Office: Dept Microbiol Biologics, 22-1 Tamagawa-cho, Minamiku Fukuoka 815-8511, Japan

ENDOH, RYOHEI, cardiologist; b. Omachi, Nagano, Japan, Apr. 1, 1954; s. Shinzi Endoh and Miharu Momose; m. Miki Kitahara, May 7, 1995; children: Maki, Ryoko. M of Medicine, Shinshu U., Matsumoto, Japan, 1981, MD, 1990. Intern Shinshu U. Hosp., Matsumoto, 1981-82, resident, 1983-84, cardiologist, 1985-87; intern Matsumoto Nat. Hosp., 1982-83; cardiologist Nagano Red Cross Hosp., 1984-85; head physician internal medicine Suwa Red Cross Hosp., 1987; head physician cardiology Showa Inan Gen. Hosp., Komagane, 1987-95; head physician internal medicine Nagano (Japan) Mcpl. Hosp., 1995—. Contbr. articles to Japan Circulation Jour., Artery, Japan Jour. Applied Physiology, Tex. Heart Inst. Jour. Fellow Japanese Soc. Internal Medicine, Japanese Circulation Soc., Japanese Assn. Acute Medicine; mem. Japanese Coll. Angiology. Office: Nagano Mcpl Hosp, 1333-1 Tomitake Nagano-shi, Nagano Japan 381

ENDRES, MATTHIAS, neurologist; b. Sigmaringen, Germany, Apr. 7, 1969; s. Otto Karl and Helga Gerda (Brunssen) E.; m. Anne-Sophie Gericke, June 26, 1998. MD, U. Hamburg, Germany, 1994. Resident U. Luebeck, Germany, 1994-96; fellow Harvard U., Boston, 1996-98; resident Humboldt U., Berlin, 1998. Recipient Oskar-Lapp award German Soc. Cardiology, 1998. Mem. Soc. Cerebral Blood Flow (Nils Lassen award 1999), Am. Heart Assn. Roman Catholic. Office: Charite-Humboldt U, Schumann Str 20/21, 10099 Berlin Germany

ENDRIZ, JOHN GUIRY, electronics executive, consultant; b. Oak Park, Ill., Jan. 10, 1942; s. John Daniel and Florence (Guiry) E.; m. Sally Jean Doubleday, July 19, 1975. BSEE, MSEE, MIT, 1965; PhD in EE, Stanford U., 1970. Guest rschr. Linkoping (Sweden) U., 1970-72; project mgr. R.C.A. Rsch. Lab., Princeton, N.J., 1972-77; engring. mgr. Varian Assocs., Palo Alto, Calif., 1977-88; v.p. engring. S.D.L., Inc., San Jose, Calif., 1988-97, v.p. power delivery bus. unit, 1997-99. Contbr. over 53 articles to profl. jours.; patentee more than 30 inventions. Mem. IEEE, S.P.I.E., Soc. Information Display. Home: 5 Heritage Ct Belmont CA 94002-2944

ENDRYS, JIRI, chemistry researcher; b. Plzen, Czechoslovakia, Dec. 15, 1940; s. Kvetoslav and Ruzena (Spurna) E.; m. Jana Kasnerova, Sept. 28, 1963; children: Alena, Zuzana. Ing. Chemistry, Inst. Chem. Tech., Prague, Czechoslovakia, 1962; PhD in Chemistry, Czechoslovak Acad. Scis., Prague, Czechoslovakia, 1967. Rsch. worker Barvy a laky, Prague, 1967-69; sr. rsch. worker Inst. Chem. Tech., Prague, 1969—; rsch. worker Spolana, Neratovice, Czechoslovakia, 1997. Contbr. articles to profl. jours. E-mail: endrysj@vscht.cz. Fax: 00420 2 24311082. Office: Inst Chem Tech, Technicka 1905, 166 28 Prague 6, Czech Republic

ENDZIŅŠ, AIVARS, chairman Latvian constitutional court; b. Riga, Latvia, Dec. 8, 1940; m. Ināra Šturma, Nov. 24, 1963; children: Arvīds, Jānis. Grad., U. Latvia Faculty of Law, 1968; PhD in Law, State U. Moscow, 1971. Main lector, dept. head law U. Latvia, 1972-90; mem. Latvian Parliament, 1990-96, chmn. legis. com., 1990-93, chmn. legal affairs com., 1993-95; acting chmn. Constitutional Ct. of Latvia, 1996-2000, chmn., 2000—; assoc. prof. Police Acad.; spl. guest status Parliamentary Assembly European Coun., 1992-95, mem. assembly, 1995-96, assoc. mem. democracy through law commn., 1992-95, mem. 1995—; head of dels. from Latvia in Parliamentary Assembly Orgn. Security & Co-operation Europe and confs. Interparliamentary Union, 1995-96. Contbr. more than 40 publs. to legal jours. and other documents. Recipient Order of Three Stars, 2000. Office: Constl Ct Latvia, Alunana St 1, LV-1010 Riga Latvia

ENENBACH, MARK HENRY, community action agency executive, educator; b. Chgo., July 28, 1949; s. Joseph Henry and Antonette Regina (Kasko) E.; children: Joy Elizabeth, Erin Regina; m. Kai Lindquist Bergin, Sept. 28, 1985; 1 child, Faith Marie. BA in Polit. Sci. with honors, Loyola U., Chgo., 1971, MA in Urban Studies with honors, 1973. Cmty. resource specialist Model Cities, Chgo., 1974-79; grad. prof. Govs. State U., Park Forest South, Ill., 1977-89; dir. energy program City of Chgo., 1980-83; prof. St. Augustine's Coll., Chgo., 1981-82; coord. cmty. svcs. Dept. Human Svcs., Chgo., 1984-91; prof. urban planning and pub. adminstrn. DePaul U., Chgo., 1987—; dir. cmty. svcs. block grant programs Cmty. and Econ. Devel. Assn. Cook County, Inc., Chgo., 1992-96, v.p./COO, 1997—; mem. adv. bd. City Colls. Chgo., 1984-88; spkr. Nat. Headstart Assn., Washington, 1995; mem. task force Ill. Dept. Commerce and Cmty. Affairs, Springfield, 1996—; spkr. Nat. Assn. State Cmty. Svcs. Programs, 2000. Pres. Lincoln Park Interagy. Coun., Chgo., 1986-91; mem. adv. bd. Salvation Army, Chgo., 1987-91. Grad. rsch. fellow Loyola U., 1972-73. Mem. Nat. Assn. Cmty. Action Agys., Ill. Assn. Cmty. Action Agys. Avocations: urban research, writing and travel in over 30 countries. Office: Cmty and Econ Devel Assn 208 S Lasalle St Ste 1900 Chicago IL 60604-1119

ENESCU, CRISAN, engineering executive, consultant; b. Cimpina, Prahova, Romania, Jan. 17, 1955; s. Stefan and Beatrice E.; m. Cristina Gutu, July 28, 1978; 1 child, Melania. MSc in Engring., Poly. U., Bucharest, Romania, 1980. Engr. Inst. Automation, IPA-SA, Bucharest, 1980-85; prin. rschr. IPA-SA, 1985-96, divsn. mgr., 1992-96; dir. Ecosys.-SRL, Bucharest, 1996; mgr. Unicontrol Engring. SRL, Bucharest. Contbr. articles to profl. jours. Mem. IEEE, Romanian Soc. for Automation and Informatics. Avocations: history, music, economy, sports. Fax: +401-222-97-73. E-mail: enescue@automation.ipa.ro. Office: Unicontrol Engring SRL, Bd Banu Manta 39 bl 30 ap21, 78171 Bucharest Romania

ENESCU, DAN MIRCEA, physician; b. Bucharest, Romania, 1952; s. Mircea Ioan and Pompilia (Anghel) E.; m. Mihaela David, Apr. 6, 1960; 1 child, Alexandra. Medicine, U.M.F., Bucharest, 1977, plastic surgeon, 1985. Gen. practitioner Tirgoviste, Romania, 1977-82; resident plastic surgeon Bucharest, 1982-85, plastic surgeon, 1985-88; exchange fellow UCLA, San Diego, 1991; cons. in plastic surgery, 1991; chief of plastic surgery Dept. for Children, Bucharest, 1989; chief of clinic plastic surgery, 1998—; mem. physicians tng. program Operation Smile, 1998; vis. prof. Internat. Cranio-Facial Inst., Dallas, 1998; burn tutorial Parkland Meml. Hosp., Dallas, 1998. Co-author: Orth. & Traumatology Ped., 1995, Emergency Med. Ped., 1997; contbr. articles to profl. jours. Mem. N.Y. Acad. Sci., E.B.A., E.C.P.B., Romanian Soc. Ped. Burns Acanta (pres. 1997), Nat. Soc. Plastic Surgery (sec. 1997), Plastic Surgery Commn. of Colegiul (sec. 1997). Achievements include establishment of first skin bank in Romania. Avocations: music, philosophy, child protection. Office: SCCC Gr Alexandrescu, Bd Iancu De Hunedoara 30-32, Bucharest Romania

ENG, CATHERINE, health care facility administrator, physician, medical educator; b. Hong Kong, May 20, 1950; came to U.S., 1953; d. Doi Kwong and Alice (Yee) E.; m. Daniel Charles Chan; 1 child, Michael B. BA, Wellesley Coll., 1972; MD, Columbia U., 1976. Diplomate Am. Bd. Internal Medicine, Am. Bd. Gastroenterology; cert. added qualifications geriatrics. Intern in internal medicine Presbyterian Hosp./Columbia, Presbyterian Med. Ctr., 1976-77, resident in internal medicine, 1977-79; fellow in gastroenterology/hepatology N.Y. Hosp./Cornell U. Med. Coll., 1979-81; instr. medicine Cornell U. Coll. Medicine, N.Y.C., 1980-81; staff physician On Lok Sr. Health Svcs., San Francisco, 1981-86, supervising physician, 1986-91, med. dir., 1992—; asst. clin. prof. dept. family and cmty. medicine U. Calif., San Francisco, 1986-95, asst. clin. prof. dept. medicine, 1992-95; assoc. clinical prof. dept. medicine, Univ. Calif., San Francisco, 1995—; primary care specialist Program of All-inclusive Care for the Elderly, San Francisco, 1987-94; asst. chief dept. medicine Chinese Hosp., San Francisco, 1993-98, chmn. com. credentials, 1994—. Instr. BLS Am. Heart Assn., San Francisco, 1988-92; mem. nominating com. YWCA of Marin, San Francisco, San Mateo, 1991-95; mem. mgmt. com. YWCA-Chinatown/North Beach, San Francisco, 1989-95; bd. dirs. Chinatown Cmty. Children's Ctr., San Francisco, 1987-90. Durant scholar Wellesley Coll., 1972. Fellow ACP; mem. Am. Geriatrics Soc., Am. Soc. Aging, Am. Gastroent. Assn., Calif. Med. Assn. (assoc.), San Francisco Med. Soc. (assoc.), Sigma Xi, Alpha Omega Alpha. Avocations: reading, hiking. Home: 130 Dorchester Way San Francisco CA 94127-1110 Office: On Lok Sr Health Scvs 1333 Bush St San Francisco CA 94109-5691

ENG, CHARIS EU LI, oncologist, geneticist; b. Singapore, Jan. 17, 1962; s. SooPeck and Siok Mui (Lee) E. BA, U. Chgo., 1982, PhD, 1986, MD, 1988. Diplomate Am. Bd. Internal Medicine and Med. Oncology. Med. resident Beth Israel Hosp., Boston, 1988-91; clin. fellow Dana-Farber Cancer Inst., Boston, 1991-95, Harvard Med. Sch., Boston, 1988-93; CRC Dana-Farber fellow U. Cambridge, Eng., 1992-95; instr. Harvard Med. Sch., Boston, 1994-95, asst. prof. medicine, 1995-98; staff physician Dana-Farber Cancer Inst., Boston, 1995-98; assoc. prof. medicine, clin. cancer genetics dir. Ohio State U., Columbus, 1999—. N.Am. editor, cancer genetics editor Jour. Med. Genetics, 1998—. Recipient Upjohn travel award, 1991. Fellow ACP; mem. Alpha Omega Alpha, Phi Beta Kappa, Sigma Xi. Office: Human Cancer Genetics Prgm Ohio State U 420 W 12th Ave # 690 Columbus OH 43210-1214

ENGALYTCHEV, VALI FATEKHOVICH, academic administrator; b. Tashkent, Uzbekistan, Apr. 30, 1953; s. Engalytchev Fatekh Shakirovich and Busya Pinkhusovna (Zaretskaya) E.; m. Natalia Nikolaevna Trofimova, Feb. 17, 1979; children: Maria, Ekaterina, Mikhail. Diploma Forensic Psychology Expert, Ctrl. Severo-Kaukaskaja, Rostov-on-Don, Russia, 1996; cert. State Employee, Pres. Russian Fedn., Moscow, 1995; PhD in Psychology, Tbilisi State U., Ga., 1983. Sr. lectr. Rep. Pedagogical Inst. Russian Lang. and Lit., Tashkent, Uzbekistan, 1984-87, assoc. prof., 1987-89; psychologist Sch. # 217, Tashkent, Uzbekistan, 1989-90; assoc. prof. Kaluga (Russia) State Pedagogical U., 1990—, head lab. for forensic psychology studies, 1995—, head psychology dept., 1993—, dir. law psychology program; cons. Kaluga (Russia) Region Office of Pub.

Prosecutor; mem. Expert Coun. for Conflict Resolution, Min. Fuel Energy, Moscow. Author: Forensic Psychology Evaluation: Methodical Handbook 2nd edit., 1997, The English Language Handbook for Psychology Department Students, 1996, A Sign of Silent Thought: Essays on Non-Verbal Communication, 1991. Founder, head coun. Civic Initiative for Perestroika, Tashkent, Uzbekistan, 1988; founder, dir. Noosphere Inst., Kaluga, Russia, 1995—. Mem. Russian Psychol. Soc., Am. Psychol. Assn., Kaluga Psychol. Soc., Univ.'s Psychology Depts. Assn. Avocations: internet, reading, swimming, travel. Home e-mail: vali@kaluga.ru. Office e-mail: psy-law.kaluga.ru. Fax: 7 (08422) 33328. Home: 85 S Razin St Apt 64, 248002 Kaluga Russia

ENGAMMARE, MAX ANDRE CLAUDE, publishing executive, researcher; b. Paris, Feb. 26, 1953; arrived in Switzerland, 1976; s. Pierre Arthur Jean and Monique Adrienne Juliette (Pouchet) E.; m. div. 1991; children: Anne Florence, Valerie Marie; m. Isabelle Malaise Engammare, July 24, 1993; children: Stanislas, Agrippa. MS in Psycho-Pedagogy, U. Geneva, 1983; MS in Theology, U. Lausanne, 1987; PhD in Theology, U. Geneva, 1992. Educator Les Glaciers, Gryon, Switzerland, 1976-87; asst. U. Geneva, 1987-88; doctor U. Mainz, Germany, 1989-90; asst. U. Geneva, 1991-92, rschr., 1993—; dir. Pub. House Droz, Geneva, 1995—; nat. editor Scholars of Early Modern Studies, 1993—; exec. bd. Fisier, 1996—, Soc. Francaise D'Etude du Seizieme Siecle, 1997—. Author: Qu'il me Baise Des Baisiers De Sa Bouche Le Cantique Des Cantiques A La Renaissance, 1993, Lire Le Cantique A La Renaissance, 1992; editor: Les Sermons de Jean Calvin Sur La Genese, 1999; contbr. more than 40 articles and 50 book reviews. Mem. CAS. Avocations: mountain climbing, paragliding. Office: Droz, 11 Rue Massot, 1206 Geneva Switzerland

ENGBER, CHERYL ANN, language educator, linguist; b. East Chicago, Ind., Oct. 12, 1945; d. James Ward and Beryl Ann (Crowe) Biddle; m. Michael David Engber, Nov. 25, 1967; children: Sara Ann, Kimberly Sue. BA in Spanish with honors, Ind. U., 1967, PhD in Linguistics, 1992, MA in Spanish, 1974; MA in Tchg. ESL, Ball State U., 1979. Instr. Spanish Anderson (Ind.) U., 1979-82; assoc. instr. intensive English program Ind. U., Bloomington, 1983-86, adminstrv. asst. com. for R & D, 1989-91, instr. semi-intensive English program, 1991-93; assoc. prof. linguistics Truman State U., Kirksville, Mo., 1993—; instr. ESL Ind. U., Kuala Lumpur, Malaysia, 1985-86; grader for Test of Written English Ednl.. Testing Svc., Princeton, N.J., 1989—; asst. to editor Studies in Second Lang. Acquisition Ind. U., 1987-89; spkr. in field. Contbr. Understanding English: A Listening Approach to ESL, 1983; contbr. articles to profl. jours. Founder Muncie (Ind.) Internat. Ctr., 1974; vol. tchr., founder internat. summer workshops for children, Muncie, 1977; deacon, elder, mem. com. First Christian Ch., Bloomington, Ind., 1987-92. Ind. U. fellow, 1982; Truman State U. grantee, 1994. Mem. Linguistic Soc. Am., Tchrs. ESL, Am. Assn. for Applied Linguistics, Nat. Coun. Tchrs. English, Phi Beta Kappa, Phi Kappa Phi. Avocations: travel, gardening, gourmet cooking. Office: Truman State Univ Divsn Lang and Lit McClain Hall 310 Kirksville MO 63501

ENGBLOM, LARS AAKE, communications educator; b. Joenkoping, Sweden, May 5, 1943; s. Arvid and Svea (Blaaberg) E.; m. Christina Hoegberg, Sept. 9, 1968; children: Jakob, Samuel, Cecilia. PhD in Econ. History, Gothenburg (Sweden) U., 1981. Reporter, prodr. Swedish TV Co., Gothenburg, 1968-80; mgr. Swedish TV Co., Falun, 1981-83, Vaexjoe, 1983-88; mng. dir. Nordic House, Reykjavik, Iceland, 1989-93; asst. prof. Joenkoeping U., 1994-98, Gothenburg U., Sweden, 1998—. Named Knight of the Order of Falcon, Iceland. Office: Gothenburg U, Box 713, SE-40530 Göteborg Sweden

ENGDAHL, RICHARD ALAN, management educator, consultant; b. Anderson, Ind., Jan. 26, 1941; m. Margaret Denise Engdahl, Jan. 5, 1977; children: Lee Joseph, Alison Kelin. BS Architecture-Design, U. Mich., 1963, MBA, 1965; PhD, U. Wash., 1986. Registered orgnl. devel. cons. Med. adminstr. U. Mich. Med. Ctr., Ann Arbor, 1961-65; mktg. mgr. Westinghouse Air Brake Corp., Peoria, Ill., 1966-67; commd. med. svc. corps officer U.S. Army, 1967, advanced through grades to lt. col., 1982; med. adminstr. U.S. Army Med. Dept., worldwide, 1967-76; cons. human resource systems Hdqrs. U.S. Army, Washington, 1976-79; cons. orgnl. devel. Tripler Army Med. Ctr., Honolulu, 1979-82; teaching assoc. U. Wash. Sch. Bus., Seattle, 1982-86; prof. mgmt. U. N.C., Wilmington, 1986—; cons. and owner Orgnl. Imagineering, 1980—; pres., CEO Virtual Pubs., Ltd., 1999—. Assoc. editor Orgn. Devel. Jour., 1990-95. Bd. dirs. Downtown Area Revitalization Effort, Wilmington, 1987—; pres. DARE, Inc.; apptd. by gov. to bd. govs. N.C. Quality Leadership Found., coun. chair, 1997-98. U. Mich. scholar, 1961-65, U. Wash. scholar, 1983-84. Mem. Acad. Mgmt., Soc. Mgmt. Assn., Am. Mgmt. Assn., So. O.D. Interest Group, Devel. Inst. (jour. reviewer 1983—), Mensa, Wilmington Quality Found. (chair 1994), Beta Gamma Sigma. Avocations: sailing, scuba diving, golf, electroncis, home design and renovation. E-mail: engdahlr@worldnet.att.net. Home: Cheshire Pl 6048 Wrightsville Ave Wilmington NC 28403-3540 Office: Univ NC Cameron Sch Bus Adminstrn Wilmington NC 28403

ENGE, VERNON REIER, editor health care publications; b. Bismarck, N.D., Dec. 12, 1942; s. Vernon Lewis and Aurella Luella (Potter) E.; m. Mary C. Mortensen, Nov. 29, 1968; children: Eric Vernon, Evan Morten. BS, BA, Dickinson State U., 1964; MA, N. D. State U., 1979. Instr. Mandan (N.D.) H.S., 1965-74; night editor Mandan Pioneer, 1974-75; pub. info. office Bismarck (N.D.) Region Social Svcs., 1976; instr. Valley City (N.D.) H.S., 1976-82; instr. tech. writing Miles City (Mont.) C.C., 1982-83; gen. reporter Richland Free Press, Sidney, Mont., 1983-84; city editor, health & sci. editor Evening Phoenix, Phoenixville, Pa., 1984-87; editor Advance for Respiratory Care Practitioners Merion Publs. Inc., King of Prussia, Pa., 1988—; editor Advance for Mgrs. of Respiratory Care Merion Publs. Inc., King of Prussia, 1992—; founding editor of several other health care mags. Merion Publs. Inc., King of Prussia, 1988—. Mem. Minimum Wage Bd., Bismarck, N.D., 1975; del. to Dem. state conv., 1979. Named Outstanding Young Educator, Mandan Jaycees, 1974. Mem. Elks. Methodist. Achievements include: development of a regional health care publication to a 19 publication network of nat. influence. Avocations: music, literature, art. Home: 34 Fords Edge Royersford PA 19468-2666 Office: Merion Publs Inc 2900 Horizon Dr Kng Of Prussa PA 19406-2651

ENGEL, DAVID LEWIS, lawyer; b. N.Y.C., Mar. 31, 1947; s. Benjamin and Selma (Fruchtman) E.; m. Edith Greetham Smith, June 9, 1973; children: Richard William, Jonathan Martin. AB in Gen. Studies in Econ. cum laude, Harvard U., 1967, JD magna cum laude, 1973; Disting. Naval grad., U.S. Naval Officer Candidate Sch., 1969. Bar: Mass. 1975. Law clk. to Judge Henry J. Friendly U.S. Ct. Appeals (2nd cir.), N.Y.C., 1973-74; assoc. Goodwin, Procter & Hoar, Boston, 1974-76, 79-80; asst. prof. law Stanford U., Calif., 1976-79; ptnr. Berman, Dittmar & Engel, P.C., Boston, 1980-84, Bingham Dana LLP, Boston, 1984—. Contbr. article to Stanford Law Rev., 1979; pres. Harvard Law Rev., 1972-73. Mem. bd. visitors Stanford U. Law Sch., 1982-84; bd. dirs. Project Joy, 1995—. Lt. (j.g.) USNR, 1969-71. Named John Harvard scholar, Harvard Coll. scholar, Nat. Merit scholar, 1964-67; recipient Sears prize, 1968, John Bingham Hurlbut award, 1979. Mem. ABA, Boston Bar Assn. (working group of task force on revision of Mass. corp. statute 1987—), Phi Beta Kappa. Office: Bingham Dana LLP 150 Federal St Boston MA 02110-1713

ENGEL, ERIC, geneticist; b. Geneva, Switzerland, Oct. 12, 1925; s. Alphonse and Henriette (Pasche) E.; m. Mireille de Montmollin, Mar. 22, 1950 ; children: Oliver, Severine, Fabienne. MD, U. Geneva, 1951. From asst. prof. to prof. medicine Vanderbilt U., Nashville, 1963-78; prof. medicine and genetics U. Geneva, 1978-91, hon. prof., 1991—; instr. medicine U. Harvard, Boston, 1962-63; rsch. fellow Mass. Gen. Hosp., Boston, 1960-62. Fellow Am. Soc. Clin. Investigation, Am. Coll. Med. Genetics; mem. Am. Soc. Human Genetics. Avocations: music, painting, literature. Home: La Grangette Faseol, 32550 Haulies France Office: Divsn Med Genetics, CMU 1 Rue Michel Servet, CH 1211 Geneva 4, Switzerland

ENGEL, JÜRGEN JOSEF KARL, architect; b. Dusseldorf, Nordrhein-Westfalen, Germany, June 10, 1954; s. Wilhelm and Marlies Engel; div.; children: Lucas, Isabel. Diploma in arch., Tech. U. Braunschweig, 1976, Tech. U. Aachen, 1979; MS in Arch., MIT, 1982. Freelance arch. Steidle & Ptnr., Munich, 1977, Schneider-Wessling, Cologne, 1980; owner Office/Archtl. Firm, Cologne, 1982-86; office head Ungers Archs., Frankfurt, 1986-89; ptnr. Found. Office KSP Engel and Zimmermann Archs. BDA, Frankfurt, 1990—; mem. Frankfurt City Town Planning Com., 1990—. Contbr. articles to profl. jours. Mem. BDA Assn. German Archs. (chmn. 1998—), Deutscher Werkbund. Office: KSP Engel und Zimmerman Gmbtt, Hanauer Landstrasse 287-289, D-60314 Frankfurt Hessen, Germany

ENGEL, RALPH MANUEL, lawyer; b. N.Y.C., May 13, 1944; s. Werner Herman and Ruth Fredericke (Friedlander) E.; m. Diane Linda Weinberg, Aug. 10, 1968; children—Eric M., Daniel C., Julie R. BA in Econs. with highest honors, NYU, 1965, JD, 1968. Bar: N.Y. 1968, U.S. Supreme Ct. 1972. Assoc. Gilbert, Segall and Young, N.Y.C., 1968-71, Trubin Sillcocks Edelman & Knapp, N.Y.C., 1971-76; assoc., then ptnr. Summit Rovins & Feldesman and predecessor firms, N.Y.C., 1976-91; ptnr. Rosen & Reade, LLP, N.Y.C., 1991—; lectr. Sch. Law, Fordham U., 1990-91. Contbr. articles to legal and other publs.; editor-in-chief The Commentator, NYU, 1968. Mem. Planning Com., Larchmont, N.Y., 1992—. Fellow Am. Coll. Trust and Estate Counsel; mem. N.Y. State Bar Assn. (trust and estate law sect. com. on practice and ethics 1991—, elder law sect., com. on guardianships and fiduciaries 1991-97, com. on estates and tax planning 1997—), Assn. Bar City of N.Y. (com. on estate and gift taxation 1992-95, chmn. subcom. on splitting and combining trusts 1994-95, chmn., subcom. on spousal rights 1994-95, com. on trusts, estates and surrogate's cts. 1997-2000), N.Y. County Lawyers' Assn. (sect. on estates, trusts and surrogate's court practice 1999—), Estate Planning Coun. Westchester County (bd. dirs. 1985-91). Home and Office: 6 Rockwood Dr Larchmont NY 10538-2537 Office: 757 3rd Ave New York NY 10017-2013

ENGEL, TALA, lawyer; b. N.Y.C.; d. Volodia Vladimir Boris and Risia (Modelevska) E.; m. James Colias, Nov. 22, 1981 (dec. Nov. 1989). AA, U. Fla., 1952; BA in Russian and Spanish, U. Miami, 1954; JD, U. Miami, Coral Gables, 1957; postgrad., Middlebury Coll., 1953. Bar: Fla. 1957, U.S. Dist. Ct. (so. dist.) Fla. 1957, U.S. Dist. Ct. (no. dist.) Ill. 1962, U.S. Supreme Ct., 1965, D.C. 1982. Pvt. practice Miami, Fla., 1957-61, Chgo., 1966-86, 90-93; pvt. practice immigration atty. Washington, 1987-89, 93—; atty. Immigration and Naturalization Service, Chgo., 1961-62; parole agt. Ill. Youth Commn., Chgo., 1963-66. Editor The Lawyer, 1956; mem. editl. bd. Miami Law Quar. and Alpha Lambda Delta, 1955-56. Bd. dirs. Cordi-Marian Settlement, Chgo., 1977-93. Named One of 2000 Outstanding Women of 20th Century, Dictionary Internat. Biography, 2000. Mem. Dist. Columbia Bar Assn., Ill. Bar Assn. (gen. assembly 1984-86), Chgo. Bar Assn. (devel. of law com. 1985-87), Chgo. Bar Found., Fed. Bar Assn., Fla. Bar Assn., Am. Immigration Lawyers Assn., Nu Beta Epsilon. Avocations: traveling, theater, singing, writing, Russian and Spanish langs., computers. Home and Office: 2800 Quebec St NW Apt 1027 Washington DC 20008-1237

ENGEL, WALBURGA See VON RAFFLER-ENGEL, WALBURGA

ENGEL, WILLIAM KING, neurologist, educator; b. St. Louis, Nov. 19, 1930; s. William Ernst and Opal (King) E.; m. Valerie Askanas; children: W. Keith, Peter J., Bradford C., Eve M. Kerr. B.A., Johns Hopkins U., 1951; M.D., C.M., McGill U., 1955; M.D. (hon.), L'univ. d'Aix Marseille II, 1987. Diplomate: Am. Bd. Neurology and Psychiatry, Pan. Am. Med. Assn. (hon. life mem.). Intern U. Mich. Hosp., 1955-56; clin. assoc. Nat. Inst. Neurol. Diseases and Blindness, 1956-59; clin. clk. Nat. Hosp., London, 1959-60; with Nat. Inst. Neurol. Diseases and Stroke, 1960-81, chief med. neurology, 1963-78, chief neuromuscular diseases, 1978-81; clin. prof. neurology George Washington U., 1969-81; prof. neurology and pathology, chief div. neuromuscular diseases, dept. neurology U. So. Calif. Sch. Medicine, Los Angeles, 1981—; mem. med. bd. NIH, 1968-69;; founding dir. U. So. Calif. Neuromuscular Center, Hosp. of Good Samaritan, 1981—; mem. med. adv. bd. St. Jude's Children's Rsch. Hosp., Memphis, 1970-76, Myasthenia Gravis Found., 1970—, L.A. chpt. Muscular Dystropy Assn., 1981—, Amyotrophic Lateral Sclerosis Nat. Found., 1971-85, Amyotrophic Lateral Sclerosis Soc. Am., 1980-85, mem. sci. adv. bd., 1982-85; vis. prof., invited lectr., advisor internat. congresses in Europe, S.Am., Can., Australia, Far East; cons. Nat. Naval Med. Ctr. Former Mem. editorial bd.: Archives of Neurology; contbr. numerous papers to profl. lit., poems to mags. Past pres. Citizens Assn., Bethesda, Md., Longhouse chief YMCA Indian Guides, 1965-66; past chmn. troop com. Boy Scouts Am.; mem. edn. adv. bd. Phronesis, Spain; nat. corp. mem. Muscular Dystrophy Assn., 1985-88, nat. v.p. 1988— , med. adv. bd. Los Angeles chpt., 1981—, bd. dirs. 1985—. Recipient Meritorious Service medal USPHS, 1971, Gaetano Conte Gold medal for clin. rsch., 1999, various awards from Italian me . socs. Fellow Am. Acad. Neurology (S. Weir Mitchell award 1962; pres. VI Internat. Congress Neuromuscular Diseases 1986); mem. AMA, Histochem. Soc., Am. Soc. Cell Biology, Am. Assn. Neuropathologists, Soc. for Neurosci., World Commn. Neuromuscular Disease (exec. com.), Am. Neurol. Assn., L.A. County Med. Assn., Sociètè Belge d'Electromyographie (assoc.), Asociación de Distrofia Muscular de la Republica Argentina (hon. pres.), Sociètè Française de Neurologie (hon.). Office: U So Calif Neuromuscular Ctr Good Samaritan Hosp 637 Lucas Ave Los Angeles CA 90017-1912

ENGELAND, UWE, physicist; b. Wyk Auf Fohr, Germany, Nov. 12, 1967; s. Gunther and Friedel (Schroder) E. Diploma, Georg August U., Gottingen, Germany, 1995. Scientist Theoretical Physiks, Gottingen, Germany, 1993-95, MPI Biophys. Chem., Gottingen, Germany, 1995-96, Nuclear Medicine, Gottingen, Germany, 1996-99; cons. in field. Office: Nuclear Medicine, Robert Koch Str 40, 37075 Gottingen Germany

ENGELBART, DOUG, engineering executive; b. Portland, Oreg., Jan. 30, 1925. BSEE, Oreg. State U., 1948, D (hon.), 1994; degree in engring., U. Calif., Berkeley, 1952; PhD in Elec. Engring., U. Calif., 1955. Electronic/radar tech. USN, 1944-46; elec. engr. NACA Ames Lab., Mountain View, Calif., 1948-51; asst. prof. elec. engring. U. Calif., Berkeley, 1955-56; rschr. Stanford (Calif.) Rsch. Inst. (now SRI Internat.), 1957-59, dir. augmentation rsch. ctr., 1959-77; sr. scientist Tymshare, Inc., Cupertino, Calif., 1977-84, McDonnell Douglas ISC, San Jose, Calif., 1984-89; dir. Bootstrap Project Stanford U., 1989-90; dir. Bootstrap Project, Palo Alto, Calif., 1990-91, Bootstrap Inst., Fremont, Calif., 1991—. Contbr. numerous articles to profl. jours. Recipient Lifetime Achievement award for Tech. Excellence, PC Mag., 1987, Disting. Alumni of Yr. award Oreg. STate U., 1987, Disting. Svc. and Outstanding Contbns. in Field citation Sigma Phi Epsilon, St. Louis, 1989, Lifetime Achievement award for Vision, Inspiration and Contbn., Electronic Networking Assn., San Francisco, 1990, Software Sys. award Assn. Computing Machinery, 1990, Am. Ingenuity award Nat. Assn. Mfrs.' Congress of Am. Industry, Washington, 1991, Disting. Alumnus award U. Calif., Berkeley, 1991, Lifetime Achievement award Dominican Coll. of San Rafael, Calif., 1991, Lifetime Achievement award Price Waterhouse, Washington, 1994, cert. of appreciation Smart Valley, Inc., 1994, Editors' Choice award MacUser Awards Ceremony, 1995, SoftQuad Web award World Wide Web Conf., Boston, 1995, cert. of merit The Franklin Inst. Com. on Sci. and the Arts, 1996, Spl. award Am. Soc. for Info. Sci., 1996, Jerome H. Lemelson-MIT prize for excellence in invention and innovation, 1997; named Pioneer of the Electronic Frontier, Electronic Frontier Found., Washington, 1992; Engelbart award established in his honor Internat. Conf. on Hypertext and Hypermedia, 1994. Fellow Nat. Acad. Arts and Scis.; mem. IEEE (treas., vice chmn., chmn. San Francisco chpt. profl. group on electronic computers 1957-59, Computer Pioneer award 1993), NAS (com. on augmentation of human intellect 1989, panel on future role of computers in rsch. librs. 1968-70), Nat. Acad. Engring., Computer Profls. for Social Responsibility (adv. bd.), The Tech. Ctr. of Silicon Valley (adv. coun.), Phi Kappa Phi, Tau Beta Pi, Sigma Tau, Eta Kappa Nu, Blue Key, Sigma Xi. Achievements include visionary and pioneering work in organizational augmentation, including strategies for continuous improvement, human-tool co-evolution and interactive collaborative hypermedia computing to support the knowledge-intensive work of groups and individuals; 7 patents relating to bi-stable gaseous plasma digital devices, 12 patents relating to all-magnetic digital devices, 1 patent for invention of the Mouse. Home: 89 Catalpa Dr Atherton CA 94027-2167 Office: Bootstrap Inst 6505 Kaiser Dr Fremont CA 94555-3614

ENGELBERG, HYMAN, internist, researcher; b. N.Y.C., Oct. 7, 1913; s. Julius and Tillie (Grebel) E.; children: Michael, Alan, Lon. BA, Cornell U., 1933, MD, 1936. Intern Cedars of Lebanon Hosp., L.A., 1936-37, chief med. resident, 1939-40; asst. resident in medicine Montefiore Hosp., N.Y.C., 1937-38; sr. attending physician Cedars-Sinai Med. Ctr., L.A., 1944—; pres. Calif. Arteriosclerosis Rsch. Found., L.A., 1960—; cons. in thrombosis rsch. Stritch Sch. of Medicine, Loyola U., Maywood, Ill., 1984—. Author: Your Heart's Best Friend--The Untold Story, 1986, Cholesterol: Truth and Humbug, 1991, Heparin and the Prevention of Artherosclerosis: Basic Research and Clinical Application, 1990; contbr. more than 100 articles to profl. jours. 1st lt. USAF, 1940-44. Recipient Honor Achievement award Angiology Rsch. Found, 1969; named hon. mem. Turkish Soc. Hematology, 1987. Mem. N.Y. Acad. Scis. Jewish. Office: PO Box 16458 Beverly Hills CA 90209-2458

ENGELHARDT, HUGO TRISTRAM, JR., physician, educator; b. New Orleans, Apr. 27, 1941; s. Hugo Tristram and Beulah (Karbach) E.; m. Susan Gay Malloy, Nov. 25, 1965; children: Elisabeth, Christina, Dorothea. B.A., U. Tex., Austin, 1963, Ph.D., 1969; M.D. with honors, Tulane U., 1972. Asst. prof. U. Tex. Med. Br., 1972-75, assoc. prof., 1975-77; mem. Inst. Med. Humanities, 1973-77; Rosemary Kennedy prof. philosophy of medicine Georgetown U., 1977-82; sr. research scholar Kennedy Inst. Center for Bioethics, Washington, 1977-82; prof. depts. internal medicine, community medicine and ob-gyn. Baylor Coll. Medicine, Houston, 1983—; mem. Ctr. for Med. Ethics and Health Policy, Houston, 1983—; prof. dept. philosophy Rice U., Houston, 1983—; chmn. adv. panel on infertility prevention and treatment for office of tech. assessment of the U.S. Congress, 1986-87; vis. scholar Internat. Akad. für Philosophie, Liechtenstein, 1997, Liberty Fund, spring, 1998. Author: Mind Body: A Categorial Relation, 1973, The Foundations of Bioethics, 1986, rev. edit., 1996, Bioethics and Secular Humanism, 1991, The Foundations of Christian Bioethics, 2000; co-author: Bioethics: Readings and Cases, 1987; assoc. editor Ency. of Bioethics, 1973-78, Jour. Medicine and Philosophy, 1974-84; mem. editl. adv. bd. Quirón, 1982—, Bioethics, 1987—, Ethik in der Medizin, 1988—, Bioetica, 1993—, Christian Theology, 1997—; editor Jour. Medicine and Philosophy, 1984—, (series) Philos. Studies in Contemporary Culture, 1992—; co-editor Philosophy and Medicine series, 1974—, Clin. Med. Ethics, 1991—, Christian Bioethics, 1995—; editor: (with others) Evaluation and Explanation in the Biomedical Sciences, 1975, Philosophical Medical Ethics, 1977, Mental Health, 1978, Clinical Judgment, 1979, Concepts of Health and Disease, 1981, New Knowledge in the Biomedical Sciences, 1982, Scientific Controversies, 1987, The Use of Human Beings in Research, 1988, Sicherheit und Freiheit, 1990, Hegel Reconsidered, 1994, The Philosophy of Medicine, 2000. Mem. bioethics com. Nat. Found. March of Dimes, 1975—. Fulbright fellow, 1969-70, Woodrow Wilson vis. fellow, 1988; fellow Inst. for Advanced Studies, Berlin, 1988-89. Mem. Am. Philos. Assn., European Acad. Scis. and Arts. Home: 2802 Lafayette Houston TX 77005-3038 Office: Ctr Med Ethics Health Policy Baylor Coll Medicine One Baylor Plz Houston TX 77030

ENGELHARDT, REGINA, cosmetologist, artist, small business owner; b. Kiwerce, Poland, Oct. 1, 1928; came to U.S., 1949; d. Marian and Maria (Wardach) Engelhardt; m. Gerard Edward Twardon, May 30, 1953 (div. 1961); children: Miriam Teresa Twardon Bielski, Elizabeth Maria Twardon, Renee Marie Twardon Gilchrist. Grad., Laski Inst. Tech., 1951; lic. cosmetologist, Hamtramck Beauty Sch., 1960; art student, Mercy Ctr., 1980-84. Sec. Am. Savs., Detroit, 1950-55; cosmetologist Magic Touch Salon, Oak Park, Mich., 1960—; owner Regina's Fine Arts, Detroit, 1986—, Art Restorations, 1986—; art tchr. Farmington Activity Ctr., Farmington Hills, Mich., 1993—; spkr. in field. Artist lithographs; represented in permanent collection at Althorp Mus., Eng., 1998, also pvt. collections in U.S., Can., Poland, Eng. Mem. Dem. Nat. Com., 1996—; mem. nat. com. to preserve social security and medicare, 1993—. Recipient Gold and Silver medals Internat. Art Challenge, 1987-88, 90, Kubinski award Friends of Polish Arts, 1989, First and Fourth awards Mich. State Exhibit, 1988. Mem. Sculptores Guild of Mich., Four Octave Club, Farmington Artists Club (6 Popular Vote awards 1985, 86, 97, merit award local art exhibit 1997, two merit awards 1998), Sierra Club, Internat. Platform Assn., Nature Conservancy. Roman Catholic. Avocations: music, needlework, dance, reading. E-mail: reginaart@webtv.net. Home: 17345 Wildemere St Detroit MI 48221-2722

ENGELHARDT, ROLF-UDO, chemistry educator; b. Berlin, Jan. 22, 1935; s. Walter and Greda (Wlazil) E.; m. Ingrid Crecelius, 1961; children: Amelie, Gundula, Caroline, Miriam, Ophelia, Nikola, Samuel. Diploma, U. Freiburg, 1961, Dr.rer.nat., 1964. Prof. Free U., Berlin, 1970-71, prof. inorganic chemistry, 1971—. Co-author: Chemie in Flüss Aumoniak, 1966; author: Developments in Inorganic Nitrogren Chemistry, 1973; contbr. articles to profl. jours. Decorated Bundesverdienstkreuz am Bande (Germany). Mem. Gesellschaft Deutscher Chemiker. Avocations: canoeing, kites, string figures. Home: Goldenes Horn 25, D-12107 Berlin Germany Office: Inst Chemie Anorganische Analyt Chem, Free U Fabeckstr 34-36, D-14195 Berlin Germany

ENGELKE, JOANNA DEMBER, health products executive; b. Cin., May 19, 1960; d. William Norton and Cynthia (Fox) Dember; m. Charles William Engelke, May 17, 1987; children: Philip David, Rebecca, Elise, Marianne Florence. BA, Yale U., 1982; MBA, Harvard U., 1986. V.p., ptnr. Bain & Co., Boston, 1993-98; gen. mgr. hemostasis Dade Behring, Marburg, Germany, 1998—; Bd. dirs. HemoSense, Inc., Milpitas, Calif. Fax: 49-6421-39-4639. Home: 25 Morse Rd Newton MA 02460-2454 Office: Dade Behring Marburg GmbH, Emil-von-Behring-Strasse 76, Marburg 35047, Germany also: Die Rappenwiesen 34, 61350 Bad Homburg Germany

ENGELKING, ELLEN MELINDA, pattern company executive, real estate broker, manufacturing company; b. Columbus, Ind., May 12, 1942; d. Lowell Eugene and Marcella (Brane) E.; children: Melissa Claire Fairbanks John David Prohaska, Ellen Margaret Brunner. Student, Sullins Coll., 1961, Franklin Coll., 1961-62, Ind. U., 1963. Chmn., CEO Engelking, Inc., Columbus, Ind.; founder The FlexCell Group. Sec. Bartholomew County Rep. Party, 1976-80; chmn. bd. dirs. Jr. Achievementm 1996—; chmn. Pvt. Industry Coun. South Ctrl. Ind.; protocol hostess Pan Am. Games X, Indpls., 1987. Bd. dirs. Ind. Humanities Coun., 1997—, United Way, 2000—. Recipient Franklin Coll. Alumni Citation, 1994, Athena award Oldsmobile Inst. Am. Bank C. of C., 1995. Mem. Columbus Area C. of C. (vice chmn. bd. dirs. 1990, bd. dirs. 1997—), Centra Credit Union (bd. dirs.), Delta Delta Delta. Roman Catholic. Avocation: study and present adaptation of Shaker work ethic. Office: Engelking Inc PO Box 607 Columbus IN 47202-0607

ENGELMANN, ARNO, psychology educator; b. Berlin, Dec. 6, 1931; arrived in Brazil, 1941; s. José Salomão and Sara (Singer) E.; m. Lucy Calil, July 12, 1963. Licentiate, São Paulo (Brazil) U., 1960, BS, 1955; PhD, U. Ill., 1962, São Paulo U., 1972. Asst. in psychology FPSL São Paulo U., 1960-71; asst. in psychology Inst. Psychology, São Paulo U., 1971-72, dr.-asst., 1972-91, free docent, 1991-93, full prof. psychology, 1993—; assessor, State of San Paulo Rsch. Support Found., São Paulo, 1982-86. Author: Subjective States, 1978; editor: Wolgang Köhler, 1978; contbr. articles to profl. jours. Home: Rua da Consolação, 3617 ap. 42, 01416001 São Paulo Brazil Office: Inst Psychology-USP, Av Prof Mello Moraes, 1721, 05508900 São Paulo Brazil

ENGELMANN, RUDOLPH HERMAN, electronics consultant; b. Hewitt, Minn., Mar. 5, 1929; s. Herman Emil Robert and Minna Louise (Kniep) E.; children: Guy Robert, Heidi Louise. BA, U. Minn., 1953. Electronic designer Lawrence Livermore (Calif.) Lab., 1959-61; cons. Atlantic Rsch. Corp., Manchester, N.H., 1961-64, Gen. Radio Co., West Concord, Mass., 1963-69, Possis Engring., Mpls., 1970—, 3M Co., St. Paul, 1977-78, Pako Photo, Mpls., 1977-78, Litton Microwave, Mpls., 1977-79; Presenter papers at confs., 1988-89, 89-90. Contbr. articles to profl. jours. 1st lt. USAF, 1946-53. Achievements include developments and patents in gigahertz digital frequency scalers and counters and time interval meters, touchtone telephone for U.S. Army, automatic photographic focus control, automatic temperature monitor and control for grain and petroleum storage safety and volume correction, optical character recognition, high efficiency battery charging systems, end-of-charge detector, rudderless flight control, ultra lightweight muscle prostheses, flight controls, power management, stealth penetrating radar, high efficiency shape memory alloy modulation and linear circuitry, high-efficiency electronic orthetic muscle, digitally variable 90db A.C. power source, raster scanning microscope, linear wave blood pump.

Office: World Effort Found 1171 Bush St Apt 2 San Francisco CA 94109-5926

ENGELMANN, UWE, medical informatics scientist, consultant; b. Barbis, Germany, June 22, 1955; s. Werner H. and Vera O. (Wolf) E.; m. Astrid Brüggemann, Aug. 6, 1986; children: Mareike, Niels. Diploma in Med. Informatics, U. Heidelberg, Germany, 1983, PhD, 1990. Cert. in med. informatics. Cons. U. Heidelberg, 1978, BMW AG, Munich, 1985-86; assoc. prof. Fachhochschule des Landes Rheinland-Pfalz, Pfalz, Germany, 1984-87; owner, CEO, Interactive Sys., Heidelberg, 1986-92; sr. rsch. scientist German Cancer Rsch. Ctr., Heidelberg, 1987—; cons. Steinbeis-Transfer Ctr. Med. Informatics, Heidelberg, 1995—. Mem. GMDS, GI, FGK, BVMI, IEEE Computer Soc., Assn. for Computing Machinery, German Roentgen Assn. Avocations: juggling, crop circle research. Office: German Cancer Rsch Ctr, Im Neuenheimer Feld 280, D-69120 Heidelberg Germany

ENGER, EDWARD HENRY, JR., editor, writer; b. Mpls., Mar. 16, 1930; s. Edward Henry Sr. and Anastasia (Barber) E.; m. Carolyn Sue Bush, June 1, 1964. BS in Edn., U. Minn., 1952. Cert. tchr., Calif. Tchr. Downers Grove (Ill.) Pub. Sch., 1956-58; editor Harper & Row, Evanston, Ill., 1958-62; author Harper & Row, N.Y.C., 1975-78; editor Silver Burdett Co., Morristown, N.J., 1962-68, Dell Pub. Co., N.Y.C., 1968-75; author Nat. Textbook Co., Chgo., 1979-81; editorial dir. Amsco Sch. Publs., N.Y.C., 1982-97. Author: Writing by Doing, 1981, (textbook series) Language Basics, 1975-78. Served to cpl. U.S. Army, 1954-56, Korea. Mem. Nat. Council Tchrs. English. Democrat. Avocations: gardening, cooking, hiking, jogging.

ENGGAARD, KNUD, politician; b. Odder, Denmark, June 4, 1929; s. Jens Nielsen and Anna (Skovsgaard) E.; m. Elsebeth Andersen, Dec. 1, 1962; children: Thomas, Jakob, Christian. MS in Engring. Sci., Royal Tech. U., Copenhagen, Denmark, 1954. With Swedish Engring. Co., 1956-58; engr. Royal Danish Airforce Material Command, 1958; chmn. Liberal Youth of Denmark, Denmark, 1959-62, Danish Youth Council, Denmark, 1962-64; M.P. Liberal Party, Denmark, 1964-77, 79-81, 84-98, chmn. liberal group, 1970-71, 73-77, vice chmn., 1978-82; minister of interior Denmark, 1978-79, 86-87, minister of energy, 1982-86, minister of econ. affairs, 1987-88, minister of def., 1988-93; chmn. Copenhagen Telefon Co., 1974-78; pres. Nordic Coun., 1976-77, 96-97; bd. dirs. Nat. Bank, 1970-72, 74-75, Royal Mortgage Bank, 1970-78; bd. dirs. Copenhagen Port Authorities, 1970-78, chmn. def. com., 1993-98. Served as lt. Army Tech. Corps (Res.) 1955. Office: Melbyvej 8, 2740 Skovlunde K, Denmark

ENGIN, NUR, engineer, researcher; b. Ankara, Turkey, Sept. 16, 1970; s. Oktay and Semanur Engin; m. Marc de Wolf, Jan. 26, 1996. BS, Mid. East Tech. U., Ankara, Turkey, 1993, MS, 1996. Tchg. asst. Mid. East Tech. U., Ankara, 1993-96; rsch. asst. Twente U., Enschede, 1996—; rschr. Philips Rsch., Eindhoven. Contbr. articles to profl. jours. including Integrated Design and Test of Mixed-Signal Circuits. Mem. IEEE. Avocations: reading, travel, movies, cooking. Office: MESA Rsch Inst/U Twente, PO Box 217, 7500 AE Enschede The Netherlands

ENGLAND, JOHN MELVIN, lawyer, clergyman; b. June 29, 1932; s. John Marcus and Frances Dorothy (Brown) E.; m. Jane Cantrell, Aug. 2, 1953; children: Kathryn Elizabeth, Janette Evelyn, John William, Kenneth Paul, James Andrew, Samuel Robert. Student, Ga. State U., 1951-53; JD, U. Ga., 1956; BD magna cum laude with honors Theology, Columbia Theol. Sem., Decatur, Ga., 1964. Bar: Ga. 1959, U.S. Dist. Ct. (no. dist.) Ga. 1967, U.S. Ct. Mil. Appeals 1976, U.S. Ct. Appeals (5th cir.) 1967, U.S. Ct. Appeals (11th cir.) 1981, U.S. Supreme Ct. 1977, U.S. Dist. Ct. (mid. dist.) Ga. 1986, U.S. Dist. Ct. (so. dist.) Ga. 1991, U.S. Dist. Ct. (no. dist.) Tex. 1991; ordained to ministry Presbyn. Ch., 1964. Spl. agt. FBI, Washington, 1956-57, Indpls., 1957-59, Charlotte, N.C., 1959, Greenville, S.C., 1959-60; student supply pastor Bethel and Buford Presbyn. Chs., Atlanta, 1960-63; pastor Mullins (S.C.) Presbyn. Ch., 1964-67; asst. dist. atty. Fulton County, Ga., 1967-75; sr. ptnr. England and Weller, Atlanta, 1975-88, England, Weaver & Kytle, 1988-94, England & McKnight, 1994-2000, England & England, 2000—; legal seminar lectr. and spkr. throughout the country under auspices of Christian orgns.; spl. pros. for gov. Ga., 1976-79; spl. cons. on appellate reform Supreme Ct. Ga., 1979-80; state bar rep. to Superior Ct. Uniform Rules Com. Coun. Superior Ct. Judges, 1984, Uniform Rules Com. State Bar Ga., 1993—. Elder, tchr., evangelism coord. Presbyn. Ch. USA; chmn. Christian Bus. Men's Coms. of U.S.A., Atlanta, 1971-73, chmn. internat. conv., Atlanta, 1979, bd. dirs., 1971-81. Mem. ABA, ATLA, State Bar Ga., Atlanta Bar Assn., Lawyers Club Atlanta, Ga. Trial Lawyers Assn., Nat. Assn. Criminal Def. Lawyers, Ga. Assn. Criminal Def. Lawyers, North Fulton Bar Assn. Office: England & England 9040 Roswell Rd Ste 410 Atlanta GA 30350-1863

ENGLE, RICHARD MALLORY, academic administrator, civil engineer; b. Chgo., Jan. 5, 1933; s. Robert Henry Sr. and Faerie Josephine (Mallory) E.; m. Claudia Standish White, June 7, 1958 (div. Sept. 1990); children: Jennifer K. Radl, Diana T., Adele S.Schneider, Richard H.W. BArch, U. Ill., 1956, MS in Architecture Engring., 1957. Registered profl. engr., N.Mex. Commd. C.E. Corps. U.S. Navy, Washington, many areas, 1957; advanced through grades to commdr. U.S. Navy, retired, 1978; physical plant dir. Miami Univ., Oxford, Ohio, 1978-86; assoc. v.p. for facilities Rutgers U., New Brunswick, N.J., 1986—. Contbr. various tech. articles to profl. pubs.; presentor Software Ownership, Nat. Bur. of Standards, 1983. 1st V.P. United Fed. Credit Union, Japan, 1970-75; vol. Boy Scouts Am., 1957—; vestry Episc. Ch., various locations, 1965-66, 80-86, 88—. Decorated Navy Achievement medal; Navy Commendation medal; recipient Thanks badge, Far East Coun. Girl Scouts Am., Atsugi, Japan, 1975. Mem. NSPE, Nat. Eagle Scout Assn., Assn. of Phys. Plant Adminstrs. (Midwest v.p.1984-86). Protestant. Avocations: travel & camping, music & theater, private flying, swim official. Home: 15 Silver Holw N Brunswick NJ 08902-2664 Office: Rutgers U 82 St 1603 Piscataway NJ 08854-8037

ENGLE, SUSAN ANN, chemist; b. Hershey, Pa., Nov. 16, 1956; d. Harold Glenn Jr. and Doris Jane (Hovis) Engle; m. Scott Vincent Carney (div. Dec. 1993); children: Kristin, David; m. I. Michael Zulak, Feb. 21, 1999. BS in Chemistry, Lebanon Valley Coll., 1978; MBA, Temple U., 1985, PhD, 1995. Lab. asst. Lebanon Valley Coll., Annville, Pa., 1976-78; rsch. technician Hershey Foods, Inc., 1976-78; technician Pitman-Moore, Inc., Washington Crossing, N.J., 1978-80; chemist Pitman-Moore, Inc., Washington Crossing, 1980-81, methods devel. chemist, 1981-83, supr. methods and analysis lab., 1983-85; group leader analytical control Rorer, Inc., Fort Washington, Pa., 1987-89; sr. supr. stability Rhone-Poulenc Rorer, Inc., Fort Washington, 1989-91, quality assurance mgr., 1991-93, quality control mgr., 1993-95, acting dir. plant quality assurance and control, 1995-96; dir. quality assurance Novartis Consumer Health N.Am., Inc., Lincoln, Nebr., 1996-2000, ALZA Corp., Vacaville, Calif., 2000—. Mem. choir Jarrettown United Meth. Ch., 1991-97. Recipient Scientisic German award, 1978, Rhone Poulenc Rorer award for advancement/devel. of women, 1994; scholar Nat. Honor Soc., 1978. Mem. Am. Chem. Soc. (Phila. sect.), Am. Assn. Pharm. Scientists, Consumer Health Products Assn. (mfg. controls com.). Republican. Methodist. Avocations: golf, swimming, skiing. Office: ALZA Corp 700 Eubanks Dr Vacaville CA 95688-9470

ENGLEBERT, ANNICK REGINE, linguist; b. Brussels; d. Paul Marcel and Arlette (Merckx) E.; m. Claude Deleau, May 11, 1988 (div. 1993); children: Amélie, Amaury, Odile, Fantine, Lynric. Arts Degree, U. Brussels, 1982, PhD, 1988, Agrégé in French Linguistics, 1993. Aspirant Fonds Nat. de la Rsch. Scientifique, Brussels, 1984-88, rschr., 1990-92; rschr., asst. U. Brussels, 1993—, tchr., 1995—. Author: A Little Word "De", 1992, The French Past Participle, 1996, The French Infinity de Narration, 1997, Thesis and Computer, 1998; (software) The French Past Participle, 1992; co-author: Reading, Analyzing, Writing Scientific French Language, 1999, How to Arrange One's Ideas, 1999. Mem. Belgium Swimming League (ofcl. 1995—). Avocations: swimming, multimedia software creating, skiing cross country. E-mail: anengleb@ulb.ac.be. Home: 40 Rue du Hainaut, 1420 Braine-L'Alleud Belgium Office: U Libre de Brussels, 50 Ave Fr Roosevelt, 1050 Brussels Belgium

ENGLEMAN, CHARLES EDWARD, newspaper editor and publisher; b. Greenfield, Mo., Jan. 25, 1911; s. Franklin Pierce and Mabel Claire (Wilson) E.; m. Lela Jean Garnett; children: Carol Ann Sander, Stephen Charles. BS in Journalism, U. Okla., 1933. Reporter Daily Times-Democrat, Altus, Okla., 1934-35; news editor Daily Democrat-Chief, Hobart, Okla., 1935-36; advt. mgr. Daily News, Elk City, Okla., 1936-37; editor and pub. The Walters (Okla.) Herald, 1937-40; editor, pub., owner The Clinton (Okla.) Daily News, 1940—. Pres. Clinton Regional Hosp. Bd. Trustees, 1979-80; pres. Foss Reservoir Master Conservancy Dist. Bd. Trustees, 1956—; mem. U. Okla. Bd. Regents, 1976-83, pres. 1982-83; bd. dirs. U. Okla. Found., 1975—. Recipient Disting. Alumni award, U. Okla. Sch. Journalism, 1984, Okla. Journalism Hall of Fame award, Cent. State U., 1985, Milt Phillips award for Excellence in Newspaper Journalism, Okla. Press. Assn., 1982, Stanley Draper Disting. Editorial award, Okla. Heritage Assn., 1983, Disting. Svc. award U. Okla., 1995; named Clinton Citizen of Yr., 1988. Mem. Okla. Press Assn. (pres. 1957-58, Pres.'s award 1999), United Press Editors of Okla. (pres. 1961-62), Okla. Newspaper Found. (pres. 1985-86), Rotary (pres. Clinton chpt. 1947-48), Clinton C. of C. (pres. 1952-53), Univ. Okla. Alumni Assn. (pres. 1962-63). Democrat. Methodist. Avocations: gardening, golf, quail hunting, fishing. Home: 601 S 14th St Clinton OK 73601-4205 Office: The Clinton Daily News 522 Avant Ave Clinton OK 73601-3436

ENGLER, BRIAN DAVID, systems analyst; b. Palmerton, Pa., Oct. 9, 1947; s. David James and Doreen Estelle (Sheldon) E.; m. Margaret Mary Hurlock, Dec. 31, 1969 (div. Apr. 1981); children: Donna, David; m. Maxine Sue Richard, May 24, 1981; children: Rachel, Stacey. BS with merit, U.S. Naval Acad., 1969; MS in Ops. Rsch., Naval Postgrad. Sch., Monterey, Calif., 1978; MBA in Fin., Acctg., Marymount U., 1986. Commd. ensign USN, 1969, advanced through grades to comdr., 1983, naval flight officer, mission comdr., ops. analyst, 1969-89, ret., 1989; ops. analyst, project leader Systems Planning and Analysis., Alexandria, Va., 1989-90; asst. program mgr. Systems Planning and Analysis., Falls Church, Va., 1990-91, program mgr., 1991-2000; exec. v.p. Mil. Ops. Rsch. Soc., 2000—. Assoc. editor (alumni newsletter) O.R. News, 1976-78. Mem. Big Bros./ Big Sisters of Balt., Annapolis, Md., 1968-69; sec.-treas. bd. dirs. Gov.'s Sq. Homeowners Assn., Williamsburg, Va., 1989-97. Decorated Navy Commendation medals (2), Meritorious Svc. medal; recipient Juvenile Decency award Kiwanis Club, 1965, Cert. of Proficiency, Civil Air Patrol, 1963, Best Cadet award Temple U., 1965. Mem. Mil. Ops. Rsch. Soc. (bd. dirs. 1991—, sec.-treas. 1993-94, v.p. for adminstrn. 1994-95. v.p. fin. and mgmt. 1999-00), VFW (sr. vice comdr.), Am. Legion, Mil. Applications Soc., Inst. for Ops. Rsch. and Mgmt. Sci., Washington Inst. for Ops. Rsch. and Mgmt. Sci., Delta Epsilon Sigma. Avocations: running, sailing, reading, music, fencing, bowling. Home: 5918 Clermont Landing Ct Burke VA 22015-2565 Office: Mil Ops Rsch Soc 101 S Whiting St Alexandria VA 22304-3418

ENGLER, EVA KAY, dental and veterinary products company executive; b. Czechoslovakia, May 7, 1927; m. Alfred Engler (dec. 1979); 2 children. P-res., founder med. and dental mfg. co. Engler Engring. Corp., Hialeah, Fla., 1964—. Avocations: languages. Office: Engler Engring Corp 1099 E 47th St Hialeah FL 33013-2139

ENGLERT, ROY THEODORE, JR., lawyer; b. Alexandria, Va., Dec. 5, 1958; s. Roy Theodore and Helen Frances (Wiggs) E. AB, Princeton U., 1978; JD, Harvard U., 1981. Ct. law clk. U.S. Ct. Appeals-D.C. Cir., Washington, 1981-82; assoc. Wilmer, Cutler & Pickering, Washington, 1982-86; asst. to the solicitor gen. U.S. Dept. Justice, Washington, 1986-89; assoc. Mayer, Brown & Platt, Washington, 1989-90, ptnr., 1991—. Tech. official judo Centennial Olympic Games, Atlanta, 1996. Presbyterian. Avocation: judo. Home: 411 S Pitt St Alexandria VA 22314-3713 Office: Mayer Brown & Platt 1909 K St NW Washington DC 20006-1152

ENGLISH, BRUCE VAUGHAN, environmental consultant; b. Richmond, Va., Aug. 6, 1921; s. Pollard and Lucy Kelly (Rice) E.; m. Virginia Tejas McCall Shaw, Feb. 6, 1949. BS in Physics and Math., Randolph-Macon Coll., 1942; MS in Physics and Math., Ind. U., 1943; PhD in Physics, U. Va., 1958. Grad. asst. instr. army specialized tng. program/rsch. asst. Manhattan Dist. Engrs. Project; physics instr. Ind. U., Bloomington; asst. prof. physics army specialized tng. program Randolph-Macon Coll., Ashland, Va., 1943-44, assoc. prof., acting chmn. dept. physics, 1948-58, prof., chmn. dept., 1958-64; physicist, head high pressure lab. U.S. Navy Underwater Sound Reference Lab., Orlando, Fla., 1946-48; physicist, cons. historic preservation, pollution control and environment Ashland, 1964—; dir. Poe Found., Inc., Richmond, 1968-97, pres., 1973-92, life hon. pres., 1998—; pres., dir. Edgar Allan Poe Mus., Richmond, 1973-92; pres. Pollution Control Assocs., Richmond, 1967-70. Co-pub.: Poe's Richmond, 1978; columnist Herald-Progress, 1971—; contbr. numerous articles to Poe Messenger mag. Founding mem. Richmond Symphony, 1956; mem. Patrick Henry Scotchtown Com., Hanover County, Va., 1958—; pres. Hist. Richmond Found., 1967-70; bd. dirs. Church Hill Model Neighborhood Bd., Richmond, 1968-73; chmn. Bicentennial Com. for Hanover County, 1974-92, Drainage Com., Ashland, 1980s, Courthouse Com. for Hanover County, 1985—; lay reader, mem. vestry St. John's Ch., Church Hill, Richmond, Va., 1969-70; hon. pres. Poe Found., Inc., 1998. With USN, 1944-45. Named Hon. Citizen State of Md., 1990; Ford Faculty fellow, 1951-52, Danforth fellow, 1956-57, du Pont fellow, 1957-58. Mem. AAAS, Am. Phys. Soc., Va. Acad. Sci., Va. Hist. Soc., Nat. Trust for Hist. Preservation, Irish Georgian Soc., Cousteau Soc. (founding), Air and Waste Mgmt. Assn., Nat. Soc. for Clean Air Gt. Britain, Soc. Descendants of Peter Francisco (founder, advisor), City Tavern Club, Commonwealth Club, Farmington Country Club, Downtown Club, Phi Beta Kappa, Sigma Xi, Omicron Delta Kappa, Chi Beta Phi, Pi Delta Epsilon. Episcopalian. Achievements include research for project developing atomic bomb; increasing awareness of hazards of pollution since 1955, of Edgar Allan Poe's cosmology, cryptography, and other scientific writings.

ENGLISH, LYN DENISE, mathematician, educator; b. Brisbane, Australia; d. Brian Henry and Denise Dagmar (Milliner) E. BEd, Brisbane Coll. Advanced Edn., Australia, 1979, MEd, 1981; PhD, U. Queensland, Brisbane, 1988. Curriculum coord. dept. edn. Brisbane Coll. Advanced Edn., 1979-84, lectr., 1985-88; sr. lectr. Queensland U. Tech., Brisbane, 1989-92, assoc. prof., 1992—. Author: Mathematics Education: Models and Processes, 1995; editor, author: Mathematical Reasoning: Analogies, Metaphors, & Images, 1997, Handbook of International Research in Mathematics Education, 2000; founding editor: Mathematical Thinking and Learning: An International Journal. Mem. APA, Nat. Coun. Tchrs. Math., Internat. Group Psychology of Math. Edn. Avocations: aerobics, gardening. Office: Queensland U Tech Victoria, Park Rd Kelvin Grove, Brisbane QLD 4059, Australia

ENGLISH, MARLENE CABRAL, management consultant; b. Lawrence, Mass., Apr. 28, 1954; d. Amick John and Mary Rose (Vasconcelos) Cabral; m. Richard Gayle English, June 24, 1978. BBA, U. Mass., 1976. Acct. mgr. Revlon, Inc., N.Y.C., 1977-79; tech. rep. Rapidata, Inc., N.Y.C., 1979-80; mgr.acctg. systems group Pannell, Kerr, Forster, Dallas, 1980-83; mgmt. cons. Blythe/Nelson, Dallas, 1983-84, Prism Cons., Arlington, Tex., 1984—; sec., treas. Highland-Avery Industries, Inc., Dallas, 1988-95. Author: And God Created Woman, 1995. Tech. systems procurement & installation Rep. Nat. Conv., Dallas, 1984; dir. Faith Harvest Ministries, Inc., Dallas, 1990-95; sys. cons. Van Cliburn Internat. Piano Competition, Ft. Worth, 1985. Catholic. Avocations: antique linen restoration, gardening, writing, Christian works for children, classical piano. Home and Office: Prism Cons 4320 Rambling Creek Dr Arlington TX 76016-3418

ENGLISH, RON DALE, artist; b. Decatur, Ill., June 3, 1959; s. Jimmie Lee and Mary Etta (Parker) E.; m. Tarssa Leslie Yazadani; children: Zephyr Elizabeth, Mars Alexander. BA, U. N.Tex., 1984; MFA, U. Tex., 1986. project dir. dept. recreation and cultural affairs Jersey City (N.J.) Mus., 1995; mural project dir. Guggenheim Children's Fund, The Bronx, N.Y., 1993; design instr. Pratt Inst., N.Y.C., 1996. Art editor HYPNO Mag., 1996, AGatheringoftheTribes Mag., 1997; project dir. dept. recreation and cult. affairs Jersey City (N.J.) Mus., 1995; dir. mural project Guggenheim Children's Fund, The Bronx, N.Y., 1993; design instr. Pratt Inst., Bklyn., 1996. One-man shows include OK Harris, N.Y.C., 1989, Stockwell Gallery, N.Y.C., 1989, Robinson Galleries, Houston, 1990, 93, 96, 35 Downing Gallery, N.Y.C., 1990, Gallery Stendhal, N.Y.C., 1991, 92, 97, Toyamaya Gallery, Kobe, Japan, 1991, Clark & Co., Washington, 1992, Wunderlich Gallery, Austin, 1994, Michael Kisslinger Gallery, N.Y.C., 1994, Museum of Contemporary Art, Washington, DC, 1994, Zero-1 Gallery, L.A., 1996, Hypergroup, L.A., 1996, Green Dolphin Gallery, Palm Beach, Fla., 1996, Gallery Stendhal, N.Y.C., 1997, Alma-Ata Museum, Kazakhstan, 1997, Noiseville, N.Y.C., 1998, Angstrom Gallery, Dallas, 1998, David Leonardis Gallery, Chgo., 1999, 313 Gallery, N.Y.C., 1999, MTV, N.Y.C., 1999, Merry Karnowsky Gallery, L.A., 2000, Sam Cintron Gallery, Jersey City, N.J., 2000, numerous others; exhibited in groups shows at B-Squared, N.Y.C., 1989, Police Bldg., 1989, Harkin Gallery, N.Y.C., 1989, Ground Zero, N.Y.C., 1990, Black and White in Color, N.Y.C., 1990, Robinson Galleries, Houston, Tex., 1990, Charles Lucien Gallery, N.Y.C., 1990, The Gallery, N.Y.C., 1990, Elaine Horwitch Gallery, Scottsdale, Ariz., 1991, Riposati Gallery, Italy, 1991, Ayzenberg Gallery, L.A., 1991, Art in General, N.Y.C., 1991, Gallery Stendhal, N.Y.C., 1991, 92, 96, Laura Larkin Gallery, Del Mar, Calif., 1991, Robinson Galleries, Houston, 1991, Elston Fine Arts, N.Y.C., 1991, Arte, Javits Ctr., N.Y.C., 1992, Payton Rule Gallery, Denver, 1992, Tenth St. Gallery, N.Y.C., 1992, Westbeth Gallery, N.Y.C., 1992, Trammel Crow Pavilion, Dallas, 1992, Clark & Co., Washington, 1993, 94, Deutser Gallery, Houston, 1993, 94, Palm Beach Museum, Lake Worth, Fla., 1993, William King Regional Arts Ctr., Abington, Va., 1994, Trans Hudson Gallery, Jersey City, NJ, 1995, Museum of Contemporary Art, Washington, 1995, 96, 98, 99, Rockville Arts Place, Rockville, Md., 1995, Gallery Galgano, N.Y.C., 1996, Zero-1 Gallery, L.S., 1996, Searles/Spicer Showroom, N.Y.C., 1996, 111 Bldg., Jersey City, NJ, 1996, Ozone Gallery, N.Y.C., 1996, 97, Tribes Gallery, N.Y.C., 1996, Am. Image Gallery, N.Y.C., 1997, Tomasulo Gallery, Cranford, NJ, 1997, Westwood Gallery, N.Y.C., 1997, The Rocky Aoki Found., N.Y.C., 1997, Teatro Degli Artisti, Italy, 1997, Community Gallery, Jersey City, NJ, 1997, Random Road Modern, Cleve., 1998, Ace Gallery, N.Y.C., 1998, Merry Karnowsky Gallery, L.A., 1998, Rico Gallery, Santa Monica, Calif., 1998, David Leonardis Gallery, Chgo., 1998, McKee Gallery, N.Y.C., 1998, Pacific Design Ctr., L.A., 1998, The Alternative Mus., N.Y.C., 1998, Mass. Mus. Contemporary Art, 1999, The Lab, San Francisco, 1999, 313 Gallery, N.Y.C., 1999, numerous others; permanent exhibitions: Everhart Museum, Scranton, Pa., Whitney Mus., N.Y.C., Paterson Mus., NJ, Mus. Checkpoint Charlie, Berlin, Germany, Mus. of Contemporary Art, Paris, France, Franklin Furnace, N.Y.C., U. N.Tex., Denton; album covers The Moist Boys, The Sutcliffes, Faction Zero, Baby Drowsy, Shove It, The Retroliners, Banana Blender Surprise, Invisible Culture, The Gefkens; contbr. illustrations to numerous pubs.; TV appearances: PBS Ch. 13 News, 1987, A Current Affair, 1988, Morton Downy Jr. Show, 1989, 95, State of the Arts (BBC), 1989, Comtemporary N.Y. Artists, 1990, Downtown Tonight, 1990, Good Day NY, 1991, Fox Style News, 1991, Volcanic Video, 1991, On the Avenue, 1991, Jenny Jones, 1992, Nine Broadcast Plaza, 1992, The Real World, MTV, 1992, Naruhodo! The World (Japanese TV), 1993, On the Back Porch with Jim Swift, 1994, Art Strokes, 1995, Media TV (Bravo network), 1995, State of Mind (MSNBC), 1995, Citizen Art (PBS), 1996, The Ad and the Ego, 1997, World News Today (CNN), 1998, Talk Soup, 1998, Puck (Dutch TV), 1998, Subvertising, 1998, Ooh La La (Canadian TV), 1999, Snap Judgment (Court TV), 1999, Potpourri (KTSF), 1999; prodr.: (concept CD) Revelations Book II, 1999; designer anti-drug billboards internat. drug control program UN, N.Y. and Kazakhstan, 1997, poster Carri Fisher's Oasis Recovery Cmty., L.A., 1997, fundraising lunchbox WFMU Pub. Radio, Jersey City, 1999. Fundraiser Greenpeace, N.Y., 1986;. Grantee Artist Space, 1986, 87, N.Y. State Coun. Arts, 1988, 89, Manhattan Neighborhood Network, 1995. Avocations: music, travel. Home: 236 6th St Apt 2 Jersey City NJ 07302-2443 Studio: 111 1st St Ste 32B Jersey City NJ 07302-3058

ENGMAN, ERNST RUNE, engineering executive; b. Stockholm, Sweden, May 17, 1938; s. John and Gerda (Nilsson) E.; m. Irene Karebo Larsen; 1 child, Charlotta. MSc, Royal Inst. Technology, Sweden, 1964; MBA, U. Lund. Mng. dir. ENEA, Stockholm, Sweden, 1964-81; pres. EGH AG, Zurich, 1981—. Mem. Sjöofficerssällskapet. Avocations: golf, Thai Chi, brass orchestra, skiing. E-mail: rune.engman@telia.com. Office: EGH AG, Box 24, S-183 21 Täby Sweden

ENGQVIST, ALICE BIRGITTA, internist, gastroenterologist; b. Solna, Sweden, Mar. 17, 1940; d. Ivar Albin and Anna Maria (Sandstrom) E. Med. lic., Karolinska Inst., Stockholm, 1969. Cert. specialist internal medicine and gastroenterology. Resident Södersjukhuset, Stockholm, 1969-78, cons., 1978—. Mem. Swedish Soc. Medicine, Swedish Soc. Gastroenterology and Gastrointestinal Endoscopy, Swedish Soc. Clin. and Exptl. Hypnosis. Avocations; gardening, art, travelling. Office: Södersjukhuset, 11883 Stockholm Sweden

ENGQVIST, LARS, Swedish government official. Ministry health and social affairs Govt. of Sweden, Stockholm, 1998—. Mem. Social Democratic Party. Office: Ministry Health/Soc Affairs, Regeringstatan 30-32, S-103 33 Stockholm Sweden

ENGS, RUTH CLIFFORD, health educator, historian; b. Ridgeway, Pa., Sept. 15, 1939; d. Theodore Alexander and Elinor Kay Clifford; m. William Denis Engs, July 24, 1965 (div. 1973); m. Jeffrey Lee Franz, Oct. 2, 1987. BA, U. Vt., 1961; diploma in nursing, Merritt Coll., 1968; MA, MS, U. Oreg., 1970; EdD, U. Tenn., 1973. RN, Ind. Rsch. asst. Harvard Med. Sch., Boston, 1961-63; asst. prof. Dalhousie U., Halifax, N.S., Can., 1970-71; asst. prof. Ind. U., Bloomington, 1973-80, assoc. prof., 1980-90, prof. applied health sci., 1990—; vis. prof. U. Queensland (Australia), 1980. Author: Teaching Health Education in the Elementary Schools, 1978, Responsible Drug and Alcohol Use, 1979, Alcohol and Other Drugs: Self Responsibility, 1987, Clean Living Movements: American Cycles of Health Reform, 2000; editor: Controverseys in the Addiction Field, 1990, Women: Alcohol and Other Drugs, 1992; contbr. over 150 articles to profl. jours. Mem. Am. Sch. Health Assn., Am. Alliance Health Phys. Edn. and Recreation. Unitarian. Avocations: flying, golfing, ranching. Office: Dept Applied Health Sci Ind U Poplars 615 Bloomington IN 47405

ENGSTRAND, BEATRICE C., neurologist, educator; b. Oceanside, N.Y., July 16, 1960; d. Donald Daniel and Claudia Helen Engstrand. BA, Lehigh U., 1982; MD, Med. Coll. Pa., 1984; hon. doctorate, Lehigh U. Diplomate Am. Bd. Psychiatry and Neurology, bd. cert. in neurology; lic. physician, N.Y. Resident in medicine North Shore U. Hosp., Manhasset, N.Y., 1984-85; resident in neurology N.Y. Hosp., N.Y.C., 1985-86, SUNY Health Sci. Ctr., Bklyn., 1986-88; attending physician Met. Hosp., N.Y.C., 1988-92; asst. prof. neurology N.Y. Med. Coll., Valhalla, 1988—; pvt. practice Huntington, N.Y., 1992—; founder, pres. Neuro-Degenerative Disease Found., 1993—; presenter and lectr. in field. Author: (book) A Gift of Healing—A Legacy of Hope, 1990. Mem. adv. bd. arts and sci. Lehigh U., Bethlehem, Pa., 1992—, women's adv. study bd., 1993—; mem. legis. com. Suffolk County Med. Soc., 1994-97; com. fundraiser Gov. George Pataki Election, 1995; mem. People for Ethical Treatment of Animals, Physicians for Responsible Medicine, other animal rights groups. Recipient Woman of Distinction award Soroptomist Internat.; named one of Outstanding Young Woman of Am., 1997. Fellow Am. Acad. Neurology (diplomate); mem. AMA, ACP, Am. Med. Student Assn., Am. Acad. Neurology, Nat. Bd. Med. Examiners (diplomate), Med. Soc. N.Y. State, N.Y. County Med. Soc. (pub. rels. com.), Westchester County Med. Ctr. (bioethics com.), Bklyn. Neurol. Soc., Med. Coll. Pa. Alumni Assn., Cornell U. Alumni Assn., Rotary Club Upper Manhattan (v.p. 1990-91, pres. 1991-92, Paul Harris award 1991). Republican. Avocations: traveling, animals, languages, opera, writing. Office: 76 E Main St Ste 1 Huntington NY 11743-2837

ENGSTROM, DAN BERTIL, structural engineer, researcher, consultant; b. Stockholm, Sweden, Sept. 15, 1966; s. Bertil J. and Ia (Bjorkman) E.; m. Maud C. Willardsson, July 2, 1993. MSc, Chalmers U. Tech., Goteborg, Sweden, 1991, PhD, 1997. Co-owner IB Ingenjorsbyra AB, Billdal, Sweden, 1986—; supr. HSB Bygg AB, Goteborg, Sweden, 1991-92; rsch. asst. Chalmers U. Tech., Goteborg, Sweden, 1992-97; postdoct. rsch. fellow Royal U. Tech., Stockholm, 1999—; vis. scientist Forest Products Lab., Madison, Wis., 1996-97; tech. expert UN Indsl. Devel. Orgn., 1997—. Rsch. grantee Sweden-Am. Found., Stockholm, 1996. Mem. Swedish Assn. Civil and Structural Engrs. Achievements include Swedish Nat. (open division) and World Champion (Masters) frisbee player. Home: Eskadervagen 34, S-183 54 Taby Sweden Office: IB Ingenjorsbyra AB, Bolshedens Industrivag 27, S-427 50 Billdal Sweden

ENGUEHARD, JEAN-LUC, banker; b. Angers, Anjou, France, Jan. 10, 1950; s. Henri and Suzanne (Lainé) E.; m. Dominique Patris de Breuil, June 10, 1990; children: Joseph, Raphaël, Cyprien, Louise. Diploma, Inst. d'etudes Politique, Paris, 1973; M in Law, Paris II U., 1974; postgrad., Ecole Nat. D'Adminstrn., France, 1977. Acct. Caisse des dèpots, France, 1977-79; asst. mgr. Caisse de dèpots, Paris, 1983-89, dir., 1993—; mem. ins. dept. Caisse Nat. de Prévoyance, 1979-81; inspector de fin. Ministry of Fin., Paris, 1981-83; gen. mgr. CDC Internat., France, 1989-92; CEO Sogeposte subs. Caisse des depots and La Poste, 1999—; lectr. Inst. de etudes Politiques, de Paris, 1983-87. Author: (book) Le Sport en France, 1978. Avocations: jogging, skiing. Home: 8 Rue Cernuschi, 75017 Paris France Office: Caisse de Depots, Sogeposte, 23 Ave Franklin J Roosevelt, 75008 Paris France

ENGWIRDA, MAARTEN BOUDEWIJN, auditor; b. Tilburg, The Netherlands, June 2, 1943; s. Pieter Frans Engwirda and Theresia Petronella Van Alfen; m. Elisabeth Maria Tiddens, May 8, 1992; children: Naomi, David, Dennis. LLM, U. Groningen, 1967; postgrad., Clingendael Inst. Internat., The Hague, The Netherlands, 1968. With Ministry of Fgn. Affairs, The Hague, 1968-70, 73; policy asst. Parliamentary Group of Dem. 66, 1970-71; mem. Netherlands and European Parliament for Dem. 66, 1971-73; with Internat. Energy Agy., Paris, 1975-77; M.P. The Netherlands, 1977-89; mem. Netherlands Ct. of Auditors, 1990-95, European Ct. of Auditors, Luxembourg, 1996—. Contbr. numerous articles to profl. papers. Mem. Netherlands Student Assn. for Internat. Rels. (hon.). Home: 26 Rue des Vignes, L-6765 Grevenmacher Luxembourg Office: European Ct of Auditors, 12 Rue Alcide de Gasperi, L-1615 Luxembourg Luxembourg

ENHORNING, CONSTANCE ELISABET, broadcasting executive; b. Kristianstad, Sweden, Oct. 22, 1945; came to The Gambia, 1969; d. Tage Enhorning and Britt Wadner. Studentkompetens in English and Swedish, Latinskolan, Malmo, Sweden, 1966. Producer Radio Syd, Malmo, 1964-66, gen. mgr., Banjul, The Gambia, 1972—; kanslisekreterare Skanes Turisttrafikforbund, Malmo, 1966-69; owner, operator restaurant/disco, shop on board M/S Cheeta, Banjul, The Gambia, 1969-71. Avocation: tennis. Home and Office: PO Box 279-280, Banjul Gambia

ENKHSAIKHAN, JARGALSAIKHAN, ambassador; b. Ulaanbaatar, Mongolia, Sept. 4, 1950; m.; 6 children. Lawyer, State Inst. Internat. Rels., Moscow, 1974, PhD in Law, 1979. Sec, legal dept. Mongolia, N.Y.C., USSR, 1974-79; sec. Mongolian Mission to UN, N.Y.C., 1979-86; acting head of legal and planning depts. MFA, 1986-88; minister-counsellor Mongolian Embassy, Moscow, 1988-92; adviser Pres. of Mongolia, Ulaanbaatar, 1992-93; exec. sec. Mongolian Nat. Security Coun., Ulaanbaatar, 1993-96; permanent rep. Mongolia UN, N.Y.C., 1996—; mem. UN Gen. Assembly sessions, 1975, 79-86, 92, 96-99, v.p., 1997, chmn., 1998; rapporteur Sixth (Legal) Com. UNGA, 1979, vice chmn., 1981, chmn., 1998; vice chmn. Spl. Com. on Non-use of Force in Internat. Rels, 1983; Mongolian rep. Law of the Sea Conf., 1976-82. Contbr. articles on internat. law and internat. rels. to Mongolian publs.; also to publs. in Russia and U.S. Office: Permanent Mission Mongolia to UN 6 E 77th St New York NY 10021-1704

ENNAHAR, SAÏD, food microbiologist, researcher; b. Youssoufia, Morocco, Nov. 16, 1966; arrived in France, 1990; s. Bouchaïb Ben-Brahim and Halima Bent Ahmed Ennahar. BS, Chouaïb Doukkali U., El Jadida, Morocco, 1990; MS, Louis Pasteur U., Strasbourg, France, 1991, PhD, 1995. Tchg. and rsch. assoc. Louis Pasteur U., 1994-96, postdoctoral rschr., 1996-97; postdoctoral rschr. INRA, Jouy-en-Josas, France, 1997-98, Kyushu U., Fukuoka, Japan, 1998-2000, Nat. Grassland Rsch. Inst., Tochigi, Japan, 2000—; cons., Aerial, Strasbourg, 1995-97. Contbr. articles to profl. jours.; patentee in field. Postdoctoral fellow Inst. Nat. Recherche Agronomique, 1997-98, Japan Soc. Promotion Sci., Japan, 1998-00, Sci. Tech. Agy., Japan, 2000—. Avocations: tennis, volleyball, movies, music. Office: Louis Pasteur U Dept Chimie, 74 Route Durhin, F-67401 Illkirch Cedex France

ENNESSER, FRANÇOIS JACQUES, computer scientist; b. Saint-Ouen, France, Mar. 29, 1969; s. Gilbert Claude Eugene and Monique Christiane (Samain) E. Degree in engring. with honors, Ecole Superior Engrs., Paris, 1991; MS, U. So. Calif., 1992. Rsch. engr. I.C. Vision, L.A., 1992-93; telecom. engr., writer Nortel Matra Cellular, Paris, 1994; rsch. engr. Air Liquide, Paris, 1995-99, Bull CP8 Smartcards, Louveciennes, France, 1999—. Contbr. articles to profl. jours.; patentee gas-metal arc welding. Served with French artillery, 1993-94. Mem. IEEE, Conseil Nat. Engrs. Sci. Avocations: palmtop computing, role playing, tutoring, rowing, cycling. E-mail: F.ennesser@computer.org. Home: 19 rue des Feuillantines, F 75005 Paris France Office: Bull SC&T, Rte de Versailles BP 45, F-78431 Louveciennes France

ENNIS, THOMAS MICHAEL, management consultant; b. Morgantown, W.Va., Mar. 7, 1931; s. Thomas Edson and Violet Ruth (Nugent) E.; m. Julia Marie Dorety, June 30, 1956; children: Thomas John, Robert Griswold (dec.). Student, W.Va. U., 1949-52; AB, George Washington U., 1954; JD, Georgetown U., 1960. With Gov. Employees Ins. Co., Washington, 1956, 59, Air Transport Assn. Am., Washington, 1959-60; dir. ann. support program George Washington U., 1960-63; nat. dir. devel. Project HOPE, People to People Health Found., Inc., Washington, 1963-66; nat. exec. dir. Epilepsy Found. Am., Washington, 1966-74; exec. dir. Clinton, Eaton, Ingham Community Mental Health Bd., Lansing, Mich., 1974-83; nat. exec. dir. Alzheimer's Disease and Related Disorders Assn., Inc., Chgo., 1983-86; exec. dir., pres. The John Douglas French Alzheimers Found., L.A., 1986-96, pres. emeritus, 1996—; clin. instr. dept. cmty. medicine and internat. health Georgetown U., 1967-74; adj. assoc. prof. dept. psychiatry Mich. State U., 1975-84; lectr. Univ. Ctr. for Internat. Rehab., 1977; cons. health and med. founds., related orgns.; cons. Am. Health Found., 1967-69, Reston, Va.-Georgetown U. Health Planning Project, 1967-70. Editl. bd. Am. Jour. Alzheimer's Disease, 1997—. Mem. adv. bd. Nat. Center for the Law and the Handicapped, 1971-74; advisor Nat. Reye's Syndrome Found.; mem. Nat. Com. for Research in Neurol. Disorders, 1967-72; mem. nat. adv. bd. Developmental Disabilities/Tech. Assistance System, U. N.C., 1971-78; nat. trustee Nat. Kidney Found., 1970-74, mem. exec. com. and bd. Nat. Capitol Area chpt., pres., 1972-74; bd. dirs. Nat. Assn. Pvt. Residential Facilities for Mentally Retarded, 1970-74; bd. dirs., mem. exec. com. Epilepsy Found. Am., 1977-84, Epilepsy Center Mich., 1974-83; nat. bd. dirs. Western Inst. on Epilepsy, 1969-72; bd. dirs., pres. Mich. Mid-South Health Systems Agy., 1975-78; sec. gen. Internat. Fedn. Alzheimer's Disease and Related Disorders, 1984-86; mem. panel Alzheimer's Disease Edn. and Referral Ctr., 1990-93; mem. Calif. State Coun. on Developmental Disabilities, 1997—; med. adv. bd. EdenCare Sr. Living Svcs., advisor Ctr. Aging, Washington, 1998—. World Rehab. Fund fellow Norway, 1980. Mem. Nat. Epilepsy League (bd. dirs. 1977-78), Mich. Assn. Cmty. Mental Health (pres. 1977-79), Nat. Coalition Rsch. Neurol. Disorders (dir. at-large 1991—), Scan Health Plan (bd. govs.), Phi Alpha Theta, Phi Kappa Psi. Home and Office: 23740 Killion St Woodland Hills CA 91367-5822

ENO, PAUL FREDERICK, editor; b. Hartford, Conn., Mar. 30, 1953; s. Earl Bryan and Bernice Sarah (Landers) E.; m. Jaclyn Ann Blackmon, June 7, 1981; children: Jonathan David, Benjamin Thomas. AA, St. Thomas Sem., Bloomfield, Conn., 1973; BA in Philosophy, Wadhams Hall Coll., Ogdensburg, N.Y., 1975; postgrad., Trinity Coll., Hartford, Conn., 1976-78. Book series editor Warbrooke Pub. Ltd., Montreal, Que., Can., 1974-76; staff writer Pawtuxet Valley Daily Times, West Warwick, R.I., 1979-80; mng. editor Observer Publs., Smithfield, R.I., 1980-83; copy editor Providence Jour., 1985-91; freelance editor, writer and publisher, 1976—; owner New River Press, Woonsocket, R.I., 1990—; exec. dir. Pickering Inst. for New Eng. Studies, 1999—. Author: Best of Times, 1992, Rhode Island: A Genial History, 1994, Underhill Days, 1995, Faces at the Window, 1995, Footsteps in the Attic, 2000; editor: John Brown's Adirondack Empire, 1988, Flexography: Principles and Practices, 1990; contbr. articles to mags. Vice chmn. Cumberland Hist. Dist. Comm., 1987-92; bd. dirs. New Eng. Confedn., 1997—. With USCGR, 1983-89. Recipient medal R.I. Hist. Soc., 1987. Mem. R.I. Press. Assn. (bd. dirs., treas. 1982-89, Best Editorial of Yr. 1981, 82), Cumberland Beagle Club. Avocations: riding, boating, model railroading, shooting. Home: 645 Fairmount St Woonsocket RI 02895-4012

ENOMOTO, MAKOTO, biotechnology company executive; b. Tokyo, Jan. 26, 1929; parents Norikazu and Hisako (Nagase) Ushiki; m. Kazue Enomoto, Mar. 11, 1956; children: Ellen, Minoru. MD, U. Tokyo, 1952, PhD, 1960. Instr. U. Wis. Med. Sch., Madison, 1967-68; assoc. prof. dept. carcinogenesis U. Tokyo, 1968-72; prof. dept. pathology St. Marianna U. Sch. Medicine, Kawasaki, Japan, 1972-77; cons. pathologist Sagamihara Kyodo Hosp., Kanagawa, Japan, 1977-80; dir. dept. pathology Japan Bioassay Lab., Hatano, Japan, 1982-93; dir., mng. dir. Biosafety Rsch. Ctr., Shizuoka, Japan, 1980—; bd. dirs. Interdisciplinary Rsch. Inst. Environ. Sci., Kyoto, Japan, 1990-96; cons. pathologist Cen. Hosp. Self Def. Armed Forces Japan, Tokyo, 1977-80. Author: International Textbook of Medicine, 1980; author, editor: Color Atlas of Toxicological Pathology, 1987; contbr. articles to profl. jours. Com. for Evaluation New Drugs, Min. Health & Welfare, Tokyo, 1974-77, Com. for Evaluating Chemicals in Environment., 1978-81. Fellow NIH, 1961-64. Mem. Japan Soc. Pathology (coun.), Japan Cancer Assn. (meritorious, coun. 1954-93), Japan Soc. Toxicologic Pathology (bd. dirs.), Am. Assn. Cancer Res (corr. mem. 1982—), Am. Assn. Microbiol. (meritorious mem. 1977—). Fax: 0538 58 1243. Home: 4-9-6 Nakameguro Meguro-ku, Tokyo 153-0061, Japan Office: Biosafety Rsch Ctr Food, 582-2 Arahama Shioshinden, Shizuoka 437-1213, Japan

ENOMOTO, RYOKICHI, English literature educator; b. Tokyo, Sept. 17, 1928; s. Tomekichi and Haru Enomoto. MA, Nihon U., Tokyo, 1955. Prof. English lit. Senshu U., Tokyo, 1955-89; prof., dean Ishinomaki (Japan) Senshu U., 1989-99, prof. emeritus, 1999—. Home: Hayamiya 3-52-5, Nerimaku Tokyo 179-0085, Japan Office: Ishinomaki Senshu Univ, Miyagi Ishinomaki 986-80, Japan

ENQVIST, OVE TEODOR, career military officer; b. Helsinki, Apr. 28, 1953; s. Olle Teodor and Rut (Strangberg) E.; m. Asta Hellevi Maatta; children: Lotta,Eliisa. Grad. lt., Mil. Acad., Helsinki, 1976; staff officer, Staff Mil. Coll., Helsinki, 1985. Fort comdr. Finnish Coast Artiller Finnish Def. Forces, 1976-79, dep. battalion comdr., 1980-82; project mgr. Gen. Headquarters Finnish Def. Forces, Helsinki, 1986-91; chief divsn. dep. commandant Coast Artillery Sch. Finnish Def. Forces, 1991-94, battalion comdr., 1994-96; dep. chief, chief divsn. Gen. Headquarters Finnish Def. Forces, 1996—; cons. Coast Def. Study Group, U.S., Mil. Mus., Helsinki. Author: History of Suomenlinna Fortress, 1918-98, Coastal Guns in Finland, 1918-98; contbr. articles to profl. jours. Mem. Finnish Soc. Mil. Sci., Soc. Mil. History. Lutheran. Home: Suomenlinna C54 B11, F-00190 Helsinki Finland

ENRICO, ROGER A., soft drink company executive. Former v.p. sales and mktg. Pepsi-Cola Metropol Bottling Co. Inc., Purchase, N.Y.; now pres., chief exec. officer Pepsico Worldwide Beverages, Purchase, N.Y.; CEO Pepsico, Inc., 1994—; also chmn. bd. dirs. Office: Pepsico Inc 700 Anderson Hill Rd Purchase NY 10577-1444

ENRIQUEZ, CRISTINO CATUD, radiologist, internist, cardiologist; b. Batangas, Philippines, 1941. MD, U. of the East, Philippines, 1964. Diplomate Am. Bd. Radiology. Internist St. Mary's Hosp., Waterbury, Conn., 1965-66; res. internal med. Hosp. St. Raphael, New Haven, Conn., 1966-68; res. diagnostic radiol. Jackson Meml. Med. Ctr. U Miami, 1974-77; fellow in cardiology Baylor U., 1969-70; fellow in pulmonary disease Yale U. Hosp., 1971-72; founder Rapha Health & Longevity Inst. Fellow Am. Coll. Internat. Physicians; mem. AMA, Am. Coll. Cardiology, Am. Coll. Radiology, Interam. Coll. Radiology, Assn. Philippine Physicians in Am., Full Gospel Businessmen's Fellowship, Christian Med. and Dental Assn. Office: 808 Brickell Key Dr Apt 2908 Miami FL 33131-2691

ENRIQUEZ, JUAN CABOT, researcher; b. Mexico City; s. Antonio and Marjorie Enriquez-Savignac. BA, Harvard U., 1981, MBA, 1986. CEO, Urband Devel. Corp., Mexico City, 1988-94; peace negotiator State of Chiapas, Mex., 1994; rschr. Bus. Sch., Harvard U., Cambridge, Mass., 1996-98, rschr., mem. vis. com. David Rockefeller Ctr., 1998—; mem. genetics adv. coun. Harvard Med. Sch., Boston; mem. chmn.'s coun. Am.'s Soc. Author: Flags, borders, Anthems, and Other Myths, 2000; also articles. Office: Harvard U David Rockefeller Ctr LAS 61 Kirkland St Cambridge MA 02138-2030

ENRIQUEZ, RICARDO CABURIAN, JR., electrical engineer; b. Manila, Feb. 7, 1950; s. Ricardo Pascual and Ana Sison (Caburian) E.; m. Margie Gallego Ferrer, May 22, 1977; children: Theamarie, John Eigram, Krisheela. AA, Pamantasan Lungsod, Manila, 1969; B. of Tech. in Elec. Engring., Pamantasan Lungsod, 1971, BSEE, 1974. Prodn. planning and control engr. Beta Electric Corp., Mandaluyong, The Philippines, 1974-76, field svc. engr., 1977-83; elec. engr. EDM Switchboards, Papuan Electric Pty. Ltd., Port Moresby, Papua New Guinea, 1983-85, LM Pecor, Quezon City, Philippines, 1986-87, AG&P-AMSCO, Manila, 1987-88, E.C., Al-Jouf, Saudi Arabia, 1988—. Contbr. poetry to Tagalog and English collections. Mem. Del Rey-Camarin Homeowner's Assn., Calocan City, 1980—; active Christ the Livingstone Fellowship, Philippines, 1996—. Mem. Inst. Integrated Elec. Engrs., U.S. Chess Fedn., Filipino Computer Soc. Roman Catholic. Avocations: chess, poetry, composing songs, lawn tennis, table tennis. Home: Lot 2 Bk 14 King John Del Rey 2, Camarin Caloocan Metro-Manila, The Philippines Office: Al Jouf Elec Corp Bach A, Bldg EC Compound Box 120, Doumat Aljandal Saudi Arabia

ENSENAT, DONALD BURNHAM, lawyer, former ambassador; b. New Orleans, Feb. 4, 1946; s. A.G. and Genevieve (Burnham) E.; m. Taylor Harding, June 5, 1976; children: Farish, Will. BA, Yale U., 1968; JD, Tulane U., 1973. Bar: La. 1973, U.S. Ct. Appeals (5th cir.) 1974, U.S. Supreme Ct. 1975, U.S. Ct. Appeals (11th cir.) 1982, Tex. 1991. Legis. asst. Congressman Hale Boggs, U.S. Ho. of Reps., Washington, 1969-70, legis asst. Congresswoman Lindy Boggs, 1973-74; personal aide Hon. George Bush, Houston, 1970; asst. atty gen. State of La., New Orleans, 1975-80; assoc., dir., mng. dir. Carmouche, Gray, & Hoffman, A.P.L.C., New Orleans, 1981-89; mng. dir. Hoffman Sutterfield Ensenat, A.P.L.C., New Orleans, 1989-92, sr. dir., 1994-97; sr. counsel Locke Liddell & Sapp, PC, New Orleans, 1997—; U.S. amb. to Brunei, 1992-93. Bd. dirs. World Trade Ctr., New Orleans, chmn. fin. com., 1990-92, exec. com., 1993—, pres.-elect, 1995, pres., 1996, chmn. bd. dirs., 1997. With USAR, 1968-74. Mem. State Bar Tex., La. State Bar Assn., Maritime Law Assn. U.S., Yale Alumni Assn. La. (bd. dirs. 1976-92, 94—, pres. 1980-82), Assn. Yale Alumni (rep. 1976-79). Republican. Roman Catholic. Avocation: sports. E-mail: densenat@lockeliddell.com. Home: 1233 Harmony St New Orleans LA 70115-3422 Office: Locke Liddell & Sapp LLP 601 Poydras St Ste 2400 New Orleans LA 70130-6036

ENSENAT, LOUIS ALBERT, surgeon; b. Merida, Mexico, Oct. 24, 1916; s. Frank and Guadalupe F. (Ensenat) E.; m. Ruth Ogden, July 9, 1943; children: Gloria Louise, Tinita Ruth, Louis Albert, Rita Joan, Barbara Jean, Michael Monroe. BS, Tulane U., 1938, MD, 1941; MSc in Medicine, U. Pa., 1953. Diplomate Am. Bd. Surgery, Am. Bd. Abdominal Surgery. Intern Charity Hosp., New Orleans, 1941-42; resident surgery Charity Hosp., Monroe, La., 1942, Lakeshore Hosp., New Orleans, La.; resident surgery VA Hosp., New Orleans, La., Batavia, N.Y.; fellow in surg. pathology Tulane U. Sch. Med.; preceptorship in surgery Biloxi (Miss.) VA Hosp.; staff surg. VA Hosp., Montgomery, 1946-52; pvt. practice surgery Pasadena, Tex., 1952-62, New Orleans, 1962—; surgeon; b. Merida, Mexico, Oct. 24, 1916; s. Frank and Guadalupe F. (Ensenat) E.; B.S., Tulane U., 1938, M.D., 1941; M.Sc. in Medicine, U. Pa., 1953; m. Ruth Ogden, July 9, 1943; children—Gloria Louise, Tinita Ruth, Louis Albert, Rita Joan, Barbara Jean, Michael Monroe. Intern, Charity Hosp., New Orleans, 1941-42; resident surgery Charity Hosp., Monroe, La., 1942, Lakeshore Hosp., New Orleans, VA hosp., New Orleans, Batavia, N.Y.; fellow in surg. pathology Tulane U. Sch. Med.; preceptorship in surgery Biloxi (Miss.) VA Hosp.; staff surg. VA Hosp., Montgomery, 1946-52; pvt. practice surgery, Pasadena, Tex., 1952-63, New Orleans, 1963—; founder, adminstr. Mercy Hosp. Pasadena, 1954-63, chief surgery, 1954-63; founder, dir. Gulf Coast Home Builders, Inc.; trustee Angiology Research Found., 1986—. Trustee, Big State Factors Corp. Served from lt. (j.g.) to lt. comdr. USN, 1942-46. Decorated Purple Heart, Bronze Star. Diplomate Am. Bd. Surgery, Am. Bd. Abdominal Surgery. Fellow French Soc. Phlebology, Am. Coll. Angiology (pres.); mem. AMA, Hawthorne Surg. Soc., Am. Soc. Abdominal Surgeons, N.Y. Acad. Scis., Am. Med. Writers Assn. Author articles in field. Author articles in field. Trustee, Big State Factors Corp. Served from lt. (j.g.) to lt. comdr. USN, 1942-46. Decorated Purple Heart, Bronze Star. Fellow French Soc. Phlebology, Am. Coll. Angiology (pres.); mem. AMA, Hawthorne Surg. Soc., Am. Soc. Abdominal Surgeons, N.Y. Acad. Scis., Am. Med. Writers Assn. Home and Office: 7630 Jeannette St New Orleans LA 70118-4064

ENSLEN, PAMELA CHAPMAN, lawyer; b. Detroit, Dec. 29, 1953; d. Ralph Nicholas Chapman and Roberta Margaret Clarke McLaughlin; m. Richard Alan Enslen, Nov. 2, 1985; 1 child, Alan Gennady Robert. BMus, U. Mich., 1976, MMus, 1977; JD, Wayne State U., 1981. Bar: Mich. 1981, U.S. Dist. Ct. (ea. and we. dist.) Mich., U.S. Ct. Appeals (6th cir.), U.S. Supreme Ct. Pre-hearing atty. Mich. Ct. Appeals, Detroit, 1981-83; fed. law clk. U.S. Dist. Ct., We. Dist. Mich., Kalamazoo, 1983-85; sr. ptnr. Miller, Canfield, Paddock & Stone, Kalamazoo, 1985—; lectr., cons., arbitrator, author and mediator in field. Co-founder, bd. dirs. Community Dispute Resolution Ctr. of Kalamazoo County, 1988—; bd. dirs. Am. Cancer Soc., Kalamazoo, 1991—. Named Mich. Lawyer of Yr., Mich. Lawyers Weekly, 1998. Mem. ABA (standing com. on dispute resolution 1990-93, governing coun. dispute resolution sect. 1994-97, chair dispute resolution sect. 1997—, sect. del. House of Dels. 1999—), ATLA, Mich. Bar Assn. (counsel sect. on arbitration and alternative dispute resolution 1985—), Kalamazoo County Bar Assn. (chair law day com. 1989, bd. dirs. 1996—), Kalamazoo Trial Lawyers Assn., Women Lawyers Assn. of Mich. (regional rep. 1989-90), Nat. Order of Barristers, Pi Kappa Lambda. Democrat. Avocations: reading, music. Office: Miller Canfield Paddock & Stone 444 W Michigan Ave Kalamazoo MI 49007-3752

ENSLINGER, GARY LEE, insurance agent and executive; b. Wichita, Kans., Mar. 10, 1952; s. Joseph E. and Esther (Depperschmidt) E.; m. Terrie J. Clark, May 18, 1974; children: Sean L., Nicholas J. BS in Psychology, Newman U., 1974; MEd in Guidance and Counseling, Wichita State U., 1976. Program dir. Continuing Care Inc., Wichita, Kans., 1974-80; store owner Sunnyside Thriftway, Wichita, 1980-82; dist. mgr. United Group Assocs., Dallas, 1982-86; agt., tng. dir. Farm Bur. Kans., Wichita, 1986—, mgr. satellite office, 1994—. Mem. Wichita Assn. Life Underwriters (numerous sales awards). Roman Catholic. Avocation: restoring old cars. Office: Farm Bur 2420 S Seneca St Wichita KS 67217-2802

ENSMINGER, DALE, mechanical engineer, electrical engineer; b. Mt. Perry, Ohio, Sept. 26, 1923; s. Charles Henry and Mary Elpha (Koehler) E.; m. Lois Elizabeth Hamilton, Mar. 25, 1948; children: Martha Jean, Laura Lee, Charles Robert, Jonathan Dale, Mary Ann, Daniel Joseph. BSME, BSEE, Ohio State U., 1950, postgrad., 1950-53. Registered profl. engr., Ohio. Rschr. Battelle Meml. Inst., Columbus, Ohio, 1950, prin. rschr.; sr. rschr. Battelle Columbus Labs., mgr. ultrasonics, sr. rsch. scientist, 1984-88; cons. in field. Author: Ultrasonics, 1973, 2d edit. 1988; contbr. articles to profl. jours., chpts. to books; patentee in field; contbr., reviewer Am. Soc. Non-Destructive Testing Handbook, 1989—. Sec. Columbus Prison Assn., 1950—; dean, dir. Columbus Bible Inst., 1952-97; mem. bd. Fundamental Bapt. Mission of Trinidad and Tobago. With U.S. Army, 1943-46. Recipient Cert. of Recognition, NASA, 1975. Mem. Acoustical Soc. Am., Soc. for Non-Destructive Testing, Ultrasonic Industry Assn. Home: 198 E Longview Ave Columbus OH 43202-1236

ENTIN, STEPHEN JAY, federal agency administrator; b. New Bedford, Mass.. BAmath., Dartmouth Coll., Hanover, N.H., 1969; MA econ., U. Chgo., 1975. Staff economist Office Senator Robert Taft, Washington, 1975-76; economist Joint Economic Com., U.S. Congress, Washington, 1976-81; dep. asst. sec. economic policy U.S. Treasury Dept., Washington, 1981-88; economist Inst. Rsch. Economics Taxation, Washington, 1988-97, pres. exec. dir., 1997—; adv. Nat. Commn. Econ. Growth and Tax Reform, Washington, 1994-96; dir. Global Inst. Taxation, St. John's U., Jamaica, N.Y., 1998—. Contbg. author: (book) Empowering Health Care Consumers Through Tax Reform, 1999. Mem. Nat. Economists Club, Phi Beta Kappa. Avocations: gardening, science fiction. Fax: 202-463-6199. E-mail: erettax@ibm.net. Office: Inst Rsch on Economics Taxation 1730 K St NW Ste 940 Washington DC 20006-3868

ENTREMONT, PHILIPPE, conductor, pianist; b. Rheims, France, June 7, 1934; came to U.S., 1953; s. Jean and Renée (Monchamps) E.; m. Andree Ragot, Dec. 21, 1955; children: Félicia, Alexandre. Student, Conservatoire National Superieur de Musique, Paris, Jean Doyen. founder, artistic dir. Santo Domingo Music Festival, 1997—. Profl. debut at 17, Barcelona, Am. debut at 19, Nat. Gallery, Washington, 1953, pianist-condr. debut Mostly Mozart Festival, N.Y.C, 1971; rec. artist CBS, Teldec, EMI, Schwann and ProArte records; guest condr. Pitts. Symphony, Royal Philharm. Orch. Nat. de France, Montreal Symphony, San Francisco Symphony, Phila. Orch., Detroit Symphony, numerous others; prin. condr. Netherlands Chamber Orch., 1993—; prin.-guest condr. Israel Chamber Orch., 1994-96, condr. laureate, 1996—; lifetime mus. dir. Vienna Chamber Orch., 1975-91, chief laureate, 1991—; mus. dir. New Orleans Symphony Orch., 1981-85, Denver Symphony, 1986-89, others. Decorated Officer of the Legion of Honor, Legion of Honor, Officer de l'Order National du Merite: Austrian First Class Cross of Honor for the Arts and Scis., Comdr. in Order of Arts and Letters, 1998; A finalist Queen Elizabeth of Belgium Internat. Concours, 1952; Grand Prix Marguerite Long-Jacques Thibaud Competition, 1953; Harriet Cohen Piano medal, 1953; 1st prize Jeunesses Musicales; Grand Prix du Disque, 1967, 68, 69, 70; Edison award, 1968; Nominee Grammy award, 1972. Former mem. Academie Internationale de Musique Maurice Ravel (pres. 1975-80). Office: care Audrey Michaels 122 E 76th St New York NY 10021-2833

ENTRIKEN, ROBERT KERSEY, retired management educator; b. McPherson, Kans., Jan. 15, 1913; s. Frederick Kersey and Opal (Birch) E.; m. Elizabeth Freeman, May 26, 1940 (div. Nov. 1951); children: Robert Kersey Jr., Edward Livingston Freeman, Richard Davis; m. Jean Finch, June 5, 1954; 1 child, Birch Nelson. BA, U. Kans., 1934; MBA, Golden Gate U., 1961; postgrad., City U. Grad Sch., London, 1971-73. C.P.C.U. Ins. broker Houston, 1935-39, McPherson, Kans., 1935-39; asst. mgt. Cravens, Dargan & Co., Houston, 1939-42; br. mgr. Nat. Surety Corp., Memphis, San Francisco, 1942-54; v.p. Fireman's Fund Ins. Co., San Francisco, 1954-73; prof. mgmt. Golden Gate U., San Francisco, 1974-88; resident dean Asia programs Golden Gate U., Singapore, 1987-88; prof. emeritus Golden Gate U., 1989-97; underwriting mem. Lloyd's of London, 1985—, cons./expert witness gen. mgmt. and surety bonding, 1987-97; ret., 1997; adj. prof. Golden Gate U., San Francisco, 1953-73. Contbr. articles to trade and profl. jours. Bd. dirs., sec., treas. Northstar Property Owners Assn., Calif., 1982-86. Served to capt. USNR, 1944-73, ret., 1973. Mem. Ins. Forum San Francisco (pres. 1965, trustee 1975-78, 84-88), Surety Underwriters Assn. No. Calif. (pres. 1956), CPCU Soc. (pres. No. Calif. chpt. 1957, Ins. Profl. of Yr., San Francisco chpt. 1981, bd. dirs. 1989-93), Chartered Ins. Inst., Ins. Inst. London, Musicians' Union Local No. 6 (life), U.S. Naval Inst., Assn. Naval Aviation, Commonwealth Club, Naval Order U.S., Phi Delta Theta. Libertarian. Episcopalian. Home: 351 El Camino Del Mar San Francisco CA 94121-1130

ENTRIKEN, ROBERT KERSEY, JR., motorsport writer, retired newspaper editor; b. Houston, Feb. 13, 1941; s. Robert and Jean (Finch) (stepmother) E.; married 1972 (div. 1982); 1 child, Jean Louise; m. Sandra Jo Miller, Mar. 4, 1989; children: Caitlyn Miller, Matthew Kersey; 1 adopted child, Stephanie Lynn; 1 stepchild, Jared Ray Adamson. Student, Sch. Journalism, U. Kans., 1961-69. Gen. assignment reporter Salina Jour., Kans., 1969-71; motorsport columnist Salina Jour., 1970-83, courts reporter, 1971-82, Sunday editor, 1972-75, spl. sects. editor, 1975-94, neighbors editor, 1982-95, TV editor, 1994-95; contbg. editor Sports Car Mag., Tustin, Calif., 1972—; motorsport columnist Motorsports Monthly, Tulsa, Okla., 1983-85, Nat. Speed Sport News, 1996—; operator Ikke sa Hurtig Racing. Contbr. Performance Racing Industry mag., Sports Car World mag., Car Collector mag., Parts & People mag., Kansas! mag., Jox mag., Speedvision.com mag.; editor Kansas Motor Sports Ann., 1996. With USN, 1969-71, Guam. Mem. Am. Auto Racing Writers and Broadcasters Assn. (gen. v.p. 1982-86, Midwest v.p. 1980-82, chmn. All-Am. Team selections 1983—, chmn. Legends in Racing selections hall of fame 1989—), Ea. Motorsports Press Assn., Sports Car Club Am. (Best Story award 1972, 73, 76-78, 83-87, 89, 92, inaugural recipient Vern Jaques Sports Car Contbr. of Yr. nat. award 1999, Solo Cup nat. award 1981, England-Stripe award 1989, Nat. Solo I champion 1986, Road Racing Driver of the Yr. Salina Region 1995, Solo Driver of Yr. Wichita Region 1976, 82, Solo II Champion Kans. 1978, 84, Midwest divsn. 1984, regional exec. Kans. region 1974, founding mem.

Salina region 1990, regional exec. Salina region 1994, Midwest divsn. Mid-Am. pointskeeper 1974—, nat. pointskeeper 1995—), Soc. of Profl. Journalist Sigma Delta Chi. Avocations: sports car racing, autocrossing, skiing. Home and Office: 2731 Scott Ave Salina KS 67401-7858

ENTSCH, BARRIE, biochemist, molecular biologist; b. Townsville, Queensland, Australia, Apr. 16, 1943; s. Nicholas and Iris May (Frankling) E.; m. Margaret Elizabeth Robertson, Jan. 14, 1965; children: Nicholas, Katherine. BSc, U. Queensland, Brisbane, Australia, 1964; PhD, U. Sydney, Australia, 1972. Chemist Queensland Dept. Primary Industries, Brisbane, 1964-68; rsch. assoc. dept. biol. chemistry U. Mich., Ann Arbor, 1972-76; rsch. fellow Rsch. Sch. Biol. Scis. Australian Nat. U., Canberra, 1976-80; sr. rsch. scientist Australian Inst. Marine Scis., Townsville, 1980-84; assoc. prof. molecular and cellular biology group U. New Eng., Armidale, Australia, 1984—, head molecular and cellular biology group, 1997—; vis. lectr. dept. biol. chemistry U. Mich., Ann Arbor, 1983, 90, 94, 98; dir. Inst. Biotechnology U. New England, 1994-97. Contbr. numerous rsch. articles to biochemistry jours.; presenter papers to sci. socs. Recipient award NIH, U.S., 1992-95; Queensland Govt. fellow, 1961-63; CSIRO postgrad. studentship, 1968-72; Australian Rsch. Coun. Competitive grantee, 1987-90, 94-96, 99—. Mem. Royal Australian Chem. Inst. (chartered), Australian Soc. for Biochemistry and Molecular Biology, Australian Soc. Plant Physiologists. Avocations: photography, cinema, theatre, tennis, gardening. Office: Univ New England, Molec and Cell Biology Grp, Armidale NSW 2351, Australia

EÖRSI, ANNA, art historian; b. Budapest, Hungary, Nov. 9, 1950; d. Gyula and Marianna (Hajdu) E.; m. Jànos Körner, July 17, 1971 (div. 1987); 1 child, Julia. BA, U. Budapest, 1974. Sr. researcher dept. art history Faculty of Letters, U. Budapest, 1974—. Author: Cosimo Tura, 1976, International Gothic Style in Painting, 1986, Giovanni Arnolfini's Impalmamento Oud Holland, 1996, Haer Scala Significat Ascension Nirutum, Remarks on the Iconography of Christ Mounting on a Ladder, 1997. Mem. Hungarian Soc. for Art History. Avocation: cooking. Home: Pozsonyi ut 11/B, H1137 Budapest Hungary Office: Elte Btk Müvészettort, Pesti Barnabàs v 1-3, 1052 Budapest Hungary

EPEDO, EMMANUEL, judge. Pres. Supreme Ct., Togo. Office: Cour Supreme, Rue Albert Sarrault, BP 906, Lomé Togo*

EPHRON, NORA, writer, director; b. N.Y.C., May 19, 1941; d. Henry and Phoebe (Wolkind) E.; m. Dan Greenburg (div.); m. Carl Bernstein (div.); children: Jacob, Max; m. Nicholas Pileggi. BA, Wellesley Coll., 1962. Reporter N.Y. Post, 1963-68; free-lance writer, 1968—; contbg. editor, columnist Esquire mag., 1972-73, sr. editor, columnist, 1974-78; contbg. editor N.Y. mag., 1973-74. Author: Wallflower at the Orgy, 1970, Crazy Salad, 1975, Scribble Scribble, 1978, Heartburn, 1983, Nora Ephron Collected, 1991; screenwriter: (with Alice Arlen) Silkwood (nominated Acad. award for best original screenplay), 1983, Heartburn, 1986, Cookie, 1989, When Harry Met Sally (nominated Acad. award, BAFTA award for best screenplay), 1989, My Blue Heaven, 1990; dir., screenwriter (with Delia Ephron) This Is My Life, 1992, Mixed Nuts, 1994, Michael, 1996, You've Got Mail, 1998; co-screenwriter, dir. Sleepless in Seattle (nominated Acad. award for best original screenplay), 1993; screenwriter, producer, dir., Red Tails in Love: A Wildlife Drama in Central Park, 2000; producer, dir., Numbers, 2000; screenwriter, producer, Hanging Up, 2000. Mem. Writers Guild Am., Authors Guild, Dirs. Guild of Am., Acad. Motion Picture Arts and Scis.

EPIKHIN, VYACHESLAV MIKHAILOVICH, physicist, researcher; b. Chelyabinsk, USSR, Oct. 13, 1950; s. Mihail F. and Zoya N. (Shelamova) E.; m. Galina I. Dudenina, June 17, 1977; 1 child, Pavel V. Solid state engr.-physicist diploma, Moscow Engring.-Phys. inst., 1974, postgrad., 1976-79; PhD in Physics and Math., Nat. Sci. and Rsch. Inst. for Phys.-Tech. and Radiotech. Measurements, Moscow region, 1985. Cert. in phys. engring. Jr. rsch. scientist Nat. Sci. & Rsch. Inst. for Phys.-Tech. & Radiotech. Measure, Mendeleevo, 1979-85, sr. rsch. scientist, 1985-93, 95—; sr. rsch. scientist Inst. Space & Time Metrology, Mendeleevo, 1993-95; mem. Arrow, Mendeleevo, 1988-92; mem., cons. Fortic Ltd., Mendeleevo, 1992-95; head acousto-optic group Sigma-Optic Ltd., Mendeleevo, 1995—. Patentee in field. Individual rsch. grantee Internat. Sci. Found., 1993. Avocations: traveling, playing tennis, dogs, cars. Fax: (095) 535-91-35. E-mail: epikvm@mail.ru. Office: VNIIFTRI, Mendeleevo, Moscow Region, Russia 141570

EPLER, GARY ROBERT, physician, author, educator; b. Chico, Calif., Apr. 5, 1944; s. Deane Chandler and Kathryn Louise (McNeil) E.; m. Joan Susan Weidman, Sept. 10, 1983; children: Gregory C., Brett H. MD, Tulane U., 1971; MPH, Harvard U., 1978. Diplomate in internal medicine and pulmonary medicine Am. Bd. Internal Medicine. Intern Harlem Hosp., Columbia U., 1971-72; resident U. Hosp., Boston, 1974-76, pulmonary medicine fellowship, 1975-78; asst. prof. medicine Sch. Medicine Boston U., 1978-85, assoc. clin. prof. medicine, 1985-96; assoc. clin. prof. medicine Harvard U., Boston, 1995—; med. dir. respiratory therapy, chmn. dept. medicine New England Bapt. Hosp., Boston, 1983-98, med. dir. rehab. unit, 1983-98; parasitology rsch. fellow Tulane U., Cali, Colombia, 1969-70, USPHS, Ctrs. Disease Control, 1972-74; tuberculosis cons. CDC Vietnamese Refugee Camps, Eglin AFB, Fla. and Indiantown Gap, Pa., 1975, Cuban Refugee Camp, Indiantown Gap, 1980; med. cons. CDC, Vietnamese Refugee Programs in Hong Kong, Thailand, Philippines, Malaysia, Indonesia; vis. attending physician U. Hosp., Boston City Hops. and Boston VA Hosp., 1978-98, Brigham and Women's Hosp., Boston, 1999—; med. dir. Occupational Health Ctr., Wilmington, Mass; vis. prof. Kyoto (Japan) U., 1990; many others. Author book on diseases of bronchioles, 1994; editor book on occupational lung diseases; editl. reviewer New England Jour. Medicine, Annals of Internal Medicine, Jour. AMA, Am. Rev. Respiratory Diseases, Chest, Jour. Respiratory Medicine, Jour. Western Medicine, Jour. Rheumatology, European Respiratory Jour.; contbr. chpts. to books, more than 85 articles to sci. jours. Lt. comdr. USPHS, 1972-74. Recipient cert. of appreciation Am. Lung Assn. Mass.; named one of Outstanding Med. Specialists in U.S., Town and Country Mag., 1989. Fellow ACP, Am. Coll. Chest Physicians (chmn. com. on occupational and environ. health 1987-88, v.p. New England States chpt. 1989-91, pres. chpt. 1991-93); mem. AMA (alt. del. 1987-93), Am. Soc. Law and Medicine (treas. 1983-85, Disting. Svc. award 1985), Am. Coll. Physician Execs., Mass. Thoracic Soc. (mem. coun. 1980-84, sec.-treas. 1984-85, pres. 1986-88), Mass. Med. Soc. Office: Brigham and Women's Hosp Pulmonary/Critical Care Med 75 Francis St Boston MA 02115-6106

EPP, GARRETT WAYNE, music educator; b. Reedley, Calif., July 4, 1944; s. William "Howard" and Verna Myrtle (Janzen) E. BA in Music Edn., Bethel Coll., 1967; MusM, So. Meth. U., 1975, M Sacred Music, 1975; Mus D, U. Mo., Kansas City, 1993. Cert. elem., secondary tchr., Ind., Kans. Choral dir. grades 4-12 Stockton (Kans.) Unified Sch. Dist., 1967-70; edn. coord./counselor/tchr. Mpls. City Workhouse, 1970-73; supr. music/choral dir. grades 7-12 South Adams Schs., Berne, Ind., 1975-88; pvt. voice tchr. part-time Shawnee Mission South H.S., Overland Park, Kans., 1990-91; artist-in-residence/pvt. voice instr. Paseo Acad. Fine & Performing Arts, Kansas City, Mo., 1991-93; adj. faculty/pvt. voice instr. Kansas City (Kans.) C.C., 1993; performing arts chair/secondary choral coord./choral dir. Olathe (Kans.) North H.S., 1993—; profl. singer Kansas City (Mo.) Chorale, 1998—; profl. singer/sect. leader St. Michael's & All Angels Episcopal Ch., Overland Park, 2000—; dir. music Trinity United Meth. Ch., Kansas City (Kans.), 1989-93; founder, music dir. Kansas City Singers, 1991; guest conductor Kansas City Symphony Chorus, 1991. Ch. choir director various Kans., Ind. chs., 1966-93; founder, music dir. Stockton (Kans.) Cmty. Chorus, 1967-70; dir., conductor other singing groups, 1970-93; soloist with several major choruses; mem. chorus other groups. Recipient U. Mo. Kansas City Chancellor's Non-Resident award, 1988-90, Perkins Sch. Theology Tuition award, 1974-75, Bethel Coll. Music Theory assistantship, 1965-67. Mem. Internat. Fedn. Choral Music, Am. Choral Dirs. Assn., Music Educators Nat. Conf., Nat. Assn. Tchrs. of Singing, Nat. Educators Assn., Coll. Music Soc., Phi Kappa Phi, Pi Kappa Lambda. Mennonite. Achievements: one of 160 singers selected by audition from throughout the world to perform in Carnegie Hall with the Robert Shaw/Carnegie Hall Festival Chorus, 1990, 92, 94, 99. Avocations: biking, hiking, racquetball, cultural activities. Office: Olathe North H S 600 E Prairie St Olathe KS 66061-3355

EPPELBAUM, LEV VILEN, geophysicist, researcher, educator; b. Tbilisi, Georgia, May 18, 1959; arrived in Israel, 1990; s. Vilen Mark and Esfir Lev (Grabovetsky) E.; m. Elina Markus Kreinin, Mar. 16, 1986; children: Esfir, Tal. MSc in Geophysics, Inst. Oil and Chemistry, Baku, Azerbaijan, 1982; PhD in Geophysics, Inst. Georgian Acad. Sci. and Baku, Azerbaijan, 1989; postdoc., Tel Aviv U., 1991-92. Geophysicist Inst. Geophysics, Baku, 1982-84; rschr. Inst. Geophysics, 1984-88, sr. rschr., 1988-90; rschr. dept. geophysics Tel Aviv U., 1990-95, sr. lectr. dept. geophysics, 1995—; cons. Archeol. Authority, Jerusalem, 1994—, oil companies, environmental geophysics. Author: Interpretation of Geophysical Fields in Complicated Environments, Kluwer, 1996; contbr. articles to Geoexploration, Jour. Applied Geophysics, Geophysics, Geophys. Jour. Internat., Geoinformatics, Jour. of Geophys. Res., Geophy. Rsch. Letters, Tectonophysics, Archaeol. Prosperz., Jour. of the Prehist. Soc., Sci. Israel, others, chpts. to books. With Azerbaijan Mil., 1982. Grantee Min. Sci. Israel, 1992, Ministry Energy Israel, 1995-2000, Weitzman Inst., 1996-97, UNESCO, 1998, Tel Aviv U. grant, 1995, 97, 99, 2000. Mem. Soc. Exploratory Geophysics, N.Y. Acad. Sci., Am. Geophys. Union, Mediterranean Soc. Geologists Geophysicists, Japan Soc. Geoinformatics, Israel Geol. Soc., Planetary Soc., European Assn. of Exploration Geophysics. Jewish. Avocations: chess, fantastic literature, basketball. E-mail: levfrodo@tau.ac.il. Fax: 9723 640 9282. Home: 27 Moshe Dayan St Apt 8, 67653 Tel Aviv Israel Office: Tel Aviv U Dept Geophysics, Ramat Aviv, 69978 Tel Aviv Israel

EPPERSON, ERIC ROBERT, company executive, film producer; b. Oregon City, Oreg., Dec. 10, 1949; s. Robert Max and Margaret Joan (Crawford) E.; m. Lyla Gene Harris, Aug. 21, 1969; 1 child, Marcie. BS, Brigham Young U., 1973, M of Acctg., 1974; MBA, Golden Gate U., 1977, JD, 1981. Instr. acctg. Brigham Young U., Provo, Utah, 1973-74; supr. domestic taxation Bechtel Corp., San Francisco, 1974-78; supr. internat. taxation Bechtel Power Corp., San Francisco, 1978-80; mgr. internat. tax planning Del Monte Corp., San Francisco, 1980-82, mgr. internat. taxes, 1982-85; internat. tax specialist Touche Ross & Co., San Francisco, 1985-87; dir. internat. tax Coopers & Lybrand, Portland, 1987-89; exec. v.p., chief fin. officer Epperson Dayton Sorenson Prodns., Inc., Salt Lake City, 1989-90, Epperson Prodns., 1990-92; exec. dir. The Oreg. Trail Found., Inc., Oregon City, 1992-93; pres., chmn. bd. MFD Ltd., Portland, Oreg., 1993—; pres. Oreg. Trail Films, Ltd., 1998—, Morgan's Ferry Prodns., LLC, 1998—, Lakeboat Prodns., L.L.C., 1999—, Oregon Trail Television, Ltd., 1999, Oregon Trail Promotions, Ltd., 1999; pres. Oreg. Trail TV, Ltd., 1999—. Author: (with T. Gilbert) Interfacing of the Securities and Exchange Commission with the Accounting Profession: 1968 to 1973, 1974; producer (motion pictures) Without Evidence, 1995, Morgan's Ferry, 1999, Lakeboat, 2000; exec. producer (motion picture) Dream Machine, 1989. Scoutmaster, Boy Scouts Am., Provo, 1971-73, troop committeeman, 1973-74, 83—; mem. IRS Vol. Income Tax Assistance Program, 1972-75; pres. Mut. Improvement Assn., Ch. Jesus Christ of Latter-day Saints, 1972-74, pres. Sunday sch., 1977-79, tchr., 1974-80, ward clk., 1980-83, bishopric, 1983-87; bd. dirs. Oreg. Art Inst. Film Ctr., Oreg. Trail Coordinating Coun., Hist. Preservation League of Oreg.; vice chmn. ranch devel. com. Boy Scouts Am., Butte Creek. Mem. World Affairs Coun., Japan/Am. Soc., Internat. Tax Planning Assn., Internat. Fiscal Assn., Oreg. Trail Coordinating Coun. (exec. bd.), Oreg. Hist. Soc., U.S. Rowing Assn., Oreg. Calif. Trail Assn., Royal Photographic Soc., Commonwealth Club, Multnomah Athletic Club. Republican. Office: PMB 180 25 NW 23d Pl Ste 6 Portland OR 97210-5599

EPPERSON, JAMES ANTHONY MENDOZA, mathematics educator; b. San Antonio, Dec. 14, 1965; s. Jonas Gallego and Olga Mendoza Alvarez; m. Minerva Cordero Braña, June 19, 1999; children: Nicholas Jacob Cordero Epperson, George Alexander Vourtsanis. BS with acad. distinction, Tex. A&M U., 1987; PhD, U. Tex., 1996. Tchg. asst. dept. math. U. Tex., Austin, 1989-92, asst. instr. dept. math., 1992-95, postdoctoral fellow Charles A. Dana Ctr. for Math. and Sci., 1996-98; asst. prof. dept. math. and stats. Tex. Tech. U., Lubbock, 1998—; cons. Charles A. Dana Ctr. for Math. and Sci. Edn., Austin, 1991-95, 98-99, The Coll. Bd., Southwestern Region, Austin, 1996. Co-author: Advanced Placement Program Mathematics Vertical Teams Toolkit, 1998; contbr. chpt. to book. Active Hispanic Action Group, Lubbock, 1999. Mem. Am. Math. Soc., Math. Assn. Am. (Nat. Project NExT fellow 1998, Tex. Project NExT fellow Tex. sect. 1999), Nat. Coun. Tchr. Math., Soc. for Advancement of Chicanos and Native Ams. in Sci. Democrat. Roman Catholic. Avocations: genealogy research, reading 17th century history, listening to music, playing raquetball. E-mail: epperson@math.ttu.edu. Fax: 806-742-1112. Office: Tex Tech Univ Dept Math and Stats PO Box 41042 Lubbock TX 79409-1042

EPPERSON, JOEL RODMAN, lawyer; b. Miami, Fla., Aug. 29, 1945; s. John Rodman and Ann Louise (Barrs) E.; m. Gretchen Jean Meyer, Apr. 16, 1968; children: Joel Rodman, David Michael, Sandra Elizabeth. BS, U. South Fla., 1967; JD, South Tex. Coll., 1976. Bar: Fla. 1976, U.S. Dist. Ct. (mid. dist.) Fla. 1976, U.S. Ct. Appeals (5th cir.) 1976, U.S. Supreme Ct. 1979, U.S. Ct. Appeals (11th cir. 1991. Asst. state's atty. State of Fla., Tampa, 1976-79; ptnr. Bryant & Epperson, Tampa, 1979-86; assoc. Bruce L. Scheiner, Ft. Myers, Fla., 1987-88; ptnr. Epperson & Stahl, Ft. Myers, 1988-90, Epperson & DeMinico, Tampa and Ft. Myers, 1991-92; ptnr. Epperson & Assocs., P.A., Tampa and Ft. Myers, 1993-99, Tampa, 1999—. Capt. USMC, 1968-72. Mem. ABA, ATLA, Acad. Fla. Trial Lawyers Assn., Hillsborough County Bar Assn. Democrat. Home: 1306 Anglers Ln Lutz FL 33549-5040 Office: Epperson & Assocs 1719 W Kennedy Blvd Tampa FL 33606-1643

EPPES, WALTER W., JR., retired lawyer; b. Meridian, Miss., Oct. 9, 1929; s. Walter W. Sr. and Mary (Seymour) E.; m. Katherine Bailey, Oct. 17, 1952; children: Kathy Eppes Yarborough, Susan Eppes Whitehead. Student, U. Ala., Tuscaloosa, 1947-50; LLB, U. Miss., 1952. Bar: Miss. 1952, U.S. Dist. Ct. (so. dist.) Miss. 1952, U.S. Ct. Appeals (5th cir.) 1952. Adjuster U.S. Fidelity & Guaranty Co., Meridian, 1952-54; ptnr. Shumate & Eppes, Meridian, 1954-63, Huff, Williams, Gunn, Eppes & Crenshaw, Meridian, 1963-73, Eppes, Watts & Shannon, Meridian, 1973-95, Eppes & Carter, Meridian, 1995—. Author: (with others) Mississippi Law Institute, 1975. Pres. Roundtable Investors, Meridian, 1992. Mem. Am. Bd. Trial Advs. (diplomate), Miss. Bar (pres. 1985-86), Internat. Soc. Barristers (gov. 1968—), Internat. Assn. Def. Counsel (comm. chmn. 1960—), Downtown Club Meridian (pres. 1972), Northwood Country Club (bd. dirs. 1972). Republican. Presbyterian. Avocation: hunting. Home: 4833 15th Pl Meridian MS 39305-1736 Office: Eppes & Carter Attys PO Box 3037 Broadmoor Mart Meridian MS 39303

EPPES, WILLIAM DAVID, civic worker, curator; b. 1918; s. Talmadge DeWitt and Annie Lou (McCord) E. AB, Coll. of William and Mary, 1939; BS in LS, Vanderbilt U., 1940; student, U. Miami, U. Manchester (Eng.), 1950, Columbia U., 1950; MA, NYU, 1959; student, U. Durham, Eng., 1987. Reference asst. George Washington U., 1943-45, Calif. State U., San Francisco, 1945-46; cons. Z.D. McCord Co., San Francisco, 1945-47; head stack personnel Butler Libr. Columbia U., N.Y.C., 1954-58; assoc. prof. Kean State Coll., N.J., 1958-61; asst. libr. Cooper Union, N.Y.C., 1961-70; founder Film Classics League, St. Petersburg, Fla., 1950; co-founder Backstage Gallery, St. Petersburg Jr. Coll., 1950, Littlebury Eppes Meml. Libr., Westover Ch., Va.; adv. bd. Coral Gables (Fla.) Hist. Preservation Bd. Rev., 1979-81; trustee Greenwich Village Trust for Hist. Preservation, Inc., 1980, pres., 1980-84, 1984-90; cons. Hist. Buckingham (Va.) Inc., 1987—; hon. commr. Eleanor Roosevelt Monument Fund, Inc., N.Y.C. Author: The Empire Theatre (1893-1953), 1978, Gertrude Michael-A Star of the Golden Age of Hollywood, 1985, Montgomery (Ala.) Theatre 1822-1985, 1986; contbr. articles to mags. and hist. jours. Bd. dirs. St. Petersburg Symphony Orch., 1950-54; exec. bd. Assn. Village Homeowners, N.Y.C., 1969-82, Assocs. of Earl Gregg Swem Libr., Coll. of William and Mary, 1973-86; benefactor Jonathon Daniels Sch., Keene, N.H., 1998, Apple Hill Chamber Orch., Sullivan, N.H., 1998, Kean State Coll., 1999—; benefactor, hist. cons. Redford Performing Arts Ctr. Keene (N.H.) State Coll., 2000—; pres. coun. Va. Hist. Soc., 1982; profl. advisor Leed Plantation, Sea Island Hist. Soc., S.C. Mem. Theater Hist. Soc. (rsch. and reference com. 1977-81), Author's Guild, Inc., W&M Choir, Va. Hist. Soc. (exec. coun. 1995), Sea Island Hist. Soc. (profl. adv. bd. 2000). Episcopalian. Home: 14 Rivermead Rd Peterborough NH 03458-1701 also: 37A New St Charleston SC 29401-2405 also: 14 River Mead Rd Peterborough NH 03458-1701

EPPINK, JEFFREY FRANCIS, energy and environmental consultant; b. Whittier, Calif., Jan. 31, 1955; s. Reno Paul and Bertina (Gilje) I.; m. Sheryl Ann Baumberger, Aug. 27, 1977; children: Christina Michelle, Michael Jeffrey. BS, Calif. State Poly. U., 1978; MS, U. So. Calif., 1981; MBA, Va. Poly. Inst. and State U., 1996. Planetary scientist Jet Propulsion Lab., Pasadena, Calif., 1979-81; explorationist Chevron Overseas Petroleum Inc., San Ramon, Calif., 1981-91; project mgr. ICF Kaiser Internat., San Francisco, 1991-92; diplomacy fellow Asia Bur. U.S. Agy. Internat. Devel., Washington, 1992-93; project mgr. ICF Kaiser Internat., Fairfax, Va., 1993-98; mgr. projects and bus. devel. Advanced Resources Internat., Inc., Arlington, Va., 1998—. Mem. selection com Hubert H. Humphrey fellow, 1994, Human Resources com. Am. Geol. Inst., 1995. Mem. AAAS, KC, Am. Assn. Petroleum Geologists, Soc. Exploration Geophysicists, Internat. Assn. Energy Econs. Republican. Roman Catholic. Avocations: travel, long distance swimming, planetology, woodworking. Home: 13503 King Charles Dr Chantilly VA 20151-3325 Office: Advanced Resources Internat 1110 N Glebe Rd Arlington VA 22201-4795

EPPLE, WOLFGANG KARL, computer science engineer; b. Munderkingen, Germany, Mar. 3, 1953; s. Karl and Maria Magdalena (Beck) E.; m. Ingeborg Christina Blöchle, May 25, 1980; 1 child, Lilly. BSc in computer sci., Univ., Karlsruhe, Germany, 1980, PhD, 1985. Scientific asst. U. Karlsruhe, 1980-82, asst. prof. Robotics Inst., 1983-85; mgr. planning R&D BMW AG, Munich, 1985-88, sr. mgr. logistics & control prototype production, 1988-91; gen. mgr. industrialization BMW SA, Pretoria, South Africa, 1991-93, gen. mgr. engring. and export, 1993-95, gen. mgr. engring. and project mgmt., 1995-97; project dir. compact 3 series BMW AG, Munich, 1997—; cons. software engring. Standard Elec. Lorenz, Stuttgart, Germany, 1984-85; presenter in field. Author: Ein Verfahren zur Entwicklung von Bedienerdialogen/VDI Verlag, 1985; co-author: Einführung in die Informatik für Naturwissenschaftler & Ingenieure, 1991; contbr. over 30 articles to profl. jours. Press rep. German Christian Dem. Union, 1976-77, treas., 1978-79; pres. Com. Scientific Edn., 1983-85; pres. Eurotable, Munich, Venice, 1990-92. Lt. German Air Force, 1972-74. Mem. Gesellschaft für Informatik, Assn. Computing Machinery, Eurotable, Alumni Assn. Universitäts-Seminar der Wirtschaft. Roman Catholic. Avocations: cycling, playing saxophone, travelling, photography. Home: Kaagangerstr 134, 82279 Eching am Ammersee Germany Office: BMW AG G2-H, Postfach 400240, 80788 Munich Germany

EPPS, JAMES HAWS, III, lawyer; b. Johnson City, Tenn., Sept. 15, 1936; s. James Haws and Anne Lafayette (Sessoms) E.; m. Jane Mahoney, Oct. 9, 1976; children from previous marriage--James Haws IV, Sara Stuart. B.A., U.N.C., 1955-59; J.D., Vanderbilt U., 1962. Bar: Tenn. 1962, U.S. Dist. Ct. Tenn. 1962, U.S. Ct. Appeals (6th cir.) 1971, Interstate Commerce Commn. Bar 1962, U.S. Supreme Ct. 1967. Prin. Epps & Epps, Johnson City, Tenn.; city atty. Johnson City, 1967—, Johnson City Bd. Edn., 1967-86; spl. counsel State of Tenn., 1966-70; former gen. counsel Appalachian Flying Svc. Inc., ET&WNC Transp. Co., Inc. First bd. govs. Transp. Law Jour. Past bd. dirs. Washington County Mental Health Assn., East Tenn. and Western N.C. Transp. Co., East Tenn. and Western N.C. R.R., Tennolina Corp., Appalachian Air Lines, Inc., Appalachian Flying Svc., Inc., Farmers and Mchts. Bank, Limestone, Tenn., Tenn. Mental Health Assn., budget com. United Fund of Johnson City, 1964-68, Assault Crime Counsel Early Support Svcs. Inc., Safe Passage Inc., Johnson City Homeless Coalition, Home Base Adv. Coun.; former legal adviser Appalachian Council Girl Scouts U.S.A.; mem. Tenn. Law Revision Commn., 1970-71; legal counsel Salvation Army, mem. adv. bd. 1974—, exec. com. 1977—, 1st v.p. adv. bd. 1991, pres. adv. bd. 1993, 94, mem. property com.; chmn. Family Violence Coun.; mem. Civil Def., 1967—; chmn. Washington County for Tenn. Leukemia Soc., 1991; mem. exec. com. Washington County Dem. Party, Tenn. Bicentennial Commn., exec. and fin. coms. Fellow Tenn. Bar Found.; mem. ABA, Fed. Bar Assn., Nat. Orgn. Legal Problems Edn., Nat. Assn. R.R. Trial Counsel, Internat. Mcpl. Lawyers Assn., (stata chmn. Tenn. 1988-89, ethics and environ. coms. 1989—, regional v.p. 1989-92, chmn. resolutions com. 1989-90, chmn. dues and alternatives revenue 1996-97, budget and fin. 1996—, mem. federalism com. 1996—, state league counsel rev. com. 1997, awards com., 1999—, lectr., trustee, 1992—, third v.p. 1999—), Nat. Legal Aid Defender Assn., Tenn. Bar Assn., Am. Judicature Soc., Washington County Bar Assn. (past pres.), Tenn. Mcpl. Attys. Assn., Assn. ICC Practitioners (past com. profl. ethics and grievences), Transp. Lawyers Assn., Motor Carrier Lawyers Assn., Am. Counsel Assn., Johnson City C. of C. (Disting. Service award 1968), Internat. Platform Assn., Lawyers Com. for Civil Rights Under Law, World Peace Through Law Ctr., Tenn. Lung Assn., Tenn. Correctional Assn., Tenn. Taxpayers Assn. (past bd. dirs.), Tennesseans for Better Transp., U.S. Supreme Ct. Hist. Soc., Def. Research Inst., Tipton Haynes Hist. Assn. (past dir.); Clubs: Hurstleigh, J.C. Country, Unaka Rd. and Gun, Highland Stable, North Johnson City Bus. (dir., past pres. 1966-67), Nat. Lawyers, East Tenn. State U. Centry, Boys'Club (charter) (Johnson City/Washington County). Lodges: Masons, Elks (legal counsel 1963-67), former Kiwaniian; Phi Delta Phi, Phi Delta Theta. Episcopalian. Clubs: Hurstleigh, J.C. Country, Unaka Rd. and Gun, Highland Stable, North Johnson City Bus. (dir., past pres. 1966-67), Nat. Lawyers, East Tenn. State U. Centry, Boys' Club (charter) (Johnson City/Washington County). Lodges: Masons, Elks (legal counsel 1963-67), former Kiwaniian. Office: 115 E Unaka Ave Johnson City TN 37601-4623 also: PO Box 2288 Johnson City TN 37605-2288

EPRIGHT, CHARLES JOHN, retired aerospace engineer; b. Bklyn., Jan. 11, 1932; s. Charles and Margaret Mary (Tripoli) E.; m. Mary Lucy Bono, May 29, 1954; children: Daniel John, Michael James, Marisa Epright Becker, Victoria Epright Carmona, Maria Carmela. BS in Math., U. Nev., 1965; MS in Engring. Mgmt., Northeastern U., 1971. Sr. engr. Raytheon, Andover, Mass., 1970-78, Delmo-Victor, Belmont, Calif., 1978-79; advanced systems engring. specialist Lockheed Missile and Space Co., Austin and Sunnyvale, Tex. and Calif., 1979-87; engring. scientist Tracor Aerospace, Austin, 1987-89; staff engr. Lockheed Engring. and Sci. Co., Houston, 1989-99. Civic adv. Salem-in-Action, N.H., 1977-79; dir. Reachout, Salem, 1976-79; cmty. action com. mem. N.H. Com. for Adopted and Foster Children, Manchester, 1978-79, Runaway Hotline, Austin, 1984-88, 99—, Middle Earth Spectrum Shelter, 1987-89; mem. pub. responsibility com. Mental Health/Mental Retardation, Austin, 1988-89; bd. dirs., v.p. Assn. Retarded Citizens, 1989-93; mem. outreach Covenant House Tex., Houston, 1990-99. With USAF, 1950-70. Decorated Legion of Merit; recipient Family of Yr. award Sons of Italy, 1968, 69. Mem. Air Force Assn. (life), DAV, Am. Legion. Roman Catholic. Lodge: KC (grand knight 1968-69). Avocations: stamp collecting, photography, collecting old books. Home: 7500 Bender Dr Austin TX 78749-3105

EPSTEIN, JONATHAN DANIEL, journalist; b. Schenectady, N.Y., July 20, 1971; s. Gilbert Howard and Celia (Feiner) E. BA in Polit. Sci., History, U. Rochester, N.Y., 1993; MS in Print Journalism, Columbia U., N.Y.C., 1994. Reporter Am. Banker, Washington, 1994-96, deputy sect. editor, 1996-97; reporter News Journal, Wilmington, Del., 1997—. Cmty. bd. mem. U. Del. Hillel, Newark, 1998—. Fellow Stonier Grad. Sch. Banking, Newark, 1997. Mem. Soc. Profl. Journalists. Jewish. E-mail: jepstein@wilmingt.gannett.com. Office: News Journal 950 W Basin Rd New Castle DE 19720-1006

EPSTEIN, JUDITH ANN, lawyer; b. L.A., Dec. 23, 1942; d. Gerald Elliot and Harriet (Hirsh) Rubens; m. Joseph I. Epstein, Oct. 4, 1964; children: Mark Douglas, Laura Ann. AB, U. Calif., Berkeley, 1964; MA, U. San Francisco, 1974, JD, 1977. Bar: Calif. 1978, U.S. Dist. Ct. (no. dist.) Calif 1978, U.S. Supreme Ct. 1983, U.S. Ct. Appeals (9th cir.) 1984. With social svcs. dept. Sutter County, Yuba City, Calif., 1964-66; bus. devel. assoc. Yuba County C. of C., Marysville, Calif., 1968-70; rsch. clk. Calif. Supreme Ct., San Fransisco, 1977; ptnr. Crosby, Heafey, Roach & May, Oakland, Calif., 1978-91; gen. counsel and sec. Valent USA Corp., 1991-98; fellow The Commonwealth Club of Calif., 1999—; lectr. U. Calif. Grad. Sch. Journalism in Media Law, Berkeley, 1987-91; bd. dirs. Sierra Pacific Steel, Hayward, Calif.; adj. prof. U. San Francisco, 1999—. Bd. dirs., v.p. Oakland Ballet, 1980-92; mem. bd. counselors U. San Francisco Sch. Law, 1994; trustee U. San Francisco, 1996—; bd. dirs. San Francisco Bay area Girl Scouts U.S., 1998—, East Bay Cmty. Found. Recipient Pres.'s award Oakland Ballet, James Madison Freedom of Info. award Soc. Profl. Journalists, 1992; award for Disting. Achievement, Girl Scouts U.S., 1995. Fellow Am. Bar Found.;

mem. Calif. Women Lawyers Assn., Alameda Bar Assn., Berkeley Tennis Club.

EPSTEIN, LEE JOAN, political science educator; b. N.Y.C., Mar. 17, 1958; d. Kenneth Maurice and Ann (Buxbaum) Spole; m. Jay Stuart Epstein, June 21, 1980. BA magna cum laude, Emory U., 1980, MA, 1982, PhD, 1983. Mallinckrodt Disting. Univ. prof. polit. sci. Washington U., St. Louis, 1998—, prof. law, 2000—. Author: Conservatives in Court, 1985; co-author: Constitutional Law for a Changing America, 1992, Supreme Court and Legal Change, 1992, The Choices Justices Make, 1998; contbr. articles to profl. jours., chpts. in books. Mem. Am. Polit. Sci. Assn., So. Polit. Sci. Assn., Midwest Polit. Sci. Assn., Law and Soc. Assn., Pi Sigma Alpha, Alpha Epsilon Phi. Jewish. Avocations: skiing, tennis. Office: Washington U Dept Polit Sci PO Box 1063 Saint Louis MO 63188-1063

EPSTEIN, MICHAEL ALAN, lawyer; b. N.Y.C., June 26, 1954; s. Herman and Lillian (King) E. BA, Lehigh U., 1975; JD, NYU, 1979. Bar: N.Y., 1980, US. Dist. Ct. (so., ea. dists.) N.Y., 1980. Ptnr. Weil, Gotshal & Manges, N.Y.C., 1979—; lectr. in field. Author: Modern Intellectual Property, 1984, 3d edit., 1994, International Intellectual Property, 1992; editor: Corporate Counsellors Deskbook, 1982, 3d edit., 1990, Biotechnology Law, 1988, The Trademark Law Revision Act, 1989, Trade Secrets, Restrictive Covenants and Other Safeguards, 1986, Online-Internet Law, 1997, Epstein on Intellectual Property, 1998; co-editor, mem. editl. bd. Jour. Proprietary Rights, The Computer Lawyer, The Intellectual Property Strategist, The Cyberspace Lawyer; contbr. articles to profl. jours. Trustee Jonas Salk Found., Am. Health Found. Donald L. Brown fellow in trade regulation NYU Sch. Law, 1978-79. Mem. ABA, N.Y. State Bar Assn. Home: 1020 Park Ave New York NY 10028-0913 Office: Weil Gotshal & Manges 767 5th Ave Fl Concl New York NY 10153-0119

EPSTEIN, MURRAY, medical educator; b. Tel Aviv, Aug. 11, 1937; came to U.S., 1940; s. Louis and Susanna (Mendelowitz) E.; m. Nina Nilsson, June 25, 1978; children: David L., Susanna R., Jonathan M. BA, Columbia Coll., 1959; MD, Columbia U., 1963. Diplomate Am. Bd. Internal Medicine, Am. Bd. Nephrology. Fellow in nephrology Peter Bent Brigham Hosp., Boston, 1966-68; med. investigator USAF Sch. Aerospace Medicine, Brooks AFB, Tex., 1968-70; asst. prof. medicine U. Miami, Fla., 1970-74, assoc. prof. medicine, 1974-78, prof. medicine, 1978—; staff physician VA Med. Ctr., Miami, Fla., 1970—. Author: Hypertension: Practical Management, 1988; editor: The Kidney in Liver Disease, 1978, 83, 88, 96, Calcium Antagonists in Clinical Medicine, 1992, 2d edit., 1997, Angiotensin II Receptor Antagonists, 2000; contbr. over 350 articles to profl. jours. Maj. USAF, 1968-70. Recipient med. investigatorship Howard Hughes Med. Inst., 1972-76, Disting. Scientist award Nat. Kidney Found., 1990. Fellow ACP; mem. Am. Soc. Clin. Investigation, Am. Physiol. Soc., Am. Soc. Nephrology. Achievements include research in pathogenesis and management of hypertension, renal function in diseases characterized by abnormal volume regulation, the role of the renin-angiotensin-aldosterone system, edematous disorders, and renal complications of liver disease. Office: VA Med Ctr Nephrology Sect 1201 NW 16th St Miami FL 33125-1624

EPSTEIN, WILLIAM LOUIS, dermatologist, educator; b. Cleve., Sept. 6, 1925; s. Norman N. and Gertrude (Hirsch) E.; m. Joan Goldman, Jan. 29, 1954; children—Wendy, Steven. AB, U. Calif., Berkeley, 1949, MD, 1952. Mem. faculty U. Calif., San Francisco, 1957—; assoc. prof. div. dermatology U. Calif., 1963-69, prof. div. dermatology, 1969—, dir. dermatol. rsch., 1957-70, acting chmn. div. dermatology, 1966-69, chmn. dept. dermatology, 1970-85; cons. dermatology Outpatient Dept.; cons. various hosps. Calif. Dept. Public Health; cons. Food and Drug Adminstrn., Washington, 1972—, Dept. Agriculture, 1979; dir. div. research Nat. Program Dermatology, 1970-73; Dohi lectr., Tokyo, 1982; Beecham lectr., 1988-89; Nippon Boehringer Ingelheim lectr. 18th Hakone Symposium on Respiration, Japan, 1990. Decorated medal of honor Order of the Rising Sun, gold rays with neck ribbon (Japan). Mem. AAAS, AMA, Am. Soc. Cell Biology, Am. Acad. Dermatology and Syphlology (nominating com. 1984), Pacific Dermatologic Assn., Am. Fedn. Clin. Rsch., Soc. Investigative Dermatology (bd. dirs., pres. 1985), Am. Dermatol. Assn., Assn. Profs. Dermatology (sr. mem.), Dermatology Found. (pres. 1986-87), Phi Beta Kappa, Sigma Xi. Home: 267 Golden Hinde Psge Corte Madera CA 94925-1953

ERAKOVIĆ, VESNA, pharmacologist, researcher; b. Rijeka, Croatia, Aug. 8, 1966; d. Andrija and Marija (Bilić) E. MD, Rijeka Med. Sch., 1990, M Biomed. Scis., 1995, PhD in Biomed. Sci., 1998. Resident Clin. Hosp. Ctr., Rijeka, 1990-91; rsch. asst. Rijeka Med. Sch., 1992-2000; head Pharmacodynamics Lab., PLIVA-Rsch. Inst., Zagreb, Croatia, 1998—. Contbr. articles to profl. rsch. jours. Recipient rsch. grant Austrian Govt., Graz, 1995. Mem. Soc. for Neurosci., Fedn. European Biochem. Socs. (travel grants 1995, 96), Croatian Soc. Clin. Pharmacology and Therapy. Avocations: travel, languages, books, arts, walking. Home: Lipa 40/a, 51000 Rijeka Croatia Office: PLIVA-Rsch Inst, Prilaz Baruna Filipovica 25, 10000 Zagreb Croatia

ERASMUS, DESMOND, manufacturing executive; b. Durban, Natal, South Africa, Feb. 14, 1947; s. Carl and Nora Vernon (Hobson) E.; m. Angela Heather Gorman, Jan. 10, 1976; children: James, Matthew, Tessa. Mng. dir. ef exec. Redex, Johannesburg, South Africa, 1976—; mng. dir. Holt Lloyd Internat., 1976—, Turtleline, 1984-96, Holts, South Africa, 1994—; divsn. chief Morganite Consumer Products, 1986-94; dir. Protector Gard-Rite, 1990-92, Rocol, 1990-94. Chmn. McAuley House Convent, Johannesburg, 1991—. Capt. Natal Mounted Rifles, 1965-82. Recipient John Chard medal, 1978. Mem. Country Club Johannesburg, Durban Country Club. Avocations: golf, trout fishing. Office: Holts, PO Box 8883785, South Hills 2136, South Africa

ERASMUS, LOUISA HELENA, director human resources consulting firm; b. Soekmekaar, Gauteng, South Africa, Sept. 11, 1971; d. Barend Frederik and Jannetje (Kuiper) E. BCom, U. Pretoria, 1992; cert. mgmt., Henley U., 1999. IT support Nissan, Pretoria, South Africa, 1993-94; sr. cons. Andersen Cons., Pretoria, 1994-96; dir. Mandevco Cons., Pretoria, 1996—. Mem. Computer Soc. South Africa, Inst. Dirs.

ERAUW, JOHAN ACHIEL, lawyer, educator, commercial arbitrator; b. Flanders, Belgium, Sept. 29, 1948; m. Riet Zegers; children: Eva-Maria, Liesbeth. Candidate in law, U. Ghent, Belgium, 1969, M in law, 1972; PhD maxima cum laude, U. Ghent, 1981. Rsch. asst. Law Sch., Tübingen (Germany) U., 1972-73; lawyer Ghent Bar, 1973-75, Brussels Bar, Dieux, Geens & Ptnrs.; asst. prof. Law Sch., U. Ghent, 1973-81, prof. internat. law, 1981—; co. legal counsel C&A Belgium, 1988-95; counsel for legis. on pvt. internat. law Belgian Ministry of Justice, 1996—; vis. prof. U. Fla., Am. U., Washington, U. Shanghai; hon. prof. East China U. of Law, Shanghai, 1995; arbitrator in internat. comml. litigation ICC-Paris and CEPANI-Brussels, World Intellectual Property Orgn., Geneva; arbitrator CIETAC-Beijing; cons. UNCITRAL; counsel to UN Internat. Trade Com.; spkr., lectr. in field. Author: De Onrechtmatige Daad in het Inernationaal Privaat-recht, 1982, Internationaal Privaatrecht: De Bronnen, 1982, De Bron van het Vreemde Recht Vloeit Overvloedig, 1984, Beginselen van Internationaal Privaatrecht, 1985, Bronnen van Internationaal Privaatrecht, 1991, 97; (with N. Wattè) Les Sources du Droit International Prive (Belge et Communautaire), 1993; editor: Europese Basisteksten Voor de Praktijk, 1989, 95; co-editor: Liber Memorialis François Laurent (1810-1887), 1989; mem. editl. bd. 5 law revs.; contbr. 100 articles to profl. jours. and books. Pvt. Belgian Army, 1973-74. Recipient Quintennial award Belgian U. Found., 1983; Fulbright scholar U. Minn., 1983. Mem. Internat. Bar Assn., Internat. Law Assn., Internat. C. of C. (arbitration, Paris, Brussels), Fulbright Alumni Assn. (past pres. and sec.). Office: U Ghent Law Sch, Universiteitstraat 4, B-9000 Ghent Belgium

ERB, PETER A. L., immunology professor, researcher; b. Walenstadt, St. Gallen, Switzerland, Sept. 5, 1942; s. Felix and Irene (Hoffmann) E.; m. Karin E. Herrmann, Aug. 29, 1967; children: Thomas, Stefan. PhD, Univ., Basel, Switzerland, 1969. Postgrad. Microbiology, Basel, 1970-72, U. Coll., London, 1973-75; head Immunology U., Basel, 1976-77, lctr., 1977-88, prof., 1988—; head Immunology U., Basel, 1976, Hiv Confirmatory Laboratory, 1986; cons. Swiss Nat. Sci. Funds, 1985. Editor: Immunology Letter, 1998; contbr. articles to profl. jours. Active Swiss HIV Commn., 1993, Swiss HIV Cohort Study, 1990. Recipient Amerbach Prize award, U. Basel, 1978. Mem. Am. Soc. Microbiology, British Soc. Immunology, European Soc. Clin. Microbiolgy and Infectious Diseases. Avocations: reading, bicycle riding, traveling. Office: Inst Med Microbiology, Petersplatz 10, CH4003 Basel Switzerland

ERBATUR, OKTAY, chemistry educator; b. Yozgat, Turkey, May 27, 1947; s. Cevdet and Saliha Erbatur; m. Nevin Gaye Bulut, Dec. 10, 1975; 1 child, Osman Cuneyt. BS in Chemistry, Middle East Tech. U., Ankara, Turkey, 1971, MS in Chemistry, 1973; PhD in Chemistry, Cukurova U., Adana, Turkey, 1982. Tchg. and rsch. asst. Hacettepe U., Ankara, 1973-75; rschr. Petrochem. Co., Ankara, 1975-77; from instr. to assoc. prof. Cukurova U., Adana, 1977-92, prof., 1992—; cons. Synthetic Fiber Co., Adana, 1988-99; advisor to sci., engring., environment and agrl. rsch. groups Turkish Sci. and Tech. Rsch. Coun., Ankara, 1988—. Contbr. chpts. to books. Pres. Turkish Chemists Assn., Ankara, 1973-75; mem. exec. com. Turkish U. Assts. Assn., Ankara, 1973-75. Fellow Brit. Coun., Salford, U.K., 1978, Brit. Coun., Birmingham, U.K., 1981, Internat. Devel. Rsch. Ctr., Sherbrooke, Can., 1983. Mem. Am. Chem. Soc. (fuel divsn., analytical chemistry divsn., environ. chemistry divsn.). Avocations: playing basketball. E-mail: erbatur@mail.cu.edu.tr. Fax: 90-322-338-6070. Office: Dept Chemistry, Cukurova Univ, 01330 Adana Turkey

ERBIL, HUSNU YILDIRIM, surface and polymer physical chemist, researcher; b. Izmir, Turkey, Mar. 15, 1954; s. Ibrahim Esber and Ummahan (Kizildemir) E.; m. Serap Kincak, Dec. 15, 1980; childrne: Ayberk, Billur; m. Ayse Cecen, May 18, 1994; children: Beril, Onur. BSc in Chem. Engring., Istanbul (Turkey) U., 1977; MSc in Polymer Chemistry, Aston U., Birmingham, Eng., 1978; PhD in Phys. Chemistry, Istanbul Tech. U., 1985. Project engr. PETKIM Petrochems. Co., Aliaga, Turkey, 1979; asst. rschr. TUBITAK, Marmara Rsch. Inst., Gebze, Turkey, 1979-83; rschr. Aston U., 1983; sr. rschr. TUBITAK, Marmara Rsch. Inst., 1984-89; rsch. cons. TUT Adhesives Co., ERAY Ltd., Istanbul, 1990-92; assoc. prof. TUBITAK, Marmara Rsch. Inst., 1992-98; prof. phys. chemistry Kocaeli (Turkey) U., 1998—. Author: Vinyl Acetate Emulsion Polymerization and Copolymerication with Acrylic Monomers, 2000; contbr. 2 chpts. CRC Handbook of Surface and Colloid Chemistry, 1997; contbr. articles to scientific publs. Recipient rsch. scholarship Brit. Coun., Birmingham, Eng., 1983; rsch. fellow Royal Soc. Eng., 1998—. Mem. Am. Chem. Soc., Internat. Assn. Celloid and Interface Scientists, Turkish Chamber Engrs., Marmara Sailing Club. Avocations: reading, chess, table tennis. Home: Toren Sokak No:19 C D:13, 80620 Levent Istanbul Turkey Office: Kocaeli U Faculty Sci, Dept Chemistry, 41430 Izmit Kocaeli, Turkey

ERBSEN, CLAUDE ERNEST, journalist; b. Trieste, Italy, Mar. 10, 1938; came to U.S., 1951, naturalized, 1956; s. Henry M. and Laura Elena (Treves) E.; m. Jill J. Prosky, July 16, 1959; 1 dau., Diana Lisa; m. Hedy Miriam Cohn, Apr. 7, 1970; children—Allan Henry, Michael David. BA cum laude, Amherst Coll., 1959; Inter-Am. Press Assn. scholar, U. Andes, Bogota, Colombia, 1960. Reporter-printer Amherst Jour.-Record, 1955-57; staff reporter El Tiempo, Bogota, 1960; with AP, 1960-1965; newsman in AP, N.Y.C., Miami, Fla., Washington; to chief of bur. Brazil, 1965-69; exec. rep. for Latin Am., 1969-70; bus. mgr., adminstrv. dir. AP-Dow Jones Econ. Report, London, 1970-75; dep. dir. world services AP, N.Y.C., 1975-80; v.p., dir. AP-Dow Jones News Services, 1980-87; v.p., dir. world services AP, N.Y.C., 1987—; bd. dirs. World Press Inst., St. Paul. Served to lt. USNR, 1961-65. Recipient San Giusto D'Oro award City of Trieste, 1995. Mem. Internat. Press Inst., Coun. Fgn. Rels., World Assn. of Newspapers, U. Club. Home: 27 Stratton Rd Scarsdale NY 10583-7556 Office: AP 50 Rockefeller Plz New York NY 10020-1605

ERBSLOEH, JOACHIM, retired obstetrician/gynecologist, educator; b. Wuppertal-Barmen, Germany, Sept. 28, 1909; s. Walter and Laura (Brink) E.; m. Sybil Louise Bannister, May 9, 1936 (div. 1936); 1 child, Erik; m. Agnes Emma, Baroness of Puttkamer, Dec. 23, 1942 (dec. 1995). MD, U. Bonn, Germany, 1930; prof. (hon.), U. Kiel, Germany, 1966. Med. diplomate. Med. asst. pediat. clinic, Frauenklinik Krankenhaus Schneidemühl, Danzig, Germany, 1933-34; physician State Frauenklinik, Danzig, 1934-38; physician surg. clinic Med. Acad., Danzig, 1938-39; med. supt. Mcpl. Hosp. for Women, Danzig, 1939-44; supr. ob-gyn., dir. nurses sch. hosp. Bad Oldesloe, Germany, 1947-74; supt. ob-gyn. dept. City Hosp., Bad Berleburg, Germany, 1980-81; med. supt., dir. maternity nurses, Bromberg (Germany) Mcpl. Lying-In Hosp. and Gynecology Clinic, 1939-45; dir. ward Diaconissen Hosp., Bromberg, 1939-45. Author: Über die röntgenologischen Darstellungsmöglichkeiten des weibl. Genital-apparates mit Hilfe von Jodö 2nd Jodsol, 1951, Die Frau als Mutter, 1953, rev. edit., 1966, Gynäkologische Röntgendiagnostik, 1954, Diagnostico Radiologico en Ginecologia, 1958; co-author: (with W. Hangarter) Der Rheumatismus in der Frauenheilkunde und Geburtshilfe, 1966; contbg. author: Psychotherapie (J.H. Schultz), 1952; contbr. over 150 articles to profl. jours. Mem. Supreme Coun. for Europe, 1978. Recipient Gran Croce s. Merito d. Lavoro Italian Acad. per lo Svil. Ec. e. So., 1979. Fellow Internat. Coll. Surgeons; mem. Internat. Assn. for Protection of Life (hon., Madeleine Rousseau prize 1979, supreme coun. 1979), N.Y. Acad. Scis., German Soc. Gynecology, German Soc. Radiology, Univ. Soc. Kiel, Berufsverband der Frauenärzte, Schleswig-Holsteinischer Landesausschuss für Krebsbekämpfung u. Krebsforschung, Deutsche Gesellschaft für Gynäkologie und Geburtshilfe. Evangelical. Avocations: music therapy, chromotherapy, psychotherapy, Zen Buddhism. Home: Travenhoehe 14, D-23843 Bad Oldesloe Germany

ERCEG, DAMIR, pharmacologist; b. Mostar, Croatia, June 20, 1965; s. Mile Erceg and Jelka Mandich. MD, U. Zagreb, 1990, MS, 1993; postgrad., U. Cardiff, 1996-98. Intern DZ Vrgorac KBC Rebro, Zagreb, 1991; gen. practice DZ Vrgorac, 1992; rschr. Pliva Rsch. Inst., Zagreb, 1993, head of pharmacology, 1994-97, clin. rsch. coord., 1997—. Contbr. articles to sci. and profl. jours. Mem. Croatian Soc. Clin. Pharmacology and Therapeutics, Internat. Union of Pharmacologists, British Assn. Pharmaceutical Physicians, Am. Acad. Pharmaceutical Physicians. E-mail: erceg@pliva.hr. Home: Marjanovicev Prilaz 2/9, Zagreb 10000, Croatia Office: Pliva Pharm Industry Inc, Ulica grada Vukovara 49, Zagreb 10000, Croatia

ERCEL, GAZI, banker. Gov. Ctrl. Bank of the Republic of Turkey, Ankara, 1996—. Office: Turkiye Cumhuriyet Merkez Bankasi AS, Head Office Istikal Cad 10, Ulus Ankara 06100, Turkey*

ERDELYI, EILEEN EDITH, financial planner and advisor; b. Glendale, Calif., Aug. 12, 1951; m. Alex Erdelyi, Jr., Dec. 11, 1971; children: Stephen Alex, Diana Lynn, Brian R. Cert. real estate salesperson, Lumbleau Real Estate Sch., L.A., 1985; stock market investment cert., Pacific Sch. Fin., Pasadena, Calif., 1985; cert. fin. planning program, U. So. Calif., 1987; cert. fin. planner, Coll. Fin. Planning, Denver, 1988; AAS, Palomar Coll., San Marcos, Calif. Lic. real estate salesperson, Calif.; CFP; lic. series 63 and 7 Nat. Assn. Securities Dealers; lic. in health and disability ins., life agt. Calif. Supervising clk. dept. pub. social svcs. and dept. probation Los Angeles County, L.A., 1969-75; broker assoc. Red Carpet Real Estate, Tujunga, Calif., 1986-88; assoc. fin. advisor prudent planning-alliance adv. group NBC Employees Fed. Credit Union, Burbank, Calif., 1988-89; fin. advisor, affiliate Alliance Adv. Group, Inc., Chatsworth, Calif., 1989-94; real estate sales assoc. Key Real Estate, Escondido, Calif., 1989-94; fin. advisor Capital Planning Concepts, San Diego, 1994-95; sr. fin. advisor Alliance Adv. & Securities, Inc., Escondido, 1995—. Former press chmn., treas., v.p., pres. Sunland Woman's Club Jrs. of Calif. Fedn. Woman's Clubs, 1978-88, also former bd. dirs. Verdugo Met. dist. Avocations: gardening, water sports, creative writing. Address: PO Box 300822 Escondido CA 92030-0822 Office: 3390 Auto Mall Dr Ste 200 Westlake Vlg CA 91362-3657

ERDÉLYI, LAJOS DEZSÖ, educator, invertebrate neurobiologist; b. Nagykörös, Pest, Hungary, Apr. 26, 1934; s. Lajos Erdélyi and I. Karai; children: Lajos Andras, Szabolcs Peter. Diploma, U. Szeged, 1956, Dr. univ., 1961; PhD, Hungarian Acad. Sci., 1984. Lectr. Dept. Anatomy Histology and Embriology, Szeged, Hungary, 1956-63, lectr. II, 1963-67; gast scientist Dept. of Animal Physiology, Alexandria, Egypt, 1965-66; sr. lectr. Dept. of Animal Physiology, Szeged, 1967-84; gast rschr. Max-Planck Inst. Abt. Neurochemie, Göttingen, 1980-81; reader Dept. of Comparative Physiology, Szeged, 1984—; dep. head Dept. of Comp. Physiology, 1985-88, head, 1988-94; chmn. Bd. of Biol. Depts., Szeged, 1991-94. Co-author: Practices in Comparative Animal Physiology, 1986, Physiology I. II., 1991. Recipient Award Ministry of Edn., 1989. Mem. Internat. Soc. for Invertebrate Neurobiology, European Neuroscis. Assn., N.Y. Acad. Sci. Avocations: gardening, dogs and cats. Home: Lengyel udvar 10, H-6729 Szeged Hungary

ERDELYI-TOTH, VALERIE AGATHA, chemist, reseacher; b. Budapest, Hungary, Feb. 26, 1937; d. John and Cornelia (Luft) Toth; m. Kalman Erdelyi, Aug. 5, 1962; children: Frank Kalman, Gabriel John. Degree in Chem. Engring., Tech. U., Budapest, 1962, PhD, 1979. Mem. staff CHINOIN, Budapest, 1955-57, prodn. engr., 1962-67, rsch. chemist, 1967-70; sr. rsch. fellow Nat. Inst. Oncology, Budapest, 1970—, head lab pharm., 1986—, dep. dir., 1992-2000; mem. bd. Soc. Chemotherapy, Hungary, 1992—. Contbr. chpts. to books and articles to profl. jours. Recipient grant SEA, 1979, Wellcome, 1980, Lilly, 1984. Mem. N.Y. Acad. Sci., Hungarian Soc. Chemistry, Hungarian Soc. Oncology. Roman Catholic. Avocations: playing piano, painting, reading, travelling. Office: Nat Inst Oncology, Rath Gy u 7-9, 1122 Budapest Hungary

ERDEM, ATILLA, neurosurgeon, educator; b. Gaziantep, Anatolia, Turkey, Nov. 7, 1954; s. Mahmut Sevket and Nezihe (Kuyumcu) E.; m. Hatice Rana Erdem, July 15, 1982; 1 child, Mehmet Can. MD, U. Ankara, Turkey, 1977. Med. diplomate. Resident neurosurgery dept. Ankara U., 1977-83, neurosurgeon, cons., 1983-90, assoc. prof. neurosurgery dept., 1990-96, prof. in neurosurgery, 1996—; bd. dirs. Epilepsy Surgery Program, Ankara. Collaborator: Microneurosurgery IV B, 1996. Mem. Turkish Neurosurg. Soc. Avocations: playing guitar, photography. Home: Name Sokak Önder, Apt 27/7, 06450 Dikmen Ankara, Turkey Office: Ibn-i Sina Hastahanesi, Nörosirürji Kl, 06100 Samanpazari Ankara, Turkey

ERDMAN, BARBARA, visual artist; b. N.Y.C., Jan. 30, 1936; d. Isidore and Julia (Burstein) E. Postgrad., Chinese Inst., 1959-60; BFA, Cornell U., 1956. Visual artist Santa Fe, 1977—; guest critic Studio Arte Centro Internat., Florence, Italy, 1986; guest lectr. Austin Coll. Sherman, Tex., 1986; mem. Oracle Conf. Polaroid Corp., nationwide, 1986-88. One-woman shows include Aspen Inst., Baca, Colo., 1981, Scottsdale (Ariz.) Ctr. for Arts, 1988, AAAS, Washington, 1994; exhibited in group shows, 1959—, including AAAS, 1994, Wichita Falls Art Mus., Tex., 1996, San Bernardino County Mus., 1998; represented in permanent collections N.Mex. Mus. Fine Arts, Santa Fe, IBM, N.Y.C.; author: New Mexico USA, 1985. Bd. dirs. N.Mex. Right to Choose, Santa Fe, 1981-87, Santa Fe Ctr. for Photography, 1983, pres. bd. 1985-89; mem. N.Mex. Mus. Found., Albuquerque Mus. Found. Mem. Art Student's League (life), Soc. for Photographic Edn. (guest lectr. 1987), Santa Fe Ctr. for Photography (pres., bd. dirs. 1984-89), Am. Coun. Arts. Avocations: ceramics, textiles, cats. Home and Office: 1070 Calle Largo Santa Fe NM 87501-1090

ERDMANN, CHRISTINE ANNE, epidemiologist; b. Nov. 5, 1967. BA, U. Wis., 1990; MPH, U. Calif., Berkeley, 1995. Scientist Lawrence Berkeley (Calif.) Nat. Lab., 1997—. Office: Mailstop 50-B 3238 Lawrence Berkeley Nat Lab Berkeley CA 94720-0001

ERDMANN, WLODZIMIERZ STEFAN, biomechanist, researcher; b. Torun, Poland, Sept. 3, 1949; s. Jan and Zofia (May) E.; m. Alicja Ewa Nowak, Oct. 7, 1972; children: Piotr, Agnieszka. M of Phys. Edn., Piasecki U. Sch. Phys. Edn., 1971; PhD, Piasecki U. Sch. Phys. Edn., Poznan, 1976; postgrad., Gdansk Tech U., 1984-85; DSc, Wrocl U.Sch. of Phys. Edn., 1996. Asst. Sniadecki U. Sch. of Phys. Edn., Gdansk, 1971-76, asst. prof., 1977-84, assoc. prof., 1985-96, prof., 1997—; vis. prof. U. Tokyo, 1997; dir., chmn. Lab./Dept. of Biomechanics Sniadecki U. Sch. of Phys. Edn., 1971—, dep. head Inst. of Biol. Scis., 1978-81, dir. Ctr. of Locomotion Rsch., 1993—, v.p. pro-rector Sniadecki U., 1997-99. Author: Sport Sciences in Poland and East Europe, Biomechanics and Locomotion, 1997, (in Polish) By the Word and by the Picture, 1994, Investigation on Geometric and Inertial Quantities of the Male Trunk Obtained by Computerized Tomography Method, 1995, Biomechanics. A Guide to the Laboratory Experiments, 1999; contbr. articles to profl. jours.; patentee in field. Recipient Distinction award Ministry of Labor, Chief Work Inspector, 1995, Individual Ministry award Ministry of Phys. Culture and Tourism, 1998. Mem. Internat. Soc. of Biomechanics, Internat. Soc. of Biomechanics in Sports (dir. 1992-94), Polish Soc. of Biomechanics (mem. coun. 1987—, sec. 1988-96), N.Y. Acad. Scis. Avocations: journeys, music, physical recreation, reading, biographical books. E-mail: werd@awf.gda.pl. Home: Kurpinskiego 16 M 8, 80-169 Gdansk Poland Office: Sniadecki U Sch Phys Edn, Wiejska 1, 80-336 Gdansk Poland

ERDÖ, SÁNDOR LAJOS, pharmacologist; b. Budapest, Hungary, Nov. 6, 1954; s. Sándor and Mária (Kis) E.; m. Ágnes Erdöné-Rigó, Sept. 30, 1978; children: Gábor, Andrea, Rebeka. MSc, U. Medicine, Budapest, 1978, PhD, 1980; Habilitation, Hungarian Acad. Sci., Budapest, 1987. Rschr. Gedeon Richter Co., Budapest, 1978-80, sr. rschr., 1980-87; sr. rschr. U. Göttingen, Germany, 1987-92; head lab. Chinoin Co., Budapest, 1992-95; dep. dir. sci. BIOREX R & D Co., Veszprém, Hungary, 1996-97, dir. R&D, 1997-98; mng. dir., pres. ERDO Pharma, Ltd., Budapest, Hungary; vis. prof. U. Rome, 1986; chief advisor Gedeon Richter Co., 1992. Editor: Gabaergic Mechanisms in the Mammalian Periphery, 1986, Gaba Outside the CNS, 1992; contbr. over 100 rsch. articles to profl. publs.; patentee in field. Recipient 3 awards Hungarian Nat. Socs., 1979-85. Mem. Internat. Soc. Physiol. Sci. (O'Fenn award 1986), Internat. Brain Rsch. Orgn., European Soc. Neurochemistry (hon. lectr. 1986).

ERDOGDU, FERRUH, agricultural and biological engineering educator; b. Eregli, Turkey, Oct. 19, 1970; s. Feran and Aynur Erdogdu. BS in Food Engring., Hacettepe U., Ankara, Turkey, 1992; M of Engring., U. Fla., 1996, PhD in Agrl. and Biol. Engring., 2000. Food engr. Ersu Fruit Juice Inc., Eregli, 1992-93; rsch. asst. Mersin (Turkey) U., 1993-94; postdoctoral rschr. in biol and agrl. engring. U. Calif., Davis, 2000—. Contbr. articles to sci. jours. Acad. scholar Turkish Ministry Nat. Edn., 1994. Mem. Inst. Food Technologists, Am. Soc. Agrl. Engrs., Inst. Thermal Processing Specialists, Soc. for Indsl. and Applied Math. Fax: 352-392-4092. E-mail: ferruherdogdu @yahoo.com. Office: U Calif Davis Biol and Agrl Engring Badner Hall Davis CA 95616

EREGIE, CHARLES OSATANDE, pediatrician, consultant; b. Bewin, Nigeria, July 27, 1956; s. Richard Iduorobo and Grace Amenaghawon (Obaseki) E. B in Medicine, U. Benin Sch. Medicine, 1981; B in Surgery, 1981. Internship U.Teaching Hosp., Benin City, Nigeria, 1981-82; nat. youth svc., 1982-83, sr. house officer, 1983-84, registrar, 1984-86, sr. registrar II, 1986-87, sr. registrar I, 1987-89, lectr. in Pediatrics, cons., 1989-90, sr. cons. Pediatrics, head of dept., 1990-91; chief cons. Pediatrics, head of dept. Specialist Hosp. Dept. Pediatrics, Yola, Nigeria, 1991—. Contbr. articles to profl. jours. Mem. AAAS, N.Y. Acad. Sci. Avocations: music, dancing, football, reading. Home: 7 Ewasede St, Benin City Republic of South Africa Office: U Benin Coll Med Scis, Inst Child Health, PMB 1154 Benin City Edo State, Nigeria

EREMEEV, IGOR PETROVICH, physicist, researcher; b. Sverdlovsk, USSR, Aug. 29, 1936; s. Peter Ivanovich E. and Elena Ivanovna ShaBalova; m. Galina Mikhailovna Elusova, Apr. 2, 1970 (div. Aug., 1993); 1 child, Peter. Cert. Music Sch., Ural States Conservatoire, Sverdlovsk, USSR, 1951; diploma, Ural Poly. Inst., Sverdlovsk, USSR, 1960; Degrees Candidate & Dr. Phys.-Math. Sci., Supreme Cert. Com., 1974, 2000. Engr. Kurchatov Inst. Atomic Energy, Moscow, 1960-66, researcher, 1967-76, sr. researcher, 1977-89; chmn. com., people dep. Moscow City Coun., 1990-93; founder, pres. Internat. Bus. Nucleonic, Moscow, 1994—; del. USSR Am. Leadership Conf., Washington, 1990. Contbr. more than 70 articles to profl. jours.; patentee in field. Atty. B.N. Yeltsin Elections of USSR People Deps., Moscow, 1989. Recipient USSR State prize Govt. of USSR, 1973. Mem. Swiss Neutron Scattering Soc. Avocations: piano, marathon pacing, ski running, water skiing, down hill skiing. Home: 36 Birjusov St Apt 102, 123060 Moscow Russia Office: Internat Bus Nucleonic, 1 Kurchatov Sq, 123182 Moscow Russia

EREMIN, YURI ALEXANDER, mathematician, consultant; b. Moscow, Russia, Oct. 5, 1947; s. Alexander Peter and Lidia Vasil (Yakovleva) E.; m. Natalia Vladimir Grishina, Aug. 18, 1952; children: Helen, Oleg. MS in

Physics, Moscow State U., 1972, PhD, 1976, DSc, 1989. Rschr. Computer Ctr. Moscow State U., 1975-78, sr. rschr., 1978-82, sr. rschr. applied math. and computer sci., 1982-93, rsch. prof. applied math. and computer sci., 1993—; cons. ADE Corp., Westwood, Mass., 1993—. Author: Discrete Sources Method in EM Scattering, 1992; contbr. articles to profl. jours. including Computer Phys. Comm., Applied Optics, among others. Grantee Russian Found. for Basic Rsch., 1996, Volkswagen Found., 1995, INTAS, 1997. Mem. N.Y. Acad. Scis. Office: Moscow State U Appl Math, Vorobyov Hills, 119889 Moscow Russia

EREMINA, OLGA YURIEVNA, entomologist, researcher; b. Moscow, Apr. 11, 1953; d. Yuri Michailovich Pjatin and Kira Genrichovna Bergman; m. Vladimir Vasilievich Eremin, Oct. 15, 1971; children: Nick, Marina. MS, Agrl. Acad., Moscow, 1980; postgrad., Rsch. Inst. Chem. Plant Protn., Moscow, 1980-85; PhD, Moscow State U., 1987; D of Biol. Sci., All-Russian Rsch. Inst. Plant Protection, St. Petersburg, 1996. Lab. asst. Rsch. Inst. Chem. Plant Protection, Moscow, 1970-81; rsch. scientist All-Russian Rsch. Inst. for Nature Protection, Moscow, 1981-87; sr. rsch. scientist Rsch. Inst. Disinfectology, Moscow, 1987-93, leading rsch. scientist, 1993—; mem. sci. coun. Rsch. Inst. Disinfectology, 1997—. Contbr. articles to profl. jours.; patentee in field. Grantee Internat. Sci. Found., Moscow, 1993, 93-95, Russian Fundamental Rsch. Found., Moscow, 1997—. Mem. Russian Entomology Soc. Russian Orthodox. Avocations: dogs, reading, travel. Home: Graivoronskaya St 8-1-96, 109518 Moscow Russia Office: Sci Rsch Inst Disinfectology, Nauchny proezd 18, 117246 Moscow Russia

EREN, HALIT, engineering educator; b. Sept. 1, 1950. B in Engrng., Sheffield U., 1973, M in Engrng., 1975, PhD, 1978; diploma bus. and adminstrn., Curtin U., 1998. Lectr. WAIT, Kalgoorlie, Australia, 1982-86; lectr. Curtain U., 1986—, head electronics engrng., 1995—; profl. cons. to pvt. and govt. agys. in instrumentation control and process control. Contbr. articles to profl. jours., encys. and books. Officer, 1976-77. Grantee Australian Govt. and pvt. orgns. Mem. IEEE, IEE. Avocations: martial arts, marathon running, travel, reading. Office: Curtain U Tech, Sch Elec Comp/ Engr Kent St, Bentley 6102, Australia

EREN, ZEYNEP, artist; b. Ankara, Turkey, Apr. 16, 1954; d. Cemil Cahit Eren and Hicran Yilmaz. BA, Ankara U., 1978. Ethnology diplomate. Mus. asst. Gen. Directorate Antiquities and Mus. Ministry of Culture, Ankara, 1978-84; freelance artist Ankara, 1984—. One-woman shows include: Turkish-French Cultural Assn., Ankara, 1981, Underwater Archaeology Mus., Bodrum, Turkey, 1983, Hoby Fine Arts Gallery, Istanbul, Turkey, 1984, East Ins. Art Gallery, Ankara, 1985, The Door Gallery Bar, Marmaris, Turkey, 1985, Harmony Art Gallery, Ankara, 1988, Am. Turkish Soc. Turkish Ctr., N.Y.C., 1989, Toyan Exhbn. Gallery, Ankara, 1991, Black/White Spl. Things, Ankara, 1993, 95; exhibited in group shows at Dost Sanat Ortami, Ankara, 1983, Sema Yazar Youth Found. Mixed Painting Exhbn., 1991, Turco-Brit. Assn. Art Gallery, 1992, Castle Art House, Antalya, 1993, Black/White Spl. Things, 1993-94; prin. works include (hammer copper works) Antakya (Turkey) State Properties Hotel, Gen. Directorate State Water Resources, Ankara, (ceramic wall panels) Grand Hotel Sauna, Ankara, Gen. Directorate State Water Resources Lodgements, Ankara, Gen. Directorate State Hwys. Guesthouse, Ankara, Izmir (Turkey) Bread Factory, Eryaman Housing Social Complex, Ankara, Numune Hosp., Ankara, Hyatt Regency Hotel, Istanbul, Orhan Ağaçli Resort Facilities, Aksaray, Turkey, others, (stained glass) Taris Union Guesthouse, Ankara, Ministry of Customs and Fin., Ankara, Tibas Bus. Ctr., Ankara, Eryaman Housing Social Complex, Ankara, pvt. collections, (sculpture) PET Holding, Ankara, City Hosp. (wall ceramic), Ankara, Jaser Palace (glass work), Bethlehem, 1999, World Bank (wall ceramic), Ankara, 1999. Mem. SANART. Avocations: archaeology, psychology, literature, music, cinema. Home: And Sokak 18/1 Çankaya, Ankara Turkey

ERENPREISA, JEKATERINA ARON, cell biologist; b. Drepropetrovsk, Ukraine, Feb. 13, 1945; arrived in Latvia, 1947; d. Aron Liebmann and Zisel Sokol; m. Valery Tcherniak, Oct. 5, 1963 (div. Sept. 1972); m. Janis Olgerds Erenpreiss, Dec. 27, 1972 (dec. Dec. 1996); children: Ilja, Janis, Juris. MD, Riga (Latvia) Med. H.S., 1968, PhD, 1971, habilitation, 1991. From jr. to sr. scientist Latvia Inst. Exptl. Clin. Medicine, Riga, 1968-93; leading rschr. A. Kirchenstein Inst. Microbiology and Virology, Riga, 1993-96, lab. dir., 1997—; leading rschr. Latvian U. Biomedicine Ctr., 2000—. Author: Chromatin Organization in Interphase Cell Nucleus, 1990; contbr. articles to profl. jours. Active Popular Front, 1988-90. Mem. Latvian Morphologists Soc. (bd. dirs.), Internat. Union Against Cancer, European Soc. Analytical Pathology, Latvian Acad. Sci. (corr.). Achievements include discovery of cooperative character of cell nucleus structure. Office: Latvian U Biomedicine Ctr, Ratsupites 1, LV-1067 Riga Latvia

ERGEC, RUSEN, law educator, lawyer; b. Istanbul, Turkey, Jan. 3, 1952; arrived in Belgium, 1967; s. Abdurrahman Ergec and Fikriye Unsel. Degree in polit. sci., U. Brussels, 1975, M in Internat. Law, 1976, degree in law, 1981, PhD in Public Law, 1985. Asst. prof. U. Brussels, 1981-86, prof. law, 1986—, dir. Inst. European Studies, 1990-91, dir. Ctr. of Human Rights; counsel De Bandt, Van Hecke & Lagae, Brussels, 1991—; ptnr. Landwell, 2000—; v.p. Inst. of Human Rights; parliamentary advisor Belgian Parliament, 1985-86; dirs. com. Ctr. for the Study of Federalism, Brussels, 1988; presenter Conf. on Security and Coop. in Europe, Prague, Czech Republic, 1992. Author: Human Rights Under Exceptional Circumstances, 1986 (Alice Seghers award 1987), European Convention on Human Rights, 1990, Introduction to Public Law, 1995, International and European Protection of Human Rights. Recipient René Marcq award U. Brussels, 1981. Mem. Trans European Policy Assn., Brussels Bar Assn., French Soc. Internat. Law. Avocations: reading, jogging. Office: U Brussels Sch of Law, Ave Franklin Roosevelt 50 CP 137, B-1050 Brussels Belgium

ERGENÇ, MUSTAFA NIDA, lawyer; b. Istanbul, Turkey, Aug. 19, 1946; s. Ahmet Nesimi and Hatice Sabiha (Ates) E.; m. Hatice Aysun Süzer, Sept. 22, 1982; 2 children by previous marriage. Degree, U. Istanbul, 1971. Tax officer Istanbul Municipality, 1968-72; pvt. practice Istanbul, 1974—. Author: The Law of Execution and Bankruptcy, 1991. Mem. Tennis, Fenncing, Mountaineering Club, Besiktas Gymnastic Club, Yesilyurt Sport Club. Islam. Home: B-6 # 10, Halkali Cad Toplukonutlar, Yesilkoy Turkey Office: Ergeng Hukuk Burosu, Cumhuriyet Caddesi 12/3, 80200 Istanbul Turkey

ERGENZINGER, KLAUS, physicist; b. Stuttgart, Germany, Oct. 8, 1966; s. Richard and Ruth (Burkhardt) E.; m. Margit J. Klemp, Sept. 11, 1998; 1 child, Christoph. Diploma in physics, U. Heidelberg, Germany, 1993; PhD in Physics, U. Zurich, Switzerland, 1996. Devel. engr. Infineon, Munich, 1997, project leader CAD, 1998-2000; project leader EUV lithography Carl-Zeiss, Oberkochen, Germany, 2000—; sci. cons. Patentee double exposure in microlithography, halfstepping; contbr. articles to profl. jours. Swiss Nat. Sci. Found. scholar, 1993-96. Mem. Soc. Photo-Industry Engrs., German Phys. Soc.

ERGIN, M.T., physician and surgeon; b. Istanbul, Turkey, Feb. 22, 1927; came to U.S., 1954; s. Sabri and Hacer (Daryal) E.; m. Florence M. Roman; children: Meliha Ellen, Tahsin Mark, Tarik John, Turhan Michael (dec.). MD, U. Istanbul, 1950. Diplomate Am. Bd. Surgery; cert. in laser surgery, laparoscopic surgery, advanced laparoscopic surgery. Rotating intern J.J. McCook Meml. Hosp., Hartford, Conn., 1955-56, asst. resident in surgery, chief resident, 1956-57; resident in surgery Hartford Hosp., 1957-61; pvt. practice surgery Hartford; active staff dept. surgery Hartford Hosp., 1961—, sr. attending surgeon, 1976—; active attending surgeon U. Conn. Sch. Medicine, 1969—, clin. assoc., 1970-82, asst. clin. prof. surgery, 1982-89, assoc. clin. prof., 1989-92, clin. prof. surgery, 1992—; attending surgeon Conn. Children's Med. Ctr. Recipient Presdl. Sports award, 1973; rsch. grantee Hartford Hosp., 1959, 59-65, U. Conn. Sch. Medicine/NSABP, 1985—, U.S. Dept. Health and Human Svcs./Nat. Cancer Inst., 1986, Yale U. Sch. Medicine/Nat. Cancer Inst., 1986, Hartford Hosp., 1990, 85-92. Fellow ACS (state chmn. commn. on cancer, cancer liaison program 1991—, on cancer Conn. chpt. 1991—, exec. com. 1991—, Recognition of Svc. award 1991), Royal Med. Soc. London (sec. on oncology); mem. Conn. Soc. Am. Bd. Surgeons, Conn. Med. Soc. (chmn. cancer coord. com. 1986-89), Hartford County Med. Assn., Hartford Med. Soc., New Eng. Cancer Soc., Pan Am. Med. Assn., Am. Cancer Soc. (bd. dirs. Hartford chpt. 1974-82, chmn. svc. com. 1977-80, mem. med. affairs com. 1988—, bd. dirs. Conn. divsn. 1986—, v.p. bd. dirs. 1989—, exec. com. 1986—, v.p. Conn. divsn. 1989-91, chmn. exec. com. 1991—, pres. Conn. divsn. 1991—, Conn. Divsn. Svc. award 1988, 90, Cert. of Merit, 1988, Leadership medal 1993, St. George Nat. Medal 1993), Internat. Soc. Lymphology, Conn. Oncology Assn., N.Y. Acad. Scis., Am. Radium Soc., Am. Soc. Clin. Oncology, Gastro Intestinal Tumor Study Group, Ea. Coop. Oncology Group, Internat. Soc. for Study of Comparative Oncology, Am. Assn. for Cancer Rsch., Soc. Head and Neck Surgery, Soc. Surg. Oncology. Office: 85 Seymour St Ste 511 Hartford CT 06106-5524 also: 30 W Avon Rd Avon CT 06001-3678

ERHARDY, CLAUDIUS, entertainment company executive; b. N.Y.C., July 14, 1958; arrived in France, 1973; s. Joseph P. Herzbrun and Melanie Van Muyden; m. Elizabeth Naudin; children: Audrey, Maureen, Romain, Lucas. Computers and video games purchasing dir. Fnac, Paris, 1979-89; electronics purchasing dir. Toys R Us, Paris, 1989-90; calculators, phones, computers & video games purchasing dir. Auchan-Boulanger, Lille, France, 1990-93; product dir. Bandai, Paris, 1993-99; v.p. France Disney Interactive, Paris, 1999—. Avocations: drums, movies, 4-wheel drive, disc jockey. Fax: 33 1 34739356. E-mail: claudius.erhardy@disney.com. Office: Disney Interactive, 50 ave Montaigne, 75008 Paris France

ERIBO, FESTUS, mass communication educator, journalist; b. Benin City, Edo, Nigeria, June 16, 1950; came to the U.S., 1985; s. Wilfred Omovbe and Grace Iroguehi Eribo; m. Luba N. Eribo, Aug. 24, 1978; children: Brenda, Hilda. MA, Leningrad (Russia) State U., 1979; PhD, U. Wis., 1989. Tchr. Edo Coll., Benin City, 1971; pub. rels. mgr. Ribway Group Cos., Benin City, 1971-73; prin. info. officer Dept. Info., Benin City, 1980-89; asst. prof. East Carolina U., Greenville, 1990-95, assoc. prof., 1995—. Co-author: Window on Africa: Democratization and Media Exposure, 1993, Press Freedom and Communication in Africa, 1997; author: In Search of Greatness: Russia's Communications with Africa and the World, 2000. Mem. Assn. for Edn. in Journalism and Mass Comm. Home: 402 Lancelot Dr Greenville NC 27858-8647 Office: Dept Comm East Carolina Univ Greenville NC 27858

ERIÇ, RAUF HÜRMAN, metallurgical engineering educator; b. Gallipoli, Turkey, Sept. 19, 1951; s. Mustafa Ihsan and Fatma Nilufer (Dalmis) E.; m. Nurhan Coban, Jan. 19, 1976; children: Ihsan Berkin, Nilufer Birce. BSc in Engrng., Middle East Tech. U., Ankara, Turkey, 1973, MSc in Engrng., 1975, PhD, 1979. Registered profl. engr. Project engr. Ministry of Nat. Resources and Energy, Ankara, Turkey, 1973-74; rsch. asst. Middle East Tech. U., Ankara, Turkey, 1974-78, instr., 1978-80, asst. prof., 1980-83, assoc. prof., 1983-85; sr. lectr. U. Witwatersrand, Johannesburg, South Africa, 1985-88, acting head dept., 1987-88, 90, prof., 1989, chamber of mines prof., 1991, dept. head, 1991-95, dep. dean faculty of engrng., 1995-97, dir. materials rsch. ctr., 1995—; head sch. process and materials engrng. U. Witwatersrand, 1998—; industry cons., 1986—; cons. Mintek (Coun. for Minerals Tech.), Randburg, South Africa, 1988—; vis. prof. Delft U. Tech., The Netherlands, 1998. Co-author: Mineral and Metal Extraction: An Overview, 1994; contbr. over 100 sci. and tech. articles to profl. jours. and conf. proceedings. Lt. Army, 1975, Turkey. Recipient Gold plate Chamber of Chem. and Metall. Engrs., 1985, Stainless Steel plate Asilcelik Steel Works, 1984, Silver medal South African Inst. Mining and Metallurgy, 1992, Gold plate for contbns. as advisor/cons. to Turkish metall. industry, 1997. Fellow South African Inst. Mining and Metallurgy; mem. TMS, Can. Inst. Metallurgists, N.Y. Acad. Scis. Avocations: photography, geography. Home: 66 Queen Alexandra Rd Lombardy E, Johannesburg 2090, South Africa Office: U Witwatersrand Sch Process and Materials Engrng, Private Bag 3, Johannesburg WITS 2050, South Africa

ERIC, SO SHING-YIT, publisher; b. Canton, China, Mar. 24, 1957; arrived in Hong Kong, 1967; s. So and Mui (Shui-Fong) Yan; m. Lau Wai-ming Linda, Mar. 31, 1957; children: Joanna, Clement. BD, Chung Chi Coll., Hong Kong, 1985; M of Theology, South East Asia Grad. Sch., Hong Kong, 1994. Program sec. Hong Kong Coun. of Ch. of Christ in China, 1985-86; rschr. Hong Kong C.T. Ch., 1987-88, pastor, 1988-89; minister-in-charge Hong Kong Chi Ch., 1990-94; pub. Chinses Christian Lit. Coun., Hong Kong, 1994-99; gen. sec. Hong Kong Christian Coun., 1999—. Office: 9/F Christian Ecumen Bldg, 33 Granville Rd, Kowloon Hong Kong

ERICHSEN, JONATHAN THOR, neuroscientist, educator; b. Washington, Sept. 8, 1950; s. Hans Skabo and Ruth Elsie (Henderson) E. AB summa cum laude, Harvard U., 1972; DPhil, Oxford (Eng.) U., 1979. Postdoctoral fellow SUNY, Stony Brook, 1979-82, rsch. asst. prof., 1983-95; sr. lectr. Cardiff (Wales) U., 1995—. Contbr. articles to profl. jours.; patentee in field. Recipient scholarship Marshall Commn., 1972-75; Danforth fellow, 1975-79. Mem. Assn. for Rsch. in Vision and Ophthalmology, Internat. Brain Rsch. Orgn., Soc. for Neurosci., Assn. for the Study of Animal Behavior, Phi Beta Kappa. Avocations: hiking, bell ringing. Office: Cardiff (Wales) U, King Edward VII Ave, Cardiff Wales

ERICKSON, ARTHUR CHARLES, architect; b. Vancouver, B.C., Can., June 14, 1924; s. Oscar and Myrtle (Chatterson) E. Student, U. B.C., Vancouver, 1942-44; B.Arch., McGill U., Montreal, Que., Can., 1950; LL.D. (hon.), Simon Fraser U., Vancouver, 1973, U. Man., Winnipeg, Can., 1978, Lethbridge U., 1981; D.Eng. (hon.), Novia Scotia Tech. Coll., McGill U., 1971; Litt.D. (hon.), U. B.C., 1985. Asst. prof. U. Oreg., Eugene, 1955-56; assoc. prof. U. B.C., 1956-63; ptnr. Erickson-Massey Architects, Vancouver, 1963-72; prin. Arthur Erickson Architects, Vancouver, 1972-91, Toronto, Ont., Can., 1981-91, Los Angeles, 1981-91; prin. Arthur Erickson Archtl. Corp., Vancouver, 1991—. Prin. works include Can. Pavilion at Expo '70, Osaka (recipient first prize in nat. competition, Archtl. Inst. of Japan award for best pavilion), Robson Square/The Law Courts (honor award), Mus. of Anthropology (honor award), Eppich Residence (honor award), Habitat Pavilion (honor award), Sikh Temple (award of merit), Champlain Heights Cmty. Sch. (award of merit), San Diego Conv. Ctr., Calif. Plz., L.A., Fresno City Hall, Can. Embassy, Washington, MacMillan Bloedel Bldg., Roy Thompson Hall, Bank of Can.; subject of Time mag. cover article and New Yorker profile; contbr. articles to profl. publs. Mem. com. on urban devel. Coun. of Can., 1971; bd. dirs. Can. Conf. of Arts, 1972; mem. design adv. coun. Portland Devel. Commn., Can. Coun. Urban Rsch.; trustee Inst. Rsch. on Pub. Policy. Capt. Can. Intelligence Corps., 1945-46. Recipient Molson prize Can. Coun. Arts, 1967, Triangle award Nat. Soc. Interior Design, Royal Bank Can. award, 1971, Gold medal Tau Sigma Delta, 1973, residential design award Can. Housing Coun., 1975, August Perret award Internat. Union Archiects Congress, 1975, Chgo. Architecture award, 1984, Gold medals Royal Archtl. Inst. Can., 1984, French Acad. Architecture, 1984, Pres. award excellence Am. Soc. Landscape Architects, 1979; named Officer, Order of Can., 1973, Companion Order of Can., 1981. Fellow AIA (hon., Pan Pacific citation Hawaiian chpt. 1963, gold medal 1986), Royal Archtl. Inst. Can. (recipient award 1980); mem. Royal Inst. Brit. Archs., Archtl. Inst. B.C., Royal Inst. Scottish Archs. (hon.), Coll. d'arquitectos de España (hon.), Coll. d'archictectos de Mex. (hon.), Royal Can. Acad. Arts (academician), Heritage Can., S.F.U. Faculty Club. Office: Arthur Erickson Archtl Corp, 1672 W 1st Ave, Vancouver, BC Canada V6J 1G1

ERICKSON, EDWARD LEONARD, biotechnology company executive, consultant; b. Chgo., Dec. 7, 1946; s. Leonard Gerald and Eleanore Antoinette (Picek) E.; m. Helen Leonora Masten, Dec. 29, 1979. BS in Math., Ill. Inst. Tech., 1968, MS in Math., 1970; MBA in Gen. Mgmt., Harvard U., 1980. Mktg. rep. IBM, Miami, Fla., 1975-76; sr. systems engr. Advanced Tech., Inc., McLean, Va., 1976-78; cons. Bain & Co., Boston, 1979-80; sr. assoc. Resource Planning Assocs., Washington, 1980-82; dir. RPA Mgmt. Cons., London, 1982-83; dir. corp. devel. Amersham Internat. plc., Little Chalfont, Eng., 1983-86, gen. mgr. internat. ops., 1986-88; v.p. fin. ops. The Ares-Serono Group, Boston, 1988-90; pres. Serono-Baker Diagnostics (The Ares-Serono Group), Allentown, Pa., 1990-91; pres., chief exec. officer, dir. Cholestech Corp., Hayward, Calif., 1991-93; pres., CEO, DepoTech Corp., La Jolla, Calif., 1993-98, also bd. dirs.; chmn., pres., CEO Immunicon Corp., 1998—. Contbr. articles to profl. jours. Lt. USN, 1970-75. John L. Loeb fellow Harvard U., 1980, George F. Baker scholar, 1980, NASA fellow, 1968-70. Mem. Am. Soc. Clin. Oncology (affiliate), Am. Assn. Pharm. Scientists. Republican. Avocations: tennis, skiing. Home: 6887 Tohickon Hill Rd Pipersville PA 18947-1415

ERICKSON, GARWOOD ELLIOTT, computer consulting company executive; b. Little Silver, N.J., Jan. 8, 1946; s. Gustaf Walter and Martha Lake (Adams) E.; m. Carol Wyborski, July 21, 1973; children: Christopher Lake, Jason Edward. AB, Dartmouth Coll., 1967; BE, Thayer Sch. Engring., 1968, ME, 1969; MBA, U. Mich., 1974. Systems analyst Ford Motor Co., Dearborn, Mich., 1969-72, sect. supr., 1972-82, mgr., 1982-83; corp. dir. mgmt. info. svcs. Hoover Universal, Ann Arbor, Mich., 1983-86; corp. dir. mgmt. info. svcs. Vickers, Inc., Troy, Mich., 1986-89, dir. sales, 1989-90, dir. quality mgmt., 1990-93; chief info. officer R.L. Polk & Co., Taylor, Mich., 1993-96; owner Great Lakes Technols. Group, Southfield, Mich., 1996—. Sec. Trayer Lakes Cmty. Assn., Ann Arbor, 1977. Advanced Rsch. Projects Agy. fellow, 1967-69. Mem. Dartmouth Club (pres. Ann Arbor 1982-86). Office: 26999 Central Park Blvd Ste 380 Southfield MI 48076-4178

ERICKSON, LYNN EDWARD, non-commissioned officer, human resource manager; b. Baldwin, Wis.; s. Morris Albert and Mary Irene Erickson; m. Kathleen Elizabeth E., Sept. 15, 1979. BS, U. Wis., River Falls, 1977; MA, Webster U., 1995. Enlisted U.S. Army, 1979; pers. generalist U.S. Army, Ft. Campbell, Ky., 1981-83; pers. supr. 8th Inf. Divsn. Hdqs., Bad Kreuznach, Germany, 1983-86, Hdqs. Support Troops, Aberdeen Proving Ground, Md., 1986-89, 569th Pers. Svc. Co., Augsburg, Germany, 1989-92; pers. cons. U.S. Army Readiness Group, Ft. Sam Houston, Tex., 1992-95; pers. mgr. 1st Med. Group, Ft. Hood, Tex., 1995-98; 1st sgt., human resource mgr. Operational Test Command, Ft. Hood, Tex., 1998—. Mem. Leadership Killeen (Tex.), 1999. Mem. VFW. Republican. Roman Catholic. Avocations: reading, fishing, golfing, travel. E-mail: leekee50@vvm.com. Home: 10528 Sorrento Dr NW Albuquerque NM 87114-3804 Office: Operational Test Command Bldg 91012 Fort Hood TX 76544

ERICKSON, RALPH D., retired physical education educator, small business owner, consultant; b. Beresford, S.D., June 25, 1922; s. John Henning and Ester Christina (Lofgren) E.; m. Nancy Erickson, Sept. 1949 (div. 1961); m. Patricia Erickson, Apr. 1973 (div. 1975); m. Karen Ann Erickson, June 1, 1989; 1 child, Karina Ann. BS in Phys. Edn., Northwestern U., 1949, MA in Edn., 1953. Swim instr., coach Chgo. Park Dist., 1946-54; social studies tchr., swim coach Elmwood Park (Ill.) High Sch., 1954-65; swimming, water polo coach Loyola Univ., Chgo., 1965-87, assoc. prof. phys. edn., 1971-87; salesman Alexander Hamilton Inst., Chgo., 1966-69; tchr. Chgo. Bd. Edn., 1969-70; bd. dirs. Capital Investments & Ventures Corp., Santa Ana, Calif., 1983-93, Cosmopolitan Comm., Santa Ana, 1991-93; vice chmn. Internat. Profl. Assn. Diving Inst., Santa Ana, 1966-93. Author: Under Pressure, 1961, Discover the Under Water World, 1971, V/W Navigation, 1972, Search and Recovery, 1973. Sgt US Army, 1942-45. Recipient Reach Out award Diving Equipment Mfg. Assn.; named to Ill. H.S. Swimming Coaches Hall of Fame, 1982, Athletic Hall of Fame Loyola U. Chgo., 1986. Mem. Profl. Assn. Diving Instrs. (co-founder). Home and Office: 17307 Whippoorwill Trl Leander TX 78645-9734

ERICKSON, W(ALTER) BRUCE, business and economics educator, entrepreneur; b. Chgo., Mar. 4, 1938; s. Clifford Eric and Mildred B. (Brinkmeier) E. BA, Mich. State U., 1959, MA, 1960, PhD in Econs., 1965. Rsch. assoc. subcom. on antitrust and monopoly U.S. Senate, 1960-61; asst. prof. econs. Bowling Green (Ohio) U., 1964-66; asst. prof. bus. and govt. Coll. Bus. Adminstrn., U. Minn., Mpls., 1966-70; assoc. prof. Coll. Bus. Adminstrn., U. Minn., 1971-75, prof. dept. mgmt., 1975—, prof., chmn. dept. mgmt., 1977-80, co-chmn., then chmn., 1988-92; bd. dirs. various bus., non-profit and venture capital orgns.; cons. rock salt antitrust cases for atty. gens. Mich., cons. rock salt antitrust cases for atty. gens. Calif., Ill., Wis., Minn.; cons. U.S. Justice Dept. Author: An Introduction to Contemporary Business, 4th edit., 1985, Government and Business, 1980, 2d edit., 1984, International Business, 1998; co-author: International Business, 1998; bd. editors Antitrust Law and Econs. Rev., Jour. Indsl. Orgn.; contbr. articles to profl. jours. Bd. dirs. Found. for Constl. Edn. and the Citizens League, 1991-92; mem. ethics com. Ebenezer System, Minn. Mem. Am. Econ. Assn., Royal Econ. Soc. Office: Carlson Sch Mgmt 321 19th Ave S Minneapolis MN 55455-0438

ERICSON, MAGDA VERA, physicist; b. Tunis, Tunisa, Dec. 18, 1929; d. Victor and Dora (Coen) Galula; m. Torleif Ericson, Aug. 8, 1957; children: Sandra, Axel. B, Ecole Normale, Paris, 1953; PhD, Sorbonne, Paris, 1958. Attachee de recherches CNRS, Paris, 1953-59; fulbright fellow MIT, Cambridge, 1959-60; assoc. prof. U. Lyon, France, 1960-67; prof. U. Lyon, 1967—; rsch. assoc. MIT, Cambridge, 1969-70; visitor CERN, Geneva, 1963—. Contbr. numerous articles to profl. jours. Recipient Palmes Academiques award Min. Edn., 1978, Prix De La Charlonie Acad. Sci., Alexander Humboldt award Humboldt Found. Home: de Bude N1, 1202 Geneva Switzerland Office: CERN, 23 Geneva Switzerland

ERICSON, PHYLLIS JANE, psychologist, psychotherapist, consultant; b. Ft. Worth, Aug. 16, 1947; d. John H. and Charlotte Marie (Turner) E.; divorced; children: Colleen Nichole Christensen, Sean Matthew Murphy Pass. B. Gen. Studies in Bus. Mgmt. and Advt., U. Tex., Arlington, 1981; MA in Psychology and Psychotherapy, Antioch U., 1990; Grad. in Psychology, Union Inst., Cin., 1995. Lic. profl. counselor, marriage and family therapist, chem. dependency counselor, Tex.; cert. nat. and neurolinguist programming master strategist. Clk.-typist Gen. Dynamics Corp., Ft. Worth, 1965-69; counselor Snelling & Snelling Pers., Ft. Worth, 1970-72; account exec. Ft. Worth Star Telegram, 1972-79; v.p., prin. Ericson Assocs., Inc., Hurst, Tex., 1979-83; account exec. L.A.Times, Times Mirror Corp., 1983; nat. advt. dir. Baker Comm., Beverly Hills, Calif., 1984; owner, prin., builder GE Rehabs, Ft. Worth, 1984-86; counselor Comprehensive Counseling (later Ctrl. Psychol. Svcs.), Hurst, 1988-91; dir., counselor, cons., awareness counseling of DFW Ctrl. Psychol. Svcs., St. Marteen, Netherlands Antilles & Ft. Lauderdale, Fla., 1988—; counselor J. Marszalek & Assoc., Dallas, 1984-87, Wynrose Outpatient Program, Arlington, Tex., 1988-89, HCA Richland Hosp., North Richland Hills, Tex., 1988-89; crisis intervention counselor Suicide and Crisis Ctr., Dallas, 1987-88; pvt. practice Ctr. for Counseling Devel. Svcs., Ft. Worth, 1987-88; group facilitator, clin. cons. Bedford Meadows Hosp., 1989-91; instr. psychology dept. Tex. Wesleyan U., 1989; mem. allied staff, group facilitator Charter Hosp.-Grapevine, Tex., 1991-92. Mem. The Am. Psychotherapy Assn. (diplomat). Avocations: travel, education, writing, lecturing, water and snow sports. Address: 1100 E Lamar Blvd Apt 4 Arlington TX 76011-4322

ERICSON, RUTH ANN, psychiatrist; b. Assaria, Kans., May 15; d. William Albert and Anna Mathilda (Almquist) E. Student, So. Meth. U., 1945-47; BS, Bethany Coll.; MD, U. Tex., 1951. Intern Calif. Hosp., L.A., 1951-52; resident in psychiatry U. Tex. Med. Br., Galveston, 1952-55; psychiatrist Child Guidance Clinic, Dallas, 1955-63; clin. instr. Southwestern Med. Sch., Dallas, 1955-72; practice medicine specializing in psychiatry Dallas, 1955-2000; cons. Dallas Intertribal Coun. Clinic, 1974-81, Dallas Ind. Sch. Dist., U.S. Army, Welfare Dept., Tribal Concerns, Alcoholism, Adv. Bd. Intertribal Coun. Recipient Disting. Svc. Awd., Am. Med. Women's Assn., 1999, Alumni award of merit Bethany Coll., Lindsborg, Kans., 2000. Fellow Am. Geriatrics Assn., Royal Soc. Medicine; mem. So. Med. Assn. (life), Tex. Med. Assn. (life), Dallas Med. Assns. (life), Am. Psychiat. Assn. (life), Tex. Psychiat. Assn., North Tex. Psychiat. Assn., Am. Med. Women's Assn. (Disting. Svc. award 1999), Dallas Area Women Psychiatrists, Alumni Assn. U. Tex. (Med. Br.), Navy League (life), Air Force Assn., Tex. Archaeol. Soc. (life mem.), Dallas Archaeol. Soc. (hon. life mem., pres. 1972-73, 82-84, 89-91, 97-99, archival rschr., pres. 1997-99), South Tex. Archaeol. Soc., Tarrant County Archeol. Soc., El Paso Archeol. Soc., N.Mex. Archaeol. Soc., Paleopathology Soc., Internat. Psychogeriatric Assn. (Famous Women of the 20th Century), Alpha Omega Alpha, Delta Psi Omega, Alpha Psi Omega, Pi Gamma Mu, Lambda Sigma, Alpha Epsilon Iota, Mu Delta. Lutheran. Home: 4007 Shady Hill Dr Dallas TX 75229-2844

ERICSSON, ANDERS P.E., film and theatre department administrator; b. Jönköping, Spåland, Sweden, May 1, 1952; s. Helge and Inga (Lindkvist) E.; m. Elisabeth Barbro Gleisner, May 24, 1997; children: Eric, Axel. BA, U. Stockholm, 1984. Adminstr. Swedish Radio/TV, Stockholm, 1984-85; head dept. Stockholm Cultural Dept., 1985-86; editor Swedish Film Inst., Stockholm; head film and theatre dept. City of Skövde, Sweden, 1988—; CEO Filmstudion, Vällingby, Stockholm, 1985-86, Skövde, 1991-96, Skövde Film Festival, 1989—. Contbr. articles to profl. jours. Recipient award Royal Dramatic Theatre, Stockholm, 1992. Avocations: film, theatre, music,

wine, food. Home: Äsketorpsvagen 5, S-541 36 Skövoe Västra Götaland, Sweden Office: City of Skövoe, Fredsgatan 4, S-541 83 Skövoe Västra Götaland, Sweden

ERICSSON, BERNT OLOF, chief engineer; b. Frösön, Jämtland, Sweden, Jan. 31, 1933; s. Olof Irenikus and Signe Birgitta (Johnson) E.; m. Inger Rålin, Sept. 3, 1966 (dec. Nov. 29, 1991); children: Mats, Karin. MSc in Chem. Engring., Chalmers U., Gothenburg, Sweden, 1956, DSc, 1962. Lab. mgr. Fors Co. Pulp Mills, Köpmanholmen, 1957-59; rsch. engr. Swedish Forest Products Lab., Stockholm, 1959-62; postdoctoral fellow U. Wash., Seattle, 1962-64; sr. chem. engr. VBB AB, Stockholm, 1964-77, prin. engr., 1977-80, chief engr., 1980—; assoc. prof. Royal Inst. Tech., Stockholm, 1965-75; lectr. at confs. worldwide. Contbr. numerous articles to profl. jours. Recipient Arthur Sidney Bedell award Water Environ. Fedn., 1987, Water Conservation award Boliden-Kemira, 1985; Sweden-Am. Found. scholar, 1962, Swedish Forest Products Lab. scholar, 1961. Mem. Swedish Assn. for Water (editl. com. 1969-95), Swedish Assn. Chem. Engrs. (com. bd. mem. 1979-94), Internat. Water Supply Assn. (com. bd. mem. 1982—), Internat. Desalination Assn. (bd. dirs. 1978-81). Office: SWECO/VBB Viak AB, PO Box 34044, S-10026 Stockholm Sweden

ERICSSON, MATS FOLKE GERHARD, insurance company executive; b. Stockholm, Apr. 15, 1954; s. Folke G. and MayBritt V. (Akesson) E.; m. Eva B. Bengtsson, Mar. 29, 1986; children: Daniel, Camilla, Sara. Claims adjuster Folksam Ins., Stockholm, 1975-80; dist. mgr. Trygg-Hansa Ins., Stockholm, 1980-83, asst. v.p. mktg., 1983-87; pres. Spennare Expo, Stockholm, 1987-89; regional mgr. Trygg-Hansa, Stockholm, 1989-91, mktg. mgr., 1992-98; pres. Lansforsakringar Halland, Halmstad, Sweden, 1998—; cons. in field. Author: In Search of Knowledge of Advertising and Marketing, 1988. Mem. Sondrum Tennis Club, Exec. Club, Jobs and Soc. Halland, Ringenas Golf Club. Avocations: tennis, travel. Home: Gustaf Janssons v 21, 302 40 Halmstad Sweden Office: Lansforsakringar, Box 518, 301 80 Halmstad Sweden

ERIE, STEVEN PHILIP, political science educator; b. Bakersfield, Calif., Jan. 28, 1946; s. Harlan Eugene Erie (dec.) and Carmen Joyce (O'Brien) Barr. BA, UCLA, 1967, MA, 1969, PhD, 1975. Asst. prof. pub. adminstrn. U. So. Calif., L.A., 1975-78; asst. prof. polit. sci. SUNY, Albany, 1978-80; policy analyst U.S. Dept. Health and Human Svcs., Washington, 1980-81; asst. prof. U. Calif. San Diego, La Jolla, 1981-89, assoc. prof. polit. sci., adj. prof. history, 1989—; cons. L.A. Pub. Commn. on County Govt., 1975-76, Ednl. Testing Svc., Princeton, N.J., 1989-91; cons. RAND, Santa Monica, 1997—, Metropolitan Forum Project, L.A., 1997—, L.A. Econ. Devel. Corp., 1999—, Orange County Bus. Coun., 1998—; sr. fellow So. Calif. Studies Ctr., L.A., 1997—. Author: Rainbow's End, 1988 (Best Book on Urban Politics, Am. Polit. Sci. Assn. 1989, Robert Park award Am. Sociology Assn. 1989); contbg. editor Metro Investment Report, 1994—; mem. editl. adv. bd. U. Press of Va., Charlottesville, 1993—. Active Citizens Charter Reform Com., San Diego, 1993, 98-00, Pacific Coun. on Internat. Politics, 1998—, San Diego Dialogue, 1995—, Citizens Coordinate for Century Three, San Diego, 1996; bd. dirs. Water and Power Assocs., L.A., 1994—, Gov.'s Commn. on Bldg. for 21st Century, 1998—; mem. Pacific Coun. on Internat. Policy, 1998—. Charles F. Scott Meml. fellow UCLA, 1972-78: Faculty fellow Nat. Assn. Schs. of Pub. Affairs and Adminstrn., Washington, 1980-81; Faculty Rsch. grantee Calif. Policy Seminar, Berkeley, 1990, 94. Mem. Am. Polit. Sci. Assn. (exec. coun. urban politics sect. 1989-91, chair book prize com. 1991), Western Polit. Sci. Assn., Orgn. Am. Historians, Calif. Hist. Soc. Avocations: reading, tennis, swimming. Office: Univ Calif San Diego Dept Polit Sci La Jolla CA 92093

ERIKSEN, ERIK FINK, endocrinologist, osteoporosis researcher; b. O. Jerstal, Denmark, Feb. 8, 1953; s. Christian Frede and Signe (Fink) E.; m. Karin Fink, July 19, 1975; children: Morten Fink, Mads Fink. MD, Aarhus U., Denmark, 1980; D of Med. Sci., Aarhus U., 1989. Diplomate Endocrinology and Internal Medicine. Cons. Aarhus (Denmark) U. Hosp., 1980-82; rsch. fellow Aarhus Amtssygehus, 1982-85; postdoctoral fellow Mayo Clinic, Rochester, Minn., 1985-87; clin. fellow Aarhus U. Hosp., 1987-89, asst. prof. internal medicine, 1989-96, assoc. prof. internal medicine, 1996—, cons. endocrinology and internal medicine, 1994, chmn. dept. endocrinology, 1995. Author: Osteoporosis, 1992, Histomorphometry, 1993; mem. editl. bd. Osteoporosis Int., 1989, Bone, 1988, Bone Mineral Rsch., 1988-98, Scandinavian Jour. Musculoskeletal Rsch., 1992; sci. editor European Jour. Clin. Investigation; contbr. articles to profl. jours. Mem. European Calcified Soc., Danish Soc. Internal Medicine, Danish Endocrine Soc. (bd. dirs.), Am. Soc. Bone and Mineral Rsch. (Young Investigator award 1987), Danish Bone and tooth Soc. (chmn.), Internat. Osteoporosis Found. (mem. scientific adv. com.). Office: Aarhus Amtssygehus Univ/Endocrinology Dept, Tage Hansensgade 2, DK-8000 Århus Denmark

ERIKSEN, POUL SINDBERG, medical consultant; b. Naestved, Denmark, May 4, 1944; s. Knud and Karen Sindberg (Hansen) E.; m. Lis Vangedal, Aug. 28, 1976; children: Mikkel, Thomas. MD, U. Copenhagen, 1971, cert. gen. practioner, 1976; DMSci., U. Lund, Sweden, 1984. Sr. house officer St. Joseph Hosp., Copenhagen, 1971-76; sr. registrar dept. ob-gyn. U. Hosp. Hvidovre, Copenhagen, 1976-82, Hilleroed (Denmark) County Hosp., 1982-83; sr. registrar dept. ob-gyn. U. Hosp. Herlev, Copenhagen, 1983-86, cons., 1986-94; cons. Ctrl. Hosp. Naestved, 1994-95; cons. dept. ob-gyn. King Faisal Specialist Hosp. and Rsch. Ctr., Riyadh, Saudi Arabia, 1995-97; head ob-gyn. dept. Ctrl. Hosp., Naestved, 1998—. Lt. Royal Danish Marines, 1973-74. Grantee Danish Med. Coun., 1980, 81, Danish Med. Sci. Rsch. Coun., 1991, U. Lund, 1985. Avocations: golf, oenology, gastronomy. E-mail: psi@cn.stam.dk. Fax: 45-55-77-3432.

ERIKSON, G(EORGE) E(MIL) (ERIK ERIKSON), anatomist, archivist, historian, educator, information specialist; b. Palmer, Mass., May 3, 1920; s. Emil and Sofia (Gustafson) E.; m. Suzanne J. Henderson, Apr. 23, 1950; children: Ann, David, John, Thomas. BS, Mass. State Coll. (now U. Mass.), 1941; MA in Biology, Harvard U., 1946, PhD in Biology, 1948. Reader in history of sci. and learning Harvard U., 1943-45, asst. prof. gen. edn. in biology, 1949-52, lectr. anthropology, 1965; instr. anatomy Harvard Med. Sch., 1947-49, rsch. fellow anatomy, 1949-52, assoc. in anatomy, 1952-55, asst. prof. anatomy, 1955-65, assoc. curator Warren Anat. Mus., 1961-65; prof. med. sci. Brown U., Providence, 1965-90, prof. emeritus, 1990—, chmn. sect. morphology, 1968-85, co-chmn. sect. population biology, morphology & genetics and chmn. for anatomy, 1985-90; visiting prof., Dept. Anatomy and Cellular Biology Harvard U. Med. Sch., 1990-91; visiting lectr. in surgery Med. Sch. Harvard U., 1991—; anatomist dept. surgery Mass. Gen. Hosp., Boston, 1990—; pres. Erikson Biographical Institute, Inc., Providence, 1990—; adv. bd. Reed Elsevier, 1990; anatomist various Boston hosps., 1952-82, Mass. Gen. Hosp. Sch. Med. Illus., 1947-60, Mass. Gen. Hosp., 1990—, Lahey Clinic, Boston, 1947-60; anatomist depts. surgery, orthopedics & rehab., and neurosurgery R.I. Hosp.; cons. anatomist Surg. Techniques Illus., 1976-80; cons. Dorlands Illus. Med. Dictionary; Rockefeller Found. cons. med. and pub. health, S. Am., 1959; specialist State Dept., Brazil, 1962, (Fulbright Fellow); adj. mem. faculty R.I. Sch. Design, 1970—; Kate Hurd Mead lecturer Coll. Physicians Phila., 1977; Raymond C. Truex lecturer Hahnemann U. Sch. Med., 1985; adj. mem. faculty R.I. Sch. of Design, Providence, 1970—. Sheldon traveling fellow, Cent. Am., 1946; Guggenheim fellow, S. Am., 1949. Mem. Am. Assn. Phys. Anthropologists (archivist and co-historian 1981—), History Sci. Soc. (life mem.), Am. Assn. Anatomists (historian and archivist 1972-86, archivist 1986-90, historian and archivist 1990—), Am. Assn. History Medicine (council 1972-74), Oral Hist. Assn., Assn. of Anatomy Chairmen (emeritus), Alpha Omega Alpha Honor Med. Soc. (faculty election 1957). Achievements include special research in new world primates and gen. intellectual history, especially biology and medicine, developing database on over 420,000 careers without limits of time, place, or field with extensive institutional, subject, geographical analyses. Office: Brown U Sch Medicine Providence RI 02912-0001 also: Erikson Biog Inst 242B Meeting St Providence RI 02906-2221

ERIKSON, RICHARD ALAN, history educator, artist; b. Burbank, Calif., Sept. 19, 1944; s. Wilbert Leroy and Ruth (Evans) E.; m. Kathryn Irene Erikson, Apr. 14, 1976; children: John, Stephanie, Alan. BA, U. Redlands, 1966; MA, U. So. Calif., 1972. Cert. secondary tchr., Wash. History tchr. Glendale (Calif.) Unified Schs., 1967-76, Bremerton (Sch.) Sch. Dist., 1976-77; history and art tchr. Ctrl. Kitsap Schs., Silverdale, Wash., 1977—; guest lectr. Pacific Oaks Coll., Bellevue, Wash., U. Wash., Seattle; guest spkr. Ctrl. Wash. U., Ellensburg; co-founder Alley Cat Games, Inc., 1999. One-man show Bainbridge Island Art Gallery, 1984. Democrat. Avocations: oil and watercolor painting, sailing, reading. Home: 11220 186th Ave KPN Gig Harbor WA 98329 Office: Ridgetop Jr HS 10600 Hillsboro Dr NW Silverdale WA 98383-7713

ERIKSON, THOMAS (KARL PEHR), shipbroker; b. Stockholm, Sweden, Mar. 4, 1939; s. Ake Karl Lennart and Marna (Nilsson) E.; m. Christina Hardelin, Dec. 30, 1965; children: Catherine, Charlotte. Supply officer Motor Torpedo Boat Divsn., 1962-64; paymaster H.M. Destroyer, Södermanland, 1963; econ. Salen Shipping, 1965-70; chartering mgr. Salen Reefer, 1970-78; shipbroker Sven Salen AB, 1978-82, shipbroker (RoRo), 1982-83; mng. RoRo Salen Dry Cargo, 1983-84; mgr. RoRo Projects Stockholm Chartering, 1985—. Comdr. Royal Navy Res., Sweden, 1973. Mem. Naval Officers Club, Stora Sallskapet, Timmermansorden (knight). Avocations: golf, sailing, skiing.

ERIKSON, UNO EUGEN, diagnostic radiology educator, dean; b. Uppsala, Sweden, June 15, 1930; s. Georg Eugen and Dagny Katarina (Johansson) E.; m. Britt Elisabeth Håkansson, July 27, 1930 (div. 1965); 1 child, Eva; m. Birgit Rydén, Feb. 26, 1966; children: Per, Anna. Grad. in medicine, Uppsala (Sweden) U., 1954, MD, 1959, PhD, 1965. Prof. and chmn. in diagnostic radiology Uppsala (Sweden) U., 1982-93, dean med. faculty, 1993-96; pres. Swedish Soc. Med. Radiology, 1988. Co-editor Annal Radiol et Jour. de Radiologie, 1977, Acta Radiologica, 1983-93. Recipient The Boris Rajewsky medal EAR, 1997. Fellow Cardiovasc. and Interventional Radiology Europe (disting.); mem. European Assn. Radiology (vice chmn. edn. com. 1990-94, pres. edn. com. 1995—). Home: Konsumvägen 33A, S-75645 Uppsala Sweden Office: Dept Diagnostic Radiology, Univ Hosp, S-75185 Uppsala Sweden

ERIKSSON, DONALD GORDON, finance company executive; b. Johannesburg, South Africa, June 25, 1945; s. Eric Gordon and Isobel Jessie (Campbell) E.; m. Rosemary Joan Wright Eriksson, Oct. 23, 1971; children: Deborah, Warren, Trent. Cert. in Theory, Witwatersrand U., Johannesburg, 1969. Chartered acct. Audit clk. Coopers & Lybrand, South Africa, 1964-69; sr. audit. Coopers & Lybrand, London, 1970-71; audit mgr. Coopers & Lybrand, South Africa, 1972-75, audit ptnr., 1976-90; cons. South Africa, 1991-92; mng. dir. Commercial Union Group Svcs., South Africa, 1991-98; CFO Commercial Union of South Africa, 1993—; exec. ptnr. Coopers & Lybrand, South Africa, 1987-90; trustee Babcock Africa, South Africa, 1983—; pres. Johannesburg Chartered Accts. Soc., 1985-86; councillor Inst. Dirs., South Africa, 1987—. Chmn. Northcliff Nursery Sch., Johannesburg, 1979-83, Cliffview Sch. Bd., Johannesburg, 1984-87; councillor Northcliff Union Ch., Johannesburg, 1992—. Mem. Bryanston Golf Club, Inst. Dirs. Anglican. Avocations: cycling, swimming, golf, sports. Office: Commercial Union, 26 Loveday St, Johannesburg South Africa

ERIKSSON, OVE ERIK, botany researcher, educator; b. Stockholm, July 6, 1935; s. Ragnar Erik Albert and Gunhild Linnea (Jansson) E.; m. Birgitta Pettersson, July 30, 1960; children: Erik, Mats, Leif. BSc, U. Uppsala, Sweden, 1960, PhLic, 1965, PhD, 1967. Lectr. Umeå U., 1967-95, prof. dept. ecol. environ. sci., 1995—; mem. editl. adv. bd. Mycotaxon, 1990-99; convenor symposia various internat. congresses. Author: The Families of Bitunicate Ascomycetes, 1981; founder, co-editor jour. Systema Ascomycetum, 1982-98; founder jour. Myconet, 1997—. Mem. Brit. Mycological Soc. (Centenary mem. 1996), Internat. Assn. Plant Taxonomy, Swedish Bot. Soc., Internat. Mycol. Assn. (exec. com. 1990-94). Home: Smörbäcksv 26, SE-90592 Umeå Sweden Office: Umeå U, Dept Ecol Environ Sci, SE-90187 Umeå Sweden

ERIKSSON, SVEN-ERIK, neurologist; b. Stockholm, Dec. 22, 1949; s. Arne Erik and Kerstin Linnea (Jönsson) E.; m. Kristina Marianne Zackrisson, June 17, 1972; children: Emma, Jakob, Susanna. MD, Karolinska Inst., Stockholm, 1975; qualification as specialist in neurology, Univ. Hosp., Linköping, Sweden, 1981. House officer Gävle (Sweden) Hosp., 1975-77; sr. house officer Univ. Hosp., Linköping, 1977-78, registrar, 1979-81, asst. physician dept. neurology, 1981-83, ward physician dept. neurology, 1983-84; chief physician divsn. neurology dept. medicine Falu Hosp., Falun, Sweden, 1984-92, Falun, 1993—; chief physician divsn. neurology dept. medicine Mälar-Hosp., Sweden, 1992. Contbr. articles to profl. publs. Mem. Swedish Soc. Medicine, Swedish Neurology Soc. Avocations: physical exercise, skiing. Office: Falu Hosp, 791 82 Falun Sweden

ERIKSSON, ULF, artist, consultant; b. Helsingborg, Sweden, Nov. 4, 1942; s. Karl-Erik Wihelm and Evy Linnea (Nordborg) E.; m. Ananya Ponsovit; children: Ulrika, Frederik, Tobias, André, Angelica. Degree in engring., Helsingborg Tech. Sch., 1969. Dir., cons. Studio Ulf Eriksson, Teckomatorp, Sweden, 1961—; cons. Konstnarernas Riks-Organisation, Sweden, 1985. Represented in numerous pvt. and pub. collections including Libr. of Congress, Washington, Met. Mus., N.Y.C., Boston Mus., Bklyn. Mus., N.Y. Pub. Libr., Art Inst., Mpls., Biblioteque Nat., Paris, Swedish Nat. Mus., Stockholm, Mus. of Archives, Lund, Sweden, Hamburg (Germany) Kunst Halle, Rheinland-Ffalz State Collection, Preusicher Kultur Mus. Am Ostwald, Dortmund, Germany, Kupferstick Samlung, Albertina, Vienna, Austria, Tokyo U. Art Collection, Univ. Art Collection, Kuala Lumpur, Malaysia, others; author: Fragment, 1973; contbr. articles to profl. jours.; prodr., cameraman, actor: (TV film) A Moment in Time, 1989; cameraman, visual creator: (TV film) The World of Kjell Ringi, 1986. Co-founder Ship to Bosnia, 1996-98. Grantee Statens Konstråd, Stockholm, 1973, Rheinland Pfalz grantee Bad Munster Am Stein Ebernberg, Germany, 1975; recipient Elsa Killbergs award Helsingborg Town, 1965-67. Fellow Lions. Avocations: studying antiquities, Asian art and philosophy, golf, fishing. Home and Studio: Karlsgatan 43, PO Box 107, 26020 Teckomatorp Sweden

ERIKSSON-BIQUE, SIRKKA-LIISA ANNELI, mathematics educator; b. Palkane, Finland, Jan. 8, 1958; d. Jalmari Viljam and Bertta Maria (Ojanpera) E.; m. Stephen Francis Michael Bique, Sept. 21, 1986; children: Anna-Maria, Sylvester, Linda. MA, U. Tampere, 1980; PhD, U. Joensuu, 1984. Jr. rschr. Acad. of Finland, Helsinki, 1986-88; asst. U. Joensuu, 1989, lectr., 1990, 91, chief asst., 1991-92, assoc. prof., 1993-98; sr. rschr. scholarship The Acad. of Finland, Helsinki, 1992-93, sr. fellow, 1998—. Contbr. articles to profl. jours.; reviewer Zentralplat fur die Mathematik, 1990, Math Revs. Rsch. grant The Acad. of Finland, 1986, 92, 98; scholarship The Vilho, Yrjo, Kalie Vaisala Found., 1991. Mem. Am. Math. Soc., Math. Assn. of Am., Finnish Math. Soc. Lutheran. Avocations: cross country skiing, swimming, walking, reading. Office: U Joensuu, PO Box 111, 80101 Joensuu Finland

ERION, CAROL ELIZABETH, music educator; b. Quincy, Ill., Jan. 16, 1943; d. Alva Eugene and Margaret Althea (Kaempfer) McKenney; m. David F. Erion, June 19, 1965; children: Elizabeth Celia Erion Matthews, Paul Frederick. MusB, Oberlin Coll., 1965; MusM, New England Conservatory Music, 1982; cert., U. Toronto, Ont., Can., 1978, Mozarteum Acad. Music, Salzburg, Austria, 1979. Music tchr. Montessori Sch. No. Va., Annandale, 1972-84, St. Agnes Episcopal Sch., Alexandria, Va., 1984-85, The Sidwell Friends Sch., Washington, 1985-87; music and fine arts tchr. Arlington (Va.) Pub. Schs., 1988—; music dir. All Saints Episcopal Ch., Alexandria, 1983-90; workshop clinician various music edn. orgns. in U.S., 1980—; adj. prof. George Mason U., Fairfax, Va., 1983—; cons. WETA-TV, Washington, 1987. Author: Tales to Tell, Tales to Play, 1982; contbr. articles to profl. jours. Humanities fellow Coun. Basic Edn., 1989. Mem. NEA, AAUW, ASCD, Am. Recorder Soc., Am. Orff Schulwerk Assn. (pres. 1993-95), Arlington Edn. Assn. (pres. 1998-2000). Democrat. Episcopalian. Home: 19 W Linden St Alexandria VA 22301-2621

ERKAN, SEMIH, agricultural engineer, researcher; b. Konya, Turkey, Aug. 1, 1951; s. Selahattin and Seniha (Arslan) E.; m. Mualla Ari, May 27, 1993; 1 child, Selin. Degree in agrl. engring., Ege U., Izmir, Turkey, 1973, degree in plant pathology, 1974, 76, PhD, 1984. Cert. plant virologist. Assoc. prof. Ege U., 1984-87, prof., 1987-93, mem. sci. and tech. ctr., 1993-95, v.p. grad. sch., 1999—; mem. Turkish Phytopathology Bd., Izmir, 1980-85; head project detection of seed pathogens, 1990—; vis. rschr. viruses of lettuce, 1988. Author: Molecular Biology, 1993, Seed Pathology, 1998. Lt. land forces Turkish armed forces, 1973-75. Mem. Phytopathol. Soc. (Young Rschr. award 1981), Biology Soc. Muslim. Avocations: football, walking, travel, visiting exhibitions. Office: Ege U Ziraat Faculty, Bitki Koruma Bolumu, 35110 Bornova-Izmir Turkey

ERKMEN, AYDAN MÜSERREF, electrical engineering educator; b. Ankara, Turkey, Aug. 15, 1956; d. Neset Mehmet and Ayten (Süngü) A.; m. Ismet Erkmen, July 10, 1978; children: Baris, Burcu. BSc with high honors, Bosphorous U., Istanbul, 1978; MSc, Drexel U., 1981; PhD, George Mason U., 1989. Undergrad. teaching asst. math. dept. Bosphorous U., Istanbul, 1976-78; teaching asst. elec. and computer engring. dept. Drexel U., Phila., 1979-80, rsch. asst., 1980-81; rsch. asst. Sch. Info. Tech. and Engring., George Mason U., Fairfax, Va., 1986-89; asst. prof. dept. elec. engring. Mid. East Tech. U., Ankara, 1989-91, assoc. prof., 1991—; electronics student rsch. group advisor, Mid. East Tech. U., 1993-99, mem. edn. com., 1992—. Author: Advances in Automation and Robotics, 1990, Intelligent Systems: Safety Reliability and Maintainability Issues, NATO ARW, 1993, Sensor and Data Fusion, SPIE Milestone Series, Vol. MS 124, 1996; co-editor Internat. Jour. Intelligent Mchanics: Design and Production; assoc. editor Internat. Jour. Robotics and Automation; mem. editl. bd. IEEE Robotics and Automation Mag., 2000—; contbr. chpt. to book and articles to profl. jours. Mem. IEEE (student br. counselor Mid. E. Tech. U. 1992—), IEEE Robotics and Automation Soc. (mem. adminstrn. com. 1996-98, 2000—, co-chair edn. com. 1998—, long range planning com. 2000—), Sci. and Tech. Rsch. Coun. Turkey (exec. com. modern mfg. systems 1992-96, elec., electronics and informatics grand com., 1994-98), Turkish Tech. Devel. Found. (indsl. project reviewer 1995, 99), Internat. Fedn. Automatic Control (adminstrv. com. 1997—), Turkish Chamber of Elec. Engrs., Eta Kappa Nu. Avocations: swimming, tennis, skiing, mountain bicycling. Home: Dumluca Sok No 10, 06530 Ankara Turkey Office: Mid East Tech U, Dept Elec Engring, 06531 Ankara Turkey

ERKTIN, AYSE HASOL, architect; b. Istanbul, Turkey, Oct. 24, 1964; d. Dogan and Ayse Hayzuran (Yunt) Hasol; m. Mehmet Erktin, June 22, 1990; 1 child, Ali. BS, Istanbul Tech. U., 1986; MDesS, Harvard U., 1988; MBA, Bogazici U., Turkey, 1991. Asst. editor Yapi Mag., Turkey, 1985-87; ptnr. HAS Mimarlik, Ltd., Turkey, 1988—. Mem. Istanbul Project Mgmt. Assn. (v.p. 1999—), Harvard Club of Turkey (v.p. 1996—). Office: HAS Mimarlik Ltd, Kaya Aldogan Sok 15, 80600 Zincirlikuyu Istanbul Turkey

ERLANDER, SVEN BERTIL, academic administrator, educator; b. Halmstad, Sweden, May 25, 1934; s. Tage and Aina (Andersson) E.; m. Lillemor Sandahl; children: Charles, Kim, Gunnel, Inger. Licentiate, Stockholm U., 1964, Doctor of Philosophy, 1968. Asst. to prof. Stockholm U., 1959-68, docent, 1969-70; prof. Linköping (Sweden) U., 1971—, pres., 1983-95. Mem. Royal Swedish Acad. Engring. Scis., Math. Programming Soc., Ops. Research Soc. Am., Am. Math. Soc. Home: Hedborns Gata 13, 58437 Linköping Sweden Office: Linköping U, 58183 Linköping Sweden

ERLANDSEN, THOR EGIL, marine engineering company executive; b. Arendal, Norway, June 29, 1959; s. Egil and Rigmor (Myge) E.; m. Siv Astri Tønnessen, July 29, 1962 (div. March 1999); children: Linn Cecilie, Thom Christer, Morten Andreas. Degree in mech. and design engring., Agder Regional Coll., 1982, postgrad., 1977-88; postgrad., Norwegian State Tech. Inst., Chartered Engrs. Assn. Tech. mgr. Jorgensen & Vik/Watercraft A/S, Norway, 1982-85; sr. project engr., project mgr. Ugland Engring. A/S, Norway, 1986-96; project mgr. Marine Tech. A/S, Norway, 1996-97; gen. mgr. Marine Engring. A/S, Grimstad, Norway, 1997—; asst. project mgr. Ugland Engring. A/S, Norway, 1989-90; project mgr. Pennecon Ugland Loading Sys., Inc., Norway and Can., 1994-96, Aker Maritime Pusnes A/X, 1996-97, 97-99; lectr. in field. With Norwegian Army, 1979-80. Avocations: motorboating, sailing, skiing. Home: Moy Moner, N-4890 Grimstad Norway Office: Marine Engring A/S, Televeien 1 PO Box 238, N-4891 Grimstad Norway

ERLANGER, BERNARD FERDINAND, biochemist, educator; b. N.Y.C., July 13, 1923; s. Leo and Frieda (David) E.; m. Rachel Fenichel, June 23, 1946; children—Laura, Louis, Leon. BS with highest honors, CCNY, 1943; MA, NYU, 1949; PhD, Columbia U., 1951. Chemist U.S. Indsl. Chems. Co., Inc., Newark, 1943-44; tech. adviser Manhattan Project, U.S. Army, Los Alamos, 1944-46; prodn. mgr. Hexagon Labs., Inc., N.Y.C., 1946-48; faculty Columbia, 1951—, prof. microbiology, 1966—; vis. scientist Instituto Superiore di Sanita, Rome, 1961-62, Inst. Cell Biology, Shanghai, People's Republic of China, 1978; mem. Fulbright-Hays Award Com., 1966-72; invited expert analyst biochem. and molecular biology edit. Chemtracts; mem. study sect. neurol. C, NIH, 1985-88. Recipient 600th Anniversary medal Copernican Med. Acad., Cracow, Poland, 1979,Sigma Alpha/Mu Gamma award N.Y. Heart Assn., Townsend Harris medal CUNY, 1995; Fulbright scholar U. Republic of Uruguay, 1967, Guggenheim fellow Inst. Phys.-Chem. Biology, Paris, 1969, Am. Cancer Soc. scholar Pasteur Inst., Paris, 1979. Recipient Physicians and Surgeons Disting. Svc. award Columbia U., 1996. Mem. Am. Chem. Soc., Am. Soc. Biol. Chemists, Biochem. Soc., N.Y. Acad. Scis. (mem. conf. com. 1978), Soc. Exptl. Biol. Medicine (assoc. editor proceedings 1981-88), Harvey Soc., Am. Soc. Immunologists, N.Y. Heart Assn., Am. Soc. Photobiology, Phi Beta Kappa, Sigma Alpha Mu (Gamma award). Achievements include research on mode of action of antibiotics and on cancer; investigation of mechanisms of enzyme catalysis, immunochemistry of macromolecules concerned with genetics immunology of fullernes, photoregulation, biological receptors. Home: 16316 15th Dr Flushing NY 11357-2935 Office: Columbia U 701 W 168th St New York NY 10032-2704

ERLICH, HAGGAI, historian, educator; b. Tel Aviv, Mar. 29, 1942; s. Hanock and Judith (Rosiner) E.; m. Hanna Schneller, July 23, 1967 (div. 1983); children: Ori, Shiri, Yoav; m. Yocheved Liberman, May 20, 1984; 1 child, Omri. BA, Tel Aviv U., 1966; MA, Hebrew U., Jerusalem, 1969; PhD, Sch. Oriental/African Studies, London, 1973. Lectr. Tel Aviv U., 1973-78, sr. lectr., 1978-83, assoc. prof., 1983-92, full prof., 1992—. Author: Ethiopia and Eritrea-Ras Alula 1875-1897, 1982, The Struggle Over Eritrea 1962-1978, 1983, Students and University in Egyptian Politics, 1989, Ethiopia and the Middle East, 1994, The Nile-Histories, Cultures, Myths, 1999. Rsch. acad. officer Israeli Def. Force, 1978-91. Recipient awards Brit. Coun., 1970, U.S. Inst. of Peace, 1987, 98, Israeli Sci. Acad., 1995. Avocation: tennis. Office: Dept Middle Ea & African, Tel Aviv Univ, 69978 Tel Aviv Israel

ERLING, SPENCER, steel contracting executive, civil engineer; b. Johannesburg, South Africa, Jan. 12, 1946; s. Herbert and Cynthia Erling; m. Hazel Joan Kirkel, Feb. 7, 1971; children: Ghita, Toni. BSCE, U. Witwatersrand, South Africa, 1966. Registered profl. engr., South Africa; chartered engr., U.K. Design engr. Dorman Long Africa, South Africa, 1967; project engr. Speedy Welders, South Africa, 1969-75, mng. dir., 1976-89; tech. mgr. Girder Naco (Pty.) Ltd., South Africa, 1989-97, tech. dir., 1997—; bd. dirs. Girder Naco (Pty.) Ltd., Erling Rishon (Pty.) Ltd., South Africa. Chmn. Emmarentia Residents Assn., Johannesburg, 1988-89. Lt. South African Def. Force, 1968. Fellow South African Instn. Civil Engrs.; mem. Instn. Structural Engrs. (assoc.), South African Inst. Steel Constrn. (bd. dirs. 1977-99). Mem. Dem. Party of South Africa. Jewish. Avocations: cycling, hiking, sports, wildlife. Office: Girder Naco Pty, PO Box 14127, Wadeville 1422, Republic of South Africa

ERLYKIN, ANATOLY DMITRIEVICH, physicist; b. Moscow, Jan. 23, 1936; s. Dmitry Ivanovich and Ekaterina Filippovna (Iljicheva) E.; m. Margarita Evgenievna Shevtsova, Feb. 8, 1959 (div. 1971); 1 child, Zurabova Julia Anatolievna; m. Svetlana Konstantinovna Machavariani, Oct. 16, 1971; 1 child, Uliana Anatolievna. Grad., U. Moscow, 1959; PhD (hon.), P.N. Lebedev Phys. Inst., Moscow, 1968, DS (hon.), 1986. Sr. engr. Inst. Thermotechnique, Moscow, 1959, jr. rsch. assoc., 1959-60, group leader, 1960-61; jr. rsch. assoc. P.N. Lebedev Phys. Inst., 1964-73, sr. rsch. assoc., 1973-80, leading rsch. assoc., 1980-86, head rsch. assoc., 1986—. Contbr. over 200 articles to sci. jours. Avocations: tennis, music. E-mail: A.D.Erlykin@durham.ac.uk. Fax: 44-0191-374-3749. Office: U Durham Phys Dept, Sci Labs South Rd, Durham DH1 3LE, England

ERMA, REINO MAURI, lawyer, university chancellor emeritus; b. Tampere, Finland, Apr. 8, 1922; s. Edvin Eugen and Ida Irene (Haapala) E.; m. Hilkka Marjatta Ahjo, Jan. 5, 1946; children: Juhani, Sinikka, Anneli,

Tapio. LLM, Helsinki U., 1944, Licentiate in Laws, 1948, LLD, 1955. With KOP Bank, Helsinki, 1947-70, dir., 1960-70; prof. bus. law Faculty Econs. and Administrn. U. Tampere, 1970-84, rector, 1976-81, chancellor, 1984-90. Author: Contract of Work, 1955, General Conditions for the Building Contracts, 1974, 91, Legal Aspects of Subcontracting, 1975, General Conditions for the Delivery of Goods between Finland and CMEA Countries, 1980, Banking Laws, 1986, Legal Handbook of Foreign Trade, 1989, 94; co-author: (with A. Guttorm and L. Lehtinen) Arbitration in Finland and in Russia, 1999. Served with Finnish Army, 1940-44. Decorated Comdr. Order first cl. Finnish White Rose, Cross of Freedom, Medal of Freedom. Mem. Internat. Law Assn., Arbitration Assn. Finland, Rotary (past pres.). Home: Mustanlahdenkatu 1 B 87, 33210 Tampere Finland Office: Law Office Erma Toimisto, Mustanlahdenkatu 1 B 95, 33200 Tampere Finland

ERMAKOV, EVGENII IVANOVICH, biologist, agrophysicist, ecologist; b. Rzhaksa, Tambov, USSR, June 4, 1929; s. Ivan Jakovlevich and Anna Ivanovna (Uvarova) E.; m. Ludmila Petrovna Kuchumova, Apr. 5, 1956 (dec. Mar. 1992); 1 child; m. Zoja Pavlovna Grebienkina, June 10, 1997. BS, Agrl. Inst., Ordzhonikidze, USSR, 1953; PhD, Agrophysical Rsch. Inst., Leningrad, USSR, 1976. Jr. rschr. Agrophysical Rsch. Inst., Leningrad, USSR, 1958-61; sr. rschr. Agrophysical Rsch. Inst., Leningrad, 1961-76, lab. head, 1976-82, vice dir., 1982—. Contbr. over 280 articles to sci. jours; holds 70 patents in field. Recipient Honoured of State award, Russian Govt., Moscow, 1996; named Honored Scientist of the Russian Fedn., Russian Govt., Moscow, 1996. Fellow Russian Acad. Agrl. Scis.; mem. N.Y. Acad. Scis. Avocations: classical music, sports. Fax: 7 (812) 534 1900. Home: 19-2 Sikeiros Str Apt 55, 194354 Saint Petersburg Russia Office: Agrophysical Inst, 14 Grazhdansky Prospect, 195220 Saint Petersburg Russia

ERMERT, LEANDER, pathologist; b. Irmgarteichen, Germany, May 9, 1963; s. Heinrich and Maria (Wolf) E.; m. Monika Jost, Mar. 4, 1994. MD, U. Giessen, 1993, DSc, 1996. Rschr. U. Giessen, Germany, 1993—. Mem. Am. Thoracic Soc., U.S. and Can. Acad. of Pathology. Office: U Giessen, Aulweg 123, 35385 Giessen Germany

ERMINI, FLAVIO, publisher; b. Verona, Italy, Dec. 15, 1947; s. Andrea Ermini and Lina Caliari; m. Nadia Scutari, Jan. 23, 1971 (div. 1996); 1 child, Amanda. Diploma in acctg., U. Verona, Italy. Editor Mondadori, Verona, 1968—; pub. Anterem, Verona, 1976—. Author: (poetry books) Roseti e Cantiere, 1980, Epitaphium Blesillae, 1982, Thaide, 1983, Idalium, 1986, Segnitz, 1987, Delosea, 1989, Hamsund, 1991, Antlitz, 1994, Karlsar, 1998. Avocations: literature, philosophy. Home and Office: Via San Giovanni in Valle 2, 37129 Verona Italy

ERMOLIEV, YURI MICHAILOVICH, mathematician, researcher; b. Karachev, Briansk, Russia, Nov. 3, 1936; s. Michail Nickiforovich and Lidia Nickolaevna (Gustiakova) E.; m. Ljudmila Grigorievna Tovstucha, May 4, 1963; 1 child, Ermolieva Tatjana. Mathematician, U. Kiev, Ukraine, 1959, candidate degree, 1964, DSc in Math., 1972, full prof., 1974. Rschr. Inst. Cybernetics, Kiev, Ukraine, 1960-72; head rsch. dept. Inst. Cybernetics, Kiev, 1972-79, 84-91; project leader Internat. Inst. Applied Systems Analysis, Laxenburg, Austria, 1979-84, 91—. Author: Stochastic Programming Methods, 1976, The Finite Difference Method in Optimal Control, 1978, Stochastic Methods in Economics, 1979, Nondifferentiable and Stochastic Optimization in Physics, 1995. Ukraine State prize in sci., State Com., Kiev, 1978, USSR State prize in sci., State Com., Moscow, 1981; Kjell Gunnarson's Risk Mgmt. prize The Swedish Ins. Soc., Stockholm, 1997. Mem. Acad. Scis. Kiev, Ukraine (academician 1988). Avocations: downhill and water skiing, biking, music, painting. Office: Int Inst Appl Syst Analysis, Schloss, A-2361 Laxenburg Lwr Aust, Austria

ERNESTA, L., library director; b. Victoria, Mahe Island, Seychelles, May 14, 1946; d. Jean-Baptiste and Isabelle Fairy (Moustache) Rosette; m. Donald Robert Ernesta, Dec. 24, 1970; children: Keddy, Lindy, Leroy. Diploma in Social and Cmty. Devel., Internat. Social Tng. Inst.; Diploma in Librarianship, Manchester Poly. Sch. Libr. Cert. tchr. Tchr. Ministry of Edn., Seychelles, 1968-79, librarian, 1980-83, sr. librarian, 1983-87; asst. dir. Nat. Lib., Victoria, Mahe, Seychelles, 1987—. Mem. Lib. Assn. U.K., Seychelles Lib. Assn. (chmn. 1990-92, vice-chmn. 1992-94, mem. coun. 1994—). Roman Catholic. Avocations: reading, gardening. Office: Nat Libr, PO Box 45 Francis Rachel St, Victoria Mahe Seychelles

ERNI, DOMINIQUE, plastic surgeon; b. Sursee, Lucerne, Switzerland, Dec. 24, 1959; s. Hans and Mireille (Carron) E. MD, U. Berne, Switzerland, 1984. Intern in gen. surgery Regional Hosp., Wolhusen, 1985-87, U. Hosp., Basel, 1989-90; resident in plastic surgery Inselpital U. Hosp., Berne, 1991-96, sr. resident, 1998—; rsch. fellow U. Calif., San Diego, 1997. Contbr. articles to profl. jours. Swiss Nat. Found. for Rsch. grant, 1998. Mem. Swiss Soc. Plastic Surgery (Promotion prize 1991), Swiss Soc. for Rsch. in Surgery, European Soc. for Microcirculation. Avocations: chess, sailing, biking, golf, skiing. Home: Kreuzhubel 28, 6208 Oberkirch Switzerland Office: Inselpital Univ Hosp, Dept Plastic Surgery, 3010 Berne Switzerland

ERNST, DANIEL PEARSON, lawyer; b. Des Moines, Sept. 30, 1931; s. Daniel Ward and Thea Elaine (Pearson) E.; m. Ann Robinson, April 14, 1956; children: Ellen, Daniel R., Ruth Ann. BA, Dartmouth Coll., 1953; JD, U. Mich., 1956. Bar: Iowa 1956, Ill. 1964, Mich. 1980. Assoc. Clewell Cooney & Fuerste, 1960-64; ptnr. Nelson Stapleton & Ernst, Stapleton & Ernst, Stapleton Ernst & Sprengelmeyer, East Dubuque, Ill., Nelson Stapleton & Ernst & Sprengelmeyer, Dubuque, Iowa, 1964-79; pvt. practice Dubuque, 1979-80; ptnr. Ernst & Cody, Dubuque, 1981-84, Daniel P. Ernst, P.C., Dubuque, 1984-90, Vincent Roth & Ernst, P.C., Galena, Ill., 1991; pub. defender State of Iowa, Dubuque, 1991-96; pvt. practice Dubuque, 1997—; U.S. trustee 1979-91. Capt. USAF, 1957-60. Mem. ABA, Iowa State Bar Assn. (bd. govs. 1985-89), Dubuque County Bar Assn. (2d v.p. 1979-80, 1st v.p. 1980-81, pres. 1981-82), Ill. State Bar Assn., Jo Daviess County Bar Assn., State Bar Assn. Mich., Grand Traverse-Leelanau-Antrim Bar Assn. Democrat. Avocations: swimming, sailing. Office: Attorney-at-Law 899 Mount Carmel Rd Dubuque IA 52003-7946

ERNST, EDZARD, medical educator; b. Wiesbaden, Hessen, Germany, Jan. 30, 1948. MD, Munich U., 1976, PhD, 1985. Prof. U. Hannover, Germany, 1989-90, U. Vienna, Austria, 1990-93; prof. complementary medicine U. Exeter, Eng., 1993—; vis. prof. Royal Coll. Phys. Surgeons Can. Editor: Fibrinogen a New Cardiovascular Risk Factor, 1992, Advances in Idiopathic Low Back Pain, 1993, Complementary Medicine: An Objective Appraisal, 1996, Homeopathy: A Critical Appraisal, 1998, Acupuncture: A Scientific Appraisal, 1999, Herbal Medicine: A Concise Overview for Professionals, 2000; editor-in-chief Perfusion Med. Jour., Focus on Alternative Complementary Med. Jour. Recipient Sci. prize Zeitschrift für Allgem. Medicine, Germany, 1984, Kneipp prize, Germany, 1984, Prize der Stadt Bad Kissingen, Germany, 1990. Fellow Royal Coll. Physicians Edinburgh; mem. N.Y. Acad. Scis., Royal Soc. Medicine. Office: U Exeter Sch Postgrad MedHealth Scis, 25 Victoria Park Rd, Exeter EX2 4NT, England

ERNST, JOHN LOUIS, management consultant; b. Pine Bluff, Ark., Dec. 24, 1932; s. Albert C. and Christine (Vinent) E.; m. Lois R. Geraci, June 12, 1971; children: Ann Marie, Catherine Teresa, Laura Elizabeth, Christine Margaret. BS, Spring Hill Coll., Mobile, Ala., 1954; postgrad., Georgetown U. Law Sch., 1956-57. Stockbroker Washington Planning Co., 1957-58; pub. rels.-sales exec. Am. Airlines, Washington, Phila. and N.Y.C., 1958-62; account exec. Ted Bates Advt. Agy., N.Y.C., 1962-65; sr. v.p., mgmt. dir. Marschalk Advt. Agy., N.Y.C., 1965-68; dir. Interpub. Svc. Corp., 1967-69; sr. v.p., mng. dir. McCann-Erickson Advt. Agy., N.Y.C., 1969-70; pres. Ernst-Van Praag, N.Y.C., 1970-75; chmn. bd. A.V.E. Corp., N.Y.C., 1974-75, Advt. to Women, Inc., N.Y.C., 1975-86; pres. Bellvinent Communications, Inc., N.Y.C., 1986—, Art Vault Internat., N.Y.C., 1996—. Capt. USMC, 1954-57. Mem. Amyotrophic Lateral Sclerosis (Lou Gehrig's Disease) Assn. (chmn. bd. dirs., CEO Greater N.Y.C. chpt. 1997—), Players Club. Address: 20 Monroe Ave Spring Lake NJ 07762-1717

ERNST, KURT WILHELM, retired chemical engineer, researcher; b. Göttingen, Germany; s. Karl Wilhelm and Alwine Dorette (Dorenwell) E.; m. Ursula Emmy Schäfer, Mar. 6, 1959; children: Frank, Katrin. Degree in lab. chemistry, Max Planck Assn., Göttingen, 1956; degree in chem. engrng., Fachhochschule Beuth, Berlin, 1959. Analytical chemist H.C. Starck, Goslar, Germany, 1959-61; mgr. Deutsche Novopan, Göttingen, 1961-66, dir. R & D, 1966-79, gen. mgr., 1984-89; engring. mgr. Glunz AG, Hamm, Germany, 1979-84; environ. mgr. Glunz AG, Hamm, 1991-93; gen. mgr. Glunz Consult, Meppen, Germany, 1989-91. Co-author: (with H.J. Deppe) Technologie der Spanplatten, 1964, 4th edit., 1999, MDF-Mitteldichte Faserplatten, 1996; contbr. articles to profl. jours.; inventor in field. Fax: 49 551796431. Home: Mittelberg 39, 37085 Göttingen Germany

ERNST, OLIVIER JEAN, radiologist; b. Roubaix, France, Dec. 2, 1961; s. Marc and Josette (Dumont) E.; m. Sophie Chantal Tirloy, Sept. 26, 1992; children: Simon, Mathilde, Florian. MS, U. Paris, 1988, Faculty Medicine, Lille, France, 1991; MD, Faculty Medicine, Lille, France, 1997, PhD, 1999. Resident Centre Hospitalier Universitaire, Lille, France, 1986-91, radiologist, 1994—. Author: IRM de l'abdomen, 1993; contbr. articles to profl. jours., chpts. to books. Fellow CHRU, 1991-94. Mem. Soc. French Radiologists. Avocation: amateur radio. Home: 2 rue de la Philanthropie, F-59700 Marcq-en-Baroeul France Office: CHRU de Lille Radiologie, 1 place de Verdun, F-59037 Lille France

ERNST, RANDYL ALLEN, engineer; b. Reading, Pa., Sept. 3, 1954; s. Allen O. and Gladys Ernst; m. Teresa M. Gallen, Apr. 30, 1977; children: Christopher, Jason. BSME, Temple U., 1987. Project mgr. Perley-Halladay, Malvern, Pa., 1987-88; project engr. Gilbert Commonwealth, Reading, Pa., 1988-90; project mgr. RPA Assocs., Inc., Wyomissing, Pa., 1990—. Designer animal isolation cubicle and animal rsch. kennels; co-designer preparative chromatography solvent delivery sys. Mem. Internat. Soc. Pharm. Engrs. Avocations: boating, fishing. Office: RPA Assocs Inc 716 N Park Rd Wyomissing PA 19610-2912

ERNST, RICHARD ROBERT, chemist, educator; b. Winterthur, Zurich, Switzerland, Aug. 14, 1933; s. Robert and Irma (Brunner) E.; m. Magdalena Kielholz, Oct. 9, 1963; children: Anna Magdalena, Katharina Elisabeth, Hans-Martin Walter. Diploma Chemistry, ETH-Zurich, 1956, DSc in Tech., 1962; PhD (hon.), ETH-Lausanne, Switzerland, 1986, Technische Hochschule, Munich, 1989, U. Zurich, 1994, U. Antwerp, 1997, U. Cluj-Napoca, 1998, U. Montpellier, 1999. Scientist ETH-Zurich, 1962-63, privatdozent, 1968-70, asst. prof., 1970-72, assoc. prof., 1973-76, prof., 1976—; scientist Varian Assocs., Palo Alto, Calif., 1963-68; cons. Spectrospin AG, Fällanden, Switzerland, 1978—, v.p. bd. dirs. Numerous inventions, patents in field. 1st lt. ACS-Dienst, 1953-88, Swiss mil. Recipient Silver medal ETH-Zurich, 1962, Ruzicka prize, 1968, Gold medal Soc. Magnetic Resonance in Medicine, San Francisco, 1983, Benoist prize Swiss Fedn. Confedn., Berne, 1986, Kirkwood award Yale U., 1989, Ampere prize, 1990, Wolf prize in chemistry, 1991, Louisa Gross Horwitz prize Columbia U., 1991, Nobel prize in chemistry, 1991, award for Achievements in Magnetic Resonance EAS, 1992. Mem. NAS (India), Deutsche Akademie Leopoldina, Acad. Europaea, Schweizerische Chemische Gesellschaft, Royal Soc. London, Österreichische Gesellschaft für Analytische Chemie, Am. Phys. Soc., U.S. Nat. Acad. Sci., Am. Acad. Arts and Scis., Schweizerische Akademie d. Tech. Wiss., Russian Acad. Scis. Avocations: Tibetan art, music. Office: Lab F Phys Chem ETH-Zentrum, 8092 Zurich Switzerland

ERNTELL, MATS THORE HENNING, physician, consultant; b. Karlskrona, Blekinge, Sweden, July 8, 1951; s. Thorsten and Rut (Hansson) E.; m. Ann Britt, Nov. 5, 1998; children by previous marriage: Rebecka, Filip. MD, Lund (Sweden) U., 1976, PhD, 1987. Intern Halmstad (Sweden) Hosp., 1976-78, cons., 1989—; resident dept. infectious diseases Lund U., 1978-82, specialist, 1982-89. Contbr. articles to profl. jours. Mem. Swedish Med. Assn., Swedish Assn. Infectious Diseases (treas. 1994—), European Soc. Clin. Microbiology and Infectious Diseases. Avocations: tennis, family, travel. Office: Halmstad Hosp, Dept Infectious Diseases, S-30185 Halmstad Sweden

ERNY, PIERRE JEAN PAUL, ethnologist, educator; b. Colmar, Alsace, France, July 7, 1933; s. Charles and Madelaine (Bronner) E.; m. Marie-Antoinette Weibel, Aug. 22, 1963; children: Benoît, Mathieu, Marie-Claire. D in Psychology, U. Strasbourg, France, 1965, D in Religious Sci., 1970, PhD in Ednl. Sci., 1978. Prof. Koupela, Burkina Faso, 1958-60; psychol. rschr. Brazzaville, Congo, 1963-65; maître de confs. U. Strasbourg, 1965-70; prof. U. Officielle du Congo, Lubumbashi, Zaire, 1970-71, U. Nat. du Zaire, Kisangani, 1971-73, U. Nat. du Rwanda, Butare, 1973-76, U. Marc Bloch, Strasbourg, 1976—; dir. Inst. d'Ethnologie U. des Scis. Humaines, Strasbourg, 1984-93. Author: The Child in African Traditional Thought, 1968, The Child and His Environment in Africa, 1972, The First Steps in the Life of the African Child, 1973, Rwanda 1994,: Keys to Understand the Drama of a People, 1994, Clés pur une Anthropologie ouverte, 1998, Ecoliers d'hier en Afrique Centrale, 1999, La maison du sculpteur. Ethnographie d'une enfance alsacienne ordinaire, 1999, Contes, Mythes, Mystères, 2000, Enfants du ciel et de la Verre, Essais d'authropologie religieuse, 2000. Home: 6 Rue Victor Huen, 68000 Colmar Alsace, France

EROGLU, HUDAVERDI, paper technologist, educator; b. S. Koçhisar, Ankara, Turkey, Apr. 10, 1948; s. Bektas and Hatice (Toptas) E.; m. Refiye Pamir, June 18, 1971; children: Cengiz Alp, Burtay Hatice. Diploma in forest engrng., Forestry Faculty, Istanbul, Turkey, 1969; diploma in paper chemistry, Ecole Francaise de Papeterie, Grenoble, France, 1976. Cert. forest engr. Rschr. Ecole Francaise de Papeterie, Grenoble, 1971-76; rsch. asst. Black Sea U., Trabzon, Turkey, 1976-81, assoc. prof., 1981-87, prof., 1987-95; prof. Karaelmas U., Zonguldak, Turkey, 1995—; head dept. Forestry Faculty, Trabzon, Turkey, 1986-89, vice dean, Bartin, Trukey, 1995-97, head dept., 1995-97; dir., pres. Profl. Sch., Bartin, 1997-99. Author: Papermaking Technology, 1990, Fiberboard Manufacturing, 1999. Organizer Paper Recycling, Istanbul, 1998. Lt. Turkish Army, 1969-71. Scholar Turkish Sci. Coun., 1969-75. Mem. Turkish Pulp and Paper Orgn., Turkish Forestry Assn., N.Y. Acad. Scis. Achievements include invention of Soda Oxygen Pulping of Wheat Straw, MDF Production from Straw. Avocations: music, tennis, chess, trekking. Home: 20 Sokak, Bahçelievler Turkey Office: Bartin Orman Fakultesi, Dept Forest Product, 74100 Bartin Turkey

ERÖSS, KLÁRA, chemistry educator, researcher; b. Debrecen, Hajdu, Hungary, May 28, 1936; d. István and Ilona (Török) E.; m. József Kiss, Aug. 4, 1963; children: Sándor Kiss, Zsuzsanna Kiss. Degree in Chem. Engring., Tech. U., Budapest, 1959. Sr. lectr. Tech. U., 1962-69, lectr., 1969-92, prof., 1992—; educator Inst. Analytical Chemistry, Budapest, 1962—. Contbg. author to several textbooks; contbr. articles to profl. jours.; lectr. in field. Recipient Excellent Work award Ministry of Culture and Edn., 1985. Mem. Spectrochem. Orgn., Orgn. Hungarian Chemistry. Avocations: gymnastics, gardening, listening to music. Home: Attila 65, 1013 Budapest Hungary Office: Tech U Inst Analytical Chem, Gellert Terr 4, 1502 Budapest Hungary

EROSTYAK, JANOS, physicist; b. Gyula, Bekes, Hungary, Nov. 21, 1961; s. Janos and Zsuzsanna (Konyecsni) E.; m. Andrea Buzady, Nov. 6, 1992; children: Janos, Zita. MS, Jozsef Attila U., Szeged, Hungary, 1984, PhD, 1998. Asst. prof. Janus Pannonius U., Pecs, 1984-98, assoc. prof., 1998—. Author: (book) Optics, 1995, 99. Avocation: numismatics. Office: U Pecs, Ifjusag 6, Pécs H-7624, Hungary

ERRICKSON, BARBARA BAUER, component based software company executive; b. Pitts., Apr. 5, 1944; d. Edward Ewing Bauer and Margaret J. McConnell; m. James Jay Burcham, June 30, 1966 (div. May 1972); children: James Jay II, Linda Lee; m. William Newel Errickson, Apr. 9, 1976 (div. Feb. 1987). BA, U. Ill., 1966; MBA, So. Meth. U., 1981. Programming trainee Allstate Ins. Co., Northbrook, Ill., 1973; programmer, team leader Motorola, Inc., Chgo., 1974-78; supr. systems Tex. Instruments, Dallas, 1978-81, product line mgr. worldwide shipping systems, 1981-83, product line mgr. shipping, inventory systems, 1983-84, mgr. mktg. info. systems, 1985, mgr. benefit systems, 1986-89, mgr. S.W. case cons. and edn., 1990-97; western area advanced practices mgr. Sterling Software Inc., Plano, Tex., 1997; western area N.Am. tch. svcs. mgr. Sterling Software Inc., Plano, 1997-99; exec. advisor Castek Software Factory, Toronto, Can., 1999—; dir., billing and software developer Spring Park Home Owners, Garland-Richardson, Tex., 1984—, pres. and chmn. fin., 1985, v.p. legal, 1986. Active Dallas Women's Ctr., 1984—; mem. bus. adv. council So. Meth U. Bus. Adv. Program; mem. bus. adv. coun. El Centro Coll. Rehab. for Physically Challenged Through Data Processing, 1987—; chmn. control and adminstrn./mktg. United Way, 1986-89. Recipient Women in Leadership cert. YWCA Met. Chgo., 1977. Mem. Am. Mgmt. Assn., Am. Women in Computing (bd. dirs. 1987—, pres. 1989), Community Assns. Inst., So. Meth. U. MBA Soc., Gleneagles Country Club, Beta Gamma Sigma. Republican. Presbyterian. Avocations: sailing, horseback riding, running, oil painting, cycling. Home: 5676 Gleneagles Dr Plano TX 75093-5973 Office: 6501 Westin Pkwy Ste 210 Cary NC 25513

ERRINGTON, JEFFERY, molecular microbiology researcher; b. Gateshead, Eng., May 3, 1956; s. Sydney and Elizabeth (Wright) E.; m. Veronica Mary Geoghegan, Apr. 24, 1982; children: Sinead Elizabeth Mary, Niamh Veronica Claire. BSc, U. Newcastle-upon-Tyne, Eng., 1977; PhD, Thames Poly., London, 1981. Rsch. fellow U. Oxford, Eng., 1981-85, Royal Soc. rsch. fellow, 1985-89, Univ. lectr., 1989-97, prof. microbiology, 1997—, BBSRC sr. rsch. fellow, 1997—; tutorial fellow Magdalen Coll., Oxford, 1989—; cons. Apcel Ltd., Slough, Eng., 1987; dir., chmn. Prolysis Ltd., 1998—; trustee EPA Cephalosporin Fund., 1999—. Mem. editl. bd. Jour. Bacteriology, Washington, 1992-94, Molecular Microbiology, Oxford, 1997—, Current Opinion in Microbiology, 1998—; contbr. some 110 articles to profl. jours.; holder 4 patents pending. Recipient John Corran prize U. Newcastle-upon-Tyne, 1977. Mem. Soc. for Gen. Microbiology, Am. Soc. for Microbiology, Genetical Soc. Avocations: soccer, piano, travel, sub aqua. Office: Sir Wm Dunn Sch Pathology, S Parks Rd, Oxford OX1 3RE, England

ÉRSEK, TIBOR, plant pathologist; b. Kecskemét, Hungary, May 8, 1945; s. Tibor I. Sándor and Terézia (Kulcsár) É; m. Ágnes Palojtay, Feb. 23, 1974; children: Zsuzsanna, Lilla. Student, József Attila U., Szeged, Hungary, 1970; PhD, Hungarian Acad. Sci., Budapest, 1978, DSc, 1991. Rsch. asst. Plant Protection Inst., Budapest, 1970-73, rsch. assoc., 1973-79, sr. rschr., 1980-91, scientist, head plant pathology dept., 1995—; vis. scholar plant pathology dept. U. Mo., Columbia, 1991-94. Author, editor: (in Hungarian) Pathogens and Infected Plants, 1985, Plant Pathogenic Microorganisms, 1998; contbr. articles to profl. jours.; mem. editl. bd. Acta Phytopathologica et Entomologica Hungarica, 1986—. Recipient Outstanding Rschr. award Ministry of Agr., 1981; grantee U.S.-Hungarian Sci. and Tech. Joint Fund, 1995-99. Fellow Hungarian Agrl. Soc. (Linhart György award 2000); mem. Hungarian Acad. Scis. (plant protection com. 1996—, gen. microbiology com. 1997—). Mem. Hungarian Democratic Forum. Avocations: photography, travel, writing fiction. Office: Plant Protection Inst, Herman Ottó 15, 1022 Budapest Hungary

ERSKINE, SHEENA CHRISTINE, retired educator, researcher; b. Edinburgh, Scotland, Apr. 16, 1946; d. William and Christina Gardner (Johnston) Yule; m. Norman Alexander Erskine, Dec. 18, 1965; 1 child, Neil. Diploma in Tchg., Dundee (Scotland) Coll. Edn., 1966, diploma in Learning Support, 1974; MEd with honors, Dundee U., 1987. Cert. tchr., Scotland. Tchr. infants Fife Coun., Glenrothes, Scotland, 1966; tchr. Borders Coun., Hawick, Scotland, 1967-72; tchr. spl. edn. needs Dundee Coun., 1972-74; tchr.-in-charge Assessment, Treatment & Observation Ctr., Dundee, 1975-88; profl. asst. Tayside Edn. Dept., Dundee, 1988-94, ret., 1994; cons. Cambridge (Eng.) Edn. Consultants Ltd., 1992—. Author, editor: (poetry) Internal Landscapes, 1991; co-editor: Gender Issues in International Education: Beyond Policy and Practice, 1999; contbr. articles to profl. jours. Recognition for svcs. to edn. Her Majesty Queen Elizabeth II, 1994.

ERSKINE FAVRE, BARBARA L., media relations executive; b. Hartford, Conn., July 26, 1955; d. H. Craig Bell and Arlene Erskine; m. Stephane Taboulet, Feb. 24, 1978 (div. Feb. 1985); m. Gilbert Georges Favre, Sept. 19, 1992 (dec. 1998). BA, Sarah Lawrence Coll., 1976; cert. Inst. of French Studies, NYU, 1979, postgrad., 1983. Adminstr. Inst. of French Studies, NYU, 1978-84; asst. to fgn. affairs columnist Flora Lewis N.Y. Times Paris Bur., 1985-90; dir., mem. exec. bd. World Econ. Forum, Geneva, 1990—, dir., 1997-2000; guest Women's World Leadership Coun., 2000—. European editor Wired mag., 2000—. Mem. World Editors Forum, Press Club of Switzerland. Democrat.

ERTAS, ISMET, retired educator; b. Ordu, Turkey, Sept. 3, 1932; s. Abdurrahman and Ayse Hatice (Guner) E.; m. Aybuke Engin, Aug. 23, 1963; children: Ayla Yildiz, Engin Deniz, Elif Belkis, Merih Nihan. BS, Istanbul U., Turkey, 1954, PhD, 1959. Asst. Inst. Exptl. Physics, Istanbul U., Turkey, 1954-59; asst. prof. Inst. Exptl. Physics, Ege U., Izmir, Turkey, 1960-66, assoc. prof., 1966-81; prof. dept. physics Ege U., Izmir, Turkey, 1981—; head exptl. physics Ege U., 1969-81, dir. fundamental sci. inst., 1981-82, dean faculty sci., 1982-94, dir. grad. sch. natural and applied sci., 1994-99. Author: Laboratory of Experimental Physics, 8th edit., 1999, Experimental Physics I, 7th edit., 2000, Experimental Physics II, 3d edit., 1996, Laboratory of Modern and Experimental Physics, 1973, Laboratory of Modern Physics, 1991, The First 25 Years of Ege University Faculty of Sciences, 1992; contbr. articles to profl. jours.; editor Jour. Faculty Sci., 1982-94. Lt. Turkish Army, 1959-60. Govt. The Netherlands scholar, Leiden U., 1964-65. Mem. Turkish Phys. Assn., Turkish History Sci. Soc., Spectroscopy Assn., Cultural & Progress Found. Province Ordu. Islam. Avocation: photography. Home: Hurriyet Cad No 84, Bornova Izmir 35030, Turkey Office: Ege Univ, Fen Fakultesi Fizik Bolumu, Bornova Izmir 35100, Turkey

ERTL, DORIS ELISABETH, anesthesiologist; b. Amberg, Germany, Jan. 24, 1952; d. Josef and Annelies (Eder) E. MD, Ludwig-Maximilians U, Munich, 1977. Intern Hosp. Rotthalmunster, Bavaria, 1978, Hos. Barmherzige Bruder, Munich, 1978-81; anesthesiologist Pasing Hosp., Munich, 1981—. Contbr. articles to profl. publs. Mem. N.Y. Acad. Scis., German Assn. Anesthesiologists. Avocations: travel, golf. Home: Egenhofen 18, 82152 Planegg Germany Office: Hosp Munich-Pasing, Steinerweg 5, 81241 Munich Germany

ERTL, GERHARD, institute director; b. Stuttgart, Germany, Oct. 10, 1936; s. Ludwig and Johanna (Schneider) E.; m. Barbara Maschek; children: Julia Christine, Mathias. Diploma Physics, Tech. U. Stuttgart, 1961; D Natural Scis., Tech. U. Munich, 1965; PhD (hon.), U. Bochum, 1992, U. Munster, 2000. Asst., lectr. Tech. U. Munich, 1965-68; prof. Tech. U. Hannover (Germany), 1968-73, U. Munich, 1973-86; dir. Fritz Haber Inst., Berlin, 1986—; vis. prof. Calif. Inst. Tech., Pasadena, 1976-77, U. Calif., Berkeley, 1981-82. Author books and articles on chemistry and physics of surfaces. Recipient P.W. Emmett award Am. Catalysis Soc., 1979, C.F. Gauss medal Braunschweig Acad. Scis., 1985, Liebig medal German Chem. Soc., 1987, Mittasch medal German Soc. Chem. Engrs., 1990, Leibniz prize German Sci. Found., 1991, Hewlett Packard prize European Phys. Soc., 1992, Japan prize Sci. and Tech. Found. of Japan, 1992, Bunsen medal German Soc. Phys. Chemistry, 1992, Medard W. Welch Award, Am. Vacuum Soc., 1995, Wolf prize Chemistry, Wolf Found., Israel, 1998, Karl Ziegler prize, German Chem. Soc., 1998. Fellow Royal Soc. Edinburgh (hon.); mem. Am. Acad. Arts & Scis. (fgn. hon. mem.). Office: Fritz Haber Inst, Faradayweg 4-6, 14195 Berlin Germany

ERTUR, OMER SELCUKHAN, United Nations official, educator; b. Istanbul, Turkey, July 2, 1944; s. Mustafa Arif and Fatma (Bedia) E.; m. Margaret Rozelle O'Bryan, April 29, 1967 (div. April 1972); 1 child, Suzan; m. Kathleen Ann Palmer, May 28, 1978; 1 child, Adam. BA, Memphis State U., 1970, MA, 1973; PhD, Portland State U., 1978. Urban planner Columbia Region Assn. of Govts., Portland, 1972-74; rsch. assoc. Portland State U., 1974-78; urban planner CH2M-Hill Internat., Saudi Arabia, 1978-81; regional planner UNCHS/Habitat, Nairobi, 1982-84; prof. Iowa State U., Ames, 1981-88; country dir. UNFPA, Sudan, Nepal, 1988-94; resident coord./rep. UN/UNDP, Turkmenistan, 1994-99; resident rep. UNFPA, Vietnam, 1999—; masters program coord. pub. adminstrn. Portland State U., 1974-75; grad. program coord. cmty. and regional planning Iowa State U., 1984-88; urban planning adv. Metropolitan Municipality, Istanbul, Turkey, 1987-88. Author, editor: Population and Human Resources Development in the Sudan, 1994; contbr. articles to profl. jours. Recipient Doctoral Rsch. fellow Clark Found., 1977, Tchg. fellow U. N.-Tokten, 1986. Avocations:

music, reading, walking. Office: UNFPA- Vietnam PO Box 20 New York NY 10163-0020

ERUL, ALI OMER, insurance company executive; b. Phila., Aug. 27, 1964; s. Ömer Mustafa E. and Zeynep (Yazici) Davran; m. Arzu Elif Sakarya, Oct. 28, 1988; 1 child, Cemre. Avocations: reading, driving, trekking.

ERUMSELE, ANDREW AKHIGBE, development policy analyst; b. Auchi, Nigeria, Nov. 18, 1944; came to U.S., 1966; naturalized, 1971; s. Erumsele Bello and Itete (Isadoh) Iyoke; m. Mary Catherine Wimbley, Dec. 6, 1969 (div. 1975); 1 child, Uwadia Alexis; m. Laura Ann Stepanski, Jan. 21, 1987 (div. 1996); children: Ashley Idiagbon, Tristan Iyoke. BA magna cum laude, Loyola U., L.A., 1969; MPA, UCLA, 1971; MA, Am. U., 1974, PhD, 1977. Leadership fellow L.A. County Planning Commn., 1969-70; rsch. fellow UN Inst. for Tng. and Rsch., 1970; mem. staff U.S. Congrl. Commn. on Reorgn. of D.C. Govt., 1972-73; mgmt. and policy analyst U. D.C., Washington, 1973-97, also asst. to dean Coll. Life Scis., asst. to dean Coll. of Arts and Scis., 1994-97; founder, pres. Devel. Analytics, Inc., 1983—; exec. dir. Inst. Nigerian Affairs, 1992—; cons. Internat. City Mgmt. Assn., Orgn. of African Unity, Inst. for Public Adminstrn.; mem. World Affairs Coun., Washington. Spl. corr. for various African newspapers. Univ. scholar Nigerian Govt. scholar UCLA; recipient Hall of Nations award Am. U., Washington, 1972. Mem. Am. Soc. for Pub. Adminstrn., Acad. Polit. Sci., Soc. for Internat. Devel., Am. Soc. for Internat. Law, Pi Gamma Mu. Democrat. Moslem. Office: PO Box 39067 Washington DC 20016-9067

ERVE, RUUD H.G.P. VAN, orthopaedic surgeon; b. Arnhem, Gelderland, The Netherlands, Nov. 1, 1964; s. Dre Van and Bep Van (Kevenaar) E.; m. Jane Van Kerkdyk, Apr. 20, 1990; children: Daphne, Annouck. BA, Cath. U. Nymegen, The Netherlands, 1990; MD, State U. Groningen, The Netherlands, 2000. Resident in orthpaedics Acad. Hosp. Groningen, 1996-2000; orthop. surgeon Deventer Ziekenhuis, The Netherlands, 2000—. Contbr. articles to profl. jours. 1st lt. The Netherlands Mil. Police, 1990-92. Mem. Dutch Orthop. Residents Soc. (bd. dirs. 1997-99), Dutch Orthop. Soc. (ednl. bd. 1997-99). Office: Deventer Hosp. PO Box 5001, 7400GC Deventer The Netherlands

ERVIN, ANTHONY, Olympic athlete; b. Burbank, Calif., May 26, 1981. Recipient Gold medal 50-meter freestyle Sydney Olympics, 2000. Office: USA Swimming 1 Olympic Plz Colorado Springs CO 80909-5746*

ERVIN, BILLY MAXWELL, aerospace executive; b. Dante, Va., July 29, 1933; s. Willie Beldon and Ollie Lowel (Biggs) E.; m. Barbara Frances Walsh, June 27, 1971; 1 child, Honore McDonough; 1 stepchild, Kerry Thompson. BS, U.S. Naval Acad., 1955; grad., Navy Nuclear Power Training, 1961; M in Marine Affairs, U. R.I., 1971; MBA, U. Mass., 1989. Commd. ensign USN, 1955, advanced through grades to capt., 1975; chief engr. aircraft carrier USN, Pacific, 1969-70; destroyer capt. USN, Atlantic/Pacific, 1971-73; project mgr. USN, Washington, 1973-78, head logistics br., 1978-80, head rsch. and devel. br., 1980-82; insp. gen. Europe USN, London, 1982-85; ret. USN, 1985; adminstr. Baystate Eye Care, P.C., Springfield, Mass., 1986-88; mgr. engrng. adminstrn. and planning Kaman Aerospace Corp., Bloomfield, Conn., 1990-92; chief oper. officer Conn. Orthopaedic and Sports Medicine Ctr., Vernon, CT, 1992-97; bus. mgr. engrng. Kaman Aerospace Corp., Bloomfield, 1997—. Decorated Bronze Star; recipient Meritorious Svc. Medal award Pres. of the U.S., 1985. Mem. Naval War Coll. Found., Navy League, St. Andrew's Soc., Clan Irwin Assn. Avocations: antique cars, genealogy. Home: 20 Magnolia Ter Springfield MA 01108-2512 Office: Kaman Aerospace Corp PO Box 2 Bloomfield CT 06002-0002

ERVIN, PATRICK FRANKLIN, nuclear engineer; b. Kansas City, Kans., Aug. 4, 1946; s. James Franklin and Irma Lee (Arnett) E.; m. Rita Jeanne Kimsey, Aug. 12, 1967; children: James, Kevin, Amber. BS in Nuclear Engrng., Kans. State U., 1969, MS in Nuclear Engrng., 1971; postgrad., Northeastern U., 1988. Registered profl. engr., Ill., Colo., Calif., Idaho, Wash.; cert. paleontology paraprofl., Colo. Reactor health physicist Dept. Nuclear Engrng. Kans. State U., Manhattan, 1968-69, rsch. asst. Dept. Nuclear Engrng., 1969-72, sr. reactor operator, temp. facility dir. Dept. Nuclear Engrng., 1970-72; system test engr. Commonwealth Edison Co., Zion, Ill., 1972-73, 73-74; shift foreman Commonwealth Edison Co., Zion, 1973, shift foreman with sr. reactor operator lic., 1974-76, prin. engr., 1976-77, acting operating engr., 1977; tech. staff supr. Commonwealth Edison Co., Byron, Ill., 1977-81; lead test engr. Stone & Webster Engrng. Corp., Denver, 1982-83, project mgr., 1982-95, ops. svcs. supr., 1982-86, asst. engrng. mgr., 1986-89, cons. engr., 1989-94; sr. cons., 1994-96; decommisioning program mgr. Rocky Flats Closure project Kaiser-Hill Co., Denver, 1996—. Contbr. articles to profl. jours. Served with U.S. Army N.G., 1971-77. Mem. Am. Nuclear Soc. (Nat. and Colo. chpts.), Am. Nat. Standards Inst. (working group on containment leakage testing). Independent. Roman Catholic. Avocations: paleontology, hunting, fishing, camping, stamp collecting. Home: 2978 S Bahama St Aurora CO 80013-2340 Office: Kaiser Hill Co 10808 Highway 93 # B Golden CO 80403-8200

ERWA, EL-FATIH MOHAMED AHMED, diplomat. Rep. to UN, Govt. of Sudan. Office: Permanent Mission of Sudan 655 3rd Ave Ste 500-510 New York NY 10017-5617

ERWIN, ALEXANDER, federal official; b. Jan. 17, 1948. B in Econs. with honors, U. Natal, South Africa, 1978. Lectr. dept. econs. U. of Natal, 1971-78; trade unionist, 1977-93, economist; dep. min. Ministry of Fin., 1994-96; min. Ministry of Trade and Industry, Pretoria, South Africa, 1996—; mem. Inst. Indsl. Edn., 1973-75; vis. lectr. Ctr. for So. African Studies, U. York, 1974-75; gen. sec. Trade Union Adv. and Coordinating Coun., 1977-79, Fedn. South African Trade Unions, 1979-83; nat. edn. office Nat. Union Metalworkers, 1988-93; interim exec. mem. African Nat. Congress, So. Natal Region, 1989, br. exec. mem., Western Areas Br., 1990-91; COSATU rep. on Nat. Econ. Forum; pres. UN Conf. on Trade and Devel., 1996-2000. Editor African Nat. Congress's Reconstruction and Devel. Program. African Nat. Congress. Office: Pvt Bag X274, 11th Fl Prinsloo St, Pretoria 0001, South Africa

ERWIN, GOODLOE Y., physician, land company executive; b. Athens, Ga., June 14, 1919; s. Howell Cobb and Llucy Gratten (Yancey) E.; m. Patricia Graham, Sept. 27, 1947; children: Alexander Wales, Charles Graham, Leslie Erwin Moose, Catharine. BS in Chemistry, U. Ga., 1940; MD, Emory U., 1943. Diplomate Am. Bd. Internal Medicine. Intern Grady Meml. Hosp., Atlanta, 1944; resident in medicine VA Hosp., Salt Lake City, 1947-48; pvt. practice internal medicine St. Marys Hosp., Athens Ctrl. Hosp., 1948-87; pres. Erwin Land Co., Athens, 1987—; dir. respiratory therapy dept. Athens Gen. Hosp., 1963-75, dir. CCU, 1965-70. Pres. Athens Hist. Soc., 1992-94; bd. dirs. Athens Cmty. Chest, 1950-60. 1st lt. M.C., U.S. Army, 1944-46, ETO. Fellow Am. Coll. Chest Physicians, Am. Coll. Cardiology; mem. Ga. Heart Assn. (pres. 1957-58, Disting. Svc. award 1964), Ga. Lung Assn. (pres. 1973-74), Ga. Soc. Internal Medicine (pres.), Phi Beta Kappa, Alpha Omega Alpha. Baptist. Avocations: genealogy, golf, swimming. Home: 354 Milledge Cir Athens GA 30606-4334

ERWIN, JOAN LENORE, artist, educator; b. Berkeley, Calif., Feb. 12, 1932; d. Ralph Albert and Dorothy Christine (Wuhrman) Potter; m. Byron W. Crider, Jan. 28, 1956 (div. May 1975); children: Susan Lynne Crider Adams, Gayle Leann Crider; m. Joseph G. Erwin Jr., May 28, 1976; children: Terry, Ray, Steve, Tim. BS, U. So. Calif., 1954; MS in Sch. Adminstrn., Pepperdine U., 1975. Cert. tchr., Calif.; registered occupational therapist, Calif. Occupational therapist Calif. State Hosp., Camarillo, 1955-56, Harlan Shoemaker Sch., San Pedro, Calif., 1956-57; tchr. Norwalk (Calif.) Sch. Dist., 1957-59, Tustin (Calif.) Sch. Dist., 1966-68, Garden Grove (Calif.) Sch. Dist., 1968-92; freelance artist Phelan, Calif., 1976—; comml. artist Morningstar Creations, Fullerton, Calif., 1982-92; substitute tchr. Snowline Sch. Dist., Phelan, Calif., 1994—; owner, artist Plumfrog Creations, Phelan, 2000—; artist Y.U.G.O., Los Alamitos, 1977-87; organizer 34th Annual Open Internat. Exbhn. Art, San Bernardino County Mus., 1999. Pet portrait artist, U.S. and Eng., 1978-85; author, artist Biblical coloring books, 1985-90; exhibited in group shows San Bernardino County Mus., Redlands, Calif., Riverside Art Mus. Bd. dirs. San Bernardino County Mus., Fine Arts Inst. Calif. Elks scholar, 1952-53; grantee Ford Found., 1957-58, Mentor Tchr. Program, 1986. Republican. Baptist. Avocations: gardening, travel. Home: 10080 Monte Vista Rd Phelan CA 92371-8371

ERWIN, ROBERT BARTLEY, insurance agent, retired; b. Urbana, Ohio, Apr. 6, 1936; s. William E. and Asenath A. (Barger) E.; m. Nancy Lou LeFever, Nov. 16, 1956; children: Charyl, Linda, Jeffrey. Grad. high sch., Urbana, Ohio. Cert. life underwriter. Retail sales mgmt. G.C. Murphy Co., Bellefontaine, Ohio, 1954-56, Dee's, Bellefontaine, 1956-60; ins. agt. Nationwide Ins., Bellefontaine, 1960-97; retired, 1997; Pres., dir., Faith Rsch. Inc., Jewett, Ohio, 1990—; pres. OALU/NALU, Bellefontaine, 1985—; speaker in field. Past pres., endowment chair Tecumseh coun. Boy Scouts Am., Springfield, 1990; campaign chmn., pres. United Way Logan County, Bellefontaine, 1979-80; chmn. exec. com. Logan County Rep. Party. Mem. Nat. Assn. Life Underwriters, Masons, York Rite, Scottich Rite, Shriners, Elks, Kiwanis (past pres., past lt. gov.). Methodist. Avocations: boating, fishing, golf. Office: Erwin Ins Agy 143 E Chillicothe Ave Bellefontaine OH 43311-1957

ERYOMIN, ALEXANDER NIKOLAEVICH, bio-organic chemistry researcher; b. Mogilev region, Belarus, Mar. 27, 1947; s. Nikolayi Fedorovich and Pavlina Albertovna (Grinfeld) E.; m. Maria Mikhailovna Artemochkina, Oct. 29, 1967 (div. Feb. 1995); children: Alexander, Dmitriy. Degree in Biology, Byelorussian State U., Minsk, Belarus, 1971-76; PhD, Inst. Bio-organic Chemistry, Minsk, Belarus, 1980, D in Chemistry, 1993. Cert. sci. rschr. Sci. collaborator Inst. Bio-organic Chemistry, Byelorussian Acad. Scis., 1976-85, sr. sci. collaborator, 1985-94, leading sci. collaborator, 1994—. Contbr. articles to profl. jours. 2d lt. Belarus Mil., 1967-69. Avocations: philathelia, theosophy. Home: Raduzhnaya St 6-55, 220020 Minsk Belarus Office: Nat Acad Scis Inst Bio-org Chem, Kuprevicha St 5/2, 220141 Minsk Belarus

ERZHEMSKY, GEORGE L., conductor, psychologist; b. Petrograd, Russia, Dec. 24, 1918; s. Lev D. Rafalovich and Aleksandra N. Erzhemskaya; m. Tatiana N. Lavrova, May 12, 1953; 1 child, Marina. Diploma in piano, Leningrad Conservatoire, 1941, diploma in conducting, 1955, DA, 1973; D Psychol. Scis., St. Petersburg State U., 1994. Concertmaster Bashkir Opera Ballet and Theatre, Ufa, Russia, 1944-45, chief condr., 1953-54; chief condr. Leningrad Theatre of Musical Comedy, 1945-46; condr. Acad. Maly Opera and Ballet Theater, Leningrad, 1946-73; prof. Leningrad Conservatoire, 1973-83, St. Petersburg U. Humanities and Social Scis., 1995—; performing condr. with various symphony orchs. and opera theatres, Moscow, St. Petersburg, Volgograd, Rostov-on-don, Ulianovsk, Irkutsk, Russia, 1983—. Condr., dir. new prodn. opera Aihylu, 1954 (prize and diploma Ministry of Culture, 1954), over 100 opera and ballet performances; author: Psychology of Conducting Practice, 1983, Regularities and Paradoxes of Conducting Practice (in Russian), 1993, Psychological Paradoxes of Conducting, 1998. Comdr. Russian armed forces, 1942-44. Recipient 9 Govt. medals Govt. of Russia, 1945-98, Order of Great Patriotic War, Govt. of Russia, 1945; named Honored Art Worker, Russia, 1953, Hon. Academician, Internat. Acad. Psychol. Scis., 1994, Internat. Acmeologic Acad., 1997, Baltic Pedagogical Academy. Mem. Russian Theatre Soc., N.Y. Acad. Scis. Avocations: writing books and research articles. Home: 28/11 Novgorodskaya St F14, 193124 Saint Petersburg Russia Office: St Petersburg U Humanities, 15 Fuchika St, 192238 Saint Petersburg Russia

ESAKI, LEO, physicist, foundation executive; b. Osaka, Japan, Mar. 12, 1925; came to U.S., 1960; s. Soichiro and Niyoko (Ito) E.; m. Masako Kondo, May, 31, 1986; children from previous marriage: Nina Yvonne, Anna Eileen, Eugene Leo. B.S., U. Tokyo, 1947, Ph.D., 1959. With Sony Corp., Japan, 1956-60; with Thomas J. Watson Research Center, IBM, Yorktown Heights, N.Y., 1960-92; IBM fellow Thomas J. Watson Research Center, IBM, 1967-92, mgr. device research, 1965-92; dir. IBM-Japan, 1975-92; pres. U. Tsukuba, Ibaraki, Japan, 1992-98; chmn. Sci. and Tech. Found. of Ibaraki, 1998—; pres. Shibaura Inst. of Tech., Tokyo, ach, 2000—. Recipient Stuart Ballantine medal Franklin Inst., 1961, Japan Acad. award, 1965, Nobel prize in physics, 1973; decorated Order of Culture Govt. of Japan, 1974, Grand Cordon Order of Rising Sun, 1998. Fellow IEEE (Morris N. Liebman Meml. prize 1961, Medal of Honor 1991), Am. Phys. Soc. (councillor-at-large 1971-74, internat. prize for new materials 1985, Japan prize, 1998), Japan Phys. Soc., Am. Vacuum Soc. (bd. dirs. 1973-74); mem. NAS (fgn. assoc.), NAE (fgn. assoc.), Am. Acad. Arts and Scis., Am. Philos. Soc., Max-Planck Gesellschaft, Russian Acad. Scis. (fgn.), Academia Nacional de Ingenieria Mex. (corr.), Japan Acad. Achievements include discovery of Esaki tunnel diode, 1957, pioneering research of semiconductor superlattices and quantum wells. Home: 2484 Uenomuro, Tsukuba Ibaraki 305-0023, Japan Office: Shibaura Inst of Tech, Minato-ku, Tokyo 108-8548, Japan also: Tsukuba Internat Congress, 2-20-3 Takezono, Tsukuba Ibraaki 305-0032, Japan also: PO Box 851 Katonah NY 10536-0851

ESASHI, YOHJI, plant physiologist, environmental biologist; b. Sendai, Miyagi, Japan, Mar. 28, 1933; s. Katsutaro and Yukiko (Takahashi) E.; m. Setsuko Tsukamoto, June 10, 1958; children: Mari, Takuji. Bachelors degree, Tohoku U., Sendai, 1955, Masters degree, 1957, PhD, 1961. Cert. biologist. Tech. ofcl. Tohoku U., Sendai, 1960-62, asst., 1962-69, assoc. prof., 1969-74, prof., 1974-95, hon. prof., 1995—; cons. Dainihon Ink & Chems. Inc., Sakura, Japan, 1985-96, FAO, Rome, 1989-91; commr. Sci. Coun. Japan, Tokyo, 1981-87; head Japan Wood Seed Rsch. Inst., 1996—. Author 12 books; contbr. articles to profl. jours.; patentee in field. Commr. Nat. Broadcasting Soc., Sendai, 1990. Mem. Japanese Soc. Plant Physiologists (councilor 1973-96), Bot. Soc. Japan (councilor 1989-95). Avocation: Go. Home: Aobaku Ohtemachi, 980-0805 Sendai Miyagi, Japan Office: Tohoku U, Gikaigan 10, 290 Ichihara Chiba 290-0058, Japan

ESCAF, SAFWAN J., surgery educator, urology educator; b. Alepo, Syria, June 28, 1951; arrived in Spain; s. Ihsan H. Escaf and Kauzida F. Barmidah; m. Conchita M. Robles, July 18, 1953; children: Eduardo, Andrés. MD, Coll. Medicine, Oviedo, Spain, 1979, PhD, 1990. Urology resident Ctrl. Hosp., Oviedo, 1980-85, chief sect. urology, 1994-97; attending urologist San Agustin Hosp., Aviles, Spain, 1985-93; prof. surgery, urology Ctrl. Hosp., Coll. Medicine, Oviedo, 1994—. Contbr. articles to profl. jours. Mem. European Urol. Assn., Am. Urol. Assn., Spanish Urol. Assn. Office: Coll Medicine Oviedo Univ, Julian Claveria 6, 33006 Oviedo Asturias, Spain

ESCALANTE-RAMIREZ, VLADIMIR, astronomer; b. Mexico City, May 9, 1958; s. Hernan and Estela (Ramirez) E. BS in Physics, Nat. U. Mexico, Mexico City, 1982; PhD in Astronomy, Harvard U., 1988. Assoc. prof. Nat. U. Mex., Inst. Astronomy, Mexico City, 1988—. Contbr. articles to profl. jours. Recipient Gabino Barreda medal, Nat. U. Mex., 1982. Mem. Am. Phys. Soc., Fedn. Am. Scientists, Mexican Soc. Physics. Office: Nat U Mex Inst Astronomy, AP Postal 70-264, 04510 Mexico City Mexico

ESCALET, FRANK DIAZ, art gallery owner, artist, educator; b. Ponce, P.R., Mar. 16, 1930; s. Frank Thillet and Concepcion Rodriquez (Diaz) E.; m.Shirley Leslie Fanner, Sept. 29, 1953 (div. Aug., 1955); children: Judith Alicia, Sudan Edith Escalet Barry; m. Marjorie Janet Gaydash-Huebner, July 19, 1964; 1 child, Frank Daniel (dec.). Owner, operator Talent Shop, N.Y.C., 1955-58, House of Escalet, N.Y.C., 1958-71, Pandora's Box, Eastport, Maine, 1971-73, Cobbler's Bench Art Gallery, Pembroke, Maine, 1973-82, House of Escalet Gallery, Kennebunkport, Maine, 1982-84, House of Escalet Studios, Kennebunkport, 1984—; tchr. leathercraft Pasamaquoddy Reservation, Perry, Maine, 1971-72, Vocat. Sch. for Retarded Children, Calais, Maine, 1972-73. One-man traveling show Czechoslovakia, Russia, Poland, Yugoslavia, Hungary, Ukraine, 1991—; represented in permanent collections at Naprstkovo Mus., Prague, Union of Artists, Moscow, Bratslavia Primitive Mus., Slovakia, Frydek-Mistek Mus. No. Moravia, Museo Chicano, Phoenix, S.E. Tex. Art Mus., Beaumont, Arch. M. Huntington Gallery, Austin, Tex., Housatonic Mus., Bridgeport, Conn., Orgn. of Am. States Art Mus., Washington, Marywald(N.Y.) Sisters Ctr., Mus. City N.Y., 1998; featured on pub. TV, 1978, 82, 89; works in permanent collection Mus. City of N.Y., Ellen Noel Mus. Art of Permian Basin, Odessa, Tex.; artist: Song and Dance Man acrylic, 1996. With US Air Force, 1947-54. Recipient numerous internat. and U.S. awards. Avocations: photography, antiques, gardening, traveling, reading. Home and Office: House of Escalet Studios PO Box 26 13 Fletcher St Kennebunk ME 04043-6705

ESCARON, PIERRE CAMILLE, engineering executive; b. Tours, France, Jan. 13, 1937; s. Paul André and Madeleine Berthe (Fouché) E.; m. Marianne Virginia Mattucci, July 25, 1964; children: Anne, Patrick, Claire. BA, Wash. State U., 1962; Engr., ECAM, Cath. Sch. Arts and Trad, Lyons, France, 1960. Quality mgr. Schlumberger, Houston, 1985-86, mfg. engrng. mgr., 1986-88; ops. mgr. Schlumberger, Oxnard, Calif., 1988-93; mfg. mgr. Daniel, Larbert, Scotland, 1993-94; ops. mgr. Weston, Farnborough, Eng., 1994-96; divsn. mgr. Maulde & Renou, Saint Quentin, France, 1996-97; cons. Schlumberger, Agoura Hills, Calif., 1993. Translator: Electronics Book, 1962; patentee in oilfield equipment and instrumentation. Pres. Alliance Francaise, Houston, 1983-84. Lt. French Mil., 1962-64. Mem. ASME. Avocations: painting, computers, photography, biking, skiing. Home: 27525 Freetown Ln Agoura Hills CA 91301-3560

ESCARRAZ, ENRIQUE, III, lawyer; b. Evergreen Park, Ill., Aug. 30, 1944; s. Enrique Jr. and Mary Ellen (Bandy) E.; children from previous marriage; Erin Christine, Martina Mary; m. Patricia Jane Escarraz; children: Sarah Ellen, James Lee, Jason F. BA, U. Fla., 1966, JD, 1968. Bar: Fla. 1969, U.S. Dist. Ct. (so. and mid. dists.) Fla. 1969, U.S. Ct. Appeals (5th cir.) 1971, U.S. Ct. Appeals (11th cir.) 1981. VISTA atty. Community Legal Counsel, Chgo., 1968-69; mng. atty. Fla. Rural Legal Services, Ft. Myers, 1969-71; pvt. practice law St. Petersburg, Fla., 1971-82, 85-87, 88—; ptnr. Anderson & Escarraz, St. Petersburg, 1982-85; asst. gen. counsel U. South Fla., 1987-88; assoc. James L. Eskald Law Office, Largo, Fla., 1988; part-time atty. Pub. Defender's Office Fla. 6th Cir., St. Petersburg, 1973-74; bd. dirs. Gulf Coast Legal Svcs., Inc., 1989—, pres., 1994-96. Vol. Cmty. Law Prog., Inc.; coord. James B. Sanderlin for Judge, Pinellas County, Fla., 1972-76; mem. ACLU Legal Panel, St. Petersburg, 1972—; cooperating atty. NAACP Legal Panel, St. Petersburg, 1972—; cooperating atty. NAACP Legal Def. Edn. Funds, Inc., N.Y.C., 1973—; pres. Creative Care, Inc., Clearwater, Fla., 1974-80; mem. allocations com. United Way, Pinellas County, 1976, 1978-81; pres., treas. Cmty. Youth Svcs., Inc., St. Petersburg, 1977-82; co-chmn. Blue Ribbon Com. Pinellas County Dem. Exec. Com., 1977-82; mem. Fla. HRS Dist. V Adv. Coun., Pinellas County, 1982, St. Petersburg Human Rels. Rev. Bd., 1984, 90—, St. Petersburg Adult Cmty. Band, 1989—, Greater St. Petersburg Second Time Around Marching Band, 1990-92; mem. adv. bd. Jacquelyn Elvera Hodges Johnson Fund, 1990—. Mem. ABA, ATLA, FBA, Nat. Assn. Social Security Claimant Reps., Pinellas County Trial Lawyers Assn., St. Petersburg Bar Assn. (pro bono com. 1988, 95—), Bayshore Runners Club, Greater Pinellas County Dem. Club (sec.-treas. 1989-97, bd. dirs. 1997—), Road Runners Club Am. Office: 2121 5th Ave N Saint Petersburg FL 33713-8013 also: PO Box 847 Saint Petersburg FL 33731-0847

ESCASSUT, ALAIN PAUL, mathematician, educator; b. Gouzon, France, Nov. 18, 1943; s. Alfred and Marie-Louise (Monnet) E. Lic. in Math., U. Bordeaux, France, 1965, D of State, 1972. Asst. prof. U. Bordeaux, 1969-84, assoc. prof., 1984-87; prof. U. Blaise Pascal, Clermont-Ferrand, France, 1987—; charge d'enseignment U. Paris Sud, Orsay, France, 1973-74; vis. asst. prof. Princeton (N.J.) U., 1981. Author: Contbr. articles to profl. jours. Mem. Am. Math. Soc., Soc. Math. de France. Home: 286 Rue du Montant, 63110 Beaumont France Office: U Blaise Pascal Lab de Math Pure, Les Cézeaux, 63177 Aubiere France

ESCHE, CLEMENS, dermatologist, immunologist; b. Berlin, May 12, 1966; came to U.S., 1996; s. Dieter and Ingrid (Pindt) E. MD, U. Cologne, Germany, 1994. Resident dept. dermatology U. Kiel, Germany, 1993-94, U. Berlin, 1994-95, U. Düsseldorf, Germany, 1995-96; rsch. assoc. U. Pitts. Cancer Inst., 1996-2000, instr., 2000, asst. prof., 2000—. Recipient Ausbildungsstipendium Es 132/1-1 Deutsche Forschungsgemeinschaft, 1996-98, ADO-Vortrags prize German Dermatol. Oncology Assn., 1998, Presl. award Soc. Biol. Therapy, 1998, Travel award PsychoNeuroImmunology Rsch. Soc., 1999; Advanced Polymer Sys. rsch. fellow Derm. Found., 1999-2000. Mem. Soc. for Investigative Dermatology (Albert M. Kligman award 1998, 2000), Am. Assn. Cancer Rsch., Am. Assn. Immunologists. Achievements include finding that tumors induce apoptosis in dendritic cells, that cytokine interleukin-12 induces accumulation of dendritic cells in vivo, and that cytokine flt3 ligand inhibits growth in murine melanoma and lymphoma. Avocation: flute. Fax: 801-912-5342. E-mail: ce@usa.com. Home: 12 Oakland Sq Pittsburgh PA 15213-4116 Office: U Pitts Cancer Inst 300 Kaufmann Bldg 3471 5th Ave Pittsburgh PA 15213-3215

ESCHENMOSER, ALBERT, chemist; b. Erstfeld, Aug. 5, 1925; s. Alfons and Johanna (Oesch) E.; m. Elizabeth Baschnonga, 1954; 3 children. Dr. Nat. Sci., Swiss Fed. Inst. Tech., 1951; student Collegium Altdorf, Kantonsschule St. Gallen, ETH Zurich; Dr.rer.nat. (hon.), U. Fribourg, 1966; DSc (hon.), U. Chgo., 1970, U. Edinburgh, 1979, U. Bologna, 1989, U. Frankfurt, 1990, U. Strasbourg, 1991, Harvard U., 1993, Scripps Rsch. Inst., La Jolla, 2000. Privatdozent organic chemistry Swiss Fed. Inst. Tech., 1956, assoc. prof., 1960, prof. organic chemistry, 1965; prof. Skaggs Inst. Chem. Biology Scripps Rsch. Inst., La Jolla, Calif., 1996. Contbr. articles to profl. jours. Recipient Kern award Swiss Fed. Inst. Tech., 1949, Werner award Swiss Chem. Soc., 1956, Ruzicka award Swiss Fed. Inst. Tech., 1958, Fritzsche award Am. Chem. Soc., 1966, Marcel Benoist prize Swiss Govt., 1973, R.A. Welch award in Chemistry, Houston, 1974, Kirkwood medal Yale, 1976, A.W.V. Hofmann-Denkmunze, GDCh., 1976, Dannie Heinemann prize Akademie der Wissenschaften Göttingen, 1977, Davy medal Royal Soc. London, 1978, Tetrahedron prize Pergamon Press, 1981, G. Kenner award U. Liverpool, 1982, Arthur C. Cope award Am. Chem. Soc., 1984, Wolf prize for chemistry, Wolf Found., Israel, 1986, Cothenius medal Leopoldina Halle, 1991, Orden Pour le mérite fur Wissenschaften und Künste, 1992, Oesterreichisches Ehrenzeichen für Wissenschaft und Kunst, 1993, Nakanishi prize Chem. Soc. Japan, 1998, Paracelsus prize Swiss Chem. Soc., 1999. Mem. Am. Acad. Arts and Scis. (fgn.), Nat. Acad. Scis. U.S. (fgn. assoc.), Akademie der Wissenschaften (corr. mem. Göttingen), Deutsche Akademie der Naturforscher Leopoldina (Halle), Royal Soc. (fgn. London), Pontifical Acad. (Vatican), Acad. Europe (London), Croatian Acad. Sci. Arts (corr. mem. Zagreb). Home: Bergstrasse 9, 8700 Kuesnacht Switzerland Office: ETH Laboratory Oraganic Chemistry, Universitaetstr 16, CH 8092 Zurich Switzerland

ESCHER, ROBERT F.A., hematologist, researcher; b. Sion, Switzerland, June 4, 1965; s. Rudolf and Augusta (Pfammatter) E.; m. Geneviève Delaloye, Dec. 5, 1992; children: Anaïs, Cyril, Chloé. MD, U. Berne, Switzerland, 1992; postgrad., U. Zurich, Switzerland, 1997. Med. asst. U. Berne, 1993-96; postgrad. fellow Univ. Hosp. Berne, 1996-97, asst. in hematology, 1998—. Patenee recombinant anti-glycoprotein IIb/IIIa autoantibodies, 1997. Lt. sanitary troups Swiss armed forces, 1997—. Recipient Travel award Am. Soc. Hematology, 1996, 97, 98. Mem. AAAS, Verband Schweizer Assistenz-und Oberärzte, Foederatio Medicorum Helveticorum. Avocations: piano, jogging. Home: Dufourstr 41, 3005 Berne Switzerland Office: Univ Hosp, 3010 Berne Switzerland

ESCLOPÉ, ALAIN, foreign diplomat; b. Claira, France, May 18, 1942. Mem. European Parliament, 1999—, mem. com. on regional policy, transport and tourism, substitute com. on culture, youth, edn., the media and sport; mem. Group for a Europe of Democracies and Diversities; mem. delegation for relations with the mem. states of ASEAN, S.E. Asia and the Republic of Korea. *

ESCOBAR, FREDY GUSTAVO, oil company executive; b. Cochabamba, Bolivia, July 6, 1951; s. Raul and Celina (Rosas) E.; m. Frida Ugarte; children: Raul, Gustavo, Daniela. Degree, Coll. La Salle, 1970; BS, U. Mex., 1975, MS, 1981. Chief Petroleum Engrng. Dept., Santa Cruz, Bolivia, 1986-88; dir. Nat. Petroleum Engrng. Direction, Santa Cruz, 1988-89; advisor, pres., mgr. Nat. Oil Co., Santa Cruz, 1990-93; from dir. exploration & exploitation to v.p. Nat. Oil Co., Santa Cruz, La Paz, Bolivia, 1993-97; CEO, gen. mgr. Canadian Energy Enterprises, Oil and Gas Co., Santa Cruz, 1998—; cons. Petrolex Oil & Gas, Santa Cruz, 1989-93. Avocations: soccer, basketball. Home: Calle Senda #50, Santa Cruz Bolivia Office: TPFB, Calle Bueno #185 PO Box 401, La Paz Bolivia

ESCOTET, MIGUEL-ANGEL, psychologist, educator; b. Leon, Spain, Mar. 27; came to U.S., 1967; s. Miguel and Mercedes (Alvarez) E.; m. Martha Ardila, Dec. 21, 1963; 1 child, Marta I. Student, Poly. Zulia, Madrid, 1958-60; lic. in clin. psychology, Javeriana U., Bogota, Colombia,

1964; MA in Psychology, Edn., U. Tex., 1969; PhD in Psychology, Rsch., U. Nebr., 1972; D (hon.), Maran U., Brazil; hon. degree, Palermo U., Buenos Aires. Acad. dean U. Oriente, Cumana, Venezuela, 1970-72; pvt. practice Miami, Madrid, Caracas, 1972-93; assoc. prof. Fort Lewis Coll., Durango, Colo., 1972-74; sub-sec. edn. Min. Edn., Caracas, Venezuela, 1974-76; v.p. Open U. Venezuela, Caracas, 1976-81; vis. prof. Fla. Internat. U., Miami, 1981-83, prof., dir. IIDE grad., 1993—; sec. gen. Orgn. Iberoam. States, Madrid, 1983-88; pres. Iberam. U., Salamanca, Spain, 1988-91; spl. adv. UNESCO, Paris, 1991-93; cons. UNESCO, Paris, 1976—, World Bank/Internat. Bank, Washington, 1976-82; adv. bd. UNESCO Higher Edn., Paris, 1992—. Author: Learning for the Future, 1993, University and Future, 1996, The End of the University, 1997, Auto-Evaluacion Universitaria, 1998; editor: Cultural and Social Foundations of Education, 1997. Pres. The Escotet Found., 1997—. Recipient Andres Bello Gold award Pres. Venezuela, 1986, Gold medal Orgn. Iberoam. States, 1988. Mem. Am. Psychol. Assn., Latin Am. Assn. Edn. (v.p. 1991—), Latin Am. Assn. Psychology (pres. 1986-90), Comparative Internat. Edn. Soc., Club Rome. Avocations: chess, cycling, jai-lai, ecology. Office: Fla Internat U Zeb 345A Univ Park Miami FL 33199-0001

ESCOTT, SHOOLAH HOPE, microbiologist; b. Stamford, Conn., May 20, 1952; d. Robert R. and Fanny (Levy) E.; m. Joseph J. Sulmar, Sept. 6, 1992. Cert. med. tech., St. Vincent's Hosp., Bridgeport, Conn., 1974; BS, U. Conn., 1974; MS, Northeastern U., Boston, 1985. Cert. med. technologist. Clin. lab. scientist NCA, 1976; med. technologist St. Elizabeth's Hosp., Boston, 1976, Harvard U. Health Svcs., Cambridge, Mass., 1976-79; med. technologist microbiology lab. New Eng. Deaconess Hosp., Boston, 1979-84; supr. microbiology Norwood (Mass.) Hosp., 1984-87; adminstrv. supr. microbiology labs. Med. Ctr. Ctrl. Mass., Worcester, 1991-96; supr. microbiology lab. Worcester Meml. Hosp., Worcester, 1987-91; mgr. microbiology Meml. Hosp., 1996-98; regional coord. northeast office Nat. Lab. Tng. Network, Boston, 1998—. Named Nat. Merit Scholar, 1970; grantee, 1970. Mem. Am. Soc. Clin. Pathologists, Am. Soc. for Microbiology, Am. Soc. for Microbiology, N.E. Assn. for Clin. Microbiology and Infectious Disease (bd. dirs. Mass. chpt. 1989-91, 99-2000, treas. 1991-93, pres.-elect 1993-94, pres. 1994-95, past pres. 1995-96). Achievements include study of parasites of South East Asian refugees; the culturing of genital mycoplasmas in low birth weight neonates and poster at Nat. ASM on C.Difficile toxin detection, poster at Nat. ASM on premier EHEC Kit for shiga-toxin producing e-coli. Avocation: travelling in Europe. Office: NE Office NLTN St Lab Inst 305 South St Boston MA 02130-3515 Address: 3 Viles Rd Lexington MA 02421-5515

ESCOURROU, GISELE MARIE, geography educator; b. Suresnes, France, Apr. 11, 1933; d. Hubert Eugene Levasseur and Marie Louise Prodhomme; m. Pierre Louis Escourrou, Sept. 3, 1960; 1 child, Nicole. Superior, U. Paris (France) Sorbonne, 1959, agregation, 1960, doctor, 1967; doctor, U. Paris (France) Sorbonne, 1975. Prof. Lycee, Caen, France, 1960-63, Corbeil, France, 1963-67; asst. Faculte de Lettres, Paris, 1967-70; maitre asst. Paris (France) IV Sorbonne, 1970-76; prof. Paris VIII, St. Denis, France, 1976-86; prof. Paris (France) Sorbonne, 1986-93, prof. emeritus, 1993; dir. Ctr. de Climatologie et d'Hydrologie Appliquees, Paris; mem. Jury Agregation, Paris, 1987-91; pres. Com. of Climatology, Paris, 1988-92. Author: Climatologie Pratique, 1978, Climat et Environnement, 1980, Le Climat de la France, 1982, Le Climat et la Ville, 1991, Transports, Contraintes Climatogies et Pollutions, 1996. Named officer Palmes Academiques, 1985. Roman Catholic. Office: Inst Geography, 191 rue St Jacques, 75005 Paris France

ESCRIBANO-MARTINEZ, JULIO, molecular biologist; b. Albaceie, Spain, May 25, 1962; s. Julio Escribano-Sajardo and Maria-Juana Martinez-Denia; m. Marieta Alfaro-Aroca, June 27, 1992; children: Marta, Alicia. BS, U. Complutense, Madrid, 1988, PhD, 1992. Assoc. rschr. U. Castilla-La Mancha, Albacete, Spain, 1994-95, assoc. prof., 1995—. Contbr. articles to profl. jours. Pre-doctoral fellow Ramon y Cajal Hosp., Madrid, 1988-92, postdoctoral fellow Yale U., New Haven, 1992-94. Mem. Spanish Biochem. Soc., Assn. Rsch. in Vision and Ophthalmology, Spanish Genetics Soc. Home: Alcalde Martinez de la Ossa, 02001 Albacete Spain Office: Inst Desarrollo Regional, Facultad de Mediciua, Campus Univ, 02071 Albacete Spain

ESCUDERO, JUAN, solicitor; b. Torrelavega, Spain, Apr. 13, 1967; s. Eleuterio Escudero and Margarita Herreros. Lic., U. Liège, Belgium, 1991; diplome d'etudes superieures Européennes, U. Nancy, France, 1993, diplome d'etudes approfondies, 1993. Bar: Madrid, Spain; practicing solicitor. Lawyer Membrillera & Rodriguez Molnar, Madrid, 1995-97; ptnr. Estudio Juridico Almagro, Madrid, 1997—. Mem. Internat. Bar Assn. (com. bus. law sect.). Avocations: skiing, travel, tennis, horse riding. Office: Estudio Juridico Almagro, Consuegra, 3, E-28036 Madrid Spain

ESFANDIARY, DARA SADIGH, information technology executive; b. Tehran, Iran, July 7, 1964; s. Mohsen Sadigh and Mary (Nieradka) E.; 1 child, Lily Veronica. BS, George Washington U., 1990. Asst. dir. budget Sch. Gov. and Bus. Admintrn. George Washington U., Washington, 1986-87; software programming, systems analysis cons. Davison Assocs., Washington, 1987-89; sr. computer specialist Orkand Corp., Washington, 1989-91; dir. devel. Elm Svcs. Corp., Rockville, Md., 1991-92; v.p., chief info. officer Software Engring. Solutions Corp., Washington, 1992-94; ADP sect. leader U.S. Dept. of Interior/Fish Wildlife Svc., Washington, 1994—; info. sys. and bus. tech. cons. SES Corp., Washington, 1985—, leadership tng., 1996—, knowledge discovery and data visualization cons., 1997—; parliamentary procedure trainer, pres. Free & Wild Club Toastmasters Internat., Washington, 1995. Contbr. articles to profl. jours. Participant Re-enactment of Laying U.S. Capital/Cornerstone, Washington, 1995. Mem. IEEE, Am. Mgmt. Assn., Mensa, Toastmasters Internat. (chpt. pres. 1995, head fraternal orgn. 1996-97). Avocations: scuba diving, tennis, Tae Kwon Do, skiing, opera. Home: 4401 Sedgwick St NW Washington DC 20016-2713 Office: Fish and Wildlife Svc 4401 Fairfax Dr Ste 140 Arlington VA 22203-1610

ESHAGIAN, JOSEPH, ophthalmologist; b. Iran, Mar. 15, 1951; s. Ebrahim and Touran (Monasebian) E. BS with honors, U. Mich., 1971; MD, SUNY, Syracuse, 1975. Diplomate Am. Bd. Ophthalmology. Intern U. Mich. Hosp., Ann Arbor, 1975-76; resident in ophthalmology U. Iowa Hosp., Iowa City, 1976-79, assoc. dept. ophthalmology, 1979; practice medicine specializing in ophthalmology, L.A., 1980—. Contbr. articles to med. jours. Mem. AMA, Am. Acad. Neurology, Assn. Rsch. in Vision and Ophthalmology., Am. Assn. Ophthalmology, Contact Lens Assn. Ophthalmologits, Med. Eye Svcs. Calif., Am. Acad. Ophthalmology, Calif. Med. Assn., Los Angeles County Med. Assn., Am. Soc. Contemporary Ophthalmology, Internat. Glaucoma Congress. Office: 1211 N Vermont Ave Ste 200 Los Angeles CA 90029-1748

ESHEL, RE'UVEN, researcher, mechanical engineering educator; b. Haifa, Israel, Nov. 12, 1936; s. Shimon Fritz and Margot (Levy) Aschner; m. Ruth Ratner, June 17, 1962; children: Nurith, Ya'el, Ronen. BSc, Technion, Haifa, Israel, 1958, DSc Tech., 1963. Head aeromechanics divsn. Rafael, Haifa, 1977-81, head missile divsn., 1982-86, v.p., 1987-94; vis. prof. U. Calif., Berkeley, 1981-82, McGill U., Montreal, Que., Can., 1986-87; dir. Technion R&D, Haifa, 1994-97; adj. prof. Technion, 1970—; vis. prof. Tel Aviv U., 1998—; cons. Min. of Def., Tel Aviv, 1994—; bd. dirs. Dimotech Ltd., Haifa. Contbr. articles to profl. jours.; author numerous reports in field. Mem. Civil Guard, Haifa, 1970-84. Reserve Officer Israel Air Force, 1971-90. Mem. Am. Def. Preparedness Assn., Assn. U.S. Army, MIT-Enterprise-Forum, Soc. Rsch. Adminstrs., Israeli Assn. Dirs., N.Y. Acad. Sci. Jewish. Avocations: sports, travel, music. Home: PO Box 820 Denya, Haifa 34987, Israel

ESHKOLI, HAVA WAGMAN, historian, educator; b. Tel-Aviv, Israel, Apr. 28, 1944; d. Meir and Hana (Bart) Wagman; m. Abraham Eshkoli, July 13, 1965; children: Izhak, Nir, Halel, Meir. BA, Bar-Ilan U., Ramat-Gan, Israel, 1966, MA, 1976, PhD, 1988. Cert. tchr., Israel. Tchr. high sch. Ramat-Gan, 1963-79; tchg. asst. Bar-Ilan U., Ramat-Gan, 1979-89, lectr., 1989-95; sr. lectr. Levinsky Coll. Edn., Tel-Aviv, 1991—; rsch. fellow Internat. Ctr. Holocaust Studies, Yad-Vashem, 1995-97; sr. rschr. Finkler Inst./Bar-Ilan U., Ramat-Gan, 1988—, coord. inter-deptl. seminar, 1991—; cons. Beit-Haedut, Nir-Galim, Israel, 1993-98; lectr. in field. Author: Silence: Mapai and the Holocaust, 1939-42, 1994; editor: The Reconstruction of Religious Zionism in Europe After the Holocaust; contbr. articles to profl. jours. Recipient Warman Essay prize Bar-Ilan U., 1967, Dvorzecki prize Yad-Vashem, 1978, Egit prize, The Histadrut (Gen. Fedn. Labor), 1990; Meml. Found. for Jewish Culture grantee, 1982-85. Fellow Internat. Ctr. Holocaust Studies; mem. Hist. Soc. Israel, World Union of Jewish Studies. Jewish. Avocations: reading novels and biographies, swimming, gymnastics. Home: 3 Keren Hayesod St, 44235 Kefar Sava Israel Office: Finkler Inst Holocaust Rsch, Bar-Ilan Univ, 52100 Ramat Gan Israel

ÉSIK, OLGA, radiation oncologist; b. Szeged, Hungary, 1950; d. Zoltán and Olga (Pongó) É; m. Lajos Tron; 1 child. MD, Albert Szent-Györgyi Med., Szeged, 1974; PhD, Hungarian Acad. Scis., Budapest, 1989, DSc, 2000. Lic. internist, med. oncologist, radiation oncologist. Trainee dept. internal diseases Mcpl. Hosp., Kaposvár, Hungary, 1975-79; asst. dept. radiology Albert-Szent-Györgyi Med. U., Szeged, 1979-90; prin. asst. dept. radiation oncology Uzsoki Hosp., Budapest, Hungary, 1990-92; dep. dept. head dept. radiotherapy Nat. Inst. Oncology, Budapest, 1992-2000; full prof., chmn. dept. radiotherapy Semmelweis U., Budapest, 2000—. Editor: Yearbook of the Hungarian Society for Radiation Oncology, 1995; mem. editl. bd. Strahlentherapie und Onkologie, 1996—. Grantee Govt. of Japan. Mem. Hungarian Soc. Radiation Oncology (sec. 1992-96, pres. 1996-2000), Hungarian Soc. Oncologists (bd. dirs. 1995—), European Soc. Therapeutic Radiology and Oncology (bd. dirs. 1998—). E-mail: esik@oncol.hu. Office: Semmelweis U Faculty Health, Ráth György u 7-9, H-1122 Budapest Hungary

ESÎN, HÜSEYÎN TUGRUL, trading and travel company executive; b. Istanbul, Turkey, Dec. 31, 1962; s. Numan S. and Aynur (Yalçin) E.; m. Hatice Pinar Can, June 9, 1990; children: Onur, Cem, Kaan. Student, Rochester Inst. Tech., 1982 84; degree in econs. and adminstrv. scis., Bosphorus U., Istanbul, 1986. Bd. dirs. Esin Internat. Transport and Trading Co., Istanbul, 1978—, Esin Tourism, Istanbul, 1986—; vice chmn. Esin Fgn. Trade, Istanbul, 1991—. Mem. Fgn. Econ. Rels. Bd. With Turkish Army, 1987. Mem. Jr. Chamber Internat. Turkey (exec. v.p.), Young Businessmen Assn. of Turkey, Turkish Assn. Travel Agys., Bosphorus U. Alumni Assn., Maharishi Mahesh Yogi TM Assn., Turkish Tourism Investors Assn., Young Businessman Assn. Turkey, Turkish Industrialists Businessmens Assn., Turkish Clothing Mfrs., Bosphorus Textile Group, Industrialists-Businessman Assn. Merter, World Econ. Forum Turkey (assoc. mem.), Internat. Apparel Exporters Assn., Alumni of Internat. Sch. of Geneva, T.E.D. Club, Internat. Forewarders Club, Internat. Apparel Fedn., Istanbul German-Turkish C. of Industry and Commerce, Kemer Golf and Country Club, Turkish Am. Bus. Forum, British C. of C., French C. of C., Istanbul Aviation Club. Avocations: travel, tennis, skiing, social clubs, swimming. Office: Esin Internat Transport and Trade Co, Topcu Cad Uygun Apt No 2 K2, 80090 Istanbul Turkey

ESKEW, BENTON, judge; b. Bastrop, Tex., Sept. 2, 1961; s. Charles Allen and Vina M. (Sims) E. BBA, Baylor U., 1984, JD, 1986. Bar: Tex., U.S. Dist. Ct. (no. and we. dists.) Tex.; ordained Bapt. minister. Assoc. McCamish, Ingram, Martin & Brown, Austin, Tex., 1986-88, Naman, Howell, Smith & Lee, Austin, 1989-91; ptnr. Eskew & Goertz, Bastrop, Tex., 1992-94; judge Bastrop County, Tex., 1994—. Bd. dirs. Child Protective Svcs. Bd., Bastrop, 1994—, Bastrop Boys and Girls Club, 1998—. Mem. Bastrop C. of C., Masons, York Rite, Scottish Rite, Shriners, Lions Club, Kiwanis Club. Home: PO Box 1120 Bastrop TX 78602-1120 Office: Bastrop County Ct Law 804 Pecan St Bastrop TX 78602-3846

ESKIN, MEHMET, psychologist; b. Oct. 15, 1963; s. Mustafa Ali and Saniye (Yildirim) E.; m. Zeliha Tekeli, Apr. 24, 1961; children: Berke, Ege. BSc in Psychology, Mid. East Tech. U., Ankara, Turkey, 1987, MSc in Clin. Psychology, 1989; postgrad., Oslo (Norway) U., 1990; PhD, Stockholm U., 1995. Rsch. asst. Mid. East Tech. U., 1987-89; doctoral asst. Stockholm U., 1991-95, rsch. fellow, 1995-96; psychologist Stockholm County Coun., 1996-97; lectr. Koç U., Istanbul, Turkey, 1997-98, Istanbul Bilgi U., 1999—; dir., cons. Diyalog, Istanbul, 1999—. Contbr. articles to profl. jours. Recipient stipend Swedish Found. for Rsch. and Internat. Coop., 1997-99; fellow Stockholm U., 1995-96; grantee Swedish Inst., 1992-95. Mem. Swedish Psychol. Assn., Turkish Psychol. Assn., N.Y. Acad. Scis. Avocations: reading, jogging. Office: Diyalog, Bagdat Cad # 441 D2, Suadiye Istanbul Turkey

EŠKINJA, IVAN, chemistry educator; b. Prizren, Yugoslavia, May 15, 1934; s. Rudolf and Katica (Bobanović) E.; m. Ljerka Kralj, Dec. 28, 1963; children: Mirela, Maja. BSc in Chemistry, U. Zagreb, Croatia, 1959, MSc in Chemistry, 1968, PhD in Chemistry, 1972. Tech. advisor Pobjeda, Zagreb, 1960-62; tech. mgr. Geoistraživanje, Zagreb, 1969-72; prof. faculty chem. engring. and tech. U. Zagreb, 1972—. Author: Qualitative Inorganic Chemical Analysis, 1982, Undergraduate Instrumental and Process Analysis. Mem. Croation Chem. Soc., Croatian Air Polution Prevention Assn., Croatian Soc. Chem. Engring. and Tech., Croatian Soc. Plastic and Rubber. Roman Catholic. Avocation: electrotechnology, mechanics, sailing, playing basketball. Home: Hećimovićeva 2, 10000 Zagreb Croatia Office: U Zagreb Fac Chem Eng Tech, Marulićev Trg 19, 10000 Zagreb Croatia

ESKOV, ALEXEI GRIGOREVICH, physicist; b. Sorochinsk, Orenburg, Russia, Oct. 31, 1945; s. Grigorii Matveevich and Vera Filippovna (Goncharova) E.; m. Lioubov Petrovna Djakova, Aug. 22, 1974; 1 child, Mikhail. M.Physics, Novosibirsk State U., Russia, 1969; PhD of Physics, Kurchatov Inst. Atomic Energy, Moscow, 1975. Engr. Inst. Nuclear Physics, Novosibirsk, 1969-71; sr. rschr. Troitsk (Russia) Innovation and Fusion Rsch. Inst., 1971—. Contbr. articles to profl. jours. Soros Found. grantee, 1994. Avocations: mountain skiing, chess. E-mail: eskov@triniti.ru. Home: Shkolnaja 4-46, 142092 Troitsk Moscow, Russia Office: Troitsk Innovation/Fusion, Rsch Inst, 142092 Troitsk Moscow, Russia

ESLAKE, SAUL RICHARD, economist; b. 1958. B in Econs. with honors, U. Tasmania, 1979. Chief economist McIntosh Securities, Melbourne, Australia, 1986-91, Nat. Mutual, Melbourne, 1991-95, ANZ Bank, Melbourne, 1995—; dir. Gascor, Melbourne, 1994-97, North-East Health Care Network, Melbourne, 1995-97, Australian Housing and Urban Rsch. Inst., 1998—; chief exec. Victorian Audit Commn., Melbourne, 1992-93. Fellow Securities Inst. of Australia (nat. councillor 1995-97), Econs. Soc. of Australia, Australian Inst. Mgmt. (assoc.); mem. Australian Inst. Co. Dirs. Fax: 61-3-92735711. E-mail: eslakes @anz.com. Office: Aust/NZ Banking Group, 100 Queen St, Melbourne 3000, Australia

ESMAEL, HARESAD, manufacturing executive; b. Kuala Lumpur, Malaysia, Sept. 5, 1956; s. Esmael Casem and Elizabeth Abdul. MBA, Harvard U., 1987. Mgr. Camburt S/B, Kuala Lumpur, 1987-92, mng. dir., 1992—. Muslim. Avocations: reading, swimming, golf, traveling, sightseeing. Home: 3 JLN Jaya, Bandar Tun Razak Cheras, Kuala Lumpur 56000, Malaysia Office: Camburt SDN BHD, PO Box 12905, Kuala Lumpur 50792, Malaysia

ESMAILZADEH, EBRAHIM, mechanical engineering educator, consultant; b. Mashhad Khorasan, Iran, Apr. 6, 1944; s. Mohammad and Fakhrolsharieh (Riaz) E.;m. Rouhangiz Daei Sadeghi, July 15, 1977; children: Reza, Ali. BSc with honours, U. London, 1967, MPhil, 1969, PhD, 1971. Chartered engr., U.K. Lab. instr. U. London, 1967-71; asst. prof. Arya-Mehr U. Tech., Tehran, 1971-75; vis. assoc. prof. MIT, Cambridge, Mass., 1976-77; prof. Sharif U. Tech., Tehran, 1980-89, univ. disting. prof., 1992-97, v.p., 1979-80; vis. prof. U. Victoria, Can., 1990-91, 97—; rsch. advisor Ministry of Heavy Industry, Iran, 1982-84; tech. cons. in field. Author textbooks and jour. articles on mech. engring.; mem. editl. bd. nat. and internat. jours.; spkr. in field. Named Excellent Prof., Iranian Soc. Mech. Engrs., 1994, Exemplar Prof. of Iranian Univs., 1993. Fellow Instn. Mech. Engrs. Eng., ASME; mem. Soc. Automotive Engrs., Iranian Acad. Scis. Tehran (chair mech. engring. dept. 1995-97), Iranian Soc. Control and Instrumentation Engrs. (dir. 1994). Avocations: chess, photography, music, ball games, skiing. Home: 2365 Lam Cir Apt 1302, Victoria, BC Canada Office: U Victoria, PO Box 3055, Victoria, BC Canada V8W 3P6

ESMEIN, JEAN CHARLES, Japanologist; b. Poitiers, France, Dec. 1, 1923; s. Paul Edmond Esmein and Marcelle Marie-Louise Roux; m. Claude Suzanne Estève, Aug. 4, 1945; children: Pierre, Bernard. Cadet, The Naval Coll., Toulon, France, 1942; diploma in Japanese, Ecole Nat. Langues Orientales, Paris, 1956; advanced mgmt. program, Stanford Inst., INSEAD, Fontainebleau, France, 1979; LittD, U. Paris VII, 1983. Chartered Japanese interpreter. Officer French Navy, 1942-58; mgr. Bull Corp. Japan, Tokyo, 1958-65; press attaché French Fgn. Office/French Embassy, Beijing, 1965-68; dir. credit Lyonnais Bank and UBAF Bank, Tokyo, 1970-79; lectr. Ecole Sci. Politiques, 1983-93; vis. prof. Nat. Sch. Adminstrn., Paris, 1980-81. Chmn. Conf. IFAC on Environ. Systems Planning, Design and Control, 1977; mem. Com. Sci. de la Fondation pour Etudes de Défense Nat., 1987; elected rep. Coun. Superieur des Français de l'Etranger, Paris, 1972-75, 82-84. Decorated Croix de Guerre, officier Légion d'Honneur; recipient Jean Mermoz Lit. prize, UCTF, Paris, 1979. Mem. Marine Acad., Strategic Mgmt. Soc. (founder), Assn. Computing Machinery, The Folklore Soc. Japan. Avocations: history, computer-aided musical composition. Home: Rue Gay Lussac 25, 75005 Paris France Office: Rue St Cosme 30, 95270 Luzarches France

ESMIEU, DOMINIQUE M., market research executive; b. Marseille, France, Feb. 25, 1955; s. Louis Jacques and Lucie Marie (Imbert) E.; m. Gita Chari, May 26, 1979; children: William, Shanti, Florence. Diploma in engring., Paris Chemistry and Physics, 1979, Diplome d'Etudes Appronfondies in Analytical Chemistry, 1979, Test English Fgn. Lang., 1979. Rsch. engr. Rhone Poulenc Pharms., Vitry, France, 1979-84; R&D rsch. engr. Colgate Palmolive, Courbevoie, France, 1984-87, tech. coord., 1987-89, exec. dir. mktg. rsch., 1989—. Mem. European Soc. Market Rsch. Avocations: tennis, jogging, mountain biking, photography. Office: Colgate Palmolive, 55 Blvd Mission, 92401 Marchand France

ESONU, BABINGTON ONYEMAECHI, animal scientist, educator; b. Umuahia, Abia, Nigeria, Mar. 6, 1957; s. John Onwusonye and Rose Onyecherelam (Mbakwe) E.; m. Roseline Ugo Ezema, Dec. 10, 1983; five children. B in Agrl. Tech., Fed. U. Tech., Owerri, Nigeria, 1987, MSc in Animal Sci., 1991, PhD in Animal Sci., 1996. Higher live stock supt. Nat. Root Crops Rsch. Inst., Umudike, Nigeria, 1982-84; lectr. II Michael Okpara Coll. Agr., Owerri, 1988-91; asst. lectr. Fed. U. Tech., Owerri, 1992-94, lectr. II, 1994-97, lectr. I, 1997-99, sr. lectr., 1999—; cons. MBA Farms, Umuahia, Nigeria, 1987-88, Selins Farms, Umuahia, 1987-88, Jacob Farms Plc, Owerri, 1996—; chmn. saat siwes com. Fed U. Tech., Owerri, 1996—. Contbr. articles to profl. jours. Deacon, sec. Assemblies of God Ch., Ebgu-Owerri, 1991—; spl. marshal Fed. Road Safety Corps, Owerri, 1994—; chmn. bd. govs. Assemblies of God Bethel Jr. Sem., Owerri, 1997—; facilitator Nat. Youth Svc. Corps, Owerri, 1998—. Recipient Postgrad. award Fed. Govt. Nigeria, 1990-91;. Mem. Nigerian Soc. Animal Prodn. (cert. 1997), African Network Rural Poultry Dev., N.Y. Acad. Sci. Avocations: soccer, singing, swimming, reading. Office: Fed U Tech Dept Animal Sci, PMB 1526, Owerri Imo, Nigeria

ESPALDON, ERNESTO MERCADER, plastic surgeon, former senator; b. Sulu, Philippines, Nov. 11, 1926; arrived in Guam, 1963; s. Cipriano Acuna Espaldon and Claudia (Cadag) Mercader); m. Leticia Legaspi Virata, May 31, 1952; children: Arlene Espaldon Ramos, Vivian Espaldon Wolff, James, Diane, Karl, Ernesto Jr. AA, U. Philippines, Manila, 1949; MD, U. Santo tomas, Manila, 1954; postgrad. in gen. surgery, U. Okla., 1959; postgrad. in plastic and recon. surgery, Washington U., St. Louis, 1961. Diplomate Am. Bd. Plastic Surgery. Plastic surgeon Guam Meml. Hosp., Agana, 1963—, chief surgery, 1965-69; pres., plastic surgeon Espaldon Clinic, Agana, 1969—; senator Guam Legislature, Agana, 1974-80, 86-92, chmn. Com. on Health, Welfare and Ecology and Com. on Ethics and Standards, 1974-80; vis. prof. Bicol Med. and Edn. Ctr., Legaspi City, The Philippines, 1980—; cons. plastic surgery U.S. Naval Hosp., Guam, 1972-76; chmn. com. on advance health care Assn. Pacific Islands Legislators, 1988-92, Coll. Assurance Plan Pre-Need Ednl. Plan, Guam, 1979-85, dir. Coll. Assurance Plan Pension, Philippines, 1982—, Coll. Assurance Plan, Philippines, 1980—, Citizens Security Bank, Guam, 1990-98. Author: With The Bravest, 1996. Pres., founder Guam Balikbayan Med. Mission, Agana, 1974—; organizer, co-founder Aloha Med., Mission, Honolulu, 1982—. Guerrilla comdr. Sulu (Philippines) Area Command, 1943-46, 2d lt. Philippine Army, 1946-47. Recipient Thomas Jefferson award for pub. svc., Am. Inst. Pub. Svc., Washington, and Honolulu Advertiser, 1983, Raja Baguinda award for humanitarian svc. 6th Centennial Celebration of Islam in The Philippines, 1980; named Most Outstanding Filipino Overseas Philippine Govt. and Philippine Jaycees for Pub. Svc., 1982, Most Outstanding Cmty. Filipino Leader of Guam Philippine-Am. Cmty., 1979, Man of Yr. and Disting. Svc. award Inst. Philippine Am. Affairs, Hawaii, 1983; named Most Outstanding Alumni Achiever for Humanitarian Svc., U. Santo Tomas, 1981, Ernesto M. Espaldon profl. chairship in plastic and reconstructive surgery U. Santo Tomas, 1995. Fellow ACS, Philippine Coll. Surgeons; mem. AMA, Pan Pacific Surg. Assn., Guam Med. Soc. (pres. 1970-72, chief del. to AMA 1973-76), KC. Republican. Roman Catholic. Home: PO Box Ce Agana GU 96932-8982 Office: GCIC Bldg Ste 709 Agana GU 96910

ESPAR, WILLIAM GEORGE, interventional cardiologist; b. Michigan City, Ind., Oct. 17, 1960; s. William George and Margaret Mary (Nadaf) E.; m. Camelia Rada Naddaf, Aug. 4, 1990; children: Jessica, Matthew, Michelle. BA, Ind. U., 1983; MD, Am. U. Caribbean, Plymouth, Montserrat, 1988. Diplomate in internal medicine and cardiovasc. medicine Am. Bd. Internal Medicine. Resident in internal medicine Hennepin County Med. Ctr., Mpls., 1990-92; fellow in cardiology U. Colo. Health Scis. Ctr., Denver, 1993-96, fellow in interventional cardiology, 1995-96; interventional cardiologist Heart and Circulation Clinics, Merrillville, Ind., 1996-98; med. dir. Ind. Inst. Cardiology, Michigan City, 1998—, dir. coronary interventions, 1998—; co-dir. cardiology St. Anthony Meml. Hosp., Michigan City, 1998—. Contbr. articles to profl. jours. Fellow ACP. Roman Catholic. Avocations: bicycling, swimming, piano, movies. Office: Ind Inst Cardiology 1507 Wabash St Ste 400A Michigan City IN 46360-4361

ESPENLAUB, MARGO LINN, women's studies educator, writer, artist; b. Decorah, Iowa, May 1, 1944; d. Lloyd Wilson and Margaret Mary (Seegmiller) Ruid; m. Alan Ludwig Espenlaub, Aug. 8, 1988; children: Arn R. Johnson, Cara C. Johnson. BA in Philosophy, U. Colo., 1983, M in Humanities, 1985; PhD in Women's Studies, The Union Inst. Grad. Sch., 1995. Assoc. dir. student devel., mem. faculty U. Denver, The Women's Coll.; colloqium coord. Front Range Feminist Scholars, Denver, 1991-98; faculty coord. TWC Student Writer's Club. Co-author: Women's Studies: Thinking Women, 1993; gen. editor Voices of the Women's Coll., 1999, Voices 2000. Mem. biomed. ethics com. Kaiser Permanente, Denver, 1986-96. Mem. Nat. Women's Studies Assn., Colo. Women's Agenda, Women's Caucus for Art (Colo. chpt.), Front Range Women in the Visual Arts, Colo. Mountain Club. Avocations: drawing, writing, hiking, snow shoeing. Office: U Denver Womens Coll 7150 Montview Blvd Denver CO 80220-1866

ESPEY, LINDA ANN GLIDEWELL, accountant; b. Birmingham, Ala., Aug. 11, 1944; d. Emmett O'Neal and Iola Florence (Harris) Glidewell; m. Lindsey Stribling Smith, Nov. 5, 1966 (div. Dec. 1990); 1 child, Lindsey Nelson; m. Charles G. Espey, Sept. 11, 1997; 1 stepchild, Heidi Espey Holladay. BA cum laude, Birmingham-So. Coll., 1984. Stenographer Cook's Pest Control, Decatur, Ala., 1962, Nelson-Weaver Cos., Birmingham, Ala., 1963-69; resident mgr. Twin Homes of Mt. Brook, Ala., 1966-69; bookkeeper, sect. to v.p. Molton, Allen & Williams, 1969-72; sec. quality assurance dept. So. Co. Svc., Birmingham, 1972-74, sec. sys. constrn. budget, 1974-82, sr. sec. treasury dept., 1982-83; jr. acct. major projects-acctg. Ala. Power Co., Birmingham, 1983-87, sr. acct. fuel dept., 1987-90, sr. acct. stats. dept., 1990-92; fin. adminstr., comptr. Ala. Bapt., Inc., Birmingham, 1992-99; bus. revenue tax compliance officer Shelby County, 1999—. Asst. treas. So. Co. Svcs. State and Fed. PAC,, Ala. PowerCo. State and Fed. PAC. Mem. Am. Soc. Women Accts., The Club, Inc., Alpha Lambda Delta, Birmingham So. Alumni Assn. (coun. mem.). Baptist. Avocations: travel, culinary art, walking, fishing.

ESPIDEL, JOUSSEF EVELIO, research scientist; b. La Victoria, Jan. 1, 1956; s. Evelio Magsimo and Flor Maria (Masmud) E.; m. Aida Fulgencia Portes, July 21, 1979; 1 child, Anita Fozie Espidel Portes. BSc, U. Essex, Colchester, Eng., 1978; grad. diploma, U. East Anglia, Norwich, Eng., 1980,

MSc, 1981; PhD, U. Durham, Eng., 1990. Rschr. in nuclear magnetic resonance Inst. Venezolana de Investigaciones Cientificas, Caracas, Venezuela, 1981-86, Petroleos de Venezuela S.A. INTEVEP, Los Tegues, Venezuela, 1990-92, 96—; head molecular characterization unit Petroleos de Venezuela S.A. INTEVEP, Los Tegues, 1992-95. Co-author: (book chpt.) Developments in Petroleum Science, 1999. Recipient Premio Nacional de Ciencias al Mejortrabajo de Quimica, Consejo Nacional de Investigación Tecnologia, 1996. Mem. Royal Soc. Chemistry (Eng.). Roman Catholic. Office: INTEVEP SA Dept Anal/Eval, Postal 76343, 1070A Caracas Venezuela

ESPINO, MARTIN, business consultant; b. Jalapa, Veracruz, Mex., Dec. 7, 1940; s. Neftali E. and Concepcion Hernandez; m. Alma Maria Medina, Jan 16, 1965; children: Martin, Oscar, Alma Patricia. Bus. Adminstrn., Monterrey Inst. Tech., Mex., 1962, M in Mgmt., 1973; U. Adminstrn. Splst., U. Calif., 1966; M in Orgn. Devel., Pepperdine U., 1978. Dean Sch. Bus. U. Veracruz (Mex.), Jalapa, 1964-68, 71-72; orgn. mgr. Hylsa, Monterrey, Mex., 1969-71, procurement mgr., 1972-75, orgn. devel. mgr., 1975-87; dir. corp. quality Alfa Group, Monterrey, Mex., 1987-92; pres. Benchmarking of Mex., Monterrey, 1992—; cons. U. Monterrey, Mex., 1970-71; prof. Monterrey Inst. Tech., 1970-71, U. Ams., Puebla, Mex., 1973-74; internee U. Wis., Milw., 1967. Recipient Proteo award Profls. en Desarrollo Organizacional, 1988. Mem. Met. Quality Coun. (pres. 1991-93), Prodeo (pres. 1984-85). Roman Catholic. Avocations: painting, reading. Home: Rio Necaxa #1121 Valle Ote, 66269 San Pedro NL, Mexico Office: Benchmarking de Mex, Via Augusta #120-3, 66220 San Pedro NL, Mexico

ESPINOLA-ZAVALETA, NILDA GLADYS, cardiologist; b. Trujillo, Peru, Feb. 3, 1960; arrived in Mexico, 1990; d. Marcelino Teofilo Espinola-Rodriguez and Maria Elva Zavaleta-Flores. Student, Acad. Medicine, Cracow, Poland, 1981-86; Doctorate in Med. Sch., Acad. Medicine, Warsaw, Poland, 1989; postgrad., Nat. Inst. Cardiology, Mexico City, 1990-93. Cert. Mexican Coun. Cardiology. Asst. prof. Banach Hosp., Warsaw, 1986-89; cardiology resident Nat. Inst. Cardiology, Mexico City, 1990-93, echocardiography trainee, 1993-94, staff physician, 1994—; prof., lectr. Internat. Congress Pneumology and Cardiology, 1988-89, 94-98, Nat. Congress Cardiology, 1990, 93, 95-99; cardiologist Gustavo Guerrero Hosp., Mexico City, 1993—, Medica Sur Hosp., Mexico City, 1994—, Am. Brit. Cowdray Hosp., Mexico City, 1997—; echocardiographer Santa Monica Hosp., Mexico City, 1997—. Contbr. chpt. to book and articles to profl. jours. Charity cons. Gustavo Guerero Hosp., Mexico City, 1991—. Recipient recognition for efficiency and quality in benefity of patients NIH, Mexico, 1999—; named Nat. Investigator, Nat. Sys. Rsch., Mexico, 1998—, Sr. Investigator, NIH, Mexico, 1999—. Mem. Mexican Soc. Cardiology, Mexican Soc. Hypertension, Peruvian Soc. Cardiology. Roman Catholic. Avocations: reading, movies, aerobic exercise, knitting, crocheting. Office: Nat Inst Cardiology, Juan Badiano #1, 14080 Mexico City Tlalpan, Mexico

ESPINOSA, ALVARO FELIPE, entrepreneur, artist; b. Stanford, Conn., Aug. 14, 1959; s. Alvaro Felipe and Eugenia Claiborne (Carver) E.; m. Laura Diann Pierce, Dec. 19, 1981 (div. Aug. 1994); 1 child, Katherine Margaret. MScA, Ctrl. Mich. U., 1988; BSc in Journalism, U. Colo., 1982. Human resources adminstr. Libr. Congress, Washington, 1986-89; dir. Genesys Health Sys., Grand Blanc, Mich., 1989—; v.p. Applied Resources Unlimited, Boulder, Colo., 1994—; pres. Three Stones Inc., Saginaw, Mich., 2000—. Author numerous poems; prin. works include various bronze sculptures. Sgt. U.S. Army, 1983-86. Mem. Soc. Human Resource Mgmt. E-mail: Pespinosa@compuserve.com. Office: Three Stones Inc 6360 Fox Glen Dr Apt 2 Saginaw MI 48603-4323

ESPINOZA, ROBERTO CARLOS, advertising agency executive; b. Lima, Peru, Aug. 20, 1971; s. Luis Espinoza Canales and Ana Irma Hernandez. Grad., Peruvian Advt. Inst., Lima, 1995. Media asst. Creativity/Young & Rubicam, Lima, 1996, Grey-Peru, Lima, 1996; media supr. asst. JWT Peru, Lima, 1996-97; media cons. A.C. Nielsen, Lima, 1997; media dir. JWT Bolivia, 1998; media cons. A.C. Nielsen, Lima, 1997. Avocations: soccer, tennis, reading marketing books. E-mail: rceh@mixmail.com. Office: JWT Bolivia, Lisimaco Gutierrez 513, Sopocachi La Paz, Bolivia

ESPIROTO SANTO, GABRIEL, NATO official, military officer; b. Bragança, Portugal, Oct. 8, 1935; m. Maria Antoinette Marcelo; 3 children. Grad., Portuguese Mil. Acad., 1957. Commd. 2d lt. Portuguese Armed Forces, 1957, advanced through grades to gen., 1997, early assignments include tng. and command posts, later in several tng. and staff posts with Army Staff Coll., also with Cabinet Army Chief of Staff, Staff Chief of Def., with mil. staff of Pres. of Republic, later dep. comdr., comdr. Army Anti-Aircraft Def. Tng. Ctr., Army Hdqrs., 1981, exec. asst. to Army Chief of Staff, 1987-91, Portuguese mil. rep. to NATO Mil. Com., 1991-94, quartermaster gen. to Army, dep. chief of Army Staff, 1994-97, chief of Army Staff, 1997-98, Portuguese Chief of Def., 1998—. Decorated Order of Aviz, Mil. Merit and Order of Cruzeiro do Sul, Order of Merit Militar of Spain, others. Mem. Portuguese Nat. Geographic Soc., History Soc. Office: Armed Forces of Portugal, Ave Ilha de Madeira, 1400 Lisbon Portugal also: NATO Hdqrs, Blvd Leopold III, 1110 Brussels Belgium*

ESPOSITO, ANTONIO, physics engineer; b. Napoli, Italy, Jan. 12, 1963; s. Nicola Esposito and Veturia Orsi; m. Hiroko Suzuki. D of Engring., U. Naples, 1993. Owner bus. in high tech security systems, 1983-87; profl. rugby player CUS team/Univ. Sport Ctr., 1984-90; rschr. Consiglio Nazionale delle Ricerche (CNR), Napoli, 1992-95, European Orgn. for Nuclear Physics (CERN), Geneva, 1997, Electrotech. Lab., Tsukuba, Japan, 1995-99; physics project and R&D scientist Tech. U. of Munich, Garching, Germany, 1999—; com. mem. Italian Embassy, 1996; coord. European project on monitoring with Cryogenic Detectors for Accelerators; co-chair first bilaterial symposium Japan-Italy in Tokyo. Contbr. articles to profl. jours.; patentee in field. Pres. Russian Vodka Ceremony, Tsukuba, 1995—. Achievements include reaching the national second league with CUS Rugby team, 1987; 100 clients per year in high-tech security business; design of ultra-fast superconductive Josephson digital circuit; development of theoretical new models for the RMQT (Resonant Macroscopic Quantum Tunneling) effect, 1991-93; responsibility for developing and building first cryogenic silicon detector in world for high-energy particles CERN experiment COMPASS (Common Muon Proton Apparatus for Structure and Spectroscopy). Avocations: musician, playing football, painting, cuisine. Fax: 0049-89-289-12570. Office: Tech U Munich E-18 Dept Physics, James Frank Strasse, D-85747 Garching Germany also: CERN, EP Divsn, CH-1211 Geneva 23, Switzerland

ESPOSITO, CIRO, virologist and researcher; b. Naples, Italy, Nov. 11, 1954; s. Pasquale and Concetta (Marigliano) E.; m. Silvana Morelli, Mar. 28, 1985; children: Davide, Claudio, Nadia. MD, U. Naples, 1983; Specialist in Virology, U. Messina, Italy, 1986. Med. diplomate, 1983. Asst. oncol. virology Naples U., 1983-85; asst. Local Health Unit, USL 41, Naples, 1985-88; rsch. fellow dept. haematology U. Cambridge, Eng., 1988-89; rsch. assoc. HIV Screening Group, Naples, 1989-92; rsch. fellow Rome Health Superior Inst., ISS, Naples, 1992-94; asst. D. Cotugno Hosp. for Infectious Disease, Naples, 1993-94, 1st asst., 1994—; cons. Italian Pharmacotherapic Inst., Rome, 1987—, Immuno Pharmacology Rsch., Catania, Italy, 1988-96; vice dir. Italian Assn. for Virus Study and Rsch., Naples, 1989—; cons. Aversa Psychiat. Hosp., Justice Minister, Rome, 1991—; check dr. Nat. Inst. for Social Security, 1988-91; on call physician Local Health Unit, USL 36, 1992-93. Author: (booklet) Etiopathogenesis of Viral Hepatitis, 1989, Progress in Viral Hepatitis Study, 1996; editor: (pamphlet) HIV Infection and AIDS, 1991. Hon. mem. Concilium Sanitatis Italicum, Avezzano, Italy, 1987; mem. De Beaumont Bonelli Found. for Cancer, Naples, 1983-88; mem. com. Italian Assn. for Viral Study and Rsch., 1989—; hon. mem. Christian Knights of Labor, Rome, 1994. Recipient Cilifrese award Tumor Prevention Assn., Rome, 1987, Abroad honor Edn. Minister, Rome, 1988, Great Cross of Pub. Health award Roman Acad., 1992, Gold Hercules award Internat. Acad., Rome, 1993, Gold Little Horse award European Union, Rome, 1996. Mem. N.Y. Acad. Scis., Italian Soc. Immuno-Oncology (sec. 1990—), European Soc. for Clin. Virology. Achievements include research on efficacy of hepatitis A vaccine in prevention of secondary hepatitis A infection. Avocations: soccer, swimming, tennis. Office: D Cotugno Hosp, Via G Quagliariello 54, 80131 Naples Italy

ESPOSITO, LARRY WAYNE, planetary astronomer; b. Schenectady, N.Y., Apr. 15, 1951; s. Albert and Beverly Jane (DeLaMater) E.; m. Diane Marie McKnight, July 24, 1975; children: Rhea, Ariel. SB in Math., MIT, 1973; PhD in Astronomy, U. Mass., 1977. Research assoc. Lab. Atmospheric and Space Physics U. Colo., Boulder, 1977—, lectr., 1979-84, assoc. prof. dept. astrophys., planetary and atmospheric scis., 1984-95, prof., 1995—; prin. investigator NASA, Cassini Space Mission, 1990—; investigator Pioneer Venus, Pioneer Saturn, Voyager, Galileo, Mars Observer, USSR Phobos and Mars 1994 spacecraft missions, 1977—; mem. NASA Planetary Atmospheres Mgmt. Ops. Working Group, 1981-84, Nat. Acad. Scis. Space Sci. Bd. com. on planetary and lunar exploration, 1982-86, chmn. 1989-92; dep. chmn. Nat. Acad. Scis. Space Sci. Bd. task group on planetary exploration, 1984-86; chair Europa Planetary Protection Task Group, 1999-2000, Task Group Forward Contamination Europa, 1999-2000. Contbr. articles to sci. publs. Recipient Exceptional Sci. Achievement medal NASA, 1986, Richtmyer Lecture award Am. Assn. Physics Tchrs. and Am. Phys. Soc., 1991. Mem. Am. Astron. Soc. (div. planetary scis. com. 1983-86, H.C. Urey prize 1985), Internat. Astron. Union, Am. Geophys. Union, Internat. Council Sci. Unions (exec. mem. com. space research). Methodist. Club: Boulder Go. Achievements include discovery of Saturn's 4th ring, 1979 (as part of the Pioneer Saturn Team), first Hubble Space Telescope observations of Venus, 1995. Office: U Colo CB392 Lab Atmosphere Spc P Boulder CO 80309-0001

ESQUENAZI, SALOMON, ophthalmologist; b. Bogota, Colombia, Sept. 29, 1961; s. Isidoro and Ketty (Tarragano) E.; m. Olga Bibas, June 7, 1986; children: Isi, Karina, Becky. MD, Rosario U., Bogota, 1985, postgrad., 1989. Diplomate Colombian Bd. Ophthalmology. Intern San Jose Hosp., Bogota, 1986-88, chief resident, 1988-89; ophthalmologist Barraquer Clinic, Bogota, 1989; instnl. mem. Fundacion Santa Fe, Bogota, 1989—; med. dir. Centro Oftalmologico, Bogota, 1993—. Contbr. articles to profl. jours. Mem. Am. Soc. Cataract and Refractive Surgery, Internat. Soc. Refractive Keratoplasty, Soc. Ophthalmology Bogota. Liberal. Jewish. Office: Centro Oftalmologico Olsabe, Calle 120 #8-62, Bogota Colombia

ESQUIBEL, EDWARD V., psychiatrist, clinical medical program developer; b. Denver, May 28, 1928; s. Delfino C. and Beatrice (Solis) E.; m. Elaine F. Telk (div. 1961); children: Roxanne, Cyndi, Allen, James; m. Lillian D. Robb, 1961; children: Amanda, Ramona. MD, U. Colo., 1958. Diplomate Am. Bd. Psychiatry and Neurology. Assoc. chief svc. Ill. State Psychiat. Inst., Chgo., 1964-66; dir. undergrad. program psychiatry, asst. prof. psychiatry Chgo Med. Sch., 1966-68; cons. and supr. group therapy Lake County Mental Health Clinic, Gary, Ind., 1968-72; pvt. practice Daytona Beach, Jacksonville, Fla., 1972-82; chief forensic svcs., dir. div. maximum security and inst. rsch. Colo. State Hosp., Pueblo, 1981; assoc. clin. prof. psychiatry Quillen-Dishner Coll. Medicine, Johnson City, Tenn., 1982-84; clin. psychiatrist VA Outpatient Clinic, Riviera Beach, Fla., 1984-86; mental health coord., supr. VA, Pensacola, Fla., 1986-88; assoc. chief staff, ambulatory care VA Med. Ctr., Ft. Lyon, Colo., 1988-90, Carl Vinson VA Med. Ctr., Dublin, Ga., 1990-91; staff physician VA Med. Ctr., Sheridan, Wyo., 1993—; chief psychiat. svcs. VA Med. Ctr., Lake City, Fla., 1993-94; contract physician, 1995—. Contbr. articles to profl. jours. Sgt. U.S. Army, 1948-52. Recipient Plaque Recognition award Southeastern Psychiat. Inst., 1964, Internat. Pers. Creative award, 1972, Key to City Daytona Beach, 1975, Hosp. Dirs. commendation VA, 1991. Avocations: gardening, arts and crafts, reading. Home and Office: 801 Gospel Island Rd Inverness FL 34450-3592

ESREY, WILLIAM TODD, telecommunications company executive; b. Phila., Jan. 17, 1940; s. Alexander J. and Dorothy (B.) E.; m. Julie L. Campbell, June 13, 1964; children: William Todd, John Campbell. BA, Denison U., Granville, Ohio, 1961; MBA, Harvard U., 1964. With Am. Tel & Tel. Co., also N.Y. Tel. Co., 1964-69; pres. Empire City Subway Ltd., N.Y.C., 1969-70; mng. dir. Dillon, Read & Co. Inc., N.Y.C., 1970-80; exec. v.p. corp. planning United Telecommunications, Inc., Westwood, Kans., 1980-81, exec. v.p., chief fin. officer, 1981-82, 84-85; pres., chief exec. officer United Telecommunications, Inc., 1985—; pres. United Telecom Communications, Inc., Kansas City, Mo., 1982-85; chmn., chief exec. officer Sprint Corp., Westwood, Kans., 1990—; bd. dirs. Earthlink Network, Inc., Exxon Corp., Duke Energy Corp., Gen. Mills, Inc., Everen Capital Corp. Bd. dirs. Midwest Rsch. Com. for Econ. Devel. Mem. Mission Hills Country Club, River Club, Links Club, Kans. City Country Club, Phi Beta Kappa. Office: Sprint 2330 Shawnee Mission Pkwy Westwood KS 66205-2090

ESSA, MOHAMMED HUSSEIN, environmental engineer, researcher; b. Bur-Hakaba, Somalia, Oct. 10, 1953; s. Ali Hussein and Daud Ebla (Ahmed) E.; m. Mariam Mohammed, Oct. 15, 1978; children: Shukri, Ayan, Abdulwali, Hafsa, Asma. BSCE, Somali Nat. U., Mogadishu, Somalia, 1988; MSCE, King Faud U. Petroleum/Mineral, Dhahran, Saudi Arabia, 1993. Quantity surveyor Hamar Co., Mogadishu, 1973-83; irrigation engr. Geddtop Co., Mogadishu, 1988-90; lectr. SNU, Mogadishu, 1988-90; rsch. asst. King Fahd U. Petroleum & Minerals, Dhahran, 1991-93, rsch. engr., 1994—. Contbr. articles to profl. jours. Avocations: reading, sports. Office: King Fahd U Petroleum, Dept Civil Engring, Dhahran 31261, Saudi Arabia

ESSANDOH, HILDA BRATHWAITE, kindergarten educator; b. N.Y.C., Feb. 19, 1925; d. Charles Christopher and Millicent Marian (Boxill) Brathwaite; m. Samuel O. Essandoh, June 11, 1959; children: Millicent Efua, Yvonne Araba, Dorothy Esi. BA, Hunter Coll., 1959; MS, Bank Street Coll. Edn., 1976, profl. diploma in supervision-adminstrn., 1980. Cert. nursery, kindergarten, 1st-6th grades, sch. adminstrn. and supervision. Tchr. kindergarten N.Y.C. Bd. Edn., 1962-91. Recipient Ely Trachtenberg award. Home: 548 W 165th St New York NY 10032-4942

ESSAWI, TAMER AHMAD, education educator; b. Jerusalem, Dec. 28, 1948; s. Ahmed Ali and Fatma Hassan Alyan E.; m. Jumana Hassan Odeh, Oct. 15, 1982; children: Dana, Tala. BS, Grove City Coll., 1973; MSc, Leningrad State U., 1978; PhD, Acad. of Med. Sci., 1981. Lectr. Birzeit U., Palestine, 1973-75, Bethlehem U., 1975-76; asst. prof. Birzeit U., Palestine, 1982—; chmn. biology and biochemistry dept. Birzeit, Palestine, 1997—, med. technology, 1999; mem. Acad. Coun., Birzeit U., 1996-99, Coun. for Higher Edn., Ramallah, Palestine, 1985-88. Mem. adv. com. for Palestenian Peace Delegation, Jerusalem, 1991-95, Jerusalem com., 1996—, Bd. for Peace and Democracy, Jerusalem, 1992—. Mem. ASM. Avocations: reading, swimming, hiking. Home: Jerusalem 54963, Palestine Office: Birzeit Univ, Biology/Biochem Dept, 14 Birzeit Palestine

ESSELBACH, MATTHIAS, physicist; b. Thueringen, Germany, Oct. 30, 1969; s. Hans-Georg and Ilse (Krueger) E. Diploma, U. Jena, 1994. Scientific collaborator U. Jena, Germany, 1994—. Home: Fr Ebert Str 1, Koenitz 07336, Germany Office: U Jena Inst Applied Optics, Max Wien Platz 1, Jena 07743, Germany

ESSÉN, HANNO FREDRIK BENGTSSON, mechanical engineering educator; b. Stockholm, Sept. 27, 1948; s. Bengt R-Son and Venla Alberta (Gebhard) E. PhD, U. Stockholm, 1979. Lectr. U. Stockholm, 1984-88; sr. lectr. Royal Inst. Tech., Stockholm, 1988—. Author: Basic Mechanics, 1993. Vice chmn. Swedish Sceptics, Stockholm, 1984—. Mem. European Phys. Soc. Avocation: football (soccer). Office: KTH, Dept Mechanics, S-100 44 Stockholm Sweden

ESSER, CARL ERIC, lawyer; b. Montclair, N.J., Feb. 12, 1942; s. Josef and Elly (Graber) E.; m. Barbara A. B. Stelzer, Oct. 12, 1968; children: Jennifer, Eric, Brian. AB, Princeton U., 1964; JD, U. Mich., 1967. Bar: Pa. 1967. Assoc. firm Reed Smith Shaw & McClay LLP, Phila., 1967-72, ptnr., 1973—. With USMCR, 1960-66. Mem. ABA, Pa. Bar Assn., Phila. Bar Assn., Pa. Soc. Healthcare Attys. (bd. dirs.), Pa. Lawyers Fund for Client Security (bd. dirs., chmn.), Octavia Hill Assn. (bd. dirs., asst. sec.), Racquet Club, Penllyn Club (bd. govs.), Mfrs. Golf and Country Club. Republican. Office: Reed Smith Shaw & McClay LLP 2500 One Liberty Pl Philadelphia PA 19103

ESSER, FRANZ MARTIN, chemist; b. Munich, Germany, July 31, 1939; s. Franz Joseph and Hedwig Mechthild (Schuler) E.; m. Nobue Kawashige, Feb. 18, 1971; children: Rika, Erik,. Diploma, Tech. U., Munich, Germany, 1970; PhD, Tech. U., Berlin, 1973. Lab. tech. Australian Nat. U., Canberra, 1961-64; head lab. Boehringer, Ingelheim, Germany, 1974-99; rschr. on work of artist Franz J.E. Contbr. articles to profl. jours. Mem. European Peptide Soc. Avocation: city guide.

ESSER, JAMES MARK, cardiovascular and interventional radiologist; b. Madison, Wis., Aug. 1, 1960; s. John Michael Esser and Helen Josephine (Brown) Butterworth. MD, SUNY, Buffalo, 1985. Diplomate Am. Bd. Radiology, Nat. Bd. Med. Examiners. Transitional resident John Burns Sch. Medicine-U. Hawaii, Honolulu, 1985-86, asst. clin. instr. surgery, 1985-86; resident in diagnostic radiology Beth Israel Med. Ctr.-Mt. Sinai Sch. Medicine, N.Y.C., 1986-90; fellow in vascular and interventional radiology St. Luke's-Roosevelt Hosp., N.Y.C., 1990-91; clinical fell. Cardiovasc. and Interv. Rad., Columbia COll. of Physicians and Surgs., 1990-91; attending staff emergency dept. Bellevue Hosp., N.Y.C., 1988-91; attending radiologist Elmhurst Hosp., N.Y.C., 1990-91, St. Mary's Hosp., West Palm Beach, Fla., 1991-92, Med. Ctr. Hosp., Punta Gorda, Fla., 1992-93, Welborn Hosps. & Clins., Evansville, Ind., 1993-94, St. Mary's Med. Ctr., Evansville, 1993—, Cmty. Meth. Hosp., Henderson, Ky., 1994—, Perry County Meml. Hosp., Tell City, Ind., 1995—, St. Mary's Ctr. for Her, Evansville, 1995—, Vencor Hosp., Louisville, 1998—, Jasper Meml. Hosp., Jasper, IN, 1998—, Wellington Regional Med. Ctr., West Palm Beach, FL, 1998—. Pres., v.p. N.Y.C. Soc. Physicians for Social Responsibility, 1987-90. Clin. fellow Columbia Coll. Physicians and Surgeons, 1990-91. Mem. AAAS, Am. Coll. Radiology, Radiol. Soc. N.Am., Soc. Cardiovasc. and Interventional Radiology, Am. Roentgen Ray Soc., Ky. Med. Assn., Henderson County Med. Soc., N.Y. Roentgen Soc., Nat. Trust Historic Preservation. Roman Catholic. Avocations: jogging, surfing, rock climbing. Home and Office: PO Box 495 Henderson KY 42419-0495

ESSER, JOSEF LAMBERT, educator, political scientist; b. Aachen, Germany, Apr. 12, 1943; s. Josef and Maria (Kaussen) E.; m. Rita Witt, Mar. 25, 1970. Doctor, U. Konstanz, Germany, 1974. Asst. clk. Aachen, 1959-67; rschr. U. Constance, Germany, 1974-80; prof. U. Frankfurt, Germany, 1981—. Editl. bd. Zeitschrift für Internationale Bezieheungen, other; contbr. articles to profl. pubs. Avocations: music, sports. Home: Bross Str 5, 60487 Frankfurt am Main Germany Office: U Frankfurt, Robert Mayer Str 5, 60054 Frankfurt am Main Germany

ESSEX, ELIZABETH ANNETTE, physicist, researcher; b. Grafton, NSW, Australia, Apr. 21, 1940; d. Charles William and Edna Marjorie (Munday) E.; m. Harvey Alan Cohen; children: David, Alexander, Raymond, Zara. BS with honors, U. New Eng., Armidale, Australia, 1961; PhD, U. New Eng., 1966. Lectr. U. West Indies, Jamaica, 1966-68; rsch. scientist James Cook U., Australia, 1968; lectr. La Trobe U., Australia, 1969-72; sr. lectr. La Trobe U., 1972—. Contbr. articles to profl. jours. Fellow Australian Inst. Physics; mem. Inst. Physics, Am. Geophys. Union. Home: 15 Shorts Rd, Eltham 3095 VIC, Australia Office: Sch Physics, La Trobe U, Bundoora 3083 VIC, Australia

ESSIEN, AKANEREN IDEM, animal scientist; b. Ndon Obodom, Nigeria, Mar. 10, 1952; s. Idem and Jenny (Udosen) E.; m. Nessie Sam Ayanam, Apr. 18, 1981; children: Anietie, Utibe. BSc, U. Ibadan, 1976, MSc, 1980, PhD, 1983. Agrl. officer, tutor Coll. Agriculture, Obubra, Nigeria, 1977-79; rsch. asst. dept. animal biology U. Pa., Phila., 1982; lectr. agriculture U. Cross River State, Uyo, Nigeria, 1984-89; from sr. lectr. animal sci. to prof. U. Calabar, Nigeria, 1990—; dean, faculty of agr. U. Calabar, 1994-95, 1998—; monitoring scientist Fed. Ministry Industry & Technology, Lagos, Nigeria, 1994; vis. scholar dept. animal sci. U. Uyo, 1996-97. Mem. Nigerian Soc. Animal Prodn., Animal Sci. Assn. Nigeria, N.Y. Acad. Scis. Avocations: scrabble, table tennis, current affairs, Christian music, reading. Home: Ndon Obodom Village, Akwa Ibom State Nigeria Office: Univ Calabar Fac of Agr, PMB 1115, Calabar Nigeria

ESSIEN, PRINCE UWEM EKPO, lawyer, consultant; b. Nung Oku Ekanem, Akwa Ibom, Nigeria, Apr. 14, 1940; s. K. Chief Ekpo and Alice (Ebong) E.; m. Unwa Ekanem, May 5, 1965 (div. June 1965); 1 child, Kufreabasi; m. Eno Udom Sept. 9, 1968; m. Eno Udom, Sept. 19, 1968; Benedicta Effiong, Jan. 17, 1981; children: Nsikanagasi, Udeme, Idongesit, Akaninyene, Ekaete, Ekamma, Oto-Drong. LLB (hon.), Ahmadu Bello U., Zaria, Nigeria, 1971; BA, Nigeria Law Sch., Lagos, Nigeria, 1972. Cert. barrister, solicitor Supreme Ct. Nigeria. Dep. solicitor Ministry Justice, Calabar, Nigeria, 1981; legal mgr. NNPC, Lagos, Nigeria, 1988-90, gen. mgr. legal divsn., 1990-93; group mgr., legal sec. corp. NNPC, Lagos, Abuja, Nigeria, 1993-96; group GM, sec. to corp. NNPC, Abuja, Nigeria, 1997-99; prin. cons. Essien, Johnz Assocs., Abuja, Nigeria, 1999—; chmn. Staff Home Ownership Scheme Co. NNPC, Lagos, 1997-99; mem. Staff Pensions bd. NNPC, Lagos, 1997-99; dir. Baywood Continental Ltd. Lagos, 1999—; cons. Drake Oil Ltd., Lagos, 1999—. Founder Quaiboe Ch. APAPA, Lagos, 1964; gen. sec. Inst. Adminstrn. Students Union, Zaria, Nigeria, 1969-70; nat. treas. Nat. Union Nigerian Students, Zaria, 1969-70; founder, pres. AWAARFA Devel. Assn., Algos, 1987. Obong Ifiok King of Wisdom award Onna local govt. area award Akwaibom, Nigeria, 1998, Obong Ifiok award Use-Offot UYO Akwaibom, Nigeria, 1998, Merit award Law Soc. U. Uyo, Nigeria, 1999. Mem. Nigerian Bar Assn., Internat. Bar Assn., 1986—, Am. Bar Assn., 1990—. Pentecostal. Avocations: reading, swimming, traveling, African/Classical music. Home: Plot 24 84 Cadastral Zone A Maitama, Abuja Nigeria Office: Essien John & Assocs, Ste BS 109 Bane x Plz PO Box 4250, Garki Abuja Nigeria

ESSLER, WILHELM KARL, philosophy educator; b. Gross Glockersdorf, Czechoslovakia, Apr. 27, 1940; arrived in Fed. Republic Germany, 1946; s. Franz and Anna (Schnörch) E.; m. Uta Wieland; children: Gabriele A., Ulrike R. PhD, U. Munich, 1964. Asst. philosophy faculty U. Munich, 1963-66, 67-69, dozent, 1969-75, assoc. prof., 1975-79; prof. dept. philosophy U. Frankfurt, 1979—; lectr. Hägerström Lectures, U. Uppsala, 1984; vis. lectr. dept. philosophy U. Pa., Phila., 1966; vis. prof. dept. philosophy U. Tübingen, Fed. Republic Germany, 1971-72, U. Trier, Fed. Republic Germany, U. Hamburg, Fed. Republic Germany, 1974, U. Frankfurt, 1978-79. Author: Introduction to Logic, 1966, Philosophy of Science, Vols. I-IV, 1970-79, Analytical Philosophy, 1972; (with others) Fundamentals of Logic, Vols. I-II, 1983, 91; editor Erkenntnis-Internat. Jour. Analytic Philosophy, 1974—, also others; contbr. numerous articles to profl. jours. Town councillor City of Günzburg, Fed. Republic Germany, 1972-78; dist. councillor Dist. of Günzburg, 1978-79. Mem. Internat. Inst. Philophy Paris (corr.). Mem. Social Dem. Party Germany. Avocations: iai-do, Buddhist philosophy. Home: Nelkenweg 12, D-8870 Günzburg Federal Republic of Germany Office: U Frankfurt Dept Phil and History, PO Box 111932 Box 776, D-60054 Frankfurt 11, Federal Republic of Germany

ESSMYER, MICHAEL MARTIN, lawyer; b. Abilene, Tex., Dec. 6, 1949; s. Lytle Martin Essmyer and Roberta N. Essmyer Nicholson; m. Cynthia Rose Piccolo, Dec. 27, 1970; children: Deanna, Mike, Brent Austin. BS in Geology, Tex. A&M U., 1972; postgrad., Tex. Christian U., 1976; JD summa cum laude, South Tex. Coll. Law, 1980. Bar: Tex. 1980, U.S. Dist. Ct. (no., so., ea. we. dists) Tex. 1982, U.S. Ct. Appeals (5th cir.) 1981, U.S. Ct. Appeals (9th cir.) 1990, U.S. Ct. Appeals (1st cir.) 1993, U.S. Ct. Appeals (7th cir.) 1995, U.S. Ct. Appeals (fed. cir.) 1985, U.S. Ct. Claims, 1981, U.S. Supreme Ct. 1991. Briefing atty. Supreme Ct. Tex., Austin, 1980-81, Haynes & Fullenweider, Houston, 1981-89, Essmyer & Hanby, Houston, 1989-92; atty. Essmyer & Assocs., Houston, 1992-94; pres. Essmyer & Tritco, LLP, Houston, 1994-95, Essmyer, Tritco & Clary, LLP, Houston, 1995-99, Essmyer & Tritco, LLP, Houston, 1999—. Lead article editor South Tex. Law Jour., 1979. Dem. candidate for state rep., Bryan, Tex., 1972; del. Dem. Party, Houston, 1982, 84; precinct chmn. Harris County Dem. Exec. Com., Houston, 1983-86. Capt. USAF, 1972-78. Nat. Merit Scholar, 1968-72. Mem. ABA, Houston Bar Assn., Tex. Trial Lawyers Assn. (assoc. dir. 1996—), Harris County Trial Lawyers Assn. (dir. 1997—), Assn. Trial Lawyers Am., Tex. Criminal Def. Lawyers Assn., Tex. Bar Found., Harris County Criminal Lawyers Assn. (dir. 1986-87), Fed. Bar Assn., Houstonian Club, The Doctor's Club of Houston. Roman Catholic. E-mail: essmyer@flash.net. Home: 1122 Glourie Dr Houston TX 77055-7506 Office: Essmyer & Tritico LLP 4300 Scotland St Houston TX 77007-7328

ESSY, AMARA, Ivorian government official; b. Bouaké, Ivory Coast, Dec. 20, 1944; s. Bakary and Korotoumou (Ouattara) E.; m. 1971; children:

Nicolas, Abdoulaye, Myriam, Mathy, Adama, Ismaël, Leila. LLB, Carnegie Inst. Geneva, postgrad. degree in pub. law. With Dept. Econ. Relations, Tech. and Econ. Cooperation, Côte d'Ivoire, 1970; 1st counselor Côte d'Ivoire Embassy, Brazil, 1971-73; counselor Côte d'Ivoire Mission to UN, N.Y.C., 1973-75; ambassador to Switzerland, 1975-81; ambassador to UN N.Y.C., 1981-90; ambassador to Argentina, 1981-83, ambassador to Cuba, 1983-88; pres. UN Security Coun., 1990; min. fgn. affairs Govt. of Côte d'Ivoire, 1990—; pres. 49th session UN Gen. Assembly, 1994-95. Named to Order Nat. Ivoirien. Avocations: jogging, soccer, bicycling. Office: Ministry of Fgn Affairs, 06 BP 368, Abidjan 06, Côte d'Ivoire

ESTABROOK, ROBERT HARLEY, journalist; b. Dayton, Ohio, Oct. 16, 1918; s. Charles and Christianne M. (Harley) E.; m. Mary Lou Stewart, Dec. 22, 1942; children: John Stewart, James Ross, David Morse, Margaret Harley. AB, Northwestern U., 1939; postgrad., Am. Press Inst., Columbia, 1947; LHD (hon.), Colby Coll., 1972. City editor Emmet County Graphic, Harbor Springs, Mich., 1936; editor Daily Northwestern, Northwestern U., 1938-39; reporter Cedar Rapids (Iowa) Gazette, 1939-40, editorial writer, 1940-42; editorial writer Washington Post, 1946-53, editor editorial page, 1953-61; corr. Washington Post, London, 1961-62, chief fgn. corr., 1962-65, UN and Can. corr., 1966-71; editor, pub. Lakeville (Conn.) Jour., 1971-86, pub. emeritus, cons., 1987—; lectr. journalism U. Md., 1948-49; India Editor Exchange Program, 1987. Served from pvt. to capt. AUS, 1942-46; in charge Army newspaper and radio sta. 1945, Brazil. Recipient John Peter Zenger award U. Ariz., 1979, Eugene Cervi award, 1980, Horace Greeley award, 1980, Yankee Quill award Acad. New Eng. Journalists, 1983; named to New Eng. Cmty. Newspaper Hall of Fame, 2000. Mem. Nat. Conf. Editorial Writers (founder, life mem. pres. 1951), Council Fgn. Relations, Conn. Council on Freedom of Info. (chmn. 1981-82, Stephen Collins award, 1989), New Eng. Press Assn. (pres. 1983), Rotary Club, Phi Beta Kappa, Sigma Delta Chi (award for best editorial 1954), Deadline Club (Pulitzer Prize juror 1988, 89, award for UN corr. 1969, Golden Quill award for best editorial 1973, 78, Herbert Brucker award 1977), Delta Tau Delta. Unitarian. Office: Lakeville Jour 33 Bissell St Lakeville CT 06039-1212

ESTEBAN, HERNANI PATRICIO, business administration educator; b. Batan, Aklan, The Philippines, July 20, 1919; s. Jose Esteban and Rita Patricio; m. Teresita Lagniton, Jan. 24, 1954; children: Honorita, Cecilia, Victor, Juancho, Theresa. BS in Commerce, Far Ea. U., Manila, 1947, MSBA, 1953; PhD in Bus. Adminstrn., U. St. Thomas, Manila, 1956, PhD in Psychology, 1978. Profl. cert. of accreditation World Edn. Svcs., Inc. Chief clk. Base S U.S. Army, Cebu, The Philippines, 1945-46, clk., 1946-47; pers. asst. USAF, Angeles, The Philippines, 1947-52, employee utilization officer, 1952-54, tech. asst., 1954-55; prof. lectr. Poly., U. of The Philippines, Manila, 1972—; participant with distinction IMPACT II, internat. mgmt. seminar Ind. U. Grad. Sch. Bus., 1963; dean faculty grad. studies Far Ea. U., Manila, 1968-69, Philippine Coll. Commerce, Manila, 1969-70; v.p. for acad. affairs Poly., U. of The Philippines, Manila, 1970-72; v.p. for adminstrn. with rank of prof. U. of City of Manila, 1972-81; guest spkr. Kiwanis Internat., Denver, 1957, Rotary of Duluth, 1957; participant Am. Soc. Tng. Dirs., Ft. Worth, 1957. Contbg. writer profl. publs. Lt. col. Army Armed Forces of The Philippines, 1994—, ret.; combat sgt. USAF, 1941-46. Recipient Citation of Recognition, USAID, 1963, Citation of Achievement U.S. Govt. of Internat. Coop. Adminstrn., 1963; vis. grantee U.S. Govt. of Internat. Coop. Program, Dallas, 1957. Mem. APA, ABI, IBC, Am. Ex-Prisoners of War (life), Sr. Citizens Club of Calif. Democrat. Roman Catholic. Avocations: writing articles, reading, hiking, watching movies, dancing. Fax: (632) 373-2572. E-mail: juancho@portalinc.com. Home: 42 Bulletin St W Triangle, 1104 Quezon City The Phillipines Office: Polytechnic U Grad Sch, Sta Mesa, Manila Philippines

ESTEFAN, NABIL, business and finance executive; b. Beirut, July 30, 1956; came to U.S., 1980; s. Joseph George and Marie (Zahr) E.; m. Fadia Elia, July 26, 1980; children: Kareem, Dana. BA in Bus. Adminstrn. summa cum laude, New Eng. Coll., Sussex, Eng., 1980; MBA Fin. and Investments summa cum laude, George Washington U., 1982. CPA, Md. Bank analyst Standard & Chartered Bank, Beirut, 1973-75; fin. analyst Internat. Fin. Svcs., Washington, 1985-86; contr. Online Computer Sys., Inc., Germantown, Md., 1986-91, v.p. fin., 1991-93; CFO Reed Tech. and Info. Svcs., Ft. Washington, Pa., 1993-96; v.p. fin. Pepsi-Cola Internat., Somers, N.Y., 1996-97; dir. planning Pepsi-Cola Internat., Somers, 1997; pres., owner Optimum Capital Mgmt., 1998—. Mem. AICPA, Am. Mgmt. Assn. Avocations: skiing, tennis, reading, classical music, opera. Home: 1114 Hillcrest Rd Narberth PA 19072-1224

ESTEFAN, SELIM FAHMY, chemistry educator; b. Quena, Egypt, Nov. 10, 1936; s. Fahmy Estefan and Liza Ibrahim (Michael) Saleh; m. Evone Habib Jacoub; children: Mickel, Mark, Mirand. BSc, Cairo U., 1960, MSc, 1965, PhD, 1970; hon. diploma of sci., World Cultural Coun., 1989. Demonstrator Egypt Atomic Energy, Cairo, 1960-62; rsch. asst. Nat. Rsch. Ctr., 1962-70, rschr., 1970-75, assoc. prof., 1975-80, rsch. prof., 1980—, dept. head, 1996; cons. Lake Qarun Project, Fayoum, Egypt, 1973-84, Ministry of Electricity, Cairo, 1986-93, Egypt Sulphur Project, Cairo, 1984-92, Egypt Phosphate Project, Cairo, 1978-82. Contbr. over 130 articles to profl. jours.; patentee in field. Mem. Sixth Oct. Sporting Club (cultural advisor), Can. Inst. Mining and Metallurgery, Scientific Profl. Syndicate, Sigma Xi. Coptic Orthodox. Avocations: exploratory tours, music, humanities. Home: 12 Nawal St #12 Agouza, Cairo Egypt Office: Nat Rsch Ctr, Tahreer St, Cairo 12622, Egypt

ESTELLA, MARGARITA M., research scientist; b. Zaragoza, Spain, Sept. 24, 1930; d. Jose Bermudez de Castro Estella and Angela Marcos. Lic., U. Complutense Madrid, 1954, D of History, 1974. Becario C.S.I.C., Madrid, 1957; prof. U. Complutense Madrid, 1964-66; collaborator sci. C.S.I.C., Madrid, 1972-87; sci. investigator Centro de Estudios Historicos, Madrid, 1987—. Author: Escultura Barroca de Marfil en Espana: las escuelas europeas y las coloniales, 1984 (2 vols.), Juan Bautista Vazquez el Viejo en Castilla y America, 1990, Los Leoni, escultores entre Espana e Italia en el Catalogo con estudios de Urrea, Moran, Tarraga, Cano, Coppel, 1994, La Imagineria de los Retablos de la Capilla del Condestable de la Catedral de Burgos, 1995. Roman Catholic. Home: C Jose Ortega y Gasset 17, 28006 Madrid Spain Office: Centro Estudios Historicos, Duque de Medinaceli 6, 28014 Madrid Spain

ESTEP, LAWRENCE ROBERT, videographer, photographer; b. New Albany, Ind., Mar. 15, 1973; s. Karen Sue (Estep) Spry. Grad. h.s., New Albany. Pub. svc. dir. WNAS Radio/TV, New Albany, 1989-90, weather dir., 1989-91, ops. dir., 1990-91; weather dir., master control operator WBNA-TV, Louisville, 1992-95, pub. svcs. dir., 1993-95; master control operator WFTE-TV, Salem, Ind., 1996-99, Sta. WDRB-TV, Louisville, 1996-99; owner Estep Enterprises, Crawfordsville, Ind., 1999—; radio announcer, news asst. WIMC/WCVL, Crawfordsville, Ind., 1999—. Mem. Warn Weather Group, Am. Legion Post 42, Sons of the Am. Legion (squadron comdr. 1983-84, dir. Alert Ind. Tornado Rsch. 1992-96), Montgomery County EMA. Avocations: severe weather rsch., hot air ballooning, amusement parks, photography, NASCAR. E-mail: wxguy@webtv.net. Home and Office: 2002 Waterford Ct Apt D Crawfordsville IN 47933-3287

ESTEP, MYRNA LYNNE, systems analyst, philosophy educator; b. Whitesville, W.Va., Jan. 7, 1944; d. Modest Schaeffer and Mary Magdalene E.; m. Richard Keith Schoenig, June 5, 1971; 1 child, Debora Lynne. BA, Ind. U., 1970, MS, 1971, PhD, 1975; postgrad., U. Tex., 1993 . Assoc. instr. Ind. U., Bloomington, 1972-75; asst. prof. U. Tex., San Antonio, 1975-78; rsch. edn. specialist Acad. Health Scis., San Antonio, Tex., 1979-84; program systems analyst, field researcher USMC, U.S. Navy, Quantico, Va., 1984-87; grad. faculty, advisor U. Zimbabwe, 1987-89; rsch. systems analyst San Antonio, 1990—; adj. faculty in philosophy U. of Incarnate Word, San Antonio, 1996-99, Our Lady of the Lake U., San Antonio, 1996-98; grad. faculty U. Zimbabwe, Harare; advisor to ministries of higher edn. and labour, manpower planning and social welfare, Zimbabwe, 1987-89. Author: The Relation Between Theoretical and Procedural Knowing, 1975; co-editor: (with E.S. Maccia and others) Women and Education, 1975; reviewer for jours.; contbr. sci. papers and monographs to profl. publs., including Feminista: The On-Line Jour. of Feminist Reconstrn., 1998 . Recipient Best Paper award U. Vienna, Austria, 1992. Mem. AAAS, Internat. Soc. Gen. Systems Rsch., Austrian Soc. Cybernetics, Math. Assn. Am., N.Y. Acad. Sci., Phi Kappa Phi. Home: 16022 Oak Grove Dr San Antonio TX 78255-1128

ESTERHAI, JOHN LOUIS, JR., surgeon, medical educator; b. Phila., Oct. 23, 1946; s. John Louis and Louise K. (Moyer) E.; m. Carol Jean Keely, Apr. 12, 1969; children: Staci June, Gregory Wayne. BA, Gettysburg Coll., 1968; MD, Temple U., 1972. Intern in surgery Temple U. Health Sci. Ctr., Phila., 1973; flight surgeon USAF, Kadena AFB, Okinawa, Japan, 1973-76; resident in orthop. surgery U. Pa. Sch. Medicine, 1977-80; asst. prof. orthopedic surgery Hosp. U. Pa., Phila., 1980-87, assoc. prof. orthopedic surgery, 1987-2000, prof. orthopedic surgery, 2000—. Editor: Musculoskeletal Infection, 1992. Maj. USAF, 1973-76. Recipient award Am. Orthopedic Assn., 1989, Assn. Bone and Joint Surgeons, 1994. Fellow Am. Acad. Orthopedic Surgeons, ACS; mem. Internat. Soc. Fracture Repair, Orthopaedic Rsch. Soc., Musculoskeletal Infection Soc. (pres. 1997-98). Office: Hosp U Pa Dept Orthopaedic Surgery 3400 Spruce St Philadelphia PA 19104-4206

ESTERHAMMER, ANGELA, literary theorist, educator; b. Toronto, Ont., Can., Nov. 20, 1961; d. Hermann and Marianne (Schittich) E.; married, Feb. 20, 1989. BA, U. Toronto, 1983; postgrad., U. Tübingen, Germany, 1983-84; PhD, Princeton U., 1990. Asst. prof. U. Western Ont., 1989-94, assoc. prof., 1994-99, prof., 2000—, chair Dept. of Modern Langs., 2000—; vis. prof. Freie U., Berlin, 1996-98. Author: Creating States: Studies in the Performative Language of John Milton and William Blake, 1994, The Romantic Performative: Language and Action in British and German Romanticism, 2000; translator (and introduction): Two Stories of Prague by R.M. Rilke, 1994; contbr. articles to profl. jours. Alexander von Humboldt Found. rsch. fellow, Freie U. Berlin, 1996-97, Whiting Fellow in Humanities, 1988; recipient John Charles Polanyi prize Govt. of Ont., 1990, Toronto Arts Awards Found. Protégé award, 1988. Mem. MLA, N.Am. Soc. for Study of Romanticism (founding mem.), Can. Comparative Lit. Assn., Internat. Comparative Lit. Assn. Mem. United Ch. of Can.

ESTERHÁZY, PETER, author; b. Hungary, Apr. 14, 1950; m. Gitta Reén; 4 children. Grad., U. Budapest, Hungary, Eötvös Loránd U. Writings include: (fiction) Fancsikó and Pinta, 1976, Don't Be A Pirate on Papal Waters!, 1977, Production-Novel (Little Novel), 1979, Indirect, 1981, Who Can Guarantee the Lady's Safety?, 1982, Transporters, 1983, Little Hungarian Pornography, 1984, Helping Verbs of the Heart, 1985, 17 Swans, 1987, Certain Adventure, 1989, Hrabal's Book, 1990, The Glance of Countess Hahn-Hahn, 1991, A Woman, 1995; (play) Daisy: opera semiseria in one act, 1984, Farewell Symphony, 1994, She Loves Me, 1995; (other writings) The Stuffed Swan, 1988, The Wonderful Life of the Little Fish, 1991, From the Ivory Tower, 1991, Notes of a Blue Stocking, 1994. Recipient Attila József prize, Lajos Kossuth prize. Office: Hungarian Writers Fedn, Bajza-utca 18, 1062 Budapest Hungary*

ESTES, ANDREW HARPER, lawyer; b. Pecos, Tex., Dec. 16, 1956; s. Bobby Frank and Gayle (Harper) E.; m. Deidre Dement, Mar. 19, 1976; children: Andrew Kimble, Jada Catherine. BA, Tex. Tech U., 1977; JD, Baylor Sch. Law, 1979. Bar: Tex. 1980, U.S. Dist. Ct. (no. dist.) Tex. 1980, U.S. Dist. Ct. (we. dist.) Tex. 1981, U.S. Ct. Appeals (5th cir.) 1982, U.S. Supreme Ct. 1983, U.S. Tax Ct., U.S. Ct. Appeals (10th cir.) 1987. Ptnr. Lynch, Chappell & Alsup P.C., Midland, Tex., 1980—; mem. admissions com. Dist. 16, State Bar Tex., 1982-85, bd. dirs., 1999—. Mem. Tex. Tech. U. Coll. Edn. Devel. Coun., Lubbock, 1986-87; vol. Big Bros., Midland, 1983—, bd. dirs., 1985-89; bd. dirs. Hearthstone Temporary Children's Shelter, 1988-92. Named Big Brother of Yr., Big Bros./Big Sisters of Midland, 1985; recipient Trimble Vol. Svc. award, Leadership Midland Alumni, 1986, Pro Bono Atty. award West Tex. Legal Svcs., 1991. Mem. ABA, Midland County Young Lawyers Assn. (sec., treas. 1987-88, Outstanding Young Lawyer of Midland County 1992), Midland County Bar Assn. (sec., treas. 1987-88, v.p. 1992-93, pres. elect. 1993-94, pres. 1995-96), State Bar Tex. (Dist. 16B grievance com. 1990-93, chmn. 1992-93, bd. dirs. 1999—), Tex. Young Lawyers Assn. (bd. dirs. 1987-89), Tex. Bd. Legal Specialization (cert.), Phi Delta Phi. Presbyterian. Home: 1404 Princeton Ave Midland TX 79701-5760 Office: Lynch Chappell & Alsup PC The Summit Bldg 300 N Marienfeld St Fl 7 Midland TX 79701-4345

ESTES, CARL LEWIS, II, lawyer; b. Ft. Worth, Feb. 9, 1936; s. Joe E. and Carroll E.; m. Gay Gooch, Aug. 29, 1959; children: Adrienne Virginia, Margaret Ellen. B.S., U. Tex., 1957, LL.B., 1960. Bar: Tex. 1960. Law clk. U.S. Supreme Ct., 1960-61; assoc. firm Vinson & Elkins, Houston, 1961-69; ptnr. Vinson & Elkins, 1970—. Bd. dirs. Houston Grand Opera Assn., Houston Arboretum. Fellow Am. Bar Found., Tex. Bar Found.; mem. ABA, Internat. Bar Assn., Am. Law Inst., Am. Coll. Probate Counsel, Tex. Bar Assn., Internat. Fiscal Assn., Internat. Acad. Estate and Trust Law. Fellow Am. Bar Found., Tex. Bar Found.; mem. ABA, Internat. Bar Assn., Am. Law Inst., Am. Coll. Probate Counsel, Tex. Bar Assn., Internat. Fiscal Assn., Internat. Acad. Estate and Trust Law, Asia Soc. (bd. dirs.). Office: Vinson & Elkins 3300 First City Towers Houston TX 77002

ESTES, DOUGLAS LEE, motel owner; b. Oakland, Calif., Sept. 12, 1944; s. Elmer Leroy and Patricia Lillian (Hansen) E.; Justine Nell Pinard, Mar. 5, 1977; children: Jordan, Aaron, Natasha, Allison. BS in Bus. Adminstrn., U. S.D., 1966; MS, U. Wyo., 1971. Teaching asst. U. Wyo., 1969-70; devel. dir. Yankon Sioux Tribe, Wagner, S.D., 1970-71; price analyst Cost of Living Council, Washington, 1972-74; fin. analyst Fed. Energy Office, Washington, 1974-75; owner, mgr. Sands Motel, Wall (S.D.) Motel, Wall Super 8 Motel, 1975—; bd. dirs., treas. BED Co., Full House, Inc., S.D. Vending, Inc. Bd. dirs. S.D. Bldg. Authority, Pierre, 1983—; Rep. committeeman, Pennington County, 1978-86; mem. Black Hills Badlands and Lakes Assn., 1976—, bd. dirs., 1995—; bd. dirs. S.D. Tourism Adv. Bd., Pierre, 1980—; chmn. S.D. Mktg. Task Force, 1986-87. With U.S. Army, 1967-69. Mem. Am. Legion (post comdr. 1980-81), Wall C. of C. (bd. dirs. 1984—), Wall Hospitality Assn. (v.p. 1986, 87, 88), S.D. Innkeppers Assn. (bd. dirs.), Beta Gamma Sigma. Methodist. Avocations: jazz music, community theatre. Office: Sands Motel 804 Glenn St Wall SD 57790

ESTES, JACK CHARLES, oil service company executive, scientist; b. Rogers, Ark., Apr. 7, 1935; s. Jack Russell and Merle Clara (White) E.; m. Sandra Jean Reeves, Nov. 10, 1961; children: Michael Lynn, David Russell, Cristi Yvonne. BS in Engring., U. Tulsa, 1965. Computer engr. Remington Rand Univac, Illion, N.Y., 1960; rsch. tech. Pan Am. Petroleum Corp., Tulsa, 1960-65, rsch. engr., 1965-76; rsch. supr. Amoco Prodn. Co., Tulsa, 1976-89; pres. Environ. Drilling Tech., Inc., Tulsa, 1990—; prin. Estes Consulting Group, Tulsa, 1999—. Contbr. articles to profl. jours.; patentee in field. With USAF, 1955-59. Mem. ASME, N.E. Okla. Sq. Dance Assn. (bd. dirs. 1989-92), Am. Petroleum Inst. (chmn. internat. subcom. 13 1982-85, vice chmn. com. 13 1986-89, task group chmn. 1989—, Svc. award 1991), Internat. Drilling Contractors (chmn. drill bit standardization task group 1973-80), Am. Mgmt. Assn., Soc. Petroleum Engrs. (tech. editor Jour. Petroleum Tech. 1977-78, Svc. award 1985, program com. 1989-92), Am. Chem. Soc. (Svc. award 1984), Sci. Rsch. Soc. (internat. sci. fair judge), Sigma Xi.

ESTES, LAURIE LYNN, educational program developer and administrator; b. Concord, N.H., Nov. 13, 1960; d. Elwood LeRoy and Francis Marion (Carver) E. BA, Mt. Holyoke Coll., 1986; MDiv, U. Chgo., 1996. Performing arts adminstr. U. Maine, Orono, 1980-83; sr. program adminstr. Boston Ctr. for Adult Edn., 1987-91; asst. to dir. internat. initiative Coun. for A Parliament of the World's Religioun, Chgo., 1995-98; dir. New Beginnings program for immigrants and refugees Loyola U., Chgo., 1988-99; Inst. World Spirituality, Chgo., 1999; asst. to pres. Maximum Entropy, Inc., Chgo., 1999—; Human Rights liason UN, N.Y.C., Stanford U., South Africa, Brazil, etc., 1996—. Francis Perkins fellow, 1984-86. Mem. Am. Assn. Religion (com. on psychology and religion 1994-98), United Religions Initiative (charter mem.). Episcopalian. Avocations: reading aloud, volunteer work, writing and editing. E-mail: llynnestes@yahoo.com.

ESTES, MOREAU PINCKNEY, IV, real estate executive, lawyer; b. Nashville, Oct. 10, 1917; s. Moreau Pinckney III and Lillian (Cole) E.; m. Bertha Lewis, Jan. 14, 1941; children: Moreau Pinckney V, Robert Lewis, Victoria Susanne. Student, Vanderbilt U., 1935-36; LLB, Cumberland U., 1938. Bar: Tenn. 1938. Sole practice law Nashville, 1938-41, bldg. contractor, 1940-43, 46-53; dir. Davidson County Farm Bur., Nashville, 1950-56; v.p. Davidson Farmers Coop., 1955-56; gen. mgr. Harpeth Valley (Tenn.) Utilities Dist., 1963-67; founder, pres. Hillsboro-Harpeth Corp., 1964—; founder, sec.-treas. Alpha Publishing Co., Brentwood, Tenn., 1986—, also bd. dirs.; founder, owner Realty Investment Co., Nashville, 1964—. Mem. residents adv. bd. Tenn. Selective Svcs. System, 1941; atty. property div. State of Tenn., 1963-67, property adminstr., 1964-67; asst. commr. Tenn. Dept. Conservation, 1975; Dem. primary cand. U.S. Ho. of Reps., 1950; del. State Dem. Conv., 1951; sec. Williamson County Dem. Primary Commn., 1967-69; asst. dir. communications Tenn. Dem. Gubernatorial Campaign, 1974; Williamson County coord. Tenn. Dem. Primary Gubernatorial candidate, 1978; middle Tenn. coord. Dem. Primary and Gen. Election Gubernatorial candidate, 1982; bd. stewards, Sunday sch. tchr. Hobson Meth. Ch., 1940-42, 46-50; founder, chmn. bd., 1st pres. Rivermont Watershed Dist., Davidson County, Tenn., 1990-94; apptd. col., aide de camp Staff of Tenn. Gov. Frank Clement, 1963-67, Gov. Ray Blanton, 1975-79, Gov. Lamar Alexandar, 1979-87. Served to 1st lt. Signal Corps U.S. Army, 1942-46, with Res., 1946-51. Named Nashville Mcpl. Tennis Singles and Doubles champion, 1939, 40, Middle Tenn. Singles and Doubles Mcpl. Tennis champion, 1940. Mem. Nashville Home Builders Assn. (pres. 1950), Tenn. Horsemen's Assn. (dir. 1964), Tenn. Hist. Soc., Tenn. Bar Assn., Nashville Bar Assn., Bibl. Archaeology Soc., Nat. Audubon Soc., Smithsonian Assocs., Vanderbilt U. Alumni Assn., Nat. Geographic Soc., SAR, Internat. Bible Assn., Nature Conservancy, Sierra Club, Am. Legion, Wildwood Swimming and Tennis Club (founder, 1st chmn.), Delta Kappa Epsilon. Democrat. Methodist. Home: 6434 Panorama Dr Brentwood TN 37027-4823

ESTES, NATHAN ANTHONY MARK, III, cardiologist, medical educator; b. Newport, R.I., Aug. 20, 1949; s. Nathan Anthony Jr. and Ione (Lewis) E.; m. Noël Evangeline Thorbecke, June 22, 1974; children: Elise Thorbecke, N.A. Chace, Kathryn Elizabeth. BA cum laude, U. Pa., 1971; MD magna cum laude, U. Cin., 1977. Diplomate Am. Bd. Internal Medicine, Am. Bd. Cardiovascular Disease, Am. Bd. Cardiac Electrophysiology. Med. intern New Eng. Deaconess Hosp.-Harvard Med. Sch., Boston, 1977-78, med. resident, 1978-80; fellow in cardiology New Eng. Med. Ctr.-Tufts U., Boston, 1980-82; fellow in electrophysiology Mass. Gen. Hosp.-Harvard Med. Sch., Boston, 1982-83; dir. cardiac arrhythmia New. Eng. Med. Ctr. Svc., Boston, 1983-96, dir. heart station, 1983-91; assoc. prof. medicine Tufts U. Sch. Med., Boston, 1983-90, prof., 1990-96, chief New Eng. Cardiac Arrythmia Ctr., 1996-97; chief New. Eng. Arrhythmia Ctr., Boston, 1996—, Lifespan Cardiac Arrhythmia Consortium, Boston, 1998; ednl. cons., 1985-96; mem. internat. safety monitoring bd. 3M Pharms., Mpls., 1990-96; co-chmn. pubs. com. NIH, Bethesda, 1993-96; chmn. instl. rev. bd. Tufts U. Sch. Medicine, 1996—. Contbr. over 200 articles to sci. jours.; contbr. over 30 chpts. to books; editor books, 1994-96; editl. bd. Jour. Interventional Electrophysiology, 1995—, Pacing and Cardiac Electrophysiology, 1995—, Jour. Cardiovasc. Electrophysiology, Am. Jour. Sports and Medicine, 1998, Am. Jour. Cardiology. Vestry mem. Trinity Ch., Newton, Mass., 1985-87; coach Baystate Tournament of Champions, Waltham, Mass., 1990-94; judge N.H. Racing Assn., Lincoln, 1993-95; bd. trustees Moses Brown Sch., Providence, R.I., 1997—. Fellow Am. Coll. Cardiology; mem. Am. Heart Assn. (chmn. bd. trustees Boston chpt. 1998, vice chair New Eng. affiliate 1999, pres.-elect New Eng. affiliate 2000, coun clin. cardiology), N.Am. Soc. Pacing and Electrophysiology (chmn. publs. com.), New Eng. Electrophysiology Soc. (pres. 1994-97), Alpha Omega Alpha. Episcopalian. Avocations: sailing, skiing, tennis, running. Office: New Eng Med Ctr 750 Washington St Boston MA 02111-1526

ESTES, RICHARD MARTIN, lawyer; b. N.Y.C., June 27, 1933; s. Jack Estes and Irene Eva (Dessauer) Schwarz; m. Pamela Jane Graine, Mar. 18, 1965; children: Kenneth Murray, William Jonathan, Jessica Jane. BA, Yale Coll., 1955; LLB, Columbia U., 1959; LLM in Taxation, NYU, 1962. Bar: N.Y. 1959, Fla. 1976; U.S. Supreme Ct. 1962. Assoc. White & Case, N.Y.C., 1959-62, Root, Barrett, Cohen Knapp & Smith, N.Y.C., 1962-65; asst. tax counsel Rockefeller Family & Assocs., N.Y.C., 1965-68; tax counsel Bear, Stearns & Co., N.Y.C., 1968-70; assoc. to ptnr. Spear & Hill, N.Y.C., 1970-75; founding ptnr. Christy & Viener, N.Y.C., 1976-98, Salans, Hertzfeld, Heilbronn, Christy & Viener, N.Y.C., 1999—; lectr. in field. Contbr. articles to profl. jours. Trustee, sec., nomination com. N.Y.C. Police Found., 1971—; bd. mem., v.p., sec. Yale Project 55, Inc., N.Y.C., 1993—; trustee, treas. 1010 Tenants Corp., N.Y.C., 1988—. Maj. USAR, 1955-65. Honored as co-founder N.Y.C. Police Found., 1991. Mem. ABA, Assn. of the Bar of the City of N.Y. (libr. com.), N.Y. State Bar Assn. (tax sect.), Fla. Bar Assn., Univ. Club (coun., libr. and art com. 1976—), Grolier Club, Harmonie Club, Beach Point Club. Avocations: antiquarian book collector, fitness, reading, travel. Office: Salans Hertzfeld Heilbronn Christy & Viener 620 5th Ave New York NY 10020-2402

ESTEVE, PERE, foreign diplomat; b. Barcelona, Spain, Dec. 26, 1942. Mem. European Parliament, 1999—, com. fgn. affairs/human rights/common security/def. policy, substitute com.citizens' freedoms/rights/justice/home affair; mem. Group of the European Liberal, Democrat and Reform Party; mem. delegation to the EU-Bulgaria Joint Parliamentary Com. Mem. Catalan Dem. Convergence. *

ESTIEVENART, GEORGES, executive director. B. Elem. Math., U. Troyes, 1960; Degree in German, The Sorbonne, Paris, 1963, Higher Diploma in Sec. Tchg. of German, 1965. Asst. for French Goethe-Schule, Karlsruhe, Germany, 1963-64; tchr. german various secondary schs. Min. of Edn., France, 1964-69; asst. faculty of arts U. Nancy, 1969-70; tchr. german Ecole Militaire Interarmes de Coëtquidan, France, 1970-71; head asst. del. Inst. d'Etudes Politiques, Strasbourg, France, 1971-74; adminstr. Directorate Gen. for Budgets, then Devel. Commn. of European Communities, Brussels, 1974-81; chargé de mission Delegation l'Aménagement du Territoire and Régional, Paris, 1981-83; gen. sec. Internat. Ctr. for Higher Studies in Mediterranean Agronomy, Paris, 1983-85; adminstr. Directorate Gen. for External Rels. Commn. of European Communities, Brussels, 1985-88, prin. adminstr., 1985-89, head sector environment, 1989-90, head sector drugs, 1990-91, head unit abolition of frontier controls on persons, 1991-93, head unit Drugs and Drugs Monitoring Ctr., 1993—, permanent corr., 1990-94; dir. European Monitoring Ctr. for Drugs and Drug Addiction, Lisbon, 1994—. Contbr. numerous articles to profl. jours. Office: EMCDDA, Rua Cruz Sta Apolonia 23-25, P1149045 Lisbon Portugal

ESTOR, ANNEMARIE, literature and science researcher, poet; b. Gouda, The Netherlands, Apr. 24, 1973; d. Bernard Cornelis Estor and Anna Maria Catharina Wilhelmina Kessels. BA, U. Maastricht, 1992, MA, 1996. Rsch. fellow U. Leiden, 1996—. Author: (Dutch) Afternoon, 1996, Space, 1997, Under Tealeaves, 1999; contbr. articles to profl. jours. Encouragement grant NWO, 1997, grant for Internat. scholarship, 1998, 99. Mem. MLA, Soc. for Lit. and Sci., First European Conf. Soc. for Lit. and Sci. (co-organizer 1998—). Avocation: classical singer (opera). Office: Dept English U of Leiden, PO Box 9515, NL2300RA Leiden The Netherlands

ESTRADA, JOSEPH MARCELO EJERCITO, Philippine government official; b. Tondo, Manila, The Philippines, Apr. 19, 1937; m. Luisa Pimentel; children: Jinggoy, Jacqueline, Jude. Student, Ateno de Manila U., Mapua Inst. Tech.; PhD, U. Pangasinan. Film actor, late 1950s; mayor San Juan, The Philippines, 1969-86; chmn. com. on cultural communities, com. on rural devel., com. on pub. works Senate, 1987-92, vice chmn. coms. on health, natural resources, ecology and urban planning, 1987-92; chmn. Presdl. Anti-Crime Commn., 1992—; fomer v.p., now pres. Govt. of The Philippines, Manila, 1992—; pres. Joseph Estrada Prodns. Inc., San Juan Police and Fire Trust Fund; pres., founder Movie Workers Welfare Found.; pres., adv. Philippine Motion Pictures Prodrs. Assn.; gov. Film Acad. of the Philippines. Founder, pres. ERAP sa Mahihirap Found., San Juan Progress Found., San Juan Police and Fire Trust Fund, Friends of Joseph Estrada burial assistance program; founder, hon. chmn. Philippine Druge Abuse Resistance Edn., Inc. (PHILDARE). Recipient Best Actor award 5 times, Best Picture award 5 times, Pub. Adminstrn. award Ten Outstanding Young Men, 1972; named to FAMAS Hall of Fame, 1981, 84, one of Three Outstanding Senators of Yr., Free Press, 1989, Outstanding Mayor and Foremost Nationalist, Inter Provincial Info. Svc., 1971. Mem. Partido Ng Masang Pilipino. Achievements include establishment of first San Juan Mcpl. High Sch., Agora Complex, a modern slaughterhouse, Govt. Ctr. with Post Office, a min-pk., improved roads and alleys, improved and renovated school bldgs., new schs.,

health ctrs. barangay halls and playground; relocation of squatter families; computerization of real estate tax; establishment of MOWELFUND; assistance to movie pers. Office: Office of the President/Presidencial Guest House, Malacanang Palace Compound J P Laurel St. San Miguel Manila The Philippines*

ESTRADA-FLORES, SILVIA, science educator; b. Tlalnepantla de Baz, Mex., Apr. 13, 1967; d. Marcial Estrada-Omaña and Graciela Flores-Gomez. BSc in Food Engring., Fac. Estudios Sup. Cuautitlan, Mex.; PhD, Massey U., Palmerstown North, New Zealand. Cert. in food engring. Lectr. asst. Cuautitlan campus Nat. U. Mex., 1990-92, lectr. in food tech. Cuautitlan campus, 1992-96, assoc. prof. Cuautitland campus, 1996—; cons. CONESAL, Mex., mem. nat. group rschrs. CONACYT, Mex., 1999. Contbr. articles to rsch. jours. Recipient Merit award: Best Student of Food Engring. in Mex., Nat. Arts, Scis. and Tech. Sch., Nat. Coun. Sci., and Mex. Newspaper, 1991, scholar UNAM, 1992. Avocations: weight training, karate, music, computers. E-mail: strada@servidor.unam.mx. Home: C Izcalli, Av de los Reyes 19 D 104, Mexico City CP 54700, Mexico Office: Centro Invest Teoricas, Av 1o de Mayo S/N, Mexico City CP 54700, Mexico

ESTRIN, EMMANUIL ISAAKOVICH, physicist; b. Moscow, May 19, 1931; s. Isaak Evseevich and Esfir Solomonovna (Judina) E.; m. Galina Antonovna Gritsuk, Aug. 21, 1955. MSc, Moscow Inst. Steel, 1954; PhD, Ctrl. Rsch. Inst. Iron & Steel, 1963; D in Physics, Inst. Phys. Metallurgy, 1976. Jr. researcher Inst. Phys. Metallurgy Ctrl. Rsch. Inst Iron Steel Industry, Moscow, 1954-63, sr. researcher, 1963-91, leading researcher, 1991—, prof., 1996—; chief researcher Rsch. Ctr. for Superhazardous Materials, Troitsk, Russia, 1997—. Editor Soviet physics abstracts, 1964-94; contbr. numerous articles to sci. and profl. jours. Avocations: skiing, water travel. Home: 3 Parkovaya st 22 Apt 3, 105043 Moscow Russia Office: Ctr Rsch Inst Iron Steel, Industry 2-nd Baumanskaya 9/23, 107005 Moscow Russia

ESTRIN, GENRIKH YAKOVLEWITSH, structural engineer, researcher, administrator; b. Moscow, Nov. 5, 1933; s. Yakov Lwowitsh and Fayna Moyseewna (Birulina) E.; Nina Grigoriewna Brezgunova, Dec. 10, 1960; 1 child, Sergey. Degree in civil engring. with honors, Moscow Inst. Civil Engrs., 1955; postgrad., All-Union Sci. Rsch. Inst., Moscow, 1976. Constrn. chief MK 38, Moscow, 1955-68; head group Ctrl. Sci. Rsch. Inst., Moscow, 1972-73, chief specialist, 1973-76, sr. sci. worker, 1976-88, head divsn. structural engring., 1988—. Author: Progressive Steel Constructions, 1971, Joints of the Steel Building Constructions, 1992; contbr. articles to profl. jours. Recipient medals Exhbn. of Nat. Economy Achievements, Moscow, 1977-90; grantee Internat. Sci. Found., 1992. Mem. N.Y. Acad. Scis. Avocations: swimming, travel. Office: TsNJJ Promzdaniy, Dmitrovskoe Chausse 46-2, 127238 Moscow Russia

ESTRIN, MORTON, pianist, music educator; b. Burlington, Vt., Dec. 29, 1923; s. Nathan and Gertrude Ada (Lapidow) E.; m. Eleanor Sylvia Glassman, June 17, 1944 (div. Nov. 1986); 3 children: Steven Paul (dec.), Coren Gail, Robert Alan; m. Roberta Barbara Green Zaltzman, Dec. 28, 1986. Student, NYU, 1942-44; pvt. study, Vera Maurina Press, 1941-49. Prof. music Hofstra U., Hempstead, N.Y., 1958—; pvt. tchr., Hicksville, N.Y., 1941—. Debut Town Hall, N.Y.C., 1949; tours of U.S. and Europe; appeared in Carnegie Hall, Lincoln Ctr., Merkin Hall, N.Y.C.; performed all 24 Preludes by Rachmaninoff Nat. Gallery Art, Washington, Alice Tully Hall, N.Y.C., 1985; CDs include Etudes, Opus 8, Scriabin, 1989, Suite in D minor Opus 91, Raff, 1989, Sonata in G, Tchaikowsky, 1991, Six Etudes, Rubinstein, 1991; 5 CDs issued by Sync Labs. (Connoisseur Soc.) of music by Rachmaninoff, Brahms, others, 2000. Mem. Am. Fedn. Musicians, AAUP, Bohemian Club N.Y., Pi Kappa Lambda. Home: 9 Clotilde Ct Hicksville NY 11801-5515

ESTY, DANIEL CUSHING, lawyer; b. Boston, June 6, 1959; s. John Cushing and Katharine (Cole) E.; m. Elizabeth Henderson, Oct. 20, 1984. AB, Harvard U., 1981; BA, Oxford U., 1983; JD, Yale U., 1986. Bar: Calif. 1986, U.S. Ct. Internat. Trade 1987, D.C. 1988, U.S. Dist Ct. D.C. 1988. U.S. Ct. Appeals (Fed. Cir.) 1988. With Arnold & Porter, Washington, 1986-89; spl. asst. to adminstr. EPA, Washington, 1989-90, dep. chief of staff, 1990-91, dep. asst. adminstr. for policy, 1991-93; sr. fellow Inst. for Internat. Econs., Washington, 1993-94; dir. Yale Ctr. for Environ. Law and Policy, New Haven, Conn., 1994—; assoc. dean Yale Sch. Forestry and Environ. Studies, 1998—. Home: 213 Preston Ter Cheshire CT 06410-3138 Office: Yale Ctr for Environ Law and Policy 205 Prospect St New Haven CT 06511-2106

ETCHEGARAY, ROGER CARDINAL, archbishop; b. Espelette, France, Sept. 25, 1922; s. Jean-Baptiste and Aurélie (Dufau) E. Ed. Petit Séminaire, Ustaritz, France, Grand Séminaire, Bayonne, France; PhD (hon.) St. John's U. Ordained priest Roman Cath. Ch., 1947; served diocese of Bayonne, 1947-60; asst. sec. then sec.-gen. French Episcopal Conf., 1961-70, pres., 1975-81; consecrated archbishop of Marseilles (France), 1970-85; prelate Mission of France, 1975-81; elevated to Sacred Coll. of Cardinals, 1979; pres. Council European Episcopal Conf., 1971-79; pres. Pontifical Coun. for Justice and Peace, 1984—; pres. Pontifical Coun. Cor Unum, 1984-95, Ctrl. com. for the Jubilee of the Holy Year 2000, 1994; mem. Congregation for Evangelization of Peoples, Congregation for Cath. Edn., Supreme Tribunal Apostolic Signatura, Pontifical Coun. for Christian Unity, Pontifical Coun. for Social Communications, Adminstrn. of Patrimony of the Holy See. Author: Dieu à Marseille, 1976, J'avance comme un âne, 1984, L'Evangile aux couleurs de la vie, 1987, Jésus, vrai homme, vrai Dieu, 1997. Decorated Grand Cross Nat. Order Fed. Rep. Germany, Grand Cross Nat. Order Hungary; named Comdr. Legion of Honor France. Mem. French Acad. Social Scis. Address: Palazzo San Calisto 16, 00153 Rome Italy*

ETENG, ENO EBRI, psychiatrist; arrived in Eng., 1954; s. Eno Ebri and Aquo Ubi Eteng; m. Valerie Jean Nuttall, Jan. 8, 1970; children: Matthew, Helen, Paul. MB ChB, Leeds (Eng.) U., 1957; diploma in psychiat. medicine, Royal Coll. Physicians & Surgeons, Eng. Jr. house officer, 1958; sr. house officer in medicine Manchester, Eng., 1959; registrar in psychiatry Derby/Blackburn, Eng., 1960-62; sr. registrar in psychiatry Warrington, Eng., 1962-64; sr. med. officer Home Office, Prison Dept., U.K., 1964-82; sr. clin. lectr., cons. psychiatrist U. Calabar, Nigeria, 1982-85, prof. emeritus, 2000—; cons. psychiatrist U.K., 1986—; clin. tutor Mental Retardation Bd., Bedfordshire, Eng., 1990-92. Contbr. articles to profl. jours. Fellow Royal Soc. Medicine, Royal Coll. Psychiatrists, Royal Soc. Arts; mem. Brit. Med. Assn. Christian. Avocations: gardening, visiting cathedrals, bibliography, music, countryside walking.

ETESSAMI, HIRBOD (HIRI ETESSAMI), endodontist, educator; b. Tehran, Jan. 31, 1965; came to U.S., 1978; s. Abdollah and Mahin Etessami; m. Jacqueline Etessami, Aug. 21, 1993; children: Noah, Jonah. Student, Georgetown U., 1982-85; DDS, U. So. Calif., 1989, Cert. in Advanced and Surg. Endodontics, 1991. Endodontist in pvt. practice, L.A., 1991—; pres., CEO, founder Mymoneysworth.com; clin. instr. U. So. Calif. Sch. Dentistry, 1991—, UCLA Sch. Dentistry, 1993—. Bd. dirs. Beth Jacob Congregation, Beverly Hills, Calif., 1995—; bd. dirs. L.A. Mozart Orch., 1995-96; mem. ethics com. U. So. Calif. Dental Sch., 1985-91. Mem. ADA, Calif. Dental Assn., Am. Assn. Endodontics, Alpha Omega (pres. chpt. 1989). Jewish. Avocations: playing Santour (hammer/dulcimer), Archeology, theology, politics. Office: 9201 W Sunset Blvd Ste 908 Los Angeles CA 90069-3710

ÉTÈVENAUX, JEAN, editor; b. Oyonnax, Ain, France, Apr. 28, 1947; s. Fernand and Huguette (Gentaz) É.; m. Joëlle Duclos, Sept. 26, 1970; children: Hugues, Florence, Jean-Axel, Astrid. Diploma, Inst. Polit. Studies, Lyon, France, 1969; D in History, U. Jean Moulin, Lyon, France, 1980. Head libr. U. Lubumbashi, Democratic Republic of the Congo, 1971-75; editor Le Jour. Rhône-Alpes, Lyon, 1977-87, Missi, Lyon, 1992—, Pôle et tropiques, Lyon, 1996—. Author: Mademoiselle de Quincié, 1989, Les Grandes Heures de Lyon, 1992 (Prix du Livre du Conseil Gén. du Rhône 1992), Jean Moulin, 1994 (Feuille d'or Livre sur la Place Nancy 1994), La Cuisine lyonnaise, 1996. Prin. pvt. sec. City Perpignan, France, 1995. Recipient Grand Prix d'Ornano du Souvenir Napolénien, 1964. Mem. Assn. Auteurs et Ecrivains Lyonnais, Lions, Accademia internazionale Greci-Marino. Roman Catholic. Avocations: philately, reading, comics. Home: 49 Rue du Grand Roule, F 69350 La Mulatière France Office: 31 Rue du Plat, F 69002 Lyon France

ETHERINGTON, EDWIN DEACON, lawyer, business executive, educator; b. Bayonne, N.J., Dec. 25, 1924; s. Charles K. and Ethel (Bennett) E.; m. Katherine Colean, Sept. 11, 1953; children: Edwin Deacon Jr., Kenneth C. (dec.), Marion L. (dec.), Robert M. B.A. with honors and distinction, Wesleyan U., 1948; J.D., Yale U., 1952. Bar: D.C 1953, N.Y. 1955. Asst. dean, instr. English, Wesleyan U., 1948-49; asst. instr. Yale Law Sch., 1951-52; law clk. to judge Ct. Appeals, Washington, 1952-53; asso. Wilmer & Broun, Washington, 1953-54, Milbank, Tweed, Hope & Hadley, N.Y.C., 1954-56; sec. N.Y. Stock Exchange, 1956-58, v.p., 1958-61; ptnr. Pershing & Co., 1961-62; pres. Am. Stock Exchange, 1962-66; pres. Wesleyan U., Middletown, Conn., 1966-70, now pres. emeritus; pres. Nat. Center for Voluntary Action, Washington, 1971, chmn., 1972; chmn. bd. advisors U.S. Trust Co. of Fla.; chmn. Conn. Gov.'s Commn. on Svcs. and Expenditures, 1971-72, Nat. Advt. Rev. Bd., 1973-74. Named Conn. Citizen of Yr., 1973. Mem. Order of Coif, Yale Club, Black Hall Golf Club, Old Lyme (Conn.) Country Club, Old Lyme Beach Club, Island Club (v.p.), Jupiter Island (Fla.) Club, Hobe Sound (Fla.) Yacht Club (bd. dirs.), Hobe Sound (Fla.) Golf Club, Seminole Golf Club, North Palm Beach (Fla.) Club, Phi Beta Kappa Assocs., Phi Beta Kappa, Kappa Beta Pi, Phi Delta Phi. Congregationalist. Home: 102 Bassett Creek Trl Hobe Sound FL 33455-2201 also: 46 Billow Rd Old Lyme CT 06371-2503

ETHERINGTON, NORMAN ALAN, history educator; b. Mt. Vernon, Wash., June 27, 1941; arrivedin Australia, 1968; s. Robert Andrew and Marion Nell (Garlick) E.; m. Margaret Susan Brock, June 19, 1980; children: Nathan Harry, Ben Karl. BA, Yale U., 1963, MA, 1966, MPhil, 1968, PhD, 1971. Instr. history Yale U., New Haven, 1963-64, asst. dir. dept., 1966-67; lectr. history U. Adelaide, Australia, 1968-73, sr. lectr., 1974-78, reader, 1979-89; prof. U. Western Australia, Perth, 1989—; chmn. bd. Constl. Mus., Adelaide, 1978-81, History Trust, Adelaide, 1981-87. Author: Preachers, Peasants and Politics, 1978, Theories of Imperialism, 1983, Rider Haggard, 1983, Peace, Politics and Violence in the New South Africa, 1992. Councillor Adelaide City Coun., 1985-87, alderman, 1987-89; bd. dirs. Adelaide Symphony Orch., 1986-89. Fellow Royal Hist. Soc., London, 1988, Acad. Social Scis. in Australia, 1993. Mem. Australian Hist. Assn. (pres. 1994-96), African Studies Assn. (pres. Australia 1986-88). Avocations: music, cabinet making. Home: 14 Campbell St, Perth Subiaco WA 6008, Australia Office: U Western Australia, History Dept, Perth Nedlands WA 6009, Australia

ETKIND, PAUL, epidemiologist, health facility administrator; b. New Haven, Conn., Aug. 18, 1952; s. Herbert and Mae Etkind; m. Sue Carole Etkind, June 5, 1988; 1 child, Mollie. BA, Clark U., 1974; MPH, Yale U., 1976, DrPH, 1998. Rsch. asst. Sch. Pub. Health Harvard U., Boston, 1976-77; epidemiologist Mass. Dept. Pub. Health, Boston, 1977-82, sr. epidemiologist, 1984-86, dir. immunization program, 1986-88, dir. epidemiology program, 1988-91, dir. divsn. STD prevention, 1991—. Contbr. articles to profl. jours. V.p. Temple Shalom, Milton, Mass., 1998—. Mem. APHA, Am. STD Assn., Nat. Coalition STD Dirs. (chair-elect 1998-2000, chair 2000—), Mass. Pub. Health Assn. Office: Mass Dept Pub Health 305 South St Boston MA 02130-3515

ETO, HAJIME, information scientist, educator; b. Tokyo, June 16, 1935; s. Yoshio and Kikuko (Tamari) E. BA, U. Tokyo, 1959, MA, 1962; MS, U. Calif., Berkely, 1967; PhD, Tokyo Inst. Tech., 1979. Rschr. Hitachi Ltd., Tokyo, 1962-76; prof. U. Tsukuba, Japan, 1976-99, Chiba Keizai U., Japan, 1999—; prof. emeritus U. Tsukuba, 1999—. Author, editor: R & D Management Systems in Japanese Industry, 1984, R & D Strategies in Japan, 1993; mem. editl. bd. Scientometrics Jour., 1979—, Human Sys. Mgmt., 1980-84, Internat. Jour. of the Sci. of Scis., 1994—, Internat. Jour. Svc. Tech. & Mgmt., 1998—; contbr. sci. articles to profl. jours. Recipient Fulbright scholarship U.S.-Japan Edn. Com., 1966. Mem. AAAS, Internat. Soc. Scientometrics and Informetrics (mem. coun. 1993—, mem. editl. bd. 1995—), Japan Assn. for Philosophy Sci. (mem. coun. 1970-92), Japan Soc. for Sci. Policy (bd. dirs. 1994-96, coun. 1997—), Assn. of France on Cybernetics, Econs. and Tech. (mem. editl. bd. 1985—), N.Y. Acad. Sci. Home: Nakano 3-43-17-305, Nakano-ku Tokyo 164-0001, Japan

ETO, MORIFUSA, chemistry educator; b. Isahaya, Nagasaki, Japan, Feb. 20, 1930; s. Soroku and Hatsu (Kikuchi) E.; m. Tadako Ishida, Dec. 28, 1958; children: Nozomu, Megumu. MS, Kyushu U., Fukuoka, Japan, 1952, PhD, 1962. Instr. Kyushu U., Fukuoka, 1957-63, assoc. prof., 1963-77, prof. agrl. chemistry, 1977-93, prof. emeritus, 1993—; pres. Miyakonojo (Japan) Nat. Coll. Tech., 1993-98; prof. emeritus, 1998—; pres. Kyushu Women's U., Kitakyushu, 1999—; vis. assoc. prof. U. Calif., Berkeley, 1973-74; vis. prof. Ctrl. China Normal U., Wuhan, 1995, Nankai U., Tianjin, 1995. Author: Organophosphorus Pesticides, 1974; author, editor Bioorganic Chemistry of Pesticides, 1985, A New Turn in Pesticide Sciences, 1987. Mem. task group WHO, IPCS Environ. Health Criterir, Geneva, 1990; chmn. Com. for Pesticide Use Guidelines, Kumamoto, Japan, 1990; mem. Com. for Environ. Hazards, Fukuoka, 1992. Recipient Japan Agrl. Sci. award Fedn. Japanese Agrl. Sci. Socs., Tokyo, 1981, medal with purple ribbon Govt. of Japan, 1996, award Kyushu Soc. Engring. Edn., 1999. Mem. Agrl. Chem. Soc. Japan (chmn. West Japan br. 1981-83, agrl. chemistry award 1963), Am. Chem. Soc. Internat. (Agrochemicals Rsch. award 1993), Pesticide Sci. Soc. Japan (pres. 1989-91, Disting. Svc. medal 2000). Achievements include invention of insecticide salithion. Home: 34-2 Aoba-7 Higashi-ku, Fukuoka 813-0025, Japan

ETO, SHINKICHI, educator; b. Mukden, China, Nov. 16, 1923; s. Toshio and Nui (Yamashita) E.; m. Kazuko Ohno, July 16, 1949; children: Hikaru, Mari, Izumi. LLB, U. Tokyo, 1948. Assoc. prof. dept. internat. rels. U. Tokyo, 1957-67, prof. dept. internat. rels., 1967-84; pres. Asia U., Tokyo, 1987-95; chancellor Toyo Eiwa Ednl. Instn., Tokyo, 1998—; vis. prof. Peking U., 1997—; chair Tokyu Scholarship Found., 1996—. Author: East Asian Political History, 1979, International Relations, 1982, A Biography of Satow Eisaku, 1989; co-translator: My Thirty-Three Years' Dream, 1982. Recipient Purple Ribbon Order Japanese Govt., 1993, Fukuoka Asian Culture Prize Fukuoka Prefectural Govt., 1997. Mem. Japan Fedn. of Unesco Assns. (adviser 1978—), Japanese Soc. of Asian Studies (pres. 1986—), Japan Assn. of Internat. Rels. (dir. emeritus 1992—), Japan Assn. of Internat. Law (hon. dir. 1994—), Japan Assn. of the UN (dir. 1982—). Home: 4-46-9 Kugayama Suginami-ku, Tokyo 168-0082, Japan Office: Toyo Eiwa, 5-14-40 Roppongi Minatoku, Tokyo 106-8507, Japan

ETSOU-NZABI-BAMUNGWABI, FREDERIC CARDINAL, archbishop; b. Mazalonga, Zaire, Dec. 3, 1930. Titular bishop of St. Lucy, archbishop of Kinshasa, elevated to the Sacred Coll. Cardinals, 1991. Office: Archevegne, BP 8431, Kinshasa Democratic Republic of Congo*

ETTER, CHRISTIAN, financial and economic diplomat; b. Romanshorn, Switzerland, Jan. 6, 1953; came to U.S., 1996; s. Kurt E. and Lucie Etter-Heiz; m. Dorothée Etter-Huber; children: Bettina, Benjamin. M in Econs., Bus., and Law, U. Bern, Switzerland, 1978; D in Econs., U. Bern, 1984; student mgmt., U. Rochester, 1977. Economist Ministry of Agriculture, Quebec, Can., 1977, Fed. Office Industry and Labor, Bern, 1978-79; rsch., tchg. asst. dept. econs. U. Bern, 1979-85; head divsn. Fed. Office for Fgn. Econ. Affairs, Bern, 1985-96; econ. minister Embassy of Switzerland, Washington, 1996-2000; head task force EFTA Third Country Negotiations, State Sec. Econ. Affairs, Bern, 2000—; head Swiss del. to GATS/WTO, Geneva, 1991-96; lectr. U. St. Gallen, Switzerland, 1997—. E-mail: christianetter@was.rep.admin.ch. Office: Embassy of Switzerland 2900 Cathedral Ave NW Washington DC 20008-3499

ETTERER, SEPP, industrial relations consultant; b. Munich, Aug. 31, 1944; came to U.S., 1955, naturalized, 1962; s. Josef and Ingeborg Anna (Fierlings) E.; m. Judith Annette Shell, Feb. 25, 1978; children, Johnathan Sepp, Julia Anne, Joseph William; children from previous marriage: Victoria Marie, Christina Diane, Kurt. BSEE, Mich. State U., 1966. Lic. comml. pilot. Assoc. ele. engr. Boeing Co., 1966-67; pulp mill supr., plant safety engr. Procter & Gamble Co., 1970-76; sr. safety rep. Bechtel Power Co., 1976-77; plant safety supt. Hooker Chems. & Plastics Corp., 1977-78; indsl. relations dir. Interstate Lead Co. Inc., Leeds, Ala., 1978-85; regional personnel and safety dir. Structl. Steel Fabrication div. Trinity Industries, Inc., Birmingham, Ala., 1985-89; safety mgr. freight car div. Trinity Industries, Bessemer, Ala., 1989-94; pres. Safety Maintenance Orgn., Inc., Birmingham, 1994—; inds. rels. cons.; v.p. Le Marche aud Fleurs, Inc., 1986-97. Author: Take It—It's Yours, 1975, Sky Pig, 1976, Equity 5, 1980, (software) SMOsys M7 Indsl. Rels. Mgmt., 1995. Capt. USAF, 1967-70. Mem. Am. Soc. Safety Engrs. (past pres.), Am. Indsl. Hygiene Assn., Air and Water Mgmt. Assn., Soc. for Human Resource Mgmt. Home: 1315 Wickford Rd Birmingham AL 35216-2903 Office: PO Box 661333 Birmingham AL 35266-1333

ETTIGHOFFER, DENIS CHARLES, management and organization consultant; b. Lourdes, France, Apr. 6, 1943; s. Marianne Caroline Ettighoffer; div., 1975; children: Sandrine, Sophie, Florian, Benjamin (dec.); m. Dominique Villanova; children: Camille, Jean François. Diploma in mktg. and strategy, Ctr. Hauts Etudes, Paris, 1978. Tech. mgr. Sereb Aerospatial, Bordeaux, France, 1965-69; comml. engr. Rank Xerox, Paris, 1969-77, Gamma Consultants Internat., Paris, France, 1977-79; head of automation dept. XI Conseil, France, 1979-81; head news info. com. techs. dept. Bossard Cons., Paris, 1981-92; pres. Eurotechnopolis Inst., Paris, 1992—; pres. automation dept. Assn. Française Cybernetique Econ. Tech., Paris, 1979-83; pres. V.O.C. (Virtual Orgn. Cons.), Paris, 1999—. Author: Virtual Enterprise and New Ways of Working, 1992 (trans. 4 langs.; 3d Millenium Mgr. prize 1993, Rotary Club prize 1998), The Future Office, 1994, eBusiness Generation, 1999 (Rotary Club prize 1999); co-author: Work in the 21st Century, 1995, The Chronos Syndrome, 1998; editor: Dunod, 1998, Meta.organizations, Village Mondial, 2000. Avocations: music, reading, surfing the Internet. E-mail: eurtechn@francenet.fr, ettighof@francenet.fr. Home and Office: 12 Rue des Bourdonnais, 78000 Versailles France

ETTINGER, JOSEPH ALAN, lawyer; b. N.Y.C., July 21, 1931; s. Max and Frances E.; children: Amy Beth, Ellen Jane. BA, Tulane U., 1954, JD with honors, 1956. Bar: La. 1956, Ill. 1959. Asst. corp. counsel City of Chgo., 1959-62; pvt. practice, Chgo., 1962-73, 76-80; sr. ptnr. Ettinger & Schoenfield, Chgo., 1980-92; pvt. practice, Chgo., 1993—; assoc. prof. law Chgo.-Kent Coll., 1973-76; chmn. Village of Olympia Fields (Ill.) Zoning Bd. Appeals, 1969-76; chmn. panel on corrections Welfare Coun. Met. Chgo., 1969-76; spl. state appellate defender State of Ill., 1997-98. Contbr. articles to profl. publs. Capt. JAGC, U.S.Army, 1956-59. Recipient svc. award Village of Olympia Fields, 1976. Mem. Chgo. Bar Assn., Assn. Criminal Def. Lawyers (gov. 1970-72).

ETTL, ARMIN, ophthalmologist, plastic eye surgeon; b. Strass, Austria, Feb. 13, 1962; s. Siegfried and Herta (Jobstl) E.; m. Karin Leibetseder, Mar. 27, 1999; 1 child, Alexander. MD, U. Graz, Austria, 1987. Intern Greys Hosp., Pietermaritzburg, South Africa, 1988-89; asst. U. Innsbruck, Austria, 1989-94; cons. ophthalmic surgeon Gen. Hosp., St. Polten, Austria, 1995-96; head dept. Neuro-Ophthalmology, Strabismus, Oculoplast, Orbital Surgery Gen. Hosp., St. Polten, 1996—; lectr. ophthalmology U. Innsbruck, 1999—. Author: High Resolution MRI Anatomy of the Orbit, 1999; contbr. articles to profl. jours. Fellow Orbital Ctr., Amsterdam, The Netherlands, 1995, Moorfields Eye Hosp., London, 1995. Mem. Am. Acad. Ophthalmology, European Soc. Plastic & Reconstructive Surgery, Austrian Soc. Ophthalmology. Avocation: piano. Office: Grillparzerstr 2A, A-3100 Saint Polten Austria also: Allg Krankenhaus, Dept Neuro-Ophthalmology, A-3100 Saint Polten Austria

ETTL, WOLFGANG JOHANN, actuary, educator, researcher; b. Vienna, Austria, May 24, 1955; s. Anton and Hedwig (Wecker) E.; m. Eva Maria Miglbauer, Oct. 15, 1985; children: Richard, Anna, Andreas. PhD of Math., U. Vienna, Austria, 1978; diploma vers. math., Tech. U. Vienna, habilitation of actuarial math., 1988. Asst. prof. actuarial dept. Tech. U., Vienna, 1978-88, assoc. prof. actuarial math., 1988—; chief actuary Bank of Austria, Vienna, 1985—, Ins. Group of Austrian Industries Group, Vienna, 1989—, Unilever Pension Fund, 1989—; cons. Benefits & Pension Funds, Ins. Compensation, 1980—. Author: Rechnungsgrundlagen fur die Pensions Versicherung, 1989; co-author: Recht des betrieblichen Altersversorgung, 1989, 90. Mem. Assn. German Actuaries, Assn. Swiss Actuaries, Assn. Austrian Actuaries. Roman Catholic. Avocations: children, sailing, skiing. Office: Consulting Actuaries W Ettl, Hausergasse 26, A-3400 Klosterneuburg Austria

ETTWIG, VOLKER, management consultant; b. Alpen, Germany, Jan. 18, 1968; s. Heinrich Peter and Mary Sibylle (Anhuf) E. Diplom Kaufmann, U. Cologne, 1994; CEMS-Master, Stockholm Sch. Econs., 1994; PhD, U. Dortmund, 1997. With Volkswagen AG, Wolfsburg, Germany, 1995-96; mgr. IBM Cons. Group, Mainz, 1997—; sr. IBM cons. Author: Process Control of Group Technological Assembly Systems, 1998; contbr. articles to profl. jours. Dep. chmn. Young Liberales, Wolfsburg, 1996. With German Air Force, 1987-88. Mem. PIM & CEMS Student and Alumni Assn. (bd. dirs. 1993-94). Home: Vor der Frecht 12, 55128 Mainz Germany Office: IBM Consulting Group, Hechtsheimer Str K St 8870, 55131 Mainz Germany

ETZEL, ALAN EMERY, editor, educator; b. Waterville, Maine, Apr. 9, 1946; s. Bernard Adam and Elizabeth (Emery) E.; m. Liisa Kristiina Ruoho, Apr. 14, 1984; 1 child, Peter Kristian. BA, Tufts U., 1968; postgrad., UCLA, 1973-74. Tchr. Peace Corps, Chad, 1968-70; instr. Hambakis Sch., Rethymnon, Crete, Greece, 1971-73, Northrop Corp., Dhahran, Saudi Arabia, 1974-84, Josbel Oy, Helsinki, Finland, 1985-87; dir. HTI-Tekniikka Oy, Helsinki, 1987-89; tech. editor, writer Helsinki, 1989—; dir. Josbel Oy, Helsinki, 1992-2000; tech. writer ICL Data, 2000—. Author several books on tech. lang. instrn. (Merit award, 1984). Bd. dirs. Friends of the English Sch., Helsinki, 1991-93. Mem. Rotary (v.p. Helsinki 1991-92, pres. 1992-93). Home: Kaskenpolttajantie 12 A, 00670 Helsinki Finland Office: ICL Invia Oyj, PO Box 458, FIN00101 Helsinki Finland

ETZIONI-HALEVY, EVA, political sociology educator; b. Vienna, Mar. 21, 1934; arrived in Israel, 1945; d. Solomon Horowitz and Irene esther (Pudles) Glückson; m. Zvi Halevy; children: Ethan, Oren, Tamar. BA, Hebrew U., Jerusalem, 1955; MA, Tel-Aviv U., 1969, PhD, 1971. Sr. lectr. dept. sociology Tel-Aviv U., 1976-78; sr. lectr. sociology Australian Nat. U., Canberra, 1978-84, reader in sociology, 1985-89; prof. polit. sociology Bar-Ilan U., Ramat Aviv, Israel, 1989—. Co-author: Who is the Israeli Student?, 1973, Political Culture in Israel, 1977; co-editor: Social Change: Sources, Patterns and Consequences, 1973; author: Political Manipulation and Administrative Power -- A Comparative Study, 1979, Social Change: The Advent and Maturation of Modern society, 1981, Bureaucracy and Democracy: A Political Dilemma, 1985, The Knowledge Elite and the Failure of Prophecy, 1985, National Broadcasting Under Siege: A Comparative Study, 1987, Fragile Democracy: The Use and Abuse of Power in Western Societies, 1989, The Elite Connectionm: Problems and Potential of Western Democracy, 1993, The Elite Connection and Democracy in Israel, 1993, Place at the Top: Elites and Elitism in Israel, 1997; editor: Classes and Elites in Democracy and Democratization, 1997, The Divided People, 2000; contbr. numerous articles to profl. jours., chpts. to books. Fellow Acad. of the Social Scis. in Australia. Office: Bar-Ilan University, Dept Sociology, 52900 Ramat Gan Israel

ETZKOWITZ, HENRY, educator, consultant; b. N.Y.C., July 9, 1940; s. Benjamin and Mary E.; m. Michelle Baker; 1 child, Alexander. BA, U. Chgo., 1962; PhD, New Sch. U., 1969. Assoc. prof. SUNY, Purchase, N.Y., 1972—; dir. Sci. Policy Inst. Author: The Second Academic Revolution: MIT and the Rise of Entrepreneurial Science, 2001; co-author: Public Venture Capital, 2000, Athena Unbound: the Advancement of Women in Science and Technology, 2000. E-mail: henryetzkowitz@earthlink.net. Home: 325 Riverside Dr New York NY 10025-4162 Office: Science Policy Inst SUNY Purchase NY 10577

ETZOLD, HERMAN ALBERT, clergyman, theology educator; b. Farrar, Mo., Mar. 10, 1915; s. Martin Gottlieb and Selma Bertha (Stueve) E.; m. Mabel Marie Traugott, Aug. 31, 1942; children: Thomas, Mary Vanagas, Elisabeth Schroeder, Rhoda Finck, Bonnie Johnson, Rachel Eaton, Peter. MS in Edn., Ind. U., 1970; MST, Luth. Sch. Theology, Chgo., 1972; DMin, Concordia Theol. Sem., Ft. Wayne, Ind., 1985. Ordained to ministry Lutheran Ch., 1942. Pastor Signal Hill Luth. Ch., Belleville, Ill., 1942-48, St. Stephen Luth. Ch., St. Louis, 1948-53, Trinity Luth. Ch., Bloomington, Ill.,

1953-60, Our Savior Luth. Ch., St. Charles, Mo., 1960-62; prof., dean of students Concordia Coll., Ft. Wayne, 1962-77; prof. St. Paul's Coll., Concordia, Mo., 1977-78; prof. theology Concordia U., Seward, Nebr., 1978—; sr. mentor Calif. Luth. U., Thousand Oaks, Calif., 1983; vis. prof. Christ Coll., Irvine, Calif., 1983-84; v.p. Ctrl. Ill. dist. Luth. Ch.-Mo. Synod, Springfield, 1957-60; mem. Bd. Luth. World Relief, St. Louis, 1957-68. Author sermons in 10 vols. of Concordia Pulpit, devotions in Portals of Prayer, articles on Luth. confessions in The Lutheran Witness, 1971. Mem. 4th of July Planning Com., Seward, 1980-83. Aid Assn. for Luths. study grantee, 1964-85. Mem. Kiwanis Club. Democrat. Avocations: gardening, travel, computer. Home: 445 N Columbia Ave Seward NE 68434-1601

EU, KONG-WENG, consultant surgeon; b. Singapore, July 21, 1962; s. Tak-Chee Eu and Kwai-Yeau Wong; m. Christina Yu-Lin Chia; children: Ernest, Elizabeth, Elaine. MBBS, Nat. U. Singapore, 1986, M in Med. (Surgery), 1991. Resident in Surgery Singapore Gen. Hosp., 1986-91; brigade med. officer Ministry Defense, Singapore, 1987-89; surgical registrar Royal Infirmary, Edinburgh, Scotland, 1992-93; clin. fellow Cleveland Clinic, 1993-95; sr. registrar Singapore Gen. Hosp., 1995-96; cons. Singapore Gen. Hosp., 1997—; dir. Colorectal Cancer Rsch., Sinagpore Gen. Hosp., 1995—. Extensive contbr. articles to profl. jours. Speaker in field. Capt. Ministry Defense, Singapore, 1987—. Recipient Distinction award Nat. Safety First Coun., 1978, Meritorious award Sch. St. John's Ambulance Cadet Corp., 1978, Singapore Govt. Pub. Svc. Commn. award 1981-85; Singapore Govt. Ministry Health trainee; Japan Surg. Soc. Travel grantee, 1994, Nat. Med. Rsch. Coun. grantee, Singapore, 1997, Johnson & Johnson Edn. grantee, 1994, Singapore Cancer Soc. grantee, 1997. Fellow Royal Coll. Surgeons Edinburgh, Internat. Coll. Surgeons, Acad. of Medicine (Singapore); mem. Am. Soc. Colon and Rectal Surgeons, Cleve. Clinic Found. Alumni. Avocations: swimming, soccer, billiards. Home: 18 Mei Hwan Rd, Singapore 568320, Singapore Office: Dept Colorectal Surgery, Singapore Gen Hosp, Singapore 169608, Singapore

EUBANK, STEPHEN REID, lawyer; b. Lynchburg, Va., July 21, 1969; s. Robert Leland and Carolyn Austin Eubank; m. Rebecca Helen Robbins, July 1, 1995. BA, William & Mary, 1991; JD, U. Richmond, 1994. Bar: Va. 1994, U.S. Ct. Appeals, 1994, U.S. Dist. Ct., west dist., Va., 1996. Assoc. J. Thompson Shrader & Assocs., Amherst, Va., 1994-99; sec. Amherst (Va.) Nelson Bar, 1995-97, v.p., 1998, pres., 1999; team mem. J&DR Ct. Calendar Mgmt., Richmond, Va., 1998. Editor: (journal) U. Richmond Law Review, 1993-94; (book) VA Lawyer, 1995-97; contbr. articles to profl. jours. Mem. Quaker Meml. Presbyn. Ch., Lynchburg, Va., 1980-99, Amherst (Va.) Hist. Soc., 1995-99. Recipient Bankruptcy Book award Lawyers Coop. Pub. Co., 1994. Mem. Va. State Bar Assn. Avocations: history, reading, travel, home improvement. Office: J Thompson Shrader & Assocs PC 330 S Main St Amherst VA 24521

EUBANKS, RONALD W., lawyer, broadcaster; b. Montgomery, Ala., Sept. 17, 1946; s. William Shell and Violet Lavern (Walker) E.; 1 child, Edward Todd; m. Anna Shaw; stepdaughter, Jennifer Shaw. Student, Auburn U., 1964-65; BA, U. Ala., 1968; JD, U. Utah, 1974. Bar: Utah 1974, Nebr. 1979, Minn. 1983, Wash. 1985, U.S. Ct. Appeals (10th cir.) 1977, U.S. Ct. Appeals (8th cir.) 1979, U.S. Supreme Ct. 1977, U.S. Ct. Appeals (9th cir.) 1985. Gen. mgr. Sta. WVMI and Sta. WQID, Biloxi Gulfport, Miss., 1968-71; with FCC, Washington, 1974-75; assoc. Hansen & Hansen, Salt Lake City, 1975-77; with law dept. Union Pacific R.R., Omaha, 1977-83; asst. gen. counsel Burlington No. R.R. Co., St. Paul, 1983-84, gen. counsel western region, 1984-87; v.p. law and corp. affairs Glacier Park Co., 1987-88; exec. v.p. Ecos Corp., 1988; CEO Capital Comms., Montgomery, 1991-97; pres. ET Comms., Montgomery, 1988-97; sr. regional v.p. So. Star Comm., 1997—; dir. Camas Prairie R. R., Longview Switching Co. Co-author: Practical Law in Utah, 1978, Defense of Mary Carter, 1984; contbr. articles to profl. publs. Bd. dirs., mem. exec. com., legal counsel Utah Boys Ranch, Salt Lake City, 1977-79; bd. dirs. Children and Youth Svcs., Salt Lake City, 1977-84, Nebr. affiliate Am. Diabetes Assn., 1982-83, Greater Montgomery Sickle Cell Found., 1990—, Ala. Broadcasters Assn., 1998—, Oreg.-Wash. R.R., 1984-87, Camas Prairie R.R., 1984-87, Longview Switching Co., 1984-87; chmn. Wash. R.R. Assn., 1984-87; co-chmn. Montgomery Father and Son Banquet Com., 1993—; bd. dirs., mem. exec. com. Montgomery Mental Health Assn., 1995—, treas., 1996—; bd. dirs., mem. exec. com. Montgomery Area Coun. on Aging, 1998-99; bd. advisors, dept. comm. Ala. State U., 1995—. Recipient Friend of Youth award YMCA, 1993; named Role Model of Yr. Southlawn Sch., 1996-97. Mem. ABA (sect. on litigation, coms. on publs. and trial techniques, sect. on tort and ins. practice, com. on r.r. law), Washington State Bar Assn., Seattle-King County Bar Assn., Wash. R.R. Assn. (chmn. 1984-87), Def. Rsch. Inst. (chmn. com on r.r. law 1984-86, mem. com. on practice and procedure), Jason's Soc., Phi Alpha Delta, Alpha Tau Omega. Presbyterian. Home: 9750 Vaughn Rd Pike Road AL 36064-2751 Office: Capital Comm 648 Perry St Montgomery AL 36104

EUDY, JAMES DOUGLAS, molecular biologist; b. Henderson, Nebr., Oct. 5, 1961; s. Monroe Jefferson and Myrtle Elizabeth E. BS, U. Nebr., 1988; PhD, U. Nebr. Med. Ctr., Omaha, 1995. Postdoctoral fellow Dept. Pathology U. Nebr. Med. Ctr., Omaha, 1995-98, rsch. instr. Dept. Pathology, 1998-99; asst. prof. Ctr. for Human Molecular Genetics, Omaha, 1999—; tchg./student U. Nebr. Med. Ctr., 1998—;. Contbr. articles to profl. jours. 1st pl. in Midwest Med. Student Rsch. Forum, Creighton U., 1994. Mem. AAAS, Am. Soc. Human Genetics. Avocations: guitar, reading. E-mail: jdeudy@unmc.edu.

EUGSTER, CARL, investment company executive; b. Landquart, Switzerland, Aug. 3, 1923; s. Conrad Heinrich and Maria (Büsch) E.; m. Suzanne Jaeger, July 2, 1924; children: Carl Andreas, Johannes Martin, Barbara Susanna. Doctorate, U. Zurich, Switzerland, 1952. Dir. corp. devel. J.R. Geigy S.A., Basel, Switzerland, to 1970; dir. corp. devel., econ. policy rsch. CIBA-Geigy, Basel, 1970-83; chmn. Marigen SA, Riehen, Switzerland, 1983—. Contbr. articles to profl. jours.; patentee in field. Avocation: mountaineering. Home: Hackbergstrasse 40, CH-4125 Riehen Switzerland

EULDERINK, FRITS, pathologist; b. Enschede, The Netherlands, Sept. 5, 1934; s. Barend Fredrik and Hendrika Maria (Wijk) E.; m. Alice Josien Schukkink, Feb. 1, 1960 (div. 1989); children: Frits, Josien Henriette Maryse, Erik Aernout; m. Marianna Sergeevna Rusakova, June 28, 1989. MD, U. Amsterdam, The Netherlands, 1960; D, U. Leiden, The Netherlands, 1971. Resident in pathology U. Leiden, 1961-65; pathologist Lab. for Pathology, Dordrecht, 1965-67; cons. pathology dept. U. Leiden, 1969-73, prof. pathology dept., 1973-99; pathologist Delft, 1991-99; ret., 1999; com. on pathology European League Against Rheumatism, 1973-97, sec. 1980-91. Contbr. articles to profl. jours. Capt. Med. Corps, Netherlands Mil., 1960-61. Mem. Leiden Gerontol. Circle (founder, chmn. 1981-91). Office: U Leiden, Pathology Dept, PO Box 9603, 2300 RC Leiden The Netherlands

EUN, MOO-YOUNG, genetics researcher; b. Iksan, Chonbuk, Republic of Korea, Jan. 30, 1950; m. Hyun-Hee Cho, Jan. 7, 1978; children: Na-Rae, Mi-Rae. BS, Chonbuk Nat. U., 1972, MS, 1978; PhD, La. State U., 1980. Jr. rschr. Honam Crop Experiment Sta., Rural Devel. Adminstrn., Iksan, 1971-82, sr. rschr., 1982-84; sr. rschr. Agrl. Scis. Inst. Rural Devel. Adminstrn., Suwon, Republic of Korea, 1985-91; dir. Molecular Genetics divsns. Agrl. Biotech. Inst., Suwon, Republic of Korea, 1991-94; dir. Cytogenetics divsn. Nat. Inst. Agrl. Sci. & Tech., 1995-99, dep. dir. gen., 1999—; program leader Korea Rice Genome Rsch. Program, Suwon, 1994—; working group mem. Internat. Rice Genome Sequencing Project, 1998—. Author: Plant Biotechnology Applicaiton, 1992; editor-in-chief Rural Devel. Adminstrn. Jour. Agrl. Scis., 1992; editor Korean Jour. of Breeding, 1992; patentee (6) in field (Korean). Recipient Outstanding Rsch. Offical award Prime Minister of Korea, 1983; U.S. AID fellow, N.Y., 1978-80. Mem. Korean Breeding Soc. (exec. bd., editor), Korean Soc. Crop Sci. (exec. bd.), Korean Soc. Plant Tissue Culture (exec. bd.), Korean Soc. Molecular Biology. Fax: 82-331-290-0307. Office: Nat Inst Agrl Sci & Tech Rural Devel Adm, Seodun-Dong, Suwon 441-707, Republic of Korea

EUTHYMTOU, PARASKEVI, physics educator; b. Athens, Greece, May 14, 1923; s. Constantin-Athanasios and Anna Dimitrios (Mouzaki) E. BSc in Physics, Athens U., 1947, PhD in Physics, 1952, diploma Radioelectricity, 1954. From asst. to prof. in chair, Physics Dept. Athens U., 1948-82, prof. physics solid state sect. physics dept., 1981—, dir. solid state physics sect., 1982-86, leader semiconductor group, 1961—. Author 5 books; contbr. papers to profl. jours. and internat. confs. Grantee, Nat. Acad. Scis. (U.S.), U. Ill., Urbana, 1957-58, Greek Atomic Energy Com., Reading, Eng., and Ecole Normales, Paris, 1960, Fulbright, U. Syracuse (U.S.), N.Y., 1964-65, Internat. Atomic Energy Com., Reading, Eng., 1966, Cultural Exchange Program, Romania, 1972, Hungary, 1976. Mem. AAAS, Union of Greek Solid State Physicists (pres., leader bilateral rsch. programs and seminars), N.Y. Acad. Scis., European Phys. Soc., Materials Rsch. Soc. Home: Dimitrakopoulou 17, 11742 Athens Greece Office: Athens U/Dept Physics, Solid State Sect Solonos 104, 10680 Athens Greece

EUVRARD, GEORGE JOHN, education educator; b. East London, S. Africa, Oct. 19, 1954; s. John Delville and Nancy Joy (Trollope) E.; m. Gwenda Joan Day, Dec. 16, 1977; children: Mandy-Jayne, Jonathan, Benjamin. BA, Rhodes U., S. Africa, 1976; B in Edn., UNISA, S. Africa, 1983; MA, Rhodes U., 1987; PhD, UNISA, 1994. Registered counselling psychologist, S. Africa Med. & Dental Coun. Lectr. Tech. Inst., S. Africa, 1976-82; tchr./counsellor York H.S., George, S. Africa, 1979-84; lectr. Rhodes U., S. Africa, 1986-94; sr. lectr. Rhodes U., 1994-95, head edn. dept., 1995—, prof. edn., 1999—; counselling psychologist, pvt. practice, Grahamstown, 1988—, edn. cons., Ea. Cape, 1986—, rsch. cons., Ea. Cape, 1995—, mgmt. cons., Ea. Cape, 1990—. Contbr. articles to profl. jours. Chmn. governing coun., Victoria Primary Sch., Grahamstown, 1992-96, Cape Coll. of Edn., Ft. Beaufort, 1996—; chmn. steering com., Murray and Roberts chair of environ. edn., Grahamstown, 1992—. Avocations: family, running, hockey, cycling, music. Home: 8 St Aidans Ave, 6139 Grahamstown S Africa Office: Rhodes U, Somerset St, 6140 Grahamstown S Africa

EUZEBY, JACQUES ACHILLE, veterinarian; b. Bagnols-sur-Cèze, Gard, France, Nov. 8, 1920; s. Ernest and Marie-Louise (Payan) E.; m. Renée Gayte, May 20, 1944; children: Alain, Jacqueline, Jean, Chantal, Claude, Florence. MD, Veterinary Sch., Lyon, France, 1942; Lic. Sci. Agrégation Ecoles Vet., Facultèdes Sciences, Paris, 1947; Dr. Honoris Causa, U. Turin, Italy, 1969, U. Timisoara, Romania, 1995; Hon. Prof., U. Asuncion, Paraguay, 1978. Maitre-asst. parasitology Ecole Veterinaire, Lyon, France, 1946-51, maitre de conf., 1952-55, prof., 1955-88, hon. prof., 1988—. Author 21 books on the subject of parasitic diseases, parasitic zoonses and med. mycology; contbr. articles to profl. jours. Mem. Acad. Medicine, Vet. Acad. France, Acadèmie Royale des Scs. Veterinaires d'Espagne. Liberal Party. Roman Catholic. Home: Rue Vauban #149, 69006 Lyon France Office: Ecolel Veterinaire de Lyon, BP 83, 69280 Marcy-l'Etoile France

EVA, EHRLICH, economist; b. Budapest, Hungary, June 18, 1932; s. Ehrlich Zoltan and Iren (Hermann) E.; m. Sandor Piukovics, Aug. 22, 1957 (div. 1970); m. Gabor Revesz, Dec. 31, 1971. MA of Econ., Budapest U., 1958; PhD, Karl Marx U., Budapest, 1975. Research scientist Hungarian Nat. Planning Office, Budapest, 1959-79; sr. rsch. prof. Inst. World Econs. of Hungarian Acad. Sci., Budapest, 1979—; dir. UN Econs. Commn. of Europe, Geneva, 1980-82; various U.S. univs., 1984, Geneva, 1968; vis. prof. St. Anthony's Coll., Oxford, 1974. Author: International Analyses to be Used in Hungarian Long-Term Planning, 1968, Japan: A Case of Catching Up, 1979; co-author: Infrastructure, 1975, Hungary and Prospects 1985-2005, 1995, Infrastructure: Strategic Issues for Hungary's Accession to the EU, 1998. Recipient prize Hungarian Acad., 1990, Szédeny prize, 1998. Mem. European Econ. Assn. Avocations: sports, music. Home: Felsozol dmali ut 17, 1025 Budapest Hungary Office: Inst World Econs, Országház-utca 30 PO Box 936, 4535 Budapest Hungary

EVANGELISTA, LINDA, model; b. St. Catherine's, Ont.; m. Gerald Marie (div.). Model Elite Model Mgmt. Corp. Appearances include Gianni Versace shows, (video) George Michael's Freedom, Unzipped, 1995, Catwalk, 1995, The Loss of Sexual Innocence, 1999, New Kid on the Block, 1999. Recipient Spl. Lifetime Achievement award VH1 Fashion and Music Awards, 1997. Office: Wilhamenas Womens Divsn 300 Park Ave South New York NY 10010*

EVANGELOU, ALECOS COSTA, Cyprian government official; b. Kato Lakatamia, Cyprus, July 23, 1939; 3 children. Called to bar Gray's Inn, London, 1967; with Nicosia (Cyprus) Dist. Adminstrn.; from law officer to atty. Office Atty. Gen., Cyprus; with min. fin. Govt. Cyprus, min. justice and pub. order, 1993-97; former chair Appropriate Authority Intellectual Property; pres. Supreme Sports Tribunal, Cyprus Radio-TV Authority, 1998. Avocation: advocate. Office: Eagle Star House, Kyriacos Matsis Ave No 16, 1082 Nicosia Cyprus Home: PO Box 29238, 1623 Nicosia Cyprus

EVANGELOU, GRIGORIOS NIKOLAOS, surgeon; b. Thessaloniki, Macedonia, Greece, Aug. 4, 1930; s. Nikolaos and Efrosini (Kaliperi) E.; m. Evgenia Daroglou, July 12, 1969; children: Efrosini, Nikolaos. MD, U. Thessaloniki, 1954. Med. diplomate. Dir. pers. NATO, Izmir, Turkey, 1957-59; chief Surg. Dept., Ioannina, Greece, 1964-66; chief surg. dept. Mil. Hosp., Alexandroupolis, Greece, 1967-71, 401 Gen. Mil. Hosp., Athens, 1971-75, 424 Gen. Mil. Hosp., Thessaloniki, 1976-78, NIMTS Hosp., Athens, 1979-85, 91-97; assoc. prof. U. Athens, 1977-97. Contbr. articles to profl. jours. Brig. M.C., Greek mil., 1981. Fellow ACS; mem. Hellenic Surg. Soc. (v.p.), European Assn. Endoscopic Surgery and Other Interventional Techniques, Hellenic Surg. Soc. (pres.). Home: 5 Kondylaki Filothei, 15237 Athens Greece Office: NIMTS Hosp, 10 Monis Petraki, 11521 Athens Greece

EVANS, ALAN GEORGE, electrical engineer; b. Upland, Pa., June 8, 1942; s. Thomas Leslie and Jennie E.; m. Barbara Lee Kilhefner, June 26, 1965; children: Christopher Alan, Jennifer Lee. BSEE, Widener U., 1964; MSEE, Drexel U., 1967, PhD, 1972. Asst. engr. Phila. Electric Co., 1964-70; computation analyst Material Scis. Corp., Blue Bell, Pa., 1970-72; tchg. asst. Drexel U., Phila., 1965-72; assoc. engr. Calspan Corp., Cheektawaga, N.Y., 1972-74; asst. prof. U.S. Naval Acad., Annapolis, Md., 1983-84; electronic engr. Naval Surface Warfare Ctr., Dahlgren, Va., 1974—; symposium tech. com. Inst. Navigation, Alexandria, Va., 1974—; mem. U.S. Def. Mapping Agy., Arlington, Va., 1986-92, U.S. Nat. Geodetic Survey, Rockville, Md., 1985. Contbr. articles to profl. jours. Sec. Sch. Adv. Coun., LaPlata, Md., 1984-91; asst. leader 4-H, LaPlata, 1982-89; active parent bd. U. Del., 1994-95. Recipient R&D award U.S. Def. Mapping Agy., 1988, Disting. Alumni award Chichester H.S., Pa., 1986, fellowship and teaching assistantship Drexel U., 1965-71. Fellow Internat. Assn. Geodesy (spl. study group 1986—); mem. IEEE, Inst. Navigation (bd. dirs. coun. 1996-97, exec. com. internat. satellite tech. conf. 1996-98), Sigma Xi. Republican. Achievements include patents in field; rsch. in the application of global positioning system satellites in area of relative positioning, in signal multipath, signal processing, receiver devel. and geodetic measurements. Home: 7455 Woodhaven Dr La Plata MD 20646-4008 Office: Naval Surface Warfare Ctr 17320 Dahlgren Rd Dahlgren VA 22448-5150

EVANS, ANDREW LLOYD, pediatrician; b. Cardiff, Wales, U.K., Sept. 19, 1953; s. Aneurin Lloyd and Harriet (Lewis) E. BA, Cambridge U., Eng., 1975; MA, Cambridge U., 1979, MD, 1993; BM BCh, Oxford, U.K., 1978. Sr. registrar Hammersmith Hosp., London, 1987-90; cons. pediatrician Royal Free Hosp., London, 1990—; chmn. Child Devel. and Disability Group, U.K., 1992-98; treas. European Acad. Childhood Disability , 1996—; exec. com. Brit. Assn. of Comm. Child Health, 1993-98; mem. standing com. on childhood disability Royal Coll. of Paediatrics and Child Health, 1995—. Contbr. articles to profl. jours. Fellow Royal Coll. Physicians/London, Royal Coll. Pediats. and Child Health; mem. Physiol. Soc. Avocation: opera. Office: Royal Free Hosp/Dept Child, Pond Street, NW3 2QG London United Kingdom

EVANS, BARRY CRAIG, financial services company exexutive; b. Cin., Dec. 12, 1944; s. Tracy Warren and Dorothy N. (Burton) E.; m. Judith R. Jacobs, Apr. 28, 1984. BS in Bus., Miami U., Oxford, Ohio, 1967. CLU. Ptnr. Evans & Co., Cin., 1971-81; dir. agt. devel., dir. advanced underwriting Mass. Mut. Life Ins. Co., Cin., 1980-83; br. office mgr. Office Supervisory Jurisdiction Mut. Svc. Corp., Cin., 1982-89, Fahnestock & Co., Inc., Cin., 1991-98; assoc. gen. agt. Cen. Life Assurance Co., Cin., 1989-92; chmn., pres., CEO Evans Fin. Group, Cin., 1983—; pres. Cin. Fin. Cons., Inc., 1980-98; registered prin., br. mgr. Raymond James Fin. Svcs., Inc., 1998—. Apptd. bd. dirs. Cin. State Tech. and C.C., 1995-98; mem. ACS Heritage League; chmn.-bd. dirs. Linton Chamber Music Series, 1998—, Cin. Choral Soc., 1982-84; bd. dirs. Sch. Lay Ministry Ch., 1988-89, co-chmn. fund raising com. bldg. expansion, 1990-91, chmn. bldg. expansion com., 1989-91; mem., Hyde Park Cmty. United Methodist Ch., Ch. coun., co-chmn. Congregational Care Commn.; mem. The Taft Mus. 60th Anniversary Com., 1991-92; mem. exec. com./trustee Am. Cancer Soc., Hamilton County unit, trustee Ohio Divsn.; bd. dirs., chmn. planned and major gifts com.; bd. dirs. Cin. State Tech. and C. of C. Found., 1996-98; trustee Cin. State Found., 1996-98; bd. dirs. Tin Foor Found. Capt. USAF, 1967-71, Vietnam. Decorated Bronze Star, Air Force Commendation medal. Mem. Soc. Fin. Svc. Profls. (pres. Cin. chpt. 1987-88), Chamber Music Am., Am. Coll. CLU/ChFC Golden Key Soc. (benefactur), Internat. Assn. Fin. Planning (pres. Cin. chpt. 1987-88), Nat. Assn. Life Underwriters, Million Dollar Round Table (life), Cin. Estate Planning Con. (pres. 1988-89), Cin. C. of C., Bankers Club (life, chmn. emeritus bd. govs.), Pres. Club Miami Univ. (Oxford, Ohio), Trout Unltd., Ducks Unltd., Fedn. Fly Fishers (life), Buckeye United Fly Fishers, Ohio Gun Collectors Assn. (life), NRA (life), Fairfield Sportsmen's Assn., Milford Gun Club, Box 13 Assocs. (fire divsn. Cin.). Republican. Avocations: fly fishing, woodworking, cello, skeet shooting, photography. Office: Evans Fin Group 414 Walnut St Ste 1205 Cincinnati OH 45202-3913

EVANS, BILLY JOE, chemistry educator, consultant; b. Macon, Ga., Aug. 18, 1942; s. Will and Mildred (Owens) E.; m. Adye Bel Sampson, Aug. 31, 1963; children: William Joseph, Carole Elizabeth. BSc in Chemistry summa cum laude, Morehouse Coll., 1959-63; PhD in Chemistry, U. Chgo., 1968. Asst. prof. Howard U., Washington, 1969-70; asst. prof. chemistry U. Mich., Ann Arbor, 1970-73, assoc. prof., 1973-79, prof., 1979—; dir. Program Scholarly Rsch. Ubran/Minority High Sch. Students, Ann Arbor, 1980—, Comprehensive Studies Program, Ann Arbor, 1984-85; cons. Nat. Bur. Stds., Washington, 1970-80, Ford Motor Co., Detroit, 1977, U.S. Geol. Survey, Washington, 1977-81. Contbr. articles to profl. jours. Bd. dirs. Detroit Met. Sci. and Engrng. Fair, 1983, Cranbrook Inst. of Sci., 1989-95; judge Southeastern Mich. Sci. and Engrng. Fair, Ann Arbor, 1983—. Fellow Woodrow Wilson Found., 1963, Nat. Rsch. Coun. Can., 1968-69, Alexander von Humboldt Found., 1977-78; recipient Catalyst medal Chem. Mfrs. Assn., 1995, Presdl. Mentoring award, 1998. Mem. Am. Phys. Soc., Am. Chem. Soc. (nat. award 1997), Mineral. Soc. Am., Am. Geophys. Union, U. Mich. Rsch. Club (pres. 1984-85), Exchange Club, Phi Beta Kappa, Phi Kappa Phi. Home: 810 Oxford Rd Ann Arbor MI 48104-2637 Office: U Mich Dept Chemistry 930 N University Ave Ann Arbor MI 48109-1001

EVANS, BRIAN DAVID, librarian; b. London, May 29, 1937; s. Herbert George and Ellen Eliza (Smith) E.; m. Gillian Chambers, June 21, 1958 (dec. 1979); children: Timothy Huw, Simon David, Kate Rebecca. BA, Open U., Eng., 1980. Libr. Clapham Libr., London, 1964-65, Earlsfield Libr., London, 1965-67; reference and info. svcs. libr. Havering Ctrl. Libr., London, 1967-95; cons. local historian; editor Local Govt. Annotations, 1969—, Romford Record, London, 1969—; columnist Havering Recorder Newspaper, 1995-97; lectr. in field. Author/compiler: Bygone Romford, 1988, Hornchurch and Upminster, 1990, Bygone Dagenham and Rainham, 1992, Romford, Collier Row and Gidea Park, 1994, also 20 other books. Hon. life. mem. Romford Hist. Soc., 1990—. Mem. Libr. Assn. (assoc.), Nat. Trust (life), Gt. Ea. Ry. Soc., Nondescripts, Rotary (pres. Romford 1996-97, pub. rels. officer 1997—). Avocations: local history, walking, cartophily, reading. Office: Havering Recorder, River Chambers High St, Romford Essex RM1 1TX, England

EVANS, CHARLES WILLIAM, mathematician, educator; b. Newbury, Eng., Dec. 31, 1942; s. Charles William George and Gwendoline Celia (Jones) E.; m. Rosemary Joan Lanfear, Dec. 17, 1966 (div. 1973); children: Ivan Peter, Miranda Lesley; m. Jean Turton, Sept. 15, 1973; children: Edwin Charles Lorance, Caroline Madeleine Jean. BA, U. Southampton, 1965, MSc, 1967, PhD, 1978. Asst. lectr. Southampton (Eng.) Coll. Higher Edn., 1966-67; asst. lectr. Portsmouth (Eng.) Coll. Higher Edn., 1967-68, lectr., 1968-72; sr. lectr. Portsmouth Polytech., 1972-95; prin. lectr. U. Portsmouth, 1995—, head divsn. math. and statistics, 1997; vice-chmn. Wessex br. Inst. Math. and Applications, 1980-83, chmn., 1983-84, sec.-treas. 1991-94, chmn., 1996-97. Author: Engineering Mathematics, 1989, 3d edit., 1997; contbr. articles to profl. jours. Fellow inst. Math. and Its Applications (coun. 1994-97); mem. London Math. Soc., Am. Math. Soc. Roman Catholic. Office: U Portsmouth Comp Sci Math, Mercantile Ho Hampshire Ter, Portsmouth PO1 2EG, England

EVANS, CHRISTOPHER ROBIN, ecologist, researcher; b. Bournemouth, Dorset, Eng., Aug. 29, 1950; s. Arthur John and Iris Beatrice Ivy (Haines) E.; m. Judith Ann Webb, May 15, 1971; children: Emma, Matthew, Paul. BSc, Southampton Coll., 1981; PhD, U. Southampton, 1989; MA, U. London, 1990; BSc with honors, Open U., 1994; cert. coastal zone mgmt., Bournemouth U., 1998. Proprietor C.R. Evans Farmhouse Restoration, Bournemouth, Dorchester, Eng., 1982-86; exec. officer Bermuda Lobster project U. Southampton, 1986-89; co-proprietor Dorset Natural Resources and Environment Cons., Bournemouth, 1989-94, 97—; mgr. rsch. and mgmt. br. Nat. Fisheries Authority, Papua New Guinea, 1994-96; ind. rschr. dept. oceanography Southampton Oceanography Ctr., 1997—; chief fishery/wildlife biologist Dep. Mar. Wildlife Resources, Pago Pago, Am. Samoa, 2000—; intern Bermuda Biol. Sta. Rsch., 1986-87; assoc. fisheries cons. MacAlister Elliott & Ptnrs.,Lynington, 1999—; instr. Bournemouth Coll., 1994; course tutor aquatic habitat conservation mgmt. U. Southampton, 1998. Contbr. articles to profl. jours. Baptist. Avocations: shore walking, forest walking, travel, reading, writing. Home: 2 Edgehill Rd Winton, Dorset Bournemouth BH9 2PQ, England Office: U Southampton Oceanograph Ctr, Sch Earth & Ocean Sci, Southampton SO14 3ZH, England Office: Dept Mar Wildlife Resources PO Box 3730 Pago Pago AS 96799-3730

EVANS, DAVID ALAN PRICE, physician; b. Birkenhead, England, Mar. 6, 1927; s. Owen and Ellen (Jones) E. BSc with 1st class hons., U. Liverpool, Eng., 1948; MBChB, U. Liverpool, 1951, MSc, 1957, MD, 1959, PhD, 1965, DSc, 1981. House physician, house surgeon U. Liverpool Tchg. Hosp., 1951-52, med. registrar, 1955-58, 59-60; fellow Johns Hopkins U., 1958-59; lectr. U. Liverpool, 1960-62, sr. lectr., 1962-78, prof., 1968-72, chmn., dir., 1972-83, emeritus prof., 1994—, sr. physician dept. medicine, 1999—; dir. medicine Riyadh (Saudi Arabia) Armed Forces Hosp., 1983-99; vis. prof. Karolinska U., Stockholm, 1968, Johns Hopkins U., Balt., 1972, Sir Henry Dale Meml. lectr., 1972, U. Mich., Ann Arbor, 1982, U. Berne, Switzerland, 1981; Poulson Meml. lectr. Oslo U., 1972; Walter Idris Jones meml. lectr. U. Wales, 1972; Watson Smith lectr. Royal Coll. Physicians, London, 1976. Author: Genetic Factors in Drug Therapy: Clinical and Molecular Pharmacogenetics, 1993; scientific editor Saudi Med. Jour., 1983-93; mem. editl. bd. Pharmacogenetics, 1991—; contbr. articles to profl. jours. Capt. Royal Army Med. Corps., 1953-55. Holt fellow U. Liverpool, 1952-53, Johns Hopkins Hosp. fellow, 1958-59; recipient Thornton prize Ea. Psychiatric Assn. Fellow Royal Coll. Physicians; mem. Assn. Physicians Great Britain Ireland, British Med. Assn., Johns Hopkins, Soc. Scholars (life). Presbyterian. Fax: 00 966 1 478 4057. E-mail: dapevans@kfsh-hub.kfshrc.edu.sa. Home and Office: Riyadh Armed Forces Hosp, C123 PO Box 7897, Riyadh 11159, Saudi Arabia

EVANS, DAVID EDGAR, plant biologist, researcher; b. Birmingham, Eng., July 29, 1957; s. Edgar and Grace Marion (Holtham) E.; m. Margaret Patricia Adkin, July 27, 1985; children: Robert, Rachel, Sarah. BSc with honors in Botany, U. Wales, Aberystwyth Dyfed, 1978, PhD, 1981. Botany fellow Dept. Plant Scis. U. Oxford, Eng., 1983-88, Royal Soc. U. rsch. fellow, 1988-92; Royal Soc. U. rsch. fellow Oxford Brookes U., 1992-98, sr. lectr., 1998—. Assoc. editor Jour. Exptl. Biology, 1992—; editor: Endocytosis, Exocytosis and Vesicle Traffic in Plants, 1991. Rsch. grantee Agr. and Foods and Biotech. and Biol. Scis. Rschs. Couns. Avocations: reading, walking. Home: 19 Littleworth Rd, Wheatley Oxon OX33 1NW, England Office: Oxford Brookes U, Gipsy Lane Campus, Headington OX3 0BP, England

EVANS, DAVID JOHN, computing educator; b. Llanelli, Wales, Sept. 30, 1928; s. Stanley and Margaret Ann (King) E.; m. Naldera Owens, Aug. 6, 1955; children: Neil Wyn, Tracy Susanne (dec.), Clare Joanne. BSc in Math., U. Coll. Wales, Aberystwyth, 1949; MSc in Engring., Southampton (Eng.) U., 1956; PhD, Manchester (Eng.) U., 1963; DSc, U. Wales, 1985;

DSc (hon.), Tech. U. Iasi, Romania, 1995. Aerodynamist Rolls Royce, Hucknall, U.K., 1952-53; sr. mathematician Rolls Royce, Derby, U.K., 1955-57; rsch. asst. Southampton U., 1953-55; rsch. fellow Manchester U., 1957-65; dir. computing lab. Sheffield (U.K.) U., 1965-72; prof. computing Loughborough (U.K.) U., 1972-96, prof. emeritus, 1996—; prof. computing Nottingham Trent U., U.K., 1996—l; dir. Parallel Algorithms Rsch. Ctr., Loughborough U., 1989-96; vis. prof. Wuhan U., China, 1985-95. Author: Preconditioning Methods, 1983, Systolic Algorithms, 1992, Group Explicit Methods, 1996; editor Internat. Jour. Computer Math. With RAF, 1950-52. Fellow Brit. Computer Soc., Inst. Math. and Applications (chartered). Avocation: music. Office: Nottingham Trent U, Burton St, Nottingham NG1 4BU, England

EVANS, DAVID JOHN ALEXANDER, geography educator; b. Welwyn Garden City, Eng., Oct. 10, 1959; s. William Albert and June Margot (Hickson) E.; m. Tessa Jane Fenoughty, June 20, 1992; children: Tara Ann Hope, Charlotte Elizabeth. BA with honors, U. Wales, Lampeter, Wales, 1982; MS, Meml. U., St. John's, Can., 1984; PhD, U. Alta., Edmonton, Can., 1988. Lectr. King's Coll., London, 1989-90; lectr. U. Glasgow, 1990-96, sr. lectr., 1996-99, reader, 1999—. Author: (book) Glaciers and Glaciation, 1998; editor: (book) Cold Climate Landforms, 1994; contbr. articles to profl. jours. Fellow Royal Geograph. Soc.; mem. Quaternary Rsch. Assn., Brit. Geomorphology. Rsch. Group. Avocations: cricket, mountain walking, antique buses, Land Rovers. Office: Dept Geography, U Glasgow, Glasgow G12 8QQ, Scotland

EVANS, DAVID SEAMUS, health organization researcher; b. Neath, Wales, Feb. 8, 1966; arrived in Ireland, 1997; s. Ieuan Morgan and Susan Celine (McLaughlin) E.; m. Eileen Teresa Rowley, Sept. 18, 1998. BSc, U. Ulster, 1987; MSc, Cranfield U., 1989, PhD, 1992. Rsch. officer U. Ulster, Belfast, Ireland, 1993-97, Western Health Bd., Galway, Ireland, 1997—. Editor (conf. proc.): Transport Options for Belfast, 1996, New Urban Transport Systems, 1995, Urban Transport and the Environment, 1995, European Peripherality, 1994, others. Mem. Chartered Inst. of Transport. Office: Western Health Bd, Merlin Park Reg Hosp, Galway Republic of Ireland

EVANS, DOUGLAS HAYWARD, lawyer; b. Providence, R.I., July 21, 1950; s. Jerrold Merton and Gladys Jean (Snelgrove) E.; m. Sarah Edwards Cogan, May 28, 1983; children: Anne Morrill, Thomas Taylor Seelye, Elizabeth Hayward. AB, Franklin & Marshall Coll., 1972; JD, Cornell U., 1975. Bar: N.J. 1975, U.S. Dist. Ct. N.J. 1975, N.Y. 1976, U.S. Dist Ct. (so. dist.) N.Y. 1991. Assoc. Windels, Marx, Davies & Ives, N.Y.C., 1975-85; assoc. Sullivan & Cromwell, N.Y.C., 1985-90, spl. counsel, 1990—; faculty NYU Inst. Fed. Taxation, N.Y.C., 1984; counsel, treas., pres. St. David's Soc. State of N.Y., N.Y.C., 1985—; bd. dirs. Friends of Washington Sq. Park, 1989—, Washington Sq. Assn., 1992—, 1st Presbyn. Ch. Nursery Sch., 1999—. Co-Author: Estate Accounting, 1980, Probate and Estate Administration, 1982, Administration of Estates, 1985, Settling An Estate, 1989; Editor-in-Chief and Co-Author: Probate and Administration of New York Estates, 1995; also articles. Trustee Franklin & Marshall Coll., 1994—, Grace Ch. Sch., N.Y.C., 1997—, vice chmn., 2000—; mem. Ch. Club of N.Y., Salmagundi Club, N.Y.C. Fellow Am. Coll. of Trust and Estate Coun.; mem. ABA, N.J. Bar Assn., N.Y. State Bar Assn. (estate litig. and adminstrn. of trusts and estates com., com. on Cont. Legal Edn.; chmn. 1991-94), N.Y. County Lawyers Assn. (not-for-profit com.), Phi Beta Kappa, Phi Delta Phi, Phi Alpha Theta, Pi Gamma Mu. Episcopalian. Home: 43 Fifth Ave New York NY 10003-4368 Office: Sullivan & Cromwell 125 Broad St Fl 28 New York NY 10004-2489

EVANS, EDWARD FRANK, educator; b. Birmingham, England, Mar. 30, 1936; s. Frank and Kathleen (Oakden) E.; m. Diana Marguerite Price, July 20, 1963; children: Nicola Jane, Jonathan Andrew. BS, U. Birmingham, England, 1957, Mc ChB, 1960, PhD, 1965, DS, 1988. Reader Keele U., England, 1973-78, prof., 1978—, head dept. comm. & neurosci., 1982-93, dean faculty scis., 1984-87; vis. assoc. NINDB, NIH, Betjesda, Md., 1965-67. Contbr. articles to profl. jours. Gov. Wrekin Coll., 1984-96, Clayton High Sch., 1980-85. Recipient TS Littler prize Brit. Soc. Audiology, 1973, James Yearsley medal Royal Soc. Medicine, 1989, Rayleigh Gold medal Inst. Acoustics, 1994; rsch. fellow U. Birmingham, England, 1961-65, sr. rsch. fellow Keele U., 1967-73. Fellow Royal Coll. Physicians, Inst. Acoustics; mem. Brit. Soc. Audiology. Mem. Ch. of England. Avocations: sailing, boat restoration, theatre, opera. Office: Keele U, Keele ST5 5BG, England

EVANS, ESSI H., research scientist; b. Bad-Schwalbach, Germany, Jan. 12, 1950; came to U.S., 1951, naturalized, 1957; d. John H. (b. Horst H. Jahn) and Jean E. (von Schwerin); m. Everett M. Turner Jr., Aug. 16, 1974. BS in Agr., U. Md., 1972; MS in Animal Sci., U. Guelph, 1974, PhD in Animal Sci., 1976. Polymer chemist Monarch Rubber Co., Balt., 1972; rsch. asst., tchg. asst. U. Guelph, Ont., 1972-76; project dir. animal nutrition Can. Packers Inc., Toronto, Ont., 1976-85, tech. mgr. animal nutrition and animal health, 1986-89, rsch. mgr., 1989-90, gen. rsch. and nutrition mgr. shur-gain divsn., 1990-93, mgmt. dir., 1993-2000, v.p. Shur Gain, 2000—; farm cons.; guest lectr. Hubbard Farms fellow, 1975-76; NRC Indsl. postdoctoral fellow, 1976-79. Contbr. articles to sci. jours. and profl. and sci. confs. James Harris scholar, U. Md., 1972; recipient Hamilton Milk Prodrs. award, 1973, 74; Ont. Ministry of Agr. and Foods Provincial Lottery grantee, 1980-83. Mem. AAAS, Am. Soc. Animal Sci., Am. Dairy Sci. Assn., Am. Assn. Vet. Nutritionists, Coun. for Agrl. Sci. and Tech., Nat. Feed Industry Assn., Can. Feed Industry Assn. Republican. Home: 64 Scugog St, Bowmanville, ON Canada L1C 3J1 Office: Shur-Gain Div Maple Leaf Fd, 30 Eglinton Ave W Ste 300, Mississauga, ON Canada L5R 3E7

EVANS, EVAN, petroleum executive; b. N.Y.C., May 19, 1925; s. John William Jr. and Therese Rosemary (Guilfoyle) E.; m. Natalie Coe Holbrook, Feb. 20, 1968; children: Megan, Meredith, Rhys, Valerie, Cynthia, David. Student, St. Lawrence U., 1942-43, 46, BS, 1949; BS, MIT, 1951. Engr. Calif. Tex. Oil Corp., N.Y.C., 1951-55, Bahrain, 1955-57; refinery ops. asst. Calif. Tex. Oil Corp., N.Y.C., 1957-60, Rotterdam, 1960-62; refinery plant mgr. Calif. Tex. Oil Corp., Lebanon, 1963; refinery specialist Calif. Tex. Oil Corp., N.Y.C., 1963-65; refinery project mgr. King Wilkinson, Antwerp, Belgium, 1966-68; v.p. United Refining Co., Warren, Pa., 1972-81, dir., 1974-81, 96—; pres. Kiantone Pipeline, 1970-81; v.p. Western Crude Oil Inc., 1981-83; pres. Wesco Internat. Inc., 1981-83, Holvan Properties Inc., Madison, Conn., 1985—; dir. U.S. Energy Sys., 1995—, Belgian Refining Corp., 1993-96, Alexander-Allen Inc., 1994—. Chmn. Am. Sch. Rotterdam, 1961-62. With USN, 1943-46. Mem. N.Y. Athletic Club. Address: 331 Old Toll Rd Madison CT 06443-1710

EVANS, FRANCES JOANNE, publishing company administrator, publisher; b. Weston-Super-Mare, Somerset, Eng., Apr. 29, 1969; d. Idris and Moyra Alice (Thomas) E. BA with honors, South Bank U., London, 1992; European Bus. Cert., F.H. Pforzheim, Germany, 1993. Asst. planner BBDO, Hamburg, Germany, 1993-94; strategic planner FCB, Hamburg, Germany, 1994-96; product mgr. Marquard Media, Munich, 1996-97; gen. mgr. Marquard Media, Budapest, Hungary, 1998—. Avocations: sailing, skiing, fitness, socializing. Office: JMG Magazin Kiado Ket, Hajogyari Sziget 213, 1033 Budapest Hungary

EVANS, FRANKLIN BACHELDER, marketing educator emeritus; b. Chgo., Feb. 9, 1922; s. Franklin B. and Arline (Brown) E.; m. Barbara V. Both, Sept. 16, 1943; children: Mary A., Amy B., Geoffrey B., Christopher G. A.A., U. Chgo., 1941, A.B., 1943, M.B.A., 1954, Ph.D., 1959. Asst. prof. mktg. U. Chgo., 1957-64; prof. mktg. U. Hawaii, 1964-69; prof. advt. Northwestern U., 1969-80, prof. emeritus, 1981—; cons. to bus. and industry; researcher on consumer motivation. Contbr. articles to profl. jours. Served with AUS, 1943-45, CBI. Decorated Bronze Star. Home: 17046 Lloyds Byu Apt 416 Spring Lake MI 49456-9274

EVANS, G. ANNE, lawyer; b. Eastland, Tex., Feb. 24, 1954; d. Travis Clay and Maude Velma (DeMoss) E.; children: Courtney Faith, Alexandria Brooke. BA in Psychology, U. Nebr., Omaha, 1988; JD, U. Nebr., Lincoln, 1991. Bar: Nebr. 1991, U.S. Dist. Ct. Nebr. 1991, U.S. Ct. Appeals (8th cir.) 1992. Pvt. practice, Omaha, 1991—. Mm. Nat. Assn. Criminal Def. Lawyers, Nebr. State Bar Assn., Nebr. Criminal Def. Attys. Assn., Am. Inns of Ct. (co-founder Omaha chpt.), Golden Key, Phi Alpha Delta, Psi Chi. Democrat. Mem. Christian Science. Avocations: theatre, hiking, climbing, calligraphy.

EVANS, GARETH, Australian government and international official; b. Melbourne, Victoria, Australia, Sept. 5, 1944; m. Merran Anderson, Jan. 15, 1969; 2 children. BA, U. Melbourne, honours law degree; MA, Oxford (Eng.) U. Lectr., sr. lectr. law U. Melbourne, 1971-76; senator for Victoria, Australian Parliament, 1978-96, mem. opposition ministry, spokesman on atty.-gen. matters, 1980-83, atty.-gen., 1983-84, min. for resources and energy, 1984-87; dep. leader of govt. in Senate, 1987-93; min. for transport and communications, 1987-88, min. for fgn. affairs, 1988-96; leader of govt. in Senate, 1993-96; dep. leader opposition spokesman on treasury matters, 1996-98; mem. House of Reps., 1996-99; pres., CEO Internat. Crisis Group, Brussels, 1999—. Co-author: Australia's Constitution: Time for Change?, 1983, Australia's Foreign Relations in the World of the 1990s, 1991, 2nd edit., 1995; author: Cooperating for Peace, 1993. Avocations: travel, golf, reading, opera.

EVANS, HENRY JOHN, geneticist; b. Llanelli, Wales, Dec. 24, 1930; s. David and Gwladys May (Jones) E.; m. Gwenda Rosalind Thomas, 1956 (dec. 1974); children: Paul, Hugh, John, Owen; m. Roslyn Rose Angel, Sept. 11, 1975. BSc, U. Wales, Aberystwyth, 1952, PhD, 1955; DSc (hon.), U. Edinburgh, 1996. Scientist Med. Rsch. Coun., Harwell, Eng., 1955-64; prof. genetics U. Aberdeen (Eng.), 1964-69; dir. Med. Rsch. Coun. human genetics unit Western Gen. Hosp., Edinburgh, 1969-95; mem. sci. coun. Alberta (Can.) Heritage Found. for Med. Rsch., 1986-99; chmn. sci. coun. Cancer Rsch. Campaign, London, 1990-95, v.p. 1995—; chmn. Caledonian Rsch. Found., Edinburgh, 1990—; chmn. bd. govs. Beatson Inst. Cancer Rsch., Glasgow, Scotland, 1992-99. Contbg. editor numerous articles for profl. jours.; lectr. in field. Decorated Comdr. Order of the Brit. Empire (Eng.). Fellow Inst. of Biology, Royal Coll. Physicians (Eng.), Royal Coll. Surgeons (Eng.); mem. Edinburgh New Club. Home: 45 Lauder Rd, Edinburgh EH9 1UE, England Office: MRC human genetics unit, Western Gen Hosp Crewe Rd, Edinburgh EH4 2XU, Scotland

EVANS, J. GARY, psychologist, educator; b. Darlington, S.C., Nov. 24, 1949; s. James G. and Mary Evelyn Evans; m. Judy Field Evans, Dec. 20, 1972. BA magna cum laude, Ga. So. Coll., 1972, cert. edn. specialist, 1977, MEd, 1975; PhD, Ga. State U., 1988. Diplomate Am. Bd. Profl. Psychology; cert. dir. pupil pers., sch. psychologist; lic. psychologist, Ga. Program evaluator, psychologist Child Devel. Ctr., Dublin, Ga., 1973-74; program sch. psychologist Comprehensive Psycho-Ednl. Svcs., Valdosta, Ga., 1975-77; outpost ctr. coord., psychologist Comprehensive Psycho-Ednl. Svcs., Tifton, Ga., 1977-80; assoc. sch. psychologist Gwinnett County (Ga.) Pub. Schs., 1980-85, coord. psychol. svcs., 1985-94; asst. prof. Ga. State U., Atlanta, 1994—; asst. prof. divsn. ednl. studies Emory U., Atlanta, 1993-94; presenter in field. Contbr. articles to profl. jours. Mem. psychoednl. adv. com. Ga. State Dept. Edn., 1979-80, psychol. report writing com., 1987-88; mem. devel. com. Ga. Sch. Psychologists Evaluation Instrument, 1987-89; mem. sch. psychology revision com. Tchr. Cert. Test, 1988-89, chair State Adv. Panel for Spl. Edn., 1993-94. Recipient award of appreciation Big Bros./Big Sisters, 1980. Mem. APA, Am. Acad. Sch. Psychology (sec. 1999—), Nat. Assn. Sch. Psychologists (parliamentarian 1976-77, regional rep. 1977-78, 83-84, 92-94, editor newsletter 1978-79, pres. 1979-80, rsch. chmn. 1980-81, legis. chmn. 1981-83, 90-92, chmn. profl. stds. 1988-89, 97-98, co-chair redistricting com. 1989-90, chair univ. trainers com. 1999—, Del. Appreciation cert. 1983), Phi Delta Kappa, Kappa Delta Phi. Avocation: marathon running. Address: 1611 Wickersham Pl Suwanee GA 30024-2806

EVANS, JAMES HAYS, photographer; b. Carrollton, Mo., Apr. 12, 1937; s. James Earl and Selma Ethel (Hays) E.; m. Anna Gale Block, Dec. 23, 1960; children: Amy Denise Jackson, Alecia Lou Stultz. Student, Colo. Sch. Mines, Golden, 1954-55; AB, U. Mo., 1959; MA, Northeast Mo. State U., 1964. Cert. secondary sch. educator, Mo. Owner, operator Evans Photography, St. Clair, Mo., 1953—; instr. scis. Westran Sch. Dist., Huntsville, Mo., 1959-63, St. Clair (Mo.) R XIII Schs., 1963-64; head sci. dept. Mary Knoll Jr. Seminary, Chesterfield, Mo., 1964-69, Villa Duchene Acad., St. Louis, Mo., 1969-70, Visitation Acad., St. Louis, 1970-73; sales engr. von Weise Gear Co., St. Louis, 1973-80; product engr. White Rogers (divsn. Emerson Elec.), St. Louis, 1980-81. Alderman City of St. Clair, 1966-70, Mayor City of St. Clair, 1971-75; treas. St. Clair Hist. Mus., 1988-2000, Wedding and Portrait Photograph Internat. Mem. Profl. Photographers Am., Profl. Photographers Mo., Profl. Photographers Greater St. Louis (past. sec., 2nd v.p.), Rotary Club (sec.-treas. 1995-96, v.p. 1996-97, pres. 1997-98), Greater St. Louis Profl. Photographers (sec. 1997-2000, 2nd v.p. 2000—), Huntsville Lodge. Avocations: woodworking, gardening, photography. Home and Office: Evans Photography 335 E Springfield Rd Saint Clair MO 63077-1731

EVANS, JOHN DAVIES, archaeologist; b. Jan. 22, 1925; s. Harry and Edith (Haycocks) E.; m. Evelyn Sladdin, 1957. BA, U. Cambridge, 1948, MA, 1950, PhD, 1956, LittD, 1979; Dr. h.c., U. Lyon, 1983. Fellow, Brit. Inst. Archaeology, Ankara, Turkey, 1951-52; research fellow Pembroke Coll., Cambridge, 1953-56; prof. prehistoric archaeology London U., 1956-73, prof. archaeology, dir. Inst. Archaeology, 1973-89, prof. emeritus, 1989—; pres. Prehistoric Soc., 1974-78; pres. Council Brit. Archaeology, 1979-82; mem. permanent council Internat. Congress Prehistoric and Protohistoric Scis., 1975—, pres., 1982-85; chmn. area archaeol. adv. com. for Southeast Eng., 1975-79; chmn. Treasure Trove Reviewing Com., 1988-96; mem. Royal Commn. on the Hist. Monuments of Eng., 1985-92. Decorated Order Brit Empire. Fellow Brit. Acad.; mem. German Archaeol. Inst., Soc. Antiquaries of London (pres. 1984-87). Author: Malta (Ancient Peoples and Places Series), 1959; (with A.C. Renfrew) Excavations at Saliagos, near Antiparos, 1968; The Prehistoric Antiquities of the Maltese Islands, 1971; contbr. articles to profl. jours. Home: Melbury Cottage, 5 Love Ln, Shaftesbury Dorset SP7 8BG, England*

EVANS, JOHN DERBY, telecommunications company executive; b. Detroit, June 3, 1944; s. Edward Steptoe and Florence (Allington) E.; m. Susan Blair Allan, Apr. 7, 1973 (div. Nov. 1986); children: John Derby, Courtenay Boyd. AB, U. Mich., 1966. Pres. Evans Comm. Sys. Inc., Charlottesville, Va., 1970-72; v.p., gen. mgr. Capitol Cablevision Corp., Charleston, W.Va., 1972-76; regional mgr. Am. TV and Comm. Corp., Denver, 1974-76; exec. v.p., COO Arlington (Va.) TeleCom. Corp., 1976-83; pres. Arlington Cable Ptnrs. Ltd., 1983-94, Suburban Cable Ptnrs., Brooklyn Pk., Minn., 1985-89, Hauser Comm., N.Y.C., 1985-94, Evans Telecomm. Co., 1983—; chmn., CEO Waterford Marine Inc., Key West, Fla., 1996—; staff asst. sec. planning and devel. Dept. HEW, Washington, 1976; bd. dirs. Eisenhower World Affairs Inst., chmn. strategic planning com., 1997—, vice chmn. 1999—; vice chmn. bd. dirs. Signature Theater, Inc., Arlington, Va., Cable Satelliter Pub. Affairs Network (C-SPAN), exec. com., 1982-93, 98—, chmn., 1991-93, chmn. fin. com., 1997—; pres. Montgomery Cablevision (LP), Rockville, Md., 1986-94, Washington Metro Cable Club, 1981—; bd. dirs. Falcon Comm. Co., L.A., Falcon Cable TV, 1998-2000, Sierraware Inc., Sacremento, Calif., 1999—; GBR scientific, 1999—, Sierraware Inc., Sacramento, 1998-2000, GBR Sci. Co., Balt.; v.p. North Ctrl. Cable Comm. Co., Roseville, Minn., 1986-92; mng. gen. ptnr. Waterford Farm Partnership, Middleburg, Va., 1993—; Siciliano forum lectr. U. Utah, 1998; future makers lectr. Emory U., 1999. Trustee C-Span Ednl. Found., 1994—, Signature Theater, Arlington; chmn. bd. trustees Evans Found., 1994—; chmn. Cancer/AIDS Rsch. Network, Balt.; mem. steering com. Inst. Human Virology U. Md., Balt.; bd. dirs. Internat. Cancer and AIDS Rsch. Found., Hollings Cancer Ctr., Charleston, S.C.; adv. com. AIDS Rsch. Inst. U. Calif., San Francisco; mem. vis. com. Coll. LS and A, U. Mich., 1994—, mem. president's adv. bd., 1998—, mem. commn. on info. tech., 2000—; chmn. Waterford Found., 2000—; lectr. Inst. of the Humanities, U. Mich., 2000. Mem. Nat. Cable TV Assn. (nat. chmn. awards com. 1981, bd. dirs. 1982—, chmn. govt. rels. com. 1985-86, chmn. elections, bylaws com. 1991-97, mem. regulatory policy com. 1991-95, mem. conv. com. 1999-00, Pres. award 1979, Vanguard award 1984, convention com. 1998—), Va. Cable Assn. (bd. dirs. 1979—, v.p. 1982, pres. 1983, 84), Asia-Pacific Conf. Sci. and Tech. Leaders (U.S. del. 1996), Fisher Island (Fla.) Club, Caribbean Acad. of Sci. (U.S. del. 10th ann. meeting 1998), Farmington Country Club, Boars Head Sports Club (Charlottesville), Wintergreen (Va.) Sports Club, Washington Golf and Country Club (Arlington), Cable TV Adminstrn., Mktg. Soc. (bd. dirs. 1985). Republican. Episcopalian. Home and Office: Waterford Farm PO Box 1082 Rte 709 Middleburg VA 20118

EVANS, JOHN WINTON, engineering educator, consultant; b. Fosston, Minn., June 8, 1957; s. Winton Lowell and Jean (Larson) E.; m. Jillian Youngeun Shin, July 8, 1977; children: Christopher, Raina. BSME, U. Nebr., 1983; MS, U. Iowa, 1987; PhD, Johns Hopkins U., 1994. Engr. Rockwell Internat., Cedar Rapids, Iowa, 1983-87; engring. group leader Unisys Corp., Goddard Space Flight Ctr., 1987-91; program mgr. NASA, Washington, 1991-97; vis. prof. Inst. Advanced Engring., Seoul, Korea, 1995—; rsch. cons. Daewoo Electronics, Seoul, 1995—; mem. STAR panel Dept. Def., 1993; sponsor, advisor NSF, Japan Tech. Evaluation Ctr., 1994; mem. com. White House Nat. Econ. Coun., 1994; presenter in field. Editor: Quality Conformance and Qualification of Microelectronics, 1994, Product Integrity and Reliability in Design, 1999; contbr. articles to profl. jours., chpt. to books. Vol. tchr. Kyonggi-do Soungnam (Korea) Sch. Dist., 1997. Mem. IEEE (mem. orgn. com. electronic packaging adv. com., internat. reliabiligy physics symposium 1993), ASME. Avocations: skiing, hiking, camping. Office: Inst Advanced Engring, Yongin PO Box 25, Kyonggi-do 449-860, Korea

EVANS, JOYCE EVANS, administrative assistant; b. Dodgeville, Wis., Mar. 18, 1942; d. Alvin Herman and Leona Sophia (Harms) Christianson; m. Ronald Warren Evans, Jan. 22, 1939; children: Renee, Douglas, Staci. Sec. Iowa County Nurse, Dodgeville, Wis., 1959-62, Gen. Hosp., Dodgeville, 1964-65, Dodgeville Clinic, 1965-67; officer mgr. Petrolane Gas Svc., 1972-82; student records sec. Dodgeville H.S., 1985—. Mem. ch. choir Grace Luth. Ch., Dodgeville, 1960—, organizer Befrienders, 1996—; scout leader Boys Scouts Am., Dodgeville, 1967-75, Girl Scouts U.S., Dodgeville, 1969-72. Named Friend of Edn. Congressman Klug, 1994. Avocations: reading, music. Office: Dodgeville HS 912 W Chapel St Dodgeville WI 53533-1022

EVANS, LARRY, mycologist, restauranteur; b. Decatur, Ill., Mar. 6, 1955. BA in Botany, U. Mont., 1979. Cert. tchr. Taxonomist, tree salesman 4E's Trees, Decatur, 1968-82; lang. facilitator Phoenix Internat. Cons., Tokyo, 1983-85; tchr. Dae Won Wei Gook Ohakyo, Seoul, Republic of Korea, 1985-87; freelance writer Missoula, Mont., 1991-93; lectr. U. Mont., Missoula, 1994—; owner Black Day Cafe, Missoula, 1997—; cons., Missoula, 1991—. Author: Hey Now Hitchhikers!, 1981; columnist Mushroom Jour., 1998—. Mem. N.Am. Mycol. Assn., Pacific N.W. Key Coun., Western Mont. Mycol. Assn. (dir. 1991—), Missoula Farmers Market.

EVANS, LAWRENCE E., lawyer, educator; b. Houston, Mar. 30, 1950; s. Lawrence Edgar and Edith (Kinzy) E.; m. Nancy Campbell, Aug. 20, 1977; children: Christopher, Laura. BA, Washington & Lee U., 1973; JD, South Tex. Coll., 1977. Bar: Tex. 1977, Mo. 1989. Lawyer Gunn, Lee & Miller, Houston, 1977-88, Herzog, Crebs & McGhee, St. Louis, 1988-2000, Blackwell, Sanders, Peper, Martin LLP, St. Louis, 2000—; adj. prof. Washington Univ. Sch. of Law, St. Louis. Mem. Metro. Bar Assn. St. Louis (chmn. Patent, Trademark and Copyright sect. 1994), Internat. Trademark Assn., Am. Intellectual Property Law Assn. Office: Blackwell Sanders Peper Martin LLP 720 Olive St Ste 2400 Saint Louis MO 63101

EVANS, LAWRENCE JACK, JR., lawyer, judge; b. Oakland, Calif., Apr. 4, 1921; s. Lawrence Jack and Eva May (Dickinson) E.; m. Marjorie Hisken, Dec. 23, 1944; children: Daryl S. Kleweno, Richard L., Shirley J., Coursey, Donald B. MA, Am. U., Beirut, 1951; grad., Command and Gen. Staff Coll., 1960; PhD, Brantridge Forest Sch., Sussex, Eng., 1968; JD, Ariz. State U., 1971; grad., Nat. Jud. Coll., 1974. Diplomate Near East Sch. Theology, Beirut, 1951; bar: Ariz. 1971, U.S. Dist. Ct. Ariz. 1971, U.S. Ct. Claims 1972, U.S. Customs Ct. 1972, U.S. Tax Ct. 1972, U.S. Ct. Customs and Patent Appeals 1972, U.S. Ct. Appeals (9th cir.) 1972, U.S. Supreme Ct. 1975. Enlisted USN, 1938-41; enlisted U.S. Army, 1942-44, commd. 2d lt., 1944, advanced through ranks to lt. col., 1962; war plans officer G-3 Seventh Army, 1960-62; chief, field ops. and tactics divsn. U.S. Army Spl. Forces, 1963, chief spl. techniques divsn., 1964, unconventional warfare monitor, 1964-65; ops. staff officer J-3 USECOM, 1965-68; mem. Airborne Command Post Study Group, Joint Chiefs of Staff, 1967, ret., 1968; mem. faculty Ariz. State U., 1968; sole practice law, cons. on Near and Middle Eastern affairs, Tempe, Ariz., 1971-72, 76—; v.p., dir. Trojan Investment & Devel. Co., Inc., 1972-75; active Ariz. Tax Conf., 1971-75; mem. adminstrv. law com., labor mgmt. rels. com., unauthorized practice of law com. Ariz. State Bar. Author: Legal Aspects of Land Tenure in the Republic of Lebanon, 1951, International Constitutional Law (with Helen Miller Davis) Electoral Laws and Treaties of the Near and Middle East, 1951; contbr. articles to mags., chpts. to books. Chmn. legal and legis. com. Phoenix Mayor's Com. to Employ Handicapped, 1971-75; active Tempe Leadership Conf., 1971-75; chmn. Citizens Against Corruption in Govt., 1976-95; mem. Princeton Coun. on Fgn. and Internat. Studies, 1968; comdr. Ranger Area-Ariz. Ranger Region-West, 1993—. Decorated Silver Star, Legion of Merit, Bronze Star, Purple Heart, Combat Infantryman badge, Master Pharachutist badge, Aircrewman badge; named Outstanding Adminstrv. Law Judge for State Svc. to U.S., 1974; named to U.S. Army Ranger Hall of Fame, 1981. Fellow Coll. of Rites of U.S.A.; mem. Ranger Bns. Assn. World War II (life), Temple Rep. Mens Club (v.p. bd. dirs. 1971-72), U.S. Army Airborne Ranger Assn. (life), Mil. Order Purple Heart (life), NRA (offcl. referee, life), Masonic Order of the Bath, The Philatethes Soc., Ye Ancient and Old Order of Corks, Order of the Secret Monitor, BL (twice past master Thunderbird Lodge #48 Phoenix, past master Ariz. Rsch. Lodge #1), Order Ky. Cols., Sovereign Mil. Order of Temple of Jerusalem (grand advocat pro tem 1993, grand officer 1993), Knight Commdr. Grace Sovereign Mil. Order St. John of Jerusalem (Knights Hospitallers), Grand Chpt. Royal Arch Masons Ariz. (grand lectr.), Fraternal Order of Medieval Knighthood, Internat. (sovereign venerable master Ariz. Coll. 1988-93, supreme sovereign grand master 1991), YR (past high priest, past thrice illustrious master, twice eminent past comdr., Knight Templar Cross of Honor, 1988, Orator Order of High Priesthood, Grand Chpt. YRM 1989, pres. Grand Coun. Holy Order of High Priesthood of Ariz. 1996-97, York Rite Mason of Decade, Scottsdale YRB 1989), SR (32, ritual dir.), Chief Adept Ariz. Coll. Socs., Rosicruceana in Civitatibus Foederatis IX Degree, Grand Commandery of Knights Templar of Ariz. (grand insp. gen. 1990-91), Grand Royal Arch Masons Ariz. (grand lectr. 1995-96), Masons (knight U.S.A., Chevalier and Ami du Patriarchate, KCM Ordo Sancti Constantini Magni), Order of Secret Monitor, So. Calif. Rsch. Lodge, Royal Order of Scotland, Comdr. Ranger Area-Ariz. (Ranger Region-West Red 1993), Mil. Order of World Wars (historian, archivist), The Nat. Sojourners Inc., United Assn. (life, local #469 Phoenix), Phi Delta Phi, Delta Theta Phi, Alpha Rho of Theta Chi. Episcopalian. Home: 539 E Erie Dr Tempe AZ 85282-3712

EVANS, LOUISE, investor, retired psychologist, philanthropist; b. San Antonio; d. Henry Daniel and Adela (Pariser) E.; m. thomas Ross Gambrell, Feb. 23, 1960. BS, Northwestern U., 1949; MS in Clin. Psychology, Purdue U., 1952, PhD in Clin. Psychology, 1955. Lic. Marriage, Family and Child Counselor Calif.; Nat. Register of Health Svc. Providers in Psychology; lic. psychologist, Calif., N.Y. (inactive); diplomate Clin. Psychology, Am. Bd. Profl. Psychology. Intern clin. psychology Menninger Found. Topeka (Kans.) State Hosp., 1952-53; postdoctoral fellow clin. child psychology Menninger Clinic, Topeka, 1955-56; staff psychologist Kankakee (Ill.) State Hosp., 1954; head staff psychologist child guidance clinic Kings County Hosp., Bklyn., 1957-58; dir. psychology clinic Barnes-Renard Hosp.; instr. med. psychology Sch. Medicine Washington U., 1959; clin. rsch. cons. Episc. City Diocese, St. Louis, 1959; pvt. practice clin. and cons. psychology Fullerton, Calif., 1960-92; fellow Internat. Coun. Sex Edn. and Parenthood, 1984, Am. U., Washington; psychol. cons. Fullerton Cmty. Hosp., 1961-81; staff cons. clin. psychology Martin Luther Hosp., Anaheim, Calif., 1963-70; nat. and internat. lectr clin. psychology schs. and profl. groups, 1950—; charperson, participant psychol. symposiums, 1956—; guest spkr. clin. psychology civic and cmty. orgns., 1950—. Contbr. articles on clin. psychology to profl. pubs. Elected to Hall of Fame Ctrl. H.S., Evansville, Ind., 1966; recipient Svc. award Yuma County (Ariz.) Head Start Program, 1972, Statue of Victory Personality of Yr. award Centro Studi E. Ricerche Delle Nazioni, Italy, 1985, Alumni Merit award Northwestern U. Coll. Arts and Scis., 1997; named Miss Heritage, Heritage Publs., 1965. Fellow AAAS (emeritus), APA (clin. divsn. psychology of women divsn., divsn. psychotherapy, cons. divsn., dir. exec. bd. 1976-79), Acad. Clin. Psychology,

Am. Assn. Applied and Preventative Psychology (charter), Royal Soc. Health England (emeritus), Internat. Coun. Psychologists (dir. 1977-79, sec. 1962-64, 73-76), Am. Orthopsychiat. Assn. (life), World Wide Acad. Scholars of N.Z. (life), Am. Psychol. Soc. (charter), L.A. Soc. Clin. Psychologists (exec. bd. 1966-67); mem. AAUP (emeritus), Calif. State Psychol. Assn. (life, ins. com, 1961-65), L.A. County Psychol. Assn. (emeritus), Orange County Psychol. Assn. (charter founding mem., exec. bd. 1961-62), Orange County Soc. Clin. Psychologists (founder, exec. bd. 1963-65, pres. 1964-65), Am. Pub. Health Assn. (emeritus), Internat. Platform Assn., N.Y. Acad. Scis. (emeritus), Purdue U. Alumni Assn. (life mem., pres. coun., dean's club pacesetters, Citizenship award for Contbns. to Mental Health Fields 1975, Disting. Alumni award, 1993, Old Master, 1993), Northwestern U. 1851 Soc. (Coll. Arts and Scis. Merit award 1997), Ctr. Study Presidency, Soc. Jewelry Historians USA (charter), Alumni Assn. Menninger Sch. Psychiatry, Sigma Xi (emeritus), Pi Sigma Pi (pres. 1947-48, sec. 1946-47). Achievements include development of innovative theories and techniques of clinical practice; acknowledged pioneer in development of psychology as science and profession both nationally and internationally, and in marital and family therapy, and in consulting to hospitals and clinics. Office: PO Box 6067 Beverly Hills CA 90212-1067

EVANS, MARK RUSSELL, physician, researcher; b. London, July 21, 1957; s. Russell Wilmot and Pamela Muriel (Hayward) E. MB, ChB, U. Liverpool, Eng., 1982, MD, 1997. House officer, sr. house officer Univ. Teaching Hosps., Liverpool, 1982-85; registrar Plymouth (Eng.) Hosps., 1985-87; sr. house officer in pediatrics Westminster Children's Hosp., London, 1988-89; clin. rsch. fellow St. George's Hosp., London, 1989-96; lectr. medicine Sch. Med. Scis. U. Sci. and Technology, Kumasi, Ghana, 1996-98; hon. lectr. London Sch. of Hygiene & Tropical Medicine, 1998-99; specialist registrar infectious diseases/tropical medicine Hosp. for Tropical Diseases, London, 1998-99; Barnett Christie lectr. Brit. Info. Soc., 1999; SpR second to CDSC, London. Recipient award for distinction in obstetrics and gynecology U. Liverpool, 1982. Fellow Royal Soc. Tropical Medicine and Hygiene; mem. Royal Coll. Physicians (diploma in tropical medicine and health, diploma in child health). Anglican. Avocations: windsurfing, tennis, paragliding, mediaeval history study, travel. Office: Divsn Infectious Diseases, Jenner Wing SGHMS Cranmer Ter, London SW17 0RE, England

EVANS, MARTIN G., management educator; b. Cardiff, Wales, Nov. 28, 1939; s. Griffith Thomas and Dorothea F.N. (Bradley) E.; m. Nancy R. Remage, Aug. 3, 1968; children: Lisa, Katherine. Prof. U. Toronto Rotman Sch. Mgmt., 1966—; adj. prof. Harvard U. Sch. Pub. Health, Boston, 1999—. Contbg. author: Variations in Organizational Science: A Conference in Honor of Donald T. Campbell, Thousand Oaks, California, 1999; contbr. articles to prof. jours., including Can. Jour. Adminstrv. Scis., Am. Psychologist, Orgnl. Behavior and Human Performance. Fellow APA, Am. Psychol. Soc.; mem. Acad. Mgmt. (co-webmaster rsch. methods divsn.). E-mail: evans@mgmt.utoronto.ca. Office: U Toronto, Rotman Sch Mgmt, Toronto, ON Canada M5S 3E6

EVANS, MARY SONIA, sociologist; b. Chemsford, Essex, Eng., Aug. 24, 1946; d. Frances M. and Monica E. (Warwick) Evans; m. David george Morgan, Dec. 19, 1983; children: Thomas James, James Alexander. BSc, London Sch. Econs., 1967, MSc, 1968; DPhil, U. Sussex, 1975. Lectr. econs. U. Kent, Canterbury, Eng., 1971-95, prof., 1995—; vis. fellow Harvard U., Boston, 1978-79. Author: Jane Austen and the State, 1986, A Good School, 1987, An Introduction to Contemporary Feminist Thought, 1997, Missing Persons/The Impossibility of Auto/Biography, 1999. Treas. Women's Studies Network Assn., London. Fellow Royal Soc. of Arts; mem. Brit. Sociol. Assn. Home: Patrixbourne Lodge, Canterbury Kent CT4 5BP, England Office: Univ of Kent, Canterbury Kent CT2 7NY, England

EVANS, MICHAEL ROBERT, educational consultant, writer; b. Watford, Eng., Mar. 10, 1942; s. Eric Butler and Irene Nora (Lumm) E.; m. Penelope Sarah Lang, July 26, 1969; children: Rebecca, Charlotte. Cert. Edn., U. London, 1964; Advanced Diploma in Edn., U. Sussex, 1970. Tchr. Oxhey Wood Sch., Watford, 1964-70; dep. head Cowley Hill Sch., Boreham Wood, 1970-74; headmaster Barton Sch., Cambridge, U.K., 1975-95; freelance ednl. consultancy, 1995—; co-ptnr. Madingley Pre-Preparatory Sch., Cambridge, 1997—; mem. several nat. coms. Royal Soc. for the Prevention of Accidents, 1981—, chmn. nat. safety edn. com., 1991-96; educator health and safety; vol. tchr., cons. Brit. Execs. Svc. Overseas, Sofia, Bulgaria, 1995; freelance writer in field, including courses and material on quitting smoking. Author: (books) Safety on Educational Visits, 1994, History of Barton School, 1992; contbr. articles to profl. jours. Ch. warden St. Mary's Ch., Comberton, Cambridge, 1991—; chmn. Brit. Heart Found., Cambridge Com., 1982—; mem. Ely Diocesan Synod, 1997—. Mem. Soc. Authors, Nat. Assn. Head Tchrs., European Fedn. Freelance Writers. Mem. Ch. of England. Avocations: writing, foreign travel, gardening, photography, family life. E-mail: mre@scribbletalk.co.uk.

EVANS, MORGAN D., physicist; b. N.Y.C., July 12, 1965; m. Susan Mary Fournier, June 7, 1997; 1 child, Nathaniel Alexander. BS in Physics, Rennselear Poly. Inst., 1987; MS in Physics, U. Mass., 1990; PhD in Physics, U. Fla., 1994. Indsl. physicist Boreas, Inc., Billerica, Mass., 1995-96, Varian IIS, Gloucester, Mass., 1996—. Home: 2 Rockwood Heights Rd Manchester MA 01944-1028 Office: Varian IIS 35 Dory Rd Gloucester MA 01930-2236

EVANS, MYRON WYN, physicist; b. Craigcefnparc, Wales, May 26, 1950; came to U.S., 1986; s. Edward Ivor and Mary (Jones) E.; m. Laura Jean Joseph, Feb. 18, 1988. BSc, Aberystwyth U., Wales, 1971, PhD, 1974, DSc, 1977. Jr. rsch. fellow Wolfson Coll., Oxford, 1975; advanced fellow Sci. and Engring. Rsch. Coun., Aberystwyth, 1978-83; vis. scientist Cornell U., 1989-92, U. Zurich, 1989-90; prof. Alpha Found., Budapest, Hungary, 1995—; dir. Alpha Found. Inst. for Advanced Study, 1998—; nat. com. British Sci. and Engring. Rsch. Coun.; rsch. assoc. Pa. State U., 1992; 1st sci. coord. European Molecular Liquids Group, 1980; sr. assoc. Pa. State U., 1990; sci.-tech. advisor Plaid Cymru, 1991; vis. prof. Trinity Coll., Dublin, 1985, IBM, Kingston, N.Y., 1986, York U., Toronto, 1995, Indian Statis. Inst., Calcutta, 1995; vis. scientist U. Pisa and Scuala Normale Superiore, 1980, U. Zurich, 1990, Cornell U., 1989, 91. Editor Modern Nonlinear Optics, 1997, The Enigmatic Photon, 1994-99, monographs Wiley World Sci. and Kluwer; author: The Enigmatic Photon, 5 vols. 1994-99, Molecular Dynamics, 1982, Molecular Diffusion, 1984, Memory Function Approaches to Stochastic Problems in Condensed Matter, 1985, Dynamical Processes in Condensed Matter, 1985, Simulaton and Symmetry in Moledular Diffusion and Spectroscopy, 1992, The Photon's Magnetic Field, 1992, The Photomagneton in Quantum Field Theory, 1994, Water in Biology, Chemistry and Physics, 1996, Classical and Quantum Electrodynamics and the B Field, 1999; contbr. articles to profl. jours. Leverhulme fellow, Humboldt fellow, Brit. Imperial Chem. Industries fellow, 1974, NRC Can. fellow, 1974, Jr. Rsch. fellow Wolfson Coll., Oxford, 1975, Brit. Ramsay Meml. fellow, 1976, IBM fellow; recipient Harrison Meml. prize Royal Soc. Chemistry, London, 1978, Meldola medal, 1979, Disting. Am. Scientist award Assn. Disting. Am. Scientists, 2000. Mem. Optical Soc. Am., Am. Inst. Physics, N.Y. Acad. Scis., Sigma Pi Sigma. Republican Nationalist. Avocations: poetry, landscape photography, athletics. Home: 82 Lois Ln Ithaca NY 14850-6247 Office: Alpha Found Inst Physics, 11 Rutafa St, Budapest Hungary

EVANS, PAMELA R., marketing executive; b. Hoisington, Kans., Aug. 25, 1957; d. John Roy and Sarah Mace (Alder) E. BS in Bus., U. Kans., 1980. Sales rep. Home & Automotive Products div. Union Carbide Corp., Seattle, 1981; dist. sales mgr. Home & Automotive Products div. Union Carbide Corp., Syracuse, N.Y., 1981-82; mktg. assoc. Home & Automotive Products div. Union Carbide Corp., Danbury, Conn., 1982-84, assoc. product mgr., 1984; asst. product mgr. Grocery Products div. Ralston Purina, St. Louis, 1984-85, product mgr., 1985-86; product mgr. Eveready Battery Co. subs. Ralston Purina, St. Louis, 1986-88, group dir. mktg., 1988-90; dir. mktg. Consumer Products div. Esselte Pendaflex, 1990-91; dir. new bus. devel. Olympus Am., Inc., Woodbury, NY, 1991-92; v.p. mktg. consumer products group Olympus Am., Woodbury, NY, 1992-95; pres. blueprints, inc., New Hope, Pa., 1995—, The SJI Cos., St. Louis, 1998—. Bd. advisors Sentry Group, Electri-Cord Mfg. Co. Avocations: music, sports, reading, photography. Office: 2300 Locust St Saint Louis MO 63103-1512

EVANS, PAUL, osteopath; b. Nutley, N.J., May 23, 1950; m. Roxanne Romack. BS cum laude in Biology, U. Miami, 1972; DO, Phila. Coll. Osteopathic Med., 1979. Diplomate Am. Bd. Family Practice, Nat. Bd. Osteo. Examiners; cert. Am. Osteo. Bd. Family Practice. Commd. 2d lt. U.S. Army, 1972, advanced through grades to col., 1995; ret., 1998; asst. chief mil. pers. U.S. Army Med. Svc. Corps, Frankfurt, Fed. Republic Germany, 1972-75; intern Letterman Army Med. Ctr., San Francisco, 1979-80; resident in family practice Womack Army Community Hosp., Ft. Bragg, N.C., 1980-82; dir. family practice quality assurance Tripler Army Med. Ctr., Hawaii, 1982-84, dir. residency tng. dept. family practice, 1984-86; asst. prof. family practice, physician Uniformed Svcs. U. Health Scis., F. Edward Hebert Sch. Med., Bethesda, Md., 1986-92, clerkship dir., 1986-88, dir. continuing med. edn., 1987-91, asst. prof. mil. and emergency medicine, 1991-92; chief dept. family practice Reynolds Army Community Hosp., Ft. Sill, Okla., 1992-94, chief primary care, 1994-95, chief dept. family practice and cmty. medicine, 1994-95, chmn. rsch. com., dir. hosp. continuing med. edn., 1992-95, dir. physicians asst. tng. program, dir. quality improvement, 1992-94; tchg. chief dept. family practice Madigan Army Med. Ctr., Tacoma, Wash., 1995-97, dir. primary care projects Tricare N.W., 1997-98, dir. primary care, mem. exec. bd. dirs., exec. adv. coun.; clin. assoc. prof. of family medicine U. Wash., 1996-98; assoc. dean curricular affairs Okla. State U. Coll. Osteopathic Med., Tulsa, 1998—, assoc. prof. family med., exec. coun. curriculum com., learning resources com., 19985, dir. Dept. Edn. Resources and Devel., 1998—; presenter, lectr., cons. in field; mem. part-time clin. faculty, family practice residency DeWitt Army Hosp., Ft. Belvoir, Va., 1986-89, 91-92, Malcolm Grow USAF Med. Ctr., Andrews AFB, Md., 1989-91. Reviewer Am. Family Physician, Patient Care, Military Medicine, Family Medicine, Farmly Practice Mgmt.; contbr. articles to profl. publs. Asst. med. dir. Old Dominion 100 Mile Run, Front Royal, Va., 1990, med. dir., 1991; asst. med. dir. Am. Diabetes Assn. Youth, Honolulu, 1984, med. dir., 1985. USUHS grantee. Fellow Am. Acad. Family Physicians; mem. Am. Osteo. Assn., Am. Coll. Osteo. Family Physicians, Uniformed Svcs. Acad. Family Physicians (chmn. edn. com. 1993-97, sec.-treas. 1997-98), Soc. Tchrs. Family Medicine (mem. genogram rsch. com. 1989-94, mem. managed care com. 1997—), Amer. Osteo. Assn., Amer. Coll. Osteo. Family Phys., Okla. Osteo. Assn., Phila. Coll. Osteo. Medicine Alumni Assn. (life), Omicron Delta Kappa, Alpha Epsilon Delta. Avocations: bicycling, downhill skiing, scuba diving, collecting salt water fish, finch breeding. Home: 3909 S Sequoia Ave Broken Arrow OK 74011-1146 Office: Okla State U Coll Osteo Medicine 1111 W 17th St Tulsa OK 74107-1800

EVANS, PAUL ANTHONY LEE, management educator, consultant; b. Harrogate, Eng., Apr. 13, 1946; arrived in France, 1974; s. Frank Lee and Pamela Roberts (Ogden) E.; m. Bente Riisgaard Jensen, Aug. 5, 1967; children: Christine, Natasha. BA in Law, Pembroke Coll., Cambridge U., 1967; postgrad., Bus. Sch., Copenhagen, 1969; MBA, INSEAD, Fontainebleau, France, 1970; PhD, MIT, 1974. Acctg. asst. Howarth & Co., Gatodma, Zimbabwe, 1963-64; cons. Pugh Roberts, Cambridge, Mass., 1972-74; from asst. prof. to assoc. prof. INSEAD, 1974-83, prof. orgnl. behavior, 1983—; vis. scholar U. So. Calif., L.A., 1983-84; project dir. Royal Dutch/Shell, The Hague and London, 1988-89; founder, bd. dirs. European Human Resource Forum, Bristol, Eng., 1991—; cons., advisor to sr. mgmt. World Bank, Eastman Kodak, Ciba-Geigy, Apple, Shell, numerous others. Author: Must Success Cost So Much?, 1980; author, editor: Human Resource Management in International Firms, 1989; producer, performer in ednl. video Managing People, 1990. Mem. Human Resource Planning Soc. (bd. dirs. 1988-92). Avocations: scuba diving, skiing, garden design. Office: INSEAD, Blvd de Constance, 77300 Fontainebleau France

EVANS, PAUL VERNON, lawyer; b. Colorado Springs, Colo., June 19, 1926; s. Fred Harrison and Emma Hooper (Austin) E.; m. Patricia Gwyn Davis, July 27, 1964; children: Bruce, Mike, Mark, Paul. B.A. cum laude, Colo. Coll., 1953; J.D., Duke U., 1956. Bar: Colo. 1956, U.S. Dist. Ct. Colo. 1956, U.S. Supreme Ct. 1971, U.S. Ct. Appeals (10th cir.) 1974. Field mgr. Keystone Readers Service, Dallas, 1946-50; sole practice Colorado Springs, 1956-60; ptnr. Goodbar, Evans & Goodbar, 1960-63; sr. ptnr. Evans & Briggs Attys., Colorado Springs, 1963-95; city atty. City of Fountain, Colo., 1958-62, City of Woodland Park, Colo., 1962-78; atty. Rock Creek Mesa Water Dist., Colorado Springs, 1963—. Author instruction materials. Precinct com. man Republican Com., Colorado Springs, 1956-72. Served with USNR, 1944-46, PTO. Recipient Jr. C. of C. Outstanding Achievement award, 1957. Mem. Colo. Mining Assn., Am. Jud. Soc., ABA, Colo. Bar Assn. (com. chmn. 1966-67, 84), El Paso County Bar Assn. (com. chmn. 1956—0, Assn. Trial Lawyers Am., Colo. and Local Trial Lawyers, Tau Kappa Alpha (pres.), Phi Beta Kappa. Republican. Club: Optimist (pres. 1966-67). Home: 244 Cobblestone Dr Colorado Springs CO 80906-7624 Office: 227 E Costilla St Colorado Springs CO 80903-2103

EVANS, R. MONT, state legislator; b. Montpelier, Idaho, Jan. 9, 1947; m. Cheryl Evans; 4 children. BA in Polit. Sci. and History, Brigham Young U.; MSW, U. Utah. Social worker, adminstr. Utah Dept. Corrections; mem. Utah Ho. of Reps., 1986-96; mem. Utah State Senate, 1996—, mem. transp. and pub. safety com., mem. transp. and environ. quality appropriations com., chair state and local affairs com. Mem. Riverton (Utah) City Coun., 1983-86; trustee, chmn. Riverton Arts Coun., 1983-87; trustee Riverton Hist. Soc.; mem., chmn. Riverton City Planing and Zoning Commn., 1982-84. Recipient Total Citizen award Utah C. of C., 1992. Republican. Mormon. Home: 1599 Big Var Way Riverton UT 84065-4003

EVANS, RICHARD H., aerospace executive; b. Blackpool, 1942; married; 3 children. Grad., Royal Masonic Sch., Hertfordshire. With fin., contracts and costing br. Ministry Transport and Civil Aviation; with Ministry Tech.; govt. contracts officer Ferranti, Manchester, 1967-69; contracts officer mil. aircraft divsn. Brit. Aircraft Corp., Warton/Lancashire, 1969-78; comml. dir. Warton divsn. Brit. Aerospace, 1978-81, asst. mng. dir., 1981-83; dir. Panavia Aircraft GmbH, 1981-83; dep. mng. dir., mem. aircraft group bd. Brit. Aerospace Warton, 1983-86; dep. mng. dir., mng. dir. designate mil. aircraft divsn. Brit. Aerospace, 1986-87; mktg. dir. Brit. Aerospace Plc, 1987-88; chief exec. Brit. Aerospace Plc, London, 1990-98, now also bd. dirs.; chmn. Brit. Aerospace Def. Cos., 1988-90, British Aerospace Plc, 1999—, BAE Sys. Recipient CBE. Office: BAE Sys/Warwick House, PO Box 87 Aerospace Ctr, Hampshire GU14 6YU, England*

EVANS, RICHARD JOHN, historian; b. Woodford, Essex, Eng., Sept. 29, 1947; s. Ievan Trefor Evans and Evelyn Jones; m. Elin Hjaltadottir, 1976 (div. 1992); life ptnr. Christine Corton; children: Matthew John Corton Evans, David Corton Evans. MA, Oxford U., 1973, DPhil, 1973; DLitt, U. East Anglia, U.K., 1990. Lectr. in history U. Stirling, U.K., 1972-76; lectr. in European history U. East Anglia, Norwich, 1976-83, prof. European history, 1983-89; prof. history Birkbeck Coll., U. London, 1989-98, vice-master, 1993-98, acting master, 1997-98; prof. modern history U. Cambridge, Eng., 1998—; hon. fellow Jesus Coll., Oxford U., 1998—. Author: Death in Hamburg, 1987 (Wolfson Literary award for History 1987, William H. Welch medal Am. Assn. for History of Medicine 1988, Medaille fur Kunst und Wissenschaft der Freien - und Hansestadt Hamburg 1993), Rituals of Retribution, 1996 (Fraenkel prize for Contemporary History 1994), others. Fellow Gonville and Caius Coll., Cambridge. Fellow Br. Acad., Royal Soc. of Lit., Royal Hist. Soc. Avocations: cooking, playing the piano, reading, gardening. Office: Gonville & Caius Coll, Cambridge CB2 1TA, England

EVANS, ROBERT VINCENT, sales and marketing executive; b. Mobile, Ala., Sept. 21, 1958; s. William Alexander Evans and Katherine Barbara (Doerr) Davidson; children: James Vernon, Chelsea Marie. BS in Computer Info. Systems, Regis U., Denver, 1987, BS in Tech. Mgmt., 1987; postgrad. in Mgmt., U. Wash., 1995. Electrician Climax (Colo.) Molybdenum Co., 1978-82; applications engr. Honeywell, Inc., Englewood, Colo., 1982-83, sales engr., 1983-87; systems engr. Apple Computer, Inc., Seattle, 1987-88; regional systems engring. mgr. Apple Computer, Inc., Portland, Oreg., 1988-96; dist. sales mgr. Apple Computer, Inc., Seattle, 1997—. Author: Anthology of American Poets, 1981. Dir. Operation Lookout, Seattle, 1989; mem. Rep. Nat. Com.; commr. dist. chmn. Boy Scouts Am. Recipient USMC Blues award, Marine Corps Assn. Leatherneck award, 1977, Denver Post Outstanding Svc. award, 1983, N.Y. Zool. Soc. Hon. medal, James West fellowship award, Paul Harris fellowship award, Silver Beaver award Boy Scouts Am., 1998. Mem. Am. Mgmt. Assn., Am. Platform Assn., Mensa, Rotary, Kiwanis. Republican. Mem. Northwest Cmty. Ch. Avocations: reading, church ministry, family activities. Office: Apple Computer Inc PO Box 40355 Bellevue WA 98015-4355

EVANS, ROBIN JOHN, electrical engineer; b. Melbourne, Victoria, Australia, Oct. 29, 1947; s. Roger Johnn and Joyce Doris (Bee) E.; m. Margaret Anne Lee, Feb. 8, 1969; children: Jamie Scott, Jacqueline Louise. BEE, U. Melbourne, Australia, 1969; MEE, U. Newcastle, Australia, 1973, PhD in Elec. Engring., 1975. Engring. officer, flight lt. RAAF, Australia, 1969-74; rsch. fellow MIT, Cambridge, Mass., 1975-76, Cambridge (Eng.) U., 1976-77; prof. U. Newcastle, Australia, 1986-91, U. Melbourne, Australia, 1992—. Co-editor: (book) Automatic Control: 12th IFAC World Congress, 6 Vols., 1994; contbr. over 100 articles to profl. internat. jours. Fellow Acad. Tech. Sci. & Engring., Instn. Engrs. Australia. Avocation: sailing. Office: U Melbourne Dept Elec Engr, Grattan St, Parkville VIC 3052, Australia

EVANS, ROGER LYNWOOD, scientist, patent liaison; b. Ipswich, Suffolk, Eng., June 25, 1928; came to U.S., 1953; s. Evelyn Jesse and Ethel Jane (Woods) E.; m. Jane Adelaide Baird, Nov. 24, 1954 (div. 1976); children: Robert Malcolm Baird, Roderick Lawrence Woods, Alison Clare; m. Wendy Dorothy Grove, Apr. 11, 1977. BA in Natural Sci., Oxford (Eng.) U., 1953, MA, 1955, DPhil in Natural Sci., 1958; MS in Inorganic Chemistry, U. Minn., 1955. With chem. and radiopharm. R & D dept. 3M Co., St. Paul., 1958-77, patent liaison, 1977-91; developer intellectual property initiative, tech. devel. dept., 1992-93; cons. 3M, 1993-99; originator 3M Richard G. Drew Creativity Award, 1970, program cons., 1995—. Founder, editor Newsletter of the Tech. Forum, 1971-93; inventor, writer, producer series of videos on intellectual property topics. Mem., chmn. Mendota Heights Planning Commn., 1962-68, Sunfish Lake Planning Commn., 1968-84, Dakota County Planning Commn., Minn., 1965-72. 2d lt. Brit. Army, 1946-49, Eng. Anglican. Avocations: photography, amateur opera singer, travel, writing. Home and Office: 9965 Rich Valley Blvd Inver Grove Heights MN 55077-4529

EVANS, THOMAS EDGAR, JR., title insurance agency executive; b. Toronto, Ohio, Apr. 17, 1940; s. Thomas Edgar and Sarah Ellen (Bauer) E.; m. Cynthia Lee Johnson, Feb. 23; children: Thomas Edgar, Douglas, Melinda, Jennifer. BA, Mt. Union Coll., 1963. Tchr. Lodi, Ohio, 1963-64; salesman Simpson-Evans Realty, Steubenville, Ohio, 1964-65, Shadron Realty, Tucson, 1965-67; real estate broker, co-owner Double E Realty, Tucson, 1967-69; escrow officer, br. mgr., asst. county mgr., v.p. Ariz. Title Ins., Tucson, 1969-80; pres. Commonwealth Land Title Agy., Tucson, 1980-82, also dir.; pres. Fidelity Nat. Title Agy., 1982-90; bd. govs. Calif. Land Title Assn., 1990—; exec. v.p. Fidelity Nat. Title Ins. Co., 1990-92; v.p. Inland Empire Divsn. Fidelity Nat. Title, 1991-93, pres. Orange County divsn., 1993-2000, exec. v.p., regional mgr., 2000—; bd. dirs. Western Fin. Trust Co., Fidelity Nat. Fin. Inc., Fidelity Nat. Title Ins. Co., Fidelity Nat. Title Agy. Pinal, The Griffin Co., Computer Market Place, Inc., e Market Place; bd. dirs., chmn. bd. Cochise Title Agy., TIPCO; v.p., dir. A.P.C. Corp. Named Boss of Yr., El Chaparral chpt. Am. Bus. Women's Assn., 1977. Mem. Calif. Land Title Assn. (pres. 1995-96), So. Ariz. Escrow Assn., So. Ariz. Mortgage Bankers Assn. (bd. dirs. 1982-85), Ariz. Mktg. Bankers Assn., Old Pueblo Businessmen's Assn. Tucson, Tucson Bd. Realtors, Ariz. Assn. Real Estate Exchangors (bd. dirs. 1968-69), Land Title Assn. Ariz. (pres. 1984), So. Ariz. Homebuilders Assn., Tucson Real Estate Exchangors (pres. 1968), Pacific Club, Ctr. Club, Old Pueblo Courthouse Club, La Paloma Club, Ventana Country Club, Centre Ct. Club, Coto de Casa Country Club, Elks Club, Pima Jaycees (dir. 1966), Sertoma (charter pres., chmn. bd. Midtown sect. 1968-70), Sunrise Rotary, Old Pueblo Club, South Coast Repertory (trustee 1996-2000), Blue Key, Sigma Nu. Home: 28861 Glen Rdg Mission Viejo CA 92692-4301 Office: 4050 Calle Real Ste 210 Santa Barbara CA 93110-3413

EVANS, THOMAS PASSMORE, business and product licensing consultant; b. West Grove, Pa., Aug. 19, 1921; s. John and Linda (Zeuner) E.; m. Lenore Jane Knuth, June 21, 1947; children: Paula S., Christina L., Bruce A., Carol L. BS in Elec. Engring., Swarthmore Coll., 1942; M in Engring., Yale U., 1948. Registered profl. engr., Pa. Engr. atomic power divsn. Westinghouse Electric Corp., Pitts., 1948-51; dir. R&D AMF, Inc., N.Y.C., 1951-60; dir. rsch. O.M. Scott & Sons Co., Marysville, Ohio, 1960-62; v.p. R&D W.A. Sheaffer Pen Co., Fort Madison, Iowa, 1962-67; dir. rsch. Mich. Tech. U., Houghton, 1967-80; dir. rsch., mem. faculty Berry Coll., Mt. Berry, Ga., 1980-88; prof. bus. adminstrn. Berry Coll., Mt. Berry, 1980-86. Author, patentee in field. Lt. USN, 1943-46. Mem. IEEE, AAAS. VFW, Am. Forestry Assn., Nat. Defense Industl. Assn., Am. Phys. Soc., Soc. Plastics Engrs., Yale Sci. and Engring. Assn., Nat. Coun. Univ. Rsch. Adminstrs., Air Force Assn., Am. Legion, High Mus. Art, Hunter Mus. Art, Nat. Trust Hist. Preservation, Yale Club of Ga., Sigma Xi, Tau Beta Pi. Home: 1220 Broadrick Dr Apt 1222 Dalton GA 30720-2809

EVANS, TREVOR MILLS, retired solicitor, retired coroner; b. Swansea, Wales, Sept. 28, 1924; s. William Arthur and Alma (Mills) E.; m. Margaret Jones, October 10, 1952; children: Eifrion Mills, Susan Alma, Adrian Mills, Meirion Mills. Degree, Swansea Grammar Sch. Asst. Signode Ltd, Wales, 1940-42; solicitor Sydney G. Thomas & Co., Wales, 1946-60, ptnr., 1960-88, cons., 1988-91; Her Majesty's coroner, South Powys, Wales, 1966-89. Chmn. Welsh Kennel Club. Mem. The Law Soc., Chartered Inst. Secs. (assoc.), Chartered Inst. Taxation (assoc.). Avocations: breeding, judging and exhibiting dogs, photography, male choral performance. Home: Plasnewydd, Broadway, Builth Wells LD2 3DB, Wales

EVANS, VALERIE MARIE, association executive; b. Balt., Nov. 25, 1965; d. John Henry and Esther Marie Walker; m. Larry Allen Evans, Apr. 29, 1994; 1 child, Bianca M. BA in Comms., Morgan State U., Balt., 1988. Dir. membership Soc. for In Vitro Biology, Landover, Md., 1983-99, Howard County Assn. Realtors, Columbia, Md., 1988-93; dir. Am. Assn. Physics Tchrs., College Park, Md., 1999—. Active Voices for Children, Columbia, 1991. Mem. Am. Soc. Assn. Execs., Greater Washington Soc. Assn. Execs. (chair membership com. 1988—). Avocations: exercise, walking, reading. E-mail: vevans@aapt.org. Office: Am Assn Physics Tchrs One Physics Ellipse College Park MD 20740-3845

EVANS, WALTER REED, retired engineering executive, consultant; b. El Paso, Tex., Oct. 25, 1921; s. Charles Reed and Ruby Estelle (Simpson-Rountree) E.; m. Frances Adelaide Lounsbury, Jan. 15, 1942 (dec. 1975); children: Sandra Frances, Roger R., Sharon A.; m. Dorothy May Cuthbertson, 1975; stepchildren: Jack W., William D., Charles T. Rogers. BS in Mech. Engring., U. Tex. Registered profl. engr. La., Tex. Engring. and mech. supr. Celanese and Exxon Corps., Tex. and Venezuela, 1948-57; plant mgr., pres. Falcon Chem. Corp., Lake Charles, La., 1957-59; cons. SIP, Inc., Houston, 1960-62; instrument engr. Exxon, Aruba, 1963; mech. mgr. Exxon, Malaga, Spain, 1964-65; chief engr. Exxon, West Pakistan, 1966-71; divsn. head Exxon, Sriracha, Thailand, 1972; project mgr. S & B, Inc., Houston, 1973-79; mech. mgr. Arabian Am. Oil Co., Ras Tanura, Saudi Arabia, 1979-81; pvt. practice mech. engring. cons., 1982-88; Tex. state coord., lobbyist ASME, Austin, 1988-94; prof., competency monitor Tex. State Bd. Engring. Registration, 1995-99; founder, v.p. Structural Metals, Inc. divsn. Comml. Metals, Inc., Seguin, Tex., 1947-48; trustee Teal Petroleum Co. divsn. W.R. Grace Co., 1975-79; mechanic aircraft engine, Kelly Field, Tex. Author: Aircraft Engine Overhaul, 1942. With Tex. N.G., 1938-42; lt. USAAF, 1942-44, ETO. Fellow ASME (life); mem. NSPE (life), NRA, Squires Bus. Men's Orgn., Austin Amateur Radio, Men's Garden Club, Austin Rifle Club. Republican. Episcopalian. Avocations: hunting, fishing, stamp/coin collecting, gardening, reading. Home and Office: 11279 Taylor Draper Ln Apt 329 Austin TX 78759-3965

EVANS, WILLIAM DOUGLAS, psychologist, researcher; b. Seattle, June 6, 1962; s. William B. and Lucille W. E.; m. Heidi Anne Nasstrom, May 22, 1999. BA, Reed Coll., 1984; MA, The Johns Hopkins U., 1988, PhD, 1991. Vis. lectr. U. Md., Balt., 1988-91; rsch. assoc. Westower Cons., Washington, 1991-93; rsch. officer Acad. Ednl. Devel., Washington, 1993-97, pres., 1997—; dir. rsch. Prospect Assocs., Silver Spring, Md., 1998—; cons. in field. Contbr. articles to profl. jours. Mem. Am. Pub. Health Assn., Am. Ednl. Rsch. Assn., Am. Psychological Assn., Am. Evaluation Assn. Avocations: cycling, history, baseball, music. E-mail: devans@prospectassoc.com. Office: Prospect Assocs 10720 Columbia Pike Ste 500 Silver Spring MD 20901-4400

EVDOKIMOV, VALERI, andrologist, researcher; b. Moscow, Nov. 28, 1940; s. Vasili and Anna (Garova) E.; m. Irina Neischtat, May 5, 1973 (div. Aug. 1982); 1 child, Kirill. MD, I.M. Sechenov Inst., Moscow, 1969. Scientist, rschr. Inst. of Epidemiology and Microbiology, Moscow, 1969-82; leading scientist, rschr. S.R. Inst. of Urology of the Health Ministry, Moscow, 1982—. Co-author: Manual of Urology, 1998; contbr. more than 70 articles to profl. jours. Mem. N.Y. Acad. Scis., Russian Assn. Human Reprodn. Avocations: volleyball, swimming. Home: Verkhnaya Maslovka 20-27, 125083 Moscow Russia Office: 3 Parkovaya Str 51, 105425 Moscow Russia

EVEN, FRANCIS ALPHONSE, lawyer; b. Chgo., Sept. 8, 1920; s. George Martin and Cecilia (Neuman) E.; m. Margaret Hope Herrick, Oct. 16, 1945; children: Janet Beth, Dorothy Elizabeth. B.S. in Mech. Engring, U. Ill., 1942; J.D., George Washington U., 1949. Bar: D.C. bar 1949, Ill. bar 1950. Engr. GE, 1945-49; ptnr. Fitch, Even, Tabin & Flannery (patent and trademark law), Chgo., 1952—. Mem. bd. edn., River Forest, Ill., 1963-69; trustee West Suburban Hosp., Oak Park, Ill., 1974-77; mem. bd. Ill. State Hist. Soc., 2000—. With combat engrs. AUS, 1942-45. Fellow Am. Coll. Trial Lawyers (emeritus); mem. ABA, Am. Intellectual Property Law Assn. (bd. mgrs. 1963-66), Ill. Bar Assn., Chgo. Bar Assn., Intellectual Property Law Assn. Chgo. (bd. mgrs. 1972-73, pres. 1874), No. Ill. Ct. Hist. Assn. (pres.), Union League Club (Chgo.), Oak Park (Ill.) Country Club, River Forest Tennis Club, Chgo. Literary Club. Republican. Home: 1018 Park Ave River Forest IL 60305-1308 Office: 120 S La Salle St Chicago IL 60603-3403

EVERAERT-DESMEDT, NICOLE, semiotics educator; b. Brussels, July 31, 1947; d. André and Marie-Henriette (Lostrie) Desmedt; m. Guy Everaert; children: Michaël, Florence. Grad. in Italian lang.-philosophy-lit., Cath. U. Louvain, Belgium, 1969, PhD in Social Comm., 1984. Prof. semiotics U St. Louis, Brussels, 1988—; particiant confs. and workshops in semiotics. Author: La communication publicitaire. Etude Sémio-pragmatique, 1984, Sémiotique du récit, 1988, Le processus interprétatif. Introduction à la sémiotique de Ch. S. Peirce, 1990, Magritte ou risque de la sémiotique, 1998; author approximately 50 papers on semiotics. Mem. Internat. Assn. for Semiotic Studies. Avocations: arts, cinema, literature, Médias, Reiki. Home: Rue de la Hutte 23, 6142 Leernes Belgium Office: Fac Univs St Louis, Blvd du Jardin Botanique 43, 1000 Brussels Belgium

EVERBACH, OTTO GEORGE, lawyer; b. New Albany, Ind., Aug. 27, 1938; s. Otto G. and Zelda Marie (Hilt) E.; m. Nancy Lee Stern, June 3, 1961; children: Tracy Ellen, Stephen George. BS, U.S. Mil. Acad., 1960; LLB, U. Va., 1966. Bar: Va. 1967, Ind. 1967, Calif. 1975, Mass. 1978. Counsel CIA, Langley, Va., 1966-67; corp. counsel Bristol-Meyers Co., Evansville, Ind., 1967-74, Alza Corp., Palo Alto, Calif., 1974-75; sec., gen. counsel Am. Optical Corp., Southbridge, Mass., 1976-81; assoc. gen. counsel Warner-Lambert Co., Morris Plains, N.J., 1981-83; v.p. Kimberly-Clark Corp., Neenah, Wis., 1984-86, sr. v.p., gen. counsel, 1986—, sr. v.p. law & govt. affairs, 1988—. Served with U.S. Army, 1960-63. Mem. Am. Bar Assn., Mass. Bar Assn., Ind. Bar Assn., Calif. Bar Assn. Office: Kimberly-Clark Corp DFW Airport Sta PO Box 619100 Dallas TX 75261-9100

EVERETT, DONNA RANEY, business educator; b. Corpus Christi, Tex., May 30, 1939; d. Donald Wayne and Zora Lee (Wynne) Raney; div.; 1 child, Donna Melinda. BA, Phillips U., Enid, Okla., 1961; MS, U. Houston, 1983, EdD, 1988. Various positions various orgns., Tex., 1965-80; adj. prof. U. Houston, 1983-88; asst. prof. bus. Tex. Tech U., Lubbock, 1988-89, Lamar U., Beaumont, Tex., 1989-90; asst. prof. bus. edn. Tex. Tech U., Lubbock, 1990-93; assoc. prof. bus. and mktg. edn. Ea. N.Mex. U., Portales, 1993-94; asst. prof. bus. edn. U. Mo., Columbia, 1994-96, Morehead State U., Morehead, Ky., 1996—; sponsor Zeta Kappa chpt. Pi Omega Pi, Phi Beta Lambda; co-sponsor Gamma Chi, Delta Pi Epsilon; undergrad. mentor, 1996. Troop leader Girl Scouts U.S., Ft. Worth and Lake Jackson, Tex., 1964-80, dir. tng. Lake Jackson coun., 1980-82. Recipient curriculum devel. award Tex. Higher Edn. Coordinating Bd., 1987-88, outstanding article award Nat. Assn. Bus. Tchrs. Edn. Rev., 1992, Outstanding Paper award Orgn. Systems Rsch. Assn., 1997, Dean's Excellence in Tchg. award Coll. Bus./Morehead State U., 1999; named Outstanding Faculty Mem., Tex. Tech U., 1991. Mem. Am. Ednl. Rsch. Assn. (bus. edn. and inf. sys. spl. interest group), Internat. Soc. Tech. in Edn., Tex. Bus. Edn. Assn. (editor 1988-93, Collegiate Bus. Tchr. of Yr. dist. 4 1988, dist. 17 1992), Nat. Bus. Edn. Assn. (mem. computer enrichment task force), Tex. Computer Edn. Assn., Ky. Bus. Edn. Assn., S.W. Fedn. Adminstrv. Disciplines (Disting. Paper award 1989, 93, 2000), Am. Vocat. Assn. (com. mem. 1990-95), Delta Pi Epsilon (pres. Alpha Gamma chpt. 1988-89), Phi Delta Kappa (sec. Alpha Mu chpt.). Avocations: travel, reading.

EVERETT, JAMES JOSEPH, lawyer; b. San Antonio, May 7, 1955. BA, St. Mary's U., San Antonio, 1976; JD, Tex. So. U., 1980. Bar: U.S. Dist. Ct. Ariz. 1987, U.S. Tax Ct. 1980, U.S. Ct. Appeals (9th cir.) 1988. Sr. trial atty. IRS, Phoenix, 1980-87; ptnr. Brnilovich & Everett, Phoenix, 1987-89; owner Law Offices of James J. Everett, Phoenix, 1989—; of counsel Broadbent, Walker & Wales, 1991-95. Mem. ATLA, ABA (bus. and tax sects.), Fed. Bar Assn., Tex. Bar Assn., Ariz. Bar Assn., State Bar Ariz. (cert. tax specialist), Maricopa County Bar Assn., Ariz. Tax Controversy Group, Valley Estate Planners (Phoenix), Ctrl. Ariz. Estate Planners, Ariz. Soc. Boutiques, St. Thomas Moore Soc. Office: 608 E Missouri Ave Phoenix AZ 85012-1377

EVERHART, THOMAS EUGENE, retired university president, engineering educator; b. Kansas City, Mo., Feb. 15, 1932; s. William Elliott and Elizabeth Ann (West) E.; m. Doris Arleen Wentz, June 21, 1953; children—Janet Sue, Nancy Jean, David William, John Thomas. AB in Physics magna cum laude, Harvard, 1953; MSc, UCLA, 1955; PhD in Engring., Cambridge U., Eng., 1958. Mem. tech. staff Hughes Research Labs., Culver City, Calif., 1953-55; mem. faculty U. Calif., Berkeley, 1958-78, prof. elec. engring. and computer scis., 1967-78, Miller research prof., 1969-70, chmn. dept., 1972-77; prof. elec. engring., Joseph Silbert dean engring. Cornell U., Ithaca, N.Y., 1979-84; prof. elec. and computer engring., chancellor U. Ill., Urbana-Champaign, 1984-87; prof. elec. engring. and applied physics, pres. Calif. Inst. Tech., Pasadena, 1987-97; pres. emeritus Calif. Inst. Tech., Pasadena, 1997—; fellow scientist Westinghouse Rsch. Labs., Pitts., 1962-63; guest prof. Inst. Applied Physics, U. Tuebingen, Germany, 1966-67, Waseda U., Tokyo, Osaka U., 1974; vis. fellow Clare Hall, Cambridge, U., 1975; chmn. Electron, Ion and Photon Beam Symposium, 1977; cons. in field; mem. sci. and ednl. adv. com. Lawrence Berkeley Lab., 1978-85, chmn., 1980-85; mem. sci. adv. com. GM, 1980-89, chmn., 1984-89, bd. dirs., 1989—; bd. dirs. Agilent Technologies Inc., Saint-Gobain Corp., Reveo, Inc., Raytheon Co., Hughes Electronics Co., Elec. Power Rsch. Inst.; tech. adv. com. R.R. Donnelly & Sons, 1981-89; sr. sci. advisor W.M. Keck Found., 1997—; pro-vice chancellor Cambridge U., 1998. Chmn. Sec. of Energy Adv. Bd., 1990-93; bd. dirs. KCET, 1989-97, Corp. for Nat. Rsch. Initiatives, 1990—, Electric Power Rsch. Inst., 1998—; trustee Calif. Inst. Tech., 1998—; mem. bd. overseers Harvard U., 1999—. Marshall scholar Cambridge U., 1955-58, NSF sr. fellow, 1966-67, Guggenheim fellow, 1974-75. Fellow IEEE, AAAS, ASEE, Royal Acad. Engring.; mem. NAE (ednl. adv. bd. 1984-88, mem. com. 1984-89, chmn. 1988, coun. 1988-94, 96—), Microbeam Analysis Soc. Am., Electron Microscopy Soc. Am. (coun. 1970-72, pres. 1977), Coun. on Competitiveness (vice-chmn. 1990-96), Assn. Marshall Scholars and Alumni (pres. 1965-68), Athenaeum Club, California Club, Sigma Xi, Eta Kappa Nu. Home: PO Box 1639 Santa Barbara CA 93116-1639 Office: Calif Inst Tech Office Pres Emeritus/202-31 1200 E California Blvd Pasadena CA 91125-0001

EVERLY, GEORGE STOTELMYER, JR., psychophysiologist, educator; b. Balt., May 31, 1950; s. George Stotelmyer and Kathleen Webster E.; children: Marideth, George III, Andrea. BS, U. Md., 1972, MA, 1974, PhD, 1978; postdoctoral tng., U. Miami, 1983-85, Harvard U., 1985-86. Lectr. U. Md., College Park, 1975-80; assoc. prof. psychology, dir. psychophysiology lab. Loyola Coll., Balt., 1980-85, prof. psychology, 1985—; dir. psychol. svcs. div. Homewood Hosp. Ctr. Johns Hopkins Health System, Balt., 1990-92; CEO, chmn. bd. dirs. Internat. Critical Incident Stress Found., Balt., 1989-95; chmn. emeritus, 1995—; CEO, Inst. Advanced Studies Crisis and Disaster Mgmt., Balt., 1995—; vis. scholar Harvard U., 1985-87, vis. lectr. medicine Harvard Med. Sch., 1987-88; NGO rep. to UN, 1997—; mem. adj. faculty Johns Hopkins U. Sch. Hygiene and Pub. Health, 1998—;. Author: Occupational Health Promotion, 1985; The Nature and Treatment of the Stress Response, 1981, Psychotraumatology, 1995, Innovations in Disaster and Trauma Psychology, 1995; The Stress Mess Solution, 1980; co-author: Controlling Stress and Tension, 1979; Experiencing Health, 1985; Personality and Its Disorders, 1985, The Assessment of Human Stress, 1987, Clinical Guide to Treatment of the Human Stress Response, 1989; founding and exec. editor Internat. Jour. Emergency MEntal Health, 1999—; rschr., developer The Everly Behavioral Survey, 1982. Recipient cert. of honor Balt. City Police Dept., 1981, Prof.'s medal Weiner U., Lima, Peru, 1997. Fellow Acad. Psychosomatic Medicine, Am. Inst. Stress (trustee); mem. APA, Soc. Behavioral Medicine, Am. Acad. Behavioral Medicine.

EVERS, KATHINKA BIRGITTA, science administrator, philosophy researcher; b. Lund, Scania, Sweden, Oct. 17, 1960; d. Jan Karl Allan and Birgitta Viveca (Siversson) E. Student, Balliol Coll., Oxford, Eng., Australian Nat. U., Canberra; PhD, U. Lund, 1991. Post-doctoral rsch. fellow U. Tasmania, Hobart, Australia, 1992-93; philos. cons. UNESCO, Paris, Seoul, 1993-97; assoc. fellow Balliol Coll., Oxford, 1994; post-doctoral rsch. fellow Human Rights Ctr., U. Essex, Eng., 1996; exec. dir. SCRES/ICSU standing com. responsibility & ethics in sci. Internat. Coun. Sci., Oslo, 1997—; freelance journalist, Sweden, France, U.K., 1986-99; field agt. South Pacific Inst., Australian Nat. U., Canberra, 1991; cons. TMV, Stockholm, 1992; philos. cons. in field. Author: Plurality of Thought, 1991, Why Tolerance?, 1997. Rsch. grantee Wallenberg Inst., Lund, 1992-93, HSFR, Stockholm, 1995-96. Mem. AAAS, Philosophy Soc. (chair 1991-92). Avocations: hang gliding, trekking, dancing, literature, music. Office: PO Box 522, 0105 Oslo Norway

EVERS, ROBERT JAMES, real estate sales and development executive; b. Buffalo, N.Y., June 17, 1932; s. Joseph Daniel and Mary Gertrude (McCarthy) E.; m. Donna Lee Arduin, Aug. 31, 1963; children: Christina Marie, Andrea Katherine, John Robert. BA in Econs., St. Bonaventure U., 1958; MBA, Stanford U. Secretariat Atomic Energy Commn., Washington, 1958-60; with Rockwell/Gen. Dynamics, Washington and Calif., 1960-69; mng. dir. Arcata Mgmt., Menlo Park, Calif., 1969-72; dir. opers. Pres.'s Policy Internat. Econ. Coun., Washington, 1974-76; exec. v.p. Can Mfrs. Inst., Washington, 1976-78; pres. Evers Devel., Chevy Chase, Md., 1980—; dir., treas. Evers & Co. Real Estate, Washington, 1986—. Republican. Roman Catholic. Office: Evers & Co Real Estate 4400 Jenifer St NW Washington DC 20015-2113

EVERS, TERRY N., university administrator, consultant; b. Ft. Hood, Sept. 17, 1950; d. Mayron Daniel and Ruby Nellene Evers; m. Laurence H. Hurley, Dec. 26, 1995. BA, U. Tex., El Paso, 1972; MEd, S.W. Tex. State U., 1992. Exec. asst. to pres. Office of the Pres., U. Tex., Austin, 1993-98, spl. asst. to the pres., 1998—; cons., Tex., 1999—. Mem. State Employee Charitable Campaign Local Com., 1999-2000. Mem. Nat. Assn. Presdl. Assts. in Higher Edn., Psi Chi, Kappa Delta Pi. Avocations: writing, watercolor painting, harp. E-mail: tevers@mail.utexas.edu. Office: Univ Tex Austin Office of the Pres Austin TX 78712

EVERSOLE, KELLYE ANNE, government relations and public affairs consultant; b. Wichita Falls, Tex., Apr. 28, 1958; d. John Lewis and Frankye Louise (Atchley) E. BA (hons.), George Washington Univ., 1983. Staff asst. U.S. Senator David Boren, Washington, 1979-81, legis. asst., 1981-88; profl. staff mem. U.S. Senate Com. on Agriculture, Nutrition and Forestry, Washington, 1988-89; exec.dir. Federal Crop Ins. Commn, Washington, 1989-90; pres. Eversole Assocs., Chevy Chase, Md., 1991—; cons. Nat. Corn Growners Assn., St. Louis, Mo., 1995—, Am. Seed Trade Assn., Washington, 1998—. Appt. mem. USTR/USDA Agriculutral Policy Adv. Com., Washington, 1994-98. Recipient Outstanding Performance award Nat. Corn Growers Assn., 1999. Mem. Soc. WOmen Environmental Profls. (founding, bd. dirs.), ABA AGricultural Mgmt. Task Force Adv. com. Office: Eversole Assocs 3208 Park View Rd Chevy Chase MD 20815-5644

EVERT, CHRISTINE MARIE (CHRIS EVERT), retired professional tennis player; b. Ft. Lauderdale, Fla., Dec. 21, 1954; d. James and Colette Evert; m. John Lloyd, Apr. 17, 1979 (div.); m. Andy Mill, July 30, 1988; children: Alexander James, Nicholas Joseph, Colton Jack. Amateur tennis player, until Dec. 1972, profl. tennis player, 1972-89, ret. from tennis, 1989; owner Evert Enterprises/IMG, Boca Raton, Fla., 1989—; Olympics commentator CBS Sports, 1992; commentator NBC Sports tennis events; winner numerous tournaments including U.S. Jr. Championship, 1970, 71, U.S. Open, 1975, 76, 77, 78, 80, 82, Wimbledon Singles, 1974, 76, 81, doubles, 1976, Australian Open, 1982, 84, French Open Singles, 1974, 75, 79, 80, 83, 85, 86, Virginia Slims, 1972, 73, 75, 77, 87, European Women's Open, Geneva, 1987, Eckerd Open, 1987; spl. advisor to U.S. Nat. Tennis Team by U.S. Tennis Assn.; bd. dirs. Internat. Tennis Hall of Fame; trustee Womens Sports Found. Star 3 vols. VCR instrnl. tennis tapes, 1991—; corp. spokesperson and rep., appearing in TV commls. and print advertisements; host and organizer Chris Evert Pro-Celebrity Tennis Classic, 1989, 90, 92, 93, 94, 95, 96, 97, 98, 99. Founder Chris Evert Charities, Inc., Healthy Start. Recipient Lebair Sportsmanship trophy, 1971; named Female Athlete of Yr. AP, 1974, 75, 77, 80, Athlete of Yr. Sports Illustrated, 1976, Greatest Woman Athlete of Last 25 Years Women's Sports Found., 1985, Flo Hyman award Women's Sports Found., 1990, Providencia award Palm Beach County Conv. and Visitors Bur., 1991; named one of Top 10 Romantic People of 1989, Korbel; inducted Madison Sq. Garden Walk of Fame, 1993, inductee, Internat. Tennis Hall of Fame, 1995. Mem. U.S. Lawn Tennis Assn. (Top Women's Singles Player award 1974), Nat. Honor Soc., Fla. Sports Found. (bd. dirs.), Women's Tennis Assn. (pres. 1982-91, exec. com., Sportmanship award 1979, Player Svc. awards 1981, 86, 87). *

EVERT, SANDRA FLORENCE (WHEELER), medical/surgical nurse; b. Saginaw, Mich., Sept. 18, 1949; d. Charles William and Florence Arlene (Babcock) Wheeler; m. Raymond Clyde Evert, Jan. 20, 1968; children: Christine Michelle, Raymond Clyde II. AD cum laude, Lansing C.C., 1986. Med./surg. staff nurse E.W. Sparrow Hosp., Lansing, Mich., 1986—. Mem. First United Pentecostal Ch. of Grand Ledge, Mich. Mem. Apostolic Ch. Avocations: camping, Bible reading, Christian music, family, church functions. Home: 10 Willard Ct Grand Ledge MI 48837-1356

EVESQUE, PIERRE HENRI, physics researcher; b. Neuilly, Seine, France, Dec. 26, 1951; s. Jacques François and Nicole Odette (Schulz-Robellaz) E.; m. Claire Françoise Bompaire, Oct. 8, 1981. Grad. in physics, Ecole Superieure Physique et Chimie Industrielles de Paris, Paris, 1976; D degree, U. Paris VI, 1979, D in Physics, 1984. Researcher ESPCI, Paris, 1976-77, asst. prof., 1977-78; researcher Nat. Ctr. for Sci. Rsch., Paris, 1980-93; dir. rsch. Nat. Ctr. for Sci. Rsch., Châtenay-Malabry, 1993—; postdoctoral fellow UCLA, 1984-85; cons. European Space Agy., Paris, 1990-93; cons. Pont-à-Mousson, 1990-91. Editor Powders and Grains, 1993—; contbr. articles to profl. jours. Coun. mem. Fac. Libre de Théologie Réformée, Aix-en-Provence, France, 1987—. With France Air Army, 1978-79. Mem. Am. Phys. Soc., Materials Rsch. Soc., Soc. Française de Physique, Assn. pour l'Etude de la Micromécanique des Milieux Granulaires (editor 1990). Presbyterian. E-mail: evesque@mssmat.ecp.fr. Office: CNRS Lab Mécanique/Structures Materiaux, Ecole Ctrl Paris, 92295 Chatenay-Malabry France

EVETT, RUSSELL DOUGHERTY, internist, educator; b. Norfolk, Va., Feb. 1, 1932; s. Edward Hall and Elizabeth (Dougherty) E.; m. Mary Gail Kirby, Aug. 18, 1956; children: Stephen, Anne, Gail, John. BS, Randolph-Macon Coll., 1953; MD, Med. Coll. Va., 1957; MS in Medicine, Mayo Clinic and U. Minn., 1963. Diplomate Am. Bd. Internal Medicine. Intern DePaul Hosp., Norfolk, 1957-58; fellow in internal medicine Mayo Clinic, Rochester, Minn., 1960-63; pvt. practice internal medicine Norfolk, 1964—; pres. med. staff Leigh Meml. Hosp., Norfolk, 1970-72; chmn. dept. internal medicine Norfolk Gen. Hosp., 1972-74; assoc. prof. medicine Eastern Va. Med. Sch., 1974— ; mem. staff Med. Center Hosps., DePaul Hosp.; mem. Va. Health Info. Bd., 1997—; mem. Med. Coll. Va. Bd., 1998—. Served with USNR, 1958-60. Mem. Va. Health Info. Bd., 1997—, Norfolk Cmty. Svcs. Bd., 2000—. Served with USNR, 1958-60. Fellow ACP (Laureate award 1997); mem. Va. Gastroenterol. Soc. (pres. 1975-77), Norfolk Acad. Medicine (pres. 1976-77), Med. Soc. Va. (pres. 1994-95), AMA (alt. del. 1985-95, del. 1995-99), Va. Health Info. Bd., Norfolk Cmty. Svcs. Bd., So. Med. Assn., Norfolk Yacht and Country Club, Harbor Club, Phi Beta Kappa, Omicron Delta Kappa, Alpha Omega Alpha. Methodist. Home: 6147 Studeley Ave Norfolk VA 23508-1044 Office: 530 Wainwright Bldg Norfolk VA 23510

EVGENEV, MICHAEL BORIS, health facility administrator; b. Moscow, Aug. 7, 1944; s. Boris Sergei and Olga Yakovlovna (KLalmanovich) E.; Evgeneva Ludmila (div. 1998); children: Alexi, Peter, Nicholas. M, Moscow Ped. Inst., 1967; PhD, Inst. Devel. Biol., Moscow, 1970; D of Biology, Inst. Molecular Biology, Moscow, 1979. Rsch. scientist Inst. Devel. Bilogy, Moscow, 1970-78; sr. scientist Inst. Molecular Biology, Moscow, 1978-84, leading scientist, head group, 1984-90; head lab. Inst. Cell Biophys., Moscow, 1995—; vis. prof. Johns Hopkins U., 1990-95. Contbr. articles to profl. jours. Grantee NIH, 1995, 97, Howard Hughes Med. Inst., 1997. Mem. Russian Genetics Soc., N.Y. Acad. Scis. Avocations: sports, books, classical music. Home: Apt 127, Cheruyakbovskaya str 4, 125319 Moscow Russia Office: Inst Cell Biophys, Institutskaya str 3, 142292 Moscow Russia

EVGENY, POZHIDAEV, physical chemistry educator, university dean; b. Yalta, Crimea, USSR, Sept. 30, 1937; s. Dmitry Pozhidaev and Xenia Vorobiova; m. Natali Podrez, June 19, 1982; 1 child, Alexandra. Grad. in engring. and chemistry, Mendeleev's Chem.-Tech. Inst., Moscow, 1959; D Tech. Sci., Moscow Inst. Electronics-Math., 1982. Mem. faculty Moscow Inst. Electronics and Math., 1980—, prof. phys. chemistry, 1983—, head dept., 1980-92, dean Faculty Info. and Telecom., 1992—. Contbr. over 100 articles to sci. jours., including Phys. Stat. Solid, Acta Polymerica, Russian acad. jours. Named Honored Man of Sci. and Sci. Engring., Russian Fedn., 1996, govtl. prize, 1997. Mem. Russian Acad. Quality Problems, Fishing Club. Home: 12-2-24 Stroykovskaya St, 109316 Moscow Russia Office: Moscow Inst Elect and Math, 3/12 B Trekhsviatitelsk per, 109028 Moscow Russia

EVLOGIEVA, MARIANA PETROVA, publisher; b. Montana, Bulgaria, Oct. 1, 1964; d. Peter and Tsetska (Gavrilova) Grigorov. M in Philology, Sofia U., 1988, M in Journalism, 1989. Editor BEA, Sofia, Bulgaria, 1988-91, Pres-Esperanto Ltd., Sofia, 1991-92; pres. Interpres Publ. House, Sofia, 1992—; chief editor Bulgarian Esperantist Rev., Sofia, 1992-93, Bus. Club Rev., Sofia, 1994, AmUzE Rev., 1999—; editor 7 Days Teletext, Sofia, 1996—. Author: Esperanto for Beginners, 1991; contbr. articles to profl. jours. Mem. Union Bulgarian Journalists, Union Bulgarian Esperantists. Office: Interpres, Drushba-2 PK 18, 1582 Sofia Bulgaria

EVRARD, SERGIO GUSTAVO, physician, psychiatrist, consultant; b. Buenos Aires, Nov. 1, 1967; s. Carlos Enrique Gustavo and Neva Etra (Ottini) E. MD, U. Buenos Aires, 1996. Asst. prof. histology, cell biology and embriology U. Buenos Aires, 1988—, head practical works histology, cell biology, embriology, 1996—; resident in psychiatry Hosp. Braulio A. Moyano, Buenos Aires, 1996-2000, cons. psychiatrist, 2000—; cons. psychiatrist Min. de Salud y Acción Social, Buenos Aires, 1996-2000; presenter in field. Presenter in field. Recipient Diploma de la Fundacion Bolsa de Comercio, Buenos Aires, 1986. Mem. Soc. Argentina Wernicke-Kleist-Leonhard, Assn. Argentina de Psiquiatras. Avocations: photography, diving, sailing, swimming. E-mail: sevrard@intramed.net.ar. Home: Zabala 2473 4o A, Buenos Aires 1426, Argentina Office: Hosp Braulio A Moyano, Brandsen 2570, Buenos Aires 1287, Argentina

EVSEEVA, LYUDMILA EVGENIYEVNA, physicist, researcher; b. Moscow, Aug. 27, 1952; d. Evgeniy Vasilyevich and Ida Mihaylovna (Levinskaya) Sadchikov; m. Viacheslav Evgenievich Evseev, 1974 (div. 1983); 1 child, Sergey; m. Viktor Fiodorovich Zinchenko, 1983 (div. 1998); 1 child, Yuliya. Diploma in physics, Byelorussian State U., Minsk, Belarus, 1974. Jr. rschr. Heat & Mass Transfer Inst., Minsk, 1974-88, rschr., 1988—. Contbr. articles to profl. jours. Office: Heat & Mass Transfer Inst, P Brovki 15 Acad Sci, 220072 Minsk Belarus

EWALDS-KVIST, BÉATRICE MARIANNE, psychology educator, researcher; b. Porvoo, Finland, Aug. 30, 1945; d. Toivo Erik and Gunvor (Hällfors) Ewalds; m. Mårten Oskar Rudolf Kvist, May 29, 1971; children: Sebastian, Wilhelm. MA, Åbo Akademi U., Turku, Finland, 1978; lic., Åbo Akademi U., 1980, PhD, 1985. Lic. psychologist. Demonstrator Åbo Akademi U., 1977-84, lectr., 1984-88, asst. in psychology, 1988-90, chief asst., 1992-93; asst. prof. dept. psychology Å Akademi U., 1996—; docent Åbo Akademi U., 1996—; sr. mistress Pargas, Finland, 1993-95; chief asst. dept. psychology Turku U., 1999—. Contbr. articles to profl. jours. Grantee Ministry Edn., Helsinki, 1989.

EWALT, JACQUELYN MARIE, biologist; b. Pitts., May 20, 1968; d. Thomas A. and Veronica Ewalt. BS, La Roche Coll., Pitts., 1991; student, Duquesne U., 1993. Biology lab. asst. La Roche Coll., 1990-91; environ. chemistry Allegheny County Health Dept., Pitts., 1992; gen. biology lab. instr., faculty liasion Duquesne U., Pitts., 1992-93; molecular biology rsch. asst. MaGee Womens Rsch. Inst., Pitts., 1993-95; with client collections dept. Quest Diagnostics Inc. (formerly Corning Clin. Labs.), Pitts., 1995-97, biologist microbiology lab., 1997-99, virology lab., 1999—; sci. teaching asst. La Roche Pre-Coll. Program, Pitts., 1991; judge Pitts. Regional Sci. and Engring. Fair. fol. histology lab. Ohio Valley Gen. Hosp., McKees Rocks, Pa., 1991; judge Pjas local competition Holy Trinity Sch., McKees Rocks, 1993, 94, 95, Pitts. Regional Sci. and Engring. Fair; vol. Carnegie Sci. Ctr., Pitts. Named faculty scholar Duquesne U., 1992-93; recipient Best Composition award Nat. Aviary Photo Contest. Mem. AAAS, Am. Inst. Biol. Scis., Nat. Audubon Soc., Pitts. Zool. Soc. Avocations: art, music, theater, photography. Home: 5 Sterling Dr Coraopolis PA 15108-3511

EWELL, A. BEN, JR., lawyer, businessman; b. Elyria, Ohio, Sept. 10, 1941; s. Austin Bert and Mary Rebecca (Thompson) E.; m. Suzanne E.; children: Austin Bert III, Brice Ballantyne, Harrison Dale, Jonathan Eli. BA, Miami U., Oxford, Ohio, 1963; JD, Hasting Coll. Law, U. Calif., San Francisco, 1966. Bar: Calif. 1966, U.S. Dist. Ct. (ea. dist.) Calif. 1967, U.S. Supreme Ct. 1982, U.S. Ct. Appeals (9th cir.) 1967. Pres. A.B. Ewell, Jr., A. Profl. Corp., Fresno, 1984-98, The Clarksfield Co., Inc., Fresno, 1989—; formerly gen. counsel to various water dists. and assn.; gen. counsel, chmn. San Joaquin River Flood Control Assn., 1984-88; CEO Millerton New Town Devel. Co., 1988-94, chmn., 1994-96; pres. Millerton Open Space and Natural Resource Plan, 1999—; regional v.p. Western Water Co., 1999—; mem. task force on prosecution, cts. and law reform Calif. Coun. Criminal Justice, 1971-74; mem. Fresno Bulldog Found., Calif. State U.; mem. San Joaquin Valley Agrl. Water commn., 1979-88; co-chmn. nat. adv. coun. SBA, 1981, 82, mem. 1981-87; bd. dirs. Fresno East Cmty. Ctr., 1971-73; mem. Fresno County Water Adv. Com., 1989, Fresno Cmty. Coun., 1972-73; chmn. various area polit. campaigns and orgns., including Reagan/Bush, 1984, Deukmejian for Gov., 1986; mem. adv. com. St. Agnes Med. Ctr. Found., 1983-89; trustee U. Calif. Med. Edn. Found., 1989-90, Fresno Met. Mus. Art, History and Sci., active, 1989—, mem. adv. coun., 1993-94· bd. dirs. Citizens for Cmty. Enrichment, Fresno, 1990-93; mem. Police Activities League, 1995—, Fresno Conv. and Visitors Bur., 1997—; bd. dirs. Fresno Volleyball Club, 1998—. Bd. dirs. fresno Volleyball Club, 1998—, pres., 1999—. Mem. Millerton Lake C. of C., Brighton Crest Country Club (pres. 1989-96), Cooper River Country Club, Phi Alpha Delta, Brighton Crest Golf and Country Club, Sigma Nu. Congregationalist. Office: 410 W Fallbrook Ave Ste 102 Fresno CA 93711-5830

EWEN, H.I., physicist; b. Chicopee, Mass., Mar. 5, 1922; s. Arthur and Ruth Frances (Fay) E.; m. Mary Ann Whitney, Feb. 11, 1956; children: Donald, Jim, Bruce, Mark, David, Deborah, Daniel, Rebecca. BA, Amherst Coll., 1943; MA, Harvard U., 1948, PhD, 1951. Mem. faculty Amherst Coll., 1943; co-dir. Harvard Radio Astronomy Program, 1952-58, rsch. assoc. astronomy dept., 1958-65, assoc., 1965-80; v.p. Millitech Corp., South Deerfield, Mass., 1989-2000; rsch. prof. Sch. Engring. U. Mass., 2000—; pres. Ewen Knight Corp., Weston, Mass., 1952-88, Ewen Dae Corp., 1958-88, E.K. Assocs., 1993—; sci. advisor to Cin. Electronics Corp. for USAF Air Weather Svc.; mem. Global Solar Radio Telescope Network, 1977-86. Contbg. author: Advances in Microwaves, vol. 5, 1970, Electromagnetic Sensing of the Earth from Satellites, 1967, Geoscience Instrumentation, 1974, also articles; co-discoverer 21 cm interstellar hydrogen line, 1951; remote sensing of atmospheric ozone distribution (resonant line at 102 GHz), 1966. Served to lt. USNR, 1943-46. NRC fellow, 1946-49; recipient svc. award Harvard Coll., 1977. Fellow AAAS (life), IEEE (Morris E. Leeds award

1970), Am. Acad. Arts and Scis.; mem. Am. Astron. Soc. (Tinsley prize 1988), Phi Beta Kappa, Sigma Xi. E-mail: docewen@crocker.com.

EWEN, PAMELA BINNINGS, lawyer; b. Phila., Mar. 22, 1944; d. Walter James and Barbara (Perkins) Binnings; m. Jerome Francis Ayers, Aug. 22, 1965 (div. July 1974); 1 child, Scott Dylan; m. John Alexander Ewen, Dec. 13, 1974. BA, Tulane U., 1977; JD cum laude, U. Houston, 1979. Bar: Tex. 1979, U.S. Dist. Ct. (so. dist.) Tex. 1981, U.S. Ct. Appeals (5th cir.) 1981. Law clk. Harris, Cook, Browning & Barker, Corpus Christi, Tex., 1977-79; assoc. Kleberg, Dyer, Redford & Weil, Corpus Christi, 1979-80; atty. law dept. Gulf Oil Corp., Houston, 1980-84; assoc. Baker & Botts, L.L.P., Houston, 1984-88, ptnr., 1988—. Author: Faith On Trial, 1999. La. Legis. scholar, New Orleans, 1976-77. Mem. ABA (forum com. on franchising 1983-85, corp., banking, bus. law sect., 1984—, law practice mgmt. sect., subcom. Women Rainmakers Assn.), Am. Petroleum Inst. (spl. subcom. to gen. com. on law, com. on product liability 1982-85), Tex. State Bar (com. on uniform communal code 1988—), Tex. Assn. Bank Coun. (bd. dirs. 1994-97), Jr. Achievement S.E. Tex. (bd. dirs. 1997—), Order of Barons. Office: Baker & Botts 3000 1 Shell Plz Houston TX 77002

EWERT, JÖRG-PETER, neurobiologist, researcher; b. Danzig, Poland, Apr. 26, 1938; German citizen; s. Erich and Liselotte (Dubois) E.; m. Sabine Beate Schuchardt, Sept. 16, 1967; children: Jörg Christian, Inga Mareen. Biologist, U. Göttingen, Germany, 1958-65, Dr. rer.nat., 1965, Staatsexamen, 1967. Sci. asst. Tech. U., Darmstadt, Germany, 1966-70; dozent Tech. U., Darmstadt, 1970-71; rsch. fellow Foundations' Fond, Belmont, Mass., 1970-71; assoc. prof. Tech. U., Darmstadt, 1971-72; prof. chair zoology/physiol. U. Kassel, Germany, 1973—; dir. NATO-ASI, Kassel, 1981; chmn. Senat, U. Kassel, 1987-88. Author: (textbook) Neuroethology, 1980, Neurobiology of Behavior, 1998, Sensory and neurophysiology, 1992. Chmn. Ethics Comm. for Animal Protection, 1995-96. Recipient award for Scientific Movie, Assn. for Media In Sci., Amsterdam, 1994, award for artificial neuronal net, German-Austrian U., 1993. Fellow AAAS; mem. Soc. Neurosci., Internat. Soc. Neuroethology (founding com.). Avocations: painting, fitness tng., sports cars. Office: U Kassel, Heinrich-Plett-Strasse 40, D-34132 Kassel Germany

EWIG, BRENT MATTHEW, health policy analyst; b. Milw., Oct. 15, 1971; s. Glenn and Shirlee (Mahr) E. BA in English, Valparaiso U., 1993; MS, Johns Hopkins U., 2000. Intern The White House, Washington, 1993; govt. liaison InterHealth, Washington, 1994-96; sr. dir. access policy Assn. State and Territorial Health Officials, Washington, 1996—. Mem. APHA, Am. Soc. Assn. Execs., Nat. Rural Health Assn. Democrat. Lutheran. Office: ASTHO 1275 K St NW Ste 800 Washington DC 20005-4091

EWING, BLAIR GORDON, federal official; b. Kansas City, Mo., Dec. 3, 1933; s. Lynn Moore and Margaret (Blair) E.; m. Barbara F. Thompson, Jan. 3, 1959 (div. Nov. 1991); children: Blair Gordon, Chatham Boyd; m. Martha L. Brockway, April 30, 1994. AB, U. Mo., 1954; postgrad. (Rotary Found. fellow), U. Bonn (Germany), 1957-58; AM, U. Chgo., 1960. Reporter Chgo. City News Bur., 1958-59, UPI, 1959-60, Traffic World Mag., 1960-61; instr. polit. sci. Chgo. City Jr. Coll., 1961-62, SUNY, Binghamton, 1962-67; planning and mgmt. cons. Harold Wise and Assocs., Washington, 1967-69; program analyst Office of Asst. Sec. HEW, Washington, 1969-70; dir. criminal justice planning D.C. Govt., 1970-72; dir. dept. pub. safety Met. Washington Coun. of Govts., 1972-74; dir. planning and evaluation div. U.S. Dept. Justice, Washington, 1974-78; dep. dir. Nat. Inst. Law Enforcement and Criminal Justice, Dept. Justice, 1976—; acting dir., 1977-79; asst. dir. U.S. Office Pers. Mgmt., Washington, 1979-81, dep. dir., 1981-83; sr. exec. U.S. Office Mgmt. and Budget, 1983-86; dir. Mgmt. Improvement, Dept. Def., 1986-98; adj. prof. Law Ctr. Georgetown U., 1971-74. Author: Peace Through Negotiation: The Austrian State Treaty, 1966; contbr. articles to profl. jours. Mem. Montgomery County (Md.) Human Rels. Commn., 1975-76; mem. Montgomery County Bd. Edn., 1976-98, pres., 1982-83, 90-91; elected mem. coun. Montgomery County, Md, 1998. With U.S. Army, 1954-56. Woodrow Wilson fellow, 1956-57; recipient disting. svc. award Office Pers. Mgmt., 1981, U.S. Dept. Def. Disting. Civilian Svc. award, 1990, Presdl. Rank award Meritorious Sr. Exec., 1990. Mem. Phi Beta Kappa. Democrat. Episcopalian. Home: 3 Park Valley Rd Silver Spring MD 20910-5424 Office: Montgomery County Coun 100 Maryland Ave Rockville MD 20850-2322

EWING, ELISABETH ANNE ROONEY, priest; m. James E. Ewing. Student, Mt. San Antonio Coll., 1978. Ordained to ministry Evang. Episcopal Chs., 1998. Pastor, gen. overseers, CEO St. Matthew Living Cathedral, N.Y.C., 1998—; mem. Rand Rsch. Corp.; mem. diplomat cir. L.A. World Affairs Coun. Co-editor: Church History, 1996-98, The Church Visible, 1996-98, Life After Death, 1996-98, Bible Lessons, 1996-98; assoc. editor Pinnacle Today Internat. Mag., St. Matthew Publs., St. Matthew Tribune. Mem. Knights of Malta (Dame). Office: St Matthew Cathedral 10736 Jefferson Blvd Ste 145 Culver City CA 90230-4969

EWING, JAMES E., priest; m. Elisabeth Anne Rooney. Ordained to ministry Evang. Episcopal Chs., 1951. Sr. pastor, gen. overseer St. Matthew Living Cathedral, N.Y.C.; mem. Rand Rsch. Corp.; mem. diplomat cir. L.A. World Affairs Coun.; rsch. bd. dirs. Am. Biog. Inst./Internat. Biog. Ctr. Author, editor: Church History, The Church Visible, Life After Death, Bible Lessons. With USAF, 1953-57. Mem. Knights of Malta, Sovereign Order St. John of Jerusalem. Office: St Matthew Cathedral Ste 145 10736 Jefferson Blvd Culver City CA 90230-4969

EWING, KY PEPPER, JR., lawyer; b. Victoria, Tex., Jan. 7, 1935; s. Ky Pepper and Sallie (Dixon) E.; m. Almuth Rott, Apr. 6, 1963; children: Kenneth Patrick, Kevin Andrew, Kathryn Diana. B.A. cum laude, Baylor U., 1956; LL.B. cum laude, Harvard U., 1959. Bar: D.C. 1959, U.S. Supreme Ct 1963. Assoc. firm Covington & Burling, Washington, 1959-64; partner firm Prather, Seeger, Doolittle, Farmer & Ewing, Washington, 1964-77; dep. asst. atty. gen. antitrust div. Dept. Justice, Washington, 1978-80; ptnr. Vinson & Elkins, Washington, 1980—; dir. Washington Inst. Fgn. Affairs. Co-editor-in-chief: State Antitrust Practice and Statutes, 3 Vols., 1990; mem. antitrust adv. bd. Antitrust and Trade Regulation Report Bur. Nat. Affairs, 1990—; mem. edit. bd. Antitrust Report Matthew Bender & Co., 1993—. Pres. Potomac Valley League, 1977, Carderock Springs Citizens Assn., 1975-78. Fellow Am. Bar Found.; mem. ABA (chmn. legis. com. antitrust sect. 1987-91, coun. antitrust sect. 1991-94, fin. officer antitrust sect. 1994-96, chmn. FTC/Dept. Justice working group 1994-97, mem. ho. of dels. 1996-98, vice chair antitrust sect. 1998-99, chair elect antitrust sect. 1999-2000, chair antitrust sect. 2000—), D.C. Bar Assn., Am. Soc. Internat. Law, Internat. Bar Assn. (editl. adv. bd. Bus. Law Internat.), Inter-Am. Bar Assn., Met. Club. Democrat. Episcopalian. Home: 8317 Comanche Ct Bethesda MD 20817-4561 Office: Vinson & Elkins 1455 Pennsylvania Ave NW Fl 7 Washington DC 20004-1013

EWING, MICHAEL SNYDER, producer, film company executive; b. Kalamazoo, Mich., Mar. 29, 1960; s. Robert Earl and Juan Marie Snyder. Student, We. Mich. U., 1979, Am. Acad. Dramatic Arts, N.Y.C., 1980, Stella Adler Conservatory, N.Y.C., 1979-81, Actors Studio, N.Y.C., 1981, Stella Adler Conservatory, N.Y.C., 1980-84. Theater dir., co-prodr. L.A., 1985, N.Y.C., 1986-87; asst. to prodr. Paramount Pictures, L.A., 1988; asst. prodr. Paramount Pictures, 1989-90, assoc. prodr., 1991-95; co-prodr. Warner Bros., 1995-96; pres. Greenhaven Films, L.A., 1995—. Dir., co-prodr. (plays) World Premiere, Tigers Wild, L.A., 1985, N.Y.C., 1986-87; asst. to prodr. (film) The Naked Gun: From the Files of Police Squad, 1988; asst. prodr.: (film) Nothing But Trouble, 1990, Crazy People; assoc. prodr.: Naked Gun 2-1/2: The Smell of Fear, 1991, Naked Gun 33 1/3: The Final Insult, 1993, Tommy Boy, 1994; co-prodr.: (film) My Fellow Americans, 1995-96, Nutty Professor 2, 1998-99; exec. prodr.: The Incredible Shrinking Man, 2000. Office: Nutty Professor II/Universal Studios 100 Universal City Plz Bldg 506 Universal City CA 91608-1002

EWING, MICHAEL THOMAS, marketing educator, consultant, researcher; b. Pieter Maritzburg, Kwa-Zulu, South Africa, Dec. 17, 1967; arrived in Australia, 1996; s. Donald Kirkwood and Anne Ethel (Styles) E.; m. Lee-Ann Chambers, July 9, 1994; 1 child, Thomas Kirkwood. B.Com., U. Natal (South Africa), 1991; M.Com., U. Pretoria (South Africa), 1993, PhD, 1996. Mktg. rsch. mgr. Ford, South Africa, 1992-95; lectr. Curtin U., Perth, Australia, 1996-98; sr. lectr. Curtin U., Perth, 1998—; assoc. faculty Inst. Mktg. Mgmt., Johannesburg, South Africa, Henley Mgmt. Coll., Eng., 1999—; presenter in field. Contbr. articles to profl. jours., chpts. to books. Lt. South African Def. Force, 1986-87. Recipient Nat. Colours (judo) South African Univs. Sports Coun., 1991. Fellow Am. Mktg. Assn., Acad. Mktg. Sci., Assn. Consumer Rsch. Roman Catholic. Avocations: golf, fly-fishing, writing. Office: Curtin U Tech Sch Mktg, GPO Box u1987, 6845 Perth Western Australia, Australia

EWING, PATRICK ALOYSIUS, professional basketball player; b. Kingston, Jamaica, Aug. 5, 1962; m. Rita Ewing; children: Patrick Aloysius, Randi. BFA, Georgetown U., 1985. Basketball player New York Knickerbockers, N.Y.C., 1985—; mem. U.S. Olympic Basketball Teams (received Gold medal), 1984, 92. Named to Sporting News All-Am. 2nd team, 1983-84, Sporting News All-Am. 1st Team, 1985, All-Star team, 1986, 88-93; recipient Naismith award, 1985; named NCAA Disvn. I Most Outstanding Player, 1984, Sporting News Coll. Player of Yr., 1985, NBA Rookie of Yr., 1986, Sporting News Coll. Player of Yr., 1985, All-Defensive 2nd team, 1988, 89, 92, All-NBA 2nd team, 1988, 89, 91, 92, All-NBA 1st team, 1990, NBA All-Star team, 1986-95. Player NCAA divsn. I championship team, 1984; holder NBA Finals series record most blocked shots (30), 1994; co-hlder NBA finals single-game record most block shots (8), 1994. Office: Seattle Super Sonics Key Arena 351 Elliott Ave W ste 500 Seattle WA 98119

EXBRAYAT, JEAN-MARIE, biologist, researcher, histology educator; b. Besseges, Gard, France, Mar. 30, 1952; s. Fernand and Marie-Rose (Vitalis) E.; m. Pascale Pionchon, Sept. 16, 1978; children: Philippe, Jean-François. Grad., Acad. Montpellier, France, 1970; MS, U. Montpellier, 1974, PhD, 1977; DSc, U. Paris, 1986. Maitre-asst. Cath. U., Lyon, France, 1979-86, lectr., 1986-87, prof., 1987—, dean sci. faculty, 1997—; dir. Ecole Pratique Hautes Etudes, Lyon, France, 1991—. Author: Cahier de l'Institut Catholique de Lyon, 1993; co-author: Evolution Biologique, 1989, Ecotoxicity of Chemicals to Amphibians, 1992, L'origine es espèces aujourd'hui, 1995, L'evolution biologique, science, histoire ou philosopie?, 1997, Les Gymnophiones, 2000, Methodes classiques de visualisation du genome en microscopic photonique, 2000. Decorated Chevalier Acad. Palms. Mem. AAAS, French Herpetological Soc. (gen. sec. 1991-97), Zool. Soc. France, Societas Europaea Herpetologica, N.Y. Acad. Scis. Roman Catholic. Fax: 33-04-72-32-50-66. Office: Cath Univ, 25 Rue Du Plat, 69288 Lyon France

EXCELL, PETER STUART, electronics and electrical engineering researcher; b. London, June 27, 1948; s. Henry Michael and Elna Haf (Williams) E.; m. Dianne Suffield Excell, Apr. 3, 1982; 2 children. BSc, Reading U., Eng., 1970; PhD, Bradford U., Eng., 1980. Chartered engr., U.K Engring. Coun. Researcher Bradford (Eng.) U., 1971-79, lectr., 1979-85, sr. lectr., 1985-89, reader, 1989-99, head of dept., 1996-97, dep. dir. telecomms. rsch. ctr., 1997—, prof., pers. chair in applied electromagnetics, 1999—; cons. Oil, Computer and Mobile Comms. Industries, Eng., 1975—. Contbr. articles to profl. jours. Grantee Engring. and Phys. Scis. Rsch. Coun., Eng., 1977—, European Union, 1993—. Fellow IEE; mem. IEEE (sr.), Remote Sensing Soc. Achievements include pioneer use of magnetic-resonance image of human head to model absorption of microwaves in tissue, use of parallel supercomputers for such work and development of hybrid computer method to optimise simulation of mobile telephone and human head. Office: U Bradford, Telecomms Rsch Ctr, Bradford BD7 1DP, England

EXE, DAVID ALLEN, electrical engineer; b. Jan. 29, 1942; s. Oscar Melvin and Irene Marie (Mattis) E.; m. Lynn Rae Roberts (dec.); m. Mary Ann Savilla; children: Doreen Lea, Raena Lynn. BSEE, S.D. State U., 1968; MBA, U. S.D., 1980; postgrad., Iowa State U., 1969-70, U. Idaho, 1978-80. Registered prof. engr., Idaho, Oreg., Minn., S.D., Wash., Wyo., Utah, N.Y., Ind. Wis. Applications engr. Collins Radio, Cedar Rapids, Iowa, 1969-70; dist. engr. Bonneville Power Adminstrn., Idaho Falls, Idaho, 1970-77; instr. math. U. S.D., Vermillion, 1977-78; CEO EXE Engring., Idaho Falls, 1978-83, Greenfield, Minn., 1985—; safety mgr. CPT Corp., Eden Prairie, Minn., 1983-85; owner, CEO Exe Inc., Eden Prairie, 1983—; chmn. bd. Applied Techs. Idaho, Idaho Falls, 1979—; chmn., CEO Azimuth Cons., Idaho Falls, 1979-81; v.p. D & B Constrn. Co., Idaho Falls, 1980-83; bd. dirs., v.p., COO Nat. Multi-Housing Corp., 1989. Tech. advisor Nat. Earth Day, 1991; apptd. Minn. State Bd. Profl. Engrs., 1991. With USN, 1960-64. Mem. IEEE, IEEE Computer Soc., NSPE, Am. Cons. Engrs., Nat. Contracts Mgrs. Assn., Mensa, Am. Legion, VFW, Masons, Elks. Fax: 763-477-9991; email: dexe@execinc.net. Office: Indsl Engring Inc 7934 Cedar St Rockford MN 55373-8405

EXERGIAN, FLORIN EDUARD, physician, surgeon, researcher; b. Bucharest, Romania, Jan. 8, 1949; s. Eduard N. and Ana D. (Mihailescu) E.; m. Virginia Ileana C. Coman, Mar. 19, 1977; 1 child, Ana Maria. MD, Bucharest Inst. Medicine and Pharmacy, 1972. Gen. practitioner Radomiresti, Romania, 1972-75; resident Prof. Ghe Marinescu Hosp., Bucharest, 1975-80, neurosurgeon, 1980-90; sr. neurosurgeon Prof. Dr. D. Bagdasar Hosp., Bucharest, 1990—, chief spinal surgery dept., 1999—; concept and project mgr. Computing Ctr., Bagdasar Hosp., 1986-89, 95—, assoc. prof. Neurosurgical Clinic, 1997—; cons. Higher Forensic Commn., Romania, 1999—, Biotehni, France. Contbr. articles to profl. jours. Pres. S.Trauma Found., Bucharest. Recipient Ann. award Armenian's Union, 1996. Mem. N.Y. Acad. Scis., Romanian Acad. Med. Scis. Avocations: music, computer science, parapsychology. Home: Str V Voiculescu 25, Sector 3, Bucharest Romania Office: Hosp Prof D Bagdasar, Sos Berceni 10-14 Sector 4, Bucharest Romania

EXNER, OTTO, chemist; b. Prague, Nov. 14, 1924; s. Otto Karel and Ludmila (Homolkova) E.; m. Radmila Brunclikova, Dec. 14, 1957; children: Zuzana, Marketa. Engr., Inst. of Chem. Tech., Prague, 1949; Dr. Technology, Inst. of Chem. Technology, Prague, 1951; DS, Czechoslovak Acad. Scis., Prague, 1961; D (hon.), U. Pardubice, 2000. Rsch. scientist Rsch. Inst. of Pharmacy, Prague, 1950-53, Czechoslovak Acad. of Scis., Prague, 1954-92; scientific adviser Czech Acad. of Scis., Prague, 1993—; external prof. Slovak Tech. U. Bratislava, Slovakia, 1974-83; vis. prof. U. Bologna, Italy, 1983, U. Nice, France, 1991, 95. Author: (books) Dipole Moments in Organic Chemistry, 1975, Correlation Analysis of Chemical Data, 1988; contbr. articles to profl. jours. Recipient gold medal Slovak Tech. U., Bratislava, 1989, Heyrovsky medal Czech Acad. Scis., Prague, 1991, medal for merit U. Paris, 1991, Votocek medal Inst. Chem. Tech., Prague, 2000; named fellow Czech Learned Soc., 1997. Mem. Czech Chem. Soc. (hon.). Office: Inst Organic Chemistry & Biochem, Flemingovo n 2, 16610 Praha 6 Czech Republic

EXNER, PAVEL VLADIMIR, physicist, researcher, educator; b. Prague, Czechoslovakia, Mar. 30, 1946; s. Vilém and Marie (Karvánková) E.; m. Jana Wiendlová, Oct. 1, 1971; children: Milena, Hana, Věra. MSc in Theoretical Physics, Charles U., Prague, 1969, doctorate, 1970; DrSc, Joint Inst. Nuclear Rsch., Dubna, Russia, 1990. Asst. prof. theoretical physics Charles U., 1970-76, rsch. assoc., 1976-78; rsch. fellow Joint Inst. Nuclear Rsch., Dubna, 1978-86, head dept. math. physics, 1986-90; chief rsch. scientist Nuclear Physics Inst., Prague, Czech Republic, 1990—; vis. prof. Ctr. of Theoretical Physics Nat. Ctr. Sci. Rsch., Marseille, France, Inst. for Math. Ruhr U., Bochum, Germany, E. Schrödinger Inst., Vienna, Austria. Author: Open Quantum Systems and Feynman Integrals, 1984; co-author: Hilbert Space Operators in Quantum Physics, 1994; contbr. over 100 articles to profl. jours. Mem. Internat. Assn. Math. Physics, Union of Czech Mathematicians and Physicists (Young Physicist's 1st prize 1975), Am. Math. Soc., Doppler Inst. for Math. Physics. Avocations: literature, arts, classical music, mountain hiking. Home: V olšinách 120, 10000 Prague Czech Republic Office: Nuclear Physics Inst, Czech Acad Sci, 25068 Řež Czech Republic

EYADEMA, ETIENNE GNASSINGBE, president of Togo; b. Pya, Lama-Kara, Dec. 26, 1937; s. Gnassingbé and N'Danida Eyadéma. Served with French Army, including service in Indo-China, Dahomey, Niger, Algeria, 1953-61; now pres. Republic of Togo, Lomé; commd. Togolese Army, 1963; army chief-of-staff of Togo, 1965—, seized power, 1967, pres. of Togo, minister of def., 1967, 81—. Decorated officer Order Nat. de Mono; chevalier Légion d'Honneur (France). Office: Office of President, Palais Presidential Ave de la Marina, Lomé Togo*

EYBL, VLADISLAV, pharmacologist; b. Pisek, Czechoslovakia, June 20, 1932; s. Antonin and Marie E.; m. Marie Lucakova, May 7, 1958; 1 child, Vladislava. MD, Charles U., 1957, PhD, 1964; DSc, Czech Acad. Sci., 1985. From asst. prof. to prof. med. faculty Charles U., Pilsen, Czech Republic, 1957—. Avocation: music. Office: Charles Univ, Med Faculty in Pilsen, 30166 Pilsen Czech Republic

EYCKMANS, LUC A. F., medical institute administrator; b. Antwerp, Belgium, Feb. 23, 1930; s. Robert F. J. and Alice L. (Van Genechten) E.; m. Godelieve Cornelissen, July 15, 1957; children: Bob, Marc, Monique, Wim, Christiane, Johan,, Lilian. MD, Katholieke Univ., Leuven, Belgium, 1954; postgrad., Inst. Tropical Medicine, Antwerp, Belgium, 1957; PhD, Katholieke Univ., Leuven, 1972; D. (hon.), U. Lille (France), 1989. Resident in internal medicine Katholieke U. Leuven, 1954-57, 60-61; physician Cath. Missions, Kisantu, Congo, 1957-60; fellow in medicine Baylor U. Med. Ctr., Dallas, 1961-63, Cornell U. Med. Ctr., N.Y.C., 1963-64; asst. prof. U. Leuven, 1965-72; prof. internal medicine U. Antwerp, 1973-76; dir., prof. Inst. Tropical Medicine, Antwerp, 1976-95; sec.-gen. TROPMEDEUROP, Europe, 1983-89; exec. dir. Francqui Found., 1992—. Contbr. articles to profl. jours., chpts. to books. Major Medic Belgian mil. res., 1989. Named Grand-Officer, Order of the (Belgian) Crown. Mem. Belgian Soc. Tropical Medicine (sec.-gen. 1976-95), Royal Acad. Overseas Scis. (Belgium), Nat. Acad. Medicine (corr., Paris), Royal Soc. Tropical Medicine and Hygiene (hon., London), Soc. de Pathologie Exotique (hon., Paris), Academia Europaea. Home: Wildenhoge 26, B 3020 Winksele-Herent Belgium Office: Francqui-Found, Defacqz St 1, B1000 Brussels Belgium

EYDE, GEORGE F., real estate developer; b. Lansing, Mich., Apr. 28, 1935; s. Sam A. and Eva A. (Nouhan) E.; m. Mary Ann Christensen, Dec. 18, 1969; children: Evemarie, George M., Sarah, Nathaniel, Nancy, Nicholas. Student, Mich. State U., East Lansing. Cert. builder, Mich.; lic. real estate agt., Mich. Ptnr. Eyde Co., East Lansing, 1958—; land developer, 1958—; mem. corp. devel. coun. WKAR-TV. Bd. dirs. St. Thomas Sch. Athletic Coun.; pres. Lansing Cath. Cen. Athletic Assn. With Mich. N.G., 1958-64. Mem. Lansing C. of C. (bd. dirs., pres.), Greater Lansing Home Builders Assn., Nat. Assn. Realtors, Mich. Home Builders Assn., City of East Lansing Bus. Assn., Downtown Mchts. Assn. of lansing, Internat. Coun. of Shopping Ctrs. Avocations: racquetball, hand ball, bicycling. Home: PO Box 4218 East Lansing MI 48826-4218 Office: Eyde Co 4660 S Hagadorn Rd Ste 660 East Lansing MI 48823-6804

EYDEN, BRIAN PHILIP, tumor diagnostician, medical researcher; b. Burton-upon-Trent, Eng., Nov. 25, 1947; s. Alfred and Sarah Ellen (Tivey) E.; m. Freda Elizabeth Hamilton, Nov. 29, 1975; children: Joanna Maxine, Suzanne Hamilton. BSc, U. London, 1969; PhD, U. Glasgow, Scotland, 1974. Postdoctoral rsch. fellow U. Glasgow, 1972-75; EEC rsch. fellow Ctr. Nuc. Studies, Mol, Belgium, 1975-78; clin. scientist Christie Hosp., Manchester, Eng., 1978—. Author: Organelles in Tumor Diagnosis: an Ultrastructural Atlas, 1996; co-author: Handbook of Diagnostic Electron Microscopy for Pathologists-in-Training, 1996; contbr. over 125 rsch. articles to sci. pubs. including Ultrastructural Pathology, Histopathology, Jour. Clin. Pathology, Am. Jour. Surg. Pathology, others. Mem. Soc. Ultrastructural Pathology. Socialist. Avocations: playing piano, orchestral music, photography. Home: 3 Cherry Lane, Cheshire Sale M33 4NF, England Office: Christie Hosp NHS Trust, Wilmslow Rd, Manchester M20 4BX, England

EYHERABIDE, JUAN JOSE, education educator; b. Balcarce, Argentina, Jan. 27, 1944; s. Hector Eduardo and Joaquina (Ezcurdia) E.; m. Margarita Vitale, July 28, 1944; children: Esteban, Mercedes, Santiago. Agrl. Engr., Faculty of Agrl. Scis., Argentina, 1967. Extensionist Inta, Balcarce, Argentina, 1967-71; farms mgr. Balcarce, 1971-76; field rschr. Imperial Chem. Industry, Balcarce, 1976-80; prof. Nat. U. of Mar Del Plata, Argentina, 1980—. Author: (books) Toxicidad Vegetal para el Ganado, 1991, Problematica y Control de Malezas en Papa, 1995, Bases para el manejo del Maiz, el Girasol, y la Soja, 200. Mem. AAAS, N.Y. Acad. Scis., Weed Sci. Soc. Am. Roman Catholic. Avocations: squash, jogging. Office: Facultad de Ciencias, Agrarias CC 276, Buenos Aires, 7620 Balcarce Argentina

EYJÓLFSSON, REYNIR HALLDÓR, science administrator; b. Haugar, Skriddalur, Iceland, Mar. 19, 1937; s. Eyjolfur Halldorsson and Kristin Einarsdottir; m. Helga Vilhjalmsdottir, Dec. 15, 1962 (dec. June 1990); 1 child, Kristin. MS in Pharmacy, Pharm. U., Copenhagen, 1964; PhD, Pharm. U., 1968. Provisor State Import Pharms., Reykjavik, Iceland, 1964-65; amanuensis Pharm. U., Copenhagen, 1968-70; quality rsch. mgr. Pharmaco Ltd., Reykjavik, 1971-75; official Ministry of Health, Reykjavik, 1976-81; drug formulation mgr. Delta Ltd., Hafnarfjordur, Iceland, 1982—. Author: Cyanogenic Glycosides in Nature, 1968; co-author: Recent Advances in Chemistry of Cyanogenic Glycosides, 1970; contbr. articles to profl. jours. Grantee Danish Ministry Edn., 1965-68. Home: Eyrarholt 6, IS 220 Hafnarfjordur Iceland Office: Delta Ltd, Reykjavikurvegur 78, IS 220 Hafnarfjordur Iceland

EYMAN, RUSSELL GARDNER, periodontist; b. Tallahassee, Fla., Mar. 21, 1944; s. David Russell and Eleanor Mildred (Gardner) E.; m. Jan Rene Oxner (div. Oct. 1996); children: Jeanne K., Ann T. DDS, Emory U., 1969; MS, U. Tex., Houston, 1976. Commd. 2d lt. USAF, 1969, advanced through grades to col., dental officer, 1969-79, ret., 1979; periodontist Warner Robins, Ga., 1979—. Mem. adminstrv. bd. Trinity United Meth. Ch., Warner Robins, Ga., 1993-95. Fellow Ga. Dental Assn., 1990. Mem. ADA (pres. Ga. chpt. 1969—), Am. Acad. Periodontology, So. Acad. Periodontology (editor 1992-97), Am. Coll. Dentistry, Internat. Coll. Dentists, Ga. Acad. Dental Practice, Warner Robins C. of C. (dir. 1995-96). Republican. Avocations: golf, skiing. Home: 2301 Houston Lk Rd Perry GA 31069 Office: 225 Carl Vinson Pkwy Warner Robins GA 31088-5831

EYMIEU, ALEX, management consultant; b. Tours, France, Sept. 1, 1969; s. Guy E. and Eliane (Le Roy de Lanauze Moline) E.; m. Miao Chuan Wang, Sept. 6, 1995; children: Delphine, Camille. BA, Weller Internat. Mgmt., France, 1990; Cert., McLaren Coll. Bus., San Francisco, 1991. Export mgr. EFI France, Metz, 1991-92, EFI Taiwan, Taipei, 1992; import mgr. Icok Corp., Taipei, 1992-96; cons. TAO Taiwan, Taipei, 1996-98, mgmt. cons., 1998—. Mem. Am. C. of C. Taipei (membership com.), European Coun. for Commerce and Trade, French C. of C. in Taiwan. E-mail: AlexEymieu@mail.net.tw. Office: TAO Taiwan, Ste 1021, Min Chuan East Rd Sect 3, Taipei Taiwan

EYRAUD, HENRI LOUIS CHARLES, chemical engineer; b. Saint-Chamond, France, June 23, 1920; s. Henri Adolphe and Georgette Marie Marcelle (Malecot) E.; m. Odette Julie Jacob Eyraud, July 19, 1945; children: Christian, Lysiane, Denis, Jean-Michel, Claudine. Degree in Phys. Sci., U. Lyon, 1944; degree in Chemistry, 1945, PhD in Physics, 1949. Asst. prof. U. Lyon, 1948-58; assoc. prof., 1958-60, prof., 1960-86, prof. emeritus, 1986-90; mem. coun. Superior U., 1977-82; cons. French Atomic Energy Commn., 1955-86, Tissmetal-Lionel Dupont Co., 1960-81, Krebs Co., 1995-98; head of dept. of mechanical and civil engring., Nat. Inst. Applied Scis. of Lyon, 1960-67; pres. Assn. for Applied Rsch. and for Continuing Edn., 1966-90, Ecoprocess Ltd. Co., 1991. Author: Acta Metallurgica, 1974, Thermochimica Acta, 1986, Jour. Membrane Sci., 1992, Filtration and Separation, 1993; contbr. articles to profl. jours. Decorated officer Nat. Order of Merit, comer. Order Palmes Academiques (France); recipient Herpin prize Académie des Sciences Belles-Lettes et Arts of Lyon, 1992. Mem. Internat. Rotary Club, N.Y. Acad. Scis. Achievements include research in thermogravimetry, thermoporometry, permporometry, wet electrostatic precipitators; inventor electromigration of the grain boundaries of a massive metal. Avocations: fishing, gardening. Office: Ecoprocess SA, 55 Rue Joliot Curie, 69005 Lyon France

EYSENCK, MICHAEL WILLIAM, psychologist, educator; b. London, Feb. 8, 1944; s. Hans Jurgen and Margaret Malcolm (Davies) E.; m. Mary Christine Kabyn, Mar. 22, 1975; children: Fleur Davina Ruth, William James Thomas, Juliet Margaret Maria. BA, U. London, 1965, PhD, 1973. Lectr. Birkbeck Coll., U. London, 1965-81, reader, 1981-87; prof. psychology Royal Holloway and Bedford New Coll., U. London, 1987—. Author: Human Memory: Theory, Research and Individual Differences, 1977, Attention and Arousal: Cognition and Performance, 1982, A Handbook of Cogni-

tive Psychology, 1984, (with others) Personality and Individual Differences, 1985, The Psychology of Happiness: Facts and Myths, 1990 (with others) Cognitive Psychology: A Student's Handbook, 1990, Anxiety: The Cognitive Perspective, 1992, Principles of Cognitive Psychology, 1993, Perspectives on Psychology, 1994, Individual Differences: Normal and Abnormal, 1994, Simply Psychology, 1996, Anxiety and Cognition: A Unified Theory, 1997, Psychology: An Integrated Approach, 1998, Psychology: Student's Handbook, 2000, (with others) Psychology for AS Lead, 2000; editor: European Jour. Cognitive Psychology, 1989-92. Mem. European Soc. for Cognitive Psychology (mem. adv. bd. 1985—), Brit. Psychol. Soc. (chmn. cognitive psychology sect. 1982-87). Avocations: tennis, travel, walking, golf. Office: U London Royal Holloway & Bedford New Coll, Egham Hill, Egham Surrey TW20 0EX, England

EYSKENS, ERIK JOANNES, surgeon, educator; b. Leuven, Belgium, July 20, 1935; s. Gaston and Gilberte (DePetter) E.; m. Julie Ponet, Oct. 16, 1965; children: Patricia, Werner, Thomas. PhD, Catholic U. of Leuven, Belgium, 1960, Specialist in Surgery, 1966, D Surg. Sci., 1972. Asst. prof. Catholic U. of Leuven, 1972; prof. U. Antwerp, Belgium, 1992—; chief dept. of surgery St. Vincent Hosp., Belgium, 1980-92; v.p. med. dept. U. Antwerp, 1986-88; chief surgery dept. Univ. Hosp., Antwerp, 1992; chmn. med. com. U. Hosp. Antwerp, 1997—. Author: Leerboek Chirurgie, 1983, 4th rev. edit. 1997; author, editor: Codex Medicus, 1985, 10th rev. edit. 1996; contbr. articles to profl. jours. Mem. Acad. De Chirurgie, Royal Acad. Medicine, Nat. and Internat. Surgical Assn., DePrince (Antwerp), Order the Crown (comdr. 1989), Order of Leopold (officer). Roman Catholic. Home: Troyentenhoflaan 14, 2600 Antwerp Belgium Office: U Hosp Antwerp, Wilrijkstraat 10, 2650 Edgem Antwerp Belgium

EYT, PIERRE ETIENNE LOUIS, archbishop; b. Laruns, Basses-Pyrénées, France, June 4, 1934; s. Jean and Joséphine (Gabastou) E. Student, Inst. Études Juridiques et Économiques, Pau, France, Inst. Catholique, Toulouse, France; PhD in Theology, Gregorian U., Rome. Ordained priest, 1961. Chaplain Ch. Saint-Louis des Français, Rome, 1963; prof. dept. theology U. Toulouse, France, 1967-72; vice rector Inst. Catholique, Toulouse, 1972-75, rector, 1975-81; rector Inst. Catholique, Paris, 1981-86; asst. archbishop Bordeaux, France, 1986-89, archbishop, 1989—; cardinal, 1994—; mem. Commn. Théologique Internat., 1980, Sacré Congrégation pour l'Edn. Catholique, Rome, 1989—; pres. Union des Établissements d'Enseignement Supérieur Catholique, 1985; spl. sec. Synod Bishops, 1987. Author: Je Crois En Dieu, 1985, L'Avenir de l'Homme, 1986; contbr. numerous articles to philos. and theol. jours. Named Chevalier des Palmes Académiques, Officier du Mérite de la République Fédéral d'Allemagne, 1979. Office: Archevêché, 183 Cours de la Somme BP 79, 33034 Bordeaux France*

EYTON, JOHN TREVOR, senator, business executive; b. Quebec, Que., Can., July 12, 1934; s. John and Dorothy Isabel (dec.) E.; m. Barbara Jane Montgomery, Feb. 13, 1955; children: Adam Tudor, Christopher Montgomery, Deborah Jane Findlay, Susannah Margaret Belton, Sarah Elizabeth Gould. BA, U. Toronto, Can., 1957, LLB, 1960; LLD, U. Waterloo, 1992. Bar: Ont. 1962, created Queen's Counsel. Read law Tory, Tory, DesLauriers & Binnington, Toronto, Ont., 1960-62, assoc., 1962-67, ptnr., 1967-79; pres., CEO Brascan Ltd., Toronto, 1979-90, chmn., 1990-98; chancellor U. King's Coll., Halifax, N.S., Can., 1996—; senator Senate of Can., Ottawa, Ont., Can., 1990—; mem. bd. Brascan Corp., Toronto; bd. dirs. Brascan Corp., Ivernia West Plc., Gen. Motors of Can. Ltd., M.A. Hanna Co., Noranda Inc., Coca Cola Enterprises Inc., Trilon Fin. Corp., IMAX Corp. and Toronto 2008 Olympic Bid Corp.; chmn. bd. govs. Can. Sports Hall of Fame; adv. bd. Nestle. Gov. Can. Olympic Found.; exec. com. Brit. N.Am. Com. Decorated Order of Can., 1986. Mem. Upper Can. Law Soc., Can. Bar Assn., Toronto Club, York Club, Caledon Mountain Trout Club, Devil's Pulpit Golf Club (Caledon), The Rideau Club (Ottawa), Royal Palm Yacht and Country Club (Boca Raton). Progressive Conservative. Anglican. Avocations: ski, golf. Home: Tudorcroft RR 2, Caledon, ON Canada L0N 1C0 Office: Brascan Corp, 181 Bay St Ste 4400, Toronto, ON Canada M5J 2T3 also: Senate of Can, Parliament Bldgs Rm 561-S, Ottawa, ON Canada KTA UA4

EYZAGUIRRE, JOSE MARIA, lawyer; b. Santiago, Chile, Oct. 31, 1936; s. Jose Maria and Sara (Garcia de la Huerta) E.; m. Carmen Baeza Alamos, Aug. 27, 1961; children: José María, Sebastián, Carmen, Cristóbal, Nicolás y Catalina. Secondary Lic., Colegio San Ignacio, Santiago; Degree in Law, Cath. U., 1960. Lawyer, Supreme Ct. of Chile. Prof. law Cath. U., Santiago, 1965; ptnr. Claro y Cía, Santiago, 1968—. Pres. Com. to Draft Property Clause in Constn., Santiago, 1974-77; mem. Civil Code Reform Com., Santiago, 1980-86. Mem. Chilean Bar Assn., Internat. Bar Assn., Interam. Bar Assn. (coun. mem.). Renovación Nacional Party. Roman Catholic. Office: Claro Y Cia, Gertrudis Echenique 30 Las Condes, Santiago Chile

EZAKI, YASUO, ecologist; b. Osaka, Japan, Dec. 12, 1951; s. Zenichi and Hisako (Tatsumi) E.; m. Fujiyo Noguchi, Mar. 24, 1985; children: Junpei, Shujiro. BS, Kyoto Univ., Kyoto, Japan, 1976, MS, 1978, D in sci., 1985. Lectr. Ritsumeikan Univ., Kyoto, 1989; supr. Hyogo Prefectural Bd. of Edn., Kobe, Japan, 1989-92; chief researcher Mus. of Nature and Human Activities, Hyogo, Sanda, Japan, 1992; assoc. prof. Himeji Inst. Tech., Sanda, Japan, 1992—, prof., 1999; com. mem. Stork Reintroduction Hyogo Prefecture, Kobe, Japan, 1992—. Author: Animal Societies, 1994; editor: The Ecology and Mating System of The Great Reed Warbler, 1995, Conservation of Biological Communities in Rivers, Ponds and Paddy Field, 1998; contbr. articles to profl. jours. Adv. Off. of Kinki Dist. Min. of Construction, 1993—. Fellow Ornithological Soc. Japan; mem. Ecological Soc. Japan, British Ornithologists Union. Avocations: badminton, sightseeing in historical places, bird-watching. Office: Himeji Inst Tech, Yayoi-Ga-Oka 6, 669-1546 Sanda Japan

EZCURRA, MARIA CRISTINA, physician, researcher; b. Burnos Aires, Argentina, Apr. 29, 1954; d. Oscar and Hilda (Gonzalez) E.; m. Eduardo Pedro Strusi, Feb. 26, 1981. BS, Buenos Aires Nat., Argentina, 1972, MD, 1978. Med. Diplomate 1978, Infectious Diseases Diplomate 1984. Resident in infectious diseases Muniz Hosp., Buenos Aires, Argentina, 1979-83, resident chief in infectious diseases, 1983-84; attending physician Clinicas Hosp., Buenos Aires, Argentina, 1985-96, French Hosp., Buenos Aires, Argentina, 1988-92; asst. prof. in infectious diseases Buenos Aires (Argentina) U., 1993-99; chief in infectious disease unit French Hosp., Buenos Aires, Argentina, 1992—. Co-author: Infectologia, 1994, Posgrado en Cirigua Maxilogalia, 1998; contbr. articles to profl. jours. Recipient Annual Award in Infectious Diseases, Clinicas Hosp., 1993. Mem. Argentine SOc. Infectious Diseases, Jour. Infectologia y Microgiologia Clinica. Avocations: swimming, reading, snorkeling. Home phone: 54 1 4775-4666.

EZE, FRIDAY CHINYERE, gynecologist; b. Ahoada, Rivers, Nigeria, June 11, 1933; s. Enoch Ugoma Nune and Naomi (Okporo) E.; m. Rosaline Nkem Nwugo, June 11, 1978; m. Rosaline Nkem Nwugo, June 11, 1978; 7 children. MB BChir, Glasgow (Scotland) U., 1964. Gen. practitioner Ministry of Health, Nigeria, 1965-73, cons., 1978-83; chief med. dir. Victory Clinics Ltd., Port Harcourt, Nigeria, 1984—. Commr. of Fin., Rivers State, Nigeria, 1983. Fellow Royal Coll. Ob-Gyn. London, MCOA; mem. AAAS, Brit. Med. Assn., Soc. Gynecology Obstetrics of Nigeria. Anglican. Avocations: reading, table and lawn tennis. Office: Victory Clinics Ltd, 175 King Perekule St, Port Harcourt Nigeria

EZEAKU, LEVI CHUKWURA, economist, educator; b. Agulu, Anaocha, Nigeria, Mar. 10, 1945; s. Festus Moha Ezeaku and Lucy Amodo Adi; m. Irene Delunebechukwu Obi, June 27, 1970; children: Chidinma, Chinomnso, Ogochukwu, Kosieme, Chisomje. BSc in Econs., U. Nigeria, 1973; MSc, London Sch. Econs., 1977; PhD (hon.), World U., Ariz., 1986. Planning officer East Ctrl. State Govt., Enugu, Nigeria, 1974; jr. fellow U. Nigeria, Nsukka, 1974-76, asst. lectr., 1977-78; from lectr. I to reader Anambra State Coll. Edn., Awka, Nigeria, 1978-90, head dept., 1978-82, dean faculty, 1980-87; sr. lectr. Nnamdi Azikiwe U., Awka, 1990—, head dept. econs., 1990-95; cons. Crownbank Corp., Anambra, 1996—. Co-author, editor Principles and Practice of Management and Business Studies, 1986; author: Commerce for the Certificate Year, 1980, When Will the Messiah Come, 1992, Introduction to Microeconomic Principles, 1994. Chmn. adv. com. on econ. and fin. matters Anambra State Govt., 1992-93; patron Boys and Girls Brigade, St. Stephen's Parish, Agulu, Nigeria, 1995—; chmn. St. Stephen's Ch. Parish, Agulu, 2000. Fellow Internat. Biog. Assn. (mem. hon. adv. bd.). Anglican. Avocations: gardening, writing, music. Home: No 1 Nwagene Rd, Ifiteani Agulu Box 47, Agulu Anaocha Nigeria Office: Nnamdi Azikiwe U Awka, PMB 5025, Awka Anambra Nigeria

EZEANYIKA, LAWRENCE UCHENNA SUNDAY, biochemistry educator; b. Enugu, Nigeria, Dec. 18, 1960; s. Innocent Uzoetuo and Anderline Adadinma (Umeagukwu) E. BSc, U. Nigeria, Nsukka, 1985, MSc, 1989, PhD, 1995. Demonstrator U. Nigeria, Nsukka, 1987-89, sr. lectr., 1999—; lectr. II U. Maiduguri, Nigeria, 1990-96; lectr. I U. Maiduguri, 1996-99. Contbr. articles to profl. jours. Scholar Fed. Govt. Nigeria, 1987, Commonwealth, 1992. Roman Catholic. Avocations: football, table tennis, reading novels, listening to Christian music, singing. Office: Dept Biochemistry, Univ Nigeria, Nsukka Enugu, Nigeria

EZELL, JAMES NORMAN, II, environmental engineer; b. York, Ala., Aug. 14, 1947; s. James Norman and Peggy (Tillery) E.; m. Carolyn Breckinridge Woltz, Jan. 15, 1972; 1 child, Jonathan. BA, U. Ala., Tuscaloosa, 1969, MS in Engring., 1991. Cert. profl. engr., Ala. Art dir. U. Ala. TV, Tuscaloosa, 1969-72; owner Ezell Artist's Materials, Tuscaloosa, 1971-77; drafting supr. Almon Assocs., Inc., Tuscaloosa, 1977-88, engr., 1988-92, engr., assoc., 1992-97, ptnr., corp. sec., 1997—, also bd. dirs.; cons. Ala. Dept. Transp., Montgomery. Photographer Highlights for Children, 1990. Host father Acad. Yr. Am., Tuscaloosa, 1995, 96; mem. curriculum com. Ala. Sch. Fine Arts, 1998. Methodist. Avocations: book collecting, antiques, photography. Fax: 205-349-2107. Office: Almon Assocs Inc 2008 12th St Tuscaloosa AL 35401-2904

EZENWA, IKECHUKWU VINCENT, forage scientist, educator; b. Aba, Abia State, Nigeria, July 25, 1964; s. Ezenwa Eugene Nwafor and Maria Nwakaku Nwafor; m. Ebele Uzoamaka Onwumbiko, June 17, 1995; children: Chibuikem Chisom, Amarachukwu Chibuzo. BS in Animal Sci., U. Ibadan, Nigeria, 1986, MS in Agronomy, 1988, PhD, 1995. Rsch. asst. and assoc. Internat. Livestock Rsch. Inst., Ibadan, 1986-92; rsch. assoc. Internat. Inst. ropical Agr., Ibadan, 1992; lectr. II forage sci. U. Ibadan, 1993—, rep. of congregation, 1996-98; grad. assoc. Internat. Livestock Rsch. Inst., Addis Ababa, Ethiopia, 1988-92; Japan Sci. and Tech. Agy. fellow Nat. Grassland Rsch. Inst., Nishinasuno, Tochigi, 1998-2000; cons. assisted agrl. devel. project World Bank, Oyo State, Nigeria, 1996. Contbr. articles to sci. jours., including Tropical Grasslands, Bull. Animal Health and Prodn. in Africa, Agroforestry Sys. Rsch. grantee Internat. Found. for Sci., Sweden, 1997-98; Japan Sci. and Tech. Corp. and Japan Internat. Sci. and Tech. Exch. Ctr. fellow, Tsukuba, 1998-2000. Mem. AAAS, Am. AGronomy Soc., Crop Sci. Soc. Am., Soil Sci. Soc. Am., Tropical Grassland Soc. Australia, N.Y. Acad. Scis. Avocations: tennis, soccer. Fax: 81-287-36-6629. E-mail: ikeezenwa@hotmail.com. Home: U Ibadan, Dept Agronomy, Ibadan Iti St, Nigeria Office: Nat Grassland Rsch Inst, Senbonmatsu 768, Tochigi Nishinasuno 329-2793, Japan

EZENWA, JOSEPHINE NWABUOKU, social worker; b. Oct. 20, 1959; d. Igwe Silas O. and H.R.H. Veronica A. Ezenwa; children: Bryan, Brenda, Sean. BA Psychology & Human Svcs. with honors, Fontbonne Coll., St. Louis, 1980; MSW, Washington U., St. Louis, 1981; postgrad., St. Louis U., 1991-93. Rsch. dir. Nat. Benevolent Assn., St. Louis, 1981-89; tchr. University City Sch. Dist., 1989-94; therapist Presbyn. Children's Home, St. Louis, 1994-95; nephrology social worker St. Louis Regional Med. Ctr., 1995-97; founder, chair St. Louis Regional Med. Ctr. Dialysis Support Group, 1995-97; social worker St. Louis U. Hosp., 1997; CEO, pres. BBS Care U.S.A., Inc., St. Louis, 1997—; founder/chair St. Louis Regional Med. Ctr. Dialysis Support Group, 1995-97; chair long range planning com. Washington U.; presenter in field. Mem. NASW, NAFE, Coun. Nephrology Social Workers, Nat. Assn. Forensic Counselors, Nat. Assn. Cognitive Behavioral Therapists, Washington U. Sch. Social Work Alumni Assn. (bd. dirs.), Creve Coeur-Olive C. of C., Lions Club. Avocations: choreography, fashion consulting, event coordinating, design, travel. Office: St Louis U Hosp 3536 Vista at Grand Saint Louis MO 63110 also: BBS Care USA Inc 8420 Delmar Blvd Ste 505 Saint Louis MO 63124-2180 also: BBS Care USA Inc 8420 Delmar Blvd Ste 505 Saint Louis MO 63124-2180

EZEONU, FRANCIS CHUKWUEMEKA, biochemist, educator; b. Lagos, Nigeria, Oct. 25, 1963; s. Francis Iwegbunam and Josephine Amaechi (Obiefuna) E.; m. Jane Nkoli Oraka, Aug. 5, 1994; children: Kenechukwu, Kosisochukwu. BSc with honors, Anambra State U. Tech., Enugu, Nigeria, 1986; MSc, U. Ibadan, Nigeria, 1988; PhD, Nnamdi Azikiwe U., Awka, Nigeria, 1992. Grad. demonstrator U. Ibadan, 1988; asst. lectr. Anambra State U. Tech., Enugu, 1989-90, lectr. II, 1990-93; lectr. I Nnamdi Azikiwe U., Awka, 1993-96, sr. lectr., 1996—; mem. governing coun. Nnamdi Azikiwe U., 1997—. Co-author: Xenobiotics and Drug Action, 1997; contbr. articles to profl. jours. Pres. students union Anambra State U. Tech., 1985; br. sec. acad. staff union of univs. Nnamdi Azikiwe U., 1992-94. Recipient Profl. Svc. award Rotaract Dist. 9140, Nigeria, 1995. Mem. Biochem. Soc. Nigeria, Found. for African Devel. Through Internat. Biotechnology. Office: Nnamdi Azikiwe U, Applied Biochem PMB 5025, Awka Anambra, Nigeria

EZERSKAYA, ELENA VLADIMIROVNA, physicist; b. Kharkov, Ukraine, May 5, 1957; d. Vladimir Osiphovich and Valentina Aleksandrovna (Fedorets) E.; m. Vladislav Olegovich Cheranovskii, June 27, 1992. MS, Kharkov State Univ., Kharkov, 1979, PhD, 1985, docent, 1994. Researcher Kharkov State Univ., 1982-89, docent, 1989—. Contbr. articles to profl. jours. Office: Kharkov State Univ, Svoboda Sq 4, 61077 Kharkov Ukraine

EZHOV, YURI VLADIMIROVICH, retired mechanical engineer; b. Ufa, USSR, Apr. 14, 1926; s. Vladimir Maximovich and Maria Mikhailovna (Batrakova) E.; m. Zlata Mikhailovna Chadova, 1948 (div. 1963); m. Victoria Ivanovna Perevalova, 1963 (div. 1982); m. Lidia Ivanovna Rezvanova, 1982; children: Tatjana, Elena, Galina; 1 stepchild, Olga. Degree in mech. engring., Ural Poly. Inst., Sverdlovsk, USSR, 1948. Engr., designer Mech. Works of Dalstroy, Komsomolsk on Amur, USSR, 1948-54, Works of Low Voltage Equipment, Ufa, 1955-56, Works # 161, Ufa, 1956-57; sr. engr., designer Proekt-Inst. Sverdniptimash, Sverdlovsk, 1958-61, Exptl. Design Bur. Lighting, Ufa, 1967-69; engr. designer Ural br. NIAT, 1961-67; engr. designer Ufa Motor Works, 1969-85; locksmith Ufa Apparatus-Bldg. Works, Ufa, 1985-87; patient lift operator Hosp. No. 21, Ufa, 1987-93. Contbr. articles to profl. publs.; patentee in field. Mem. Bashkortostan-USA Soc. Avocations: radio, photography, motorcycling, amateur radio. Home: 50 Yrs USSR St 48 252, 450071 Ufa Russia

EZRATTY-BADER, MYRIAM, judge; b. Nice, Alpes-Maritimes, France, Dec. 7, 1929; m. José Ezratty, June 8, 1956. Diplome law, U. Aix-En-Provence, licenciate letters. Assigned to bench prosecutor's office Région de Nancy, Région Parisienne, 1953-58; bureau head Mgmt. of Edn., Mgmt. Civil Affairs and Seal Justice Min., 1958-74; tech. cons. Cabinet Simone Veil, 1974-79; pres. Ct. Appeals, Paris, 1979-81; dir. edn. oversight, 1981-83, dir. penitentary adminstrn., 1983-86; gen. counsel Supreme Ct., 1986-88; 1st pres. Paris Ct. Appeals, 1988-96, hon. 1st pres., 1997—. Mem. Franco-Brit. Jurists Soc., pres. bd. dirs., Internat. Ctr. for Prevention of Crime. Office: Cour D'Appel, 34 Quai de Orfevres, 75055 Paris France also: Internat Ctr for Prevention of Crime, 507 place d'Armes, Montreal, PQ Canada

ÉZSIÁS, ANDRÁS, consultant maxillofacial surgeon; b. Budapest, Hungary, Nov. 1, 1953; s. Brunó György and Maria Magdolna (Herczeg) É.; m. Zsuzsanna Bártfai (div. 1986); 1 child, Dániel; m. Edina Érsek, 1990; children: Monica, Alexandra, Mark. DMD, Semmelweis U., Budapest, 1977, MD, 1981; spl. cert. in gen. surgery, Postgrad. Inst. of Budapest, 1986; spl. bd. cert. in oral and maxillofacial surgery, Royal Coll. Surgeons England, Specialist Tng. Authority, UK, 1996; postgrad. trainee surgeon, Janos Hosp., Budapest, Hungary, 1981-86. Diplomate European Bd. Oro-Maxillofacial Surgery (fellow). Sr. house officer Liverpool (Eng.) Dental Hosp., 1988-90, St. Lawrence Hosp., Chepstow, Wales, 1990; registrar Queen Alexandra Hosp., Portsmouth, Eng., 1991-92, St. Lawrence Hosp. Chepstow and U. Hosp. Wales, Cardiff, 1992-94; sr. registrar Cheltenham Gloucester Hosps., Eng., 1994-95, John Radcliffe Hosp., Oxford, Eng., 1995-98; cons. Prince Charles, Princess of Wales & Royal Glamorgan Hosps., Wales, 1998—; tchr. undergrad. program Janos Tchg. Hosp., Hungary, 1981-86, Univ. Hosp. Wales, Cardiff, 1993-94, Oxford U., 1995-98; lectr. Sch. Nursing, Portsmouth, Eng., 1991-92. Contbr. articles to profl. jours. Sub-lt. Hungarian Army Med Corps, 1981-82. Fellow Royal Coll. Surgeons Eng., Royal Coll. Surgeons Edinburgh, Internat. Assn. Oral and Maxillofacial Surgeons, British Assn. Oral and Maxillofacial Surgeons, European Assn. for Cranio-Maxillofacial Surgery, Brit. Assn. Head and Neck Oncologists, European Acad. Facial Plastic Surgery. Roman Catholic. Avocations: travel, mountain climbing. Office: Prince Charles Hosp, Maxillofacial Unit, Merthyr Tydfil CF 47 9 DT, Wales

EZZAT, EMILE MICHEL, airline company executive; b. Cairo, Egypt, Jan. 25, 1936; s. Michel Rizkalla and Eugine (Henen) E.; m. Sylvia Henry Archache, Apr. 27, 1963; children: Mike, Carin. Grad., U. Tex. Ticket office mgr. S.A.S., Cairo, 1954-58; dist. sales mgr. S.A.S., Alexandria, Egypt, 1959-67; gen. sales mgr. S.A.S., Cairo, 1968-80; gen. mgr. Egypt and Sudan S.A.S., 1981—, gen. mgr. Egypt, Sudan, Ethiopia, Djibouto, Saudi Arabia, Kuwait, Bahrain, Dubai, Sharjan, Abu Daubi, Oman, Qajar, South and North Yemen, 1989—. Vice chmn. Bd. Airline Reps., Egypt. Recipient Aviation Award, Ministry of Civil Aviation, Cairo, 1977; Hon. Disting. Citizen, State of Wash., Seattle, 1983. Fellow Rotary Club; mem. Maadi Sporting Club, Maadi Yacht Club, Auto Club. Avocations: tennis, reading. Office: Scandinavian Airlines, 2 Champollion St, Cairo Egypt

EZZINE, JELEL, engineering educator, consultant; b. Nabeul, Tunisia, Jan. 17, 1959; s. Mohamed E. and Saida El-Adjmi. BS, Ecole Nat. d'Ingenieurs Tunis, Tunisia, 1982; MSEE, U. Ala., Huntsville, 1985; PhD, Ga. Inst. Tech., 1989; Habilitation Universitaire, 2000. Asst. prof. King Fahd U. Petroleum and Minerals, Dhahran, Saudi Arabia, 1989-95; acting chmn., 1991; maître asst. Ecole Nat. d'Ingénieurs de Tunis, Tunisia, 1995—; vis. rsch. prof. Dartmouth Coll., Hanover, N.H., 1998—, Automation and Robotics Rsch. Inst. U. Tex.-Arlington, Ft. Worth, 1998; cons. Inst. Regional Scis. Informatiques et Telecomms., Tunis, Tunisia, 1996-98, Group Chimique Tunisien, Gabes, 1996-98; spkr. in field. Editor: The Arabian Jour. Scis. and Engring., 1993; contbr. articles to profl. jours., chpts. to books. Founding mem. Nabeul 21 (Tunisia), 1998; mem. The Balaton Group, 1998. Fellow Jemison Inst.; mem. IEEE (sr. mem., CEB assoc. editor), Assn. Splsts. Electricien Tunisie (gen.sec. 1996—), Internat. Fedn. Automatic Control. Muslim. Avocations: astronomy, reading, exercising. E-mail: jelel.ezzine@ieee.org. Home: 47 Ave Habib Karma, 8000 Nabeul Tunisia Office: ENIT, BP # 37, 1002 Tunis-Belvédere Tunis, Tunisia

FABBRINI, SERGIO, political science educator; b. Pesaro, Marche, Italy, Feb. 21, 1949; s. Gino and Sisla (Cavazza) F.; m. Manuela Cescatti, Mar. 26, 1956; children: Federico, Sebastiano. Diploma in Sociology cum laude, Trento U., Italy, 1973. Asst. in polit. economy Faculty of Econs., Trento U., 1974-76; asst. in polit. economy and sociology Faculty of Sociology, Trento U., 1977-81, tenured researcher in polit. studies, 1982-91, prof. pub. policy, 1991-93; prof. internat. rels. Naples U., 1993-96; prof. polit. sci. Trento U., 1996—; prof. comparative politics U. Calif., Berkeley, 1996, 97; chmn. European Consortium for Polit. Rsch. Standing Group on Am. Politics Promoter, 1988-93; vis. prof. U. Calif., Berkeley, Harvard U. Author: American Neoconservatism, 1986, Politics and Social Change, 1988, Citizen's Politics, 1991, American Presidentialism, 1993, Which Democracy? 1994, 3rd edit., 1999, The Rules of Democracy, 1997, The Democratic Prince, 1998, (with S. Vasallo) The Government, 1999, Internal Vetoes and External Pressures: The Italian Political Change, 2000, Pressures and Vetoes: Political Change in Italy, 2000; contbr. articles to sci. jours. NATO sr. fellow U.S. and Italian Rsch. Com. fellow U. Calif., Berkeley, 1982, 88, IGS fellow U. Calif., Berkeley, 1991. Mem. Am. Polit. Sci. Assn., Soc. Italiana Scienza Politica, Internat. Polit. Sci. Assn. Avocations: swimming, mountaineering, classical music. Home: via Milano 13, 38100 Trento Italy Office: Trento U Faculty Sociol, via Verdi 26, 38100 Trento Italy

FABER, JOSEF IVAN, neurologist; b. Czech Budejovice, Czech Republic, June 25, 1935; s. Josef and Terezie (Kocmoudova) F.; m. Vera Pavlina Maskova, Mar. 19, 1971; children: Martina, Marketa, Vit. MD, Charles U., Czech Republic, 1959. Medical diplomate. Secondary doctor Hosp., Strakonice, Czech Republic, 1959-66; secondary doctor of neurol. dept. Charles U., Praha, 1966-71, rschr. neurol. dept., 1971-82; leading rschr. neurol. dept. Charles U., 1986—, prof. neurology, 1993—; rschr. Psychiat. Rsch. Inst., Praha-Bohnice, 1982-86; cons. Faculty Hosp., Prague 2, 1986—. Contbr. articles to profl. jours. Capt. Czech Air Forces, 1982. Mem. Czech Soc. for Clin. Neurophysiology (pres. 1990-92), Czech Ligue Epilepsy, Czech Med. Assn. Roman Catholic. Avocations: astronomy, sports, swimming, fencing, tourism. Home: Janackovo nabrezi 51, 150 00 Prague 5 Czech Republic Office: Neurol Dept/Charles U, Katerinska 30, 120 00 Prague 2 Czech Republic

FABER, MARC, investment company executive; b. Switzerland, Feb. 28, 1946; arrived in Hong Kong, 1973; m. Supatra Srinark Faber; 1 child, Nantamada. PhD in Econs., U. Zurich, Switzerland, 1970. With White Weld & Co., N.Y.C. and Zurich, 1970-78; mng. dir. Drexel Burnham Lambert Ltd., Hong Kong, 1978-90, Marc Faber Ltd., Hong Kong, 1990—; dir. Baring Chrysalis Fund, Baring Taiwan Fund, Income Ptnrs. Global Strategy Fund, Framlington Eastern Europe Fund, Buchanan Spl. Emerging Mkts. Fund, Hendale Asia Fund, Indian Smaller Cos. Fund, Regent Magna Europa Fund PLC, Tellus Capital. Author: The Great Money Illusion, 1988, Riding the Millenium Storm; editor, author: The Gloom, Boom & Doom Report, 1980—. Mem. Swiss Acad. Ski Club, SC18 Italy,. Office: Marc Faber Ltd 16 Queen's Rd, 2705 New World Tower, Hong Kong Hong Kong

FABER, ROBERT CHARLES, lawyer; b. N.Y.C., June 26, 1941; s. Sidney G. and Beatrice (Siebert) F.; m. Carol Z. Zimmerman, Aug. 15, 1965; 1 child, Susan Faber. BA, Cornell U., 1962; JD, Harvard Law Sch., 1965. Bar: N.Y. 1966; U.S. Dist. Ct. (so. dist.) N.Y. 1967; U.S. Ct. Appeals (2nd cir.); U.S. Ct. Appeals (fed. cir.) 1982; U.S. Supreme Ct. 1971; U.S. Patent and trademark Office 1967. Atty., ptnr. Ostrolenk, Faber, Gerb & Soffen, LLP, N.Y.C., 1965—; lecturer Practicing Law Inst., N.Y.C., 1974—. Author: Landis on Mechanics of Patent Claim Drafting, 3d edit. 1990, 4th edit. 1996. Mem. Am. Intellectual Property Law Assn., N.Y. Intellectual Property Law Assn., Harvard Club of N.Y. Office: Ostrolenk Faber Gerb & Soffen LLP 1180 Ave of Americas New York NY 10036-8401

FÁBIÁN, ISTVÁN, chemist, educator; b. Debrecen, Hungary, June 4, 1956; s. József and Józsefné (Muszka Erzsébet) F.; m. Livia Szabó, Aug. 18, 1979; children: Ákos István, Ádám András. MSc in Chemistry, Lajos Kossuth U., Debrecen, 1980, PhD in Chemistry, 1982; CSc in Chemistry, Hungarian Acad. Sci., Budapest, 1992. Postdoctoral fellow Max Planck Inst. for Biophys. Chemistry, Göttingen, Germany, 1983-84; asst. prof. dept. inorganic and analytical chemistry Lajos Kossuth U., Debrecen, 1985-87, 91-93, assoc. prof., 1994—; Alexander von Humboldt fellow U. Witten-Herdecke Inst. for Inorganic Chemistry, Witten, 1992-93; vis. rsch. prof. dept. chemistry Miami U., Oxford, Ohio, 1988-91; mem. editl. bd. Jour. Inorganic Reaction Mechanisms. Contbr. articles to profl. jours. Mem. Hungarian Chem. Soc., Hungarian Humboldt Soc. Avocations: history, politics, modern music. Office: U Debrecen, Dept Inorg/Analytic Chem, H-4010 Debrecen Hungary

FABIÁN, JOSEF, microbiologist, researcher; b. Střítež, Moravia, Czech Republic, May 27, 1930; s. Josef and Rose (Vilémová) F.; m. Mary Rajchertová, July 16, 1960; children: Ann, Libor. Engring. Diploma, Agrl. U., Brno, Czech Republic, 1953; PhD, Chem. Technol. U., Prague, Czech Republic, 1957. Doctoral asst. Rsch. Inst. Food Tech., Prague, 1953-58; rsch. scientist Inst. Microbiology, Czech Acad. Sci., Prague, 1958-73, rsch. scientist enzyme and biotech. group, 1991—; A.v.Humboldt fellow Max Planck Inst., Munich, 1969-70; staff Rsch. Inst. Cann. Ind., Prague, 1973-90; rsch. inst. peptides biochem. group Inst. Organic Chemistry/Biochemistry, Czech Acad. Sci., Prague, 1993—. Contbr. articles to profl. jours.; patentee (25+) in field. Recipient Silver medal World Congress Refrigeration, 1963. Mem. Am. Soc. Cryobiology. Avocation: music composition. Home: Roztylské nám 298/40, 141 00 Prague 4, Czech Republic Office: Inst of Microbiology Czech Acad Scis, Videňská 1083, 142 20 Prague 4, Czech Republic

FABIAN, LASZLO, marketing and public relations executive; b. Budapest, Feb. 16, 1966; s. Laszlo and Maria (Kalman) F.; m. Terezia Horvath, Aug. 20, 1994; 1 child, Csenge. BA in Bus. Adminstrn., Coll. Fgn. Trade,

Budapest, 1989; MBA, U. Pitts., 1995. Mktg. dir. Kontrax Ltd., Budapest, 1988-92; client svc. mgr. Saatchi & Saatchi, Budapest, 1993-94; mktg. dir. Recognita Corp., Budapest, 1994-95; mktg. and pub. rels. dir. Synergon Ltd., Budapest, 1995—; cons. Toboz Advt., Ltd., Budapest, 1997—. Editor (mag.) Magasyn, 1997—. Avocations: cars, yachting, skiing. Office: Synergon, Baross u 91-95, Budapest 1047, Hungary

FABIANO, BRUNO, industrial engineer, researcher; b. Rome, Sept. 24, 1961; s. Sebastiano and Maria (Cheracci) F. Degree in chem. engring., U. Genoa, Italy, 1988; PhD in Environ. Tech. and Economy, U. Rome La Sapienza, 1996. Cert. engr., fire prevention expert, environ. acoustic expert. Adminstrn. councilor Sci. Inst. Due Isar srl, Savona, Italy, 1989-96; contract prof. process industry plant Genoa U., 1996, postdoctoral rschr., 1997-98, contract prof. bus. economy and mgmt., 1999, assoc. rschr., 1999—; cons. Sertubi Spa, Trieste, Italy, 1999, Cogefarimpresit Spa Fiatimpresit Group, Turin, Italy, 1996-97, Esso Italia Spa, Savona, 1996, Italcementi Spa, Bergamo, Italy, 1995. Contbr. articles to profl. jours., chpt. to book. Fellow European Fedn. Chem. Engring. (mem. loss prevention working panel 1996); mem. Italian Assn. Chem. Engring., Inst. Chem. Engrs. (mem. loss prevention panel 1997). Avocations: skiing, fishing, snowboarding. Office: U Genoa Chem/Process Engr, Via Opera Pia 15, 16145 Genoa Italy

FABINYI, GAVIN CHRISTOPHER ANDREW, neurological surgeon; b. Melbourne, Victoria, Australia, May 12, 1946; s. Andrew and Elizabeth (Robinson) F.; m. Jan Piper, Nov. 16, 1973; children: David Charles Andrew, Michael Gavin Nicholas, Helen Olivia, Jan. MBBS, U. Melbourne, 1970. Med. officer Alfred Hosp., Melbourne, 1971-72; sr. prosector in anatomy U. Melbourne, 1973; neurosurgical registrar Royal Melbourne Hosp., 1974-77, neurosurgeon, 1980-87; sr. registrar in neurosurgery Radcliffe Infirmary, Oxford, Eng., 1977-80, Manchester (Eng.) Royal Infirmary, 1977-78; dir. neurosurgery Austin & Repatriation Gen. Hosp., Melbourne, 1987—; nat. dir. Australian Brain Found., 1987-94; neurosurg. mem. Psychosurg. Rev. Bd., Victoria, Australia, 1994. Mem. editl. bd. Jour. Clin. Neurosciences, 1993-2000; contbr. numerous articles to profl. jours. Royal Australasian Coll. Surgeons rsch. grantee, 1988; grantee NHMRC, 2000. Fellow Royal Australasian Coll. Surgeons (dep. chmn. neurosurg. bd. 1988-96); mem. Neurosurg. Soc. Australasia (exec. com. 1984-94, pres. 1992-94). Avocations: reading, neurosurgical history, court tennis, philosophy. Home: 264 Domain Rd, South Yarra 3141 Victoria, Australia Office: Austin Hospital, Dept of Neurosurgery, Heidelberg 3084 Victoria, Australia

FABIUS, LAURENT, politician, former prime minister of France; b. Paris, Aug. 20, 1946; s. Andre' and Louise (Mortimer) F. Student Institute d'etudes politiques, Paris, Ecole normale Supérieure. Ecole nationale d'administration, 1971-73. Aditor, Conseil d'Etat, France, 1973—; 1st asst. to mayor of Grand Quevilly, France, 1977—; dep. Seine-Maritime, France, 1978-81; sec. Nat. Socialist Party and press charge, 1979; ministry del. Ministry of Economy and Fin., for Budget, France, till 1983; minister of industry and research, France, 1983-84; prime minister of France, 1984-86; pres. Nat. Assembly, 1988-92; 1st sec. Socialist Party, 1992, 93; mem. European Parliament, 1989, 91; pres. Socialist Group in Parliament, 1995. Author: La France inequal, 1975, Le Coeur du Futu, 1985, C'est eu Allant vers la Mer, 1990, Les Blessures de la Verité; minister of finance, France, 2000—. Office: Ministry of Economy Finance & Industry, 139 rue de Bercy, 75572 Paris Cedex 12, France*

FABRA, PAUL ANDRE, journalist, columnist; b. Paris, Dec. 21, 1927; s. Jean and Andree (L'Honorey) F; 1 child, Marie-Helene. Student, Faculte de Droit, Paris; Inst. d'Etudes Politiques, Paris. Journalist l'Enterprise, Paris, 1953, La Vie Française, Paris, 1954-61, Le Monde, Paris, 1961-93, 93—. Contbr. essays Wall St. Jour., other profl. publs.; translated and published Capital for Profit The Triumph of Ricardian Political Economy Over Marx and the Neoliberal, 1990. Recipient Chevalier de la Legion d'Honneur, Prix Jacques Rueff, 1979. Office: Les Echos, 46 rue La Boetie, 75009 Paris France

FABRE, ALAIN, electrical engineering educator; b. Perpignan, France, June 23, 1947; s. Augustin François and Josette (Teis) F. MS in Electronics, U. Bordeaux (France), 1972, PhD, 1974. Asst. prof. electronics U. Oran, Algeria, 1974-87; asst. prof. electronics Ecole Centrale Paris, 1987-95, head analogue integrated circuits design group, 1988-95; prof. electronics Ecole Nat. Supérieure d'Electronique et de Radioelectricite de Bordeaux, 1995—; rsch. on design of high speed analog RF integrated circuits with the telecom. circuits and sys. group (TCS) at microelectronics lab., U. Bordeaux I. Patentee in field; guest editor Analog Integrated Cirs. and Signal Processing, Current Mode Circuits, March and May, 1995; contbr. articles to profl. jours. Mem. IEEE (sr.). Avocations: swimming, yoga, walking, painting, photography. Office: Lab IXL U Bordeaux, 351 Cours de la Liberation, 33405 Talence France

FABRE, CLAUDE P., physicist, researcher, educator; b. Paris, Apr. 23, 1951; s. Maurice F. and Jacqueline S. (Gasc) F.; m. Francoise Berger, Dec. 18, 1976. Agregation in Physics, Ecole Normale Superieure, Paris, 1974; degree, U. Paris 6, 1974, U. Paris 6, 1981. Rsch. attache Nat. Ctr. for Sci. Rsch., Paris, 1974-81, charge of rsch., 1981-86, dir. rsch., 1986-96; prof. U. Pierre et Marie Curie, Paris, 1996—, prof. physics, 1997—; assoc. prof. Ecole Polytechnique, Paris, 1986-98. Author: (handbook) Introduction to Lasers and Quantum Optics; editor: (sci. collection of books) Knowledge of Today; contbr. over 100 articles to profl. jours. Recipient Fabry de Gramont prize French Optical Soc., 1991. Mem. Optical Soc. Am., European Phys. Soc., European Optical Soc. Office: Laboratoire Kastler Brossel, Universite PM Curie Case 74, 75252 Paris France

FABRE, SERGE JEAN, physician; b. Salles-Curan, Aveyron, France, Feb. 28, 1926; s. Albert Léon and Olympe Julienne (Niel) F.; m. Sabine Nelly Husquin, Sept. 14, 1949; children: Raphaêl, Marie, François, Anne, Marc, Pierre, Elisabeth. PCB, Faculté des Sciences, Montpellier, France, 1945; MD, Faculté de Médecine, Montpellier, France, 1960. Intern Hosp. Montpellier, 1947; resident Faculté de Médecine, 1953; chef de clinique Faculté de Médecine, Montpellier, 1960-63; prof. Faculté de Médecine, Dakar, Sénégal, 1967-71, Sch. of Med., Constantine, Algeria, 1963-67, Ctr. Hosp. Régional, Montpellier, 1971—. Fullbright grantee, Duke U., 1958-59. Mem. Médecins du Monde. Roman Catholic. Home: Ave des Quakers, 30111 Congénies, Gard France

FABRI, PETER JEFFREY, surgeon, educator; b. Dec. 9, 1947; m. Sharon E. Schur. BA, Northwestern U., 1969; MD, Loyola U., Maywood, Ill., 1973. Assoc. prof. surgery Ohio State U., Columbus, 1984-86; prof. surgery U. South Fla. Coll. Medicine, Tampa, 1986—, program dir. gen. surgery residency, 1988-94, prof. dept. pharmacology and therapeutics, 1990—, dir. divsn. general surgery, 1992-94, assoc. dean clin. affairs, 1993—; chief surgery James A. Haley Vets. Hosp., Tampa, 1986—, interim chief of staff, 1991-92; pres. Am. Soc. for Parenteral and Enteral Nutrition, 1995. Author Nutrition in Inflammatory Bowel Disease, 1992, Replacement of Central Vascular Catheters, 1993, The Remedial Year in Surgical Training: An Institutional Experience, 1997, The Endocrine Surgeon and Endocrine Neopolasms, 1997. Chmn. field adv. com. in surgery Dept. Vets. Affairs, Washington, 1996; mem. spl. task force in surgery Undersec. Dept. Vets. Affairs, Washington, 1998. Mem. AMA, Am. Coll. Surgeons, Am. Cancer Soc., Am. Surg. Assn., Endocrine Surgeons (program dir. 1992), Phi Sigma Kappa. Avocations: sailing, skiing, reading. Office: James A Haley Vets Hosp 13000 Bruce B Downs Blvd Tampa FL 33612-4745

FABRIKANT, CRAIG STEVEN, psychologist; b. Buffalo, Jan. 8, 1952; s. Benjamin and Laurine Miriam (Zucker) F.; m. Carol Diane Golub, Nov. 6, 1977; children: Chad Adam, Carly. BA, Fairleigh Dickinson U., 1974, MA, 1977; PhD, Fla. Inst. Tech., 1983. Intern in psychology N.J. Dept. Human Svcs., Trenton, 1977-78; clin. psychologist North Jersey Devel. Ctr., Totowa, 1978-85, Cedar Grove Residential Ctr.; chief psychologist Hackensack (N.J.) Med. Ctr., 1985-96; pvt. practice, 1984—; adj. instr. Montclair State Coll., 1980-82; part-time instr. Fairleigh Dickinson U.; cons. psychology N.J. Dept. Labor and Industry, Newark, 1980—. Author profl. papers. Mem. APA, Assn. Advancement Behavior Therapy, N.J. Psychol. Assn. Home: 750 Martin Ave Oradell NJ 07649-2300 Office: 106 Old Hook Rd Westwood NJ 07675-2421

FABRIKESI, EUGENIA-THEODORA, physicist; b. Athens, Greece, Oct. 2, 1950; d. Otto-Peter and Theodora (Vasilopoulou) F.; m. Alexander Serafetinides, Dec. 27, 1979; children: Andreas, Otto. Diploma, U. Athens, 1973; M.Sc., U. Essex, Colchester, England, 1974; D., U. Essex, 1981. Researcher Nat. Defence Rsch. Centre, Athens, 1978-84; head. physics dept. Nat. Defence Rsch. Centre, 1984—; cons. MOD, Athens, 1980—. Contbr. articles to profl. jours.; translator: Optics and Lasers, 1986. Grantee for post studies NATO, 1975-78. Mem. Inst. Physics (U.K.) (Greece). Avocations: stamp collecting, coin collecting, match boxes collecting, swimming. Home: Riga Fereou 11, 15121 Athens Pefki, Greece Office: Nat Defence Rsch Centre, Amygdaleza, 13600 Athens Greece 13600

FABRIS, FRANCESCO, information specialist, educator; b. Triest, Italy, Apr. 19, 1959; s. Antonio and Albina (Peric) F.; m. Clementina Frescura, Aug. 4, 1984; children: Gloria, Alida, Gerson. Degree in electronics engring., Trieste U., 1986, PhD, 1989. Asst. prof. Udine U., 1991-98, assoc. prof., 1998—. Contbr. articles to profl. jours. including Jour. Info. and Optimization Scis. and IEEE Transactions on Info. Theory. Recipient Marconi Italiana award, 1986, Bruno Maestro Found. award, 1989. Mem. IEEE, Associazione Elettrotecnica Elettronica Italiana. Avocations: hands-on activities, diving, collecting stamps. Office: Udine U Dept Math & Info, via delle Scienze 206, 33100 Udine Italy

FABRIZIO, GIUSEPPE AURELIANO, electronics researcher; b. San Remo, Imperia, Italy, July 29, 1971; arrived in Australia, 1976; s. Antonio Leonardo and Giovanna (Fiorellini) F. B of Engring., U. Adelaide, Australia, 1993. Cert. elec. and electronic engr. Engr. Graphic Electronic Industries, Adelaide, 1993-94; rschr. Def. Sci. and Tech. Orgn., Adelaide, 1994—, Ctr. for Sensor Signal and Info. Processing, Adelaide, 1994—. Contbr. papers and articles to profl. jours. and confs. Avocations: tennis, soccer, volleyball, cycling, bushwalking. Home: 13 Taworri Rd Fairview Park, 5126 Adelaide Australia

FABRY, ALAIN, business executive; b. Bourg-en-Bresse, France, Feb. 2, 1945; s. Henri and Charlotte (Clerc) F.; m. Joëlle Audras, May 4, 1969; children: Laurent, Natthieu. Grad., Inst. d'Etudes Politiques, Lyon, France, 1968; Doctor in Law, U. Lyon, 1972. Lectr. U. Law, Madagascar, 1969-70, Lyon, France, 1971-74; dir. planning and devel. New City Agy., Lille, France, 1974-78; advisor to the min. of equipment Cairo, 1979-81; dir. Internat. Lyonnaise des Eaux, Singapore, Paris, London, 1982-92; v.p. bus. devel. Dumez Constrn., France, 1992-95; sr. v.p. internat. affairs Suez-Lyonnaise des Eaux, 1995—; dir. Safege, France, 1995, Soc. des Euax du Nord, Lille, 1997, Propar Co., France, 1997. Mem. Assn. Française des Ville Nouvelles (bd. dirs. 1996), Medef Internat. (bd. dirs. 1999). Avocations: travel, historical monuments, music, Nordic skiing. Office: Suez Lyonnaise des Eaux, 1 rue d'Astorg, 75008 Paris France

FACCHI, PAOLO, language philosophy educator; b. Casatenovo, Lombardia, Italy, Mar. 20, 1927; s. Gaetano and Alessandra (Porro) F.; m. Emilia Ravani, 1954 (dec. 1993); 1 chld, Alessandra. Degree in Philosophy, U. Milan, 1949. Contbr. articles to profl. jours. Home: via Castelbarco 7, 23880 Casatenovo Italy Office: Dept Philosophy, U Trieste, 34123 Trieste Italy

FACHET, JÓZSEF, immunologist, pathophysiologist, educator; b. Munkács, Czechoslovakia, Aug. 20, 1935; s. József and Olga (Gombos) F.; m. Judit Gönczó, Sept. 1, 1971; children: Gergó, Boldizsár, Imola. MA summa cum laude, Med. U. Sch., Budapest, Hungary, 1959; PhD in Hungarian Acad. Sci., U. Budapest, 1973, DMSc, 1994. Rschr. rsch. inst. exptl. medicine Hungarian Acad. Sci., Budapest, 1959-73; head immunogenetic rsch. unit Biol. Rsch. Ctr. Hungarian Acad. Sci., Szeged, Hungary, 1973-80; med. prof. dept. pathophysiology Univ. Med. Sch., Debrecen, Hungary, 1980—, dir. dept. pathophysiology and immunology, 1980-2000. Contbr. chpts. to book in field. Postgrad. fellow Med. Rsch. Coun. of Can., 1965-66; postgrad. rsch. fellow Wellcome Trust, Glasgow (Scotland) U., 1969-70; vis. fellow Internat. Soc. Promotion of Scis. (Japan), 1978. Mem. Hungarian Immunology Soc. (exec. com. 1980-88), Hungarian Allergy Soc., Hungarian Physiol. Soc. (exec. com. 1978—). Roman Catholic. Avocations: travel, music, books. Home: 117 Böszörményi St, H-4032 Debrecen Hungary Office: U Debrecen Med & Health Sci Ctr Dept Immunology, 98 Nagyerdei Allee, H-4012 Debrecen Hungary

FACHIMA, SHOSHANNA GISSELLE, musician; b. N.Y.C., Aug. 30, 1953; arrived in Israel, 1968; d. Jacob John and Beatrice Bayle (Mann) Rosner; m. Simon Fachima; 1 child, Jacob. BA, Bar Ilan U., Ramat Gan, Israel, 1979, MA, 1982; PhD, Bar Ilan U. & Tel Aviv U., Ramat Gan, Tel Aviv, Israel, 1985; MA, Rubin Acad., Ramat Aviv, Israel, 1982; MOIF, FIBA, IBA, Oxford, Eng., 1996. Lectr. and rschr. Bar Ilan U., Ramat Gan, Israel, 1979-85; libr. of music Bar Ilan U., Ramat Gan, 1980-82; prin. alto Tel Aviv Philharmonic Choir, 1980-85; prin. recorder player Consort of Old Music, Bar Ilan, 1979-85; sales mgr. Steiner Music Supply, Tel Aviv, 1982-86; owner, artist Artgrafika, Ganay Tikva, Israel, 1989—. Artist: works exhibited in one person shows Hong Kong, 1992, Panama City, 1992, 99, 2000, Santiago, Chile, 1995, N.Y.C., 1993-2000, Miami, Fla., 1995, Casa Blanca, Morroco, 1996, West Orange, N.J., 1996, Jerusalem, 1997-99, Maseilles and Leone, 1997, Paris, 1995-2000, London, 1995-97, Sydney and Melbourne, Australia, 1996; author: (books) Gematriya Secrets in the Torah, 1995, Gemitriya Secrets of Hebrew Alphabet, 1997. Kidney donor, Tel Aviv, Israel, 1982. Grantee Rotary Club Tel Aviv, 1982. Mem. N.Y. Acad. Scis. Jewish. Avocations: gourmet cooking, chess, art collecting. Home: POB 564, 55105 Ganay Tikva Israel

FACHIN, STEFANO, economics and statistics educator, consultant; b. Rome, May 12, 1959; s. Gino and Silvana (Candotti) F.; m. Elena Forte, Oct. 2, 1996; 1 child, Paolo B. Laurea, U. La Sapienza, Rome, 1983; PhD, U. Cambridge, Eng., 1989. Lectr. U. La Sapienza, 1991—; cons. Fininvest, Milan, Italy, 1992-93, Ministry of Treasury, Rome, 1995—, Fiat, Turin. Contbr. articles to Oxford Bull Econs. and Stats., Jour. of Forecasting, Applied Econs. Letters, Applied Econs. Grantee Adam Smith Fund, U. Cambridge, 1984, Einaudi Found., Turin, Italy, 1985-86. Mem. European Econ. Assn. Roman Catholic. Avocations: mountaineering, wine tasting. Home: Largo Pannonia 48, 00183 Rome Italy Office: U La Sapienza, P Le A Moro 5, 00185 Rome Italy

FACHNIE, H(UGH) DOUGLAS, film manufacturing company official; b. Windsor, Ont., Can., Sept. 8, 1952; came to U.S., 1957; s. Harold Lennox Fachnie and Mary Jane (Schultz) MacKenzie. B Gen. Studies, U. Mich., 1973. Salesman Quarry, Inc., Ann Arbor, Mich., 1974; store mgr. Quarry, Inc., Ann Arbor and Saginaw, Mich., 1974-77; dist. mgr. Fotomat Corp., San Diego, 1977-80; dir. ops. Fotomat Corp., Wilton, Conn., 1980-81, dir. merchandising, 1981-83; mgr. optical products Fuji Photo Film U.S.A., Inc., N.Y.C., 1983-84; product mgr. consumer film Fuji Photo Film U.S.A., Inc., Elmsford, N.Y., 1984-89, sr. product/packaging mgr. film and one-time use cameras, 1989-94, mktg. mgr. consumer photo, 1995-97, 98-00; comml. planning and logistics mgr. profl. and photofinishing Fuji Phot Film USA, Inc., Elmsford, N.Y., 1998-2000, dir. mktg., color paper and chems., comml. imaging divsn., 2000—. Mem. AAAS, Photog. Mktg. Assn., Digital Imaging Mktg. Assn., Am. Prodn. and Inventory Control Soc. Republican. Avocations: home maintenance, flying, photography, audiophile, curling. Home: 30 Fleetwood Dr Danbury CT 06810-7010 Office: Fuji Photo Film USA Inc 555 Taxter Rd Elmsford NY 10523-2394

FACINI, CHRISTINA J., secondary education educator; b. Smithtown, N.Y., Dec. 19, 1968; d. Aldo Louis and Gilda Maria F.; m. James Paul Lull, June 29, 1996. BSEE, SUNY, Buffalo, 1991; MA in Math., SUNY, Stony Brook, 1998. Cert. tchr., N.Y. Adj. prof. SUNY, Farmingdale, 1993; tchr. Comsewogue Union Free Sch. Dist., Port Jefferson Sta., N.Y., 1993-94, Hampton Bays (N.Y.) Union Free Sch. Dist., 1994—; adj. prof., instr. Southampton (N.Y.) Coll., 1998—. Mem. IEEE. Avocations: walking, needlepoint, reading. Office: Hampton Bays Secondary Sch 88 Argonne Rd Hampton Bays NY 11946

FACORELLIS, YORGOS EVANGELOS, archeometrist; b. Athens, Greece, May 23, 1960; s. Evangelos and Alkaterini (Kontogeorgis) F.; m. Fotini Ioannis Mourtou, Sept. 12, 1992; children: Orestes, Artemis. Diploma in food tech., Tech. Inst. Athens, 1982; B in Chemistry, U. Thessaloniki, 1986; DESS in Archaeometry, U. Bordeaux, 1989; PhD, U. Patras, 1996. Assoc. researcher Nat. Ctr. Scientific Rsch. Demokritos, Athens, 1990—; assoc. prof. Technol. Edn. Inst. Athens Sch. Conservation Antiquities and Works of Art, Athens. Mem. Assn. Greek Chemists, Assn. Greek Food Techs., Greek Soc. Archaeometry (treas. 1990-99, pres. 1999—). Avocations: poetry writing, hiking, archaeology, gardening. E-mail: yfacorellis@ims.demokritos.gr and yfacorellis@yahoo.com. Home: Koundouriotou 15, 145 63 Kifissia-Athens Greece

FADARISHAN, STEPHEN ROBERT, systems engineer; b. Scranton, Pa., Nov. 24, 1953; s. Steve and Grace Catherine (Mack) F.; m. Ines Fernandez, June 25, 1988. BS in Elec. Engring., Pa. State U., 1982. Lic. gen. radiotelephone operator with ship radar endorsement FCC.; EIT. Design engr. Locus Inc., State College, Pa., 1982-84, Gen. Instruments, Hatboro, Pa., 1984-86; sr. engr. Norden Systems, Norwalk, Conn., 1986-89; contract software engr. Westinghouse, Balt., 1989-91, Boehringer Mannheim, Indpls., 1991-92; tech. advisor in engring. standards Cummins Engine Co., Columbus, Ind., 1992—; cons. Watermark, Inc., Ft. Wayne, Ind., 1991—. Mem. Homeowners Orgn., Greenwood, Ind., 1993—. Mem. Letters of Commendation, USN, 1975, 77. Mem. IEEE, Assn. for Info. and Image Mgmt., Soc. for Tech. Comm., Eta Kappa Nu. Achievements include development of process and system implementation which converts existing corporate documents for electronic distribution via the corporate intranet web. Avocations: cross-country skiing, reading. Office: Cummins Engine Engring Standards Box 3005 M/C 50111 Columbus IN 47202-3005

FADER, SHIRLEY SLOAN, writer; b. Paterson, N.J.; d. Samuel Louis and Miriam (Marcus) Sloan; m. Seymour J. Fader; children: Susan Deborah, Steven Micah Kimchi. BS, MS, U. Pa. Writer, journalist, author Paramus, N.J.; chmn., coord. ann. writers seminar Bergen C.C., 1973-76. Author: (books) The Princess Who Grew Down, 1968, From Kitchen to Career, 1977, Jobmanship, 1978, Successfully Ever After, 1982 (Brit. edit. 1985), Wait a Minute: You Can Have It All, 1993, paperback edit., 1994; (columns) Jobmanship, People and You, Family Weekly mag., 1971-82, How to Get More From Your Job, Glamour mag., 1978-81, Start Here, Working Woman mag., 1980-88, Work Strategies, Working Mother mag., 1987-88, Women Getting Ahead, Ladies Home Jour., 1980-90, How Would You Handle It, New Idea mag., 1984—, Moving Up, Woman mag., 1989-90, Career Expert "Ask the Experts", Woman's World mag., 1992-95; contbg. editor Family Weekly, 1971-82, Glamour mag., 1978-81, Working Woman mag., 1980-88, Working Mother mag., 1987-88, Ladies Home Jour., 1980-90, Woman mag., 1989-90; contbr. articles on career, relationships and travel to mags. worldwide. Mem. Authors Guild, Am. Soc. Journalists and Authors (moderator ann. writer's conf. 1971-2000, nat. v.p. 1976-77, mem.-at-large nat. exec. coun. 1976-78, 83-86, nat. sec., mem. exec. coun. 1995-96), Nat. Press Club, Newswomen of N.Y. Address: 377 Mckinley Blvd Paramus NJ 07652-4725

FADNAVIS, NITIN WASANTRAO, chemist, researcher; b. Hyderabad, India, Oct. 31, 1954; s. Wasantrao Vitthairao and Kumudini Fadnavis; m. Geeta Nitin Mahabale, Apr. 6, 1982; 1 child, Mihir. BSc in Physics, Chemistry, and Math., Inst. Sci., Nagpur, Maharashtra, India, 1974, MSc in Organic Chemistry, 1976, PhD in Organic Chemistry. Jr. rsch. fellow U. Grants Commn., New Delhi, 1976-78; sr. rsch. fellow CSIR, New Delhi, 1978-80; postdoctoral rsch. assoc. in chemistry U. Groningen, The Netherlands, 1981-84; chemistry lectr. Dharampeth Coll. Sci., Nagpur, 1984-85; pool officer Indian Inst. Chem. Tech., Hyderabad, 1985-86; postdoctoral rsch. assoc. Inst. for Polymere ETH, Zurich, 1986-87; scientist B Indian Inst. Chem. Tech., Hyderabad, 1987—, scientist E-1, 1997; cons. M/S Kopran Ltd., Mumbai, India. Contbr. articles to profl. jours. including Jour. Am. Chem. Soc., Jour. Organic Chemistry, Biotech. Progress. Recipient Nat. Merit scholarship Govt. India, 1970-74; sr. rsch. fellow Coun. Sci. and Indsl. Rsch., 1978-80. Mem. All India Biotech. Assn., Analytical Soc. India. Avocations: reading, writing short stories and plays in Marathi, acting in amateur theatre. E-mail: fadnavisnw@yahoo.com. Office: Indian Inst Chem Tech, Biotransformations Lab, Hyderabad 500007, India

FADNER, WILLARD LEE, physics educator, researcher; b. Racine, Wis., Aug. 10, 1933; s. Glenn Roland and Evelyn Hannah (Larsen) F.; m. Alice J. Lienhard, June 27, 1959; children: Jenette Marie Dunworth, Peter Willard. BSEE, Purdue U., 1955; MS in Physics, U. Wis., 1962; PhD in Physics, U. Colo., 1971. Project engr. A.C. Electronics, Milw., 1958-62; project asst. U. Wis., Madison, 1962-64; instr. Mankato (Minn.) State U., 1964-68; from rsch. asst. to rsch. assoc. U. Colo., Boulder, 1968-72, instr., 1971-72; from asst. prof. to assoc. prof. U. No. Colo., Greeley, 1972-80, prof., 1980—, chair dept. physics, 1991—; faculty senator U. No. Colo., Greeley, 1991-98; book reviewer, jour. referee in field. Contbr. numerous articles to profl. jours. including Nuclear Physics, Phys. Rev., Physics Letters, Am. Jour. Physics; contbr. photography articles to Shutterbug mag. ElectroOptics Lab. grantee Eastman Kodak, U. No. Colo., 1988, Computer Enhanced Phys. Labs. NSF—Leadership in Lab. Devel. grantee U. No. Colo., 1992-94. Achievements include development on the Generalized Correspondence Principle; work on wave-particle duality for photons; work on educational value of undergraduate research. Avocation: photography. Office: U No Colo Dept Physics Greeley CO 80639-0001

FADUL, JAMAL MAKKI, physician, nephrologist; b. Khartoum, Sudan, June 14, 1956; arrived in Sweden, 1992; s. Makki AlHanafi and Rabiha Hamad (AlTtahir) F.; m. Nahala Hassan Mahmoud, Apr. 1, 1993; 1 child, Mohammad. MB BCh, U. Alexandria, Egypt, 1982; PhD, Uppsala (Sweden) U., 1997. Intern Khartoum Tchg. Hosp., 1983-84, med. officer, 1984-85; registrar Ajman Hosp., United Arab Emirates, 1985-92; mem. staff med. dept. Univ. Hosp., Uppsala, 1997—. Contbr. articles to profl. jours. Mem. Swedish Soc. Nephrology, Swedish Soc. Physicians, Uppsala Physician Union. Mem. Sudanese Dem. Party. Muslim. Avocations: football, tennis, music, reading novels. Home: Vaktargatan 30A, 123, 754 22 Uppsala Sweden Office: Univ Hosp Dept Medicine, 751 85 Uppsala Sweden

FAERMAN, SILVIA FABIANA, lawyer; b. Buenos Aires, Dec. 7, 1957; d. Jaime and Zulema (Kohen) F. LLB, U. Buenos Aires, 1984. Jr. lawyer Marval & O'Farrell, Buenos Aires, 1984-87, sr. lawyer, 1987-91; sr. assoc. Marval, O'Farrell & Mairal, Buenos Aires, 1991-97; head of legal dept. Kearney & MacCulloch, Buenos Aires, 1997—; vis. scholar Southwestern U. Sch. Law, 1996; founder, factotum lunching events IP Lawyers Cir., Buenos Aires, 1986—; guest lectr. Southwestern U. Sch. Law, 1996-97, guest prof., 1996-97; lectr., spkr. nat. and internat. congress and seminars on intellectual property, 1987—; advisor Fundación Universitaria del Rio de la Plata, 1996—; adj. assoc. prof. Southwestern U. Sch. of Law, 1998—; co-dir. of summer program in Buenos Aires, Southwestern U. Sch. Law, 1999, 2000. Contbr. articles to profl. jours. Recipient travel scholarship Fundación Universitaria Del Rio de La Plata, 1986. Mem. Internat. Assn. for Protection of Indsl. Property, Interam. Assn. for Indsl. Property, Argentine Assn. for Agts. of Indsl. Property. Jewish. Avocations: language, art, letterwriting, jogging, traveling. Home: Las Heras 3923 11th Fl AptE, 1425 Buenos Aires Argentina

FAESSLER, PETER ERNST, historian, educator; b. Oberkirch, Germany, Oct. 23, 1964; s. Ernst and Gisela (Wamsler) F.; m. Anke Scharrahs, Aug. 20, 1969; 1 child, Anna Caroline. MD, U. Freiburg, 1995. Scientific collaborator Heidelberg Acad. Scis., Germany, 1992, U. Freiburg, Germany, 1993-94; asst. prof. Tech. U. Dresden, Germany, 1994—. Author: Hans Spemann 1869-1941, 1997. Avocations: soccer, singing. Home: Hertelstrasse 16, 01307 Dresden Germany Office: Tech U Dresden, Mommsenstr 13, 01069 Dresden Germany

FAGAN, CIARAN PIUS, biochemist, educator; b. Newry, No. Ireland, July 30, 1956; s. Gerard and Catherine (McCourt) F.; m. Margaret McKee, May 24, 1986; children: Olga, David. BA, Trinity Coll., Dublin, Ireland, 1978, PhD, 1982. R&D supr. WBE Ltd., Dublin, 1981-84; scientist Noctech Ltd., Galway, Ireland, 1984-87; postdoctoral NIHE, Dublin, 1987-89; lectr. DCU, Dublin, 1989—. Author: (chpt.) Lyophilization of Proteins, 1996, Storage of Pure Proteins, 1996, (book) Stabilizing Protein Function, 1997. Mem. Biochem. Soc., Irish Rsch. Scientists' Assn. Roman Catholic. Avocations: reading, swimming. Office: Dublin City Univ, Sch Biotech, Dublin 9, Ireland

FAGAN, FREDERIC, neurosurgeon; b. Bklyn., Oct. 18, 1935; s. Jack and Sophie (Altschuler) F.;m. Donna Fagan, Mar. 1, 1969; children: Gabrielle, Samantha. BA, Ohio State U., 1958. Intern Santa Monica (Calif.) Hosp., N.Y.C., 1959; resident N.Y. Hosp., N.Y.C., Calif., 1960; cons. AMA, L.A., 1980—. Dir. Smithsonian Assocs., Washington, 1995, U.s. Holocaust Meml. Mus., Washington, 1995. Named Surgeon of Yr. MacMillan Industries, Santa Clara, Calif., 1989. Mem. N.Y. Acad. Scis., NRA (dir. 1995). Home: 11102 Excelsior Dr Apt 9E Norwalk CA 90650-5646 Office: Woodruff Hosp 3800 Woodruff Ave Long Beach CA 90808-2125

FAGAN, JAY, social work educator; b. Phila., Mar. 28, 1952; s. Robert and Irene Fagan; m. Josephine D. Fagan, Feb. 27, 1983; children: Anna, Lisa. BA, Trinity Coll., Hartford, Conn., 1973; MSW, U. Pa., 1977; D of Social Work, Columbia U., 1988. Social worker Phila. Psychiat. Ctr., 1974-79, Cath. Social Svcs., Levittown, Pa., 1979-81, Staten Island Aid, Inc., 1981-85, Edwin Gould Svcs. for Children, New Hyde Park, N.Y., 1985-87; lectr. U. Pa., Phila., 1988-90; assoc. prof. Temple U., Phila., 1990—; social worker Wordsworth Acad. Day Sch., 1988-92; panelist grant rev. panel Univ./Head Start Partnerships: Translating Rsch. into Practice, 1996, Local Rsch. Partnerships for Early Head Start Programs, 1996; presenter in field. Editor: Clinical and Educational Interventions for Fathers, 2000; contbr. articles to profl. jours. Grantee Commn. on Nat. and Cmty. Svc., 1992, HHS, Washington, 1995, 96. Mem. Nat. Coun. on Family Rels. Home: 8300 Brookside Rd Elkins Park PA 19027-1904 Office: Temple U Ritter Hall Annex 5th Fl Philadelphia PA 19122

FAGBAMI, AYODELE ADEDAYO, agronomy educator, environmentalist; b. Ikun-Akoko, Nigeria, May 25, 1943; s. Peter Fagbami Ajiye and Ruth Duduyemi (Balogun) Fagbami; m. Bisola Adeolu Shokoya, Sept. 18, 1969; children: Olusoji, Feyisara Esan, Adebowale, Olorunnimbe. BSc, Ibadan (Nigeria) U., 1968; PhD, Aberdeen (Scotland) U., 1972. U. Ibadan, 1972-79, Sr. lectr., 1979-84, reader, 1984-87, prof. agronomy, 1987-92, 97—; dir. land use planning Nat. Agrl. Devel. Authority, Abuja, Nigeria, 1992-96; cons. Regional Ctr. Tng. in Aerospace Surveys, Ile-Ife, Nigeria, 1988, Fed. Agrl. Co-ordinating Unit/World Bank, Ibadan, 1986-87, Shell Petroleum Devel. Co, Warri, Nigeria, 1980-83; resource person Internation Inst. Tropical Agr., Ibadan, 1989-93. Contbr. articles to profl. jours., chpt. to book. Dir. Wemaboard Estates, Lagos, Nigeria, 1980; sec. Akoko Devel. Group, Nigeria, 1989-97. Fulbright fellow, Mich. State U., 1984; Salzburg Seminar fellow, 1985, 97; Commonwealth Scholarship, 1969-72. Mem. Nigerian Soc. Remote Sensing (pres. 1991—), Soil Sci. Soc. Nigeria, Sr. Staff Club. Roman Catholic. Avocations: photography, travel, fast walking, table tennis. E-mail: afagbami@mail.skannet.com. Home: 58 Adebiyi St Off Ring Rd, GPO Box 36508, Ibadan Oyo, Nigeria Office: U Ibadan, Dept Agronomy, Ibadan Oyo, Nigeria

FAGER, EVERETT DEAN, minister; b. Redkey, Ind., Apr. 6, 1947; s. Luther Von and Nola Marceil (Elliott) F.; m. Kathy Jo McKean, Mar. 17, 1973 (div. Aug. 1989); children: Holly Renee (dec.), Ryan Christopher; m. Janet A. Caskey, June 12, 1993; children: Benjamin Dean, Sarah Ashley; stepchildren: Eric, Mike, Nick Caskey. BA, U. Evansville, 1969; ThM, Boston U., 1972; D of Ministry, Drew U., 1981. Ordained to ministry Meth. Ch. as elder, 1973. Youth and edn. min. First United Meth. Ch., Decatur, Ind., 1972-76, St. Mark's United Meth. Ch., Decatur, 1972-76; min. Albany (Ind.) United Meth. Ch., 1976-82, Osceola (Ind.) United Meth. Ch., 1982-86; sr. pastor Taylor Chapel United Meth. Ch., Ft. Wayne, Ind., 1986-91; assoc. dir. for local ch. ministries North Ind. Conf., 1991-94; ptnr. GROW Ministries, Ft. Wayne, 1983-93; pastor Main St. United Meth. Ch., Peru, Ind., 1994—; chaplain Jaycees, Decatur, 1975-76; mem. area comm. com. United Meth. Ch., 1980-86, conf. comm. chair., 1980-86, 94—; mem. conf. program com. United Meth. Ch., 1984-90; assoc. faculty Bethel Coll., Mishawaka, Ind., 1985-86; chmn. Membership Recruitment Task Force Ch. Builders of Ft. Wayne Dist., 1987-91; mem. com. on Investigation N. Ind. Conf. United Meth. Ch., 1988-91, chair Kokomo dist. com. on superintendency, 1998—; bd. dirs. Assoc. Chs. Allen County, Ft. Wayne, 1988-91. Chmn. Walkathon, Adams County March Dimes, Decatur, 1973-75; mem. Publicity Com. Osceola Days, 1984-86; vice chmn. Osceola Bd. Zoning Appeals, 1985-86; mem. new ch. devel. task force North Ind. U. Meth. Ch., 1989-93; mem. local coord. coun. Gov.'s Task Force for a Drug-Free Ind., 1994—; mem. C.O.M.P.A.S.S., 1995—. Named Outstanding Young Man Am., Jaycees, Decatur, 1975; recipient Ch. Growth awards N. Ind. Conf. United Meth. Ch., 1988. Mem. Peru Min. Assn. (pres. 1995-96), Rotary (Sgt.-at-Arms 1998-99, chaplain 1999—). Democrat. Home: 363 W 3rd St Peru IN 46970-1961

FAGERBERG, JAN CHRISTER, clinical scientist; b. Stockholm, Jan. 27, 1962; s. Bengt and Erna (Klingbeil) F.; m. Catharina von Bornstedt; 1 child, Mikaela. MD, Karolinska Inst., Stockholm, 1988, PhD, 1995. Intern Motala Hosp., Sweden, 1988-90; registrar Karolinska Hosp., Stockholm, 1990-95, cons., 1995-98, chief physician, 1998-99; asst. med. dir. Roche AB, Stockholm, 1999-2000; clin. scientist oncology global drug devel. F. Hoffmann-LaRoche Ltd., Basel, Switzerland, 2000—; cons. in field. Contbr. articles to profl. jours. Mem. Swedish Soc. Medicine, Swedish Soc. Oncology, Cancer Soc. Stockholm, European Soc. Therapeutic Radiology and Oncology. Office: F Hoffmann-LaRoche Ltd, PDC2 Bldg 52/1215, CH-4070 Basel Switzerland

FÄGERLIND, INGEMAR EMANUEL, education educator; b. Fredsberg, Sweden, Dec. 26, 1935; s. John Emanuel and Elsa Linnea (Andersson) F. BA, U. Stockholm, 1964, Lic. Degree in Edn., 1968, PhD in Edn., 1975. Elem. sch. tchr. Falköping, Solna, Sundbyberg, 1958-63; rschr./adminstr. Stockholm Sch. Edn., 1963-73; asst. prof. Inst. Internat. Edn. Stockholm U., 1975-83, prof. edn., chair dept., 1983—, dir. Inst. Internat. Edn., 1982—; adv. prof. East China Normal U., Shanghai, 1997; cons. Swedish Internat. Devel. Authority, World Bank, UNDP, UNESCO, European Union in Botswana, Ethiopia, Zambia, Zimbabwe, Pakistan, China, Kazakstan, Kyrgistan, Turkmenistan, Belarus, South Africa; coord. European Union network in comparative edn., 1998—. Author/co-author 10 books incl. Education and National Development, A Comparative Perspective, 1983, 2d edit., 1989; Higher Edn. at Crossroads, Tradition or Transformation, 1999, Swedish editor Scandinavian Jour. Edn., 1989-95. Mem. Stockholm Inst. for Internat. Econ. Studies (bd. dirs.), Nordic Internat. and Comparative Edn. Soc. Lutheran. Avocations: classical roses, gardening. Home: Järntorget 85, 106 91 Stockholm Sweden Office: Inst Internat Edn, Stockholm Univ, 10691 Stockholm Sweden

FAGERMAN, PETER WILHELM, transportation and logistics consultant; b. Helsinki, Finland, Mar. 4, 1942; s. Curt W. and Inger Y. (Sundman) F.; m. Barbara Ann Gleason, Jan. 22, 1972; children: Camilla, Alex, Robert. Cert. shipping and internat. trade, London Sch. Fgn. Trade, 1966; student, NYU, 1971-72; cert. intercultural skills, Abo Akademi U., Turku, 1998. Mem. internat. sales staff Nordisk Transport & Spedition Ab, Stockholm, 1969-70; acting gen. mgr./export traffic Nordisk Transport, Inc., N.Y.C., 1970-73; sales mgr. liner dept. Oy Victor Ek Ab, Helsinki, 1973-75; mng. dir. Finnfreight Oy, Helsinki, 1975-79; pres. Finnish Import Svcs. Ctr., Inc., N.Y.C., 1979-82; exec. v.p. Distbn. Svcs. Internat., Inc., Elizabeth, N.J., 1982-83; mng. dir., ptnr. Interfreight Oy and Oy Fagerman & Co Ab, Helsinki, 1984-92; dir., dir. sea/air/liner dept. DFDS Transport Oy, Helsinki, 1992-97; cons. Oy Fagerman & Co Ab, Kauniainen, 1997—. Mem. Finnish Am. Club (bd. dirs. 1987-89, 96-98, chmn. 1989), Finnish Am. C. of C. (bd. dirs. 1980-83), Finnish Freight Forwarders Assn. (airfreight com. 1996—). Avocations: bridge, badminton. Home: Richardsgr 4D, 02700 Grankulla Finland Office: D Fagerman Co, PO Box 27, 02701 Kauniainen Finland

FAGERSTRÖM, BJÖRN ROBERT, company executive; b. Eskilstuna, Sörmland, Sweden, May 5, 1928; arrived in Eng., 1978; s. Hjalmar and Greta (Fall) F.; m. Anna Curman, Apr. 14, 1962; children: Annika, Cecilia, Carl. BA, U. Lund, Sweden, 1951, M.Polit. Economy, 1952; MBA, U. Gothenburg, Sweden, 1954. Asst. to fin. dir. Uddcholm AB, Sweden, 1954-56; asst. to fin. dir. FACIT AB, Sweden, 1956-58, asst. to mng. dir., 1958-61; mktg. mgr. farm divsn. ALFA Laval, Stockholm, 1962-65, dir. corp. planning and devel., 1966-71; mng. dir. Societé ALFA Laval, Paris, 1971-72, Alfa Laval Pty. Ltd., Sydney, Australia, 1972-78, Alfa Laval Co. Ltd., London, 1978-84; pres. Alfa Laval Inc., Ft. Lee, 1984-88; chmn. trustees Alfa Laval Pension Fund, 1995—. Bd. dirs. Swedish Conservative Party, London, 1995—. Sweden-Am. Found. scholar, 1961. Mem. Swedish Golfing Soc. (treas. 1994—). Avocations: investments, golf, gardening, stamps. Home phone and fax: 01784-43287 or 01784-439257. . Home: Parrock Lodge, Bjorn Fagerstrom, Englefield Green, Surrey TW20 OJU, England

FAGERSTRÖM, RITVA KYLLIKKI, psychiatrist, psychotherapist, psychologist, researcher; b. Korpilahti, Finland, Mar. 28, 1943; m. Raimo Eino Uolevi Lehto, July 11, 1991. BA, U. Helsinki, 1971, MA, 1972, lic. in philosophy, 1977, MD, 1983; PhD, U. Tartu, 1996. Asst. psychiatrist Psychiat. Clinic/The Hosp. of U. of Helsinki, 1979-85; psychiatrist The Mehiläinen Clinic, Helsinki, 1985—; spl. reader Psychol. Reports and Perceptual and Motor Skills, 1993-95. Contbr. more than 55 articles to profl. jours. Mem. N.Y. Acad. Scis. Avocations: reading, traveling.

FAGGIANI, SERGIO MARIA, physics educator; b. Milan, Italy, Jan. 17, 1932; s. Dalberto and Elsa (Donzelli) Faggiani; m. Maria Cariboni, Aug. 1, 1960. Degree in Physics, U. Genoa, Italy, 1955. Asst. prof. U. Rome, 1958-70; prof. U. Cagliari, Italy, 1970-71, U. Pisa, Italy, 1971—; dir. Dept. Energetics, Pisa, 1988-94; pres. Italian Thermotech. Assn.-Tuscan sect., 1973-81; pres. Italian Union Thermofluiddynamics, 1990-98. Author: Complementi di Fisica tecnica, 1989; contbr. numerous articles to profl. jours. Mem. ASME, Lions. Home: Via Gamerra 6, 56100 Pisa Italy Office: U Pisa, Via Diotisalvi 2, 56100 Pisa Italy

FAGHIH, NEZAMEDDIN, engineering educator; b. Estahban, Fars, Iran, July 29, 1953; s. Rokneddin and Homayoun Soltan (Enayat) F.; m. Leyla Sarfaraz, Sept. 23, 1954; children: Rose-Taj, Ali. BSc, Surrey (Eng.) U., 1976, MSc, 1977, PhD, 1980; diploma, Internat. Ctr. Theor. Physics, 1990. Chmn. Iranian Rsch. Orgn. for Sci. and Tech., 1980-84; asst. prof. Maryland U., 1985-86; asst. prof. Shiraz U., Iran, 1986-94, dept. chmn., 1989-94, main libr. chmn., 1994-95; assoc. prof. Shiraz U., 1995-2000, prof., 2000—; cons. Sina Chem. Industries, Iran, 1983-84; sci. bd. Internat. Power Conf., Iran, 1987—, Maintenance Congress, Iran, 1993—, Indsl. Safety Congress Iran, 1995—. Author: (books) Maintenance Engineering, 1989 (Book of Yr. prize 1990, min. of higher edn.), Science in the Mathnawi of Maulawi, 1992 (Selected book 1993), Occupational Stresses, 1997, Love and the Entity, 1997, Control Systems, 1997, Quality Control, 1998, The Fundamentals of System Simulation, 1999, The Transfer of Science and Technology, 2000, Dynamic Systems: Fundamentals and Identifications, 2000; editor: Procs. Internat. Power Conf., 1988, 89, 93, Procs. of Indsl. Tech. in Fars Province, 1995 (prize 1995); assoc. editor Jour. Social Scis. and Humanities, 1997. Rep. Third World Remote Sensing Assn., 1988; bd. dirs. Estahban Devel. Orgn., Iran, 1993; chmn. PTA (Shiraz U. Sch.), Iran, 1992; mem. adv. bd. Com. Against Harmful Work, Iran, 1994. Grantee: Shirz U., Iran, 1988, 90, 93, 95; UNESCO grant, Internat. Ctr. for Theoretical Physics, Italy, 1988, 90. Mem. IEEE, Am. Math. Soc., N.Y. Acad. Scis., Inst. Indsl. Engrs., others. Avocations: reading, poetry, travel, gardening, riding. Home: End of Abrishami Ave, No 56 New 35 Metri Ave, 71447 Shiraz Fars, Iran Office: Shiraz Univ, Tappeh Eram, 71944 Shiraz Fars, Iran

FAGIOLO, VINCENZO CARDINAL, archbishop; b. Segni, Italy, Feb. 5, 1918. Ordained priest Roman Cath. Ch., 1943. Prelate auditor Roman Rota, 1967-71; ordained archbishop Chieti-Vasto, 1971; sec. Congregation Insts. Consecrated Life & Socs. Consecrated Life, 1984-90; pres. Pontificial Coun. for the Interpretation of Legislative Texts, Rome, 1991-94; created and proclaimed cardinal, 1994; pres. disciplinary commn. Roman Curia, 1990—. Office: Via Rusticucci 13, 00193 Rome Italy*

FAGOONEE, INDURLALL, science educator, researcher; b. Curepipe, Mauritius, Feb. 21, 1950; m. Premila Gaya, Aug. 15, 1975; children: Lina, Nishley. Lic. in Sci., U. Paris VI, 1974; M in Animal Biology, U. Paris XI, 1975, D in Specialite, 1978; MS in Marine Sci., U. Miami, 1984. Chartered biologist, U.K. Prof. U. Mauritius, 1977—, now pro-vice-chancellor for curriculum devel. and quality; advisor marine resources and environ. Ministry of Agr., Mauritius, 1988-90; cons. SIgma Consulting Engrs., Mauritius, 1989, World Bank, UNESCO, FAO, UN Devel. Program. Mem. editl. bd. Insect Sci. and Application; contbr. articles to profl. jours. Asst. instr./dive master Nat. Assn. Underwater Instrs. Fellow Inst. Biology U.K., Royal Entomol. Soc. U.K.; mem. N.Y. Acad. Scis. Avocations: reading, swimming, hiking, Internet, scuba diving. Office: Univ Mauritius, Ctrl Adminstrn, Reduit Mauritius

FAHED, CHARBEL DAWOOD, ophthalmologist; b. Ashcout, Lebanon, Oct. 15, 1951; s. Dawood Tamer and Daad Yousef (Dariane) F.; m. Victoria Mary-Hala Chebaya, Oct. 4, 1981; children: Dawood, John, Joseph, Mariam, Anna, Grace. BS, Am. U., Beirut, 1976, MS, 1977, MD, 1980. Clin. instr. ophthalmology Am. U., Beirut, 1984-85, assoc., 1985-88; dir. ophthalmology Ctr. Hosp. St. Georges, Ajaltoun, Lebanon, 1984—; part time cons. Eye & Ear Hosp., Naccash, Lebanon, 1995—; med. dir. Najjar Found., Beirut, 1986—; br. dir. ForeSight Found., Beirut, 1992—; moderator multiple local symposiae. Contbr. articles to profl. jours. Mem. Am. Acad. Ophthalmology, Soc. of Ophthalmology, Am. U. Beirut Alumni. Roman Catholic. Avocations: tennis, swimming, classical music. Home: El Jisr, Ashcout Kisrouan Lebanon Office: Eye & Ear Hosp Internat, Naccache 70-933, Lebanon also: St George Hosp, Ajaltoun Lebanon

FAHEY, JOHN JOSEPH, Australian government official; b. New Zealand, Jan. 10, 1945; s. Stephen and Annie F.; m. Colleen McGurran, 1968; 3 children. Grad., Chevalier Coll. Mem. Parliament of N.S.W., 1984-95; min. indsl. rels. and employment, 1988-90, min. assisting premier of N.S.W., 1988-90, min. indls. rels., furthur edn., tng. and employment, 1990-92, premier and treas., 1992, premier and min. econ. devel., 1993-96, fed. min. fin., 1996—. Avocation: following sports. Office: Min for Fin and Adminstrn, Parliament House Ste M651, Canberra ACT 2600, Australia*

FAHIM, AYMAN EKRAM, physician, medical educator, researcher; b. El-Menia, Egypt, Apr. 5, 1970; s. Ekram Fahim Mesiha and Nawal Wahba Bishara. MBBCh (MD), Suez Canal U., 1993, MS in Occupl. Medicine, 1999. Asst. lectr. occupl. medicine Suez Canal U., Ismaila, Egypt, 1996—. Office: Faculty of Medicine, Suez Canal Univ, Ismailia Egypt

FAHIMI, H. DARIUSH, medical educator, pathologist; b. Tehran, Iran, May 7, 1933; arrived in U.S., 1958; s. Reza and Touran (Teimuri) F.; m. Marlis Frielinghaus, May 15, 1964 (div. 1983); children: Isabelle, Marcus. MD, U. Heidelberg, Fed. Republic of Germany, 1957. Diplomate Am. Bd. Pathology. Intern SUNY, Bklyn., 1959-60; jr. resident Mallory Inst. Pathology, Boston, 1960-61, chief and sr. resident, 1961-64; rsch. fellow Med. Sch. Harvard U., Boston, 1963-64; rsch. assoc. U. Brussels, 1964-66; asst. prof. pathology Harvard Med. Sch., 1966-69, assoc. prof. pathology, 1970-74; vis. prof. U. Heidelberg, 1974-75, prof., chmn. dept. anatomy and cell biology, 1975—; teaching fellow Tufts U. Med. Sch., Boston, 1959-62, Harvard U. Med. Sch., 1962-63; dean Preclin. Scis., Faculty of Medicine, U. Heidelberg, 1987-89. Editor: Peroxisomes in Biology and Medicine, 1987; contbr. articles to profl. jours. NIH rsch. grantee, 1972-77. Mem. AAAS, Am. Soc. Cell Biology, Am. Assn. Pathologists, German Soc. Cell Biology (pres. 1987-90), Histochem. Soc. (coun. mem. 1989—, pres. 1993-95), Internat. Fedn. of Societies for Histochemistry and Cytochemistry (gen. sec. 1992-96), Soc. Histochemistry (hon.). Avocations: tennis, skiing. Office: U Heidelberg, Im Neuenheimer Feld 307, 69120 Heidelberg Germany

FAHLBECK, REINHOLD HANS, legal studies educator; b. Stockholm, July 9, 1938; s. Erik and Gertrud F.; m. Marie Christine Anckarsvard, June 8, 1963. BA, U. Lund, 1963, LLB, 1967, LLM, 1972, LLD, 1974. Faculty dept. bus. econs. U. Lund (Sweden) Law Sch., 1963-66, asst. prof. pvt. law, 1974-78, assoc prof., 1978-80; pvt. practice Stockholm, 1967-77; prof. labor law Stockholm Sch. Econs., 1980—; chmn. India-Bangladesh sect. Emmaus-Swallos, Caritas Lund; vis. prof. Sophia U., Tokyo, 1989, 94, Stanford Law Sch., 1990, Jagiellonian U., Crakow, Poland, 1992. Mem. editl. bd. Internat. Jour. Comparative Labour Law and Indsl. Rels., Holland, Comparative Labor Law and Policy Jour. Zorn fellow, 1981. Fellow Am. Coun. Learned Socs., Japan Found.; mem. U.S. Nat. Acad. Arbitrators (fgn. corr.). Home: 26 Nyckelkroken, S226 47 Lund Sweden Office: Stockholm Sch Econs, Box 6501, S113 83 Stockholm Sweden

FAHMY, GAMAL MOHAMAD, plant ecologist; b. El-Minya, Egypt, May 10, 1955; s. Mohamad Fahmy and Atteyat Osman Abd El-Rahim; m. Manal Salah El-Deen Osman, June 6, 1990; children: Hussein, Fatemah. BSc in Botany and Chemistry, Cairo U., Giza, Egypt, 1976, MSc in Plant Ecology, 1980, PhD in Plant Ecology, 1987. Demonstrator of botany Faculty of Sci., Cairo U., Giza, Egypt, 1976-80, asst. lectr., 1980-87, lectr. botany, 1987-93, assoc. prof., 1993-2000; prof. Faculty of Sci., Cairo U., Giza, 2000—; asst. lectr. German Acad. Exch. Svc., Tech. U. Munich, 1983-85; rsch. scientist Acad. Sci. Rsch. and Tech., Cairo, 1993-95. Contbr. articles to profl. jours. Recipient Encouraging prize Cairo Univ., 1998. Mem. Egyptian Botanical Soc., German Botanical Soc., Internat. Assn. Ecology, Internat. Allelopathy Soc., Botanical Soc. Am., Syndicate of Sci. Professions. Avocations: biographies, photography, classical and light music, desert excursions, fishing. Office: U Cairo Faculty of Sci, Dept Botany, 12613 Giza Egypt

FAHMY, SHERIF MEDHAT, chemist, educator; b. Cairo, Jan. 19, 1975; s. Medhat Mohamed and Olfat Rashad (Ibrahim) F. BSc in Chemistry, Cairo U., 1996, Pre-Master in Chemistry with honors, 1998, MSc in Chemistry with honors, 1999. Demonstrator chemistry dept. faculty sci. Cairo U., 1996—. Mem el-Zamalek Club. Democrat. Muslim. Avocations: reading, listening to music, computers, football. Home: 3 Kadri St, El-saida Zainab, Cairo 12613, Egypt Office: Cairo U Faculty Sci, El-gamaa St, Giza Egypt

FAHNER, HAROLD THOMAS, marketing executive; b. Detroit, Sept. 4, 1940; s. Harold L. and Beatrice H. (Craig) F.; m. Patricia A. Churchvara, Aug. 25, 1962; children: Michael, Janet Peter. BS in Econs., U. Detroit, 1962. With sales dept. Dun & Bradstreet, Inc., N.Y.C., 1963-67; mgr. sales tng. Blue Cross-Blue Shield, Detroit, 1967-70; mgr. sales, mgmt. tng. A. O. Smith Harvestore Products, Inc., Arlington Heights, Ill., 1970-76, dist. sales mgr., 1976-77, eastern regional mgr., 1977-79; mktg. cons., 1980-82; v.p. mktg. Neuero Corp., West Chicago, Ill., 1982-85; v.p. sales & mktg. Atwater Group, Inc., Mpls., 1985-87; v.p. corp. mktg., Blue Cross/Blue Shield of Fla., Inc., Jacksonville, Fla., 1988—; mem. bd. trustees grad. sch. sales mgmt. and mktg. Syracuse U.; instr. Internat. Sales Mgmt. Inst.; lectr. in field. Author: The Problem Solving Approach to Selling, 1975, The Sales Manager's Model Letter Book, 1976, 2d edit., 1987, Successful Sales Management, 1983. Mem. Am. Mktg. Assn., Am. Advtg. Fedn. (bd. dirs. Jacksonville chpt.), Sales & Mktg. Execs. Assn. Internat. (pres. Jacksonville chpt.). Home: 1601 Ocean Dr S Jacksonville FL 32250-6362 Office: Blue Cross Blue Shield 8900 Freedom Commerce Pky Jacksonville FL 32256-8264

FAHS, JOHN DAVID, bank executive; b. Rockford, Ill., July 20, 1959; Arrived in Norway, 1985; s. Eldon Eugene and Joan Adelle (Eby) F.; m. Merethe Giske, May 20, 1983; children: Benjamin, Sarah. B in Polit. Sci., Manchester Coll., 1983; M in Internat. Mgmt., Am. Grad. Sch. Internat. Mgmt., 1984; postgrad., London Bus. Sch., 1994-95. Cert. fin. risk mgr. Global Assn. of Risk Profls. Asst. FX dealer Den Norske Credit Bank, Oslo, Norway, 1985; various staff positions in internat. and investment banking Den Norske Credit Bank, Oslo, 1986-93; head middle office Den Norske Credit Bank, London, 1993-96, derivatives dealer, 1996-97; dir. market risk mgmt. CIBC Wood Co. PLC, London, 1997-98; head of middle office Christiania markets Christiania Bank og Kreditkasse ASA, Oslo, 1998—. Treas. Nordberg Day Care Ctr., Oslo, 1989-90. Mem. Norwegian-Am. C. of C., ACI Fin. Markets Assn., Global Assn. of Risk Profls. Avocations: reading, music, bicycling, cross-country skiing. E-mail: john.fahs@markets.kreditkassen.no. Office: Christiania Markets, Middelthunsgate 17, Sentrum Oslo 0107, Norway

FAHY, JOSEPH WILLIAM, JR., newspaper reporter; b. Oldenburg, Ind., Mar. 15, 1954; s. Joseph William Fahy Sr. and Ruth Evelyn Pedigo; children: Joseph W. III, John P., Catherine L. AB in English, U. Notre Dame, 1976. Staff writer Virginian-Pilot and Ledger-Star, Norfolk, Va., 1983, 84-89, Hartford (Conn.) Courant, 1984, Indpls. News, 1989-95, Indpls. Star and News, 1995-99, Indpls. Star, 1999—. Recipient Heart of Am. award Am. Legion, 1999, 1st pl. award in investigative reporting Ind. Soc. Profl. Journalists, 1999, 1st pl. award for feature series Ind. AP Mng. Editors, 1994. Roman Catholic. E-mail: jfahy@starnews.com. Home: 5630 Carrollton Ave Indianapolis IN 46220-3152 Office: Indpls Star 307 N Pennsylvania St Indianapolis IN 46204-1819

FAIFMAN, MARK PETROVICH, physicist, researcher; b. Baku, USSR, Apr. 10, 1947; s. Peter Mosesovich and Margareta Markovna (Gorenstein) F.; m. Eugenia Felixovna Rakita, Dec. 4, 1971; children: Michael, Helena. M Physics, Azerbaijan State U., Baku, USSR, 1969; PhD in Physics and Math., Joint Inst. for Nuclear Rsch., Dubna, USSR, 1978. Rschr. Joint Inst. for Nuclear Rsch., Dubna, 1973-79; jr. scientist Kurchatov Inst. Atomic Energy, Moscow, 1979-86, sr. scientist, 1986-96, asst. head divsn. for theoretical rsch. Russian Rsch. Ctr., 1996—. Contbr. articles to profl. jours. Avocations: listening to classical music, fiction reading, tourism. Office: Russ Rsch Ctr Kurchatov Ins, Kurchatov Sq 46, 123182 Moscow Russia

FAIG, WOLFGANG, civil engineer, engineering educator; b. Crailsheim, Germany, Apr. 27, 1939; married; 3 children. Diploma Ing, Tech. U. Stuttgart, 1962; Dr Ing, U. Stuttgart, 1969; MScE, U. N.B., Fredericton, Can., 1965. Rsch. assoc. photogrammetry dept. civil engring. U. N.B., 1965, Inst. Applied Geodesy, Stuttgart, Germany, 1966-69; asst. prof. civil engring. U. Ill., Champaign-Urbana, 1970-71; from asst. prof. to assoc. prof. survey and photogrammetry U. N.B., 1971-78, prof. survey engring., 1978—, assoc. dean engring., 1981-90, dean engring., 1990-99; chmn. Working Group V-2 Internat. Soc. Photogrammetry and Remote Sensing, 1972-76, nat. reporter, 1980—; vis. prof. sch. survey U. NSW, Sydney, Australia, 1984-85, Faculty Engring. Survey, Wuhan Tech. U. Survey and Mapping, 1986; active in internat. rels. Nat. Sci. and Engring. Rsch. Coun. Can., 1988-93; commd. Can. Lands Surveyor. Mem. Am. Soc. Photogrammetry and Remote Sensing (Talbert Abrams grand award 1995), Can. Inst. Geomatics, Assn. Profl. Engrs. N.B. (2d v.p. 1994), Assn. N.B. Land Surveyors (hon.). Achievements include rsch. in self-calibration of amateur cameras and their use for precision photogrammetry; modeling of vastly different observables; four-dimensional photogrammetry in deformation studies; digital photogrammetry. Office: U New Brunswick, PO Box 4400, Fredericton, NB Canada E3B 5A3

FAIN, RICHARD DAVID, cruise line executive; b. Boston, Oct. 9, 1947; s. Morton Edgar and Libby Miriam (Winer) F.; m. Colleen Jo Ferris, July 27, 1969; children: Julie Meredith, Sara Elizabeth, Benjamin Alfred, Jessica Lynn. BS, U. Calif., Berkeley, 1969; MBA, U. Pa., 1972. Mgr. internat. fin. IU Internat. Corp., Phila., 1972-75; joint mng. dir., dir. Gotaas Larsen Shipping Corp., London, Eng., 1975-88; chmn., chief exec. officer Royal Caribbean Cruise Line, Miami, Fla., 1988—; chmn. Internat. Coun. Cruise Lines, Washington, 1993-95; bd. dirs. Assurance Foreningen Gard, SunTrust Bank, Miami, Semi-conductor Packaging Materials, Inc. Chmn. Greater Miami Conf. and Visitors Bur., 1995-97; trustee U. Miami, United Way Miami. Decorated Legion of Honor (France); named ARC Humanitarian of Yr., Dade County, Fla. Mem. Chaine de Rotisseurs. Home: 700 Arvida Pkwy Miami FL 33156-2325

FAINBERG, VALENTIN, chemical engineer, writer, playwright; b. Leningrad, Russia, Dec. 20, 1934; arrived in Israel, 1991; s. Samuel and Olga (Tyukhtyaev) F.; m. Ludmila Khodakovsky; children: Larry, Eugen. MA in Engring., Tech. U., Tallinn, Estonia, 1956; PhD, Acad. Mgmt., St. Petersburg, Russia, 1964; DSc, Acad. Scis., Tallinn, 1974. Engr. Kiviter Co., Kohtla-Yazve, Estonia, 1956-61; assoc. prof. Acad. Mgmt., St. Petersburg, 1964-76, leading scientist, 1976-89, prof., 1989-91; scientist Technion, Haifa, Israel, 1991-98; vice mayor City of Haifa, 1998—. Author: Chemistry and Technology of Shale Tar, 1976, Like a Lightning, 1977, The Real Man, 1978, Justus Liebig, 1982, Oil Shale Chemistry, 1985, History of Russian and Soviet Censorship, 1985, One must go away, 1988, The Delights of Adultery, 1997, Four walls and one passion, 1997; editor Israeli Repatriate Scientist Jour., 1995—, Twenty Two, 1996—; mem. editl. bd. Energy Sources Jour., 1994—, Oil Shale Jour., 1996—; patentee in field; contbr. over 70 articles to profl. jours., 100 articles to newspapers; plays presented in various theaters. Fellow Union Russian Writers; mem. Union Russian Theatre Workers, Israeli Fedn. Writer Unions, Assn. Immigrant Scientist (v.p. 1996—). Israel ba-Aliya. Avocations: theater, literature, fine arts, travel. E-mail: fainberg@ladpc.gov. Home: 53-19 Beit Lehem St, 35568 Haifa Israel Office: Haifa 14 Hassan Shukry, PO Box 4811, 31047 Haifa Israel

FAINGOLD, EDUARDO DANIEL, language and linguistics educator, researcher; b. La Plata, Argentina, Sept. 6, 1958; came to U.S., 1990; s. Enrique and Annie (Turkenich) F.; m. Sonia D. Hocherman; 1 child, Noam. BA in English and French, Hebrew U., Jerusalem, Israel, 1984, MA in English, 1987; PhD in Linguistics, Tel-Aviv U., 1992. Vis. scholar Tech. U. Berlin, 1988-89, UCLA, 1990-92, SUNY, Stony Brook, 1992-95; asst. prof. U. Tulsa (Okla.), 1995—; advisor to UNESCO, 1998; guest prof. Hebrew U. Jerusalem, Israel, 1996. Author: The Case for Fusion: (Jewish) Ladino in the Balkans and the Eastern Turkish Empire, 1989, Child Language, Creolization and Historical Change, 1996; guest editor: S.W. Jour. Linguistics, 1997, mem. editl. bd., 1997—; book rev. editor: Southwest Jour. of Linguistics, 1999-01; contbr. book reviews, articles to profl. jours. Book publ. grantee German Sci. Found., 1996, faculty rsch. grantee U. Tulsa, 1996-2000, Salzburg Seminar grantee, 1999, Nat. Endowment for Humanities grantee, 2000; recipient Fozis Rsch. prize, 1989, Tel-Aviv U. Cultural Doctoral prize, Tel-Aviv, 1991, Teaching award Teaching and Technology, U. Tulsa, 1997. Mem. MLA, Am. Assn. Tchrs. Spanish and Portuguese, Internat. Clin. and Linguistics Assn., Linguistic Assn. S.W., Linguistic Soc. Am., Internat. Linguistic Assn. Office: U Tulsa 600 S College Ave Tulsa OK 74104-3126

FAINSILBER, ADRIEN, architect; b. Le Nouvion, Aisne, France, June 15, 1932; s. Sigismond and Fanny (Moconci) F.; m. Julia Frances Berg, July 16, 1961; children: Olivier, Laura, Simon. Diplomé par le gouvernement, Ecole Nat. Superieure Beaux, Paris, 1960. In-charge studies Paris Region Devel. and Town Planning Inst., 1965-70. Prin. works include U. Villetaneuse, U. Tech. Compiegne, Oise, Evy Hosp., Essone, LA Geode Parc de la Villette, Paris, City of Sci., La Villette, Paris, Water Treatment Plant, Valenton, France, Mus. Fine Arts, Clermont, Ferrand, Unedic Headquarters, Paris Town Hall, Sarthe Children's Hosp., Toulouse Mus. Modern and Contemporary Art, Strasbourg Inst., others. Recipient Bronze medal Soc. Encouragement Art and Industry, 1973, Prix UIA Auguste Perret, 1990, Legion d'Honneur Ordre des Arts et des Lettres Grand Prix Nat. d'Architecture, 1986. Mem. Acad. of Architecture (Silver medal 1982), Soc. Francaise d'Urbanistes, French Soc. Architects, Brit. Soc. Architects, Cercle D'Etudes Architechurales, Internat. Acad. Architecture, Architects Couns. (pres. 1986-88). Office: 7 rue Salvador Allende, 92000 Nanterre France

FAIR, ALAN DEREK, physician; b. Feilding, New Zealand, May 9, 1921; arrived in Japan, 1953; s. Ernest and Ethel Maud (McNabb) F. MB, ChB, U. New Zealand, 1945. Med. officer Brit. Hosp., Paris, 1950, UN Korean Reconstrn. Agy./UN Civil Assistance Command, Korea, 1951-53; physician Tokyo Med. and Surg. Clinic, 1953-70, med. dir., 1970-98, sr. ptnr., 1998—; attending physician Internat. Cath. Hosp., Tokyo, 1953—. Contbr. articles to profl. jours. including Brit. Med. Jour. and Japan Med. Jour. Capt. New Zealand Army, 1946-47. Decorated Order of the Brit. Empire (Eng.). Mem. Brit. Med. Assn., Aerospace Med. Assn., Am. Assn. Pediat., Royal Soc. Medicine (Eng.), Tokyo Club (com. mem. 1989—), Tokyo Am. Club, Carlton Club (London). Anglican. Avocations: reading, music, golf. Home: Minato-ku, 2-13-12-310 Moto-Azabu, Tokyo 106-0046, Japan Office: Tokyo Med & Surg Clinic, 3-4-30 Shiba Koen, Bldg 32 Tokyo 105-0011, Japan

FAIR, KIMBERLY ROLLINS, chemist; b. Logan, W.Va., Jan. 12, 1971; d. Johnny Mac and Brenda (Podunavac) Rollins; m. Kennith Allen Fair Jr., Aug. 10, 1991; 1 child, Megan Nicole. BS in Chemistry, Lenoir-Rhyne Coll., Hickory, N.C., 1996. Pharmacy IV technician Frye Regional Med. Ctr., Hickory, 1992-98; chemist Hickory Springs Mfg. Co., Conover, N.C., 1998—. Mem. Am. Chem. Soc. Office: Hickory Springs Mfg Co PO Box 2948 Hickory NC 28603-2948

FAIR, MARCIA JEANNE HIXSON, retired educational administrator; b. Scobey, Mont.; d. Edward Goodell and Olga Marie (Frederickson) Hixson; m. Donald Harry Mahaffey (div. Aug. 1976); 1 child, Marcia Anne (dec.); m. George Justin Fair, Mar. 26, 1997. BA in English, U. Wash.; MA in Secondary Edn., U. Hawaii, 1967. Cert. secondary and elem. tchr. and adminstr. Tchr. San Lorenzo (Calif.) Sch. Dist., 1958-59; tchr. Castro Valley (Calif.) Sch. Dist., 1959-63, vice prin., 1963-67; vice prin. Sequoia Union High Sch. Dist., Redwood City, Calif., 1967-77, asst. prin., 1977-91, ret., 1991; tchr. trainer Project Impact Sequoia Union Sch. Dist., Redwood City, 1986-91; mem. supr.'s task force for dropout prevention, 1987-91, Sequoia Dist. Goals Commn. (chair subcom. staff devel. 1988); mentor tchr. selection com., 1987-91; mem. Stanford Program Devel. Ctr. Com., 1987-91; chairperson gifted and talented Castro Valley Sch. Dist.; mem. family svcs. bd., San Leandro, Calif. Vol. Am. Cancer Soc., San Mateo, Calif., 1967, Castro Valley, 1965; Sunday sch. tchr. Hope Luth. Ch., San Mateo, 1970-76; chair Carlmont H.S. Site Coun., Belmont, Calif., 1977-91; mem. Nat. Trust for Hist. Preservation; project initiator, dir. Bridle Trails Cmty. Club Neighborhood Beautification, project dir., 1999—. Recipient Life Mem. award Parent, Tchr., Student Assn., Belmont, 1984, Svc. award, 1989, Exemplary Svc award Carlmont High Sch., 1989, 92; named Woman of the Week, Castro Valley, 1967, Outstanding Task Force Chair Adopt A Sch. Program San Mateo (Calif.) County, 1990. Mem. ASCD, AAUW, DAR, Assn. Calif. Sch. Adminstrs. (Project Leadership plaque 1985), Sequoia Dist. Mgmt.Assn. (pres. 1975, treas. 1984-85), Met. Mus. Art, Smithsonian Instn., Libr. of Congress Assocs. (charter), Am. Heritage - The Soc. of Am. Historians, Internat. Platform Assn., Animal Welfare Advocacy, Woodrow Wilson Internat. Ctr. Scholars, Nat. Geographic Soc., The Nat. Mus. Women in the Arts, Am. Mus. Natural History (charter mem.), Delta Kappa Gamma, Alpha Xi Delta (Order of Rose award 1997). Avocations: oil painting, travel, tap dancing, redecorating, writing poetry.

FAIRALL, ANTHONY PATRICK, astronomer, planetarium director, writer; b. London, Sept. 15, 1943; arrived in South Africa, 1948; s. Sydney Richard and Christine Winifred (Eddington) F.; m. Delphine Ann O'Brien, July 8, 1972 (div. Oct. 1996); children: Lara Rosemary, Richard Craig, David Burton Jonathan; m. Pamela Alexandra Craib, Nov. 16, 1996; children: Desmond Cameron, Elizabeth Pamela. BSc, U. Cape Town, South Africa, 1965, BSc with honors, 1966; PhD, U. Tex., 1970. Tchg., grad. asst. U. Texas, Austin, 1967-70; lectr. U. Cape Town, 1970-76, sr. lectr., 1976-82, assoc. prof., 1982-97, prof., 1997—; lectr. South African Mus., Cape Town, 1965-66, dir., 1988—. Contbr. articles to profl. jours. Grantee in field. Mem. Astron. Soc. So. Africa (pres. 1983-84), Royal Astron. Soc. (assoc.). Avocations: hiking, water sports, cycling. Home: 59 Albion Rd, Rondebosch 7700, South Africa Office: U Cape Town, Dept Astronomy, Rondebosch 7700, South Africa

FAIRBAIRN, EDUARDO M.R., civil engineer, educator, consultant, researcher; b. Rio de Janeiro, Brazil, Oct. 25, 1951; s. Arnoldo Hasselmann and Regina M.M.R. (Moraes-Rego) F.; m. Branca Bastos Americano, June 15, 1985; children: Alberto A., Marcela A. Degree in engring., U. Federal Rio de Janeiro, 1973, MSc, 1978; D in Engring., U. Paris VI, 1984. Prof. UCP, Petropolis, 1976-80; asst. rschr. CEBTP, Paris, 1980-84; assoc. prof. U. Federal Rio de Janeiro, 1984—, head structural divsn., 1986-88, head civil engring. dept., 1997—; vis. rschr. LCPC, Paris, 1992-94. Author: Computer Vision for Measuring Structural Deformations, 1995; inventor in field; contbr. more than 60 articles in profl. jours. Mem. ASCE, RILEM, ABB. Avocations: karate, skiing, photography, literature, guitar. Office: Coppe/UFRJ-PEC, Caixa Postal 68506, 21945970 Rio de Janeiro Brazil

FAIRBRIDGE, RHODES WO., geologist, educator; b. Pinjarra, Australia, May 21, 1914; s. Kingsley Ogilvie and Ruby Ethel (Whitmore) Fairbridge; m. Dolores Gloria Carrington, June 19, 1943; 1 child, Kingsley Carrington Fairbridge. BA, Queens U., 1936; BS, Oxford U., 1938; DS, U. West Australia, 1942; PhD, U. Gotenburg, Sweden, 1977. Field geologist Iraq Petroleum Co., Middle East, 1938-40; lectr. U. W. Australia, Nedlands, 1946-53; prof. Columbia U., N.Y.C., 1955-82; vis. prof. U. Ill., Urbana, 1953-54, Sorbonne U., Paris, 1961, U. Cologne, Germany, 1977; vis. scientist NASA, N.Y., 1983—. Editor: (vol. and series) Ency. Earth Sci. Series, 24 vols. 1966-99 (Disting. Ref. award Geol. Info. Soc. 1999). Lt. USAF, PTO, 1942-46. Fellow Geol. Soc. Am. (sr.); mem. Geol. Assn./London, Sedimentology Soc., Coastal Edn. & Rsch. Found. (v.p. 1983—), Geol. Soc. of France (hon. life mem.), Internat. Union for Quaternary Rsch. (life). Avocation: travel. Home: 420 Riverside Dr Apt 2B New York NY 10025-7749 Office: PO Box 801 Amagansett NY 11930-0801

FAIRCHILD, JOSEPH VIRGIL, JR., accounting educator; b. New Orleans, Nov. 26, 1933; s. Joseph Virgil and Georgiana Malone (Bourgeois) F.; m. Judith Champagne, Aug. 12, 1961; children: Georgianna, Joseph, Benjamin. BS in Geology, La. State U., 1956, MBA, 1963, PhD, 1975. CPA, La. Geologist United Core, Inc., Houston, 1956-57; assoc. acct. Humble Oil & Refining Co., New Orleans, 1963-64; ptnr. L.A. Champagne & Co., Baton Rouge, 1964-69; pvt. practice acctg. Thibodaux, La., 1969-2000; ret., 2000; asst. prof. acctg. Nicholls State U., Thibodaux, 1969-75, assoc. prof., 1975-76, prof., 1976-84, Disting. prof. acctg., 1984—, asst. dean Coll. Bus., 1985-86, dir. grad. bus. studies, 1982-85; rsch. reviewer USAF Bus. Rsch. Mgmt. Ctr., Wright-Patterson AFB, Ohio, 1974-84; cons. Def. Sys. Mgmt. Coll., Ft. Belvoir, Va., 1980-81; faculty senate v.p. govt. com., chmn. dean's search com.; vis. prof. Henderson State U., Arkadelphia, Ark., 2000—. Author: (with others) The Acquisition and Distribution of Commercial Products, 1980, 1985-86, 1986-87, 1987-88 and 1988-89 Income Tax Guides for State Legislators; contbr. articles to profl. jours.; actor: (TV, movies) The Kingfish-TNT, Orleans-CBS, Deadman Walking; (plays) South Pacific, Arsenic and Old Lace, Brigadoon, Damn Yankees. Mem. St. Genevieve Sch. Bd., Thibodaux, 1979-83, E.D. White Cath. H.S. Bd., 1985-87, chmn. fin. com., 1985-87; lector St. Genevieve Ch., 1975—, choir, 1989—. 1st lt. USAF, 1957-60, lt. col. USAFR ret. Trueblood Prof. Touche-Ross Found., N.Y.C., 1987. Mem. AICPA, Soc. La. CPA's (lectr. seminars, La.'s Outstanding Acctg. Educator 1994), Am. Acctg. Assn., Nat. Assn. Accts., Nicholls State U. Alumni Assn. (Hon. Alumnus award 1991, Case Educator of Yr. 1994). Roman Catholic. Avocations: flying, skiing, photography, fishing. Home: 412 Plater Dr Thibodaux LA 70301-5616 Office: Nicholls State U Dept Acctg Thibodaux LA 70310-0001

FAIRCHILD, PHYLLIS ELAINE, school counselor; b. Franklin, La., Feb. 23, 1927; d. Joseph Virgil and Georgiana (Bourgeois) F. BS in Chemistry and Biology, U. Southwestern La., 1946; postgrad., La. State U., 1949-50, MEd in Guidance, 1966. Cert. chemistry, biology, gen. sci., Spanish and social studies tchr., counselor, La. Tchr. sci. St. Mary Parish Sch. Bd., Franklin, 1952-58, counselor, 1977-82; tchr. sci. Am. Dependent Schs., Yokohama, Japan, 1958-60, London, Lakenheath, Eng., 1960-61, Ramey AFB, PR, 1961-62; tchr. sci. Norfolk (Va.) City Schs., 1962-63, Iberville Parish Sch. Bd., Plaquemine, La., 1963-66; tchr. sci., counselor East Baton Rouge Parish Sch. Bd., Baton Rouge, 1966-77; counselor Hanson Sch. Bd., Franklin, 1982-94, 96-98; ret., 1998; mem. adv. com. La. Dept. Edn., Baton Rouge, 1976, 78. Mem. La. Landmarks Soc., Cath. Daugs. Am. (co-chmn. religious litergy 1992-94), Fortnightly Lit. Club (pres. 1982-83), Sigma Delta Pi, Pi Gamma Mu, Kappa Kappa Gamma, Delta Kappa Gamma (chmn. membership, scholarship, profl. affairs, 1971-77, parliamentarian 1996-98). Avocations: reading, walking, piano, writing. Home: 214 Morris St Franklin LA 70538-6127

FAIRCLOUGH, SIR JOHN W., science administrator; b. Thirsk, Eng., Aug. 23, 1930; m. Margaret Ann; 3 children. BScTech, Manchester U., 1954; DSc (hon.), Southampton, 1983, U. Cranfield, 1987, U. Manchester, 1988, U. Aston, 1990; DTech (hon.), Loughborough, 1990; DSc (hon.), Ctrl. London Polytechnic, 1991, City Univ., 1992, Manchester Mcpl. Univ., 1992. With Ferranti Ltd. UK, Ferranti Electric USA, 1954-57, IBM Lab., Poughkeepsie, N.Y., 1957-59; project mgr. IBM UK Labs. Ltd., 1959-64, lab. dir., 1964-68; dir. data processing mktg. and svc. IBM UK, 1969-70; lab. dir. IBM Lab., Raleigh, N.C., 1970-72; v.p. comm. systems IBM, 1972-74; chmn. IBM UK Labs. Ltd., 1974-82, dir. mfg. and devel., chmn., 1982-86; chief sci. advisor U.K. Cabinet Office, London, 1986-90; chmn. Rothschild Ventures Ltd., 1990-98; non-exec. dir. Oxford Instruments Group, 1990-98; bd. dirs. Psion Plc, Prince of Wales Innovation Initiative; adv. coun. sci. and tech., energy rsch. and devel., 1986-89; adv. bd. rsch. couns., 1986-89; bd. govs. European Joint Rsch. Ctr. 1986-89, com. rsch. on sci. and tech., 1986-89; trustee Found. Mental Health, 1997-99; gov. Inst. Expert Witness; chmn. Opsys plc Smart Chem. Co., Ltd. Patentee in field; author, co-author of over 20 pubs. Named Freeman City of London, 1989, Knight Bachelor, 1990. Fellow Inst. Elec. Engring U.K., Brit. Computer Soc. (pres. 1986), Royal Acad. Engring. U.K., Nat. Acad. Engring., Portsmouth Polytechnic (hon.), Inst. Civil Engrs. (hon.), Inst. Mech. Engrs. (hon.); mem. Inst. Elec. Engrs., Company Info. Technologists, Royal Soc. Arts and Mfg. Avocations: gardening, carpentry. Home: The Old Blue Boar, St Johns St, Winchester SO23 0HF, England also: Flat 3/57 Millbank, London SW1, England

FAIRCLOUGH, JONATHAN HOLDEN, software engineering consultant; b. Leigh, Lancs., Eng., Apr. 7, 1954; s. John Holden and Ethel Ruby (Norman) F.; m. Rachel Marion Henderson, Sept. 2,1978; children: Iain, Alexander, Selena. BA, U. Cambridge, Eng., 1975; MSc, U. London, 1981. Tchr. Univ. Tutorial Coll., London, 1975-77, King Harold Sch., Waltham Abbey, Eng., 1978-80; higher sci. officer SERC, Chilton, Eng., 1980-85; sr. sci. officer SERC, Hawaii, 1985-89; prin. cons. Logica, Leatherhead, Eng., 1990-93; quality mgr. Anite Systems, Woking, Eng., 1994-99; U.K. expert on ISO/TC176/SC2/WG17; cons. Original Ltd., Guildford Surrey, 1999—; chmn. BSi/QS/1/-/7, London, 1995—; convenor Software Engring. Standards User Group, Woking, 1996—. Co-author, editor: Software Engineering Standards, 1994, Software Engineering Guides, 1995; author articles. Fellow Royal Astron. Soc.; mem. IEEE, Brit. Computer Soc. Mem. Labour Party. Home and Office: 131 Stoke Rd, Guildford Surrey GU1 1ET, England

FAIRHEAD, JAMES DEREK, geophysics educator, university director; b. Barnet, Herts, Eng., Nov. 19, 1944; s. Leonard Charles Thomas and Rhoda Helen (Palin) F.; m. Christine Ann Cheesewright, July 29, 1972; children: Helen Louis, Alexander James. BS, Durham (Eng.) U., 1967; MS in Geophysics, Newcastle upon Tyne (Eng.) U., 1968, PhD in Geophysics, 1975. Lectr. U. Leeds (Eng.), 1972-86, sr. lectr., 1986-92, prof. applied geophysics, 1992—, mng. dir. GETECH divsn., 1986—. Contbr. more than 60 articles to profl. jours. Recipient medal Bur. Gravity Internat., 1994. Mem. S.E.G. (Spl. Commendation 1999), E.A.G.E., A.A.P.G. Anglican. Avocation: golf. Office: GETECH c/o Sch Earth Scis, U Leeds, LS2 9JT Leeds W Yorkshire, England

FAIRLEIGH, JAMES PARKINSON, music educator; b. St. Joseph, Mo., Aug. 24, 1938; s. William Macdonald and Mable Emily (Parkinson) F.; m. Marlane Alberta Paxson, June 25, 1960; children: William Paxson, Karen Evelyn. MusB, U. Mich., 1960; MusM, U. So. Calif., 1965; PhD, U. Mich., 1973. Instr., asst. prof. Hanover (Ind.) Coll., 1965-75; assoc. prof. R.I. Coll., Providence, 1975-80; prof., head music dept. Jacksonville (Ala.) State U., 1980—; dir. of music First Presbyn. Ch., Anniston, Ala., 1981—; presenter, lectr. at meetings of profl. orgns., 1974-99. Contbr. articles to profl. jours., mags., 1966—. Served to 1st lt. U.S. Army, 1960-62. Mem. Am. Musicol. Soc., Ala. Music Tchrs. Assn. (cert., treas. 1982-86, 1st v.p. 1986-88, pres. 1988-90), Coll. Music Soc. (southern chpt. exec. bd. 1996-98), Music Tchrs. Nat. Assn. (cert.), Assn. Ala. Coll. Music Adminstrs. (sec., treas. 1985-89, pres. 1989-91), Phi Beta Kappa, Phi Kappa Phi, Pi Kappa Lambda, Phi Eta Sigma, Phi Mu Alpha Sinfonia. Republican. Avocations: waterkiing, swimming, backpacking. Home: 512 Fairway Dr SW Jacksonville AL 36265-3301 Office: Jacksonville State U Dept Music Jacksonville AL 36265

FAIRWEATHER-TAIT, SUSAN JANE, nutritionist; b. King's Lynn, Norfolk, Eng., July 17, 1949; d. Arthur Leslie and Mildred Joan (Woodward) Fox; m. Philip Andrew Fairweather-Tait, Aug. 15, 1980 (dec. Jan. 1983); m. Christopher Bruce McEvoy, May 17, 1986; 1 child, Andrew James. BSc, U. London, 1973, MSc with distinction, 1974, PhD, 1978, DSc, 1996. Lectr. Middlesex Poly., London, 1974-77; demonstrator King's Coll., London, 1976-77; rsch. nutritionist Beecham Products, London, 1978-79; sr. sci. officer Inst. of Food Rsch., Norwich, Eng., 1979-86, prin. rsch. scientist, 1986—, head diet health and consumer sci. divsn., 1999—; lectr. U. East Anglia, Norwich, 1990—, hon. chair Sch. Health, 1998—; mem. com. on dietary reference values Com. Med Aspects of Food Policy, London, 1987-92; mem. task force on iron Brit. Nutrition Found., London, 1992-95; mem. biovailability of nutrients task force Internat. Life Sci. Inst. Europe, Brussels, 1992—. Contbr. articles to profl. jours., chpts. to books. Recipient BNF Nutrition prize, 1997; European Union Project grantee, 1989—, Med. Rsch. Coun. grantee, London, 1994—, Biotech. and Biol. Scis. Rsch. Coun. grantee, 1996—. Mem. Nutrition Soc., Am. Inst. Nutrition, European Acad. Nutritional Scientists. Avocations: literature, art, antiques, opera, gardening. Office: Inst of Food Research, Norwich Rsch Pk, Norwich NR4 7UA, England

FAISAL, FARHAD, physics educator; b. Pabna, Bengal, Bangladesh, Nov. 3, 1939; arrived in Germany, 1974; s. Bande Ali Ahmed and Rausanara (Begum) Ahmed; m. Wanda Maria Mafezzoni, Aug. 1974; 1 child, Ahmed Aldo. Student, Edward Coll., Pabna, Bangladesh, 1958; BSc, Dhaka (Bangladesh) U., 1961, MSc, 1962; PhD, London U., 1967. Rsch. asst. Atomic Energy Authority, Harwell, Eng., 1967-69; resident rsch. fellow NASA, Md., 1969-71; rsch. assoc. U. Pitts., 1971-73; prof. physics U. Bielefeld, Germany, 1974—. Contbr. over 100 articles to rsch. publs. Kali Narayan scholar Dhaka U., 1961; postdoctoral fellow U.S. Acad. Scis., 1969. Mem. Deutsche Hochschul Lehroe Verband, N.Y. Acad. Scis. Office: Univ Bielefeld, Universitat Str 25, D-33615 Bielefeld Germany

FAISS, ROBERT DEAN, lawyer; b. Centralia, Ill., Sept. 19, 1934; s. Wilbur and Theresa Ella (Watts) F.; m. Linda Louise Chambers, Mar. 30, 1991; children: Michael Dean Faiss, Marcy Faiss Ayres, Robert Mitchell Faiss, Philip Grant Faiss, Justin Cooper. BA in Journalism, Am. U., 1969, JD, 1972. Bar: Nev. 1972, D.C. 1972, U.S. Dist. Ct. Nev. 1973, U.S. Supreme Ct. 1977, U.S. Ct. Appeals (9th cir.) 1978. City editor Las Vegas (Nev.) Sun, 1957-59; pub. info. officer Nev. Dept. Employment Security, 1959-61; asst. exec. sec. Nev. Gaming Commn., Carson City, 1961-63; exec. asst. to gov. State of Nev., Carson City, 1963-67; staff asst. U.S. Pres. Lyndon B. Johnson, White House, Washington, 1968-69; asst. to exec. dir. U.S. Travel Adminstrn., Washington, 1969-72; ptnr., chmn. adminstrv. law dept. Lionel, Sawyer & Collins, Las Vegas, 1973—; mem. bank secrecy Act Adv. Group U.S. Treasury. Co-author: Legalized Gaming in Nevada, 1961, Nevada Gaming License Guide, 1988, Nevada Gaming Law, 1991, 95, 98. Recipient Bronze medal Dept. Commerce, 1972, Chris Schaller award We Can, Las Vegas, 1995, Lifetime Achievement award Nev. Gaming Attys. Assn., 1997; named One of 100 Most Influential Lawyers in Am. and premier U.S. gaming atty., Nat. Law Jour., 1997. Mem. ABA (chmn. gaming law com. 1985-86), Internat. Assn. Gaming Attys. (founding, pres. 1980), Nev. Gaming Attys. Office: Lionel Sawyer & Collins 300 S 4th St Ste 1700 Las Vegas NV 89101-6053

FAISSNER, HELMUT CARL, physics educator; b. Kempten, Allgäu, Germany, May 5, 1928; s. Ludolf and Dorothea (Dengler) F.; m. Ursula Kammann, Aug. 15, 1953; children: Andreas, Wolfgang, Cordelia. Diploma in Physics, U. Heidelberg, Germany, 1952, D Natural Sci., 1952; D Natural Sci. (hon.), U. Tübingen, Germany, 1996; Rhein-Westfäl Inst. Tech. Asst. Max-Planck Inst. Med. Forsch., Heidelberg, 1952-56, U. Tübingen, 1956-58; rschr. CERN, Geneva, 1958-64; prof. Rhein-Westfalen Inst. Tech., Aachen, Germany, 1964-93, prof. emeritus physics, 1993—, rector, 1969-70. Author: Polarisation of Nucleons by Scattering, 1961; co-editor: Procs. of the Internat. Neutrino Conf., 1977, 6th Topical Workshop on Proton-Antiproton Collider Physics, 1987. Recipient Max-Born prize German and English Phys. Soc., 1980. Fellow Am. Phys. Soc.; mem. German Phys. Soc., Lions Internat. Mem. Social-Democratic Party of Germany. Roman Catholic. Avocation: listening to classical music. Home: Eupener Str 285a, 52076 Aachen Germany Office: III Physics Inst Physics Ct, Rhein-Westfäl Inst Tech, 52056 Aachen NRW, Germany

FAIVRE, ANTOINE, educator; b. Reims, France, June 5, 1934; s. André and Madeleine (Clour) F. Diploma, Ecole Pratique Hautes Etudes, 1965; doctor of letters, U. Paris-Sorbonne, 1969. Rschr. C.N.R.S., France, 1965-69; assoc. prof. U. Paris, 1969-72; prof. in German Lang. and Lit. U. Bordeaux, 1972-85, U. Rouen, 1985-90; prof. religious studies Ecole Pratique des Hautes Etudes, Sorbonne, 1979—, chair history esoteric and mystical currents in Europe. Author: Access to Western Esotericism, 1996, Philosophie de la Nature, 1995, The Golden Fleece and Alchemy, 1995, The Eternal Hermes, 1996; editor (series) Cahiers de l'Hermétisme, 1978—, A.R.I.E.S., 1985—. Maj. French Army, 1971-91. Recipient Palmes Académiques Bd. of Edn., 1981. Mem. Am. Acad. of Religion. Avocation: history of cinema. Home: 8 Chemin Scribe, 92190 Meudon France Office: EPHE (V) - Sorbonne, 45 rue des Ecoles, 75005 Paris France

FAIVRE-DUBOZ, GUY MARIE FRANCOIS, retired oil company executive; b. Fez, Morocco, Mar. 25, 1936; s. Jean and Henrietta (Cucherousset) Faivre-Duboz; m. Liliane Bigot, Aug. 16, 1960; children: Luc, Eric. B, Lycee, Fez, 1954. Chief acct. Oil Cy, Paris, 1962-65, in-charge acctg. orgn., 1966-72, auditor, mgr., 1973-76, audit dept. mgr., 1977-81, fin. dept. mgr., 1982-2000. Served to lt. French Inf., 1959-62. Decorated Valeur Militaire, 1962. Mem. Internal Auditors Inst.

FAIZ, MOHAMED M., physicist, researcher; b. Jaffna, Sri Lanka, Apr. 2, 1959; s. Mohamed and Fowzia (Aboobucker) Meeransahib; m. Thasmina Sellathamby, Dec. 17, 1987; children: Sajid, Nida, Huda. BS, U. Jaffna, 1981; MS, U. Ill., 1987, PhD, 1992. Lectr. U. Jaffna, 1981-83, Eastern U., Sri Lanka, 1983-85; rsch. asst. Argonne Nat. Lab., Chgo., 1988-92, postdoctoral fellow, 1992-94; asst. prof. King Fahd U. Petroleum & Minerals, Dhahran, Saudi Arabia, 1994-2000; assoc. prof. King Fahd U. Petroleum & Minerals, Dhahran, 2000—. Mem. Am. Physical Soc. Office: King Fahd U Petroleum & Minerals, Physics Dept, 1152 Dhahran Saudi Arabia

FAJARDO, BEDA GAVINO, lawyer; b. Gubat, Sorsogon, Philippines, Nov. 4, 1943; s. Jacinto Jarabejo Fajardo and Adelfa Azul Gavino; m. Rafaelita Gonzales Faustino, Aug. 16, 1973; children: Rafaela Margarita, Christian, Juan Paolo. BA, U. Philippines, 1964, LLB, 1968; postgrad., Harvard U., 1990, Tulane U., 1999. Assoc. atty. Teves Campos Mendoza & Hernandez, Manila, 1970-71; sr. assoc. Salcedo Del Rosario Bito & Misa, Manila, 1971-75; ptnr. Montilla Linsangan Reloj & Fajardo, Manila, 1976-90; mng. ptnr. Fajardo Law Offices, Makati, Philippines, 1990—; arbitrator Constrn. Industry Arbitration Commn.; dir. Australian Power and Water Philippines, Inc. Author: Tetley's Maritime Liens and Claims, 2d edit., 1998. Mem. Presdl. Commn. for Better Adminstrn. of Justice/created by Pres. Corazon Aquino, 1990; nominee Philippine Constnl. Commn., 19973; candidate for Congress, 1998; trustee Philippine Dispute Resolution Ctr. Inst., 1998-99; dir. Philippine Inst. of Constrn. Arbitrators, 1998-99. Named Outstanding Sorsoganon in Law, Province of Sorsogon, 1995, Outstanding Sen., Philippine Jaycees, 1990. Mem. Rotary of Manila (chair justice com. 1999). Avocations: reading history books, watching hist. movies, gardening, swimming, jogging. Home: 972 Aurora Blvd, 1109 Quezon City/Manila Philippines Office: Fajardo Law Office/7th Flr, Cityland Condo 10/Twr 2, 1200 Makati City/Manila Philippines

FAJARDO, HERMINIA ROSALES, company executive; b. Pateros, Manila, Jan. 19, 1929; m. Luzmindo Boza Fajardo; children: Maria Angelica Pormarejo, Maria Paula Teresa Acuña, Jose Maria, Andres Maria. BS in Pharmacy, Manila Ctrl. U., 1950; BSChE, Mapua Inst. Tech., Manila, 1954; diploma, Rsch. Inst. Mgmt. Sci., Delft, The Netherlands, 1959; MBA in Indsl. Mgmt., Quezon City, 1967; PhD in Commerce, U. Santo Tomas, Manila, 1979. Market rschr. E.R. Squibb & Sons, Inc., Makati, The Philippines, 1955; sr. indsl. engr. Indsl. Devel. Ctr., Manila, 1955-62; mem. faculty indsl. chemistry Mapua Inst. Tech., 1955-65; v.p., gen. mgr. Sehwani, Inc., Pasig City, The Philippines, 1962-69; assoc. dir. Inst. for Small Scale Industries U. of The Philippines, Quezon City, 1969-78; ops. dir. Resource Cons. Internat., Inc., Makati, 1978-82; exec. v.p. Apparrel Tech. and Mgmt. Svcs. Inc., Pasig City, 1987-89; chmn., pres. Profl. Inst. for Mgmt. Advancement, Quezon City, 1993-96; prof. ops. mgmt. Coll. Bus. Adminstrn. U. of The Philippines, 1979-95, professorial lectr., 1994-97; mem. faculty Grad. Sch. Bus. and Econs. De La Salle U., Manila, 1995—; cons. Marikina (The Philippines) Shoe Trade Commn., 1974-80; sr. cons. Bus. Rsch. Found., Quezon City, 1972-90; supervising cons. Commn. on Small and Medium Industries, Makati, 1978-79; UNIDO cons. Directorate Gen. for Small Industries, Ministry of Industry, Govt. of Indonesia, Jakarta, 1982-85, Govt. of Sierra Leona, Freetown, 1991, Nat. Indsl. Devel. and Fin. Orgn., Freetown, 1991, Royal Hashemite Kingdom, Amman, Jordan, 1995; mgmt. cons. Indsl. Govt. Bd. Govt. of Sri Lanka, Moratuwa, 1986; cons. tech. park project U. of The Philippines, 1988-90; macro indsl. econs. expert Asian Devel. Bank, Pasig City, 1989-90; cons. materials mgmt. sys. Atlas Fertilizer Corp., Toledo City, The Philippines, 1990; sr. fellow sci. and tech. Dept. Sci. and Tech., Taguig, The Philippines, 1994; nat. cons. on people with disabilities Interdepartmental Project on Urban Informal Sector, Makati, 1995; cons. small and medium enterprise devel. Philippine C. of C. and Industry, Manila, 1994-98; cons. on ops. mgmt. Nat. Econ. Enterprise Devel. Program, Presdl. Coun. for Countryside Devel., Bacolod City, The Philippines, 1995;

chair/resource person numerous confs., seminars or workshops in field. Contbr. articles to profl. publs. Bd. dirs., sec. Philippine com. UNIFEM, 199498. Fellow Netherlands Bur. for Tech. Assistance, 1959, Oversas Tech. Coop. Agy., 1970, UNIDO, 1974, U.S. AID, 1976, UN Devel. Fund for Women, 1993; grantee U.S. AID, 1965, UNIDO, 1975. Mem. Profl. Inst. Mgmt. Advancement (chmn., pres. 1993-96), Small Enterprise Rsch. and Devel. Found. (trustee 1990-91), Mfg. Industry Roundtable (exec. com. mfg. linkage program 1989—), Women for Women Found., Zonta (internat. dist. 17 chair status of women com. 1991-94, exec. dir. Found. 1990—, chair internat. dist. 17 status of women com. 1994-96, 2000-02, coord. svc. com. internat. area 1 1992-94, Spl. Svc. award 1991), Zonta Internat. (area 5 dir. dist. 17 1998-2000), Zonta Found. Philippines Inc. (pres.). Home: 14 Twinpeaks Dr Blue Ridge, Quezon City Manila 1109, The Philippines

FAJARDO, ROMEO VELASCO, ophthalmologist, educator; b. Malolos, Bulacan, The Philippines, Mar. 8, 1927; s. Justo Bulaong and Maria Cruz (Velasco) F.; m. Narcisa Lacson Quiaoit, Dec. 30, 1961; children: Moises Romeo, Maria Florentina, Therese Narcisa, Raymond Bonifacio. AA, U. of the Philippines, Manila, 1947, MD, 1952. Diplomate in Ophthalmology Am. Bd. Ophthalmology, Philippine Bd. Ophthalmology. Resident in ears, eyes, nose and throat Philippine Gen. Hosp., Manila, 1953-58; resident in ophthalmology Wills Eye Hosp., Phila., 1958-60; instr. ophthalmology U. of The Philippines, Manila, 1961-66, from asst. to assoc. to full prof., 1966-92; rsch. ophthalmologist Inst. Ophthalmology, Manila, 1965-92; prof. emeritus in ophthalmology U. of The Philippines, Manila, 1992—; cons. ophthalmology Philippine Gen. Hosp., Manila, 1961—, Manila Drs. Hosp., Manila, 1991—; chmn. dept. ophthalmology Philippine Gen. Hosp. and U. of The Philippines, Manila, 1988-91, Manila Drs. Hosp., 1998—; Luis Santos and Jose Rizal lectr. Philippine Acad. Ophthalmology, 1979, 85, Presdl. lectr., 1976, 98; Zuellig-Pharma Industries professorial chair U. of The Philippines, Manila, 1983, U.P. Diamond Jubilee professorial chair, 1989, 90, 91, De Ocampo Rsch. professorial chair, 1992. Editor: Practice Guidelines in Ocular Inflammation, 1999; editor-in-chief: (textbook) Philippine Textbook of Ophthalmology (Golden Book award), 1981, (jour.) Philippine Jour. Ophthalmology, 1969—; inventor in field. Pres. San Isidro Cath. Cmty. Assn., Manila, 1979—, West Pura Cir., Quezon City, The Philippines, 1987—; pres. Tierra Homeowners Assn., Quezon City, 1991. Recipient Alcond Rsch. award Philippine Acad. Ophthalmology, 1976, 78, 82, 84, 88, 92. Fellow Philippine Coll. Surgeons (emeritus), Philippine Acad. Ophthalmology (pres. 1975-76, Merit award 1980), Am. Acad. Ophthalmology; mem. Internat. Ocular Inflammation Soc. (councillor 1991—), Philippine Ocular Inflammation Soc. (pres. 1997—), Philippine Med. Assn. (pres. Manila chpt. 1953—, emeritus), Asian-Pacific Acad. Ophthalmology (councillor 1981—, pres. XVII congress 1999, Disting. Svc. award 1999). Roman Catholic. Avocations: reading, writing. Home: 3 Maria Eva, 1107 Quezon City The Philippines Office: Manila Drs Hosp, 667 United Nations Ave, 1000 Manila The Philippines

FAKAE, BARINEME BEKE, veterinary surgeon, educator; b. Bori, Ogoni, Nigeria, Mar. 26, 1956; s. Beke Faribo and Elinah Oroni (Uwa) F.; m. Dorothy Barine Obuh, Aug. 18, 1978; children: Tuamene, Lenu, Lebia, Suanu, Niabari. DVM, U. Nigeria, Nsukka, 1982, MSc, 1986; PhD, U. Edinburgh, Scotland, 1993. Registered vet. surgeon, Nigeria. Petroleum insp. Mines and Power, Nigeria, 1975-76; vet. officer Nat. Youth Corp, Calabar, Nigeria, 1982-83; grad. asst. U. Nigeria, 1983-86, lectr. II, then lectr. I, 1986-93, sr. lectr., 1993—; head dept. vet. parasitology and entomology U. Nigeria, 1995-96, cons. Vet. Tchg. Hosp., 1993—. Contbr. articles to sci. jours. Bd. dirs. Scripture Union Press and Books Ltd., Nigeria, 1998; mem. visitation panel Fed. Ministry of Edn., Nigeria, 1999. Traveling fellow Brit. Coun., Nottingham, Eng., 1993, Wellcome Trust, Aberyswyth, Wales, 1999; 3rd World vis. scientist Royal Soc., Aberyswyth, 1998. Mem. Nigerian Soc. for Animal Prodn., Brit. Soc. Parasitology, World Assn. Vet. Educators. Avocations: table tennis, music, computer graphics. E-mail: misunn@aol.com. Office: Univ Nigeria, Dept Vet Parasit/Entom, Nsukka Nigeria

FAKAFANUA, TUTOATASI, Tongan government official; b. Jan. 20, 1962; married; 3 children. B in Commerce, U. Otago, Dunedin, New Zealand, 1983, LLB, 1987; LLM (hon.), U. Auckland, New Zealand, 1991; DMin, Faith Evang. Luth. Sem., Tacoma, 2000. Lay preacher Free Wesleyan Ch.; law clerk, barrister and solicitor Clive Edwards & Co., Auckland, 1987-89; mem. bd. dirs. Tonga Devel. Bank; crown counsel Crown Law Dept., Tonga, 1991; min. labor, commerce, and industries Govt. Tonga, Nuku'alofa, 1991—. Mem. Legis. Assembly, Privy Coun. and Cabinet, dep. min. finance, registrar of cos., registrar of inc. socs., 1991—, min. fin., treas., commr. Inland Revenue, contr. post office, min.-in-charge statistics dept. Office: Min Finance, PO Box 87 Vuna Rd, Nuku'alofa Tonga

FAKHRO, SAMIR QASIM, technology educator, computer company executive; b. Manama, Bahrain, Dec. 21, 1953; s. Qasim Ahmad and Aysha Mohammad Fakhro; m. Faiqa A. Abdul Rahman; 1 child, Aysha. BSc in Elec. Engring., Am. U. Beirut, 1975; MSc in Elec. Engring., U. Mich., Ann Arbor, 1976, PhD in Elec. Engring., 1980. Chmn. computer sci. sect. Gulf Polytechnic, 1980-81, head engring. depts., 1982-85, asst. to dean engring. affairs, 1985-87, assoc. prof. elec. engring and computer applications, 1987; asst. to pres. U. Bahrain, 1987-89, v.p. adminstrn. and fin., 1989-95, advisor to pres. on info. tech. matters, 1996-97, prof. elec. engring. and computer applications, 1993—; chmn. Qasim Ahmad Fakhro Group of Cos., Bahrain, 1995—; dep. dir. gen. Asia region Internat. Biog. Centre, Cambridge, Eng., 1995—; dep. gov. Am. Biog. Inst., N.C., 1995—; prof., dep. chmn. bd. trustees Mediterranean U. Sci. and Tech., Valencie, Spain, 1995—; cons. UNESCO, 1986—; cons. Assn. Arab Univs., Jordan, 1993-94, Ednl. Devel. Centre, U.S.A., 1992—, Internat. Assn. Edn., Tng. & Comm. Techs., France, 1994—, Arab Ctr. Strategic Studies, Egypt, 1994—, Qatar Ctr. Futuristic Studies, 1998—; presenter various rsch. confs.; mem. rsch. bd. advisors Am. Biog. Inst., N.C., 1995; mem. nat. computer licensing com. Govt. Bahrain, 1985—; mem. Nat. Com. for Assessment of Tech. Qualifications of Acad. Degrees Holders in Bahrain, 1985-96; sr. cons., mem. Nat. Computer Edn. Com., 1985—; chmn. computers and info. systems com. Arabian Gulf U., 1987, ex-mem. com. for introduction computers in spl. edn., 1987; nat. rep. UNESCO's intergovtl. informatics program, 1990—, Regional Info. Tech. and Software Engring. Centre, 1992—; mem. organizing com. Middle East Conf. on Info. Tech., Bahrain; chmn. evaluation com. for awarding The Crown Prince Prize to Best Bahraini Rschr. in field of Sci. and Tech., 1994-95; mem. organizing com. Middle East Conf. on Info. Tech., Bahrain., 1994-95; chmn. com. Crown Prince Award Prize, 1994, 95; chmn. com. Univ. Faculty Acad. Promotions, 1996, 97; dep. chmn., founder Al Nadeem Info. Tech., Bahrain, 1995—. Trustee U. Sci. and Tech., Yemen Republic, 1997—. Recipient rsch., tuition and teaching fellowships U. Mich., Ann Arbor, 1976-79, scholarships Ministry of Edn., 1970-75, 75-76. Mem. IEEE, Am. Soc. Engring. Edn., Am. Assn. Physics Tchrs., Bahrain Soc. Engrs., Internat. Coun. on Edn. for Teaching, Internat. Assn. for Edn., Tng. and Comm. Techs., France, N.Y. Acad. Sci. and Tech. Avocations: table tennis, swimming, walking, reading. Home: PO Box 633, Manama Bahrain Office: U Bahrain, PO Box 32038, Manama Bahrain

FAKOUSSA, THOMAS AWAD, pilot, safety educator; b. Port Said, Egypt, May 19, 1948; arrived in Germany, 1956; s. Hassan Awad and Gisela Nadia (Telschow) F.; m. Claire Woolford, Sept. 15, 1980; children: Rebecca, Olivia. Lic. airline pilot. Capt. German Lufthansa, 1977-95; founder Personal Resource Mgmt. Tng. for Safer Pilots; founder Creative Learning Assn., 1992-95; mgr. Awareness Tng., 1995—.

FALANGAS, COSTAS, hotel executive; b. Athens, Attika, Greece, July 7, 1975; s. John Falangas and Maria Pologeorgis. Cert. in French, Inst. Française D'Athenes, Greece, 1991; cert. Deutsch ALS Fremdsprache, Goethe Inst. Chania-Crete, Greece, 1991; cert. in English, Greece, 1992; diploma, Ctr. Internat. Glion, Switzerland, 1996. Asst. fin. mgr. Hotel de la Tremoille, Paris, 1995; gen. mgr. Bali Paraside Beach, Rethymno, Greece, 1996—; v.p. M. Pologeorgis S.A., Bali, Greece, 1996-99. Cpl. Greek Army, 1998. Mem. Greek Tourist Orgn., Tourism 12 Months in Crete. Democrat. Greek Orthodox. Avocations: drawing, architecture, painting, culture, reading. Home: 1 Kondylaki 8, 74100 GR Rethymno Greece Office: Bali Paradise Beach Hotel, Resort D'Bungalow, 74057 Bali Greece

FALASCHI, PAOLO, internist, educator; b. Offagna, Ancona, Italy, Oct. 2, 1947; s. Vittorio and Iole (Provaroni) F.; m. Maria Costanza Tonnini; 1 child, Giulia Maria. MD, U. Rome, 1972. Med. diplomate. Intern, resident Policlinico Umberto I, Rome, 1972-75; postdoctoral fellow in endocrinology U. La Sapienza, Rome, 1972-75, asst. prof., 1976-79, 81-82; vis. fellow St. Bartholomew's Hosp., London, 1976-77; vis. asst. prof. Mt. Sinai Sch. Medicine, N.Y.C., 1980-81; assoc. prof. Second U. Naples, Italy, 1988-99; prof. endocrinology Campus Biomedico, Rome, 1996—; assoc. prof. internal medicine, 2nd faculty medicine U. La Sapienza, Rome, 1999—. Contbr. over 300 articles to profl. jours. Roman Catholic. Avocations: reading, golf, travel. Home: Via Tor Fiorenza 13, 00199 Rome Italy Office: Via Dora 1, 00197 Rome Italy

FALCAM, LEO A., Micronesian government official. V.p. Federated States of Micronesia, 1997—. Office: Office of the Pres, POB PS-53 Palikir, Pohnpei 96941, Federated States of Micronesia

FALCÃO, JOSÉ FREIRE CARDINAL, archbishop; b. Ereré, Ceará, Brazil, Oct. 23, 1925; s. Otávio Freire de Andrade and Maria Falcão Freire. Lic. in Philosophy, Seminary, Fortaleza, Brazil, 1945, lic. in Theology, 1949. Priest Limoeiro do Norte, 1949-67, bishop, 1967-71; archbishop Teresina, 1971-84; archbishop Brasila, 1984—, cardinal, 1988—. Address: QL 12-Cj12 Lote 1 Lago Sul, 71600-325 Brasilia Brazil Office: Curia Arquidiocesana, Av L2 Sul Q 601, 70200-610 Brasília Brazil*

FALCO, GÉRARD, economic information manager; b. Paris, Feb. 14, 1940; s. Jean Jacques and Marina (Kamenka); m. Helène Lucie Viviand, Dec. 11, 1971; children: Nadine, Isabelle. Degree in engring., Ecole Superieure Informatique Electonique Automatisme, France, 1966. Attaché Ecole des Hautes Etudes Commericales, France, 1967-68, info. mgr., 1968-70, adminstrv. mgr. fin. Ctr. Calculations, 1970-72; under-dir. info. C. of C. & Industry, Paris, 1975-80, adj. dir. info., 1980-87, dir. econ. info., 1987—; adminstrator HPM; chargè de cours Ecole Nat. Superieure Techniques, Avancees, France, 1972; sec. gen. (hon.) Assns. Telefirm, Telexport and Audite; mem. com. Français pour l'Audio Visuel. Editor Orgn. Internat. Info., Info. and the Mgr. Active mcpl. coun. of mayor Marnes la Coquette, 1989-95. Knight Nat. Order of Merit (France). Mem. Ctr. Francais du Droit de Copie (adminstr.). Home: 19 Ave Etienne de Moutgolfier, 92430 Marnes la Coquette France Office: C of C, 27 Ave de Friedland, 75008 Paris France

FALCO, MATHEA, lawyer, educator; b. Montgomery, Ala., Oct. 15, 1944; d. Maceo and Kathleen (Fream) Falco; m. Peter Tarnoff, June 11, 1982; 1 child, Benjamin Tarnoff. BA cum laude, Radcliffe Coll., 1965; JD, Yale U., 1968. Bar: D.C. 1968, U.S. Supreme Ct. 1969, Calif. 1984. Chief counsel, staff dir. U.S. Senate Juvenile Delinquency Subcom., Washington, 1971-74; rsch. fellow, spl. asst. to Pres., Drug Abuse Coun., Washington, 1974-76; asst. sec. of state Dept. State, Washington, 1977-81; counsel Pub. Utilities Commn., San Francisco, 1982-86; cons. Carnegie Corp. N.Y., N.Y.C., 1987-92; pres. Drug Strategies, Washington, 1993—. Author: Making of A Drug-Free America; Programs That Work, 1992, 94. Trustee Radcliffe Coll., Cambridge, Mass., 1967-79; mem. bd. overseers Harvard U., Cambridge, 1985-91, Coun. Fgn. Rels. Office: Drug Strategies 1575 Eye St NW Washington DC 20005-1105

FALCONE, ROBERT EDWARD, surgeon; b. Sulmona, Italy, Apr. 12, 1950; s. Joseph and Sophie (Kosier) F.; 1 child, Melissa. Student, Cleve. State U., 1968-71; BA in Chemistry magna cum laude, Kent (Ohio) State U., 1973; MD cum laude, Ohio State U., 1976, postgrad., 1987-90. Mem. staff and teaching faculty Grant Med. Ctr., Columbus, Ohio, 1981—, dir. trauma svcs., 1985-98, dir. surg. ICU, med. dir. life flight, 1988-95, chmn. dept. surgery, 1989-90, med. co-dir. med flight; v.p. trauma and critical care svcs. Grant/Riverside Med. Ctr. Hosps., 1998-99, sr. v.p. trauma, 1999—; chmn. Ohio Com. on Trauma, 1994—; chmn. nutritional support com. Riverside Meth. Hosp., Columbus, 1983-84; med. dir. Franklin County Paramedic Sch., Columbus, 1992-95; clin. assoc. prof. Ohio State U. Coll. of Medicine, Columbus, 1985—; surg. product advisor Ethican, Inc., 1984-85, Bd. Cardiosurgery, Inc., 1986-87; lectr. in continuing medicine edn. Merck Sharp and Dohme, Inc., 1986—, Squibb & Sons, Inc., 1989—, Roerig Divsn. Pfizer, Inc., 1994—. Contbr. numerous articles to profl. jours. Fellow ACS, Soc. Critical Care Medicine; mem. Am. Assn. Surgery for Trauma, Pan-Am. Trauma Soc., Soc. Internat. de Chirurgie, Ea. Assn. Surgery for Trauma, Ctrl. Surg. Assn., Alpha Omega Alpha, Sigma Psi. Avocations: music, art, Martial arts. Office: Grant Med Ctr 111 S Grant Ave Columbus OH 43215-4701

FALCONER, IAN ROBERT, university researcher; b. Walton-on-Thames, Surrey, England, May 12, 1935; arrived in Australia, 1960; s. Robert H. and Lilian W.F.; m. Mary E. Roff, Sept. 20, 1958; 3 children. BSc, U. Nottingham, Eng., 1957, DSc, 1971; PhD, U. Aberdeen, Scotland, 1960; diploma in theology, Australia Coll. Theology, 1991; DSc (hon.), Prince of Songkla U., Thailand. Cert. chartered chemist, chartered biologist. Lectr. Waite Agrl. Inst., South Australia, 1960-64; from lectr. to reader in animal biochem. U. Nottingham, 1964-71; chmn. acad. bd. U. New Eng., NSW, Australia, 1983-85, pro vice-chancellor, 1988-90, dean of scis., 1990-92, emeritus prof., 1997—; dep. vice chancellor acad. U. Adelaide, Australia, 1992-97, rsch. project leader blue-green algal toxins drinking water, 1997—; vis. prof. U. Reading, Eng., 1977; vis. fellow Clare Hall. Cambridge (Eng.) U., 1986, Australian Nat. U., 1998; cons. Internat. Devel. Program, Australia, 1975—. Author: Mammalian Biochemistry, 1969, Lactation, 1971, Algal Toxins in Seafood and Drinking Water, 1993; editor Environ. Toxicology, 2000—. Fellow Royal Soc. for Chemistry, Australian Inst. Biology (pres. 1997-99); mem. Internat. Soc. Toxinology, Australian Soc. for Biochemistry and Molecular Biology. Avocations: bush walking, fishing. Fax: 61 2 6251 7621. Home: 44 Mirning Crescent, Aranda ACT 2614, Australia Office: U Adelaide Med Sch, Dept Clin & Exptl Pharmacol, Adelaide 5005, Australia

FALCONER, KAREN ANN See DAVIS, KAREN ANN

FALCONER, KENNETH JOHN, mathematician, researcher, educator; b. Hampton, U.K., Jan. 25, 1952; s. Angus Duncan and Ivy Magdalene (King) F.; m. Isobel Jessie Nye, July 15, 1978; children: Benedict, Jennifer. BA, U. Cambridge, Eng., 1974, MA, 1978, PhD, 1978. Rsch. fellow Corpus Christi Coll., Cambridge, 1977-80; lectr. U. Bristol, U.K., 1980-87, reader, 1987-93; prof. U. St. Andrews, Fife, Scotland, 1993—, head pure math., 1995—; vis. prof. Oreg. State U., 1985-86. Author: The Geometry of Fractal Sets, 1985, Fractal Geometry-Mathematical Foundations and Applications, 1990, Techniques in Fractal Geometry, 1997; co-author: (with H. Croft and R. Guy), Unsolved Problems in Geometry, 1992; editor Jour. London Math. Soc., 1990-99; contbr. over 70 articles to profl. jours. Fellow Royal Soc. Edinburgh; mem. Edinburgh Math. Soc. (mem. com. 1996-99), Long Distance Walkers Assn. (chair 2000—). Avocations: long distance walking, hill walking, choral singing. Home: Lumbo Farmhouse, St Andrews, Fife KY16 8NS, Scotland Office: U St Andrews Math Inst, N Haugh St Andrews, Fife KY16 9SS, Scotland

FALCONER, ROGER ALEXANDER, water engineering educator, consultant; b. Carmarthen, Wales; s. Cyril Thomas (dec.) and Winifred Matilda Mary (Rudge) F.; m. Nicola Jane Wonson, Apr. 30, 1977; children: James Alexander Hayward, Simon Alexander Thomas, Sarah Alexandra Maureen. BSc in Engring. with honors, Kings Coll., London, 1973; MSCE, U. Wash., Seattle, 1974; PhD, Imperial Coll., London, 1976; D of Engring., U. Birmingham, Eng., 1992; DSc in Engring., U. London, 1994. Lectr. civil engring. U. Birmingham, 1977-86; prof. water engring. U. Bradford, Eng., 1987-97, head of dept. civil and environ. engring., 1997; Hyder prof. environ. water mgmt. Carfiff Univ., Cardiff, 1997—. Author books on environ. water mgmt.; contbr. over 160 articles to profl. jours. Recipient Ippen award Internat. Assn. Hydraulic Rsch., The Netherlands, 1991. Fellow ASCE (assoc. editor 1994—), Instn. Civil Engrs. (chartered, Telford Premium 1994, Vernon-Harcourt lectr. 1994), Chartered Instn. Water and Environ. Mgmt., Royal Acad. Engring. (Silver medal 1999), City and Guilds Inst. London, internat. Assn. Hydraulic Rsch. (coun. mem.), Chartered Inst. Environ. Water Mgmt. (coun. mem.). Avocations: music, walking, cycling, travel. E-mail: falconerra@cardiff.ac.uk. Home: Hatherton, Radyr Court Rd Llandaff, Cardiff CF5 2QF, United Kingdom Office: Cardiff Sch Engr/Cardiff U, PO Box 686, Cardiff CF24 3TB, United Kingdom

FALDO, NICK (NICHOLAS ALEXANDER FALDO), professional golfer; b. Hertfordshire, Eng., July 18, 1957; m. Gill Faldo; children: Natalie, Matthew, Georgia. Profl. golfer PGA, 1976—; mem. European Ryder Cup Team, 1977, 79, 81, 83, 85, 87, 89, 91, 93, 95, 97, World Cup Team, 1977, 91, 98, Dunhill Cup Team, 1985, 86, 87, 88, 91, 93, Nissan Cup Team, 1986, Kirin Cup Team, 1987, Four Tours Championship Team, 1990. Winner Brit. Open, 1987, 90, 92, Brit. Youths Amateur Championship, 1975, English Amateur Championship, 1975, Colgate PGA Championship, 1978, Brit. PGA Championship, 1978, 80, 81, Car Care Plan Internat., 1984, Spanish Open, 1987, French Open, 1988, Volvo Masters, 1988, Volvo PGA Championship, 1989, Dunhill Brit. Masters, 1989, Peugeot French Open, 1989, Suntory World Match Play, 1989, The Masters, 1989, 90, Irish Open, 1991, Carroll's Irish Open, 1992, 93, Brit. Open, 1992, Scandinavian Masters, 1992, GA European Open, 1992, Toyota World Matchplay, 1992, Johnnie Walker Classic, 1993, Doral/Ryder Open, 1995; named European Rookie of Yr., 1977; recipient MBE award, 1987; leading money winner European Tour, 1983, 92, winner Master Tourn., 1996, Nissan Open, 1997, elected World Golf Hall of Fame, 1997. Office: care IMG 1 Erieview Plz Ste 1300 Cleveland OH 44114-1715

FALK, DIANE M., research director, librarian, editor, writer; b. N.Y.C.; d. Leon H.E. Falk and J. Constance Moorehead (Lilienthal) Stephenson. BA in English and World Lit., Columbia U., 1973, MLS, 1979. Text editor, bibliog. enhancement N.Y. Times Info. Svc., Inc., N.Y.C., 1980—; rsch. libr., documents analyst Atlantis Energy and Minerals, N.Y.C., 1980-81; project coord. for legal dept. GAF Corp., N.Y.C., 1981-82; cataloger Exxon Edn. Found., N.Y.C., 1982; indexer, fact-checker H. W. Wilson & Co., Bronx, N.Y., 1982; bibliog. orgn. The Rockefeller Found., N.Y.C., 1983; info. specialist Harkavy Info. Svc., N.Y.C., 1983, 84, Newsworld Comm., N.Y.C., 1985; dir. rsch., head libr. The World & I Mag., Washington, 1986—; Copy editor, rsch. mgr. HSA-UWC, N.Y.C. and Washington, 1974-75, 86; reference asst. Lehman Libr., Columbia U., N.Y.C., 1978; rsch. libr., documents analyst UN Ctr. for Transnational Corps., 1979. Contbr. articles to profl. jours. English and comms. prof., vol. United to Serve Am., Washington Saturday Coll., Howard U., Washington, 1992—; ofcl. tour guide Washington Times Found. and Corp.; conf. coord. Internat. Acad. Arts, Literary, Bus., Legal and Polit. Groups and Issues, 1991—; instr., conf. demonstrator for internet and other knowledge mgmt. tech. rsch. resources. Recipient Corp. award Washington Times Corp., 1997. Mem. ALA, Spl. Librs. Assn., D.C. Libr. Assn., Intellectual Freedom Interest Group (chairperson 1996-97), Rsch. and Reference Interest Group, Women's Fedn. for World Peace (sec. D.C. chpt. 1993), Internat. Leadership Seminars (staff vol. 1991—), Internat. Fedn. for World Peace (signature campaign staff 1990-91, vol. 1990—, acting sec. 1993—), The Prosperity Coun. (editor newsletter 1991). Avocations: photography, arts, travel, writing. E-mail: dmfalk@worlddandimag.com, research@worldandimag.com, library@worldandimag.com. Home: 508 Columbia Rd NW Washington DC 20001-2904 Office: The World & I Mag Libr and Rsch Dept 3600 New York Ave NE Washington DC 20002-1947

FALK, GATHIE, artist; b. Alexander, Manitoba, Canada, Jan. 31, 1928; s. Cornelius and Agatha (Penner) F.; m. Dwight Allen Swanson, Nov. 11, 1974 (div. 1978. Student, U. Brit. Columbia, 1956-65. One-man shows include Canvas Shack, 1965, Odalesque Gallery, 1967, Douglas Gallery, Vancouver, 1968, Can. Cultural Ctr., Paris, 1974, Bau-Xi Gallery, Vancouver, 1976, Nat. Gallery Tour, 1976-77, Forest City Gallery, London, Ont., 1977, Edmonton Art Gallery, 1978, Artcore, Vancouver, 1978, UBC Art Gallery, 1980, U. So. Alberta, Lethbridge, 1980, Glenbow Mus., Calgary, 1980, Equinox Art Gallery, Vancouver, 1981, 82, 83, 85, 87-99, Isaacs Gallery, Toronto, 1982, 84, 87, 88, 90, Painting Retrospective Art Gallery of Greater Victoria, 1985, 24 Yr. Retrospective Vancouver Art Gallery, 1985, 49th Parallel, N.Y.C., 1987, Wynick Tuck Gallery, Toronto, 1992, René Blouin Gallery, Montreal, 1998, Rimouski Art Gallery, Quebec, 1999, Vancouver Art Gallery, 2000; exhibited in group shows at Burnaby Art Gallery, 1964, 69, 73, 75, 80, Montreal Mus. Fine Arts, 1967, 70, 74, Nat. Gallery of Can., 1975, 84, Art Gallery of Greater Victoria, 1973, 74, 79, Douglas Art Gallery, 1968, 69, Agnes Etherington Art Centre, Kingston, 1972-78, Edmonton U. Art Gallery, Alta. Coll. Art, Calgary, 1981, Musee d'art de Saint-Laurent, Que., 1981, Norman Mackenzie Art Gallery, Regina, Nickle Art Mus., 1982, The Art Gallery at Harbour Front, Toronto, 1977, 85, VAG, 1983, Centre Internat. d'Art Contemporaia d'Montreal, 1985, Toyama, Japan, 1987, Touring Billboards, 1987, 88, Glenbow Art Gallery, Calgary, 1999, Windsor Art Gallery, 1999, represented in permanent collections Indusman Collection, Ringhouse, Can. Comml. and Indsl. Bank, Art Gallery of Ont., Nat. Gallery, Art Bank, Vancouver Art Gallery. Grantee Can. Council, 1967, Can. Council Arts Bursary, 1968, 69, 71, 2 murals at Dept. External Affairs Bldg., Ottawa, 1973, mural Vancouver Credit Union Bldg., 1979, mural Canadian Embassy, Washington, 1988. Recipient Sun award, 1968, Sr. Can. Coun. award, 1980. Office: Equinox Gallery, 2321 Granville St., Vancouver, BC Canada V6H 3G3

FALK, HEINZ, organic chemistry educator; b. St. Pölten, Austria, Apr. 29, 1939; s. August and Luzie (Mörtl) F.; m. Rotraud Strohbach, Feb. 10, 1966; 1 child, Alexander. PhD, U. Vienna, Austria, 1966. Asst. U. Vienna, 1964-75, lectr., 1972, assoc. prof., 1975-79; prof. U. Linz, 1979—. Author: The Chemistry of Linear Oligopyrroles, 1989; co-editor Chemistry Monthly; contbr. more than 260 articles to profl. jours. Recipient prize Sandoz, 1977. Mem. Austrian Acad. Scis. (Ernst Späth prize 1976), N.Y. Acad. Scis., Am. Soc. Photochem. Photobiology, European Soc. Photochem. Photobiology, Gesellschaft Österr Chemiker (v.p. 1989-95), Gesellschaft Deutscher Chemiker. Avocations: glider plane flying, hiking, collecting minerals and fossils, ancient Egypt. Office: U Linz Johannes Kepler U, Altenbergerstr 69, A-4040 Linz Austria

FALK, HEINZ FRED, company executive, physicist; b. Berlin, Aug. 21, 1938; s. Max Otto and Erna Marie (Fasching) F.; m. Karin Christa Kupsch, Apr. 7, 1978; children: Urte, Franka, Martin. Diploma in Physics, Humboldt-U., Berlin, 1961, Dr.rer.nat., 1966, Dr.sc.nat., 1977; Prof. Physics (hon.), Acad. Scis., Berlin, 1980; Hon. Prof. Degree, Mercator U., Duisburg, Germany, 1990. Lectr. Humboldt U., Berlin, 1961-64; rsch. scientist Acad. Scis., Berlin, 1964-86, dep. dir., 1986-89; mng. dir. Spectro Analytical Instruments, Kleve, Germany, 1989—. Mem. Rotary. Avocations: tennis, jogging, classical music. Home: Spielberg 9, 47533 Kleve Germany Office: Spectro Analytical Instru, Boschstr 10, 47533 Kleve Germany

FALK, ROBERT BARCLAY, JR., anesthesiologist, educator; b. Lancaster, Pa., July 1, 1945; s. Robert Barclay and Miriam (Neff) F.; m. Carol Anne Gundel, May 30, 1970; 1 child, Juliana Gundel. BA, Franklin and Marshall Coll., 1967; MD, Jefferson Med. Coll., 1971. Diplomate Am. Bd. Anesthesiology. Intern Conemaugh Valley Meml. Hosp., Johnstown, Pa., 1971-72; resident in anesthesiology M.H. Hershey Med. Sch. Hosp., 1974-77; ptnr. Anesthesia Assocs., Lancaster, 1977—, sr. v.p., 1993-94, pres., 1994—; staff anesthesiologist Lancaster Gen. Hosp., 1977—, vice chmn. dept. anesthesiology, 1984-85, chmn., 1985-92; clin. asst. prof. dept. anesthesiology Hershey (Pa.) Med. Sch., 1977—. Contbr. articles to profl. jours. Participant alumni phonathon Franklin and Marshall Coll., 1978-81, vice chmn., 1981, chmn., 1983, mem. alumni admissions com., 1977-79, chmn., 1980-87, chmn. 20th reunion gift com.; mem. Lancaster Regional Alumni Coun., 19987-91, trustee athletic com., 1988-96, 98; mem. Lancaster Area Arts Coun., 1989-91; Sunday sch. tchr. Trinity Luth. Ch., Lancaster, 1977-80; bd. dirs. Lancaster Summer Arts Festival, 1981—, v.p., 1982-84, pres., 1985-90; bd. dirs. Pa. Acad. Music, 1991—, vice-chmn., 1991-92, chmn., 1993—. Lt. M.C., USNR, 1972-74. Mem. Am. Soc. Anesthesiologists, Pa. Soc. Anesthesiologists, Intenat. Anesthesia Rsch. Soc., Pa. Med. Soc., Lancaster Country Club, Hamilton Club (v.p. 1995-97, pres. 1997-99), Masons, Shriners, Chaine des Rotisseurs. Republican. Home: 1025 Marietta Ave Lancaster PA 17603-3106 Office: Anesthesia Assocs 133 E Frederick St Lancaster PA 17602-2222

FALKMAN, SUSAN ANN, sculptor; b. Davenport, Iowa, Mar. 9, 1945; d. Robert Andrew Fries and Corinne La Du; m. Edwin G. Falkman, 1966 (div. 1971); m. Dean E. Johnson, April 1, 1989 (div. 2000); 1 child, Ian. BSc, U. Ill., 1967. Independent study work Nicoli Studio, Carrara, Italy, 1978-80, Studio Sarzanini, Carrara, Italy, 1980-81, Studio Carrione, Carrara, Italy, 1982-85; artist in residence Lincoln Ctr. for Arts, Milw., 1985-90, Carving Studio, West Rutland, Vt., 1993-94, 1999-2000. Prin. works include signa-

ture large scale sculpture Sharon Lynn Wilson Ctr. for the Arts, Waukesha County, Wis. public marble sculptors Aubagne, France, 1986, Barossa Valley, Australia, 1988; creator travelling exhibition Body Memories, 1994, video, 1995. Vol. Peace Corps., Liberia, West Africa, 1968-69; plan commr. City of Mequon, Wis., 1990-98. Recipient First Prize Purchase award City of Carrara, Italy, 1980, City of Digne, France, 1983, Creator of Diamond award Gov. State of Wis., 1995; named Sacajewea artist Profl. Dimensions, Milw., 1997. Mem. Unitarian Ch. Avocations: tai chi, zen meditation, natural landscaping. Home: 1531 W Bonniwell Rd Mequon WI 53097-1719

FALKMER, URSULA GERDA, oncology educator, physician; b. Hof, Bavaria, Germany, Mar. 27, 1943; arrived in Sweden, 1964; d. Christian Kadner and Erna (Sünderhauf) K.; m. Åke Askensten, 1967 (div. 1987); children: Ann-Eva, Henry; m. Sture Emil Falkmer, July 29, 1989. MB, U. Freiburg (Germany), 1964; MD, Karolinska Inst., Stockholm, 1984; PhD, Karolinska Inst., 1989. Registered physician, Sweden; splst. clin. oncology, Sweden and Norway. Intern in clin. oncology Karolinska Hosp., Stockholm, 1984, resident in clin. oncology, asst. prof., 1992-99; sr. physician Radiumhemmet Karolinska Hosp., 1993-96; chief physician Cancer Clinic U. Hosp., Trondheim, Norway, 1996-99; prof. oncology, head physician, med. dir. Cancer Clinic U. Hosp., Trondheim, 2000—; chairperson Norwegian Neuroendocrine Tumor Group, 1999—. Contbr. about 100 articles to med. jours. Grantee Swedish and Norwegian cancer rsch. founds., Swedish Med. Rsch. Coun., 1993. Mem. Norwegian and Swedish Physicians' Assns., Swedish Soc. medicine, European Soc. Pathology, Swedish Soc. Oncology, Norwegian Soc. Oncology, European Assn. Palliative Care, European Neuroendocrine Tumour Network. Avocations: rural life, gardening, skating, cross country skiing. Home: Trollahaugen 44, N-7018 Trondheim Norway Office: Kreftavelingen, Regionsykehuset, N-7006 Trondheim Norway

FALKNER, NOREEN MARGARET, English language educator; b. Dunkirk, N.Y., Apr. 21, 1945; d. Edward John and Marie Catherine (Fern) Roman; m. William Jackson III, Aug. 2, 1974; 1 child, Jessica Hayes. BS in English, Art and Edn., U. Dayton, 1966; MS in English and Drama Edn., SUC, Buffalo, 1971. Cert. tchr. N.Y. 7th and 8th grade lang. arts tchr. Clinton Jr. H.S., Buffalo, 1967; 7th grade English tchr. Amsdell Heights Jr. H.S., Hamburg, N.Y., 1967-68; 10th, 11th, 12th grade English tchr. Frontier Ctrl. H.S., Hamburg, 1968—, English dept. chairperson, 1974-96; prom advisor Frontier Ctrl. H.S., 1968-72, cheerleading advisor, 1969-74, dist. devel. coun., 1983-85, dist. lang. arts com. chairperson, 1981-83, PTSA, 1968—, nat. honor soc. selection com., 1980-96, play dir. and advisor, 1968-74; English dept. chairpersons of Erie County, Buffalo, 1986-96. Co-editor: (cookbook) Great Lake Effects: Buffalo Beyond Winter and Wings, 1997 (1st place Tabasco award Mid-Atlantic states 1998); contbr. articles to The Central Parker. Vol. Jr. League of Buffalo, 1981—; mem. Nat. Coun. of English Tchrs., 1986—, Nardin Parent Coun., Buffalo, 1986—. Mem. Youngstown Yacht Club, Delta Kappa Gamma (Theta chpt.). Democrat. Roman Catholic. Avocations: walking, reading, writing, decorating, knitting. Home: 349 Woodbridge Ave Buffalo NY 14214-1516 Office: Frontier Ctrl High Sch S4432 Bay View Rd Hamburg NY 14075-1335

FALKNER, WILLIAM CARROLL, lawyer; b. Baird, Tex., Mar. 26, 1954; s. Vernon Lee and Eunice Vera (Fore) F.; m. Linda May (Tilley), May 23, 1987; children: Heather Lynn, Holly Ann. BA in Govt., Tarleton State U., Stephenville, Tex., 1976; JD, Stetson U., Gulfport, Fla., 1984. Bar: Fla. 1984, U.S. Dist. Ct. (mid. dist.) Fla. 1985, U.S. Ct. Appeals (11th cir.) 1985. Asst. co. atty., sr. asst. co. atty. Pinellas County Atty.'s Office, Clearwater, Fla., 1985—. Editor Res Ipsa, Clearwater, Fla., 1992-93; contbr. articles to profl. jours. Lt. col. U.S. Army Res., 1976—. Mem. ABA, Fla. Bar Assoc., Clearwater Bar Assoc. Baptist. Avocations: reading, writing, sports, biblical studies. Office: Pinellas County Atty's Office 315 Court St Clearwater FL 33756-5165

FALKOWSKI, MARY GERARD, elementary principal; b. Wilmington, Del., Jan. 10, 1935; d. Frank Saczyn and Maryanne (Licka) F. BS in Edn., Villanova (Pa.) U., 1969, MA in Adminstrn., 1974. Joined Sisters of St. Benedict, 1952. Tchr. grades 2 - 8 St. Elizabeth Elem. Sacred Heart, Wilmington, 1954-67; elem. prin. St. Elizabeth Elem., Wilmington, 1968—. Recipient Pacem in Terris award, Disting. Grad. award St. Hedwig's. Fellow Nat. Assn. Elem. Sch. Prins., Nat. Cath. Edn. Assn., Del. Assn. Elem. Sch. Prins., Mid. State Assn. Elem. Schs.; mem. Cath. Elem. Prins. Orgn. (pres. 1972, treas. 1994-96, Prin. of Yr. 1993). Democrat. Roman Catholic. Avocations: walking, woodwork, bicycling, sewing, decorating. Home: 803 S Broom St Wilmington DE 19805-4244 Office: St Elizabeth Elem 1500 Cedar St Wilmington DE 19805-4294

FALKOWSKI, THERESA GAE, chemistry educator; b. El Paso, Tex., Mar. 19, 1958; d. Chester Doan and Patricia Ann Harman; m. Henry Steven Falkowski, May 16, 1981. AA, Potomac State Coll., 1978; BA, W.Va. U., 1980. Lab. asst. Potomac State Coll., Keyser, W.Va., 1977-78, gen. chem. prep rm. mgr., 1986—, chem. lab. instr., 1995-99; chem. lab. tchg. asst. W.Va. U., Morgantown, 1981-83, chem. lab. tech., 1981-85, adj. instr. chemistry, 1999—; cons. USS N.C. Battleship Meml., Wilmington, 1981—; mem. haz-mat response team Potomac State Coll., 1993—. Author: Clark Hall of Chemistry: A Pictorial History, 1996, Laboratory Manual for Chemistry 12, 1996; illustrator: Laboratory Manual for Chemistry 15/16, 1991. Mem. Am. Chem. Soc., W.Va. Acad. Sci., Carnegie Mus. Natural History and Sci. Ctr., The Nat. Maritime Ctr., The N.C. Aquarium Soc., The Mote Marine Lab. Avocations: model building, World War II history, aircraft identification, science fiction. Office: Potomac State Coll Fort Ave Keyser WV 26726

FALL, ATLEY See BALL, WILLIAM LEE

FALL, CHEIKH IBRAHIMA, banking executive; b. Louga, Senegal, Oct. 1, 1947; m. Marième Diouma Faye, 1972; 3 children. Fin. analyst ops. dept. Banque oeust-africaine de développement, 1978-79, with rural devel. and infrastructural ops. dept., 1979-81, officer-in-charge of dept., 1981, dir. of dept., 1981-85, dir. loans and equity dept., 1985-86; dir. office or pres. African Devel. Bank, 1986-92, dir. co. programs South Region dept., 1992-95, officer-in-charge of adminstrv. and gen. svcs. and restructu, 1995-96; sec.-gen. African Devel. Bank, Abidjan, Ivory Coast, 1996-99; v.p., corp. sec. The World Bank Group, 1999—. Avocations: music, golf, reading. Fax: (202) 522-1640. Office: The World Bank Group 1818 H St NW Rm Mc12205 Washington DC 20433-0001

FALLACI, ORIANA, writer, journalist; b. Florence, Italy, June 29, 1930; d. Edoardo and Tosca (Cantini) F. Grad., Liceo Classico Galileo Galilei, Italy; student, U. Florence Faculty Medicine, 1946-48; Litt.D. (hon.), Columbia Coll., Chgo., 1977. Editor, spl. corr. Europeo Mag., Milan, Italy, 1958-77; collaborator with major publs. throughout world, including Look mag., 1977-96, Life mag., 1977-96, The Washington Post, 1977-96, N.Y. Times, 1977-96, London Times, 1977-96; writer, 1996—; dir. Rizzoli Pubs. Corp. Author: (novels) Penelope alla guerra, 1962 (pub. as Penelope at War, 1966), Lettera a un bambino mai nato, 1975 (pub. as Letter to a Child Never Born, 1976), Un uomo: romanzo, 1979 (pub. as A Man, 1980; Viareggio prize), In'shallah, 1990 (Hemingway prize 1991, Super Bancarella prize 1991); (nonfiction) I sette peccati di Hollywood, 1958, Il sesso inutile, 1961 (pub. as The Useless sex, 1964), Gli antipatici, 1963 (pub. as The Egoists, 1965), Se il sole muore, 1965 (pub. as If The Sun Dies, 1967), Niente a cosi sia, 1969 (pub. as Nothing, and So Be It, 1972; Bancarella prize 1971), Quel giorno sulla Luna, 1970, Intervista con la Storia, 1974 (pub. as Interview with History, 1976); audio: Oriana Fallaci reads Letter to a Child Never Born, 1993. Recipient St. Vincent award for journalism, 1971, 73. Office: Rizzoli 31 W 57th St Fl 4 New York NY 10019-3496 also: RCS Rizzoli Libri, Via Mecenate 91, 20138 Milan Italy*

FALL CREEK, STEPHANIE JEAN, state agency administrator; b. Springfield, Mo., May 6, 1950; d. Martha Jean (Barton) Wertz; m. Jerry R. Tillman, 1987; children: Ernest, Daniel, Christopher, Joseph; stepchildren: Shannon, Tiffanie. AB in History, U. Okla., 1972; MSW in Social Welfare, U. Calif., Berkeley, 1974, DSW in Social Welfare, 1984. Dir. Inst. for Geron. Research and Edn., N.Mex. State U., Las Cruces, 1983-87, N.Mex. State Agy. on Aging, Santa Fe, 1987-91; dir. Office of Planning N.Mex. Dept. of Health, 1991-92; dir. div. long term care N.Mex. Dept. Health, Albuquerque, 1992—; exec. dir. Fairhill Inst for the Elderly, Cleve.; pres. Fallcreek & Assocs., Santa Fe, 1982—; sr. assoc. Age Wave Inc., Emeryville, Calif., 1985-87; cons. various hosps. and health care orgns.; speaker confs. and trade shows; guest radio and TV programs on aging. Author: (with others) A Healthy Old Age: A Sourcebook for Health Promotion with Older Adults, Health Promotion and Aging: Strategies for Action, Health Promotion and Aging: A National Resource of Selected Programs; also articles and book chpts. Bd. dirs. Nat. Assn. State Units of Aging, 1987-91, S.W. Soc. on Aging, 1988-90, Am. Soc. on Aging, 1992—; treas. Dome Found., 1990—. Danforth fellow, 1972-78. Mem. Geron. Soc. Am., Am. Soc. on Aging, Am. Assn. Ret. Persons (mem. nat. adv. com. Nat. Resource Ctr. on Health Promotion and Aging), Nat. Council on the Aging, Soc. for Values in Higher Edn., Nat. Assn. Social Workers, AAUW, Nat. Assn. of State Units on Aging, SW Soc. on Aging. Office: Fairhill Ctr 12200 Fairhill Rd Cleveland OH 44120-1013

FÄLLDIN, NILS OLOF THORBJÖRN, former Prime Minister of Sweden, retired farmer; b. Högsjö, Sweden, Apr. 24, 1926; s. Nils Johan Fälldin and Hulda Katarina Olsson; m. Rut Solveig, Feb. 25, 1956; children: Eva, Niklas, Pontus. Farmer Ås, Högsjö, Sweden, 1956-90; councillor Local Govt., Högsjö rural dist., 1951-68; mem. Swedish Riksdag, 1958-64, 67-85; chmn. numerous coms. and investigations; party chmn. Swedish Center Party, 1971-85; prime min. Govt. of Sweden, Stockholm, 1976-78, 79-82; chmn. Bd. Nordiska Muséet, Stockholm, 1986-96, Swedish Telecom/Telia, Stockholm 1988-95, Föreningen Norden, Stockholm, 1988-2000, Föreningenbanken AB, Stockholm, 1992-96; mem. Olof Palme Cmmn., Stockholm, 1987-88; chmn. Del. Info. Measures furthering European Integration, Stockholm, 1992-94. Contbr. articles to profl. jours. Decorated grand cross Order of White Rose (Finland), grand officer of Royal Norwegian Order of Merit, 1999; recipient H.M. The King's medal 12th Class with chain, 1986. Home: Ås, S-870 16 Ramvik Sweden

FALLER, DOROTHY ANDERSON, international agency administrator; b. Chgo., July 6, 1939; d. Albert T. and Lillian G. (Chalbeck) Anderson. Student, Ill. Wesleyan U., 1956-59; AB, U. Ill., 1959-60; MSSA, Case Western Res. U., 1975. lic. social worker; m. Adolph Faller, Sept. 5, 1959; children: Carl, Kurt. Child welfare worker Klamath County Pub. Welfare Commn., Klamath Falls, Oreg., 1960-67; social svc. cons. Ind. State Dept. Pub. Welfare, 1968-72; adminstrv. asst. Berea (Ohio) Children's Home, Berea, 1974; rsch. asst. Case Western Res. U. Sch. Applied Social Scis., 1975, Mandel Sch. Applied Social Scis.; social svcs. supr. Ohio Dept. Pub. Welfare, Cleve., 1975-81; exec. dir. Cleve. Internat. Program, 1981-99, 1981-99; sec. gen., CEO Coun. Internat. Programs USA, 1999—; cons. to Cleve. Found., Am. Sickle Cell Anemia Found., John A. Yankey & Assocs.; field instr. Case Western Res. U., 1976-77, lectr., 1981; dir. African Internship Project Substance Abuse Prevention, 1992-95; dir. Ghana Conf., 1995; mem. adv. coun. Mandel Ctr. Non-Profit Orgns., 1995-96, Case Western Res. U., Nat. Network Social Work Mgrs., Nat. Bd. Editor, contbr. Ohio Children's Budget Project: A Public Policy Study, 1975. Bd. dirs. West Shore Unitarian Ch., 1978-81, 2000—, Volgograd Free Speech Forum, 1995—. Hon. by Fulbright Assn., 1999. Mem. Acad. Cert. Social Workers (cert.), Nat. Assn. Social Workers (unit chair state bd., exec. com. nat. bd. dirs. 1985-88, chmn. Internat. Activities Com. of Nat. Bd. 1986-89, program com. 1989-91, del. Internat. Fedn. Social Workers, Sweden, 1988, Cleve. unit Social Worker of Yr. 1986, del. from Ohio to del. assembly 1990, conf. chair ann. mtg. profession 1993), Nat. Bd., Nat. Network of Social Work Mgrs., Case Western Res. U. Sch. Applied Social Scis. Alumni Assn., Sigma Kappa (pres. 1959), Alpha Lambda Delta (pres. 1956). Home: 6889 Columbia Rd Olmsted Falls OH 44138-1523 Office: 1700 E 13th St Ste 4ME Cleveland OH 44114-3238

FALLER, JÓZSEF, surgeon, gastroenterologist, educator; b. Szombahely, Hungary, Oct. 11, 1936; s. József and Mária Faller; m. Edit Szeidl, Nov. 29, 1962. MD, U. Medicine, Budapest, Hungary, 1961; PhD, Hungarian Acad. Sci., Budapest, 1977, DSc, 1996. Registrar County Hosp., Mosonmagyaróvár, Hungary, 1961-62; asst. Surg. Anatomical Inst. Med. U., Budapest, 1963-65; asst. prof. 1st Surg. Dept. Med. U., Budapest, 1966-76, 1st asst. prof., 1976-81; assoc. prof. 1st and 3rd Surg. Dept. Med. U., Budapest, 1981-86; prof. surgery, head dept. 2nd Surg. Dept. Med. U. and St. John Hosp., Budapest, 1987-98, with 1997—; nat. del. o/CICD, 1988—. Editor Magyar Sebészet, 1981-90, editor-in-chief, 1990—; mem. editl. bd. Croatian Jour. Surgery, 1992—. Mem. Hungarian Surg. Soc. (gen. sec. 1983-86, pres. 1999—, medal of Balassa Janos 'memory 1997), N.Y. Acad. Scis. Avocations: gardening, playing tennis, music, theater. Home: Kökörcsin 9, H-1113 Budapest Hungary Office: Semmelweis Med Sch Dept Sur, Kútvölgyi út 4, H-1125 Budapest Hungary

FALLER, RHODA DIANNE GROSSBERG, lawyer; b. N.Y.C., Dec. 21, 1946; d. Benjamin and Marion (Mediasky) Sragg; m. Stanley Grossberg, Apr. 12, 1973 (div. Oct. 1983); children: Joseph Seth, Daniel Benjamin; m. Bernard Martin Faller, May 31, 1987. BS, SUNY, Stony Brook, 1967; MS, Pace U., 1973; JD, N.Y. Law Sch., 1978. Bar: N.Y. 1979, N.J. 1979, U.S. Dist. Ct. N.J. 1979, Fla. 1980, U.S. Dist. Ct. (ea. and so. dists.) N.Y. 1982, Ky. 1996, U.S. Dist. Ct. (ea. dist.) Ky. 1997. Assoc. Fuchsberg & Fuchsberg, N.Y.C., 1982-91, DeBlasio & Alton, P.C., N.Y.C., 1991-95, Rhoda Grossberg Faller, Esq., Teaneck, 1995-96, Becker Law Office, Louisville, Ky., 1997-2000; pvt. practice Louisville, 2000—. Mem. Assn. Trial Lawyers Am., Nat. Assn. Women Bus. Owners, Ky. Acad. Trial Attys., Ky. Bar Assn., N.Y. State Trial Lawyers Assn., N.Y. State Bar Assn., Fla. Bar Assn., Louisville Bar Assn., Women Lawyers Assn. Democrat. Jewish. Home: 213 Mockingbird Gardens Dr Louisville KY 40207-5718 Office: Law Office of Rhoda Faller PLLC 500 W Jefferson St Louisville KY 40202-2823

FALLER, THOMPSON MASON, philosophy educator; b. Louisville, Apr. 26, 1938; s. Louis Joseph and Katherine Thompson Faller; m. Madeleine O'Brien, Aug. 22, 1969; 1 child, Thompson Mason II. BA, St. Mary's Coll., 1962; MA, Xavier U., 1964; PhD, U. Salzburg, Austria, 1969. From instr. to prof. U. Portland, Oreg., 1964—; instnl. rev. bd. mem. Providence Health Sys., Portland, 1990—; animal rsch. rev. com. mem. Oreg. Health Scis. U., Portland, 1991—. Authro: Axiology: F. Brentano, 1983; contbr. chpts. to books. Chair com. for scholars Reagan/Bush Election Com., Washington, 1984-88; pres. Portland-Sapporo Sister City Assn., 1987—; com. mem. Portland Sister City Coun., 1998—; v.p. Cascade Coun. Boy Scouts, Portland, 2000—. Recipient Pilgrim shell Patriach of Jerusalem, Jerusalem, 1996; named Danforth Assoc., Danforth Found., St. Louis, 1976, J.F. Kennedy Man of Yr., KC, Portland, 1993; Fulbright fellow, Washington, 1968-69. Mem. AAUP, Nat. Assn. Bds. Edn. (chair exec. com. 1991—), Nat. Cath. Edn. Assn. (bd. dirs. 1994—), Nat. Assn. Fgn. Student Affairs, Internat. Ho. of Japan, Knights of Malta (knight), Knights of the Holy Sepulchre (knight), Delta Epsilon Sigma. Roman Catholic. Avocations: raquetball, classical music, football, traveling. E-mail: faller@up.edu. Home: 4684 NW Brassie Pl Portland OR 97229-0901 Office: Univ Portland 5000 N Willamette Blvd Portland OR 97203-5798

FALLET, TRULS RUGLAND, electrical and petroleum engineer; b. Oslo, Mar. 30, 1941; s. Toralf Henrik and Margit (Rugland) F.; m. Karen Haasted (div. 1980); m. Karen Hassel, Jan. 5, 1985. MSc, Tech. U., Norway, 1966. Tech. mgr. Noratom, Oslo, 1973-77; pres. A/S Fartskriver, Oslo, 1977-78; editor Elektro, Oslo, 1978-85; scientist SINTEF, Oslo, 1985-87, rsch. dir., 1987-92, prin. scientist, 1992—; bd. dirs. AFU Electronics, Oslo, 1987—, Monitec, Trondheim, Norway, 1988-90. Author: High Temperature Electronics, 1997; patentee electromagnetic data transmission in oil wells, water/oil contact level gauge, inflow control system for multilateral oil wells. Scientist Norwegian Def. Rsch. Establishment, 1966-73, Oslo, Kjeller. Mem. Soc. Profl. Elec. Engrs., Soc. Automatic Control Engrs., Soc. Petroleum Engrs. (bd. dirs. 1996—). Home: Rosenborg gt 22, N-0356 Oslo Norway Office: Sintef E & K, PO Box 124, N-0314 Oslo Norway

FALLIN, BARBARA MOORE, human resources director; b. Paducah, Ky., Nov. 12, 1939; d. James Perry Moore and Margaret Arminta (Winn) Kastner; m. Jon Ball, Jan. 21, 1961 (div. July 1963); m. Ralph Daniel Fallin, May 23, 1965; children: Wade, Cathi, Cindy Pergrim, Danielle. Student, Fla. Christian Coll., 1957-58. Cert. sr. profl. in human resource mgmt. Exec. asst. to contr. The Borden Co., Tampa, Fla., 1958-65; mktg. asst. Martin-Marietta Corp., Shalimar, Fla., 1965-71; asst. to pres. Browning-Marine, Ft. Walton Beach, Fla., 1973; pers. coord. Keltec Fla., Shalimar, 1974-78; pers. mgr. Metric Systems Corp., Ft. Walton Beach, 1979-87, pers. dir., 1987-92; dir. human resources Metric Sys. Corp., Ft. Walton Beach, 1992—; mem. Job Svc. Employer Com., Ft. Walton Beach, 1985—; mem. adv. bd. Bay Area Vocat.-Tech. Ctr., Ft. Walton Beach, 1988-92; mem. adv. bd. Okaloosa Applied Tech. Ctr. Sch. Adv. Coun., 1995-98, chmn., 1997-98; bd. dirs. Pvt. Industry Coun., 1996—, vice chmn., 1998-99, chmn. 2000—. First mistress Krewe of Bowlegs, Ft. Walton Beach, 1983-84, first lady to Cap'n Billy Bowlegs XXXII, 1986-87; mem. citizens adv. com. U. West Fla., Pensacola, 1991-97; mem. funds distbn. com. Okaloosa County United Way, 1990-93; mem. BNA's Pers. Policies Forum, 1995-96; mem. Pacesetters fund raiser team Salvation Army Capital Campaign, 1996-97. Mem. NAFE, Soc. Human Resource Mgmt. (Emerald Coast chpt. pres. 1986-88, bd. dirs. 1988-92), Nat. Mgmt. Assn., Ft. Walton Beach C. of C. (hosts com. 1991—), Laureate Gamma Phi (exec. bd. dirs. 1996-97, sec. 1997-98, Valentine queen 1997, v.p. 2000-2001). Republican. Presbyterian. Avocations: collecting penquins and camels, making scrapbooks. Office: Metric Sys Corp 645 Anchors St NW Fort Walton Beach FL 32548-3803

FALLMANN, WOLFGANG FRANZ, electronics educator; b. Waidhofen-Ybbs, Austria, Feb. 4, 1937; s. Friedrich and Leopoldine (Germershausen) F. PhD in Physics, U. Vienna, Austria, 1965. Sci. coworker L. Boltzmann Soc., Vienna, 1965-67; asst. U. Vienna, 1967-72, U. Tech., Vienna, 1972-76; assoc. prof. microelectronics U. Tech., 1976-98, head microelectronics-semicondr. tech. divsn., 1994-98, head Inst. Elec. Engring. and Electronics, 1999; head Inst. Applied Electronics and Quantumelectronics U. Tech./Mem. Inst. Indsl. Electronics and Material Sci., 2000—; sr. rsch. assoc. U. Sheffield, Eng., 1969-70, U. Newcastle upon Tyne, Eng., 1970-71; v.p. Internat. Hans-Hass-Inst. f. energon rsch., 1999—; mem. steering com. Micronanoelectronics Engring. Conf., 1988—. Contbr. articles to sci. jours., including Solid State Electronics, Physics Letters, Thin Solid Films, Jour. Vacuum Sci. Tech.B., Microelectronic Engring.; co-patentee in field. Recipient Theodor Koerner award Theodor Koerner Soc., 1968. Mem. Austrian Phys. Soc., German Phys. Soc., Soc. for Microelectronics (pres. 1990-94, v.p. 1995-98), head inst. Lithogr. rsch. E. Schroedinger Soc., 1990—, Soc. Sci. and Tech. Documentation (pres. 1998—), Int. Hans-Hass Inst. f. Engeron Rsch. (v.p. 1999—). Roman Catholic. Avocations: music, photography, cycling. Fax: 43-1-58801-36699. E-mail: wolfgang.fallmann@tuwien.ac.at. Home: Weyringergasse 27/10, A-1040 Vienna Austria Office: U Tech, Gusshausstrasse 27/29, A-1040 Vienna Austria

FALLON, ELDON E., judge; b. New Orleans, Feb. 16, 1939; s. Edward and Delia (Koster) F.; m. Cecile Fallon, Sept. 28, 1967. BA, Tulane U., 1960, JD, 1962; LLM, Yale U., 1963. Bar: La. 1962. Assoc. Kierr & Gainsburgh, 1962-66; ptnr. Gainsburgh, Benjamin & Fallon, New Orleans, 1966-95; judge U.S. Dist. Ct., New Orleans, 1995—; adj. prof. Tulane U. Author: Trial Handbook For Louisiana Lawyers, 1981; contbr. articles to profl. jours. Fellow Am. Bar Found., Am. Coll. Trial Lawyers, La. Bar Found. (bd. dirs., pres. 1995-96); mem. La. Bar Assn. (sec. treas. 1984, pres. 1985-86). Office: US Courthouse 500 Camp St New Orleans LA 70130-3313

FALLON, PAT, artist, art educator; b. Cartagena, Colombia, Nov. 2, 1939; (parents Am. citizens); d. Carlos Fallon and Maureen (Bryne) Fallon Laird; m. Ronald Patrick Conner, Dec. 26, 1960 (div. June 1976); children: Hadley Kathryn Conner, Kenneth Fallon Conner. BA, Antioch Coll., 1962; BFA, Cleve. Inst. Art, 1980; MFA, Kent State U., 1982. Office mgr. cmty. govt. Antioch Coll., Yellow Springs, Ohio, 1961-62; camp dir. Camp Fire Girls, Dayton, Ohio, 1963-65; tchr. painting Valley Art Ctr., Chagrin Falls, Ohio, 1973-74, Shaker Heights (Ohio) Adult Edn., 1973-77; tchg. asst. Cleve. Inst. Art, 1976-80; grad. asst. art dept. Kent (Ohio) State U., 1980-82; gallery mgr. Kuban Gallery Fine Art, Cleve., 1982-83; gallery dir. Ursuline Coll., Cleve., Ohio, 1983-89; adj. prof. art Ursuline Coll., Pepper Pike, Ohio, 1989-94, assoc. prof., 1994-99; prof. Art Dept. Ursuline Coll., Pepper Pike, 2000—; coord. N.E. exhibit New Orgn. Visual Arts-NOVA, Cleve., 1974-75; mem. editl. adv. bd. Collegiate Press, 1990-98; art dept. chair Ursuline Coll., Cleve., 1998—; presenter in field. One-woman shows include Wasmer Gallery, Ursuline Coll., 1997, In Town Club, Cleve., 1997; exhibited in group shows at Canton (Ohio) Art Inst., 1981, Kuban Galleries, Cleve., 1983, Collector's Gallery, Dayton, 1983, Bonfoey Gallery, Cleve., 1983, Cleve. Inst. Art, 1985-87, Ursuline Coll., 1989, 91, 93, 95, 97, Willoughby (Ohio) Fine Arts Ctr., 1992, Cleve. Mus. Art, 1993, Hallinan Ctr., Case Western Res. U., Cleve., 1995, The Black Box, Cleve., 1996, Cleve. State U., 1996, Nat. Exhibit on Homeless, Cleve., 1999—, Internat. Touring Exhibit Toledo Lake Erie Coun., 1999-2000, Here Here Gallery, 1999-2000; represented in permanent collections, including Nat. U. Ireland, Sligo; sabbatical year multi-media project exhbns. on homeless; contbr. articles to profl. jours. Vol., advisor art com. N.E. Ohio Coalition for Homeless, Cleve., 1996-97. Fellow Ohio Humanities Coun., 1986-94. Mem. Coll. Arts Assn., Founds. in Art Theory and Edn., Amnesty Internat. Democrat. Roman Catholic. Home: 3300 Kenmore Rd Shaker Hts OH 44122-3462 Office: Ursuline Coll 2550 Lander Rd Cleveland OH 44124-4318

FALLON, PETER, poet, editor, publisher; b. Germany, 1951. Grad., Trinity Coll., Dublin, Ireland. Writer-in-residence Trinity U.; founder Gallery Press; poet-in-residence Deerfield Acad., Mass.; Heimbold prof. Irish studies Villanova U., Pa. Author: (poems) the Speaking Stones, Winter Work, The News and Weather, Eye to Eye, The Deerfield Series: Strength of Heart, News of the Worls, 1993, News of the World: Selected and New Poems, 1998 (Irish Times Book of the Yr.). Recipient O'Shaughnessy Poetry award Irish Am. Cultural Inst. E-mail: galleryWindigo.ie. Home: Loughcrew Oldcastle, County Meath Ireland

FALLS, KATHLEENE JOYCE, photographer; b. Detroit, July 3, 1949; d. Edgar John and Acelia Olive (Young) Haley; m. Donald David Falls, June 15, 1974; children: Daniel John, David James. Student, Oakland Community Coll., 1969-73, Winona Sch. Profl. Photography, 1973-80; degree in photography, Winona Sch. Profl. Photography, 1988, 90. Lic. ham radio-technician class. Printer Guardian Photo, Novi, Mich., 1967-69; printer, supr. quality control N.Am. Photo, Livonia, Mich., 1969-76; free lance photographer Livonia, 1969-76; owner, pres. Kathy Falls, Inc., Carleton, Mich., 1976—; instr. digital imaging Monroe County (Mich.) C.C., 1994—; instr. Monroe County Community Coll. Continuing Edn., 1981-83; nat. artisan judge Congl. High Sch. Art Competition, 1985—; owner Picture Perfect, Carleton, 1987; co-owner Haleys Gift Shoppe, Dundee, Mich., 1989; pub. info. officer Am. Radio Relay League, 1998—. Author: (booklet) Emergency Photo-Retouching for Photographers, 1988; editor The Hertzian herald, 1998; contbr. articles to profl. jours.; represented in spl. categories in the Nat. Loan Collection, Profl. Photographers Am., 1980, 81, 83, 87; represented in permanent Collections Monroe County Hist. Mus., Archives Notre Dame; newsletter editor Hertzian Herald. Catechist St. Parick's Ch., Carleton, 1984-87, mem. parish coun., 1998—; active Big Bros. and Big Sisters, Monroe, 1986-87; corr. sec. Monroe Women's Ctr., 1986-88; mem. Amateur Radio Emergency Svc.; bd. dirs. Ladies Ancient Order of Hibernians. Recipient Photographic Craftsman degree, 1989, numerous awards granted by profl. photographic orgns.; editor: Hertzian Herald. Mem. NAFE, Am. Soc. Photographers, Detroit Profl. Photographers Assn. (bd. dirs. 1987—, artisan chmn. 1981-82, Best of Show award 1981, 83), Profl. Photographers Mich. (artisan chair 1982-83, Best of Show award 1976, 81, Artist of Yr. 1980, 91), Profl. Photographers Am. (cert. profl. photog. specialist, photographic specialist degree 1988), Am. Photog. Artisans Guild (coun. mem., bd. dirs. 1987—, pres. 1992, Photog. Artisan degree 1989, Artisan Laurel degree 1991), Monroe County Fine Arts Coun. (pres. 1998-99, 99—), Monroe C. of C. (chmn. council women bus. owners), Nat. Orgn. Women Bus. Owners, Profl. Photographers Am. (Photog. Craftsman degree 1990), Monroe County Radio Comms. Assn., Toastmasters, Internat. Club, Ladies Ancient Order of Hibernians (bd. dirs. 1998-99), Scarab Club Detroit. Republican. Roman Catholic. Club: Monroe Camera. Avocations: guitar, piano, drawing, travel, camping. Home and Office: 14940 Carpenter Rd Camden MI 49232

FALOLA, TOYIN, history educator; b. Jan. 1, 1953; s. James and Grace N. Falola; m. Florence Falola, July 25, 1981; children: Dolapo, Bisola, Toyin. BA, U. Ife, Ile-Ife, Nigeria, 1976, PhD, 1980. Prof. U. Ife, 1977-90, York U., North York, Ont., Can., 1990-91; prof. U. Tex., Austin, 1991—, Frances H. Nalle Centennial prof. history. Author: Decolonization and Development Planning, 1996, Religious Militancy and Self-Assertion, 1997, Violence in Nigeria, 1998; editor African Econ. History, African History and

the Diaspora Series, The History of Nigeria, 1999, Tradition and Change in Africa, 2000, The Culture and Politics of Money Among the Yoruba, 2000. Mem. Am. Hist. Assn., African Studies Assn., Ife Humanities Soc., Hist. Soc. Nigeria. Office: U Tex Dept History Austin TX 78721

FALTEJSEK, JIŘÍ, quality assurance professional; b. Hradec Králové, Czech Republic, Jan. 9, 1958; s. Rudolf and Jarmila (Štěpánová) F.; m. Miroslava Straková, July 7, 1984; children: Zuzana, Vit. MA, Czech Tech. U., Prague, 1982. Cert. chem. engring., quality mgr. Analytical chemist Nuclear Rsch. Inst., Řež, Czech Republic, 1982-85, sci. worker, 1985-91, quality mgr., 1995-97; sci. worker Czech Environ. Inst., Prague, 1992-94, Inst. Nuclear Physics, Řež, 1994-95; quality assurance mgr. Radioactive Waste Repository Authority, Prague, 1997—. Co-author Interactive program for evaluation of circle analysis. Mem. Czech Soc. Quality. Fax: 420-2-24907604. E-mail: faltejsek@rawra.cz. Office: RAWRA-SURAO, Gorazdova 24, CZ 120-0 Prague Czech Republic

FALUS, FERENC, health care company executive, consultant; b. Budapest, Hungary, July 23, 1950; s. Miklos and Katalin (Neulander) F.; m. Vera Piszker; children: Daniel, Anna. MD, Semmelweis Med. Sch., Budapest, 1975. Cert. chest physician. Physician Nat. Ambulance Svc., 1975-77, Nat. Koranyi Inst., 1977-89; head dept. RCU Semmelweis Med. Sch., 1989-94; mgr., med. dir. Harris Health Svcs., Hungary, 1994—. Exec. v.p. Soros Found. Health Programme, Budapest, 1996. Mem. Assn. Hungarian Home Health and Hospice (pres. 1995). E-mail: ffalus@compuserve.com. Office: PO Box 227, H-1536 Budapest Hungary

FALUYI, AKINSOLA OLUSEGUN, human resources development consultant, corporate professional; b. Ibadan, Oyo, Nigeria, Nov. 13, 1934; s. Nathaniel Ogundare and Victoria Adebisi (Thompson) F.; m. Theresa Ololade Ajai; children: Oluseun, Olukunle, Akindiji, Oluyemisi, Olufemi, Olusiji, Abayomi, Olumuyiwa. BS, Loughborough (Eng.) U., 1958. Registered profl. engr., Nigeria. Engr. Univ. Coll. Hosp., Ibadan, Nigeria, 1960-62; asst. to chief engr. Dunlop Nigerian Industries Ltd., Ikeja, 1962-64, svcs. engr., 1964-65; chief engr. Lagos (Nigeria) U. Teaching Hosp., 1965-75; mng. dir. Atess Ltd., Lagos, 1980—; prin. ptnr. Edison Group Ptnrs., 1976-79; dir. Studies Atess Inst., Lagos, 1984—, Sigma Petroleum Ltd., 1998—. Author: (booklet) The Nigerian Engineer and the Challenges of a Depressed Economy, 1986, journal Hosp. Engr., 1973. Mem. Nat. Commn. for Right Hand Traffic, Nigeria, 1970-72; sec. Com. on the Re-Orgn. of Structure of Electricity Supply Industry in Nigeria, 1979; pres. Coun. Registered Engrs. of Nigeria, 1988-91; mem. Nat. Com. on Engring. Infrastructure, 1990. Recipient Merit award Excellence for Disting. Svc. to Tech., 1997. Fellow Brit. Instn. Hosp. Engrs., Nigerian Assn. Health Engring. (hon., pres. 1974-78), Nigerian Soc. Engrs. (sec.-gen. 1978-81, v.p. 1984, pres. 1985-85, merit award 1983); mem. Internat. Fedn. Hosp. Engring. (coun. 1972-89), Brit. Engring. Coun. (chartered engr. 1970), Acad. Engring. (found. v.p. 1998). Jehovah's Witness. Avocation: reading. Office: Atess Inst, 16 Ogunlana Dr, Surulere Lagos Nigeria also: PO Box 7127, Marina Lagos

FALVEY, PATRICK JOSEPH, lawyer; b. Yonkers, N.Y., June 29, 1927; s. Patrick J. Falvey and Nora Rowley Falvey; m. Eileen Ryan, June 29, 1963; 1 child, Patrick James. Student, Iona Coll., 1944-47; JD cum laude, St. John's U., Jamaica, N.Y., 1950. Bar: N.Y. 1951, U.S. Supreme Ct. 1972. Law asst. Port Authority of N.Y. and N.J., 1951, atty., 1951-65, chief condemnation and litigation, 1965-67, asst. gen. counsel, 1967-72, gen. counsel, 1972-91, gen. counsel, asst. exec. dir., 1979-87, dep. exec. dir., 1987-91, spl. counsel, 1991—; advisor U.S. del. to UN Com. on Internat. Trade Law, U.S. State Dept. Pvt. Trade Law; advisor to U.S. del. UN diplomatic confs. on treaty on liability of ops. of transport terminals, N.Y. County Lawyers Assn., 1992—. With USN, 1945-46. Recipient Howard S. Cullman Disting. Svc. medal Port Authority of N.Y. and N.J., 1982, 91; Loftus award and Trustee's Honoree Iona Coll., 1982. Fellow Am. Bar Found.; mem. ABA (chmn. urban state and local govt. law sect. 1983-84, vice-chmn. model procurement code project 1979—, sect. del. 1987-90, Award for Lifetime Achievement in Local Law 2000), FBA, Airport Operators Coun. Internat. (legal com.), Assn. Bar City N.Y., N.Y. County Lawyers Assn., Nat. Inst. Mcpl. Law Officers, Internat. Assn. Ports and Harbors (hon., legal counsellors com., arbitrator, mediator trade and comml. matters, cons. transp. and trade studies), Woodlawn Comm. Assn. (counsel 1996-2000, bd. dirs. 2000—). Address: PMB 81 Pondfield Rd Ste 338 Bronxville NY 10708-3818

FALZON, MICHAEL, politician; b. Gzira, Malta, Aug. 17, 1945; s. Francis Falzon and Esther Cauchi; m. Mary Anne Aquilina, Apr. 5, 1970; 1 child, David. BArch, U. Malta, 1969. Registered profl. architect and civil engr. Min. devel. of infrastructure Malta, 1987-92, min. for environment, 1992-94, min. edn. and human resources, 1994-96; chmn. Water Svcs. Corp., Malta, 1999—. Gen. sec. Nationalist Party Youth Movement, Malta, 1974; info. sec. Nationalist Party, Malta, 1976. Roman Catholic. Office: Water Svcs Corp Head Office, Qormi Rd, LQA 05 Luqa Malta*

FAMÀ, FRANCESCO, ophthalmologist, researcher; b. Taormina, Messina, Italy, Apr. 10, 1967; s. Silvestro and Rita (Scaffidi) F.; m. Stefania Patti, Apr. 2, 1997. MD, U. Messina, Italy, 1990, ophthalmologist, 1994, M in Diagnostic Techniques in Ophthalmology, 1996, M in Mountains Medicine and Ophthalmology, 1997. Resident Eye Inst., Messina, Italy, 1990-94; rschr. Uveitis Ctr., Messina, Italy, 1991-97; asst. Eye Mil. Svc., Messina, Italy, 1994-97; dir. Eye ML Svc., Catanzaro, Italy, 1997—; cons. Chirone, Messina, 1993—; dir. Eye Diagnostic Ctr., Messina, 1995-99. With Italian Army (med. br.), 1994—. Recipient Casà award Sicilian Ophthal. Soc., 1995. Mem. Italian Opthalmol. Soc., Assn. Profl. Italiana Med. Oculisti, N.Y. Acad. Scis., Am. Assn. Advacement Sci. Home: Via Metastasio 21, 95014 Giarre Catana Sicily, Italy Office: Viale San Martino 14, 98124 Messina Sicily, Italy

FAMERÉE, JOSEPH FLORENT, theologian, educator; b. Emptinne, Namur, Belgium, Sept. 29, 1955; s. Gustave Raymond and Maria Victorine (Eloy) F. Grad. in classical philology, Notre-Dame de la Paix, Namur, 1975; M of Classical Philology, Cath. U. Louvain, Belgium, 1977, ThM, 1987, PhD in Theology, 1992. Tchr. Ancient Greek Profondeville (Belgium) H.S., 1977-85; Cath. priest Arbre (Belgium) Parish, 1986-90; rschr., asst. faculty theology Cath. U. Louvain, 1989-95, prof. theology, 1995—; rschr. Inst. Religious Sci., Bologna, Italy, 1990, Aristotle U., Thessaloniki, Greece, 1994; vis. fellow St. Vladimir's Orthodox Theol. Faculty, Crestwood, N.Y., 1994. Author: L'ecclésiologie d'Yves Congar, 1992; editor: Concile Vatican II et Eglise Contemporaine, 1991, 93, Démocratie dans les Églises, 1999; contbr. articles to profl. jours. Fulbright-Hays rsch. scholar, 1994. Mem. European Soc. Cath. Theology, Internat. Editl. Bd. History Vatican II, Theology Soc. Louvain (sec. 1992—). Office: Faculty Theology Cath U, Grand-Place 45, B-1348 Louvain-la-Neuve Belgium

FAMIGLIETTI, NANCY ZIMA, computer executive; b. Hartford, Conn., Nov. 10, 1956; d. Jospeh and Angeline (Morello) Zima; m. Arthur R. Famiglietti Jr., May 23, 1981. BA in Math., Computer Sci., Eastern Conn. State Coll., Willimantic, 1978. Sr. programmer analyst Hamilton Standard, Windsor Locks, Conn., 1978-82; system analyst Cigna Corp., Hartford, 1982-83, system designer, 1983-86, lead system designer, 1986-89; system advisor Aetna Life & Casualty Co., Hartford, 1989-93, system adminstr., 1993-94, sr. sys. adminstr., 1994-95, bus. sys. mgr., 1995-98; with Hartford Life, Windsor, Conn., 1998, bus. cons., 1998-2000, team leader, 2000—. Active Windsor (Conn.) Hist. Soc. Mem. Kappa Mu Epsilon. Avocations: reading, walking, crafts, swimming, bicycling. Home: 81 Mcgrath Rd South Windsor CT 06074-1123

FAMILUSI, JULIUS BABASHOLA, pediatrics educator, pediatric neurology consultant; b. Lagos Island, Nigeria, Feb. 16, 1934; s. Gilbert Fajaiyeyomi and Leah Oretipe (Fagbo) F.; m. Mobolaji Adetinrin Aderemi, Apr. 3, 1964; children: BAmidele, Titilayo, Akinbowale, Ajibola, Opeyemi. MB, BChir, London U., 1962. Lectr. U. Ibadan, Nigeria, 1969-72; sr. lectr. U. Ibadan, 1972-76, prof. pediat., 1976—; prof. pediat. King Saud U., Riyadh, Saudi Arabia, 1989-92, U. Zimbabwe, 1996-98; cons. pediat. neurologist UCH, Ibadan, 1969—; provost Coll. Health Scis., Lautech, 1993-94; dep. provost U. Ibadan, 1980-82, head dept. pediat., 1977-80. Chmn. Cerebral Palsy Assn. of Nigeria, 1996—. Spl. fellow in pediat. neurology Rockefeller Found., 1972-73, Heinz fellow Brit. Pediat. Assn., 1974, sr. African fellow Fulbright Found., 1983. Fellow Royal Coll. Pediat. (Glasgow, Scotland), Nigerian Coll. Pediat., West African Coll. Pediat.; mem. Pediat. Assn. Nigeria (pres. 1986-89), Internat. Child Neurology Assn. (v.p. 1998—), World Fedn. Neurology. Methodist. Avocations: horticulture, swimming, table tennis, reading, music. Home: 1 16th Ave Oluyole Estate, Ibadan Nigeria Office: Dept Pediat, University College Hosp, PMB 5116 Ibadan Nigeria

FAMMERÉE, RICHARD ARTHUR, poet, composer, performing artist. BA, Beloit Coll. Former chmn. art. dept. The Found., Chgo.; former pres. Chgo. Artists Coalition; former dir. Chgo. Arts Emerging, BHF Atelier, Chgo.; dir. Poetry in Process, 1996—, Nomadica, 1996—. Author: Lessons of Water and Thirst, 2000, poems; editor Lap of Poetica Literary Jour., 1997-98; dir. Poetry and Its Music International, 1999—, Sacred Site, 1999—, Voice Palace, 2000—; co-dir: Linnaeus & Fammerée, 1996—. Avocations: world travel, French studies.

FAN, CHANGXIN, electrical engineering educator; b. Beijing, Sept. 12, 1931; s. Jiqing and Lizhen (Chen) F.; m. Xinru Lu, Jan. 19, 1957; 1 child, Hongmin. Grad., Beijing U., 1952. Teaching asst. Xidian U., Xi'an, People's Republic China, 1952-62, lectr. elec. engring., 1962-78, assoc. prof., 1978-82, prof., 1982—; chmn. acad. com. China Nat. Key Lab. ISN, 1994—. Author: Principles of Communications, 1984 (nat. award 1988), Engineering Matrix Methods, 1988, Introduction to Digital Communications, 1977, Digital ASIC Design, 1993; contbr. articles to profl. jours. Bd. dirs. Shaanxi br. China Internat. Culture Exch., Xi'an, 1985. Recipient Excellent Prof. award Xidian U., 1985. Fellow IEEE, Chinese Inst. Electronics, Inst. Elec. Engrs., China Inst. Communications (bd. dirs. 1980—). Avocation: travel. E-mail:chxfan@ieee.org. Office: Xidian U Dept Info Engring, 2 Taibai Nan Rd, Xian Shaanxi 710071, China

FAN, CHONG CHENG, educator, researcher; b. Jiangsu, China, Aug. 12, 1937; s. Ch'uan Fan and Marie Tuan Sun; m. Qing Yu Zhu, April 28, 1968; 1 child, Ke-fang Fan. Graduate, Tsinghua U., Beijing, China, 1958. From asst. to assoc. prof. Tsinghua U., Beijing, China, 1958-89, prof., 1989—; cons. Da Tang Telecom., China, 1998—, Zhongxing Telecom., China, 1999—. Author: Guided-Wave Optics, 1988 (Outstanding Textbook award 1992). Recipient Outstanding Rschr. award State Commn. Sci. and Tech., 1996, Advancement in Sci. and Tech. award The State Edn. Commn., Beijing, 1996, 97, Nat. Invention award, 1997. Mem. IEEE, Optical Soc. Am., Chinese Inst. Electronics, China Inst. Comm. (vice chmn. profl. com. optical comm. Avocations: music, reading. E-mail: deefcc@mail.tsinghua.edu.cn. Office: Dept Electronic Engineering, Tsinghua Univ, Beijing 100084, China

FAN, HONGGANG, mechanical engineer, researcher; b. Hanchuan, Hubei, China, Apr. 15, 1970; came to U.S., 1997; s. Chunsheng Fan and Houmei Zhao; m. Feng Guo, July 18, 1999. BSME, Xi'an (China) Jiaotong U., 1991, PhD in Mech. Engring., 1995. Postdoctoral fellow Korea Advanced Inst. Sci. and Tech., Taejon, 1996-97; rsch. fellow dept. mech. engring. U. Mo., Rolla, 1997-98; rschr. dept. mech. engring. So. Meth. U., Dallas, 1998—. Contbr. articles to sci. jours., including Jour. Material Processing Tech., Jour. Physics D: Applied Physics, Metall. and Materials Trans. B., Jour. Engring. Manufacture, Numerical Health Transfer, Jour. Heat and Mass Transfer, Electric Welding Machine, Welding Tech., Jour. Naval Acad. Engring., Jour. Xi'an Jiaotong U. Mem. ASME (paper presenter ann. meeting 1999, Best Rsch. award 1999). E-mail: honggang@seas.smu.edu. Home: PO Box 751662 Dallas TX 75275-1662 Office: So Meth U Dept Mech Engring 3100 Smu Blvd Dallas TX 75205-6314

FAN, LILY XIAOMING, fashion designer; b. Shanghai, China, July 21, 1956; d. XinYa and QingYun (Ai) F. BS, Shanghai Mech. Inst. Tech., 1982; MS, CUNY, 1989. Engr. Wedgco, Gaithersburg, Md., 1989-91, RTKL Assocs., Balt., 1991-92; design trainee Ulla-Maija, N.Y.C., 1994-95; patternmaker Alvina Valenta, Babylon, N.Y., 1995-96; owner Manhattan Fashion Studio, Flint, Mich., 1996—; lead designer Four Seasons Bridal Shows, Grand Rapids, Mich., 1998-99. Named best new Mich. bridal designer Bride & Groom Publs., 1998. Avocations: interior design, music, tennis, scuba diving. Office: Manhattan Fashion Studio 4036 Grand Blanc Rd Swartz Creek MI 48473-9165

FAN, XIJUN, education educator; b. Yuncheng, China, Oct. 8, 1947; s. Hanting and Errui (Liu) F.; m. Shufen Tian, May 31, 1971; children: Yalin, Binghui. BSc, Beijing Normal U., 1970; MSc, Shandong Normal U., 1981. Lectr. Liaocheng (China) Edn. Coll., 1972-75, Shandong Normal U., Jinan, Cina, 1983-88; assoc. prof. Shandong Normal U., Jinan, 1988-93, prof., 1993—; vis. scholar Beijing U., 1986-87; sr. vis. scholar Ariz. State U., Tempe, 1993-97. Contbr. articles to profl. jours. Recipient Sci. and Tech. Progress award Edn. Com. of Shandong Province, 1990, 92, Sci. and Tech. Progress award of Shandong Province, 1999. Mem. Chinese Optical Soc., Chinese Phys. Soc., Optical Soc. Am.adr. E-mail: xijun@jn-public.sd.cninfo.net. Office: Shandong Normal U, East Wenhua Rd, Jinan, Shandong Prov China 250014

FAN, YEUK HON JOHN, engineering executive; b. Hong Kong, May 27, 1960; s. Pui Chung and Sui Kwan (Lau) F.; m. Nap Shan Chan, Nov. 12, 1989; children: Sharon, Cleopatra. Higher diploma, Hong Kong Polytechnic, 1983, Assoc., 1985; MBA, U. Okla., 1994, MA in Econs., 1996. Chartered engr. Chief rep. in China Swire Engring., Ltd., Guangzhou, 1997—; asst. engr. Shinryo Corp, Hong Kong, 1985-87; engr. Welcome Engring Ltd., Hong Kong, 1987-89; resident engr. Wong & OoYang (HK) Ltd., Hong Kong, 1989-91; contracts mgr. Taikoo Engring. Ltd., Hong Kong, 1991-94; project mgr. Swire Pacific Ltd., Hong Kong, 1995-97; asst. gen. mgr. Swire Engring., Ltd., 1997—; chief rep. in China Swire Engring., Ltd., Beijing, Shanghai; tech. dir. Zenith Bldg. Svcs. Ltd., Hong Kong, 1994. Mem. ASME, ASHRAE, Chartered Instn. Bldg. Svcs. Engrs., Hong Kong Instn. Engrs. Methodist. Avocations: swimming, bridge, tourism, music. Home: 10B Glory Heights, 52 Lyttelton Rd, Hong Kong Hong Kong Office: 6th Fl Warwick House, E Tai Koo Pl, Quarry Bay Hong Kong

FAN, YONG-KANG, surgeon, educator; b. Shanghai, Nov. 2, 1931; s. Aiwen Fan and Li-jun Zhao; m. Bing-shi Bao, May 30, 1957; children: Zuwei, Joy G. MD, Shanghai Med. U., 1953. Vis. surgeon 1st Hosp. of Shanghai Textile, 1964-79, vice chief surgeon, 1979-87, chief surgeon, 1987—; prof. surgery Shanghai 2d Med. U., 1989-96, Anhui (China) Med. U., 1994-96; vice dir. 1st Hosp. of Shanghai Textile, 1980-95, cons., 1996-99, v.p. med. assn., 1989-96; cons. Med. Rsch. Ctr. of Harvard Sch. Pub. Health/1st Hosp. Shanghai Textile, 1996-99. Contbr. articles to profl. jours.; chief editor Med. Jour. of Shanghai Textile, 1995-99. Recipient award for disting. contbr. in med. sci. State Coun. of China, 1993. Home: House 24 Ln 163, Chang Shu Rd, Shanghai 200031, China Office: 1st Hosp Shanghai Textile, 1291 Jiang Ning Rd, Shanghai 200060, China

FAN, Z. HUGH, chemist, biomedical engineer; b. Qidong, Jiangsu, China, Jan. 23, 1966; came to U.S., 1994; BSc, Yangzhou Tchr.'s Coll., 1985; PhD, U. Alta., Edmonton, Can., 1993. Lectr. Yangzhou Tchr.'s Coll., 1985-89; postdoctoral fellow Iowa State U., Ames, 1994-95; mem. tech. staff Sarnoff Corp., Princeton, N.J., 1995-2000; prin. scientist Aclara BioScis. Inc., Mountain View, Calif., 2000—. Mem. AAAS, Am. Chem. Soc., Electrochem. Soc. Achievements include patents for miniaturized analyzer, biochip, microfluids. Office: Aclara BioScis Inc 1288 Pear Ave Mountain View CA 94043-1432

FANCHER, PAUL STRIMPLE, research scientist; b. San Antonio, Jan. 5, 1932; s. Paul and Katherine Althea (Johnson) F.; m. Mary Kuhns, June 26, 1954; children: Katherine, Janet, Louise, Rebecca. BS in Engring., U. Mich., 1953, MS in Engring., 1959, Profl. Degree, 1964. Rsch. asst. U. Mich., Ann Arbor, 1957-59, rsch. assoc., 1959-61, assoc. rsch. scientist, 1961-70, rsch. scientist, 1970-98, sr. rsch. scientist, 1998—; mem. sci. com. Vehicle Sys. Dynamics, Cranfield, Eng., 1991-95; mem. exec. com., dir. rsch. Gt. Lakes Ctr. for Truck and Transit Rsch., Ann Arbor, 1994-99. Contbr. articles to profl. jours. With U.S. Army, 1953-56. Fellow Soc. Automotive Engrs. (chmn. vehicle dynamics com. 1992—); mem. Internat. Assn. Vehicle Sys. Dynamics. Avocations: gardening, traveling, fishing. E-mail: fancher@umich.edu. Office: Univ Mich Transp Rsch Inst 2901 Baxter Rd Ann Arbor MI 48109-2150

FANCHI, JOHN RICHARD, industrial technologist, educator, physicist; b. Pontiac, Ill., Nov. 17, 1952; s. John Anton and Shirley Mae (Andersen) F.; m. Katherine Frances Goedecke, Aug. 22, 1976; children: Anthony Clifford, Christopher John. BS in Physics, U. Denver, 1974; MS in Physics, U. Miss., 1975; PhD in Physics, U. Houston, 1977. Rsch. asst. Denver Rsch. Inst., 1970-74; rsch. engr. Getty Oil Co., Houston, 1978-79, Cities Svc. Co., Tulsa, 1979-81; sr. engr. Keplinger & Assocs., Tulsa, 1981-84; advanced sr. engr. Marathon Oil Co., Littleton, Colo., 1984-95, Houston, 1995-98; pres. Access Pubs., Denver, 1990-93; prof. Colo. Sch. Mines, Golden, 1998—; co-owner Fanchi Enterprises Cons., 1998—; adj. prof. physics U. Tulsa, 1980-81; vis. scientist Colo. Alliance for Sci., Denver, 1989-95; lectr. Arapahoe C.C., 1992; instr. engring. and math. U. Houston, 1996-97. Author: Parametrized Relativistic Quantum Theory, 1993, Principles of Applied Reservoir Simulation, 2d edit., 2000, Math Refresher for Scientists and Engineers, 2d edit., 2000, Integrated Flow Modeling, 2000; referee Soc. of Petroleum Engrs., 1981—, Founds. of Physics Jour., 1988—; contbr. over 40 articles to profl. jours. Cen. com. Colo. Reps., Denver, 1974; coord. coun. Littleton Pub. Schs., 1989-91, v.p., sch. bd., 1993-95; coach YMCA, Littleton, 1987-92; chmn. accountability com. Runyon Elem. Sch., Littleton, 1990-91. U. Miss. fellow, 1974-75, U. Houston, 1975-77; Colo.-Wyo. Acad. Sci. grantee, 1972. Mem. Am. Phys. Soc., Soc. Petroleum Engrs., Internat. Assn. Relativistic Dynamics (co-founder, pres. 1998-2002). Lutheran. Achievements include development of widely used software models of fluid flow in porous media; pioneered devel. of parametrized relativistic quantum theory; application of high technology to model performance and manage devel. of world-class size oil and gas fields; research on the effect of laser radiation on chemical reactions. Home: 180 Eagle Dr Golden CO 80403-7775

FANDINO, JAVIER, physician; b. Cartagena, Colombia, Dec. 3, 1968; s. Jaime and Margaret Marie (Merz) F. MD, U. Javeriana, Bogota, Colombia, 1992. Resident U. Hosp. Zurich, 1994-95, 95-96, U. Bern, Switzerland, 1994-95. Neurol. fellow U. Va., Charlottesville, 1998-99, U. Cin., 1999. Mem. Swiss Med. Assn., Swiss Neurosurg. Assn., Am. Heart Assn., Cardiovascular Group Switzerland. Avocations: cello, sailing. Office: U Hosp Zurich Dept Neurol, Fravenflinilstrasse 24, 8091 Zurich Switzerland

FANELLI, MICHAEL PAUL, music educator; b. Evanston, Ill., Feb. 12, 1943; s. George and Gloria (Del Carlo) F.; m. Carla Jean Saiger, May 28, 1978. BMus, U. Ill., 1968, EdD in Music Edn., 2000; MA in Music History, U. Mo., 1981. Cert. tchr. K-12, Mo., Iowa. Instr. of double bass U. Mo., Columbia, 1968-74; double bass artist-in-residence Stephens Coll., Columbia, 1968-75; profl. double bassist St. Louis Philharmonic, 1975-83; instr. instrumental music Sch. Dist. of the City of Ladue, Mo., 1983-87; instr. of music U. No. Iowa, Cedar Falls, 1987—; instr. of double bass Grinnell (Iowa) Coll., 1996—; founder, music dir. No. Iowa Jr. Orchestra, Cedar Falls, 1990-92; music dir. No. Iowa Youth Orchestra, 1994—; distance learning instr. music iowa Comms. Network, U. No. Iowa, 1995—; adv. bd. Iowa Alliance for Arts Edn., Des Moines, 1994—. Contbr. articles to profl. jours.; contbg. author: American String Teacher, 1997. Double bassist U. Ill., U.S. State Dept. tour of S.Am., 1964. Microcomputer grantee U. No. Iowa, Cedar Falls, 1989, 92, 95-98. Mem. Iowa String Tchrs. Assn. (pres. 1996-98, Disting. Svc. award 1992, Cert. for Outstanding Contbn. 1996), Iowa Sch. Orchestra Assn. (pres. 1992-96), Am. String Tchrs. Assn. (editl. com. 1997—, Outstanding Contbr. 1995-97), Suzuki Assn. of the Americas (column editor 1992—), Mo. String Tchrs. Assn. (sec.-treas. 1983-87), Kappa Delta Pi. Avocations: Am. art history, photography, fly fishing. Home: 203 Parkgate Rd Cedar Falls IA 50613-1953 Office: Univ No Iowa Price Lab Sch Cedar Falls IA 50613

FANG, CUI CHANG, mechanics educator, scientist; b. Cixi, Zhejiang, China, Sept. 23, 1928; s. Yong Tang Fang and Guang Ming Wang; m. Li Li Huang, Feb. 9, 1957; children: Zigang, Zihan, Zitao. BS, Tsinghua U., Beijing, 1950. Asst. mechanics Tsinghua U., 1950-54, lectr. mechanics, 1954-61, assoc. prof. mechanics, 1961-86, prof. mechanics, 1986; prof. mechanics Beijing Grad. Sch. China U. Mining, 1987—, tchr. doctoral students Beijing Grad. Sch., 1990—; mem. compiling group exptl. stress analysis China Great Ency. Press, 1979—. Author: Moire Method of Strain Analysis, 1983; co-author: Handbook on Strength Design and Test of Aeroengine, 1984 (Sci. and Tech. Progress award China Aviation Industry Ministry 1986, Nat. Sci. and Tech. Progress award China State Sci. and Tech. Commn. 1987), Experimental Stress Analysis, 1984, Contemporary Photomechanics, 1990; contbr. author: China Great Encyclopaedia, 1985; chief editor: Strength of Materials, 1964; editor: Advanced Engineering Mechanics, 1990. Recipient Beijing Sci. and Tech. Achievements award Beijing Mcpl. Govt., 1980, Outstanding Contbns. to Devel. of Chinese Higher Edn. award State Coun. China, 1992—. Mem. Chinese Soc. Mechanics. Avocations: taijiquan, qigong, music. Home: Tsinghua Univ, Apt 502-1 W Bldg 43, Beijing 100084, China Office: China U Mining at Beijing, D 11 Xueyuan Rd, Beijing 100083, China

FANG, HUNG-YUAN, educator; b. Taiwan, China, Oct. 23, 1945; m. Han-Jean Wong; children: Yu-Jen, Yi-Jen, Chia-Jen. B, Nat. Taiwan U., 1970, M, 1973; M, MIT, 1980; PhD, Chung Yuan Christian U., 1993. Chem. engr. Chinese Petroleum Corp., Chia-Yi, Taiwan, 1973-81, asst. mgr., 1981-86, dept. mgr., 1986-94; prof. Nat. Kaohsiung Inst. Marine Tech., 1994-95, Nat. Yunlin U Sci. & Tech., Toulin, China, 1995—; cons. Devel. Ctr. for Biotech., Taipei, 1993-95; cons. devel. Taiwan Salt Indsl. Corp.; part time prof. Nat. Chia-Yi Agrl. Inst., 1986—. Contbr. articles to profl. jours. Recipient Excellence Performance award Indsl. Waste Minimization, 1992, Tech. Achievement award Chinese Agrl. Chem. Soc., 1986, Disting. Youth medal Taiwan Gov., 1977. Mem. Chinese Inst. Environ. Engring., Chinese Inst. Food Sci. and Tech., Chinese Agrl. Chem. Soc. Avocations: antique and stamp collecting, table tennis. Fax: 886-5-2231815. Home: no 7-2 Lane 37 Wufeng S Rd, 600 Chia-Yi Taiwan Office: Nat Yunlin U Sci and Tech, 123 Univ Rd Sect 3, 640 Touliu Yulin, Taiwan

FANG, JI-QIAN, medical statistics educator; b. Shanghai, July 6, 1939; m. Mei-Ying Gong; 2 children. BS in Math., Fudan U., Shanghai, 1961; PhD in Biostats., U. Calif., Berkeley, 1985. Lectr. dept. biomath. Beijing Med. U., 1961-85, prof., dir. dept. biomath. and biostats., 1985-90; prof., dir. dept. med. stats. Sun Yat-Sen U. Med. Scis., Guangzhou, China, 1991—; vis. prof. U. Kent, Canterbury, Eng., 1987-88, Nat. U. Australia, Canberra, 1990; adj. prof. Chinese U. Hong Kong, 1993—. Author: Multi-State Survival Analysis, 1986 (Disting. Rsch. award Min. Pub. Health), Sequential Discriminant Analysis, 1988 (Disting. Rsch. award Mcpl. Govt.), Statistical Methods for Cancer Research, 1992 (Disting. Rsch. award Min. Pub. Health), Medical Statistics and Computer Experiment, 1997 (Guangdon Provincial Govt. award for Disting. Tchg. Arts). Fellow Royal Stats. Soc.; mem. Internat. Biometric Soc. (coun. mem.), Inst. Math. Stats. Avocations: drama, writing. Office: Sun Yat-Sen U Med Scis, Dept Med Stats, 510080 Guangzhou Guandong, China

FANG, JOONG, philosopher, mathematician, educator; b. Piongyang, Korea, Mar. 30, 1923; came to U.S., 1948, naturalized, 1962; s. Gabiong and Igab (Kim) F.; children: Eva Maria, Guido Andreas. Student, Chuo U., Tokyo, 1939-41; BS, Coll. Tech. Seoul, Korea, 1944; MA, Yale U., 1950; PhD, U. Mainz, Germany, 1957. Asst. prof. math. Jinhae Coll., also U. Pusan, Korea, 1945-48, Valparaiso (Ind.) U., 1958-59, St. John's U., 1959-61, U. Alaska, 1961-62; assoc. prof. No. Ill. U., 1963-67; prof. math. and philosophy Memphis State U., 1967-73; prof. philosophy Old Dominion U., Norfolk, Va., 1974-90; prof. emeritus Old Dominion U., 1990—; vis. prof. U. Münster, Germany, 1971. Author: Das Antinomienproblem, 1957, Abstract Algebra, 1963, Kant-Interpretationen, I, 1967, Numbers Racket: The Aftermath of "New Math", 1968, Towards a Philosophy of Modern Mathematics, I. Bourbaki, 1970, II. Hilbert, 1970, Mathematicians from Antiquity to Today, I, 1972, Sociology of Mathematics and Mathematicians, 1975, The Illusory Infinite: A Theology of Mathematics, 1976, Logic Today, Basics and Beyond, 1979, Linguistic Sense of the Japanese (in Japanese), 1984, Between Mathematics and Sociology, I. The Needham Question, 1994, II. The Birth of Exact Sciences, 1994, III. Fad, Fashions and Fallacies, 1994, Kant and Mathematics Today, 1997; editor: Philosophia Mathematica, 1964-92. Mem. Am. Math. Soc., Am. Philos. Assn. Address: 9745 Oak View Dr North VA 23128-9041

FANG, REMI (RONG FANG), physicist, educator; b. Ping-Jiang, Hunan, China, Aug. 10, 1958; arrived in France, 1989; s. Kui and Ruizhi (Xiong) F. Grad., Tsinghua U., Beijing, 1982; postgrad., Inst. High Energy Physics,

Beijing, 1985; Dr, U. Louis Pasteur, Strasbourg, France, 1997. Lectr. U. Sci. and Tech. China, Hefei, 1985-89; vis. assoc. prof. Paris U., 1989-91; vis. scholar Ctr. Nuclear Rsch., Strasbourg, France, 1991-93; engr. Aerial Irradiation Ctr., Strasbourg, France, 1993—. Contbr. articles on physics of diffusion, surface charging and electrodynamics to profl. jours. Mem. AAAS, N.Y. Acad. Scis. Avocations: music, dance, swimming. Home: 14 rue Marivaux, 67200 Strasbourg France Office: Aérial, 19 rue de Saint-Junien BP23, 67305 Schultigheim Cedex, France

FANG, SHU-CHERNG, industrial engineering and operations research educator; b. Nantou, Republic of China, June 14, 1952; came to U.S., 1976; s. Shao-Han and Lei Fang; m. Chi-Hsin Chao. BS in Math., Nat. Tsing-Hua U., Republic of China; MS in Math., Johns Hopkins U.; PhD in Indsl. Engring., Northwestern U. Asst. prof. U. Md., Balt., 1979-80; sr. staff mem. AT&T Engring. Rsch. Ctr., Princeton, N.J., 1980-85; supr. AT&T Bell Labs., Holmdel, N.J., 1985-88; dept. chief AT&T Corp. Hdqrs., Berkeley Heights, N.J., 1986-87; prof. N.C. State U., Raleigh, 1988—, dir. ops. rsch., 1990—, Walter Clark chair prof., 1996—; cons. AT&T Advanced Decision Support Systems, Berkeley Heights, 1988-90, Rsch. Triangle Inst., Raleigh, 1988-90. Author: Introduction to Fiber Optical Communications, 1986; Linear Optimization: Theory and Algorithms, 1993, Entropy Optimization and Mathematical Programming, 1997; contbr. more than 100 articles to profl. jours. Cray Rsch. Inc. grantee, 1990-95; Murphy fellow Northwestern U., 1977, Hopkins fellow Johns Hopkins U., 1976; recipient AT&T Tech. Achievement award, 1984, IBM Global Partnership award 1998, N.C. State Outstanding Rsch. award, 1997-98. Fellow N.C. Supercomputing Ctr.; mem. Ops. Rsch. Soc. Am., Inst. Indsl. Engrs. (sr. mem.), Assn. Chairpersons Ops. Rsch. Depts. (sec.-treas. 1990-91, v.p. 1991-92, pres. 1992—), Honor Soc. Ops. Rsch. (faculty mem.). Office: NC State U PO Box 7906 Raleigh NC 27695-0001

FANG, YUNG-SHOW, civil engineering educator; b. Taipei, Taiwan, May 25, 1954; s. Liang-Chin and Yea-Ja (Yeh) F.; m. Huei-Ling Yang, Oct. 11, 1987; children: Jane-Wen, Jane-Ching. B of Engring., Chung-Yuan U., 1976; M of Engring., U. S.C., 1979; PhD, U. Wash., Seattle, 1983. Assoc. prof. dept. civil engring. Nat. Chiao Tung U., Hsin-Chu, Taiwan, 1983-94, prof., 1994—; vis. assoc. prof. dept. of structural engring. Cornell U., Ithaca, N.Y., 1985; dir. Inst. of Civil Engring. Nat. Chiao Tung U., 1994-96. Contbr. articles to profl. jours. 2nd lt. Taiwanese Army, 1976-78. Recipient Outstanding Rsch. award Nat. Sci. Coun., 1998. Mem. ASCE, Internat. Soc. of Soil Mechanics and Geotech. Engrs., Taiwan Geotech. Soc., Chinese Inst. Civil Hydraulic Engring. (editor-in-charge), Tau Beta Pi. Achievements include rsch. on earth pressure against retaining structures, contbr. to a new method to estimate ground settlement due to tunneling in urban areas. Fax: 886-3-571-6257. E-mail: ysfang@cc.nctu.edu.tw. Office: Nat Chiao Tung Univ/Civil Engring, 1001 Ta Hsueh Rd, Hsinchu 30050, Taiwan

FANG, YUN-ZHONG, biochemist, educator; b. Nanjing, China, Aug. 16, 1919; s. Han Fang and Shu-Zhi; m. Ai-Hua Wu, Sept. 9, 1948; three children. B in Agriculture, Northwestern Agrl. Coll., 1942. Asst. rschr. Northwestern Agrl. Coll., China, 1942-44; rschr. Med. Coll. Nat. Def., China, 1945-47; lectr. Nantong Med. Coll., China, 1948-49; assoc. prof. Nat. Acad. Med. Scis., China, 1950-51, Acad. Mil. Med. Scis., China, 1952-82; prof. Beijing Inst. Radiation Medicine, China, 1982—. Editor: Medical Enzymology, 1983, Free Radicals and Enzymes, 1989, Advances in Free Radical Biology and Medicine, 1991, Advances in Free Radical Life Sciences, 1993-96. Home: 27 Tai-Ping Rd, 100850 Beijing China

FANG, ZHAOHONG, engineering educator; b. Hongjiang, Hunan, China, Nov. 9, 1945; s. Youhe Fang and Meiru Lu; m. Yizhu Hu, Sept. 9, 1973; 1 child, Liang. Grad., Tsinghua U., Beijing, 1968, MSc, 1981; PhD, Tsinghua U., 1987. Engr. Lijin (China) Textile Mill, 1968-78; from asst. prof. to prof. Shandong Inst. Civil Engring., Jinan, China, 1981-92; prof. Shandong Inst. Civil Engring., Jinan, 1992—, head dept. urban constrn., 1994-95, dean of studies, 1995-96, v.p., 1996—; vis. scholar U. Manchester, U.K., 1986, U. British Columbia, Can., 1993. Editor Ency. Chem. Engring., 1994; contbr. articles to profl. jours. Recipient Sci. Tech. award State Edn. Commn. China, 1993, Sci. and Tech. Commn. Shandong Province, 1996, Min. Constrn. China, 1996. Avocations: Go. Office: Shandong Inst Civil Engring, 47 Heping Rd, Jinan Shandong Province 250014, China

FANG, ZHENHE, physics educator, academic administrator; b. Shanghai, Dec. 23, 1944; s. Xihuang and Fengzhi (Ye) F.; m. Rongying Bian, Jan. 1, 1972; children: Lunhao, Guanghao. BS, Shanghai U. Sci. and Tech., 1966; MIEE, Instn. Elec. Engrs. Asst. prof. Shanghai U. Sci. and Tech., 1967-77, lectr., 1978-87, assoc. prof., 1988-95; prof., dir. Inst. Shanghai U., 1995—. Author: The Fundamental of Information Superhighway, 1996, Leaping on Information Age, 1999; patentee digital gyro simulator. Recipient Sci. Rsch. award State Planning Commn., China, 1989. Mem. Shanghai Assn. Inertial Tech. (standing com.), Shanghai Assn. Infrared and Remote Sensing, Microwave Remote Sensing Br. (standing com.). Home: Bldg B No 323, Fan yu Rd, 200052 Shanghai China Office: Shanghai Inst Elec Physics, No 39 Chen Zhong Rd, 201800 Shanghai China

FANOS, KATHLEEN HILAIRE, osteopathic physician, podiatrist; b. Bremerhaven, Germany, Aug. 18, 1956; came to U.S., 1957; d. Homer Dantangelo and Ilse Helmar (Ochs) F. AAS in Music, Nassau C.C., Garden City, N.Y., 1976; BS in Music Edn., Hofstra U., 1978, postgrad., 1978-79; D Podiatric Medicine, Coll. Podiatric Med. and Surg., Des Moines, 1987; DO, Coll. Osteo. Med. and Surg., Des Moines, 1994. Diplomate Am. Bd. Internal Medicine. Tchr. music McKenna Jr. H.S. and Eastlake Elem. Sch., Massapequa, N.Y., 1978-79; musician numerous profl. orgns., N.Y., Iowa, 1979—; preceptorship in podiatry Bayshore, N.Y., 1987-88; pvt. practice podiatry Hyde Park, West Roxbury and Brookline, Mass., 1988-91, Des Moines, 1991-92; resident in internal medicine Winthrop U. Hosp., Mineola, N.Y., 1994-97; internist Cmty. Med. Assocs., Jackson, N.J., 1997—; ins. med. examiner Portamedic, Burlington, Mass., 1988-91. Mem. AMA, ACP (assoc.), Am. Bd. Internal Medicine, Am. Soc. Internal. Medicine, Am. Osteo. Assn., Am. Coll. Osteo. Family Physicians, N.Y. State Internal Medicine Soc., Phi Theta Kappa, Pi Kappa Lambda, Sigma Sigma Phi, Phi Delta Epsilon. Avocations: music, tennis, bowling, skiing, travel.

FANT, ALFRED EDWARD, JR., computer science educator; b. Houston, Aug. 8, 1953; s. Alfred Edward and Christine Clara (Goodwin) F.; m. Patricia Jean Rutledge, Nov. 25, 1983 (div. 1999); 1 child, James Edward. B in Astronomy, U. Tex., Austin, 1977; B in Computer Sci., St. Edward's U., 1981; M in Computer Sci. Tech., Boston U., 1988; D in Computer Sci. Edn., Nova Southeastern U., 1993. Cert. secondary computer sci. tchr., Tex., microsoft trainer, 1997. USARP rsch. scientist U. Tex. Applied Rsch. Labs., McMurdo, Antarctica, 1977-79; computer programmer Applied Rsch. Labs. U. Tex., Austin, 1979-82; computer sci. instr. Hyde Park Bapt. Schs., Austin, 1982-84, U.S. Dept. of Def. Dep. Schs., Schweinfurt, Fed. Republic Germany, 1984-89; contr. manned spaceflight NASA, Houston, 1989-95; prof. computer sci. IBM, Austin, 1996—. Contbr. articles to BYTE Mag., Sky and Telscope, MicroComputing, Power/Play Jour., 73 Mag. Active with Boy Scouts Am., 1965--; cadette troop leader Girl Scouts Am., 1979--. Recipient Antarctica Service medal U.S. Congress, 1978, Eagle Scout Boy Scouts Am., 1971, Lifetime Girl Scout membership Girl Scouts Am., 1982, Woodbadge World Orgn. of Scouting Movement, 1977. Mem. Am. Astron. Soc. Baptist. Achievements include first construction of 1MHz radio telescope in Antarctica; first design of cheap computer braille writing for the blind. Home: PO Box 26284 Austin TX 78755-0284 Office: IBM-Tivoli Sys Austin TX 78759

FANTA, JAN, surgeon; b. Prague, Czech Republic, Dec. 18, 1950; s. Josef Fanta and Božena Žáryová Budinská; m. Dana Vitová, Oct. 6, 1977; children: Barbara, Klára. MD, Charles U., Prague, 1975. Houseman anaesthetist 1st Surg. Clinic, Prague, 1976; house surgeon 3rd Surg. Clinic, Prague, 1977-85, resident surg. officer, 1985-86, head surgeon of Tchg. Hosp., 1986-89, asst. prof., 1989-93; head Surg. Clinic 3rd med. Faculty, Prague, 1993—; active mem. European Laser Assn., Prague, 1992-94; mem. Czech Surg. Com., Prague, 1993-95; pres. surg. grant com. Health Ministry of Czech Republic, 1999—. Mem. editl. bd. Jour. Sukl, 1996—. Grantee Ministry of Health, Prague, 1995, 96, 97, 98, 99. Office: Surg Clinic, Šrobárova 50, 100 34 Prague Czech Republic

FANTANA, NICOLAIE LAURENTIU, electrical engineer, researcher; b. Nasaud, Romania, Dec. 11, 1950; s. Ion and Sanziana (Pascu) F.; m. Ana-Maria Ciortea, July 24, 1976; children: Antoniu, Horatiu. Diploma in engring., Poly. U. Timisoara, Romania, 1974, PhD in Engring., 1985. Rsch. engr. Electromotor Co., Timisoara, 1975-78; asst. prof. Faculty Elec. Engring., Poly. U. Timisoara, 1978-90, assoc. prof., 1990-91; vis. scientist U. Karlsruhe, Germany, 1991-92; sr. sci. rschr. Asea Brown Boveri Corp. Rsch., Heidelberg, Germany, 1992—; with Internat. Conf. Large High Voltage Electric Sys. Contbr. articles to sci. jours.; patentee in field. Recipient Disting. Asst. Prof. award Ministry of Edn., Romania, 1985. Mem. IEEE. Avocations: music, travel. E-mail: fantana@decrc.abb.de. Fax: 49-6221-596353. Office: Hauselgasse 39, Heidelberg 69124, Germany

FANTI, STEFANO, nuclear medicine physician; b. Bologna, Italy, Apr. 28, 1964; s. Marino Fanti and Maria Teresa Gamberini. MD, U. Bologna, 1991. Cert. specialist nuclear medicine, 1996. Physician nuclear medicine S. Orsola-Malpighi Hosp., Bologna; co-dir nuclear medicine Hesperia Hosp., Modena, Italy, 1997-98; physician nuclear medicine Maggiore Hosp., Bologna, 1998-99. Author: Nuclear Medicine Semeiology of Kidney, 1994, Nuclear Medicine Imaging of Central Nervous System, 1999; contbr. articles to profl. jours. Postdoctoral fellow S. Orsola-Malpighi, Bologna, 1992-96, rsch. fellow, 1996-97. Mem. Soc. Nuclear Medicine, European Assn. Nuclear Medicine. Office: S Orsola-Malpigni Nuclear Medicine Dept, via Albertoni 15, 40138 Bolgona Italy

FANUEL, BONGINKOSI, military officer; b. Piet Retief, South Africa, Sept. 22, 1969; s. Jane Fanuel; m. Nontobeko Maluli, Mar. 31, 1994; 2 children. Diploma in wildlife mgmt., Pretoria (South Africa) Tech., 1992. Advanced to capt. SANDF, Ermelo, South Africa, 1987—, platoon sgt., 1988-96, platoon comdr., 1997-98, tng. officer, 1999—. Lutheran. Avocations: watching television, table tennis, reading.

FANUELE, FRANK JOHN, engineering executive; b. N.Y.C., June 19, 1938. BSEE, Rensselaer Poly. Inst., 1960. Elec. engr. GE, 1960-64; project engr. Fairchild Electrometrics Corp., 1964-69; sys. engring. mgr. Mech. Tech. Inc., 1969-84; tech. sales mgr. Brown & Sharpe Mfg. Co., 1984-86; tech. mktg. mgr. Robotic Vision Sys., 1989; pres. Fanuele Enterprises, Albany, N.Y., 1986—. Achievements include transforming state of the art research and development activities into practical implementation in military, aerospace, automotive sectors and general factory automation. Office: Fanuele Enterprises 256 Partridge St Albany NY 12208-2624

FANUS, PAULINE RIFE, librarian; b. New Oxford, Pa., Feb. 14, 1925; d. Maurice Diehl and Bernice Edna (Gable) Rife; m. William Edward Fanus, June 20, 1944; children: Irene Weaver, Larry William, Daniel Diehl. BS, Pa. State U., 1945; MLS, Villanova U., 1961; postgrad., Temple U., 1986—. Periodical libr. Tex. Coll. Arts Industries, Kingville, 1945; tchr. nursery sch. Studio Sch., Wayne, Pa., 1953-55; libr. circulation, reference Franklin Inst., Phila., 1963-66; asst. libr. Ursinus Coll., Collegeville, Pa., 1966; catalog libr., instr. Eastern Coll., St. Davids, Pa., 1967-71; head libr. Agnes Irwin Sch., Rosemont, Pa., 1971-93, head libr. emeritus, 1993—. Book reviewer The Book Report. Mem. AAUP (chpt. sec. Eastern Coll. 1970-71). Home: 78 Holly Dr New Holland PA 17557-9476

FAQUIH, OSAMAH JAAFAR, bank executive; b. Almadina Almonwara, Saudi Arabia, 1943; s. Jaafar Ibrahim Faquih; 5 children. BA in Acctg. and Bus. Adminstrn., U. Riyadh, Saudi Arabia, 1969; MBA, U. Ariz., 1973. Instr. faculty adminstrv. scis. U. Riyadh, 1969-71, lectr. faculty adminstrv. scis., 1974-75; dir. capital and loan dept. Saudi Fund for Devel., Riyadh, 1975-80; asst. dep. fin. minister Internat. Devel. Coop., Riyadh, 1981-83, dep. fin. minister, 1983-90; dep. minister of fin. Nat. Economy/Arab Monetary Fund, 1990-94; chmn. bd. dirs., dir.-gen. Arab Monetary Fund, United Arab Emirates, 1989-94; CEO, chmn. bd. dirs. Arab Trade Fin. Program, United Arab Emirates, 1989-94; pres. Islamic Devel. Bank, Jeddah, Saudi Arabia, 1994-95; min. commerce Govt. of Saudi Arabia, Riyadh, 1995—; chmn. bd. govs. OPEC Fund for Internat. Devel., Vienna, Austria, 1982—; chmn. bd. dirs. Gulf Agy. in Egypt, 1984-92; chmn. governing coun. Common Fund for Commodities, 1988-92. Contbr. articles to profl. publs. Office: Ministry Commerce, PO 1774 Airport Rd, Riyadh 11162, Saudi Arabia*

FARA, LAURENTIU VLADIMIR, physics educator, researcher; b. Bucharest, Romania, Oct. 11, 1944; s. Dumitru and Silvia (Gherghinescu) F. MS, Bucharest U., 1967; PhD, Inst. Atomic Physics, Bucharest, 1982. Asst. lectr. physics dept. Bucharest Poly. U., 1968-78, lectr., 1978-90, prof. physics, 1990—; pres. Nat. Agy. Renewable Energy, Bucharest, 1993—. Author: Solar Energy Conversion: Principles and Applications, 1982, Solar Thermal Storage: Applications in Agriculture, 1991; contbr. over 150 sci. articles to nat. and internat. jours.; editor-in-chief: Solar Energy for Sustainable Development jour. Mem. bd. Internat. Energy Found.; mem. Internat. Steering Com. World Renewable Energy Congress; instl. mem. EUFORES. Recipient Dragomir Hurmuzescu prize for contbn. in solar energy field Romanian Acad., Bucharest, 1985. Fellow European Phys. Soc. (bd. dirs. 1993—), European Optical Soc. (adv. bd. mem. 1993—), Internat. Solar Energy Soc. (chair Romanian sect. 1992—, editor-in-chief Romanian Solar Energy Soc. newsletter); mem. N.Y. Acad. Scis., Nat. Geog. Soc. Orthodox. Avocations: energy policy, history, philosophy, music, tourism. Home: Argentina Str 19 Sector 1, RO-71206 Bucharest Romania Office: Bucharest Poly U Physics Dp, 313 Splaiul Independentei Sector 6, RO-77206 Bucharest Romania

FARABET, TRISTAN, beverage company executive; b. Boulogne, France, Sept. 21, 1966; s. René and Anne (Jeramec) F.; m. Florence Rouvier, Feb. 16, 1991; 1 child, Clemence. Degree, HEC, France, 1988. Cons. Bain & Co., London and Paris, 1988-92; nat. vending mgr. Coca-Cola, Paris, 1993-95, dir. planning, 1995-97, dir. fin. svcs., 1996—, dir. S.W. region, 1998—. Home: 79 Rue Ducau, 33000 Bordeaux France Office: Coca-Cola Enterprise, BP 102, 33704 Merignac France

FARAG, M. SAMIR, psychologist, consultant; b. Gharbia, Egypt, Nov. 2, 1940; m. Zeinab Saad El Sobtasy, Mar. 23, 1978; children: Hend, Yasmin. BS in Mil. Scis., Mil. Faculty, Cairo, 1958; BA in Psychology, Ain-Shams U., Cairo, 1974, MA in Psychology Loyalty, 1982, PhD in Psychology Egyptian Personality, 1988. Lic. psychotherapist; cert. total quality mgmt. Staff pers. dept. Nat. Def. Coun. Egypt, 1966-74, dir. psychology dept., 1975-83; v.p. Inst. for Strategic Scis., Cairo, 1984-88; cons. Mgmt. Devel. Ctr., Cairo, 1990—; mgrs. selection Assessment Ctr., Cairo, 1975—; vis. prof. Inst. for Strategic Scis., Cairo, 1988—; psychotherapist Pvt. Ctr., Cairo, 1995—. Author: Sadat & Peace Initiative, 1978, Loyalty Between Psychology and Koran, 1989. With Egyptian Mil. Forces, 1958-66. Recipient Order of Merit, Pres. Nasser, 1959, Order of the Republic, Pres. Mubarak, 1988. Mem. Egyptian Assn. Family and Social Conflict Resolution (mem. directorate), Arab Mgmt. Assn., APA (internat. affiliate), Internat. Assn. Applied Psychology, Internat. Assn. Cross-Cultural Psychology, World Islamic Assn. for Mental Health (mem. directorate). Muslim. Avocations: arts, ping-pong. Fax: 002 02-3494125, 00202-3609342. E-mail: mdci@idsc.gov.eg. Home: 1 Mohamed Afify St, Hegaz Sq, Heliopolis Cairo, Egypt

FARAG, MAHMOUD MOHAMED, engineering educator; b. Cairo, May 27, 1937; s. Mohamed D. and Kamla M. (Hassan) F.; m. Penelope Joan Gretchen Plant, March 23, 1964; children: Sherif, Sophie. BS in Engring., Cairo U., 1959; M in Metallurgy, Sheffield U., England, 1962; PhD, Sheffield U., 1965. Asst. prof. Ain Shams U., Cairo, 1965-70; assoc. prof. Ain Shams U., 1970-71; assoc. prof. Am. U. in Cairo, 1971-75, prof., 1975—, chmn. engring. dept., 1984-85, vice provost, 1992—; con. Continental Can Co., Stamford, Conn., 1981-85; dir. Engring. Svcs. AUC, Cairo, 1983—; prin. investigator Schlumberger Oil Co., Hartford, Conn., 1985-87; bd. dirs. Sornaga, Cairo, 1992—. Author: Materials and Process Selection, 1979, Selection of Materials, 1989, Materials Selection for Engineering Design, 1997; contbr. articles to profl. jours. Chair Com. on Environment, AUC-Cairo, 1992—. Recipient C.M. Desch award Sheffield U., 1969, Egyptian State award for Promotion of Sci. Govt. of Egypt, 1975, 1st Order of Merit for Arts and Scis. Govt. of Egypt, 1975. Mem. ASME, AIME (Metallurgy Soc.), Egyptian Soc. for Engrs. Avocations: painting (oils and watercolors), sculpture (metal and stone), classical music. Home: 6 El Zahraa St, Dokki Cairo Egypt Office: Am University in Cairo, 113 Kasr El Aini St PO Box 2511, Cairo Egypt

FARAG, RADWAN SEDKEY, chemist, educator; b. Cairo, Nov. 27, 1941; s. Sedkey Farag and Fathia Allam (Ali) Mohamed; m. Fatma Mahmoud El-Shishi, Aug. 8, 1967; 1 child, Mohamed. BSc, Cairo U., 1963, MSc, 1966; PhD, London U., 1974. Demonstrator Faculty of Agr., Cairo U., Giza, 1963-67, assoc. lectr., 1967-74, lectr., 1974-79, assoc. prof., 1979-84, prof., 1984—, head biochem. dept., 1988-94, dir. ctrl. lab., 1975-95; mem. Nat. Com. Biochem. & Molecular Biology. Egypt, 1997. Author: Chromotographic Analysis, 1990, Lipids, 1991, Physical and Chemical Analysis of Fats and Oils, 1995, Principles of Biochemistry, 1999; contbr. articles to profl. jours.; editl. bd. New Egyptian Jour. Medicine, 1993—. Bd. dirs. Open Ctr., Cairo U., 1988-94; mem. Nat. Ency., 1989, 92. Recipient Egyptian State award Egyptian Acad. Sci. Rsch. and Tech., 1978, 84, 20th Century award Achievement IBC, Cambridge, England, 1997. Mem. AAAS, Am. Oil Chemist Soc., Egyptian Orgn. for Standardization and Quality Control, N.Y. Acad. Sci., Internat. Assn. for Cereal Sci. and Tech. France, Nat. Geographic Soc. Avocations: football, handball, squash, swimming. Home: 7 Dr Ibrahim St, El Sahafeen City Giza, Egypt Office: Cairo University, El Gamma St Faculty of Agriculture, Giza Egypt

FARAH, FUAD SALIM, dermatologist; b. Haifa, Palestine, 1929. MD, Am. U., Beirut, 1954. Diplomate Am. Bd. Dermatology. Internship Am. U., Beirut, Lebanon, 1954-55; residency Am. U., Beirut, 1955-56; res. internal medicine Am. U., Beirut, Lebanon, 1956-57; fellowship Barnes Hosp., 1957-59; dir. immunology rsch. & tng. ctr. WHO, Beruit, Lebanon, 1970-76; physician SUNY Upstate Med. Ctr., Syracuse, chief sect. dermatology, 1976-99; pvt. practice Syracuse; instr. dept. medicine Am. U., Beirut, 1959-60, asst. prof., 1960-66, assoc. prof., 1966-74, prof., 1976. Fellow Am. Acad. Dermatology; mem. Internat. Soc. of Tropical Medicine, Soc. for Investigative Dermatology. Fax: 315-422-3129. Office: The Hill Med Ctr 1000 E Genesee St Syracuse NY 13210-1892 also: Upstate Med Ctr 750 E Adams St Syracuse NY 13210-2306

FARAH, KIMBERLY SUE, chemistry educator, researcher; b. Morristown, N.J., Apr. 6, 1962; d. Basil Said and Barbara (Donald) F. BS, Va. Tech. U., 1984; MSE, U. Lowell, 1989; PhD, U. Mass., 1993. Asst. prof. Lasell Coll., Newton, Mass., 1993-98, assoc. prof., dept. head, 1998—; faculty cons. Kennedy-Western U., Thousand Oaks, Calif., 1994-99; mem. adv. bd. exercise physiology Lasell Coll., Newton, 1995-99. Author: (book chpt.) Advances in Applied Spectroscopy, 1997; contbr. articles to profl. jours.; mem. editl. bd. Microchemical Jour., Lake Charles, La., 1997-99. Mem. scholarship com. Girl Scouts Am., Manchester, N.H., 1996-99. 1st lt. U.S. Army, 1984-88, Korea, Ala. Grantee State St. Found., Boston, 1995-97. Mem. Am. Chem. Soc., Soc. for Applied Spectroscopy. Avocations: horseback riding, flute, biking. E-mail: kfarah@nh.ultranet.com.

FARAONE, TED, public relations executive, consultant; b. Providence, Feb. 21, 1956; s. Raffaele Pietro and Jennie (Landi) F.; m. Teri Dickstein, June 1, 1988. BA, Columbia U., 1978. Publicity dir. Sta. WNYC Radio-TV, N.Y.C., 1979-81; press rep. Sta. WNBC-TV, N.Y.C., 1981-82, Sta. WCBS-TV, N.Y.C., 1982-83; dir. press rels. Sta. WCAU-TV, Phila., 1983-86, Sta. WBBM-TV, Chgo., 1986-87; pres. Faraone Comm., Inc., N.Y.C., 1987-93; vice chmn. Faraone Comm., Inc., 1994, chmn., 1995—; founder, ptnr. Ingenio, 1999—. Editor: mag. Sta. WNYC Program Guide, 1979-81. Mem. NATAS (mem. bd. govs. N.Y. chpt. 1993—, sec. 1995-97, v.p. 1997—), NARAS, Acad. of TV Arts and Scis., Internat. Radio and TV Soc., Pub. Rels. Soc. (accredited), Counselors Acad., Writers and Artists for Peace in Mid-East, Eastern Packard Club (dir. 1998—), Friars Club (N.Y.C.), Phi Beta Kappa. Office: Faraone Communications Inc 75 W End Ave New York NY 10023-7853

FARAONE, TERI, public relations executive; b. N.Y.C., July 6, 1953; d. Seymour and Marilyn (Lutsky) Dickstein; m. Ted Faraone, June 1, 1988. BA, Kean Coll. of N.J., Elizabeth, 1979; MA, CUNY, 1996; postgrad., Columbia U., 1999—. Asst. mgr. Citicorp, N.Y.C., 1982-88; mgr. Faraone Comms., N.Y.C., 1988-92, dir. acct. svcs., 1990-92, v.p., 1992-94, pres., 1994—. Mem. NATAS. Office: Faraone Communications Inc 75 W End Ave New York NY 10023-7853

FARAUT, JEAN-PIERRE, hotel owner and developer; b. Nice, France, Sept. 16, 1944; s. Jean and Anne-Marie F.; m. Suzy Patricia Gillen, Aug. 19, 1967; children: Philippe P., François William. Degree in law, U. Aix en Provence, 1967. V.p. Hotels de la Cite, Paris, 1969-74, ptnr., gen. mgr., 1975-79; gen. mgr. Sopag Cons., Paris, 1978-85; v.p. devel. Imperial Hotel Corp., 1987-88; chmn. Hotels de la Ville, Paris, 1985-89; pres. Hotelinvest, Paris, 1989—; bd. dirs. Hotel Royal Monceau, Paris; expert witness Paris Appellate Ct., 1986—. Contbr. articles on hotel industry to trade publs. Town councilman, Town of Biarritz, France, 1970-76; judge, Tribunal de Commerce, Paris, 1977-80. With French armed forces, 1968. Roman Catholic. Avocation: golf. Office: 12 Ave Matignon, 75008 Paris France

FARB, THOMAS FOREST, financial executive; b. N.Y.C., Oct. 28, 1956; s. Peter and Oriole (Horch) F.; m. Stacy Siana Valhouli, Apr. 29, 1961; children: Peter Forest Valhouli-Farb, Siana Louisa Valhouli-Farb, Andreas John Valhouli-Farb. AB, Harvard U., 1980. Rsch. assoc. Mass. House Ways and Means Com., Boston, 1976-78; asst v.p. Bank of Boston, 1980-83; v.p., CFO and gen. mgr. ea. ops. Symbolics, Inc., Burlington, Mass., 1983-89; sr. v.p., CFO & controller Airfund Corp., Lexington, Mass., 1989-92; v.p. corp. devel., chief fin. officer and treas. Cytyc Corp., Marborough, Mass., 1992-94; exec. v.p., CFO, treas. Interneuron Pharms., Inc., Lexington, Mass., 1994-98; gen. ptnr., CFO Summit Ptnrs., Boston, 1998—; bd. dirs. HNC Software, Inc., San Diego, Redwood Trust, Inc., Mill Valley, Calif., Saf-T-Med. Inc., Barrington, Ill. Mem. Fin. Execs. Inst., Bus. Assocs. Club, Treas. Club Boston, Newcomen Soc. Home: 1228 Lowell Rd Concord MA 01742-5527 Office: Summit Partners 600 Atlantic Ave Fl 28 Boston MA 02210-2211

FARBER, DONALD CLIFFORD, lawyer, educator; b. Columbus, Nebr., Oct. 19, 1923; s. Charles and Sarah (Epstein) F.; m. Ann Eis, Dec. 28, 1947; children: Seth, Patricia. BS in Law, U. Nebr., 1948, JD, 1950. Bar: N.Y. 1950. Assoc. Newman, Hauser & Teitler, N.Y.C., 1950-58; sole practice N.Y.C., 1958-80; of counsel Conboy, Hewitt, O'Brien & Boardman, N.Y.C., 1980-84; ptnr. Tanner Propp Fersko & Sterner, N.Y.C., 1984-95, Farber & Rich LLP, N.Y.C., 1995-98; of counsel Hartman & Craven LLP, N.Y.C., 1998—; prof. law York U., Toronto, Ont., Can., 1970, 72-73; prof. theatre law Hofstra Law Sch., Hempstead, N.Y., 1974-75; prof. New Sch. for Social Rsch., N.Y.C., 1972—, Hunter Coll., 1978. Author: From Option to Opening, 1968, 4th edit., 1st Limelight edit., 1988, Producing on Broadway, 1969, Actor's Guide: What You Should Know About the Contracts You Sign, 1971, Producing, Financing and Distributing Film, 1973, 2d edit., 1991, The Amazing Story of the Fantasticks: America's Longest Running Play, 1991, Producing Theatre: A Comprehensive Legal and Business Guide, 1981, 3d Limelight edit., 1997, Common Sense Negotiation-The Art of Winning Gracefully, 1996; gen. editor (10 vol. series, author theatre vol.) Entertainment Industry Contracts-Negotiating and Drafting Guide. With AUS, 1941-44, ETO. Mem. Order of Coif, Hon. Law Soc. Fax: (212) 223-7561. Home: 14 E 75th St New York NY 10021-2657 Office: Farber & Turek 750 Lexington Ave Ste 600 New York NY 10022-1200

FARBER, GEORGE ALLAN, dermatologist; b. Miami, Fla., Jan. 4, 1934; s. Charles R. and Clara M. (Milman) F.; m. Nancy Graves, Dec. 26, 1955; children: George Allan, Michael G., Jeffrey N., Guy C., Scott O. BS, La. State U., 1955, MD, 1959. Diplomate Am. Bd. Cosmetic Surgery. Intern So. Bapt. Hosp., New Orleans, 1959-60; resident Charity Hosp. of New Orleans, 1963-66; commd. 2d lt. M.C. USAF, 1955, advanced through grades to lt. col., 1965; chief aviation medicine and mil. pub. health Luke AFB, Phoenix, 1960-63; flight surgeon, chief dermatology and syphilology 12th USAF Hosp., Cam Ranh Bay, Vietnam, 1966-67; chief dermatology svc., cons. to Surgeon Gen. S.E. region USAF Med. Referral Ctr., Keesler AFB, Miss., 1967-70; ret. USAF, 1970; asst. prof. medicine Tulane U. Sch. Medicine, New Orleans, 1970-75; assoc. prof. Tulane U. Sch. Medicine, 1976-84; pvt. practice dermatology, 1970—; clin. assoc. prof. dermatology Tulane U. Sch. Medicine, New Orleans, 1975—; mem. staff Kenner Regional Ctr. Hosp., 1994—; past mem. staff Charity Hosp. New Orleans, East Jefferson Hosp., So. Bapt. Hosp., Kenner (La.) Regional Med. Ctr.; prof., med.

dir. resident and postgrad. accredited tng. program Gulf South Med. and Surgery Inst., Kermer, La.; mem. profl. staff Kenner Dermatology Clinic; ret. dir. Fairground Corp., New Orleans; mem. courtesy staff Northshore Regional Med. Ctr., Slidell, La.; bd. dirs. La. Divsn. Am. Lukemia Soc. Mem. Kenner Med. Soc. (founder, sec./treas. 1998), N.Am. Acad. Cosmetic and Reconstructive Surgery (founder, bd. dirs., pres. 1998-99), Am. Soc. Dermatologic Surgery (co-founder, past officer and dir.), Am. Acad. Cosmetic Surgery (co-founder, past officer and dir.), Am. Bd. Cosmetic Surgery (co-founder, past officer and dir.). Home: 5 Chateau Petrus Dr Kenner LA 70065-2058 Office: Gulf South Med Surg Inst 200 W Esplanade Ave Ste 106 Kenner LA 70065-2473

FARELL CUBILLAS, ARSENIO, Mexican government official. Comptroller gen. Govt. of Mex., Mexico City. Office: Office of Comptroller Gen, Avenida Insurgentes 1735, 10 Piso Mexico City 01020, Mexico*

FARES, MIKHAEL ISSAM, bank executive; s. Issam Fares and Oumayma Farah; m. Lara Rizk. Pres. Fares Found., Lebanon, 1984—; dir. Wedge Bank M.E., Lebanon, 1985-96; chmn. Wedge Bank M.E., 1991-96; dir. Wedge Bank Switzerland, 1985-94, chmn., 1991-96, corp. investment adviser, 1987—; dir. Wedge Group Internat., Tex., 1987—, Lebanon Holding, Luxembourg. Bd. visitors Fletcher Sch. of Law and Diplomacy, Mass., 1992—; internat. adv. coun. Am. Univ. Beirut, N.Y., 1992—; bd. trustees Balamand Univ., Lebanon, 1994—, Am. Univ. Beirut, 1996—.

FARGHALI, HASSAN, pharmacologist, administrator, educator; b. Manfalot, Assiut, Egypt, June 6, 1943; arrived in Czech Republic, 1981; s. Hassan and Naima Abd El Shafi; m. Jana Brantova, Oct. 10, 1950; children: Omar, Hany. PhD, Charles U., Czech Republic, 1973; DSc, Charles U., 1996. Diplomate in pharmacology (med. scis.). Asst. prof. U. Basarh, Iraq, 1977-81; rschr. Acad. Sci. Czechoslovakia, 1981-86; postdoctoral fellow U. Medicine and Dentistry N.J., 1986-87; assoc. rsch. prof. U. Pitts., 1988-92; assoc. prof. Faculty of Medicine Charles U., Prague, 1994-97, chmn., prof., 1997—; rsch. cons. Acad. Scis. of Czech Republic, 1997—. Contbr. chpts. to books, articles to profl. jours. Mem. Czech Pharmacol. Soc. Avocations: jogging, reading novels, listening to classical and space music. Home: Piscita 331 Jahodnice, 19800 Prague 9, Czech Republic

FARHUD, D. D., genetics educator, academic administrator. MD, U. Erlangen, Germany, 1969; PhD in Human Genetics and Anthropology, U. Mainz, Germany, 1972, BSc in Psychology, 1973. Founder, prof., head dept. human genetics and anthropology Tehran (Iran) U. Med. Scis., 1973—; founder, dir. Genetic Clinic, Tehran, 1981—; mem. expert adv. panel human genetics WHO, Geneva, 1976—; mem. com. ethics human genetics, 1994—; founder, dir. Ctr. Human Genetic Rsch., Maternity Hosp., Tehran, 1977; guest prof. Ctr. Handicapped Children, U. Munich, 1989-90. Editor-in-chief Iranian Jour. Pub. Health, 1981—, Jour. Ecology, 1986-89; co-editor: Biological Dictionary, English-Persian, 1981-91; mem. biol. com.: Larger Persian Encyclopedia, 1992—; mem. adv. bd. Jour. Acad. Scis., 1995—; contbr. articles to profl. jours. Recipient Kharazmi Internat. Sci. prize, 1990. Fellow Third World Acad. Scis.; mem. Iranian Acad. Scis., Iranian Genetics Soc. (sec. 1974—). Office: Tehran U Med Scis, Sch Pub Health, Tehran Iran

FARIAS, ROBSON FERNANDES DE, chemistry educator; b. Nova Iguacu, Brazil, Jan. 30, 1967; s. Romeu Fernandes de Farias and Raimunda Leite da Costa. B Chemistry, U. Rio Grande do Norte, Brazil, 1991, M Chemistry, 1993; D Chemistry, U. Estadual de Campinas, 2000. Prof. UF de Roraima, Brazil, 1994—. Author: Quimica, ensino & Cidadania, 1999; contbr. articles to profl. jours. With Brazilian Navy, 1986-87. Mem. Assn. Bras. Análise Termica e Calorime Tria, Soc. Brasileira de Quimica (regional sec., Best Work award materials sect. 1999), N.Y. Acad. Scis. Avocations: history, astronomy, tennis, psychology. Fax: 55 95 623-9075. Office: Dept Quimica UFRR, 69310270 Boa Vista Roraima Brazil

FARIAS BOUVIER, NESTOR, consulting company executive; b. Santa Fe, Argentina, July 23, 1941; s. Americo Farlas and Nelly Bouvier Samyn; m. Marina Lopez Anadon (div.); m. Maria Elena Daro, June 6, 1988; children: Gaston, Martina. Degree in chem. engring., U. Nat. Litoral, Santa Fe, 1964; MBA, Iese. Navarra U., Barcelona, Spain, 1968. Pres., CEO Sapin Ltd., Brazil, 1973-78; pres. Sapin S.A. Bus. Cons., Buenos Aires, 1975—, Petroquimica Bahia Blanca, Buenos Aires, 1984-87; pres., CEO Austral Airlines, Buenos Aires, 1987-89; CEO, bd. dirs. Met. Railway SA, Argentina, 1992-94; CEO DGT Electronics S.A., Argentina, 1977-99; pres. Nucleo Electrca S.A., 2000—. Contbr. papers on bus. policy/mgmt. to profl. jours. Industry sec. Argentine Govt., 1985. Roman Catholic. Avocations: tennis, skiing, horseback-riding. Office: Sapin SA Bus Cons, Cordoba 669 8, 7054 Buenos Aires Argentina

FARICY, JOHN HARTNETT, JR., lawyer; b. Augsburg, Germany, Nov. 5, 1955; came to U.S., 1956; s. John Hartnett and Mary Helen Sarah (Bowe) F. BA, Tulane U., 1977; JD, William Mitchell Coll. Law, St. Paul, 1982. Bar: Minn. 1982, U.S. Dist. Ct. Minn. 1983, U.S. Ct. Appeals (2d cir.) 1987, U.S. Supreme Ct. 1988. Ptnr. Faricy & Roen, P.A., Mpls., 1996—. Mem. Univ. Club of St. Paul. Office: Faricy & Roen PA 150 S 5th St Minneapolis MN 55402-4200

FARINA, JOHN, lawyer; b. Rockville Center, N.Y., Oct. 20, 1959; s. Joseph P. Farina and Marilyn A. Echkoff; m. Julia Pressly, May 30, 1987; children: Matthew, Timothy, Nicholas. BA, Villanova U., 1981; JD, Suffolk U., 1985. Bar: Mass. 1985, Fla. 1986. Law clk. U.S. Ct. Appeals (4th dist.), West Palm Beach, Fla., 1985-86; assoc. Winthrop Stimson Putnam & Roberts, Palm Beach, Fla., 1986-90, Edwards & Angell, Palm Beach, 1990-94; ptnr. Boyes & Farina, West Palm Beach, 1994—; mem. Fla. Probate Rules Com., Fla. Bar Greivance Com., 1998—. Mem. Palm Beach County Bar Assn. Avocations: trap and skeet shooting, running, tennis. Home: 131 Thornton Dr Palm Bch Gdns FL 33418-8089 Office: Boyes & Farina PA 1601 Forum Pl Ste 900 West Palm Beach FL 33401-8105

FARIÑA, JULIANA, pathologist; b. Badajoz, Spain; d. Adolfo Fariña and Juliana Olaya Gonzalez; m. Jeronimo Buencuerpo, 1974; children: Juliana, Jeronimo. MD, Dr. Medicina Sch., Madrid, 1970, physician, 1976. Diplomate Spanish Bd. Pathology Anatomy. Fellow pathol. anatomy Clinic Hosp., Madrid, 1970-73, mem. med. staff, 1973-77; aggregate prof. Med. Sch. Cordoba, Spain, 1977-78; aggregate prof. U. Complutense, Madrid, 1978-83, prof., head Sch. Medicine, 1983—; prof., head dept. pathology II Hosp. Clinico, Madrid, 1983—; pres. Nat. Commn. Postgrad. Formation in Pathology, 1996—; pres. sci. com. Virtual Congress Hispanoamericano, 1997—. Author, editor: anatomia Patologica, 1990, Citopatologia Respiratoria y Pleural, 1996; rschr. in field; mem. editl. bd. rev. Patologia, 1996—; inventor new autopsy method. Mem. com. Coord. Investigation U. Hosp., 1999; mem. tech. com. Clin. Hosp., Madrid, 1997—; mem. coun. Med. Sch., U. Complutense, 1996—. Recipient scholarship award Found. Marquesa de Pelayo, 1972. Mem. Spanish Soc. Pathology (dir. com. 1980-84), N.Y. Acad. Scis., Internat. Acad. Pathology, Royal Medicine Acad. Avocations: oil painting, writing, basketball, music, walking. Home: Miloca 32, 28230 Las Rozas de Madrid Spain Office: Hosp Clinico, Plaza Cristo Rey S/N, 28040 Madrid Spain

FARINE, PIERRE ANDRE, microelectronics engineer; b. Chaux-de-Fonds, Neuchatel, Switzerland, Mar. 4, 1953; s. Andre and Anna (Puglisi) F.; m. Mary Maitre, Aug. 26, 1978; children: Gael, Marc, Emilie. BS in Microtech. Engring., Ecole Tech. Superieure, Le Locle, Switzerland, 1974; MS in Microtech. Engring., U. Neuchatel, 1978, PhD, 1984. Project mgr. U. Neuchatel, 1984-85, Asulab SA, Neuchatel, 1985-87; dept. mgr. R&D Labs. of the Swatch Group, Asulab SA, Marin, 1987—; assoc. prof. Swiss Fed. Inst. Tech., Lausanne, 1986-87. Contbr. articles to profl. jours. including IEEE Transactions on Signal Processing, European Solid State Circuit Conf., Inst. Navigation GPS Conf. and Congres Europeen de Chronometrie; patentee in field. Mem. IEEE. Roman Catholic. Avocations: swimming, tennis, downhill skiing, cross-country skiing. Office: Asulab SA, Rue des Sors 3, 2074 Marin Switzerland

FARIZ, ZIAD, banker. Gov. Ctrl. Bank Jordan, Amman, 1996—. Office: Ctrl Bank Jordan, POB 37, Amman 11118, Jordan*

FARJAT, GÉRARD, law educator; b. Dijon, France, Mar. 25, 1929; s. Robert and Maria (Perie) F.; m. Alice Leberger, Oct. 27, 1951; children: Frédéric, Emmanuelle. LLD, U. Dijon, 1961, postgrad., 1963. Magistrate Tribunal, Saint-Claude, France, 1957; prof. law U. Dijon, France, 1958-63, U. Phnom-Penh, Cambodia, 1964-68, U. Nice, France, 1968-74, 76—, U. Tunis, Tunisia, 1975-76. Author: L'Ordre Public Économique, 1963, Droit Privè de l'économie, 1975, Droit économique, 1982; contbr. articles to profl. jours. Decorated Legion D'Honneur, 1982. Mem. Assn. Internat. Droit Economique (pres. 1982-92, editor rev. 1992—). Avocations: sailing, skiing. Home: 2 Rue Offenbach, 06000 Nice France Office: U Nice Faculty of Law, 7 Ave Robert Schuman, 06050 Nice France

FARKAS, ABRAHAM KRAKAUER, urban developer, educator; b. Dunkirk, N.Y., Oct. 31, 1947; s. Louis Ari and Hedy (Krakauer) F.; m. Pamela Ann Price, June 15, 1970; children: Madeleine, Uri, Jacob. BA in Polit. Sci., Purdue U., 1969, MA in Am. Studies, 1971; PhD in Am. Studies, U. Minn., 1976. Asst. prof. housing and pub. policy U. Tenn., Knoxville, 1976-80; dir. community devel. and planning City of Ft. Wayne, Ind., 1980-83; mgr. econ. devel. City of Seattle, 1983-85; exec. dir. planning and devel. City of Eugene, Oreg., 1985-98; devel. dir. Portland Devel. Commn., 1998—; mem. bd. advisors for housing and mktg. Oreg. State U., Corvallis, 1990-94; leader Am. delegation for urban econ. devel. in former East German cities, 1997. Editor Housing and Society, 1980; contbr. articles to profl. jours. Bd. dirs. Temple Beth Israel, Eugene, 1990-91, Networking for Youth, Inc., 1993-98, Eugene YMCA, 1993-98, Jewish Fedn. Lane County, 1995-98, Oreg. Holocaust Resource Ctr., 2000—. Lilly fellow, 1979; Tenn. Endowment for Humanities grantee, 1978. Mem. Urban Land Inst., Nat. Community Devel. Assn. (bd. dirs. 1982), Coun. for Urban Econ. Devel. (treas. N.W. chpt. 1986-87, nat. bd. dirs. 1995—). Jewish. Avocations: tennis, running, chess, golf, bike touring. Office: Portland Devel Commn 1900 SW 4th Ave Portland OR 97201-5350

FARKAS, ATTILA, cardiologist; b. Szombathely, Vas, Hungary, 1963; s. Miklos and Miklosne (Kelemen) F. MD, Med. U., Pecs, Hungary, 1987; MA, Eotvos L. U., Budapest, 1996; MD, Karl Franz U., Graz, Austria, 1995; European cardiologist diploma, Sophia Antipolis, France, 2000. Physician Markusovszky Hosp., Szombathely, Hungary, 1987-92, cons., 1992-95, 1995—, sr. cons., 1997—; lectr. Pecs Med. U., Szombathely, 1996—; mem. controlling dept. Markusovszky Hosp., 1999—. Author: (book) Cardiac Emergencies, 1996, (multimedia CD) Treatment of Cardiac Emergencies, 1998. Sec. Internat. Cmty. Hungarian Med. Chamber, 1995—; pres. newly-joined members Working Group of PWG of European Union, 1996—; mem. support fund cmty. of permanent working group of European Hosp. Doctors, 1997—; pres. econs. and law cmty. Vas County Med. Chamber, 1998—. Grantee Hungarian-Austrian Govt., Graz, 1997, Rotary Internat. Group Study Exch., Australia, 1999, Austrian Soc. of Cardiology Study, 1993. Mem. Hungarian Soc. Cardiology, Hungarian Soc. for Med. Informatics, Austrian Soc. Cardiology. Office: Markusovszky Hosp III, Bel Markusovszky 3, H-9701 Szombathely/Vas Vas, Hungary

FARKAS, CAROL GARNER, nurse, administrator; b. N.Y.C., Apr. 26, 1936; d. Charles Harry and Phyllis (Levine) Schotland; m. Theodore Arthur Garner, 1956 (dec. 1971); children: Charles Hugh Farkas Garner, Judi Beth Garner Farkas, Andrea Lee Garner Farkas Krupen; m. Robin Lewis Farkas, Oct. 17, 1972; adopted children: Bradford Lewis Farkas, Andrew Lawrence Farkas. BSN with distinction, Cornell U., 1976; MPH, Columbia U., 1980. Nursing dir. Am. Inst. Life Threatening Illness and Loss Columbia Presbyn. Med. Ctr., N.Y.C., 1980—; del. white House Conf. Aging, N.Y. State Gov.'s Conf. Aging; mem. N.Y. State Hospice Adv. Group, 1979-81; mem. adv. com. office health mgmt. N.Y. State Dept. Health, 1979-81; mem. select com. financing and licensure, com. legis. edn. Nat. Hospice Orgn., 1980—; vol. adminstr., practitioner in sympton control psychiatry dept. Meml. Sloan-Kettering Cancer Ctr., N.Y.C., 1981-96; mem. Choice in Dying, 1991-92, Nat. Coun. Death and Dying, 1990-91, Soc. Right to Die, 1982-90; co-chair med. student conf. nursing com. Columbia Presbyn., N.Y.C., 1992. Co-editor: Nursing and Thanatology, 1982; contbr. articles to profl. publs., chpts. to books. Bd. mem. N.Y. State Task Force on Life and the Law, 1994-97. Mem. Sigma Theta Tau. Fax: 307-734-8006. E-mail: rfarkas@inventfund.com. Home: PO Box 9223 485 Indian Springs Dr Jackson Hole WY 83002

FARKAS, GYULA, surgeon, educator; b. Kolozsvár, Hungary, Oct. 14, 1941; s. Gyula and Adrienne Pozsonyi F.; m. Yvette Mándi, Aug. 21, 1968; children: Gyula, Yvette. Diploma in medicine, Szeged, Hungary, 1967, gen. surgeon, 1971, gastroenterologist, 1998; PhD, Budapest, Hungary, 1984, DSc, 1997. Diplomate. Asst. prof. Szeged, 1972-80, lectr., 1980-86, assoc. prof, 1986-96, prof., 1996—. Author: Surgical Oncology, 1976, 97, Pacreatic Disease: Towards the Year of 2000, 1998. Recipient Markusovsky award Budapest, 1979, Dr. Petri Med. Sci. award Budapest, 1992. Mem. European Soc. Organ Transplantation, Internat. Soc. Surgery, World Assn. Hepato-Pancreato-Biliary Surgery. Avocations: music, history. Home: Oroszlán U.4, H-6720 Szeged Hungary Office: Dept Surgery PO Box 427, U Szeged Faculty Medicine, 6701 Szeged Hungary

FARKAS, HENRIETTE, physician, researcher; b. Budapest, Oct. 15, 1958; d. Miklos and Miklose (Benefy Margit) F.; m. Istváan Hosszu; 1 child, Gergely. MD, Semmelweis U. of Med. Scis., Budapest, 1982, PhD, 1998. Sr. cons. ORFI, Budapest, 1982-98, Semmelweis U. Med. Scis., Budapest, 1998—. Mem. IGSC, EAACI. Office: Semmelweis U Med Scis, Kutvolgyi, 1125 Budapest Hungary

FARKAS, ISTVÁN, agricultural studies educator; b. Sormás, Hungary, June 28, 1951; s. István and Ilona (Németh) F.; m. Mária Fekete, Sept. 7, 1974; children: Zsuzsa, Kata. MSc, Tech. U., Budapest, Hungary, 1975, spl. engring. degree, 1976, dr.techn., 1977; PhD, Acad. Scis., Budapest, 1985, DSc, 1993; habil techn., U. Agr., Gödöllö, Hungary, 1994. Rsch. fellow U. Agr., Gödöllö, 1975-80, PhD fellow, 1980-83, asst. prof., 1983-86, assoc. prof., 1986-94, prof., head dept., 1994—; vis. rschr. Tech. U., Helsinki, Finland, 1990; vis. prof. U. Agr., Vienna, Austria, 1990-91; coord. Joule project EU, Gödöllö, 1994-97, dir. Tempus project, 1995-98. Editor ISES World Congress Procs., 1993; guest editor spl. issue Drying Tech. Jour., 1994-96, MATCOM, COMAG; patentee complex solar drying sys. Mem. IFAC Agrl. TC (chmn. 1996—), ISES (Europe governing bd. 1993—), EFCE Drying WP (chmn. 1996-2000). Avocations: excursions, swimming, reading. Home: Fácán sor 60, H-2100 Godollo Hungary Office: U Agr, Szent Istvan Univ, Páter K ul, H-2103 Godollo Hungary

FARKAS, JOZSEF BELA, chemical engineer, educator; b. Budapest, Hungary, June 4, 1933; s. Bela and Ida (Piri) F.; m. Piroska Anna Csentes, Sept. 21, 1957; children: Kinga, Csilla, Balazs. Diploma in engring., Technical U., Budapest, 1956, DEng, 1964; PhD in Food Microbiology, Hungarian Acad. Scis., 1968, DS in Food Sci., 1978. Asst. sci. officer Rsch. Inst. Canning, Meat and Refrigeration, Budapest, 1957-59; sci. officer, SSO Ctrl. Food Rsch. Inst., Budapest, 1959-69, head dept. microbiology, 1969-72, dep. dir., 1972-86; dir. Internat. Facility Food Irradiation Tech., Wageningen, The Netherlands, 1980-85; prof. food sci. U. Horticulture & Food, Budapest, 1986—, head dept. food tech., 1986-93, vice rector, 1993-96; bd. mgr. Internat. Food Irradiation Project, Karlsruhe, Germany, 1972-80; chmn. food adv. bd. Minitry of Agr., Budapest, 1993—, chmn. codex alim. Hungary, 1994—. Author: Irradiation of Dry Food Ingredients, 1988; co-author: Testing Methods in Food Microbiology, 1984; guest editor Internat. Jour. Food Microbiology, 1994; regional editor Radiation Physics and Chemistry, 1995. Recipient Eijkman Found. award, 1992, Szechenyi award, 1999. Mem. Hungarian Acad. Scis. (vice chmn. com. food sci. 1991—), Hungarian Sci. Soc. for Food Industry (mem. exec. com. 1956, co-pres. 1998—, Sigmond Kosutany award 1974, 92), Hungarian Microbiol. Soc. (co-chmn. food microbiology 1985—, Manninger award 1993). Avocations: gardening, natural history books. Home: Ady Endre 19, H-1221 Budapest Hungary Office: Szent Istvan U, Menesi Ut 45, H-1118 Budapest Hungary

FARKAS, MARIA MARGIT, physician, educator; b. Szekesfehervar, Fejer, Hungary, Aug. 13, 1934; d. Janos Farkas and Margit Szabo; m. George Boros, Aug. 8, 1959. MD, Med. U., Pecs, Hungary, 1958, cert. specialist clin. lab., 1962; cert. specialist nuclear medicine, Med. U., Budapest, Hungary, 1982; PhD, Sci. Qualifications Com., Budapest, 1977. Cert. habilitation Med. U., Pecs, 1995. Asst. prof. Med. U., Pecs, 1958-78; head physician clin. lab. Pulmonol Hosp., Mosdos, Hungary, 1978-83, County Hosp., Kaposvar, Hungary, 1983—; sci. com. County Hosp., Kaposvar, Hungary, 1985—; spl. head physician Nat. Health Svc., Kaposvar, 1991—; bd. dirs. Hungarian Clin. Lab. Assn.; rep. Somogy County Pecs Acad. com., 1996—, prof. U Med. Sch. Pecs Faculty Health Sci., Pecs, Hungary, 1995—. Co-author: Pathophysiology, 1979; contbr. articles to profl. jours. Avocations: journeys, photography. Office: County Hosp, Dept Nuclear Medicine Tallian Gy 20, H-7401 Kaposvar Somogy, Hungary

FARKAS, MICHAEL LASZLO, plastic and reconstructive surgeon; b. Budapest, Hungary, Oct. 3, 1946; arrived in Switzerland, 1956; m. Silvia Maria Vieli, May 21, 1971; children: Nandor Imre, Tivadar Ivo. MD, U. Zurich, Switzerland, 1974. Diplomate Am. Bd. Plastic and Reconstructive Surgery. Intern St. Vincent's Med. Ctr., Bridgeport, Conn., 1974-75; resident in surgery Spital Limmattal, Schlieren, Switzerland, 1975-77, St. Vincent's Med. Ctr., 1977-80, Yale U. Med. Ctr., New Haven, Conn., 1977-80; chief resident St. Vincent's Med. Ctr., 1980-81; resident in plastic surgery Duke U. Med. Ctr., Durham, N.C., 1981-82, clin. instr. plastic surgery, 1983; pvt. practice Bern, Switzerland, 1984—. Author: Querschnittanatomie zur Computertomographie, 1986. Office: Waldhoeheweg 6, CH-3013 Bern Switzerland

FARLEY, BENJAMIN WIRT, religious studies educator, writer; b. Manila, The Philippines, Aug. 6, 1935; s. Wirt Pamplin and Bessie (Campbell) White F.; m. Alice Anne Gamble; children: John David, Bryan Kirk. AB, Davidson Coll., 1958; BD, Union Theol. Sem., Richmond, Va., 1963, ThM, 1964, PhD, 1976. Ordained to ministry Presbyn. Ch., 1963. Instr. Lees-MacRae Coll., Banner-Elk, N.C., 1973-74; asst. prof. bible, religion, philosophy Erskine Coll., Due West, S.C., 1974-78, assoc. prof., 1978-84, Younts prof., 1985—, chair bible, relgion, philosophy dept., 1978-91. Author: The Hero of St. Lo, 1986, Mercy Road, 1986, The Providence of God, 1988, Corbin's Rubi-Yacht, 1992, In Praise of Virtue, 1994, Son of the Morning Sky, 1999; translator, editor: Calvins Sermons on the Ten Commandments, 1980, Calvin's Treatises Against the Anabaptists and Against the Libertines, 1982; co-translator: Calvin's Ecclesiastical Advice, 1991; contbr. articles to profl. jours. Chair Bi-Racial Com., Franklin, Va., 1967-68, pres. of the Calvin Studies Soc. in America, 1997—. Named Writer of the Season, Nostalgia mag., 1990; Fund for Theol. Edn. fellow, 1970; Thomas Carey Johnson scholar Union Theol. Sem., 1963. Mem. Am. Philos. Assn., Calvin Studies Soc. (pres. 1997—), Coloquium on Calvin Studies, Internat. Calvin Congress, Omicron Delta Kappa. Republican. Avocations: golf, sailing, hunting, fishing, hiking.

FARLEY, REGINALD R., minister of industry and international business; b. Barbados, June 26, 1961; married. Edn. Degree, U. W. Indies, 1983, BS, 1988. Tchr., 1978-90; bus. devel. officer Barbados Indsl. Devel. Corp., 1989-92; exec. dir. Barbados C. of C. and Industry, 1992-94; leader Senate, Barbados, 1994-99; min. industry and internat. bus Govt. of Barbados, Bridgetown, 1994—; mem. parliament, 1999—. Office: Min Industry/Internat Bus, Upton, Saint Michael Barbados

FARLEY, THOMAS T., lawyer; b. Pueblo, Colo., Nov. 10, 1934; s. John Baron and Mary (Tancred) F.; m. Kathleen Maybelle Murphy, May 14, 1960; children: John, Michael, Kelly, Anne. BS, U. Santa Clara, 1956; LLB, U. Colo., 1959. Bar: Colo. 1959, U.S. Dist. Ct. Colo. 1959, U.S. Ct. Appeals (10th cir.) 1988: Dep. dist. atty. County of Pueblo, 1960-62; pvt. practice Pueblo, 1963-69; ptnr. Phelps, Fonda & Hays, Pueblo, 1970-75, Petersen & Fonda, P.C., Pueblo, 1975—; bd. dirs. Pub. Svc. Co. Colo., Denver, Wells Fargo Pueblo, Wells Fargo Sunset, Found. Health Systems, Inc., Colo. Public Radio. Minority leader Colo. Ho. of Reps., 1967-75; chmn. Colo. Wildlife Commn., 1975-79, Colo. Bd. Agr., 1979-87; bd. regents Santa Clara U., 1987—; commr. Colo. State Fair; trustee Cath. Found. Diocese of Pueblo, Great Outdoors Colo. Trust Fund. Recipient Disting. Svc. award U. So. Colo., 1987, 93, Bd. of Regents, U. Colo., 1993. Mem. ABA, Colo. Bar Assn., Pueblo C. of C. (bd. dirs. 1991-93), Rotary. Democrat. Roman Catholic. Office: Petersen & Fonda PC 215 W 2nd St Pueblo CO 81003-3251

FARMAN-FARMAIAN, GHAFFAR, investment company executive; b. Tehran, Iran, Jan. 14, 1930; s. Abdol Hossein Mirza and Massoumeh (Tafreshi) F-F.;m. Jahan Aalam, Aug. 5, 1956; children: Massoumeh, Amir Hossein, Ali Reza, Afsar. D.L.C. with honors, Loughborough (Eng.) Coll., 1951; MS, U. Ill., 1953; PhD, U. Calif., Berkeley, 1958. Head power div. Karadj Water & Power Orgn., Tehran, 1961-64; mem. Iranian Nat. Com. on Electro-Tech. Standards, Tehran, 1966-79; pres. Armed Forces Communication & Electronic, Tehran, 1970-71; chmn. IEEE, Tehran, 1972-73; mem. Iranian Nat. Com. on Energy Ministry of Water and Power, Tehran, 1972-79; co-founder, chmn. ASEA Iran Co., Tehran, 1973-79; vice chmn. Bank of Tehran, 1973-79; co-founder, bd. dirs. Tehran Ins. Co., 1975-79; pres. Univest Corp., N.Y.C., 1982—, Astle Properties Inc., Houston, 1989—. Author tech. papers. chmn., bd. trustees Community Sch., Tehran, 1975-79. Recipient 1st prize Inst. Elec. Engrs., 1956, 57, Alfred Nobel prize Am. Inst. Civil Engrs., 1958. Mem. IEEE (life), Armed Forces Communication & Electronic Assn. (life). Avocations: financial planning, tennis, hiking. Office: PO Box 3221, CH-1211 Geneva 3 - Rive, Switzerland

FARMER, MARTHA KNIGHT, academic administrator, executive; b. Roanoke, Ala., July 21, 1938; d. Edward Wilson Jr. and Bobbie (Neely) Knight; m. Claude William Farmer Jr., Oct. 10, 1958; children: Claude William III, Andrea Elizabeth. BS, U. Ala., 1960, MSc, 1965; PhD, U. S.C., 1977. CPA, Ga. Tchr. math. Aiken (S.C.) Jr. High Sch., 1964-66; from instr. to prof. Sch. of Bus. Adminstrn., Augusta (Ga.) Coll., 1966-94, coord. acctg., MIS and bus. law depts., 1982-85, acting assoc. dean, 1985-86, acting dean, 1986-88, dean, 1988-91, 93-94; acting pres. Augusta (Ga.) Coll., 1991-93; staff acct. Baird and Co., CPAs, Augusta, 1970-71; pres. Castleton State Coll., 1994—; mem. exec. com., treas. Vt. Higher Edn. Coun., 1995-96, v.p., 1996-97, pres., 1997-98. editl. advisor Soc. for Advancement of Mgmt. Advanced Mgmt. Jour., North Dalmouth, Mass., 1990-92. Bd. dirs. Augusta chpt. ARC, 1992-94, Banker's First, Augusta, 1993-94, Rutland Econ. Devel. Corp., Vt., 1996—, Calvin Coolidge Meml. Found., 1997—; mem. cmty. adv. bd. Jr. League Augusta, 1992-94. Mem. Am. Acctg. Assn. (com. rels. 2-yr. faculty), Ga. Soc. CPAs (sec.-treas., v.p., program chair Augusta chpt., pres. 1983-87), So. Bus. Adminstrn. Assn. (exec. com. 1988-94, sec.-treas. 1990-92, v.p. for programs 1993-94), Edn. Found. Ga. Soc. CPAs (bd. dirs. 1988-94), Rutland Area Vis. Nurses Assn. (bd. dirs. 1997—), Augusta C. of C. (econ. devel. com. 1988-92, chair existing industry com. 1989-90, bd. dirs. 1989-91, 93-94, vice chmn. edn. com. 1991, exec. com. 1992-94, treas. 1994), Rotary, Phi Kappa Phi (editl. advisor Nat. Forum 1989-93). Avocations: cooking, walking, reading, traveling. Home: PO Box 1425 Castleton VT 05735-1425 Office: Castleton State Coll Castleton VT 05735*

FARNELL, GRAEME, publisher; b. Glasgow, Scotland, July 11, 1947; s. Wilson Elliott and Mary Montgomerie (Crichton) F.; m. Jennifer Gerda Huddlestone, July 19, 1970; 1 child, Paul. MA, Edinburgh (Scotland) U., 1970; diploma in film, London Film Sch., 1972. Asst. keeper Mus. East Anglican Life, Stowmarket, U.K., 1973-76; curator Inverness Mus. and Art Gallery, U.K., 1976-79; dir. Scottish Mus. Coun., Edinburgh, U.K., 1979-86; dir. gen. Mus. Assn., London, 1986-89; mng. dir. Heritage Devel. Ltd., Milton Keynes, Eng., 1989—. Author: The American Museum Experience, 1986; editor: Handbook of Grants, 1990, 93; editor Heritage Devel., 1989—, European Heritage Directory, 1998, Heritage Retailing, 1999—, Heritage Bus., 1999—; contbr. articles to profl. jours. Traveling scholar Smithsonian Instn., Washington, 1984. Fellow Mus. Assn., Royal Soc. Arts. Avocations: Baroque opera, travel. Home: Shenley Lodge, 8 Faraday Dr, Milton Keynes MK5 7DA, England Office: Heritage Devel, Witan Ct 301 Upper 4th St, Milton Keynes MK9 1EH, England

FARNEN, RUSSELL FRANCIS, political scientist, educator; b. New Haven, Apr. 18, 1933; s. Russell and Anna (Ryan) F.; m. Christa Sigrid, Sept. 21, 1979; children: Edward Reid, Monika K. Germaine.8. BS, Ctrl. Conn. State U., 1957; MA, Syracuse U., 1960, PhD, 1963. Instr. Syracuse (N.Y.) U., 1957-60; asst. prof. U. Fla., Gainesville, 1960-64; assoc. examiner Ednl. Testing Svc., Princeton, N.J., 1964-67; assoc. prof. polit. sci. Vanderbilt U., Nashville, 1967-72; prof. polit. sci. James Madison U., Harrisonburg, Va., 1972-77, SUNY, Saratoga Springs, 1977-81, U. Conn., Storrs,

1981—; cons. U.S. Dept. Edn., Washington, 1994—; vis. scholar Harvard Sch. Pub. Health, Boston, 1989—. Author: Integrating Political Science, Education, and Public Policy, 1990; co-author: The Authoritarian Personality Revisited, 2000; co-editor: Democracy, Authoritarianism and Education, 2000; mng. editor Politics, Groups and the Individual, 1997—; editl. contbr. Nationalism Identity and Emnicity, 1994, Democraty, Socialization and Conflicting Loyalties in East and West, 1997, Politics, Sociology and Economics of Education, 1998. Cpl. U.S. Army, 1950-51. Mem. Internat. Polit. Sci. Assn., AAUP, APA. Democrat. Avocations: golf, tennis, swimming, jogging. E-mail: htfdadm2@uconnvm.uconn.edu. Office: U Conn 85 Lawler Rd West Hartford CT 06117-2620

FARNHAM, CLAYTON HENSON, lawyer; b. New Brunswick, N.J., Aug. 18, 1938; s. Richard Bayles and Naomi Shropshire (Henson) F.; m. Katharine Gross, Sept. 16, 1967; children: Julia Kernan, Richard Bayles II. BA, U. of the South, 1961; LLB, U. Ga., 1967. Bar: Ga. 1968, U.S. Dist. Ct. (no., so. and mid. dists.) Ga. 1968, U.S. Supreme Ct. 1978, U.S. Dist. Ct. (no. dist.) Miss. 1978, U.S. Ct. Appeals (5th. cir., 11th cir.) 1968, (4th cir.) 1980, U.S. Ct. Appeals (8th cir.) 1992. Law clk. to judge U.S. Dist. Ct., Atlanta, 1967-69; from assoc., to ptnr. Swift, Currie, McGhee & Hiers, Atlanta, 1969-82; ptnr. Drew, Eckl & Farnham, Atlanta, 1982—. Contbr. articles to profl. jours. Lt. (j.g.) USNR, 1961-64. Mem. ABA (coun. TIPS sect. 1989-92), Internat. Assn. Def. Counsel (com. chmn. 1987-89), Ansley Golf Club, Lawyer's Club Atlanta, Old War Horse Lawyer's Club. Home: 30 Inman Cir NE Atlanta GA 30309-3332 Office: Drew Eckl & Farnham 800 W Peachtree St NW PO Box 7600 Atlanta GA 30357-0600

FARNHAM, THOMAS JAVERY, historian; b. Bennington, Vt., May 7, 1938; s. Harold Frederick and Marjorie Lucille (Javery) F.; children: Jonathan, Christopher, Julia; m. Gwen Davis, Mar. 19, 1983; stepchildren: Andrew Davis, Jennifer Davis. BA, Ohio Wesleyan U., 1959; MA, U. N.C., 1961, PhD, 1964. Asst. prof. Moorhead (Minn.) State Coll., 1964-66; mem. faculty dept. history So. Conn. State U., New Haven, 1966—, prof., 1971—; pres. TLI Assocs., Inc., 1987-91; pres. Trent Bridge Co., 1991—. NEA fellow, 1969-70, Early Am. Industries fellow, 1982, Robert Newman fellow, 1991-92. Pres. Jones County Hist. Soc. Mem. Assn. Study Conn. History, New Haven Colony Hist. Soc. (dir., v.p.), Orgn. Am. Historians, New Bern Hist. Soc. Author: Regulators of North Carolina, 1971; A Child I Set Much By, 1976; Weston: The Forging of a Connecticut Community, 1979; Upper State Street: Our History, 1982, Fairfield: The Biography of a Community, 1989, Southern Connecticut State University: A Centennial History, 1993; co-author: New Haven: An Illustrated History, 1981. Office: PO Box 430 Pollocksville NC 28573-0430

FARNHAM, TIMOTHY, training and education administrator; b. Arlington, Calif., Mar. 1, 1947; s. Jack Pershing and Joyce Maureen (Evans) F.; m. Sue Ann Newton Frantz, Oct. 25, 1969 (div. Jan. 1975); children: Kevin, Kara; m. Paula Eleen Kerner, Nov. 25, 1978; children: Melinda, Elyse. BBA summa cum laude, Nat. U., 1990. Equipment engr. Pacific Bell, San Diego, 1980-86, design engr., 1986-87; mgr. instrn. and devel. Bellcore, Lisle, Ill., 1987-89, mgr. tng. and edn., 1991-95; tech. engr. Pacific Bell, San Ramon, Calif., 1989-91, 95-96; regional mgr. new tech. and applied R & D Teleport Comm. Group, Walnut Creek, Calif., 1996-99; dir. tng. and edn. Telecordia Techs. Inc., 1999—; lead presenter wireless comm. curriculum Bellcore; presenter tech. confs., orgns. including UN APEC Agy., Bangkok, USTA Showcases, Western Comm. Forum, Network '90s Conf., San Francisco, Expo Comm, Mex., Mexico City, Inst. for Internat. Rsch., Beverly Hills, Calif. Contbr. articles to profl. conf. procs. Sgt. USAF, 1965-68. Mem. IEEE, N.Y. Acad. Scis. Avocations: reading, playing guitar, genealogy research. Office: 863 Dover Cir Benicia CA 94510-3651

FARNSWORTH, BRUCE NORMAN, obstetrician/gynecologist; b. Sydney, Australia, Dec. 24, 1956; s. Yvonne Maree Moraza, Oct. 23, 1983; children: Louise, Karen, Raymond, Clare. MBBS, U. Sydney, 1981; MRACOG, RACOG, Australia, 1987; MRCOG, RCOA, London, 1988; FRACOG, RACOG, Australia, 1989. Resident doctor Westmead Hosp., Sydney, 1981-87; sr. registrar Royal United Hosp., Bath, U.K., 1988; vis. specialist Manning Base Hosp., Taree, Australia, 1989—; dir. Mayo Pvt. Hosp., Taree, 1997—, CMS Computers, 1996—; Australian rep. ObGyn Net, 1996—. Author med. rsch. papers, publs. Sec. Manning Med. Staff Coun., 1995-97, Australia Assn. Ambulatory Vaginal Surgeons, 1998—. Mem. Australian Med. Assn., Fertility Soc. Australia, Nat. Assn. Spec. Ob/Gyn. Avocations: computers, electronics. Office: 54 Commerce St, 2430 Taree/NSW Australia

FARNSWORTH, STEPHEN JAMES, political science educator, writer; b. Burlington, Vt., Apr. 25, 1961; s. Willis H. and Margaret L. Farnsworth. BA in Govt., Dartmouth Coll., 1983; BA in History, U. Mo., Kansas City, 1990; MA in Govt., Georgetown U., 1993, PhD in Govt., 1997. Staff reporter Kansas City Star & Times, 1985-90; nat. econs. corr. Fairchild News Svc., Washington, 1990-93; rschr. Ctr. for Study of Responsive Law, Washington, 1993-94; lectr. Georgetown U., Washington, 1994-95; sr. lectr. polit. sci. Mary Washington Coll., Fredericksburg, Va., 1995, instr. polit. sci., 1996-97, asst. prof. polit. sci., 1997—. Columnist Richmond Times-Dispatch, 1999, N.Y. Times, 1994; contbr. articles to profl. jours. Mem. Am. Polit. Sci. Assn., Midwest Polit. Sci. Assn., So. Polit. Sci. Assn. Office: Mary Washington Coll 1301 College Ave Fredericksburg VA 22401-5300

FARNSWORTH, T. BROOKE, lawyer; b. Grand Rapids, Mich., Mar. 16, 1945; s. George Llelwyn and Gladys Fern (Kennedy) F.; children: Leslie Erin, T. Brooke. BS in Bus., Ind. U., 1967; JD, Ind. U., Indpls., 1971. Bar: Tex. 1971, U.S. Dist. Ct. (so. dist.) Tex. 1972, U.S. Tax Ct. 1972, U.S. Ct. Appeals (5th cir.) 1977, U.S. Ct. Appeals D.C. Cir. 1977, U.S. Supreme Ct. 1978, U.S. Ct. Appeals (11th cir.) 1982, U.S. Dist. Ct. (we. dist.) Tex. 1988, U.S. Dist. Ct. (no. dist.) Tex. 1994. Adminstrv. asst. to treas. of State of Ind. Indpls., 1968-71; assoc. Butler, Binion, Rice, Cook & Knapp, Houston, 1971-74; counsel Damson Oil Corp., Houston, 1974-78; prin. Farnsworth & Assocs., Houston, 1978-90, Farnsworth & von Berg, Houston, 1990—; bd. dirs., corp. sec. Lomax Exploration, Inc. Contbr. articles on law to profl. jours. Mem. ABA, Fed. Bar Assn., State Bar Tex., Houston Bar Assn., Fed. Energy Bar Assn., Assn. Trial Lawyers Am., Tex. Trial Lawyers Assn., Comml. Law League Am., Petroleum Club (Houston), Champions Golf Club. Republican. Mem. Christian Ch. Home: 6206 Memorial Dr Houston TX 77007-7020 Office: Farnsworth and von Berg 333 N Sam Houston Pkwy E Ste 30 Houston TX 77060-2414

FARNWORTH, ALAN, pilot; b. Leigh, Eng., July 24, 1964; s. Roy and Patricia (Mawson) F.; m. Tina Joanna Cavanagh, June 16, 1990; children: Sarah Adele, Steven Thomas. D Engring. Bus. Mgmt., U. Warwick, 1998. Lic. airline transport pilot. Flt. test engr. Brit. Aerospace, Chester, Eng., 1985-90, mgr. aircraft testing, 1990-94; product unit exec. Brit. Aerospace, Chester, 1995-97; project mgr. Airbus Delivery Ctr. Airbus Industrie, Toulouse, France, 1994-95; capt. British Regional Airlines, Manchester, Eng., 1998—; chief ground instr. 632 VGS, U.K., 1995-99. Flight lt. Royal Air Force, 1987-92. Mem. Royal Aeronat. Soc. Avocation: aviation. Office: British Regional Airlines, Olympic Ho Manchest Airport, M90 1JE Manchester Cheshire, England

FARON, FAY CHERYL, private investigator, writer; b. Kansas City, Mo.; d. Albert David and Geraldine Fay (Morgan) F. Student, Glendale (Ariz.) C.C., 1967-68, Ariz. State U., 1968-71, U. Ariz., 1971-72. Lic. pvt. investigator, Calif. Owner Monogramation, San Francisco, 1976-80; assoc. prodr. Sta. KGO-TV, San Francisco, 1980-81, Power/Rector, San Francisco, 1982-83; owner Office in the City, San Francisco, 1982-83, The Rat Dog Dick Detective Agy., San Francisco, 1983—; lectr., guest spkr. San Francisco U., 1984—, San Francisco Assn. Legal Assts., 1984—, Commonwealth Club San Francisco, 1987, Calif. Collectors Coun., San Francisco, 1992—, Book Passage Mystery Writers Conf., 1997-99. Author: A Private Eye's Guide to Collecting a Bad Debt, 1991, Missing Persons, 1997; author/editor: The Instant National Locator Guide, 1991, 2nd edit., 1993, 3rd edit, 1996, Rip-Off, 1998; columnist Ask Rat Dog, 1993—; host, writer: (Court TV Crime Story Spl.) Rip-Offs and Scams, 2000. Co-founder, pres. bd. ElderAngels, San Francisco. Subject of Jack Olsen's book, Hastened to the Grave, 1998. Mem. Nat. Assn. Investigative Specialists, Nat. Assn. Bunco Investigators (asst.), Profls. Against Confidence Crimes (asst.), Sisters in Crime. Avocations: biking, camping, horseback riding, river rafting, travel.

FAROOQ, AFGAN, chemistry educator, researcher; b. Gujrat, Punjab, Pakistan, Apr. 27, 1965; s. Muhammad and Bibi Akbar. BSc with honours in Chemistry, U. Karachi, Pakistan, 1989, MSc in Organic Chemistry, 1990, PhD in Organic Chemistry, 1997; postgrad., U. Karachi, 1997-98; MPhil in Molecular Scis., U. Sussex, Brighton, Eng., 1994; postgrad., Hokkaido U., Sapporo, Japan, 1998—. Chartered chemist, London. Jr. rsch. fellow H.E.J. Rsch. Inst. Chemistry, U. Karachi, 1990-92, sr. rsch. fellow, 1994-98; rsch. assoc. Lab. Ecol. Chemistry Hokkaido U., Sapporo, Japan, 1998—; Participant confs. in field. Contbr. over 40 articles to sci. jours., including Current Organic Chemistry, Planta Medica, Jour. Natural Products, Phytochemistry, also chpts. to books. Active in conservation Wild Life, Eng., 1994—. Scholar Brit. Coun., 1992; fellow Japan Soc. for Promotion Sci., Tokyo, 1998-00. Fellow Third World Acad. Scis.; mem. Royal Soc. Chemistry, Am. Chem. Soc., Phytochem. Soc. N.Am., Chem. Soc. Pakistan, Internat. Union Pure and Applied Chemistry, Japan Soc. for Biosci., Biotech. and Agrochemistry. Achievements include research on isolation, structure elucidation and biotransformation studies of medicinally important natural products of microbal, medicinal plants and animals of marine and terrestrial origins. Avocations: playing tennis hockey, travel, bird watching, reading and writing poetry. Fax: 92-21-4963373. E-mail: farooq@abs.agr.hokudai.ac.jp. Home: Gujrat Plz, Jamia Masjid Rd, Karachi 7, Pakistan Office: U Karachi Rsch Chemistry, Internat Ctr Chem Scis, Karachi 75270, Pakistan

FAROOQI, ZUBAIR AHMAD, language educator, journalist; b. Sabarhad, Jaunpur, India, Sept. 10, 1943; s. Nizamuddin Farooqi and Tahira Khatoon; m. Farzana Begum; children: Ahmad Salman, Maryam. BA, U. Delhi, India, 1970, MA in Arabic, 1973; PhD in Arabic, Jamia Millia Islamia, Delhi, 1984. Translator, broadcaster Arabic unit All India Radio, 1971-76; lectr. in Arabic Jamia Millia Islamia U., Delhi, 1976-80, reader, 1980-93, prof., 1994—. Editor Arabic Jour., 1996—, Thaqafatul Hind Quar. Arabic; contbr. articles to profl. jours. Recipient cert. Honor Pres. India, 1999. Avocations: reading, classical poetry, composing poetry. Home: 6 Zakir Bagh, M.A. Jauhar (Okhla) Rd, New Delhi 110025, India Office: Jamia Millia Islamia, Dept Arabic, Jamia Nagar 110025, India

FAROOQUE, ABUJAFAR MOHAMMAD, financial educator; b. Chittagong, Bangladesh, Jan. 12, 1952; s. Abu and Rakiba (Hannan) Salek; m. Shamim Akhtar; 1 child, Sadia. BA with honors, U. Punjab, Pakistan, 1973; MS, U. Wisc. Madison, 1978. Vis. scholar B.I.D.S., Bangladesh, 1979; dep. chief Ministry of Fisheries, Bangladesh, 1979-81; asst. prof. U. Chittagong, Bangladesh, 1981—; mem. interministerial task force, Bangladesh, 1980. Recipient Interwing scholarship, D.P.I., Pakistan, 1969. Mem. Am. Alumni Assn., Old Faujian Assn. Avocations: writing, music, travel, cricket. Office: Dept Economics, U Chittagong, Chittagong Bangladesh

FAROOQUI, ISHTIAQ UDDIN, company executive; b. Karachi, Pakistan, June 19, 1973; s. Ashfaq Uddin and Baderun Nisa Farooqui. BSc with honors, U. Karachi, 1994, MSc in Food Microbiology, 1995; MBA in Quality Mgmt. and Mktg., Hamford U., Karachi, 1999. Sales exec. Internat. Food Establishment, Sharjah, United Arab Emeritus, 1996-97; microbiologist Parke Davis & Co., Karachi, 1997-98; brand mgr. Uniferoz, Karachi, 1998—. Recipient scholarship Hamford U., Karachi, 1998. Mem. Am. Soc. Microbiology, Gulshan-e-Maymar Club (joint sec., Best Team Leader 1999). Avocation: playing table tennis. E-mail: ishtiaq@messagez.com. Home: C-11, Sector X-1, Gulshan-e-Maymar, Karachi 75340, Pakistan Office: Uniferoz Block 7 & 8, 38 Darul Aman Soc, Karachi Sind, Pakistan

FARQUHAR, DORIS IRENE DAVIS, academic administrator; b. Wharton, Tex., Apr. 4, 1946; d. Charles Roy Davis and Pauline Maxine Tyson Powers; m. 1966 (div. 1981); children: Marcus Lea, Davis Carlton. Student, Southwest Tex. State, 1964-67. Licensed pvt. pilot. Dir. radiology grad. med. edn. M.D. Anderson Cancer Ctr., Houston, 1969-72; dir. grad. med. edn. Baylor Coll. Medicine, Houston, 1972-78; dir. acad. affairs med. sch. U. Tex., Houston, 1978-93; dir. acad. affairs dept. surgery sch. medicine Yale U., New Haven, 1993-99; instr. surgery Va. Commonwealth U. Med. Coll. Va., Richmond, 1999—; cons. quality assurance improvement WHO, 1997—. Author: Chapter 10 Directory to GME, 1994. Mem. Assn. Am. Med. Colls. (task force GME 1991-95, steering com. GME 1995-97), Assn. Hosp. Med. Educators (bd. dirs. 1993-95, sec.-treas. 1993-95), Houston Livestock Show & Rodeo (life). Avocations: horses, flying, needlepoint. Office: Va Commonwealth U/Med Coll Va Dept Surgery Richmond VA 23298

FARQUHAR, ROBERT MICHAEL, lawyer; b. Chelsea, Mass., Apr. 28, 1954; s. Robert Vociel and Helen Margaret (Stevens) F.; m. Carol Elizabeth Auch, Dec. 16, 1978; children: Stephanie Elizabeth, Andrew Michael. BS, So. Meth. U., 1977, JD, 1980. Bar: Tex. 1980, U.S. Dist. Ct. (no. and ea. dists.) Tex. 1980, U.S. Ct. Appeals (5th and 11th cirs.) 1980, U.S. Supreme Ct. 1990; cert. bus. bankruptcy law Tex. Bd. Legal Specialization. Assoc. Carter Jones MaGee Rudberg Moss & Mayes, Dallas, 1980-82; ptnr. Johnson & Cravens, Dallas, 1982-88; shareholder Winstead Sechrest & Minick, P.C., Dallas, 1988—. Mem. ABA, Dallas Bar Assn. Republican. Episcopalian. Avocations: bicycling, computers. Office: Winstead Sechrest Minick PC 1201 Elm St Ste 5400 Dallas TX 75270-2199

FARR, CHARLES SIMS, lawyer; b. Hewlett, N.Y., June 29, 1920; s. John Farr and Hazel (Zealy) Sims; m. Mary Randolph Rue, Dec. 21, 1946 (dec. Dec. 1980); children: Charles Sims, Virginia Farr Ramsey, Randolph Rue, John II; m. Muriel Tobin Byrnes, Oct. 13, 1990. Student, Princeton U., 1938-40; LLB, Columbia U., 1948. Bar: N.Y. 1949, Fla. 1984. Assoc. White & Case, N.Y.C., 1948-58, ptnr., 1959-88, of counsel, 1989-92, ret.; mem. bd. visitors Columbia U. Sch. Law. Contbr. articles to profl. publs. Chmn. Commonwealth Fund, N.Y.C., 1976-93; trustee St. Luke's-Roosevelt Hosp. Ctr., 1968-92, Gen. Theol. Sem., 1968-77, N.Y. Zool. Soc., Kent Sch.; mem. bd. fgn. parishes Protestant Episcopal Ch., 1954-78, pres., 1977; chancellor to pres. bishop Protestant Episcopal Ch. in U.S.A., 1977-85; vestryman St. James' Ch., N.Y.C., 1966-76, sr. warden, 1973-76, jr. warden, 1984-86; mem. coun. Rockefeller U., 1980-92. Lt. Comdr. USN, 1941-45, ETO, MTO, PTO. Recipient medal Columbia U. Alumni Assn., 1977. Fellow Am. Coll. Probate Counsel (regent 1960-75), Am. Bar Found.; mem. Assn. of Bar of City of N.Y., Century Club (trustee 1992-95), Links Club, River Club, Pilgrims Club, Yeamen's Hall (S.C.). Republican. Home: PO Box 9455 900 Yeomans Hall Rd Charleston SC 29410 also: 200 E 66th St Apt E802 New York NY 10021-9192

FARRALL, HAROLD JOHN, retired accountant; b. Harvard, Nebr., Mar. 25, 1918; s. John William and Olive Almira (Frazell) F. BSBA, Nebr. U., 1940. Clerk teletype ctr. Bur. Aeronautics, Washington, 1946-47; cost acct. Bur. Reclamation Br. Office Region 7, Grand Island, Nebr., 1948-53; fin. officer Bur. Reclamation Br. Office Region 7, Ainsworth, Nebr., 1953-54; payroll acct. to supervisory operating acct. Bur. Reclamation Hdqs. Region 7, Denver, Colo., 1955-72; accts. payable supr. Dutton-Lainson Co., Hastings, Nebr., 1974-85; ret., 1985. Author: The Rise and Fall of the United States, 1990, 2d edit., 1998. With U.S. Army, 1941-45. Regents scholarship U. Nebr., 1936. Mem. DAV, VFW, Am. Legion, Ind. order of Odd Fellows, Fed. Govt. Accts. Assn., Mensa. Avocation: big band music.

FARRAR, DONNA BEATRICE, hospital official; b. Ayer, Mass., Feb. 4, 1950; d. Raymond H. and Shirley E. (Perham) F. B Music Edn., U. Mass., 1971; MDiv, Bangor Theol. Sem., 1979; D Ministry, Christian Theol. Sem., 1987; M Family Studies, U. Ky., 1997. Tchr. music Billerica (Mass.) Pub. Schs., 1971-76; chaplain intern various hosps., Bangor, Maine, 1979; assoc. pastor Emanuel United Ch., Hales Corners, Wis., 1980-82; chaplain resident Ind. U & Meth. Hosp., Indpls., 1982-85; assoc. chaplain Ohio State U. Hosp., Columbus, 1985-87; assoc. dir., dir. Ind. U. Med. Ctr., Indpls., 1987-92; dept. dir. U. Ky. Hosps., Lexington, 1992—. Vol. reader Ombudsman Agy., Lexington, 1995. Mem. Am. Assn. Marriage & Family Therapists. Democrat. Mem. Christian Ch. Avocations: reading, felines, dancing, travel, art. Office: U Ky 800 Rose St # H-118 Lexington KY 40536-0001

FARRAR-HOCKLEY, ANTHONY HERITAGE, defense consultant, historian; b. Coventry, Eng., Apr. 8, 1924; s. Arthur and Agnes Beatrice (Griffin) F-H.; m. Margaret Bernardette Wells, July 7, 1945 (dec. Aug. 1981); 2 children; m. Linda Wood, Dec. 10, 1983. LittB, Oxford (Eng.) U., 1974. Ofcl. historian U.K. Cabinet Office, London, 1978-95. Author: Edge of the Sword, 1954, The Somme, 1964, Death of an Army, 1968, Airborne Carpet, 1969, War in the Desert, 1969, General Student, 1973, British in The Korean War, 2 vols., 1990, 94, Army in the Air, 1994; editor, The Commander, 1957; contbr. to numerous mil. and hist. jours. Gen. Brit. Army, 1979-83, comdr.-in-chief Allied Forces No. Europe. Decorated 4 stars, Mil. Cross, Disting. Svc. Order (2). Fellow Royal Soc. of Arts. Office: c/o Nat Westminster Bank, Wellington St, Aldershot Hants GU11 1YJ, United Kingdom

FARRÉ, JEAN ANTOINE, physical science educator; b. Toulouse, France, Sept. 4, 1935; s. Antoine François and Carmena (Reale) F.; divorced; children: Jacqueline (dec.), Frederic; m. Jacqueline Lucienne Joubert, July 15, 1975; children: Rémi, Bertrand, Pascale. BS, U. Paul Sabatier, Toulouse, 1966, MS, 1969, PhD, 1980. Asst. prof. U. Paul Sabatier, 1966-72, asst. prof. II, 1974-84; head elec. dept. Instituto de Technologia, Caracas, Venezuela, 1972-74; dir. sci. ctr. Jolimont, Toulouse, 1984-86; prof., head electronic dept. Supaero, Toulouse, 1986, head CIMI rsch. group, 1989; cons. Drire/Anvar, France, 1992-94. Patentee in field; contbr. numerous articles to profl. jours. With France mil. svc., 1961-62. Recipient Chevalier de l'ordre des Palmes Academiques award, 1993. Mem. Internat. Soc. Optical Engrng. Avocations: astronomy, old optical instruments, small mechanics, small wood models. Office: Supaero, 10 Av Ed Belin BP 4032, 31055 Toulouse France

FARRE GOMIS, ANTONIO J., pharmaceutical company executive; b. Barcelona, Spain, Feb. 13, 1944; s. Jose Farre and Antonia Gomis; m. Maria Escofet, July 31, 1971; children: Anna, Cristina. Degree in chem. engring., Chem. Inst. Sarrià, Barcelona, 1966, PhD, 1985. Staff R&D HOSBON, Barcelona, 1968-70, head pharmacology, 1970-74; head pharmacology VITA, Barcelona, 1974-85; head pharmacology ESTEVE, Barcelona, 1985-91, head biol. divsn. R&D, 1991—. Contbr. articles to profl. jours. Mem. Am. Soc. Pharm. and Exptl. Therapeutics, Internat. Union Pharmacy (councillor gastrointestinal sect. 1994—), Barcelona Pharm. Soc. Office: ESTEVE SA, MDD Montserrat 221, 08041 Barcelona Spain

FARRELL, GEORGE KEVIN, manufacturing executive; b. Pitts., June 10, 1958; s. George Thomas and Gertrude Helen Farrell; m. Sandra Lee Farrell, Sept. 8, 1989; children: Jacqueline, Victoria, George. BS, Grove City Coll., 1980; MBA, U. Pitts., 1991. With Dynamet Inc., Washington, Pa., 1980—, supt. rolling mill, 1987-90, mgr. ops., 1991-94, gen. mgr. fine wire and shapes divsn., 1995-2000; dir. ops. Perryman Co., Houston, Pa., 2000—. Mem. Assn. Iron and Steel Engrs., Internat. Titanium Assn. Home: 18 Midway Rd Pittsburgh PA 15216-1316 Office: The Perryman Co 213 Vandale Dr Houston PA 15342

FARRELL, GREGORY ALAN, biomedical engineer; b. Bklyn., May 12, 1942; s. Edmond William and Edna Florence (Williams) F.; m. Mary Louise Lupiani, Sept. 3, 1966; children: Juliana Eden, Cristina Elizabeth. BSME, Cooper Union, 1964; MS in Biomed. Engring., Columbia U., 1972, postgrad., 1972—. Mech. engr. Gen. Dynamics, San Diego, 1964-65, Rochester, N.Y., 1965-67; rsch. asst. Columbia U. Med. Sch., N.Y.C., 1968-69; instr. pathology N.Y. Med. Coll., 1969-72; rsch. engr. Technicon Instruments Corp., Tarrytown, N.Y., 1972-82; mgr. mech. engring. Baker Instruments Corp., Allentown, Pa., 1982-84, prin. mech. engr., 1984-86; prin. engr. Nat. Patent Devel. Corp., N.Y.C., 1986-87; project engr. Bayer Diagnostics (formerly Miles Diagnostics) (formerly Technicon Instruments), Tarrytown, 1987-90, new product devel. mgr., 1990—; prin. staff engr. Tarrytown, 2000—. Patentee in field; contbr. articles to profl. jours. Winner med. design excellence award, Indsl. Designers Soc. Am., 1998. Democrat. Roman Catholic. Achievements include product devel. of several automated clin. hematology and other instruments. Home: 447 Hillcrest Rd Ridgewood NJ 07450-1520 Office: Bayer Diagnostics 511 Benedict Ave Tarrytown NY 10591-5005

FARRELL, JOHN LINDSAY, construction executive; b. Sydney, NSW, Australia, Nov. 1, 1931; s. Arnold Simpson and Dorothy Maude (Hart) F.; m. Margaret Hesling, Aug. 20, 1955; children: Linda, Richard, Mark, Paul. Clk. of Works cert., 1952, bldg. cert., 1961. Clk. of works CML Ins., Sydney, 1979-80; clk. of works Qantas, Sydney, 1980-81, The Land Corp., Sydney, 1982-84, Grosvenor Consultants, Sydney, 1984-88, Kumagai Gumi, Sydney, 1988-93, Prominent Internat., Sydney, 1996—. Compiler: Farrell & Farrelly Convict Index, 1788-1853, 1988. Fellow Clk. of Works Inst. of Australia (sec./treas. 1972-97, plaque 1997). Mem. Ch. of Christ. Avocations: hist. rsch., writing, Bible study.

FARRELL, JOHN STANISLAUS, manufacturing company executive; b. County Down, No. Ireland, May 19, 1931; arrived in Can., 1931, naturalized, 1931; s. George Stanislaus and Agnes Anna (McCartney) F.; m. Vyra June white, Aug. 7, 1959; children—John McCartney, Lizanne Jennifer. BASc in Elec. Engring., U. Toronto, 1956. Registered profl. engr., Can. With ITT Can., Ltd., Montreal, Que., Can., 1962-69; dir. avionics and transmission ITT Can., Ltd., 1968-69; mktg. dir. Leigh Instruments, Ltd., Carleton Place, Ont., 1969-70; gen. mgr. Leigh Instruments, Ltd., 1970-73; pres., chief exec. officer Gestalt Internat. Ltd., Vancouver, B.C., Can., 1973-76; v.p. Cornat Industries, Ltd., Vancouver, 1976-78; sr. v.p. Versatile Corp., Vancouver, 1978-86; exec. dir. Rimquest Internat., Vancouver, 1986-88; pres. Versatech Trading and Devel. Corp., Vancouver, 1988—, also bd. dirs.; chmn., dir. Auspulp Pty. Ltd., Australia, Jara Mgmt. Inc., U.S.; bd. dirs. Versatech Trading and Devel. Corp., Vancouver, Tikal Resources Corp., Calgary, Alta., Can. Chmn. Resource Svcs. Australia, Sydney. With RCAF, 1950-59. Mem. Profl. Engrs. of Ont. Club: Vancouver Lawn Tennis and Badminton.

FARRELL, PAUL NOEL, communications company executive; b. Dublin, Ireland, Dec. 15, 1970; s. Noel and Rosaleen (O'Dea) F. Diploma in mktg., Carlow (Ireland) Inst. Tech., 1992; BA, BS, U. Glamorgan, Dublin; MBA, St. Ambrose U., 1998. Mktg. mgr. Bus. & Tech. Ctr., Carlow, 1992-96; mkt. analyst Lee Enterprises, Davenport, Iowa, 1997-98; mktg. mgr. MCI World Com, Dublin, 1999—; pvt. mkt. rschr., Carlow, 1994-96. Mem. AMA, Delta Mu Delta. Avocations: golf, soccer, walking, reading. Office: MCI World Com, Erne St, Dublin 2 Ireland

FARRELL, SHARON ELAINE, real estate broker; b. Boston, Nov. 8, 1941; d. Winston Cushman and Evelyn (Murphy) Lawson; m. James E. Waldron, Oct. 15, 1961 (div. Apr. 1987); children: Peter M., Kathleen M.; m. Richard J. Farrell, May, 1994. AA, Massasoit Community Coll., 1984; grad., Realtors Inst., 1987; BS, Stonehill Coll., 1998. Cert. residential specialist. Adminstrv. asst. Bus. Svcs. Office, Massasoit C.C., Brockton, Mass., 1983—; assoc. broker Anderson Real Estate, Inc., East Bridgewater, Mass., 1984—. Den mother Cub Scouts Boy Scouts Am., East Bridgewater, 1972-76, den leader, coach, 1976-78; mem. com., 1978-79. Mem. Am. Soc. Notaries (life), Nat. Assn. Realtors, Mass. Assn. Realtors, Nat. Assn. Cert. Residential Specialists, Mass. Assn. Cert. Residential Specialists, Green Key Soc., Beta Xi, Theta Alpha Kappa. Roman Catholic. Avocations: reading, travel. Home: 10 Colewood Rd East Bridgewater MA 02333-1687 Office: Anderson Real Estate Inc 406 Central St East Bridgewater MA 02333-2020

FARRELL, TERESA JOANNING, lawyer; b. L.A., Sept. 17, 1958; d. Harold T. and Helen Dolores Joanning; m. Michael P. Farrell, Oct. 18, 1986. BA, U. Calif., San Diego, 1980; JD, U. Calif., 1986. Bar: Calif. 1986, U.S. Dist. Ct. (ctrl. dist.) Calif. 1987. Assoc., spl. counsel Gibson, Dunn & Crutcher LLP, Irvine, Calif., 1986-98, ptnr., 1999—. Bd. dirs. Second Harvest Food Bank, Orange, Calif., 1993—, The Harvesters, Newport Beach, Calif., 1993—. Mem. Calif. State Bar Assn. (real property sect.), Internat. Coun. Shopping Ctrs. Office: Gibson Dunn & Crutcher LLP 4 Park Plz Ste 1400 Irvine CA 92614-8557

FARREN, CONOR KEVIN, psychiatry educator, researcher; b. Dublin, Ireland, Oct. 26, 1961; camd to U.S., 1993; s. Andrew Kevin and Moya Theresa (Mayes) F.; m. Anne Marie Neary, Apr. 24, 1992; children: Ciara Marie, Annemarie Patricia. MB, BCh, Nat. U. Ireland, Dublin, 1985; PhD, Trinity Coll. Dublin, 1997. Diplomate Am. Bd. Psychiatry and Neurology. Asst. prof. psychiatry Yale U., New Haven, 1993-99; assoc. prof. Mt. Sinai Sch. Medicine, N.Y.C., 1999—; assoc. dir. addiction psychiatry Bronx (N.Y.) VA Med. Ctr., 1999—; mem. sci. adv. bd. Nat. Inst. Alcoholol Abuse

and Alcoholism, Washington, 1999. Mem. editl. bd. Alcohol and Alcoholism, Cardiff, Wales, 1998—; 1st editor CNS Spectrums, 2000; contbr. numerous articles to med. jours., chpts. to books. Recipient new investigator award Assn. for Med. Edn. and Rsch. in Substance Abuse, 1996. Fellow Royal Coll. Physicians Ireland; mem. Am. Psychiat. Assn., Am. Acad. Addiction Psychiatry, Rsch. Soc. on Alcoholism, Royal Coll. Psychiatrists. Roman Catholic. Achievements include patent in pharmacology field. E-mail: conor.farren@med.va.gov. Home: 421 Park Ave Rye NY 10580-1211 Office: Bronx VA Med Ctr Divsn Addiction Psychiatry 130 W Kingsbridge Rd Bronx NY 10468-3904

FARRINGTON, BERTHA LOUISE, nursing administrator; b. Poteet, Tex., Jan. 20, 1937; d. Leonard Gilbert and Janie (Hernandez) Lozano; m. James Charles Farrington, Jan. 30, 1965; children: Mark Hiram, Robert Lee. BSN, Tex. Women's U., 1960; NP, U. Tex., 1984. RN, Tex. Charge nurse emergency rm. Parkland Meml. Hosp., Dallas; head nurse emergency rm./day surgery Bapt. Meml. Hosp., Pensacola, Fla.; asst. dir. health svcs. U. Tex. Southwestern Med. Ctr., Dallas, dir. student health svcs. cons. Student Health Com. Office: 5323 Harry Hines Blvd Dallas TX 75390-7208

FARSCHTSCHI, ABBAS, engineering educator; b. Teheran, Iran, Jan. 9, 1945. Dr INg. Habil. Wiss./akad.rat Tech. U. Clausthal, Germany, 1971-77; prof. Arya-Mehr U., Isfahan, Iran, 1977-78; entwicklungs-ing. BBC Mannheim, Germany, 1979-85; Wiss. mitarbeiter Sigri GmbH, Meitingen, Germany, 1985-87; acad. dir./PD Tech. U., Munich, Germany, 1987-93; Univ. prof. Tech. U. Chemnitz, Germany, 1993—. Home: Lenbachstr 2F, 86415 Mering, Bayern Germany

FARSI, FUAD ABD AL-SALAM, federal official; b. 1946. MA in Polit. Sci., Portland U., 1971; PhD in Polit. Sci., Duke U., 1976. Asst. prof. King Saud U., 1976; asst. dep. min. Ministry Industry, 1977, dep. min., 1979; dep. min. Ministry Info., Riyadh, Saudi Arabia, 1980; min. Ministry Info., Riyadh, 1995—. Office: Ministry of Information, Nasseriya St, Riyadh 11161, Saudi Arabia*

FARUQUI, AZHAR MASOOD A., cardiologist, educator; b. Karachi, Sindh, Pakistan, June 10, 1948; s. G.N. and S.B. Faruqui; m. Shahida A. Ahmed, May 2, 1971; children: Najmus, Ainul, Raquib. MBBS, Dow Med. Coll., 1971. Diplomate Am. Bd. Internal Medicine, Am. Bd. Cardiovascular Disease. Resident, fellow Emory U. Sch. Medicine, Atlanta, 1972-76; tutor in cardiology Royal Postgrad. Med. Sch., London, 1976; asst. prof., dir. cath lab. Emory U. Sch. Medicine, Atlanta, 1977; from asst. prof. to prof. cardiology Nat. Inst. Cardiovascular Diseases, Karachi, 1978-96, exec. dir., chmn. acad. faculty, 1996—; vis. prof. Aga Khan U., Karachi, 1985—, Cromwell Hosp., London, 1995—, Emory U. Sch. Medicine, 1994; dean faculty of cardiology Coll. Physicians and Surgeons, Karachi, 1995—. Editor Pakistan Heart Jour.; former assoc. editor Asia Pace Newsletter, Jour. Pakistan Med. Assn.; contbr. over 200 articles to med. jours. Advisor in field WHO, Geneva, 1989—. Fellow Am. Heart Assn. (coun. mem.), Am. Coll. Cardiology, Pakistan Acad. Med. Scis., Nat. Acad. Med. Scis. Pakistan, Coll. Physicians and Surgeons Karachi (hon.), Royal Coll. Physicians and Surgeons Can.; mem. Pakistan Cardiac Soc. (mem. coun. 1978—), Pakistan Hypertension League (founder, pres. 1996—). Avocations: travel, writing, think tanks. Office: Nat Inst Cardivasc Dis, Rafiqui Shaheed Rd, Sindh Karachi 75510, Pakistan

FARWELL, WALTER MAURICE, vocalist, educator; b. Sidney, Iowa, Mar. 29, 1928; s. Clyde Ross and Erma Leona (Liggett) F. B.Mus.Edn., U. Mo., Kansas City, 1950; MA, U. Iowa, 1953. Vocal music tchr. pub. schs., Fayette, Iowa, 1953-59; head voice tchr. Wartburg Coll., Waverly, Iowa, 1960-61; vocal music tchr. pub. schs., Tipton, Iowa, 1961-67; music educator pub. schs., Davenport, Iowa, 1967-90; choir dir. Meth. Ch., Fayette, Tipton, 1953—; vocal soloist, 1953—; organist Replacement Tng. Ctr., Ft. Bragg, N.C., 1951-52. Author: (4 vols.) History of Fremont County, Iowa, 1968-91; contbr.: Bells of Stony Creek, 1994; editor: Court Records Atchison County, Mo. (pamphlet), 1985; cons. (county history) Thumbprints in time, 1996; contbr. historical articles to profl. pubs. Cpl. U.S. Army, 1950-52. Recipient Am. Legion award, 1941. Mem. NEA, Davenport Area Ret. Tchrs. Assn., Fremont County Hist. Soc. (charter). Methodist. Avocation: historical and genealogical research. Home: 549 E 4th St Tipton IA 52772-1933

FASANO, ANTHONY VINCENT, chiropractor; b. Montclair, N.J., Dec. 28, 1936; s. Benjamin and Rose (Formiglia) F.; m. Linda Lorraine Jacobsen, Dec. 4, 1965; children: Steven Michael, Dana Nicole. BA, U. No. Colo., 1964; PhD, Loyola U., Chgo., 1971; D. Chiropractic, Pa. Chiropractic Coll., 1987. Diplomate Am. Acad. Pain Mgmt. Instr. anatomy Phila. Col. Osteo Medicine, Phila., 1971-72; asst. prof. anatomy N.J. Med. Sch., Newark, 1972-80; assoc. prof. anatomy Fairleigh Dickinson U. Sch. Dentistry, Hackensack, N.J., 1980-84; prof., chmn. basic sci. div. Pa. Chiropractic Coll., Phila., 1984-87; pvt. practice Langhorne, Pa., 1987—; vis. prof. St. George (Granada) U. Sch. Medicine, 1984, 99; guest lectr. Internat. Symposium of Implantology, N.Y.C., 1989; tchr. rev. classes continuing edn. courses for chiropractors Nat. Bd. Exam., 1987—. Author: (with others) Second International Symposium on the Red Blood and Lens Metabolism, 1980; contbr. articles to profl. jours. 1st aid officer Cheesequake Vol. 1st Aid Squad, Old Bridge, N.J., 1978—; bd. dirs. Big Brother/Big Sister, Middlesex County, N.J., 1978-87; trainer Hot Line, Maywood, Ill., Old Bridge, 1969-78; mgr./coach Little League/Soccer League, Old Bridge, 1977-80. With USNR, 1954-62. NDEA fellow U.S. Dept. Edn., 1968-71. Mem. N.Y. Acad. Scis., Pa. Chiropractic Fedn., Am. Alliance Massage Profls. (v.p. 1982—), Am. Running and Fitness Assn. (profl.), Internat. Chiropractic Assn. Democrat. Roman Catholic. Address: 250 W Ridge Pike Limerick PA 19468-1764

FASCIOTTI, VITTORIO, mechanical engineer; b. Milano, Aug. 1, 1930; s. Luigi and Maria (Chiapello) F. D in Ingegneria Meccanica, Politecnico, Milano, 1956; postgrad., Scuola teologica dei cappuccini, Trento, Italy, 1973. Vice capo reparto produzione tubi Falck, Milano, 1956-57; servizio progettazione meccanica Edison Chimica, Milano, 1958-59; progettazione turbine Escher Wyss, Zurich, Switzerland, 1960-61; libero traduttore, 1962-69; redattore Neue Stadt Verlag, Munchen, 1969-71, direttore, 1972-80; direttore editoriale Città Nuova Editrice, Roma, 1981—. Roman Catholic. Avocations: sport, musica. Office: Citta Nuova Editrice, Via degli Scipioni 265, I-00192 Rome Italy

FASKE, DONNA See KARAN, DONNA

FASOL, KARL HEINZ, educator; b. Vienna, Jan. 29, 1927; s. Theodor and Fanny Amalia (Laschtowiczka) F.; m. Ilse Maria Boltzmann, June 6, 1953; children: Gerhard Ludwig, Roland Arthur, Dieter Bernhard. Dipl.engr., Tech. U. Vienna, 1951, Dr.tech., 1955. Asst. prof. Tech. U., Vienna, 1966-69; prod. U. Bochum, Germany, 1969—; vis. prof. numerous schools in various countries; cons. in field. Contbr. articles to profl. jours., 5 books. Mem. IEEE, Rotary. Office: U Bochum, D-44780 Bochum Germany

FASSETT, FRANCES NICHOLAS (KITTY FASSETT), pianist, record producer; b. Louisville, Sept. 15, 1933; d. Charles and Frances (Allen) Nicholas; m. Richard Ashford Lee, Aug. 27, 1955 (div. 1975); children: Frances Lee Davis, Edward Ashford Lee, Maria Catalina Ryan; m. Stephen Bryant Fassett, Dec. 4, 1975 (dec. Mar. 1980). BA with honors, Vassar Coll., 1955; BMus, P.R. Conservatory of Music, San Juan, 1965, MMus, 1966. Founder, dir. Waldo Theatre, Inc., Waldoboro, Maine, 1990—. Home and Office: 3630A Brownsboro Rd # 300 Louisville KY 40207-1861

FASSINO, PIERO FRANCO RODOLFO, government official; b. Avigliana, italy, Oct. 7, 1949; married. Degree in polit. sci. Various apptd. positions Turin Fedn. Italian Communist Party, 1971-83, sec., 1983-87; mem. Nat. Coun. PCI (Turin Fedn. Italian Communist Party), 1983-87, mem. nat. secretariat, 1987, head of party, 1988; min. Ministry Fgn. Trade, Rome, 1998—; min. justice. Town counselor, Turin, 1975-80, 85-90, provincial counselor, 1980-85. Office: Via Anenula, 00186 Rome Italy*

FASSLABEND, WERNER, Austrian government official; b. Marchegg, Austria, Mar. 5, 1944; married; 2 children. JD, U. Vienna, 1970. Pvt. practice Vienna; product mgr., sales dir. Henkel-Persil, until 1972; mem. coun. Marchegg, 1972—; chmn. local br. Austrian People's Party, 1980—, dist. chmn., 1984—; chmn. for Lower Austria Ganserndorf, 1984—; provincial chmn. for Lower Austria, dep. chmn. profl. employees' sect. Austrian Fedn. Workers and Employees (affiliation of Austrian People's Party), 1985—; mem. parliament, 1987-90, mem. parliamentary nat. def. com.; fed. min. def. Austria, 1990—, 3d pres. parliament, 2000—. Office: 1017 Wien Parlament, 1030 Vienna Austria

FASSOIS, SPILIOS D., mechanical engineering educator; b. Patras, Greece, July 27, 1958; s. Demetrios S. and Elli G. (Karka) F.; m. Sophia F. Deli, July 14, 1984; children: Elli, Demetrios. Diploma in Mech. Engring., Nat. Tech. U. Athens, 1982; MSc in Mech. Engring., U. Wis., 1984, PhD in Mech. Engring., 1986. Rsch. asst. U. Wis., Madison, 1983-86; faculty mech. engring. U. Mich., Ann Arbor, 1986-94, U. Patras, 1992—; rsch. project leader Ford Motor Co., Dearborn, Mich., 1989-90, 91, 92, Eastman Kodak, Rochester, 1989-92, Whirlpool, Mich., 1990, H.S.A.P., Athens, 1996—, Hellenic Aerospace Industry, Greece, 1998—, Hellenic Railways, 1998—. Assoc. editor ASME Jour. of Dynamic Sys., Measurement and Control, 1995—; mem. editl. bd. Mech. Sys. and Signal Processing Acad. Press, 2000—; contbr. articles to profl. jours. Recipient Excellence in Teaching award U. Mich., 1990, Exxon Outstanding Tchg. award, 1987, 88; Ford Motor Co. grantee, 1991. Mem. ASME, IEEE, ASA. Avocations: photography, history, travel. Home: 18 Feidiou Str, GR26500 Rion Greece Office: U Patras, Dept Mech/Aeronautical Engring, GR 26500 Patras Greece

FASSOULIS, SATIRIS GALAHAD, communications company executive; b. Syracuse, N.Y., Aug. 19, 1922; s. Peter George and Anastasia P. (Limpert) F. BA, Syracuse U., 1945. V.p. Commerce Internat. Corp., 1949-75; chmn. Global Comm. Co., N.Y.C., 1976—, Global Def. Products Inc., N.Y.C., 1976—; dir Comml. Exports (Overseas) Ltd., U.K., CIC Internat. Ltd., N.Y.C.; dir. Colombia Technology Corp., Colombia Energy Corp. Mem. U.S. Congl. Adv. Bd.; bd. dirs. Better Life Enterprises for the Blind, Inc. 1st lt. USAAF, 1941-45. Decorated Purple Heart, Air medal with 3 oak leaf clusters, Prisoner of War medal. Mem. N.Y. C. of C., Am. Def. Preparedness Assn., Navy League U.S., Armed Forces Comm. and Electronics Assn., U.S. Naval Inst., Air Force Assn., Assn. of U.S. Army, Internat. Platform Assn., N.Y. Athletic Club, Order of Ahepa. Republican. Episcopalian. Home: 20 Waterside Plz New York NY 10010-2612 Office: Ste 33A 20 Waterside Plz Apt 33A New York NY 10010-2617

FATEMI, SAEID KHAN, language educator, writer; b. Yazd, Iran; s. Mohammad Ali and Saltanat Fetemi; m. Minoo Varzegar; children: Delaram, Arezou. BA in French Lang. Lit., U. Tehran, 1947, BA in Law, 1947, PhD in Persian Lit., 1950; PhD in Comparative Lit., Sorbonne, 1953. Assoc. prof. U. Tehran, 1953-65, prof., 1965—; translator of French into Persian UNESCO; vis. prof. Princeton U., Kent State U. Author: Greek and Roman Mythology, A Collection of Poems; author, translator: Formation of the Rural Education; translator (books) Human Rights, Human Against Ignorance; chief editor Bakhtare-Emruz Daily Newspaper, Tehran; translator Courier, Payam; editor PAYAM; contbr. 500 articles to nat. and internat. profl. jours.; presented papers at nat. and internat. confs. Leader Iran-e-Emruz Polit. Party, 1978-80; elected mem. supreme coun. Nat. Front Iran, 1960—; del. Internat. Ct. Justice; polit. prisoner, 1953-62. Mem. Internat. Coun. Philosophy and Human Scis., Assn. Writers and Poets. Avocations: reading, writing. Home: 277 Prospect Ave Hackensack NJ 07601-2512

FATHALLA, MAHMOUD FAHMY, obstetrics and gynecology educator; b. Abu-Hammad, Sharkiah, Egypt, May 1, 1935; s. Fathalla Ibrahim Elsayed and Fatima Mahmoud Helmy; m. Wafaa Ahmed Hammad, Oct. 4, 1964; children: Mohammed, Ahmed. MB, BChir, Cairo U., 1957, diploma of surgery, 1960, D in Ob-Gyn., 1962; PhD, Edinburgh (Scotland) U., 1967; Doctorate (hon.), Uppsala (Sweden) U., 1991, Helsinki (Finland) U., 2000. Asst. prof. ob-gyn. Facylty of Medicine, Assiut (Egypt) U., 1968-72, prof. ob-gyn., 1972—, dean, 1978-86; chmn. bd. dirs. Program for Appropriate Tech. in Health, Seattle, 1979-80, 83-86; chmn. internat. med. adv. panel Internat. Planned Parenthood Fedn., London, 1986-93; responsible officer for R&D spl. program of human reproduction, WHO, Geneva, 1986-88, dir. spl. program of human reproduction, 1989-92, mem. expert adv. panel on maternal and child health, 1984-86; sr. advisor The Rockefeller Found., N.Y., 1992-99. Editor (spl. issue World Report on Women's Health) Internat. Jour. Gynecology and Obstetrics, 1994. Hon. fellow ACOG, 1985; fellow ad Eundem Royal Coll. Ob-Gyn., 1990. Mem. Internat. Fedn. Gynecology and Obstetrics (pres. 1994-97). Office: Assiut U Hosp Dept Ob-Gyn, PO Box 30, Assiut Egypt

FATHAUER, THEODORE FREDERICK, meteorologist; b. Oak Park, Ill., June 5, 1946; s. Arthur Theodore and Helen Ann (Mashek) F.; m. Mary Ann Neesan, Aug. 8, 1981. BA, U. Chgo., 1968. Cert. cons. meteorologist. Rsch. aide USDA No. Dev. Labs., Peoria, Ill., 1966, Cloud Physics Lab., Chgo., 1967; meteorologist Sta. WLW Radio/TV, Cin., 1967-68, Nat. Meteorol. Ctr., Washington, 1968-70, Nat. Weather Svc., Anchorage, 1970-80; meteorologist-in-charge Nat. Weather Svc., Fairbanks, Alaska, 1980-98, lead forecaster, 1998—; instr. U. Alaska, Fairbanks, 1975-76, USCG Aux., Fairbanks and Anchorage, 1974—; specialist in Alaska meteorology. Contbr. chpt to book Denali's West Buttress, 1997, Living With the Coast of Alaska, 1997; contbr. articles to weather mags. and jours. Bd. dirs. Fairbanks Concert Assn., 1988—; bd. dirs. No. Alaska Combined Fed. Campaign, 1996—, campaign chmn., 1996-97; bd. dirs. Friends U. Alaska Mus., 1993—, pres., 1993-95, sec. 1997-98; bd. visitors U. Alaska Fairbanks, 1995—; bd. dirs., sec. Fairbanks Symphony Assn., 1994—; bd. trustees U. Alaska Found., 1997—, mem. coll. fellows, 1993—, exec. com., 1997—, vice chair, 1998-99, chair, 2000—; mem. adv. bd. Salvation Army Fairbanks Corps, 1997—. Recipient Outstanding Performance award Nat. Weather Service, 1972, 76, 83, 85, 86, 89, Fed. Employee of Yr. award, Fed. Exec. Assn., Anchorage, 1978. Fellow Am. Meteorol. Soc. (TV and radio seals of approval), Royal Meteorol. Soc.; mem. AAAS, Am. Geophys. Union, Western Snow Conf., Arctic Inst. N.Am. (exec. sec. U.S. Corp. 1998—), Oceanography Soc., Can. Meteorol. and Oceanographic Soc., Greater Fairbanks C. of C., Am. Sailing Assn. Republican. Lutheran. Avocations: reading, music, skiing, canoeing. Home: PO Box 80210 Fairbanks AK 99708-0210 Office: Nat Weather Svc Forecast Office Internat Arctic Rsch Ctr U Alaska PO Box 757345 Fairbanks AK 99775-7345

FATHY, MOOSA, judge. Chief justice High Ct.- Maldives; now mem. Adv. Coun. on Jud. affairs; now pres. Supreme Coun. Islamic Affairs, Male. Office: Min Justice-Islamic Affairs, Ibrahimee Magu, Male 20-05, Maldives*

FATÔME, MARC LUCIEN, research scientist, administrator, consultant; b. Cherbourg, France, Apr. 17, 1937; s. Marcel François and Colette (Despax) F.; m. Annick Christiane Bertho, June 28, 1962. MD, U. Bordeaux, France, 1962; diploma in Radiobiology, U. Paris 6, 1969, PhD, 1980. Commd. ensign French Navy, 1963, advanced through grades to gen., 1991; physician B.S.L. Ship, 1963-65; physician, tchr. Mil. Atomic Sch., Cherbourg, 1965-67; rsch. asst. Mil. Health Svc. Rsch. Inst., Clamant, France, 1968-71, radiobiology rschr., 1971-88, chief dept. radiobiology, 1988-97; sci. dir. Mil. Health Svc. Rsch. Inst., Grenoble, France, 1995—; French cons. NATO, Brussels, 1974-96; mem. sci. bd. U. Grenoble, 1995—; mem. sci. bd. radioprotection com. Electricite de France, Paris, 1996; mem. pedagogic bd. Nat. Diploma of Superior Study in Radiology and Radioprotection, U. Grenoble, 1995—. Recipient Silver medal of honor Mil. Health Svc., 1995; decorated officer Nat. Order of Merite, 1992, officer Legion of Honor, 1997. Fellow European Soc. Radiobiology, French Soc. Therapeutic Chemistry, French Soc. Radioprotection. Avocations: walking, bridge, reading, music. Home: 2 Allee de la Roseraie, 38240 Meylan France Office: CRSSA BP 87, 24 Ave Maquis Gresivaudan, 38702 La Tronche Cedex, France

FATOUROS, ARGHYRIOS ATHANASIOU, international law educator; b. Athens, Greece, Sept. 19, 1932; s. Athanasios A. and Eudocia (Sakalis) F.; m. Naomi-Andrée Feldman, Dec. 18, 1960 (div. Apr. 1975); children: Eudocia-Sophia, Thanos; m. Anna Frangoudaki, Mar. 4, 1983. Diploma, U. Athens, 1955; M in Comparative Law, Columbia U., 1956, LLM, 1957, JSD, 1962. Lectr. faculty of law U. Western Ont., London, Cna., 1960-62, asst. prof., 1962-63; asst. prof. Ind. U. Sch. Law, Bloomington, 1964-66, assoc. prof., 1966-68, prof., 1968-80; prof. faculty of law U. Thessaloniki, Greece, 1980-90; prof. faculty polit. sci. and pub. adminstrn. Nat. U. Athens, 1990—; permanent rep. of Greece to Orgn. Econ. Coop. and Devel. (OECD), Paris, 1982-85; dir. Ctr. Internat. and European Econ. Law, Thessaloniki, 1986-89; mem. Permanent Ct. of Arbitration, The Hague, The Netherlands, 1985—. Author: Government Guarantees to Foreign Investors, 1962; co-author: Public International Law, 1983-91; editor, contbr.: Transnational Corporations: The International Legal Framework, 1994; mem. adv. bd. ICSID Review. Sec. gen. Ministry of Edn., Athens, 1989-90; Minister of Justice, Athens, 1996. With Hellenic Navy, 1957-60. Mem. Inst. Internat. Law, Am. Soc. Internat. Law, Hellenic Soc. Internat. Law and Rels. (pres. 1987-89). Fax: 301-32-52-352. Home: Ipitou 21, 105 57 Athens Greece Office: U Athens Faculty Polit Sci, Omirou 19, 10672 Athens Greece

FATOUROS, DIMITRIS, architect; b. Athens, Aug. 20, 1928; s. Athanasios D. Fatouros and Eudocia S. Sakkais; m. Evangeli A. Tressou. Diploma in Architecture, Nat. Tech. U., Athens, 1952, postgrad., 1956-59. Sr. asst. Sch. of Architecture Nat. Tech. U., Athens, 1954-56; assoc. prof. Sch. of Architecture Aristotole Nat. U., Thessaloniki, Greece, 1959-65, prof., 1965-96, prof. emeritus, 1996—; vis. fellow Sch. of Architecture Yale U., 1966-67; dean Sch. of Engring. and Architecture Aristoteles U. Thessaloniki, 1967-68, 77-78, rector, dir. lab. design, 1961-96; min. of edn., Athens, 1993-94. Architect: Nat. Gallery/Athens (1st prize nat. competition 1957), others: author: (book) A Syntax of the Architecture Design, 1995. Chmn. Nat. Ctr. Social Rsch., Athens, 1981-89, Cmty. Culture Cons., Brussels, 1988-90. Ensign Greek Mil., 1952-54. Mem. Nat. Assn. Greek Arch. (pres. 1973-74, 74-75). Home: 15 Kodrou Str, 105 58 Athens Greece

FATTA, DESPO COSTA, chemical engineer; b. Famagusta, Cyprus, Oct. 4, 1970; arrived in Greece, 1988.; d. Costas Stavrou and Andri Panagioti Orphanidou F. Diploma in chemical engring., Nat. Tech. U., Greece, 1993; MSc with honors, European Assn. Environ. Mgmt., Edn., 1995; PhD, Nat. Tech. U., Greece, 1998. Cert. chemical engr., Tech. Chamber of Greece, Cyprus. Scientific assoc. Nat. Tech. U., Greece, 1998—; lectr. seminars in field. Contbr. articles to profl. jours. Recipient scholarship State Inst. Greece, 1988-93, European Union, Brussels, 1994-95, Leventis Found., Greece, 1996-98. Christian Orthodox. Avocations: foreign languages, piano, gym, literature. Office: Nat Tech U, 9 Heroon Polytechniou, 15773 Athens Greece

FATULLAYEV, ELDAR GURBAN, engineer, educator, researcher; b. Baku, Azerbaijan, Mar. 12, 1942; s. Gurban Fetulla oglu and Fatma Mutellim gizi (Aslanova) F.; m. Dilshad Yunus Babayeva, Dec. 10, 1971; 2 children. Engr., Tech. Inst., Baku, 1960-65; PhD, Poly. Inst., St. Petersburg, Russia, 1971-74. Worker Oil and Chem. Inst., Baku, 1959-60; engr. Technology Mech. Engring. Sci. Rsch., Baku, 1965-69; asst. prof. Tech. U., Baku, 1984-97, dean of faculty, 1994-95; assoc. prof. Cries U., Turkey, 1997—; Contbr. articles to profl. jours. Chmn. bd. Azerbaijan Nat. Front, Tech. U., 1989-96. Avocations: gardening, horseback riding, baking bread. Home: Mirza Aga Aliev 235, 370014 Baku Azerbaijan Office: H Javid Ave 25, 370602 Baku Azerbaijan

FATUZZO, CARLO, member European Parliament; b. Genoa, Italy, Mar. 14, 1944. Mem. European Parliament, Brussels, 1999—; mem. com. on employment and social affairs, substitute mem. com. on environ., pub. health and consumer policy, mem. del. to European Union-Russian parliamentary cooperation com. Mem. Group of European People's Party (Christian Dems.) and European Dems. Office: European Parliament, Rue Wiertz ASP 12E254, B-1047 Brussels Belgium*

FAU, DANIEL ROGER, biologist, researcher; b. Bois-Colombes, Paris, France, July 7, 1948; s. Paul F. and Odette (Boulanger) F.; m. Anne-Christine Tatinclaux, June 1, 1996; 1 child, Anne-Cécile. M of Physiology, U. Paris, 1969, D of Univ., 1973, DSc, 1981. Cert. rsch. scientist. Rschr. Nat. Ctr. Sci. Rsch., Paris, 1973-81, 85-88; vis. prof. U. Calif., Davis, 1982-84; rschr. Nat. Inst. Sci. Rsch. Medicine, Clichy-Paris, 1989—; cons. Elf, Paris, 1979-82, P. Fabre, France, 1995-97. Contbr. articles to profl. jours. Grantee NSF, 1982-84. Mem. Am. Soc. Nutritional Scis., N.Y. Acad. Scis., Sigma Xi. Office: Rsch Unit 481, Hopital Beaujon, F92118 Clichy France

FAUB, KENNETH JAMES, school nurse practitioner; b. Pitts., Sept. 5, 1942; s. Kenneth John and Emma L. (Morgan) F. Diploma, St. John's Gen. Hosp., Pitts., 1970; BSN, Carlow Coll., 1985; MSN in Nursing Edn., Duquesne U., 1995. Cert. ARC disaster nurse, emergency/primary care nurse practitioner, sexually transmitted disease specialist, AIDS educator, sch. nurse practitioner. Charge nurse emergency room St. John's Gen. Hosp., 1970-75; head nurse Family Are Ctr., 1975; nurse practitioner, sexually transmitted disease clinic Allegheny County Health Dept., Pitts., 1976-93; nurse practitioner Pitts. Bd. Pub. Edn., 1989—; pub. speaker on health-related topics. Instr. first aid, automated external defibrillator, CPR and disaster health svcs., ARC; merit badge counselor Boy Scouts Am.; mem. human resource availability list Nat. Red Cross. Mem. Nat. Sch. Nurse Practitioner Assn., Pitts. Sch. Nurse Orgn., Pa. Sch. Nurse Practitioners Orgn., Am. Acad. Nurse Practitioners, St. John's Gen. Hosp. Alumni Assn., Carlow Coll. Alumni Assn., Duquesne U. Alumni Assn., Allegheny U. Nursing Alumni Assn., Allegheny Gen. Hosp. Alumni Assn., Sigma Theta Tau, Acacia.

FAUCHERON, JEAN-LUC OLIVIER, surgeon; b. Verzy, Marne, France, Jan. 17, 1959; s. Jean-Marie Maurice and Bernadette Marie-Paule (Gavroy) F.; m. Odile Marie-Louise Bosseaux, July 22, 1994; children: Olivier, Richard, Henri, Berengere. MD, U. Paris, 1988, Manchester (Eng.) U., 1989; Diploma Advanced Rsch., U. Marseille, France, 1993. Chief resident in surgery U. Paris, 1988-94; cons. anatomy St. Antoine Hosp., Paris, 1990-94; cons. Michallon Hosp., Grenoble, 1994—; asst. prof. U. Grenoble, 1994—. Author: Rob and Smith Operative Surgery, 1993. Capt. French Mil., 1980. Recipient Duval-Marjolin Price award, 1988, Laureat, French Nat. Soc. Gastroenterology, 1990; grantee British Coun., 1989. Avocations: skin diving, tennis, making champagne. Home: 2 C Chemin Maupertuis, 38240 Meylan Isere, France Office: Michallon Hosp 12 eme C, BP 217 Grenoble Isere, France

FAUCONNIER, GUIDO ALFONS JOZEF, communications educator, consultant; b. Brussels, Dec. 14, 1935; s. Marcel and Lucie (Van Tomme) F.; m. Francine Van Eyken, May 5, 1960; children: Marc, Erik, Kristien An. MA in Polit. and Social Sci., U. Leuven, Belgium, 1957, MA in Bus. Adminstrn., 1960, PhD in Polit. and Social Sci., 1961. Human resource mgr. Hosp. Leuven, 1959-60; pub. rels. officer Dept. State, State of Belgium, 1960-64, U. Leuven, 1965-68; prof. Royal Mil. Acad. Belgium, 1964-66; prof. U. Leuven, 1968—, pres. Media Ctr., 1988—; hon. prof. Royal Mil. Acad., Belgium, 1966; vis. prof. U. Rome, 1983-84, U. Pretoria, South Africa, 1974-75, U. Gent, Belgium, 1997-98; pres. Flemish Media Coun., Belgium, 1987-95, Consumption Coun. Belgium, State Dept. Econ. Affairs, 1984-87; mem. Rsch. Coun. U. Leuven, 1987-90, 96-99, Nat. Coun. Sci. Rsch., Brussels, 1990-95. Author: The Advertising Business in Belgium, 1961 (Frans Theelen award 1961, Jean Marie Huyghe award 1962), Mass Media and Society, 1971, General Communication Theory, 1982; co-author: Advertising Theory, 1993, Public Relations Theory, 1982. Recipient fellowship U.S. Dept. State, 1976, Francqui chair Francqui Found., Ghent, Belgium, 1998. Roman Catholic. Avocation: gardening. Office: U Leuven Dept Comm Scis, Van Evenstraat 2A, 3000 Leuven Belgium

FAUL, GARY LYLE, electrical engineering supervisor; b. Clarksburg, W.Va., Nov. 5, 1939; s. Lyle Joseph and Irene (Hadden) F.; m. Edith Uvenzia Kelly, Nov. 26, 1966. BSEE, AS in Instrumentation and Control, Cleve. State U., 1966; AS in Mktg. Mgmt., ICS, 1969. Lic. FCC 1st class. Engr., project mgr. Bailey Controls, Wickliffe, Ohio, 1962-77; engr. Davey McKee, Independence, Ohio, 1977-78; engr., supr. Ariz. Pub. Svc., Phoenix, 1978—; prin., cons. engr. Advanced Systems Design, Phoenix, 1982—; owner I&C Consulting Firm Advanced Sys. Design. Contbr. tech. papers to jours. Vol. Child Ctr., Phoenix, 1986, Kids Voting, Phoenix, 1992; parade marshall Fiesta Bowl, Phoenix, 1991. With U.S. Army, 1959-65. Mem. Instruments Soc. Am. (ISA E.G. Bailey award). Republican. Office: Ariz Pub Svc Co MS3888 PO Box 53999 2124 W Cheryl Dr Phoenix AZ 85021-1808

FAULKNER, DONALD JACK, astronomer; b. Brisbane, Queensland, Australia, Mar. 31, 1937; s. Ormsby Jack and Edna Zillah (Fletcher) F.; m. June Elizabeth Gray, July 29, 1961; children: Mark Wesley, Timothy Michael, Alexandra Jane. BSc with honors, U. Queensland, 1959, MSc, 1960; PhD, Australian Nat. U., Canberra, 1964; DSc, U. Queensland, 1983. Rsch. asst. physics dept. Univ. Coll., London, 1964-65; Queen Elizabeth fellow Mt. Stromlo Observatory Australian Nat. U., Canberra, 1965-68, fellow, 1968-75, acad. dir. Supercomputer Facility, 1987-89, sr. fellow Mt. Stromlo and Siding Spring Observatories, 1975-98, assoc. dir., 1994-98; vis. fellow Joint Inst. for Lab. Astrophysics, Boulder, Colo., 1976; sr. vis. fellow sci. rsch. coun. physics dept. Univ. Coll., London, 1975. Contbr. articles to profl. jours. Lay preacher Uniting Ch. in Australia, Canberra, 1965—. Recipient scholarships U. Queensland, 1954, 57, Dulcie Evelyn Williams Math. prize, 1957; Queen Elizabeth II fellow Australian Govt., 1965; Nat. Bur. Standards fellow U. Colo., 1976. Fellow Royal Astron. Soc., Astron. Soc. Australia (coun. mem. 1975-76, 83-86, sec. 1971-73, v.p. 1987-89, pres. 1989-91); mem. Internat. Astron. Union. Avocations: public lecturing, painting, gardening, lay preaching. Office: Australian Nat U, Cotter Rd Mt Stromlo Observatory, Weston ACT 2611, Australia

FAULKNER, HERBERT WILLIAM, tourism management educator; b. Bowral, Australia, Apr. 19, 1945; s. Arthur and Gweneth (Wilkinson) F.; m. Shirley Anne Alexander, May 11, 1968; children: Joanne, Benjamin, Katharine. BA in Geography, U. New England, Armdale, Australia, 1972, BA with honors, 1974; PhD, Australian Nat. U., 1979. Tchr. N.S.W. Dept. Edn., Armidale, 1965, 68-73; nat. svcman. Australian Army, 1966-67; rsch. scholar Australian Nat. U., Canberra, 1974, 77-78; lectr. Warnambool Inst. Advanced Edn., Australia, 1975-76, U. Wollongong, Australia, 1979-81; prin. rsch. officer Bur. Transport Econs., Canberra, 1981-83; dir. Commonwealth Dept. Sport Recreation and Tourism, Canberra, 1983-87; inaugural dir. Commonwealth Bur. Tourism Rsch., Canberra, 1987-93; prof. Griffith U., Gold Coast, Australia, 1993—; dir. Ctr. for Tourism and Hotel Mgmt. Rsch., Griffith U., 1993—; dep. CEO Coop. Rsch. Ctr. Sustainable Tourism, 1993—. Avocations: weightlifting, gardening, surfing. Home: 2 Georgina St, 4210 Oxenford Australia Office: Ctr Tourism/Hotel Mgmt, Gold Coast Mail Ctr, 4217 Gold Coast Australia

FAULKNER, KEITH, clinical scientist, consultant; b. Wakefield, Eng., July 1, 1956; s. Kenneth and Doreen (Land) F.; m. Susan Lesley Kirkham, Oct. 16, 1982. BS in Physics (hon.), Imperial Coll., 1977, A.R.C.S. in Physics, 1977; MS in Physics, St. Bartholomew's Hosp., London, 1978; PhD in Medicine, Manchester U., 1984. Basic grade physicist Christie Hosp., Manchester, 1978-83, sr. grade physicist, 1983-86; prin. grade physicist Northern Regional Health Authority, Newcastle upon Tyne, 1986-90, cons. clin. sci., 1990-98; dir. quality assurance Northern and Yorkshire, 1998—; contractor CEC Radiation Protection Program, Brussels, 1988-91, 92-95; cons. IAEA, Vienna, 1991-2000. Editor: Computers in Diagnostic Radiology, 1990, Radiation Protection in International Radiology, 1995, Safety in Diagnostic Radiology, 1995. Mem. L.H. Gray Trust, Eng., 1991. Recipient Founders prize Inst. Phys. Sci. in Medicine, Founders prize Soc. for Radiol. Protection, Sir William Lee Rsch. prize No. Regional Health Authority, Newcastle upon Tyne, 1990, 91. Fellow Inst. Phys. Scis. in Medicine, Inst. Physics; mem. Hosp. Physicists' Assn., Brit. Inst. Radiology (Barclay prize 1992), Soc. for Radiation Protection. Avocations: golf, bridge. Office: Newcastle Gen Hosp, Newcastle Gen Hosp, Quality Assurance Ref Ctr, Newcastle upon Tyne NE4 6BE, England

FAULKNER, ROBERT LLOYD, advertising executive, graphic designer; b. Chgo., Nov. 8, 1934; s. L. Lester and Agnes Elizabeth (Irons) F.; m. Elizabeth Alice Thomas, June 14, 1958; children: Anne Elizabeth, Lynn Marie, Thomas Robert. BFA in Advt. Design, U. Ill., 1958. Account exec. Brad Sebstad Advt., Chgo., 1966-67; sr. account exec. D'Arcy Advt. Co., Chgo., 1967-70; v.p. Wm. A. Robinson Inc., Northbrook, Ill., 1970-71; nat. mdse. and promotion mgr. James B. Beam Distilling Co., Chgo., 1971-73; v.p. Coord. Advt., Chgo., 1973-77, Grant/Jacoby Inc., Chgo., 1977-79, Kennedy Advt., Chgo., 1979-86; exec. v.p. Kamen/Faulkner Inc., Chgo., 1986-89; pres., owner Bob Faulkner Corporation, Western Springs, Ill., 1989—; course coord., advt. lectr. grad. level advt. courses Northwestern U. and Roosevelt U., Chgo., 1980-85. Author: Learn to Cross Country Ski, 1976; co-author: Cross-Country Skiing for Everybody, 1975. Dir. Western Springs Hist. Soc., 1992-95; mem. Illegitimate Theatre of Western Springs. Recipient numerous advt. awards. Mem. Bus. Mktg. Assn. (Cert. Bus. Communicator), Nat. Ski Patrol (life), Model T Ford Owners Assn., Sports Car Club Am., Portage Lake Yacht Club. Episcopalian. Avocation: fine art painting. Home: 4050 Central Ave Western Springs IL 60558-1110

FAULQUES, ERIC CLAUDE, physicist, researcher; b. Setif, Algeria, Mar. 16, 1958; s. Claude Bernard and Nicole (Nadaud) F.; m. Christine Cauneau, June 9, 1990. MSc, U. Orleans, 1979; DEA in Materials Scis., U. Paris, 1980; PhD in Physics, U. Nantes, 1986, Degree in Gemmology, 1998. Attaché of rsch. CNRS, Orsay, France, 1982-84; rschr. CNRS, Nantes, 1984-87, group leader, 1988—; postdoctoral rschr. U. Vienna, Austria, 1987-88; vis. scientist LBNL, Berkeley, Calif., 1990-91; assoc. mem. Specializing Coun. on Condensed Matter Physics, Bulgarian Acad. Scis., Sofia, 1997. Author: (book) Spectroscopy of Superconducting Materials; editor Am. Chem. Soc. Symposium Series 730, 1999. Fulbright scholar, 1990; recipient NATO award, 1990. Mem. Soc. Francaise de Physique, Am. Chem. Soc. (organizer symposium 1998). Roman Catholic. Avocations: gemmology, hiking, trekking, painting. Home: 1 Blvd Pasteur, 44100 Nantes France Office: Inst des Matèriaux JR, 2 Rue de la Houssinière, F-44322 Nantes France

FAUNDEZ, JULIO, law educator, international law consultant; b. Santiago, Chile, July 13, 1945; s. Julio Faundez and Adriana Bravo; m. Anne Bosman, Aug. 30, 1979; children: Daniel, Antonia. LLB, Cath. U. Chile, 1969; LLM, Harvard U., 1970, SJD, 1972. Sr. rsch. fellow Inst. Internat. Studies, U. Chile, Santiago, 1972-73; lectr. law U. Warwick, Coventry, Eng., 1974-88, sr. lectr., 1989-91, reader, 1992-94, prof., 1995—; legal cons. UN Inst. Tng. and Rsch., Geneva, 1993, ILO, Geneva, 1994, Inter-Am. Devel. Bank, Washington, 1994; adv., counsel for Govt. of Namibia on Kasikili Island Dispute, 1995; contbr. external svcs. on internat. law topics BBC. Author: Marxism and Democracy in Chile: from 1932 to the fall of Allende, 1988, Independent Namibia: Succession to Treaty Rights and Obligations, 1989, Affirmative Action: International Perspectives, 1994; editor: Good Government and Law, 1997. Mem. Internat. Law Assn., Am. Soc. Internat. Law. Office: U Warwick, Sch Law, Coventry CV4 7AL, England

FAUNTLEROY, DON EDWARD, photography director; b. Pasadena, Calif., May 5, 1953; s. Donald and Frances (Shiro) F.; m. Susan Emma Ducat, June 4, 1976 (Div. Feb. 1986); m. Lesley-Anne Down, Sept. 27, 1986; children: Season Marie, Juliana, George Edward; 1 stepchild, Jack Friedkin. Asst. camera Internat. Photographers, 1973-85; camera operator Guild Local 600, L.A., 1985-89, dir. photography, 1989—. Mem. Am. Soc. Cinematographers. Democrat. Roman Catholic. Avocations: photography, tennis, skiing.

FAURE, FELIX L., retail executive; b. Pamiers, France, Mar. 31, 1925; s. Jean and Louise (Ibry) F.; m. Annie Medeville (div. 1981); 1 child, Dominique; m. Suzanne Girard; 1 child, Frederic. Degree, Ecole Superior de Commerce, 1945; degree in law, Faculte de Droit, 1946. Pres. UNIMAG Faure, Pamiers, France, 1960—, UNIMAG Midi Pyrenees, Auch, France, 1975; cons. Bank of France, Foix, 1960—. Club: France U.S.A. Office: UNIMAG Faure, 10 Place de la Republique, 09100 Pamiers France

FAURRE, PIERRE LUCIEN, business executive; b. Paris, Jan. 15, 1942; s. Lucien Marie and Anne Jeanne (Dame) F.; m. Pierrette Claudine Mome, July 24, 1962; children: Pierre, Sylvie. Degree in engring., Ecole Polytechnique, Paris, 1962; PhD, Stanford U., 1967; doctorate, U. Paris, 1972. Asst. mgr. Centre D'Automatique Ecoles des Mines, Paris, 1967-71; sci. dir. IRIA, Rocquencourt, France, 1971-72; exec. sec. gen. SAGEM, Paris, 1972-83, exec. v.p., CEO, 1983-87, chmn. bd., CEO, 1987—; chmn. bd., chief exec. officer SAT, 1988-98; prof. math. Ecole Polytechnique, Paris, 1982-93, chmn. bd. 1993—. Author: Navigation inertielle optimale, 1971, Elements d'Automatique, 1974, 2d edit., 1984, Elements of System Theory, 1977, Operateurs rationnels positifs, 1979; also articles. Decorated officer Ordre Nat. du Merite, Officer Legion of Honor; recipient prix Laplace, 1962, prix Constantin de Magny, 1979, Académie de Sciences, prix Science et Défense, 1984. Mem. French Nat. Acad. Scis., Acad. Europaea, Internat. Acad. Astronautics, Soc. Math. de France. Home: 14 rue Fresnel, 75116 Paris France Office: SAGEM, 6 ave d'Iena, 75116 Paris France

FAUSER, BART CLEMENT JOHANNES MARIA, gynecologist, educator; b. Utrecht, The Netherlands, July 25, 1954; s. Karel C.M. and Loni M. Fauser; children: Sjoerd, Bobbie. MD, U. Nymegen, The Netherlands, 1979, PhD, 1985. Rsch. fellow U. Nymegen, 1980-81; resident in oby/gyn. Groot Ziekengasthuis, Den Bosch and U. Nijmegen, The Netherlands, 1981-86; asst. prof. Erasmus U., Rotterdam, The Netherlands, 1986-91, sect. head reproductive endrocrinology and fertility, 1991-97; dir. divsn. reproductive medicine Erasmus U. Med. Ctr., Rotterdam, 1997—, prof., 1997—; vis. prof. Stanford U., Palo Alto, Calif., 1993-95; prof. Free Univ., Brussels, 1995—; chmn. Stichting Voortplantings Geneeskunde Rotterdam, 1990—. Author, editor books and chpts.; contbr. 200 articles to profl. jours. 1st lt. Royal Dutch Army, 1979-80. Fulbright Rsch. scholar U. Calif., San Diego, 1987-88. Mem. Netherlands Orgn. Sci. Rsch., European Soc. Human Reproduction and Embryology (chmn. spl. interest group reproductive endocrinology 1995—). Fax: 31-10-436-7306. E-mail: fauser@gyna.azr.nl. Home: Rott Ryweg 176, 3042 AT Rotterdam The Netherlands Office: Dykzigt U Hosp Ob-Gyn Erasmus U, Dr Molewaterplein 40, 3015 GD Rotterdam The Netherlands

FAUSER, BERTFRIED, physicist, researcher; b. Speyer, Germany, Nov. 28, 1962; s. Rudolf Eugen and Dorothea Ida (Neth) F.; m. Mechthild Riehle, Jan. 4, 1994; 1 child, Pauline Ariadne. Diploma, U. Tübingen, Germany, 1985, diploma in physics, 1990, D in Natural Scis., 1996. Asst. U. Tübingen, Germany, 1987-88, U. Túbingen, Physics Inst., Germany, 1988-96; staff U. Konstanz, Germany, 1998—. Office: Univ Konstanz, Fak Physics Fach M 678, 78457 Konstanz Germany

FAUST, NAOMI FLOWE, education educator, poet; b. Salisbury, N.C.; d. Christopher Leroy and Ada Luella (Graham) Flowe; m. Roy Malcolm Faust, Aug. 16, 1948. AB, Bennett Coll; MA, U. Mich., 1945; PhD, NYU, 1963. Elem. tchr. Pub. Schs. Gaffney (S.C.); tchr. English, French, phys. edn. Atkins H.S., Winston-Salem; instr. English Bennett Coll. and So. U., Scotlandville, La., 1944-46; prof. English Morgan State Coll., Balt., 1946-48; tchr. English Greensboro (N.C.) Pub. Schs., 1948-51, N.Y.C. Pub. Schs., 1954-63; prof. edn. Queens Coll. of CUNY, Flushing, 1964-82; writer, lectr., poetry readings, 1982—; lectr. in field. Author: Discipline and the Classroom Teacher, 1977; (poetry) Speaking in Verse, 1974, All Beautiful Things, 1983, And I Travel by Rhythms and Words, 1990; contbr. poetry to jours. Named Tchr.-Author of 1979, Tchr.-Writer; recipient Cert. of Merit for Poem Cooper Hill Writers Conf., 1970, Achievement award L.I. br. AAUW, 1985, Poet of the Millennium award Internat. Poets Acad.; named Internat. Eminent Poet, Internat. Poets Acad. Mem. AAUP, Acad. Am. Poets, Nat. Coun. Tchrs. English, Nat. Women's Book Assn., Nat. Assn. Univ. Women (L.I. br.), World Poetry Soc. Intercontinental, N.Y. Poetry Forum, NAACP, United Negro Coll. Fund, Alpha Kappa Alpha, Alpha Kappa Mu., Alpha Epsilon. Home: 11201 175th St Jamaica NY 11433-4135

FAUST, WILLIAM ROSCOE, physicist; b. Shawnee, Okla., Mar. 9, 1918; s. Hugh Graham and Bertha Adele (Weinmann) F.; m. Mary Cone Dees, Jan. 29, 1942; children: Hugh H., Margaret Adele, Mary Elizabeth. BSEE, Okla. State U., 1939; MSEE, Ill. Inst. Tech., Chgo., 1941; PhD in Physics, U. Md., 1949. Physicist Naval Rsch. Lab., Washington, 1941-55; assoc. supt. Radiation Divsn. Naval Rsch. Lab., 1956-64, supt. Application Rsch. Divsn., 1964-69, assoc. dir. rsch., 1969-72, ret., 1972; chief nuclear rsch. Convair, Ft. Worth, 1955-56. Contbr. articles to profl. jours.; patentee in field. Mem. Sons Am. Revolution, Prince Georges County, Md., 1980—. Fellow Am. Phys. Soc., Wash. Acad. Sci., Philos. Soc. Washington; mem. AAAS. Home: 1665 Heather Ln Huntingtown MD 20639-4108

FAUSTI, LUIGI, bank company executive; b. Ancona, Italy, Mar. 9, 1929; m. Eliana Antognoli; 3 children. Degree in law, U. Rome; D in Econs. honoris causa, 2nd U. Naples, 1996. With Banca Comml. Italiana, Milan, 1947—, dep. gen. mgr., 1984-87, gen. mgr., 1987-90, mng. dir., 1990-94, former chmn., mng. dir., hon. chmn., bd. dirs.; vice chmn. Compagnie Monegasque de Banque, Monaco, ASSIBA, Milan; bd. dirs. Mediobanca, Milan, Assn. Bancaria Italiana, Rome, Assn. Interessi Met., Milan, Inst. Europeo di Oncologia, Milan, Found. "Rosselli", Turin, ISPI, Milan, ASSONIME, Rome. Avocations: gourmet foods, sea fishing. *

FAUSTO, RUI, chemistry educator, researcher; b. Coimbra, Portugal, Jan. 7, 1961; s. António Armando and Maria da Conceição (Ribeiro) Lourenço; m. Maria De Fátima Leitão, Nov. 24, 1985; 1 child, Ana Sofia. PhD in Chemistry, Portugal, 1988. Asst. lectr. U. Coimbra, Portugal, 1985-87, prof. chemistry, 1988—, pres. acad. coun. Faculty of Scis. and Tech., 1996-2000. Editor: Recent Experimental and Computational Advances in Molecular Spectroscopy, 1993, Low Temperature Molecular Spectroscopy, 1996. Mem. IUPAC, Portuguese Soc. Chemistry, European Photochemistry Assn. Avocations: rock band piano player, painter. Office: U Coimbra, Dept Chemistry, P-3049 Coimbra Portugal

FAUSTOV, RUDOLF NIKOLAEVICH, theoretical physicist, researcher; b. Moscow, July 1, 1938; s. Nikolai Fedorovich and Nina Mikhailovna (Dvoryankina) F.; m. Natalia Samoilovna Vologjanina, Feb. 27, 1965; children: Alexei, Nikolai. Diploma in physics, Moscow State U., 1961; PhD in Theoretical Physics, Jt. Inst. for Nuclear Rsch., Dubna, USSR, 1965, DSc in Theoretical Physics, 1972. Sr. researcher lab. theoretical physics Jt. Inst. for Nuclear Rsch., Dubna, 1961-76; sect. leader State Com. for Stds., Rsch. Inst., Moscow, 1976-89; prin. researcher Sci. Coun. for Cybernetics, Moscow, 1989—; prof. Moscow State U., 1979—; cons. Gt. Russian Encyclopaedia, Moscow, 1976—; lectr. Internat. Sch. Physics, Italy, 1987, 89, Ettore Majorana, Enrico Fermi, etc. Editor: Quantum Metrology and Fundamental Constants, 1981; contbr. articles to profl. jours. Grantee Govt. of Russia, Moscow, 1994, 97, 2000 Russian Found. for Fundamental Rsch., Moscow, 1993, 96, 2000 DAAD, Bonn, Germany, 1996. Mem. Russian Phys. Soc., Internat. Union of Pure and Applied Physics (Commn. on Symbols, Units, Nomenclature, Atomic Masses and Fundamental Constants 1996—). Avocation: collecting science and fiction books. Office: Russian Acad Scis Sci Coun, Cybernetics Vavilov Str 40, 117333 Moscow Russia

FAUTH, DIETMAR, telecommunications industry executive, consultant; b. Stuttgart, Germany; s. Otto and Gertrud (Oberst) F.; m. Ursula Wolfart, Oct. 15, 1992. MS, Oreg. State U., 1976; Phd, U. Stuttgart, Germany, 1984. Software developer Siemens AG, Munich, Germany, 1984-89; mgr. Siemens AG, Munich, 1990-96, sr. cons., 1996-99, dir., 1999—; cons. Open Softward Found., Cambridge, Mass., 1989-90. Contbr. articles to profl. jour. Avocations: tournament chess, hiking, skiing, French wines. Home: Kleinstr 48, 81379 Munich Germany Office: Siemens ICN ISA, Hofmannstr 51, 81359 Munich Germany

FAVA, GIOVANNI CLAUDIO, member European Parliament; b. Catania, Italy, Apr. 15, 1957. Mem. European Parliament, Brussels, 1999—; mem. com. on regional policy, transport and tourism, substitute mem. com. on fisheries and com. on fgn. affairs, human rights, common secueity, and def. policy, mem. del. for rels. with countries C.Am. and Mex. Mem. roup of Party of European Socialists. Mem. Democratic Left Party. Office: Dem Left Region Secretariat, Corso Calatafimi 633, I-91100 Palermo Sicily, Italy*

FAVA, MAURIZIO, hospital administrator, researcher; b. Valdagho, Italy, May 8, 1956; came to U.S., 1985; s. Ezio Fava and Olga Danieli; m. Stefania Lamon, May 18, 1985; 1 child, Giovanni. Med. degree, U. Padua, Italy, 1982. Dir. depression rsch. program Mass. Gen. Hosp., Boston, 1990-94, dir. depression clin. and rsch. program, 1994—; assoc. prof. psychiatry Harvard Med. Sch., Boston, 1994—. Co-editor: (book) Research Designs and Methods in Psychiatry, 1992. DuPont-Warren fellow Mass. Gen. Hosp., 1988. Mem. Am. Psychiat. Assn., Am. Coll. Neuropsychopharmacology. E-mail: mfava@partners.org. Office: Mass Gen Hosp ACC 812 15 Parkman St Boston MA 02114-3117

FAVEREAU, OLIVIER, economics educator; b. Paris, May 28, 1945; s. Pierre and Claude (Guillaume) F.; m. Catherine Balbarie, June 24, 1976; children: Marie, Amelie, Julie, Peggy. Diploma, Inst. D'Etudes Polits., 1966; PhD, U. Paris, 1982. Asst. prof. U. Paris X, 1971-83; prof. U. Le Mans, 1984-87, U. Paris X, 1988—; dir. CNRS Rsch. Unit, 1994—. Coauthor: Analyse Economique des Conventions, 1994. Home: 8 Rue Ernest Renan, 92130 Issy-Les-Mx France Office: U Paris X, 200 Av De La Republique, 92001 Nanterre France

FAVIER, DOMINIQUE, editor, journalist; b. Saint-Maur, France, June 26, 1948; s. Alphonse and Suzanne (Chassagnon) F.; m. Michèle Seguy, Feb. 20, 1950; children: Manuela, Jeremy. Baccalaureate, Lyceé J.J. Rousseau, Thonon, France, 1967; lic. German, U. Limoges, France, 1973. Journalist L'Echo du Centre, Limoges, 1975-82, chief editor, 1982-88; editor Bovins Limousins, Limoges, 1988—. Mem. French Soc. Agrl. Journalists (adminstr. 1992—), Limousin Press Club (sec. 1988-93). Home: 4 cours Bugeaud, 87000 Limoges France Office: France Limousin Selection, Lanaud, 87220 Boisseuil France

FAVIS-MORTLOCK, DAVID THOMAS, geomorphologist; b. Romford, Essex, Eng., Aug. 27, 1953; s. Ronald James and Joan Agnes (Favis) Mortlock. BA, U. Lancaster, 1975; PhD, U. Brighton, 1994. Programmer Redman Heenan Engrs., Worcester, Eng., 1976-78; project leader Rural Warwickshire Agy., Stoneleigh, Eng., 1982-85; supr. Countryside Rsch. Unit, Brighton, Eng., 1985-86; dir. tng. Brighton Computer Tng. Ctr., 1987-88; owner, sr. cons. Jupiter Computer Cons., Brighton, 1988-94; rsch. scientist U. Oxford, Eng., 1993-2000; lectr. phys. geography Queen's U. Belfast, No. Ireland, 2000—; vis. prof. USDA, 1996. Editor: Modelling Soil Erosion by Water, 1998; contbr. articles to profl. jours. Mem. Internat. Geosphere-Biosphere Programme-Global change and Terrestrial Ecosystems Soil Erosion Network, Brit. Geomorphological Rsch. Group, Brit. Soc. for Soil Sci., Am. Geophys. Union, Soil and Water Conservation Soc. Avocations: playing fiddle, reading, meditating. Fax: 44(0)28 90321280. E-mail: d.favis-mortlock@qub.ac.uk. Office: Sch Geography, Queens Univ Belfast, Belfast BT7 1NN, Northern Ireland

FAVORS, WILLIE JAMES, chemist; b. Sumter, S.C., Dec. 28, 1960; s. Monroe Glover and Mary Virginia Favors; m. Melanie Nicole Whities, June 27, 1997; children by previous marriage: Willie James Jr., James Anthony, Joseph Clarence. BS cum laude, S.C. State Coll., 1983. Tchr. chemistry DePaul High Sch., Wayne, N.J., 1985-86; adhesives chemist Caschem Inc., Bayonne, N.J., 1986-90; sr. rsch. chemist Facile Holdings, Inc., Paterson, N.J., 1990-91—; rsch. assoc. Frito-Lay Inc., Plano, Tex., 1992-98; lab./process svcs. mgr. M&M/Mars, Albany, Ga., 1998—. Assoc. Sunday sch. tchr. Salem Bapt. Ch., Sumter, 1978—. 2d lt. U.S. Army, 1983-85. Mem. AAAS, Am. Chem. Soc., Am. Inst. Chemists, Inst. Food Technologists, Am. Soc. Microbiologists, Am. Assn. Cereal Chemists, Internat. Assn. Food Protection, Phi Beta Sigma, Beta Kappa Chi. Democratic. Achievements include research with others toward patent for re-enterable encapsulants for telecommunications; for moisture cured adhesives in recreational surfaces. Office: M&M/Mars 1209 W Oakridge Dr Albany GA 31707-5303

FAVRE, JACQUES, neurosurgeon; b. Neuchâtel, Switzerland, Apr. 7, 1964; s. Pierre and Michéle (Cottini) F.; m. Nicole Sanceau, Oct. 24, 1991; children: Léa, Brendan. Cert. in parasitology, U. Neuchâtel, 1986; MD, U. Lausanne, Switzerland, 1988. Neurosurgery resident Ctr. Hospitalier Universitaire Vaudois, Lausanne, 1989-90, 91-94; surgery resident Neuchâtel, 1990-91; fellow in functional neurosurgery Oreg. Health Sci. U., Portland, 1995-96, clin. assoc. prof., 1999—. Author: (computer software) Pharmacology of Diuretics, 1988, NeuroStereo, Interspike, 1990-96; contbr. articles to profl. jours. and books. Mem. European Soc. Stereotactic and Functional Neurosurgery, Am. Soc. Stereotactic and Functional Neurosurgery, World Soc. Stereotactic and Functional Neurosurgery. Avocations: snowboarding, mountains, computers, squash. Home: Chemin de Cotterd 11, 1820 Territet Switzerland Office: Riviera Hosp Dept Neurosurg, via Belmont, 1820 Montreux Switzerland

FAVRE, JUNE MARIE, actress, singer; b. Clay County, Kans., June 14, 1937; d. Riley Otto and Edythe May (Constable) Woellhof; m. Joseph Jean Favre, Jan. 16, 1957 (dec. Jan. 1988). Cert. respiratory therapist. Owner N.Y. Connection, Denver, 1979-92; event coord. Colo. Contemporary Dance, Denver, 1993; exec. dir. Joey Favre Humanities Ctr., Denver, 1988—; guest artist Met. State Coll., Denver, 1977, N.Mex. State Theatre, Raton, 1974; founder, actor The Third Eye Theatre, Denver, 1966-78; cons. First Night Colo., Denver, 1994; publicist Gypsy Prodns., Denver, 1992, 93. Author (children's theatre) A Christmas Carol, 1994. Recipient Writing award Fla. Citrus Dept., 1991, Rocky Mountain Women's Inst. Associateship award, 1995, Mayor's Award for Excellence in the Arts, 1996, Editor's Choice award The Poetry Guild, 1998. Mem. AFTRA, The Friday Club. Avocations: playing piano, developing arts programs for children.

FAVREAU, DONALD FRANCIS, corporate executive; b. Cohoes, N.Y., Sept. 7, 1919; s. Alphonse Emille and Millie Loretta (Smith) F.; m. Helen Patricia Rafferty, June 2, 1945; 1 dau., Susan Debra. BA, Knox Coll., 1949; MA, SUNY, 1954; exec. devel. diploma, Cornell U., 1965. Prof. mil. sci. LaSalle Inst., Troy, N.Y., 1949-54; mgr. tng. Ford Motor Co., Cleve., 1954-57, Am. Bosch Arma Corp., Garden City, N.Y., 1957-59; asst. to v.p. Royal Metal Corp., N.Y.C., 1959-60; mgr. personnel devel. N.Y. Stock Exchange, N.Y.C., 1960-62; manpower coord. N.Y. State Dept. Labor, 1962-65; prof., assoc. dir. SUNY, Albany, 1965-69, dir. Center for Exec. Devel. and Pub. Safety Mgmt., 1969-82; dean SUNY Coll. Gen. Studies, Albany, 1982-83; prof. emeritus SUNY, Albany, 1983—; pres., CEO Don Favreau Assocs., 1983—; adj. instr. Western Res. U., 1952-54; adj. prof. C.W. Post Coll., 1975—; vis. lectr. Colo. State U., 1970-82; cons. in field; co-chmn. Wingspread Conf., 1966; prin. presenter Williamsburg Conf. of Nat. Fire Svc. Orgns., 1970; prin. presenter NAS Conf., 1967. Author: Wingspread: Fire Service Administration Education and Research, 1967, Crisis in Fire Service: Education Dimensions, 1967, Fire Service Higher Educational Programs, 1969, Introduction to Fire Protection, 1972, Criminal Victimization of the Elderly, 1977, Modern Police Administration, 1978; appeared in film Billy Bathgate, 1991. Active Saratoga Performing Arts Ctr.; bd. dirs. Nat. Alliance Bus., 1979—, metro dir., 1985—; vice-chmn. Pvt. Industry Coun., Albany, 1980—; v.p. N.E. N.Y. Alliance of Bus., 1982—, pres., 1991-93; bd. dirs. Vis. Nurse Assn. of Albany, 1984—; dep. sheriff Niagara County, N.Y., 1974. 1st lt. AUS, 1943-46. Named hon. citizen Ville de Lafayette, hon. citizen New Orleans, 1968; recipient commendation Pres. Carter, 1978, Pres. Reagan, 1992, N.Y. State Police, 1973, Wichita State U., 1967, U. Maine, 1970, Internat. Assn. Police Chiefs, 1974, SUNY, Albany, 1983, Internat. Right of Way Assn., 1975, Merit cert. State of N.Y., 1983; named hon. fire chief City and County of Denver, 1983, col. State of La., aide de camp to Gov., 1968; hon. criminal sheriff Parish of Orleans, New Orleans, 1968. Mem. VFW, AAUP, NEA, Internat. Fire Adminstrn. Inst. (exec. dir. 1965-73), Am. Mgmt. Assn., Nat. Fire Protection Assn., Internat. Assn. Chiefs of Police, N.Y. State Assn. Fire Chiefs, Soc. Advancement of Mgmt., Am. Soc. Tng. Dirs., Nat. Assn. 10th Mountain Divsn. Assn. (bd. dirs., membership chmn. N.Y. chpt.), Friends of St. Patrick (dir.), Internat. Fedn. Mountain Soldiers, Am. Legion (U.S. Normany com. 1989), United Univ. Professions, 10th Mountain Divsn. Colo. Hut Assn., Assn. U.S. Army, Elks, Sigma Nu, Colo. Hist. Soc., U. Albany Alumni Assn., Siwash Athletic Club, N.Y. State Troopers Assn., Humane Soc. U.S., Sierra Club, The Wilderness Soc., Adirondack Mountain Club, Knox Coll. Fifty Year Club. Avocations: skiing, trout fishing, mountaineering. Home: 32 Hemlock Dr Clifton Park NY 12065-4846

FAVREAU, SUSAN DEBRA, management consultant; b. Cleve., Dec. 15, 1955; d. Donald Francis and Helen Patricia (Rafferty) F. Cert., N.Y. State Police Acad., 1974; student, Cornell U., 1984, SUNY, 1986. Comms. specialist N.Y. State Police, Loudonville, 1974-87, comms. specialist div. hdqrs., 1987-98; mgmt. cons., sec.-treas., dir. Don Favreau Assocs., Inc., Clifton Park, N.Y., 1983-86, v.p., 1986—; comms. specialist divsn. hdqrs. N.Y. State Police, Albany, 1987-98, sys. support specialist divsn. hdqrs., 1998—; adj. faculty Internat. Assn. Chiefs of Police; NYSPIN coord. FBI/Nat. Crime Info. Ctr. cert. program, 1986—. Author: Teamwork in the Telecommunication Center, 1986, One More Time: How to be a Mature and Successful Telecommunications Manager, 1987, Law Enforcement Terminal Security, 1991; also NYSPIN cert. manuals. Recipient Dirs. commendation N.Y. State Police Acad., 1977, commendation N.Y. State Police, 1978, Supt.'s commendation, 1986, Y2K commendation Gov. George Pataki, 2000.

Mem. NAFE, N.Y. State Civil Svc. Assn., Emergency Communicators Profl. Assn. (adv. bd.), Colonie Police Benevolent Assn. (hon.), Am. Soc. Law Enforcement Trainers, Assoc. Pub. Safety Communications Officers (planning commn. Atlantic chpt. 1991, registration chair ann. NE conf. 1991), N.Y. State Troopers Police Benevolent Assn. (hon.), Nat. Bus. Women Am., Internat. Assn. Chiefs Police, Am. Horse Shows Assn., Am. Soc. Law Enforcement Trainers, Capital Dist. Hunter/Jumper Coun. Republican. Roman Catholic. Avocations: equestrienne, target shooting, reading, sewing. Home: 60 Tallow Wood Dr Clifton Park NY 12065-2825 Office: Hdqrs NY State Police State Office Bldg Campus Bldg # 22 Albany NY 12226

FAW, RICHARD EARL, nuclear engineering educator; b. Ohio, June 22, 1936; s. Robert Harvey and Mary Elizabeth (Baird) F.; m. Beverly A. Giltner, Mar. 25, 1961; children: Jennifer, Andrew. BSChemE, U. Cinn., 1959; PhD in Chem. Engring., U. Minn., 1962. Cert. chem. engr., Ohio, nuclear engr., Kans. Prof. nuclear engring. Kans. State U., Manhattan, 1968-2000. Author: Radiological Assessment, 1992; co-author: Principles of Radiation Shielding, 1984, Radiation Shielding, 1996; contbr. articles to profl. jours. Capt. U.S. Army, 1962-64. Mem. Am. Nuclear Soc. (profl. excellence award 1986), Health Physics Soc., Am. Assn. Physicists in Medicine. Methodist.

FAWCETT, BRIAN CHARLES, atomic physicist, researcher; b. Oswestry, Eng., Sept. 17, 1929; s. Charles Harrisson and Agnes Kate (England) F.; m. Marie-Thérèse Galliaerde, Jan. 2, 1952; children: Miriam, Pierre, Anita. BSc, U. London, 1962, DSc, 1971. Rsch. asst. Mullard Rsch. Lab., Eng., 1956-58; exptl. officer Atomic Energy Authority, Eng., 1958-68; prin. sci. officer Sci. Rsch. Coun., Eng., 1968-90. Contbr. over 120 articles to profl. jours. Avocations: caravanning, satellite reception, chess. Office: Sci Rsch Coun, Rutherford Appleton Lab, Chilton OX11 0QX, England

FAWCETT, CHRISTOPHER BABCOCK, civil engineer, construction and water resources company executive; b. N.Y.C., Dec. 17, 1951; s. George Gifford Fawcett Jr. and Andi Adams Emerson; m. Nina Beth Williamson, June 20, 1986 (div. Aug. 1993); 1 child, Kyle Christopher Adams. Student, U. Okla., 1969-72, Concordia U., Montreal, Que., Can., 1979-81; BS, Clarkson U., 1984. Lic. civil engr.; registered civil engr., N.Y. Owner C.B.F. Handyman Co., N.Y.C., 1974-77; v.p., gen. mgr. Fawcett & Fawcett, Inc., N.Y.C., 1977-84; project mgr. U.S. Army Corps Engrs., N.Y.C., 1985-86; asst. project mgr. N. Kruger Constrn., Inc., Locust Valley, N.Y., 1986-87; project mgr., engr. Finch, Pruyn & Co., Inc., Glens Falls, N.Y., 1987-98; propr. Caton Hill Enterprises, 1992—. Founder, chmn. Tri-County Nat. Engrs. Week and Nat. Jr. H.S. Mathcounts Competition programs, Glens Falls, 1987-98; founding sponsor Challenger Ctr. for Space Sci. Edn. Mem. NSPE, ASCE, Am. Welding Soc., Am. Concrete Inst., Nat. Space Soc. (charter), Engrs. for Edn., Assn. State Dam Safety Ofcls., Constrn. Specifications Inst., Order of Engr., Cousteau Soc., Greenpeace. Avocation: scuba diving. Office: Caton Hill Enterprises 14 Lake Ave Glens Falls NY 12801-2229

FAWCETT, JOHN SCOTT, real estate developer; b. Pitts., Nov. 5, 1937; s. William Hagen and Mary Jane (Wise) F.; m. Anne Elizabeth Mitchell, Dec. 30, 161; children: Holly Anne, John Scott II (dec.). BS, Ohio State U., 1959. Dist. dealer rep. Shell Oil Co., San Diego, 1962-66; dist. real estate rep. Shell Oil, Phoenix, 1967-69; region real estate rep. Shell Oil, San Francisco, 1970-71; head office land investments rep. Shell Oil, Houston, 1972-75; pres., CEO Marinita Devel. Co., Newport Beach, Calif., 1976—; lectr. in land devel. related fields. With U.S. Army, 1960-61. Named Ky. Col., Gov. Ky., 1996. Mem. Internat. Platform Assn., Internat. Coun. Shopping Ctrs., Internat. Right of Way Assn., Internat. Inst. Valuers, Inst. Bus. Appraisers, Nat. Assn. Rev. Appraisers and Mortgage Underwriters, Am. Assn. Cert. Appraisers, Urban Land Inst., Nat. Assn. Real Estate Execs. (pres. L.A. chpt. 1975), Calif. Lic. Contractors Assn., Bldg. Industry Assn., U.S. C. of C., Town Hall of Calif., Ohio State U. Alumni Assn., Toastmasters (pres. Scottsdale Ariz. club 1968, pres. Hospitality T club 1964), U. Athletic Club, Phi Kappa Tau. Republican. Roman Catholic. Avocations: antiques, tennis, skiing. Home: 8739 Hudson River Cir Fountain Vly CA 92708-5503 Office: Marinita Devel Co 3835 Birch St Newport Beach CA 92660-2600

FAWCETT, MARIE ANN FORMANEK (MRS. ROSCOE KENT FAWCETT), civic leader; b. Mpls., Mar. 6, 1914; d. Peter Paul and Mary (Stepanek) Formanek; m. Roscoe Kent Fawcett, Mar. 16, 1935; children: Roscoe Kent, Peter Formanek, Roger Knowlton II, Stephen Hart. Grad. high sch., Mpls.; cert., Harvard U., 1976-83. Chmn. of vols. Merry Go Round Club House and Mews, Greenwich, Conn., 1949-92, trustee, 1948-90, v.p., bd. dirs., 1949—, corr. sec., 1992—, chmn. entertainment, 1970-90; bd. dirs., vol. chmn., corr. sec. Nathaniel Witherell Hosp., Greenwich, 1952—, chmn. vols., 1956-89, corr. sec. aux. bd., 1956-94; bd. dirs., corr. sec. Nathaniel Witherell Auxiliary Hosp., 1952—; chmn. vols. Greenwich Hosp., 1953-54; dist. chmn. ARC, Community Chest, Mental Health, 1946-50; vol. mentally retarded children Milbank Sch., Greenwich, 1958-92. Bd. dirs. Cerebral Palsy, Greenwich Symphony, 1956—, Greenwich Symphony Guild, 1956—, Putnam Indianfield Sch.; bd. dirs., corr. sec. Merry Go Round Mews, 1949—; bd. dirs. Multiple Sclerosis Soc., 1948—, v.p., 1970, corr. sec., 1958—; active drives for ARC, Community Chest, Leukemia, Muscular Dystrophy, Mental Health, Mentally Retarded Children Milbank Sch.; bd. dirs. Merry-Go-Round News for the Elderly, 1948—, Nathaniel Witherell Hosp. for Elderly, 1952—, Greenwich Symphony Guild, 1956—, Travel Club Greenwich, 1982—; participating mem. Huxley Inst. Biosocial Rsch.; mem. polo com. Susan Cancer Fund, Pegasus Therapeutic Riding and Rusk Inst. Rehab. Medicine; trustee Menninger Found., Topeka. Named Woman of Year, Soroptomist Club, 1967; recipient Community Svc. award United Cerebral Palsy Assn. Fairfield County, 1972, Fund Drive award Cerebral Palsy, 1970, citations for 36 yrs. outstanding vol. svcs. Nathaniel Witherell Hosp. Aux., Conn. Dept. Health, 1977. Mem. Internat. Platform Assn., The Woman's Club of Greenwich, Travel Club of Greenwich (corr. sec., bd. dirs. 1982—), Charles F. Menninger Soc. (mem. Roll of Nonor 1998, Sustaining Excellence award). Home: 4452 Portland Ave Minneapolis MN 55407-3548 Address: 8141 12th Ave S Minneapolis MN 55425-1055

FAWCETT, SHERWOOD LUTHER, research laboratory executive; b. Youngstown, Ohio, Dec. 25, 1919; s. Luther T. and Clara (Sherwood) F.; m. Martha L. Simcox, Feb. 28, 1953; children: Paul, Judith, Tom. BS, Ohio State U., 1941; MS, Case Inst. Tech., 1948, PhD, 1950; hon. degrees, Ohio State U., Gonzaga U., Whitman Coll., Otterbein Coll., Detroit Inst. Tech., Ohio Dominican Coll. Registered profl. engr., Ohio. Mem. staff Columbus Labs. Battelle Meml. Inst., 1950-64, mgr. physics dept., 1959-64; dir. Pacific Northwest Labs., Richland, Wash., 1964-67; trustee Battelle Meml. Inst., Columbus, Ohio, 1968-92, exec. v.p., 1967-68, CEO, 1968-84, pres., 1968-80, chmn., 1981-84, chmn. bd. trustees, 1985-87; assoc. trustee Columbus, Ohio, 1987-94; chmn. bd. dirs. Transmet Corp. With USNR, 1941-46. Decorated Bronze Star; recipient Washington award Western Soc. Engrs., 1989. Mem. AIME, NSPE, Am. Phys. Soc., Am. Nuclear Soc., Am. Phys. Soc., Sigma Xi, Tau Beta Pi, Delta Chi, Sigma Pi Sigma. Home: 1852A Riverside Dr Columbus OH 43212-1875 Office: Transmet Corp 4290 Perimeter Dr Columbus OH 43228-1036

FAWELL, HARRIS W., lawyer, former congressman; b. West Chicago, Ill., Mar. 25, 1929; m. Ruth Johnson, 1954; children: Richard, Jane, John. Student, Naperville North Central Coll., 1949; LL.D., Chgo. Kent Coll. Law, 1952. Ptnr. Fawell, James & Brooks, Naperville, Ill., 1954-84; mem. Ill. Senate, Springfield, 1963-77; gen. counsel Ill. Assn. Park Dists., 1977-84; mem. 99th-105th Congresses from 13th Ill. dist., 1985-98; of counsel James, Gustafson & Thompson, 1999—; mem. Edn. and the Workforce Com., chmn. subcom. on employer-employee rels.; mem. House Sci. Com. Office: 1001 E Chicago Ave Ste 103 Naperville IL 60540-5500

FAWZI, AHMED, botanist, educator; b. Cairo, Egypt, Oct. 21, 1937; s. Abdel-Hamid Fawzi and Tafida Mahmoud Hasanein; m. Soheir Yehya El-Hakim, Feb. 14, 1971; 1 child, Mennatalla. B Agr., Cairo U., 1958, MS in Agr., 1966, PhD in Agr., 1974. Asst. rschr. Nat. Rsch. Ctr., Cairo, 1967-74, rschr., 1974-79, assoc. rsch. prof., 1979-84, prof., 1984—, head dept. botany, 1997—; executive mgr. micronutrients project, Egypt, 1981—; cons. Chemonics, Egypt, 1995, German-Egypto Project on Seed Improvement, 1996, Sudanese-German Project on Support for Horti. Crop Growers, Khartoom, Sudan, 1987; presenter in field. Contbr. to book: World Fertilizer Use Manual, 1991; contbr. articles to profl. jours. Avocations: swimming, soccer, television, music. Home: 129 Abd El-Hamid Badawy # 7, Cairo Egypt Office: Nat Rsch Ctr, El Tahreer, Cairo Egypt

FAXON, ALICIA CRAIG, art educator; b. N.Y.C., July 27, 1931; d. William Donald and Clara Alicia (Harnecker) Craig; m. Richard Bremer Faxon, Feb. 21, 1953; children: Richard Paul, Thomas Hardwick. AB, Vassar Coll., 1952; MA, Radcliffe Coll., 1953, Boston U., 1971; PhD, Boston U., 1979; DHL (hon.), Simmons Coll., 1998. Lectr. New Eng. Sch. Art and Design, Boston, 1974-77; acting dir. Danforth Mus., Framingham, Mass., 1977; teaching assoc. Boston U. Sch. for Art, 1978-79; vis. lectr. Simmons Coll., Boston, 1979-80, asst. prof. art, 1980-86, assoc. prof., 1986-91; chmn. dept. art and music, 1987-93, prof. art, 1991-93, alumnae endowed chair, 1992-93; lectr. Sch. for Lifelong Learning, Harvard U., Cambridge, Mass., 1978-80; program chmn. Women's Studies Adv. Bd., 1982-84; R.I. editor Art New Eng., 1994-99. Author: Catalog Raisonné of Prints of J.-L. Forain, 1982, Pilgrims and Pioneers, 1987, Dante Gabriel Rossetti, 1989; co-author: (with Liana Cheney and Kathleen Russo) Self-Portrait of Woman Painters, 2000; co-editor (with Susan Casteras) Pre-Raphaelite Art in its European Context, 1995; mem. editl. bd. Woman's Art Jour., 1989—. Mem. acquisitions com. Danforth Mus., 1974-89, trustee, 1975-77. Recipient Nan award for art criticism Art New Eng., 1987; grantee Nat. Endowment for Arts, 1982, Simmons Coll., 1984, NEH, 1989, 92. Mem. Coll. Art Assn. (chmn. preRaphaelite session 1990), Women's Caucus for Art (program co-chmn. 1986-88), Victorian Soc., 19th Century Art Historians Group, Vassar Coll. Alumnae Assn. Democrat. Episcopalian. Avocations: travel, writing.

FAXON, BRAD, professional golfer; b. Oceanport, NJ, Aug. 1, 1961; m. Bonnie Faxon (div.); children: Melanie, Emily, Sophie Lee. B in Econs., Furman U., 1983. Member PGA, professional golfer, 1983-. Co-sponsor Billy Andrade/Brad Faxon Charities for Children, 1991—; co-host CVS Charity Classic, 1999. Winner Provident Classic, 1986, Buick Open, 1991, New England Classic, 1992, The International, 1992, Heineken Australian Open, 1993, Freeport-McDermott Classic, 1997, B.C. Open, 1999. Achievements include being ranked 7th on PGA tour, 1992; mem. (nat. teams) Walker Cup, 1983, Ryder Cup, 1995, 97, Dunhill Cup, 1997, (PGA tour charity team) JCPenney Classic, 1999. Address: PGA 100 PGA Tour Blvd Ponte Vedra Beach FL 32082

FAY, TONI GEORGETTE, communications executive; b. N.Y.C., Apr. 25, 1947; d. George E. and Allie C. (Smith) Fay. BA, Duquesne U., Pitts., 1968; MSW, U. Pitts., 1972, MEd, 1973; cert., Yale U. Drug Dependence Unit, 1973. Caseworker N.Y.C. Dept. Welfare, 1968-70; regional commr. Gov. Pa. Coun. Drugs and Alcohol, 1973-76; dir. social svcs. Pitts. Drug Abuse Ctr., 1972-73; dir. planning and devel. Nat. Coun. Negro Women, 1977-79; exec. v.p. D. Parke Gibson Assocs., 1979-82; mgr. cmty. rels. Time Inc. (now Time-Warner Inc.), N.Y.C., 1982-83, dir. corp. cmty. rels. and affirmative action, 1983-93, v.p., corp. officer, 1993—. Bd. dirs. UNICEF, Congl. Black Caucus Found., NAACP Legal Def. Fund Bd., Franklin and Eleanor Inst., Apollo Theatre Found.; apptd. bd. advs. Nat. Inst. Literacy, 1996—. Named Woman of Yr., Pitts. YWCA, 1975, N.Y. Women's Forum; recipient Twin award YWCA of USA, 1987; named one 100 Top Women in Bus., Dollars and Sense Mag., 1986. Office: Time Warner Bldg 75 Rockefeller Plz New York NY 10019-6990

FAYARD, THIERRY HUBERT, radio astronomy engineer, inventor; b. Dakar, Senegal, Jan. 17, 1960; s. Jean Marc and Elizabeth (Bucquet) F. BS, Montgeron Lycee, 1979; M in Theoretical Physics, Pierre and Marie Curie U., Paris, 1984; D in Astronomy, Paris Observatory, 1989. Tchr. Coll. Bellevue, Yerres, 1982-83, Lycee St. Pierre, Brunoy, 1983-84; scientist Inst. Geographique Nat., Paris, 1985-89; project mgr. Centre Nat. Etude Spatiale, Toulouse, 1989—. Contbr. articles to profl. jours. including Astronomy & Astrophysics, Proc. European VLBI, and Transputer Application & Sys. Recipient award European Space Agy., 1985. Mem. Connaissance Echange Devel. (pres. 1990), Franco Tibetan Help. Achievements include patents in sharp audiovisual electronic sys. with piezo electric components and digital signal processing technics for audio studio recording; first devel. precise reliable location of pulsar 1937 + 214 by VLBI; set up a solar energy workshop in India for refugees. Office: Centre Nat Etude Spatiale, 18 av Belin, 31055 Toulouse France

FAYE, BERNARD JOANNES, animal production professional, researcher; b. Lyon, France, June 12, 1950; s. Raymond Louis and Denise Gilberte (Giraud) F.; m. Odile Jeanne-Emilie Chevallier, Apr. 28, 1973; children: Sylvain, Mariama, Fabrice. D in Vet. Medicine, Vet. Sch., Lyon, 1974; MSc, Clermont (France) U., 1979-80; PhD, U. Paris XII, 1995; State Doctorate, U. Montpellier, France, 1998. Tech. asst. Livestock Svc., Awassa, Ethiopia, 1976-77, Niamey, Niger, 1977-79; head biochem. nutrition svc. NVI, Debre Zeit, Ethiopia, 1981-83; head lab. ecopathology INRA, Theix, France, 1983-96; head animal prodn. dept. CIRAD, Montpellier, 1996—; vet. inspector Inst d'Elevage et de Medecine Veterinaire des Pays Tropicaux, Awassa and Debre Zeit, Ethiopia, 1976-83, Inst. Nat. de la Recherche Agronomique, Theix, 1983-88, sr. scientist, 1988-96; sr. scientist Centre de Cooperation Internat. pour la Recherche Agronomique et le Devel., Montpellier, 1996-98. Author: Ethiopian Farmers, 1991, Animal Ecopathology, 1994, Guide for Camel Farming, 1997; editor (spl. issue) The International Symposium on Animal Ecopathology and Farm Mgmt., 1994; mem. editl. bd. The Addis News, 1997-98. Pres. Ngo Assn., Clermont, France, 1986-96; adminstr. Vets. Sans Frontieres, Lyon, 1990-96. Recipient Malbrant-Feunten, Acad. Vet. France, 1996. Mem. Assn. pour l'Etude de l'Epidemiologie des Maladies Animals (adminstr. 1994-97), Internat. Found. for Scis. (advisor 1990-98). Avocations: walking, reading, photography. Office: CIRAD-EMVT, Campus Internat Baillarguet, 34032 Montpellier Herault, France

FAYED, RAMZI, academic administrator, educator; b. Cairo, Aug. 19, 1938; s. Mohamed Riad and Mary Elizabeth (Quegan) F.; m. Anne Elizabeth Johnson, Aug. 19, 1966. BS, Manchester U., 1961, MS, 1963, PhD, 1968. Rsch. statis. officer Brit. Motor Agts. Assn., 1961-65; CEO Brit. Motor Industry, 1966-68; sr. lectr. U. NSW Sch. Mktg., Sydney, Australia, 1971-73, acting head, 1971-72; chmn., mng. dir. Fayed Assocs. Pty. Ltd., Sydney, Australia, 1973-97; faculty dir. Internat. Mktg. Inst., Australia, 1984-88, prof., head., 1991—; hon. prof. Charles Sturt U., 1992—; hon. cons. Royal Agrl. Soc. NSW, 1972-96; mem. NSW Dairy Promotional Coun., 1978-81; cons. Victorian Totalizator Agy. Bd., 1980-81; judge Hoover Mktg. Awards, 1972-73; chmn. Nat. Mktg. Conf. Australia, 1979-83. Contbr. articles to profl. jours. Hon. dir. nat. bd. Australian Travel Industry Assn., 1974-85; adv. Assn. Cons. Engrs. Australia, 1988-90, Law Soc. NSW, 1984-90. Fellow Australian Inst. Mgmt., Australian Inst. Co. Dirs. Office: 25 Bligh St Ste 803, Sydney New South Wales 2000, Australia

FAYET, MICHEL, mechanics educator; b. Mayet de Montagne Allier, France, Mar. 25, 1941; s. François Fayet and Thérèse (Perenchio) Houdot; m. Nicole Pieve, Mar. 31, 1969; children: Pascale, Anne. Degree in engring., Ecole des Arts et Métiers, Paris, 1964; PhD, Nat. Inst. Applied Sci., Lyon, 1990; Habilitation, Nat. Inst. Applied Sci., 1996. Tchr. secondary edn. France, 1964-78; prof. Nat. Inst. Applied Sci., Lyon, 1978-93, dir. mechanics rigid solid team, 1993—. Contbr. articles to Mechanism and Machine Theory, European Jour. Mechanics. Achievements include patents for Sphero Trochoidal of Spatial Scanner, Generalised Pantograph, research in rigid body dynamics, creation of the global inertia tensor notion, new formula in plane kinematics, analysis of over constrained mechanisms in view to transforming them in non overconstrained ones, paradoxical mechanisms of RCRC type, biomechanics, dynamics of semi-free mechanisms. Home: 2 chemin des Mouilles, 69130 Ecully France Office: Nat Inst Applied Sci, 20 av A Einstein Bat 302, 69621 Villeurbanne Cedex, France

FAYETTE, KATHLEEN OWENS, lawyer; b. N.Y.C., Feb. 28, 1939; d. Edward Francis and Margaret Grace (Quigley) Owens; m. Alan Gerard Fayette, June 15, 1963; children: Stephen, Suzanne, Christopher. AB, Marymount Coll., N.Y.C., 1960; JD, Pace U., White Plains, N.Y., 1979. Asst. MHLS atty. Appellate divsn. N.Y. State Supreme Ct., N.Y.C., 1979-82; instr. law Interboro Inst., 1983-84; ct. liaison Project Greenhope, N.Y.C., 1985-87; dir. alternative to incarceration N.W. Bronx Cmty. and Clergy Coalition, N.Y.C., 1987-89; ct. liaison Children's Village, Dobbs Ferry, N.Y., 1989-91; pvt. practice, 1998—; lectr., cons. on the legal rights of the mentally disabled; cons. alternative incarceration. Author: The Bar is Closed, 1986; columnist You and the Law, 1982-83. Cons., dir. Bishop-Browne Project, Fla., 1994—; pro bono child welfare advocate Guardian ad Litem Program, Fla., 1992—. Mem. Pace U. Sch. Law Alumni Assn., Marymount Coll. Alumni Assn. Roman Catholic. Avocations: curling, skeet shooting, scuba diving. Fax: 561-451-3035. Office: 1515 N Federal Hwy Ste 300 Boca Raton FL 33432-1994

FAYNZILBERG, ALEKSANDR, mathematician; b. Odessa, Ukraine, Nov. 1, 1917; arrived in U.S., 1992; s. Marc and Marianne (Landman) F. Mathematician, aerodynamics, Moscow Univ., 1938, D of math., 1952. Asst. prof. Inst. of Rail Transport, Tbilisi, Georgie, 1941-44, Inst. of Chem., Moscow, 1944-53; prof. Agricultural Acad., Moscow, 1953-92; ret., 1992. Contbr. over 100 articles to profl. jours. Mem. N.Y. Acad. Scis.

FAYO, ANTHONY THOMAS, research scientist; b. Cornwall, N.Y., Aug. 12, 1966; s. Thomas Louis and Margaret Joy (Perno) F.; m. Corinne Renee Luckfield, Apr. 6, 1991. AS in physics, Dutchess C.C., 1987; BS, U. Albany, 1989. Mass spectral interpretation specialist Hewlett Packard. Chemist Camo Labs., Inc., Poughkeepsie, N.Y., 1989-90; group leader chemist Pace, Inc., Wappingers Falls, N.Y., 1990-92; mass spectrometry supr. Northeast Analytical, Inc., Schenectady, N.Y., 1992-93; rsch. scientist N.Y. State Dept Health, Albany, 1993—. Recipient Citizenship award New Paltz Knights of Columbus, 1984. Roman Catholic. Avocations: softball, tennis, hockey, music. Home: 91 Whitney Dr Valatie NY 12184-5245 Office: NY State Dept Health Empire State Plaza PO Box 509 Albany NY 12201-0509

FAYOLLE, ALAIN, business educator; b. Saint-Etienne, France, Dec. 19, 1952; s. Pierre and Christine (Postareme) F.; m. Monique Magand, Aug. 31, 1974; children: Pierre-Alain, Francoise. Degree in engring., C.E.S.I., Lyon, France, 1981; DESS, U. Lyon 3, 1990, DEA, 1992, DSc, 1996; European engr. degree (hon.), CNISF/FEANI, Paris, 1994. Engr. Richier, St. Etienne, France, 1981, Laurent, St. Etienne, 1982; engr., cons. Icare, Lyon, 1982-87; pres., CEO Meta Concept, St. Etienne, 1987-91; prof. EM Lyon, 1991—; cons. Stratequip, St. Etienne, 1990-98. Author: L'ingénieur Entrepreneur Francais, 1999; contbr. articles to profl. jours., chpt. to book. Mem. ICSB, Acad. Mgmt., Acad. Entrepreneuriat. Home: 9 rue Crillon, 69006 Lyon France Office: EM Lyon BP 174, 23 Ave Guy de Collongue, 69132 Ecully Cedex France

FAYZILBERG, EMANUIL, physicist; b. Odessa, Ukraine, Feb. 14, 1914; came to U.S., 1992; s. Marc Faynzilberg and Marianne Landman. Graduate, Power Engring. Inst., Moscow, 1935; D. in Engring, Polytech. Inst., Tbilisi, Georgia, 1944. Engr. metalworking factory, Saint Petersburg, Russia, 1936-69; asst. prof. Engring. Naval Sch., Saint Petersburg, Russia, 1939, Inst. Rail Transport, Tbilisi, Georgia, 1941-44; prof., faculty head Inst. Rail Transport, Moscow, 1949-65, Acad. Transport, Saint Petersburg, 1945-48, Inst. Mgmt., Moscow, 1966-76; prof. Inst. Building, Moscow, 1977-79; prof. Inst. Info., Moscow, 1980-91, retired, 1991. Contbr. over 90 articles to profl. jours. and books. Mem. N.Y. Acad. Sci.

FAZEKAS, BÉLA, veterinarian, researcher; b. Besenyötelek, Hungary, Sept. 24, 1955; s. Lajos Fazekas and Klára Magyar; m. Mária Kis, Oct. 20, 1979; children: Béla, Enikö. DVM, U. Vet. Sci., Budapest, Hungary, 1979; PhD, Pannon U. Agr., Keszthely, Hungary, 1998. Rsch. fellow Rsch. Inst. Vet. Sci., Budapest, 1979-81; lab. vet. Vet. Inst., Debrecen, Hungary, 1981-87, head of chemistry dept., 1987—; judicial vet. cons. Vet. Inst., Debrecen, 1981—. Contbr. articles to profl. jours. Avocation: gardening. Office: Vet Inst, Bornemissza u 3-7, 4031 Debrecen Hungary

FAZEKAS, ISTVA'N, mathematician, educator; b. Eger, Hungary, May 17, 1954. PhD, Kossuth U., 1986. Asst. Kossuth U., Debrecen, Hungary, 1978-82, asst. prof., 1982-90, assoc. prof., 1990—; dept. head Kossuth U., Debrecen, 1994—; rschr. Agrl. U., Wageningen, The Netherlands, 1993; assoc. prof. Odense (Denmark) U., 1997; dept. head Agrl. U., Debrecen, 1995-99. Editor: Optimization of Stochastic Systems, 1990. Mem. Bolyai Math. Soc. Home: Tessedik 206, 4032 Debrecen Hungary Office: U Debrecen, PO Box 12, 4010 Debrecen Hungary

FAZEKAS, TAMÁS, physician, cardiology educator; b. Kiskunfélegyháa, Hungary, May 4, 1950; s. Lajos Fazekas and Klára Gödry; m. Andrea Selmeczi, Sept. 25, 1982 (div. 1996); children: Tamás, Bence; life ptnr., Gizella Liszkai. MD, Albert Szent Györgyi U., Szeged, Hungary, 1974; PhD in Medicine, Hungarian Acad. of Scis., 1985. Lectr. 1st dept. internal medicine Szent-Györgyi U. Med. Sch., 1975-83, asst. prof., 1984-95, assoc. prof., 1995-96; prof., chief Békés County Tchg. Hosp., Gyula, Hungary, 1997—; vis. prof. Okla. U. Health Scis. Ctr. Coll. Medicine, Oklahoma City, 1992. Author, editor: Magnesium in Biological Systems, 1994, Cardiac Electrophysiology and Arrhythmology (in Hungarian), 1999; reviewer Circulation; contbr. numerous articles to profl. jours. Fellow European Soc. Cardiology; mem. N.Am. Soc. Pacing and Electrophysiology, Hungarian Soc. Internal Medicine, Hungarian Soc. Cardiology (leader working group on arrhythmia 1994—). Avocation: history of cardiology/arrhythmias. Home: Batthyány 31, H-6722 Szeged Hungary Office: Dept Cardiology, Semmelweis St 1, H-5700 Gyula Hungary

FAZELBHOY, ALIFF SULTAN, lawyer; b. Mumbai, India, Aug. 19, 1965; s. Sultan Hussein and Rehmat Sultan F.; m. Nazima Aliff Shaikm, May 23, 1993; children: Rahil, Neher. BCom, Bombay U., Mumbah, India, 1985, LLB, 1988; LLM, Cambridge U., England, 1991. Articled clk., paralegal Hooseinally Visram & co., Mumbai, 1987-90; assoc. solicitor Bhatt & Saldanha, Mumbai, 1990-92; sr. assoc. solicitor Thakker & Thakker, Mumbai, 1992-95; ptnr. ARA Law, Mumbai, 1996—. Author: Transfer Pricing, 1997, Taxation of Trusts, 1999. Recipient ODA scholarship Cambridge Commonwealth Trust, 1990. Mem. Bombay Inc. Law Soc., Willingdon Sports Club. Avocations: bridge, scrabble, swimming. Office: ARA Law, Agra Bldg Fl 1 121 MG Rd, Mumbai 400023, India

FAZELI, POOYA, editor; b. Tehran, Iran, June 27, 1970; s. Ghassem and Robi (Eizadi) F. BS, U. Washington, 1989; MS, Yale U., 1991; PhD, Harvard U., 1997. Editor-in-chief Stanford Med. Rev., Stanford, Calif., 1998—; pres. Stanford Med. Rev. Assn., 1998—; cons. USMEDEX, N.Y.C. Co-author: (book) Cracking the Boards: USMLE Step 1, 1998. Lear scholar Stanford Med. Sch., 1997; recipient Spl. Vol. award Future's Program, Somerville, Mass., 1993. Mem. AMA, ACP, Santa Clara Valley Med. Assn. Avocations: photography, biking, travel. E-mail: fazeli@stanford.edu. Home: Rains 16F 704 Campus Dr Stanford CA 94305 Office: Stanford Med Rev Assn M 105 Stanford Med Sch Stanford CA 94305

FAZHANG, DING, publishing executive. Pub. exec., chief editor Xin Min Wan Bao, Shanghai, China; v.p. Wenhui Xinmin United Press Group, Shanghai, China. Office: Wenhui Xinmin United Press, 755 Wei Hai Lu, Shanghai Peoples Republic of China

FAZIO, ANTONIO, bank executive; b. Alvito, Italy, 1936; m. Maria Cristina Rosati; children: Annamaria, Giovanni Battista, Valeria Maria, Maria Chiara, Eugenia. Grad., U. Econs. and Bus., 1960; postgrad., MIT, 1962-63, 66-67; degree in econs. (hon.), U. Bari; degree in lit. (hon.), Johns Hopkins U., Bologna; degree in polit. sci. (hon.), U. Macerata; degree in statis. and econ. (hon.), Sacro Cuore U., Milan; degree in law (hon.), U. Cassino; degree in computer engring. (hon.), U. Lecce. Collaborator econometric rsch. office Bank of Italy, Rome, 1961-66, dep. office chief rsch. dept., 1972, head rsch. dept, 1973-79, ctrl. mgr. econ. rsch., 1980, dept. dir. gen., 1982-93, gov., 1993—; coun. mem. European Monetary Inst., 1994-98; governing coun., gen. coun. European Ctrl. Bank, 1998—; chmn. Italian Fgn. Exch. Office; Gov. for Italy at IBRD (World Bank), Internat. Fin. Corp., Internat. Devel. Agy., MIGA, ADB; mem. Group Twenty, Group Ten and Group Seven (Fin.); bd. dirs. Bank for Internat. Settlements, Nat. Rsch. Coun. Decorated grand cross Order of Merit (Italy); Paul Harris fellow Rotary Internat. *

FAZIO, D. FREDRICO, lawyer; b. Bradford, Pa., July 25, 1940; s. Joseph Richard and Florence Fazio; m. Nancy Kretzschmar, May 4, 1963; children: Joseph R. III, Quinn. BS, Fla. State U., 1962; JD, U. Miami, Fla., 1967. Bar: Fla. 1967, U.S. Dist. Ct. (so. dist.) Fla. 1967. Assoc. Hawkesworth &

Kay, Miami; ptnr. Fazio, Dawson, DiSalvo, Cannon, Abers & Podrecca, Ft. Lauderdale, Fla., 1969—; bd. dirs. Lucor, Inc. Mem. Downtown Devel. Authority, Ft. Lawderdale, 1992—, chmn., 1995, also sec. of bd.; bd. dirs. Boys Town of Fla., 1969-89. Mem. Am. Bd. Trial Advocates (pres., bd. dirs. 1992—), Ocean Reef Club. Avocations: golf, sailing. Home: 2887 Riverland Rd Fort Lauderdale FL 33312-4456 Office: Fazio Dawson DiSalvo Cannon Abers & Podrecca 633 S Andrews Ave Ste 500 Fort Lauderdale FL 33301-2862

FAZIO, FERRUCCIO, nuclear medicine educator; b. Garessio, Cuneo, Italy, Aug. 7, 1944; m. Margherita Colnaghi; children: Alessandro, Arianna. Degree in medicine and surgery, U. Pisa, Italy, 1968, splty. in nuclear medicine, 1970, splty. in respiratory diseases, 1975; MD (hon.), U. Lund, Sweden, 1992. Resident in internal medicine U. Pisa Med. Sch., 1968-71, asst. prof., 1972-77; rschr. CNR, Pisa, 1972-77, sec. com. for biology and medicine, 1981-94; cons. in nuclear medicine Med. Rsch. Coun. cyclotron unit Hammersmith Hosp., London, 1977-80; sr. lectr. medicine and radiology U. London, 1977-80; assoc. prof. nuclear medicine U. Milan, 1979-87, prof., 1987—, mem. adminstrv. bd., 1986-90; mem. Nat. Health Coun., Italy, 1990-93; dir. PET Cyclotron Ctr., San Raffaele Hosp., Milan, 1990—; dir. Consiglio Nazionale delle Ricerche Inst. Neuroscis. Bioimaging, Milan, 1994—. Contbr. over 300 articles to internat. med. jours. Lt. Italian Army, 1970-71. Mem. Italian Assn. Nuclear Medicine. Avocations: skiing, mountain climbing, diving, fishing, cooking. Office: Hosp San Raffaele Nucl Med, Via Olgettina 60, 20132 Milan Italy

FAZIO, PETER VICTOR, JR., lawyer; b. Chgo., Jan. 22, 1940; s. Peter Victor and Marie Rose (LaMantia) F.; m. Patti Ann Campbell, Jan. 3, 1966; children: Patti-Marie, Catherine, Peter. AB, Coll. of Holy Cross, Worcester, Mass., 1961; JD, U. Mich., 1964. Bar: Ill. 1964, U.S. Dist. Ct. (no. dist.) Ill. 1965, U.S. Ct. Appeals (7th cir.) 1972, U.S. Supreme Ct. 1977, D.C. 1981, U.S. Ct. Appeals (D.C. cir.) 1988, Ind. 1993. Assoc. Schiff, Hardin & Waite, Chgo., 1964-70, ptnr., 1970-82, 84—; exec. v.p. Internat. Capital Equipment, Chgo., 1982-83, also bd. dirs., 1982-85, sec., 1982-87; bd. dirs. Planmetrics Inc., Chgo., 1984-92, Chgo. Lawyers Commn. for Civil Rights Under Law, 1976-82, co-chmn., 1978-80; bd. dirs. Seton Health Corp. No. Ill., Chgo 1987-90, vice chmn., 1989-90. Trustee Barat Coll., Lake Forest, Ill., 1977-82; bd. dirs. St. Joseph Hosp., Chgo., 1990-95, mem. exec. adv. bd., 1984-89, chmn., 1986-89; vice chmn. bd. dirs. Cath. Health Ptnrs., 1995-99, chmn., 1999—; dir. exec. com. Ill. Coalition, 1994—, N.W. Ind. Forum, 1994-98. Mem. ABA (coun. 1991-94, chmn. sect. pub. utility, transp. and comm. law), FBA, Ill. Bar Assn., Chgo. Bar Assn., Fed. Energy Bar Assn., Edison Electric Inst. (chmn. legal com.), Am. Gas Assn. (legal com.), Am. Soc. Corp. Secs., Met. Club, Econ. Club Chgo., Comml. Club Chgo. Office: Schiff Hardin & Waite 6600 Sears Tower 233 S Wacker Dr Chicago IL 60606-6473

FAZIO, VIC, former congressman; b. Winchester, Mass., Oct. 11, 1942; m. Judy Kern; children: Dana Fazio, Anne Fazio (dec.), Kevin Kern, Kristie Kern. BA, Union Coll., Schenectady, 1965; postgrad., Calif. State U., Sacramento. Journalist, founder Calif. Jour.; congl. and legis. cons., 1966-75; mem. Calif. State Assembly, 1975-78; mem. 96th -103rd Congresses from Calif. 3rd Dist., 1979-98; former chmn. Dem. Congl. Campaign Com.; chmn. Dem. caucus, house steering policy com.; mem. legis. br. appropriations subcom., ranking mem. appropriations subcom. energy and water; mem. Ho. budget com. 97th-100th Congress; majority whip-at-large 96th-105th Congress; also co-chmn. Fed. Govt. Svcs. Task Force 96th-101st Congresses, former chmn. bipartisan com. on ethics; mem. appropriations com. 105th Congress; sr. ptnr. Clark & Weinstock, Washington, 1999—; former mem. Sacramento County Charter and Planning Commns. Bd. dirs. Asthma Allergy Found., Jr. Statesman, Nat. Italian-Am. Found. Coro Found. fellow; named Solar Congressman of Yr. Mem. Air Force Assn. Office: Clark & Weinstock Inc 52 Vanderbilt Ave New York NY 10017-3808

FAZZALARI, NICOLA LORENZO, biomedical scientist; b. Adelaide, Australia, Nov. 2, 1950; s. Ilario and Grazia (Caruso) F.; m. Louise Francis Fairchild, June 29, 1985; children: Rebecca Alice, Miranda Claire. B Applied Sci., U. Adelaide, 1971, BSc with honors, 1973, grad. diploma in edn., 1974, PhD, 1987. High sch. tchr. South Australian Edn. Dept., Adelaide, 1975-77; med. scientist Inst. of Med. and Vet. Sci., Adelaide, 1978-82, sr. med. scientist, 1982-87, prin. med. scientist, 1987-97, chief med. scientist, 1997—; sr. rsch. assoc. orthopedics Royal Adelaide Hosp., 1989—; sr. lectr. U. of Adelaide, 1991—. Contbr. articles to profl. jours. Commonwealth scholarship Australian Govt., 1970, John Darlby scholarship, 1971; postdoctoral fellowship Henry Ford Hosp., 1991-92. Mem. Rotary Internat., Orthopaedic Rsch. Soc. Office: Inst Med and Vet Sci, Frome Rd, Adelaide 5000, Australia

FDIDA, SERGE, computer science educator; b. Suresnes, France, Aug. 30, 1959; s. Elie and Dolly (Nahum) F. Diploma, U. Paris VI, 1982, PhD, 1984, Habilitation, 1989. Asst. prof. computer sci. U. Paris VI, Paris, 1983-88, assoc. prof. computer sci., 1988-91, prof. computer sci., 1995—; prof. computer sci. U. Paris V, Paris, 1991-95; head Masi and LIP6-CNRS Network Team, Paris, 1990—; visitor IBM, U.S.A., 1995. Author: Modeles de Systemes et Reseaux, 1989, Des Autoroutes de l'Information au Cyberespace, 1997; editor: MTPE '87, 1987, HPN '94, 1994, PCN '95, 1995, ECMAST '97, 1997, NGC '99 Networking, 2000; contbr. articles to profl. jours. Mem. IEEE (sr.), Assn. for Computing Machinery. Home: 18 rue des Pivoines, 94140 Alfortville France Office: Univ Paris VI, Lip6 4 Place Jussieu, 75005 Paris France

FEARING, WILLIAM KELLY, art educator, artist; b. Fordyce, Ark., Oct. 18, 1918; s. George David and Frankie (Kelly) F. BA, La. Tech. U., 1941; MA, Columbia U., 1950. Classroom tchr. Windfield Pub. Schs., La., La., 1942-43; prodn. illustrator Consolidated Vultee Aircraft, Fort Worth, 1943-45; prof. art Tex. Wesleyan Coll., Fort Worth, 1945-47; prof. art U. Tex., Austin, 1947-87, Ashbel Smith prof., 1983—, Ashbel Smith prof. emeritus, 1987—. Author: (with C.I. Martin and E. Beard) Our Expanding Vision, 1960, The Creative Eye, 1969, 2d edit., 1979, (with E. Beard, N. Krevitsky, C.I. Martin) Art and the Creative Teacher, 1971, (with E.L. Mayton, B. Francis, E. Beard) Helping Children See Art and Make Art, 1982, (with E.L. Mayton and R. Brooks) The Way or Art Inner Vision Outer Expression, 1986; guest editor Tex. Quar., Creativity and the Human Spirit, vol. XVI, 1978; one man shows include El Paso Mus. Art, Esther Bear Gallery, Santa Barbara, 1964, Gallery Visual Arts, La. Tech. U., Ruston, 1966, U. Tex. Art Mus., Austin, 1967, Ft. Worth Art Ctr., 1969, Witte Meml. Mus., San Antonio, 1969, U. Tex. Art Mus., Austin, 1974, Mary Moore Gallery, LaJolla, 1975, Mary Moffett Gallery, La. Tech. U., 1976, DuBose Gallery, Houston, 1977, L and L Gallery, Longview, 1975, 78, Retrospective Spencer Gallery, Fine Arts Ctr., U. Ark.-Monticello, 1981, Mary Moffett Gallery, Sch. Art and Arch., La. Tech. U., 1981, Old Jail Art Ctr., Albany, Tex., 1985, Marion Koogler McNay Art Mus., San Antonio, 1986, Valley House Gallery, Dallas, 1992, 96, Robinson Galleries, Houston, 1995, Flatbed Press and Gallery, Austin, 1995, 97, Pascal/Robinson Galleries, Houston, 1999; exhibited in group shows at Carnegie Inst., Pitts., 1955, 56, 57, Pa. Acad. Art, Phila., 1954-56, Mus. Fine Arts, Houston, 1956-57, Dallas Mus. Fine Art, 1956-57, Munson-Williams-Proctor Inst., Utica, 1956-57, Edwin Hewitt Gallery, N.Y.C., 1957, Dallas Mus. Fine Art, 1958, Am. Fedn. Art, 1958, Mus. Fine Art of Little Rock, 1961, Colorado Springs Art Ctr., 1961, 63, Philbrook Art Ctr., Tulsa, 1963, Fort Worth Art Ctr., 1963, U. Ill., Urbana, 1955, 59, 63, Denver Art Mus., 1963, U. Ariz. and Ark Art Ctr.,1964-65, N.Y. World's Fair, Tex. Pavillion, 1964, Tex. Pavillion Hemistair, San Antonio, 1968, Tex. Tech U. Mus. Art, Lubbock, 1978, U. Tex.-Austin, 1979, Art Gallery Sch. Art and Architecture, La. Tech. U. Ruston, 1984, Jack S. Blanton Mus. Art (formerly Archer M. Huntington Art Gallery), U. Tex.-Austin, 1963-82, 83-91, 92-98, 99, Longview Mus. and Arts Ctr., Tex., 1962, 63, 75, 85, 90, 91, Amarillo Art Ctr., Tex., 1988, Dallas Mus. Fine Arts, 1991, Robinson Gelleries, Houston, 1993,94, 96, 97, 98, 99, Valley House gallery, Dallas, 1994-99, Flatbed Press and Gallery, Austin, 1996, 97, 98, 99, 2000, Ga. Art Mus., U. Ga., Athens, 1997, Marion Koogler McNay Art Mus., San Antonio, 1997, 98, 99, 2000, Mus. of Big Bend, Sul Ross State U., Alpine, Tex., 1998, Nancy Wilson Scanlon Gallery, Helms Fine Art Ctr., Austin, 1999, Austin Mus. Art, 2000. Mem. Nat. Soc. Lit.. and Arts, Austin Mus. of Art, Tex. Art Edn. Assn., Phi Kappa Phi. Home: 914 Calithea Rd Austin TX 78746-2716

FEARS, JESSE RUFUS, historian, educator, academic dean; b. Atlanta, Ga., Mar. 7, 1945; s. Emory Binford Fears; m. Charlene Louise Bauer, July 6, 19 66; children: Laura Elizabeth, Jesse Rufus IV. BA summa cum laude, Emory U., 1966; MA, Harvard U., 1967, PhD, 1971. Asst. prof. classical langs. Tulane U., New Orleans, 1971-72; asst. prof. history Indiana U., Bloomington, 1972-75, assoc. prof. history, 1975-80, prof. history, 1980-86; prof., chair classical studies Boston U., 1986-90, assoc. dean Coll. Liberal Arts, 1987-89, dir. humanities found., 1988-90; dean Coll. Arts and Scis. U. Okla., Norman, 1990-92, prof. Classics, 1990—, G.T. and Libby Blankenship prof. history of liberty, 1992—, dir. Ctr. for History of Liberty, 1992—. Author: Princeps A Diis Electus, 1977, (monographs) The Cult of Jupiter, 1981, The Theology of Victory, 1981, The Cult of Virtues, 1981; editor: (3 vols.) Selected Writings/Lord Acton, 1985-88; contbr. chpts. to books, numerous articles to profl. jours. Bd. dirs. Okla. Sch. Sci./Math., Oklahoma City, 1990—. Recipient Judah P. Benjamin award; Danforth fellow Danforth Found., 1966-71; fellow Am. Acad. in Rome, 1969-71, Guggenheim Found., 1976-77, Howard Found., 1977-78, Alexander Von Humboldt, 1977-78, 80-81, Ctr. for History of Freedom, Wash. U., 1989-90; grantee Am. Philos. Soc., 1972, 79, NEH, 1974, Am. Coun. Learned Soc., 1979, Woodrow Wilson, 1983, Kerr Found., 1994, 99, Zarrow Found., 2000. Mem. AAUP, Am. Philol. Assn., Classical Assn. Middle West and South, Archaeol. Inst. of Am., Phi Beta Kappa, Golden Key Nat. Honor Soc. Office: U Okla Dept Classics Ctr History of Liberty Kaufman Hall Norman OK 73019

FEAST, MICHAEL WILLIAM, astronomer, researcher; b. Deal, Kent, Eng., Dec. 29, 1926; s. Frederick and Dorothy Marguerite (Knight) F.; m. Elizabeth Constance Maskew, Apr. 28, 1962; 3 children. PhD, U. London, 1949; DSc (hon.), U. Cape Town, 1993. Fellow Nat. Rsch. Coun., Ottawa, Can., 1949-51; astronomer Radcliffe Obs., Pretoria, South Africa, 1952-74; astronomer South African Astronomical Obs., Cape Town, 1974-76, dir., 1976-92; hon. prof. U. Cape Town, 1983—. Contbr. articles to profl. jours. Fellow Royal Soc. South Africa (gen. sec. 1985-86, treas. and v.p. 1989-90); mem Acad. Sci. of South Africa, Internat. Astronomy Union (v.p. 1979-85, pres. commn. on stellar spectra 1967-70, pres. commn. on variable stars 1970-76), Royal Astronomy Soc. (assoc., editor 1993—), South Africa Inst. Physics (coun. 1993-99, De BeersGold medal 1992), South Africa Astronomy Soc. (past pres., Gill medal 1983). Home: 12 Meadow Rd, Rosebank 7700, South Africa Office: U Cape Town, Astronomy Dept, Rondebosch 7701, South Africa

FEATHER, NORMAN THOMAS, psychology educator, researcher; b. Sydney, NSW, Australia, July 27, 1930; s. Thomas William and Lilian (England) F.; m. Daryl Raynes; children: Mark William, Norman. BA, U. Sydney, Armidale, Australia, 1951, diploma in edn., 1952; MA with honors, U. New Eng., Armidale, Australia, 1958; PhD, U. Mich., 1960. From lectr. to assoc. prof. U. New Eng., Armidale, 1952-67; found. prof. psychology The Flinders U. South Australia, Adelaide, 1968-2000; prof. emeritus, 2000—; vis. prof. U. Mich., Ann Arbor, 1962, 67, Harvard U., 1974; del. in humanities and social scis. to China as guest of Chinese Govt., 1980. Author: Values in Education and Society, 1975, The Psychological Impact of Unemployment, 1990, Values, Achievement, and Justice, 1999; editor: Expectations and Actions, 1982, Australian Psychology, 1985, (with John W. Atkinson) A Theory of Achievement Motivation, 1966; contbr. more than 200 articles to profl. jours. Fulbright scholar, 1958, 67; grantee Brit. Coun., 1984, 87; recipient Disting. Alumni award U. New Eng., 1998. Fellow Australian Psychol. Soc. (pres. 1978-79, Disting. Sci. Contbn. award 1999), Acad. Social Scis. in Australia, Soc. for Psychol. Study of Social Issues, Soc. for Personality and Social Psychology. Avocations: music, art, tennis, swimming. Home: 15 High St Unley Park, Adelaide SA 5061, Australia Office: The Flinders U S Australia, Sch Psychology GPO Box 2100, Adelaide SA 5001, Australia

FEATHER, PETER MILTON, economist, researcher; b. Madison, Wis., Feb. 3, 1963; s. Milton S. and Betty L. F.; m. Kelli L. Dannar, Apr. 15, 1987 (div. June 1992). BS, U. Mo., 1985, MS, 1988; PhD, U. Minn., 1992. Resource economist Econ. Rsch. Svc. USDA, Washington, 1992—. Contbr. articles to profl. jours. Mem. Am. Agrl. Econs. Assn., Assn. Environ. and Resource Economists. Avocations: bicycling. Home: 912 Plum St SW Vienna VA 22180-6505 Office: USDA-ERS 1800 M St NW Washington DC 20036-5802

FEATHERMAN, BERNARD, steel company executive; b. May 3, 1929; m. Sandra Green, May 29, 1958; children: Andrew C., John James. BS, Temple U., 1951; postgrad., Grad. Bus. Sch., 1951-52, Law Sch., 1952-54, Wharton Sch., U. Pa., 1965-66. Chmn. bd. dirs. Western Metal Bed Co., Phila., 1978-86; with CIATEQ USA, Inc., 1995-98; dir. Pa. Steel and Aluminum Corp. (now Pa. Steel Corp.), Bensalem, Pa., 1972—. Wardwell Retirement Complex, Saco, Maine, 1998—, Counselling Svcs., Inc., Saco, 1998—, Newsletter Pub. Co., Phila. Contbr. articles to profl. jours.; inventor electronics locking locker. Mem. exec. bd. Southeast chpt. Nat. Found. March of Dimes, 1969-82, vice-chmn., 1978-80; pres. Phila. Assn. for Retarded Citizens, 1975-77, trustee, 1983-96; trustee Phila. Devel. Disabilities Corp., 1991-96, Equity 591 F8AM, 1990-92; chmn. Mayor's Adv. Com. on Mental Health-Mental Retardation, Phila., 1979-92, bd. dirs. 1993; mem. tax policy and budget rev. com. City of Phila., fiscal adv. com., 1990; bd. dirs. Costar, Inc., 1989-92; co-chmn. Mayor's Sml. Bus. Adv. Com., Phila., 1979-92, mem., 1979-95; del. White House Conf. on Sml. Bus., 1980, Pa. del., 1995, vice-chmn., 1986; chmn. sml. bus. coun. Dem. Nat. Com., 1982-84; fin. chmn. Pa. Dem. Orgn., 1985-86; mem. adv. bd. Coll. Liberal Arts and Scis., Temple U., 1982-91, chmn. incubator program, 1989-91, chmn. Entrepreneurial Inst., 1990; co-dir. Enterpreneurial Inst. U. New Eng., 1996-98; adv. bd. West Chester (Pa.) State U. Bus. Sch., 1986-87, Frankford Hosp., 1983—; steering com. entrepreneurial forum Drexel U. Bus. Sch., 1988-91; chmn. 3d Congl. Sml. Bus. Coun., Phila., 1984-88; bd. dirs. Phila. Citywide Devel. Corp., 1984-96; bd. dirs. Phila. Loan Fund, Inc., 1987-88. Recipient award of appreciation Sml. Bus. Coun., Dem. Nat. Com., 1983; Gold medal of Honor Adult Trainees Found., Phila., 1976; citation White House Conf. on Sml. Bus., 1980; named Entrepreneur of Yr. Mid Atlantic Region Supporter of Entrepreneurship, 1990, Ea. Pa. Sml. Bus. Adv. of Yr. SBA, 1991. Mem. Assn. of Steel Distbrs. (nat. pres. 1975-76, 86-87, named Steel Distbr. of Yr. 1976), Inst. Am. Entrepreneurs (life), Shelving Mfrs. Assn. (nat. chmn. 1977-78), Pa. Soc., Assn. Steel Distbrs. (nat. pres. 1975-76, 86-87, Hunting Park-Germantown Bus. Assn. (pres. 1986-96), Rotary, Masons (trustee), B'nai Brith (pres. 1980-82, Nat. Youth Svcs. award Quaker City lodge 1985). Home: PO Box 428A Kennebunkport ME 04046-1728

FEATHERMAN, SANDRA, university president, political science educator; b. Phila., Apr. 14, 1934; d. Albert N. and Rebe (Burd) Green; m. Bernard Featherman, Mar. 29, 1958; children: Andrew Charles, John James. BA, U. Pa., 1955, MA, 1978, PhD, 1978. Asst. prof. dept. polit. sci. Temple U., Phila., 1978-84, assoc. prof., 1984-91, asst. to pres., 1986-89, pres. faculty senate, 1985-86, dir. Ctr. Pub. Policy, 1986-91; vice chancellor acad. adminstrn., prof. polit. sci. U. Minn., Duluth, 1991-95; pres. U. New Eng., Biddeford, Maine, 1995—. Author: Jews, Black and Ethnics, 1979, Race and Politics at the Millenium, 2000; contbr. articles to profl. jours. Bd. dirs. Citizens Com. Pub. Edn. Phila., 1977-89, pres., 1979-81; pres. Pa. Fedn. C.C.; trustee C.C. Phila., 1970-92, chmn. bd. trustees, 1984-86; life trustee, v.p. Samuel Fels Found., 1978—; bd. dirs. United Way SE Pa., 1977-89, United Way Pa., 1981-84, Maine Civil Liberties Union, 1995-97, U. New Eng., Guld of Maine Aquarium; pres. Girls Clubs Am., Phila., 1971-73, mem. nat. bd., 1971-74; mem. Pa. Coun. Arts, 1979-83; nat. bd. dirs. Women and Founds.-Corp. Philanthropy, 1986-91; v.p. Jewish Cmty. Rels. Coun., 1982-89; spkr. Commonwealth Pa. Humanities Coun., 1988, 90, 91; bd. govs., mem. exec. com. Am. Assn. Colls. Osteopathic Medicine, also sec.; bd. dirs. Kennebec Girl Scout Coun. Recipient Brooks Graves award Pa. Polit. Sci. Assn., 1982, City of Phila. Cmty. Svc. award, 1984, Women's Achievement award YWCA, 1989, Adminstr. of Yr. award minn. Women in Higher Edn., 1994. Mem. AAUW (bd. dirs. Phila. chpt. 1975-78, 80-91, pres. 1984-86, nat. chair internat. fellowships panel 1987-91, nat bd. dirs. 1993—, Outstanding Woman award 1986), Am. Polit. Sci. Assn., Maine Ind. Colls. Assn. (pres. 1998—), Greater Portland Alliance Colls. and Univs. (pres. 1997-98), Maine Ind. Colls. Assn. (pres. 1998—). Office: U New Eng Hills Beach Rd Biddeford ME 04005-9526

FEATHERSTONE, WILLIAM EDWARD, geodesy educator; b. Clatterbridge, U.K., Aug. 14, 1967; s. James Alfred Featherstone and Barbara Elizabeth (Thomson) Owen; m. Annabel Kate Davies, Jan. 9, 1998; 1 child, Thomas George. BSc with honors, U. Newcastle-upon Tyne, 1988; DPhil, U. Oxford, 1992. Tutor U. Oxford, 1985-88; sr. rsch. fellow Curtin U. of Tech., Australia, 1992-93, lectr., 1993-94, sr. lectr., 1994-97, assoc. prof., 1998—; vis. prof. De Montfort U., Leicester, Eng., 1999—; cons. in field; councillor Inst. of Surveyors, Australia, 1996-99; acad. bd. Curtin U. Tech., 1997—. Author: GPS Surveying, 1996, The Role of the Earth's Gravity Field in Surveying, 1997. Harper-Somers fellow U. Newcastle, 1998; grantee Australian Rsch. Coun., 1992—. Fellow Royal Astronomical Soc., Internat. Assn. Geodesy; mem. Australasian Surveying and Mapping Lectrs. Assn. (pres. 1995—), Mapping Sci. Inst., Inst. Engring. Surveyors. Avocation: squash raquets. Home: 30 Potts St, Melville Heights, Perth 6156, Australia Office: Curtin U Tech, Kent St Bentley, Perth 6052, Australia

FEAVEARYEAR, JOHN EDGAR, aerospace systems engineer; b. London, Dec. 28, 1933; arrived in U.S., 1959; s. Albert Edgar and Ruby Lousa (Castleton) F.; m. Kate Elizabeth Pert Feavearyear, July 27, 1957; children: Sara, Susan, Simon, David. MA, Trinity Coll., Cambridge, Eng., 1958; BA, 1956. Engr. IBM, 1965-72; project mgr., 1972-82, functional mgr., 1982-91; engring. dir. Eng., 1991-94; project dir. Loral, Eng., 1994-96; tech. dir. Lockheed Martin Fed. Sys., Owego, N.Y., Eng., 1996-2000; dir. advanced programs aerospace sys. Lockheed Martin Fed. Sys., Owego, N.Y., 2000—; tech. bd. mem. Soc. British Aerospace Cos., London, 1995-99. Mem. IEEE (sr.). Republican. Episcopalean. Home: 12 King Point Cir S Owego NY 13827-1146 Office: Lockheed Martin Int Sys PO Box 41 Owego NY 13827-0041

FEAZELL, VIC, lawyer; b. Monroe, La., June 8, 1951; 1 child, Gregory Victor. BA, Mary Hardin Baylor Coll., 1972; JD, Baylor U., 1979. Bar: Tex. 1979, U.S. Ct. Appeals (5th cir.) 1988, U.S. Dist. Ct. (no. dist) 1988, U.S. Dist. Ct. (so. dist), 1989. Dir. drug abuse treatment program Mental Health-Mental Retardation, Waco, Tex., 1975-79; pvt. practice Waco, 1979-82; dist. atty. McLennan County, Tex., 1983-88; pvt. practice Austin, Tex., 1989-94; of counsel Rosenthal and Watson, Austin, 1995—; pres. McLennan County Peace Officers Assn., Waco, 1984-87; pro bono def. counsel Henry Lee Lucas, 1989-94; expert legal corr. O.J. Simpson Trial, KTBC T.V. Primary character: Careless Whispers, 1986 (Edgar award 1986); exec. prodr. Rhinos the Movie, Natural Selection, Blood Sweat and Teeth, Rage in the Cage; pres. One Horn Prodns.; contbr. articles to profl. jours. Del. State Dem. Conv., Houston, 1988. Named Outstanding Young Alumni, U. Mary Hardin Baylor, Belton, Tex., 1985, Peace Officer of Yr., Waco JC's, 1986. Mem. Nat. Assn. Criminal Def. Lawyers (life), Tex. Trial Laywers Assn., Tex. Criminal Def. Lawyers Assn., State Bar Tex., Bar of U.S. Fifth Cir. Avocation: flim making. E-mail: vic@vicfeazell.com.

FECANIN, MARY ELLEN, secondary education educator; b. Passaic, N.J., Sept. 20, 1963; d. Ernest J. and Mary E. (Enerson) F. BS, Douglas Coll., 1985; MA, Montclair State Coll., 1989. Tchr. biology, sci. dept. chairperson St. Mary H.S., Rutherford, N.J.; tchr. sci., chairperson sci. dept. St. Rose H.S., Belmar, N.J., 1990-97, Manchester Twp. High Sch., 1997—. Frances B. L'Hommedieu Acad. scholar, Douglass Coll. Essay scholar. Mem. Assn. for Supervision and Curriculum Devel., N.J. Sci. Tchrs. Assn., Nat. Cath. Edn. Assn., N.J. Edn. Assn., Omicron Nu. Home: 33 Decatur Ave Seaside Park NJ 08752-1250

FEDA, JAROSLAV, soil scientist; b. Ostrava, Moravia, Czech Republic, Mar. 5, 1929; s. Frantisek and Helena (Burianová) F.; m. Dagmar Koštálová, Apr. 16, 1955; 1 child, Helena. Engring. Degree, Czech Tech. U., 1953, PhD, 1957; DSc, Czech Acad. Scis., 1986. Asst. prof. Czech Tech. U., Prague, 1951-53, assoc. prof., 1966—; scientist Czech Acad. of Sci., Prague, 1956-69, chief scientist, 1969—, resident coord., 1968-89, head of lab., 1992—; rsch. fellow Czech Acad. Sci., Prague, 1956—; found. expert Škoda works, Ranchi, India, 1961-62; prof. Basrah U., Iraq, 1966-68. Author: (book) Stress in Subsoil, 1978, Mechanics of Particulate Materials, 1982 (Czech Lt. award 1975), Creep of Soils, 1992; contbr. to profl. jours. Sci. mem. Czech. Com., Prague, 1958-81; mem. Czech Union of Civil Engrs., Prague, 1992—. Recipient Czechoslovak Acad. of Sci. award, Prague, 1984, Silver medal of S. Bechyně, Czech Acad. Sci., 1989, others. Mem. Internat. Soc. SMFE (chmn. Czech and Slovak com. 1992-99). Avocations: sports, skiing, mountaineering, bicycling, lit. Office: Inst Theor Appl Mechanics, Prosecka 76, 190 00 Praha 9, Czech Republic

FEDER, ROBERT, lawyer; b. N.Y.C., Nov. 29, 1930; s. Benjamin and Bertha (Bloodstein) F.; m. Marjorie Feder, Dec. 3, 1950; children: Susan E., Judith D., Benjamin D., Jessica R., Abigail M. BA cum laude, CCNY, 1953; LLB, Columbia U., 1953. Bar: N.Y. 1953, U.S. Tax Ct. 1956, U.S. Dist. Ct. (so. dist.) N.Y. 1973. V.p., gen. counsel Presdl. Realty Corp., White Plains, N.Y., 1953-71; ptnr. Cuddy & Feder & Worby, White Plains, 1971—; bd. dirs. Westchester County (N.Y.) Legal Aid Soc., 1972—, pres., 1974-78; adj. prof. sch. bus. Columbia U., 1988-89; bd. dirs. Presdl. Realty Corp. (Amex), Interplex Industries, Inc., Healthstar Network, Inc. Pres., White Plains Community Action Program, 1967-69; bd. dirs. White Plains Hosp. Ctr., 1978—, also sec., treas., chmn. 1992-97; commr. White Plains Housing Authority, 1984—; trustee SUNY-Purchase Coll. Found., 1988—, vice-chmn., 1995—; adj. prof. Pace U. Law Sch., 1985-87. Mem. ABA, N.Y. State Bar Assn., White Plains Bar Assn., Westchester County Bar Assn., Am. Coll. Real Estate Lawyers. Home: 9 Oxford Rd White Plains NY 10605-3602 Office: Cuddy & Feder & Worby 90 Maple Ave White Plains NY 10601-5105

FEDERICI, WILLIAM VITO, newspaper reporter; b. Bklyn., June 22, 1931; s. Theodore and Margaret (DeMaio) F.; m. Arlene Ann McAuliffe, Oct. 1, 1955 (dec.); children: William Theodore, Robert Gerard. Student, Hofstra Coll., 1949-50, St. John's U., 1954-56. With N.Y. Daily News, 1950—, nat. corr., until 1965, spl. reporter, 1965-72, asst. city editor in charge investigations, 1975-79, Bklyn. editor, 1979—; dir. spl. projects Office Spl. State Prosecutor, N.Y.C., 1972-75; exec. dir. corp. affairs Bklyn. Union Gas Co., 1987—. Author series on child abuse which initiated N.Y. laws to protect children, 1969. Served with USN, 1950-54, Korea. Recipient several journalism awards, including George Polk award Long Island U., 1970, Sigma Delta Chi award for met. reporting, 1975.

FEDERICO, PANFILO BENNY, mechanical engineer; b. Pettorano, Aquila, Italy, Aug. 9, 1964; came to U.S., 1979; s. Luigi Pietro and Anna (Federico) F.; m. Nancy Celeste Mills, Feb. 9, 1991; children: Sara Ana, Gabriella, Gino. BSME, Worcester Poly. Inst., 1987, MSME, 1993. Engring. office mgr. GIW, Augusta, Ga., 1997; sr. design engr. MPMW, Mobile, Ala., 1997—. 1st lt. USAR, 1983-91. Mem. ASME, Soc. Automotive Engrs. Republican. Roman Catholic. Home: 13040 State Route 359 Uniontown KY 42461-9702 Office: MPMW 905 S Ann St Mobile AL 36605-4770

FEDERMAN, JACOB, cardiologist; b. Ainring, West Germany, Oct. 31, 1946; arrived in Australia, 1947; s. Chaim and Freda (Kagan) F.; m. Rachel Gerczuk, Jan. 23, 1972; children—Dean Elliot, Simone Lisa. M.B.B.S., U. Melbourne, 1970. Diplomate Australian Bd. Cardiology. Med. intern Royal Melbourne (Australia) Hosp., 1971; med. resident, registrar Alfred Hosp., Melbourne, 1972-74, research fellow cardiology, 1975-77; fellow cardiology Mayo Clinic, Rochester, Minn., 1977-79; cardiologist, cardiology dept. Alfred Hosp., Melbourne, 1979—, resident med. staff, 1979—; tchr. med. students Monash U., 1979—. Contbr. articles to cardiac jours. Nat. Heart Found. Australia travel grantee, 1977. Fellow Royal Australian Coll. Physicians, Am. Coll. Cardiology; mem. Australian Med. Assn., Brit. Med. Assn., Australian and New Zealand Cardiac Soc., Am. Soc. Echocardiography, Australian Soc. Ultrasound in Medicine. Jewish. Avocations: golf, tennis, table tennis, chess. Home: 5 Hart St, Caulfield, Melbourne 3161, Australia Office: Alfred Hosp Cardiology Dept, Commercial Rd Prahran, Melbourne 3181, Australia

FEDIN, ALEXANDER VICTOROVICH, research scientist, educator; b. Kovrov, Russia, Jan. 27, 1960; s. Victor Alexandrovich and Lydia Pavlovna (Zabotina) F.; m. Irina Yureivna Bykova, July 17, 1998; 1 child, Maria Alexandrovna. Degree in engring., Poly. Inst., Kovrov, Russia, 1983; DS Inst. Gen. Physics, Russian Acad. Sci., Moscow, 1994. Engr. JSC Degtyarev

Plant, Kovrov, 1983-87; engr. State Tech. Acad., Kovrov, 1987-91, assoc. prof., 1994-96, head dept., 1996—, chmn. state exam. com., 1998—. Patentee laser devices (4). Mem. trade union com. State Tech. Acad., 1999. NATO grantee, 1999. Home: Schorsa Str House 1 Apt 37, 601900 Kovrov Russia Office: State Tech Acad, 19 Mayakovsky St, 601910 Kovrov Russia

FEDIRKO, VIKTOR MYKOLAJOVYCH, physician, researcher; b. Kamjanka-Buz'ka, Lviv, Ukraine, Oct. 25, 1946; s. Mykola Ivanovych and Ganna Mychajlivna (Krush) F.; m. Ljudmyla Volodymyrivna Sytar, June 5, 1971; 1 child, Natalija Viktorivna. Diploma, Lviv Tech. U., Ukraine, 1969; PhD, Nat. Acad. Scis. of Ukraine, Karpenko Physico/Mech. Inst., 1977, DS, 1991, Sr. Scientist, 1990, Prof., 1993. Scientist Nat. Acad. of Scis. of Ukraine/Physico-Mech. Inst., Ukraine, 1972-79, sr. scientist, 1979-86, chief of lab., 1986-89, head of dept., 1989—; prof. Lviv State Agrl. U., 1994-96, 98-99. Author: (books) Thermal Processing of Titanium and Aluminium Alloys in Vacuum and Inert Environment, 1987, Nitriding of Titanium and Its Alloys, 1995. Avocations: hunting, fishing. Office: Nat Acad Scis Ukraine/Karpe, Phys-Mech Inst/5 Naukova St, 79601 Lviv Ukraine

FEDORE, RONALD J., telecommunications company executive; b. Bklyn., Feb. 19, 1948; s. Francis G. and Sylvia C. (Hornack) F.; m. Dorothy J. Cooke, Sept. 18, 1971; children: Craig, Carolyn, Christopher. BS in Physics, Drexel U., 1971. Sr. systems analyst Cir. F Industries, Trenton, N.J., 1971-74, Gould Inc., Langhorn, Pa., 1974-75; project analyst Catalytic Inc., Phila., 1975-79; mgr. mgmt. info. systems Siemens Info. System, Boca Raton, Fla., 1979-82, mgr. mgmt. info. system devel., 1982-86; project mgr. methods/procedures Tel Plus Comms. Co. div. Siemens, Boca Raton, Fla., 1986-91, mgr. bus. adminstrn., 1991-93; project mgr. Bus. Solutions Rolm, A Siemens Co., Santa Clara, Calif., 1993-95; spl. events v.p. Employee Club, 1993-99; mgr. comms. programs Siemens Bus. Comms. Systems, Inc., 1995-99; mgr. electronic info. delivery Siemens Info. and Comm. Networks, 1999—; export compliance ofcl. Siemens/Tel Plus, Boca Raton, 1986-93, mem. svc. com., 1984-93; rep. to various local charities. Creator, dir. Flamingo Strut parade, 1987-89. Mem. Boca Raton Cmty. Rels. Bd., 1989-91; candidate for Boca Raton City Coun., 1991; mem. site coun. Dublin (Calif.) H.S., 1993-96; mem. parish coun. St. Raymond Ch., 1994-99, pres., 1996-99; mem. Diocesan Pastoral Coun., Oakland Diocese, 1998—. Recipient Outstanding Leadership award, Boca Raton C. of C., 1989, Spl. Svc. cert. U.S. Atomic Energy Comm., 1968; named Person of Yr., Boca Raton C. of C., 1988. Home: 11897 W Vomac Rd Dublin CA 94568-1048 Office: Siemens Info and Comms Networks 4900 Old Ironsides Dr Santa Clara CA 95054-1811

FEDORENKO, OLGA A., physicist; b. Chelyabinsk, Russia, June 4, 1945; d. Alexandr Yegorovich and Zinaida Andreevna F.; m. Yuriy Veniaminovich Kulish, Nov. 24, 1967; children: Elena, Tatyana. Physics, Kharkov State U., Ukraine, 1968; PhD (hon.), Inst. Single Cryst., 1987. Cert. solid state physics. Engr. Inst. Single Crystals, Kharkov, 1969-73, jr. rschr., 1973-88; sr. rschr. Inst. Single Crystals, 1988—. Contbr. articles to profl. jours. Grantee Soros Found., 1993. Mem. Internat. Soc. Optical Enging. Avocations: reading, travel, knitting, needlework. Office Fax: 308349. E-mail: fedorenko@isc.kharkov.com. Office: NTC Inst Single Crystals, 60 Lenin Ave, 61001 Kharkov Ukraine

FEDOROV, A.S., researcher; b. Pushchino, Moscow, Russia, May 11, 1972; s. Sergey and Olga (Zubtsova) F. MS, Moscow State Acad. of Fine Soil Tech., 1996. Rsch. trainee Inst. Soil Sci. and Photosynthesis, Russian Acad. Sci., Pushchino, 1996-98; jr. rschr. Inst. Basic Biol. Problems, Russian Acad. Sci., Pushchino, 1998—. Contbr. articles to profl. jours. Mem. Am. Soc. Microbiology. Office: Inst Basic Biol Problems, Russian Acad Sci, 142290 Pushchino Moscow, Russia

FEDOROV, LEV MIKHAILOVICH, biologist, researcher; b. Toguchin, Russia, Sept. 13, 1951; s. Mikhail Antonovich Fedorov and Valentina Nikolaevna (Tulupova) Bobrova; m. Galina Lukinichna Burlina, Oct. 30, 1976; children: Natalia, Ivan. Degree in qualified biologist, M.V. Lomonosov State U., Moscow, 1982; PhD in Biology, Russian Acad. Scis., Moscow, 1987. Jr. scientist Rsch. Ctr. Med. Genetics, Russian Acad. Med. Scis., Moscow, 1987-90, sr. scientist, 1990-92; postdoctoral fellow Max-Planck Inst. for Immunbiology, Freiburg, Germany, 1993-94, Inst. Med. Radiation and Cell Rsch., U. Wuerzberg, Germany, 1995—. Contbr. articles to profl. jours. Sgt. Soviet Army, 1972-74. Avocations: sports, fishing. Office: Inst Med Rad & Cell Rsch, Versbacher St 5, 97078 Würzburg Bayern, Germany

FEDOROV, MIKHAIL PETROVICH, engineering educator; b. Tallin, USSR, May 11; s. Peter Antoninovich and Natalja Vladimirovna (Orlovskaja) F.; m. Kira Nikolaevna Volodenkova; children: Maria, Peter, Nikolay. MS, State Tech. U., St. Petersburg, 1969, Grand Doctor, 1985, PhD, 1974. Asst. prof. State Tech. U., St. Petersburg, 1969-76, assoc. prof., 1976-86, prof., 1986, dean dept. of hydrotechnics, 1986-96, 1st v.p., 1996—. Author: (textbooks) Principles of Hydraulic and Hydrotechnik Engineering, Ecology for Engineers, 1992, Ecological Engineering, 1995. Recipient medal of honor Govt. of Russian Fedn., 1994, Sign of Honor, Govt. of USSR, 1986. Mem. Internat. Assn. for Hydraulic Rsch., Russian Assn. of Hydrotechnic Engrs. (pres.). Avocation: ice fishing. Office: State Tech Univ, Polytekhnickeskaya Str 29, 195251 Saint Petersburg Russia

FEDOROV, SERGEY MARK, dermatologist, academic administrator; b. Moscow, Aug. 5, 1951. Student, Med. U., Moscow, 1974; PhD, Inst. Dermatology, Moscow, 1989. Scientific worker Inst. Dermatology, Moscow, 1977-88, head dept., 1988—. Author: Laser Treatment in Dermatology, 1996, Immunology in Psoriasis, 1997, Dermatological and Sexual Transmitted Diseases, 1996, Professional Dermatoses, 1997. Mem. Russian Soc. Dermatoveneorology (bd. dirs. 1991—). Avocation: tennis. Home: 12-42 Novinsky Blvd, 121069 Moscow Russia Office: Inst Dermatology, 3 Kozolenko str, 107076 Moscow Russia

FEDOROV, VICTOR VASILIEVICH, library director; b. Krasnogorosk, Russia, Mar. 12, 1947; s. V.V. and E.P. Fedorov; m. Fedorova Galina Ivanovna Efimova, Jan. 31, 1997; children: Dmitrij, Maria. Degree in econs., Leningrad Inst. Fin. & Economy, Russia, 1971, PhD in Econs., 1974. Head deputy editor Country Youth mag., 1980-85; head editor, then dir. Molodaia Gvardia, 1989-97; deputy dir. the Russian State Libr., 1997-98, dir., 1998—. Mem. editl. bd. Biblioteka. Deputy Soviet Pskov region, 1969-77; mem. ctrl. com. Young Communist League, 1977-80; mem. presidium All-Russia Soc. for Nature Protection, 1978-80. Mem. Russian Libr. Assn., Russian Union Journalists. Fax: 095-913-6933. Office: Vozdvizhenka 3/5, Moscow 101000, Russia

FEDOROWSKI, JERZY ANDRZEJ, paleontology educator, university official; b. Brześć n/B., Poland, Sept. 5, 1934; s. Zygmunt and Marianna (Tokarska) F.; m. Mirosława Krystyna Klepacka, Aug. 9, 1955; children: Bożena, Marta, Anna. MS, U. Warsaw, Poland, 1958; PhD in Paleontology, Jagiellonian U., Cracow, Poland, 1963; DSc, A. Mickiewicz U., Poznan, Poland, 1971. Scientist Polish Acad. Scis., Poznan, 1958-70, head lab., 1970-76; head lab. A. Mickiewicz U., 1976-87, prof. paleontology, 1971—, head dept., 1987-90, rector, 1990-96; rsch. assoc. Smithsonian Instn., Washington, 1974; mem. Main Coun. Polish Univs., Warsaw, 1982-85; cons. Can. Geol. Survey, Calgary, Alta., 1986-87; chmn. sci. coun. Inst. Paleobiology, 1990-97. Author monographs; contbr. articles to sci. jours. Head univ. subcomm. Solidarity, 1980-89; mem. Lech Wałesa's Citizens Com., 1989-90. Fellow Smithsonian Instn., 1972. Mem. Internat. Assn. for Study Fossil Cnidaria (pres. 1979-83, v.p. 1983-95), Polish Geol. Soc. (hon.; pres. Poznan br. 1985-91), Polish Acad. Scis. (geol. com. 1990—), Polish Acad. Letters and Arts, Paleontol. Soc. Avocations: wildlife photography, especially flowers, classical music. Home: Lisowskiego 6/1, 61-606 Poznań Poland Office: Inst Geol Adam Mickiewicz U, Makow Polnych 16, 61-606 Poznan Poland

FEDORSKI, JERZY, horse genetics educator, researcher; b. Wroclaw, Poland, Mar. 8, 1947; s. Zbigniew and Maria (Konopinska) F.; m. Hanna Graczyk, June 3, 1975; children: Aleksandra, Zbigniew. MSc, U. Wroclaw, 1970, DSc, 1975. Asst. U. Wroclaw, 1970-74, adj., 1975-80; jr. lectr. U. Szczecin (Poland), 1981-87, lectr., 1988-89; lectr. U. Christian-Albrechts, Kiel, Fed. Republic of Germany, 1991-92; entrepreneur, 1993—. Author: Rearing Horses, 1977, Practising with Rearing Horses, 1980. Roman Catholic. Home: Dorfstrasse 21 A, 24878 Jagel Germany

FEDORTSEVA, REGINA FEDOROVNA, biologist; b. Leningrad, Russia, Mar. 26, 1940; d. Fedor Alekseevitch and Elfrida Ivanovna (Trummal) Kazakov; m. Oleg Evgenjevitch Fedortsev, Mar. 8, 1964. MS, U. Leningrad, Russia, 1966; PhD in Biology, Inst. Cytology Acad. Sci., Leningrad, 1974. Jr. rschr. Inst. Cytology, Leningrad, Russia, 1972-82; sr. rschr. Inst. Cytology, St. Petersburg, Russia, 1982-93; head lab., sr. scientific rschr. All-Russian Ctr. Ecol. Biol. Medicine, St. Petersburg, Russia, 1993-97, All-Russian Ctr. Emergency & Radiation Medicine, St. Petersburg, Russia, 1997—; mem. acad. bd. Inst. Cytology, 1972-82. Contbr. articles to profl. jours.; inventor in field. Mem. European Cytogeneticists Assn., European Soc. Human Genetics, Internat. Soc. Hematology. Avocation: collecting Easter eggs. Home: 74 Cryboedova Apt 31, 190068 Saint Petersburg Russia Office: All Russian Ctr, 4/2 Lebedeva St, 194044 Saint Petersburg Russia

FEDOSOV, EUGENI ALEXANDROVICH, aviation system company executive; b. Moscow, May 14, 1929; s. Alexander Ephimovich F. and Nadezda Anempodistovna Smirnova; m. Lidia Petrovna Vasilyeva, July 23, 1955; 1 child, Verzun Vera Eugenievna. Diploma, Moscow High Tech. U., 1952; PhD in Tech. Scis., Moscow, 1967, Prof. in Tech. Scis., 1969. Sr. lab. technician Moscow High Tech. U., 1953-56; head dept. GosNIIAS, Moscow, 1956-59, dep. dir., 1959-70, dir. gen., 1970—; mem. scientific and tech. bd. of the pres. Co-author: Dynamics of anlaog linear systems with determined and random parameters, 1974, Self-Guided Systems Design, 1975, Terminal Location Control Systems in Counteracting Environment, 1989, Aircraft Building of Russia, 1995, Dynamic Design of Automatic Monoeuverable Aircraft Control Systems, 1997, Intellectual Control of Dynamic Systems, 2000. Dep. Moscow City Coun., 1970-74, 74-78, 78-82. Recipient Order of the Badge of Honour, 1966, Order of Lenin, 1971, 83, Lenin prize, 1976, Hero of Socialist Labour, 1983, Gold Medal, 1983. Mem. Russian Acad. Scis. (chmn. scientific bd. mech. engring., echs and control processes dept., academician, sec. dep., gen. editor Control Systems theory jour., Big Gold medal of academician petrov B.N. 1986). Avocations: tennis. Office: GosNIIAS, 7 Victorenko St, 125319 Moscow Russia

FEDOTOV, VASILIY IVANOVICH, technical specialist; b. Mariupol, Ukraine, Oct. 15, 1941; s. Ivan Efimovich and Feodosiya (Rozhchenko) F.; m. Marina Vladimirovna Borislavskaya, Feb. 13, 1971; Andrey, Alina. Grad., Poly. Inst., Kiev, Ukraine, 1965, postgrad., 1971; PhD, Polit. Inst., Kiev, 1975. Sci. assoc. Sr. Poly. Inst., Kiev, 1971-78, Sr. Agrl. Acad., Kiev, 1978-87; chief dept. Inst. Nipifeft, Niznevartovsk, Russia, 1987-92; main specialist Obyedinenie Neftepribor, Kiev, 1992—. Patentee in field. Mem. N.Y. Acad. Scis. Avocations: music, sports, books. Home: Rusanovskiy Blvd 1 ky 111, 02154 Kiev 154, Ukraine Office: Obyedinene Neftpribor, Lenina 17/2 Kv 175, 626440 Nirnevartovsk Russia

FEDROWITZ, CHRISTIAN HARRY, electrical engineer, educator; b. Herchweiler, Kusel, Germany, Dec. 29, 1960; s. Gerhard Josef and Elisabeth Maria F.; m. Heike Mueller, July 7, 1989; children: Amelie Sophie, Daniel Maximilian. Diploma in engring., U. Siegen, Germany, 1987, DEng., 1994. Rsch. asst. U. Siegen, 1987-95, sr. lectr. data processing, 1995—, head rsch. group, 1995—; pres. DIMAS Digital Mfg. Svcs. GmbH, Siegen, 1994—; spkr. in field. Author: PC-based Offline Programming, 1994. Mem. IEEE, Verein Deutscher Ingenieure, Gesellschaft Informatik, Assn. Computing Machines, Arbeitsgemeinschaft Simulation. Office: U Siegen FB 12 PD, Hoelderlinstrasse 3, D 57068 Siegen NRW, Germany

FEDULIN, ALEKSANDER ALEKSEEVICH, historian, educator; b. Moscow, Nov. 25, 1959; s. Aleksei Egorovich and Lidiya Andreevna (Kovaliova) F. Grad., Moscow State Hist. and Archive Inst., 1985, postgrad., 1987-89. Chief ednl. dept. Moscow State Hist. and Archieves Inst., 1989-91; dean of faculty Moscow State Acad. of Svc., 1991, vice rector Rector Inst. of Tourism and Hospitality, 1991-98; vis. prof. Ind. U., 1990-91. Author: Foundation and Development of the Social Partnership in Russia, 1999, The Foreign Experience of the Social Partnership and Possibilities of its Adoption to Russian Reality, 1999. Grantee IREX, 1990. Avocations: listening to music (clarinet). Home: Vasilia Petuskova Str 7-56, Moscow Russia Office: Inst Tourism/Hospitality, 11 Botanicheskaya Str, 127427 Moscow Russia

FEDULINA, TATIANA GERMANOVNA, chemist; b. Leningrad, Russia, Oct. 19, 1951; d. German Waxman and Elisaveta Ekimova; m. Mikhail Alekseevich Fedulin, Jan. 4, 1980; 1 child, Andrew. Diploma, Leningrad State U., 1973; PhD, Acad. Forestry, Leningrad, 1986. From jr. rschr. to assoc. prof. Acad. Forestry Leningrad, 1973—. Office: St Petersburg Acad Forestry, Institutsky per 5, 194021 Saint Petersburg Russia

FEES, JAMES RICHARD, investment banker, corporate director, entrepreneur; b. Fairbury, Nebr., Sept. 21, 1931; s. Robert Anthony and Mildred Pauline (Holtz) F.; m. Francine; children: Christina Marie, Eric (dec.). BA, U. Notre Dame, 1957; diplom Arabic, Georgetown U., 1959; diploma French, Alliance Francaise, Paris, 1965. Diplomat Dept. State, Washington, Arab countries, Switzerland, 1960-80; CEO Tradeco, Ltd., Geneva, Nassau, 1980-96; chmn. Tradeco Group, Ltd., London, Beijing, The Hague, 1998—; pres. 100 Internat., London, 1998—; mem. bd. advisors Union Bank, Algiers, 1994—; bd. dirs. Bd. Walk A.G., Zug, Switzerland, 1996—; ptnr. Merchant Ivory Fin. Ptnrs. LDC, 1994-96, Tradeco Software Techs., Ltd., London; chmn. Tradeco Techs., Ltd., Brit. V.I., 2000—; chmn., founder Boardwalk Ltd., Bermuda, 2000—. Mem. Rep. Senatorial Inner Circle, Washington, 1981—, founder Rep. Presdl. Group, 1982—, internat. chmn. Reps. Abroad, 1987-89; bd. dirs. Reps. Abroad, 1984-93, bd. advisors 1994-96; dir. Federated League Ams. Around the Globe, 1991-93; prodr. Sovereign Nation Conf. World Peace and Good Health, Plymouth, Mass., 2000. Served with AUS, 1953-55. Mem. World Econ. Forum., Am. Club (Brussels pres. 1991, also Geneva). Roman Catholic. Fax: 44-207-546-8570. E-mail: jrfees@tradecogroup.com. Office: Tradeco Group Ltd, 10 Stratton St, London W1X 5FD, England

FEFFERMAN, HILBERT, government official, lawyer; b. N.Y.C., June 5, 1913; s. Jacob and Sarah F.; m. Helen Libby Relkin, June 16, 1940. BS, NYU, 1934; JD, Harvard U., 1937. Bar: N.Y. 1938, U.S. Supreme Ct. 1953. Pvt. practice N.Y.C., 1938-41; atty. U.S. Housing and Home Fin. Agy., Washington, 1941-59, asst. gen. counsel for legislation, 1960-62, assoc. gen. counsel for ops., 1962-67; chief legislative counsel HUD, Washington, 1967-72; cons. Housing and Devel. Legislation, Bethesda, Md., 1973—; lectr., vis. prof. city planning MIT, Cambridge, Mass., 1973-76. Contbr. articles to profl. jours. Recipient Disting. Svc. award HUD, 1968. Home and Office: 5661 Bent Branch Rd Bethesda MD 20816-1049

FEHER, ISTVAN M., philosopher, educator; b. Budapest, Hungary, 1950; s. Miklos Feher and Magda Herzfeld. MA, ELTE U., Budapest, 1974, ELTE U., Budapest, 1977; PhD, ELTE U., Budapest, 1979; DSc, Acad. Scis., Budapest, 1990. Rsch. asst. ELTE U., 1977-81, asst. prof., 1981-87, assoc. prof., 1987-92, prof., 1992—, head dept., 1990-97, dir. grad. program hermeneutics, 1992—. Author: Jean-Paul Sartre, 1980, Martin Heidegger, 1984, 2d edit., 1992, On the Meaning of Life: Between Rationalism and Irrationalism, 1991, Heidegger and Scepticism: From Sceptical Doubt to Hermeneutic Question, 1998; editor: Wege and Irrwege des neuren Umganges mit Heideggers Werk, 1991, Heidegger, The Concept of Time, 1992, Sartre, on Liberty, 1992. Husserl, Philosophy as Strict Science, 1993; coeditor: Zeit und Freiheit, 1999. Grantee Croce Found., Naples, Italy, 1983-84, Humboldt Found., Bochum, Germany, 1986-87, Tubingen, Germany, 1996, Am. Coun. Learned Socs. U. Va., 1992-93, German Acad. Exch. Svc., Munich, 1986; hon. mem. Centro Studi Umanistici, Calabria, Italy, 1990. Mem. Hungarian Acad. Scis. (mem. philosophy com.), Hungarian Phil. Assn. (gen. sec. 1990-95), Internat. Schelling Soc. (sci. adv. bd. 1986—), Heidegger Studies (sci. adv. bd. 1989—), Mesotes Itinerari Filosofi (sci. adv. bd. 1991—), Internat. Soc. Hermeneutics & Sci. (sci. adv. bd. 1994—), German-Hungarian Soc. Philosophy (pres. 1995—). Office: ELTE U Philosphy Dept, PO Box 107, H-1364 Budapest Hungary

FEHÉR, OTTÓ, management consultant; b. Budapest, Hungary, Apr. 19, 1954; s. Imre and Anna (Berkes) F.; m. Margit Surányi, Mar. 15, 1985. Diploma in vehicle engring., Tech. Coll. Transport-Comm., Budapest, 1975; diploma in sys. analysis engring., Tech. U. Heavy Industry, Dunaujváros, Hungary, 1979. Cert. quality mgmt. sys. engr. Plant engr. IKARUS Co., Budapest, 1975-79; mgmt. cons. SZENZOR Ltd., Budapest, 1979-87, Coopsys. Ltd., Budapest, 1987-91; dir. SIRIUS Ltd., Budapest, 1991—; lectr. Tsukuba (Japan) U., 1990; seminar lectr. ALL-Russia Inst. Light Alloys, Moscow, 1994, 97; award com. Internat. Inst. for Applied Sys. Analysis-Shoji Shiba, Budapest, 1995—. Co-author: TQM Handbooks, 1989, 91; contbr. articles to profl. jours. Mem. Hungarian Assn. for Overseas Tech. Scholarship Soc. (pres. 1990-96), Hungarian Quality Club. Avocation: mind technology development. Office: SIRIUS Ltd, Laborc köz 25/A, 1037 Budapest Hungary

FEHÉR, OTTÓ, retired physiologist; b. Debrecen, Hungary, Feb. 4, 1927; s. Andor Fehér and Erzsébet Nagy; m. Márta Jókay, 1948 (div. 1959); children: Zsigmond, Péter; m. Anna Szabo, 1959 (div. 1973); 1 child, Zsófia; m. Gabriella Könyves, 1975; 1 child, Andrea. MD, U. Med. Sch., Debrecen, 1951, clin. lab. specialist, 1962. Med. diplomate. Asst. dept. physiology U. Med. Sch., Debrecen, 1951-61, lectr. dept. physiology, 1962-67; prof. J.A. Univ., Szeged, 1967-96; ret., 1996; dir. dept. Comparative Physiology, Szeged, 1967-88. Co-author: (with Gy Adám) Textbook of Comparative Physiology (2 edits.), Practical Exercises in Comparative Physiology; contbr. over 100 articles to profl. jours. Recipient Acad. prize Hungarian Acad. Scis., 1977. Mem. Hungarian Physiol. Soc. (presdl.), Hungarian Neurosci. Soc., Hungarian Biol. Soc. Home: Sarkantyu u 39, H-6771 Szeged Hungary

FEHLING, JÜRGEN DETLEV, classics educator; b. Berlin-Zehlendorf, Berlin, Germany, June 10, 1929; s. August Wilhelm and Anna Margarete (Bahr) F.; m. Antje (Gerfin), Mar. 16, 1968; children: Ludwig Wilhelm, Ludmilla. PhD in Classics, U. Kiel, Germany, 1955, Habilitation, 1964. Sci. asst. U. Kiel, 1956-66, lectr. classics, 1966-70, prof., 1970—. Author: Wiederholungsfiguren, 1969, Quellenangaben Herodots, 1971 (English edit. 1989), Ethologische Überlegungen, 1974, Amor und Psyche, 1977, Die 7 Weisen und die frühgriechische Chronologie, 1985, Ursprüngliche Geschichte vom Fall Trojas, 1991, Materie u. Weltbau in d. Zeit der frühen Vorsokr., Wirklichkeit u. Tradition, 1994. Mem. Mommsen Gesellschaft, Soc. Linguistica Europaea. Avocations: languages, zoology. Office: U Kiel Inst Altertumskunde, Leibnizstrasse 8, D-24098 Kiel Germany

FEHLMANN, RICHARD, mathematician; b. Schöftland, Aargau, Switzerland, Feb. 13, 1953; s. Kurt and Doris (Vollenwyder) F. PhD, U. Zurich, Switzerland, 1980. Lehrbeauftragter U. Zurich, 1984-85; assoc. prof. U. Jyvaskyla, Finland, 1985; guest mathematician U. Helsinki, Finland, 1986-87; rschr. Nokia Rsch. Ctr., Helsinki, 1988-95, prin. scientist, 1995—; vis. prof. U. Minn., 1981-82. Mem. Am. Math Soc., Suomen Matemaattinen Yhdistys. Office: Nokia Rsch Ctr, PO Box 407, 00045 Nokia Group Helsinki, Finland

FEHR, GREGORY PARIS, marketing and distribution company executive; b. Urbana, Ill., Nov. 10, 1943; s. Orval Joachim and Cuba Lucile (Paris) F.; m. Sharon Louise Burba, Jan. 21, 1965 (div. Jan. 1975); children: Kristina K., Gregory Tyson Howard; m. Kathleen Lorretta Meyers, Aug. 10, 1990. BS in Indsl. Engring., Okla. U., 1967; MBA, Drake U., 1977. Registered profl. mech. engr. Iowa, Okla., Ala.; cert. corrosion technologist. From engr. to sr. project engr. Fisher Controls Co., Marshalltown, Iowa, 1967-77; fgn. liaison GE, Portland, Maine, 1977-79; gen. mgr. Arabian Am. Oil Co., Dhahran, Saudi Arabia, 1979-81; v.p. Oil Tech. Svcs., Houston, 1981-85; mgr. materials engring. Standard Oil Prodn. Co., Houston, 1985-86; mgr. nuclear products Wyle Labs., Huntsville, Ala., 1986-88; sr. materials engr. Sci. Applications Internat., Las Vegas, Nev., 1988-96; v.p. GPF Mktg. and Distbn., Las Vegas, 1988—; sr. project mgr. Converse Cons. S.W., Inc., Las Vegas, 1996—; cons. task groups Am. Petroleum Inst., 1983-86, Electric Power Rsch. Inst., San Mateo, Calif., 1986-89; chmn. employee adv. coun. Sci. Applications Internat., Las Vegas, 1992. Contbr. articles and tech. papers to profl. jours. Pres. Marshalltown Tennis Assn., 1972-73; head swim coach YMCA/YWCA, Marshalltown, 1973-74; mem. adv. bd. Marshalltown C.C., 1975. Mem. NSPE, ASME, Nat. Assn. Corrosion Engrs., Am. Petroleum Inst., Am. Soc. Nondestructive Testing. Avocations: skiing, scuba diving, sailing, photography.

FEHR, MANFRED, engineering educator, researcher; b. Jena, Thuringen, Germany, Mar. 25, 1936; arrived in Can., 1961; arrived in Brazil, 1978; s. Kurt and Elisabeth (Haase) F.; m. Giomar Esther Yemail, Oct. 30, 1971; children: Mario, Monica. BS, Laval U., Québec, Can., 1967, PhD, 1977; MS, U. Alta. (Can.), Edmonton, 1969. Registered profl. engr. Québec, Alta., São Paulo, Minas Gerais (Brazil). Process engr. Noranda Mines, Valleyfield, Can., 1967; lectr. Univ. Indsl. de Santander, Bucaramanga, Colombia, 1969-72, Univ. Cen. Venezuela, Caracas, 1972-73, Inst. Algérien du Pétrole, Algiers, Algeria, 1977-78; asst. prof. Unicamp, Campinas, Brazil, 1978-82; mktg. mgr. Codetec, Campinas, Brazil, 1980-81; postdoct. fellow Kungliga Tekniska Hogskolan, Stockholm, 1990; rsch. engr. Canmet, Montreal, 1992-93; prof. U. Fed. de Uberlandia, Uberlandia, Brazil, 1982—; cons. Can. U. Svc. Overseas, 1972, Codetec, Brazil, 1980, Styrelsen Teknisk Utveckling, Stockholm, 1990, City Hall, Uberlandia, Brazil, 1992, Hydro Québec, Montreal, 1992-93, Min. Edn., Brasilia, Brazil, 1992-95, Gesellschaft fuer technische Zusammenarbeit, Eschborn, Germany, 1987, Environ. Protection Agy., Araguari, Brazil, 1997. Author: Reasons and Procedures For Staff Evaluation, 1995; contbr. over 180 articles to jours. and congress procs. consular warden Canadian Embassy, Brasilia, Brazil, 1991-96. Scholar Union Carbide Can., Ottawa, 1963; rsch. grantee Nat. Rsch. Coun., Brasilia, Brazil, 1985. Mem. Brazilian Assn. Chem. Enging. (pres. 2 local chpts. 1980-85), Tchrs.' Union (treas. 1995-96), Brazilian Postal Chess Club, Assn. Profl. Engrs., Assn. Profl. Chemists. Mem. Nat. Party (Winnipeg). Avocations: chess, swimming, jogging, reading, writing. Home: Caixa postal 811, 38400 974 Uberlândia MG, Brazil Office: Federal University, Caixa postal 593, 38400 974 Uberlândia MG, Brazil

FEHR, URY ERNST, marketing executive; b. Jerusalem, Israel, July 18, 1936; s. Joachim and Miriam (Shaltiel) F.; m. Gila Lachmann Yossour (div. 1985); children: Yael, Rahm, Oded; m. Brunhild H. Weber, 1989; children: Victoria. MSc, U. Md., 1963; PhD, UCLA, 1966. Computer programmer, systems analyst, 1959-62; asst. engr. UCLA, 1963-66, asst. geophysicist, 1966-67; asst. rsch. prof. U. Columbia, N.Y.C., 1967-70; pres. IASL, N.Y.C., 1970-73; mng. dir. Hachel Internat., Iran, Europe, 1974-79; exec. v.p. N.E.B.-S.A., Europe, 1979-84, pres., 1984—; mng. dir. Dr. Fehr GmbH, Germany, 1980; vis. prof. internat. mktg. various European Univs., 1980-82; spkr. in field. Contbr. articles to profl. jours. Fellowship HTI, 1963-65; scholarship UCLA, 1963-65. Mem. AAAS, N.Y. Acad. Sci., New Millenium Com. Avocations: special art collection, stamps, music, several sports. Home and Office: Wilhelm-Busch Strasse 16, 65479 Raunheim Germany

FEHRENBACH, T(HEODORE) R(EED), author, businessman; b. San Benito, Tex., Jan. 12, 1925; s. T.R. and Rose Mardel (Wentz) F.; m. Lillian Breetz, Aug. 22, 1951. BA magna cum laude, Princeton U., 1947. Field supr. Travelers Ins. Co., San Antonio, 1954-56; owner ind. ins. agy. San Antonio, 1956-69; mng. trustee Fehrenbach Trusts, 1970—; pres. Royal Poinciana Corp., San Antonio, 1971-92. Author: This Kind of War, 1963, This Kind of Peace, 1966, Lone Star (PBS TV Series 1985-86), 1968, Fire and Blood, 1973, Comanches, 1974, Seven Keys to Texas, 1983, Texas: A Salute From Above, 1985, others; contbr. numerous articles, stories to mags., U.S. fgn. periodicals. Mem. Tex. 2000 Commn., 1981-82; chmn. Tex. Hist. Commn., 1987-91. 1st lt. AUS, 1943-46, lt. col., 1950-53, Korea. Recipient Freedoms Found. award, 1965, Evelyn Oppenheimer award, 198, citations Tex. Ho. of Reps., 1969, 73, Tex. Legislature, 1977; T.R. Fehrenbach Book awards created in his honor Tex. Hist. Commn., 1986; named Disting. Citizen, San Antonio, 1973, Knight of San Jacinto. Fellow Am. Numismatic Soc., Tex. State Hist. Assn.; mem. Philos. Soc. Tex., Authors Guild, Sci. Fiction Writers Am., Conopus Club, Argyle Club, Torch Club, Princeton Club of N.Y.C., Garden of the Gods Club (Colo.). Republican. Episcopalian. Home: 131 Mary D Ave San Antonio TX 78209-5667 Office: 5108 Broadway St # San San Antonio TX 78209-5746

FEI, LIN, engineering educator, engineering executive; b. Ningbo, Zhejiang, China, Oct. 15, 1957; s. Shen Shen F. and Ai Mei Zhou; m. Jiu Ru Chen, Jan. 27, 1986; 1 child, Xi. BS in Physics, Fu Dan U., Shanghai, China, 1982; Promotion, Munich U., 1987-89; Mittlestufe III, Goethe-Inst.

Freiburg, Germany, 1987. Sr. engr. in laser and optoelectronics. Asst. rschr. N. China No. 3, Tianjin, China, 1982-86; vis. scholar Max-Planck Inst. Quantumoptik, Munich, 1987-89; rschr. Inst. Chem. and Phys. Engring., Tianjin, China, 1989-91, assoc. prof., 1992—; vice mng. dir., sales mktg. mgr. Lexel Laser Beijing Co. Ltd., 1995-99; product mgr. Cantronic Sys. Inc., 2000—; cons. as liaison Venture Capital Conss., Encino, Calif., 1996; rschr. in field. Mem. edtl. bd. China Laser Focus, The Buyer Guide, 1998; Inventor in field. Recipient Second prize Communicate of Saving Electricity and Energy, 1992, First place Photography Com. Shen-Jian, 1993. Fellow Fed. Com. Tianjin Youth. Avocations: swimming, music, dancing, table-tennis, photography. Fax: 604-294-6518. E-mail: linfei@cantronic.com. Office: 116-3823 Hennig Dr, Burnaby, BC Canada V5C 6P3

FEI, MINRUI, automation educator; b. Shanghai, July 8, 1961; s. Chun Fei and Ruixia Zhang; m. Chenqing Zhou, Feb. 10, 1989; 1 child, Zixiang. BSc, Shanghai U. Tech., 1984, MSc, 1992; DSc, Shanghai U., 1997. Cert. tchr., China. Asst. instr. Shanghai U. Tech., 1984-89, lectr., 1990-93; prof. automation Shanghai U., 1994—, asst. dir. Sch. Automation, 1996-97, exec. dep. dir. Sch. Automation, 1998-99, exec. dep. dir. Sch. Mechatronical Engring. & Automation, 1999—; mem. Com. Heat Processing Automation, China, 1996—; mem. com. Intelligent Automation, China, 1998—; mem. com. Automation Application, China, 1998—. Mem. editl. bd. Jour. Shanghai U., 1997—; contbr. articles to sci. jours., including Control Theory and Applications, Control and Desicion, Acta Simulata Systematica Sinica, Chinese Jour. Sci. Instrumentation. Named Outstanding Youth Tchr., Govt. of Shanghai, 1993, 95, 97, 99. Mem. IEEE, Internat. Fedn. Automatic Control, Automation Soc. China, Instrument Soc. China, Chinese Assn. Sys. Simulation (trustee 2000—). Avocations: art, music. Office: Shanghai U Dept Automation, 149 Yanchang Rd, Shanghai 200072, China

FEI, YIJIAN, ophthalmologist, biomedical researcher; b. Luzhou, Sichuan, China, June 12, 1962; came to the U.S., 1993; s. Kaili Fei and Zhizheng Fu; m. Yueyi Zhang, Aug. 7, 1987; children: Tianming, Benjamin. MD, Luzhou Med. Coll., 1983; M in Med. Sci., West China U. Med. Scis., Chengdu, China, 1986. Resident, instr. dept. ophthalmology West China U. Med. Scis., Chengdu, 1984-88, asst. prof. dept. ophthalmology, 1988-92; vis. rsch. scientist U. Eye Hosp., Tübingen, Germany, 1992-93; rsch. fellow dept. opthalmology Med. Coll. Ga., Augusta, 1993-98; rsch. assoc. dept. ophthalmology and visual sci. Yale U., New Haven, 1998—. Author: Degenerative Retinopathies: Advances in Clinical and Genetic Research, 1991 (award Assn. Sci. and Tech., Chengdu, 1992), Retinal Diseases: Clinical and Basic Research, 1995; contbr. articles to profl. jours. Recipient Outstanding Young Scholar Acad. award West China U. Med. Scis., Chengdu, 1988, Outstanding Rsch. award Assn. Sci. and Tech. Chengdu City, 1989, Advancement Sci. and Tech. award Govt. Sichuan Province, Chengdu, 1993; named Outstanding Rschr., U.S. Immigration and Naturalization Svc., Tex., 1996; rsch. fellow Acad. Exch. Svc. Germany, Bonn, 1992. Fellow Chinese Assn. Ophthalmic Genetics (Outstanding Rsch. award 1987); mem. AAAS, Chinese Assn. Retinal Diseases, Assn. for Rsch. in Vision and Ophthalmology, N.Y. Acad. Scis. Achievements include introduced the modern molecular genetic and recombinant DNA technologies into the scientific communities of eye research in China; applied genetic linkage analysis and candidate gene approach to find out the genetic causes or molecular defects of some blinding or debilitating retinal diseases; successfully generated mouse models for the study of human retinal function, development and diseases. Avocations: reading, sports, listening to music, fishing, traveling. Home: 95 Kaye Vue Dr Apt 2L Hamden CT 06514-2332 Office: Dept Ophthalmology/Visual Sci Yale Univ Sch of Medicine 330 Cedar St New Haven CT 06510-3218

FEICHTINGER, FRIEDRICH, metallurgical engineer; b. Ried Im Innkreis, Austria, May 5, 1945; arrived in South Africa, 1978; s. Fritz and Maria (Diermaier) F.; m. Margit Groinigg, June 30, 1978; children: Silke, Kerstin. Diploma in engring., U. Mining and Metallurgy, Leoben, Austria, 1973; diploma, Tech. U., Aachen, Germany, 1975; Dr.mont., U. Mining and Metallurgy, Leoben, Austria, 1978. Technologist ironmaking Iscor Ltd., Vanderbijlpark, Republic of South Africa, 1978-81, sr. technologist ironmaking, 1981-85, supt. process devel., 1985-94, exec. mgr. iron and steel foundry, 1993-94; mng. dir. IHME CC, Vanderbijlpark, 1994—. Contbr. articles to profl. jours. Mem. N.Y. Acad. Scis., Internat. Rsch. Circle Prodn. Dynamics (coord. 1986—). Avocations: wildlife, photography, gardening, horse-riding, reading. Office: IHME CC, 7 Offenbach, Vanderbijlpark 1911, South Africa Home: Gartenweg 3, A-3950 Ehrendorf Austria

FEIFEL, HARTMUT, physician, dentist, researcher; b. Aalen, Germany, Mar. 2, 1959; s. Konrad and Dorothee (Schiele) F.; m. Susanne Weag, July 14, 1983; children: Johannes, Anna, Maria, Matthias. Lic. in dentistry, U. Tübingen, 1985, lic. in medicine, 1986, MD, 1986, DDS, 1987, PhD, 1994. Resident dept. oral and maxillofacial surgery Mcpl. Hosp. Karlsruhe, Germany, 1986-87, Katharinen Hosp., Stuttgart, Germany, 1987-91, Tübingen, Germany, 1991; asst. in oral and maxillofacial surgery Ulm, Germany, 1991, Karlsruhe, 1992; asst. prof. dept. oral, maxillofacial-facial plastic surgery Rhenish Westphalian U. Tech., Aachen, Germany, 1992-98; assoc. prof. Rhenish Westphalian U. Tech., Aachen, 1998—. Contbr. articles to profl. jours. Mem. Fed. Assn. German Oral and Maxillofacial Surgeons, German Soc. Implantology, German Soc. Oral and Maxillofacial Surgery, German Soc. Osteology, German Soc. for Plastic and Reconstructive Surgery, German Dental Soc., European Assn. for Cranio-Maxillofacial Surgery, Internat. Assn. Oral and Maxillofacial Surgeons. Roman Catholic. Avocations: classical music, sports. Home: Kirchrather Str 33, 52074 Aachen Germany Office: U Tech Dept Oral Maxillofac, Surgery Pauwelsstr 30, 52074 Aachen Germany

FEIGEN, RICHARD L., art dealer, collector, author; b. Chgo., Aug. 8, 1930; s. Arthur P. and Shirley (Bierman) F.; m. Sandra Elizabeth Canning Walker, Feb. 23, 1966 (div. 1978); children: Philippa Canning, Richard Wood Bliss; m. Margaret Langan Culver, Sept. 12, 1998. B.A., Yale U., 1952; M.B.A., Harvard U., 1954. Asst. treas. Beneficial Standard Life Ins. Co., Los Angeles, 1955-56; mem. N.Y. Stock Exchange, 1956-57; pres., dir. Richard L. Feigen & Co., Inc., N.Y.C. and London, 1957—; mem. com. works fine art N.Y. State Office Bldg., Harlem; lectr. in field. Author: Tales from the Art Crypt, 2000; contbr. articles to art publs. Candidate, del. Dem. Nat. Conv., 1972; trustee John Jay Homestead Assn., Katonah, N.Y., 1979-90, Lincoln U., Pa., 1988-92; trustee, mem. pres.'s coun. U. South Fla. Fellow Mpls. Soc. Fine Arts, Met. Mus. Art, Art Inst. Chgo.; mem. Art Dealers Assn. Am. (bd. dirs. 1972-76, 97-99), Harvard Bus. Sch. Assn., Arts Club, Casino Club. Home: Cantitoe House Cantitoe Rd Katonah NY 10536-9718 also: 960 5th Ave New York NY 10021-1708 Office: 34 E 69th St New York NY 10021-5016

FEIGHNER, GEORGE CHRISTY, laboratory owner, chemist; b. Chgo., Feb. 9, 1926; s. Christy J. and Alice M. (Arnold) F.; m. Ruth J. Zink, July 15, 1945; children: Diane R. Libby, George Jr., Eric R. BS in Chemistry, U. Mich., 1949, MS in Organic Chemistry, 1950; postgrad., Okla. State U., 1950-60. Rsch. chemist Continental Oil Co., Ponca City, Okla., 1950-55, rsch. group leader, 1955-60, rsch. sect. head, 1960-65; project coord. Continental Oil Co., Saddlebrook, N.J., 1966-67; mgr. customer svc. lab. Continental Oil Co., Taterboro, N.J., 1966-67; owner, mgr. Sci. Svcs., Oakland, N.J., 1972-74; mng. ptnr. Maner Co., Oakland, 1977-93; pres. Sci. Svcs. S/D Inc., Sparrowbush, N.Y., 1994—; v.p. Argeo Inc., Pearl River, N.Y., 1990—. Contbr. articles to profl. jours. and chpts. to books. Mem. sch. bd. McCord Dist., Osage County, Okla., 1951-56. With USNR, 1943-45. Mem. AAAS, ASTM (chmn. 1988-95, award of merit 1998), Am. Chem. Soc. (sect. chmn. 1965), Am. Oil Chemists Soc. (past sect. officer), Soc. Cosmetic Chemists. Republican. Lutheran. Achievements include research on synthesis of dodecyl benzene, manufacture of detergent alkylate, a novel synthesis of higher aluminum alkyls, redeposition of natural soils in a home laundry test, soiled cloths used in testing, detergency properties of mono and dialkylated mono and disulfonated diphenyloxide surfactants; 22 patents in purification of alkaryl sulfonates, alkyl phenols, separation of terephthalic, isophthalic and benzoic acids, transalkylation of aromatic hydrocarbons, alkyl chlorides of molecular weight 300-500, production of dinonylnaphthalenes sulfonates, dialkylnaphthalenes, multistage alkylation of aromatic hydrocarbons, preparation of alkyl aryl hydrocarbos, preparation of alkyl aryl hydrocarbons, continuous neutralizing of sulfonated oil, sepration of a-Olefins from hydrocarbon mixtures, process for preparation of high molecular weight aluminum alkyls, detergent alkylate and the sulfonate derivative, oxidation of aromatic hydrocarbons, linear alkyl benzene process; avocations: golf, gardening, gems and minerals. E-mail: sssdinc@warwick.com. Office: Sci Svcs S/D Inc PO Box 778 Sparrow Bush NY 12780-0778

FEIGIN, GEORGY ARONOVICH, otorhinolaryngologist, educator; b. Namangan, Uzbekistan, Apr. 23, 1929; s. Aron M. and Rahel M. Feigin; m. Lola N. Feigin; children: Mikhail, Dmitry. MD, Med. U. Tashkent, Uzbekistan, 1953. Otorhinolaryngologist Begobot, Uzbekistan, 1953-56; postgrad. rsch. Med. U. Tashkent, 1953-56, assoc. prof., 1959-64; head dept. otorhinolaryngology Bishkek (Kyrgyzstan) Med. U., 1977-97; head, course in otorhinolaryngology and head and neck surgey Kyrgyz Ctr. Advanced Tng. for Med. Pers., Bishkek, 1997—. Author numerous books, including Prevention and Treatment of Functional Disturbances after Laryngeal Resection, 1974, Throat Defects in Laryngeal Cancer Surgery, 1978, Acute Stenosing Laryngotracheobronchitis in Children, 1981, Basics of Clinical Pharmacology for ENT Doctors, 1985, Hemorrhage and Thrombosis in ENT Diseases, 1989, Tracheotomy and Tracheostomy, 1993, Vasomotor Rhinitis, 1994, Rhinitis in Children, 1995; contbr. over 160 articles to profl. jours., chpts. to books. Recipient medal for valorous svc. during WWII. Mem. Am. Acad. Otorhinolaryngology-Head and Neck Surgery (corr.), Internat. Acad. Otorhinolaryngology-Head and Neck Surgery, Kyrgyz Assn. Otorhinolaryngology Drs. (chmn. 1964—). Avocation: gardening. Home: 127 Chui Prospect # 176, 720011 Bishkek Kyrgyzstan Office: 1 Togolok Moldo St, 720000 Bishkek Kyrgyzstan

FEIGON, JUDITH TOVA, ophthalmologist, surgeon, educator; b. Galveston, Tex., Dec. 2, 1947; d. Louis and Ethel Feigon; m. Nathan C. Goldman; children: Michael G., Miriam G. AB, Barnard Coll., Columbia U., 1970; postgrad., Rice U., U. Houston, 1970-71; MD, U. Tex., San Antonio, 1976. Diplomate Am. Bd. Ophthalmology. Intern Mt. Auburn Hosp., Cambridge, Mass.; intern, clin. tchg. fellow Harvard U. Med. Sch., 1976-77; resident in ophthalmology Baylor Coll. Medicine, Houston, 1977-80, fellow in retina, 1980-82, clin. faculty, 1982-95; asst. prof. ophthalmology U. Tex. Med. Br., Galveston, 1982-85, clin. asst. prof., 1985-91, clin. assoc. prof., 1992—; pvt. practice medicine specializing ophthalmology, vitreoretinal diseases, surgery, Houston, 1983—; physician advisor to Houston br. Tex. Soc. to Prevent Blindness, 1987-89, also bd. dirs.; mem. staff Meth., St. Lukes, Tex. Children's, John Sealy, St. Joseph's Hosp., Park Plaza; clin. faculty Baylor Coll. Medicine, 1992-95. Contbr. articles to profl. publs. Mem. Assn. Am. Physicians and Surgeons, Am. Acad. Ophthalmology, Tex. Med. Assn. Houston Ophthal. Soc., Harris County Med. Soc., U. Tex. San Antonio Alumni Assn., Vitreous Soc., Tex. Ophthalmol. Assn. Office: 7515 Main St Ste 650 Houston TX 77030-4599

FEILD, CHARLES ROBERT, pediatrician, educator; b. Little Rock, May 16, 1953; s. Robert Mills and Irene (Edwards) F.; m. Christina Reid Docherty, Nov. 20, 1981; children: Daniel Robert, Hannah Christina. Student, Hendrix Coll., 1971-74; MD, U. Ark., 1978. Diplomate Am. Acad. Pediatrics; lic. physician, Ark.; cert. advanced trauma life support. Intern and resident in pediatrics U. Ark. for Med. Scis., Ark. Children's Hosp., 1978-81; pediatric registrar Guy's Hosp., London, 1981; fellow, hon. pediatric registrar Inst. Child Health-U. London-Hosp. for Sick Children, 1982; clin. asst. prof. pediatrics U. Ark. for Med. Scis., 1981-82, asst. prof. pediatrics, 1982-85, 88-92, assoc. prof. pediatrics, 1992—, chief community pediatrics and pub. policy dept. pediatrics, 1991—; attending physician Ark. Easter Seals Residential Facility, 1983-85, 88—; chief Exceptional Family Mem. Svc., 1985-88; attending pediatrician Ctrs. for Youth and Families, Little Rock, 1992—; mem. exec. com. Ark. Children's Hosp. Med. Staff, 1990-93, program chmn. 1992-93; mem. ACH outpatient care com., student promotions com. Coll. Medicine, U. Ark. for Med. Scis., 1991-96; adj. assoc. prof. Coll. Nursing, UAMS, 1995—; prin. investigator Comprehensive Child Devel. Project Dept. Health Human Svcs., 1995-98, exec. dir., UAMS Devel. Start Progs., 1998. Contbr. articles to med. jours. Bd. dirs. Hillcrest Hist. Neighborhood Resident's Assn.; camp physician Quapaw coun. Boy Scouts Am.; mem. ops. coun. Remmel Child Devel. Ctr., Little Rock. Grantee Robert Wood Johnson Found., 1990, 92 U.S. Dept. Housing and Urban Devel., 1991, commty. access to Am. Acad. of Peds. Child Health Hall of Fame, 1997. Fellow Am. Acad. Pediatrics (regional dir. Community Access to Child Health program 1993-2000, mem., facilitator State Community Access to Child Health program 1989—); mem. So. Soc. Pediatric Rsch., Am. Sch. Health Assn., Ambulatory Pediatric Assn., Nat. Health Policy Coun. (mem. steering com. 1993—), Ctrl. Ark. Pediatric Soc. (v.p. 1992-93, pres. 1993-94), Ark. Perinatal Assn. Methodist. Office: Ark Children's Hosp South Campus Rm 610 800 Marshall St Little Rock AR 72202-3591

FEIN, PATRICK LOUIS-MARIE, French language educator; b. London, June 6, 1938; arrived in South Africa, 1988; s. Henry Charles and Suzanne (Lehalle) F.; m. Nicoletta Jane Carloni, Dec. 3, 1983. BA with honors in French, U. Hull, Eng., 1962; PhD in French Lit. Studies, London U., 1982. Asst. lectr. U. Aberdeen, Scotland, 1965-68; lectr./sr. lectr. Univ. Coll./ Univ. Rhodesia, Zimbabwe, 1968-88; prof. and head dept. French Rhodes U., Grahamstown, South Africa, 1988—, head Sch. Langs., 1998—; external examiner in French U. Natal, 1977-81, U. Botswana, 1988, 89, U. Lesotho, 1988-90, U. Zimbabwe, 2000—. Author: Women of Sensibility or Reason: The Function of the Feminine Characters in the Novels of Marivaux, Diderot, Crébillon fils, Duclos and Laclos. Decorated Chevalier in the Order of the Palmes Académiques, French Govt., 1985, Chevalier in Order of Constantine the Great Chancellory of the Order, 1987; recipient Sr. Visitor award Voltaire Found., Linacre Coll., Oxford, 1987. Home: Valmont II Schapenberg Estate, 54 Bizweni Ave, Somerset West 7129, Republic of South Africa Office: Rhodes Univ French Studies, Sch Langs PO Box 94, Grahamstown 6140, Republic of South Africa

FEIN, RONNIE, writer, journalist; b. N.Y.C., June 5, 1943; d. William and Lily (Hoffman) Vail; m. Edward Fein, Nov. 15, 1969; children: Meredith, Gillian. BA, Northwestern U., 1964; LLB, NYU, 1967. Atty. Chadbourne, Parke, Whiteside & Wolff, N.Y.C., 1967-70, Rosenman, Colin, N.Y.C., 1970-71; dir. Ronnie Fein Sch. Creative Cooking, Stamford, Conn., 1971—; freelance demonstrator cooking, dept. stores various locations, 1971—; journalist Stamford Trader, 1980-81, The Advertiser, New Canaan, 1981-98, Times-Mirror newspapers, 1984—, Consumer's Digest Mag., 1989—, Darien Times, 1993-98, Newsday, 1995—, Hersam-Acorn newspapers, 1997-98, L.A. Times Syndicate, 1999—, Westport Mag., 1999—, Greenwich Mag., 1999—; contbg. editor The New Cook's Catalogue, 2000; talk show host The New WNLK, Norwalk, Conn., 1984. Author: The Complete Idiot's Guide to Cooking Basics, 1995, 3d edit., 2000. Alumni admissions dir. Fairfield County, Northwestern U., Evanston, Ill., 1985-98. Fellow Conn. Womens Culinary Alliance (charter, newsletter co-chmn. 1988-89, pres. 1996-97). Home: 32 Heming Way Stamford CT 06903

FEINBAUM, GEORGE, internist, endocrinologist; b. Samarkand, Uzbekistan, July 31, 1945; came to the U.S., 1965, naturalized, 1972; s. Joseph and Cyrla (Szoken) F.; 1 son, Livius. Student, Med. Acad. Wroclaw, Poland, 1963-65, Queens Coll., 1966-70; MD, Albert Einstein Coll. Medicine, 1973. Diplomate Am. Bd. Internal Medicine. Intern Met. Hosp. Ctr., N.Y.C., 1973-74, resident in internal medicine, 1974-76, fellow in endocrinology and metabolism, 1976-77; pvt. practice in internal medicine and endocrinology Bklyn., 1977—; asst. in medicine Brookdale Hosp. Med. Ctr., Bklyn. Fellow ACP; mem. Kings County Med. Soc., Endocrine Soc., N.Y. Acad. Scis., Mensa. Office: 3245 Nostrand Ave Brooklyn NY 11229-3716 also: 934 Manhattan Ave Brooklyn NY 11222-5915

FEINBERG, RICHARD ALAN, clinical psychologist; b. Oakland, Calif., Aug. 12, 1947; s. Jack and Raechel Sacks (Hoff) F. BA, Calif. State U.-Hayward, 1969; MA in Clin. Psychology, Mich. State U., 1972, PhD, 1979; Nat. Register of Health Service Providers in Psychology, 1980. Instr., Merritt Coll., Oakland, 1975-76; clin. psychologist Highland Gen. Hosp., Oakland, 1976-79; asso. Lafayette Center Counseling and Edn., 1978-79; clin. psychologist Tri-City Mental Health Center, Fremont, Calif., 1979-81, dir., 1981-86; pvt. practice clin. psychology, 1976—; participant profl. conf. USPHS fellow, 1969-71. Mem. Am. Psychol. Assn., Calif. Psychol. Assn. Jewish. Office: 38950 Blacow Rd Ste D Fremont CA 94536-7379

FEINBERG, RICHARD E., international political economy educator; b. N.Y.C., Jan. 10, 1947. BA, Brown U., 1969; PhD, Stanford U., 1978. Formerly exec. v.p., dir. Overseas Devel. Coun., Washington; former pres. Inter-Am. Dialogue, Washington; spl. asst. to President U.S., sr. dir. Inter-Am. Affairs Nat. Security Coun., Washington, 1993-96; now vis. fellow Inst. Econ.; dean Grad. Sch. Internat. Rels. and Pacific Studies U. Calif., San Diego, 1993-96, prof. internat. polit. economy, dir. APEC Study Ctr., 1996—. Author over 100 books and articles, including The Intemperate Zone: The Third World Challenge to U.S. Foreign Policy, Subsidizing Success: The Export-Import Bank in the U.S. Economy, Summitry in the Americas: A Progress Report, 1997. Office: PO Box 80213 San Diego CA 92138-0213

FEINBERG, ROBERT JULIAN, judge; b. Plattsburgh, N.Y., Feb. 13, 1924; s. Benjamin Franklin and Leah (Mendelsohn) F.; m. Laurie Covert, Mar. 22, 1974. BA, Yale U., 1945, JD, 1947. Bar: N.Y. 1948; cert. circuit ct. civil mediator 1994, Fla. Assoc. Costello, Cooney & Fearon, Syracuse, N.Y., 1947-50; mem. Feinberg, Jerry & Lewis, Plattsburgh, 1950-60; sole practice Plattsburgh, 1961-67; mem. Jerry, Lewis, Feinberg & Lyon, Plattsbugh, 1967-70; judge Clinton County (N.Y.) Ct. and Family Ct., Plattsburgh, 1970-88; civil mediator Circuit Ct. Fla., Delray Beach, 1994—; asst. atty. gen. N.Y. State, 1948; mem. N.Y. State Assembly, 1957-64. Mng. editor Yale Law Jour., 1946-47. Mem. N.Y. State Bar Assn., Clinton County Bar Assn. (past pres.), Am. Judges Assn., Rotary (past pres.) Elks (past dist. dep., grand exalted ruler), Masons (32 deg.), Shriners, Moose, B'nai B'rith (past pres.), Yale Club N.Y.C., Grad. Club (New Haven, Conn.), Delray Beach (Fla.) Club. Republican. Jewish. Address: PO Box 827 Plattsburgh NY 12901-0827 Also: PO Box 1220 Delray Beach FL 33447-1220

FEINBERG, ROBERT S., plastics manufacturing company executive, marketing consultant; b. Newark, May 14, 1934; s. Clarence Jacob and Sabina (Zorn) F.; BA in English, BS in Chemistry, Trinity Coll., Hartford, Conn., 1955; MBA in Mktg., Fairleigh Dickinson U., 1966; advt. diploma Assn. Indsl. Advt., 1967, advt. diploma N.Y. Inst. Advt., 1967; Pres., Trebor Assocs. and Trebor Plastics Co., Teaneck, N.J., 1961—; mktg. cons. computer software Zettler Softwear Co., Burroughs Corp.; sr. council Yankelovich, Skelly and White, Inc.; cons. Greenwich Assocs.; co-chmn., ptnr. Edgeroy Co., Inc., Ridgefield and Palisades Park, N.J., 1973—; co-chmn., ptnr. LeMont Sales Co., Teaneck, 1973—; cons. plastic formulations W.R. Grace, Endicott Johnson, Brown Shoe Co., U.S. Shoe Co., Ciba, Uniroyal. Mem. Soc. Plastics Engrs. (sr.), Sporting Goods Mfrs. Assn., Sell Overseas Am., U.S. Profl. Tennis Assn., Bergen County Tennis League (v.p.). Club: Ahdeek Tennis. Author: Olympia Shoe Co., 1966; co-inventor Edgeroy Ball Press (Internat. Tennis Hall of Fame, Newport, R.I.); patentee in polymer and mech. engring. fields. Home: PO Box 273 Teaneck NJ 07666-0273

FEINENDEGEN, LUDWIG EMIL, retired hospital and research institute director; b. Garzweiler, Germany, Jan. 1, 1927; s. Ludwig and Rosa (Klauth) F.; m. Jeannine Gemuseus; children: Dominik, Christophe. MD, U. Cologne, Germany, 1952; postgrad. med. tng., U. Hosp., Cologne. St. Peter's Gen. Hosp., New Brunswick, N.Y., St. Cornelius Hosp., Viersen, Germany, St. Vincents Hosp., N.Y.C., 1952-58; Asst. physician, scientist med. dept. Brookhaven Nat. Lab., Upton, N.Y., 1958-63; sci. officer European Atomic Energy Commn., Brussels, Belgium, 1962-67; sci. officer lab. Pasteur de l'Inst. du Radium, Paris, France, 1964-67; dir. inst. medicine rsch. ctr. Jülich GmbH., Germany, 1967-93; prof., dir. nuclear medicine U. Hosp. Düsseldorf, Germany, 1967-93, prof. emeritus, 1993—; prof. emeritus Cath. U., Seoul, Korea, 1991—; rsch. collaborator med. dept. Brookhaven Nat. Lab., Upton, N.Y., 1963-93, sr. scientist, 1993-98, rsch. collaborator, 1998—; assignee Dept. of Energy, Washington, 1994-98; Fogarty scholar NIH, Bethesda, 1998—; mem. Nat. Coun. on Radiation Protection and Measurements, Com. 24, U.S., 1969-79; mem. adv. coun. Fed. Ministry Health, Bonn, Germany, 1972-93; mem. Internat. Commn. on Radiol. Protection Com. 2, Eng., 1973-85; mem. sci. coun. dept. for radiation hygiene Fed. Office Health, Berlin, Bonn, 1973-89; Fed. Office Radiol. Protection, 1990-94; mem. coun. sci. and lit. Goethe Inst., Munich, 1978-87; mem. Internat. Commn. on Radiation Units and Measurements, 1982—; adv. coun. Fed. Ministry Def., Bonn, 1983—; A.C. Helmholtz prof. U. Wis. Med. Sch., 1983. Mem. civil def. commn. Fed. Ministry of Interior, Bonn, Germany, 1974-2000; mem. commn. experts "Rsch. Baden-Württemberg," Ministry Sci. and Arts, Stuttgart, Germany, 1988-89; mem. com. ann. Lindau meetings Nobel Laureates, 1979—. Decorated Comdr.'s Cross Order of Merit, Germany, 1994; recipient G.V. Hevesy lecture medal, 1990, C.W. Röntgen medal City of Remscheid, Germany, 1991, State prize Northrhine-Westfalia, 1991, E. and F. Wachsman prize German Röntgen Ray Soc., 1994, Hanns Langendorff medal Assn. German Radiation Protection Physicians, 1995; Damon Runyon fellow, 1962; Dr. Robert K. Match Disting. scholar L.I. Jewish Med. Ctr., 1989, NIH Fogarty Scholar, 1998-99. Fellow European Soc. Cardiology; mem. Rhine-Westfalian Acad. Scis. (class for natural scis., engring. and econs. 1971—), German Soc. Nuc. Medicine (hon. 1998—), Rotary (dist. gov. 1992-93). E-mail: feinendegen@gmx.net. Office: Brookhaven National Lab Brookhaven Nat Lab Medical Dept Upton NY 11973 Office: Heinriche-Heine U/Nuc Med, Rsch Ctr Juelich, 52425 Juelich Germany also: Wannental 45, 88131 Lindau Germany

FEINER, AVA SOPHIA, public affairs and management consultant, economist; b. Bklyn., Feb. 13, 1950; d. Ignace and Lola (Pasternak) F.; m. Clifford Douglas Stromberg, June 25, 1972; children: Kimberly Greta, Eric George. BA summa cum laude, Yale U., 1971; MA, Harvard U., 1974, PhD in Govt., 1978. Legis. asst. to U.S. Senator Bill Bradley, Washington, 1979-82; dir. internat. trade policy U.S. C. of C., Washington, 1982-83, mgr. internat. policy dept., 1983-85; corp. program dir. IBM, Washington, 1985-87, corp. dir. pub. affairs, trade and investment, 1987; pres. Feiner Pub. Affairs Cons., Washington, 1988—; co-founder, dir. Washington Alive! Inc., 1989-90; pres. Washington Networks, 1990—; teaching fellow Harvard U., Cambridge, Mass., 1972-74; lectr. nat. and internat. politics and econs., 1978—; bd. dirs., World Trade Forum, Washington, 1987-89. Co-author: American Excellence in A World Economy, 1987; contbr. articles on econs., trade, fgn. policy to various publs. Del. to Atlantic Coun. Young Leadership Program, Wis. and Can., 1978, 80, Aspen Inst. Exec. Seminar, 1982, Germany-U.S. Young Leadership Conf., San Francisco, 1982, Harbor Sch. Bd., 1992-93; co-chair Holton-Arms Sch. Silent Auction, 1995-96; mem. adv. com. Cmty. Homeowners, 1999—. Fgn. Policy fellow Brookings Instn., 1975-76, guest scholar, 1976-77; Carnegie Endowment for Internat. Peace fellow, 1975-76. Mem. Coun. Fgn. Rels. (task force on women 1988-91, term membership com. 1988-91, internat. affairs fellows com. 1991-95, Washington program adv. com. 1995-98), Trade Policy Forum, Phi Beta Kappa. Avocations: photography, karate, swimming, bicycling, tennis.

FEINERMAN, ELI, agricultural economist, educator; b. Kfar Yehezkel, Israel, Oct. 31, 1946; s. Uzi and Hannah (Bernstein) F.; m. Dvora Kanzuker (dec. June 1987); children: Ofer, Gili, Uzi; m. Patricia Lewis; children: Eli, Maya. BS in Agrl. Econs., Hebrew U. of Jerusalem, Rehovot, Israel, 1972, MS in Agrl. Econs., 1975, PhD in Agrl. Econs. and Mgmt., 1980. Lectr. dept. agr. econ. and mgmt. Hebrew U. of Jerusalem, 1984-90, sr. lectr., 1991-95, chmn. dept. agr. econ. and mgmt., 1992-96, assoc. prof., head dept. agr. econ. and mgmt., 1996—; vis. asst. prof. Iowa State U., 1988-89, vis. assoc. prof., 1989-96; chmn. referee com. agrl. econs. chief Israel Ministry of Agr., 1991—; com. mem. Ministry of Agr., Ministry of Environment and Water Commn., 1991—. Contbr. chpts. to books, more than 40 articles to profl. jours. Capt. Israeli Def. Force, 1964-67. Grantee Lady Davis Fund, 1980, Maurichio Richter Fund, 1985, Walter and Elise Haas, 1986; named Yekutiel Federman chair in Hotel Mgmt., 1999. Mem. Am. Agr. Econs. Assn. Avocations: exercise, nature trips, singing, reading. Office: Dept Agrl Econs and Mgmt, Hebrew U Jerusalem Box 12, 76100 Rehovot Israel

FEINGOLD, MORDECHAI, historian, researcher, educator; b. Haifa, Israel, Aug. 25, 1951; s. Yaakov Ullman and Leah Skopol Feingold; m. Carol Lynne Magun, Aug. 20, 1972; children: Yaakov, Ariella. BA, Hebrew U. Jerusalem, Israel, 1972, MA, 1976; DPhil, Oxford (Eng.) U., 1980. Jr. fellow Harvard U., Cambridge, Mass., 1981-84; asst. prof. Boston U., 1984-88; prof. history Va. Poly. Inst., Blacksburg, 1988—; vis. prof. Caltech, Pasadena, Calif., 1994, History of Sci. Soc., 1992-93. Author: The Mathematicians' Apprenticeship, 1984; author, editor: Before Newton: The Life and Times of Isaac Barrow, 1990; co-editor: In the Presence of the Past, 1991, The World of William and Mary, 1996. Wissenschaftskolleg fellow,

Berlin, 1996-97; Dibner Inst. fellow MIT, 1994-95, 99-2000. Office: Va Poly Inst Lane Hall Blacksburg VA 24061-0227

FEINSTEIN, ALEJANDRO, astronomer educator; b. La Plata, Argentina, May 30, 1929; s. Leon Nicolas and Berta (Levin) F.; m. Angeles Baigorri, Aug. 20, 1933; children: Carlos, Miguel, Guillermina. D in Astronomy, Astron. Obs., La Plata, Argentina, 1960. Observer, asst. astronomer Astron. Obs., La Plata, Argentina, 1948-56; instr. Astronomy Obs., La Plata, Argentina, 1952-56, tech. asst., 1956-62, asst. prof. astrophysics, 1962-63, prof. astrophysics, 1963-96, prof. emeritus, 1996; career scientist Nat. Rsch. Coun., Argentina, 1961—, sr. rschr., 1983—. Author: Astronomia Elemental, 1969-87, Una visita al universo conocido, 1994, Astronomia General: aspecto global del Universo, 1996, Objetiro Universo: manual de Astronomie elemental, 1999; contbr. more than 120 rsch. papers to sci. mags. Recipient Premio Buenos Aires Province to Astronomical Rsch., 1990, Premio Soc. Cientifica Arg. Astronomia, 1995, Premio Dr. Ricardo Platzeck, Academia Nacional de Ciencias Exactas, Fisicas y Naturales, 1996. Fellow Royal Astonomical Soc.; mem. Assn. Argentina Astronomical, Internat. Astronomical Union. Office: Observatorio Astronomico, Paseo del Bosque, 1900 La Plata Argentina

FEINSTEIN, MARTIN, performing arts consultant, art director; b. N.Y.C., Apr. 12, 1921. BSS, CCNY, 1942; MA, Wayne State U., 1943; MusD (hon.), Cath. U. Am., 1980, Shenandoah Coll. & Conservatory, 1983; LHD (hon.), Am. U., 1991; DFA, U. Md., 1995. Publicity dir. Hurok Concerts, N.Y.C., 1945-50, v.p., 1950-71; vis. prof. Yale U., New Haven, 1971-73; exec. dir. performing arts John F. Kennedy Ctr., Washington, 1972-80; pres., CEO Nat. Symphony, Kennedy Ctr., Washington, 1980-81; gen. dir. Washington Opera, 1980-95, cons., 1995—; sr. cons. U. Md. Performing Arts Ctr., College Park, 1995-2000, artistic dir., 1998-99, adj. prof., 2000—. Decorated commendatore Republic of Italy; cross of officer Order Arts and Letters (France); Grand Decoration of Honor for Svcs. (Austria), officer Order of Merit (Germany); recipient medal Nat. Soc. Lit. and the Arts, 1977, award of Contbns. in Field of Dance Am. Assn. Dance Cos., 1979, Townsend Harris medal CCNY, 1977, John Cranko medal, Stuttgart, 1979, Myrtle Wreath award Washington Hadassah, 1982, Amphion award Memphis Symphony, 1983. Office: U Md Rm 2110 Performing Arts Ctr College Park MD 20742-1620

FEINZIG, STUART C., financial planner; b. Brookline, Mass., June 9, 1946; s. Abraham and Shirley C. Feinzig; m. Dorothy P. Feinzig, May 20, 1984; children: Adam, Cara, Barry Kottler, Nina Kottler. AS, Northeastern U., Boston, 1971. Cert. fin. cons. V.p. sales mktg. Charrette Corp., Woburn, Mass., 1967-83; fin. planner New Eng. Adv. Corp., Newton, Mass., 1985—. Host radio program Saturday Financial Workshop, 1998. Coach Sudbury (Mass.) Soccer and Baseball, 1979-85. Mem. Internat. Assn. Fin. Planners, Fin. Svc. Profls., Boston Life Underwriters Assn. Avocations: golf, tennis, gardening, travel, photography. E-Mail: scfneag@aol.com. Office: New Eng Adv Group 75 Wells Ave Newton MA 02459-3296

FEI-PENG, LEE, physician, otolaryngologist, medical educator; b. Chia-I, Taiwan, Republic of China, May 10, 1956; s. Lee Kim-Bo and Chu Chi; m. Tsai Min-O; children: Shin-Hwa Lee, Chua-Yun Lee. MD, Taipei Med. Coll., 1980. Resident dept. of ENT Chang Gung Meml. Hosp., Taipei, 1980-86, attending physician dept. ENT, 1986-92; lectr. Chang Gung Med. Coll., Taoyuan, Taiwan, 1989-94, Taipei Med. Coll., 1994-95; chief ENT dept. Taipei Med. Coll. Hosp., 1994—; assoc. prof. Taipei Med. Coll., 1995—. Bd. editor Jour. of Otolaryngological Soc. of the Republic of China, 1991-98; contbr. articles to profl. jours. Ensign Navy, Taiwan. Mem. Taiwan Otolaryngological Soc. (gen. sec. 1998—), Otolaryngological Soc. of the Republic of China (Excellence paper prize 1988), N.Y. Acad. Sci. Buddhist. Office: Dept ENT Taipei Med Coll, 252 Wu Shin St, Taiepei 110, Taiwan

FEISTAUER, MILOSLAV, mathematician, educator; b. Náchod, Czech Republic, Feb. 8, 1943; s. Miloslav and Helena (Hejnová) F.; m. Jaroslava Rykrová, June 22, 1971; children: Jana, Petra. Master's degree, Charles U., Prague, Czech Republic, 1965, PhD, 1972, DSc, 1990. Asst. prof. Charles U., Prague, 1966-88, assoc. prof., 1988-91, prof., 1991—; vis. prof. U. Del., Newark, 1991, U. Karlsruhe, Germany, 1992, U. Heidelberg, Germany, 1993, U Tex., Austin, 1998, U. Houston, 1998; head Inst. Numerical Math., Charles U., Prague, 1994—; mem. sci. coun. Faculty Math. and Physics, Prague, 1993—; cons. Škoda Co., Pilsen, Czech Republic, 1976—. Author: Mathematical Methods in Fluid Dynamics, 1993; contbr. articles to profl. jours. Mem. Gesellschaft für Angewandte Mathematik und Mechanik (Czech com. 1994), European Consortium for Math. in Industry (Czech com.), Am. Math. Soc. Avocations: history of art, music, playing violin and viola. Office: Charles U Faculty Math and Physics, Charles U Fac Math/ Physics, Sokolovska 83, 186 00 Prague 8, Czech Republic

FEIT, GLENN M., lawyer; b. Elizabeth, N.J., Oct. 16, 1929; s. Charles Theodore and Beatrice (Esther) F.; m. Rona F. Gottlieb, June 14, 1953 (div. 1974); children: Glenn M., John Paul, Adam Gibbs (dec.); m. Barberi Platt Paull. BS in Econ., U. Pa., 1951; JD magna cum laude, Harvard U., 1957. Bar: N.Y. 1958, U.S. Dist. Ct. (2d dist.) 1959). Assoc. Cravath, Swaine & Moore, N.Y.C., 1957-64; ptnr. London, Buttenwieser & Chalif, N.Y.C., 1965-70, Feit & Ahrens, N.Y.C., 1970-88, Feit & Shor, N.Y.C., 1988-89, Proskauer Rose LLP, N.Y.C., 1989—; bd. dirs. C&D Techs., Inc., Blue Bell, Pa., Blair Industries, Inc., Scott City, Mo.; sec. Charterhouse Group Internat., Inc., N.Y.C. Mem. editl. bd. Harvard Law Rev., 1955-57. Bd. dirs. Friends of the IDF, N.Y.C. Lt. USN, 1951-54. Mem. ABA, Assn. Bar City N.Y., Aircraft Owners and Pilots Assn., Exptl. Aircraft Assn., Tailhook Assn., Harvard Club, Seaplane Pilots Assn., N.Y. Yacht Club, Doubles. Office: Proskauer Rose LLP 1585 Broadway Fl 27 New York NY 10036-8299

FEIZI, TEN, physician, researcher, educator; b. Nicosia, Cyprus, May 26, 1937; s. Mehmet Feizi and Zehra Aziz. MB, BChir, Royal Free Hosp., London, 1961, MD, 1969. Ho. officer, registrar in surgery and hematology Royal Free & Hammersmith Hosps., London, 1961-65; rsch. fellow in medicine Royal Free Hosp., London, 1965-68; guest investigator, asst. prof. Rockefeller U., N.Y.C., 1968-73; head glycoconjugates sect. Med. Rsch. Coun. Clin. Rsch. Ctr., Harrow, Eng., 1973-94; dir. Med. Rsch. Coun. Glycosciences Lab. Imperial Coll. Sch. Medicine, Harrow, 1994—, prof. glycosciences, 1997—; hon. cons. physician Northwick Pk. Hosp., Harrow, 1973—; cons. Adv. Coun. Sci. & Tech. Rev. Carbohydrate Sci., Eng., 1990; mem. divsn. medicine rsch. com. Imperial Coll. Sch. Medicine, London, 1997—. Fellow Royal Coll. Physicians, Royal Coll. Pathologists; mem. AAAS, Brit. Soc. Immunology, Am. Assn. Immunologists, Biochemical Soc. Fax: 020-8869-3455. Home: 94 Brunswick Rd, London W5 1AE, England Office: Imperial Coll Sch Medicine, Northwick Pk Campus, Harrow HA1 3UJ, England

FEJES, PAL, chemical reseracher; b. Mako, Hungary, Jan. 13, 1931; s. Pal Fejes and Irma Vrecznik; m. Margit Fabian (div. 1983); 1 child, Krisztina; m. Judit Szava, 1984. Degree in chemistry, U. Veszprem, Hungary, 1957, MS in Applied Math., 1963, Doctor of the Hungarian Acad. Sci., 1965, Dr.phil.habil., 1995. Head of dept. Ctrl. Rsch. Inst., Budapest, Hungary, 1957-69, Rsch. Inst. Isotopes, Budapest, Hungary, 1969-71; prof. chem. tech. U. Szeged, 1971. Contbr. over 250 articles to profl. jours., 7 books. Avocations: roses, ancient history, epigraphy. Office: Jozsef Attila U, Rerrich B Ter 1, 6720 Szeged Hungary

FEJFAR, ANTONÍN, physicist; b. Počátky, Pelhřimov, Czech Republic, June 22, 1962; s. Antonin and Dagmar (Zabloudilová) F. RNDr., Charles U., Prague, 1986, CSc, 1991; grad. internat. course, Osaka (Japan) U., 1992. Asst. tchr. Charles U., Prague, 1991, 1993-94; rsch. student Kyoto (Japan) U., 1991-93; scientist Inst. Physics, Acad. of Scis., Prague, 1994—; organizer internat. summer schs. of thin film physics Castle Chlum u Třeboně, 1991, 94. Contbr. articles to profl. jours.; editl. bd. Československy Časopis Pro Fyziku, 1991-95. Office: Inst Physics Acad Scis, Cukrovarnická 10, 162 00 Prague 6, Czech Republic

FEJFAR, ZDENĚK MIROSLAV, cardiologist; b. Libáň, Bohemia, Czechoslovakia, Oct. 14, 1916; s. Václav Fejfar and Ružena (Appeltová) Fejfarová; m. Marie Hana Hanková, Mar. 20, 1943. D of Gen. Medicine, Charles U., Prague, Czechoslovakia, 1945; DSc, Czechoslovakian Acad. Scis., Prague, 1959. House physician Charles U., 1945-46, registrar, 1947-51, lectr. med. faculty, 1950-59, prof. internal medicine, 1965—; Brit. Council scholar London, 1946-47; sr. research worker Inst. for Cardiovascular Research, Prague, 1951-59; chief med. officer in charge cardiovascular diseases unit WHO, Geneva, 1959-73; sr. research worker Inst. for Clin. and Experimental Medicine, Prague, 1973-99. Author and editor 25 books and more than 600 sci. articles. Recipient J.E. Purkyně medal Pres. Czechoslovakian Republic, 1966, citation of internat. achievement Am. Heart Assn., 1977, Gold medal Slovak Med. Soc., 1981. Fellow Royal Soc. Medicine; mem. Czechoslovakian Soc. Cardiology (hon.), Peruvian Soc. Cardiology (hon.), Swiss Soc. Cardiology (hon.), Am. Coll. Cardiology (hon., Disting. Service award 1974), French Soc. Cardiology (corr.), Brit. Soc. Cardiology (corr.). Club: Slavia (Prague). Avocations: hiking, music. E-mail: feifar@mediclub.cz. Home: Menšikovská 18, 16000 Prague Czech Republic

FEJTL, MICHAEL, science administrator, neuroscientist; b. Vienna, Austria, Mar. 14, 1961; s. Walter and Gertrude Fejtl. Degree in Biochemistry, HBLVA, Vienna, 1980; PhD, U. Vienna, 1989; asst. prof., SUNY, Albany, 1996. Student asst. U. Vienna, 1986-87; rsch. affiliate Wadsworth Labs., Albany, N.Y., 1990-91, 93-95; Erwin Schrödinger fellow Austrian Rsch. Found., Vienna, 1991-93; rsch. scientist Wadsworth Labs., Albany, 1994-96; head of electrophysiology Natural and Med. Scis. Inst., Reutlingen, Germany, 1997-99; head biol. rsch. and application Multi Channel Sys., Reutlingen, 1999—. Co-author: (book chpt.) Single Channel Studies in Molluscan Neurons, 1996. Internat. Brain Rsch. Orgn. travel grantee, 1994. Avocations: music, paragliding, classical guitar, performing arts. Fax: 49 7121 503011. E-mail: fejtl@multichannelsystems.com. Office: Multi Channel Sys, Markwiesenstrasse 55, 72770 Reutlingen Germany

FEKETE, BÉLA, internist, immunologist; b. Sátoraljaujhely, Borsod, Hungary, Dec. 21, 1941; s. Béla and I. (Sáfár) F.; m. Julianna Petrányi, June 9, 1967 (div. 1990); children: Zsófia, Zsuzsa. MD, Debrecen (Hungary) Med. Sch., 1967; PhD, Hungarian Acad. Scis., Budapest, 1974, DMSc, 1984. Cert. internist; cert. immunologist. Resident dept. internal diseases Med. Sch., Debrecen, 1967-73; rsch. fellow Hôpital Necker, Paris, 1974; clin. assoc. Semmelweis U. Medicine, Budapest, 1975-77; rsch. assoc. Nat. Inst. Pulmonology, Budapest, 1977-80; chief physician Ctrl. State Hosp., Budapest, 1980-88; prof. Semmelweis U. Medicine, Budapest, 1988—; cons. Coll. Experts Clin. Immunology Semmelweis U. Medicine, Budapest, 1994-97, Coll. Experts Exptl. Clin. Immunology Semmelweis U. Medicine, Budapest, 1995—; vis. scientist Mt. Sinai Med. Sch., N.Y., 1986, 89. Contbr. numerous articles to sci. publs., 12 chpts. to books. Recipient Diploma Sub Auspiciis Rei Publicae, Supreme Presidium Hungary, 1968. Mem. Hungarian Soc. Immunology, Hungarian Soc. Internal Medicine, Hungarian Soc. Med. Writers. Avocations: connections between medicine and humanities, gardening. E-mail: serendip@mail.matav.hu. Office: Semmelweis U 3rd Dept Internal Diseases, 4 Kutvölgyi Ut, 1125 Budapest Hungary

FEKETE, FERENC, urologist; b. Leningrad, Russia, Jan. 31, 1958; arrived in Hungary, 1960; s. Ferenc and Yvetta (Buzsinsky) F.; m. Katalin Tomasovsky, Mar. 15, 1986; children: Sylvia, Andras, Attila. MD, Semmelweis Med. U., 1982, urologist, 1987. Intern 2d Clinic of Surgery, Postgrad. Med. U., Budapest, 1980-82; clin. physician, asst. prof. Clinic of Urology, Postgrad. Med. U., Budapest, 1982-93; med. dir. Mr. Clinic, Budapest, 1993—; cons. urology Soviet Embassy, Budapest, 1989-93; med. expert Nat. Netherlanden, Budapest, 1993-95; cons. urologist Clinic of Urology, Semmelweis Med. U., Budapest, 2000—. Author: Impotencia, 1995, Erectile Dysfunction, 1999. Mem. European Assn. Urology, Hungarian Assn. Urology, Hungarian Assn. Sexology. Avocations: tennis, skiing, playing electric guitar. Home: Fo u 28, 1011 Budapest Hungary Office: Mr Clinic, Szilagyi 37-39, 1026 Budapest Hungary

FEKLISOVA, OLGA VLADIMIROVNA, physicist, researcher; b. Noginsk, Russia, Feb. 5, 1961; d. Vladimir Ivanovich Feklisov and Svetlana Nikolaevna (Kolodyajnaya) F.; m. Dmitry Vladimirovich Tolmachev, July 2, 1993. MS, Moscow State U., 1985; PhD (hon.), Inst. Microelec. Tech., Chernogolovka, Russia, 1998. Tng. rschr. Inst. Microelec. Tech., 1985-87, engr., 1987-89, jr. sci. rschr., 1989-97, sci. rschr., 1997—. Contbr. articles to profl. jours. NATO grantee, 1997, Deutsche Forschungsgemeinschaft grantee, 1997-98, 2000—. Avocations: boat tourism, bicycling, art, music. Home: Klyuchik 3-154, 142407 Noginsk Russia Office: Inst Microelec Tech, 142432 Chernogolovka Russia

FELAND, JOHN MORGAN, III, military officer, educator; b. Russelville, Ark., May 1, 1972; s. John Morgan II and Ginger (Jones) F. SB, MIT, 1994; MSME, Stanford U., 1996, postgrad. Robotics engr. MIT Artificial Intelligence Lab., Cambridge, Mass., 1992; robotics rschr. Kawasaki Heavy Industries, Nishi Akashi, Japan, 1993; design engr. Dart Container Corp., Mason, Mich., 1994; tchg. asst. dept. mech. engring. Stanford (Calif.) U., 1995-96; design engr. IDEO Product Devel., Palo Alto, Calif., 1995-96; MASINT sys. mgr. Nat. Air Intelligence Ctr., Dayton, Ohio, 1997-99; instr. USAF Acad., Colo., 1999—; cons. JMF Designs, Colorado Springs, Colo. Contbr. articles to profl. jours. Student mentor Cheyenne Elem. Sch., Colorado Springs, 2000; advisor Boy Scouts Am., Colorado Springs., 2000. Decorated Air Force Commendation medal; recipient Merit award Lincoln Found. Design Competition, 19965. Mem. ASME, Soc. Automotive Engrs., Am. Soc. for Engring. Edn., Internat. Soc. for Sci. of Engring. Design. Democrat. Methodist. Avocations: product development, sailing, road and mountain cycling, gourmet cooking. Home: 5750 Grapevine Dr Colorado Springs CO 80918-7675 Office: HQ USAFA/DFEM 2354 Fairchild Dr U S A F Academy CO 80840

FELBER, SONJA VERONIKA, mechanical engineer; b. St Poelten, Austria, Mar. 21, 1965; d. Johann and Edeltraud (Funk) E. Grad., U. Technology Vienna, 1992, DSc, 1994. Rsch. scientist OMV, Vienna, Austria, 1991-92; asst. U. Technology Vienna, 1993—. Mem. Austrian Welding Found., Austrian Iron and Steel Inst. Achievements include new findings in crack-arrest test methods CTOD tests, on thermomechanical treated steels, on pressure vessel steels, and simulation of heat affected zones. Office: Vienna U Tech, Dept Materials Sci/Testing, Karlsplatz 13, A-1040 Vienna Austria

FELBER, STEPHAN RUDOLF, neurologist, radiologist, educator; b. Erlangen, Germany, Oct. 11, 1957; s. Rudolf and Ingeburg (Fleischer) F.; 1 child, Sebastian. MD, U. Innsbruck, Austria, 1984. Resident neurology U. Innsbruck, Austria, 1984-91; resident radiology U. Innsbruck, 1994—; resident neuroradiolgy U. Homburg, Germany, 1992-93; dir. neurology and spectroscopy dept. magnetic resonance U. Innsbruck, Austria, 1989—, asst. prof. neurology, 1994—, cons. neurologist, dept. neurology, 1991—, cons. radiologist, dept. radiology II. Editor: 3D Magnetic Resonance, 1994; inventor and patentee in field. Recipient award of intensive care medicine Austria, 1993, award of the Austrian Soc. of Stroke, Austria, 1994, 97.

FELBINGER, THOMAS WOLFGANG, physician, researcher; b. Augsburg, Bavaria, Germany, Apr. 21, 1966; s. Hubert and Hertha (Jakob) F. MD, U. Ulm, 1993. Intern U. Munich Hosp., 1993-95, resident in anesthesiology, 1995-00; rsch. fellow Harvard Med. Sch., Boston, 2000—. Author: (with others) Nutrition in Clinical Practice, 2000, among others; contbr. articles to profl. jours. Recipient Sci. award European Soc. Intensive Care Medicine, 1998, Respiratory Care Specialty award Soc. Critical Care Medicine, 1999; rsch. grantee German Rsch. Soc., 2000. Mem. European Soc. Anesthesiologists. Avocations: sailing, skiing, opera music. Office: U Munich Hosp Dept Anes, Marchioninistr 15, 81377 Munich Bavaria, Germany

FELCHT, UTZ-HELLMUTH, pharmaceutical executive, chemist; b. Iserlohn, Westfalen, Germany, Jan. 8, 1947; s. Guenther Hellmuth and Elisabeth (Moenks) F.; m. Christel Messer, 1973; 1 child, Patrick-Oliver. P-rediploma, Mainz U., Germany, 1970; Diploma in Chemistry, U. Saarbrücken, Germany, 1973; PhD in Chemistry, Kaiserlautern U., Germany, 1976; PhD (hon.), Rostock U., Germany, 1996. Scientific asst. chemistry dept. Kaiserslautern U., 1976-77; head lab. synthetic chemistry Hoechst AG, Frankfurt, 1977-80; head alkylose rsch. dept. Kalle Plant Hoechst AG, Wiesbaden, Germany, 1980-84; mem. corp. staff dept. Hoechst AG, Frankfurt, 1985-86, head corp. rsch., 1986-88; exec. v.p., pres. advanced tech. group Hoechst Celanese Corp., Bridgewater, N.J., 1988-91; dir. bd. Hoechst Japan Ltd., 1990-98; chmn. mgmt. bd. SKW Trostberg Aktiengesellschaft, 1998—; mem. scientific adv. bd. Bavarian Prime Min., 1992—; chem. supervisory bd. SGL Carbon Inc., 1994—, AgrEvo, Inc., 1994-97; IPO SGL Carbon, AG, DECHEMA; prof. (hon.) tech. organic chemistry Munich U., 1999. Mem. German Assn. Chem. Process Equipment, Chem. Tech., Biotech., Rsch. Assn. Bd. German Chem. Industry, Convent Tech. Sci. Avocations: literature, history, tennis, golf. Office: SKW Trostberg AG, Dr Albert Frank Str 32, 83308 Trostberg Bavaria, Germany

FELCMAN, JUDITH, chemistry educator; b. Rio de Janeiro, Brazil, May 3, 1941; d. Jacob and Dora Ostrower; m. Elias Felcman, Mar. 10, 1962; children: Giselle, Rosane. BS, U. Brazil, Rio de Janeiro, 1962; MS, Cath. U. Rio, Rio de Janeiro, 1980, ScD, 1983. Pharmacist Jewish Hosp. of Rio, Rio de Janeiro, 1973-77; auxiliar prof. Cath. U. Rio, Rio de Janeiro, 1978-84, asst. prof., 1984-88, assoc. prof. chemistry, 1988—; rschr. in bioinorganic chemistry. Author: Cromo, 1988; contbr. sci. articles to profl. publs., chpts. to books. Mem. Wizo-Women Internat. Zionist Orgn., Israel, 1963—. Mem. Am. Chem. Soc., Royal Soc. Chemistry, N.Y. Acad. Scis., Brazilian Soc. Chemistry. Office: PUC-RJ Dept Chemistry, Rua Marques de S Vicente 225, 22453900 Rio de Janeiro Brazil

FELD, THOMAS ROBERT, academic administrator; b. Carroll, Iowa, Sept. 30, 1944; s. Edward Martin and Elaine (Wirtz) F.; m. Donna Jean Jorstad, June 1, 1968; children: Jacqueline Joan, William Jay. BA, Loras Coll., 1966; MA, No. Ill. U., 1969; PhD, Purdue U., 1972. Instr. Loras Coll., Dubuque, Iowa, 1966-70; v.p. Lea Coll., Albert Lea, Minn., 1972-73; v.p. Cen. Meth. Coll., Fayette, Mo., 1973-76, acting pres., 1976-77; pres. Mt. Mercy Coll., Cedar Rapids, Iowa, 1977-99; ret., 1999; bd. dirs. Assn. Mercy Colls., Washington, D.C., Norwest Bank. Bd. dirs. Iowa Coll. Found., Des Moines, 1977—, chmn., 1988-89; bd. dirs. Assn. Retarded Citizens, Cedar Rapids, 1979-85. Recipient Poetry award Am. mag., 1966, Teaching award Purdue U., 1971, Outstanding Fundraiser award Nat. Soc. Fundraising Execs., 1996; named Outstanding Young Dem. of Iowa, State Dems., 1965, knight Order Holy Sepulchre, 1992, Knight Comdr., 1996. Mem. CMC Colls. Assn. (bd. dirs., pres. 1979-80, 84-85, 88-89), Iowa Coordinating Coun. Postsecondary Edn. (chmn. bd. dirs. 1985-86), Assn. Mercy Colls. (exec. com. 1985—, bd. dirs.), Nat. Assn. Intercollegiate Athletics (chmn. bd. dirs. 1986-89, 94—, Hall of Fame 1996), Iowa Assn. Ind. Colls. and Univs. (chmn. bd. dirs. 1984-85), Nat. Assn. Ind. Colls. and Univs. (bd. dirs. 1990-93), Rotary (bd. dirs. 1993-97, pres. 1995—). Democrat. Roman Catholic. Avocations: golfing, fishing, poetry. Home: 4404 Hickory Wind Ln Marion IA 52302-9600 Office: Mt Mercy Coll Office of Pres Cedar Rapids IA 52402

FELDER, MYRNA, lawyer; b. N.Y.C., Apr. 19, 1941. BA magna cum laude, Brown U., 1961; JD cum laude, NYU, 1971. Bar: N.Y. 1971, U.S. Dist. Ct. (so. and ea. dists.) N.Y. 1974, U.S. Ct. Appeals (2nd cir.) 1977, U.S. Supreme Ct. 1978. Ptnr. Raoul Lionel Felder P.C., N.Y.C., 1972—; lectr., cons. in field; mem. N.Y. State Civil Practice Adv. Com., chair subcom. on matrimonial procedures, 1983—. Editor-in-chief: The Matrimonial Strategist, 1985-89; bimonthly columnist New York Law Jour.; contbr. chpts. to books. Mem. ABA, N.Y. State Bar Assn. (chair cts. of appellate jursidiction com. 1988-92), Assn. Bar City of N.Y., Women's Bar Assn., State N.Y. (dir. 1980-85, chmn. com. on matrimonial law 1984-85, pres. 1986-87), N.Y. Women's Bar Assn. (pres. 1976-77), Order of the Coif, Phi Beta Kappa. Home: 60 Sutton Pl S Apt 19as New York NY 10022-4168 Office: Raoul Lionel Felder PC 437 Madison Ave New York NY 10022-7001

FELDER, RAOUL LIONEL, lawyer; b. N.Y.C., May 13, 1934; s. Morris and Millie (Goldstein) F.; m. Myrna Felder, May 26, 1963; children: Rachel, James. BA, NYU, 1955; JD, NYU, Switzerland, 1959; postgrad., U. Bern, Switzerland, 1955-56; hon. degree of fellow in jurisprudence, Oxford U., 1995. Bar: N.Y. 1959, U.S. Dist. Ct. (so. and ea. dists.) N.Y. 1962, U.S. Ct. Appeals (2d cir.) 1962, U.S. Supreme Ct. 1970. Pvt. practice N.Y.C., 1959-61, 64—, asst. U.S. atty., 1961-64; mem. faculty Practicing Law Inst., 1979, Marymount Coll., 1982-85, Ethical Culture Sch., 1981, 82; moderator Nat. Conf. on Child Abuse, 1989; apptd. to N.Y.C. Cultural Affairs Adv. Commn., 1995—, State Commn. on Child Abuse, 1996. Author: Divorce: The Way Things Are, Not the Way Things Should Be, 1971, Lawyers Practical Handbook to the New Divorce Law, 1981, Raoul Felder's Encyclopedia of Matrimonial Clauses, 1990, updated, 1991—, Getting Away with Murder, 1996, Restaurant Guide to Los Angeles and New York, 1996, Survival Guide to New York, 1997; columnist Fame mag., 1988-92, Am. Women Mag., 1994, N.Y. Daily News Sundays, 1995; contbr. articles on law to profl. jours. and N.Y. Times; editorials to Newsweek mag., Harper's Bazaar mag., Newsday newspaper, N.Y. Post, The Guardian (London), Penthouse mag., Cosmopolitan mag., N.Y. Times; columnist Am Spectator mag., 1999—, Washington Times, 1999—; commentator Cable News Network, 1989, BBC World Wide, 1994, 95, 97, Crossing the Line, 1997-99, The Felder Report, 1998-99; guest commentator Court TV, 1992, bd. advisors, 1992-95, editl. contr.; (documentary) Survival Guide to New York, 1998; host (TV series) Metrolaw, 1995-99; host (radio talk show) The Felder Report, 1997—, TalkAmerica. Chmn. Nat. Kidney Found. Auction, also N.Y. Fund; chmn. Dinner Jerusalem Reclamation Project; grand marshall U.S.A. Day Washington, Israel Day Parade, N.Y.C.; bd. dirs. Big Apple Greeters, 1997-99, Cop Care, Hosp. Audiences Inc., Nat. Kidney Found., N.Y.C. Econ. Devel. Corp., 2000—; mem. Govs. Commn. on Child Abuse, 1989; hon. N.Y. City Police Comms., 2000. Named Man of Yr. Bklyn. Sch. for Spl. Children, Met. Geriatric Ctr., Shield Inst., 1997; recipient Defender of Jerusalem medal, 1990, Crimebusters award Take Back N.Y., 1996. Mem. ABA (judge nat. finals client counseling competition), Assn. of Bar of City of N.Y. (spl. com. matrimonial law 1975-77), N.Y. State Trial Lawyers Assn. (past chmn. matrimonial law 1974-75), Am. Arbitration Assn., N.Y. Women's Bar Assn., Minion of the Stars (chmn. bd. 1993). Home: 60 Sutton Pl S New York NY 10022-4168 Office: 437 Madison Ave New York NY 10022-7001

FELDERSTEIN, STEVEN HOWARD, lawyer; b. Rochester, N.Y., Oct. 28, 1946; s. Lester and Ruth (Tatelbaum) F.; m. Sandra Lynn Goldman, Aug. 26, 1969; 1 child, Janis. BA, SUNY, 1968; JD, U. Calif., San Francisco, 1973. Bar: Calif. Law clk. U.S. Dist. Ct., Sacramento, 1973-75; ptnr. Felderstein Rosenberg & McManus, Sacramento, 1978-86, Diepenbrock, Wulff, Plant & Hanmegan, LLP, Sacramento, 1986-98, Felderstein Willoughby & Pascuzzi LLP, Sacramento, 1999—. Contbr. articles to profl. jours. Bd. trustees Jewish Fedn. Sacramento Region, 1990-95. Mem. Calif. Bar Assn. (uniform comml. code com. bus. sect. 1983-85, insolvency com., comml. law com. 1999—), Calif. Continuing Edn. of Bar (lectr. 1987—), Practicing Law Inst. (lectr. 1995—), Am. Coll. Bankruptcy, Calif. Bankruptcy Forum (v.p. 1998, pres. 1998-99). Fax: 916-329-7435. E-mail: sfelderstein@fwplan.com. Office: Felderstein Willoughby & Pascuzzi LLP 400 Capitol Mall Ste 1450 Sacramento CA 95814-4434

FELDKÄMPER, LUDGER BERNHARD, religious organization executive; b. Mesum, Germany, May 16, 1937. Licentiate of Sacred Theology, Pontifical Gregorian U., Rome, 1964; Licentiate in Sacred Scripture, Pontifical Bibl. Inst., Rome, 1966, Dr. Sacred Scripture, 1977. Ordained priest, Roman Cath. Ch., 1963. Prof. sacred scripture Immaculate Conception Sch. Theology, Vigan, The Philippines, 1978-83, dean of students, 1968-69, spiritual dir., 1969-72; founder, dir. John Paul I Bibl. Ctr., Vigan, 1979-83; sec.-gen. Cath. Bibl. Fedn., Stuttgart, Germany, 1984—. Author: Der betende Jesus als Heilsmittler nach Lukas, Veröffentl des Missionspriesterseminars St. Augustin 19, 1978, Bibeltheologische Überlegungen zum Begriff der Evangelisierung anhand von LK 4, 16-30, 1981, Basic Bible Seminar Handbook for Core Teams. Mem. Cath. Bibl. Assn. of Am. Home: Neckarstrasse 9, D-70736 Fellbach-Öffingen Germany Office: Catholic Biblical Fedn, Postfach 10 52 22, D-70045 Stuttgart Germany*

FELDMAN, EDUARD BENJAMINOVICH, chemical physicist, researcher; b. Port Arthur, China (Soviet mil. base), Mar. 18, 1947; s. Benjamin Bencianovich and Masha Borukhovna (Rubinchik) F.; m. Galina Sergeevna Sidorenko, Oct. 23, 1971; children: Dmitry Eduardovich, Konstantin Eduardovich. Diploma in honor, Moscow Inst. Physics and Tech., 1971; PhD, Inst. Chem. Physics, Moscow, 1976; DSc, Inst. Chem. Physics,

Chernogolovka, Russia, 1992. Jr. rschr. Inst. Chem. Physics, Russian Acad. Scis., Chernogolovka, 1971-80, sr. rschr., 1980-92, leading rschr., 1992—, head lab. modelling phys.-chem. processes, 1998; prof. All-Union Poly. Inst., Moscow, 1980-87; cons. Soviet sci. program on magnetic disks, Moscow, 1988-91, Russian NMR Ctr., Moscow, 1997—; vis. prof. Sherbrooke (Que., Can.) U., 1995-97, Eidgenössische Technische Hochschule, Zurich, Switzerland, 1998; vis. prof. Eidgenössische Technische Hochschule, Zürich, 1998. Contbr. articles to sci. jours., including Phys. Letters A., Chem. Physics Letters, Jour. Chem. Physics; patentee in field. Named Outstanding Scientist of Russia, 1994, 97, 2000; Soros grantee Internat. Sci. Found., 1994, grantee Russian Fund for Basic Investigation, 1995, 98. Mem. Russian Acad. Scis. (magnetism coun. 1988—). Office: Russian Acad Scis, Inst Chem Physics, 142432 Chernogolovka Moscow, Russia

FELDMAN, FRANKLIN, lawyer, printmaker; b. N.Y.C., Nov. 12, 1927; s. Reuben and Anne (Schulman) F.; m. Naomi Goldstein, June 3, 1956; children: Sarah, Eve, Jacob. BA, NYU, 1948; LLB, Columbia U., 1951. Bar: N.Y. 1952. Mem. office Gen. Counsel, USAF, Dept. Def., Washington, 1951-53; atty. office gen. counsel to gov. State of N.Y., Albany, 1954; assoc. Stroock & Stroock & Lavan, N.Y.C., 1955-64, ptnr., 1965-88, counsel, 1989—; cons. Temp. N.Y. Commn. on Constl. Conv., 1967; lectr. in law Columbia Law Sch., 1979—; bd. dirs. Ctr. for Book Arts. Editor-in-chief Columbia U. Law Rev., 1950-51; author: (with Stephen E. Weil) Art Works: Law, Policy and Practice, 1974, Art Law, 1986 (Best Law Book Published in 1986, Scribes); contbr. articles to profl. jours. Trustee Am. Jewish Hist. Soc., Waltham, Mass., 1987-96. 1st lt., USAF, 1951-53. Yaddo Fellow, Saratoga Springs, 1983. Fellow Am. Bar Found.; mem. N.Y. State Bar Assn., Assn. of Bar of City of N.Y. (chmn. art com. 1968-71), Internat. Found. Art Rsch. (pres. 1971-76, bd. dirs. 1976-96), Internat. Art Loss Register, Ltd., Soc. Am. Graphic Artists, Century Assn., Pvt. Art Dealers Assn., Inc. (counsel, dir. 1993—), Grolier Club. Jewish. Home: 15 W 81st St New York NY 10024-6022 Office: Stroock & Stroock & Lavan 180 Maiden Ln Fl 17 New York NY 10038-4937

FELDMAN, JAVIER, communications executive; b. Cordoba, Argentine, May 17, 1974. Telecomm. engr., San Martin Sch., Argentine, 1991. Cell planning engr. Telecom Personal, Argentina, 1998. Avocations: sports. Home: Marcelo T De Alvear, 5000 Cordoba Argentina

FELDMAN, JEFFREY, investment company executive; b. N.Y.C., Sept. 13, 1947; s. Harry and Birdie F.; m. Judith Ellen, May 29, 1969; children: Helene, Scott. BA, Queens Coll., 1969; MBA, St. Johns U., 1973. Chmn., CEO Cralin and Co., N.Y.C., 1975-86; pres., CEO Cyberia Capital, N.Y.C., 1989-95, Superior St. Capital, N.Y.C., 1995—. Republican. Jewish. Office: Superior St Capital 17 State St New York NY 10004-1501

FELDMAN, OFER, political scientist; b. Tel Aviv, Feb. 27, 1954; arrived in Japan, 1982; s. Arie and Shulamit (Rinde) F.; m. Rie Ote Feldman, Feb. 18, 1988; children: Utai, Iri. BA, U. Tel Aviv, 1979; MA, Hebrew U. Jerusalem, Israel, 1982; PhD, U. Tokyo, 1987. Vis. researcher Keio U., Japan, 1987-88; assoc. prof. Ibaraki U., Japan, 1988-92; fgn. prof. U. Tsukuba, Japan, 1992-95; assoc. prof. Naruto U. Edn., Japan, 1995—; elected mem. Governing Coun., ISPP, 1993-95, Exec. Com., Psychopolitics Rsch. Group, IPSA, 1994—, chair, 2000—; exec. editor Politics, Group and the Indiv., Internat. Jour., 1995-2000. Author: Ningen Shinri to Seiji, 1989, Imeji de Yomu Nagatacho, 1992, Politics and the News Media in Japan, 1993, The Political Personality of Japan, 1999; author, contbr.: Seiji Gaku Neumon, 1992; editor: Political Psychology in Japan, 1999; co-editor: Politically Speaking, 1998, Beyond Public Speech and Symbols, 2000. With Israel Def. Forces, 1973-76. Recipient Eric Erikson award Internat. Soc. Polit. Psychology, 1993. Mem. Internat. Soc. Polit. Psychology, Am. Polit. Sci. Assn., Japan Polit. Sci. Assn., Internat. Polit. Sci. Assn. Home: 4501 Naruto U Residence, 168-2 Satoura, Naruto-shi 772, Japan Office: Naruto U of Edn, Takashima, Naruto-shi 772, Japan

FELDMAN, ROBERT HARRY, health psychology educator; b. Bklyn., Feb. 10, 1943. PhD, Syracuse U., 1974. Asst. prof. psychology SUNY Coll. at Utica/Rome, 1974-77; postdoctoral fellow in health psychology U. Conn. Med.-Dental Sch., 1977-78; asst. prof. Johns Hopkins U., Balt., 1978-79; asst. prof. dept. health edn. U. Md., College Park, 1979-84, assoc. prof., 1984-90, prof., 1990—. Author: Occupational Health Behavior, 1985. Grantee Adminstrn. on Aging, 1989. Office: U Md Dept Health Edn College Park MD 20742-0001

FELDMAN, ROGER DAVID, lawyer; b. N.Y.C., Apr. 7, 1943; s. Louis and Dora (Goldsmith) F.; m. Gail Steg, May 31, 1969; children: Rebecca, Seth. AB, Brown U., 1962; LLB, Yale U.; MBA, Harvard U. Bar: N.Y. 1966, D.C. 1977. Ops. rsch. analyst Office Asst. Sec. Def., Washington, 1967-68; staff asst. Office of Pres. U. S., Washington, 1968-69; assoc. LeBoeuf Lamb Leiby & MacRae, 1969-75; ptnr. Le Boeuf Lamb Leiby & MacRae, 1977-83; dep. asst. adminstr. FEA, Washington, 1975-77; mng. ptnr. project fin. group Nixon Hargrave Devans & Doyle, Washington, 1983-89; head ptnr. project fin. group McDermott Will & Emery, Washington, 1989-97; chair project fin. group Bingham Dana LLP, 1997—; mem. fin. adv. bd. EPA, 1989-92; bd. dirs. R.J. Rudden & Assocs. Inc., Cogeneration Inst., pub.-pvt. venture divsn. Am. Road and Transp. Builders, 1991-93, N.E. Energy and Commerce Assn., Water Industry Coun.; pres. Nat. Coun. for Pub. and Pvt. Partnerships, 1983-98, chair, 1998—. Author: (with others) Infrastructure Finance: Tools for the Future, 1988, Public-Private Ventures in Transportation, 1990, Comprehensive Guide to Water and Wastewater Finance, 1991, Privatization of Public Utilities, 1995, Privatization, 1995; mem. bd. editors Yale Law Jour., 1964-65, Jour. Project Fin., 1995—, Contrn. Bus. Rev., 1992—; Washington editor Cogeneration and Power Marketing Monthly Letter, 1987-98, Mcht. Power Monthly, 1998—, Strategic Planning for Energy and the Environment, 1992— (Author of the Yr. 1998), Power Marketers Assn. Mag., 1999—; contbr. articles to profl. jours. Mem. ABA (chmn. energy law com. 1980-83, alt. energy sources com. 1981-84, 86-90, chmn. environ. values com. 1983-89, com. on privatization 1985-90, chmn. energy fin. 1990-91), Fed. Energy Bar Assn. (chmn. cogeneration com. 1981-82), Nat. Coun. for Pub.-Pvt. Partnerships (Outstanding Contbn. to Privatization award), N.Y. Bar Assn., D.C. Bar Assn. (chair internat. fin. and investment com. 1998—), Assn. Energy Engrs. (Cogeneration Profl. of Yr. 1990), Phi Beta Kappa. Office: Bingham Dana LLP 1120 20th St NW Ste 800 Washington DC 20036-3406

FELDMANN, HARALD, psychiatrist, psychopathology researcher; b. Celle, Germany, June 14, 1925; s. Heinrich and Gertrud (Schlemm) F.; m. Regine Schmidt, Mar. 22, 1973; children: Ingrid, Eckart, Annette Christiane. Med. diploma, U. Goettingen, 1952, MD, 1955. Head physician Psychiat. Clinic U. Goettingen (Fed. Republic Germany), 1970-79, prof. psychopathology, 1979-90, head Psychopathol. Rsch. Ctr., 1979-90. Author: Hypochondriasis, 1972, Manual of Medical Psychology, 1983, Psychiatry and Psychotherapy, 1984, Mimesis and Reality, 1988, (with J.M. Broekman) Representation and Meaning, 1990, Rape and Its Psychological Sequelae, 1992; contbr. articles on psychopathology to med. jours. Home: Ludwig Beck-Strasse 13, D-37075 Goettingen Germany

FELDSTEIN, JOSHUA, educational administrator; b. Russia, Apr. 12, 1921; came to U.S., 1939, naturalized, 1944; s. Cemach and Fania B. Feldstein; B.S., Delaware Valley Coll., Doylestown, Pa., 1952; M.S., Rutgers U., 1956, Ph.D., 1962; m. Miriam Myzel, Dec. 24, 1944; children: Theodore Lee, Daniel Ethan. Instr. horticulture Delaware Valley Coll., 1952-56, asst. prof., 1956-60, assoc. prof., 1960-65, prof. horticulture, from 1965, dept. chmn., 1959-69, chmn. plant sci. div., 1966-73, assoc. dean, 1969-73, dean, 1973-75, pres. Delaware Valley Coll. Sci. and Agr., 1975-87, pres. emeritus, 1987—, interim pres., 1995-97; coord. nat. tchg. fellowships, student fin. aid, chmn. admissions, curriculum, athletics, student affairs, acad. standard coms. Accorded Legion of Honor membership by Chapel of Four Chaplains, Phila., 1974; recipient award Pa. Future Farmers Am., 1980. Mem. Am. Soc. Hort. Sci. (L.M. Ware Disting. Teaching award), Am. Inst. Biol. Scis., Eastern Assn. Coll. Deans and Advs. to Students, Soil Conservation Soc. Am., Pa. Assn. Colls. and Univs., Commn. of Ind. Colls. and Univs. Jewish. Author (with N.F. Childers): Effect of Irrigation on Fruit Size and Yield of Peaches in Pennsylvania, 1957; Peach Irrigation in a Humid Region, 1964; Effects of Irrigation on Peaches in Pennsylvania, 1965.

FELDTKELLER, ERNST (JOHANNES), retired solid-state physicist; b. Berlin, Oct. 19, 1931; s. Richard and Elisabeth (Kessler) F.; m. Karin Heinze; children: Martin, Andreas. Diplom-physiker, Tech. U., Stuttgart, Germany, 1957; Dr.rer.nat., U. Göttingen, Germany, 1959. Rschr. Siemens AG, Munich, 1959-71; head dept. Siemens Ag, Munich, 1971-83, referee for sci. and tech., 1983-92; ret., 1992; lectr. Tech. U., Munich, 1967-86. Author: Dielektrische und Magnetische Materialeigenschaften, 1973, 74, Zur Situation von Spondyloarthritis-Patienten, 1999; editor Pioniere der Wissenschaft bei Siemens, 1999; contbr. articles to profl. jours. Recipient Bundesverdienstkreuz, Fed. Republic Germany, 1995, Ehrenmitgliedschaft, Deutsche Vereinigung Morbus Bechterew, 1996. Mem. Deutsche Physikalische Gesellschaft, Deutsche Vereinigung Morbus Bechterew (sci. editor newsletter 1981—), Ankylosing Spondylitis Internat. Fedn. (v.p. 1992—). Lutheran. Avocations: music, painting.

FELGAR, RAYMOND E(UGENE), pathologist, medical educator; b. Mt. Pleasant, Pa., Mar. 2, 1963; s. Samuel Hurst and Anna June (Stull) F. BS in Microbiology with honors, Pa. State U., 1985; PhD in Pathology, U. Pitts., 1990, MD, 1992. Diplomate Am. Bd. Pathology in Anatomic and Clin. Pathology. Resident in anatomic and clin. pathology U. Pa. Med. Ctr., Phila., 1992-96; fellow in hematopathology dept. pathology Vanderbilt U., Nashville, 1996-98; dir. hematopathology and clin. flow cytometry Hahnemann Hosp., Phila., 1998; asst. prof. dept. pathology and lab medicine MCP-Hahnemann Sch. Medicine, Phila., 1998; dir. clin. flow cytometry lab., hematopathologist and co-dir. hematopathology Strong Meml. Hosp., Rochester, N.Y., 1998—; asst. prof. Dept. Pathology & Lab. Medicine U. Rochester Sch. Medicine & Dentistry, 1998—. Contbr. articles to profl. jours., chpt. to book. NIH med. scientist tng. fellow, 1987-92. Mem. AMA, Coll. Am. Pathologists, Am. Soc. Clin. Pathologists, Am. Soc. Hematology, U.S. and Can. Acad. Pathology, Soc. for Hematopathology, European Assn. for Hematopathology, Eastern Coop. Oncology Group (pathology com.), Children's Oncology Group, Pa. State U. Alumni Assn., Phi Beta Kappa.

FELGRAN, STEVEN DAVID, economist; b. N.Y.C., July 1, 1953; s. Howard H. and Ilse H. (Sturm) F.; m. Hilary Ann Macht, June 13, 1999. BA, U. Pa., 1975; MA in Econs., Yale U., 1978, MPhil in Econs., 1978, PhD in Econs., 1982. Analyst Congl. Budget Office, Washington, 1975-76; cons. Arthur D. Little, Inc., Cambridge, Mass., 1981-83; economist Fed. Res. Bank of Boston, 1983-89; prof. Coll. Bus. Adminstrn. Northeastern U., Boston, 1989-93; sr. mgr. Economic Cons. Svcs./KPMG, N.Y.C., 1993-97, ptnr., 1997—. Contbr. numerous articles to profl. jours., mags. and newspapers. Mem. ABA, Am. Econ. Assn., Phi Beta Kappa. Avocations: theater, musical comedy, historic preservation and restoration, Civil War era, travel. Office: KMPG 345 Park Ave Fl 35 New York NY 10154-0004

FELHOFER, MARYLOUISE KATHERINE, nursing administrator; b. Milw., June 30, 1952; d. Charles Walter and Tillie Elizabeth (Hrymnak) Tomasicyk; m. Paul Robert Felhofer, Aug. 12, 1977. BSN, Alverno Coll., Milw., 1974; MS in Nursing Adminstrn., U. Md., Balt., 1991. RN, Md.; cert. profl. in healthcare quality. Commd. ensign USN, 1972, advanced through grades to capt., 1997; staff and charge nurse Naval Regional Med. Ctr., Orlando, Fla., 1974-77; instr., adminstrv. officer Naval Officer Indoctrination Sch., Newport, R.I., 1977-81; charge nurse, relief dept. head, supr. Naval Hosp., Great Lakes, Ill., 1981-86; head command quality assurance dept. Naval Hosp., Guam, 1986-89; head command quality assessment dept. Nat. Naval Med. Ctr., Bethesda, Md., 1991-93; head orgnl. performance improvement customer support br. Navy Bur. Medicine and Surgery, 1994-95, head tricare quality br., 1995-96; dir. nursing adminstrv. matters, quality mgmt. specialist Office of Naval Med. Insp. Gen., 1996-99; head clin. ops. Mil. Med. Support Office, 1999—; U.S. Navy Medicine fellow Joint Commn. on Accreditation of Healthcare Orgns., 1993-94. Decorated Navy Commendation medals (3), Navy Meritorious Svc. medals (2); recipient various awards. Mem. Nat. Assn. for Healthcare Quality, Assn. Mil. Surgeons U.S., Navy Nurse Corps Assn., Nurses Alumnae Assn. U. Md., Sigma Theta Tau, Delta Epsilon Sigma, Kappa Gamma Pi, Phi Kappa Phi. Avocations: reading, cooking, gardening, traveling.

FELICI, ANGELO CARDINAL, religious organization executive; b. Segni, Italy, July 26, 1919. Ordained priest Roman Cath. Ch., 1942. Elected archbishop of Cesariana Numidia, 1967; consecrated bishop, 1967; apostolic nuncio The Netherlands, Portugal, France; created cardinal, 1988; prefect Congregation for Causes of Sts, Vatican City; pres. Pontifical Cmmn. Ecclesia Dei, Vatican City, 1995—. Office: Piazza Citta Leonina 9, 00193 Rome Italy*

FELICIANO, DONNA-CELESTE DAVID, lawyer, educator; b. Manila, The Philippines, July 1, 1968; d. Pablo Aguila and Cristina Juliana (David) F.; m. Ramon Alberto Ysmael Buenbrazo Gatmaytan, Dec. 20, 1995. BA in Econs. with distinction, Assumption Coll., Manila, The Philippines, 1988; LLB, U. The Philippines, Manila, 1992. Bar: The Philippines. Energy regulatory officer I Energy Regulatory Bd., The Philippines, 1990; lectr. Assumption Coll., Manila, 1992-94, City Coll. of Manila, The Philippines, 1996—; assoc. Juan T. David Law Office, Manila, 1993—; ptnr. David, Feliciano, Gatmaytan & Feliciano Law Office, Manila, 1999—; mem. Peláez, Gregorio, Sipin, Bala, & Robles, 2000—; advisor Hukvets Assn., The Philippines, 1993—. Contbr. papers to profl. jours. Human rights advocate, Manila. Internat. Bar Assn. scholar London, 1994. Mem. Integrated Bar of the Philippines (chpt. sec. 1999—). Roman Catholic. Avocations: swimming, dancing, singing, writing, travel. Home: 1 Don Roman St D Enrique Ht, Commonwealth Ave, Quezon City 1119, The Philippines Office: Juan T David Law Office, 1614 San Lazaro St Sta, Cruz Manila 1003, The Philippines

FELIPO, VICENTE, biomedical researcher; b. Tabernes Blanques, Valencia, Spain, May 12, 1957; s. Vicente Felipo and Maria Amparo Orts; m. Amelia Benavent, Apr. 14, 1984; children: Amelia, Maria del Mar. Lic. Chem., Valencia U., Spain, 1979, PhD in Chemistry, 1983. Predoctoral fellow Inst. Investigaciones Citolog, Valencia, 1980-85, postdoctoral fellow, 1986-89, staff researcher, 1990—. Editor: Cirrhosis, Hepatic Ency., 1990, Cirrhosis, Hyperammon, 1993, Hepatic Ency., Hyperammon, Ammonia Toxicity, 1994, Neurochem. Rsch., 1994, Metabolic Brain Disease, 1994, Advances in Cirrhosis, Hyperammonemia and Hepatic Encephalopathy, 1997, Internat. Jour. Molecular Medicine, 1997, Analytical Pharmacology, 1997. Mem. Internat. Soc. Neurochem., Soc. Neurosci., N.Y. Acad. Sci. Office: Instit Investig Citologicas, de la FIB Amadeo de Saboya 4, Valencia 46010, Spain

FELIU, VICENTE, electrical engineering educator, dean; b. Figueras, Gerona, Spain, Sept. 23, 1957; s. Sebastian Feliu and Maria Teresa Batlle; m. Maria Isabel, Apr. 6, 1984; children: Adrian, Daniel. M Indsl. Engring., Poly. U., Madrid, 1979, PhD in Elec. Engring., 1982; M Physics, Open U., Madrid, 1986. Asst. prof. elec. engring. Open U., 1980-86, assoc. prof., 1986-90, prof., 1990-94, head dept., 1991-94; prof. indsl. engring. Castilla-La Mancha U., Ciudad Real, Spain, 1994—, dean Sch. Indsl. Engring., 1994—. Contbr. articles to sci. jours., including IEEE Trans. Robotics and Automation, Jour. Robotic Sys., IEEE Trans. Automatic Control, IEEE Trans. Sys., Man and Cybernetics, Automatica, Corrosion Sci., Materials and Structures; patentee for sensors of corrosion in structures. Postdoctoral Fulbright scholar Carnegie Mellon U., Pitts., 1987-89. Mem. IEEE, Internat. Fedn. Automatic Control. Avocations: reading, tennis. Office: ETSII/U Castilla-La Mancha, Campus Universitario S/N, 13071 Ciudad Real Spain

FELIX, DAVID, retired economics educator, consultant; b. N.Y.C., June 10, 1918; s. Oscar and Jenny Felix; m. Gretchen Schafer, Aug. 20, 1945; children: Tonia, Gianna. BA, U. Calif., Berkeley, 1942; MA, U. Calif., 1947, PhD, 1955. Vis. asst. prof. econs. U. Wash., Seattle, 1950-52; prof. econs. Wayne State U., Detroit, 1954-63, Washington U., St. Louis, 1964-88; prof. emeritus, 1988—; vis. rsch. fellow Ctr. U.S.-Mex. Studies, U. Calif., 1984, vis. rsch. assoc. Ctr. Internat. Affairs, Harvard U., 1967-68; cons. UNDP, 1994-96, UN Econ. Commn. L.Am., 1974. Editor: Debt and Transfiguration, 1990; contbr. ove 26 articles to profl. jours. Lt., USN, 1942-46. Fulbright fellow, 1967, 91. Mem. Am. Econ. Assn., Econ. History Assn. (editl. bd. 1978-84), L.Am. Studies Assn. (editl. bd. 1970-72), Washington U. Prof. Emeritus Assn. (coun. 1990-91, pres. 1992). Avocations: tennis, gardening, travel. E-mail: felix@wueconc.wustl.edu. Office: Washington U Dept Econs One Brookings Dr Saint Louis MO 63130

FELIX, JULIAN, physicist, educator; b. Cd Obregón, Sonora, Mexico, Feb. 16, 1961; s. Rafael and Guadalupe (Valdez) F. BSc, E.S.F.M. IPN, Mexico City, 1985; MSc, Cinvestav Ipn, Mexico City, 1986; DSc, U. Mass., Leon, Mexico, 1994. Lectr. physics ESFM IPN, Mexico City, 1985, Cinvestav IPN, Mexico City, 1986, Itson, Cd Obregón, Mexico, 1987-90; guest scientist Fermilab, Batavia, 1991, 96; vis. scholar U. Mass., Amherst, 1992-94; lectr. physics, rschr. Inst. Physics, U. Guanajuato, Leon, 1990—; rschr. Expt. BNL-766 Nevis Labs., 1991—, Expt. FNAL-690 FERMILAB, 1990—, Expt. FNAL-871 FERMILAB, 1996—; cons. CONACyT, Mexico City, 1996; co-dir. ICFA 97-Sch., León, 1997. Contbr. articles to profl. jours. Mem. Nat. Sys. Rschrs. Avocations: writing, painting. Office: Inst Física U Guanajuato Lomas, del Bosque 103 Col Lomas del, Campestre 37150 León Mexico

FELIX, KELVIN EDWARD, archbishop; b. Roseau, Dominica, Feb. 15, 1933; s. Edward Mosley and Melanie (Cadette) F. Student, Sem. St. John Vianney, Trinidad and Tobago, 1951-56; diploma in adult edn., St. Francis Xavier U., N.S., Can., 1963, LLD (hon.), 1986; MA in Sociology and Anthropology, U. Notre Dame, 1967; postgrad., U. Bradford, Eng., 1967-70. Ordained priest Roman Cath. Ch., 1956. Assoc. pastor Roman Cath. Ch., Dominica, 1956-62; lectr., tutor U. West Indies and Sem., Trinidad and Tobago, 1970-72; assoc. gen. sec. Caribbean Conf. Chs., Trinidad and Tobago, 1975-81; archbishop of Castries St. Lucia, 1981—; cons. Pontifical Coun. for the Family, Roman Cath. Ch., Rome, 1988. Granted OBE by Queen Elizabeth II, 1992, COR UNUM by Holy Father John Paul II, 1994-99. Fax: 758-452-3697. E-mail: archbishop@candw.lc. Office: Archbishop s Office, PO Box 267, Castries Saint Lucia

FELIX, VALTER NILTON, surgeon, researcher; b. Santo André, Sao Paulo, Brazil, May 29, 1951; s. Walter and Otilia (Rogatto) F. Grad. Med. Sch., Sao Paulo U., Santo André, 1975; MD, Sao Paulo U., 1987, PhD, 1994. Cert. specialist in surgery, video-surgery, gastroenterology and intensive care. Resident Sao Paulo U. Med. Sch., 1976-78, observer, 1979-80, vol. physician, 1981-82, prof. surgery, 1983—; cons. Rsch. Nat. Coun. Brazilia, 1987—; sci. dir. Brazilian Digestive Motility Soc., Sao Paulo, Sao Paulo Intensive Care Soc. Editor: Adult/Pediatric Intensive Medicine, 1997; assoc. editor Brazilian Archives of Digestive Surgery. Recipient Brazilian Book Coun. honor, 1993; Rsch. Nat. Coun. grantee, 1987. Mem. Internat. Gastro-Surg. Club (Greece), Internat. Soc. Surgery (Japan), Critical Care Soc. (U.S.). Roman Catholic. Avocations: literature movies, theater, informatics, sports. Office: R Frei Caneca 1407 cj 221, 01307003 São Paulo Brazil

FELIZARDO, JOÃO, judge. Chief justice Supreme Court of Angola, Luanda. Office: Supreme Ct, Rua 17 de Setembro 1er andr, Palacio do Povo Luanda, Angola*

FELKER, WILLIAM H. (B. C. STUVINSKI), filmmaker, videomaker; b. Rockford, Ill., Oct. 14, 1953; s. Robert Hugh and Suzanne (Billig) F.; m. Janell Ann Schwartz, Sept. 20, 1975; children: Sage Brook, Ruth Rama, Alexandra Alta. BFA, Mpls. Coll. Art and Design, 1976. Owner B.C. Stuvinski Prodns., Mpls., 1976-78; with prodn. dept. EMCOM, Mpls., 1978-79; owner House of Cinemagraphics, Mpls., 1979—; gaffer Feature, Comml. and Indsl. Prodn. Svcs., 1975—; prodn. mgr. Paisely Pk. Enterprises, 1992-93; dir. photography Godfathers Pizza, 1995—; lighting dir. ITVA Awards, 1995, SmithKline Beecham, IBM, SuperValue, Bell Mus. Filmmaker: Voices, 1970, Field Animation Series, 1972, The Cave, 1974, What??, 1975, Phenomena 24, 1976, Dialetic Complex, 1976, Pink Movie, 1976, Turn Off After Viewing, 1976, Bridge, 1977, Five Bridge Installation Allusions, 1977, Factors of Six by David Means, 1979, L.A.S.E.R., 1979; (with Janell Felker) A Matter of Time, 1976, Cloud Gel, 1977, Sand Animation, 1977, Green Movie, 1977, The Circus is Kinder, 1977, Nine States of Motion, 1977, Landscape, 1978-90, Scrim Film, 1978, Desert, 1979, Bucolics, 1979, Homage to the 41 Sperm Whales That Beached on the Eve of the Signing of the Strategic Arms Limitation Treaty (SALT II), 1980; (with Jack Becker and Janell Felker) Upsidedownandbackwards, 1976; electric dept. Purple Rain, 1984, Here on Earth, 1999, Drop Dead Gorgeous; dir. photography: Breakfast on Broadway, 1988, Live Action, 1990-91, Pillsbury Spots, 1999, The Private Public, 2000; dir. lighting and sound Letter Press Printing, 1978, Picasso, 1980; dir. lighting Too Far, Too Fast, 1989, Swedish TV in American, 1993, Marraige Day, Mall of America, Dr. John Grey, 1996, Bell Live, 1995-2000; 1st asst. camera 2nd unit Home Town Boy Makes Good, 1989, The Come Back, Get Off, 1991, Organ Grinder, 1991; 2d asst. Divine Madness, 1980; dir., cameraman, editor AT&T Mpls. Tower: Time Lapse Documentary, 1989-91; dir. spl. effects photography, assoc. producer Resident Alien, 1990-91; lighting dir. Violet the Organ Grinder, Housestyle, 1991, Bell Live, 1994, Children's Home Society Korea and U.S., 1996; assoc. producer What About Bob, 1991-92; lighting dir., camera operator Meantime, 1990, Prince concerts and videos, 1991-92; prodn. mgr. Sacrifice of Victor, 1992; post prodn. mgr. Three Chains o' Gold, 1992, Undertaker, 1992;co-dir., dir. photography, editor Stu and Bink, 1993-97; editorial svcs., Simple Plan, 1998, Sugar and Spice, 1999; camera operator, gaffer The Visionary, 1995; camera operator, 1st asst. camera 2d unit Mallrats, 1995; helicopter camera operator In the Line of Duty, 1995; electrician Feeling Minnesota, 1995; 2d asst. camera Mighty Ducks, 1995; 2d unit gaffer, video colorist Grumpier Old Men, 1995; gaffer Psychic Friends Network, Mall of America, 1996: cinematographer NBA Jam, 1993. Recipient Jerome Found. grant, 1978, Minn. State Arts Bd. grant, 1978, NEA grants, 1978, 92. Mem. AICP, Ind. Feature Project North. Home and Office: 4802 Quail Ave N Minneapolis MN 55429-3739

FELL, CHRISTOPHER TAYLOR, film festival director; b. Bradford, Yorkshire, Eng., Feb. 25, 1969; s. John Holt and Susan (Ratcliffe) F.; m. Isma Almas Khan, Dec. 19, 1992; children: Natashs Almas, Jovairia Sultana. Mgr. Bradford Playhouse, 1992-94; programmer Nat. Mus. Photography, Film and TV, Bradford, 1994-99; dir. Leeds (Eng.) Internat. Film Festival, 1999—. Avocations: architecture, scriptwriting, travel. Office: Leeds Internat Film, Festival, Town Hall, Yorks Leeds LS1 3AD, England

FELL, RILEY BROWN, lawyer; b. New Orleans, Apr. 28, 1921; s. William Riley Brown and Lucy Agnes (Alcantara) F.; m. Mildred Elizabeth Gause, Aug. 21, 1947 (dec. July 1995); children: Damon, Martha, Mark, Michael, Brigid, James (dec.), Monica, Mary, Grace, Gerard. BSME, La. Poly. Inst., Ruston, 1943; LLB, Tulane U., 1947. Bar: La. 1947, Okla. 1961, U.S. Ct. Appeals (5th and 10th cirs.), U.S. Supreme Ct. 1957, U.S. Dist. Ct. (we. and ea. dists.) La., U.S. Dist. Ct. (no. and ea. dists.) Okla., U.S. Dist. Ct. (so. dist.) Ill., U.S. Dist. Ct. (so. dist.) Miss., others. Lawyer Hunt Oil Co., Shreveport, 1947-55, The Ohio Oil Co., Shreveport, Tulsa, 1955-63; divsn. atty. Marathon Oil Co., Tulsa, 1963-72; gen. counsel Loop Inc., New Orleans, 1972-79; ptnr. Barham & Churchill, New Orleans, 1979-82; sole practice law New Orleans, Tulsa, 1982—; legal com. Interstate Oil Compact Commn., Tulsa, 1966-70, New Orleans, 1973-81. Served in U.S. Navy, 1944-45. Mem. ABA, Am. Petroleum Inst. (chmn. subcom. 1969-81), Serra Club. Republican. Roman Catholic. Avocations: church choir, cooking, aerobics, mentoring, tutoring. Home: 4231 S Sandusky Ave Tulsa OK 74135-2860

FELL, SAMUEL KENNEDY (KEN FELL), infosystems executive; b. Wilmington, Del., Oct. 6, 1944; s. S. Kennedy and Anna Elizabeth (Alford) F.; m. Diana Marie Dickson, May 8, 1965; children: Melissa Ann, Michael Kennedy. BSBA, Oklahoma City U., 1983; postgrad. in bus., John F. Kennedy U.; grad. exec. mgmt. program, Duke U., 1991. Mgmt./data processing sys. designer/implementor Gen. Motors Corp., Detroit and Oklahoma City, 1967-81; v.p. info. systems Totco Divsn. Baker Internat., Norman, Okla., 1981-85; v.p. computer info. Cleve. Pneumatic subs. Pneumo Abex Corp. div. IC Industries, 1985-88; sr. dir. systems devel. Sprint, Kansas City, Mo., 1988-95; sr. v.p. product devel., exec. bd. mem. SynQuest, Inc., A Warburg Pincus Co., 1995-2000; CIO NYISO, Schenectady, N.Y., 2000—. Mem. Data Processing Mgrs. Assn., Oracle Users Group, Soc. Info. Mgrs.

FELLENIUS, KERSTIN BIRGITTA, special education educator; b. Stockholm, June 24, 1941; m. Göran Lars, June 11, 1967; children: Charlotta, Kristina. Spl. Tchr. for Visually Impaired, U. Stockholm, 1966, Spl. Tchr. for Learning Disabilities, 1971, Studies in Edl. Rsch., 1988; PhD, 1999. Tchr. Compulsary Sch., Stockholm, 1962-65; spl. tchr. Tomteboda Sch. for the Blind, Solna, Sweden, 1966-81; itinerant tchr. for visually impaired Stockholm, 1981-84; low vision therapist Tomteboda Resource Ctr., Stockholm, 1984-89; rschr. Stockholm Inst. Edn., 1990—, lectr., 1995—.

Author: (book) The Reading Skills of Visually Impairment, 1996. Office: Stockholm Inst Edn, Box 47308 Dept Spl Edn, S-10074 Stockholm Sweden

FELLER, JULIAN ASHLEY, orthopedic surgeon; b. Sydney, Australia, Sept. 24, 1959; s. Bruno and Margaret Meredith (Yates) F.; m. Toni Frances Hinton, 1992. MB BS with honors, Monash U., Melbourne, Victoria, Australia, 1982. Intern Alfred Hosp., Melbourne, 1983, 1983-86; basic surg. trainee Alfred Hosp., 1987-91; orthopaedic resident Victorian Tng. Program, 1987-90; fellowship in knee surgery Austin Hosp., Melbourne, 1991, orthopedic surgeon, 1992—; assoc. prof. Sch. Physics La Trobe U., Melbourne, 2000—. Contbr. articles to profl. publs. Australian Physiotherapy Rsch. Found. grant, 1993. Fellow Royal Australasian Coll. Surgeons; mem. Australian Orthopedic Assn., Australian Med. Assn., Australian Knee Soc., Am. Acad. Orthopedic Surgeons, European Soc. Sports Traumatology, Knee Surgery and Arthroscopy, We. Pacific Orthopedic Assn., Internat. Soc. Arthroscopy, Knee Surgery, Orthopaedic Sports Medicine. Home: 133 Wattle Valley Rd, Camberwell 3124, Australia Office: La Trobe U, Med Ctr, Bundoora Victoria, Australia 3083

FELLER, WINTHROP BRUCE, physicist; b. Cleve., Nov. 1, 1950; s. Robert William and Virginia Adele (Winther) F.; m. Lydia M. Conca, Aug. 14, 1988; 1 child, Daniel James. SB, MIT, 1974; postgrad., Yale U., 1974-75. Lectr. in physics and astronomy Northwestern U., Evanston, Ill., 1977-83; sr. scientist Galileo Corp., Sturbridge, Mass., 1984-92; v.p., chief scientist Nova Sci., Inc., 1993—; ptnr. Emission Sys., L.L.C. Contbr. articles to profl. jours. Recipient R&D 100 award R&D mag.; grantee NASA, ARPA, NIH, NSF, Dept. Energy, Dept. Def., Dept. Commerce. Mem. AAAS, Am. Phys. Soc., Am. Philos. Assn., Optical Soc. Am., Soc. Photo-Optical Instrumentation Engrs. (session co-chmn. detector conf.), Fedn. Am. Scientists, Union Concerned Scientists. Achievements include patents in microchannel plate field; development of low noise, conductively cooled, neutron-, hard x-, and gamma ray sensitive microchannel plate detectors, lobstereye x-ray telescope optics, digital readout systems, electron-beam lithography sources, x-ray lithography optics, mammography imaging, quantum computing, x-ray and neutron focusing microchannel lens, others; research on detectors for EUV and x-ray astronomy, space plasma detectors, mass analysis of biomolecules, and the philosophy of science. Home: 50 Shanda Ln Tolland CT 06084-3951 Office: Nova Sci Inc PO Box 928 Sturbridge MA 01566-0928

FELLNER, ANDRZEJ, navigator, educator; b. Cracow, Poland, Apr. 8, 1955; s. Tadeusz and Lucyna (Urbańska) F.; m. Jolanta Lukasik, Sept. 6, 1980; children: Katarzyna, Joanna, Radoslaw. Navigation Engr., Aviation Acad., Deblin, Poland, 1978; M, U. Cracow, 1988; D, Acad. Defence, Warszawa, Poland, 1991; grad., NATO Sch., Oberammergen, Germany, 1992, Def. Sch. Langs., Beaconsfield, U.K., 1995. Cert. engr., navigation, aviation, satellite technique. Asst. Aviation Acad., Deblin, 1978-85, lectr., 1985-88, old lectr., 1989-91, sr. prof., 1991-95, prof., 1996—; prof. U. Wilno/Litwoi, 1993; cons. Air Force Tech. Inst., Warszawa, 1985—; mem. com. space and satellite rsch. Polish Acad. Scis., Warszawa, 1995, mem. com. navigation sect. com. geodesy, 1987; with Nato Sch. Supreme Hdqrs. Europe, 1992—, Def. Sch. Langs., Beaconsfield, Eng., 1995—. Author: Polish Air Force, 1995 (distinction 1996); contbr. articles to profl. jours.; inventor in field. Wing comdr. Aviation Acad., 1993. Mem. Royal Inst. Navigation, Nat. Geog. Soc., European Geophys. Soc., Polish Astronautical Soc. Avocations: travel, books, animals, flowers. Home: Ul Urbanowicza 9m2, 08-521 Deblin 3, Poland Office: Aviation Acad, 08-521 Deblin 3, Poland

FELLOWS, ESTHER ELIZABETH, musician, music educator; b. Miami, Ariz., Nov. 5, 1952; d. John Wilmont and Flora Elizabeth (Eyestone) Walker; m. James Michael Fellows, Aug. 20, 1976; children: Joy Christine, Rachel Lindsay, Daniel Matthew, Jessica Grace. B in Music Edn., U. Colo., 1975. Co-dir. Children's Piano Lab. U. Colo., Boulder, 1975-76; instr. So. Calif. Conservatory Music, Sun City, 1976-78; pvt. instr. Ft. Lauderdale, 1978-84; instr. Ft. Lauderdale Christian Sch., 1981-83; sect. violinist Okla. Sinfonia/Tulsa Ballet, 1984—, Bartlesville (Okla.) Symphony, 1990—; pvt. instr. Broken Arrow, Okla., 1984—; pvt. instr. Ft. Lauderdale, 1978-84. Mem. Music Tchrs. Nat. Assn. (cert. piano, violin and viola), Okla. Music Tchr. Assn., Suzuki Assn. Am., Hyechka Music Club Tulsa, Tulsa Accredited Music Tchrs. Assn. (chair scholarship com.). Avocations: biking. Home: 19821 S Harvard Ave Mounds OK 74047-5049

FELS, GERHARD, economist; b. Baumholder, Germany, June 17, 1939; s. Karl Ludwig and Frieda (Schug) F.; m. Waltraut Endres, Mar. 31, 1962; children: Joachim, Florian, Katrin. Diploma in Econs., U. Saarbrücken, Fed. Republic Germany, 1965; D. in Econs., U. Saarbrücken, 1969. Economist Inst. für Weltwirtschaft, Kiel, Fed. Republic Germany, 1969-71, head dept. I, 1971-83, v.p., 1976-83, dir., prof., 1978-83; mng. dir. Inst. der deutschen Wirtschaft, Cologne, Fed. Republic Germany, 1983—; mem. German Coun. Econ. Experts, 1976-82; mem. Com. for Devel. Planning, UN, 1978-82, Group of Thirty, 1988—. Contbr. articles to profl. jours. Chair Aufsichtsrat Hannoversche Leben. Lt. German Army, 1959-60. Mem. Aufsichtsrat Bayerische Rückversicherung, Aufsichtsrat Oppenheim Kapitalanlagegesellschaft, Beirat der MZM Nestlé. Office: Inst deutschen Wirtschaft, Gustav Heinemann Ufer 84-88, D 50968 Cologne Germany

FELSBURG, DAVID F., engineering executive, educator; b. Wilmington, Del., July 3, 1946; s. Francis Edward and Alice Jenny (Biscoe) F.; m. Donna Kay Knapp, Sept. 17, 1966; children: Michelle A., David W., Daniel E., Darrell B., Darren T. BS in Electronics Engring., N.Mex. State U., Las Cruces, 1975; M in Engring., U. Utah, 1980; grad., So. Bapt. Sem. Ext., Colorado Springs, 1985. Ordained pastor So. Bapt. Ch., 1981. Chief technician, sys. trainer 1961 Comm. Squadron, Clark AFB, The Philippines, 1969-73; dir. plans and programs 4754 Radar Evaluation Squadron, Hill AFB, Utah, 1976-79; dir. USAF/FAA Joint Ops. for Atmospheric Def. Hdqs. N.Am. Aerospace Def. Command, Colorado Springs, 1979; comdr., dir. comms. sys. 47 Comms. Group, Cheyenne Mountain AFB, Colo., 1979-81; dept. head math., football defensive line coach USAF Acad., Colorado Springs, 1981-85; sr. program mgr., dir. ops. CTA Inc., Boston, 1985-89; v.p., dir. ops. CTA Inc. Northeastern Region, Boston, 1989-97; exec. v.p., COO, co-founder Paloma Sys., Inc., Alexandria, Va., 1997—. Author: New Christians Everyday, 1987; author, editor 24 tech. bus. proposals, 1985—; lectr. in field. Interim pastor Faith Evangelical Ch., Melrose, Mass., 1996-97; pastor, tchr., evangelist, seminar leader Bapt. Chs., N.Mex., Tex., Miss., Utah, Colo., Mass., N.H., Maine, Conn., R.I., Vt., Va., 1973—; founder Eton Park Home Owners Assn., Alexandria, 1998; founder, pastor Alexandria Bible Chapel, Alexandria, 1997, Wilmington Bible Chapel, Mass., 1990; platinum mem. Republican Nat. Com., Washington, 1993—. Mem. IEEE, Nat. Def. Indsl. Assn. (chpt. pres. 1995-98, pres. award 1996-97), Air Force Comms. Electronics Assn. and Air Force Assn., Assn. of Old Crows. Republican. Southern Baptist. Avocations: preaching and teaching Bible, golf. E-mail: palomadff@aol.com. Fax: 703-658-1475. Home: 6504 Nightwind Ct Alexandria VA 22312-2247 Office: Paloma Sys Inc 7002 Evergreen Ct Annandale VA 22003-3227

FELSCH, KARL-OTTO, mechanical engineering educator, scientist; b. Dermbach, Germany, Nov. 3, 1928. Dr.Ing., U. Fridericiana, Karlsruhe, Germany, 1965, Dr.Ing.habil., 1971. Asst. U. Fridericiana, Karlsruhe, Germany, 1956-61, 1st asst., 1961-72, acad. dir., 1972-74, prof., 1974; coleader Inst. Fluid Mech. & Fluid Machinery, Karlsruhe, Germany, 1974-94; leader divsn. boundary-layer Theory & The Labs., Karlsruhe, Germany, 1974-79, leader divsn. fluid machinery, 1979-94, cons. engr., 1994—. Contbr. articles to profl. jours. Mem. Gesellschaft Angewandte Mathmatik und Mechanik.

FELSENHARDT, PHILIPPE GERARD, educator; b. Tours, France, Nov. 11, 1956; arrive in U.S., 1991; s. Robert Judas and Wanda F.; m. Alexandra Nicolette Felsenhardt, Feb. 15, 1991; 1 child, Wanda Amandine. Alumnus, Ecole De Louvre, Paris, 1977; JD, Univ. Paris X, Paris, 1981, DEA, 1983. Researcher CNRS, Paris, 1981-83; sales rep. Industrial Communication, Paris, 1987-89; legal adv. Bongrain S.A., Paris, 1983-87; mktg. mgr. Culture & Communications, Brussels, Belgium, 1989-91; sales assoc. Mayor's Jewelers, Miami, Fla., 1991-92; pvt. bank rep. Banque Nationale De Paris, Miami, 1992-95; asst. dir. MIBS Univ. S.C., Columbia, 1995—; hon. consul for France, S.C., 1999. Res. lt. Airforce Commandos, 1980-81, France. Avocations: swimming, reading, spend time with family. E-mail: felsenha@sc.edu. Home: 1004 Rockwood Rd Columbia SC 29209-2440 Office: MIBS Darla Moore Sch Bus 1705 College St Columbia SC 29208-0001

FELSENTHAL, STEVEN ALTUS, lawyer; b. Chgo., May 21, 1949; s. Jerome and Eve (Altus) F.; m. Carol Judith Greenberg, June 14, 1970; children: Rebecca Elizabeth, Julia Alison, Daniel Louis Altus. AB, U. Ill., 1971; JD, Harvard U., 1974. Bar: Ill. 1974, U.S. Dist. Ct. (no. dist.) Ill. 1974, U.S. Ct. Claims 1975, U.S. Tax Ct. 1975, U.S. Ct. Appeals (7th cir.) 1981. Assoc. Levenfeld, Kanter, Baskes & Lippitz, Chgo., 1974-78, ptnr. Levenfeld & Kanter, Chgo., 1978-80; ptnr. Levenfeld, Eisenberg, Janger, Glassberg & Lippitz, Chgo., 1980-84; sr. ptnr. Sugar, Friedberg & Felsenthal, Chgo., 1984—; lectr. Kent Coll. Law, Ill. Inst. Tech., Chgo., 1978-80. Mem. ABA, Ill. State Bar Assn., Chgo. Bar Assn., Chgo. Coun. Lawyers, Harvard Law Soc. Ill., Phi Beta Kappa. Clubs: Standard, Harvard (Chgo.). Office: Sugar Friedberg & Felsenthal 30 N La Salle St Ste 2600 Chicago IL 60602-2506

FELTON, SAMUEL PAGE, biochemist; b. Petersburg, Va., Sept. 7, 1919; s. Samuel S. and Pearl (Williams) F.; m. Helen Florence Martin, Dec. 31, 1955; 1 child, Samuel Page. Degree in pharmacy, U.S. Army, San Francisco, 1942; BS in Chemistry, U. Wash., 1951, postgrad., 1954. Chief technician U. Wash., Seattle, 1952-59, rsch. assoc., 1959-62, sr. rsch. assoc., 1976—, dir. ctr. facilities lab. anesthesiology, 1969-73, dir. water quality lab., 1973-83, dir. biochem. lab. sch. of Fisheries, 1983-85; emeritus, micro-nutrition, rsch. and health in salmonids Sch. Fisheries, U. Wash., Seattle, 1985—; asst. mem., asst. to dir. divsn. biochemistry Scripps Clinic and Research Found., La Jolla, Calif., 1962-66; asst. biochemist Children's Orthopedic Hosp., Seattle, 1966-68; vis. scientist Va. Inst. Marine Scis. at Coll. William and Mary, Williamsburg, 1985. Mem. bd. of adjustments City of Edmonds, Wash., Shoreline Mgmt. Commn., Snohomish County, Wash. Served to sgt. MC, U.S. Army 1941-45. Fellow Am. Inst. Chemists; mem. Am. Chem. Soc., Am. Inst. Fishery Research Biologists, N.Y. Acad. of Scis., Soc. Exptl. Biology and Medicine. Avocations: sailing, music, travel. Office: U Wash Fisheries Rsch & Teaching PO Box 355100 Seattle WA 98195-5100

FELTS, MARGARET "GEORGE" CLEMEN, environmental engineer, consultant; b. Ft. Worth, Tex., Dec. 16, 1950; d. Arthur Taylor and Jane Jolliffe Clemen; m. Robert Louis Felts; children: Shane, Jonathan, Julia. BA Orgn. Communications, Eckerd Coll., St. Petersburg, Fla., 1973; BS Petroleum Engring., La. Tech., Ruston, La., 1977; MS Energy Engring., LaSalle U., 1989; JD, U. Pacific, 2000. Registered environ. assessor, Calif.; registered environ. mgr., Nat. Registered Environ. Profls.; lic. gen. contractor, Calif. Engr. AMOCO Oil Co. Refinery, Yorktown, Pa., 1977-80; process engr. Celanese, Vernon, Tex., 1980-82; energy spl. Calif. Energy Commn., Sacramento, 1982-84; energy cons., owner Clemen Co., Sacramento, 1984-89; chief engring. divsn. Environ. Mgmt., McClellan AFB, Sacramento, 1985-89; owner, mgr. Clemen Environ. Svcs., 1989-92; pres. Invictus Corp., Wilton, Calif., 1992—; dir. Calif. Superfund Program Calif. Dept. Toxic Substances Control, 1993-95; pres. Noesis, 1995—; litigation cons. Pvt. Attys. in Calif.; CEO Oil-Gasoline.com., Inc., 1999—; expert witness FERC; expert witness natural resources and utilities coms. Calif. State Assembly; cons., expert witness Calif. Pub. Utilities Commn., Calif. Energy Commn. Author: Studies and Testimonies for Calif. Pub. Utilities Com., FERC, Citizen's Energy Coun., 1984-89; article, Oil & Gas Jour., 1985; paper, Soc. of Petroleum Engring., 1986. Recipient Lee Community Leadership Award, Eckerd Coll., 1973. Assoc. mem. Soc. of Petroleum Engrs. Presbyterian. Office: Noesis Corp 9156 Tavernor Rd Wilton CA 95693-9659

FELTZ-CORNELIS, CHRISTINA VAN DER, psychiatrist, epidemiologist; b. Terneuzen, The Netherlands, May 17, 1962. MD, MSc, U. Amsterdam, The Netherlands, 1988, cert. psychiatrist, 1992; cert. epidemiologist, Free U. Amsterdam, 1996. Cons. psychiatrist Free U. Amsterdam, 1992-98, pvt. psychiat. svc. for family practice, 1998—; coord. rsch. group on epilepsy, cognition and psychopathology Int. Epilepsy, Heemstede, The Netherlands, 1999—. Author: (with M.Cox and B. Terluin) Somantisation, 1999; contbr. articles to med. jours., including Internat. Jour. Psychiatry in Medicine, British Jour. Oral and Maxillofacial Surgery; speaker in field. Mem. Assn. Advancement Philosophy and Psychology, Assn. Epidemiology.

FENAUT, JEAN-MICHEL, bank executive; b. Reims, Marne, France, Feb. 17, 1956; s. Pierre-Joseph and Bernadette (Lardeux) F.; m. Christine Helene Jacques, July 19, 1980; children: Pierre-Alain, Juliette. Student, Ecole Nat. Superieure De Chimie, Paris, 1979, Inst. Adminstrn. Entreprises, Paris, 1981; diploma, Ctr. Etudes Supérieures Bancaires, Paris, 1986. Prodn. mgr. Thomson/CSF, Paris, 1980-82; comml. mgr. Banque Régionale d'Escompte et de Dépôts, Paris, 1982-85, internat. mgr., 1985-88, sr. rep., 1991-99; sr. rep. Banque Régionale d'Escompte et de Dépôts, London, 1988-91; dir. ctrl./com. mgr. Banque de L'Union Maritme et Financiere, Paris, 1999—; tchr. Inst. Superieur de Gestion, Paris, 1983-86. With French Air Force, 1979-81. Mem. Fgn. Banks Assn., Lombard Assn., Anglo-French C. of C., Nat. Liberal Club, Overseas Club, Club Europeen de Londres (London, pres. 1990-91). Roman Catholic. Home: 20 Allee de Marly, 92500 Rueil Malmaison France Office: BRED, 18 Quai de la Rapee, 42 rue Maurice Thorez, 92000 Nanterre France

FEND, THOMAS, physicist; b. Hofheim, Germany, Apr. 17, 1962; s. Herbert Martin Anton and Inge Theresia (Etten) F.; m. Mandana Asgari, Mar. 5, 1992; children: Jonas, Helena. Diploma, Univ., Koln, Germany, 1990; PhD, Univ., Duisburg, Germany, 1995. Scientific asst. German Aerospace Ctr., Koln, Germany, 1991-94; scientist DLR, Koln, Germany, 1995-99. Author: Ermudungsverhalten con C/C, 1996l inventor in field. Social worker GWK, Koln, 1981-82; team mgr. TTC Esch, Koln, 1982-90. Mem. ISES. Avocations: soccer, sailing, athletics. Home: Haupt Strasse 112, 51143 Koln Germany Office: DLR, Liner Hoehe, 51147 Koln Germany

FENECH, JOSEPH, Maltese government official, lawyer; b. Apr. 2, 1931. BA with honors, Royal U. of Malta, 1952, LLD, 1955. m. Marlene Ellul; 3 children. Ptnr. Fenech and Fenech Advocates, 1956—; sec. Nationalist Parliamentary Group, 1976-87; parliamentary sec. for offshore activities and maritime affairs Govt. of Malta, Valletta, 1987-92, min. justice, 1992-95; mem. Assembly Coun. of Europe, 1995-96; mem. exec. com. Nationalist Party, 1969-96; mem. Broadcasting Authority, 1972-75; bd. govs. Internat. Maritime Law Inst. of Malta, 1989-97. Mem. coun. U. Malta, 1972-75. Mem. Malta Football Assn., Internat. Bar Assn. Office: 198 Old bakery St, Valletta Malta

FENECH ADAMI, EDWARD, prime minister of Malta; b. Birkirkara, Malta, Feb. 7, 1934; s. Luigi Fenech Adami and Josephine Pace; m. Mary Sciberras, June 27, 1 965; children: John, Joseph, Michael, Maria, Luigi. Began studies at St. Aloysius Coll., Birkirkara, Malta; BA, U. Malta, Valletta, 1955; LLD, U. Malta, 1958. Bar: Malta 1959. Adv. Valletta, 1959—; ptnr. Ganado and Assocs., Valletta, 1961-77; mem. gen. coun. and exec. com. Nationalist Party, 1961—, pres. Birkirkara sect., 1961-69; M.P., 1969—; opposition spokesman on labor and social svcs. Parliament, Valletta, 1971-77; leader opposition Parliament, 1977-82, 83-87, 1996-98; prime minister Malta, 1987-92, 92-96, 1998—; asst. sec. gen. Nationalist Party, 1962-75, also pres. gen. and administrv. couns., 1975-77, Party leader, 1977—; v.p. European Union Christian Dems., Brussels, 1979—. Mem. Nationalist Party (Christian Democrat). Roman Catholic. Home: 92 Main St, Birkirkara Malta Office: Office of the Prime Min, Auberge de Castille, Valetta CMR02, Malta

FENELEY, MARK ROGER, consultant urological surgeon; b. Bristol, Eng., Sept. 8, 1961. BChir, U. Cambridge (Eng.), 1986, MB, 1987, MD, 1996. Sr. registrar St. Bartholomew's Hosp., London, 1994-99; postdoctoral fellow in oncologic urology James Buchanan Brady Urol. Inst./Johns Hopkins Med. Instns., Balt., 1999—. Editor-in-chief (internet site) Uro-Reviews, 1996; contbr. numerous articles to profl. jours. Fellow Royal Coll. Surgeons Eng. (Hunterian prof 1997), Royal Soc. Medicine; mem. Brit. Assn. Urol. Surgeons (assoc.). Office: Nottingham City Hosp, Dept Urology Hucknall Rd, Nottingham NG5 1PB, England

FENG, CHUDE, engineering educator, ceramics engineer; b. Shanghai, China, Aug. 24, 1944; s. Zhihong Feng and Ruidi Ye; m. Xingchun Chen, Jan. 1, 1972; 1 child, Yan Feng. BS, U. Sci. and Tech. China, 1967; MS Shanghai Inst. Ceramics, Chinese Acad. Scis., 1981, PhD, 1985. Cert. in materials sci. and engring. Rsch. asst. Shanghai Inst. Ceramics, 1981-83, asst. prof., 1983-89, assoc. prof., 1989-94, prof., 1994—. Mem. Shanghai Space Soc. (mem. coun. 1996—), Chinese Advanced Soc. (mem. coun. 1996—). Avocations: bridge, table tennis. Fax: +86-21-62513903. E-mail: cdfeng@sunm.shcnc.ac.cn. Officec: Shanghai Inst Ceramics, 1295 Dingxi Rd, Shanghai 20050, China

FENG, CHUNFENG, engineering researcher; b. Zhejiang, China, June 6, 1966; s. B.M. and H.Z. (Wang) F.; m. L. Tan, Nov. 18, 1991; 1 child, Berthy Tianyu. B of Engring., Zhejiang U., 1987; M of Engring., Katholieke U. Leuven, 1995, PhD, 1998. Rsch. fellow Nanyang Technol. U., Singapore, 1998—. Contbr. articles to profl. jours. Mem. The Metals, Minerals, Materials Soc. E-mail: c feng@bigfoot.com. Home: 34300-A4 Park East Dr Solon OH 44139 Office: Sch Mech/Prodn Engring, Nanyang Technol Nanyang Ave, 639798 Singapore Singapore

FENG, PING-CHUNG, retired editor; b. Cheng-de, Hubie, China, Mar. 11, 1924. BS, BA, St. John's U., Shanghai, 1949. Editor People's Med. Pub. House, Beijing, 1953-82, ret., 1982. Editor med. texts and reference books; contbr. articles to profl. jours. Trustee World Constitution and Parliament Assn., Colo., 1985-95. Officer Chinese armed forces, 1943-45. Mem. World Citizens Assn., Campaign for a More Democratic UN (mem. internat. steering com. 1987—), UMANO Found., N.Y. Acad. Scis. Avocations: music, sports, art, literature. Home: No 101 Bldg 1 Dist 3, Anbuili, 100101 Chaoyang Dist Beijing, China

FENG, QI-YUAN, physicist, educator, researcher; b. Dafengcun Village, Quanjiao, Aug. 14, 1935; s. Feng jin-hau and Feng Cheng-Shi; m. Jun-hu Wang, May 6, 1961; children: Lu, Di. Grad., Beijing Fgn. Lang. Inst., 1956, Moscow State U., 1960. Asst. Inner Mongolia U., Huhehaote, China, 1960-77, lectr., 1978-79, assoc. prof., 1980-86, prof., 1987—; prof., doctoral tutor Huazhong U. Sci. and Tech., Wuhan, China, 1986-89; vis. prof., doctoral tutor Moscow State U., 1991-93, St. Peterburg (Russia) U., 1992-93, Vilnius U. Lithuania, 1992-93. Author: Laser Physics, 1990; contbr. over 150 articles to profl. jours. Recipient prize Inner Mongolia Sci. and Tech. Progress, 1989. Fellow Internat. Soc. Optical Engrs.; mem. Chinese Physics Soc. (tchg. com. 1985), Chinese Optical Soc. (dir. laser com. 1987). Avocations: gardening, collecting postage stamps, reading philosophy, history, music. Office: Inner Mongolia U, Dept Physics, Huhehaote City 010021, China

FENG, SARAH, international relations director; b. Taipei, Taiwan, Sept. 22, 1962; d. Fen and Sue (Chao) F. M Sociology, Western Ill. U., 1991. Account exec. Chinese TV, Washington, 1991-93; dir. Eastern TV, Taiwan, 1993—. Leader ET TV crew to Can. for filming, 1996; chief planner Brit. Movie Week in Taipei, 1996, French Movie Month in Taipei, 1996. Avocations: travel, dining and wine, dancing, socializing, reading. Office: Eastern TV 9E-10, Ln 609, Sec 5 Chung Hsin Rd, San Chung 241, Taiwan

FENG, SHIWEI, computer scientist, educator; b. Heilongjiang Province, China, May 8, 1961; parents Rufu Feng and Shuying Gao; m. Yuhui Wei, Mar. 12, 1992; 1 child, Ruirui. BS, Jilin U., 1983, MS, 1986; PhD, Beijing Poly. U., 1999. From asst. prof. to assoc. prof. Beijing Poly. U., 1986—. Avocations: swimming, fishing, films. Office: Beijing Poly U, 100 Pingleyuan St, Chaoyang Beijing China 100022

FENG, WENQING, physicist; b. Zhang Jingang, Jiangsu, China, Oct. 1, 1936; s. Hexiang and Lushi (Lu) F.; m. Yuqing Wang; children: Jiangyi, Jianghjui, Jiangnin. BS, N.-W. Indsl. U., Xi'an, China, 1961. Asst. rschr. Beijing Inst. Physics, 1961-65; asst. rschr. Kunming (China) Inst. Physics, 1965-68, head lab. no. 2, 1968-92, head project, 1982-98, vice chmn. sci. and tech. com., 1999—; master designer Chinese N. Indsl. Corp., Beijing, 1988-97; editor infrared technique Chinese N. Indsl. Corp., Beijing, 1981—. Recipient 1st Class award Guang Hua Sci. and Tech. Com., 1991, Nat. Sci. Technique Com., 1995. Mem. Soc. PhotoúOptical Instrument Engrs., Chinese Optical Soc. (derector 1985—, editor Infrared & Millimeter Waves 1986-99), Yunnan Optical Soc. (derector 1986—). Avocations: badminton, music. Office: 31 Jiao Chang E Rd, Kunming 650223, China

FENG, XIANGDONG (SHAWN) (SHAWN FENG), chemist; b. Lingling, Hunan, China, July 27, 1956; came to the U.S., 1982; s. Hui Feng and Yuying Jiang; m. Meiling Gong, Dec. 26, 1984; children: Melinda G., Stephanie G. BS, Hunan Normal U., Changsha, Hunan, China, 1978; MS, Cath. U. Am., 1984, PhD, 1988. Lectr. Hunan Normal U., Changsha, 1978-82; rsch. asst., tchg. asst. Cath. U. Am., Washington, 1982-88; postdoctoral fellow Vitreous State Lab., Washington, 1988-89, rsch. scientist, 1989-91; chemist Argonne Nat. Lab., Chgo., 1991-94; sr. rsch. scientist project mgr. Pacific N.W. Nat. Lab., Richland, Wash., 1995-97, staff scientist, project mgr., 1997-98; Glass Core Tech. chair, sr. rsch. assoc. Ferro Corp., 1998—; mem. tech. program organizing com. Am. Nuclear Soc., La Grange Park, Ill., 1996. Contbr. chpts. to books and articles to profl. jours.; patentee in field. Named Hon. Prof., Human Normal U., 1995, China Inst. Atomic Energy, Beijing, 1995; recipient Outstanding Performance award Pacific N.W. Nat. Lab., 1997, Materials Sci. award U.S. Dept. Engry, 1998, Alumni Outstanding Achievement award in sci. Cath. U. Am., 1998, Discover Mag. award, 1998, R&D 100 award, 1998; grantee Dept. Energy, Washington, 1992—. Fellow Am. Ceramic Soc. (symposium chair for tech. meetings 1989—, fed. liaison com. 1996—); mem. Am. Chem. Soc., Materials Rsch. Soc. (tech. program com. 1995). Achievements include development of specialty glass/ceramics; development of thermodynamic models based on glass structure for the prediction of glass properties from composition; development of advanced composite and polymeric materials for water purification and recycle, catalysis, drug delivery, industrial coatings and semiconductor applications. Avocations: jogging, table tennis, swimming, bicycling, computers.

FENG, XIAO, chemical engineering educator; b. Xi'an, Shaanxi, China, Feb. 27, 1953; d. Li-Sheng and Fu-Hua (Zhao) Feng; m. Xi-Zhe Wang, Aug. 19, 1977; 1 child, Wang Yu-Fei. BS, Xi'an Jiaotong U., 1982, MS, 1985, PhD, 1990. Asst. prof. Xi'an Jiaotong U., 1985-87, lectr., 1990-92, assoc. prof., 1992-98, prof. chem. engring., 1998—. Author: Principles and Technology of Energy Conservation in Chemical Industry, 1998; contbr. articles to profl. jours. China Energy Rsch. Assn. (v.p. thermodynamics and engring. application com. 1997—). Avocations: reading, collecting stamps. Office: Xi'an Jiaotong Univ, Dept Chem Engring, Xi'an 710049, People's Republic of China

FENG, XI-QIAO, research scientist; b. Suning, China, May 2, 1968; s. Guo-An and Xiu-Ying (Cao) F.; m. Shu-Xian Wu, Oct. 1, 1994; 1 child, Min-Xing. B, Tsinghua U., Beijing, 1990, M, 1991, PhD, 1995. Rsch. asst. Tsinghua U., Beijing, 1991-94, lectr., 1994-95; assoc. prof., 1999—; rsch. scientist Inst. Mechanics, Darmstadt, Germany, 1997-99; bd. dirs. Tsinghua U. Author: Damage Mechanics, 1997; contbr. articles to profl. jours. Monitor Tsinghua U., 1992-94. Recipient AbH award, 1997; China Nuclear Industry Co. grantee, Beijing, 1996, China Post-Dr. Sci. Found. grantee, Beijing, 1996; postdoctoral fellow Tsinghua U., 1995-97. Avocations: bridge, Go, table tennis. Office: Tsinghua U, Dept Engring Mechanics, Beijing 100 084, China

FENG, YANGZHENG, medical researcher; b. Lantian, Shaanxi, China, Sept. 28, 1950; came to U.S., 1992; s. Zhenmin Feng and Qingfang Yang; m. Huimin Zhang; 1 child, Tom (Shi). MD, Xi'an (Shaanxi) Med. U., 1978, postgrad., 1981-82; postgrad., Shanghai Med. U., 1991. Intern dept. medicine Shaanxi Provincial Hosp., 1979-80; intern Guangdong Ctr. Prevention and Treatment Occupl. Diseases, 1983; studied ultrasonic diagnosis, Beijing, 1984; resident dept. medicine Xi'an 521 Hosp., 1983-87; attending physician, asst. prof. Inst. Indsl. Health, Ministry Machinery and Electronics Industry China, Xi'an, 1987-91, vice chief physician, assoc. prof., 1991-92, vice chmn. dept. function exam., 1987-90, chmn. dept. occupl. health, 1990-92, guider MA/PhD postgrad. degree in cardiovasc. pharmacology, 1990-92; rsch. assoc. dept. pharmacology and toxicology U. Miss. Med. Ctr., Jackson, 1992-94, rsch. assoc. dept. psychiatry and human behavior, 1994-97, med. rschr. dept. pediat., 1997—; reporter Chinese Jour. Indsl. Medicine,

1990—; adjuster Jour. Indsl. Hygiene and Occupl. Diseases, 1991—; spl. journalist Jour. Qigong, 1988—; participant numerous symposia and confs., including Fedn. Am. Socs. for Exptl. Biology, New Orleans, 1993, Anaheim, Calif., 1994, Am. Soc. for Pharmacology and Exptl. Therapeutics, San Francisco, 1993, Am. Soc. Neurosci., Miami Beach, Fla., 1994, Washington, 1996, L.A., 1998. Contbr. over 100 articles and abstracts to sci. jours., including Jour. Indsl. Health and Occupl. Diseases, Chinese Jour. Indsl. Hygiene and Occupl. Diseases, Jour. Nature, Jour. Med. Electronic Impedance, Chinese Jour. Integrated Traditional and Western Medicine, Chinese Jour. Clin. Pharmacology, Shaanxi Medicine Jour., Jour. Explosives, Chinese Jour. Indsl. Medicine, Jour. Health Toxicology, Jour. Heart Function, Jour. Xi'an Med. U., Jour. Hippophae, European Jour. Pharmacology, Brain Rsch. Bull., Pharmacol. Biochem. Behavior, Life Sci., Jour. Pharmacol. Experimental Therapeutics, Jour. Biomed. Sci., Jour. Sex and Marital Therapy, Jour. Chromotography B., Jour. Psychiat. Rsch., Critical Care Medicine, Neurochem. Rsch., Biol. and Pharm. Bull.; editor bok chpts. Recipient 2d prize Acad. Prevention and Treatment Occupl. Diseases, 5th Ministry Machinery Industry China, 1986; outstanding rschr. award Shaanxi Bur. Weapon Industry, 1986, advanced rschr. award, 1987, 2d prize, 1990, advanced worker prize, 1991, Labor Model award, 1991; 1st prize for excellent paper Shaanxi Assn. for Pharmacy, 1991; 4th and 3d prizes for excellent paper on nature sci. Shaanxi Province, 1991, Outstanding Rsch. award Shaanxi Provincial Soc. Sci. and Tech., 1991, 3d prize progress in sci. and tech. Ministry Machinery Industry China, 1991, 3d prize progress in sci. and tech. Com. Edn. Shaanxi Province, 1994, Recent Famous Scientist in China award Sichuang People's Publ. House, 1995, 3d Prize of Progress in Sci. and Tech. Ministry of Machinery and Electonics Industry, China, 1996. Mem. Soc. for Neurosci., Chinese Soc. for Preventive Medicine (com. mem. sect. labor health Shaanxi br.). Chinese Soc. for Weapon Industry (com. mem. sect. labor and environ. protection), Chinese Soc. for Physiopathology, Chinese Assn. for Qigong Sci. (adjuster found. com., Qigong Sci. Rsch. award 1990), Chinese Soc. for Preventive Medicine, Chinese Soc. for Pathologic Physiology, Chinese Soc. for Physiology. Avocations include working out nation's health standard of nitroglycerin in the air of workplaces; research on evaluations of industrial hygiene and clinical and pharmacological studies on the cardiotonic effects of total flavones of hippophae Rhamnoides L., mechanisms of action of butorphanol, glutamate in opioid dependence, imidazoline receptors in depression, hypoxic ischemic encephalopathy in newborn. Home: 432 Fairfield Dr Madison MS 39110-8595 Office: U Miss Med Ctr Dept Pediat 2500 N State St Jackson MS 39216-4500

FENG, YOU-MIN, biochemist, researcher; b. Hebei, China, Dec. 18, 1936; s. Nai-Zhang Feng and Su-Zhen Li; m. Wen-Qin Li, June 10, 1965; children: Ji, Yan. BSc, Beijing U., 1964. Rsch. asst. Shanghai Inst. Biochemistry, Academia Sinica, Shanghai, China, 1964-78, rsch. assoc., 1978-82; vis. scientist Dept. Biochemistry, U. Miami & Sloan Kettering Ctr., N.Y.C., 1982-84; assoc. prof. Shanghai Inst. Biochemistry, Academia Sinica, 1985-90; vis. scientist VA Med. Ctr., Miami & Joslin Diabetes Ctr., Boston, 1990-91, Institut Curie, Orsay, France, 1992, 97; prof., head rsch. group insulin and related growth factors State Key Lab. Molecular Biology, Shanghai Inst. Biochem., 1991—. Avocation: ancient history of China. Office: Shanghai Inst. Biochemistry, 320 Yue Yang Road, 200031 Shanghai China

FENGER, CLAUS, pathologist, cytologist; b. Copenhagen, Denmark, Aug. 20, 1939; s. Niels Viggo Fenger and Helen Gorm Hansen; m. Lise Blicher Grunnet do (div.); 1 child, Niels; m. Inger de Fine Licht, April 30, 1994. Diploma, Aurehøj, Denmark, 1957; MD, Copenhagen U., 1967; D in Med. Sci., 1987. Chief pathologist Ctrl. Hosp., Holstebro, Denmark, 1978-81, U. Hosp., Odense, Denmark, 1981-99; prof. U. Hosp., Odense, 1999—. Author: (with others) WHO Histological Typing of Intestinal Tumors, 1989, Who Histological Typing of Oesophageal and Gastric Tumors, 1990, Histology for Pathologists, 1997. Mem. European Soc. Pathology, Danish Soc. Cancer Rsch. Avocations: art, history, nature. Office: Odense U Hosp, Winsløwparken 15, DK5000C Odense Denmark

FENNEBRESQUE, KIM SAMUEL, investment banker; b. N.Y.C., Mar. 20, 1950; s. John Drouet and Frances Jane (Campbell) F.; m. Deborah Anne Johnson, Sept. 8, 1979; children: Quincy Campbell, John Drouet II. AB, Trinity Coll., 1972; JD, Vanderbilt U., 1975. Bar: Conn. 1975, N.Y. 1977. Assoc. Day, Berry & Howard, Hartford, Conn., 1975-76, Simpson, Thacher & Bartlett, N.Y.C., 1976-77; assoc. The First Boston Corp., N.Y.C., 1977-81, v.p., 1981-85, mng. dir., 1985-90; gen. ptnr. Lazard Freres & Co., N.Y.C., 1991—; pres. SG Cowen Securities, N.Y.C. Mem. Piping Rock Club, Racquet and Tennis Club, Links Club, St. Anthony Hall Lodge. Republican. Address: 1221 Ave of the Americas New York NY 10020*

FENNELL, CHRISTINE ELIZABETH, healthcare system executive; b. Providence, July 14, 1948; d. Edmond John and Geraldine Mary (Goodenough) F. BS cum laude, Nat. Coll, Denver, 1983. Activity dir. Turtle Creek Convalescent Centre, Ft. Wayne, Ind., 1974-76; co-owner, operator Trail Ridge Welding, Estes Park, Colo., 1976-77; accounts mgr. Mayfair Women's Clinic, Denver, 1977-80; asst. adminstr. Ob-Gyn. Assocs., Aurora, Colo., 1980-82; admissions supr. St. Anthony Hosp. Sys., Denver, 1982-86; adminstr. Parkside Lodge of Colo., Thornton, 1986-89; ops./fin. mgr. Colo. Biodyne, Inc., Denver, 1989-90; adminstr. Kimberly Quality Care, Denver, 1990-93; br. mgr. Preferred Home Health Care, Inc., Lafayette, Ind., 1993-95; regional ops. dir. Arcadia Health Svcs., Inc., Southfield, 1995—; part-time instr. Nat. Coll., Denver, 1983-84. Contbr. articles to profl. jours. Bd. dirs. S.W. Denver Community Mental Health Svcs., 1986. Mem. Denver Bus. Women's Network (pres. 1986-87), Colo, Coun. Hosp. Admitting Mgrs. (v.p. 1985-86), Rotary Club. Avocations: target shooting, horseback riding, tennis. Office: Arcadia Health Svcs Inc 26777 Central Park Blvd Southfield MI 48076-4162

FENNELLY, NIAL, international justice; b. 1942. MA in Econs., Univ. Coll., Dublin. Barrister-at-law, sr. counsel; chmn. Legal Aid Bd., Bar Coun.; advocate gen. Ct. of Justice of European Cmtys., Luxembourg, 1995—. Office: Ct Justice European Cmtys, Palais de Cour de justice, Kirchberg L-2925, Luxembourg*

FENNER, RONALD JOHN, agricultural scientist, researcher; b. Bromborough, Wirral, U.K., Oct. 21, 1934; arrived in Zimbabwe, 1958; s. Joseph Bell and Norah May (Davis) F.; m. Jane Kennett, July 26, 1958 (div. Sept. 2, 1976); children: Mark Robert, Paul Anthony, Nicolette Jane; m. Elspeth Hogarth Robertson, June 3, 1978. BSc with honors, U. Reading, U.K., 1958. Analytical chemist and adv. officer Chemistry and Soil Rsch. Inst., Harare, Zimbabwe, 1958-64, officer-in-charge, soil testing and chemistry sect., 1964-74, head corp. rsch. team, 1974-78, head dept. rsch. and specialist svcs., 1978-83, asst. dir. crop rsch., 1983-87, dir., 1987-94; cons. agrl. rsch. mgmt., 1994—; bd. govs. So. African Centre for Coordination of Agrl. Rsch., Gaborone, Botswana, 1976-94; mem. bd. mgmt. Tobacco Rsch. Bd., Harare, 1976-94, Tea Rsch. Found., Mulange, Malawi, 1983-94; mem. Agrl. Rsch. Coun., Harare, 1987-94; mem. standing com. Rsch. Coun. Zimbabwe, 1992-94; mem. coun. Standards Assn. of Zimbabwe, 1993-94. Asst. editor Zimbabwe Jour. Agrl. Rsch., 1990; editor Zimbabwe Agrl. Jour., 1978. Mem. Zimbabwe Archery Assn. (v.p. 1994-96), Crop Sci. Soc. Zimbabwe, Soil Sci. Soc. Zimbabwe (hon., life.). Anglican Ch. Fax: 263-4-870657. Home: 13 Harare Dr Borrowdale, Harare Zimbabwe

FENNIRI, HICHAM, chemist, educator; b. Salé, Morocco, Mar. 27, 1966; came to the U.S., 1994; s. Cherif Fenniri and Latifa Essyad; m. Jillian M. Buriak, June 5, 1995; 1 child, Miriam Zaynab. BSc, U. Louis Pasteur, Strasbourg, France, 1989, DEA, 1990, PhD, 1994. Asst. prof. Purdue U., West Lafayette, Ind., 1997—. E-mail: hf@purdue.edu. Office: Purdue Univ 1393 HC Brown Lab West Lafayette IN 47907-1393

FENSHAM, PETER JAMES, science educator; b. Melbourne, Victoria, Australia, Oct. 26, 1927; s. Horace James and Freda (Giles) F.; m. Dorothy Christine Fairweather, Apr. 3, 1954; children: Rachel, Mark, Roderick, Patrick. BS, U. Melbourne, 1948, MS, 1950; PhD, Bristol U., 1953, Cambridge U., 1958. Lectr., reader U. Melbourne, 1956-67; prof. of sci. edn. Monash U., Melbourne, 1967-92; dean Faculty of Edn./Monash U., 1982-88; vis. prof. Stanford U., 1963, U. B.C., Can., 1991, Seoul Nat. U., Korea, 1995, U. of Leeds, Eng., 1987, 89, 95, U. East Anglia, Eng., 1978, U. Ill., 1978. Editor/author: The Content of Science, 1994, Development and Dilemmas in Science Education, 1998, Science and Technology in Post Compulsory Education, 1995; contbr. articles to profl. jours. Chair Victorian Coun. for Environ. Edn., Melbourne, 1989-93; mem. State Bd. of Edn., Victoria, 1983-86; cons. UNESCO, Thailand, 1975, Philippines, 1983, Vietnam, 1996. Mem. Order of Australia. Mem. Australian Labor Party. Mem. Uniting Ch. of Australia. Avocations: bush walking, wood, croquet. Home: 20 Stanley Ave, 3130 Blackburn Victoria, Australia

FENSTAD, JENS ERIK, mathematics educator; b. Trondheim, Norway, Apr. 15, 1935; s. Erik and Margit (Wullum) F.; m. Grete Usterud Hansen, Jan. 28, 1939; children: Anne Marie, ERik, Hakon. Mag. Scient., U. Oslo, 1959. Prof. math. U. Oslo, 1968—; chmn. Natural Sci. Rsch. Coun. Norway, 1985-89; vice rector U. Oslo, 1989-93; pres. Internat. Union of History and Philosophy of Sci., 1991-95; chief academic advisor Nordic Acad. Advanced Study, 1994-96; sci. advisor Norwegian Fgn. Office, 1994—. mem. sci. com. NATO, 1992—, European Sci. and Tech. Assembly EC, 1994-99; chmn. Physical and Engring. Scis. Com. European Sci. Found., 1995-99; mem. exec. bd. dirs. Internat. Coun. Sci. Unions, 1996-99; mem. UNESCO World Commn. on Ethics of Sci. Knowledge and Tech., 1998—. Author: General Recursion Theory, 1980; Nonstandard Methods in Stochastic Analysis and Mathematical Physics, 1986, Situations, Language and Logic, 1986. Mem. Norwegian Acad. Letters and Sci., Academia Europaea. Office: U Oslo Inst Math, PO Box 1053 Blindern, 0316 Oslo 3, Norway

FENTON, ALEXANDER, writer; b. 1929. Sr. asst. editor Scottish Nat. Dictionary, Edinburgh, 1955-59; asst. keeper Nat. Mus. Antiquities Scotland, Edinburgh, 1959-75, dep. keeper, 1975-78, dir., 1978-85; rsch. dir. Nat. Mus. Scotland, 1985-89; dir. European Ethnological Rsch. Ctr., 1989—; lectr. U. Edinburgh, 1958-60, 74-80; prof. Scottish ethnology, dir. Sch. Scottish Studies, 1990-94; hon. prof. Royal Scottish Acad., 1996—; editor The Review of Scottish Culture, 1984—. Author: The Various Names of Shetland, 1973, 2d edit., 1977, Scottish Country Life, 1976, 3d edit., 1999, A Guide to the Black House at 42 Arnol, Lewis, 1978, The Northern Isles: Orkney and Shetland, 1978, new edit., 1997, Continuity and Change in the Building Tradition of Northern Scotland, 1979, (with Bruce D. Walker) The Rural Architecture of Scotland, 1981, The Shape of the Past, 2 vols., 1985-86, Wirds an' wark 'e seasons roon on an Aberdeenshire Farm, 1987, Country Life in Scotland: Our Rural Past, 1987, The Turra Coo, 1989, Scottish Country Life, 1989, On Your Bike: Thirteen Years of Travelling Curators, 1990; author: (with others) Studies in Folk Life, 1969, The Scottish Tradition, 1974, The Union of 1707: Its Impact on Scotland, 1974, Folklore Today: A Festschrift for Richard M. Dorson, 1976, The Making of the Scottish Countryside, 1980, From the Stone Age to the 'Forty-Five: Studies Presented to R. B. K. Stevenson, 1983, The Fishing Culture of the World, 1984, Farm Servants and Labour in Lowland Scotland, 1984, Fermfolk and Fisherfolk, 1990, Essays on the Music, Poetry and History of Scotland and England, 1990, Scottish Culture, 1991, Loch Ness and Thereabouts, 1992, Scotland and the Sea, 1992, Creativity and Tradition in Folklore, 1992; editor (with Alan Gailey), contbr.: The Spade in Northern and Atlantic Europe, 1970; editor (with Hermann Pálsson), contbr.: The Northern and Western Isles in the Viking World: Survival, Continuity, and Change, 1984; editor (with Geoffrey Stell), contbr.: Loads and Roads in Scotland and Beyond: Road Transport Over Six Thousand Years, 1984; editor (with Eszter Kisbán), contbr. Food in Change: Eating Habits from the Middle Ages to the Present Day, 1986; editor (with Janken Myrdal), contbr.: Food and Drink and Travelling Accessories: Essays in Honour of Goesta Berg, 1988; editor (with others), contbr.: Land Transport in Europe, 1973, Building Construction in Scotland: Some Historical and Regional Aspects, 1976; contbr., section editor: Manual of Curatorship: A Guide to Museum Practice, 1992, Craiters...or Twenty Buchan Tales, 1995. Office: care Nat Mus Scotland, Chambers St European Ethnol Rsch Ctr, Edinburgh EH1 1JF, Scotland

FENTON, THOMAS TRAIL, journalist; b. Balt., Apr. 8, 1930; s. Matthew Clark and Beatrice (Trail) F.; m. Simone France Marie Lopes-Curval, Jan. 10, 1959; children: Ariane France, Thomas Trail. AB, Dartmouth Coll., 1952; PhD (hon.), U. Balt., 1999. Mem. staff Balt. Sun, 1961-70, chief Rome bur., 1966-68, chief Paris bur., 1968-70; reporter-producer Rome bur. CBS News, 1970-73, corr. Tel Aviv bur., 1973-77, corr. Paris bur., 1977-79; chief European corr. CBS News, London, 1979-94, Moscow, 1994-96, London, 1996—. assignments include 1967 Middle East War, 1968 Paris Peace Talks, 1971 Indo-Pakistan War, 1973 Middle East War, 1979 takeover of the Am. Embassy in Tehran, 1985 Geneva Summit, 1989-90 Revolution in Ea. Europe, 1990 Gulf Crisis, Moscow Coup, 1991, Collapse of Communism and the Soviet Union, German Nationalism, 1992, War in Former Yugoslavia, 1992, War in Chechnya, 1995, 1991 Persian Gulf War, Balkans War, 1999, death of Princess Diana, 1997. Served with USN, 1952-61. Recipient Overseas Press Club awards for articles from Paris, 1968, for coverage Indo-Pakistan War, 1971, Mid. East War, 1973, Sadat visit to Jerusalem, 1977, Mountbatten funeral, 1980, hunger in Africa, 1981, radio documentary series, 1992, Emmy awards NATAS for bombing of Marines in Beirut, 1983, for assassination in Indira Gandhi, 1984, 2 Emmy awards for death of Princess Diana, 1998, DuPont award, 1990, Weintal award Georgetown U., 1999. Mem. Soc. the Cin., Internat. Inst. Strategic Studies, Royal Inst. Def. Studies, Assn. Am. Corrs. London, Assn. de la Presse Presdl. Paris. Office: care Fgn Desk CBS News 524 W 57th St New York NY 10019-2902

FENWICK, PETER BROOKE CADOGAN, neuropsychiatrist, consultant; b. Nairobi, Kenya, May 25, 1935; s. Anthony and Betty (Darling) F.; m. Elizabeth Isobel Roberts, May 18, 1963; children: Annabelle Sarah, Natasha Jane, Tristram Nicholas. MB, BChir, Cambridge (Eng.) U., 1960; DPM, U. London, 1966; FRC Psych., 1984. House physician, med. officer St. Thomas' Hosp., London, 1960-62; gen. practice Nairobi, Kenya, 1962-63; house physician Hillingdon Hosp., 1963; SHO Midd Hosp., London, 1963-64; MRC Nat. Hosp., London, 1964-65; clin. asst. Middlesex Hosp., London, 1965-67; registrar Maudsley Hosp., London, 1967, sr. registrar, 1969-72, hon. cons., 1976; cons., 1996-97; hon. rschr. Broadmoor, Berkshire, Eng., 1972-74; sr. lectr. Inst. Psychiatry, London, 1974—; cons. Radcliff Infirmary, Oxford, Eng., 1989—, St. Thomas Hosp., London, 1974. Recipient award Wellcome Found., Crocher Found. Avocations: flying single engine aircraft, hill walking, fishing, reading, music. Home: 42 Herne Hill, SE24 9QP London England

FÉNYES, TIBOR, retired nuclear physicist; b. Biharkeresztes, Bihar, Hungary, May 4, 1929; s. Kálmán and Matild (Seregély) F.; m. Elisabeth Rupp (dec. 1986); 1 child, Zsuzsanna Hajnalka. Diploma, Kossuth U., Debrecen, Hungary, 1952, Dr. (Univ.), 1960; Dr. Phys. Sci., Hungarian Acad. Sci., Budapest, Hungary, 1971; Titular prof., Kossuth U., Debrecen, 1979. Asst., docent Kossuth U., Debrecen, Hungary, 1951-62; head nuclear spectroscopy Dept. Inst. Nuclear Rsch., Debrecen, Hungary, 1962-94; sr. rschr. Joint Inst. Nuclear Rsch., Dubna, Russia, 1963-66, 68-71; vis. rschr. U. Ky., Lexington, 1979; ret., 1995; pres. Nuclear Structure Com., Joint Inst. Nuclear Rsch., Dubna, 1977-82, Nuclear Physics Sect. of Eötvös R. Phys. Soc., Budapest, Hungary, 1985-90, Phys. Sect. of Debrecen Acad. Com., 1985-90; mem. directional Coun. of Inst. Nuclear Rsch., Debrecen, 1990-94. Contbr. more than 160 sci. articles to profl. jours. Recipient prize of Joint Inst. for Nuclear Rsch., 1972, Acad. prize Hungarian Acad. Sci., 1972, Order of work award Presidium of Hungarian Republic, 1981, prize of Inst. Nuclear Rsch., 1982, Szalay prize Inst. Nuclear Rsch., 1990, Phys. main prize Hungarian Acad. Sci., 1991; decorated Order of Hungarian Rep., Officer's Cross, 1996. Mem. Eötvös R. Phys. Soc. Avocations: tennis, tourism. Home: Mikszáth u 7 fszt 3, H-4032 Debrecen Hungary Office: Inst Nuclear Rsch, Hungarian Acad Sci, H-4001 Debrecen Hungary

FENZY, ALBERT JEAN, gastroenterologist, consultant; b. Douai, Nord, France, Sept. 4, 1934; s. Raymond and Eugenie (Lefebure) F.; m. Anne-Marie Decaudin, Oct. 16, 1959; children: Martine, Aude, Anne-Catherine. MD, U. Lille (France), 1962; qualified in gastroenterology, U. Paris, 1963, qualified in radiology, 1971. Extern Hopitaux Lille, 1955-58; resident in internal medicine Hopitaux Reims (France), 1958-64; asst. Ctr. Lutte Contre Cancer, Reims, 1964-80; chief clinic U. Reims Faculty Medicine, 1964-69; pvt. practice, Reims, 1965—. Contbr. articles to med. jours. Served with Health Service, Algeria, 1961-63. Decorated chevalier Ordre Nat. du Merite (France). Fellow Royal Soc. Medicine (U.K.); mem. Nat. Soc. Digestive Endoscopy, Nat. Soc. Coloproctology, Am. Soc. Colon and Rectal Surgeons Rsch. Found., French Nat. Soc. Gastroenterology, Syndicat Nat. Medecins Exerçant en Groupe (v.p. Paris 1976-84). Avocations: skiing, philosophy. E-mail: fenzyalbert@wahadoo.fr. Home: l4 Rue Vautier-Le-Noir, 51100 Reims France Office: Groupe Med St Remi, 22 Rue Simon, 51100 Reims France

FEOFANOV, KONSTANTIN ANATOLYEVICH, sociologist, consultant, researcher, educator; b. Tambov, Russia, Apr. 28, 1970; s. Anatoly M. and Anna S. (Potlova) F.; m. Feofanova (Burnashova) Irina V., Feb. 20, 1998. BA in Mgmt., Open U. Great Britain, Moscow, 1992; MA in Sociology, Moscow State U., 1992, PhD in Sociology, 1994. Lectr. Open Bus. Sch., Open U. Great Britain, Moscow, 1992-97; sr. lectr. sociology Moscow State U., 1995-97; mktg. dir. Media Arts Adtv., Moscow, 1995-97; asst. prof. Stankin Moscow State Technol. U., 1996—; vis. scientist, rschr. Free U. Berlin, 1997-98; chief coord. Vol. Group for Risk Rsch., Moscow, 1995—; cons. Link Mgmt. Consulting, Zhukovsky, Moscow Region, 1992-97; dep. gen. dir. NAST Independent Agy. of Social Techs., Moscow, 1999—. Inventor in field of sociol. rsch. (prize 1995). Rsch. grantee Russian Sci. Found. and Ford Found., N.Y.C.-Moscow, 1994, German Svc. Acad. Exch., Bonn, 1997. Mem. N.Y. Acad. Scis., Advt. Rsch. Found. Chgo. Avocation: travel. Fax: 7 095 2484383. Home: Vostochnaya St 2/5/71, 109280 Moscow Russia Office: Stankin Moscow State Univ, Vadkovsky per 3, 101472 Moscow Russia

FEOFILOV, GRIGORI ALEXANDROVITCH, physicist, researcher; b. Leningrad, Russia, Mar. 30, 1950; s. Alexandr Ilyich Fedorov and Nina Grigorievna Feofilova; m. Violetta Pavlovna Taran, Aug. 26, 1972; 1 child, Artem. Grad., Leningrad State U., 1973, PhD, 1977. Jr. sci. rschr. Leningrad State U., 1977-87; sr. sci. rschr. St. Petersburg (Russia) State U., 1987—; mem. collaboration bd., mem. tech. bd., project coord. internat. scientific collaboration ALICE, CERN, Geneva, 1992-2000; sci. leader project #345 Internat. Sci. and Tech. Ctr., Brussels, 1996-98, project leader, 2000—; mem. internat. sci. adv. com. VIII Internat. Wire Chamber Conf., Vienna, Austria, 1998. Contbr. articles to profl. jours. Mem. Communist Party Soviet Union, Leningrad, 1980-90. Recipient grant Internat. Sci. and Tech. Ctr., Brussels, 1996, 2000. Avocations: cross country skiing, painting, wooden house construction. Office: St Petersburg State Univ, Ulyanovskaya Str 1, 198904 St Petersburg Russia

FEOLA, DAVID CRAIG, secondary school administrator; b. Akron, Ohio, Oct. 14, 1954; s. Thomas and Mary (Koci) F. BA in Edn., U. Akron, 1976, MA in Edn., 1979, PhD, 1999. Tchr. math. Akron Pub. Schs., 1976-86, asst. prin., 1986-95; asst. prin. Revere H.S., Richfield, Ohio, 1995—; part-time prof. U. Akron, 1997—; math./computer cons. Assocs.: Programs for Learning, Akron, 1991—. Interviewer People to People, Akron, 1994—; vol. for homeless Gennesaret, Inc., Akron, 1997. Named Top Asst. Prin., Akron Edn. Assn., 1995. Mem. ASCD, Nat. Assn. Secondary Sch. Prins., Ohio Assn. Secondary Sch. Prins., Akron Adminstrs. Assn. (treas. 1986-95), Akron City Club, Pi Lambda Theta. Democrat. Congregationalist. Avocations: travel, computers, woodworking, reading, outdoor sports. Home: 1864 Gless Ave Akron OH 44301-3238 Office: Revere High Sch 3420 Everett Rd Richfield OH 44286-9712

FERAN, RUSSELL G., sales executive; b. New Orleans, Oct. 1, 1948; s. Fred and Jean (Zyslina) F.; m. Phyllis Sobel, 1973; 1 child, Leslie. BS in Indsl. Engring., La. State U., 1973. Cert. audio cons.; cert. technician Nat. Assn. Bus. and Ednl. Radio. Engr. South Cen. Bell. Telephone Co., New Orleans, 1973-75; SMIA mgr. Tandy Corp., Fort Worth, 1975-87; regional sales mg. Internat. Union Police Assns., Alexandria, Va., 1987-93; regional mgr. S.W. Pub., Phoenix, 1993—; bd. dirs. Book Rack Metairie, La., Crohn's & Colitis Found. Am.; cons. Vietnam Vets. Am., Washington, 1987—; arbitrator Better Bus. Bur. New Orleans, 1984-90. With USMC, 1967-70. Mem. Am. Philatelic Soc., Vietnam Vets. Am., Patrolman's Assn. New Orleans (hon. life 1988), Westside Amateur Radio Club (pres. 1983-85), JWV-USA (post # 580), Am. Radio Relay League (DCXX award 1971), Delta DX Assn., B'nai B'rith (pres. lodge # 182 1986-88, 93-95, v.p. New Orleans coun. 1990-92). Avocations: philately, amateur radio (W5RGF; ex-WA5OXK). Home: 101 Fairway Dr New Orleans LA 70124-1016 Office: RGF Enterprises Inc 2305 Metairie Rd Metairie LA 70001-5533

FERBER, MARKUS, member European parliament; b. Augsburg, Fed. Republic Germany, Jan. 15, 1965. Mem. European Parliament, Augsburg, Germany, 1999—; mem. Group of the European People's Party (Christian Democrats) and European Democrats; mem. com. on budgets; substitute mem. com. on regional policy, transport and tourism, delegation to the European Econ. Area Joint Parliamentary Com. Office: Peutinger Strabe 11, D-86512 Augsburg Germany

FERBER, ROBERT RUDOLF, physics researcher, educator, science administrator; b. June 11, 1935; s. Rudolf F. and Elizabeth J. (Robertson) F.; m. Eileen Merhaut, July 25, 1964; children: Robert Rudolf, Lynne C. BSEE, U. Pitts., 1958; MSEE, Carnegie-Mellon U., 1966, PhD in Semiconductor Physics, 1967. Registered profl. engr., Pa. Mgr. engring. dept. WRS Motion Picture Labs., Pitts., 1954-58, sec., 1959-76, v.p., 1976-79; sr. engr. Westinghouse Rsch. Labs., Pitts., 1956-67; mgr. nuclear effects group Westinghouse Elec. Corp., Pitts., 1967-71; mgr. adv. engr. energy projects Westinghouse Elec. Corp., East Pittsburgh, 1971-77; photovoltaic materials and collector rsch. mgr. Jet Propulsion Lab., Pasadena, Calif., 1977-85, SP100 Project contract tech. mgr., 1985-90, asst. project mgr. Spaceborne Imaging Radar, 1990-96, Earth Observing Sys. microwave limb sounder radiometer mgr., 1995-99, mgr. FIRST HIFI project amplifier devel. task, 2000—; v.p. Executaire Inc., Pitts., 1960-64; pres. Tele-Cam Inc., Pitts., 1960-78. Editor: Transactions of the 9th World Energy Conf. 1974, Digest of the 9th World Energy Conf., 1974. Contbr. articles to profl. jours.; patentee in field. Mem. Franklin Regional Sch. Dist. Bd., Murrysville, Pa., 1975-77. Fellow Buhl Found., 1965-66, NDEA, 1976-77. Mem. IEEE (sr.), ASME (chmn. 1986 Solar Energy divsn. conf.). Republican. Lutheran. Home: 5314 Alta Canyada Rd La Canada Flintridge CA 91011-1606 Office: Jet Propulsion Lab 4800 Oak Grove Dr Pasadena CA 91109-8001

FERCHER, ADOLF FRIEDRICH, science educator; b. Knittelfeld, Styria, Austria, Dec. 18, 1939; s. Ferdinand and Maria (Reissner) F.; m. Inge Greil, May 23, 1946; 1 child, Sonja. Ing., HTL, Klagenfurt, Austria, 1959; Dipl.ing., Tech. U., Vienna, Austria, 1968, Dr.techn., 1972. Jr. scientist Carl Zeiss, Optics, Oberkochen, Germany, Germany, 1968-75; assoc. prof. U. Essen, Germany, 1975-86; prof. U. Vienna, Austria, 1986—; head Inst. Med. Physics, Vienna, 1986—. Author: Medizinische Physik; contbr. articles to profl. jours. Fellow European Neuro-Ophthal. Soc.; mem. Austrian Soc. Med. Physics (pres. 1993-94), Biomed. Optics Soc./Soc. Photo-Optical Instrumentation Engrs., Deutsche Gesellschaft fuer Angewandte Optik. Avocations: architecture, winter sports. Home: Hassreitersteig 3/11, Wien A 1230, Austria Office: Inst Med Physics, Waehringer Strasse 13, Wien A 1090, Austria

FERDERBER-HERSONSKI, BORIS CONSTANTIN, process engineer; b. Craiova, Romania, May 17, 1943; came to U.S., 1980; s. Boris Modest and Anetta (Mihail) F.; m. Alexandra Ionescu; children: Boris Constantin Jr., Alexandru Vlad. MS in Process Engring., Poly. Inst., Bucharest, Romania, 1968; diploma fgn. trade, Romanian U., Bucharest, 1975. Registered profl. engr., Romania; engr.-in-tng., N.J. Plant engr. Pham. Complex, Bucharest, 1968-69, plant mgr., 1969-73; prin. engr. Indsl. Export Import, Bucharest, 1973-75, fgn. trade diplomate, 1975-80; sr. process engr. Foster Wheeler Corp., Livingston, N.J., 1980-85; projects mgr. CPC Internat./Best Foods, Fairfield, N.J., 1985-91; sr. process engr., project mgr., engring. mgr. Aqualytics, Inc., Morristown, N.J., 1991-99; engr., mgr., tech. dir. Ameridia, Tokuyama, Japan, Eurodia, France, 1999—; founder, pres. B.F.H. Design Corp., 1984—. Inventor in field. Mem. Rep. Nat. Com., Washington, 1981. Mem. AIChE, Instrument Soc. Am., Am. Rowing Assn. Avocations: electronic applications, water and snow skiing. Home: 122 Dupont Ave Hopatcong NJ 07843-1705

FEREIG, SAMI M., civil engineer; b. Cairo, May 6, 1946; arrived in Can., 1971; naturalized citizen, 1976; s. Mohamed Fereig and Faika Ahmed Sami; m. Catherine Mary Harries, Feb. 7, 1977; children: Omer, Maryam, Salem. BS with honors, Ain Shams U., Cairo, 1968; MS, Assiut U., 1971; PhD, Waterloo U., 1975, MA, 1978. Registered profl. engr., Can., Egypt. Tchg. and rsch. asst. Assiut U., 1968-71; rsch. asst. Waterloo U., 1971-75; sr.

engr. J.D. Lee Engring., Brantford, Can., 1975-79; asst. prof. engring. Kuwait U., 1979-84, assoc. prof. engring., 1985-95, asst. vice-rector for planning, 1986-87, prof. engring., 1996—; sr. bridge engr. C.C. Parker, Hamilton, Can., 1990-91; sr. cons. Ahmed Farid Mustafa, Medina, Saudi Arabia, 1980—, Projacs, Kuwait City, 1985—, Office of Consultation and Career Devel., Kuwait U., 1987—; cons. to various pvt. and pub. sector orgns., 1986—; vis. sr. lectr. U. Birmingham, 1997—; session chmn. 6th Internat. Conf. on Composites Engring., Fla., 1999, 34th Internat. Soc. of Mini- and Micro-Computers Conf., Lugano, Switzerland, 1987; vis. prof. U. Waterloo, Can., Nihon U., Japan, Pa. State U., Drexel U., U. Wis., Madison, others. Contbr. articles to profl. jours. Coord. and instr. Office of Profl. Devel., Kuwait U., 1985—; pub. spkr. Nat. Contract Mgmt., Kuwait, 1998-99, Kuwait Engring. Soc., 1982—; head tech. com. Cooperative Soc. of Housing for Egyptians Working in Kuwait, 1985-87. Recipient Indsl. fellowship Nat. Rsch. Coun. Can., Ont., 1975-77; rsch. grantee Kuwait U., 1984-98. Mem. Internat. Coun. for Bldg. Rsch., Assn. Profl. Engrs. Ont., ASCE, Syndicate Egyptian Engrs., Am. Concrete Inst. Islamic. Avocations: travel, collecting Oriental rugs, computers, stamp collecting. Office: Kuwait Univ/Dept Civil Engr, PO Box 5969, 13060 Kuwait State of Kuwait

FERENCZ, CHARLOTTE, pediatrician, epidemiology and preventive medicine educator; b. Budapest, Hungary, Oct. 28, 1921; came to U.S., 1954; d. Paul Ferencz and Livia deFekete. BSc, McGill U., 1944, MD, CM, 1945; MPH, Johns Hopkins U., 1970. Cert. pediatrics Royal Coll. Physicians and Surgeons, Can., pediatric cardiology Am. Bd. Pediatrics. Demonstrator McGill U., Montreal, 1952-54; asst. prof. pediatrics Johns Hopkins U., Balt., 1954-58, U. Cin., 1959-60; asst. prof. SUNY, Buffalo, 1960-66, assoc. prof., 1966-73; assoc. prof. epidemiology and preventive medicine U. Md. Sch. Medicine, Balt., 1973-74, prof., 1974-98, prof. pediatrics, 1985—, prof. emeritus, 1998—; Prin. investigator population based study Etiology of Congenital Heart Disease, 1981-89; mem. epidemiology and disease control study sect. NIH, 1984-88; pres. Delta Omage Alpha chpt. Pub. Health Soc., 1990-92. Recipient M.E.S. Abbott scholarship McGill U., 1943-45, M.E.R.I.T. award Nat. Heart, Lung & Blood Inst., 1987, Fogarty Internat. Ctr. Health Sci. Exchange award NIH, 1988, Helen B. Taussig award Am. Heart Assn. Md. Affiliate, 1991, Achievement award Univ. Ctr. Life Scis., Balt., 1993. Fellow Am. Acad. Pediatrics (Spl. Achievement award Md. chpt. 1994), Am. Coll. Cardiology; mem. Teratology Soc. Democrat. Office: U Md Sch Medicine 660 W Redwood St Baltimore MD 21201-1541

FERENCZ, ROBERT MARK, mechanical engineer; b. Cleve., Mar. 28, 1957; s. Bruce Joseph Ferencz and Catherine Rose Wheeler; 1 child, Stephen. BSCE, Case Western Res. U., 1980; MSCE, Stanford U., 1981, MSME, 1984, PhD in Mech. Engring., 1989. Engr., analyst Lawrence Livermore (Calif.) Nat. Lab., 1980-83, engr., code developer, 1984-89, project leader, 1998—; mgr. quality assurance Centric Engring. Sys., Inc., Stanford, Calif., 1990-93; dir. software devel. Centric Engring. Sys., Inc., Santa Clara, Calif., 1994-96; v.p. R&D Centric Engring. Sys., Inc., Sunnyvale, Calif., 1996-98. Contbr. chpt. to textbook and handbook in field. Coach youth soccer league, Livermore, 1997-99. Mem. AIAA, ASME, Am. Acad. Mechs., Soc. Indsl. and Applied Math., Sigma Xi, Tau Beta Pi. Uniterian. Avocations: performing arts, history. Fax: (925) 423-4096. E-mail: ferencz1@llnl.gov. Home: # 109 1821 Mill Springs Cmn Apt 109 Livermore CA 94550-3178 Office: Lawrence Livermore Nat Lab PO Box 808 L-125 Livermore CA 94551-0808

FERET, ADAM EDWARD, JR., dentist; b. Newark, Mar. 5, 1942; s. Adam Edward and Bronislawa Anne (Szorc) F. BA (athletic scholar), Seton Hall U., 1963; DMD, U. Medicine & Dentistry of N.J., 1967. Pvt. practice Westfield, N.J., 1972—. With USNR, 1967-70. Fellow Am. Acad. Gen. Dentistry; mem. ADA, N.J. Dental Assn., L.D. Pankey Study Club, Soc. Oral Physiology and Occlusion, Quest Study Club, Internat. Coll. Oral Implantologists, Am. Soc. Oral Implantology, Central Dental Soc., Balloon Fedn. Am., Polish-Am. Guardian Soc., Polish Falcons of Am., Copernicus Soc. Am., Toastmasters, Psi Omega. Roman Catholic. Home and Office: 440 E Broad St Westfield NJ 07090-2124

FERGUS, GARY SCOTT, lawyer; b. Racine, Wis., Apr. 20, 1954; s. Russell Malcolm and Phyl Rose (Muratore) F.; m. Isabelle Sabina Beekman, Sept. 28, 1985; children: Mary Marckwald Beekman Fergus, Kirkpatrick Russell Beekman Fergus. SB, Stanford U., 1976; JD, U. Wis., 1979; LLM, NYU, 1981. Bar: Wis. 1979, Calif. 1980. Assoc. Brobeck, Phleger & Harrison, San Francisco, 1980-86, ptnr., 1986—, mng. ptnr. products liability, ins. coverage, environ. and antitrust/appellate practices, 1996-2000, mng. ptnr. internet and E-commerce team, 2000—. Arch. computerized case mgmt. sys. Vol. San Francisco Leadership. Mem. ABA. Home: 3024 Washington St San Francisco CA 94115-1618 Office: Brobeck Phleger & Harrison 1 Market Plz Ste 341 San Francisco CA 94105-1420

FERGUSON, ANDREW SIMON CROCKER, holistic enterprise development consultant, author; b. Sevenoaks, Kent, Eng., Feb. 4, 1947; s. Ian Charles Alexander and Margery Constance Campbell (Crocker) F.; m. Jyoti Sakhuja, Aug. 7, 1976 (div. June 1983); children: Lorna Shashi, William John Graham;. MA, Oxford (Eng.) U., 1969. Cert. in mktg., bus. counselling, group tng. facilitation. Asst. brands mgr. BOCM Silcock Ltd., Basingstoke, Eng., 1969-71; mktg. officer Lever Indsl. Ltd., London, 1971-74; mktg. mgr., dir. Pertwee Group Ltd., Colchester, Eng., 1974-80; propr. Ferguson Mktg., London, 1980-87; tng. dir. Urbed Ltd., London, 1985-87; founder, dir. Breakthrough Ctr. Ltd., London and Elgin, Scotland, 1988; chartered marketer. Author: Breakthrough, 1988, Creating Abundance, 1992; co-author: Brainwave Holistic Marketing Directory, 1992, Lifeshift: Doing the Dream, 1999; bus. editor: Be Your Own Boss Careers Book, 1988-89. Trustee London Ecology Ctr., 1990-94. Scholar Tonbridge Sch., Kent, 1960; exhbn. scholar Worcester Coll., Oxford U., 1965. Mem. Chartered Inst. Mktg., Inst. Bus. Advisers. Avocations: green issues, jazz, holistic lifestyles, personal spiritual growth. Office: Breakthrough Ctr, Wester Marchhead, IV30 8XE Elgin Moray, Scotland

FERGUSON, CLEVE ROBERT, lawyer, educator; b. Long Beach, Calif., Dec. 31, 1938; s. Frank H. and Ruth S. Ferguson; m. Kathryn Jane Weaver, Apr. 10, 1965 (div. June 25, 1995); children: Sharon Anne, Robert Timothy; m. Peggy Burke Daniell, Nov. 19, 1995. AB in Econs., U. So. Calif., 1961, JD, 1965. Bar: Calif. 1966, U.S. Dist. Ct. (ctrl. dist.) Calif. 1966, U.S. Ct. Appeals (9th cir.) 1987, U.S. Supreme Ct. 1975. Assoc. Musick, Peeler & Garrett, L.A., 1965-69, Hayes & Hume, Beverly Hills, Calif., 1969-74; pvt. practice Pasadena/Claremont, Calif., 1974—; adj. prof. physics and astronomy U. La Verne (Calif.), Calif., 1993—, adj. prof. civil procedure and law and motion Coll. Law, 1994—; mem. Alcohol and Drug Abuse Com. Calif. State Bar, 1990-91; instr. astronomy and bus. law Chapman U., 1992-93; mem. adv. bd. La Verne Coll. Law, 1998—; arbitrator Am. Arbitration Assn., Nat. Arbitration Forum. Editor: Tall Tales and Memories, 1987. Mem. Stony Ridge Obs., 1985—, pres., 1994-97; co-founder, bd. govs. Mt. Wilson (Calif.) Inst., 1987—; lectr., cons. Californians for Redevel. Edn., South Gate, 1996—; bd. dirs. Clan Fergusson Soc. N.Am., 1987—, pres. elect.; mem. L.A. Opera League. With U.S. Army, 1961-62. Decorated knight Knights Templar of Jerusalem, Grand Priory of the Scots, 1998—. Fellow Soc. Antiquaries of Scotland; mem. Univ. Club Pasadena, Univ. Club Claremont, L.A. Copyright Soc., Beta Theta Pi (past pres.). Avocations: astronomy, mountaineering, dry fly fishing, skiing. Office: C Robert Ferguson Atty at Law 237 W 4th St Claremont CA 91711-4710

FERGUSON, DAVID WINDSOR STUART, environmentalist; b. San Francisco; s. Willliam and Doris Mary Ferguson. BA, Bard Coll., N.Y.C., 1960. artistic dir. Theatre Forum, N.Y.C., 1966-69. Editor-in-chief Box 749 Mag., N.Y.C., 1972-79; author: (play) Widow's House, 1974; composer: (string quartet) Mary Maud, In Memory, 983; author: The Mind Conscripted, 1994. Pres. West 400 Block Assn., N.Y.C., 1970-72; pres. North River Housing Devel. Fund corp., N.Y.C., 1974—; founding bd. mem. Housing Devel. Fund Coop. Coalition, 1994—; sec. Croton Watershed, Clean Water Coalition, Bedford, N.Y., 1999. Mem. Printable Arts Soc. (pres. 1974-99). Democrat. Episcopalian. Avocations: reading science, big bang. Home: 411 W 22nd St New York NY 10011-2519

FERGUSON, DEBBIE, Olympic athlete. Winner Gold medal 4x100 meter relays Sydney, 2000. Office: Bahamas Amateur Athletic Assn, PO Box 55, Nassau 5517, Bahamas*

FERGUSON, JAMES CLARKE, mathematician, algorithmist; b. Spokane, Wash., June 23, 1938; s. James Forsythe and Dorothy Eileen (Dillon) F. MS in Math., U. Wash., 1963; PhD in Math., U. N.Mex., 1984. Sci. programmer Boeing, Seattle, 1960-64; staff mem. GE Tech. Mil. Planning Office, Santa Barbara, Calif., 1964-66; mathematician TRW, Inc., Redondo Beach, Calif., 1966-71, Teledyne-Ryan Aero., San Diego, 1971-77; staff mem. Los Alamos (N.Mex.) Nat. Lab., 1977-85; sr. scientist Tektronix, Beaverton, Oreg., 1985-87, BBN Systems and Techs. Corp., Bellevue, Wash., 1987-92; with Point Control, Eugene, 1993-94, Camax Mfg. Technologies, Eugene, 1994-95; mathematician SDRC/Camax, Eugene, 1995—; cons. in field, 1975-87. Co-author: Key Works in Geometric Modeling, 1991, Fundamental Developments of Computer Aided Geometric Modeling, 1992; contbr. articles to profl. jours. Recipient advanced study fellowship, Los Alamos Nat. Lab., 1981. Mem. Assn. Computing Machinery, Soc. Indsl. and Applied Math. Achievements include introduction of parametric curve and surface techniques into computer aided geometric design field; complete classification of parametric planar cubics; application of parametric curve techniques to problem of shape preservation.

FERGUSON, JOHN BARCLAY, biology educator; b. Balt., July 5, 1947; s. John Miller and Helen (Sucro) F.; m. Jane Hough, June 28, 1970 (div. 1987); children: Hallam H., Gillian D.; m. Valeri J. Thomson, July 1, 1988; children: Samantha T., Fiona T. BS, Brown U., 1969; PhD, Yale U., 1973. Asst. prof. Bard Coll., Annandale, N.Y., 1977-83, assoc. prof., 1983-92, prof., 1992—, health professions advisor, 1985—. Contbr. to Microsoft Encarta 97 CD-ROM, 1 book and articles to profl. jours. Bd. trustees Ch. St. John Evangelist, Barrytown, N.Y., 1988—. NIH Postdoctoral fellow, 1974-76. Mem. AAAS, Am. Soc. Microbiology, N.Y. Acad. Scis., Sigma Xi. Home: 1469 Annandale Rd Red Hook NY 12571-3200 Office: Bard Coll Dept Biology Annandale On Hudson NY 12504

FERGUSON, JOHN DUNCAN, medical research educator; b. Saskatoon, Sask., Can., Aug. 20, 1929; s. George Alexander and Urdine (LeValley) F.; m. Tamara van den Bergh, Sept. 12, 1958. MA, U. Toronto, Ont., Can., 1956; PhD, Columbia U., 1966. Project dir. Bur. Applied Social Rsch., Columbia U., N.Y.C., 1958-64; asst. prof. Northeastern U., Boston, 1966-68; from assoc. prof. to prof. U. Windsor, Ont., 1968—; mem. assoc. med. staff Harper Hosp., Detroit, 1982-2000. Author reports in field. Grantee Ont. Cmty. and Social Svcs. Ministry, 1991-93. Presbyterian. Home: 1516 Iroquois Ave Detroit MI 48214-2747 Office: U Windsor, Windsor, ON Canada N9B 3P4

FERGUSON, JUDITH LYNNE, bookkeeper, poet, lyricist; b. Syracuse, N.Y., Oct. 22, 1950; d. John Henry Burton and Arlene Elizabeth Harmon; children: Angel, Gordon, Christina. Cert. of Completion, Comml. Trades Inst., Little Falls, N.J. Acctg. clk. Jostens, Memphis, 1983-85; bookkeeper Padgett Bus. Svcs., Augusta, Ga., 1985-89; office mgr. K-Testing Lab., Inc., Memphis, 1989-94; accounts payable corp. office Memphis Lamp Inc., 1996-98; dir. purchasing corp. office Damar Worldwide, Inc., Memphis, 1998-99. Author: (poetry book) Unsung Heroes and More, 1997; songwriter: A Real Man, 1998, The Unstamped Letter, 1998, I Thank the Lord, 1998, Broken Vows and Broken Chains, 1999, My son, 1999, My Heart Goes Tock-Tick, 1999, Destiny, 1999. Recipient Editors Choice award Nat. Libr. Poetry, 1997, 9 Editors Choice awards, 1998. Mem. Internat. Soc. Poets, Songwriters Club Am. Avocations: reading, writing. Home: 9735 Passaic Dr # A Hudson FL 34667-3439

FERGUSON, KAREN ANDREA, clinical psychologist; b. Watertown, N.Y., Feb. 1, 1963; d. Herbert Allan and MArlene Jane Berkoff; m. A. Stewart Ferguson, Oct. 3, 1992; 1 child, Zoey Tausani. BA in Neurol. Sci., Brown Univ., 1985, BS in Psychology, 1985; MA in Psychology, Case Western Res. U., 1989, MFA in Modern Dance, 1992, PhD in Psychology, 1994. Psychology trainee Metrohealth Med. Ctr., Cleve., 1987-90; psychology intern Case Western Res. U., Cleve., 1990-92, Izack Walton Killam Children's Hosp., Nova Scotia, Can., 1992-93, U. Coll. Health Svcs. Ctr., Denver, 1993-94; psychology cons. Am. Samoa Govt., 1994-97; clin. mgr., psychologist Southcentral Found., Anchorage, Alaska, 1997—. Psychology cons. Cath. Social Svcs.--Immigrant and Refugee Programs, Anchorage, 1998—, hon. bd. dirs., 1999—. Grantee IWK Children's Hosp., 1993. Mem. APA, Am. Orthopsychiatry Orgn, Counselor Cert. Orgn. Am. Samoa (pres. 1996-97). Avocations: modern dance, hiking. Home: 4327 Birch Run Dr Anchorage AK 99507-3755 Office: Southcentral Found 4320 Diplomacy Dr Anchorage AK 99508-5925

FERGUSON, MICHAEL ANTHONY JOHN, molecular parasitologist, educator; b. Bishop Auckland, Durham, Eng., Feb. 6, 1957; s. Anthony John Alexander and Pamela Mary (Gray) F.; m. Sheila Duxbury, May 21, 1982 (div. 1988); m. Maria Lucia Sampaio Güther, Oct. 24, 1992; 1 child, John Alexander. BSc, U. Manchester Inst. Sci. and Tech., Eng., 1979; PhD, U. London, 1982. Postdoctoral fellow Rockefeller U., N.Y.C., 1982-85, Oxford (Eng.) U., 1985-88; lectr. U. Dundee, 1988-91, reader, 1991-94, prof., 1994—. Recipient award Internat. Glycoconjugate Orgn., 1999. Fellow Royal Soc. Edinburgh (Makdougal-Brisbane medal 1996), Royal Soc. London; mem. Biochem. Soc. (Colworth medal 1991), Brit. Soc. for Parasitology, European Molecular Biology Orgn.

FERGUSON, R. NEIL, computer systems consultant; b. Dallas, June 22, 1952; s. Roy and Hellon Ferguson; m. L. Jean Ferguson, Aug. 12, 1977; 1 child, Rheachel Claire. BA in Psychology, U. Tex., 1976; grad., Winfield Sch. Race Driving, 1984. Systems engr. EDS, Dallas, 1976-77; systems programmer Collins Radio/Rockwell Internat., Richardson, Tex., 1977-78; systems programmer/analyst Moore Bus. Systems, Denton, Tex., 1978-79; supr., computer graphics Atlantic Richfield Co., Dallas, 1979-85; software engring. specialist E-Systems, Inc., Garland, Tex., 1986-90; dir. product mgmt., graphics and database systems MPSI, Inc., Irving, Tex., 1990-92; pvt. practice computer cons. Lewisville, Tex., 1990—; owner Computer Sys. Svc. & Cons. Co.; tech. program dir. Internat. Microcomputer Exposition, Dallas, 1978. Vol. computer sys. adminstr. Trinity Presbyn. Ch. Recipient Golden Eagle award Am. Acad. Achievement, Tymshare award Tymshare Corp., Panasonic Sci. Achievement award Matsushita Electric Corp. of Am. and Jr. Engring. Tech. Soc., NASA award, Dallas County Med. Soc. award, 1st Place award in math. and computers 21st Internat. Sci. Fair; featured in Grolier's Sci. Ency. supplement, 1967; named Regional Class Champion, Sports Car Club of Am. Mem. Assn. for Computing Machinery, Spl. Interest Group on Computer Graphics, Am. Congress Surveying and Mapping, Am. Soc. Photogrammetry and Remote Sensing. Avocations: exotic sportscar restoration, stamp collecting, scale model car construction, wrist and pocket watch collecting and restoration. Home and Office: 1097 Holly Ln Lewisville TX 75067-5711

FERGUSON, ROBERT, financial services executive, educator, writer; b. N.Y.C., Nov. 24, 1937; s. Lawrence and Claire (Billingheimer) F.; m. Catherine Latil, July 7, 1961 (div. Dec. 1982); children: Anne, Alice, Magali, Jose; m. Magali Vigo, Apr. 26, 1991. BA, Columbia U., 1959; M of Philosophy, NYU, 1983, PhD, 1987. V.p. Bradford Trust Co., N.Y.C., 1977-78, Coll. Retirement Equities Fund, N.Y.C., 1978-82; exec. v.p. Leland O'Brien Rubinstein Assocs., N.Y.C., 1982-91; pres. Axiomatic Sys., N.Y., 1986—; vice chmn. SuperShare Svcs., L.A., 1989-91; assoc. prof. fin. Fordham U. Sch. Bus., N.Y.C., 1991-98; adj. assoc. prof. fin. Columbia U. Sch. Bus., 1987-90; bd. dirs. SuperShare Svcs. Corp., L.A., vice chmn. 1989-91. assoc. editor Fin. Analysts Jour., 1974—; mem. adv. bd. Jour. Performance Measurement; contbr. articles to profl. jours. With USAR. Mem. Fin. Analysts Fedn. (Graham & Dodd award 1961, 78, 80), Investment Tech. Assn. (chmn. bd. 1975), Inst. for Quantitative Rsch. in Fin. (chmn. 1974-75). Avocation: aviation.

FERGUSON, SARAH, The Duchess of York; b. London, Oct. 15, 1959; d. Ronald Ivor Ferguson and Susan Mary (Fitzherbert Wright) Barrantes; m. Andrew, Duke of York, July 23, 1986 (div. 1996); children: Beatrice Elizabeth Mary, Eugenie Victoria Helena. Student, Hurst Lodge, Sunningdale, Eng., Queen's Secretarial Coll., London. Author: Budgie the Little Helicopter, 1989, Budgie at Bendick's Point, 1989, Budgie Goes to Sea, 1991, Budgie and the Blizzard, 1991, Victoria and Albert-Life at Osborne House, Travels with Queen Victoria, My Story, 1996. Recipient Mother Hale award, 1996. Address: Simon & Schuster Publicity Dept Ste C3A 1230 Avenue Of The Americas Fl Concl New York NY 10020-1586*

FERGUSON, WENDELL, private school educator; b. Sandersville, Ga., May 6, 1954; d. Isadore and Willie Mae (Roberts) Jordan; m. Larry Brown Sr., May 28, 1971 (div. Dec. 1985); children: Larry Brown Jr., Dwyne Lamont Brown, Anthony Patrick Brown; m. Jerry Lang Ferguson, Sept. 28, 1992 (div.). Diploma, Alphena C.C., 1972; student, Ga. State U., 1983-87; diploma in Info. Tech., Macon State Coll., 2000. Sales clk. U.S. NAS, Albany, Ga., 1972-74, 76-77; substitute tchr. Ga. Dept. Edn., Houston County, 1976-77; nutritionist (nursery) Howard AFB, Panama Canal, 1980; joined Sweet Adelines, Inc., Tulsa, 1981; data entry operator dept. budget mgmt. Atlanta City Hall, 1982; mgr., operator Atlanta Connections, 1982-83; asst. supr. micro-film Ga. Dept. Revenue, Atlanta, 1986-88; promotional sales rep. RG Clothier/L.B. Holyfield, Atlanta, 1992-95; substitute tchr. Old Nat. Christian Acad., College Park, Ga., 1995—; loan broker Cherokee Funding Inc., Thomaston, Ga., 1989—; with Dells' Clevor Enterprises, 2000; co-prodr., writer, owner Jeri-Del Prodns., Atlanta. Actress, singer, dancer various prodns. (Irving Berlin award 1982); author: Times In Life, 1996. Vol. persona bus. broker Asst. Sec. of State, Atlanta, 1994, J.D. Sims Recreation Ctr., 2000, Atlanta; coord. nominees judgeship position Fayette, Pike, Upson & Spaulding Counties, Ga., 1992; surveyor for st. lights, Atlanta, 1982; vol. Fulton County Dept. Parks and Recreation, Burdett Gym, 1996—; active We Are Today and Tomorrow; founder Steadfast Children Learning Systems Atlanta Coalition of Chs., 1997. Recipient Gold Seal award Mayor William Campbell, 1997. Democrat. Avocations: horseback riding, chess, painting, cooking, tennis. E-mail: dellthangs@yahoo.com. Home: PO Box 55486 Atlanta GA 30308-5486

FERGUSSON, DAVID ANDREW NAPIER, ethicist, physician; b. Cuckfield, Eng., Mar. 4, 1951; s. David Napier and Stella Kate (Chamberlain) F.; m. Catrin Sian Thomas Fergusson, Aug. 2, 1975; children: Hannah Claire, Alexander Napier. BSc in Physiology (hon.), U. London, 1972; MB BS, St. Thomas' Hosp. U. London, 1975. House physician St. Thomas' Hosp., London, 1976; house surgeon Croydon (Eng.) Gen. Hosp., 1976; sr. house. physician, 1977, registrar in medicine, 1977-79; prin. in gen. practice Brook Lane Med. Mission, Bromley, Eng., 1979-89; gen. sec. Christian Med. Fellowship, Eng., 1989-99; chmn. Hope Healthcare Opposed to Euthanasia, London, 1991—; med. adv. Christian Action Rsch. & Edn., 2000—; treas., 1992-94, sec., 1994-95 Human Values in Health Care Forum, London. Author: He Sent Them Out, 1988; contbg. author: Christian Choices in Healthcare, 1995; editor: Health: The Strength To Be Human, 1993. Chmn. Local Divsn. of British Med. Assn., Bromley, 1994. Recipient Musgrave scholarship St. Thomas' Hosp., London, 1971, John Mellanby scholarship, St. Thomas' Hosp., London, 1971. Mem. Christian Brethren. Avocations: reading detective fiction, watching motor racing, church.

FERINGA, BEN LUCAS, chemist, educator; b. Emmen, Drenthe, The Netherlands, May 18, 1951; m. Elisabeth Bootsma, June 21, 1984; children: Femke, Hannah, Emma. Grad. in Chemistry, U. Groningen, The Netherlands, 1974, PhD, 1978. Rsch. chemist Shell Rsch., 1978-84; lectr. chemistry U. Groningen, 1985-88, prof., 1988—; vis. prof. U. Leuven, 1998. Contbr. over 200 articles to profl. jours., chpts. to books; patentee in field. Recipient Pino Gold medal Italian Chem. Soc., 1997. Roman Catholic. Office: Univ Groningen Dept Chem, Nijenborgh 16, 9747 AG Groningen The Netherlands

FERLAN, IGOR, biochemist; b. Maribor, Slovenia, Feb. 1, 1948; s. Maks and Bosiljka (Vavpotič) F.; m. Aleksandra Stopar, Oct. 11, 1977; children: Petra, Joy. BSc in Biochemistry, U. Ljubljana, 1971, MSc in Biochemistry, 1973, PhD, 1977. Lectr. biochemistry U. Ljubljana, 1971-76; asst. prof. biochemistry Inst. Jozef Stefan, Ljubljana, 1976-79, assoc. prof., 1982-83; rsch. assoc. Okla. Med. Rsch. Found., Oklahoma City, 1979-80; exch. assoc. prof. dept. pharmacology U. Ariz., Tucson, 1980-82; rsch. sci. collaborator Tech. U. Braunschweig, Germany, 1983-85; team leader in process control and release analytics of native and recombinant proteins Biochemie GmbH, Kundl, Austria, 1985—; prof. biochemistry/biotech. U. Ljubljana, 1991—. Reviewer papers for pub. BBA, 1977—. Recipient Presern's award for entomology U. Ljubljana, 1970, Presern's award for physiology U. Ljubljana, 1971. Achievements include discovery of one the most potent animal toxins from sea anemone Actinia equina, named Equinatoxin. Home: Liesfeld 157, A-6250 Kundl Tirol, Austria Office: Biochemie GmbH, A-6250 Kundl Tirol, Austria

FERMANIS, ERNEST GEORGE, urologic surgeon; b. N.Y.C., May 15, 1944; s. George Anastasios and Georgia Martha Fermanis; m. Pauline Angelique Papageorgopoulos Moore, Feb. 20, 1982; children: Nicole Elaine, Alexis Georgette. BS cum laude, CUNY, 1966; MA cum laude, Columbia U., 1969; MD, Vanderbilt U., 1974. Diplomate Am. Bd. Urology, Nat. Bd. Med. Examiners. Intern Albert Einstein Med. Sch. Montefiore Med. Sch., N.Y.C.; resident NYU Med. Ctr.; assoc. clin. prof. urology, urologic surgeon Crawford Long Hosp. of Emory U., Atlanta, 1982—. Columbia U. scholar, 1966-69. Mem. AMA, AMA Southeastern Sect., Am. Urol. Assn., Am. Urol. Assn. Southeastern Sect., Ga. Urol. Assn., Med. Assn. Ga., Atlanta Urol. Assn., Med. Assn. Atlanta, Am. Hellenic Ednl. Progressive Assn., Lions Club, Phi Beta Kappa. Greek Orthodox. Avocations: reading, pets, swimming, fishing.

FERNALD, JAMES MICHAEL, professional engineer; b. Portsmouth, N.H., Oct. 12, 1964; s. R. Alden and Ruth Ann (Conlon) F. BS in Aerospace Engring., Syracuse U., 1986; BSME, U. N.H., 1992. Engring. technician Aquidneck Mgmt. Assn., Middleton, R.I., 1988; engr. Life Cycle Engring., Inc., Portsmouth, 1988-95, P.R. Sherman, Inc., Woburn, Mass., 1995-96, NESLAB Instruments, Inc., Newington, N.H., 1996—. Treas. troop 164 Boy Scouts Am., Portsmouth, 1989-91; bd. dirs. Ranger Found., 19995, Piscataqua Maritime Commn., 19985. Mem. Syracuse U. Alumni Assn., Golden Key, Tau Beta Pi (pres. 1991-92), Theta Chi. Roman Catholic. Avocations: chess, golf, raquetball, skiing. Office: NESLAB Instruments Inc 25 Nimble Hill Rd Newington NH 03801-2794

FERNANDES, GEORGE, federal official; b. Bangalore, Karnataka, India, June 3, 1930; married; one son. Student, St. Peter's Seminary, Bangalore. Journalist, trade union organizer; founding pres. All India Radio Broadcasters and Telecasters Union; pres. All India Railwaymen's Fedn., 1973-74; mem. Nat. Com. Socialist Party India, 1955-77, Bombay Mcpl. Cooperation, 1961-68; elected to Lok Sabha, 1967; chmn. Socialist Party India, 1973-77; founding mem. Janata Party, 1977; min. comm., 1977, min. industry, 1977-79; joint gen. sec. Janata Party, 1985-86; min. railways, 1989-90; founder Samata Party, 1994; min. def., 1998—. Mem. Samata Party. Office: Ministry of Defense, south Block 11, New Delhi 110 011, India*

FERNANDES, JEANNE MARY, human resource administrator; b. Nairobi, Kenya, May 21, 1948; came to U.S., 1984; d. John Joseph and Joan Bertha (Correya) Athaide; m. Leonard Maurice Fernandes, Oct. 17, 1970; children: Donna Michelle, Nigel Leonard. Royal Soc. arts Diploma, Kenya Poly., 1965. Sec. East African Community, Nairobi, Kenya, 1966-67; exec. sec. East African Airways, Nairobi, 1968-69; adminstrv. asst. to M.D. Cadbury Schweppes, Nairobi, 1969-73; exec. sec. Pfizer Africa Middle East M.C., Nairobi, 1973-79, pers. adminstr., 1979-84; internat. pers. specialist Pfizer, Inc., N.Y.C., 1984-87, sr. pers. assoc., 1987-91, assoc. pers. mgr., 1991-92, pers. mgr., 1992-98, dir. employee resources and comms., 1999—. Mem. NAFE, Am. Fedn. Police, Am. Mgmt. Assn., N.Y. Personnel Mgmt. Assn., Nat. Fgn. Trade Coun. (immigration com.). Roman Catholic. Avocations: music, dancing, reading. Home: 27 Ballaro Dr Huntington CT 06484-2424 Office: Pfizer Pharmaceuticals 42nd St New York NY 10017

FERNANDES, SYLVESTER VALENTINE, physician, educator, researcher; b. Goa, India; arrived in Australia, 1970; s. Desiderio Raphael and Petolina (Coutinho) F.; m. Celine Marie Demelo; children: Ryelen, Kersten, Keyoren, Meyrelle. BS with honors, Bombay U., 1963, MB, BS, 1969. Med. diplomate. Registrar Queen Victoria Hosp., Australia, 1970-72, Newcastle Hosp., Australia, 1974-75; sr. registrar Area Health Authority, Sheffield and Leeds, Eng., 1975-79; otorhinolaryngologist, head and neck surgeon Kurri Hosp., Australia, 1979—, Toronto Hosp., Australia, 1989—, John Hunter Hosp., Australia, 1990—; lectr. in anatomy Grant Med. Sch., India, 1969-70; demonstrator in anatomy Monash Med. Sch., Australia, 1972-73; fellow in anatomy Newcastle Med. Sch., 1985-87, clin. lectr. in otorhinolaryngology, head and neck surgery, 1991—. Contbr. articles to profl. jours. Fellow Royal Coll. Surgeons (Edinburgh), Royal Australasian Coll.

Surgeons, Am. Coll. Surgeons; mem. Coll. Physicians and Surgeons; mem. Australian Soc. Otolaryngology-Head and Neck Surgery, Am. Acad. Otolaryngology-Head and Neck Surgery, 1989, Australasian Acad. Facial Plastic Surgery (found.), Am. Acad. Facial Plastic and Reconstructive Surgery. Avocations: painting, running professional skills courses, surfing the internet, hobby mathematics. Office: 22 Kelton St, NSW 2285 Cardiff Australia

FERNANDES, ULPIO, Cape Verde government official. Former min. fin., min. def., min. presidency of coun. of mins. Republic of Cape Verde, now adj. min. to prime min., min. of defense, 2000S. Office: Ministry Nat Def, Vaveza Palacio do Giverno, Praia 91, Cape Verde*

FERNÁNDEZ, ALBERTO ANTONIO, security professional; b. Santiago de Cuba, Oriente, Cuba, May 21, 1945; came to the U.S., 1962; s. Carlos and Lydia (Sotera) F.; m. Alexis Quesada, July 19, 1968 (div. July 1984); children: Gyselle, Alexander; m. Rebeca Perez, Sept. 7, 1984; 1 child, Yanelle. Computer programmer, Fla. Computer Coll., 1968; police officer, Metro Dade Police Acad., 1970; AA, Miami (Fla.) Dade C.C., 1973; BS in Criminology, Fla. Internat. U., 1994; drug enforcement spl. agt., DEA Spl. Tng. Sch., 1977. Lic. pvt. investigator, Fla. Police officer Metro Dade Police, Miami, 1969-75; spl. agt. Drug Enforcement Adminstrn., 1976-88; ret., 1988; chief security advisor A.P.A. Internat. Airline, Miami, 1995-96, Faucett Internat. Airline, Miami, 1995-96, Servivensa Internat. Airline, Miami, 1996. Author (movie script) The Challenge, 1993, (screenplay) Between Two Worlds, 1997. Recipient Recognition award for fighting against drugs Dominican Govt., 1987, Outstanding Law Enforcement award U.S. Dept. Justice, 1988; named Police Officer of Yr., Kiwanis Club, Miami, 1971. Mem. Assn. Former Fed. Narcotic Agts., Fla. Internat. U. Alumni. Avocation: reading.

FERNÁNDEZ, ALBERTO LUIS, psychologist; b. Córdoba, Argentina, May 5, 1969; s. Juan and Nellida Del Valle (Montes) F.; m. Maria Elena Marquís, May 16, 1997. M.Psychology, U. Córdoba, 1993. Psychologist Alcoholism Inst., Córdoba, 1993—; clin. neuropsychologist Neurscis. Inst., Córdoba, 1995—; prof. psychology U. Córdoba, 1995—; co-advisor CO.NI.COR, Córdoba, 1999. Contbr. articles to profl. jours. Mem. APA (internat. affiliate). Avocations: playing music, soccer, science fiction, films. Office: Instituto de Neurociencias, Arquitecto thays 60, 5000 Cordoba Argentina

FERNANDEZ, ALVARO LUIS, imagenologist, educator; b. Manzanillo, Granma, Cuba, Oct. 31, 1948; s. Alvaro and Felicita (Viera) F.; m. Denia Borges, Dec. 24, 1976; children: Maria Del Carmen, Karel. MD, Oriente U., Santiago de Cuba, Cuba, 1974; postgrad., Oriente U., Manzanillo, 1984. Imagenologist, chief of radiology Ministry of Health, Puerto Padre, Cuba, 1974-78; imagenologist Cubatecnica, Ghadames, Libya, 1978-81; resident in imagenology Oriente U., Manzanillo, 1981-84; imagenologist specialist Ministry of Health, Manzanillo, 1984—; instr. U. Oriente, Manzanillo, 1986, chief diagnostic dept., 1991-99, asst. prof. medicine, 1998—; head radiol. dept. Celia Sanchez Hosp., Manzanillo, 1989-90. Roman Catholic. Avocations: bioethics, stamps, baseball, reading. Home: PO Box 171, 87510 Manzanillo Granma Cuba Office: Hosp Celia Sanchez Manduley, Circunvalacion Ave, 87510 Manzanillo Granma Cuba

FERNANDEZ, ARTURO AQUILINO, political scientist, educator, researcher; b. Buenos Aires, June 5, 1940; s. Aquilino Fernandez and Laura Celestina Buscarini; m. Margarita Elena Rozas, Nov. 1, 1980; children: Monica, Gonzalo. Grad. in law, U. Buenos Aires, 1964; M Polit. Sci., U. Louvain, Belgium, 1969, PhD in Polit. Sci., 1976. Lectr. U. del Salvador, Buenos Aires, 1970-76; rschr. Nat. U. Rosario, Argentina, 1972-93, lectr., 1984-93, dean Faculty Polit. Sci., 1990-94; principal rschr. Ctr. Labor Studies and Rsch.-Nat. Coun. Sci. and Tech. Rsch., Buenos Aires, 1993—; lectr. U. Buenos Aires, 1993—, dir. sci. polit. dept., 2000—; vis. prof. various univs., Algeria, 1977-79, Peru, 1981-83, Venezuela, 1982, Belgium, 1993, France, 1998. Author: Practicas Sociales del Sindicalismo, 1985, Sindicalismo e Iglesia, 1990, Movimientos Sociales en America Latina, 1991, Flexibilizacion Laboral y Crisis del Sindicalismo, 1997, Crisis y decadencia del Sindicalismo Argentino, 1998. Mem. Argentine Soc. Polit. Analysis (pres. 1993-95, 2000—), Internat. Polit. Sci. Assn. Mem. Frepaso Party. E-mail: gfrolm@infovla.com.ar. Home: Borges 2308 Piso 1, 1425 Buenos Aires Argentina Office: CEIL-PIETTE, Saavedra 15, 1083 Buenos Aires Argentina

FERNANDEZ, ELENA MERCEDES, agricultural scientist, educator, researcher; b. Villa Marma, Cordoba, Argentina, Nov. 27, 1956; d. Cruz Rosa and Lucia (Brignone) Fernandez. Agro-Engr., Rmo Cuarto Nat. U., Argentina, 1983; D in Agrl. Sci., Sao Paulo State U., Brazil, 1996. 2d asst. tchr., agronomy and vet. faculty Rmo Cuarto Nat. U., 1982, asst. tchr., 1985-88, asst. prof., 1988-99, dir. plant prodn. dept., 1997-98, emeritus, 1999—; Author: Field Crop Research, 1987, Pesquisa Agropecuaria Brasilera, 1999, Seed Science and Technology, 1999. E-mail: efernandez@ayv.unrc.edu.ar. Office: Rmo Cyarto Nat U/Agr/Vet, RN 36 km 601, Rmo Cuarto Cordoba Argentina 5800

FERNÁNDEZ, JORGE EDUARDO, radiation physicist; b. Cordoba, Argentina, July 14, 1953; arrived in Italy, 1987; s. Aquilino Jorge and Maria Teresa (Invitti) F.; m. Teresita Accietto, Apr. 15, 1977; children: Ignacio Javier, Martin Andres. B, Liceo Gen. Paz, Cordoba, 1970; Lic. in Physics, U. Cordoba, 1977, PhD in Physics, 1985; Laurea in Physics, U. Bologna, Italy, 1991. Undergrad. asst. U. Cordoba, 1973-77, teaching asst., 1977-85, rschr. Atomic & Nuclear Spectroscopy Group, 1977-85, assoc. prof., 1985-93; vis. prof. U. Bologna, 1989-91; rsch. staff mem. Conicet, Buenos Aires, 1985-93; vis. rschr. Nuclear Engring. Lab. U. Bologna, 1987-93, rschr., 1994—, prof. in charge, 1997—; rschr. Nat. Inst. Physics of Matter (INFM), 1994—; rsch. grp. resp. INFM, 1997—; cons. Turin (Italy) Poly., 1989-90, Fiat Ferroviaria, Savigliano, Italy, 1989-93, Enel, Milan, Italy, 1992-93, Boliden Mineral, Skelleftehamn, Sweden, 1993-95, ICS-UNIDO, Trieste, Italy, 1998-99; chmn. European conf. EDXRS-98, 1998. Author computer code SHAPE, 991, MSXRF, 1997, Vector MC, 1998; mem. editl. bd. X-Ray Spectrometry, 2000—; contbr. articles to profl. jours. Assoc. mem. Internat. Centre Theoretical Physics IAEA/UNESCO, Trieste, Italy, 1991. Mem. AAAS, Am. Phys. Soc., Internat. Radiation Physics Soc., Argentine Med. Physics Soc., Argentine Phys. Soc., N.Y. Acad. Scis. Avocations: travel, music, computers. Home: Massarenti 96, 40138 Bologna Italy Office: U Bologna Nuclear Engring Lab, Via Dei Colli 16, 40136 Bologna BO, Italy

FERNÁNDEZ, JULIO ANGEL, astronomer, educator; b. Montevideo, Uruguay, Mar. 12, 1946; s. Jose Fernández and Carminda Alves. Lic. in Astronomy, Faculty Humanities and Scis., Montevideo, 1974. Asst. prof. astronomy U. Uruguay, Montevideo, 1970-76, prof. astronomy, 1987—; vis. astronomer Nat. Observatory, Madrid, 1979; rschr. Max-Planck Soc., Katlenburg-Lindau, Germany, 1980-83; vis. prof. U. Brazil, Rio de Janeiro, 1984-86; mem. adv. bd. Planetary and Space Sciences jour., 1993-98. Author (chpt.) Encyclopedia of Planetary Sciences, 1997, (chpt.) Encyclopedia of the Solar System, 1999. Mem. Internat. Astronomical Union (small bodies names com. 1997—), Internat. Astron. Union Commn. (organizing com. 1994—, Asteroid 5996 named in honor Julio Angel 1996), Astronomical Soc. Uruguay (pres. 1994-98), Planetary Soc. Avocations: history of science, environmental issues, hiking, soccer. Office: Dept Astronomia Faculty Sci, Igua esq Mataojo, 11400 Montevideo Uruguay

FERNANDEZ, LINDA FLAWN, entrepreneur, social worker; b. Tampa, Fla., Sept. 14, 1943; d. Frank and Rose (D'Amico) F.; 1 child, Marci. B.S., U. South Fla., 1965; M.S., U. Nev., 1976. Social worker Hillsborough County, Tampa, Fla., 1965-67; parole officer adult div. Fla. Parole Commn., Tampa, 1967-69; dir. social services Sunrise Hosp., Las Vegas, Nev., 1969-78; ind. real estate investor, Fla. and Nev., 1965—; pres. Las Vegas Color Separations, Inc., 1978—, Las Vegas Typesetting, Inc., 1983—; LMR Enterprises, Inc., Las Vegas, 1984—; sec.-treas. Sierra Color Graphics, Inc., Las Vegas, 1983—. Founder, organizer Human Relations, pet mascots for elderly; team ofcl. girls' softball, 1985; mem. Clark County Citizens Com. Efficiency and Cost Reduction, 1991; vice-chmn. Citizens Com. Efficiency and Cost Reduction, 1992. Recipient numerous awards Ad Club Fedn. Mem. Las Vegas C. of C. (congl. com.) Women's Las Vegas C. of C., Ad Club Fedn., Citizens for Pvt. Enterprise, U.S. C. of C. Avocations: tennis; water skiing. Office: 3351 S Highland Dr Ste 210 Las Vegas NV 89109-3430

FERNANDEZ, MARY JOE, professional tennis player; b. Dominican Republic, Aug. 19, 1971; d. Jose and Sylvia F. 3rd ranked woman USTA; winner women's doubles (with Patty Fendick) Australia Open, 1991; gold medalist women's doubles Olympic Games, Barcelona, Spain, 1992, Atlanta, 1996; winner (with Davenport) French Open doubles Paris, 1996; mem. winning U.S. Fed Cup Team Atlantic City, N.J., 1996. Ranked # 8 World Tennis Assn. Tour, 1995, # 1 USA Women, 1995. *

FERNANDEZ, PATRICK JOSEPH, engineering executive; b. Singapore, May 22, 1954; arrived in Australia, 1974; s. Martin and Irene Fernandez; m. Asha Cherian; 1 child, Pravin Cherian-Fernandez. B in Engring., U. West Australia, 1980, M in Engring., 1989; MBA, U. New So. Wales, 1990. Cert. profl. engr., Australia. Project engr. Pub. Works Dept., Perth, Australia, 1981-85; process design engr. Water Authority of Western Australia, Perth, 1985-88; fin. analyst Tech. & Industry Devel. Authority, Perth, 1988; assoc. Infrastructure Devel. Corp., Sydney, Australia, 1990; bus. mgr. Sydney Water Corp., 1991-94; sr. rsch. assoc. grad. sch. bus. U. Sydney, 1994-96; dir. CTC Consultants, 1995-99; mgr. KPMG Cons.; sr. mgr. Arthur Andersen, 2000—; cons. Trade Practices Commn., Sydney, 1989. Served to lt. Singapore armed forces, 1973-74. Mem. ASME, Inst. Engrs., Grad. Mgmt. Assn., Australian Grad. Sch. Mgmt. Alumni Assn. (bd. dirs. 1991-93). Avocations: bush walking, antique furniture. Home: 24 Arkland St, Cammeray Sydney 2062, Australia Office: U Sydney, Arthur Andersen, 363 George St, Sydney 2000, Australia

FERNANDEZ, ROMEO JOHANN IBARDALOZA, lawyer; b. Manila, The Philippines, May 25, 1965; Romeo Rodriguez and Luz (Ibardaloza) F.; m. Cecilia Melita Relova, July 24, 1993; children: Beatrice Marie, Adrian Joseph. BA in Econs., U. The Philippines, 1986; LLB, Ateneo de Manila, 1990. Assoc. Castillo Laman Tan & Pantaleon, The Philippines, 1990-94, Quisumbing Torres & Evangelista, The Philippines, 1994; ptnr. Poblador Bautista & Reyes Law Offices, Makati, The Philippines. Placed 6th 1990 Bar Exams. Supreme Ct., The Philippines, 1991. Mem. KC. Roman Catholic. Office: Poblador Bautista & Reyes, 5th Fl Sedcco I Bdg Rada St, Makati Metro Manila, The Philippines

FERNANDEZ-BALLESTEROS, ROCÍO, psychologist, sociologist, educator, researcher; b. León, Spain, Mar. 21, 1939; d. Hermógenes Fernandez and Dolores Ballesteros; m. Carlos Giménez, Oct., 1959; 1 child, Mario. Lic. in polit. sci., U. Madrid, 1960, diploma in psychology, 1969; diploma in sociology, Internat. U. Rome, 1962; PhD cum laude, Complutense U., Madrid, 1973. Asst. Autonoma U., Madrid, 1972-74, assoc. prof., 1974-76, prof., 1979—, dir. gerontology programs, 1990—; assoc. prof. Nat. U. Distance Edn. (Open U.), Madrid, 1976-77; prof. Complutense U., Madrid, 1979-80; dir. dept. diagnosis Autónoma U. Madrid, 1980-83, dean faculty psychology, 1983-87; expert UNESCO, France and Venezuela, 1984—; evaluator European Union, Belgium, 1995; vis. prof. U. Hawaii, 1986, 88, 90, U. Costa Rica, 1987, Belgrano U., 1989, U. Simon Bolivar, 1991, U. S. Fla., 1996; vis. prof., evaluator Kuwait U., 1995.. Author: Psychodiagnostic, 1980, Myth and Reality About Health and Aging, 1992; co-editor: Behavioral Assesment, 1981; editor: Psychological Assessment, 1994; editor-in-chief European Jour. Psychol. Assessment, 1992—; mem. edtl. bd. World Psychology, 1995—, European Psychologist, 1996—. Recipient INSERSO Inst. award, 1989, Caja Madrid Found. award, 1992; grantee Caja de Ahorros y Monte de Piedad de Madrid, 1970-73, USA-Spain Joint Com., 1979, Nat. Rsch. Agy., Ministry Edn. and Sci., 1979-83, 83-86, Nat. Inst. Social Svcs., 1986-89, 90-92, 92-94, European Commn.: Concerted Action on Gerontology, 1993-96, 97—. Mem. European Assn. Psychol. Assessment (pres. 1990—), IAAP (mem. exec. com. 1990—, pres. divsn. 2 1994—), Spanish Fedn. Psychol. Assn. (exec. 1995—). Avocations: sailing, scuba diving, waterskiing. Office: Autonoma U Madrid, Campus Cantoblanco, 28049 Madrid Spain

FERNANDEZ DEL RIO, JOSE ENRIQUE, communications engineer, researcher; b. Santoña, Spain, Dec. 28, 1965; s. Jose Fernandez Martin and Maria Teresa del Rio Huerta. BS in Physics with honors, U. Cantabria, Santander, Spain, 1992, MSEE, 1994; PhD in Elec. Engring., U. Cantabria, 1997. Grad. rsch. asst. U. Cantabria, 1992-94, 95-97; vis. scholar Syracuse (N.Y.) U., 1994-95; engr. antennas for satellite design Rymsa Co., Madrid, 1997-2000; assoc. prof. Univ. Europea de Madrid, 1999—. Contbr. articles to sci. jours. including Digital Signal Processing, others. Vol. Office Internat. Svcs., Syracuse U., 1995. Rsch. fellow Marcelino Botin Found., Santander, 1993-96. Mem. NY Acad. Scis. Avocations: nature, walking, reading science books, spectator sports.

FERNANDEZ DOMÍNGUEZ, MANUEL ANTONIO, biology educator, environment education researcher; b. Santiago, Spain, Sept. 16, 1955; s. Manuel Fernández Iglesias and Soledad Domínguez Míguez. Grad. in biol. scis., U. Santiago, 1977; grad. in environ. edn., Univ. Edn. by Distance, Madrid, 1992. Tchr. biology I.B. Sánchez Canton, Pontevedra, Spain, 1978-80; head dept. I.B.A. Estrada, Spain, 1980-86, Inst. Ednl. Scis. Xelmírez I, Santiago, 1986—; prof. natural scis. Santiago U., 1997—; coord. environ. edn. ICE, Santiago U., 1988—. Author: Eurosurvey Galicia: An Analysis of the Representations and attitudes of Galician Students About Environment, 1997, Environmental and Health Scis., 1998, Saving Energy as a Contribution to the Environment, 1998, (textbook) Health and Environmental Sciences, 1999, (brochures) Don't Waste Energy, 1999; contbr. articles to mags.; editor procs. internat. event on biodiversity and tourism Bictur 98, 1999. Sec. Nova Escola Galega, Santiago, 1982-85; coord. Taller A Curuxa, Santiago, 1988-98. Recipient Premio Experiencias Educativas Santillana, 1985, 1st Premio Certame Ecologia Penas de Rodas, 1993, Premio Projectos Educativos Europeos, 1998. Mem. Fedn. Ecologista Gallega. Avocations: rock music, mountain climbing, South American literature, foreign languages. Home: Rua Atenas 8C-2oC, 15703 Santiago A Coruna, Spain Office: Inst Ed Scis, Xelmírez I, Poza de Bar S/N, 15705 Santiago A Coruna, Spain

FERNÁNDEZ-FERNÁNDEZ, FRANCISCO JOSÉ, internist; b. Ferrol, Coruna, Spain, Dec. 1, 1964; s. Alejandro and Angustias (Fernandez-Rodriguez) Fernandez-Garcia. MD, U. Santiago de Compostela, Ferrol, 1988. Resident internal medicine Ferrol, Spain, 1990-94, specialist in internal medicine, 1995—; mem. dept. internal medicine Hosp. Arquitecto Marcide, Ferrol. Contbr. articles to profl. jours. Home: Linares Rivas No5-2o, 15407 Narón Spain Officee: Hosp Arquitecto Marcide, Dept Internal Medicine, 15405 Ferrol Spain

FERNÁNDEZ-GONZÁLEZ, JUSTO, lawyer, legal assistance director; b. San Gaspar, Jalisco, Mexico, Oct. 18, 1952; came to U.S., 1966; s. Feliciano and Paula (González) Fernández; m. Bernice Armijo-Fernández, Feb. 1984 (div.); children: Justo, Natalia, Maclovio, Rene. AA, Reedley Coll., 1973; BA, UCLA, 1976, student, 1978; JD, U. Calif. Hastings, San Francisco, 1981. Bar: Tex. 1983, U.S. Ct. Appeals (5th cir.) 1984, U.S. Dist. Ct. (no. and we. dists.) Tex. 1986, U.S. Supreme Ct. 1990. Staff atty. North Ctrl. Tex. Legal Aid, Dallas, 1984-86; staff atty. El Paso (Tex.) Legal Assistance, 1986, supr., 1986-87, dep. dir., 1987-89, exec. dir., 1989—. Bd. dirs. Tex. Legal Svcs. Ctr., Austin, 1986—, Ctr. de Medico Del Valle, El Paso, 1990—, Alternative Dispute Resolution, El Paso, 1989—, Project Adv. Group region 7, Washington, 1985—; adv. com. United Way, El Paso, 1990. Reginald Heber Smith fellow Legal Svcs. Corp., Washington, 1981-84; named Most Outstanding Atty. North Cen. Legal Svcs., Dallas, 1985, Atty. of Yr., Tex. Clients Coun., 1992. Mem. Tex. Bar Assn., Fed. Bar Assn., Mexican-Am. Bar, Coll. of the State Bar. Avocations: jogging, swiming, reading, raising pigeons. Home: 2325 San Diego Ave El Paso TX 79930-1322 Office: El Paso Legal Assistance 1301 N Oregon St El Paso TX 79902-4025

FERNANDEZ LONG, HILARIO, civil engineer; b. Bahia Blanca, Buenos Aires, Sept. 12, 1918; s. Segundo and Maria Esther (Rodriguez) Fernandez Long; m. Nidia Elsa de Rioja; children: Maria Elena, Pablo, Marcelo, Maria Clara, Miguel. Degree civil engring., U. Buenos Aires. Prof. U. Buenos Aires, 1957-66, dean faculty of engring., 1962-65, pres., 1965-66; ptnr. Fernandez Long & Reggini, Buenos Aires, 1957—. Mem. Academia Nacional de Ciencias Exactas, Fisicas y Naturales, Am. Soc. Civil Engrs., Academia Nacional de Educacion. Avocations: game of go, reading Chinese. Home: Ave 75 N 330, Necochea, 7630 Buenos Aires Argentina

FERNÁNDEZ MARTIN, FERNANDO, foreign diplomat; b. Santa Cruz de la Palma, Tenerife, Spain, May 29, 1943. Mem. European Parliament, 1999—, vice-chmn. com. on devel. and coop., substitute com. on regional policy, transport and tourism; mem. Group of the European People's Party (Christian Democrats) and European Democrats; mem. Mems. from the European Parliament to the Joint Assembly of the Agreement between the African, Caribbean and Pacific States and the EU. Mem. People's Party. *

FERNANDEZ MIRABAL, JAIME DAVID, government official; b. Salcedo, Oct. 15, 1956; s. Jaime Fernandez Camilo and Dedé Mirabal Reyes; m. Lissie Campos, 1988; 1 child, Adriana. BA in Agronomy, Superior Inst. Agr.; MD, Inst. Tech. Santo Domnigo. Cons. European Union, UN; senator Salcedo Province, 1990; v.p. Govt. Dominican Republic. Mem. Party Dominican Liberation. Office: Office VP, Palacio Nacional, Avenida Mexico No 15, Santo Domingo Dominican Republic*

FERNANDEZ-PRINI, ROBERTO JOSÉ, chemist; b. Buenos Aires, June 1, 1937; s. Cèsar Eloy and Esther (Prini) F.; m. Sara Inés Casás, Nov. 9, 1962; children: Joaquin Patricio, Maria. B, Coll. Nat. Buenos Aires, 1955; D, U. Buenos Aires, 1964. Prof. U. Chile, Santiago, 1966-69; rsch. assoc. U. Md., Balt., 1969-70; prof. U. Buenos Aires, 1971-74, 84—; sr. rschr. Inst. Indsl. Tech., Buenos Aires, 1974-77, Commn. Nat. Atomic Energy, Buenos Aires, 1977—; sr. scientist Nat. Rsch. Coun., Buenos Aires, 1988; dept. head U. Buenos Aires, 1984-93, dir. inquimae, 1991—. Author: Physical Chemistry of Organic Solvents, 1973, High Temperature Agueous Solutions, 1992; mem. internat. adv. bd. Jour. Chem. Thermodynamics, 1998—. V.p. Internat. Assn. Properties Water and Steam, 1995-96, pres., 1997—; councellor Acad. Coun. Faculty Scis., U. Buenos Aires, 1991-94. Recipient award of Merit KONEX Found., Buenos Aires, 1983, Prof. H.J. Schumacher award Argentina Chem. Assn., 1997; IUPAC fellow, 1997. Avocation: sailing. Home: 11 de septiembre 927 1 B, 1426 Buenos Aires Argentina Office: Commn Nat Atomic Energy, Av Libertador 8250, 1429 Buenos Aires Argentina

FERNANDEZ REYNA, LEONEL, president of the Dominican Republic; b. Santo Domingo, Dominican Republic, Dec. 26, 1953. BA, U. Autónoma Santo Domingo, JD cum laude, 1978. Coord. Dominican Liberation Party, sec. gen., com. leader, mem. ctrl. com., 1983, mem. polit. com., 1990; dir. internat. affairs Press Dept.; editor-in-chief polit. rev. Teorí y Acción; pres. Govt. Dominican Republic, 1996—. Office: Office Pres Palacio Nacionl, Calle Moisés Garcia, Santo Domingo Dominican Republic*

FERNANDEZ-VELAZQUEZ, FERNANDO JOSE, optometrist, consultant; b. Madrid, Spain, Aug. 24, 1965; s. Fernando Fernandez-Salgado and Maria Velazquez-Gutierrez; m. Maria Jose Fernandez-Fidalgo, Dec. 16, 1995. Diploma in Optics, U. Complutense, Madrid, 1987; DOptometry, New Eng. Coll. Optometry, Boston, 1992. Diplomate in basic and clin. scis. Nat. Bds. Optometry, U.S., Internat. Bds. Examiners in Optometry; cert. specialist in refractive surgery. Prof. Centro Boston de Optometria, Spain, 1993-96; dir. Centro Fernandez-Velazquez, Spain, 1995—; cons. Laboratorios Lentiflex, Madrid, 1998—; panelist, eye care divsn. Biocompatilibities, Farnham, Eng., 1999. Author: Miopia Media Baja: Su Correccion, 1999, also articles. Fellow Internat. Assn. Contact Lens Educators Australia, Am. Acad. Optometry; mem. Internat. Soc. Refractive Surgery, Spanish Soc. Myopia (pres. 1998—). Avocations: trekking, mountain biking. Office: Centro Fernandez-Velazquez, Ferraz 2, 28008 Madrid Spain

FERNANDO, DARREL ANANDA, anatomy educator; b. Kandy, Sri Lanka, July 11, 1939; arrived in Australia; s. Henry and Lydia Fernando; m. Carmen Loos; children: Sunara, Renuka. B in Vet. Sci., U. Sri Lanka, 1957; PhD, U. London, 1962. Sr. lectr. vet. anatomy U. Sri Lanka, 1962; sr. lectr. in human anatomy U. NSW, Australia, 1966-98, U. Western Sydney, Australia, 1998—. Home: 2 Liguria St, Sydney NSW 2034, Australia Office: Faculty Health, U Western Sydney, Campelltown NSW, Australia

FERNANDO, FRANK MARCUS, bishop; b. Chilaw, Sri Lanka, Oct. 19, 1931; s. Elaris and Mary Bridget (Pinto) F. BA, U. London, 1959; B Philosophy, Propaganda Fide, Rome, 1953, Lic. Theology, 1957. Ordained to priesthood, Roman Catholic Archdioce of Colombo, Sri Lanka, 1956. Elected aux. bishop Roman Cath. Archdioce of Colombo, 1965, consecrated bishop, 1965; co-adjutor bishop of Chilaw Roman Cath. Diocese of Chilaw, 1968, bishop of chilaw, 1972; pres. Cath. Bishop's Conf. of Sri Lanka, 1979-89; chmn. Cath. Nat. Com. for Social Com., Sri Lanka, 1989—. Author books in Sinhala, Radhaguru Chintha and others. Avocations: writing, pub. speaking. Home: Bishops House, Puttalam Rd, Chilaw/NW Province Sri Lanka

FERNANDO, NEIL VERNON PATRICK, medical educator, academic administrator; b. Colombo, Sri Lanka, May 18, 1928; arrived in Malaysia, 1983; s. P. Nataniel and Rose Mabel (Wickramaratne) F.; m. Kalyani Gamage Haththotuwa, Oct. 22, 1957; children: Michael, Patrick, Kevin, Danny, Kenneth. B in Medicine and Surgery, U. Ceylon, Colombo, Sri Lanka, 1953; PhD in Pathology, U. Toronto, Ont., Can., 1963. Supernumeray pathologist Gen. Hosp. of Colombo, 1963-67; provincial pathologist Galle (Sri Lanka) Dept. of Health, 1967-69; pathologist U. Teaching Hosps., Kandy, Sri Lanka, 1970-76, Colombo, 1976-83; assoc. prof. Sch. of Med. Scis. U. Sains Malaysia, West Malaysia, 1983-93, head pathology dept., 1985-89; prof. pathology, internat. student advisor St. Georges U. Sch. Medicine, Grenada, West Indies, 1993—. Social worker. Mem. Christian Ch. Office: St Georges U Sch Medicine, Dept Pathology, Saint Georges Grenada, West Indies

FERNEDING, STEPHAN, corporate lawyer; b. Lingen, Emsland, Germany, Dec. 14, 1964; s. August and Christa (Hörnschemeyer) F. Grad. 1st law exam., U. Göttingen (Germany), 1992; grad. 2d law exam., Ministry of Justice, Hannover, Germany, 1995. Mng. dir. Nanofilm Tech. GmbH, Göttingen, 1992—; law ptnr. Ferneding & Ptnr., Göttingen, 1995-2000; mng. dir. Halcyonics, Göttingen, 1996—; CEO NFT-LLC, L.A., 1996—; atty. Montano & Co., Port of Spain, Trinidad, 1995; cons. Benedicta & Assoc., Jakarta, Indonesia, 1995, Jr. Chamber Internat. dist. Goettingen (chmn. 1998-99); chmn. Measurement Valley e.v., 1998-2000; lectr. U. South of Lower Saxony, 1998—. Lectr. in adult edn., Göttingen, 1995—. With German Army, 1985-86. Bavarian Found. law scholar, 1989. Mem. Assn. Young Entrepreneurs, Jr. Chamber Internat. Avocations: Judo, skiing, in-line-skating, classical music. Home: Theaterplatz 9A, 37073 Göttingen Germany Office: Nanofilm Tech GmbH, Anna-Vandenhoeck-Ring 5, 37081 Göttingen Germany

FERNG, YUH MING, research scientist; b. Kaoshung, Taiwan, Republic of China, Dec. 25, 1964; s. Hann Ji and Feng Ching (Kuang) F. BS, Tsing-Hua U., Hsin Chu, 1986, PhD, 1990. Assoc. engr. Inst. Nuclear Energy Rsch., Lungton, 1990—. Contbr. articles to profl. jours. including Nuclear Engring. and Design, Nuclear Sci. and Engring., Nuclear Tech., Corrosion. Recipient Best Paper of Yr. award Chung-Hwa Nuclear Soc., 1st class rsch. prize Taipower Co., 1997, rsch. prize Nat. Sci. Coun., 1998. Mem. Phi Tau Phi. Avocations: reading, sports, studying. Office: Inst Nuclear Energy Rsch, 1000 Wenhua Rd, PO Box 3-3, Lungtan Taiwan Republic of China

FERNICOLA, NILDA ALICIA GALLEGO GÁNDARA DE, pharmacist, biochemist; b. Bahia Blanca, B.A., Argentina, Jan. 9, 1931; d. Francisco and Alicia (Gándara) Gallego; m. Lucio Fernicola, Jan. 2, 1964; 1 child, Pablo Francisco. BS in Pharmacy, U. Buenos Aires, Argentina, 1955, BS in Biochemistry, 1959, PhD in Pharmacy and Biochemistry, 1962. Analyst Nat. Chemistry Office, Buenos Aires, Argentina, 1957-67; instr. Coll Pharmacy & Biochemistry, U. Buenos Aires, 1962-75; prof. U. Sao Paulo, Brazil, 1976-82, prof. postgrad. courses environ. toxicology/health/environ., 1982-93, prof. postgraduate course, 1996—, adv. master and PhD degrees, 1996—; team leader Fundacentro, Sao Paulo, 1975-76; head toxicology divsn., agy. for environ. control. Companhia de Tecnologia de Saneamento Ambiental, Sao Paulo, 1976-82, head human toxicology, 1991-93, toxicology tech. asst., 1995-97; head human toxicology and environ. health. divsn. CETESB, 1997—; toxicologist cons. PanAm. Health Orgn./WHO, 1982-91; mem. rsch. group Nat. Coun. Science, Tech., Rsch., Buenos Aires, 1967; short-term cons. PanAm. Health Orgn./WHO, Colombia, Bogota, 1993-95. Co-author: Nociones Básicas de Toxicologia, 1985, Toxicologia Ocupacional , 1989;

contbr. articles to profl. jours. Recipient award Argentina Congress, 1975. Mem. Argentinian Acad. Environ. Sci., Toxicology Soc. Panama (founder), Brazilian Toxicology Soc. (bd. dirs. Sao Paulo 1992-93), Sociedade Brasileira de Toxicologia/Brazilian Toxicolgy Soc. (v.p. 2000—), Internat. Life Sci. Inst. (coun. mem. 2000—), Revista Brasileira Toxicologia (bd. advs. 1996—), Revista Farmacia e Bioquimica da Universidade Sao Paulo (bd. advs. 1996—), N.Y. Acad. Scis., European Socs. Toxicology, XI Brazilian Congress Toxicology. Fax: 55-11-3030-6986. E-mail: nildaf@cetesb.br. Office: CETESB, Ave Frederico Herman 345, 05489-900 São Paulo SP, Brazil

FEROZ, EHSAN HABIB, accounting educator, researcher, writer; b. Chittagong, Bangladesh, Jan. 9, 1952; came to U.S., 1979, permanent resident, 1983, naturalized, 1990; s. Mohammad Obaidul and Sabera (Begum) Hakim; m. Kishwar Sultana Beg, Oct. 16, 1982; children: Rubens, Jonas, Amran. BA with honours, U. Dacca, 1972, MA first class first, 1974; MA, Carleton U., 1978; PhD, U. Chgo., 1982. Cert. fraud examiner; cert. govt. fin. mgr. Asst. prof. acctg. SUNY, Buffalo, 1983-86; asst. prof. acctg. CUNY, Baruch, 1986-89; vis. asst. prof. acctg. Carlson Sch. of Mgmt. U. Minn., 1989-91, assoc. prof. acctg., assoc. mem. grad. faculty, 1991-93, prof. acctg., assoc. mem. grad. faculty, 1993—; invited guest Ctr. For Internat. Studies, MIT, 1979; disting. faculty mentor U. Minn., 1990, 91; faculty mentor sch. bus. and econs., mem. honors and awards com., dean search com., outcome measures com., student behavior judiciary com., libr. policy com. U. Minn., Duluth, spl. project assoc. of vice-chancellor for acad. adminstrn., spring, 1995; invited presenter Jour. Acctg. Rsch. Conf., 1991; invited nominator Seidman Disting. Award in Polit. Economy, 1991, 92. Contbr. numerous articles to profl. jours., including Advances in Acctg., Acctg. Horizons, Australian Jour. Mgmt., Acctg. Orgns. and Soc., Acctg. Rev., Jour. Acctg. Rsch., Jour. Bus. Fin. and Acctg., Pub. Adminstrn. Quarterly, Fin. Accountability and Mgmt., Jour. Acctg. Abstracts, IEEE Transactions on Neural Networks, Encyclopedic Dictionary of Acctg.; mem. editl. bd. Internat. Jour. Acctg., Internat. Jour. Acctg. and Bus. Soc., Rsch. in Govtl. and Non Profit Acctg. Bd. dirs. Duluth Children's Mus., 1996—; mem. affirmative action rev. com. Minn. Edn. Assn., 1996-98. Mem. Assn. Govt. Accts., Assn. Cert. Fraud Examiners, Acad. Internat. Bus., Am. Acctg. Assn. (rsch. com. GNP sect. 1982-93, fin. com. 1992), Minn. Coun. Acctg. Educators. Avocations: walking, swimming, classical music. Office: U Minn-Dept Acctg 125 Sch Bus and Econs 10 University Dr Duluth MN 55812-2403

FERRAGUT, JUAN, pediatrician; b. Palma de Mallorca, Spain, Sept. 18, 1942; s. Rafael Ferragut and Margarita Martí; m. Carmen Elena Diago, Aug. 31, 1969; children: Rafael, Margarita, Josemaria, Carmen, Juan Ignacio, Pedro. Bachelor's degree, La Salle, Palma de Mallorca, 1960; MD, U. Navarra, Pamplona, Spain, 1967, PhD, 1970. Pediat. resident Hosp. St. Raphael, New Haven, Conn., 1970-71; pediat. resident St. Christopher's Hosp. for Children, Phila., 1971-72, resident in pediat. endocrinology, 1972-73; med. adjunto in pediats. Hosp. Infantil La Fe, Valencia, Spain, 1973-77, chief pediat. sect., 1977-78; chief pediat. sect. Hosp. Son Dureta, Palma de Mallorca, 1978—. Mem. Mallorca Pro-Vida, Palma de Mallorca, 1979. Sgt. Spanish Cavalry, 1966-69. Mem. Spanish Soc. Pediat. Endocrinology. Roman Catholic. Avocations: soccer, music, swimming, traveling. Home: General Riera 44 4th A, 07003 Palma de Mallorca Spain Office: Hosp Son Dureta, Andrea Doria 53, 07014 Palma de Mallorca Spain

FERRAIOLI, ARMANDO, biomedical engineering company executive; b. Foggia, Italy, Mar. 19, 1949; s. Alfonso and Luisa (Taurino) F. m. Maria T. Kindjarsky-D'Amato, Aug. 30, 1976; children—Solange A.P., Naike M.L., Anika M.V. Dr. Ing., U. Naples, 1973; M.Sc. in Bioengring., U. Strathclyde, 1974; Ph.D., U. Southampton, 1981. Registered profl. engr., Salerno, Italy; chartered engr., Gt. Britain. Regional mgr. Gambro Soxil SpA, Bari, Naples, Italy, 1982-84; cons. Studio di Ingegneria Medica, Cava del Tirreni, 1984—; biomed. researcher, designer hosp. structures, Italy. Mem. adv. bd. Italian biomed. jours.; contbr. over 50 articles on biomed. engring. to profl. jours.; book review editor for various jours. Internat. Brit. Council grantee, 1974-78. Mem. IEEE, Instn. Elec. Engrs. Gt. Britain, Associazione Elettrotecnica Italiana, Biol. Engring. Soc. Gt. Britain, Association for the Advancement of Med. Instrumentation, Biomed. Engring. Soc., Associazione Italiana di Ingegneria Medica e Biologica, Centro Nazionale Edilizia e Tecnica Ospedaliera. Home: Via V Veneto 23/A, 84013 Cava dei Tirreni Italy Office: Corso Italia n 232, 84013 Cava dei Tirreni Italy*

FERRAND, LOUIS GEORGE, lawyer; b. East Grand Rapids, Mich., Apr. 12, 1942; s. Louis George and Margaret Louise (LaBour) F.; m. Mary Eleanore Braseth, Oct. 25, 1969; children: Anne Elizabeth, Gregory Louis, Jacqueline Louise. BA, Alma Coll., 1964; JD, U. Mich., 1971. Bar: Mich. 1971, D.C. 1974, U.S. Supreme Ct. Pres., co-founder Cornerstone Project, Inc., Bklyn., 1966; vol. Peace Corps., Dominican Republic, 1966-68, trainer, 1968; dir. manpower programs Grand Rapids CAP, Mich., 1969-70; trial atty. Dept. Justice, Washington, 1971-76; counsel for civil rights Dept. Labor, Washington, 1976-81, dep. assoc. solicitor for civil rights, 1981-87, dep. assoc. solicitor for mine safety and health, 1987-88; of counsel Newman & Newell, 1988-89; sr. atty. Orgn. of Am. States, 1990-94, prin. atty., 1994—. Bd. dirs. Ayuda, Inc., 1988—, chair legal affairs and personnel coms., exec. com.; bd. dirs. Parklawn Recreation Assn., Alexandria, Va., 1982-84, No. Va. Meml. Soc., 1991-95, Arlington Retirement Housing Corp., 1988-93; chmn. social responsibilities com. Unitarian Ch., Arlington, Va., 1981, co-chmn. capital fund dr., 1993-94; co-founder, bd. dirs. Fondo Quisqueya Found., Inc., 1993—, treas., 1992—; co-founder, bd. dirs. Friends of Williamsburg Rowing, Inc., 1993-97, treas. 1993-95; leader cub scout pack George Washington dist. Boy Scouts Am., 1984-86; basketball coach Recreational League, 1983-89; trustee Unitarian Ch. of Arlington, 1984-87, chmn. bd. trustees, 1986-87; bd. dirs. T.C. Williams H.S. Track Boosters, 1992-97, treas. 1992-95, co-pres. 1995-96; bd. dirs. MOAS Found., 1997—, treas. 1999—; bd. dirs. I-A Bar Found., 1995—; incorporator, bd. dirs. Young Americas Bus. Trust, Inc., 1999—, vice chair, 1999—. Mem. Fed. Bar Found. (adv. 1994—), Fed. Bar Assn. (bd. dirs. D.C. chpt. 1986—, officer 1988-94, pres. 1993-94, nat. cir. officer 1993-97, nat. coun. mem. 1993-99, chair fed. career svc. divsn. 1996-99, co-chmn. nat. conv. com. 1989), D.C. Bar Assn., Mich. Bar Assn., Inter-Am. Bar Assn. (asst. sec. 1989-91, co-chmn. labor law sect. 1986-91, asst. treas. 1993-94, sec. gen. 1995—, mem. exec. com. 1995—, coun. mem. 1995—), Fed. Am. Inns of Ct. (charter mem., master 1989—, program chmn. and counselor, 1998-99, pres. 1999—). Avocations: reading, tennis, swimming, bike riding, travel. Office: Orgn of Am States Office Sec Gen Legal Svcs Washington DC 20006

FERRAND, LUDOVIC OLIVIER, psychologist, researcher; b. Châlons en Champagne, France, July 3, 1967; s. Jean-Pierre and Janine (Paris) F. MD in Cognitive Sci., Ecole Hautes Etudes Scis Soc., Paris, 1992, PhD in Psychology, 1994. Cert. psychology. Postdoctoral fellow U. Birmingham, Eng., 1995; rsch. scientist U. René Descartes, France, 1996—; prof. psychology Ecole de Psychologues Praticiens, Paris, 1996—. Autor: (with J. Segui) Leçons de parole, 2000; contbr. articles to profl. jours. Recipient cogniscis. grant CNRS, 1995. Mem. European Soc. Cognitive Psychology, Exptl. Psychology Soc., Psychonomic Soc. Home: 23-27 Rue Hallé, 75014 Paris France Office: LPE U René Descartes, 71 Ave Edouard Vaillant, 92774 Boulogne-Billancourt France

FERRANDO, JOSE, medical educator; b. Simat de Valldigna, Valencia, Spain, Aug. 20, 1937; s. Jose Ferrando and Carmen Cucarella; m. Alejandra Marrades, June 26, 1965; children: Carmen, Inmaculada et Alejandra. MD, Valencia U., 1961. Resident Hosp. of Delemont, Switzerland, 1962-63; assoc. physician, dept. gastroenterology Hosp. Clinic U., Valencia, Spain, 1964-70; dept. endoscopy chmn. Hosp. Clinic U., Valencia, 1970—; pres. Nat. Endoscopical Congress, Valencia, 1986, Nat. Spanish Congress Gastroenterology, Valencia, 1987. Author: Normal and Pathologic Appearances of the Gastrointestinal Tract and Liver, 1990. Mem. Internat. AGA, Spanish Soc. Gastroenterology (pres. 1993-94, Gold medal 1988, 91), Spanish Soc. Endoscopy, Spanish Soc. Hepatology, Valencien Soc. Gastroenterology (Gold medal 1991). Avocations: tennis, fishing. Home: Av Barón de Carcer 49, 46001 Valencia Spain Office: Hosp Clinico Univ, Av Blasco Ibañez 17, 46010 Valencia Spain

FERRANTE, AUGUSTO VITTORIO, engineering educator, researcher; b. Piove di Sacco, Padua, Italy, Aug. 5, 1967; s. Eugenio Ferrante and Annamaria Deganello. Laurea, U. Padova, 1991, PhD, 1995. Asst. prof. U. Udine, Italy, 1995-98; assoc. prof. U. Politecnico of Milan, 1998—. Contbr. articles to profl. jours. Inst. Aldo Gini scholar, 1993; grantee Consiglio Nazionale Delle Ricerche, 1996. Avocations: tennis, skiing. Home: V Matteotti 26, 25026 Conselve Padova, Italy Office: U Padua, V Gradenigo 6/A, 35131 Padua Veneto, Italy

FERRANTI, THOMAS, JR., lawyer; b. S.I., N.Y., Mar. 14, 1969; s. Thomas and Janet Rose (Giordano) F.; m. Renée Esposito, July 11, 1998. BA, St. John's U., N.Y.C., 1991, JD, 1994. Bar: N.Y. 1995, N.J. 1995, D.C. 1995. Dietary aide S.I. (N.Y.) U. Hosp., 1987-1993; intern Dept. of Investigation, N.Y.C., 1990, Justice Finnegan, N.Y. State Supreme Ct., Queens, 1990; legal intern Macy's Northeast, N.Y.C., 1991, N.Y.C. Coun., S.I., 1992; intern Supreme Ct. trial divsn. Richmond County Dist. Atty., S.I., 1993-94; tchr. law Monsignor Farrell H.S., S.I., 1994-95; pvt. practice, S.I., 1995—; lawyer, witness Criminal Trial Inst., St. John's U., 1991-94, Civil Trial Inst., 1991-94; tutor, counselor Student Network Accessing Counselor Program, 1991-94; fire fighter N.Y.C. Fire Dept., 1993—. Gen. mgr., pres. Sta. WMOC, S.I., 1989-91. St. John's U. scholar, 1988-91. Mem. ABA, N.Y. State Bar Assn., Nat. Italian-Am. Bar Assn., Golden Key, Lambda Kappa Phi, Kappa Gamma Pi, Iota Alpha Sigma (pres. 1990-91). Roman Catholic. Avocations: aquarium hobbyist, weight training, science fiction, coin collecting, travel. Fax: 718-317-5294. Home and Office: 99 Pitney Ave Staten Island NY 10309-1918

FERRARA, SERGIO, physicist, educator; b. Rome, Italy, May 2, 1945; s. Oliviero and Adriana (Ciccaleni) F.; m. Rosanna Senzio-Savino, Dec. 9, 1970; children: Flaminia, Federica. Laurea in physics, Univ. Rome, 1968. Researcher Nuclear Energy Nat. Com., Frascati, Italy, 1970-76; rsch. dir. Nat. Inst. Nuclear Physics, Frascati, Italy, 1976-93; intern researcher European Lab. Particle Physics, Geneva, 1981—; prof. physics Univ. Calif., L.A., 1985—; rep. of Ministry of Industry Nat. Inst. Nuclear Physics Coun., Rome, 1984-90; mem. scientific com. CNRS, Paris, 1989-91, deputy divsn. leader CERN, Geneva, 1995-97; mem. NATO scientific panel, NATO, Brussels, Belgium, 1996—; prof. physics, Italy, 1980. Co-author: Nuclear Physics, 1974, The Physical Review, 1976; co-editor: Unification of Fundamental Interactions, 1981; editor: Supersymmetry & Supergravity, 1988. Recipient Grand Prix Scientifique Union des Assurances de Paris, 1991, Dirac Medal and Prize UNESCO-IAEA, 1993. Mem. Italian Phys. Soc., Italian Assn. Internat. Civil Servants. Avocations: tennis, soccer, gastronomy. Office: TH Divsn CERN, 1211 Geneva 23, Switzerland

FERRARI, ATTILIO, astronomy educator; b. Turin, Italy, May 10, 1941; s. Secondo and Bianca (Quaglino) F.; m. Gabriella Mortara, Apr. 29, 1967; children: Raffaele, Monica. Laurea in Physics, U. Turin, 1964. Asst. prof. U. Turin, 1964-70, assoc. prof., 1970-85, prof., 1986—; assoc. researcher Ctr. Nazionale Ricerca, Turin, 1970-83; vis. scientist MIT, Cambridge, Mass., 1970-71; vis. prof. U. Chgo., 1998—; dir. Osservatorio Astronomico, Turin, 1986—, Consorzio Spaziale, Turin, 1990—; fellow Princeton (N.J.) U., 1968-70. Editor: Astrophysical Jets, 1982. Mem. Italian Astronom. Soc., Turin Acad. Scis., Internat. Astronom. Union. Home: Via Botero 19, I-10122 Turin Italy Office: Osservatorio Astron Torino, Strada Osservatorio 20, I-10025 Pino Torinese Turin, Italy

FERRARI, LEONARDO, physics educator, researcher; b. Parma, Italy, Feb. 1, 1943; s. Ruggero and Evelina (Artoni) F.; m. Annalisa Spadoni, June 20, 1970; 1 child, Maria Chiara. Degree in physics, U. Parma, 1968. Lectr. U. Parma, 1968-70, reader, 1971-80, assoc. prof., 1980—; fellow Consiglio Nazionale Ricerche, Parma, 1970-71. Mem. Italian Physics Soc., Italian Math. Union. Achievements include prediction of the transient negative electron mobility in Xe; analysis of relaxation processes of electrons and ions in gases; work on improved solutions of the Boltzmann equation for electrons and ions in gases; analysis of the reliability of the Fokker-Planck equation for heavy particles in gases and solution of the same equation; formulation of the kinetic and transport theory for a quasi-Rayleigh gas; derivation of differential kinetic equations for a Rayleigh gas with inelastic collisions. Office: U Parma Dept Physics, Parco Area delle Scienze 7A, I-43100 Parma Italy

FERRARI, LUCA, geologist, researcher; b. Milan, Lombardy, Italy, Apr. 12, 1961; s. Ambrogio and Maria Luisa (Pedraglio) F.; m. Guillermina Rosas Lopez, Jan. 24, 1998; 1 child, Daniela. BSc, U. Milan, 1986, PhD, 1992. Cons. geologist Comision Fed. de Eelectricidad (Mex.), Morelia, 1992, 93, Orgn. Latinoamericana de Energial Autonomous, Quito, Ecuador, 1993, Sante Fe Gold Corp., San Luis Potosi, Mex., 1994, IAEA, Wien, Austria, 1994; postdoctoral fellow Nat. Autonomous U. Mex., Guanajuato, 1995-97, rschr., 1997-98, dep. dir. Inst. Geology, 1998—. Editor Tectonophysics; editor in chief Revista Mexiana de sociedad Geologica Mexiana and Inst. de Geologia, 1998—, Geol. Soc. Am., 1998—; contbr. more than 35 articles to profl. jours. Grantee Sistema Nacional de Investigadores, 1997. Mem. Sociedad Geologica Mexicana, Union Geofisica Mexicana (treas. 1999—), Mex. Acad. Sci., Am. Geophys. Union, Geol. Soc. Am. Avocations: travel, music. Office: UNAM/Inst Geologia, Cd Univ/Apdo Postal 70-296, Mexico City 04510, Mexico

FERRARI, PAOLO, physician, nephrologist; b. Berne, Switzerland, Feb. 1, 1962; s. Carlito and Valeria (Cadola) F.; m. Elizabeth R. Culley, Mar. 30, 1996; 1 child, Oliver. MD, U. Berne, Switzerland, 1988. Intern U. Berne, 1988-89, resident in medicine, 1989-92, resident in nephrology, 1992-94; rsch. officer Monash U., Melbourne, Australia, 1994-96; sr. med. officer U. Berne, 1997-99, assoc. prof., 1999—; con. nephrology U. Berne, 1997—. Contbr. articles to profl. jours. Lt. Swiss Army, 1987-99. Recipient award Balli Found., Switzerland, 1994, award Clöetta Found., Zurich, 1997, Astra award Swiss Soc. Hypertension, 1999. Mem. Internat. Soc. Nephrology, Am. Soc. Nephrology, N.Y. Acad. Scis. Avocations: computer/information technology, travel, music, skiing. Office: Univ Hosp, Freiburgstrasse 10, 3010 Berne Switzerland

FERRARI, RONALD LESLIE, engineering educator; b. Romford, U.K., Feb. 3, 1930; s. Guiseppe Cesare and Christina Alice (Sandeman) F.; m. Judith Margaret Wainwright, Sept. 5, 1959; children: Richard M., Eleanor J., Susan P., Diana M. BSc in Math. and DIC, Imperial Coll., London U., 1951; LGSM, Guildhall Sch. of Music, 1959; MA, Cambridge U., 1965, ScD, 1994. Sci. officer Hirst Rsch. Ctr. of G.E.C. Ltd., Wembley, U.K., 1956-65; lectr. engring. Cambridge U., 1965-90; fellow Trinity Coll., Cambridge, 1966—. Author: Introduction to Electromagnetic Fields, 1975; (with P.P. Silverster) Finite Elements for Electrical Engineers, 1983, 3d edit., 1996; editor: (with A.K. Jonscher) Problems in Physical Electronics, 1973; contbr. articles to profl. jours. Flying officer Royal Air Force, U.K., 1951-56. Fellow Instn. Elec. Engrs. (London). Avocations: choral and instrumental music, hill walking. Office: Cambridge Univ, Trinity Coll, Cambridge CB2 1TQ, England

FERRARI BRAVO, GIULIANO, political scientist, educator; b. Venice, Italy, Apr. 12, 1942; s. Alberto and Dina (Bontae) F-B.; m. Francesca Guarnieri, March 25, 1968; children: Nicolò, Jacopo, Martino. Liceo Classico, P. Orseolo II, Venice, Italy, 1960; Laurea cum laude, U. Padua, Italy, 1965; PhD in Polit. Sci., Cambridge U., Eng., 1977. Rsch. student Inst. des Scis. Politiques, Paris, 1968, U. Cambridge, Eng., 1968-74; lectr. U. Padua, Italy, 1984—; rsch. fellow European Univ. Inst., Florence, 1985. Author: (books) San Francisco, 1981, J.M. Keynes, 1990; editor: J.M. Keynes, Corrispondenza Politica, 1995; contbr. articles to profl. jours. Mem. Legambiente, Padua, Italy, 1999. Recipient Jean Monnet fellowship European Univ. Inst., Florence, Italy, 1985-86. Mem. Sparkman and Stephens Assn. Avocation: sailing. Office: U Padua Dept Internat Study, Via del Santo 28, 35100 Padua Italy

FERRARI BRAVO, LUIGI, judge; b. Aug. 5, 1933. Asst. prof. U. Naples, 1956-61; prof. law U. Bari, 1961-74, dir. Inst. Internat. Law, 1968-74; prof. internat. law Istituto Univ. Orientale, Naples, 1962-68, prof. internat. orgns., 1974-76, dean dept. polit. sci., 1975-76; prof. EC law H.S. Pub. Adminstrn., Rome, 1965-79; full prof. EC law U. Rome, 1979-82, prof. pub. internat. law, prof. internat. law, 1982—; judge Internat. Ct. Justice, 1995-97; pres. Internat. Inst. Unification Pvt. Law, Rome, 1995—; judge European Ct. Human Rights, Strasbourg, France, 1998—; lectr. Hague Acad. Internat. Law, 1975, 82. Contbr. articles to profl. jours. Mem. Inst. Internat. Law, Am. Soc. Internat. Law, Italian Bar Assn., Internat. Law Assn., Soc. Francaise Drot Internat., Inst. de droit Internat. Office: Registry of European Ct, Human Rights, F-67075 Strasbourg Cedex, France*

FERRARO, JOHN FRANCIS, business executive, financier; b. N.Y.C., Jan. 3, 1934; s. John Anthony and Angelina Figliola; children: Elizabeth Ann, John Robert, Laura Marie, Rosemary. B.S.I.E. with honors and distinction, NYU, 1962. With United Technologies Corp., Windsor Locks, Conn., 1962-66; sr. project engr. United Techs. Corp., Windsor Locks, Conn., 1962-64, chief research and devel. promotion, 1964-66; founding ptnr. P.M.C. Corp., 1966-78; chmn. bd., chief exec. officer Thermodynetics, Inc.; pres. Spectrum Inc., 1966—, also dir.; pres. Pioneer Capital Corp.; mng. dir. Pioneer Ventures Assocs. L.P.; bd. dirs. Turbotec Products, Inc., Xtec Corp., Am. Interactive Media, Inc., Fidelity First Fin. Corp., Am. Shopping Mall, Inc. Contbr. numerous articles on bus., fin. and stock market to fin. publs., 1966-81; contbg. editor: Handbook of Wealth Management, 1977. Chmn. Congl. Com. for Appointees to USAF Acad., 1980; commr. Devel. Agy., Enfield, Conn., 1981; trustee Suffield (Conn.) Acad., 1980-93, chair budget and fin. com., 1987-92; trustee Birth Right, Conn., 1970-80; mem. exec. com. Holy Family Retreat League, 1984-88; mem. Gov.'s Task Force for Mfg. State of Conn., 1989-91; mem. bd. advisors St. Joseph's Residence, Conn., 1991—; trustee Western New Eng. Coll., 1997—. 1st lt. USAF, 1954-58. Decorated Meritorious Service medal. Mem. Psi Upsilon, Suffield Country Club. Home: 86 Berkshire Ave Southwick MA 01077-9642 Office: 651 Day Hill Rd Windsor CT 06095-1719

FERRAZ, FRANCISCO MARCONI, neurological surgeon; b. Floresta, Pernambuco, Brazil, Aug. 14, 1951; came to U.S., 1976. Student, Colegio Nobrega, Recife-Brazil, 1967-69; MD, Faculdade de Medicine da Universidade Federal de Pernambuco-Brazil, 1975. Diplomate Am. Bd. Neurol. Surgery, 1987. Intern, Jamaica Hosp., N.Y.C., 1976-77; resident Georgetown U. Med. Ctr. and Affiliated Hosps., Washington, 1977-82; pvt. practice medicine specializing in neurol. surgery, Washington, 1982—; staff Georgetown U. Hosp., 1982—, Arlington Hosp., 1982—; chief divsn. neurosurgery, faculty clin. instr. Georgetown U. Sch. Medicine, 1982—; faculty clin. assoc. prof. George Washington Sch. Medicine, 1994—; cons. in health care fin., internat. health care. Contbr. articles to profl. jours. Fellow ACS, Internat. Coll. Surgeons; mem. AMA, Am. Assn. Neurol. Surgeons, Pan Am. Med. Soc., D.C. Med. Soc., Arlington Med. Soc., Neurosurg. Soc. of D.C., Washington Acad. Neurosurgery, Congress of Neurol. Surgery. Home: 1004 Utterback Store Rd Great Falls VA 22066-1527 Office: 611 S Carlin Springs Rd Ste 105 Arlington VA 22204-1061

FERRAZZI, ENRICO, obstetrical educator; b. Cardano, Lombardy, Italy, Apr. 11, 1953; s. Guseppe and Carmela (Testa) F. Diploma cum laude, Med. Sch., Milan, 1978, Diploma in Ob/Gyn cum laude, 1982. Rsch. fellow Nat. Coun. of Rsch., Milan, 1983-86; cons. dept. ob/gyn. ISBM San Paolo, Milan, 1986-95; assoc. prof. U. Milan/ISBM San Paolo, 1996—; prof., chmn. dept. ob/gyn ISBM L. Sacco, U. Milan. Contbr. articles to profl. jours. Mem. Italian Soc. Ob/Gyn., Lombard Soc. of Ob/Gyn (sec. 1989-96), Study Group on Biophys. Technologies of the Italian Soc. Ob/Gyn. (sec. 1995), World Soc. Perinatal Med. (ednl. com. 1999). Avocations: tennis, horseback riding, photography. Office: U Milan Dept Ob/Gyn, ISBM L Sacco Via GB Grassi 75, 20157 Milan Italy

FERRE, SYLVIE, art agent; b. Lyon, France, Apr. 20, 1951; d. Noel Ferre and Colette Boge Favrot; m. Alain Buisson, Sept. 5, 1970 (div. June 1973); 1 child, Nicolas. Student, Faculte Lyon II, 1989-90. Model Weill/Cardin, France, 1971-80; with pub. rels. dept. Promo 2000, I.P.S., Lyon, 1975-85; radio spkr. Radio 2000, Vienne, France, 1986-89; art agt. Lyon and Paris, 1989—; participant conf. in Drouot-Richelieu: The Meeting of the Art Contemporary Market, Paris, 1995; curator of show "Poesie Sonnee", Lyon, France, 1995, Sound Poetry, Action Poetry/with Ecrits-studio in Villa Gillet, Lyon, 1995, performance of Brian Connolly (Belfast) in Nat. Art Sch. of Lyon, 1996, Fluxus Happening & Co. Gallery Art-Themes, Lyon, 1996, Polysonneries, Internat. Live Art Festival, , Lyon, 1999—, Mus. Ernst, Budapest, 1999; lectr. South Korea and Japan, 1996, others. Contbg. editor: Poesie Contemporaine, 1999; contbr. articles to publs. Mem. Lyon Art Contemporain (v.p. 1991—). Avocations: fitness, photography, jazz, skiing, cooking. Home and Office: 34 Quai Saint-Antoine, 69002 Lyon France

FERREE, JOHN NEWTON, JR., fundraising specialist, consultant; b. Wadesboro, N.C., Nov. 21, 1946; s. John Newton and Mary Cleo (Tice) F.; m. Ginger Ann Rogers, June 6, 1969 (div. 1991); m. Patricia Gayle Kruger, Nov. 19, 1994. AA, Bluefield (Va.) Coll., 1966; BA, Baylor U., 1968; JD, Samford U., 1975. Bar: Ala. Contr. Aetna Life Ins. Co., Seattle, 1972; atty. Ferree & Armstrong, Alabaster, Ala., 1975-82; exec. dir. Northwest Bapt. Found., Portland, Oreg., 1982-84; asst. v.p. Harris Trust Co. of Ariz., Scottsdale, 1984; v.p. Bapt. Found. of Ariz., Phoenix, 1985-89; dir. planned giving Phoenix Children's Hosp., 1989-91; pres. Scottsdale (Ariz.) Healthcare Found., 1991—; bd. dir. Nat. Com. Planned Giving, 1994-96; bd. dirs. FBI Citizen's Acad. Found., v.p. 1994-96, 98-99, Charitable Accord, v.p., 1996-99; instr. Cannon Sch. Found. Mgmt., 1995—; adj. prof. Ariz. State U., 1998—; cons. in field. Named Ariz. Profl. Fundraiser of Yr., 1996. Mem. Nat. Soc. Fund Raising Execs. (pres. 1990), Planned Giving Roundtable of Ariz. (pres. 1992, 97), Assn. for Healthcare Philanthropy. Republican. Baptist. Office: Scottsdale Healthcare Found 10001 E 92d St Ste 121 Scottsdale AZ 85258-4530

FERREIRA, ANNE, foreign diplomat; b. Saint-Quentin, France, Mar. 18, 1961. Mem. European Parliament, 1999—, mem. com. on budgetary control; substitute com. on agr. and rural devel.; Mem. Group of the Party of European Socialists. Socialist Party. *

FERREIRA, ANTÓNIO GUILHERME, psychiatrist, psychology educator; b. Lisbon, Portugal, Mar. 27, 1937; s. Guilherme and Sara (Domingues) Ferreira; m. Maria do Rosário Vieira Coelho, Dec. 26, 1963; children: Guilherme Manuel, Antonio Artur, Luisa Isabel. MD, U. Lisbon, 1962; DSc in Psychiatry (hon.), Sciccuna Internat. U., Lavalleta, Malta, 1989. Resident in gen. practice Santa Maria Hosp., Lisbon, 1962-64, resident in psychiatry, 1964-67; cons. in psychiatry Lisbon Ctrl. Dispensary, 1968; cons. in psychiatry Miguel Bombarda Hosp., 1969-78, head svc., 1978, head psychiat. dept., 1978-87, head tng. program dept., 1982-92, dir. hosp., 1987—, clin. dir., 1988-97; prof. Superior Inst. for Applied Psychology, Lisbon, 1980—, Modern Univ., 1998—; temp. advisor WHO; standing com. pres. Internat. Non-govermental Organ. Concerned with Mental Health Issues, 1990-93. Co-author: Social Psychiatry and World Accords, 1992; mem. editl. bd. Social Psychiatry (Jour. World Assn. for Social Psychiatry), Mediterranean Jour. Social Psychiatry, Psicopatologia, dir. Grupanálise; also articles. Recipient Dr. Leonidas A. Finiffes award Pierides Found. Larnaca, Cyprus, 1981. Fellow World Assn. for Social Psychiatry (pres. 1988-92, plaque 1992), Portuguese Assn. for Social Psychiatry (gen. sec. 1973-75, pres. 1975-85, hon. pres. 1986—), Mediterranean Socio-Psychiat. Assn. (v.p. 1980-95, pres. elect 1995-99, pres. 2000—); mem. Portuguese Assn. Group Analysis (pres. 1981-94), Group Analytic Soc. (London), Internat. Assn. Group Psychotherapy (bd. dirs. 1976-86, 95—), Portuguese Psychiat. Assn. (speaker pres. gen. assembly 1991), Portuguese Soc. of Psych. Epid. (pres. auditor's com. 1988-91), Portuguese Soc. of Epidemiology, Portuguese Br. of World Assn. for Psycho Soc. Rehab. (pres. auditor's com. 1997—), N.Y. Acad. Scis., Internat Govtl. Orgn. Avocations: history, philosophy, literature, music, opera. Office: Miguel Bombarda Hosp, R Almeida Amaral 1, 1199 Lisbon Codex Lisbon Portugal

FERREIRA, CARLOS JOSÉ GALAMBA, social foundation administrator; b. Lisbon, Portugal, Sept. 18, 1925; s. José António Bragança Ferreira and Irene Galamba Vieira Braganca Ferreira. Elec. engring. degree, Oporto (Portugal) U., 1948. Cert. engring.; ordained priest Olivais Sem., 1954. Collaborator Obra da Rua, Paço de Sousa, Portugal, 1954-56, dir., 1956—. Collaborator: (jour.) O Gaiato, 1954, dir., 1956. Home and Office: Casa do Gaiato, 4560 Paço de Sousa Portugal

FERREIRA, EDUARDO DE SOUSA, economics educator, researcher; b. Lisbon, Portugal, Feb. 15, 1936; s. Luis Ferreira Pires and Beatriz de Sousa (Monteiro) Ferreira; m. Karin Renate Paul, Mar. 19, 1965 (div. 1978); children: Anja, Boris, Ruth-Iana, Alexej, Jan, Deborah, Rute Telma; m. Elisabeth Bammel; 3 children. Diploma Econs., Karl-Ruprecht Univ., Heidelberg, Germany, 1969, D of Polit. Sci. Dr. rer. pol., 1974. Researcher

Karl-Ruprecht Univ., Heidelberg, 1970-74; prof., chair internat. econs.and European econ. integration Inst. Superior Economia e Gestao, Lisbon, 1976—; founder, dir. Ctr. Studies of Internat. Economies Inst. Superior Economia e Gestão, Lisbon, 1978—; guest prof. econs., head dept. econs. and bus. Autonomous U. Luis de Camoes, Lisbon, 1991; vis. prof. U. Pa., 1989; participant numerous confs. and seminars in Europe, Africa, U.S., Mex.; cons. UNESCO, 1973-74; coord. projects of European Union for the reform of the studies of econs. and bus. in Budapest, Hungary and Saratov, Russia. Author: Portuguese Colonialism from South Africa to Europe, 1972, Portuguese Colonialism in Africa: The End of an Era, 1974, Structures of Dependency-Economic Relations between German Federal Republic and Angola and Mozambique, 1975, Portugal and Neo-Colonialism, 1975, The Portuguese Economy in the Last Decades of the "Estado Novo": The Decay of Coporativism, 1975, Economic Integration, 1983, Conflict and Change in Portugal, 1974-84, 1985, Portugal, Africa and EEC, 1985, Closing the Migratory Cycle, 1986, The European Community and the Mediterranean, 1992, Portugal Today and Pressures for Change, 1993, Portugal Hoje, 1995, Hermes Unveiled Lessons on International Trade, 1997, Análise Sócio-Económica da Comunidade Portuguesa em França, Grundlagen der National Ökonomie (in Portuguese), 1999, Avaliação Da Comunidade Portuguesa Em França, 1999, Economics and Migrants, 2000, A Successful Irrigation: The Portuguese in France, 2000; co-founder, co-editor Estudos de Economia jour.; co-founder, dir. Galileu-Jour. of Econs. and Law. Co-founder, pres. Info. Bur. Southern Africa, Bonn, Germany, 1971-75. Mem. Assn. Fellows Portugese-Am. Found. (co-founder, pres.), Heidelberg Alumni Internat. (co-founder), Assn. Fellows of Deutscher Akademischer Austauschdienst (co-founder, pres.). Roman Catholic. Avocations: drawing, book-binding, collecting old bibles. Office: Inst Economia e Gestao, Rua Miguel Lupi 20, P-1300 Lisbon Portugal

FERREIRA, HENDRIK CHRISTOFFEL, electrical and electronic engineering educator; b. Germiston, Gauteng, South Africa, July 17, 1954; s. Thomas Ignatius and Aletta Susanna (Boshoff) F.; m. Hester Susanna Potgieter, Dec. 6, 1986. BSEE, U. Pretoria, South Africa, 1976, MS in Electronic Engring., 1978, DSc in Engring., 1980. Registered profl. engr., South Africa. Vis. rschr. Linkabit, San Diego, 1980-81; consulting engr. GHM, Pretoria, South Africa, 1981-83; sr. lectr. RAU, Johannesburg, South Africa, 1983-84, assoc. prof., 1985-89, prof., 1989—; chmn. dept. elec. engring. RAU, 1993-99. Jour. reviewer; contbr. articles to profl. jours. Recipient Presdl. award for young rschrs. Found. Rsch. Devel., Pretoria, 1989. Fellow Photog. Soc. South Africa; mem. IEEE, South African Inst. Elec. Engrs. (assoc. editor 1985—, guest editor 1993, editor in chief 1997—), Suid-Afrikaanse Akademie vir Wetenskap en Kuns, Math. Soc. Am. Avocations: photography, tennis. Office: Rand Afrikaans Univ, Box 524 Auckland Park, Johannesburg 2006, South Africa

FERREIRA, ISABEL MARIA MERCÊS, materials engineering researcher; b. Caldas da Rainha, Leiria, Portugal, July 29, 1964; d. Clementino Santos and emilia Matilde (Mercês) F. Engring. degree, U. Nova Lisbon, Portugal, 1989. Asst. in engring. Faculty Sci. and tech., U. Nova Lisbon, Monte Caparica, 1990—. Office: U Nova Lison Fac Sci/Tech, Quinta da Torre, 2825 Monte Caparica Almada, Portugal

FERREIRA, JOAO CARLOS ESPINDOLA, mechanical engineering educator; b. Rio de Janeiro, Dec. 30, 1962; s. Edison and Neusa (Espindola) F.; m. Isolda Vieira de Oliveira, Mar. 24, 1987; children: Paulo Bernardo, Ana Clara. BS, Cath. U., Rio de Janeiro, 1984, MS, 1986; PhD, U. Manchester Inst. Sci. Tech., Eng., 1991. Rsch. asst. Cath. U., Rio deJaneiro, 1983-84, U. Manchester Inst. Sci. Tech., Manchester, 1988-90; asst. prof. Cath. U., 1991-93; adj. prof. Fed. U. Santa Catarina, Brazil, 1993—; coord. Machine Tool Labs Fed. U. Santa Catarina, Brazil, 1994-98, coord, Mfg. Lab., 1994—; postdoctoral Pa. State U., 1999. Contbr. articles to profl. jours., chpts. to books. CAPES scholar, Rio de Janeiro, 1984-86, CNPq, Manchester, 1986-90, overseas rsch. scholar CVCP, Manchester, 1988-90. Mem. Soc. Mfg. Engrs., Brazil Soc. Mech. Engring. Baptist. Office: U Fed Santa Catarina, GRUCON Caixa Postal 476, 88040900 Florianópolis Brazil

FERREIRA, LUIS JORGE, engineering educator; b. Lisbon, Portugal, May 17, 1950; arrived in Australia, 1982; s. Jorge Correia and Juvenalia Rio (Apolinario) F.; children: Abilio, Charles. BSc, Queen Mary Coll., London, 1974; MSc, U. Westminster, London, 1976; PhD, U. Leeds, Eng., 1984. Transport planner Johannesburg (South Africa) City Coun., 1977-79; rsch. officer Leeds U., 1979-82; rsch. fellow U. Adelaide, Australia, 1982-84; mgr. R&D Australian Nat., Adelaide, 1984-89; mng. cons. Travers Morgan Pty., Adelaide, 1989-90; sr. planner Power & Water Authority, Darwin, Australia, 1990-91; assoc. prof. Queensland U. Tech., Brisbane, Australia, 1991—. Author: (book) Directory of Transport and Transport Related Courses, 1993, (book chpt.) Exploring Tertiary Teaching, 1992; editor: Techniques for Evaluating Transport Projects and Plans Workshop, 1992; co-author: Queensland Transport, 1997;ng,es—Planning and Practice; contbr. papers and articles to profl. jours. Fellow Instn. Engrs. Australia (mem. nat. com. on transport, mem. nat. com. on rwy. engring.), Chartered Inst. Transport. Roman Catholic. Avocation: reading. Home: 10 Canterbury Pl The Gap, 4061 Brisbane Australia

FERREIRA, MARYNA RAS, dental educator; b. Uniondale, South Africa, Sept. 17, 1925; d. Jacobus Ignatius and Susanna Magdalena (Kritzinger) F.; m. Leslie Errol Kent, Mar. 30, 1957 (dec. 1991); 1 child, Jonathan James. BS, U. Stellenbosch, 1945, MS, 1946; BChD, U. Pretoria, 1952, MDent, 1976; PhD (hon.), Med. U. So. Africa, 1996. Lectr. faculty of dentistry U. Pretoria, South Africa, 1953-71, sr. lectr., head divsn. dental materials, 1972-75, assoc. prof., head divsn. dental materials, 1976-90, prof., 1982-90, emeritus prof., 1991—; prof. faculty of dentistry MEDUNSA, Pretoria, 1992-97; mem. advice com. for dentistry South Africa Bur. Stds., Pretoria, 1972-89, mem. specifications dental materials com., 1972-90; mem. sr. faculty com. faculty dentistry U. Pretoria, 1975-77, 88-90, mem. rsch. com., 1981-90, supr., external examiner, 1974-95. Contbr. articles and abstracts to profl. jours. Mem. Dental Assn. South Africa (Middleton-Shaw Rsch. award 1976), Internat. Assn. Dental Rsch. (life), Dental Materials Group (life). Avocations: music, poetry, theater, wildlife. Office: U Pretoria Faculty Dentistr, PO Box 1266, Pretoria 0001, South Africa

FERREIRA, PAULO C., bank executive. CEO Banco Do Brasil, Brasilia, Brazil. Office: Banco Do Brasil Setor, Bancario Edeficio Sede III, 70089900 Brasilia Brazil

FERREIRA-DA-COSTA, HUMBERTO MEDEIROS, radiologist, stomatologist; b. Lisbon, Portugal, Feb. 20, 1931; s. Fernando and Maria Julieta de Medeiros (da Costa) F.; m. Elsa Pessoa Dec. 28, 1959; children: Luis, Jorge. BS, Fac. Med. Lisbon, Portugal, MD, 1957. Private practice Lisbon, 1952; radiology educator Fac. Med. Lisbon U., 1978—, chmn. radiology dept., 2000—. Avocation: music. Home: Av 5 de outubro 158-6, 1050-062 Lisbon Portugal Office: Clinica Estomatologica Prof, Av Elias Garcia 76 2CDE, 1050-100 Lisbon Portugal

FERREIRA FERNANDES, ELIS SIMONE, agricultural products executive; b. Loanda, Brazil, Aug. 22, 1966; d. Ary Ferreira and Niuza Souza (Lima) Freitas; m. Sandro Rogerio Fernandes, Nov. 12, 1999. Grad., Maringá (Brazil) U., 1989; postgrad., Cambridge U., London, 1996, Fisk Instn., São Paulo, 1997; MS, Inbrape, Mga, 1999. Tchr. Fisk Instn., Maringá, 1987-91, instr., 1991-95; sales trader Cocamar, Maringá, 1991-95, exec. officer, 1996—; cons. Fisk Instn., 1996—. Avocations: reading, swimming, films, foreign languages. Office: Cocamar Estrada, Oswaldo Moraes Correa 1000, 87065240 Maringá Brazil

FERRELL, CHARLES MADISON, retired nuclear engineer, health physicist; b. Clarksburg, W.Va., Apr. 30, 1928; s. Benjamin Franklin and Mary Ethlyn (Selby) F.; m. Donnie Sue Thompson, Aug. 30, 1957; children: Donald Franklin, Jeffrey Madison, Kimberly Marilyn. BS, Salem (W.Va.) Coll., 1950; postgrad., Vanderbilt U., 1954-55, W.Va. U., 1955-56, U. Md., 1959-61. Phys. scientist U.S. Army Chem. Corps, Edgewood, Md., 1951-52; physicist U.S. Army Chem. Corps, Frederick, Md., 1953-54; radiol. physicist U.S. AEC, Oak Ridge, 1956-57, Germantown, Md., 1957-74; nuclear engr. U.S. NRC, Bethesda and Rockville, Md., 1974-95; cons., 1995—. Co-author 5 U.S. Nuclear Regulatory publs. Dist. advancement chmn. Seneca Dist. coun. Boy Scouts Am., 1993-96. With U.S. Army, 1950-52. U.S. AEC radiol. physics fellow, 1954-55; recipient Silver Beaver award Boy Scouts Am., 1998, numerous vol. svc. awards including Nat. Assn. of Retired Fed. Employees State of Md. award, 1997, City of Gaithersburg,Md. People of Character award, 1997. Mem. Health Physics Soc., Shriners. Methodist. Achievements include design of instrumentation to measure thermal radiation from nuclear tests; evaluation of radioactive sealed sources and devices for AEC licenses; evaluation of shipping casks for spent reactor fuel; tech. asst. to AEC office of Hearing Examiner on Contract Appeal cases and nuclear power reactor licensing; evaluation of power reactor site safety and design basis accidents. Avocations: woodworking, target shooting, hunting, reading Civil War history. Home: 227 Rolling Rd Gaithersburg MD 20877-2041

FERRELL, GENE HILLIARD, architect; b. Albany, Ga., May 21, 1933; s. Robert and Lugenia (Chatman) F.; m. Alfreda Marguerita Duster, Sept. 23, 1955 (div. Oct. 1977); children: Steven, Kenneth, Janean; m. Myrna Jocille Seedborg, June 5, 1980. BArch, U. Mich., 1956; Cert. Air Base Engr., Air U., 1957. Registered arch., Calif. 2d Lt. AFROTC, 1956; arch. Paul R. Williams, FAIA and Assocs., L.A., 1958-72; v.p., dir. prodn. Jenkins-Fleming, Archs. Inc., Beverly Hills, Calif., 1972-77; project mgr. Renardet S.A., Riyadh, Saudia Arabia and Geneva, 1977-83, Obermeyer Project Mgmt., Riyadh, 1983-86; arch., engr. Al Mashrik Constrn. Co., Riyadh, 1986-93; sr. arch. Dar Al Riyadh Cons., 1993-97; cons. Parsons Internat. Ltd., Manila, 1997-98; arch. mgr. specialty project Dar Al Riyadh Cons., 1998—. Coach Ladera Little League Baseball, L.A., 1968, 69.; sponsor Baldwin Hills Football, L.A., 1969, 70, 71—. Capt. USAF, 1956—. Recipient Regents Alumni scholarship U. Mich., 1951-56. Mem. Soc. Am. Mil. Engrs. Republican. Avocations: reading, physics, math, computer programming. Office: Dar Al Riyadh Cons, PO Box 5364, 11422 Riyadh Saudi Arabia

FERRELL, MILTON MORGAN, JR., lawyer; b. Coral Gables, Fla., Nov. 6, 1951; s. Milton M. and Annie (Blanche) Bradley; m. Lori R. Sanders, May 22, 1982; children: Milton Morgan III, Whitney Connolly. BA, Mercer U., 1973, JD, 1975. Bar: Fla. 1975. Asst. state's atty. State's Atty.'s Office, Miami, 1975-77; ptnr. Ferrell & Ferrell, Miami, 1977-84; sole practice Miami, 1985-87; ptnr. Ferrell & Williams, P.A., Miami, 1987-90, Ferrell & Fertel, P.A., Miami, 1990-98, Ferrell Schultz Carter & Fertel P.A., 1999-2000, Ferrell Schultz Carter Zumpano & Fertel, P.A., 2000—. Trustee Mus. Sci. and Space Transit Planetarium, 1977-82; mem. Ambs. of Mercy, Mercy Hosp. Found., Inc., 1985-94; trustee, mem. legal com., chair com. U. Miami Project to Cure Paralysis, 1985-94; bd. trustees Eaglebrook Sch., 1995-98, Robinson Charitable Found., 1993—. Fellow Nat. Assn. Criminal Def. Lawyers, Am. Bd. Criminal Lawyers (bd. govs. 1981-82, sec. 1983-84, v.p. 1984-86, pres. 1987-88); mem. ABA (grantee 1975), Fla. Bar Assn. (jury instrns. com. 1987-88, chmn. grievance com. 11-L 1989-91), Dade County Bar Assn. (bd. dirs. 1977-80), mem. Performing Arts Ctr. Found. Greater Miami, Bath Club (bd. govs. 1992-95), Miami Club, Banker's Club, Cat Cay Yacht Club, Inc. (bd. dirs. 1997—, treas. 1998-99, pres. 1999—), Indian Creek Country Club, LaGorce Country Club, Fisher Island Club. Home: Bay Point 4511 Lake Rd Miami FL 33137-3372 Office: Ferrell Schultz Carter Zumpano & Fertel PA 201 S Biscayne Blvd Fl 34 Miami FL 33131-4332

FERRELL, PAUL CLEVELAND, writer; b. Morehouse, Mo., Aug. 17, 1943; s. Sherman Gentry and Virginia Irene (Brawley) F.; m. Wanda Darlene Jones, Nov. 27, 1963. Student, Mineral Area Jr. Coll., Flat River, Mo., 1965-66, U. Mo., S.E. Mo. State U. Registered technologist Am. Radiol. Soc. Head radiology dept. Madison Meml. Hosp., Fredericktown, Mo., 1965-66; ambulance attendant Pub. Emergency Svc., Sikeston, Mo., 1970-73; tchr. math. Sikeston Pub. Schs., 1978-80, vocat. instr., 1980-85; ghost writer Sikeston, 1981-84; author Bloomfield, Mo., 1985—; mem. adv. bds. Vocat. Edn., Sikeston, 1980-85; lectr. in math., health and philosophy. Author: Diet and the Cardiovascular Condition, 1995, The Utopian Cause, 1996, Night Reader I, 1997, Night Reader II, 1997, Morehouse Missouri, 1997, vol. 2, 1998, Night Reader III, 1998, Good Son/Bad Son, 1999, others; ghost writer, editor: The Headlee Anthology, 1984; author cultural newsletter The Plow and the Stars, 1992-93; inventor game Choice and Chance, 1992. Served with USN, 1966-70, Vietnam. Mem. Am. Registry Radiol. Technologists. Avocations: local history, visual and performing arts. Office: The Plow and the Stars 21212 County Road 510 Bloomfield MO 63825-8500

FERRELL, ROBERT HUGH, historian, educator; b. Cleve., May 8, 1921; s. Ernest Henry and Edna Lulu (Rentsch) F.; m. Lila Esther Sprout, Sept. 8, 1956; 1 dau., Carolyn Irene. BS in Edn., Bowling Green State U., 1946, BA, 1947, LLD (hon.), 1971; MA, Yale U., 1948, PhD, 1951. Intelligence analyst U.S. Air Force, 1951-52; lectr. in history Mich. State U., 1952-53; asst. prof. history Ind. U., 1953-58, asso. prof., 1958-61, prof., 1961-74, Disting. prof., 1974-88, emeritus, 1988—; vis. prof. Yale U., 1955-56, Am. U. at Cairo, 1958-59, U. Conn., 1964-65, Cath. U. Louvain, Belgium, 1969-70, Naval War Coll., 1974-75, U.S. Mil. Acad., 1987-88. Author: Peace in Their Time, 1952, American Diplomacy in the Great Depression, 1957, American Diplomacy: A History, 1959, 4th edit., 1987, Frank B. Kellogg and Henry L. Stimson, 1963, (with M.G. Baxter and J.E. Wiltz) Teaching of American History in High Schools, 1964, George C. Marshall, 1966, (with R.B. Morris and W. Greenleaf) America: A History of the People, 1971, (with others) Unfinished Century, 1973, Harry S. Truman and the Modern American Presidency, 1983, Truman: A Centenary Remembrance, 1984, Woodrow Wilson and World War I, 1985, Harry S. Truman: His Life on the Family Farms, 1991, Ill-Advised, 1992, Choosing Truman: The Democratic Convention of 1944, 1994, Harry S. Truman: A Life, 1994, The Strange Deaths of President Harding, 1996, The Dying President: Franklin D. Roosevelt, 1998, The Presidency of Calvin Coolidge, 1998, Truman and Pendergast, 1999; editor: Off the Record: The Private Papers of Harry S Truman, 1980, The Autobiography of Harry S. Truman, 1980, The Eisenhower Diaries, 1981, Dear Bess: The Letters from Harry to Bess Truman, 1983, (with Samuel Flagg Bemis) American Secretaries of State and Their Diplomacy, 10 vols., 1963-85, Banners in the Air: The Eighth Ohio Volunteers and the Spanish-American War, 1988, Monterrey is Ours!, 1990; Truman in the White House: The Diary of Eben Ayers, 1991, (with L.E. Wikander) Grace Coolidge: An Autobiography, 1992, Holding the Line: The Third Tennessee Infantry 1861-64, 1994; Truman and the Bomb, 1996, (with Joan Hoff) Dictionary of American History Supplement, 2 vols., 1996, FDR's Quiet Confidant: The Autobiography of Frank C. Walker, 1997, The Kansas City Investigation, 1999, A Youth in the Meuse-Argonne: A Memoir of World War I, 1917-1918, 2000. Served with USAAF, 1942-45. Mem. Soc. Historians Am. Fgn. Relations, Am. Hist. Assn. Home: 512 S Hawthorne Dr Bloomington IN 47401-5024 Office: Dept History Ind U Bloomington IN 47405

FERRER, JAIME SORIA-GALVARRO, dermatologist; b. Valparaiso, Chile, Mar. 19, 1944; s. Jaime Ferrer and Marina Soria-Galvarro; m. María Yimena Klapp Hepp, Mar. 21, 1970; children: Jaime Andrés, Juan Carlos, Lorena. MD, U. Chile, Santiago, 1968, pediatrician, 1970, dermatologist, 1976. Med. diplomate; cert. dermatologist. Academic Cath. U., Chile, 1970-71; asst. prof. U. Chile, 1980-85; dir. Corp. Nacional del Cancer, Chile, 1986—. Contbr. articles to med. jours. Fellow Chilean Soc. Dermatology, Soc. Pediat. Dermatology. Office: Hernando de Aguirre 194 31, Santiago Chile

FERRER, JORGE ANTONIO, ophthalmologist; b. Montevideo, Uruguay, Mar. 27, 1921; s. Francisco Ferrer and Elena Ruiz; m. Rosa María Rebés; children: Jaime, Isabel, Jorge, Elena, Bárbara. MD, U. Montevideo, 1950. Asst. prof. U. Fla., Gainesville, 1971-73; head sect. Clinica Barraquer, Barcelona, Spain, 1973-75; prof., chmn. Residencia Valle Hebron, Barcelona, 1980-91; pvt. practice ophthalmology Barcelona, 1954—. Author: Estrabismo & Amblyopia, 1972. Mem. Real Club Maritimo. Avocations: sailing, history. Office: Via Augusta 143, 08021 Barcelona Spain

FERRERI, MICHAEL VICTOR, optometrist; b. Park Ridge, Ill., May 15, 1967; s. Samuel Joseph and Dolores Jean (Liebich) F.; children: Christopher, Anthony. BS in Biol. Scis., U. Calif., Irvine, 1989; OD, So. Calif. Coll. Optometry, 1993. Cert. therapeutic optometrist, Calif., Tex. Extern Ctr. for the Partially Sighted, Santa Monica, Calif., 1992-93; pvt. practice, Long Beach, Calif., 1993—; assoc. optometrist Antelope Mall Vision Ctr., Palmdale, Calif., 1995-99; color vision analysis cons. Dept. Health and Human Svcs., Long Beach, 1994-97; participating doctor Vision USA, Long Beach, 1995—. Contbr. articles to profl. jours. Mem. Rep. Nat. Com., 1991—; v.p. congregation Grace Luth. Ch., Long Beach, 1996-99, also elder. Recipient Corning Low Vision award Corning Optics, Anaheim, Calif., 1993, Vision Therapy Enhancement cert. So. Calif. Coll. Optometry, Fullerton, 1993, appreciation cert. for outstanding contbns. to Save Your Vision Week, U.S. Senate, 1997, gov.'s letter of commendation for organizing coloring and essay contest for sch. children State of Calif., 1997, appreciation certificate Calif. Optometric Assn., 1998. Mem. Am. Optometric Assn. (contact lens sect.), Calif. Optometric Assn., Fellowship of Christian Optometrists, Optometric Ext. Program (clin. assoc.), Rio Hondo Optometric Soc. (treas. 1997-99). Avocations: camping, golfing, watersports. Home: PO Box 217 Corona CA 92878-0217 Office: Hour Eye Care 5724 E 7th St Long Beach CA 90803-2002

FERRER MALLOL, MARIA-TERESA, director, researcher; b. Barcelona, Spain, Aug. 25, 1940; d. Joan Ferrer Pacreu and Rosa Mallol Balló. BA, U. Barcelona, 1963, PhD, 1984. From colaboradora cientifica to investigadora Consejo Superior de Investigaciones Cientificas, Barcelona, 1972-89, investigadora, 1989—; dept. head Consejo Superior de Investigaciones Cientificas, Barcelona, 1979-84, 99—; dir. Inst. Milá y Fontanals, Barcelona, 1985-94; dir. review Anuario de Estudios Medievales, 1983—. Author: (with A. Garcia Sanz) Assegurances i canvis marítims medievals a Barcelona, 1983, Els sarraïns de la Corona catalano aragonesa en el s.XIV.Segregació i discriminació, 1987, La frontera amb l'Islam en el segle XIV. Cristians i sarraïns al País Valencià, 1988, Organització i defensa d'un territori fronter-er.La governació d'Oriola, 1990. Recipient Iniciación a la Investigación, Minister Edn., 1964-65, Formación Personal Investigador award Minister Edn., 1968-71. Mem. Inst. Estudis Catalans, Spanish Medieval Studies Assn. (vocal of exec. 1993—). Home: C Córsega 180 pral 2a, 08036 Barcelona Spain Office: Inst Milá y Fontanals, CSIC C Egipcíaques 15, 08001 Barcelona Spain

FERRERO-WALDNER, BENITA-MARIA, minister of foreign affairs; b. Salzburg, Sept. 5, 1948. LLD, U. Salzburg, 1970. Mgr. export co. Germany, 1971-78; sales mgr. N.Y., 1978-81; asst. mgr. Germany, 1981-83; with Austrian Embassy, Madrid, 1983, Fed. Ministry Fgn. Affairs, Austria, 1984-86; 1st sec. Austrian Embassy, Dakar; councillor econ. affairs Austrian Embassy, Paris; min. pleinpotentiary Fed. Ministry Fgn. Affairs, head mission, chargé d'affaires ad interim, dep. chief protocol, state sec., 1995-97, 1997-2000, fed. min., 2000—; chief of protocol UN, N.Y.C., 1994-95. Office: Fed Ministry Fgn Affairs, Ballhausplatz 2, A-1014 Vienna Austria*

FERRETTI, FULVIO, purchasing manager; b. Alessandria, Italy, Aug. 7, 1960; s. Franco and Franca (Milanese) F.; m. Manuela Francesconi, June 21, 1991 (div. Mar. 1995). Degree in Engring., Politecnico U., Torino, Italy, 1987. Project mgr. NDC Tech., Torino, Italy, 1988-91; purchaser Zanussi Elettrodomestici St., Pordenone, Italy, 1991-94; purchasing mgr. Electrolux AB, Revin, France, 1995-96; exec. purchasing mgr. Piaggio Spa, Pontedera, Italy, 1996-98, Ferrari Spa Racing Dept., Maranello, Italy, 1999—.

FERRETTI, GABRIELE, physicist; b. Premosello, Italy, Mar. 24, 1963; s. Ernesto and Rosalia (Gualea) F.; m. Hazel Ann Hift, Aug. 21, 1993. BS, U. Pavia, Italy, 1987; M degree, U. Rochester, N.Y., 1990, PhD, 1993. Rsch. fellow Chalmers U., Göteborg, Sweden, 1993-95, Uppsala (Sweden) U., 1995-97; rschr. SISSA, Trieste, Italy, 1997-99, Chalmers U., Sweden, 1999—. Rush Rees fellow U. Rochester, 1988-91. Mem. N.Y. Acad. Scis. Office: Inst Theoretical Phys, Chalmers U, 41296 Goteberg Sweden

FERREYRA, ELIDA VIRGINIA CIGNOLI DE, chemistry researcher; b. Capital Federal, Argentine, Jan. 29, 1941; d. Pedro and Angela Maria (Poggio) Cignoli; m. Jorge Horacio, May 15, 1971 (dec. 1996); children: Pablo Damián, Leandro Tomás, Roxana Mabel. MS, U. Buenos Aires, 1965, PhD in Scis., 1976. Rsch. asst. CITEFA, Argentina, 1966-74, rsch. assoc., 1974-81, prin. rschr., 1981—. Contbr. articles to profl. jours. ICRETT fellowship Internat. Union Against Cancer, 1979; recipient Bernardo Houssay CEDIQUIFA, 1996. Mem. Argentina Chem. Assn., Argentina Toxicol. Assn., N.Y. Acad. Sci. Roman Catholic. Avocations: playing piano, riding horses. Office: CITEFA, Zufriategui 4380, 1603 Villa Martelli Argentina

FERRI, CHARLES F., journalist; b. Utica, N.Y., May 10, 1950; s. Charles J. and Helen Baehlert; m. Rite Raaschou; 1 child, Marie Celeste. BBA, St. John Fisher Coll., 1972. Cert. secondary English tchr., N.Y., Danish as second lang. tchr., Voksen Pedagogiske Inst. Corr. Quick Frozen Foods Internat., 1983—, Pvt. Label Internat, 1983—; local corr. AP, 1989; fin. editor Ritzaus Bur., 1989-94; corr. fininicial/commodities news WVD-Vereinigte Wirtschaftsdienste, 1994-96, Knight-Ridder Fin. News (now Bridge News), 1996-98; corr. econ., polit. and legal news LRP Publs. EuroWatch, 1990-99; stringer Newsweek, 1988—; corr. radio and music industries Music & Media, 1994—, Billboard, 1994—, MusikIndustrien, 1997—. Author books for adolescent readers: Only in the Movies, 1983, Only a Dream, 1984, Under Egetraeet Sesam, 1986, Bogtrolden Apostrof, 1986, Den Onde Går Igen, 1987, Horror at Remsen High, 1992, Over the Line, 1992, Moonstruck, 1994, Pink Paradise, 1995, Love Ties, 1995, The Ghost of Rock 'n' Roll, 1997, Burning Love, 1999, (under pseudonym of Anthony Wile) Search for a Song, 1997. Mem. com. Copenhagen '96, Cultural Capital of Europe, 1993-94. Mem. Dansk Journalistsforsbund, Foreign Press Assn. (bd. dirs. 1990-91, co-chmn. 1992-93, chmn. 1993-94). Fax: 45 3391 1613. Address: Hardangerade 4 1 th, 2100 Copenhagen 0, Denmark

FERRI, ENRICO, member European Parliament; b. La Spezia, Italy, Feb. 17, 1941. Mem. European Parliament, Brussels, 1999—; vice chmn. com. on citizens' freedoms and rights, justice and home affairs, substitute mem. com. on legal affairs and internal market, substitute mem. com. on regional policy, transport and tourism, mem. dels. to parliamentary cooperation coms. and dels. for rels. with Kazakhstan, Kyrgyzstan, Uzbekistan, Tajikistan, Turkmenistan, and Mongolia. Mem. Group of European People's Party (Christian Dems.) and European Dems. Mem. Forza Italia Party. Office: Piazza Repubblica 1, I-54027 Pontremoli (MS) Italy*

FERRIBY, PETER GAVIN, librarian; b. Saginaw, Mich., July 11, 1953; s. Donald Harold and Sally Ann Ferriby; m. Rochelle Ann Stackhouse, May 30, 1981; children: Luke Kim, Leah Hwang, Benjamin Bae. BA magna cum laude, Hope Coll., 1976; MDiv, Princeton Theol. Sem., 1980; MS, Columbia U., 1987; PhD, Princeton Theol. Sem., 2000. Campus pastor Southampton (N.Y.) Coll., 1980-81; co-pastor First Congl. Ch., United Ch. of Christ, Reed City, Mich., 1982-85; cataloger Drew U. Libr., Madison, N.J., 1986-93; cataloging assoc. Firestone Libr. Princeton (N.J.) U., 1993-94; editor Consortium Rhode Island Acad. and Rsch. Librs. Union List of Serials Brown U., Providence, 1996-98; head tech. svcs. The Burke Libr. Union Theol. Sem., N.Y.C., 1998—; catalog cons. Providence Coll., 1997-98. Trustee Reed City Pub. Libr., 1983-85, Pelham (N.Y.) Pub. Libr., 1987-90. Mem. ALA, Am. Soc. Info. Sci., Libr. and Info. Tech. Assn., Assn. for Libr. Collections and Tech. Svcs., Am. Guild Organists, Phi Beta Kappa, Beta Phi Mu. Episcopalian. Avocations: rowing, bicycling, swimming. E-mail: pferriby@panix.com and pferriby@uts.columbia.edu. Fax: 212-280-1456. Office: Burke Libr Union Theol Sem 3041 Broadway at 121st St New York NY 10027

FERRIER, JOSEPH JOHN, atmospheric physicist; b. Weehawken, N.J., Jan. 28, 1959; s. Henry Pierre and Josephine (Logalbo) F. BS, Columbia U., 1980; MS, NYU, 1983. Sci. programmer Sigma Data Svcs. Corp., N.Y.C., 1980-81; programmer/analyst M/A-Com Info. Systems, Inc., N.Y.C., 1981-86; atmospheric physicist, planetary group mgr. Centel Fed. Svcs. Corp., N.Y.C., 1986-89, Hughes Aircraft Co., N.Y.C., 1989-94; atmospheric physicist, planetary group mgr., interdisciplinary group mgr. S.S.A.I., N.Y.C., 1994-2000; atmospheric physicist, sr. group mgr. S.G.T. Inc., N.Y.C., 2000—. Mem. AAAS. Office: NASA/GISS 2880 Broadway New York NY 10025-7848

FERRIGNO, GIANCARLO, bioengineering educator, researcher; b. Pozzuoli, Italy, Mar. 3, 1958; s. Domenico and Luisa (Conte) F.; m. Sabrina Labignan, June 8, 1985. Laurea Diploma in Electronic Engring., Poly. U., Milan, Italy, 1983, PhD in Boengring., 1990. Rsch. fellow Bioengring. Ctr., Pro Jeventute Found., Milan, 1983-84, sr. rschr., 1984-90; rschr. bioengring.

dept. Poly. U., Milan, 1990-98, assoc. prof., 1998—, leader artificial neural networks in integrated ergonomics, 1997-99; advisor Interuniv. Ctr. for Rsch. and Study in Movement Physiology, Parma, Italy, 1990—. Author articles; patentee in field. Recipient Carlo Luigi Rossi prize Elsag, 1984; Italian Space Agy. grantee, 1999, others. Avocations: long distance running, skiing, trekking, swimming. E-mail: ferrigno@biomed.polimi.it. Office: Poly U, Piazza L da Vinci 32, Milan Italy

FERRIN, ALLAN HOGATE, architect; b. N.Y.C., Oct. 24, 1951; s. Allan Wheeler and Barbara (Hogate) F.; m. Barbara Lorayne Weaver, May 1, 1976; children: Leigh, Ellen. Student, Princeton U., 1969-72; BA in Chinese, U. Wis., 1973; MArch, U. N.Mex., 1975. Registered architect, Wash., Ala., Oreg. Draftsman Amrep. Corp., Albuquerque, 1975-76, Mitchell Assocs., Albuquerque, 1976-77; architect Jorge del la Torre, Albuquerque, 1977-78, John Graham Co., Seattle, 1978-79; project dir. Charles Kober Assocs., Seattle, 1979-85; ptnr. Carlson/Ferrin Assocs., Seattle, 1985-93; pres. Hogate Properties, Inc., 1994—. Bd. dirs. Gainsborough Condominium Assn., Seattle, 1986-91; trustee Bainbridge (Wash.) Performing Arts Coun., The Arboretum Found., 1996-98; planning commnr. Bainbridge Island, 1995-2000; trustee The Bush Sch., 1999—. Mem. Urban Land Inst., Internat. Coun. Shopping Ctrs. Office: Hogate Properties Inc 1017 Minor Ave Apt 1001 Seattle WA 98104-1303

FERRIS, PATRICK JAMES, biologist; b. Omagh, Northern Ireland, Oct. 8, 1972; s. James Patrick and Mary Josephine (O'Kane) F. BSc, U. Ulster, 1995; MSc, U. Strathclyde, 1996. Rschr. Trinity Biotech, Dublin, 1993-94; from rsch. scientist to sr. scientist FAS Med., London, 1996—. Mem. Inst. Biology. Roman Catholic. Home: 42 Rogers Rd, Tooting London SW17 0EA, England

FERRIS, ROGER PATRICK, architect; b. Buffalo, Jan. 3, 1952; s. Herbert Parkhill and Dolores (Murphy) F.; m. Yvonne DeHaas, May 20, 1995. BA, La Salle Coll., 1974; postgrad., Columbia U., 1977-78; M in Design, Harvard U., 1982. Registered arch., Conn., N.Y., Mass., Vt., Maine, N.H., Ill., Tex., N.Mex., Washington, Va., N.C., Pa., R.I., N.J., Fla., S.C., N.C.; cert. Nat. Coun. archtl. Registration Bds. Arch. Victor Christ-Janer & Assocs., new Canaan, Conn., 1974-78; prin. Landworks Assocs., Southport, Conn., 1978-80, Ferris Franzen Assoc., Southport, 1980-82, Ferris Architects, Westport, Conn., 1982-98, Roger Ferris & Ptnrs., Westport, Conn., 1998—. Co-editor: Architectural Practices in the Nineties, 1996. Recipient Progressive Architecture Citation award, 1991, Outstanding Design award James Beard Found., 1997; Loeb fellow in advanced environ. design Grad. Sch. Design Harvard U., 1991, 92. Mem. Am. Planning Assn., Royal Inst. Brit. Architects, AIA (cert., New England Regional Award of Excellence in Architecture, 1985, 94, 96, 97, 99, Builders Nat. Design and Planning award 1988, 90-92, 94, 98, Design Award Conn. chpt. 1985-86, 89, 93-94, 96-98, New Eng. Regional award for excellence in arch.), Nat. Trust for Hist. Preservation, Conn. Trust for Hist. Preservation (Conn. Preservation Design award 1994). Office: Roger Ferris & Ptnrs 90 Post Rd E Westport CT 06880-3409

FERRO, ELIZABETH KRAMS, lawyer; b. Cheverly, Md., Oct. 14, 1948; d. Harry Francis and Jeanne Elizabeth (Edwards) Krams; children: Stephen Christopher, Elizabeth Juliet, Alexander Eli; m. Jose M. Ferro, Oct. 7, 1994. BS magna cum laude, U. Md., 1977; JD, George Washington U., 1982. Bar: D.C. 1983. Adminstr. Raleigh Stores Corp., Washington, 1973-83; atty. Lansfam Mgmt. Corp., Balt., 1983-2000, corp. sec., 1986-2000. V.p., dir. Sidney Lansburgh III Found., 1989—; bd. dirs. Debel Foods Corp., Elizabeth, N.J., 1986. Mem. ABA, D.C. Bar Assn., Alpha Sigma Lambda, Phi Kappa Phi. Roman Catholic. Home: 10210 Riggs Rd Hyattsville MD 20783-1213 Office: Lansfam Mgmt Corp 300 E Lombard St Ste 1900 Baltimore MD 21202-6739

FERRO, MARC ROGER, historian; b. Paris, Dec. 24, 1924; s. Jacques and Nelly (Firman) F.; m. Vonnie Blondel, Feb. 7, 1948. Student, U. Grenoble, France, 1942-44, U. Sorbonne, 1942-44; D honoris causa, U. Moscow. Prof. Lyceé d'Oran, Algérie, 1948-56; attaché de recherches CNRS, Paris, 1960-64; dir. d'etudes EHESS, Paris, 1964—; co-dir. Les Annales, Paris, 1970—; maitre de conferences Ecole Polytechnique, Paris, 1970-92; pres. Assn. pour la Recherche a 'l'EHESS, Paris, 1992—. Author: Cinema and History, 1976, 93, Great War, 1914-1918, 1995, Colonization: A Global History, 1997, Les Sociétès Malades du Progres, 1998. Active Mil., 1944. Named Officer de l'Ordre, Nat. du Merite, 1995. Avocation: cooking. Office: EHESS, 54 blvd Raspail, 75006 Paris France

FERRY, JOAN EVANS, school counselor; b. Summit, N.J., Aug. 20, 1941; d. John Stiger and Margaret Darling (Evans) F. BS, U. Pa., 1964; EdM, Temple U., 1967; postgrad., Villanova U., 1981. Cert. elem. sch. tchr., elem. sch. counselor. Indsl. photographer Bucksco Mfg. Co., Inc., Quakertown, Pa., 1958-59; math. and German tutor St. Lawrence U., Canton, N.Y., 1959-61; research asst. U. Pa., Phila., 1963; tchr. elem. sch. Pennridge Schs., Perkasie, Pa., 1964-74, 75-77, elem. sch. counselor, 1981—; pvt. practice counselor, real estate partnership Perkasie, 1981—; chair child study team Perkasie Elem. Sch., 1988-94; tutor math., German, St. Lawrence U., Canton, N.Y., 1959-61; supervisory tchr. East Stroudsburg U., Pennridge Schs., 1971-74; research asst. U. Pa., Phila., 1963; mem. acad. coms. for Pennridge Schs.; adj. faculty Bucks County Community Coll., 1983—; instr. Am. Inst. Banking, 1982—; notary pub., 1986—; mcpl. auditor, sec. bd. auditors, 1984-90, mcpl. auditor 1990—, chmn. bd. auditors 1990—; cons. in field. Author (with others) Life-Time Sports for the College Student: A Behavioral Objective Approach, 1971, 3d rev. edit. 1978, Elementary Social Studies as a Learning System, 1976. Vol. elem. sch. counselor Perkasie, 1979-80; mem. Hilltown Civic Assn., 1965-70, 92—; exec. com. chairperson Hilltown PTO, 1965-73; soloist Good Shepherd Episcopal Ch. Choir, Hilltown, 1964-77; steering com. Perkasie Sch., 1989-95; poll watcher, 1993; med. vol. Olympics, Atlanta, 1996; vol. Dublin Ambulance Squad, 1996—, House Rabbit Soc., Chadds Ford, Pa., 1998—, Special Olympics World Games, Summer, North Carolina, 1999, Silverdale Quick Response Med. Svc., 1999; mem. Dublin Vol. Fire and Ambulance Co., Silverdale Fire Co., Silverdale, Pa.; mem. prin.'s round table Perkasie (Pa.) Sch., 1997; vol. House Rabbit Soc. Southeastern Pa./Del. Foster Home and Sanctuary, Chadds Ford, Pa., 1998—; vol. marshal First Union USPro Championship Cycling Race, Phila., 1999, 2000; vol. spl. driver Bush Family and Friends at Rep. Nat. Conv., Phila., 2000. NSF grantee, Washington, 1972-73, Philanthropic Edn. Orgn. grantee, Doylestown, Pa., 1982; recipient Judith Netzky Meml. Fellowship award B'nai B'rith, Phila., 1979; Durning scholar Delta Delta Delta, Arlington, Tex., 1981, Am. Mgmt. Assns. scholar, N.Y.C., 1983, Statesman's award World Inst. Achievement, 1989, Achievement award Women's Inner Circle, 1990, Golden Acad. award for lifetime achievement, 1991; named to Internat. Tennis Hall of Fame, 2000 Notable Am. Women Hall of Fame, 1989, Cmty. Leaders of Am. Hall of Fame, 1990, Internat. Book of Honor Hall Of Fame, 1990, Internat. Bus. & Profl. Women's Hall of Fame, 1994, Lifetime Achievement Acad. Humane Soc. of U.S., Internat. Honor Soc. In Edn., Certificate of appreciation in recognition and acknowledgement for outstanding service and dedication as a member of the 1996 Atlanta Olympics Med. Team, 1997, Certs. of Appreciation Spring Mountain Ski Patrol, 1997, Honorary Educator certificate, St. Joseph's Indian Sch., 1996, ARC, 1986, Cert. Achievement in Recognition of Contbn. as Med. Svcs. Vol. at 1996 Centennial Olympic Games, 1996, Honor Award for Svc. to Edn. and Tchg. Profession, 1996, 99, award for Outstanding Svc. to Edn. Pennridge Schs., 1999, Certificate of appreciation for dedication to the success of the 1999 Special Olympics World Summer Games, 1999. Fellow Internat. Biog. Assn.; mem. AAUW, NEA, NAFE, Humane Soc. U.S., World Inst. Achievement, Pa. State Edn. Assn. (polit. action com. for edn., chair Pennridge Schs. 1986—, del. leadership conf. 1987, 89, Honor award for svc. to edn. and tchg. profession, 1996, 99), Pennridge Edn. Assn. (faculty rep. 1986-88, exec. coun. 1986—, negotiations resource com. 1987-89, 1990-93, steering com. Perkasie Sch. 1989-95, chairperson Child Study Team, 1988-94, Instructional Support Team, 1992—, selection com. for asst. supt. Pennridge Schs. 1993, selection com. for prin. Perkasie Sch. 1994, prin. round table 1997—), Am. Inst. Banking (chairperson 1987), U.S. Tennis Assn. (hon. life), Pa. and Mid. States Tennis Assn. (hon. life), U.S. Profl. Tennis Registry, Mid. States Profl. Tennis Registry, Women's Internat. Tennis Assn., Nat. Ski Patrol (Svc. Recognition award 1994), Spring Mountain Ski Patrol (Outstanding Aux. 1993, MOM Dedication award 1995, Outstanding Svc. and Dedication award 1996, 98, certificate of appreciation, 1997, svc. award, Nat. Ski Patrol, 1999), Pa. Elected Women's Assn., Bucks County Assn. Twp. Ofcls., Bucks County Sch. Counselors Assn., Pa. Sch. Counselors Assn., Pa. Assn. Notaries, Am. Soc. Notaries, Internat. Fedn. Univ. Women, Internat. Platform Assn., World Inst. Achievement, Am. Biog. Inst. Rsch. Assn. (rsch. bd. advisors, bd. govs. 1989—), World Inst. of Achievement, Lifetime Achievement Acad., Rails-to-Trails Conservancy, World Wildlife Fund, Bucks County Sch. Counselors Assn., Highpoint Athletic Club, Pennridge Cmty. Rep. Club. (recording sec. 1986-91, publicity chmn. 1991-92, Pen care chmn. 1992—), Assn. Tennis Profls. Tour Tennis Ptnrs., Sierra Club, The Nature Conservancy, Nat. Wildlife Fedn., John Wayne Found., Mediterranean Club, Nockamixon Boat Club, Peace Valley Yacht Club, Kappa Delta Pi. Episcopalian. Avocations: archery, flying, music, parasailing, photography. Home: 834 Rickert Rd Perkasie PA 18944-2661 Office: Pennridge Schs 601 N 7th St Perkasie PA 18944-1507

FERSON, LU ANN, medical and surgical nurse; b. Girard, Kans., June 12, 1935; d. Sammy M. and Lilly H. (Coury) F. Diploma, St. John's Sch. Nursing, Joplin, Mo., 1961; BSN, Mo. So. State Coll., 1990; postgrad., U. Mo., Kansas City, 1998—. Staff nurse operating room St. John's Hosp., Joplin, Mo., 1961-62; pvt. duty nurse N.Y. State Registry, L.I., 1964-68; psychiat. therapist Ansonia, Conn., 1969-72; staff nurse surg. dept. Waterbury (Conn.) Hosp., 1972-76; staff nurse urology dept. St. John's Med. Ctr., Joplin, 1976-79; IV nurse Danbury (Conn.) Hosp., 1980-85, McCune Brooks Hosp., 1986-88, HMSS, Inc., Lenexa, Kans., 1989-90; clin. coord. IV therapy home care dept. Mt. Carmel Hosp., Pitts., Kans., 1990-95; IV specialist, nurse mgr. Joplin (Mo.) Home Therapeutics, 1995-96; IV nurse Homebound Med., Joplin, 1996-99, Regal Home Care, Neosho, Mo., 1999—; clin. instr. for practical nursing McCune Brooks Hosp., Mt. Carmel Hosp.; lectr. in field. With USN, 1962-64. Mem. ANA, Intravenous Nurses Soc., Nursing Honor Soc. of Mo. So. State Coll. Home: 2555 E 11th St Joplin MO 64801-5378

FERTIG-DYKES, SUSAN BEATRICE, communications executive, human resources professional, community and civil society facilitator; b. Panay, The Philippines, Jan. 9, 1944; d. Claude Edward and B. Laverne (Shockley) Fertig; m. George Middleton Dykes III, Sept. 18, 1965; children: George M. Dykes IV, Dirk Fertig Dykson. BA in Comm., U. Mo., 1982. Cert. trainer in Technologies of Participation. Freelance writer, dir. producer Kansas City, Mo., 1981-83; dir. pub. svc. Sta. KSHB-TV, Kansas City, Mo., 1982-83; dir. broadcast svc. VA, Washington, 1983-86; pres., CEO Victoria Prodns., Ltd., Alexandria, Va., 1986-89; dir. media info. Bicentennial Presdl. Inaugural com., Washington, 1988-89; resume review Office Presdl. Personnel The White House, Washington, 1989; dir. policy, spl. projects Office Human Resources & Adminstrn. Dept. Vets. Affairs, Washington, 1989; dir. pub., visual comm. USDA, Washington, 1989-93; pres., CEO Fertig Comms., Alexandria, Croatia, 1993-96; CEO, bd. dirs. Fertig & Assocs. Internat., Zagreb, Croatia, 1993-96; dir. Inst. Cultural Affairs, Zagreb, Croatia, 1993-96, Inst. Cultural Affairs: Bosnia & Herzegovina, Sarajevo, 1996-97; internat. bd. dirs. ICA Internat., Brussels, 1994-98; mgr., pub. rels., human resource devel., civil soc. initiatives World Vision Internat., Bosnia and Herzegovina, 1997-99; internat. recruiter World Vision Internat., Washington, 1999—; chmn. Philippine Festival Commn., Washington, 1992, 1st v.p. 1994, pres.-elect, 1995; pres.-elect, chmn. Internat. Gold Screen Film/Video Competition, Nat. Assn. Govt. Communicators, 1994; talent, script cons., writer/prodr. Hrvatska Radio-Televizija, 1994-96; script cons. Jadran Film, Zagreb, 1994-96; dep. head ICA observer delegation to UN Internat. Conf. on Women, Beijing, 1995; participant numerous confs.; presenter in field. Ofcl. U.S. observer XVI Internat. Film Competition, Berlin, 1990; judge XVII Internat. Film Competition, Berlin, 1992, Internat. Contest Agrarian Cinema & Video, Zaragosa, 1992; judge Golden Eagle awards Coun. Internat. Non-Theatrical Events (CINE), 1992—, adv. coun., 1993—; judge Festival Internat. du Court Metrages de Mons, Belgium, 1994. Active Christ Ch., Alexandria, Va., 1983—; chmn. coord. George Bush for Pres., Alexandria, 1987-88; surrogate speaker women's groups Bush/Quayle and Victory 88, Washington; campaign tours N.H. primaries, 1988; mem. Pres.'s Club Rep. Nat. Com., Washington, 1984; bd. dirs. Found. for Aid to the Philippines, 1991-92; precinct chair George W. Bush for Pres., Alexandria, 2000; del. 8th dist. and state Rep. Convs., 2000. Mem. Assn. Philippine Am. Women (pres. 1991-93), Women in Film & Video, Alexandria Rep. City Com., Filipino-Am. Rep. Coun., Philippine Heritage Fedn., Rep. Nat. Com. (life). Episcopalian. E-mail: sfd@gmdtech.com Fax: 202-547-0973; 703-751-7626. Home: 205 S Yoakum Pky Apt 1021 Alexandria VA 22304-3826 Office: World Vision US 220 I St NE Washington DC 20002-4362

FERTNER, ANTONI, electrical engineer; b. Krakow, Poland, Oct. 8, 1950; s. Antoni and Janina (Zaleska) F.; m. Jolanta Sekowska, 1993. MSc, U. Mining and Metallurgy, Krakow, 1973; PhD, Warsaw Polytech. Inst., 1978. Rsch. engr. Inst. Nuclear Physics and Techniques, Krakow, 1973-74, Inst. Radioelectronics and Warsaw Polytech., Warsaw, 1974-78; asst. prof. Polish Acad. Sci., Krakow, 1978-79; teaching asst. Royal Inst. Tech., Stockholm, Sweden, 1981-82; scientist Swedish Inst. Microelectronics, Stockholm, 1982-90, Catella Generics AB, Stockholm, 1990-91, Ericsson Telecom AB, Stockholm, 1991—; expert algorithm devel., numerical analysis and optimization. Office: Ericsson Telecom AB, S-12625 Stockholm Sweden

FERVEUR, JEAN-FRANÇOIS, behavioral geneticist, researcher; b. Laxou, Lorraine, France, Oct. 5, 1956; s. Paul and Suzanne (Mourot) F.; m. Robyn Tracey Leonard, Aug. 6, 1996; children: Celia, Guilhem, Thibault. PhD in Biology, U. Paris VII, 1990; habilitation, U. Paris XI, Orsay, 1997. Tchr. biology French Cooperation Ministry, Bangui, 1979-81; tchr. biology Ministry Fgn. Affairs, Algeria, 1982-83, Singapore, 1983-85; rschr. biology CNRS, Gif-sur-Yvette, France, 1985-90; rsch. dir. Nat. Ctr. Sci. Rsch., Orsay, 1993-98, Dijon, France, 1998—; postdoctoral fellow Roche, Nutley, N.J., 1991-93. Recipient award Human Frontier Sci. Program, Strasbourg, France, 1994-97. Mem. Soc. Neuroethology, Soc. Neuroscis.

FESENKO, SERGUEI VIKTROVICH, radioecologist; b. Simpheropol, Grimia, Ukraine, Sept. 17, 1955; s. Victor Pavlovich and Margorita Dmitrievna (Rikova) F.; m. Galina Alexeevna Gribova, Aug. 28, 1981; 2 children. Diploma of Grad., Moscown Engrng. Phys. Inst., 1978, Moscow State U., 1982; PhD in Physics, Moscow State U., 1985; ScD in Biology, Russian Inst. Agrl. Radiology, Obninsk, 1997. Scientist Russian Inst. Agr. Radiology, Obninsk, 1983-85, sr. scientist, 1985-88, prin. scientist, 1988-91, head of lab., 1991-98, dep. dir., 1998—; lectr./prof. Inst. Power Engrng., Obninsk, 1990-92. Author: Agricultural Radioecology, 1991; contbr. articles to profl. jours. 1st lt. Russian Army, 1972-76. Recipient Prize Laureate Acad. Klechkovsky, 1997; Russian Acad. Sci. grantee, 1997. Mem. Internat. Union Radioecology, Nuclear Soc. Russian Fedn. Avocations: tennis, chess, skiing. Home: Marksa 78 app 168, 249020 Obninsk Kaluga, Russia Office: Russian Inst Agrl Radiology Agzoecol, Kievskay, 249020 Obninsk Kaluga, Russia

FESSAS, THEODORE DEMETRIOS, information technology executive; b. Thessaloniki, Greece, Apr. 11, 1951; s. Demetrios Theodore and Helen Aristomenis (Giannoupoulou) F.; m. Efi Sofoklis Koutsoureli; 2 children. Degree in mech. engrng., Nat. Tech. U., Athens, 1974; MSc in Thermodynamics, U. Birmingham, Eng., 1975. Asst. prof. NTU, Athens, 1976-81; engrng. cons. Athens, 1976-81; founder, CEO Infoquest, Athens, 1981—. Mem. Assn. Info. Tech. Enterprises (pres. 1995-99). Office: Infoquest SA, 25 A Pantou St, 17671 Athens Greece

FETISOVA, ZOYA GRIGORIEVNA, physicist; b. Moscow, Sept. 26, 1941; d. Grigory Ivanovich Eremin and Evdokiya Kapitonovna Astakhova; m. Igor Nikolaevich F., Dec. 9, 1931; 1 child, Sergei Igorevich. MS, Moscow State U., 1966, PhD, 1974, DS, 1984. Rschr. Russian Acad. Scis./Russian Inst. Molecular Biology, Moscow, 1966-70; sr. rschr. Interfaculty Lab. Moscow State U., 1970-77; prin. rschr./A.N. Belozersky Inst. Physico-Chem. Biology Moscow State U., Moscow, 1977-93; head of lab. Moscow State U., 1993—; mem. A.N. Belozersky Inst. Directorate, Moscow, 1979—; councillor Scientific Coun. of A.N. Belozersky Inst., Moscow, 1978—, United Scientific Coun. of Moscow State U., 1992—. Contbr. articles to profl. jours. Com. Ministry of Higher Edn. of Russia, Moscow, 1979-81. Recipient prize Soviet Union Ministry of Higher Edn., Moscow, 1975; grantee Internat. Sci. Found., 1993, Russian Govt., Russian Found. for Basic Rsch., Moscow, 1994-2001. Avocation: world travel. Fax: 07-095-9393181. Office: MV Lomonosov Moscow State U, AN Belozersky Inst Physico-Chem Biology, 119899 Moscow Russia

FETTER, WILLIAM ALLAN, computer graphics executive; b. Independence, Mo., Mar. 14, 1928; s. William Herbert and Edna Katherine (Werner) F.; m. Darlene Glea Wyss, Aug. 20, 1950 (div. 1962); 1 child, William Arnold (dec.); m. Barbara Ann Shaffer, Dec. 21, 1963; children: Brant Shaffer, Elena Katherine (twins). Student, Kansas City Jr. Coll., 1945-46, Kansas City U., 1948-49; BFA, U. Ill., 1952. Supr. computer graphics The Boeing Co., Wichita, Kans. and Seattle, 1959-69; v.p. Graphcomp. Scis., Newport, Calif., 1969-70; chmn. design dept., lectr. So. Ill. U., Carbondale, 1970-77; pres. So. Ill. Rsch. and Corp. Office, Carbondale, Ill., 1977—; also bd. dirs. So. Ill. Rsch. and Corp. Office (SIROCO), Bellevue, Redmond, Wash.; owner ORIGIN, Bellevue, Redmond, 1982—; presenter 3D conf. U. Tokyo, 1992; spkr. in field. Author: Human figures for Designers by Computer, 1983, Computer Graphics in Communication, 1964; author (TV program) Computer Graphics, The Accurate Eye, 1975; exhibited in show Mus. Modern Art, N.Y.C., 1976; patentee in field. Bd. dirs. Com. on Handicapped, Park Forest, Ill., 1957-58, Master Resources Council Internat., Seattle, 1980—; mem. UNESCO TACT Task Force, Washington, 1975-85. With U.S. Army, 1946-48; 2nd lt. USAFR, 1952-57. Recipient Cert. Merit Internat. Graphic Design, 1967, Letter Commendation USAF, Boeing Airplane Co., 1962, Bronze Medal Nat. and Regional Soc. Art Dirs., 1963-79. Fellow AIAA (assoc.); mem. Internat. Design Conf. (presenter 1976, 78), Soc. Info. Display, Indsl. Designers Soc. Am., N.W. Human Factors Soc., Mus. Modern Art Club, Alfa Romeo Owner's Club.

FETTEROLL, EUGENE CARL, JR., human resources professional; b. Hartford, Conn., Mar. 8, 1935; s. Eugene Carl and Gladys Marion (Crilley) F.; m. Barbara Ann Meeker, June 15, 1957; children: Eugene Carl III, Douglas Alan, Steven Joseph, Gary Michael. BA, U. Conn., 1957; MEd, Suffolk U., 1973. Supt. customer svc., mgr. pers. svcs., dir. tng. Boston Gas Co., 1957-76; dir. Ea. Enterprises, Boston, 1977-81; dir. Associated Industries of Mass., Boston, 1981-87, v.p. human resources, 1987-89; pres. Fetteroll Assocs., South Portland, Maine, 1989—; tng. cons. Associated Industries of Mass., Boston. Author: Growing Teams, 1993; editor: Trainer's Resource, 1989. Vol. United Way, Mass. and R.I., 1965—; vice chmn. bd. trustees Medfield (Mass.) Pub. Libr., 1966-70; chmn. Sch. Land Acquisition Com., Medfield, 1963-65; bd. dirs. Growth Opportunity Alliance Lawrence/Quality Productivity Competitiveness, Salem, N.H. Mem. ASTD (pres. Mass. chpt. 1972-73, Bay Colonies chpt. 1981-82, mem. nat. ethics com. 1986—, Torch award 1979), Mass. Coalition for Adult Edn., Mass. Arms Collectors. Republican. Roman Catholic. Avocations: collecting antique powder flasks, photography, travel. Fax: 207-741-9031. E-mail: genefett@maine.rr.com. Home and Office: Fetteroll Assocs PO Box 2887 S Portland ME 04116-2887

FETTERS, DORIS ANN, retired secondary education educator; b. Bklyn.; d. John Joseph and Loreta Gertrude (Stratford) F. BA, Calif. State Coll., L.A., 1952. Cert. gen. secondary tchr. Tchr. Temple City (Calif.) H.S., 1954-55, L.A. City Schs., 1955-56; vice consul 3d sec. of embassy Dept. of State, Washington, 1957-60; tchr. U. Rafael Landivar, Guatemala, 1960-63, L.A. Unified Schs., 1964-90. Mem. Am. Fedn. Tchrs., United Tchrs. L.A. Democrat. Roman Catholic. Avocations: gardening, arts and crafts, reading.

FETTWEIS, GERHARD PAUL, engineering educator; b. Antwerp, Mar. 16, 1962; s. Alfred Leo and Jane Lois (Piaskowski) F.; m. Priska Maria Beck, June 26, 1986; children: Felisa, Clara, Alice, Charlotte. MS, Aachen (Germany) U. Tech., 1986, PhD, 1990. Rsch. scientist Aachen U. Tech., 1986-90; vis. scientist IBM Rsch., San Jose, Calif., 1990-91; scientist TCSI Corp., Berkeley, Calif., 1991-94; prof., chair Dresden (Germany) U. Technology, 1994—; mem. tech. adv. bd. Inst. for Semiconductors, Frankfurt, Oder, Germany, 1996—. Assoc. editor: IEEE Transactions on Circuits and Systems II, 1992-95; contbr. articles to profl. jours. Recipient Alcatel-Sel award, 1995, Microelectronics award German Microelectronics Soc., 1993. Mem. IEEE (Solid-State Circuits Soc. Bd., Comm. Soc. Bd.), German EE Soc. (system theory com. 1996—). Avocations: family activities, skiing, outdoor activities, music. Office: Dresden U Tech, Mobile Comms Systems, 01062 Dresden Germany

FETTWEIS, GÜNTER BERNHARD LEO, mining engineering educator; b. Düsseldorf, Germany, Nov. 17, 1924; came to Austria, 1959; s. Ewald Ignaz Maria and Anna Maria (Leuschner-Fernandes) F.; m. Alice Yvonne Frieda Maria, Apr. 23, 1949; children: Astrid Maria Barbara, Raimund Ewald Rudolf, Annette Alice, Ursula Melanie. Diploma in engring., Tech. U., Aachen, Germany, 1950, DEng, 1953, DEng (hon.), 1980; D (hon.), Tech. U., Miskolc, Hungary, 1987, U. Petrosani, Romania, 1996, Mining U., Moscow, 1999. Sci. asst. Tech. U., Aachen, 1950-53; jr. mining inspector State of Nordrhein-Westfalia, Dortmund, Germany, 1953-55; mining engr. Mining Co. Neue Hoffnung, Oberhausen, Germany, 1955-57, prodn. mgr., 1957-59; prof. mining engring., head dept. mining and mineral econs. Montan U., Leoben, Austria, 1959-93, prof. emeritus, 1993—; v.p. Internat. Organizing Com. of World Mining Congress, 1974—. Contbr. about 220 articles to profl. jours., also several books. Recipient awards states of Austria, Germany, Poland and Vatican. Mem. Austrian Acad. Scis., Polish Acad. Scis., Hungarian Acad. Scis. (hon.), Academia Scientiarum et Artium Europaea Salzburg, Russian Acad. Natural Scis., Russian Acad. Mining Scis., European Acad. Scis., Arts and Letters, Paris, Mining Assn. Austria (v.p. 1964-95), N.Y. Acad. Scis., Explorers Club (N.Y.), Lions Club. Roman Catholic. Home: Gasteigergasse 5, A-8700 Leoben Austria Office: Montanuniversität, Franz-Josef-Str 18, A-8700 Leoben Austria

FETZER, JAMES HENRY, philosopher, educator; b. Pasadena, Calif., Dec. 6, 1940; s. Henry Jr. and Eleanor Atwood (Waterhouse) F.; m. Janice Elaine Morgan, June 12, 1977. AB in Philosophy magna cum laude, Princeton U., 1962; MA in History and Philosophy of Sci., Ind. U., 1968, PhD in History and Philosophy of Sci., 1970; postgrad., Columbia U., 1968-69. Asst. prof. U. Ky., Lexington, 1970-77; vis. assoc. prof. U. Va., Charlottesville, 1977-78; vis. assoc. prof. U. Cin., 1978-79, vis. NSF rsch. prof., 1979-80; vis. lectr. U. N.C., Chapel Hill, 1980-81; vis. assoc. prof. New Coll. of U. South Fla., Sarasota, 1981-83, MacArthur vis. disting. prof. arts and scis., 1983-84; adj. prof. U. South Fla., Tampa, 1984-85; vis. prof. U. Va., Charlottesville, 1984-85; postdoctoral fellow Wright State U., Dayton, Ohio, 1986-87; prof. philosophy U. Minn., Duluth, 1987-96, dept. chmn., 1988-92, disting. McKnight prof., 1996—; rsch. scholar New Coll. U. South Fla., Sarasota, 1985-86; postdoctoral fellow Wright State U., Dayton, Ohio, 1986-87; Landsdowne lectr. U. Victoria, Can., 1992. Author: Scientific Knowledge, 1981, AI: Its Scope and Limits, 1990, Philosophy and Cognitive Science, 1991, 2d edit., 1996, Philosophy of Science, 1993, Computers and Cognition, 2000; co-author: Glossary of Cognitive Science, 1993, Glossary of Epistemology/Philosophy of Science, 1993; editor: Principles of Philosophical Reasoning, 1984, Sociobiology and Epistemology, 1985, Aspects of AI, 1988, Probability and Causality, 1988, Epistemology and Cognition, 1991, Foundations of Philosophy of Science, 1993, Assassination Science, 1998, The Philosophy of Carl G. Hempel, 2000, Science, Explanation, and Rationality, 2000; co-editor: Philosophy, Language, and AI, 1988, Philosophy, Mind and Cognitive Inquiry, 1990, Definitions and Definability, 1991, Program Verification, 1993, The New Theory of Reference, 1998; co-editor Synthese, 1990-99; founder, book series editor: Studies in Cognitive Systems, 1986—, Explorations in Philosophy, 1994—; founder, editor: Minds and Machines, 1989—. With USMC, 1962-66. Recipient Dickinson prize Princeton U., 1962, Medal of U. Helsinki, Finland, 1990. Mem. AAUP, AAAS, Am. Philos. Assn., Internat. Soc. for Human Ethology, Soc. for Machines and Mentality (founder), Philosophy of Sci. Assn., Assn. Computing Machinery, Human Behavior and Evolution Soc. Office: U Minn Dept Philosophy Duluth MN 55812

FEUCHTENBERGER, PAT WALTMAN, professional artists administrator; b. Jacksonville, Ill., Feb. 7, 1933; d. Floyd Augustus and Hazel Ophelia (Ford) Waltman; m. Trealy Vinton Pennington, Feb. 13, 1953 (div. Jan. 1961); children: Gregory Vinton, Gary Lee, Mark Randall; m. Charles William Feuchtenberger, Jan. 24, 1962. MusB, St. Louis Inst. Music, 1964; MA, Radford U., 1977. Chmn. piano dept. Bluefield (Va.) Coll., 1980-82, Concord Coll., Athens, W.Va., 1982-84; dir. Feuchtenberger Artists Mgmt., Bluefield, 1983—, 1983—; music tchr., pvt. practice as music coach,

Bluefield, 1960—; founder, dir. Fine Arts Preparation Dept., Bluefield Coll., 1980-82; speaker Career Day Radford (Va.) U., 1989; adjudicator Nat. Piano Guild Festivals, 1986—. Activist Freedom in the Arts, Va., Washington, 1989; bd. dirs. Bluefield Found. Mem. Nat. Assn. Mgmt. and Presenters, Nat. Fedn. Music Clubs, Nat. Coll. Musicians, Internat. Soc. Performing Arts, Am. Symphony Orch. League, Am. Organists Guild, Assn. Performing Arts Presenters, Western Alliance Arts Adminstrs., So. Arts Fedn., Mid-Am. Arts Alliance, Va. Music Tchrs. Assn., Phi Kappa Phi. Presbyterian. Home: 804 Fincastle Dr Fincastle Estates Bluefield VA 24605

FEUERHERM, KURT KARL, artist, educator; b. Mar. 22, 1925; s. Erich Max and Erna Martha (Koenig) F.; divorced; children: Karl, Lisa, Eric. BFA, U. Buffalo, 1950; MFA, Cranbrook Acad. Art, Bloomfield Hills, Mich., 1951; fellow, Yale U., 1952. Instr. in painting Rochester (N.Y.) Inst. Technology, 1953-54, Meml. Art Gallery, Rochester, 1955-71; asst. prof. U. Rochester, 1956-71; conservator ICA Lab Oberlin (Ohio) Coll., 1972; assoc. prof. Monroe Conn. Coll., Rochester, 1972-73, Empire State Coll., Rochester, 1973-87; instr. internat. program Polimoda, Firenze, Italy, 1995-97; owner Guttenberg's Book Store, Rochester, 1983-86, Kurt Feuerherm Bookseller, Rochester, 1986-88, Hopper's, Rochester, 1980-83; vis. prof. painting Rochester Inst. Technology, 1976-85, mentor Empire State Coll., 1973-85; adj. faculty Monroe C.C., 1973-75; vis. prof. painting U. Wash., Seattle, 1969, numerous others.; judge for various local art exhibits; demonstrator painting techniques at various confs. One-man show Village Gate Gallery, 2000; group shows include Meml. Art Gallery Lending and Sales Gallery, Rochester, 1960-86, Arena Exhbn., M.A.G., Rochester, 1974-93, Syracuse (N.Y.) State Fair, 1957-62, Everson Mus. of Art, Syracuse, 1957-70, Chautaugua (N.Y.) Exhibit Am. Art, 1969, others; one-man shows include Malton Gallery, Cin., 1978, 81, 82, Oxford Gallery, Rochester, 1974, 76, 78, 80, 83, 87, 90, East-West Gallery, Victor, N.Y., 1997, others: represented by Secrest Gallery, No. Turo, Mass., Turtle Gallery, Deer Isle, Maine, others; several archtl. commns. With U.S. Army, 1943-45, ETO. Recipient scholarships Cranbrook Acad. Art, 1950-51, Norfolk Art Sch., 1950, Yale U., 1951-52, numerous painting prizes including Lillian Fairchild award U. Rochester, 1958, Henri Projansky award Rochester Finger Lakes Exhbn., 1969; represented in corp. collections including Lincoln First Bank, Rochester, Gannett Newspapers, Rochester, The Norry Corp., Rochester, Marine Midland Bank, Rochester, Security Trust Bank, Rochester, Rochester Savs. Bank, Cen. Trust Bank, Rochester, others. Home: PO Box 936 South Wellfleet MA 02663-0936

FEUERLEIN, WILHELM EGIDIUS, psychiatrist; b. Nurnberg, Bavaria, Germany, Oct. 11, 1920; s. Ludwig and Francisca (Albrecht) F.; m. Elvira Eugenie Durr; m. Gertraud Troll; children: Claudia, Albrecht, Prisca. MD, U. Erlangen, Germany, 1948; Priv. Dozent, U. Munich, 1969, Prof. Extraordinaire, 1975. Medical diplomate. Resident in internal medicine Regional Hosp., Coburg, Germany, 1948-49; resident/sr. physician Nurnberg Psychiat. Hosp., 1949-60; pvt. practice Neurology Psychiat., Furth, 1960-64; head psychiat. outpatient dept. Max Planck Inst. Psychiatry, Munich, 1964-85, retired, 1986—; temporary advisor WHO, Geneva, 1975-85; mem. Enquete Com. German Bundestag, 1970-75. Contbr. articles to profl. jours. Recipient award German Coun. on Addiction Problems, 1974. Mem. Bavarian Acad. Occupl. Social Medicine (mem. bd. 1981-85), German Soc. Addiction Rsch. and Therapy (pres. 1978-82), Am. Soc. Addictive Medicine, German Soc. Psychiat. Psychotherapy Neuroscis. Home: Heinrich-Laube-Weg 10, D-81925 Munich Germany Office: Max Planck Inst Psychiatry, Kraepelinstr 2, D-80804 Munich Germany

FEUERSTEIN, R. HORST, bank executive; b. Oberaudenhain, Germany, Feb. 8, 1942; s. Hans Georg and Ursula Ilse (Friedrich) F.; m. Nina Michajliczenko, 1977; children: Tatiana, Stefan, Maike. MA in Econs., U. Kiel, Germany, 1967, PhD in Agrl. Econs., 1970; postdoctoral student, U. Calif., Berkeley, 1971-72. Asst. prof. agrl. econs. U. Kiel, U. Göttingen, Germany, 1967-73; young profl., then sr. economist The World Bank, Washington, 1973-80; sr. economist European Investment Bank, Luxembourg, 1980-85, head of energy divsn., 1985-93, dir., projects dir., 1994—, dir. ops. eval., 2000—. Office: European Investment Bank, 100 Blvd Konrad Adenauer, 2950 Luxembourg Luxembourg

FEUGHELMAN, MAX, biophysicist; b. Czernovitz, Romania, Dec. 7, 1921; arrived in Australia, 1928; s. Avram and Rosa (Feldstein) F.; m. Dorothy Jean Adams, Jan. 11, 1947; children: Diana, David. BS with 1st class honors, U. Sydney, N.S.W., Australia, 1942, ScD, 1976; Diploma of Radio Engring., Sydney Tech. Coll., 1945. Civilian instr. radio physics Royal Australian Air Force, Sydney, 1941-42; prodn. engr. Amalgamated Wireless Valve Co., Sydney, 1942-47; lectr. physics N.S.W. Inst. Tech., Sydney, 1947-51; rsch. scientist Divsn. of Textile Physics, CSIRO, Sydney, 1951-68; prof. textile physics F.A.I.P., Sydney, 1968, U. N.S.W., Sydney, 1968-81; indsl. cons. Sydney, 1981—; cons. on phys. properties of hair Reckitts & Colman, Sydney, 1981—, Zotos Corp., Stamford, Conn., 1981—; chief cons. Fibrous Keratin Cons., Sydney, 1981—; dir. Fibrous Keratin Pty. Ltd.; prof. emeritus U. N.S.W., 1982—. Author: Mechanical Properties and Structure fo Alpha-Keratin Fibres: Wool, Human Hair and Related Fibres, 1997; contbr. over 150 articles to profl. jours., chpts. to books. Fulbright Vis. scholar U. Utah, 1975; S.G. Smith Meml. medal Textile Inst., Manchester, U.K., 1990. Mem. Botany Bay Beef and Burgundy Club (past food master). Achievements include 2 patents; research on relationship between the molecular and near-molecular structure of the alpha-keratin fibres (wool, hair, etc.), and their macro physical properties.

FEUILLET, JACK, educator; b. Chartres, France, Oct. 27, 1942; s. René and Louise (Lebrun) F.; m. July 25, 1973; children: Irène, Isabelle, Thierry. Diplômes de russe et de bulgare, École Nationale des Langues Orientales, Paris, 1967; Licence et Maîtrise d'allemand, Paris, 1968; Agrégation d'allemand, 1970; Docteur en Etudes Slaves, Paris, 1973, Docteur ès lettres, 1982. Asst. et maitre asst. de linguistique allemande Univ., Nantes, France, 1970-78; prof. of bulgare Inst. Nat. Langs. et Civilisations Orientales, Paris, 1978—; dir. Ctr. d'Etudes Balkaniques, Paris, 1980-89. Author: Introduction à l'analyse morphosyntaxique, 1988, Linguistique diachronique de l'allemand, 1989, Linguistique synchronique de l'allemand, 1991, Grammaire Structurale de l'allemand, 1993, Grammaire synchronique du bulgare, 1996, Grammaire historique du bulgare, 1999. Mem. Soc. Linguistique Paris. Home: 19 rue du Calvaire de Grillaud, 44100 Nantes France Office: INALCO, 2 rue de Lille, 75007 Paris France

FEULNER, EDWIN JOHN, JR., research foundation executive; b. Chgo., Aug. 12, 1941; s. Edwin John and Helen J. (Franzen) F.; m. Linda C. Leventhal, Mar. 8, 1969; children: Edwin John III, Emily V. BS, Regis Coll., 1963; MBA, U. Pa., 1964; PhD, U. Edinburgh, 1981; hon. degree, Nichols Coll., 1981, Universidad Francisco Marroquin, Guatemala City, 1982, Hanyang U., Seoul, Korea, 1982, Bellevue Coll., Nebr., 1987, Gonzaga U., 1992, Grove City Coll., 1994, Pepperdine U., 2000. Richard Weaver fellow London Sch. Econs., 1965; pub. affairs fellow Hoover Instn., 1965-67; rsch. analyst Rep. Conf. U.S. Ho. of Reps., 1968-69; confidential asst. to sec. def. Melvin Laird, 1969-70; campaign mgr. Crane for Congress Com., 1972; adminstrv. asst. to U.S. Congressman Philip M. Crane, 1970-74; exec. dir. Rep. Study Com., Ho. of Reps., 1974-77; pres. Heritage Found., Washington, 1977—; chmn. Inst. European Def. and Strategic Studies, 1977-96; counselor to v.p. candidate Jack Kemp, 1996; U.S. adv. com. pub. diplomacy USIA, 1982-94, chmn., 1982-91; nat. adv. bd. Ctr. for Edn. and Rsch. in Free Enterprise, Tex. A&M U.; Disting. fellow mobilization concepts Devel. Ctr. Nat. Def. U., 1983-89; mem. Pres.'s Commn. on White House Fellows, 1981-83, Exec. Com. of the Presdl. Transition, 1980-81, U.S. Delegation to IMF/World Bank, 1974-76, Carlucci Commn. on Fgn. Assistance, 1983, U.S. Commn. Improving Effectiveness of UN, 1989-93, Internat. Fin. Inst. Adv. Commn., 1999-2000; pub. del. UN 2d Spl. Session on Disarmament, 1982; White House cons. on domestic policy, 1987; mem. adv. com. Am. Polit. Channel, 1994-96; vice-chmn. Nat. Commn. on Econ. Growth and Tax Reform, 1995-96, Congrl. Policy Adv. Bd., 1997—, Internatl. Fin. Insts. Advisory Commn., 1999-2000. Author: Congress and the New International Economic Order, 1976, Looking Back, 1981, Conservatives Stalk the House, 1983, The March of Freedom, 1998, Intellectual Pilgrims, 1999, Leadership for America, 2000; contbr. articles to profl. jours., newspapers, chpts. to books. Trustee Lehrman Inst., 1981-90, Sarah Scaife Found., 1988—, St. James Sch., 1990-98, Sequoia Nat. Bank, 1987-99, Regis U., 1991—, Internat. Rep. Inst., 1995—, Acton Inst., 1995—; vice-chmn. bd. Aequus Inst., 1989—, Intercollegiate Studies Inst., 1979—, chmn., 1989-93; vice-chmn. bd. dirs. Roe Found., 1983—; mem. exec. com. Coun. Nat. Policy; trustee Am. Coun. Germany, N.Y., 1982-92; Found. Francisco Marroquin; trustee Inst. Rsch. Econs. Taxation, 1980-87; chmn. Citizens for Am. Edn. Found., 1985-89; vice chmn., trustee Manhattan Inst. Policy Studies, 1977-86; mem. coun. acad. advisors Bryce Harlow Found.; bd. visitors George Mason U., 1996—, trustee, Natl. Chamber Founds., 1998—. Recipient Washington award Freedom Found., 1979, 80, Disting. Alumni award Regis U., 1985, Superior Pub. Svc. award Dept. of Navy, 1987, Presdl. Citizens medal, 1989, Dir.'s Svc. award USIA, 1992, Thomas Jefferson Servant Leadership award Coun. Nat. Policy, 1996, Free Enterprise Man of Yr., Tex. A&M U., 1985, Man of Yr., Wharton Sch., 1993; decorated Order of Brilliant Star with Grand Cordon, Rep. of China. Mem. Am. Econs. Assn., Internat. Inst. Strategic Studies, U.S. Strategic Inst., Inst. d'Etudes Politques, Phila. Soc. (treas. 1964-79, pres. 1982-83), Mont Pelerin Soc. (treas. 1979-96, pres. 1996-98), Internat. Com. of the G.K. Chesterton Soc. (chmn. 1989-92), Belle Haven Country Club, Union League (N.Y.C.), Met. Club, Reform Club (London), Bohemian Club (San Francisco), Knights of Malta, Knights of the Holy Sepulchre, Alpha Kappa Psi. Republican. Roman Catholic. Office: The Heritage Found 214 Massachusetts Ave NE Washington DC 20002-4958

FEURING, MARTIN, physician, researcher; b. Giessen, Germany, Sept. 25; s. Rudolf and Johanna (Schar) F. Grad., Landgraf-Ludwig-Schule, Giessen, 1983; MD, 1995. Civil servant Giessen, 1984; physician Med. Policlinic U. Marburg, 1994-96, Ctr. Transfusion Medicine, U. Mainz, Germany, 1996, Inst. Clin. Pharmacology Klinikum, Mannheim U. Heidelberg, Germany, 1996—. Contbr. articles to profl. jours. Home: Zur Napoleons Nase 12, 35435 Wettenberg Germany Office: Inst Clin Pharmacology, Theodor-Kutzer-Ufer, 68167 Mannheim Germany

FEYTEN, CARINE MARIE, foreign language educator, translator, researcher; b. Mechelen, Belgium, Mar. 14, 1958; came to U.S., 1983; d. Edgard and Viviane (Limbourg) F. B.A. in Germanic Philology, Cath. U. Louvain, 1980, M.A. in Germanic Philology, 1981; cert. in edn. Univ. Ibero-Americana (Mex.), 1981; PhD in Interdisciplinary Edn., U. South Fla., 1983. Translator Industry and Minister of European Affairs, Brussels, 1976—; tchr.'s asst. high sch., Tournai, Belgium, 1979; lectr., asst. Facultés Universitaires Saint Louis, Brussels, 1978-80; lang. teaching cons., educator Inlingua Internat. Sch. Langs., Brussels, 1981-83; grad. research asst. U. South Fla., Tampa, 1983-86, adj. prof., 1986—, fgn. lang. supervising prof., 1986-88, asst. prof. fgn. lang. edn., 1987-94, assoc. prof., dir. fgn. lang. edn., 1994-00, chair dept. secondary edn., 1999—; vis. prof. 1987-88, Katholieke U. Leuven, Belguim, 1996-97; French tutor, 1984—. Recipient Study Scholarship award for Venezuela, 1980; Research Scholarship award for Spain, 1980; Outstanding Student award Cath. U. of Louvain, 1981. Fellow Linguistic Soc. Am. (fellow, 1985), Am. Council Teaching Fgn. Langs., Fla. Fgn. Lang. Assn. (Wershow award 1996), Nat. Assn. Female Execs., Tesol, Gulf-Tesol, Phi Kappa Phi. Roman Catholic. Avocations: classical guitar; gymnastics; travel; languages; gourmet cooking. Office: U South Fla Edu 162 4202 E Fowler Ave Tampa FL 33620-8000

FEZIA, CORRADO, chemist; b. Alessandria, Italy, Feb. 25, 1954; s. Giuseppe and Domenica Giuliana (Biscussi) F.; m. Daniela Maria Sissizio, July 10, 1983; 1 child, Paola Giulia. Degree in chemistry, U. Genoa, Italy, 1979. Chemistry tchr. II Sch., Alessandria, 1980-81; analyst I.V.I., Quattordio, Italy, 1981-83, PPG Industries, Quattordio, 1983—. Avocation: cycling. Home: via Ernesto Cabruna 3/C, 15100 Alessandria Italy Office: PPG Industries Italia, Via Serra 1, 15028 Quattordio Italy

FIALA, ALOIS, engineering educator; b. Telnice, Moravia, Czech Republic, June 21, 1946; s. Jan and Marie (Praxová) F.; m. Věra Neugebauerová, Jan. 15, 1972; children: Veronika, Magdalena. MS, Tech. U., Brno, Czech Republic, 1969, PhD, 1973. Asst. lectr. Tech. U., Brno, 1973-80, assoc. prof., 1980—, head dept., 1980—; auditor Czech Accreditation Inst., Prague, 1991—; cons. in field, 1990—. Author: Quality Management Through ISO 9000, 1997; contbr. articles to profl. jours. Mem. Czech Soc. Quality, Assn. Cons. to Bus. Roman Catholic. Avocation: gardening. Office: Vysokè Ucení Tech, Technická 2, 616 69 Brno Moravia Czech Republic

FIALA, PAVEL, electrotechnics educator; b. Kraslice, Czech Republic, Mar. 24, 1964; s. Jana Najsrová, Dec. 9, 1966. Dipl. engr., Tech. U. Fei Brno, Czech Republic, 1988; cert. in engring. high voltage apparatus, Tech. U., Brno, PhD, 1999. Expert asst. Rsch. Inst., Brno, 1988-90, Tech. U. Fei Brno, 1990—; rschr., cons. Lab. Optimalization Electro-Mech. Sys., Brno, 1993—; founder PMO-FEM (Project Model by Optimisation Finite Element Method, 2000. Avocations: electrotechnics, photography, music, sports, travel.E-mail: fialap@utee.fee.uutbr.cz. Office: Tech Univ Fei Brno, UTEE Technická 118, 61600 Brno Czech Republic

FIALAIRE, JACQUES, educator, researcher; b. Villefranche, Franc, Aug. 8, 1956; s. Jean and Aimée (Vert) F.; m. Ghislaine Figuero, Dec. 19, 1981; 1 child, Michel. D Pub. Law, U. Paris I, 1987; habilitation for rsch. mgt., U. Nantes, France, 1994. Legal worker Specialized Fin. Agy., Paris, 1979-82; legal worker Edn. Dept., Paris, 1982-88, staff asst., 1988-90; tchr., rschr. U. Nantes, 1990—. Author: L'Ecole En Europe, 1996, Le Droit des Services Publics locaux, 1998; author, dir.: Locaux et Temps Scolaires à L'Heure de la Décentralisation, 1997. Fellow French Inst. Adminstrv. Scis. (corr.), European Partnership Civil Svcs. (corr.). Avocations: reading, walking, bicycling. Office: Chemin Censive du Tertre, BP 81307, 44313 Nantes Cedex 3 France

FIBIGER, BO, media researcher; b. Skive, Denmark, Feb. 19, 1945; s. Eigil and Aase (Kofoed) F.; m. Helle Sinding Kjaer; children: Anne Mette, Lisbet. Degree, Aarhus U., 1971. Assoc. prof. Aarhus U., 1971—. Author: Partipolitisk Kommunikation, 1971, TV Og Politik, 1981, 80'Ernes Massemedier, 1987; editor: Fremtidens Elektroniske Massemedier, 1979, Design of Multimedia, 1997, The Semiotics of Multimedia, 1998. Mem. Local Coun., Roende, 1982-89, County Coun., 1994—; com. chmn. environ. and traffic, 1998—. Mem. SMID. Office: Aarhus U, Aabogade 34, 8200 Aarhus Denmark

FICARA, ROBIN, fine art consultant; b. Hartford, Conn., Aug. 6, 1956; d. Joseph P. Ficara and Joan E. O'Brien. BFA, Md. Inst. Art, 1978; MFA, Otis Art Inst., 1980. Libr., archives L.A. Louver, Venice, Calif., 1989-94; assoc. dir. sales George Stern Fine Arts, W. Hollywood, Calif., 1995-97; prin. Robin Ficara Fine Art, L.A., 1997—. Mem. Mus. Latin Am. Art, L.A. County Mus. Art. Mem. Network Exec. Women Hospitality. Fax: (323) 782-9989. Office: PMB # 360 8391 Beverly Blvd Los Angeles CA 90048-2633

FICCAGLIA, LESLIE M., psychologist, portrait artist; b. Huntington, N.Y., Oct. 3, 1943; d. Sewall M. and L. Lillian (Bartok) Pastor; m. Anthony W. Ficcaglia, Nov. 4, 1968; children: Jeremy Clinton, Linnet Kyung. BA in Psychology, NYU, 1965; MA in Psychology, Western Wash. U., Bellingham, 1971; student, Rowan Coll., Glassboro, N.J., 1984. Cert. sch. psychologist. Clin. psychologist Eastern Diagnostic and Evaluation Ctr., Phila., 1968; staff clin. psychologist Vineland (N.J.) State Sch., 1970-74; staff psychologist Cumberland County Hosp., Hopewell Twp., N.J., 1974-81; sch. psychologist Downe Twp. Bd. Edn., Newport, N.J., 1981-2000; grantswriter Downe Twp. Bd. Edn., Newport, 1990-2000; portrait artist Minnamuska Creek Studio, Port Elizabeth, N.J., 1995—. Developer website; author newspaper articles, booklet "What's This ADD?". Mem. Maurice River Twp. Planning Bd., 1979-98, chair, 1990-98; mem. Cumberland County Planning Bd., Bridgeton, N.J., 1982—, vice chair, 1988—; mem. N.J. State Pinelands Commn., New Lisbon, 1996—; trustee Assn. N.J. Environ. Commns., Mendham, 1995-99, adv. bd., 2000—; trustee Citizens United to Protect the Maurice River and Its Tributaries, 1999—; mem. Del. Bayshore adv. bd. Nature Conservancy, 1998—; chmn. Riverfront Renaissance Ctr. Arts, Millville, N.J., bd. dirs., 1999—. Recipient Outstanding Svc. award Cumberland County Bd. Freeholders, 1991. Mem. N.J. Planning Ofcls., Nat. Assn. Sch. Psychologists, Am. Soc. Portrait Artists, Phi Delta Kappa. Avocations: land use planning, environmental issues. Home: Minnamuska Creek Farm and Studio Port Elizabeth NJ 08348-0027

FICHSEL, HELMUT THILO LUDWIG, pediatrician, consultant, researcher; b. Rudolstadt, Thueringen, Germany, Apr. 25, 1930; s. Karl Hermann Otto and Margarete Martha Lilly (Rosenstiel) F.; m. Christa Erna Herta Plieth, Dec. 20, 1956; children: Markus, Gabriele. MD, U. Heidelberg, 1955. Intern U. Kinderklinik, Heidelberg, 1955; intern U. Kinderklinik, Bonn, 1955-56, resident, 1956-68, sr. physician, 1968-80, chief neuropediat., 1980-95; prof. pediat. U. Bonn-Pediat. U. Hosp., 1980, chief of neuropediats., 1980-95. Editor, author: Aktuelle Neuropadiatrie 86, 1987; co-author: Die Epilepsien, 1994. Recipient Alfred Hauptmann prize Stiftung Michael, Int. Liga Ag Epilepsy, 1980, Bundesverdienstkreutz, German Govt., 1997. Mem. Soc. for Neuropediat., Internat. Assn. Child Neurology, Soc. for Child Health, also others. Avocations: history, archeology, modern literature. Home: Langenbergsweg 98, D-53179 Bonn Germany

FICICIOGLU, CEM NESET, gynecologist; b. Ankara, Turkey, Jan. 17, 1961; s. Tarik and Solmaz (Ozaydin) F.; m. Filiz Diniz, Sept. 15, 1988; 1 child, Burak. MD, U. Cerrahpahsa, 1984; PhD, Marmara U., 1995. Physician Health Ministry Health Ctr., Erzurum, Istanbul, Turkey, 1984-86; from asst. ob-gyn. to assoc. prof. and clin. chief Zeynep Kamil Maternity Hosp., Istanbul, 1986—; dir. rep. endocrinology infertilitiy NF-ET Zeyney Kamil Maternity Hosp.; cons. in field. Mem. Electron Microscopy Orgn., Turkish Gyn. Fedn., ESHRE, Turkish Med. Assn. Office: Bagdat Cad No 272/10, 81060 Istanbul Turkey

FICKER, TOMÁŠ, physics educator; b. Svitavy, Czech Republic, Sept. 12, 1953; s. Jan and Františka (Vystavělová) F.; m. Věra Šmídová, Dec. 30, 1982; three children. Physicist, U. J.E. Purkyně, Brno, Czech Republic, 1977; RNDr, Charles U., Prague, 1981; CSc, Czechoslovak Acad. Sci., Prague, 1983. Phys. diplomate. Rschr. Czechoslovak Acad. Sci., Prague, 1977-83; asst. prof. Tech. U., Brno, 1983-92, assoc. prof., 1992—; mem. internat. adv. panel Physics Edn., 1996—. Contbr. articles to profl. jours. Grantee Tempus The European Cmty., 1993, Deutscher Akademischer Austauschdienst-German Acad. Exch. Svc., 1994, Nat. Grant Agy. of the Czech Republic, 1997. Avocations: reading, bicycling. Home: Mutěnická 1, CZ-62800 Brno Czech Republic Office: Physics Dept FAST VUT, Žižkova 17, CZ-60200 Brno Czech Republic

FICKINGER, WAYNE JOSEPH, communications executive; b. Belleville, Ill., June 23, 1926; s. Joseph and Grace (Belton) F.; m. Joan Mary Foley, June 16, 1951; children: Michael, Joan, Jan, Ellen, Steven. BA, U. Ill., 1949; MS, Northwestern U., 1950. Overnight editor United Press, Chgo., 1950-51; spl. project writer Sears-Roebuck & Co., Chgo., 1951-53; account exec. Calkins & Holden Advt. Agy., Chgo., 1953-56; account supr. Foote, Cone & Belding Advt. Agy., Chgo., N.Y.C., 1956-63; sr. v.p. J. Walter Thompson Co., Chgo., 1963-72; exec. v.p., dir. U.S. Western div. J. Walter Thompson Co., 1972-75, pres. N.Am. divsn., 1975-78; pres., chief operating officer J. Walter Thompson Co. Worldwide, 1978-79; pres. JWT Group, Inc., 1979-82, trustee retirement fund, dir., mem. exec. com., 1980-82; mng. dir. Spencer Stuart & Assocs., 1982-83; vice chmn., dir. Bozell, Jacobs, Kenyon & Eckhardt Inc., Chgo., 1984-89; pres. Mid-Am. Com., Chgo., 1989-93; exec. v.p., dir. Monroe Comm. Corp., 1992—; v.p., dir. Adams Comm., 1994—; mem. adv. bd. Phase One Inc.; bd. dirs. Alford Group, Inc. Fundraising cons. Nat. Mental Health Assn., 1970; comm. counselor Cook County (Ill.) Rep. Orgn., 1970; bd. dirs. Off-the-Street Club, Chgo., 1974-77, Mundelein Coll., 1985-91, United Cerebral Palsy, 1986, Chgo. Conv. and Tourists Bur., 1986-90, Columbia Coll., Chgo., 1990-95, Am. Inst. Hadron Therapy; chmn. Chgo. Funding Statue of Liberty, 1986, March of Dimes, 1987, Mayor's Chgo. Tourism Com., 1990-92; mem. steering com. El Valor, 1997-98. With USNR, 1943-46. Recipient Five-Year Meritorious Service award A.R.C., 1963, Service award Mental Health Assn., 1970. Mem. Am. Assn. Advt. Agys., Council on Fgn. Relations (Chgo. com.), Sigma Delta Chi, Alpha Delta Sigma. Clubs: Exmoor Country (Highland Park, Ill.); N.Y. Athletic; Mid-Am. (Chgo.), Internat. (Chgo.). Office: 350 S Beverly Dr Ste 300 Beverly Hills CA 90212-4817

FIDALSKI, JONEZ, agronomist, researcher; b. Chapeco, Brazil, May 23, 1965; s. Armando and Lidia F.; m. Maria Gracas Garcia Iglesias Fidalski, Jan. 14, 1995; 1 child, Ana Carolina Iflesias Fidalski. Student, U. Fed. Santa Catarina, Brazil, 1987. Cert. agronomist engr. Rschr. Inst. Agronomics of Parana, Paranavia, Brazil, 1988—. Contbr. articles to profl. jours. E-mail: fidalski@pr.gov.br. Fax: 00-55-0444231157.

FIDELMAN, URI, educator, philosopher, neuropsychologist; b. Haifa, Israel, May 19, 1936; s. Mordechai and Sophie (Morgenstern) F.; m. Tsipora Yafe (dec.); children: Tsufit, Peli. MSc, Hebrew U., Jerusalem, 1966; DSc, Technion Israel Inst. Tech., Haifa, 1982. Instr. gen. studies. Office: Technion Israel Inst Tech, Dept Humanities and Arts, Haifa 32000, Israel

FIDLER, CHARLES ROBERT, electrical engineer; b. Park Ridge, Ill., July 7, 1964; s. Charles Ezra and Shirley Ann (Skerce) F.; m. Mary Beth Olson, Mar. 16, 1991; children: Ashley Paige, Charles Robert Jr. BSEE, Ill. Inst. Tech., 1986. Registered profl. engr., Ill. Student surface warfare officer sch., commd. ensign USN, Orlando, Fla., 1986; advanced through grades to lt. USN, 1990; student Navy nuclear power sch. USN, Orlando, 1986; student Navy nuclear prototype USN, Idaho Falls, Idaho, 1986-87; student surface warfare officer sch. USN, San Diego, 1987-88; anti-submarine warfare officer USS Cushing, San Diego, 1988-90; reactor plant shift supr. USS Enterprise, Norfolk, Va., 1990-91; prin. engr. ABB Impell Corp., Chgo., 1991-93; sr. engr. Vectra, Chgo., 1993-96; supr. maintenance planning and support Nebr. Pub. Power Dist. Cooper Nuc. Sta., 1996, sr. rector ops. cert., 1996, plant performance supr., 1998, asst. maintenance mgr., 1998, asst. to plant mgr., 2000—. Contbr. articles to profl. jours. Acolyte in Cath. Ch., 2000. Lt. comdr. USNR, 1996. Mem. IEEE, Am. Nuclear Soc., Naval Inst., Naval Reserve Assn., Am. Soc. Naval Engrs. Home: 1315 S 3d St Nebraska City NE 68410-3613 Office: Nebr Pub Power Dist Cooper Nuc Sta PO Box 98 Brownville NE 68321-0098

FIEBIGER, CHRISTEL, member of the European parliament; b. Uenze, Brandenbrg, Germany, Dec. 29, 1946. Mem. European Parliament, Gross Warnow, Germany, 1999—; mem. Confederal Group of the European United Left/Nordic Green Left; mem. com. on agr. and rural devel.; substitute mem. com. on the environ., pub. health and consumer policy; mem. delegations to the parliamentary cooperation coms. and delegations for rels. with Ukraine, Belarus and Moldova; substitute mem. delegation to the EU-Poland Joint Parliamentary com. Office: Dorfstrabe 36a, D-19357 Gross Warnow Germany*

FIECHTER, GEORGES ANDRE, multinational company executive; b. Sept. 12, 1930; s. Jacques Rene and Marie Okhanoff F.; m. Francoise Forest, 1955 (dec. 1994); children: Benoit, Bettina, Gilles (dec. 1992); m. Michele Brolliet-Clerc, 1996. Student, Swiss Fed. Inst. Tech., Zurich, 1948, Internat. Mgmt. Devel. Inst., Lausanne, 1961; MA Internat. Rels., U. Geneva, 1956, DPolit.Sci., 1973. Exec. sec. Swiss Polit. Sci. Assn., Geneva, 1955-58; head press and info. depts. Internat. Com. Red Cross, Geneva, 1956-58; sec. gen. Internat. Mgmt. Devel. Inst., Lausanne, 1958-61; with leading watch cos. U.K., U.S., Brazil/Switzerland, 1961-77; cons. to dir. Grad. Inst. Internat. Studies and moderator Latin Am./study group, Geneva, 1971-73; dir. Isopublic S.A. div. Gallup, Zurich, 1970-77; dir. M.K.S. Finance S.A., Geneva, 1984-96; owner Integrated Fiduciary Trust-Mgmt. Svcs., Geneva, 1990—; chmn. Atlanticomnium S.A., Geneva, 1984—; European dir. Simonsen Associados, Sao Paulo, 1977—; cons. in asset mgmt., portfolio mgr., Geneva, Monte Carlo, Brazil 1979—. Author: Brazil Since 1964 - Modernization under a Military Regime, 1975, Les Hommes d'Etat celebres de 1920 à nos jours., 1977, Criteras d'evaluation des investissements prives suisses sur le devel., 1969; contbr. articles to profl. jours. Comdr. Nat. Order Rio Branco, Brazil. Grantee Ford Found., 1973. Fellow Chartered Inst. Mktg. (London), Inst. Dirs. (London); mem. Mktg. Comms. Execs. Internat. (Swiss chpt. Geneva), Swiss Group Ind. Fin. Advisors, IMD Internat. Alumni Assn., ECOLINT Alumni Assn., Swiss Press Assn., Am. Internat. Club (Geneva), Golf Club of Geneva. Home: Residence Constellation/11, CH-3963 Crans sur Sierre Switzerland also: 14, chemin de Conches, CH-1231 Conches Geneva Switzerland Office: c/o Fidurhone SA, 8 Rue Muzy, CH 1207 Geneva Switzerland also: PO Box 3262, CH 1211 Geneva 3, Switzerland

FIECHTER, JEAN-JACQUES, historian; b. Alexandria, Egypt, May 25, 1927; s. Jacques-René and Marie (Okhanoff) F.; m. Claudine Sauthier, 1959 (div. 1977); children: Jean-Marie, Claude-Nicolas. MA in History, U. Lausanne, Switzerland, 1950; PhD in History cum laude, U. Lausanne, 1965. CEO, pres. Blancpain Watches, 1950-80; dir. dep. gen. mgr. Swiss Watch Industry Corp., 1960-80; ind. historian, 1981—. Author: French Socialism from Dreyfus Case to World War I, 1965, An American Diplomat during the French Terror, 1983 (History Great prize Bern State), Napoleon Amazon: Regula Eugel Memorial, 1985, Duke of Lauzun - General Biron Memorial, 1986, The American Campaign of Rochambeau Officers, as Per Their Diaries, 1990, The Firing Abbeys of the State of Vaud, 1991, The Baron Pierre-Victor de Besenval, 1993 (Gen. History prize French Acad. 1994), The Harvest of the Gods, 1994; Death by Publication, 1995 (France's Grand prize for detective fiction), A Masterpiece of Revenge, 1996 (Grand prize Bern State). Fellow Soc. Belles Lettres Switzerland; mem. PEN (mem. com. 1980—). Avocations: submarine archeology, skin diving, skiing. Home: 80 Rte Geneve, 1028 Preverenges Switzerland

FIEDEROWICZ, WALTER MICHAEL, lawyer; b. Hartford, Conn., Aug. 23, 1946; s. Michael and Sylvia Christine (Ramunno) F.; m. Gerry Prattson, June 1, 1968; children: Michael, Catherine. B.A., Yale U., 1968; J.D. (Dupont fellow), U. Va., 1971. Bar: Conn. 1971, U.S. Supreme Ct. 1977. Mem. firm Cummings & Lockwood, Stamford, Conn., 1971-76, ptnr. firm, 1979-88, of counsel, 1989-91; pres. Covenant Mut. Ins. Co., Hartford, 1985-92; White House fellow U.S. Dept. Justice, Washington, 1976-77; spl. asst. to Atty. Gen., Dept. Justice, Washington, 1976-77; assoc. dep. Atty. Gen., 1977-79; bd. dirs. Photronics, Inc., First Albany Corp., Compensation Value Alliance, Hematech, Cyagra; chmn. CDT Corp., Meacock Capital. Mem. editorial bd.: Va. Law Review, 1969-71. Mem. grad. coun. Loomis-Chaffee Sch. Bd.; trustee Conn. Trust for Hist. Preservation. Mem. ABA, Conn. Bar Assn., Order of the Cof, Hartford Golf Club, Citrus Club, Univ. Club. Roman Catholic. Home: 39 Painter Hill Rd Woodbury CT 06798-1517

FIEDLER, ANDREAS ERICH, mamagement consultant; b. Hannover, Germany, Mar. 11, 1964; s. Wolfgang and Ilse (Daasch) F.; m. Ulrike Haenchen, May 30, 1998; 1 child, Markus. BA in Mgmt., U. Frankfurt, Germany, 1991. Ind. mgmt. cons. Frankfurt, Germany, 1992-93; mng. dir. Northwest Controlling Corp. Ltd., London, 1993—. Avocations: classical music, travel. Office: NW Controlling Ltd, 2 Old Brompton Rd Ste 289, SW7 3DQ London England

FIEDLER, CHRISTIAN, aerospace engineer; b. Hanover, Lower Saxony, Germany, June 17, 1964; s. Kurt Werner and Heide (Frerichs) F.; m. Ute Catrin Koehler, Sept. 9, 1988. Diploma, Tech. U., Brunswick, Germany, 1989; D Engring., U. Fed. Armed Forces, Hamburg, Germany, 1993. Rsch. asst. U. Fed. Armed Forces, Hamburg, 1990-93; sr. rsch. asst. U. Stuttgart, Germany, 1993-95; project mgr. aircraft evaluation and concepts Lufthansa German Airlines, Hamburg, 1995-96; project mgr. engring. coord. Lufthansa Technik, Frankfurt, Germany, 1996-98, sect. mgr. work package and capacity planning, 1998-2000; dir. technical support Fairchild Dornier Aerospace, Wessling, Germany, 2000—; vis. asst. prof. Ga. Inst. Technology, Atlanta, 1994. Author: (book) Boundary Element Methods in Statics and Dynamics, 1997. Recipient Outstanding Student Performance award Govt. of Lower Saxony, 1988; Jr. World Champion, Eight/Rowing, Internat. Rowing Fedn., 1982. Mem. Hamburg and Germania Rowing Club. Avocations: piano, rowing, mountain hiking. Office: Dornier Fairchild GmbH, Postfach 1103, D-82230 Wessling Germany

FIEDLER, HANS JOACHIM, soil science educator; b. Düsseldorf, Germany, Dec. 30, 1927; s. Gustav and Henriette (Meinert) F.; m. Edith Skolaude; children: Karin, Ulrike. Dr.rer.nat., U. Jena, Germany, 1951, Dr.rer.nat. habil., 1957; Dr.rer.silv. (hon.), U. München, Germany, 1988; Dr.rer.nat. (hon.), U. Trier, Germany, 1989; Dr.rer.silv. (hon.), U. Uppsala, Sweden, 1995. Asst. U. Jena, 1951-57; docent U. Rostock, Germany, 1957-59; prof. U. Dresden, Germany, 1959-95; dean U. Dresden, 1963-65, 90-95; mem. Dresden Tech. U., 1995—; expert of the German cmty. of rsch. Deutsche Forschungsgemeinschaft, Bonn, 1992—. Author, editor: Soil Use and Soil Protection, 1990, Physiology and Ecology of Trees, 1992, Trace Elements in the Environment, 1993, Environmental Protection, 1996, Methods of Soil Biology, 1997, Pedology, 2000; mem. editl. bd. Jour. Plant Nutrition Soil Sci., 1990-2000, Geochemistry, 1978—, Archives of Nature Conservation and Landscape Rsch., 1990—. Named hon. mem. European Inst. Postgrad. Studies, Dresden, 1997. Mem. Soil Sci. Soc. Germany (hon.), Saxony Acad. Sci. Leipzig, German UNESCO Commn., German Found. Environment. Avocations: musical instruments, gardening. Home: Donndorfstr 18, D-01217 Dresden Germany

FIEDLER, KLAUS, physician, educator; b. Altruppin, Germany, Feb. 1, 1938; s. August and Helene (Selig) F.; m. Renate Fiedler; 1 child, Kay. MD, Humboldt U., Berlin, 1962. Physician Hosp. Berlin-Buch, 1962-63; dir. Inst. Pub. Hygiene, Berlin/Friedrichshain, 1964-78, Berlin-Marzahn, 1979-89; dir. Inst. Pub. and Hosp. Hygiene, Jena, 1989—. Author/editor: Hygienepraxis; author: Hygiene/Präventivmedizin/Umweltmedizin, 1995, Gesundes Wohnen, Wohnmedizin im Alltag, 1997. Mem. German Soc. Housing Medicine (v.p. 1994—), Profl. Orgn. of Physicians of Hygiene and Environ. Medicine (bd. dirs. 1992—), Soc. Hygiene and Microbiology, Soc. Hygiene and Environ. Medicine (chmn. com. of housing medicine 1995—), Soc. Hygiene (chmn. dept. health housing environment 1983-89). Avocation: art history. Office: Inst for Allgemeine Krankenhaus a Umwelthygiene, Fürstengraben 23, Jena 07740, Germany

FIEDLER, WALTER, retired zoo director, educator; b. Gross-Harras, Austria, Aug. 8, 1922; s. Hans and Therese (Asperger) F. PhD, U. Vienna, 1950. With Anat. Inst., Frankfurt, Germany, 1950-51, 57-59, Zool. Inst., Fribourg, Switzerland, 1951-53; with Zool. Gardens, Basel, Switzerland, 1953-54, Zurich, 1954-55; with City Libr., Graz, Austria, 1956-57; collaborator expdn. to Ethiopia of Anat. Inst. Frankfurt-Main, 1955-56; zoo dir. Tiergarten Schönbrunn, Vienna, Austria, 1959-87, ret., 1988; lectr. U. Vienna, 1969-81, prof., 1981—. Contbr. articles on anatomy of vertebrates, primatology, and zoobiology to profl. jours., chpts. to books. Mem. Friends of Tiergarten Schönbrunn, Vienna, Vienna Aquarium, Haus des Meeres, and other zoo socs. Served with German Army, 1941-45. Decorated Goldenes Ehrenzeichen and Grosses Ehrenzeichen für Verdienste (Austria), Goldenes Ehrenzeichen (Vienna); recipient award Theodor Körner Fond, Vienna, 1955, 57. Mem. Osterreichische Gesellschaft für Vogelkunde (pres. 1976-86), Assn. German Speaking Zoo Dirs. (pres. 1976-78), Assn. Anatomists Alpine Countries, Internat. Assn. Zoo Dirs., Zool.-Bot. Soc. Austria (pres. 1985—), Zool. Soc. Germany, Zool. Soc. Switzerland, Internat. Primatol. Soc., German Mammal. Soc. (3d pres. 1986-96), Am. Mammal. Soc. Vienna, Anat. Soc. Germany, Austrian Soc. Hist. Scis. (v.p. 1992—), Brit. Fauna Preservation Soc., Nat. Geog. Soc. (hon.), Österr. Gesellschaft für Vogelkunde, Assn. German Speaking Zoo Dirs., Internat. Assn. Zoo Dirs. Roman Catholic. Home: Schloss Schönbrunn, Apothekertrakt 12, A-1131 Vienna Austria

FIEDLER, ZDDENEK JOSEF, physician, geneticist, researcher; b. Hradec Kralove, Czech Republic, Jan. 23, 1966; s. Zdenek and Vlasta (Stepanek) F. MD, Charles U., Prague, Czech Republic, 1990, PhD, 1997. Physician Univ. Hosp., Hradec Kralove, 1991—; genetics rschr. Carhles U., Hradec Kralove, 1998—, U. Pardubice, Czech Republic, 1999. Author: Construction of the Recombinant DNA, 1997. 2d lt. Arty. Regt., Czech Army, 1990-91. Mem. Czech Hussite Ch. Home: Pod Zameckem 1520, 500 12 Hradec Kralove Czech Republic Office: University Hospital, Heyrovskeho, 500 05 Hradec Kralove Czech Republic

FIEL, MAXINE LUCILLE, journalist, behavioral analyst, lecturer; b. N.Y.C.; d. William Jack and Rowena (Burton) Stempel; m. David H. Fiel; children: Meredith Susan, Lisa Beth. Student in psychology and humanities, NYU. Nat. columnist, contbg. editor Mademoiselle Mag., N.Y.C., 1972—; nat. columnist Womens World, Englewood, N.J., 1979-89; contbg. editor Overseas Promotions, N.Y.C., 1979—; articles and features editor Japanese Overseas Press, 1976—; feature editor N.Y. Now, N.Y.C., 1980-91; contbg. editor Woman's World mag., 1979-89, Bella mag., Eng., 1987-89; nat. columnist First mag. for women, 1989-91; founder Starcast Astrological Svcs., Floral Park, N.Y., 1993—; cons. legal profession jury selection, 1984—; mktg. cons. Imperial Enterprises, Tokyo and Princeton, N.J., 1983—; cons. spokesperson Rowland Co., N.Y.C., 1972-81, Allied Chem. Co., N.Y.C., 1972-75; lectr., cons. Atlanta and Fla. Bar Assns., 1986—; creator Touch Game Parker Bros., Salem, Mass., 1971-76; behavior analystand communications advisor multi-nat. bus. corps.; cons. Chesebrough-Ponds, Footwear Coun., Grand Marnier Liquor; founder Starcast Astrological Svcs., 1993; pres. Interglobal Mktg. Co., 1999. Pioneer field of polit. body lang., 1969; author: Lovescopes, 1998, The Little Book of Body Language, 1998; contbr. articles to News Am., L.A. Times, Newhouse News Svc., Newspaper Enterprise Assocs., King Features, Borderland Mag.; TV appearances on morning and afternoon shows including A Current Affair, The Regis Philbin Show, Eyewitness News, Cable News Network, Tonight Show, Today Show, Good Morning Am., Joan Rivers Show, Jenny Jones, Entertainment Tonight, Hard Copy, Inside Edition, BBC Breakfast Show, Good Morning Japan, many others; appears in daily segment Good Morning Japan; columnist I'M Mag. Japan, 1997—; own daily TV show on Nippon Network, Japan, 1989—. Active Sister Cities, Tokyo and N.Y.C.; charter mem. Elem. Sch. Cultural Exchange, Toyko and N.Y.C., Ctr. Environ. Edn.; bd. dirs. Periwinkle Prodns. Anti-Drug Abuse, N.Y.C. Recipient Achievement award field behavioral sci. and photojournalism, Tokyo, 1974, Outstanding Rsch. award field psychology of gesture, Tokyo, 1976, Outstanding Achievement award Internat. Conf. Soc. Para-Psychology, 1974-75; honored guest at award dinner for involvement and support in the merging of Eye Rsch. Inst. Boston and Harvard Med. Sch., 1991. Mem. AFTRA, Internat. Found. Behavioral Rsch. (past v.p.), Nat. Writers Assn. (profl.), Profl. Writers Assn., Authors Guild, Authors League, World Wildlife Fund, Whale Protection Fund, Cousteau Soc., Nature Conservancy, Greenpeace, People for Ethical Treatment Animals, Humane Assn. U.S., Sea Shepherd Conservation Soc., Defenders of Wildlife, Guiding Eyes for Blind, Braille Camps for Blind Children, Save the Children, Lotos Club (N.Y.C.), East End Yacht Club (Freeport, N.Y.). E-mail: intrglobal@aol.com. Office: 338 Northern Blvd Ste 3 Great Neck NY 11021-4808

FIELD, ALEXANDER JAMES, economics educator; b. Boston, Apr. 17, 1949; s. Mark George and Anne (Murray) F.; m. Valerie Nan Wolk, Aug. 8, 1982; children: James Alexander, Emily Elena. AB, Harvard U., 1970; MS, London Sch. Econs., 1971; PhD, U. Calif., Berkeley, 1974. Asst. prof. econs. Stanford (Calif.) U., 1974-82; assoc. prof. Santa Clara (Calif.) U., 1982-88, acad. v.p., 1986-87, prof., chmn. dept. econs., 1988-93, assoc. dean Leavey Sch. Bus. and Adminstrn., 1993-96, dean, 1996-97, Michel and Mary Orradre prof. econs., 1992—; mem. bd. trustees Santa Clara U., 1988-91. Author: Educational Reform and Manufacturing Development in Mid-Nineteenth Century Massachusetts, 1989, Altruistically Inclined: Evolutionary Theory, the Behavioral Sciences, and the Origin of Complex Social Organization; author, editor: The Future of Economics, 1995; assoc. editor Jour. Econ. Lit., 1981-98, 99—; editor Rsch. in Econ. History, 1993—; mem. editl. bd. Explorations in Econ. History, 1983-89. Recipient Nevins prize Columbia U., 1975; NSF rsch. grantee, 1989. Mem. Phi Beta Kappa, Beta Gamma Sigma. Home: 3762 Redwood Cir Palo Alto CA 94306-4255 Office: Santa Clara Univ Dept Econs Santa Clara CA 95053-0001

FIELD, AMANDA KATHERINE, writer, editor; b. Santa Monica, Calif., Sept. 14, 1974; d. Richard Clark and Barbara (Butler) F. BA in English, Amherst Coll., 1996; postbaccalaureate cert. in Fine Arts, Brandeis U., 1998. Kindergarten tchr. Turningpoint Sch., Bel Air, Calif., 1996-97; tchr. asst. Brandeis U., Waltham, Mass., 1997-98; graphic artist Platinum Tech., San Francisco, 1998; pre-sch. tchr. Glen Park Pre-Sch., San Francisco, 1999; mng. editor ZYZZYVA, San Francisco, 2000—. Office: 1236 3d Ave #3 San Francisco CA 94122-2705

FIELD, ANTHONY, accountant, theatre consultant; b. London, Aug. 16, 1928; s. Charles and Zelda (Robinson) F. D. Litt., City U., London, 1987; DFA, Linfield Coll., 1995. Audit clk. J. Hulbert Grave & Co., London, 1950-56; fin. dir. Chesterfield Properties Ltd., London, 1956-58, Arts Coun. Gt. Britain, London, 1958-85; vice-chmn. Theatre Projects Cons. Ltd., London, 1985—. Author, prodr: The West End Salutes Leonard Bernstein, 1988; prodr.: Tea and Sympathy, 1958, Cat on a Hot Tin Roof, 1958, A View from the Bridge, 1958, I'm Not Rappaport, 1988, The Fifteen Streets, 1988, Staring at the Sun, 1998. Chmn. Liverpool Inst. Performing Arts, Ltd., 1990—, Lyric Hammersmith, 1985-91; trustee Chichester Festival Theatre, Eng., 1991-97; magistrate S.W. London, 1968-77; vis. magistrate Wandsworth Prison, 1974-77. Recipient C.B.E. Queen Elizabeth, 1984. Fellow Inst. Chartered Accts. Jewish. Home: 152 Cromwell Tower, Barbican London EC2Y 8DD, England Office: Theatre Projects Cons Ltd, Charlton King's Rd, NW5 25W London England

FIELD, BARRY ELLIOT, internist, gastroenterologist; b. Hartford, Conn., Apr. 21, 1947; s. Arnold and Selma (Nechrich) F.; m. Julie Farr, Jan. 6, 1991; children: Rachel Elizabeth, Hannah Margaret, Miles Jay. BA (scholar), Harvard U., 1968; MD, Albert Einstein Coll. Medicine, 1972. Intern in pediat. Montefiore Hops., Bronx, N.Y., 1972-73; intern in medicine Met. Hosp., N.Y.C., 1973-74, resident in medicine, 1974-76; fellow in gastroenterology Harbor Gen. Hosp., Torrance, Calif., 1976-78; pvt. practice in internal medicine and gastroenterology North Tarrytown, N.Y., 1978—; dir. medicine Phelps Meml. Hosp., North Tarrytown. Mem. Am. Gastroenterol. Assn., Alpha Omega Alpha. Office: 777 N Broadway Ste 305 Tarrytown NY 10591-1040

FIELD, COLIN DAVID, neuropsychologist; b. Caulfield, Victoria, Australia, Mar. 10, 1956; s. Peter Colin and Audrey Violet (Russell) F.; m. Pamela Lesley Giles, Jan. 7, 1978 (div. Oct. 1989); two children; m. Belinda Vera Coyte, Feb. 19, 1995; four children. B of Behavioral Scis. with honors, La Trobe U., Bundoora, Australia, 1978; MS in Clin. Neuropsychology, U. Melbourne, Parkville, Australia, 1981; BL with honors, Deakin U., Geelong, Australia, 1990. Registered psychologist South Australia. Clin. neuropsychologist Hillcrest Hosp., Adelaide, Australia, 1982-88, 88-91, North Brisbane Hosps. Bd., Brisbane, Australia, 1988; pvt. practice in clin. neuropsychology Adelaide, 1984—; sr. clin. neuropsychologist Statewide Mental Health Svc., Glenside Hosp., Adelaide, 1991—, Repatriation Gen. Hosp., Daw Park, Australia, 1991—; lectr. Flinders U. of South Australia, 1997—. Editor: (book) Brain Impairment, 1986, Brain Impairment in the Elderly; contbr.: (book) The Primal Whimper, 1989; assoc. editor: Australian Psychologist, 1996—. Justice of peace, South Australia, 1984. Fellow Australian Psychol. Soc. (mem. coun. 1985-94, chairperson divsn. profl. affairs 1990-94, rep. Nat. Office of Overseas Skills Recognition working group for Devel. of Competency Stds. for Profession of Psychology 1992-93); mem. Australian Soc. for Study of Brain Impairment, Internat. Neuropsychol. Soc. Anglican. Avocations: reading, folk music, family history. Office: Glenside Hosp Psychol Dept, PO Box 17, Eastwood 5063, Australia

FIELD, DAVID ELLIS, lawyer; b. Washington, Feb. 3, 1953; s. Ellis Arrington and Phyllis Martina (Anderson) F. BA, U. Va., 1975, MEd, 1976; JD, George Mason U., 1983. Bar: Va. 1983, D.C. 1990, Md. 1991, U.S. Dist. Ct. (ea. dist.) Va. 1984, U.S. Ct. Appeals (4th cir.) 1985. Assoc. Law Offices Alphonse Audet, Fairfax, Va., 1984; asst. commonwealth's atty. Office of Fairfax County, Va., 1984-87; assoc. Miller & Bucholtz, P.C., Reston, Va., 1987-89, Falcone & Rosenfeld, Ltd., Fairfax, 1989, Lewis, Dack, Paradiso, O'Connor & Good, Wasington, 1989-91, Deckelbaum, Ogens & Fischer, Wasington, 1991-92; atty. Alan S. Toppelberg & Assocs., Washington, 1992-94; ptnr. Field & Cram, Fairfax, Va., 1994-98; pvt. practice Fairfax, Va., 1998-99; staff counsel AllState, Falls Church, Va., 1999—; asst. city atty. City of Fairfax, 1988-89. Mem. Am. Arbitration Assn., Fairfax Bar Assn., Delta Theta Pi. Democrat. Presbyterian. Office: # 175 3141 Fairview Park Dr Ste 175 Falls Church VA 22042-4507

FIELD, HEATHER KATHLEEN, humanities educator; b. York, Eng., Feb. 11, 1950; arived in Australia, 1976; d. Charles Lawrence and Kathleen Mary North; 1 child, Anderida Artemisia. BSc, Loughborough (U.K.) U. Tech., 1972; diploma, U. Amsterdam, The Netherlands, 1984; M Agrl. Sci., La Trobe U., Melbourne, Australia, 1988; MA, Australian Nat. U., Canberra, 1990; diploma, U. Amsterdam, The Netherlands, 1984; PhD, U. New Eng., Armidale, Australia, 1998; Grad. Cert. in Higher Edn., Griffith, Brisbane, Australia, 1999. ECC liaison officer Meat and Livestock Commn., Bletchley, U.K., 1975-76; economist Thomas Borthwick (Australasia) Pty., Melbourne, 1977-78; tutor in econs. La Trobe U., 1978-83; sr. rsch. officer Ctr. European Agrl. Studies Wye (U.K.) Coll., 1984-85; sr. rsch. officer Australian Bur. Agrl. and Resource Econ., Canberra, 1985-90; dir. Industry Commn., Canberra, 1990-92; sr. lectr. Griffith U., Brisbane, Queensland, Australia, 1992—. Contbr. articles to profl. publs. Postgrad. scholar Netherlands Univs. Found. for Internat. Cooperation, 1983; recipient Profl. Excellence award Am. Agrl. Econs. Assn., 1990. Mem. Contemporary European Studies Assn. Australia (bd. dirs. 1996), European Contemporary Studies Assn. Home: 30 Aylton St, Coopers Plains Queensland 4108, Australia Office: Griffith U Dept Humanities, Nathan 4111, Brisbane Queensland, Australia

FIELD, HERMANN HAVILAND, architect, educator, author; b. Zurich, Switzerland, Apr. 13, 1910; s. Herbert Haviland and Nina (Eschwege) F.; m. Kate Margaret Thornycroft, June 14, 1940; children: Hugh, Alan, Alison. BA cum laude, Harvard U., 1933; postgrad., Harvard Grad. Sch. Design, Cambridge, 1932-34; diploma in architecture, Swiss Fed. Poly. Inst., Zurich, 1936. Resident architect Roche Products Ltd., Welwyn Garden City, Eng., 1936-38; field rep. Czech Refugee Trust Fund, Poland and Eng., 1939-40; site planner Tuttle, Seelye, Place & Raymond, N.Y.C., 1941-45; dir. research Raymond & Rado, Architects, N.Y.C., 1945-47; dir. bldg. plans Case Western Res. U., Cleve., 1947-49; victim of kidnapping in Cold War incident, secretly held in Polish prison cellar Miedzeszyn, 1949-54; preparation of prison novels London, 1955, Boston, 1956-60; dir. planning office Tufts-New England Med. Ctr., Boston, 1961-72; founder, dir. grad. program in urban, social and environ. policy, prof. environ. planning Tufts U., Medford, Mass., 1972-78, prof. emeritus polit. sci., 1978—. Author: (with Stanislaw Mierzenski) Angry Harvest, 1958, German, Swedish, English, Polish edits., 1958-62, also cons. on film, 1984, Duck Lane, 1961, (with Frank Thibodeau) Sustaining Tomorrow, 1984, 2d edit., 1985, (with Kate Field) Departure Delayed, German and Polish edits., 1996, 97, Trapped in the Cold War, 1999; contbg. author: Problems of Pediatric Hospital Design, 1965, Evaluation of Hospital Design, 1982, Environment and Cognition, 1973; contbr. articles to profl. jours. Chmn. planning bd. Shirley, Mass., 1984-86, 89-93, vice-chmn., 1986-89; active Devens Enterprise Commn., 1995—, Hist. Dist. Commn., Shirley, 1973-88, Conservation Commn., Shirley, 1970-83, Cambridge, 1975-81; dir. Nashua River Watershed Assn., Fitchburg, Mass., 1981-85, Coolidge Ctr. Environ. Leadership, Cambridge, 1983-89; del. Internat. Conf. Sustainable Devel., Ottawa, 1986; v.p., dir. Mass. Assn. Conservation Commn., Medford, 1976-85. Recipient Environ. Leadership award New Eng. Environ. Network, 1987, Conservation award Nashua River Watershed Assn., 1988, Lifetime Preservation award Mass. Hist. Commn., 1990, Quality of Life award N.E. Regional Coun., AIA, 1993. Fellow AIA; mem. Am. Inst. Cert. Planners (charter 1978—), Boston Soc. Architects (dir. 1968-70, sec. 1970-74), Boston Archtl. Ctr., Internat. Union Conservation Nature (planning commn. 1978—), Sierra Club, Appalachian Mountain (Boston) Club. Avocations: managing wildlife sanctuary, writing autobiographical manuscript. E-mail: hfield@bicnet.net. Home and Office: Valley Farm 110 Center Rd Shirley MA 01464-2106

FIELD, JULIA ALLEN, planner, strategist, writer; b. Boston, Jan. 5, 1937; d. Howard Locke and Julia Wright (Field) Allen. BA cum laude, Harvard U., 1960; postgrad., Harvard Grad. Sch. Design, 1964-65, Pius XII Grad. Art Inst., Florence, Italy, 1961, Walden U. Inst. Adv. Studies, 1983-89. Cons. to archtl. and environ. firms, 1964-69; cons. Forestry Dept. of Simla, India, 1969-70; founder, v.p. Black Grove, Inc., Miami, Fla., 1970-80; founder, pres. Amazonia 2000, Bogota, Colombia, 1970-72; leader Task Force Amazonia 2000, DAINCO, 1977-78; elected pres. Found. Amazonia 2000 in Gen. Assembly, Leticia, Colombia, 1979—; pres. Acad. Arts and Scis. of the Ams., Miami, Fla., 1979—; mem. Presdl. Com. on Innovative Tech. Devel. Group of Yr. 2000, Colombia, 1971-74; mem. Man and Biosphere com. UNESCO, Colombia, 1972-78; mem. Task Force on Colonization Report to Pres. of Colombia, 1973; cons. So. Unified Command, Republic of Colombia, 1981-86; Hon. Nat. Insp. resources and environment Republic of Colombia, 1982—; mem. bd. visitors Duke U. Primate Ctr., 1979-82; prin. spkr. at internat. seminars and congresses. Author: Amazonia 2000, 1978, Amazonia as a World Model, 1972. Mem. City of Miami Bicentennial Com., 1975-76; coord. Cmty. of Man Task Force, Miami, 1975-76; mem. Blueprint for Miami 2000, 1982-85; adv. Tech. Jour., Delhi, India, 1985-86; participant Only One Earth Forum, UN Environ. Programme/Rene Dubos Ctr., N.Y.C., 1987, 15th Internat. Human Unity Conf., New Delhi, 1988; founder Amacayacu Nat. Park, Amazonia, Colombia, 1975; creator, builder with other scientists Villa Ciencia, Rio Cotuhe, Colombia, 1975; signed Third Amazon World Model Accord for Amazonia 2000 with IGAC and DAINCO, Colombia, 1988-93. Fellow Royal Geog. Soc. (London) (life); mem. Internat. Assn. Hydrogen Energy, EarthJustice Legal Def. Fund, Nature Conservancy, Friends of Earth, Friends of Worldwatch, Nat. Resources Def. Coun. Fax: 305-667-8426. Home and Office: 9450 Old Cutler Rd Miami FL 33156-2242

FIELD, MARSHALL, business executive; b. Charlottesville, Va., May 13, 1941; s. Marshall IV and Joanne (Bass) F.; m. Joan Best Connelly, Sept. 5, 1964 (div. 1969); 1 child, Marshall; m. Jamee Beckwith Jacobs, Aug. 19, 1972; children: Jamee Christine, Stephanie Caroline, Abigail Beckwith. BA, Harvard Coll., 1963. With N.Y. Herald Tribune, 1964-65; pub. Chgo. Sun-Times, 1969-80, Chgo. Daily News, 1969-78; dir. Field Enterprises, Inc., Chgo., 1965-84; dir., mem. exec. com. Field Enterprises, Inc., 1965-84, chmn. bd., 1972-84; chmn. bd. The Field Corp., 1984—; chmn. bd. Cabot, Cabot & Forbes, 1984—, chmn. exec. com., 1985-89, sr. dir., chief exec. officer, 1989—; pub. World Book-Childcraft Internat. Inc., 1973-78, dir., 1965-80. Bd. trustees Art Inst. Chgo., Chgo. Pub. Libr. Found., Rush-Presbyn.-St. Lukes Med. Ctr., Chgo. Cmty. Trust; vice-chmn. bd. trustees Field Mus. Natural History; bd. dirs. First Nat. Bank Chgo., 1970-85, Field Found. Ill., Lincoln Park Zool. Soc., World Wildlife Fund, Atlantic Salmon Assn., Mac Neal Found.; adv. bd. Brookfield Zoo; active Chgo. Orchestral Assn. Mem. Nature Conservancy, River Club, Chgo. Club, Comml. Club, Harvard Club, Racquet Club, Onwentsia Club, Jupiter Island Club, Shore Acres Club. Office: 225 W Wacker Dr Ste 1500 Chicago IL 60606-1235

FIELD, SALLY, actress; b. Pasadena, Calif., Nov. 6, 1946; m. Steve Craig, Sept. 1968 (div. 1975); children: Peter, Eli; m. Alan Greisman, Dec. 1984 (div. 1994); 1 son, Samuel. Student, Actor's Studio, 1973-75. Starred in TV series Gidget, 1965, The Flying Nun, 1967-69, The Girl With Something Extra, 1973; film appearances include The Way West, 1967, Stay Hungry, 1976, Heroes, 1977, Smokey and the Bandit, 1977, Hooper, 1978, The End, 1978, Norma Rae, 1979 (Cannes Film Festival Best Actress award 1979, Acad. award 1980), Beyond the Poseidon Adventure, 1979, Smokey and the Bandit II, 1980, Back Roads, 1981, Absence of Malice, 1981, Kiss Me Goodbye, 1982, Places in the Heart, 1984 (Acad. award for best actress 1984), Murphy's Romance (also exec. producer), 1985, Surrender, 1987, Punchline, 1987 (also prodr.), Steel Magnolias, 1989, Soapdish, 1991, Not Without My Daughter, 1991, Homeward Bound: The Incredible Journey, 1993 (voice only), Mrs. Doubtfire, 1993, Forrest Gump, 1994; TV movies include Maybe I'll Come Home In the Spring, 1971, Marriage: Year One, 1971, Home for the Holidays, 1972, Bridges, 1976, Sybil, 1976 (Emmy award 1977), A Woman of Independent Means, 1994; prodr. Dying Young, 1991, Eye for an Eye, 1995, Homeward Bound II: Lost in San Francisco, 1996, Merry Christmas George Bailey, 1997, From The Earth to the Moon, 1998, A Cooler Climate, 1999.

FIELDEN, JONATHAN MARK, anesthetist, intensivist; b. Yorkshire, Eng., Sept. 9, 1963; s. Barry Fielden and Margaret (Shaw); m. Catherine Ruth Emerson, July 10, 1965; 1 child, Alexander. BSc with honors, Bristol (Eng.) U., 1985, M.B.Ch.B., 1988. Sr. house officer medicine Bristol U., 1989-91; sr. house officer anesthetics Southmead Hosp., Bristol, 1991-92, R.U.H. Bath, Eng., 1992-93; provisional fellow St. Vincent's Hosp., Sydney, Australia, 1994-95; specialist registrar/registrar S.W. Anesthetic Rotation, 1993-96; specialist registrar Wessex Anesthetic Rotation, 1996-98; cons. in anaesthesia and intensive care medicine Royal Berkshire Hosp., Reading, U.K., 1998—, clin. dir. emergency srvs., 2000—. Fellow Royal Coll. Anesthetists (mem. coun. 1997—); mem. Royal Coll. Physicians, BMA (mem. coun. 1992-94, 96-98, chmn. elect west berks divsn. 2000). Mem. Ch. of England. Avocations: opera, hill walking, property renovation. E-Mail: Jonathan.F@ukgateway.net. Home: 6 Water Rd, Reading RG30 2NN, England

FIELDING, ELIZABETH BROWN, education educator; b. Ligonier, Ind., Feb. 17, 1918; d. Herbert Benjamin and Roberta (Franklin) B.; m. Frederick Allan Fielding, May 23, 1942 (wid. July 1962); children: Elizabeth Enndriss

Fielding, Frederick Allan Fielding, Jr. BA, Smith Coll., 1939; MA, U. San Francisco, 1975. Cert. tchr. com. colls., Calif. Field staff mem. San Francisco Bay Girl Scout Assn., 1963-69; exec. dir. Tri-City Project on Aging, Rodeo, Calif., 1970-73; tchr., cons. various univs., 1974-98; mem. curriculum com. U. Calif., Berkeley, 1979-80; chair edn. programs Diablo Valley Found. on Aging, Walnut Creek, Calif., 1980s. Author: The Memory Manual: 10 Simple Things You Can Do to Improve Your Memory After 50, 1999, Teacher's Guide to The Memory Manual, 2000; contbr. articles to profl. jours. Chair Mental Health Task Force, County Coun. for Aging, Contra Costa County, 1974-76; mem. Sr. Svcs. Commn., City of Lafayette, Calif., 1981-2000; pres. bd. dirs. Calif. Specialists on Aging, Calif., 1976-79. Mem. Western Gerontol. Assn. (now Am. Soc. on Aging), Internat. Transactional Analysis Assn. Avocations: writing fiction, genealogy, art appreciation, bird watching. Home: 3170 Plymouth Rd Lafayette CA 94549-3236

FIELDING, STUART, psychopharmacologist; b. Bronx, N.Y., Oct. 31, 1939; s. Harry and Ethel (Weisberg) Feinblatt; m. Maralyn J. Lowy, Aug. 26, 1962; children: Kimberly Ellen, Bradford Scott. BA, Monmouth Coll., 1962; MS, Howard U., 1964; PhD, U. Del., 1968. Mgr. psychopharmacology rsch. Ciba-Geigy Corp., Summit, N.J., 1967-75; assoc. dir. pharmacology Hoechst-Roussel Pharms., Inc., Somerville, N.J., 1975-76, assoc. dir. biol. sci., mgr. pharmacology, 1977-84, dir. pharmacology, 1984-86, dir. biol. rsch., 1987-89; v.p. R & D, dir. Interneuron Pharms., Inc., Lexington, Mass., 1989-92; chmn., CEO Bio-Enhancement Systems Corp., Morris Plaines, N.J., 1992—. Editor: (book) Psychopharmacology of Clonidine, 1981, (book series) Industrial Pharmacology: A Monograph Series, 1974-79, (jour.) Drug Devel. Rsch., 1980-92; contbr. articles to profl. publs. Fellow Am. Psychol. Assn.; mem. Am. Chem. Soc., Am. Soc. Pharmacology and Exptl. Therapeutics, Soc. Neurosci. Home and Office: 16 Bromleigh Way Morris Plains NJ 07950-1642

FIELDS, BERTRAM HARRIS, lawyer; b. Los Angeles, Mar. 31, 1929; s. H. Maxwell and Mildred Arlyn (Ruben) F.; m. Lydia Ellen Minevitch, Oct. 22, 1960 (dec. Sept. 1986); 1 child, James Eldar, m. Barbara Guggenheim, Feb. 21, 1991. B.A., UCLA, 1949; J.D. magna cum laude, Harvard U., 1952. Bar: Calif. 1953. Practiced in Los Angeles, 1955—; assoc. firm Shearer, Fields, Rohner & Shearer, and predecessor firms, 1955-57, mem. firm, 1957-82; ptnr. Greenberg, Glusker, Fields, Claman & Machtinger, 1982—. Author: (as D. Kincaid) The Sunset Bomber, 1986, The Lawyer's Tale, 1992, (as B. Fields) Royal Blood Richard III and the Mystery of the Princes, 1998; mem. bd. editors: Harvard Law Rev., 1953-55. Bd. dirs. U. So. Calif. Annenberg Sch. Comm. 1st. lt. USAF, 1953-55, Korea. Mem. ABA, L.A. County Bar Assn., Coun. Fgn. Rels. Achievements include being the subject of profiles Calif. Mag., Nov. 1987, Avenue Mag., Mar. 1989, Am. Film Mag., Dec. 1989, Vanity Fair Mag., Dec. 1993, Harvard Law Sch. Bull., spring 1998, London Sunday Telegraph, June 1999, Sunday New York Post, July 1999. Office: Greenberg Glusker Fields Claman & Machtinger Ste 2000 1900 Avenue Of The Stars Los Angeles CA 90067-4590

FIELDS, STUART HOWARD, labor relations specialist; b. Chgo., Dec. 15, 1943; s. Albert B. and Cecelia (Kessler) F.; m. Birgit Willeke, Dec. 5, 1971; children: Jessica N., Jascha D. BS, UCLA, 1965; MS, U. Calif., Northridge, 1968. Cert. tchr. and instr., Calif. Labor rels. specialist Hughes Tool Co., Culver City, Calif., 1970, Dept. of the Navy, Point Mugu, Calif., 1971-76; employee rels. specialist Agrl. Rsch. Svc., Hyattsville, Md., 1976-81; labor rels. specialist Agrl. Rsch. Svc., 1981-84, Pub. Health Svc., Rockville, Md., 1985-86; employee rels. specialist Def. Nuclear Agy., Bethesda, Md., 1986-88, Consumer Product Safety Commn., Bethesda, 1988-89, U.S. Dept. Commerce, Washington, 1989-97; sr. paralegal Gagliardo & Zipin, Attys. at Law, Silver Spring, Md., 1997—; labor rels. specialist IRS, Washington, 1997—; presdl. classroom instr.; cons. in field. Author: Requirements for Top Positions in Personnel Administration, 1968. Lt. U.S. Army, 1968-70. Mem. Soc. Fed. Labor Relations Profls., Jewish Community Ctr., Mensa. Democrat. Avocations: classical music, coin collecting, tax law, basketball. Home: 9449 Reach Rd Potomac MD 20854-2853 Office: IRS 1111 Constitution Ave NW Washington DC 20224-0001

FIENNES, JOSEPH, actor; b. Salisbury, Wiltshire, Ireland, May 27, 1970. Student, Guildhall Sch. Music and Drama. With Royal Shakespeare Co. Appeared in The Woman in Black, A Month in the Country, Son of Man, Les Enfants du Paradis, Troilus and Cressida, The Herbal Bed; films include Vacillations of Poppy Carew, 1995, Stealing Beauty, 1996, Shakespeare in Love, 1998 (Screen Actors Guild awards 1999, Chgo. Film Critics Assn. award 1999, Broadcast Film Critics Assn. award 1999, Nominee Brit. Acad. award 1999, Nominee Block Buster Entertainment award 1999), Elizabeth, 1998, Martha, Meet Frank, Daniel and Laurence, 1998, Rancid Aluminum, 1999, Forever Mine, 1999, Enemy at the Gates, 2000. Office: Ken McReddie Ltd, 91 Regent St, W1R 7TB London England*

FIERHELLER, GEORGE ALFRED, corporate director; b. Toronto, Apr. 26, 1933; s. Harold Parsons and Ruth Hathaway (Bauld) F.; m. Glenna E. Fletcher, Apr. 17, 1957; children: Vicki Elaine, Lori Ann. BA, U. Toronto, 1955; LLD, Concordia U.; DSLitt, Trinity Coll., U. Toronto. With IBM, Toronto, 1955-58, account mgr., 1962-65, mktg. mgr., 1966-68; founder, pres. Sys. Dimensions Ltd., Ottawa, Ont., 1968-79; pres., CEO Rogers Cable TV Broadcasting Co. Ltd., Vancouver, B.C., Can., 1979-85, Cantel Inc., Toronto, 1985-90; chmn., CEO Roger Cantel Mobile, Inc., 1990-93; vice chair Rogers Comm., Inc., Toronto, 1993-96; pres. Four Halls Inc., Toronto, 1997—; bd. dirs. Extendicare Inc., Rogers Cantel Inc., GBC N.Am. Fund Inc., Telesys. Internat. Wireless, N.V., Sierra Sys., Ont. Exports Inc.; pres. Bd. of Trade of Met. Toronto, 1996-97. Contbr. articles to profl. jours. Gen. chmn. United Appeal Campaign, Ottawa, 1972; chmn. campaign Carleton U., 1975-77, also chmn. bd. govs., 1977-79; mem. adv. com. Norman Paterson Sch. Internat. Affairs; bd. dirs., v.p. United Way Ottawa, 1975-79 (United Way of Can. highest award 1998); Opera Ottawa, 1970-71; trustee, mem. exec. com. Nat. Arts Ctr., 1973-79; trustee Royal Ottawa Hosp., 1978-79, Vancouver Gen. Hosp. Found., 1981-85; mem. Vancouver Centennial Commn., 1983-84; bd. govs. Simon Fraser U., Vancouver, 1981-84; chmn. United Way Vancouver, 1981; chmn. B.C. Coun. of 80's, 1980-83; chair United Way Met. Toronto, 1994-96, chmn. gen. campaign, 1991; chmn. Vision 2000, 1990-91; trustee Sunnybrook Hosp. Found., 1993—, McMichael Can. Art Collection, 1993-99; chair Trinity Coll. Campaign, 1996-99. Decorated mem. Order of Can., 2000; recipient Award of Merit, City of Toronto, 1991, Award of Excellence, Can. Wireless Ind. Assn., 1996; named to Can. Info. Tech. Hall of Fame, 1998. Mem. Can. Info. Processing Soc. (pres. 1970-71), World Pres. Orgn., Chief Execs. Orgn., Can. Assn. Data Processing Svc. Orgns., Assn. Cert. Computer Profls. (founding com.), Can. Ctr. for Philanthropy (bd. dirs. 1987-91), Bus. Coun. on Nat. Issues, Cellular Telecom. Industry Assn. (bd. dirs. 1986-94), Smart Toronto (chmn. 1996), Greater Toronto Mktg. Alliance (chair 1997—), Vancouver Club, Rideau Club, Granite Club, Nat. Club, Rosedale Golf Club. Home: 24 Pearwood Crescent, Toronto, ON Canada M3B 2C2 Office: Four Halls Inc, 121 King St W Ste 2525, Toronto, ON Canada M5H 3T9

FIERO, PATRICK, physician; b. Bklyn., May 10, 1954; s. Phillip and Concetta (Amato) F.; m. Rose Passalacqua, Jan. 24, 1976; children: Jared, Jenna, Patrick Jr., Kendra Marie. BA, NYU, 1976; MD, U. Northeast, Tampico, Mex., 1980. Diplomate Am Bd. Ob-Gyn. Resident physician Bklyn. (N.Y.) Jewish Hosp., 1980-81, St. Vincent's Med. Ctr. of Richmond, Staten Island, N.Y., 1981-86; attending physician Staten Island Ob-Gyn. Assocs., 1986-91; pvt. practice Staten Island, N.Y., 1991—. Mem. Richmond County Med. Soc., N.Y. State Med. Soc. Republican. Roman Catholic. Avocations: books, swimming, cars, collectibles. Office: Patrick Fiero MD 4308 Richmond Ave Staten Island NY 10312-6239

FIERRO, ALFREDO EMILIO, marketing professional, consultant; b. San Salvador, El Salvador, Aug. 22, 1965; s. Emilio and Susana Teresa (Gonfiotti) F.; m. Marcela Monica Gargiulo, Aug. 10, 1994 (div. 1998). Degree in bus. adminstrn. with honors, U. Catolica Argentina, Buenos Aires, 1989. Area dir. internat. mktg. Sade Indsl. Group, Buenos Aires, 1988-92; export trader SA Alba, Buenos Aires, 1992-94; comml. officer Brit. Embassy, Buenos Aires, 1994—. Mem. Am. Mktg. Assn., Asociacio Argentina de Mktg. Roman Catholic. Avocation: reading. Office: Brit Embassy, Dr Luis Agote 2412, 1425 Buenos Aires Argentina

FIETSAM, ROBERT CHARLES, accountant; b. Oct. 18, 1927; s. Celsus J. and Viola (Ehret) F.; m. Miriam Runkwitz, Apr. 12, 1952; children: Robert C., Guy P., Nancy A., Lisa R. BS, U. Ill., 1955. CPA, Mo., Ill. Claims adjuster Ely & Walker Dry Goods, St. Louis, 1947-48; acct. Price Waterhouse & Co., 1949-54; staff acct. J.W. Boyle & Co., East St. Louis, 1955-59; owner R.C. Fietsam, CPA's, Belleville, Ill., 1959-68, mng. ptnr., 1969—; Mem. Belle-Scott Com., 1979—; bd. dirs, pres. Belleville Ctr., Inc., 1980-81; mem. Ill. Pub. Accts. Registration Com., 1985-87. Bd. dirs. Meml. Hosp., 1982-85, Meml. Found., Inc., 1986-91, Bellville Hosp. Golf Classic, mem., 1983-91, chmn. 1986-91, Ill. Bd. Examiners, 1994—, vice chair, 1997-98, chair 1998-99, coun. v.p., pres. St. Paul United Ch. of Christ, 1969-73; mem. accountancy com. U. Ill., St. Louis. With USAF, 1951-53. Mem. AICPAs (coun. 1981-84, 85-90), Ill. CPA Soc. (pres. so. chpt. 1972-73, Mr. Southern Chpt. award 1976, state bd. dirs. 1979-81, sr. v.p. 1987-88, pres. 1988-89, bd. dirs. 1989-90, hon. mem. 1992, ICPAC PAC 1979-92, chmn. PAC 1989-92, Pub. Svc. award 1982-83), Nat. Assn. State Bds. Accountancy (del. 1994—), Mo. Soc. CPA's, U. Ill. Greater Belleville Illini Club (past pres.), Belleville C. of C. (pres. 1973-74), Belleville Jr. C. of C. (life, key Man award 1959-60, Outstanding Citizen award 1976), Belleville Econ. Progress, Inc. (Ambassadors 1973—), U. Ill. Alumni Assn. (life), Lambda Chi Alpha Alumnae Assn., St. Clair County Club. Optimists (life, Belleville Chpt. pres. 1979-80, Disting. Pres. award 1979-80, Optimist of Yr. Belleville, 1977, Ill. Dist. 1980), Elks. Home: 23 Persimmon Rdg Belleville IL 62223-3946 Office: 325 W Main St Belleville IL 62220-1571

FIGADERE, BRUNO ALAIN MARIE, chemist, educator; b. Boulogne, France, May 29, 1960; s. Michel Andre Marie and Nicole Raymonde Marie (Rocard) F. Maitrise Organic Chemistry, U. P&M Curie, Paris, 1983, PhD in Organic Chemistry, 1987; Habil., U. Paris-SUD, 1993. Rschr. U. Calif., Riverside, 1988-90; head of rsch. in chemistry 2ème Classe CNRS, Chatenay-Malabry, France, 1990-93, head of rsch. in chemistry 1ère Classe, 1993—; lectr. Faculty of Pharmacy, U. Paris-SUD, 1992—. Contbr. articles to profl. jours.; patentee in field. Ligue Nationale Contre Le Cancer grantee, 1993-96, Nat. Ministry of Edn. grantee, Paris, 1992—; recipient Bronze medal CNRS, 1994, award Societe Chimie Therapeutique, 1995. Mem. French Chem. Soc., Am. Chem. Soc. Avocations: horseback riding, rock climbing, skiing, sailing. Home: 11 bis Rue de la Remarde, 91530 St Cheron France 92220 Office: CNRS Faculty of Pharmacie, 5 Rue J B Clement, Chatenay-Malabry France 92290

FIGGIS, BRIAN NORMAN, chemistry educator; b. Sydney, NSW, Australia, Mar. 27, 1930; s. John Norman Eric and Dorice Birrell (Hughes) F.; children: Honor Lesley, Benjamin Wiley. MSc, U. Sydney, 1952; PhD, U. NSW, 1956; DSc, U. Western Australia, 1966. Chief chemist M.S.S. Recording Co., Slough, U.K., 1956; post-doctoral fellow U. Coll. London, 1957-58, lectr., 1959-62; reader U. Western Australia, Perth, 1963-68, prof. of chemistry, 1969—; air pollution coun. State Govt., Perth, 1976-82; Australian rsch. coun. Fed. Govt. of Australia, 1986-90. Author: Introduction to Ligand Fields, 1966, Ligard Field Theory and Its Applications, 2000; editor Transition Metal Chemistry, 1982-86; contbr. more than 200 articles to profl. jours. Fellow Royal Australian Chem. Inst., 1964; recipient Walter Burfitt prize Royal Soc. NSW, 1986. Fellow Australian Acad. Scis., Royal Australian Chem. Inst. (H.G. Smith medal 1990, Inorganic medal 1986); mem. Royal Soc. Chemistry. Avocation: DIY. Home: 9 Hamersley St, Cottesloe Australia 6011 Office: U Western Australia, Stirling Hwy, Nedlands Australia 6907

FIGGS, LINDA SUE, educational administrator; b. Westhope, N.D., Dec. 19, 1946; d. Clifford James and Ethel Grace (Geise) Drake; m. Tom R. Figgs, Dec. 27, 1969. Student, Minot State U., 1964-66; B.Music Edn., U. Kans., 1968, M.Music Edn., 1972, EdD, 1978; postgrad., U. del Valle de Mex., 1996, Habla Hispana Lang. Inst. San Miguel de Allende, Guanajuato, Mex., 1997. Cert. secondary music tchr., ednl. adminstr., Kans., Iowa, Nebr., N.D. Music tchr. Jefferson County N. High Sch., Winchester, Kans., 1968-76, 89-91, supr. student tchrs., 1970-75; rsch. asst. to assoc. dean of edn. U. Kans., Lawrence; prin. McKinley Elem., Liberal, Kans., 1992-95, Maynard Elem., Emporia, Kans., 1995-96, Stanton Street Early Childhood Ctr., 1995-96; gen. dir. Academia Cultural de Espanol, San Miguel de Allende, Mex., 1997—; rsch. asst. Sch. Edn., U. Kans., Lawrence, 1977; piano tchr. Toon Shop, Atchison, Kans., Leavenworth, Kans.; music tchr. Little Flower Sch., Minot, N.D., Effingham, Kans.; mgr. music store, Effingham; sec. humanities Minot State U.; counselor Internat. Music Camp, Dunseith, N.D., Midwestern Music and Art Camp, Lawrence; summer counselor, unit leader Nat. Music Camp, Interlochen, Mich.; sponsor 5th grade Positive Peer Group; mem. edn. adv. panel TeleKansas Alliance; mem. U.S. D.480 Action Team Mem., McKinley Action Team Mem.; reader adv. bd. S.W. Daily Times; chmn. rural residency coordinating team Chamber Music Am. and NEA; mem. tech. com. for Unified Sch. Dist. 480 and McKinley Quality Performance Accreditation Team; elem. adminstrn. rep. Stakeholders Com., Sch. Site Coun., strategic planning teams Unified Sch. Dist. 480, McKinley preassessment team, 504 team, intensive assistance team, skunk works, supervision, stakeholders, McKinley Drug Team; bd. dirs., patron, docent Baker Arts Ctr.; coord. ESL and migrant summer sch.; coord. for Unified Sch. Dist. 253 Migrant/ESL program, 1995—; 1st grade prin. rep. for Supt.'s Curriculum Coun. for Sci., elem. prin. rep. sci. com. Singer, pianist, dir. San Miguel Chorale; contbr. articles to profl. publs. Bd. dirs. Am. Youth Symphony Band and Orch., Nebr., 1970-76; music dir. United Meth. Ch., Atchison, 1988-92; mem. choir United Meth. Ch., Liberal, 1992-95; choir dir. 1st Christian Ch., Liberal, 1995, McKinley Elem. PTA, S.W. Kans. Humane soc.; bd. dirs. Cmty. Concert, 1994-95; vol. Mid Am. Air Mus.; mem. 500 Club, Leadership Liberal, 1995, Leadership Emporia, 1996, Maynard Elem. PTO, Maynard Elem. Sch. Site Coun., Flint Hills Humane Soc., SOS, Emporia Arts Coun., Emporia Area Friends of the Zoo. Mem. ASCD, NEA, AAUW (edn. and scholarship com.), Nat. Assn. Elem. Sch. Prins., United Sch. Adminstrs., Kans. Assn. Sch. Adminstrs., Kans. ASCD, Kans. Assn. Elem. Sch. Prins., Kans. Edn. Assn., Nat. Mid. Sch. Assn., Kans. Assn. Mid Level Edn., Kans. Reading Assn., Knas. Reading Coun., Profl. Devel. Coun. (co-pres., insvc. com.), U. Kans. Alumni Assn. (life), S.W. Symphony Soc. (pres. 1993-95), Assn. Cmty. Art Agys. Kans., Emporia Area C. of C. (bus. edn. com.), Sigma Alpha Iota, Pi Kappa Lambda, Phi Delta Kappa. Presbyterian. Avocations: reading, walking, piano performance, computers, stained glass. Address: 1007 Dickinson Rd Effingham KS 66023-5130

FIGUEIRA, FERNANDO FARIA ANDRADE, neurologist, researcher; b. Rio de Janeiro, Feb. 26, 1950; s. Alacil Andrade and Maria Aparecida Faria Andrade (Faria) F.; m. Etna Medeiros Moura, Oct. 19, 1974; children: Rafael, Gustavo, Raquel. MD, Rio de Janeiro U., 1974. Intern, resident Hosp. Miguel Couto, 1974-77; chief dept. neurology Hosp. da Penitencia, Rio de Janeiro, 1984—, med. dir., 1996—, head multiple sclerosis, head stroke rsch. and mgmt. teams, 1999—. Contbr. numerous articles to profl. publs. Fellow Royal Soc. of Medicine (London, U.K.); mem. Brazilian Soc. Cerebrovascular Disease (regional dir. 1994-96), Brazilian Acad. Neurology (sr. mem. 1988—), Am. Soc. Neuroimaging (fgn.), European Neurol. Soc. Office: Hosp de Penitencia, Rua Conde de Bonfim 1033, 20530 Rio de Janeiro Brazil

FIGUEIRA, THOMAS JOHN, classics educator; b. N.Y.C., Dec. 30, 1948; s. Charles Philip Figueira and Marion Catherine Gentile; m. Sarah George, Aug. 14, 1976; children: Elizabeth Anne, Julie Rose, Charles Francis. BA, Fordham U., 1970; PhD, U. Pa., 1977. Vis. asst. prof. classics Stanford U., Palo Alto, Calif., 1977-78; asst. prof. classics Dickinson Coll., Carlisle, Pa., 1978-79, Rutgers U., New Brunswick, N.J., 1979-85; assoc. prof. classics and ancient history Rutgers U., New Brunswick, 1985-91, prof. classics and ancient history, 1991-99, prof. II classics and ancient history, 1999—. Author: Aegina, 1981, Athens and Aigina in the Age of Imperial Colonization, 1991, Excursions in Epichoric History, 1993, The Power of Money: Coinage and Politics in the Athenian Empire, 1998. Rsch. fellow Fulbright Found., Athens, Greece, 1976-77, Summer fellow NEH, Harvard U., 1981, Jr. Rsch. fellow Ctr. for Hellenic Studies, Harvard U., Washington, 1982-83, Rsch. fellow John Simon Guggenheim Found., N.Y.C., 1984-85. Roman Catholic. E-mail: figueira@rci.rutgers.edu. Fax: 732-932-9246. Home: 4 Barnett Rd Lawrenceville NJ 08648-3122 Office: Rutgers Univ Dept Classics 131 George St New Brunswick NJ 08901-1414

FIGUEIREDO, PAULO COSTA, educator; b. Lisbon, Portugal, Apr. 12, 1963; s. Cesar and Sara (Sequeira) F.; m. Maria Margarida Goncalves. BSc, U. Lisbon, 1987, PhD, 1994. Postdoctoral fellow ULP, Strasbourg, France, 1994-95; assoc. prof. U. Lusofona, Lisbon, 1996—. Sgt. Portuguese Army, 1989. Fellow MFCA (coord. 1998—); mem. N.Y. Acad. Scis., Planetary Soc.

FIGUERAS, MARIA JOSE, microbiologist, educator; b. Tarragona, Spain, Mar. 17, 1956; d. Aldredo Figueras and Josefa Salvat; m. Klaas Braaksma, June 17, 1985; children: Gerrit, Saskia. B Biology, U. Barcelona, Spain, 1979, D Biology, 1986. Jr. lectr. in biology U. Barcelona, 1979-83, lectr. in biology, 1983-87, assoc. prof., 1988-92; assoc. prof. U. Rovira Virgili, Spain, 1992—; cons. WHO/UN Environ. Microbiol. Quality of Recreational Waters, 1993-99; advisor European Commn. DGXI Recreational Waters, 1999. Author: Atlas of Clinical Fungi. Rsch. grantee Ministry of Health, Spain, 1996-98, 99—, Catalan Govt., Spain, 1996, 99. Mem. Am. Soc. Microbiology, Brit. Mycological Soc. Avocations: travel, furniture restoration, gardening. Office: Dept Biology/Microbiology, Sant Llorenc 21, 43201 Reus Spain

FIGUEROA, DORYS, military officer; b. Rio Piedras, P.R., Aug. 7, 1970; d. Valentin Miranda and Dora Zeno. B Chemistry, U. P.R., Rio Piedras, 1993; MPA, Jacksonville State U., 1997. Commd. 2d lt. U.S. Army, 1993, advanced through grades to capt.; battalion chem. officer 1-501st AVN BN, Yongsan, Korea, 1994-95; co. exec. officer B/82d Chem. Batallion, Ft. McClellan, Ala., 1995-96; platton leader 11th CM Cp/84th CM BN, Ft. McClellan, 1996-97; asst. regiment chem. officer 2d Armored Cavalry Regiment, Ft. Polk, La., 1998-2000; co. comdr. 87th CM CO/2d ACR, Ft. Polk, 2000—. Avocations: crocheting, playing guitar.

FIGUEROA, KIMBERLY SUSAN, hotel and recreation executive; b. July 7, 1964; m. Alex Figueroa; 1 child: Austin James. BA, Miami U., Oxford, Ohio. Cert. activity cons. Dir. Inova Health Care, Fairfax, Va., 1987-89, Marriott Internat., Ft. Belvoir, Va., 1989-91; mgr. Marriott Internat., Arlington, Va., 1995—; cons. HCR, Toledo, 1991-95; educator, cons. Therapeutic Leisure Cons., Springfield, Va., 1998—. Recipient Cmty. Involvement award (11) Va. Health Care Assn., 1989, 91, 96, 97, 98, 99. Mem. Nat. Assn. Activity Profls. (treas. 1999—, bd. dirs.), Nat. Certification Coun. for Activity Profls. (v.p. 1993-99, bd. dirs.), Va. Assn. Activity Profls. (pres. 1995—, sec. 1993, bd. dirs.). Home: 6816 Jerome St Springfield VA 22150-2010

FIGUEROA HIGUEROS, JUAN CARLOS, electrical engineer; b. Guatemala City, Guatemala, Sept. 27, 1968; s. Carlos Fugueroa Aguja and Bessie Higueros Figueroa. BSEE, U. Kans., 1991. Automations sys. project mgr. Aerolux S.A., Guatemala, 1992-96, Trane Cen. Am., Guatemala, 1997-2000. Mem. Assn. Energy Engrs. Home: PO Box 661447 Miami FL 33266-1447 Office: Trane Cen Am, 18 Calle 19-44 Zona 10, 01010 Guatemala Guatemala

FIGUEROA MARTINEZ, BLANCA, psychologist, consultant; b. Huanuco, Peru, Feb. 2, 1948; f. Antonio Figueroa Verastegui and Blanca Esperanza Martinez Rosazza; m. J. Eduardo Godenzi Diaz, May 8, 1982. BS, Lima H.S., Peru, 1965; B in Psychology, U. Nat. Mayor San Marcos, Peru, 1982; MA in Psychology, U. Oreg., Eugene, 1974, doctoral studies, 1974. Counselor Lane County Juvenile Dept., Eugene, Oreg., 1973-74; chief of psychology Senati, Lima, Peru, 1975-78; rschr. U. Del Pacifico, Lima, Peru, 1983; trainer INFOM, Lima, Peru, 1984-85; rschr. Min. de la Presidencia, Lima, Peru, 1986-90; prof. PUC, Lima, Peru, 1980-85; psychologist CGR, Lima, Peru, 1995-98; counselor pvt. practice, Lima, Peru, 1979—; group cons. SUNAT, Lima, Peru, 1993, M.E.M., Lima, Peru, 1994. Cons. group dynamics, orgnl. devel. Cath. Parish, Surco-Lima, Peru, 1999—. Fulbright scholarship, Eugene, Oreg., 1972--74. Mem. Assn. of Psychologists, Col. of Psychologists of Peru.. Roman Catholic. Avocations: tennis, reading, art galleries, architecture, walking. Home phone: 448-3603. Home and Office: 4444 Av Alfredo Benavides, Lima 33, Peru

FIGWER, JAROSŁAW PIOTR, control engineering researcher; b. Oświecim, Poland, Sept. 11, 1962; s. Józef and Jadwiga (Steczek) F.; m. Romana Kowalska, Aug. 15, 1988; children: Piotr, Maciej. MSc, Silesian Tech. U., Poland, 1986, PhD, 1992. Registered control engr. Asst. prof. Silesian Tech. U., Gliwice, Poland, 1986—. Co-author: Advanced Control with Matlab and Simulink, 1995; contbr. articles to profl. jours. Roman Catholic. Avocations: stamp collecting, swimming. E-mail: jfigwer@i-a.polsl.gliwice.pl. Office: Silesian Tech U Inst Automa, Akademicka 16, 44-100 Gliwice Poland

FIIFI-YANKSON, ALEXANDER, quantity surveyor, researcher; b. Kumasi, Ashanti, Ghana, May 13, 1957; s. Kwesi and Theresa (Eshun) Yankson; m. Mabel Gifty Biney, Feb. 19, 1984; children: Mame Ekua Anowah, Papa Kwesi Sonsomir, Louise Naana Figyina, Alexander Jr. BSc with honors in Bldg. Tech., U. Sci. & Tech., Kumasi, 1982; postgrad. diploma, Inst. Housing Studies, Rotterdam, Holland, 1985; cert. housing, Bldg. Ctr. Japan, Tokyo, 1988; profl. diploma, Ghana Instn. Surveyors, 1988. Cert. cross-cultural mgmt. Asst. quantity surveyor Archl. & Engring. Svcs. Corp., Accra, Ghana, 1984-87, quantity surveyor, 1987-88; regional quality surveyor Archl. & Engring. Svcs. Corp., Sunyani, Ghana, 1989-95, head project planning and coord. unit, 1996; regional quantity surveyor Archl. & Engring. Svcs. Corp., Koforidua, 1997—. Mem. Ghana Instn. Surveyors, Full Gospel Men's Fellowship Internat. (voice dir. 1992-96). Mem. Ch. of Pentecost Internat. Avocations: reading, stamp collecting. Home: Bungalow No A2, Akwadum Rd PO Box, KF 2230 Koforidua Ghana Office: Archtl & Engring Svcs Ltd, PO Box 702, Koforidua E/R Ghana

FIJN, ROEL, clinical pharmacologist; b. Hattem, Gelderland, The Netherlands, Aug. 12, 1973; s. Hendrik Dirk and Adriana Antonia (van Rosmalen) F.; m. Janneke van Oers, Apr. 12, 1978. MPharmSc, U. Groningen, The Netherlands, 1996, RPh, 1997, postgrad., 2000. Cert. pharmacoepidemiologist, clin. pharmacologist. Jr. pharmacoepidemiologist U. Groningen, 1997-98, sr. pharmacoepidemiologist, 1998-2000. Contbr. articles to profl. jours. Mem. Internat. Soc. for Pharmacoepidemiology, European Soc. for Clin. Pharmacy, European Soc. for Clin. Pharmacology and Therapeutics. Fax: 31 50 3632772. Office: U Groningen Dept Pharmacoep, A Deusinglaan 7, 9713 AV Groningen The Netherlands

FIKIORIS, GEORGE JOHN, researcher; b. Boston, Dec. 3, 1962; Arrived in Greece, 1998; s. John George and Avgi (Andronikos) F.; m. Spyridoula Konstantinidou, May 1, 1993; 1 child, John. Diploma, Nat. Tech. U. Athens, Greece, 1986; SM, Harvard U., 1987, PhD, 1993. Cert. in engring. Rsch./tchg. asst. Harvard U., Cambridge, Mass., 1987-93; electronics engr. Air Force Rsch. Lab., Hanscom AFB, Mass., 1993-98; rschr. Nat. Tech. U. Athens, 1999—. Contbr. articles to profl. jours. Mem. IEEE, Am. Math. Soc., Sigma Xi. Home: 25A Solomou St, GR 15233 Halandri Athens, Greece Office: Nat Tech U Athens, Dept Elec & Computer Engrin, GR 15773 Zografou Athens, Greece

FIKS, ARSEN PHILLIP, retired physician, researcher; b. Odessa, Ukraine, Apr. 23, 1930; came to U.S., 1978; s. Phillip G. and Klara M. (Kolkin) F.; m. Eva Bubis, Sept. 16, 1951 (div. Sept. 1979); 1 child, Vitaly; m. Irina Bozilenko, June 20, 1984; 1 stepchild, Marina. MD, Odessa Med. Sch., 1952, PhD, 1972. Pathologist, dept. chief pathomorphology State Oncology Hosp., Odessa, USSR, 1956-77; sr. pathologist Ill. Inst. Tech. Rsch. Inst., Chgo., 1979-84; rsch. assoc. cytology U. Chgo., 1989-92; sr. cytotechnologist Roshe BioMed. Labs., Northbrook, Ill., 1989-92; cytotechnologist MatPath, Inc., Wood Dale, Ill., 1992-2000; ret., 2000; pathologist Kiev Radio-Oncology Inst., 1960-61, Moscow Oncology Ctr., 1964, Leningrad Inst. Oncology, 1968, The Armed Forces Inst. Pathology, Washington, 1980, U. Chgo., 1986; rschr. in pathology, oncology, the history of medicine and biology, cosmobiology, history of scis., and self-experimentation. Contbr. more than 100 articles to profl. jours. including Archives Pathology, Clin. Surg., Problems Oncology, Urology, Breast Cancer Rsch. and Treatment, among others. Recipient Highest Category Pathologist award State Pub. Health Office, 1969. Mem. Internat. Soc. for Chronobiology, Internat. Acad. Cytology, Internat. Acad. Pathology, Am. Assn. for Cancer Rsch. Avoca-

tion: classical music. Home: 360 E Randolph St Apt 1108 Chicago IL 60601-7333

FILA, JOSEPH DUNCAN, marketing and sales executive, public relations executive, real estate broker; b. Elizabeth, N.J., Jan. 2, 1950; s. Joseph Charles and Agnes McCallum (Muller) F.; m. Ann Therese Scott, Dec. 11, 1971; children: Dawn Nicole, Daniel Aaron. Comm. dir. Better World Inst., Miami, 1973-74; graphic designer ID Assoc., Miami, 1974-76; pres. Conceptum, Inc., Miami, 1976-87; assoc. Radian Realty Corp., Miami, 1982-85, Income Realty Corp., Miami, 1985-87; exec. v.p. Cervera Real Estate, Miami, 1987-91; v.p. Markets Abroad, Inc., Espoo, Finland, 1987-91; pres. Fila Assoc., Inc., Miami, 1987-96; v.p. mktg. and sales Bldg. Inspection Svcs., 1991-95; broker assoc. Cervera Real Estate, Miami, 1991—; dir. mktg. and sales Vidicomp, Miami, 1995-97; N.Am. sales dir. Aethra Telecomm., Miami, 1998-2000; v.p., gen. mgr. Audio Visual Solutions Corp., 2000—; trustee So. Fla. Ctr. Theol. Studies, Miami, 1989-96; assoc. Bus. Coun. Internat. Understand., N.Y.C., 1989—; guest instr. U. Miami, 1986-88. Editor Rotary Caribbean Chronicle, 1985-88. Pres. Elephant Forum, Miami, 1990-92; del. White House Conf. Small Bus., Washington, 1986, Curacao (N.Am.) Symposium Free Enterprise Caribbean, 1984; spl. advisor Sec. Commerce Fla. VOICE Program, Miami, 1987-90; committeeman, membership chmn. Rep. Party Dade County, Miami, 1988-96; mem. Fla. del. Rep. Nat. Conv., 1992; scoutmaster Boy Scouts Am., 1973-85; mem. Am. Forum, 1993-98. Mem. Soc. Broadcast Engrs., Internat. TV Assn., Bldg. Industry Assn. South Fla., Fla. Motion Picture and TV Assn., Coral Gables C.C. (chmn. Caribbean rels. and pub. rels. coms. 1980-85), Finish Am. C. of C. (bd. dirs.), Rotary (pres. Miami West club 1987-88, chmn. dist. pub. rels. com. 1983-84, comm. dir. Fla./Caribbean project 1983-88, internat. pub. rels. consultative com. 1988-89, dist. comm. chmn. 2000—), Miami Club (dir. 1996-98). Avocations: archery, fishing, camping, travel, motorcycling. Fax: (305375-0655. E-mail: jaddfila@earthlink.net. Home: 16423 SW 111th Ave Miami FL 33157-2828 Office: Audio Visual Solutions 928-930 N Federal Hwy Hollywood FL 33020

FILAKOVSKY, KAROL, aerodynamics educator, researcher; b. Velka Lodina, Slovakia, Dec. 14, 1935; s. Jozef and Margita (Rendosova) F.; m. Pavla Valouskova, Apr. 11, 1964; children: Karol, Ivan. Diploma in engring., Mil. Acad., Brno, Czechoslovakia, 1961, PhD, 1973; diploma in math., U. Brno, 1970. Asst. lectr. Mil. Acad., Brno, 1961-69; rschr. Mil. Rsch. Inst., Brno, 1970-72; rschr. Tech. U., Brno, 1973-82, assoc. prof., 1980-86, lectr., prof., 1987—, head dept. aircraft, 1983-91, dean Faculty Mech. Engring., 1985-89. Mem. Czech Soc. for Wind Energy (mem. top com. 1994-96). Home: Loosova 2, 638 00 Brno Czech Republic Office: Tech U, Technicka 2, 616 69 Brno Czech Republic

FILATOV, VLADIMIR VICTOROVICH, electrical and nuclear scientist, engineer; b. Borovsk, Kaluga, Russia, June 24, 1961; s. Victor Petrovich and Lidiya Ivanovna (Zvonilina) F.; m. Marina Evgenievna Pronina, Sept. 19, 1981; children: Valentin, Philipp. Diplom Engr., Bauman Higher Tech. Sch., Moscow, 1984; PhD, Efremov Inst., St. Petersburg, Russia, 1997. Engr. Efremov Inst., St. Petersburg, 1984-88, design engr., 1988-91, scientist, 1991-98, sr. scientist, 1998—, leader project of neutron source based on Tokamak, 1994-98. Contbr. articles to profl. jours. Sec. Group of Young League, St. Petersburg, 1985-88; soccer coach, sport organizer Iskra Sport Club, St. Petersburg, 1986-91. Internat. Sci. Found. grantee, 1994. Orthodox Ch. Avocations: books, soccer playing, nature, theatre, cinema. Home: App 142, Sadovaya 18 Metallostroy, 189631 Saint Petersburg Russia

FILATOVA, NADEZHDA IVANOVNA, geologist, laboratory administrator, researcher; b. Moscow, Russia, May 2, 1933. Degree in Geology, Prospecting Inst., Moscow, 1955, PhD in Geology, 1966, prof. D in Geology, 1985. Cert. in geol. engring. Chief geol. team Ministry of Geology, Moscow, 1956-85; chief of rsch. lab. Inst. Lithosphere, Moscow, 1985—. Author: Perioceanic Volcanic Belts, 1988; contbr. articles to profl. jours. Avocations: nature, travel, skiing. E-mail: filatova@ibran.ru. Office: Lithosphere/Russian Acad Sc, Staromonetney per 22, 109180 Moscow Russia

FILATOVA, NATALIA PETROVNA, cardiologist researcher; b. Khabarovsk, Russia, July 21, 1945; d. Peter Prokhorovich Filatov and Khava Savelievna Simkho. MD, First Med. Inst., Moscow, Russia, 1968, PhD, 1981. Highest qualification in cardiology Ministry of Medicine, 1996. Physician City Hosp. N32, Moscow, 1968-72; postgrad. student First Med. Inst., Moscow, 1972-74, cardiologist, 1974-82; rschr. All-Russian Ctr. for Prevention Medicine, Moscow, 1982-89, sr. rschr., 1989-97; cardiologist Health Ctr. for Cardiac Diseases, Moscow, 1997—; cons. Nat. Rsch. Ctr. for Endocrinology, Moscow, 1997-99. Contbg. author: Preventive Pharmacology in Cardiology, 1988; contbr. numerous articles to profl. jours. Mem. Assn. Cardiologists, Acad. Scis. N.Y. Avocations: travel, hiking. Home: Second Setunsky str 4 65, 119136 Moscow Russia Office: Health Ctr Cardiac Diseases, Acad Anokhin str 22/1, 117602 Moscow Russia

FILBY, IVAN LEONARD, academic administrator; b. King's Lynn, England, Apr. 20, 1962; s. Leonard William and Mary Elizabeth (Day) F.; m. Kathie Susanne Taggart, July 26, 1991; children: Samuel, Katie. BS in Mgmt. & Adminstrv. Scis., Aston U., Birmingham, England, 1984, PhD, 1990; MA, Dublin U., 1993. Lectr. bus. studies Trinity Coll., Dublin, 1989-99, dir. internat. student affairs, 1999—, chair Irish Coun. for Internat. Students; vis. prof. U. Anahuac, Mexico City, Mex., 1999; dir. Cornerstone Christian Ch., Dublin, 1993; expert European Commn., Brussels, 1994—. Contbr. articles to profl. jours. Office: Trinity Coll, Dublin 2, Ireland

FILDES, RICHARD JAMES, lawyer; b. N.Y.C., Nov. 9, 1952; s. Edgar E. and Lucille (Sanna) F.; m. Deborah D. Davenport, June 21, 1979; children: Matthew, Melissa, Heather. BS in Psychology and Econs. magna cum laude, Duke U., 1974; JD cum laude, U. Fla., 1977. Bar: Fla. 1977. Ptnr. Lowndes, Drosdick, Doster, Kantor & Reed, Orlando, Fla., 1977—, also bd. dirs., mem. mgmt. com.; past pres. Fla. Citrus Sports Assn., Inc.; trustee, dir. at large Fla. Citrus Sports Found., Inc. Mem. Lake Nona Club. Democrat. Roman Catholic. Avocations: golf, working out, fishing, reading, running. Office: Lowndes Drosdick Doster et al 215 N Eola Dr Orlando FL 32801-2095

FILE, JOSEPH, research physics engineer; b. Lecce, Italy, May 6, 1923; s. Carlo and Laura (Nuzzi) F.; m. Dorothy Richards, Sept. 2, 1944; children: Joseph C., Laurel M., Jeannette. BME, Cornell U., 1944; MS, Columbia U., 1958, PhD, 1967; Dr.Physics, U. Lecce, Italy, 1978. Design engr. Petro Chem. Devel. Co., N.Y.C., 1946-56; rsch. sr. Princeton (N.J.) U., 1956—; advisor N.E. region Fed. Lab. Consortium, 1992—; ofcl. U.S. rep. 2d Atoms for Peace Conf., Geneva, 1958; Def. Dept. appointee Employer Support for the Guard and Res., 1995. Contbr. articles to profl. jours. Pres. Marine Corps Scholarship Found., 1965-75, chmn. bd. dirs., 1975-94, chmn. emeritus. Col. USMCR, 1942-74; PTO, Korea. Decorated comdr. Order of Italian Republic; Fulbright fellow, 1978. Roman Catholic. Achievements include patent on bending free D, shaped magnetic coils for fusion reactors, and fabrication and operation of world's first sixth order superconducting magnet now used on MRI imaging devices. Office: PPPL Princeton U Princeton NJ 08543

FILEP, LÁSZLÓ, mathematics educator; b. Császló, Hungary, Dec. 6, 1941; s. Gusztáv Filep and Margit Irén Kósa; m. Sarolta Dömötör, Dec. 25, 1966. M in Math. and Physics, Lajos Kossuth U., Debrecen, Hungary, 1964, degree in math., 1978, PhD in Math., 1995; diploma in math., Loránd Eötvös U., Budapest, Hungary, 1973. Tchr. secondary sch., Nyíregyháza, Hungary, 1964-73; lectr. Bessenyei Coll. Edn., Nyíregyháza, 1973-83, assoc. prof., 1983-87, 94-95, prof., head quality assurance unit, 1994—; lectr. Al-Fateh U., Tripoli, Libya, 1987-90, 92-94. Author: History of Numerals, Hungarian edit., 1982, Bulgarian edit., 1988, 2d Hungarian edit., 1999, Game Theory, 1985, Queen of Sciences-Development of Mathematics, 1997; contbr. articles to profl. jours. Adv. bd. internat. study group History and Pedagogy Math.; mem. Internat. Commn. History Math., Global Alliance Transnational Edn. Mem. János Bolyai Math. Soc. Mem. Calvinist Ch. Avocations: history, politics, traveling. Office: Coll Nyiregyhaza, Sóstói ut 31b, H 4400 Nyiregyháza Hungary

FILEVICH, ALBERTO, physicist, researcher, educator; b. Cordoba, Argentina, Feb. 10, 1938; s. Alejandro and Fanny (Israilevich) F.; m. Clelia Chamatropulos, May 9, 1967; children: Oscar, Jorge, Elisa. Elec. engr., U. Cordoba, Argentina, 1962; licenciado en fisica, U. Cuyo, Bariloche, Argentina, 1963, doctor en fisica, 1974; licenciado en ciencias, Faculty Scis. U. Chile, Santiago, 1972. Tchr. Cordoba, Cuyo, Buenos Aires (Argentina) U., 1957-65; rsch. fellow Bariloche (Argentina) Inst., 1964-66; rsch. staff mem. Chile U. Cyclotron Lab., Santiago, 1967-74; rsch. staff mem. physics dept., Synchrocyclotron lab., Tandar Lab. Comision Nacional de Energia Atomica (Argentina), Buenos Aires, 1974—, head exptl. divsn., 1980-84; visiting rschr. Atomfysik Inst., Stockholm (Sweden) U., 1968-71, Brookhaven Nat. Lab., Upton, N.Y., 1978-80, Manne Siegbahn Inst., Stockholm (Sweden) U., 1989-91; expert mission IAEA, Vienna, Austria, La Habana, Cuba, 1989; rsch. fellow Nat. Rsch. Coun. Argentina, Buenos Aires, 1992—; invited prof. Inst. des Scis. Nucleaires, Grenoble, France, 1993; mem. Pierre Auger Collaboration, 1995-99; site mgr. So. Auger Obs. for High-Energy Cosmic Radiation. Inventor in field; contbr. articles to profl. jours. Fellow CONICET, Argentine Phys. Assn., CNEA's Profl. Assn. Avocations: diving, music, electronics, reading, computing. Home: Pringles 3268, 1602 Florida Argentina Office: CNEA Atomic Energy Commn, Ave Libertador 8250, 1429 Buenos Aires Argentina

FILHO, WALDIR SILVA, military educator; b. Cachoeiro de Itapemirim, Brazil, Dec. 6, 1960; s. Waldir and Nilza (Moreira) Silva; d. Regina Lucia Allemand Mancebo, Sept. 6, 1986; 1 child, Pedro A.M. Student, Academia Militar das Agulhas Negras, Brazil, 1985, Escola Aperfeicoamento Oficias, Brazil, 1993, U.S. Army Armor Sch., 1995. Commd. officer Brazilian Army Cavalry, 1985, advanced through grades to maj., 1998; platoon leader, co. comdr. 1st Regimento de Cavalaria, Ponta Porã, Brazil, 1986-92; helicopter pilot, flight instr. Centro de Instrucão de Aviacao do Exerito, Taubate, Brazil, 1992-96; tank co. comdr. 1st Regimento de Carros de Combate, Rio de Janeiro, 1996; exec. officer, instr. Centro de Instrução de Blindados, Brazil, 1997—. Author of mil. manuals for Brazilian Army. Active Brazilian Bapt. Conv., 1975. Avocations: scuba diving, fishing, horses. Office: CIbld, Av Brasil 25540, 21615331 Rio de Janeiro Brazil

FILIMONOV, MIKHAIL ANATOLYEVITCH, investment company executive; b. Odessa, Ukraine, Oct. 26, 1956; came to the U.S., 1971; s. Anatoly M. and Ludmila G. (Yankelevitch) F.; m. Lena Vayman (div.); 1 child, Alexandra K. AAS, N.Y. Tech. Coll., 1982; BS, Baruch Coll., 1983. V.p. Arnhold & S. Bleichroder, N.Y.C., 1983, Cresvale Internat., London and N.Y.C., 1984; 1st v.p. Quadrex Securities, N.Y.C., 1985-87; v.p. Baring Securities, N.Y.C., 1987-90; first v.p. London Investment Trust Am., Inc., N.Y.C., 1990-92; chmn., chief investment officer, CEO Alexandra Investment Mgmt. (formerly Hermes Capital Mgmt.), N.Y.C., 1992—; bd. dirs. Alexandra Global Investment Fund, Brit. Virgin Islands. Republican. Office: Alexandra Investment Mgmt 237 Park Ave Fl 9 New York NY 10017-3140

FILIMONOVA, GALINA F., medical educator; b. Vyshnij Volotchek, Tver, Russia, Sept. 20, 1940; d. Filipp F. and Maria G. Trjapochkina Filimonov; m. Ivan B. Tokin, Sept. 22, 1967; children: Ivan, Anna. MD, Med. Inst., Leningrad, Russia, 1963, DSc, 1967. Cert. excellent med. diplomate. Scientist Inst. Obstetrics-Gynecology Acad. Med. Sci., Leningrad, 1963-72; head lab. cytology Inst. Marine Biology, Murmansk, 1972-82; asst. pof. State Med. Acad., St. Petersburg, Russia, 1982-86, prof., 1986—. Author: (books) Digestive System of Echinoderms, 1978 (premium and diploma of cola divsn. Acad. Sci. 1979), Modelling of Some Liver Functions, 1993, (with I. B. Tokin) Mercury Dynamics in Human Body, 1994, Intestinal Epithelium: Proliferation, Regulation, Apoptosis, 1997. Named Hon. Citizen, local govt., Severomorsk, 1980; grantee Internat. Sci. Found., 1994, German Radiation Rsch. Soc., 1995. Mem. Soc. Ecology and Ecotoxicology (v.p. 1997—, grantee 1997), Soc. Anatomists, Histologists and Embryologists of USSR. Orthodox. Avocation: painting. Office: State Med Acad, Piscarevskij Prosp 47, Saint Petersburg 195067, Russia

FILIP, FLORIN-GHEORGHE ION, information scientist, researcher; b. Bucharest, Romania, July 25, 1947; s. Ion Gheorghe and Georgeta Petre (Marinescu) F.; m. Georgeta Gheorghe Georgescu, Aug. 10, 1974; children: Mihai-Florin, Christian-Ioan, Gabriel-Gheorghe. MSc, Tech. U. Bucharest, 1970, PhD, 1982. Rsch. engr. Rsch. Inst. for Informatics, Bucharest, 1970-79, sr. researcher, 1979-85, head rsch. lab., 1985-91, dir., 1991-97, sci. dir., 1997—; coord. nat. rsch. and devel. program in informatics, Nat. Coun. for Rsch. and Devel., Bucharest, 1993-94. Co-author: Hierarchical Real Time Systems, 1986, Industrial Informatics, 1997; contbr. articles to profl. jours.; editor-in-chief Informatics and Control Publs., 1991—. Mem. Nat. Coun. Sci. and Tech., Romanian Forum for Information Soc. (v.p. 1997), Romanian Acad. (v.p. 2000—), N.Y. Acad. Scis., Romanian Soc. for Automation and Tech. Info. (v.p. 1992—). Avocations: history, opera, tennis. Office: Rsch Inst for Informatics, M Averescu Ave 8-10, 71316 Bucharest Romania

FILIP, HENRY (HENRY PETRZILKA), physicist; b. Chgo., Mar. 29, 1920; s. Joseph and Aloisie (Filip) Petrzilka; m. Marie Louise Krajcovic, Sept. 17, 1957; children: Henry Jr., Frederick, Marie Louise; 1 stepchild, Jan Janecka. BS, Ill. Wesleyan U., 1944. Tech. asst. Fermi Pile, Manhattan Project U. Chgo., 1944; rsch. asst. atom bomb external trigger system Los Alamos (N.Mex.) Nat. Lab., 1944-49, rsch. asst. internal neutron source for atom bomb, 1949-56, exptl. researcher Rover program Flyable Nuclear Reactor, 1956-72, exptl. researcher isotope separation program, 1972-84, exptl. physicist x-ray analysis of atomic explosions, 1984-85; exptl. physicist Western Rsch. Corp., San Diego, 1985; exptl. physicist Star Wars Laser System Jan Bec Corp., San Diego, 1985-88; cons. x-ray analysis Los Alamos Nat. Lab., 1984-85, Western Rsch. Corp., San Diego, 1984-85. Mem. Pierottis Clowns. Mem. Palisade Lions (bd. mem. 1989-92), Los Alamos Rotary (pres. 1983-87), Los Alamos Kiwanis (hon.). Democrat. Avocations: woodworking, golf, skiing. Home: PO Box 38 362 W 1st St Palisade CO 81526-8781

FILIP, KAREL, health facility administrator; b. Česká Lípa, Czechoslovakia, Feb. 1, 1951; s. Karel and Vlasta (Nejedlá) F.; m. Helena Sobelová, June 28, 1973; children: Helena, Karolína. MD, Charles U., Prague, Czech Republic, 1975, PhD, 1988. Resident Dist. Hosp. Mimoň, Czech Republic, 1975-79, gen. practitioner, 1979-80; postdoctoral rsch. fellow Inst. Clin. and Exptl. Medicine, Prague, 1981-87, rschr., 1987-91, pres., 1991—; presenter in field. Contbr. articles to profl. jours. Capt. Czechoslovakian Air Force, 1975-76. Home: K Novému Dvoru 41, 142 00 Prague 4 Czech Republic Office: Inst Clin & Exptl Medicine, Vídeňská 800, 140 00 Prague 4 Czech Republic

FILIPOVSKY, JAN, physician, educator; b. Plzen, Czech Republic, July 4, 1958; s. Alexandr and Olga (Mrazova) F.; m. Helena Krausova, Dec. 7, 1986; children: Tereza, Eva. MD, Charles U., Plzen, Czech Republic, 1985; PhD, Charles U., Prague, Czech Republic, 1997. House officer U. Hosp., Plzen, 1985-90, sr. lectr., 1992-98, assoc. prof., 1998—; rsch. fellow INSERM, Paris, 1990-92; rsch. cons. Les Laboratoires Servier, Prague, Czech Republic, 1995—. Contbr. articles to profl. jours. including Cardiology, Hypertension, Internat. Jour. Obesity, and Jour. Hypertension. Mem. French Soc. Arterial Hypertension, European Soc. Hypertension, Czech Soc. Cardiology. Avocation: classical music. Home: Purkynova 31, 30136 Plzen Czech Republic Office: U Hosp 2d Dept Internal Med, E Benese 13, 30599 Plzen Czech Republic

FILIPPELLI-DIMANNA, LESLIE PAMELA, fundraiser; b. Providence, R.I., Apr. 5, 1966; d. Louis Pasquale and Virginia Rose (Giannamore) F.; m. Giampiero DiManna, Oct. 22, 1994. BA in Comms./Pub. Rels., R.I. Coll., 1988; MBA, Bryant Coll., 1992, Cert. Advanced Grad. Studies, 1999. Cert. fundraising exec. Nat. Soc. of Fundraising Execs. Dir. of devel. ARC of No. Bristol County, Attleboro, Mass., 1992-94, SENECA Health System, Narragansett, R.I., 1994-97; pres. VNA Found., Providence, 1997—. Mem. Nat. Soc. Fundraising Execs. (bd. dirs. R.I. chpt. 1996-98), Assn. Healthcare Philanthropy, New Eng. Assn. Healthcare Philanthropy. Roman Catholic. Office: VNA Found 167 Point St Providence RI 02903-4771

FILIPPOV, ANDREY ALEXANDROVICH, medical microbiologist, researcher; b. Nakhodka, USSR, Aug. 10, 1956; s. Alexander Fiodorovich and Alexandra Vasilievna (Smirnova) F.; m. Larisa Mikhailovna Fiodorova, May 15, 1982; children: Alexander, Mikhail. Diploma in Therapeutics, Med. Inst., Saratov, Russia, 1979; PhD, Anti-Plague Inst., Saratov, Russia, 1983, diploma Specialist Dangerous Infections, 1983. Jr. scientist Anti-Plague Inst., Saratov, 1983-87, chmn. Inter-Inst. Coun. Young Scientists, 1987-89, sr. scientist, 1987-98, head scientist, 1998-99, promoter PhD competitors, 1992—, mem. Inter-Inst. Sci. Problem Com., 1994—, head dept., 1999—; lead author joint rsch. project U. Calif., Livermore, 1998—. Author: Contributions to Microbiology and Immunology, 1995; contbr. articles to profl. jours. Grantee Internat. Sci. Found., 1993, Internat. Sci. Found. and Russian Acad. Natural Scis., 1994, Russian Found. Basic Rsch., 1996. Mem. Russian Soc. Microbiologists, Russian Soc. Geneticists, Am. Soc. for Microbiology. Mem. Orthodox Ch. Avocations: collecting books, listening to classical and modern music, fishing. Home: Knyazevsky vzvoz 3/5, 410002 Saratov Russia Office: Russian Rsch Anti-Plague Inst, Universitetskaya Str 46, 410005 Saratov Russia

FILIPPOV, BORIS, astrophysicist; b. Cherlak, Omsk, Russia, Sept. 1, 1951; s. Petr Filippov and Filippova Varaksina Ekaterina; m. Olesya Martsenyuk, Oct. 1, 1986; children: Aglaya, Polina. Diploma in Physics, Moscow State U., 1975; PhD in Physics and Math., Pulkovo Observatory, St. Petersburg, Russia, 1984; Sr. Rsch. Scientist, Inst. of Terrestrial Magnetism, Russian Acad. of Scis., Troitsk, Moscow, 1994, DSc in Physics and Math., 1998. Rsch. scientist Inst. Terrestrial Magnetism, Ionosphere/Russian Acad. Sci., Troitsk, Moscow, 1975-96, sr. rsch. scientist, 1987-93, head Lab. of Solar Activity, 1993—; head expedition for solar eclipse observations Russian Acad. of Scis., Vietnam, 1995, Russia, 1997, Romania, 1999. Co-author: (book) Magnetic Fields of Solar Active Regions, 1992; contbr. articles to profl. jours. Rsch. grantee Am. Astron. Soc., 1992, Russian Found. for Basic Rsch., Moscow, 1993, 96. Mem. European Astron. Soc. Avocation: physics. E-mail: bfilip@izmiran.troitsk.ru. Home: Pushkov St 3 Apt 3, 142 190 Moscow Troitsk, Russia Office: Russian Acad Scis, Izmiran, 142 190 Moscow Troitsk, Russia

FILIPPOV, GENNADIY MIKHAILOVICH, physicist, educator; b. Cheboksary, Russia, Jan. 20, 1938; s. Mikhail Egorovitch and Maria Vasilievna (Baimekova) F.; m. Valentina Grigorjevna Agafonova, May 12, 1963 (div. Oct. 1966); children: Mikhail, Pavel; m. Nina Vasilievna Gudz', June 27, 1978; children: Maria, Anna. Physicist, Moscow State U., 1961, MSc in Physics, 1968; PhD in Physics, Tomsk (Russia) State U., 1992; habilitation, Chuvash State U., Cheboksary, Russia, 1994. Head of rsch. group ECBA, Moscow, 1964-69; tchr. Chuvash State U., 1969-71, lectr., 1971-94, prof., 1994—; cons. Experience Constrn. Bur. Automatization, Moscow, 1964-69; head physics dept. Chuvash State U., 1976—. Contbr. articles to profl. jours. Grantee Russian Found. Basic Rsch., Moscow, 1997. Mem. Internat. Assn. Math. Physics. Avocations: gardening, car travel. Home: Apt 71, Gagarin-St 45, 428022 Cheboksary Russia Office: Chuvash State U Theor Phys, Moscovskiy prospect 15, 428015 Cheboksary Russia

FILIPPOV, VLADIMIR MIKHAYLOVICH, federal official; b. 1952. Rector U. People's Friendship, 1993-98; min. Ministry of Edn., Moscow, 1998—. Office: Ministry of Edn, Ul Ljusinovskaya 51, 113833 Moscow 113833, Russia*

FILIPSKI, JAN FELIKS, molecular biologist, pharmacologist; b. Warsaw, Oct. 14, 1940; s. Czeslaw and Irena Felicja Aniela (Zakrzewska) F.; m. Elizabeth S. Jablonska, Mar. 18, 1979; children: Zuzanna Irena, Mateusz Jan. MSc in Chemistry, Silesian Polytechnic, Gliwice, 1963, PhD in Chemistry, 1969. Asst. Silesian Med. Sch., Zabrze, 1963-67; rsch. officer Inst. Oncology, Gliwice, 1967-77; sr. scientist Inst. Nat. de la Santé et de la Recherche Med. (INSERM), Paris, 1983—; prof. biol. scis. Wroclaw U., 1999—; vis. scientist Nat. Cancer Inst., NIH, Bethesda, Md., 1977-83; invited lectr. Med. Sch., Paris, 1990—; mem. adv. bd. European Jour. Biochemistry, Zurich, 1985-95; mem. sci. contact expert L'Academie des Scis., Paris, 1992—. Contbr. numerous articles to profl. jours. including Sci., Nature, Biochemistry and Jour. Molecular Biology. Fellow WHO, 1971; recipient Pres.'s award Nat. Rsch. Coun. Can., 1989; grantee Groupement de Recherches et d'Etudes sur les Genomes, 1993. Avocations: playing piano, skiing, swimming, hiking. Home: 6 Ave de la Porte Brancion, 75015 Paris France Office: Institut J Monod, 2 Pl Jussieu Tour 43, 75251 Paris France

FILJAR, RENATO, information technology specialist, consultant; b. Kalinovac, Croatia, Oct. 13, 1963; s. Ivan and Mira (Hrvatic) F. BSc in Elec. Engring., Zagreb U., 1987, MSc in Elec. Engring., 1994. R&D engr. Koncar Elektronics and Computers, Zagreb, 1987-91; ind. GPS applications engr. Kalinovac, 1991-96; tchr. Mid. Tech. Sch., Djurdjevac, 1991-96; ind. cons. for GPS applications Kalinovac, 1996—; sr. telecom. engr. Jadranski Naftovod, Zagreb, 1996—; invited lectr. Mid. Tech. Sch., Djurdjevac, 1998—; ind. cons., Kalinovac, 1996—. Contbr. articles to profl. jours. including Jour. Navigation. Mem. Royal Inst. Navigation, N.Y. Acad. Scis., Croatian Soc. Elmar, Meteorol. and Navigational Soc. (founder, chmn. bd. Kalinovac 2000—). Avocations: amateur radio, hill walking, travelling, photography, books. Home: Dravska 44A, 48361 Kalinovac Croatia Office: Jadranski Naftovod, Terminal Virje, 48326 Virje Croatia

FILKER, HANS GEORG, city administrator; b. Schwarzenberg, Germany, Dec. 29, 1949; s. Hans Georg and Lotte (Rauchfuss) F.; m. Claudia Berndt, Oct. 15, 1957; children: Maren, Judith, Mikko, Mathis, Lukas, Samuel. Theol. exam., Luth. Ch. Rhineland, Germany, 1977. Asst. prof. Kirchliche Hochschule, Wuppertal, Germany, 1977-80; youth pastor Synod of Barmen, Wuppertal, 1980-89; chief exec. dir. Berlin City Mission, 1989—. Author: Bis das der Trott uns scheidet, 1997; editor: Bitte Kommen Sie zu Sache, 1992. Mem. Assn. Germany City Missions (pres. 1990—), City Mission World Assn. (dir. 1994—), Ak ev. Unternehmer, Rotary, European Assn. of City Missions (pres. 1998—). Office: Berlin City Mission, Lenaustr 4, D 12047 Berlin Germany

FILLAUX, FRANCOIS JOSEPH, research chemist; b. Paris, Mar. 12, 1942; s. Fernand Georges and Yvonne Jenny (Cusin) F.; m. Joelle Lafore, July 2, 1971; children: Judith, Clara, Thomas. Engring. degree, Sch. of Physics and Chemistry, Paris, 1967; DSc, U. Paris, 1972. With dept. rsch. Ctr. Nat. de la Recherche Sci., Paris, 1969-77; head dept. rsch. Ctr. Nat. de la Recherche Sci., Thiais, France, 1978-84, dir. rsch., 1985—. Contbr. over 100 articles to profl. jours. and books. Home: 32 rue du Javelot, 75645 Paris cedex 13, France Office: LADIR-Ctr Nat Recherche Sci, 2 rue Henry Dunant, 94320 Thiais France

FILLEY, CHRISTOPHER MARK, neurologist; b. Saranac Lake, N.Y., July 31, 1951; s. Giles Franklin and Mary Brown (Klinefelter) F. BA, Williams Coll., 1973; MD, Johns Hopkins U., 1979. Diplomate Am. Bd. Psychiatry and Neurology. Intern U. Conn., Farmington, 1979-80; resident in neurology U. Colo., Denver, 1980-83; behavioral neurology fellow Boston U., 1983-84; from instr. to asst. prof. neurology U. Colo. Sch. Medicine, Denver, 1984-91, assoc. prof. neurology, 1991-97, prof. neurology, 1997—; prin. investigator studies in Alzheimers Disease NIH, Bethesda, Md., 1991-94. Author: Neurobehavioral Anatomy, 1995, Best Doctors in America, 1996-97, 1998-99; contbr. articles to profl. jours. Health com. Denver Found., 1995-98. Mem. Am. Acad. Neurology, Am. Neurol. Assn., Internat. Neuropsychol. Soc., Behavioral Neurology Soc., Colo. Soc. Clin. Neurologists. Avocations: piano, hiking, reading, guitar, skiing. E-mail: christopher.filley@uchsc.edu. Office: Univ Colo Behavioral Neurology Sect 4200 E 9th Ave Denver CO 80220-3700

FILLIOS, LOUIS CHARLES, retired science educator; b. Boston, July 1, 1923; s. Charles Louis and Pagona (Kefalas) F.; m. Iphigenia Loomis, June 15, 1947; children: Despena, Diana, Hilary. AB, Harvard, 1948, MS, 1953, ScD, 1956. Rsch. assoc., then assoc. Harvard U., 1956-60; asst. prof. physiol. chemistry MIT, 1961-64, assoc. prof., 1964-66; assoc. rsch. prof. biochemistry and pathology Boston U. Sch. Medicine, 1966-68; prof. nutritional sci. Boston U., 1968-94; prof. biochemistry Boston U. Sch. Medicine, 1970-94; dir. divsn. basic sci. Boston U. Sch. Medicine (Sch. Grad. Dentistry), 1970-75, chmn. dept. nutritional scis., 1973-94; prof. emeritus Boston U., 1994—; chmn. Mass. Task Force Nutrition and Aging, 1970-71; cons. Mass. Office of Elder Affairs, 1971-73; co-chmn. nutrition sect. White House Conf. Aging, 1971-72; cons. VA, Bedford, Mass., 1982-87; mem. pres.'s adv. coun. Hellenic Coll., 1968-73. Author numerous research articles fields biochemistry, pathology and nutrition; contbr. sci. and profl. jours. 1st lt.

USAAF, 1943-45. Decorated DFC, Air Medal with 3 oak leaf clusters (7 battle stars); recipient Outstanding Educator of Am. award Boston U., 1972, Spl. Honor, 1995. Fellow AAAS, Am. Heart Assn. (established investigator 1961-66); mem. Am. Inst. Nutrition (chmn. fellow award com. 1978-81), Am. Soc. for Nutritional Scis., Sigma Xi (Harvard chpt.), Omicron Kappa Upsilon (hon.). Home: 19 Eliot Rd Lexington MA 02421-5630

FILLMORE, JOHN DILLON, artist; b. Canoga Park, Calif., Nov. 24, 1951; s. Herbert Peter and Patricia Louise (Dillon) F. BFA, Art Ctr. Coll. Design, Hollywood, Calif., 1973. Fine artist, designer Chris O'Connell Inc./Ancient Echoes/Martex, Santa Fe, N.Mex., 1989-95; freelance fine artist Santa Fe, Tarzana, 1974—. Recipient Hubbard Art award for excellence, 1991. Republican. Roman Catholic. Avocations: art history, collecting art and books.

FILONOV, MICHAIL RUDOLF, chemist, researcher; b. Priluky, USSR, May 29, 1961; s. Rudolf Michail and Nadia Nicolay (Kicha) F.; m. Elena Vladimir Soloviyova, Oct. 29, 1985; 1 child, Andrew. Degree in engring., Moscow Steel and Alloys Inst., 1984, PhD, 1989. Sr. rsch. worker Moscow Steel and Alloys Inst., 1989-93, prof., 1993—. Author: Theoretic and Experimental Researches of Metallurgical Processes, 1989, Scientific Schools of Moscow Steel and Alloys Institute, 1997; contbr. articles to profl. jours. Mem. State Sci.-Tech. Assn. Thermosynthesis (exec. dir. 1993—). Avocation: fishing. Office: Moscow Steel Alloys Inst, Leninsky Prospect 4, Moscow Russia

FILOV, VLADIMIR ALEXANDROVICH, biologist, researcher; b. Leningrad, USSR, Dec. 23, 1930; s. Alexandr Ivanovich and Olga Dmitrievna (Angelova) F.; m. Nelly Dmitrievna Kirillova, Nov. 25, 1953 (dec. Oct. 1954). Diploma, Tech. U., Leningrad, 1955, U. Leningrad, 1959; PhD, Med. U., Leningrad, 1960; DSc, U. Leningrad, 1970. Sci. worker Inst. Hygiene Labour, Leningrad, 1955-61; sr. sci. worker Inst. Cytology, Leningrad, 1961-63; head dept. Inst. Oncology, St. Petersburg, 1963—; dir. Inst. Libr. Acad. Sci. USSR Leningrad, 1980-88, Inst. for Xenobiotics of RANS Ltd., St. Petersburg, 1996—; pres. ASGL-Rsch. of New Antotumoral Preparations, St. Petersburg, 1999—. Author: Transformations and Determination of Industrial Organic Poisons in Organisms, 1971, Determination of Industrial Inorganic Poisons in Organisms, 1975, Pharmacokinetics, 1980, Quantitative Toxicology, 1980; editor, author: Harmful Chemical Substanctes, Vols. 1-7, 1988-98, Basis of General Industrial Toxicology, 1976; inventor sehydrinum, dioxadet (anticancer drugs), biosynthesis of NAD in tumor cells, and olipyphat (anticancer drug); contbr. more than 300 articles to profl. jours. Grantee State of Russia, 1994—, Russian Acad. Natural Scis., 1996; recipient Hon. Promoter of Sci. of Russia, Pres. of Russia, 1996. Mem. Russian Acad. Natural Scis., Russian Soc. Toxicology (presidium 1980—), Russian Soc. Pharmacology, Russian Soc. Oncology. Avocations: travel, collecting teapots. Office: Inst Oncology, Leningradskaya St 68, 189646 Saint Petersburg Russia

FILPI, ROBERT ALAN, lawyer; b. Chgo., Oct. 8, 1945; s. John Andrew and Eunice Lorraine (Taylor) F.; m. Janice Elizabeth Crusoe, June 24, 1967; children—Jennifer Anne, Christopher Alan, Emily Elizabeth. B.A. in History, magna cum laude, Harvard U., 1967; J.D., Northwestern U., 1970. Bar: Ill. 1970, U.S. Dist. Ct. (no. dist.) Ill. 1971, U.S. Ct. Appeals, 7th cir. 1971, U.S. Supreme Ct. 1975. Asst. U.S. atty. No. Dist. Ill., Chgo., 1971-75; dep. chief U.S. atty. No. Dist. Ill., Civil Divsn., Chgo., 1975-76; ptnr. Stack & Filpi, Chgo., 1976—. Assoc. editor Jour. Criminal Law, Criminology and Police Sci., 1969-70. Coach, Spring Lake Sports League, Lincolnshire, Ill., 1984-91 ; mem. Village of Lincolnshire Plan Commn., 1984-94 . Recipient Hyde prize Northwestern U. Sch. Law, 1967. Mem. Chgo. Bar Assn. Clubs: Union League, Harvard. Office: 140 S Dearborn St Ste 411 Chicago IL 60603-5201

FILSON, RICHARD PAUL, science educator; b. Long Beach, Calif., Dec. 3, 1943; s. John Pierce and Maxine (DeArmond) Filson; m. Ann Marshall, Mar. 18, 1967; children: Michael Andrew, John Benjamin. BA in Zoology, U. Calif., Davis, 1966; MS in Biol. Sci., Oreg. State U., 1971. Cert. secondary sch. tchr., Calif. Tchr. biol. sci. Edison H.S., Stockton, 1966-70; tchr. biology Stockton (Calif.) Continuation Sch., 1971-73; tchr. physics Edison H.S., Stockton, 1973-75, tchr. biology, 1975-91, tchr. sci. and biology, dept. chmn., 1991—; cons. Dober, Lidsky, Craig and Assocs., Belmont, Mass., 1997-99; inst. dir. nat. leadership program for tchrs. Woodrow Wilson Nat. Fellowship Found., Princeton, N.J., and Stockton, 1998-2000. Contbr. articles to sci. publs. Officer San Joaquin Audubon Soc., Stockton, 1971-74; docent Oak Grove Regional Pk., Stockton, 1979-86; adult leader, trainer Boy Scouts Am., Stockton, 1980—. Woodrow Wilson Nat. Fellowship Found. fellow, 1995, 97; Access Excellence fellow Genentech Corp., San Francisco, 1996; named Outstanding Sci. Tchr., Sigma Xi, U. of Pacific, 1988. Mem. Nat. Sci. Tchrs. Assn., Nat. Assn. Biology Tchrs., Am. Inst. Biol. Sci., Calif. Biology Edn. Assn. (pres. 1993-96), Calif. Sci. Tchrs. Assn. (h.s. dir. 1994-98, pres.-elect 1999—), Valley Assn. Sci. Tchrs. (pres. 1989-91, award of excellence 1993). Democrat. Avocations: fly fishing, bird watching, backpacking, skiing. E-mail: dfilson@inreach.com. Home: 3710 Wood Duck Cir Stockton CA 95207-5232 Office: Edison HS 1425 S Center St Stockton CA 95206-2016

FIMREITE, NORVALD, environmental science educator; b. Sogndal, Norway, May 12, 1935; s. Jens and Anna (Barsnes) F.; m. Solveig Marie Ruud Fimreite, June 25, 1966; 1 child, Gyril. MSc, Agrl. U. Norway, 1961; PhD, U. Western Ontario, Can., 1971. Cons. Norwegian Water Resources, Oslo, Norway, 1962-64, State Plant Protection Inst., Norway, 1964-67; PhD studies U. Western Ontario, London, Can., 1967-70; sr. ecologist Acres Internat. Ltd., Niagara Falls, Can., 1970-72; assoc. prof. U. Tromso, Norway, 1972-80; prof. Telemark Coll., Norway, 1981—; mem. bd. U. Tromso, Norway, 1974-76, Norwegian Rsch. Coun., Oslo, Norway, 1981-82, Norwegian Assn. Rsch. Workers, 1992-96. Contbr. scientific articles to profl. jours. Home: Ovre Borgvin 33, 3800 Bo Norway Office: Telemark Coll, Hallvards Eikas Plass, 3800 Bo Norway

FINAURI, GRACIELA MARIA, foreign service professional; b. Buenos Aires, June 18, 1956; d. Gerardo and Norma Mercedes (Burich) F. Student in law, Cath. U. Buenos Aires, 1985. Adminstr. protocol dept. Ministry of Fgn. Affairs, Buenos Aires, 1979-85, pvt. sec. min., 1985-87; pvt. sec. amb. Embassy of Argentina, Rome, Italy, 1987-91; pvt. sec. min. Ministry of Internal Affairs, Buenos Aires, 1993-95; chief of protocol Senate of Argentina, Buenos Aires, 1995-98; pvt. sec. to v.p. Argentine Republic, Buenos Aires, 1995-98; attaché Mission of Argentina to UN, N.Y.C., 1998—. Roman Catholic. E-mail: gmf@mrecic.gov.ar. Office: Mission of Argentina to UN One UN Plz 25th Fl New York NY 10017

FINCH, LAWRENCE N., II, computer scientist, consultant; b. Bklyn., June 26, 1943; s. Lawrence N. and Amelia Julia (Weiss) F.; m. Patricia Moldauer, June 20, 1976 (div. July 1980); m. Wanda Richards, Sept. 27, 1981; 1 child, Abigail Emily. BEE, NYU, 1966; MS in Computer Sci., Stevens Inst. Tech., 1978. Engr. Airborne Instruments Lab., Deer Park, N.Y., 1966-70, Republic Electronic Industries Corp., Farmingdale, N.Y., 1970-73; tech. staff Schering Pharm., Bloomfield, N.J., 1973-74; regional analyst mgr. computer div. Tex. Instruments, Clark, N.J., 1974-80; v.p., tech. dir. Prolifics, N.Y.C., N.J., 1980—. Recipient NSF rsch. grant, 1965. Achievements include patent for fixed compound lens scanning microwave antenna with moveable feed. Office: Prolifics 116 John St New York NY 10038-3300

FINCH, PETER JOHN, insurance company executive, lecturer; b. Kingston, Surrey, Eng., Apr. 17, 1948; s. Richard Stuart and Charlotte Betsy Finch; m. Angela Ruth Watkins, 1967 (div. 1984); m. Carol Joyce Wilson, June 1986; children: James Douglas, Sophie Claire. Chartered insurer. Dir. M&G Life Assurances Co. Ltd. M&G Pensions & Annuity Co. Ltd., Chelmsford, Eng., 1979-93; pensions tech. mgr. M&G Ltd., Chelmsford, 1988—; bd. dirs. CII Enterprises Ltd., London. Hon. editor Jour. Chartered Ins. Inst., 1996—. Mem. Chartered Ins. Inst. (assoc.; chmn. mktg. com. 1996—), Securities Inst., Ins. Inst. of Chelmsford (dep. pres. 1996-97, pres. 1997-98, v.p. 1998—), Burnham Sailing Club. Avocations: sailing, mountain biking, canaling. Office: M&G Ltd, Victoria Rd, Chelmsford Essex CM1 1FB, England

FINCH, RUTH W., photographer; b. Rochester, N.Y., Feb. 27, 1916; d. Orator Frank and Persis Earle (Davis) Woodward; m. E.C. Kip Finch, Nov. 24, 1951 (dec. Dec. 1988); children: Ruth Persis Simons, Earle Kip Finch. BA, Bryn Mawr (Pa.) Coll., 1937. Asst. editor Golf World, 1948-50; photographer Am. Indians, travel, nature. Treas. Conn. Conservation Assn., Bridgeport, Conn., 1988—. Mem. U.S. Golf Assn. (com. mem. 1953-62), Colonial Dames (N.Y.C.), New Canaan (Conn.) Country Club, New Canaan Garden Club. Republican. Episcopalian. Avocations: golf, travel, writing.

FINCHER, GEOFFREY BRUCE, biochemist; b. Melbourne, Australia, May 14, 1946; s. Frederick Lionel and Betty Lorraine (Lobb) F.; m. Janice Norma Berkley, May 7, 1977; children: Amelia Jane, Andrew Charles, Hugh Edward. B of Agrl. Sci., U. Melbourne, 1967, PhD, 1973. Tchg. fellow McGill U., Montreal, Can., 1975-76; from lectr. to reader La Trobe U., Melbourne, 1977-92; prof. plant sci. U. Adelaide, Australia, 1993-2000, assoc. dean rsch., 1995-97; coord. S.E. Australian Malting Barley Improvement Program, 1992-94; vis. scientist Carlsberg Lab., Denmark, 1983; sr. vis. scientist Sainsbury Lab., U.K., 1990. Contbr. articles to profl. jours. Fellow Royal Australian Chem. Inst. (chmn. cereal chemistry divsn. 1995-99); mem. Melbourne Cricket Club. Avocations: music, sports, squash. Office: Univ Adelaide Waite Campus, Dept Plant Sci, Glen Osmond SA 5064, Australia

FINCK, JEAN-DANIEL, bioengineering executive, researcher; b. Strasbourg, Alsace, France, Nov. 5, 1953; s. Hans Herbert and Jeanne (Hervieu) F.; m. Marianne Prigent, July 3, 1975 (div. May 17, 1986); children: Yann, Sébastien; m. Véronique Sylvie Bentz, Sep. 4, 1993. BS, Gymnase Jean Sturm, 1972; M in Biochemistry, U. Louis Pasteur, 1976; Biomed. Engring. Degree, INSA, 1979, D in Engring., 1983. Engr. Elf Bio Recherches, Toulouse, France, 1980-85; bacterial fermentation mgr. Sanofi Elf Bio Recherches, Labege, France, 1986-91, process devel. and prodn. mgr., 1992-98; internat. dir. Sanofi Recherche Labege Biotech. Devel., 1998—. Inventor and patentee in field. With French Air Force, 1976-77. Mem. Am. Soc. Microbiology, French Soc. Microbiology, Groupe Français de Génie de Procede. Avocations: sailing, fishing, games. Office: Sanofi Recherche Labege, BP 137 Voie 1, Labége Innopole 31676, France

FINCK, KEVIN WILLIAM, lawyer; b. Whittier, Calif., Dec. 14, 1954; s. William Albert and Ester (Gutbub) F.; m. Kathleen A. Miller, Oct. 7, 1989. BA in History, U. Calif., Santa Barbara, 1977; JD, U. Calif., San Francisco, 1980. Bar: Calif. 1980. lectr. Internat. Bar Assn., Learning Annex. Author: California Corporation Start Up Package and Minute Book, 1982, 9th edit., 1998; contbr. articles to various profl. jours. Avocations: hiking, golf, skiing. Office: Ste 1670 Two Embarcadero Ctr San Francisco CA 94111

FINDER, ROBERT ANDREW, pharmaceutical company executive; b. Washington, Mo., Apr. 27, 1947; s. Richard Joseph and Jeanette Mary (Graser) F.; m. Sheryl Jean Johnson, Feb. 6, 1971. B in Chem. Engring., U. Detroit, 1970. Process engr. Monsanto-J.F. Queeny Plant, St. Louis, 1970-71, prodn. supr., 1975-79, project mgr., 1980-81; engring. supt. Monsanto-Trenton (Mich.) Plant, 1981-82, gen. supt. mfg., 1982-85; mng. dir. Monsanto Chems. Thailand, Bangkok, 1985-89; chmn. bd., mng. dir. Rhone-Poulenc Thai Industries Ltd., Bangpoo Samutprakarn, Thailand, 1989-91; dir. mfg. Rhone-Poulenc Inc., Princeton, N.J., 1992-93; v.p. mfg. and process tech. Ecogen, Inc., Langhorne, Pa., 1993-95; v.p. ops. Purepac Pharm. (Faulding, Inc.), Elizabeth, N.J., 1995-99; COO, gen. mgr. Faulding China and Orals Pharms., Adelaide, Australia, 1999-2000; pres., COO Asia Pacific Faulding Pharm., Adelaide, 2000—; mem. pres.'s cabinet U. Detroit, 1988—. Life mem. World Wild Life Fund, Bangkok, 19885. Lt. U.S. Army, 1971-74. Mem. AIChE, Am. Philatelic Soc., Bangkok Sports Club. Fax: 61 8 8281 6878. Office: FH Faulding, 1538 Main North Rd, Salisbury South SA 5106, Australia

FINDLAY, RICHARD MARTIN, entertainment lawyer; b. Torphins, Aberdeen, Scotland, Dec. 18, 1951; s. Ian Macdonald Semple and Kathleen (Lightfoot) F. LLB, Aberdeen U., 1973. Trainee solicitor Wilsone & Duffus, Advocates, Aberdeen, 1973-75; asst. solicitor Maclay Murray & Spens, Glasgow, 1975-79; ptnr. Ranken & Reid, S.S.C., Edinburgh, 1979-90; entertainment lawyer, ptnr. Tods Murray, W.S., Edinburgh, 1990—; mem Bus. in the Arts Placement Scheme, 1994; assoc. Theatrical Mgmt. Assocs., 1996—; part-time lectr. on law of film Napier U., 1997. Mng. editor i-2-i the Bus. Jour. for the Internat. Film Industry, 1995. Bd. dirs. Gallus Theatre Co., Ltd., 1996-98, Dance Base, Ltd., 1997-98, Lothian Gay and Lesbian Switchboard, Ltd., 1998—, The Royal Lyceum Theatre Co., Ltd., 1999—, Audio Description Film Fund, 2000—; trustee Peter Darrell Trust, 1996—. Mem. Internat. Assn. Entertainment Lawyers, Internat. Entertainment and Multimedia Law and Bus. Network, Internat. Bar Assn., Writers Guild, New Producers Alliance, Scottish Media Lawyers Assn., Inst. Art and Law, Brit. Acad. Film and TV Arts (mgmt. com. 1998—). Avocations: theatre, film, music, photography, Scottish culture. Address: 66 Queen St, Edinburgh EH2 4NE, Scotland

FINDLEY, GARY LEE, chemistry educator; b. Little Rock, Dec. 29, 1952; s. Willis Winn and Wanda Jean (Kissinger) F.; m. Anna Marie Tringali, June 16, 1975; children: Jean-Marie, Helen Ann. BS, U. Ark., 1974; PhD, La. State U., 1978. Assoc. prof. NYU, 1982-86; adj. assoc. prof., CAMD project dir. La. State U., Baton Rouge, 1986-89; adj. prof. U. Ark., Little Rock, 1989-92; adj. prof. U. La., Monroe, 1992-95, assoc. prof., 1995-98, prof., 1998—. Author: The Geometry of Genetics, 1989; editor: Photophysics and Photochemistry in the Vuv, 1985; editor Wiley-Interscience Monographs in Chemical Physics, N.Y.C., 1984—; contbr. articles to profl. jours. Scheuer fellow NYU, 1984, fellow Deutscher Akademischer Austauschdienst, 1986. Fellow Am. Inst. of Chemists; mem. Am. Chem. Soc., Am. Phys. Soc. Achievements include research in the applications of group theory to the genetic code. Office: Dept Chemistry U La At Monroe Monroe LA 71209-0001

FINDLEY, JOHN ALLEN, JR., publishing executive; b. Fulton, Mo., Feb. 25, 1951; s. John Allen and Naomi Joan (Reker) F.; m. Oneida Lynn Blackwell, Dec. 4, 1993; children: John III, Hugh. Student, U. Mo., 1973; AB, Westminster Coll., 1973. Sales rep. Kingdom Daily News, Fulton, 1973-74; advt. dir. Colo. Daily, Boulder, 1974-76; advt. sales rep. Dallas Times Herald, 1976-77, advt. sales mgr., 1977-80, dir. consumer mktg., 1981-83, dir. circulation, 1983, dir. retail advt., 1983-84; regional sales mgr. Times Mirror Nat. Mktg., 1984-86; v.p. mktg. So. Conn. Newspapers, Stamford, 1986-88, sr. v.p. mktg. and prodn., 1989-93; pres. Charleston (W.Va.) Newspapers, 1993-97; pub., CEO Long Beach (Calif.) Press-Telegram, 1998—. Bd. govs. Calif. State U., Long Beach; bd. dirs. Long Beach Coun., Boy Scouts Am., Long Beach Found., Long Beach Venture Forum. Mem. Newspaper Assn. Am., Internat. Newspaper Promotion Assn., Sigma Chi. Office: 604 Pine Ave Long Beach CA 90844-0003

FINE, A(RTHUR) KENNETH, lawyer; b. N.Y.C., June 29, 1937; s. Aaron Harry and Rose (Levin) F.; m. Ellen Marie Jensen, July 11, 1964; children: Craig Jensen, Ricki-Barie, Desiree-Ellen. AB, Hunter Coll., 1959; JD, Columbia U., 1963; CLU, Coll. Ins., 1973; diploma, Command and Gen. Staff Coll., 1978. Bar: N.Y. 1974; registered rep. and limited prin. Nat. Assn. Securities Dealers, Inc. Joined U.S. Army N.G., 1955, advanced through grades to maj., 1973, ret., 1980; cons. U.S. Life Ins. Co., N.Y.C., 1970-74, atty., 1975-78, asst. gen. counsel, 1978; asst. counsel USLIFE Corp., N.Y.C., 1978-79, assoc. counsel, 1979-93; v.p., counsel Western Res. Life Assurance Co. Ohio, Clearwater, Fla. Mem. ABA, Soc. Fin. Svc. Profls., N.Y. State Bar Assn., N.G. Assn. U.S., Militia Assn. N.Y. (chmn. vet. officers com. 1981-90), Am. Legion (7th regt. post), Ret. Officers Club St. Petersburg, Fla. Republican. Lutheran. Home: 5953 36th Ave N Saint Petersburg FL 33710-1835 Office: Western Res Life Assurance Co of Ohio PO Box 5068 Clearwater FL 33758-5068

FINE, JO RENÉE, management executive; b. June 19, 1943; d. Ruby Arthur and Tillie Fern (Goldman) F.; m. Edward Trieber, Apr. 12, 1981; 1 child, Jessica. BA, Smith Coll., 1965; MA, NYU, 1968, PhD, 1973. Probation officer N.Y.C. Office Probation, 1966; rsch. asst. NYU, N.Y.C., 1966-68; assoc. rsch. scientist Inst. Devel. Studies, N.Y.C., 1968-73, rsch. scientist, 1973-77; program analyst N.Y. State Dept. Mental Health, N.Y.C., 1977-78; pvt. practice psychotherapy N.Y.C., 1978-81; pres. CVM Prodns., Inc., N.Y.C., 1978-92; dir. Ctr. for Diversity and Quality Mgmt. Cicatelli Assocs., N.Y.C., 1992-96; exec. v.p., dir. tng. Harris Rothenberg Internat., N.Y.C., 1996—; adj. asst. prof. dept. ednl. psychology, NYU, 1973-76, adj. asst. prof. ednl. comm. and tech., 1988-95; cons. to bds. edn., N.Y.C., also greater met. area, 1973-92, tng. cons., 1990-96. Co-author: The Synagogues of New York's Lower East Side, 1978. Bd. dirs. Project People Found. Mem. APA, ASTD (sr. v.p. N.Y. met. chpt.), Am. Jewish Com. (v.p. N.Y. chpt., nat. bd. govs.). Home: 55 W 16th St New York NY 10011-6305 Office: Harris Rothenberg Internat 99 Wall St Fl 8 New York NY 10005-4389

FINE, PETER LAWRENCE, anesthesiologist, educator; b. N.Y.C., Nov. 1, 1967; s. Stephen Lewis and Joan Susan F.; m. Lauren Gee Leong, May 5, 1994; 1 child, Max William. BS, U. Mich., 1989, MS, 1989; MD, NYU Sch. Medicine, 1993. Diplomate Am. Bd. Anesthesiology. Intern NYU Med. Ctr., N.Y.C., 1993-94; resident Yale-New Haven Hosp., New Haven, Conn., 1994-97; instr. Anesthesiology Yale-New Haven Hosp., 1997; asst. prof. Anesthesiology U. Medicine & Dentistry N.J./N.J. Med. Sch., Newark, 1997—. Mem. AMA, Am. Soc. Anesthesiology, Internat. Anesthesia Rsch. Soc., Soc. Cardiovascular Anesthesiologists, Soc. Pediatric Anesthesiologists. Jewish. Avocations: bicycling, computers, model railroading, sailing, skiing. E-mail: finepl@umdnj.edu. Office: U Medicine & Dentistry NJ Med Sch Dept Anesthesiology 185 S Orange Ave Newark NJ 07103-2757

FINE, RICHARD ISAAC, lawyer; b. Milw., Jan. 22, 1940; s. Jack and Frieda F.; m. Maryellen Olman, Nov. 25, 1982; 1 child, Victoria Elizabeth. BS, U. Wis., 1961; JD, U. Chgo., 1964; PhD in Internat. Law, U. London, 1967, cert., 1965, 66; cert. comparative law, Internat. U. Comparative Sci., Luxembourg, 1966; diplôme supérieur, Faculté Internat. pour l'Enseignement du Droit Comparé, Strasbourg, France, 1967. Bar: Ill. 1964, D.C. 1972, Calif. 1973. Trial atty. fgn. commerce sect. antitrust divsn. U.S. Dept. Justice, 1968-72; chief antitrust divsn. L.A. City Atty.'s Office, also spl. counsel gov. efficiency com., 1973-74; prof. internat., comparative and EEC antitrust law U. Syracuse (N.Y.) Law Sch. (overseas program), 1970-72; individual practice Richard I. Fine and Assocs., L.A., 1974—; mem. antitrust adv. bd. Bur. Nat. Affairs, 1981—; bd. dirs. Citizens Island Bridge Co., Ltd., 1992—; vis. com. U. Chgo. Law Sch., 1992-95; hon. consul gen. Kingdom of Norway, 1995—. Contbr. articles to legal publs. Bd. dirs. Retinitis Pigmentosa Internat., 1985-90. Mem. ABA (chmn. subcom. internat. antitrust and trade regulation, internat. law sect. 1972-77, co-chmn. com. internat. econ. orgn. 1977-79), ATLA, Am. Soc. Internat. Law (co-chmn. com. corp. membership 1978-83, exec. coun. 1984-87, budget com. 1992-97, regional coord. for L.A. 1994—, 1995 ann. program com. 1994-95, corr. editor Internat. Legal Materials 1983—), Am. Fgn. Law Assn., Internat. Law Assn., Brit. Inst. Internat. and Comparative Law, State Bar Calif. (chmn. antitrust and trade regulation law sect. 1981-84, exec. com. 1981-87), L.A. County Bar Assn. (chmn. antitrust sect. 1977-78, exec. com. sect. internat. law 1993—, treas. 1997), Ill. Bar Assn., Am. Friends London Sch. Econs. and Polit. Sci. (bd. dirs. 1984—, chmn. So. Calif. chpt. 1984—, chmn. L.A. adv. com.), L.A. World Affairs Coun. (internat. cir. 1990—), Phi Delta Phi. Office: 1840 Century Park E Ste 1050 Los Angeles CA 90067-2101

FINEBERG, ROBERT ALAN, lawyer; b. Portland, Maine, May 29, 1948; s. Samuel and Lillian (Smith) F.; m. Virginia June Brealey, Aug. 22, 1970; children: Cynthia Joy, Daniel Harwood. BA, U. Conn., 1970; JD, Temple U., 1975. Bar: Pa. 1976, N.J. 1976, U.S. Dist. Ct. (ea. dist.) Pa. 1976, U.S. Dist. Ct. N.J. 1976, U.S. Supreme Ct. 1981; cert. civil trial atty. Assoc. Charles Blasband, Norristown, Pa., 1975-76, Perskie & Callinan, Wildwood, N.J., 1976-79; sole practice Wildwood, 1979-81; ptnr. Fineberg & Rodgers, North Wildwood, N.J., 1981-89; sole practice Cape May Courthouse, 1989—; solicitor Borough of Avalon, N.J., 1979-87, Borough of Wildwood Crest, N.J., 1985-89, Bd. of Edn. of City of Cape May, N.J., 1983-91, City of Cape May, 1991-99, City of Cape May Hist. Preservation Commn., 1999—. Bd. dirs. Assn. for Retarded Citizens of Cape May County, Rio Grande, N.J., 1982-87, Cape May Jazz Festival; pres. Wildwood Crest Civic Assn., 1985-87; mem. Bd. Edn. Middle Township, N.J., 1990—. Mem. ATLA, ABA, N.J. State Bar Assn., Assn. N.J. Trial Lawyers, Cape May County Bar Assn., N.J. Inst. Mcpl. Attys., Phi Beta Kappa, Phi Kappa Phi, Delta Sigma Rho, Pi Sigma Alpha. Democrat. Jewish. Clubs: Union League (Cape May County, N.J.). Lodge: Lions. Home: 24 Chestnut Ave Cape May Court House NJ 08210-2623 Office: 208 N Main St Cape May Court House NJ 08210-2122

FINEMAN, S. DAVID, lawyer; b. Phila., Oct. 23, 1945. BA, Am. U., 1967; JD with honors, George Washington U., 1970. Bar: Pa. 1971, U.S. Dist. Ct. (ea. dist.) Pa., U.S. Ct. Appeals (3d cir.) Pa. 1980. Trial atty. Defender Assn., Phila., 1971-72; law clk. Superior Ct. Commonwealth, Pa., 1972-73; mng. ptnr. Fineman & Bach, P.A., Phila., 1981—, Fineman & Bach, Phila., 1987—; instr. bus. law Temple U., 1974-83; mem. Phila. Planning Commn., 1989-91; mem. Industry Policy Adv. Com. to Advise Sec. of Commerce on Internat. Trade Issues, 1994-98. Bd. govs. U.S. Postal Svc., 1995—, chmn. compensation com., 1997—. Mem. ABA, Phila. Bar Assn., Pa. Bar Assn., Pa. State Trial Lawyers Assn., Def. Rsch. Inst. Home: 335 Woodley Rd Merion Station PA 19066-1430 Office: 1608 Walnut St Ste 19 Philadelphia PA 19103-5443

FINGELKURTS, ALEXANDER ALEXANDROVICH, psychophysiologist, researcher; b. Krasnodar, Russia, Nov. 23, 1969; s. Alexander Adamovich and Tatyana Mihailovna Fingelkurts. BD, Orthodoxy U., Moscow, 1992; MS in Physiology, Moscow M.V. Lomonosov State U., 1995, PhD, 1998. Rschr. Moscow M.V. Lomonosov State U., 1992-98; sr. cons. on psychophysiology specialized Recruitment Svc., Moscow, 1995; cons. microstructural EEE analysis Medico-diagnostic Ctr. Armed Forces Gen. Staff on Russian Fedn., Moscow, 1996; sci. cons. Mag. "Arhidom," 1999—, Mag. "Interier," 2000—. With USSR Infantry, 1987-89. Recipient Russian Fedn. Pres. scholar, 1998. Avocations: painting, dancing. Office: Moscow State U, Dept Human Physiology, Vorobiovy Gory Moscow 119899, Russia

FINGELKURTS, ANDREW ALEKSANDROVICH, research scientist; b. Krasnodar, Russia, Nov. 23, 1969; s. Alexander Adamovich and Tatyana Mihayilovna Fingelkurts. BS in Historico-Theology, Orthodoxy U., Moscow, 1992; MS in Physiology, M.V. Lomonosov Moscow State U., 1995, PhD in Psychophysiology, 1998. Sr. lab. asst. entomology faculty Kuban Agrl. Inst., Krasnodar, 1987; sr. rsch. asst. State Sci. Ctr. Russian Fedn.-Inst. Med. and Biol. Problems, Moscow, 1990-92; sr. rschr. human physiology dept. biol. faculty Moscow State U., 1992-93, 95—, cons. on psychophysiology, rschr., prof. asst., 1994-96; sr. cons. on microstructural analysis EEG Medico-Diagnostic Ctr. Gen. Staff Armed Forces Russian Fedn., Moscow, 1996-98; sr. cons. on psychophysiology Unistaff, Moscow, 1994-95; sci. advisor Arhidom Jour., Interier Jour., 1997—. Pvt. USSR Infantry, 1987-89. Recipient award Pres. Russian Fedn., Moscow, 1998. Mem. Internat. Brain Rsch. Orgn., Orgn. Human Brain Mapping, N.Y. Acad. Scis. Avocations: painting, dancing. E-mail: fintw@hotmail.com. or brain@brain.ru. Office: Moscow State U Human Phys Biol Faculty, Vorobiovy Gory, 119899 Moscow Russia

FINGER, DAVID, manufacturing executive, marketing professional; b. New Bedford, Mass., Nov. 9, 1947; s. Louis and Dianne F.; 3 children. AA, Roger Williams U., 1970, BA, 1972, MA, 1974. V.p. mktg., sales mgr. Fibre Leather Mfg. Corp., New Bedford, Mass. Office: Fibre Leather Mfg Corp 686 Belleville Ave New Bedford MA 02745-6093

FINGER, IRIS DALE ABRAMS, elementary school educator; b. Ironton, Ohio, Jan. 22, 1939; d. Frank Abrams and Pearl (Moore) Schwab; m. Robert James Roderick Sr., July 20, 1957 (div. Nov. 1971); children: Robert James Roderick Jr., Elizabeth Ann Roderick Travis; m. Henry Waterman Bromley Jr., May 14, 1972 (div. June 1987); child: Henry Waterman Bromley III; m. Grover Cleveland Finger III, Apr. 1, 1989. Degree in early childhood and elem. edn., U. South Fla.; degree in design, Jackson Coll., Honolulu. Cert. middle sch. math. tchr.; cert. TESOL. Children's libr. Ft. Myers (Fla.) Pub. Libr., 1955-57; workmen's compensation payroll adminstr. San Diego, 1964-66; permanent substitute tchr. Sigsbee Elem. Sch., Key West, Fla., 1968-70; part-time libr. Danielson (Conn.) Libr., 1970-71; residential design Bateman Homes, Leigh Acres, Fla., 1971-72; structural steel designer So. Machine and Steel, Ft. Myers, 1972-73; dir. Ft. Myers Bus. Coll., 1973-77; structural prestress concrete designer Southland Prestress, Dean Steel and Kirby MaCumber Steel, 1977-83; tchr. Lee County Sch. Bd., Ft. Myers, 1983—, team leader, math. coach, 1983, 94-95; with Bonita Spring Mid. Sch., 1994-96, equity coord., 1995-96. Pres. PTA, Key West, 1966-68, Fla. Art League,

Ft. Myers, 1984-86; dir. Ft. Myers Bus. Coll., 1973-77; hosp. nurse ARC, 1964-66; med. evac for Vietnam wounded Philippine Islands Subic Hosp. Recipient Pres. Regan Achievement award NEA, 1976, Pres. Johnson People to People award and plank award for sch. constrn. at San Meguel, the Philippines, 1960. Mem. NEA, Fla. Tchrs. Profession, Tchrs. Assn. Lee County, Rep. Assembly, Fla. Math. Coun., Lee County Math. Coun., Pioneer Club Ft. Myers, Navy Wives and Navy Relief Soc., VFW Aux., Am. Legion, Alpha Delta Kappa. Republican. Methodist. Avocations: arts and crafts, reading, vacationing at the beach, family socials, swimming. Home: PO Box 7068 Naples FL 34101-7068 Office: Bonita Springs Mid Sch Terry St Bonita Springs FL 30000

FINGER, ROBERT ROY, marketing executive; b. Lancaster, Pa., Jan. 28, 1952; s. John LeFever and Pauline Irene (Scott) F.; m. Denise A., May 22, 1971; children: Jennifer, Robert, Claire, Andrew. AA, Franklin & Marshall Coll., 1976; BS, Elizabethtown Coll., 1979; MBA, Lebanon Valley Coll., 1995; PhD in Internat. Mktg., Harrington Ctr. Internat. Studies, London. Dispatcher Pa. Power & Light, Lancaster, 1975-79, sr. residential cons., 1985-92, bus. cons, 1992-95; pres., fin. sec. Internat. Brotherhood Elec. Workmen, Allentown, Pa., 1979-85; dir. mktg. Superior Walls Am., New Holland, Pa., 1995-97, 1998—; pres. Superior Walls Systems, Oxford, N.C., 1997-98, dir. mktg. Mem. Nat. Assn. Home Builders, Bldg. System Coun., Am. Concrete Inst., Precast Concrete Inst., Concrete Found. Assn., Sales and Mktg. Execs. (Command Performance award 1998). Republican. Roman Catholic. Avocations: family, singing. Home: 32 Greenfield Rd Lancaster PA 17602-3386 Office: Superior Walls Am 937 E Earl Rd New Holland PA 17557-9597

FINGER, WILFRIED BERND, marketing professional; b. Berlin, Germany, Apr. 29, 1948; s. Alfred Hermann Wilhelm Finger and Eva Brigitte (Nowak) Schulze; m. Betty Pius Isaac, Sept. 5, 1972; 1 child, Freddie. Grad. secondary sch., Berlin. Sales rep. Rex-Rotary GmbH, Berlin, 1968-72, sales mgr., 1972-76; exec. Redisko Büromaschinen GmbH, Berlin, 1976—. Avocations: speculation, music, windsurfing, tennis, art. Home: Brandaustr 16, 12277 Berlin Germany Office: Redisko Büromaschinenvertrieb & Svc GmbH, Kolonnenstrasse 33, 10829 Berlin Germany

FINI, GIANFRANCO, member European Parliament; b. Bologna, Italy, Jan. 3, 1952. Mem. European Parliament, Brussels, 1999—; mem. com. on environ., pub. health and consumer policy, com. on employment and social affairs, substitute mem. del. for rels. with Israel. Mem. Union for Europe of Nations Group. Mem. Nat. Alliance Party. Office: Sec di Alleanza Nazionale, Via della Scrofa 39, I-00186 Rome Italy*

FINIGAN, TIMOTHY JOSEPH, priest, editor; b. London, July 1, 1958; s. John Patrick and Dorothy Frances (Martin) F. MA with first class honors, Corpus Christi Coll., Oxford, Eng., 1980; diploma in Latin Letters, Plus XII Sch. Latin Letters, Rome, 1984; STL, Gregorian U., Rome, 1985. Ordained priest Roman Cath. Ch., 1984. Asst. priest Sacred Heart Parish, Camberwell, Eng., 1985-91, Our Lady and St. Philip Neri, Sydenham, Eng., 1991-94; parish adminstr. St. Joh Fisher, Thamesmead, Eng., 1994-97; dean of studies permanent diaconate program Southwark Roman Cath. Diocese, London, 1987-99; parish priest Our Lady of the Rosary, Blackfen, England, 1997—; webmaster Faith Keyway Trust Web Site (Internet), 1994-99. Editor Faith Mag., 1991-99. Mem. edn. com. Southwark Edn. Authority, 1988-91; chair govs. St. John Fisher Sch., 1995-97; co. sec. Thamesmead Christian Cmty. Ltd., 1995-97; trustee Faith-Keyway Trust, 1985—; chair govs. Our Lady of the Rosary Cath. Primary Sch., 1997—; trustee Guild of Our Lady of Ransom, 1997—; trustee Cath. Internet Trust, 2000—. Home: 330 A Burnt Oak Ln, Kent DA15 8LW, England

FINK, AARON HERMAN, box manufacturing executive; b. Union City, N.J., Apr. 1, 1916; s. Jacob and Tessie (Dubow) F.; m. Roslyn Lamb, Dec. 6, 1942; children: Eliot, Illene. AB, Johns Hopkins U., 1938; PhD in Bus. Adminstrn. (hon.), Hamilton State U., 1977, Marquis Guiseppe Scichules U., 1985. Treas. Associated Mills, 1938-45, now dir.; v.p., gen. mgr. Essex Paper Box Mfg. Co., Newark, 1945-48, pres., 1948—; pres. Internat. Gift Box Co., Newark, 1948—, The Aaron Fink Group, Newark, 1989—; U.S. del. Conf. Mfrs., Paris, 1954, Spl. Econ. Mission to Italy, 1954. Mem. AIAA, N.J. Paper Box Mfg. Assn. (trustee), N.J. Box Craft Bur. (pres.), Am. Soc. Quality, TAPPI, NAM, Am. Mgmt. Assn. (pres.'s assoc.), AIM (fellow pres.'s coun., adv. bd.), Nat. Soc. Bus. Budgeting, Confrerie de la Chaine des Rotisseurs, Am. Material Handling Soc., Am. Forestry Assn., Am. Soc. Advancement Mgmt., Nat. Paper Box Assn. (dir., assoc. chmn. met. divsn., chmn. plant ops. and manpower), Am. Geophys. Union, Am. Ordnance Assn., N.Y. Acad. Scis., Nat. Space Inst., Fedn. Aeronautique Internat., Seaview C. of C. Assn. N.J., Princeton Club, World Trade Club, Johns Hopkins Club (N.Y.C.), Crestmont Country Club (gov. Great Oak), Essex Club (Newark), Broken Sound Golf Club (Boca Raton, Fla.), Le Mirador Country Club (Lake Geneva, Switzerland), Seaview Country Club, Boca Raton Resort and Club. Home: 5 Evans Ct Lakehurst NJ 08733-3340 Office: 281 Astor St Newark NJ 07114-2822

FINK, ANTHONY LAWRENCE, chemistry educator, researcher; b. Hertford, Eng., Jan. 25, 1943. BSc, Queen's U., Kingston, Ont., Can., 1964; PhD, Queen's U., 1968. Prof. U. Calif., Santa Cruz, 1969—; vis. fellow All Souls Coll., Oxford, 1981. Contbr. sci. articles to profl. pubs. Office: U Calif Dept Chemistry and Biochemistry Santa Cruz CA 95064

FINK, BERND, orthopedic surgeon; b. Bonn, Germany, Sept. 23, 1964; s. Wilfried and Hedwig (Jäntgen) F.; m. Claudia Olga Elfriede Hinze, July 29, 1994. MD, U. Bonn, Germany, 1989; habilitation, 1999. Resident in surgery Alfried Krupp von Bohlen and Halbach Hosp., Essen, Germany, 1990-91; resident in trauma surgery BG Trauma Hosp., Hamburg, Germany, 1991-93; resident in orthopedic surgery Heinrich-Heine U., Dusseldorf, Germany, 1993-96; fellow in orthopedic surgery Univ. Hosp. UKE, Hamburg, 1997—. Contbr. articles to profl. jours. Mem. Deutsche Gesellschaft fur Orthopeadie u. Traumatologie, Assn. for the Application of the Methods of Ilizarov, German Orthop. Rsch. Soc., Assn. Orthop. Rheumatology, European Rheumatoid Arthritis Surg. Soc. Avocations: tennis, skiing. Office: U Hamburg Orthopedic Dept, Martini Strasse 52, 20246 Hamburg Germany

FINK, GEORGE, medical scientist; b. Vienna, Austria, Nov. 13, 1936; s. John and Theresa (Weiss) F.; m. Ann E. Langsam, Feb. 22, 1959; children: Naomi Jane, Jerome Emmanuel. MB, BChir, Melbourne U., Australia, 1960, MD, 1978; D.Phil., Oxford U., Eng., 1967, MA, 1976. Sr. lectr. dept. anatomy Monash U., Clayton, Australia, 1968-71; ofcl. fellow, tutor physiol. scis. and medicine Brasenose Coll., Oxford U., 1974-80, lectr., 1971-80; dir. brain metabolism unit Med. Rsch. Coun., Edinburgh, Scotland, 1980-99; hon. prof. pharmacology U. Edinburgh, 1984-99; v.p. rsch. Pharmos Corp., 1999—. Editor: Neuropeptides: Basic and Clinical Aspects, 1982, Neuroendocrine Molecular Biology, 1986, Neuropeptides: A Methodology, 1989, Encyclopedia of Stress, 2000; editor-in-chief: Ency. of Stress, 2000; contbr. over 340 articles to sci. jours. on neuroendocrinology, neuroendocrine molecular biology and psychoneuroendocrinology. Fellow Royal Soc. Edinburgh, Royal Coll. of Physicians of Edinburgh; mem. Physiol. Soc., Soc. Endocrinology, Endocrine Soc., Soc. Neurosci., Internat. Brain Rsch. Orgn., Anatomical Soc., European Neurosci. Assn. (mem. coun. 1980-82, 93—), European Neuroendocrine Soc. (pres. 1991-95), Physiol. Soc., Pharmacol. Soc. Avocations: reading, skiing, diving. Fax: 972 8 940-9686. Office: Pharmos Corp, Kiryat Weizmann, Removot 76326, Israel

FINK, GERHARD, educational administrator, author; b. Fürth, Bavaria, Germany, Nov. 29, 1934; s. Hans and Kaethe (Schem) F.; m. Marlies Juffa, July 21, 1964; children: Gernot, Martin. PhD, U. Erlangen, Germany, 1960, state exam., 1962. Master Gymnasium Marktredwitz, 1962-70; tchr. trainer Willstätter Gymnasium, Nürnberg, Germany, 1969-99, asst. headmaster, 1970-99. Author Greek and Latin textbooks including Cursus Latinus, Novus, Continuus, Kantharos, 1971—, Who's Who in Ancient Mythology?, 1993; numerous others; translator: Metamorphoses (Ovidius), 1989, Dialogues (Seneca), 1992, Die schönster Sagern der Antike, 1999. Lutheran. Avocation: entomology. Home: Pommelsbrunner Strasse 18, D-90482 Nürnberg Bavaria, Germany

FINK, JAMES BREWSTER, geophysicist, consultant; b. Los Angeles, Jan. 12, 1943; s. Odra J. and Gertrude (Sloot) F.; m. Georgeanne Emmerich, Aug. 24, 1970; 1 child, Jody Lynn. BS in Geophysics and Geochemistry, U. Ariz., 1969; MS in Geophysics cum laude, U. Witwatersrand, Johannesburg, Transvaal, Republic of South Africa, 1980; PhD in Geol. Engring., Geohydrology, U. Ariz. 1989. Registered profl. engr., Ariz., N.Mex.; registered land surveyor, Ariz.; registered profl. geologist, Wyo.; cert. environ. inspector. Geophysicist Geo-Comp Exploration, Inc., Tucson, 1969-70; geophys. cons. IFEX-Geotechnica, S.A., Hermosillo, Sonora, Mex., 1970; chief geophysicist Mining Geophys. Surveys, Tucson, 1971-72; research asst. U. Ariz., Tucson, 1973; cons. geophysics Tucson, 1974-76; sr. minerals geophysicist Esso Minerals Africa, Inc., Johannesburg, 1976-79; sr. research geophysicist Exxon Prodn. Research Co., Houston, 1979-80; pres. Geophynque Internat., Tucson, 1980-90, hydroGeophysics, Inc., Tucson, 1990—; cons. on NSF research U. Ariz., 1984-85, adj. lectr. geol. engring., 1985-86, assoc. instr. geophysics, 1986-87, supr. geophysicist, geohydrologist, 1986-88, bd. dirs. Lab. Advanced Subsurface Imaging, 1986—; v.p. R&D Alternative Energy Engring., Inc., Tucson, 1992—, also bd. dirs.; v.p. Reclamation Svcs., Inc., 1995—, also bd. dirs.; v.p. Catalina Marble Inc., 1996—; lectr. South African Atomic Energy Bd., Pelindaba, 1979; cons. Argonne Nat. Lab., 1992-93, Los Alamos Nat. Lab., 1987—; v.p. Rincon Stock Yard, 1997—. Contbr. articles to profl. jours. Served as sgt. U.S. Air NG, 1965-70. Named Airman of Yr., U.S. Air NG, 1967. Mem. Soc. Exploration Geophysicists (co-chair internat. meetings 1980, 81, 92, sr. editor monograph 1990, reviewer), Am. Geophys. Union (reviewer), European Assn. Exploration Geophysicists, Assn. Ground Water Scientists, Nat. Water Well Assn. (reviewer), Mineral and Geotech. Explorationists, Ariz. Geol. Soc., Ariz. Water Well Assn., Environ. and Engring. Geophys. Soc., Pres.'s Club U. Ariz. Republican. Avocations: reading, computers, natural sciences, genealogy. Home and Office: Hydrogeophysics Inc 5865 S Old Spanish Trl Tucson AZ 85747-9487

FINK, JÖRG HERMANN, physicist, educator; b. Stuttgart, Germany, Jan. 24, 1938; s. Hermann and Lore (Nagel) F.; m. Ellen Margret Genz, Feb. 27, 1970; children: Till, Judith. Diploma in Physics, U. Munich, 1963, PhD, 1966; D in Habilitation, U. Karlsruhe, Germany, 1988. Scientist FZ Karlsruhe, 1966-78, FZ Jülich, Germany, 1978-82, FZ Karlsruhe, 1982-93; dir. IFF/IFW Dresden, Germany, 1994—; prof. Tech. U. Dresden, 1994—. Editor Z. Phys. B. Jour., 1994—, Reports of Progress in Physics, 1993—; contbr. numerous articles to profl. jours. Mem. Am. Phys. Soc., European Phys. Soc., Deutsche Physikalische Gesellschaft. Office: IFW Dresden, Postfach 270016, D-01171 Dresden Germany

FINK, JOSEPH RICHARD, academic administrator; b. Newark, Mar. 20, 1940; s. Joseph Richard and Jean (Chorazy) F.; m. Donna Gibson, 1965 (div. 1986); children: Michael, Taryn; m. Christine Gaudenzi, oct. 4, 1992; children: Madison, Joseph. AB, Rider U., 1961; PhD in Am. History, Rutgers U., 1971; DLitt (hon.), Rider U., 1982, Coll. of Misericordia, 1992, Golden Gate U., 1994. Asst. then assoc. prof history Immaculata (Pa.) Coll., 1964-72, adminstrv. asst. to pres., 1969-72; dean of Arts & Scis. City Colls. Chgo., 1972-74; pres. Raritan Valley Coll., Somerville, N.J., 1974-79, Coll. Misericordia, Dallas, 1979-88, Dominican U of Calif, San Rafael, 1988—; pres. Regional Planning Coun. Higher Edn., Region 3/Northeastern Pa., 1986-88. Mem. exec. com. Philharm. Soc. Northeastern Pa., 1986-89; bd. dirs. Marin Symphony, 1989-99, San Francisco Ballet, 1994-97, Ind. Coll. No. Calif., 1992—, Marin Forum, 1991—, Guide Dogs for the Blind, 1994-97; bd. dirs. Am. Land Conservancy, 1995—, exec. com.; mem. campaign cabinet United Way San Francisco, 1990; bd. dirs. North Bay Coun., 1993—, chmn., 1996, exec. com. Mem. Nat. Assn. Ind. Colls. and Univs. (secretariat 1986), Nat. Assn. Intercollegiate Athletics (pres.'s adv. coun. 1986), Am. Coun. on Higher Edn. (commn. leadership devel. higher edn. 1978-82, commn. on internat. edn. 1993-96, acad. adminstrn. fellow 1974-75), Assn. Mercy Colls. (pres. 1985-87, exec. com. 1981-87), Coun. for Ind. Colls. (bd. dirs. 1989-92), Am. Hist. Assn., World Affairs Coun. No. Calif. (bd. dirs. 1990-96), Commonwealth Club Calif. (quar. chmn. 1989, chmn. Marin County chpt. 1989—, bd. dirs. 1992—; exec. com. 1997—). Home: 900 Green St San Francisco CA 94133-3600 Office: Dominican Coll of San Rafael 50 Acacia Ave San Rafael CA 94901-2230

FINK, MICHAEL KARL, internist, hematologist, oncologist; b. Heidelberg, Germany, Aug. 29, 1945; s. Erwin and Maria Fink. MD, U. Heidelberg, 1971; Dr.med.habil., U. Munich, Germany, 1990. Resident Klinikum Grosshadern, Munich, 1978-88; asst. med. dir. Klinikum Fürth, Germany, 1989—; privatdozent U. Erlangen, Germany, 1991. Author: Cancer Research, 1982; co-author Internat. Jour. of Cancer, 1985 (Vincenz Czerny award German Soc. for Hematology and Oncology). Recipient Internat. Proficiency badge for glider piloting Fedn. Aero. Internat., 1984. Avocation: gliding. Office: Klinikum, Jakob-Henlestr, 90744 Fuerth Germany

FINK, STANLEY, investment executive; b. Manchester, Eng., Sept. 15, 1957; s. Louis and Janet Fay (Stone) F.; m. Barbara Toni Paskin, June 28, 1981; children: Alexander, Gabriella, Jordan. BA in Law, Trinity Hall, Cambridge, Eng., 1979. Chartered acct. Audit sr. Arthur Andersen, London, 1979-82; fin. planning mgr. Mars Confectionery, Slough, Eng., 1982-83; v.p. Citibank NA, London, 1983-86; fin. dir. ED&F Man (Group) plc, London, 1987-96; mng. dir. ED&F Man Investment Products, Pfaffikon, Switzerland, 1996-99, London, 1999—. Mem. Inst. Chartered Accts. Jewish. Avocations: skiing, golf, tennis. Office: ED&F Man Group PLC, Sugar Quay Lower Thames St, London EC3R 6D4, England

FINKEL, FEDERICO, physicist, educator; b. Colchester, Essex, Eng., Mar. 4, 1970; arrived in Spain, 1976; s. Carlos Finkel and Sara Morgenstern; m. Ana Puche, July 24, 1997. Lic. Phys. Sci., U. Complutense, Madrid, 1993; PhD in Physics, U. Complutense, 1997. Asst. prof. U. Complutense, Madrid, 1997—. Contbr. articles to profl. jours.; reviewer Am. Math. Soc., 1997—. Predoctoral scholar U. Complutense, 1994-95, Spanish Ministry of Edn., 1996-97, postdoctoral scholar Imperial Coll., London, 1999. Avocations: strategy games, skiing, reading.

FINKEL, VITALY ALEXANDROVICH, physicist, researcher, educator; b. Kharkov, Ukraine, May 23, 1934; s. Alexander Moiseyevich and Anna Pavlovna (Livshitz) F.; m. Olga Mikhailovna Sukhareva, Oct. 3, 1963; 1 child, Tatyana V. BSc, Kharkov (Ukraine) State U., 1957, DSc, 1974; candidate sci., Nat. Sci. Ctr. Inst. Physics & Tech., Kharkov, 1963. Young rschr. Nat. Sci. Ctr., Kharkov Inst. Physics & Tech., 1957-60, rschr., 1960-63, sr. rschr., 1963-88, head lab., 1988—; asst. prof. Kharkov State U., 1963-81; prof. Kharkov Poly. U., 1987-90. Author: High-temperature X-ray Crystallography, 1968, Low-temperature X-ray Crystallography, 1971, Structure of Rare Earth Metals, 1978, High-temperature Superconductors: Physical Metallurgy, Technology, Application, 1993. Mem. Am. Phys. Soc., Internat. Union Crystallography. Home: Apt 11, 3 Potebni St, UA 61002 Kharkov Ukraine Office: Nat Sci Ctr Kharkov Inst Phys Tech, 1 Academicheskaya St, UA 61108 Kharkov Ukraine

FINKELSTEIN, ALLEN LEWIS, lawyer; b. N.Y.C., Mar. 19, 1943; s. David and Ella (Miller) F.; m. Judith Elaine Stutman, June 20, 1964 (div. Mar. 1980); children: Jill, Jennifer; m. Shelley Gail Barone, June 15, 1980; 1 child, Amanda. BS, NYU, 1964; JD, Bklyn. Law Sch., 1967; MBA, L.I. U., 1969. Bar: N.Y. 1968, U.S. Dist. Ct. (ea. and so. dists.) N.Y. 1973, U.S. Ct. Appeals (2d cir.) 1973, U.S. Supreme Ct. 1976, U.S. Tax Ct. 1979. Ptnr. Finkelstein, Bruckman, Wohl, Most & Rothman, N.Y.C., 1974-97; sr. ptnr. Pressman Finkelstein, N.Y.C., 1997-99; ptnr. Schwarzfeld Ganfer & Shore, N.Y.C., 1999—; asst. prof. L.I. U., N.Y.C., 1969-73, adj. assoc. prof., 1973-74; bd. dirs. Amotrophic Lateral Sclerosis Assn. Mem. ABA (bus. law and family law sect.), N.Y. State Bar Assn., Assn. of Bar of City of N.Y., Queens County Bar Assn. Jewish. Lodge: Masons. Home: 425 E 63rd St New York NY 10021-7804 Office: Schwarzfeld Ganfer & Shore 360 Lexington Ave New York NY 10017-6502

FINKELSTEIN, JOSEPH SIMON, lawyer; b. Vineland, N.J., Feb. 28, 1952; s. Absalom and Goldie (Cukier) F.; m. Sara M. Green, May 30, 1976; children: Adam, Julia, Seth. BA, Rutgers U., 1973; JD, U. Pa., 1976. Bar: Pa. 1976, N.J. 1976, U.S. Supreme Ct. 1982. Assoc. Wolf, Block, Schorr and Solis-Cohen, Phila., 1976-85, ptnr., 1985—. Mem. exec. bd. young leadership coun. bd. Fedn. Jewish Agys., Phila., 1986-88; mem. Nat. Young Leadership cabinet United Jewish Appeal, 1987-91; pres. Perelman Jewish Day Sch., 1996-99; bd. dirs. Temple Beth Hillel, Beth El, State of Israel Bonds, Phila.; mem. Wexner Heritage Found., 1991-95; exec. com., bd. dirs., chair funds. distbn. United Way of Southeastern Pa., 1997-99; trustee Jewish Fedn. of Greater Phila., 1996—. Recipient New Life/New Leadership award State of Israel, 1989, Hearts of Gold award United Way, Southeastern Pa., 1999. Mem. ABA, Internat. Coun. Shopping Ctrs., Pa. Bar Assn., N.J. Bar Assn., Phila. Bar Assn., Pa. Land Title Assoc. Home: 716 Oxford Rd Bala Cynwyd PA 19004-2112 Office: Wolf Block Schorr & Solis-Cohen LLP 1650 Arch St Fl 22D Philadelphia PA 19103-2029

FINKELSTEIN, SYDNEY DAVID, pathologist, educator; b. Montreal, Que., Can., Jan. 11, 1953; came to the U.S., 1982; s. Aron and Riva Finkelstein; m. June 20, 1976; children: Veronija Jane, Michaela Liana. MD, McGill U., Montreal, 1977. Asst. prof. Hahnemann U., Phila., 1982-89; assoc. prof. Brown U., Providence, 1989-93, U. Pitts., 1993—. Mem. U.S. and Can. Assn. Pathology. E-mail: finkelsteinsd@msx.upmc.edu. Home: 311 Marberry Dr Pittsburgh PA 15215-1437 Office: U Pitts Med Ctr 200 Lothrop St Pittsburgh PA 15213-2546

FINKING, GERALD, physician, researcher; b. Menden, Germany, May 9, 1960; s. Alfred and Christiane (Gampe) F.; m. Carola Schnitz, Dec. 28, 1998. ThM, U. Muenster, Germany, 1987; MD, U. Ulm, Germany, 1996. Singer Opera Choir, Muenster, Germany, 1983-87; journalist Westfaelische Nachrichter Muenster, 1987-92; physician, rschr. dept. cardiology U. Ulm, 1996—. Contbr. articles to profl. jours. Mem. Fed. Dem. Party, Ulm, 1992—, Amnesty Internat., 1994—, Franz Weber Found., Lausanne, Switzerland, 1995—. Avocations: singing, dancing, diving, skiing. Home: Heilmeyersteige 158/4, 89075 Ulm Germany Office: Univ Ulm, Robert-Koch-Str 8, 89081 Ulm Germany

FINKS, ROBERT MELVIN, paleontologist, educator; b. Portland, Maine, May 12, 1927; s. Abraham Joseph and Sarah (Bendette) F. B.S. magna cum laude, Queens Coll., 1947; M.A., Columbia U., 1954, Ph.D., 1959. Lectr. Bklyn. Coll., 1955-58, instr., 1959-61; lectr. Queens Coll., CUNY, 1961-62, asst. prof., 1962-65, acting chmn., 1963-64, assoc. prof. geology, 1966-70, prof., 1971—; geologist U.S. Geol. Survey, 1952-54, 63—; research assoc. Am. Mus. Natural History, 1961-77, Smithsonian Instn., 1968—; doctoral faculty CUNY, 1983—; cons. in field. Author: Late Paleozoic Sponge Faunas of the Texas Region, 1960; Editor: Guidebook to Field Excursions, 1968; Contbr. articles profl. jours. Queens Coll. Scholar, 1947. Fellow AAAS, Geol. Soc. Am., Explorers Club; mem. AAUP, Paleontol. Soc. (vice chmn. Northeastern sect. 1977-78, chmn. 1978-79), Paleontol. Assn. Britain, Soc. Econ. Paleontologists and Mineralogists, Internat. Palaeontol. Assn., Geol. Soc. Vt. (charter mem.), Planetary Soc. (charter), Phi Beta Kappa (v.p. Sigma chpt. N.Y. 1993-95, pres. 1995-99), Golden Key (hon.), Sigma Xi (exec. sec. Queens Coll. chpt. 1982-85). Office: Queens Coll CUNY Sch Earth and Environ Scis Flushing NY 11367

FINLAYSON, BRIAN LESLIE, geographer, educator, consultant; b. Rockhampton, Australia, Mar. 29, 1945; s. Roy and Ivy (Shanks) F.; m. Fiona McIntyre Harris, Sept. 21, 1974; children: Iain James, Ailsa Jane. BA in Geography with honors, U. Queensland, Australia, 1970; PhD, U. Bristol, Eng., 1976. Departmental demonstrator, lectr. Sch. Geography Jesus Coll., Oxford (Eng.) U., 1974-78; reader in geography, adj. reader civil and environ. engring. U. Melbourne, Australia, 1979—, head dept. geography, 1991-93, 2000—. Office: U Melbourne, Dept Geography and Environ Studies, Parkville 3052, Australia

FINLEY, GEORGE ALVIN, III, wholesale executive; b. Aurora, Ill., Apr. 25, 1938; s. George Alvin, II, and Sally Ann (Lord) F.; m. Sue Sellors, June 20, 1962 (dec. 1995); m. Phyllis Ann Finley; children: Valerie, George Alvin IV. BBA, So. Meth. U., 1962; postgrad. Coll. Grad. Program, Ford Motor Co., 1963. Rep. for Europe Finco Internat., 1959-61; trainee Ford Motor Co., Dearborn, Mich., 1962-63; v.p. mktg. Internat. Motor Cars, Oakland, Calif., 1963-64; Sequoia Lincoln lease mgr. Internat. Motor Cars, Oakland, 1965; regional mgr. Behlen Mfg. Co., Dallas, 1965-67; pres. C C Distbrs., Corpus Christi, Tex., 1967—; guest instr. Sch. Bus., So. Meth. U., pres., 1986-91, Nueces River Authority, 1975—; bd. dirs. Contract Svcs. Assn. Am. Sec. Bd. Washington, MD Anderson Hosp. U. Tex., Christus-Spohn Health Sys., McDonald Obs., U. Tex., exec. com.; mem. Del Mar Coll. Found. Mem. Tex. Wholesale Hardware Assn. (pres. 1991-92), Nat. Assn. Wholesalers, Am. Supply Assn., Wholesale Distbrs. Assn. (bd. dirs. 1994—), Impact Industries Inc. (chmn. bd. Sandwich, Ill. 1986-93), Nat. Retail Hardware Assn., Internat. Hardware Distbrs., Rotary Internat., State Bar of Tex. (grievance com. 1995—), Phi Delta Theta. Democrat. Methodist. Achievements include assisted in design, engring., production, mktg. Apollo Automobile, 1963-64. Home: 3360 Ocean Dr Corpus Christi TX 78411-1457 Office: PO Box 9153 210 Mcbride Ln Corpus Christi TX 78408-2298

FINLEY, LEWIS MERREN, financial consultant; b. Reubens, Idaho, Nov. 29, 1929; s. John Emory and Charlotte (Priest) F.; m. Virginia Ruth Spousta, Feb. 23, 1957; children: Ellen Annette Kraner, Charlotte Louise. Student pub. schs., Spokane. With Household Fin. Co., Portland, Oreg. and Seattle, 1953-56, Doug Gerow Fin., Portland, 1956-61; pres. Family Fin. Planners Inc., Portland, 1961—; assoc. broker Peoples Choice Realty, Inc., Milwaukie, Oreg., 1977-82, Lewis M. Finley, Real Estate Broker, Inc., 1982—; standing trustee Chpt. 13, Fed. Bankruptcy Ct., Dist. of Oreg., 1979. Author: The Complete Guide to Getting Yourself Out of Debt, 1975. With U.S. Army, 1951-53. Mem. Oreg. Assn. Credit Counselors (past pres.), N.W. Assn. Credit Counselors (past treas.), Am. Assn. Credit Counselors (v.p. 1982-85), Authors Guild, Nat. Assn. Realtors, Masons (past master), Shriners. Republican. Methodist. Home: 3015 SE Riviere Dr Portland OR 97267-5548 Office: PO Box 12287 Portland OR 97212-0287

FINLEY, MARGARET MAVIS, retired elementary school educator; b. Jackson, Mich., Dec. 2, 1927; d. Allen Aaron and Minnie Mavis (Graham) Lincoln; m. Duane Douglas Finley, Aug. 23, 1952; 1 child, Linda Louise. BS, Ea. Mich. U., 1960; postgrad., Pepperdine U., 1968-72. Cert. tchr., Mich., Calif. Tchr. Jackson Sch. Dist., 1960-67, Pomona (Calif.) Sch. Dist., 1967-88; vol. proofreader Calif. Assn. Ind. Bus., Inc. Editor Calif. Ret. Tchrs. Assn. Divsn. 82 Newsletter; contbr. poetry and articles to profl. jours. Mem. AAUW, Calif. Ret. Tchrs. Assn., Calif. Tchrs. Assn. (life). Avocations: writing, reading, hiking, travel, theater. Home: 1072 Cypress Point Dr Banning CA 92220-5404

FINN, ADAM HUGH RODERICK, pediatrician; b. Canterbury, Eng., May 26, 1959; s. Hugh Roderick and Muriel Enid (Dale) F.; m. Sarah Jane (Webb), May 28, 1988; children: Thomas, James, Henry. MA, Cambridge U., 1980; MB BCh, Oxford U., 1983; PhD, U. London, 1993. Fellow infectious diseases Children's Hosp. of Phila., 1987-88; lectr. immunology Inst. Child Health, London, 1988-92; sr. lectr. in pediat. immunology U. Sheffield, Eng., 1992—; hon. cons. pediat. immunology Children's Hosp., Sheffield, 1992—; dir. Sheffield Inst. for Vaccine Studies, 1996—; sec. Brit. Pediat. Immunology and Infectious Disease Group, 1992-98; assoc. editor Archives of Disease in Childhood, 1996—. Contbr. articles to books and pubs. in field. Fellow Royal Coll. Pediatrics and Child Health; mem. Brit. Soc. Immunology, European Soc. Pediat. Infectious Diseases (sec. 2000—), European Soc. Immunodeficiency. E-mail: a.finn@shef.ac.uk. Office: U Sheffield Dept Ped/Childrens Hosp, Divsn Child Health, S10 2TH Sheffield England

FINN, BRENDAN PETER, school psychologist; b. Somerville, Mass., Oct. 31, 1960; s. Brendan Augustus and Edith Marjorie (Goggin) F.; m. Carolyn Heising, July 9, 1988 (div. Dec. 1997); 1 child, Peter. BS magna cum laude, Northeastern U., 1990, MEd, 1993, cert. advanced grad. study, 1993. Cert. sch. psychologist, Mass., Iowa. Warehouse asst. mgr. Harvard Coop. Soc., Cambridge, Mass., 1979-93; sch. psychologist Heartland Area Edn. Agy., Johnston, Iowa, 1993—; presenter in field. Mem. Nat. Assn. Sch. Psychologists, Iowa Sch. Psychologists Assn., Phi Kappa Phi. Roman Catholic. Avocations: music, sports, reading. Home: 1503 Grand Ave Ames IA 50010-5350 Office: Heartland Area Edn Agy # 11 511 S 17th St Ames IA 50010-8125

FINN, SHANE DARREN, product development manager, design engineer; b. Sydney, NSW, Australia, Aug. 13, 1961; s. Paul Alywne and Sonya Jean

(Gorlick) F.; m. Gayle Mary Hanschen, Dec. 5, 1987; children: Aiden Trent, Ashleigh Erin, Brent Alexander. B of Engring., Capricornia Inst. Adv. Edn., Rockhampton, Australia, 1984, B Applied Sci. in Math. and Computing, 1988; Grad. Diploma of Mgmt., U. Coll. Ctrl. Queensland, Rockhampton, Australia, 1990. Power electronics engr. Gayrad Internat., Brisbane, Australia, 1984-87; sr. power electronics design engr. Maitec, Sydney, Australia, 1987-89, tech. dir., 1989-93; mgr. electronic product devel ResMed, Sydney, Australia, 1993-99, mgr. IT, 1999—; invited spkr. Electricity Tech. Adv. Ctr., Sydney, 1991-94, Sydney Electricity, 1992-94; com. mem. Stds. Australia, Sydney, 1992-94; cons. in field, 1992—. Patents include Auto-Calibrations of Pressure Transducer Offset, 1996 and Continuous Positive Airway Pressure Treatment Apparatus, 1996; author: (jour.) Conf. Proceedings, IEE-APEC, 1993. Mem. IEEE. Avocations: acoustics, music, chaos theory, scalar design, flight simulation. Home: 40 Leone Ave, Baulkham Hills, Sydney 2153, Australia Office: RESMED # 97 Waterloo Rd, North Ryde, Sydney NSW 2113, Australia

FINNBERG, ELAINE AGNES, psychologist, editor; b. Bklyn., Mar. 2, 1948; d. Benjamin and Agnes Montgomery (Evans) F.; m. Rodney Lee Herndon, Mar. 1, 1981; 1 child, Andrew Marshal. BA in Psychology, L.I. U., 1969; MA in Psychology, New Sch. for Social Rsch., 1973; PhD in Psychology, Calif. Sch. Profl. Psychology, 1981. Diplomate Am. Bd. Forensic Examiners, Am. Bd. Forensic Medicine, Am. Bd. Med. Psychotherapists and Psychodiagnosticians, Am. Bd. Disability Analysts, Am. Bd. Psychol. Specialties, Prescribing Psychologists Register; lic. psychologist, Calif. Rsch. asst. in med. sociology Cornell U. Med. Coll., N.Y.C., 1969-70; med. abstractor USV Pharm. Corp., Tuckahoe, N.Y., 1970-71, Coun. for Tobacco Rsch., N.Y.C., 1971-77; editor, writer Found. of Thanatology Columbia U., N.Y.C., 1971-76, cons. family studies program cancer ctr. Coll. Physicians & Surgeons, 1973-74; dir. grief psychology and bereavement counseling San Francisco Coll. Mortuary Scis., 1977-81; rsch. assoc. dept. epidemiology and internat. health U. Calif., San Francisco, 1979-81, asst. clin. prof. dept. family and cmty. medicine, 1985-93, assoc. clin. prof., dept. family and cmty. medicine, 1993—; active med. staff Natividad Med. Ctr., Salinas, Calif., 1984—, chief psychologist, 1984-96; profl. adv. coun. Am. Bd. Disability Analysts; asst. chief psychiatry svc. Natividad Med. Ctr., 1985-96, acting chief psychiatry, 1988-89, vice-chair medicine dept., 1991-93, sec.-treas. med. staff, 1992-94; cons. med. staff Salinas Valley Meml. Hosp., 1991—, Mee Meml. Hosp., 1996-97; dir. tng. Monterey Psychiat. Health Facility, 1996-97, chief clin. staff, 1996-97; expert cons. Calif. Bd. Psychology. Editor: The California Psychologist, 1988-95; editor Jour. of Thanatology, 1972-76, Cathexis, 1976-81. Govs. adv. bd. Agnews Devel. Ctr., San Jose, Calif., 1988-96, chair, 1989-91, 94-95. Fellow Prescribing Psychologists Register (diplomate); mem. APA, Nat. Register Health Svc. Providers in Psychology, Calif. Psychol. Assn. (Disting. Svc. award 1989), Soc. Behavioral Medicine, Mid-Coast Psychol. Assn. (sec. 1985, treas. 1986, pres. 1987, Disting. Svc. to Psychology award 1993), Forensic Mental Health Assn. Calif., Western Psychol. Assn., Assn. Advancement Behavior Therapy, Am. Med. Writers Assn., Assn. Treatment Sexual Abuses, Soc. for Personality Assessment, Internat. Rorschach. Soc., Internat. Soc. Police Surgeons.

FINNEMANN, NIELS OLE, media scientist, educator; b. Aarhus, Denmark, July 19, 1945; s. Viggo and Ingeborg (Finnemann) Nielsen; children: Rune, Torin. Degree in Lit., U. Aarhus, 1972, MA, 1982, DrPhil, 1994. Rsch. fellow Aarhus U., 1972-79; writer Aarhus, 1986-88; lectr. Aarhus U., 1986-88, 91-95; rsch. fellow Ctr. for Cultural Rsch., Aarhus, 1988-91; sr. lectr. Aarhus U., 1996-97, dir. Ctr. for Cultural Rsch., 1997-2000; editor Modtryk Publ., Aarhus, 1972-79, Ctr. for Cultural Rsch., 1989-91; vis. rsch. fellow Oslo (Norway) U., 1992. Author: A History of the Ideas of Danish Social Democratic Movement, 1985, Thought, Sign & Machine, 1994; editor: Theories & Technologies of the Knowledge Society, 1991, Modernity Modernised. Centre for Cultural Research, 1997; guest editor (periodical) AI & Society No. 4.4, 1990. Mem. Internat. Assn. for Media and Comm. Rsch., PEN Club Denmark. E-mail: finnemann@imv.au.dk. Office: Aarhus U Dept Info/Med Stud, Niels Juelsgade, DK8200 Arhus Denmark

FINNEY, ALAN, film company executive; b. Melbourne, Victoria, Australia, Feb. 2, 1945. LLB, Melbourne U., 1969. Exec. dir. Hexagon Prodns., Melbourne, 1971-80; mgr. nat. sales and mktg. Roadshow Film Distbrs., Melbourne, 1980-87, gen. mgr. distbn. and mktg., 1988-89, exec. dir., 1989-91, mng. dir., 1991-96; mng. dir. Australian Prodn. Village Roadshow Ltd., Melbourne, 1996-98; v.p., mng. dir. Buena Vista Internat. (Australia and New Zealand), Melbourne, 1998—. Assoc. prodr. feature films, including Alvin Purple, Alvin Purple Rides Again, Petersen, End Play, Eliza Fraser, 1970s; co-exec. prodr.: (feature film) Diana & Me, 1997; co-exec. prodr.: (feature film) The Craic, 1999. Fax: 613 9826 5984. E-mail: alan.finney@disney.com. Office: Buena Vista Internat, Level 4 650 Chapel St, 3141 South Yarra Victoria, Australia

FINNEY, DAVID JOHN, biometrician; b. Warrington, Eng., Jan. 3, 1917; s. Robert George Stringer and Bessie Evelyn (Whitlow); MA, ScD, Cambridge U.; DSc (hon.), City U., London, Heriot-Watt U., Waterloo U., Nat. Faculty Agr., Gembloux; m. Mary Elizabeth Connolly, Apr. 11, 1950; children: Deborah J.C. Finney Langston, Robert F.J., Katharine A. Finney Hankins. Asst. statistician Rothamsted Exptl. Sta., 1939-45; lectr. Design and Analysis Sci. Expt. Oxford U., 1945-54; reader, then prof. stats. U. Aberdeen (Scotland), 1954-66; prof. stats. U. Edinburgh, 1966-84; dir. stats. unit Agrl. and Food Research Council, 1954-84; dir. Internat. Stats. Inst. Research Centre, 1987-88; frequent cons. UN Food and Agr. Orgn., Indian Coun. Agrl. Rsch., 1951-90; vis. prof. Harvard U., 1962-63, vis. scientist Internat. Rice Research Inst., 1984-85; cons. UN World Health Orgn. Decorated Comdr. Order Brit. Empire. Fellow Royal Soc., Royal Soc. Edinburgh, Royal Statis. Soc. (past pres.), Am. Statis. Assn.; mem. Internat. Statis. Inst., Biometric Soc. (past pres.). Anglican. Author books, articles on stats. and applications biol. sci. Fax: 44-131-667-0135. Home: 13 Oswald Court S Oswald Road, Edinburgh EH9 2HY, Scotland

FINNEY, ESSEX EUGENE, JR., retired agricultural research administrator; b. Powhatan, Va., May 16, 1937; s. Essex Eugene Sr. and Etta Francis (Burton) F.; m. Rosa Ellen Bradley, June 13, 1959; children: Essex Eugene III, Karen Renee Finney Shelton. BS, Va. Poly. Inst., 1959; MS, Pa. State U., 1960; PhD, Mich. State U., 1963. Agrl. engr. U.S. Dept. Agr., Beltsville, Md., 1965-77, asst. dir., 1977-83, assoc. dir., 1983-87; assoc. area dir. U.S. Dept. Agr., Phila., 1987-89; Beltsville area dir. U.S. Dept. Agr., 1989-92; assoc. admin. Agrl. Rsch. Svc. U.S. Dept. Agr., Washington, 1992-95; ret., 1995; sr. policy analyst Office of Sci. and Tech. Policy, Washington, 1980-81; mem. bd. on agr. NRC, 1997—. Author: Quality Control, 1973; editor: (CRC handbook) Transportation & Marketing, 1981. Councilman Town of Glenarden, Md., 1975; sec. County Fedn. of Civic Assns., Md., 1973. Lt. U.S. Army, 1963-65. Princeton fellow Princeton U., 1973-74; recipient Outstanding Engring. Alumni award Pa. State U., 1985, Adminstrn. award Gamma Sigma Delta, U. Md., 1985, Outstanding Alumni award Pa. State U. Coll. Agr., 1993. Fellow Am. Soc. Agrl. Engrs. (bd. dirs. 1970-72); mem. NAE, AAAS.

FINNEY, FRANK WILLIAM, JR., literature educator, poet; b. Boston, Feb. 28, 1956; s. F.W. and Janet Ann (Waters) F.; m. Piyachat Ruengvisesh, May 1, 1992; 1 child, Elise Le Fay. BA magna cum laude, U. Mass., Boston, 1987; MA in English, Simmons Coll., Boston, 1992, MPhil in English with distinction, 1994. Lectr. lit. Thammasat U., Bangkok, Thailand, 1995—. Author: Fragments from the Smoked-Glass Elephant Bank, 1990; The Dissolution of the Sparkling Bridge, 1997; poetry pub. numerous jours. including The Plaza, Tokyo, Green Mountains Review, Potpourri, Paris/Atlantic, Verandah, ORBIS, Poetry Nottingham Internat., Offerta Speciale, Italy, Medicinal Purposes, RE:AL-The Journal of Liberal Arts, Rockford (Ill.) Rev., The Macguffin, Iota, Pennine Ink, Aireings, Dry Creek Rev., Great Midwestern Quar., Midwest Poetry Rev., Free Lunch, numerous others. Recipient Poetpourri Spl. Merit Award for Poetry, 1994, Staple Open Poetry Competition prize, Eng., 1997, Scottish Internat. Poetry Competition diploma prize, 1997. Mem. The Poetry Soc. (London). Office: Thammasat Univ, Tha Prachan, Bangkok 10200, Thailand

FINNEY, JOHN EDGAR, III, food products executive; b. Hominy, Okla., Oct. 13, 1943; s. John Edgar and Ella Frances (Beckett) F.; m. Claudia Maddalena, Aug. 29, 1965 (div. Nov. 1979); children: Kristen, Eric; m. Tiare Richert, Oct. 18, 1980; children: Thomas Beckett, Elizabeth Stuart. BA, Okla. State U., 1965; JD, Stanford U., 1968. Bar: Colo. 1969, Hawaii 1969, U.S. Dist. Ct. Hawaii 1970, U.S. Ct. Appeals (9th cir.) 1970, Calif. 1974. Assoc. law Carlsmith, Carlsmith, Wichman Case, Honolulu, 1970-73; ptnr. law Augustine & Delafield, San Diego, 1973-75; pres., chief exec. officer Pentagram Corp., Honolulu, 1976-90; pres. Indsl. Income Property Inc., Honolulu, 1992—, also bd. dirs.; bd. dirs. Offshore Holdings Inc. Bd. dirs., bd. visitors Stanford (Calif.) U. Law Sch., 1986-93, USAF Pacific Adv. Bd., Hickam AFB, Honolulu, 1987-89, Hawaii Maritime Ctr., Honolulu, 1988-90. Capt. USMC, 1968-75. Named Okla. Ambassador, State of Okla., 1989; recipient Community Svc. award Aloha United Way, Honolulu, 1988, Community Svc. award Burger King Corp., San Francisco, 1987. Mem. Young Presidents' Orgn. (chmn. 1983-84), World Presidents' Orgn., Okla. Cattlemen's Assn., Stanford Univ. Assocs., Outrigger Canoe Club. Avocations: lit., canoe racing, rugby, skiing. Home: 155 Dowsett Ave Honolulu HI 96817-1109 Office: Indsl Properties Inc Honolulu HI 96813-3107

FINNIS, JOHN MITCHELL, legal philosopher, educator; b. Adelaide, Australia, July 28, 1940; s. Maurice Meredith Steriker and Margaret McKellar (Stewart) F.; m. Marie Carmel McNally, June 20, 1964; children: Rachel, John-Paul, Catherine, Maria, Jerome, Edmund. LLB, U. Adelaide, 1961; DPhil, Oxford U., 1965. Bar: London 1970. Assoc. U. Calif., Berkeley, 1965-66; fellow U. Coll., Oxford, Eng., 1966—; lectr. in law Oxford U., 1967-72, reader in law, 1972-89, prof. law and legal philosophy, 1989—; prof. law U. Malawi, 1976-78; Biolchini Prof. Law Notre Dame Law Sch., 1995—; spl. advisor fgn. affairs com. Ho. of Commons, London, 1980-82; cons. Pontifical Commn. Iustitia et Pax, Vatican City, 1977-89; mem. Pontifical Coun. Iustitia et Pax, 1990-95; mem. Internat. Theol. Commn., Vatican, 1986-92; Huber disting. vis. prof. Boston Coll. Law Sch., 1993-94. Author: Natural Law and Natural Rights, 1980, Fundamentals of Ethics, 1983, Nuclear Deterrence, Morality and Realism, 1987, Moral Absolutes, 1991, Aquinas: Moral, Political, and Legal Theory, 1998. Mem. joint bioethical com. Cath. Bishops Eng. and Wales, Scotland and Ireland, 1981-88; vice chmn. Linacre Ctr. (for Med. Ethics), London, 1986-96. Fellow The Brit. Acad. Roman Catholic. Office: Univ Coll, Oxford OX1 4BH, England also: Univ Notre Dame Law School Notre Dame IN 46556

FINNIS, MICHAEL WILLIAM, physics educator; b. Margate, Kent, Eng., Sept. 14, 1949; s. Neville William and Mabel Anne (Gibson) F.; m. Viola Susanne Marten, Apr. 12, 1990; 3 children. BA, U. Cambridge, Eng., 1971; PhD, U. Cambridge, 1974. Higher sci. officer AEA, Harwell, U.K., 1974-78, sr. sci. officer, 1978-86, profl. grade 1, 1986-89; scientist Fritz-Haber-Inst., Berlin, 1988-90; leader theory group Max-Planck-Inst. Metallforschung, Stuttgart, Germany, 1990-95; prof. atomistic theory of materials Queen's U. of Belfast, U.K., 1995—. Rsch. grantee Engring. and Phys. Scis. Rsch. Coun., 1997—, European Cmty., 1998—. Fellow Inst. Physics. Avocations: playing viola da gamba and recorder. Office: Queen's U of Belfast, Dept Physics, Belfast BT7 1NN, United Kingdom

FINOCCHIARO, ALFONSO G., bank executive; b. Catania, Italy, Aug. 20, 1932; came to U.S., 1960; s. Giovanni and Giuseppina (Cavalieri) F.; m. Diana Louise Cavagnolo, May 14, 1960; children: John Paul, Carol Anne. D in Polit. Sci., U. Catania, 1958; MBA in Internat. Fin., Pace U., 1967. V.p. Chem. Bank, N.Y.C., 1966-77; pres., gen. mgr. Conn. Bank Internat., N.Y.C., 1977-78; exec. v.p., regional dir. Banco Portugues do Atlantico, N.Y.C., 1978-95; dir. BPA Futures Cayman, 1989-96, Internat. Strategy Svcs., 1990-96; vice-chmn. BPA Brazil, 1993-96; dir. BPA Overseas Ltd., 1993-96; advisor to bd. dirs. Banco Portugues do Atlantico, Lisbon, Portugal, 1996-97; chmn., CEO FINAB Internat. Corp. Svc. Ltd., 2000—; bd. dirs. BPD Internat. Bank, N.Y.C., Alfie Internat., Inc., So. Fin. Bank, Warrenton, Va.; advisor to bd. dirs. Banco Internat. do Funchal, Lisbon, Portugal, 1997—. Mem. Friends of Queen Catherine, Inc., chmn. fin. com., trustee, 1988—. Decorated comdr. Order Infante D. Henrique (Portugal). Fellow Internat. Mgmt. and Devel. Inst. (Leadership award); mem. Portugal C. of C. (bd. dirs., pres. 1978-98), Am. Portuguese Soc. (v.p., bd. dirs. 1979—), Global Leadership Inst. (bd. dirs. 1991—), Internat. Mgmt. and Devel. Inst, European-Am. C. of C. in the U.S. (v.p., bd. dirs. 1991-98). Republican. Roman Catholic. Avocations: piano, music, travel, foreign affairs.

FINSINGER, JOERG EUGEN, economics educator; b. Ettlingen, Fed. Republic Germany, Oct. 28, 1950; s. Otto and Margarete (Killian) F.; m. Yvette Gisele Gourdin, Aug. 9, 1987; 1 child, Adrien. MS in Math., Ohio State U., Columbus, 1975; PhD in Econs., Bonn U., Fed. Republic Germany, 1979; Habilitation, Bern (Switzerland) U., 1983. Rsch. fellow Internat. Inst. Mgmt., Berlin, 1979-83; lectr. Bern U., 1983-85; prof. bus. U. Lüneburg, Fed. Republic Germany, 1985-90; prof. U. Hohenheim, Stuttgart, Fed. Republic Germany, 1990-91, U. Vienna, Austria, 1991—; vis. prof. U. Calif., Santa Barbara, 1986, U. Jongji, Shanghai, 1988, U. Miami, Coral Gables, Fla., 1989, U. Vienna, 1990; cons. expert pvt. firms, 1983-89; expert witness Fed. Govt., 1983-98, Energiekommission, Switzerland. Author: Insurance, 1985, Verbraucherschutz, 1988, Markt und Regulierung, 1999; author and editor books, editorial bd. scholarly jours. Recipient awards from founds. Mem. Am. Econ. Assn., Royal Econ. Soc., Verein fur Socialpolitik, European Assn. Law and Econs., Austrian Acad. Scis. Office: U Vienna Inst Betriebsuirtsdiaft Lehve, Berggasse 17/17, A-1090 Vienna Austria

FINTON, MICHAEL JAMES, neuropsychologist; b. St. Joseph, Mich., Aug. 11, 1964; s. David Carlisle and Karen Kay Finton; m. Sara Elizabeth Finton, May 22, 1993; children: Caitlyn Joy, Christopher Michael. BS, Ind. U., 1987; MusM in Trombone Performance, Mich. State U., 1989, MA, 1992, PhD, 1995. Predoctoral intern VA Med. Ctr. Memphis, 1994-95; postdoctoral fellow Mayo Clinic, Jacksonville, Fla., 1995-97; coord. neuropsychology svcs. Wallace-Kettering (Ohio) Neurosci. Inst., 1997—; active med. staff Kettering Med. Ctr., 1998—; cons. Mercy Med. Ctr., Springfield, Ohio, 1999—. Recipient grant HCR Manor Care Found., 1999. Mem. APA (Blue Ribbon award 1998, 99), Internat. Neuropsychol. Soc., Nat. Acad. Neuropsychology. Avocations: rowing, astronomy, music. E-mail: michael.finton@ketthealth.com. Office: Wallace Kettering Neurosci Inst 3533 Southern Blvd Ste 5200 Kettering OH 45429-1275

FIODOROVA, NADEJDA NIKOLAEVNA, science educator; b. Astrakhan, Russia, Jan. 15, 1936; s. Nikolay Ignatievich Fiodorov and Alexandra Ivanobna Malinina; m. Juriy Vasilievich Bolotnicov, June 23, 1960 (dec. 1993); 1 child, Igor. Masters degree, Med. Inst. Ijevsk, Russia, 1967; doctor's degree, Med. U., Moscow, 1995. Asst. Med. Inst., Astrakhan, Russia, 1966-81; asst. prof. Tech. U., Astrakhan, 1982-94, prof., 1995—; physician Oil Worker's Hosp. Guriev, Kazakhstan, 1960-62. Author: The Basis of Biology, 1997 (Adminstn. grant 1999); contbr. articles to profl. publs. Grantee Astrakhan Region Adminstrn., 1999. Mem. Russian Acad. Natural Scis., N.Y. Acad. Sci., Internat. Acad. of Coun. of Europe. Avocations: reading, traveling, pets. Home: Liakhova St 3, Apt 27, 414040 Astrakhan Russia Office: Astakhan State Tech U, Tatisheva St 16, 414025 Astrakhan Russia

FIOLITAKIS, EMMANUEL, chemical engineer, researcher; b. Tylissos, Crete, Greece, Oct. 11, 1946; arrived in Germany, 1970; s. Georgios and Maria (Astyrakaki) F.; m. Eleni Dagtzidi, Aug. 29, 1970; children: Maria, Andreas. Chemistry diploma, U. Thessaloniki, Greece, 1969; chem. engring. diploma, U. Erlangen, Germany, 1971, PhD in Engring., 1976, habilitation, 1981. Asst. prof. U. Erlangen, 1976-81; rsch. fellow Forschungszentrum Jülich, Germany, 1982-86; R&D engr. Dynamit Nobel AG, Troisdorf, Germany, 1987-88, Degussa-Huels, Marl, Germany, 1989—. Contbr. articles to profl. jours.; patentee in field. Active Greek Army, 1969-70. Mem. AAAS, The Planetary Soc., N.Y. Acad. Scis., Dechema, Verein Deutscher Ingenieure. Avocation: music. Home: johannesstr 2, D-48249 Duelmen Germany Office: Degussa-Huels, Paul-Baumann-Str 1, D-45764 Marl Germany

FIONDELLA, ROBERT WILLIAM, insurance company executive; b. Bristol, Conn., May 19, 1942; s. Sisto William and Theresa (Nestico) F.; m. Carolyn Brozinski; children: Robert J., Jeffrey. A.B., Providence Coll., 1964; J.D., U. Conn., 1968. Computer programmer-analyst Travelers Ins. Co., Hartford, Conn., 1965; atty. Danaher, Lewis, Tamoney, Hartford, Conn., 1968-69; atty. law dept. Phoenix Mutual Ins. Co., Hartford, Conn., 1969-72, asst. counsel, officer, 1972-74, assoc. counsel, 1974-75, investment counsel, 1975-77, 2d v.p., counsel, 1977, v.p., gen. counsel, 1978-81, sr. v.p.-gen. counsel, 1981-83, exec. v.p. individual ins., 1983-87, pres., 1987-89, bd. dirs., pres., COO, 1989-92, pres., prin. oper. officer, 1992-94; chmn. bd., CEO Phoenix HomeLife Mutual Ins. Co., Hartford, Conn., 1994—; bd. dirs., pres. PML Internat. Ins. Ltd., Phoenix Investment Ptnrs. Ltd; bd. dirs. Life Ins. Coun. N.Y., The Advest Group, Phoenix Investment Ptnrs. Ltd., PXRE (formerly Phoenix Reins.), Phoenix Equity Planning Corp., Am. Phoenix; bd. dirs., pres. Phoenix Am. Life Ins. Co.; bd. dirs., chmn. bd. dirs. Phoenix Charter Oak Trust; bd. dirs. St. Francis Hosp. and Med. Ctr. Chmn. ea. regional fundraising Little League Ctr., Bristol; mem. Britol City Coun., 1969-71, Bristol Urban Renewal Commn., 1971-76; mem. steering com. Mayor Peter's Hartford AmeriCorps, 1995—; chmn. Bristol Retirement Bd., 1978-83; coach Edgewood Little League, Bristol, 1984-85; bd. dirs. St. Francis Hosp. and Med. Ctr., 1992—, Spl. Olympics World Summer Games, 1995—, Spl. Olympics Internat., 1996—, Barnes Group Inc., 1997—; mem. cabinet Conn. Children's Ctr. Campaign for Our Children, 1995—; mem. adv. bd. WKND Greater Hartford Initiative; co-chmn. Cmty. Cancer Ctr. Bldg. Fund, Johnson Meml. Mem. Conn. Bar Assn., Conn. Bus. and Industry Assn. (bd. dirs.), Greater Hartford C. of C. (bd. dirs., chmn. 1997—). Home: 29 Summerberry Cir Bristol CT 06010-2957 Office: Phoenix Home Life Mutual Ins Co One American Row Hartford CT 06102

FIORATO, ADELIN CHARLES, Romance languages educator; b. Sant'Ambrogio, Veneto, Italy, Apr. 5, 1924; arrived in France, 1932; s. Angel and Emily (Padovani) F.; m. Jacqueline Grégoire, Dec. 1, 1950 (dec. 1981); children: Catherine, Renaud; m. Corinne Lucas, May 25, 1985. BA, U. Paris, 1948; MA, Clermont U., 1949; Agregation, U. Paris, 1952, Docteur d'Etat, 1978. Secondary sch. tchr. Lycée Condorcet, Paris, 1951-59; asst. prof. U. Nancy, France, 1959-66; asst. prof. Romance langs. U. Chgo., 1966-67; prof., head Italian dept. U. Clermont, 1967-70; prof. U. Paris III, 1970-88, head Italian dept., 1970-74, head adults formation dept., 1978-81, v.p., 1982-85, responsible for rsch. seminars CIRRI, 1985-91, seminars CRIRC, head CNRS, 1986-99. Author: Bandello entre l'histoire et l'écriture, 1979; editor author: Discours littéraires et pratiques politiques, 1987, L'image de l'autre européen, 1991, La Table et Ses Dessous, 1999, others. Lt. Navy, 1969. Mem. Assn. for Diffusion of Italian Lang. in France (pres. 1981-90). Avocations: choral singing, novel writing. Home: 45 Quai de la Seine, 75019 Paris France Office: U Sorbonne Nouvelle, 17 rue de la Sorbonne, 75005 Paris France

FIORAVANTI, DOMENICO, olympic athlete; b. Novara, Italy, May 31, 1977. Mem. swim team Italy; winner 100 meter breaststroke European Championship, 1999, 2000, second pl. 200 meter breaststroke, 2000; winner gold in 100 meter breaststroke Olympics, Sydney, Australia, 2000, winner gold in 200 meter breaststroke, 2000. Office: Fedn Italiana Nuoto Stadio, Olimpico Curva Nord, 00194 Rome Italy*

FIORE, COLLEEN MARY, professional society administrator; b. Watertown, N.Y., May 4, 1969; d. Edward Francis Van Emmerik and Donna Roe Buske; m. James R. Fiore, Mar. 20, 1993; 1 child, Mikaela. BS, Roosevelt U., 1992. Cert. meeting profl. Program coord. Soc. Actuaries, Schaumburg, Ill., 1992-94; meeting coord. Soc. Actuaries, Schaumburg, 1994-97, meeting mgr., 1997—. Mem. Am. Soc. Assn. Execs., Profl. Conv. Mgmt. Assn. Office: Soc of Actuaries #800 475 N Martingale Rd Ste 800 Schaumburg IL 60173-2226

FIORENTINI, STEFANO, tax lawyer, consultant; b. Rome, Apr. 12, 1955; s. Renato and Anna (Coppola) F.; m. Carla Pignataro, Oct. 23, 1986; 1 child, Arianna. Law degree, U. Rome, 1977. Asst. Associazione Bancaria Italiana-Italian Banks Assn., Rome, 1978-82; sr. asst. Associazione Nazionale Co Struttori Edili Assn. of Bldg. Enterprises, Rome, 1982—; cons. in field; tchr. Luiss U. Postgrad. Sch. Author: The Substitutive Tax on Medium-Long Term Loans, 1983, International Conventions on Double Taxation, 1984, Taxation in Italy of Non-Resident Subjects, 1988. Mem. Internat. Fiscal Assn., Mensa. E-mail: fiostef@tiscalinet.it. Home and Office: Studio Fiorentini, 45 Via Nizza, 00198 Rome Italy

FIORENTINO, CARMINE, lawyer; b. Bklyn., Sept. 11, 1932; s. Pasquale and Lucy (Coppola) F. LL.B., Blackstone Sch. Law, Chgo., 1954, John Marshall Law Sch., Atlanta, 1957. Bar: Ga, D.C., U.S. Supreme Ct., U.S. Dist. Ct. D.C., U.S. Ct. Appeals (2d cir.), U.S. Dist. Ct. (no. dist.) Ga., U.S. Ct. Appeals (5th cir.), U.S. Ct. Claims. Mem. N.Y. State Workmen's Compensation Bd., N.Y. State Dept. Labor, 1950-53; ct. reporter, hearing stenographer N.Y. State Com. State Counsel and Attys., 1953; public relations sec. Indsl. Home for Blind, Bklyn., 1953-55; legal stenographer, researcher, law clk., Atlanta, 1955, 57-59; sec. import-export firm, Atlanta, 1956; sole practice, Atlanta, 1959-63, 73—; atty., advisor, trial atty. HUD, Atlanta and Washington, also legal counsel Peachtree Fed. Credit Union, 1963-74; acting dir. Elmira (N.Y.) Disaster Field Office, HUD, 1973; former candidate U.S. Adminstrv. Law Judge. Recipient State of Victory World Culture prize. Mem. Smithsonian Instn., pres., dir., gen. counsel The Hexagon Corp., Republican Nat. Com., Rep. Presdl. Task Force, Nat. Hist. Soc.; Inducted into Rep. Presdl. Legion Merit, 1993; Life Dynamics fellow; mem. Atlanta Hist. Soc., Atlanta Bot. Gardens, Am. Mus. Natural History, Mus. Heritage Soc. Mem. ABA, Fed. Bar Assn., Atlanta Bar Assn., Decatur-DeKalb Bar Assn., Am. Judicature Soc., Old War Horse Lawyers Club, Assn. Trial Lawyers Am., AAAS, Internat. Platform Soc., Nat. Audubon Soc. Presbyterian. Clubs: Toastmasters, Gaslight, Sierra. Writer non-fiction and poetry; composer songs and hymns. Home and Office: 4717 Roswell Rd NE Apt R4 Atlanta GA 30342-2915

FIORETTI, ROBERT WILLIAM, lawyer; b. Chgo., Mar. 8, 1953; s. Edward E. and Helene (Krypcio) F. BA, U. Ill., 1975; JD, No. Ill. U., 1978. Bar: Ill. 1978, U.S. Dist. Ill. 1978, N.Y. 1981, U.S. Supreme Ct. 1981. Asst. corp. counsel City of Chgo., 1978-82, sr. supervising atty., 1982-86; litigation chief Shain, Firsel & Burney, Chgo., 1986-88; ptnr. Fioretti & Des Jardins Ltd., Chgo., 1989—; adj. prof. law No. Ill. U., 2000—; appointed Ill. Supreme Ct. com. on character and fitness, 2000—. Contbr. articles to law rev. Bd. dirs. Historic Pullman Found. (exec. bd. 1995—), Chgo., 1992-00, pres., 1995—; mem. pres.'s coun. U. Ill. Found., Champaign, 1993—; mem. bd. visitors No. Ill. U., DeKalb, 1992—, mem. alumni coun. Coll. law, 1991-00, pres. alumni coun., 1994-98; bd. dirs. Chgo. Vol. Legal Svcs., 1997—, v.p. devel., 1999—; mem. adv. bd. St. Mary Nazareth Hosp., 1999—; bd. dirs. One Historic Blvd., treas., 1999—; mem. Friends of 5 Hosp.; appointed spl. asst. states atty. of Cook County, 1992-95, spl. asst. atty. gen., 1990—; pres. Historic Pullman Found., 1995-2000. Named Outstanding Young Alumni No. Ill. U., 1994, Outstanding Alumni, 1999, Disting. Svc. award, 1999. Mem. FBA (bd. dirs.), Chgo. Athletic Assn. (bd. dirs. 1993-97, v.p. 1995-97), No. Ill. U. Alumni Assn. (bd. dirs. 1997—, v.p. 1999, pres. 2000—). Office: Fioretti & Des Jardins Ltd 8 S Michigan Ave Chicago IL 60603-3357

FIORI, FRANCESCO, member European Parliament; b. Voghera, PV, Italy, Apr. 14, 1953. Mem. European Parliament, Brussels, 1999—; mem. com. on agr. and rural devel., com. on industry, external trade, rshc. and energy, mem. substitute del. for rels. with countries of S.Am. and MERCOSUR. Vice chmn. group of European People's Patry (Christian Dems.) and European Dems. Mem. Forza Italia Party. Office: European Parliament, Rue Wiertz ASP 9E114, B-1047 Brussels Belgium*

FIORINA, CARLETON S. (CARLY FIORINA), computer company executive; b. Austin, Tex., Sept. 6, 1954; married. BA in Medieval History and Philosophy, Stanford U., 1976; MBA, U. Md., 1980; MSc, MIT, 1989; postgrad., UCLA. Account exec. Long Lines AT&T, 1980, sr. v.p. Global Mktg., pres. Atlantic and Canadian Region; v.p. Corp. Ops. Lucent Technologies, group pres. Global Svc. Provider; pres., CEO Hewlett-Packard, Palo Alto, 1999—, chmn. bd. dirs., 2000—; bd. dirs. Kellogg Co., Merck & Co., Inc., Power Up; elected U.S. China Bd. Trade. Named one of Fortune Mag. Most Powerful Women in Am. Bus. Office: Hewlett-Packard 3000 Hanover St Palo Alto CA 94304-1181*

FIORINI, VITTORIO, airworthiness and engineering educator; b. Ferrara, Italy, June 21, 1931; s. Fabio and Maria (Tenani) F.; m. Enrica Baratelli, June 30, 1973; children: Maria Cecila, Fabio. Degree in mech. engring., U. Bologna, 1954; degree in aeronautical engring., Turin Poly. U., 1955; MS in

Aeronautics, Calif. Inst. of Tech., 1960; PhD, Aeorspace Engring. Sch., Rome, 1971. Tech. dir. Registro Aeronautico Italiano, Rome, 1972-92, ctrl. dir. R&D, 1993-97; asst. prof. Aerospace Propulsion, Rome, 1975-78; prof. helicopter propulsion Aerospace Engring. Sch., 1980-98; mem. com. on aircraft noise ICAO CAN, 1969-85; Italian mem. com. on aviation environ, protection ICAO CAEP, 1988-98; Italian mem. Airworthiness Com., 1990-98, Joint Aviation Authorities, 1986-97, exec. bd., 1996. Contbr. articles to sci. jours. Under lt. Italian Air Force, 1956-57. Mem. Am. Helicopter Soc., Italian Assn. Aeronautics nd Astronautics. Roman Catholic. Avocations: skiing, sailing. Home: Via Cassia 701/R1, 00189 Rome Italy

FIOROT, DINO, political scientist; b. Treviso, Italy, Aug. 21, 1919; s. Giovanni and Cesira (Furlan) F.; m. Carmen Meo. BA, U. Padova, 1944. Prof. U. Padova, Italy, 1954-55, 68-96, U. Mogadishu, Somalia, 1955-67; prof. emeritus U. Padova, 1996—.

FIRBAS, WILHELM, physician, anatomy educator; b. Vienna, Austria, Feb. 4, 1939; s. Wilhelm and Hildegard (Hälbig) F.; m. Brigitte Kurzmann, Aug. 1, 1964 (wid.); children: Christa, Ulrike. D of Medicine, U. Vienna, 1964. Asst. prof. anatomy U. Vienna, Vienna, 1964-82, prof., 1982—, head dept. anatomy, 1983—. Author: Radiologic Anatomy, 1977 (Book Fair award 1980), Neuroanatomy, 1988; contbr. numerous articles to profl. publs. Recipient award Wander Corp., 1968. Mem. Am. Assn. Clin. Anatomy, German Anat. Assn., Deutsche Ornithologen Gesellschaft, Gesellschaft Arzte Wien. Office: Dept Anatony, Währingerstrasse 13, Vienna Austria A-1090

FIREHOCK, BARBARA A., interior designer; b. Alexandria, Va., Feb. 2, 1944; d. George W. Jr. and Geraldine Tinsley (Wallin) Sickler; m. Scott Walton Ripley, Dec. 27, 1966 (div.); m. Raymond B. Firehock, Jr.; 1 child, Christopher Francis. BA, U. N. Tex., 1966; postgrad., U. Md., 1976-77. Vol. Peace Corps, Colombia, 1967-69; owner Walnut Hill Interiors, LaPlata, Md., 1981—; instr. in interior design Charles County C.C., LaPlata, 1990; site supr./interior design internship U. Md., College Park, 1992; program com. Matawoman Creek Arts Ctr., Charles County, Md., 1995-96; fundraiser The Gallery Com. of Charles County, 1988-94; interior designer Fredericksburg Area Svc. League Decorator Showhouse, 1997—, So. Md. Decorator Showhouse, 1998. Design work featured in Town and Country, 1997, Community Carousel Weekly Show/Prestige Cable, Fredericksburg, The Maryland Independent, 1991, The Maryland House and Garden Pilgrimage, 1995-96, Traditional Home, 1999. Spl. events chair Charles County Garden Club of Md.; chair Christ Ch. Concert Series, LaPlata, 1995. Named Woman of Yr. Bus. and Profl. Women, Charles County, 1982. Fellow Nat. Trust for Hist. Preservation (nat. capitol area fellow, design assoc.); Mem. ASID, Interior Design Soc. (pres. Md. chpt.), AAUW (pres., v.p., cultural chair Charles County chpt.), Chi Omega (rush info. chair for So. Md. 1993-98). Democrat. Episcopalian. Avocations: horseback riding, gardening, needlework, genealogy. Office: Walnut Hill Interiors PO Box 1451 La Plata MD 20646-1451 also: 330 Vine St Staunton VA 24401-4354

FIRESTONE, KAREN BETH, research scientist, educator; b. Washington, Sept. 11, 1963; arrived in Australia, 1991; d. Allan and Barbara (Spielman) F.; m. Warwick D. Greville, Jan. 4, 2000. BS, Va. Poly.. Inst. and State U., 1985; MS, U. Md., 1989; PhD, U. NSW. Tchg. asst. U. Md., College Park, 1988-89; field rschr. various orgns., Australia, 1989-90; rschr. Nat. Wildlife Fedn., Washington, 1991; field rschr. U. Sydney, Kosliusko Nat. Pk., Australia, 1991; rsch. officer Zool. Parks Bd. of NSW, Australia, 1991—; lectr. Tech. and Further Edn., Australia, 1997—; hon. vis. fellow U. NSW, 1992-94. Contbr. articles to profl. jours. Mem. Soc. for Conservation Biology (1st place oral paper award 1998), Australian Mammal Soc. (Bolliger award 1999), Genetics Soc. of Australia, Royal Zool. Soc. NSW, Australasian Wildlife Mgmt. Soc. Avocations: cycling, kayaking, gardening, bushwalking, reading. Office: Conservation Rsch Ctr, PO Box 20, NSW Mosman 2088, Australia

FIRESTONE, ROGER MORRIS, computer scientist; b. Washington, Aug. 23, 1945; s. Linn Jacob and Regina Caroline (Steiner) F. AB summa cum laude, ScM, Brown U., 1967; MS, NYU, 1969, PhD, 1971; MBA, U. St. Thomas, St. Paul, 1976. Mgr. tech. planning Sperry Corp./Unisys Corp., St. Paul, then Blue Bell, Pa., 1969-86; mem. tech. staff MRJ Inc., Oakton, Va., 1987-92; assoc. dir. engring. svcs. Maden Tech. Cons. Inc., Arlington, Va., 1992-93; sys. engr. V Cray Rsch., Washington, 1995; sr. scientist Comm. Techs., Herndon, Va., 1996-97; software arch. Teknowledge, Fairfax, Va., 1997-2000; info. sys. engr. lead Mitre Corp., McLean, Va., 2000—. Composer, arranger, performer orchestral, concert band, wind quintet and chamber music; contbr. articles to Scottish Rite Jour. (George Washington medal 1991). Rep. precinct capt. Devolites campaign, Fairfax County, Va., 1997. Mem. Masons (past lodge master, past coun. grand master). Jewish. Avocations: theatre (acting), amateur astronomy. E-mail: rfire@cais.net. Home: 10159 Turnberry Pl Oakton VA 22124-2847 Office: Mitre Corp 1820 Dolly Madison Blvd Mc Lean VA 22102

FIROOZABADY, EBRAHIM, plant scientist; b. Kangavar, Iran, Mar. 1, 1952; came to U.S., 1976; s. Khosrow and Tavous (Gharloghi) F.; m. Nickoo Tavassoli, Oct. 2, 1976; children: Amy, Yasmin, Navid. BS, U. Tehran, Iran, 1975; MS, U. Calif., Davis, 1978, PhD, 1982. Postdoctoral assoc. U. Nebr., Lincoln, 1982-84; rsch. scientist Agrigenetics, Madison, Wis., 1984-86, sr. rsch. scientist, 1986-88; prof. U. N.Mex., Las cruces, 1989; group rsch. scientist DNA Plant Tech., Oakland, Calif., 1989-93, prin. rsch. scientist, 1993—. Contbr. chpts. to books, numerous articles to profl. jours. Mem. Soc. for In Vitro Biology (plant divsn. v.p. 1994-96, symposium chmn. congress 1991—, plant program com. 1990—). Achievements include research in genetic engineering of different crop plants including pineapple, carnation, rose, banana, papaya, chrysanthemum, cotton, tomato, sunflower, alfalfa and tobacco; production of new cultivars by genetic engineering; inventor/patentee in field. Avocations: gardening, camping, skiing. Office: DNA Plant Tech 6701 San Pablo Ave Ste B Oakland CA 94608-1244

FIRSOV, BORIS MAXIMOVICH, sociologist, educator; b. Salsk, Russia, June 22, 1929; s. Maxim Feodorovich and Lidiya Efimovna (Muzhenkova) F.; m. Galina Stepanovna Valyavskaya, June 5, 1954. MS, Electrotech. Inst., Leningrad, Russia, 1954; Candidate in Sci., State U., Leningrad, Russia, 1969; DS, USSR Acad. Scis., 1979. Dir. TV Studio, Leningrad, 1962-66; head dept. Inst. Sociology Rsch. USSR Acad. Scis., 1969-75, head dept. Inst. Sociology-Econ. Problems, 1975-84, leading rschr. Inst. Ethnography, 1984-89; dir. Inst. Sociology Russian Acad. Scis., St. Petersburg, 1989-95; rector European U. at St. Petersburg, St. Petersburg, 1996—; cons. Lenfilm Studio, Leningrad, 1969-85; vis. prof. U. Tampere, Finland, 1974, U. Music and Theatre, Hannover, Germany, 1993-94; cons. sociologist Union Theatre Workers, Russian Fedn., 1979-88. Author: Television from a Sociologist's Vision, 1972, Ways of the Development of Mass Media, 1977; author, editor: On Qualitative Characteristics of the St. Petersburg Population, 1996; co-author: (with I. Kisseleva) Folkways of Russian Peasants, 1994. Dep. City Coun. People's Deputies, Leningrad, 1961-65; chairperson European U. Orgns. Com., St. Petersburg, 1992-95; mem. State Duma Pub. Commn. on Sci., Moscow, 1996-99. Recipient fellowship UNESCO, Paris, 1972. Mem. Union Russian Cinematographists, Union Theatre Workers, VI World Congress Ctrl. and Ea. European Studies (internat. program com. 1996—), Finnish Ctr. for East European and Russian Studies (mem. adv. com. 1996—). Avocations: reading, theatre, international tourism. Office: European Univ, 3 Gagarinskaya St, 191187 Saint Petersburg Russia

FIRTH-COZENS, JENNY, psychologist, consultant; b. Oxford, U.K., Feb. 17, 1942; d. George Samuel Cozens and Malvina Haldane; m. John Antony Firth, Oct. 6, 1966; children: Robert Antony, Ben Oliver. BA, Open U., U.K., 1976; BSc (hon.), U. Hull, U.K., 1979; MSc in Clin. Psych., U. Leeds, U.K., 1981; PhD, U. Sheffield, U.K., 1990. Chartered clin. psychologist, chartered occupational psychologist. Clin. rsch. scientist Med. Rsch. Coun. U. Sheffield, U.K., 1981-87; clin. lectr. U. Leicester, U.K., 1987-89; orgnl. devel. specialist Yorkshire Regional Health, Harrogate, U.K., 1989-91; lectr. U. Leeds, U.K., 1991-93, prin. rsch. fellow, 1993-98; lead for clin. effectiveness NHS Exec., Durham, U.K., 1993-98; dir. Clin. Psychology and Health Care Rsch. Ctr. U. Northumbria, U.K., 1998—; cons. NHS Exec., Leeds, U.K., 1994-98, North Thames Postgrad. Med., London, 1997-98; advice columnist Good Housekeeping, London, 1988-97. Author: Nervous Breakdown: What Is It?; What Causes It? Who Will Help?, 1993; Audit for Mental Health Services, 1994; editor: Stress in Health Professionals, 1999; contbr. articles to profl. jours. Grantee NHS R&D, 1993, 2000, Dept. Health, Sperrin & Lakeland Trust, 1999. Fellow British Psychology Soc., Royal Soc. Arts. Avocations: painting, gardening. Office: Ctr for Clin Psych, Univ Northumbria, Newcastle upon Tyne NE77XA, England

FIŠAR, ZDENEK, biophysicist, researcher; b. Krnov, Czech Republic, Dec. 3, 1956; s. Josef and Marie (Zumrová) F.; m. Andrea Trachtulcová, Dec. 30, 1981; 1 child, Matej. Grad., Charles Univ., Prague, 1980; PhD, Acad. Sci., Prague, 1986. Scientist Microbiol. Inst. Acad. Sci., Novy Hrádek, 1981-85, Inst. Landscape Ecology Acad. Sci., Česke Budějovice, 1985-89, 1st Medical Faculty Charles Univ., Prague, 1989—. Contbr. articles to profl. jours. Mem. Czech Neuropsychopharmacol. Soc., World Fedn. Soc. Biol. Psychiatry, Soc. Biol. Psychiatry, Czech Soc. Biochem. Molecular Biology, Czech and Slovak Neurochem. Soc. Baha'i. Avocation: computers, Internet. Home: Na Kocince 6, 160 00 Prague 6 Czech Republic Office: Charles Univ Psychiatric Rsch Lab, Ke Karlovu 11 1st Med Faculty, 120 00 Prague 2 Czech Republic

FISCH, CHARLES, physician, educator; b. Nesterov (Zolkiew), Poland, May 11, 1921; s. Leon and Janette (Deutscher) F.; m. June Spiegal, May 23, 1943; children: Jonathan, Gary, Bruce. AB, Ind. U., 1942, MD, 1944; MD (hon.), U. Utrecht, The Netherlands, 1983. Diplomate Am. Bd. Internal Medicine, Am. Bd. Cardiovasc. Medicine (mem. 1977-82). Intern St. Vincent's Hosp., Indpls., 1945; resident in internal medicine VA Hosp., Indpls., 1948-50; fellow gastroenterology Marion County Gen. Hosp., Indpls., 1950-51; fellow in cardiology Marion County Gen. Hosp., 1951-53; asst. prof. medicine Ind. U. Med. Sch., 1953-59, assoc. prof., 1959-63, prof., 1963—, disting. prof., 1975, dir. cardiovasc. divsn., 1963-90, disting. prof. emeritus, 1990—; dir. Krannert Inst. Cardiology, 1953-90; mem. cardio-renal adv. com. HEW-FDA, 1973-77, 79—; Connor lectr. Am. Heart Assn., 1980; chmn. manpower rev. com. Nat. Heart, Lung and Blood Inst., 1985-89; Charles Fisch chair in cardiology Ind. U. Author: Electrocardiography of Arrythmias, 1989; co-editor Digitalis, 1969, Cardiac Electrophysiology and Arrythmias, 1991; contbr. articles to med. jours.; mem. editorial bd. Am. Heart Jour., 1967—, Am. Jour. Electrocardiology, 1967—, Coeur et Medicine Interne, 1970—, Am. Jour. Medicine, 1973—, Circulation, 1977—, Am. Jour. Cardiology, 1967—; assoc. editor Am. Jour. Cardiology, 1977—. Capt. M.C. AUS, 1946-48. Recipient James Herrick award Am. Heart Assn. Fellow ACP, Am. Coll. Cardiology (pres. 1975-77, dir., chmn. publ. com. 1988-94, Gifted Tchr. award 1993), World Congress Cardiology (v.p. 1986); mem. Am. Fedn. Clin. Rsch., Ctrl. Soc. Clin. Rsch., Am. Physiol. Soc., Assn. Univ. Cardiologists, Assn. Am. Physicians, N.Am. Soc. for Pacing and Electrophysiology (Dist. Tchr. award 1994). Home: 7901 Morningside Dr Indianapolis IN 46240-2526 Office: Ind U Med Ctr Krannert Inst Card 1111 W 10th St Indianapolis IN 46202-4800

FISCHBACH, RUTH LINDA, ethics educator, social scientist, researcher; b. N.Y.C., June 7, 1940; d. Edward Joseph and Bess (Wolsk) Zeitlin; m. Gerald David Fischbach, July 8, 1962; children: Elissa, Peter, Mark and Neal (twins). Attended, Mt. Holyoke Coll., 1958-60; BS, RN, Cornell U., 1963; MS, Boston U., 1975, PhD, 1983; MPE, Washington U., 1990. Dir. patient edn. Beth Israel Hosp., Boston, 1978-80; postdoctoral fellow Washington U. Sch. Medicine, St. Louis, 1983-86, asst. rsch. prof., 1986-90, asst. dean, 1989-90; asst. prof. Harvard Med. Sch., Boston, 1990-98; sr. advisor for biomed. ethics Office of Dir. for Extramural Rsch./NIH, Bethesda, Md., 1998—; dir. Program in Practice of Sci. Investigation Harvard Med. Sch., 1990-98, Program for Humanities in Medicine Washington U. Sch. Medicine, 1988-90; reviewer University-wide AIDS Rsch. Program State Calif., 1995; adv. bd. Beth Israel Clin. Investigator Tng. Program, Boston, 1995—; bd. dirs. Pub. Responsibility in Med. and Rsch., Boston, 1992—. Producer: (dramatization) Miss Evers' Boys, 1993; editl. bd. Sci. & Engring. Ethics, 1994—; contbr. articles to profl. jours., chpts. to books. Pres. Lincoln Sch. PTA, Brookline, Mass., 1978-80; vol. Mass. Coalition of Battered Women Svc. Groups, Boston, 1993-98; bd. dirs. Joint Com. on Status of Women, Boston, 1990-97; trustee Penzance Point, 1998—; bd. trustees Parc Simerset Condominium, Chevy Chase, Md. Fellow Exec. Inst. of Advanced Study, St. Louis, 1988. Mem. Applied Rsch. Ethics Nat. Assn. (bd. dirs. 1994—), Mass. Bioethics Forum (bd. dirs. 1994—), Md. Mothers of Twins (pres. 1969-70), Sigma Theta Tau. Avocations: horticulture, travel, music. Home: 5630 Wisconsin Ave Apt 1502 Chevy Chase MD 20815-4458 Office: 1 Center Dr Msc 0152 Bethesda MD 20892-0001

FISCHER, AARON JACK, accountant; b. Chgo., Feb. 6, 1947; s. Ralph Hyman and Florence Idel (Kaufman) F.; m. Robin Gail Cole, Jan. 23, 1972; children: Amy Lauren, Michael Kenneth. BS in Commerce, DePaul U., 1969. CPA, Ill.; diplomate Am. Bd. Forensic Accts., Am. Bd. Forensic Examiners. Staff acct. BDO Seidman, Chgo., 1969-79, ptnr., 1979-86, tech. dir. acctg., auditing sec midwest regional, 1986-89; ptnr. Drobny and Fischer CPA (now Adler Drobny Fischer LLC), Crystal Lake, Ill., 1990—. Bd. dirs. Young Men's Jewish Coun., 1978-79. Mem. AICPA, Ill. Soc. CPA (acctg. principles com. 1978-80, ethics com. 1980-82), Am. Coll. Forensic Examiners, Twin Orchard Country Club. Home: 2243 Elm Ridge Dr Northbrook IL 60062-6507*

FISCHER, ALAIN, physician; b. Paris, Sept. 11, 1949; s. Alfred and Jacqueline (Faucheur) F.; m. Anne-Marie Horowitz, June 27, 1973; children: Nicolas, Fabien. MD, U. Paris V, 1979; PhD, U. Paris VII, 1979. Resident Paris Hosp., 1975-79, asst. prof., 1981-84, assoc. prof., 1984-87, prof., 1988—; head clin. pediatric immunology unit INSERM, Paris, 1996—, dir., 1991—. Contbr. articles to profl. jours. Advisor Min. Rsch., Paris, 1999. Avocations: reading, mountain activities. Home: 64 Rue La Colonie, 75013 Paris France Office: INSERM Hosp Necker, 149 Rue De Sevres, 75015 Paris France

FISCHER, ANDREA, German government official. Min. of health Govt. of Germany. Office: Ministry of Health, Am Probsthor 78A, 53121 Bonn Germany

FISCHER, AUGUST A., publishing executive. CEO News Internat. News Corp, London, 1990-95; COO News Corp; CEO Axel Springer Verlag AG, Germany, 1997—; chmn. Axel Springer Verlag AG. Office: Axel Springer Verlag AG, Axel-Springer-Platz 1, D-20350 Hamburg Germany

FISCHER, BERND JURGEN, history educator; b. Bunde, Westphalen, Germany, Jan. 27, 1952; came to U.S., 1961; s. Emil and Gertrud (Einars) F. BA, U. Calif., Santa Barbara, 1973, MA, 1975, PhD, 1982. Asst. prof. European history Ctrl. Mich. U., 1982-83; instr., chair social sci. divsn. Wenatchee Valley Coll., 1983-86; asst. prof. Ea. European history U. Western Ont., London, Can., 1986-87, McGill U., Montreal, 1988, U. Hartford, Conn., 1989-93; prof. history Ind. U., Ft. Wayne, 1993—, mem. exec. com. Russian and East European Inst., 1994-96; mem. adv. bd. Ctr. for Albanian Studies, U. London. Author: King Zog and the Struggle for Stability in Albania, 1984 (transl. into Albanian 1996), Albania At War, 1939-1945, 2000; contbg. author: Eastern European Nationalism in the 20th Century, 1995; editor: Albanian Studies: International Registry of Scholars and Research, 1998—; editor CLIO Jour. Lit., History and Philosophy of History, 1995—; also articles. Rsch. grantee Am. Coun. Learned Socs., 1989, NEH, 1992; travel grantee Mellon Found., 1995. Mem. Soc. for Albanian Studies (exec. com. 1990—, v.p. 1998—), Internat. Assn. for S.E. European Studies (exec. bd., U.S. com. 1993—). Avocations: travel, tennis, skiing. Home: 1517 Columbia Ave Fort Wayne IN 46805-5218 Office: Ind U Dept History Fort Wayne IN 46805

FISCHER, CLARE, composer; b. Durand, Mich., Oct. 22, 1928; s. Cecil Harold and Luella Blanche (Roussin) F.; children: Lee Clare, Brent Sean Cecil, Tahlia Georgienne Marguerite Bianca; m. Donna Van Ringelesteyn. MusB in Music Composition and Theory, Mich. St. U., 1952, MusM, 1955; MusD (hon.), Mich. State U., 1999. Arranger albums for Donald Byrd, George Shearing, Dizzy Gilespie, The Hi-lo's, Singers Unlimited, Cal Tjader, João Gilberto, Charles Lloyd , Chaka Khan, Prince, Michael Jackson, Robert Palmer, Paul McCartney, Paula Abdul, Earl Klugh, The Jacksons, most recent albums: Lembranças and Just Me- Solo Piano Excursions on Concord Records, Memento on Discovery, Rockin' in Rhythm on JVC Records, The Latin Side, Clare Fischer's Jazz Corps and Symbiosis; arranger movies for Prince; composer orchestral The Duke, Sweé Pea and Me, Tahlia, Sonatine for Clarinet and Piano, Time-piece, Suite for Cello and String Orch., and numerous others. E-mail: clarefischer@thegrid.net.

FISCHER, DUNCAN KINNEAR, neurosurgeon; b. Chapel Hill, N.C., Sept. 14, 1957; s. Newton Duchan and Janet (Jordan) F.; m. Anne Holmes Billington, Sept. 10, 1983; children: Luke Duncan, Kent Billington, Duncan Newton II. AB, Princeton U., 1979; MPhil, Yale U., 1982, MD, PhD, 1986. Cert. in neurosurgery. Intern in surgery Baylor Coll. Medicine Affiliated Hosps., Houston, 1986-87, resident in neurosurgery, 1987-92; rsch. assoc. Baylor Coll. Medicine, Houston, 1988-92; neurosurgeon San Angelo (Tex.) Cmty. Med. Ctr. and Neurosurg. Ctr., 1992—. Contbr. numerous articles to profl. publs. Med. Scientist Tng. Program scholar NIH, ACS scholar. Fellow ACS; mem. Harvey Cushing Soc., Am. Assn. Neurol. Surgeons, Sigma Xi, Phi Beta Kappa. Republican. Episcopalian. Office: 3515 Executive Dr San Angelo TX 76904-6883

FISCHER, EDMOND HENRI, biochemistry educator; b. Shanghai, Republic of China, Apr. 6, 1920; came to U.S., 1953; s. Oscar and Renée (Tapernoux) F.; m. Beverley B. Bullock. Lic. es Sciences Chimiques et Biologiques, U. Geneva, 1943, Diplome d'Ingenieur Chimiste, 1944, PhD, 1947; D (hon.), U. Montpellier, France, 1985, U. Basel, Switzerland, 1988, Med. Coll. of Ohio, 1993, Ind. U., 1993, U. Bochum, Germany, 1994. Pvt. docent biochemistry U. Geneva, 1950-53; research assoc. biology Calif. Inst. Tech., Pasadena, 1953; asst. prof. biochemistry U. Wash., Seattle, 1953-56, assoc. prof., 1956-61, prof., 1961-90, prof. emeritus, 1990—; mem. exec. com. Pacific Slope Biochem. Conf., 1958-59, pres., 1975; mem. biochemistry study sect. NIH, 1959-64, symposium co-chmn. Battelle Seattle Rsch. Ctr., 1970, 73, 78; mem. sci. adv. bd. Biozentrum, U. Basel, Switzerland, 1982-86; mem. sci. adv. bd. Friedrich Miescher Inst., Ciba-Geigy, Basel, 1976-84, chmn., 1981-84; mem. bd. sci. govs. Scripps Rsch. Inst., La Jolla, Calif., 1987—, Basel Inst. for Immunology, 1996—; bd. govs. Weizmann Inst. Sci., Rehovot, Israel, 1997—. Contbr. numerous articles to sci. jours. Mem. sci. council on basic sci. Am. Heart Assn., 1977-80, sci. adv. com. Muscular Dystrophy Assn., 1980-88. Recipient Lederle Med. Faculty award, 1956-59, Guggenheim Found. award, 1963-64, Disting. Lectr. award U. Wash., 1983, Laureate Passano Found. award, 1988, Steven C. Beering award, 1991, Nobel prize in Physiology or Medicine, 1992. Fellow Am. Acad. Arts and Scis.; mem. NAS, AAAS, AAUP, Am. Soc. Biol. Chemists (coun. 1989-93), Am. Chem. Soc. (adv. bd. biochemistry divsn. 1962, exec. com. divsn. biology 1969-72, monograph adv. bd. 1971-73, editl. adv. bd. Biochemistry, 1961-66, assoc. editor 1966-91), Swiss Chem. Soc. (Werner medal), Spanish Royal Acad. Scis. (fgn. assoc.), Venice Inst. Sci., Arts and Letters (fgn. assoc.), Japanese Biochem. Soc. (hon.). Achievements include cellular regulation by phosphorylation/dephosphorylation cycle. Office: U Washington Med Sch PO Box 357350 Seattle WA 98195-7350

FISCHER, EDMUNDO IGNACIO, cardiologist, researcher; b. Gualeguaychu, Entre Rios, Argentina, Aug. 26, 1953; s. Ildo Alberico Cabrera and Luisa Fischer. MD, La Plata (Argentina) U., LaPlata, Argentina, 1978; cardiologist, El Salvador, Argentina, 1983. Med. diplomate. Cardiologist La Plata City Faculty Medicine, Argentina, 1972-78, asst. in anatomy, 1978; chief of residents FaValoro Found., Buenos Aires, 1978-81, staff hemodynamic, 1981-83, chief cardiovascular care, 1982, sr. investigator, 1984—; cons. Bakker Rsch. Ctr., Holland, 1987-94; prof. El Salvador, Argentina, 1989-93; rschr. Inst. Nat. de la Sante et la Rsch. Med.-Conicet Agreement, France-Argentina, 1989-97, Consejo Nat. Investigation Sci. & Tech., Argentina, 1993-97. Editor: Cardiac Failure, 1989, Physiopathologie of Traitent de l'Insuffisance Cardiaque Severe, 1996, others. Sponsor Hosp., Entre Rios, 1991-97, Libr., Buenos Aires, 1993-97, Sch., Entre Rios, 1994-97. Recipient Cino del Duca Found. award, Paris, 1988, 93; Med. Rsch. grant Found. pour la Rsch. Med., Paris, 1991. Fellow Am. Coll. Cardiology (assoc.), N.Y. Acad. Sci.; mem. French Soc. Cardiology. Avocations: fishing, riding, flying. Office: Favaloro Found, Solis 453, 1078 Buenos Aires Argentina

FISCHER, ERNST OTTO, chemist, educator; b. Munich, Germany, Nov. 10, 1918; s. Karl T. and Valentine (Danzer) F. Diplom, Munich Tech. U., 1949, Dr. rer. nat., 1952, Habilitation, 1954, Dr. rer. nat. h.c., 1972, D.Sc.h.c., 1975, Dr. rer. nat. h.c., 1977, Dr.h.c., 1983. Assoc. prof. inorganic chemistry U. Munich, 1957, prof., 1959; prof. inorganic chemistry inst. Munich Inst. Tech., 1964—. Author: (with H. Werner) Metall-pi-Komplexe mit di- und oligoolefischen Liganden, 1963; transl. Complexes with di- and oligo-olefinic Ligands, 1966; Contbr. (with H. Werner) numerous articles in field to profl. jours. Recipient ann. prize Göttingen Acad. Scis., 1957, Alfred Stock Meml. prize Soc. German Chemists, 1959, Nobel Prize in Chemistry, 1973; Am. Chem. Soc. Centennial fellow, 1976. Mem. Bavarian Acad. Scis., Soc. German Chemists, German Acad. Scis. Leopoldina, Austrian Acad. Scis. (corr.), Accademia Nazionale dei Lincei, Italy (fgn.), Acad. Scis. Göttingen (corr.), Am. Acad. Arts and Scis. (fgn., hon.), Chem. Soc. (hon.). Achievements include special research in organometallic chemistry: metal pi complexes of arenes, olefins, carbene and carbyne complexes with metals, ferrocene type sandwich compounds, metal carbonyls. Home: 16 Sohnckestrasse, D-81479 Munich Germany Office: Chemistry Inst, Lichtenbergstrasse 4, D-85747 Garching Germany

FISCHER, EUGENE RANDOLPH, farmer; b. Mexico, Mo., Sept. 17, 1952; s. William Eugene Fischer and Luellua Melinda Schwartz; m. Kathryn Jean Lawrence, June 30, 1984; 1 child, Randolph William. Grad., Montgomery County R-II H.S., Montgomery City, Mo., 1971. Farmer, 1975—. Republican. Lutheran.

FISCHER, FRED WALTER, physicist, engineer, educator; b. Zwickau, Germany, June 26, 1922; s. Fritz and Louiska (Richter) F.; m. Yongja Kim, Oct. 1, 1970. BS in Mech. Engring., Columbia U., 1949, MS, 1950; MS in Physics, U. Wash., 1957; D in Elec. Engring., Tech. U. Munich, 1966. Analyst Boeing Co., Seattle, Munich, Bonn, Germany, 1950-84; cons. Boeing Co., Seattle, 1984-88; owner Fischer Cons., 1984-88; instr. physics, math., and engring. North Seattle Community Coll., 1973-93; guest tchr. Perkins Sch. Author: Analysis for Physics and Engineering, 1982, Renaissance Mathematics, 1992. First v.p., trustee Wedgwood Cmty. Coun.; mem. Wedgwood Elem. Sch. Site Coun., Eckstein Middle Sch. Site Coun. With AUS, 1943-46. Boeing scholar Max Planck Inst. Plasma Physics, 1964-65. Mem. AAAS, N.Y. Acad. Sci., Mercedes Benz Club (Seattle sect. bd. dirs.), Sigma Xi (life). Office: North Seattle CC 9600 College Way N Seattle WA 98103-3514

FISCHER, GEORG JOHANN, priest, theology educator; b. Feldkirch, Austria, June 5, 1954; s. Robert and Frieda (Wieser) F. B in Philosophy, U. Munich, 1976; M in Theology, U. Innsbruck, 1980; Lic. in Sacred Scripture, Pontificial Bibl. Inst., Rome, 1983, D in Sacred Scripture, 1988; Habilitation, U. Graz Faculty of Theology, 1993. Ordained priest Roman Catholic Ch., 1981. Asst. Gregoriana, Rome, 1985-87; tchr. U. Innsbruck, Austria, 1988-93, U. Munich Faculty Philosophy, 1989-93; dozent U. Innsbruck, 1993-95, prof., 1995—, chmn., dir. Old Testament Inst., 1995—; speaker, presenter confs., workshops and tng. programs for Bible groups, etc. author: Jahwe Unser Gott, 1989, Das Trostbüchlein, 1993, commentary on Jeremiah, 1995; co-author: Auf Dein Wort Hin, 1995. Mem. Mountain Rescue Force, Innsbruck, 1977—. Mem. Soc. of Jesus, Karl-Rahner Stiftung (bd. dirs.). Roman Catholic. Avocations: climbing, skiing, biking, violoncello. Office: Inst Alttestamentl, Karl-Rahner Platz 1, Innsbruck A-6020, Austria

FISCHER, HARALD ROBERT, biomedical engineer, researcher; b. Saulgau, Germany, Apr. 26, 1966; s. Franz Josef and Lydia Maria (Winter) F. Degree in Engring., U. Karlsruhe, Germany, 1993, Doctorate in Engring., 1997. Cert. med. engr. Group leader med. engring. Rsch. Ctr., Karlsruhe, 1997-98, head med. engring. divsn., 1998-99, dir. Inst. Med. Engring. and Biophysics, 1999—; lectr. in field. With German Mil., 1985-86. Avocations: diving, golfing. Home: Neue-Anlage-Str 63, 76135 Karlsruhe Germany Office: Rsch Ctr Karlsruhe, PO Box 3640, 76021 Karlsruhe Germany

FISCHER, JAN MARIE CYRIL, physicist; b. Prague, Czech Republic, Apr. 26, 1932; s. Jan Albert Leo and Bozena Ladislava (Zeniskova) F.; m. Jana Jisova, March 7, 1959; children: Tomas, Marketa, Pavel, Jitka. M of Physics, Charles U., Prague, Czech Republic, 1954, PhD, 1963, DS, 1991.

Jr. scientist Joint Inst. Nuclear Rsch., Dubna, Russia, 1957-61; scientist Inst. Phys., Acad. Scis., Prague, Czech Republic, 1962-65, head dept. particle physics, 1968-72, sr. scientist, 1973—; assoc. prof. Charles U., Prague, 1996—; vis. scientist Internat. Ctr. Theoretical Physics, Trieste, Italy, 1965-67, C.E.R.N., Geneva, Switzerland, 1972-73, 95, U. du Languedoc, Montpellier, France, 1988. Author: Insights into the Microworld, 1986; author papers on high energy particle scattering and on quantum chromodynamics. Mem. European Phys. Soc. (coun. mem. 1977-81, 91-95, pub. com. 1990-95). Roman Catholic. Avocations: astronomy, ancient Latin and Greek languages. E-mail: fischer@fzu.cz, also: fischerj@mail.cern.ch. Home: Srobarova 34, CZ-10100 Praha 10, Czech Republic Office: Inst Physics Acad Scis, Na Slovance 2, CZ-18221 Praha 8, Czech Republic

FISCHER, JÖRG GERARD, accountant; b. Johannesburg, South Africa; s. Jürgen and Ingeborg Fischer; m. Helga Veronica Reichert, Dec. 13, 1997. B Commerce, U. Witwatersrand, Johannesburg, 1991, B Acctg. with honors, 1992; postgrad., U. South Africa, Johannesburg, 1997. Article clk. Ernst & Young, Johannesburg, 1993-95, audit mgr., 1995-97; mgr. fin. control Std. Corp. and Merchant Bank, Johannesburg, 1997, fin. mgr. fgn. exch., 1998, head treasury fin. mgmt. and reconciliations, 1999—. Mem. Inst. Chartered Accts. (chartered), Johannesburg Country Club. Avocations: golf, dog trainer, gym, cycling, cricket. Home: PO Box 30973, 1684 Kyalami Republic of South Africa Office: Std Corp and Merchant Bank, PO Box 61344, 2107 Marshalltown Republic of South Africa

FISCHER, JOSEF "JOSCHKA", German vice chancellor. Fgn. min. Govt. of Germany; now vice chancellor Govt. of Germany, Berlin. Office: Office Federal Chancellor, Schlossplatz 1, 10178 Berlin Germany*

FISCHER, KLAUS ULRICH, computer scientist; b. Konstanz, Germany, June 14, 1958; s. Albert and Alice (Kohl) F. Diploma, Tech. U., Munich, 1985, Doctorate, 1992. Rsch. scientist Tech. U., Munich, 1986-91; sr. rschr. German Rsch. Ctr. Artificial Intelligence GmbH, Saarbrücken, Germany, 1992—; spokesman Special Interest Group for Distributed Artificial Intelligence, 1995—. With German Air Force, 1985-86. Avocations: dancing, music. Office: German Rsch Ctr Artf Intell, Stuhlsatzenhausweg 3, 66123 Saarbrücken Germany

FISCHER, KLAUS-DIETRICH, educator; b. Meissen, Germany, June 23, 1948; s. Karl Heinz and Ingeborg (Wieland) F.; m. Jennifer Anne Brown, Aug. 11, 1973; 1 child, Johanna Colleen. MA, Freie U., Berlin, 1976, DPhil, 1980. Jr. lectr. Freie U., 1976-81, asst. prof., 1981-87; prof. U. Mainz (Germany), 1987-93, sr. lectr., 1993—; vis. prof. Hannah Found., London, Ont., 1991-92; cons. in field. Author: Pelagonius, Ars Veterinaria, 1981, (with P.-P. Corsetti and G. Sabbah) Bibliographie des Textes Médicaux Latins, 1997, author supplement, 2000; editor: (with P. Potter and D. Nickel) Text and Tradition: Studies in Ancient Medicine and its Transmission, 1998. E-mail: kdfisch@mail.uni-mainz.de. Office: Medizinhistorisches Inst, Am Pulverturm 13, 55101 Mainz Germany

FISCHER, LENI, international association executive. Assembly pres. Coun. of Europe, 1998-99; honorary chmn. Council of Europe. Office: Council Europe, 67075 Strasbourg Cedex, France*

FISCHER, MANFRED MANUEL, geography educator; b. Nürnberg, Germany, Feb. 25, 1947; s. Johann and Erna (Hafner) F.; m. Elisabeth Fischer, Oct. 11, 1995; children: David Nuno, Daniel Duarte. Degree, U. Erlangen, Fed. Republic Germany, 1974; PhD, U. Erlangen, 1975; Habilitation, U. Vienna, Austria, 1982. Asst. prof. U. Vienna, 1975-82, assoc. prof., 1982-88, chmn. study programs bd., 1985-88; prof., dir. dept. econ. geography Vienna U. Econs. and Bus. Adminstrn., 1988—; vis. prof., U. Hamburg, Fed. Republic Germany, 1977-82, Oskar Lange Acad. Econs., Wroclaw, Poland, 1978, U. Calif., Santa Barbara, 1988. Co-editor: Recent Developments in Spatial Data Analysis, 1984, Regional Labour Markets, 1987, Spatial Choices and Processes, 1990, Geographic Information Systems, Spatial Modelling and Policy Evaluation, 1992, Technological Change, Economic Development and Space, 1995, Spatial Analytical Perspective on GIS, 1996, Classics in Regional Science: Regional Housing and Yabun Markets, 1996, Recent Developments in Spatial Analysis, 1997, Innovation, Networks and Localities, 1999, Spatial Dynamics of European Integration, 1999; mem. editl. adv. bd. Jour. Environ. Planning A, 1983-93; editor Jour. Geog. Sys., 1999—; cons. editor Geog. Analysis, 1985—, Sistemi Urbani, 1988—; assoc. editor Annals Regional Sci., 1989—, Papers in Regional Sci., 1991—. Mem. Internat. Geographical Union (chmn. commn. on math. models 1988-92), Internat. Eurasian Acad. Sci., Austrian Acad. Scis., Koninklije Nederlandse Akademie von Weterschapen, Regional Sci. Assn. (exec. com. European organizing com. 1986-99). Office: Vienna U Econs Bus Adminstr, Rossauer Lande 2311, A 1090 Vienna Austria

FISCHER, PETER, engineering researcher; b. Steyr, Austria, Nov. 3, 1963; s. Engelbert and Margarete (Schmutzhart) F. Degree, Engring. Sch. Steyr, 1983; diploma in engring., Tech. U., Graz, Austria, 1990; DSc in Engring., Tech. U. Graz, 1998. Rsch. assoc. Inst. Internal Combustion Engines and Thermodynamics, Graz, 1988-89; rsch. asst. Faculty of Structural Engring., Innsbruck, Austria, 1990-92; tchg. asst. U. Innsbruck, 1992-93; rsch. assoc. Rsch. Cooperation AVL-LIST GmbH Graz Inst. Engring. Mechanics, Graz and Innsbruck, 1993-95; computation specialist, rsch. advisor, project mgr. Engring. Tech. Ctr., Steyr, 1995—; rsch. supr. Tech. U. Graz, 1995—, U. Linz, Austria, 1997—. Recipient Engring. award Victor-Kaplan Found., Vienna, Austria, 1988, Rsch. award Austrian Automotive Industry Assn., 1999. Mem. N.Y. Acad. Scis., Österreichischer Verein für Kraftfahrzeugtechnik, Verein Deutscher Ingenieure. Avocations: rock and ice climbing, high altitude Alpine climbing, white water canoeing, motor biking. Home: Brunnerstrasse 6, A-4400 Steyr St Ulrich Austria Office: Tech Zentrum Steyr, Schönauerstrasse 5, A-4400 Steyr Austria

FISCHER, PETER HEINZ, public affairs and communications specialist; b. Nuremberg, Ger., Feb. 17, 1942; came to U.S., 1950, naturalized, 1956; s. Hans and Helen (Müller) F.; m. Marianne Dee, Apr. 22, 1964; children: Christopher, Melanie. BA in English and Journalism, Stephen F. Austin U., 1964. Cert. pub. relations, 1976. Editor, Shell Oil Co., Houston and Deer Park, Tex., 1964-69, regional editor, New Orleans, 1969-71, pub. relations rep., 1971-78, sr. pub. relations rep., 1978-81, mgr. community relations southeast, 1981-82, mgr. nat. news media relations, Houston, 1982-83, sr. staff environ. pub. affairs rep., Shell Products, 1983-87; mgr. community relations central/east region, 1987-90; projects mgr. mktg. and communications rsch. Shell Oil Co., Houston, 1990—93; mktg. and comm. cons., 1993—. Mem. East Harris County Mfrs. Assn. (past chmn. pub. rels. com.), Tex. Chem. Coun. (pub. affairs com., Disting. Svc. award 1988), Chem. Mfrs. Assn. (pub. opinion rsch. task group 1991), Pub. Rels. Soc. Am. (accredited, Colo. chpt.), Rocky Mt. Pub. Rels Assn., Evergreen C. of C. (dir.), Rocky Mtn. Pet Dealers Assn. (dir.). Republican. Contbr. articles to profl. jours. Home: 3578 S Saddle Rd Evergreen CO 80439-8508

FISCHER, RUSSELL LEONARD, public relations executive; b. E. Orange, N.J., Feb. 4, 1958; s. Harold Martin and Annette Carol Fischer. BA, Boston U., 1980; JD, Antioch U., Washington, 1984. Importer, retailer, owner Fendi of Short Hills, N.J., 1982-92; pub. rels. dir., v.p. IME-Xaminations, Elizabeth, N.J., 1994—. Vol. World Trade Orgn., N.Y.C., battered wives Unity Group, Short Hills, 1995-98; mem., delegate reform coun. Am. Jewish Congress, N.Y.C., 1991; mem., adv. bd. Am. Assn. Reform Judaism, Washington, 1995-99; alumni advisor, pres. South Fla. chpt. Boston U. Alumni Assn., 2000—; mem. Heritage Soc. Congregation Emanu-El, N.Y.C. Recipient Meritorious and Outstanding Cmty. Svc. award Am. Nat. Red Cross, 1976. Mem. N.J. Importers Assn. (v.p. 1989-90), Crestmont Country Club, Williams Island Club, World Trade Ctr. Club. Avocations: sculpture.

FISCHER, STANLEY, economist, educator; b. Lusaka, Zambia, Oct. 15, 1943; came to U.S., 1966, naturalized, 1976; s. Philip and Ann (Kopelowitz) F.; m. Rhoda Keet, Dec. 12, 1965; children: Michael Adam, David Benjamin, Jonathan Phillip. BSc, London Sch. Econs., 1965, MSc, 1966; PhD, MIT, 1969. Fellow U. Chgo., 1969-70, asst. prof. econs., 1970-73; assoc. prof. MIT, 1973-77, prof., 1977—, Killian prof., 1992-94; chief economist, v.p. devel. econs. World Bank, 1988-90; 1st dep. mgr. dir. IMF, 1994—; vis. sr. lectr. Hebrew U. Jerusalem, 1972; fellow Ctr. for Advanced Studies Hebrew U., 1976-77; vis. fellow Hoover Instn., Stanford U., 1981-82; cons. on Israeli economy Dept. State, 1984-87, 91-94; cons. IMF, 1991-92. Author: Indexing Inflation and Economic Policy, 1986, (with R. Dornbusch and R. Schmalensee) Economics, 1988, (with O. Blanchard) Lectures in Macroeconomics, 1989, (with R. Dornbusch and R. Startz) Macroeconomics, 7th edit., 1998; editor Nat. Bur. Econ. Rsch. Macroecons. Ann., 1986-94; contbr. articles to profl. jours. Guggenheim fellow. Fellow Econometric Soc.; mem. Am. Acad. Arts and Scis., Coun. on Fgn. Rels. Office: 12-300 F IMF Washington DC 20431-0001

FISCHER, STEVEN THOMAS, film producer, director; b. Balt., June 10, 1972; s. Thomas William and Marjorie Lynne (Kadlec) F. Prodr., dir. Blue Dog Prodns. and Cinema and Radio Ventures, Inc., Crofton, Md., 1990—; dir. series of TV commls. TCI Comms., 1996. Writer, dir., prodr.: (corp. films) I.W.S., 1995 (Internat. TV Assn. Festival 1995) The Introvideo, 1995, Why Should I Worry About Lead?, 1996, This is CLEARCorps, 1997, (television) Hole in My Hair, 1996, Live at Christmas Palace, 1996, Those Guys, 1997, Comic Strips Remembered, 1997, Celebrate the Freedom, 1998, Crab Talk, 1998, Food Luring, 1998, It's Baroque, 1998, There's A Looney in the Family, 1998, Good Intentions, 1998, Too Weird for a Saturday, 1998, Live at Marcie's Dinner Theatre, 1998; actor: (TV show) cartoon TV shorts, 1996, 97, 98, In A Minute: Hole In My Hair, Those Guys, Comic Strips Remembered, Crab Talk, Food Luring, Avalon, 1989, In A Minute, 1996, Lead Instructor Workshop, 1998, Next Day Blinds, 1998, I-Rides, 1999, The FBI Files, 1999, Points of Light, 1999, The Hollow Man, 1999, (radio) The Quest for Character, 1993, The Bird Caller, 1994, Why Everyone Should Learn to Read, 1996, Memorial Day Tribute, 1996, The Perfect Piece of Toast, 1996, Hole in My Hair, 1996, The In a Minute Intro, 1996; animation dir.: Mr. Lumpy, 1997 (Internat. TV Assn. Festival 1997), Wally the Green Monster, 1999; prodr. This is ClearCorps., 1997; camera operator: Survivors of the Shoah, 1996, The Ro Show, 1996, Making Change, 1996, Erase the Hate, 1997; fl. dir.: Sports Spotlight, 1995, 96, Public Safety Today, 1995; illustrator: The Cows of Gambrills, 1994, The Porch Light's On, But Nobody's Home, 1990, The Happy Sportsman's Guide to..., 1992, Early Morning Blues, 1994, Videogram, 1997, Scenes from Steve's Set, 1997, 98, 9-1-1 Mag., 1994, 97, Chalk Boards, 1996, 99, Dialogue, 1996-2000, various singles, 1994; asst. dir.: Your Turn, 1996; author, illustrator: There's a Blue Dog Under My Bed, 1991; uncredited prodn. The Ink Thief, 1993, First Night Promo, 1994; First Nat. Bank Promo, 1995, Injury Prevention for the Elderly, 1995, Pulmonary Rehab., 1995, The Shadow of a Gunman, 1995, others; writer, prodr., dir.: editor: films including The Day I Lost My Sanity and Baked a Cake, 1993, A Visit to Earth, 1994, Portrait of a Lady, 1994, Man in the Hall, 1995, Jets, 1995, (video) painting with Jon Ross, 1995, The Pessimist, 1996, Eating Lunch Alone with Myself, 1996, (video) Diary Goes to Washington, 1997, others, corp. films and videos; writer, prodr., dir. tv prodns. including Sports Highlights, 1995, Live at Christmas Palace, 1996, Those Guys, 1997, It's Baroque, 1998, numerous others, radio shows. Mem. Internat. Animated Film Soc., Internat. TV Assn. (Festival award 1995, 97), Directors Guild Am., Am. Film Inst., Ind. Feature Project, Ind. Feature Film Group. Avocations: music, writing. Office: Cinema & Radio Ventures Inc PO Box 3866 Crofton MD 21114-3866

FISCHER, TIMOTHY, government official; b. New South Wales, May 3, 1946; s. J.R. F.; m. Judy Brewer, 1992; 2 child. Grad., Xavier Coll., Melbourne, Australia, 1963. Farmer Boree Creek, Australia, 1964-65, 70; mem. parliament Govt. of Australia, 1970-80, nat. party whip, 1981-84, shadow min. vets. affairs, 1985-90, shadow min. energy and resources, 1990-93, shadow min. trade, 1993-96, dep. prime min., 1996-99; fed. mem. Farrer, 1999—. With Royal Australia Regiment, 1966-69. Avocations: chess, tennis, trekking, bushwalking in Bhutan.

FISCHER, WILLIAM SAMUEL, composer, lecturer; b. Shelby, Miss., Mar. 5, 1935; s. Robert A. and Willye (Samuels) F.; m. Dolores Labrie, Feb. 14, 1934; children: Darius, Marc, Bryan, Paul. MusB, Xavier U., New Orleans, 1956; MusM, Colo. Coll., 1962. Dir. band, choir Christianburg Inst., Cambria, Va., 1957-58, St. Landry Parish, Opelousas, La., 1958-62; faculty music Xavier U., 1962-66, High Sch. of Music and Art, N.Y.C., 1969-76; dir. music Atlantic Rec. Co., N.Y.C., 1967-71, record producer, 1975-76; record producer Fantasy Rec. Co., Berkeley, Calif., 1976-79; freelance composer, arranger N.Y.C., 1967—; lectr. N.Y.C.; cons. bd. of Edn., N.Y.C. Composer (opera music) Gospel Spirit, 1966, Mass For a Saint, Concerto, The cross Bronx Concerto for Violin and Orch. Concert Music for Saxophone and Orch., 1996; author, composer (songs for choirs) Gospel Spirit, 1974; author: The Heart of Creativity, 1986, other books on film music and sound. Mem. The LeBeau Mass com. for celebration 100 years of ch. established 1897 Immaculate Conception, St. Landry Parish, La. Served to corp. USMC, 1956-57. Recipient Deutsches Akademische Austaudienst award Fed. Republic of Germany, 1966; grantee Fulbright Found., 1965, Austrian govt., 1965. Mem. Internat. Platform Assn., ASCAP. Roman Catholic. Avocation: astronomy.

FISCHER, WOLFGANG BERND, chemist; b. Rastatt, Germany, July 17, 1962. Diploma, U. Heidelberg, 1988, DSc, 1991. Postdoctoral rschr. Boston U., 1992-93, U. Essen, Germany, 1993-94, Tech. U. Dresden, Germany, 1994-98; rsch. fellow U. Oxford, England, 1998-2000; univ. lectr. U. Oxford, 2000—. Mem. Gesellschaft Deutscher Chemiker, Biophys. Soc. USA, Marie Curie Fellowship Assn. Avocations: jogging, skiing. Office: U Oxford Dept Biochemistry, South Parks Rd, OX1 3QU Oxford England

FISCHER-APPELT, PETER, academic administrator; b. Oct. 28, 1932; s. Hans and Margret (Appelt) Fischer-Appelt; m. Hildegard Zeller, oct. 17, 1959; children: Andreas, Bernhard, Dorothee. Student, U. Tubingen, Heidelberg and Bonn, 1953-60; Dr.theol., U. Bonn, 1965; L.H.D. (hon.), Temple U., 1983; LittD (hon.), Purdue U., 1992; LLD (hon.), Ind. U., 1992; D (hon.), Technol. U., Sofia, 1992, U. Varna, 1992, U. Sofia, 1994. Comml. apprentice William Prym, Stolberg, 1951-53; sci. asst./Faculty Protestant Theology U. Bonn, 1961-70; ordained to ministry Protestant Ch. of Rhinelands, 1966; minister Cologne-Mulheim, 1964-65; co-founder, chmn. Bundesassistentenkonferenz, Bonn, 1968-69; pres. U. Hamburg, 1970-91; chmn. bd. trustees UNESCO Inst. for Edn., Hamburg, 1992-96; mem. German UNESCO Commn., 1991—; chmn. bd. trustees Hans-Bredow-Inst. Rundfunk und Fernsehen, 1970-91; dep. chmn. bd. trustees Inst. Friedensforschung und Sicherheitspolitik, 1970-91; chmn. Wissenschaftskommn. Versuch fur das Fernstudium im Medienverbund, 1975-80; adv. bd., dep. chmn. Zentrale Vergabestelle Studienplatze, 1973-92; trustee Hochschul-Informationssystem GmbH, 1969-92, Deutscher Akad. Austauschidienst, 1973—; chmn. coun. Inter-Univ. Centre Postgrad. Studies, Dubrovnik, Croatia, 1981-98; mem. standing conf. on univ. problems Coun. Europe, chmn., 1989-90; chmn. Higher Edn. Legis. Reform Program Ctrl. & Ea. Europe Coun. Europe, 1991-2000; pres. Int. Found. Cyril and Methodius, Sofia, 1992-98; trustee Weisse Rose Stiftung, Munich; mem. jury DAG-Fernsehpreis, 1981-91; bd. dirs. Found. for Internat. Exch. of Sci. and Cultural Info. by Telecomms., 1982-98. Author, editor in field. Recipient Gold medal Bulgarian Acad. Scis., 1981, medal Pro Cultura Hungarica, 1988, Horseman of Madara, 1st edit. Fax: 49-4106-78637. Home: 22 Waldweg, D-25451 Quickborn-Heide Germany

FISCHER-RASMUSSEN, WIGGO, obstetrician, gynecologist; b. Naestved, Denmark, May 25, 1935; s. Ulrich and Bodil I.M. (Axel Jensen) Fischer-R.; m. Lieselotte Niemann; children: Torsten, Mads, Mikkel. MD, U. Copenhagen, 1961, D of Med. Sci., 1972. Cert. specialist obs.-gyn., Danish Nat. Health Bd., 1973. Registrar Hosps., Copenhagen, 1961-68; rsch. fellow, resident, sr. registrar obs.-gyn. U. Copenhagen, 1968-76; sr. cons. U. Copenhagen, Hvidovre Hosp., 1976-97; sr. cons. urogynecology U. Copenhagen, Rigs Hosp., 1997—; sr. lectr. obs-gyn. U. Copenhagen, 1989-97; chief obs.-gyn. dept. KFCH, Gizan, Saudi Arabia, 1983; pres. Danish Soc. Obs.-Gyn., 1992-94, 94-96; bd. dirs. Fedn. Scandinavian Socs. Obs.-Gyn., 1992-98; mem. Patient Injury Appeals Bd., Danish Min. Health, 1997—. Author: (textbook) Gynaekologi og Obstetrik, vol. I, 1982, vol. II, 1986, Obstetrik & Gynaekologi, 1996; co-author: (textbook) Kirurgisk Kompendium, 1988, 96, Gynaekologi, 1990, 98, Obstetrik, 1993; assoc. editor Acta Obstetricia et Gynecologica Scandinavica, 1992-94, 99—, chief editor, 1994-98; contbr. articles to profl. jours. Lt. surgeon Royal Danish Navy, 1962-64. Home: Fagerbo 19, DK-2950 Vedbaek Denmark Office: Rigshospitalet, Univ Copenhagen Dept Ob-Gyn, DK2100 Copenhagen Denmark

FISCHMAN, ALAN JAY, nuclear medicine physician, researcher; b. N.Y.C., May 2, 1952; s. Lawrence Ira and Ray Ann Fischman. BS, Bklyn. Coll., 1972; PhD, Rockefeller U., 1978; MD, Yale U., 1981. Diplomate Am. Bd. Nuclear Medicine. Resident in internal medicine Tulane U., New Orleans, 1982-84; resident in nuc. medicine Mass. Gen. Hosp., Boston, 1984-86, chief resident in nuc. medicine, 1986-87, dir. nuc. medicine, 1992—; instr. radiology Harvard Med. Sch., Boston, 1986-88, asst. prof. radiology, 1988-91, assoc. prof. radiology, 1991—; mem. sci. adv. bd. Dyax Inc., Cambridge, Mass., 1997—. Contbr. over 300 articles to profl. jours.; inventor in field; mem. editl. bd. Jour. Nuc. Medicine, Reston, Va., 1993—, Clin. Positron Emission Tomography, N.Y.C., 1997—, Internat. Jour. Molecular Medicine, Athens, Greece, 1997—. Grantee NIH, Bethesda, Md., Dept. Energy, 1989, 96, others. Mem. Sigma Xi. Avocations: photography, reading. Office: Mass Gen Hosp 55 Fruit St Boston MA 02114-2696

FISCHMEISTER, MARTIN FRANZ, surgeon; b. Linz, Austria, Dec. 16, 1946; s. Viktor Moritz and Hermine (Staffelmayr) F.; m. Monika Lackinger, Apr. 28, 1972; children: Florian, Stefan, Sebastian, Martina. Dr. univ. med., U. Vienna, 1972; Diploma in Hosp. Mgmt. Artz in ausbildung Unfallkrankenhaus Linz, 1972-80, registrar, 1980-84, cons., 1984—; instr. deutschsprachige Arbeitsgemeinschaft fü Arthroskopie. Contbr. articles to profl. jours.; patentee in field. With Austrian mil., 1975-92. Mem. numerous nat. and internat. med. and scientific orgns. Roman Catholic. E-mail: m.fischmeister@netway.ot. Office: Unfallkrankenhaus, Blumauerplatz 1, A 4020 Linz Austria

FISCUS, JAMES RONALD, telecommunications consultant; b. Bellevue, Pa., July 12, 1965; s. James Ronald Sr. and Cathy Ann (Grove) F.; m. Patricia Ann Cannon, Feb. 29, 1992. Installer USMC, Camp Pendleton, Calif., 1984-88, ATIMCO Network Svcs., Inc., Pitts., 1988-99; cons. Pitts., 1999—. Mem. Allegheny County, Pa. Rep. Com., Ross Twp. Rep. Com. Served to cpl. USMC, 1984-92, USMCR, 1990-92. Roman Catholic. Avocations: dogs, spectator sports, collecting coins. Home: 3315 Maple Rd Pittsburgh PA 15237-2413

FISCUS, PHILIP WAYNE, underwriter; b. Hastings, Nebr., Nov. 8, 1955. BA, Calif. State U., Northridge, 1978. CPCU. Underwriter St. Paul Fire and Marine Ins. Co., 1978-80, sr. underwriter, 1980-84, underwriter dir., 1984-92; v.p. Reliance Nat., N.Y.C., 1992-94; sr. v.p. Minet, Inc., N.Y.C., 1994-95; v.p. Chubb Group of Ins. Cos., Warren, N.J., 1995—. Contbr. articles to profl. jours. Mem. AAAS, Biotechnology Industry Assn. (host com. 1993-98), Risk and Ins. Mgmt. Soc. (assoc.). E-mail: pfiscus@chubb.com. Office: Chubb & Son Inc 15 Mountainview Rd Warren NJ 07059-6711

FIŠER, ANTONÍN, veterinarian, educator; b. Šlapanice u Brna, Moravia, Czech Republic, Apr. 22, 1934; s. Antonín and Ružena (Hofírková) F.; m. Renata Hauptová, Nov. 11, 1961 (div. 1966); m. Jana Nečasova, Sept. 21, 1966; children: Regina, Ivana. DVM, Vet. U. Brno, Czech Republic, 1958, Candidate Scis., 1970, DSc, 1992. Diplomate vet. medicine. Vet. surgeon Regional Vet. Dept. Liberec, 1958-62; asst. Inst. Animal Hygiene, Vet. U. Brno, 1962-79, 84-88, docent, 1988-93, head, 1990—, prof., 1993—; prof. Vet. Sch. Alger, Algeria, 1979-84; cons. Ministry Agr., State Vet. Dept., Prague, 1970—. Co-author: Animal Hygiene, 199, 70; contbr. articles to profl. jours. Recipient hon. awards Ministry Agr. State Vet. Dept., Prague, Czech Republic, 1976, Czech Agr. Acad., Prague, 1989. Mem. Czech Bioclimatological Soc. of Czech Acad. Scis., Soc. Vet. Physicians. Avocations: music, literature, Brno orchestra, violin playing. Home: Nadražni 112, 66451 Šlapanice u Brna Moravia, Czech Republic

FISH, HOWARD MATH, aerospace industry executive; b. Melrose, Minn., Aug. 1, 1923; s. Nathaniel and Louise Magaret (Gaetz) F.; m. Jamie Katherine Tom, May 15, 1948; 1 child, Howard Math Jr. Student, Air Command and Staff Coll., 1954; MBA, U. Chgo., 1957; postgrad., Armed Forces Staff Coll., 1960, Air War Coll., Montgomery, Ala., 1964; MAIA, George Washington U., 1964. Enlisted USAF, 1942, commd. 2d lt., 1944, capt., 1950, col., 1965, advance through grades to lt. gen., 1974, retired, 1979; deputy asst. sec. defense internat. security affairs Dept. Defense, Washington; asst. vice chief of staff USAF, Washington; chmn. U.S. Mil. Delegation to UN; v.p. internat. LTV Aerospace and Defense Co., 1980-82, Loral Corp., 1992-96; sr. advisor Internat. Lockheed-Martin Missiles and Fire Control, Dallas, La., 1996—; mem. Def. Policy Adv. Com. on Trade, Washington, 1987-94; chmn. Am. League for Exports and Security Assistance, Washington, 1986-94, Wash. Inst. Fgn. Affairs, 1996—. Decorated Def. DSM, Air Force DSM, Legion of Merit, DFC, Air medal, Purple Heart, POW medal. Mem. Am. Def. Preparedness Assn. (chmn. internat. div. 1984-94), Army Navy Club, Air Force Assn., Washington Inst. Fgn. Affairs, Beta Gamma Sigma. Roman Catholic. Avocations: tennis, fishing. Home: 1192 County Rd 456 Thorndale TX 76577-5215 also: 1233 Capilano Dr Shreveport LA 71106-8286

FISH, MARK, soccer player. Defender Bolton Wanderers, Eng.; with SS Lazio, Rome. Address: SS Lazio, Via de Santa Cornelia 14, 00060 Formello-Roma Italy*

FISHBEIN, MEYER HARRY, archivist; b. N.Y.C., May 6, 1916; s. Jacob Fishbein and Celia Weinstein; m. Evelyn Rose Centner, Mar. 30, 1946; children: Daniel Eli, Diane Hanna. B in Social Sci., Am. U., 1950, MA, 1954, postgrad., 1954-56. Archivist Nat. Archives, Washington, 1940-57, chief bus. econs. br., 1957-61, sr. records appraisal specialist, 1962-67, dir. records appraisal divsn., 1967-75, dir. mil. archives divsn., 1975-80; prof. Am. U., Washington, 1977-81; cons. in field, 1981—; prof. Cath. U. Am., Washington, 1999—; com. automation Internat. Coun. Archives, 1972-80; spkr. in field. Author: Guidelines for Administering Machine Readable Records, A Model Curriculum for Education for Archivists in Automation, 1985, Essays on Statistical History in Paperback and on History in Books; editor: The National Archives and Statistical Research, 1973; contbr. articles to profl. jours. Bd. dirs. Ellis Island Restoration Commn., 1984—. With U.S. Army, 1943-46. Recipient Diploma for Innovations in Archives, Internat. Coun., 1984. Fellow Soc. Am. Archivists (hon., Lifetime Achievement award 1996); mem. Internat. Coun. Archives (hon.), Cosmos Club. Avocations: swimming, dancing. Home and Office: 5005 Elsmere Ave Bethesda MD 20814-5728

FISHE, GERALD RAYMOND AYLMER, engineering executive; b. Farnham Royal, Eng., Feb. 22, 1926; s. Daniel Hamilton and Dorothy Vida (Norton) F.; m. Patricia Ann Roach, Aug. 18, 1949; children: Martha Vida Bindshedler, Raymond Patrick Hamilton, G. Keith Hamilton. BS in Mech. Engring., Duke U., 1949. Registered profl. engr. Fla., Ga., Iowa (inactive Ala., Mo., Tenn. W.Va.). Project engr. E.I. DuPont de Nemours & Co., Martinsville, Va., 1952-58; architect's staff engr. So. Ill. U., Carbondale, 1958-63; sec. Adair Brady & Fishe, Inc., Lake Worth, Fla., 1965-66; chief engr. Gamble Pownall & Gilroy, Ft. Lauderdale, Fla., 1963-65; cons. forensic engr. Ft. Lauderdale, 1966—; Pres. Fishe and Kleeman, Inc., Ft. Lauderdale, 1974-85, Fidelity Inspection & Svc. Co., Ft. Lauderdale, 1983-91, Farletot Found., Inc., Ft. Lauderdale, 1985-91. Patentee in field. With U.S. Army, 1944-45. Fellow Internat. Inst. Forensic Engring. Scis., Nat. Acad. Forensic Engrs., Am. Acad. Forensic Scis. (chmn. engring. sect. 1988-89, bd. dirs. 1990-93); mem. ASHRAE, Constrn. Specification Inst., Nat. Fire Protection Assn. Republican. Episcopalian. Home: 2031 SW 36th Ave Fort Lauderdale FL 33312-4208 Office: GRA Fishe Cons Engr PO Box 478 Fort Lauderdale FL 33302-0478

FISHEL, ANDREW S., director, federal; b. Apr. 7, 1948; married, 1969. BA, Am. U., 1969; EdD of Am. Politics and Edn., Columbia U., 1975; MEd, Am. U., 1970. Legis. planning coord. U.S. Dept. HEW, Washington; mgmt. dir. Office for Civil Rights U.S. Dept. Edn., Washington; dir. fin. and resource mgmt. EEOC, Washington, 1982-89; mng. dir. FCC, Washington, 1989—. Co-author: (with Jan Pottker) Sex Bias in the Schools: The Research Evidence, 1977, National Politics and Sex Discrimination in Schools, 1996. Recipient Quality Improvement Prototype award Office Mgmt. and Budget, 1987, Outstanding Mgr. award ASTD, 1992, Disting.

Svc. medal FCC, 1992. Office: Fed Comm Commn 445 12th St SW Washington DC 20024-2101

FISHER, ALAN HALL, guidebook writer; b. Evanston, Ill., July 16, 1945; s. Howard Taylor and Marion Ethel (Hall) F.; m. Margaret Ellen Williams, July 3, 1974; children: Ellen Williams, Howard Williams. BA, Harvard U., 1967; JD, Boston U., 1977. Bar: Md. 1977. English tchr. Trinity-Pawling (N.Y.) Sch., 1967-68, Acton (Mass.)-Boxborough H.S., 1968-70; rsch. asst. Harvard U., Grad. Sch. Design, Cambridge, Mass., 1971-72; assoc. Venable, Baetjer and Howard, Balt., 1977-80; guidebook writer Balt., 1980—. Author: Country Walks Near Boston, 1976, 86, 2000, Country Walks Near Baltimore, 1981, 88, 93, 2000, Country Walks Near Philadelphia, 1983, 94, Country Walks Near Washington, 1984, 96, Country Walks Near Chicago, 1987, Day Trips in Delmarva, 1992, 98. Home and Office: 1430 Park Ave Baltimore MD 21217-4230

FISHER, ALLAN CAMPBELL, railway executive; b. Westerly, R.I., Aug. 9, 1943; s. Arthur Chester and Norma Jean (Campbell) F.; m. Ellen Tryon Roop, June 14, 1969; children: Bradford Booth, Katherine Thayer. BA in Econs., St. Lawrence U., 1965; MS in Transp., Northwestern U., 1970. Rsch. economist GM Rsch. Labs., Warren, Mich., 1969; mgmt. trainee Penn. Ctrl., 1970; asst. trainmaster Penn. Ctrl., Chgo., 1970-71; trainmaster Penn. Ctrl., Toledo, 1971-72; terminal trainmaster Penn. Ctrl., Elkhart, Ind., 1972; trainmaster Penn. Ctrl., Cleve., 1972-74, asst. terminal supt., 1974; terminal supt. Penn. Ctrl., Balt., 1975-76, Conrail, Conway, Pa., 1976; supt. N.J. divsn. Conrail, Elizabethport, 1977; supt. Lehigh divsn. Conrail, Bethlehem, Pa., 1978; regional supt. ops. improvement ctrl. region Conrail, Pitts., 1978-80, dir. budget control, 1980-82; regional supt. indsl. engring. So. region Conrail, Indpls., 1982-83; sys. dir. oper. rules Conrail, Phila., 1983—. Served with U.S. Army, 1966-67, Vietnam. Decorated Bronze Star medal; Urban Transp. fellow, 1969. Mem. NAS (com. Transp. Rsch. Bd.), Women's Transp. Seminar, Trans. Rsch. Forum, Internat. Assn. Oper. Officers, Am. Inst. Indsl. Engrs. (sr.), Am. Assn. R.R. Supt. (bd. mem.), Oper. Rules Assn. (past chmn.), Norac Rules Com. (chmn.), Ea. Code Oper. Rules Com. (chmn.), Mayflower Descs. (life), Phila. Boys Choir and Men's Chorale (bd. dirs., Man. of Yr. 1989-91, 98), Masons, Sigma Chi. Home: 215 Poplar Ave Wayne PA 19087-3503 Office: 1000 Howard Blvd Mount Laurel NJ 08054-2355

FISHER, ANDREW, IV, newswriter, television producer; b. Richmond, Va., Jan. 15, 1944; s. Andrew III and Dorothy Dale (Crannis) F.; m. Sharon Mary Cozza, Aug. 16, 1969. BA, Columbia U., 1965. News anchor Sta. WIP Radio, Phila., 1965, investigative reporter, 1968-69; writer, editor WNEW News, N.Y.C., 1969-74; overnight news anchor Sta. WNEW-AM, N.Y.C., 1974-79; morning news anchor Sta. WNEW-FM, N.Y.C., 1979-81; radio news corr. NBC News, N.Y.C., 1981-89, prin. news writer Today Show, 1990-99; fin. journalist, Bus. Ctr. CNBC, 1999—; adj. prof. journalism Columbia U., N.Y.C., 1989-90; guest lectr. Rutgers U., New Brunswick, N.J., 1984, NYU, 1978, 80. Network radio anchor Winter Olympics, Calgary, 1988, Summer Olympics, Seoul, 1988; host/prodr. Andy Fisher Reporting on Religion, 1986-89, Catch of the Day, 1985-88; corr. The Source Report, 1981-88; contbr. Marketplace, Am. Pub. Radio, 1989, More Holy Humor, 1997, Dick Clark's American Bandstand: An Anniversary Celebration of Music and Dance, 1997; reporter/prodr. Sunday News Closeup, 1969-79; consulting editor Joyful Noiseletter, Kalamazoo, Mich., 1988—; writer (TV spl.) Christmas in Rockefeller Ctr., NBC-TV, 1999. Founding patron Flying Boat Mus., Foynes, Ireland, 1990—; mem. various coms. Episcopal Diocese, Newark, 1982-87; lay reader Ch. of Saviour, Denville, N.J., 1982-87; clk. vestry St. Peter's Ch., Morristown, N.J., 1979; mem. Denville Hist. Soc. Recipient Headliner Reporting award Nat. Headliners Club, 1985, Media award Am. Women in Radio & TV, 1985, Media award N.Y. State Bar Assn., 1985, Gold medal Internat. Radio Festival, 1989. Mem. Am. Fedn. TV & Radio Artists, Actors Fund (life), Boston Street Railway Assn., Fellowship Merry Christians (bd. dirs.), N.Y.C. Transit Mus. (sustaining), N.Y. Acad. Scis., Writers Guild Am., Indian Lake Cmty. Club, Albany Acad. Alumni Assn., Ancient Order of Hibernians. Office: CNBC 2200 Fletcher Ave Fort Lee NJ 07024-5005

FISHER, ANDREW TAYLOR, computer software developer; b. Oakland, Calif., Nov. 22, 1950; s. Walter Dummer Fisher and Marjorie Catherine Lynis Smith. BA in Computer Studies, Northwestern U., 1988. Programmer Health Info. Reporting Co., Chgo., 1988-90; programming cons. Blue Cross and Blue Shield Assn., Chgo., 1990-91; programmer ACCO USA, Wheeling, Ill., 1992; programmer, tech. writer Healthcare Transformations, Hobart, Ill., 1992-93; programming cons. Abbott Labs., Abbott Park, Ill., 1993, tech. writing cons., 1995; programming cons. A.C. Nielson, Bannockburn, Ill., 1993-94; data mgmt. software devel. cons. Amoco, Chgo., 1995; programming contractor Northrop Grumman, Rolling Meadows, Ill., 1996; database programmer, tech. writer The Good Group, Inc., Evanston, Ill., 1997-2000. Recipient Steve Sutton Meml. award Chgo. Metro. Ski Coun., 1996. Mem. Nutrition for Optimal Health Assn. (wood apple award 1998), Union of Concerned Scientists of Northwestern U., Worldwatch Inst., Students for Ecological and Environ. Devel. (founder, 1st pres. 1986-88), Greenpeace, Sierra Club, Snowseekers Club (recording sec. 1995-96). Democrat. Mem. Unitarian Ch. Avocations: choral singing and acting, long distance biking, skiing, sailing, web site designing. E-mail: afisher02@sprynet.com. Home: 1630 Chicago Ave Apt 1510 Evanston IL 60201-4595

FISHER, ANN L., pro tem judge; b. Reading, Pa., Mar. 31, 1948; d. William E. and Florence (Makowiecki) Lewis; m. Donald E. Fisher, Dec. 27, 1965 (div. July 1986); children: Caroline E., Catherine E., John Michael (dec.); m. David H. DeBlasio, May 28, 1988; 1 child, Michael Joseph DeBlasio. BS in Liberal Studies, Oreg. State U., 1975; JD, Willamette U., 1983. Bar: Oreg. 1984, U.S. Dist. Ct. Oreg. 1984, U.S. Ct. Appeals (9th cir.) 1984, Wash. 1987, U.S. Dist. Ct. (we. dist.) Wash. 1987, U.S. Dist. Ct. (ea. dist.) Wash. 1996, U.S. Ct. Appeals (fed. cir.) 1996. Atty. Spears, Lubersky, Portland, Oreg., 1983-85, Greene & Markley, Portland, Oreg., 1985-89; asst. gen. counsel Portland GE, 1988-93; atty. Schwabe, Williamson & Wyatt, Portland, 1993-96; founder Ann L. Fisher Legal and Consulting Svcs., Portland, 1996—; pro tem judge Multnomah County Cir. Ct., Portland, 1995—; spkr. on corp. ethics, 1993-95; spkr. on energy issues, 1997—. Contbg. author: (treatise) ABA Year in Review, 1994, 95, Fed. Energy Bar Yr. Rev., 1997. Mem. ABA, FBA (vice chmn. electric power com. sect. natural resources, energy and environ. law, vice chmn. gas pipelines com. 1994-96), Wash. State Bar Assn., Oreg. State Bar (legis. exec. com. of adminstrv. law sect. 2000—), Oreg. Bar Assn. (ins. and bar sponsored program com. 1985-87, sec. 1986-87, chmn. 1987-88, MCLE bd. 1991-94, sec. 1992-93, chmn. 1993-94, Disciplinary Bd. Region 5 1991-97, chair 1996, 97, ethics com. 1998—), Multnomah Bar Assn. (membership com. 1987-89, Multnomah Lawyer publ. com. 1994-96, chair 1995-96, professionalism com. 1997-99), Fed. Energy Bar Assn. (electric utility regulation com. 1996-99, ethics com. 1999—), NW Energy Assn. (sec., treas. 1999-2000). Avocations: reading, writing, computers, golf, family activities. E-mail: afisher1@uswest.net. Fax: (503) 223-2305. Office: Ann L Fisher Legal and Cons Svcs 1425 SW 20th Ave Ste 202 Portland OR 97201-2485

FISHER, ANTHONY COLIN JOSEPH, priest, ethicist; b. Sydney, NSW, Australia, Mar. 10, 1960; s. Colin George and Maria Gloria (Maguregui) F. BA with honors, U. Sydney, 1982, LLB, 1984; B of Theology with honors, Melbourne Coll. Divinity, Australia, 1990; DPhil, U. Oxford, Eng., 1995. Ordained Cath. priest, 1991. Lawyer Clayton Utz, Sydney, 1984; Dominican friar, 1985—, priest, 1991—; rsch. officer Uniya-Social Rsch. Ctr., Sydney, 1991-92; rsch. assoc. John Plunkett Bioethics Ctr., Sydney, 1996—; Episcopal vicar for health care Archdiocese of Melbourne, 1997—; lectr. in ethics Australian Cath. U., Melbourne, 1995—; cons. Cath. Bishops of Australia, Eng., Wales, Scotland, and Ireland, 1990—; mem. ethics coms. several hosps., 1995—; provincial councillor Order of Friars Preachers, Australia, 1997—; chaplain State Parliament of Victoria, 1997—; mem. Senate of Priests, Melbourne, 1998—; dir. Ea. Palliative Care Inc., 1999—; mem. Infertility Treatment Authority Victoria, 1999—; chaplain various groups, 1986—. Author: (books) Abortion in Australia, 1985, IVF: The Critical Issues, 1989, I Am a Stranger: Will You Welcome Me?, 1991; contbr.: (books) A History of Solicitors in New South Wales, 1984, To the Unborn with Love, 1990, Examining Euthanasia: Legal, Ethical and Clinical Perspectives, 1995, Beyond Mere Health: Theology and Health Care in a Secular Society, 1996, Relevant Ethical Issues in Health Care, 1996, (encys.) Australian Dictionary of Biography, 1986, Principles of Health Care Ethics, 1993, Encyclopaedia of Applied Ethics, 1998; contbr. articles to profl. jours. and conf. procs. Recipient Pres.'s prize Yarra Theol. Union, Melbourne, 1990, Mary Philippa Brazil award, 1997; Brewster scholar Univ. Coll. Oxford, Eng., 1993; Ian Potter Found. grantee, 1998; 21st Century Trust Traveling fellow, 1998. Mem. Australian Bioethics Assn., Moral Theology Assn. Australia, Soc. for Protection of the Unborn Child (U.K.), Cath. Health Care Assn. Victoria (exec. com. mem., dir. 1998—), Fellowship of Cath. Scholars. Avocations: prayer, religious community life. Office: Australian Cath U, 115 Victoria Parade, 3065 Fitzroy Melbourne Victoria, Australia

FISHER, BART STEVEN, lawyer, educator, investment banker; b. St. Louis, Feb. 16, 1943; s. Irvin and Orene (Moskow) F.; m. Margaret Cottony, Mar. 1, 1969; 1 child, Ross Alan. AB, Washington U., 1963; MA, Johns Hopkins Sch. Advanced Internat. Studies, 1967, PhD, 1970; JD, Harvard U., 1972. Bar: D.C. 1972. Assoc. Patton, Boggs & Blow, Washington, 1972-78, ptnr., 1978-94; ptnr. Arent Fox Kintner Plotkin & Kahn, Washington, 1994-95; mng. ptnr. Capital House, LLC, 1995—; of counsel Porter, Wright, Morris & Arthur, 1996—; adj. prof. internat. rels. Georgetown U. Sch. Fgn. Svc., Washington, 1974-82, 97; profl. lectr. internat. rels. Johns Hopkins U. Sch. Advanced Internat. Studies, 1983-96, George Mason U., 1991, 93; chmn., bd. dirs., CBQ, Inc., exec. br. Webcasting Corp. Author: The International Coffee Agreement, 1972, (with John H. Barton) International Trade and Investment: Regulating International Business, 1986; editor: Regulating the Multinational Enterprise, 1983, Barter in the World Economy, 1985. Pres. Aplastic Anemia Found. Am. Inc., Balt., 1983-92, pres. emeritus, 1993; bd. dirs. Nat. Marrow Donor Program, Marrow Found., Aplastic Anemia Found., The Inst. at Mars Hill Coll.; program com. Georgetown Leadership Sem., Washington, 1981—; pres. Capital Baseball, Inc.; ex-officio bd. govs. Internat. Practice sect. Bar Va.; participating mem. Internat. Trade Working Group, Pres. Coun. on Year 2000 Conversion. Recipient Dean's Cert. Appreciation Georgetown U. Sch. Fgn. Svc., Washington, 1984. Mem. ABA, Internat. Bar Assn., Am. Soc. Internat. Law (rapporteur, panel trade policy and insts. 1974-77), Va. State Bar (bd. govs. internat. law sect.), Wash. Fgn. Law Soc., Parkville Post Am. Legion, Great Falls Swim and Tennis Club Va. Jewish. Home: 9009 Potomac Forest Dr Great Falls VA 22066-4110 Office: Porter Wright Morris & Arthur 1919 Pennsylvania Ave NW Washington DC 20006-3434

FISHER, CHARLES HAROLD, chemistry educator, researcher; b. Hiawatha, W.Va., Nov. 20, 1906; s. Lawrence D. and Mary (Akers) F.; m. Elizabeth Dye, Nov. 4, 1933 (dec. 1967); m. Lois Carlin, July 1968 (dec. June 1990); m. Elizabeth Snyder Kiser, Nov. 29, 1991. BS in Chemistry, Roanoke Coll., 1928, ScD (hon.), 1963; MS in Chemistry, U. Ill., 1929, PhD, 1932; DSc (hon.), Tulane U., 1953. Tchg. asst. in chemistry U. Ill., Urbana, 1928-32; instr. Harvard U., 1932-35; rsch. group leader U.S. Bur. Mines, Pitts., 1935-40; head carbohydrate divsn. Ea. Regional Rsch. Ctr. USDA, 1940-50; dir. So. mktg. and nutrition rsch. div. So. Regional Rsch. Ctr., USDA, New Orleans, 1950-72; adj. rsch. prof. Roanoke Coll., Salem, Va., 1972—; established The Elizabeth Snyder Fisher Scholarship, Roanoke Coll., 1992. Coauthor: Profiles of Eminent American Chemists, 1988; contbr. over 200 articles to profl. jours. Co-inventor 72 patents. Pres. New Orleans Sci. Fair, 1967-69; bd. dirs. Salem Hist. Soc., 1982-85, Salem Ednl. Found., 1991—; established Lawrence D. and Mary A. Fisher Scholarship Roanoke Coll., 1978, Lois Carlin Fisher Scholarship, 1991. Recipient So. Chemists award, 1956, Herty medal, 1959, Chem. Pioneer award Am. Inst. Chemists, 1966; named Polymer Science Pioneer, 1981, Roanoke Coll. medal, 1996; named to Hall of Fame, Salem Ednl. Found., 1996; The Charles H. Fisher Lecture established in his honor Roanoke Coll., 1990. Mem. AAAS, Am. Inst. Chemists (hon., pres. 1962-63, chmn. bd. dirs., Presdl. citation of merit, 1986), Oil Chem. Soc., Am. Chem. Soc. (dir. region IV 1969-71), Chemurgic Coun. (dir.), Am. Assn. Textile Chemists and Colorists, Hidden Valley Country Club (Salem, Va.), Cosmos Club (Washington), Internat. House, Round Table Club (New Orleans); Chemists Club (N.Y.C.). Achievements include co-invention of acrylic rubber.

FISHER, DALE DUNBAR, animal scientist, dairy nutritionist; b. Lewisburg, Pa., Feb. 13, 1945; s. Glenn Murray and Elsie May (Bryson) F.; divorced; children: Elsie Maria, Maria Vanessa. BS in Animal Sci., Pa. State U., 1967, MS in Animal Industry, 1978, PhD in Animal Industry, 1980. Vol. animal husbandry Peace Corps, Ciudad Quesada, Costa Rica, 1967-71; area animal husbandry-pasture specialist Costa Rican Ministry of Agr., Ciudad Quesada, 1971-73; vis. scientist Internat. Ctr. for Tropical Agr., Cali, Colombia, 1973-75; animal nutritionist Co-op. Feed Dealers, Inc., Chenango Bridge, N.Y., 1981—. Contbr. articles to profl. jours. Eva B. and G. Weidman Groff Meml. scholar Pa. State U., 1979. Mem. Am. Soc. Animal Sci., Am. Dairy Sci. Assn., Am. Soc. Agronomy, Am. Acad. Vet. Nutrition, N.Y. Acad. Scis., Am. Coll. Nutrition, Sigma Xi, Phi Kappa Phi, Gamma Sigma Delta. Democrat. Avocations: jogging, reading. Home: 578 Chenango St Binghamton NY 13901-2134 Office: Coop Feed Dealers Inc PO Box 670 Chenango Bridge NY 13745-0610

FISHER, DAVID ISA, law educator; b. Boston, Sept. 9, 1956; arrived in Sweden, 1982; s. Franklin S. and Helen (Hochs) F.; m. Ingela Friberg, June 20, 1996. BA, Fordham U., 1979; JD, NY Law Sch., 1981; LLD, Stockholm U., 1990. Bar: N.Y., 1982. Staff atty. N.Y. State Divsn. Criminal Justice Svcs., 1982; rsch. assoc. Faculty Law Stockholm U., 1991-96, assoc. prof., 1998—. Author: Prior Consent to International Direct Satellite Broadcasting, 1990, Defamation via Satellite: A European Law Perspective, 1998; translator: (dictionary) English Law Dictionary, engelsk-svensk-engelsk, 1989. Office: Stockholm U, Faculty Law, 106 91 Stockholm Sweden

FISHER, DELBERT ARTHUR, physician, educator; b. Placerville, Calif., Aug. 12, 1928; s. Arthur Lloyd and Thelma (Johnson) F.; m. Beverly Carne Fisher, Jan. 28, 1951; children: David Arthur, Thomas Martin, Mary Kathryn. BA, U. Calif., Berkeley, 1950; MD, U. Calif., San Francisco, 1953. Diplomate Am. Bd. Pediat. (examiner 1971-80, mem. subcom. on pediat. endocrinology 1976-79). Intern, resident in pediat. U. Calif. Med. Ctr., San Francisco, 1953-55; resident in pediat. U. Oreg. Hosp., Portland, 1957-58; from asst. prof. to assoc. prof. pediat. Med. Sch. U. Ark., Little Rock, 1960-67, prof. pediat., 1967-68; prof. pediat. UCLA, 1968-73, prof. pediat. and medicine Med. Sch., 1973-91, prof. emeritus, 1991—; chief, pediat. endocrinology Harbor-UCLA Med. Ctr., 1968-75, rsch. prof. devel. and perinatal biology, 1975-85, chmn. pediat., 1985-89, sr. scientist Rsch. and Edn. Inst., 1991—; dir. Walter Martin Rsch. Ctr., 1986-91; pres. Nichols Inst. Reference Labs, San Juan Capistrano, Calif., 1991-93; pres. acad. assocs., chief sci. officer Nichols Inst., San Juan Capistrano, Calif., 1993-94; pres. acad. assocs., chief sci. officer Quest Diagnostics-Nichols Inst., San Juan Capistrano, Calif., 1994-97, sr. sci. officer, 1997-98, chief sci. officer, 1998-99; v.p. sci. and innovation Quest Diagnostics Inc., 1999—; cons. genetic disease sect. Calif. Dept. Health Svcs., 1978-98; cons. genetic disease sect. Calif. Dept. Dept. Health Svcs., 1978—; mem. organizing com. Internat. Conf. Newborn Thyroid Screening, 1977-88. Co-editor: Pediatric Thyroidology, 1985, 7 other books; editor-in-chief Jour. Clin. Endocrinology and Metabolism, 1978-83, Pediat. Rsch., 1984-89; contbr. chpts. to numerous books, over 500 articles to profl. jours. Capt. M.C., USAF, 1955-57. Recipient Career Devel. award NIH, 1964-68. Mem. Inst. Medicine NAS, Am. Acad. Pediat. (Borden award 1981), Soc. Pediat. Rsch. (v.p. 1973-74), Am. Pediat. Soc. (pres. 1992-93), Endocrine Soc. (pres. 1983-84, Williams Leadership award 1998)), Am. Thyroid Assn. (pres. 1988-89), Am. Soc. Clin. Investigation, Assn. Am. Physicians, Lawson Wilkins Pediatric Endocrine Soc. (pres. 1982-83), Western Soc. Pediat. Rsch. (pres. 1983-84), Phi Beta Kappa, Alpha Omega Alpha. Home: 24582 Santa Clara Ave Dana Point CA 92629-3031 Office: Quest Diagnostics-Nichols Inst 33608 Ortega Hwy San Juan Capistrano CA 92675-2042

FISHER, DONALD WAYNE, medical association executive; b. Pitts., Mar. 2, 1946; s. David H.W. and Jean K. F.; children by previous marriage: Kimberly Elizabeth, Jeffrey Wayne. A.A., Hinds Jr. Coll., 1966; B.S. in Biology and Chemistry, Millsaps Coll., 1968; M.S. in Anatomy, U. Miss., 1970, Ph.D. in Anatomy, 1973; postgrad. in assn. mgmt., U. Md., 1977-79. Cert. assn. exec. Instr. dept. chemistry and biology Hinds Jr. Coll., Raymond, Miss., 1968-74; instr. dept. anatomy U. Miss. Sch. Medicine, Jackson, 1973-74; co-dir. and exec. officer physician asst. program U. Miss. Sch. Medicine, 1972-74; asst. professorial lectr. George Washington U. Sch. Medicine, 1974—; exec. dir. Assn. Physician Asst. Programs, Arlington, Va., 1974-80, Am. Acad. Physician Assts., Arlington, 1974-80; pres., CEO Am. Med. Group Assn., Alexandria, Va., 1980—; pres., CEO Am. Group Practice Corp., Inc., 1989, treas. polit. action com., 1980—; mem. Nat. Commn. on Allied Health Edn., 1977-80; mem. adv. com. for tng., devel. and utilization of physician extenders Systems Scis., Inc., 1975-80; pres. Am. Acad. Physician Assts. Ednl. and Rsch. Found., 1977-80; sec., treas. Am. Group Practice Found., 1980—; mem. Am. Express Health Care Faculty, 1985-88. Robert Wood Johnson Found. grantee, 1973-80. Mem. Am. Soc. Assn. Execs. (govt. rels. com. 1980—), Assn. Am. Med. Colls., AAAS, Am. Internat. Health Alliance (bd. dirs. 1992—, treas. 1995—), Greater Washington Soc. Assn. Execs., Fairfax County Hosp. Assn., Arlington (Va.) C. of C. Home: 3814 Ivanhoe Ln Alexandria VA 22310-2170 Office: Am Med Group Assn 1422 Duke St Alexandria VA 22314-3403

FISHER, EDGAR JACOB, JR., religious organization administrator; b. Istanbul, Turkey, June 3, 1919; came to U.S., 1934; s. Edgar Jacob and Elisabeth Fehr Fisher; m. Mildred Anne Hill, Dec. 18, 1948 (dec. Oct. 1975); m. Constance Fleming Warwick, July 26, 1980; 1 child, Elisabeth Anne. BS, William and Mary Coll., 1942. Adminstrv. asst. Near East Coll. Assn., N.Y.C., 1945-48; dir. Va. Coun. on Health and Med. Care, Richmond, Va., 1948-84; v.p., treas., bd. dirs. Cross-Over Ministry, Richmond, 1982—; vis. lectr. Ea. Va. Med. Sch., Med. Coll. Va./Va. Commonwealth U., Va. Sch. Medicine. Bd. mem., cons. Keep Virginia Beautiful, Richmond, 1960—; bd. mem. Needle's Eye Ministries, Richmond, 1980—, Med. Soc. Va. Found., Ctrl. Va. Health Edn. Ctr., Va. League for Nursing, Va. Thanksgiving Festival, Blue Cross Va., Richmond Area Rehab. Ctr.; sec., bd. mem. Westminster Presbyn. Homes; hon. bd. mem. Easter Seal Soc. Va.; mem. adv. com. Va. Assn. Women and Hwy. Safety Leaders, Va. Solicitation of Contbns. Law; cons. Ea. Va. Med. Sch.; ecumenical rels. divsn. Hanover Presbytery; mem. health info. com. Va. Lung Assn.; active Hunger Task Force for Hanover Presbytery, Engrs. Club Richmond; mem. task force com. on placement svcs. Nat. Health Coun., del.-at-large; mem. investigational rev. bd. Va. Heart Inst.; lay trustee Va. Recreation and Pks. Soc.; elder St. Giles' Presbyn. Ch.; others. Lt. USN, 1942-45. Recipient Disting. Svc. award Med. Soc. Va., Richmond, 1957, Disting. Svc. to Rural Va., Va. Farm Bur. Fedn., 1974, Friends of Nursing award Va. League for Nursing, Richmond, 1972, Cert. Appreciation, Va. Pharm. Assn., 1984, Cert. of Appreciation Am. Cancer Soc.-Va. Divsn., 1977. Mem. Va. Soc. Assn. Execs. (life), Richmond Pub. Rels. Assn. (treas., 2d v.p., 1st v.p., pres.), Kappa Alpha Order, Omicron Delta Kappa. Republican. Avocations: gardening, wood working. Home: 8008 Cameron Rd Richmond VA 23229-8402

FISHER, EDWARD ALLEN, educator, physician, biochemist; b. N.Y.C., Nov. 5, 1950; s. Bernard S. and Renee (Nissim) F.; m. Catherine Williams, Jan. 20, 1977 (div. 1980); 1 child, Matthew; m. Jill F. Feltheimer, Nov. 3, 1985; children: Laura, Claudia. BA, Harpur Coll., 1971; MPH, U. N.C., 1978; MD, NYU, 1975; PhD, MIT, 1982. Diplomate Am. Bd. Pediatrics. Resident in pediatrics Duke U. Med. Ctr., Durham, N.C., 1975-77; fellow nutrition and metabolism Boston Children's Hosp., 1978-81; med. staff fellow NIH, Bethesda, Md., 1981-84; asst. prof. pediatrics U. Pa., Phila., 1984-87; asst. prof. biochemistry and medicine Med. Coll. Pa., Phila., 1987-91, assoc. prof. biochemistry and pediatrics, 1991-95; dir. lipoprotein rsch. Mount Sinai Cardiovascular Inst., 1995—; prof. medicine, pediatrics and cell biology Mount Sinai Sch. of Medicine, 1999—. Contbr. articles to profl. jours. USPHS postdoctoral fellow, 1977-78, 78-81, 81-84; NIH grantee, 1989—. Fellow Am. Heart Assn. (coun. arteriosclerosis), Am. Coll. Nutrition; mem. AAAS, Am. Soc. Cell Biology. Avocations: family vacations, music. Home: 188 Rock Creek Ln Scarsdale NY 10583-7416 Office: Mount Sinai Med Ctr Box 1269 One Gustave L Levy Pl New York NY 10029

FISHER, EUGENE, marketing executive; b. Sept. 30, 1927; s. Morris and Sarah (Edelstein) F.; m. Joline Cobb, July 28, 1856 (dec.); children: Robin Downing, Amy Homer, Douglas; m. Penny Blanchard, Dec. 18, 1988. PhB, U. Chgo., 1945, MBA, 1948. With Brunswick Corp., Lake Forest, Ill., 1955-95; dir. mktg. planning bowling divsn. Brunswick Corp., Lake Forest, 1955-72, dir. corp. mktg. rsch., 1972-87, corp. mktg. dir., 1987-95; pres. Fisher Mktg. Intelligence, Inc., 1982—; guest lectr. in field. Mng. editor Profile Mag., 1988-98; prodr. Chgo. Maritime Festival, 1988-91, Brunswick 150th Anniversary Exhbn., 1995, Chgo. Cultural Ctr. Mem. civic planning com. Ill. State Hist. Soc., 1994—; mem. U. Chgo. Class of 1945 reunion com., 50th reunion dinner chmn., 1995, 55th reunion program chmn., 2000; bd. dirs 2626 Lakeview Condominium Assn., 1995-2000, pres. 1996-2000. Mem. Am. Mktg. Assn., Chgo. Maritime Soc. (bd. dirs. 1991-95), Nat. Bowling Coun. (mktg. com. 1975-83), Phi Sigma Delta. Fax: 773-281-0822. E-mail: Fishermarketing@webtv.net. Home and Office: Apt 4103 2626 N Lakeview Ave Chicago IL 60614-1832

FISHER, GEORGE MYLES CORDELL, photographic imaging company executive, mathematician, engineer; b. Anna, Ill., Nov. 30, 1940; s. Ralph Myles and Catherine (Herbert) F.; m. Patricia Ann Wallace, June 18, 1965; children: Jennifer, Barcy, William. BS in Engring., U. Ill., 1962; MS in Engring., Brown U., 1964, PhD in Applied Maths., 1964-66. Mem. tech. staff Bell Telephone Labs., Murray Hill, N.J., 1965-67; supr. Bell Telephone Labs., Holmdel, N.J., 1967-71; dept. head Bell Telephone Labs., Indpls., 1971-76; dir. mfg. systems Motorola Inc., Schaumberg, Ill., 1976-77; asst. dir. mobile ops. Motorola Inc., Ft. Worth, 1977-78; v.p. portable ops. Motorola Inc., Ft. Lauderdale, Fla., 1978-81, v.p. paging divsn., 1981-84; asst. gen. mgr. comm. sector Motorola Inc., Schaumburg, 1984-86, sr. exec. v.p., 1986-88, pres., CEO, 1988-90, chmn., CEO, 1990-93; chmn., pres., CEO Eastman Kodak Co., Rochester, N.Y., 1993-97, chmn., CEO, 1997-99; chmn. Nat. Acad. Engring., 1999-2000; bd. dirs. AT&T, GM, Delta Air Lines, Inc., Eli Lilly & Co.; chmn. EKC Bd., 1999-2000. Contbr. articles on continuum physics; 3 patents in optical wave guides and digital communications. Mem. U. Ill. Found., Nat. Merit Scholarship Bd., Chgo., 1986—. Recipient M. Eugene Merchant Mfg. medal ASME/SME, Am. Soc. Mfg. Engrs., 1994. Mem. IEEE. Office: Eastman Kodak Co 343 State St Rochester NY 14650-0001 Address: PO Box 546 Pittsford NY 14534-0546

FISHER, JAMES W., JR., management consultant; b. Aug. 14, 1942; s.James W. and Virginia (Gustafson) F.; m. Hannelore enke, Aug. 15, 1966; children: Julia, Heidi, Michael, Elke. BA cum laude, Princeton U., 1964; MBA, Harvard U., 1966. With GM, Detroit, 1970-73, Ford Motor Co., Detroit, 1973-80; dir. compensation and benefits Air Products and Chems., Inc., Allentown, Pa., 1980-87, corp. dir. orgn. planning and human resources devel., 1987-92, dir. human resources rsch., 1992-94; pres. James Fisher Co., Ltd., Emmaus, Pa., 1991-98, Victoria Beach, N.S., Can., 1998—; cons. in field. Series editor, contbg. author Guidelines for CEOS, 1999—. Office: James Fisher Co Ltd, Box 2294, Victoria Beach, NS Canada B0S 1K0

FISHER, JOHN MORRIS, association official, educator; b. Fairhaven, Ohio, Apr. 20, 1922; s. Marion Hays and Bessie (Morris) F.; AB, Miami U., Oxford, Ohio, 1947; postgrad. Bklyn. Law Sch., 1950-51, Northwestern U., 1954-55; LLD (hon.), Nasson Coll., 1972; m. Thelma Ison, Feb. 2, 1947; children: Steven Roger, Linda Lucille. With Belden Mfg. Co., Richmond, Ind., 1941; spl. agt. FBI, 1947-53; exec. staff asst. to v.p. personnel and employee rels. Sears Roebuck & Co., Chgo., 1953-57, chmn. security com., 1957-61; oper. dir. Am. Security Coun., 1956-57, pres., chief exec. officer, 1957-87, chmn., chief exec. officer, 1987—; pres. Am. Rsch. Found., 1961-90; pres., chief exec. officer Am. Security Coun. Found., 1962-87, chief exec. officer, 1987-92, chmn., 1992—; pres. Communications Corp. Am., 1972-80, chmn., 1980—; pres. Am. Coalition Patriotic Socs., 1978-91; adminstrv. chmn. Coalition for Peace Through Strength, 1978—; dir. Ctr. for Internat. Security Studies, 1977-83; organizer, pres. Fidelifax, Inc., 1956-57; chmn. merc. div. Nat. Safety Coun., 1959-60, 1st vice chmn. trades and svcs. sect., 1961-62. Chmn. Chgo. Retail Safety Conf., 1959-60; spl. adviser Ill. Supt. Pub. Instrn., 1963-64; cons. to Gov. Fla.; cons. to chmn. com. cold war edn. Nat. Gov.'s Conf., 1962-65, Ill. CD Adv. Council, 1965-68; pres. Am. Council World Freedom, 1971-72; mem. exec. com. Nat. Captive Nations Com., 1968-70. Bd. visitors Freedoms Found., 1964-65; bd. dirs. Am. Fgn. Policy Inst., 1976-84, Security and Intelligence Fund, 1976-84, James Monroe Library, 1977-85; pres. Culpeper Meml. Hosp. Found., 1984-86; exec. chmn. U.S. Congl. Adv. Bd., 1982—; chmn. Nat. Security Caucus Found., 1997—. 1st lt. USAAF, 1943-45. Decorated Air medal with clus-

ters; recipient 10th Anniversary medal and scroll Assembly Captive European Nations, Order Lafayette Freedom award, 1973, Disting. Service award Chapel of 4 Chaplains, 1979, others. Mem. Am. Soc. Indsl. Security (dir. 1959-62), Phi Kappa Tau. Republican. Presbyterian. Club: Kingsmill Country (Williamsburg, Va.). Office: Am Security Coun Found Wash Comm Ct Boston VA 22713 Home: 212 Richard Brewster Rd Williamsburg VA 23185-6532

FISHER, KING, retired marine contracting company executive; b. Port Lavaca, Tex., Jan. 14, 1916; s. Charles Everett and Kittie (Moss) F.;. Student pub. schs., Port Lavaca. m. Jewel Tanner, Aug. 13, 1937; children: Ann Fisher Boyd, Linda Fisher LaQuay. Pres. King Fisher Marine Svc., Inc., Port Lavaca, 1941-96, chmn. bd., 1959-98, cons., 1998; marine cons., 1998—; corp. sec. pres. Fisher Channel & Dock Co., Port Lavaca, 1954—; bd. dirs. First Nat. Bank of Port Lavaca, Seaport Bank, Seadrift, Tex. Inducted into Pipeliners Hall of Fame, 1997, Rivers and Harbors Hall of Fame, 1998. Mem. Tex. Mid-Coast Water Devel. Assn., Gulf Coast Intracoastal Canal Assn., Port Lavaca C. of C. Home: Fisher Rd Chocolate Port Lavaca TX 77979 Office: PO Box 166 Port Lavaca TX 77979-0166

FISHER, MARGARET CATHARINE, pediatrician, epidemiologist, educator; b. York, Pa., Mar. 1, 1949; d. Robert Foster Fisher and Miriam Arlene (Miller) Coryell. BA summa cum laude, Susquehanna U., 1971; MD, UCLA, 1975. Diplomate Am. Bd. Pediats., sub-bd. pediat. infectious disease. Resident in pediat. St. Christopher's Hosp. for Children, Phila., 1975-78, fellow pediat. infectious disease, 1978-80, hosp. epidemiologist, 1980-98; asst. prof. pediat. Temple U., Phila., 1980-86, assoc. prof., 1986-94; assoc. prof. pediat. Med. Coll. Pa./Hahnemann Sch. Medicine, Phila., 1994-97, prof., 1997—; chmn. dept. pediat. Monmouth Med. Ctr., Long Branch, N.J., 2000—; cons. Temple U. Hosp., Phila., 1985-95. Contbr. articles to profl. jours. Pres. St. Christopher's Hosp. for Children Med. Staff, 1995-97. Fellow Am. Acad. Pediat. (editl. bd. Pediatric UPDATE 1993—, mem. com. on infectious diseases 1996—), Pediat. Infectious Disease Soc., Infectious Diseases Soc. of Am.; mem. Soc. Hosp. Epidemiologists, Am. Soc. Microbiology. Avocations: reading, jigsaw puzzles. Office: Monmouth Med Ctr Dept Pediatrics Long Branch NJ 07740

FISHER, MARGARET ELEANOR, psychologist, lawyer, arbitrator, mediator, educator; b. 1927; d. John T. and Mary (Worden) F. BS cum laude in Psychology, Seton Hall U., 1958; postgrad., U. Paris, 1958, Carl Jung Inst., Switzerland, 1958-59, NYU, 1959-60, U. Md., 1960-63; MA magna cum laude in Ednl. Psychology, San Diego State U., 1966; postgrad. (NDEA grantee), U. Alaska, 1965, MBA, MPA, 1991; Phd cum laude in Psychology, U. Wash., 1970; JD magna cum laude, La Salle U., 1993. Lic. pilot comml. helicopter, fixed wing, psychologist, Mass., Ind., Alaska. Resident counselor Children's Ctr., N.Y.C., 1959-60; tchr. Am. Dependent's Schs., Okinawa, Germany, Turkey, Fran, 1960-64; tchr. English as fgn. lang. Jean Giraudoux Lycée, Chateauroux, France, 1963-64; tchr. English and French Sweetwater Sch. Dist., Chula Vista, Calif., 1964-66; asst. to editor Rev. of Ednl. Rsch. Jour., Seattle, 1967-68; psychologist vocat. rehab. program Edmonds Sch. Dist., Lynnwood, Wash., 1968-70; cons. psychologist Charles Denny Youth Ctr., Everett, Wash., 1969-71; instr. psychology Seattle Cmty. Coll., 1971; asst. prof. dept.social scis., humanities and edn. Purdue U., Lafayette, Ind., 1971-72; lang. evaluation specialist Def. Lang. Inst., Monterey, Calif., 1972; rsch. psychologist U. Calif., San Francisco, 1972; asst. prof. psychology U. Calif., Santa Cruz, 1973, Mass. State Colls., 1973-76; pvt. practice psychology Mass., 1976-78; psychologist N.Y. State Dept. Mental Hygiene, 1978, Alaska divsn. mental health Harborview Devel. Ctr., Valdez, 1978-79, Alaska Pychiat. Inst., Anchorage, 1979-95; psychologist, atty. Alaska Psychol., Arbitration & Mediation Svcs., Inc., 1995—; adj. prof. law and psychology La Salle U. Contbr. articles to psychol. and law jours. Mem. Alaska State Bd. Psychologists and Psychol. Assocs. Examiners, 1984-88; arbitrator, mediator forensic psychologist Am. Arbitration Assn., Soc. Profl. in Dispute Resolution. Amb. to Mauritius, Anchorage organizing com. 1994 Winter Olympics, 1988—; pres. Internat. Coun. Psychologists, 1992, world area chairs coord.; capt. CAP, Alaska, 1987—. With Civil Air Patrol. Recipient Internat. travel award Purdue U., 1972, scholarly support award Mass. State Coll., 1974, 75, 76. Fellow Am. Coll. Forensic Examiners (diplomate, cert. forensic examiner); mem. APA, DAR, Alaska Psychol. Assn., Internat. Coun. Psychologists (past pres. 1992), Mensa. Home and Office: # 345 3421 E Tudor Rd # 345 Anchorage AK 99507-1282

FISHER, MARK JAY, neurologist, neuroscientist, educator; b. Bklyn., Aug. 23, 1949; s. Ralph Aaron and Dorothy Ann (Weissman) F.; m. Janeth Godeau, Aug. 5, 1994. BA in Polit. Sci., UCLA, 1970; MA in Polit. Sci., U. S.D., 1972; MD, U. Cin., 1975; JD, Loyola U., 1997. Diplomate Am. Bd. Psychiatry and Neurology. Intern UCLA Sepulveda VA Hosp., 1975-76; resident UCLA Wadsworth VA Med. Ctr., 1976-79, chief resident, 1979-80; faculty mem., dir. stroke rsch. program U. So. Calif. Sch. of Medicine, L.A., 1980-98, prof. neurology, 1995-98; dir. residency tng. program U. So. Calif. Sch. Medicine, L.A., 1992-96; chmn. dept. neurology U. Calif. at Irvine, Orange, 1998—, prof. neurology and anatomy and neurobiology, 1998—. Editor: Medical Therapy of Acute Stroke, 1989. Recipient Tchr. Investigator award NIH, Bethesda, Md., 1984-89, Program Project grantee, 1994-99. Mem. Am. Acad. Neurology, Am. Neurol. Assn., Am. Heart Assn. (stroke coun.), Nat. Stroke Assn., Internat. Soc. for Thrombosis and Haemostasis, State Bar of Calif. Office: U Calif Irvine Dept Neurology 101 The City Dr S Orange CA 92868-3201

FISHER, MARSHALL LEE, operations management educator; b. Wyandotte, Mich., Feb. 19, 1944; s. Gary Hamilton and Bernice (Druckenbrod) F.; m. Geraldine Ann DeFusco, Nov. 18, 1967; children: Kara, Kimberly, Tobin. BSEE, MIT, 1965, MIT, 1969; PhD, MIT, 1970. Asst. prof. mgmt. sci. Grad. Sch. Bus., U. Chgo., 1970-75; vis. prof. (asst.) dept. ops. rsch. Cornell U., Ithaca, N.Y., 1974-75; assoc. prof. Wharton Sch., U. Pa., Phila., 1975-79, prof. ops. and info. mgmt., 1979-86, co-dir. Fishman-Davidson for Svc. and Ops. Mgmt., 1986—; Thomas Henry Carroll-Ford Found Found. vis. prof. bus. adminstrn. Harvard Bus. Sch., Boston, 1996; cons. Dupont, NASA, Dept. Def., Exxon, FritoLay, Navistar, Air Products & Chems., Inc., USM Corp., Scott Paper, Campbell Soup, Gen. Motors, Spiegel, IBM, Ahold, Allied Signal, others. Editor: Mgmt. Sci, 1979-87, SIAM Jour. Algebraic and Discrete Methodis, 1980-87; contbr. articles to profl. jours. Recipient E. Grosvenor Plowman award Nat. Council Phys. Distbn. Mem. Inst. Mgmt. Sci. (Mgmt. Sci. Practice prize 1983, pres. 1988-89), Math. Programming Soc., Ops. Rsch. Soc. Am. (Lanchester prize 1977), Nat. Acad. Engring. (elected), Sigma Xi. Office: U Pa Wharton Sch Dept Ops and Info Mgmt 3620 Locust Walk Philadelphia PA 19104-6302

FISHER, NANCY DEBUTTS, library director; b. Pitts., Apr. 10, 1945; d. Jacob John DeButts and Marie Christine Grills; m. Bruce C. Fisher, May 29, 1971. BS, Cleve. State U., 1968; MSLS, Case We. Res. U., 1973. Reference libr. Cleve. Heights-Univ. Heights Pub. Libr., 1968-79; mgr. Beachwood (Ohio) br. Cuyahoga County Pub. Libr., 1980-90; dir. Wickliffe (Ohio) Pub. Libr., 1990—. Key communicator Wickliffe City Schs., 1992; bd. dirs. Wickliffe Civic Ctr. Inc., 1999—; mem. adv. coun. Wickliffe United Way, 1991—, Holden Aboretum Warren H. Corning Libr. adv. com., 1999; Case Western Res. Univ. Libr. Sci. alumni planning com., 1997—. Mem. ALA, Ohio Libr. Coun., Cleve. Area Met. Libr. Sys. (bd. dirs. 1994-96), Wickliffe C. of C. (v.p. 1998-99, Civic Leader of Yr. 1999, pres. elect 2000), Rotary (pres. 1992-94), Lake County C. of C. Bd. E-mail: fisherna@oplin.lib.oh.us. Home: 939 Stuart Dr South Euclid OH 44121-3425 Office: Wickliffe Pub Libr 1713 Lincoln Rd Wickliffe OH 44092-2499

FISHER, PAUL CARY, writing supplies company executive; b. Lebanon, Kans., Oct. 10, 1913; s. Carey A. Fisher and Alice Bales-Fisher; children: Terry Hough, Cary Fisher, Pomm Hepner, Marteen Moore, Morgan Fisher, Scott Fisher. BS, Kans. State U., 1939. Gen. mgr. Butter-Nut Bakery, Cedar Rapids, Iowa, 1936-38, Aetna Ball Bearing Co., Chgo., 1952-45; pres. Fisher-Armour Mfg. Co., Chgo., 1945-50; owner Fisher Pen Co., Boulder City, Nev., 1950—. Dem. presdl. candidate, N.H. Primary, 1960. Named Small Bus. Person of Yr., State of Nev., U.S. Small Bus. Adminstrn., 1980, Exporter of Yr., Gov.'s Office State of Nev., 1995, 97, Inventor of Yr. Nev. Tech. Coun., 1998. Mem. Boulder city Rotary, Phi Kappa Phi. Avocations: handball, tennis, chess. Office: Fisher Pen Co 711 Yucca St Boulder City NV 89005-1905

FISHER, PETER, physics educator; b. Subiaco, Australia, Nov. 4, 1930; s. Lewis and Lucy Elizabeth (Wright) F.; m. Nora Smith, Jan. 6, 1956; children: Kimberley Anne, Susan Elizabeth, John Lockburn. BSc, U. Western Australia, 1951, BSc with honors, 1952, PhD, 1956. Rsch. assoc., asst. prof. Purdue U., West Lafayette, Ind., 1956-58, asst. prof., 1959-62, assoc. prof., 1962-68, prof., 1968-75, vis. prof., 1979; prof. U. Wollongong, NSW, Australia, 1974—. Contbr. articles on solid state physics to profl. jours. Hackett scholar U. Western Australia, 1952, ICIANZ scholar, 1954, 55; Fulbright scholar Purdue U., 1956-58. Fellow Am. Phys. Soc., Australian Inst. Physics (chmn. N.S.W. br. 1981); mem. Inst. Physics, Australian Inst. Nuclear Sci. and Engring. (pres. 1991). Anglican. Avocations: cycling, tennis, fishing. Home: 17 Elizabeth St, Mangerton NSW 2500, Australia

FISHER, RICHARD B., investment banker; b. Phila., July 21, 1936; s. Ernest W. and Doris Virginia (Rans) F.; m. Emily Hargroves, Sept. 7, 1957; children: R. Britton, Catherine Curtis, Alexander Dylan. A.B., Princeton U., 1957; M.B.A., Harvard U., 1962. Mng. dir. Morgan Stanley & Co., Inc., N.Y.C., 1970—, pres., 1984-91, chmn., 1990-97; chmn. exec. com. Morgan Stanley Dean Witter & Co., N.Y.C., 1997-2000, chmn. emeritus, 2000—; chmn. Institutional Securities and Investment Banking Group, 1999, chmn. emeritus, 2000. Trustee Bar Coll.; chmn. Rockefeller U., Bklyn. Acad. of Music Endowment Trust, Urban Inst. Mem. Nat. Golf Links, Blin Brook Club, Lyford Cay Club, Mid Ocean Club, Meadow Brook Club. Office: Morgan Stanley Dean Witter & Co 1585 Broadway Fl 40 New York NY 10036-8200

FISHER, ROBERT CHARLES HARU, publishing company executive, editor; b. Burlington, Iowa, Mar. 3, 1930; s. Ray Erwin and Blanche Columbia (Brolin) F. B.A. cum laude, Harvard U., 1955; postgrad., Columbia U. Law Sch., 1955-56, Tokyo U., 1957-59. Analyst, adjutant gen's. office U.S. Army, Kansas City, Mo., 1949-50, Washington, 1950-51; adv. Prime Minister Takeo Miki of Japan, 1957-64; Far Eastern rep. Fodor Travel Guides, Tokyo, 1959-64; exec. editor Fodor Travel Guides, N.Y.C., 1964-66, 75-77; exec. v.p. Fodor Travel Guides, 1975-77, pres., 1977-80; exec. editor Fodor Travel Guides, London, 1966-74; v.p. David McKay Co., N.Y.C., 1976-80; pres. Fisher Travel Guides, 1980-88; gen. editor Crown Insider's Travel Guides, 1988-89; editorial dir. Gault Millau Guides, 1989-90; cons. Simon & Schuster, N.Y.C., 1990-92; editorial dir. Maco Comm., N.Y.C., 1992-94; exec. editor Arthur Frommer, Inc., N.Y.C., 1995—; Founder, dir. Kansas City Open Forum, 1949-50; bd. dirs. Internat. Assn. Med. Assistance to Travelers, 1972—, v.p., 1985—; chmn. Hotel and Restaurant Unsafe Food Labeling Action com., 1995—; pres. Fisher Publs. Inc., 1997—. Author: Picasso, 1967, Klee, 1967, Guide to Japan, 1981, Insider's Guide to Japan, 1986; co-author: Off-Season Riviera, 1997, Off-Season London, 1999. Served with CIC U.S. Army, 1952-54, Korea. Balt. Scholarship Fund grantee for study in Japan, 1956-59. Mem. Japan Soc. (N.Y.), Internat. House of Japan, Soc. Am. Travel Writers (dir. 1978-80, v.p. 1981-83, pres. 1983-84), N.Y. Travel Writers Assn. (pres. 1979-81); British Guild Travel Writers (chmn. 1970-71), Soc. Am. Travel Writers Found. (pres. 1985-90). Clubs: Harvard of N.Y.C, Am. of Japan.

FISHER, SHIRLEY IDA A., photography and humanities educator; b. Cleve., Aug. 7, 1935; d. E. and I. (Morley) F. BFA, Ohio U., 1957, MFA, 1959; postgrad., U. Calif., Berkeley, 1964—, U. Calif., Santa Cruz, 1964—. Instr. Detroit Community Ctr., 1960-63; med. photographer Ford Hosp., Detroit, 1961-63; comml. photographer Detroit, 1960-63; photo producer San Jose State U., 1963-70, prof. photography, 1966-67; prof. digital photography and humanities, coord. dept. De Anza Coll., Cupertino, Calif., 1967-99, founder digital photography dept., 1985-99; photojournalist to Mexican, Puerto Rican and Costa Rican dept. tourism; photographer in over 64 countries; owner Hispanic and Anglo Publs., San Jose, 1986—, World Images Photography, Cupertino, 1963—; 1st invited Am. photographer to Ecuador. Work in internat. mus., embassies, bi-nat. ctrs. and pvt. collections; author, editor: Argentine and Chilean Photo, 1984, Cinco de Mayo en San Jose, 1987; author/editor/photographer: El Die de/as Muertos, 1999; author/editor/photographer, The Sea, 2000; editor: Self Reflections, 1987. Am. participant USIS serving in Ecuador, Uruguay, Chile, Bolivia, Venezuela, Brazil, Argentina, 1981-86. Mem. Soc. Photog. Edn., Sister Cities San Jose (Calif.), Friends of Photography, Peninsula Advt. Photographers Assn., South Bay Bookies Art Caucas, Adobe Users Group, Phi Theta Kappa, Kappa Alpha Mu. Avocations: travel, writing, photographic exhibiting and theme projects, private photo classes, metaphysics. E-mail: worldimages@yahoo.com. Home and Office: PO Box 1081 Cupertino CA 95015-1081

FISHER, WAYNE, lawyer; b. Cameron, Tex.. BBA cum laude, Baylor U., 1959, LLB, 1961. Bar: Tex. 1961, U.S. Dist. Ct. (so. dist.) Tex. 1961, U.S. Ct. Appeals (5th and 11th cirs.) 1982, U.S. Supreme Ct. 1982, U.S. Dist. Ct. (ea. and we. dists.) 1983, U.S. Dist. Ct. (no. dist.) Tex. 1988, U.S. Dist. Ct. Ariz. 1990, U.S. Claims Ct. 1990; cert. personal injury trial law specialist Tex. Bd. Legal Specialization. Assoc. Fulbright & Jaworski, Houston, 1961-66; founder, ptnr. Fisher, Boyd, Brown, Boudreaux & Huguenard, LLP, Houston, 1966—; mem. dist. ct. adv. group U.S. Dist. Ct. (so. dist.) Tex. 1991; spkr. in field. Contbr. articles to profl. jours. Bd. dirs. South Tex. Coll. Law, 1986—, Houston Symphony Orch., 1987—; state membership chair The Supreme Ct. Hist. Soc., 1992. Recipient Disting. Alumni award Baylor U., 1991. Fellow Am. Coll. Trial Lawyers (complex litigation com., spl. problems in the adminstrn. justice com., regent 1993—), Internat. Acad. Trial Lawyers (bd. dirs. 1985—, admissions com. 1985-86, sec.-treas. 1989-91, dean of acad. 1991-92, pres. 1993), Am. Bd. Trial Advs., Inner Circle Advs., Tex. Bar Found. (sec., bd. dirs. 1973-74); mem. ATLA, ABA (tort and ins. practice sect., trial techniques com., aviation and space law com., professionalism com., chmn. task force on the size of civil juries in fed. cts.), Am. Judicature Soc., State Bar Tex. (dir. 1972-75, spl. com. to study disciplinary procedures 1973-74, chmn. adminstrn. justice com. 1975-76, personal injury trial law adv. commn. 1978-80, com. on fed. laws and regulations affecting the bar 1990—, pres.-elect 1980-81, pres. 1981-82), Tex. Trial Lawyers Assn. (pres. 1974-75), Houston Trial Lawyers Assn. (pres. 1971-72), Houston Bar Assn., Internat. Acad. Trial Lawyers (pres. 1993-95), Supreme Ct. Hist. Soc. Found. (state chair La., Miss. and Tex.). Office: Fisher Boyd Brown Boudreaux & Huguenard LLP Riviana Bldg 14th Fl 2777 Allen Pkwy Houston TX 77019-2141

FISHER, WESLEY ANDREW, research administrator, Eurasian studies specialist; b. N.Y.C., Oct. 23, 1944; s. Mitchell Salem and Esther (Oshiver) F.; m. Regine Rayevsky, Sept. 15, 1979; children: Maxim, Katya. BA, Harvard U., 1966; M Phil. in Sociology, Columbia U., 1976, PhD with distinction, 1976, cert. Russian Inst., 1976. Instr. Dept. Sociology, W. Averell Harriman Inst., Columbia U., N.Y.C., 1972-76, asst. prof., 1976-80, adj. assoc. prof., 1981-87; assoc. chmn. Dept. Sociology, Columbia U., N.Y.C., 1980-81; sec. Am. Council Learned Socs. Commns. with USSR Internat. Rsch. & Exch. Bd., N.Y.C. and Princeton, N.J., 1981-89, asst. dir. and dir. Soviet programs, 1989-93; dep. dir. Rsch. Inst., U.S. Holocaust Meml. Mus., Washington, 1993-97, acting dir., 1997, spl. asst. to mus. dir., 1997-98; cons. Sakharov Mus., Russia, 1997—; dir. internat. programs U.S. Holocaust Meml. Mus., Washington, 1999-2000, dir. external affairs, 2000—; guest lectr. Foreign Svc. Inst. U.S. Dept. of State, 1976-83; visiting lectr. New Sch. for Social Rsch., 1978-79; rsch. fellow philosophy faculty Moscow (USSR) State Univ., 1970-71, Ctr. for the Study of Population, Moscow State Univ., 1976-86; liaison Soviet Union, Am. Sociological Assn., 1976-86; rep. to intergovernmental task force Internat. Coop. on Holocaust Edn., Remembrance and Rsch., 1998—. Author: The Moscow Gourmet: Dining Out in the Capital of the USSR, 1974, The Soviet Marriage Market: Mate Selection in Russia and the USSR, 1980, Social Stratification and Mobility in the USSR, 1973, A Scholar's Guide to the Humanities and Social Sciences in the Baltics and the Soviet Union, 1992, International Directory of Organizations in Holocaust Education, Remembrance, and Research, 1998; contbr. articles, revs., guidebooks to acad. and profl. jours. Advisor Program for Soviet Emigre Scholars, Nat. Jewish Welfare Bd., Hebrew Immigrant Aid Soc.; bd. dirs. N.Y. Assn. for New Americans; rep. intergovernmental task force Internat. Coop. Holocaust Edn., Remembrance, and Rsch., 1998—. Recipient Herbert H. Lehman fellowship in Pub. and Internat. Affairs,1966, Foreign Area fellowship Ford Found., 1970, two Fulbright-Hays fellowships, 1970-71, 76-77. Mem. Am. Assn. for the Advancement of Slavic Studies, Am. Sociol. Assn., Harvard Club of N.Y.C., Fulbright Assn., Phi Beta Kappa. Jewish. E-mail: wfisher@ushmm.gov. Home: 5920 Edson Ln N Bethesda MD 20852-2932 Office: US Holocaust Meml Museum 100 Raoul Wallenberg Pl SW Washington DC 20024-2126

FISHER, WILLIAM HENRY, education educator; b. York, Pa., July 4, 1912; s. Charles Henry and Mary Naomi (Light) F.; m. Christine Albers, June 25, 1938 (dec. Nov. 1959); 1 child, Charles Albers; m. Ruth Dyer, Dec. 27, 1962. BA in Sociology, Secondary Edn., U. Wash., 1935, MEd, 1943; DEd in Social Studies Edn., Columbia U., 1949. Tchr. social studies Wapato (Wash.) Sr. High Sch., 1936-39, Kirkland (Wash.) Sr. High Sch., 1939-44, Fieldston Sch. of The Ethical Culture Soc., N.Y.C., 1945-47; asst. prof. edn., sociology Eastern Wash. State U., Cheney, 1947-50; asst. prof., supr. student tchrs. U. Ariz., Tucson, 1950-51, Temple U., Phila., 1951-52, Wilkes Coll., Wilkes-Barre, Pa., 1952-53; curriculum dir. Las Vegas (N.Mex.) Pub. Schs., 1953-56, supt. schs., 1956-61; assoc. prof. edn. U. Tex., El Paso, 1961-67, assoc. prof., 1967-71; prof. U. Mont., Missoula, 1971—; vis. prof. (summers) Highlands U., Las Vegas, N.Mex., 1950-55, U. N.Mex., Albuquerque, 1961, Western State Coll., Gunnison, Colo. (summers) 1960, 63, 66, Eastern Ill. U., Charleston, 1967, U. Fla. Gainesville, 1971, U. Tenn., Knoxville, 1976; v.p. student council Tchrs. Coll., Columbia, 1946-47; appointed to commn. to revise the high sch. Phys. Edn. Curriculum, N.Mex., 1954-56; pres. Coop. Program in Ednl. Adminstrn., N.Mex., 1960-61; program chmn. Trans-Pecos Edn. Conf. U. Tex., El Paso, 1963-65; chmn. umbrella com. supporting grad. programs Sch. Edn. U. Mont., 1966-78; chair-discussant numerous nat. and regional meets; instr. in field, Mont. Contbr. numerous articles to profl. jours. Mem. AAUP (pres. U. Tex.-El Paso chpt. 1964-65), Soc. Philosophy and History of Edn. (panel mem. ednl. philosophy meeting 1996), Philosophy of Edn. Soc. (presenter papers ann. meetings), Am. Ednl. Studies Assn., Western Social Sci. Assn. (chair, panelist ann. meetings Am. studies sect.), Phi Delta Kappa, Kappa Delta Pi. Home: 604 Plymouth St Missoula MT 59801-4129 Office: U Mont Sch Edn Missoula MT 59812-0001

FISHKIN, SHELLEY FISHER, English language educator; b. N.Y.C., May 9, 1950; d. Milton and Renée B. Fisher; m. James S. Fishkin; children: Joseph, Robert. BA, Yale Coll., 1971; MA, Yale U., 1974, MPhil, 1974, PhD, 1977. Assoc. Chubb fellow Yale Coll., New Haven, 1974-85, dir. Poynter fellowship in journalism, 1980-85, vis. lectr., 1981-84; sr. lectr. Am. studies U. Tex., Austin, 1985-89, prof. Am. studies, 1993—, prof. English, 1994—. Author: From Fact to Fiction: Journalism and Imaginative Writing in America, 1985 (Frank Luther Mott award Nat. Journalism Scholarship Soc. 1986), Was Huck Black? Mark Twain & African American Voices, 1993 (Outstanding Acad. Book award CHOICE), Lighting Out for the Territory: Reflections on Mark Twain and American Culture, 1997; editor: The Oxford Mark Twain, 1996; co-editor: Listening to Silences: New Essays in Feminist Criticism, 1994, People of the Book: Thirty Scholars Reflect on Their Jewish Identity, 1996, (book series) Race and American Culture, 1993, Encyclopedia of Civil Rights in America, 1998. Recipient Disting. Acad. Specialist award U.S. Info. Agy., 1994, H. Ransom Tchg. award Coll. Liberal Arts, 2000; Am. Coun. Learned Socs. fellow, 1987-88; Fulbright Disting. lectr., 1999. Mem. MLA (exec. coun. nonfiction prose divsn 1991-95), Am. Studies Assn. (nominating com. 1990-92, internat. com. 1993-96, program com. 1995, nat. coun. 2000—), Mark Twain Cir. Am. (pres. 1998-2000), Charlotte Perkins Gilman Soc. (co-founder, exec. dir. 1990-98). Office: Dept Am Studies U Tex Austin TX 78712

FISIAK, JACEK, university administrator, educator; b. Konstantynow, Poland, May 10, 1936; s. Czeslaw and Jadwiga (Pasnicka) F.; m. Liliana Sikorska, Aug. 21, 1999. MA, U. Warsaw, Poland, 1959; PhD, U. Lodz, Poland, 1962; DLitt, A. Mickiewicz U., Poznan, Poland, 1965; DHC (hon.), U. Jyvaskyla, Finland, 1984. Asst. lectr. U. Lodz, 1959-63, adj. prof., 1963-65, docent, 1965-67; docent A. Mickiewicz U., 1965-71, head Sch. English, 1965, prof., 1971—, head dept. English, 1965—, pres., rector, 1985-88, minister of edn., 1988-89; vis. prof. U. Kans., Lawrence, 1970, U. Fla., Gainesville, 1974, SUNY, 1975, Am. U., Washington, 1979-80, 91-92, U. Kiel, Fed. Republic of Germany, 1979, U. Vienna, 1983, 89, 90, U. Zurich, Switzerland, 1984, 94, U. Tromso, Norway, 1985, U. Jyvaskyla, Finland, 1987, U. Saarbrucken, Fed. Republic of Germany, 1990, 93, U. Bamberg (Germany), 1994. Author and editor of 33 books, including: A Short Grammar of Middle English, 1968, 7th rev. edit., 1996, A Bibliography of Writings for the History of English, 1987, An Outline History of English, 1996, others; editor jours. Folia Linguistica Historica, Studia Anglica Posnaniensia, Papers and Studies in Contrastive Linguistics; contbr. more than 100 articles to profl. jours.; mem. numerous editorial bds. Chmn. com. on modern langs. and lit. Ministry Higher Edn., 1974-88. Recipient Comdrs. Cross of Order Polonia Restituta with Star, 1996, Comdrs. Cross of Order Lion of Finland Pres. of Finland, 1980, Order of Brit. Empire, Queen of England, 1981, Officer's Cross of Palmes Académique, 1989; others. Mem. Internat. Assn. Univ. Profs. of English (pres. 1974-77), Internat. Assn. Hist. Linguistics (v.p. 1979-81, pres. 1981-83), Soc. Linguistica Europaea (v.p. 1973, 83-84, pres. 1982-83), Polish Acad. Scis. (chmn. com. on modern langs. and lit. 1981-93), Internat. Fedn. Modern Lang. Tchrs. (sec. gen. 1980-83), Academia Europaea, Acad. of Finland, Norwegian Acad. Avocations: sports, modern history. Office: A Mickiewicz U, Wieniawskiego 1, 61-712 Poznan Poland

FISICHELLA, GIANCARLO, race car driver; b. Rome, Jan. 14, 1973. Race car driver, 1992—. 12-time winner Italian minikart class championships, 1984, 8-time winner Italian cadets class championship, 1985, 13-time winner, 1986, Italian champion, 1988; regional jr. class champion, 1987, 2d karting internat. class European Championship, 1989, 91, 1st Intercontinental championship, Hong Kong, 1989, 22 wins Italian championship Kart 100cc, 1989, 2 wins Italian F3, 1993, F3 Italian Champion, 1994, 4 podium finishes ITC/DTM, 1995, 6 podium finishes ITC/DTM, 1996, 8 Grand prizes F1 with Minardi, 1996, 2 podium finishes F1 with Jordan, 1997, 2 podium finishes F1 with Benetton, 1998, 2 podium finish F1 with Benetton, 1998, podiums in Monaco and Can. F1 Benetton, 2000.

FISK, DORIS ROSALIE SCANLAN, volunteer; b. Mpls., Aug. 20, 1915; d. Arthur William and Lea Marie (Beauchaine) Scanlan; m. Ellsworth William Fisk, Aug. 31, 1942; children: Gregory, Janine, Marilyn, Kathleen. Student, Mpls. Bus. Coll., 1935, U. Minn., 1940, San Antonio Jr. Coll., 1964. Hosp. vol. ARC, 1940-71; vol. Audie Murphy Vets. Hosp., 1972-80; med. transcriber Radiology Assocs., San Antonio, 1962-64; nurse office mgr. for surgeon San Antonio, 1964-77; vol. Sr. Svc. Orgn., San Antonio, 1970—; vol., fund raiser Vis. Nurse Assn. S.W. San Antonio, 1992-97; vol. Quantum Brookhollow Med. Ctr., 1999—. Sec. vol. Demo-Ne Demos, San Antonio, 1960-64; pres. YWCA Wives, San Antonio, 1964-65, Espada Mission Aux., San Antonio, 1965-66; chair March of Dimes, San Antonio, ARC, 1940-1971, chmn. of vols.; vol. usher and seamstress Harlequin Theatre, from 1971; treas. altar soc. St. Mary's Cath.Ch., 1984-92; pres. flu shot prog. VNA, vol. Brookhollow Libr., 1995-96; chmn. Brooke Gen. Hosp. Vols. Recipient Golden Globe award Vol. Vis. Nurse of the Yr., San Antonio, 1993, Gold Key ring J.C. Penney; Letter of Congratulation, Pres. Clinton. Mem. AAUW, La Societé Francaise Canadian, Ret. Sr. Vols. (bd. mem. 1996—), Officers Wives Club (tour guide 1996-97, tel. chairperson 1999-2000, 2000-2001), Smithsonian Instn., Williamsburg, Met. Mus., Beta Sigma Phi (life). Democrat. Roman Catholic. Avocations: travel, reading, sewing. Home: Apt 32 4707 Broadway St San Antonio TX 78209-6240

FISK, EDWARD RAY, retired civil engineer, author, educator; b. Oshkosh, Wis., July 19, 1924; s. Ray Edward and Grace O. (Meyer) Barnes; married, Oct. 28, 1950; children; Jacqueline Mary, Edward Ray II, William John, Robert Paul. BCE, Marquette U., 1949; student, Fresno (Calif.) State Coll., 1954, UCLA, 1957-58. Registered profl. engr., Ariz., Calif., Colo., Fla., Idaho, Ky., La., Mont., Nev., Oreg., Utah, Wash., Wyo.; lic. land surveyor, oreg., Idaho; lic. gen. engring. contractor, Calif.; cert. arbitrator Calif. Constrn. Contract Arbitration Com. Engr. Calif. Div. Hwys., 1952-55, Bechtel Corp., Vernon, Calif., 1955-59; project mgr. Toups Engring. Co., Santa Ana, Calif., 1959-61; dept. head Perliter & Soring, Los Angeles, 1961-64; Western rep. Wire Reinforcement Inst., Washington, 1964-65; cons. engr. Anaheim, Calif., 1965; assoc. engr. Met. Water Dist. So. Calif., 1966-68; chief specification engr. Koebig & Koebig, Inc., Los Angeles, 1968-71; mgr. constrn. services VTN Consol., Inc., Irvine, Calif., 1971-78; pres. E.R. Fisk Constrn., Orange, Calif., 1978-81; corp. dir. constrn. mgmt. James M. Montgomery Cons. Engrs., Inc., Pasadena, Calif., 1981-83; v.p. Lawrence, Fisk & McFarland, Inc., Santa Barbara and Orange, 1983—; pres. E.R. Fisk & Assocs., Orange, 1983—, Gleason, Peacock & Fisk, Inc., 1987-92; v.p. constrn. svcs.

Wilsey & Hamm, Foster City, Calif., 1993-94; adj. prof. engring., constrn. Calif. State U., Long Beach, 1987-90, Orange Coast Coll., Costa Mesa, Calif., 1957-78, Calif. Poly. State U., Pomona, 1974; instr. U. Calif., Berkeley, Inst. Transportation Studies, 1978—, engring. prof. programs U. Wash., 1994—, internationally for ASCE Continuing Edn.; former mem. Calif. Bd. Registered Constrn. Insps. Author: Machine Methods of Survey Computing, 1958, Construction Project Administration, 1978, 82m,88, 92, 97, Construction Engineers Complete Handbook of Forms, 1981, 92, Resident Engineers Field Manual, 1992; co-author: Contractor's Project Guide, 1988, Contracts and Specifications for Public Works Projects, 1992. Served with USN, 1942-43, USAF, 1951-52. Fellow ASCE (life fellow, past chmn. exec. com. constrn. divn., former chmn. nat. com. inspection 1978—), Nat. Acad. Forensic Engrs. (diplomate); mem. Orange County Engring. Council (former pres.), Calif. Soc. Profl. Engrs. (past pres. Orange County), Structural Engrs. Assn. Calif. (engrs. joint contracts documents com. 1993-95), Am. Arbitration Assn. (nat. panel), U.S. Com. Large Dams, Order Founders and Patriots Am. (past gov. Calif.), Soc. Colonial Wars (dep. gov. gen. Calif. chpt.), S.R. (past dir.), Engring. Edn. Found. (trustee), Tau Beta Pi. Home: 1792 N Ridgewood St Orange CA 92865-4454

FISK, MERLIN EDGAR, judge; b. Great Falls, Mont., Mar. 18, 1921; s. Edgar Anson and Eleanor Sybil (Worden) F.; m. Margery Anne Hall, May 27, 1942; children: Mary Dana, Catherine, Anne, Elizabeth. BSChemE, Mont. State U., 1942. Tech. adminstr. Lago Oil & Transport Co., Ltd. subsidiary Exxon Corp., Aruba, Aruba Netherlands Antilles, 1942-62; v.p., gen. mgr. Antilles Chem. Co. subsidiary Exxon Corp., 1962-64; dir. mfg. Esso Pappas Indsl. Co., Athens, Greece, 1964-67; gen. mgr. Essochem, S.A. subsidiary Exxon Corp., Madrid, 1967-69; mgr. ops. and planning Essochem, S.A. subsidiary Exxon Corp., Brussels, 1969-71, ret., 1971; judge probate div. State of Conn., Newtown, 1979-91; ret., 1991; pres. judge Conn. Probate Assembly, 1990-91. Mem. Commn. on Aging, Newtown, 1987-99; trustee Cyrenius H. Booth Libr., Newtown, 1975-95, 97—; bd. dirs. Newtown Meals on Wheels, Inc., 1974-93, Recording for the Blind, Inc. Conn. chpt., New Haven, 1975-92, Waterbury (Conn.) Ballet Co., 1987-97. Mem. Am. Arbitration Assn. (comml. panel 1991-98), Men's Literary and Social Club of Newtown (pres. 1984-85). Republican. Episcopalian. Avocations: golf, gardening, reading.

FISUN, OLEG IVANOVICH, physicist; b. Kemerovo, Russia, Feb. 20, 1946; s. Ivan Vladimirovich and Maria Ivanovna Fisun; m. Tatjana Valentinovna Telejnikova, Jan. 16, 1971; children: Gleb, Svjatoslav. MS, Kiev U., 1970; PhD, Inst. Electrodynamics, 1973. Postdoctoral fellow, rsch. assoc., lab. head Inst. Modeling Problems, Kiev, Russia, 1973-86; Head dept. synergetics, sci. dir. State Inst. Physics and Tech., Moscow, 1987—; rsch. assoc. Inst. fur Theoretische Physik lund Synergetik, Stuttgart, Germany, 1979-80; prof. Kurchatov Inst. Atomic Energy, Moscow, 1983. Mem. N.Y. Acad. Scis., Ecol. Acad. Russian Fedn. Office: State Inst Physics & Tech, Prechistenka str 13/7, 119034 Moscow Russia

FITCH, EDWARD HAROLD, industry consultant; b. Sydney, New South Wales, Australia, May 27, 1929; s. Edward William and Dorothy Alice (Rice) F., m. Gretchen Anne Cole, Aug. 20, 1965; children: Nancy Alice, Lincoln Gray. With Qantas Airways, Sydney, 1946-89, mgr. cargo services, 1983-89; dir. Infofreight Internat., Mascot, NSW, 1989—; cons. to Australian Law Reform Commn., 1988-89, Australian airfreight industry, 1989—. Mem. Australian Inst. Materials Mgmt., Airfreight Acad. Australia (dir. 1982-99), Internat. Air Transport Assn. (com. chmn. 1980-93). Club: Royal Motor Yacht. Avocations: boating. Home: 47 Whale Beach Rd, Avalon Beach, New South Wales 2107, Australia Office: PO Box 561, Avalon Beach NSW 2107, Australia

FITCH, RACHEL FARR, health policy analyst; b. July 27, 1933; d. Allen Edward and Rosie Leola (Jones) Farr; m. Coy Dean Fitch, Mar. 31, 1956; children: Julia Anne, Jaquelyn Kay. Student, Little Rock U., 1965-67; BS, St. Louis U., 1974, MS, 1976, PhD, 1983. RN, Mo. Psychiat. staff nurse VA Ft. Root Hosp., North Little Rock, Ark., 1954-57; surg.-med. staff nurse St. Vincent Infirmary, Little Rock, Ark., 1957-65; acute care nurse Georgetown U. Hosp., Washington, 1968-69; pub. health nurse to adminstr. South office Vis. Nurse Assn. Greater St. Louis, 1970-73; cons. in edn. St. Louis City Health Dept., 1977-80; rsch. specialist Sen. John C. Danforth, St. Louis, 1980; owner RFF Assocs., 1983-86; project dir. study of infant mortality in city of St. Louis, 1978. Mem. community health edn. com. Am. Heart Assn., 1977-87; bd. dirs. LWV of Mo., 1984—, editor newspaper, 1984-87, dir. health issues, 1987-99, 1st v.p. 1999—; chmn. Mo. Consumer Health Care WATCH, 1996—; mem. adv. com. Mo. Medicaid Consumer, 1996-97; mem. Mo. Welfare Coord. Com., 1997-99, Mo. Dept. Ins., 2000—. Mem. Am. Pub. Health Assn., Acad. Polit. Sci., Grand Jury Assn. St. Louis (bd. dirs.), Woman's Club (St. Louis U. Sch. Medicine, past pres.), Sigma Theta Tau. Address: 23 Lenox Pl Saint Louis MO 63108-1901

FITCH, VAL LOGSDON, physics educator; b. Merriman, Nebr., Mar. 10, 1923; s. Fred B. and Frances Marion (Logsdon) F.; m. Elise Cunningham, June 11, 1949 (dec. 1972); children: John Craig (dec. 1987), Alan Peter; m. Daisy Harper Sharp, Aug. 14, 1976. B. of Engring., McGill U., 1948; Ph.D., Columbia U., 1954. Instr. Columbia, 1953; instr. physics Princeton, 1954-56, asst. prof., 1956-59, assoc. prof., 1959-60, prof., 1960—, Class 1909 prof. physics, 1968-76, Cyrus Fogg Bracket prof. physics, 1976-84, James S. McDonnell Distinguished Univ. prof. physics, 1984—; Mem. Pres.'s Sci. Adv. Com., 1970-73. Trustee Asso. Univ., Inc., 1961-67. Served with AUS, 1943-46. Recipient Research Corp. award, 1967; E.O. Lawrence award, 1968; Wetherill medal Franklin Inst., 1976; Nobel prize in physics, 1980; Grad. Alumnus award Am. Assn. State Colls. and Univs., 1984; Nat. Medal of Sci., 1993; Sloan fellow, 1960. Fellow Am. Phys. Soc. (pres. 1987-88); mem. Am. Acad. Arts and Scis., Nat. Acad. Sci., Am. Philos. Soc. Office: Princeton U Dept Physics PO Box 708 Princeton NJ 08544-0001

FITE, GILBERT COURTLAND, historian, educator, retired; b. Santa Fe, Ohio, May 14, 1918; s. Clyde Fite and Mary Jane McCardle; m. Alberta June Goodwin, July 24, 1941; children: James Franklin, Jack Preston. BA, U. S.D., 1941, MA in History, 1941, LittD (hon.), 1975; PhD, U. Mo., 1945, HHD (hon.), 1983; LittD (hon.), Seattle Pacific U., 1962. From asst. prof. to profl. U. Okla., Norman, 1945-68, George Lynn Cross prof. history, 1968-71; pres. Ea. Ill. U., Charleston, 1971-76; Richard B. Russell prof. history U. Ga., Athens, 1976-86, prof. emeritus, 1986—. Author: Peter Norbeck: Prairie Statesman, 1948, Mount Rushmore, 1952, George Peek & The Fight for Farm Parity, 1954, The Farmer's Frontier, 1865-1900, 1966, American Farmers: The New Minority, 1981, Cotton Fields No More, Southern Agriculture, 1865-1980, 1984, Richard B. Russell, Senator from Georgia, 1993, others; contbr. over 50 articles to profl. jours. Trustee Phillips U., Enid, Okla., 1969-76, Lexington (Ky.) Theol. Sem., 1972-76. Fulbright scholar, 1962-63, 69-70; Guggenheim Found. fellow, 1964, Ford Fellow, 1954-55; named to S.D. Hall of Fame, 1990. Mem. Agrl. History Soc. (pres. 1960-61), So. Hist. Assn. (pres. 1974), Western History Assn. (pres. 1985-86), Phi Alpha Theta (pres. 1981-83). Methodist. Avocations: photography, golfing, traveling. Home: 4 Fite Cir Bella Vista AR 72714-5528

FITES, DONALD VESTER, retired tractor company executive; b. Tippecanoe, Ind., Jan. 20, 1934; s. Rex E. and Mary Irene (Sackville) F.; m. Sylvia Dempsey, June 25, 1960; children: Linda Marie. BS in Civil Engring., Valparaiso U., 1956; MS, MIT, 1971. With Caterpillar Overseas S.A., Peoria, Ill., 1956-66; dir. internat. customer divsn. Caterpillar Overseas S.A., Geneva, 1966-67; asst. mgr. market devel. Caterpillar Tractor Co., Peoria, 1967-70; dir. Caterpillar Mitsubishi Ltd., Tokyo, 1971-75; dir. engine capacity expansion program Caterpillar Tractor Co., Peoria, 1975-76, mgr. products control dept., 1976-79; pres. Caterpillar Brasil S.A., 1979-81; v.p. products Caterpillar Tractor Co., Peoria, 1981-85, exec. v.p., 1985-89; pres., chief opd. officer Caterpillar Inc., Peoria, 1989-90, pres., COO, 1989-90, chmn., CEO, 1990-99, also bd. dirs.; mem. bd. dirs. Oshkosh Truck Corp., 2000S; bd. dirs. Caterpillar Inc., Wolverine Worldwide, Mobil Corp., AT&T, Ga.-Pacific Corp.; past chmn. Equip. Mfg. Inst. Trustee Farm Found., 1985—, Meth. Med. Ctr., 1985—, Knox Coll., 1986—; chmn., nat. adv. bd. Salvation Army, 1985—, adminstrv. bd. 1st United Meth. Ch., 1986—; bd. dirs. Valparaiso U., Keep Am. Beautiful; past chmn. U.S.-Japan Bus. Coun. Mem. Agrl. Roundtable (chmn. 1985-87), SAE, ACTPN, Bus. Coun., Bus. Roundtable (past chmn.), Nat. Assn. Mfrs. and Bus. Coun., Nat. Fgn. Trade Coun., Mt. Hawley Country Club, Creve Coeur Club, Country Club of Peoria. Republican. Office: Oshkosh Truck Corp 2307 Oregon Street Oshkosh WI 54902*

FITOUSSI, JEAN-PAUL SAMUEL, economist; b. Aug. 19, 1942; s. Joseph and Mathilde (Cohen) F.; m. Annie Krief, July 11, 1964; children: Lisa, David. Student, U. Paris, 1961-63; licencie in Econs., U. Strasbourg, 1966, D d'Etat in Econs., 1971, Agrege in Econs., 1973; D Honoris Causa, U. Buenos Aires. From asst. to hon. dean Louis Pasteur U., Strasbourg, France, 1968-77, hon. dean, 1977—; prof. European U. Inst., 1979-83, Inst. d'Etudes Politiques de Paris, 1983—; cons. EEC, 1978-82, 84—; dir. Bur. Theoretical and Applied Econs., U. Strasbourg, 1974-82, rsch. dept. Observatoire Francais des Conjonctures Econs., 1982-89, pres. 1990—; adv. com. Econ. and Social Scis. Rsch. Coun., U.K., 1986; mem. French Nat. com. Sci. Rsch., 1987-90; bd. dirs. GAN Ins. Co. Author: Inflation, Equilibre et Chomage, 1973, Le Fondement microeconomique de la theorie Keynesienne, 1974; co-author: (with E. Phelps) The Slump in Europe, 1988, Le débat interdit, 1995, (with P. Rosanvallon) Le Nouvel Age des Inégalités, 1996, (with Jean-Paul Fitoussi) Rapport siu l'État de l'Union Européenne, 2000; editor: (with E. Malinvaud) Unemployment in Western Countries, 1980, Modern Macroeconomic Theory, 1984, (with M. de Cecco) Monetary Theory and Economic Institutions, 1986, (with P.A. Muet) Macrodynamique et déséquilibres, 1986, A L'est en Europe, 1991, (with alii) Competitive Disinflation, 1993, Economic Growth, Capital and Labour Markets, 1995. Decorated Chevalier de L'Ordre Nat. du Mérite; recipient prize Acad. Scis. Morales et Politiques, 1974. Mem. Internat. Assn. Applied Econometrics, Internat. Econ. Assn. (gen. sec. 1984, European chpt., French chpt. prize 1972, Am. chpt.). Office: Observatoire Francais des Conjonctures Economiques, 69 quai d'Orsay, 75007 Paris France

FITREMANN, JEAN-MICHEL, psychologist, writer; b. Boulogne Billancourt, France, Aug. 4, 1944; s. Robert H. and Nicole (Bigard) F.; m. Barbara Schasseur, July 13, 1991 (div. Apr. 1994). MA, U. Pierre et Marie Curie, Paris, 1965; PhD, U. Pierre et Marie Curie, 1977; D in Clin. Psychology, U. Denis Diderot, Paris, 1994. Lic. psychotherapist. Reader U. Pierre et Marie Curie, 1967-75, asst. prof., 1975-78; chargé de mission sci. direction Nat. Ctr. Sci. Rsch. (CNRS), Paris, 1978-80; prof. Ecole Nat. Superieure de Mécanique, Paris, 1978-80; cons. Soc. Nat. Estudes Construction de Noteurs d'Avious, Melun, France, 1980-82, various oil cos., France, Germany, Norway, 1968-86; psychotherapist Nantes, France, 1986—; cons. verious engring. cos., Europe, U.S., 1966-86; rsch. dir., Hydrosci., Nantes, 1980-86. Contbr. articles to profl. jours. Served with French Army, 1967-68. Mem. European Assn. Psychotherapy, Syndicat Nat. des Psychologues. Achievements include work on theory of 2-phase flow, psychoanalytic theory of the body and the psychic structure, rsch. in trance and psycho-religious phenomena promotes structural psychology and structural psychotherapy. E-mail: jmf@structuralpsy.org. Office: 1 rue de Verdun, F-44000 Nantes France

FITTON, HARVEY NELSON, JR., former government official, publishing consultant; b. Washington; s. Harvey Nelson and Ada Hortense (Marshall) F.; m. Bernice Jeanette Sutton, Jan. 8, 1946 (dec. Sept. 1998). Student, Nat. Acad. Theater, 1940; degree in Am. Studies, George Washington U., 1949, MA in Am. Lit. and Cultural History, 1956; postgrad., Am. U., 1963. Editor, rsch. asst. Nat. Acad. Scis., Nat. Rsch. Coun., Washington, 1949-56; med. writer and editor NIH, Bethesda, Md., 1956-58; info. specialist farmer cooperative svc. USDA, Washington, 1958-61, publs. editor office of info., 1961-63, chief editorial br. office of info., 1963-66, head pub. divsn. office govtl. and pub. affairs, 1966-84, dep. dir. of info., office govt. and pub. affairs, 1984; cons. in writing, editing, publishing and continuing edn. Washington, 1985—; instr. USDA Grad. Sch., Washington, 1962-92, chmn. editl. adv. com., 1976-85, mem. comm. skills adv. com., 1986-97. Editor, rsch. asst. Atlas of Tumor Pathology, 1949-56; editor NIH Record, 1956-58; contbr. articles to profl. jours. Pres. Clermont Woods Community Assn., Fairfax County, Va., 1968, No. Va. Family Svc., Falls Church, 1972-73; elder local Presbyn. Ch. With USN, 1942-45. Recipient Horace Hart award Edn. Coun. of Graphic Arts Industry, 1980; inductee Internat. Poetry Hall of Fame, 1996. Fellow Soc. for Tech. Comm. (pres. Washington chpt. 1972-73, asst. to pres. for recognition programs 1976-77); mem. Acad. Am. Poets, Internat. Soc. Poets, Haiku Soc. Am., Agrl. Communicators in Edn. (pres. Washington chpt. 1968, Spl. Achievement award 1986), Nat. Assn. Govt. Communicators (pres. Washington chpt. 1979, nat. pres. 1980, mem. editl. bd. Govt. Comm., 1994—, Communicator of Yr. 1984), St. Andrews Soc., Nat. Assn. Scholars, Assn. Lit. Scholars and Critics, Toastmasters (pres. Alexandria chpt. 1959-60), SAR. Avocations: gardening, tap dancing and singing, book collecting, writing poetry. Home and Office: 5624 Glenwood Dr Alexandria VA 22310-1323

FITTRO, RONALD G., JR., healthcare executive, consultant; b. Charleston, W.Va., July 13, 1957; s. Ronald G. Fittro and Leona Gladys Craner. AS, C.C. Allegheny County, Pitts., 1981; BSN, U. Pitts., 1990, MSN, 1992. Assoc. chief nurse VA Med. Ctr., Pitts., 1992-95; DON, VA, Bklyn., 1995-97; mgr. United Healthcare, N.Y.C., 1997-99; CEO Genro Assocs., 1999—. Coord. combined fed. campaign United Way. Mem. ANA, Sigma Theta Tau.

FITZALAN-HOWARD, BENNETT-THOMAS HENRY ROBERT, consultant, public administration and policy analyst, political theorist, theologian, philosopher; b. Geneva, Oct. 10, 1955; came to U.S., 1959; s. S. and A. (Argyle-Campbel) FitzA.-H. BA, BS, Union Coll., Albany, N.Y., 1973; BA, Union Coll., 1973; MDiv, NBTS, 1978; MS, Rutgers U., 1980; MA, Russell Sage Coll., 1987; postgrad., NYU, 1989, Yale U., 1989. Cert. fin. analyst, broker; cert. min. Bride in the Light New Testament Ministry. Adminstrv. analyst Todd Logistics, Inc., N.J., and Saudi Arabia, 1980-81; owner, cons. Fitz Co., Internat., Albany, 1981—; mem. N.Y. Merc. Exch.; insr. Gaton Sch., Yale U., 1987-89, NYU, 1987-89. Author: Expropriation Predictability and Politics, 1979, The Politics of the U.S. Budget, 1987, The Courts in a Democratic System, 1987, White House-Wall Street: The October 87 Crash and the Post Regan Persidency, 1987, The Politics of Deficits, 1988, Enemyless: Can We Survive?, 1989, Responsibility and Accountability: The Forgotten Cornerstones of Democracy, 1990, The Eagle and the UN: Is the US Mature Enough to be the Sole Super-Power?, 1998: contbg. author: Toward a Global Government, 1972, Conservetism: New World Order?, 1990, Tory vs. Labour: Tory: The New English Order, 1992, Hyperinflation, 1992, Eschatology Now, 1992, Eschatology and Current Events, 1992, Bride in the Light: New Testament Church, The Opened Seals of Revelation. Active local ARC, RP Found. With U.S. Army, 1974-77. Mem. AIGA, AAAS, APA, SAR, VFW, Acad. Polit. Sci. (life), Am. Philatelic Soc. (life). Am. Vietnam Vets. Assn., Audubon Soc., Am. Numismatic Assn. (life), Fin. Analysts Fedn. (at large), Fin. Execs. Inst. (at large), Nat. Assn. Securities Dealers (at large), N.Y. Mercantile Exchange, Am. Enterprise Inst., Brookings Inst., Am. Legion, MENSA, Am. Soc. Internat. Law, Am. Bach Found., Am. Soc. Info. Sci., Blind Vets. Assn. (life), Am. Conservative Union, Nat. Press Club, Equestrian Club, Gideons, Mus. Modern Art, Barons of Magna Carta. Avocations: oriental antiques and silver, British stamps and coins, photography, reading, piano and cello. E-mail: Norfolk90@aol.com.

FITZ-CARTER, ALEANE, elementary education educator, composer; b. Council Bluffs, Iowa, July 24, 1929; d. Andrew Wilburt and Beatrice Mildred (Maddox) Fitz; m. James Benny Carter, Dec. 10, 1958 (wid. Aug. 1964); children: Angel Beatrix, Angel Sherrie. BSEd, U. Nebr., 1956. Elem. sch. tchr. Omaha Pub. Schs., 1956-69; instr. Black history and music U. Nebr., Omaha, 1970-74; nat. faculty mem. Gospel Music Workshop Am. Inc., 1986; music tchr. Ascension Luth. Sch., L.A., 1990-94; minister of music Messiah Luth. Ch., L.A., 1996—; church musician Tamarind Seventh Day Adventist Ch., Compton, Calif., 1997—; performing artist Nebr. Arts Coun., Omaha, 1980—, Iowa Arts Coun., Des Moines, 1998—; tchr. adult edn. L.A. Unified Schs., 1998—; ednl. cons. Torrance (Calif.) Unified Schs., 1997—; program prodr. KETV TV, Omaha, 1970-73; radio talk show host, KOWH Radio, Omaha, 1973-74; comms. cons. Mayor's Human Rels. Bd., Omaha, 1970-73; midwest bd. rep. Nat. Black Media Coalition, Washington, 1973-76, others; tchr. Black Awareness Opportunities Industrialization Ctr., 1969-74; instr. history of jazz, Oasis, L.A., 1997—; arranger, librettist, lyricist, elocutionist, storyteller, lectr. in field. Founder, dir. Omaha Gospel Choir, 1965-68; recs. include I Love Jesus, 1965, A Mighty Fortress, 1986; peformer (one-woman show) Rosa Parks, 1979—, Omaha Junior Theater, 1980-85; actresss appearing in I Elvis, Hard Copy, 1992, Ice Cube video Dead Homie MTV, 1990; music dir. stage show One Last Look, Marla Gibbs Theater, 1990; contbr. articles to profl. jours.; composer: One Child, 1993, (sacred hymns) Psalm 91, 1993-97; Children's TV workshop: Strawberry Square II: Take Time, NETV, Lincoln, NE, 1983; invited by South African churches of KwaZulu Natal and African Enterprises to do a piano performance for country's celebration of 1st yr. anniversary freedom at Durban, South Africa, 1995; recordings include LP I Love Jesus Omaha Gospel Choir, 1965, A Mighty Fortress CD, piano instrumental, 1986. Presenter for Soul Food history abroad including Ghana, Spain, Morocco, England, South Africa; presentation vis. with Huell Howser, KETV; founder, dir. Omaha gospel choir, 1965-68. Recipient Comty. Christian Leadership award Salem Baptist Ch., Omaha, Nebr., 1937, Woman in Fine Arts award Alyce Wilson Womens Ctr., Omaha, 1987, 5 yr. ACT-SO award NAACP, Omaha, 1986, Outstanding Songwriter award, 1987-88, Psalm 91 Song of Yr. award Thurston Frazier Chorale, 1987, Nebr. Chpt. GMWA award, 1987-88, Fine Arts award Bethesda Seventh Day Adventist Ch., 1988, Comty. Guest Day Bethesda Seventh Day Ch., Omaha, Nebr., 1988, Outstanding Svc. award L.A. Union Seventh Day Acad., 1992, Creativity in music award Thurston Frazier Chorale, GMWA, 1993, Svc. Above Self award Rotary, 1995, Svc. comty. award Salem Baptist Mission, Norfolk, Nebr., 1995, Svc. Above Self award Rotary Club Watts-Willowbrook, Calif., 1995; grantee L.A. Dept. Cultural Affairs, L.A. Dept. of Cultural Affairs grantee; nominee Best Supporting actress Great White Hope Ctr. Stage, Omaha, Nebr., 1982. Mem. Nebr. Congress of Parents and Tchrs. (hon. life mem.), Sigma Gamma Rho, Gamma Beta Sigma Chpt., Sigma Gamma Rho, Gamma Beta Sigma. Avocations: walking, swimming, cooking. Home: 200 E Hyde Park Blvd Apt 2 Inglewood CA 90302-5545

FITZGERALD, GERALD, writer, director, actor; b. Tyler, Tex., Aug. 14, 1959; s. Truman D. and Eddie Ruth Fitzgerald. AA, Tyler Jr. Coll., 1982; BFA, Stephen F. Austin State U., Nacogdoches, Tex., 1986. Freelance video editor Fitzvizion, Dallas, 1986-91, actor-writer, 1991-97; tech. writer AutoTester, Dallas, 1995-96; rsch. specialist NationsBank, Dallas, 1996-98; dir. rsch. Wilmington Inst., Addison, Tex., 1998—; dir. Tyler Film Soc., 1981-93; dir. new play reading series Pegasus Theatre, Dallas, 1997-2000. Author: (plays) Some Show, 1990, Journey to the Center of the Earth, 2000, (video) Fritz Finger's Frivolous Flottila of Fun, 1990 (Crystal awad Cable Access Dallas 1990); prodr. (video) To the Newlyweds, 1989 (Crystal award Cable Access Dallas 1989). Mem. ASCAP, Dramatists Guild, Playwrights Project, S.T.A.G.E., Alpha Chi. Avocations: astrology, dining with friends, web-surfing, cinema. Home: PO Box 822781 Dallas TX 75382-2781 Office: Wilmington Inst 1530 Dallas Pky Ste 150 Addison TX 75001

FITZGERALD, HAROLD KENNETH, social work educator, consultant; b. Lakewood, Ohio, Apr. 28, 1921; s. Edward James and Julia Florence (Klell) F.; m. Caroline Lee Graham, May 31, 1951; children: Mark, Matthew, Mary, Maura, Kristin. AB, John Carroll U., 1942; MSSW, Cath. U. of Am., 1948, DSW, 1953. Social worker ARC, Cin., 1950-53; exec. dir. Cath. Social Svcs., Atlanta, 1953-56; dir. social services Muscular Dystrophy Assn. of Am., N.Y.C., 1957-58; regional cons., survey dirs. Am. Found. for the Blind, N.Y.C., 1958-66; assoc. dir. Commn. on Standards and Accreditation for the Blind, N.Y.C., 1963-66; prof. social work Syracuse (N.Y.) U., 1966-88, prof. emeritus, 1988—; dir. internat. projects Coun. on Social Work Edn., N.Y.C., 1956-67; bd. dirs. Lighthouse, Syracuse, 1967-90, Cen. N.Y. Assn. for Hearing Impaired, Syracuse, 1976-90, Support, 1990-96, Aurora, 1991—; cons. Nat. Conf. Cath. Charities, Washington, 1966-80, UN, Teheran, Iran, 1975-76. Contbr. articles to profl. jours. Mem. Commn. on Peace and Social Justice, Diocese of Syracuse, 1989-91. Lt. USN, 1943-46. Mem. NASW, AAUP, N.Y. State Assn. Human Svcs. (bd. dirs. 1980-93), Internat. Assn. Schs. Social Work, Inter Univ. Consortium Internat. Social Devel. Roman Catholic. Avocations: skiing, swimming. Home and Office: 301 Greenwood Rd Syracuse NY 13214-2327

FITZGERALD, JAMES FRANCIS, cable television executive; b. Janesville, Wis., Mar. 27, 1926; s. Michael Henry and Chloris Helen (Beiter) F.; m. Marilyn Field Cullen, Aug. 1, 1950; children: Michael Dennis, Brian Nicholas, Marcia O'Loughlin, James Francis, Carolyn Jane, Ellen Putnam. B.S., Notre Dame U., 1947. With Standard Oil Co. (Ind.), Milw., 1947-48; pres. F.-W. Oil Co., Janesville, 1950—, Total TV, Inc. (cable TV Systems), Wis., 1965-86; bd. dirs. Milw. Ins. Co., Bank One, Janesville N.A.; chmn. bd. Golden State Warriors, Oakland, Calif., 1986-95, Total TV Calif., 1987-96. Bd. govs., chmn. TV com. NBA; chmn. bd., pres. S.P.A.C.E. Inc. subs. Milw. Bucks NBA team, 1976-85; chmn. Greater Milw. Open (PGA Tournament), 1985, Notre Dame Bus. Adv. Coun., 1989—. Served to lt. (j.g.) USNR, 1944-46, 51-53. Mem. Chief Execs. Forum, World Bus. Coun., Wis. Petroleum Assn. (pres. 1961-62), Janesville Country Club, Castles Pines Golf Club, Vintage Club (pres. 1989-91), San Francisco Golf Club, El Dorado Country Club. Roman Catholic. Home and Office: PO Box 348 Janesville WI 53547-0348

FITZGERALD, JOHN EDWARD, III, lawyer; b. Cambridge, Mass., Jan. 12, 1945; s. John Edward Jr. and Kathleen (Sullivan) FitzG. BCE, U.S. Mil. Acad., West Point, N.Y., 1969; JD, M in Pub. Policy Analysis, U. Pa., 1975. Bar: Pa. 1975, N.Y. 1978, Calif. 1983, U.S. Supreme Ct. 1991. Commd. 2d lt. U.S. Army, 1969, advanced through grades to capt., 1971, resigned, 1972; assoc. Saul Ewing Remick & Saul, Phila., 1975-77, Shearman & Sterling, N.Y.C., 1977-78; atty., dir. govt. rels. and pub. affairs Pepsico, Inc., Purchase, N.Y., 1978-82; sr. v.p., dept. head Security Pacific Corp., Los Angeles, 1982-83; ptnr. Schlesinger, FitzGerald & Johnson, Palm Springs, Calif., 1983-87; mng. ptnr. FitzGerald & Assocs., Palm Springs, 1987—; judge pro tem Desert Jud. Dist.; lectr. Calif. Continuing Edn. of the Bar; trustee Nat. Coun. Freedom Found., Valley Forge, Pa. Bd. dirs., chmn. Palm Sprngs Boys and Girls Club, Desert Youth Found.; chmn., pres. United Way of the Desert; mem. Com. of 25, Palm Springs; trustee, v.p., Palm Springs Desert Mus.; pres. exec. bd. Coachella Valley coun. Boy Scouts Am. Named Palm Springs Disting. Citizen of Yr., 1999; recipient Friend of Youth award Boys and Girls Clubs, 1998, Disting. Eagle award Boy Scouts Am., 1999. Mem. ABA, Calif. Bar Assn., Desert Bar Assn. (trustee, chmn. cmty. law sch.), Riverside County Bar Assn., Orange County Bar Assn., Assn. Trial Lawyers Am., Calif. Trial Lawyers Assn. (lectr.), Am. Arbitration Assn. (arbitrator), O'Donnell Golf Club, Desert Bus. Roundtable, World Affairs Coun., Lincoln Club of the Coachella Valley (vice chmn. bd. dirs., jud. nomination com.). Office: Ste 105 3001 Tahquitz Canyon Way Palm Springs CA 92262-6900

FITZGERALD, KEVIN MICHAEL, lawyer, mediator; b. Kansas City, Kans., May 10, 1956; s. Thomas Francis and Theresa Ann (Grosdidier) FitzG.; m. Susan Patricia Parker, June 21, 1980; children: Kathryn Ann, Shannon Elizabeth, Erin Parker. BBA, U. Tex., Arlington, 1981; JD, U. Ark., 1985. Bar: Mo. 1985, U.S. Dist. Ct. Mo. 1985, U.S. Ct. Appeals (8th cir.) 1985. Assoc. Taylor, Stafford, Woody, Cowherd and Clithero, Springfield, Mo., 1985-90; ptnr. Taylor, Stafford, Woody, Clithero and FitzGerald, Springfield, 1990—. Mem. Mo. Bar Assn., Springfield Met. Bar Assn. (sec. 1997, chmn. alternative dispute com. 2000), Legal Aid Southwest Mo. (bd. dirs. 1993-96), Nat. Diocesan Attys. Assn. Office: Taylor Stafford Woody Clithero & FitzGerald 3315 E Ridgeview St Ste 1000 Springfield MO 65804-4083

FITZGERALD, NIALL, food products executive; b. Sept. 13, 1945; s. William FitzGerald and Doreen Chambers; m. Monica Cusack, 1970; 3 children. Student, St. Munchins Coll., Limerick; MComm, Univ. Coll. Dublin, Ireland, 1986. With Unilever, 1968—, Unilever N.Am., 1978-80; CEO foods Unilever, South Africa, 1981-85; group treas. Unilever, 1985-86, fin. dir., 1987-89, exec. dir., 1987-96; exec. dir. Unilever Detergents, 1992-95; vice chmn. Unilever PLC, London, 1994-96, chmn., 1996—; bd. dirs. Prudential Corp., Bank of Ireland. Fellow RSA. Avocation: observing humanity. Office: Unilever, PO Box 68 Blackfriars, London EC4P 4BQ, England*

FITZGERALD, PAUL, business executive, consultant; b. Melbourne, Australia, Jan. 7, 1955; s. Les James and Maureen (Bowman) F.; m. Diane Henry, Dec. 10, 1998; children: Madeline, Hannah. BA in Sociology, La-Trobe U., Melbourne, 1977, Diploma of Edn., 1977; Diploma of Applied Psychology, Northwestern U., 1972; MBA, SUNY, 1981. Mgr. Tangentyere Coun., Alice Springs, Australia, 1982-83; exec. officer Illawarra Cmty. Hunting Truste, NSW, Australia, 1983-84; dir. Equasearch Cons.

Melbourne, 1985-94; CEO, Yorke Regional Devel. Bd., 199-496; strategic planner various state govts., 1996-97; CEO, Jobfutures Ltd., Sydney, Australia, 1997—; bd. dirs. Group Investment, Sydney; trustee Com. for the Econ. Devel. of Australia; bd. dirs. Ctr. for Corp. Rsch., Sydney, 1990-92. Co-author: Guide to Informed Giving, 1989; author reports. Harkness Found. fellow, 1981-82. Avocations: sailing, camping, film. Home: 5 Hansard St, Zetland NSW 2017, Australia Office: Jobfutures Ltd, Level 15/323 Castlereagh St, 2000 Sydney NSW, Australia

FITZGERALD, PETER GOSSELIN, senator, lawyer; b. Elgin, Ill., Oct. 20, 1960; s. Gerald Francis and Marjorie (Gosselin) F.; m. C. Nina Kerstiens, July 25, 1987; 1 child, Jake Buchanan. AB, Dartmouth Coll., 1982; cert. of attendance, Aristotelian U., Salonica, Greece, 1983; JD, U. Mich., 1986. Bar: Ill. 1986, U.S. Dist. Ct. (no. dist.) Ill. 1986. Assoc. Isham, Lincoln & Beale, Chgo., 1986-88; ptnr. Riordan, Larson, Bruckert & Moore, Chgo., 1988-92; mem. Ill. Senate, 1993-98, chmn. state govt. ops. com., 1997-98; U.S. senator from Ill., 1999-; counsel Harris Bankmont, Inc., 1992-96; bd. dirs. Harris Bank Palatine N.A., 1993-98. Translator: Dartmouth Classical Jour., 1982. Pres. Young Rep. Orgn., Palatine, Ill., 1988; bd. dirs. north ctrl. Ill. region Children's Home and Aid Soc. Rotary Found. internat. grad. scholar, 1982-83. Mem. Ill. State Bar Assn., Econ. Club Chgo., Inverness Golf Club, Union League Club. Roman Catholic. Office: US Senate 555 Dirksen Bldg Washington DC 20510-0001

FITZGERALD, ROBERT DENHAM, anesthesiologist, researcher; b. Vienna, Austria, May 15, 1959; s. Ernest Denham and Gertrude Friederike (Eder) F.; m. Annelies Stefaner, Mar. 30, 1990. MD, U. Vienna, 1984. Resident in anesthesia U. Vienna, 1984-93; rsch. asst. Inst. Gen. and Comparative Physiology, Vienna, 1985-86; intern U. Vienna Med. Sch., 1986-89; rsch. fellow A.C. Burton Vascular Biology Labs., London, Ont., Can., 1993-96; cons. dept. anesthesia U. Vienna, 1993-96; rsch. dir. Ludwig Boltzmann Inst., Vienna, 1996—; dir. cardiovascular anesthesia divsn. dept. anesthesia Lainz Hosp., Vienna, 1996—. Contbr. articles to profl. jours. Recipient award Govt. Can., 1993, Critical Care Rsch. award Am. Coll. Chest Physicians, 1996. Fellow Austrian Soc. Anesthesia and Intensive Care (treas. 1997—); mem. European Soc. Intensive Care Medicine. Office: Ludwig Boltzmann Inst, Wolkersbergenstrasse 1, A-1130 Vienna Austria

FITZGERALD, ROBERT HANNON, JR., orthopedic surgeon; b. Denver, Aug. 25, 1942; s. Robert Hannon and Alyene (Webber) Fitzgerald Anderson; m. Lynda Lee Lang, Apr. 27, 1968 (div. 1984); children: Robert III, Shannon, Dennis, Katherine, Kelly; m. Jamie Kathleen Dent, Mar. 9, 1985; children: Brian, Steven. BS, U. Notre Dame, 1963; MD, U. Kans., 1967; MS, U. Minn., 1974; Magistri Artivum, U. Pa., 1995. Instr. orthop. surgery Mayo Med. Sch., Rochester, Minn., 1974-77, cons. orthop. surgery, 1974-89, asst. prof., 1977-82, assoc. prof., 1982-86, prof., 1986-89, chief adult reconstructive surgery, 1987-89, dir. orthop. rsch., 1988-89; prof. chmn. dept. orthop. surgery Wayne State U. Sch. Med., 1989-95; chief orthop. surgery Hutzel Hosp., 1989-95, Detroit Receiving Hosp., 1989-95; orthopedist-in-chief Detroit Med. Ctr., 1989-95, chmn. coun., specialist-in-chief, 1993-95; chmn. dept. orthop. surgery U. Pa. Sch. Med., Phila., 1995-99; chief orthop. surgery Hosp. U. Pa., Phila., 1995—; P.B. Magnuson prof. bone and joint surgery U. Pa. Sch. Med., Phila., 1996—; chief orthop. surgery Phila. Veterans Med. Ctr.; Bd. dirs. Hutzel Hosp., 1989-95; dir. Penn. Orthop. Inst., U. Pa. Health Sys., 1997—; cons. Ctr. Disease Control, Atlanta, 1981—, NIH, 1987; chmn. orthop. study sect., 1989-91. Assoc. editor Jour. Orthop. and Traumatology, 1978—, Jour. Bone Joint Surgery, 1982-86, Clin. Orthop. and Related Rsch., 1988—; editor Seminars in Arthroplasty, 1993—; trustee Jour. Bone Joint Surgery, 1987-92, sec. 1988-92, Hutzel Hosp., 1989-95. Served to capt. USAF, 1968-70. Decorated Air Commendation medal; recipient Kappa Delta award for Musculoskeletal rsch., 1983. Fellow Am. Acad. Orthop. Surgeons, Phila. Coll. Physicians; trustee Lourdes H.S. Devel. Bd., Rochester, 1982-88; mem. AMA, Am. Orthopedic Assn., Rsch. Soc., Assn. Bone and Joint Surgeons, Interurban Ortho Soc., Internat. Soc. Microbiology, Zumbro County Med. Soc., Min-Da-Man Orthop. Soc., Minn. Orthopedic Soc., Am. Soc. Microbiology, N.Y. Acad. Scis., Am. Hip Soc. (Stinchfield award 1985, Charnley award 1986, 95, pres. 1993-94), Internat. Hip Soc., Am. Orthop. Assn. (N.Am. traveling fellow 1974, Am. Brit. Can. traveling fellow, 1981), Surg. Infection Soc. (charter mem.), Clin. Orthop. Soc., Internat. Soc. Orthop. Surgery and Traumatology, Mid-Am. Orthop. Soc. (bd. dirs. 1989-93, 94—, pres. elect 1994, pres. 1996), Detroit Acad. Orthop. Surgery, Mich. Orthop. Soc., Mich. State Med. Soc., Detroit Acad. Med., Pa. Orthop. Soc., Phila. Orthop. Soc. (bd. dirs. 1998—), Phila. Acad. Med., bd. devel. Mayo Clinic, 1984-87, St. John's Ch., 1988-89, bd. edn. St. John's Grade Sch./Jr. H.S., Rochester, 1983-87, Interurban Club, Sigma Xi, Kappa Delta, Alpha Epsilon Delta. Republican. Roman Catholic. Avocations: cross-country and downhill skiing. Home: 1218 Country Club Rd Gladwyne PA 19035-1418 Office: U Pa Dept Orthopaedic Surgery Sch Medicine II Silverstien Pavilion 3400 Spruce St Philadelphia PA 19104-4206

FITZGERALD, TIM K., writer, political organizer; b. San Jose, Calif., Jan. 3, 1946; s. Ralph George and Bernice Christine (Huston) F. BA, San Jose State Coll., 1971, San Jose State U., 1980; MA, San Jose State U., 1985, San Jose State U., 1997. Treas. Associated Students San Jose State Coll., 1969-70; camp bus. mgr. Boy Scouts Am., Sonora, Calif., 1973; co. budget analyst Allstate Equity Investments, San Jose, 1980; adminstrv. asst. Summer Employment of Youth program CETA, San Jose, 1981; pres. Corp. for Shared Responsibility, San Jose, 1983-84; rschr. San Jose, 1992-96; owner/operator Raccoon Pubs., San Jose, 1991-92; freelance writer San Jose, 1986—, rschr., 1992-96; adminstrv. trustee Inst. for Social Orgnl. Rsch., San Jose, 1992-94, 98—; instr. Cerro Coso C.C., Mammoth Lakes, Calif., 1998-2000. Author: Essays in Capitalism, 1986, Inner City, 1993, Twilight in the Afternoon, 1997, Critical Mass: Prospects for a New World Order, 1998, The Quest, 2000, (narrative) Trail to Black Mountain, 1978, (poetry) Impressions from Idle Rock, 1981; host. (talk show) KSJS Radio, San Jose, 1995-97; corr. Mono County Rev. Herald, 1997-98. Mgr., candidate for State Assembly, San Jose, 1994, for San Jose City Coun., 1982, for Mono County Bd. Edn., 1998; delegate Green Party Nat. Conv., 2000; co-coord. State Green Party Platform, Calif., 1993, State Green Party campaigns and candidates, Calif., 1995-97; elected mem. Green Party County Coun., Santa Clara County, Calif., 1992-94, Mono County, 2000—; vol. Cmty. Companions, Inc., San Jose, 1990-91; commr. City of San Jose Disability Adv., 1993-97, vice chair, 1997; mem. task force on poverty Santa Clara County, 1995-97; mem. Mono County Mental Health Adv. Bd., 1998—, chair, 1999—. Advanced cadet U.S. Army ROTC, 1966-67. Mem. Am. Acad. Poets, Nat. Writers Union, Fellowship of Reconciliation, Commonwealth Club, Sierra Club, Tau Delta Phi. Lutheran. Avocations: hiking, wilderness photography, chess, bridge. Office: Inst for Social Organizational Rsch PO Box 3504 Mammoth Lakes CA 93546-3504

FITZGERALD, WILLIAM JOSEPH, surgeon; b. Boston, Oct. 6, 1962; arrived in Australia, 1973; s. William Joseph and Anita (Magee) F.; m. Nadine Dianne Robinson, July 25, 1987; children: Liam, Caitlin (twins), Ellen. MB, BS with honors, U. Queensland, 1986. Intern Princess Alexandra Hosp., Queensland, Australia, 1987-88; resident Princess Alexandra Hosp., 1988-90; surgical registrar Mater Hosp., Brisbane, Australia, 1991-94; cons. surgeon, 1995—. Fellow Royal Australian Coll. Surgeons; mem. Australian Med. Assn., Australian Assn. Surgeons, Australian Doctors Fund, mem. Prin. Surgeons of Australia, Gen. Surgeons of Australia. Avocations: tennis, golf.

FITZMAURICE, LAURENCE DORSET, bank executive; b. Worcester, Mass., Aug. 7, 1938; s. John Vincent and Alice (Earle) F.; m. Ann McQuaid, Apr. 15, 1961; children: Laura, Peter, Meghan. BS in Mgmt., Babson Coll., 1959; postgrad. in law, Boston Coll., 1961. Prodn. control Sylvania, Needham, Mass., 1959-61; divsn. controller EG&G, Inc., Bedford, Mass., 1961-69; asst. corp. controller Tyco Labs., Waltham, Mass., 1970; corp. controller Analog Devices, Norwood, Mass., 1971-73; v.p. fin. Balco, Inc., Newton, Mass., 1974-75; comptroller Commonwealth of Mass., Boston, 1976-78, commr. of revenue, 1978; sr. cons. Am. Mgmt. Systems, Arlington, Va., 1979; prin. cons. Boston, 1980-81; v.p. State St. Bank & Trust Co., Boston, 1982—; adj. prof. Northeastern U. Grad. Sch. Polit. Sci., Boston, 1977-78; mem. faculty New Eng. Coll. Fin., 1998—; mem. Bd. Bank Incorp., Boston, 1978. Commr. Mass. State Lottery, Braintree, 1976-78; sec. Mass. Housing Fin. Agy., Boston, 1978; pres. Human Rels. Svc., Wellesley, Mass., 1988-89, trustee, 1986—; bd. dirs. Social Policy Rsch. Group, Boston, 1981-92, Boston Mcpl. Rsch. Bur., 1985—, exec. com. 1999—; mem. allocations com. United Way of Mass. Bay, 1998, multi-yr. audit task force, 1999—; bd. overseers USS Constitution Mus., 1999—. Cpl. USMCR, 1957-63. Democrat. Roman Catholic. Club: Union of Boston. Avocations: tennis, golf.

FITZPATRICK, CHRISTINE MORRIS, legal administrator, former television executive; b. Steubenville, Ohio, June 10, 1920; d. Roy Elwood and Ruby Lorena (Mason) Morris; student U. Chgo., 1943-44, U. Ga., 1945-46; m. T. Mallary Fitzpatrick, Jr., Dec. 19, 1942; 1 child, Thomas Mallary III. BA, Roosevelt U., 1947; postgrad. Trinity Coll., Hartford, Conn., 1970. Assoc. dir. Joint Human Rels. Project, City of Chgo., 1965-66; tchr. English, Austin Sch. for Girls, Hartford, 1966-70; promotion coord. Conn. Pub. TV, Hartford, 1971-72, dir. community rels., 1972-73, v.p., 1973-77; pub. rels./pub. affairs cons. Commonwealth Edison Co., Chgo., 1977-79; dir. spl. events Chgo. Public TV, 1979-84; v.p. Fitzpatrick Group, Inc., Chgo., 1986-88; adminstrv. dir. Fitzpatrick Law Offices, 1988-94, Fitzpatrick Eilenberg & Zivian, 1994-96; adminstrv. dir. Fitzpatrick Law Offices, Chgo., 1997-99, 2200 Ventures LLC, Chgo., 1999—; v.p. Pub. Rels. Clinic Chgo., 1980-81. Bd. advisers Greater Hartford Mag., 1975-77; bd. dirs. World Affairs Ctr., Hartford, 1975-77; mem. adv. coun. Am. Revolution Bicentennial Commn. Conn., 1975-77. Mem. Pub. Rels. Soc. Am. (dir. Conn. Valley chpt. 1976-77), Am. Women in Radio and TV (New Eng. chpt. pres. 1976-77), LWV (Chgo. chpt. pres. 1962-64, Hartford chpt. v.p. 1971-73). Home: 5518 S Harper Ave Chicago IL 60637-1830

FITZ-PATRICK, DAVID, endocrinologist, educator; b. Burnley, Lancashire, England, Sept. 1, 1951; came to U.S., 1975; s. Malcolm Milligan and Ada (Maguire) F.; m. Elizabeth Joaquin, Dec. 30, 1972; children: Ian Rodney, Claire Larissa. MB, BS, U. Newcastle-Upon-Tyne, England, 1974. House officer Newcastle (England) Gen. Hosp., 1974-75; resident in internal medicine U. Md. Hosp., Balt., 1975-77; fellow in endocrinology McGill U., Montreal, Que., Can., 1977-81; cons. physician Straub Clinic and Hosp, Honolulu, 1981-91, chief of endocrinology, 1986-91; asst. clin. prof. medicine John Burns Sch. Medicine, Honolulu, 1982-95, assoc. clin. prof., 1995—; med. dir. Diabetes and Hormone Ctr. of Pacific, Honolulu, 1990—, East-West Med. Rsch. Inst., 1999—; mem. house of dels. Hawaii Med. Assn., 1987-90; med. adv. com. Bd. Med. Examiners, Hawaii, 1989—; founding mem., bd. dirs. Juvenile Diabetes Found., Honolulu, 1989-92 (Geraldine Fleming Meml. fellowship 1980-81); dir. East-West Med. Rsch. Inst., 1999—. Mem. editl. bd. Endocrine Practice, 2000—; contbr. articles to profl. jours.; founder, editor Diabetes & Endocrinology Home Page on Internet. Dir. The Straub Found., Honolulu, 1984-90. Rsch. scholar McGill U., 1979-80. Fellow Am. Coll. Physicians (mem. coun. 1990-93, Gov's. prize 1986), Am. Coll. Endocrinology; mem. Am. Diabetes Assn. (pres. 1984-86, 93-94), The Endocrine Soc., Am. Soc. Internal Medicine, Am. Assn. Clin. Endocrinologists (state chair 1992-96, 98—). Avocations: reading, family, tennis, golf. Office: 1329 Lusitana St Ste 304 Honolulu HI 96813-2411

FITZPATRICK, JAMES DAVID, lawyer; b. Syracuse, N.Y., Oct. 21, 1938; s. William Francis and Margaret Mary (Shortt) F. BS, Holy Cross Coll., Worcester, Mass., 1960; JD, Syracuse U., 1963. Bar: N.Y. 1963, U.S. Dist. Ct. (no. dist.) N.Y. 1965. Assoc. Bond, Schoeneck & King, Syracuse, N.Y., 1963-76, mem., 1976-88, ptnr., 1988—; pres. Hiscock Legal Aid Soc., Syracuse, 1975-76; faculty Nat. Bus. Inst., Eau Claire, Wis., 1990—; del. Russian Conf. on Banking-The Kremlin, Moscow, 1992, 93. Mem. presdl. Roundtable, Washington, 1991-92; founding mem. pres.'s task force Nat. Coalition Against Pornography, Common Cause; chmn. adv. bd. Rep. Nat. Coms., 1994; mem. The Studio Mus. in Harlem, Am. Mus. Nat. History; founding mem. Am. Air Mus.; nat. adv. coun. USN Meml. Found. Recipient Afghanistan Freedom Fighter award Afghan Mercy Fund, 1989, Rep. Senatorial Medal of Freedom, Honored Friend of El Salvador award, 1991, Wisdom award of Honor, Wisdom Soc. for Advancement of Knowledge, Learning and Rsch. in Edn., named to Wisdom Hall of Fame, 1999. Mem. ABA, NAACP, N.Y. State Bar Assn., Onondaga County Bar Assn. (chmn. real estate com. 1990-96), Internat. Bar Assn., Am. Land Title Assn., UN Assn. of U.S.A., Habitat for Humanity Internat., Amnesty Internat. U.S.A., Nat. Audubon Soc., Ctr. for Nat. Independence in Politics, Smithsonian Nat. Assocs., Nat. Trust for Hist. Preservation, Navy League U.S., World Future Soc., Ams. Guild, Internat. Platform Assn. (spkr. Internat. Youth Ctr., New Delhi), Inst. Global Ethics, World Jurist Assn. Republican. Roman Catholic. Avocations: housing education, reading, walking. Home: 201 Croyden Rd Syracuse NY 13224-1917 Office: Bond Schoeneck & King 1 Lincoln Ctr Fl 18 Syracuse NY 13202-1324

FITZPATRICK, MATTHEW JOSEPH, financial services company executive; b. Kittery, Maine, Sept. 2, 1971; s. Richard Michael and Jane Ellen (Caron) F.; m. Deborah Marie, Oct. 26, 1996. BS, Providence Coll., 1993; MBA, Boston Coll., 1999. Mktg. coord. Sea Beam Instruments, Walpole, Maine, 1993-94; customers svc. specialist Fidelity Investments, Boston, 1995-96, assoc. client svc. mgr., 1997-98; implementation project mgr. Fidelity Investments, Marlboro, Maine, 1999. Mem. Omicron Delta Epsilon. Roman Catholic. Avocations: personel investing, european history, softball. E-mail: mfitz22@yahoo.com. Home: 6 Larson Rd Milford MA 01757-3723 Office: Fidelity Investments 300 Puritan Way # Mm3L Marlborough MA 01752-3076

FITZPATRICK, PHILIP J., judge, lawyer; b. Bronxville, N.Y., Aug. 21, 1945; s. Francis J. Fitzpatrick and Florence I. Tompkins; m. Gene F. Rybicki, July 25, 1970 (div. July 1985); 1 child, Matthew. BA cum laude, Georgetown U., 1967; JD cum laude, Boston U., 1973. Sole practice Jeffersonville, Vt., 1974-90; probate judge Lamoille County, Vt., 1988—; sr. ptnr. Fitzpatrick & Hobart, Jeffersonville, 1990—. Mem. Vt. Probate Judges Assn. (pres. 1998—). Avocations: reading, landscaping, writing poetry. Home: PO Box 368 Hyde Park VT 05655-0368

FITZPATRICK, THOMAS BERNARD, dermatologist, educator; b. Madison, Wis., Dec. 19, 1919; s. Joseph J. and Grace (Lawrence) F.; m. Beatrice Devaney, Dec. 27, 1944; children: Thomas B., Beatrice, John, L. Scott, Brian. BA with honors, U. Wis., 1941; MD, Harvard U., 1945; fellow, Mayo Found., 1948-51; PhD, U. Minn., 1952; fellow, Commonwealth Fund, Oxford, 1958-59; DSc (hon.), U. Mass., 1987, U. Rochester Med. Sch., 1996. Intern 4th (Harvard) Med. Service, Boston City Hosp., 1945-46; biochemist Army Med. Ctr., Md., 1946-48; asst. prof. dermatology U. Mich. Med. Sch., 1951-52; prof., head divsn. dermatology U. Oreg. Med. Sch., 1952-58; Edward Wigglesworth prof. dermatology Harvard Med. Sch., 1959-87, prof. emeritus, 1987—, head dept., 1959-87; chief dermatology svc. Mass. Gen. Hosp., Boston, 1959-87; Prosser White orator St. John's Dermatol. Soc., London, 1964; Dohi internat. exch. lectr. dermatology, Japan, 1969; spl. cons. USPHS, NIH; cons. in dermatology Brigham and Women's Hosp., Children's Hosp. Med. Ctr., Boston, 1962—; mem. sci. adv. bd. EPA, 1985; mem. climatic impact com., chmn. health effects NAS; pres. Dermatology Found., 1971, Internat. Pigment Cell Soc., 1978-81, Assn. Profs. Dermatology, 1983. Chief editor: Dermatology in General Medicine, 1971, 4th edit., 1993; mem. editl. bd. New Eng. Jour. Medicine, 1961-69; editor Year Book Dermatology, 1984-97, Fitzpatrick's Dermatology in General Medicine, 5th edit., 1999; columnist Boston Globe, 1984—. Capt. MC U.S. Army, 1946-48. Decorated Officer Order of Rising Gold Rays (Japan), 1986; recipient Mayo Found. Alumni Rsch. award, 1951, Outstanding Achievement award U. Minn. Bd. Regents, 1964, Myron Gordon award 6th Internat. Pigment Cell Conf., 1965, Disting. Svc. award Dermatology Found., 1989, U. Wis., 1983, award for discovery of PUVA photochemotherapy for psoriasis Nat. Psoriasis Found., 1993, Nat. Med. Rsch. award Nat. Health Coun., 1994, Discovery award Dermatology Found., 1997, Mentor award Am. Skin Assn., 2000; Established Thomas B. Fitzpatrick prof. dermatology and endowed chair Harvard U., 1987, Thomas B. Fitzpatrick profl. chair, 1990. Fellow Am. Acad. Dermatology (hon., master, past bd. dirs.); mem. NAS (mem. inst. medicine 1994), Royal Soc. Medicine (hon.), Am. Acad. Arts and Scis., Assn. Am. Physicians, Soc. Investigative Dermatology (hon., pres. 1959-60, Stephen Rothman award, gold medal 1970), Am. Soc. for Clin. Investigation (emeritus 1965), Brit. Assn. Dermatology (hon.), South African Dermatol. Soc. (hon.), Med. Assn. Israel Dermatol. Soc. (hon.), St. John's Hosp. Dermatol. Soc. (London, hon.) Argentina, Danish, Italian, Finnish, German, Polish, Austrian, Mex. dermatol. socs. (hon.), Pacific Dermatologic Assn. (hon.), French Soc. Dermatology and Syphiligraphy (fgn. corr.), Australasian Coll. Dermatologists, Alpha Omega Alpha. Home: 209 Newton St Weston MA 02493-2338 Office: Mass Gen Hosp Dermatology Svc 55 Fruit St Boston MA 02114-2696

FITZPATRICK, WHITFIELD WESTFELDT, lawyer; b. New Orleans, Jan. 31, 1942; s. William Harry and Frances (Westfeldt) F.; m. Jean Phipps, July 6, 1984. BA, Washington & Lee U., 1964; JD, Tulane U., 1967; LLM, Grenoble U., France, 1969, Doctorate, 1972. Bar: La. 1967, Va. 1972, N.Y. 1974, U.S. Dist. Ct. (ea. dist.) La. 1974, D.C. 1975, U.S. Dist. Ct. (we. dist.) La. 1975, U.S. Ct. Appeals (5th cir.) 1975. Law clk. Supreme Ct. Commonwealth of Va., Norfolk, 1969-70; assoc. Coudert Bros., N.Y.C., 1972-74; sr. assoc. Phelps, Dunbar, Marks, Claverie & Sims, New Orleans, 1974-76; counsel Mobil Oil Corp., New Orleans, 1976-79, Mobil North Sea Ltd., London, 1979-82; gen. counsel The Hague, Netherlands, 1982; sr. counsel, asst. sec. Mobil Exploration and Producing U.S., Inc., Midland, Tex., 1987-89; asst. sec. Mobil Producing Tex. and N.Mex., Inc., Midland, 1987-89; with direction juridique Elf Aquitaine, Europe and U.S. coord., 1989-94; spl. advisor to dir. of comml. and lic. adminstrn. divsn. ELF Petroleum Norge, 1994-97; exec. v.p. and gen. counsel Fountain Oil Inc., 1997—. Contbr. articles to profl. pubs. Named Mem. Soc. of the Friends of the Legion of Honor, Ordres de Chevalerie; Grenoble U. Law Sch. scholar, 1967-69; fellow Govt. of France, 1970-72. Mem. ABA, Maritime Law Assn., Internat. Bar Assn., La. Bar Assn., Va. Bar Assn., N.Y. Bar Assn., D.C. Bar Assn., chmn. Am. Coordinating Coun. of Norway, Boston Club of New Orleans, Racquet and Tennis Club of N.Y., Royal Auto Club of London, Soc. Colonial Wars, Societé des Amis du Musée National de la Légion d'Honneur. Avocations: golf, skiing, reading, tennis. Home: Camilla Collets vei No 8, 0285 Oslo Norway Office: Fountain Oil Inc, Skysstasjon 11-B, PO Box 87, 1371 Asker Norway

FITZSIMMONS, DEBRA C., art educator, artist; b. Chgo., Dec. 24, 1951; d. Edwin Steven and LaVerne Ruth Tanski; m. John R. Fitzsimmons, July 16, 1974; children: Jill A., John R. III. BFA, So. Ill. U., 1973; MEd, Carthage Coll., 1995; MFA, No. Ill. U., 1997. Art tchr. Gorham (Ill.) Unit Dist., 1973, Dongola (Ill.) Unit Dist., 1973-79, Mundelein (Ill.) H.S., 1991—. Exhibited in numerous shows, 1997-99. Exhbn. chmn. Midwest Pastel Juried Show, St. Charles, Ill., 1991; conf. presenter Edn. for Global Involvement, Chgo., 1995, Midwest Conf. Asian Affairs, Macomb, Ill., 1995. Recipient Best of Show award Coll. of Lake County, 1991. Mem. NEA, Nat. Art Edn. Assn. (conf. presenter 1998), Ill. Art Edn. Assn., Ell. Edn. Assn., Midwest Pastel Soc., Figurative Art League. Avocations: drawing, painting. Office: Mundelein HS 1350 W Hawley St Mundelein IL 60060-1504

FITZWANGA, NASHON, lawyer; b. Kisumu, Nyanza, Kenya, July 26, 1947; s. James Fitzwanga and Hellena Kaiser; m. Margaret Bulage Kabazzi; children: Kaiser, Nakili, Victoria, Dalla, Hiro. BA with honors, U. Nairobi, Kenya, 1973; BL, U. London, 1979; LLM, U. Nottingham, Eng., 1992; PhD in Internat. Law, Matriculation Knightsbridge U., Eng., 1997. Cert. in internat. law, jud. arbitration, land econs., valuation surveying. Regional dir. Martin Heymann Group of Cos., Uganda, 1973-74; chief estate rating surveyor East African Econ. Comty., Tanzania, 1974-77; estate and rating surveyor Kenya Govt. Parastatal, 1978-79; mng. dir. Urban Associated Surveyors Ltd., Kenya, 1980-84; regional rep. Internat. Law Assn. Del. to UN, U.K., 1985—; ad hoc dir.-gen. Environ. Disaster Rsch. Found., Kenya, 1992—; panel jud. arbitrator Regional Ctr. for Coml. Arbitration, Cairo, 1986—, World Arbitration Reporter Parker Sch. of Fgn. and Comparative Law, Columbia U., N.Y.C., 1989—, Coml. Arbitration Panel of Supreme Ct. of Egypt, Cairo, 1995—, Permanent Ct. of Arbitration, Pt. Louis, Mauritius, 1996—. Author: (monograph/jour.) The Legal Position of UN Security Coun. Resolution 748 Against Libya in Lockerbie PanAm Bombing, 1993 (banner and cert. of appreciation Rotary Internat.), The Legal Status of the Doctrine of Exclusive Econ. Zone in Internat. Law, 1990, Law and Practice of the UN Security Coun. in Maintenance of Internat. Peace and Security, 1996 (banner of appreciation Rotary Internat. 1996). Com. mem. Rural Devel. Focus of Office of Pres. of Kenya, 1985. Mem. Internat. Law Assn. (sr. mem.), Internat. Bar Assn. (sr. mem.), Chartered Inst. Arbitrators (sr. mem.). Home: Coral Dr PO Box 95057, Mombasa Kenya Office: Park Place, St James St, London SW1 1LR, England

FITZ-WILLIAMS, MCFAULAND PATRICK, surgeon, educator, cardiothoracic and vascular surgical consultant; b. Sekondi, Ghana, Oct. 6, 1940; s. McFauland Patrick and Margaret Kra (Ashun) F.-W.; children: Margaret, Marianne, McFauland Jr., Peter, Issac, Joseph, Edna, Debora. MD with honors, Lvov State Med. Inst., Ukraine, USSR, 1969, diploma in gen. surgery with honors, 1971; Cand. Med. Scis. in Cardiovasc. Surgery, Acad. Med. Scis., Moscow, 1979; cert. in gen. cardio-thoracic surgery, 2d Moscow-Pirogov Med. Inst., 1984. Intern Lvov State Med. Inst., 1969; initiator tropical medicine course, then med. officer Effia-Nkwanta Group Hosps., Sekondi, 1971-74, registrar surg. dept., 1974; sr. med. officer, gen. surgeon Ashanti Goldfields Corp. Mines Hosp., Obuasi, Ghana, 1974-76; initiated specialist course cardiothoracic-vascular surgery Acad. Med. Scis., Moscow, 1976-79; cardiothoracic surg. specialist Korle Bu Tchr. Hosp., Accra, Ghana, 1980-90; gen. practice medicine Accra, 1990—; cardiothoracic surg. cons.; vis. cons. Narh-Bita Hosp., Tema, Ghana; med.-officer in charge Eikwe Cath. Mission Hosp., Nzima, Ghana, 1974; surgeon-in-charge Bolgatanga (Ghana) Govt. Hosp., 1974; conf. presenter in field; facilitator, pub. lectr. on health matters. Contbr. articles to med. jours.; patentee in field. Mem. choir St. Paul's Pro-Cathedral Cath. Ch., Sekondi; patron St. Jude's Martyrs of Uganda Cath. Ch. Choir, Mamprobi, Ghana; mem. Christian Aid and Svcs. Found; past pres. Ghana-USSR Friendship Soc., patron. Decorated knight comdr. Mystical Order St. Peter (London). Mem. Royal Soc. Tropical Medicine and Hygiene, Royal Commonwealth Soc., Internat. Cardiac Pacing Soc. (regional rep.), Ghana Med. Assn., N.Y. Acad. Scis., Internat. Union against Tb and Lung Diseases, All Soviet Soc. Surgeons, Brit. Thoracic Soc., Pan-African Cath. Doctors Guild, All Soviet Soc. Pulmonologists, Soviet Trained Ghanaian Grad. Assn. (past v.p.), Fijai Old Students Assn. (nat. pres.), Nat. Geog. Soc., YMCA (life Accra). E-mail: newachi@ghana.com. Home and Office: PO Box MS 14, Achimota Via New Achimota v Accra Ghana

FIX, DOUGLAS MARTIN, electrical engineer; b. Lincoln, Nebr., Oct. 20, 1953; s. Raymond Harold and Juliana Marie (Spatz) F. BSEE, BSCS, U. Colo., 1979; MSEE, Southern Meth. U., 1983. Registered profl. engr. Tex. Computer ops. Seismograph Svc. Corp., Denver, 1974-78, seismic analyst, 1978-80; design engr. Tex. Instruments, Dallas, 1980-85, sr. engr., 1985-88, lead engr., 1988—; adj. prof., Eastfield Coll., Mesquite, Tex., 1983—; cons. Computers U2, Allen,Tex., 1990—. Contbr. article to profl. jours.; patentee digital video monitor interface arch., hardware ind. device interface. Elder, tchr. Zion Luth. Ch., Dallas, 1992—; crime watch coord. Neighborhood Homeowners, Dallas, 1988. Recipient Sundstrand scholarship Sundstrand Corp., 1978. Mem. IEEE, Eta Kappa Nu (sec. 1978), Soc. Info. Display, Mensa, Tau Beta Pi. Republican. Lutheran. Achievements include research in digital pll clocking for TV synch signal processor and preprocessor designs for 4 classified military projects. Avocations: snow skiing, water skiing, foreign travel, classical music, theater. Home: 761 Livingston Dr Allen TX 75002-5229 Office: Texas Instruments 13510 N Central Expy Dallas TX 75243-1108

FIX-BONNER, HANS, educator; b. Muenchweiler, Germany, Mar. 1, 1947; s. Ludwig and Anna (Emanuel) F.; m. Maria Bonner, June 13, 1978. MA, U. Saarland, Germany, 1972, Dr.p., 1978. Asst. prof. U. Bonn, Germany, 1979-89; prof. U. Greifswald, Germany, 1990—, dean, 1994-96; vis. prof. U. Minn., Mpls., 1984-86. Feodor Lynen fellow Avh Found., U. Minn., 1984-86. Home: R Breitscheid Str 8, D-17489 Greifswald Germany Office: Ernst Moritz Arndt U, D-17487 Greifswald Germany

FIXEN, RANDALL ROBERT, academic director; b. Marshall, Minn., July 15, 1959; s. Robert LeRoy Sr. and Jeanette Marie Fixen; m. Ahna Lynn Halbakken, July 15, 1989; children: Christopher Aaron, Mariah Lynn. BA, S.W. State U., 1983; MA, U. N.D., 1985, PhD, 1992. Cert. vocat. guidance counselor. Coor. alcohol and drug prevention U. N.D., Grand Forks, 1985-86, dir. internat. student affairs, 1985-90; dir. counseling, housing, student activities, acad. advisement, intramurals Lake Region State Coll., Devils Lake, 1992—; v.p. N.D. State Housing Officers, Devils Lake, 1995—; pres.

N.D. State Housing Officers, 1998—. Pres. bd. United Way, Devils Lake, N.D., 1994; mem. Devils Lake Sch. Bd., 1997—; problem capt. Odyssey of the Mind, Devils Lake, 1996—; 3rd chair trumpet Devils Lake Elks Band, 1992—. Mem. Am. Counseling Assn., Am. Vocat. Assn., Nat. Assn. Fgn. Student Affairs (chairperson region IV 1990-91, career svcs. grant for internat. students 1988), N.D. Counseling and Personnel Assn., Optimist Club. Avocations: fishing, reading, travel. E-mail: fixenra@stellarnet.com, fixenr@lrsc.nodak.edu. Home: 818 5th St Devils Lake ND 58301-2611 Office: Lake Region State Coll 1801 College Dr Devils Lake ND 58301-1598

FIXOT, BERNARD, book publisher; b. Villejuif, France, Oct. 6, 1943; s. Louis Fixot and Marthe Courtin; m. Valérie-Anne Giscard D'Estaing, Dec. 4, 1987; children: Guillaume, Iris. V.p. sales Gallimard Group, France, 1972-77, Hachette Livres Group, France, 1978-80; pres., CEO, Editions No 1, France, 1977-86, Editions Fixot, France, 1987-99, Editions Robert Laffont, France, 1993-99, T.F.1 Editions, France, 1988—. Office: Editions XO, Tour, Montparnasse 33 Av du Maine, 75755 Paris Cedex 15, France

FIZER, JOHN, literature educator; b. Myrcha, Carpathia, Ukraine, June 13, 1925; came to U.S., 1949; s. Michael I. and Maria A. (Balazh) F.; m. Maria K. Uhnenko, Nov. 21, 1930; children: Andrew, George, Natalie, Irene. PhD, U. Munich, 1949; MA, Columbia U., 1952, PhD, 1960; Dr. Honoris Causa, U. Kyiv-Mohyla, Ukraine, 1996. Asst. prof. U. Notre Dame, South Bend, Ind., 1954-60; assoc. prof. Rutgers U., New Brunswick, N.J., 1960-65, prof. literature, 1965—; vis. prof. Northwestern U., Evanston, Ill., 1961, 63, 64-65, Columbia U., N.Y.C., 1988, Warsaw U., 1984; cons. UN U., Tokyo, 1984-85; analyst Harvard U., Cambridge, Mass., 1952, Princeton (N.J.) U., 1954. Author: Psychologism and Psychoaesthetics, 1981, Alexander A. Potebnia's Psycholinguistic Theory of Literature, 1988, Psychologizm i Psychoestetyka: Krytyczna Analyza Zwiazkow, 1991. Numerous grants in field. Home: 26 Bedford Rd Somerset NJ 08873-1623

FIZIEV, PLAMEN PETKOV, theoretical physics educator; b. Stara Zagora, Bulgaria, Mar. 10, 1948; s. Petko Ganev and Elena Christova (Trendafilova) F.; m. Tsvetanka Yankova Stavreva, Apr. 2, 1977; 1 child, Petko Plamenov. MS, U. Sofia, Bulgaria, 1971; PhD, Joint Inst. Nuclear Rsch., Dubna, Russia, 1988. Cert. physicist. Sci. rschr. U. Sofia, 1972, asst., 1974-80, asst. prof., 1988-90, prof. physics, 1990—; sci. rschr. Joint Inst. Nuclear Rsch., Dubna, Russia, 1980-87. Contbr. articles to profl. jours. Lt. Bulgarian Nat. Army, 1972-73. Recipient gold medal Ministry Edn. Bulgaria, 1966. Mem. Union Bulgarian Scientists, Union Bulgarian Physicists. Avocation: classical music. Home: Vhod G Ap 102, JK Nadejda 5, Blok 527, 1229 Sofia Bulgaria Office: U Sofia Faculty Physics, 5 James Bourchier, 1164 Sofia Bulgaria

FJELD, BJORN OYVIND, religious organization executive; b. Skien, Norway, 1945; m. Reidun Fjeld, 1968; 3 children. Cand. in Theology, Det teologiske Menighetsfakul., Oslo, 1971; DMin, Trinity Evang. Div. Sch., 1993. Tchr. in theology, 1971-76, pastor, 1976-81; pres. Norwegian Covenant Ch., 1982-96; sec.-gen. Internat. Fedn. of Free Evang. Chs., 1986-98, pres., 1998—; sec. Christian Coun. Norway, 1996-97; pres. Ansgar theol. Sem., Kristiansand, 1997—. Home: Nedre Brattbakken 12, N-4635 Kristiansand Norway Office: Ansgar Theological Seminary, F Fransons Vei 4, N-4635 Kristiansand Norway

FJELDSTAD, LISE, actress; b. Oslo, June 17, 1939; d. Oivin and Julie Fjeldstad; m. Per Sunderland; children: Peik, Blomma. Student, Artium, Oslo, 1958, Dramaschool of Norway, 1961-63. Actress Det Norske Teatret, Oslo, 1963-71, T.V. Theatre, 1971-74, Nat. Theatre, Oslo, 1975—. Stage roles include Rosalinde in As You Like It, Desdemonia in Othello, Hedda in Hedda Gabler, Solveig in Peer Gynt, Nora in A Doll's House, Mrs. Alvig in Ghosts, Irene in When We Dead Awaken, Mary in Mary Queen of Scots, Elisabet in Don Carlos, Martha in Who's Afraid of Virginia Woolf, Blanche in Streetcar Named Desire, Alice in Dance of Death, also several leading roles in film, TV and radio. Recipient Best Actress award Swedish Film Inst., 1982, Norwegian Film Inst., 1991. Mem. Royal Norwegian St. Olav's Guard. Home: Prof Dahlsgt 27, 0353 Oslo Norway Office: Nat Theatre, Oslo Norway

FJERDINGSTAD, ERIK, environmentalist, educator; b. Virum, Copenhagen, Denmark, Oct. 4, 1940; s. Einar Svend Age and Else Emilie Sophie (Andersen) F. PhD, Copenhagen U., 1966. Adj. faculty Virum (Denmark) State H.S., 1966-72; assoc. prof. Copenhagen U., 1972-80; ret., 1981; lectr. AugKragh Inst., Copenhagen, 1973-80. Contbr. articles to profl. jours. With Danish Civil Def., 1967-75. Scholarship Nordic Sch. Pub. Health U. Gothenburg, 1972. Mem. AAS, AAAS, N.Y. Acad. Scis., Danish Soc. Material Sci. Lutheran. Avocations: reading, travel, mountaineering, photography. Home: Bredebovej 23 Imt, DK-2800 Kings Lyngby Denmark

FLACH, FREDERIC FRANCIS, psychiatrist; b. N.Y.C., Jan. 25, 1927; s. George Raymond and Margaret (Donovan) F.; m. Patricia Anne Kane, June 23, 1951 (div. 1966); children: Frederica, Christopher, Geraldine, Andrew, Winifred; m. Joyce Elizabeth Rasmussen, Sept. 9, 1971. BA summa cum laude, St. Peter's Coll., Jersey City, 1947; MD, Cornell U., 1951. Diplomate Am. Bd. Psychiatry and Neurology. Intern second med. div. Bellevue Hosp., N.Y.C., 1951-52; from resident to chief resident psychiatry Payne Whitney Clinic, N.Y.C., 1953-58; pvt. practice N.Y.C., 1958—; attending psychiatrist N.Y. Presbyn. Hosp., N.Y.C., 1962—, St. Vincent's Hosp., N.Y.C., 1974—; adj. assoc. prof. psychiatry Cornell U. Med. Coll., N.Y.C., 1962—; program dir. Directions in Psychiatry, N.Y.C., 1981—; chmn. The Hatherleigh Co., Ltd., 1990—. Author: The Secret Strength of Depression, 1974, Choices, 1976, Fridericus, 1980, Resilience, 1988, Rickie, 1990, Take Command, 1994, The Secret Strength of Angels, 1998, Faith, Healing, and Miracles, 2000, others. Lt. (j.g.) USNR, 1945-46. Knight Equestrian Order of the Holy Sepulchre of Jerusalem, 1999. Fellow Am. Psychiat. Assn. (life). Roman Catholic. Avocations: travel, swimming, reading. Office: 420 E 51st St New York NY 10022-8014

FLACHSMANN, JEAN-PAUL, finance company executive; b. Zurich, Switzerland, Jan. 4, 1936; s. Jean and Isabelle (Fluehler) F.; m. Helena Papadimitriou, Mar. 29, 1969; children: Isabelle, Jannis. BA, U. St. Gall, Switzerland, 1961; MS in Econs., U. Paris, 1962. Bus. cons. Betriebswissenschaftiches Inst. der Eidgenoessischen Tech. Hochschule, Zurich, 1963-68; dir. Ratiomatic AG, Zug, Switzerland, 1969-72; v.p. Fin. Investment Bank, Zurich, 1972-78; pres., chmn. Atlas Fin. Ltd., Zug, 1978-99; chmn. Atlas Europe Ltd., Vaduz, Liechtenstein, 1980-99, Tele Discount Ltd., Zug, Switzerland, 1996-99. Inventor in field. Vice chmn. Swiss People's Pary, Zug, 1994-98; spkr. People's Party in parliment,Canton Zug, 1994-98; councillor and dir. construction, planning and environ. to Canton Zug, 1999—; pres. found HumanVita, Zug, 1996-98. Recipient Silver medal Internat. Invention Fair, Basle, Switzerland, 1983, Geneva, Switzerland, 1984. Fellow Swiss Union Sports, Music Theater Soc. Zug. Office: Atlas Europe Ltd, Baarerstrasse 57, 6300 Zug Switzerland

FLACK, RONALD DAVID, diplomat, public service educator, banker; b. Cloquet, Minn., Feb. 3, 1934; s. John and Marian Gladys (Steidl) F.; m. Danièle Guigard, Mar. 11, 1961; children: Jean-Marc, Claire-Paule. BA, U. Minn., 1960. Joined Fgn. Svc., Dept of State, Washington, 1962; 3rd sec. Am. Embassy, Athens, Greece, 1963-65; 2nd sec. Am. Embassy, Manila, The Philippines, 1965-69, Abidjan, Ivory Coast, 1969-70; 1st sec. Am. Embassy, Paris, 1970-73, Algiers, Algeria, 1973-75; counselor Am. Embassy, Athens, 1976-80; permanent rep. UN, Geneva, Switzerland, 1983-87; dep. amb. Am. Embassy, Copenhagen, 1987-90; min. counselor U.S. Mission to OECD, Paris, 1990-95; diplomat in residence NYU, N.Y.C., 1995-97; vice chmn. Taylor Cos., Washington, 1998—. Bd. dirs. Internat. YMCA, N.Y.C., 1997. Mem. Danish Am. Soc., Scandinavian Am. Soc. Home: 1750 P St NW Washington DC 20036-1340 Office: Taylor Cos 1215 19th St NW Washington DC 20036-2401

FLAGG, E(LOISE) ALMA WILLIAMS, educational administrator; b. City Point, Va., Sept. 16, 1918; d. Hannibal Greene and Caroline Ethel (Moody) Williams; m. J. Thomas Flagg, Jr., June 24, 1942 (dec. Apr. 1994); children: Thomas L., Lois Luisa. BS, Newark State Coll., 1940, LittD (hon.), 1968; MA, Montclair (N.J.) State Coll., 1943; EdD, Columbia U., 1955. Tchr., Washington, 1941-43; with Newark Pub. Schs., 1943-83, vice-prin., 1963-64, prin., 1964-67, asst. supt., 1967-78, dir., 1978-83; bd. dirs. Krueger-Scott Mansion Cultural Ctr., Share-N.J., v.p., 1996—; cons. edn., 1972—; adj. instr., spkr. in field, poet-in-residence various pub. schs. Author: (poetry) Lines and Colors, 1979, Feelings, Lines, Colors, 1980, Twenty More with Thought and Feeling, 1981, Lines, Colors, and More, 1998; editor: Cardiac Valve Bioprosthesis. Mem. Newark Bicentennial Commn. Recipient various profl. awards; E. Alma Flagg Sch. erected, 1984; E. Alma Flagg Scholarship Fund established, 1984. Mem. NAACP (life), LWV (pres. Newark 1982-84), AAUW, ASCD, N.J. Hist. Soc., Nat. Soc. Study of Edn., Nat. Coun. Tchrs. of English, Nat. Assn. Negro Bus. and Profl. Women's Clubs (Truth award, 1985) Nat. Coun. Tchrs. of Math., Nat. Alliance Black Sch. Educators, Nat. Coun. Negro Women (life), Newark Sr. Citizen's Commn. (editl. cons. 1989—), Alpha Kappa Alpha (life), Kappa Delta Pi. Presbyterian. Home: 67 Vaughan Dr Newark NJ 07103-3470

FLAGG, HELEN CLAWSON, writer; b. Netcong, N.J., May 27, 1921; d. Clyde Leroy and Rose Ann (Wood) Wilgus; m. Raymond E. Clawson, Feb. 7, 1942 (dec. May 1988); children: Lana Hope (Mrs. Dale Hope), Rory Zane; m. Allen Macomber Flagg, Nov. 16, 1991. Student, Rutgers U., 1941-42. CEO, ATS Corp., nat. placement co., Ft. Collins, Colo., 1976-80; pres. Status Unltd., pub. rels., Ft. Collins, 1982-90; fin. planner Waddell & Reed, Ft. Collins, 1984-90; stockbroker Dean Witter, Clearwater, Fla., 1990-91; fin. planner, ins. rep. Walnut Street Securities, Clearwater, 1992-95; former pub. spr. on fin. and religious subjects. Author: Joy in the Morning, 1995; contbr. numerous articles to newspaper and mags., including Fortune mag. Cons., historian Presbyn. Ch., Clearwater, 1995-99; supporter numerous civic orgns; sec. Altrusa, Ft. Collins, 1976-80. Mem. NAFE. Republican. Avocations: writing, poetry, reading history. Home: PO Box 8041 Radnor PA 19087-8041

FLAHERTY, CHARLES FOSTER, JR., psychology educator, researcher; b. Hyannis, Mass., June 25, 1937; s. Charles Foster Sr. and Helen Claire (White) F.; m. Mary Dempsey; children: Brendan Thomas, Jennifer Ellen. BA, Northeastern U., 1964; MA, U. Wis., 1967, PhD, 1968. Prof. psychology Rutgers U., New Brunswick, N.J., 1968—, chmn. psychology dept., 1978-80, 83-86, 91—, assoc. dean arts and scis., 1987-88; reviewer NSF, Animal Learning and Behavior, Am. Jour. of Psychology, Jour. of Comparative Psychology. Author: Learning and Memory, 1977, Animal Learning and Cognition, 1985, Incentive Relativity, 1996; co-editor Current Topics in Animal Learning, 1991. Served with USAF, 1955-59. Grantee NSF, NIMH, Charles and Johanna Busch, 1983—. Mem. AAAS, Soc. for Neurosci., Psychonomic Soc., N.Y. Acad. of Scis., Am. Psychol. Soc., Acad. Behavioral Medicine Rsch., Pavlovian Soc. Republican. Office: Rutgers U Psychology Dept New Brunswick NJ 08903

FLAHERTY, DAVID PETER, academic administrator; b. Northwick, England, Feb. 17, 1946; s. Nellie F.; m. Susan Clark, Nov. 16, 1974 (div. Nov. 1996); three children. BA, Open U., 1990, MBE, 1999. Stoneman, swimming pool supervisor Northwich Coun., England, 1966-73; asst. mgr. leisure ctr. Winsford Coun., England, 1973-74; from mgr. leisure ctr. to asst. head sports divsn. Vale Royal Coun., Northwich, 1974-96; leisure and recreation mgr. Sir John's Deane's Coll., Northwich, 1996=98; profl. trainer assessor, martial arts coach, 1998. Appointed mem. of the Order of the British Empire in Queens Birthday Honours, 1998. Fellow Br. Assn. Phys. Tng.; mem. Inst. Leisure & Amenity Mgmt., Inst. Sport & Mgmt. Assn.

FLAHERTY, JOHN PAUL, JR., state supreme court chief justice; b. Pitts., Nov. 19, 1931; s. John Paul and Mary G. (McLaughlin) F.; m. Linet Flaherty; 7 children, 2 stepchildren. BA, Duquesne U., 1953; JD, U. Pitts., 1958; LLD (hon.), Widener U., 1993. Bar: Pa. 1958. Pvt. practice Pitts., 1958-73; mem. faculty Carnegie-Mellon U., 1958-73; judge Ct. Common Pleas Allegheny County, 1973-79, pres. judge civil divsn., 1978-79; justice Supreme Ct. Pa., 1979-96, chief justice, 1996—; USIA speaker in Far East, 1985-86. Mem. Pa. Hist. Soc.; bd. visitors U. Pitts. Sch. Law; chair Pa. County Records Com. Recipient Medallion of Distinction U. Pitts., 1987, Judicial award Pa. Bar Assn., 1993, Pres. award Pa. Bar Assn., 1999; named Man of Yr. in law and govt., Greater Pitts. Jaycees, 1978, named to Century Club of Disting. Alumni, Duquesne U., 1994. Mem. Pa. Acad. Sci. (chmn. hon. exec. bd. 1978-89, Disting. Alumnus award 1977), Am. Law Inst., Pa. Soc., Mil. History Soc. Ireland, Friendly Sons St. Patrick, Am. Legion. Office: Pa Supreme Ct 6 Gateway Ctr Pittsburgh PA 15222-1318

FLAJŠHANS, MARTIN, fish geneticist; b. Prague, Czech Republic, Jan. 16, 1964; s. Pavel and Helena (Bartoničková) F.; m. Markéta Převrátilová, Oct. 29, 1988; 1 child, Ludvík. Diploma Ing., U. Agr., Prague, 1986. Fellow Rsch. Inst. Fish Culture and Hydrobiology, Vodňany, Czech Republic, 1986-90, R&D scientist, 1990—, dept. head dep., 1993—; invited scientist Mus. Nat. d'Histoire Naturelle, Paris, 1994, 95; cons. fish introduction com. Ministry Agr., Prague, 1993—, Genetic Resources Coun., 1995—; chmn. Breeding Coun., Fisheries Assn. of Czech Republic, Č. Budějovice, Czech Republic, 1995—; invited scientist Institut für Gewässerökologie und Binnenfischerei, Berlin, 1997. Co-author: Atlas of Common Carps, 1995; editor-in-chief Bull. Vyzkumny ustav rybársky a hydrobiologicky Vodnany, 1994—; co-editor Fish Reproduction, 1992; editor Procs. of Sci. Papers to 75th Anniversary of Rsch. Inst. Fish Culture and Hydrobiology, 1996. Mem. Network Tropical Aquaculture Scientists, N.Y. Acad. Scis., Czech Zool.Soc. Avocations: wine growing, gardening, ornithology, literature. Office: Rsch Inst Fish Culture & Hydrobiology, U South Bohemia Dept Fish Genetics, 389 25 Vodňany Czech Republic

FLAMMANG, DANIEL, cardiologist, internist, researcher, consultant; b. Rochefort, Namur, Belgium, Mar. 11, 1947; s. Paul and Aline (Berguet) F.; m. Anne Marie Rassat, Sept. 4, 1971; children: Gaelle, Benoit, Isabelle. MD magna cum laude, Louvain U., Belgium, 1971, diploma in internal medicine, 1977, diploma in cardiology, 1977; diploma in internal medicine, Paris U., 1977, diploma in cardiology, 1977. Cert. med. dr. with spltys. in internal medicine and cardiology. Intern, then resident Univ. Hospitals, Louvain, Paris, France, 1971-75, fellow, 1975-77; head assoc. dept. cardiology Angouleme (France) Gen. Hosp., 1977-84, dept. head cardiology, 1984—, asst. prof. faculty of medicine, 1993—; clin. expert Nat. Dept. Health, Paris, 1983—; assoc. dir. State Doctorate in Med., Nantes U., Poitiers U., France, 1978—, Clin. Med. Edn., Bordeaux U., France, 1996—; sci. cons. med. companies, U.S., 1985—. Software devel. inventor Management of Medical Recordings, 1996; patentee in field; contbr. articles to profl. jours. Young Investigator award European Soc. Cardiology, Amsterdam, The Netherlands, 1976. Mem. French Soc. Cardiology, European Soc. Cardiology, Assn. Libre de Cardiologie. Office: Angouleme Gen Hosp, Dept Cardiology, 16470 Saint Michel France

FLAMMER, AUGUST, psychology educator; b. Zuzwil, St. Gallen, Switzerland, Mar. 4, 1938; m. Silvia Meyerhans; children: Monica, Ivo, Pascal. Diploma in applied psychology, U. Fribourg, Switzerland, 1966, PhD in Exptl. Psychology, Philosophy, 1970, DrHabil in Exptl. and Ednl. Psychology, 1974. Lectr. U. Basel, Switzerland, 1973-75; lectr. U. Fribourg, 1973-75, prof., 1975-83; lectr. U. Bern, Switzerland, 1975-83; prof. U. Bern, 1983—, chmn. dept. psychology, 1988-89, 96-98, dean Faculty Philosophy, 1990-91; ednl. counselor Wangen/Olten, Switzerland, 1967-68. Author: Experiencing One's Efficacy, 1990, Theories of Development, 1996, Introduction to the Psychology of Social Discourse, 1997; author, editor: The Adolescent Experience, 1999. Bd. dirs. Swiss Acad. Humanities and Social Scis., 1979-85, Swiss Nat. Sci. Found., 1981-92. Recipient Students' strain in Switzerland and Norway award Swiss NSF, 1993-96, Mastering Life in Japan and in Switzerland award Swiss NSF, 1995-98; Adolescent Vandalism grantee Swiss NSF, 1996-99. Mem. APA, Internat. Soc. for the Study Behavioral Devel., Swiss Psychol. Assn. Home: Brunnenhofstrasse 17, 3065 Bolligen Bern, Switzerland Office: Univ Bern Dept Psychology, Muesmattstrasse 45, 3000 Bern 9, Switzerland

FLANAGAN, CLYDE HARVEY, JR., psychiatrist, psychoanalyst, educator; b. Louellen, Ky., Aug. 21, 1939; s. Clyde H. Sr. and Ruby Marie (Caldwell) F.; m. Gloria Kay Glymph, June 1,1961 (div. Feb. 1974); children: Clyde H. III, Christpher Shane; m. Carol Anne Ross, Apr. 13, 1974; children: Patrick Ross, Colleen Helen. BS, Maryville Coll., 1962; MD, U. Tenn. Med. Unit, Memphis, 1966. Cert. Am. Bd. Psychiatry and Neurology in Adult, Child, Adolescent Psychiatry; diplomate Nat. Bd. Med., Am. Bd. Forensic Medicine. Commd. 2d lt. U.S. Army, 1965, advanced through grades to col., 1980; rotating med. intern U.S. Army Tripler Gen. Hosp., Honolulu, 1966-67; gen. psychiatry resident U.S. Army Walter Reed Gen. Hosp, Washington, 1967-69, child psychiatry resident, 1969-71; asst. chief child guidance svc. Walter Reed Army Med. Ctr., Washington, 1971-80; chief cmty. mental health activity Ft. Belvoir, Va., 1980-86; asst. head tri-svc. alcohol rehab. dept. Nat. Navy Hosp., Bethesda, Md., 1986-88, ret., 1988; dir. gen. psychiat. residency program W.S. Hall Psychiat. Inst., Columbia, S.C., 1988-92; prof. dept. of psychiatry/behavioral sci. Sch. Medicine U. S.C., Columbia, 1988—, dir. divsn. psychoanalysis dept. psychiat./behavioral sci., 1992—; candidate in psychoanalysis Washington Psychoanalytic Inst., 1978-88; tng. and supervising analyst U. N.C./Duke PSA Ednl. Program, Chapel Hill, 1991—. Contbr. chpt. to books in field. Recipient Tchr. Yr. award Resident's Gen. Psychiat. Rsch. Program William S. Hall Psychiat. Inst., 1995, Spl. Alumni citation Maryville Coll., 2000. Fellow Am. Psychiat. Assn., Am. Acad. Child and Adolescent Psychiatry (Franklin Robinson award 1975), Am. Coll. Forensic Examiners, Am. Bd. Forensic Medicine; mem. Am. Psychoanalytic Assn. (councilor 1989—, cert. in adult, adolescent, and child psychoanalysis Bd. Profl. Stds. 1991), Am. Coll. Psychiatrists (comm. pub. edn. 1998-99, Laughlin fellow selection com. 2000—), N.C. Psychoanalytic Soc. (councilor 1989-98), S.C. Psychiat. Soc. (membership chmn. 1991—), Am. Group Psychotherapy Assn. (founder, cert. group psychotherapist), Internat. Psychoanalytic Assn., Am. Assn. Child Psychoanalysis. Avocations: fishing, boating, collecting stamps, books, and coins. Office: U SC Sch Medicine Dept Neuropsychiatry 3555 Harden Street Ext Ste 104A Columbia SC 29203-6894

FLANDERS, ELEANOR CARLSON, community volunteer; b. Spearville, Kans., Mar. 27, 1916; d. Carl Edward and Laura Rebecca (Pine) Carlson; m. Laurence Burdette Flanders, Jr., June 6, 1941; children: Laurel F. Umile, John C., Lynette F. Moyer, Paul L. BA, cert. journalism, U. Colo., 1938; family inst. cert., Vassar Coll., 1958. Examiner of credits U. Colo., Boulder, 1938-41; stock market analyst trust dept. First Nat. Bank, Longmont, Colo., 1970-85; landlady, investor St. Vrain Hist. Soc., Longmont, 1952—; vice pres. elect, St. Vrain Valley Sch. Bd., 1978-84. Contbr. articles to profl. jours. Precinct worker, del. Rep. Party, Longmont and Boulder, 1941—; club leader 4-H Boulder County, 1947-63; pres., charter mem. Boulder County Mental Health Clinic, 1947-60; mem. PEO Sisterhood, 1948—; trustee, mem. investment com. First Congl. Ch., Longmont, 1960—; North Colo. area rep. Am. Field Svc., Longmont, 1965-70; coord. tutoring program Boulder County Juvenile Ct., 1965-81; trustee, farm mgr. Carl and Laura Carlson Trust, Oberlin, Kans., 1971-85; trustee, dir. Colo. 4-H Youth Fund, Ft. Collins, 1973-86; trustee, investment counsel Am. Mothers Endowment Fund, N.Y.C., 1979-90; active St. Vrain Edn. Found. Endowment Fund, Longmont, 1985—; trustee, bd. dirs. Longmont Cable Trust, 1986-88; nat. treas. Am. Mothers, N.Y., 1988-90; elected 2-term dir. St. Vrain Valley Sch. Bd., 1978-86. Mem. AAUW (charter), U. Colo. Alumni Assn. (dir., sec. 1950-58), St. Vrain Hist. Soc. (dir., pres. 1970—), St. Vrain Valley Edn. Found. (founder, dir., pres. 1984—), Sunshine Club (pres. 1947—). Avocations: gardening, travel, duplicate bridge, reading, writing. Home: 917 W 3rd Ave Longmont CO 80501-5413

FLANDRE, DENIS GEORGES, microelectronics researcher and educator; b. Charleroi, Hainaut, Belgium, Jan. 29, 1964; s. Guy and Josette (Leclercq) F.; m. Florence A. Donck; children: Raphaël, Emma, Marjolaine. Degree in Elec. Engring., U. Catholique de Louvain, Belgium, 1986, PhD, 1990. Rschr. Inst. Pour L'Encouragement De La Recherche Scientifique Dans L'Industrie Et L'Agriculture, Brussels, 1986-90; vis. scientist Centro Nacional De Microelectronica, Barcelona, Spain, 1990-91; sr. rsch. asst. Fonds Nat. Recherche Scientifique, Brussels, 1991-93; rsch. assoc. Fonds Nat. Recherche Scientifique, Belgium, 1993-99, sr. rsch. assoc., 1999—; founder, tech. cons. CISSOID Co., 2000; contractor European Commn. Eureka/Esprit/Eurimus/IST Projects, 1993—; lectr. U. Cath. Louvain, Belgium, 1994-99; adv. bd. mem. European Commn. High Temperature Electronics Network of Excellence, 1996—; vice co-chmn Union Radio-Scientifique Internat. Conf., Internat. Symposium Signals, Sys. & Electronics, Pisa, Italy, 1998; prof. U. Cath. Louvain, Belgium, 1999—; lectr. Europractice org. Silicon-on-Insulator, 1998—. Contbr. articles to profl. jours. Sub-lt. Belgian Landforce Tech. Dept., 1988-89. Recipient Siemens Biennal award, Belgium, 1992, Wernaers prize, Belgium, 1997, Prof. R. Van Geen prize, 1999; Sci. fellow NATO, Spain 1990; Travel grantee Fonds Nat. Recherche Scientifique, Grenoble, France, 1993. Mem. IEEE, Brazilian Microelectronics Soc. (lectr. 1994). Office: Microelectronics Lab UCL, Place du Levant 3, 1348 Louvain-La-Neuve Belgium

FLANDROIS, SERGE EUGENE, chemist; b. Sainte Cecile, Vendee, France, Mar. 15, 1940; s. Eugene and Eugenie F.; m. Monique Marie Favereau, Sept. 3, 1962; children: Guillaume, Julien. BS, Bordeaux U., 1961, PhD, 1964, DS, 1967. Rsch. fello CNRS, Bordeaux, 1969-78; rsch. dir. CNRS, 1978—; postdoctoral fellow A. Von Humboldt, Gottingen, Germany, 1971-72; cons. Accatel-Alsthom, Paris, 1992—; chmn. French Group of Intercalation, 1988-91. Editor: (book) Chemical Physics of Intercalation, 1988; 5 patents on batteries; editl. bd. Jour. Carbon, 1987—. Recipient Millet-Ronssin award French Acad. of Scis., Paris, 1994. Mem. French Chem. Soc. Achievements include contbns. to structure and properties of intercalation compounds, mechanism of intercalation Li-ion batteries. Office: Ctr de Recherche P Pascal, Ave Albert - Schweitzer, 33600 Pessac France

FLANIGAN, ROBERT CHARLES, urologist, educator; b. Lima, Ohio, May 2, 1946; children: Nancy, Charles. BA in Chemistry, Coll. of Wooster, 1968; MD, Case Western Res. U., 1972. Resident in surgery and urology Case Western Res. U., 1972-78; vol. asst. prof. urology U. Nebr., 1978-80; asst. prof. surgery U. Ky. Med. Ctr., Lexington, 1980-84, assoc. prof. surgery, 1984-86; prof. urology, chmn. dept. Loyola U. Med. Ctr., Maywood, Ill., 1986—; chief urology Hines VA Hosp., 1986—; trustee Am. Bd. Urology. Officer M.C., USAF, 1978-80. Recipient Cardinal's Medallion, Archdiocese of Chgo., 1995. Fellow ACS; mem. Am. Urol. Assn., Am. Assn. Genito-Urinary Surgeons, Soc. Pelvic Surgeons, Am. Soc. Transplant Surgeons, Chgo. Urol. Soc. (past pres.), Soc. Univ. Urologists (sec.-treas.), Soc. Urologic Oncology (sec.), Loyola U. Physicians Found. (v.p. 1995—).

FLANNAGAN, LARNELL DANIEL, academic administrator; b. Jan. 31, 1953. BS, Va. State U., 1975; MS, SUNY, Brockport, 1980; EdD, SUNY, Buffalo, 1987. Tchr. Rochester (N.Y.) City Schs., 1975-87; asst. dean Erie C.C., Buffalo, 1988-89; dept. chair Hampton (Va.) U., 1989-93; assoc. for rsch. SUNY Sys. Adminstrn., Albany, 1993-98, liaison assoc., 1998—. Recipient Disting. Svc. awards, N.Y. Urban League, 1977-85; scholar Fulbright-Hays, 1993. Home: 4091 Warrior Trl Stone Mountain GA 30083-3126

FLANSBURGH, EARL ROBERT, architect; b. Ithaca, N.Y., Apr. 28, 1931; s. Earl Alvah and Elizabeth (Evans) F.; m. Louise Hospital, Aug. 27, 1955; children: Earl Schuyler, John Conant. BArch, Cornell U., 1954; MArch, MIT, 1957; S.C.M.P., Harvard U. Sch. Bus., 1982. Job capt., designer The Architects Collaborative, Cambridge, Mass., 1958-62; partner Freeman, Flansburgh & Assos., Cambridge, 1961-63; prin. Earl R. Flansburgh & Assocs., Cambridge, 1963-69, pres., dir. design, 1969—; bd. dirs. daka, Inc.; exec. v.p. Environment Systems Internat., Inc.; vis. prof. archtl. design Mass. Inst. Tech., 1965-66; instr. art Wellesley Coll., 1962-65, lectr. art, 1965-69; cons. Arthur D. Little, Inc., Cambridge, 1964-70. Archtl. works include Weston (Mass.) High Sch. Addition, 1965-67, Cornell U. Campus Store, 1967-70, Cumnock Hall, Harvard U. Bus. Sch, 1973-75, Acton (Mass.) Elementary schs, 1966-68, 69-71, Wilton (Conn.) High Sch, 1968-71, 14 Story St. Bldg, 1970, Boston Design Ctr., 1985-86, Glenwood Sch., Dallas, 1985-88, New Univ. No. B.C., Prince George, Can., 1991—, Boston Coll. Law Sch., 1992—; exhibited works Light Machine I, IBM Gallery, N.Y.C., 1958, Light Machine II, Carpenter Center, Harvard, 1965, 5 Cambridge Architects, Wellesley Coll., 1969, Work of Earl R. Flansburgh and Assos, Wellesley Coll., 1969, New Architecture in New Eng, DeCordova Mus., 1974-75, Residential Architecture, Mead Art Gallery, Amherst Coll., 1976, works represented in, 50 Ville del Nostro Tempo, 1970, Nouve Ville, New Villas, 1970, Vacation Houses, 1970, Vacation Houses, 2d edit., 1977, Interior Design, 1970, Drawings by American Architects, 1973, Interior Spaces Designed by Architects, 1974, New Architecture in New England, 1974, Great Houses, 1976, Architecture Boston, 1976, Presentation Drawings by American Architects, 1977, Architecture, 1970-1980, A Decade of Change, 1980, Old and New Architecture, A Design Relationship, 1980, 25

Years of Record Houses, 1981, School Ways: The Planning and Design of American Schools, 1992; Author: (with others) Techniques of Successful Practice, 1975. Chmn. architecture com. Boston Arts Festival, 1964, Downtown Boston Design adv. com.; bd. dirs. Cambridge Ctr. Adult Edn.; pres. Downtown North Boston, 1994—; trustee Cornell U., 1972—; chmn. bldgs. and properties com., 1976-87; mem. exec. com. acad. affairs com.; class sec. SCMP VII Harvard Bus. Sch., 1982-89. 1st lt. USAF, 1954-56. Recipient design awards Progressive Architecture, design awards Record Houses, design awards AIA, design awards City of Boston, design awards Mass. Masonry Inst., spl. design citations Am. Assn. Sch. Adminstrs., spl. 1st prize Buffalo-Western N.Y. chpt. AIA Competition., Walter Taylor award Am. Assn. Sch. Adminstrs., 1986, William Candill award Am. Coll. & Univ. Mag., 1993, Award of Honor, Boston Soc. Archs., 1999; Fulbright Rsch. grantee Bldg. Rsch. Sta., Eng., 1957-58. Fellow AIA, Nat. Acad. Design; mem. Royal Inst. Brit. Architects, Boston Soc. Architects (chmn. program com., 1969-71, commr. pub. affairs 1971-73, commr. design 1973-74, dir. 1971-74, pres. 1980-81), Boston Found. Architecture (treas. 1984-89), Cornell U. Coun., Quill and Dagger Soc., St. Botolph Club, Tau Beta Pi. Home: 225 Old County Rd Lincoln MA 01773-4601 Office: 77 N Washington St Boston MA 02114-1908

FLAØYEN, ARNE, veterinarian; b. Melhus, Norway, July 27, 1962; s. Åge and Jarldis (Eidsmo) F. Cand. Med. Vet., Norwegian Coll. Vet. Medicine, Oslo, 1989; Dr. scientiarium, Norwegian Coll. Vet. Medicine, 1991, Dr. med. vet., 1993. Assoc. prof. Norwegian Coll. Vet. Medicine, Oslo, 1993-96; head sect. toxicology Nat. Vet. Inst., Oslo, 1996—. Lt. Norwegian Army. Avocation: outdoor activities. Office: Nat Vet Inst, PO Box 8156 Dep, N-0033 Oslo Norway

FLASCHEN, DAVID JENKIN STEWARD, marketing executive; b. Summit, N.J., Dec. 10, 1955; s. Steward Samuel and Joyce Davies Flaschen; m. Deborah Nordwall, Apr. 7, 1984; children: Katherine Skylar, David Jenkin Steward Jr. BA, Brown U., 1977; MBA, U. Pa., 1982. Profl. athlete N.Am. Soccer League, Chgo., 1977-79; mgr. product mktg. IBM, Princeton, N.J., 1982-84; materials mgr. Gavilan, Sunnyvale, Calif., 1984; corp. v.p., divsn. gen. mgr. Dataquest, San Jose, Calif., 1985-89; asst. to pres. Dun and Bradstreet Corp., N.Y.C., 1989-91; v.p. software svcs. IMS Internat., London, 1991-93; pres., COO A.C. Nielsen N.Am., Schaumberg, Ill., 1993-95; chmn., CEO Donnelly Mktg. Inc., Naperville, Ill., 1996-97; pres., CEO Thomson Fin., Boston, 1997-99; spl. ptnr. One Liberty Ventures, Boston, 2000—; bd. dirs. DM Holdings Inc., Chgo., Paychek, Inc., Rochester, SI Ventures, Fla., Buyerzone.com, Cambridge, Mass. Fund raiser United Way, Chgo., 1993, 94, 95; bd. dirs. Jobs for Mass., 1998—; bd. advisors Jobs for Mass., 1997-99, CEOs for a Fundamental Change in Edn., 1998—, Mayor's Econ. Adv. Coun., 1999—. Recipient Forty Under 40 award Crain's Mag., 1994; mem. All Star Soccer Team, Nat. Collegiate Athletic Assn., 1977. Mem. Direct Mktg. Assn., Kenilworth (Ill.) Club (bd. dirs. 1996-97). Avocations: contemporary art, champagne cap collecting. Home: 180 Clyde St Chestnut Hill MA 02467-2904

FLASCHEN, STEWARD SAMUEL, high technology company executive; b. Berwyn, Ill., May 28, 1926; s. Hyman Herman and Ethel (Leviton) F.; m. Joyce Davies, Apr. 21, 1949; children: John, Sheryl, David, Evan. BS in Chemistry, U. Ill., 1947; MA, Miami U., Oxford, Ohio, 1948; PhD in Geochemistry, Pa. State U., 1953. Supr. rsch. dept. Bell Telephone Labs., Murray Hill, N.J., 1952-59; dir. phys. scis., R & D semiconductor products div. Motorola, Inc., Phoenix, 1959-64; sr. v.p., gen. tech. dir., mem. corp. policy bd. ITT Corp., N.Y.C., 1964-86; pres. Flaschen & Davies, New Canaan, Conn., 1986—; chmn. Transwitch Corp., Shelton, Conn., 1988—; chmn. Telco Systems Corp., 1992—, Norwood, Mass.; bd. dirs. Sipex Corp., Billerica, Mass., Merrill Lynch Venture Capital, N.Y.C., Advanced Tech. Venture Ptnrs., Boston, San Jose, Calif., Sipex Corp., Billerica, Mass.; lectr. Pace U. Grad. Sch. Bus. Author: Search and Research, 1965; also articles; patentee in field. Mem. Scottsdale Bd. Edn., 1960-64. Served with USNR, 1944-46. Fellow Am. Inst. Chemists, IEEE, Pa. State U. Alumni; mem. AAAS, Electromech. Soc. Am., Am. Ceramic Soc., Indsl. Research Inst., N.Y. Acad. Scis., Univ. CLub. Avocations: family, exercise.

FLASINSKI, MARIUSZ STANISLAW, computer science researcher; b. Bochnia, Cracow, Poland, May 20, 1960; s. Stanislaw and Wladyslawa (Kruczek) F.; m. Kinga Myszka, Jan. 19, 1985; children: Piotr, Zofia. MPh in Computer Sci., Jagiellonian U., Cracow, 1984; PhD in Computer Sci., Tech. U. Mining & Metallurgy, Cracow, 1988, DSc in Computer Sci., 1993. Asst. researcher Jagiellonian U., Cracow, 1984-88, asst. prof., 1989-91, head artificial intelligence systems dept., 1994—, prof., 2000—; vis. prof., expert system project cons. Deutsches Elektronen Synchrotron, Hamburg, Germany, 1992-94; mfg. systems cons. Qumak Internat., Cracow, 1994-98; IT cons. CERN, Geneva, 1997; dir. gen. TCH Cons., Cracow, 1999—; mem. electrotechnics and computer sci. com., automatic control and robotics com. Polish Acad. Scis. Author: Pattern Recognition, 1991, Introduction to Analytical Design of Information Systems, 1997; contbr. over 100 articles to profl. jours.; co-editor Machine Graphics and Vision Internat. Jour., 1994—. Roman Catholic. Avocations: playing piano, accordion, singing, riding bicycle. Office: Jagiellonian Univ, Nawojki 11, 30-072 Cracow Poland

FLATEN, ROBERT ARNOLD, retired ambassador; b. Mpls., May 21, 1934; s. Arnold Wangensten and Evelyn (Solberg) F.; m. Carroll Jean Johnson, Dec. 22, 1956; children: Kristin, Karen, Sonia, Arne. BA, St. Olaf Coll., Northfield, Minn., 1956; MA, George Washington U., 1961. Vice consul Am. Consulate, Strasbourg, France, 1962-63, Peshawar, Pakistan, 1964-66; 2d sec. Am. Embassy, Tel Aviv, 1966-69, dep. chief mission, 1982-86; Fgn. Svc. insp., legis. mgmt. officer, office dir., dep. asst. sec. U.S. Dept. State, Washington, 1970-82, office dir., 1987-90; amb. to Rwanda Am. Embassy, Kigali, 1990-93. Chair exec. com. Peace Prize Forum, 1996. 2d lt. USAF, 1956-59. Mem. Am. Fgn. Svc. Assn., Minn. Internat. Ctr., Immortal Chaplains Found., UN Assn./Minn. Home: 5008 90th St E Northfield MN 55057-4349

FLATTAU, PAMELA EBERT, research psychologist, consultant; b. Chgo., Dec. 24, 1946; d. Raymond Clarence and Sylvia Anne (Jones) E.; m. Edward Samuel Flattau, Feb. 1, 1977; children: Jeremy Paul, Victoria Celeste. BSc with honors, U. Leeds, Eng., 1969; MS, U. Ga., 1972, PhD, 1974. Congrl. sci. fellow AAAS-APA, Washington, 1974-75; staff officer NAS/NRC, Washington, 1975-81, sr. staff officer, 1985-90, unit dir., 1990-95; policy analyst NSF, Washington, 1981-85; pres. Flattau Assocs. LLC, Washington, 1995—; mem. exec. com. Coun. Profl. Assns. for Fed. Stats., Washington, 1986-87. Editor: Research Doctorate Programs in U.S., 1995; author, editor series Biomed and Behavioral Research Personnel 1975-80, 1994; author, contbr.: Science and Engineering Indicators Series, 1981-85. Bd. dirs. Assn. Advancement Psychology, Washington, 1980-82. Mem. AAAS, APA (travel grantee 1992, 2000, Young Psychologist 1976), Am. Psychol. Soc., Soc. for Social Studies of Sci., Human Resources Planning Soc., Sigma Xi. Office: Flattau Assocs LLC 5335 Wisconsin Ave NW Ste 440 Washington DC 20015-2052

FLATTÉ, STANLEY MARTIN, physicist, educator; b. Los Angeles, Dec. 2, 1940; s. Samuel and Henrietta (Edelstein) F.; m. Renelde Marie Demeure, June 26, 1966; children: Michael, Anne. BS, Calif. Inst. Tech., 1962; student, NYU, 1960-61; PhD, U. Calif.-Berkeley, 1966. Research particle physicist Lawrence Berkeley Lab., Calif., 1966-71; asst. prof. physics U. Calif.-Santa Cruz, 1971-73, assoc. prof., 1973-78, prof., 1978—; dir. Ctr. for Studies of Nonlinear Dynamics La Jolla Inst., 1982-86, dept. chmn., 1986-89; cons. phys. oceanography and underwater sound U.S. Govt.; vis. researcher, Cern, Geneva, 1975, Scripps Inst. Oceanography, 1980, Cambridge U., Eng., 1981. Author: (with others) Sound Transmission Through a Fluctuating Ocean, 1979; contbr. (with others) articles profl. jours. Woodrow Wilson fellow, 1962; NSF fellow, 1962-66; Guggenheim Found. fellow, 1975. Fellow AAAS, Am. Phys. Soc., Acoustical Soc. Am., Optical Soc. Am.; mem. Am. Geophys. Union, Sigma Xi (pres. Santa Cruz chpt. 1999—). Achievements include discovery of cusp phenomenon in particle physics; developed methods for using sound and light waves to probe statis. atmosphere, ocean and earth processes. Office: Univ Calif Physics Dept Santa Cruz CA 95064

FLATTERY, THOMAS LONG, lawyer, legal administrator; b. Detroit, Nov. 14, 1922; s. Thomas J. and Rosemary (Long) F.; m. Gloria M. Hughes, June 10, 1947 (dec.); children: Constance Marie, Carol Dianne Lee, Michael Patrick, Thomas Hughes, Dennis Jerome, Betsy Ann Sprecher; m. Barbara J. Balfour, Oct. 4, 1986. BS, U.S. Mil. Acad., 1947; JD, UCLA, 1955; LLM, U. So. Calif., 1965. Bar: Calif. 1955, U.S. Patent and Trademark Office 1957, U.S. Customs Ct. 1968, U.S. Supreme Ct. 1974, Conn. 1983, N.Y. 1984. With Motor Products Corp., Detroit, 1950, Equitable Life Assurance Soc., Detroit, 1951, Bohn Aluminum & Brass Co., Hamtramck, Mich., 1952; mem. legal staff, asst. contract adminstr. Radioplane Co. (divsn. Northrop Corp.), Van Nuys, Calif., 1955-57; successively corp. counsel, gen. counsel, asst. sec. McCulloch Corp., L.A., 1957-64; sec., corp. counsel Technicolor, Inc., Hollywood, Calif., 1964-70; successively corp. counsel, asst. sec., v.p., sec. and gen. counsel Amcord, Inc., Newport Beach, Calif., 1970-72; v.p., sec., gen. counsel Schick Inc., L.A., 1972-75; counsel, asst. sec. C.F. Braun & Co., Alhambra, Calif., 1975-76; sr. v.p., sec., gen. counsel Automation Industries, Inc. (now PCC Tech. Industries Inc. a unit of Penn Cen. Corp.), Greenwich, Conn., 1976-86; v.p., gen. counsel G&H Tech., Inc. (a unit of Penn Cen. Corp.), Santa Monica, Calif., 1986-93; temp. judge Mcpl. Ct. Calif. L.A. Jud. Dist. and Santa Monica Unified Cts., 1987—; settlement officer L.A. Superior and Mcpl. Cts., 1991—; pvt. practice, 1993—; panelist Am. Arbitration Assn., 1991—; jud. arbitrator and mediator Alternative Dispute Resolution Programs L.A. Superior and Mcpl. Cts, 1993—, Calif. Ct. Appeals 2d Appellate Dist., 1999—. Contbr. articles to various legal jours. Served to 1st lt. AUS, 1942-50. Mem. ABA, Nat. Assn. Secs. Dealers, Inc (bd. arbitrators 1996, mediators 1997), State Bar Calif. (cochmn. corp. law dept. com. 1978-79, lectr. continuing legal edn. program), L.A. County Bar Assn. (chmn. corp. law dept. com. 1966-67), Century City Bar Assn. (chmn. corp. law dept. com. 1979-80), Conn. Bar Assn., Santa Monica Bar Assn. (trustee 1999—, chmn. alt. dispute resolution sect. 2000—), N.Y. State Bar Assn., Am. Soc. Corp. Secs. (L.A. regional group pres. 1973-74), L.A. Intellectual Property Law Assn., Am. Ednl. League (trustee 1988—, sec. 1998—), West Point Alumni Assn., Army Athletic Assn., Friendly Sons St. Patrick, Jonathan Club (dir. 1996-99), Braemar Country Club, Phi Alpha Delta. Roman Catholic. Home and Office: 439 Via De La Paz Pacific Palisades CA 90272-4633

FLAUTRE, HÉLÈNE, foreign diplomat; b. Bapaume, France, July 29, 1958. Mem. European Parliament, 1999—, mem. com. on employment and social affairs, substitute com. on industry, external trade, rsch./energy; mem. Group of the Greens/European Free Alliance; vice-chmn. delegation for relations with the Maghreb countries and the Arab Maghreb Union; substitute delegation to the EU-Turkey Joint Parliamentary Com. Office: Parlement européen, Rue Wiertz ASP 8G169, B-1047 Brussels Belgium*

FLAVIN, D. AESCHLIMAN, artist, lecturer, educator; b. June 6, 1931; d. Herman G. and Elsie Aeschliman. Student, Washington U., St. Louis, St. Louis C.C., Leon Cooper Art Sch. Lectr. on Georgia O'Keefe and Mary Cassatt. One woman shows include Jr. League St. Louis, 1987; group shows include Christ in Art Festival Kirkwood United Meth. Ch., 1983, So. Watercolor Soc., 1987, 90, 93, Luth. Women's Missionary League, 1991, Ste. Genevieve Galleria, Mo. Athletic Assn., Springfield (Mo.) Art Assn., Gallery 100-Midwest Minis, Cape Girardeau, Mo., 1993, Ralston Purina, St. Louis, 1993, St. Peter's (Mo.) Cultural Arts Ctr., Monday Club Webster Groves (Mo.); represented in pub. and pvt. permanent collections in U.S., Can., China, France. Art chmn. Mo. 8th dist. Federated Women's Club, art chmn. Nat. League of Am. PEN Women; artist coord. Mo. Bapt. Hosp., 1987-90. Recipient signature award So. Watercolor Soc., 1987, 90, Grumbacher award for best of show Artworld, 1987; named Artist of Yr., Soc. Ind. Artists, 1982, 85, Woman of Day award. Mem. Nat. League Pen Women (art chmn. St. Louis br.), St. Louis Artist Guild, So. Watercolor Soc. (signature), Am. Women in the Arts. Address: PO Box 230109 Saint Louis MO 63123-0809

FLECHNER, ROBERTA FAY, graphic designer; b. N.Y.C., June 7, 1949; d. Abraham Julius and Evelyn (Medwin) F. BA, CCNY, 1970; MA, NYU, 1972; cert. Printing Industries Met. N.Y., N.Y.C., 1974, 75, 79. Researcher, asst. editor Arno Press, N.Y.C., 1970-73; free-lance editor Random House, N.Y.C., 1973-74, graphic designer/compositor coll. dept., 1984-88; graphic designer Core Communications in Health, N.Y.C., 1974-76; prodn. mgr. Heights-Inwood News, N.Y.C., 1976-77; art dir., graphic designer Jour. Advt. Research, N.Y.C., 1976-81; prin., graphic designer/compositor Roberta Flechner Graphics, N.Y.C., 1976—; graphic designer/compositor W. W. Norton & Co., Inc., 1977—, McGraw Hill, Inc., 1990-94; mech. artist Fawcett, N.Y.C., 1979-80; graphic designer Avon Internat., N.Y.C., 1982; art dir., compositor, layout artist Source: Notes in the History of Art, N.Y.C., 1982—; graphic designer John Wiley & Sons, Inc., N.Y.C., 1985. Designer stationery, 1979 (Art Direction mag., Creativity-cert. distinction 1979). Art dir. enviroNews, N.Y. State Atty. Gen.'s Environ. Protection Bur., N.Y.C., 1977-78. Mem. Graphic Artists Guild, NOW, Women's Nat. Book Assn. (cons.), Nat. Assn. Female Execs., Women's Caucus for Art, Am. Inst. Graphic Arts, CCNY Alumni, NYU Alumni. Office: 10615 Queens Blvd Flushing NY 11375-4365

FLECK, STEPHEN, psychiatrist; b. Frankfort-am-Main, Germany, Sept. 18, 1912; came to U.S., 1935; s. Georg and Anna (Beer) F.; m. Louise Harlan, Oct. 13, 1945 (dec. 1992); children: AnnaLou F.J. Singer, Stephen H., Carra Rockwood. Cand. Medicine, J.W. Goethe U., Frankfort, Fed. Republic of Germany, 1931-33; postgrad., U. Amsterdam, 1933-35; MD, Harvard U., 1940. Diplomate Nat. Bd. Med. Examiners, Am. Bd. Psychiatry and Neurology. Intern Beth Israel Hosp., Boston, 1940-42; clin. trainee Henry Phipps Psychiat. Clinic, Johns Hopkins Hosp., Balt., 1946-48, asst. internal medicine, Commonwealth fellow, 1948-49; asst. prof. psychiatry U. Wash., Seattle, 1949-53; psychiatrist-in-chief Psychiat. Inst., Yale U., New Haven, 1953-83, prof. psychiatry and pub. health Sch. Medicine, 1963-83, prof. emeritus, 1983—; psychiatrist-in-chief Conn. Mental Health Ctr., New Haven, 1969-83; cons. Bridgeport (Conn.) Mental Health Ctr., 1983-95; mem. adv. bd. Whiting Forensic Inst., Middletown, Conn. 1957; mem. Hamden (Conn.) Mental Health Commn., 1970-86. Served to maj. U.S. Army, 1942-46. Fellow Am. Psychiat. Assn. (life), Group for Advancement Psychiatry (life); mem. AMA, Am. Pub. Health Assn., Western New England Psychoanalytic Soc., Conn. Psychiat. Soc. (pres. 1966-67), Conn. Pub. Health Assn. (hon.). Office: Yale U Sch Medicine 25 Park St Rm 608 New Haven CT 06519-1189

FLECKINGER-PELLÉ, JACQUELINE J., mathematician, educator; b. Niort, France, Feb. 20, 1944; d. Jacques J. and Renee (Pierre) Pellé; m. Robert Fleckinger, Feb. 27, 1965; 1 child, Sylvie. Ed., France. Mem. faculty Inst. Preparation l'Enseignement Secondaire, Rouen, France, 1964-65, Orsay, France, 1965-68; asst. Faculte des Scis., Tunis, Tunisia, 1968-70, Inst. Nat. Polytechnique, Toulouse, France, 1970-79; maitre asst. Inst. Nat. Polytechnique, Toulouse, 1979-84, maitre de conferences, 1985-88; prof. U. Toulouse 1, 1988—, head math. dept.; maitre de conferences Ecole Nationale Supérieure de l'Aeronautique et l'Espace, Toulouse, 1973-78, prof., 1979-90. Contbr. articles to profl. publs. Mem. Am. Math. Soc., French Math. Soc., Tunisian Math. Soc. Fax: 33 561128562. E-mail: jfleck@univ-utse1.fr. Home: 41 Rue Boyssonne,, 31400 Toulouse, France

FLEGAL, A(RTHUR) RUSSELL, JR., toxicologist, geochemist, educator; b. Oakland, Calif., Aug. 30, 1946; s. Arthur Russell Sr. and Barbara Flegal; m. Brenda Dolan, Dec. 18, 1970; children: Heather Dolan, John Arthur. BA, U. Calif., Santa Barbara, 1968; MS, Moss Landing (Calif.) Marine Labs., 1976; PhD, Oreg. State U., 1979. Rsch. assoc. Moss Landing Marine Labs., 1981-85; vis. rsch. assoc. Calif. Inst. Tech., Pasadena, 1981-93; assoc. rsch. geochemist U. Calif., Santa Cruz, rsch. geochemist, 1988-92, chair environ. toxicology, 1992—, assoc. dean natural sci. divsn., 1994—; vis. scientist Swiss Fed. Inst. Tech., Zurich, Switzerland, 1988, Lawrence Livermore (Calif.) Nat. Labs., 1988-96, Centre Nationale de Reserche Scientifique, 1998; mem. com. Nat. Rsch. Coun., Washington, 1989-93, Intergovt. Oceanographic Commn., Paris, 1989—; cons. EPA, Washington, 1989-98. Contbr. chpts. to sci. texts, sects. to ency.; contbr. more than 100 articles to profl. jours. Post doctoral fellow Calif. Inst. Tech., 1980, Rsch. fellow, 1980-81. Office: U Calif Environ Toxicology Santa Cruz CA 95064

FLEGEL, ULLA, internist; b. Linz, Austria, Oct. 22, 1939; d. Hannes Flegel and Hilde Flegel-Herbrich; m. Franz Kissler, Jan. 21, 1967 (div. Oct. 1970); m. Erich Macho, May 27, 1994 (dec. Oct. 1994). MD, U. Vienna, Austria, 1965. Resident Karst, Vienna, 1965-69; internist 1st Med. Clinic, Vienna, 1969-76; cons. internist ENT Clinic, Vienna, 1976—; head Office for Internal Medicine, Vienna, 1976—. Participant Olympic Games, Tokyo, 1964. Mem. Vanswieten Gesellschaft, Soc. for Internal Medicine, Zonta Club. Avocations: athletics, literature, theatre, music, arts.

FLEGEL, WILLY A., immunohematologist, physician; b. Dieburg, Germany, June 3, 1960; s. Willy E. and Anna (Rotsch) F. MD magna cum laude, U. Frankfurt, Germany, 1986; habilitation, U. Ulm, Germany, 1998. Intern U. Frankfurt, Main, Germany, 1984-85; resident U. Ulm, Germany, 1985-91; rsch. assoc. U. Calif., San Diego, 1991-93; head immunohematology German Red Cross Blood Ctr., Ulm, 1993—. Contbr. chpts. to books and articles to profl. jours. Mem. German Soc. Immunology, Am. Soc. Microbiology, Am. Assn. Blood Banks. Roman Catholic. Avocation: piloting. E-mail: waf@ucsd.edu. Office: U Ulm, Helmholtzstrasse 10, D-89081 Ulm Germany

FLEHARTY, MARY SUE, administrative assistant; b. Lincoln, Nebr., Aug. 13, 1962; d. Joseph Patrick and Joy Lou (Harnish) Huntley; m. Bradley Daryle Osborne, Mar. 26, 1983 (div. June 1988); m. Terry Lester Fleharty, Aug. 13, 1990. Student, Lincoln Sch. Commerce, 1996-97. Loan processor Am. Charter Fed. Savings and Loan, Lincoln, 1981-84; pub. broadcast exchange operator, sec. Lincoln Clinic, P.C., 1989-91; PBX operator, sec. Woods Park Med. Mgmt. Inc., Lincoln, 1991-93; data reporting asst. Harris Tech. Group, Lincoln, 1993; lease coord. Progressive Lease, Inc., Lincoln, 1993; PBX comms. specialist Branker Buick, Lincoln, 1994-97; sec., receptionist Reel Quick, Inc., Lincoln, 1997-98; case mgmt. sec. Madonna Rehab. Hosp., Lincoln, 1998-2000; exec. adminstrv. asst. Nebr. Heart Inst., Lincoln, 2000—. Vol. ARC, Lincoln, 1977—, chmn., 1983-84, pres. Lincoln Fire Dept. Aux., 1993; cert. EMT; notary public Nebr., 1993—; mem. Benevolent Patriatric Order of Does, 1998—, inner guard, 1999, sec., 2000. Named Outstanding Vol. ARC, 1985. Mem. NAFE, Benevolent Patriotic Order of Does (inner guard 1999, sec. 2000—). Republican. Presbyterian. Avocations: church handbell ringing, shuffleboard, playing pool, bowling, gardening. E-mail: mfleharty@neheart.com. Fax: 402-483-8708. Office: Nebr Heart Inst 1500 S 48th St Ste 712 Lincoln NE 68506-1225

FLEISCHER-RIEVESCHL, ELLEN LEE, real estate agent; b. Cin., Dec. 15, 1945; d. Leo Simon and Janet Fleischer; m. George Rieveschl, Jr. BA in Mgmt. Econs., U. Cin., 1968. Pub. rels. Cin. Gas and Electric CO., 1968-71; campaign coord. Taft for Senate, Cin., 1971-72; new bus. devel. profl. Fifth Third Bank N.A., Cin., 1973-77; mktg. mgr. Williamsburg Mgmt., Cin., 1984-86; real estate agt. Sibcy Cline Realtors, Ft. Mitchell, Ky., 1986-91, Re/Max Affiliates, Ft. Mitchell, 1992—; artist, Cin., 1978-85; mem. Kenton Boone Bd. Realtors, Northern Ky. Exhibitor watercolor abstracts various galleries in Cin., Naples and Coral Gables, Fla., N.Y.C.; author essay, Congl. Record, 1st pl. award, 1968. Divsn. leader United Way; mem. steering com. Emery Soc. for Children's Hosp. Mem. Ky. Assn. Realtors, Nat. Assn. Realtors, Million Dollar Club, Friends of Covington, No. Ky. Heritage League, Cin. Art Mus., Cin. Symphony Com., Forward Quest of Covington, Omicron Delta Epsilon. Avocations: horseback riding, walking, swimming, travel, painting. Home: 100 Riverside Pl Covington KY 41011-1718

FLEISCHHACKER, W. WOLFGANG, psychiatrist, educator, scientist; b. Baden, Austria, Apr. 29, 1953; s. Walter and Hedwig (Laschitz) F.; m. Astrid Fleischhacker, Aug. 29, 1987; children: Nicolas, Sebastian. MD, Innsbruck (Austria) U., 1978. Head dept. biol. psychiatry Innsbruck U. Clinics, 1993—; prof. psychiatry Innsbruck U., 1993—, head Inst. Profl. Comm. and Psychotherapy, 1999—. Co-author: Pharmakotherapie in der Psychiatrie, 1991, Lehrbuch der Psychiatrie, 1997; editor: Kombinations therapie in der Psychiatrie, 1990, Die Behandlung der Schizophrenien: State of the Art, 1998; contbr. articles to profl. jours. Fulbright scholar Hillside Hosp. 1987-88. Mem. European Coll. Neuropsychopharmacology, Coll. Internat. Neuropsychopharmacology, Austrian Schizophrenia Soc. (pres. 1997-99), Austrian Soc. Neuropsychopharmacology and Biol. Psychiatry (pres. 2000—), EU Group for Rsch. in Schizophrenia (chmn. 1997—). Office: Dept Psychiatry, Anichstrasse 35, 6020 Innsbruck Austria

FLEISCHHAUER, CARL-AUGUST, judge of international court of justice; b. Düsseldorf, Dec. 9, 1930; s. Kurt and Leonie (Schneider-Neuenburg) F.; m. Liliane Sarolea, 1957; 2 children. Student, U. Heidelberg, U. Grenoble, U. Paris, U. Chgo. Rsch. fellow Max-Planck Inst. Comparative Fgn. Pub. Law and Internat. Law, Heidelberg, 1960-62; with Fgn. Svc. of Germany, 1962-83, legal adviser fed. fgn. office, 1975, legal adviser, dir.-gen. legal dept., 1976; under-sec.-gen. legal affairs, legal counsel UN, 1983-94; judge Internat. Ct. Justice, 1994—. Contbr. articles to profl. jours. Recipient various decorations. Avocations: modern history, literature. Office: care Internat Ct Justice, Peace Palace, 2517 KJ The Hague The Netherlands

FLEISCHMAN, KEITH MARTIN, lawyer; b. Newark, June 13, 1958. BA, U. Vt., 1980; JD, Calif. Western U., 1984. Bar: N.Y. 1985, U.S. Dist. Ct. (so. dist.) N.Y. 1986, U.S. Ct. Appeals (2d cir.) 1989, U.S. Ct. Appeals (11th cir.) 1995, U.S. Ct. Appeals (4th cir.) 1999, U.S. Supreme Ct. 2000. Asst. dist. atty. Bronx (N.Y.) County Dist. Atty., Rackets and Maj. Offense, 1984-88; trial atty. U.S. Dept. Justice, Dallas Bank Fraud Task Force, Washington, 1988-90; asst. U.S. atty. U.S. Atty. Office, Dist. Conn., 1990-92; trial lawyer, ptnr. Milberg Weiss Bershad Hynes & Lerach LLP, N.Y.C., 1992—; inst., lectr. trial practice U.S. Dept. Justice, Washington, 1990-91. Coord. com. mem. New England Bank Fraud Task Force, Dist. Conn., 1990-92. Avocations: skiing, climbing. Office: Milberg Weiss Bershad Hynes & Lerach LLP One Pennsylvania Plaza New York NY 10119

FLEISHER, ANDREW ROY, engineer, investor, business consultant; b. Key West, Fla., Aug. 25, 1953; arrived in Australia, 1988; s. Oscar Teller, Jr. and Ruth (Schechter) F.; 1 child, Carla. BS in Engring., Calif. State U., San Jose, 1986. Gen. mgr. Sun King Enterprises Ltd., Honiara, Solomon Islands, 1986; contractor Project Mgmt. and Tech. Documentation, Sydney, Australia, 1988-90, cons., contractor, project mgr., 1992—; mgr. bus. devel. Porgera Joint Venture, Porgera, Papua New Guinea, 1990-92. Avocations: sailing, motorcycling. Office: GO Box 3879, Sydney NSW 2001, Australia

FLEISHER, ERIC WILFRID, retired foreign service officer; b. Washington, Jan. 31, 1926; s. Wilfrid and Greta Agda (Sundberg) F.; m. Elizabeth Fredrikson, Dec. 22, 1948 (div. 1974); children: Emily Susanne, Eric Torsten; m. Thale Gunneng, Aug. 5, 1974 (dec. Feb. 2000); 1 child, Arne Ericsson. Cert., U. Stockholm, 1948; BA, George Washington U., 1950; PhD, U. Lund, Sweden, 1953. Orientation officer U.S. Displaced Persons Commn., French Zone, Germany, 1950-51; program and ops. officer Refugee Relief Dept. State, Washington, 1954-55, intelligence rsch. analyst, 1955-58; polit. officer Am. Embassy, Copenhagen, Denmark, 1959-63; consul Faroe Islands, 1959-63; polit. counselor Helsinki, Finland, 1964-69; dep. country dir., then dir. Nordic countries Washington, 1969-73; press attache Am. Embassy, Stockholm, 1974-76; spl. asst. human rights and refugee affairs Washington, 1977-80, fgn. affairs cons., sr. cons., 1980—. Author: Viking Times to Modern, 1953; translator, editor: Scandinavia in Great Power Politics, 1905-1908, 1958; contbr. articles to various publs. 1st lt. U.S. Army, 1944-47, Tokyo. Mem. Am. Fgn. Svc. Assn., Diplomatic and Consular Officers Ret., Am. Scandinavian Found. Avocations: hiking, hunting, photography. Home: 8300 Thoreau Dr Bethesda MD 20817-3164 Office: Rm 5151 SA2 Dept State Washington DC 20522-6001

FLEISHER, FREDERIC ELLIOTT, communications executive; b. Tokyo, Jan. 31, 1933; s. Wilfrid and Greta (Sundberg) F.; divorced; children: Linn M., Rebecca M. BA, U. Stockholm, 1951, MA, 1954, PhD, 1967. Lectr. Scandinavian lit. U. Stockholm, 1967-71; producer, dir. TV programs Sta. TRU-TV, Stockholm, 1968-77; lectr. Am. lit. U. Stockholm, 1970-71; producer, dir. TV programs Sveriges Utbildningsradio (Swedish Ednl. Broadcasting Co.), Stockholm, 1978-90, head internat. rels., 1990-98; cons., 1998—. Contbr. articles to profl. jours.; co-host internat. prodn. sessions, Munich, 1993, 94, Berlin, 1995, 97, Fla., 1995, Bern, 1996, Chgo., 1996, Pa. State U., 1997, Phoenix, 1997; mem. editl. bd. Ednl. Media Internat., 1993—. Jury mem. MediaNet Awards, 1994, Rotterdam Market, 1998, Rotterdam Erasmus, 1998; jury pres. Basle Ednl. Awards, 1997. Recipient Poetry Translations award Sweden, 1964; various grants. Mem. Internat. Coun. Ednl. Media (exec. com. 1991-98), European Broadcasting Union (program com. for edn. 1995-98). Home: Norrbackagatan 17, SE 113 41 Stockholm Sweden Office: Telenor vision Intermedia, Vretenvaegen 12, SE-

17154 Solna Sweden also: Viking Vision, St Olofs Vaeg 10, 27736 Vitaby Sweden

FLEISHER, JERRILYN, financial planner; b. Phila., May 7, 1952; d. Earl D. and Bette (Romisher) F.; m. Steven M. Bierman, May 28, 1978; 1 child, Emily Larissa. BA, Dickinson Coll., 1973; MBA, Wharton Sch. U. Pa., 1975. Promotion analyst Gillette Co., Boston, 1975-77; product mgr. Chesebrough Ponds Co., Greenwich, Conn., 1977-80, Loreal Co., N.Y.C., 1980-81; account exec. Futterman Orgn., N.Y.C., 1981-83; fin. cons. Shearson Lehman Bros., Greenwich, 1983-92; pres. Fin. Views, Greenwich, 1992—. Mem. Internat. Bd. CFPs, Phi Beta Kappa. Home: 17 Ivanhoe Ln Greenwich CT 06830-3925

FLEISHMAN, PHILIP ROBERT, internist; b. Hartford, Conn., Apr. 17, 1935; s. Morris and Anna Lillian (Farber) F.; m. Anita Rose Coopersmith, Oct. 18, 1964; children: David, Beth, Rachael. BS, Trinity Coll., Hartford, 1957; MD, SUNY, Bklyn., 1961. Diplomate Am. Bd. Internal Medicine. Practice specializing in internal medicine East Islip, N.Y., 1967—; attending physician, dir. medicine Southside Hosp., Bay Shore, N.Y., 1993—; attending physician Good Samaritan Hosp., W. Islip, N.Y.; v.p. med. bd. Southside Hosp., 1986-89; pres., 1989—; clin. asst. prof. SUNY Med. Sch., Stony Brook, 1967—; asst. dir. medicine, 1988—, dir. med. sch., 1993—; founder, co-dir. diabetic clinic Southside Hosp.; also bd. dirs., 1999—; bd. dirs. Southlake Hosp., 1998—. Contbr. articles to profl. jours. Co-author, chmn. constn. and bylaws Pro-Arts Group Islips, 1979; asst. basketball coach Police Athletic League, 1979; v.p., trustee Bay Shore Jewish Ctr., 1979—, pres., 1988-90; bd. dirs. Southside Hosp., 1998—. Capt. M.C. U.S. Army, 1965-67. Fellow ACP; mem. AMA, Am. Diabetes Assn., N.Y. State Med. Soc., N.Y. State Soc. Internal Medicine (past chpt. pres.), Suffolk County Med. Soc. Office: 45 E Main St East Islip NY 11730-2502

FLEITH, DENISE SOUZA, psychology educator; b. Rio de Janeiro, July 8, 1962; d. Alcir and Lucy (Souza) F. Degree psychology, U. Brasilia, 1985, tchrs. cert. psychology, 1985, M in Psychology, 1990; PhD, U. Conn., 1999. Psychologist Ministry of Army, Brasilia, 1988-91; asst. prof. U. Brasilia, 1991-99, assoc. prof., 1999—; ad hoc reviewer Psychology: Theory and Research, 1992-93; head sch. and devel. psychology dept. U. Brasilia, 1994-95. Co-author: Dealing with Emotions, Playing with Ideas, 1999; contbr. articles to profl. jours. Doctoral scholarship Coordination of U. Pers. Devel., 1995-99; recipient Extraordinary Expense award Rsch. Found./U. Conn., 1998. Mem. Am. Psychol. Assn., Nat. Assn. for Gifted Children (grad. student rsch. grant 1998), WCGTC. Avocations: exercising, traveling, reading. Home: SQN 202 bloco H apt 504, 70832080 Brasilia DF, Brazil Office: Inst Psicologia, U Brasilia, 70910900 Brasilia Brazil

FLEMING, ALAN FREDERICK, hematologist; b. Tunbridge Wells, Eng., June 30, 1931; s. Thomas and Helen (Butler) F.; m. Jean Leonora Ainsley, Sept. 5, 1958 (div. Nov. 1992); children: Neil, Andrew, Ian; m. Moyra Claire Cornhill, Jan. 22, 1993; children: Alan, Helen. BA, Cambridge U., 1953, MB, BChir, 1957, MA, 1958, MD, 1968. Arnold Yeldham and Mary Raine sr. rsch. fellow U. Western Australia, Perth, 1966-69; reader, prof. hematology Ahmadu Bello U., Zaria, Nigeria, 1970-85; dep. dir. rsch. Tropical Diseases Rsch. Ctr., Ndola, Zambia, 1985-88; vis. scientist Deutsches Primatenzentrum, Göttingen, Germany, 1989; prof. hematology So. African Inst. Med. Rsch., Johannesburg, South Africa, 1990-94; dir. lab. svcs. U. Tchg. Hosp., Lusaka, Zambia, 1995-98; vis. prof. pediatrics Yale U., New Haven, 1980; hon. sr. lectr. Liverpool (Eng.) Sch. Tropical Medicine, 1987-92; hon. prof. hematology U. Zambia, 1985-88, 95-98; Alwyn Zoutendyk meml. lectr. South African Inst. Med. Rsch., Johannesburg, 1994, Kunle Ijaiya meml. lectr. Ahmadu Bello U., Zaria, 1984.; vis. prof. tropical diseases U. Witwatersrand, Johannesburg, South Africa, 1995-98; vis. lectr. tropical hematology, London Sch. Hygiene and Tropical Medicine, 1998—; hon. prof., head dept. tropical medicine U. Witwatersrand, 1994. Editor: Sickle-Cell Disease, 1982, Epidemiology of Haematological Disease, 1992; co-editor: The Global Impact of AIDS, 1988. Mem. com. Leukemia Fund Zambia, 1995-97. Fellow Royal Coll. Pathologists Eng., Nat. Med. Coun. Nigeria, West African Coll. Physicians, Royal Soc. Medicine, Royal Soc. Tropical Medicine and Hygiene (regional sec. 1994); mem. Sickle Cell Club Nigeria (pres. 1974-83), Internat. Soc. Hematology, Internat. Soc. Blood Transfusion. Avocations: walking, history, Baroque music, viewing architecture, 18th Century literature. E-mail: a.fleming@virgin.net. Home: Kilmersdon Common Farmhouse, Common Ln Holcombe, Bath BA3 5QB, England

FLEMING, ALICE CAREW MULCAHEY (MRS. THOMAS J. FLEMING), writer; b. New Haven, Dec. 21, 1928; d. Albert Leo and Agnes (Foley) Mulcahey ; m. Thomas J. Fleming, Jan. 19, 1951; children: Alice, Thomas, David, Richard. AB, Trinity Coll., 1950; MA, Columbia U., 1951. Author: The Key to New York, 1960, Wheels, 1960, A Son of Liberty, 1961, Doctors in Petticoats, 1964, Great Women Teachers, 1965, The Senator from Maine: Margaret Chase Smith, 1969, Alice Freeman Palmer: Pioneer College President, 1970, Reporters At War, 1970, General's Lady, 1971, Highways into History, 1971, Pioneers in Print, 1971, Ida Tarbell, The First of the Muckrakers, 1971, Nine Months, 1972, Psychiatry, What's it All About?, 1972, The Moviemakers, 1973, Trials that Made Headlines, 1974, Contraception, Abortion, Pregnancy, 1974, New on the Beat, 1975, Alcohol: The Delightful Poison, 1975, Something for Nothing, 1978, The Mysteries of ESP, 1980, What to Say When You Don't Know What to Say, 1982, The King of Prussia and a Peanut Butter Sandwich, 1988, George Washington Wasn't Always Old, 1991, What, Me Worry?, 1992, P.T. Barnum: The World's Greatest Showman, 1993, A Century of Service, 1998; editor: Hosannah the Home Run!, 1972, America Is Not All Traffic Lights, 1976; contbr. articles to mags. Nat. bd. dirs. Medic Alert Found. U.S., 1991-97, vice chmn., 1996-97, past. chmn. N.Y. regional bd.; mem. pres.'s coun. United Hosp. Fund. Recipient Nat. Media award Family Svc. Assn. Am., 1973, Alumnae Achievement award Trinity Coll., 1979, Nat. Vol. of Yr. award Medic Alert Found., 1991, 93. Mem. PEN, Authors Guild. Address: 315 E 72nd St New York NY 10021-4625

FLEMING, DONALD HARNISH, historian, educator; b. Hagerstown, Md., Aug. 7, 1923; s. Donald Harnish and Luciphene (Beery) F. A.B., Johns Hopkins U., 1943; A.M., Harvard U., 1944, Ph.D., 1947. With Brown U., 1947-58, successively lectr., asst. prof., asso. prof., 1953-55, prof. history, 1955-58; prof. history of sci. Yale U., 1958-59; vis. prof. Harvard U., 1958-59, prof. history, 1959-70, Jonathan Trumbull prof. Am. history, 1970—; dir. Charles Warren Center for Studies in Am. History, 1973-80. Author: John William Draper, 1950 (Beveridge prize Am. Hist. Assn.), William Henry Welch and the Rise of Modern Medicine, 1954; co-author: Glimpses of the Harvard Past, 1986; co-editor: Perspectives in American History, 1967-80, 85—, The Intellectual Migration: Europe and America, 1930-1960, 1969. Fellow Am. Acad. Arts and Scis.; mem. History of Sci. Soc., Antiquarian Soc. Home: 221 Mount Auburn St Cambridge MA 02138-4874

FLEMING, HORACE WELDON, JR., higher education administrator, educator; b. Elberton, Ga., Jan. 14, 1944; s. Horace Weldon Sr. and Alma G. (Dove) F.; m. Orene Stephens Greene, Feb. 8, 1970; children: Susan Renee, Patrick Weldon. BA, U. Ga., 1965, MA, 1966; PhD, Vanderbilt U., 1973. Mem. faculty Clemson (S.C.) U., 1971-87; chief economist U.S. Senate Judiciary Com., 1981; staff dir. Office of Pres. Pro Tem U.S. Senate, 1981-82; founding dir. Strom Thurmond Inst. Govt. and Pub. Affairs, Clemson, 1982-90; exec. v.p. U. of the Pacific, Stockton, Calif., 1990-92; exec. v.p., provost Mercer U., Macon, Ga., 1992-96; pres. U. So. Miss., Hattiesburg, 1997—; cons. to fed., state and local govt. agys. on fin., orgn. and mgmt., energy and water policy; frequent media columnist and spkr.; bd. dirs. Miss. Tech., Inc., Inst. for Tech. Devel., 1997—. Charter trustee Dropout Prevention Fund, 1986-90, The Palmetto Project, 1987-90; v.p. Hill Found., 1982-96; mem. Pres.'s Nat. Vol. Adv. Coun., 1986-89; mem. Assembly on the Future of S.C., 1988; mem. Gov.'s Transition Task Force on Govt. Reform, 1986-87; mem. S.C. Reorgn. Commn., 1987-90; mem. Stockton-San Joaquin (Calif.) Conv. and Visitors Bur., 1990-92; mem. Vision 2000 task force Stockton Bus. Coun., 1990-92; bd. visitors Air U., 1998—. Capt. U.S. Army, 1969-71, Vietnam. Recipient Order of Palmetto, S.C., 1990, award of merit S.C. Water Resources Commn., 1990, Palmetto Pride award The Palmetto Project, 1990, others; Faculty fellow Leadership Hilton Head Island, 1989. Mem. Scabbard and Blade, Blue Key, Tiger Brotherhood, Phi Mu Alpha, Pi Sigma Alpha, Sigma Phi Epsilon, Omicron Delta Kappa, Phi Kappa Phi, numerous orgns. in higher edn. Office: U So Miss PO Box 5001 Hattiesburg MS 39406-1000

FLEMING, IAN, chemistry educator, researcher; b. Kingswinford, Eng., Aug. 4, 1935; s. David Alexander and Olwen Lloyd (Jones) F.; m. Joan Mor Irving, Aug. 3, 1959 (div. July 1962); m. Mary Lord Bernard, Nov. 12, 1965. BA, Cambridge (Eng.) U., 1959, PhD, 1963, ScD, 1982. Rsch. fellow Pembroke Coll., Cambridge, 1962-64, fellow, 1964—; univ. demonstrator Cambridge U., 1964-65, asst. dir. rsch., 1965-80, univ. lectr., 1980-86, reader in organic chemistry, 1986-98, prof. organic chemistry, 1998—; vis. prof. chemistry U. Wis., Madison, 1980, Harvard U., Cambridge, Mass., 1990. Author: Selected Organic Syntheses, 1973, Frontier Orbitals and Organic Chemical Reactions, 1976, Pericyclic Reactions, 1998; co-author: Spectroscopic Methods in Organic Chemistry, 1st edit. 1966, 2d edit. 1973, 3d edit. 1980, 4th edit. 1987, 5th edit. 1995, Spectroscopic Problems in Organic Chemistry, 1967. Fellow Royal Soc.; mem. Royal Soc. Chemistry (Tilden Lectr. 1981, prize for organic synthesis 1983), Am. Chem. Soc. Avocations: movies, music. Office: Cambridge U Dept Chemistry, Lensfield Rd, Cambridge CB2 1EW, England

FLEMING, JANE WILLIAMS, retired educator, writer; b. Bethlehem, Pa., May 26, 1926; d. James Robert and Marion Pauline (Melloy) Groman; m. George Elliott Williams, July 2, 1955 (div. July 1965); children: Rhett Dorman, Santee Stuart, Timothy Cooper; m. Jérome Thomas Fleming, Sept. 25, 1980. BS, UCLA, 1951; MA, Calif. State U., Long Beach, 1969. Tchr. San Diego Unified Sch Dist., 1951-55, Costa Mesa (Calif.) Sch. Dist., 1955-56, Long Beach (Calif.) Sch. Dist., 1956-58, 62-87, 90-92; ret. Author: Why Janey Can't Teach, 2000. Mem. Phi Kappa Phi, Ret. Tchrs. Assn., UCLA Alumni Assn., Planetary Soc. (charter), Mus. of Tolerance. Avocations: theater, travel. E-mail: jwilli5687@aol.com. Address: PO Box 13053 Belmont Shore CA 90803-8053

FLEMING, JOHN MITCHEL, psychologist, researcher; b. Dublin, July 6, 1957; s. John Mitchel Fleming and Ann Marie Simpson; m. Mary Bernadette Hickey; children: John, Clodagh. BA, Trinity Coll., Dublin, 1978, PhD, 1997. Registered psychologist. Trainee psychologist St. John of God Bros., Dublin, 1978-80; clin. psychologist Daus. of Charity, Dublin, 1980-87, sr. clin. psychologist, 1988—; part-time lectr. Univ. Coll., Dublin, 1986—, Trinity Coll., Dublin, 1997—. Mem. Psychol. Soc. Ireland (registered, pres. 1986-87), Psychologists for Peace (treas. 1987—). Roman Catholic. Avocation: painting. Home: 86 Roselawn Rd Castleknock, Dublin 15, Ireland Office: Daus of Charity Svcs, St Vincents Ctr Navan Rd, Dublin 15, Ireland

FLEMING, MARJORIE FOSTER, freelance writer, artist; b. Phila., Sept. 12, 1920; d. Major Bronson and Helen Margaret (Vertner) Foster; m. John Joseph Hundermark, Sept. 24, 1949 (div. Sept. 1955); children: John Foster Hundermark, David Laurence Hundermark; m. Paul Stewart Fleming, May 6, 1961. BA, Ursinus Coll., 1942; studied painting with Morris Blackburn, Cheltenham Ctr. Arts, with R. Goldman; studied painting with Paul Wieghardt, Cheltenham Twp. Ctr. for Arts; studied with Paul Wieghardt, Chgo. Art Inst. Cert. tchr. Cost acct. Philco Corp., Phila., 1942-43; asst. bank auditor Liberty Title and Trust, Phila., 1943-44; asst. dept. spl. events Phila. Evening Bulletin, 1945-47; asst. stage TV and radio show prodr. Phila., 1947-49; Appeared on Wit's End (live pilot TV show), 1948, guest Poetry Today, Sta. WRTN radio, N.Y.C., 1997; adult edn. studies Temple U. Pierce Business Coll, Cheltenham H.S., Oak Ln. Co. Day Sch., Cheltenham Adult Sch., Arthur Murray Dance Sch. Contbr. Northwest Herald, Crystal Lake, Ill., 1996—. Vol. occupl. therapist ARC. Mem. Internat. Poetry Mus., Internat. Libr. Poetry, Internat. Soc. Poets (inducted into Hall of Fame Mus.), Poetry Guild, Am. Diabetes Assn., Cheltenham Ctr. Arts, Kappa Delta Chi, Omega Chi. Republican. Methodist. Avocations: sculpture, photography, creative needlework, pianist, collecting sheet music. Home: 82 Holly Dr Crystal Lake IL 60014-5022

FLEMING, MARY LINDA, statistician; b. Little Rock, Aug. 17, 1938; d. Roy Francis Fleming and Florence Combs Mills; m. Hugh Noel Beam, June 4, 1958 (div. Apr. 1968); children: Linda Leigh Kiener, John David Beam. BS, Midwestern U., Wichita Falls, Tex., 1969, MS, 1971; MPH, U. Okla., 1975, PhD, 1978. Biostatistician Okla. Rsch. Found., Oklahoma City, 1971-79; dir. geol. info. sys. U. Okla., Norman, 1979-87; master tchr. New Covenant Acad., Lexington, Ky., 1987-88; prof. stats. Ea. Ky. U., Richmond, 1988-93, chair math., stats., and computer sci., 1993-98; dir. programs Am. Statistical Assn., Alexandria, Va., 1998—. Choral singer Lexington Singers, 1988-96; mentor Ky. Acad. Sci., 1992. Recipient Outstanding Alumnus award Midwestern U., 1999. Mem. Am. Statistical Assn., Nat. Coun. Tchrs. Math., Math. Assn. Am. Avocations: jogging, gardening, singing. E-mail: mary@amstat.org. Office: Am Statistical Assn 1429 Duke St Alexandria VA 22314-3461

FLEMING, ROBERT, investment company executive; b. Sept. 18, 1932; s. Philip and Joan Cecil (Hunloke) Fl; m. Victoria Margaret Aykroyd, 1962; 3 children. Grad., Eton Coll., Eng., Royal Mil. Acad., Sandhurst, Eng. With The Royal Scots Greys, 1952-58, Robert Fleming, 1958—; dep. chmn. Robert Fleming Holdings, London, 1986-90, chmn., 1990-97; retired; chmn. Robert Fleming Holdings, 1999—; bd. dirs. Robert Fleming Trustee Co., 1961—, chmn., 1985-91; bd. dirs. Robert Fleming Investment Trust, 1968—, Robert Fleming Holdings, 1974—, Glenshee Chairlift Co. Ltd., 1995—. High sheriff, 1980, Oxfordshire, Eng., dep. lt., 1990. Avocations: hunting, fishing, music. Office: Robert Fleming Holdings Ltd, 25 Copthall Ave, London EC2R 7DR, England*

FLEMING, SIDNEY HOWELL, psychiatrist, educator; b. Lubbock, Tex., May 22, 1938; d. McKinley and Wilna Adrian (Simer) Howell; m. J.D. Fleming, Jr., June 28, 1960; 1 child, Julie Adrianne. BA, Agnes Scott Coll., Decatur, Ga., 1959; MD, Emory U., 1964. Diplomate Am. Bd. Psychiatry and Neurology. Intern Emory U./Va. Hosp., Atlanta, 1964-65, resident in psychiatry, 1965-68; mem. faculty Emory U. Med. Sch., 1968—, assoc. prof. psychiatry, 1975—; chmn. Pres.'s Commn. on Status of Women, 1984-85. Grantee NIMH, 1969-71. Mem. Am. Coll. Psychiatry, Am. Psychiat. Assn. (editl. bd. on curriculum on psychol. of women and men 1979-81, com. on women 1985-90), Assn. Acad. Psychiatrists, Ga. Psychiat. Assn., Med. Assn. Ga., Druid Hills Club. Republican. Address: 1248 Oxford Rd NE Atlanta GA 30306-2610

FLEMING, STEVEN DENIS, scientific director; b. London, Oct. 30, 1956; s. Denis Frank Appleby and Elizabeth Sheila May Fleming; m. Jane Harrod, Nov. 1, 1985; children: Aaron, Reuben, Emily. BSc in Zoology (hons.), UCNW Bangor, Wales, 1979; MSc, City of London Polytechnic, 1982; PhD, U. Sheffield, 1987. Sci. officer Dept. Physiology Inst. of Psychiatry, London, 1980-81; sci. officer Vision Rsch. Unit The Rayne Inst., St. Thomas' Hosp., London, 1981-82; SERC postgrad. studentship Dept. Human Metabolism U. Sheffield, Eng., 1983-87; rsch. officer U. Sydney, Australia, 1987-89; Wellcome Trust lectr. U. Bristol, Eng., 1989-90; rsch. assoc. U. Leicester, Eng., 1990-92; lectr. U. Nottingham, Eng., 1993-97; sci. dir. Westmead Fertility Ctr., Sydney, 1998—; prin. lectr., sr. tutor U. Nottingham, 1993-97; summer sch. convenor U. Goteborg, Sweden, 1994-96; spl. guest lectr. Univ. Coll. London, 1996-97; sr. lectr. U. Sydney, 1998—. Contbr. numerous articles to profl. jours. Recipient Travel grant Soc. for Study of Fertility, 1992, Univ. Major Equipment grant, 1993, The First Olympus BX Travel award, 1994, Organon Sponsorship of Master's Degree Course Brochure, 1994, Organon Sponsorship of Master's Degree Summer Sch., 1995. Mem. Fertility Soc. Australia, ALPHA, Scientists in Reproductive Tech., Soc. for Study of Fertility, Soc. for Endocrinology, Brit. Fertility Soc. Avocation: photography (winner N. Sydney Bicentennial Photographic Competition). Office: U Sydney Dept Ob-Gyn, Westmead Hosp, Sydney 2145, Australia

FLEMMING, GUNTHER, meteorologist; b. Waltershausen, Germany, June 1, 1933; s. Hans and Hildegard (Scharfe) F.; m. Maria Holtsch, June 9, 1961; children: Georg, Johannes. Diploma, U. Leipzig, 1957, DSc, 1962. From asst. to prof. U. Technology, Dresden, Germany, 1957—. Author: Climate, Environment, Man, 1979, 2d edit., 1990, Forest, Weather, Climate, 1982, 3d edit., 1994, Introduction to Applied Meteorology, 1991. Mem. German Meteorol. Soc. (silver medal 1990). Avocations: classical music, singing, dancing, hiking, fine arts. Home: Dorfhainer Str 6, D 01189 Dresden Germany

FLERKÓ, BÉLA, anatomist, educator; b. Pécs, Hungary, June 14, 1924; s. Béla and Etelka (Teimel) F.; m. Vera Bárdos, July 23, 1951. MD, Univ. Med. Sch., Pécs, 1948; PhD, Hungarian Acad. Sci., Budapest, 1956, DSc, 1967; PhD (hon.), U. Kuopio, Finland, 1982. Instr. dept. anatomy Univ. Med. Sch., Pécs, 1948-51, asst. prof., 1951-61, assoc. prof., 1961-64, prof., 1964-94, prof. emeritus, 1994—, dir. dept. anatomy, 1964-92, rector med. sch., 1979-85. Contbr. articles to profl. jours.; co-author: Hypothalamic Control of the Anterior Pituitary, 1962, 3d edit., 1972. Med. lt. Hungarian Army Res., 1953. Recipient Nat. award Hungarian Govt., 1978, Albert Szent-Györgyi award, 1992, Mid Cross of Order of Hungarian Rep., 1995. Mem. Hungarian Soc. Endocrinology (pres. 1973-81), Internat. Soc. Neuroendocrinology (pres. 1988-92, G. Harris Meml. Lecture 1979), Hungarian Acad. Scis., Academia Europaea. Avocations: classical music, photography. Office: Univ Medical Sch Dept Anatomy, Szigeti ut 12, H-7643 Pécs Hungary

FLEROV, VLADIMIR ILJA, physicist, researcher; b. Irkutsk, Russia, Aug. 11, 1938; s. Ilja Vasilij and Natalija Akim (Klimova) F.; m. Galina Konstantin Djomina, Sept. 14, 1937; children: Alexei, Nelija. Student, Latvian U., 1960; Dr. in Physics, Inst. Physics, Latvia, 1980. Technician, engr. Semicondr. Plant, Latvia, 1960-64; rschr. Inst. Physics, Latvia, 1964-92, Nuclear Rsch. Ctr., Latvia, 1992—. Author: (with Konjaev and Surikov) TV Sensors of Imagination in Radiation Fields, 1989; contbr. articles to profl. jours. Recipient medal for development of virgin land, Russia, 1956. Mem. Christian-Democracy Party. Avocations: biking, literature, dogs, travel, conferences. E-mail: vflerov@sal.lv. Home: 31 Dzirnavu St #24, LV-1010 Riga Latvia Office: Inst Physics, 32 Miera St, LV-2169 Salaspils 1, Latvia

FLETCHER, BRADY JONES, vocational education career specialist; b. Natchitoches, La., Apr. 17, 1928; d. Louis Benjamin and Isadore Hannah (Stephens) Jones; m. Donald Greene Fletcher, Aug. 13, 1950; children: Donald Bruce, Nathan Louis, Debra Patrice. BA, Clark Coll., 1950; MA (fellow), Howard U., 1953; postgrad. (NDEA fellow), Ind. U., 1965; EdS in Guidance, George Washington U., 1967, EdD, 1977. Tchr. math. and sci. Fairmont Heights (Md.) High Sch., 1951-54; tchr. math. and sci. Douglas High Sch., Upper Marlboro, Md., 1955-57, Prince George's County (Md.) Pub. Schs., 1951-59, Banneker Jr. High Sch., Washington, 1959-63; chmn. guidance dept. Garnet/Patterson Jr. High Sch., 1963-67; counselor Lincoln Jr. High Sch., D.C. pub. schs., 1967-69, Kensington (Md.) Jr. High Sch., 1969-73, Banneker Jr. High Sch., 1975-77; career edn. specialist Montgomery County (Md.) Schs., 1973-75; counselor Frederic Douglass Middle Sch., Indpls., 1999—; cons. Md. State Dept. Edn., 1973, Balt. City Pub. Schs., 1973, Balt. County Pub. Schs., 1973, D.C. Pub. Schs.; mem. adv. com. for spl. needs population Montgomery Coll., Rockville, Md., Am. Coll. Testing Bd., Washington, 1987—; project dir. InterAmerica Rsch. Assoc., Inc., Rosslyn, Va., 1977. Editor: Career Edn., 1973-75; Increasing Collaboration in Career Education (2 vols.). Rep. to Cmty. Action Bd. for Montgomery County Edn. Assn.; dir. D.C. Summer Youth Job Program, 1981; tech. cons., del. to Russia, Czech Republic and Poland with citizen amb. program People to People Internat., 1993. Inst. Ednl. Leadership fellow, summer 1984, Montgomery County Vocat. Assessment Ctr. (recipient dedicated service award 1987); recipient Educators award Clinton A.M.E. Ch., 1988, Multicultural Counseling award Founders of Orgn., 1987, award Montgomery County Coun., 1990; resolution in her honor Md. State Senate, 1990; Adminstr. of Yr. for I-Star Program, Ind. Say No to Drugs, 1994; named Alumnus of Yr. George Washington U., 1999, keynote spkr. opening conf. edn. and tech.; inducted into Hall of Fame, Englewood H.S., Chgo., 1999. Mem. AACD (Nat. award for govt. rels.), Am. Pers. and Guidance Assn. (Human Rels. Com. award 1974, editor conv. newsletter 1983), Am. Assn. Specialists in Group Work (nat. chairperson human rels. 1993, Recognition award 1993), Md. Pers. and Guidance Assn. (award 1975), Nat. Capital Pers. and Guidance Assn. (award 1975-76), Ind. Counseling Assn. (v.p. ctrl. chpt. 1992), Ind. Sch. Counselors Assn., Ind. Career Devel. Assn. (Ind. sch. counselor), Ind. Multicultural Assn., D.C. Assn. Counseling and Devel. (pres. 1986-87, del. to North Atlantic region assembly, recipient award disting. profl. leadership 1987, award for profl. devel. of assn. 1986, trustee 1988-89, co-chairperson govt. rels. com., Nat. awards Govt. Rels. Com. Boston 1989 and Cin. 1990), Nat. Vocat. Guidance Assn., Assn. Non-White Concerns, Nat. Assn. Career Edn., Nat. Sch. Counselor Assn., Internat. Platform Assn., Indpls. Urban League, Alpha Kappa Alpha, Phi Delta Kappa. Home: 7340 Steinmeier Dr Indianapolis IN 46250-2567

FLETCHER, DAVID RALPH, civil engineer; b. Geneva, Ill., Oct. 29, 1953; s. Ralph Earl and Katherine Caroline (Thetard) F. BS in Civil and Environ. Engring., U. Wis., 1983, MS in Civil and Environ. Engring., 1986. From project leader to chief geographic info. sys. sect. Wis. Dept. of Transp., Madison, 1984-92; pres. Geog. Paradigm Computing, Madison, 1992-95; assoc. dir. Alliance for Transp. Rsch.-U. Wis., Albuquerque, 1996-99; pres. Geog. Paradigm Computing, Albuquerque, 1999—; instr. engring. devel. U. Wis., Madison, 1988-91; instr. internat. programs Fed. Hwy. Adminstrn., Washington, 1990-94; chmn. panel 20-27 Transp. Rsch. Bd., Washington, 1990—, task force geog. info. sys., 1996—, co-chmn. com. A5015. Author: Handbook of Integrated Transportation Information Systems, 1996. Mem. ASTM, Wis. Land Info. Assn. (pres. 1989-90), Urban Regional Info. Sys. Assn., Tau Beta Pi, Chi Epsilon. Achievements include development of the fundamental interface between linear and spatial info. between vector and photographic images; development of dynamic segmentation; design of geographic info. sys. for transp. Office: Geog Paradigm Computing PO Box 40483 Albuquerque NM 87196-0483

FLETCHER, HOMER LEE, librarian; b. Salem, Ind., May 11, 1928; s. Floyd M. and Hazel (Barnett) F.; m. Jacquelyn Ann Blanton, Feb. 7, 1950; children—Deborah Lynn, Randall Brian, David Lee. B.A., Ind. U., 1953; M.S. in L.S, U. Ill., 1954. Librarian Milw. Pub. Library, 1954-56; head librarian Ashland (Ohio) Pub. Library, 1956-59; city librarian Arcadia (Cal.) Pub. Library, 1959-65, Vallejo (Calif.) Pub. Library, 1965-70; city librarian San Jose, Calif., 1970-90, ret., 1990. Contbr. articles to profl. jours. Pres. S. Solano chpt. Calif. Assn. Neurol. Handicapped Children, 1968-69; mem. Presbyn. Ch. Sunnyvale, 1997. Served with USAF, 1946-49. Mem. ALA (intellectual freedom com. 1967-72), Calif. Library Assn. (pres. pub. libraries sect. 1967), Phi Beta Kappa. Democrat. Presbyterian. Home: 7921 Belknap Dr Cupertino CA 95014-4973

FLETCHER, JOHN FREDERICK, accountant; b. Feckenham, Eng., Apr. 3, 1948; s. John and Iris (Glover) F.; m. Winifred Susan Case, Mar. 16, 1969; 4 children. Cert. Inst. Credit Mgmt., Inst. Adminstrv. Accts. Mgr. S. Wall & Sons Ltd., Redditch, Eng., 1966-72; mgr. A&F Sanders Ltd., Birmingham, Eng., 1972-74; fin. dir., export shipping mgr. Inductotherm Europe Ltd., Droitwich, Eng., 1974—; dir. Electric Melting Svcs. Co. Ltd., Sheffield, Eng., 1996—. Mem. Brit. Rabbit Coun. (nat. treas. 1993—), Feckenham Cricket Club (mem. exec. com., treas. 1987—). Conservative. Salvation Army. Home: 30 Showell Rd, The Ridings Droitwich Wors WR9 80Y, England Office: Inductotherm Europe Ltd, The Furlong, WR9 9AH Droitwich England

FLETCHER, JOHN PERRY, vascular surgeon, educator; b. Perth, Australia, Sept. 25, 1946; s. Roland Melbourne and Dorothy Kitty Matilda (Playle) F.; m. Isabelle Beryl Violet Duplex, Jan. 22, 1969; children: John Nicholas, Isaac Alexander. MB BS, U. Western Australia, 1970; MD, U. Sydney, Australia, 1989, M of Surgery, 1992. Diplomate in diagnostic ultrasound. House officer Napier (New Zealand) Hosp., 1970; med. officer 2d Mil. Hosp., Ingleburn, Sydney, Australia, 1971-72; surg. registrar Royal Prince Alfred Hosp., Sydney, 1972-75, Stoke Mandeville Hosp., Aylesbury, Eng., 1975-77; fellow Cleve. Clinic, 1977-78; sr. lectr. in surgery U. Sydney and Westmead Hosp., 1978-88, assoc. prof., 1988-97, prof., 1997—. Contbr. chpts. to books, articles to profl. jours. Capt. M.C., Royal Australian Army, 1971-72. Fellow Royal Australasian Coll. Surgeons, Royal Coll. Surgeons; mem. Surg. Rsch. Soc. Australasia (pres. 1997-98), Internat. Union of Angiology (v.p. 1998-2000), Internat. Soc. for Cardiovascular Surgery, Australasian Soc. Ultrasound in Medicine, Australasian Soc. Thrombosis and Haemostasis, Australian Soc. Parenteral and Enteral Nutrition, Australian and New Zealand Soc. Phlebology. Avocations: music, opera, cricket, football, running, travel. Office: U Sydney Dept Surgery, Westmead Hosp, Westmead NSW 2165, Australia

FLETCHER, KENNETH BOYD, business executive, entrepreneur; b. Denver, Nov. 25, 1974; s. Loren Edward and Holly (Donaldson) F. BA in Econs., BA in Internat. Rels., U. Pa., 1997. Mem. e-commerce com. SBA, Washington, 1999, program analyst, 1997-99, bus. recruiter trade missions, 1998-99; dir. CAPITAL venue, LLC, Hampton, N.H., 1999—; asst. cons. Keiloch Consulting, Washington, 1997—. Author, editor, inventor (small bus. exporter database) Trade Mission Online, 1999. Mem. N.Am. Assn. Tech. Profls. (bd. dirs. 2000—). Democrat. Congregationalist. Avocations: international trade, foreign policy, snow skiing, sailing. Office: CAPITAL venue LLC 86 Putnam Ave Cotuit MA 02635-2817

FLETCHER, NEVILLE HORNER, physicist; b. Armidale, NSW, Australia, July 14, 1930; s. Alleine Horner and Florence Mabel (Glass) F.; m. Eunice Marian Sciffer, Sept. 2, 1953; children: Robin, Anne, John. BSc, Sydney U., 1951, DSc, 1973; MA, Harvard U., 1953, PhD, 1955; Research engr. Clevite Transistor Products Co., Boston, 1953-55; research scientist Australian Commonwealth Sci. and Indsl. Research Orgn., 1956-60; mem. faculty U. New Eng., Armidale, 1960-83, prof. physics, 1963-83, emeritus prof., 1983—, dean Faculty Sci., 1963-65, pro vice-chancellor, 1968-72, chmn. profl. bd., 1970-72; dir. Inst. Phys. Scis., Australian Commonwealth Sci. and Indsl. Rsch. Orgn., 1983-88, chief rsch. scientist, 1988-95; vis. fellow Australian Nat. U., 1995—; mem. Australian Research Grants Com., 1974-78; JSPS prof. Hokkaido U., 1975; mem. Internat. Commn. on Acoustics, 1985-90; chmn. Antarctic Sci. Adv. Com., 1990-96. Recipient Edgeworth David medal Royal Soc. NSW, 1963; Nuffield fellow, 1966; Frank Knox fellow Harvard, 1952; decorated Order of Australia, 1990. Fellow Australian Acad. Sci. (sec. phys. scis. 1980-84, Lyle medal 1993), Inst. Physics London, Australian Inst. Physics (pres. 1981-83), Acoustical Soc. Am. (Silver medal in musical acoustics 1998), Australian Acad. Technol. Sci. and Engring., Australian Acoustical Soc. Author: The Physics of Rainclouds, 1962; The Chemical Physics of Ice, 1970; Physics and Music, 1976, Acoustic Systems in Biology, 1992; co-author: The Physics of Musical Instruments, 1990, 2nd edit., 1998, Principals of Vibration and Sound, 1994; contbr. numerous articles to profl. jours. Office: Australian Nat Univ, Rsch Sch Physics Scis, Canberra ACT 0200, Australia

FLETCHER, SARAH LEE, retired elementary education educator; b. Webb, Ala., May 7, 1925; d. James Harvey and Emma Freddie (Scarborough) Lee; m. Gaston Maurice Fletcher, June 24, 1948; children: S. Daphne, Lee Maurice, Timothy J. Student, Bob Jones Coll., 1943-44, assoc. bus. cert., 1947; student, Calhoun Coll., 1968-70, Troy State U., 1970-72; BRE, Bethany Theol. Seminary, 1995, MRE, 1996. With Atlanta and St. Andrews Bay Rwy. Co., 1944-46; sec. to pub. Dothan (Ala.) Eagle, 1947-48; tchr. Morgan County Schs., Decatur, Ala., 1967-69, Newton (Ala.) Pub. Schs., 1969-72, Trinity Christian Schs., Oxford, Ala., 1972-73, Berachah Christian Acadamy, Huntsville, Ala., 1973-75; sec. Dominion Textile, Yarmouth, Nova Scotia, 1975-76; tchr. Mueller Christian Sch., Miami, 1976-79, Berean Christian Sch., Dothan, 1979-86, Grace Bible Acad., Dothan, 1987-90, Clinton Christian Acad., Upper Marlboro, Md., 1990-91; cons. Mary Kay Cosmetics, 1982—. Author: To Love Again, 1996; compiler, contbg. author: (book of short stories) The Set of the Sails, 1997; contbr. articles to Christian papers and mags. Active in ch. Mem. Troy State U. Creative Writing Club, Dothan Creative Writing Group. Baptist. Avocations: helping the elderly, writing, walking, speaking. Home: 1119 Garden Ln Dothan AL 36301-3407

FLETCHER, WARRICK JEFFREY, marine biologist. BSc, U. Melbourne, Victoria, Australia, 1979, BSc with honors, 1980; PhD, U. Sydney, N.S.W., Australia, 1985. Biologist Dept. Fisheries, Queensland (Australia) Dept. Primary Industries, Brisbane, 1985-88; biologist Dept. Fisheries, Western Australia, 1988-92, sr. rsch. scientist, 1992-96; dir. rsch. N.S.W. Fisheries, Cronulla, 1996—. Mem. Australian Soc. Fish Biology. Office: NSW Fisheries, 202 Nicholson Parade, NSW Cronulla 2230, Australia

FLETCHER ARANCIBIA, PABLO ENRIQUE, internal medicine endocrinology physician, educator; b. Panama, Apr. 15, 1928; s. Paul and Juana (Arancibia) Fletcher; m. Lilia Vasquez, Jan. 19, 1953; children: Juana E., Pablo E., Eduardo E., Lilia E. BS cum laude, Inst. Nat., Panama, 1946; MD cum laude, U. Autonoma de Mexico, Mexico City, 1953. Med. diplomate. Intern Hosp. Santo Tomas, Panama, 1953-54; resident in internal medicine Inst. de la Nutricion, Mexico City, 1954-56; fellow in endocrinology Mass. Gen. Hosp., Boston, 1956-58; chief endocrinology Social Security Hosp., Panama, 1960-89, chief dept. medicine, 1979-85; chief prof. medicine U. Panama, Panama, 1976—, dir. Ctr. of Endocrinology, 1981—; v.p. Panamerican Endocrinology Fedn., 1982-90; med. dir. Social Security Hosp., Panama, 1984-85; adj. prof. medicine U. Miami, Fla., 1989—; nat. health dir. Social Security Panama, 1989-94. Chief editor: Revista Medica-Caja de Seguro Social, Panama, 1982-85; editor: Acta Endocrinological Panamericana, 1969-72; contbr. numerous articles to profl. jours. Treas. Asociacion Medica Nacional de Panama, 1953-54; pres. Asociacion de Medicos, Odontologos y Afines de la Caja de Seguro Social, Panama, 1964-65, Fedn. Internal Medicine Socs. Ctrl. Am., 1969-71, Soc. Bolivariana de Endocrinologia, South Am., Panama, 1971-73. Recipient Best Tchr. award U. Panama, Gold medal U. Panama, 1995. Fellow ACP (gov. 1979-93, Laureate and Masters awards 1995); mem. AAAS, Am. Thyroid Assn., Am. Diabetes Assn., Am. Endocrine Soc., N.Y. Acad. Scis., British Endocrine Soc., Fedn. Panamericana de Endocrinologia (pres. 1982-90), Assn. Panama de Endocrinologia y Metabolismo (pres. 1980-83), Soc. Panamena Medicina Interna (pres. 1971-73), Internat. Soc. Internal Medicine, Latin Am. Soc. Thyroid, Latin Am. Soc. Diabetes, Internat. Diabetes Fedn., Internat. Coun. for Control of Iodine Deficiency Disorders, Internat. Endocrine Soc., N.Y. Acad. Scis. Roman Catholic. Avocations: lecturing, swimming. Home: Calle Septima PO Box 4127, Altos del Golf 12, Panama City Panama

FLETTNER, MARIANNE, opera administrator; b. Frankfurt, Germany, Aug. 9, 1933; d. Bernhard J. and Kaethe E. (Halbritter) F. Bus. diploma, Hessel Bus. Coll., 1953. Sec. various cos., 1953-61, Pontiac Motor Div., Burlingame, Calif., 1961-63; sec. Met. Opera, N.Y., 1963-74, asst. co. mgr., 1974-79; artistic adminstr. San Diego Opera, 1979—. Avocations: traveling, hiking, swimming, cooking. Home: 4015 Crown Point Dr San Diego CA 92109-6270 Office: San Diego Opera 1200 Third Ave 18th Fl San Diego CA 92101-4112

FLEUTRY, MICHEL, technical translator; b. Vernon, France, Oct. 7, 1931; s. Marcel and Marie (Lagrené) F.; m. Jeanne Collignon, Mar. 6, 1971; children: Eric, Frank. Student, Conservatoire Nat. Art Metiers, 1958. Specialist rsch. lab. Recherches Balistiques et Aérodynamiques, Vernon, 1954-60, engr., tech. translator, 1960-65; tech. translator European Launcher Devel. Orgn., Paris, 1965-68, Soc. Européenne de Propulsion, Paris, 1974-75; scientific and linguistic cons. Office Nat. d'Etudes et de Recherches Aérospatiales, 1976-80; tech. translator Vernon, 1980—. Author: Dictionnaire Encyclopédique d'Electronique, 1991. Avocations: do it yourself, railways modeller, sports, touring. Office: La Maison du Dictionnaire, 98 Blvd Montparnasse, 75014 Paris France

FLEW, ANTONY (GARRARD NEWTON), philosophy educator emeritus; b. London, Feb. 11, 1923; s. Robert Newton and Alice Winifred Flew; m. Annis Ruth Harty Donnison, 1952; children: Harriet Rebecca, Joanna Naomi. Student, Sch. Oriental and African Studies, London; MA with 1st class honors, St. John's Coll., Oxford, 1948; DLitt, U. Keele, Eng., 1974. Lectr. philosophy Oxford (Eng.) U., Christ Ch., 1949-50; lectr. moral philosophy U. Aberdeen, Scotland, 1950-54; prof. philosophy U. Keele, 1954-71, U. Calgary, Alta., Can., 1972-73; prof. philosophy U. Reading, Eng., 1973-82, emeritus prof., 1983—; vis. prof. NYU, 1958, Swarthmore Coll., 1961, U. Pitts., 1965, U. Malawi, 1967, U. Md., 1970, SUNY, Buffalo, 1971, U. Calif., San Diego, 1978-79; Gavin David Young lectr., U. Adelaide, 1963; part-time prof. York U., Toronto, 1983-85; Gifford lectr. St. Andrews, 1986; Disting. rsch. fellow social philosophy and policy ctr. Bowling Green State U., 1986, 87, 88, 89, 90, 91-92; participant numerous talks and discussions on radio and TV, Eng., Zambia, Australia, Can., U.S. Author: A New Approach to Psychical Research, 1953, Hume's Philosophy of Belief, 1961, God and Philosophy, 1966, Evolutionary Ethics, 1967, An Introduction to Western Philosophy, 1971, Crime or Disease?, 1973, Thinking About Thinking, 1975, The Presumption of Atheism, 1976, Sociology, Equality and Education, 1976, (with T.B. Warren) The Warren-Flew Debate, 1977, A Rational Animal, 1978, Philosophy: An Introduction, 1979, The Politics of Procrustes, 1981, David Hume: Philosopher of Moral Science, 1986, The Logic of Mortality, 1987, Power to the Parents: Reversing Educational Decline, 1987, (with G. Vesey) Agency and Necessity, 1987, Equality in Liberty and Justice, 1989, (with Terry Miethe) Does God Exist?, 1991, Thinking About Social Thinking, 1992, Atheistic Humanism, 1993, Shephard's Warning: Setting Schools Back on Course, 1994, Darwinian Evolution, 1997, Philosophical Essays, 1998, How to Think Straight, 1998; editor: Logic and Language Vol. 1, 1951, Vol. 2, 1953, New Essays in Philosophical Theology, 1955, Essays in Conceptual Analysis, 1956, Hume on Human Nature and Understanding, 1962, Body, Mind and Death, 1964, Malthus: An Essay on the Principle of Population, 1971, A Dictionary of Philosophy, 1979, Philosophical Problems of Parapsychology, 1987, Hume's Inquiry Concerning Human Understanding, 1988; mem. editl. bd. Sociol. Rev., 1954-71; mem. editl. adv. bd. Question, 1958-70; cons. editor Humanist, 1972-81, Jour. Critical Analysis, 1974—, Hume Studies, 1976-94, Jour. Libertarian Studies, 1976—. With intelligence RAF, 1943-45. Recipient Praise of Reason award, 1985, Disting. Rsch. fellow Social Philosophy and Policy Ctr. Bowling Green State U., 1986-91, Richard M. Weaver award, 1998, James Wilbur award, 1999. Fellow Acad. Humanism (laureate); mem. Mind Assn., Rationalist Press Assn. (v.p. 1972-88), Freedom Assn. (mem. coun.), Vol. Euthanasia Soc. (chmn. exec. com. 1976-79), Aristotelian Soc. Office: 26 Alexandra Rd, Reading Berks RG1 5PD, England

FLICK, ARNOLD L., retired physician, community activist; b. L.A., May 1, 1930; s. Samuel and Pearl Flick; m. Nancy Flick; children: Susan, Rachel, Sarah. BS, UCLA, 1950; MD, U. Chgo., 1954. Cer. Am. Bd. Internal Medicine, Am. Bd. Gastroenterology. Clin. prof. medicine U. Calif., San Diego, 1968-91; med. dir. Smoking Rsch., San Diego, 1966-68; pvt. practice San Diego, 1961-98; cmty. activist Citizens for Fully Informed Vote, San Diego, 1999—. Jewish. Avocations: biking, hiking, tennis, violin.

FLICK, CHARLOTTE, human services administrator; b. Sioux City, Iowa, Aug. 13, 1950; d. Patrick Leo Flick and Kathryn Irene Gentry; children: David, Neil. BS, U. Nebr., Omaha, 1988, MPA, 1997. Paralegal Legal Aid Soc., Omaha, 1990-98; project dir. Urban League Nebr., Omaha, 1999—; chair health com. S. Omaha Cmty. Care Coun., 1999-2000, Omaha Healthy Start, 2000, bd. dirs.; gov. appointed commr. Nebr. Commn. Status Women, 2000—. Nominating com. Juvenile Diabetes Found. Mem. Lions (2d v.p. Omaha Westside chpt. 2000—). Home: 5206 Bedford Ave Omaha NE 68104-3548 Office: Urban League Nebr 3024 N 24th St Omaha NE 68110-2026

FLICK, THOMAS MICHAEL, mathematics educator, educational administrator; b. Covington, Ky., July 14, 1954; s. Thomas Lawrence and Crystel (Moore) F.; m. Jeanine M. Moran, Nov. 23, 1991. BS, No. Ky. U., 1976, MA, 1981; MEd, Xavier U., 1977; PhD, Southeastern U., 1979; EdD, U. Sarasota, 1989. Cert. secondary tchr., Ohio, Ky. Assoc. vice prin., dean, chmn. math., prin. summer sch. Purcell Marian High Sch., Cin., 1977-89; asst. prof. Xavier U., Cin., 1989-95, assoc. prof., 1995—; lectr. astronomy Wilmington Coll., Ohio, 1977-78, engring. and nat. sci., U. Cin., 1979—. Author: Guidelines for Astronomy Courses, 1976, 78, (with J. Ventre & J. Boothe) Astronomy Teaching Handbook, 1992, Introduction to the Universe, 1991, 93, Eclipses: Presentations for Educators, 1999; contbr. articles to profl. jours. Guest lectr. Cin. Nature Ctr., Milford, 1976—; chmn. edn. Astron. League, Washington; tchr. Super Saturday Program for Gifted and Talented., Cin., 1983; commn. mem. Archdiocese Cin., 1986. Recipient Ohio NSF Presdl. Award for Excellence in Math. Edn., 1986, Greater Cin. Found./GE grantee, 1987. Mem. Ohio Coun. Tchrs. Math. (contest coord. 1983—, Outstanding Math. Tchr. award 1982), Nat. Astron. League (v.p. 1980-82, chmn. edn. 1975—), Nat. Coun. Tchrs. Math., Math. Assn. Am., Ohio Acad. Sci. (Jerry Acker Outstanding Math. Tchr. award 1986-87), Sigma Xi (Outstanding Math. Tchr. award 1985), Pi Mu Epsilon. Roman Catholic. Club: Midwestern Astronomers. Avocations: golf, piano, bicycling, model railroading. Home: 1720 Monticello Dr Fort Wright KY 41011-3765 Office: Xavier U Dept Edn 3800 Victory Pkwy Dept Edn Cincinnati OH 45207-1035

FLICKINGER, DON JACOB, patent agent; b. Massillon, Ohio, Dec. 31, 1933; s. John Jacob and Elizabeth Ann (Slinger) F.: m. Sonja Loy Jersild (dec. Aug. 1987); 1 child, Packy J. Flickinger. Student, Kent (Ohio) State U., 1951-54, U. Ariz., 1958; BA, Ariz. State U., 1963, MA, 1964. Bar: U.S. Patent and Trademark Office, 1973. Apprentice tool and die maker Spun Steel Corp., Canton, Ohio, 1951-54; staff Ariz. State U., Tempe, 1963-65; law clerk, paralegal Drummond, Cahill & Phillips, Phoenix, 1966-73; reg. patent agent Drummond, Nelson & Ptak, Phoenix, 1973-77, self employed, Phoenix, 1977-94; counsel Parsons & Goltry, Phoenix, 1995—; lectr., instr. Patent Seminars & Courses, Phoenix, 1977—; staff Rio Salado C.C., Phoenix, 1982-84. Patentee Collapsible Dust Pan, Hort. Growing Unit. Comdg. officer Poolee Enrichment Program, Family Marine Force, Poolee Assistance Co., Phoenix; sponsor Thunderbird Little League, Phoenix, 1985, 86, 87; big brother Valley Big Brothers, Phoenix, 1968-70; participant, staff Valley Big Bros./Big Sisters Fish-a-Ree, 1984-87; judge Crown Royal Kinetic Contraption Compeition, 1990. With USMC, 1954-57. Am. Soc. Tool. scholar, Tucson, 1960; recipient Disting. Svc. cert. Valley Big Brothers, Phoenix,1970, Honor award Westside Area Career Project, Glendale, 1981. Mem. BBB, NRA (endowment), Nat. Wildlife Fedn. (leaders club), Am. Legion, Ariz. Heritage Alliance, Phoenix Symphony Guild, Sundome Performing Arts Assn., Wilderness Soc., Nature Conservancy, Sea Shepard Conservation Soc., Legal Defense Fund, Defenders of Wildlife, Am. Legion, Mensa, Kappa Delta Pi. Republican. Buddhist. Avocations: philosophy, reading, woodworking, arts & crafts, fishing. Office: Parsons & Assocs 340 E Palm Ln Ste 260 Phoenix AZ 85004-4530

FLIEGER, STANISLAW KOSTKA, veterinarian; b. Witkowo, Poland, May 23, 1936; s. Franciszek and Ludwika (Ciesnik) F.; m. Anna Maria Pasek, Aug. 4, 1962; children: Piotr, Pawel. DVM, Agrl. Acad. Lublin, Poland, 1962, PhD, 1969. Specialist in autonomic nervous system. Asst. Agrl. Acad. Lublin, Poland, 1964-69, lectr., 1970-76, asst. prof., 1976-86, prof. assoc., 1986-98, head Inst. Animal Anatomy, 1995—, pro-rector of students, 1987-90, 93-96, prof., 1999—. Author: Splanchnology of Domestic Animals, 1995, Peripherial Nervous System in Domestic Animals, 1995; contbr. articles to profl. jours. Mem. Polish Anat. Soc. (pres. Lublin sect. 1980-83), Polish Soc. Vet. Scis., European Anat. Soc. Democrat. Roman Catholic. Avocations: classical music, literature. Home: B Chrobrego 2/21, 20-611 Lublin Poland Office: Faculty Vet Medicine, Akad Rolnicza W Lublinie, 20-033 Lublin Poland

FLIGGE, JÖRG, librarian, library director; b. Königsberg, Germany, Dec. 1, 1940; s. Armin and Ursula (Schroeter) F.; m. Gabriele Edner, July 6, 1968; children: Christina, Claudia. PhD, U. Bonn, Germany, 1972. Cert. sci. libr. Jr. libr. Univ. Libr., Bonn, 1972-74; libr. adminstr. Univ. Libr., Duisburg, Germany, 1974-77, head libr. adminstr., 1978-79, dep. dir., 1979, libr. dir., 1980; dep. dir. City Libr., Duisburg, 1983-90; dir., ltd. libr. dir. Bibliothek der Hansestadt Lübeck, Germany, 1990—; mem., head commn. AV-media in librs. German Libr. Inst., Berlin, 1980-90; mem. exec. bd., treas. Bibliotheca Baltica, Stockholm, Sweden, 1992—; mem. German-Russian Libr. Commn. Restitution, Berlin, Germany and St. Petersburg, Russia, 1993—. Author: Herzog Albrecht von Preussen und der Osiandrismus, 1972; author, editor: Bibliotheca Baltica, 1994, Stadt und Bibliohek, 1997; contbr. articles to profl.jours. Active Gesellschaft zur Beförderung gemeinnütziger Tätigkeit, Lübeck, 1991—. Mem. Verein Deutscher Bibliothekare, Verein der Bibliothekare an Öffentlichen Bibliotheken, Rotary. Lutheran. Avocations: music, studying cultural history. Home: Hermann-Lönsweg 24, 23562 Lübeck Germany Office: Bibliothek der Hansestadt Lübeck, Hundestr 5-17, 23552 Lübeck Germany

FLINDELL, EDWIN FREDERICK, III, retired musicologist, choral conductor, organist; b. San Antonio, Feb. 27, 1926; s. Edwin Frederick Jr. and Katherine Reid (Darby) F.; m. Susan Reinoehl, Feb. 1948 (div. Mar. 1953); 1 child, Carolyn; m. Ingrid Dieckmann, Sept. 8, 1964; children: Grace, Theodore. Student, Dartmouth Coll., 1943-44; AB, Yale U., 1947; tchg. cert., Peabody Conservatory, Balt., 1952; AM, U. Pa., 1957, PhD, 1959. Tchr. Dobbins Tech. H.S., Phila., 1959-60, Roxborough H.S., Phila., 1961-62; fellow Humboldt Found., Göttingen, Germany, 1962-64; asst. prof. SUNY, Plattsburgh, 1964-68; assoc. prof. Franklin Pierce Coll., Rindge, N.H., 1968-71; tchr., organist, choral condr. Evang. Konsistorium, Berlin, 1971-91; faculty pres. World Campus Afloat, Chapman Coll., Orange, Calif., 1968-69; asst. prof. (on leave) N.H. Coll., Manchester, 1969-71; asst. prof. Schiller Coll., Berlin, 1973-74; assoc. prof. (on leave) U. Nev., Las Vegas, 1978-79. Contbr. articles to profl. jours., including Acta Musicologia, Musica Disciplina, BACH; arranger 9 Negro spirituals, 1977-78. With USAAF, 1944-45. Fulbright scholar, Göttingen, 1960-61; summer rsch. fellow SUNY, 1965, 66, 68. Mem. Am. Musicological Soc., Dartmouth Club Germany (v.p. 1998—). Avocations: ping pong, swimming, sailing. Home: Kaiserkorso 5, 12101 Berlin Germany

FLINK, STANLEY EDGAR, writer, public affairs consultant; b. Newark, May 28, 1924; s. Julius Edward and Frances (Heyman) F.; m. Mary Hilson, 1949 (div. 1961); children: Wendy, Steven; m. Joy Reynolds, May 24, 1975. BA, Yale U., 1945 W (WWII); postgrad., Oxfor (Eng.) U., 1947. Corr. Time Inc., L.A., 1949-58; assoc. producer NBC-TV, N.Y.C., 1958-61; producer, writer CBS-TV, N.Y.C., 1961-63; chief exec. officer, cons. pub. affairs London, 1963-72; first dir. Office of Pub. Info. and Alumni Communications Yale U., New Haven, Conn., 1972-80; pres. Stanley Flink Assocs., Hamden, Conn., 1981—; dir. Nat. Theater of the Deaf, Chester, Conn., 1985—; ptnr. Benton and Flink Prodns., N.Y.C., 1987—; asst. prof. NYU Sch. Journalism and Mass Communication, 1985—; lectr. Yale U., 1998—. Author: But Will They Get it in Des Moines, 1960, Sentinel Under Siege: The Triumphs and Troubles of America's Free Press, 1996; editor: (book) Wildlife Crisis, 1968, Yale Alumni Mag., 1976-79. 2d lt. U.S. Army, 1943-47, PTO. Mem. Yale Club of N.Y.C. (bd. dirs.), New Haven Yale Club. Avocation: tennis. Home and Office: 49 Deepwood Dr Hamden CT 06517-3414

FLINN, CHARLES GALLAGHER, lawyer, priest; b. Ft. Lauderdale, Fla., Feb. 22, 1938; s. Robert Galloway and Gertrude (Gallagher) F. AB, Princeton U., 1959; LLB, U. Va., 1962; BD, U. London, 1980; ThM, Westminster Theol. Sem., 1994. Bar: Fla. 1962, Va. 1962, U.S. Supreme Ct. 1966, D.C. 1970; ordained to ministry Episcopal Ch. as deacon, 1991, as priest 1992. Assoc. Charles B. Fulton, Esq., West Palm Beach, Fla., 1962-63; asst. counsel Office Gen. Counsel U.S. Dept. Navy, Washington, 1963-71; asst. commonwealth's atty. County of Arlington, Va., 1971-72, asst. county atty., 1972-75, dep. county atty., 1975-81, county atty., 1981-93; atty. Arlington Sch. Bd., 1981-93; curate Grace Episcopal Ch., Brunswick, Md., 1991-93; vicar Trinity Episcopal Ch., Monmouth, Ill., 1994-96; vice-chancellor Episcopal Diocese, Quincy, Ill., 1996—; vis. lectr. in biblical lang. Reformed Theological Seminary, Orlando, Fla., 1997—; adj. faculty Protestant Episcopal Theol. Seminary, Va., Alexandria, 1999—. Mem. Va. Local Govt. Attys. Assn. (bd. dirs. 1988-92), Va. Coun. Sch. Bd. Attys. (dir.-at-large 1988-93).

FLINN, ROBERT STURDIVANT, composer, import executive; b. Alberta, Va., June 20, 1940; s. Meade Flinn and Mary Frances Shepard. Student, The Coll. William and Mary, 1963-65. Composer (song) Forever August Moon, 1970 (Popular Song award ASCAP 1997, 98, 99, 2000). Mem. ASCAP, Brunswick County Historical Soc. (life), Clan Montgomery Soc. Internat. (life), The Jamestowne Soc. (life), St. Andrew's Soc. Williamsburg. Episcopalian. Avocations: travel to europe, historical society tours, local tourism endeavors, dancing to big band music. Home: Merry Hill 119 Church St Alberta VA 23821-2029

FLINT, DOUGLAS J., business executive. Chartered acct. Peat Marwick Mitchell & Co.; ptnr., 1988-95; group fin. dir. HSBC Holdings plc, London, 1995—; bd. dirs. HSBC Holdings plc, HSBC Investment Bank Holdings plc, HSBC Bank Malaysia Berbad, HSBC Argentina Holdings S.A., HSBC Bank USA, others. Office: HSBC Holdings plc, 10 Lower Thames St, London EC3R 6AE, England

FLINT, HARRY JAMES, microbiologist; b. London, Jan. 5, 1951; s. Harry Edgar Flint and Marion Winifred (Austin) Shaw; m. Janet Elizabeth Hines, July 15, 1978 (div. Apr. 1993); children: Kathryn Elisabeth, Harry Christopher; m. Irene Stewart Mands, July 19, 1993; 1 child, Rowan Marjory. BSc, Edinburgh (Scotland) U., 1972, PhD, 1977. Lectr. U. Nottingham, Eng., 1976-80, U. of W.I., Barbados, 1980-82; rsch. fellow Edinburgh U., 1982-85; sr. sci. officer Rowett Rsch. Inst., Aberdeen, Scotland, 1985-89, prin. sci. officer, 1989—, group leader microbial genetics, 1993—, div. head, 1998—; hon. sr. lectr. U. Aberdeen, 1992-2002. Contbg. author: (book) The Rumen Microbial Ecosystem, 2d edit., 1997, also 18 book chpts. on symposium procs.; contbr. articles and papers to sci. jours.; mem. editl. bd.: Applied and Environ. Microbiology, 1997-2000; assoc. editor Anaerobe, 2000—. Mem. Genetical Soc., Soc. for Gen. Microbiology. Avocations: hill walking, ornithology, sailing. Office: Rowett Rsch Inst, Greenburn Rd Bucksburn, AB21 9SB Aberdeen Scotland

FLINT, STEPHEN ERNEST, architect; b. Fairbury, Ill., May 2, 1957; s. Ernest Worth and Elizabeth Nellie Flint; m. Diana Lynne Cox, Aug. 30, 1980; children: Chadwick Stephen, Elizabeth Jordan. A. So. Ill. U., 1977; BArch, U. Ill., Chgo., 1984. Lic. arch., Ill. Draftsman Johns-Manville, Hodgkins, Ill., 1977-78, Perkins & Will, Chgo., 1978-84, Alan R. Yore Assocs., Arlington Heights, Ill., 1985-86; job capt. Jensen & Fore Archs., Oak Brook, Ill., 1986-88; prin. ARCON Assocs., Inc., Lombard, Ill., 1988—; tchr. jr. achievment Glenn Westlake Mid. Sch., 1998—. Vice-chmn. Lombard Planning Commn., 1987—; chmn. sites and markers com. Lombard Hist. Soc., 1997—. Mem. Lombard Area C. of C. & Industry (v.p. 1997—), Lombard Rotary. Republican. Methodist. Fax: 630-495-2178. Home: 812 S LaLonde Ave Lombard IL 60148 Office: ARCON Assocs Inc 420 Eisenhower Ln N Lombard IL 60148-5404

FLIPPEN, EDWARD L., lawyer; b. Richmond, Va., Dec. 2, 1939; s. Hannie Thomas Flippen; m. Pearcy light, Feb. 14, 1970; children: Elizabeth Hunter, Margaret Harlan. BS, Va. Commonwealth U., 1965; MBA, Coll. of William and Mary, 1967, JD, 1974. Bar: Va. 1974, N.C. 1981. Gen. atty. Va. State Corp. Commn., Richmond, 1975-78, assoc. gen. counsel, 1978-80, dep. gen. counsel, 1980; asst. gen. counsel Duke Power Co., Charlotte, N.C., 1980-81, assoc., 1981-83; ptnr. Mays & Valentine, LLP, Richmond, 1983-99, McGuireWoods, LLP, Richmond, 1999—; lectr., U. Va. Sch. Law, 1978-82; adj. law prof. Coll. of William and Mary, 1996—, Washington & Lee U., 1997—, Univ. Richmond, 2000—; vis. fellow U. London, 1998-99; chmn. Gov's. Blue Ribbon Commn. Higher Edn., 1998-2000. Author: Practical Networking: How to Give and Get Help with Jobs, 2000. bd. visitors Va. Commonwealth U., Richmond, 1994, rector, 2000—; adv. bd. Va. Ctr. on Aging, Richmond, 1994-98; trustee River Rd. United Meth. ch., Richmond, 1995-98; bd. MCV Hosps. Authority, 2000—. With U.S. Army, 1958-61. Mem. Va. State Bar (chmn. adminstrv. law sect., 1986-87), Soc. for Advanced Legal Studies (assoc. fellow). Republican. Avocations: writing, teaching, assisting others in job placements. Office: McGuireWoods LLP One James Ctr 901 E Cary St Richmond VA 23219-4057

FLISHER, ALAN JOHN, psychiatry educator, clinician, researcher; b. Cape Town, We. Cape, S. Africa, Apr. 16, 1957; s. William John and Lillian Jeanne (Elder) F.; m. Merunisa Mohamed. MS, U. Cape Town (S. Africa), 1981, MB, Ch.B., 1988, MMed, 1994, PhD, 1996. cert. clin. psychologist, med. practitioner, psychiatrist S. African Med. and Dental Coun. Med. officer Red Cross War Meml. Children's Hosp., Cape Town, S. Africa, 1990-91; registrar U. Cape Town, 1991-95; lectr., splst., clinician U. Cape Town and Red Cross War Meml. Children's Hosp., 1995—; postdoct. rsch. scientist Columbia U., N.Y.C., 1994-95; assoc. prof. U. Cape Town, 1998—; head psychiat. emergency svc. Crook Schuur Hosp., 1999—; rsch. scientist N.Y. State Psychiat. Inst., N.Y.C., 1994-96; vis. asst. prof. pub. health Columbia U., N.Y.C., 1996. Contbr. articles to profl. jours. Chairperson Orgn. Appropriate Social Svcs. in S. Africa, We. Cape, 1990-92. Post-Intern scholarship Med. Rsch. Coun., 1990, postdoct. overseas scholar, 1994-95; recipient Andries Blignaut award Best Mulit Authored Pub. S. African Med. Jour., 1993. Fellow Coll. Psychiatrists Coll. Medicine S. Africa; mem. Coll. Paediatricians Coll. Medicine S. Africa (diplomate), Soc. Psychiatrists S. Africa. Avocations: reading history, playing clarinet, jogging. Home: 1 Highfield Rd, 7780 Rosebank We Cape, South Africa Office: Groote Schuur Hosp, Dept Psychiatry, 7925 Observatory We Cape, South Africa

FLISS, ALBERT EDWARD, JR., molecular neuroscientist; b. Harrisburg, Pa., Nov. 8, 1959; s. Albert Edward and Irene (Pierlioni) F.; m. Makiko

Suzuki Fliss, Sept. 10, 1994; 1 child, Nicholas Fliss. BS, U. Ctrl. Fla., 1982; MS, Mount Sinai Sch. of Medicine, 1997, PhD, 1998. Rsch. assoc. USDA, Orlando, Fla., 1984-85; biol. scientist U. Fla., Gainesville, 1985-88, USDA, Gainesville, 1988-89; rsch. assoc. U. Fla., Gainesville, 1989, sr. biologist, 1989-92; sr. scientist BioNebraska, Inc., Lincoln, Nebr., 1992; rsch. assoc. Tex. A&M U., College Station, 1992—; rsch. scientist U. Md. Sch. of Medicine, Regeneron Pharm., Tarrytown, N.Y., 1993-95; CEO, pres. Designer Genes, Inc., Gainesville, 1990—. Contbr. articles to profl. jours. Recipient Superior Accomplishment award U. Fla., 1990. Mem. Lambda Chi Alpha, Omicron Delta Kappa. Democrat. Roman Catholic. Home: 6491 Lacelike Row Columbia MD 21045-4625

FLITNER, ANDREAS H., education educator; b. Jena, Thuringen, Germany, Sept. 28, 1922; s. Wilhelm and Elisabeth (Czapski) F.; m. Sonia Christ, Aug. 14, 1950; children: Elisabeth, Margarete, Cornelia, Christine, Michael, Ursula, Gabriele. Tchr. degree, U. Hamburg, 1950; MA, U. Basle, 1951, PhD, 1951; Dr. habil., U. Tubingen, 1955. Lectr. dept. German lang. U. Cambridge, Eng., 1950-51; asst., lectr. Leibniz-Kolleg, U. Tubingen, 1951-53; prof. edn. U. Erlangen, 1956-58, U. Tubingen, 1958-88; hon. prof. U. Jena, 1991—. Author: Konrad...Uber Erziehung und Nicht-Erziehung, 1985, 9th edit., 1998, Für das Leben oder für die Schule? Pädagog u polit Essays, 1987, Reform der Erziehung - Impulse des 20 Jahrhunderts, 1992, 4th rev. edit., 1999; editor: Wilhelm von Humboldt: Werke in fünf Banden, 5 vols., 1961-83; co-editor: Wege aus der Ausbildungskrise, 1999, Optik-Technik-Soziale Kültur: Siegfried Czapski, Weggefälerse und Nachfolger Ernst Abbes, 2000. Mem. Akademie fur Bildungsreform (chmn. 1984—), Akademie gemeinn. Wissenschaften Erfurt, Academia Europaea. Home: Im Rotbad 43, 72076 Tübingen Germany

FLOCH, FRANÇAIS EDOUARD, toxicologist; b. Petit-Couronne, Normandie, France, Dec. 27, 1943; s. Francais M. and Maria (Vidalich) F.; m. Roseline S. Reynard, July 17, 1965 (div. June 1995); children: Stephanie, Nicolas; m. Arielle M. Gard, Sept. 28, 1996; 1 child, Alice. Lic. in Agronomy, U. Lille, France, 1967, M Biology, 1968, M in Human Biology, 1971, diploma in Human Biology, 1972; PhD in Biology, Pasteur Inst., 1968. Cert. toxicologist. Asst. prof. INSEARM, Lille, 1967-70; rschr. faculty medicine U. Lille, 1970-73; confirmed rschr. S.U. Rhone Poulenc, Paris, 1973-78; head immunology lab. Rhone Poulenc, Paris, 1979-83, dir. immunology, 1984-87; dir. pharmacology Solvay, Lyon, France, 1988-93; expert toxicologist Rhodia, Lyon, 1994—; cons. inflamation Rhone Poulenc, Paris, 1981-87, cons. allergy, 1984-87; mem. aliment safety CSHPF, Hygiene Coun., Paris, 1994-97; mem. polluted scis. and emergencies Ministry Environ., Paris. Editor: Pharmacoloty of Immunoregulation, 1976; patentee in field. Mem. Parents/Sch., Paris, 1975-79; pers. del. Trade Union, Paris, 1978-82. Mem. French Soc. Immunology, European Soc. Toxicology, N.Y. Acad. Scis. Roman Catholic. Avocations: water painting, walking skying, gardening. Office: Rhodia CRL BP62, 85 Ave des Freres Perret, 69192 Saint Fons France

FLOCH-BAILLET, DANIELE LUCE, ophthalmologist; b. Brest, France, Jan. 9, 1948; d. Herve Alexandre and Lucie (Henry) Floch; m. Gilles Pierre Baillet, Dec. 6, 1980; 1 child, Victoire-Amelie. MD, Med. U. Brest, 1972. Cert. in ophthalmology, 1975. Med. cons. ophthalmology Brest Hosp., 1976-85; gen. practice ophthalmology Landivisiau, France, 1977—; researcher ophthalmic bacteriology, 1985—. Author: (with P. Francois) Nosological Outlines from Coats, 1975, Exsudation from Coats, 1976. Mem. French Ophthalmologist Soc., European Contact Lenses Soc. Ophthalmologists, Nat. Syndicat French Ophthalmology, Contact Lens Assn. Ophthalmologists, Assn. Ophthalmologic Improvement from East-Paris. Roman Catholic. Home: 11 Rue Creach Joly, 29600 Morlaix France Office: 7 Rue Georges Pompidou, 29400 Landivisiau France

FLODGREN, BOEL, university president, law educator; b. Örebro, Sweden, Nov. 17, 1942; d. Wilhelm T.L. and Maj (Fagerlin) Ohlsson; m. Per Flodgren, May 27, 1967; children: Tove, Erik, Johan. JD, Lund U., Sweden, 1978. Prof. law Lund U., 1987—, pres., 1992—. Office: Lund Univ, PO Box 117, SE-22100 Lund Sweden

FLOM, ROBERT MICHAEL, interior designer; b. Grand Forks, N.D., Oct. 27, 1952; s. John Nicholai and Irene Magdaline (Miller) F.; m. Holly Suzanne Schue, July 20, 1975 (div. June 1986); m. Margaret Elizabeth Moon, Oct. 15, 1988; children: Amy Michelle Moon, Jamie Bryant Moon. Student, Western Tech., 1970-71, U. N.D., 1980-83, LaSalle U., 1994-95, Century U., 1996—. Asst. food and beverage mgr. Holiday Inn/Topeka Inns, Denver, 1970-71; interior designer, fl. mgr. Crossroads Furniture, Grand Forks, 1972-85; store mgr. Greenbaums, Tacoma, 1986-88, interior designer, 1986—; tng. advisor Greenbaums, Bellevue, Wash., 1988—. Mem. Am. Soc. Interior Designers (allied mem.), Autism Soc. Tacoma-Pierce County (treas. 1991—). Avocations: reading, cycling, cross-country skiing, hiking, woodworking. Home: 6816 47th St W Tacoma WA 98466-4912 Office: Greenbaums 929 118th Ave SE Bellevue WA 98005-3889

FLOOD, A. L. (AL FLOOD), retired bank executive; b. Monkton, Ont., Can., 1935; married; 4 children. Grad. program for mgmt. devel., Harvard U. Various mgmt. positions corp. & credit ops. Can. Imperial Bank of Commerce, Toronto, 1951-74; area exec. U.S.A. and Latin Am. Can. Imperial Bank of Commerce, 1974-78, gen. mgr. U.S.A. and Latin Am., 1978-79, v.p. corp. banking, 1979-80, v.p. U.S. ops., 1980-83, sr. v.p. U.S. ops., 1983-84, head internat. ops., 1984, exec. v.p., 1984-86, pres., 1986-92, chmn., CEO, 1992-99, ret., 1999, also bd. dirs.; bd. dirs. Noranda Inc. Trustee Talisman Energy Inc.; hon. chmn. Bus. Coun. on Nat. Issues. Office: Can Imperial Bank Commerce, Commerce Court, Toronto, ON Canada M5L 1A2

FLOOD, DIANE LUCY, marketing communications specialist; b. Plainfield, N.J., June 13, 1937; d. William Edward and Lucy (Dycker) Flood. BA, Vassar Coll., 1959; postgrad., Fontainebleau Sch. Fine Arts, France, 1961. Advt. prodn. aide indsl. chem. divsn. Am. Cyanamid Co., Wayne, N.J., 1959-62, prodn. supr., 1962-64, creative coord. organic chems. divsn. advt., 1964-66, design art and copy mgr., 1966-70, advt. rep., 1970-72, advt. rep. paper, process chems. and resins, indsl. chem. divsn., 1972-77, advt. coord. water treating, mining, paper, oil recovery chems., 1977-83, mgr. mktg. comms. indsl. products div., 1983—, mgr. mktg. comms. Venture Chems. divsn., 1986-87, Chem. Products and Indsl. Products divsn., 1987-89, mgr. mktg. comms. Chem. Products Indsl. Products and Interna, 1989-90, mgr. mktg. comms. Chem. Group, 1990-93; mgr. Global Mktg. Comms. Cytec Industries Inc., West Paterson, N.J., 1993-99; retired Am. Cyanamid Co., Wayne, N.J., 1999; comms. cons. 1999—. Past dir., v.p., past pres. 103 Gedney St. Owners Co-op, 1985-92; mem. consistory First Reformed Ch., Nyack, N.Y. Mem. 1st Ref. Ch. Home: 103 Gedney St Apt 3C Nyack NY 10960-2227 Office: 103 Gedney St Lbby Office Nyack NY 10960-2238

FLOOD, GREGORY CHARLES, human resources management specialist; b. Yonkers, N.Y., Sept. 4, 1946; arrived in Italy, 1980; s. Harold Austin and Anne Marie (Wallace) F.; m. Catherine Virginia Predham, Dec. 9, 1967. BS, SUNY Albany, 1973. Personnel tech. Rensselaer County Civil Svc. Commn., 1974-77; from personnel adminstr. to assoc. program budget coord. N.Y. State Dept. Edn., Albany, 1977-80; establishments officer to chief pers. policy, planning, establishments svcs. Food & Agriculture Orgn. UN, Rome, 1980—; sec. FAO Fin. Com., 1998—. Pres. East Greenbush (N.Y.) Rep. Club, 1974; vol. firefighter East Greenbush Fire Dept., 1974-80. Served in U.S. Navy, 1966-70. Mem. Am. Soc. Pub. Adminstrn., Internat. Personnel Mgmt. Assn., Am. Club Rome (treas. 1995-96, pres. 1996-98). Roman Catholic. Avocations: reading, computer programming, badminton, stage craft. Home: Via dei Pescatori 983/E/1, 00125 Rome Italy Office: Food and Agriculture Orgn UN, Via delle Terme di Caracalla, 00100 Rome Italy

FLOOD, HENRY, non-profit organization executive; b. Charleston, S.C., Nov. 26, 1949; s. Joseph Harrison Jr. and Patricia (Johnson) F.; m. Nilde Martinez, Oct. 21, 1990. Student, Charleston So. U., 1968-70, Coll. of Charleston, 1970-74; MA in Legal Studies, Antioch U., 1985. Admitted to St. Regis Mohawk Bar. Dir. rsch. Edn1. Svcs. Inst., Arlington, Va., 1985; cons. Constn. Bicentennial Commn., Washington, 1986-88; dir. R & D, Falmouth Inst., 1988-92; program specialist Adminstrn. for Native Ams., Washington, 1992-93; devel. specialist, spl. counsel St. Regis Mohawk Tribe, Hogansburg, N.Y., 1993-97; pres. Self-Determination Inst., Aventura, Fla., 1993—; v.p. DKW Internat., Miami, Fla., 1996—; prin. drafter Mohawk constn. and laws, 1993-97. Author: Writing and Revising Constitutions in Indian Country, 1998; contbg. editor Value Engrng. Digest, 1981-88. Pres. Com. To Incorporate Folly Beach, S.C., 1973. Recipient cmty. leadership award City of Folly Beach, 1973, cert. of merit Del. Assn. for Pub. Adminstrn., 1978. Mem. St. Regis Mohawk Bar Assn., Toastmasters (area 3 gov., dist. 47). Episcopalian. Avocations: reading, writing, music, public speaking. Office: 20533 Biscayne Blvd Ste 224 Aventura FL 33180-1529

FLOOD, JOE EMERSON, secondary education educator; b. Miles, Tex., Aug. 6, 1933; s. O.Z. and Cleo Bell (Tidwell) F.; m. Maria Peppas, Dec. 20, 1940; 1 child, Anastasia. BA, Howard Payne Coll., Brownwood, Tex., 1959; MEd, Howard Payne Coll., 1965; MS in Internat. Rels., Troy (Ala.) State U., 1992; adminstr.'s cert., U. Tex., Brownsville, 1995. Tchr. Flour Bluff ISD, Corpus Christi, Tex., 1959-64; tchr. Dept. Def. Dependents Schs., Kubasaki, Japan, 1965-67, Praia, Portugal, 1967-68, Subic Bay, The Philippines, 1968-69, Ramstein, Germany, 1969-94; tchr. Brownsville (Tex.) ISD, 1994—; asst. instr. Howard Payne Coll., Brownwood, 1964-65; chairperson social scis. dept. Ramstein Jr. H.S., 1973-74, dir. talented and gifted history program, 1985-94; dir. Russian Tours, Ramstein, 1986-93; chairperson history dept. Alternative Edn. Ctr., Brownsville, 1994-98; asst. instr. English Mich. State program Univ. Ryukyus, Okinawa, Japan, 1966. Parish coun. pres. St. Nicholas Ea. Orthodox Ch., Kapaun AS, Germany, 1989-90; charter mem. Ramstein Coun. Internat. Rels. Sgt. U.S. Army, 1953-56. Recipient Grammata award Orthodox Ch. Am., 1989. Mem. Overseas Fedn. Tchrs. (mem.-at-large, exec. com.), Ramstein Fedn. Tchrs. (pres. 1975). Democrat. Avocations: Russian history, travel, gardening, cooking. Home: 510 Alokee Ct Lake Mary FL 32746-2218

FLOOD, PATRICK CHRISTOPHER, business educator, researcher, corporate speaker; b. Drogheda, Leinster, Ireland, Apr. 22, 1961; s. Bartholomew and Catherine (Ellis) F.; m. Patricia Mary Quinn; children: Christopher, Patrick Ellis. B.Comm., U. Coll. Dublin, 1981, M.B.S., 1982; PhD, London Sch. Econs., 1988. Brit. coun. scholar London Sch. Econs., 1984-86; lectr., sr. lectr. U. Limerick, 1986-93, assoc. prof. human resource mgmt., 1997—, prof. orgnl. behavior, head rsch. program Irish Mgmt. Inst., 1994—; fellow in orgnl. behavior London Sch. Bus., 1994—; mem. editl. bd. Bus. Strategy Rev., 1996—. Joint editor Jour. Irish Bus. and Adminstrv. Rsch., 1991—; co-author: Personnel Management in Ireland, 1990, Continuity and Change in Employee Relations in Ireland, 1994, Managing Without Traditional Methods, 1996, The European Union and the Employment Relationship, 1997, Managing Strategy Implementation, 2000, Attracting and Retaining Knowledge Workers, 2000, Effective Top Management Teams, 2000. Fulbright scholar, U. Md., 1993, Human Capital and Mobility scholar European Commn., London Bus. Sch., 1994-96; recipient Award for Excellence in Rsch. U. Limerick, 1998, Tchg. Excellence award, 1998. Mem. Internat. Assn. for Indsl. Rels., Strategic Mgmt. Soc., Irish Assn. for Indsl. Rels., Brit. U. Indsl. Rels. Assn., Acad. Mgmt., Friends of LSE in Ireland (chair). Roman Catholic. Avocations: walking, oil painting, swimming, travel, gardening. Office: University of Limerick, Plassey Park, Limerick Ireland

FLORATOS, EMMANUEL, physicist; b. Athens, Greece, Nov. 26, 1947; s. Gerasimos and Zoe (Tambiskou) F.; m. Harikleia Tzortzi, Dec. 28, 1967; children: Maria, Zoe. BSc in Math., U. Athens, 1969, PhD in Theoretical Physics, 1973. Fellow European Coun. Nuclear Rsch., Geneva, 1976-78; rsch. assoc. Nat. Coun. Scientific Rsch., Paris, 1978-80, Ecole Normale Superieur, Paris, 1980-81; assoc. scientist U. Berne (Switzerland) Inst. Theoretical Physics, 1981-83; prof. physics U. Crete, Iraklion, 1983-2000; dir. Inst. Nuclear Physics, Athens, 1995—, U. Athens, 2000—; nat. rep. Cern Coun., 1994—;. Contbr. articles to profl. jours. Christian Orthodox. Avocations: piano, athletics. Home: Roumelis 26C, 15341 Aghia Paraskovi Greece Office: Inst Nuclear Physics NRC, Phys Sci Dept, 15310 Aghia Paraskevi Greece

FLORATOS, EVANGELOS JACOB, coffee company executive; b. July 22, 1936; s. Jacob Evangelos and Maria George (Sourmelis) F.; m. Stavroula Iliopoulos, July 22, 1972; 1 child, Maria. Student pub. schs. Chmn. ABEEA, SA, coffee mgrs., Patras, 1975—; founder, pres. Patras Bus. & Innovation Ctr., 1991—, Ctr. for Support of Small & Medium Enterprises, Patras, 1993—; pres. Co. for Mgmt. of Cmty. Programs of Western Greece, Peloponnese and Ionian Islands, 1997—; pres., founder's mem. Achaia Coop. Bank, 1994—; founder's mem. Union of Coop. Banks in Greece, 1995, pres., 1996—; pres., founder's mem. Patras Circuit SA, 1995—. Mayor Patras, 1999—. With Greek Air Force, 1957. Mem. Panhellenic Assn. Coffee Traders (gen. sec.), Patras C. of C. (cons.), Lions. (v.p. Pitras), Achaia C. of C. (pres. 1988-99, 1st v.p.). Green Orthodox.

FLORE, PATRICE, physiologist; b. Tain l'Hermitage, France, Oct. 26, 1964; d. Luigi and Linda (Dinino) F.; m. Magali Boutinaud; 1 child, Sacha. Student, Joseph Fourier U., Grenoble, France, 1982-90; PhD, Joseph Fourier U., 1990. Home: 6 Rue Commandantlenoir, 38130 Echirolles France Office: Medical Air, 50 Rue de L'Industrie, 38420 Domene France

FLOREA, VIOREL GRIGORE, cardiologist, researcher, educator; b. Straseni, Moldova, Jan. 8, 1964; s. Grigore Hristofor and Vera Dmitry (Sturza) F.; m. Natalia Dmitry Saina, Oct. 26, 1985; children: Alexander, Victor. Grad., Kishinev State Med. Inst., 1988; MD, Cardiology Rsch. Ctr., Moscow, 1990, PhD, 1992, DSc, 1997. Intern Cardiology Rsch. Ctr., Moscow, 1988-90, fellow, 1990-93; asst. prof. Med. U. of Moldova, Kishinev, 1993-98, assoc. prof., 1998—; rsch. fellow Nat. Heart and Lung Inst., London, 1998-2000; postdoctoral assoc. U. Minn., Mpls., 2000—. Contbr. articles to profl. jours. Mem. Working Group on Heart Failure, Cardiac Rehab. and Exercise Physiology, European Soc. Cardiology (rsch. fellow 1997, European cardiologist 2000), N.Y. Acad. Scis. Avocations: sports, reading, tourism. E-mail: flore022@tc.umn.edu. Home: G Asachi St 62 Apt 43, Chisinau 2028, Moldova Office: VA Med Ctr Cardiology 111-C One Veterans Dr Minneapolis MN 55417

FLORENCE, KENNETH JAMES, lawyer; b. Hanford, Calif., July 31, 1943; s. Ivy Owen and louella (Dobson) F.; m. Verena Magdalena Demuth, Dec. 10, 1967. BA, Whittier Coll., 1965; JD, Hastings Coll. Law U. Calif., San Francisco, 1974. Bar: Calif. 1974, U.S. Dist. Ct. (ctrl. dist.) Calif. 1974, U.S. Dist. Ct. (ea. and so. dists.) Calif. 1976, U.S. Dist. Ct. (no. dist.) Calif. 1980, U.S. Ct. Appeals (9th cir.) 1975, U.S. Supreme Ct. 1984. Dist. mgr. Pacific T&T, Calif., 1969-71; assoc. Parker, Milliken, et al, L.A., 1974-78; ptnr. Dern, Mason, et al, 1978-84, Swerdlow Florence Sanchez & Rathbun A Law Corp., Beverly Hills, 1984—; pres. Westside Legal Services, Inc., Santa Monica, Calif., 1982-83. Served to lt. USNR, 1966-69, Vietnam. Col. J.G. Boswell scholar, 1961. Mem. ABA (co-chmn. state labor law com. 1988-91). Democrat. Office: Swerdlow Florence Sanchez & Rathbun 9401 Wilshire Blvd Ste 828 Beverly Hills CA 90212-2921

FLORENZ, KARL-HEINZ, member of European parliament; b. Neukirchen-Vluyn, Belgium, Oct. 22, 1947. Mem. European Parliament, Brussels, 1999—; mem. Group of the European People's Party (Christian Democrats) and European Democrats; mem. com. on the environ., pub. health and consumer policy; substitute mem. com. on budgets; mem. delegation for rels. with the countries of South Asia and the South Asia Assn. for Regional Cooperation (SAARC). Office: Europaisches Parlament, Rue Wiertz ASP 10#162, B-1047 Bruxelles Belgium*

FLORENZANO, FRANCESCO, academic administrator, psychologist; b. Albanella, SA, Italy, July 31, 1957; s. Giuseppe and Carlotta (Gatto) F. Degree in Psychology, U. Rome, 1981. Rschr. I.S.S., Rome, 1984; mem. dept. stats. LABOS, Rome, 1987; rschr. E. Coun., Italy, 1990-91; pres. Popular U. Rome, 1996—, Italian Fedn. Continuing Edn., 1998; prof. Med. Sch., Rome, 1986-88; relator Sec. de Estado da Saude, São Paulo, Brazil, 1988, USL Terni, Italy, 1996; chmn. IRCSS Fatebrne Fratelli, Rome, 1989-91. Contbr. articles to profl. jours. Office: Popular Univ Rome, via Del Corso 101, 00186 Rome Lazio, Italy

FLORES, PHILIP JOSEPH, bank executive; b. San Francisco, Nov. 14, 1949; s. Edward Philip and Orlean Marie F.; BS, UCLA, 1971; MBA with honors, U. So. Calif., 1973. Exec. v.p. Guam Savs. & Loan Assn., Agana, Guam, 1973-80, pres., 1980-99, also chmn. bd.; pres., CEO, chmn. BankPacific, 1999—; pres., chmn. bd. Marianas Fin. Corp., Pacific Basin Investment Corp., Casa De Flores Inc., Guahan Travel, Inc.; chmn., pres., chief exec. officer Fin. Properties Investment Corp., Our Lady of Peace Meml. Plans, Inc., Guam Dry Cleaners, Inc., Fabriclean Guam Ltd., Dustax Guam Ltd.; bd. dirs. Guam Port Authority; pres., chmn. bd. Troser Art, Inc., Connoisseurs Art, Inc. Named Guam Bus. Exec. of Yr., 1985. Mem. Guam Savs. and Loan Commn.; chmn. Campaign to Elect Ben Blaz to U.S. Congress, 1982, 84, 86; mem. pvt. industry council Guam-White House Exec. Com., 1982; mem. nat. steering com. Fund for Am.'s Future, 1986—; mem. Rep. Nat. Com.; del. Rep. Nat. Com., 1988; chmn. Rep. Party of Guam, 1989—; past pres., chmn. Our Lady of Peace Meml. Gardens; pres. Guahan Waste Control. Mem. Guam C. of C. (chmn. 1986), Jaycees. Roman Catholic. Clubs: Rotary (pres.). Home: 123 Ocean View Dr Agana GU 96922-1503 Office: 151 Aspinall Ave Agana GU 96910-5156

FLORESCU, RADU RADU, East European history educator; b. Bucharest, Romania, Oct. 23, 1925; s. Radu Alexander and Vera Marie Florescu; m. Nicole Elizabeth Michel, Dec. 2, 1951; children: Nicholas, John, Radu, Alexandra. BA, Oxford (Eng.) U., 1951, MA, 1951, BLitt, 1951; PhD, Ind. U., 1962. Instr. Boston Coll., Chestnut Hill, Mass., 1953-56, asst. prof., 1956-62, assoc. prof., 1962-89, prof., 1989-97, prof. emeritus, 1997—; dir. East European Rsch. Ctr., Boston, 1968—; cons. US Embassy, Bucharest, 1969, Senator Edward Kennedy, Boston, 1989, U.S. Dept. State, Washington, 1953—; mem. consul of Romania, Boston, 1996. Co-author: In Search of Dracula, 1975, Dracula Prince of Many Faces, 1989, In Search of Dracula, 1994 (award Dracula Soc. 1997); author: Frankenstein, 1975, The Struggle Against Russia in Romania, 1989, Essays on Romanian History, 1999. Hon. sec. Oxford Soc., New Eng., 1968-88. Recipient Gladstone Meml. prize, 1948; Fulbright fellow, 1967, 68; sr. fellow St. Antony Coll., 1973-74. Fellow Romanian Acad. Soc. (sr.); mem. Soc. Romanian Studies (pres., bd. dirs. 1989). Democrat. Avocations: bicycling, tennis, table tennis, skiing. Home: James Landing 48 Ladds Way Scituate MA 02066-1901 Office: Consulate of Romania Harbor Tower I 85 East India Rowe 4H Boston MA 02110

FLORES FACUSSE, CARLOS ROBERTO, country president, publisher; b. Tegucigalpa, M.D.C., Honduras, Mar. 1, 1950; m. Mary Carol Flake; children: Mary Elizabeth, Carlos David. BS in Indsl. Engring., La. State U., MS in Internat. Econs. and Fin., PhD (hon.). Past prof. Sch. Bus. Adminstrn. Nat. U. Honduras, C.Am. Sch. Banking; co-owner, mgr. Periódicos y Revistas, S.A., also exec. bd. dirs.; pub. Diario La Tribuna; co-owner, mgr. LITHOPRESS Indsl.; past congressman to Nat. Assembly Govt. of Honduras, past congressman dept. Francisco Morazá, past pres. Liberal Coun., past rep. to Liberal Convention, past min. presidency, pres. of congress, 1995-98, pres., 1998—; bd. dirs. Honduran Inst. Soc. Security, Ctrl. Bank Honduras, Nat. Inst. Profl. Tng. Author: Working Together Towards the Future of Honduras. Past presdl. candidate Liberal Party; past pres. exec. coun. Liberal Party Honduras; past gen. coord. Movimiento Liberal Florista; fin. sec. Nat. Directorate Movimiento Liberal Rodista. rep. Mem. Nat. Assn. Industries, Indsl Engrs. Assn. Honduras, Honduran Coun. Pvt. Sector, Honduran Inst. Interam. Culture., Rotary. Office: Casa Presdl Centro Office Pres. Civico Gubernamental, Tegucigalpa DC, Honduras

FLOREY, ANDRÉ BERNARD, chemical laboratory administrator, consultant; b. Sierre, Valais, Switzerland, Nov. 21, 1948; s. Albert and Rosalie (Pitteloud) F.; m. Angèle Bruchez, Aug. 24, 1974; children: Nathalie, Guillaume. Diploma in Engring., Ecole Polytech. Fed. Lausanne, Switzerland, 1973, DSc in Chemistry, 1979. Lab. chief Alusuisse, Sierre, Switzerland, 1976-90, lubricants specialist, 1991—. Pres. Gen. Coun., Sierre, 1990-96. Mem. Jeune Chambre Internat. Mem. Christian Democracy. Roman Catholic. Home: Sous-Géronde 93, CH-3960 Sierre Valais, Switzerland

FLOREY, JERRY JAY, aerospace and management consultant; b. Geddes, S.D., Apr. 3, 1932; s. Henry Clifford and Lizzie M. Florey; m. Mary E. Richey, Sept. 17, 1955; children: Glenn David, Janet Renee. BSChemE, Oreg. State U., 1955. Cert. in electronics. From research engr. to engrng. supr. Rockwell Internat., Canoga Park, Calif., 1955-66; sr. project engr. Rockwell Internat., Downey, Calif., 1966-67; successively engrng. mgr., engrng. dir., chief engr. space sys. electronics divsn. Rockwell Internat., Seal Beach, Calif., 1967-85, dir. advanced systems, rsch. and tech., 1985-89; propulsion sys. specialist, sr. staff mgr. strategic planning and market analysis McDonnell Douglas Space Co., Huntington Beach, Calif., 1989-95; cons. McDonnell Douglas, 1995-96; mgmt. cons., 1996—; participant on several industry workshop panels which advised USAF regarding its mil. space systems tech. planning activities. Mem. editl. bd. Aerospace Am. Scoutmaster Boy Scouts Am., Costa Mesa, Calif., 1970; mem. Republican Presdl. Task Force; del. at large Rep. Platform planning com. Recipient Astronaut Person Achievement award NASA, 1969, NASA Cert. Appreciation Marshall Space Flight Ctr., Huntsville, Ala., 1972, Skylab Achievement award NASA, 1973, AIAA and USAF Recognition of Svc. certs. AFSTC, 1985, Apollo Achievement award NASA, Washington, 1969. Fellow AIAA (assoc., bd. dirs., nat. space and missile systems tech. activities com., fin. and internat. membership coms.); mem. Nat. Mgmt. Assn., Nat. Mktg. Soc. Am., U.S. Space Found. Home: 2085 Goldeneye Pl Costa Mesa CA 92626-4770

FLOREZ, JUAN BAUTISTA, physics educator; b. Armenia, Colombia, Oct. 12, 1954; s. Gonzalo and Isabel (Moreno) F.; m. Maria del Socorro Galvis, Feb. 12, 1981; 1 child, Andrea Carolina. Grad. in Physics, U. Quindio, Armenia, 1979; MSc in Physics, U. Antioquia, Medellin, Colombia, 1985; PhD in Physics, Cinvestav, Mexico City, 1993. Chief dept. physics U. Nariño, Pasto, Colombia, 1994—; cons., researcher U. Nariño, Pasto, 1987, also bd. dirs. Contbr. articles to profl. jours. Mem. Colombian Phys. Soc. Avocations: music, dancing, reading. Office: U Nariño, Ciudad Univ.-Torobajo, San Juan de Pasto 1175, Colombia

FLORI, ANNA MARIE DIBLASI, nurse anesthetist, educational administrator; b. Amsterdam, N.Y., Oct. 29, 1940; d. Tony and Maria (Macario) DiBlasi; children: Tammy, Tina, Toni; m. Gilberto Flori, May 24, 1986. Grad., Albany Med. Ctr. Sch. Nursing, 1962, Fairfax Hosp. Sch. Nurse Anesthetists, Va., 1972; BS in Anesthesia, George Washington U., 1979; M. in Bus. and Pub. Adminstrn., Southeastern U., Washington, 1982; PhD, Columbia Pacific U., 1983. Cert. registered nurse anesthetist. Staff nurse West Seattle Gen. Hosp., 1962-64; office nurse Filmore Buckner, M.D., Seattle, 1964-66; staff nurse anesthetist Fairfax Hosp., 1972-73; staff nurse anesthetist Potomac Hosp., Woodbridge, Va., 1973, chief nurse anesthetist, 1973—; dir. Potomac Hosp. Sch. for Nurse Anesthetists and Sch. for Nurse Anesthesia; faculty mem. Columbia Pacific U., 1973-90; chief nurse anesthetist No. Va. Anesthesia Assn., 1988—; guest lectr. No. Va. Community Coll., Inservice Potomac Hosp., George Washington U.; coord. Free Clinic Prince William County, Woodbridge, Va. Contbr. books on anesthesia. Mem. Am. Assn. Nurse Anesthetists, Va. Nurse Anesthesia Assn., Nat. Italian Am. Found. Home: 12954 Pintail Rd Woodbridge VA 22192-3831

FLORI, JEAN-BAPTISTE, judge. Pres. Tribunal Superieur d'Appel Mayotte. Office: BP 106, Tribunal Superieur d'Appel, 97600 Mamoudzou Mayotte*

FLORIAN, MARIANNA BOLOGNESI, civic leader; b. Chgo.; d. Giulio and Rose (Garibaldi) Bolognesi; BA cum laude, Barat Coll., 1940; postgrad. Moser Bus. Sch., 1941-42; m. Paul A. Florian III, June 4, 1949; children: Paul, Marina, Peter, Mark. Asst. credit mgr. Stella Cheese Co., Chgo., 1942-45; With ARC ETO Clubmobile Unit, 1945-47; mgr. Passavant Hosp. Gift Shop, 1947-49; pres., Jr. League Chgo., Inc., 1957-59; pres. woman's bd. Passavant Hosp., 1966-68; bd. dirs. Northwestern Meml. Hosp., 1974-81, mem. exec. com., 1974-79; pres. Women's Assn., Chgo. Symphony Orch., 1974-77, founder WFMT/CSO Radiothon, 1976; chmn. Guild Chgo. Hist. Soc., 1981-84, trustee Chgo. Hist. Soc., 1981-84; life trustee Orchestral Assn., v.p. 1978-82, vice chmn. 1982-86, mem. exec. com. 1978-87; mem. women's bd. U. Chgo.; mem. vis. com. dept. music U. Chgo., 1980-90; pres. bd. dirs. Antiquarian Soc. of Art Inst., 1989-91. Recipient Citizen Fellowship, Inst. Medicine Chgo., 1975, Presdl. Commendation for leadership and svc. Barat Coll., 1990. Clubs: Friday (pres. 1972-74), Contemporary; Winnetka Garden.

FLORIAN, VICTOR, psychologist, researcher, educator; b. Bucharest, Romania, May 17, 1945; arrived in Israel, 1959; s. Ahron and Ema Flori-

an. BA, Hebrew U., Haifa, Israel, 1969; MA, Bar-Ilan U., Raman Gan, Israel, 1972, PhD, 1979. Instr. Bar-Ilan U., 1971-79, sr. lectr., 1983-87, assoc. prof., 1987-92, prof., 1992—; lectr. Haifa U., 1980-83, sr. lectr., 1983-87; cons. Rehab. Svcs., Israel Def. Ministry, Haifa, 1974-80; rehab. cons., supr. United Israeli Kibutz Fedn., Ramat-Gan, 1980-91; rehab. psychologist Israel Min. Labor, Tel Aviv, 1971-76; vis. scientist, lectr. CUNY, summer 1987; vis. scholar U. Minn., summer 1994; chair Peleg-Bilig Ctr. Study of Family Well-Being Bar Ilan Univ., Israel, 1998—. Contbr. numerous articles to profl. jours. Fulbright fellow, 1982-83; USIA grantee, 1994. Office: Bar-Ilan U, Dept Psychology, 52900 Ramat Gan Israel

FLORIDA, RICHARD LOUIS, economics educator; b. Newark, Nov. 26, 1957; s. Louis and Eleanor F. BA, Rutgers Coll., 1979; MPh, Columbia U., 1984, PhD, 1986. Prof. Ohio State U., Columbus, 1984-87; H. John Heinz III prof. regional econ. devel. Carnegie Mellon U. Sch. Pub. Policy and Mgmt., Pitts., 1987—; adj. scholar Am. Enterprise Inst., Washington; vis. prof. MIT, John F. Kennedy Sch. Govt. Harvard U.; adv. White House Office of Sci. and Tech.Policy, U.S. Dept. Commerce, U.S. Congress, state and local govts., Govt. of Can., EU, Govt. of Japan, multinat. corps. Author: Beyond Mass Production, 1993, The Breakthrough Illusion, 1990, Industrializing Knowledge: University-Industry Linkages in Japan and the United States, 1999; contbr. 75 articles to profl. jours., newspapers including The N.Y. Times, The Wall St. Jour., U.S. News and World Report; commentator on PBS documentaries about U.S. economy, global competitiveness, future of jobs. Active Cooun. Gt. Lakes Govs.; bd. dirs. TeamPa., Pa.'s 21st Century Environ. Commn. Office: Carnegie Mellon U Heinz Sch 5000 Forbes Ave Pittsburgh PA 15213-3890

FLORIN-CHRISTENSEN, ALEJO, physician; b. Buenos Aires, Jan. 30, 1946; p. Vladimiro Florin and Nora Christensen. MD, U. Buenos Aires, 1968. Consejo de Certificación de Profesionales Médicos, Buenos Aires. Resident in internal medicine CEMIC, Buenos Aires, 1969-72, chief resident in internal medicine, 1972-73, attending physician, 1976—, staff mem. dept. medicine endocrinology, 1976—, head sect. endocrinology, 1980—; asst. clinician Nuffield Dept. Clin. Biochemistry, The Middlesex Hosp., U. London, 1973-75; vis. rsch. worker Middlesex Hosp., London, 1973-75, U. Oxford, Eng., 1974, NYU Med. Sch., 1977-78. Contbr. articles to profl. jours. Recipient A. Parodi prize CONICET, Buenos Aires, 1973; Wellcome fellow London, 1973, J.S. Guggenheim fellow, N.Y., 1978. Fellow Sociedad Argentina de Investigación Clínica; mem. Soc. Nuclear Medicine, The Endocrine Soc. Avocations: horse riding, swimming, polo, rowing. Office: CEMIC, Bustamante 2560, 1425 Buenos Aires Argentina

FLORIS, FRANS, geoscientist; b. Haarlem, The Netherlands, Apr. 12, 1965; s. Lou and Tinie (De Reuver) F.; m. Diana Verbeem,Dec. 1, 1989; children: Zefanja, Rebecca, Sarah. MS, Delft U. Technology, 1987, PhD, 1991. Rschr. NITG-TNO, Delft, 1991-99, head of sect., 1999—; conf. com. mem. EAGE, Houten, The Netherlands, 1999; keynote spkr. Statoil Rsch. Summit, Trondheim, 1999; invited lectr. U. Utrecht, 1999. Author: (book) Two-Phase Flow in Porous Media, 1991; contbr. articles to profl. jours. Head usher, Living Water Ch., Delft, 1992—. Avocations: soccer, ice-skating. Home: Churchilllaan 21, 2625 GS Delft/Zuid-Holland The Netherlands Office: Netherlands Inst App GeoSci, PO Box 6012, 2600 JA Delft/Zuid-Holland The Netherlands

FLORKOWSKI, WOJCIECH JAN, economics educator; b. Leszno, Poland, Oct. 4, 1954; came to the U.S., 1981; s. Henryk and Irena J. Florkowski; m. Malgorzata Florkowska, June 23, 1979. Diploma, Akad. Economiczna, Poznan, Poland, 1978; MS, U. Ill., 1983, PhD, 1986. Trainee economist Karolew (Poland) State Farm, 1978; economist Stadnina Koni, Racot, Poland, 1978-80; export advisor Regional Bd. Agr. Coops., Leszno, 1980-81; grad. rsch. asst. U. Ill., Urban-Champaign, 1981-86; assoc. prof. U. Ga., Griffin, 1986—; mem. promotion and edn. com. Ga. Agrl. Commodity Com. for Pecans, 1995—; cons. supplemental nutrition Ministry Agr. and Food Economy, Warsaw, Poland, 1996; presenter produce quality workshop Wincenty Witos Found., Lublin, Poland, 1997; presenter farm mgrs. from Ukraine workshop Cochran Fellowship Program, Griffin, Ga., 1998. Contbr. chpts. to books and articles to profl. jours. Co-founder, v.p. Assn. Agrl. Economists and Agribusiness, Poland, 1993-95. Recipient Recognition award Ga. Pecan Growers Assn., Inc., 1996, 1st place poster competition So. Agrl. Econ. Assn., Greensboro, N.C., 1996, Best Ext. Publ. award Am. Assn. Hort. Sci., 1997, Commemorative medal Rector Poznan Agrl. U., 1999. Mem. Am. Agrl. Econ. Assn., Am. Soc. Hort. Sci. (so. region), European Assn. Agrl. Economists, So. Agrl. Econ. Assn., Western Agrl. Econ. Assn., Food Distbn. Rsch. Soc. E-mail: wflorko@gaes.griffin.peachnet.edu. Office: Univ Ga Agr and Applied Econs 1109 Experiment St Griffin GA 30223-1731

FLORY, MARGARET MARTHA, retired religious organization administrator; b. Wauseon, Ohio, May 13, 1914; d. Arthur Henry and Laura Grace (Gorsuch) F. BA, Ohio U., 1936, MA, 1938; postgrad., Union Theol. Seminary, 1940-43; LLD, Maryville Coll., 1988. Teaching fellow Ohio U., Athens, 1936-38, dir. Westminster Found., 1940-44; tchr. Bainbridge (Ohio) High Sch., 1938-39; mem. drama and speech faculty Ala. State Coll., Montevallo, 1939-40; Eastern area sec. Presbyn. Ch. Nat. Hdqrs., N.Y.C., 1944-51, staff student world rels., 1951-68, staff new dimension in mission, 1969-73; staff ecumenical sharing program dir. Presbyn. Ch. U.S.A., 1973-80; short-term tchr. missions and ecumenical rels. San Francisco Theol. Sem., 1979-80, min. in residence Pacific Sch. Religion, Berkeley, Calif., 1981; mem. Stony Point (N.Y.) ctr. program staff Presbyn. Ch. U.S.A., 1981-87; ret., 1987. Author: Moments in Time, 1995, From Past to Future: Experiments in Global Bridging, 1997, Dear House, 2000; contbr. articles to profl. jours. Active Pres. Kennedy's Women's Com. on Civil Rights, 1963; trustee Maryville (Tenn.) Coll., 1963-78; pres. bd. trustees World Student Christian Fedn., N.Y.C., 1968-90; coun. ch. rels. Warren Wilson Coll., N.C., 1993—. Named Outstanding Alumnae Ohio U.; recipient Human Rights award Korean Christian Scholars, 1985, Woman of Faith award Presbyn. Women, 1987, Cert. of Appreciation Silliman U., 1981; conf. hall named in her honor John Knox Internat. Studies Ctr., Geneva, 1993. Mem. AAUW (exec. bd.), Assn. for Women's Edn. in Asia (pres. 1973-85), Ch. Relationships with Eastern Europe, Ch. Women United, Phi Beta Kappa. Avocations: reading, theater, walking, gardening, floral decoration. Home and Office: 276 College Walk Ln Brevard NC 28712-3161

FLOSSE, GASTON, senator, French Polynesian federal official; b. Rikitéa, Mangaréva, Gambier Islands, June 24, 1931; m. Marie-Jeanne; children: Vera, Joan, Reginald, Jacqueline, Hinérava, Christina, Cora. Mayor City of Pirae, Society Islands, 1965-2000; govt. advisor, 1965-67; mem. Assemblée Territoriale de Polynésie, 1976-77; dep. French Polynisia, 1978-82, 86, 93; v.p. Govt. Coun. of Polynesia, 1982-84; mem. European Parliament, 1984-86; pres. Territorial Govt. of French Polynesia, 1984-87, 91—; sec. state to min. Ministry of Overseas Ters., 1986-88; senator, 1998—; mem. law. commn. French Senate. Office: Office of the President, BP 2551, Papeete French Polynesia

FLØTTRE, NILS HENRIK, secondary education educator; b. Tønsberg, Norway, Mar. 31, 1941. MSc in Phys. Chemistry, U. Oslo, 1969. Lectr. Manglerud Upper Secondary Sch., Oslo, 1966-70, Oppegård Upper Secondary Sch., 1970-79, Nøtterøy Upper Secondary Sch., Borgheim, Norway, 1979—; mem. Nat. Evaluation Bd. Chemistry, Physics, 1980-85, 91-94; educator del. 1st Internat. Space Camp, Huntsville, Ala., 1990. Co-author: Space Matter Time, 1979, Facts in Physics and Chemistry, 1983; author: Natural Science, 1994, 2d edit., 1997, Orbital Motion, 1993, Man in Space, 1993, Rockets, 1993, Satellites and Applications, 1995, Chemistry 2KJ, 1997, Chemistry 3KJ, 1998. Recipient award for outstanding tchg. in physics Norwegian Phys. Soc., 1999. Mem. Norwegian Non-Fiction Writers and Translators Assn. Home: Langivkveien 46, N-3145 Tjøme Norway

FLOWER, WALTER CHEW, III, investment counselor; b. New Orleans, Mar. 3, 1939; s. Walter Chew II and Anne Elisa (Lusk) F.; m. Ella Smith Montgomery, Dec. 21, 1966; children: Anne Stuart, Lindsey Montgomery. BA in Econs., Tulane U., 1960; MBA in Fin., Harvard U., 1964. Cons. AID, State Dept., 1964-65; fin. analyst Delta Capital Corp., New Orleans, 1965-66; v.p., mng. partner Loomis Sayles & Co. Inc., New Orleans, 1967-78; pres. Walter C. Flower & Co., Investment Counsel, New Orleans, 1978—; dir. Starmount Cos.; vice chair Tulane Med. Ctr.; bd. dirs. Longue Vue Found., 1983—; dir GPOA Found., 1985—; vestryman, mem. parish council Trinity Ch., 1978—; dir., fin. adv. Jr. League New Orleans, 1978-82; fin. adv. Hermann Grima Hist. House, 1978—, Beauregard House, 1979—, Metairie Park Country Day Sch., 1991—, New Orleans Mus. Art, 1998—. Lt. USNR, 1960-62. Mem. Boston Club, La. Club., Pickwick Club, New Orleans Lawn Tennis Club, So. Yacht Club (New Orleans), Fishers Island Yacht Club, Stratford Club, Lakeshore Club, Wyvern Club, Confrerie Des Chevaliers Du Tastevin, Phi Beta Kappa. Office: 408 Magazine St New Orleans LA 70130-2435

FLOYD, JEANNE, professional society administrator; b. New Bedford, Mass.; d. Alfred Oscar and Irene Fournier Morel; m. Harry Joseph Floyd Jr., Aug. 8, 1964; 1 child, Jason Alfred. BS, Coll. of Notre Dame of Md., 1982; MS, U. Md., 1984; PhD, Pa. State U., 1993. Asst. dir. Psychogeriatric Clin., Johns Hopkins Med. Instns., Balt., 1979-88; dir. programs and svcs. Pa. Nurses Assn., Harrisburg, 1988-95; exec. dir. Midwest Alliance in Nursing, Indpls., 1995-97; dir. rsch. and evaluation Sigma Theta Tau Internat., Indpls., 1997—. Contbr. articles to profl. jours., including Am. Jour. Gerontological Nursing, Reflections, Synergy. Mem. adv. bd. Friends of Strand Theater, York, Pa., 1994-95, Nursing 2000, Indpls., 1995-97. Lt. Nurses Corp., USAF, 1962-64. Mem. Am. Soc. Assn. Execs. (cert.), Ind. Soc. Assn. Execs. Roman Catholic. Avocations: gardening, exercising, antiquing. E-mail: floyd@stti.iupui.edu. Home: 5681 Guilford Ave Indianapolis IN 46220-3266 Office: Sigma Theta Tau Internat 550 W North St Indianapolis IN 46202-3191

FLOYD, JOHN DAVID, theology educator, minister; b. Lockesburg, Ark., Sept. 28, 1934; s. William Chaney Floyd and Alice Thadine (Park) Trammell; m. Helen Nutt, June 3, 1955; children: Elizabeth Ann Stivers, John Paul. BA, Ouachita Bapt. U., 1952-56; BD, Southwestern Bapt. Theol. Sem., 1962, M in Div., 1969; ThD, Mid-Am. Bapt. Theol. Sem., 1976; post doctoral studies, Fuller Theol. Sem., 1980-81. Ordained to ministry Bapt. Ch., 1952. Pastor various So. Bapt. Chs., 1952-65; missionary Fgn. Mission Bd. So. Bapt. Conv., Philippines, 1965-75; v.p. adminstrn., prof. missions Mid-Am. Bapt. Theol. Sem., Memphis, 1975-84; dir. missionary enlistment Fgn. Mission Bd. So. Bapt. Conv., Richmond, Va., 1984-85; v.p., dir. of D of Ministry program Mid-Am. Bapt. Theol. Sem., Memphis, 1985-93; dir. fgn. mission bd. for europe The Southern Baptist Convention, 1993-2000; v.p. Mid-Am. Bapt. Theol. Sem., 2000—; head Missionary Dept. Mid-Am. Bapt. Theol. Sem., Memphis, 1977-84, cons. ch. growth, 1979-84, dir. sch. world missions, 1982-84. Editor: Inductive Bible Study Series, 1970, 1971 Church Growth Survey in the Philippines, 1972, Modern Cults, 1979; editor numerous articles Mid-Am. Bapt. Theol. Jour., 1976-86. Campaigner Rep. Party in Va., Richmond, 1984-85. Served as 1st lt. inf. U.S. Army, 1957-59. Recipient Eye of the Eagle award 101st Airborne Div. Ft. Campbell, 1984, Key to the City award Booneville City Govt., 1982. Mem. Am. Assn. Missiologists, Assn. Mission Profs., Internat. Missiological Soc., Nat. Planned Giving Assn., Am. Mgmt. Assn. Home: care Fgn Mission Bd 2533 Brotherwood Cv Collierville TN 38017-8972 Office: Mid-Am Bapt Theol Sem 2216 S Germantown Rd Germantown TN 38138-3804

FLOYD, JOHN MILLICE, engineering executive, educator; b. Bedford, Eng., Jan. 30, 1941; s. Millice Alfred and Alice (Case) F.; m. Carolyn Isobel Taylor, Dec. 10, 1966; children: Joshua William, Lachlan John, Fergus Patrick, Eliza Gweneth Alice. BSc in Metallurgy, U. Melbourne, Australia, 1963, MSc in Metallurgy, 1965; PhD in Metallurgy, London U., 1970; diploma, Imperial Coll. Sci. and Tech., London, 1970. Exptl. officer Commonwealth Sci. and Indsl. Rsch. Orgn., Melbourne, 1965-66, rsch. scientist, 1970-81; prin., then chmn. Ausmelt, Melbourne, 1981-94; professorial rsch. fellow U. Melbourne, 1983-87, professorial assoc., 1987—. Contbr. numerous articles to sci. publs.; patentee equipment and methods for metal recovery by smelting. Decorated Order of Australia; recipient Clunies-Ross Nat. Sci. and Tech. award, Australia, 1995. Fellow Australian Acad. Tech. Sci. and Engring., Australian IMM (chmn. procs. com. 1985-87, Pres.'s award 1997), IMM (London); mem. CIM (Toronto), Metals Soc. of AIME. Avocations: farming, surfing, swimming. Home: PO Box 117, Victoria Upper Beaconsfield 3808, Australia Office: Ausmelt Ltd, 12 Kitchen Rd, Victoria Dandenong 3175, Australia

FLOYD, WALTER LEO, lawyer; b. St. Louis, May 29, 1933; s. Walter L. Sr. and Estelle E. (Kiess) F.; children: Michael W., Mary Ann, Mark L.; m. Patricia A. Knapko, Sept. 3, 1994. BS, St. Louis U., 1955, LLD, 1959. Bar: Mo. 1959, Ill. 1959, U.S. Dist. (ea. dist.) Mo. 1959. Owner The Floyd Law Firm P.C., St. Louis, 1959—. Contbr. articles to profl. jours. Fellow: Orgn. Nat. Bd. Trial Advocacy; mem. Mo. Assn. Trial Attys. (sec. 1961, v.p. 1962, 85), Am. Trial Lawyers Assn. (lectr.), Mo. Bar Assn., Ill. Assn., Phi Delta Phi. Democrat. Unitarian. Address: Floyd Law Firm 8151 Clayton Rd Ste 202 Saint Louis MO 63117-1111

FLUCKEY, EUGENE BENNETT, retired navy officer, author; b. Washington, Oct. 5, 1913; s. Isaac Newton and Luella (Snowden) F.; m. Marjorie Palmer Gould, June 6, 1937 (dec. Sept. 17, 1979); 1 child, Barbara Ann Fluckey Bove; m. Eleanor Margaret Wallace McAlpine, Aug. 20, 1980. BS, U.S. Naval Acad., 1935; M Design Engring., Navy Postgrad. Sch., 1943; student, Nat. War Coll., 1959. Commd. ensign USN, 1935; submarine capt. USS Barb WWII; advanced through grades to rear adm. USN, 1960; NATO comdr. in chief Iberian Atlantic Area; ret., 1972. Author: Thunder Below!, 1992 (Samuel Eliot Morison prize as best book on naval subjects 1993). Decorated Congl. Medal of Honor, Navy Cross (4), Knight of Malta, St. John of Jerusalem, grand cross Medal of Knights St. Catherine of Sinai; Fluckey Hall, Nuclear Submarines Combat Tng. Ctr., Groton, Conn., named in his honor 1989; Fluckey Hall, new hdqs. U.S. Comdr. Submarines Western Pacific named in his honor, Yokosuka, Japan, 1996, Knight of St. George the Martyr, Knight of St. Lazarus, Knight of Don Carlos I of Portugual. Home: 1016 Sandpiper Ln Annapolis MD 21403-4633

FLUECKIGER, CLAUDE RENÉ, marketing executive; b. Basel, Switzerland, Dec. 13, 1952; s. René Robert and Marceline Odette (Roth) F.; m. Susan Katherine Schuhmacher; children: Ellen, Matthew, Patrick. M Agronomy, Swiss Fed. Inst. Tech., Zurich, 1977, PhD in Sci., 1982. Asst. to CEO Novindustra Basel, Switzerland, 1977-78; asst. Swiss Fed. Inst. Tech., Zürich, Switzerland, 1978-82; project leader Ciba, Basel, Switzerland, 1983-91, head crop mgmt., 1991-96; head crop mgmt. Novartis, Basel, Switzerland, 1996-97; dir. mktg. Novartis Crop Protection, Inc., Greensboro, N.C., 1997—; Trainer CIBA Mgmt. Basic Course, 1994-96; food inspector, Magden, Switzerland, 1990-94. Contbr. over 60 articles to profl. jours.; patentee in field. Mem. Entomological Soc. (Swiss chpt., bd. mem. 1989-95, Am. chpt.), Schweizer Verband Ingenieur-Agronomen Lebensm-Ingenieure, Gesellschaft Studierender Eidg. Technischen Hochschule, Sigma Xi. Office: Novartis Crop Protection In PO Box 18300 Greensboro NC 27419-8300

FLUEGEL, WALTER GENO, urban planner; b. Pekin, Ill., Aug. 10, 1963; s. Walter John and Frances F.; m. Karyn Marshall, Dec. 28, 1997; children: Brandy, Hunter. BA in Urban and Regional Planning, U. Ill., 1989. Planner City of Boca Raton, Fla., 1990; exec. dir., project mgr. Ft. Lauderdale (Fla.) Downtown Devel. Auth., 1991; planner Highlands County, Sebring, Fla., 1991-92; dir. of planning/assoc. planner City of Plantation, Fla., 1992-96; pres. Fluegel Devel. Cons., Sunrise, Fla., 1996-99; dir. of planning Keith & Assocs., Pompano Beach, Fla., 1999—. Vice-pres. Palm Beach Culver Alumni Club, Fla., 1999; mem. Broward County Tech. Adv. Com., Ft. Lauderdale, 1996; sec. United Meth. Men, Boca Raton, 1990; sr. rep. U. of Ill. Student Planning Orgn., Champaign-Urbana, Ill., 1986. Mem. AICP, Am. Planning Assn. Avocation: hockey. E-mail: wfluegel@aol.com. Office: Keith & Assocs 301 E Atlantic Blvd Pompano Beach FL 33060-6643

FLÜGELMAN, MÁXIMO ENRIQUE, financier, composer; b. Buenos Aires, Nov. 2, 1945; s. Cirilo and Matilde (Rhein) F. Lic. es Sci. Econ., U. Geneva; diploma in econ. policy, Cath. U., Buenos Aires; MBA, Harvard U.; BM, Manhattan Sch. Music; M in Composition, Juilliard Sch. Credit officer Citibank, Buenos Aires and N.Y.C., 1970; sr. investment officer World Bank Group Internat. Fin. Corp., Washington, 1972-77; internat. mgr., chief external funding, negotiator Nat. Devel. Bank, Buenos Aires, 1981-84; v.p. banker 1st Chgo. Internat. Capital Markets Group, Chgo. and N.Y.C., 1985-89; v.p., mem. exec. com. Inter-Am. Investment Corp., Washington, 1989-94; sr. advisor Earth Scis. & Techs. Inc., 1995-97; ptnr. M.A.P.A., Inc., 1998—; mem. ofcl. Argentine del. to IMF/World Bank meetings, Inter Am. Devel. Bank gen. assemblies; lectr. Buenos Aires Nat. U., Cath. U., Washington. Author: Argentina and the Debt Crisis, 1983; contbr. articles on internat. fin. and arts to profl. jours. including La Nacion, Ambito Financiero; musical compositions include Symphonic Variants for orch., Concertino for woodwinds and orch., Piano sonata, Sonatina per corde for string orch., Sea Sonnets for soprano and orch., Sonatina for chamber orch., Rhapsody for Cello and Orch., Concerto for Piano and String orch.; chamber works performed at Aspen Festival, Latin Am. Chamber Music Festival, Quinteto Rego, Argentina; orchestral works performed Indpls. Symphony, Interam. Festival Orch., Kennedy Ctr., Washington, Carnegie Hall, N.Y.C., Northwestern U. Orch., Nat. Argentine Symphony, Buenos Aires Philharm. at Teatro Colon, Conn. Chamber Orch., Fla. Philharm. Recipient 14th ann. contemporary orchestral composition award Ind. State U./Indpls. Symphony; 1st prize LRA Argentine State Radio Chamber Orch. composition contest, Outstanding Young Musician of Yr. award Argentine Jr. C. of C.; Amigos dela Musica composition contest Indpls. Symphony; finalist Nissim Orchestral Composition Competition; fellow Bunge and Born Found. Mem. ASCAP, Argentine Coun. on Fgn. Rels., Teatro Colón Found. (trustee, founding), A. Ginastera Found. (dir.), Soc. Argentina de Autores y Compositores, Soc. Rural Argentina, Cosmos Club (Washington), Doubles, Harvard Club (N.Y.C.), Club Nautico San Isidro (Buenos Aires). Home: Apt 1110 2801 New Mexico Ave NW Washington DC 20007-3940

FLUGGER, PENELOPE ANN, banker; b. Chgo., June 26, 1942; d. William and Florence Bernadette (Brongiel) Grabos; B.S., U. Ill., 1964; M.B.A., Baruch Coll., 1971; CPA, N.Y., Ill.; m. Robert John Flugger, July 11, 1970. Sr. mgr. Price Waterhouse Co., N.Y.C., 1964-75; with Morgan Guaranty Trust Co., 1975-98, auditor, 1982-94, sr. v.p., 1982-94, mng. dir., 1994-98; mem. N.Y.C. Audit Com., Fin. Exec. Inst. Mem. AICPAs, Inst. Mgmt. Accts., Fin. Execs. Inst., N.Y. State Soc. CPAs, Ill. State Soc. CPAs.

FLYNN, DANIEL FRANCIS, investment company executive; b. Hartford, Conn.; s. Daniel C. and Frances E. (Hurley) F.; m. Barbara L. Quinn, June 12, 1965; children: Daniel C., Garrett S., Laura D. BA, Coll. of the Holy Cross, 1956; JD, U. Conn., 1962. Bar: Conn. 1962. Chmn., CEO John G. Martin Found., Farmington, 1969—; dir., chmn., CEO, pres. JCI Corp., Farmington, Conn., 1968—, Resources Mgmt. Corp., Farmington, 1976—; dir., chmn., CEO Resources Investment Co., Farmington, 1977—, RMC Realty Co., Farmington, 1985—; former dir. Security-Conn. Life Ins. Co. Former regent, mem. exec. com. U. Hartford, former chmn. resources com., mem. com. regent mems., mem. investment com.; trustee, mem. exec. com. Horace Bushnell Mem. Hall Corp.; bd. vis. Barney Sch.; hon. life mem., bd. mgrs. Silver Hill Found., Inc., past dir., past dir. devel. com.; mem. exec. com., past pres. U. Conn. Law Sch. Found., Inc.; trustee Conn. Policy and Econ. Coun., Inc.; corporator St. Francis Hosp. and Med. Ctr.; founding trustee John G. Martin Scholarship Trust; spl. gifts chmn. United Way Hartford; former trustee Hartford Art Sch.; past pres. Westmont Residents' Assn.; mem. Pres. Coun. Coll. Holy Cross. Mem. Am. Soc. Internat. Law, Am. Judicature Soc., Am. Assn. Individual Investors, Conn. Bar Assn., Newcomen Soc. Am., Twentieth Century Club. Office: Resources Mgmt Corp 2 Batterson Park Rd Farmington CT 06032-2553

FLYNN, ELIZABETH ANNE, advertising and public relations company executive; b. Washington, Aug. 21, 1951; d. John William and Elizabeth Goodwin (Mahoney) F. AA, Montgomery Coll., Rockville, Md., 1972; BS in Journalism, U. Md., 1976; postgrad., San Diego State U., 1976. Writer, researcher Sea World, Inc., San Diego, 1977-79; sr. writer Lane & Huff Advt., San Diego, 1979-80; account exec. Kaufman, Lansky, Baker Advt., San Diego, 1980-82; mng. dir. Excelsior Enterprises, Beverly Hills, Calif., 1983-84; sr. account exec. Berkhemer & Kline, Inc., L.A., 1985; pres. Flynn Advt. & Pub. Rels., L.A., 1985—; cons. Coca-Cola Bottling Co. L.A., 1982-84; U.S. corr. Aeronovum mag., 1990-98; v.p. mktg. Graffiti Prevention Systems, L.A., 1990-91; dir. new bus. devel. BBDO Hispanica, L.A., 1992-93; pub. rels. dir. Regional Organ Procurement Agy. So. Calif., UCLA Med. Ctr., 1994-97, pub. info. officer/cons. Cmty. Devel. Dept. City of L.A., 1998-2000. Bd. dirs. Friends of Reconstructive Surgery, Beverly Hills, 1983-89, Nat. Kidney Found., 1994, Nat. Orgn. for Renal Diseases, L.A., 2000—, So. Calif. Coalition on Donation, 1994-97, also mem. steering com., 1995-97; sec. Nat. Coun. Local Coalitions, 1995-97; comms. com. Assn. organ Procurement Orgns.; cons. Rotary Internat. Give of Yourself program, 1993—; media cons. divsn. transplantation HHS, 1994-98; found. rels. mgr. Juvenile Diabetes Found. Internat., 2000. Mem. Nat. Orgn. Women Bus. Owners. Address: Flynn Advt & Pub Rels 1440 Reeves St Ste 104 Los Angeles CA 90035-2950

FLYNN, RALPH MELVIN, JR., sales executive, marketing consultant; b. Winchester, Mass., May 2, 1944; s. Ralph Melvin and Mary Agnus (Giuliani) F.; m. Rose Marie Petrock (div. 1988); children: John Patrick, Marc Jeffery; m. Carolyn F. Lee; 1 child, Sean Michael. Engr. Bell Tel. Labs., Holmdel, N.J., 1966-68; tech. coord. Expts. in Art and Tech., N.Y.C., 1968-69; exec. v.p. Bestline Products, San Jose, Calif., 1969-73; pres. Internat. Inst. for Personal Achievement, Palo Alto, Calif., 1975-76, Diamite Corp., Milpitas, Calif., 1977-84; dir. mktg. IMMI, Campbell, Calif., 1973-77; v.p. internat. Neo-Life Co., Fremont, Calif., 1984—; pres. Ultra Promotions, Los Gatos, Calif., 1988-89, Score Publishing, Saratoga, Calif., 1987—; tech. cons. Robert Rauschenberg, N.Y.C., 1968; cons. Std. Oil Co., San Francisco, 1975, I.B.C., Geneva, 1984-88, 1st Interstate Bank, L.A., 1985, Ray Rossi, Design Environs., Los Altos Hills, Calif., 1995; pres. CoffeeSociety.com Your Online Cofffee Store, 1999—; lectr. in field. Author: The Only Variable, 1985, Navigating towards Success, 1986; contbr. articles to profl. publs. Named adm. State of Nebr., 1987; Joseph Kaplan Trust scholar, 196l. Mem. Direct Selling Assn., Coffee Soc. (founder 1988), Rolls Royce Owners Club. Republican. Avocations: music, sailing, art, interior design, classic automobiles. Office: Coffee Soc 21265 Stevens Creek Blvd Cupertino CA 95014-5715

FLYNN, VERNON JAMES HENNESSY, barrister; b. London, 1966. MA, Trinity Coll., Cambridge, Eng., 1989. Bar: London. Comml. law tutor London Sch. Econs., 1990-91. Recipient Denning scholarship Lincoln's Inn, 1991, Hardwicke scholarship Sir Thomas Moore award, Lincoln's Inn, 1990, sr. scholarship Whittaker Scholar, Trinity Coll., others. Office: Essex Ct Chambers, 24 Lincolns Inn Fields, WC2A 3ED London England

FLYNT, CLIFTON WILLIAM, computer programmer, software designer; b. Waterville, Maine, Feb. 7, 1953; s. Jerrold Miller and Alta Livia (Marasi) F.; m. Carol Ann Clapper, May 1, 1993. BS in Biochemistry, SUNY, Syracuse, 1975, postgrad., 1975. Chemist SUNY, Syracuse, 1975-77, Gelman Sci., Ann Arbor, Mich., 1978-79; programmer Applied Dynamics, Ann Arbor, 1979-81, GeoSpectra, Ann Arbor, 1981-83, BioImage, Ann Arbor, 1983-86; cons. Resource One, Chgo., 1986-88; sr. programmer Cimage, Ann Arbor, 1988-90; project leader, v.p. Veracity, Inc., Walled Lake, Mich., 1990-92; mem. tech. staff Computational Bioscis. Inc., 1992-93; sr. applications software engr. Applied Intelligent Systems, Inc., Ann Arbor, Mich., 1993-96; sr. rsch. engr. First Virtual Holdings, Inc., San Diego, 1996-97; pres. Flynt Cons. Svcs., 1997-99, Noumena Corp., Dexter, MI, 2000—; mem. tech. resource com. Arbornet, Ann Arbor, 1986-90; vis. lectr. Grinnell (Iowa) Coll., 1999; spkr., conductor workshops in field. Author: Tcl/Tk for Real Programmers, 1998, (computer aided instrn. packages) Tcl Tutor; author articles and procs. Mem. IEEE, Am. Chem. Soc., Assn. Computing Machinery. Avocations: songwriting, woodworking, guitar.

FO, DARIO, playwright; b. San Giano, Italy, Mar. 24, 1926. Grad., Acad. Fine Arts, Milan, Brera Art Acad. m. Franca Rame; 1 child. Co-founder I Dritti revue co., 1953; artistic dir. Chi l'ha visto?, 1959; founder with Rame Compagnia Dario Fo-Franca Rame, 1959, Nuova Scena theatre cooperative; founder La Comune theatre collective, Milan, 1970-73. Writings include: (plays) Poer nano ed altre storie, 1952, Il dito nell'occhio, 1953, I sani da legare, 1954, Ladri, manichini e donne nude, 1957, Comico finale, 1958, Gli arcangeli non giocano a flipper, 1959, Aveva due pistole con gli occhi bianchi e neri, 1960, Chi ruba un piede è fortunato in amore, 1961, Teatro comico, 1962, Isabella, tre caravelle e un cacciaballe, 1963, Settimo, ruba un po'meno, 1964, La colpa è sempre del diavolo, 1965, Ci ragiono e canto, 1966, La Signora è da buttare, 1967, Grande pantomima con bandiere e pupazzi piccoli e medi, 1968, Legami pure che tanto io spacco tutto lo stesso, 1969, Mistero Buffo, 1969, L'operaio conosce 300 parole il padrone 1000 per

questo lui è il padrone, 1969, Morte accidentale di un anarchio, 1970, Vorrei morire anche stasera se dovessi pensare che non è servito a niente, 1979, Tutti unitti!, Tutti insieme! Ma scusa, quello non è il padrone?, 1971, Fedayn, 1972, Pum pum! Chi e? La polizia, 1972, Ordine! Per Dio.000.000.000, 1972, basta con i fascisti, 1973, Guerra di popolo in Cile, 1973, The Bawd, 1973, Porta e belle, 1974, Non si paga, non si paga, 1974, Canzoni e ballate, 1974, Il caso Marini, 1974, Il fanfari rapito, 1975, La guillarata, 1975, La marijuana della mamma è la piú bella 1976, (with Franca Rame) Tutta casa, letto e chiesa, 1977, Storia della tigre et altre storie, 1978, Betty, 1980, Clascon, trombette e pernacchi, 1981, Storia vera di Piero d'Angera: che alla crociata non c'era, 1981, Una madre, 1982, (with Rame) Fabulazzo osceno, 1982, (with Rame) Coppia aperta, quasi spalancata, 1983, Quasi per caso una donna: Elisabetta, 1984, The History of Masks, 1984, Diario di Eva, 1984, Hellequin, Harlekin, Arlechino, 1985, (with Rame) 25 monologhi per una donna, 1989, Una giornata qualunque, 1986, Il ratto della Francesca, 1986, La parte del Leone, 1987, Lettera dalla Cina, 1989, Il papa e la strega, 1989, Zitti! stiamo precipitando, 1990, Johan Padan a la descoverta de le Americhe, 1991, (with Rame) Parliamo di donne: L'eronia—grassa è bello, 1991; (screenplay) Lo svitato, 1956; (radio play series) Poer nano ed altre storie, from 1951; (teleplays) Monetine da 5 lire, 1956, Chi l'ha visto?, 1959, (with Rame) Il teatro di Dario Fo, 1977, (with Rame) Buona sera, 1979-80, La professione della Signora Warren, 1981, The Tricks of the Trade, 1985, (variety show) Transmissione forzata, 1988, (with Rame) Una lepre con la faccia da bambina, 1989, (with Rame) Coppia aperta, 1990, Settimo ruba un po'meno, 1991, Mistero Buffo, 1991; (other writings) Manuele minimo dell'attore, 1987, Dialogo provacatorio sul comico, il tragico, la follia e la ragione, 1990; (adaptation) La storia di un soldato (Igor Stravinsky), 1978, (with Rame) L'opera della sghignazzo (John Gay), 1981; (play collections) Le commedie I-IX, 1966-91, Compagni senza censura 1, 1970, 2, 1972, Il teatro politico di Dario Fo, 1977; dir. plays: Gli amici della battoneria, 1962, Chi ruba un piede è fortunato in amore, 1963, La passeggiata della domenica, 1967, Enzo Jannacci: 22 canzioni, 1968, La storia di un soldato, 1978, L'opera della sghignazzo, 1981, Tutta casa, letto e chiesa, 1986, Il barbiere di siviglia, 1987, 88, 89, 90, 92, Gli arangeli non giocano a flipper, 1987, Il medico per forza/Il medico volante, 1990, 91, Isabella, tre caravelle e un cacciaballe, 1992. Recipient Sonning award Denmark, 1981, Obie award, 1987, Nobel prize for Literature, 1997. Office: Michael Imison Playwrights Ltd, 28 Almeida St, London N1 1TD, England also: C T F R, Viale Piave 11, 20129 Milan Italy*

FOBES, JOHN EDWIN, international organization official; b. Chgo., Mar. 16, 1918; s. Wilfred and Mable (Skogsberg) F.; m. Hazel Ward Weaver, June 7, 1941; children: Patricia Cleveland, John Geoffrey Weaver. BS cum laude, Northwestern U., 1939; MA, Tufts U., 1940; HHD (hon.), Bucknell U., 1973. With Bur. Budget, Washington, 1942, 46-48; secretariat prep. commn. of UN, London, 1945; exec. sec. UN advisory group of experts on adminstrn., pers. and budgetary questions, 1946; adviser Pan Am. Union, 1947-48; with ECA, Marshall Plan, 1948-52; attache U.S. del. to NATO and OEEC, Paris, 1952-55; dir. Office Internat. Adminstrn., Dept. State, Washington, 1955-59, spl. asst. to asst. sec. state, 1959-60; asst. dir. Tech. Cooperation Mission to India, 1960-62; dep. dir. AID Mission to India, 1962-64; asst. dir. gen. UNESCO, Paris, 1964-70, dep. dir. gen., 1970-77; vis. rsch. scholar Ind. U., Harvard, 1970; vis. scholar Duke U., Durham, 1978-82; vis. lectr. U. N.C., Chapel Hill, 1981-82; adj. prof. Western Carolina U., 1983-90. Pres. Am. Libr. in Paris, 1968-70. Mem. advisory com. UN Gen. Assembly, 1955-60; chmn. U.S. Nat. Commn. for UNESCO, 1980-81. Served as maj. USAAF 1942-46, ETO. Clarion Dewitt Hardy scholar Northwestern U., 1939. Fellow World Acad. Arts and Scis.; mem. Acad. Coun. on UN, Internat. Studies Assn., World Futures Studies Fedn. U.S. Assn. for Club of Rome (chmn. 1982-88), Club of Rome, Assn. for Promotion of Humor in Internat. Affairs (co-founder), Ams. for Universality of UNESCO (founder, chmn.), UN Assn. (nat. coun.), Phi Beta Kappa. Home: 28 Beaverbrook Rd Asheville NC 28804-1502

FOCAS, CARALAMPO, transport advisor; b. Athens, Aug. 19, 1960; arrvived in U.K., 1979; s. Anghelos Phocas and Anna Caralampe-Focá. MA in Sociology, U. Aberdeen, Scotland, 1983; MSc in Transport Planning, Poly. Cen. London, 1984; PhD, London Sch. Econs., 1987. Lectr. Thames Poly., London, 1985-86, City of London Poly., 1986-87; rschr. London Strategic Policy Unit, 1987-88; transport advisor London Rsch. Ctr., 1988—. Author: Top Towns, 1995, A Comparison of World Transport Systems, 1998. Recipient Apple Excellence award Apple Bus. Mag., 1991; Rees Jeffreys scholar, 1984-87. Office: London Rsch Ctr, sitias 2, SE1 7SZ Athens 11523, Greece

FOCKLER, HERBERT HILL, foundation executive; b. Summersville, W.Va., Feb. 18, 1922; s. William Okey and Annie Lee (Fitzwater) F.; m. Mary Hildegarde Ziegler, May 15, 1950; 1 child, Herbert. BA, W.Va. U., 1947, MA, 1948; cert., Oxford (Eng.) U., 1948, Harvard U., 1949. Adminstr. library Princeton (N.J.) U., 1952-54, Library of Congress, Washington, 1956-58; advisor White House Confs., Washington, 1959-60; exec. NIH, Bethesda, Md., 1961-69; chmn. Sci. and Tech. Coms., Washington, 1969-70; exec. dir. Sci. Founds., Washington, 1971-72; trustee, chmn. Am. Arts Internat. Found., Washington, pres., 1984—, also bd. dirs.; trustee Nat. Mus. of Health and Medicine Found., 1989—; chmn., trustee World Tech. Found., Washington, 1988-89; bd. dirs. Nat. Info. Tech. Ctr., 1992—; advisor NSF, 1975, White House Conf. on Bus., 1975, 78, Montgomery Coll., Rockville, Md., 1978, World Bank, 1986, Winston Churchill Found., 1988, various pub. scos., 1989—, various tech. industries, 1986—, IMF, 1991; mem. adv. coun. Coolfont Found., Berkeley Springs, W.Va., 1980-87; mem. Presdl. Rsch. Group; assoc. Woodrow Wilson Internat. Ctr., 1988—; mem. Bd. on Sci. Edn. Editor: Contemporary South, 1968, also conf. records and newsletters; author sci. research reports and bibliographies. Adv. Stanford U., 1967-69; trustee Threshold Environ. Found., Washington, 1969-75, Nat. Mus. Health and Medicine Found., 1989-90, adv. coun., 1991—; mem. pres.'s coun. Shenandoah Coll., Winchester, Va., 1982-87; mem. Found. Advancement Edn. in Scis., 1980—, Joint Bd. Edn. in Sci. and Engring., 1991—; bd. dirs. Nat. Mus. of Lang., 1999—, Global Children's Health Fund, 1999—. Served as staff sgt. U.S. Army, 1941-45. Mem. AAAS, Acad. Polit. Sci., Am. Polit. Sci. Assn., Washington Acad. Scis. (bd. dirs. 1992—), U.N. Assn., Smithsonian Assocs., Am. Assn. Mus., Nat. Trust Historic Preservation, Libr. Congress Assocs., Colonial Williamsburg Found., Fgn. Policy Inst., World Affairs Coun., Policy Studies Orgn., Found. for Advancement Edn. in Sci., Internet Soc., Smithsonian Assocs., Am. Film Inst., Am. Assn. Mus., Nat. Trust Hist. Preservation, Harvard Club, Princeton Club, W.Va. Club, W.Va. Acad. Sci., Nat. Press Club. Clubs: Harvard U., Princeton U., W.Va. (Washington). Home and Office: 10710 Lorain Ave Silver Spring MD 20901-1512

FODA, RABIZ NASIR, industrial engineer; b. Bombay, India, May 14, 1949; arrived in Can., 1994; s. Nasir Huseinibhai Foda and Amena (Yahya) Khairullah; m. Nermin Zoyeb Kantawala, Dec. 5, 1977; children: Maria, Zulqarnain, Farzeen. B Tech. with honors, Indian Inst. Tech., Bombay, 1973; grad. diploma in mgmt. studies, U. Bombay, 1981. Sr. asst. engr. Tata Electric Cos., Bombay, 1973-85; elec. engr. Sceco-Western Region, Jeddah, Saudi Arabia, 1985-92, mem. corp. tech. mgmt. group for transmission dept., 1986-90, chief of sub-stations, 1990-92, acting dir. transmission, 1989-92; sr. engr. SBG-Indsl. Power Projects, Jeddah, 1993-94, Elecsar Engring. Ltd., Can., 1995-99, Atomic Energy Can. Ltd., Mississauga, Ont., Can., 1999—; cons. for energy conservation Econ. Cons., Bombay. Contbr. articles to profl. publs. Mem. IEEE (sr.), N.Y. Acad. Scis., Project Mgmt. Inst., India Forum, Embassy of India, Jeddah (mng. com. 1990—), Soc. Power Engrs. India, Econ. Forum of Indian Expatriates (mem. exec. com. 1987-88), Indian Inst. Tech. Alumni Assn. Can. (mem. exec. com. 1996—). Avocations: painting, reading, music, tennis, swimming. Home: 27-3360 Council Ring Rd, Mississauga, ON Canada L5L 2E4

FODIMAN, AARON ROSEN, publishing executive; b. Stamford, Conn., Oct. 10, 1937; s. Yale J. and Thelma F. BS, Tulane U., 1958; LLB, NYU, 1960, MBA, 1961; grad., L'Academie de CuisineCanardier, Washington, 1977. Bar: N.Y. 1960, D.C. 1961, Va. 1965. With FTC, Washington, 1961-65; practiced in Arlington, Va., 1965-78; pres. Fast Food Operators, Inc., N.Y.C., 1978-84, Hampton Healthcare, 1984-91, Kapok Tree Restaurants, Tampa Bay Publs., 1986—. Author: Life is not an Illusion, it Just Looks That Way, 1998; pub., editor: Tampa Bay Mag.; TV host local sports show, Dine Line, Tampa Bay Mag.;. Bd. dirs. Tampa Players Inc., Washington Ballet, Manhattan Punch Line Theatre, Kent Jewish Cmty. Ctr.; pres. Dunedin Art Ctr., Bay Ballet Theatre; chmn. Pinellas County Arts Coun., Golda Meir Ctr., Bay Ballet Theatre, A Taste of Pinellas; cmty. advisor Clearwater Dunedin Jr. League; mem. adv. bd. Am. Film Inst.; chmn. Ford Presdl. Campaign, 1976; advisor Fed. Res. Bank Atlanta; participant Leadership Pinellas; participant, founder Leadership Tampa Bay, Nat. Conf. Christians and Jews; Pinellas County amb. to Ringling Mus. Art. Recipient Hyam Soloman Freedom award, 1974, Miniature Palette award Miniature Art Soc. of Fla., 1987, Order of Salvador medal Dali Mus., 1989, Lifetime Achievement award Internat. Restaurant and Hospitality Rating Bur., 2000; honoree award winner Friends of Arts Pinellas County, Svc. to Mankind award Sertoma Club; knighted as Baron Order of St. John of Jerusalem, 1999. Mem. Pinellas County Restaurant Assn. (pres.), Tampa Bay Restaurant Assn. (pres.), Fla. Restaurant Assn. (bd. dirs.), Tampa Bay Food and Wine Soc. (pres.).

FODOR, GÁBOR BÉLA, chemistry educator, researcher; b. Budapest, Hungary, Dec. 5, 1915; came to U.S., 1969, naturalized, 1976; s. Domokos Victor and Paula Maria (Bayer) F.; m. Ana Maria Ruiz. Cand. Ing., Poly. Tech. Inst., Graz, Austria, 1934; PhD, Szeged U., Hungary, 1937; DSc, Acad. Scis., Budapest, 1952; PhD (hon.), Szeged U., Hungary, 1994. Demonstrator Szeged U., Hungary, 1935-38, from assoc. prof. to prof., 1945-57; rsch. chemist Chinoin Pharm. Ltd., Budapest, Hungary, 1938-45; head stereochemistry Lab. of Acad., Budapest, Hungary, 1958-65; prof. Laval U., Que., Can., 1965-69; Centennial prof. chemistry W.Va. U., Morgantown, 1969-86, prof. emeritus, 1986—; prof. emeritus József Attila U., Szeged, Hungary, 1990—; project dir. Nat. Found. Cancer Research, Bethesda, Md., 1977-86; vis. prof. U. Munich, 1966, Stevens Tech., Hoboken, 1968, Darmstadt, THD, 1975-76. Author: Organische Chemie I-II, 1966; contbr. articles to prof. jours.; patentee in field. Recipient Kossuth prize Budapest, 1950, 54, Silver medal U. Helsinki, 1958, Golden diploma U. Szeged, 1988, Diamond diploma U. Szeged, 1998, Albert Szent-Györgyi medal, Szeged, Hungary, 1992; overseas fellow Churchill Coll., Cambridge, Eng., 1961—. Mem. Am. Chem. Soc., Can. Inst. Chemistry, Am. Inst. Chemists, Chem. Soc. London, Hungarian Acad. Sci., Sigma Xi. Roman Catholic. Office: West Va U Dept Chemistry Morgantown WV 26506-6045

FODY, EDWARD PAUL, pathologist; b. Balt., June 11, 1947; s. Edward Paul and Frances Dorothy (Schultz) F.; m. Nancy June Keipe, July 19, 1974. BS, Duke U., 1969; MS, U. Wis., 1971; MD, Vanderbilt U., 1975. Diplomate Am. Bd. Pathology. Resident in pathology Vanderbilt U. Hosp., Nashville, 1975-78; fellow in chemistry U. Tex. Med. Sch., Houston, 1979-80, asst. prof. pathology, 1980-81; chief lab. VA Hosp., Little Rock, 1981-87; assoc. prof. pathology U. Ark. Med. Sch., Little Rock, 1981-87; dir. pathology Bethesda Hosp., Cin., 1987-96; dir. pathology dept. Erlanger Hosp., Chattanooga, 1996—. Editor, author: Clinical Chemistry, 1984, chpt. to book. Fellow Coll. Am. Pathologists, Am. Soc. Clin. Pathologists; mem. AMA, Am. Assn. for Clin. Chemistry, Am. Soc. for Microbiology, Tenn. Med. Assn., Hamilton County Med. Soc. Republican. Lutheran. Avocations: boating, photography. Home: 408 Gentlemens Rdg Signal Mountain TN 37377-3250 Office: Erlanger Hosp Dept Pathology 975 E 3rd St Dept Chattanooga TN 37403-2163

FOELDES, CSABA, linguist, educator; b. Bácsalmás, Hungary, June 8, 1958; s. János and Margit (Kappeller-Szekeres) F. MA in German Russian Langs., Lajos Kossuth U., Debrecen, Hungary, 1981, PhD in Gen. Linguistics, 1983; PhD in Germanic Studies, Friedrich-Schiller U., Jena, Germany, 1987; degree in contrastive linguistics, Hungarian Acad. Sci/Humanities, Budapest, 1987; Dr. habil. in German Linguistics, U. Debrecen, 1997. Lectr. Tech. Coll., Kecskemét, Hungary, 1981-85; head German dept. Tchr. Tng. Coll., Szeged, Hungary, 1985-99; prof., head German dept. Veszprém (Hungary) U., 1996—, dir. Inst. Philology, 1999—; guest prof. linguistics Zurich U., 1993, Humboldt guest-rschr., Inst. German Lang., Mannheim, Germany, 1995-96; guest prof. German linguistics Halle U., Germany, 1998; bd. dirs. Inst. German Langs. Mannheim; pres. sect. langs. and literatures Hungarian Acad. Scis. and Humanities Veszprem, 1999—. Author: Deutsch-ungarisches Wörterbuch sprachwissenschaftlicher Fachausdrücke, 1991, Mehrsprachigkeit, Sprachenkontakt und Sprachenmischung, 1996, Deutsche Phraseologie kontrastiv: intra und interlinguale Zugänge, 1996, Linguistisches Wörterbuch Deutsch-Ungarisch, 1997; co-author: Umgang mit der Umgangssprache, 1991, Deutsche Rundfunksprache in mehrsprachiger Umwelt, 1995, Német-magyar nagyszótár, 1998, Magyar-német nagyszótár, 1998. Pres. Assn. Germans in Csongrad County, Szeged, Hungary, 1995-96. Soc. Modern Philology, Hungary Assn. Tchrs. German (sec. 1989—), Internat. Vereinigung für germanische Sprach- und Literaturwissenschaft, Soc. Hungarian Germanists (v.p.), Hungarian Humboldt-Assn., N.Y. Acad. Scis. Home: Szivárvány u 25, H-6725 Szeged Hungary Office: U Veszprém Dept German, Füredi u 2 Pf 158, H-8201 Veszprém Hungary

FOERST, JOHN GEORGE, JR., fundraising executive; b. Queens, N.Y., June 8, 1927; s. John George and Mary Elizabeth (McGinn) F.; m. Marion Theresa Cassidy, June 27, 1953; children: Gerard M., Kathryn J. BA, St. Johns U., Queens, 1950. Regional rep. Nat. Found. for Infantile Paralysis, N.Y.C., 1950-52; campaign dir., v.p. Cmty. Counselling Svc., N.Y.C., 1952-59, v.p., asst. to pres., 1965-69, pres., 1969-87, chmn., 1987-96, chmn. emeritus, 1997—; pres. John G. Foerst, Inc., N.Y.C., 1959-65. Contbg. author: complete Guide to Corporate Fund Raising, 1982. Bd. dirs. St. Francis Hosp., Roslyn, N.Y., 1972—, The Ctr. for Devel. Disabilities, Woodbury, N.Y., 1974-87, Nat. Ctr. for Disability Svcs. Inc., Albertson, N.Y., 1988-99, Cath. Health Sys. of L.I., 1998-99, Help for the Poor Found., 1998-99, Mid-Atlantic Hosp. Trust, Bermuda; trustee Pope John Paul II Libr. and Cultural Ctr., Washington, 1998—, Telicare, Uniondale, N.Y.; chmn. Am. Assn. Fund Raising Counsel, N.Y.C., 1982; mem. Cardinal's Com. of Laity, Roman Cath. Archdiocese N.Y., 1984—. Mem. Union League, Knights of Malta. Republican. Home: 77 Dover Rd Manhasset NY 11030-3717 Office: Community Counselling Svc Co 350 5th Ave Ste 7210 New York NY 10118-7299

FOERSTER, DAVID WENDEL, JR., counselor, consultant, human resources specialist; b. Jacksonville, Fla., Jan. 7, 1953; s. David Wendel Foerster and Estelle Jones Williams. BA cum laude, U. Fla., 1977. Cert. and registered gen. mediator Supreme Ct. of Ga. Founding dir. Addictive Disease Resouce Ctr., Atlanta, 1979-84; founding exec. dir., crisis mediator Resource Ctr., Atlanta, 1984—; cons. Womble, Carlylse, Sandridge & Rice, Atlanta, Godwin Assocs., King & Spalding, Altell, Taylor & Mathis, State Bar Ga., Shepard Spinal Hosp., Altell PortmanHoldings Ltd., Wachovia Corp., Sun Trust Bank, The Kroger Co., Atlanta Humane Soc.; lectr. Ga. State U., Atlanta, 1984—, Atlanta Pub. Schs.; vice-chmn. Lawyers Assistance Com., 1997-98. Contbr. articles to profl. jours.; interviewee, expert CBS, PBS, ABC, CNN, Bus. Week, Wall Street Jour., Atlanta Jour. Cosntn., 1978—. Bd. dirs. Resource Ctr., Atlanta, 1984—; instr. All Saints Episcopal Ch., Atlanta, 1985—. Recipient merit award Mended Hearts, Inc., 1985; grantee HBO, 1987; Frederick G. Storey Will Watt Fellow, 1995; Paul Harris fellow, 1994. Mem. ACA, Ga. Addiction Counselors Assn., Ga. Employee Assistance Forum, Nat. Assn. Addiction Counselors, Employee Assistance Profl. Assn., Am. Mgmt. Assn., Inst. Student Leadership. Avocations: classical music, reading, photgraphy. Office: Resource Ctr 2921 Piedmont Rd NE Ste D Atlanta GA 30305-2785

FOFIE, AKOSUA GYAMFUAA, publishing executive; b. Brosankro, Ghana, July 29, 1957; d. Kofi Fofie and Abena Amoam; m. Nana Opoku Fofie; children: Adwoa Oforiwaa, Pokuaa Ankama. Student, Adabie Comml. Coll., Kumasi, 1972-75. Mng. dir. Beginners Publ., Accra, Ghana, 1987—. Author: The Tested Love, 1989, The Forbidden Love, 1990, Because She Was a Woman, 1990, Murder at Sunset, 1991, Only the Fittest Can Survive, 1991, You Can't Always Win, 1992, One More Chance, 1992, Suffered Because of Love, 1996, The Agony of an African Woman, 1996, The Price of Jealousy, 1997, The Game is Patience, 1997, Desperate Intervention, 1998, Heaven Will Judge Her Differently, 1998; author: 57 Supplementary Workbooks for Children; author 20 children's story books. Named Publisher of Yr. Ghana Book Devel. Coun., 1999. Mem. Ch. of Pentecost. Office: Beginners Publ, Cantonments, CT 785 Accra Ghana

FOGARTY, EDWARD MICHAEL, lawyer; b. Woonsocket, R.I., Feb. 25, 1948; s. Raymond Henry and Mary (Hogan) F.; m. Gail Higgins, Jan. 8, 1977. BA, Providence Coll., 1969; JD, Georgetown U., 1972. Bar: R.I. 1972, D.C. 1973, U.S. Supreme Ct. 1977. Law clk. U.S. Dist. Ct. R.I., Providence, 1972-73; assoc. Wilkinson, Cragun & Barker, Washington, 1973-79, ptnr., 1979-82; ptnr. Baenen, Timme, De Reitzes & Middleton, Washington, 1982-83; counsel Spriggs & Hollingsworth, Washington, 1983-98; legal counsel to speaker R.I. Ho. of Reps., Providence, 1987-93; legal counsel to majority leader R.I. Senate, Providence, 1993—; arbitrator R.I. Superior Ct., 1989—. Trustee Festival Ballet of R.I., 1988—, pres., 1994-96. Mem. ABA, R.I. Bar Assn. (ho. dels. 1992-94), Am. Arbitration Assn. (nat. panel of arbitrators 1985-96), Univ. Club. Democrat. Roman Catholic. Home: 488 Lloyd Ave Providence RI 02906-4550 Office: 309 State House Providence RI 02903

FOGARTY, GERARD JOSEPH, psychology educator; b. Murwillumbah, NSW, Australia, Feb. 21, 1950; s. John Patrick and Rosina Mary (Burns) F.; m. Julie Christine Long, Jan. 4, 1974; children: Lucinda, Sam, Andrew. BA with honors, U. New Eng., Australia, 1973, diploma in Edn., 1974; PhD, U. Sydney, Australia, 1984. Registered psychologist, Australia. Tchr. H.S., NSW Edn., 1974-76; rsch. student U. Sydney, 1977, tutor, 1978-83; trainer Australian Mutual Provident Soc., Sydney, 1984; mgr. tng. AMP Soc., Sydney, 1985-87; prin. lectr. U. So. Queensland, Australia, 1988-97, prof. psychology, 1997—; mem. Psychyologists' Registration Bd. Queensland. Contbr. articles to profl. jours. Mem. coun. Royal Queensland Lawn Tennis Assn., 1989-93, Relationships Australia, 1990-94; cons. Australian Def. Force, 1993—. Recipient Australian Postgrad. Rsch. award Australian Govt., 1980-84. Mem. Australian Psychol. Soc. (profl. devel. and tng. com. 1991-98, mem. adv. group directorate of sci. affairs 1999—), Australian Ins. Industry, Heads of Schs. of Psychology (chairperson 1999—), N.Y. Acad. Scis. Avocations: tennis, golf, surfing, travel. Office: Univ So Queensland, Baker St, Toowoomba Queensland 4350, Australia

FOGARTY, JANET E., lawyer; b. Cambridge, Mass., June 16, 1950; d. Frederick A. and Joan Burgess; m. William L. Fogarty, June 7, 1969; 1 child, William P., II. BS, U. San Francisco, 1985, JD, 1991. Bar: Calif. Real estate salesperson Westborough Realty, South San Francisco, 1977-81; v.p., office mgr. Real Vest Realtors, Millbrae, Calif., 1985-87; real estate broker Real Vest Realtors, Millbrae, 1981-90; assoc. Lillick & Charles, San Francisco, 1991-93; of counsel Lakin Spears, Palo Alto, Calif., 1993-96, Deborah Wilder & Assocs., Burlingame, Calif., 1996-98, Fogarty & Watson LLP, Burlingame, 1998—; city rep., dir. City/County Assn. Govts., 1991-94; chmn. Growth Mgmt. Policy Com., 1992-95; instr. San Jose (Calif.) State U., 1999. Mayor City of Millbrae, 1990-91, 93-94, mem. City Coun., 1987-95; bd. dirs. Bay Area Air Quality Mgmt. Dist., San Francisco, 1992-96; bd. dirs., chmn. San Mateo Transit Dist., San Carlos, Calif., 1975-85, chmn., 1980-81; bd. dirs. Multi-City TSM Agy., South San Francisco, 1993-95, chmn., 1993-95. Mem. Soroptimist (pres. 1990-91, Woman Distinction award 1995), Rep. Women's Fedn., Calif. Elected Women's Assn., Calif. Women Lawyers, Millbrae C. of C. (chmn. 1999-2000), San Mateo County Visiting Nurses Assn. Hospice (chmn. 1997—), Visiting Nurses Assn./Home Hospice Northern Calif. (regional found. bd. 1998—, sec. 2000). Republican. Roman Catholic. Avocations: reading, politics, travel. Home: 1126 Hillcrest Blvd Millbrae CA 94030-2235 Office: Fogarty & Watson LLP 1633 Bayshore Hwy Ste 329 Burlingame CA 94010-1515

FOGARTY, STEPHEN JAMES, medical association administrator; b. Melbourne, Australia, Oct. 17, 1940; s. Tom and Barbara Emily (Campbell) F.; m. Patricia Ann Darbyshire Fogarty, Nov. 24, 1962; children: Sarah, David, James, Simon. Secondary edn., Melbourne Grammar Sch., Australia, 1950-58. Sr. rep. Nestle Co., Melbourne, Australia, 1965-73; regional sales mgr. Baxter Healthcare, Melbourne, Australia, 1973-81; mkt. R & D mgr. Terumo Corp., Melbourne, Australia, 1981-85, nat. sales mgr., 1985-92; gen. mgr. Terumo Corp., Sydney, Australia, 1992—; vis. lectr. Coll. of Pharmacy, Melbourne, Australia, 1978-81; chmn. Med. Industry Assn. of Australia, Sydney, 1996—; bd. dirs., vice-chmn. Monash U. Ctr. for Biomed. Engring., Melbourne, Australia, 1994—. Fellow Australian Inst. Co. Dirs., Australian Inst. of Mgmt.; mem. Royal Melbourne Golf Club, Melbourne Cricket Club. Avocations: swimming, reading, golf, gardening. Office: Terumo Corp, 5 Thomas Holt Dr, North Ryde 2113, Australia

FOGARTY, THOMAS JAMES, surgery educator; b. Cin., Feb. 25, 1934; s. William Henry and Anna Isabella (Ruthemeyer) F.; m. Rosalee Mae Brennan, Aug. 28, 1965; children: Thomas James Jr., Heather Brennan, Patrick Erin, Jonathan David. BS in Biology, Xavier U., 1956; MD, U. Cin., 1960; D (hon.), Xavier U., 1987. Intern U. Oreg. Med. Sch., Portland, 1960-61, resident, 1962-65, instr. surgery, 1967-68; chief resident, instr. surgery divsn. cardiovascular surgery Stanford (Calif.) U. Med. Ctr., 1969-70, asst. prof. surgery, 1970-71, asst. clin. prof. surgery, 1971-73; cardiovascular surgeon pvt. practice, Stanford, 1973-78; pres. med. staff Stanford U. Med. Ctr., 1977-79; cardiovascular surgeon pvt. practice, Redwood City, Calif., 1978-93; dir. cardiovascular surgery Sequoia Hosp., Redwood City, Calif., 1980-93; prof. surgery Stanford U. Med. Ctr., 1993—; bd. dirs. Acorn Cardiovascular Inc., Satellite Dialysis Ctrs., Inc.; co-founder, bd. dirs. AneuRx, Inc., Biopsys Med., Inc., Cardiac Pathways, Inc., Emergency Med. Sys., Windy Hill Tech., Inc., Gen. Surg. Innovations, Inc., LocalMed, Inc., Vital Insite, Inc., Raytel Med. Corp., Cardiovascular Imaging Sys., Inc., Devices for Vascular Intervention, Inc., Hancock Labs., Imagyn Med., Inc., Physiometrix, Inc., Ventritex, Inc., Xenotech; mem. scientific adv. bd. Autogenics, BioLink Corp., Cardio Thoracic Sys., Inc., bd. dirs.; pres., founder Fogarty Engring., Inc.; co-founder, sr. ptnr. Three Arch Ptnrs. Contbr. articles to profl. jours.; patentee in field. Fellow U. Cin. Coll. Medicine, Good Samaritan Hosp., 1961-62, Nat. Heart Inst. Surgery br., Bethesda, Md., 1965-67, rsch. fellow divsn. cardiovascular surgery Stanford Med. Ctr., 1968-69; recipient AstroLobe award Roger Bacon High Sch., 1974, Disting. Alumnus award U. Cin. Med. Sch., 1989, Lifetime Achievement award Phoenix Hall of Fame, 1997; named Inventor of Yr., San Francisco Patent and Trademark Assn., 1980. Mem. AMA, ACS, Am. Assn. Thoracic Surgery, Am. Bd. Thoracic Surgery, Am. Coll. Physican Inventors, Am. Heart Assn. (grantee), Am. Inst. Med. and Biol. Engring., Assn. for Advancement Med. Instrumentation, Med. Device Mfrs. Assn., Am. Med. Polit. Action Com., Am. Surg. Assn., Internat. Soc. Endovascular Surgery, Western Thoracic Surg. Soc., Calif. Med. Soc., Pacific Coast Surg. Assn., San Francisco Surg. Soc., San Mateo County Med. Assn., Santa Clara County Med. Assn. (Achievement award in medicine), Internat. Soc. Cardiovascular Surg. (N.Am. chpt.), Soc. Clin. Vascular Surgery, Soc. Vascular Tech., Soc. Thoracic Surgeons, Soc. Vascular Surgery (past pres. 1995), Copco Lake Sportsmen Assn., Santa Cruz Mountain Winegrowers Assn., South Skyline Assn., Sports Car Club Am., Rapley Trail Improvement Assn., Soc. Med. Friends of Wine. Republican. Avocations: hunting, fishing, pond gardening, woodworking, geneology. Office: 3270 Alpine Rd Portola Vally CA 94028-7523

FOGEL, ESTHER MARIAN, veterinary researcher; b. Bklyn., July 23, 1917; d. Chone and Rebecca (Kaplan) Fogel; m. Seymour Roseig, Jan. 21, 1967. Cert., Med. Assts. Sch., N.Y.C., 1967; student, Orange County Community Coll., Middletown, N.Y., 1967-68. Cert. clin. lab. technician, N.Y. Gen. lab. technician Arden Hill Hosp., Goshen, N.Y., 1967-68; tech. rsch. asst. Lamont-Doherty Geol. Obs., 1968-70. Democrat. Achievements include research on the organism saccharomyces cerevisiae in its inactive dry state as brewers yeast or bakers yeast, and its ability to repel the parasites, fleas and ticks from domestic pets through a biochemical process of metabolism in conjunction with meat protein: the end product as CO(NH2)2" in solution in sweat; a coincidental process of coat pigment losses in both dogs and cats fed the initial Yeast was resolved by adjusting the B, A, D Vitamins and Calcium.

FOGEL, IRVING MARTIN, consulting engineer; b. Gloucester, Mass., Apr. 15, 1929; s. Jacob and Ethel (David) F.; children: Ethan, Ronit. BS, Ind. Inst. Tech., 1954, D of Engring. (hon.), 1982. Registered profl. engr., 22 states, Israel. Civil engr. Ill. Hwy. Dept., Peoria, 1954-55; field engr. Peter Kiewit Sons Co., East Gary, Ind., 1955; field engr., progress engr., cost engr. Peter Kiewit Sons Co., Ogdensburg, N.Y., 1955-56; supt. grading and paving Merritt, Chapman & Scott, Binghamton, N.Y., 1956; cost engr. Drake-Merritt, Goose Bay, Labrador, 1956-57; constrn. mgmt. engr. Mil. Estimating Corp., Madrid, Spain, also P.I., 1957-58; project mgr. Ministry of Def., State of Israel, 1958-59, Frederic R. Harris (Holland) N.V., The Hague, also Tehran, Iran, 1959-61, Solel Boneh & Assocs., Addis Ababa, Ethiopia, 1961-63; asst. to tech. dir. Frederic R. Harris, Madrid, 1963-64; chief engr. McKee-Berger-Mansueto, Inc., N.Y.C., 1964-65, v.p. constrn. mgmt., 1965-

69; pres. Fogel & Assocs., Inc., N.Y.C., 1969—; lectr. Author guides and handbooks on constrn. bus., latest being Construction Owner's Handbook of Property Development, 1992; contbr. articles to profl. jours. Fellow ASCE (life); mem. NSPE, Am. Arbitration Assn., Am. Assn. Cost Engrs. Internat. Home: 404 E 79th St New York NY 10021-1466 Office: 168 5th Ave New York NY 10010-5910

FOGEL, JEREMY DON, judge; b. San Francisco, Sept. 17, 1949; s. Daniel and Gladys (Caplan) F.; m. Kathleen Ann Wilcox, Aug. 20, 1977; children: Megan, Nathaniel. AB, Stanford U., Palo Alto, Calif., 1971; JD, Harvard U., 1974. Bar: Calif. 1974, U.S. Dist. Ct. (no. dist.) Calif. 1974. Atty. Smith, Johnson, Fogel and Ramo, San Jose, 1974-78; dir. atty. Mental Health Advocacy Project, San Jose, 1978-81; exec. dir. Santa Clara County Bar Assn. Law Found., San Jose, 1980-81; judge Santa Clara County Mcpl. Ct., San Jose, 1981-86, Santa Clara County Superior Ct., San Jose, 1986-98, U.S. Dist. Ct. (no. dist.) Calif., 1998—; faculty Calif. Continuing Jud. Studies Prog., Berkeley, 1987—. Contbr. articles to profl. jours. Recipient Service award, Mental Health Assn., Santa Clara County, 1980, Honors award Legal Advocates Children and Youth, 1997; named Judge of Yr., Consumer Attys. Calif., 1997. Mem. Calif. Judges Assn. (v.p. 1990-91, exec. bd. 1988-91, chair jud. ethics com. 1987-88, discipline and disability com. 1991-93, jud. discipline adv. panel 1992-98, Pres.'s award 1997). Office: US Dist Ct 280 S 1st St Rm 4050 San Jose CA 95113-3095

FOGEL, RICHARD, lawyer; b. Bklyn.; m. Sheila Feldman; children: Bruce, Lori Ellen. BA, York Coll., CUNY, 1971; JD, N.Y. Law Sch., 1974. Bar: N.J. 1976, U.S. Dist. Ct. N.J. 1976, N.Y. 1981, U.S. Tax Ct. 1977. Tax law specialist IRS, Newark, 1975-77; sr. pension cons., atty. N.Y. Life, N.Y.C., 1977-81; pvt. practice, Franklin, N.J., 1981-85, Wayne, N.J., 1985-88, McAfee, N.J., 1988—; lectr. Inst. for Continuing Legal Edn., Newark, 1977—; mem. adj. faculty Upsala Coll., East Orange, N.J., 1978-88; presenter 34th ann. meeting. Internat. Soc. for Systems Scis., Portland State U., 1990. Recipient Certs. of Appreciation, IRS, Newark, 1977, Inst. Continuing Legal Edn., Newark, 1981-82, 84, Cert. in Recognition of Accomplishments, Coop. Extension Cook Coll., Rutgers U., 1982, Disting. Grad. award York Coll., 1984, Founder's Day Dist. Alumni award, 1992. Home: 28 Elizabeth Dr Sussex NJ 07461-3402 Office: Vernon Colonial Pla PO Box 737 Rt 94 Mc Afee NJ 07428

FOGEL, ROBERT WILLIAM, economist, educator, historian; b. N.Y.C., July 1, 1926; s. Harry Gregory and Elizabeth (Mitnik) F.; m. Enid Cassandra Morgan, Apr. 2, 1949; children: Michael Paul, Steven Dennis. AB, Cornell U., 1948; AM, Columbia U., 1960; PhD, Johns Hopkins U., 1963; MA, U. Cambridge, Eng., 1975, Harvard U., 1976; DSc, U. Rochester, 1987, U. de Palermo, Argentina, 1994, Brigham Young U., 1995. Instr. Johns Hopkins U., 1958-59; asst. prof. U. Rochester, 1960-64; Ford Found. vis. research prof. U. Chgo., 1963-64, asso. prof., 1964-65, prof. econs., 1965-69, prof. econs. and history, 1970-75; prof. econs. U. Rochester, 1968-71, prof. econs. and history, 1972-75; Taussig research prof. Harvard U., Cambridge, Mass., 1973-74; Harold Hitchings Burbank prof. polit. economy, prof. history Harvard U., 1975-81; Charles R. Walgreen Disting. Svc. prof. Am. instns. U. Chgo., 1981—; Pitt prof. Am. history and insts. U. Cambridge, 1975-76; chmn. com. math. and statis. methods in history Math. Social Sci. Bd., 1965-72; rsch. assoc. Nat. Bur. Econ. Rsch., 1978—, dir. DAE program, 1978-91; dir. Ctr. for Population Econ., Chgo. Author: The Union Pacific Railroad: A Case in Premature Enterprise, 1960, Railroads and American Economic Growth: Essays in Econometric History, 1964, (with others) The Reinterpretation of American Economic History, 1971, (with others) Dimensions of Quantitative Research in History, 1972, (with S.L. Engerman) Time on the Cross: The Economics of American Negro Slavery, 1974, Ten Lectures on the New Economic History, 1977, (with G.R. Elton) Which Road to the Past? Two Views of History, 1983, Without Consent or Contract: The Rise and Fall of American Slavery, Vol. 1, 1989, (with others) Vols. 2-4, 1992. Gilman fellow, 1957-60, Social Sci. Rsch. Coun. fellow, 1960, Ford Found. Faculty Rsch. fellow, 1970; Faculty Rsch. grantee, 1966, NSF grantee, 1967, 70, 72, 75, 76, 78, 92, 93, 94, 95, 96, Fulbright grantee, 1968, NIH grantee, 1991, 92, 93, 94, 95, 96; recipient Arthur H. Cole prize, 1968; Schumpeter prize, 1971; co-recipient The Bancroft prize, 1975, Gustavus Myers prize, 1990; Nobel Prize in Econ. Sci., Nobel Foundation, 1993. Fellow Econometric Soc., Royal Hist. Soc., AAAS; corr. fellow Brit. Acad.; mem. European Acad. Arts, Scis. and Humanities, Am. Econ. Soc. (pres.-elect 1997), Royal Econ. Soc., Econ. History Assn. (trustee 1972-81, pres. 1977-78), Econ. History Soc., Am. Hist. Assn., Assn. Am. Historians, Social Sci. History Assn. (pres. 1980-81), Agrl. History Soc., Am. Acad. Arts and Scis., Nat. Acad. Scis., Population Assn. Am., Internat. Union for Sci. Study of Population, Phi Beta Kappa. Office: U Chgo Grad Sch Bus Ctr for Population Econ 1101 E 58th St Chicago IL 60637-1511

FOGELBERG, PAUL ALAN, continuing education company executive; b. St. Paul, May 18, 1951; s. Harry William and Dorothy Marie (Dokmo) F.; m. Melissa Rosanne Ormsbee, Oct. 1980; children: Emily Lauren, Julia Christine, Sara Ellen. BS, U. Minn., 1975; JD, Hamline U., 1978. Pub. affairs asst. The Pillsbury Co., Mpls., 1974-75; dir. Nat. Practice Inst., Mpls., 1978-81; CEO The Profl. Edn. Group, Inc., Minnetonka, Minn., 1981—. Mem. Hamline U. Pres. Club, Hamline U. Sch. Law Alumni Assn. (Disting. Svc. 1988, pres. 1985-86), Cen. States Dressage and Combined Training Assn. (bd. dirs.), Opportunity Internat. Minn. Presbyterian. Office: The Profl Edn Group Inc 12401 Minnetonka Blvd Minnetonka MN 55305-3994

FOGELBERG, PAUL ERIK, retired geography educator, university official; b. Pori, Finland, Aug. 26, 1935; s. Harald Fogelberg and Viva Hernberg; m. Maj-Britt Nielsen, Sept. 15, 1962; children: Nina, Heidi, Ville. MSc, U. Helsinki, 1962, PhD, 1970. Assoc. prof. U. Oulu, Finland, 1981-82; asst. U. Helsinki, 1963-80, prof. geography, 1982-98, vice rector, 1992-98. Editor Fennia, 1972-78, Boreas, 1974-88. Ensign Finnish Army, 1955-56. Mem. European Assn. Sci. Editors (pres. 1991-94), Internat. Assn. Univs. (dep. bd. 1995-00). Avocations: wind music, gardening. Home: Putousrinne 1G, FIN-01600 Vantaa Finland

FOGELMARK, STAFFAN J.H., Greek studies educator; b. Fryksande, Varmland, Sweden, Apr. 12, 1939; s. Olof J.D. and Signe L.A. Fogelmark; m. Christina E. Liljewalch, Feb. 20, 1968; children: Erik, Klara, Karl. BA, Lund (Sweden) U., 1964, MA, 1968, PhD, 1972. Reader in Greek Lund U., 1972-85, sr. lectr., 1985-96; prof. Greek U. Gothenburg, 1997—; fellow Ctr. for Hellenic Studies, Harvard U., 1973-74; Charles Gordon Mackay lectr. U. Edinburgh, 1979. Author: Studies in Pindar, 1972, Chrysaigis IG 12:5, 611, 1975, Flemish and Related Panel-Stamped Bindings, 1990; contbr. articles to profl. jours. including Harvard Studies in Classical Philology, Hermes, L'Antiquité Classique, Scandia. Recipient The Gleerup award New Soc. Letters at Lund, 1992, Disting. Tchg. award Student Union Lund U., 1995; rsch. grantee Swedish Coun. for Rsch. in the Humanities, 1991-93. Mem. Am. Philol. Assn., Bibliog. Soc., Biblio. Soc. Am., Cedant Curae Soc. Avocations: music, mountaineering, Renaissance books and paintings. Home: Gerdagatan 8, SE-22362 Lund Sweden Office: U Gothenburg, Box 200, SE-40530 Gothenburg Sweden

FÖGER, KARL, chemistry scientist; b. Stams, Tirol, Austria, Oct. 19, 1948; arrived in Australia, 1975; s. Karl Johann and Josefa (Pramstaller) F.; m. Annemarie Wild, Mar. 19, 1977; 1 child, Lydia. PhD in Chemistry, U. Innsbruck, Austria, 1975. Scientist divsn. materials sci. and tech. Commonwealth Sci. and Indsl. Rsch. Orgn., Melbourne, Australia, 1975-81, sr. scientist, 1981-86, prin. scientist, 1986-92, sr. prin. scientist, 1992—; dep. dir. R & D, Ceramic Fuel Cells Ltd., Melbourne, 1992—; vis. prof. Stanford (Calif.) U., 1983-84; numerous conf. presentations in field. Contbg. author: Catalysis: Science and Technology, 1984; contbr. over 100 articles to sci. jours. Fellow Royal Australian Chem. Inst. Roman Catholic. Avocations: history, music, tennis, skiing. Home: 2 Macartney Ave, Kew Vic 3101, Australia Office: CSIRO Divsn Materials Sci, 170 Browns Rd, Noble Park VIC 3174, Australia

FOGERTY, JAMES EDWARD, archivist, state official; b. Mpls., Jan. 26, 1945; s. Robert P. and Ralpha Chamberlain (James) F. B.A., Coll. St. Thomas, 1968; M.L.S., U. Minn., 1972. Regional ctrs. dir. Minn. Hist. Soc., St. Paul, 1972-76, field dir., 1976-79, dep. state archivist, 1979-86, head aquisitions and curatorial dept., 1986—; sec.-treas. Midwest Archives Conf., Chgo., 1977-81, pres., 1983-85. Author: Collecting Phil Spector, 1991; editor: Oral History Collections of the Minnesota Historical Society, 1984; contbr. articles to Am. Archivist, Midwestern Archivist, History News, others. Fellow Soc. Am. Archivists; mem. Internat. Coun. Archives (U.S. rep., com. on oral sources), Oral History Assn., Midwest Archives Conf., Am. Assn. For State and Local History, Phi Alpha Theta. Office: Minn Hist Soc 345 Kellogg Blvd W Saint Paul MN 55102-1906

FOGH-ANDERSEN, NIELS, laboratory director; b. Frederiksberg, Denmark, Apr. 10, 1950; s. Poul and Birgit (Duelund) F.; m. Kirsten Clemmesen Fogh-Andersen, Oct. 23, 1981. MD, Copenhagen U., 1975, PhD, 1988. Dir. lab. Herlev (Denmark) Hosp., 1985—. Office: Herlev Hosp 54 M1, Herlev Ringvej 75, DK2730 Herlev Denmark

FOGLIETTA, THOMAS MICHAEL, diplomat, former congressman; b. Philadelphia, Pa., Dec. 3, 1928; s. Michael and Rose (Buttari) F. B.A., St. Joseph's Coll.; postgrad., Temple U. Bar: Pa., U.S. Supreme Ct. Pvt. practice law Phila.; mem. 97th-105th Congresses from 1st Pa. dist., Washington, D.C., 1981-97, Phila. City Coun.; U.S. amb. to Italy U.S. Dept. State, Rome, 1997—; mem. subcom. Mil. Constrn. Transp. Appropriations, Congl. Human Rights Caucus, Congl. Arts Caucus, Congl. Narcotics Caucus, Congl. Hispanic Caucus; founder and chmn., Congl. Urban Caucus, Congl. Black Caucus. Mem. Dem. Study group. Democrat. Roman Catholic. Office: US Amb to Italy William J Green Bldg 10402 US State Dept Washington DC 20521-9500

FOGLIZZO, THIERRY NICOLAS, astrophysicist; b. Paris, Sept. 16, 1967; s. René and Edith (Reyne) F.; m. Diana Saundby, Nov. 23, 1995; children: Laszlo, Garance. Degree in engring., Ecole Poly., France, 1990; PhD in Astrophysics, U. Paris, 1994. With Max Planck Astrophysik, Munich, 1994-96; astrophysicist Commissariat à l'Energie Atomique, Saclay, France, 1996—. Office: CEA, Svc d'Astrophysique, 91191 Gif-sur-Yvette France

FOHL, TIMOTHY, consulting and investment company executive; b. Pitts., Apr. 21, 1934; s. Edward Zinn and Dorothy (Umbenhauer) F.; m. Nancy Lee Hattox, Apr. 15, 1961; children: Nicholas, Jeffrey, Peter. AB, Dartmouth Coll., 1956; MS, MIT, 1959, PhD, 1963; postgrad. exec. devel. program, Whittemore Sch. Bus. and Econs., 1977. Rsch. scientist Itek Corp., Lexington, Mass., 1962-63; rsch. scientist Mt. Auburn Rsch. Assos., Newton, Mass., 1963-68, prin. scientist, dir., 1968-72; with GTE Products Corp., Danvers, Mass., 1972-79, mgr. new product devel. lighting group, 1977-82, mgr. engring. devel., 1982-85, dir. engring. devel., 1985-88; scientist GTE Labs., Inc., Waltham, Mass., 1988-92; pres. Tech. Integration Group, Carlisle, Mass., 1992—; v.p. Light Time in Space, Inc., 1993—. Contbr. articles to profl. jours.; patentee in field. Pres., trustee Carlisle Conservation Found., 1972-79; v.p. Carlisle Trails Assn., 1975—; fin. chmn. Town Republican Com., 1980. Recipient Leslie H. Warner Tech. Achievement award, 1990. Mem. Mass. Bus. Roundtable. Home: 681 South St Carlisle MA 01741-1517

FOK, DENNIS WAI-KEE, design director, educator; b. Hong Kong, Sept. 20, 1952; s. Dao-Wah and Lin-Foon (Tam) F.; m. Catherine Chiu-Sheung Tsang, Jan. 6, 1979; children: Julian Chung-Hang, Valerie Tung-Tung. Higher Diploma in Design, Hong Kong Poly., 1975; MA in Interior Design, Leicester (Eng.) Poly., 1979. Sr. set designer Comml. TV Ltd., Hong Kong, 1975-76; interior design Jens Munk Ltd., Hong Kong, 1976-77; project designer Dale Keller & Assocs. Ltd., Hong Kong, 1979-81; interior designer The Hong Kong Land Co. Ltd., 1981-87; design dir. Dennis Fok Design Ltd., Hong Kong, 1987—; bd. dirs. Avanti Trading Ltd., Hong Kong, Efflex Trading Co., Hong Kong. Interior designer Marco Polo (HK) Hotel, 1988, Maxim's Caterers Ltd., 1988, 89, 97, Crown Motors Ltd., 1992, Patong Thai Restaurant, 1994, Mandarin Oriental HK, Ltd., 1995, 96, 97, Adidas Asia/Pacific Ltd., 1996, Wah Nam Group Ltd., 1997, Golden Lion Group Ltd., 1998, Club de Millennium, 1999, Lee Kum Kee Guest House, 1999, P&O Travel Ltd., 2000, Royal Motor Boutique Ltd., 2000, many others; also various residential design projects. Mem. Chartered Soc. Designers, Hong Kong Jockey Cub, Internat. Assoc. Clubs (U.K.). Avocations: color perspectives, painting, international travel. Office: Dennis Fok Design Ltd Fl 5, 282 Lockhart Rd, Wanchai Hong Kong

FOK, THOMAS DSO YUN, civil engineer; b. Canton, China, July 1, 1921; came to U.S., 1947, naturalized, 1956; s D. H. and C. (Tse) F.; m. Maria M.L. Liang, Sept. 18, 1949. B.Eng., Nat. Tung-Chi U., Szechuan, China, 1945; M.S., U. Ill., 1948; M.B.A. Dr. Nadler Money Marketeer scholar, NYU, 1950; Ph.D., Carnegie-Mellon U., 1956. Registered profl. engr., N.Y., Pa., Ohio, Ill., Ky., W.Va., Ind., Md., Fla. Structural designer Lummus Co., N.Y.C., 1951-53; design engr. Richardson, Gordon & Assocs., cons. engrs., Pitts., 1956-58; assoc. prof. engring. Youngstown U., Ohio, 1958-67, dir. computing ctr., 1963-67; ptnr. Cernica, Fok & Assocs., cons. engrs., Youngstown, Ohio, 1958-64; prin. Thomas Fok & Assocs., cons. engrs., Youngstown, Ohio, 1964-65; ptnr. Mosure-Fok & Syrakis Co., Ltd., cons. Engrs., Youngstown, Ohio, 1965-76; cons. engr. to Mahoning County Engr. Ohio, 1960-65; pres. Computing Systems & Tech., Youngstown, Ohio, 1967-72; chmn. Thomas Fok and Assocs., Ltd., cons. engrs., Youngstown, Ohio, 1977—. Contbr. articles to profl. jours. Trustee Pub. Libr. of Youngstown and Mahoning County, 1973—; trustee Youngstown State U., 1975-84, chmn., 1981-83; mem. Ohio State Bd. Registration for Profl. Engrs. and Surveyors, 1992-96. Recipient Walter E. and Caroline H. Watson Found. Disting. Prof.'s award Youngstown U., 1966, Outstanding Person award Mahoning Valley Tech. Socs. Council, 1987. Fellow ASCE; mem. Am. Concrete Inst., Internat. Assn. for Bridge and Structural Engring., Am. Soc. Engring. Edn., Nat. Soc. Profl. Engrs., AAAS, Soc. Am. Mil. Engrs., Ohio Acad. Sci., N.Y. Acad. Sci., Sigma Xi, Beta Gamma Sigma, Sigma Tau, Delta Pi Sigma. Lodge: Rotary. Achievements include development of a design method by computer for a solid-ribbed tied, through arch Ft. Duquesne Bridge; development of Analysis of Continuous Truss by Digital Computer. Home: 325 S Canfield Niles Rd Youngstown OH 44515-4020 Office: 3896 Mahoning Ave Youngstown OH 44515-3022

FOKKEMA, DOUWE WESSEL, literature educator; b. Utrecht, The Netherlands, May 4, 1931; s. Dirk and Gijsbertha Catharina (Van der Meulen) F.; m. Elrud Ibsch; children: Aleide, Diederik. MA in Dutch Lang. and Lit., U. Amsterdam, The Netherlands, 1956; postgrad., Leiden (The Netherlands) U., 1953-56, PhD in Chinese Lit., 1965; postgrad., U. Calif., Berkeley, 1963-64; PhD (hon.), U. Silesia, Poland, 1995. Civil servant East European desk Ministry of Fgn. Affairs, The Hague, The Netherlands, 1959-63, civil servant East Asian desk, 1964-66; chargé d'affaires Netherlands Diplomatic Mission, Peking, 1966-68; rsch. assoc. in comparative lit. Utrecht (The Netherlands) U., 1968-71, assoc. prof. comparative lit., 1971-80, prof. comparative lit., 1980-96, dir. Rsch. Inst. for History and Culture, 1987-94, chmn. bd. Netherlands Grad. Sch. for Lit. Studies, 1995-96; chair steering com. rsch. program on the culture of the Netherlands in European context Netherlands Orgn. for Sci. Rsch., Utrecht, 1990—. Author: Literary Doctrine in China, 1965, Report From Peking, 1972, (novel) Zichtbare Steden, 1993, Marco's Missie, 1999, 5 others; co-author Theories of Literature in the 20th Century, 1977, 4th edit., 1995, Modernist Conjectures, 1988, Knowledge and Commitment, 2000, 13 others. Decorated ridder in de Order Oranje-Nassau (Netherlands). Mem. Internat. Comparative Lit. Assn. (pres. 1985-88, hon. pres. 1988), Brit. Comparative Lit. Assn., Internat. Assn. for Semiotic Studies, Deutsche Gesellschaft für Semiotik, Portuguese Comparative Lit. Assn. (hon.), South-African Comparative Lit. Assn. (hon.), Academia Europaea, Netherlands Assn. Comparative and Gen. LIt. (pres. 1975-81). Office: Utrecht U, Kromme Nieuwe Gracht 29, 3512 HD Utrecht The Netherlands

FOKUO, EMMANUEL ADU, mechanical engineer; b. Mampong-Ashanti, Ghana, Apr. 18, 1954; s. Samuel Kwaku Fokuo and Adwoa Sika; m. Dora Afua Pokuaah, Dec. 31, 1984; children: Ebenezer Adu Dwomoh, Rhoda Adu Fokuo. B in Engring., Sunyani Tech. Inst., 1972; Mech. Engring., Sch. Mines, 1974, Takoradi Poly. Inst., 1976. Maintenance trainee Volta Aluminium Co. Ltd., Tema, Ghana, 1976-78; mech. technician Mim Timber Co. Ltd., Ghana, 1978-79; plant engr. Trasacco Furniture Ltd., Accra, Ghana, 1979; plant and mech. engr. Poku Transport Industries Ltd., Kumasi, Ghana, 1979-85, asst. tech. and prodn. mgr., 1985-87; mech. engr. Ehwia Wood Products Ltd., Ghana, 1988-89, acting chief engr., 1989-94, chief engr., product mgr., 1994-98; head kiln drying dept. Wood Industries Tng. Ctr., Ghana, 1998—; tutor mech. engring. dept. Kumasi Poly. Inst., 1982. Designer Dimension-Push Bench, Circular Saw Machine. Methodist. Avocations: reading, writing, riding, photography. Home: RBR 2 Kofiase Rd, Mampong-Ashanti Ghana also: Plot 18 Block U, Asokwa, Kumasi Ghana Address: PO Box 9004, Ahensan, Kumasi Ghana also: Plot 17 Block Q, Ayigya, Kumasi Ghana

FÖLDES, ENIKÖ, chemist; b. Zirc, Hungary, May 22, 1944; s. Ferenc and Judit (Tóth) F. Chem. engr., Chem. U. of Veszprém, 1967; specialized engr., Tech. U., 1970; PhD, Hungarian Acad. Sci., 1984. Chem. engr. ORION Radio and TV Factory, Budapest, 1967-72; rschr. Rsch. Inst. for Plastics, Budapest, 1972-84; sr. rschr. Ctrl. Rsch. Inst. Chem., Budapest, 1984—; vis. rschr. Polytech. U., Bklyn., 1988; cons. Tech. U. of Budapest, 1995—. Contbr. articles to profl. jours. Mem. SPE, Hungarian Chem. Soc. Office: Chem Rsch Ctr, Hungarian Acad Sci POB 17, 1525 Budapest Hungary

FÖLDES, ISTVÁN B., physicist, researcher; b. Budapest, Hungary, Sept. 2, 1954; s. István and Edit (Beregi) F.; m. Maria Eszenyi; 1 child, David. Dipl.Phys., Lóránd Eötvös U., Budapest, 1977, Dr.rer.nat., 1980. Rschr. Ctrl. Rsch. Inst. Physics, Budapest, 1980-84, 86-88; Max-Planck stipendiate M.P. Inst. f. Quantenoptik, Garching, Germany, 1984-86; sr. sci. co-worker KFKI-Rsch. Inst. Particle and Nuclear Physics, Budapest, 1989-91, 94—; guest rschr. Max-Planck Inst. f. Quantenoptik, Garching, 1991-93; lectr. Szeged (Hungary) U., 1998—. Contbr. over 40 articles to profl. jours. Mem. European Phys. Soc., Roland Eötvös Phys. Soc. (Selenyi prize 1997). Avocations: sports, literature, music, philosophy. Office: KFKI-Rsch Inst Particle Phy, Konkoly-Thege 29-33, H-1125 Budapest Hungary

FOLDES, LUCIEN PAUL, economics educator; b. Vienna, Austria, Nov. 19, 1930; s. Egon and Marta (Landau) F. B in Commerce, U. London, 1950, Diploma in Bus. Adminstrn., 1951, MSc., 1952. Asst. lectr. econs. London Sch. Econs., 1951-52, 54-55, lectr. econs., 1955-61, reader econs., 1961-79, prof. econs., 1979-96, prof. emeritus econs., 1996—. Author articles to profl. jours. Served to lt. British Army, 1952-54. Rockefeller Travelling fellow, 1962. Fellow Royal Econ. Soc.; mem. Am. Econ. Assn., Inst. Math. Stats., London Math. Soc, Royal Statistical Soc. Avocation: math. analysis. Office: London Sch Econs, Houghton St, London WC2A 2AE, England

FOLEY, EUGENE ARTHUR, accountant, consultant; b. San Jose, Calif., May 6, 1953; s. Eugene Frank and Shirley Ann (Merrill) F.; m. Elaine Sayre, July 9, 1995; children: Eugene Welles, Patrick Michael, Brian Ross. BSBA, U. Hartford, 1976; MS in Taxation, Golden Gate U., 1979; MDiv, Princeton Theol. Sem., 1994; M of Acctg., Rutgers U., 2000. CPA, Calif., N.J.; cert. mgmt. acct., info. systems auditor, computer profl., internal auditor, networking specialist. Acct. J.K. Lasser et al, San Jose, 1976-79; internal auditor Carter Hawley Hale, Los Angeles, 1979-81; lectr., asst. prof. Calif. State U., Sacramento, 1979-84; owner, cons. E.A. Foley Accountancy, Sacramento, 1981-84; corp. audit mgr. Emhart Corp., Farmington, Conn., 1984-86; controller Powers Mfg. div. Emhart Corp., Elmira, N.Y., 1986-88; owner, cons. Foley Cos., Elmira, N.Y., 1988-92; asst. prof. Rider U., Lawrenceville, N.J., 1992-94; asst. Christian edn. Cold Spring Presbyn. Ch., 1993-96; pastor Court House Presbyn. Ch., 1996-2000; tchr. Cape May County Tech. Sch., N.J., 1999—; pvt. practice Eugene A. Foley, CPA, North Cape May, N.J., 2000—; mcpl. auditor, contr. State of N.J., Camden, 2000—; bus. mgr. Calif. Polit. Rev., 1987—. Sec.-treas., exec. dir. Elmira YMCA, 1986-87; treas. Supreme Ct. Project, Calif., 1985-86; v.p. fin., 1987, treas., 1988, Sullivan Trail Council Boy Scouts Am., dist. commr. George Washington Coun., 1992-94, So. N.J. Coun., 1994-96, dist. exec., 1996-99; treas. Calif. Pub. Policy Found., 1987—; mgr., CFO Lower Township, N.J., 1996-97; commr. Learning for Life/Venturing, 1999—. Recipient Whitney M. Young Jr. Svc. award Boy Scouts Am., 1989. Mem. Am. Inst. CPA's, Calif. Soc. CPA's, Inst. Internal Auditors (cert.), Inst. Mgmt. Accts., EDP Auditors Assn., Mensa, Am. Numismatic Assn., Am. First Day Cover Soc., Am. Topical Assn. (life), Nat. Assn. Comm. Systems Engrs., Masons, Scottish Rite. Lodges: Masons, Scottish Rite. Avocations: coin collecting, genealogy. Home and Office: 7 Sheriff Taylor Blvd North Cape May NJ 08204-4476

FOLEY, JOHN MILES, English language and classical studies educator; b. Northampton, Mass., Jan. 22, 1947; s. Cornelius Burns and Eleanor Margaret (Broggi) F.; m. Anne Marie Conlisk, July 30, 1983; children: Elizabeth Anne, Isaac Michael, John Miles Jr. AB in Physics, Math., and Chemistry, Colgate U., 1969; MA in English Lit., U. Mass., 1971, PhD in English and Comparative Lit., 1974. Asst. prof. English Emory U., Atlanta, 1974-79; fellow Harvard U., Cambridge, Mass., 1976-77, 80-81; from assoc. prof. to prof. U. Mo., Columbia, 1981—, prof. English and classics, 1985—, Witt Byler endowed chair in the humanities, 1985—, Curators' prof. classical studies and English, 1998—; vis. prof. U. Belgrade, Serbia, 1980. Author: The Theory of Oral Composition, 1988, Traditional Oral Epic, 1990, Immanent Art, 1991, The Singer of Tales in Performance, 1995, Teaching Oral Traditions, 1998, Homer's Traditional Art, 1999, others; contbr. articles to profl. jours. Fellow Am. Folklore Soc., Russian Acad. Scis., Internat. Folklore Fellows (Finland); mem. MLA (exec. com. 1985-89, 87-91, 89-93, 98—). Avocation: languages. Office: U Mo Ctr for Studies in Oral Tradition 316 Hillcrest Hall Columbia MO 65211-6280

FOLEY, JOHN PATRICK, media analyst, lecturer, consultant, advocate; b. London, Nov. 18, 1954; s. James and Bridget May (O'Connor) F.; m. Viorela Dediu, Sept., 1989 (div. Aug. 1994); 1 child, James-Augustine. BA, Oxford (Eng.) U., 1977; MA, Lancaster (Eng.) U., 1978. Comml. liaison Gestetner Internat., London, 1979-81; operational rsch. analyst Thorn EMI, London, 1981-83; corp. planner Total Oil, London, 1983-86; dir. Saladin Inc., London, 1986-88; mgr. Coopers & Lybrand, London, 1988-93; mng. dir. Convergent Decisions Group, London, 1993—. Author: Digital Terrestrial Television in Europe, 1996, 2d edit., 1998. Chmn. Families Need Fathers Charity, London, 1997-99; policy dir. Nat. Coun., 1999—; networker Prostate Cancer Soc.; founder The Separation Orgn. Ltd., 1999. Liberal Democrat. Roman Catholic. Avocations: media, reading, chess, cycling. Office: CDG, PO Box 14505, London SW15 3WG, England

FOLEY, MARTIN JAMES, lawyer; b. Nebr., Nov. 7, 1946; s. James Gleason and Mary Elizabeth (O'Brien) F.; m. Linda Sivyer; children: James Gleason II, Daniel Patrick, Ryan Edward, Michelle Sivyer. Cert. Completion, Cambridge U., 1967; BA in Philosophy, U. So. Calif., 1968, JD, 1974, MBA, 1975. Bar: Calif. 1975, U.S. Dist. Ct. (cen. dist.) Calif. 1975, U.S. Dist. Ct. (ea., so. and no. dists.) Calif. 1980, U.S. Ct. Appeals (9th cir.) 1980, U.S. Ct. Fed. Claims 1991, U.S. Supreme Ct. 1990. Acct. Ford Motor Co., San Jose, Calif., 1968, cost analyst, 1970-71; assoc. Adams, Duque & Hazeltine, 1975-80; sr. ptnr. Bryan, Cave, McPheeters & McRoberts, L.A., 1980-89, Sonnenschein Nath & Rosenthal, L.A., 1990—; mem. bd. govs. Gen. Alumni Assn., U. So. Calif., 1982-84, ct. appt. settlement officer Calif. State, 1992-94, U.S. Dist. Ct. (cen. dist.), 1998—; lectr. groups and profl. confs. Contbr. articles to profl. jours. Served to lt. (j.g.) USNR, 1968-70. Mem. ABA (numerous coms.), Calif. Bar Assn. (conf. of dels. 1979-93), L.A. County Bar Assn., Jonathan Club (L.A.), Annandale Golf Club (Pasadena, Calif.). Republican. Roman Catholic. Office: Sonnenschein Nath Rosenthal 601 S Figueroa St Ste 1500 Los Angeles CA 90017-5720

FOLEY, PATRICIA JEAN, accountant; b. Bridgeport, Conn., Jan. 12, 1956; d. John Edward and Louise (Caselli) F. AA, Housantonic C.C., 1978; BS, Cen. Conn. State Coll., 1980; MBA, U. Hartford, 1996. CPA, Conn. Staff acct. Spitz, Sullivan, Wachtel & Falcetta, Hartford, Conn., 1981-82, client acct., 1982-85, sr. acct., 1985-87, supr., mgr., 1987-97; mgr. Falcetta Wachtel & Knochenhauer LLC, Bloomfield, Conn., 1997-98; prin. Patricia J. Foley, CPA, Newington, Conn., 1998—; mem. Acctg. Del. to Russia, Ukraine & Estonia Citizens Amb., 1993. Pres. Woodsedge Condominium Assn., Newington, Conn., 1989-92, treas., 1985-92; dir. Friends of Lucy Robbins Welles Libr. of Newington, 1996—, sec., 1998-99, membership co-chair, 1999—. Mem. AICPA (mgmt. adv. svc. com. 1987—, info. tech. divsns., 1992—), Conn. Soc. CPAs, Am. Women Soc. CPAs, Cmty. Assn. Inst. (membership chair Conn. chpt. 1991-92), Nat. Assn. Women Bus. Owners. Home: 35 Woodsedge Dr Apt 1B Newington CT 06111-4271 Office: 35-1B Woodsedge Dr Newington CT 06111-4271

FOLEY, THOMAS STEPHEN, diplomat, former speaker House of Representatives; b. Spokane, Wash., Mar. 6, 1929; s. Ralph E. and Helen Marie (Higgins) F.; m. Heather Strachan, Dec. 1968. B.A., U. Wash., 1951,

LL.B., 1957. Bar: Wash. Ptnr. Higgins & Foley, 1957-58; dep. pros. atty. Spokane County, Spokane, 1958-60; asst. atty. gen. State of Wash., Olympia, 1960-61; spl. counsel interior and insular affairs com. U.S. Senate, Washington, 1961-64; mem. 89th-103rd Congresses from 5th Wash. dist., Washington, D.C., 1965-94, House majority whip, 1981-86; House majority leader 89th-103rd Congresses from 5th Wash. dist., Washington, 1987-89; speaker U.S. Ho. of Reps., Washington, 1989-94; ptnr. Akin, Gump, Strauss, Hauer & Feld, Washington, 1995-97; chmn. Pres.'s Fgn. Intelligence Adv. Bd., 1995-97; U.S. amb. to Japan U.S. Dept. State, Tokyo, 1997—; instr. law Gonzaga U., 1958-60; mem. bd. advisors Ctr. Strategic and Internat. Studies; mem. adv. council Am. Ditchley Found. Author: Honor in the House. Bd. overseers Whitman Coll.; bd. advisors Yale U. council; bd. dirs. Council on Fgn. Relations. Mem. Phi Delta Phi. Democrat. Office: US Embassy, 1-10-5 Akasaka, Minato-ku Tokyo 107-8420, Japan

FOLEY, VIRGINIA SUE LASHLEY, counselor, international training consultant; b. Richmond, Ind., May 1, 1942; d. Robert E. and Flora Rose (Johnson) Lashley; m. Laurence Michael Foley Sr., Jan. 28, 1968; children: Megan Leigh, Jeremie Beth, L. Michael Jr. BA, Hanover Coll., 1964; MS, San Francisco State U., 1969. Cert. profl. counselor and internat. mental health tng. cons. Vol. Peace Corps, Danao City, The Philippines, 1964-66; counselor, tng. cons. In Touch Found., U.S. Peace Corps., Asian Devel. Bank, Manila, 1981-85, Internat. Sch., 1981-85; counselor, tng. cons. to Overseas Briefing Ctr. U.S. Dept. of State, Washington, 1988-90; counselor, mental health cons. U.S. State Dept./U.S. Peace Corps, La Paz, Bolivia, 1990-92; mental health coord. U.S. Embassy, Lima, Peru, 1992-94; counselor, mental health tng. cons. Aetna/HAI, Lima, Peru, 1994-96, Harare, Zimbabwe, 1996—. Author: Leisure Time Activities for Families in Manila, 1983; (manuals) Career Development Manual, 1984; writer mags. What's On in Manila, 1983-85, Off Duty Mag., 1985, USAID Frontlines, 1991-94, Lima Times, 1994, Fgn. Svc. Jour., 1996; contbr. articles to mags. Mem. U.S. Embassy Mental Health Com. Recipient award of recognition Bukidnon State Coll., The Philippines, 1985. Mem. Am. Counseling Assn., Internat. Assn. Marriage and Family Counselors, Assn. Boliviana de Psicologia Humanista (founding mem.), Am. Women's Club (co-pres. 1998—). Avocations: instrumental music, art, crafts, hiking, literature. Address: USAID Amman Unit 70205 Box 6 APO AE 09892-7206

FOLGATE, CYNTHIA A., domestic violence systems coordinator, educator; b. Chgo., Jan. 27, 1950; d. William C. and Cassie Edna (Sisemore) F. BA, No. Ill. U., 1974, MA, 1983. Sec. No. Ill. U., DeKalb, 1974-80, 83-84, instr., 1984-92; outreach coord. Safe Passage, DeKalb, 1992-96, crisis intervention/outreach coord., 1996-97, systems advocacy coord., 1997—; coord. DeKalb County Domestic Violence Initiative, 1998—; instr. Waubonsee C.C., Sugar Grove, Ill., 1990—; mem. DeKalb County Domestic Violence Forum, 1990-91. Mem., bd. deacons 1st Congregational United Ch. of Christ, DeKalb, 1989-92; speech cons. for various election campaigns, DeKalb County, 1988-90; coord. DeKalb County Domestic Violence Initiative, 1998—. Mem. Friends of Barb City Manor. Democrat. Office: Safe Passage PO Box 621 Dekalb IL 60115-0621

FOLGUERA, JAIME, lawyer; b. Madrid, Apr. 4, 1954; s. Jose Fulguera and Pilar Crespo; m. Blanca Sanchez-Velasco; children: Blanca, Jose. Law degree, U. Autonoma, Madrid, 1997. Ptnr. Uria & Menendez, Madrid. Author: El Control de Concentraciones en la Union Europea, 1999. Office: Uria & Menendez, Jorge Juan 6, 2800 Madrid Spain

FOLIAS, CHRISTOS, member European Parliament; b. Thessaloniki, Greece, Feb. 14, 1951. Mem. European Parliament, Brussels; mem. com. on industry, external trade, rsch. and energy, com. on budgetary control, chmn. substitute del. for rels. with Switzerland, Iceland and Norway. Mem. Group of European People's Party (Christian Dems.) and European Dems. Mem. New Democracy Party. *

FOLIĆ, RADOMIR J., structural engineering educator; b. Šaptej, Serbia, Yugoslavia, Apr. 12, 1940; s. Jovo and Milica (Ćulafić) F.; m. Danica Čvorović, July 9, 1963 (div. 1973); children: Mirjana, Boris; m. Nadja Kurtović, Feb. 25, 1978; 1 child, Milica. Grad. engr., U. Belgrade, Yugoslavia, 1963, DEng, 1983; M. U. Zagreb, Croatia, 1974. Registered profl. engr. Prin. engr. "Put"-Rd. Co., Priština, Yugoslavia, 1963-67; asst. prof. engring. U. Belgrade, Pristina, 1967-72; prin. designer URBIS-Design & Rsch. Co., Novi Sad, Yugoslavia, 1972-80; asst. prof. tech. scis. U. Novi Sad, 1980-84, assoc. prof. tech. scis., 1984-88, prof., 1988—, dean faculty tech. scis., 1986-88; sci. advisor Inst. Testing Materials and Structures, Belgrade, Yugoslavia, 1992—; head Inst. Indsl. Bldg., Novi Sad, 1981-86, 89—. Author: (with others) of 380 papers including: Computer-aided Analysis and Design of CS, 1984, 1990, Demountable Concrete Structures, 1985, Numerical Models in Geomechanics, 1986, Failure to Concrete Structures, 1993, 96, Structural Faults and Repair, 1987, 89, 95, 97, 99; contbr. articles to profl. jours.; patentee in field. Mem. Soc. Structural Engring. Serbia-Belgrade (pres. 1989-99), Internat. Union Testing and Rsch. Labs. Materials and Structures (mem. damage classification concrete tech. com.), Internat. Assn. for Bridge and Structural Engring., Am. Concrete Inst. Office: U Novi Sad Faculty Tech Scis, Trg Dositeja Obradovica 6, 21000 Novi Sad Serbia, Yugoslavia

FOLK, JERRY LEE, ecumenical leader; b. St. Marys, Ohio, July 3, 1937; s. Harold Rollo and Olive Alilian (Stoker) F.; m. Kathryn Ann Chociej, May 13, 1972; children: Stephanie Margaret, Christopher John. BA, Capital U., Colombus, Ohio, 1959; MDiv, Wartburg Theol. Sem., Dubuque, Iowa, 1963; ThD, Karl Eberhard U., Tuebingen, Germany, 1970. Ordained to ministry Evang. Luth. Ch. Am., 1967. Pastor St. John's Luth. Ch., Steubenville, Ohio, 1967-72; prof. religious studies, peace studies Bethany (W.Va.) Coll., 1972-76; dir. Shalom Ctr., Sioux Falls, S.D., 1976-87; exec. dir. Commn. Ch. Soc., Evang. Luth. Ch. Am., Chgo., 1987-92; lead pastor St. John's Luth. Ch., Madison, Wis., 1992-94; exec. dir. Wis. Coun. Chs., Sun Prairie, 1994—; adj. faculty Luther Theol. Sem., St. Paul, 1976-87; assoc. prof. religion Augustana Coll., Sioux Falls, 1976-87; dir. Peace and Justice Mins., Mpls., 1981-83; vis. prof. Luth. Sch. Theology, Chgo., 1985-86; mem. ch. world svc. bd. Nat. Coun. Churches, 1996 -99, mem. ecumenical networks commn., 1996-99; mem. Nat. Farm Worker Ministry Bd., 1995—. Author: Worldly Christians, A Call to Faith, Prayer and Action, 1983, Doing Justice, Doing Theology, 1991; author, editor: Peaceways, 1983. Mem. Mayor's Fair Housing Commn., Steubenville, 1968-72; bd. dirs. United Brotherhood Coun., Sioux Falls, 1976-80; co-founder, bd. dirs. S.D. Peace and Justice Ctr., Watertown, 1980-87. Luth. World Fedn. scholar, 1963-65; recipient Outstanding Social Min. award Ea. Dist. Am. Luth. Ch., 1972. Mem. Nat. Assn. Ecumenical Staff, Fellowship Reconciliation, Luth. Peace Fellowship, Ch. Labor Network. Avocations: swimming, gardening. Home: 614 Division St Madison WI 53704-5514 Office: Wis Coun Chs 750 Windsor St Sun Prairie WI 53590-2149

FOLK, KATHERINE PINKSTON, English language educator, writer, journalist; b. Corsicana, Tex., Feb. 8, 1925; d. Lucian Albert and Katherine (Shell) Pinkston; m. Elmer Ellsworth Folk, Apr. 21, 1946; children: Russell Harter, David Shell, Barbara Kay Folk Nowotny. BA in Journalism, Tex. Tech. U., 1946; postgrad., U. Houston, 1960-71. Reporter Scurry County Times, Snyder, Tex., 1946; dir. advt. Dunlaps Dept. Store, Lubbock, Tex., 1946; instr. English Odessa (Tex.) Coll., 1948-53; dir. communication, editor Viva Mag. Houston Met. Ministries, 1979-80; dir. communication for continuing edn. Houston Community Coll. System, 1989-90, instr. English, 1980—; auditor creative writing Rice U., Houston, 1966; tutor English Spring Br. Ind. Sch. Dist., Houston, 1970-75. Contbr. articles to popular mags. Ann. sponsor Odessa Coll., 1950-53; mem. Harris County Heritage Soc., Houston, 1985-91, Nat. Fedn. Rep. Women, Houston, 1987-99, literacy chair, 1999, Country Playhouse Little Theatre, 1987-96; bd. dirs. Spring Br. YWCA, Houston, 1990-91. Mem. AAUW, Jr. League Houston (patron tea rm.), Nat. Fedn. Press Women, Soc. Chldren's Book Writers, Romance Writers Am., Delta Delta Delta (chmn. scholarship com. 1972). Episcopalian. Avocations: writing, reading, walking, music, travel. Office: Houston C C Sys 22 Waugh Dr Houston TX 77007-5813

FOLKE, JENS, chemist, consultant, educator; b. Copenhagen, Aug. 16, 1953; s. Ivan and Lena (Andersen) F.; m. Karen Vinther, Jan. 19, 1985; children: Christian, Emil. MSc in Organic Chemistry, Biochemistry, U. Copenhagen, 1980; DSc in Environ. Chemistry, Tech. U. Chalmers, U. Goteborg, Sweden, 1985; M in Environ. Mgmt., Tech. U. Denmark, 1998; postgrad., U. Wash., Ctr. for Inland Waters, Burlington, Ont., Can. Registered environ. auditor Environ. Auditors Registration Assn. Chemist Occupl. Health Inst., Copenhagen, 1980-81, Water Quality Inst., Horsholm, Denmark, 1981-85; cons. COWI, Lyngby, Denmark, 1986-91; dir. MFG, Gilleleje, Denmark, 1991—; cons. clients including Danish Nat. Agy. for Environ. Protection, Nordic Coun. Mins., ECC, Ministry of Environ., Ont. and Alta., U.S. EPA, UN and World Bank orgns., cos. including Air Liquide, Eka Nobel, Novo Nordisk, Procter & Gamble, StoraCell, others; external prof. ecotoxicology U. Roskilde, Denmark, 1991-94, external prof. social sci. and tech., 1995—; mem. sci. and concertation coms. on organic micropollutants in aquatic environ. EEC Directorate, 1981-86. Contbr. articles to sci. jours., conf. procs. Recipient Hede-Nielsen prize, 1984; U. Cambridge scholar, 1979. Mem. TAPPI (Best Tech. Paper environ. conf. gen. category 1992, 95), Environ. Auditors Registration Assn., Danish Assn. Consulting Engrs., Danish Soc. Profl. Engrs. (mem. com. sector chem. engring. 1983-93). Avocation: classical chamber music. Home and Office: Ostergade 16, 3250 Gilleleje Denmark

FOLKE, PETERSON KARL, mechanical engineer, educator; b. Jonkoping, Sweden, Dec. 4, 1935; s. Karl and Margareta P.; m. Bjook, Nov. 5, 1965. Grad., KTH, Sweden. Prof. Royal Inst. Technology, Stockholm, Sweden, 1977—. Home: Enebyberg sv 41, S 18248 Enebyberg Sweden

FOLKMAN, JUDAH, surgeon, researcher; b. Cleve., Feb. 24, 1933; s. Jerome D. and Bessie F.; m. Paula Prial, 1960; 2 children. BA, Ohio State U., 1953; MD, Harvard U., 1957. Intern then asst. resident surgery Mass. Gen. Hosp., Boston, 1957-60, sr. asst. resident surgery, 1962-64, chief resident, 1964-65; asst. surgeon Boston City Hosp., 1965-66; from instr. to assoc. in surgery Harvard U. Med. Sch., 1965-67, prof. surgery, 1967—, Julia Dyckman Andrus prof. pediat. surgery, 1968—, prof. anatomy and cellular biology, 1989—; assoc. dir. Sears Surg. Labs., 1966-67; sr. surgeon Hosp. Med. Ctr., Boston, 1968-81; sr. assoc. surgery, dir. Surg. Rsch. Labs., Boston, 1981—; chief resident pediat. surgery Phila. Children's Hosp., 1969; rschr. in field. First to theorize that cancer cells needed to create their own blood supply in order to survive. Lt. USN, 1960-62. Recipient Career Devel. award NIH, 1966, Lila Gruber award Am. Acad. Dermatology, 1974, Sheen award Am. Cancer Soc., 1989, Internat. award Gairdner Found., 1991, Wolf award Wolf Found., 1992, Lucian award Royal Coll. Surgeons Can., 1993, Steiner award Josef Steiner Found., 1994, Cancer Rsch. award Bristol-Myers, 1995, Ernst Schering award, Germany, 1996, Massry prize Meira and Shaul Massry Found., 1997, Pincus award Worcester Found. Biomed. Rsch., 1998; fellow Am. Cancer Soc. Mem. ACS, NAS, Am. Surg. Assn., Assn. Acad. Surgery, Soc. Univ. Surgeons, Am. Acad. Pediat., Am. Pediat. Surg. Assn., Mass. Med. Soc., Allen O. Whipple Soc. Address: Honeywell 103 Children's Hosp 300 Longwood Ave Boston MA 02115-5724*

FOLKS, CATHALIN BUHRMANN, English language educator; b. Aurora, Ill., Jan. 27, 1947; d. Donald C. and June D. Buhrmann; m. Matthew A. Folks, Aug. 4, 1969. BA, U. Calif., Santa Barbara, 1969; MA in Folklore, Ind. U., 1970, MA in English, 1974, PhD in English, 1989. Assoc. prof. English Cleve. (Tenn.) State Cmty. Coll., 1978-92; prof. English Pellissippi State Tech. Cmty. Coll., Knoxville, 1992—. Contbr. articles to profl. jours. Mem. AAUP, New Chaucer Soc., Nat. Coun. Tchrs. English, Langland Soc., 2-Yr. Coll. English Assn., Cmty. Coll. Humanities Assn., Smoky Mountains Hiking Club (hike leader conservation activities 1980—). Avocations: hiking, reading, gardening, travel, being a grandmother. Office: Pellissippi State Tech CC PO Box 222990 Knoxville TN 37933-0990

FOLLETT, KENNETH MARTIN, author; b. Cardiff, Wales, June 5, 1949; s. Martin D. and Lavinia C. (Evans) F.; m. Mary Emma Ruth Elson, Jan. 5, 1968 (div. 1985); children: Emanuele, Marie-Claire; m. Barbara Broer, Nov. 8, 1985. BA, U. Coll., London, 1970. Reporter, music columnist South Wales Echo, 1970-73; reporter Evening News, London, 1973-74; editorial dir. Everest Books Ltd., London, 1971-75, 87-96, dep. mng. dir., 1976-77; pres. The Dyslexia Inst.; chair Nat. Year of Reading, 1998-99; mem. coun. Nat. Literary Trust. Author: The Shakeout, 1975, The Bear Raid, 1976, Secret of Kellerman's Studio, 1976, Eye of the Needle, 1978 (Edgar award Best Novel), Triple, 1979, The Key to Rebecca, 1980, The Man from St. Petersburg, 1982, On Wings of Eagles, 1983, Lie Down with Lions, 1985, The Pillars of Earth, 1989, Night over Water, 1991, A Dangerous Fortune, 1993, Pillars of the Almighty, 1994, A Place Called Freedom, 1995, The Third Twin, 1996, The Hammer of Eden, 1998, Code to Zero, 2000; (as Martin Martinsen) The Power Twins and the Worm Puzzle, 1976; (as Symon Myles) The Big Needle, 1974, The Big Black, 1974, The Big Hit, 1975; (as Bernard L. Ross) Amok: King of Legend, 1976, Capricorn One, 1978; (as Zachary Stone) The Modigliani Scandal, 1976, Paper Money, 1977; screenwriter: Fringe Banking, 1978, A Football Star, 1979, Lie Down with Lions, 1987. Fellow U. Coll. London. Fellow Royal Soc. Arts. Office: PO Box 4, Stevenage SG3 6UT, England

FOLLICK, EDWIN DUANE, law educator, chiropractic physician; b. Glendale, Calif., Feb. 4, 1935; s. Edwin Fullford and Esther Agnes (Catherwood) F.; m. Marilyn K. Sherk, Mar. 24, 1986. BA, Calif. State U., L.A., 1956, MA, 1961; MA, Pepperdine U., 1957, MPA, 1977; PhD, DTh, St. Andrews Theol. Coll., Sem. of Free Prot. Episc. Ch., London, 1958; MS in Libr. Sci., U. So. Calif., 1963, MEd in Instructional Materials, 1964, AdvMEd in Edn. Adminstrn., 1969; postgrad., Calif. Coll. Law, 1965; LLB, Blackstone Law Sch., 1966, JD, 1967; DC, Cleve. Chiropractic Coll., L.A., 1972; PhD, Academia Theatina, Pescara, 1978; MA in Organizational Mgmt., Antioch U., L.A., 1990. Tchr., libr. adminstr. L.A. City Schs., 1957-68; law librarian Glendale U. Coll. Law, 1968-69; coll. librarian Cleve. Chiropractic Coll., L.A., 1969-74, dir. edn. and admissions, 1974-84, prof. jurisprudence, 1975—, dean student affairs, 1976-92, chaplain, 1985—, dean of edn., 1989—; assoc. prof. Newport U., 1982; extern prof. St. Andrews Theol. Coll., London, 1961; dir. West Valley Chiropractic Health Ctr., 1972—. Contbr. articles to profl. jours. Chaplain's asst. U.S. Army, 1958-60. Decorated cavaliere Internat. Order Legion of Honor of Immaculata (Italy); Knight of Malta, Sovereign Order of St. John of Jerusalem; Knight Grand Prelate, comdr. with star, Order of Signum Fidei; comdr. chevalier Byzantine Imperial Order of Constantine the Gt.; comdr. ritter Order St. Gereon; chevalier Mil. and Hospitaller Order of St. Lazarus of Jerusalem (Malta); numerous others. Mem. ALA, NEA, Am. Assn. Sch. Librarians, L.A. Sch. Libr. Assn., Calif. Sch. Libr. Assn., Assn. Coll. and Rsch. Librarians, Am. Assn. Law Librarians, Am. Chiropractic Assn., Internat. Chiropractors Assn., Nat. Geog. Soc., Internat. Platform Assn., Phi Delta Kappa, Sigma Chi Psi, Delta Tau Alpha. Democrat. Episcopalian. Home: 6435 Jumilla Ave Woodland Hills CA 91367-2833 Office: 590 N Vermont Ave Los Angeles CA 90004-2115 also: 7022 Owensmouth Ave Canoga Park CA 91303-2005

FÖLLMI, BEAT A., musicologist, theologian; b. Zurich, Switzerland, June 9, 1965; s. Arthur and Iris (Grenacher) F.; m. Bettina Zinnenlauf, Sept. 28, 1991. DrPhil in Musicology, U. Zurich, 1995; postgrad., U. Strasbourg, France, 1997-2000. Asst. for N.T. studies faculty theology U. Zurich, 1990-96; editor Edit. Oecumenical Ch. History of Switzerland, Interconfessional Hist. and Theol. Com., Berne, 1991-95; editl. asst. Complete Works of Othmar Schoeck, Othmar Schoeck Soc., Zurich, 1988—; dir. Carciofoli Pub. House, Zurich, 1990—. Author, translator plays and novels. Mem. Othmar Schoeck-Gesellschaft (mem. com. 1995—), Am. Musicology Soc., Musikforschende Assn. der Schweiz. Avocations: cooking, travel. E-mail: beat.foellmi@bluewin.ch. Office: Othmar Schoeck-Gesellschaft, Florhofgasse 11, Zurich Switzerland 8001

FOLTER, ROLAND, book historian, rare books company executive, bibliographer; b. Fulda, Fed. Republic Germany, May 27, 1943; s. Heinz and Annemie (Bennewitz) F.; m. Siegrun Heinecke, Aug. 28, 1967 (dec. 1988); m. Mary Ann Kraus, Apr. 29, 1989; 1 child, Elizabeth. MA, Brown U., 1967, PhD, 1969. Rare books cataloger Yale U., New Haven, Conn., 1966-68; prof. U. Ill., Urbana, 1969-77; dir. H.P. Kraus Rare Books, N.Y.C., 1977—; jury Internat. League Antiquarian Booksellers Prize for Bibliography. Author: Deutsche Dichterbibliotheken, 1975, The Gutenberg Bible in the antiquarian book trade, 1999; co-author: Bibliography: Its History, 1984; contbr. to ency. and articles to profl. jours. Violinist Frankfurt (Germany) Youth Symphony Orch., 1960-65. Fellow Brown U., 1968, Faculty fellow U. Ill., 1970-75. Fellow Pierpont Morgan Libr.; mem. Bibliog. Soc. Am. (coun. 1982-90), N.Y. Philharm. Soc., Assn. Internat. de Bibliophilie, Maximilian Gesellschaft, Gesellschaft der Bibliophilen, Antiquarian Booksellers Assn. Am., Old Book Table (pres. 1995-97), Yale Libr. Assocs., Princeton Club. Avocations: violin, chamber music, book collecting, mountaineering. Office: H P Kraus Rare Books 16 E 46th St New York NY 10017-2404

FOLTINEK, HERBERT, language and literature educator; b. Vienna, Austria, Apr. 29, 1930; s. Helmut and Elisabeth Charlotte (Jaeschke) F.; m. Elisabeth Sengstschmid, Feb. 14, 1964. PhD, U. Vienna, 1954. Lectr. in German U. Cambridge, Eng., 1957-59; lectr. U. Vienna, 1960-65, assoc. prof., 1966-69, prof. English and Am. lang. and lit., 1969—. Author: Vorstufen zum Viktorianischen Realismus, 1968, Susan Ferrier: Marriage, 1977, George Eliot, 1982, Charles Dickens und der Zwang des Systems, 1987; co-editor: Jour Sprachkunst, 1982—. Mem. Modern Humanities Rsch. Assn., Austrian Acad. Scis. Lutheran. Home: Ferrogasse 48/7, A-1180 Vienna Austria Office: U Vienna Dept English, Universitaetscampus AAKH/Hof 8, Spitalgasse 2-4 A-1010 Vienna Austria

FOLZ, JEAN-MARTIN, automotive company executive; b. Strasbourg, France, Jan. 11, 1947; s. Robert Folz and Marianne (Bock) F.; m. Marie-Claire Picardet, 1968; 2 children. Ed., Ecole Ste.-Genevieve, Versailles, Ecole Polytechnique. Advisor Office of Min. of Commerce and Crafts, 1974-75; asst. dir. Office of Min. for Quality of Life, 1976-77; dir. Office Sec. of State, Ministry of Industry, 1977-78; factory mgr. Rhone-Poulenc Polymeres, St. Fons, France, 1979-80; dep. gen. mgr. Rhone Poulenc Spl. Chems., 1981-84; mng. dir. Jeumont-Schneider, 1984-87; CEO Péchiney, 1987-91; pres. Le Carbone Lorraine, 1987-91; CEO Eridiana, 1991-95; pres. Bégin-Say PSA Peugeot-Citroen, 1991-95; chair directorate PSA Peugeot Citroën, 1995-96, dir. automotive divsn., 1996-97, pres., 1997—, pres. Automobiles Peugeot, 1997—, pres. Automobiles Citroën, 1997—. Franco-Japanese House scholar, 1970-71. Office: 75 Ave de la Grande Armee, Paris 75116, France

FOMEL, BORIS MARK, physicist, consultant; b. Saratov, Soviet Union, July 26, 1935; arrived in Israel, 1995; s. Mark Avra'am and Sophi Levi (Kohen-Tzadik) F.; m. Ella Yisai Sverdlov, Dec. 23, 1961; m. Nadejda Dimirty Utkin, May 15, 1990; 1 child, Mark. MSc in Physics, Saratov U., 1958; PhD in Tech. Sci., Novosibirsk U., 1968. Sr. engr. Rsch. Lab. Electronics Industry, Ulyanvsk, 1958-60, Rsch. Lab. Aerospace Industry, Saratov, 1960-63; prof. physics Novosibirsk State U., 1969-95; group leader Budker Inst. Nuclear Physics, Novosibirsk, 1969-95; pres. Prudence Software Ltd., Jerusalem, Israel, 1996—; vis. prof. Weizmann Inst. Sci., Rechovot, 1996-97; spkr. week radiophysics sem. Budker Inst. Nuclear Physics, 1985-95; mem. sci. coun. for control dept. high energy physics Russian Acad. Scis., Moscow, 1978-85; coord. collaboration between Budket Inst. Nuclear Physics and European Orgn. for Particle Physics Novosibirsk-Geneva/Russia-Switzerland, 1993-95; cons. Digitran, Simulation Sys., Logan, Utah, 1996. Author: Methods of the Nonlinear Oscillations Theory, 1970; editor Computing in Accelerators, Conceptual Design and Constrn., 1987-95; inventor hierarchical integrated sys. for problem-oriented software devel.; contbr. articles to profl. jours. Founder, pres. Family Sports and Health Club of Three Generations, Novosibirsk, 1985-95, dir., lectr. fitness courses, 1983-93. Grantee Soros Found., 1995, Ministry of Industry and Trade (Israel), 1996-98. Mem. N.Y. Acad. Scis. Avocations: mountain climbing, skiing, tennis, history of religions. E-mail: fomel@jsi.co.il. Office: Prudence Software Ltd, 8 Hamarpeh St, 91450 Jerusalem Israel

FOMICHOV, SERGIY KONSTANTINOVICH, engineering educator, consultant; b. Kiev, Ukraine, USSR, June 2, 1954; s. Konstantin Sergievich and Valentina Pavlovna (Mosheykina) F.; m. Nataliya Ivanivna Skryabina, Aug. 5, 1994; children: Alina, Julia. BS in Mech. Engring., Nat. Tech. U. Ukraine, USSR, 1976; MS in Mech. Engring., Nat. Tech. U. Ukraine, 1978, PhD in Tech.Sci., 1985. Engr. Nat. Tech. U. Ukraine, Kiev, USSR, 1978-79; asst. prof. Nat. Tech. U. Ukraine, Kiev, 1979-81, assoc. prof., 1986-96, prof., 1996—; prof. tech. sci. Russian Acd. Oil and Gas, 1994; head methodol. commn. tech. com. TK-78 tech. diagnostic and non-destructive testing State Com. Ukraine for Standardization, Metrology and Certification, Kiev, 1985—; vice-dir. Ukrainian Welder's Cert. Com., Kiev, 1994-99; expert of the Sci. Project Nat. Tech. U. of Ukraine. Author: Quality Control of Welding, 1983, Trunk Pipeline Repair Work, 1996, Basics of Quality Management, 1999; patents for method and device for stress measurement of ferromagnetic materials, device for treatment of welds, method for electrochem. protection of metal units from corrosion, others. Recipient medal Nat. Econ. Exhibn., 1980, award for Best Metal Work Ministry Edn., 1981, award for Achievements in Quality Ukrainian Union Experts and Consultants, 1999. Mem. Ukrainian Mktg. Assn. (head quality mgmt. com. 1996—), Ukrainian Assn. for Quality (head Professors in Quality club 1999—), N.Y. Acad. Scis. Avocations: mountain skiing, tourism, climbing, numismatics, Russian history. Office: Nat Tech U Ukraine, 37 Pobedy Str, 253056 Kiev Ukraine

FOMIN, VALERY PROKOPIEVICH, astrophysicist; b. Siktivkar, Komi, Russia, Mar. 23, 1944; s. Prokopi Vasilievich and Alexandra Andreevna (Kokovkina) F.; m. Vera Nikolaevna Bocharova, Oct. 25, 1969; children: Sergey, Elena. Engr.-physicist, Leningrad Polytech. Inst., Russia, 1969; DSc, Leningrad Physics Tech. Inst., Russia, 1979. Engr. Crimean Astron. Observatory, Nauchny, Crimea, Ukraine, 1969-72; sr. engr. Crimean Astron. Observatory, Nauchny, 1972-75, scientist, 1975-79, sr. scientist, 1979—. Contbr. Over 85 articles to astrophysical and physical jours. Grantee U.S. Civilian Rsch. & Devel. Found., 1997-99. Mem. Internat. Astron. Union. Home: Bldg 6A Flat 5, 334413 Nauchny Crimea, Ukraine Office: Crimean Astrophys Observtry, 334413 Nauchny Crimea, Ukraine

FOMIN, VLADIMIR MIKHAILOVICH, physicist, researcher, educator; b. Kishinev, Moldova, Nov. 1, 1953; s. Mikhail Georgievich and Maria Afanasievna (Shinkarenko) F.; m. Eugenia Davidovna Lvovskaia, Apr. 25, 1997; children: Karina, Maria, Mikhail. MSc cum laude, State U. Kishinev, 1975, PhD, 1978; Habilitation, Acad. Scis. Moldova, Kishinev, 1990. Sr. sci. rschr. State U. Moldova, Kishinev, 1978-87, from asst. prof. to prof., 1981-95, prof., 1995—, chief lab., 1987-91, prin. scientific rschr., 1991—; univ. prof. Supreme Attestation Commn. Moldova, Kishinev, 1999; vis. prof. U. Antwerp, Belgium, 1995-98, 2000—; vis. rschr. Tech. U., Eindhoven, The Netherlands, 1998-99. Co-author: Transport and Optical Properties of Semiconductors in Strong Fields, 1986, Vibrational Excitations, Polarons and Excitons in Multi-Layer Structures and Superlattices, 1990; contbr. over 100 articles to profl. jours. Recipient Moldova State prize, 1987; A. von Humboldt Found. fellow U. Halle-Wittenberg, Germany, 1993-94, Diploma of a Discovery Acad. Nat. Sci. Russia, 1999. Mem. German Phys. Soc., European Phys. Soc., Am. Phys. Soc., Phys. Soc. Moldova. Avocations: operas, symphonic music, photography, swimming. Office: Dept Natuurkunde U Antwerp, Universiteitsplein 1, B 2610 Antwerp Belgium

FOMINE, SERGUEI, chemical engineer, educator; b. Moscow, Aug. 20, 1961; arrived in Mex., 1993; s. Mikhail and Galina (Kulik) F.; m. Lioudmila Frolova, June 1, 1982; 1 child. MS, Moscow Inst. Fine Chem. Tech., 1984; PhD, Kharpov Inst. Phys. Chemistry, 1989. Rschr. Karpov Inst. Phys Chemistry, 1984-93; from asst. prof. to prof. Nat. Autonomous U. Mex., 1993—. Author: Photonic and Optoelectronic Polymers, 1997; contbr. articles to profl. jours. Mem. Mex. Chem. Soc. E-mail: fomine@servidor.unam.mx. Office: Nat Autonomous U Mexico, Cir Ext s/n CU Coyoacan, 04510 Mexico City Mexico

FONDA, JANE, actress; b. N.Y.C., Dec. 21, 1937; d. Henry and Frances (Seymour) F.; m. Roger Vadim (div.); 1 child, Vanessa; m. Tom Hayden, Jan. 20, 1973 (div.); 1 child, Troy; m. Ted Turner, Dec. 21, 1991. Student, Vassar Coll. Appeared on Broadway stage in There Was a Little Girl, 1960, The Fun Couple, 1962; appeared in Actor's Studio prodn. Strange Interlude, 1963; appeared in films Tall Story, 1960, A Walk on the Wild Side, 1962, Period of Adjustment, 1962, Sunday in New York, 1963, In the Cool of the Day, 1963, The Love Cage, 1963, La Ronde, 1964, Cat Ballou, 1965, The Chase, 1966, Any Wednesday, 1966, The Game Is Over, 1967, Hurry Sundown, 1967, Barefoot in the Park, 1967, Barbarella, 1968, Spirits of the Dead, 1969, They Shoot Horses, Don't They?, 1969, Klute, 1970 (Acad. award best actress), Steelyard Blues, 1973, A Doll's House, 1973, The Blue Bird, 1976, Fun with Dick and Jane, 1976, Julia, 1977, also producer Coming Home, 1978 (Acad. award best actress), California Suite, 1978,

Comes a Horseman, 1978, also producer The China Syndrome, 1979, Electric Horseman, 1979, Nine to Five, 1980, On Golden Pond, 1981, Rollover, 1981, The Dollmaker, 1984 (ABC-TV, Emmy award best actress), Agnes of God, 1985, The Morning After, 1986 (Acad. award nomination best actress), Old Gringo, 1988, Stanley and Iris, 1990, producer Lakota Woman, 1994; (TV miniseries) A Century of Women, 1994; author: Jane Fonda's Workout Book, 1981, Women Coming of Age, 1984, Jane Fonda's New Workout & Weight-Loss Program, 1986, Jane Fonda's New Pregnancy Workout & Total Birth Program, 1989, Jane Fonda Workout Video, 12 additional videos. Recipient Golden Apple prize for female star of yr. Hollywood Women's Press Club, 1977, Golden Globe award, 1978; rated no. 1 heroine of young Ams., U.S. News Roper Poll., 1985, 4th most admired woman in Am., Ladies Home Jour. Roper Poll, 1985. Office: CAA care Kim Hodgert 9830 Wilshire Blvd Beverly Hills CA 90212-1804

FONDILLER, SHIRLEY HOPE ALPERIN, nursing educator, journalist, historian; b. Holyoke, Mass.; d. Samuel and Rose (Sobiloff) Alperin; m. Harvey V. Fondiller, Dec. 27, 1957 (div. June 1984); 1 child, David Stewart. BS, Columbia U., 1962, MA, 1963, MEd, 1971, EdD, 1980. Dir. ednl. adminstrs., cons. and tchrs. sect. Am. Nurses Assn., N.Y.C., 1964-66, coord. careers program, 1967-70, coord. clin. sessions, 1971-72; editor Am. Nurse, Kansas City, Mo., 1975-78; assoc. prof., asst. to dean for spl. projects Rush-Presbyn.-St. Luke's Med. Ctr., 1979-86; exec. dir. Mid-Atlantic Regional Nursing Assn., N.Y.C., 1986-89; adj. assoc. prof. Columbia U., 1986—; founder, prin. Pub. for Health Dimensions, phd, 1990—. Author of books; contbr. articles to profl. jours. Fellow Am. Acad. Nursing; mem. Kappa Delta Pi, Sigma Theta Tau.

FONG, BERNARD W. D., physician, educator; b. Honolulu, May 18, 1926; s. Leonard K. and Francis C. Fong; m. Roberta Wat, Aug. 14, 1950; children: Phyllis K., Jeffrey S., Camille K., Allison K. BS, Bucknell U., 1948; MD, Jefferson Med. Coll., 1952. Diplomate Am. Bd. Internal Medicine. Intern Germantown Hosp., Phila., 1952-53; chief med. resident Germantown Hosp., 1953-55; teaching fellow cardiology Jefferson Med. Coll. Hosp., Phila., 1955-56; attending physician Queen's Med. Ctr., Honolulu, 1956—, St. Francis Hosp., Honolulu, 1956-89; clin. prof. medicine U. Hawaii, Honolulu, 1982—; med. dir. medicare part B Aetna Ins. Co., Hawaii, Guam, 1988-97, Transamerica Occidental Life Ins. Co., Hawaii and Guam, 1997-2000, Noridian Govt. Svcs., Hawaii and Guam, 2000—; adv. coun. Nat. Heart, Lung and Blood Inst., NIH, Bethesda, Md., 1976-80, chmn. 3d forum on cardiovascular risk factors, 1985; adv. com. cardiovascular risk factors in minorities NIH, 1976-89; pres. Triple C, 1996—. Pres. Hawaii Heart Assn., Honolulu, 1962-63; bd. dirs. Am. Heart. Assn., N.Y.C., 1963-66; pres. Chung Shan Assn., Honolulu, 1969-70, United Chinese Soc. Hawaii, Honolulu, 1973-74; 1st v.p. Wong Leong Doo Benevolent Soc., Honolulu, 1973—; 1st v.p. Ocean View Cemetery, Honolulu, 1973—. With USNR, 1944-46, PTO. Fellow ACP (bd. govs. 1972-76, inaugural laureate internal medicine Hawaii chpt. 1986), Am. Coll. Cardiology (bd. govs. 1992-96, chairperson 1995-96, trustee 1997—), Am. Coll. Chest Physicians; mem. Am. Soc. Internal Medicine (pres. Hawaii chpt. 1980-82). Republican. Roman Catholic. Home: 97 Dowsett Ave Honolulu HI 96817-1107 Office: 1380 Lusitana St Ste 706 Honolulu HI 96813-2443

FONG, HIRAM LEONG, former senator; b. Honolulu, Oct. 15, 1906; s. Lum Fong and Chai Ha Lum; m. Ellyn Lo; children, Hiram, Rodney, Marie-Ellen Fong Gushi, Marvin-Allan (twins). AB with honors, U. Hawaii, 1930, LLD, 1953; JD, Harvard U., 1935; LLD, Tufts U., 1960, Lafayette Coll., 1960, Lynchburg Coll., 1970, Lincoln U., 1971, U. Guam, 1974, St. John's U., 1975, Calif. Western Sch. Law, 1976, Tung Wu (Soochow) U., Taiwan, 1978, China Acad., Taiwan, 1978; LHD, L.I. U., 1968. With supply dept. Pearl Harbor Navy Yard, 1924-27; chief clk. Suburban Water System, 1930-32; dep. atty. City and County of Honolulu, 1935-38; founder, ptnr. law firm Fong, Miho, Choy & Robinson, until 1959; founder, chmn. bd. emeritus Finance Factors, Grand Pacific Life Ins. Co.; founder, chmn bd. Finance Investment Co., Market City, Ltd., Fin. Enterprises Ltd.; pres. Ocean View Cemetery, Ltd.; owner, operator Sen. Fong's Plantation and Gardens, Honolulu; dir. numerous firms, Honolulu; hon. cons. China Airlines. Mem. Hawaii Legislature, 1938-54, speaker, 1948-54; mem. U.S. Senate, 1959-77, Post Office and Civil Service Com., Judiciary Com., Appropriations Com., Spl. Com. on Aging; U.S. del. 150th Anniversary Argentine Independence, Buenos Aires, 1960, 55th Interparliamentary Union (World) Conf., 1966, Ditchley Found. Conf., 1967, U.S.-Can. Inter-Parliamentary Union Conf., 1961, 65, 67, 68, Mex.-U.S. Inter-Parliamentary Conf., 1968, World Interparliamentary Union, Tokyo, 1974; mem. Commn. on Revision Fed. Ct. Appellate System, 1975—; Active in civic and service orgns.; v.p. Territorial Constl. Conv., 1950; del. Rep. Nat. Conv., 1952, 56, 60, 64, 68, 72; founder, chmn. bd. Fin. Factors Found.; founder, pres. Hiram & Ellyn Fong Found.; founder, pres., chmn. bd. Market City Found.; hon. co-chmn. McKinley High Sch. Found., 1989; bd. visitors U.S. Mil. Acad., 1971—, U.S. Naval Acad., 1974—. Served from 1st lt. to maj. USAAF, 1942-44; ret. col. USAF Res. Recipient award NCCJ, 1960, Meritorious Svc. citation Nat. Assn. Ret. Civil Employees, 1963, Horatio Alger award, 1970, citation for outstanding svc. Japanese Am. Citizens League, 1970, award Am. Acad. Achievement, 1971, Outstanding Svc. award Orgn. Chinese Ams., 1973, award Nat. Soc. Daus. Founders and Patriots Am., 1974, cert. Pacific Asian World, 1974, Citizen Among Citizens award Boys & Girls Clubs of Hawaii, 1991, Disting. Alumnus award U. Hawaii Alumni Assn., 1991, Kulia I Ka Nu'u award Pub. Schs. Hawaii Found., 1992, Dedication and Support Svc. award McKinley Found., 1995, ABOTA-Hawai'i Ha'aheo award, 1997; named to Jr. Achievement Hawaii Bus. Hall of Fame, 1995; decorated Order of Brilliant Star with Grand Cordon Republic of China, 1976, Order of Diplomatic Svc. Merit, Gwanghwan Medal Republic of Korea, 1977; Univ. of Hawaii Colls. of Arts and Scis. Hiram L. Fong Endowment in Arts and Scis., 1995; recipient nat. Outstanding Citizen Achievement award Orgn. Chinese Ams., Inc., 1996; named Model Chinese Father of Yr., United Chinese Soc., 1996. Mem. Am. Legion, VFW, Lambda Alpha Internat. (Aloha chpt.), Phi Beta Kappa. Congregationalist. Home: 1102 Alewa Dr Honolulu HI 96817-1507

FONG, SIMON CHI CHIU, educator, research scientist; b. Hong Kong, Nov. 16, 1969; s. David Kum Ming Fong and Regina Siu Ling Kwong. B in Computer Sys. Engring. with honors, La Trobe U., Melbourne, Vic., Australia, 1993, PhD, 1998; M in Bus. Sys., Monash U., Melbourne, Vic., Australia, 1998. Cert. JAVA developer Inst. Sys. Sci., Nat. U. Singapore. Analyst programmer Creative Software Techs., Melbourne, 1993-94; tchg. asst. La Trobe U., Melbourne, 1994-96; sys. engr. Singapore Network Svcs., 1997; integrated comm. specialist Hong Kong Telecom., 1998; asst. prof. Nanyang Technol. U., Singapore, 1998—; cons. Inthenet Tech., Melbourne; sr. cons. CoRe Solutions, Hong Kong; presenter in field. Contbr. articles to Jour. Computer Sys. Sci. and Engring., Computer Comm.-Elsevier Sci., Australian Computer Sci. Comms. Recipient Australian Postgrad. Rsch. award Australia Rsch. Coun., Melbourne, 1995-97. Mem. IEEE Comm. Soc., Australian Soc. Telecom. Avocations: skiing, photography, reading, model making. E-mail: fong simon@hotmail.com. and fong@latcs1.lat.oz.au. Fax: 65 7926559. Home: 24 Beckett St, Balwyn VIC 3103, Australia Office: Nanyang Technol Univ, Sch Applied Sci Nanyang Ave, Singapore 639798, Singapore

FONSECA, GELSON, JR., diplomat. Rep. from Brazil UN, N.Y.C. Office: Permanent Mission of Brazil 747 3rd Ave Fl 9 New York NY 10017-2803*

FONSECA, JOSE LUIS CARDOZO, chemistry educator, researcher; b. Angra dos Reis, Brazil, Nov. 20, 1961; s. Jose Augusto and Antonia (Cardozo) Fonseca; m. Marcia Rodrigues Pereira, June 22, 1991; 1 child, Mariana Rodrigues. Diploma in chem. engring., Fed. U. Rio de Janeiro, 1985, MSc in Polymer Sci. and Tech., 1990; PhD in Chemistry, U. Durham, Eng., 1994. Cert. chem. engring. R&D chem. engr. Sociedade Anonima Cortume Carioca, Rio de Janeiro, 1985-88; post-doctorate staff Sao Carlos (Brazil) Inst. Physics, 1994-96; lectr. dept. chemistry Fed. U. Rio Grande do Norte, Natal, Brazil, 1996—. Contbr. articles to profl. jours. Sci. Productivity grantee Conselho Nacional de Desenvolvimento Cientifico e Tecnoligico, 1997—. Avocation: pipe smoking. E-mail: jlcf@ufrnet.ufrn.br and fonseca@linus.quimica.ufrn.br. Fax: 55 84 211 9224. Home: Rua Praia de Pititinga 9107, 59092350 Natal RN, Brazil Office: U Fed Rio Grande do Norte, Campus Univ Lagoa Nova 1662, 59072970 Natal RN, Brazil

FONTAINE, GUY HUGUES, cardiologist, researcher; b. Corbeil-Essonnes, Ile de France, France, Dec. 24, 1936; s. Andre and Gisele (Maisonneuve) F.; m. Ilfat Masri; children: Nadia, Marc, Florence, Corinne. MD with high distinction, U. Paris, 1966; PhD with high distinction, U. Paris XI, Orsay, France, 1991. Attache cons. Paris Hosp., 1979—; co-dir. dept. clin. electrophysiology Hosp. Jean Rostand, Ivry sur Seine, France, 1979; vis. prof. U. Ariz. Health Scis. Ctr., Tucson, 1986; U. Shanghai, 1990—; frequent consultant in ARVD and electrophysiological treatment for patients internationally; organizer chmn. Internat. Symposium on Fulguration and Laser in Cardiac Arrhythmias, Paris, 1985, Arrhythmogenic Right Ventricular dysplasia/cardiomyopathy, 1996; rsch. dir. U. Paris, 1993; co-chmn. World Congress on Catheter Ablation, 1986; mem. sci. bd. World Congress on Cardiac Arrhythmias, 1996—. Author: The Essential of Cardiac Pacing, (with others), 1976, rev. 3d edit., 1985; co-editor: L'essentiel sur L'enregistrement de l'Holter de l'ECG, 1983, Cardiac Pacemakers, 1985, Ablation in Cardiac Arrhythmias, 1987, Cardiac Arrhythmias, Recent Progress in Investigation and Management, 1988, Les Troubles du Rythme Cardiaque, 1993, Arrhythmobenic Right Ventricular Cardiomyopathy and Related Disorders, 2000; contbr. 739 papers to profl. jours., sci. confs. etc., 361 of which were written in English; mem. editl bd. Cardiovascular Reports (Germany), Heart and Vessels (Japan), Jour. Cardiovascular Electrophysiology (U.S.), Annales Cardiol. Angéiol. (France), Rhythmology, (Can.), Revista Latina de Cardiologia (Argentina), Hertz (Germany), Stimucoeur (France); reviewer for 114 internat. med. jours.; lectr. in France and abroad on cardiac treatment especially treatment of cardiac arrhythmias and arrhythmogenic Right Ventricular Cardiomyopathies; about 20 lectrs. yearly 1968—; patentee in field. Named 4th Murray Kornfeld Meml. Lectr., Am. Coll. Chest Physicians, Boston, 1989; recipient Master Tchr. award Cardiovascular Revs. and Reports, 1990, prix Electicité-Santé, Paris, 1992; co-recipient Found. Pr. Pierre Rijlant prize, Belgian Royal Acad. Medicine, 1995, Golden Caduceus, Assistance Pub. des Hopitaux de Paris, 1997. Fellow European Soc. Cardiology, Am. Coll. Cardiology, Am. Heart Assn. Coun. of Clin. Cardiology (internat.); mem. French Soc. Cardiology (Medtronic prize 1994), Internat. Soc. and Fedn. of Cardiology (co-chmn. working group on cardiomyopathy/dysplasia 1991—), Unit 451 affiliation, Bul. Acad. Nat. Medicine Paris. Office: Hosp Jean Rostand, 39-41 rue Jean le Galleu, 94200 Ivry Sur Seine France

FONTAINE, JEAN-PAUL, physician; b. Versailles, Yvelines, France, Apr. 29, 1943; s. Paul and Jeanne (Coustans) F.; m. Vanina Bonelli, Oct. 12, 1968; children: Anne-Laure, Isabelle, Paul-Vincent, Francois-Xavier. MD, U. Reims, France, 1974, Med. Pedagogy Cert., 1990. Gen. practice medicine Reims, 1974—; physician attaché Hosp. Ctr., Reims, 1974-76; adj. instr. physiopathology Tech. High Sch., Reims, 1976—, Coll. Med., U. Reims, 1980-90; mem. Med. Order Coun., 1978-90. Author: Le Livre des Livres, 1994; mem. editl. bd. Revue française de Généalogie, 1982-93; editor: Le Bibliophile Rémois, 1985—. Mem. Nat. Acad., Amis de la BM de Reims (chmn. 1993—). Roman Catholic. Lodge: Round Table. Avocations: history of book, bibliophily. Home and Office: 19 Blvd Doumer, 51100 Reims France

FONTAINE, MARCEL, law educator; b. Stanleyville, Congo, Oct. 30, 1936; s. Jean Fontaine and Simone Hendrichs; m. Amelie Lauve, Aug. 7, 1961 (div. 1986); children: Alex, Joel, Anne, Nicole; m. Jelena Koch, May 16, 1986. LLM, U. Liege, 1960, M in Econs., 1962, PhD in Law, 1967. Asst. U. Liege, 1960-69; prof. law U. Louvain, Belgium, 1969—; dir. ctr. droit obligations U. Louvain, 1974—, pres. grad. program ins. law, 1995—; vis. prof. various univs., 1977—. Author: The Theory of Workable Competition, 1962, Contracts Between Oil Companies and Oil Retailers, 1962, The Legal Nature of Credit Insurance, 1966, Insurance Law, 2d edit., 1996, Consumer Law in Belgium and Luxembourg, 1981, (with Th. Bourgoignie) The Law of International Contracts, 1989; contbr. articles to profl. jours. Am. Field Svc. scholar, 1953-54; recipient European Bernheim award, 1955. Mem. Internat. Ins. Law Assn. (presdl. coun.), Unidroit (corr.), Inst. World Bus. Law Internat. C. of C. (mem. coun.). Avocations: astronomy, music. Office: Univ Louvain Law Sch, Pl Montesquieu 2, 1348 Louvain-la-Neuve Belgium

FONTAINE, MAURICE ALFRED, ecophysiologist, oceanographer, molysmologist, biologist; b. Savigny-sur-Orge, Essonne, France, Oct. 28, 1904; s. Émile and Lea (Vadier) F.; m. Yvonne Broca, Aug. 2, 1928; 1 child, Yves Alain. ScD, Faculty of Scis., Paris. Chef de travant Faculty of Scis., Paris; head of conf. Faculty of Pharmacy; dir. lab. Ecole Pratique des Hautes Etudes, Paris, 1946; prof., dir. Inst. Oceanographique, Paris, 1957-68, 75-84; pres. Soc. Européenne d'Endocrinologie comparée, Paris, 1969; dir., prof. Mus. Nl d'Histoire naturelle, Paris, 1966-71. Author: Physiologie, 1969, Rencontres insolites d'un biologists autour du monde, 1999; contbr. over 432 articles to profl. jours. Decorated Comdr. Legion d'Honneur, France, 1977, Comdr., Ordre de Sahametrei, Cambodia, 1966, Ordre de St. Charles, Monaco, 1972; recipient Grand Prix d'Oceanographie, Prince Albert 1st, Monaco, 1996. Mem. Acad. Agr., Acad. Medicine Paris (pres.), Acad. Scis. Paris, N.Y. Acad. Scis., Pacific Sci. Assn., Ecophysiology Soc. (founder, pres. 1974), Club Des Explorateurs. Avocation: thalassoethics. Home: 25 Rue Pierre Nicole, 75005 Paris France Office: Inst Oceanographique, 195 Rue Saint-Jacques, 75005 Paris France

FONTAINE, NICOLE, foreign diplomat; b. Granville-Ymauville, France, Jan. 16, 1942. Mem. European Parliament, pres.; mem. of the bur. Group of the European People's Party (Christian Democrats) and European Democrats. *

FONTAINE, PIET FRANCISCUS MARIA, retired history educator; b. Amsterdam, The Netherlands, Apr. 11, 1921; s. Frans and Berta (Kannegieter) F.; m. Anneke Thomassen, Apr. 16, 1952; children: Resian, Britt, Bernadet, Relinde, Filip. MA, U. Amsterdam, 1947, D, 1954. Rschr. Netherlands State Inst. War Documentation, Amsterdam, 1947-48; tchr. history Ignatius Coll., Amsterdam, 1948-75, Fons Vitae, Amsterdam, 1949-51; tchr. trainer U. Amsterdam, 1961-70, State U. Utrecht, The Netherlands, 1970-83. Author: (in Dutch) The Council of State 1588-1590, 1954, The Origination of History, 1985, Hitler the Unknown, 1992, (in English) The Light and the Dark: A Cultural History of Dualism, 15 vols., 1986-2000, Mythical Eyes. History, Counter-History and Myth, 1998. Mem. N.Y. Acad. Scis. Roman Catholic. Avocations: music, photography, walking, cycling. Home: Johan Ramaerstraat 9 HS, 1065 GA Amsterdam The Netherlands

FONTAINE-BAYER, LUCETTE BLANCHE, educator; b. Albert, Somme, France, June 30, 1934; d. Wilhelm and Marcelle Angèle (Audegond) Bayer; m. Michel Joseph Fontaine, Aug. 22, 1960; children: Marc Luc, Anne Marcelle. Student, Ecole Normale Supérieure, Fontenay-Aux-Roses, France, 1955; Agrégation, Sorbonne, France, 1960. With Lycée de Jeunes Filles, Amiens, France, 1960-62, Lycé3e Pilote, Enghien-les-Bains, 1962-73, Ecole d'Interprétariat, Paris, 1964-66, Faculté de Nanterré, France, 1964-66, Lycée Louis Thuillier, Amiens, 1973-94. Author: (book) Le Chasse-Marée de Picardie, 1993 (book of short stories and poems) Petite Suite en Noir et Blanc, 1999, (book chpt.) Cheval et Société, 1995; contbr. articles to profl. jours. Decorated Chevalier, Ordre des Palmes Académiques, 1994. Mem. Assn. des Membres de L'Ordre des Palmes Academiques (bd. dirs. 1994—), Assn. des Amis du Musée de la Voiture et du Tourisme (bd. dirs. 1995), Soc. des Antiquaires de Picardie, 1994. Avocations: children, nature, animals, history, art. Home: 9 rue Dufour, 80000 Amiens Somme, France

FONTANA, BERNARD LEE, retired anthropologist, writer, consultant; b. Oakland, Calif., Jan. 7, 1931; s. Bernard Campion and Hope Mary (Smith) F.; m. Hazel Ann McFeely, June 27, 1954; children: Geoffrey Earl Francis, Nicholas Anthony, Francesca Ann. BA, U. Calif., Berkeley, 1953; PhD, U. Ariz., 1960. Field historian U. Ariz., Tucson, 1960-62, 78-92; ethnologist Ariz. State Mus., Tucson, 1962-78; writer, cons. Tucson, 1992—; lectr. anthropology dept. U. Ariz., 1962-78; expert witness Papago Tribe of Ariz., Sells, 1962-64; pres. Ariz.-Sonora desert Mus., Tucson, 1983-85; cons. San Xavier Dist. Tohono O'Odham Nation, Tucson, 1992-93, KUAT-TV, Tucson, 1996. Author: Tarahumara: Where Night Is The Day Of The Moon, 1979 (Border Regional Libr. Assn. award 1979), Of Earth and Little Rain: The Papago Indians, 1981 (Border Regional Libr. Assn. award 1981), Entrada: The Legacy of Spain and Mexico in the United States, 1994, A Guide to Contemporary Southwest Indians, 1999; editor: Before Rebellion, 1996. Active western regional adv. com. Nat. Pk. Svc., San Francisco, 1974-76; sheriff Tucson Corral of the Westerners, 1976; sec. Patronato San Xavier, Tucson, 1989—. Calif. Alumni scholar U. Calif. Alumni Assn., Berkeley, 1948; pre-doctoral fellow Wenner Gren Found. for Anthrop. Rsch., 1959; recipient Ben Avery award Ariz. Clean and Beautiful, 1994, Ariz. Gov. Hist. Preservation award Ariz. Heritage Found., 1995. Fellow Ariz. Nev. Acad. Sci.; mem. Soc. For Hist. Arch. (life, pres. 1970, J. C. Harrington medal 1992), Ariz. Arch. and Hist. Soc. (pres. 1960-61, editor 1958-60, Victor R. Stoner award 1990), Am. Soc. for Ethnohistory (pres. 1965, editor 1969-72), S.W. Pks. and Monuments Assn. (life, vice chmn. 1988, Edward Danson award 1989, Emil Haury award 1991). Avocation: philately. Home and Office: 7710 S Mission Rd Tucson AZ 85746-7143

FONTANA, JOSI DOMINGOS, scientist, educator; b. Itapui, Sao Paulo, Brazil, July 31, 1944; s. Ricardo and Maud (Spirandelli) F.; m. Christine Krawiec, Mar. 16, 1973; children: Claudio, Milene. Degree in Pharmacy and Biochemistry, Fed. U. Parana, Curitiba, Brazil, 1975, MSc in Biochemistry, 1975; PhD, U. Buenos Aires, 1980. Postdoctorsl fellow Divsn. Biol. Scis., Nat. Rsch. Coun., Ottawa, Ont., Can., 1986; scientist, prof. Fed. U. Parana, 1964—; cons. BioFill Produtos Biotecnologicas SA, Curitiba, 1989-91. Contbr. articles to profl. jours. Pres. deliberating coun. Scout Group N.S. Medianeira, Curitiba, 1993. Recipinet Dr. Nilo Cairo prize, 1971, medal Fed. Coun. Pharmacy, 1971. Mem. Assn. Profs. Fed. U. Parana (sec. 1981-82), Brazilian Soc. Biochemistry and Molecular Biology (sec. 1984). Roman Catholic. Avocation: Caribbean music. E-mail: jfontana@bio.ufpr.br. Home: 345, Rua Pres Epitacio Pessoa, 82530 Curitiba, Parana Brazil Office: UFPR Poly Ctr, Jardim das Americas, Curitiba, Parana 81531, Brazil

FONTANA, MARIO H., nuclear engineer; b. West Springfield, Mass., Mar. 30, 1933; s. Remo and Sabina F.; m. Sue Janeway, Apr. 12, 1958; children: Richard, Edward. BS, U. Mass., 1955; MS, MIT, 1957; PhD, Purdue U., 1968. Registered engr., Tenn. Mem. rsch. staff Oak Ridge (Tenn.) Nat. Lab., 1957-63, 65-81, asst. dir. nuc. safety rsch., 1968-72, head advanced concepts devel. engring. tech. divsn., 1972-81, asst. to dir. engring. tech. divsn., 1990-92, group leader advanced concepts, 1963-64; group leader Advanced Concepts, 1993-94; instr. Purdue U., Oak Ridge, Tenn., 1964-65; dir. industry degraded core program Tech for Energy, Inc., Knoxville, Tenn., 1981-84; v.p. engring. Energex Oak Ridge, 1984-85; dir. nuclear safety tech. IT Corp. and Tenera, L.P., Knoxville, 1985-90; sr. scientist Avco Rsch. and Advanced Devel., Wilmington, Mass., 1963-64; cons. AEC, Washington, 1972-73, Nuc. Regulatory Commn., Washington, 1979-81, 91—, U.S. Dept. Energy, Washington, 1986-89; adj. prof. U. Tenn., 1995—; mem. Adv. Com. on Reactor Safeguards, 1995-99. Author more than 100 reports and articles. Fellow Am. Nuclear Soc. (chmn. nuclear reactor safety divsn. 1972-73, 94-95); mem. AAAS, ASME, Am. Mgmt. Assn., Soc. Risk Analysis, Rotary Internat., Sigma Xi, Tau Beta Pi. Achievements include patents for method of arc synthesis of uranium carbide from UF6 and Graphite, others. Office: Oak Ridge Nat Lab PO Box 2009 Oak Ridge TN 37831-2009

FONTANA, OLIVIER FREDERIC, marketing manager; b. France, July 5, 1968; m. Tanja Mecava, July 27, 1996; children: Maxime, Ambre. MSEE, Ecole Superieure d'Ingenieurs en Electrotechniques et Electronique, Marne la Vallee, France, 1992; MBA, Erasmus U., The Netherlands, 1998. Sales engr. Factory Sys., Emerainville, France, 1993, regional sales mgr., 1993-96; bus. devel. mgr. Philips Digital Networks, Eindhoven, The Netherlands, 1998, market group mgr., 1999—.

FONTANA, PEDRO, bank executive; b. Barcelona, Spain, May 30, 1952; s. Jose M. and Pilar Fontana; m. Maria Jose Gregori, June 8, 1985; children: Maria Jose, Pedro. MBA, Esade, Barcelona, 1974, Harvard U., 1976. Chief exec. Banca Mas Sardá, Barcelona, 1983-89, NH Hoteles, Barcelona, 1989-90; dir. gen. COOB-92, Barcelona, 1990-93; chief exec. Turisme de Barcelona, 1993-94; pres. Banca Catalana, Barcelona, 1994-2000; dir. gen. BBVA Catalunya, 2000—; bd. dirs. Areas S.A. Bd. dirs. Círculo de Economía, Barcelona, 1996—, Escuela Administración Empresas, Barcelona, 1991—; pres. Consell Social U. Barcelona. Orden Isabel la Católica, Kingdom of Spain, 1992, Orden Olímpica Plata, Internat. Olympic Com., 1992, Orden Olímpica, Spanish Olympic Com., 1992. Mem. C. of C. (plenary), Econ. Commn. C. of C. (pres. 1994—), R.C. Tenis Barcelona (bd. dirs. 1993).

FONTANGES, ROBERT, microbiologist, immunologist, consultant; b. Belleville, France, Nov. 22, 1928; s. Louis and Fernande (Bouquin) F.; m. Josette Crôtte, July 18, 1952; children: Guillemette,Thierry, Arnaud. MD, U. Lyon, France, 1953, D es Scis., 1965; Diploma, Inst. Pasteur, Paris, 1961. Cert. serologist, microbiologist, immunologist, cellular physiologist. Head chem. microbiology divsn. Svc. Santé Armées, Lyon, 1963-86; maitre de confs. U. Grenoble and Lyon, France, 1965-71; dean physiology and psychophysiology U. Lyon, 1971-77, prof., 1971-93; dir. rsch. ctr., gen. medicine inspector Svc. Santé Armées, Paris, 1986-88; hon. prof. gen. medicine Cellular Physiology Lab., U. Lyon, Villeurbanne, France, 1993—; pres. Centre de Bioexperimentation, Valbex, U. Lyon I; cons. aerosols, immunomodulators, vaccinations; cons. fermentation, bacteria, viruses, sterilization, solid/liquid plants for the pharma. and biotech industry. Contbr. more than 300 articles to internat. publs. Decorated officer Legion of Honor, Mil. Merit Cross, Comdr. Order Nat. Merit (France), comdr. Order Acad. Palmes (France); comdr. Nat. Order Niger; recipient vermeil medal Svc. Santé des Armées; Paul Harris fellow Rotary Internat., 1999. Mem. Rotary (pres. 1998-99). Avocation: movies, travel. Home: 24 rue Comdt Faurax, 69006 Lyon France

FONTANI THOMAS, LAURA, consultant; b. Florence, Italy, Feb. 9, 1962; m. Gerassimos Thomas; 1 child, Mara. BA, U. Mass., 1984; M of Internat. Affairs, Columbia U., 1986. Gen. securities registered rep. Nat. Assn. Securities Dealers; options and futures registered rep. Chgo. Bd. of Trade. Asst. rschr. UN Econ. Commn. for Europe, Geneva, summer 1983; rsch. fellow Coun. for Religion and Internat. Affairs, summer 1985; fixed income salesperson Morgan Stanley, London, 1986-92; head of fixed income sales, v.p. J.P. Morgan, Brussels, 1992-98; mng. dir., founder LF Fin. Mkts. Tng. and Cons., 1998—. Contbr. short stories to anthologies (Serenissima Lit. prize 1995). Mem. Associazione Toscani in Belgio, Columbia Club Belgium (mem. bd.). Avocations: writing, reading, skiing. E-Mail: laura.fontani@skynet.be. Office: 22A Square De Meeus, 1040 Brussels Belgium

FONTENOT, DOMINIC NICHOLAS, mathematician, writer; b. Detroit, Dec. 24, 1948; s. Edgis Joseph and Ida Mae (Billeaudeau) F. BS in Maths., Wayne State U., 1971. Computer programmer Jet Propulsion Lab., Pasadena, Calif., 1982-84; software engineer Def. Satellite Program, West Lake Village, Calif., 1984-89; software engr. Xerox Corp., 1990-92. Author: God's Fingerprint Prayer: Petition or Contact The Supreme Court Ain't Supreme. Mem. Ancient Hermetic Order of Asclepius. Avocations: philosophy, astrology, alchemy, herbalism, calendars. E-mail: tunafish@onebox.com.

FONTENOT, JACKIE DARREL, safety and health consultant; b. Leesville, La., Sept. 22, 1946; s. Oliver Huel and Ida Cora (Abshier) F.; m. Carolyn Luetta Brown, Jan. 2, 1968 (div. Dec., 1968); 1 child, Duane Alan; m. Hilda Marie Lopez, June 7, 1969; 1 child, Kayla Marie. Student, San Houston State U., 1964-66, Lee Coll., 1989-91. Cert. safety profl. (bd. cert. safety profls.); hazard control mgr. (bd. hazard control mgmt.); authorized crane inspector; cert. instr.; approved profl. source Tex. Workers Comp. and Field Safety Rep. Commn. Safety engr. Brown & Root, Monroe City, Tex., 1968-70; field safety rep. Tex. Gulf Sulphur Co., Fannett, Tex., 1970-72; plant safety supr. NL Baroid, Channelview, Tex., 1972-73; prodn. dept. safety coord. NL Baroid, Houston, 1973-76, regional safety mgr., 1976-81; mgr. safety and health NL Baroid Petroleum Svcs., Houston, 1981-86, NL Petroleum Svcs., Houston, 1986-88, Baroid Corp., Houston, 1988-91; safety and health cons. pvt. practice, Anahuac, Tex., 1991—; mem. indsl. com. NFPA, Boston, 1976—; instr. driver safety-fire suppression Tex. Safety Assn., Tex. A&M Extension Svc., 1976—; project dir. Tex. A&M Indsl. Fire Sch., master instr., 1993—; cert. instr. MSHA; speaker in field. Contbr. articles to Safety Coun. Newsletter, 1982-93. Sch. bd. trustee, Anahuac Ind. Sch. Dist., 1981-93; umpire Anahuac Youth Athletic Assn., 1980-82; Anahuac vol. fireman, 1976-86. Recipient Instr. Achievement award Tex. Safety Assn., Austin, 1977. Mem. Am. Soc. Safety Engrs. (nominated for Safety Profl. of Yr. Gulf Coast chpt. Houston 1986), Nat. Safety Coun. (chmn. petroleum sect. 1981—, Masons (past master lodge #995). Avoca-

tions: fishing, hunting. Home and Office: PO Box 1207 Anahuac TX 77514-1207

FONTÈS, BÉATRICE LILIANE, marketing professional; b. Metz, Lorraine, France, Aug. 30, 1956; d. Jacques Gabriel and Jeannine (Noirez) F. Degree, Inst. U. of Tech., France, 1977, U. Censier, Paris, 1980. Market rsch. cons. Figesma Conseil, Paris, 1977-83; market rsch. mgr. Application des Gaz, Paris, 1983-97; market rsch. exec. IFEM, Paris, 1997—. Avocation: classical singing. Home: 100 Blvd Massena, 75013 Paris France Office: ADG, IFEM, 4 rue du Dahomey, 75011 Paris France

FONTES, F. JAIME NOVAIS, telecommunications company executive; b. Oporto, Portugal, July 3, 1952; s. Wilson and Maria Fernanda (Campos) F.; m. Elsa Maria Magalhães, Apr. 5, 1975; children: João Tiago, Liliana. Lic., Oporto U., 1974. Tchr. U. Coimbra, Portugal, 1974-80, U. Oporto, 1980-83; cons. Telefones Lisboa e Porto, 1980-90, dir., 1990-94; dir. Portugal Telecom, Oporto, 1994-96, head of dept., 1996—; tchr./cons. Ednl. Inst., Oporto, 1986-88. Mem. Ordem Engenheiros, Automobile Club of Portugal (fellow). Home: Rua do Souto 81-5D, 4470 Maia Portugal Office: Portugal Telecom, Rua João de Deus 636, 4101 Porto Codex Oporto Portugal

FONTES, PAULO A., surgeon, educator; b. Sao Paulo, Brazil, Jan. 20, 1962; s. Paulo B. and Midlred (Chaves) F.; m. Monica M. Mollerstrand, Sept. 9, 1991; children: Rafaella M., Karl Liam M. MD, Sao Paulo State U., 1985. Bd. cert. gen. surgery Brazilian Coll. Surgeons. Intern Sao Paulo State U. Sch. Medicine, Botucatu, Brazil, 1984-85; resident Prof. Edmundo Vasconcelos Hosp., Sao Paulo, 1986-88, mem. med. staff, 1990-91, supr. gen. surgery residents, 1990-91; rsch. fellow Sao Paulo Fed. U., 1990-91; rsch. fellow U. Pitts. Med. Ctr., 1991-93, vis. asst. prof. surgery, 1993-96, clin. fellow, 1996-98, attending surgeon, assoc. prof., 1998—; dir. S. & Am. divns. U. Pitts. Med. Ctr. Oversease Inc., 1998—. Contbr. articles to profl. jours. Recipient Bradesco Found. prize, 1988, 89; scholar Sao Paulo State Govt., 1980-85. Avocations: sailing, biking, working out, surfing. Fax: 412-647-5480. Home: 522 Gettysburg St Pittsburgh PA 15206-4548 Office: U Pitts Med Ctr 4C Falk Clinic 3601 5th Ave Pittsburgh PA 15213-3403

FONTES, WAGNER, biology educator; b. São Paulo, July 14, 1963; s. Belchor and Edmea (Albano) F.; m. Mariana de Souza Castro. MD, U. São Paulo, 1987; PhD, U. Brasília, Brazil, 1996. Surgeon Clinic Hosp., U. São Paulo, 1987-91; assoc. rschr. U. Brasília, 1992-96, prof., 1997—. Contbr. articles to profl. jours.; inventor in field. 1st ltd. Brazilian Air Force, 1988. Recipient Trauma Project award Support Program for Sci. and Tech., 1999. Mem. Brazilian Soc. for Biochemistry and Molecular Biology. Avocations: electronic assemblies, computers, swimming. Office: U Brasília, UnB-ICC Cellular Biol, 70910900 Brasília DF, Brazil

FONTINOY, CHARLES-MARIE, retired Oriental studies educator; b. Stavelot, Belgium, Mar. 12, 1920; s. Charles-Henry and Marie-Eugènie (Gouders) F. Lic. in Philosophy and Letters, State U. Liege, 1941, D in History and Oriental Lit., 1963. Tchr. Athénée Royal of Aywaille, Belgium, 1945-66; prof. State U. Liege, 1966-85, chmn. dept. Oriental studies, 1980-85. Author: Le duel dans les langues sémitiques, 1969; contbr. articles to profl. jours. Decorated grand officer Order of Leopold II (Belgium); recipient Bourses ppur missions à l' étranger Comm. Mixte des Echanges Culturels Franco-Belges, Paris, 1954, 55, 57, 59, 66. Bourse de recherche Partrimoine de l'Univ. de Liege, 1960. Mem. Soc. Bibl. Lit., Inst. Iudaicum (mem. com.), Soc. Belge d'études Orientales (mem. com.). Roman Catholic. Avocations: literature, psychology, ornithology. Home: La Bovière 3, 4920 Aywaille Belgium

FONTY, BERNARD-JACQUES, obstetrician; b. Angers, France, May 20, 1941; s. Pierre-Emile and Fernande-Celuta (Dorland) F.; m. Godeleine Faugeron, Oct. 29, 1966 (div. Apr. 1978); children: Nicolas, Simon; m. Annie-Marie Payen, May 15, 1983; 1 child, Alexandre. MD, U. Paris, 1971. Intern Paris Hosp., 1968-72, asst., 1972-79; head of clinic U. Paris, 1972-79; practice medicine specializing in obstetrics Paris, 1979—. Author: Bonjour l'Aurore, 1987; contbr. articles to profl. jours. Roman Catholic. Home and Office: 71 Blvd Raspail, 75006 Paris France

FONVIELLE, CHARLES DAVID, lawyer; b. Melbourne, Fla., Dec. 28, 1944; s. Charles David Fonvielle Jr. and Margaret Jordan Palmer; m. Deborah Konas, July 25, 1970; children: C. Caulley, D. Jordan. BA, U. Fla., 1968; JD, Fla. State U., 1972. Bar: Fla. 1972, U.S. Dist. Ct. (no., mid. and so. dists.) Fla. Asst. pub. defender Fla. Pub. Defender Assn., Tallahassee, 1972-74; pvt. practice Tallahassee, 1974-77; ptnr. Thompson, Wadsworth, Messer, Turner & Rhodes, Tallahassee, 1977-80, Green & Fonvielle, Tallahassee, 1980-84, Green, Fonvielle & Hinkle, Tallahassee, 1984-85, Fonvielle Hinkle & Lewis, Tallahassee, 1985—. Bd. dirs. Fla. State U. Coll. of Law, endowed prof. litigation. Mem. ALTA (sustaining), Tallahassee Bar Assn. (bd. dirs. 1978-79), Acad. Fla. Trial Lawyers (Eagle sponsor 1990—), Nat. Bd. Trial Advocacy (cert.), Fla. Bar Assn. (bd. legal specialization and edn. 1991—), Fla. State U. Pres.'s Club (bd. visitors). Avocations: physical fitness, flying, spearfishing, sports cars. Office: Fonvielle Hinkle & Lewis 3375 Capital Cir NE Ste A Tallahassee FL 32308-3778

FOO, SIANG HENG, human resource director; b. Singapore, Nov. 28, 1949; s. Kia Beng and Juat Eng (Fuah) F.; m. Jee Kiat Wong, Nov. 4, 1978; children: Vincent, Desmond, Derek. BS, U. Singapore, 1971; BS (hon.), 1972, MS, 1976. Personnel officer Singapore Airlines Ltd., 1978-80; personnel mgr. Singapore Press Holdings Ltd., 1980-88, Philips Singapore Pte Ltd., 1988-90; sr. mgr. pers. and adminstrn. Abacus Distrbn. Systems Pte, Ltd., Singapore, 1990-96; human resource dir. Asia Pacific Synposys Singapore Pte Ltd., Singapore, 1996-97, Origin Tech. Pte Ltd., Singapore, 1997—. Lt. Singapore Armed Forces, 1975-78. Rsch. scholarship U. Singapore, 1972. Mem. Am. Mgmt. Assn., Singapore Human Resources Inst., Nature Soc. Singapore, Singapore Recreation Club. Avocations: reading, jogging, badminton, collecting first day covers, travel. Home: Apt Blk 79 Marine Dr 07-30, Singapore 440079, Singapore Office: Origin Technology Pte Ltd, 8 Temasek Blvd 07-01, Singapore 038988, Singapore

FOOKES, ERIC GEOFFREY VINCENT, software developer; b. Woerden, Holland, The Netherlands, Apr. 14, 1964; arrived in Switzerland, 1967; s. Geoffrey Alan F. and Catharina Maria (Groenendijk) F.; m. Satu Sinikka Vainio, Aug. 1, 1987; children: Lisa, Tania. BSc, U. Geneva, 1988, MSc, 1991. FNRS asst. U. Geneva, 1990, rsch., tchg. asst., 1993-97; tchr. Normaalikoulu, Turku, Finland, 1991-92; software developer Geneva, 1991—. Developer software on the Internet. Avocations: photography, travel, cycling, skiing. Office: Av Eugene-Pittard 22T, 1206 Geneva Switzerland

FOOKES, PETER GEORGE, engineering geologist, educator; b. Essex, Eng., May 31, 1933; s. George Ernest and Ida Corina Fookes; m. Edna May Nix, July 25, 1987; children: by former marriage: Jennifer, Gregory, Timothy, Anita, Rosemary. BSc with honors, Queen Mary Coll., London U., 1960, PhD, 1967, DSc in Engring., 1979. Chartered engr. U.K. Rsch. asst. Brewing Industry Rsch. Foun., 1950-54; sr. technician Chelsea Coll., London U., 1956-57; field engring. geologist Binnie and Ptnrs., London, 1960-65; lectr. Imperial Coll., London U., 1966-71, cons. engring. geologist, 1971—; vis. prof. London U., 1979-96, City U., 1991—; hon. prof. Birmingham U., 1999—, Newcastle U., 1993-96. Author: over 150 papers and books. Recipient several awards including Wm. Smith medal Geol. Soc., 1985, 1st Glossop medal, 1997. Fellow Inst. Geology, Geol. Soc., Instn. Mining and Metallurgy, Royal Acad. Engring.; mem. Geologists Assn., Instn. Civil Engrs. (assoc. George Stephenson Gold medal 1990). Avocations: industrial archaeology, canal boats. Address: Lafonia, 11A Edgar Rd, Winchester, Hampshire S023 9SJ, England

FOONG, BRENDA MEE LAI, media planner; b. Kuala Trengganu, Malaysia, Apr. 16, 1973; d. Francis Chee Wai Foong and Peck Choo Chee. BA with honors, U. So. Miss., 1998. Mentor Cosmotots IQ Devel. Ctr., Kuala Lumpur, Malaysia, 1994-95; rsch. asst. Cooke Libr. U. Miss., 1996-97, photographer, 1996-98; media planner Mindshare Singapore/Ogilvy & Mather, Singapore, 1998—. Avocations: music, reading. Office: Mindshare Singapore, 5 Temasek Blvd # 06-01 Suntect CityTower, Singapore 038985, Singapore

FOOT, HUGH CORRIE, psychology educator; b. Northwood, Middlesex, Eng., June 7, 1941; s. John Lovell and Bertha Lillian (Corrie) F.; m. Daryl Madeleine May, Dec. 14, 1968; children: Jonathan Stuart, Caroline Louise. BA in Psychology, U. Durham, Eng., 1962; PhD in Psychology, U. St. Andrews, Scotland, 1967. Rsch. fellow U. Dundee, Scotland, 1965-68; lectr. in psychology U. Wales, Cardiff, 1968-77, sr. lectr., 1977-88, reader, 1988-92; prof., psychology dept. head U. Strathclyde, Glasgow, Scotland, 1992—. Editor: (books) Pedestrian Accidents, 1982, Children Helping Children, 1990, Friendship and Social Relations in Children, 1995, Humour and Laughter: Theory, Research and Application, 1996. Grantee: Econ. and Social Rsch. Coun., Swindon, Eng., 1986-87, U. Strathclyde, Glasgow, Scotland, Dept. of Transport, London, 1995-97. Fellow Brit. Psychol. Soc. (chartered psychologist). Avocations: walking, tennis, gardening, wild life. Office: U Strathclyde Psychol Dept, 40 George St, Glasgow G1 1QE, Scotland

FOOT, MICHAEL RICHARD DANIELL, historian; b. London, Dec. 14, 1919; s. Richard Cunningham and Nina (Raymond) F.; m. Philippa Ruth Bosanquet, June 21, 1945 (div. 1959); m. Elizabeth Mary Irvine King, Apr. 1, 1960 (div. 1972); children: Sarah, Richard; m. Mirjam Michaela Romme, Mar. 25, 1972. BA, MA, New Coll., Oxford, Eng., 1945, BLitt, 1950. Prof. modern history U. Manchester, Eng., 1967-73; dep. warden Wiston (Eng.) House, 1973-75. Author: The Gladstone Diaries, Vols. 1-4, 1968-74, SOE in France, 1966, Resistance, 1977; co-editor: Oxford Companion to the Second World War, 1995, others. Maj. Royal Arty., 1939-45. Decorated Croix de Guerre, officer Order Orange-Nassau. Mem. Savile Club, Spl. Forces Club. Home: Martins Cottage, Nuthampstead Royston Herts SG8 8ND, England

FOOTE, NATHAN MAXTED, retired physical science educator; b. Woodlawn, Pa., Oct. 8, 1913; s. Myron Tinkham and Ada May (Maxted) F.; m. Laura Belle Gruey, Sept. 5, 1936; children: Jonathan W., L. Nadine, Frances C., Willard G. AB, DePauw U., 1935; MS, Purdue U., 1939. Jr. chemist U.S. FDA, Phila., 1939-40; Rsch. engr. RCA, Camden, N.J., 1940-49; rsch. scientist Colgate Palmolive, Jersey City, N.J., 1950-52; rheologist B.F. Goodrich Chem. Co., Avon Lake, Ohio, 1953-58; acting head, Dept. Physics Baldwin Wallace Coll., Berea, Ohio, 1958-60; vis. asst. prof. Physics Pa. State U., University Park, 1960-61; asst. prof. Physics, Behrend Coll. Pa. State U., Erie, 1964-78, ret., 1979; assoc. prof. Phys. Sci. SUNY, Geneseo, 1961-64. Author: Industrial and Engineering Chemistry, 1944, Industrial and Engineering Chemistry, 1947. Del. Ohio Coun. Am. Bapt. Men, 1955-58. Mem. AAAS, Am. Chem. Soc. (50 Yr. award 1993), Sigma Xi. Avocations: stratospheric chem. change, lawn bowling. Home: 14 E Main St Lot B Mount Dora FL 32757-3470

FOOTE, ROBERT LEONARD, oncologist, educator, researcher; b. Payson, Utah, Dec. 18, 1957; s. Leonard H. and Lauana (Whitaker) F.; m. Kally Rae Henderson, Apr. 20, 1979; children: Catherine Anne, Anthony Leonard, Robert Tyler, Ralph Andrew, Patrick Henderson, Thomas James. BS in Chemistry, Brigham Young U., 1980; MD, U. Utah, 1984. Diplomate Nat. Bd. Med. Examiners, Am. Bd. Radiology. Intern LDS Hosp., Salt Lake City, 1984-85; resident in radiation oncology Mayo Grad. Sch. Medicine, Rochester, Minn., 1985-88; Mayo Found. scholar U. Fla., Gainesville, 1988, clin. fellow in oncology, 1988; sr. assoc. cons. Mayo Clinic, Rochester, 1988-91, cons., 1991—; from instr. to assoc. prof. oncology Mayo Med. Sch., Rochester, 1988-99, prof., 1999—; trustee Albert Lea (Minn.) Med. Ctr., 1997—. Contbr. articles to med. jours., including Jour. Neurosurgery, Cancer. Cubmaster, instnl. rep. Boy Scouts Am., Rochester, 1985—; bishop LDS Ch., Rochester, 1996—. Named Mayo Fellow Assn. Tchr. of Yr., Mayo Found., 1990, 95, 97, 2000. Mem. Am. Soc. for Therapeutic Radiology and Oncology, Am. Coll. Radiology, Sigma Xi. Avocations: coin and rare book collecting. Office: Mayo Clinic 200 1st St SW Rochester MN 55905-0002

FOOTE, WARREN EDGAR, neuroscientist, psychologist, educator; b. Boston, Nov. 5, 1935; s. Warren Edgar and Edith Irene (Landry) F.; B.A., Hamilton Coll., 1958; M.A., Boston U., 1960; Ph.D., Tufts U., 1965; m. Cynthia Sue Hall, July 21, 1973; children: Pamela Fowler, Sarah Canby, Julia Landry, Christopher Warren. Research assoc. Harvard U. Med. Sch., 1966-67, vis. asst. prof. psychology, 1970-73, asst. prof., 1974-83, assoc. prof., 1983—; USPHS postdoctoral fellow Yale, 1967-69; research scientist Norwich (Conn.) State Hosp., 1969-70; sr. Fulbright scholar Max-Planck Inst., Munich, Germany, 1973-74; assoc. psychologist Mass. Gen. Hosp., Boston, 1974—, psychologist, 1984-95, sr. psychologist, 1995—; cons. Gen. Foods Corp., 1970-74, Neurotech Corp., 1987-88. Served with M.C., AUS, 1959-60. Recipient McCurdy prize Mass. Soc. Research in Psychiatry, 1962; sr. Fulbright fellow, 1973-74; Nat. Inst. Neurol. Disease and Stroke grantee, 1974-77; NIMH grantee, 1970-73; Nat. Eye Inst. grantee, 1979—; Wayland Pub. Sch. Found. advisor, 1982—; Nat. Inst. Communicative Disorders and Stroke grantee, 1983—. Mem. AAAS, N.Y. Acad. Scis., Soc. Neurosci., Am. Psychol. Assn., Sigma Xi. Club: Harvard (Boston). Contbr. articles, revs. to profl. jours. Home: 5 Hilltop Park Wilbraham MA 01095-1753 Office: Mass Gen Hosp PO Box 70 Boston MA 02114

FORBES, BRYAN, film director, writer; b. London, July 22, 1926; s. Theo and Katy (Seaton) Clarke; m. Nanette Newman, Aug. 27, 1955; children: Sarah Kate Amanda, Emma Clempson. D (hon.), London U., Sussex U. Founder Beaver Films; chief exec., head prodn. EMI/MGM. Actor films including The Small Back Room, and 20 others; co-prodr./writer The Angry Silence (British Acad. award for best screenplay, nominated Acad. Award, Critics prize Berlin Film Festival); writer, actor The League of Gentleman; dir. Whistle Down the Wind; writer, dir. The L-Shaped Room, Seance on a Wet Afternoon (British Acad. award for best screenplay, Edgar award), King Rat, The Whisperers, Deadfall, The Raging Moon, The Naked Face; prodr., dir. The Wrong Box; dir. The Madwoman of Chaillot, The Stepford Wives; prodr. The Go-Between, The Railway Children, The Tales of Beatrix Potter; co-author, dir. The Slipper and the Rose, The Sunday Lovers, Menage a Trois; writer/prodr./dir. International Velvet; author: The Distant Laughter, Familiar Strangers, Intemation Velvet, The Rewrite Man, the Endless Game, A Song at Twilight, The Twisted Playground, Partly Cloudy, Quicksand and the Memory of all That, (short stories) Truth Lies Sleeping, (autobiography) Notes For a Life, A Divided Life, Ned's Give-Biography of Dame Edith Evans, That Deopicable Race-A History of The British Ading Tradition. Service British Army Intelligence Corps, 1943-47. Scholarship The Royal Acad. of Dramatic Art. Mem. British Screenwriters Guild (founder, ex-pres.), Nat. Youth Theatre of Great Britain (pres.), The Beatrix Potter Soc. (past pres.). Avocations: collecting books, gardening. Home: 7 X Pines Lake Rd, Wentworth, Surrey GU25 4QP, England

FORBES, JOHN EDWARD, financial consultant; b. Chgo., Sept. 18, 1925; s. Harry Charles and Jeanette Anne (Field) F.; m. Dorsey Connors, Aug. 10, 1961. Student, Rensselaer Poly. Inst., 1943-44, Franklin and Marshall Coll., Lancaster, Pa., 1943; BA, Monmouth Coll., 1949; postgrad., Northwestern U., 1949-50. Account exec. and commodity mgr. Merrill Lynch, Pierce, Fenner and Smith, Inc., Chgo., 1949-61; pres. San Jose Cigarette Co., Calif., 1958-68; account exec. Hornblower & Weeks, Hemphill, Noyes, Inc., Chgo., 1961-71, assoc. resident mgr., 1971-75, v.p., resident mgr., 1975-78; corp. v.p. Loeb, Rhoades, Hornblower & Co., Chgo., 1981—, Shearson Lehman Bros., Chgo., 1961—; sr. v.p. fin. cons. Salomon Smith Barney, Chgo., 1995—; pres. 227 E. Delaware Corp, Chgo., 1980-86; bd. dirs. Trend Industries, Chgo. Lt. USN, 1943-46, PTO. Clubs: Econ., Chgo. Bond, Hundred Club of Cook County, Tavern (pres. 1981-82), Saddle and Cycle (bd. dirs. 1983-86). Lodge: Soc. St. Andrew. Home: 227 E Delaware Pl Chicago IL 60611-7758 Office: Smith Barney Inc 10 S Wacker Dr Fl 2800 Chicago IL 60606-7438

FORBES, JOHN FRANCIS, government official; b. Ossining, N.Y., Aug. 19, 1946; s. Frank Joseph and Sara A. Forbes. BA, Marist Coll., 1968; MBPA, Southeastern U., Washington, 1981; MA, Boston U., 1986. Spl. agt. U.S. Customs Svc., Rouses Point, N.Y., 1972-73; spl. agt. enforcement U.S. Customs Svc., Buffalo, 1974-78; sr. spl. agt. U.S. Customs Svc., Reston, Va., 1978-82; customs rep. U.S. Customs Svc., Bonn, Fed. Republic Germany, 1982-87; program mgr. U.S. Customs Svc., Washington, 1987-88, chief gen. smuggling sect., 1988, chief gen. smuggling br. fin. investigations divsn., 1988-91, investigator senate permanant subcom. on investigations, fin. investigation div., 1992-94, with customs congl. affairs, 1994; with group IV-El Dorado task force U.S. Customs Svc., N.Y.C., 1994-99; mem. banking subcom. on oversight and investigation U.S. Ho. of Reps., 1999—; spl. agt. Drug Enforcement Agy., Rouses Point, 1973-74; investigator Senate Permanent Subcom. on Investigations, 1992-94. Contbr. articles to profl. mag. Mem. Nat. Trust for Hist. Preservation, Washington, Friends of Kennedy Ctr., Washington. 1st lt. U.S. Army, 1968-71, Vietnam. Mem. VFW, Internat. Police Assn., Assn. Cert. Fraud Examiners, Fraternal Order of Police, World Affairs Coun. Washington, Fed. Law Enforcement Officers Assn., Wilson Ctr. Assocs., Lincoln Soc., Cousteau Soc., World Future Soc., The Acad. of Polit. Sci., ASPA, Fed. Planning Network, Nat. Capitol Hist. Soc. Roman Catholic. Avocations: running, reading, scuba diving, cross country skiing. Office: House Banking Com Subcom Oversight & Invest House Ford Anx Rm 139 Washington DC 20515-0001

FORBES, LARRY DOUGLAS, economist; b. Norfolk, Va., Sept. 16, 1951; s. Oswell Harris and Sara Frances Forbes; m. Michele Lyons, Nov. 24, 1993. AA, Coll. of The Albemarle, Elizabeth City, N.C., 1971; BSBA, Old Dominion U., 1988; MA in Mgmt., Regent U., 1998. Cert. econ. developer, Am. Econ. Devel. Coun. Legis. asst. Va. Gen. Assembly, Richmond, 1983-88; sr. trade analyst Va. Dept. World Trade, Norfolk, 1986-90; dir. ops. Alliance Europe, Norfolk, 1990-93; sr. internat. trade economist Va. Econ. Devel. Partnership, Richmond, 1993—. Author, editor: (series) Virginia in a Global Economy, 1987, 90, 93, 99. Vice chmn. Portsmouth (Va.) Dem. Party, 1993; bd. dirs. Indsl. Devel. authority, New Kent County, Va., 2000—. Sgt. 1st class, USAR, 1971-96. Recipient Best of Class award for industry study, Am. Econ. Devel. Coun., 1999, Superior award for industry study, 1996. Mem. Nat. Assn. Bus. Econs., Internat. Trade Data Users Group, Va. Assn. Economists, Va. Econ. Developers Assn., Richmond Assn. Bus. Economists (bd. dirs. 1998-00).. United Methodist. Avocations: golf, fishing, gardening. E-mail: lforbes@yesvirginia.org. Home: 7465 Pinehurst Dr Quinton VA 23141-1521 Office: Va Econ Devel Ptnership 901 E Byrd St Richmond VA 23219-4069

FORBES, PETER, architect; b. Berkeley, Calif., May 22, 1942; s. John Douglas and Margaret (Funkhouser) F.; m. Patricia Ann Marsh, Aug. 27, 1966 (div. 1982); children: Alexander John, Anne deMarken; m. Erica Longfellow deBerry, July 21, 1990; 1 child, Allegra Longfellow. BArch, U. Mich., 1966; MArch, Yale U., 1967; Dr. Engring. Tech. (hon.), Wentworth Inst. Tech., 1991. Registered architect, Mass., Va., Calif., Maine, R.I., N.Y., Mich., Conn., D.C.; cert. Nat. Council Archtl. Registration Bds. Project designer Skidmore, Owings & Merrill, Chgo., 1965-66; assoc. ptnr. PARD Team, Inc., Boston, 1967-71; pres. Forbes Hailey Jeas Erneman, Inc., Boston, 1972-80, Peter Forbes and Assoc., Inc., Boston, 1980—; mem. Commonwealth of Mass. Designer Selection Bd., 1986-89; mem. Spl. Commn. Concerning State and County Bldgs., 1978-81; bd. dirs. continuing edn. Boston Archtl. Ctr.; vis. critic U. Mich., 1980-82, Cath. U. Am., Rome, 1982; vis. lectr. Cath. U., Washington, 1997; lectr., vis. critic Va. Poly. Inst. and State U., 1989-92, 96, Columbia U., 1984; vis. critic N.C. State U., 1997; Thomas S. Monaghan Disting. vis. prof. U. Mich., 1987; vis. prof. Harvard U., 1989, 91, 94, G. Truman Ward vis. lectr. Va. Poly. Inst. and State U., 1996; vis. lectr. Lawrence Tech. U., 1996, Evergreen State Coll., 1996, U. B.C., 1996; guest lectr. Boston Mus. Fine Arts, 1997, Guido A. Binda vis. lectr. U. Mich., 1997. Author: Ten Houses: Peter Forbes and Associates, 1995; exhbns. include Cath. U. Am., 1982, 97, U. Mich., 1982, 87, 97, Va. Poly. Inst. and State U., 1983, Boston Athenaeum, 1986, Harvard U., 1986, Lawrence Tech. U., 1996; contbr. articles to profl. jours. Recipient Record House award, 1983, 86, 87, 89, New Eng. Design awrd, 1986, 87, 89, 91, 94, 96, 97, 98, Archtl. Excellence award Am. Inst. Steel Constrn., 1987, Tucker award Bldg. Stone Inst., 1987, 90, Best and Brightest award, 1995, Honor award Am. Wood Inst., 1989, Nat. Housing Design award, 1990, Silver award Indsl. Designers Soc. Am., 1993, 94, Am. Arch. award Chgo. Athenaeum Mus. Arch. and Design, 1999. Fellow AIA (nat. jud. coun. 1987—, Nat. honor award 1986, 92, New Eng. regional coun./design award 1986, 87, 89, 91, 94, 96, 97, 98, Washington D.C. merit award 1994; Excellence in Arch. award Maine chpt. 1995), Boston Soc. Archs. (bd. dirs., commr. pub. affairs, chmn. ethics com., v.p., pres. 1988-89, Excellence in Arch. award 1988-89, 91-94, 98, Honor award 1995, 97, 98, Excellence in Housing design award 1996, 98), Soc. Archtl. Historians (life), Century Club, Newport Reading Rm., Racquet and Tennis Club, Nat. Tennis Club, Yale Club, Boston Athenaeum. Home: Greenings Is Southwest Harbor ME 04679 Home (winter): Viale Giovanni Milton 65, 50129 Florence Italy Office: Peter Forbes and Assocs PO Box 100 Seal Harbor ME 04675-0100

FORBES, SARAH ELIZABETH, gynecologist, real estate corporation officer; b. Currituck, N.C., May 4, 1928; d. Dexter and Mary (Brock) Forbes. BA, U. Rochester, 1949; MD, Med. Coll. of Va., 1954. Diplomate Am. Bd. Ob-Gyn. Intern Norfolk (Va.) Gen. Hosp., 1954-55; resident ob-gyn Johnston-Willis Hosp., 1955-56; resident ob-gyn Norfolk Gen. Hosp., 1956-57, chief resident, 1957-58; pvt. practice gynecologist Newport News, Va., 1958—; pres., real estate investor Mary B. Forbes Land Corp., Newport News, 1972—; pres. Sebrof Corp., Newport News, 1978—, Haras, Inc., Newport News, 1984—, S.S. U.S., Inc., Newport News, 1984—; bd. dirs. Family Planning Coun.; mem. teaching staff ob-gyn dept. Riverside Hosp. Pres. Peninisula Soc. for Prevention Cruelty to Animals, 1966—; mem. adv. bd. Peninisula chpt. Parents without Ptnrs.; bd. dirs. Newport News chpt. Am. Cancer Soc., pres., 2d v.p., 1971-72, 1st v.p., 1972-73, pres., 1973-74, chmn. rsch., 1961-69; candidate for Newport News City Coun., 1986; bd. dirs. Va. Peninsula Boys and Girls Club, 1991-99, 1st v.p., pres. Va. Peninsula Boys and Girls Club, 2000—. Recipient AMA Physicians Recognition award for Continuing Edn., 1973-76, Twin award Va. Peninsula YWCA, 1987, Medallion award Peninsula Boys and Girls Club, 1993; named Woman of Yr. for Peninsula Area, 1975. Mem. Va. Peninsula Acad. Medicine (pres. 1973-74, v.p. 1972-73, sec., treas. 1971-72); fellow AMA, Va. Med. Soc., Newport News Med. Soc. Am. Coll. Ob-Gyn, Tidewater Ob-Gyn Soc. Office: 12420 Warwick Blvd Newport News VA 23606-3001

FORCEVILLE, CHARLES JOSEPH, humanities educator; b. Heemstede, The Netherlands, Aug. 18, 1959; s. Charles and Johanna Theodora Catharina (Van Rossum) F.; life ptnr. Gesina Maria van Altena. Grad., Vrye U., Amsterdam, 1981, Doctorate, 1988, PhD, 1994. Freelance translator The Netherlands, 1988-90; rschr. Netherlands Orgn. Wetenschappelyk Onderzoek, 1990-94; lectr. Vrye U., 1991-99; rschr. Onderzoekschool Literatuur Wetenschap, Ryks U., Leiden, The Netherlands, 1996-98; reviewer English-lang. lit. Dutch newspaper Trouw, 1988—; lectr. U. Amsterdam, 1999—. Author: Pictorial Metaphor in Advertising, 1996; book rev. editor Metaphor and Symbol, 1999—; contbr. articles to profl. jours. Harting scholar U. Durham, Eng., 1982-83; grantee Can. Fed. Govt., 1990, 93. Avocations: visiting art galleries, film, friends, eating out, collecting Jacques Brel records. Office: U Amsterdam/Dept Film/TV, Nieuwe Doelenstraat 16, 1012 CP Amsterdam The Netherlands

FORD, AUSTIN MCNEILL, clergyman; b. Decatur, Ga., Feb. 6, 1929; s. Harold Augustus and Elizabeth Austin Ford. AB, Emory U., 1950; MTh, U. of South, 1953. Ordained to ministry, Episcopal Ch., 1963. Asst. St. Luke's Ch., Atlanta, 1953-55; rector St. Bartholomew's Ch., Atlanta, 1955-67; founder, dir. Emmaus Ho., Atlanta, 1967-96; ret., 1996; pres. Ga. Coun. Human Rels., Atlanta, 1966-72, Met. Coun. Interracial Equality, Atlanta, 1970-74; mem. Nat. Commn. Internat. Yr. of Child, Atlanta, 1980-82. V.p. Gate City Day Nursery Assn., Atlanta, 1965-98; bd. dirs. Atlanta Boy Choir, Atlanta Opera Bd. Democrat. Episcopalian.

FORD, BETTY BLOOMER (ELIZABETH FORD), former First Lady of United States, health facility executive; b. Chgo., Apr. 8, 1918; d. William Stephenson and Hortence (Neahr) Bloomer; m. Gerald R. Ford (38th Pres. U.S.), Oct. 15, 1948; children: Michael Gerald, John Gardner, Steven Meigs, Susan Elizabeth. Student, Sch. Dance Bennington Coll., 1936, 37; LL.D. (hon.), U. Mich., 1976. Dancer Martha Graham Concert Group, N.Y.C., 1939-41; fashion dir. Herpolscheimer's Dept. Store, Grand Rapids, Mich., 1943-48; dance instr. Grand Rapids, 1932-48; chmn. bd. dirs. The Betty Ford Ctr., Rancho Mirage, Calif. Author: autobiography The Times of My Life, 1979, Betty: A Glad Awakening, 1987. Bd. dirs. Nat. Arthritis Found. (hon.); trustee Martha Graham Dance Ctr., Eisenhower Med. Ctr., Rancho Mirage; hon. chmn. Palm Springs Desert Mus.; nat. trustee Nat. Symphony Orch.; bd. dirs. The Lambs, Libertyville, Ill. Episcopalian. Home: PO Box 927 Rancho Mirage CA 92270-0927

FORD, EDWIN ROE, engineering company executive; b. Brownfield, Tex., May 26, 1943; s. J.B. and Leila (Flache) F.; m. Regina L. Ford; children: Bryan, Brody. BSCE, Tex. A&M U., 1970, postgrad. studies, 1974. Registered profl. engr., Tex.; registered pub. land surveyor, Tex. Design engr. Urban Engring., Corpus Christi, Tex., 1970-78; v.p. Comprehensive Design, Inc., New Braunfels, Tex., 1978-80; pres. Ford Engring., Inc., San Antonio, 1980—; founder CivilCadd, Inc.; city engr. City of Schertz, Schertz, Tex., 1978—, City of Converse, Converse, Tex., 1984—, City of Marion, Marion, Tex., 1987—. Bd. mem. New Braunfels Youth Soccer Assn., New Braunfels, Tex., 1980-84; sponsor, Converse Little League, Inc., Converse, Tex., 1986—. 1st Lt. U.S. Army, 1966-69. Mem. NSPE, Consulting Engring. Coun. of Tex., Tex. Soc. Profl. Engrs. (Young Engr. of Yr. award 1976), ASCE (pres. 1976), Tex. Soc. Civil Engrs. (pres. 1976), Tex. Soc. Pub. Land Surveyors, Profl. Engrs. Pvt. Practice, Peacock Alumni Assn. (bd. dirs. 1989—), Peacock Mil. Acad. Alumni Assn. (life, bd. dirs.), Lions, Jaycees. Office: Ford Engring Inc 10927 Wye St Ste 104 San Antonio TX 78217-2642

FORD, GERALD J., bank executive. B in Econs., So. Meth. U., 1966, JD, 1969. Bar: Tex. Chmn., CEO First Gibraltar Bank, Tex., 1988-93; chmn. bd. dirs. First Madison Bank; pres., owner Madison Fin., Inc.; founder First United Bank Group, Inc.; chmn., CEO First Nationwide Bank, 1994, Calif. Fed. Bank, 1997, Golden State Bancorp, 1998—. Named Among 40 Most Generous, Fortune Mag., 1998. Office: Golden State Bancorp Inc 135 Main St San Francisco CA 94105-1812*

FORD, GERALD RUDOLPH, JR., former President of United States; b. Omaha, July 14, 1913; s. Gerald R. and Dorothy (Gardner) F.; m. Elizabeth Bloomer, Oct. 15, 1948; children: Michael, John, Steven, Susan. A.B., U. Mich., 1935; LL.B., Yale U., 1941; LL.D., Mich. State U., Albion Coll., Aquinas Coll., Spring Arbor Coll. Bar: Mich. 1941. Practiced law at Grand Rapids, 1941-49; mem. law firm Buchen and Ford; mem. 81st-93d Congresses from 5th Mich. Dist., 1949-74, elected minority leader, 1965; v.p. U.S., 1973-74, pres., 1974-77; del. Interparliamentary Union, Warsaw, Poland, 1959, Belgium, 1961, Bilderberg Group Conf., 1962; dir. The Travelers, Inc.; adv. dir. Tex. Commerce Bancshares, Inc., Am. Express Co.; mem. internat. adv. coun. Inst. Internat. Studies. Served as lt. comdr. USNR, 1942-46. Recipient Grand Rapids Jr. C. of C. Distinguished Service award, 1948; Distinguished Service Award as one of ten outstanding young men in U.S. by U.S. Jr. C. of C., 1950; Silver Anniversary All-Am. Sports Illustrated, 1959; Distinguished Congressional Service award Am. Polit. Sci. Assn., 1961, Medal of Freedom, 1999, Congressional Gold Medal, 1999. Mem. Am., Mich. State, Grand Rapids bar assns., Delta Kappa Epsilon, Phi Delta Phi. Republican. Episcopalian. Clubs: University (Kent County), Peninsular (Kent County). Lodge: Masons. Office: PO Box 927 Rancho Mirage CA 92270-0927*

FORD, GORDON BUELL, JR., English language, linguistics, and medieval studies educator, author, retired hospital industry accounting financial management executive; b. Louisville, Sept. 22, 1937; s. Gordon Buell Sr. and Rubye (Allen) F. AB summa cum laude in Classics, Medieval Latin, and Sanskrit, Princeton U., 1959; AM in Classical Philology and Linguistics, Harvard U., 1962, PhD in Linguistics, Slavic and Baltic Langs. and Lits., 1965; postgrad., U. Oslo, 1962-64, U. Sofia, Bulgaria, 1963, U. Uppsala, Sweden, 1963-64, U. Stockholm, 1963-64, U. Madrid, 1963. CPA. Yeager, Ford, and Warren Found. Disting. prof. Indo-European, Classical, Slavic, and Baltic linguistics, Sanskrit, and Medieval Latin Northwestern U., Evanston, Ill., 1965—; Lybrand, Ross Bros., and Montgomery Found. Disting. prof. English and linguistics U. No. Iowa, Cedar Falls, 1972—; sr. exec. v.p. for real estate accounting fin. mgmt. Gorgay, Inc., The Real Estate Co., Louisville, 1976-77, also bd. dirs.; sr. exec. v.p. for reimbursement and rates acctg. fin. mgmt. hosp. acctg. divsn. Humana, Inc., The Hosp. Co., Louisville, 1978-93; ret., 1993; dir. Southeastern Investment Trust, Inc., Louisville, 1976—; ret., 1993; rsch. prof. The Southeastern Investment Trust, Inc. Rsch. Found., Louisville, 1976—; vis. prof. Medieval Latin, U. Chgo., 1966—; vis. prof. linguistics U. Chgo., Downtown Ctr., 1966—; prof. English evening divs. Northwestern U., Chgo., 1968-69, prof. anthropology, 1971-72. Author: The Ruodlieb: The First Medieval Epic of Chivalry from Eleventh-Century Germany, 1965, The Ruodlieb: Linguistic Introduction, Latin Text with a Critical Apparatus, and Glossary, 1966, The Ruodlieb: Facsimile Edition, 1965, 3d edit. 1968, Old Lithuanian Texts of the Sixteenth and Seventeenth Centuries with a Glossary, 1969, The Old Lithuanian Catechism of Baltramiejus Vilentas (1579): A Phonological, Morphological, and Syntactical Investigation, 1969, Isidore of Seville's History of the Goths, Vandals, and Suevi, 1966, 2d edit. 1970, The Letters of Saint Isidore of Seville, 1966, 2d edit. 1970, The Old Lithuanian Catechism of Martynas Mazvydas (1547), 1971, others; translator: A Concise Elementary Grammar of the Sanskrit Language with Exercises, Reading Selections, and a Glossary (Jan Gonda), 1966, The Comparative Method in Historical Linguistics (Antoine Meillet), 1967, A Sanskrit Grammar (Manfred Mayrhofer), 1972; contbr. numerous articles to many scholarly jours. Appointed to Hon. Order Ky. Cols. (life). Mem. Linguistic Soc. Am. (life, Sapir life patron), Internat. Linguistic Assn. (life), Societas Linguistica Europaea (charter, life), Am. Philol. Assn. (life), Classical Assn. of the Atlantic States (life), Classical Assn. of the Middle West and South (life), Classical Assn. of N.Eng. (life), Medieval Acad. of Am. (life), Renaissance Soc. of Am. (life), MLA (life), Am. Assn. Tchrs. Slavic and East European Langs. (life), Am. Assn. Advancement Slavic Studies (life), Am. Coun. Tchrs. Russian (life), Assn. for Advancement Baltic Studies (life), Inst. Lithuanian Studies (life), Tchrs. of English to Speakers of Other Langs. (charter, life), SAR (life), Princeton Club (N.Y.C., Chgo.), Princeton Alumni Assn. (Louisville), Harvard Club (N.Y.C., Chgo., Louisville, Lexington, Ky.), Pres.'s Soc. Bellarmine Coll. (life), Louisville Country Club, KC (life), Phi Beta Kappa (life). Baptist. Home: 3619 Brownsboro Road Louisville KY 40207-1863 also: PO Box 2693 Clarksville Br Jeffersonville IN 47131-2693

FORD, HARRIET-LYNN, English educator; b. Wichita Falls, Tex., May 27, 1952; d. Wesley Craig and Alice Ann Stallcup; 1 child, Michael Adam Brown; m. John Ceburn Ford Jr., Aug. 20, 1983. BA in English Edn., Okla. Ctrl. State U., 1977, MA in English, 1979. Adj. instr. Pellissippi State Tech. C.C., Knoxville, Tenn., 1989-90, instr. to assoc. prof. English, 1990-99, interim dept. head acad. devel. divsn., 1994-95, program coord. for remedial and devel. English, 1995—. Co-editor, co-author: (textbook) Preparing for College Writing, 1996; editor, co-author: Preparing for College Writing, 1997, 2d edit., 1999. Docent Knoxville Zoo, 1990-97. Mem. AAUP (chpt. pres.), AAUW, Nat. Coun. Tchrs. English. Avocations: reading, Celtic music, golf. Office: Pellissippi State Tech CC Hardin Valley Rd Knoxville TN 37933

FORD, HARRISON, actor; b. Chgo., July 13, 1942; m. Mary Ford; children: Willard, Benjamin; m. Melissa Mathison; children: Malcolm, Georgia. Ed., Ripon Coll. Appeared in motion pictures including: Dead Heat on a Merry-Go-Round, 1966, Luv, 1967, The Long Ride Home, 1967, Getting Straight, 1970, Zabriske Point, 1970, The Conversation, 1974, American Graffiti, 1974, Star Wars, 1977, Heroes, 1977, Force 10 From Navarone, 1978, Hanover Street, 1979, Frisco Kid, 1979, Apocalypse Now, 1979, The Empire Strikes Back, 1980, Raiders of the Lost Ark, 1981, Blade Runner, 1982, Return of the Jedi, 1983, Indiana Jones and the Temple of Doom, 1984, Witness, 1985, Mosquito Coast, 1986, Frantic, 1988, Working Girl, 1988, Indiana Jones and the Last Crusade, 1989, Presumed Innocent, 1990, Patriot Games, 1992, The Fugitive, 1993, Clear and Present Danger, 1994, Sabrina, 1995, A Hundred and One Nights, 1995, Devil's Own, 1996, Air Force One, 1997, Six Days Seven Nights, 1998, Random Hearts, 1999, What Lies Beneath, 2000; appeared in TV movie James A. Michener's Dynasty, 1976; numerous TV appearances including Judgement: The Court-Martial of Lt. William Calley, 1975, The F.B.I., Gunsmoke, The Virginian, The Possessed, Young Indiana Jones Chronicles.

FORD, SIR HUGH, mechanical engineer; b. July 16, 1913; s. Arthur and Constance F.; m. Wynyard Scholfield 1942 (dec. Oct. 1991; 2 children; m. Thelma Morgan Jensen, Nov. 30, 1993. Attended City and Guilds Coll., U. London; DSc in Engring., PhD; DSc (hon.), Salford, 1976; QUB, 1977, Ashton, 1978, Bath, 1978, Sheffield, Sussex. Practical trainee GWR Locomotive Works, 1931-36; rsch. into heat transfer, 1936-39; R. and Eng. Imperial Chem. Industries, Northwich, 1939-42; chief engr. tech. dept. Brit. Iron and Steel Fedn., 1942-45; then head mech. working div. Brit. Iron and Steel Rsch. Assn., 1945-47; reader in applied mechanics U. London Imperial Coll. of Sci. and Tech., 1948-51, prof., 1951-69, head dept. mech. engring., 1965-78, prof. mech. engring., 1969-80, prof. emeritus, 1981—, pro-rector, 1978-80; chmn. Sir Hugh Ford and Assocs., Ltd.; dir. Air Liquide U.K. Ltd., 1976-95; tech. dir. Davy-Ashmore Group, 1968-71; dir. Herbert Ltd., 1972-79; SRC, 1968-72 (chmn. engring. bd.); ARC, 1976-82. Author: Advanced Mechanics of Materials, 1963; author profl. papers. Created Knight, 1975; recipient James Watt Internat. Gold medal, 1985; Whitworth scholar. Fellow Royal Soc. (council 1973-74), Inst. Mech. Engrs. (council, v.p. 1972, 75, sr. v.p. 1976, pres. 1977-78, Thomas Hawksley gold medal 1948), Royal Acad. Engring. (v.p. 1982-84), ICE, CGI, Inst. Metals (pres. 1963, Robertson medal); mem. Welding Inst. (pres. 1983-85), Brit. Assn. (pres. sect. 6 1975-76), ASME (hon.), New Inst. Materials (pres. 1985-87), Athenaeum Club.

FORD, JEAN ELIZABETH, former English language educator; b. Branson, Mo., Oct. 5, 1923; d. Mitchell Melton and Annie Estella (Wyer) F.; m. J.C. Wingo, 1942 (div. 1946; m. E. Syd Vineyard, 1952 (div. 1956); m. Vincent Michel Wessling, Feb. 14, 1983 (div. Dec. 1989). AA in English, L.A. City Coll., 1957; BA in English, Calif. State U., 1959; MA in Higher Edn., U. Mo., 1965; postgrad., UCLA, 1959-60, U. Wis. Law Sch., 1970, U. Mo. Law Sch., 1970, U. Wis., 1966. Cert. English tchr., real estate broker, Mo. Dance instr. Arthur Murray Studios, L.A., 1948-51; office mgr. Western Globe Products, L.A., 1951-55; pvt. dance tchr., various office jobs L.A., 1955-59; social dir. S.S. Matsonia, 1959; social worker L.A. County, 1959-61; 7th grade instr. Carmenita Sch. Dist., Norwalk, Calif., 1961-62; English instr. Leadwood (Mo.) High Sch., 1962-63; dance instr. U. Mo., 1963-66, SW Mo. State U., 1966-68, NW Mo. State U., 1970-76, Johnson County Community Coll., 1976-77; tax examiner IRS, Kansas City, Mo., 1978-80; tax acct. Baird, Kurtz & Dobson, Kansas City, Mo., 1981; dance tchr. Singles Program Village, Presbyn. Ch., Kans., 1981-96; substitute tchr. various sch. dists., 1976-85; dance chmn. Mo. Assn. Health, Phys. Edn. and Recreation, 1965-66, 68-69, dance chmn. ctrl. dist. AAHPER, 1972-73; vis. author Young Author's Conf., Ctrl. Mo. State U., 1987, 88, 89; speaker Am. Reading Assn., Grandview, Mo., 1990; real estate sales agt., Kansas City, 1980-84; real estate sales broker, Mo., 1990—, Kans., 1990-2000; pvt. practice tax acct., dance tchr., 1984—. Author, pub.: Fish Tails and Scales, 1982, 3d edit., 2000. Mem. Village Presbyn. Ch., Prairie Village, Kans. Mem. Am. Contract Bridge League, Kansas City Ski Club, U.S. Amateur Ballroom Dancers Assn., Inc. (assoc.). Democrat. Presbyterian. Avocations: tennis, swimming, skiing, sailing, bridge. Home and Office: 9528 Manning Ave Kansas City MO 64134-2229

FORD, JONATHAN MARCUS, historian, educator; b. Brisbane, Australia, May 4, 1957; s. John Montague and Hazel Evelyn (A'Beckett) F.; m. Brenda Joy Biggs, Dec. 17, 1988; 1 child, Leela Rhiannon. Diploma in tchg., U. Ctrl. Queensland, Australia, 1978; BA, U. Ctrl. Queensland, 1981; PhD, U. Queensland, 1995. Organizer Postgrad. Students' Assn. U. Queensland, 1981-91; tutor Dept. Employment, Edn. and Tng., Australia, 1989, U. Queensland, 1990-91, Sunshine Coast U., Australia, 1996, Queensland U. Tech., 2000; mem. acad. bd. U. Queensland, 1989-91; hist. cons. The Seven Network, Australia, 1995, Mil. Mus. of the Pacific Ltd., Australia, 1996, Game Rsch. Design, U.S., 1996, Brisbane City Coun., 1997, 98, Carson Group, 1998. Author: Allies in a Bind, 1996; contbr. articles to profl. jours. Candidate Australian Labor Party, Queensland, 1986; sec. Australian Inst. Internat. Affairs, Queensland, 1988-90. Served with Australian mil., 1978-81. John Treloar rsch. grantee Australian War Meml., Canberra, 1992; 1st Mil. Dist. Sgts.' Club scholar U. Queensland, Brisbane, 1984. Mem. Australian Hist. Assn., Queensland Studies Ctr., Profl. Historians Assn. (founding pres.), Am. Civil War Round Table of Australia. Roman Catholic. Avocations: music, reading, bushwalking. Home: 7 Station Ave Northgate, Brisbane 4013, Australia

FORD, KENNETH WILLIAM, physicist; b. West Palm Beach, Fla., May 1, 1926; s. Paul Hammond and Edith (Timblin) F.; m. Karin Stehnike, Aug. 27, 1953 (div. 1961); m. Joanne Baumunk, June 9, 1962; children: Paul T., Sarah E., Caroline A., Adam B., Jason L., Ian L.; 1 stepdau., Nina Tannenwald. Student, John Carroll U., 1945, U. Mich., 1945-46; AB, Harvard Coll., 1948; PhD, Princeton U., 1953. Rsch. asst. Los Alamos Sci. Lab., 1950-51; rsch. assoc. Princeton U., Princeton U., 1951-52; from rsch. assoc. to assoc. prof. Ind. U., 1953-58, asst. prof. physics, 1954-57; from assoc. prof. to prof. Brandeis U., 1958-64; prof. U. Calif., Irvine, 1964-70, chmn. dept. physics, 1964-68; prof. physics U. Mass., Boston, 1970-75; pres. N.Mex. Inst. Mining and Tech., Socorro, 1975-82; exec. v.p. U. Md., Adelphi, 1982-83; pres. Molecular Biophysics Tech. Inc., 1983-85; edn. officer Am. Phys. Soc., 1986-87; exec. dir. Am. Inst. Physics, 1987-93; tchr. Germantown Acad., 1995-98; sci. program dir. David and Lucile Packard Found., 1998-99; tchr. Germantown Friends Sch., 2000—; mem. Commn. Coll. Physics, 1968-71. Author: The World of Elementary Particles, 1963, Basic Physics, 1968, Classical and Modern Physics, 3 vols., 1972-74; (with John Wheeler) Geons, Black Holes, and Quantum Foam: A Life in Physics, 1998; mem. editl. bd. Phys. Rev., 1960-62, The Physics Tchr., 2000—; contbr. articles to profl. jours. With USNR, 1944-46. Fulbright fellow Max Planck Inst., Germany, 1955-56, NSF sr. postdoctoral fellow Imperial Coll. London, 1961-62, MIT, 1962. Fellow AAAS (coun. del. physics electorate 1983-86), Am. Phys. Soc. (chmn. forum on physics and soc. 1981, councilor 1984-87); mem. Am. Assn. Physics Tchrs. (pres. 1972, Disting. Svc. citation 1976), Fedn. Am. Scientists.

FORD, MARCIA MARIE, financial consultant; b. Kenmore, N.Y., Jan. 8, 1956; d. Zigmund S. and Clara A. (Slaga) Klimek. BS, State U. Coll., Buffalo, 1977; MBA, Rochester Inst. Tech. With Buffalo (N.Y.) Savs. Bank; acctg. asst. State U. Coll., Buffalo; with dept. computer sci. Rochester (N.Y.) Inst. Tech.; fin. analyst NCR, Dayton, Ohio, Xerox Corp., Rochester; fin. cons. Cigna Fin. Advisors Inc., Ford, Steinberg & Assocs., Inc., Rochester; pres. Ford & Assocs., Inc., Rochester. Bd. mem., family wish grantor, chmn. nominating com., fin. com., program devel. com. Make-A-Wish Found. Western N.Y., 1995-97. Mem. Internat. Assn. Fin. Planners, Nat. Life Underwriters, Rochester Life Underwriters. Office: 170 Packe HS Landing Fairport NY 14450-6208 Address: PO Box 66208 170 Packetts Landing Fairport NY 14450

FORD, MARK LEE, aerospace engineer, scientist; b. Toronto, Ont., Can., Jan. 8, 1966; s. Jeffrey Theo Maurice and Elaine Joan Maude (de Lang) F. BSc, U. Toronto, 1989; MS, Boston U., 1993, PhD, 1996. Cert. engr. Grad. rsch. fellow Boston U., 1992-93, Am. Chem. Soc.-Petroleum Rsch. Fund fellow, 1993-96; U.S. Nat. Sci. Found. fellow Ministry Internat. Trade and Industry, Tsukuba, Ibaraki, Japan, 1996-98; rsch. cons., sci. collaborator Mech. Engring. Lab., Tsukuba, 1994; mgmt. cons., 1998—; investigator in field. Contbr. articles to profl. jours. and mags. Vol. Aijien Children's Home and Orphanage, Tsukuba, 1997—. Mem. AIAA, ASME, Am. Phys. Soc., Am. Astronautical Soc., Asiatic Soc. Japan, Tau Beta Pi. Achievements include research and development of stratospheric airships as aerospace platforms; co-derivation of Ford-Nadim equation for thermocapillary migration of drops. Avocations: swimming, sailing, flying, cooking. E-mail: mozart@bu.edu.

FORD, PETER FLETCHER, writer; b. Harpenden, England, June 3, 1936; s. Fletcher Calvert and Muriel Mary (Mayo-Smith) F.; m. Laura Cecile Geeve, Aug. 28, 1960 (div. Apr. 1991); children: Piers, Julian, Isabel. Editor Cassell, London, 1958-61; sr. copy editor Penguin Books, Harmondsworth, Eng., 1961-64; sr. editor Thomas Nelson, London, 1964-70; freelance writer, editor, 1971—; cons. Quartet Books, London, 1971-95. Author: (retelling for children) The Elephant Man, 1983, A Collector's Guide to Teddy Bears, 1990; co-author: All About Drugs, 1970, (with Max Wall) The Fool on the Hill, 1975, Topolski's Buckingham Palace Panoramas, 1977, The Picture Buyer's Handbook, 1988, Rings and Curtains: The Personal and Family Memoirs of Albert Whiteley, 1992; (with Dr. Michael Howell) The True History of the Elephant Man, 1980, rev. edits., 1983, 92, Medical Mysteries, 1985 (pub. in U.S. as The Beetle of Aphrodite and Other Medical Mysteries, 1985; pub. in paperback as The Ghost Disease and Twelve Other Stories of Detective Work in the Medical Field, 1986); contbg. author: (with Anthony Feldman) Scientists and Inventors, 1979; translator (with Kenneth Mitchell) History of the International: World Socialism 1943-68; compiler The Monkey's Paw and Other Stories, 1994; editor, introduction: A Willingness to Die (by Brian Kingcome), 1999. Mem. London Libr. With Royal Artillery, 1955-56, Malaya. Mem. Brit. Assn. Soc. Authors, N.Y. Acad. Scis., Folklore Soc. Avocations: walking, book collecting, theatre, music. Home and Office: The Storehouse, Longhope Stromness, Orkney KW16 3PQ, United Kingdom

FORD, ROBERT DAVID, lawyer; b. New Orleans, Oct. 30, 1956; s. Thomas Paul and Inez Mary (Rodriguez) F.; m. Jean Ann Burg, May 5, 1979; children: Robert David Jr., Charlene Elizabeth, Timothy Michael. BA, U. New Orleans, 1978; JD, Loyola U., 1983. Bar: La. 1983, U.S. Dist. Ct. (ea. dist.) La. 1983, U.S. Dist. Ct. (mid. dist.) La. 1997, U.S. Ct. Appeals (5th cir.) 1985. Claims rep. State Farm Mut. Auto Ins. Co., Metairie, La., 1978-80; assoc. Hammett, Leake & Hammett, New Orleans, 1983-86; ptnr. Thomas, Hayes, Beahm & Buckley, New Orleans, 1986-95; mem. Chehardy, Sherman, Ellis, Breslin & Murray, Metairie, La., 1995-96; ptnr. Hailey, McNamara, Hall, Larmann & Papale, Metairie, 1996—. Mem. ABA (coms. on health law, profl. liability and products liability litigation 1992, subcoms. on hosp. and clinic med. devices and med. malpractice liability 1992), La. Bar Assn., La. Assn. Def. Counsel, Am. Soc. Law and Medicine, La. Soc. Hosp. Attys. of La. Hosp. Assn., Def. Rsch. Inst., Phi Kappa Theta, Pi Alpha Delta. Republican. Roman Catholic. Avocations: golf, softball. Home: 8 Caney Ct Kenner LA 70065-3944 Office: Hailey McNamara Hall Larmann & Papale 1 Galleria Blvd Ste 1400 Metairie LA 70001-7543

FORD, WILLIAM CLAY, JR., automotive executive; b. May 3, 1957; marrried;. BA, Princeton U., 1979; MS in Mgmt., MIT, 1984. Prodn. planning analyst, advisor vehicle devel. design ctr., mfg. engr. auto assembly divsn., mgr. Ford Motor Co., N.Y., 1979-82; mem. nat. bargaining team Ford/UAW labor talks, mktg. strategy analyst No. Am. Auto Opns., advt. specialist Ford Motor Co., 1982-83, internat. fin. specialist, mem. fin. staff, 1984-85, planning mgr. car prodn. devel., 1985-86, dir. com. vehicle mktg. Europe divsn., 1986-87, chmn., mng. dir. Switzerland divsn., 1987-89, mgr. heavy truck engr. and mfg. Ford Truck Opns., 1989-90, dir. bus. strategy Ford Auto Group, 1990-91, exec. dir. bus. strategy Ford Auto Group, 1991-92, gen. mgr. climate control divsn., 1992-94, v.p. com. tracking vehicle ctr. Ford Auto Opns., 1994-95, chmn. fin. com., 1995-99, chmn. bd., 1998—; vice chmn. Detroit Lions; mem. fin. com., properties com. NFL. Chmn. bd. trustees Henry Ford Mus., Greenfield Village; trustee Henry Ford Health Sys., Detroit Renaissance, Conservation Internat.; mem. World Econ. Forum's Global Leaders for Tomorrow; vice-chmn., bd. dirs. Greater Downtown Partnership Inc., Detroit. Alfred P. Sloan fellow MIT, 1983-84. Office: Ford Motor Co 1 American Rd Dearborn MI 48126-2798

FORDHAM, CHRISTOPHER COLUMBUS, III, university dean and chancellor, medical educator; b. Greensboro, N.C., Nov. 28, 1926; s. Christopher Columbus and Frances Long (Clendenin) F.; m. Barbara Byrd, Aug. 16, 1947; children: Pamela Fordham Richey, Susan Fordham Crowell, Betsy Fordham Templeton. Cert. in medicine, U. N.C., 1949; MD, Harvard U., 1951. Diplomate Am. Bd. Internal Medicine. Intern Georgetown U. Hosp., 1951-52; asst. resident Boston City Hosp., 1952-53; prof. medicine emeritus U. N.C. Sch. Medicine, 1993—; sr. asst. resident N.C. Meml. Hosp., Chapel Hill, 1953-54; fellow in medicine U. N.C. Sch. Medicine, 1954-55, instr. medicine, 1958-60, asst. prof., 1960-64, assoc. prof., asst. dean, Sch. Medicine, 1964-68, prof., assoc. dean, 1968-69; acting asst. sec. for health Dept. HEW, Washington, 1977; dean Sch. Medicine U. N.C., 1971-79; prof. medicine U. N.C. Sch. Medicine, 1971—, vice chancellor for health affairs, 1977-80, chancellor, 1980-88, chancellor emeritus and prof. medicine, 1988-93, chancellor emeritus, dean emeritus, prof. medicine emeritus, 1993—; prof. medicine, v.p. for medicine, dean Sch. Medicine, Med. Coll. Ga., Augusta, 1969-71; practice medicine, specializing in internal medicine Greensboro, N.C., 1957-58; chair Gov.'s Com. on N.C. Awards, 1993—. Bd. dirs. Royal Soc. Med. Found., N.Y.C., 1990-95; chmn. N.C. Awards Com., 1993—. Officer USAF, 1955-57. Master ACP; fellow AAAS; mem. AAUP, AMA (spl. award 1990), Nat. Assn. State Univs. & Land Grant Colls. (chair coun. univ. governance 1990-91), N.C. Med. Soc., So. Soc. Clin. Investigation, Am. Soc. Nephrology, Am. Fedn. Clin. Rsch., Soc. Health and Human Values, Am. Assn. Med. Colls. (exec. coun. 1975-78, rep. liaison com. med. edn. 1977-79), Am. Assn. Med. Coll. So. Regional Deans (chmn. 1972-73, 75-76, chmn. nat. coun. deans 1977), N.Y. Acad. Scis., Inst. Medicine of Nat. Acad. Sci. (council 1985-90), Elisha Mitchell Sci. Soc., Order Golden Fleece, Sigma Xi, Alpha Omega Alpha. Office: Univ NC Sch Medicine Campus Box 7000 Rm 5023 Clin Wing Chapel Hill NC 27514

FORDHAM, PAUL ELLIS, adult education educator, consultant; b. Great Ellingham, Norfolk, Eng., Dec. 26, 1925; s. Robert Ross and Gertrude Lily (Ellis) F.; m. Sheila Moonyeen Morgan, June 17, 1950 (div. Sept. 27, 1978); children: Edmund, Simon; m. Ada Alison Dickins, June 29, 1981. BA, U. Leeds (Eng.), 1950. Lectr. adult endn. U. Nottingham (Eng.), 1951-61, Makerere U. Coll., Kampala, Uganda, 1961-62; prin. Coll. Social Studies, Kikuyu, Kenya, 1962-66; dir. Inst. Adult Studies U. Coll., Nairobi, 1966-68; prin. sec. home civil svc. Govt. of U.K., 1968-71; dir. dept. adult edn. U. Southampton (Eng.), 1971-89; dir. Internat. Ctr. Edn. in Devel. U. Warwick (Eng.), 1989-94, cons. INCED dept. cont. edn., 1994—; Chair exec. com. Nat. Inst. Adult Cont. Edn., Leicester, Eng., 1983-86; personal chair prof. adult edn. U. Southampton (Eng.), 1980, prof. emeritus, 1989; prof. (hon.) U. Warwick, 1989-2000. Author: Geography of African Affairs, 1965, 68, 72, 74, Participation, Learning and Change, 1980; co-author: Learning Networks in Adult Education, 1979, Adult Literacy: A Handbook for Development Workers, 1995, A Chance to Change, 1998. Mem. Commonwealth Assn. Edn. and Tng. of Adults (hon. life, sec.-gen. 1988-90), Royal Commonwealth Soc., Nat. Inst. Adult Cont. Edn. (hon. life). Mem. Soc. Friends. Avocations: walking, travel, jazz, natural history. Home: 2 Bishopstone Town Walls, Shrewsbury SY1 1UE, England Office: U Warwick, INCED Dept Cont Edn, Coventry CV4 7AL, England

FORDICE, PATRICIA OWENS, civic leader, former state first lady; b. Jackson, Miss., Nov. 27, 1934; d. Lloyd Leon and Veo (McLelland) Owens; m. Daniel Kirkwood Fordice, Aug. 13, 1955 (div. Feb. 2000); children: Angela Leigh, Daniel Kirkwood III, Hunter Lloyd, James Owens. Student, Christian Coll., Columbia, Mo., 1952-53, Memphis State U., 1953-54. First lady State of Miss., Jackson, 1992-2000; host radio talk show. Responsible for art exhibit Palaces of St. Petersburg Russian Imperial Style, Jackson, 1996, Splendors of Versailles exhbn., Jackson, 1998; creator Spendors of Miss. Project, Bucks for Books; host, hon. chmn. Internat. Ballet Competition, 1998, also mem. bd.; founder Miss. Gov.'s Initiative for Vol. Excellence Awards; creator SAFETY (Securing Brighter Future for Today's Youth); creator women's health initiative Heart of Miss. Women; hon. chmn., spokesperson for Friends of Children's Hosp.; spokesman Miss. Div. Tourism; hon. chmn. Spl. Olympics, Very Spl. Arts, Miss. Family for Kids; organizer fight against breast cancer Miss. Florist Assn., 1995, Miss. chpt. Am. Cancer Soc., also hosps. and clinics; co-host Power of One, Miss. Woman's Conf., from 1996; co-chmn. abstinence program Miss. Dept. Human Services; hon. pres. Gulf Pines coun. Girl Scouts U.S.A., 1994; past pres. Ofcl. Miss.'s Women's Club; hon. chmn., mem. founding bd. Miss. Commn. Volunteerism, 1993—; active Miss. Blood Svcs.; bd. dirs. Hospice Care Found., Vicksburg, Miss.; active Salvation Army; vol. Toys for Tots; participant Gateway Rescue Mission, 1998, Habitat for Humanity; keyperson key arts program Miss. Arts Commn.; spkr. to numerous chambers of commerce orgns., Rotary and Lions clubs, other civic and charitable groups; vol. Rankin County Human Resource Ctr.; promoter Good Neighbor Day; lobbyist for Medicare coverage of arthritis drugs; hon. chmn. emeritus of bd. Commn. for Internat. Cultural Exch.; bd. dirs. Miss. Symphony; Internat. Ballet Competition; amb. Ageless Heroes awards program Blue Cross & Blue Shield Miss.; spokesperson Arthritis Found; also others. Decorated knight Sovereign Order of Orthodox Knights Hospitaller of St. John of Jerusalem; named Miss.'s Outstanding Philanthropist, 1996; recipient Communicator award Soil and Water Conservation Soc., 1997, Need Knows No Svc. award Salvation Army, 1997, award as outstanding leader and vol. Miss. Blood Svcs., 1998, medal of honor DAR, 1999, medal of excellence Miss. U. for Women, 1999, Steward of Arts and Edn. award Phi Theta Kappa, 1999, Keep Ms Beautiful Louise Godwin award for excellence, 1999; inducted into Miss. Family for Kids' Hall of Fame, 1997. Mem. Nature Conservancy (life), Girl Scouts U.S.A. (life), United Meth. Women (life), Garden Club Soc. Miss. (life), Vicksburg Jr. Aux. (life, pres. 1970). Home: 207 Winter Teal Ct Madison MS 39110-9652

FORE, ANN, counselor, educator, country dance instructor; b. Artesia, N.Mex., July 16, 1948; d. Stanley William and Jackie (Hightower) Blocker; divorced; 1 child Richard Todd. BS, Eastern N.Mex. U., Portales, 1971, MA, 1976. Instr. sociology Eastern N.Mex. U., Clovis, 1974; counselor, instr. So. Plains Jr. Coll., Plainview, Tex., 1975-76; drug and alcohol counselor U.S. Dept. Army, Ft. Hood, Tex., 1976-77; group leader Forest Svc., USDA, Estacada, Oreg., 1980-81; owner Women's Issues Counseling Svcs., Salem, 1985—; tchr. country western ptnr. dancing and line dancing various ednl. settings, Salem, Oreg., Portland C.C., Salem Keizer Schs. Author: founder, adminstr. award-winning, nationally televised country dance team Koda Kountry Drifters. U. N.Mex. rsch. dept. grantee, 1972; recipient Star award United Country/Western Dance Coun., 1998. Mem. APGA, Willamette Writers Assn., Nat. Tchrs. Assn. for Country/Western Dance Instrs., Internat. Platform Assn. Republican. Christian. Avocations: reading, camping, photography, public speaking. Home and Office: PO Box 13851 Salem OR 97309-1851

FOREJT, JIŘÍ F., geneticist; b. Pardubice, Czech Republic, Dec. 28, 1944; s. František and Stanislava Forejt; m. Marie Kotfaldová, Apr. 22, 1972; children: Kamila, Alena. MD, Charles U., Prague, 1968, DSc, 1991; PhD, Acad. Scis., Prague, 1975. Cert. physician. Postdoctoral fellow Acad. Sci. Prague, 1969-75, head dept., 1981—; vis. rsch. fellow Institut Pasteur, Paris, 1980; vis rsch. scholar Imperial Cancer Rsch. Fund, London, 1989; vis. prof. Princeton U., 1992-93, vis. rsch. scholar, 1993-94, 96-97; head subcontract NIH grant, 1992-97; head com. Czech Grant Agy., Prague, 1995-98. Contbr. articles to sci. jours. Decorated Officer Internat. Mammalian Genome Soc.; Internat. rsch. scholar Howard Hughes Med. Inst., 1995—. Mem. Czech Biol. Soc., Czech Biochem. Soc., European Molecular Biology Orgn., Czech Learned Soc. Home: Zapasnicka 880, 102 00 Prague 10, Czech Republic Office: Inst Molecular Genetics, Videnska 1083, 142 20 Prague 4, Czech Republic

FOREMAN, ALFRED G., theologian, philosopher; b. Sulfur, La., Mar. 19, 1960; s. Grover Foreman and Stella Kibodeaux. BA, U. La., Lafayette, 1987; MA, Liberty U., 1991. Founder S. La. Weather Sta., Crowley, 1986—; pastor Ch. of God, Crowley, 1986—; dir. La. Philos. Inst., Crowley, 1989-99; lectr. Islamic Ctr., Lafayette, La., 1983-84, La. Philos. Inst. Humanities, Crowley, 1993—. Dir. S. La. Weather Jour., 1986—. Mem. Internat. Palm Soc. (La. and Calif. chpts.). Home: 130 Palms Rd Crowley LA 70526-1907

FOREMAN, DEBORAH DELORES, social work administrator, consultant; b. Manhanten, N.Y., July 2, 1954; d. Donald K. Williams and Barbara (Skinner) Partee; m. Phillip Clayton Foreman, June 30, 1979; children: Deidra Sheno, Phylicia Casey. BSW, Norfolk State U., 1976; MSW, Va. Commonwealth U., 1985; DEd, Nova Southeastern U., 1995. Lic. social worker, D.C. Eligibility worker Norfolk, Va., 1976-77; supr. casework Saja Runaway House, Washington, 1976; social worker I Norfolk Social Svcs., 1977-79; social worker II Fairfax (Va.) Dept. Human Svcs., 1979-84; dir. summer camp for spl. children 4-H Va. Tech. U., Falls Church, summer 1996; social work adminstr. Fairfax County Pub. Schs., 1984—; founder/program mgr. Ptnrs. in Home Sch. Edn. Parent Program, 1993—; mem. adv. bd. George Mason U., Fairfax, 1994-95. Chair Africare/Jumoke Com./Cmty., Fairfax, 1990-92; v.p. Jack and Jill Am., Fairfax, 1990-91; co-chair Farifax Domestic Violence Coaltion, 1990-91. Named one of Outstanding Young Women Am., 1987; recipient Fitz Turner award Va. Edn. Assn., 1991, Vol. of Yr. Wesley Housing Devel., 1995. Mem. AAUW (No. Va. online br. co-pres. 1995-97, panel mem. for career grants 1999-00), ASCD, Va. Assn. Univ. Women (chair resolution com. 1997-88), Fairfax Assn. Sch. Social Workers (chair diversity com. 1997—), George Mason Honor Soc., Phi Delta Kappa. Democrat. Baptist. Avocations: volunteering in the community, collecting shells, reading romantic novels, organizing family gatherings, visiting beaches. Home: 4729 Irvin Sq Alexandria VA 22312-2233 Office: Fairfax County Pub Schs 6520 Diana Ln Alexandria VA 22310-3012

FOREMAN, JOHN PATRICK, electrical engineer; b. Lake Charles, La., Aug. 16, 1954; s. John Calvin Foreman and Daisy Mae (Finley) Foreman Milsted. BSEE, McNeese State U., Lake Charles, 1976. Registered profl. engr., Tex., Calif., La., Oreg., Mass., Wash. Elec. engr. Fluor Engrs. & Contractors, Houston, 1977-83, Jacobs Engring. Group, Houston, 1983, Burgess & Niple, Ltd., Houston, 1984-86; project mgr. Turpin & Rattan Engring., San Diego, 1986-92, TH Rogers & Assocs., Oakland, Calif., 1993, Alfa Tech. Consulting Engrs., San Jose, Calif., 1994-99, TKG Consulting Engrs., San Diego, 2000—. Mem. IEEE, NSPE, Tex. Soc. Profl. Engrs. Democrat. Roman Catholic. Avocations: darts, skiing, volleyball, softball, martial arts. Home: 1065 15th St Apt 209 San Diego CA 92101-5791 Office: TKG Consulting Engrs 4370 La Jolla Village Dr San Diego CA 92122-1250

FOREMAN, PHILIP FRANK, mechanical engineer; b. Exning, Suffolk, Eng., Mar. 16, 1923; s. Frank and Mary (Chapple) F.; m. Margaret Cooke, Oct. 19, 1971; 1 child, Grahame Philip. DLC with honors, Loughborough (Eng.) Coll., 1943, DTech (hon.), 1983; DSc (hon.), Queen's U., Belfast, No. Ireland, 1976; DUniv, Open U., London, 1985. Sr. sci. officer Royal Naval Sci. Svc., London, 1943-58; mgr. Short Bros. & Harland, Belfast, 1958-67; CEO Short Bros. Plc, Belfast, 1967-83, chmn., CEO, 1983-88; cons. engr. Foreman Assocs., Holywood, No. Ireland, 1988—; non-exec. dir. Simon Engring. Plc., Stockport, Eng., 1987-92, Ricardo Group Plc, Shoreham, Eng., 1988-91, chmn., Hinckley, 1991-97; non-exec. dir. Brit. Standards Instn., 1986-98, pres. 1991-98; chmn. Progressive Bldg. Soc., Belfast, 1987-99. Mem. senate Queen's U. Belfast, 1992—; dep. lt. City of Belfast, 1975-98; freeman City of London, 1980. Decorated Comdr. Brit. Empire, Knight Bachelor. Fellow Instn. of Mech. Engrs. (pres. 1985), Royal Aero. Soc. (hon., Gold medal 1980), Royal Acad. Engring. Office: Foreman Associates, 26 Ballymenoch Rd, Holywood BT18 0HH, Northern Ireland

FOREST, EVA BROWN, songwriter, producer; b. Ontario, Va., July 7, 1941; d. William Butler and Ruth Pauline (Simpson) Brown; m. Willie J. Forest Jr., Sept. 16, 1961; children: Gerald, Darryl, Angela. AA, Bismarck (N.D.) State Coll., 1981; BSN, U. Mary, Bismarck, 1984. RN, Colo. Charge nurse St. Alexius Med. Ctr., Bismarck, 1984-85, Cedars Health Care Ctr., Lakewood, Colo., 1989-90; staff devel. coord. Park Avenue Bapt. Home, Denver, 1990-91; supr., charge nurse Cedars Health Care Ctr., Lakewood, Colo., 1991—; charge nurse Villa Manor Health Ctr., Lakewood, Colo., 1991-93; charge nurse Stovall Care Ctr., Denver, 1995-96, supr., 1997-98, supr., charge nurse, 1999—. Songwriter, prodr., 1999; recorded (CD) God Has Begun a Good Work in Me, 1999. Vol. for cultural exch. lang., culture and fashions YWCA, Kano, Nigeria; vocalist gospel music workshop, N.D.; pianist adult and children's choir, N.D.; mem. MADD, Habitat for Humanity Internat., HALT, Vols. of Am. Mem. Nat. Multiple Sclerosis Soc., DAV Commdrs. Club.

FOREST, FRED, artist; b. Mascara, Algerie, June 7, 1933; s. Armand Forest and Yvonne Molla; m. Sophie Lavaud; 1 child, Adrien. D d'Etat, Sorbonne (France) U. Prof. Ecole Nat. D'Art, Cergy, 1975-93; prof. titulaire, chair des scis. de info. U. Nice Sophia Antipolis. Home: Territoire du Ml, 60540 Anserville Oise, France

FOREST, PHILIP EARLE, housing finance consultant; b. San Mateo, Calif., Dec. 4, 1931; s. Percy Egbert and Charlotte Elizabeth (Copeland) F.; m. Sally Annette Cauble, Apr. 30, 1988. BS, U. Md., 1972. Enlisted U.S. Army, 1950, advanced through grades to maj., 1964; various pos. FHA, HUD, Washington, 1966-77; spl. asst. to asst. sec. for housing HUD, Washington, 1977-78, spl. asst. to dep. asst. sec. for single family housing, 1978-83, spl. asst. to undersec., 1979, acting dep. asst. sec. for single family housing, 1980-81; housing and housing finance cons. Arlington, Va., 1983—. Author: Building the Single Family Loan Package, 1988, Collection Department Responsibilities and Operations, 1986, Processing the Loan, 1986, FHA/VA Servicing Handbook, 1990, Mortgage Loan Servicing, 1994. Pres. Columbia (Md.) Commuter Bus Corp., 1975-83. Mem. Mortgage Bankers Assn. Am. (assoc. single family and loan adminstrn. coms. 1983—), Nat. Assn. Rev. Appraisers and Mortgage Underwriters (sr., registered mortgage underwriter 1983-93), Appraisal Inst. (affiliate 1998-99), Md.-Nat. Capital Bldg. Industry Assn. (fin. com. 1984—), Nat. Assn. Home Builders (standing com. housing fin. 1989-91, 93-2000, single family govtl. subcom., vice-chmn. 1990, chmn. 1991, single family subcom., vice-chmn. 1995, chmn. 1996, task force on crisis in fin. housing prodn., chmn. HUD subcom. 1990, task force on internat. bus. devel. 1991, internat. housing com. 1998—), Am. Alliance for Loan Mgmt. (incorporator, dir., exec. v.p. 1989—).

FOREST, SAMUEL CHRISTOPHE, mechanical engineer, researcher; b. Bourg-en-Bresse, France, July 20, 1968; s. Rene Jean-Victor and Colette (Rigollet) F.; m. Bettina Rosemarie Klein; children: Florent, David. Degree in civil engring., L'Ecole des Mines de Paris, 1992, PhD, 1996. Chief of rsch. CNRS, Evry, France, 1996. Contbr. articles to profl. jours. Mem. MECAMAT (adminstrn. coun. 1998—), Euromech. Avocations: chamber music, cinema, literature. E-mail: samuel.forest@mat.ensmp.fr. Office: ENSMP/CNRS BP 87, Ctr des Matériaux, F-91003 Evry France

FOREST, VIANNEY, archeozoologist, veterinarian; b. Lyon, France, Oct. 31, 1960; s. Robert and Marie-Joseph (Ollier) F. Lic. in biology, U. Lyon, 1981; DVM, E.N.V.L., Lyon, 1987. Vet. cons. L.B.F., Aixen, France, 1987-88; pvt. practice vet. surgery Montpellier, France, 1989-93; archeozoologist AFAN/CNRS, Montpellier, 1993—. Lt. French vet. svc., 1986-87.

FORESTER, JEAN MARTHA BROUILLETTE, innkeeper, retired librarian, educator; b. Port Barre, La., Sept. 7, 1934; d. Joseph Walter and Thelma (Brown) Brouillette; m. James Lawrence Forester, June 2, 1957; children: Jean Martha, James Lawrence. BS, La. State U., 1955; MA (Carnegie fellow 1955-56), George Peabody Coll. Tchrs., 1956. Libr. Howell Elem. Sch., Springhill, La., 1956-58; asst. post libr. Fort Chaffee, Ark., 1958; command libr. Orleans Area Command, U.S. Army, Orleans, France, 1958-59; acquisitions libr. Northwestern State U., Natchitoches, La., 1960; serials libr. La. State U., New Orleans, 1960-66; mem. faculty La. State U., Eunice, 1966-85, asst. libr., 1972-85, assoc. libr., 1985-87, acting libr., 1987-88, dir. libr., 1988-89, libr. emeritus, 1989—; asst. prof., 1972-85, faculty senator, 1978-80, 85-86, 87-89; innkeeper Crown'n'Anchor Inn, Saco, Maine, 1989—. Co-author: Robertson's Bill of Fare; contbr. articles to profl. jour. Active Eunice Assn. Retarded Children. Mem. La. Libr. Assn. (sect. sec. 1971-72, coord. serials interest group 1984-85), UDC, Delta Kappa Gamma (chpt. parliamentarian 1972-74, rec. sec. 1984-86), Alpha Beta Alpha, Phi Gamma Mu, Phi Mu, Order Eastern Star. Democrat. Baptist.

FORFAR, JOHN COLIN, cardiologist, consultant; b. Edinburgh, Scotland, Nov. 22, 1951; s. John Oldroyd and Isobel Mary (Fernback) F.; m. Susan Claire Chambers, 1979 (div. 1986); 1 child, Katriana Louise. BS with 1st class honors, U. Edinburgh, 1972, MB BChir, 1975, MD, 1985, PhD, 1984; MA, Oxford U., 1985. Cert. specialist cardiologist. Physician in tng. Royal Infirmary, Edinburgh, 1975-79; Brit. Heart Found. lectr. U. Edinburgh, 1979-82; lectr. cardiovasc. medicine U. Oxford, 1983-84; sr. med. registrar John Radcliffe Hosp., Oxford, 1984-85; clin. reader cardiovasc. medicine U. Oxford, 1985-86; cons. physician, cardiologist John Radcliffe Hosp., Oxford, 1986—; hon. sr. lectr. U. Oxford, 1994—; chair Cardiac Clin. Ctr., 1998—; mem. com. on safety medicines Medicines Commn., 1998—. Author 8 book chpts.; contbr. numerous articles to med. jours. Fellow Royal Coll. Physicians Edinburgh, Royal Coll. Physicians London. Office: John Radcliffe Hosp, Dept Cardiology, OX3 9DU Oxford England

FORGÁCS, IVÁN, physician, medical educator; b. Budapest, Hungary, Feb. 12, 1933; s. Andor and Erzsébet (Mezei) F.; married; 1 child, Balázs. MD, Med. U., Budapest, 1957; degree as specialist, Postgrad. Med. U., Budapest, 1961; PhD, Hungarian Acad. Scis., Budapest, 1966. Lectr. medicine Semmelweis Med. U., Budapest, 1951-74, dir., 1974-76, prof., 1979-81; dep. dir. gen. Ministry of Health, Budapest, 1976-82; prof., head Postgrad. Med. U., 1982—, rector, 1990-93; prof., dir. Inst. Pub. Health Szentgyörgyi A. Med. U., Szeged, Hungary, 1996-98; advisor to Min. of Health, 1982-90; commr. Ministry of Welfare, 1994-96; mem. exec. bd. WHO, Geneva, 1984-87; exec. bd. mem. Hungarian Health Rsch. Coun., 1986-90, 94—. Author: Health, Health Care, and Social Services, 1989, Hungary: The Quest for HFA, 1990, Primary Health Care in Hungary, 1992. Mem. Assn. Schs. Pub. Health in the European Region (pres. 1987-88), Assn. for Med. Edn. in Europe (mem. adv. bd. 1984-88), Hungarian Assn. Med. Edit. (pres. 1980-99). Office: Semmelwei U Fac Health Sci, PO Box 112, H-1389 Budapest Hungary

FORGAS, JOSEPH PAUL, psychology; b. Budapest, Hungary, May 16, 1947; arrived in Australia, 1969; s. Paul and Anna (Orszagh) F.; m. Letitia Jane, Mar. 16, 1974; children: Paul Joseph, Peter John. BA, Macquarie U., 1972, Macquarie U., 1973; DPhil, Oxford U., 1977, DSc, 1990. Lectr. U. New So. Wales, Sydney, Australia, 1977-80, sr. lectr., 1980-82; prof. U. Giessen, Germany, 1982-85, U. New So. Wales, 1985—. Author: Social Episodes, 1979, Interpersonal Behavior, 1985; editor: Social Cognition, 1981, Emotion & Social Judgment, 1991, Feeling and Thinking: The Fole of Affect in Social Cognition, 2000. Recipient grad. award, German Acad. Exch. Svc., 1975, The Light Found., Oxford, England, rsch. prize, Alexander van Humboldt Found., 1993, early career award, Australian Psychol. Soc., 1980. Fellow Acad. Social Scis. in Australia; mem. Soc. Exptl. Social Psychology, Internat. Soc. for Rsch. on Emotion, Am. Psychol. Assn. Roman Catholic. Avocations: gliding, collecting old cameras, travel. Office: Dept Psychology, U New South Wales, Sydney 2052, Australia

FORGÓ, FERENC, economics educator; b. Pècs, Hungary, Apr. 16, 1942; s. Ferenc F. and Margit (Kerènyi) Hetènyi; m. Erzsèbet Kiss, May 27, 1966; children: Ferenc, Erzsèbet. MS, U. Econs., Budapest, Hungary, 1965, PhD, 1974. From asst. prof. to assoc. prof. U. Econs., Budapest, Hungary, 1965-91, prof., 1992—; vis. prof. Rutgers U., Camden, N.J., 1984-85, U. So. Calif., L.A., 1993-94; chmn. dept. math., computer sci. U. Econ., 1987-96, dept. ops. rsch., 1995—. Author: Nonconvex Programming, 1988; co-author: Einführung in die Spieltheorie, 1983, Introduction to the Theory of Games, Concepts, Methods, Applications, 1999. Mem. Hungarian Soc. for Econ. Modelling (pres. 1990-91), Math. Programming Soc., Econometric Soc. Avocations: tennis, chess. Home: Napvirág 19, 1025 Budapest Hungary Office: U Econs Dept Ops Rsch, Fövamtér 8, 1093 Budapest Hungary

FORINA, MARIA ELENA, gifted education educator; b. Santiago, Cuba, Apr. 10, 1942; came to U.S., 1972; d. Jorge Fernando and Maria Elena (De Gongora) Chaves; m. Antonio Forina, May 28, 1961; children: Maria Elena, Amalia, Jose, Jorge Antonio. AA, Somerset County Coll., 1975; BS magna cum laude, U. Tex. Pan Am., Edinburg, 1982, M in Gifted Edn., 1995. Cert. elem. tchr., bilingual tchr., gifted edn. tchr., Tex.; SOI cert. trainer. 1st grade tchr. Pharr-San Juan-Alamo (Tex.) Ind. Sch. Dist., 1981-83, gifted edn. resource tchr., 1983-88, 6th grade gifted edn. tchr., 1988—, AMS writing trainer, 1991—. Eucharistic minister Resurrection Cath. Ch., Alamo, 1982—, CCD tchr., 1986—, mem. blue ribbon com., 1988—, mem. pastoral coun., 1993-97; mem. adv. bd. Lalo Arcaute Pub. Libr., 2000—. Mem. ASCD, Nat. Coun. Tchrs. Math., Nat. Coun. Tchrs. English, Tex. Assn. for Gifted and Talented, Phi Kappa Phi, Delta Kappa Gamma. Republican. Avocations: classical music, opera, reading, gourmet cooking. Home: 842 Fannin Box 3901 Alamo TX 78516 Office: Alamo Mid Sch 1819 W Us Highway 83 Alamo TX 78516-2102

FORISTER, MATTHEW LEWIS, ecologist; b. Ojai, Calif., June 19, 1974; s. Glen Warren and Ann Clement Forister. BA in English writing, U. San Francisco, 1995; postgrad., U. Calif., Davis, 1997—. English tchr. Peace Corps, Fastiv, Ukraine, 1995-97; ecol. field rschr. U. Calif., Davis, 1996—. Univ. scholar U. San Francisco, 1992; fellow U. Calif., Davis, 1997. Avocations: folk music (guitar, electric bass). E-mail: mlforister@ucdavis.edu.

FORKIN, JOHN RICHARD, company director; b. Wirksworth, Great Britain, Aug. 12, 1960; s. Richard and Ann Forkin; m. Alice Forkin. Student, City of London U., 1981. Chmn. UN Youth, 1980-82; mgr. Cmty. Transport, Derby; dir. CVS, Derby, 1987-92; strategy dir. S. Derby Chamber, 1993—; dir. Derby Pride, 1992-97, Derbyshire Careers Svcs., Cromford, 1993-99. Mem. Prince's Trust Derbyshire. Avocations: maps, Derby County FC. Fax: 44 1332 299962. E-mail: johnf@sdchamber.co.uk. Office: SD Chamber, St Helen's St, Derby DE1 3GY, England

FORLEO, ROMANO C., gynecologist; b. Bologna, Italy, Nov. 12, 1933; s. Ascanio and Angiola (Bartolini) F.; m. Giulia Pagliai, Sept. 24, 1959; children: Patrizia, Pier Francesco. MD, U. Florence, 1958; PhD in OB-GYN, 1965, PhD in Endocrine Gynecology, 1968. Resident U. Florence, 1958-64; rsch. fellow in ovarian endocrinology London, 1962-63; asst. prof. U. Florence, 1965-68, U. Rome, 1968-72; prof. postgrad. sch. ob-gyn. I Univ., Rome, 1968-72, prof. sexology faculty psychology, 1975-78; prof. postgrad. ob-gyn. Cath. U., Rome, 1972-80; prof. postgrad. sch. ob-gyn. II Univ., Rome, 1980—, prof. history of medicine, faculty of medicine, 1996—; head dept. ob-gyn. Fatebenefratelli Hosp., Rome, 1972-97, cons. gen. direction for edn. and orgn. dept. gyn., 1997—. Contbr. numerous scientific publications including books on physiopathology of reproduction, gynecological surgery, medical care in childbirth, sex education, childbirth care and educational books for adolescents; also contbr. numerous articles to newspapers. Senator Italian Republic, 1992-94, mem. Labour Commn.; mem. DC's Ethics and Devel. Nat. Commn., 1992-93; mem. constituency Italian Popular Party, 1993; mem. Nat. Com. Christian-Social Movement, 1994—. Decorated Order of Merit of Italian Republic. Mem. Italian Soc. Ob-Gyn., World Soc. Sexology (past pres.), Adolescent Gynecology Soc. (gen. sec. 1991-99), Italian Soc. Sterility and Fertility, Acad. Sanitarial Art, Sci., Nat. Bioethical Com., Order of Journalists, Movement of Italian Cath. Adult Scouts, Nat. Com. Bioethics. Fax: 39.06.6539989. E-mail: rcforleo@mclink.it. Home: Via Lungarina 65, 00153 Rome Italy Office: European Hosp, Via Portuense 700, 00149 Rome Italy

FORM, FREDRIC ALLAN, accountant; b. Bklyn., Mar. 2, 1942; s. Milton and Tedde (Bilus) F.; m. Jo Ann August, Aug. 29, 1964; 1 child, Andrew. BBA, Pace U., 1970. Sr. acct. S.P., N.Y.C., 1963-69, Cooper & Co., N.Y.C., N.Y., 1963-69; pvt. practice pub. acctg. Levittown, N.Y., 1969—. Bd. dirs. Wantagh Cmty. Arts Program, Inc., 1980-84; bd. dirs., treas. Ctrl. Nassau County React, Inc., 1979-82; treas. Your, Ours, Mine Cmty. Ctr., Levittown, 1987-93, Levittown C.C., 1992—; v.p. Reli React, Inc., 1983-91, treas., 1983—. Named Small Businessman of Yr., Levittown C.C.. Mem. Nat. Soc. Pub. Accts. (2d v.p. 1983-85, v.p. 1985-86, pres. 1986-87, bd. dirs. Nassau-Suffolk chpt. 1986-92, pres. 1992-94), Kiwanis (treas. Levittown club 1988-89, 97—). Office: 2950 Hempstead Tpke Levittown NY 11756-1383

FORMAN, EDGAR ROSS, mechanical engineer; b. Camden, N.J., Oct. 5, 1923; s. Edgar Charles and Annie (Baragwanath) F.; m. Alma Kuppinger, Sept. 26, 1953; children: Bruce, Dianne. BSME, Drexel U., 1950, MBA, 1953. Project engr. Penn Instrument div. Burgess Manning Co., Phila., 1950-55; application engr. Moore Products Co., Phila., 1955-59; chief instrument engr. Catalytic Co., Phila., 1959-67, mgr. mgmt. sys. dept., 1967-71; supervising instrument engr. United Engrs. & Constructors, Inc., Phila., 1971-78; mgr. instrument and controls dept. Day & Zimmermann, Inc., Phila., 1987-89; dir. Automation Tech., 1989-93; cons., 1993—; guest lectr. U.S. Naval Acad., Sun Oil Co., U. Del. Contbr. articles to profl. jours. Past mem. Boy Scouts Am.; mem. pres. coun. Spring Garden Coll., 1979-83, chmn. indsl. adv. com., 1984-89; past pres. Erdenheim Civic Assn. Served with AUS, 1943-46. Fellow Instrument Soc. Am. (Phila. sect. pres. 1960, past chmn. edn. commn., v.p. dist. 2 1982-84, chmn. food and pharm. div., 1986-87, nat. v.p. 1989-93, mem. nat. honors and awards com. 1993-96, Eckman award 1982, Man of Yr. 1987, Golden Achievement award 1995, Outstanding Svc. award 1990, China visitation team 1996, Engrs. Week liaison 1997-2000, founder Outstanding Tech. Achievement award 1998, cert. instr. 1998-2000, Dist. 2 Svc. award 1999); mem. ASME (life, past chmn. dynamic sys. and controls div., old guard com.), NSPE (pres. Valley Forge chpt. 1982-83, county Mathcounts coord. 1994-95, Engrs. Week coun. 1990-99, Man of Yr. award Del. Valley Engrs. 1990), Masons, Scottish Rite, Shriners, Commandry, Alpha Phi Omega (nat. pres.), Pi Tau Sigma (pres.), Pi Nu Epsilon. Episcopalian. Office: Process Automation Tech 702 Avondale Rd Glenside PA 19038-7337

FORMAN, HOWARD IRVING, lawyer, former government official; b. Phila., Jan. 12, 1917; s. Jacob and Dora (Moses) F.; m. Ada Pressman, Aug. 2, 1938; children: Kenneth J., Harvey R. BS in Chemistry, St. Joseph's Coll., 1937; LLB, Temple U., 1944; MA, U. Pa., 1949, PhD, 1955. Bar: D.C. 1945, Pa. 1973. Rsch. chemist Frankford Arsenal, Dept. Army, Phila., 1940-44; patent atty. Frankford Arsenal, Dept. Army, 1944-46, chief patents br., 1946-56; asst. dir. Pitman-Dunn Rsch. Labs., 1955-56; lectr. polit. sci. Temple U., 1956-63; from patent atty. to trademark and internat. corp. counsel Rohm and Haas Co., Phila., 1956-76; dep. asst. sec. U.S. Dept. Commerce, Washington, 1976-81; also dir. Office of Product Standards Policy; chmn. interagy. com. on standards policy Weiser, Stapler & Spivak, Phila., 1974-76; head. U.S. dels. to UN internat. confs., Geneva, 1976-81; sec., dir. Rohm & Haas Asia, Inc., 1973-76; v.p., gen. counsel, dir. Brilliant Internat., Inc., Bala-Cynwyd, Pa., 1974-83; sec., dir. Far East Chem. Services, Inc., Wilmington, Del., 1973-76; Rohm and Haas Far East Chem. Services, Inc., GmbH, Zug, Switzerland, 1975-76; dir. U.S. Pharm. Corp., 1975-83; pvt. practice Phila., 1981—; advisor to asst. sec. for econ. affairs relative to internat. intellectual property matters Dept. State, 1968-72; orginator Internat. Lab. Accreditation world-wide biennial confs. (ILAC), 1977—; chmn. ANSI accredited stds. com., Z21, on performance and installation gas burning appliances and accessories, 1981-97. Author: Inventions, Patents and Related Matters, 1957, Patents-Their Ownership and Administration by the U.S. Government, 1957; Editor: Patents, Research and Management, 1961, The Law of Chemical, Metallurgical and Pharmaceutical Patents, 1967; author plays: The Birth of the American Patent System, 1976, The Birth of the American Patent and Copyright Systems , 1990.; contbr. to publs. in field. Bd. dirs. Lower Moreland Twp. Sch. Bd., Montgomery County, Pa., 1969-75; bd. dirs. Eastern Montgomery County Vocat.-Tech. Sch., 1969-75, sec., 1970-75; bd. dirs. Warminster (Pa.) Gen. Hosp., 1983-91; emeritus dir. Allegheny United Hosps., Inc., 1991-94; life trustee Med. Coll. Pa. and Hahnemann U. Hosps., 1994-98. Recipient Robert J. Painter Meml. award Stds. Engring. Soc.-ASTM, 1978, Leo B. Moore award Stds. Engring. Soc., 1981. Fellow Am. Inst. Chemists; mem. ABA, FBA, AAAS, ASTM (hon. life, bd. dirs. 1985-87), Internat. Assn. Protection Indsl. Property, Am. Nat. Stds. Inst. (bd. dirs. 1977-80, Finegan Stds. medal 1996), Nat. Coun. Patent Law Assn. (chmn. 1967-68), Am. Chem. Soc., Sci. Rsch. Soc. Am., Am. Assn. Lab. Accreditation (dir. 1983-91), Am. Patent Law Assn. (bd. mgrs. 1970-73), Am. Coll. Legal Medicine, Phila. Bar Assn. (sec. 1973-74, com. on jurimetrics, tech. and patents, v.p. 1975), Phila. Patent Law Assn. (pres. 1964-66), Licensing Execs. Soc., Stds. Engring. Soc. (Robert J. Painter Meml. award 1978, Leo B. Moore award 1981), Franklin Inst. (vice chmn. Futures Ctr. campaign), Nat. Lawyers Club, Gas Appliance Mfrs. Assn. (meritorious svc. award 1996), Am. Soc. Gas Engrs. (hon.), Sigma Xi. Achievements include being the principal draftsman, prime mover in devel. original OMB Circular A-119 which established nat. policy calling for primary dependence of Fed. Govt. on private sector standards orgns. for devel. of standards required for procurement and regulatory purposes by govt. agencies. Fax: (215) 947-5036. Home: 1033 Corn Crib Dr Huntingdon Valley PA 19006-3335 Office: Albidale-Windmill Circle PO Box 66 Huntingdon Valley PA 19006-0066

FORMAN, ROBERT GRAHAM, obstetrician-gynecologist; b. Manchester, Lancashire, Eng., Jan. 22, 1956; s. Morris and Hilda (Doran) F.; m. Nathalie Helene Loreille, Sept. 19, 1986; children: Louis-Eliott, Paul Emile. MBBS, Middlesex Hosp. Med. Sch., London, 1978; MD, U. London, 1988. Clin. chief Hosp. Antoine Beclere, Clamart, France, 1985-88; clin. lectr. John Radcliffe Hosp., Oxford, Eng., 1988-90; cons. in ob-gyn. St. Thomas Hosp., London, 1990-95; dir. Ctr. for Reproductive Medicine, 1996—. Author: Drug Induced Infertility and Sexual Disfunction, 1996; contbr. 50 articles to profl. jours., 1985—. Insp. Human Fertilization and Embryology Authority, London, 1995—. Named. Dr. of Yr. BUPA Med. Found., London, 1992; travelling fellow Med. Rsch. Coun., Paris, 1985. Fellow Royal Coll. Ob-gyn. (mem. European com. 1993-95). Avocations: wine, European cinema.

FORMÁNEK, JIŘÍ, physicist, educator; b. Pardubice, Czech Republic, Feb. 25, 1936; s. František and Marie (Kainová) F.; m. Hana Pešlová, Apr. 28, 1961; 1 child, Eva. CSc, Tech. U., Prague, 1966; PhD, Charles U., Prague, 1976, ScD, 1981. Asst. prof. Tech. U., Prague, 1960-66; fellow CERN, Geneva, 1966-67; lectr. U. Md., Washington, 1969; rschr. Rutherford Lab., Chilton, Eng., 1974-75; docent Charles U., Prague, 1976-81, prof. physicist, 1981—, vice dean Faculty Math. and Physics, 1976-85, dir. Nuclear Ctr., 1985-90; head high energy physics dept. Czech Acad. Sci., 1987-90. Author: Introduction to Quantum Theory, 1983 (Min. of Edn. prize 1986), Relativistic Quantum Mechanics and Quantum Field Theory, 1998; contbr. articles to profl. jours. Recipient Award of Czech Lit. Fund, 1984, Nat. Prize of Czech Republic, 1985, Silver medal Czech Acad. Scis., 1986. Mem. Czech Acad. Sci. (corr.). Office: Charles Univ Nuclear Ctr, V Holešovičkách 2, CZ 18000 Prague 8, Czech Republic

FORMENTO, DANIEL, radio company executive, writer; b. Pitts., Aug. 11, 1954; s. Stephen P. and Betty Jean (McCorkle) F.; m. Alison Ashley, Oct. 7, 1995; children: Alexander Daniel, Natalie Annette. Grad. high sch., Mt. Lebanon, Pa. Program mgr. The Source/NBC Radio Network, N.Y.C., 1979-82; prin. Dan Formento Prodns., N.Y.C., 1982-84; pres. Radio Today Entertainment, N.Y.C., 1984—, West Hill Studios, N.J., 1993—; v.p., creative dir. ABC Radio Network, 1998. Author: Rock Chronicle, 1982; producer radio programs including Flashback, 1984 , Rock Stars, 1985—, Walter Cronkite's 20th Century, 1988, Pop Quiz, 1992—; radio comml. Grog Shop, 1976 (Aftra award 1976); announcer radio feature Today in Rock History, 1979—; TV comml. Short Cuts, 1989—; producer radio feature One Minute With, 1976 (Golden Quill award 1976), Pop Quiz, 1992— (Internat. Radio Festival of N.Y. grand award 1992). Democrat. Avocations: swimming, tennis, audio enthusiast. Office: ABC Radio Network 444 Madison Ave New York NY 10022-6903

FORMIGUINHA See ZAGALLO, MARIO JORGE LOBO

FORMO, BRENDA TERRELL, travel company executive; b. Greensboro, N.C., May 18, 1946; d. Walter C. Terrell and Eunice W. Kirkman; m. Robert A. Formo, Oct. 14, 1978; 1 child, Eric Victor. BSBA, East Carolina U., 1968; MA in Bus. Adminstrn., Webster U., 1977; postgrad., 1970, 72, 77, 84, 87; grad., Army War Coll., 1990. Commd. 2d lt. U.S. Army, 1969, advanced through grades to col., 1991, ret., 1993; acctg. instr. U.S. Army Fin. Sch., Ft. Harrison, Ind., 1969-71; women's officer recruiter U.S. Army Kansas City Recruiting Main Sta., 1971-73; recruiting ops. officer U.S. Army SW Recruiting Command, San Antonio, 1973-75; area comdr. U.S. Army San Antonio Dist. Recruiting Command, 1975-77; chief pay and examination divsn. U.S. Army Fin. and Acctg. Office, Yongsan, Korea, 1977-78; asst. chief acctg. U.S. Army Mil. Dist. Washington Fin. and Acctg. Office, 1978-80; banking officer U.S. Army Europe Office of the Dep. Chief of Staff for Resource Mgmt., 1980-84; fin. and acctg. officer Def. Nuclear Agy., 1984-87; investigator Office of Dept. of the Army Inspector Gen., 1987-91; chief programs and analysis divsn. Dept. Army Office of Dep. Chief of Staff for Logistics, 1991-93; fin. mgmt. cons., 1993-96; co-founder, pres. BRE Travel, 1996—. Pres. Browne Acad. PTA, Alexandria, Va., 1987; active Guilford Coll. United Meth. Ch., Greensboro. Decorated Legion of Merit with oak leaf cluster (2 awards), Meritorious Svc. medal with 3 oak leaf clusters (4 awards), Army Commendation medal with 4 oak leaf clusters (5 awards). Mem. Am. Soc. Travel Agts., Assn. of the U.S. Army, Terrell Soc. Am., Cardinal Golf and Country Club (Greensboro). Address: 4116 Obriant Pl Greensboro NC 27410-8372

FORMOLI, TAREQ AHMAD, environmental research scientist, consultant; b. Kabul, Afghanistan, Mar. 22, 1954; s. Wali Ahmad and Maliha F.; m. Shahnaz Lali Formoli, Jan. 10, 1987; children: Waleed, Shakeel, Sheena. BS, Kabul U., Afghanistan, 1977; MS, Calif. State U., Fresno, 1982. Inspector Calif. Dried Fruit Assn., Fresno, 1982-83; chemist Dept. Water Resources, Los Banos, Calif., 1994-95; pesticide scientist Calif. Dept. Food and Agr., Sacramento, 1985-93; assoc. environmental rsch. scientist Calif. Environment Agy., Sacramento, 1993—; bd. dirs. mem. Afghan Devel. Assn., Peshawar, Pakistan, 1996—; adv. bd. Soc. Afghan Vols. for Environ., Peshawar, Pakistan, 1997—. Founder, editor: Afghanistan Horizon, 1985; author: An Overview and Assessment of Afghanistan's Environment, 1994. Recipient Cert. Appreciation Mercy Hosps. Found., Sacramento, 1985, Afghan Devel. Assn., Pakistan, 1997, Customer Svc. Calif. Environmental Protection Agy., Sacramento, 1998. Mem. Calif. Assn. Profl. Scientist, 1991—. Avocations: basketball, travel, science fiction movies. E-mail address: tformoli@cdpr.ca.gov. Fax: (916) 445-4280. Home: 1714 Ladino Rd Sacramento CA 95864-1626

FORNACE, ALBERT J., JR., medical researcher; b. Phila., Apr. 5, 1949; s. Albert J. and Frances H. (Langan) F.; m. Arlene V. Ferretti, Feb. 6, 1951; children: Kimberly M., Kyrstin L.R., Mark E. BS, Pa. State U., 1970; MD, Jefferson Med. Coll., 1972. Diplomate Anatomic Pathology. Med. intern George Washington U. Hosp., 1972-73; pathology resident Brigham & Womens Hosp., Boston, 1975-78; clin. fellow Harvard U., Boston, 1975-79; rsch. fellow Harvard Sch. Pub. Health, Boston, 1976-79; med. rschr. Nat. Cancer Inst., NIH, Bethesda, Md., 1979-85, sr. med. scientist, 1985—, chief gene response sect. DBS, 1995—; authority in molecular radiobiology and molecular oncology. Mem. numerous editl. bds. of profl. jours.; contbr. articles to profl. jours. Capt. USPHS, 1984—. Office: Nat Cancer Inst Divsn Of Basic Sci # 37-5c09 Bethesda MD 20892-0001

FORNACIARI PASSANO, MARCO, agronomist, researcher, wine producer; b. Rome, Aug. 24, 1958; s. Carlo Fornaciari and Magda da Passano; m. Francesca Fanini, Aug. 29, 1992; children: Benedetta, Giacomo. Agrl. degree, U. Perugia, Italy, 1985. Univ. rschr. dept. plant biology U. Perugia, 1990—. Office: Dept Plant Biology, Borgo XX Giugno 74, 06121 Perugia Italy

FORNATTO, ELIO JOSEPH, otolaryngologist, educator; b. Turin, Italy, July 2, 1928; came to U.S., 1953; s. Mario G. and Julia (Stabio) F.; m. Mary Elizabeth Pearson, Dec. 17, 1960; children: Susan, Robert, Daniel. MD, U. Turin, Italy, 1952. Diplomate Am. Bd. Otolaryngology. Intern Edgewater Hosp., Chgo., 1956-57; resident U. Ill., Chgo., 1953-56; chief otolaryngologist Elmhurst (Ill.) Clinic, 1958—; sr. otolaryngologist Elmhurst (Ill.) Meml. Hosp., 1964—; med. dir. Chgo. Eye Ear Nose Throat Hosp., 1966-69; clin. asst. prof. Loyola U., Chgo., 1967-87; bd. dirs. DuPage County unit Am. Cancer Soc., 1977-94; chmn. Elmhurst Clinic, 1980-89. Founder Centurion Club, Deafness Research Found., N.Y.C., 1960—. Recipient Disting. Svc. award Elmhurst Meml. Hosp., 1994. Mem. AMA, Ill. Med. Soc., Am. Acad. Facial Plastic and Reconstructive Surgery, Am. Acad. Otolaryngologic Allergy, Am. Acad. Otolaryngology and Head and Neck Surgery. Roman Catholic. Avocations: music, bicycling. Home: 200 W Jackson St Elmhurst IL 60126-4807 Office: Elmhurst Clinic 172 Schiller St Elmhurst IL 60126-2885

FORNE, MARC, Andorran government official. Head. of govt. Govt. of Andorra, Andorra la Vella. Office: Office of Exec Coun, C. Prat de la Crev 62-64, Andorra la Vella Andorra*

FORNI, GAETANO, museologist, historian; b. Milan, Dec. 28, 1926; s. Mario Carlo Forni and Giulia Cernuschi; m. Francesca Pisani, July 24, 1952; children: Mario, Giulia, Vittore, Emilia, Michelangelo, Alessandra. D. U. Milan, 1951. Head master Agr. Sch., S. Maria Versa, Italy, 1963-65; prin. E. Scaetta Sch., Milan, 1966-67, D. Birago Sch., Milan, 1968-92; sci. contbr. Lombardy Mus. History Agr. Milan U., 1993—; joint mgr. Rivista di Storia Dell' Agr., Firenze, Italy, 1993—. Joint editor: 2500 anni di Cultura della Vite nell'ambito alpino e Cisalpino, 1996, Alle Radici della Civiltá del Vino in Sicilia, 1999; joint editor Acta Museorum Italicorum Agriculturae, 1977—. Counselor Roman Cath. U. H.S. Tchrs., Milan, 1993—. Mem. Italian Assn. for the Ethno-Anthropological Scis. (counselor), Assn. Internat. Mus. (hon.). Roman Catholic. Avocation: mountaineering. Home: Keplero 33, 20124 Milan Italy Office: Mus Lombardo Storia Agr, Casella Postale 908, 20101 Milan Italy

FORO, LYNDA J., humane organization director; b. Buffalo, Aug. 6, 1941; d. Chauncey B. Sturgess and Dorothy May Griffin; m. Bradley R., Dec. 9, 1960 (div. 1974); children: Gwyn Denise, Craig Bradley. BA, U. Md., 1976; AA, Montgomery Coll., 1974; cert. in nonprofit mgmt., Ariz. State U., 1995. Founder, pres. Doing Things for Animals, Sun City, Ariz., 1994—; dir. The Pet Savers Found., Pt. Washington, N.Y., 1999—. Editor: (quar. newsletter) No-Kill News, (nat. directory) No-Kill Directory, 2000; prodr. No-Kill Conf. Hosp. corpsman USN, 1959-61. Recipient Humane Achievement award Humane Coalition of Mass., 1997. Mem. Soc. Animal Welfare Adminstrs. E-mail: lyndaf@petsavers.org. Office: Doing Things for Animals 59 S Bayles Ave Port Washington NY 11050-3728

FOROS, MARKOS APOSTOLOS, shipping company executive, real estate company executive; b. Chios, Greece, Oct. 18, 1948; s. Apostolos Markos and Fani Apostolos (Andreadis) F.; m. Marianna Giannoulos, Nov. 7, 1978; children: Stella, Constantina, Stephanie. BS in Econs., London Sch. Econs./Polit. Sci., 1972; MBA, Harvard U., 1974. Asst. to the pres. C. Paul Luongo Co., Boston, 1973; account officer The First Nat. Bank of Chgo., 1974-76; CFO The Chandris Group of Cos., N.Y.C., London, Piraeus, 1976-92; pres. Celebrity Cruises Mgmt. Inc., Piraeus, Greece, 1992—; mng. dir. Chandris (Hellas) Inc., 1998. Mem. Hellenic Soc. for the Protection of the Environ. and the Cultural Heritage, Athens, 1986. Fellowship Inst. of Commerce. Mem. British Inst. of Mktg., British Inst. of Mgmt., Mgmt. Cons., Assn. of the Socs. Anonymes, Greek Passenger Shipowners Assn. (v.p.), Propeller Club (gov.), Hellenic Ch. Shipping (coun. mem., marine arbitrator, mem. governing body). Office: Internat Cruises SA, 95 Akti Miaouli St, 18538 Piraeus Greece

FOROUGHBAKHCH, RAHIM, biologist, researcher; b. Fasa, Fars, Iran, Apr. 13, 1949; arrived in Mexico, 1980; s. Hassan Foroughbakhoh and Iran Pournavab; m. Eticia Amira Hauad, Nov. 7, 1981; children: Rashid, Farid, Karim. Degree in Biology, U. Tabriz, Iran, 1975; M in Applied Ecology, U. Montpellier, France, 1978, DS, 1981; postgrad., Nat. Inst. Agronomy, Montpellier, 1993. French lang. diplomate U. Poitiére, France, 1975, Ecofisiologist diplomate Nat. Ctr. Sci. Rsch., Montpellier, 1976; cert. natural resource engring. U. Tex., 1994. Rsch. asst. U. Tabriz, 1973-74, ecol. advisor, 1974-75; rsch. advisor U. Montpellier, 1978-81; formal prof. forestry mgmt. U. Nuevo Leon, Linares, Mexico, 1981-91; prof. biometry U. Nuevo Leon, Linares, 1982-83, prof. agroforestry introduction, 1985-91, prof. agroforestry mgmt., 1987-91, prof. statis. methods, 1988-91, prof. exptl. design, 1988-91; prof. biostatis. analysis U. Nuevo Leon, Monterrey, Mexico, 1992—; prof. advanced ecology U. Nuevo Leon, Monterrey, 1995—, prof. ecosystems mgmt., 1995—, prof. exptl. design, 1996-97, prof. applied stats., 1997—; head agroforestry dept. U. Nuevo Leon, Linares, 1987-91; mem., adviser acad. and rsch. coun. U. Neuvo Leon, Linares, 1989-91, others; rsch. prof. Pub. Edn. Secretariat, Mexico City, 1989, Nat. Inst. Agronomy, Montpellier, 1993, U. Nuevo Leon, Monterrey, Mexico, 1994; mem. orgns. com. audit agroforestry Nat. Inst. Agronomy, Montpellier, 1993; mem. orgns. com. Leucaena R&D workshop Forestry Inst. Bogor, Indonesia, 1994; prof. in rsch. methodology U. Chapingo, Mexico City, 1994-95, prof. in aird lands mgmt., 1994-96, mem. orgns. com. I Congress in arid lands mgmt., 1997; mem. com. for evaluation the innovation prize in sci. and tech. Nat. Coun. Sci. and Pub. Edn. Secretariat, Mexico City, 1998; mem. com. for evaluation fgn. scholarship Nat. Coun. Sci. and Tech., Mexico City, 1998, cons., mem. biology sci. rsch. com., 1995-98. Editor: Experimental Design University of Nuevo Leon, 1996, Applied Manual of Quattro-Pro University of Nuevo Leon, 1997, Statgraphics: Application and Uses, University of Nuevo Leon, 1998; mem. editl. coun. Environ. Quality Jour., Tech. Inst. Monterrey, 1995—, Biol. Publs. Jour., U. Nuevo Leon, Monterrey, 1995—; contbr. chpts. to books and articles to profl. jours. Mem. Rotary Club, Colinas Sport Club. Avocations: cycling, long walks, basketball. Home: Jean Racine 1502, 64640 Monterrey Mexico Office: Univ Nuevo Leon, Ciudad Univ AP F 2, 66450 San Nicolas Graza, Mexico

FORRAI, GEORGE, pediatrician, human geneticist, researcher; b. Budapest, Hungary, May 23, 1930; s. Ödön and Margit (Mocsári) F.; m. Klára Vadász; children: Gábor, Péter. MD, Med. U., Budapest, 1954; PhD, Hungarian Acad. Scis., Budapest, 1986. Cert. specialist in pediatrics. Asst. prof. Med. U. Pediat. Clinic No II, Budapest, 1954-63; family pediatrician local govt., Budapest, 1963-95; assoc. prof. Haynal Imre Med. U., Budapest, 1982—; pvt. practice Budapest, 1996—. Author some 400 biomed. and/or ednl. articles, books, chpts. of books in many langs. and pub. in 11 countries. Mem. Internat. Assn. Human Biologists, Internat. Directory Human Geneticists. Home: Alig utca 5, 1132 Budapest Hungary Office: Vezér utca 156, 1148 Budapest Hungary

FORREST, DAVID VICKERS, psychiatrist, educator; b. N.Y.C., July 8, 1938; s. Melbourne Arthur and Cleo Florence (Garello); m. Lynne Putnam Stetson; children: Daniel Stetson, Susannah Nissly. AB summa cum laude, Princeton U., 1960; MD, Columbia U., 1964, cert. in psychoanalysis, 1974. Cert. in psychiatry Am. Bd. Psychiatry and Neurology. Intern in medicine St. Luke's Hosp., N.Y.C., 1964-65; resident in psychiatry N.Y. State Psychiat. Inst., Columbia Presbyn. Med. Ctr., N.Y.C., 1965-68; chief psychiatric clinic 935th Med. Det. (KO) 93d Evacuation Hosp., Long Binh, Vietnam, 1968-69; chief psychiatric consultation Letterman Army Med. Ctr., San Francisco, 1969-70; pvt. practice psychiatry N.Y.C., 1970—; mem. psychiatry faculty Columbia U., N.Y.C., 1970—, dir. edn. ednl. rsch. dept. N.Y. State Psychiat. Inst., 1970-77; assoc. prof. clin. psychiatry Columbia U., Coll. Physicians and Surgeons, N.Y.C., 1984—; faculty psychoanalytic ctr. Columbia U., Coll. Physicians and Surgeons, 1974—, liaison psychiatrist neurology, 1977—; clin. prof. of psychiatry Columbia U., Coll. Physicians and Surgeons, N.Y.C., 2000—; lectr. psychiatry U. Saigon Med. Sch., Vietnam, 1968-69; lectr. abnormal psychology Far East div. U. Md., Long Binh, Vietnam, 1969. Author: Selected American Expressions, 1974, 76, 82; co-author: Treating Schizophrenic Patients, 1983, (video cassette series) Electronic Textbook of Psychiatry, 1972-77; co-author, pub: The Ballet Company Game, 1973; founding editor, pub. Spring: The Jour. of the E. E. Cummings Soc., N.Y.C., 1980—; editor: Neural Net News, N.Y. State Psychiat. Inst., 1989-91; technical cons. Star Trek TV series, 1997—; contbr. articles to profl. jours., textbooks. Psychiat. cons. N.Y.C. Ballet Co., 1973; first aid instr. Boy Scouts Am., 1983—. Capt. USAF, 1968-70, Vietnam. Decorated Bronze Star; Gen. Motors nat. scholar. Fellow Am. Psychiat. Assn., Am. Coll. Psychiatrists, Am. Acad. Psychoanalysis (program chair), Am. Coll. Psychoanalysts (program chair 1987-89, bd. regents 1989-92, v.p. 1993, pres.-elect 1994, pres. 1995), Explorers Club; mem. Am. Acad. Neurology (assoc.), N.Y. Clin. Soc. (v.p. 1995, pres. 1996). Episcopalian. Avocations: invention, discovery, magic. Office: 133 E 73rd St Ste 211 New York NY 10021-3556 also: 155 W 68th St Apt 1219 New York NY 10023-5818

FORREST, GAIL, human resources executive; b. McAllen, Tex., Apr. 18, 1955; d. Richard Baker Forrest and Diane Mattison. BA, U. So. Calif., 1977; postgrad., George Washington U., 1978-82; MBA, U. Md., 1987. Editl. asst. ABA, Washington, 1977-78; pers. asst. UNISYS Corp., McLean, Va., 1978-80; pers. asst. UNISYS Corp., McLean, 1981-82, corp. dir. compensation and adminstrn., 1983-87, dir. pers., 1988-89, dir. human resources, 1989-90, dir. ops., 1991-94; dir. human resources Ameritech corp., 1994-97, Sears Corp., 1997—; cons. in field. Mem. Soc. Human Resource Mgmt., Chgo. Execs. Club. Republican. Methodist. Home: 235 Bryant Ave Glen Ellyn IL 60137-5547 Office: Sears Roebuck 3333 Beverly Rd Hoffman Est IL 60179-0001

FORREST, HERBERT EMERSON, lawyer; b. N.Y.C., Sept. 20, 1923; s. Jacob K. and Rose (Fried) F.; m. Marilyn Lefsky, Jan. 12, 1952; children: Glenn Clifford, Andrew Matthew. Student, CCNY, 1941, Ohio U., 1943-44; BA with distinction, George Washington U., 1948, JD with highest honors, 1952. Bar: Va. 1952, D.C. 1952, U.S. Supreme Ct. 1956, Md. 1959, U.S. Ct. Appeals (D.C. cir.) 1953, (1st cir.) 1992, (2d cir.) 1971, (3d cir.) 1957, (4th cir.) 1956, (5th cir.) 1981, (7th cir.) 1996, (8th cir.) 1991, (9th cir.) 1994, (11th cir.) 1981. Plate printer Bur. Engraving and Printing, Washington, 1942-43, 1946-52; law clk. to chief judge Bolitha J. Laws U.S. Dist. Ct., Washington, 1952-55; pvt. practice Washington, 1952-87; with Welch & Morgan, 1955-65; with Steptoe & Johnson, 1965-85, of counsel, 1986-87; trial atty. fed. programs br. civil divsn. U.S. Dept. Justice, Washington, 1987—; chmn. adv. bd. D.C. Criminal Justice Act, 1971-74; sec. com. admissions and grievances U.S. Ct. Appeals, D.C., 1973-79; title-1 audit hearing bd. U.S. Office Edn. HEW, 1976-79; edn. appeals bd. U.S. Dept. Edn., 1979-82; mem. Lawyer's Support Com. for Visitors Service Center, 1975-87. Contbr. articles to legal jours.; advisory bd.: Duke Law Jour, 1969-75. Pres. Whittier Woods PTA, 1970-71. Served with F.A., Signal Corps U.S. Army, 1943-46. Recipient Walsh award in Irish history, 1952, Goddard award in commerce, 1952. Fellow Am. Bar Found. (life), ABA (council 1972-75, 1981-84, budget officer 1985-88, vice chmn. task force on sect. devel. 1987-89, chmn. com. on agy. rule making 1968-72, 1976-81, chmn. membership com. 1984-85, editor ann. reports 1973-88, adminstrv. law sect., fellow adminstrv. law and regulatory practice, mem. comm. com. public utilities law sect., vice chmn. industry regulation com. 1985-86, chmn. comm. subcom. 1983-85, antitrust law sect., internat. law sect., sec. judicial adminstrn., sect. sci. and tech., comm. forum); mem. George Washington Law Assn., Am. Judicature Soc., Va. State Bar Assn., Fed. Bar Assn. (chmn. jud. rev. com. 1981-85, vice chmn. adminstrv. law sect. 1985-87), Fed. Comm. Bar Assn. (del. to ABA Ho. Dels. 1979-81, exec. com. 1967-71, 76-84, v.p. 1981-82, pres. 1982-83, chmn. telecomm. com. 1983-87), D.C. Bar Assn. (past sec., exec. com.), NAM, Nat. Conf. Bar Pres., Washington Council Lawyers, Legal Aid and Pub. Defender Assn., Am. Arbitration Assn. (comml. panel 1976-87), D.C. Unified Bar (bd. govs. 1976-79, chmn. com. on employment discrimination complaint service 1973-79, chmn. task force on services to public 1974-78, chmn. com. on appointment counsel in criminal cases 1978-88, co-chmn. com. on participation govt. employees in pro bono activities 1977-79), Broadcast Pioneers, Order of Coif, Phi Beta Kappa, Pi Gamma Mu., Artus, Phi Eta Sigma, Phi Delta Phi. Democrat. Lodge: B'nai Brith. Home: 8706 Bellwood Rd Bethesda MD 20817-3033 Office: US Dept Justice 901 E St NW Rm 1050 Fed Washington DC 20004-2037

FORREST, RICHARD DUNCAN, physician, writer, educator; b. London, Apr. 28, 1945; arrived in Sweden, 1971; s. John Orchover and Irene (Leanse) F.; m. Riitta Maaret Helena Järventaus; children: Victoria, Emilia, Mia. MB, BS, Guy's Hosp., London, 1968, MD, 1987. Diplomate Nat. Bd. Health and Welfare, Sweden. Cons. physician Cen. Hosp., Boden, Sweden, 1979-88, cons. clin. chemist, 1988-90; pvt. practice Luleå, Sweden, 1990—; CEO Forrest Lab. Svc. AB, Luleå, Sweden, 1994-2000; mng. dir. Forrest Med. Info., 1987-2000. Author: Dr. Forrest's Diabetes Guide, vol. 1, 1994, vol. 2, 1995, 2d edit., 2000, Practical Guide to Erectile Dysfunction and Diabetes, 1999; contbr. articles to profl. jours. Mem. Royal Coll. Physicians, Royal Coll. Surgeons, Swedish Med. Assn. Avocations: rock & roll record and memorabilia collector. Office: Fagerlinsvägen 3, SE-97239 Luleå Sweden

FORRESTAL, ROBERT PATRICK, banker, lawyer; b. N.Y.C., Oct. 31, 1931; s. Patrick A. and Lillian D. (Moran) F.; m. Wilma Anderson, Sept. 29, 1956; 1 child, Renee Marie. BA, St. John's U., 1953; JD, Georgetown U., 1961. Bar: D.C. 1961, U.S. Supreme Ct. 1964. Atty. Spencer & Whalen, Washington, 1961-64; atty. Fed. Res. Bd., Washington, 1964-68, asst. sec., 1968-70; v.p., gen. counsel Fed. Res. Bd., Atlanta, 1970-74; sr. v.p., gen. counsel Fed. Res. Bank of Atlanta, 1974-79, 1st v.p., 1979-83, pres., 1983-95; ptnr. Smith, Gambrell and Russell, Atlanta, 1996—; bd. dirs. ING Corp., Genuine Parts Co., Equifax Corp., ING Ins. Co. Bd. dirs. Leadership Atlanta, 1971-73, Child Svcs. and Family Counseling Ctr., Atlanta, 1974-81, Ga. Worlds Congress Inst., 1979-83, United Way of Met. Atlanta, 1984-90, So. Ctr. for Internat. Studies, 1986-94; bd. sponsors Atlanta Symphony Orch., 1973-75; divsn. chmn. United Way, Atlanta, 1980-81; bd. dirs., exec. com. Ga. State U., Atlanta, 1972-83, chmn. recognition fund, 1975, chmn. trustees, 1976-78, mem. bd. advisors Coll. Bus. Adminstrn.; bd. dirs. Ctrl. Atlanta Progress, Piedmont Hosp. Found.; trustee Atlanta Arts Alliance, Oglethorpe U.; mem. adv. bd. Atlanta Humanities Program; bd. visitors Emory U., 1986-89, Berry Coll., 1987-89, Ga. State U. Sch. Law; mem. bd. councilors Carter Ctr.; active Friends of Piedmont Hosp., Piedmond Med. Care Found. Lt. USN, 1953. Fulbright scholar, 1953. Mem. Atlanta C. of C. (bd. dirs. 1984-87, 93-94), Rotary (bd. dirs. 1985-88, 93—), World Trade Club of Atlanta. Home: 3949 Vermont Rd NE Atlanta GA 30319-1212 Office: Smith Gambrell & Russell 1230 Peachtree St NE Ste 3100 Atlanta GA 30309-3592

FORRY, JOHN INGRAM, lawyer; b. Washington, Feb. 9, 1945; s. John Emerson and Marion Carlotta (MacArthur) F.; m. Carol Ann Micken, Jan. 12, 1980; children: Alicia Ann, Camilla Lorraine. BA, Amherst Coll., 1966; JD, Harvard U., 1969. Bar: Calif. 1970, D.C. 1998, N.Y. 1998, U.S. Tax Ct. 1977, U.S. Supreme Ct. 1975. Founding ptnr. Forry Golbert Singer & Gelles, L.A., 1973-80; sr. ptnr. Morgan, Lewis & Bockius, L.A., 1980-97, McDermott, Will & Emery, N.Y.C., 1997-98, Ernst & Young LLP, N.Y.C., 1999—. Co-author, editor: A Practical Guide to Foreign Investment in the United States, 1979, 3d edit., 1989, 4 other books; contbr. over 40 articles to profl. jours. Co-founder Forry Fund in Philosophy and Sci., Amherst (Mass.) Coll., 1984—; mem. adv. group to U.S. Commr. of Internal Revenue, Washington, 1985-86. Mem. Internat. Bar Assn., Internat. Fiscal Assn., other bar assns. Republican. Roman Catholic. Avocations: philosophical implications of scientific developments, automobile racing, mountain climbing, scuba diving. Fax: 212-773-6760. Office: Ernst & Young LLP 787 7th Ave Fl 23 New York NY 10019-6018

FORSBACH, RALF, historian; b. Siegburg, Germany, Mar. 21, 1965; s. Hans Günter and Christine (Böckem) F. MA, U. Bonn, Germany, 1990, PhD, 1995. Jr. rsch. fellow U. Rostock, 1995-97, U. Bonn, 1997—. Author: (biography) Alfred Von Kiderlen-Wächter, 2 vols., 1997. Mem. Soc. Supporters Cologne Cathedral, 1991. Mem. Union Historians Germany. Roman Catholic. Home: Cecilienstr 29, 53721 Siegburg Germany Office: Historisches Seminar, Konviktstr 11, 53113 Bonn Germany

FORSBERG, K. HAAKAN, electronic design engineer; b. Helsingborg, Sweden, May 9, 1969. MSc in Computer Sci. and Engring., Linkoping U., 1997; postgrad., Chalmers U. Tech., Gothenburg, Sweden, 1998—. Electronics engr. Spectronic, Helsingborg, 1991-96; electronic design engr. Ericsson Saab Avionics AB, Jonkoping, 1996—. 2d lt. Swedish Mil. Res. Mem. IEEE, IEEE Computer Soc., IEEE Lasers and Electro-Optics Soc., Optical Soc. Am. Avocations: cycling, cooking, computer programming. E-mail: rapid@ce.chalmers.se. Office: Chalmers U Tech, Dept Computer Engring, SE-41296 Gothenburg Sweden

FORSBERG, PETER, professional hockey player; b. Ornskoldsvik, Sweden, July 20, 1973. Profl. hockey player MODO Hockey Swedish League, 1990-94, Swedish Olympic Team, 1994, Quebec Nordiques, Colo. Avalanche, 1994—. Named to Swedish League All-Star team, 1991-92; named Swedish League Player of Yr., 1993-94, NHL Rookie of Yr., Sporting News, 1994-95; recipient Calder Meml. award 1994-95; mem. Gold Medal winning Swedish Olympic Team, 1994. Office: c/o Colorado Avalanche 1635 Clay St Denver CO 80204-1743

FORSBERG WARRINGER, GUNNEL, retired museum director, writer; b. Stockholm, Aug. 28, 1939; d. Tore Erik Ragnar and Margit Linnea Cecilia (Orth) Forsberg; m. Rune Oskar Fredrik Warringer. BA, U. Uppsala, Sweden, 1964; MA, Royal Acad. Art/Arch. Sch., Stockholm, 1980. Mus. curator Kalmar (Sweden) Läns Mus., 1964-77, first mus. curator, 1977-81, asst. mus. dir., 1981-98; Editor, author: Kalmar Lan 1965-72, 1980-97, Kalmar Stads Historia, 1971-85; author: Kalmar, idyller till 1974, 1974, Lindbomska gården i Säter En historisk-teknisk förundersökning, 1981, Sekelskiftets Kalmar i Emil Blombergs bilder. Bok utgiven av Natur & Kultur, 1983, Byggarnas hus. Bok utgiven av Kalmar Läns Byggmästarförening, 1987, Kvarteret Repslagaren, Kvarnholmen, Kalmar, Bok utgiven av Konsthögskolans arkitekturskola i Stockholm, 1988, Jenny Nyström-konstnärinna, 1992, God Jul med Jenny Nyström, 1996, 2nd edit., 1999, Året runt-från jul till jul med Jenny Nyström, 1997, Första året, 1998, 2nd edit., 1998, others; contbr. articles to profl. jours. cons. in restoration Kalmar Castle, 1966-94; cons. The Coun. of Kalmar Cathedral, 1971-94; fellow Com. for Eketorps Fortress Future, Öland, 1972-98; exec. officer Jenny Nystroms and Curt Stoopendaal's Found., Kalmar, 1984-97; cons., fellow Assn. of Castles and Mus. Around the Baltic, Malbork, Poland, 1991-97. Pres., fellow Swedish Humanistic Assn., Kalmar, 1976-94; charter pres. Zonta, Kalmar, 1992-94; historicus, editor St. Christopher's Gille, Kalmar, 1994; sec. Jenny Nyström's Vänner, Stockholm, 1994. Scholar Sodermanl/Närkes Nation, Uppsala, 1964, Uppsala U., 1962, 63, 64, 66. Mem. Swedish Mus. Assn. Lutheran. Avocations: art and craft activities, nature walks, embroidery. Home and Office: Kaggensgatan 6, 392 32 Kalmar Sweden

FORSGREN, KLANE F., oil company executive, consultant; b. Preston, Idaho, Sept. 10, 1936; s. John Clifford Forsgren and Mary Oneta Fuhriman; m. Eva Kaye Glover, June 5, 1961; children: Karrie, Kelson, Kurtis, Kyle, Kathryn, Kaelyn, Keith, Kamille. B of Engring. Sci. Chem. Engring., Brigham Young U., 1961; M of Engring. Sci. Chem. Engring., U. Ill., 1963, PhD in Chem. Engring., 1965. Registered profl. engr., Pa., Idaho, Utah, Wyo. Rsch. assoc. Rohm & Haas, Phila., 1965-68; lab. head Rohm & Haas, 1968-72, mgr. product devel., 1972-75; consulting engr. Forsgren-Perkins Engring., Resburg, Idaho, 1975-81; v.p. engring. Forsgren Assocs., Resburg, 1981-91; mgr. environ. and engring. Sinclair Oil Corp., Salt Lake City, 1991-94, v.p. engring., environment health and safety, 1994—. Author: (book chpts.) Effective Project Management Through Applied Cost and Schedule Control, 1995. Pres. Utah Indsl. Energy Users Assn., Salt Lake City, 1987-88. Mormon. Avocations: fishing, woodworking, foreign travel. E-mail: kforsgren@sinclairoil.com. Home: 137459 1500E Bountiful UT 84010

FORSGREN, PER GUNNAR, power company research and development executive; b. skelleftea, Sweden, Oct. 10, 1932; s. Gunnar and Signe (Nilsson)

F.; m. Vivan Adelina Markgren, Aug. 4, 1957; 1 child, Patrik. MSEE, Chalmers Tech. U., 1968. Rschr. CTH/ASEA, Vattenfall, Sweden, 196-70; rsch. mgr. IKO/ITT, Sweden, 1970-72; cons. Vega Cons., Stockholm, 1972-75; rsch. mgr. Stockholm Energi, 1975-92, Forsgren Utueckling FoU, 1992—; sector chmn. SEF, Stockholm, 1987-92, bd. dirs.; mem. rsch. coun. VAST, 1978-92. Author book; contbr. numerous articles to profl. jours. Sgt. Swedish Army, 1952-72. Mem. IEEE (sr.; treas.-sec. 1993). Avocations: sailing, gardening. Home: Grastensvagen 12, 18734 Taby Sweden Office: Krafthuset FoU, Grastensu.12, 18734 Taby Sweden

FORSHAW, JEFFREY ROBERT, physics educator, researcher; b. Leigh, Lancashire, Eng., Feb. 26, 1968; s. Thomas and Sylvia Ann (Swallow) F.; m. Gail Marie Bradbrook, Nov. 21, 1998. BA with honors, Oxford (Eng.) U., 1989; PhD, Manchester (Eng.) U., 1992. Higher sci. officer Rutherford-Appleton Lab., Eng., 1992-95; rsch. fellow U. Manchester, Eng., 1995—. Author: Quantum Chromodynamics and The Pomeron, 1997. Fellow U.K. Inst. Physics, 1999; recipient Maxwell medal U.K. Inst. Physics, 1999. Avocations: rock climbing, yoga, running long distance. Office: U Manchester Dept Physics, Brunswick St, Manchester M13 9PL, United Kingdom

FORSHAY, STEVEN R., marketing professional, consultant; b. Knoxville, Tenn., Nov. 17, 1942; s. Raymond Leroy and Majorie Zoe Forshay; m. Judith Ann West, Sept. 7, 1963; children: Steven William, Ann Marie, Sarah Lewis. BS, U. Tenn., 1964; MBA, U. Tenn., Chattanooga, 1972. Mfg. engr. Am. Lava Corp., Chattanooga, 1967-75; indsl. ceramic sales staff 3M-Tech. Ceramics, Sunnyvale, Calif., 1976-78; mktg. mgr. 3M-Tech. Ceramics, St. Paul, 1979-89; bus. mgr. 3M-Tech. Ceramics, Dusseldorf, Germany, 1990-94; mktg. ops. staff 3M-New Products Dept., St. Paul, 1995—; mktg. cons. in field. Chmn. staff parish Centennial United Meth., Roseville, Minn., 1988, chmn. long range planning, 1996. Capt. U.S. Army, 1964-66. Mem. Am. Ceramic Soc., Am. Soc. Metals, Am. Inst. Indsl. Engrs., Internat. Soc. Hybrid Microelectronics (com. chair 1976-78), Kiwanis Club Signal Mountain (pres. 1975-76). Avocation: international travel. Home: 19 Spring Farm Ln North Oaks MN 55127-2142 Office: 3M 9E 10 Bldg 220 Saint Paul MN 55144-0001

FORSHEY, TIMOTHY ALLAN, lawyer; b. Urbana, Ill., Apr. 25, 1961; s. Thomas Collins Forshey and Paula Jean (Upp) Baker; m. Shannon Marie Gillham, May 11, 1996. BA, Ill. Wesleyan U., 1983; MS, N.E. Mo. State U., 1986; JD, U. Ill., 1989. Bar: Ariz. 1990, Ill. 1990, Colo. 1999. Student prosecutor Champaign County State's Atty. Office, Champaign, Ill., 1987-89; atty. Jones, Skelton and Hochuli, Phoenix, 1989-91, Goldstein, Kingsley & McGroder, Phoenix, 1991-93, Matz & Rubin, Phoenix, 1993-95, Timothy A. Forshey P.C., Phoenix, 1995-97, Davis, McKee & Forshey P.C., Phoenix, 1997—. Vol. Am. Kidney Found., Phoenix, 1989—, March of Dimes, Phoenix, 1989—; approved atty. NRA, Washington, 1995—; head coach, mem. adv. bd. Pop Warner Football, Phoenix, 1990. Mem. ATLA, U.S. Practical Shooting Assn., Ariz. State Bar Assn., Ill. State Bar Assn., Maricopa County Bar Assn., Mensa. Republican. Avocations: target shooting, hunting, camping, reading, theater. Office: Davis McKee & Forshey 5333 N 7th St Ste A201 Phoenix AZ 85014-2821

FORSLID, ANDERS, veterinarian, educator; b. Mariestad, Sweden, Mar. 17, 1955; s. Svante and Margareta (Johansson) F.; m. Anna Ingvar, Mar. 30, 1985; children: Louise, Erik, Gustav. DVM, Swedish U. Agrl. Scis., Uppsala, 1984; PhD, Swedish U. Agrl. Scis., 1987. Rschr. Swedish Meat Rsch. Inst., 1985-87, head of dept., 1987-94; univ. veterinarian, head of dept. lab. animal sci. Lund U., 1994—; assoc. prof. Swedish U. Agrl. Scis., Uppsala, 1992. Mem. Swedish Soc. for Veterinary Medicine (bd. dirs. 1996—, chmn. lab. animal sect. 1996—). Office: Dept Lab Animal Sci, Lund U Sölvegatan 10, S-223 62 Lund Sweden

FORSLIND, BO, biophysicist, educator; b. Stockholm, Jan. 28, 1934; s. Erik and Kivi Signe (Kivijärvi) F.; m. Gudrun Birgitta Bergendahl (div. 1985); children: Björn, Karin. MD, Karolinska Inst., Stockholm, 1965, PhD, 1970. Assoc. prof. Karolinska Inst., Stockholm, 1971—, prof., 1998-99, prof. emeritus, 1999—; part-time pvt. practice, Stockholm, 1972—; vis. scientist Nat. Inst. Police Sci., Tokyo, 1985, Csiro Parkville, Melbourne, Australia, 1986. Author: Electron Microscopy, 1981. Mem. European Soc. Dermatol. Rsch., European Hair Rsch. Soc. (treas. 1990-93). Avocations: sailing, music, jazz, string quartet. Fax: 46 8 650 3790. Home: Kungsholmsgatan 22, S-112 27 Stockholm Sweden Office: Karolinska Inst, Dept Med Biochem/Biophysics, Exptl Dermatology Rsch Gr, S-171 77 Stockholm Sweden

FORSON, BARNABAS, English language educator; b. Kwanyako, Ghana, Jan. 27, 1937; s. Edward Anokye and Kate Manko (Amoah) F.; m. comfort Yirenkyiwa Amoa, Aug. 8, 1964; children: Eva, Annemarie, David. BA with honors in English, U. Ghana, Legon, 1965, MA in Linguistics, 1968; MA in Linguistics, UCLA, 1976, PhD in Linguistics, 1979. Primary sch. tchr. Presbyn. Sch., Aperade, Ghana, 1956-57; tchr. Sch. for Blind, Akropong, Ghana, 1960-61; jr. lectr. math. Presbyn. Tchr. Tng. Coll., Aburi, Ghana, 1961-62, 65-66, 68-70; rsch. fellow Lang. Ctr., U. Ghana, Legon, 1970-75, 79-88, dir., 1980-82, 86-88; sr. lectr. English lang. U. Swaziland, Kwaluseni, 1988-90; assoc. prof. English U. Venda, Thohoyandou, South Africa, 1990-93, prof., head English, 1993—. Co-author: An English Course for Primary Schools, 1975, revised, 1982, English for Junior Secondary Schools, 1988; chmn. edtl. bd. Christian Messenger, 1983-88. Chmn. lit. com. Presbyn. Ch. Ghana, Accra, 1983-88. Recipient rsch. scholarship West African Linguistics Soc., Ibadan, Nigeria, 1968-69, scholarships Brit. Coun., Accra, 1973, African-Am. Inst., N.Y.C., 1975-79. Mem. English Acad. South Afria, Conf. Profs. English. Avocations: lettering, calligraphy. Home: 10 Block Q, Sibasa 0970, South Africa Office: U Venda, PO Box 188, Legon Ghana

FORSSELL-ARONSSON, EVA BIRGITTA, physicist, researcher; b. Göteborg, Sweden, July 2, 1961; d. John Björn and Birgitta Ingegerd (Nilsson) Forssell; m. Dan Åke Vilhelm Aronsson, June 13, 1987. MS in Engring. Physics, Chalmers U. Tech., Göteborg, 1986; PhD in Radiation Physics, Göteborg U., 1992. Asst. prof. Göteborg U., 1985-90, sr. lectr., 1991-92, 93—, assoc. prof., 1995—, sr. rschr. Swedish Nat. Cancer Soc., 1996—; hospital physicist Sahlgrenska U. Hosp., Göteborg, 1985-90, 92-93; dir. studies dept. radiation physics Göteborg U., 1991-92, 93-96, prof., 2000—. Avocation: music. Home: Lekskolegatan 11, S-431 42 Mölndal Sweden Office: Dept Radiation Physics, Sahlgrenska U Hosp, S-413 45 Göteborg Sweden

FORSTER, DAVID M.C., neurosurgeon; b. Jerusalem, Palestine, Aug. 20, 1935. MA, Emmanuel Coll/St. Thomas Hosp., Cambridge and London, Eng., 1959, MB BChir, 1960. House surgeon St. Thomas Hosp., London, 1960; house physician Lewisham Gen. Hosp., 1960; house ob-gyn St. Thomas Hosp., London, 1961; resident in neurosurgery Royal Hallamshire Hosp., 1964-68; asst. overlakare Karolinska Hosp., Stockholm, 1969-73; cons. neurosurgeon Royal Hallamshire Hosp., Sheffield, Eng., 1974—; dir. Nat. Ctr. Stereotactic Radiosurgery. Fellow Royal Coll. Surgeons London. Home: Half Acre 49 Church Ln, Dore Sheffield S17 3GT, England Office: Royal Hallamshire Hosp, Glossop Rd, Sheffield S10 2JF, England

FÖRSTER, ECKART HERIBERT, philosophy educator; b. Bremen, Germany, Jan. 12, 1952; s. Heribert and Ingeburg (Hüneken) F.; m. Gita Satterlee van Heerden, Apr. 27, 1996; 1 child, Kira. BPhil, Oxford U., 1979, DPhil, 1982. Lectr. Balliol Coll., Oxford, Eng., 1980-82, Harvard U., 1982-83; asst. prof. Stanford U., 1983-90, assoc. prof., 1990-96, prof., 1996; prof., endowed chair U. Munich, 1996—; vis. prof. Princeton U., 1988-89, U. Fed., Porto Alegre, Brazil, 1998, Ohio State U., Columbus, 1999; chair dept. philosophy U. Munich, 1998—. Author: Kant's Final Synthesis, 2000; editor: Kant's Transcendental Deductions, 1989, Kant's Opus Postumum, 1993, (series of books) Stanford Studies in Kant and German Idealism; contbr. articles to profl. jours. Adv. bd. Stanford Humanities Ctr., 1994-96. Rhodes scholar Rhodes Trust, 1976; fellow Am. Coun. Learned Socs., 1985, Stanford Humanities Ctr., 1987. Mem. Oxford Soc. (hon. sec. German br. 1997—), Am. Philos. Assn., Hölderlin Gesellschaft, Bavarian Acad. Sci. (Jacobi commn., Schelling commn.). Office: U Munich, Geschwister-Scholl-Platz 1, 80539 Munich Germany

FORSTER, HAMISH, engineer; b. Blackburn, Lancashire, Eng., Sept. 7, 1969; came to U.S., 1999; s. William Toshach Forster and Eileen Barbara Walker. B in Engring., U. London, 1990, MSc, 1991; PhD, U. Leeds, Eng., 1996. Registered chartered engr. Rsch. fellow U. Leeds, 1996-97; biomaterials engr. Smith & Nephew Group Rsch. Ctr., York, Eng., 1997-99; sr. rsch. engr. Smith & Nephew Orthopaedics, Memphis, 1999—; orthopaedic com. mem. Brit. Stds. Inst., London, Internat. Stds. Orgn., Geneva; biomaterials spl. interest group mem. Inst. Physics & Engring. in Medicine, York. Mem. Instn. Mech. Engrs., Inst. Materials, Inst. Physics and Engring. in Medicine. Avocations: Tae Kwon Do, mountain biking, snowboarding, adventure travel. E-mail: hamish.forster@smith-nephew.com. Fax: 901-399-6020. Office: Smith & Nephew Orthopaedics 1450 E Brooks Rd Memphis TN 38116-1804

FORSTER, JEAN-CHARLES, consumer products company executive; b. Besançon, France, Apr. 22, 1968; came to U.S., 1995; s. Jacques and Nicole (Socié) F. Diploma, Weller Internat. Bus. Sch., Dijon, France, 1991; MBA, Stirling (Eng.) U., 1992. Export mgr. Cottet S.A., Morez, France, 1993-95; v.p. Cottet U.S., Mamaroneck, N.Y., 1995—. Avocations: cigars. Office: Cottet Morel USA 500 W Main St Wyckoff NJ 07481-1406

FORSTOT, STEPHAN LANCE, ophthalmologist; b. N.Y.C., Aug. 19, 1943; s. Shepard and Edith Forstot; m. Lynne Rochelle Bitton, June 15, 1945; children: Michele, Jordan. AB, Princeton U., 1965; MD, Johns Hopkins U., 1969. Diplomate Am. Bd. Ophthalmology. Ophthalmologist Corneal Cons. of Colo., Denver, 1982—; ophthalmologist U. Colo. Sch. of Medicine, Denver, 1976-82, clin. prof., 1982—. Contbr. articles to profl. jours. Recipient Honor award Am. Acad. Ophthalmology. Mem. Contact Lens Assn. of Ophthalmology (bd. dirs. 1985-87), Internat. Soc. Refractive Surgery (bd. dirs. 1995-96). Avocation: tennis. Office: Corneal Cons of Colo 8381 Southpark Ln Littleton CO 80120-4508

FORSYTH, ELLIOTT CHRISTOPHER, French language educator; b. Mt. Gambier, Australia, Feb. 1, 1924; s. Samuel and Ida Muriel (Brummitt)F.; m. Rona Lynette Williams, May 29, 1967; children: Alison Wendy, Fiona Katharine. BA in French with honors, U. Adelaide, Australia, 1947, diploma in edn., 1950; doctorate, U. Paris, 1954. Tchr. French lang. The Friends' Sch., Hobart, Tasmania, Australia, 1947-49; from lectr. to sr. lectr. U. Adelaide, 1955-66; found. prof. French La Trobe U., Melbourne, Victoria, Australia, 1966-87, prof. emeritus, 1988—; vis. prof. U. Wis., Madison, 1963-65; vis. prof. U. Melbourne, 1992. Author: La Tragédie Française, 1962; editor: Jean de la Taille, 1968, Concordance des 'Tragiques' d' A. d'Aubigné, 1984; co-editor: Baudin in Australian Waters, 1988; contbr. articles on Agrippa d'Aubigné to profl. publs., 1979-88. Named Officier des Palmes Acad., French Govt., 1971, Comdr. des Palmes, 1983. Fellow Australian Acad. Humanities (v.p. 1973-74), Australian Coll. Edn. Mem. Uniting Ch. Australia. Avocations: photography, music. Home: 25 Jacka St, North Balwyn Victoria, Australia 3104

FORSYTH, KEVIN DOUGLAS, child health educator; b. Auckland, New Zealand, June 20, 1953; s. Douglas Gordon and Marion Pathenah (Young) F.; m. Johanna Hanff, Jan. 20, 1976; children: Karl, Jantina, Anton, Stefan. MB ChB, Otago U., 1977, MD, 1987; PhD, Flinders U., 1991. Lectr. U. London, 1987-89; dir. of immunology Childrens Hosp., Perth, Australia, 1990-92; prof., head child health Flinders U. of South Australia, 1993—; chair ednl. IT com. Flinders U. Sch. Medicine, 1998—; chmn. South Australian Immunisation Forum, 1993—; bd. dirs. Nat. Childhood Immunisation Com., Australia, 1995-97, Child Health Coun., South Australia, 1994-98, Ch ildrens Interests Bur., Australia, 1994—; chair Pediat. Interactive Edn. Consortium, Australia and New Zealand, 1995—, Pediat. Professorial Heads Com., Australia and New Zealand, 1996—, exec. mem. Internat. Pediatric Chairs Assoc., 1998—. Contbr. articles to profl. jours. Commonwealth Sr. fellowship British Coun., 1995, Commonwealth fellowship, 1987-89. Fellow Royal Australian Coll. of Physicians, Coll. of Australian Physician, Royal Coll. of Pathologists and Austrasian, Australian Coll. of Pathology. Baptist. Office: Flinders Med Ctr Dept Pediatrics, Bedford Park, Adelaide SA 5042, Australia

FORSYTHE, PATRICIA HAYS, development professional; b. Curtis, Ark.; d. John Chambers and Flora Jane (Eby) Hays; m. Kurt G. Pahl, Dec. 15, 1962 (div. Dec. 1980); children: Thomas Walter, Susan Clara; m. Robert E. Forsythe, June 20, 1981; 1 child, Nathaniel Ryan. BA, Calif. State U., Los Angeles, 1974; MSLS, U. So. Calif., 1976. Asst. to dir. devel. office The Assocs., Calif. Inst. Tech., Pasadena, 1978-81; exec. dir. Iowa City Pub. Library Found., 1982-89; dir. devel. Hoover Presdl. Libr. Assn., West Branch, Iowa, 1989-94, exec. dir., 1994—. Contbr. articles to profl. jours. Recipient Outstanding Fund Raising Exec. award Ea. Iowa, 1990, honorary Paul Harris fellow, 1994. Mem. ALA, LWV (editor 1985-87), Nat. Soc. Fund Raising Execs. (bd. dirs. 1987-89, chmn. Ea. Iowa Philanthropy Day 1990-91, bd. dirs. Ea. Iowa chpt. 1986-91), Assn. Am. Execs., Blacksmith Assn. N.Am., Iowa City C. of C., West Branch C. of C. (bd. dirs.), Iowa Life Shares Assn. (bd. dirs., pres. 1995-96), Libr. Adminstrn. and Mgmt. Assn., Johnson County Area Women's Network, Hancher Guild (audience devel. 1981-85, pres. 1985-86), Univ. Athletic Club, Rotary (program chair 1992-98, permanent fund chair 1999—). Congregationalist. Avocations: travel, writing, cooking, drama. Home: 1806 E Court St Iowa City IA 52245-4643 Office: Hoover Presdl Libr Assn PO Box 696 West Branch IA 52358-0696

FORSYTHE, RANDALL NEWMAN, paralegal, educator; b. Hammond, Ind., Mar. 24, 1959; s. Perry Newman and Elwanda (Cox) F.; children: Kenneth Newman, Keith Randall. AA in Law Enforcement, Calumet Coll., Whiting, Ind., 1979, BA in Criminal Justice magna cum laude, 1982, BS in Mgmt. magna cum laude, 1982; Lawyer's Asst. Cert., Roosevelt U., Chgo., 1986. Labor leader/painter Inland Steel Co., East Chicago, Ind., 1978-86; ins. and securities rep. Primerica, Portage, Ind., 1984-91; paralegal Katz, Brenman & Angel, Merrillville, Ind., 1987-91, Komyatte & Freeland, P.C., Highland, Ind., 1991—; coord. paralegal divsn. Sawyer Coll., Merrillville, 1989-92, paralegal instr., 1989—; ct. apptd. spl. advocate Juvenile divsn. Lake County Superior Ct., Gary, Ind., 1987—. Manuscript/book reviewer West Pub. Co., St. Paul, 1991—. Parliamentarian Orchard Dr. Bapt. Ch., Hammond, Ind., 1981-91. Mem. Assn. Trial Lawyers Am., Nat. Assn. Legal Assts., Ind. Legal Assts. (Ind. Legal Asst. of Yr. 1990, liaison to nat. orgn. 1989-92, 97). Avocations: coaching children's Little League baseball, basketball, football teams, adult softball, hunting, fishing, camping. Office: Komyatte & Freeland PC 9650 Gordon Dr Highland IN 46322-2909

FORSYTHE, VELMA BROWN, accountant, consultant, English language educator; b. California, Pa., Apr. 27, 1928; d. Ernest and Anne Leyland Brown; m. Forrest Evans Forsythe, Aug. 6, 1950 (dec. Oct. 1982); children: Leslie Ann, Lynn Allyson. BS in Bus. Edn., Ind. (Pa.) U., 1950; student various univs. and colls., Pa. and Wis., 1952-96. High sch. tchr. bus. edn. Pa. and Ohio, 1954-58; v.p., tax preparer Kincaid Tax Svc., Akron, Ohio, 1968-74; pub. acct. Pitts. and Akron, 1974-82; controller Holiday Inn, Dubois, Pa., 1982-86; asst. controller Radisson Hotel, Lexington, Ky., 1986-87; asst. to pres. Petroleum Inc.-Jadel Inc., Clearfield, Pa., 1987-88; acct., cons. Forsythe Bus. Svcs., Dubois, 1982—; tchr. ELI Ulaanbartar, Mongolia, 1999—. Vol. Internat. Exec. Svc. Corps., Egypt, Ghana, Slovak Republic, Stanford, Conn., 1992—; lay missionary fin. and edn. United Meth. Ch. Uganda, Mozambique, 1991—; missionary amb. to Indonesia, 1998; vol. exec. Citizens Democracy Corps, Republic of Georgia, Spring, 2000, Russia, Summer 2000. Mem. AAUW (program chair 1997-99, Woman of Yr. award 1998), Kappa Delta Pi, Delta Sigma Epsilon. Republican. Methodist. Avocations: travel, reading, hiking, canoeing. Home and Office: 717 Treasure Lk Du Bois PA 15801-9019

FORT, ARTHUR TOMLINSON, III, physician, educator; b. Lumpkin, Ga., Sept. 24, 1931; s. Thomas Morton and Gladys (Davis) F.; m. Jane Wilmer McClelland, June 15, 1957; children: Abby Lucinda, Arthur Tomlinson IV, Juliana Melody, Ernest Arlington, II. BBA, U. Ga., 1952; MD, U. Tenn., 1962. Diplomate: Am. Bd. Ob-Gyn, Am. Bd. Family Practice. Intern, then resident in ob-gyn U. Tenn.-City of Memphis Hosp., 1962-66; asst. prof. U. Tenn. Med. Sch., 1966-70; prof. ob-gyn, head dept. Sch. Medicine La. State U., Shreveport, 1970-73; prof. maternal-child health and family planning, head program family health Sch. Pub. Health Tulane U., 1973-74; practice medicine specializing in rural family medicine Vacharie, La., 1974-79; prof. ob-gyn and family medicine, head dept. family medicine and comprehensive care Sch. Medicine La. State U., Shreveport, 1980—. Author articles in field. Adv. bd. mem. State of La. Dept. Health and Human Resources, 1986-88. With USAF, 1952-57. Recipient Golden Apple Teaching award Student AMA, 1969, Golden Apple Teaching award Western Interstate Commn. on Higher Edn., 1973. Fellow Am. Coll. Ob-Gyn, Am. Acad. Family Practice; mem. AMA. Office: PO Box 33932 Shreveport LA 71130-3932

FORT, IVAN, chemical engineer, researcher; b. Praha, Czech Republic, May 28, 1938; s. Jan and Marie (Slavikova) F.; m. Edita Pesanova, Nov. 26, 1962; children: Pavla, Petr. DiplIng, Inst. Chem. Tech., Praha, 1961, PhD, 1966; DSc, Czech Tech. U., Praha, 1990. Asst. prof. Inst. Chem. Tech., Praha, 1961-86; rsch. worker Czech Tech. U., Praha, 1986-90, prof. chem. engring., 1990—. Leading rsch. worker. Grantee NSF, 1990; European Union, 1993, 98, Czeck Grant Agy., 1993, 96, 98, NATO, 1998. Fellow Czech Soc. Chem. Engrs.; mem. European Fedn. Chem. Engring. (sci. sec. 1978—), Prague Inst. Chem. Tech. (sci. com. 1990—). Mem. Civic Dem. Party. Avocations: jogging, classic music, farming. Office: Czech Tech U, Technicka 4, 16607 Prague Czech Republic

FORT, ROBERT BRADLEY, minister; b. Portsmouth, Va., Dec. 27, 1948; s. Richard Gould and Hazel Naomi (McBride) F.; m. Esther Faith Hardin, June 10, 1967; children: Yvonne René, Nathan Michael. Ordained to ministry United Evang. Ch., 1973. Evangelist United Evang. Chs., Monrovia, Calif., 1966, nat. youth dir., 1968-70, asst. to the pres., 1970-73, Calif. dist. supt., 1973-75; evangelist Assemblies of God, Springfield, Mo., 1976-78; sr. pastor Lynden (Wash.) Assembly of God, 1978-81, County Christian Ctr., Bellingham, Wash., 1981-87, First Assembly of God, Salinas, Calif., 1988—; exec. dir. Life Mgmt. Sems., Salinas, 1989—; pres. Fort Ministries, Salinas, 1967—; exec. v.p., chmn. bd., CEO United Evang. Chs., Hollister, Calif., 1996—; plenary spkr. World Congress Evang. Chs., Nairobi, Kenya, Africa, 1993. Composer Love was the Color, 1980 (Grand prize Music City Songfest, Nashville, 1981); singer, musician 15 records. Chmn. resolutions com. NorCal/Nev. Dist. of the Assemblies of God, 1997-2000. Republican. Office: Fort Ministries PO Box 1000 San Juan Bautista CA 95045-1000

FORTE, LORD CHARLES (BARON FORTE), hotel and catering company executive; b. Nov. 26, 1908; m. Irene Mary Chierico, 1943; 6 children. Ed. Alloa Acad., Dumfries Coll., Mamiani, Rome. Dep. chmn. Trust House Forte PLC, 1970-78, chief exec., 1971-78, exec. chmn., 1978-81, chmn., 1982-92, pres. 1992-96; mem. consultative adv. com. to Ministry Food, 1946; mem. London Tourist Bd.; pres. Italian C. of C. for Gt. Britain, 1952-78, Westminster C. of C., 1983-86; contbr. articles to catering trade papers. Decorated grand officier Ordine al Merito dell Repubblica Italiana, cavaliere di Gran Croce della Repubblica Italiana; decorated knight, 1970. Fellow Catering Inst. (exec. com.), Brit. Inst. Mgmt., Royal Soc. Arts. Clubs: Carlton, Caledonian.

FORTÉ, DEBRA BROOKS, municipal government official; b. Lake Charles, La., Aug. 14, 1957; d. Richard L. and Bess (Rollins) Brooks; m. Terry L. Cole, Aug. 14, 1977 (div. 1987); 1 child, Brooklyn MacKenna; m. James D. Forté, June 4, 1987. BS in Acctg., McNeese State U., 1978; MPA, U. North Tex., 1989. Acctg. supr. City of Lake Charles, La., 1978-83; finance officer City of La Porte, Tex., 1983-85; dir. of finance City of McKinney, Tex., 1985-90; fiscal and human resources dir. City of Euless, Tex., 1990-95; asst. city mgr. City of Lubbock, Tex., 1995-97, 1st asst. city mgr., 1997—; chair pub. adminstrn. alumni adv. bd. U. North Tex., Denton, 1993-97; adj. prof. MPA program DBU, 1993. Co-author: Texas Municipal Clerks Certification, 1993; contbr. articles to profl. jours. Chair edn. com. Susan G. Komen Breast Cancer Found., Lubbock, 1995—, Leadership Tex. class, 1997. Named MPA Program Alumna of Yr., U. North Tex., 1993; LBJ Sch. Pub. Affairs schoalr, 1992. Mem. Govt. Fin. Officers Assn. (prs. 1991, exec. bd. U.S. and Can. 1994-97, Outstanding Fin. Officer 1989, award of Excellence 1988, 90), Tex. Mcpl. League, Internat. City/County Mgmt. Assn., Tex. City Mgmt. Assn. (fundraising com.). Avocations: running, scuba diving, skiing, family travel. Home: 6808 Nashville Ave Lubbock TX 79413-6032 Office: City of Lubbock 1625 13th St Lubbock TX 79401-3830

FORTELNY, IVAN, polymer physicist; b. Třebíč, Czech Republic, Nov. 13, 1946; s. Antonín and Zdenka (Stejskalová) F. MSc, Masaryk U., Brno, Czech Republic, 1970; PhD, Charles U., Prague, Czech Republic, 1974. Asst. Inst. Macromolecular Chemistry, Acad. Sci. Czech Republic, Prague, 1970-74, rsch. fellow, 1974-82, sr. rsch. fellow, 1982-95; chief rsch. fellow, 1995—. Contbr. articles and revs. to sci. jours. Avocation: hiking. Home: Myslikova 5, 11000 Praha 1, Czech Republic Office: Inst Macromol Chem Acad Sci, Heyrovského n2, 16206 Prague 6, Czech Republic

FORTENBAUGH, SAMUEL BYROD, III, lawyer; b. Phila., Nov. 6, 1933; s. Samuel Byrod Jr. and Katherine Francisca (Wall) F.; children: Samuel Byrod IV, Cristina Fortenbaugh Alemany, Katherine Dooley, Francesca Cowden. BA, Williams Coll., 1955; LLB, Harvard U., 1960. Bar: N.Y. 1961, U.S. Dist. Ct. (so. dist.) N.Y. 1961. Assoc. Kelley Drye & Warren, N.Y.C., 1960-69, ptnr., 1970-79; ptnr. Morgan, Lewis & Bockius, N.Y.C., 1980—; bd. dirs. Baldwin Tech. Co., Inc., Norwalk, Conn., Goodman Equipment Corp., Chgo.; bd. dirs., sec. Furgueson Capital Mgmt. Inc., N.Y.C.; chmn. bd. dirs., sec. Wall Industries, Inc., Kannapolis, N.C.; chmn. bd. dirs. Knight Textile Corp, Saluda, S.C.; trustee Patroni Scholastici, New Brunswick, N.J., 1978—, sec. 1985—; lectr. profl. seminars. Contbr. articles to profl. jours. Mem. ABA, Assn. of Bar of City of N.Y. (mem. Young Lawyers com. 1962-65, corp. law com. 1976-79, com. on securities regulation 1982-85, chmn. com. on issue distbn. of securities 1984-85), Racquet and Tennis Club, N.Y. Yacht Club, Bay Head (N.J.) Yacht Club, Indian Harbor Yacht Club (Greenwich, Conn.), Phi Beta Kappa. Office: Morgan Lewis & Bockius LLP 101 Park Ave Fl 45 New York NY 10178-0002

FORTEY, RICHARD ALAN, paleontologist; b. London, Feb. 15, 1946; s. Frank and Margaret Zander (Wilshin) F.; m. Bridget Elizabeth Thomas, Sept. 12, 1968 (div. 1975); 1 child, Dominic; m. Jacqueline Francis, June 25, 1977; children: Rebecca, Julia, Leo. BA, Cambridge U., Eng., 1968, MA, 1971, PhD, 1971, DSc, 1985. Rsch. fellow Natural History Mus., London, 1970-73, sr. sci. officer, 1973-77, prin. sci. officer, 1978-86, sr. prin. sci. officer, 1986-91, individual merit promotion, 1991—; Howley vis. prof. Meml. U., Nfld., 1977-78; vis. prof. paleobiology Oxford U., 2000—. Author: Fossils: The Key to the Past, 1982, The Hidden Landscape, 1993 (Natural World Book of Yr. award 1993), Life: An Unauthorized Biography, 1997. Fellow Linnean Soc. London, Geol. Soc. London (pres. 1994-96, Lyell medal 1996), The Royal Soc. Mem. Labour party. Avocations: mushrooms, writing humor. Office: The Natural History Mus, Cromwell Rd, SW7 5BD London England

FORTEZA, BARTOMEU, philosophy educator; b. Felanitx, Baleares, Spain, June 17, 1939; s. Bartomeu Forteza and Elisa Pujol; m. Ma Dolores González, Jan. 22, 1977; children: Ricardo, Maria, B. Israel. Licentiate philosophy, Gregorian U., Rome, 1977, U. Barcelona, Spain, 1978; PhD, U. Barcelona, 1993. Tchr. H.S. Boscan, Barcelona, 1978-81, H.S. Cardedeu, Spain, 1981-82, H.S. CanTunis, Barcelona, 1982-86, H.S. Les Marine, Castelldefels, Spain, 1986-95; mem. rsch. group U. Barcelona, 1995—; prof. Ramon Llull U., Barcelona, 1999-2000; mem. Inst. Sci. Edn., U. Autónoma, Barcelona, 1982-88; head master H.S. Les Marines, Castelldefels, 1992-94; prof. philosophy and enterprise U. Barcelona, 1997-98; course mgr. Fund Bosch Gimpena, Barcelona, 1998-99. Author: Objectivity in the Linguistic Philosophy of Thomas Hobbes, 1999; translator, editor: Thomas Hobbes: Liberty and Necessity, 1991, The Hobbes: El Cuerpo, 2000; contbr. articles to profl. jours. Mem. Catalan Soc. Philosophy, N.Y. Acad. Scis. E-mail: bfortesa@pie.xtec.es. Home: c/ Camp 14, 08021 Barcelona Spain

FORTI, LENORE STEIMLE, business consultant; b. Houghton, Mich., Sept. 9, 1924; d. Russell Nicholas and Agnes (McCloskey) Steimle; m. Frank Forti, May 29, 1950 (dec.). BBA summa cum laude, Northwood U., 1973, Dr.Laws, 1969. Asst. corp. sec., purchasing agt. Fed. Life & Casualty Co., Detroit, 1942-53; supr. sectl. J.L. Hudson Co., Detroit, 1953-57, adminstrv. asst. to exec. v.p., 1957-86; instr. Wayne State U. and U. Mich. Adult Edn., Detroit, 1958-71; creator, dir. Seminars for Profl. People, 1971—. Co-author: The Professional Secretary; contbr. articles to profl. jours. Asst. bus. dir. planning City of Detroit for Civil Def.; chmn. bd. trustees PSI Rsch. and

Ednl. Found.; trustee PSI Retirement Home Complex, Albuquerque; elected dir. Property Owners and Residents Assn., Sun City West Mcpl. Govt., 1994-97; past pres. Women's Bd. Northwood U., Midland, Mich.; pres. parish coun. Our Lady of Lourdes Ch., Sun City West, Ariz., 1988, pres. ladies guild, 1990, pres. singles club, 1995; 1st v.p. Vol. Bur. of Sun Cities, 1989; bd. dirs. Sun City West Cmty. Fund, 1998-99; bd. dirs., 2d v.p. Sun City West Found., 1998—. Elected One of Detroit's Top Ten Working Women, 1969; elected to Exec. and Profl. Hall of Fame. Mem. Internat. Assn. Adminstrv. Profls. (internat. pres. 1967-69), Future Secs. Assn. (nat. coord.), Lioness Club (pres. 1991-92), Sun City West Singles Club (pres. 1988). Republican. Roman Catholic. Avocations: golf, bridge, Mah Jongg, line dancing. Home and Office: 12613 W Seneca Dr Sun City West AZ 85375-4635

FORTI, WILLIAM BELL, business executive, inventor; b. Washington, Dec. 6, 1941; s. Francis and Margaret Lee (Bell) F.; m. Martha Louise Goding; children: Scott, Jennifer, Meredith, Kimberly, Mark, Andrea. BS, U. Richmond, 1963, MComm., 1964. Fin. analyst SEC, Washington, 1964-66; economist Joint tax, House judiciary, Senate commerce coms. U.S. Congress, Washington, 1966-71; from sr. staff exec. to exec. v.p. Bendix Corp., Southfield, Mich., 1971-75; mgr. bus. devel. projects Internat. Paper Co., N.Y.C., 1975-78; dir. planning, bus. devel. positions Gen. Dynamics, St. Louis, Md., 1978-92; founder, chmn. William Mark Corp., Claremont, Calif., 1992—. Patentee for flying sports products. Mem. World Affairs Coun., L.A., 1997; co-chmn. L.A. County Aerospace Task Force, L.A., 1999; participant current strategy forum Naval War Coll., R.I., 2000, nat. security forum Air War Coll., Maxwell AFB, Ala., 1997. Recipient Recognition of Dedicated Svc. County of L.A., 1992, Recognition of Contribution Naval War Coll. Found., 1997, Joint Civilian Orientation Conf., 1999. Mem. NSTA, Def. Orientation Conf. Assn. (bd. dirs. 1999—), Claremont U. Club (asst. treas. 1994—), Radio Controlled Hobby Trade Assn., Kite Trade Assn., Claremont C. of C., Rotary. Republican. Avocations: travel, reading, hiking, golf, skiing. Office: William Mark Corp 112 Harvard Ave Claremont CA 91711-4716

FORTIER, JEAN-MARIE, retired archbishop; b. Que., Can., July 1, 1920; s. Joseph and Alberta (Jobin) F. Student, Grand Sem. Que., 1940-45; L.Th., Laval U., Que., 1945; postgrad., U. Louvain, Belgium, 1946-48; Licentiate in Ch. History, Gregorian U., Rome, 1950. Ordained priest Roman Catholic Ch., 1944; sec. to bishop of Hearst, Ont., Can., 1945-46; tchr. ch. history Grand Sem. Que., 1950-60; consecrated bishop Ste. Anne de la Pocatiere, Que., 1961-65, Gaspe, Que., 1965-68; archbishop Sherbrooke, Que., 1968-96, archbishop emeritus, 1996—; mem. Congregation for Sacraments and Divine Cult, 1975-84; v.p. Can. Cath. Conf., 1971-73, pres., 1973-75; pres. Comité Episcopal des Communications Sociales, 1976-84; v.p. l'Assemblee des Evêques du Quebec, 1981-85, pres., 1985-89. Mem. Knights Holy Sepulchre of Jerusalem, Assn. Eveques de Que. (pres. 1985-89), Assn. des Chevaliers de Colomb de Que., Filles d'Isabelle. Address: 2 rue Port Dauphin CP 459, Quebec, PQ Canada G1R 4R6

FORTIER, L. YVES, barrister; b. Quebec City, Que., Can., Sept. 11, 1935; s. Francois and Louise (Turgeon) F.; m. C. Carol Eaton, Sept. 26, 1959; children: Michel, Suzanne, Margot. BA summa cum laude, U. Montreal, 1955; BCL, McGill U., 1958; BLitt, Oxford U., 1960, LLD (hon.), 1989, 92, 93, 99. Created Queen's counsel, 1976. Sr. ptnr., chmn. Ogilvy, Renault Advs., Barristers and Solicitors, Montreal, 1960—, on leave; Can. amb. to UN N.Y.C., 1988-92; counsel for Can. in Can.-USA, Gulf Maine Case in World Ct., 1984, Royal Commns., Commn. Inquiry War Criminals, Commn. Inquiry Lang. Air Traffic Control, Commn. Inquiry R.C.M.P.; mem. Permanent Ct. Arbitration The Hague, 1984-89; pres. London Ct. Internat. Arbitration, 1998—; chief negotiator Can.-France fishing dispute, 1987-89, Can.-U.S. Pacific Salmon Treaty dispute, 1993-98; Can.'s chief del. to 43d, 44th, 45th, 46th sessions of UN Gen. Assembly, Can. rep. UN Security Coun., 1989-90; v.p. UN 45th Gen. Assembly; gov. Hudson's Bay Co.; bd. dirs. Royal Bank Can., Nortel Networks Corp., Nova Chems. Corp., duPont Can. Inc., Southam Inc. Bd. dirs. Can. Inst. Advanced Legal Studies, Internat. Peace Acad., UN Internat. Sch., Montreal Gen. Hosp. C.D. Howe Inst., Clin. Rsch. Inst., Can. Found. for AIDS Rsch. Decorated officer and companion Order of Can.; Rhodes scholar, 1960. Mem. ABA (hon.), Can. Bar Assn. (pres. 1982-83, founding dir. Law for Future Fund), Internat. Commn. Jurists (Can. sect.), Internat. Law Assn. (Can. br.), Am. Coll. Trial Lawyers (regent 1991-95), Internat. Assn. Permanent Reps. to UN (exec. bd.), Mount Royal Club, Univ. Club, Montreal Indoor Tennis Club, Hermitage Country Club, The Brook Club (N.Y.). Roman Catholic. Avocations: tennis, squash, skiing, golf. Home: 19 Rosemount Ave, Westmount, PQ Canada

FORTIER, QUINCY ERNEST, retired obstetrician, gynecologist; b. Auburn, Mass., Sept. 16, 1912; s. Edgar Quincy and Nina (Chase) F.; children: Carlene, Renee, Kathleen, Annette, Quincy, Dana, Sonia, Nannette. BS, U. S.D., 1941; MB, U. Minn., 1944, MD, 1945. Diplomate Am. Bd. Ob-Gyn. Intern Wichita Falls (Tex.) Clinic Hosp., 1945; surgeon Combined Metals Reductions Co., Pioche, Nev., 1945-50; teaching fellow dept. ob-gyn U. Minn., Mpls., 1951-55; commd. capt. USAF, 1958, advanced through grades to col.; chief ob-gyn. Ramey AFB, P.R., 1955-59; comdr. 468th Med. Svcs. Flight, Nellis AFB Hosp., Las Vegas, 1960-72; ret. USAF, 1972; adj. clin. prof. ob-gyn U. Nev. Med. Sch., Las Vegas and Reno, 1984—, resident ob-gyn, 1955-57; assoc. emeritus prof. of ob-gyn U. Nevada Medical Sch., 1994; owner, chief physician Women's Hosp., Las Vegas, 1958-70; emeritus asst. prof. Ob-Gyn U. Nev. Med. Sch., 1995, ret.; owner hosp., Pioche, 1945-50, univ. physician, instr. hygiene U. Nev., Reno, 1950-51; adj. clin. prof. ob.-gyn. U. Nev. Med. Sch., Reno, 1982—. Trustee So. Nev. Meml. Hosp., Las Vegas, 1960-62; candidate Nev. Legislature, 1962; fund raiser, donor of sch. bldg. and property Luth. Jr. and Sr. High Schs., Las Vegas. Fellow Am. Coll. Ob-Gyn; mem. AMA, VFW, Am. Fertility Soc., Pacific Coast Fertility Soc., Res. Officers Assn., Armed Forces Med. Soc., Aerospace Med. Assn., Nev. State Med. Assn. (Dr. of Yr. 1991), Clark County Med. Assn., Masons, Shriners. Republican. Episcopalian. Home and Office: 1431 Wengert Ave Las Vegas NV 89104-3351

FORTINA, ANTONIO FORMIA, orthopedic surgeon; b. Novara, Italy, July 29, 1952; s. Mario Boschi and Renata Vittonatto (Formia) F.; m. Michela Pesce Genta, June 3, 1978; children: Elisabetta, Giorgio. MD, U. Torino, Italy, 1977, degree in orthopedics, 1981, degree in physiotherapy, 1984. Prof. orthopedic diseases Regional Sch. Physiotherapy, Novara, 1988-89, 91-92, 94-95; asst. orthopedist Hosp. Novara, 1978-88, sub-chief orthopedics dept., 1989-95; in charge Integrated Orthopedic Activities Orgn., 1995-2000; prof. orthopedic diseases U. Ea. Piedmont, 1998-2000; in charge outpatient dept. orthopedic diseases ASL Novara, 2000—; tutor U. Torino, 1996-98, U. Ea. Piedmont, 1998—; lectr. in field; prof. orthopedic diseases U. Novara, 1998-99. Contbr. to numerous sci. revs. and publs. including Encyclopedia Medica Italiana, 1987—. Chief med. staff Iris Oleggio Football Club, 1982-95. Recipient medal Nobile Collegio Caccia, 1977. Mem. Italian Soc. Orthopedics and Traumatology, Italian Soc. Phys. and Rehab. Medicine, Italian Soc. Sport Traumatology, Italian Soc. Medicine and Surgery Foot, Fedn. Medico-Sportiva Italiana, Club Italiano Chirugia del Ginocchio. Roman Catholic. Avocations: cycling, history. Home: Viale Pasquali 15, 28100 Novara Italy

FORTINA, FABIO, entrepreneur; b. Varese, Italy, May 11, 1957; arrived in Austria, 1996; s. Piero Fortina and Linda Piantanida; m. Christin Rauch, Jan. 17, 1995; 1 child, Nathalie. BS, Salzburg U., Austria, 1980; MBA, NYU, 1989. Promotion dir. RJR Nabisco Europe, Geneva, Switzerland, 1984-91; divsn. gen. mgr. Estée Lauder, Milan, 1991-93; mng. dir. Pomellato, Milan, 1993-95, RAMS, Innsbruck, Austria, 1995—; cons. Olympic Games, 1992, 94, 98. Lt. Italian Armed Forces, 1980. Recipient cert. of appreciation Order of the Sons of Italy in Am., 1983. Home: Karl Kapferer Str, 6020 Innsbruck Austria

FORTNER, ROSANNE WHITE, environmental science educator; b. Logan, W.Va., Nov. 13, 1945; d. William Edward and Annabel (Blevins) White; m. Richard Donald Fortner, Aug. 20, 1966; children: Christopher Neil, Craig Michael. BA, W.Va. U., 1967; MA, Oreg. State U., 1973; EdD, Va. Poly. Inst. and State U., 1978. Curriculum developer NSTA, Washington; curriculum cons. U.S. Nat. Park Svc., Washington; edn. coord. Ohio Sea Grant Coll. Program, Columbus; prof. natural resources Ohio State U., Columbus; assoc. dir. F.T. Stone Lab., Put-in-Bay, Ohio; dir. Earth Sys. Edn. Program, Columbus, Ohio. Author: (with Mayer) The Great Lake Erie; author, editor nine vols. curriculum activities for Earth Sys. Edn.; editor: Proceedings of 2d Internat. Conf. on Geosci. Edn.; exec. editor Science Activities; contbr. numerous articles on edn. and communication to profl. jours. Recipient Rsch. award N. Am. Assn. for Environ. Edn., 1992, Disting. Alumni award Va. Poly. Inst. and State U., 1989; Ohio Sea grantee, 1981-2000, grantee Nat. Estuarine Sanctuary, George Gund Found., Ohio Bd. Regents, Spencer Found., Great Lakes Protection Fund, NSF; named 1st Edn. Liaison Nat. Oceanic and Atmospheric Adminstrn. Fellow AAAS Edn. Secretary; mem. Nat. Marine Educators Assn. (pres.), Coalition Earth Sci. Edn. (bd. dirs.), N.Am. Assn. Environ. Edn. (bd. dirs.), Ohio Acad. Sci. (v.p.).

FORTNEY, THOMAS KENT, cost and petroleum engineer, management consultant; b. Douglas, Ariz., June 22, 1947; s. Thomas Hayes Fortney and Edna (Cosper) Randall. BA, No. Ariz. U., 1970, MA, 1973; M Internat. Mgmt., Am. Grad. Sch. Internat. Mgmt., Glendale, Ariz., 1980; BS in Petroleum Engring., U. Okla., 1990; attended, Heriot-Watt Univ., Edinburgh, Scotland. Cert. cost engr. Internat. Cost Engring. Coun. Mgmt. cons. Lorer and Assocs., Orange, Calif., 1981-84; cons. to Stockmar Corp., Fortney Cons., Long Beach, Calif., 1984-85; prodn. analyst E.F. Brady Constrn., L.A., 1985-87; cons. Santa Fe Drilling, London, 1990-91; mgmt. and engring. cons. Fortney Cons., Flagstaff, Ariz., 1990-91; oil well fire fighter and driller Santa Fe Drilling, Kuwait, 1991-92; cost and mgmt. cons. Fortney Cons., Mesa, Ariz., 1992-96; cons. Santa Fe North Sea Brit. Gas, Shell Oil, Brit. Petroleum, 1996; inventory control supr. Sphere Supply, Houston, 1997—; project engr. Modec, USA, Houston, 1997; wellsite supr. OGCI, Houston, 1997; tech. engr. Geodiamond, Smith Internat., Houston, 1998; project controls engr./chevron LL652 Kvaertner Cons., Houston, 1999—; cons exec. v.p. Santa Fe Drilling, 2000—; advisor Western Leisure Travel, Salt Lake City; drilling cons. Nigus Corp., Lagos, Nigeria, 1990; cons. Santa Fe-North Sea in Cost Eng., Drilling Eng., Organizational Behavior, Aberdeen, Scotland, 1996, 99; turnkey estimator, Santa Fe, Venezuela. Vol. St. Vincent DePaul Shelters, World Vision Internat. Mem. Am. Assn. Cost Engrs. (cert., bd. dirs. Gulfcoast chpt.), Soc. Petroleum Engrs., Profl. Mgmt. Inst. Democrat. Baptist. Avocations: model ship building, computers, weight lifting. Home: 8455 Will Clayton Pkwy Apt 207 Humble TX 77338-5803

FORTOV, VLADIMIR E., physicist, researcher; b. Noginsk, Moscow Region, Russia, Jan. 23, 1946; s. Eugeny and Galina (Muha) F.; m. Tatjana Fortova, Jan. 28, 1967; 1 child, Svetlana. BSEE, Moscow Inst. Physics & Tech., 1968, PhD, 1971. Researcher, chief of labs. Inst. Chem. Physics USSR Acad. Scis, Chernogolovka, 1971—, Inst. High Temps. USSR Acad. Scis., Moscow, 1988-90; dir. High Energy Density Rsch. Ctr., Moscow, 1990—; min. sci and tech Govt. Russia, Moscow, 1996-98. Author: Physics of Nonideal Plasma, 1990, Material Dynamics at Intense Impulse Loading, 1992. Chmn. Russian Fund Basic Rsch., Moscow, 1993-97; v.p. Russia Acad. Sci., 1999—. Recipient USSR State award for Physics & Math., USSR Gov., 1986, USSR Red Bunnet orden, 1987, Merit for Fatherland, 1997, Bridgman award, 1999. Mem. Russian Acad. Sci., Internat. Unit of High Pressure Rsch. (v.p. 1993—), N.Y. Acad. Scis., Am. Phys. Soc., European Acad. Sci., Internat. Planetary Soc. Avocations: skiing, sailing. Office: Inst Problems Chem Physics RAS, Chernogolovka, Moscow 142432, Russia

FORTSON, LAURA ROGERS, educational consultant; b. Demorest, Ga., Sept. 15, 1915; d. Jonathan Clark and Mary Floyd (Blackshear) Rogers; m. Edwin B. Fortson, Jan. 23, 1943; children: Mary Lillian, Edwin Jr., Clark. BFA, U. Ga., 1936, MA in Art Edn., 1958, EdD in Early Childhood Edn., 1969. Cert. elem. edn. Dir. Children's Studio for the Creative Arts, Athens, Ga.; kindergarten project dir. U. Ga. R & D Ctr., Athens, 1966-69; primary tchr. Clarke County Sch. Dist., Athens, 1975-83; cons. on kindergarten and primary edn./program devel., 1983—, tchr. coll. courses in early childhood edn., 1983—, also in-svc. tchg. tng. Sr. co-author: Early Childhood Curriculum: Open Structures for Integrative Learning, 1995; contbr. chpts. to textbooks and articles to profl. jours. Named for Excellence in Contbn. to Arts Edn. Mem. Assn. Childhood Edn. Internat., Nat. Assn. Edn. Young Children, Nat. Coun. Tchrs. English, Internat. Reading Assn., Delta Kappa Gamma. Home and Office: 310 Milledge Hts Athens GA 30606-4930

FORTUNATO, JOSE MANUAL CARDOSO, marketing executive; b. Porto, Portugal, Oct. 16, 1968; s. Jose Manual and Helena (Cimaral) F.; m. Mafalda Duarte Carvatho, Oct. 1999. Grad in econs., FEP, Porto, 1991; MBA, INSEAD, 1993. Analyst CISF-BCP, Porto, 1991-93; mgr. Sonae Comercio Svcs., Porto, 1994-96; mktg. mgr. Banco Espirito Santo, Lisboa, 1996-99, Modelo Continente, Porto, 1999—. Avocation: sports. Office: Sonae Comercio Svcs, Rua Joao Mendonca 529 6, 4460 Senhora da Hora Portugal

FORTUNATO, MARIO DAVID CARDOSO, scientific researcher; b. Porto, Portugal, Apr. 12, 1970; s. Jose Soares and Helena Manuela (Cardoso) F. Rschr. Fac. Medicina, Porto, Portugal, 1992-93; technician I.P.O., Porto, Portugal, 1993-94; rschr. Fac. Medicina, Porto, Portugal, 1994-99. Home: Rua Do Campo Alegre, 4150 Porto Portugal Office: Servico Fisiologia, Alameda Hernani Monteiro, 4200 Porto Portugal

FORTUNE, ANNE E., social worker, educator; b. New Haven, June 27, 1945; d. Mark and Mary (Sutherland) F. Student, Am. Coll. in Paris, 1963-64; BA, U. Chgo., 1970, MA in Social Work, 1975, PhD, 1978. Action rsch. coord., rsch. asst. Woodlawn Exptl. Schs. Project, Chgo., 1968-71; tester Woodlawn Mental Health Ctr., Chgo., 1969; rsch. assoc. Looking Glass, vol. runaway ctr. Travelers Aids Soc. Metro. Chgo., 1971-73; rsch. asst. Ctr. Study of Welfare Policy U. Chgo., 1973-74, rsch. asst. Social Svcs. Fall-Outs Project, 1974-75, rsch. assoc., clin. supr. Task-Centered Treatment Project, 1974-77; asst. prof. George Warren Brown Sch. Social Work Washington U., St. Louis, 1977-82; assoc. prof. Sch. Social Work Va. Commonwealth U., Richmond, 1982-89; from assoc. prof. to prof. Sch. Social Welfare SUNY, Albany, 1989—. Co-author: Research in Social Work, 1999, Teaching Research: An Instructor's Manual for Research in Social Work, 1999; editor: Task-Centered Practice with Families and Groups, 1985; co-editor: Multicultural Issues in Social Work, vol. II, 1998; contbr. numerous articles to profl. jours., chpts. to books. Mem. NASW (comms. com. 1997—), Coun. Social Work Edn., Acad. Cert. Social Workers, Soc. for Social Work and Rsch. E-mail: rfortune@albany.edu. Office: Sch Social Work Suny Albany Albany NY 12222-0001

FORTUNE, HUBERT HOLMES, business owner; b. Edinburgh, Midlothian, Scotland, July 20, 1951; s. Hubert Hildebrand and Elizabeth McCann (Holmes) F. BEd, Edinburgh U., 1975. Tchr. geography Lothian Region Dept. Edn., Edinburgh, 1975-77, 1979-81, 84-88, prin. tchr. geography, 1988-92; prin. tchr. geography St. Mary H.S., Highgate, Jamaica, W.I., 1977-79; edn. officer UNICEF U.K. com. UN, Edinburgh, 1981-84; bus. owner Mr. H.H. Fortune, Edinburgh, 1992—. Author: (booklet) Many Cultures Together, 1982-83. Chmn. opening/closing ceremonies Internat. Youth Yr., Edinburgh Gathering, 1983-84; chmn. Japan Edn. Group for Lothian Region, 1983-84; helper/advisor Cmty. Rels. Coun., Edinburgh, 1973-75; v.p., treas. Moray House Students Rep. Coun., Edinburgh, 1973-75. Recipient Annabella G. Clark prize Moray House Coll. Edn., 1975. Mem. Scottish Episcopal Ch. Avocations: travel, classical music and opera, rugby, antiques, paintings.

FORTUNOV, VALENTIN IVANOV, publishing company executive, journalist; b. Bourgas, Bulgaria, Aug. 15, 1957; s. Ivan Stoyanov and Zlata Peneva (Dobreva) F.; m. Diana Slavtcheva Vasileva, Dec. 15, 1984; children: Ivan, Zlatena, Alexander. M, Sofia (Bulgaria) U., 1985. Ind. journalist Sofia, 1978-84; corr. Mladej, dayly, Sofia, 1984-89; dir. Dolphin Press Pubs., Bourgas, 1990-94; chmn. Dolphin Press Group, Bourgas, 1994—. Gen. editor: International Dictionary of Finance, 1991, International Dictionary of Management, 2 vols., 1992, International Dictionary of Law and Commerce, 10 vols., 1993, International Dictionary of Banking and Insurance, 3 vols., 1994, Internat. Dictionary of Marketing and Advertising, 2 vols., 1997, Econ. Ency. Grand Delfina, 1999; web host Grand Delfina On-Line, 2000. Mem. Golden Dolphin Club (pres. 1997—). Christian. Avocations: motoring, gardening. Office: Dolphin Press Group, 19 Christo Botev St, 8000 Bourgas POB 296, Bulgaria

FOSCHI, PIER LUIGI, cruise company executive; b. Milan, Italy, Sept. 25, 1946; s. Ubaldo and Ester (Dominici) F.; m. Liliana Vercesi, Feb. 22, 1969; children: Massimo, Lorenzo. Degree in fin. and acctg., Tech. Inst., Milan, 1969. Computer programmer PTT (SIP), Milan, 1964-70; orgn. and sys. mgr. F.B.M. Mech. Constrn., Milan, 1970-74; EDP mgr. Otis Italy, Milan, 1974-77, info. and sys. dir., 1977-82, fin. dir., 1982-85; contr., treas. Otis Elevator European Ops., Paris, 1985-88; mgr. dir. SELIT subs. of Otis, Milan, 1988-90; sr. v.p. Otis Elevator Pacific Asia Ops., Hong Kong, 1990-95; exec. v.p. Otis Elevator Pacific Asia Ops., Singapore, 1995-97; chmn., CEO, Costa Cruises, Genoa, Italy, 1997; cons. in EDP, Milan, 1972-75. Avocations: golf, reading, opera, tennis. Office: Costa Crociere Spa, via XII Ottobre 2, 16121 Genoa Italy

FOSS, ALEXANDER JAMES EASTERBROOK, ophthalmic surgeon consultant; b. London, Apr. 16, 1961; s. Arthur Alexander and Ursula (Clare) Gathercole) F.; m. Fiona Allison Simpson, May 14, 1988; children: Iain, James, Clare. BA, Oxford (Eng.) U., 1983, BM BCh, 1986, MA, 1991, DM, 1996. House officer John Radcliffe Hosp., Oxford, 1986-87; house officer Royal Berkshire Hosp., Reading, 1987; sr. house officer Guy's Hosp., London, 1987-88; registrar Oxford Eye Hosp., 1988-90, Moorfield Eye Hosp., London, 1991-97; cons. Queen's Med. Ctr., Nottingham, Eng., 1997—. Contbr. articles to profl. jours. Fellow Royal Coll. Ophthalmology; mem. Royal Coll. Physicians. Office: Queens Med Ctr, Nottingham NG7 2UH, England

FOSS, JOHN HOUSTON, writer, consultant, educator; b. Cleveland, June 20, 1925; s. Clifford Paul and Isabella Har (Bull) F.; m. Jean Willard, Oct. 26, 1985. BS in Agriculture, Wash. State U., 1951; MA in Am. Lit., Duke U., 1953. Tech. writer Douglas Aircraft Co., El Segundo, Calif., 1954-56; cons., writer Palos Verdes Estates, Calif., 1956-79, Seattle, 1979-84; mgr. tng. programs Am. Radio Relay League, Newington, Conn., 1984-87; pvt. practice pubs. cons. N.Y.C., 1987—; adj. vis. instr. U. S.C., Beaufort, 1992-93; asst. prof. English Calif. Lut. Coll., Thousand Oaks, 1953-54; cons. Green River C. C., Auburn, Wash., 1981-83. Editor: (coll. textbook) Horseshoeing Theory and Hoof Care, 1977; editor (coll. textbook) Anatomy and Physiology of Farm Animals, 1965; contbr. articles to profl. jours. Pres. Southland Juvenile Found., Inc. With U.S. Army, 1943-46; with USCG Aux., 1997—. Mem. Am. Radio Relay League, Am. Horse Shows Assn., Am. Horse Protection Assn. (dir. 1991-2000), Authors Guild, Authors League Am., Phi Gamma Delta. Republican. Avocations: amateur radio, chess, bicycling, skiing. Home and Office: 15 Pier Pointe New Bern NC 28562-8820

FOSS, KARL ROBERT, auditor; b. Aug. 26, 1938; s. Robert Henry and Ethel Caroline (Huston) F. Student, U. Wis., 1956-59, 62; BS, Madison Bus. Coll., 1961. Auditor Wis. Dept. Revenue, Madison, 1962-95; owner, mgr. LIST, Middleton, Wis., 1968-76; Bd. dirs. Middleton Hist. Soc., 1976-93, v.p., 1980; legis. adv. Old Car Hobby, 1971—. Co-recipient Spl. Interest Autos Appreciation award, 1971. Mem. Wis. Automobile Clubs in Assn. Inc. (co-founder 1971, bd. dirs. 1971—, pres. 1972-74, 77-78, 80, 86-87, v.p. 1975-76, 79, 85, 95-2000), Oldsmobile Club Am. (nat. dir. 1973-85, treas. 1981-85), Contemporary Hist. Vehicle Assn., Studebaker Drivers Club, Nash Car Club Am., Crosley Car Club, Antique Automobile Club Am., Vintage Chevrolet Club of Am., The Marmon Club, Model T Ford Club Am. Pub.; Suppliers List, 1968, Suppliers List Directory, 1969. Home: 1619 Middleton St Middleton WI 53562-3723

FOSS, LUKAS, composer, conductor, pianist; b. Berlin, Germany, Aug. 15, 1922; came to U.S. from Paris, 1937, naturalized, 1942; s. Martin and Hilde (Schindler) F.; m. Cornelia Brendel, Sept. 1951; 2 children. Student, Paris Lycée Pasteur, 1932-37; grad., Curtis Inst. Music, 1940; spl. study, Yale U., 1940-41; pupil of, Paul Hindemith, Julius Herford, Serge Koussevitzky, Fritz Reiner, Isabelle Vengerova; hon. doctorate, Yale U., 1991; 15 other hon. doctorates. Former prof. UCLA (in charge orch. and advanced composition); faculty Harvard U., 1970-71; prof. of composition Boston U., 1992—; founder Ctr. Creative and Performing Arts, Buffalo U.; vis. prof. Carnegie Mellon U., Pitts., 1987-90; composer in residence Tanglewood, 1989, 90; Mellon lectr. Nat. Gallery, Washington, 1987. Former condr., music dir., Buffalo Philharmonic; music dir., condr., Bklyn. Philharmonic, 1971-90, condr. laureate, 1990—; music dir., condr. Milw. Symphony Orch., 1981-86, condr. laureate, 1986—; orchestral compositions performed by many major orchs.; best known works include (opera) Griffelkin, Baroque Variations (orch.), Echoi (4 instruments), Time Cycle (songs with orch.), Renaissance concerto (flute and orch.); orch., chamber music, ballets, works commd. by, League of Composers, Nat. Endowment for Arts, N.Y. Arts Coun., NBC opera on TV, Am. Choral Condrs. Assn., Ind. U., 1979 Olympics, Boston Symphony, Chgo. Symphony; (recipient N.Y. Critic Circle citation for Prairie 1944, Soc. for Pub. Am. Music award for String Quartet in G 1948, Rome prize 1950, Horblit award for Piano concerto #2 1951, Naumburg Rec. award for Song of Songs 1957, Creative Music grant Inst. Arts and Letters 1957, N.Y. Music Critics Circle award for Time-Cycle orch. songs 1961, for Echoi 1963, Ditson award for condr. who has done the most for Am. music 1973, N.Y.C. award for spl. contbn. to arts 1976, ASCAP award for adventurous programming 1979, CRI rec. award for Thirteen Ways of Looking at a Blackbird 1979). Guggenheim fellow, 1945; Creative arts award Brandeis U., 1983; Laurel leaf award Am. Composers Alliance, 1983. Mem. Am. Acad. of Arts and Letters.

FOSSATI, HUMBERTO MARIO, electrical engineer, researcher; b. Bryan, Tex., Nov. 16, 1965; s. Humberto and Nancy Miryam (Tejada) F. BS in Elec. Engring., Tex A&M U., 1987, MS, 1989; postgrad., Rice U. Staff engr. Space Sta., IBM, Houston, 1989-93; staff engr. LAMPS, IBM/Loral Fed. Systems, Owego, N.Y., 1993-95; project engr. Compaq Computer Corp., Houston, 1995-97, multimedia architect portable PC divsn., 1997-99, program mgr. advanced technology, 1999—; rschr. Pleiades Rsch., 1989-96. Contbr. articles to profl. jours. Rice U. fellow, 1992; NSF grantee Tex. A&M U., 1987-89. Mem. IEEE, Sigma Xi. Republican. Roman Catholic. Avocations: collecting stamps, playing tennis, soccer, swimming. Home: 8206 Turnmill Ct Spring TX 77379-7161 Office: Compaq Computer 20555 SH 249 MS 120304 Houston TX 77070

FOSSE, ERIK, surgeon, educator, consultant; b. Oslo, Dec. 2, 1950; s. Nils and Elizabeth (Hammer) F.; m. Carolyn Midsem, Aug. 23, 1977; children: Hilde Midsem, Eivind. MD, U. Oslo, 1976, PhD, 1987. Resident dept. surgery Lovisenberg Hosp., Oslo, 1982-84; asst. prof. dept. surgery Ullevold Hosp., Oslo, 1984-87, sr. resident, 1987-90, cons., 1991-94; cons. Rikshosp., Oslo, 1994-97, head of dept. interventional ctr., 1995—. Author: War Surgery, 1995; contbr. articles to profl. jours.; musician, singer Rett Opp Fra Elva, 1997. Pres. Norwegian Aid Com., Oslo, 1983—. Lt. col. Norwegian Army, 1994—. Recipient Palestinian Humanitarian award Palestinian Red Crescent Soc., 1984. Mem. European Assn. Cardiothoracic Surgery, European Assn. Cardiovascular Surgery, Scandinavian Assn. Thoracic Surgery, European Assn. Endoscopic Surgery, Norwegian Assn. Cardiothoracic Surgery. Avocation: guitar. Home: Maridals vn 71, 0458 Oslo Norway Office: Interventional Ctr, Rikshopitalet, 0027 Oslo Norway

FOSSEEN, NEAL RANDOLPH, business executive, former banker, former mayor; b. Yakima, Wash., Nov. 27, 1908; s. Arthur Benjamin and Florence (Neal) F.; m. Helen Witherspoon, Sept. 26, 1936; children: Neal Randolph Jr., William Roger. BA, U. Wash., 1930; LD (hon.), Whitworth Coll., 1967. With Wash. Brick, Lime & Sewer Pipe Co., 1923-32, v.p., 1932-38; pres. Wash. Brick & Lime Co., 1938-58; dir. Securities Intermountain Co., 1954-71; v.p., dir. Old Nat. Bank Wash., 1958-68; v.p., dir. Wash. Bancshares, 1968-71, vice chmn., 1971-72, chmn. bd., pres., 1972-73; dir. Utah-Idaho Sugar Co., 1968-79, 1st Nat. Bank Spokane, 1972-79; dir. Spokane Indsl. Park, 1959-72, treas., 1959-66; dir. North Coast Life Ins. Co., 1965-76, Quarry Tile Co., 1965-68, Day Mines, Inc., 1968-81; chmn. emeritus, dir. Old Nat. Bancorp., 1973-77; pres. 420 Investment Co., 1982-84; hon. dir. Met. Mortgage Co., 1995—. Mem. exec. com. Expo '74; mem. adv. bd. Mus. Native Am. Culture, 1957-81; mayor City of Spokane, 1960-67, mayor emeritus, 1967—; mem. adv. bd. emeritus Spokane Intercollegiate Rsch. and Tech. Inst., 1993-96; past chmn. adv. bd. Wash. State Inst. Tech.; bd. dirs., past pres. coun. Boy Scouts Am.; bd. dirs. Wash. Rsch. Coun., sec., 1968-74;

bd. dirs. YMCA, 1969-80, Pacific Sci. Found., 1970-73, Mountain States Legal Found., 1979-85; mem. adv. bd. Grad. Sch. Bus., U. Wash., 1974-81, emeritus, 1981—; mem. adv. bd. dept. history, 1981—; chmn. Regent Gonzaga U., 1948-61, emeritus, 1961—, benefactor, (hon.) LD, 1999; mem. adv. bd. Coll. Engring., Wash. State U., 1949-79; hon. trustee Found. N.W.; trustee Rockwood Cmty. Found., 1993-97, Gonzaga Dussault Found., Fosseen-Kusaka Disting. Professorship, Jackson Found. Scholarship, U. Wash., 1998; mem. adv. bd. Advanced Tech. Ctr., 1989-94, Mukogawa Fort Wright Inst., Whitworth Coll. Internat. Mgmt., City Innovation; founding. dir. Athetic Round Table. Col. USMCR, ret. Recipient Shrine award El Katif Temple, 1974, Non Sibi, Sed Patriae award Marine Corps. Res. Officers Assn., Outstanding Svc. award Fairchild AFB, Spokan Mcpl. League, Forward Spokane award Spokane County Hotel and Restaurant Coun., Liberty Bell award Spokane County Bar Assn., Book of Golden Deeds, Exchange Club, Sister City Outstanding Svc. award Town Affiliation Assn., Disting. Citizen award Ea. Wash. U., 1982, Founders Day award, 1994, Disting. Citizen award Air Force Air Mobility Command, 1995, Citizen League Lifetime Svc. award, 1997, Inland N.W. Philanthropy award Found. N.W., 1999; named hon. citizen Nishinomiya, Japan; inducted to Inland N.W. Hall of Fame. Mem. VFW, Ret. Officers Assn., Assn. Wash. Bus. (past pres.), Spokane C. of C. (v.0. 1946-51), Spokane-Nishinoniya Sister City Soc. (pres.), Srs. N.W. Golf Assn. (gov.), Mil. Order World Wars (Perpetual), Order of the Rising Sun (Japan), Balboa de Mazatlan Club (Mex.), Spokane Club (life), Spokane Country Club (life), Prosperity Club, Travellers Century Club, Spokane Ski Club, Rotary (Paul Harris fellow, benefactor), Beta Theta Pi (Oxford Cup award), Alpha Kappa Psi. Home: Rockwood Manor 701 2903 E 25th Ave Spokane WA 99223-4992

FOSSEL, ERIC THOR, medical biophysicist; b. Mpls., Dec. 11, 1941; s. Spencer M. and Jane (Nelson) F.; m. Anne H. Plant, June 14, 1964 (div. 1981);children: Karin, Lars; m. Jan McQuere McDonagh, Jan. 6, 1982; 1 child, Jonathan. MS in Chemistry, Yale U., 1966, MPhil, 1967; PhD in Chemistry, Harvard U., 1970, MTS, 2000. Assoc./biology, chemistry Harvard Coll., Cambridge, Mass., 1974-75; lectr. biophysics Harvard Med. Sch., Boston, 1975-76, asst. prof. biophysics, 1976-83, asst. prof. radiology, 1983-85, assoc. prof. radiology, 1985-95; dir. radiol. rsch. Beth Israel Hosp., Boston, 1987-95; vis. scientist Francis Bitter Magnet Lab./MIT, 1976-83; cons. Inst. for Clin. Applications, Boston, 1990-93; pres. Strategic Sci. & Tech., Inc., 1995—. Contbr. articles to profl. jurs. Am. Heart Assn. established investigator, 1978-83. Mem. Am. Fedn. Clin. Rsch., Assn. of Univ. Radiologists, Soc. of Magnetic Resonance in Medicine (founding mem.), Biophys. Soc., Fellowship of Soc. St. John the Evangelist. Republican. Episcopalian. Achievements include patents for NMR cancer blood test, major unique trans-dermal drug delivery system. Office: Strategic Sci & Tech Inc 892 Worcester St Wellesley MA 02482-3718

FOSSUM, ROBERT MERLE, mathematician, educator; b. Northfield, Minn., May 1, 1938; s. Inge Martin and Tina Otelia (Gaudland) F.; m. Cynthia Carol Foss, Jan. 30, 1960 (div. 1979); children: Karen Jean, Kristin Ann; m. Barbara Joel Mason, Aug. 4, 1979 (div. 1993); children: Jonathan Robert, Erik Anton; m. Robin Karyl Goodman, Aug. 10, 1997. BA, St. Olaf Coll., 1959; AM, U.Mich., 1961, PhD, 1965. Instr. U. Ill., Urbana, 1964-66; asst. prof. U. Ill., 1966-68, assoc. prof., 1968-72, prof. math., 1972—; lectr. Aarhus U., Denmark, 1971-73, Copenhagen U., Denmark, 1976-77; vis. prof. Université de Paris VI, 1978-79, Oslos U., 1968-69. Contbr. numerous articles to profl. jours. Recipient Disting. Alumni award Northfield H.S.; Fulbright grantee Oslos U., 1967-68. Fellow AAAS, N.Y. Acad. Scis., Internat. Assn. of Math. Physics, Soc. for Indsl. and Applied Math., Am. Math. Soc. (assoc. sec. ctrl. sect. 1983-87, sec.-designate 1988, sec. 1989-99), Dansk Matematisk Forening, Inst. Algebraic Meditation (sec.), Swedish Math. Soc., Det Kongelig Norske Videnskabers Selskab (elected natural scis. sect.), Phi Beta Kappa, Sigma Xi. Democrat. Lutheran. Club: Heimskringla (Urbana). E-mail: r-fossum@uiuc.edu. Office: U Ill Dept Math 1409 W Green St Urbana IL 61801-2943

FOSTER, BRIAN DUANE, biologist, consultant; b. Sacramento, 1961; s. Duane Ray and Loretta Margaret Foster. BA, Point Loma Coll., 1983; PhD, Vanderbilt U., 1991. Postdoctorate staff The Scripps Rsch. Inst., LaJolla, Calif., 1991-93; cons. San Diego, 1993—; cons. endangered species monitoring Calif. Dept. Fish and Game, San Diego, 1993-97, USN, San Diego, 1994—. Contbr. articles to profl. jours. Spokesperson No on Proposition 4 Campaign, Calif., 1998. Recipient Grad. Rsch. assistantship Vanderbilt Grad. Sch., Nashville, 1988; grad. fellow Vanderbilt U., Nashville, 1984; rsch. grantee Am. Cancer Soc., Nashville, 1990, postdoctoral tng. grantee NIH, LaJolla, 1991. Mem. AAAS, Am. Ornithologists Union, Wilson Ornithological Soc., Cooper Ornithological Soc., Assn. Field Ornithologists, Colonial Waterbird Soc. Democrat. Avocations: birding, hiking, fishing. Home: 129 1/2 D Ave Coronado CA 92118-1334

FOSTER, DALE WARREN, political scientist, educator, management consultant, real estate broker, accountant; b. Bryan, Tex., Mar. 7, 1950; s. William Henry and Maysie Blanche (Hembree) F. BBA, Tex. A&M U., 1972, MA, 1979, Cert. in Profl. Teaching, 1987; BS, U. Houston, 1981, MEd, 1983; AAS, Houston C.C. Sys., 1982. Cert. in property mgmt. Dept. mgr. J.C. Penney Co., Bryan, 1973-74; shopper advt. mgr. Harte-Hanks Newspapers/Daily Eagle, Bryan, 1975-76; bus. mgr., contr. S.M. Hardee Enterprises, College Station, Tex., 1976-78; ops. mgr. Western Food Svcs., Inc., Pasadena, Tex., 1978-80; internal auditor Hermann Hosp., Houston, 1980-82; high sch. tchr. Cypress-Fairbanks Independent Sch. Dist., Houston, 1983-84; alternative sch. tchr. Alief Independent Sch. Dist., Houston, 1984-88; gov. prof. Houston C.C. System, 1980—, chmn. govt. dept. co-op program, 1992—; lead instr. Houston C.C. Sys., 1993—; supr. student tchr. U. Houston, 1989-90; adj. instr. North Harris County Coll., Houston, 1983-96; fin. cons. Pro-Trac Econ. Planning Adv. Bd., Denver, 1985-86; Presdl. Scholars lectr. Minority Students Honors Program, Houston, 1986-89; coord. legis. practicum Harris County Congl. Internship Program, 1988—; exch. tchr., The Netherlands, 1992. Co-editor textbook supplement, curriculum guide, departmental political reader; author classroom instructional project. Mem. adv. com. Hermann Affiliated Fed. Credit Union, Houston, 1980-82; mem. fin. coun. Harris County Dem. Com., 1991-93; mem. dean's coun. U. Houston, 1992-96; trustee, treas. Wilmington-Barnard Found., 1992—. Named Tchr. of Yr., Cy.-Fair H.S., 1984, Alief Individualized Study Ctr., 1987, Master Tchr. Nat. Leadership Inst. U. Tex., Austin, 1991, host tchr. Washington Week Intern Program, 1995; recipient Adj. Teaching and Comty. Svc. award North Harris County Coll. Dist., 1990, Teaching Excellence medal Nat. Inst. Staff and Orgn. Devel., 1991, 98; Fulbright scholar, 1992, 98; Robert A. Taft fellow L.B.J. Sch. Pub. Affairs, 1995, Fulbright-Hays fellowship U.S. Dept. Edn., 1998. Fellow Am. Bd. Master Educators; mem. ASCD, Tex. Jr. Coll. Tchrs. Assn., Tex. Coun. Social Studies, Inst. Mgmt. Accts., Internat. Platform Assn., Am. Fin. Assn., Fulbright Assn., Houston C.C. Sys. Faculty Assn. (treas. 1997—, Outstanding Tchr. award 1991, Tchr. of Yr. 1997), Phi Theta Kappa, Alpha Phi Omega, Kappa Delta Pi. Democrat. Baptist. Avocations: travel, reading, bowling, water sports, outdoor activities. Office: Houston C C NW 5514 Clara Rd Houston TX 77041-7204

FOSTER, DAVID RAMSEY, soap company executive; b. London, May 24, 1920; (parents Am. citizens); s. Robert Bagley and Josephine (Ramsey) F.; m. Anne Firth, Aug. 2, 1957 (dec. June 1994); children: Sarah, Victoria; m. Alexandra Chang, May 24, 1996. Student in econs., Gonville and Caius Coll., Cambridge (Eng.) U., 1938. With Colgate-Palmolive Co. and affiliates, 1946-79; v.p., gen. mgr. Europe Colgate-Palmolive Internat., 1961-65; v.p., gen. mgr. household products divsn. parent co. Colgate-Palmolive Internat., N.Y.C., 1965-68, exec. v.p., 1968-70, pres., 1970-75, CEO, 1971-79, chmn., 1975-79. Author: Wings Over the Sea, 1990. Trustee Woman's Sport Found. Served to lt. comdr. Royal Naval Vol. Res., 1940-46. Decorated Disting. Svc. Order, D.S.C. with bar, Mentioned in Despatches (2); recipient Victor award City of Hope, 1974, Herbert Hoover Meml. award, 1976, Adam award, 1977, Harriman award Boys Club N.Y., 1977, Charter award St. Francis Coll., 1978, Walter Hagen award, 1978, Patty Berg award, 1986, Commr.'s award LPGA, 1995. Mem. Soc. Mayflower Descs., Hawks Club (Cambridge U.), Royal Ancient Golf Club (St. Andrews, Scotland), Royal Cinque Ports Golf Club (life), Sunningdale Golf Club, Swinley Forest Golf Club (U.K.), Sankaty Head Golf Club, Racquet and Tennis Club (N.Y.C.), Mission Hills Country Club, Bally Bunion Golf Club (life). Home: 540 Desert West Dr Rancho Mirage CA 92270-1310

FOSTER, DOUGLAS TAYLOR, lawyer, investor; b. L.A., Oct. 30, 1927; s. James Taylor Foster and Irene Eve Ericksen; m. Nita Burt Peterson, July 3, 1951 (div. May, 1975); children: Jane Taylor Dickson, Stephanie Foster Abram. BA in Econ. and Bus., U. Wash., 1950; JD, Stanford U., 1956. Bar: Calif. 1957, U.S. Dist. Ct. (so. dist.) Calif. 1957, U.S. Ct. Appeals (9th cir.) 1959, U.S. Dist. Ct. (no. dist.) Calif. 1969, U.S. Supreme Ct. 1971, U.S. Dist. Ct. (ea. dist.) Calif. 1985. From assoc. to ptnr. Farrand, Fisher & Farrand, L.A., 1956-66; legal counsel McClatchy Newspapers and Broadcasting, Sacramento, Calif., 1967-81; ptnr. Diepenbrock, Wulff, Plant & Hannegan, Sacramento, 1981-84; lawyer pvt. practice, Sacramento, 1985—; sec. bus. and corp. sect. L.A. County Bar Assn., 1966. Candidate L.A. County Rep. Ctrl. Com., San Marino, Calif., 1965. Lt. USN, 1950-53, Korean War. Mem. ABA, ATLA, Calif. State Bar, Sacramento County Bar Assn., Calif. Trial Lawyers Assn., Consumer Attys. of Calif., Capital City Trial Lawyers Corp., Consumer Attys. of Sacramento County, Rotary Club Arden-Arcade, Seattle Yacht Club, Sacramento Yacht Club, Sutter Club, Am. Trial Lawyers Am. Presbyterian. Achievements include succesful defense of cable television license, Lake of the Pines Development, No. Calif., involving first judicial interpretation and ruling under the Cable TV Act of 1984 in U.S. Dist. Ct. (ea. dist.) Calif., 1986. Avocations: boating, tennis, golf, bridge, other sports. Office: Douglas F Foster Esq 2625 Fair Oaks Blvd Ste 1 Sacramento CA 95864-4936

FOSTER, DUDLEY EDWARDS, JR., musician, educator; b. Orange, N.J., Oct. 5, 1935; s. Dudley Edwards and Margaret (DePoy) F. Student Occidental Coll., 1953-56; AB, UCLA, 1957, MA, 1958; postgrad. U. So. Calif., 1961-73. Lectr. music Immaculate Heart Coll., L.A., 1960-63; dir. music Holy Faith Episcopal Ch., Inglewood, Calif., 1964-67; lectr. music Calif. State U., L.A., 1968-71; assoc. prof. music L.A. Mission Coll., 1975-83, prof., 1983—, also chmn. dept. music, 1977—; mem. dist. acad. senate L.A. Community Colls., 1991-92; mem. acad. senate L.A. Mission Coll., 1993-97; dir. music 1st Luth. Ch., L.A., 1968-72. Organist, pianist, harpsichordist; numerous recitals; composer O Sacrum Convivium for Trumpet and Organ, 1973, Passacaglia for Brass Instruments, 1969, Introduction, Arioso & Fugue for Cello and Piano, 1974. Fellow Trinity Coll. Music, London, 1960. Recipient Associated Students Faculty award, 1988. Mem. Am. Guild Organists, Am. Musicol. Soc., Nat. Assn. of Scholars, Acad. Senate, Town Hall Calif., L.A. Coll. Tchrs. Assn. (pres. Mission Coll. chpt. 1976-77, v.p., exec. com. 1982-84), Mediaeval Acad. Am. Republican. Anglican. Office: LA Mission Coll Dept Music 13356 Eldridge Ave Sylmar CA 91342-3200

FOSTER, EDWARD PAUL (TED FOSTER), process industries executive; b. Pawtucket, R.I., Aug. 23, 1945; s. Edward Francis and Vivian Adrienne (Davagne) F.; m. Barbara Philomena Cook, Dec. 17, 1965 (div. Apr. 1978); children: Edward Robert, Gwendolyn Lucy; m. Johanna Helena Klaassen, June, 1985 (div. 1988). BSChemE with distinction, U. R.I., 1967; MSChemE, Worcester Poly. Inst., 1970; MBA, Lehigh U., 1981. Mfg. melting engr. Corning Glass Works, Central Falls, R.I., 1966-67; group leader rsch. and devel. The Babcock & Wilcox Co., Alliance, Ohio, 1968-71; mgr. tampella process The Babcock & Wilcox Co., Barberton, Ohio, 1972-74; from comml. devel. engr. to dir. bus. devel. in gases, metallurgy, coal, energy, chems. and polymers, and environ. areas Air Products and Chem., Inc., Allentown, Pa., 1974—; cons. U.S. Army Natick (Mass.) Lab., 1966-67. Contbr. articles to profl. jours.; patentee in field. Chmn. fin. Unitarian Ch., Bethleham, Pa., 1985, chmn. social, 1983-84. NDEA fellow HEW, 1967-69; ROTC scholar U.S. Army, 1965, Nat. Merit scholar, 1963. Mem. AIChE, Comml. Devel. Assn. (vice chmn. fall meeting 1996, nat. program chmn. 1997-99, bd. dirs.), Am. Chem. Soc., Comml. Devel. and Mktg. Assn. (bd. dirs. 2000—), Phi Kappa Phi, Tau Beta Pi, Theta Chi. Avocations: tennis, downhill skiing, sailing, biking. Home: 6023 Fairway Ln Allentown PA 18106-9610 Office: Air Products and Chems 7201 Hamilton Blvd Allentown PA 18195-1526

FOSTER, GEOFFREY, microbiologist, researcher; b. Perth, Scotland, Dec. 5, 1957; s. John Wallace and Mary Helen (Matchett) F.; m. Thelma Margaret Thomson, Aug. 23, 1985; children: Audrey, Gregor, Eilidh. Higher nat. cert. in med. lab. scis., Dundee (Scotland) Coll. Tech., 1981; spl. exam. fellow Inst. Biomed. Scis., Glasgow (Scotland) Coll. Tech., 1983. Cert. biomed. scientist. Asst. sci. officer East of Scotland Coll. Agr., Perth, 1974-83; sci. officer North of Scotland Coll. Agr., Aberdeen, 1983-87; higher sci. officer Scottish Agrl. Coll., Inverness, 1987-98, regional lab. supr., 1998—. Author numerous papers in field. Fellow Inst. Biomed. Scis.; mem. Am. Soc. for Microbiology, Soc. for Anaerobic Microbiology, Soc. Gen. Microbiology. Office: Stratherrick Rd, Inverness 1V2 4J2, Scotland

FOSTER, GEORGE MCCLELLAND, JR., anthropologist; b. Sioux Falls, S.D., Oct. 9, 1913; s. George McClelland and Mary (Slutz) F.; m. Mary Fraser LeCron, Jan. 6, 1938; children: Jeremy, Melissa Bowerman. BS, Northwestern U., 1935; PhD, U. Calif. at Berkeley, 1941; DHL (hon.), So. Meth. U., 1990. Instr. Syracuse U., 1941-42; lectr. UCLA, 1942-43; vis. prof. U. Calif.-Berkeley, 1953-55, prof. anthropology, 1955-79, prof. emeritus, 1979—, chmn. dept., 1958-61; acting dir. Mus. Anthropology, 1955-57; lectr. pub. health, 1955-64; anthropologist Inst. Social Anthropology, Smithsonian Instn., 1943-52, dir., 1946-1952; field rsch. Calif. Indians, 1937, Spain, 1949-50, Mexico, 1940—; adviser AID, India-Pakistan, 1955, Afghanistan, 1957, Zambia, 1961, 62, Nepal, 1965, Indonesia, 1973-74, WHO, Sri Lanka, 1975, Malaysia, 1978, India, 1979, 80, 81, Manila, 1983; adviser UNICEF, Geneva, 1976. Author: Traditional Cultures and the Impact of Technological Change, 1962, Tzintzuntzan: Mexican Peasants in a Changing World, 1967, Applied Anthropology, 1969, (with B. Anderson) Medical Anthropology, 1978, Hippocrates' Latin American Legacy, 1993, others, also monographs and articles. Recipient Berkeley citation, 1979; Guggenheim fellow, 1949; fellow Center for Advanced Study in Behavioral Scis., 1969-70. Fellow Am. Anthrop. Assn. (pres. 1970, Disting. Service award 1980); mem. Southwestern Anthrop. Assn. (Disting. Research award 1981), Nat. Acad. Scis., Am. Acad. Arts and Scis., Soc. Applied Anthropology (Malinowski award 1982). Club: Cosmos (Washington). Home: 790 San Luis Rd Berkeley CA 94707-2030

FOSTER, JODIE (ALICIA CHRISTIAN FOSTER), actress; b. L.A., Nov. 19, 1962; d. Lucius and Evelyn (Almond) F.; 1 child, Charles. BA in Lit. cum laude, Yale U., 1985. Acting debut in TV show Mayberry, R.F.D, 1969; numerous other TV appearances including My Three Sons, The Courtship of Eddie's Father, Gunsmoke, Bonanza, Paper Moon, 1974-75; TV spl. The Secret Life of T.K. Dearing, 1975, A Salute to Martin Scorsege, 1997; TV movies Rookie of the Year, Smile, Jenny, You're Dead; motion picture appearances Napoleon and Samantha, 1972, Menace on the Mountain, One Little Indian, 1973, Tom Sawyer, 1973, Kansas City Bomber, 1972, Bob & Carol & Ted & Alice, 1973, Alice Doesn't Live Here Anymore, 1974, Taxi Driver, 1976 (Acad. award nominee for Best Supporting Actress), Echoes of a Summer, 1976, Bugsy Malone, 1976, Freaky Friday, 1976, Moi, Fleur Bleue, 1977, Casotto, 1977, The Little Girl Who Lives Down the Lane, 1977, Candleshoe, 1977, Foxes, 1980, Carny, 1980, O'Hara's Wife, 1982, Svengali, 1983, Hotel New Hampshire, 1984, The Blood of Others, 1984, Mesmerized, 1986, Siesta, 1986, Five Corners, 1986, Siesta, 1987, Stealing Home, 1988, Five Corners, 1988, The Accused, 1988 (Acad. award for Best Actress, 1989), Backtrack, 1989, The Silence of the Lambs, 1991 (Golden Globe award for Best Actress in Drama, 1992, Acad. award for Best Actress, 1992), Shadows and Fog, 1992, Sommersby, 1993, Maverick, 1994, Contact, 1997, Anna and The Kine, 1999; dir., actress: Little Man Tate, 1991; prodr., actress: Nell, 1994 (Acad. award nominee for Best Actress 1995); dir., prodr. Home For the Holidays, 1995; prodr. Contact, 1996; exec. prodr. (Showtime) Babydance, Waking the Dead, Anna, 1999. Recipient Golden Globe award, 1989. Office: EGG Pictures Production Co Jerry Lewis Annex 5555 Melrose Ave Los Angeles CA 90038-3112

FOSTER, JOSEPH KEVIN, IV, entertainer, scribe; b. Waterbury, Conn., Feb. 29, 1960; s. Joseph Adrian and Stella Lucia (Vicedomini) F. Prin., owner JK Enterprises, Kaweah Commonwealth, Calif., 1978—. Author: Cycling Castro's Country: The Tour de Cuba, 2000, (screenplay) 9 Dragon, 1999; photography featured in Outside Mag., Bicycling Mag., various newspapers worldwide; actor (Broadway) Go Home, Spec 5, 1983-85, (Off Broadway) various, 1980-83, (TV) Kane and Abel, 1985, (film) Friday 13th, Part 2, 1980, Daniel, 1983; active W. Thomas Littleton's Southbury (Conn.) Playhouse, 1974-78, HB Studio, N.Y.C., 1981, Stella Adler, N.Y.C., 1981, The Am. Acad. Dramatic Arts, N.Y.C., 1980-81, The Actor's Studio, N.Y.C., 1981-85. Recipient Guinness World Record award Guinness, London, 1989, Cyclist of Yr. award Cycling Industry Bicycling Mag., Emmaus, Pa., 1990. Mem. Highpointer's Club, Ch. at Kaweah. E-mail: captainamerica@kevin-foster.com. Office: JK Enterprises PO Box 72 Kaweah CA 93237

FOSTER, JOSEPH TENNILLE, JR., school administrator, teacher; b. Phila., Nov. 19, 1948; s. Annie Atkins; m. Elizabeth Huggenim, Aug. 13, 1966; children: Jamar Walter Williams, Jabari Kwasi Foster. BS, Cheyney U. Pa., Weston, 1970; MSW, Bryn Mawr Coll., 1978. Tchr. Bd. Edn., Phila., 1970-76; social worker Baptist Children's Home, Phila., 1978-79; asst. dir. Harambee Inst. Inc., Phila., 1979—; area dir. Sonny Hill League, Phila., 1972—. Mem. Omega Psi Phi, Concerned Black Men. Democrat. Methodist. Avocations: tennis, martial arts, basketball. Home: 141 N 57th St Philadelphia PA 19139-2407

FOSTER, MARK STEPHEN, lawyer; b. Edgerton, Mo., Feb. 6, 1948; s. George Elliott and Annabel Lee (Bradshaw) F.; m. Camille Pepper, June 27, 1970; children: Natalie Ashley, Stephanie Ann. BS, U. Mo., 1970; JD, Duke U., 1973. Bar: Mo. 1973, U.S. Ct. Mil. Appeals 1974, Hawaii 1975, U.S. Dist. Ct. Hawaii 1975, U.S. Dist. Ct. (we. dist.) Mo. 1977, U.S. Ct. Appeals (8th cir.) 1986, U.S. Supreme Ct. 1994. Assoc. Stinson, Mag & Fizzell, Kansas City, 1977-80, ptnr., 1980—, mng. ptnr., 1987-90, bd. dirs., 1991—, chmn. bd. dirs., 1998—; arbitration panelist Nat. Assn. Securities Dealers, N.Y.C., 1985—, Pvt. Adjudication Found., Durham, N.C., 1988—. Active Citizens Assn., Kansas City, 1982-92; pres. Spelman Med. Found., Smithville, Mo., 1984-88; bd. dirs. Alzheimers Assn. Metro. Kansas City, 1997—, 1st v.p., 1998, pres., 1999. Lt. comdr. USNR, ret. Mem. ABA, Hawaii Bar Assn., Mo. Bar Assn., Kansas City Met. Bar Assn., Am. Arbitration Assn. (panelist 1990—, large complex case adv. com. 1993—), Carriage Club (bd. dirs. 2000—), Masons. Home: 1035 W 65th St Kansas City MO 64113-1813 Office: Stinson Mag & Fizzell PC PO Box 419251 1201 Walnut St Ste 2800 Kansas City MO 64106-2117

FOSTER, NORMAN LOUIS, neurology educator, researcher; b. Jacksonville, Ill., July 27, 1951; s. Louis Palmer and Evelyn Ann (Armstrong) F.; m. Carol Marvel, Nov. 19, 1977; children: Daniel Alexander, Sarah Elizabeth. BA, MacMurray Coll., 1973, DSc (hon.), 1995; MD, Washington U., St. Louis, 1977. Diplomate Am. Bd. Psychiatry and Neurology. Straight med. intern Jewish Hosp., St. Louis, 1977-78; resident in neurology U. Utah, Salt Lake City, 1978-81; med. staff fellow NIH, Bethesda, Md., 1981-84; asst. prof. neurology U. Mich., Ann Arbor, 1984-91, assoc. prof., 1991-98, prof., 1998—, assoc. rsch. scientist Inst. Gerontology, 1995-96, sr. rsch. scientist, 1998—. Contbr. over 150 articles to med. jours., chpts. to books. Office: U Mich Dept Neurology 1920 TC 1500 E Medical Center Dr Ann Arbor MI 48109-0005

FOSTER, PETER REYNOLDS, biochemical engineer, researcher; b. Newcastle-upon-Tyne, Eng., Oct. 16, 1945; s. Harold Frederick and Elizabeth Miller (Dickson) F.; m. Gillian Mather, Feb. 14, 1983. BSc with honors, Heriot-Watt U., Edinburgh, Scotland, 1968; MSc, U. Coll., London, 1969, PhD, 1972. Chartered engr. Rschr. Scottish Nat. Blood Transfusion Svc., Edinburgh, 1973-74; head R & D Scottish Nat. Protein Fractionation Ctr., Edinburgh, 1974—. Author: Blood: Blood Products & HIV, 1994, Kirk-Othmer Encyclopedia of Chemical Technology, 1994, Engineering Processes for Bioseparations, 1994, Haemophilia, 1997; contbr. articles to profl. jours. Fellow Inst. Chem. Engrs.; mem. Brit. Blood Transfusion Soc., World Fedn. Hemophilia. Mem. Labour Party. Avocations: art, literature, football. Office: Protein Fractionation Ctr, 21 Ellens Glen Rd, Edinburgh EH17 7QT, Scotland

FOSTER, PHILLIPS WAYNE, retired adult education educator; b. Ogdensburgh, N.Y., Apr. 20, 1931; s. Eddy Elwood and Alice (Phillips) F.; m. Mary Lou Ellen Denzine; children: David, Dean, Shati. BS, Cornell U., 1953; MS, PhD, U. Ill., 1957. From asst. prof. to assoc. prof. Mich. State U., E. Lansing, 1957-61; prof. U. Md., Coll. Pk., 1961-91; ret., 1991. Mem. Rotary. Home: 7526 Sweetbriar Dr College Park MD 20740-3030

FOSTER, RUTH MARY, dental association administrator; b. Little Rock, Jan. 11, 1927; d. William Crosby and Frances Louise (Doering) Shaw; m. Luther A. Foster, Sept. 8, 1946 (dec. Dec. 1980); children: William Lee, Robert Lynn. Grad. high sch., Long Beach, Calif. Sr. hostess Mom's Food Host of Coast, Long Beach, 1945-46; dental asst., office mgr. Dr. Wilfred H. Allen, Opportunity, Wash., 1946-47; dental asst., bus. asst. Dr. H. Erdahl, Long Beach, 1948-50; office mgr. Dr. B.B. Blough, Spokane, Wash., 1950-52; bus. mgr. Henry G. Kolsrud, D.D.S., P.S., Spokane, 1958—, Garland Dental Bldg., Spokane, 1958—. Sustaining mem. Spokane Symphony Orch. Mem. NAFE, Nat. Assn. Dental Assts., DAV Aux., DAV Comdrs. Club, Wash. State Fedn. Bus. and Profl. Women (dir. dist. 6), Spokane's Lilac City Bus. and Profl. Women (past pres.), Nat. Alliance Mentally Ill, Wash. Alliance Mentally Ill, Internat. Platform Assn., Spokane Club, Credit Women's Breakfast Club, Dir.'s Club, Inland N.W. Zool. Soc., Pioneer Circle of Women Helping Women. Democrat. Mem. First Christian Ch. Avocations: gardening, reading, continuing education studies. Office: Henry G Kolsrud DDS PS 3718 N Monroe St Spokane WA 99205-2850

FOSTER, SYDNEY WILLIAM GEORGE, retired aerospace and aviation history consultant; b. London, Sept. 24, 1916; s. Sydney Amos and Nellie (Bryant) F.; m. Norma Dorreen Dight, June 27, 1942; children: Valerie Anne Dight-Foster, Michael Noel Dight-Foster. Nat. cert., Twickenham (Eng.) Tech. Coll., 1940. Chartered engr. Apprentice Gen. Aircraft Ltd., Croydon, Eng., 1932-35, draughtsman, 1935-38; sr. design draughtsman Heston Aircraft Ltd., Southall, Eng., 1938-45; tech. dir. Broadway ENG Ltd., Eng., 1945-50; ptnr. Aerospace Consultancy, Middlesex, Eng., 1950—; cons. London, 1981-90; local govt. officer London Borough Hounslow, 1971-81; lectr. on matters of aviation; mem. Air Registration Bd. Design Approval, 1959. Author ednl. films on aerodynamics, with tchg. notes, 1945; author: (monograph) Cody's Tree et al, 1997. Councillor, Parish Coun., Guildford, Eng., 1995—; mem. Guildford Environ. Forum, 1992—; mem. Farnboro Air Scis. Trust, 1996—. Lt., Home Guard, Middlesex, 1940-45, Heston Airport. Fellow Brit. Interplanetary Soc.; mem. Cody Soc. (founding mem., chmn. 1993—), Royal Aero. Soc. (assoc. fellow, Farnboro br. 1996—, Weybridge br. 1980—). Mem. Church of England. Avocations: writing, environmentalism, art, gardening, masonry, aviation history researching. Home: Ash Green, Guildford GU12 6HL, England

FOSTER, THOMAS WILLIAM, management consultant, entrepreneur; b. Columbus, Sept. 19, 1934; s. James Homer and Lucy Isabel (Perkins) F.; m. Natalie Figner, Feb. 20, 1963 (div. June 1965); m. Blanca Victoria Alvarez, Dec. 24, 1987; children: Kirsten Lee, Lucy Jeanne. BS in Mining Engring., Ohio State U., 1961; MBA, Southwestern U., 1982. CFP, Ohio, 1973; registered engr., Ohio. Explorations mgr. Anaconda Copper Corp., Tucson, 1965-68; ptnr., assoc. sr. ptnr. Arthur Young, L.A., 1968-73; pres. The Foster Orgn., Cin., Lima, Peru, 1973—; mng. dir. Foster & Foster, Wilmington, Del., 1988—, Lima, Peru, 1988—; lectr. in field. Author: English textbooks, 1988-90, Passport to English, 1990, Sales Finesse, 1995, Personal Victory, 1995, People Without Problems Are In Cemeteries, 1998; publ. Victoria Personal mag., 1995—. Mem. Family Alert, Lima, 1991—; mem., lectr. Internat. Prisoner Fellowship, Lima, 1995—. Recipient Victoria Personal award Ednl. Civic Assn., 1995, Excellence in Sales AFP Profuturo, 1995. Mem. Inst. for Mining Engrs. Peru, Am. Assn., Am. C. of C., Assn. Villa del Mar, El Bosque Country Club. Roman Catholic. Avocations: tennis, mountain climbing, scuba diving, river rafting, exploration. Home: Penthouse, Malecon de la Marina 224, 18 Miraflores Lima, Peru Office: Foster & Foster, Miguel Dasso 139 Ste 301, 27 San Isidro Lima, Peru

FOSTER, VIRGINIA, retired botany educator; b. Joseph, Oreg., Feb. 4, 1914; d. Perry Alexander and Genevieve (Shain) F. BS, U. Wash., 1949, MS, 1950; PhD, Ohio State U., 1954. Prof. Judson Coll., Marion, Ala., 1956-58; prof. Miss. State Coll. for Women, Columbus, 1958-59, LaVerne (Calif.) Coll., 1959-60, Calif. Western U., San Diego, 1960-61, Pensacola (Fla.) Jr. Coll., 1962-84. Author: (lab. manual) The Botany Laboratory, 1976, rev. edit., 1985, 3d edit., 1991. Avocations: gardening, travel, photography. Home: 9270 Scenic Hwy Pensacola FL 32514-8054

FOSTER, WALTER HERBERT, JR., real estate company executive; b. Belmont, Mass., Nov. 2, 1919; s. Walter Herbert and Gertrude (Sullivan) F.; m. Hazel Campbell, Aug. 7, 1942 (div. July 1979); children: Katherine D., Walter H. III, Stephen C., Banton T.; m. Nedra Ann Thompson, July 3, 1981; 1 child, Timothy John. Student, Harvard U., 1937-38; BS, U. Maine, 1947; grad. in real estate, Tri-State Inst., 1968-70. Cert. gen. appraiser, Maine. Owner, mgr. Foster Bros., Lyndeborough, N.H., 1947-56; ter. sales mgr. Beacon Milling Co., Oakland, Maine, 1956-64; v.p. Sherwood & Foster, Inc., Old Town, Maine, 1964-67; sales rep. Bangor (Maine) Real Estate, 1967-73; chief appraiser James W. Sewall Co., Old Town, 1970-73; mgr. J.F. Singleton Co., Bangor, 1973-80; pres. Coldwell Banker Am. Heritage, Bangor, 1980—; dean Tri-State Inst., 1981; mem. Maine Real Estate Commn., 1987-93, chmn. 1991. Mem. Rep. Nat. Com., Washington, 1980; mem. assessment bd. appeals Old Town, Maine, Holden Assessment Bd. of Appeals; bd. dirs. Penobscot Theatre, 1987-92, treas., 1989, mem. Maine State Bd. Property Rev., 1998. Capt. USAF, 1941-46, USAFR ret., 1966. Mem. Nat. Assn. Realtors (bd. dirs. 1980-81), Maine Assn. Realtors (life, bd. dirs. 1976-80, pres. 1980, Realtor of Yr. 1984), Bangor Bd. Realtors (bd. dirs. 1973-74, pres. 1976, Realtor of Yr. 1976, 84), Maine Real Estate Commn. (chmn. 1991-92), Maine State Bd. Property Tax Review, Commn. to Study Real Estate Appraiser Cert. and Licensing, Nat. Assn. Rev. Appraisers, Am. Assn. Cert. Appraisers, Res. Officers Assn., Appraisal Inst. (assoc.), Nat. Assn. Ind. Fee Appraisers (sr.), Harvard Club of Ea. Maine (treas.), Rotary (bd. dirs. local club), Am. Legion., Ret. Officers Assn. Episcopalian. Avocations: woodworking, gardening. Home: Mistover Dole Hill Rd RR 2 Box 692 East Holden ME 04429-9802 Office: Coldwell Banker Am Heritage 510 Broadway Bangor ME 04401-3468

FOSTER, WALTER HERBERT, III, mechanical and manufacturing engineer, executive; b. Old Town, Maine, Apr. 15, 1945; s. Walter Herbert Jr. and Hazel Gertrude (Campbell) F.; m. Grace Irene Damon Jordon, Jan. 22, 1965 (div. Feb. 1980); 1 child, Walter Herbert IV; m. JoAnn Mary Doherty, Feb. 21, 1996. BSME, U. Maine, 1977; MSME, Worcester Poly. Inst., 1987. Registered profl. engr. Various positions Gen. Electric, Fitchburg, Mass., 1977-80; mgr. engring. support Gen. Electric, Bangor, Maine, 1980-84; sr. engr. turbine devel. Gen. Electric, Fitchburg, 1984-85, sr. engr. Navy programs, 1985; mgr. product assurance Gen. Electric, Bangor, 1986-89; mgr. indsl. product svc. Gen. Electric, Fitchburg, 1989-91, mgr. comml. customer svc., 1991-92; product line mgr. Gen. Electric, Schenectady, 1992-93; sales mgr. Gen. Electric/Power Generation, Schenectady, 1993-95; pres., CEO Foster Steam Turbine Cons. Ltd., Jaffrey, N.H., 1995—, Foster Steam Holding Ltd., Jaffrey, N.H., 1995—, Foster Power Generation Equipment Reapplication, Ltd., Jaffrey, N.H., 1999—. Served with U.S. Army, 1965-69, Korea. Decorated Army Commendation medal. Mem. ASME. Achievements include patent for steam turbine rotor weld repair. Avocations: building, solar energy, masonry, automobiles, computers. Home and Office: 551 Thorndike Pond Rd Jaffrey NH 03452-5150

FOSTER, WILLIAM ANTHONY, management consultant, educator; b. Washington, Nov. 26, 1929; s. Willard Hill and Evelyn Marie (Serrin) F.; m. Donna Roy Hayden, Feb. 5, 1955 (div. July 1985); children: Serrin M., Donna L., Shickel, Laura A. Valentine; m. Frances Christian Meacham, Dec. 6, 1995. BS in Bus. and Pub. Adminstrn., U. Md., 1956; MSPA, Nova Southeastern U., 1975, DPA, 1977. Registered profl. engr., Calif. Dir. indsl. engring. Washington region U.S. Postal Svc., 1969-71, mgr. indsl. engring. and plant maintenance Ea. Region, 1971-72; mgr. indsl. engring. U.S. Postal Svc., Washington, 1972-80, nat. coord., 1980-83, program mgr. tng., 1983-86; pres., educator, trainer, cons. William A. Foster Assoc., Washington, 1986—; educator, trainer, cons. U.S. Postal Svc., Washington, 1983-86, Embry-Riddle U., Daytona Beach, Fla., 1993, U. D.C., Washington, 1977-83, Southeastern U., 1980; dir., mgr. ops. U.S. Postal Svc., Washington, 1962-83. Author exec. tng. books; moderator TV show (Inaugural award 1991). Charter mem. Charleston Assn., Springfield, Va., 1968-84. Mem. ASTD (com. mem. 1986—), Am. Inst. Indsl. Engrs. (govt. liaison 1976-80, Nat. award for excellence 1969), Am. Soc Pub. Adminstrn. (cons. 1980-84), D.C. Coun. Engring. and Archtl. Socs. (chmn., PBS chair 1979-81, Outstanding Svc. award 1981, Bicentennial Engring. and Archtl. award 1976). Republican. Roman Catholic. Avocations: public speaking, American history, family, travel. Home: 1441 Northgate Sq Apt 12B Reston VA 20190-3754

FOTOPOULOS, SOPHIA STATHOPOULOS, medical research scientist, administrator; b. Kansas City, Mo., Nov. 6, 1936; d. Marinos G. and Stavroula (Fotopoulos) Stathopoulos; m. Chris K. Fotopoulos, Aug. 27, 1963 (div.) *In 1909, at age nine, a loving, brilliant and motivated father, Marinos Stathopoulos, left his small village, Gardiki, for Athens to make enough money to go to the "promise land" called America to support his poor family. In 1916, he arrived in Kansas City, Missouri. His restaurant and candy store became highly successful. In 1932, he married Stavroula Fotopoulos in her village Ellinitsa, where she studied math and designed and wove dyed blankets. They had a six-month European honeymoon. Stavroula has been a doting wife, mother and grandmother. Marinos was and is a wonderful idol* BA, U. Kans., 1958, MA, 1964, PhD, 1970. Diplomate Behavioral Scis. Regulatory Bd. State of Kans., Council for Nat. Register of Health Svc. Providers. Rsch. asst. U. Kans. Med. Ctr., Kansas City, 1958-61; rsch. assoc. Inst. Cmty. Studies, Kansas City, Mo., 1965-66; lectr. U. Kans., Lawrence, 1969-70; dir. Psychophysiology-pharmacology Lab. Greater Kansas City (Mo.) Mental Health Found., 1970-73; staff assoc. neuropsychophysiology, 1973, Midwest Rsch. Inst., Kansas City, Mo., 1974-75, sr. scientist, head Psychophysiology Lab., 1975-77, assoc. dir. chem. scis. div., 1977-79, dir. life scis. div., 1979-84; dean, dir. rsch. Am. U., Washington, 1984-87; exec. v.p., CEO Immucomp, Inc., 1987-92; pres., CEO Bioactive Tech., 1992—. rsch. prof. dept. medicine Kansas U. Med. Ctr., 1987-97; spl. rev. com. Nat. Cancer Inst., 1978-98; mem. adv. com. Am. Cancer Soc., 1982-96; lectr. U. Mo.-Kansas City Sch. Medicine, 1970-84. NIH research fellow, 1962-64, HHS research fellow, 1965-69; recipient Creative Scientist award Am. Inst. Research, 1971. Mem. AAAS, Claude Bernard Soc., Internat. Soc. for Antiviral Rsch., N.Y. Acad. Scis., Biofeedback Soc. Am., Mo. Biofeedback Soc. (pres. 1979-80), Sigma Xi. Greek Orthodox. Clubs: Zonta Internat. (pres. KCII 1983-85), Philoptochos Soc. Contbr. articles to profl. jours. and books.*Ms. Fotopoulos designed an experiment (1968) controlling blood flow to kill cancer. With equipment non-existent, she attached a physiograph to a oscilloscope, measured EKG while simultaneously providing the subject heartbeat "feedback". This experiment won her the National Creative Scientist award in 1971. As a pioneer, she helped name "biofeedback" and influenced worldwide experimental and therapeutic advancement. She formed the team of Cook, Graham, Cohen and Metz. They performed cutting edge experiments including treatments for cancer, anorexia and nausea; National Breast Cancer Study; Psychophysiologic Control; Biochemical and Pshychoshysiological Effects. Since 1987, she has focused on energy mechanisms and development of natural cancer therapeutics* Office: Bioactive Tech 8433 Quivira Rd Lenexa KS 66215-2802

FOTSIS, STAVROS SPYROS, mariner; b. Mar. 3, 1937; s. Spyros Fotsis and Gianoula Martini; m. Ermioni Gogolos, Sept. 16, 1973; children: Anna, Spyros. Student, Pitman Sch. English, London, 1964-65. Ship's officer Overseas Shipping, Piraeus, Greece, 1957-64, ship's master, 1966-72; ship's master Orri Lines, Jeddah, Saudi Arabia, 1973-77, Halcoussis Shipping, Piraeus, Greece, 1978-86; resident Paphos, Cyprus, 1986-92. Author numerous poems. Recipient Dangerous Ops. award North Vietnamese Govt., 1967, Dangerous Skill Ops. award Nautical Authority of Bangladesh, 1971. Mem. Paphos C. of C. and Industry. Conservative. Greek Orthodox. Avocations: poetry; hunting. Home: Polydrosson Thesprotias44017, Tahydromeion Vrossinis, Ioannina Epirus Greece

FOTTLER, MYRON DAVID, health services educator; b. Boston, Sept. 5, 1939; s. Myron Dustin and Anna Eileen Fottler; m. Carol Ann Fottler, Aug. 11, 1972. BS, Northeastern U., 1962; MBA, Boston U., 1963; PhD, Columbia U., 1970. Asst. prof. SUNY, Buffalo, 1967-75; from assoc. prof. to prof. U. Ala., Tuscaloosa, 1976-83; prof., PhD program dir. U. Ala., Birmingham, 1983-99; prof., program dir. U. Ctrl. Fla., Orlando, 1999—; cons. numerous legal firms and corps. Author 12 books; contbr. over 20 chpts. to books and over 100 articles to profl. jours. Recipient Hayhew award Am. Coll. Health Care Execs., 1997, Outstanding Svc. award Acad. Mgmt.-Healthcare Mgmt. Divsn., 1999. Episcopalian. Avocation: tennis. E-mail: fottler@mail.ucf.edu. Office: Univ Ctrl Fla Coll Health and Pub Affairs Tr534 Orlando FL 32816-0001

FOTTRELL, EAMONN MICHAEL, psychiatrist; b. Youghal, Cork, Ireland, Nov. 21, 1935; arrived in Eng., 1966; s. Matthew and Mary (O Sullivan) F.; m. Maureen Philomena Lennon, July 21, 1973; children: Matthew, Sinead, Katie, Edward. MB, BCh, U. Coll. Cork, 1964, MD, 1980. Cert. gen. medicine; diplomat in psychol. medicine. Intern in med. surgery No. Ireland North Infirmary, 1964-65; locum gen. practitioner, 1965; sr. house officer psychiatry Cork Psychiat. Hosp., 1965-66; registrar in psychiatry West Park Hosp., Epsom, Surrey, Eng., 1966-68; vis. psychiatrist Children's Cottages for Learning Difficulties, Melbourne, Australia, 1968-69; sr. registrar psychiatry St. Thomas' Hosp., London, 1970-72, Belmont Hosp Sutton, Surrey, Eng., 1972-73; locum cons. psychiatrist Bexley (Kent, Eng.) Hosp., 1973-74; med. adminstr., cons. psychiatrist Tooting Bec Hosp., London, 1966-94; clin. dir. elderly mental health Lambeth Health Care Trust, London, 1994-99; cons. psychiatrist Lambeth Health Care Trust and St. Thomas Hosp., London, 1994-99; clin. dir. old age psychiatry, cons. psychiatrist South London and Maudsley Nat. Health Svc. Trust, 1999—. Author: Case Histories in Psychiatry, 1981, Doctor Handbook for Junior Psychiatrists in Training in Tooting Bec Hospital and St. Thomas Hospital, 1983. Trustee Spires Centre for Homeless, Hungary and Unemployed People, Streatham, 1990—. Fellow Royal Coll. Psychiatrists (exec. com. elderly psychiat. sect. 1988-92); mem. Brit. Med. Assn., Med. Campaign Against Nuclear War, Greenpeace, Oxfam.

FOTTRELL, PATRICK, biochemistry educator, university president; b. Cork, Youghal Co, Ireland, Sept. 26, 1933; s. Matthew and Mary (O'Sullivan) F.; m. Esther Kennedy, 1963; 4 children. BSc, U. Coll. Cork, 1956, MSc, 1958; PhD, U. Glasgow, 1961; DSc, Nat. U. Ireland, 1975. Sr. rsch. officer Agrl. Inst., Johnston, Ireland, 1963-65; lectr., assoc. prof. biochem. U. Coll. Galway, Ireland, 1965—; pres. Nat. U. Ireland, Galway, 1996—; vis. prof. Harvard U., 1972, 82. Contbr. articles to profl. jours. Belt Meml. fellow. Mem. Royal Irish Acad. EEC Sci. Writers. Office: Nat Univ Ireland, Galway Ireland

FOUAD, BACHTOUTI, civil engineer; b. El-Eulma, Setif, Algeria, Jan. 1, 1968; s. Bachtouti and Lecheli Fouad. Cert. pub. works engr. Engr. Pub. Works, Kouba, Algeria, 1988-93. Avocation: wood working. Home: 159 rue Bochir Gassab, 19600 El-Eulma Setif, Algeria

FOUAD, FOUAD ABDULLA, business administrator; b. Dammam, Saudi Arabia, July 6, 1951; s. Abdulla Fouad Abdul Aziz Bubshait and Maryam Hassan Sater; m. Nouriya Mohamad al-Fadhel Bahraini, 1976; children: Abdulla Fouad, Jr., Fahad Fouad, Mohamad Fouad. BBA, Am. U. Beirut. Pres., sr. exec. Abdulla Fouad Group Cos., Saudi Arabia, 1975-98, pres., COO, 1998—; dir. Mantech Co. Ltd., Abdulla Fouad-Impalloy Ltd. Co. Mem. Nat. Assn. Accts., Assn. Bus. Mgmt. Avocations: fishing, music, photography. Office: Abdulla Fouad Co Ltd, PO Box 257, Dammam 31411, Saudi Arabia*

FOUCHARD, JOSEPH JAMES, retired government agency administrator; b. Chgo., June 6, 1928; s. Joseph Narcisse and Nell Gladys (Rowe) F.; m. Martha Jean Swiney, Aug. 20, 1950; children: James M., Melissa A., Lisa E. BS in Journalism, U. Ill., 1950. Asst. news editor Champaign-Urbana Courier, Urbana, Ill., 1953-56; chief copy editor Globe-Democrat, St. Louis, 1957-60; info. officer U.S. AEC, Washington, 1960-65, asst. dir. pub. info., 1966-74; asst. dir. U.S. NRC, Washington, 1975-78, dir. pub. affairs, 1978-94, pub. affairs counsel, 1994—; pub. affairs advisor Pres.' Task Force on Chernobyl Reactor Accident, Washington, 1986, U.S. Del. to Conf. on Chernobyl Accident, Vienna, Austria, 1986, Internat. Conf. on Nuclear Info., Paris, 1993; dir. NRC info. activities Three Mile Island Reactor Accident, 1979. 1st lt. U.S. Army, 1950-53. Recipient Presdl. Meritorious Sr. Exec. award Pres. Reagan, 1988, Presdl. Disting. Sr. Exec. award Pres. Bush, 1992; Univ. scholar. Presbyterian. Home: 4840 Flower Valley Dr Rockville MD 20853-1627

FOULDS, (HUGH) JON, diversified financial services company executive; b. May 2, 1932; s. E. J. and Helen Shirley (Smith) F.; m. Berry Cusack-Smith, 1960 (dissolved 1970); 2 children; m. Helèn Senn, 1977. Student, Bootham Sch., York; MA (hon.), Salford U., 1987. Dir. Brammer PLC, 1980-91, chmn., 1988-90; dir. London Atlantic Investment Trust (now London Smaller Cos. Investment Trust plc), 1983-95, Pan-Holding SA, 1988—, Eurotunnel PLC, 1988-96, Mercury Asset Mgmt. Group PLC, 1989-98; dir., CEO 3i Group PLC (formerly Investors in Industry), 1976-88, dep. chmn., 1988-92; dir. Halifax PLC, 1986—, chmn., 1990-99; chmn. Moneygator.com. Mem. Garrick Club, Hurlingham Club, Cercle Interallié (Paris). Avocations: tennis, skiing, shooting, pictures. Office: Prince Consort House, 109-111 Farringdon Rd, London EC1R 3BW, England*

FOULDS, LESLIE RICHARD, management educator; b. Auckland, New Zealand, Aug. 28, 1948; s. Richard S. and Edith H. (Nixon) F. BSc, Auckland U., 1970, MSc with honors, 1972; PhD, Va. Poly. Inst., 1974. Lectr. Massey U., New Zealand, 1976-79; sr. lectr. U. Canterbury, New Zealand, 1980-83; prof. engring. U. Fla., 1983-85; prof. ops. mgmt. U. Waikato, New Zealand, 1985—. Author: Optimization Techniques, 1981, Combinatorial Optimization for Undergraduates, 1984, Graph Theory Applications, 1994, (with D.F. Robinson) Digraphs, 1980; editor Asia Pacific Jour. Operational Rsch., 1990—. Fellow Inst. Combinatorics and Its Applications, Winnipeg (founding); mem. New Zealand Soc. Operational Rsch. (coun.), Australasian Soc. Combinatorial Math. Avocations: philately, yoga, transcendental meditation, fine wines, travel. Office: U Waikato, Pvt Bag 3105, Hamilton 2020, New Zealand

FOULDS, WALLACE STEWART, ophthalmologist, educator, consultant; b. London, Apr. 26, 1924; s. James and Nellie Margach (Stewart) F.; m. Margaret Holmes Walls, Dec. 20, 1947; children: Iain Stewart, Margaret Elizabeth Rudd, Alison Sutherland Steadman. MB, ChB, Glasgow (Scotland) U., 1946, MD, 1958, ChM with honors, 1964; DSc (hon.), Strathclyde U., Glasgow, 1995. Resident in ophthalmology Moorfields Eye Hosp., London, 1952-54; sr. registrar U. Coll. Hosp., London, 1954-58; part time rsch. asst. Inst. Ophthalmology U. London, 1954-58; cons. ophthalmologist Addenbrooke's Hosp., Cambridge, Eng., 1958-64; hon. lectr. Cambridge U., 1958-64; Tennent prof. ophthalmology U. Glasgow, 1964-89; vis. prof. Nat. U. Singapore, 1993—; adviser in rsch. Singapore Nat. Eye Ctr. and Singapore Eye Rsch. Inst., 1993—; co-dir. Singapore Eye Rsch. Inst., 1999—. Flight lt. Royal Air Force Med. Br., 1947-49. Recipient CBE, Her Majesty Queen Elizabeth, 1988, Internat. Gold medal Singapore Nat. Eye Ctr., 1997; hon. fellow Med. and Dental Def. Union Scotland, 1994, Royal Soc. Medicine, London, 1996. Fellow Royal Coll. Surgeons Eng., Royal Coll. Ophthalmologists London (founder pres. 1988-92), Jules Gonin Soc. (v.p. 1990-94), Assn. Eye Rsch. (pres. 1988-89), Ophthal. Soc. U.K. (pres. 1984-86), Oxford Ophthal. Congress, Am. Acad. Ophthalmology, Royal Scottish Automobile Club. Author over 20 chpts. to books and over 200 articles to profl. jours. Avocations: sailing, natural history, gardening. Fax: 0141 357 4297. E-mail: wallace@wsfoulds.demon.co.uk. Home and Office: 68 Dowanside Rd, Glasgow G12 9DL, Scotland United Kingdom

FOULKE, JUDITH DIANE, health physicist; b. Bucyrus, Ohio, Nov. 22, 1945; d. Lawrence Kern Foulke and Alberta Amelia (Foulke) Houpt; m. Mark Allen Elrod, July 17, 1981. BA, St. Mary of the Springs, 1967; MS, U. Mich., 1969; PhD, Purdue U., 1973. Health physicist NASA Goddard Space Flight Ctr., Greenbelt, Md., 1969-71, U.S. Atomic Energy Commn., Washington, 1973-77; radiobiologist U.S. Nuc. Regulatory Commn., Washington, 1977-87; health physicist U.S. Dept. Energy, Washington, 1987—. Mem. Spires Brass Band, Frederick, Md. Mem. AAAS, Am. Nuc. Soc., Health Physics Soc. Democrat. Roman Catholic. Home: 10 Sunnyview Ct Germantown MD 20876-4025

FOUNTAIN, DESMOND HALE, sculptor, painter; b. Devonshire, Bermuda, Dec. 29, 1946; s. Desmond Oswald Trevor and Ruth Emily (Masters) F.; divorced; children: Annabel Emily Clare, Luke Desmond Hugh. Diploma in art and design, Exeter Coll. Art, Devonshire, Eng., 1969; cert. in edn., art. tchrs. diploma, U. Bristol, Eng., 1970. Part-time tchr. Crediten, Eng., 1970-71; temp. tchr. Blundels Sch., Tiverton, Eng., 1971; head art dept. Warwick Acad., Bermuda, 1971-74; CEO Tangible Investments Ltd., Bermuda, 1995—; founder The Sculpture Gallery at Southampton Princess Hotel, Bermuda, 1988—; cons. Polestar Corp., Bermuda, 1991—. Over one thousand sculptures, worldwide, include medallion portrait of Her Royal Highness the Princess Margaret (in silver, gold and platnum), 1984, bronze statue of Sir George Somers, 1984, life-size bronze of Mark Twain, 1995, Spirit of Bermuda (Johnny Barnes), 1998, OZ Trial Heroes, U.K., 2000. Pres. Bermuda Soc. Arts, 1975; founder Bermuda Fine Art Trust, 1981; chmn. Bermuda Nat. Gallery Com., 1986-88; pres. students guild Exeter Coll. Art, 1968-69. Art studies grantee City of Stoke-on-Trent, Eng., 1964-70; recipient award Ministry of Cmty. Culture and Info. Svcs., Bermuda, 1993. Fellow Royal Soc. Brit. Sculptors; mem. Nat. Sculpture Soc. (colleague), Royal Bermuda Yacht Club, Bermuda Boat and Canoe Club. Avocations: sailing, antiques, art collecting, sculpting, painting. Office: Sculpture Studio, PO Box FL 317, Flatts FL BX, Bermuda

FOUNTAIN, JOANNA F., library consultant, business owner; b. Huauchinango, Puebla, Mexico, May 2, 1945; d. Thomas E. and Iona F.; m. Raymond L. Schroeder, 1985; 1 child, Stacey H. Chambers. BA, Syracuse U., 1966; MLS, U. Tex., 1970; PhD, Tex. Woman's U., 1982. Libr. Emerson Elem. Sch., Miami, Fla., 1967-69; libr., dir. Oak Springs Br. Oak Springs br. Austin (Tex.) Pub. Libr., 1970-72; bilingual rsch. libr., Edn. Svc. Ctr., Region 13, Austin, 1972-76, tng. specialist, 1976-78; editorial dir. Voluntad Pubs., Austin, 1978-79; assoc. dir. for collection devel. Tex. So. U. Libr., Houston, 1981-83; dir. libr. tech. svcs. Southwestern U., Georgetown, Tex., 1983-90; adj. faculty U. Tex., Austin, 1990—; owner, sole propr. Bibliotechnics, Georgetown, 1990—; tech. svcs. libr. Austin Ind. Sch. Dsit., 1995—. Author: Headings for Children's Materials, 1993, Hey, Miss! You Got A Book For Me?, 1978, 81, Subject Headings for School and Public Libraries, 1996; editor, compiler bibliography CARTEL, 1973-76, Guide to Title VII Bilingual Bicultural Education Programs, 1973-75. Mem., officer La Sertoma, Georgetown, 1983-88. Recipient Grad. fellowship Tex. Woman's U., 1979-81, Higher Edn. Act grant U. Tex. at Austin, 1969-70. Mem. ALA. Presbyterian. Avocation: handicrafts. Home and Office: 603 Serenada Dr Georgetown TX 78628-1633

FOUQUET, ANNE (JUDY FUQUA), musician, music educator; b. Wurtland, Ky., Oct. 2, 1938; d. John Paul and Garnet May (Gibson) Hillman; m Warren Russell Fuqua, Dec. 21, 1961 (div. Dec., 1992); children: Bryan David, Faith Fuqua-Purvis, Paul Carroll. BMus., Am. Conservatory, Chgo., 1962; MMus., No. Ill. U., 1967; MFA, U. Iowa, 1971, D in Musical Arts, 1997. Organist various churches and denominations, Ill., 1960—; profl. accompanist Wis., Ill., 1970—; piano instr. Beloit (Wis.) Coll., 1972—; instr. Rockford (Ill.) Coll. Acad., 1991—; ind. instr. Keyboard Studio, Rockford, Ill., 1971—; clarinet player Rockford (Ill.) Park Band, 1995—. Composer: (song cycle soprano) Spinner of the Seasons, 1987, (suite for flute and hapsichord) Issar Suite, 1992; author: (play) Miracle of Love, 1982; (novel) If It Hadn't Been for Joel, 1980; (memoirs) Daddy Was a Farmer, Mother Was a City Girl, 1999. Mentor Helping One Student To Succeed, Structured Reading, Kishwaukee Sch., Rockford, Ill., 1997-98, adult lit. tutor READ Chatanooga, 1999—. Nominee Best Classical Pianist Rockford Area Music Industry, 1996. Mem. Am. Guild of Organists, Music Tchrs. Nat. Assn., Ill. Music Tchrs. Assn. (adjudicator 1994-97), Kishwaukee Valley Concert Band, Szuki Assn. of the Americas, Midwest Hist. Keyboard Soc., Mendelsson Club (founder composer showcase concerts Rockford 1991-97, bd. dirs. 1993-97), Am. Fedn. of Musicians, Tenn. Music Tchrs. Assn. (adjudicator 1999), Sierra Club. Avocations: hiking, langs. (German, French, Hebrew), cooking, gardening. Office: Cadek Conservatory Music U Tenn Chattanooga 724 Oak St Chattanooga TN 37403-2406

FOURCADE, RICHARD OLIVIER, urologist; b. Clermont-Ferrand, France, Mar. 28, 1944; s. Jean Roger and Colette Elisa (Brunschwik) F.; m. Daniele Chastrey, May 26, 1979; 1 child, Thierry-Marc. MD, Paris U., 1974. Chef de clinique, gynecologique asst. Assistance Publique-Hopitaux de Paris, U. Paris, 1974-75, chef de clinique, urologique asst., 1975-79; head dept. urology Hosp. Auxerre, France, 1979—; clin. researcher, main investigator numerous clin. trials; active internat. confs., Paris. Author: La Prostate-Guide Pratique, 1997; contbr. numerous articles to sci. and profl. jours. Mem. Conseil Dept. Ordre des Medecins, Syndicat des Chirurgiens Urologues Francais (v.p. 1987-96), Assn. Francaise d'Urologie (exec. bd. 1986-92, treas. 1992-98), Soc. Internat. d'Urologie, Am. Assn. Urology, European Assn. Urology (internat. rels. and pub. rels. officer 1997-2000), Regional Coun. for Continuing Med. Edn. (pres. 1997—), European Orgn. on Rsch. and Treatment of Cancer, Rotary. Home: Les Chesnez, 89000 Auxerre France Office: Ctr Hosp Svc d'Urologie, 2 Bd de Verdun, 89000 Auxerre France

FOURCARD, INEZ GAREY, foundation executive, artist; b. Bklyn.; d. George W. and Frances E. (MacDonald) Garey; student Pratt Inst., 1946-48; BFA, McNeese State U., 1963; diploma Maestro di Pitturia Arti Modernea e Contemporaneo, Salsomaggiore, Italy, 1982. Waldren Arthur Fourcard, Aug. 7, 1948; children—Chrystal Frances, Sharon Lynn, Waldren Arthur, Andrea Renee, David Marquard, Anita Lynn. Exhibited in numerous one man shows throughout U.S., also in Eng., France and Spain; 3 paintings on loan to Gov. La., 1974-77; mem. gifted and talented sect. of Spl. Edn. State of La., 1971-73; mem. adv. council Child Centered/Parent Tutored Kindergarden Program, 1974—; mem. La. Task Force for Community Edn., 1974-75; v.p. La. Assn. for Sickle Cell Anemia, 1974—; named best statewide vol.; mem. Calcasieu Parish Bicentennial Com., 1974—; exec. dir., founder Southwestern Sickle Cell Anemia Found., Lake Charles, La., 1973—, producer, dir. 7 Sickle Cell Telethons, Sta. KPLC-TV, 1980-87; bd. dirs., exec. dir., found. World Sickle Cell Anemia/Thalassemia Found.; del. to Dem. Nat. Convs., 1980, 84. Named Hon. Citizen of Fort Worth, 1977; recipient Award of Merit, Human Relations Council of Lake Charles Deanery, award for services to sickle cell disease Sigma Gamma Rho, award for community service Phi Beta Sigma, Gold medal first prize Accademia Italia della Arti e del Sarvo, Italy, 1980, Statua della Vittoria Centro Studie Richerche Delle Nazioni, Italy, 1985. Democrat. Roman Catholic. Important works include The Widow in pvt. collection Bertrand Russell Peace Found., London. Home: 1414 Saint John St Lake Charles LA 70601-2470 Office: 730 Enterprise Blvd Lake Charles LA 70601-4516

FOURNEL, PAUL LUCIEN, writer, professional society administrator; b. Saint-Etienne, France, May 20, 1947; s. Henri Alphonse and Andree Alphonsine (Granier) F.; m. Martine Fontaine, Apr. 13, 1953; children: Charlotte, Valentin. PhD, Paris X U., 1972. Editor Hachette Jeunesse, Paris, 1974-76; chief editl. svc. Ency. Universalis, Paris, 1976-78; dir. lit. Slatkine France, Paris, 1978-80; pres., dir. Editions Ramsay, Paris, 1980-89; dir. Ed. Seghers, Paris, 1989-92; pres. Soc. des Gens de Lettres de France, Paris, 1992—; assoc. prof. U. Paris III, VIII; asst. prof. Princeton (N.J.) U., U. Colo., Boulder; exec. dir. Alliance Française, San Francisco; attaché culturel au Caire. Recipient Prix del Duca, Prix FNAC, Prix Ecrivains Sportifs, Prix Goncourt de la Nouvelle Acad. Concourt, 1989. Home: 48 rue de l'Abbe Groult, 75015 Paris France Office: Amb de France, Cairo Egypt

FOURNEL FLEURY, CORINNE MARIE, veterinarian, educator; b. Taverny, Val D'oise, France, Jan. 5, 1955; d. Rene Henry and Micheline Clotilde (Sehet) Fleury; m. Francois Fournel (div. 1990); children: Sylvain, Frederique. DVM, Ecole Vet. Lyon, 1978; M in Haematology and Immunology, Claude Bernard U., 1990, PhD, 1996, HDR, 1998. Asst., asst. prof. Ecole Veterinaire, Lyon, France, 1978-91; prof. Ecole Veterinaire, Lyon, 1991—. Author: Color Atlas of Cancer Cytology of the Dog and Cat, 1994; contbr. articles to profl. jours. Mem. Am. Soc. Vet. Clin. Pathology, European Vet. Cytology Working Group (founding). Roman Catholic. Avocations: ballet, piano, gardening. Office: Ecole Vet de Lyon, PO Box 83, 69280 Marcy L'Etoile France

FOURNIER, ALBERT EDOUARD, nephrologist, medical educator; b. Calais, France, Nov. 26, 1938; s. Albert Pierre and Sabine (Six) F.; m. Jacqueline Catherine Kaponas, Apr. 14, 1973 (dec. Mar. 1988); children: Stephane, Alexandre, Sabine; m. Roxana Oprisiu, May 18, 1996; children: Eleonore, Hadrien. Student, Med. Sch. of Paris, Lille, France, 1957-62, Lycee Francais, London, 1957. Resident U. Hosp., Paris, 1964-68; fellow Mayo Clinic, 1968-69; asst. prof. U. Paris, SD; chief of clinic U. Hosp., Paris, 1969-72; prof. medicine 2nd class U. Picardie, Amiens, France, 1973—; chief of nephrology U. Hosp., Amiens, 1978—; prof. medicine 1st class U. Pi-

cardie, Amiens, 1987—. Author: Depletion Potassique, 1972, Rein et Hypertension, 1978, Vitamin D et maladie des os, 1984, also nephrology textbook, hypertension textbook; contbr. articles to profl. jours. Mem. French, European, Am. and Internat. Socs. Nephrology and Hypertension. Avocations: swimming, skiing, tennis. Office: Nephrology CHU, Hospital SUD, 80054 Amiens France

FOURNIER, GERARD FERNAND, aeroacoustician, consultant; b. Serifontaine, France, July 25, 1942; s. Andre J. and Eliane F. (Patte) F.; m. Maryse E. Nouzeran, 1962; children: Laurent, Chantal. Grad. in Engring., Poly. Inst., Grenoble, France, 1964; DSc, U. Paris, 1971. Head group plasmas and lasers Office National d'Etudes et de Recherches Aerospatiales, Paris, 1971-76, head subdivsn. directed energy, 1976-82, head divsn. acoustics, 1983-97; cons., mgr. Gerard Fournier Internat. Cons., Paris, 1990—. Sci. editor Revue de Physique Appliquee, 1984-89; patentee in field. Lt. French Air Force, 1965-66. Recipient Medaille De Vermeil, Soc. d'Encouragement pour l'Industrie Nationale, France, 1982. Mem. AIAA (aeroacoustics com. 1996-99), N.Y. Acad. Scis., Confedn. European Aerospace Socs. (aeroacoustics com. 1995—, chmn. 1997-98), Assn. Aeronautique et Astronautique de France (aerodynamics com. 1997—), French Soc. Physics. E-mail: gfic@wanadoo.fr. Home and Office: 115 Ave De La Divsn Leclerc, 92290 Chatenay-Malabry France

FOURNIER, JOSETTE, chemistry educator; b. Allauch, France, Sept. 27, 1938; m. Paul Fournier, Dec. 16, 1961; children: Meriem, Jean-Bernard. Degree in phys. scis., 1968; MS in Organic Chemistry, U. Aix-Marseille, 1970, PhD, 1972. Asst. U. d'Alger, Algeria, 1962-65, Ecole Nat. Poly., Algeria, 1965-70, U. d'Aix-Marseille, 1970-74; prof. U. d'Angers, France, 1974—. Co-author: Manuel de chimie organique, 1983, Carbocyclic Cage Compounds, 1992, Les Professeurs du CNAM, dictionnaire biographique, 1994; author: chimie des pesticides, 1988; co-author, editor: Chimie des Couleurs et des Odewes, 1993, Ecolochimie, 1994, Chimie dans la Maison, 1996, Chimie du Petit D'ejeuner, 1998. Mem. French Soc. Chemistry, IUPAC, Acad. of Angers. Roman Catholic. Avocations: mountains, scientific expositions, history of chemistry. Office: CREPA, 8 rue Becquerel, 49070 Beaucouze France

FOURNIER, MARC, foundation executive; b. Beauvais, Oise, France, May 5, 1928; s. Alexandre and Jeanne (Loix) F.; m. Henninge Astrup, May 27, 1953; children: Anne-Catherine Labuzan, Marc Alexandre, Frédéric. Dir. financier P.D.G. Copafima, Paris, 1996—, Altra Banque, Paris, 1996—; adminstr. Didot-Bottin; pres. Fondation St. Louis pour le recherche, 2000—. Office: Copafima & Altra Banque, 7 rue Lamennais, 75008 Paris France

FOURNIER, WALTER FRANK, real estate executive; b. Northampton, Mass., Feb. 26, 1912; s. Frank Napoleon and Marie Ann F.; m. Ella Mae Karrey, May 16, 1938; children: Margaret Irene, Walter Karrey. BS in Mktg., Boston U., 1939; postgrad., Anchorage Community Coll., 1963-64, Alaska Pacific U., 1964-65. Coin sales supt. Coca Cola Co., Springfield, Mass., 1939-43; electrician foreman Collins Electric Co., Springfield, 1946-48; sales coord. for pre-fabricated homes Sears Roebuck & Co., Western Mass., 1948-49; wholesale sales rep. Carl Wiseman Steel and Aluminum Co., Great Falls, Mont., 1949-51; supt. City Electric Co., Anchorage, 1951-52; owner, adminstr. Acme Electric Co., Anchorage, 1953-64; appraiser Gebhart & Peterson, Anchorage, 1964-68; broker, owner Walter F. Fournier & Assocs., Anchorage, 1968—; pres. Alaska Mortgage Cons., Anchorage, 1968-69; owner Alaska Venture Capital, 1985—. Pres. Fairview Community Council, Anchorage, 1980-81. Served with U.S. Army, 1928-31, with USN, 1944-45, PTO. Recipient Spl. Recognition award HUD, 1967. Mem. Review Mortgage Underwriters, Inst. Bus. Appraisers, Internat. Soc. Financiers, Soc. Exchange Counselors (rep. 1970), Alaska Creative Real Estate Assn. (pres. 1978, Gold Pan award 1988), Alaska Million Plus Soc. (pres. 1983). Roman Catholic. Lodge: KC. Avocations: weight lifting, flying, fishing.

FOURQUET, BERNARD JEAN, pulmonologist, consultant; b. Calais, France, Sept. 1, 1948; s. Michel Jean and Jeanne Marie (Pecherand) F.; m. Marie Jeanne Graveline, Oct. 10, 1967; children: Sandrine, Romain, Matthias. B, Lycée of Calais, 1966; MD, Centre Hop. Universitain, Amiens, 1978. Med. Diplomate bd. cert. in pulmonology. Internship Centre Hop. Universitary, Amiens, 1975-78, cons., 1978-79; pvt. practice Calais, 1980-83; cons. Centre Hop. de Calais, 1981-88, 1st consulrant, 1989—. Fellow Societe Europeene de Pneumologie, Soc. Pathologic Thoracique du Nordit, Soc. Pathologie Thracique du Nord Informatique. Avocations: horses, sailing. Home: 10 rue Philippine de Hainaut, Calais Pas de Calais 62100, France Office: Cabinet de Pneumologie, 2C rue Philippine deHainaut, Calais France 62100

FOURT, BERNARD-FRANCOIS P., retired engineer; b. Vermelles, France, Oct. 12, 1927; s. Antoine-Jean Fourt and Denise Angele Hanot-Fourt; m. Henriette Mortamet, Sept. 22, 1956; children: Benoit, Gilles, Catherine, Frederique (dec.), Jerome, Beatrice, Martin, Xavier, Marie-Laure. Degree in Elec. Engring., Ecole Supr. Electricity, Malakoff, 1952; MBA, Harvard Bus. Sch., Boston, 1955; Ancien Auditeur, IHEDN, Paris, 1969. Profl. engr. Sales engr. Le Carbone Lorraine, Paris, 1952-53; prodn. mgr. Compagnie Electromecanique and subs., Villeurbane, France, 1955-59; svc. mgr. Compagnie Electromecanique and subs., Paris, 1959-62; plant mgr. Darex, DeWalko, W.R. Grace, Epernon, France, 1962-64; internal cons. Alcatel Alsthom (formerly CGE), France, 1964-67; pres. Le Joint Français, Bezons, France, 1967-76; pvt. cons. Le Vesinet, France, 1976-88; expert at the ct. of appeal Versailles, 1978—. Lt. French Army, 1947-48, hon. maj. Roman Catholic. Avocations: golf, bridge. Home: 11 Rue des Reservoirs, Le Vesinet 78110, France

FOURTOU, JANELLY, foreign diplomat; b. Paris, Apr. 2, 1939. Mem. European Parliament, 1999—, mem. com. on legal affairs and internal mkt., mem. com. on petitions; substitute com. on culture, youth, edn., the media and sport; mem. Group of the European People's Party (Christian Democrats) and European Democrats; mem. delegation for relations with the countries of Ctrl. Am. and Mex.; substitute delegation to the EU-Lithuania Joint Parliamentary Com. Office: Parlement européen, Rue Wiertz ASP 13E150, B-1047 Brussels Belgium*

FOUSSARD, ODETTE BLANPIN, retired pharmacy educator, researcher; b. Paris, Mar. 25, 1927; d. Robert and Louise (Crosnier) Blanpin; m. Michel Foussard, July 27, 1963; children: Patrick, Sylvie, Isabelle. PhD in Pharmacy, U. Paris, 1955, Agregation of Pharmacy Pharmacodyn., 1958; Scis. degree, U. Poitiers, France, 1963; High Skilled Prof. degree (hon.), U. F. Rabelais, Tours, 1993. Intern in pharmacy Biochem. Analysis Lab., State Hosps. Broca-Bretonneau, Paris, 1948-53; supr. hormonal analysis and hematol. lab. State Hosps. La Pitie-Salpetriere, Paris, 1953-56; supr. Hormonal Explorations Lab. State Hosp. St. Antoine, Paris, 1956-59; assoc. prof. pharmacodyn. U. Tours (France) Med. and Pharmacy Sch., Faculty, 1958-64; prof. U. Tours (France) Med. and Pharmacy Sch., 1964-93, organizer, supr. pharmacodyn. cert., 1973-80; ret., 1993; pub. expert pharmacotoxicology French Ministry Health and Social Security, Paris, 1960-93; mem. sci. reading com. Lyon-Pharmaceutique, 1985—; numerous lectures to schs., hosps. and learned socs., France, Guadeloupe, Germany, 1951-98; jud. expert of pharmacology and toxicology Ct. Appeal, Orleans, France, 1985-98. Author: Common Drugs, 1996, Comfort Drugs, 1998, (with others) Fundamental Pharmacology, 1989, Medicines (Antiepileptics, Local Anesthetics), 1996; contbr. over 290 articles to sci. jours., including Jour. Pharmacologie, Anesth.-Analg., Arch. Int. Pharmacodynamy, Ann. Pharm. France, Therapie, France. Del. Dept. San. and Social Edn., Indre et Loire, France, 1963-70. Decorated chevalier Nat. Order of Merit, Legion of Honor (France), officer in order Acad. Palms (for svcs. to edn. in France); recipient gold medal State Hosps. Paris, 1952; recipient Prix Roussel, 1955, 58, Prix Helme, 1961, prize of Pharmacy Order, 1963. Mem. Acad. Scis., Arts and Lit. Touraine. Roman Catholic. Avocations: reading, lectures, documentary research in history and science. Home: 11 rue du Petit Pas d'Ane, 37300 Joué les Tours Touraine, France

FOWLER, CARL, retired educator, boxing statistician; b. St. Louis, Mar. 19, 1939; s. Cornelius and Esther (Laten) F.; m. Grace Hicks, Apr. 12, 1967 (div. Feb. 1976); children: Kinmberly, Maya; m. Marlis Lorraine Tennon, Aug. 22, 1978; 1 child, Ingrid. BS, Lincoln U., Jefferson City, Mo., 1963; MS, Govs. State U., Chgo., 1975, postgrad. Lic. pvt. investigator. Tchr. Chgo. Bd. Edn., 1965-93. Author: Boxing for Boxers, 1982; inventor computerized statis. data base system for boxing. Served with U.S. Army, 1963-65. Recipient Cert. of Merit, ARC, St. Louis, 1960. Avocation: karaoke. Home: 1545 W 120th St Chicago IL 60643-5461

FOWLER, CHARLES ALLISON EUGENE, retired architect, engineer; b. Halifax, N.S., Can., Jan. 24, 1921; s. Charles Allison and Mildred (Crosby) F.; m. Dorothy Christine Graham, Aug. 30, 1947; children: Graham Allison, Beverly Anne. BSc, Dalhousie U., 1942; B in Engring., McGill U., 1944; BArch., U. Man., 1948; DEng (hon.), Tech. U. of Nova Scotia, 1975. With C.A. Fowler, Bauld & Mitchell, Ltd. (and predecessor firms), Halifax, 1946-80; sr. ptnr. C.A. Fowler, Bauld & Mitchell, Ltd. (and predecessor firms), 1950-70, pres., 1970-80, chmn., 1980-81; pres. C.A. Fowler & Co., 1950-70, 81-95; assoc. Vaughan Engring. Assocs. Ltd., Halifax, 1992-94; ret., 1995. Prin. works include Miners Mus., Glace Bay, N.S., Dalhousie U. Fine Arts Ctr., 1970, univ. ctr. Acadia U., Acad. Ctr. at Mt. St. Vincent U., Halifax Law Cts., Canadian Martyrs Ch., Can. Permanent Bldg. Hfx., Halifax Metro Ctr., Stadacona Hosp., Victoria Gen. Hosp., Centre 200, Sydney, N.S. Past chmn. bd. dirs. N.S. Coll. Art and Design. With Can. Army, 1943-46. Fellow AIA (hon.), Royal Archtl. Inst. Can. (pres. 1965), Can. Soc. for Civil Engring.; mem. Engring. Inst. Can. (life). Mem. United Ch. Home: 2 Hall's Rd. Halifax, NS Canada B3P 1P3

FOWLER, CLARE JULIET, uro-neurology consultant; b. Bristol, Eng., July 1, 1950; d. Peter A. and Jean M. (Crum) F.; m. Christopher G. Fowler, Dec., 1975 (div. 1996); children: Alice, William. MB, BS with honors, Middlesex (Eng.) Med. Sch., 1973; MSc in Physiology, U. Coll. London, 1978. Hosp. cons. U. Coll. London Hosp., London, 1987—, St. Bartholomew's Hosp., London, 1987-89, Nat. Hosp. for Neurology and Neurosurgery, London, 1987—; dep. med. dir. U. Coll. London Hosps. Trust, 1998—. Editor: Clinical Neurophysiology, 1994, Neurology of Bladder, Bowel and Sexual Dysfunction, 1999; contbr. 27 chpts. to books on neurology of bladder and sexual function; contbr. numerous articles to profl. jours. Fellow Royal Coll. Physicians; mem. Internat. Continence Soc. (sci. com. 1995-97), Brit. Soc. Clin. Neurophysiology (sec. 1992-95), Clin. Autonomic Rsch. Soc. (chmn. 1990-92). Avocations: travel, dining out, spending time with granddaughter. Fax: 020 7813 4587. E-mail: c.fowler@ion.ucl.ac.uk. Office: Nat Hosp Neurol Neurosurg, Queen Sq, London WC1N 3BG, England

FOWLER, FREDERICK VICTOR, JR., import company executive; b. Newton, Mass., May 27, 1933; s. Frederick Victor and Priscilla (Coffin) F.; m. Nancy White, Apr. 18, 1959; children: Cynthia, Frederick III. BSBA, Boston U., 1955. Salesman Fred V. Fowler Co., Newton, 1958-69; v.p. UNA Corp., Boston, 1969-72; pres., CEO Fred V. Fowler Co., Inc., Newton, 1972—; ptnr. J-L Crescent Co., Detroit, 1988—. Col. USAF, 1955-78. Mem. Soc. Mgr. Engrs., Am. Measuring Tools Mfrs. Assn. (pres.), Nat. Machine Tool Builders Assn., Nat. Bus. Aircraft Assn., Aircraft Owners and Pilots Assn., Air Force Assn., Res. Officers Assn., Rep. 500 Club, Boston U. Alumni Club (v.p. 1975-78). Episcopalian. Avocations: flying, golf, skiing, travel. Office: Fred V Fowler Co Inc 66 Rowe St Auburndale MA 02466-1530

FOWLER, GEORGE SELTON, JR., architect; b. Chgo., Jan. 20, 1920; s. George Selton and Mabel Helena (Overton) F.; m. Yvonne Fern Grammer, Nov. 25, 1945; 1 child, Kim Ellyn. Cert. in European geo-politics and advanced language study, Hamilton Coll. (Army Specialized Tng. Program), 1944; BS in Architecture, Ill. Inst. Tech., 1949, postgrad. City and Regional Planning, 1968. Cert. Elec. Assn. Ill., 1976; reg. arch., Ill., Ohio. Co-founder, pres. The Modern Arts Press, Chgo., 1946; instr. archtl. and related engring. subjects Am. Sch. and Tech. Soc., Chgo., 1948-65; urban planner Chgo. Land Clearance Commn., 1949-50; liaison architect Chgo. Housing Authority, 1950-68, chief design-tech. divsn., 1968-80, dir. dept. engring., 1980-84; prin. George S. Fowler Architect, Chgo., 1984-90; treas., bd. dirs. Chgo. Housing Authority Credit Union, 1963-65; architect, cmty. planner and cons. Interconco., 1965-66. Author: (textbook study guide) Reinforced Concrete Design, 1959. Patentee, subcom. chmn. Mayor's Adv. Commn. to Revise the Bldg. Code, 1986-91; founder, pres., EFCO Creative Concepts Rsch., 1988—. Served with Corp. of Engrs., U.S. Army, 1942-46, group sgt. maj., 1944-46. Recipient citation for residential devel. Mayor Richard J. Daley, Chgo., 1960, Black Achievers of Industry Recognition award YMCA, Chgo., 1977; Kappa Alpha Psi grantee, 1936. Mem. Nat. Assn. Housing and Redevel. Ofcls., Internat. Platform Assn., Inventors Coun. Chgo. Home and Office: 8209 S Rhodes Ave Chicago IL 60619-5005

FOWLER, HENRY HAMILL, investment banker; b. Roanoke, Va., Sept. 5, 1908; s. Mack Johnson and Bertha (Browning) F.; m. Trudye Pamela Hathcote, Oct. 19, 1938; children: Mary Anne Fowler Smith, Susan Fowler-Gallagher, Henry Hamill (dec.). AB, Roanoke Coll., 1929, LLD, 1962; LLB, Yale U., 1932, JSD, 1933; LLD, William and Mary U., 1966, Wesleyan U., 1966. Bar: Va. 1933, D.C. 1946. Counsel TVA, 1934-38, asst. gen. counsel, 1939; spl. asst. to atty. gen. as chief counsel subcom. Senate Com. Edn. and Labor, 1939-40; spl. counsel Fed. Power Commn., 1941; asst. gen. counsel Office Prodn. Mgmt., 1941, War Prodn. Bd., 1942-44; econ. advisor U.S. Mission Econ. Affairs, London, 1944; spl. asst. to adminstr. Fgn. Econ. Adminstrn., 1945; dep. adminstr. N.P.A., 1951, adminstr., 1952; adminstr. Def. Prodn. Adminstrn., 1952-53; dir. Office Def. Moblzn., mem. NSC, 1952-53; sr. mem. firm Fowler, Leva Hawes & Symington, Washington, 1946-51, 1953-61, 64-65, undersec. Treasury, 1961-64, sec. Treasury, 1965-68; gen. partner Goldman, Sachs & Co., N.Y.C., 1969-81, ltd. ptnr., 1981—; chmn. Goldman, Sachs Internat. Corp., N.Y.C., 1969-84; dir. Corning Glass Works, U.S. and Fgn. Securities Corp., U.S. Industries Inc., Norfolk and Western Co., Trans-World Airlines. Trustee Franklin D. Roosevelt Four Freedoms Found., 1982-87, Lyndon B. Johnson Found., 1973—, Roanoke Coll., 1954—, Christ Ch., Alexandria, Va., Atlantic Coun. U.S., vice chmn., 1978—; co-chmn. Citizens Network for Fgn. Affairs, 1987—, Com. on the Present Danger, 1976-88, Bretton Woods Commn., 1985-89; chmn. bd. trustees Roanoke Coll., 1974-81; chmn. Atlantic Coun. U.S., 1973-78; chmn. bd. trustees Inst. Internat. Edn., 1972-77; mem. coun. Miller Ctr. for Pub. Affairs, U. Va., 1980-91; bd. dirs. Alfred E. Sloan Found., 1971-81, Carnegie Found. for Peace, 1974-80, Japan Soc., 1974-78. Mem. Councilor Conf. Bd. Yale Law Sch. Assn. Washington (pres. 1955), Links Club (N.Y.C.), River Club (N.Y.C.) Met. Club (Washington), Bohemian Club (San Francisco), Pi Kappa Phi, Phi Delta Phi. Democrat. Episcopalian. Home: 209 S Fairfax St Alexandria VA 22314-3303 Office: Goldman Sachs 85 Broad St New York NY 10004-2456 also: 200 E 66th St New York NY 10021-9175 *Died Jan. 3, 2000.*

FOWLER, HUGH CHARLES, rail transportation executive; b. Chgo., May 21, 1926; s. Frank Parker and Dorothy Valentine Hinckley F.; m. Shirley Sprague, July 7, 1949; children: Laurie Lynn, Hugh C. Jr. BS in Bus., U. colo., 1948. V.p. Tool & Armstrong, Inc., Denver, 1958-62, Campbell Mithun, Inc., Mpls., 1962-66; pres. Fowler & More, Inc., Denver, 1966-76; v.p. Hillsdale (Mich.) Coll., 1981-85; pres. Wishy Washy, Inc., Denver, 1985-92, Classic Schs., Inc., Denver, 1992—. Sen. Colo. Gen. Assembly, Denver, 1968-80; regent-at-large U. Colo., Boulder, 1982-89; commr. White House Pres. Scholars, Washington, 1980-92; dir., sec. Colo. Monorail Authority, Idaho Springs, 1998—. Lt. USNR, 1943-58. Republican. Presbyterian.

FOWLER, JENNEFER RAE, sculptor; b. Bay City, Tex., Feb. 14, 1973; d. Bobby Owens and Ygerne Roxanne Michalec Hubbell; 1 child, Lexis DeVoe Beauford. Student, Richland Jr. Coll., 1991, 92; BFA with honors, U. Ctrl. Ark., 1998; postgrad., U. Ark. Little Rock, 1999—. Intern, apprentice Richard Hunt Studios, Chgo., 1997; tech. asst. Chgo. Fine Art Foundry, 1997, Hunt Studios, Chgo., 1997; sculptor disability svcs. U. Ctrl. Ark., Conway, 1998; tchr. Assn. Retarded Citizens, Little Rock, 1999; mem. com. Kramer Artist Coop., Little Rock, 1997; v.p. Kramer Sch. Artist Coop. Sculptor, Moon Meditation, 1997; exhibited in group shows at U. Ctrl. Ark., Conway, 1997, 98, Womans' City Club, 1999, Ctrs. Youth and Family, 1999, Art Found., Hot springs, 1999, 2000. Scholar U. Ctrl. Ark., 1998. Mem. Art History Assn. (v.p. 1997). Democrat. Avocations: painting with oil, watercolors, acrylic; camping, canoeing, swimming, figure drawing. Home: 715 Sherman St Apt 7 Little Rock AR 72202-2685

FOWLER, JOHN ROBERT, JR., emergency medicine physician, consultant; b. Atlanta, Aug. 30, 1955; arrived in Turkey, 1990; s. John Robert and Mary Anne (Robinson) F.; m. Dianne Elaine Frierson, Dec. 22, 1981; children: Amy, Sarah, Elaine, John, Tom, Debby. BS, UCLA, 1978, MD, 1983. Diplomate Am. Bd. Emergency Medicine, Nat. Bd. Med. Examiners. Resident dept. emergency medicine U. Cin. Hosp., 1983-87, asst. clin. prof., 1987-90; mem. staff St. Luke's West Hosp., Florence, Ky., 1987-90; asst. prof. Dokuz Eylül U. Sch. Medicine, Izmir, Turkey, 1990-97; educator, consultant Ephesus Emergency Medicine Tng. and Rsch. Ctr., Izmir, 1998—; dir. emergency medicine residencey program Dokuz Eylül U., 1993-97, med. dir. paramedic tng. program, 1993-97; cons. emergency medicine residency programs Bursa and Antalya, Turkey, 1998—; cons. Turkish Ministry Health, Ankara, 1992—. Contbr. articles to profl. jours., chpts. to books. Player U.S. Nat. Rugby Team, 1980-85. Inducted into GTE Acad. All-Am. Hall of Fame, Dallas, 1999. Fellow Am. Coll. Emergency Physicians, Am. Acad. Clin. Toxicology; mem. Emergency Medicine Physicians Assn. Turkey (founder), Emergency Medicine Assn. Turkey (founder). Presbyterian. Avocations: basketball, Bible study, bicycling. E-mail: fowler@ispro.net.tr. Home: Atadan Cad No 124, 35160 Buca Izmir, Turkey Office: Ephesus Emer Med Tng & Rsch, 1457 Sk No 27, 35220 Alsancak Izmir, Turkey

FOWLER, ROBERT RAMSAY, Canadian government official; b. Ottawa, Ont., Can., Aug. 18, 1944; s. Robert MacLaren and Sheila Gordon (Ramsay) F.; m. Mary Stoker, June 13, 1981; children: Linton, Ruth, Antonia, Justine. BA, Queen's U., Kingston, Ont., 1968. Joined Fed. Pub. Svc. Can. Internat. Develop. Agy., Ottawa, 1968-69, dept. external affairs, 1969-71; 2nd sec. Can. Embassy, Paris, 1971-74; with comml. policy divsn. external affairs, 1974-76; 1st sec., counsellor Can. Permanent Mission to UN, N.Y.C., 1976-78; exec. asst. to under-sec. state, external affairs Can. Ottawa, 1978-80; asst.ssec. to cabinet, fgn. and def. policy Privy Coun. Office, Ottawa, 1980-86; asst. dep. min. (policy) Dept. Nat. Def., Ottawa, 1986-89, dep. min., 1989-95; amb. and permanent rep. UN Permanent Mission of Can. to UN, N.Y.C., 1995—. Avocation: photography. Office: Perm Mission of Canada to UN 885 2nd Ave Fl 14 New York NY 10017-2201

FOWLER, SCOTT WELLINGTON, biological oceanographer; b. Berkeley, Calif., May 31, 1941; s. Charles Arman and Inez (Hanson) F.; m. Diana Carolyn Martin, June 12, 1965; children: Tanith Nicole, Derek Martin. BA, U. Calif., 1964; MS, Oreg. State U., 1966, PhD, 1969. Lab. rsch. asst. biology dept. U. Calif., Riverside, 1964; rsch. asst. oceanography dept. Oreg. State U., Corvallis, 1964-66, 67-69; rsch. scientist Battelle N.W. Labs., Richland, Wash., 1966-67; Fulbright postdoctoral lectr. Sch. of Marine Scis. and Food Tech., Guaymas, Mex., 1969-70; head radioecology lab. IAEA Marine Environ. Lab., Monaco, 1970—; cons. Smithsonian Inst. Mediterreanian Marine Sorting Ctr., Kherredine, Tunisia, 1971, UN Environ. Program, Persian Gulf, 1980, Oman, 1980, Libya, 1982, Algeria, 1983, Somalia, 1986; expert Internat. Atomic Energy Agy., Dominican Repulic, 1993; invited prof. INRS U. Quebec, 1993—; prin. investigators numerous UN and European Union rsch. contracts; tech. sec. Group of Experts on Sci. Aspects of Marine Environ. Protection UN, 1999—. Contbr. articles to profl. jours. Predoctoral fellow U.S. Atomic Energy Commn., 1966-68; recipient Disting. Svc. award Internat. Atomic Energy Agy., 1999. Mem. Internat. Commn. for Scientific Exploration of the Mediterranean (pres. marine radioactivity com. 1979-84, 90-95, pres. environl. chemistry com. 1996—), Am. Geophys. Union, Am. Soc. of Limnology and Oceanography, Internat. Union for Conservation of Nature Commn. on Ecology, Internat. Union Radioecologists. Avocations: tennis, swimming, skiing, gardening, oenology. Home: 8 Allee des Orangers, 06320 Cap d'Ail France Office: Internat Atomic Energy Agy, Marine Environ Lab POB 800, MC98012 Monaco Monaco

FOWLER, TERRI (MARIE THERESE FOWLER), artist; b. Decatur, Ga., Sept. 26, 1949; d. John Francis and Marjorie Herndon; m. John Charles Fowler, July 29, 1972; children: Courtney Marie, Douglas Edwin. Studied with Carolyn Wyeth, Wyeth Sch. Art, 1972. speaker to arts groups, schools. One-man shows include Hampden Sydney Coll., 1973, Longwood, Coll., 1976, C&S Bank, Camden, S.C., 1979, Benfield Gallery, 1985-99; exhibited in cen. chpt. Va. Mus., 1973 (recipient award 1973), Colonial Williamsburg, 1974-77, Md. St. House, Md. St. Senate, 1983-85; works selected by Am. Heart Assn. for Holiday Card Series, 1986-87, commnd. Prince Edward County Bicentennial Com., 1976; represented in many nat. and internat. pvt. collections. Active Girl Scouts Am. ctrl. Md.; sec. citizens adv. com. Annapolis Mid. Sch. Mem. Balt. Watercolor Soc., Md. Fedn. Art. Annapolis Watercolor Club., San Diego Watercolor Soc., U.S. Naval Acad. Womens Club and Garden Club. Avocations: reading, flower arranging, gardening. Home: 123 Groh Ln Annapolis MD 21403-4008

FOWLER, WAYNE LEWIS, SR., internist; b. Topeka, Kans., Jan. 5, 1923; s. Morrill George and Grace Anna (Carlson) F.; m. Violet June Ransom, Sept. 4, 1948; children: Wayne Jr., Deborah. BS, Washburn U., 1945; MD, U. Ind., 1947. Diplomate Am. Bd. Internal Medicine. Intern Kansas City (Mo.) Gen. Hosp., 1947-48, resident internal medicine, 1948-51; internist Galvin-Haughey Clinic, Concordia, Kans., 1953-95, NCK Med. Clinic, Concordia, Kans., 1995—; past pres. med. staff St. Joseph Hosp., Concordia Kans. Capt. US Air Force, 1951-53,. Fellow Am. Coll. Physicians (Laureate award Kans. chpt. 1994), Am. Coll. Chest Physicians; mem. AMA, Cl. County Med. Soc., Kans. Med. Soc., Am. Soc. Internal Medicine, Concordia Elks, Concordia Moose, Topeka Masonic Lodge # 17, Scottish Rite Bodies Topeka, ISIS Shrine alina. Republican. Episcopalian. Avocation: amateur radio. Home: 332 W 8th St Concordia KS 66901-3406 Office: NCK Med Inc 1010 3rd Ave Concordia KS 66901-4003

FOWLER, WYCHE, JR., ambassador; b. Atlanta, GA, Oct. 6, 1940; s. William Wyche and Emelyn (Barbre) F.; 1 dau., Katherine Wyche. BA, Davidson Coll., 1962; JD, Emory U., 1969. Bar: Ga. 1970. Chief asst. to Congressman Charles Weltner, 1965; mem. Atlanta Bd. Aldermen, 1969-73; pres. Atlanta City Council, 1973-77; mem. 95th-99th Congresses from 5th Ga. Dist., 1977-87; U.S. Senator from Ga., 1987-92; with Powell, Goldstein, Frazer & Murphy, Washington & Atlanta, 1993-95; pvt. practice law, 1996; U.S. amb. Saudi Arabia, 1996—. Served in U.S. Army. Recipient Myrtle Wreath award, 1972, Congl. sunbelt coun. ann. award, 1981, Ga. Citizens Coalition on Hunger award, 1982; named Outstanding Young Man Atlanta Jaycees, 1972, Outstanding Young Man Ga. Jaycees, 1973. Mem. ABA, State Bar Ga., Phi Delta Theta. Democrat. Office: US Embassy Unit 61307 APO AE 09803-1307

FOWLES, JOHN, author; b. Essex, Eng., Mar. 31, 1926; s. Robert and Gladys (Richards) F.; m. Elizabeth Whitton, Apr. 2, 1954 (dec. 1990); m. Sarah Smith, Sept. 3, 1998. Honours degree in French, Oxford U., 1950; D.Litt., Exeter U., 1983; LittD, U. East Anglia, 1997. Author: The Collector, 1963, The Aristos, 1964, The Magus, 1966, The French Lieutenant's Woman, 1969, Poems, 1973, The Ebony Tower, 1974, Shipwreck, 1977, Daniel Martin, 1977, Islands, 1978, The Tree, 1979, Mantissa, 1982, A Maggot, 1985, Wormholes, 1998. Hon. fellow New Coll., Oxford, 1997. Office: Jonathan Cape Ltd, 20 Vauxhall Bridge RD, London SW1V 2SA, England

FOWLKES, NANCY LANETTA PINKARD, social worker; d. Amos Malone and Nettie (Barnett) Pinkard; m. Vester Guy Fowlkes, June 4, 1955 (dec. 1965); 1 child, Wendy Denise. BA, Bennett Coll., 1946; MA, Syracuse U., 1952; MSW, Smith Coll., 1963; MPA, Pace U., 1982. Dir. publicity Bennett Coll., Greensboro, N.C., 1946-47, 49-50; asst. editor Va. Edn. Bull. ofcl. organ Va. State Tchrs. Assn., Richmond, 1950-52; asst. office mgr. Cmty. Svc. Soc., N.Y.C., 1952-55; social caseworker, asst. supr. Dept. Social Svcs. Westchester County, White Plains, N.Y., 1959-67; supr. adoption svcs. Westchester County, White Plains, 1967-77, supr. adoption and foster care, 1977-89; mem. adv. bd. White Plains Adult Edn. Sch. First v.p. Eastview Jr. H.S., 1970-71; area chmn. White Plains Cmty. Chest, 1964; sec. Mt. Vernon Concert Group, 1952-54; fund raising co-chmn. Urban League Guild of Westchester, 1967; pres. White Plains Interfaith Coun., 1972-74; pres. northeastern jurisdiction United Meth. Ch., 1988-92; chmn. adminstrv. bd. Meth. Ch., 1970-72, 82-83, vice chmn., 1978-80, vice chmn. trustees, 1973-77, treas., 1978-83; lay spkr., v.p. Met. dist. United Meth. Women, 1977-79, exec. bd. N.Y. conf.; N.Y. conf. rep. Upper Atlantic Regional Sch., 1981-83, mem. nominating com., 1982-83, trustee N.Y. conf., 1982-88, pres. N.Y. conf., 1983-87; bd. dirs. Global Ministries United Meth. Ch., 1988-96, women's divsn., 1988-96, v.p., chair sect. finance women's divsn., 1992-96, supt., 1997—, chair program divsn. N.Y. conf., 1989-93; v.p. superintendency commn. Met. North Dist., 1997—; chair Episcopal residence

N.Y. Conf. Episcopancy Commn., 1997—; mem. N.Y. Conf. Bd. Ordained Ministry, 2000—; bd. dirs. Family Svc. Westchester, Bethel Meth. Home, Ossining, N.Y., White Plains YWCA, 1985-93, Scarritt Bennett Ctr., Nashville, 1990—, Gum Moon Women's Residence, San Francisco, 1992-96, White Plains-Greenburg NAACP, 1993-98. Mem. NASW, Acad. Cert. Social Workers, Jack and Jill of Am. Inc. (chpt. pres. 1954-56, regional sec.-treas. 1967-71), Nat. Bus. and Profl. Women's Club (chpt. sec. 1954-56), Internat. Platform Assn., Theta Sigma Phi (sec.-treas.), Zeta Nu Omega, Alpha Kappa Alpha (pres. 1960-64, treas. 1975-78), Regency Bridge Club (pres. 1963-65). Home: 107 Valley Rd White Plains NY 10604-2316

FOX, ALLISON MARGARET, clinical neuropsychologist; b. Sydney, Australia, July 11, 1960; d. Geoffrey Arthur and Anne Joann (Fraser) F.; m. Gregory Alan Fraser, Apr. 18, 1992; children: Ian, Matthew, Jacqueline. BSc with honors, Sydney, 1986, PhD in Psychology, 1995, M in Clin. Neuropsychology, 1998. Cert. psychologist, clin. psychologist; registered psychology NSW State Registration Bd. Rsch. asst. Prince of Wales Hosp., Sydney, 1984-87; lectr. Nat. Drug and Alchol Rsch. Ctr., Sydney, 1990-93, U. Wollongong, 1993-97, 1993-99; lectr. U. We. Australian, 1999—; hon. rsch. fellow Nat. Drug and Alcohol Rsch. Ctr., Sydney, 1993-96; neuroimaging panel mem. Neurosci. Inst. for Schizophrenia and Associated Disorders, 1994—. Contbr. articles to profl. jours. Mem. Australian Psychol. Soc., Coll. of Clin. Neuropsychologists. Avocations: reading, family. Fax: 61-2-42214163. E-mail: afox@psy.uwa.edu.au. Home: 328B Bagot Rd, Subiaco WA 6008, Australia Office: U Wollongong, Northfields Ave, Wollongong NSW 2522, Australia

FOX, BRIAN L. (MONTY FOX), automotive executive; b. Indpls., Sept. 3, 1960; s. Ralph E. and Delores L. F.; m. Mary Ann Fox (div. Oct. 19, 1995); children: Brian, Kyle, Meghan. BS, Olivet Nazarene U., 1983; exec. devel. trainee, Ford Motor Inst., Dearborn, Mich., 1986; MBA/JD, Ind. U., 1992. Cert. quality engr., lead auditor. Divsn. dir. quality Ford Motor Co., Dearborn, 1984-93; divsn. v.p. quality Gen. Corp. Automotive, Fairlawn, Ohio, 1993-95; corp. dir. quality Mishikawa Stds., Topeka, Ind., 1995-98, Southcorp Packaging, Atlanta, 1998—; arbitrator BBB Indpls., 1986—, NLRB Indpls., 1989—, Am. Arbitration Assn. Indpls., 1989—. Co-author: (book) Benchmarking, 1992; contbr. articles to profl. jours. Mem. Am. Soc. Quality Control. Mem. Ch. of the Nazarene. Avocations: following sons' sports activities, daughter's cheerleading, music, golf. E-mail: bf873744@aol.com. Home: 1201 Carson Way Apt 119 Greenwood IN 46143-2231

FOX, CARSON ALEXANDRA, artist, educator; b. Oxford, Miss., July 6, 1968; d. James Edward and Patricia (Lockhart) F.; m. David Patrick Kelly, May 23, 1998. Cert., Pa. Acad. Fine Arts, 1991; BFA, U. Pa., 1996; MFA, Rutgers U., 1999. Instr. fine arts Pa. Acad. Fine Arts, Phila., 1994—, NYU, N.Y.C., 1999—; artist-in-residence Cardiff (Wales) Inst. Higher Edn., 1993, Frans Masereel Print Ctr., Kasterlee, Belgium, 1998; lectr. in field. One woman shows at St. Conat's Art Ctr., Cardiff, 1993, Artist House Gallery, Phila., 1995, 97, 98, Rider U. Gallery, Lawrenceville, N.J., 1999, Montomery County (Pa.) Coll. Gallery, 2000; group exhbns. include Lemuria Gallery, 1991, 92, Main Line Art Ctr., 1991, 95-99, Woodmere (Pa.) Mus., 1991, Montgomery Coll., 1992, Artist House Gallery, 1992, 95-98, Llantaman Glange Arts Ctr., Cardiff, 1993, William Penn Charter Sch., Phila., 1992, 93, Nat. Mus. Wales, Cardiff, 1994, Sande Webster Gallery, 1995, 97, Mus. Am. Art, Pa. Acad. Fine Arts, 1996-98, Mason Gross Gallery, Rutgers U., 1999; represented in permanent collections at Royal Mus. Belgium, Antwerp, Phila. Mus. Art, Hofstra Mus., Hempstead, N.Y., N.J. Acad. Medicine, Princeton, Rider U., Arco Chem. Co., Phila. Cresson fellow Pa. Acad. Fine Arts; Huldah Bender Kerner scholar, 1989, Ruth and Ben Wolf Printmaking scholar, 1991; recipient Benjamin Lanard Meml. award H.M., 1990, Daniel Garber Drawing award, 1990, Ruth and Ben Wolf Printmaking prize H.M., 1990, Monotype Purchase prize, 1990, Small Black and White Print prize H.M., 1990, award for excellence in fine arts award Nat. League Am. Pen Women, 1990, Color Print Purchase prize H.M., 1991, Henry Pratt Meml. prize in printmaking, 1991, John R. Connor Meml. Prize in printmaking, 1991, Charles Toppan Drawing award, 1991, Grumbacher award for printmaking, 1992; N.J. Acad. Medicine artist's print commn., 1999. Avocation: gardening. Office: Pa Acad Fine Arts 1301 Cherry St Philadelphia PA 19107-2095

FOX, DONALD THOMAS, lawyer; b. Council Bluffs, Iowa, June 12, 1929; s. Donald and Genevieve (Tinley) F.; m. Ana Clemencia Tercero-Graham; children: Mark, Matthew, Genevieve, Melissa. AB magna cum laude, Harvard U., 1951; LLB, N.Y. U., 1956; Brevet de Traduction et de Terminologie Juridiques, U. Paris, 1957, Diplôme de Droit Comparé, 1961. Bar: N.Y. 1957, U.S. Ct. Claims 1960, U.S. Dist. Ct. (so. and ea. dists.) N.Y. 1960, U.S. Ct. Appeals (2nd cir.) 1960, D.C. 1968, U.S. Tax Ct. 1973. Instr. Inst. Comparative Law, NYU, 1957-59; assoc. Davis, Polk, Wardwell, Sunderland & Kiendl, N.Y.C., 1958-67; ptnr. Fox Horan & Camerini, LLP and predecessor firms, N.Y.C., 1968—; bd. dirs. Washington Sq. Legal Svcs., Inc., N.Y.C., 1974-85, Uniroyal Goodrich Tire Co., 1990-96, Michelin Licensing Svcs. Inc., Globalstar do Brazil, 1995-99; mem. adv. com. on history and theory Harvard U. Grad. Sch. Design, 1990—. Author: Conciliation of International Economic Disputes, 1964, Human Rights in Guatemala, 1979, Report on Contra Activity in Nicaragua, 1985, Violence in Colombia, 1989, Hungarian Constitutional Reform and the Rule of Law, 1993, Elections in Ethiopia, 1995, Elections in Nicaragua, 1996, Elections in Mexico, 1997; editor: The Cambodian Incursion: Legal Issues, 1971; mem. panel advisors Jour. Internat. Law and Politics, 1968-99; contbr. articles to legal jours. Trustee Law Ctr. Found., N.Y.U., 1975-86, chmn. campaign fund, , 1980; mem. Am. Soc., 1975—; Coun. on Fgn. Rels., 1973—. 1st lt. USAF, 1951-53. Named to Com. of Honor, Giulio Romano Exhbn., Mantova, Italy, 1989; Albert Gallatin fellow, 1978; Nat. scholar Harvard U., Root-Tilden scholar NYU, Fulbright scholar U. Paris. Fellow Am. Bar Found. (life); mem. Am. Law Inst., Am. Assn. Internat. Commn. Jurists (exec. com., bd. dirs. 1970—, chmn. 1991—), Am. Arbitration Assn. (panel arbitrators 1970—), Assn. of Bar of City of N.Y. (chmn. com. lawyers role in search for peace 1969-71, chmn. com. audit 1978-80, treas. 1982-84, chmn. com. profl. responsibility 1971-74, chmn. fin. com. 1982-84), NYU Law Alumni Assn. (pres. 1971-73), NYU Alumni Fedn. (pres. 1983-85), Humanitarian Found. for Nicaragua (exec. com. bd. dirs. 1991-96), The Century Assn. (chmn. wine com.), The DownTown Assn., Harvard Club of N.Y.C. Office: Fox Horan & Camerini LLP 825 3rd Ave New York NY 10022-7519

FOX, DUKE MELVIN, manufacturing company executive; b. Tracy, Calif., July 6, 1919; s. Hugh Stephen and Frances Irene (Thornton) F.; m. Betty Doerr, Oct. 16, 1952; 1 child, Ralph D. AA, Modesto (Calif.) Jr. Coll., 1940. Engr. Hughes Aircraft Co., Culver City, Calif., 1940-44, Douglas Aircraft, Santa Monica, Calif., 1946-48; pres., owner Fox Mfg. Co., Ft. Smith, Ark., 1948—. Patentee two-cycle motors. With USAAF, 1944-46. Mem. Acad. Model Aeros. (Hall of Fame), Soc. Mfg. Engrs. Republican. Avocations: model airplanes, music, gardening. Home: 2400 S Knoxville St Fort Smith AR 72901-7624 Office: Fox Mfg Co 5305 Towson Ave Fort Smith AR 72901-8497

FOX, J. CHARLES, environmental adminstrator; b. Aug. 2, 1960; married; 1 child. BS in Urban Geog., U. Wis., 1983. Various positions with environ. orgns. Am. Rivers, Friends of the Earth, Environ. Policy Inst., 1983-93; spl. asst. to adminstr. EPA, Washington, 1993-96; asst. sec., COO Md. Dept. Environment, Annapolis, 1996-98; environ. adminstr. EPA, Washington, 1998—. Office: EPA 401 M St SW # Mc4101 Washington DC 20460-0002

FOX, JENNIFER CARMEL, lawyer, consultant, political lobbyist; b. Melbourne, Victoria, Australia, Apr. 13, 1963; d. Kenneth Daniel and Patricia Mary (Jenkins) F. BA, U. Queensland, Brisbane, Australia, 1983, LLB, 1987. Admitted to bar as barrister and solicitor Supreme Cts. Victoria and NSW, High Ct. Australia. Judge's assoc. Supreme Ct. NSW, Sydney, Australia, 1987-89; solicitor Dibbs Crowther & Osborne, Sydney and Melbourne, 1989-92, Corrs Chambers Westgarth, Melbourne, 1992-93, Mallesons Stephen Jaques, Melbourne, 1993-95; sr. rsch. fellow U. Melbourne, 1995-96; prin. policy advisor Shadow Min. for Comm., Canberra, Australia, 1996-97; gen. counsel Macquarie Corp. Telecom., Sydney, 1997-98; prin. Fox & Assocs., Media & Telecom. Lawyers, Sydney, 1998—; cons. Cutler Hughes & Harris, solicitors, Sydney, 1998—, Baker & McKenzie, solicitors, Sydney, 1999—; mem. Pub. Interest Law Clearing House, coordinating body for pro bono legal work in NSW, 1999—. Contbg. author: (looseleaf svc.) Communications Law and Policy in Australia, 1992—; contbr. chpt. to book. Mem. Australian and New Zealand Assn. Psychiatry, Psychology and Law, NSW Medico-Legal Soc. Mem. Australia Labor Party. Roman Catholic. Avocations: mental health law reform, travel (especially Vietnam and Asia).

FOX, JOAN PHYLLIS, environmental engineer; b. Rockledge, Fla., July 16, 1945; d. John A. and Nonie L. (Knutson) Fox. BS in Physics with high honors, U. Fla., 1971; PhD in Civil/Environ. Engring., U. Calif., Bekeley, 1980. Engr. Bechtel, Inc., San Francisco, 1971-76; dir. program and prin. investigator Lawrence Berkeley Lab., 1977-81; prin. engr., pres. Environ. Mgmt., Berkeley, 1981—; guest lectr. dept. conservation and resource studies U. Calif., Berkeley, 1980-84; expert witness in litigation involving air pollution, odor, nuisance, indsl. accidents, groundwater contamination, hazardous wastes, risk assessment. Contbr. articles to profl. pubs. Grantee Dept. Energy, 1976-81, EPA, 1976-81. Mem. NAS (past mem. com. surface mining and reclamation, mem. subcom. on QA/QC of irrigation-induced water quality problems 1986-90), Am. Chem. Soc., Am. Water Resources Assn., Soc. Environ. Toxicology and Chemistry, Phi Beta Kappa, Sigma Pi Sigma. Achievements include design and development of methods to analyze air pollutants. Office: 2526 Etna St Berkeley CA 94704-3115

FOX, MILES, surgeon, urologist; b. Prague, Czechoslovakia, Feb. 22, 1927; s. Victor and Marie Fox; m. Valerie Jean Glover, Sept. 6, 1986; children: Helena, Mary Jane, Candida, Emily Susan, Anna Victoria. MB ChB, Manchester U., Eng., 1950, ChM, 1960, MD, 1965. Dir. Renal Transplant Unit Royal Hallamshire Hosp., Sheffield, Eng., 1968-83, cons. urologist, 1966—; hon. clin. lectr. in surgery U. Sheffield, 1961-92. Capt. Royal Army Med. Corps, 1951-53, Great Britain, Germany. Named Hunterian Prof. of Eng., Royal Coll. of Surgeons, 1976. Fellow Royal Coll. Surgeons; mem. Brit. Assn. of Urological Surgeons, Brit. Transplantation Soc., Brit. Med. Assn., The Transplantation Soc., Internat. Urology, Finnish Med. Assn., Brit. Microsurg. Soc. E-mail: miles.fox@sheffield.ac.uk. Office: Claremont Hosp, 401 Sandygate Rd, Sheffield S10 5UB, Great Britain

FOX, PETER KENDREW, librarian; b. Beverley, Yorkshire, Eng., Mar. 23, 1949; s. Thomas Kendrew and Dorothy (Wildbore) F.; m. Isobel McConnell, Mar. 28, 1983; children: Louise Catherine, Jennifer Clare. BA, King's Coll., London, 1971; MA, U. Sheffield, 1973. Asst. libr. officer U. Library, Cambridge, Eng., 1973-77, asst. under-libr., 1977-78, under-libr., 1978-79; dep. libr. Trinity Coll., Dublin, Ireland, 1979-84, libr., 1984-94; libr. U. Cambridge, England, 1994—; mem. An Chomhairle Leabharlanna, Dublin, 1982-94; mem. Com. on Libr. Cooperation in Ireland, 1983-94; mem. Nat. Preservation Adv. Com., London, 1984-95, Nat. Preservation Office Mgmt. Com, 1996—; chmn. Sconul Adv. Com. on Info. Svcs., London, 1987-90; mem. Wellcome Trust Libr. Adv. Com., 1996—, chmn., 2000—; mem. Lambeth Palace Libr. Com., 1996—; chmn. bd. dirs. Consortium of Univ. Rsch. Librs., 1997-2000, Brotherton Collection Adv. Com., 1999—; mem. humanities and social scis. adv. com. Brit. Libr., 2000—. Author: Reader Instruction Methods in Academic Libraries, 1974, Trinity College Library, Dublin, 1982; editor: International Conferences on Library User Education Proceedings, 1980, 82, 84, Treasures of the Library: Trinity College, Dublin, 1986, The Book of Kells, 1990, Cambridge University Library: The Great Collections, 1998. Fellow Selwyn Coll. Cambridge. Mem. Libr. Assn. U.K. (assoc.). Club: United Oxford and Cambridge U. (London). Office: Univ Libr, Univ Libr West Rd, Cambridge CB3 9DR, England

FOX, THOMAS GEORGE, health science educator; b. N.Y.C., Sept. 15, 1942; s. Thomas Peter and Alice Cecilia (Ehler) F.; m. Mary Patricia Palmer, Aug. 29, 1980; children: Christopher Adam, Thomas Andrew, Stephen Baron. BA, Coll. N.J., 1964; MEd, U. Vt., 1966; PhD, U. Mich., 1972. Asst. to dean U. Mass., Amherst, 1966; dir. counseling and student svcs. U. Mich., Ann Arbor, 1966-68, sr. adminstrv. asst. Med. Ctr., 1968-69, adminstrv. assoc., 1969-71; asst. dean Robert Wood Johnson Med. Sch., Piscataway, N.J., 1972-77, assoc. dean, 1977-83; sr. v.p. Robert Wood Johnson U. Hosp., New Brunswick, N.J., 1983-86; exec. v.p. U. Health System of N.J., New Brunswick, 1986-90; prof., v.p. devel. and univ. rels. Oreg. Health Scis. U., Portland, 1990-94; CEO Univ. Found., 1990-94; pres., CEO, Liberty Sci. Ctr., Jersey City, 1994-96; CEO, Operation Smile, Norfolk, Va., 1996-2000; sr. v.p. Advancement and Sponsored Programs, Wheeling (W.Va.) Jesuit U., 2000—; asst. prof. U. Medicine and Dentistry N.J., 1973-79, assoc. prof., 1979-83, clin. assoc. prof., 1983-90. Contbr. articles to profl. jours. Trustee Francis E. Parker Meml. Home, 1981-90, 96—. Fellow Acad. Medicine N.J.; mem. Am. Coll. Healthcare Execs.(diplomate), Am. Soc. Assns. Execs. (Key Philanthropic Orgns. Com.). Home: 11 Barrington Dr Wheeling WV 26003-6683 Office: Wheeling Jesuit Univ 316 Washington Ave Wheeling WV 26003-6295

FOX, VINCENTE, government official; b. Mexico City, July 2, 1942; s. Jose Luis Fox and Mercedes Quesada; children: Ana Cristina, Vicente, Paulina, Rodrigo. Student, Iberian Am. U.; grad., Harvard U. Pres. Mex. & Latin Am. Coca Cola Co., Mexico City; gov. Guavajuato, Mex., 1995-99; pres. elect Govt. Mex., Mexico City, 2000—. Dep. leader Nat. Action Party, Mexico City, 1988—. Office: Office of The Pres. Puerti Col San Miguel, Mexico DF 11850, Mexico*

FOXCROFT, NIGEL HOWARD, humanities educator; b. Manchester, Eng., Oct. 1, 1958; s. Ronald Joseph and Irene (Coltman) F.; m. Georgie Barna, July 28, 1979; children: Robert Nigel Craig, Roland Julian Alex. BA in Russian Studies with honors, U. Leeds, 1980; MPhil in Russian and Slavonic Studies, U. Sheffield, 1986. Grad. trainee, asst. sci. officer Brit. Libr., Boston Spa, Eng., 1980-82; Slavonic libr., lectr. Russian and English U. Szeged, Hungary, 1983-85; lectr. Russian and English Gyula Juhasz Tchr. Tng. Coll., Szeged, 1985-91; lectr. Russian and European studies U. Brighton, Eng., 1989-90, sr. lectr. Russian and European studies, 1990—, acting course leader, examinations officer, 1998—. Contbr. articles to profl. jours. Mem. Soc. for Coop. in Russian Studies, Assn. Lang. Learning, Brit. Assn. Slavonic and East European Studies, Britain-Russia Ctr. Avocations: travel, photography. Office: Sch Langs, Univ Brighton, Falmer, Brighton BN1 9PH, England

FOX-RABINOVICH, GERMAN SIMONOVICH, engineering executive; b. Moscow, Aug. 8, 1949; s. Simon and Faina (Aronova) F.; m. Gulnara Dosbaeva, Nov. 25, 1988; 1 child, Michael. Mech. Engr., Tech. U. Stankin, Moscow, 1972; PhD, All-Russian Ry. Inst., Moscow, 1983, ScD, 1993; DBA, Kennedy Western U., Calif., 1998. Lead engr. Sci. Assn. Optics, Moscow, 1972-82; prodn. engr. Plant MEMZ, Moscow, 1983-84; head of rsch. lab. Sci. Assn. Dinamo, Moscow, 1984-92; pres. Rimet, Moscow, 1992-99; rsch. scientist McMaster U., Hamilton, Canada. Contbr. articles to profl. jours.; patentee in field. Fax: gfox.mcmail.mcmaster.ca. Office: McMaster U, Hamilton, ON Canada L8S 4L7

FOY, THOMAS PAUL, lawyer, retired state legislator, retired banker; b. Silver City, N.Mex., Oct. 19, 1914; s. Thomas J. and Mary V. Foy; m. Joan Carney, Nov. 17, 1948 (dec. June 1994); children: Celia, Thomas Paul Jr. (dec.), Muffet (Mary Ann), J. Carney, James B.,. BS in Commerce, Notre Dame U., 1938, JD, 1939. Bar: N.Mex. 1946. Dist. atty. N.Mex. 6th Jud. Dist., Silver City, 1949-57; atty. Village of Bayard, N.Mex., 1954-68, Village of Ctrl., N.Mex., 1960-70; v.p., counsel, bd. dirs. Sunwest Bank, Silver City, 1946-84, chmn. bd. dirs. 1969-84, chmn. emeritus, 1984-97; state rep. Dist. 39 State of N.Mex., Grant-Hidalgo, 1971-98; chmn. jud. com. N.Mex. State Legis., Santa Fe, 1984-98; pres. Foy & Vesely and Foy, Foy & Castillo, Silver City, 1946—. 1st lt. U.S. Army, 1941-46; prisoner of war, PTO, 1942-45. Decorated Bronze Star, Purple Heart, Asiatic-Pacific Ribbon with 3 oak leaf clusters; recipient Citizen of Yr. award Silver City-Grant County C. of C., 1965, Dedication to Advancement award Trial Lawyers Assn., 1993, N.Mex. Disting. Svc. medal, 1994. Mem. ABA, N.Mex. Bar Assn. (bar commr. 1967-85, v.p. N.Mex. bar commn. 1978-79, Disting. Svc. of Laws award 1987), Am. Judicature Soc., Bataan Vets. Orgn. (state comdr. 1965-66, 98-99), KC (Grand Knight 1936-37), VFW (state comdr. 1959-60), Lions (dist. gov. 1956-57), Elks. Democrat. Roman Catholic. Avocations: football, baseball, travel, conventions. Office: Foy Foy & Castillo PC 210 W Broadway St Silver City NM 88061-5353

FOYOUZI-YOUSSEFI, REYHANEH, pharmacologist; b. Tehran, Iran, Dec. 6, 1964; arrived in Switzerland, 1983.; d. Amin and Seyedeh (Salimi-Eshkevari). Diploma of Asst. Pharmacist, Sch. Pharmacy, Geneva, Switzerland, 1988, Diploma of Pharmacy, 1991; PhD in Pharmacy, U. Geneva, Geneva, Switzerland, 1999. Pharmacist Geneva, Switzerland, 1991—. Contbr. articles to profl. jours.

FRADEANI, MAURO, dentist; b. Ancona, Italy, Oct. 12, 1951; s. Eolo and Giulia (Buffarini) F.; m. Alessandra Vitali, June 27, 1993. MD, Libera Università Degli Studi G. D'Annunzio, Chieti, 1979; DDS, Università Degli Studi, Ancona, 1983. Pvt. practice Pesaro, Italy; spl. lectr. La. State U., New Orleans, 1997. Contbr. articles to profl. jours. Mem.Italian Acad. Prosthetic Dentistry (pres. 1999—), European Acad. of Esthetic Dentistry (vice pres. 1999—), Amer. Acad. Esthetic Dentistry (active), Am. Acad. Fixed Prosthodontics, Internat. Coll. Prosthodontists. Avocations: car racing, traveling, sports journalist for private radio. Home: via Filangieri No 81, 61100 Pesaro Italy Office: Corso XI Settembre No 92, 61100 Pesaro Italy

FRADIS, MILO, physician, researcher; b. Czernowitz, Russia, Aug. 15, 1939; arrived in Israel, 1963; s. Nehemiah and Brana (Shilman) F.; m. Johanna Ana Heimowitz, Feb. 15, 1967; children: Zwi Iacob, Maya, Nehemiah-Ran. Diploma in medicine, Hebrew U., Jerusalem, 1966, MD, 1968. Completed specialization otolaryngological diseases Rothschild U. Hosp., Haifa, Israel, 1973. Fellow in ear surgery U. Tübingen, Germany, 1976-77; 1st dep. Dept. Otolaryngology Bnai Zion Med. Ctr., Haifa, 1976—; sr. lectr. Bruce Rappaport Faculty Medicine Technion-Israel Inst. Tech., Haifa, 1980—; vis. prof. in field; rschr. in field. Contbr. articles to profl. jours. Capt. Israeli Army, 1973-90. Jewish. Avocations: chess, swimming, classical music. Home: Pevsner 8, 33133 Haifa Israel Office: Bnai Zion Hosp, Golomb 47, Haifa Israel

FRAGA ESTÉVEZ, CARMEN, foreign diplomat; b. Léon, Spain, Oct. 19, 1948. Mem. European Parliament, 1999—, mem. com. on fisheries, substitute com. on agr. and rural devel.; vice-chair Group of the European People's Party (Christian Democrats) and European Democrats; mem. delegation for relations with the Maghreb countries and the Arab Maghreb Union. Mem. People's Party. *

FRAGELL, LEVI, humanism consultant; b. Nes, Romerike, Norway, Mar. 30, 1939; s. øivind and Astrid (Hansen) F.; divorced; children: Siriann, øvind, Axel. BA, U. Oslo, Norway, 1968, U. Trondheim, Norway, 1971. Journalist Oslo, 1961-64, pub. rels. officer, 1964-70; press officer Ministry of Justice, Oslo, 1973-81; sec. gen. Humanist Assn., Oslo, 1982-91, editor, 1991-97, sr. cons., 1997—; pres. Internat. Humanist and Ethical Union, London, 1987-91, 98—. Leader Action Against State Ch., Oslo, 1970-78. Recipient Internat. Humanist award Coun. for Secular Humanism, N.Y., 1999, The Taboo prize Govtl. Coun. for Psychiatry, Oslo, 1998. Home: Dyretrakket 51, 1251 Oslo Norway

FRAGOULIS, EMMANUEL GEORGE, biochemistry educator; b. Sitia, Crete, Greece, Jan. 15, 1947; s. George Emmanuel and Chrysoula Michail (Kotsifaki) F.; m. Maria-Helen-Maura Fournogeraki, Mar. 1, 1977; children: Christina, George. B in Natural Scis., U. Athens, Greece, 1972, Reader Biochemistry, 1980; D Natural Sci., U. Marburg, Germany, 1974. Rsch. asst. Inst. Physiol. Chemistry, Marburg, 1972-74; lectr. dept. biology U. Athens, 1976-79, asst. prof. dept. biochemistry, 1981-87, assoc. prof., 1987-91, prof., 1991-96, head dept. biochemistry, 1988-89, mem. senate, 1984-88, vice chmn. faculty biology, 1988-90, chmn., 1992-94; gen. sec. sci. and tech., 1996-99, head dept. biochemistry-molecular biology, 1996-97, 99—; postdoctoral fellow Max Plank Inst., Ladenburg, Germany, 1979-80; chmn. governing bd. Alexander Fleming Rsch. Ctr., 1995-96. Mem. Nat. Adv. Bd. Rsch., 1982-84, 93-96, 99—; mem. Covermedia Bd. Pasteur, 1985-87. Recipient Scholarships Deutsche Academische Austrausch Denst, 1976, European Molecular Biology Orgn., 1977, 87; Humboldt fellow Humboldt Found., 1979. Mem. Hellenic Biochem. and Biophys. Soc. (pres. 1994-96), Gesselschaft fur Biologische Chemie, European Soc. Comparative Biochemistry and Physiology. Home: Scholiou 30, 153 42 Aghia Paraskevi Atti Attiki Greece Office: Lab Biochemistry, Panepistemiopolis Kouponia, 157 01 Athens Greece

FRAIOLI, BEVERLY, bank auditor; b. Cranston, R.I., Aug. 16, 1951; d. William Cyrus Ellsworth and Hazel Sharp; m. Frank Louis Fraioli, July 19, 1975; 1 child, Jason William. BA, U. R.I., 1973; Gen. Banking Diploma, Am. Inst. Banking, 1992; Cert. Trust Auditor, Cannon Fin. Inst., 1997; Cert. Bank Auditor, Bank Adminstrn. Inst., 1997; Cert. Cmty. Bank, Ind. Bankers, Orlando, Fla., 1995. Cert. auditor. Psychiat. attendant R.I. Inst. of Mental Health, Warwick, 1974-77; treas./owner K&F Svcs., Inc., Panama City Beach, Fla., 1977-85; internal auditor Bay Bank & Trust Co., Panama City, Fla., 1986—. Vol. United Way Meals on Wheels, Panama City, 1992-93; mem. Bay County C. of C., Panama City, 1994-95; sec./band booster Panama City Christian Sch. Band, 1995-97; Sunday Sch. tchr. Cen. Bapt. Ch., Panama City, 1995—. Mem. Nat. Assn. of Trust Audit and Compliance Profls., inc. Baptist. Avocations: tracing family heritage, reading, travel, gardening. Office: Bay Bank & Trust Co 509 Harrison Ave Panama City FL 32401-2621

FRAIOLI, GAETANO, thoracic surgeon, researcher; b. Caserta, Campania, Italy, Mar. 6, 1948; s. Carmine and Vicenza (Errichiello) F.; m. Diana Insolvibile, Mar. 9, 1978; children: Valentina, Roberta. MD, U. Naples, Italy, 1973, gen. surgeon, 1979, thoracic surgeon, 1985. Asst. in emergency surgery U. Naples, 1973-74, asst. in thoracic surgery, 1975-86, asst. prof. thoracic surgery, 1986—. Med. officer Legion of Naples, 1976-77. Fellow ACCP. Avocations: sea, bricolage, computer multimediality. Home: Via V Scala 28, 80128 Naples Italy Office: U Federico II Faculty Med, Via Pansini 5, 80131 Naples Italy

FRAISSARD, JACQUES PAUL, chemistry educator, researcher; b. Oran, Algeria, Apr. 20, 1934; s. Alexandre Firmin and Paule Eudoxie (Prinet) F.; m. Michelle Fanny Parcot, Dec. 23, 1958. BSc, U. Paris, 1957, Degree in Phys. Chemistry, 1961. Rschr. French Nat. Ctr. Rsch., Paris, 1957-63; asst. prof. U. Paris, 1963-71; prof. U. Pierre and Marie Curie, France, 1971-79, full prof., 1979—; dir. Lab. Chimie des Surface, Paris, 1971—; dir. team on surfaces and interfaces CNRS, Paris, 1986—; adj. prof. U. Del., Newark, 1988; cons. Union Carbide, Tarrytown, N.Y., 1981-90, UOP, Des Plaines, Ill., 1990—, Du Pont, Wilmington, Del., 1988. Author: Chemical Equilibra in Aqueous Solutions, 1989, Catalysis: Science and Technology, vol. 10: Application of NMR Methods to Catalysis, 1996; editor Magnetic Resonance in Colloid and Interface Science, 1979, Acidity and Basicity of Solids, 1994, Physical Adsorption, 1997, others; contbr. articles to profl. jours. Pres. Club Perspectives et Realités, Hauts de Seine, 1981-95; pres. Parti Populaire pour la Démocratie Française, 1995. Recipient Award of French Acad. Scis., 1998. Mem. French Chem. Soc. (prize 1962), Am. Chem. Soc. Roman Catholic. Avocations: old cars, gardening, boating, tennis. Office: U Pierre Marie Curie Case 196, Chim Surfaces, 4 Pl Jussieu, 75252 Paris France

FRAISSE, GENEVIÈVE, mem. European Parliament; b. Paris, Oct. 7, 1948. D State, Sch. High Studies Social Scis. With CERN, 1983—, dir. rsch., 1997—; mem. European Parliament, 1999—, mem. com. on culture, youth, edn., the media and sport, mem. com. on women's rights and equal opportunities, substitute com. on legal affairs and the internal market; mem. Confederal Group of the European United Left/Nordic Green Left; mem. delegation for rels. with U.S.; former vis. prof. Rutgers U. Author: Femmes toutes mains, essai sur le service domestique, 1979, Clémence Royer philosophe et femme de sciences, 1985, Muse de la raison, démocratie et exclusion des femmes en France, 1989, La raison des femmes, 1992, La différence des sexes, 1996, Les femmes et leur histoire, 1998, (with Roselyne Bachelot) Deux femmes au royaume des hommes, 1999; co-editor: Histoire des femmes en Occident, Vol IV, 1991, L'exercice du savoir et la différence des sexes, 1991; contbr. numerous articles to various publs.; works translated into German, English, Italian, Spanish, Greek, Portuguese, and Japanese. *

FRAME, JEAN GROETZ, educator, consultant; b. Medina, Ohio, July 18, 1951; d. Edward Joseph and Gwendolyn Mae (Lindley) G.; m. Carl Ralph Frame, Dec. 10, 1983. BS, U. Akron, 1973, postgrad., 1973-83. Elem. tchr. Medina City Schs., 1973-86; sch. age tutor Nurtury Child Devel. Ctr., 1989-96; cons. to pvt. and pub. schs., individual learning tutor, 1990—; cons. staff devel. team Medina Schs., 1982-90; staff cons. Medina Drug Prevention Program, 1982-90; dir. summer sch. age program Nurtury Presch., Medina, 1980-81; writer of reading and sci. goals and curricula, 1986. Composer of musical scores, 1972, 73. Dir. music Mt. Zwingli United Ch. of Christ, 1992—; vol. story teller Westfield Elem. Sch., 1993—; elder Mt. Zwingli United Ch. of Christ, 1994-97, organist, 1997—. Jennings Found. scholar Kent State U., 1984-85. Mem. AAUW, Am. Guild English Handbell Ringers, Medina City Tchrs. Assn. (bldg. rep.), Medina City Staff Devel. Team, Kappa Delta Pi. Home: 6881 Buffham Rd Seville OH 44273-9112

FRAME, LAWRENCE MILVEN, JR., inventor; b. Adrian, Mich., Apr. 13, 1951; s. Lawrence M. Sr. and Margret L. Frame. Student, Art Instrns. Sch., Cin., North Light Sch., Cin. Gen. laborer USAF. Patentee; songwriter; author: 100% Service Connected and Social Security Disability, Golden Book of Short Stories, Part VI; art exhibited in show at Scioto Paint Valley Mental Health Ctr., 1993. With USAF, 1971-75. Recipient several art and writing awards. Mem. Am. Legion, Disabled Am. Vets. Avocations: art, writing, electrophysics. Home: 6810 1/2 County Road 26 Archbold OH 43502-9437

FRÄMLING, KARY ÅKE, researcher; b. Borgå, Nyland, Finland, Oct. 15, 1965; arrived in France, 1991; s. Bernt and Birgit Maria (Danielsson) F.; m. Marie Noelle Chantal Vignone, July 1, 1995; children: Niels Giovanni Bernt, Ottilia Birgit Givlia Sveo. MSc, U. Tech., Helsinki, Finland, 1990; diplome d'etudes approfondies, Inst Nat Sci Appliquées, Lyon, France, 1993; PhD in French, Ecole Nat. Superieure Mines, Saint Etienne, France, 1996. Software analyst Unicom Consulting oy, Espoo, Finland, 1988-89; rschr. Neste Oy, Borgå, Finland, 1990; software analyst Nokia Cellular Sys. Oy, Helsinki, 1990-91; rschr. Ecole Nat. Superieure des Mines, Saint Etienne, 1991-96; tech. mgr. Logimage Soc. Anonyme Responsabilité Limitée, Saint Etienne, 1996-98; sr. lectr. Arcada Polytech, Espoo, Finland, 1998-2000; rschr. Helsinki U. Tech., Espoo, 2000—; mng. dir. Oy Faidon AB, Helsinki, 1989—. Contbr. articles to profl. jours. Rsch. grantee Acad. Finland, 1991, Kaute Rahasto, 1992. Lutheran. Avocations: squash, skiing, sports. Home: Råbacavägen, 06650 Hammars Nyland Finland Office: Teknillinen Korkeakoulu, TKO-Laboratorio PL 5400, 02015 TKK Finland

FRAN, GRANDMA See BROWN, FRANCES LOUISE

FRANC, ALES, pharmacist, researcher; b. Kolín, Czechoslovakia, Sept. 21, 1968; s. Pavel and Daniela (Kurková) F. MS in Pharmacy, Charles U., Hradec, Czechoslovakia, 1990. Pharmacist Pharm. Svc., Prachatice, Czechoslovakia, 1990-91, Prague, Czechoslovakia, 1992; asst. Lachema, Brno, Czechoslovakia, 1992-93, rschr., 1993-94, top rschr., 1995; mem. working group in ophtolmology rsch. Vet. and Pharmacy U., Brno, 1995, cons. in diplomatheses, 1994-95. Contbr. articles to rsch. reports. Mem. Assn. Scientists and Technicians, Czech Med. Assn. Home: Purkynova 19, Brno 61200, Czech Republic Office: Lachema a s Vú, Karasek 1, Brno 62133, Czech Republic

FRANCA, JOSE-AUGUSTO, art historian, educator, author; b. Nov. 16, 1922; s. Jose M. and Carmen (Rodriques) F.; m. Marie-Therese Mandroux, 1972; 1 dau., Manuela. Diplome sociology of art, Ecole Hautes Etudes, Paris, France, 1962; D in History, U. Paris, 1962, Doctor ès Lettres, 1969. Art critic, publs. including Art d'Aujourd'hui Paris, Goya, Madrid,, Estado de Sao Paulo (Brazil), 1946—; cinema critic, 1948—; prof. sociology art, history modern art Curso de Formacao Artistica, Lisbon, 1964-70; prof. modern culture and art, head dept. U.N. Lisbon, 1974-93, prof. emeritus, 1993—; dir. Ctr. Culturel Portugues, 1983-89, C. Gulbenkian Found., Paris. Author: (novel) Natureza Morta, 1949; (play) Azazel, 1957; (short stories) Despedida Breve, 1958; (essays) Charles Chaplin, the self-made-myth, 1953; Situacao da Arte Ocidental, 1959, Une Ville des Lumieres; la Lisbonne de Pombal, 1965, Oito Ensaios sobre arte Contemporanea, 1967, A Arte em Portugal no seculo XIX, 2 vols., 1967, A Arte em Portugal no Seculo XX, 1974, Le Romantisme au Portugal, 1975, Rafael Bordalo Pinheiro, 1980, Amadeo e Almada, 1986, Historia da Arte Ocidental; 1780-1980, 1987, Os anos 2o em Portugal, 1992, Lisboa 1898, 1997, (In) definicoes de Cultura, 1997, O Palacio de S. Bento, 1999, Cem quadros Portugueses no Seculo XX, 2000, Memorias para o ano 2000, 2000. Editor; Unicornio, 1951-56; Cadernos de Poesia, 1952-53; Pintura e Nao, 1969-71; Coloquio Artes, 1970-96. City Councilor, Lisbon, 1974-75; pres. Inst. de Cultura Portuguesa, 1976-80; city dep., Lisbon, 1990-93; councilor Commn. on Hist. Monuments, 1994-96. Decorated officier Ordre National du Merite; chevalier Ordre des Arts et Lettres (France); comdr. Ordem Rio Branco (Brazil), Grand-Croix Ordem Instruccao Publica; grand-officer Ordem Infante D. Henrique; officer Ordem. Santiago (Portugal). Mem. Academia das Ciencias, Academia Nacional de Belas Artes (v.p. 1975-77, pres. 1977-80), Internat. Com. Art History, European Acad. Scis. et Lettres (v.p. 1985-2000, hon. pres. 2000—), Internat. Assn. Art Critics (v.p. 1970-73, pres. 1984-87, hon. pres. 1987—); World Acad. Scis. and Arts; Acad. Nat. Lettres et des Arts de Bordeaux; Soc. Europeene de Culture, Ateneo Veneto, Acad. Reale de San Fernando. Address: Le Pavillon, Jarzé 49140, France also: Rua Escola politecnica 49-4, 1250 Lisbon Portugal

FRANCARD, MICHEL, educator; b. Bastogne, Belgium, Mar. 17, 1952; s. Maurice and Denise (Georges) F.; m. Monique Nannan, July 17, 1976; children: Christel, Géraldine. B Linguistics, Cath U Louvain, Belgium, 1975, PhD, 1979. Prof. Cath. U. Louvain, 1990-97, prof. linguistics, 1997—. Author: Aspects de la Phonologie Générative du Français Contemporain, 1975, Le Parler de Tenneville. Introduction à l'étude Linguistique des Parlers Wallo-Lorrains, 1980 (prize Legros 1981), Dictionnaire des Parlers Wallons du Pays de Bastogne, 1994 (prize Doppagne, 1995, prize Communauté française de Belgique 1995), (book and video) Ces Belges qui parlent Français (grand prize l'A.D.M.E.S. 1994). Expert Conseil Supérieur de la Langue Française, Belgium, 1993—, Conseil des Langues Régionales Endogénes, Belgium, 1991—. Avocations: bee-keeping, gardening, ancient and baroque music.

FRANCAVILLA, DONNA T., journalist; b. Camden, N.J., Dec. 4, 1960; d. Lelio and Aurora (DeVuono) Ciccotelli; m. Thomas Louis Francavilla, May 29, 1957; children: Michael, Lisa, Jessica, Gregory. BS, Emerson Coll., Boston, 1985. Talk show prodr. WWDB-FM Talkradio, Phila., 1980-81; desk asst., prodn. asst. KYW Newsradio 1060 AM, Phila., 1981-82; talk show prodr. WRKO-AM, Boston, 1982-85; news anchor radio network Internat. Media News, Washington, 1986-88; program dir., news dir. Westinghouse WPGC AM & FM, Washington, DC, 1988-90; traffic reporter Metro Traffic Control, Phila., 1990-92; news anchor, all news radio WINZ-AM, Miami, 1993-94; news reporter NBC, WVTM-TV, Birmingham, Ala., 1996—; radio corr. CBS, 1999—, 1999—; owner Frankly Speaking Comm., LLC; participant RIAS German Journalist Exhange Program, 1999; freelance writer Birmingham Mag.; news reporter APTV Ala. Pub. TV, Montgomery. Talk show host Frankly Speaking, What Women Talk About When Men Aren't Around, Ala. Radio Network, 2000—; freelance wire svc. reporter Agy. French Press, 2000—. V.p. Greystone Ladies Club, Birmingham, 1995. Mem. Jefferson County Med. Alliance; public rels. dir., Jefferson County Med. Alliance. Roman Catholic. Avocations: exercising, dancing, skiing, cooking, writing. Home: 5079 Greystone Way Birmingham AL 35242-6456

FRANCE, DOROTHY DANIEL, minister; b. Danieltown, Va., Nov. 23, 1926; d. Arthur R. and Susan G. (Waller) Daniel; m. Carl G. France, Aug. 6, 1946 (dec. Nov. 1997); 1 child, Dorothy Gail France Frankle. BA, Bethany Coll., 1950; postgrad., William and Mary Coll., 1964, Va. Commonwealth U., 1966. Dir. Army Dir. Svcs., Camp Pickett, Va., 1944-46; tchr. Nottoway County Pub. Schs., Crewe, Va., 1950-55, Henrico Pub. Schs., Richmond, Va., 1961-63, Petersburg (Va.) Pub. Schs., 1964-68; dir. Cmty. Devel., New River Cmty Action, Radford, Va., 1969-73; min. Petunia Christian Ch., Wytheville, Va., 1969-72, Galilee Christian Ch., Wytheville, 1973-75; assoc. dir. CROP/Ch. World Svc., Va., N.C., 1975-76; dir. CROP/Ch. World Svc. for Va., Richmond, 1977-80; dir. resource devel. Va. Inst. of Pastoral Care, Richmond, 1980-81; min. Prospect Christian Ch., Dinwiddie, Va., 1982-87; dir. Refugee Resettlement CWS/EMM, Va. Coun. of Chs., Richmond, 1981-91; cons. on Am. corp. involvement in South Africa Christian Ch., Indpls., 1971. Author: Special Days of the Church Year, 1969, Newness of Life, 1970, Partners in Prayer, 1986, Welcome to the United States An Orientation Guide for Refuges, 1988, Blessed Assurance, 1999, (with Jason and David Frankle) You Might Be a Football Fan If....Simplified Game Notes for Would Be Fans, 2000; author/editor: At Christ's Table, 1997; author: (with others) Go Quickly and Tell, 1973; editl. com. Toward Better Grouping in Reading, 1968. Recipient Valiant Woman award Ch. Women United. Mem. AAUW, Va. Coalition on Nutrition, Delta Kappa Gamma (chair personal growth and devel. com. 1968). Avocations: writing, travel. Home and Office: 2968 Silver Maple Dr Fairlawn OH 44333-3295

FRANCE, JOSEPH DAVID, securities analyst; b. Smithville, Mo., July 24, 1953; s. Raymond Hughes and Bonnie Lee (Cavin) F; m. Tina Rachel Sidney; 1 child, Lucille Terrell. BS in Pharmacy, U. Kans., 1977, MBA, 1980. Chartered fin. analyst; registered pharmacist. Staff pharmacist U. Kans. Med. Ctr., Kansas City, 1977-80; securities analyst First Nat. Bank Chgo., 1980-82; securities analyst Smith Barney, Harris Upham & Co., Inc., N.Y.C., 1982-86, mng. dir., 1986-93; 1st v.p. Merrill Lynch, N.Y.C., 1993-95; sr. v.p. Dillon, Read & Co., 1995-96; dir. CS First Boston, N.Y.C., 1996—. Mem. Am. Soc. Health-Sys. Pharmacists, N.Y. Soc. Securities Analysts, Assn. for Investment Mgmt. and Rsch., Am. Math. Soc. Democrat. Jewish. Avocations: reading, computers, writing. Office: 11 Madison Ave Fl 6 New York NY 10010-3629

FRANCE-DEAL, JUDITH JEAN, language educator; b. Falls City, Nebr., June 27, 1941; d. Paris and Georgia Elizabeth (Reiger) France; m. Gary Arthur Deal, Dec. 30, 1960; children: Kevin, Timothy. Student, Bapt. Inst. Christian Workers, Bryn Mawr, Pa., 1959; grad., Liberty Bible Inst., 1994, Barbizon Sch. Modelling, 1998. Cert. and lic. chaplain. Vol. worker with many orgns., 1957—; receptionist Central Ins. Co., Omaha, Nebr., 1960-62; vol. PTA, Cub Scouts, etc., Wis., 1966-76; tchr. spl. edn. First Bapt. Ch., Dallas, 1985-88, vol. tutor ESL, 1985—; inspirational spkr.; tchr. English and Bible studies 1st Bapt. Ch., Richardson, Tex., 1989—; pres., founder God's Internat. ABCs, Inc.; model for numerous advts. and commls. Author: Center of Our Lives, 1994. Chaplain-min. to cancer patients Tulsa Cancer Treatment Ctr.; vol. chaplain Plano Specialty Hosp. Recipient numerous writing awards. Mem. Internat. Platform Assn. Republican. Avocations: sewing, reading, writing poetry, helping others, songs. Office: Gods Internat ABC 1000 14th St Ste 122 Plano TX 75074-6220

FRANCES, KATRINA See VAN ALLEN, KATRINA FRANCES

FRANCHINI, INNOCENTE, medical educator; b. Cremona, Italy, June 22, 1940; s. Giuseppe and Ester (Salotti) F.; m. Claudia Barili, Oct. 21, 1967; children: Paolo, Nicola, Maria Chiara. Degree in medicine, U. Parma, Italy, 1965, degree in endocrinology, 1967, degree in nephrology, 1971, degree in occupational medicine, 1974. Vol. asst. clin. medicine U. Parma, 1966-69, asst., 1969-73, tchr. occupational medicine, 1973-80, assoc. prof. occupational medicine, 1980-86, full prof. occupational medicine, 1986—; dir. sch. specialization occupational health U. Parma, 1986—, coord. doctorate of occupational health, 1989—. Contbr. numerous articles to profl. jours. Mem. Internat. Neurotoxic Assn., Internat. Com. Occupational Health, Soc. Italian Occupational Medicine, Assn. U. Occupational Medicine (pres.). Office: Univ Parma Medicina Lavoro, Via Gramsci 14, 43100 Parma Italy

FRANCIS, DICK (RICHARD STANLEY FRANCIS), novelist; b. Tenby, Wales, U.K., Oct. 31, 1920; s. George Vincent and Catherine Mary (Thomas) F.; m. Mary Margaret Brenchley, June 21, 1947; children: Merrick, Felix. LHD (hon.), Tufts U., 1991. Steeplechase jockey, 1946-57; journalist London Sunday Express, 1957-73. Author: (autobiography) The Sport of Queens, 1957, Dead Cert, 1962, Nerve, 1964, For Kicks, 1965 (Silver Dagger award 1965), Odds Against, 1965, Flying Finish, 1966, Blood Sport, 1967, Forfeit, 1968 (Edgar Allen Poe award 1969), Enquiry, 1969, Rat Race, 1970, Bonecrack, 1971, Smokescreen, 1972, Slay-Ride, 1973, Knock Down, 1974, Risk, 1977, Trial Run, 1978, Whip Hand, 1979 (Gold Dagger award 1980, Edgar Allen Poe award 1980), Reflex, 1980, Twice Shy, 1981, Banker, 1982, The Danger, 1983, Proof, 1984, Break In, 1985, Lester (biography of Lester Piggott), 1986, Bolt, 1986, Hot Money, 1987, The Edge, 1988, Straight, 1989, Longshot, 1990, Comeback, 1991, Driving Force, 1992, Decider, 1993, Wild Horses, 1994, Come to Grief, 1995, 2 Edgar Allen Poe award for Best Novel and Grand Master, 1996.RD To The Hilt, 1996, 10 lb. Penalty, 1997, Field of Thirteen, 1998, Second Wind, 1999, Shattered, 2000; co-editor: (with John Welcome) The Racing Man's Bedside Book, 1969, Best Racing and Chasing Stories, 1966, part II, 1969, The Dick Francis Treasury of Great Racing Stories, 1991; contbr. anthologies Winter's Crimes, 1973, Stories of Crime and Detection, 1974, Ellery Queen's Crime Wave, 1976, Ellery Queen's Searches and Seizures, 1977; contbr. articles to periodicals. Officer RAF, 1940-46. Decorated Order Brit. Empire, Nibbies award 1998; champion steeplechase jockey The Jockey Club, London, 1954. Mem. Mystery Writers Am., Crime Writers Assn., Detection Club, Racecourse Assn. Avocations: traveling, racing. HOME: care of John Johnson Ltd, 45-47 Clerkenwell Green, London ECIR OHT, England

FRANCIS, JOHN CHARLES, telecommunications professional, consultant; b. Sunderland, Eng., Feb. 8, 1957; arrived in Switzerland, 1990; s. Wilfrid and Mary (Bird) F.; m. Gabriele Maria Moshammer, Mar. 6, 1998; 1 child, Daniel. BSc with honors, U. East Anglia, Eng., 1982; MSc, Heriot-Watt U., Scotland, 1984, PhD, 1986. Rsch. assoc. Heriot-Watt U., 1984-86; founding ptnr. SLL, France, 1987-90; cons. ASCOM, Switzerland, 1991-95; project leader Swisscom, Bern, Switzerland, 1996—; exec. dir. SLL, France, 1987-92; raporteur ETSI, France, 1997-98, GSM MOU, Ireland, 1997; work package leader EU, Brussels, 1996-98. Author: (book) Causal Reasoning: A Systems Approach, 1991; contbr. papers to profl. jours. Grantee Sunderland Coun., 1979, rsch. grantee Sci. and Engring. Rsch. Coun., 1981, 82. Mem. Swiss Group Artificial Intelligence and Cognitive Sci., Gorilla Found. Avocations: musical composition, electronic music, metaphysics. Office: Swisscom Corp Tech, Ostermundigenstr 93, CH-3000 Bern Switzerland

FRANCIS, JOY N., communications engineer; b. Koltayam, Kerala, India, May 28, 1966; came to U.S., 1993; s. W. T. and Cicily (Joseph) Francis. Diploma in comm. engring., Ctrl. Poly. Tech., Tvm, India, 1985; M, St. Berchman's Coll., Chy, India, 1987. Technician PCIA, Va., 1997, Nextel Comm., Las Vegas, Nev., 1998—; sys. engr. Motorola, Algonquin, Ill., 1997, technician, Fla., Ill. Lt. N.G., 1997-98. Avocations: volleyball, basketball. Home: 3430 Polaris Ave Las Vegas NV 89102-7727 Office: Nextel Comm 5870 W Harmon Ave Las Vegas NV 89103-4885

FRANCIS, JULIAN W., bank executive. Gov. Ctrl. Bank of the Bahamas. Office: The Ctrl Bank of the Bahamas, Frederick St PO Box N4868, Nassau Bahamas*

FRANCIS, KAREN See RUGALA, KAREN FRANCIS

FRANCIS, LESLIE JOHN, theology educator, psychology researcher; b. Colchester, Eng., Sept. 10, 1947; s. Ronald Arthur and Joan Irene (Swann) F. BA in Theology, U. Oxford, Eng., 1970; BD in Theology, U. Oxford, 1990; PhD in Edn., U. Cambridge, Eng., 1976; DSc in Edn., U. Cambridge, 1997; MTh, U. Nottingham, Eng., 1976; MSc in Psychology, U. London, 1977. Leverhulme rsch. fellow London Ctrl. YMCA, 1977-82; rsch. officer Culham Coll. Inst., Abingdon, Eng., 1982-88; Mansel Jones fellow, D.J. James prof. pastoral theology Trinity Coll., Carmarthen, Wales, 1989-99; D.J. James prof. pastoral theology U. Wales, Lampeter, 1992-99; dir. Welsh Nat. Ctr. Religion Edn., prof. practical theology U Wales, Bangor, 1999—; curate Haverhill, Suffolk, Eng., 1973-77; priest-in-charge Little Wratting and Great Bradley, Suffolk, Eng., 1977-82, North Cerney and Bagendon, Gloucestershire, Eng., 1982-85; dean of chapel Trinity Coll., Carmarthen, 1994-99. Author: Teenage Religion and Values, 1995, Drift from the Churches: Attitudes toward Christianity during Childhood and Adolescence, 1996, Church Watch: Christianity in the Countryside, 1996, Personality Type and Scripture: Exploring Mark's Gospel, 1997, Gone But Not Forgotten: Church Leaving and Retaining, 1998, The Long Dinconate, 1999. Fellow Brit. Psychol. Soc., Coll. Preceptors. Anglican. Avocations: music, walking, countryside, architecture, public service vehicles. Office: U Wales Bangor, Normal Site, Bangor LL57 2PX, England

FRANCIS, LORNA JEAN, nutritionist; b. Mt. Carmel, Ill., July 2, 1955; d. Adolph William and Edna Louise (Kleinschmidt) Kirsch; m. Lionel Jackie Bush, Oct. 2, 1976 (div. Mar. 1988); children: Leah Joann, Lucas Jeffrey; m. Terry Glen Francis, Dec. 30, 1989; 1 child, Ashley Michelle. BS in Dietetics, So. Ill. U., 1976, MS in Cmty. Nutrition, 1984. Cert. nutrition support dietitian Am. Soc. Parenteral and Enteral Nutrition. Tchr.'s asst. So. Ill. U., Carbondale, 1982-84; cons. dietitian, Ill., Ind., 1984-86, Hillhaven Corp., Columbus, Ohio, 1986-89; clin. dietitian Deaconess Hosp., Evansville, Ind., 1989-91; mgr. clin. nutrition Marriott-Welborn Bapt. Hosp., Evansville, 1991-96; dept. dir. Sodexho-Marriott, Evansville, 1996-98; food svc. dir. U. Evansville, 1998—; mem. adj. faculty U. Evansville, 1989—; mem. adv. bd. Riverfront Home and Health Agy., Vincennes, Ind., 1993-97; mem. med. adv. bd. YMCA, 1998—; exam. writer Nat. League for Nursing, N.Y.C., 1991, 97. Contbr. articles to profl. jours. Co-chmn. Parent Tchr. League, Evansville Luth. Sch., 1993-95, chmn. health com., 1997; bd. dirs. Meals on Wheels, Evansville, 1994—; vol. Center City Corp., Evansville, 1996—. Mem. Am. Dietetic Assn. (registered), Ind. Cons. Dietitians (chmn. 1987-88), Ind. Nutrition Edn. Network, S.W. Ind. Dietetics Assn. (edn. chmn. 1992—, pub. rels. com. 1983-84, co-chmn. 1984-85, chmn. 1985-86). Avocations: choir, golf, gardening, reading. Home: 13325 Gilles Ln Evansville IN 47725-9580 Office: U Evansville 1800 Lincoln Ave Evansville IN 47722-0001

FRANCIS, RICHARD ANDREW, French language educator; b. Yarmouth, Eng., Apr. 19, 1942; s. Nehemiah and Flora Ruby (Cooke) F.; m. Judith Anne Sadler, July 25, 1970; children: Julia Claire, John Christopher Mark. BA, Magdalen Coll., Oxford, Eng., 1963, BLitt, 1968; PhD, U. Nottingham, 1987. Lectr. U. Nottingham, Eng., 1966-93, reader in French 18th Century studies, 1993—. Author: The Abbé Prévost's First-Person Narrators, 1993, Prévost, Manon Lescaut, 1993, Romain Rolland, 1999; translator: Romain Rolland Mahatma Gandhi Correspondence, 1976. Avocations: reading, music, general knowledge. Home: 9 Lyncombe Gardens Keyworth, Nottingham NG12-5FZ, England Office: U Nottingham Dept French, University Park, Nottingham NG7 2RD, England

FRANCIS, STEWART ALEXANDER CLEMENT, secondary education educator, retired; b. London, Feb. 25, 1938; s. Clement Alexander and Patricia Marion Margaret (Stewart) F.; m. Valerie Cecily Joan Stead, Jan. 9, 1965; children: Richard, Kate. BA honours degree in classics, Cambridge (Eng.) U., 1961, cert. edn., 1962, MA, 1965. Asst. master Mill Hill Sch., London, 1962-63; asst. master Maidenhead (Eng.) Grammar Sch., 1963-66, head lower sch., 1967-69; head English and 6th form William Penn Sch., Rickmansworth, Eng., 1969-74; dep. head Southgate Sch., London, 1974-79; headmaster Chenderit Sch., Middleton Cheney, Eng., 1979-84; headmaster Colchester (Eng.) Royal Grammar Sch., 1985-2000, ret., 2000; guest various schs. and villages, Northamptonshire and Essex, Eng., 1979—; mem. ct. U. Essex, Colchester, 1996-2000; com. mem. Bluecoat Trust, Colchester, 1985-2000. With Brit. Army, 1956-58. Winner Men's Squash Championship for Buckinghamshire, Eng., 1970. Fellow Royal Soc. Arts; mem. N.E. Essex Headtchrs. Assn. (com., pres. 1987-88), Marylebone Cricket Club, Jesters Cricket Club (com. 1966-71), London Schs. and Colls. Dining Club, Johnian Soc., U. Essex Assn., Nat. Assn. Head Tchrs., Inst. of Dirs. (assoc.). Avocations: sports, reading, sketching, art exhibitions and galleries, writing verse. Home: Willow Springs, 32 The Lane West Mersea, Essex C05 8NT, England

FRANCIS, TIMOTHY DUANE, chiropractor; b. Chgo., Mar. 1, 1956; s. Joseph Duane and Barbara Jane (Sigwalt) F. Student, U. Nev., 1974-80, We. Nev. C.C., 1978; BS, L.A. Coll. Chiropractic, 1982, Dr. of Chiropractic magna cum laude, 1984; postgrad., Clark County C.C., 1986—; MS in Bio/Nutrition, U. Bridgeport, 1990. Diplomate Internat. Coll. Applied Kinesiology, Am. Acad. Pain Mgmt., Am. Naturopathic Med. Bd.; cert. kinesiologist, applied kinesiology tchr.; lic. chiropractor, Calif., Nev. Instr. dept. recreation and phys. edn. U. Nev., Reno, 1976-80; from tchng. asst. to lead instr. dept. principles & practice L.A. Coll. Chiropractic, 1983-85; pvt. practice Las Vegas, 1985—; asst. instr. Internat. Coll. Applied Kinesiology, 1990, chmn. exam review com., 1993, chmn. syllabus review com., 1994; adj. faculty The Union Inst. Coll. of Undergrad. Studies, 1993; joint study participant Nat. Olympic Tng. Ctr., Beijing, China, 1990. Mem. editl. rev. bd. Alternative Medicine Rev., 1996; contbr. articles to profl. jours. including Internat. Coll. Applied Kinesiology. Charles F. Cutts scholar, 1980. Fellow Internat. Acad. Clin. Acupuncture, British Inst. Homeopathy (homeopathy diploma 1993); mem. Am. Chiropractic Assn. (couns. on sports injuries, nutrition, roentgenology, technic, and mental health), Nev. State Chiropractic Assn., Nat. Strength and Conditioning Assn., Gonsted Clin. Studies Soc., Found. for Chiropractic Edn. and Rsch., Internat. Chiropractors Assn., Internat. Coll. Applied Kinesiology, Internat. Fedn. Practitioners Natural Therapeutics, Nat. Inst. Chiropractic Rsch., Nat. Strength and Conditioning Assn., Am. Naturopathic Med. Assn., Nat. Acad. Rsch. Biochemists, Phi Beta Kappa, Phi Kappa Phi (v.p. 1979-80, Scholar of the Yr. award, 1980), Delta Signa. Republican. Roman Catholic. Avocations: karate, weightlifting. Home: 3750 S Jones Blvd Las Vegas NV 89103-2259

FRANCISCOLO, MARIO ENRICO, entomologist, educator, ballistics expert; b. Genoa, Liguria, Italy, Aug. 9, 1923; s. Adolfo and Dalmazia (Cappelli) F.; m. Renata Gatto, Aug. 29, 1948 (dec. Nov. 1999). D in Natural Scis., U. Genoa, 1951; cert. ballistics, Camera di Commercio, Trieste, Italy, 1976. Prof. entomology U. Genoa, 1962-66, 79-86, U. Trieste, 1967-79; v.p. Soc. Entomologica Italiana, Genoa, 1996—; cons. forensic entomology U. Genoa, 1980—; referee Asociacion Europea de Coleopterlogia, Barcelona, 1987, Entomol. Soc. Am., Lanham, Md., 1992—, The Coleopterists Soc., Natchez, 1972—. Author: Fauna Cavernicola del Savonese, 1956, Mordellidae of South Africa, 1964, Fauna d'Italia, Vol. 14, Coleoptera Hydradephage, 1979, Fauna d'Italia, Vol. 35, Coleoptera Lucanidae, 1997; contbr. more than 140 articles to profl. jours. Recipient Commendatore al Merito, Pres. Rep. of Italy, 1975. Fellow Soc. Entomologica Italiana (hon.), Royal Entomol. Soc. Avocations: classic pianoforte, hunting, target shooting, technology of ammunition and firearms. Home: Corso Firenze 44-6, I-16136 Genoa Italy Office: U Genoa Istituto di Zool, Via Balbi 5, 16100 Genoa Italy

FRANCK, ANTOINE MAURICE, marketing executive; b. Paris, Dec. 13, 1932; s. Adolphe and Nicole (Treves) F.; m. Dominique Adler, Apr. 15, 1958; children: Olivier, Nicolas. Purchaser Rotary, Paris, 1952-62; tech. asst. Camille Bloch, Switzerland, 1962; field mgr. Avery, Paris, 1963-73; mktg. mgr. Monarch, Paris, 1973-79; sales mgr. Imexco, Paris, 1980-84, Flexcon, Paris, 1987-97, Hologram Industries, Paris, 1998; with Euracli, 1998, Mistral Graphic, 2000—. E-mail: AntoineFranck1@aol.com. Home: 40 rue des Tilleuls, 92100 Boulogne-Billancourt France

FRANCK, HELMUT, internal medicine and rheumatology consultant; b. Bonn, Germany, Jan. 20, 1954; s. Paul and Hildegard (Berzen) F.; m. Beatrix Bertele, Apr. 27, 1984; children: Isabelle, Martin, Monika, Richard. BSc in Physics and Chemistry, U. Bonn, 1975, MSc in Physics and Chemistry, 1980, MD, 1982, PhD, 1983. Edil. Commn. Fgn. Med. Grads. Bonn, 1983; jr. registrar U. Bonn, 1983-84; sr. registrar U. Düsseldorf, Germany, 1984-89, cons. internal medicine & rheumatology, 1989-91; asst. med. dir. Ctr. Rheumatology, Clinic Wendelstein, WHO Ctr. Edn. Rheumatology, Bad Aibling, Germany, 1990-91; med. dir. Clinic Mayenbad, Clinic Rheumatology, Bad Waldsee, Germany, 1991-97, Phys. Therapy Ctr. Rheumatology, Bad Waldsee, 1991-97, Ctr. of Rheumatology, Oberammergau, Germany, 1997—; lectr. Sch. Phys. Therapy, Bad Waldsee, 1992-97; cons. internal medicine, rheumatology, phys. therapy and sports medicine. Contbr. articles to profl. jours. Fellow Sc. Endocrinology, Rheumatology, Sport Medicine, Internat Medicine, mem. German Soc. Rheumatology (founding mem. rehab. sect. 1994), Soc. Rheumatology (founding mem. bone sect. 1989). Avocations: sports, classic music, languages. Office: Ctr Rheumatology, Hubertusstr 40, 82487 Oberammergau Germany

FRANCO, CARLOS, professional golfer; b. Assuncion, Paraguay, May 24, 1965; m. Celsa. Profl. golfer, 1986—; mem. World Cup team, 1992; winner over Sam Torrance Dunhill Cup, 1993; winner Jun Classic, 1994, Sapporo Tokyo Open, 1995, ANA Open, 1996; runner-up Token Corp. Cup, 1997, Dydo Drinco Shizuoka Open, 1997; winner Justsystem KSB Open, 1998, Fuji Sankei Classic, 1998; mem. Internat. Pres. Cup Team, 1998; winner Compaq Classic of New Orleans, 1999, Greater Milw. Open, 1999. Avoca-

tion: fishing. Office: PGA of Am 100 Avenue Of Champions Palm Bch Gdns FL 33418-3665*

FRANCO, JOSE, astrophysicist, researcher; b. Mexico City, July 18, 1949; s. Jose and Elvira (Lopez) F.; m. Bertina Olmedo (div. 1983); m. Claudia Bodek, Oct. 18, 1985; children: Daniela, Tomas. BSc in Physics, U. Mex., Mexico City, 1975; MSc in Physics, U. Wis., 1979, PhD in Physics, 1982. Prof. astrophysics U. Mex., Mexico City, 1983—; sub.-dir. Inst. for Astronomy, Mexico City, 1993-95; vis. prof. U. São Paulo, Brazil, 1987, Max Planck Inst., Munich, 1988-89, Inst. Astrophysics, Canarias, Spain, 1992, U. La Plata, Argentina, 1996, Korea Astrophysical Observatory, 1999, gen. coord. Guillermo Haro Internat. Program on Astrophysics, 1996—. Editor: Chemical and Dynamical Evolution of Galaxies, 1991, Star Formation, Galaxies and the Interstellar Medium, 1993, Numerical Simulations in Astrophysics, 1994, Starbust Activity in Galaxies, 1997, Interstellar Turbulence, 1999; Astrophysical Plasmas, 2000, editl. bd. Cambridge Contemporary Astrophysics, 1995—. Rsch. grantee Cray Rsch. Co., 1993-95, European Econ. Comty., Belgium, 1992-94, U. Mex., 1992-95. Mem. Internat. Astron. Union, Am. Astron. Soc., Mexican Soc. Physics, Mexican Acad. Scis. Avocations: music, snorkeling. Office: U Mexico Instituto de Astronomia, Apdo Postal 70-264, 04510 Mexico City Mexico

FRANCO, MANUEL, psychiatrist, director; b. Leon, Spain, July 8, 1963; s. Manuel and Angeles (Martin) F.; m. Teresa Orihuela, Sept. 16, 1995. Bachelor, Valladolid, 1987, PhD, 1992, MD, 1992. Resident U. Hosp., Valladolid, 1988-92; prof. assoc. U. Valladolid, 1993-94; infant psychiatrist U. Hosp., Valladolid, 1993-94; head of sect. of mental health Castilla-Leon Coun., Valladolid, 1994; head of psychiatry unit Rodriguez Charorro Hosp., Zamora, 1994—; dir. mental health network Castilla-Leon, 2000; cons. Spiral Found., Oviedo, Spain, 1993-95, San Luis Hosp., Palencia, Spain, 1993-96, Feclaps, Valladolid, 1990-96; dir. Intras Found., Valladolid, 1992-96. Contbr. articles to profl. jours; designer: (software cognitive rehab.) Grachior Sys., 1999. Vol. Felclaps, 1989, sec. AEPS, Madrid, 1993. Cabo Army, 1988-89. Named Best Poster Gerotology Castilla Soc., 1994. Mem. Spanish Psychogeriatrics Soc., Am. Assn. Mental Deficiency, Internat. Psychol. Assn. Avocations: medical informatics, journeys, history. Home: Juan de Juni 3 2oB, 47006 Valladolid Spain Office: Rodriguez Chamorro Hosp, Avd Hernan Cortes 40, 49021 Zamora Spain

FRANCO, RALPH ABRAHAM, lawyer; b. Montgomery, Ala., Dec. 27, 1921; s. Abraham and Matilda (Habib) F.; m. Lila Keene, June 9, 1974; 1 stepchild, Charles Walton deCelle. BS, U. Ala., 1943; JD, U. Ala., 1948. Bar: Ala. 1948. Assoc. Hill, Hill, Carter, Franco, Cole & Black P.C. and predecessor firms, Montgomery, 1948-53, ptnr., 1953-88, stockholder, 1988—; mem. adv. bd. dirs. internal medicine residency program med. sch. U. Ala., Montgomery. Past pres. Jewish Fedn., Montgomery; bd. dirs., past pres. St. Margaret's Hosp. Found., St. Margaret's Found.; bd. dirs. Cath. Social Svc., Montgomery, pres., 1984-86, dir. emeritus; bd. dirs., pres. U. Ala. Law Sch. A Found.; bd. dirs., past pres. Etz Ahayem Synagogue. Capt. inf. U.S. Army, 1943-52, PTO, JACG, 1952-74, ret. col. Fellow Am. Bar Found.; mem. ABA, Ala. Bar Assn. (past pres. young lawyers, chmn. real property and probate sect. 1985-86), Montgomery County Bar Assn. (bd. dirs.), llth Jud. Cir. Hist. Soc. (bd. dirs. 1985—), Ala. Law Inst., Ret. Officers Assn., Blue and Gray Assn. (bd. dirs.), U. Ala. Law Sch. Alumni Assn. (past pres., bd. dirs.), Chancellors Soc. (Auburn U. Montgomery), Lions (bd. dirs. Montgomery, past pres.), Standard Country Club (bd. dirs. 1970-76). Home: 3609 Thomas Ave Montgomery AL 36111-2013 Office: Hill Hill Carter et al 425 S Perry St Montgomery AL 36104-4235

FRANCO, ROBERT, economist; b. Cairo, Aug. 11, 1941; came to U.S., 1960; s. Edgard and Speranza Franco; m. Martine Pastor, June 9, 1978; children: Erik, Arnaud. BA, U. Calif., 1963, PhD, 1970; MA, San Diego State U., 1965. Economist Transp. Inst., Washington, 1970-72; mgr. CACI, Arlington, Va., 1972-74; asst. divsn. chief IMF, Washington, 1974-94; resident rep. IMF, Senegal, 1984-87; sr. country economist World Bank, Washington, 1994-96; resident rep. IMF, Harare, Zimbabwe, 1996—; cons. OECD, Paris, 1970-74; prof. U. Md., College Park, 1970-80. Mem. Am. Econ. Assn., AAUP, Omicron Delta Epsilon. Avocations: tennis, music, fishing, boating. Home: PO Box 2960 IMF, Harare Zimbabwe Office: IMF C-200 700 19th St NW # C-200 Washington DC 20431-0001

FRANCOIS, ERIC NICOLAS, investment banking executive; b. Valence, France, July 19, 1960; s. Andre Joseph and Marlene Emilie (Martin) F.; m. Maliha Anne Perrault, July 10, 1993; children: Célia, Louis. MSc, Ecole Nat. de L'Aviation, Toulouse, France, 1983; MBA, INSEAD, Fontainebleau, France, 1988. Engr. French Civil Aviation Authority, Paris, 1983-85; project mgr. Internat. Civil Aviation Orgn., Montreal, also Dakar, Senegal, 1985-87; v.p. Credit Nat., Paris, 1988-91; gen. mgr. Jet Fin., Paris, 1991-95; mng. dir. ING Lease France, Paris, 1995—; cons. Mgmt. and Investment, Europe, Paris, 1989-91. Avocations: philosophy, sports (tennis, swimming). Home: 3 Villa Haussmann, Issy-les-Moulineaux 92130, France

FRANÇOIS-PONCET, JEAN ANDRÉ, business executive, French senator; b. Paris, Dec. 8, 1928; s. Andre and Jacqueline Constance Henriette (Dillais) F.-P.; m. Marie Therese de Mitry, Apt. 18, 1959; children: Philippe, Jacques, Florence. BA, Wesleyan U., Middletown, Conn., 1947; MA, Tufts U., 1948, U. Paris, 1949; PhD, U. Paris, 1952; postgrad., Nat. Sch. Pub. Adminstrn., 1955, Stanford U., 1971. Joined French Ministry for Fgn. Affairs, 1955; with Bur. of Sec. of State, 1956-58; sec. gen. French del. charge negotiating treaties Common Market and Euratom, 1956-57; sec. gen. charge negotiating treaties European Instns. at Ministry Fgn. Affairs, 1958-61; prof. Inst. d'Etudes Politiques de Paris, 1960; head French Assistance and Coop. Mission in Morocco, 1961-63; charge African affairs Ministry Fgn. Affairs, 1963-68; counsellor French embassy, Tehran, Iran, 1968-70; chmn. bd., pres., CEO Ets J.J. Carnaud & Forges de Basse-Indre, 1973-75; minister of state for fgn. affairs, chief coord. Presidency of French Republic, 1976-78, minister fgn. affairs, 1978-81; mem. French Senate, 1983—; reporter Le Figaro, 1984—; pres. Conseil Général, 1987—; chmn. econ. com. French Senate; bd. dirs. FMC Corp. Author: The Economic Policy of West Germany, 1970. Decorated chevalier Legion of Honor. Home: 53 Rue de Varenne, 75007 Paris France*

FRANCONI, FLORENCE, physicist; b. Tours, France, June 4, 1966; f. Jean and Monique (Moreau) F.; Laurent Lemaire, Aug. 7, 1998. PhD summa cum laude, U. F. Rabelais, Tours, France, 1994. Rsch. asst. U. Coll., London, 1994-95, Inst. Neurology, London, 1995-96; rsch. ingenior U. Angers, France, 1996—. Recipient Innovation Tec. award, 1994. Mem. Internat. Soc. for Magnetic Resonance in Medicine. Office: Svc Common RMN, 2 bd Lavoisier, 49045 Angers Cedex France

FRANCULA, NEDJELJKO, cartography educator; b. Zagreb, Croatia, June 20, 1937; s. Mate and Marija (Zupan) F.; m. Blanka Zarinac, Mar. 6, 1966. BS, Faculty Geodesy, Zagreb, Croatia, 1962; PhD, Faculty Agrl., Bonn, Germany, 1971. Scientific asst. Faculty Geodesy, Zagreb, Croatia, 1963-75, asst. prof., 1975-80, assoc. prof., 1980-85, prof., 1985—; mem. Commn. Geodesy, Zagreb, 1992—. Co-author: Multilingual Dictionary of Cartography, 1977; contbr. articles to profl. jours.; editor-in-chief Geodetski List, 1987-95. Mem. Croatian Geodetic Soc., Croatian Soc. Comm., Croatian Acad. Engring. Home: Siget 18b, 10000 Zagreb Croatia Office: Faculty Geodesy, Kaciceva 26, 10000 Zagreb Croatia

FRANETZKI, MANFRED, medical engineering executive, researcher, entrepreneur; b. Halle, Germany, May 4, 1943; s. Richard Franz and Margarete Gertrud (Gorisch) F.; m. Stella Angela Giusto. Jen. 9, 1947; children: Elisa Marlene, Richard Emanuele. Diploma in physics, Martin Luther U., Halle, 1967; DEng, Technische U., Karlsruhe, Germany, 1975. Rsch. asst. Humboldt U., Berlin, 1967-69; group, project leader Siemens Med. Engring., Erlangen, Germany, 1970-79; head basic R&D Siemens Electromedicine, Erlangen, 1979-80; head bus. unit Drug Adminstrn., Erlangen, 1980-88; head R&D dental tech. Siemens (now Sirona GmbH), Bensheim, Germany, 1989-94, head dental innovation ctr., 1994-98; pres. Ctr. for Dental Innovations GmbH, Bensheim, Germany, 1998—; asst. prof. Tech. U., Karlsruhe, 1976-78. Contbr. about 70 sci. articles on med. tech. to profl. jours.; patentee in field. Mem. European Soc. for Ergonomics in Dentistry, Lions Club. Avocations: playing musical instruments, volleyball, cycling. Home: Nussallee 9, D-64625 Bensheim Germany Office: Fabrikstrasse 37, D-64625 Bensheim Germany

FRANGESKOU, VASSILIKI, academic librarian; b. St. Constantine, Cyprus, Dec. 31, 1956; d. Andreas and Theopisti (Georgiou) F.; m. Michael Thomas Richardson, Dec. 30, 1995; children, Anna Dora and Andreas Thomas David. BA, U. Ioannina, Greece, 1978; PhD in Classics, U. Leeds, England, 1985; MA in Libr., U. Sheffield, England, 1990. Libr. U. Ioannina, Greece, 1978-79; tchr. classics Greek Hich Schs., Greece, Cyprus, 1979-81, 85-92; founder, libr. U. Cyprus, Nicosia, 1990-91, lectr., 1992-2000; libr. U. Bristol, U.K., 2000—; mem. Comm. Establishment of State Libr., Cyprus, 1994-95; vis. fellow dept. classics & ancient history Bristol U., UK, 1996, 99, 2000. Contbr. articles to profl. jours. Alexander Onassis Found. scholar, 1981-82, 88-89, A.G. Leventis Found. scholar, 1986, 87, Ctr. Hellenic Studies scholar, Washington, 1994. Mem. Am. Philological Assn., Classical Assn., Brit. Libr. Assn. Greek Orthodox. Avocations: poetry translation, crafts, photography. Office: Libr U Bristol, Tyndall Ave, Bristol BS8 1TJ, United Kingdom

FRANGOPOULOS, ZISSIMOS A., banker; b. Athens, Greece, Dec. 16, 1944; s. John and Thalia (Landi) F.; m. Ruth Snowdon Hoopes, Nov. 21, 1981. BA, Yale U., 1967; MBA, Columbia U., 1969. Lending officer Chem. Bank, N.Y.C., 1969-74; v.p. energy group Chem. Bank, London, 1974-79; sr. v.p. merchant banking Chem. Bank, N.Y.C., London, 1979-84; mng. dir., chief exec. officer Chem. Bank Internat. Ltd., London, 1981-84; sr. v.p., dir. for corp. fin. Chem. Banking Corp., N.Y.C., 1984-90, treas., 1990-92; sr. v.p., treas. Chem. Bank, N.Y.C., 1992-94; mng. dir. Chase Securities, Inc., N.Y.C., 1994-99; treas. Cancer Care Connection Inc., Newark, 2000—, also bd. dirs.; bd. dirs. Christiana Bank & Trust Co., Wilmington. Home: 17 E 96th St New York NY 10128-0783 Office: PO Box 620 Mendenhall PA 19357

FRANK, ALEJANDRO, physicist, educator; b. Monterrey, Mex., Aug. 4, 1951; s. Nathan and Martha (Hoeflich) F.; m. Monica Bolton; children: Pablo, Dan. B in Physics, Nat. Autonomous U. Mex., Mexico City, 1975, DSc in Physics, 1979. Asst. rschr. Nat. Autonomous U. Mex., 1977-79, asst. prof., 1979-82, assoc. prof., 1982-84, prof., 1987—, head dept. physics, 1989-90, 96—; vis. prof. Yale U., New Haven, 1985-86, U. Seville, Spain, 1991-92; asst. editor Revista Mex. Fisica, 1989-90. Author: Algebraic Methods in Molecular and Nuclear Structure Physics, Wiley, 1994; contbr. over 140 articles to profl. jours. Guggenheim Found. fellow, 1991; recipient Manuel Noriega prize Orgn. Am. States, 1991. Fellow Am. Phys. Soc., Mex. Phys. Soc.; mem. Mex. Acad. Sci. (Nat. Prize Exact Scis. 1989). Avocations: reading, tennis, traveling. Office: Inst Sci Nucleares Circ Ext, Nat Autonomous U Mex 70-543, 04510 Mexico City Mexico

FRANK, ANDREAS MICHAEL, neurosurgeon; b. Bad Homburg VDH, Hessen, Fed. Republic Germany, Sept. 24, 1955; s. Rudolf and Valerie Anna-Marie (Fiala) F.; m. Bettina Gabriela Heinze, Oct. 23, 1990; children: Johanna Teresa, Daniel Alexander. MD, Dusseldorf U., 1982. Cert. neurosurgeon. Resident in neurosurgery Munich (Germany) Tech. U., 1982-89, registrar, 1989—; med. advisor exec. bd. Bavarian Red Cross, Munich, 1984-91, vice physician in chief exec. bd., Oberbayern Branch, 1989—. Author: (with others) Grading in Neurosurgery, 1996, The Disc And Its Diseases Enke Verlag Stuttgart; contbr. articles to profl. jours. Physician Bavarian Red Cross, Munich, 1982—. Recipient Bronze medal of merit Bavarian Red Cross, 1989, Silver medal of merit, 1991. Mem. German Soc. of Neurosurgery (mem. adv. bd. 1994-98), German Soc. for Disaster Medicine, Internat. Back Pain Soc., German Soc. Spine Rsch. Roman Catholic. Avocations: classical music, opera, sailing, painting. Office: Dept Neurosurgery Munich Tech U, Ismaninger St 22, 81664 Munich Germany

FRANK, ANNA GLEBOVNA, physicist, researcher; b. Leningrad, Russia, Apr. 2, 1936; d. Gleb Michailovich and Lidia Borisovna (Prochorova) F.; m. Vladimir Nicolaevich Murzin, Oct. 14, 1962; children: Marina, Tatiana. MD in Physics, Moscow State U., 1959; PhD in Physics & Math., Lebedev Physics Inst., USSR Acad. Scis., Moscow, 1973; DS in Physics, Gen. Physics Inst., USSR Acad. Scis., Moscow, 1990. Jr. rsch. scientist P.N. Lebedev Phys. Inst., USSR Acad. Scis., Moscow, 1959-62, rsch. scientist, 1962-76, sr. rsch. scientist, 1976-83; sr. rsch. scientist Gen. Physics Inst., USSR Acad. Scis., Moscow, 1983-90, prin. rsch. scientist, 1990—. Editor: Gleb Michailovich Frank, 1997; contbr. articles to profl. jours. Am. Phys. Soc. grantee, 1992; Internat. Sci. Found. grantee, Moscow, 1993, 94, 95; Internat. Assn. Promotion Cooperation with Scientists of Former Soviet Union grantee, Moscow, 1994, 95, 96, 98, 99; Russian Basic Rsch. Found. grantee, 1993, 94, 95, 96, 97, 98, 99, 2000; recipient USSR State Physics prize USSR Govt., 1982. Office: Gen Physics Inst Russian, Acad Scis 38 Vavilov St, 117942 Moscow Russia

FRANK, BERNARD, lawyer; b. Wilkes-Barre, Pa., June 11, 1913; s. Abraham and Fanny F.; m. Muriel I. Levy, June 19, 1938; children: Roberta R. Penn, Allan R. PhB, Muhlenberg Coll., Allentown, Pa., 1935, LHD, 1987; JD, U. Pa., 1938; postgrad., NYU, 1940-42. Bar: Pa. 1939. Since practiced in Allentown; asst. U.S. atty. Eastern Dist. Pa., 1950-51; asst. city solicitor Allentown, 1956-60. Author articles on ombudsmen in profl. jours. Vice chmn. B'nai B'rith Nat. Commn. Adult Jewish Edn., 1959-61, chmn., 1961-63; bd. dirs. Muhlenberg Coll., 1987-93. With AUS, 1943-46. Decorated comdr. Order of North Star Sweden; recipient Disting. Service award Internat. Ombudsman Inst., 1980. Mem. ABA (chmn. com. ombudsman 1970-76, vice chmn. com. on pub. advs. and pub. representation adminstrv. law sect. 1984-92, fellow adminstrv. law and regulatory procedure sect. 2000), Internat. Bar Assn. (chmn. com. ombudsman 1973-80), Fed. Bar Assn. (chmn. com. ombudsman 1973-80), Pa. Bar Assn., Lehigh Bar Assn., Inter-Am. Bar Assn., World Assn. Lawyers, U.S. Assn. Ombudsmen (hon.), Internat. Ombudsman Inst. (hon. life mem., bd. dirs. 1978-89, pres. 1984-88), Jewish Pub. Soc. Am. (bd. dirs. 1982-99, v.p. 1986-89, 94-98, life trustee 1999—), 94th Inf. Div. (pres. 1953-54). Home: 3203 W Cedar St Allentown PA 18104-3407 Office: 640 Hamilton Mall Allentown PA 18101-2110

FRANK, FRANK, scientist; b. Berlin, Mar. 3, 1938; s. Wilhelm Frank and Anna Goeres; m. Barbara Neumann, Apr. 1, 1966 (div. June 1971); 1 child, Philipp Sebastian; m. Eva Stutzel, July 17, 1980; 1 child, Stephanie Constanze. Diploma in Physics, Tech. U., Berlin, 1964, PhD, 1979. Asst. gen. mgr. B. Halle Nachf., Berlin, 1965-70; dir. application rsch. Messerschmitt-Bolkow-Blohm, Munich, 1970-92; dir. corp. devel. Dornier Medizintechnik GmbH, Munich, 1992-96; gen. mgr. Dornier Surg. Systems GmbH, Munich, 1997-98; dir. R & D Dornier Med. Laser GmbH, Munich, 1998—; chmn. bd. Laser and Medicine Tech., Berlin. Editor: Lasermedizin jour., 1990; author: (scientific movie) The Nd: YAG Laser in Urology, 1980 (Film award German Soc. Urology 1980), The Nd: YAG Laser in Neurosurgery, 1982 (Galena D'Oro Semena Internat de Cine Medico 1983); contbr. articles to profl. jours. Mem. Am. Soc. for Laser Surgery and Medicine (charter mem.), German Soc. for Laser Medicine (com.'s gen. mgr. 1981), Laser Assn. Neurol. Surgeons Internat. (trustee). Avocations: horseback riding (dressage, jumping, cross country), coach driving, sailing. Office: Dornier Medizintechnik GmbH, Argelsreider Feld 7, D-82234 Wessling Germany

FRANK, GERALD WENDEL, civic leader, journalist; b. Portland, Oreg., Sept. 21, 1923; s. Aaron Meier and Ruth (Rosenfeld) F. Student, Stanford U., 1941-43, Loyola U., L.A., 1946-47; BA with honors, Cambridge U., 1948, MA, 1953; D Bus. Adminstrn. (hon.), Greenville (Ill.) Coll., 1971; LLD (hon.), Pacific U., 1983. Mgr. Meier & Frank Co., Salem, Oreg., 1955-65; v.p. Meier & Frank Co., Ltd., 1948-65; also bd. dirs.; pres. Gerry's Frankly Speaking, Salem, Oreg., 1996—; co-owner Gerry Frank's Konditorei, Inc., Salem, Oreg., 1982—; bd. dirs. World Masters Games 1998, Inc. Author: Where to Find It, Buy It, Eat It in New York, 11 edits., 1980—, Joan and Gerry's Little Black Book of Shopping Secrets, 1991, Friday Surprise, 1995; sr. corres. Northwest Reports, 1992-96; commentator/reporter Morning news shows KPTV, Portland, 1993—. Trustee Lorene Sails Higgins Charitable Trust, 1993-2000; chief of staff to Sen. Mark O. Hatfield, 1973-92; gen. chmn. Mark Hatfield for U.S. Sen., 1966, 72, 78, 84, 90; mem. Culver Commn. on Reorganization of U.S. Senate, 1975-76; mem. mgmt. com. U.S. Senate, 1978; active Nat. Found. Infantile Paralysis, Arthritis and Rheumatism Found., Portland C. of C., Salem Area C. of C., Sunshine Divsn., Portland Police Res., Portand Area Coun., Cascade Area Coun., Cascade Pacific Coun., Nat. Coun., Boys Scouts Am., Portland Rose Festival Assn., Jr. Achievement, Travelers Aid Soc. Portland, Nat. Mcpl. League, Salem Pub. Libr. Found., Portland United Fund, Marion-Polk Counties United Good Neighbors, Salem Gen. Hosp., Nat. Retail Merchants Assn., Citizens' Conf. for Govtl. Coop., Gov.'s Econ. Devel. Commn., Oreg. Retail Distributors' Inst., Am. Heart Soc., Oreg. Rsch. Assn., Salem 4-H Club, Willamette River Days, Salem YWCA, Willamette U. bd. trustees, League Women Voters, Oreg. Grad. Inst. Sci. & Tech., Portland Met. Futures Unltd., Inc., Marion-Salem Bldg. Study Com., Oreg. Symphony Soc., Am. Legion, Oreg. Coast Aquarium, 1990—, exec. com., U.S. Com. for UNICEF, 1990-99, Oreg. High Desert Mus., Salvation Army, Salem Art Assn., Parry Ctr. for Children, St. Vincent Hosp. & Med. Ctr., Oreg. Health Scis. U., OMSI, chair, dir., 1996-97, Oreg. Tourism Coun., chair, 1996—, Oreg. Ind. Colls. Found., AAA of Oreg., Oreg. Garden Found., Oreg. State Bar Ho. Dels., Miss Oreg. Scholarship Program. Recipient numerous awards including Silver Beaver Boy Scouts Am., 1963, Reginald H. Vincent trophy United Good Neighbor of Yr., 1980, Brotherhood Nat. Conf. Christians and Jews, Portland, 1984, Glenn Jackson leadership Willamette U., 1984, Tom Lawson McCall fellowship Pacific U., 1987. Mem. Am. Legion, Elks, Rotary (Paul Harris fellow 1986). Avocations: travel, gourmet dining. Home: 3250 Crestview Dr S Salem OR 97302-5959 Office: Gerry's Frankly Speaking Inc 2601 25th St SE Ste 500 Salem OR 97302-1287 also: PO Box 2225 Salem OR 97308-2225

FRANK, HARTMUT FRIEDRICH GUSTAV, architect; b. Koscian, Poland, Dec. 5, 1942; arrived in Germany, 1945; s. Herbert and Ursula (Claus) F.; m. Carmen Amelia Muñoz Chequer; children: Matilde, Augusta, Leonora. Degree in architecture, Tech. U., Berlin, 1969. Asst. tchr. Eidgenössische Tech. Hochschule, Zürich, Switzerland, 1970-71; lectr. Hochschule fuer Bildende Kuenste, Berlin, 1971-72; prof. Hochschule fuer Bildende Kuenste, Hamburg, 1976—; asst. lectr. dept. architecture Tech. U., Berlin, 1972-75; head dept. architecture Hochschule fuer Bildende Kuenste, Hamburg, 1977-78, v.p., 1987-89; senator founding senate Tech. U., Hamburg, 1977-82; bd. dirs. Hamburg Architecture Archives. Assoc. editor Planning Perspectives; contbr. articles to profl. jours. Mem. Assn. for Applied Arts (vice-spkr.). Studio: Eppendorfer Landstr 86, D 20249 Hamburg Germany Office: Hochschule fuer Bildende Kuenste, FB Arch, Lerchenfeld 2, D-22081 Hamburg Germany

FRANK, HARTMUT GOTTLIEB, chemistry educator, environmental scientist; b. Bernburg, Germany, Apr. 6, 1943; s. Werner G. and Emma P. (Rabe) F.; 1 child, Alexander. Diploma in Chemistry, U. Tubingen, Germany, 1969, PhD, 1973, Habilitation, 1986, Dozent, 1988. Rsch. asst. U. Tubingen, Tubingen, Germany, 1973-74; vis. asst. prof. Baylor Coll. Med., Houston, 1974-76; rsch. scientist Dept. Organic Chem., Tubingen, Germany, 1977; vis. rsch. scientist Inst. Chem. Physics Acad. Sinica, Dalian, China, 1981-83; rsch. scientist Dept. Toxicology, Tubingen, Germany, 1978-85; vis. prof. Universidade Nova de Livboa, Lisbon, Portugal, 1986—; vis. rsch. fellow Australian Nat. U., Canberra, Australia, 1987-89; lectr. Dept. Toxicology, Tubingen, Germany, 1986-93; prof., chair environ. chemistry and ecotoxicology U. Bayreuth, Germany, 1993—. Inventor: Chirasil-Val, 1978; editor, author, Chirality and Biological Activity, 1988; editor in chief Jr. High Resolution Chromatography, 1990. Recipient diploma award, Assn. Chem. Industries, 1969, Analytical Chem. award, Soc. German Chemists, 1983; Fulbright scholar, 1974. Mem. Am. Chem. Soc., Soc. German Chemists, German Soc. Pharmacol. Toxicology. Avocations: hiking, bicycling, chess. Office: U Bayreuth, Environ Chemistry, D-95440 Bayreuth Germany

FRANK, JOHN LEROY, lawyer, government executive, educator; b. Eau Claire, Wis., Mar. 13, 1952; s. George LeRoy and Frances Elaine (Torgerson) F. BS summa cum laude, U. Wis., Eau Claire, 1974; JD cum laude, U. Wis., Madison, 1977. Bar: Wis. 1977, U.S. Dist. Ct. (we. dist.) Wis. 1977, U.S. Supreme Ct. 1982. Instr. law U. Wis., Madison, 1976-77; assoc. Garvey, Anderson, Kelly & Ryberg, S.C., Eau Claire, 1977-81; legis dir., counsel Congressman Steve Gunderson, Washington, 1981-85, chief of staff, counsel, 1985-89; staff coord. 92 Group, Washington, 1987-89; paralegal instr., program dir. Chippewa Valley Tech. Coll., 1989-93, 97—; pvt. practice Eau Claire, Wis., 1990-93, 97—; counsel, minority cons. House Subcommittee on Livestock, Washington, 1993-95; counsel Congressman Steve Gunderson, Washington, 1993-97; dep. minority counsel House Com. on Agr., Washington, 1993-95, dep. chief counsel, 1995-97; commr. W. Ctrl. Wis. Regional Planning Commn., Eau Claire, 1998—; pol. analyst, commentator WEAU-TV, Eau Claire, Wis., 1998—. Named One of Outstanding Young Men in Am., U.S. Jaycees, 1977. Mem. ABA, FBA, Wis. Bar Assn., Wis. Assn. for Career and Tech. Edn. (bd. dirs. 2000—, legis. com. chair 2000—), U. Wis. Alumni Assn. (outstanding sr. arts & scis. 1974), Phi Delta Phi, Phi Gamma Delta (Durrance award 1978). Republican. Lutheran. Address: 2113 Meadow Ln Eau Claire WI 54701-7965

FRANK, JUDIT, chemical engineer; b. Pécs, Hungary, Dec. 5, 1942; d. Kálmán and Veronica (Radich) F. MS, Technical U., Budapest, Hungary, 1966, PhD, 1974. Chem. researcher CHINOIN Pharm. Chem. Works, Budapest, Hungary, 1966-69, research group leader, 1969-74, head rsch. group, 1976-86, head semisynthetic antibiotics devel., 1987-91; sci. mgr. CHINOIN, Budapest, 1992-93, strategic project mgr. AGCHEM bus. unit, 1994-96; head AGCHEM Svcs., Budapest, 1997-99, sci. adviser, 2000—; vis. scientist U. East Anglia, Norwich, Eng., 1974-75. Contbr. articles to profl. jours.; Patentee (17) patents in field. Fellow Hungarian Acad. Scis. (head rsch. group Ctr. Rsch. Inst. Chemistry, 1976-92, sec. rsch. com. antibiotics 1991-97). Avocations: traveling, skiing, swimming. Home: Szölö-Köz 2, H-1032 Budapest Hungary Office: CHINOIN AGCHEM Bus. Unit, PO Box 49, H-1780 Budapest Hungary

FRANK, LAWRENCE J., library director; b. Detroit, Oct. 9, 1943; s. George A. and Marjorie J. (McConkey) F.; m. Bonnie L. Bonsky, Aug. 4, 1973; children: Alyssa Ann, Nathan D. BA with honors, Western Mich. U., 1976, MA magna cum laude, 1977; AMLS, U. Mich., 1979; cert. pub. adm. advanced mgmt. program, Miami U., Oxford, Ohio, 1983; cert. edn., U. Wis., 1996. Pub. Librs. Profl. cert., N.Y., Librs. Permanent Profl. cert., Mich., Profl. cert., Ky. Libr. intern Ann Arbor (Mich.) Pub. Libr., 1979; reference libr. Toledo-Lucas County Pub. Libr., 1979-81; exec. dir. Amos Meml. Pub. Libr., Sidney, Ohio, 1981-85; dir. Troy (Mich.) Pub. Libr., 1985-86, Boyd County Pub. Libr., Ashland, Ky., 1986-95, St. Clair County Libr., Port Huron, Mich., 1995-99, Onondaga County Pub. Libr., Syracuse, N.Y., 1999—; tchr., missionary The Lang. Inst., Japan Luth. Ch., Tokyo and Niigata, Japan, 1968-71; cons. in libr. design and orgn., Port Huron, 1996-98. Contbr. articles to jours.; author of poems. Bd. dirs. Ky. Coun. on Econ Edn., Ashland, 1986-95; mem. steering com. U. Cin. Children's Hosp., Ashland, 1987-90; active Main St. Port Huron, 1996-98. Named Boss of the Yr., Jaycees, Ashland; Tuition scholar U. Mich., Ann Arbor, 1978-79. Mem. APHA, ALA, ACLU (ctrl. N.Y. chpt.), Libr. Adminstrn. and Mgmt. Assn., Pub. Libr. Adminstrn., N.Y. Libr. Assn. Avocations: wine and art collecting, writing, drawing, hiking, environmental design. Office: Onondaga County Pub Libr The Galleries Syracuse 447 S Salina St Syracuse NY 13202-2417

FRANK, MARTIN, geochemist; b. Pforzheim, Germany, Feb. 3, 1966; s. Helmut and Ingrid (Gellisch) F.; m. Claudia Schmengler, Sept. 7, 1994; children: Yannick, Alisa. Diploma, U. Heidelberg, 1992, PhD, 1995. Rsch. fellow U. Heidelberg, Germany, 1995-96, U. Oxford, England, 1996-99, ETH Zürich, Switzerland, 1999—. Avocations: sports, children and family, literature. Office: Inst Isotope Geol/Min Res, Dept Earth Scis ETH Zurich, N061 Sonneggstrasse 5 CH-8092, Switzerland

FRANK, MARTIN ERNST, real estate executive, writer; b. Bern, Switzerland, Sept. 26, 1950; s. Heinrich Rudolf and Hedwig Louise (Peter) F.; m. Agnes Ollennu; children: Rizvi Syed Karbalai, John William. Ed., various pub. schs.; Fed. Diploma in Horsemanship. Ptnr. DeSoto Moveis Ltd., Zurich, Switzerland, 1976—. Author: (fiction) La Mort de Chevrolet, 1981, Lobo, 1980, Six Love Stories, 1999, Little Book of Death, 2000, others. Office: DeSoto Moveis Ltd, Dahliastr 4 PO Box 72, Zurich CH-8034, Switzerland

FRANK, MARY LOU BRYANT, psychologist, educator; b. Denver, Nov. 27, 1952; d. W.D. and Blanche (Dean) Bryant; m. Kenneth Kerry Frank, Sept. 9, 1973; children: Kari Lou, Kendra Leah. BA, Colo. State U., 1974,

MEd, 1983, MS, 1986, PhD, 1989. Tchr. Cherry Creek Schs., Littleton, Colo., 1974-80; grad. dir. career devel. Colo. State U., Ft. Collins, 1980-86; intern U. Del., Newark, 1987-88; psychologist Ariz. State U., Tempe, 1988-93; assoc., lead prof. psychology Clinch Valley Coll. U. Va., Wise, 1992-96, and asst. acad. dean, 1993-95; head psychology dept., prof. North Ga. Coll. and State U., Dahlonega, 1996—; chmn. bd. regents adv. com. Psychology; instr. Colo. State U., Ft. Collins, 1981-82, counselor, 1984-85, 86-87; psychologist Ariz. State U., Tempe, 1989-92; assoc. prof. psychology Clinch Valley Coll. U. Va., 1992-96; chair adv. com. Ga. Bd. Regents, 1999—; speaker in field. Author: (program manual) Career Development, 1986; contbr. book chpts. on eating disorders and existential psychotherapy, 1996, 98, 99; reviewer Buros Mental Measurements Yearbook. Mem. Ga. Woman of the Yr. Com., 1999, 2000. Mem. APA, AACD, ACES, Southeastern Psychol. Assn. (chair undergrad. rsch. 1996—), Odeka (faculty adv.), Phi Kappa Phi, Phi Beta Kappa, Pi Kappa Delta, Psi Chi (Ga. Woman of the Yr. com. 1999, 2000). Avocations: music, hiking, reading. Office: North Ga Coll and State Uni Psychology Dept 207 Dunlap Hall Dahlonega GA 30533

FRANK, MICHAEL JOHN, training and development company executive; b. Lorain, Ohio, Aug. 10, 1943; s. Michael Norman and Patricia Bell (Robertson) F.; m. Suzanne Groce, Mar. 22, 1969; children: David Michael, Lisa Renee. BSBA, Ohio State U., 1970; postgrad., Boston Coll., 1977-80. CPA, Mich., Ohio. Staff acct. Haskins & Sells, Detroit, 1970-72; mgr. acctg. Xerox Edn. Ctr., Columbus, Ohio, 1972-74; fin. analyst Xerox Pub. Group, Stamford, Conn., 1974-76; mgr. fin. planning Ginn and Co., Lexington, Mass., 1976-81; contr. Xerox Learning Sys., Stamford, Conn., 1981-83; v.p. fin. Xerox Learning Sys., Stamford, 1983-85; v.p. fin. Learning Internat., 1985-91, CFO, 1991-96, sr. v.p. bus. devel., 1996-97; profl. svcs. mgr. Parson Group, N.Y.C. Vol. Appalachian Svc. Project, 1992-96; mem. Ridgefield Emmaus, 1990-96, chmn., 1994, 95. Served to cpl. USMC, 1963-67, Japan, South Vietnam. Mem. AICPA, Cub Scouts of Am., Harvard, Mass. (bd. dirs. 1979-80), Marine Corps League, VFW, Phi Kappa Psi, Jaycees (Columbus). Republican. Congregationalist. Home: 486 N Salem Rd Ridgefield CT 06877-2424 Office: Parson Group LLC 70 E 55th St Fl 5 New York NY 10022-3222

FRANK, PAUL MARTIN, engineering educator, scientist; b. Heidelberg, Germany, July 7, 1934; s. Otto Wilhelm and Elisabeth (Junkert) F.; m. Hildegard Katharina Faure, May 20, 1961; children: Stefan, Brigitte. Diploma in Elec. Enring., U. Karlsruhe, Germany, 1959, D in Control Engring., 1966, habil., 1973; D (hon.), GH.Asachi, Iasi, Romania, 1994, U. Haute-Alsace, Mulhouse, France, 1997, U Cluj-Napoca, Romania, 1998. Rsch. asst. U. Karlsruhe, Germany, 1959-66, jr. acad., 1966-71, sr. acad., 1971-73, dept. head dept., 1973-74, assoc., 1975-76; prof., head dept. measurement and control U. Duisburg, Germany, 1976-2000, head faculty elec. engring., 1980-81, prof. emeritus, 1999—; guest prof. U. Wash. Seattle, 1974-75, U. Strasbourg, France, 1976—; v.p. German-French Inst. Automation and Robotics, 1997-99, pres., 1999-2000, head DUI br., 1986—; co-founder assoc. Amira GMBH, Duisburg, 1986—; cons. several indsl. cos., 1972—; guest lectr. Inst. Politecnico Nat. IPN, Mex., 1976, 81, Northwestern Poly. U., Xian, China, 1983, Qinghua U., Beijing, 1985, U. Nat. Autonoma Mex., 1991. Author: Entwurf von Regelkreisen mit vorgeschriebenem Verhalten, 1974, Pulsfrequenzmodulierte Regelungssysteme, 1975, Introduction to System Sensitivity Theory, 1978, Entdeckung von Instrumentenfehlanzeigen mittels Zustandsschätzung in technischen Regelungssystemen, 1984; author, co-editor: Fault Diagnosis in Dynamic Systems, 1989; editor: Advances in Control, 1999, Issues of Fault Diagnosis for Dynamic Systems, 2000; editor-at-large European Jour. Control, 1995—; contbr. more than 420 articles to profl. jours. and internat. confs., chpts. to 29 books; co-editor 5 tech. jours.; organizer, gen. chmn. ECC 99, 1999. Recipient Louis-Pasteur medal Louis Pasteur U. Strasbourg, 1989, GH Asachi medal of merit Tech. U. GH Asachi, Romania, 1994, Felber medal in Silver, Czech Tech. U., Prague, 1996, Medal of Honour, U. Miskolc, Hungary, 1996. Fellow IEEE; mem. European Union Control Assn. (sec. 1993-95, 2d v.p. 1995-97, 1st. v.p. 1997-99, pres. 1999—), Union German Engrs., Union German Electrotech., Gesellschaft für Mess-und Automatisierungstechnik (chmn. theory and fundamentals 1987-96, bd. dirs. Fuzzy Initiative NRW 1987-98), Rotary (pres. 1994-95). Protestant. Avocations: skiing, swimming, hiking, music, home construction. Home: Am Steinwerth 4, 47269 Duisburg Germany Office: Gerhard Mercator U, Bismarck St 81, 47048 Duisburg Germany

FRANK, RICHARD DARYL, therapist; b. Melbourne, Victoria, Australia, May 30, 1938; s. August Ashley and Christina Mary (Birrel-Moore) F.; m. Marilyne Miriam Smith, Mar. 17, 1962; children: Tina Louise, Heidi Jane. Diploma in Med. Gymnastics, Inst. Phys. Culture, 1957; Diploma in Printing tech., Melbourne Sch. Printing, 1958. Cadet exec. McCarron Bird P/L, Melbourne, 1955-60; dir. Collegiate Gymnastic Equipment P/L, Melbourne, 1960-66; territory mgr./area mgr. Mobil Oil Australia P/L, Melbourne, 1967-83; gen. mgr. Premier Oil Co. Australia, Bendigo, 1983-86; clin. therapist Richard Frank, Bendigo, 1977-87, Melbourne, 1987—; dir. Australian Lubrication Cons., Melbourne, 1983-93, Brunswick Auto One, Melbourne, 1993-97; mng. dir. Forces of Nature, 2000—. Bd. dirs. Arid Lands Rsch. and Sci. Found., Melbourne, 1980-93; pres. Golden City A.U.S.S.I. Swimming, Bendigo, 1980; diving coach Bendigo Swimming Club, 1981-84; pres. Melbourne U. Motorcycle Club, 1993; master Wesley Collegians Lodge, 1990-91, 98-99. Mem. Speedway Sidecar Riders Assn. (pres. 1975), Motorcycling Australia (del. 1996-99), Massage Assn. Australia, Ortho Molecular Med. Assn., Masons (master 1990-91, 98-99), Wesley Collegians Lodge (master 1990-91, 98-99), Historic Mgmt. Com. of Victoria, Historic Motorcycle Racing Assn. Victoria (pres. 2000—). Mem. Ch. of Almighty God. Avocations: motorcycle racing, swimming, fishing, grandchildren.

FRANK, ROBERT ALLEN, advertising executive; b. Albany, N.Y., Sept. 26, 1932; s. Edward and Marian (Kostelanetz) F.; m. Cynthia Tull, Aug., 1984; children: David, Chelsea, Alison. B.A., Colby Coll., 1954; MBA, Amos Tuck Sch. Bus. Adminstrn., Dartmouth Coll., 1958. Cost control adminstr. ABC-TV, N.Y.C., 1958-59; corp. auditor CBS Inc., N.Y.C., 1959-60, TV sales svc. account exec., 1961, account exec. radio network sales, 1962-69; exec. v.p., co-founder SFM Media Corp., N.Y.C., 1969—, pres. Media Svc. div., 1981; pres., CEO SFM Media LLC, N.Y.C., 1998—. Radio-TV cons. Nat. Kidney Fund., 1974; active radio TV for various polit. campaigns including Robert Kennedy for Senator, 1964, Richard Nixon for Pres., 1972, Ford for Pres., 1976, Bush for Pres., 1980, Reagan for Pres., 1980, Du Pont for Pres., 1988; mem. Leadership Coun. Nat Rep. Congl. Com., Rep. Nat. Com., Pres.' Club, 1984-88, Rep. Nat. Senatorial Com. Inner Circle, 1985-88, Citizens for Rep. Pres. Com., 1984-88; trustee Nat. Child Labor Com., 1984-96, vice chmn., 1994-96; trustee Myasthenia Gravis Found., 1984-93. Served to capt. USAF, 1954-56. Mem. Internat. Radio-TV Soc., Amos Tuck Alumni Assn. N.Y. (pres. 1976-77, dir. 1979), Dartmouth Club (N.Y.C.), Pi Gamma Mu. Home: 35 Lounsbury Rd Ridgefield CT 06877-4710 Office: SFM Media Corp Ste 9W 1180 Avenue Of The Americas Fl 10 New York NY 10036-8405

FRANK, RONALD, chemist, researcher; b. Neuenburg, Germany, Oct. 9, 1948; s. Helmut and Edith (Bolenius) F. Diploma in Chemistry, U. Hamburg, 1974, PhD, 1979. Postdoctoral fellow U. Hamburg, 1979-80; asst. tchr. 5, 1977-79; sr. scientist GBF, Braunschweig, 1980, head project group "chem. peptide synthesis", 1985-91, head project group "constrn. of model structures", 1992-93, head rschr. group moleular recognition, 1994—, mem. sci. assembly, 1985—, co-chmn., 1990-92, chmn., 1995-97. Contbr. articles to profl. jours.; patentee in field; editl. bd. Jour. Molecular Rec., Molecular Diversity. Mem. European Peptide Soc., Am. Peptide Soc., German Chem. Soc., German Soc. for Biochemistry and Molecular Biology (WT Binder prize 1998, ACT award 1999). Avocations: philosophy, world travel. Office: GBF, Mascheroder Weg 1, D-38124 Braunschweig Germany

FRANK, RONALD WILLIAM, lawyer, financier; b. Greensburg, Pa., Mar. 11, 1947; s. William John and Louise (Mautino) F.; m. Marsha Ann Kolesar, Aug. 30, 1969. BSChemE, Carnegie Mellon U., 1969; JD, Duke U., 1972. Bar: Pa. 1972. Ptnr. Buchanan Ingersoll P.C., Pitts., 1972-93, Babst, Calland, Clements & Zomnir, P.C., Pitts., 1993-99; mng. dir. Morgan Franklin & Co., 1994—; ptnr. Reed Smith Shaw & McClay, Pitts., 2000—; bd. dirs. Morgan Franklin & Co.; sec. Nat. Roll Co. Contbr. articles to profl. jours. Chmn. nat. fund raising com., Carnegie-Mellon U., Pitts., 1983-88, bd. advisors Sch. Engring. and Sci.; mem. adv. bd. Sch. Engring., Carnegie Mellon U.; mem. bd. visitors sch. law Duke U., Durham, N.C. Mem. ABA, Pa. Bar Assn. (coun., corp. sec. 1982-85, chmn. Internat. and Comparative law sect. 1992—), Allegheny County Bar Assn., Internat. Bar Assn., Duquesne Club, Shannopin Country Club. Avocations: golf, skiing, computers, amateur radio. Home: 1675 Gloucester Ct Sewickley PA 15143-8518 Office: Reed Smith Shaw & McClay LLP 435 6th Ave Ste 2 Pittsburgh PA 15219-1886

FRANK, SERGEI, federal official; b. 1960. Min. Ministry of Transport, Moscow, 1998—. Office: Ministry of Transport, Sadovaya-Samotechnaya 10, Moscow 101433, Russia*

FRANK, SERGEY O., Russian government official. Honor Degree in Marine Navigation, Far Eastern State Marine Acad., Vladivostok, 1983; Degree in Civil and Pub. Law, Far Eastern State U., Vladivostok, 1995; grad. Higher Comml. Sch., Acad. Fgn. Trade, Moscow, 1989. Lectr., chair econs., chair navigation Far Eastern State Marine Acad., 1983-84, dep. prin., 1984-89; gen. mgr. fgn. econ. rels. dept. Far Eastern Shipping Co., 1989-91, exec. v.p. fin. and planning, 1991-95; dep. dir. maritime transport dept. Ministry of Transport of the Russian Fedn., 1995-96, dep. minister of transport, 1996-97, 1st dep. minister of transport, 1997-98, minister of transport, 1998—; chmn. bd. dirs. Aeroflot, 1999—; bd. dirs. Sovcomflot; mem. com. on econ. issues Nat. Security Coun.; vice chair Govt. Com. for Transport Policy.

FRANK, STEPHEN IRA, political science educator; b. Seattle, Oct. 14, 1942; s. Nancy Ann (Schwartz) Frank; m. Barbara Ann Covey; 1 child, Thomas Aaron. BS in Edn., History and Polit. Sci., Ctrl. Mich. U., 1966, MA in Polit. Sci., 1969; PhD in Polit. Sci., Wash. State U., Pullman, 1976. Tchr. social sci. Clarkston (Mich.) High Sch., 1967-69; instr. in polit. sci. Gogebec Community Coll., Ironwood, Mich., 1967-69, Lamar U., Beaumont, Tex., 1975-76; prof. polit. sci. N.E. La. U., Monroe, La., 1976-78, St. Cloud (Minn.) State U., 1978—; co-dir., founder St. Cloud State U. Survey. Author: (with Steven Wagner) We Shocked the World: A Case Study of Jesse Ventura's Election As Governor of Minnesota, 1999; contbr. articles to profl. jours. Mem. Am. Polit. Sci. Assn., Am. Assn. Pub. Opinion, Nat. Assn. Prelaw Advisors, Midwest Prelaw Advisors Assn. (bd. dirs.), St. Cloud State U. Faculty Assn. (pres. 1993-94), Phi Kappa Delta. Avocations: gardening, walking, reading. Office: St Cloud State U Dept Polit Sci 319 Brown Hall Saint Cloud MN 56301-4444

FRANK, THOMAS, design, construction and management executive; b. Salt Lake City, Nov. 23, 1937; s. Simon and Suzanne (Seller) F. BFA, U. Utah, 1963. Lic. contractor, Utah. Owner Thomas Frank Designers & Specifiers, Salt Lake City, 1962—; owner, pres. OmmiComputer West, Salt Lake City; bd. dirs. Silver Eagle Refining, Inc.; cons. in field; instr. design, textiles and drafting LDS Jr. Coll., Salt Lake City, 1963-86; lectr. on interior design for jr. and high schs. Bus. & Industry Coop. Edn. Program; profl. adviser interior design curriculum devel. program U. Utah; mem. inter-profl. adv. coun. Utah State Bldg. Bd.; lectr., presenter seminars in field. Contbr. articles to profl. publs. Exec. v.p. Salt Lake Art Ctr., 1977-80; spl. advisor Children's Ctr.; co-chmn. spl. events Utah divsn. Am. Cancer Soc., 1978. Recipient awards U. Utah, 1962, Utah Designers Craftsman Guild, 1962, State Fair Fine Arts, 1962, Recognition award Gov. Mrs. Scott Matheson, 1980, Honor award Utah Soc. AIA, 1982. Fellow Am. Soc. Interior Designers (nat. coun. for interior design qualification); mem. N.Am. Autocadd Users Group, Nat. Kitchen and Bath Assn. (pres. mountain states chpt. west 1991-92), Am. Soc. Interior Designers (nat. long-range planning com. 1985-87, nat. comms. area coord. 1985, nat. membership devel. com. 1986-87, nat. regional dir. 1991-92, nat. edn. com. 1981, nat. chmn. energy conservation 1980-82, nat. chpt. pres.' orientation task force 1980, nat. bd. dirs. 1977-82, chmn. regional indsl. rels. 1977-78, numerous other offices, numerous awards), AID (sec. Utah 1969-71, bd. govs. 1970-74, Utah pres. 1973-75), Nat. Coun. Interior Design Quantification. Avocations: tennis, skiing, art collecting. Home: 2360 Oakhill Dr Salt Lake City UT 84121-1520 Office: Thomas Frank Designers 3369 Highland Dr Salt Lake City UT 84106-3356

FRANK, TIBOR, historian; b. Budapest, Hungary, Feb. 3, 1948; s. Henrik and Hedvig (Flesch) F.; m. Zsuzsanna Várkonyi, Apr. 20, 1974; 1 child, Benedek. MA, Eötvös Loránd U., Budapest, 1971, DS, 1973; PhD, Hungarian Acad. Letters & Sci., Budapest, 1979; habilitation, Eötvös Loránd U., Budapest, 1996; DLitt, Hungarian Acad. Letters & Sci., Budapest, 1998. From asst. prof. to prof. Eötvös Loránd U., 1971—; chair dept. Am. Studies Eötvös Loránd U., 1992-94, dir. Sch. English and Am. Studies, 1994—; Fulbright vis. prof. U. Calif., Santa Barbara, 1987-90, dir. New Europe program, 1994-97; disting. vis. prof. U. Nev., Reno, 1990-91; cons. Nuc. Age Peace Found., Santa Barbara, 1991-96. Author: The British Image of Hungary 1865/1870, 1976, Marx és Kossuth, 1985, Egy emigráns alakváltásai, 1985, Japanese edit., 1994, Ethnicity, Propaganda Myth-Making, 1999; editor: The Origins and Originality of American Culture, 1984, Values in American Society, 1995; editor spl. issue, Hungarian Studies, Culture and Society in Early 20th Century, 1994; mem. editl. bd. Nationalities Papers, 1989—; mem. adv. bd. Hist. Abstracts, 1989-93, 2000—, European Jour. Am. Culture, 1998—. Rsch. sec. Mass Comm. Rsch. Ctr., Budapest, 1974-75; Hungarian Min. of Culture and Edn., Budapest, 1984-86. Grantee Woodrow Wilson Internat. Ctr. for Scholars, 1989, Am. Philos. Soc., 1989-90, Rockefeller Found., 1992, Széchenyi Hungarian Nat. Prof., 1997-2000, Hungarian Fulbright Bd., 1999—. Mem. European Assn. for Am. Studies (bd. 1994-2000), N.Y. Acad. Scis. Avocations: collecting manuscripts, classical music. Office: Eötvös Loránd U, Ajtósi Dürer sor 19-21, H-1146 Budapest Hungary

FRANK, WILLIAM FIELDING, computer systems design executive, consultant; b. N.Y.C., Oct. 27, 1944; s. Karl Frederick and Margaret Ruth (Denisson) F.; m. Linda Carol Hainfield, Dec. 20, 1965 (div. 1972); children: Aaron, Tobin. BA, Middlebury Coll., 1966; MA, U. Chgo., 1969; PhD, U. Pa., 1976. Assoc. prof. Oreg. State U., Corvallis, 1969-79; mem. tech. staff Bell Labs., Whippany, N.J., 1979-81; pres. Enterprise Engring. Assts. Inc., Warren, Vt., 1982-99; founder, chief scientist Cmty. Integration Tech., Manchester by the Sea, Mass., 1999—; assoc. prof. MIT, Cambridge, 1981-85; cons. Citibank, 1982—, AT&T, 1984, N.Y. Times, 1985, Bank of Am., 1985, State of Calif., 1986—, Digital Equipment Corp., 1987-89, Soviet Ministry of Trade, 1990, Bankers Trust, 1991, Fidelity Investments, 1993—, Reuters, 1996, Ameritech, 1996, NEC, 1998—, U.S. chief delegate Internat. Stnds. Orgn., 1999—; tech. adv. bd. LIMITrader, 2000—. Contbr. articles to profl. jours. Rsch. grantee NSF, 1971, 77, NEH, 1976, 81. Mem. Assn. for Computing Machinery, Computer Soc. IEEE. Republican. Congregationalist. Achievements include pioneering of object-oriented enterprise modelling, client role modelling and research in business rule driven software design. Office: FSA Ste 341 2 Portland Fish Pier Portland ME 04101

FRANK, WILLIAM NELSON, lawyer, accountant; b. Cin., June 3, 1953; s. Nelson A. and Marion A. (Kirbert) F.; m. Brenda L. Norwood, Sept. 30, 1995. Student, Capital U., 1971-74; BS in Edn., Bowling Green State U., 1975; JD, U. Toledo, 1978; postgrad., U. Cin., 1980-82. Bar: Ohio, 1978, U.S. Dist. Ct., U.S. Tax Ct., U.S. Supreme Ct.; CPA, Ohio; cert. tchr., Ohio. Asst. city prosecutor City of Columbus, Ohio, 1978-80; asst. pub. defender Hamilton (Ohio) County, 1981-84; sole practice William N. Frank, Columbus, 1978-85; regional fin. mktg. mgr. Primerica Fin. Svcs., Columbus, 1984-90, Cin., 1990-92; atty., acct. Tyirin, Benvie & Co., Cin., 1990-92; atty. Hyatt Legal Svcs., Cin., 1992-93; pvt. practice Cin., 1993—; spl. counsel to Ohio Atty. Gen., 1996—; auditor Phillip Willeke, Inc., Columbus, 1985-87; securities rep. 1st Am. Nat. Securities, Columbus, 1985-92; lectr. in law Hondros Career Ctr., 1993—, special council to the Ohio Attorney Genl., 1996—. Mem. Hamilton County Rep. Club, Cin., 1981—. Named to Hon. Order Ky. Cols. Commonwealth of Ky., 1978. Mem. AICPA, Cin. Bar Assn., Ohio Soc. CPAs, Cheviot Masons (worshipful master, master 1999), Royal Order of Scotland, Knights Templar, Royal Arch Mason, Order of Eastern Star, Shriners, Cin. Hist. Soc. (tour dir.), Order of DeMolay (chevalier degree 1972, Legion of Honor 1994), Delta Tau Upsilon, Phi Alpha Delta. Republican. Mem. Ch. of Christ. Avocations: tennis, Scottish Bagpipe musician, martial arts. Home: 3260 Milverton Ct Cincinnati OH 45248-2857 Office: 3050 Harrison Ave Cincinnati OH 45211-5752

FRANKE, JACK EMIL, foreign language educator; b. Pine Bluff, Ark., July 8, 1965; s. Ernest Rudolph and Charlotte (Harris) F.; m. Lyudmila Veniaminovna Vagun, Aug. 30, 1996; 1 child, Maria. BA, U. Tex., 1987; MA, Monterey Inst. Internat. Studies, 1992; PhD, St. Petersburg (Russia) State U., 1995. Interpreter/at-sea rep. Marine Resource Corp., Seattle, 1988-90; tng. specialist-Russian Def. Lang. Inst., Monterey, Calif., 1990-94, assoc. prof., 1997—; computer-aided lang. instrn. dir. Dept. Fgn. Langs. George C. Marshall Ctr., Garmisch-Partenkirchen, Germany, 1994-97; pres. Ganbaru Yudanshakai, Monterey. Co-author: Russian Topical Reader, 1992, (CD-ROM) Basic Military Language Course-Russian, 1993, (monograph) Multimedia as a Means of Intensifying Self-Study in the Russian Language for Foreigners, 1995, (web site) American-Russian POW/MIA Commn., 1996. With U.S. Army, 1983-85. Mem. Am. Legion, U.S. Judo Fedn., Computer-Aided Lang. Instrn. Consortium, Am. Coun. on Tchg. Fgn. Langs., Phi Sigma Iota. Republican. Russian Orthodox. Avocations: judo, weight-lifting, racquetball, travel. Fax: (831) 373-2782. E-mail: drfranke@yahoo.com. Home: 370 Clay St Apt 13 Monterey CA 93940-2254 Office: Def Lang Inst PO Box 5818 Monterey CA 93944-0818

FRANKE, RAINER SIEGFRIED, biochemist; b. Königsberg, Germany, Sept. 24, 1938; s. Siegfried Herbert Franke and Hertha Luise (Dittel) Schober; m. Renate Rathsfeld, July 15, 1965 (div. 1968); 1 child, Christian; m. Heiderose Borowski, Dec. 19, 1979. Dipl.-Chem., Tech. U., Dresden, Germany, 1963, Dr.rer.nat., 1970; Dr.sc.nat., Martin Luther U., Halle, Germany, 1972; Prof. Medicinal Chemistry, Acad. Scis., Berlin, 1978; Dr.rer.nat. habil., Martin Luther U., Halle, Germany, 1991. Asst., sr. asst. Dist. Hosp., Dresden, 1963-70; sr. asst. Humboldt U., Berlin, 1970-71; head rsch. group Inst. Molecular Biology, Berlin, 1971-74; head dept. Inst. Drug Rsch., Berlin, 1975-91, head divsn., 1990-91; dir. Consulting in Drug Design GbR, Basdorf, Germany, 1991—; lectr. Martin Luther U., Halle, 1973-77, Humboldt U., Berlin, 1979-83, Free U., Berlin, 1990. Author: Optimization Methods in Drug Research, 1980, Theoretical Drug Design Methods, 1984; contbg. author: Physicochemical Methods in Clinical Laboratories, 1969, 80, 88, Quantitative Structure Activity Analysis, 1978, Computer Aided Drug Design in Industrial Research, 1995, Bioactive Compound Design, 1996; contbr. numerous articles to sci. jours.; mem. editorial bd. several sci. jours. Recipient Buchheimer prize Pharmacol. Soc. Germany, 1975, Nat. Sci. and Tech. prize Council of State, 1979. Mem. Internat. QSAR Soc. (bd. 1991), European Fedn. Medicinal Chemistry (mgmt. com. 1986-90), Com. European QSAR Confs., Soc. Chem. Industry Eng. (pesticides group com. 1992-2000), Internat. Soc. Quantum Chemistry, AAAS, N.Y. Acad. Scis., German Soc. Pharmacology and Toxicology. Avocations: reading, music, hiking. Home and Office: Gartenstr 14, D-16352 Basdorf Germany

FRANKE, WAYNE THOMAS, retired government affairs director, consultant; b. San Angelo, Tex., June 23, 1950; s. Bernard Raymond and Henrietta Elizabeth (Kozelsky) F.; 1 child, Mauri Jane. BBA in Gen. Bus., Angelo State U., 1972. Adminstrv. clk. Gen. Telephone Co. of the S.W., San Angelo, 1968-72; comm. cons. Gen. Telephone Co. of the S.W., Irving, Tex., 1972-75; asst. govt. affairs mgr. Gen. Telephone Co. of the S.W., San Angelo, 1975-78; govt. affairs mgr. Gen. Telephone Co. of the S.W., Austin, Tex., 1976-86; govt. affairs dir. Gen. Telephone Co. of the S.W., Austin, 1986-98; owner MJWT Cons., Austin, 1998—; legis. affairs com. Tex. Indsl. Devel. Council, College Station, 1977-84, chmn., Austin, 1981-83; mem. energy and awards coms., 1978-79; mem. U.S. Speaker Jim Wright's Diplomatic Mission to Moscow, 1987. Fundraiser Boy Scouts Am., Austin, 1987-88, Austin Performing Arts Ctr., 1998-2000; loaned exec. Tarrant County United Way, 1973-74; issues mgmt. adv. coun. North Tex. Commn., Dallas, 1985-87; program chmn. John Ben Shepperd Leadership Forum, Odessa, Tex., 1986, chmn., Austin, 1987, John Ben Shepperd Alumni Forum, 1988; mem. John Ben Shepperd Governing Bd., 1990-91, chmn. fin., 1990-91, fin. com. 1990-92, adv. bd., 1991-93, vice-chmn. John Ben Shepperd Found., 1997-2000, chmn., 1998-99; corp. co-chmn. drive United Cerebral Palsy Assn., Austin area, 1990-96; mem. Hays Country Oaks Archtl. Control & Protection Com., 1993-96; steering com., fundraising Travis County Assn. Retarded Citizens; trustee West Tex. Boy's Ranch Found., 1995—, treas. exec. com., 1999—; chmn. Tex. Statehood Sesquicentennial Program, 1996; bd. dirs. Angelo State U. Ex-Students Assn., 1999—. Recipient External Team Excellence award GTE, 1992-93, Strive for Excellence award, 1992; named Lobbyist of the Year for GTE Corp., 1987, 91, 1989 Disting. Alumnus, Angelo State U.; Wayne Franke Day proclaimed by San Angelo, Tex. City Council Oct. 14, 1989, one of ten Rising Stars of Tex., Tex. Bus. mag., 1988. Mem. Tex. Assn. Bus. and C. of C. (statewide state affairs com., chmn. state affairs com. 1977-79, bd. dirs. Austin chpt. 1985-88, vice chmn. 1987), Tex. Taxpayers and Rsch. Assn. (state affairs com. 1985-97), Tex. Self-Ins. Assn. (co-chair legis. com. 1993), Homeowners Assn., West Tex. C. of C. (state affairs com., legis. adv. coun.), Bus. Ins. Consumers Assn. (exec. com. 1990-95), Lewisville/San Angelo C. of C. (amb. 1974-77, Amb. of the Yr. 1975, 76). Roman Catholic. Lodge: Optimists (sec. Irving chpt. 1973-74, v.p. youth work, 1974-75, pres., 1975, bd. dirs. San Angelo chpt. 1977, lt. gov. North Tex. dist., 1978-79). Avocations: golf, rock work, fishing, tree trimming, camping.

FRANKEL, GENE, theater director, writer, producer, educator; b. N.Y.C., Dec. 23, 1923; s. Barnet and Anna (Taleman) F.; m. Pat Ruth Carter, May 1, 1963; children: Laura Ann, Ethan-Eugene. BA, NYU, 1943. Artistic dir. Gene Frankel Theatre, N.Y.C., 1963—; exec. dir. Gen. Frankel Theatre, N.Y.C., 1973—; founding dir. Berkshire Theatre Festival, Stockbridge, Mass., 1965-66; vis. Arena Stage, Washington, 1969-71; cultural exchange dir. U.S. Dept. State, Belgrade, Yugoslavia, 1968-69; dir. Hartman Theatres, Stamford, Conn., 1976-79; vis. prof. Boston U., 1967-69, Queens Coll., N.Y.C., 1969-71, Columbia U., N.Y.C., 1972-73; cons. dir. Nat. Shakespeare Co., N.Y.C., 1966—; dir. various regional theaters, 1969-80. Dir.: Broadway, 1969 (Burns Mantle 1969, Best Play award), Emperor Jones, European tour, 1970, Oh Dad, Poor Dad, Belgrade, Yugoslavia, 1969, Lost in the Stars, Broadway, 1971, The Night That Made American Famous, 1975, Cry of Players, 1967, The Blacks, Off-Broadway, 1961 (Obie award 1963), also European tour, Brecht on Brecht, Off-Broadway, 1965, To Be Young Gifted and Black, Off-Broadway, 1970, Enemy of the People, Off-Broadway, 1969, Indians, On Broadway, 1979, Pueblo, 1981, 27 Wagons Full of Cotton, 1985, Talk To Me Like the Rain, 1985, War Play, 1986, The Marriage, 1986, Private Wars, 1987, Sister Aimee, 1987, The Dutchman, 1988, Carreno, 1989—; author, dir. The Actor Then Ma, 1979; co-author, dir.: (play/concert) Carreno, 1990, See Moscow and Die, 1991, (play) Hallowed Ground The Private Thoughts of Abraham Lincoln, 1997; author: So This is the Wicked Stage, 1993, Notes on Othello, 1998, What's Absurd About the Theatre of the Absurd?, 1998, People do Not Want to Suffer, Only Actors Do, 1999; taught and directed numerous actors and actresses including Anne Bancroft, Maya Angelou, Morgan Freeman, Vincent Gardenia, Frank Langella, Fred Gwynne, Louis Gosset, Jr., Walter Matthau, Rod Steiger, Beau Bridges, James Earl Jones, Loretta Swit, Judd Hirsh, Stacy Keach, Lee Marvin, Raul Julia, others. With U.S. Army Air Force, World War II. Recipient Lola D'Annunzio award, 1958; recipient Obie award for Volpone, Village Voice, 1958, Obie award for Machinal Village Voice, 1963, Vernon Rice award for Machinal, Drama Desk-N.Y. Post, 1963; Ford Found. fellow, 1969-71. Mem. SAG, Soc. Choreographers and Dirs., Actors Equity Assn. Office: 4 Washington Square Vlg New York NY 10012-1936 also: Gene Frankel Theatre 24 Bond St New York NY 10012-2424

FRANKEL, JENNIE LOUISE, writer; b. Chgo., Aug. 7, 1949. Student, Roosevelt U., 1968, U. Hawaii, 1969-71, Golden West Law Sch., 1976. bd. govs. Hollywood Scriptwriting Inst., Authors Guild; fashion model, singer/actor in TV commls., 1967-76, 79-81; fashion model & television commls., 1967-81. Co-author: You'll Never Make Love in this Town Again, 1996 (N.Y. Times Bestseller), Unfinished Lives, 1996, Tales From the Casting Couch, 1996; editor-in-chief Page Turner Publishing; composer network TV theme songs; model TV commls., 1967, 76, 78-81. Ace award judge Blue Ribbon Panel. With USO Vietnam Tour, 1968. Mem. Acad. TV Arts & Scis. (blue ribbon panel judge), L.A. Women in Music (bd. dirs. 1991-92), Circumnavigators Club. Avocation: comedy. Office: PO Box 346 Sedona AZ 86339-0346

FRANKEL, LESLIE FRITZ GUNTHER, stockbroker; b. Worms, Germany, July 13, 1922; arrived in South Africa, 1936; s. Richard and Sophie (Grunebaum) F.; m. Cecile Isaacs, Dec. 15, 1946; children: Sidney Lewis, Babette Jane Katz. BSc in Engring., U. Witwatersrand, Johannesburg, South Africa, 1946; PhD (hon.), Hebrew U. Jerusalem, 1983. Cert. in

engring., stockbroking. Sr. ptnr. firm of stockbrokers South Africa, 1946-94; chief exec. Kempar Group Elec. Factories, South Africa, 1950-74; chmn. Altira Group of Cos., Israel, 1977—; hon. life pres. SG Frankel Pollak Securities (Pty) Ltd., Johannesburg, 1996—; chmn. pvt. cos., South Africa, 1949—; com. mem., chmn. listings com. Johannesburg Stock Exch., 1977-81, mem., 1946—. Appointee State Pres.'s Fund, Pretoria, South Africa, 1983-92; coun. mem. U. Witwatersrand, Johannesburg, 1984-96; chmn. fund raising com. and fin. com. Johannesburg Child Welfare Soc., 1984-98, apptd. hon. v.p., 1988-94. Decorated Order for Meritorious Svc., State Pres. South Africa, 1987. Mem. Wanderers Club, Inanda Club, Houghton Golf Club. Jewish. Home: 15 Second St Abbotsford, 2192 Johannesburg Gauteng, South Africa Office: SG Frankel Pollak Securs, 2d Fl 17 Diagonal St, 2001 Johannesburg Gauteng, South Africa

FRANKEMÖLLE, HUBERT, theological educator; b. Stadtlohn, Germany, Jan. 10, 1939; s. Paul and Anna Frankemölle; m. Renate Stieler; children: Anja, Peter. BA Cath. Theology and Ancient Philology, 1968, PhD, 1972. Asst. prof. U. Münster, Germany, 1972-79; prof. Paderborn U., Paderborn, Germany, 1979—. Author: Das Taufverständnis des Paulus, 1970, Jahwe-Bund und Kirche Christi. Studien zur Form- und Traditionsgeschichte des "Evangeliums" nach Matthäus, 1974, 2d edit., 1984, Biblische Handlungsanweisungen. Beispiele pragmatischer Exegese, 1983, Der erste und zweite Petrusbrief; Der Judasbrief, 1987, 2d edit., 1990, Evangelium. Begriff und Gattung. Ein Forschungsbericht, 1988, 2d edit. 1994, Der Brief des Jakobus I-II, 1994, Matthäus-Kommentar I, 1994, 2d edit., 1999, II, 1997, Jüdische Wurzeln christlicher Theologie, 1998, Lebendige Welt Jesu und des NT. Eine Entdeckungsreise, 2000. Mem. Studiorum Novi Testamenti Societas, Arbeitsgemeinschaft der Deutschsprachigen Katholischen Neutestamentler. Office: U GH Dept Cath Theology, Bldg N 3 140, 33095 Paderborn Germany

FRANKEN, PHILIPP, molecular biologist; b. Düsseldorf, Germany, Jan. 9, 1960; s. Johannes and Anna (Breindl) F.; m. Susanne Dohr, July 2, 1988; children: Daniel, Lukas, Marie, Johanna. Diploma, U. Cologne, Germany, 1988, PhD, 1991, habilitation, 1999. Scientist Max-Planck Soc., Cologne, 1991-93, Marburg, Germany, 1995—; scientist INRA, Dijon, France, 1993-95. Contbr. articles to profl. jours.; patentee in field. Mem. Amnesty Internat.; vol. Hephata, 1980-82. Kulturförderpreis Stadt Aachen, 1984. Mem. Vereinigung für Allgem U. Agewandt Mikrobol. Avocations: violin, theatre, sports. Office: Max Planck Inst, Karl-von Frisch-Strass, D-35043 Marburg Germany

FRANKENBERG, ELIEZER, biologist, educator; b. Beirut, July 7, 1945; arrived in Israel, 1946; s. Yehudah Carl and Esther Gladis (Sarfati) F.; m. Sabina Krull, Mar. 18, 1968; children: Nirit, Gila. BSc, Hebrew U., Jerusalem, 1970, MSc, 1972, PhD, 1978; postgrad., Ruhr U., Bochum, Germany, 1979-80. Cert. in animal comm. and conservation biology. Tchg. asst. zool. Hebrew U., 1975-77; rschr. Smithsonian Instn., Washington, 1980-81; lectr. Hebrew U., Jerusalem, 1981-83; coord. wildlife protection Nature Res. Authority, Jerusalem, 1983-89, dir. dept., 1989-91, chief scientist, 1991-98; dep. chief scientist Nature & Nat. Pks. Protection Authority, Israel, 1999—; sr. rsch. assoc. Hebrew U., Jerusalem, 1983—; focal point UN Environ. Program/Conv. on Migratory Species-Conv. on Biodiversity, 1987—; mem. Man and Biosphere Com., Israel, 1992—; adj. sr. lectr. Ben Gurion U., Beer Sheva, Israel, 1997—; mem. nat. com. UNESCO, Israel, 1997—. Author: A Guide to Wildlife Protection Problem Solving, Preventing Damage and Disturbance by Wild Animals, 1989; contbr. rsch. reports to profl. jours. Master sgt. Israeli Def. Forces, 1964-66. Recipient Best Student Paper award Soc. for the Study of Amphibians and Reptiles, 1975; postdoctoral fellow Heinrich Hertz Fund, 1979. Mem. NRA (chair employees com. 1986-88), The World Conservation Union Commns., Zool. Soc. Israel (bd. dirs., contr. 1985-95), Israeli Ecology Soc. Avocation: classical music. Office: Nature/Nat Pks Protect Auth, Av Ve'Olamo St 3, 95463 Jerusalem Israel

FRANKENBERGER, JANE ROSSING, soil and water engineer; b. Northfield, Minn., Jan. 18, 1958; d. Thomas D. and Dorothy A. (Rosen) R.; m. James Rossing Frankenberger, July 22, 1996. BA in Physics and Religion, St. Olaf Coll., Northfield, 1979; MS in Agrl. Engring., U. Minn., St. Paul, 1984; PhD in Agrl. and Biol. Engring., Cornell U., 1996. Physics and math. tchr. Mennonite Ctrl. Com., Zaire, 1979-82; agrl. devel. specialist Evang. Luth. Chs. in Am., Senegal, 1985-90; asst. prof. Purdue U., 1996—. Claire Boothe Luce fellow Luce Found.-Cornell U., 1990. Mem. Phi Beta Kappa, Gamma Sigma Delta, Phi Kappa Phi, Alpha Epsilon. Home: 2640 Newman Rd West Lafayette IN 47906-4530 Office: Purdue U 1146 Agrl and Biol Engring West Lafayette IN 47907-1146

FRANKENDAL, BO ERWIN, oncologist; b. Stockholm, June 17, 1938; s. Erwin and Paula (Bluhm) Frankenthal; m. Anne-Marie Lascombe, Dec. 21, 1961; children: Erik, Christine, Bertil, Marie-Hélène. MD, Karolinska Inst., Stockholm, 1964; specialist in gynecologic oncology, Sweden, 1972, specialist in ob-gyn., 1973; PhD, Umea, Sweden, 1973. Asst. prof. U. Umea, 1973; dir. dept. gynecol. oncology Örebro, Sweden, 1974-92; chief dept. gynecol. oncology, radiumhemmet Stockholm, 1992—. Lt. Swedish Army. Avocations: history, sci. of art, gardening. Home: 16 Ångsstigen, S 17240 Sundbyberg Sweden Office: Dept Gynecol Oncology, Karolinska Sjukhuset, S 17176 Stockholm Sweden

FRANKENFELD, MIGUEL HARRY, information specialist, journalist; b. Santiago, Chile; s. Otto and Greta (Danzig) F. BA with honors, Cath. U. Chile, Santiago, 1966; MS with honors, Columbia U., 1969. Producer TV programs Ceutech-U. TV, Santiago, 1964-66; reporter Las Ultimas Noticias, Santiago, 1964-67, corr. to N.Y., 1968-69; translator UNICEF, Santiago, 1969-70; edn., sci. and culture editor OAS, Washington, 1970-76, from sr. editor to chief press divsn., 1976-90, prin info specialist, 1990-96, ret., 1996; lectr. univs., colls., h.s. groups. Author: Heart Transplants, Medical, Ethical and Economic Issues, 1989; translator: Guillain-Barré Syndrome, An Overview for the Lay Person, 1994, revised edit., 1997, How to Take Good Care of Your Heart, 1998. Active Temple Micah, Washington, 1980—; vol. tchr. Hispanic Groups, Washington, 1984—. Fellow Inter-Am. Press Assn. (Angel Ramos scholarship 1968); mem. Assn. Chilean Journalists in Washington, U.S. Holocaust Mus., Columbia U. Club (Washington). Jewish. Avocations: photography, volunteer tutoring, hiking, writing, assisting students in obtaining financial aid for college. Home: 520 N St SW Apt S-417 Washington DC 20024-4574

FRANKEVICH, EUGENE LEONIDOVICH, molecular physics educator, researcher; b. Samara, Russia, Feb. 19, 1930; s. Leonid Vladimir and Valentina Valeria (Eseleva) F.; m. Irene Peter Lenchenko, July 9, 1957; children: Tatiana, Vladimir. MS, Tech. U., St. Petersburg, Russia, 1954; PhD, Inst. Chem. Physics, Moscow, 1957, DSc, 1966. Cert. physicist. Rschr. Inst. Chem. Physics, Moscow, 1954-86, head of lab., 1970-86; prof. Inst. Physics and Tech., Moscow, 1972-93; head of lab. Inst. Energy Problems of Chem. Physics Russian Acad. Scis., Moscow, 1986—. Author: Chemical Generation and Reception of Radio Microwaves, 1994; contbr. numerous chem. physics articles, papers to profl. jours.; rschr. in field. Recipient Lenin sci. prize Russian Govt., Moscow, 1986. Mem. Russian Acad. Natural Sci. Achievements include discovery of ion-molecule reactions; magnetic field spin effects. Avocations: gardening, jogging. Office: Inst Energy Problems, Leninskii Prospect 38-2, 117334 Moscow Russia

FRANKHAM, RICHARD, conservation geneticist, educator; b. Singleton, Australia, Apr. 4, 1942; s. Ronald and Marjorie Ethel (Peel) F.; m. Helen Nancy Sheaffe, Feb. 8, 1965 (div. 1984); children: Roger, David; m. Annette Lindsay, Oct. 7, 1994. BSc in Agriculture with honors, U. Sydney, Australia, 1964, PhD, 1968. Rsch. scientist Agr. Can., Lacombe, Alta., 1967-69; postdoctoral fellow U. Chgo., 1969-71; lectr. Macquarie U., Sydney, 1971-72; sr. lectr. Macquarie U., 1973-81, assoc. prof., 1981-97, prof., 1997—; cons. animal breeding Hazett's Dunrobin Poultry Stud, 1979-85; mem. Conservation Breeding Specialist Group, World Conservation Union, Gland, Switzerland, 1992-94, 94-96, 96-98; mem. internat. program com. 2nd Internat. Conf. on Quantitative Genetics, Raleigh, N.C., 1985-87. Assoc. editor Conservation Genetics; mem. editl. bd. Genetical Rsch., Cambridge, Eng., 1996—, Animal Conservation, 1997—; contbr. articles and revs. to profl. jours. Mem. Genetics Soc. Australia (hon. treas. auditor 1973-75), Soc. for Conservation Biology (organizing com. 12th meeting 1996-98). Avocations: travel to interesting biological sites, bushwalking, movies, jazz. Office: Macquarie Univ Key Ctr, Biodiversity and Biosources, Sydney NSW 2109, Australia

FRANKL, JEANNE SILVER, association executive; A.B. in Lit. summa cum laude, Brown U., 1952; LL.B., Yale U., 1955; m. Kenneth R. Frankl; 1 dau., Kathryn. Admitted to Conn. bar, 1955, N.Y. bar, 1956; law sec. to Hon. Edmund L. Palmieri, 1955-56; atty. Port of N.Y. Authority, 1956-60; assoc. firm Rosenman Colin Kaye Petschek Freund & Emil, N.Y.C., 1960-67; chief of program planning, office of edn. liaison, City Human Resources Adminstrn., 1967-69; spl. asst. to dep. adminstr. N.Y.C. Human Resources Adminstrn., 1969-70; asst. dir. Community Sch. System Project, N.Y. Lawyers Com. for Civil Rights under Law, 1970, dir., 1970-73; counsel and law project dir. Public Edn. Assn., N.Y.C., 1973-80, exec. dir., 1980-93 ; lectr. Rutgers U. Law Sch. Edn. Law Seminar, 1972-73. Mem. Phi Beta Kappa. Home and Office: PO Box 955 67 Old Montauk Hwy Amagansett NY 11930

FRANKL, WILLIAM STEWART, cardiologist, educator; b. Phila., July 15, 1928; s. Louis and Vera (Simkin) F.; m. Razelle Sherr, June 17, 1951; children: Victor S. (dec.), Brian A. BA in Biology, Temple U., 1951, MD, 1955, MS in Medicine, 1961. Diplomate Am. Bd. Internal Medicine, Am. Bd. Cardiovasc. Disease. Intern Buffalo Gen. Hosp., 1955-56; resident in medicine Temple U., Phila., 1956-57, 59-61; faculty Temple U. Sch. Medicine, 1962-68, dir. EKG sect. dept. cardiology, 1966-68, dir. cardiac care unit, 1967-68; prof. medicine, dir. divsn. cardiology Med. Coll. Pa., Phila., 1970-79; prof. medicine, assoc. dir. cardiology divsn. Thomas Jefferson U., Phila., 1979-84; physician-in-chief Springfield (Mass.) Hosp., 1968-70; prof. medicine, co-dir. William Likoff Cardiovascular Inst. Hahnemann U., Phila., 1984-86, dir. William Likoff Cardiovascular Inst., dir. divsn. cardiology, 1986-92, Thomas J. Vischer Prof. medicine, chmn. dept. medicine, 1987-92; prof. medicine, dir. cardiovascular regional programs Allegheny U. of the Health Scis., 1992-98; dir. cardiovascular regional programs Allegheny U. Hosps., 1992-98; v.p. cardiovascular program devel. Allegheny U. Hosps. System, 1995-98; prof. medicine cardiology divsn. dept. medicine Temple U. Sch. Medicine, 1998-2000; cons. cardiology Phila. Va Hosp., 1970-79; Fogarty Sr. Internat. fellow Cardiothoracic Inst., U. London, 1978-79; pres. Pa. affiliate Am. Heart Assn., 1985-86; clin. prof. of medicine, Temple U. Sch. of Medicine, 2000—. Contbr. articles to profl. jours. Capt. (M.C.), U.S. Army, 1957-59. Cardiovascular Rsch. fellow U. Pa., Phila., 1961-62; recipient Golden Apple award Temple U. Sch. Medicine, 1967; award Med. Coll. Pa., 1972; Lindback award for distinguished teaching, 1975. Fellow ACP, Am. Coll. Cardiology (gov. Ea. Pa. 1986-89), Phila. Coll. Physicians, Am. Coll. Clin. Pharmacology (regent 1980-85, 93-98), Coun. Clin. Cardiology of Am. Heart Assn. (coun. on arteriosclerosis); mem. AAUP, AAAS, N.Y. Acad. Scis., Am. Fedn. Clin. Rsch., Assn. Am. Med. Colls., Am. Heart Assn. (bd. govs. S.E. Pa. chpt. 1972-84, pres. 1976, Pa. affiliate pres. 1984-85), Am. Soc. Clin. Pharmacology and Exptl. Therapeutics, Phila. County Med. Soc. (pres. 1993-94, 1st dist. trustee to Pa. Med. Soc. bd. trustees 1998-2001). Home and Office: 536 Moreno Rd Wynnewood PA 19096-1121

FRANKLIN, BARRY ALLAN, health facility administrator, physiologist; b. Cleve., May 23, 1948; s. Norman Paul and Lottie (Medow) f.; m. Linda Alice Dreyfuss, June 5, 1971; children: Michael, Laura. BS, Kent State U., 1970; MS in Applied Physiology, U. Mich., 1971; PhD in Physiology, Pa. State U., 1976. Coord. cardiac evaluation and reconditioning Millard Fillmore Hosp., Buffalo, 1976-77; asst. prof. medicine, exercise physiologist Case Western Res. U., Cleve., 1977-78; program dir. cardiovascular fitness and rehab. Sinai Hosp., Detroit, 1979-85; prof. biology Mercy Coll., Detroit, 1979-84; asst. prof. physiology Wayne State U., Detroit, 1979-81, assoc. prof. physiology, 1986-94, prof. physiology, 1994—; dir. cardiac rehab. and exercise labs. William Beaumont Hosp., Royal Oak, Mich., 1985—; clin. prof. exercise sci. Oakland U., Rochester, Mich., 1992—; prof. family medicine U. Mich., Ann Arbor, 1998—; cert. exercise specialist Am. Coll. Sports Medicine, 1976 (faculty examiner exercise specialist workshops, 1978-94, fellow 1982, dir. exercise specialist workshop and cert. 1982—, chmn. program dir. subcom. 1984-86, exercise specialist subcom. 1980-84, cert. program dir. 1980, chmn. 1982-84, sci. exhibits subcom. 1984, pres.-elect Midwest Regional Chpt. 1986-87, pres. 1988, adminstrv. coun. bd. trustees 1986-87, area rep. cardiopulmonary rehab. ann. meeting 1990-91, 94-96, profl. edn. com. 1989-95, v.p. 1993-95, program com. 1993-95, budget fin. com., 1994-97, chair ad hoc liason com. 1994-97); mem. exercise com. Am. Heart Assn. Mich.; mem. med. adv. bd. Nat. Alliance Cardiovasc. Technologists, 1984-86; vis. prof. U. Ill. Coll. Medicine, 1982; vis. scholar Western Mich. U., Kalamazoo, 1984; bd. trustees, v.p. Am. Assn. Cardiovasc. Pulmonary Rehab., 1985-87 (chmn. sci. sessions 1986, abstract reviewer 1986—, pres.-elect 1986-87, pres. 1987-88, program chmn. 1987, chmn. reimbursement com. 1989-91, mem. at large 1989-91, award excellence 1992); sci. adv. bd. Rockport Walking Inst., 1985-91; chmn. exercise cardiac rehab. com. Am. Heart Assn. Mich., 1986-91 (bd. trustees 1989-95, chmn. program com. 1992-93, pres.-elect 1993-94, pres. 1994-95); projects com. Rsch. Inst. William Beaumont Hosp., 1989—; mem. couns. clin. cardiology Am. Heart Assn., 1992—; sci. adv. bd. Life Fitness, 1993; mem. Gov's. Coun. Phys. Fitness, Health Sports, 1994—; invited participant NIH consensus Devel. Conf. Phys. Activity Cardiovasc. Health, 1995; sci. adv. bd. Duke U. Med. Ctr., 1997—. Author, editor over 230 articles to sci. books, jours. including American Journal of Health Promotion, American Journal of Cardiology, Journal of Cardiopulmonary Rehabilitation (review bd. 1983—, editor-in-chief 1991-95, cons. editor 1996—), Cardiopulmonary Physical Therapy Journal, Heartline, The Physician and Sportsmedicine, The Exercise Standards and Malpractice Reporter, Medicine and Science in Sports and Exercise, The Journal of Cardiovascular Nursing, others; editl. bd. mem. American Journal of Cardiology, 1994—, The Physician and Sportsmedicine, 1987—; columnist Heartland Fitness, The Detroit Free Press, 1998—. Med. adv. bd. mem. Jewish Cmty. Ctr. Met. Detroit, 1979-85, Young Men's Christian Assn. Met. Detroit, 1983-92; host dir. Nat. Multiple Sclerosis Soc., William Beaumont Hosp., 1991-93; bd. trustees Am. Heart Assn., Mich. Affiliate, 1989-98; adj. faculty Wayne State U. Sch. Medicine, U. Mich., Oakland U. Recipient George Altman award outstanding grad. sr., Kent State U., 1970, BEACON Wellness award Blue Care Network Southeastern Mich., 1991, Media award San Diego County Med. Soc., 1995, Disting. Svc. award Am. Assn. Cardiovasc. Pulmonary Rehab., Middleton, Wis., 1996, Horace Elgin Dodge Award Am. Heart Assn. Mich., 1998; Rackham Grad. Sch. fellow, U. Mich., 1970-71. Fellow Am. Coll. Sports Medicine (pres. 1999-00), Am. Assn. Cardiovasc. Pulmonary Rehab. (pres. 1988). Jewish. Avocations: distance walking, travelling, writing, golf. Home: 2853 Baltane Rd West Bloomfield MI 48323-3101 Office: Beaumont Rehabilitation & Health Ctr Cardiac Rehab 746 Purdy St Birmingham MI 48009-1797

FRANKLIN, BENJAMIN BARNUM, dinner club executive; b. Topeka, Nov. 7, 1944; s. Charles Benjamin and Margaret Lavona (Barnum) F. BA in Speech, U. Colo., 1967. With Associated Clubs, Inc., Topeka, 1967—, v.p., 1972-83, pres., 1983—; lectr., 1969-76; trustee Capper Found, 1994—, John Austin Cheley Found., 1995—. Honoree, Benjamin Barnum Franklin Day, Lima, Ohio, June 11, 1983. Editor, pub. newsletter The Dinner Gong; contbr. articles to profl. jours. Chmn. steering com. Capper Found. for Cripped Children, Topeka. Mem. Internat. Platform Assn. (gov. 1975-2000), SAR, Topeka Sales and Mktg. Execs. (bd. dirs. 1985—), Explorers Club, Am. Alpine Club, Knife and Fork Club (internat. v.p. 1991), Internat. Knife and Fork Club (pres. 1994—), Topeka Knife and Fork Club, Met. Dinner Club (pres. 1983—), Exec. Dinner Club (pres. 1983, lectr. 1969-76), Rotary (bd. dirs. 1975-78, Paul Harris fellow), Friends of Libr., Sigma Phi Epsilon. Republican. Presbyterian. Office: PO Box 4585 Topeka KS 66604-0585

FRANKLIN, BONNIE SELINSKY, federal agency administrator; b. Oakland, Calif., Mar. 17, 1944; d. Harold Joseph and Madge (Warden) Selinsky; m. Alfred Carl Franklin, Jan. 24, 1981; 1 child, Amy Beth. AB in Am. Studies, George Washington U., 1966, MBA in Acctg., 1977. Tax auditor IRS, Baileys Crossroads, Va., 1966-71; from program analyst to tax law specialist IRS, Washington, 1971-77, from program analyst appeals to chief procedures sect., 1979-82, tech. asst. to nat. chief appeals, 1985—; regional analyst conf. IRS, Atlanta, 1977-79. Chair Arlingtonians for a Better County, Arlington, Va., 1994-97, archivist, 1999-2000; active Friends of the Libr., Arlington, 1996—. Mem. LWV (treas. Arlington Va. chpt. 1998—), AAUW. Democrat. Lutheran. Avocations: reading, travel.

FRANKLIN, DOROTHY ANN, guidance counselor; b. West Point, Ky., June 30, 1938; d. Raymond and Laura B. (Robards) Williams; m. Herbert Franklin, Mar. 31, 1962; children: Marcus, Lori. BS, Ky. State U., 1960; MEd, U. Louisville, 1969; postgrad., Ind. U., 1973-74, U. Dayton. Cert. in guidance supervision. Tchr. Cardinal Cmty. High Sch., Eldon, Iowa, 1960-61; tchr., counselor Louisville/Jefferson County Schs., Louisville, 1961-72; counselor Monroe County Schs., Bloomington, Ind., 1972-74, Alachua County Schs., Gainesville, Fla., 1974-80, Franklin County Schs., Frankfort, Ky., 1980-84, Sidney (Ohio) City Schs., 1984—. Bd. trustees United Way, Sidney, 1993-96, Riverview Behavior Health Care Ctr., Sidney, 1993-96; mem. steering com., mem.-at-large City of Sidney Comprehensive Plan, 1996-97; mem. adv. bd. Bank One, Sidney, 1994-97; mem. adv. coun. Planned Parenthood, Sidney, 1993-98. Mem. AAUW, NEA, Am. Assn. Counseling Devel., Ohio Edn. Assn., Ohio Sch. Counselors Assn., Sidney Edn. Assn., Tri-County Br. NAACP, Kappa Delta Pi, Alpha Kappa Alpha. Democrat. Baptist. Avocations: real estate, reading, travel. Home: 1312 Spruce Ave Sidney OH 45365-3453

FRANKLIN, GODFREY, adult education educator; b. Ghana, West Africa; came to U.S., 1976; s. Mercy Lydia Kyeiwa-Franklin; m. Kay Tidmarsh, Dec. 29, 1973; children: Jared J., Irina T. Diploma in theology, Melbourne Coll. Div., Australia, 1973; BD, Ref. Theol. Coll., Geelong, Australia, 1975; MA, U. Ala., 1978, PhD, 1983. Ordained Reformed Presbyn. pastor, 1976. Pastor Ref. Presbyn. Ch., Selma, Ala., 1976-81; counseling psychologist U. West Fla., Pensacola, 1983-91, asst. prof. edn., 1991-95, assoc. prof., 19965, dir. Office Multicultural Studies, 19985; founding pastor Multiracial Ref. Presbyn. Ch., Pensacola, 1989—; cons. USAF S.O.S., Hurlburt Field, Fla., 1985-99. Contbr. articles to profl. jours. Recipient Golden Apple award Escambia County Sch. Sys., Pensacola, 1993, 99, Disting. Tchr. award U. West Fla., 1993, 99, Outstanding Undergrad. Tchg. and Advising award, 1994, Tchr. of Yr., 1995. Mem. ASCD, ACA, Am. Assn. Christian Counselors, Nat. Mid. Sch. Assn., African-Am. Heritage Soc. (bd. dirs.), Phi Kappa Phi. Avocations: travel, soccer, racquetball, jogging, golf. Home: 5625 Saint Adamnan Ave Pensacola FL 32503-7916 Office: Univ of West Florida 11000 University Pkwy Pensacola FL 32514-5732

FRANKLIN, H. BRUCE, language educator, writer; b. Bklyn., Feb. 28, 1934; s. Robert and Florence (Cohen) F.; m. Jane Morgan, Feb. 11, 1956; children: Karen, Gretchen, Robert Morgan. BA, Amherst Coll., 1955; PhD, Stanford U., 1961. Tugboat deckhand, mate Pa. R.R., Jersey City, 1955-56; asst. prof. English, assoc. prof. Stanford (Calif.) U., 1961-64, 65-72; asst. prof. English Johns Hopkins U., Balt., 1964-65; vis. prof. English Wesleyan U., Middletown, Conn., 1974-75; prof. English Rutgers U., Newark, N.J., 1975-87; John Cotton Dana prof. English Rutgers U., Newark, 1987—; cons. Stanford Rsch. Inst., 1962-64, Sugarloaf Films, 1993; adv. bd. mem. Vietnam Generation, 1994—. Author: The Wake of the Gods: Melville's Mythology, 1963, rev. edit., 1983, Future Perfect: American Science Fiction of the 19th Century, 1966, 4th edit., 1995, Herman Melville's Mardi: And a Voyage Thither, 1964, The Scarlet Letter, Together With Main Street, Ethan Brand, and Hawthorne's Published Critical Writings, 1967, Herman Melville's the Confidence-Man: His Masquerade, 1967, Who Should Run the Universities, 1969, From the Movement: Toward Revolution, 1971, The Essential Stalin: Major Theoretical Writings, 1905-52, 1972, Back Where You Came From, 1975, The Victim as Criminal and Artist: Literature From the American Prison, 1978, Robert A. Heinlein: America as Science Fiction, 1980, American Prisoners and Ex-Prisoners: An Annotated Bibliography of Their Writings, 1798-1981, 1982, Countdown to Midnight, 1984, Vietnam and America: A Documented History, 1985, rev. edit., 1995, War Stars: The Superweapon and the American Imagination, 1988, M.I.A. or Mythmaking in America, 1992, the Vietnam War in American Stories, Songs, and Poems, 1996, Prison Writing in 20th Century America, 1998, Vietnam and Other American Fantasies, 2000; edit. bd. cons. Sci.-Fiction Studies, 1973—; contbr. articles to profl. jours. 1st lt. USAF, 1956-59. Fellow Am. Coun. Learned Societies, 1968-69, grantee, 1967; Stanford Wilson fellow, 1960-61, Rockefeller Found. Humanities fellow, 1975-76; grantee Nat. Endowment Humanities, 1982, William Joiner Ctr., 1987; recipient Alexander Cappon prize, 1978, Eaton award, 1981, Pilgrim award, 1983, Disting. Scholar award Internat. Assn. Fantastic in Arts, 1990, Pioneer award, 1991. E-mail: hbf@andromeda.rutgers.edu. Office: English Dept Rutgers Univ Newark NJ 07102

FRANKLIN, IAN MAXWELL, medical educator; b. London, Sept. 6, 1949; s. Edwin William and Elizabeth Joyce (Kessler) F.; m. Anne Christine Bush, July 29, 1975; children: Matthew Charles Maxwell, Sophie Rose. BSc, Leeds (Eng.) U., 1971, MB, BChir, 1974; PhD, U. London, 1981. Registrar in haematology Gen. Infirmary, Leeds, 1976-77; Med. Rsch. Coun. rsch. tng. fellow U. Coll. Hosp. Med. Sch., London, 1977-80; sr. registrar in haematology U. Coll. Hosp., London, 1980-82; cons. haematologist Queen Elizabeth Hosp., Birmingham, Eng., 1982-92; cons. haematologist bone marrow transplant unit Royal Infirmary, Glasgow, Scotland, 1992-96; prof. transfusion medicine U. Glasgow, 1996—; dir. haematology Ctrl. Birmingham Health Authority, 1989-91; chmn. Study Group on Blood Banks and Bone Marrow Transplantation, Coun. of Europe, France, 1995-96; dir. Glasgow and West Scotland Blood Transfusion Svcs., Lanarkshire, Scotland, 1996-97; nat. med. and sci. dir. Scottish Nat. Blood Transfusion Svc., 1997—. Author: Sickle Cell Disease: A Guide for Patients, Careers and Health Workers, 1990; contbr. chpt. to book and articles to profl. jours. Fellow Royal Coll. Physicians (London, Glasgow and Edinburgh), Royal Coll. Pathologists; mem. Assn. Physicians of Great Britain and Ireland, Am. Soc. Hematology, Brit. Blood Transfusion Soc., Brit. Soc. for Haematology (sci. sec. 1995—). Avocations: sailing, cycling, reading, gastronomy. Office: Dept Medicine, Royal Infirmary, Glasgow G31 2ER, Scotland

FRANKLIN, JOHN ALBERT, solicitor; b. Sydney, N.S.W., Australia, May 25, 1938; s. Albert Edward and Gladys Mary (Extrem) F.; m. Anne Winifred Mellor, Sept. 30, 1966 (div. Jan. 1990); children: Michael John Macquarie, Jane, Charlotte Anne; m. Diane Rosemary Griffiths, June 24, 1989. Diploma in labour rels. and the law, Sydney U., 1978, LLM, 1989. Cert. solicitor, barrister, Australia. Exec. dir. Law Soc. Western Australia, Perth, 1978-80, Elec. Contractors Assn. N.S.W., Sydney, 1981-88; fed. sec. Elec. Contractors Assn. Australia, Sydney, 1981-88; solicitor Sydney Water, 1988-94; pvt. practice Sydney, 1968-77, 80, 1994—; in-house lawyer Switzerland Gen. Ins., 1988-89; part-time lectr. masters course in dispute resolution U. Tech., Sydney, 1992-94. Mem. Internat. Law Assn., Commn. Internat. Jusits. Avocations: swimming, golf, tennis.

FRANKLIN, MARY ANN WHEELER, educator, higher education and management consultant; b. Boston; d. Arthur E. Wheeler Sr. and Madeline Ophelia (Hall) Wheeler-Brooks; m. Carl Matthew Franklin; 1 child, Evangeline Rachel Hall Franklin. BS, U. N.H., 1942; MEd, U. Buffalo, 1948; EdD, U. Md., 1982. Cert. tchr., N.Y., Ga. Instr. sci. edn. W.Va. State Coll., 1947; tchr. gen. sci. John Marshall Jr. High Sch., Bklyn., 1952-58, 59-60; assoc. prof. sci. Elizabeth City State Coll., 1960-67; asst. dean Morgan State Coll., Balt., 1967-77; asst. dean Coll. Arts and Scis. Morgan State U., Balt., 1977-78, asst. v.p. acad. affairs, 1978-82; asst. prof. bus. Catonsville (Md.) Community Coll., 1982; asst. to dean evening and weekend coll. So. U. New Orleans, 1983-92; cons. numerous including Herford County Tchrs., Murfreesboro, N.C., 1961, St. Catherine's Sch., Elizabeth City, N.C., 1962-64, St. Elizabeth Cath. Sch., Elizabeth City; cons., bd. dirs. Archbishop Keough H.S., Balt., 1970-80, Hampton (Va.) Inst., 1971, St. Paul Coll., 1972; bd. dirs. Archbishop Keough H.S.; presenter confs., seminars and workshops; spkr. in field. Editor Morgan State U. Acad. Affairs Newsletter, 1980-82; editor, pub. Morgan State U. Catalog, 1969-82, So. U. New Orleans Catalog, 1986-84, 89-92; author: The How and Why of Testing at Elizabeth City State College, 1962, Report on Princeton University Program for Physics Teachers in HBCU's, 1964, A Descriptive Report of Pre-College Study Booster Program, 1965, 66, Learning Summer Camp Code, National Library of Poetry, 1992, Interrogations of a Metropolis of the Day, Who Are We/Who We Are, 1994. Mem. com. higher edn. Citizens League, Balt., 1979-81; assoc. dir. youth camp NCCJ, 1974-75, bd. dirs., 1969-80; dir., originator Vestibule Program and Parents Workshop for New Citizens and Residents, SUNO Summer Learning Camp, 1984-95, Ctr. Women Against Crime Conf.; pres. Lake Willow Homeowners Assn., 1994-96. Fellow NSF, Harvard U., 1958-59, Carnegie-Ford-NSF, Princeton U., 1964; recipient Education award Am. Assn. of Coll. Tchrs. Edn., 1966. Mem. AAUW, Am. Mgmt. Assn., Nat. Coun. Negro Women, Am. Assn. Higher Edn., Am. Assn. Continuing Higher Edn., Nat. Assn. Trainers and Educators for Alcohol and Substance Abuse Counselors (bd. dirs.), La. Assn. Continuing

Higher Edn., Md. Assn. Higher Edn., Urban League, Delta Sigma Theta, Phi Sigma, Pi Lambda Theta. Avocations: fine arts, portraits, pastels, listening to classical music and popular show tunes, swimming.

FRANKLIN, MARY ELIZABETH, special education educator; b. Utica, Miss., Dec. 24, 1953; d. Earl Jordan and Bettye Jean Dixon; 1 child, Portia. B.Mus.Edn., Chgo. State U., 1975; MEd, Roosevelt U., Chgo., 1977; PhD, So. Ill. U., 1987. Tchr. Chgo. pub. schs., 1975-85; asst. prof. spl. edn. U. Cin., 1987-93, assoc. prof. spl. edn., 1993—; cons. pub. schs. and U.S. Office Edn. Reviewer, assoc. editor, mem. editl. bd. profl. jours.; contbr. articles to profl. jours. Recipient grants. Mem. Coun. for Exceptional Children (pres. local chpt. 1990), Assn. for Persons with Severe Handicaps (chmn. subcom. 1989-90). Democrat. Avocations: playing piano, singing, reading, walking, swimming. E-mail: Mary.Franklin@UC.Edu. Office: U Cin Coll of Edn PO Box 210002 Cincinnati OH 45221-0001

FRANKLIN, PAUL DEANE, financial services executive, investor; b. Shreveport, La., Oct. 17, 1942; s. Paul Amerideth and Marjorie (Hyde) F.; m. Carol Fillmore Talley, Aug. 30, 1966 (div. July 1982); children: Kyle D., Sean R.; m. Barbara Joyce, Oct. 12, 1985. BS in Bus., La. Tech. U., 1964; MBA in Fin., La. State U., 1965. CFP. Pers. rep. Monsanto Co., El Dorado, Ark., 1966-68; supr. pers. Monsanto Co., Muscatine, Iowa, 1968-70; supt. pers. Monsanto Co., Stonington, Conn., 1970-71, Comml. Solvents Corp., Terre Haute, Ind., 1971-74; mgr. human resources Mobay Chem. Corp., Baytown, Tex., 1974-85; pres. Micro Energy Sys., Inc., Pitts., 1985-88; mgr. human resources Miles Inc. (name now Bayer Corp.), Charleston, S.C., 1988-95; dir. human resources Bayer Corp., Charleston, S.C., 1995-98; owner Franklin & Assocs. Inc., Charleston, 1998—. Co-chmn. United Way, Baytown, Tex., 1983-84; coach Boys Club Am., Terre Haute, 1972-74; scoutmaster Boy Scouts Am., Baytown, 1975-76; bd. dirs. Pvt. Industry Coun., Charleston County, 1994-95, Goodwill Industries of Lower S.C., Inc., 1996—, Pvt. Industry Coun. Berkeley County, 1996-98, Trident Work Force Devel. Bd., 1998-99; bd. govs. Trident Area Consortium for Tech., 1994-98. Mem. Inst. CFPs, Trident Indsl. Rels. Com., Rotary (sgt.-at-arms), Beta Gamma Sigma (scholastic achievement award 1964), Delta Sigma Pi (internat. mem.). Republican. Avocations: travel, reading, physical fitness. Home: 648 Harbor Creek Pl Charleston SC 29412-3203 Office: 147 Wappoo Creek Dr Ste 105 Charleston SC 29412-2122

FRANKLIN, ROOSEVELT, minister; b. Chattanooga, Aug. 30, 1933; s. James R. and Cora Ann (Ponds) F.; m. Darnell Pinkston, Sept. 30, 1972; children: Sophia, Siemoran Dellazar. BS, Northeastern U., 1958; MA (hon.), Savannah State Coll., 1962; M. of Cybernetics, Grad. Sch. Wicca, St. Charles, Mo. Lic. metaphysician. Pastor Free For All Bapt. Ch., Greenwood, S.C., 1959-61; radio min. Spiritual Ch., Aiken, S.C., 1961-63; nat. lectr. United Coun. Spiritual Ch., Raleigh, N.C., 1963-66; min. Holy Trinity House of God, Macon, Ga., 1966—; youth dir. Holy Trinity Ch., Macon, 1966-72, talent coord., 1966-73; dir. Spiritual Singers, 1966—; lectr. in field; world renown authority on witchcraft and transcendental meditation; expert in clairvoyance, spiritual meditation. Organizer voters registration, Macon, 1977; pub. relations vol. Nat. Dem. Party, Atlanta, 1984; bd. dirs. Retired Persons Assn., 1980—. Capt. U.S. Army, 1951-54, Korea. Named extrovert promoter Music Workshop, 1979; recipient Afro Am. Heritage award Afro Am. Heritage Mus., 1987, Golden Eagle award Macon Courier, 1988, Nat. Achievers award Nat. Black Secs. Assn., 1990, Ednl. award Ptnrs. Youth Club, 1991, Golden Eagle award 500 Black Men of Am. Club, 1992, Black Achievement award Nat. Negro Achievers Assn., 1993, Nat. Rschrs. Occult award United Spiritual Coun. Chs., 1994, Mahogany Triumph award Am. Black Affluent Assn. Am., 1995, Concerned Citizens award People in Action Club, 1996, Good Samaritan award United Youth Fellowship Club, 1997, Model Citizen's award Office of the Gov. Ga., 1997, Registered Spiritual award, Registered Psychic award and Mystic award United Spiritual Coun. Assn., 1998, Appreciation award for continuous contbns. UNCF, 1998, Commemorative award Ga. Farmer's Assn., 1998, Activist award Boys Clubs Am., 1998, Outstanding Activities award United Fraternities Am., 1998, Presdl. Acknowledgement, Nat. Assn. Disabled Persons, 1999, Dr. of Metaphysics award, Dr. of Biblical Counseling award and Dr. of Religion award, 1999. Mem. NAACP (life), SCLC (life), Inner Circle Congl. Aids, C. of C., Minister's Alliance (v.p. 1966—, Citizens award 1979), Ga. Black Am. Pageant (coord. 1980—, Leadership award 1982), Direct Sellers League, Smooth Ashlar (dist. dep. 1970—), Rolls-Royce Club, Woodsmen of Am., Pioneer Club, Shriners (nat. amb.), Masons (33 deg., sovereign grand gen. inspector), Optimist, Kiwanis, Civitan, Elks, Nat. Lodge (treas. 1987—), Potentate of the Rosicruscins, Sertoma, Lions. Democrat. Avocations: martial arts, billiards. Office: Holy Trinity House of God 280 Straight St Macon GA 31204-6100

FRANKLIN, STANLEY PHILLIP, computer scientist, cognitive scientist, mathematician, educator; b. Memphis, Aug. 14, 1931; s. Sam and Lily (Rosenblum) F.; m. Jeannie Stonebrook, Apr. 1, 1979; children—Lynn Ann, Michele Suzanne, Phillip Byron, Bruce Eric, Halli Eileen, Elena Simone, Sunny Patrice, Sam Elliot. B.S., U. Memphis, 1959; M.A., UCLA, 1962, Ph.D., 1963; NSF postdoctoral fellow, U. Wash., Seattle, 1963-64. Asst. prof. math. U. Fla., 1964-65; assoc. prof., then prof. Carnegie-Mellon U., 1965-72; prof. math., chmn. dept. math. scis. U. Memphis, 1972-84, prof. computer sci., 1984—, co-dir. Inst. for Intelligent Systems, 1987—; vis. prof. Indian Inst. Tech., Kanpur, Technion, Haifa, Israel; vis. mem. Mathematische Centrum, Amsterdam, Netherlands; condr. workshops, cons. in field. Author research papers and books in field. Served with USMCR, 1951-53. Recipient Bd. Visitors Eminent Faculty award, 1997. Mem. Assn. for Computing Machinery, Am. Assn. for Artificial Intelligence, Cognitive Sci. Soc., Internat. Neural Network Soc., Sigma Xi, Pi Mu Epsilon. Home: 5736 Rich Rd Memphis TN 38120-2086 Office: U Memphis Dept Math Sci Memphis TN 38152-0001

FRANKLIN, WILLIAM GEORGE, manufacturing executive; b. Schenectady, N.Y., Sept. 14, 1921; s. Raymond Fred and Edna Laura (Faustmann) F.; m. Florence Smith, Mar. 27, 1948; William George, Cynthia Lee; m. Frances Engwall, Jan. 30, 1995;. BS, MIT, 1943. Chem. engr. Exxon, Elizabeth, N.J., 1943-48; v.p. David Smith Steel Co., Bklyn., 1948-69; pres. Hillside Spinning & Stamping, Union, N.J., 1969—; pres. Hillside Metal Ware Co., Union, 1969—, Aero Metal Products Co., Union, 1981—. Chmn. Gov.'s Debt Collection, Trenton, N.J., 1982-83; pres. Union County Econ. Devel., Union, 1985-86; dir. YMCA, Scotch Plains, N.J., 1972-81; mem. Summit Rep. Com. Mem. Nat. Housewares Asnn., Nat. Assn. Food Equipment, Mfrs. Assn., Baltusrol Golf Club, Wyndemere Country Club. Republican. Presbyterian. Avocations: golf, model railroading, snow skiing, grandchildren, charities. Office: Hillside Spinning & Stamping Co 1060 Commerce Ave Union NJ 07083-5026

FRANKLIN, WILLIAM PRICE, computer programmer; b. Oct. 8, 1953; s. Billy Wayne Franklin and Kikue (Hanaoka) Johnston. Student, West Tex. State U., 1972-74; AS, Lakeland Coll., 1986. Data processing mgr. Customized Service Co., Inc., Amarillo, Tex., 1979-81; dist. acct. Browning Ferris, Inc., Amarillo, 1981-84; sr. programmer Fedders Air Conditioning USA Inc., Effingham, Ill., 1986-90; systems programmer Fedders N.Am., Inc., Effingham, 1990-94; systems software mgr. Fedders Corp., Effingham, 1994-99, mgr. info. systems, 1999—. Del. Tex. Rep. Conv., 1972. Roman Catholic. Avocations: motorcycles, music. Home: RR 2 Box 415B Mattoon IL 61938-9406 Office: Fedders Corp 415 W Wabash Ave Effingham IL 62401-2671

FRANKLIN-GRIFFIN, CATHY LOU HINSON, nursing educator; b. Newton, N.C., Nov. 8, 1950; d. Willie A. and Evelyn Irene (Thornton) Hinson; 1 child, John Eric; m. Harry Griffin. ADN, Western Piedmont Comm. Coll., 1971; BSN, East Carolina U.; student, Med. U. S.C.; MA, Appalachian State U., 1990. RN, N.C., S.C., Ga., Ala., N.D., Calif. Patient educator Wayne County Meml. Hosp., Goldsboro, N.C.; developer cardiac rehab. & permanent pacemaker implantation programs Wayne County Meml. Hosp., 1980-81; infection control nurse Charleston (S.C.) Meml. Hosp., 1981-83; instr. nursing United Health Careers, Inc., San Bernardino, Calif., 1986-88, Caldwell Community Coll., CCC & TI, Hudson, N.C., 1986-88; rsch. coord. weekend/evening nursing program CCC and TI, Boone, N.C., 1991-93; dean nursing & allied health Rockingham C.C., Wentworth, N.C., 1993-2000; freelance contract nurse edn. Rowan-Cabarrus C.C., 2000; contract grant writer; mem. spkr.'s bur. Rockingham C.C.; bd. dirs. Rockingham Mental Health Ctr., Free Clinic Reidsville; legis. chair N.C. ADN Coun., 1997-99, pres. N.C. Conference Dirs. of ADN Programs, 1999—; nurse educator N.C. Bd. Nursing, 2000—, bd. dirs. Author: (with others) Fundamentals of Nursing, Nursing the Whole Person; pub. CCC & TI Skillbook; editorial cons. and contbr. Mosby Nursing Texts; grants writer. Capt. fundraising for Civic Ctr.; speaker for community orgns. Named one of Outstanding Young Women of Am., 1987. Mem. ADN (mem. dirs. coun., mem. legislation com.), NCAPNES, Phi Theta Kappa, Phi Kappa Phi, Sigma Theta Tau.

FRANKS, HERSCHEL PICKENS, judge; b. Savannah, Tenn., May 28, 1930; s. Herschel R. and Vada (Pickens) F.; m. Judy Black; 1 child, Ramona. Student U. Tenn.-Martin, U. Md.; JD, U. Tenn.-Knoxville; grad. Nat. Jud. Coll. of U. Nev. Bar: Tenn. 1959, U.S. Supreme Ct. 1968. Claims atty. U.S. Fidelity & Guaranty Co., Knoxville, 1958; ptnr. Harris, Moon, Meacham & Franks, Chattanooga, 1959-70; chancellor 3d Chancery div. of Hamilton County, 1970-78; judge Tenn. Ct. Appeals, Chattanooga, 1978—; spl. justice Tenn. Supreme Ct., 1979, 86, 87; presiding judge Hamilton County Trial Cts., 1977-78; spl. judge Tenn. Ct. of Criminal Appeals, 1990-92; mem. commn. to study appellate cts., 1990-92. Served with USNG, 1949-50, USAF, 1950-54. Mem. ABA (award of merit), Tenn. Bar Assn. (award of merit 1968-69), Tenn. Bar Found., Chattanooga Bar Found., Chattanooga Bar Assn. (pres. 1968-69, Founds. of Freedom award 1986), Am. Judicature Soc., Inst. Jud. Adminstrn., Optimists (pres. 1965-66), Community Service award 1971), Mountain City Club, City Farmers Club, Phi Alpha Delta. Mem. United Ch. of Christ. Address: 540 Mccallie Ave Ste 562 Chattanooga TN 37402-2039

FRANSES, PHILIP HANS B.F., econometrics, educator; b. Wageningen, The Netherlands, Sept. 30, 1963; s. Sebastiaan P.W. and Jessy M. (Vemer) F.; m. Gabrielle Elizabeth Van Der Spoel, Nov. 5, 1993; children: Tobias, Cedric. MSc, U. Groningen, 1987; PhD, Erasmus U., 1991. Rsch. fellow Royal Acad. of Arts & Scis., Amsterdam, 1992-96; from asst. prof. to assoc. prof. Erasmus U., 1991-98, prof., 1998—, dir. of ribes, 1996-99; sec. Union of Royal Acad. Rsch. Fellows, vis. prof. Univ. Calif., San Diego, Univ. of Western Australia, Univ. Vienna; sr. rsch. fellow Tinbergen Inst. Author: Periodicity and Stochastic Trends in Economic Time Series, 1996, Time Series Models for Business and Economic Forecasting, 1998; contbr. articles to profl. jours.; assoc. editor several jours. Recipient Johannes C. Ruigrok award. Mem. Am. Statistical Assn., Econometric Soc., Royal Rowing and Yacht Club, Internat. Statistical Inst. Avocations: tennis, boxing, literature, music. Home: Waghenaerdreef 52, NL 2661 Bergschenhoek The Netherlands Office: Econometric Inst. PO Box 1738, 3000 DR Rotterdam The Netherlands

FRANSON, TIMOTHY RAYMOND, pharmaceutical company executive, physician; b. Galesburg, Ill., Oct. 6, 1951; s. Raymond L. and Elizabeth A. (Simpson) F.; m. A. Christine Hassett, Aug. 10, 1974; children: Scott, Rebecca, Melissa. BS in Pharmacy with honors, Drake U., 1974; MD with honors, U. Ill., Chgo., 1978. Diplomate Am. Bd. Internal Medicine, Am. Bd. Infectious Diseases. Res. in internal medicine U. Iowa, Iowa City, 1978-81; fellowship in infectious diseases Med. Coll. Wis., Milw., 1981-83, asst. prof. medicine, hosp. epidemiologist, 1983-86; clin. rsch. physician in infectious diseases Eli Lilly & Co., Indpls., 1986-88, dir. infectious diseases/chemotherapy, 1988-91; group med. dir. Europe Eli Lilly & Co., Windlesham, U.K., 1991-93; exec. dir. health econs. and decision sci. Eli Lilly & Co., Indpls., 1993-94, exec. dir. regulatory affairs, 1994-97, v.p. clin. rsch. and regulatory affairs, 1997—; mem. State of Wis. Pub. Health Task Force on AIDS, 1985-86; mem. European Soc. for Clin. Micro and Infectious Disease Com. on Trial Guidelines, 1991-93; mem. dean's adv. bd. Drake U. Coll. Pharmacy, Des Moines, 1996—; dir. Kerr L. White Health Rsch. Inst., Decatur, Ga., 1997—; mem. dean's devel. adv. bd. Xavier Coll. Pharmacy, La.; mem. dean's adv. coun. U. Iowa Coll. Pharmacy; bd. dirs. Villages of Ind. Editor: A Comprehensive Sourcebook for Antibiotice Review, 1987; assoc. editor: Clinical Manual of Infectious Disease, 1984; mem. editl. adv. bd. FDA Advt. and Promotion Manual, 1996—; contbr. over 60 articles to profl. jours. Chair ednl. master plan com. Eagle Union Sch. Corp., Zionsville, Ind., 1994-96, mem. supt.'s adv. bd., 1996-97; clin. lead pharm. industry FDA Modernization Act of 1997. Recipient grant NIH/NIA (Nat. Inst. on Aging), 1985-88. Fellow Am. Coll. Physicians, Infectious Diseases Soc. Am.; mem. Pharm. Rsch. and Mfg. Assn. (regulatory affairs coord. com. 1995-98, chair clin. steering com. 1997-99, sci. and regulatory exec. com. 1997-99), Rho Chi, Alpha Omega Alpha. Republican. Presbyterian. Avocation: golf. Home: 8905 Hunt Club Rd Zionsville IN 46077-8449 Office: Eli Lilly and Co Corporate # 2643324 Indianapolis IN 46285-0002

FRANSSON, IVAR S.F., marketing professional; b. Tingsryd, Sweden, June 20, 1957; s. Bertil and Inez (Svensson) F.; m. Christina Leijonhufvud, Feb. 28, 1987; children: Sebastian, Simon. Grad., U. Vaxjo, Sweden, 1984. Ombudsman CUF, Kalmar, Sweden, 1978-79; riksombudsman CUF, Stockholm, 1980-81; project leader Kooperativa Inst., Stockholm, 1984-86; project leader Foreningsbanken, Stockholm, 1986-90, head mktg., 1990-97; head mktg. Swedbank, Stockholm, 1997—. Author: Ekonomi i Sam Verkan, 1986. Sgt. Swedish Air Force, 1977-78. Mem. Sallskapet. Avocations: golf, skiing, horse riding, hunting. Office: Swedbank, Brunkebergstorg 9, 10534 Stockholm Sweden

FRANT, GRIGORY, electrical engineer, industrial consultant; b. Kishinev, Moldavia, Oct. 22, 1949; came to Israel, 1974; s. Michael and Batia (Polsky) F.; m. Bluma Koifman, July 7, 1973; 1 child, Ariel. MSc, Poly. Inst., Cheliabinsk, USSR, 1971; PhD, Columbia Pacific U., San Rafael, Calif., 1992. Sr. engr. Project Inst., Kishinev, 1973-74; elec. engr. Technion IIT, Haifa, Israel, 1974—; cons. Metals Inst., Haifa, 1974—, Exptl. Power Sta., Haifa, 1986-88. Mem. Assn. of Engrs. com. Technion IIT, Haifa, 1992—. Mem. Union of Grad. Engrs. in Israel. Jewish. Avocations: radio, sports, literature. Home: Tamar 2/7 Ramot Itzhak, 36841 Nesher 36841, Israel Office: Technion Materials Dept, Technion City, Haifa 32000, Israel

FRANTZ, ROBERT WESLEY, lawyer; b. Long Branch, N.J., Dec. 31, 1950. BS, Rutgers U., New Brunswick, N.J., 1973; JD, Rutgers U., Newark, 1977. Bar: N.J. 1977, U.S. Dist. Ct. N.J. 1977, U.S. Ct. Appeals (4th and 10th cirs.) 1978, U.S. Ct. Appeals (6th, 7th and 8th cirs.) 1979, D.C. 1980, U.S. Ct. Appeals (9th cir.) 1980, U.S. Dist. Ct. D.C. 1981. Trial atty. U.S. Dept. Justice, Washington, 1977-80; assoc. Hamel and Park, Washington, 1980-82; asst. gen. counsel Chem. Mfrs. Assn., Washington, 1982-85; counsel, environ. protection GE, Fairfield, Conn., 1985-88, Pittsfield, Mass., 1988-89; mgr. and counsel Environ. Remediation Program, Fairfield, Conn., 1989-95; mgr., sr. counsel Environ. Ops. Program, Fairfield, 1995-98; gen. mgr., counsel GE Engines Svcs., Cin., 1998—; mem. sci. adv. bd. subcom. on risk reduction options U.S. EPA, 1996—. Contbr. articles to profl. publs.; editorial bd. Rutgers Law Rev., 1976. Mem. Newtown (Conn.) Charter Revision Commn., 1986-87. Mem. ABA (exec. editor Natural Resources and Environment 1986-93, coun. mem. sect. natural resources 1993-96). Avocations: sailing, golf, skiing, bicycling, woodworking. Office: GE Engine Svcs 1 Neumann Way # Md-t164 Cincinnati OH 45215-1915

FRANTZESKAKIS, JOHN MICHAEL, civil engineering educator; b. Athens, Attika, Greece, July 13, 1930; s. Michael John and Georgia Michael (Kapidaki) F.; m. Theodora John Galati, May 11, 1960; children: Michael, Anastasia. MS, Nat. Tech. U., Athens, 1953; Cert. Transport, Bur. of Hwy. Traffic/Yale U., New Haven, Conn., 1964; PhD (with hons.), Aristotle U., Thessaloniki, Greece, 1971. Registered profl. civil engr. Traffic and transp. engr. Doxiadis Assocs., Athens, 1956-65, head transp. brn., 1965-70; founder and ptnr. J.M. Frantzeskakis & Assocs., Athens, 1971-75; ptnr. Denco Ltd., Athens, 1975-80; sr. lectr. Nat. Tech. U., Athens, 1980-85, assoc. prof., 1985-88, prof. traffic engring., 1988-97, prof. emeritus, 1997—; dean faculty civil engring., Nat. Tech. U., 1991-93, dir. dept. transp. planning and engring., 1990-91, 93-94, 96-97; advisor Ministry Mercantil Marine, Transport and Comms., Athens, 1971-72. Co-author: Transportation Planning and Engineering, 3 vols., 1980-86, Road Safety, 1994, Traffic Management, 1996; contbr. articles to profl. jours. Mem. Hellenic Inst. Transp. Engrs. (pres. 1975-76), Inst. Transp. Engrs. (life), Greek Rd Fedn. (bd. dirs. 1992-93). Home: 2 Padadiamanti Str, GR15237 Filothei Athens Greece Office: Denco Ltd, 16 Kifissias Ave, 15125 Amaroussio Athens Greece

FRANTZIDES, CONSTANTINE THEMIS, general surgeon; b. Limassol, Cyprus, Nov. 6, 1950; came to U.S., 1983; s. Themistokles and Christothea (Papageorgeou) F.; m. Eleni Kasapi, May 8, 1981; children: Alexander, Marlena. MD, U. Athens, Greece, 1976; PhD, Med. Sch. Athens U., Greece, 1987. Chief resident Athens U., Greece, 1981-82; rsch. fellow Med. Coll. Wis., Milw., 1983-84, asst. clin. prof., 1984-85, vis. asst. prof., 1986-88, asst. prof., 1989-93, assoc. prof., 1993-97; dir. minimally invasive surgery ctr. Med. Coll. Wis., 1995-97; staff surgeon Milw. Regional Med. Ctr., 1989-97, Froedtert Meml. Hosp., Milw., 1989-97; prof. surgery U. Chgo., 1997—, dir. minimally invasive surgery ctr., 1997—; chmn. divsn. surgery Louis A. Weiss Meml. Hosp., Chgo., 1998—. Author: Postcholecystectomy Syndrome, 1991, Laparoscopic and Thoracoscopic Surgery, 1995; contbr. more than 100 articles to profl. jours. Recipient Shipley medal So. Surg. Assn., Hot Springs, Va., 1985; Physicians Recognition award AMA, Chgo., 1990, 98; 1st Ind. Rsch. award NIH, 1986. Mem. ACS, Am. Gastroenterology Assn., Collegium Internat. Chirurgiae Digestivae, N.Y. Acad. Scis., Soc. Surgery Alimentary Tract, Soc. Univ. Surgeons, Colegio Brasilero de Cirurgia Digestiva (hon.), Soc. Am. Gastroenterological Surgeons, Soc. Laparoscopic Surgeons, Hellenic Surg. Assn. (hon.), Ctrl. Surg. Assn., Western Surg. Assn. Achievements include discovery of a method for intrinsic denervation of the small intestine to study the physiology of this organ; several first laparoscopic procedures performed in the world including laparoscopic pseudocystojejunostomy, laparoscopic highly selective vagatomy and laparoscopic repair of gastric perforations; invented laparoscopic inflatable balloon retractor and "atraugrip" grasping forceps. Office: U Chgo Louis A Weiss Meml Hosp Dept Surgery 4646 N Marine Dr Chicago IL 60640-5759

FRANZ, GERHARD HEINRICH, art historian; b. Dresden, Saxony, Germany, Jan. 19, 1916; arrived in Austria, 1963; s. Oswald Julius and Hedwig Maria (Wilhelmi) F.; m. Rosemarie Berdau, Sept. 27, 1929; children: Roger Alexander, Rainald Christoph, Cornelia Claudia. Dr.Phil., U. Berlin, 1939; Dr.Phil.Habil., U. Breslau, Germany, 1943. Asst. Poly. Sch., Dresden, 1940-41, German Inst. for Art History, Paris, 1943-44; docent, prof. U. Mainz, Germany, 1946-63; prof. U. Graz, Austria, 1963—. Author: Bauten und Baumeister der Barockzeit in Bohmen, 1962, Niederläändische Landschaftsmalerei im Zeitalter des Manierismus, 1968, Das Alte Indien, 1990; editor jour. Kunsthistorisches Jahrbuch Graz I-XXII, 1965-86. Lutheran. Home: Charlottendorfgasse 7, A-8010 Graz Austria Office: Karl Franzens U, Universitätsplaz 3, A-8010 Graz Austria

FRANZ, INGOMAR WERNER, physician, consultant, researcher; b. Prerow auf dem Darss, Germany, Aug. 28, 1944; s. Otto Werner and Irmgard (Heldt) F.; m. Gabriele Hein Franz, Oct. 23, 1976; children: Thorid, Göran, Ragna. MD, Free U. Berlin, 1972. Cert. cardiologist. Intern, 1972-78; assoc. prof. cardiology Free U. Berlin, 1978-86; chief rehab. clinic BFA, Todtmoos, 1986. Author: Ergometry in Hypertensive Patients, 1985, B-receptor Blockade in the Therapy of Hypertension, 1986, Hypertension and the Heart, 1991; editor: Exercise Blood Pressure in Hypertensive Patients, 1993. Recipient Hufeland prize, Colonia Co., Koln, 1982, Therapiewoche prize Karlsruhe, 1982. Mem. German Soc. Hypertension, German Soc. Cardiology, German Soc. Internal Medicine. Avocation: aerobic exercise. Office: Klinik Wehrawald der BFA, Schwarzenbacher Strabe 3, 79682 Todtmoos Germany

FRANZECK, ULRICK KLAUS, internist; b. Eschenbach, Oberpfalz, Germany, Sept. 29, 1951; arrived in Switzerland, 1988, naturalized, 1996; s. Fritz and Frieda (Scholz) F.; m. Doris Wicki, May 13, 1983; children: Florian, Fabian. Grad., Ludwigs Maximillians U., Munich, 1978, MD, 1979. Postdoctoral fellow U. Calif., San Diego, 1978-80; asst. physician U. Hosp., Zurich, Switzerland, 1981-83; physician Nat. Hosp., Hamburg, Germany, 1983-84; asst. physician Univ. Hosp., Heidelberg, Germany, 1984-88; staff physician Univ. Hosp., Zürich, 1988—; prof. vascular medicine U. Zürich, 1997—. Author: Transkutaner Sauerstoffpartialdruck, 1991; co-author: A Textbook of Vascular Medicine, 1996; contbr. over 100 articles to sci. jours. Congress sec. XVI European Conf. on Microcirculation, Zürich, 1990, Dreiländertagung Angiologie, Zürich, 1993. Staff physician Germany Mil., 1983-84. Recipient innovative instrumentation award European Soc. for Microcirculation, 1992, Senator Pütter prize, 1983, Max Ratschow prize, 1990, Georg Friedrich Götz prize, 1994, Swiss Angiology prize, 1996. Avocations: mountaineering, triathlon, arts, books, Baroque music. Office: Ctr Vasc Diseases, Stadelhoferstr 8, Ch-8001 Zurich Switzerland

FRANZETTI, CARLOS ALBERTO, composer; b. Buenos Aires, June 3, 1948; came to U.S., 1970; s. Carlos Osvaldo and Beatrice (D'Giacómo) F.; m. Maria B. Lagos, Jan. 16, 1971 (dec.); 1 child, Carlos Jr.; m. Allison Brewster, Jan. 18, 1994; 1 child, Mariana Beatriz. BA, Salvador Conservatorio, Buenos Aires, 1965; M Composition, Nacional Musics, Buenos Aires, 1969; postgrad., Julliard Sch., N.Y.C., 1990-91. Music dir. Fermata Internat., Mexico City, 1971-73, Blank Prodns., N.Y.C., 1974-80, Sorin Films, Buenos Aires, 1983-85, Havana-N.Y. Music, N.Y.C., 1985-90, Sunday Prodns., N.Y.C., 1990—; condr., composer Orquesta Nova Chamber Group, 1991; gen ptnr. Amapola Records LLC, 1998. Work includes: (film scores) Misunderstood, 1984 (Gold record 1985), Q&A, 1989, The Mambo Kings, 1991, Le Film du Roi, 1991; (other recs.) Orquesta Nova Chamber Group, 1991, 92, Tropic of Capricorn, 1993, Soundtracks and Jazz Tunes, 1994, Images Before Dawn-Symphonic Music of Carlos Franzetti, 1995, Portraits of Cuba, 1996 (Grammy award for Best Latin Jazz Performance, 1997), Obsession, 1998 (Grammy nominee best latin jazz performace 1999; arranger and conductor), Remembrances, 1998 (Grammy nominee best large jazz ensemble 1999; arranger, composer, condr. and prodr.) , Carlos Franzetti-Piano Concerto No. 2 and Symphony No. 1, 1998, Concierto del Plata, 1998; arranger, condr. MTV Unplugged Luis Alberto Spinetta, 1997; composer, arranger, condr. Tango with Stockholm Jazz Orch., 1999. Recipient Trofeu Laus award D'adgfad, Barcelona, Spain, 1988, 1st prize Competition award Promusica/Yamaha, Argentina, Billboard award, U.S.A., Clio award, 1990, Konex Found. award, 1995. Mem. SAG, AFTRA, BMI, Local 802 Musicians Union. Roman Catholic. Avocations: films, boxing, travel. Home: 749 N Broad St Apt 206 Elizabeth NJ 07208-2430

FRANZINI, LOUIS RALPH, psychology educator, clinical psychologist; b. Beaver Falls, Pa., Aug. 11, 1941; s. Louis Ralph and Martha Lavina Franzini; m. Dolores Franzini, Aug. 8, 1964 (div. Jan. 1, 1994); children: Mary Lou, Jeremy; m. Jessica S. Franzini. BS, U. Pitts., 1963; MA, U. Toledo, 1965; PhD, U. Pitts., 1968. Lic. psychologist, Calif. Prof. San Diego State U., 1969—. Author: Eccentric and Bizarre Behaviors, 1995, Convention Survival Techniques, 1997. Avocation: competitive tennis. E-mail: franzini@sunstroke.sdsu.edu. Office: San Diego State Univ 6363 Alvarado Ct Ste 103 San Diego CA 92120-4913

FRAPPAZ, DIDIER, physician; b. Lyon, France, June 17, 1953; s. Guy and Francine (Marx) F.; children: Arthur, Timothée. MD, 1980. Asst. physician St. Etienne, France, 1986-92; specialist Ctr Leon Berard, Lyon, 1992—. Mem. Internat. Soc. Pediat. Oncology, Am. Soc. Clin. Oncology. Office: Ctr Leon Berard Pediatrics, 28 Rue Laennec, 69373 Lyon Cedex 08, France

FRASCELLA, DANIEL WILLIAM, JR., scientist; b. New Brunswick, N.J., July 6, 1934; s. Daniel William Sr. and Jenny (Revere) F.; m. Mary Patricia Fitzpatrick, Sept. 2, 1956; children: Daniel III, Nancy, Thomas. BS in Pharmacy magna cum laude, Rutgers U., 1960, MS in Physiology, 1962, PhD in Physiology and Biochem., 1968. Jr. pharmacologist Carter-Wallace Pharm., Cranbury, N.J., 1960-61; rsch. assoc. U. Pa., Phila., 1962-63; rsch. fellow Rutgers U., New Brunswick, 1963-65, asst. prof., 1965-68; rsch. fellow Merck Inst. Med. Rsch., Rahway, N.J., 1968-69; asst.prof. St. John's U., Jamaica, N.Y., 1970-74; assoc. dir. Hoechst-Roussel Pharm., Somerville, N.J., 1974—; vis. assoc. prof. City U. S.I., N.Y., 1972-74; diabetes cons. Hoechst-Roussel, 1974-96, CE program devel., 1974-82; ind. med. mktg. cons. on diabetes; pres. Diabetologics, 1996—. Author: (with others) Secondary Diabetes, 1980. With USN, 1952-55. Recipient H.A.B. Dunning award Am. Pharm. Assn., 1986, Edn. award Calif. Pharm. Assn., 1985. Fellow Royal Soc. of Medicine; mem. AAAS, Am. Diabetes Assn. (profl.), Am. Coll. Clin. Pharmacology, N.Y. Acad. Sci., Sigma Xi. Republican. Roman Catholic. Avocations: early American antiques, books and paper Americana, collecting stamps. Home: 1006 Stanton Lebanon Rd Lebanon NJ 08833-3109 Office: Diabetologics PO Box 197 Stanton NJ 08885-0197

FRASCH, WERNER WILLIAM, manufacturing professional; b. Hepsisau, Baden-W., Germany, June 17, 1945; s. Wilhelm and Emma (Haas) F.; m. Gisela Irene Lausmann, June 30, 1944. Law student, Eberhard-Karls U., Tuebingen, Germany, 1974-79. Pub. rels. City of Kirchheim, Germany, 1971-73; asst. mgr. City of Kuppenheim, Germany, 1973-74; pub. Boorberg Verlag, Stuttgart, Germany, 1979—. Author: (books) Duke Ulrich of Wurtt, 1990, History of Kirchheim, 1985, King Kasimir and His Festival, 1990, Der Riese Auf Dem Reussenstein, 1997, Vom Hohenneuffer auf den Reussenstein Historische Wanderung mif Gustav Schwab, 1999. E-mail: w.frasch@boorberg.de. Home: Loewenstrasse 63, 70597 Stuttgart Germany Office: Boorberg Verlag, Scharrstr 2, 70563 Stuttgart Germany

FRASE, LAWRENCE THOMAS, phychologist, science administrator; b. Oak Park, Ill., May 10, 1935; s. Lawrence Michael and Elizabeth Grace (Stybr) F.; m. Concetta Ann Rascati; children: David, Scott. AB, U. Miami, 1959; MS, U. Ill., 1962, PhD, 1965. Asst. prof. U. Mass., Amherst, 1965-68; rschr. Bell Labs, Murray Hill, N.J., 1968-89; head basic skills Nat. Inst. Edn., Washington, 1976-78; exec. dir. rsch. Edn. Testing Svc., Princeton, N.J., 1990-99; rsch. prof. George Mason U., Fairfax, Va., 2000—. Editl. bds. of numerous jours.; author softward. Fellow Am. Assn. Advancement Sci., 1985, AAAS, 1985, Am. Phsychol. Soc., 1991. Avocations: sailing. E-mail:LFRASE@MINDSPRING.COM. Home: 40 Keats Rd Basking Ridge NJ 07920-2616

FRASER, BARRY JOHN, university administrator; b. Melbourne, Australia, Apr. 8, 1945; s. Reginald Francis and Margaret Eileen (Toohey) F.; m. Marilyn Denise Cox, Dec. 3, 1974; children: Michelle Louise, Sally Nicole. BSc, Melbourne U., 1967; BEd, Monash U., Australia, 1972, PhD, 1976. Tchr. Victoria Edn. Dept., Australia, 1969-71; sr. tutor Monash U., Melbourne, 1972-75; from lectr. to sr. lectr. Macquarie U., Sydney, 1976-81; head sch. Western Australia Inst. Tech. (now Curtin U. Tech.), Perth, 1982—, dir. Sci. and Math. Edn. Ctr., 1984—, prof. edn., 1985—. Author: Classroom Environment, 1986; Windows into Science Classrooms, 1990, Educational Environments, 1991, Improving Science Education, 1995, Gender, Science and Mathematics, 1996, Improving Teaching and Learning in Science and Mathematics, 1996, International Handbook of Science education, 1998; contbr. articles to profl. jours. Fellow AAAS, Internat. Acad. Edn., Australian Coll. Edn., Acad. Social Scis. Australia; mem. Am. Edtl. Rsch. Assn., Nat. Assn. Rsch. in Sci. Tchg., Australian Assn. Rsch. in Edn. Office: Curtin U Tech, Bentley 6102, Australia

FRASER, BRENDAN, actor; b. Indianapolis, Dec. 3, 1968. Movies include: Dogfight, 1991, Encino Man, 1992, School Ties, 1992, Twenty Bucks, 1993, Son in Law, 1993, Younger and Younger, 1993, With Honors, 1994, In the Army Now, 1994, Airheads, 1994, The Scout, 1994, The Passion of Darkly Noon, 1995, Balto (voice), 1995, Now and Then, 1995, Kids in the Hall: Brain Candy, 1996, Mrs. Winterbourne, 1996, Glory Daze, 1996, George of the Jungle, 1997, Still Breathing, 1998, Gods and Monsters, 1998, Sinbad: Beyond the Veil of Mists (voice), 1999, Ringside, 1999, Monkey Bone, 1999, Blast from the Past, 1999, The Mummy, 1999, Dudley Do-Right, 1999, Bedazzled, 2000, Monkeybone, 2000. Office: Creative Artists care Peter Levine 9830 Wilshire Blvd Beverly Hills CA 90212-1825

FRASER, ELEANOR RUTH, radiologist, administrator; b. Woodlake, Calif., May 31, 1927; d. Morton William and Dorothy Jean (Harding) F. BA magna cum laude, Pomona Coll., 1949; MD, Stanford U., 1954. Diplomate Am. Bd. Radiology. Resident in radiology Los Angeles County Hosp., L.A., 1957; radiologist St. Joseph Hosp., Orange, Calif., 1957-61; pvt. practice Anaheim, Calif., 1961-78; radiologist Radiology Nuclear Med. Group, Bakersfield, Calif., 1978-85; dir. radiology Kern Valley Hosp., Lake Isabella, Calif., 1985-2000, chief of staff, 1992-99. Mem. AMA, Calif. Med. Assn., Kern County Med. Assn., Soc. Nuclear Medicine, Kern Valley Exchange Club (sec. 1992-94), Phi Beta Kappa. Methodist. Avocations: music, writing. Home & Office: PO Box 1657 Lake Isabella CA 93240-1657

FRASER, FRANCES MARIE, artist; b. Hutchinson, Kans., May 13, 1935; d. Jacob J. and Nellie Elizabeth (Landis) Hollinger; div; children: Clinton Stevens, Joseph Michael, Jeffrey Eugene, Robert Charles, Barbara Marie, Julia Lynn. Cert. tchr., Calif. C.C., 1979. Profl. artist, instr. oil and pastel, 1975-99. Founding mem., advisor, chairperson, mentor City of Norco (Calif.) Western Art Show, 1996-99. Recipient Grumbacher Gold medallian, 1999. Mem. So. Calif. Pastel Soc. (founding mem., pres. 1992-95). Democrat. Avocations: hiking, computer. E-mail: franfraser@Yahoo.com. Home: PO Box 1331 115 Edwards Ln Vian OK 74962

FRASER, GALE WILLIAM, II, civil engineer; b. Chgo., Sept. 14, 1954; s. Gale William and Marilyn (Peeken) F.; m. Brenda Jean Trom, Sept. 6, 1974; children: Gale William III, James, Michael. BSCE, N.D. State U., 1977. Registered profl. engr., N.D., Minn., Nev. Staff engr. Houston Engring., Inc., Fargo, N.D., 1977-86; planning engr. City of Las Vegas, Nev., 1986-88; asst. gen. mgr. Clark County Regional Flood Control Dist., Las Vegas, 1988-93, gen. mgr., 1993—; vice chmn. all hazards mitigation adv. com. State of Nev., Carson City, 1999—. Mgr. Paradise Valley Am. Little League, Las Vegas, 1990—. Mem. NSPE (Young Engr. of Yr., So. Nev. chpt. 1990), ASCE, Am. Pub. Works Assn., Nat. Assn. Flood and Stormwater Agys. (co-chair flood control com. 1998—). Lutheran. Avocations: baseball, skiing, camping. Fax: 702-455-3870. E-mail: galerfc@co.clark.nv.us. Office: Clark County Reg Flood Control Dist 600 S Grand Central Pkwy Las Vegas NV 89106-4511

FRASER, GORDON MURRAY, science writer; b. Glasgow, Scotland, Feb. 23, 1943; arrived in France, 1984; s. Ralph Jack and Ray (Braverman) F.; m. Gillian Sally Harbinson, Oct. 16, 1975; children: Nathalie, Benjamin. BS, Imperial Coll., London, 1961, PhD, 1964. Mem. Royal Coll. Sci. (assoc.). Rsch. scientist Tel Aviv U., 1967-69, Sussex U., Brighton, Eng., 1969-70; journalist IPC Bus. Press, London, 1970-72; freelance journalist London, 1972-75; info. officer Rutherford Lab., Didcot, Eng., 1975-77; editor European Orgn. Nuc. Rsch., Geneva, 1977—; head publs. svc. European Orgn. Nuc. Rsch., 1979-92, editor-in-chief, 1986—. Author: The Quark Machines, 1997, Particle Century, 1998, Antimatter-The Ultimate Mirror, 2000; co-author: Search for Infinity (in 10 langs.), 1994; contbr. articles to profl. jours., mags. and newspapers. Avocations: languages, crossword puzzles. Office: European Orgn Nuc Rsch/CERN, 1211 Geneva 23, Switzerland

FRASER, JOHN FOSTER, management company executive; b. Saskatoon, Sask., Sept. 19, 1930; s. John Black and Florence May (Foster) F.; m. Valerie Georgina Ryder, June 21, 1952; children: John Foster Jr., Lisa Ann. B of Commerce, U. Sask., 1952; LLD (hon.), U. Winnipeg, 1993. Pres. Empire Freightways Ltd., Saskatoon, Sask., 1953-60, Empire Oil Ltd., Saskatoon, 1960-62, Hanford Drewitt Ltd., Winnipeg, 1962-68, Norcom Homes Ltd., Mississauga, Ont., 1969-78; pres., chief exec. officer Fed. Industries Ltd., Winnipeg, 1978-91, chmn., chief exec. officer, 1991-92, chmn. bd., 1992-95; vice chmn. Russel Metals, Winnipeg, 1995-97; chmn. bd. Air Canada, 1996—; bd. dirs. Internat. Comfort Products Corp., Bank of Montreal, Air Can., Investors Group, Inc., Can. Devel. Investment Corp., Shell Can. Ltd., The Thomson Corp., Ford Motor Co. Can. Ltd., Man. Telecom Svcs. Inc., Centra Gas Man. Inc., Coca-Cola Beverages Ltd., Inter-City Products Corp., Continental Airlines, Inc., Am. West Airlines; past chmn. Coun. for Bus. and Arts in Can. Bd. dirs., founding chmn. Assocs. Faculty of Mgmt. Studies U. Man.; past pres. Man. Theatre Centre; past bd. govs. St. John's Ravenscourt Sch., Winnipeg; mem. cultural rev. policy com. Province of Man., 1979; past pres. Royal Winnipeg Ballet, 1992-93. Decorated officer Order of Can., 1990; recipient Peter D. Curry award U. Man., 1984, Outstanding Bus. Achievement award as Citizen of Yr. Man. C. of C., 1984; named Transp. Person of Yr. Nat. Transp. Week, 1990. Mem. Am. Mgmt. Assn. (pres.'s assn.), Royal Lake of the Woods Yacht Club, Toronto Club. Progressive Conservative. Presbyterian. Avocations: boating, reading. Office: 201 Portage Ave Ste 3100, Winnipeg, MB Canada R3B 3L7

FRASER, JOSEPH ROBERT EMMOTT, physician, consultant; b. Inglewood, Victoria, Australia, Sept. 27, 1927; s. William Wilfred and Alphina Deborah (Emmott) F.; m. Muriel Ruth McKain, Jan. 20, 1951; children: Gail, Peter, Ian, David, Martin. MB, BS, U. Melbourne, Australia, 1949, MD, 1954; Hon. MD, Uppsala (Sweden) U., 1988. Medical diplomate. Cons. physician Prince Henry's Hosp., Melbourne, 1960-66, mem. exec. sr. med. staff, 1961-65; cons. physician Royal Melbourne Hosp., 1966-92, chmn. bd. med. rsch., 1984-92, head of unit, 1989-92, hon. cons. physician, 1993—; asst. dir. dept. medicine U. Melbourne, 1966-78, dep. chmn., 1978-92, hon. sr. rsch. assoc. lab. for fetal and neonatal immunology, 1993—; vis. scientist Inst. Med. and Physiol. Chemistry, Uppsala U., 1980-92; vis. assessor tertiary health and med. edn. Papua New Guinea, 1981; advisor fed. and state govts. on arbovirus disease. Contbr. chpts. to books and articles to profl. and sci. jours. Named Fgn. mem. Royal Soc. Sci., Uppsala, 1985, Order of Australia, Gov.-Gen. of Australia, 1990. Fellow Royal Australasian Coll. Physicians, Royal Coll. Physicians (London); mem. Royal Swedish Acad. Sci. (fgn. mem.), Soc. In Vitro Biol. (USA), Matrix Biology Assn. Australia and New Zealand (pres. 1978-80), Cardiac Soc. Australia and New Zealand, Australian Rheumatology Assn. Avocations: natural history, literature, snow sports. Home: 131 Manning Rd, East Malvern VIC 3145, Australia

FRASER, ROBERT WESTON, economics educator, consultant; b. Adelaide, Australia, Dec. 23, 1955; s. Murray Robert and Valma Joy (Raphael) F.; m. Hilary Denise Brumwell, June 12, 1982; children: Matthew Robert, Clair Magdalen, Adam Raphael. B in Econs. with honors, U. Adelaide, 1977; MPhil in Econs., U. Oxford, Eng., 1979, PhD in Econs., 1982. Asst. prof. U. Va., Charlottesville, 1981-82; lectr. econs. U. Western Australia, Perth, 1982-87, sr. lectr., 1988-92, assoc. prof., 1993-98, prof., 1999-2000; prof. agrl. econs. Imperial Coll. U. London, Wye, 2000—; head Agrl. and Resource Econs., U. We. Australia, 1991-2000; sub-cons. Erm-Mitchell McCotter, Perth, 1991-2000. Contbr. articles to profl. jours. Mem. Com. Inquiry into Electricity and Gas Tariffs Western Australia, 1983-85. Rhodes scholar, 1977; rsch. grant Australian Rsch. Coun., 1992, 94, 95, 98, 99, 2000, Grains R&D Com., 1997—. Mem. Australian Agrl. and Resource Econs. Soc. (treas. Western Australia br. 1993-2000, pres.-elect 1997, pres. 1998). Avocation: spending time with my children. Home: 5 Victoria Ave Claremont, 65 Eltisley Ave, 6010 Cambridge CB3 9JQ, England Office: Imperial Coll at Wye, Faculty Agr Nedlands, 6907 Kent England

FRASER, WILLIAM KERR, university official; b. Glasgow, Scotland, Mar. 18, 1929; s. Alexander and Rachel (Kerr) F.; m. Marion Anne Forbes, Apr. 6, 1956; children: Graham, Andrew, Lindsey, Douglas. MA, Glasgow U., 1949, LLB, 1951, LLD (hon.), 1982; LLD (hon.), Strathclyde (Scotland) U., 1991, Aberdeen (Scotland) U., 1993; Dhc, Edinburgh, 1995. Various positions Scottish Office, Edinburgh, 1955-78, permanent under sec. of state, 1978-88; prin., vice chancellor Glasgow U., 1988-95, chancellor, 1996—; chmn. Royal Commn. Ancient and Hist. Monuments, 1995-2000, Scotland Inheritance Fund, 1996—. Fellow Royal Coll. Physicians and Surgeons (Glasgow, hon, 1992), Royal Scottish Acad. Music and Drama (hon.), 1995; mem. New Club Edinburgh. Office: Broadwood Gifford, East Lothian EH41 4JE, Scotland

FRASER-MOLEKETI, GERALDINE, federal official; b. Landsdowne, South Africa, Aug. 24, 1960; married; 3 children. Political activist, 1974-80, in exile, 1980-90; organizer nat. office South African Communist Party Com.; dep. minister Welfare and Population Devel., 1995-96, min., 1996-99; head nat. prep. com. UN-Sponsored Internat. Conf. Women and Devel., Beijing; min. Ministry of Pub. Svc. and Adminstrn., Pretoria, South Africa, 1999—; mem. nat. exec. com. African Nat. Congress, 1998. African Nat. Congress. Office: Pvt Bag X884, Pretoria 0001, South Africa

FRASIER, RALPH KENNEDY, lawyer, banker; b. Winston-Salem, N.C., Sept. 16, 1938; s. LeRoy Benjamin and Kathryn O. (Kennedy) F.; m. Jeannine Quick, Aug. 1981; children: Karen D. Frasier Alston, Gail S. Frasier Cox, Ralph Kennedy Jr., Keith Lowery, Marie Kennedy, Rochelle Doar. BS, N.C. Cen. U., Durham, 1963, JD, 1965. Bar: N.C. 1965, Ohio 1976. With Wachovia Bank and Trust Co., N.A., Winston-Salem, N.C., 1965-70; v.p., counsel Wachovia Bank and Trust Co., N.A., 1969-70; asst. counsel, v.p. parent co. Wachovia Corp., 1970-75; v.p., gen. counsel Huntington Nat. Bank, Columbus, Ohio, 1975-76; sr. v.p. Huntington Nat. Bank, 1976-83, sec., 1981-98, exec. v.p., 1983-98, cashier, 1983-98; v.p. Huntington Bancshares Inc., 1976-86, gen. counsel, 1976-98, sec., 1981-98; sec., dir. Huntington Mortgage Co., Huntington State Bank, Huntington Leasing Co., Huntington Bancshares Fin. Corp., Huntington Investment Mgmt. Co., Huntington Nat. Life Ins. Co., Huntington Co., 1976-88; v.p., asst. sec. Huntington Bank N.E. Ohio, 1982-84; asst. sec. Huntington Bancshares Ky., 1985-97; sec. Huntington Trust Co., N.A., 1987-97, Huntington Bancshares Ind., Inc., 1986-97, Huntington Fin. Services Co., 1987-98; dir. The Huntington Nat. Bank, Columbus, Ohio, 1998—; of counsel Porter Wright Morris & Arthur LLP, Columbus, 1998—; trustee Online Computer Libr. Ctr., Inc., Columbus, 1999—, mem. fin. com., 2000—, mem. audit com., 2000—; dir. ADATOM.COM, Inc., Milpitas, Calif., 1999—, mem. compensation com., 1999—, chair audit com., 1999—. Bd. dirs. Family Svcs. Winston-Salem, 1966-74, sec., 1966-71, 74, v.p., 1974; chmn. Winston-Salem Transit Authority, 1974-75; bd. dirs. Rsch. for Advancement of Personalities, 1968-71, Winston-Salem Citizens for Fair Housing, 1970-74, N.C. United Community Svcs., 1970-74; treas. Forsyth County (N.C.) Citizens Com. Adequate Justice Bldg., 1968; trustee Appalachian State U., Boone, N.C., 1973-83, endowment fund, 1973-83, Columbus Drug Edn. and Prevention Fund, Inc., 1989-92; trustee, vice chmn. employment and Edn. Commn. Franklin County, 1982-85; mem. Winston-Salem Forsyth County Sch. Bd. Adv. Coun., 1973-74, Atty. Gen's Ohio Task Force Minorities in Bus., 1977-78; bd. dirs. Inorads Columbus, Inc., 1986-95, Greater Columbus Arts Coun., 1986-94, Columbus Urban League Inc., 1987-94, vice chmn., 1990-94; trustee Riverside Meth. Hosp. Found., 1989-90, Grant Med. Ctr., 1990-95, Grant/Riverside Meth. Hosps., 1995-97; trustee Ohio Health Corp., 1997—; dir. Cmty. Mutual Ins. Co., 1989-92, mem. audit com., 1989-92; trustee N.C. Ctrl. U., Durham, 1993—, vice-chmn., 1993-94, chmn. 1995, chair ednl. planning and acad. affairs com., 1995-98, mem. audit, devel. and personnel coms., 1998—; mem. Ohio Bd. Regents, 1987-96, vice-chmn., 1993-95, chmn., 1995-96; trustee Nat. Jud. Coll., Reno, Nevada, 1996—, fin. and audit com., 1997—, chair, 1999—, treas. 1998—, Columbus Bar Found., 1998— (fellows com. 1998—, grants com., 1998—); AEFC Pension Adminstrn. Com. defined benefit plan of the ABA, Am. Bar Endowment, Am. Bar Found., and Nat. Jud. Coll., Chgo, Ill., 1998—; trustee, mem. audit and fin. coms. Online Computer Libr. Ctr., Inc., Dublin, Ohio, 1999—. With AUS, 1958-64. Mem. ABA, Nat. Bar Assn., Ohio Bar Assn., Columbus Bar Assn. Office: Porter Wright Morris & Arthur LLP 41 S High St Ste 3100 Columbus OH 43215-6101

FRASK, ROBIN ANN KOSTANESKY, secondary school educator; b. Hazleton, Pa., Apr. 27, 1971; d. John F. and Karen A. (Brandmier) Kostanesky; m. Randy Michael Frask, July 2, 1999. BS in Edn., Mansfield U., 1993; MEd, Wilkes U., 1999. Substitute tchr. Weatherly (Pa.) Area Sch. Dist., 1994-96; substitute tchr. Hazleton (Pa.) Area Sch. Dist., 1994-96, sci. tchr., 1996—. Mem. NEA, Pa. State Edn. Assn. E-mail: rmf@ccomm.com. Home: 345 Shingle Mill Dr Drums PA 18222-1216

FRASSINELLI, GUIDO JOSEPH, retired aerospace engineer; b. Summit Hill, Pa., Dec. 4, 1927; s. Joseph and Maria (Grosso) F.; m. Antoinette Pauline Clemente, Sept. 26, 1953; children: Lisa, Erica, Laura, Joanne, Mark. BS, MS, MIT, 1949; MBA, Harvard U., 1956. Treas. AviDyne Rsch., Inc., Burlington, Mass., 1958-64; asst. gen. mgr. Kaman AviDyne divsn. Kaman Scis., Burlington, 1964-66; asst. dir. strategic planning N. Am. ACFT OPNS, Rockwell Internat., L.A., 1966-69; from mgr. program planning to project mgr. advanced programs Rockwell Space Sys. Divsn., Downey, Calif., 1970-94; ret. Rockwell Space Systems Div., Downey, 1994. Mem. Town Hall of Calif., L.A., 1970—; treas. Ecology Devel. and Implementation Commitment Team Found., Huntington Beach, Calif., 1971-75; founding com. mem. St. John Fisher Parish Coun., Rancho Palos Verdes, Calif., 1978-85. Recipient Tech. Utilization award, NASA, 1971, Astronaut Personal Achievement award, 1985. Fellow AIAA (assoc.; tech. com. on econs. 1983-87, exec. com. L.A. sect. 1987-91, 94-98), Inst. for Advancement of Engring.; mem. Sigma Xi, Tau Beta Pi. Roman Catholic. Achievements include determination of aircraft damage limits and atomic-weapon-delivery capabilities of aircraft; development of cost models to account for advances in engineering state of art, of cost prioritization techniques for space shuttle improvements, of software to produce business plans. Home: 29521 Quailwood Dr Rncho Pls Vrd CA 90275-4930

FRATESCHI, LAWRENCE JAN, economist, statistician, educator; b. Chgo., Oct. 7, 1952; s. Lawrence and Olga (Los) F. BS in Math. and Psychology, U. Ill., Chgo., 1975, MA in Econs., 1979, MS Pub. Health in Biostats. and Epidemiology, 1990, PhD in Econs., 1992. Teaching asst. dept. math, lectr. dept. info. and decision scis. U. Ill., Chgo., 1978-80, rsch. assoc. epidemiology and biostatistics Sch. Pub. Health, 1989-90; statistician Argonne (Ill.) Nat. Labs., 1980-81; asst. prof. econs. and stats. Coll. of DuPage, Glen Ellyn, Ill., 1981-86, assoc. prof., 1986-90, prof. econs., stats., 1990—; rsch. prof. epidemiology and biostats. Sch. Pub. Health U. Ill., Chgo., Ill., 1993—. Contbr. articles to profl. publs. Mem. Am. Econ. Assn., Am. Statis. Assn., Am. Pub. Health Assn., Soc. Epidemiologic Rsch., Midwest Econs. Assn., Ill. Econs. Assn., Ill. Pub. Health Assn., Phi Eta Sigma, Phi Kappa Phi, Delta Omega. Office: Coll of DuPage 425 22nd St Glen Ellyn IL 60137-6784

FRATTI, MARIO, playwright, educator; b. L'Aquila, Italy, July 5, 1927; came to U.S., 1963, naturalized, 1974; s. Leone and Palmira (Silvi) F.; children: Mirko, Barbara, Valentina. Ph.D., Ca Foscari U., 1951. Tchr., 1964-65; mem. faculty Columbia U., 1965-66; mem. Adelphi Coll., 1964-65; mem. faculty Hofstra U., 1973-74; prof. lit. New Sch. Hunter Coll., N.Y.C., 1967—; drama critic. Drama critic: Paese, 1963—, Progresso, 1963—, Ridotto, 1963—, Ora Zero, 1963—; playwright: Cage-Suicide, 1964, Academy-Return, 1967, Mafia, 1971, Races, 1972, Bridge, 1971, Eleven Plays in Spanish, 1977, Refrigerators, 1977; author: Eleonora Duse-Victim, 1981, Nine, 1982 (Tony), Biography of Fratti, 1982, A.I.D.S., 1987, V.C.R., 1988, (mus.) Encounter, 1989, Family, 1990, Friends, 1991, Lovers, 1992, Leningrad Euthanasia, 1993, Holy Father, 1994, Sister, 1995, Sacrifices, 1996, Jurors, 1997, also 8 plays in Russian, 1997, 4 plays in Japanese, 1997, 7 minidramas in Spanish, 1998, 4 plays in Spanish, 1999. Served to lt. Italian Army, 1951-53. Recipient awards for plays and musicals. Mem. Drama Desk, Am. Theatre Critics, Outer Critics Circle (v.p.). Democrat. Home: 145 W 55th St Apt 15D New York NY 10019-5355

FRAUENKRON, HELGE, physicist; b. Huckeswagen, Germany, Sept. 8, 1968; s. Guenter Robert and Inge Marta (Gerhards) F. Diploma, U. Wuppertal, Germany, 1993, PhD, 1996. Asst. U. Wuppertal, 1993-96; post doctorial High Performance Computer Ctr., Julich, Germany, 1996-99; sci. collaborator IABG, Frankfurt, Germany, 1999—. Contbr. articles to profl. jours. Avocations: chess, painting, arts.

FRAUNDORFER, MARK ROBERT, urologist; b. Eshowe, Natal, South Africa, Jan. 18, 1951; arrived in New Zealand, 1959; s. John F. and Kathleen K. (Fyfe) F.; m. Janet Griffiths; children: David, Elise. MB, B of Surgery, U. Otago, New Zealand, 1975; diploma in Hyperbaric and Underwater Medicine, Monash U., 1978; diploma, Royal Coll. Obstetricians and Gynecologists, London, 1979. Cert. scuba diving instr., launch master; lic. helicopter pilot. Externship Hope Haven Children's Hosp., 1974, 75; house surgeon Tauranga (New Zealand) Hosp., 1976-77; gen. practice Townsville, Australia, 1978; registrar in ob-gyn. Freedom Fields Hosp., Plymouth, Eng., 1979; registrar in urology Inst. Urology, St. Paul's Hosp., London, 1980, Waikato Hosp., Hamilton, New Zealand, 1981-82; registrar in gen. surgery Tauranga Hosp., 1983; registrar in urology Dunedin (New Zealand) Hosp., 1984; registrar in pediat. surgery Princess Mary Hosp., Auckland, New Zealand, 1985; registrar in urology Auckland (New Zealand) Hosp., 1985; cons. urologist Tauranga Hosp., 1986—; bd. dirs. Wakefield Hosp. Ltd., Norfolk Cmty. Hosp. Ltd., Urotech Ltd., Venturo Ltd., Nikau Properties Ltd., Promed Devels. Ltd., Promed Urology Ltd., Health-Med Group Ltd., Queen Elizabeth Hosp. Ltd., Delta Trading Ltd., Health & Hygiene Holdings and Health & Hygiene Internat., Bay of Plenty Helicopters Ltd., Highbury Nominees Ltd., Urology Svcs. Ltd., Urologic Ltd., Quadrant Enterprises, Stone Svcs. NZ Ltd., Refit NZ Ltd; spkr. in field. Author: (chpt.) Diving Safety, 1993; contbr. articles to profl. jours. With Royal Australasian Navy, 1978. Fellow Royal Australasian Coll. Surgeons; mem. Australasian Urol. Soc. (tng., edn. and acreditation com.), South Pacific Underwater Med. Soc., Am. Urol. Assn. (corr.), Endourological Soc., Assn. Salaried Med. Specialists (exec. mem. 1989-95, sec./treas. 1993-95). Home: 4C/T2 1 Marine Parade, Taurange New Zealand Office: Promed Urology Ltd, PO Box 56, Tauranga New Zealand

FRAWLEY, JOHN EDMOND, vascular and transplantation surgeon; b. Toowoomba, Queensland, Australia, May 11, 1939; s. John Joseph and Spencely May (Bremser) F.; m. Elizabeth Mary Waters, Oct. 24, 1964; children: St. John Patrick, Dominic John, Christopher Stephen, Matthew Kitto, Benjamin Peter, James Alexander, Eloise Anna. MB, BS, U. Queensland, Brisbane, 1962. Intern Princess Alexandra Hosp., Brisbane, 1963; med. officer Thursday Island Torres Strait, 1964; professorial registrar U. West Australia, Perth, 1965-67, tutor anatomy, 1966; surg. registrar Mater Misericordiae Hosp., Brisbane, 1968; sr. registrar Chelmsford (Eng.) Hosp., 1969-70, Hammersmith Hosp., London, 1969-70; lectr. surgery U. London, St. Mary's Hosp., 1970-71, U. NSW, Sydney, Australia, 1972-76; vascular/transplant surgeon U. NSW, Prince Henry Hosp., Sydney, 1972—; transplant surgeon U. Sydney, Concord Hosp., 1991—; head vascular unit Prince Henry Hosp., 1985—; chmn. dept. vascular/transplant surgery Prince of Wales Hosp., Sydney, 1993—. Contbr. articles to sci. jours. Recipient Disting. Svc. award Sydney Adventist Hosp., 1996. Fellow Royal Australasian Coll. Surgeons (transplantation sect., convenor 1979-80, com. chmn. 1994-95, cert. continuing profl. standards 1996); mem. AAAS, Internat. Soc. Cardiovasc. Surgery, Australian Med. Assn., Australian Assn. Surgeons, Stroke Soc. Australasia, Australian and New Zealand Soc. Phlebology, Transplant Soc. Australia and New Zealand, Royal Australasian Coll. Surgeons (vascular sect.), N.Y. Acad. Scis. Roman Catholic. Avocations: painting, poetry, history, literature, piano. Home: 23 Riddles Ln, NSW Pymble 2073, Australia Office: Ste 2/2 Hornsby House, 32 Florence St, NSW Hornsby 2077, Australia

FRAWLEY BAGLEY, ELIZABETH, government advisor, ambassador; b. Elmira, N.Y., July 13, 1952; m. Smith Bagley; 2 children. BA in French and Spanish cum laude, Regis Coll., 1974; JD in Internat. Law, Georgetown U., 1987. Staff Office Congl. Rels. Dept. State, spl. asst. to Amb. Sol Linowitz, congl. liaison Conf. on Security and Cooperation in Europe; amb. to Portugal Dept. State, Washington, 1993-97, former amb. to Portugal, 1997—; adj. prof. law Georgetown U. Washington. Home: 1539 29th St NW Washington DC 20007-3061

FRAWLEY-O'DEA, MARY GAIL, clinical psychologist, psychoanalyst, educator; b. Lowell, Mass.; d. John Edward and Mary Gail (Quinn) Frawley; m. Dennis Michael O'Dea, Jan. 1, 1996; 1 stepson, Daniel Patrick, 1 adopted son, Igor Ibradzic; 1 daughter, Mollie Gilmore Chun O'Dea. BA, St. Mary's Coll., Notre Dame, Ind., 1972; MBA, So. Meth. U., 1975; PhD, Adelphi U., 1988, postdoctoral diploma in psychoanalysis, 1996. Psychologist II Pomona (N.Y.) Mental Health Clinic, 1987-91; asst. clin. prof. Adelphi U., Derner Inst., Garden City, N.Y., 1989—; pvt. practice clin. psychologist/psychoanalyst New City, N.Y., 1990—; faculty supr. Minn. Inst. Contemporary Psychoanalysis, Mpls.-St. Paul, 1996—, continuing edn. faculty, N.Y. Psychol. Assn. for Psycholanalysis, 1998—; supr. and faculty Nat. Tng. Program for Psychoanalysis, N.Y. Co-author: treating the Adult Survivor of Childhood Sexual Abuse, 1994, Contemporary Psychodynamic Supervision, 2000; contbr. chpts. to books, articles to profl. jours. Mem. APA, Adelphi Soc. Psychoanalysis and Psychotherapy. Avocations: hiking, cooking, theater, symphony, reading. Home and Office: 5 Opal Ct New City NY 10956

FRAZER, STUART HARRISON, III, cotton merchant; b. Montgomery, Ala., Feb. 13, 1948; s. Stuart Harrison Jr. and Myrta Frances (Garrett) F.; m. Linda Gail Patterson, Nov. 21, 1971 (div. 1983); 1 child, Heather Allison; m. Mary Prue Coleman, Oct. 28, 1983; children: Laura Goldman, Meredith Jane. Student, Huntingdon Coll., Montgomery, 1966-68, Auburn (Ala.) U., 1970-73. V.p. Weil Bros. Cotton Inc., Montgomery, 1970-88; sr. v.p. Rollins Cotton Co., Montgomery, 1988-92, pres., 1992-94; pres. Prodn. Mktg., Montgomery, 1994—; mem. USDA adv. com. con Cotton Clasing, Washington, 1988—; bd. dirs. N.Y. Cotton Exch., Cotton Coun. Internat., Nat. Cotton Coun.; mem. agrl. adv. com. to Commodity Futures Trading Commn., Washington. Mem. YMCA Boys Work Com., pres. 1986-87. With U.S. Army, 1968-69. Mem. Am. Cotton Shippers Assn. (dir., 1st v.p. 1992, 2nd v.p. 1991, pres. 1993), Nat. Cotton Coun., Atlantic Cotton Assn. (pres. 1981-82), Montgomery Cotton Exch. (pres. 1976—), Montgomery Country Club. Episcopalian. Home: 2517 Darrington Rd Montgomery AL 36111-1527 Office: Prodn Mktg PO Box 210309 Montgomery AL 36121-0309

FRAZHO, GREGORY JOHN, non-commissioned officer; b. Detroit, Sept. 23, 1969; s. Michael Thomas and Laurene Cherie Frazho. BA in History, Mich. State U., 1992. Retail sales assoc. MC Sporting Goods, Okemos, Mich., 1992-93; enlisted USN, advanced through grades to 1st class petty officer, 1998; recruit and co. clk. Co. 951, Great Lakes, Ill., 1993; sect. leader Navy Student Co., Indpls., 1993-94; ship's journalist USS America, Norfolk, Va., 1994-96; leading petty officer, awards clk. Naval Media Ctr., Sasebo, Kyushu, Japan, 1996-98; pub. affairs officer Navy Recruiting Dist., New Orleans, 1998—. Navy recruiting rep. Mayor's Mil. Adv. Com., New Orleans, 1998—. Decorated Navy and Marine Corps Commendation medal, NATO medal. Avocations: ice hockey, in-line skating, music, mountain bike riding, comedy. E-Mail: frazhog@yahoo.com.

FRAZIER, LYN, psycholinguist; b. Madison, Wis., Oct. 15, 1952; d. Lyman Frazier. BA in linguistics, Univ. Wis., 1974; MA in linguistics, Univ. Conn., 1976, PhD in linguistcs, 1978. Prof. Univ. Mass., Amherst, 1978—; linguistics adv. bd. NSF, 1990-92; scientific adv. coun. MAx Planck Inst., for Psycholinguistics, The Netherlands, 1994-99. Author: On Sentence Interpretation, 1999; co-author: Construal, 1996; co-editor: Perspectives on Sentences Processing,1 994, Language Processing and Language Acquisition, 1990. Recipient rsch. grants Nat. Sci. Found., Nat. Inst. Health, Nat. Inst. of Mental Health, Nat. Inst. Health Training. E-mail: lyn@linguist.umass.edu. Office: Univ Mass Linguistics S Coll Amherst MA 01003

FRAZIER-CLEMONS, BRENDA, lawyer, municipal official; b. Phila., June 18, 1939; d. Paris Luster and Mattie Laura Frazier; 1 child, Robert Adam. BA, Rutgers U., 1960; MAT, U. Chgo., 1962; PhD, U. Madrid, 1965; JD, Temple U., 1987. Prof., dean Howard U., Washington, 1975-76, 79-84; legis. chief City Coun. Phila., 1988—. Chair St. Barnabas Sch., Phila., 1995-98. Fulbright fellow. Mem. Nat. Bar Assn., Temple Am. Inn Ct. (CLE coord.), Phi Beta Kappa. Fax: 215-686-1938. Office: City Coun Phila 577 City Hall Philadelphia PA 19107-3201

FREAR, JON S., pet services company executive; b. Salt Lake City, July 23, 1973; s. Joseph W. and Linda Joyce Frear; m. Angela Marie Blair, Jan. 25, 1996; children: Joshua, Brielle. Owner Rocky Mountain Kennels, Sandy, Utah, 1991-94; pres., CEO, Rocky Mountain KC Co., Salt Lake City, 1993—, Internat. League Pet Svcs., Salt Lake City, 1993—; pres. Apollo Group, Salt Lake City, 1998—. Author: (children's book) The Life of a Young Inventor, Book 1, 1996, The S.P.I.C.E. Book, 1999. Mem. LDS Ch. Avocations: writing, cooking, camping, hiking.

FREAS, GEORGE WILSON, II, computer consultant; b. Franklin, Ky., Oct. 27, 1955; s. George Wilson and Audrey Carolyn Freas; m. Cynthia Anne Fleming, Feb. 19, 1984 (div. Oct. 1990); 1 child, Alexander Morange. BS in Computer Sci., Western Ky. U., 1979; MS in Computer Sci., U. Ala., Huntsville, 1994. Pres. Synergistic Cons., Inc., Huntsville, 1991—; software cons. Bell South Telecom., Birmingham, Ala., 1995-98; software cons. Boeing Internat. Space Sta. Marshall Space Flight Ctr., Ala., 1999—; adj. prof. Am. Inst. for Computer Sci., Birmingham, Ala., 1997—. Author: Canny Canon, 1990; author: (software) GEN7 Desktop, 1993, LALL-LL(1), 1992. Home: PO Box 2885 Huntsville AL 35804-2885 Office: Synergistic Consultants Inc PO Box 18888 Huntsville AL 35804-8888

FRÉCHETTE, LOUISE, Canadian diplomat. With dept. external affairs Govt. of Can., from early 1970s, amb. to Argentina and Uruguay, 1985; asst. dep. min. for L.Am. and Caribbean Ministry of Fgn. Affairs, 1988, asst. dep. min. for internat. econ. and trade policy, 1991-92; amb. to UN, 1992-94; assoc. dep. min. Can. Dept. Fin., 1994-95, Can. Dept. of Fin., 1995; dep. minister def. Govt. of Can., 1995-98; dep. sec. gen. UN, 1998—.

FRECKELTON, IAN RICHARD, barrister; b. Durban, South Africa, May 1, 1958; s. Brian and Joan (Lloyd) F.; m. Helen Mary Maloney, Oct. 6, 1990; children: Leo Henry, Julia Millicent. BA, Sydney U., 1980, LLB, 1982; PhD, Griffith U. From legal officer to sr. legal officer Australian Law Reform Commn., Sydney, 1982-86; counsel Police Complaints Authority, Melbourne, Australia, 1986-88; barrister Melbourne, 1988—; adj. prof. law and legal studies La Trobe U., Melbourne, 1998—; prof. medicine. Monash U., Melbourne, 1999—. Author: The Trial of the Expert, 1987, Indictable Offences in Victoria, 1999, Controversies in Health Law, 1999, Victorian Criminal Law, Investigation and Procedure, Vols. 1-3, 2000; co-author: Expert Evidence, vols. 1-5, 1993—, The Law of Expert Evidence, 1999, The Expert in Criminal Law, 1999, The Expert in Family Law, 1999, Clinical Injuries Compensation: Law and Practice, 2000, Police in Our Society, 1987; editor Jour. Law & Medicine, 1993—; Editor-in-chief Psychiatry Psychology and Law, 1993—; internat. editor: Behavioral Scis. and the Law, 1998—. V.p. Victorian Coun. Civil Liberties, Melbourne, 1991-92, 96-97; mem. Social Security Appeals Tribunal, Melbourne, 1989-93, Mental Health Review Bd. Victoria, 1996—, Psychosurgery Review Bd. Victoria, 1997—, Psychologists Registration Bd. Victoria, 1999—. Mem. Australian and New Zealand Assn. Psychiatry and Psychology Law (life mem., pres. 1991-97). Avocations: swimming, chess, mediaeval music. Office: Owen Dixon Chambers, 205 William St, Melbourne VIC 3000, Australia

FRED, ROGERS MURRAY, III, veterinary oncologist; b. Leesburg, Va., July 22, 1955; s. Rogers Murray Jr. and Barbara Ann (Stewart) F.; m. Kimberly Edna Shepherd, Oct. 15, 1989; 1 child, Asa Hugh Shepherd. BS, Washington and Lee U., 1977; postgrad., U. Ga., 1979-81; DVM, Va. Poly. Inst., 1985. Staff veterinarian Abbey Animal Hosp., Balt., 1986-89; resident in vet. oncology U. Pa., Phila., 1989-91; clin. oncologist Red Bank (N.J.) Vet. Hosp. & Referral Svc., 1991—; lectr. in field. Co-author: Connective Tissues in Health & Disease, 1980. Bd. dirs. Ebenezer Chs. and Cemetery Co., Bloomfield, Va., 1986—, Monmouth Hills (N.J.), Inc. Mem. SCV (camp comdr. 1988-90), Am. Vet. Med. Assn., Vet. Cancer Soc., N.J. Vet. Med. Assn., Civil War Preservation Trust, Phi Kappa Phi, Phi Zeta. Republican. Episcopalian. Avocations: reading, walking, battlefield touring, bird watching. Home: 15 Monmouth Hills Highlands NJ 07732 Office: Red Bank Vet Hosp 210 Newman Springs Rd Red Bank NJ 07701-1465

FREDERICK, CRAIG MATTHEW, sculptor; b. New Britain, Conn., Feb. 27, 1963; s. Theodore John and Joyce Chase Frederick; m. Laura Jean Wixon, Oct. 4, 1997. BA in Geology and Biology, Skidmore Coll., 1985; MFA in Sculpture, U. Pa., 1992. Tchr. St. Mary's Hall, San Antonio, 1986-89, U. Pa., Phila., 1991, Galveston (Tex.) Coll., 1992-94; sculptor The Bob Wilson Art Foundry, Houston, 1993-94; sculptor, owner Sculpture by Craig, New Britain, 1994—; tchr. The Black Brick Studio and Gallery, Plainville, Conn., 1994—; devel. bd. mem. N.B. Landmark Com., City Hall, New Britain, 1994-95, Summer Learning Arts Mentorship, 1997; lectr. in field. One-man shows include The Colonade, Phila., 1991, The Stanley Works World Hdqrs., Farmington, Conn., 1992, The Loomis Chaffee Sch., Windsor, Conn., 1992, Two Houston Ctr., 1993, The Geary Gallery, Darien, Conn., 1996, The Black Brick Studio and Gallery, Plainville, 1997, 98; exhibited at group shows at Inst. Contemporary Art, Phila., 1990, Meyerson Gallery, U. Pa., 1991, 92, Gutman Ctr., New Hope, Pa., 1992, Galveston (Tex.) Art Ctr., 1992, Machorro Gallery, Houston, 1993, Jack Meier Gallery, Houston, 1993, Black Brick Studio and Gallery, Plainville, 1994, 96, 98, New Britain Mus. Am. Art, 1995, New Britain Art League, 1995, Pump House Gallery, Hartford, Conn., 1997, Hartford Fine Art and Framing, 1998, Pfizer, Inc., Groton, Conn., 1998, 99, Charter Oak Cultural Ctr., Hartford, 1998, Bradley Internat. Airport Exhbn. Series, 2000; represented in permanent collections New Britain Pub. Libr., Petrolios Mexicanos, Mexico City, Art Foundry Carpino, Houston, Yarde Metals, Inc., Bristol, Conn.; commissions include ctr. of downtown plz., City of New Britain, 2000. Cons., mem. Vision New Britain, 1994-97; mem. long range planning com. New Britain Mus. Am. Art, 1995-97; mem., activist New Britain Archtl. Preservation Trust, 1996-97; original mem. initial concepts The New Arch Com., New Britain, 1997-98. Holt/Dupont grantee Holt/Dupont Orgns., San Antonio, 1988. Mem. Internat. Sculpture Ctr., Greater New Britain Arts Alliance (co-founder, pres. 1996-97), Guild.Com (represented artist). E-mail: SculptByC@aol.com.

FREDERICK, LOURDUSAMY, electrical company executive; b. Tiruchirappalli, India, June 2, 1969; s. Maria Louis Lourdusamy and Lourdusamy Philomine. Diploma in elec. engring., S.J. Poly., Bangalore, India, 1988; BEE, U. Visveshvaraya, Bangalore, 1992; M in Tech., Indian Inst. Tech., Kanpur, 1998. Grad. trainee M/S Kirloskar Elec. Co. Ltd., Bangalore, India, 1992-93, design engr., 1993-96, sr. design engr., 1998—. Avocations: reading, gardening, interior decoration. Home: 3/3-114C Louis Colony, East Ambikapuram, Tiruchirappalli 620 004, India Office: Kirloskar Elec Co Ltd, Unit I PB 5555 Malleswaram, Bangalore 560 055, India

FREDERICKS, HENRY JACOB, lawyer; b. St. Louis, Dec. 1, 1925; s. Henry Jacob III and Mary Elizabeth (Pieron) F.; m. Marjorie Helen Kiely, 1951 (div. 1962; dec.); children: Joseph Henry, James Andrew, Elizabeth Ann.; m. Susan Kay Brennecke, 1971 (div. 1991); 1 child, William Michael; m. Deborah Jean Rose, 1992; 1 child, Daniel Baptise Jerome. JD, St. Louis U., 1950; postgrad., Sch. Commerce and Fin., 1945-47. Bar: Mo. 1950, U.S. Dist. Ct. (ea. and so. dists.) Mo. 1951, U.S. Ct. Appeals (8th cir.) 1978, U.S. Supreme Ct. 1986. Pvt. practice St. Louis County, 1950-80; assoc. Mark D. Eagleton, St. Louis, 1960, Goldenhersh Fredericks & Newman, St. Louis, 1961-69, Friedman and Fredericks, St. Louis, 1969-81; chief trial atty. for cir. atty. St. Louis, 1955, 1st asst. to cir. atty. Thomas F. Eagleton, 1987, spl. asst. to cir. attys., 1960-81; asst. U.S. atty. Ea. Dist. Mo., Dept. Justice, 1981—; lectr. in field; chmn. bd. Gateway Boxing Promotions, Inc. Mem. Mo. Athletic Commn., 1974-76, boxing chmn. Mo. Athletic Commn. and AAU, 1977. Served with USAAF, 1943-46, ETO. Decorated Air medal with 4 battle stars. Mem. ABA, Mo. Bar Assn., St. Louis County Bar Assn., Am. Trial Lawyers Assn., Internat. Platform Assn., St. Louis Amateur Boxing Assn., Inc. (pres.), Delta Theta Phi. Home: PO Box 612 Chesterfield MO 63006-0612 Office: US Ct and Custom House Office US Atty Saint Louis MO 63101

FREDERICKS, J. RICHARD, ambassador; b. Detroit; m. Stephanie Sorensen; children: Matthew, Colleen, Will. BA in Bus. Adminstrn., Georgetown U.; MBA, Columbia U. Securities analyst Dean Witter, 1970-77; ptnr. Shuman, Agnew & Co., 1977; ptnr. Montgomery Securities (now Bank of Am. Securities), sr. mng. dir. investment rsch.; amb. to Switzerland and Liechtenstein Bern, 1999—. Office: US Embassy, Jubilaumstr 93, 3005 Bern Switzerland*

FREDERICKS, ROBERT JOSEPH, language company executive; b. N.Y.C., Dec. 26, 1934; s. Harold D. and Mary E. (McCarthy) F.; m. Jeanette C. Kubin, July 7, 1984. BS in Chemistry, Villanova U., 1957; MS in Chemistry, St. Joseph's Coll., Phila., 1959; PhD in Chemistry, Lehigh U., 1965. Rsch. chemist GAF Corp., Easton, Pa., 1960-67; rsch. supr. Allied Chem. Corp., Morristown, N.J., 1968-72; mgr. analytical chemistry Ethicon, Inc., Somerville, N.J., 1972-74; dir. rsch. svcs. Ethicon, Inc., Somerville, 1974-76, assoc. dir. rsch., 1976-78; v.p. rsch. and devel. Surgikos, Piscataway, N.J., 1978-79, Johnson & Johnson Dental Products Co., East Windsor, N.J., 1980-82; sr. v.p. and gen. mgr. Biosci. Med. Products, Somerville, N.J., 1982-85; pres. Allen Transl. Svc., Morristown, N.J., 1985—. Author: X-Ray Diffraction for the Industrial Chemist, 1971; contbr. articles to profl. jours. Pres. Morris County Hist. Soc., Morristown, 1982-86, trustee, 1975-93; pres. Washington Assn. N.J., Morristown, 1988-92, 93-99, trustee, 1983—, trustee Craftsman Farms Found., 1994; mem. adv. bd. New Philharm., N.J., 1992-99, trustee, 1994-98, 1st v.p., 1995-98; hon. historian Twp. of Morris, 1992—. Served to lt. (j.g.) USN, 1958-60. Recipient Achievement award Washington Assn., 2000. Mem. AAAS, Am. Chem. Soc., N.Y. Acad. Scis., Am. Assn. Sovereign Mil. Order of Malta, Morristown Field Club, Morristown Club (bd. govs. 1996—, v.p. 1998, pres. 1999—), Morristown Rotary Club (bd. dirs. 1992-93), Sigma Xi, Delta Epsilon Sigma. Republican. Roman Catholic. Avocations: tennis, gardening. Home: 16 Butterworth Dr Morristown NJ 07960-2625

FREDERICKS, SHARON KAY, nurse's aide; b. Grand Rapids, Mich., July 12, 1942; d. Leroy and Edith Luella (Crawford) F. Cert. in Interior Decorating, LaSalle U., 1975; AAS, Community Svc. Asst., Kalamazoo Valley Coll., 1982; assoc. paralegal studies, Internat. Corr. Schs., Scranton, Pa., 1993; AAS in Bus. Mgmt., Davenport Coll., 1994, BBA in Bus. Adminstrn., 1997. Cashier Goodwill Industries, Battle Creek, Mich., 1963; dishwasher Woolworths, Kalamazoo, 1963; nurses aide Mary L. Bocher, Kalamazoo, 1964-69, Sisters St. Joseph, Nazareth, Mich., 1976-98; kitchen aide Saga Foods, Kalamazoo Valley C.C., 1981-82, Saga Foods, Nazareth Coll., 1983-84; ind. sales rep. Avon, 2000—. Vol. Portage Ctrl. Jr. and Sr. High Sch., 1961-62, Bronson Meth. Hosp., Kalamazoo, 1961-62; vol. nurse aide ARC, 1964-69, Bloodmobiles Bronson Meth. Hosp., 1970-75, Borgess Med. Ctr., 1977; sec.-treas. 3d Order St. Francis Secular, 1976-79, pres., dir. pres. pub. rels. and bulls., 1979-81; participant neighborhood watch Vine Neighborhood, Kalamazoo, 1985-88; vol. Cath. Family Svcs., 1991—; vol., adminstrv. aide, Kalamazoo, 1991—; vol. monitor Kalamazoo Women's Festival, 1991, 92; mem. grounds com. New Horizon Village, 1998, neighborhood watch com., 1999. Thomas F. Reed Jr. scholar Davenport Coll., 1993; recipient John Edgar Hoover gold medal, 1991; named Vol. of Month, Kalamazoo Regional Psychiat. Hosp., July 1976; named Vol. of Week, Cath. Family Svcs., Sept. 13, 1993, Oct. 1995. Mem. Davenport U. Alumni Assn. Roman Catholic. Avocations: photography, textile painting, helping people, reading, learning wildlife, environmental policies, pet policies, governmental policies. Home: 2310 Inverness Ln Apt 204 Kalamazoo MI 49048-1459

FREDERICKS, WARD ARTHUR, venture capitalist, food industry consultant; b. Tarrytown, N.Y., Dec. 24, 1939; s. Arthur George and Evelyn (Smith) F.; m. Patricia A. Sexton, June 12, 1960; children: Corrine E., Lorrine L., Ward A. BS cum laude, Mich. State U., 1962, MBA, 1963, PhD. Assoc. dir. Technics Group, Grand Rapids, Mich., 1964-68; gen. mgr. logistics systems Massey-Ferguson, Inc., Toronto, Ont., Can., 1968-69, v.p. mgmt. svcs., comptr., 1969-73, sr. v.p. fin., dir. fin. Americas, 1975—; comptr. Massey-Ferguson Ltd., Toronto, Ont., Can., 1973-75; prin. W.B. Saunders & Co., Washington, 1962—; sr. v.p. mktg. Massey.Ferguson, Inc., 1975-78, also pres., gen. mgr. tractor divsn., 1978-80; gen. mgr. Rockwell Graphic Sys., 1980-82; pres. Goss Co.; v.p. ops. Rockwell Internat., Pitts., 1980-84; v.p. Fed. MOG, 1983-84; chmn. MIXTEC Group LLC, 1998—; also dir., chmn.; prin. Venture Assocs., 1993—; dir. Polyfet RF, Inc., Venture Assocs., Badger Horthland, Inc., MST, Inc., Calif., Tech-Mark Group, Inc., Spectra Tech., Inc., Mixtec Group-Venture Capital, Inc., Unicorn Corp., Mixtec Food Group Calif., Mixtec Signal Tech., Harry Ferguson, Inc., M.F. Credit Corp., M.F. Credit Co. Can Ltd.; chmn. Produce-Careers.com., 2000—. Author: (with Edward Smykay) Physical Distribution Management, 1974; author: Management Vision, 1988, Competitive Advantage in Technology Organizations, 1986, Competitive Advantage in Technology Firms, 1996; contbr. articles to profl. jours. Bd. dirs., mem. exec. com. Des Moines Symphony, 1975-79; exec. com. Conejo Symphony, pres., 1988-90; pres. Westlake Village Cultural Found., 1991; mem. exec. com. Alliance for Arts; pres. Conejo Valley Indsl. Assn., 1990, 93; mem. Constn. Bicentennial Com., 1987-88, Ventura County Airport Commn., 1995—, La Quinta Arts Found., World Affairs Coun. of the Desert; bd. dirs. Ventura County Bus. Incubator, 1996—; v.p. Com. Leaders Club, 1988, pres., 1989-90, pres. Westlake Cultural Found., 1991; vice chair Alliance for the Arts; bd. regents Calif. Lutheran U., 1990-99, chmn. acad. affairs, 1993-99, exec. com., 1992—, chmn. acad. affairs, 1992-99, vice chmn., 1997-98; v.p. Aviation C.C. of Calif.; pres. coun. McCallen Theater, Palm Desert. Fellow Am. Transp. Assn., 1962-63, Remlose, 1962-63; mem. AAAS, IEEE, SAR, Am. Mktg. Assn., Nat. Coun. Phys. Distbn. Mgmt. (exec. com. 1974), Produce Mktg. Assn., United Fresh Fruit and Vegetable Assn., Internat. Fresh-Cut Produce Assn., Soc. Automotive Engrs., U.S. Strategic Inst., Tech. Execs. Forum (Tech. Corridor 100 award 1989), Internat. Food Mfg. Assn., Produce Mktg. Assn., Toronto Bd. Trade, Westlake Village C. of C. (chmn. 1990), Cochella Valley Community Concerts Assn. (bd. dirs. 1992-95), Old Crows, Assn. Advanced Tech. Edn., Air Force Assn., Aerospace Soc., Experimental Aircraft Assn., Mil. Order World Wars, Conf. Air Force (Col.), Westlake Village C. of C. (chmn. bd. 1990-91), Republican Ctrl. Com., State of Calif., 1993-98, Community Leaders Cluyb, Pres.'s Club Mich. State U., North Ranch Country Club, Indian Wells Country Club, Sherwood Country Club, St. Georges Club (U.K.), Aviation Country Club of Calif. (v.p. 1999, pres. 2000), Rotary, Flying Rotorians, World Affairs Coun., Beta Gamma Sigma. Lutheran. Home: 75375 Painted Desert Dr Indian Wells CA 92210 Office: 31255 Cedar Valley Dr Westlake Village CA 91362-4014

FREDGA, KERSTIN, science academy educator; b. 1935. PhD in Astrophysics, Stockholms U. Pres. Royal Swedish Acad. of Scis., Stockholm, 1994-97; prof. sci. Rymdstyrelsen, Sweden, 1973-89; rsch. assoc. NASA Goddard Space Flight Ctr., 1964-66, 68; rsch. asst. Utrecht U., 1968-71, Kungliga Tekniska Hogskolan, 1966-67, 71-73; dir. gen., chmn. of bd. Swedish Nat. Space Bd., 1989-98; prof. Alfvén lab. Royal Inst. Tech., Stockholm, 1998—. Editl. bd. chmn. Forskning och framsteg, 1981-84.

FREDRICK, SUSAN WALKER, tax company manager; b. Painesville, Ohio, Nov. 17, 1948; d. Floyd Clayton and Margaret (Merkel) Walker; m. Stephan Douglas Fredrick, Oct. 20, 1973. BS, Mt. Union Coll., Alliance, Ohio, 1970; MS, U. Conn., 1973. Research asst. Boyce Thompson Inst., Yonkers, N.Y., 1971-74; dir. quality control Lawley, Matusky, Skelly, Tappan, N.Y., 1974-75; field supr. Ecological Analysts, Middletown, N.Y., 1975-76; scientist Pandullo Quirk Assocs., Wayne, N.J., 1976-78; editor Biosis. Info. Service, Phila., 1978-80; tax preparer H&R Block, Inc., King of Prussia, Pa., 1978-80; dist. mgr. H&R Block, Inc., Malvern, Pa., 1980—; guest lectr. Temple U., 1981-86. Mem. Nat. Assn. Enrolled Agts., Pa. Soc. Enrolled Agts., Nat. Assn. Underwater Instrs. (active instr.), Keystone Divers Club (West Chester, Pa.). Avocations: scuba diving, cross-country skiing, swimming. Office: Lincoln Ct Shopping Ctr PO Box 1174 Frazer PA 19355-0949

FREDRIK, BURRY, theatrical producer, director; b. N.Y.C., Aug. 9, 1925; d. Fredric Kreuger and Erna Anita (Burry) Gerber; m. Gerard E. Meunier, Dec. 27, 1945 (div. 1949). Grad., Sarah Lawrence Coll., 1947. Ind. theatrical dir., producer U.S. and abroad, 1955—; lit. mgr., dir. Boston Post Road Stage Co., 1988-92; artistic dir. Fairfield County Stage Co. (formerly Boston Post Road Stage), 1992-93. Producer: (Broadway plays) Too Good To Be True, 1964-65 (nominated Tony award 1965), Travesties, 1975-76 (Tony award 1976), An Almost Perfect Person, 1977, The Night of the Tribades, 1978, To Grandmother's House We Go, 1981, The Royal Family, 1975-76, (off-Broadway plays) Thieves Carnival, 1955 (Spl. Tony award 1955), Exiles, 1956 (OBIE award 1956), Buried Child (Pulitzer prize 1980); dir.: (nat. tours) Misalliance, 1953, Milk and Honey, 1963, Dark at the Top of the Stairs, 1958, Dear Love, 1971, To Grandmother's House We Go, 1982, (off-Broadway prodns.) The Decameron, 1961, Catholic School Girls, 1981, (Broadway prodn.) Wild and Wonderful, 1972. Chmn. Weston Commn. for Arts, 1997-2000; mem. fin. commn./bd. trustees Long Wharf Theatre, New Haven, 1998-2000, trustee, 1999—. Home: 51 Hillside Rd N Weston CT 06883-1513

FREE, ANN COTTRELL, writer; b. June 4, 1916; d. Emmett Drewry and Emily (Blake) Cottrell; m. James Stillman Free, Feb. 24, 1950; 1 child, Elissa. Grad., Collegiate Sch. for Girls, Richmond, 1934; student Richmond divsn., Coll. William and Mary (now Va. Commonwealth U.), 1934-36; AB, Barnard Coll. Columbia U., 1938. Reporter Richmond Times Dispatch, 1938-40; Washington corr. Newsweek, 1940-41, Chgo. Sun, 1941-43, N.Y. Herald Tribune, 1943-46; pub. info. dir., China corr. UN Relief-Rehab. Adminstrn., China Mission, Shanghai, 1946-47; corr. Mid. and Near East and Europe, 1947-48; writer-photographer Marshall Plan, Washington/Western Europe, 1949-50; Washington corr. N.Am. Newspaper Alliance, 1955-60; contbg. editor Between the Species; former Washington editor EnviroSouth Quar., 1977-82; pres. Flying Fox Press. Author: Forever the Wild Mare, 1963, Animals, Nature and Albert Schweitzer, 1982, No Room, Save in the Heart, 1987, Since Silent Spring: Our Debt to Albert Schweitzer and Rachel Carson, 1992; contbr. newspapers and mags., including Washington Star and Washington Post. Mem. Friends of the Rachel Carson Nat. Wildlife Refuge (hon. founding mem.); chmn. Mrs. Roosevelt's Press Conf. Assn., 1943; cons. expert Rachel Carson Coun.; v.p. Vieques (P.R.) Humane Soc.; past coord. Albert Schweitzer Summer Fellows Program; past bd. dirs. Albert Schweitzer Fellowship; pres. Albert Schweitzer Coun. on Animals and Environment; trustee Albert Schweitzer Animal Welfare Fund; recorded oral history for Columbia U. Animal Advocacy Archives, 1999. Recipient Dodd Mead-Boys' Life Writing award, 1963, Albert Schweitzer medal, Animal Welfare Inst., 1963, Jr. Book award cert. Boys Clubs of Am., 1964, Humanitarian of Yr. awards Washington Animal Rescue League, 1971, Montgomery County Humane Soc., 1971, Washington Humane Soc., 1983, News Writing award Dog Writers Assn. Am., 1975, 78, Rachel Carson Legacy award, 1987, Disting. Alumni award The Collegiate Schs., 1992, Cert. Appreciation Dept. of Interior Fish and Wildlife Svc. for role in establishing Rachel Carson Nat. Wildlife Refuge, 1995, Lifetime Svc. award Animal Rescue League, 1997; inducted Va. Comms. Hall of Fame, 1996. Mem. Soc. Woman Geographers, Nat. Press Club, Am. News Women's Club. Home: 4700 Jamestown Rd Bethesda MD 20816-2923 also: 56 Bell's Ln Lantz Mill Edinburg VA 22824

FREE, MARY MOORE, biological and medical anthropologist; b. Paris, Tex., Mar. 6, 1933; d. Dudley Crawford and Margie Lou (Moore) Hubbard; m. Dwight Allen Free Jr., June 26, 1954 (dec.); children: Hardy (dec.), Dudley (dec.), Margery, Caroline. Student, Ward-Belmont Coll., 1951; BS, So. Meth. U., 1954, MLA, 1981, MA, 1987, PhD, 1989. Instr. So. Meth. U., Dallas, 1982-89, prof. continuing edn., 1989-90; prof. So. Meth. U., Dedman Coll., Dallas, 1990—; adj. asst. prof. dept. anthropology So. Meth. U., Dallas, 1990—; prof. Richland C.C., Dallas, 1986; house anthropologist Baylor U. Med. Ctr., mem. adv. bd. Inst. for Study of Earth and Man, 1995, preceptor clin. edn. affiliation, 1990—, chair Class 1954 sustentation drive, organ/tissue transplantation task force, 1997; cardiothoracic transplantation team Baylor U. Med. Ctr., S.W. transplantation team Baylor U. Med. Ctr./U. Tex. Southwestern Med. Sch., 1990— (cardiothoracic transplantation award for excellence in svc., 1998); adv. bd. geriatrics Vis. Nurse Assn., Dallas, 1984-91; presenter in field anthropology, medicine, women's issues; bd. Dedman Coll. SMU Excellence in Sci. Lecture Series, Dallas Soc. SMU, Collegium de Vinci, SMU; contbr. AMA/JAMA protocol on authorship; spokesperson, adv. bd. Lisa Landry Childress Found. for Organ Donation Awareness. Author: The Private World of the Hermitage: Lifestyles of the Rich and Old in an Elite Retirement Home, 1995; contbr. chpts. in sci. books, ednl. TV, and articles to Anthropology Newsletter, Am. Anthropologist, Am. Jour. Cardiology, Cahiers de Sociologie Economique et Culturelle-Ethnopsycholie, Jour. Heart Failure, Jour. Internat. Soc. Dermatology, Jour. Leadership Ctr., Baylor Health Care System; mem. editl. bd. Baylor U. Med. Ctr. Procs.; editor/contbr. Jour. Kimberly H. Courtwright and Joseph W. Summers Inst. of Metabolic Disease, BUMC, 1998; contbr. articles to profl. jours. Bd. dirs. New Hearts and Lungs, Baylor Med. Ctr., 1994—, Lisa Landry Childress Found. for Organ Donor Awareness, Victims Outreach, 1997—, Isis Soc. and internat. issues com. Baylor U. Med. Ctr.; active various svc. and social orgns. Named one of Notable Women of Tex., 1984; recipient Outstanding Svc. Cardiothoracic Transplantation award Baylor U. Med. Ctr., 1998; provide Dr. Mary Moore Free Endowment for grad. study fieldwork in anthropology So. Meth. U. Fellow Am. Anthrop. Assn., Inst. for Study of Earth and Man; mem. AAAS, Internat. Soc. Heart Failure (sci. adv. bd.), Internat. Acad. Cardiology Inc. (internat. sci. adv. bd.), Internat. Congress Heart Disease (internat. sci. adv. bd.), Internat. Soc. Heart Disease (sci. adv. bd.), Soc. Heart Edn. (sci. adv. bd.), Dallas Women's Club, Dallas Petroleum Club, Brook Hollow Golf Club, Pi Beta Phi. Methodist. Achievements include development of position of house anthropologist in non-academic medical center, community medicine program; cross-cultural research on old age, women and cardiology. Home: 4356 Edmondson Ave Dallas TX 75205-2602 Office: Baylor U Med Ctr 3500 Gaston Ave Dallas TX 75246-2096

FREEBAIRN, JOHN WILLIAM, economics educator; b. Grenfell, Australia, Mar. 21, 1944; s. William Maxwell and Bertha Elize (Schwarzlose) F.; m. Margaret Leigh Gordon, 1970; children: Kristine Tania, Pam Alice. B Agrl. Econs., UNE, 1965, M Agrl. Econs., 1968; PhD, U. Calif., Davis, 1971. Economist New South Wales Dept. Agr., Sydney, Australia, 1965-68, 72-74; rsch. fellow ANU, Canberra, Australia, 1974-76; prof., dean La Trobe U., Melbourne, Australia, 1976-84; rsch. dir. Bus. Coun. Australia, Melbourne, 1984-86; prof. econs. Monash U., Melbourne, 1986-95, U. Melbourne, 1996—; cons. govt. and pvt. industry orgns., 1974—. Author: Spending and Taxing, 1988; contbr. articles to econs. publs. Treas., Rosanne East High Sch., Melbourne, 1986-87, pres., 1987-91. Mem. Am. Econ. Assn., Econ. Soc. Australia, Australian Agrl. Econs. Soc. (pres. 1981), Am. Agrl. Econs. Assn. Office: U Melbourne, Dept Economics, Parkville Victoria 3052, Australia

FREEBODY, PETER RAYMOND, literacy and language educator; b. Sydney, NSW, Australia, Aug. 12, 1950; s. Raymond Noel and Josephine

Mary (Doyle) F.; m. Virginia Lee Thomas, May 18, 1973; children: Georgia Lee, Kelly Alexandra, Simon Patrick. BA with 1st class honors, Sydney U., 1972; PhD, U. Ill., 1980; diploma in edn., Sydney Tchr.'s Coll., 1973. Lectr. U. New Eng., Armidale, NSW, 1981-91; prof. Griffith U., Brisbane, Queensland, Australia, 1992—. Office: Griffith U Ctr, Ctr for Literacy & Lang, 4122 Brisbane Australia

FREEBORN, MICHAEL D., lawyer; b. Mpls., June 30, 1946; s. Andrew W. and Verena M. (Keller) F.; m. Nancie L. Siebel, Oct. 19, 1947; children: Christopher A., Nathan M., Joel C., Paul K. BS, USAF Acad., 1968; MBA, U. Chgo., 1975; JD, Ind. U., 1972. Bar: Ill. 1972, Ind. 1972. Assoc., ptnr. Rooks, Pitts & Poust, Chgo., 1972-83; ptnr. Freeborn & Peters, Chgo., 1983—; writer, lectr. in field. Assoc. editor Ind. Law Rev., 1970-71. Vice chmn. Voices for Ill. Children, 1993—; bd. dirs. Constnl. Rights Found. Chgo., 1996—, Chgo. Youth Ctrs., 1998—; chmn. citizens adv. coun. Ill. Coastal Zone Mgmt. Program, Chgo., 1979. Capt. USAF, 1968-72. Recipient Founders Day award Ind. U. Law Sch., 1972. Mem. Ill. Bar Assn., Ind. Bar Assn., Union League, Legal (Chgo.). Lutheran. Office: Freeborn & Peters 311 S Wacker Dr Ste 3000 Chicago IL 60606-6679

FREED, GARY E., pediatrician; b. Phila., June 30, 1947; s. Isadore and Ruth (Karp) F.; m. Suzanne Balis, June 8, 1969; children: Jennifer, Rebecca. BS, U. Pitts., 1969; DO, Coll. Osteopathic Med., 1973. Diplomate Am. Bd. Pediats. Intern Cooper Med. Ctr., Camden, N.J., 1973-74; pediatric resident Thomas Jefferson U., Phila., 1974-76; physician Haddon Pediat. Group, Hadden Heights, N.J., 1976-84; clin. dir. Am. SIOS Inst., Atlanta, 1987; dir. nursing Grody Meml. Hosp., Atlanta, 1992-96; dir. Emory Egleston Apnea Ctr., Atlanta, 1996—; dir. pediat. clerkship Emory U., Atlanta, 1993—; Pres. Am. Assn. SIDS Prevention Physicians, Atlanta, 1993, 97, 98. Author: Pediatric Clinics of North America, 1994, editor 1996. E-mail: gary.freed@choa.org. Office: Emory Univ 2030 Ridgewood Dr NE Atlanta GA 30322-1031

FREED, MELVYN NORRIS, retired higher education educator, writer; b. Kansas City, Mo., Apr. 30, 1937; s. Carl and Betty (Wachtel) F.; m. Janet Lea Triplitt, Dec. 26, 1971; children: David A., Edward L. BA in Econs. with distinction, U. Mo., Kansas City, 1959; MS in Edn., So. Ill. U., Carbondale, 1962, PhD in Higher Edn., 1965. Dir. instl. rsch. Ark. State U., Jonesboro, 1965-72, v.p. for adminstrn., 1972-76; v.p. for adminstrn. Govs. State U., University Pk., Ill., 1977-82; univ. prof., rsch. assoc. Govs. State U., University Pk., 1982-87; writer, 1987—; co-founder, past dir. measurement and rsch. So. Ctrl. Region Edn. Lab., Little Rock; past evaluator rsch. grants U.S. Office of Edn., Washington; co-founder U.S. River Acad. (chartered by Congress) in the late 1960s. Co-author: The Educator's Desk Reference, 1989 (1 of 30 Best Reference Books 1989), Business Information Desk Reference, 1991, Patient's Desk Reference, 1994, others; contbr. articles to profl. jours.; editor: Handbook of Statistical Procedures and Their Computer Applications, 1991; tool inventor. Village trustee Hazel Crest, Ill., 1997—, plan commr., 1988-97; adminstrv. asst. Congressman William Alexander, Washington, 1969; v.p., bd. dirs. Calumet Coun. Boy Scouts Am., Munster, Ind., 1978-95. Recipient U.S. Congl. citation, Washington, 1971, Silver Beaver award Boy Scouts Am., 1976, Disting. Svcs. award Ark. State U., 1975. Mem. Masonic Lodge (worshipful master), Scottish Rite of Freemasonry (named Knight Comdr. of the Ct. of Hon. 1979), Alpha Epsilon Pi (life), Phi Kappa Phi, Omicron Delta Kappa. Home: 17023 Magnolia Dr Hazel Crest IL 60429-1020

FREEDBERG, IRWIN MARK, dermatologist; b. Boston, July 4, 1931; s. Arthur Harris and Sayde Ruth (Bixby) F.; m. Irene Sybil Lisman, July 4, 1954; children—Marjorie, Kenneth, Deborah. Student, Dartmouth Coll., 1949-52; M.D., Harvard U., 1956. Intern Beth Israel Hosp., Boston, 1956-57; resident in internal medicine Beth Israel Hosp., 1957-59; resident in dermatology Mass. Gen. Hosp., Boston, 1959-62; instr. to prof. dermatology Harvard U. Med. Sch., Boston, 1962-77; prof., chmn. dept. dermatology Johns Hopkins Sch. Medicine, Balt., 1977-81; George Miller McKee prof. and chmn. dept. dermatology NYU Sch. Medicine, N.Y.C., 1981—; adv. council Nat. Inst. Arthritis, Diabetes and Digestive and Kidney Diseases, 1984-86, musculoskeletal and skin diseases, 1986-87. Contbr. articles in field to profl. jours.; editor: Jour. Investigative Dermatology, 1972-77. Guggenheim fellow, 1969-70; NIH grantee, 1962—; Am Cancer Soc., Am. Contract Bridge League faculty research asso., 1965-70. Fellow AAAS; mem. Inst. Medicine of Nat., Acad. Sci.; mem. Coun. Biologic Editors, Am. Soc. Biol. Chemistry, Am. Soc. Clin. Investigation, Soc. Investigative Dermatology (pres. 1981-82), Harvey Soc., Am. Fedn. Clin. Rsch., Assn. Am. Physicians, Assn. Profs. Dermatology (pres. 1986-88), Am. Dermatologic Assn. (treas. 1987-92, dir. 1992-97, pres. 1997-98), Am. Soc. Cell Biology, Am. Bd. Dermatology (dir. 1984-94, v.p. 1992, pres. 1993), Am. Med. Assn. (Ho. of Dels. 1990—), N.Y. Acad. Medicine (sect. on dermatology 1986-87, chmn. 1987-88), Am. Acad. Dermatology (dir. 1991-96), French Dermatology Soc. (hon.), Korean Dermatology Soc. (hon.). Home: 333 E 68th St New York NY 10021-5693 Office: 562 1st Ave New York NY 10016-6402

FREEDENBERG, DEBRA, physician, geneticist; b. N.Y.C., May 4, 1955; d. Martin and Shirley Freedenberg. PhD, MPhil, Mt. Sinai Sch. Medicine, 1979; MD, SUNY, Buffalo, 1982. Diplomate Am. Coll. Med. Genetics, Am. Acad. Pediat. Intern, residency Yale New Haven Hosp.; med. sch. faculty U. Tex. Southwestern, Dallas, 1989-92, Tex. A&M, Temple, 1993-95, U. Iowa, Iowa City, 1995-96; med. dir. Genetics Inst. Austin, Tex., 1997—. Contbr. articles to profl. jours. Fellow Am. Coll. Med. Genetics (founder); mem. Am. Acad. Pediat., Am. Soc. Human Genetics. Office: Genetics Inst Austin 900 E 30th St Ste 220 Austin TX 78705-3323

FREEDMAN, DAVID NOEL, religious studies educator; b. N.Y.C., May 12, 1922; s. David and Beatrice (Goodman) F.; m. Cornelia Anne Pryor, May 16, 1944; children: Meredith Anne, Nadezhda, David Micaiah, Jonathan Pryor. Student, CCNY, 1935-38; AB, UCLA, 1939; BTh, Princeton Theol. Sem., 1944; PhD, Johns Hopkins U., 1948; LittD, U. Pacific, 1973; ScD, Davis and Elkins Coll., 1974. Ordained to ministry Presbyn. Ch., 1944; supply pastor in Acme and Deming, Wash., 1944-45; tchg. fellow, then asst. instr. Johns Hopkins U., 1946-48; asst. prof., then prof. Hebrew and Old Testament lit. Western Theol. Sem., Pitts., 1948-60; prof. Pitts. Theol. Sem., 1960-61, James A. Kelso prof., 1961-64; prof. Old Testament San Francisco Theol. Sem., 1964-70, Gray prof. Hebrew exegesis, 1970-71, dean of faculty, 1966-70, acting dean of sem., 1970-71; prof. Old Testament Grad. Theol. Union, Berkeley, Calif., 1964-71; prof. dept. Nr. Ea. studies U. Mich., Ann Arbor, 1971-92, Thurnau prof. Bibl. studies, 1984-92, dir. program on studies in religion, 1971-91; prof., endowed chair in Hebrew Bibl. studies U. Calif., San Diego, 1987—; dir. religious studies program U. Calif., 1989-97; Danforth vis. prof. Internat. Christian U., Tokyo, 1967; vis. prof. Hebrew U., Jerusalem, 1977, Macquarie U., N.S.W., Australia, 1980, U. Queensland (Australia), 1982, 84, U. Calif., San Diego, 1985-87; Green vis. prof. Tex. Christian U., Ft. Worth, 1981; dir. Albright Inst. Archeol. Rsch., 1969-70, dir., 1976-77; centennial lectr. Johns Hopkins U., 1976; Dahood lectr. Loyola U., 1983; Soc. Bibl. Lit. meml. lectr., 1983, Smithsonian lectr., 1984; prin. bibl. cons. Reader's Digest, 1984, 88, 89, 90, 94; disting. faculty lectr. Univ. Mich., 1988; Stone lectr. Princeton Theol. Sem., 1989; Mowinckel lectr., Oslo U., 1991; lectr. Uppsala U., Sweden, 1991; vis. lectr. Brigham Young Ctr. Near Eastern Studies, Jerusalem, 1993. Author: Divine Commitment and Human Obligation, 1997, Psalm 119, 1999, The Nine Commandments, 2000; co-author: (with J.D. Smart) God Has Spoken, 1949, (with F.M. Cross, Jr.) Early Hebrew Orthography, 1952, (with John M. Allegro) The People of the Dead Sea Scrolls, 1958, (with R.M. Grant) The Secret Sayings of Jesus, 1960, (with F.M. Cross, Jr.) Ancient Yahwistic Poetry, 1964, rev. edit., 1975, 97, (with M. Dothan) Ashdod I, 1967, The Published Works of W.F. Albright, 1975, (with L.G. Running) William F. Albright: Twentieth Century Genius, 1975, 2d edit., 1991, (with B. Mazar, G. Cornfeld) The Mountain of the Lord, 1975, (with W. Phillips) An Explorer's Life of Jesus, 1975, (with G. Cornfeld) Archaeology of the Bible: Book by Book, 1976, Pottery, Poetry and Prophecy, 1980, (with K.A. Mathews) The Paleo-Hebrew Leviticus Scroll, 1985, The Unity of the Hebrew Bible, 1991, (with D. Forbes and F. Andersen) Studies in Hebrew and Aramaic Orthography, 1992, (with Sara Mandell) The Relationship between Herodotus' History and Primary History, 1993; co-author, editor: (with F. Andersen) Anchor Bible Series Hosea, 1980, Anchor Bible Series Amos, 1989, Micah, 2000; editor: (with G.E. Wright) The Biblical Archaeologist, Reader I, 1961, (with E.F. Campbell, Jr.) The Biblical Archaeologist, Reader 2, 1964, Reader 3, 1970, Reader 4, 1983, (with W.F. Albright) The Anchor Bible, 1964—, including, Genesis, 1964, James, Peter and Jude, 1964, Jeremiah, 1965, Job, 1965, 2d edit., 1973, Proverbs and Ecclesiastes, 1965, I Chronicles, II Chronicles, Ezra-Nehemiah, 1965, Psalms I, 1966, John I, 1966, Acts of the Apostles, 1967, II Isaiah, 1968, Psalms II, 1968, John II, 1970, Psalms III, 1970, Esther, 1971, Matthew, 1971, Lamentations, 1972, 2d edit., 1992, To the Hebrews, 1972, Ephesians 1-3, 4-6, 1974, I and II Esdras, 1974, Judges, 1975, Revelation, 1975, Ruth, 1975, I Maccabees, 1976, I Corinthians, 1976, Additions, 1977, Song of Songs, 1977, Daniel, 1978, Wisdom of Solomon, 1979, I Samuel, 1980, Hosea, 1980, Luke I, 1981, Joshua, 1982, Epistles of John, 1983, II Maccabees, 1983, II Samuel, 1984, II Corinthians, 1984, Luke II, 1985, Judith, 1985, Mark, 1986, Haggai-Zechariah 1-8, 1987, Ecclesiastes, 1987, 2 Kings, 1988, Amos, 1989, Titus, 1990, Jonah, 1990, Leviticus I, 1991, Deuteronomy I, 1991, Numbers 1-20, 1993, Romans, 1993, Jude and 2 Peter, 1993, Zechariah 9-14, 1993, Zephaniah, 1994, Colossians, 1995, Joel, 1995, James, 1995, Obadiah, 1996, Tobit, 1996, Ecclesiastes, 1997, Ezekiel 21-37, 1997, Galatians, 1997, Malachi, 1998, Acts of the Apostles, 1998, Exodus 1-18, 1999, Jeremiah 1-20, 1999, Mark 1-8, 2000, Numbers 21-36, 2000, 1 Peter, 2000, Isaiah 1-39, 2000, Thessalonians 1&2, 2000, Leviticus 17-22, 2000, Leviticus 23-27, 2000; editor Anchor Bible Ref. Libr., Jesus Within Judaism, 1988, Archeology of the Land of the Bible, 1990, The Tree of Life, 1990, A Marginal Jew Vol. 1, 1991, The Pentateuch, 1991, The Rise of Jewish Nationalism, 1992, History and Prophecy, 1993, Jesus and the Dead Sea Scrolls, 1993, The Birth of the Messiah, 1993, The Death of the Messiah, 2 vols., 1994, Introduction to Rabbinical Literature, 1994, A Marginal Jew, vol. 2, 1994, The Scepter and the Star, 1995, An Introduction to the New Testament, 1997, Education in Ancient Israel, 1998, Warrior, Dancer, Seductress, Queen, 1998, A History of the Synoptic Problem, 1999, editor: Eerdmans Critical Commentary, 1 and 2 Timothy, 1999, Philemon, 2000, The Letter to Philemon, 2000, Biblical Resource Series, The Parables of Jesus, 2000, The Rivers of Paradise, 2000, Eerdmans Dictionary of the Bible, 2000, (with J. Greenfield) New Directions in Biblical Archaeology, 1969, (with J.A. Baird) The Computer Bible, 1971, A Critical Concordance to the Synoptic Gospels, 1971, An Analytic Linguistic Concordance to the Book of Isaiah, 1971, I, II, III John: Forward and Reverse Concordance and Index, 1971, A Critical Concordance to Hosea, Amos, Micah, 1972, A Critical Concordance of Haggai, Zechariah, Malachi, 1973, A Critical Concordance to the Gospel of John, 1974, A Synoptic Concordance of Aramaic Inscriptions, 1975, A Linguistic Concordance of Ruth and Jonah, 1976, A Linguistic Concordance of Jeremiah, 1978, Syntactical and Critical Concordance of Jeremiah, 1978, Synoptic Abstract, 1978, I and II Corinthians, 1979, Zechariah, 1979, Galatians, 1980, Ephesians, 1981, Philippians, 1982, Colossians, 1983, Pastoral Epistles, 1984, 1 & 2 Thessalaians, 1985, Density Plots in Ezekiel, 1986, Exodus, 1987, Hebrews, 1988, Ruth, 1989, James, 1991, 1 & 2 Peter, 1991, 1, 2 & 3 John and Jude, 1991, Psalms, Job and Proverbs, 1992, Apocalypse, 1993, The Pentateuch, 1995, Aramaic Inscriptions, 1975, (with T. Kachel) Religion and the Academic Scene, 1975, Am. Schs. Oriental Research publs; co-editor: Scrolls from Qumran Cave I, 1972, Jesus: The Four Gospels, 1973, Pomegranates and Golden Bells, 1995; Reader's Digest editor: Atlas of the Bible, 1981, Family Guide to the Bible, 1984, Mysteries of the Bible, 1988, Who's Who in the Bible, 1994, The Bible Through the Ages, 1996, Complete Guide to the Bible, 1998; gen. editor: (facsimile edit.) Complete Guide to the Bible, 1998; The Leningrad Codex, 1998; assoc. editor Jour. Bible Lit., 1952-54, editor, 1955-59; cons. editor Interpreter's Dictionary of the Bible, 1957-60, Theologisches Wörterbuch des Alten Testaments, 1970-92, English Translation Theological Word-Book of the Old Testament, 1975—; editor in chief The Anchor Bible Dictionary, 6 vols., 1992; co-editor (with W.H. Propp and Baruch Halpern) The Hebrew Bible and Its Interpreters, 1990; contbr. numerous articles to profl. jours. Recipient prize in New Testament exegesis Princeton Theol. Sem., 1943, Carey-Thomas award for Anchor Bible, 1965, Layman's Nat. Bible Com. award, 1978, 3 awards for Anchor Bible Bibl. Archaeol. Soc., 1993; William H. Green fellow in Old Testament, 1944, William S. Rayner fellow Johns Hopkins U., 1946, 47, Guggenheim fellow, 1959, Am. Assn. Theol. Schs. fellow, 1963; Am. Coun. Learned Socs. grantee-in-aid, 1967, 76. Fellow U. Mich. Soc. Fellows (sr., chmn. 1980-82); mem. Soc. Bibl. Lit. (pres. 1975-76), Am. Oriental Soc., Am. Schs. Oriental Rsch. (v.p. 1970-82, editor bull. 1974-78, editor Bibl. Archeologist 1976-82, dir. publs. 1974-82), Archaeol. Inst. Am., Am. Acad. Religion, Bibl. Colloquium (sec.-treas. 1960-90). Office: U Calif San Diego Dept History 0104 9500 Gilman Dr Dept 0104 La Jolla CA 92093-5004

FREEDMAN, HARRY, composer; b. Lodz, Poland, Apr. 5, 1922; came to Can., 1925; s. Max and Rose (Nelken) F.; m. Mary Louise Morrison, Sept. 15, 1951; children: Karen Liese, Cynthia Jane, Lori Ann. Student, Winnipeg Sch. Art, 1936-40, Royal Conservatory Music, 1945-50. Musician Toronto Symphony, 1946-70; dir. Canadian Music Centre. Composer: Tableau, 1952, Images, 1958, Tokaido: chorus and wind quintet, 1964; Tangents (orch.), 1967; ballet Rose Latulippe, 1966; Toccata, 1968; Debussy orchestration Piano Preludes, 1971; children's choir Keewaydin, 1971; orch. Tapestry, 1973; Romeo and Juliet Ballet, 1973; violin and piano Encounter, 1974; clarinet Lines, 1974; orch. Nocturne 2, 1975; narrator and chamber ensemble The Explainer, 1976; Celebration (saxophone concerto for Gerry Mulligan), 1977; choir Green...Blue...White, 1978; 1-act jazz opera Abracadabra, 1979; chorus and orch. Nocturne 3, 1980; brass quintet and orch. Royal Flush, 1980; clarinet and string quartet Chalumeau, 1981; Concerto for Orch., 1982; Third Symphony, 1983; ballet Oiseaux Exotiques, 1984; narrator and orch. A Garland for Terry, 1985; string orch. Contrasts, The Web and the Wind, 1986; children's choir Rhymes from the Nursery, 1986; music theater Fragments of Alice, 1987; orch. A Dance on the Earth, 1988; Touchings, concerto for percussion ensemble and orch., 1989, marimba solo Bones, 1989, orch. Town, 1991; 2 pianos and choir, Songs from Shakespeare, 1990; soprano and string quartet Spirit Song, 1993; 22 solo strings, Indigo, 1994; Touchpoints for flute, viola and harp, 1994; soprano and lute Bright Angels, 1995; saxophone quartet, Saxtet, 1995, flute, clarinet, violin, cello, piano Blue Light, 1995; Higher, bass clarinet, and cello, 1996; orchestra and 4 choirs, Borealis, 1997, harp solo Dances, 1997, choir Voices, 1999, Marigold, concerto for viola and orchestra, 1999; 16 solo strings, Graphic 9: for Harry Somers, 2000; string quartet, Graphic 8, 2000—; also many scores for Stratford Shakespeare Festival, films, stage, TV; host Music on a Sunday Afternoon, 1987. Served with RCAF, 1942-45. Officer Order of Can., 1984; Can. Coun. sr. arts grantee, 1960, 63, 73-74, 81, 97-98; recipient Can. film awards, 1970, Composer of Yr. award Can. Music Coun., 1979, Lynch-Staunton award Can. Coun., 1998; Tanglewood scholar, 1949, Royal Conservatory scholar, 1950. Mem. Canadian League Composers (founding mem., pres. 1975-78). Address: 2407-35 Wynford Heights Crs, Don Mills, ON Canada M3C 1L1

FREEDMAN, JO ANN, toxicologist; b. N.Y.C.; m. Jonathan A. Freedman, June 28, 1959; children: Lorin John, Michael James, Noah David. BS in Chemistry, Antioch Coll.; MS in Biochemistry, U. Chgo.; PhD in Biology, Syracuse U. Bd. cert. Am. Bd. Toxicology. Rsch. asst. in molecular biochemistry Brandeis U., Waltham, Mass.; rsch.. asst. in photosynthesis Tyco Labs., Waltham; teaching asst. dept. biology Syracuse (N.Y.) U., 1977-78, 81-82, postdoctoral and rsch. assoc. Bioenergetics Lab., 1983, 87-88, rsch. asst. prof. biology, 1988-90; postdoctoral assoc. Labs. for Cell Biology, Sch. Medicine, U. N.C., Chapel Hill, 1984-85; postdoctoral fellow, rsch. assoc. dept. biol. scis. Brock U., St. Catharines, Ont., Can., 1985-87; scientist Syracuse Rsch. Corp., 1988-92; toxicologist and health assessor Agy. for Toxic Substances and Disease Registry, Atlanta, 1992—; adj. prof. Onondaga (N.Y.) Community Coll., 1988; reviewer Current Topics in Bioenergetics. Contbr. articles and abstracts to profl. jours., chpts. to books. Grantee Am. Heart Assn., 1985-86; NSF grantee, 1989-92. Mem. Am. Chem. Soc., Am. Soc. for Biochemistry and Molecular Biology, Assn. for Women in Sci., Soc. Toxicology, Internat. Assn. Women Biochemists. Address: Mail Stop E56 1600 Clifton Rd Stop E56 Atlanta GA 30333

FREEDMAN, JONATHAN WILLIAM, entertainment company executive. 2d asst. dir. Playing With Time, Toronto, Ont., Can., 1988-89; floor dir. YTV TV, Toronto, 1989-91; sr. prodr. REO TV, Toronto, 1991-94; exec. prodr. Gray Matter, Toronto, 1994-96; exec. prodr., head of prodn. Sony Computer Entertainment Europe, Leeds, Eng., 1996—. Recipient Bafta award 199, Min. of Sound award 1999. Mem. Dirs. Guild Can. Fax: 011-44(0)113-242-3671. E-mail: jonathan.freedman@psygnosis.co.uk. Office: Sony, 19-20 Park Row 4th Fl, Leeds LS1 5JF, England

FREEDMAN, MONROE HENRY, lawyer, educator, columnist; b. Mt. Vernon, N.Y., Apr. 10, 1928; s. Chauncey and Dorothea (Kornblum) F.; m. Audrey Willock, Sept. 24, 1950 (dec. 1998); children: Alice Freedman Korngold, Sarah Freedman Izquierdo, Caleb (dec. 1998), Judah. AB cum laude, Harvard U., 1951, LLB, 1954, LLM, 1956. Bar: Mass. 1954, Pa. 1957, D.C. 1960, U.S. Dist. Ct. (ea. dist. N.Y.), U.S. Ct. Appeals (D.C. cir.) 1960, U.S. Supreme Ct. 1960, U.S. Ct. Appeals (2d cir.) 1968, N.Y. 1978, U.S. Ct. Appeals (9th cir.) 1982, U.S. Ct. Appeals (11th cir.) 1986, U.S. Ct. Appeals (Fed. cir.) 1987. Assoc. Wolf, Block, Schorr & Solis-Cohen, Phila., 1956-58; ptnr. Freedman & Temple, Washington, 1969-73; dir. Stern Community Law Firm, Washington, 1970-71; prof. law George Washington U., 1958-73; dean Hofstra Law Sch., Hempstead, N.Y., 1973-77, prof. law, 1973—, Howard Lichtenstein Disting. prof. legal ethics, 1989—; Drinko-Baker & Hostetler chair in law Cleve. State U., 1992; faculty asst. Harvard U. Law Sch., 1954-56, instr. trial advocacy, 1978—; lectr. on lawyers' ethics; exec. dir. U.S. Holocaust Meml. Coun., 1980-82, gen. counsel, 1982-83, sr. adviser to chmn., 1982-87; cons. U.S. Commn. on Civil Rights, 1960-64, Neighborhood Legal Services Program, 1970; legis. cons. to Senator John L. McClellan, 1959; spl. com. on courtroom conduct N.Y.C. Bar Assn., 1972; exec. dir. Criminal Trial Inst., 1965-66; expert witness on legal ethics state and fed. ct. proceedings, U.S. Senate and House Coms., U.S. Dept. Justice, FDIC; spl. investigator Rochester Inst. Tech., 1991; reporter Am. Lawyer's Code of Conduct, 1979-81; mem. Arbitration panel U.S. Dist. Ct. (ea. dist.) N.Y., 1986—; Inaugural Wickwire lectr. Dalhousie Law Sch., N.S., 1992; lectr. S.C. Bar Found., 1993, numerous profl. confs; adv. subgroup on ethics U.S. Dist. Ct. (ea. dist.) N.Y., 1994-96. Author: Contracts, 1973, Lawyers' Ethics in an Adversary System, 1975 (ABA gavel award, cert. of merit 1976), Teacher's Manual Contracts, 1978, American Lawyer's Code of Conduct, 1981, Understanding Lawyers' Ethics, 1990, Group Defamation and Freedom of Speech—The Relationship Between Language and Violence, 1995; co-editor; columnist Cases and Controversies, Am. Lawyer Media, 1990-96, (with Supreme Ct. Justice Ruth Bader Ginsburg) Freedom, Life, & Death: Materials on Comparative Constitutional Law, 1997; television appearances include Donohue, CNN Money Line, CBS 60 Minutes, CNN Late Edition, Court TV, and others; contbr. articles to profl. jours. Recipient Martin Luther King Jr. Humanitarian award, 1987, The Lehman-LaGuardia Award for Civic Achievement, 1996. Fellow Am. Bar Found. (life); mem. ABA (ethics adv. to chair criminal justice sect. 1993—, Michael Franck award 1998), ACLU (nat. bd. dirs. 1970-80, nat. adv. coun. 1980—, spl. litigation counsel 1971-73), Am. Law Inst. (consultative group on the law governing lawyers, 1990-99, consultative group on Uniform Comml. Code art. 2 1990—), Soc. Am. Law Tchrs. (mem. governing bd. 1974-79, exec. com. 1976-79, chmn. com. on profl. responsibility 1974-79, 87-90), ABA (vice chmn. ethical considerations com. criminal justice sect. 1989-90, ethics advisor to chmn. criminal justice sect., 1993-96), N.Y. State Bar Assn. (com. on legal edn. and admission to bar 1988-92, criminal justice sect. com. on profl. responsibility, 1990-92, award for Dedication to Scholarship and pub. svc. 1997), Assn. Bar City N.Y. (com. on profl. responsibility 1987-90, com. on profl. and jud. ethics 1991-92), Fed. Bar Assn. (chmn. com. on profl. disciplinary standards and procedures 1970-71), Am. Soc. Writers on Legal Subjects (mem. com. on constitution and bylaws 1999—) Am. Jewish Congress (nat. governing coun. 1984-86), Am. Arbitration Assn. (arbitrator, nat. panel arbitrators 1964—, cert. svc. award 1986), Nat. Network on Right to Counsel (exec. bd., exec. com. 1986-90), Nat. Prison Project (steering com. 1970-90), Nat. Assn. Criminal Def. Lawyers (vice chmn. ethics adv. com. 1991-93, co-chmn., 1994), Scribes (constn. and bylaws com. 1999—). Democrat. Jewish.

FREEDMAN, WALTER, lawyer; b. St. Louis, Oct. 30, 1914; s. Sam and Sophie (Gordon) F.; m. Maxine Weil, June 23, 1940; children—Jay W., Sandra Freedman Sabel. A.B., Washington U., 1937, J.D., 1937; LL.M., Harvard, 1938. Bar: Mo., Ill., D.C. Atty. SEC, Washington, 1938-40, U.S. Dept. Interior, Washington, 1940-42; chief counsel Office Export Control, Foreign Econ. Adminstrn., 1942-44, dir., 1944-45; partner Freedman, Levy, Kroll & Simonds (and predecessor firm), Washington, 1946—; Fairchild fellow Harvard U. Law Sch., 1937-38. Editor-in-chief: Washington U. Law Quarterly, 1936-37; Contbr. articles to profl. jours. Decorated chevalier de l'Ordre de la Couronne (Belgium), 1950; recipient Disting. Alumni award Washington U. Sch. Law, 1995. Mem. Washington Bd. Trade, Am. Law Inst., ABA, Fed. Bar Assn., D.C. Bar Assn., Woodmont country Club (bd. mgrs.), Cosmos Club, Phi Beta Kappa, Omicron Delta Kappa, Phi Sigma Alpha. Jewish (trustee temple). Home: 4545 W St NW Washington DC 20007-1513 Office: 1050 Connecticut Ave NW Washington DC 20036-5303

FREEHLING, DANIEL JOSEPH, law educator, law library director; b. Montgomery, Ala., Nov. 13, 1950; s. Saul Irving and Grace (Lieberman) L. BS, Huntingdon Coll., 1972; JD, U. Ala., 1975, MLS, 1977. Ref. libr., asst. to assoc. dean U. Ala. Sch. Law, Tuscaloosa, 1975-77; assoc. law libr. U. Md., Balt., 1977-79, Cornell U., Ithaca, N.Y., 1979-82; law libr. dir., assoc. prof. U. Maine, Portland, 1982-86; law libr. dir., assoc. prof. law Boston U., 1986-92, prof., 1992—, assoc. dean for adminstrn., 1993-97, assoc. dean for info. svcs., 1999—; mem. steering com., law program com. Rsch. Librs. Group, 1989-91; treas. New Eng. Law Libr. Consortium, 1989-91; vice chair, chair-elect sect. on law librs. Assn. Am. Law Schs., 1990-91, chair, 1992. Mem. ABA (accreditation com. 1995—), Am. Assn. Law Librs. (chair acad. law librs. spl. interest sect. 1981-82, edn. com. 1982-83, membership com. 1983-84, program chair 1987-88, local arrangements co-chair 1992-93, chair mentoring and retention com. 1995-96). Home: 21A Lakeshore Rd Boxford MA 01921-1113 Office: Boston U Law Sch Pappas Law Libr 765 Commonwealth Ave Boston MA 02215-1401

FREELAND, ALAN EDWARD, orthopedic surgery educator, physician; b. Youngstown, Ohio, July 30, 1939; s. Harold Edward and Esther Amelia (Hanley) F.; m. Janis Ann Foerschl, Oct. 11, 1969; children: Matthew, Jennifer, Rebecca, Michael. BA, Johns Hopkins U., 1961; MD, George Washington U., 1965. Cert. hand surgery Am. Bd. Orthopaedic Surgery. Intern Church Home and Hosp., Balt., 1965-66; resident Johns Hopkins Hosp., Balt., 1967-70, Letterman Army Med. Ctr., San Francisco, 1973-75; prof. dept. orthopaedic surgery U. Miss. Med. Ctr., Jackson, 1978—, chief of staff, 1986-87, also bd. dirs. Rowland Med. Libr., 1996-98; chief surgery Miss. Meth. Rehab. Ctr., Jackson, 1991-93, pres. elect med. staff, 1994, pres. med. staff, bd. dirs., 1995-97. Author: Stable Internal Fixation of the Hand and Wrist, 1986, The First Twenty-Five Years: History of the American Association for Hand Surgery, 1996, Hand Fractures: Repair, Reconstruction, and Rehabilitation, 2000; mem. editl. bd. Orthopedics, Slack, Inc., 1986—, Jour. Orthopaedic Trauma, Raven Press, 1993—, Year Book of Hand Surgery, 1997—; sect. editor, sr. editor hand surgery Jour. Orthopedic Trauma, 1997—; sect. editor Hand Surgery, 1997—. Mem. Fire Protection Dist., Brandon, Miss., 1990-93. Lt. col. U.S. Army, 1971-78. Fellow Am. Acad. Orthopaedic Surgeons, Am. Orthopaedic Assn.; mem. Am. Soc. Surgery of Hand (governing coun. 1989-92), Am. Assn. Hand Surgeons (parliamentarian 1994, historian 1995, 99, exec. com., bd. dirs. 1994—, treas. 1996-98, v.p. 2000, Nat. Clinician/Tchr. of Yr. 1997), Internat. Fedn. Socs. for Surgery of Hand (chmn. bone and joint com. 1992—), Miss. State Orthopaedic Assn. (pres. 1986, pres. Jackson chpt. 1985), S.E. Hand Club (sec.-treas. 1998—). Home: 303 Swallow Dr Brandon MS 39047-6454 Office: 2500 N State St Jackson MS 39216-4500

FREELAND, JAMES M. JACKSON, lawyer, educator; b. Miami, Fla., Feb. 17, 1927; s. Byron Brazil and Mary Helen (Jackson) F.; m. Valerie; children: Carole Leigh, Thomas Byron, James Jackson Jr. AB, Duke U., 1950; JD, U. Fla., Gainesville, 1954; postgrad. fellow, Yale U. Law Sch., 1960-61. Bar: Fla. 1954. Assoc. firm Dowling & Culverhouse, Jacksonville, 1954-57; mem. faculty Law Sch. U. Fla., Gainesville, 1957-60, 61-62, 65—, prof. law, 1970-95; dir. grad. tax law program U. Fla., 1977-82, disting. svc. prof. law, 1983-94, disting. svc. prof. emeritus, 1995—; of counsel August & Kulunas, P.A., West Palm Beach, Fla., 1995—; prof. law NYU Law Sch., 1963-65; vis. prof. U. Ariz. Law Sch., Tucson, 1969-70; mem. tax faculty Practicing Law Inst., 1969-76; vis. tax prof. Leiden U., The Netherlands, 1983. Co-author: Federal Income Taxation of Estates, Trusts and Beneficiaries, 1970, 3d edit., 1998, The Florida Will and Trust Manual, 1983, The Tennessee Will and Trust Manual, 1984, Fundamentals of Federal Income Taxation, 1972, 10th edit., 1998; adv. editor Jour. Corp. Taxation, 1977—, S Corp. Tax Jour., 1989—. Served with USNR, 1944-46. Named Outstanding prof. U. Fla., 1968, Outstanding Law Prof., 1970-73, 75; Designated Disting. Service Prof. Law, 1982. Mem. ABA, Am. Law Inst., Am. Coll. Tax Counsel, The Fla. Bar Tax Sect., (Outstanding Tax Lawyer State of Fla.

1982), Am. Judicature Soc., Order of Coif, Fla. Blue Key, Phi Kappa Phi. Republican. Methodist. Home: 7700 NW 41st Ave Gainesville FL 32606-4114

FREELAND, ROBERT FREDERICK, retired librarian; b. Flint, Mich., Dec. 20, 1919; s. Ralph V. and Susan Barbara (Goetz) F.; m. June Voshel, June 18, 1948; children: Susan Beth Visser, Kent Richard. BS, Eastern Mich. U., 1942; postgrad., Washington & Lee U., 1945; MS, U. So. Calif., 1948, postgrad., 1949; postgrad., U. Mich., 1950-52, Calif. State U., 1956-58, UCLA, 1960; LittD (hon.), Linda Vista Bible Coll., 1973. Music supr. Consol. Schs. Warren, Mich., 1946-47; music dir. Carson City (Mich.) Pub. Schs., 1948-49; librarian, audio-visual coord. Ford Found., Edison Inst., Greenfield Village, Dearborn, Mich., 1950-52, Helix High Sch. Library, 1952-77; librarian, prof. library sci. Linda Vista Bible Coll., 1976—; reference libr. San Diego Pub. Libr. System, 1967-97; cons. edn., libr. and multimedia. Editor book and audio-visual aids review, Sch. Musician, Dir. and Teacher, 1950-75. Former deacon and elder Christian Reform Ch., libr., 1969-72, Classis archivist, 1991—; pub. affairs officer, sr. program officer, moral leadership officer Sq. 57 GP III, Calif. wing CAP. With USAAF, 1942-46. Named Scholar Freedoms Found., Valley Forge, Pa., 1976-80. Mem. NEA (life), ALA, Nat. Music Camp, Calif. Tchrs. Assn., Music Libr. Assn. So. Calif. (adviser exec. bd.), Calif. Libr. Assn. (pres. Palomar chpt. 1972-73), Sch. Libr. Assn. Calif. (treas. 1956-73), Calif. Media and Libr. Educators (charter mem.), Am. Legion (Americanism chmn. 22d dist. San Diego County, chmn. oratorical contest com. La Mesa post), Ret. Officers Assn., San Diego Aero Space Mus., San Diego Mus. Art, Alumnia Assn. Ea. Mich. U. Home: 4800 Williamsburg Ln Apt 223 La Mesa CA 91941-4651

FREEMAN, ANTHONY GEORGE, retired physician, consultant; b. London, Mar. 14, 1920; m. Florence Eleanor Thomas, Febr. 18, 1950; children: Michael, Susan, Elizabeth. Student, Queen's Coll., Cambridge, Eng., 1938-43; MA, MB, BChir., U. Cambridge, 1947, MD, 1950; MRCP, London, 1953, FRCP, 1972. Registrar in Pathology Bristol Royal Infirmary, 1948-50; registrar, Med. Prof. Unit Cardiff Royal Infirmary, 1950-52; sr. med. registrar, tutor in medicine U. Bristol, 1953-59; cons. physician Princess Margaret Hosp., Swindon, Wiltshire, 1959-85; hon. cons. physician Wessex Area Health Authority, 1985—; mem. ct. of examiners for fellowship Royal Coll. Surgeons, 1974-80. Author: 'D Day: the Medical aspects of 'Operation Overlord; contbr. numerous articles to profl. jours. Past pres. Anglo-Am. Med. Soc., 1960-62; founder, mem., past pres. Multiple Sclerosis Soc. and Parkinsons Disease Soc., Swindon, 1962-65. Capt. Royal Army Med. Corps., 1944-47. Fellow Royal Coll. Medicine (Eng.) (mem. coun. 1976-81), Marylebone Cricket Club. Avocations: photography, philately. Home: Meadow Rise-3 Lakeside, SN3 1QE Swindon Wiltshire, England

FREEMAN, ANTOINETTE ROSEFELDT, lawyer; b. Atlantic City, Oct. 7, 1937; d. Bernard Paul and Fannie (Levin) Rosefeldt; m. Alan Richard Freeman, June 22, 1958 (div. Apr. 1979); children: Barry David, Robin Lisa. BA, Rutgers U., 1972; JD, Ind. U., 1975; LLM, Temple U., 1979. Bar: Pa. 1975, Wash. 1992, U.S. Dist. Ct. (ea. dist.) Pa. 1976, U.S. Ct. Appeals (3d cir.) 1982. Substitute tchr. Washington Twp. Sch. Dist., Indpls., 1972; dep. prosecutor intern Marion County Prosecutor, Indpls., 1974-75; asst. dist. atty. City of Phila., 1975-76; mgr. EEO Wyeth Labs., Radnor, Pa., 1976-80, SmithKline & French Labs., Phila., 1980-82; sr. counsel SmithKline Beecham Corp., Phila., 1982-91; assoc. gen. counsel Immunex Corp., 1991—; arbitrator Am. Arbitration Assn., 1976—; Counsel Regional Interests Developing Efficient Transp., 1983-85; adv. bd. Family Svc. Phila., 1980-81, Greater Phila. C. of C., 1983; pres. Croskey Ct. Condominium Assn., 1983-87; bd. dirs. Logan Sq. Neighborhood Assn., 1983-91, pres., 1985-87; v.p., sec. Friends of Logan Sq. Found., 1985-91; counsel Hapoel Games USA; chairperson Ctr. City Coalition for Quality of Life; atty. Vol. Lawyers for the Arts, Phila., 1985-91; bd. dirs. Sr. Employment and Ednl. Svc., BathHouse Theater, 1991-99, v.p. 1994-96; bd. dirs. Bellini preview group Seattle Opera Guild, 1994-96 ; mem. Assoc. Corp. Coun. for Arts., 1992-93; mem. adv. bd. regulatory affairs cert. program U. Wash. Mem. ABA, Pa. Bar Assn., Phila. Bar Assn., Wash. State Bar Assn., Merit Employers Coun. (1st v.p. 1978-79), Phila. Women's Network, Phila. Lawyers Club, Phila. King County Med. Soc./King County Bar Assn. (med.-legal com.). Democrat. Jewish. Office: Immunex Corp 51 University St Seattle WA 98101-2936

FREEMAN, ARTHUR MERRIMON, III, psychiatry educator, dean; b. Birmingham, Ala., Oct. 10, 1942; s. Arthur Merrimon II and Katherine (Lide) F.; m. Linda Poynter; children: Arthur M. IV, Katherin Leigh, Edward Todd. AB in Philosophy, Harvard U., 1963; MD, Vanderbilt U., 1967. Diplomate Am. Bd. Psychiatry and Neurology; lic. psychiatrist, Ala., N.C., La. Asst. prof. dept. psychiatry and behavioral scis. Stanford (Calif.) U., 1974-77; prof., vice chmn. dept. psychiatry U. Ala., Birmingham, 1977-90; med. dir. Appalachian Hall Hosp., Asheville, N.C., 1990-91; prof., chmn. dept. psychiatry La. State U. Med. Ctr., Shreveport, 1991—, dean, 1993-96; regional med. dir. divsn. mental health La. Dept. Health and Hosps., 1992-94. Author: Psychiatry for the Primary Care Physician, 1979. Bd. dirs. Vols. of Am., Shreveport, 1993-96, Shreveport Symphony, C. of C., 1993-96. Lt. comdr. M.C., USN, 1972-74. Nat. Merit scholar Harvard U., 1959-63; Biochemistry fellow Karolinska Inst., Stockholm, 1965, fellow in hepatic disease Royal Free Hosp., London, 1966, Paul Harris fellow Rotary Club. Fellow APA, Am. Coll. Psychiatrists (Laughlin fellow 1971), Acad. Psychosomatic Medicine, So. Psychiat. Assn.; mem. Am. Assn. Chmn. of Depts. of Psychiatry, Biomed. Rsch. Found. N.W. La. (bd. dirs. 1993-96), La. Psychiatry Med. Assn. (pres. North La. chpt.). Home: 5929 E Ridge Dr Shreveport LA 71106-2423 Office: La State U Med Ctr Dept of Psychiatry 1501 Kings Hwy Shreveport LA 71103-4228

FREEMAN, CATHY, Olympic athlete; b. Mackay, Australia, Feb. 16, 1973. Winner Commonwealth Games, 1994; winner Silver medal 400 meter Atlanta, 1996; winner Gold medal 400 meter World Championships, 1997, 99, winner Lausanne Grand Prix 400 meter, 2000, winner Monte Carlo Grand Prix 400 meter, 2000; winner Gold medal 400 meter Sydney, 2000. Named Young Australian of Yr., 19990, Aboriginal Athlete of the Yr., 1991, Australian of the Yr., 199; first Australian woman to run under 50 seconds for 400 meters, 1996. First Aboriginal track and field athlete to represent Australia in the Olympics. Office: Athletics Australia Fawkner Tower, 431 St Kilda Rd Ste 22, Melbourne Victoria, Australia 3004*

FREEMAN, CHARLES J., financial executive, credit risk manager; b. Stamford, Conn., Feb. 15, 1958; s. Thomas Hadley and Marcia (Sanders) F.; m. Mary Ann Freeman, Aug. 29, 1981 (dec. Nov. 1999); children: Heather, Thomas. BS, Rider U., 1980; MBA, UCLA, 1983. Mgr. internat. cash mgmt. Chem. Bank, N.Y.C., 1978-81, corp. fin. assoc., 1983-85, v.p., 1988-95; M&A assoc. Citibank, N.Y.C., 1985-87; mgr. long-term fin. Merrill Lynch, N.Y.C., 1987-88; sr. v.p. Chase Manhattan Mortgage Corp., N.Y.C., 1995—; vis. lectr. numerous univs. including Princeton U., Yale U., Harvard U., London Sch. Econs., N.Y. Fed. Res. Co-author: Housing Partnerships, 1997; inventor Risk Mgmt. Sys.; contbr. articles to profl. jours.

FREEMAN, CHAS. W., JR., government official, ambassador, author; b. Washington, Mar. 2, 1943; divorced; 3 children; m. Margaret Van Wagenen Carpenter, 1993. BA, Yale U.; JD, Harvard U. Joined Fgn. Svc., 1965, assigned to India and Taiwan; Am. interpreter for Pres. Nixon, People's Republic China, 1972; vis. fellow East Asian Legal Rsch. Ctr., Harvard U., 1974-75; dep. dir. for Taiwan affairs, dir. pub. programs, dir. plans and mgmt. U.S. Dept. State, Washington, 1975-78; dir. program coord. and devel. USIA, Washington, 1978, acting U.S. coord. for refugee affairs; dir. China affairs U.S. Dept. State, 1979; dep. chief of mission Am. Embassy, Beijing, 1981, Bangkok, 1984; prin. dep. asst. sec. state for African affairs U.S. Dept. State, Washington, 1986; amb. to Saudi Arabia, Riyadh, 1989-92; asst. sec. def. The Pentagon, Washington, 1993-94; dist. fellow U.S. Inst. of Peace, Washington, 1994-95; chmn. bd. Projects Internat. Inc., Washington, 1995—; co-chmn. U.S. China Policy Found., 1996; vice-chmn. Atlantic Coun., 1997, pres. Middle East Policy Coun.; bd. dirs. Inst. for Def. Analyses; bd. dirs. World Affairs Coun. Washington, 1998; mem. bd. visitors Dept. Def. Regional Ctrs., 1998—; mem. U.S. Nat. Security Study Group, 1998—. Author: The Diplomat's Dictionary, 1994, revised edit., 1997; Arts of Power, 1997. Recipient Sec. Def. Meritorious Civilian Svc. award, 1991, Disting. Pub. Svc. awards, 1993-94, Sec. State Disting. Honor, 1991, Dir. Ctrl. Intelligence Shield Medallion award, 1991, First Class Order of Abd Al-Aziz award Saudi Arabian Govt., 1992. Mem. Am. Acad. Diplomacy, Metropolitan Club. Home: 2805 31st St NW Washington DC 20008-3524 Office: Project Internat Inc 1800 K St NW Ste 1018 Washington DC 20006-2202 also Office: Mid East Policy Coun 1730 M St NW Ste 512 Washington DC 20036-4516

FREEMAN, JAMES ATTICUS, III, lawyer, insurance and business consultant; b. Gadsden, Ala., Jan. 27, 1947; s. James Atticus and Dorothy Mae (Watson) F.; m. Judith Gail Davis, June 19, 1970; children: Gwendolyn Gail, James Atticus IV, Laura Marie. BS, Vanderbilt U., 1969, JD, 1972. Bar: Tenn. 1972. Broadcaster, newsman GE Broadcasting, Nashville, 1965-72; atty. The Murray Ohio Mfg. Co., Nashville, 1972-73, legal officer, 1973-81; asst. v.p., legal officer, asst. sec. The Murray Ohio Mfg. Co., Brentwood, Tenn., 1981-86, asst. v.p., legal officer, dir. risk mgmt., 1986-90, sec., 1988-90; of counsel Blackburn, Little, Smith & Slobey, Nashville, 1990-92; atty. Blackburn & Slobey, Nashville, 1992-94; shareholder Blackburn Slobey Freeman & Happell PC, Nashville, 1995-99, Blackburn & McCune, PC, Nashville, 1999—; pres. Litigation Mgmt. Specialists, Inc., 1989—; founder Nat. Alternative Dispute Resolution Svcs. Tenn., Inc.; bd. dirs. Some Assembly Required, Inc., Phoenix Property Mgmt. Svcs., Inc., Product Assembly, Inc.; lectr. corp. law, mem. bd. advisers Southeastern Inst. Paralegal Edn., Nashville, 1982-98); guest lectr. U. Wis. Sch. Engring., Madison, 1983—; resource cons. Med Marc Ins., 1992—. Mem. ABA, Tenn. Bar Assn., Nashville Bar Assn. (chmn. membership com. 1984, program chmn. corp. sect. 1985-86), Def. Rsch. Inst., Am. Soc. Metals (mem. adj. faculty Cleve. chpt. 1984-88), Outdoor Power Equipment Inst. (chmn. corp. counsel com. 1976-84), Bicycle Mfrs. Assn. (chmn. legal affairs com. 1978-81), Vanderbilt Alumni Assn., Risk and Ins. Mgmt. Soc. (v.p. Cumberland chpt. 1988, 89, Phi Alpha Delta. Episcopalian. Office: Blackburn and McCune PC 201 4th Ave N Nashville TN 37219-2011 also: Litigation Mgmt Specialists Two Brentwood Commons # 150 750 Old Hickory Blvd Brentwood TN 37027-4528

FREEMAN, JOEL ARTHUR, author, organizational change facilitator; b. Lewiston, Maine, July 24, 1954; s. Arthur Fickett and Katherine Ann (Schroeder) F.; m. Shirley Lee Burkhardt, Jan. 6, 1996; children: David Joel, Jesse Andrew, Jacob Edward, Shari Adelaide. MS in Pastoral Counseling, Loyola Coll., Balt., 1986; PhD in Pastoral Counseling, Evang. Theol. Sem., Dixon, Mo., 1991. Ordained to ministry Calvary Chapel Outreach Fellowship, 1975. Pastor Glorious Gospel Ch., Friendship, Maine, 1975-77, Balt., 1977-80, Columbia, Md., 1980-88; pastor Stillmeadow Christian Fellowship, Balt., 1988-93; pres. Freeman Inst., Severn, Md., 1993—; chaplain NBA Washington Wizards Basketball Team, 1979—; host radio talk show Sta. WABS, 1977-88; TV host Howard Cable Co., Ellicott City, Md., 1980-86; interviewer CBN Satellite Radio Network, 1988—; mentor, corp. chaplain The Shepherd's Guide, 1980—; chaplain Sports World Ministries, 1998—; exec. com. Jammin' Against the Darkness, 1998—. Author: The Doctrine of Fools, 1984, God Is Not Fair, 1987, Living with Your Conscience without Going Crazy, 1989, Kingdom Zoology, 1991, Return to Glory: The Powerful Stirring of the Black Man, 1997; co-prodr., co-writer (film) Return to Glory, 1998. Instr. chaplain's office Johns Hopkins U., Balt., 1977-79; mem. steering com. Word Renewal Pastor's Fellowship, Balt., 1977-83, County Exec. Prayer Breakfast, Howard County, 1983-86; area coord. Washington for Jesus, 1980. Mem. Inst. in Basic Life Principles (coord. 1979-86). Republican. Office: Freeman Inst 1103 Burkhardt Ln Severn MD 21144-2800

FREEMAN, JOHN CLINTON, meteorologist, oceanographer; b. Houston, Aug. 7, 1920; s. John Clinton and Ann (Dotson) F.; m. Marjorie Schaefer, June 14, 1947; children: John C. III, Walter H., Jill F. Hasling, Cathryn F. Disch, Helen, Paul D. BA, Rice U., 1941; MS, Calif. Inst. Tech., 1942; postgrad., Brown U., 1946-48; PhD, U. Chgo., 1952. Commd. 2d lt. USAF, 1941, advanced through grades to lt. col., 1970; weather officer U.S. Army, 1941-46; math. rschr. grad. divsn. applied math. Brown U., Providence, R.I., 1946-48; rschr. in meteorology U.S. Weather Bur., Washington, 1948-49, Inst. Advanced Study, Princeton, N.J., 1949-50, U. Chgo., 1950-52; rschr. in meteorology and oceanography, prof. Tex. A&M, College Station, Tex., 1952-55; meteorology and oceanography rschr. Gulf Cons.-NESCO, Houston, 1955-66; prof., chmn. and dir. rsch. Inst. Storm Rsch.-U. St. Thomas, Houston, 1957-88; dir. rsch., pres. Weather Rsch. Ctr., Houston, 1988—; convenor, chmn. Internat. Conf. Coastal Engring., Houston, 1984; presenter in field. Contbr. chpts. to books. Fellow Am. Meteorology Soc. (chmn. com. applied meteorology 1975-76, Meisinger award 1950, spl. award Tex. tornado radar network 1961); mem. Am. Geophys. Union, Marine Tech. Soc. (local chmn. 1970). Democrat. Church of Christ. Avocation: dog training. Office: Weather Rsch Ctr 3227 Audley St Houston TX 77098-1901

FREEMAN, JOY LYNN, counselor, psychotherapist; b. Neptune, N.J., Jan. 8, 1952; d. Benjamin Morris Edelstein and Joy Freeman; m. Kenneth G. Nelson; 1 child, Sandahl Nelson. BA in Dance and Performing Arts, Lone Mt. Coll., 1974; D of Chiropractic, N.Y. Inst. Chiropractic, 1978; postgrad., Internat. U. Profl. Studies, 1997—. Chiropractor Marin Chiropractic Ctr., Mill Valley, Calif., 1978-89, Sportech, Larkspur, Calif., 1978-89, Coast Chiropractic Ctr., Encinitas, Calif., 1978-89; pvt. practice counselor, therapist, personal coach, 1990—; spkr. in field, presenter seminars; organizer workshops and retreats; nature retreat facilitator. Columnist Am. Chiropractic, ICA Jour., Dynamic Chiropractic, 1989-98; radio interviewee.

FREEMAN, KEVIN DAVID, portfolio management executive; b. Tulsa, Aug. 17, 1961; s. Kerry Landon and Evelyn Sue (Courtney) F.; m. Marnie Renee Westfall, Jan. 29, 1999. BSBA and Econs., U. Tulsa, 1983. CFA. Pres., sr. editor, sr. market strategist DBA, The Personal Capitalist, Tulsa, 1981-91; mng. dir. Templeton Portfolio Adv., Carmel, Calif., 1991—; cons. Templeton Galbraith & Hansberger, Nassau, The Bahamas, 1990; bd. dirs. Carmel Creamery, Inc. Author: (booklet) A Common Sense Guide to Investment Profits, 1990; author, editor (newsletter) The Personal Capitalist, 1985-91. Chmn., founder Adam Smith Found., Tulsa, 1989-92; pub. policy expert-econs. The Heritage Found., Washington, 1991-92; assoc. Hillsdale (Mich.) Coll., 1996—; bd. govs. Coun. for Nat. Policy, 1998—. Recipient Double Ruby award Nat. Forensic League, 1979. Mem. Assn. Investment Mgmt. and Rsch., Internat. Soc. Fin. Analysts, Pres. Club Hillsdale Coll. Republican. Baptist. Avocations: golf, scuba diving, horseback riding, entrepreneur. Office: Templeton Portfolio Adv 26515 Carmel Rancho Blvd Carmel CA 93923-8701

FREEMAN, KURT ANDREW, psychologist, educator; b. Fullerton, Calif., Apr. 29, 1970; s. Otis Lee and Carol Therese F.; m. Johnny E. Whitted. BA, Claremont McKenna Coll., 1992; MA, W.Va. U., 1995, PhD, 1999. Behavior data specialist, clin. specialist Kennedy Krieger Inst., Balt., 1992-94; grad. clinician Univ. Affiliated Ctr. Devel. Disabilities, Morgantown, W.Va., 1995-98; intern Fr. Flanagan's Boys Home, Boys Town, Nebr., 1998-99; asst. prof. Pacific U., Portland, Oreg., 1999—. Mem. Assn. Behavior Analysis, Assn. Advancement Behavior Therapy. Avocations: mountain biking, watercolor painting. Home: 5300 Parkview Dr Apt 1081 Lake Oswego OR 97035-8727 Office: Pacific U 511 SW 10th Ave Fl 4 Portland OR 97205-2732

FREEMAN, LEONARD MURRAY, radiologist, nuclear medicine physician, educator; b. N.Y.C., Apr. 20, 1937; s. Joseph and Tillie (Krutman) F.; m. Marlene Carolyn Held, Apr. 28, 1967; children: Eric Lawrence, David Robert, Joy Esther. B.A., N.Y. U., 1957; M.D., Chgo. Med. Sch., 1961. Diplomate: Am. Bd. Radiology, Am. Bd. Nuclear Medicine. Intern Beth Israel Hosp. and Med. Center, N.Y.C., 1961-62; resident in radiology Bronx Municipal Hosp. Center, 1962-65; mem. staff Albert Einstein Coll. Medicine, N.Y.C., 1965—; co-dir. div. nuclear medicine Jacobi Med. Ctr., N.Y.C., 1965-83; dir. nuclear medicine Montefiore Med. Center, N.Y.C., 1976—, attending radiologist, 1977—; cons. nuclear medicine USPHS Hosp., S.I., N.Y., 1967-82, St. Barnabas Hosp., Bronx, 1967—, Beth Israel Hosp. and Med. Center, 1974—, Maimonides Hosp. and Med. Center, 1974-99, Bklyn. VA Hosp., 1984—; asst. instr. radiology Albert Einstein Coll. Medicine, Bronx, 1964-65, instr., 1965-67, asst. prof., 1967-72, assoc. prof., 1972-77, prof., 1977—, prof. nuclear medicine, 1983—, vice chmn. dept. nuclear medicine, 1987—; mem. adv. coun. nuclear medicine program Brookhaven Nat. Labs., Upton, N.Y., 1972-82; examiner nuclear medicine Am. Bd. Radiology. Author: Clinical Scintillation Scanning, 1969, Clinical Scintillation Imaging, 1975, Freeman and Johnson's Clinical Radionuclide Imaging, 1984; co-editor Seminars in Nuclear Medicine, 1970—, Physicians Desk Reference for Radiology and Nuclear Medicine, 1971-80; reviewer Jour. Nuclear Medicine, 1972—; editor Nuclear Medicine Ann., 1980—, Current Concepts in Diagnostic Nuclear Medicine, 1983-87, Advances in Functional Neuroimaging, 1988-90; mem. editl. bd. European Jour. Nuclear Medicine, 1979—, Jour. Nuclear Medicine and Allied Scis., 1982-96, Nuclear Medicine Communications, 1986—, Quar. Jour. Nuclear Medicine, 1996—; contbr. numerous articles to jours., also book chpts. Fellow Am. Coll. Radiology, Am. Coll. Nuclear Physicians, N.Y. Acad. Medicine; mem. AMA, Soc. Nuclear Medicine (gov. local chpt. 1973—, nat. trustee 1973-77, nat. v.p. 1977-78, nat. pres. 1979-80, chmn. pub. rels. com. 1981-91, chmn. correlative imaging coun. 1982-84, chmn. awards com. 1983-86, Disting. Edn. award 1993, Berson-Yallow award Greater N.Y. chpt. 1997), Am. Roentgen Ray Soc., Radiol. Soc. N.Am., N.Y. Roentgen Soc., L.I. Radiol. Soc., Soc. Gastrointestinal Radiologists, N.Y. State Med. Soc., New York County Med. Soc., Pan Am. Med. Assn. (hon. life), European Assn. Nuclear Medicine, Gissellschaft für Nuklearmedizin (hon. corr.), L.I. Soc. Nuclear Med. Technologists (hon. life), Alpha Omega Alpha (hon.). Home: 50 Sutton Pl S New York NY 10022-4167 Office: 111 E 210th St Bronx NY 10467-2401

FREEMAN, PATRICIA ELIZABETH, library and education specialist; b. El Dorado, Ark., Nov. 30, 1924; d. Herbert A. and M. Elizabeth (Pryor) Harper; m. Jack Freeman, June 15, 1949; 3 children. BA, Centenary Coll., 1943; postgrad., Fine Arts Ctr., 1942-46, Art Students League, 1944-45; BSLS, La. State U., 1946; postgrad., Calif. State U., 1959-61, U. N.Mex., 1964-74; EdS, Peabody Coll., Vanderbilt U., 1975. Libr. U. Calif., Berkeley, 1946-47; libr. Albuquerque Pub. Schs., 1964-67, ind. sch. libr. media ctr. cons., 1967—. Painter lithographer; one-person show La. State Exhibit Bldg., 1948; author: Pathfinder: An Operational Guide for the School Librarian, 1975, Southeast Heights Neighborhoods of Albuquerque, 1993; compiler, editor: Elizabeth Pryor Harper's Twenty-One Southern Families, 1985; editor: SEHNA Gazette, 1988-93, N.Mex. AAUW, 1999—. Mem. task force Goals for Dallas-Environ., 1977-82; pres. Friends of Sch. Librs., Dallas, 1979-83; v.p., editor Southeast Heights Neighborhood Assn., 1988-93. With USAF, 1948-49. Honoree AAUW Ednl. Found., 1979, 96; vol. award for outstanding service Dallas Ind. Sch. Dist., 1978; AAUW Pub. Service grantee 1980. Mem. ALA, AAUW (dir. Dallas 1976-82, Albuquerque 1983-85, N.Mex. 1999—), LWV (sec. Dallas 1982-83, editor Albuquerque 1984-88), Nat. Trust Historic Preservation, Friends of Pub. Libr., N.Mex. Symphony Guild, Alpha Xi Delta. Home: 612 Ridgecrest Dr SE Albuquerque NM 87108-3365

FREEMAN, RICHARD FRANCIS, banker; b. Mt. Kisco, N.Y., Apr. 19, 1934; s. Richard Francis and Nora Frances (O'Connell) F.; m. Barbara Jean Calhoun, Nov. 30, 1957; children: Kathleen, Kevin, Kelley, Keith. B.S. in Finance and Banking, Miami U., Oxford, Ohio, 1956; grad., Stonier Grad. Sch. Banking, Rutgers U., 1973. With Central Nat. Bank, Cleve., 1956-60, No. Westchester Nat. Bank, Chappaqua, N.Y., 1960-67; with State Nat. Bank Conn., Bridgeport, 1967-78, exec. v.p., dir., 1974-78; pres., chief exec. officer The Bank Mart (formerly City Savs. Bank Conn.), Bridgeport, 1978-91; pres., CEO Bridgeport Area Found., to 1999, dir., chmn., 1999—; bd. dirs. Conn. Energy Corp., So. Conn. Gas. Co., Physicians Health Svcs., Inc. Former chmn. bd. trustees Park City Hosp., Bridgeport; bd. dirs. Bridgeport Econ. Devel. Corp., Ctr. for Fin. Studies, Inc.; mem. bus. adv. coun. Miami U. Sch. Bus. Adminstrn. Office: Bridgeport Area Found 940 Broad St Bridgeport CT 06604-4813

FREEMAN, LORD ROGER NORMAN, former British government official; b. Neston, Cheshire, Eng., May 27, 1942; s. Norman James and Marjorie Hilda (Ellis) F.; m. Jennifer Margaret Watson, Feb. 15, 1969; children: Edmund Malcolm, Olivia Margaret. BA with honors, Balliol Coll., Oxford, Eng., 1964; MA, Oxford U., 1969. Mng. dir. Lehmans Bros. Inc., N.Y.C. and London, 1969-84; mem. Parliament for Kettering Govt. of U.K., 1983-97, parliamentary under sec. of state for Armed Forces, 1986-88, parliamentary under sec. of state for health, 1988-90, min. of state for pub. transport, 1990-94, min. of state for defense procurement, 1994-95, cabinet min., chancellor of the duchy of Lancaster (Office of Pub. Svc.), 1995-97; cons. Pricewaterhouse Coopers, 1997—; bd. mem., chmn. Thomson-CSF (U.K.). Named Privy Counsellor Her Majesty the Queen, 1993. Office: Thomson-CSF, 173 Blvd Haussmann, 75415 Paris Cedex 08, France*

FREESE, BARBARA TAPP, nursing educator; b. Kansas City, Mo., Oct. 1, 1944; d. Ernest M. and Marjorie (McIntosh) Tapp; m. Hal Freese, Feb. 3, 1968; 1 child, Tiffany Jo. BSN, U. Mo., 1967; MSN, Clemson U., 1980; EdD, U. Ga., 1989. Nursing faculty Lander U., Greenwood, 1975—, dean sch. nursing, 1989-2000. Contbr. articles to profl. jours. Trustee Neuman Sys. Model Group. Fellow Royal Coll. Nursing, Australia; mem. ANA, Nat. League for Nursing, Mensa, Sigma Theta Tau., Kappa Delta Pi.

FREESE, KATHERINE, physicist, educator; b. Freiburg, Germany, Feb. 8, 1957; came to U.S., 1957; d. Ernst and Elisabeth Gertrude Maria (Bautz) F.; 1 child, Douglas Quincy Adams. BA, Princeton U., 1977; MA, Columbia U., 1981; PhD, U. Chgo., 1984. Postdoctoral fellow Harvard/Smithsonian Ctr. for Astrophysics, Cambridge, Mass., 1984-85, Inst. for Theoretical Physics, Santa Barbara, Calif., 1985-87, U. Calif., Berkeley, 1987-88; asst. prof. physics MIT, Cambridge, 1988-91; prof. physics U. Mich., Ann Arbor, 1991—; gen. mem. Aspen Ctr. for Physics, 1991—. Contbr. articles to profl. jours. William Rainey Harper fellow U. Chgo, 1982; Sloan Found. fellow, 1989; Presdl. Young Investigator NSF, 1990, rsch. grantee, 1991, 94; Presdl. fellow U. Calif., 1987. Mem. Am. Phys. Soc., Assn. for Women in Sci. Democrat. Avocations: water polo, swimming, skiing, tennis. Office: U Mich Dept Physics Ann Arbor MI 48109

FREESTON, KENNETH RUSSELL, school system administrator; b. Newark, June 27, 1950; s. H. Russell and Ruth Loan (Lehr) F.; m. Cheryl Wuchter, Feb. 13, 1982; 1 child, David Kenneth. BA, Colgate U., 1972, MAT, 1973; PhD, U. Conn., 1985. Tchr. social studies West Hartford Pub. Schs. (Conn.), 1973-79, head dept. social studies, 1979-83; prin. Amity Regional Jr. H.S., Bethany, Conn., 1983-88; asst. supt. Newtown (Conn.) Pub. Sch., 1988-94; supt. Easton, Redding, Region 9, Conn., 1994—; cons. total quality mgmt., curriculum Grinnell Coll. Author: Welcome to Club Dad; contbr. articles to profl. jours. and mags. Named to Outstanding Young Men Am. U.S. Jaycees, 1981; recognized by Pres. Reagan as prin. on nat. exemplary sch., 1984. Mem. Nat. Soc. Study Edn., Nat. Assn. for Edn. Young Children, Am. Ednl. Rsch. Assn., Am. Assn. Sch. Adminstrs., ASCD (Conn. Ednl. Leader of Yr. 1997), N.E. Ednl. Rsch. Assn., Phi Delta Kappa. Episcopalian. Achievements include research in organizational behavior, leadership. Avocations: writing, antiques, photography. Home: 8 King St Newtown CT 06470-1703 Office: Bds of Edn 605 Main St Monroe CT 06468-2853

FREI, TAMA'S, journalist, reporter, anchorman; b. Pecs, Hungary, May 21, 1966; s. Tamas Frei and Judit Szili; m. Edit Schranz, Aug. 20, 1994; children: Zsófia, Balázs. Student, U. Law, Budapest, 1986-87, U. Internat. Relationship, Moscow, 1988-89; journalism diploma, Sch. Radio Journalism, Bern, Switzerland, 1991; student, U. Tenn., 1992. Media mgmt. trainee Voice of Am., U.S. Info. Agy., Washington, 1990; reporter Hungarian Radio, Budapest, 1992; anchorman Hungarian TV, Budapest, 1992-95, editor, 1994-95; editor-in-chief Action News, Budapest, 1996—. Recipient Hungarian Pulitzer prize, 1992, Opus prize, 1995, Best Hungarian TV Journalist award, 1996. Mem. Assn. Investigative Reporters and Editors, Fedn. Hungarian Journalists, Internat. Journalism Club. Avocations: tennis, skiing, diving, collecting old history books.

FREIDHEIM, CYRUS F., JR., management consultant; b. Chgo., June 14, 1935; s. Cyrus F. and Eleanor Freidheim; m. Marguerite VandenBosch; children: Marguerite Lynn, Stephen Cyrus, Scott. BSChE, U. Notre Dame, 1957; MS in Indsl. Adminstrn., Carnegie Mellon U., 1963. Plant mgr. Union Carbide Corp., Whiting, Ind., 1961; cons. Price Waterhouse, Chgo., 1962; fin. analyst Ford Motor Co., Dearborn, Mich., 1963-66; vice chmn. Booz, Allen & Hamilton, Chgo., 1966—; dir. Household Internat. Inc., 1989—, Security Capital Group, 1991—, Microage, 1988—. Author: The Trillion Dollar Enterprise, 1998. Chmn. bd. trustees Thunderbird, The Am. Grad. Sch. Internat. Mgmt.; dir. Chgo. Coun. Fgn. Rels.; trustee Rush-Presbyn.-St. Luke's Med. Ctr., 1981—; assoc. Northwestern U., 1981—; trustee Chgo. Symphony Orch.; vice chmn. bd. overseers Rush U., bd. dirs.;

trustee Brookings Instn., 1998—. With USN, 1957-61. Mem. Coun. Fgn. Rels., U.S. Japan Bus. Coun., Chgo. Club, Mid Day Club, Econ. Club, Comml. Club (Chgo.), Stanwich Club (Greenwich, Conn.), Old Elm Club, Lost Tree Club (North Palm Beach). Home: 1320 N State Pkwy Chicago IL 60610-2118 Office: 225 W Wacker Dr Chicago IL 60606-1224

FREIDLIN, IRINA SOLOMONOVNA, immunologist, consultant; b. Leningrad, Russia, Mar. 7, 1936; d. Solomon Iakovlevich and Natalia Glebovna (Ivashencova) F. Grad. physician, Med. Inst., Leningrad, 1959, PhD in Medicine, 1962, DSc in Medicine, 1974. Med. diplomate. Asst. prof. Med. Inst., Leningrad, 1964-68, assoc. prof., 1968-87, additional prof., 1987—, prof. microbiology and immunology, 1989—; head dept. immunology Inst. Exptl. Medicine Russian Acad. Med. Scis., St. Petersburg, Russia, 1991—; mem. NATO Collaborative Rsch. Project, Lauven, Belgium, 1994-95. Author: Mononuclear Phagocyte System, 1984; contbr. articles to profl. jours. WHO fellow Pasteur Inst., Paris, 1964-65, grant and title Soros Prof. Internat. Soros Sci. Edn. Program, 1995-96. Mem. Soc. Immunologists (mem. presidium St. Petersburg 1985—), Russian Soc. Immunologists (mem. presidium 1992—), Soc. Immunologists Moscow (editl. bd. Russian Jour. Immunology 1996-97), Russian Acad. Med. Scis. (corr.). Avocation: macrobiotic style of life. Home: Acad Pavlov Str 16b-I, 197022 Saint Petersburg Russia Office: Inst Exptl Medicine RAMS, Acad Pavlov Str 12, 197376 Saint Petersburg Russia

FREIHA, JUDITH ANNE SUPPLE, volunteer; b. Greenbrae, Calif., July 22, 1958; d. Frederic Edward and Helen Marilyn (Andersen) Supple; m. Bassam Said Freiha, Sept. 12, 1983; children: Hassiba Therese, Issam Elias, Elissa-Bassima. Student, Am. River Coll., Sacramento, Calif., 1978, Santa Monica Coll., 1979. Gov. Brit. Sch. Paris, Croissy-sur-Seine, 1994—; dancer, choreographer classical ballet Sacramento Ballet Co., 1969-72. Fgn. corr. Fairuz Mag., 1994—. Co-chmn. Girl Scouts USA, Paris, 1995-99, lifetime mem.; asst. dist. commr. Boy Scouts Am., Charlemagne Dist., Paris, 1996-99, hon. mem.; mem. Rep. Womens Guild, Palm Springs, Calif., 1987-99; asst. programmer films Palm Springs Internat. Film Festival, 1999—. Episcopalian. Avocation: photography for magazines, painting, modern art, writing poetry. Office: Dar Assayad SAL, PO Box 1038, Hazmieh Lebanon

FREIHERR ZU PUTLITZ, GISBERT, physics educator, foundation executive; b. Rostock, Germany, Feb. 14, 1931; s. Waldemar and Annalies (von Wolffersdorff) F.; m. Haide Beckers, July 9, 1960; children: Jasper, York, Julian. Cert. mechanic-toolmaker, IHK Nürnberg Zündapp AG, Germany, 1953; diploma in physics, U. Heidelberg, Germany, 1961; D, U. Heidelberg, 1962; JD (hon.), Boston U., 1986; D (hon.), U. Md., 1986; hon. degree, U. Fed. do Rio Grande do Sul, 1987; D (hon.), Staatsuniversität Leningrad, Russia, 1990, U. "Alisher Navoi", Samarkand, Uzbekistan, 1992, Staatsuniversität Kaliningrad, 1995, Jagiellonische U. Krakau, 1996. Asst. in physics U. Heidelberg, 1962-66, docent in physics, 1966-70, assoc. prof. physics, 1970-72, prof. physics, 1972—; sci. dir. Gesellschaft für Schwerionenforsch, Darmstadt, Germany, 1978-83; chmn. Assn. German Nat. Labs., Bonn, 1981-83, Gottlieb Daimler-und Karl Benz-Stiftung, Ladenburg, Germany, 1986—; rector U. Heidelberg, 1983-87; chmn. 4th Internat. Conf. on Atomic Physics, Heidelberg,1974, 2d German-Soviet Laserseminar, Heidelberg, 1980, 1st European Conf. on Atomic and Molecular Physics, Heidelberg, 1981, 10th Internat. Conf. on Particles and Nuclei, 1984, Linear Accelerator Conf., Darmstadt, Germany, 1984. Contbr. over 200 articles to profl. jours.; editor European Phys. Jour. Recipient Staatspreis für Mechaniker des Landes Bayern, 1953, Gold medal of honor State of Baden-Württemberg, 1988, Leo Baeck prize Ctrl. Coun. of Jews in Germany, 1989; named to Order of Merit 1st class, Fed. Republic of Germany, 1984. Fellow Am. Phys. Soc., Siliman Coll. Yale U. (assoc.), World Acad. Art and Sci., N.Y. Acad. Scis.; mem. German Physics Soc., European Phys. Soc., Deutsche Gesellschaft Naturforscher und Ärzte, Acad. Scis. Berlin, Heidelberg Acad. Scis. (pres. 2000—), Acad. Europaea, Deutsche Akademie der Naturforscher Leopoldina, Berlin-Brandenburg Acad. of Scis. (corr.). Evangelical. Office: U Heidelberg, Philosophenweg 12, 69120 Heidelberg Germany

FREIJ, GHASSAN JAMIL, executive; b. Kuwait, Aug. 1, 1959; s. Jamil and Latifeh (Abdouh) F.; m. Raeda Freij, June 5, 1994; children: Farah and Ruby (twins). B of Engring., Liverpool U., England, 1981, PhD, 1985. Rschr. Liverpool U., England, 1984-85; rsch. assoc. Cambridge U., England, 1985-88; project mgr. Philips, England, 1988-90; coord. rsch. & devel. Philips, Brussels, 1990-92; tech. dir. Erti Co., Brussels, 1992-95, dir. ops., 1995—. Recipient Overseas Rsch. Student award England Com. U. Vice Chancellors, Loverpool, 1981-84; Liverpool U. scholar, 1981-84. Avocations: skiing, water skiing, swimming, sailing, chess, cycling. Office: Ertico, Ave Louise 326, B-1050 Brussels Belgium

FREILICH, IRVIN M., lawyer; b. Ulm, Germany, Mar. 3, 1949; came to U.S., 1949; s. Charles J. and Sylvia (Schaengold) F.; m. Judith Ellen Pines, June 20, 1971; children: Jared P., Emily R. BA, U. Cin., 1971; JD, Georgetown U., 1974. Bar: N.Y. 1975, N.J. 1977, U.S. Dist. Ct. (so. and ea. dist.) N.Y. 1975, U.S. Dist. Ct. (no. dist.) N.Y. 1985, U.S. Dist. Ct. N.J. 1975, U.S. Ct. Appeals (3d cir.) 1983, U.S. Ct. Appeals (2d cir.) 1975, U.S. Ct. Appeals (D.C. cir.) 1996, U.S. Supreme Ct. 1987. Assoc. Kaye, Scholer, Fierman, Hayes & Handler, N.Y.C., 1974-77; from assoc. to ptnr. Hannoch Weisman, Roseland, N.J., 1977-90, 94-99; ptnr. Edwards & Angell, Newark, 1990-94, Robertson, Freilich, Bruno & Cohen, LLC, Newark, 1999—. Office: Robertson Freilich Bruno & Cohen LLC One Riverfront Plz Newark NJ 07102

FREIMAN, CHARLES VISVALD, engineering foundation administrator; b. N.Y.C., June 17, 1932; s. John and Selma Marie (Pupurin) F.; m. Margaret Carol Messerschmidt, June 5, 1955; children: Paul, Katherine, Barbara, John. AB, Columbia Coll., 1954; BS, Columbia U., 1955, MS, 1956, EngScD, 1961. Adj. instr. NYU and U. Conn., N.Y.C. and Stamford, 1963-65; instr. in elec. engring. Columbia U., N.Y.C., 1956-60; mgr. IBM R & D, various locations, 1960-84, IBM Computer Sci. Inst., Tokyo, 1985-87, IBM Corp. Artificial Intelligence Project Office, White Plains, N.Y., 1987-89; sec. IBM Acad. of Tech., Armonk, N.Y., 1989-90; dir. Engring. Found., N.Y.C., 1990-98; exec. dir. United Engring. Found., N.Y.C., 1998—; program chair U.S. Com. for IFIP Congresses, 1971, 74, 77; steering com. Nat. Rsch. Coun., Japanese-English Machine Translation, Washington DC, 1989-90; v.p. JETS, Alexandria, Va., 1997—; computer engring. program evaluator Accreditation Bd. for Engring. & Tech., N.Y.C., 1988-91; lectr. in field. Editor: Information Processing '71, 1971; contbr. articles to profl. jours. and conference proceedings. Chmn. United Fund, Pleasantville, N.Y., 1962; pres., treas. Luth. Congregations, N.Y., Calif., Japan, 1961—; vice-chmn. Com. on Housing for the Elderly, Pleasantville, 1968-84. Pulitzer scholar Columbia U., N.Y.C., 1950-54; Goodrich prize Columbia U., 1952; named Man of the Yr. Emanuel Evangelical Luth. Ch., Pleasantville, 1984. Mem. IEEE (sr. mem., life), N.Y. Acad. Scis., AAAS, Assn. for Computing Machinery, Sigma Xi, Tau Beta Pi, Eta Kappa Nu. Democrat. Achievements include 10 U.S. patents and author of 25 patent publications for high performance computers and protective coding. Home: 25 High Ridge Rd Ossining NY 10562 Office: United Engring Found 3 Park Ave New York NY 10016-5902

FREIMAN, LENER JOSIFOVICH, corrosion engineer; b. Moscow, Dec. 2, 1931; s. Yosif Abramovich Freiman and Olga Grigoryevna Cogan; m. Lisa Isakovna Popok, Nov. 1, 1956; children: Leonid, Valentin. Student, Moscow Inst. Steel, 1949-55; D of Chemistry, Karpov Inst. Phys. Chemistry, Moscow, 1967. From engr. to sr. engr. Kemerovo (USSR) Mech. Plant, 1955-58; from jr. rschr. to rschr. Karpov Inst. Phys. Chemistry, Moscow, 1958-67, sr. rschr., 1967-84; sr. rschr. K.D. Pamfilov Acad. Mcpl. Economy, Moscow, 1984-96, lead rschr., 1996—; chief sci. dept. COMECOA Coord. Ctr. Corrosion Protection, Moscow, 1972-80; sr. lect. Moscow Inst. Chem. Machine-Bldg., Moscow, 1976-83. Author: Potentiostatic Methods in Corrosion Investigations and Electrochemical Protection, 1972, Corrosion Protection of Underground Metallic Structures, 1990; co-editor: Corrosion Abstracts, 1984—; contbr. articles to profl. jours. Home: Grodnenskaya ul 10-109, 121471 Moscow Russia Office: KD Pamfilov Acad Mcpl Econ, Volokolamskoye shosse 116, 123371 Moscow Russia

FREIRE, JUAN JOSE, education educator; b. Madrid, Aug. 27, 1950; s. Juan Freire and Maria Angeles Gomez. BS in Chemistry, Univ. Complutense, Madrid, 1972, PhD in Chemistry, 1975. Asst. prof. U. Complutense, Madrid, 1978-92, prof., 1992—; sec. Spanish Group of Polymers, Madrid, 1989-92; postdoctoral fellow Yale U., New Haven, Conn., 1975-77. Contbr. about 100 articles to profl. jours. Mem. Am. Chem. Soc., Real Sociedad de Quimica. Avocations: sports, music, reading. Office: Dep Quimica Fisical, Univ Complutense, 28040 Madrid Spain

FREIRE, MARIA DO CARMO MATIAS, dentist; b. Inhumas, Goiás, Brazil, May 30, 1961; d. Fidelino de Souza and Josefina Matias Freire; m. José Luiz Derr, Apr. 15, 1987. M in Dental Pub. Health, U. London, 1991, PhD in Dental Pub. Health, 1999. Dentist Local Health Authority, Goiânia, Brazil, 1984-92; lectr. Dental Sch. Fed. U. of Goiás, Goiânia-Go, 1992—; pvt. practice Goiânia-Go, 1986-91. Contbr. articles to profl. jours. Scholarship British Coun., 1990, Coordenacão de Aperfeiçoament de Pessoal de Nível Superior, 1996. Avocations: cinema, travel. Office: Faculdade de Odontologia, Praça Universitária, 74605220 Gioânia Brazil

FREIRE, RUI M.S. CARDOSO, communications executive; b. Lisbon, Portugal, June 21, 1951; s. José S.C. and Maria Tereza (Soveral) F.; m.Maria-JoséR.A.P. Cardoso, June 21, 1975; children: Mafalda, Ines, Diana. Student, U. Lisbon, 1972. Journalist Motor, Lisbon, Portugal, 1983-87, Diario Motor, Lisbon, Portugal, 1986-89; editor Autosport, Lisbon, Portugal, 1987-93, editor-in-chief, 1993—. Office: Autosport, R Ruben A Leitão 2-1o, 1200 Lisbon Portugal

FREITAG, CAROL WILMA, state official, political scientist; b. Ada, Okla., July 21, 1939; d. Lowell William and Lois Marie (Robertson) Petersen; m. Henry Wesley Freitag, Dec. 20, 1961 (dec. Nov. 1985); children: Bonita Louise, Henry Lowell. Diploma in Dental Hygiene, Northwestern U., 1959; BA, Purdue U., Hammond, Ind., 1988. Registered dental hygienist, Ill. Pvt. practice dental hygiene Henry W. Freitag, D.D.S., Homewood, Ill., 1959-85; mem. group practice Chgo., 1970; faculty, interim dir. dental hygiene Prairie State Coll., Chicago Heights, Ill., 1971-72; pvt. practice James J. Kreuz, D.D.S., Homewood, 1985-90; contbr. articles to profl. jours. Chair U.S. Constn. Bicentennial Commn., Village of Matteson, Ill., 1986-89; pres. Matteson Hist. Soc., 1987-89; panel spkr. South Suburban Heritage Assn., Homewood, 1990. Calumet rep. Bicentennial Com. Purdue U., 1988; vis. com. Northwestern Dental Sch., 1997-98; mem. centennial celebration com. Bloom Twp. H.S., 2000. Recipient Key to City, Village of Matteson, 1990, Svc. award Northwestern U., 1980, Good Neighbor award Village of Matteson, 1989. Mem. AAUW, Am. Dental Hygienists' Assn. (chairperson Ann. Session Program 1975), Ill. Dental Hygienists Assn. (pres. 1968-69, bd. dirs., Merit award 1979), G.V. Black Soc. (leader, pres. 1997-2001), Evelyn E. Maas Soc. (pres. 1989-90, bd. dirs., Merit award 1993), Northwestern Dental Sch. Alumni Assn. (bd. dirs. 1969—, pres. 1977-78, v.p. 1976-77, 90-93), Acad. Polit. Sci., Sigma Phi Alpha (hon. mem. dental hygiene soc.), Alpha Chi (scholarship soc.). Avocation: travel. Home: 7926 Belle Rive Ct Tinley Park IL 60477-4583

FREITAS, ALEX ALVES, computer science educator, researcher; b. Belo Horizonte, Brazil, Dec. 18, 1964; s. Roberto de Freitas Costa and Mara Augusta Alves. BSc, FATEC-SP, Sao Paulo, Brazil, 1989; MSc, UFSCar, Sao Carlos, Brazil, 1993; PhD in Computer Sci., U. Essex, Colchester, Eng., 1997. Sys. analyst ECT-SP, Sao Paulo, 1989-90, TRF-SP, Sao Paulo, 1990-91; univ. lectr. CEFET-PR, Curitiba, Brazil, 1997-98; assoc. prof. PUC-PR, Curitiba, 1999—. Author: Scientific Book on Data Mining, 1998; contbr. articles to profl. jours. Mem. AAAI (life), The Planetary Soc. Avocations: science fiction, chess, detective novels, travel, cinema.

FREITAS, BRENO MAGALHÃES, science educator; b. Fortaleza, Ceará, Brazil, Feb. 25, 1965; s. Breno Araujo and Isabel (Magalhães) F.; m. Débora Gaspar, Sept. 10, 1994; 1 child, Douglas. BSc, Fed. U. Ceará, Fortalez, 1988, MSc, 1991; PhD, U. Wales, Cardiff, 1995. Cert. in agronomy. Rsch. asst. Brazilian Nat. Rsch. Coun.-EMBRAPA, Sobral, Brazil, 1988-89; rsch. lectr. Fed. U. Ceará, Fortaleza, 1996—; cons. High Edn. Agrl. Sch., Mossoró, Brazil, 1996-2000, Tech. Ctr. State of Ceará, Fortaleza, 1997—; rschr. Brazilian Nat. Rsch. Coun., 1996—. Author: (tech. film) Pollination, 1994; (CD-Rom) Life of Bees, 1999. Recipient Prêmio Octávio Domingues, Brazilian Soc. Animal Sci., 1992. Mem. Internat. Bee Rsch. Assn., Internat. Commn. for Plant-Bee Relationship, Beekeepers' Assn. of Ceará (pres. 1990-91). Avocations: soccer, reading, films. Office: Fed U Ceará, Dept Zoology CP 12168, 60355970 Fortaleza Brazil

FREITAS, LUIS CARLOS DA CONCEICAO, computer company executive; b. Rio de Janeiro, Apr. 11, 1951; s. Antonio and Arcelina (da Conceição) F.; m. Marcia Maria Berthold, Feb. 4, 1977; children: Rafael Berthold, Bruno Berthold. Econs., U. Fed. Fluminense, Niteroi, Rio de Janeiro, 1973; M in Econs., Fundação Getulio Vargas, Rio de Janeiro, 1975, PhD in Econs., 1984. Gen. mgr. tech. area Devel. Bank Rio de Janeiro State, Rio de Janeiro, 1975-83; mgr. new bus. devel. Brit. Am. Tobacco (Souza Cruz-Brazil), Rio de Janeiro, 1983-88; controller, 1996-98; CFO Polo Industria e Comercio (subs. Brit. Am. Tobacco), São Paulo, 1989, Industrias Alimenticias Maguary S.A. (subs. Brit. Am. Tobacc, São Paulo, 1989-92, BAT (New Zealand), Wellington, 1992-94; chief internat. auditor BATCO-Eng., Staines, 1994-96; CFO Dell Computers (Brazil), Eldorado Sul, Rio Grande do Sul, 1998—. Avocations: tennis, reading, soccer. Office: Dell Brazil, Av Indsl Belgraf, 400-Bairro Medianeira Eldorado do Sul Rio Grande do Sul, Brazil

FREIVALDS, LAILA, Swedish government official, lawyer; b. Riga, Latvia, June 22, 1942; m. Johan Hedström; 1 child. Attended, U. Uppsala, Sweden. With Dist. Ct., 1970-72, Svea Ct. of Appeals, 1973-74; reporting clk. Ct. of Appeal, 1974; counsel Västerås Rent Tribunal, 1974-75; with Riksdag Info. Office, 1975-76; sr. adminstrn. officer, head divsn. Nat. Bd. for Consumer Policies, 1976-79, dir. gen., consumer ombudsman, 1983-88; min. of justice Ministry of Justice, 1988-91, 94—; legal cons. Baker & McKenzie, Stockholm, 1992-94. Office: Ministry of Justice, Rosenbad 4, S-103 33 Stockholm Sweden

FREIWALD, DAVID ALLEN, physicist, mechanical engineer; b. Cleve., June 4, 1941; s. Harry Herman and Arline Mildred (Woehrman) F.; children: Wesley, Todd, Christopher; m. Joyce Darlyne Gross, Apr. 3, 1976. BSME, Northwestern U., 1963, PhD, 1968. Rsch. scientist Sandia Nat. Labs., Albuquerque, 1967-72; scientist, staff dir.'s office Los Alamos (N.Mex.) Nat. Lab., 1972-81; program mgr. SEA, Inc., McLean, Va., 1981-82, MRJ, Inc., Oakton, Va., 1982-85; dir., gen. mgr. Gen. Dynamics, San Diego, 1985-90; v.p.. F2 Assocs., San Diego, 1991-92, Albuquerque, 1992—; adv. bd. USAF, Washington, 1985; team leader 20-Yr. Look Ahead Study Gen. Dynamics, St. Louis, 1986-87; SMES adv. bd. Bechtel, Inc., San Francisco, 1986-87. Active N.Mex. Gov.'s Land Use Legislation Com., Santa Fe, 1971, Energy Task Force, 1973-74; pres. Whispering Ridge Homeowners Assn., 1988. Mem. Am. Def. Preparedness Assn., Marine Corps Assn., N.Mex. Acad. Sci. (pres. 1981), Tau Beta Pi, Pi Tau Sigma, Sigma Xi. Republican. Methodist. Achievements include patents pending for magnetically protected laser fusion cavity, burst laser communication mode for satellite-submarines, explosive driven shock tubes for top-atmosphere weapon effects simulation, numerous patent applications for robotic laser-based industrial decoating systems. Home: 1708 Soplo Rd SE Albuquerque NM 87123-4485 Office: 4505 Columbine NE Albuquerque NM 87113-2238

FRELINGHUYSEN, ALICE COONEY, museum curator; b. N.Y.C., Mar. 1, 1954; d. Daniel Russell and Alice (Knotts) Cooney; m. George L. K. Frelinghuysen, June 17, 1978; children: Henry, Russell. BA, Princeton U., 1976; MA, U. Del., 1978. Cert. Winterthur Program in Early Am. Culture. Asst. curator Met. Mus. Art, N.Y.C., 1980-87, assoc. curator, 1987-94, curator, 1994—; chmn. bd. trustees Am. Ceramic Circle, past pres., 1988-92; adv. coun. The Art Mus., Princeton U.; bd. advisors The Census of Stained Glass Windows in Am.; bd. dirs. Shelburne (Vt.) Mus. Author: American Porcelain, 1770-1920, 1989, American Art Pottery from the Morse Museum of American Art, 1995; co-author: Splendid Legacy: The Havemeyer Collection, 1993 (Henry Allen Moe prize N.Y. State Hist. Assn. 1994, award Met. chpt. Victorian Soc. Am. 1994), Herter Brothers: Furniture and Interiors for a Gilded Age, 1994 (Henry Russell Hitchcock award Victorian Soc. Am. 1995, Ann. Publ. award Met. N.Y. chpt. Victorian Soc. Am. 1995); contbr. articles to profl. jours. Bd. dirs. The Frelinghuysen Found., Vis. Nurse Svc. N.Y.; trustee Princeton U. Andrew W. Mellon fellow Met. Mus. Art, 1978-80. Mem. Decorative Arts Soc., Victorian Soc. in Am., Early Am. Glass Club. Office: Met Mus of Art 1000 5th Ave New York NY 10028-0113

FREMON, RICHARD C., retired infosystems specialist; b. St. Louis, May 28, 1918; s. Richard Horatio and Hazel Pauline (Rhea) F.; m. Virginia Isabelle Moore, Sept. 7, 1940; children: Carolyn E. Fremon Maycher, Richard L., James N., Nancy I. Brown. AB, Columbia U., 1939; BEE, 1940, MEE, 1944. With personnel Bell Telephones, N.Y.C., 1941-54, dir. salary adminstrn., Murray Hill, N.J., 1954-73, dir. adminstrv. systems, 1973-81; dir. computer ctr. Centenary Coll., Hackettstown, N.J., 1981-89. Contbr. chpt. to book. Trustee Sea Cliff Sch. Bd., N.Y., 1950-52; past chmn. Engring. Manpower Commn., N.Y.C., 1965. Mem. Inst. Indsl. Engrs. (sr.), Panther Valley Club. Democrat. Presbyterian. Home: 32 Barn Owl Dr Hackettstown NJ 07840-3205

FRENCH, DANA LEWIS, computer consultant; b. Stillwater, Okla., Nov. 17, 1958; s. Hilton Victor O'Daniel and Fern Ethel (Dennis) F. BS in Zoology, U. Okla., 1983, postgrad., 1983-84. Chem. engring. technician Applied Tech. Inc., Norman, Okla., 1979; sr. systems analyst Energ Analysts, Inc., Norman, 1981-89; owner French Consulting Svcs., Norman, 1989-93; sr. tech. cons. Applied Intelligence Group, Edmond, Okla., 1993—. Developer various computer programs, including Shell Curses, French Menus, KshEvents, KshSchedule, others. Mem. Open View Forum. Avocations: hang gliding, sky diving, scuba diving, snow skiing, water skiing. Office: Applied Intelligence Group 13800 Benson Rd Edmond OK 73013-6417

FRENCH, EDWARD RONALD, plant pathologist; b. Buenos Aires, Apr. 28, 1937; s. Daniel Argentino and Federica Romana (Tonizzo) F.; m. Delia G. Monar-Peralta, Mar. 9, 1968; children: Vivian Marie, Ronald David, Sandra Janice. BS, U. R.I., 1960; MSc, U. Minn., 1963; PhD, N.C. State U., 1965. Plant pathologist agrl. mission to Peru N.C. State U., Raleigh, 1965-71, asst. prof. dept. plant pathology, 1971-72; head pathology dept. Internat. Potato Ctr., Lima, Peru, 1972-91, leader disease mgmt. program, 1992-95, assoc. dir. rsch., 1996-97, scientist emeritus, 1998—; vis. prof. U. Agraria La Molina, Lima, 1967—; vis. plant pathologist Cen. Agrl. Rsch. Inst., Gannoruwa, Sri Lanka, 1980-81; vis. scientist Sta. de Pathologie Vegetale, Rennes, France, 1990; mem. Jakob Eriksson Prize Com., Stockholm, 1980—; v.p. French Realty Co., Inc., North Kingstown, R.I., 1981-99, pres., 1999—; mem. tech. adv. com. J. & A. Niederhauser Award, 2000—. Author, editor: Prospects For The Potato in the Developing World, 1972; author: (with T.T. Hebert) Metodos de Investigacion Fitopatologica, 1980; editor: (with G. Galvez) Plant Pathologists in Latin America, 1990. Pres. Tuqui Urco Housing Devel., Monterrico, Lima, 1977-78, 84-85, 93-94; pres. bd. dirs. F.D. Roosevelt Am. Sch. Lima, Camacho, 1987-89; assoc. bd. dirs. F.D. Roosevelt Ednl. Inst., Lima, 1986—; pres. Am. Sch. Lima Found., Wilmington, Del., 1990—. Named Hon. Citizen City of Huanuco, Peru, 1985; E.R. French Bd. Rm. named in his honor FDR Am. Sch. Lima, Camacho, 1989. Fellow Am. Phytopathol. Soc. (com. mem. Office Internat. Programs 1999—); mem. Internat. Soc. Plant Pathology (v.p. 1983-88, coun. 1973—), Peruvian Phytopathol. Soc. (hon.), Assn. Latin Am. Fitopatologia (hon., pres. 1970-74, 85-87, exec. sec. 1974-80, 92—), Rinconada Country Club, Club Tenis Terrazas Miraflores, R.I. Club Sports Honor Soc., Sigma Chi (magister 1958-59, Freshman award 1957, Found. award 1960), Alpha Zeta (Centennial Honor Roll 1997), Gamma Alpha, Sigma Xi (hon.), Phi Sigma (hon.), Phi Kappa Phi (hon.). Roman Catholic. Avocations: tennis, swimming. E-mail: e.french@cgiar.org. Office: Internat Potato Ctr, Apartado 1558, Lima 12, Peru

FRENCH, GARY LAWRENCE, physician, educator, researcher; b. London, Dec. 19, 1945; s. Lawrence Charles and Hazel (Thorn) F.; m. Carolyn Jane Bedingfield, July 17, 1971 (div.); children: David, Nichola; m. Pei Jun Wu, Mar. 26, 1999. BSc, St. Thomas Hosp., London, 1967; MB BS, St. Thomas Hosp., 1970; MD, London U. Intern, resident Ho Lambeth Hosp. London, Kent & Canterbury Hosp., 1970-72; asst. lectr. pathology St. Thomas Hosp., 1972-75; lectr. microbiology U. West Indies, Jamaica, 1975-77; lectr. microbiology St. Thomas Hosp., 1977-80, sr. lectr. microbiology, 1980-82; prof., chmn. dept. microbiology Chinese U. Hong Kong, 1982-90; hon. cons. Prince of Wales Hosp., Hong Kong, 1982-90; prof. microbiology, head dept. infection Guy's Kings Coll. and St. Thomas Sch. Medicine, 1990—; hon. cons., dir. Infection Ctr. Guy's and St. Thomas Hosp. Trust, 1990—. Editor Jour. Hosp. Infection, 1994-99. Fellow Royal Coll. Pathologists, Royal Coll. Pathologists Australasia, Hosp. Infection Soc. (chmn. 1999—). Avocations: walking, talking, theatre, music. Office: Dept Microbiology, St Thomas Hosp, London SE1 7EH, England

FRENCH, HAROLD STANLEY, food company executive; b. Bklyn., Oct. 2, 1921; s. Morris and Fay (Kaufman) F.; m. Claire E. Weingart, Oct. 3, 1943 (dec. Mar. 1983); children: Madelaine Diane, Janet Gail. BA, L.I. U., 1942; postgrad., NYU, 1950, Columbia U., 1960; PhD in Philosophy, Am. Coll., 1998. Asst. buyer R.H. Macy Co., N.Y.C., 1949-52; group mgr. Abraham & Straus Co., Hempstead, N.Y., 1952-54; mdse. mgr. Popular Club Plan, Passaic, N.J., 1954-60, Nat. Silver Co., N.Y.C., 1964-69; mktg. dir. Waverly Products Co., Phila., 1970-74; pres. Pet Food Industries, Inc., N.Y.C., 1974—, Harold French & Co., Inc., N.Y.C., 1974—, African Fruit Co. Inc., 1993—, Harold French Engring. Corp., 1993—; pres. King Agro-Indsl. Corp., 1986, Globe King Agro-Indsl. Co. Ltd., Nigeria, 1988—; trade agt. to Nigerian Govt., 1992—, also builder workers' housing, supplier of housing materials; founder, pres. The People Speak mag., 1995; founder, pres., pub. New Century Pub. Co. Inc., 1998. Author: Dating and Mating for Women Over 50, Over 60, Over 70, 1999, You Can be a Hero, For Men Over 50, Over 60, Over 70, 1999. Chmn., pres. The Nigeria Fund, Inc., 1989—; contbg. patron N.Y. Met. Opera, N.Y.C. Ballet; home builder for Nigerian Govt. Workers. With M.I., U.S. Army, 1943-45. Decorated Bronze Star. Home: 60 E 8th St New York NY 10003-6514

FRENCH, JOHN, III, lawyer; b. Boston, July 12, 1932; s. John and Rhoda (Walker) F.; m. Leslie Ten Eyck, Jan. 11, 1957 (div. 1961); children: John B., Lawrence C.; m. Anne Hubbell, Jan. 9, 1965 (div. 1983); children: Daniel J., Susanna H.; m. Marina Kellen, Nov. 21, 1987. BA, Dartmouth Coll., 1955; JD, Harvard U., 1958. Bar: N.Y. 1959, D.C. 1988. Assoc. Milbank, Tweed, Hadley & McCloy, N.Y.C., 1961-68, Satterlee & Stephens, N.Y.C., 1968-73; asst. gen. counsel Continental Group, Inc., Stamford, Conn., 1973-81; v.p., gen. counsel, sec. Peabody Internat. Corp., Stamford, Conn., 1981-82; ptnr. Appleton, Rice & Perrin, N.Y.C., 1982-84; ptnr. Beveridge and Diamond, N.Y.C., 1985-93, counsel, 1993-99; chmn. Tudor Assocs., LLC, N.Y.C., 1999—; exec. v.p., gen. counsel The Nat. Urban Tech. Ctr., MC, 1999; lectr. Practising Law Inst., 1979-83, Am. Law Inst., 1978; bd. dirs. Resorts Mgmt., Inc., Tudor Assocs., LLC, N.Y.C. Contbr. articles to profl. jours. Trustee Hudson River Found., YMCA-YWCA Camping Svcs. of Greater N.Y., Inc.; bd. dirs. Third St. Music Sch. Settlement House, Inc., N.Y.C., Internat. House, Inc., N.Y.C., Young Concert Artists, Inc., 33 E. 70th St. Corp., Teatro alla Scala Found.; mem. Westchester County Planning Bd., 1974-85; mem. N.Y. State Environ. Bd., 1976-88. Capt. JAGC, USAF, 1958-61. Mem. ABA, N.Y. State Bar Assn. (lectr.), Assn. of Bar of City of N.Y. (lectr.), Environ. Law Inst., Am. Soc. Corp. Secs., Met. Opera, Soc. Mayflower Descs., River Club, Harvard Club, Knickerbocker Club, The Pilgrims, Century Assn. Republican. Office: Tudor Assocs LLC 33 E 70th St New York NY 10021-4941

FRENCH, LAURENCE ARMAND, social science educator, psychology educator; b. Manchester, N.H., Mar. 24, 1941; s. Gerald Everett and Juliette Teresa (Boucher) F.; m. Nancy Picthall, Feb. 13, 1971. BA cum laude, U. N.H., 1968, MA, 1970, PhD, 1975; postdoctorate, SUNY, Albany, 1978; PhD, U. Nebr., 1981; MA, Western N.M. U., 1994. Diplomate Am. Bd. Forensic Medicine, Am. Bd. Forensic Examiners, Am. Bd. Psychol. Specialties in Forensic Psychology & Neuropsychology; lic. psychologist, Ariz. Instr. U. So. Maine, Portland and Gorham, 1971-72; asst. prof. Western Carolina U., Cullowhee, N.C., 1972-77, U. Nebr., Lincoln, 1977-80; psychologist I N.H. Hosp., Concord, 1980-81; psychologist II Laconia (N.H.) State Sch., 1981-88; sr. psychologist N.H. Divsn. for Children & Youth Svcs., Concord, 1988-89; prof., chair dept. social scis. Western N.Mex. U., Silver City, 1989—; Psi Chi Nat. Honor Soc. in psychology Western N.Mex. faculty adviser; adj. assoc. prof. U. So. Maine, 1980-84; cons. N.C. Dept. Mental Health, 1972-77, Nebr. Indian Commn., Lincoln, 1977-80, Cherokee (N.C.) Indian Mental Health Program, 1974-77; cons.

alcohol program Lincoln Indian Ctr., 1977-80; profl. adv. bd. Internat. Coll. Prescribing Psychologists. Author: The Selective Process of Criminal Justice, 1976, (with Richard Crowe) Wee Wish Tree: Special Qualla Cherokee Issue, 1976, (with Hornbuckle) Cherokee Perspective, 1981, (with Letman et al) Contemporary Issues in Corrections, 1981, Indians and Criminal Justice, 1982, Psychocultural Change and the American Indian, 1987, The Winds of Injustice, 1994, Counseling American Indians, 1997, The Qualla Cherokee Surviving in Two Worlds, 1998, Addictions and Native Americans, 2000; spl. issue editor Quar. Jour. Ideology, Vol. II, 1987; contbr. articles to profl. jours. Commr. Pilsbury Lake Village Dist., Webster, N.H., 1985-90. With USMC, 1959-63, Badge of Honor, Republic of China, 1998. Recipient Hon. medal Rep. China, 1998, Nat. Int. Drug Abuse 1st Leadership in Rsch. award, 1999; Dissertation Yr. fellow U. N.H. 1971-72, Nebr. U. System grad. faculty fellow, 1978. Fellow APA, Prescribing Psychologists Register (diplomate), Soc. Psychol. Study Social Issues, Am. Coll. Forensic Examiners (diplomate); mem. Nat. Assn. Sch. Psychologists, Veterans Foreign Wars (life), Am. Soc. Criminology (life), Internat. Coll. Prescribing Psychologists Inc. (profl. adv. bd.), Nat. Assn. Alcohol and Drug Abuse Counselors (nat. chmn., clin. issue com. 1996-98), N.Mex. Alcohol and Drug Abuse Counselors Assn. (educator of the yr. award 1997), Phi Delta Kappa (treas. 1990-91, pres. 1991-92). Office: Western NMex U Dept Social Scis Silver City NM 88062

FRENCH, MICHAEL BRUCE, marketing consultant; b. Arlington, Va., Sept. 18, 1954; s. Orville Sidney and Doris (Goldberg) F.; m. Robin Ann Abenstein, Oct. 15, 1978; children: Brian Michael, Matthew Jeffrey, Sean Thornton. BA, Princeton (N.J.) U., 1976; M in Mgmt., Northwestern U., Evanston, Ill., 1978. Brand asst., asst. brand mgr. Procter & Gamble Co., Cin., 1978-80, brand mgr., 1981-84; mktg. dir. Coca-Cola Bottling Mideast Inc. subs. P&G, Lexington, Ky., 1984-85; v.p. mktg. Coca-Cola Botting Mideast, Inc., Lexington, 1985-87; brand mgr. Coca-Cola USA, Atlanta, 1987-89; mktg. mgr. chain accounts Coca-Cola Fountain, Atlanta, 1989, dir. channel mktg., 1989-93, dir. product definition and devel., 1993, asst. v.p. mktg. ops., 1993-94, v.p. mktg., 1994-95; dir. edn. mktg. Coca-Cola USA, Atlanta, 1995-97, dir. consumer occasions mktg., non-retail, 1997-99; dir. Coca-Cola Connection, 1999-2000; sr. cons. Monitor Co., Cambridge, Mass., 2000—. Mem. Rep. Party of Ga., Atlanta, 19885; mem. baseball steering com. U. Ky., Lexington, 1986-87; fundraising chmn. Jr. Achievement of the Bluegrass, Lexington, 1986-87; chmn. pub. awareness subcom. Gov.'s Anti-Substance Abuse Commn., Frankfort, Ky., 1986-87; divsn. coord. Coca-Cola United Way Campaign, 1996. Named to Hon. Order of Ky. Cols., 1986. Mem. Princeton Club of Ga. Avocations: golf, youth baseball and basketball, reading, family. E-mail: tigers.76@gateway.net and mike french@monitor.com. Home: 75 Rodgers Rd Carlisle MA 01741 Office: Monitor Two Canal Park Cambridge MA 02141

FRENCH, RICHARD PAUL, artist; b. Aurora, Mo., Apr. 12, 1936; s. Howard William and Georgia Elizabeth (Calloway) F. BFA, U. Ariz., 1964. Prin./designer Design 2000, Providence, 1971-74; dir. packaging and graphics Raymond Loewy Internat., N.Y.C., 1974-75; corp. design dir. Rexham Corp., N.Y.C., 1975-78; acct. supr. P.W. Inc., Louisville, 1978-81; v.p. Benton & Bowles/TCA, White Plains, N.Y., 1981-82. One-man shows include Highlands Regional Art Ctr., Sebring, Fla., 1988, Oakland Park (Fla.) Pk. Libr., 1989, Flamingo Gardens Mus., Davie, Fla., 1989, Fla. Capital Bldg, Tallahassee, 1991, Fla. Collectors Gallery, 1996, 97; exhibited in group shows at Gold Coast Watercolor Soc., 1987 (Best in Show, Maj. award), 88, 90, 91, 94, Fla. Watercolor Soc., 1988, 98, 91, 94, 95, 96, 97, 98, Palm Beach Watercolor Soc., 1989, Watercolor USA, 1989, Hollywood Art Guild, 1989, 90, Internat. Soc. Marine Painters, 1989, Coral Spring Art Assn., 1990, Ft. Lauderdale Mus. Art, 1990, 94, Cultural Arts Ctr., Delray Beach, Fla., 1991, La. Watercolor Soc. Internat. Exhbn., 1992, Fells Point Art Assn., 1992, Adirondacks Nat. Exhbn. Am. Watercolors, 1992, 93, Artisphere Nat., 1993, Boca Raton Mus. Art, 1994, Art Serv, Inc., 1995, Soc. Four Arts, Palm Beach, 1997; paintings included in numerous publs.; represented in permanent collections Sun Bank/Volusia, Daytona Beach, Sunbank/South Fla., N.A., Ft. Lauderdale, Blockbuster Entertainment Corp., Ft. Lauderdale, Flamingo Gardens, Davie, Pinchevsky & Assocs., Plantation, Fla., Petereit Pharm., Hamburg, Germany, Home Savs. Bank, Hollywood, Fla., Fla. Trust for Hist. Preservation, Foley & Lardner, Tampa, The Century House, Nantucket, Mass., The Oakland Park (Fla.) Libr., City of Coral Gable, Fla., WXEL TV, West Palm Beach, Fla., Stanhan House, Ft. Lauderdale; represented in numerous pvt. collections. Bd. dirs. Oaks Owners Assn., Bradenton, Fla., 1999. With USAF, 1955-58. Recipient Career Achievement award Drury U., Springfield, Mo., 1999. Mem. Fla. Watercolor Soc. (pres. 1993, bd. dirs. 1994—). Democrat. Avocations: gardening, home remodeling, interior design. Home: 1302 Willow Oak Cir Bradenton FL 34209-7837

FRENCH, RICHARD VAUGHN, federal agency administrator; b. Beckley, W.Va., Feb. 8, 1966; s. Zina Harold and Betty Jo (Hutchison) F.; m. Jamie Lyn Hart, Oct. 12, 1996. BA in Polit. Sci., W.Va. U., 1988, MPA, 1989. Staff asst. Rep. Nick J. Rahall II, Washington, 1990; labor rels. specialist U.S. Dept. Labor, Washington, 1990-95, program mgmt. specialist, 1995-97, program analyst, 1997-98, spl. asst. to asst. sec., 1998—; spl. asst. Corp. Nat. Svc., Washington, Phila., 1997. Mem. Am. Soc. Pub. Adminstn., W.Va. Soc. Washington (1st v.p. 1997—). Office: US Dept Labor Rm S-2203 200 Constitution Ave NW Washington DC 20210-0001

FRENCH, URI SMITH, III, career officer, actor; b. Elmira, N.Y., Aug. 23, 1937; s. Uri S. Jr. and Joan (Lewis) F.; children: John Michael, Mary Catherine, Carolyn Joan; m. Linda Nelson, June 1, 1991. B cum laude in Political Sci., Benedictine Coll., 1971; MA cum laude in Mgmt., Ctrl. Mich. U., 1979; graduate, Indsl. Coll. Armed Forces, 1977. Commd. lt. U.S. Army, 1957, advanced through grades to brigadier gen., 1983; commdr. 3d Armored Divsn. Artillery, Hanau, Germany, 1980-83; chief of staff First U.S. Army, Fort Meade, Md., 1983-84; asst. divsn. comdr. 82d Airborne Divsn., Fort Bragg, N.C., 1984-86; commdg. gen. 4th Army ROTC Region, Fort Lewis, Wash., 1986-87; actor. Actor film and TV, 1995—. Republican. Avocation: golf. Home and Office: 7519 Walton Ln Annandale VA 22003-2558

FREND, WILLIAM HUGH CLIFFORD, emeritus educator, clergyman; b. Shottermill, Surrey, England, Jan. 11, 1916; s. Edwin George Clifford Frend and Edith Bacon; m. Mary Grace Crook, June 2, 1951; children: Sarah Anne, Simon William Clifford. BA, U. Oxford, Eng., 1937, DPhil, 1940, MA, 1951, DD, 1966; BD, Cambridge U., Eng., 1964; DD (hon.), Edinburgh U., 1974. Ordained to Holy Orders, Scottish Episcopal Ch., 1983. Asst. prin. War Office, London, 1940-41, War Cabinet Office, London, 1941-42; intelligence officer Polit. Warfare Exec. Office, 1942-45; info. officer Brit. Mil. Govt., Austria, 1945-46; with editorial bd. German War Document Project, 1947-51; commd. 2d lt. Brit. Army, 1947, advanced through grades to capt., ret., 1967; rsch. fellow U. Nottingham, Eng., 1951-52; Bye fellow Gonville and Caius Coll., Cambridge, Eng., 1952-54, 97; fellow Gonville and Caius Coll., Cambridge, 1956-69; lectr. faculty of div. U. Cambridge, 1954-69; prof. eccles. history U. Glasgow, Scotland, 1969-84; priest-in-charge Barnwell Group of Parishes, Peterborough, Eng., 1984-90; pres. internat. com. Eccles. Comparée, 1980-83, hon. pres., 1983—; sr. fellow Dumbarton Oaks, Washington, 1984; vis. prof. Rhodes U., Republic of S. Africa, 1964—, U. S. Africa, 1976—, John Carroll U., Cleve., 1981—. Author: The Donatist Church, 1952, Martyrdom and Persecution in Early Christianity, 1965, The Early Church, 1965, Rise of Monophysite Movement, 1972, Rise of Christianity, 1984, Saints and Sinners in the Early Church, 1985, The Archaeology of Early Christianity, 1996; editor Modern Churchman, 1964-83. Chmn. Assn. Univ. Tchrs., Scotland, 1976-78; vice chmn. Community Coun., Buchanan, Scotland, 1980-84. Recipient Territorial Efficiency Decoration War Office, 1959, 67. Fellow The Brit. Acad. (elected mem. 1983), Royal Soc. Edinburgh, Royal Hist. Soc.; mem. AAAS, N.Y. Acad. Scis., Soc. Antiquities London. Conservative. Anglican. Club: Arts & Authors (London, disting. mem.). Avocations: Romano-Brit. archaeology, gardening. Home: 31 Rectory Farm Rd, Little Wilbraham CB1 5LB, England

FRENDO, MICHAEL, parliamentarian, lawyer; b. Floriana, Malta, July 29, 1955; s. Joseph and Josephine (Felice) F.; m. Irene Brincat, July 14, 1984; children: Luke, Sara, Julia. LLD, U. Malta, 1977; LLM in European Legal Studies, U. Exeter, Eng., 1979. Tng. mgr. Thomson Internat. European Law Centre Ltd., London, 1979-82; dir. press and media Nationalist Party, Pieta, Malta, 1982-85; editl. dir. Independence Press, Pieta, Malta, 1982-85; pvt. practice Valletta, Malta, 1985-90, 96—; mem. Parliament, Valletta, 1987—; Parliamentary Sec. for Youth, Culture & Consumer Protection Maltese Govt., 1990-92; min. Youth and the Arts, 1992-94, Transport, Comms. and Tech., Valletta, Malta, 1994-96. Author: Eurolex User Manual for Conducting Computerized Legal Information Retrieval, 2 vols., 1980, Is Malta Burning?, 1981; co-author: Malta in the European Community, 1989, Malta in the Council of Europe, 1990, Europe, The Case for Membership, 1996. Active Maltese Parliament Del. to the European Parliament, 1989-90, 96—, chmn., 1990-92; mem. Parliamentary Assembly of the Coun. of Europe and its Econ. Affairs and Environ. Coms., 1989-92, E.U.-Malta Joint Parliamentary Com., 1996—; chmn. Inst. Youth Studies U. Malta, 1992-94. Mem. Christian Democrat Party. Roman Catholic. Fax: 356 245397. E-mail: mfrendo@gftlex.com. Home: Mrammiti Lourdes Ln, Saint Julian's Malta Office: Gatt Frendo Tufigno Advs, 66 Old Bakery St, Valletta VLT 09, Malta

FRENE, JEAN BAPTISTE MARIE, mechanical engineering educator; b. Longes, Rhône, France, Aug. 24, 1941; s. Joannes Antoine and Anna (Marquet) F.; m. Madeleine Geny, July 29, 1965; children: Patrick, Nathalie, Laurence. Degree in engring., Inst. Nat. Applied Sci., Lyon, France, 1966; D of Engring., U. Lyon, 1970, D of Phys. Sci., 1974; D Honoris Causa, U. Polytech. Bucharest, 1998. Asst. Inst. Nat. Applied Sci., Lyon, 1967-69, maître-asst., 1969-75; maître de conf. U. Poitiers, France, 1975-79; prof. U. Poitiers, 1979—, v.p., 1990-98; researcher lab. mech. Contact INSA, Lyon, 1966-75; researcher lab. solic mechs. U. Poitiers, 1975-85, dir., 1986-94. Author: Lubrification hydrodynamique, 1990, Hydrodynamic Lubrication, 1997; patentee hydrostatic device, 1991; contbr. numerous papers to sci. publs. With French Army, 1968-69. Decorated Chevalier Palmes Acad., 1982, Officier Palmes Acad., 1988; recipient Price of Rhone Coun. Gen., 1966, Price Montyon of Academie des Scis., 1994. Mem. ASME, Soc. Tribologists and Lubrication Engrs., Assn. U. Mechs., Soc. Tribology of France, N.Y. Acad. Scis., Assn. Française de Mécanique. Roman Catholic. Avocation: photography. Home: 9 rue du Clain, 86280 Saint Benoit France Office: U Poitiers Lab Mech Solids, SP2MI, 86960 Futuroscope France

FRENI, MIRELLA, soprano; b. Modena, Italy, Feb. 27, 1935; d. Ennio and Gianna F.; m. Leone Magiera, 1955; 1 dau., Micaela; m. Nicolai Ghiaurov. Debut as Micaela in Carmen, Modena, 1955, since has appeared in maj. opera houses throughout world including Covent Garden, 1961, La Scala, 1962, Royal Opera House, Met. Opera, 1965, Vienna State Opera, Paris Opera, Salzburg Festival, Glyndebourne Festival; appeared in film Madame Butterfly and U.S. pub. TV broadcast of The Marriage of Figaro; maj. roles include: Zerlina in Don Giovanni, Nanette in Falstaff, Mimi in La Boheme, Violetta in La Traviata, Desdemona in Otello, title role in Adriana Lecouvrer, 1994; numerous operatic recs., including Carmen (Grammy award for best opera rec. 1964). Address: care John Coast Opera Mgmt, 31 Sinclair Rd, London W14 ONS, England Address: Masstroianni Assoc 161 W 61st St Apt 17E New York NY 10023-7460

FRENK, CARLOS SILVESTRE, physics educator, consultant; b. Mexico City, Oct. 27, 1951; arrived in Eng., 1985; s. Silvestre and Alicia (Mora) F.; m. Susan Frances Clarke, Dec. 9, 1978; children: David, Stephen. BS in Theoretical Physics, U. Mex., 1976; math. tripos part III, Cambridge (Eng.) U., 1977, PhD in Astronomy, 1981. Postdoctoral rsch. fellow U. Calif., Berkeley, 1981-83; asst. rsch. physicist U. Calif., Santa Barbara, 1983-85; postdoctoral rsch. fellow U. Sussex, Eng., 1983-85; lectr. astronomy U. Durham, Eng., 1985-91; reader physics U. Durham, 1991-93, prof. physics, 1993—; cons. U.K. Rsch. Couns., Swindon, Eng., 1990—. Editor: (books) The Epoch of Galaxy Formation, 1989, Observational Tests of Cosmological Inflation, 1991; contbr. numerous sci. papers to profl. jours. Leverhulme rsch. fellow, 2000—; sr. fellow Particle Physics and Astronomy Rsch. Coun., U. Durham, 1996-99, Sir Derman Christopherson fellow, U. Durham, 1992-93, sci. rsch. fellow, Nuffield Found., 1991-92; named 16th most cited phys. scientist in U.K., 1990-99. Fellow Royal Astron. Soc.; mem. Internat. Astron. Union, Am. Astron. Soc. Mem. Labour Party. Office: U Durham Dept Physics, South Rd, Durham DH1 3LE, England

FRENKEL, DAVID-ARIE, law educator; b. Tel Aviv, Feb. 2, 1940; s. Tsvi and Eshter-Sarah (Berezovsky) F.; m. Naomi Davis, June 8, 1971; children: Esther, Tsvi, Dov, Dvora, Raya. M of Journalism, Hebrew U., 1961, LLD, 1975. Pvt. practice, 1963-69, 81-89; asst., faculty of law Hebrew U., Jerusalem, 1969-72; instr., rschr. faculty of law and Inst. Legis. Rsch. & Comparative Law, Hebrew U., Jerusalem, 1972-75; dep. legal adviser Ministry of Edn. and Culture, Israel, 1974-76; dep., then legal adviser Ministry of Health, Israel, 1976-81; legal advisor Municipality of Beer-Sheva, Israel, 1990-97; assoc. prof. law, dept. bus. adminstrn. Ben-Gurion U. Sch. Mgmt., Beer-Sheva, Israel, 1997—; external tchr. Hebrew U. Jerusalem, hadassah Med. Sch., Pub. Health Sch. and Faculty of Dental Medicine, 1978—; tutor Open U., 1993—; external tchr. Haifa U., Health Adminstrn. br., 1982-98, Bar-Ilan U., Ashelon br., 1982-91; from tchr. to sr. lectr. Ben-Gurion U., Beer Sheva, 1981-97, with faculty of tech. dept. industry and adminstrn. engring., 1986—; lectr. Hadassah Cmty. Coll., Jerusalem, 1974-87; mem. ethics com. for experiments on animals, Ben-Gurion U., Beer-Sheva, 1998—; chmn. ethics com. for Soroka U. Med. Ctr., Beer-Sheva, 1997—; judge local authorities disciplinary tribunal, 1996—. Author: Law of Cooperative Societies in Israel - Judicature and Legislation, 1966, Effect of Taxation on Registration of Rights in Land, 1972, Civil Judicature on Military and Security Matters, 1974, Law and Medicine - Military Aspects, 1985, Associations Law in Israel - The Law of not-for-profit organizations in israel, 2000; co-author: (with G. Tedeschi) Law Citations, 1972, (with A. Kirschenbaum and N. Rakover) A Guide to the Sources of the Jewish Law, 1983; (with E. Davis) The Hebrew Amulet, 1995; co-editor Health Law in Can. Jour., 1980-87; contbr. chpts. to books and articles to profl. jours. WHO fellow, 1979. Fellow Royal Soc. of Health, Royal Inst. of Pub. Health and Hygiene; mem. Am. Soc. of Law, Medicine and Ethics, Internat. Assn. of Jewish Lawyers, Soc. for Medicine and Law in Israel, World Assn. of Med. Law, Israel Bar. Office: Ben Gurion U Dept Bus Admin, Sch Mgmt, Beer-Sheva Israel

FRENKEL, JACOB AHARON, economist, educator; b. Tel-Aviv, Israel, Feb. 8, 1943; came to U.S., 1967; s. Kalman H. and Lea (Zwibaum) F.; m. Niza Yair, Sept. 3, 1968; children: Orli-Miriam, Tahl-Ida. B.A. in Econs. and Polit. Sci, Hebrew U., Jerusalem, 1966, postgrad. (fellow), 1966-67; M.A. (fellow), U. Chgo., 1969, Ph.D. in Econs. (Lilly Honor fellow), 1970. Mem. faculty Grad. Sch. Bus., U. Chgo., 1973-87, David Rockefeller prof. internat. econs., 1982-87; econ. counsellor, dir. research IMF, 1987-91; mem. faculty Tel Aviv U., 1991-96, Weisfeld prof. econs. of peace and internat. rels., 1994-96; gov. bank of Israel, Jerusalem, 1991-99; chmn. sovereign advisory group Merrill Lynch, London, 2000S; mem. G-7 Coun., adv. com. of Inst. for Internat. Econs.; mem. group of 30, disting. mem. adv. com. Korea Inst. for Global Econs.; chmn. bd. govs. Inter-Am. Devel. Bank, 1995-96 ; co-chmn. Israeli del. to multilateral peace talks on regional econ. devels., 1991—. Author numerous books on internat. and macro econs.; editor Jour. Polit. Economy, 1973-87; contbr. numerous articles to profl. jours. Decorated gran cruz Orden de Mayo al Merito (Argentina); recipient Czech Karel Englis prize in econs. Fellow Econometric Soc.; mem. Am. Acad. Arts and Scis. (fgn. hon.), Japan Soc. Monetary Econs. (hon.), Israel Assn. Grads. in Social Scis. and Humanities (hon. pres.). Office: U Chgo 1126 E 59th St Chicago IL 60637-1580*

FRENKEL, PETER, chemist; b. Minsk, Belarus, Jan. 5, 1959; came to U.S., 1991; s. Lev and Roza (Fishman) F.; m. Elena Mamaeva, Sept. 26, 1981; children: Anna, Aleksandr, Aleksey. MS in Organic Chemistry, Belarus U., Minsk, 1981; PhD in Inorganic Chemistry, Belarus Inst. Tech., Minsk, 1990. Chemist Belarus U., Minsk, 1981-84, rsch. scientist, 1984-90, sr. rsch. scientist, 1990-91; process chemist Witco Corp., Marshall, Tex., 1991-93, devel. chemist II, 1993-98, rsch. & devel. chemist III, 1996—; sr. rsch. chemist Witco Corp., Marshall, 1998-99, mgr. R&D, 1999—; cons. in field. Mem. AAAS, Am. Chem. Soc., Soc. Plastic Engrs. Achievements include inventor stabilizers for peroxydicarbonates; developed theoretical concept of the stabilization; contributor in the field of ion-exchange in molten salts; research in catalytic activity of hetropoly acids on synthesis and reactivity of organic peroxides. Avocations: music, racquetball, soccer. Office: Witco Corp PO Box 1439 Marshall TX 75671-1439

FRENTZEN, HEINZ-HARALD, race car driver; b. Mönchengladbach, Germany, May 18, 1967. Office worker Germany, 1986-87, 91-92; race car driver Jordan Mugen Honda, 1986—. German Jr. Kart Champion, 1981, vice champion German Formula Ford 1000, 1987, champion German Formula Opel Lotus, 1988, vice champion German Formula 3, Germany, 1989, 3d pl. finisher Grand Prix, Monza, Italy, 1995, 1st pl. finisher Grand Prix of San Marino, 1997, 2d pl, Magny-Cours, France, 1997, 3d pl., Belgium, Italy, Austria, Luxemburg. Avocations: dining, running, mountain biking, fitness training. Office: Ofcl Heinz-Harald Frentzen Club, c/o Fahr-Werk Waldstrasse 79, 64846 Gross-Zimmern Germany

FRENZEL, FRANCES JOHNSON, registered nurse, educator, lecturer, poet; b. Bedford, Va., Feb. 2, 1911; d. J. James and Willie Calpernia (Markham) Johnson; m. Paul H. Frenzel, Dec. 21, 1933 (dec. 1990); children: Virginia Lee Frenzel Lawrence, Helen Marie Frenzel LaGourgue. RN, Wash. Adventist Hosp., Takoma Park, Md., 1932; BS, Columbia Union Coll., 1933; real estate license, Glendale (Calif.) C.C., 1968. Cert. real estate broker. RN supr. Glendale (Calif.) Adventist Med. Ctr., 1933-34; instr. various flower show schs., Nat. Coun. State Garden Clubs, U.S. & Mex., 1951-98; flower design instr. Edinburg (Tex.) Coll., 1953; founder, chmn. World Flower Festival L.A. Garden Club and Greater L.A. Dist. Calif. Garden Clubs, Inc., 1962-98; lectr. in many states including Hawaii. Author: Arrangements on Parade, 1950; contbr. poems to books and nat. and state mags.; contbr. photographs of flower arrangements to profl. jours. Mem. City of Glendale Beautification adv. council, 1974—, L.A. County Med. Auxillary, Glendale, 1956—, pres., 1968-69; election precinct officer L.A. County, Glendale, 1956—; founder The Golden Garden Angel fund, 1998. Recipient Editor's Choice award, 1999, numerous Garden Club awards 1962-89, various other awards from organizations and Los Angeles County. Mem. Ikabana Internat. (L.A. chpt.), Internat. Soc. Poets, Judges Coun. So. Calif. (chmn. 1978-80), Judges Coun. Orange County, L.A. Garden Club (pres. 1960-62), Greater L.A. Dist. Calif. Garden Clubs (dir. 1962-64), Los Angeles County Med. Assn. Alliance (pres. Dist. IV 1968-69), Calif. Garden Clubs Inc. (life; bd. dirs., pub. rels. chmn. 1999—, co-chmn. golden gardens angel fund for bd. 1999—), Nat. Coun. State Garden Clubs Inc. (life), Internat. Soc. Poetry. Avocations: flower arranging, gardening, gourmet cooking, interior decorating, happy family. Home: 1641 Ridgeview Dr Glendale CA 91207-1041

FRENZEL, MICHAEL, holding company executive; b. Leipzig, Germany, Mar. 2, 1947. Bd. dirs. Pressag AG, Dusseldorf, Germany, 1988-92, vice-chair, 1992-93, chmn. bd., 1994—; chair bd. dirs. Amalgamated Metal Corp., plc, London; chair supervisory bd. Howaldtswerke-Deutsche Werft AG, Kiel, Preussag Stahl AG, Salzgitter; vice chair supervisory bd. VTG Vereinigte Tanklager und Transportmittel GmbH, Hamburg, Linke-Hofmann-Busch Waggon-Fahrzeug-Maschinen GmbH, Salzgitter, Creditanstalt-Bankverein AG, Vienna, PreussenElektra AG, Hannover, IVG Industrieverwaltungs AG, Bonn, Lufthansa Comml. Holding GmbH, Cologne, Thyssen Aufzuge GmbH, Neuhausen a.d.F; mem. Consultative BD Hannoversche Lebensversicherung AG, Hannover, Landesbank Rheinland-Pfalz, Mainz, Allianz AG, Hannover. Office: Preussag AG, Karl-Weichert Allee 4, 30625 Hannover Germany*

FRÈRE, BARON ALBERT, oil industry executive. Joint pres. Pargesa Holding Co., 1981—; chmn. exec. bd., mng. dir. Groupe Bruxelles Lambert (GBL) S.A., Brussels, 1987—; became pres. Petrofina S.A., 1990, now chmn.; dep. chmn. Cobepa S.A., Brussels; bd. dirs. GIB Group. Office: Cobepa SA Parc Atrium, Rue de la Chancellerie 2/1, B-1000 Brussels Belgium Office: Groupe Bruxelles Lambert SA, 24 ave Marnix, 1050 Brussels Belgium*

FREREJEAN, PIERRE EDWARD, investment management company executive; b. Paris, Oct. 16, 1954; s. Frere Jean Hunbert and Bazin Armelle Frerejean; m. Maignon Marie Christine, July 12, 1975; children: Aymeric, Adrien, Alexis, Augustin. Degree in law, Inst. Etudes Politiques Paris. Gen. mgr. Euro Pacific Advisers, Hong Kong, 1987-88; rep. dir. Iam Japan, Tokyo, 1988-90; dir. adjoint Rothschild & Co., Paris, 1994-96; pres. Funds Selection, Paris, 1996—. Mem. St. Cloud Club. Avocation: golf. Home: Av mozart 78, 75016 Paris France Office: Funds Selection, 31 rue de Labaure, 75008 Paris France

FRESCH, MARIE BETH, court reporting company executive; b. Norwalk, Ohio, Jan. 16, 1957; d. Ralph Roy and Vonda Mae (Brunkhorst) Spiegel; m. James R. Fresch, Aug. 5, 1978; 1 child, Alexandra Jane. AS in Bus., Tiffin U., 1977; cert. in ct. reporting, Acad. Ct. Reporting, 1979. Registered profl. reporter, Ohio. Ofcl. reporter Seneca County Common Pleas Ct., Tiffin, Ohio, 1979-80; owner, operator Marie B. Fresch & Assocs., Norwalk, 1980—. Coach indoor & outdoor Soccer teams, 1994—, summer softball teams, 1994—; leader Girl Scouts Am., 1998—, sch. organizer, team leader, 1997-99, parade organizer, 1998—. Recipient Cert. of Merit, Nat. Ct. Reporters Assn., 1990; named Outstanding Leader, Girl Scout Coun., 1998, Outstanding Vol., 2000. Mem. Nat. Ct. Reporters Assn., Ohio Ct. Reporters Assn. (student promotions and pub. rels. coms. 1986—, dist. rep. 1994-95, fundraising com. 1993-96), NOW (sec. Port Clinton chpt. 1984-86, treas. 1986-87, 91), Am. Legion Aux., Kappa Delta Kappa. Democrat. Methodist. Lodge: Order of Eastern Star (esther 1979-81). Avocations: target shooting, swimming, biking, gardening, hiking. Home and Office: 47 Warren Dr Norwalk OH 44857-2447

FRESCURA, FRANCO, architect; b. Trieste, Italy, Sept. 28, 1946; arrived in South Africa, 1956; s. Umberto and Fiore (Cottiero) F.; m. Lesley-Anne Morton, Nov. 28, 1970; 1 child, Gabriella Lindiwe. BArch, Witwatersrand U., Johannesburg, South Africa, 1977, MArch cum laude, 1981, PhD, 1986. Registered architect. Prin. architect Franco Frescura Architects, Johannesburg, 1977-94; lectr. U. Witwatersrand, Johannesburg, 1978-84, hon. rsch. assoc., 1994—; sr. lectr. U. Port Elizabeth, South Africa, 1985-94; dir. Environ. Devel. Unit, Port Elizabeth, 1991-94; sr. mgr. South Africa Post Office, Pretoria, 1994-99, project dir., 1999—; cons. Devel. Bank Southern Africa, South Africa, 1990-94, Harlech-Jones Architect, Port Elizabeth, 1991-94. Author: Rural Shelter, 1981 (Habitation Space Internat. award 1981), The B.O.N.C. of the C.G.H. of 1864, 1991 (Horne Meml. award 1992), A Glossary of SA'n Architectural Terms, 1989; contbr. articles to profl. jours. Del. ANC Nat. Policy Forums for Land, Housing and Culture, 1991-94, Codesa Commn. on Nat. Symbols, 1993. Recipient Herald Archtl. Heritage EPHerald, Port Elizabeth, 1988, Congress awards Philatelic Fedn. Southern Africa, South Africa, 1984, 89. Mem. South African Assn. Art Historians (life, chair Eastern province 1990-92), African Studies Assn. Atlanta, Inst. South African Architects, Artists and Writers Guild South Africa (chair 1974-75). Mem. African Nationalist Congress. Avocations: philately, photography, art, medieval music.

FRESSINAUD MASDEFEIX, CATHERINE, neurologist, researcher; b. Angers, France, Dec. 16, 1959; d. Louis Marie Henry and Lucienne Simonne (Loudenot) F.-M.; 1 child, Clara. MD with distinction, U. Limoges, France, 1988; postgrad., U. Limoges, 1990; PhD in Molecular and Cellular Biology, U. Strasbourg, 1989, Habil in Rsch. in Molecular & Cell. Bio., 1993. Intern Univ. Hosp., Limoges, 1982-86; with Neurochemistry Ctr., Strasbourg, 1986-87; intern Nat. Inst. for Sci. and Med. Rsch., Strasbourg, 1987-89; asst. chief neurology dept. Univ. Hosp., Limoges, 1990-93; mem. staff neurology dept. Médecin des Hôpitaux U. Hosp., Angers, 1994—. Contbr. numerous articles on neurology and neurochemistry to Jour. of Neurochemistry, Muscle and Nerve, Neurology, Jour. Cellular Physiology, Neurosci. Letters, Neurochemistry Internat., others. Recipient prize Ligue Francaise contre la Sclérose en Plaques, 1993; Nat. Inst. for Sci. and Med. Rsch. grantee Found. for Med. Rsch., 1990, Assn. Rsch. la Sclérose en Plaques, 1991, 93, others. Mem. French Soc. Neurology, French Neuropathology Soc., French Neuroscis. Soc., European Soc. for Neurochemistry, Am. Soc. for Neurochemistry (corr.), Internat. Soc. Neurochemistry. Avocations: painting, tennis, golf, horse riding. Fax: 33-0-2-41-35-35-94. Office: Univ Hosp Neurology Dept, 4 Rue Larrey, 49033 Angers Cedex01, France

FRETES, RICARDO EMILIO, physician; b. San Juan, Argentina, Jan. 25, 1954; s. Aldo Jorge and Amor Ana (Moreno) F.; m. Stella Maris Sanchez Correa; children: Alejandra Cecilia, Marcela Ines, Ricardo German. B, Nat. Coll., San Juan, Argentina, 1972; MD, Nat. U. Cordoba, Argentina, 1986. Asst. medicine Nat. U. Cordoba, Argentina, 1975-78, teaching asst. medicine, 1980-89, asst. prof., 1989—; cons. in field. Author: The Life in

Evolution and Ecology, 1997; co-author: (chpts.) Histological Techniques, 1991; contbr. articles to profl. jours. Coun. mem. Red Cross, Cordoba, 1996—. Grantee Conicor, Cordoba, 1991, Nat. U., Argentina, 1995—; rsch. fellow CONICET, Buenos Aires, Argentina, 1982-84, 87-89. Mem. N.Y. Acad. Scis. Roman Catholic. Avocations: tennis, volleyball, fishing. Office: Nat U COrdoba, Ciudad U, 5016 Cordoba Argentina

FRETZ, JOSEPH NELSON, art educator, artist; b. Denver, May 5, 1952; s. John Lewis and Beulah Eldora Fretz; m. Maxine Sharon Martin, Aug. 23, 1980; children: Alice Martin. BA in Psychology, Ea. Mennonite U., Harrisburg, Va., 1974; AA in Comml. Art, Rocky Mt. Coll. Art & Design, Denver, 1985. Lic. educator, Colo. Adolescent counselor Mid-Valley Treatment Ctr., Salem, Oreg., 1976-77, Looking Glass Family Svcs., Eugene, Oreg., 1978-81, Edgefield Lodge, Troutdale, Oreg., 1981-83, St. Luke's Hosp., Denver, 1983-89; freelance comml. artist Denver, 1985—; art tchr. Rocky Mt. Coll. Art & Design, Denver, 1989-98, Jefferson County Schs., Golden, Colo., 1998—; student advisor, mem. adv. bd. illustration dept. Rocky Mt. Coll. Art & Design, Denver, 1995-98. Painter Artists Mag., 1998. Artist Keep the Lights Campaign, 1992; juror Aspenfest Art Festival, Georgetown, Colo., 1993; art donor Habitat Humanity, Lakewood, Colo., 1997, Foothills Art Ctr., Golden, 1998. Recipient Pauline Law Meml. award Nat. Exhbn. Allied Artists Am., 1992, 2d pl. No. Colo. Artists Assn., 1995, Purchase award Curtis Sch. Arts & Humanities, 1996. Mem. Nat. Soc. Painters Casein and Acrylic (Best of Show 1993), Rocky Mountain Nat. Watermedia Soc. (Colo. Bank award 1995, 2d pl. 1995, 3d pl. 1997). Democrat. Mennonite. Avocations: photography, hiking/backpacking, bicycling, travel. Office: Pomona HS 8101 Pomona Dr Arvada CO 80005-2572

FREUDENBERG, KURT, accountant, finance executive; b. N.Y.C., Dec. 2, 1957; m. Janet R. Latham, Oct. 5, 1991; children: Katharine, Kyle. BS, Trenton State U., 1980; MBA, L.I. U., 1984. CPA. Sr. mgr. Deloitte & Touche, N.Y.C., 1984-95; dir. fin. Nat. Broadcasting Co., N.Y.C., 1996; v.p. acctg. Avis Rent A Car, Inc., Garden City, N.Y., 1997—. Mem. AICPA. E-mail: KFreuden@Avis.com and KurtFreude@aol.com. Home: 4 Sturbridge Ct Shoreham NY 11786-2044 Office: Avis Rent A Car Inc Garden City NY 11530

FREUDENRICH, DAVID ROBERT, civil engineer, traffic engineer; b. Pitts., Dec. 22, 1961; s. Robert David and Frances M. (Feduska) F.; m. Tara Ann Howey; 1 child, Mackenzie Lee. BS in Bioloy, Pa. State U., 1984; BS in Civil Engring. Tech., Point Park Coll., 1994. Engr. in tng. Design engr. Boswell Engring., South Hackensack, N.J., 1984-87, Travers Assocs., Clifton, N.J., 1987-89; engr. Mackin Engring. Co., Inc., Pitts., 1989; sr. planner Wilbur Smith Assocs., Pitts., 1989-94; sr. traffic engr. Maguire Group Inc., Pitts., 1994—. Chmn. computer practices group ASCE, 1991-93; info. tech. chmn. focus group Maguire Group Inc., 1998—; jr. bd. dirs. Rehab. Inst. Pitts., 1991-93; indsl. adv. bd. Point Park Coll., 1994—; co-chmn. reservations Burger King Cancer Caring Ctr.-Steeler Fashion Show Fundraiser, 1994—; mem. corp. stds. com. Maguire Group Inc., 1998—. Mem. ASCE (bd. dirs. Pitts. sect., exec. sec. Pitts. sect.), ASME, Am. Soc. Hwy. Engrs. (sr.), Inst. Transp. Engrs. (assoc.), Acoustical Soc. Am., Pitts. Squash Racquets Assoc., Corp. Computer Stds. (chair corp. info. tech.), Pitts. Regional Intelligent Transp. System (steering com.). Republican. Roman Catholic. Avocations: squash, tennis, computers, photography, gardening. Home: 106 Timberlane Dr Pittsburgh PA 15229-1059 Office: Maguire Group Inc 564 Forbes Ave Ste 1212 Pittsburgh PA 15219-2903

FREUDENTHAL, ERNEST GUENTER, technology and business educator; b. Mannheim, Germany, July 22, 1920; came to the U.S., 1937; s. Leopold and Selma (Rosenthal) F.; m. Stephanie Karlsruher, Dec. 26, 1948; children: Pamela Hausman, Joan Fraifeld. BA in Econs., Vanderbilt U., 1948, MA in Econs., 1971. Employee Werthan Industries, Nashville, 1942-44, 46-48, middle mgmt. staff, 1948-69, v.p. mfg., 1969-71, sr. v.p., 1971-90; adj. assoc. prof. bus., tech., pub. policy, indsl. mktg. Vanderbilt U., Nashville, 1971—. Mem. Bus. Res. Adv. Coun. to the Bur. Labor Statis., Washington, 1981—; chmn. Metro Social Svcs. Commn., Nashville, 1989—, Com. on Employment Projections of the Bus. Rsch. Adv. Coun., Washington, 1997—; commr. Tenn. Holocaust Commn., Inc., 1998—; mem. Holocaust Edn. Colloquium, 1999—; pres. Jewish Cmty. Ctr., Nashville, 1965-67. Staff sgt. U.S. Army, 1944-46, PTO. Recipient Sage award Coun. on Aging, Nashville, 1995. Mem. Jewish Fedn. Nashville (pres. 1974-76), The Temple (pres. 1986-88), Vanderbilt Inst. Pub. Policy Studies, Univ. Club, Phi Beta Kappa. Avocation: hiking. Home: 4406 Sunnybrook Dr Nashville TN 37205-3860 Office: Vanderbilt Univ Box 6188 Nashville TN 37235

FREUND, ECKHARD, electrical engineering educator; b. Düsseldorf, Germany, Feb. 28, 1940; s. Karl and Margret (Meya) F.; m. Brigitte Keudel; children: Viviane, Ariane. Diploma in engring., Tech. Sch. Darmstadt, Fed. Republic Germany, 1965; D Engring., Tech. U. Berlin, 1968. Scientist U. Raumfahrt, Oberpfaffenhofen, Fed. Republic Germany, 1965-70; guest prof. aero. engring. U. So. Calif., L.A., 1972-76, 83; guest scientist European Space Ops. Ctr., Darmstadt, Fed. Republic Germany, 1970-71; sci. coord. Fraunhofer Inst., Karlsruhe, Fed. Republic Germany, 1976-78; prof. dept. elec. engring. Fernuniversität, Hagen, Fed. Republic Germany, 1978-84; prof. dept. elec. engring., dir. Inst. Robotics Rsch. U. Dortmund, Fed. Republic Germany, 1985—; sci. adviser Jet Propulsion Lab., NASA, Pasadena, Calif., 1983. Author: Zeitvariable Mehrgrössensysteme, 1971, Regelungssysteme in Zustandsraum, I/II, 1986, 87; contbr. some 250 articles on robotics and automation to tech. publs. Office: Inst Robotics Rsch Dortmund, Otto Hahn Strasse 8, D 44221 Dortmund Germany

FREUND, EMMA FRANCES, medical technologist; b. 1922; d. Walter R. and Mabel W. (Loveland) Ervin; m. Frederic Reinert Freund, March 4, 1953; children: Frances, Daphne, Fern, Frederic. BS, Wilson Tchrs. Coll., Washington, 1944; MS in Biology, Cath. U., Washington, 1953; MEd in Adult Edn., Va. Commonwealth U., 1988. Tchr. math and sci. D.C. Sch. Sys., Washington, 1944-45; technician in parasitology lab. U.S. Dept. Agr., Beltsville, Md., 1945-48; histologic technician dept. pathology Georgetown U. Med. Sch., Washington, 1948-49; clin. lab. technician Kent and Queen Anne's County Gen. Hosp., Chestertown, Md., 1949-51; histotechnologist Med. Coll. Va. Hosp., Richmond, Va., 1951—; cons. profl. meetings and workshops; mem. exam. coun. Nat. Cert. Agy. Med. Lab. Pers. Co-author: (mini-course) Instrumentation in Cytology and Histology, 1985; editor Histo-Scope Newsletter. Asst. Cub Scout den leader Robert E. Lee coun. Boy Scouts Am., 1967-68, den leader, 1968-70. Mem. AAAS, NAFE, AAUW, APA, Am. Mgmt. Assn., Am. Soc. Clin. Lab. Sci. (rep. to sci. assenbly histology sect. 1977-78, chmn. 1983-85, 89-96), Va. Soc. Med. Tech. (Richmond chpt. corr. sec. 1977-78, bd. dirs. 1981-82, pres. 1984-85), Va. Soc. Histotech. (pres. 1994-96), Nat. Certification Agy. (clin. lab. specialist in histotech., clin. lab. supr. clin. lab. dir.), N.Y. Acad. Scis., Am. Assn. Clin. Chemistry (assoc.), Am. Soc. Clin. Pathologists (assoc.; cert. histology technician), Nat. Geog. Soc., Va. Govtl. Employees Assn., Nat. Soc. Histotech. (by-laws com. 1981—, C.E.U. com. 1981—, program com. regional meeting 1984, 85, 87, 97, 2000, chmn. regional meeting 1987, program chmn. state meeting 1998, 99, program chmn. regional meeting 2000, Conv. scholarship award 1997, Clin. Chemists' Recognition award 1995, 98), Am. Mus. Natural History, Smithsonian Inst., Am. Mgmt. Assn., Am. Chem. Soc., Am. Soc. Quality, Clin. Lab. Mgmt. Assn., Van Slyke Soc., Nat. Soc. Hist. Preservation, Sigma Xi, Phi Beta Rho, Kappa Delta Pi, Phi Lambda Theta. Home: 1315 Asbury Rd Richmond VA 23229-5305

FREUND, HANS-JOACHIM, physical chemist; b. Solingen, Germany, Mar. 4, 1951; s. Fritz and Lotte (Willms) F.; m. Susanne Herfurth, July 1, 1977; children: Julia, Martin, Sebastian. Diploma in chemistry, U. Cologne, Germany, 1975, D in Natural Scis., 1978, Privat-Dozent, 1983. Asst. U. Cologne, Germany, 1977-83; assoc. prof. U. Erlangen-Nurnberg, Germany, 1983-87; prof. U. Bochum, Germany, 1987-96; dir. Fritz-Haber Inst. Max-Planck-Gesellschaft, Berlin, 1996—; hon. prof. U. Bochum, Free U. Berlin, Tech. U. Berlin, Humboldt U., Berlin. Contbr. over 250 articles to internat. jours. Recipient Leibniz award Deutsche Forschungsgemeinschaft, 1995, Doktoranden Stipend, 1976, Forschungs Stipend, 1979; fellow Studienstiftung des Deutschen Volkes, 1974. Mem. Gesellschaft Deutscher Chemiker, Deutsche Bunsenges, Deutsche Physikal Gesellschaft, Am. Phys. Soc., Am. Vacuum Soc., Am. Chem. Soc., Chem. Soc. Sect. Academia Europaea, Berlin Brandenburgische Akademie der Wissenschaften. Office: Max-Planck-Gesellschaft Fritz-Haber Inst, Faradayweg 4-6, D-14195 Berlin Germany

FREUND, HERBERT RUDOLF, surgeon, educator, researcher; b. Haifa, Israel, Sept. 20, 1941; s. Kurt and Emmy (Muller) F.; m. Ruth Fisher, May 11, 1982; children: Michael-Ron, Daniel-Roy. MD, Hebrew U., Jerusalem, 1970. Resident in surgery Hadassah U. Med. Ctr., Jerusalem, 1970-75, chief physician, 1979-89, chief of surgery, 1989—; clin. and rsch. fellow Harvard U., Boston, 1977-78, U. Cin., 1978-79; assoc. prof. surgery Hebrew U., Jerusalem, 1980-83, prof. surgery, 1983—; vis. prof. U. Cin., 1983-84, Mt. Sinai Med. Ctr., N.Y.C., 1988-89, Stanford (Calif.) U., 1992, 95, 97: mem. adv. bd., chief scientist Israel Ministry of Health, 1990—; mem. med. bd. Hadassah U. Med. Ctr. Mem. editorial bd. Clin. Nutrition, Nutrition, Jour. Parenteral and Enteral Nutrition; contbr. numerous articles to profl. jours. Mem. various med./surg. orgns. and socs. Jewish. Avocation: music. Office: Hadassah U Hosp Mt Scopus, Dept Surgery, 91240 Jerusalem Israel

FREUND, ROLAND WILHELM, mathematician; b. Schweinfurt, Germany, Aug. 1, 1955; s. Wilhelm and Frieda F.; m. Susanne Ruehl, Oct. 31, 1979; children: Andreas Lance, Alexander Ray. Diploma in Math., U. Wuerzburg, Germany, 1982, PhD in Math., 1983, Habilitation in Math., 1991. Rsch. scientist NASA Ames Rsch. Ctr., Moffett Field, Calif., 1988-92; mem. tech. staff AT&T Bell Labs., Murray Hill, N.J., 1992-96; mem. tech. staff Bell Labs., Lucent Technologies, Murray Hill, 1996-99, Disting. mem. tech. staff, 1999—; vis. rsch. assoc. Stanford U., Calif., 1985-86; part-time lectr. Rutgers U., New Brunswick, N.J., 1993; adj. asst. prof. Columbia U., N.Y.C., 1995; vis. lectr. Princeton U., N.J., 1996; mem. program com. Copper Mountain Conf., 1990—. Mem. editl. bd. SIAM Jour. Numerical Analysis, SIAm Jour. on Matrix Analysis, others; contbr. more than 100 articles to profl. publs.; patentee in field; author two software packages: QMRPACK, BL-QMR, 1993, 96. Recipient Best-Paper award Cad category, Design, Automation and Test in Europe Conf., Munich, 1999, SIAM activity group on linear algebra prize Soc. for Indsl. and Applied Math., Snowbird, Utah, 1994, Heinz-Maier-Leibnitz award German Sec. of Edn. and Sci., Muenster, Germany, 1989. Mem. Soc. Indsl. and Applied Math. Avocation: cycling. E-mail: freund@research.bell-labs.com. Office: Bell Labs 700 Mountain Ave Rm 2c-525 New Providence NJ 07974-1208

FREUND, RONALD S., management consultant, marketing company executive; b. Hanford, Calif., Mar. 13, 1934; s. Wayne S. and Bluebell (McConihe) F.; m. Jane Mary Thaler, Dec. 10., 1964; children: Nancy Anne, Timothy Wayne. BA, Stanford U., 1956, MBA, 1959. Ind. economist Stanford Research Inst., Menlo Park, Calif., 1956-63; dir. bus. planning J.C. Penney Co. Inc., N.Y.C., 1963-72; pres. Corwin Co., Kansas City, Mo., 1972-85, Midpoint Nat. Inc., Kansas City, 1988—, Summit Assocs., Kansas City, 1985—; cons. Menninger Clinic, Topeka, Kans., 1991; v.p., 1991-93; chmn. exec. com. Midpoint Trade Books, N.Y.C., 1995—; cons. Nat. Renewable Energy Lab., Golden, Colo., 1987—; cons., trustee Midwest Research Inst., Kansas City, 1974—. Mem. Kansas City Club. Office: Midpoint Nat Inc 1263 Southwest Blvd Kansas City KS 66103-1901

FREUND, TAMAS F., neurobiologist; b. Zirc, Veszprem, Hungary, June 14, 1959; s. Antal Freund and Terez Lohn; m. Edina Varga, Sept. 12, 1981; children: Eva, Adam. Diploma in Biology, Eotvos U., Budapest, 1983, PhD, 1984; CSc, Hungarian Acad. Sci., Budapest, 1986, DSc, 1992. Rsch. fellow Dept. Pharmacology, Oxford, 1982-83; jr. rsch. fellow 1st Dept. Anatomy Semmelweis U., Budapest, 1983-86, rsch. fellow 1st Dept. Anatomy, 1986-89; sr. rcsh. fellow Dept. Pharmacology, Oxford, End., 1986-88; head dept. Inst. Exptl. Medicine Hungarian Acad. Sci., Budapest, 1990—, dep. dir. Inst. Exptl. Medicine, 1994—; mem. com. Med. Rsch. Coun., Hungary, 1992—; sec. Nat. Rsch. Found., Hungary, 1992-95. Editl. bd.: Neurosci. jour., 1991—, Exptl. Brain Rsch. jour., 1992—, Jour. Brain Rsch., 1992—; sect. editor Hippocampus, European Jour. Neurosci.; contbr. over 120 articles to profl. jours. and publs.; contgb. author books in field. Recipient Drs. C. and F. Demuth award Swiss Med. Rsch. Found., Switzerland, 1991, Krieg Cortical Kudos award Cajal Club, U.S.A., 1991, Krieg Cortical Discoverer award and Cajal medal, 1998; Dargut and Milena Kemali Neurosci. Found. award, 1998, Bolyai prize, Hungary, 2000; grantee Human Frontiers Sci. Program, 1991, 95, Howard Hughes Med. Inst., U.S.A., 1995. Mem. European Neurosci. Assn. (mem. program com. 1995—), Hungarian Neurosci. Soc. (sec. 1993-98), Hungarian Acad. Sci. (pres. neurosci. com. 1997—), Internat. Brain Rsch. Orgn. (exec. com. 1998—, chmn. ctrl./ea. europe regional com.). Roman Catholic. Avocation: music. Office: Inst Exptl Medicine, Szigony u 43, H-1083 Budapest Hungary

FREVERT, JAMES WILMOT, financial planner, investment advisor; b. Richland Twp., Iowa, Dec. 19, 1922; s. Wesley Clarence and Grace Lotta (Maw) F.; m. Jean Emily Sunderlin, Feb. 12, 1949; children: Douglas James, Thomas Jeffrey, Kimberly Ann. BS in Gen. Engring., MIT, 1948. Prodn. mgr. Air Reduction Chem. Co., Calvert City, Ky., 1955-61; plant mgr. Air Products & Chems., West Palm Beach, Fla., 1961-62; pres. Young World HWD, Ft. Lauderdale, Fla., 1962-66; v.p. Shareholders Mgmt. Co., L.A., 1966-73, Thomson McKinnon Secs., North Palm Beach, Fla., 1973-89, Raymond James & Assoc., West Palm Beach, Fla., 1989-91. Founder, past pres. MIT Club Palm Beach County, dir., 1976—; ednl. council mem. 1977-81. Served to 1st lt. USAF, 1943-46. Mem. Palm Beach Pundits, Circumnavigators Club. Republican. Presbyterian. Home: 883 Country Club Dr No Palm Beach FL 33408-3742

FREW, ALLAN M., aerospace executive; m. Susan Frew. BSEE, U. Mich., 1961, MSEE, 1962. Dep. gen. mgr. def. sys. divsn. TRW, Redondo Beach, Calif., 1995-98, v.p., gen. mgr., 1998—. Trustee Calif. Sci. Center, L.A., 1999—. Office: TRW Space and Tech Divsn 1 Space Park, R4 2198 Redondo Beach CA 90278

FREWIN, DEREK BRIAN, pharmacology educator, university dean; b. Badulla, Sri Lanka, Nov. 21, 1941; arrived in Australia, 1965; s. Thomas Alfred and Ruth Constance (Williamson) F.; m. Margaret Elizabeth Spencer, Dec. 13, 1967; children: Michael, Joanne, Christine. MB, BS with honours, U. Ceylon, Colombo, 1965; MB, BS, U. Adelaide, Australia, 1967, MD, 1971. Resident med. officer Royal Adelaide Hosp., 1965-66, vis. clin. pharmacologist, 1973-77, sr. vis. clin. pharmacologist, 1977—, physician in charge hypertension clinic, 1973—, bd. dirs., 1991—; postgrad. rsch. fellow in human physiology and pharmacology U. Adelaide, 1966-67, lectr., 1967-72, sr. lectr. clin. pharmacology, 1973-76, reader, 1977-88, assoc. prof., 1989-90, prof., dean Faculty Medicine, 1991—, head divsn. health scis., 1996-98; exec. dean Faculty of Health Scis., 1999—; vis. assoc. prof. Columbia U. Coll. Physicians and Surgeons, N.Y.C., 1972, 73, vis. prof., 1974, 75, 87; cons. clin. pharmacologist Queen Victoria Maternity Hosp., 1977-95, Lyell McEwin Hosp., 1983-86; mem. Lions Heart Rsch. Adv. Com., 1978-91, Sci. Adv. Com. Sudden Infant Death Syndrome, 1986-91; mem. bd. mgmt. Modbury Hosp., 1990—; bd. dirs. Queen Elizabeth Hosp., 1991-95, North Western Adelaide Health Svc., 1995—; mem. accreditation com. Australian Med. Coun., 1994-97, mem. of coun., 1998—; mem. adv. bd. divsn. human nutrition Commonwealth Sci. and Indsl. Rsch. Orgn., Australia, 1992—; also others; chair Com. of Deans of Australasian Med. Schs., 1997-99. Sub editor Australian Jour. Exptl. Biol. Med. Sci., 1983-85, dep. editor, 1986-88; mem. editl. bd. Clin. Autonomic Rsch., 1990—; mem. internat. adv. editl. bd. Archives Internat. Pharmacodynamie et de Therapie, 1986—; contbr. over 170 artices and revs. to sci. jours., chpts. to books. Med. officer South Australian Speedways, 1966-68; sr. divisional surg. St. John's Ambulance, 1968-74; mem. bd. mgmt. Port Adelaide Meth. Mission, 1974-88; pres. Intercollegians Athletics Club Adelaide, 1985-86; hon. med. officer to several nat. track and field athletics championships, 1979-87. Fellow Royal Australasian Coll. Physicians, Royal Coll. Physicians (London); mem. Australian Physiol. and Pharm. Soc. (local sec. 1967, mem. coun. 1973-75), Australian Soc. Clin. and Exptl. Pharmacologists (local sec. 1981), High Blood Pressure Rsch. Coun. Australia, Am. Hypertension Soc., N.Y. Acad. Scis., Cardiac Soc. Australia and New Zealand, Australian Med. Assn., South Australian Salaried Med. Officers Assn., Australian Soc. for Med. Rsch. Mem. Liberal Party Australia. Mem. Uniting Ch. of Australia. Avocations: tennis, music, reading. Office: U Adelaide Faculty Medicine, Office of Dean, Adelaide 5005, Australia

FREY, ANDREAS, biochemist, researcher; b. Frankfurt, Germany, Aug. 15, 1959; s. Wilhelm and Emma Gertraude (Winkel) F.; m. Barbara Sophie Charlotte Meckelein, June 30, 1995. MS, Tech. U. Darmstadt, 1986, PhD, 1991. Rsch. asst. Tech. U. Darmstadt, Germany, 1986-91; rsch. assoc. Boston U., 1991, Children's Hosp., Boston, 1992-95; rsch. assoc., instr. U. Muenster, Germany, 1995—; rsch. fellow pediatrics Harvard Med. Sch., Boston, 1992-95. Patentee in field; contbr. articles to profl. jours. With German Army, 1978-79. Grantee Bundesministerium fuer Bildung/Wissenschaft Forschung und Technologie, 1995-98, Deutsche Forschungsgemeinschaft, 1996—. Mem. German Soc. Biochemistry and Molecular Biology, German Soc. Immunology, Am. Chem. Soc., Soc. Mucosal Immunology. Home: Am Pastorenbusch 10, D-48161 Muenster Germany Office: Inst Fuer Infektiologie, Von Esmarch Str 56, D-48149 Muenster D-48149, Germany

FREY, BRUNO S., economics educator; b. Basel, Switzerland, May 4, 1941; s. Leo and Julie (Bach) F. Lic., U. Basel, 1964, D, 1965, habilitation, 1969; D (hon.), U. St. Gallen, Switzerland, 1998, U. Goteborg, 1998. Assoc. prof. U. Basel, 1969—; prof. U. Konstanz, Germany, 1970-77, U. Zürich, Switzerland, 1977—; guest prof. Stockholm U., 1982; vis. fellow All Souls Coll., Oxford (Eng.) U., 1983; fellow Wissenschaftskolleg, Berlin, 1984-85; vis. rsch. prof. U. Chgo., 1990; vis. prof. Rome U., 1996-97, Goteborg Univ., 1998, Siena, 2000. Author: International Political Economics, 1984, Muses and Markets, 1989, Economics as a Science of Human Behaviour, 1992, 2d edit., 1999, Not Just for the Money, 1997, The New Federalism for Europe: Functional, Overlapping, Competing, Jurisdictions, 1999, Art and Econs. 2000. Recipient Vernon prize Assn. for Pub. Policy Analysis, 1996; fellow U.S. Pub. Choice Soc., 1997. Mem. European Econ. Assn. (bd. dirs. 1991-95), Assn. for Cultural Econs. Internat. (exec. bd. 1993—), European Pub. Choice Soc. (coun. 1980-95). Roman Catholic. Avocation: travel. Home: Niederdorfstr 29, CH-8001 Zürich Switzerland Office: Inst Empirical Econ Rsch, Bluemlisalpstr 10, CH-8006 Zürich Switzerland

FREY, DALE FRANKLIN, financial investment company executive, manufacturing company executive; b. Lancaster, Pa., Aug. 14, 1932; s. Franklin W. and Mary A. (Strickler) F.; m. Betty Ann Heistand, Aug. 22, 1953; children—Scott, Philip, Kyle, Susan. BS in Econs., Franklin and Marshall Coll., 1954; MBA, NYU, 1957. With GE, Fairfield, Conn., 1957-97, mgr. group fin. ops., 1975-77, internat. and Can. group staff exec., internat. sector, 1977-80, v.p., treas., 1980-84, 86-93; chmn. bd., pres. GE Investment Corp., Stamford, Conn., 1984-97; bd. dirs. Praxair Inc., Danbury, Damon Runyon-Walter Winchell Cancer Rsch. Fund, Roadway Express, Akron, After Market Tech., Chgo., Cmty. Health Sys., Go Co-op, Maitland, Fla.; mem. adv. bd. NYU Stern Sch. Trustee Franklin and Marshall Coll. Capt. USAF, 1955-57. Mem. Fin. Execs. Inst. (chmn. com. corp. fin. 1983-85), Aspetuck Valley Country Club (Weston, Conn.). Clubs: Aspetuck Valley Country (Weston, Conn.). Office: care Michael Allen Co One Gorham Island Westport CT 06880

FREY, HARLEY HARRISON, JR., anesthesiologist; b. Toledo, Feb. 22, 1920; s. Harley Harrison and Mina Rosina (Wiedemann) F.; m. Jane Luceia Murray, Aug. 28, 1944 (dec. 1964); children: Richard E., Martha J., Thomas C.; m. Emma Jean Hamilton, Apr. 15, 1966; 1 stepchild, Rick A. Gregory. BS, U. Toledo, 1942; MD, U. Cin., 1945. Diplomate Am. Bd. Anesthesiology. Intern Akron City Hosp., Ohio, 1946-49; fellow anesthesia U. Minn., Mpls., 1950; hon. mem. staff St. Elizabeth Hosp. Med. Ctr., Lafayette, Ind., 1950—, Lafayette Home Hosp., 1950—. Bd. dirs. Lafayette Symphony Orch., 1952-54; counselor, committeeman Lafayette coun. Boy Scouts Am., 1955-63; ruling elder Presbyn. Ch., 1964-67, active deacon, 1991-94; bd. dirs. Lafayette Citizens Band, 1997-2000. Fellow Am. Coll. Anesthesiology; mem. Am. Soc. Anesthesiology (bd. dirs. 1965-74), Ind. Soc. Anesthesiology (pres., bd. dirs. 1961-74, Disting. Svc. award 1992), Ind. State Med. Soc. (Cert. Distinction 1995), Tippecanoe County Med. soc. (pres. 1961), Rotary (bd. dirs. 1992-95) Lafayette Country Club (bd. dirs. 1963-65). Avocations: music, painting. Home and Office: 3513 Creek Ridge Lafayette IN 47905-5619

FREY, HARRY JUHANA, neurology educator; b. Helsinki, Finland, Jan. 25, 1941; s. Carl Harry and Sirkka Annikki (Astala) F.; m. Tuula Frey, June 18, 1982; children: Carl-Harry, Carl-Johan, Lisbet. MD, U. Turku, Finland, 1966, PhD, 1971. Assoc. chief physician U. Turku, 1970-80; prof. U. Tampere, Finland, 1980—, chmn. dept. neurology, 1984—; vis. scientist Albert Einstein Coll., N.Y.C., 1972-73, Nat. Inst. Neurology, London, 1977; mem. Med. Rsch. Coun., 1985-90; vice chmn. Nordic Com. of Med. Rsch., 1989; mem. EEC workgroup European Brain Rsch. Program, 1993—; prof., faculty, bd. dirs. Grad. Sch. Neurosci., Tampere, 1994—; bd. dirs. Euroespes Found., 1992—; mgmt. com. EU-cost brain damage repair program, 1998—. Editor: Immunological Disorders of the Nervous System, 1979, Healthpanorama 2000, 1982; contbr. numerous articles to profl. jours. Bd. dirs. Internat. Grad. Sch. Neursci., Inc., 1994—. Mem. World Fedn. Neurology (nat. del. 1989—), Nordic Neurol. Soc. (bd. dirs. 1988—), Norage Soc. (v.p. 1994—), Ragnar Granit Inst. Avocations: future studies, sculpturing. Office: U Tampere Inst Clin Sci, Teiskontie 35, 33520 Tampere Finland

FREY, HOLGER, chemistry educator, researcher; b. Ellwangen, Germany, May 5, 1965; s. Hauke and Gisela (Ott) F.; m. Annette Schifferdecker, Oct. 12, 1996. Diploma in chemistry, U. Freiburg, Germany, 1990; PhD, U. Twente, 1993. Cert. chemistry prof. Asst. prof. chemistry U. Freiburg, 1993—. Contbr. numerous articles to profl. jours. Mem. Gesellschaft Deutscher Chemiker (Travel Stipend 1995, Hermann-Schnell award 1998, Internat. Union Pure and Applied Chemistry (Young Scientist World Polymer Congress award 2000), Gesellschaft Deutscher Naturforsch, USC Freiburg. Roman Catholic. Avocations: long-distance running, track and field sports, literature. Office: Freiburg Materials Rsch Ctr Inst for Makromolekulare Chem, Stefan Meier Str 21/31, 79104 Freiburg Germany

FREY, JAMES SEVERIN, educational association executive; b. Milw., Mar. 1, 1938; s. Severin Anthony and Marian Clarice (Blattner) F.; m. Margo Walther, June 29, 1963; children: Michelle Marie Frey Loberg, David James Frey. BA, Marquette U., 1960, MA, 1967; EdD, Ind. U., 1976. Asst. to dir. admissions Marquette U., Milw., 1961-66; dir. fgn. student svcs. U. Wis., Milw., 1966-71; cons. U.S. Ednl. Commn. in Japan, Tokyo, 1971-72; asst. dir. of admissions Ind. U., Bloomington, 1972-76; exec. dir. World Edn. Svcs., Inc., Milw., 1977-80; pres. Ednl. Credential Evaluators, Inc., Milw., 1980—; cons. New Zealand Qualifications Authority, Wellington, 1990, 92, So. Africa Devel. Coordinating Coun., Mbabane, Swaziland, 1983; acad. specialist U.S. Info. Agy., Iraq, 1987; field svc. cons. NAFSA, Washington, 1968-74. Author: The Educational System of Turkey, 1972, 92, Iraq, 1988; co-author, editor: The Admission and Placement of Students from Canada, 1989; co-author: Israel, 1976. Grantee Internat. Edn. Rsch. Found., 1975. Mem. NAFSA (Homer Higbee award 1991), European Assn. for Internat. Edn., Am. Assn. of Collegiate Registrars and Admissions Officers. Avocations: travel, reading history, racquetball, card playing, gardening. Office: Ednl Credential Evaluators Inc PO Box 514070 Milwaukee WI 53203-3470

FREY, JOACHIM, microbiologist and chemist; b. Zürich, Switzerland, July 21, 1951; s. Hans Fritz and Helene (Schoenborn) F.; m. Agnes Irene Kollegger, Mar. 7, 1958; children: Raphael, Sibylle. MS, U. Uppsala, Sweden, 1975; Diploma in Molecular Biology, U. Geneva, 1976, PhD, 1980; prof., U. Berne, Switzerland, 1992. Rsch. asst. U. Geneva, 1975-80, rsch. fellow, 1981-87, lectr., 1987—; rsch. assoc. Max Plack Inst., Berlin, 1980-81; prof., dir. Inst. Vet. Bacteriology, U. Berne, 1987—; cons. Intervet Internat. Boxmeer, The Netherlands, 1990—, Indo-Swiss Collaboration in Biotech., Berne, 1990—; assoc. prof. Inst. Molecular Agrobiology U. Singapore, 1995—. Author: Molecular Mechanisms of Bacterial Virulence, 1994; editor: Mycoplasmas of Ruminants, 1996, 4th edit., 2000; contbr. articles to profl. jours. Mem. Commn. for Biotech. Safety, Swiss Acad. Scis., Berne, 1990—. Recipient E.A. Stein prize U. Berne, 1994. Mem. Am. Soc. Microbiology (steering com.), Swiss Soc. Microbiology, French Soc. Microbiology. Avocations: windsurfing, skiing, hiking, music. Home: Schreinerweg 9, CH-3012 Bern Switzerland Office: Inst Veterinary Bacteriology, Laenggasstrasse 122, CH-3012 Bern Switzerland

FREYCHET, PIERRE FRANCOIS, physician, educator; b. Philippeville, Algeria, Apr. 23, 1935; s. Henri Dominique and Jeanne Marie (Stofati) F.; m. Claude Lucie Sourd, June 8, 1959; 1 child, Laurent. MD, U. Paris, 1966. Sr. resident Diabetes Ctr., Hotel Dieu Hosp., Paris, 1966-69; internat. rsch. postdoctoral fellow Diabetes Sect., NIH, Bethesda, Md., 1969-71; with Inst. Nat. de la Sante et de la Rech. Med., France, 1971—, dir. rsch. U. Nice

Med. Sch., 1975-78; assoc. prof. medicine, unit head Inst. Nat. de la Sante et de la Rech. Med., Nice, 1978-87, prof. medicine, chief internal medicine and endocrine diabetes unit, 1982-97; mem. Nat. Sci. Coun. Inst. Nat. de la Sante et de la Rsch. Med., Paris, 1978-83; mem. sci. coun., U. Nice, 1979-88; com. mem., Nat. Coun. Univs, Paris, 1983-97. Contbg. author: Insulin Receptors, 1976, Receptors for Insulin and Glucagon, 1977, Pancreatic Hormones, 1989; contbr. papers to internat. med. jours. Recipient Prix Philipeaux, French Acad. Scis., Paris, 1981, Prix de la Fondation A. Lacassagne, Coll. France, Paris, 1983, Prix de la Fondation Pour la Prevention et l'Amelioration de la Sante, Groupe des Populaires d'Assurances and Inst. France, Paris, 1986. Mem. European Assn. for Study of Diabetes (pres. 1986-89; Oskar Minkowski award 1975), French Endocrine Soc. (pres. 1988), Am. Diabetes Assn., Endocrine Soc. U.S.A., Acad. Royal Medicine Belgique. Avocations: mountain hiking, skiing. Home: 132 Ave de Brancolar, F 06100 Nice France Office: INSERM, Unit 145 Fac Medicine, F 06017 Nice France

FREYD, JENNIFER JOY, psychology educator; b. Providence, Oct. 16, 1957; d. Peter John and Pamela (Parker) F.; m. John Q. Johnson, June 9, 1984; children: Theodore, Philip, Alexandra. BA in Anthropology magna cum laude, U. Pa., 1979; PhD in Psychology, Stanford U., 1983. Asst. prof. psychology Cornell U., 1983-87, mem. faculty coun. of reps., 1986-87; assoc. prof. psychology U. Oreg., Eugene, 1987-92, prof., 1992—; mem. dean's adv. com. U. Oreg., 1990-91, 92-93, mem. exec. com. Ctr. for the Study of Women in Soc., 1991-93, mem. child care com., 1987-89, 90-91; fellow Ctr. for Advanced Study in the Behavioral Scis., 1989-90; elected mem. faculty coun. of reps. Cornell U., 1986-87; mem. dean's adv. com. U. Oreg., 1990—, exec. com. Ctr. for Rsch. Study of Women in Soc., 1991-92, Inst. of Cognitive and Decision Scis., 1991-94. Author: Betrayal Trauma: The Logic of Forgetting Childhood Abuse, 1996 (Disting. Publ. award Assn. of Women in Psychology 1997, Pierre Janet award Internat. Soc. for Study Dissociation 1997); mem. editl. bd. Jour. Exptl. Psychology: Learning, Memory, and Cognition, 1989-91, Gestalt Theory, 1985—, Jour. of Aggression, Maltreatment, and Trauma, 1997—; guest reviewer Am. Jour. Psychology, Am. Psychologist, others; contbr. articles to profl. jours. Recipient Graduate fellowship NSF, 1979-82, Univ. fellowship Stanford U., 1982-83, Presdl. Young Investigator award NSF, 1985-90, IBM Faculty Devel. award, 1985-87, fellowship Ctr. for Advanced Study in the Behavioral Scis., 1989-90, John Simon Meml. fellowship Guggenheim Found., 1989-90, Rsch. Scientist Devel. award NIMH, 1989-94, Pierre Janet award Internat. Soc. for the Study of Dissociation, 1997; other rsch. funding. Fellow AAAS, APA (liaison divsn. 35 to sci. directorate 1996—), Am. Psychol. Soc.; mem. Psychonomic Soc., Assn. for Women in Psychology, Sigma Xi. Office: U Oreg 1227 Dept Psychology Eugene OR 97403-1227

FREYD, WILLIAM PATTINSON, fund raising executive, consultant; b. Chgo., Apr. 1, 1933; s. Paul Robert Freyd and Pauline Margaret (Pattinson) Gardiner; m. Diane Marie Carlson, May 19, 1984. BS in Fgn. Svc., Georgetown U., 1960. Field rep. Georgetown U., Washington, 1965-67; campaign dir. Tamblyn and Brown, N.Y.C., 1967-70; dir. devel. St. George's Ch., N.Y.C., 1971; assoc. Browning Assocs., Newark, 1972-73; regional v.p. C.W. Shaver Co., N.Y.C., 1973-74; founder IDC, Henderson, Nev., 1974—. Inventor PHONE/MAIL program. Bd. dirs. Nev. Symphony Orch., 1994-99, N.J. Symphony Orch., 1991-94; apptd. Nev. Charitable Solicitation Task Force, 1994, pres.'s circle adv. coun. U.S. Naval Acad., 2000. Mem. Nat. Soc. Fund Raising Execs. (nat. treas. 1980-81, pres. N.Y. chpt. 1974-76, cert. 1982), Am. Assn. Fund Raising Counsel (sec. 1984-86), World Fund Raising Coun. (bd. dirs. 1995-99, treas. 1998-99), Georgetown U. (regional club coun.), N.Y. Yacht Club, Union League Club N.Y., Masons, Nassau Club, Circumnavigators Club. Achievements include the invention of the Phone Mail Program. Office: IDC 5-521 IDC Ctr 2920 N Green Valley Pkwy Henderson NV 89014-0406

FREYMOND, JEAN F., political scientist, educator; b. Lausanne, Vaud, Switzerland, May 4, 1941; s. Jacques and Antoinette (Cart) F.; m. Guadalupe Sanchez, Jan. 10, 1981; children: André Felipe, Claudia Nathalie. Licence en droit, U. Geneva, 1964; PhD in Polit. Sci., Grad. Inst. Internat. Studies, Geneva, 1974. Vis. lectr. Inst. Internat. Rels., U. W.I., St. Augustine, Trinidad and Tobago, 1973-74; co-dir. diplomatic tng. programme Grad. Inst. Internat. Studies, Geneva, 1975-79; vis. prof. El Colegio de Mex., Mexico City, 1979-80; dir. Ctr. for Applied Studies in Internat. Negotiations, Geneva, 1980—; sec. bd. Sasakawa Africa Assn., Geneva, 1987—, Bus. Humanitarian Forum, 1998—; bd. dirs. Geneva Ctr. for Security Policy, Geneva Internat. Ctr. for Humanitarian Demining. Author: Le Illéme Reich et la réorganisation économique de l'Europe (1940-1942), 1974, Political Integration in the Commonwealth, Caribbean. A Survey of Recent Attempts with Special Reference to the Associated States (1967-1974), 1980. Sec. Swiss Pugwash Group, Geneva, 1980—. Mem. Swiss Polit. Sci. Assn., Swiss Soc. for History. Home: 4 chemin des Pessules, 1296 Coppet Switzerland Office: Ctr App Studies Internat 7, bis Ave Paix Case Post 1340, 1211 Geneva Switzerland

FREYSSINET, GEORGES LOUIS, research executive; b. Saint Etienne, Loire, France, May 28, 1946; s. Joseph Freyssinet and Marie Louise Laurençon; m. Marie-Martine Hareng, Aug. 4, 1969; children: Eric, Jerome. Licence Sciences Naturelles, U. Claude Bernard, Lyon, France, 1967, Thèse 3ème Cycle, 1970, Thèse d'Etat, 1977. Asst. U. Claude Bernard, Lyon, 1964-73; maître-asst. U. Claude Bernard, Lyon-Rhône, France, 1973-76; prof. U. Claude Bernard, Lyon-Rhône, France, 1980; rsch. asst. Brandeis U., Waltham, Mass., 1977-78; vis. prof. U. Ill., Champaign, 1978-79; prof. U. Limoges, France, 1980-84; head plant molecular cell biology Rhône Poulenc Agrochimie, Lyon, 1984-92; sci. advisor Rhône Poulenc, Courbevoie, France, 1992-98; head regulatory affairs for GMO, Rhône Poulenc Agro; CEO RhoBio, 1998-2000; head of global genomics rsch. Aventis CropSci., 2000—; cons. Ministry Rsch., Paris, European Commn., Brussels; chmn. Plant Indsl. Platform,Netherlands, 1996-2000. Author: The Biology of Euglena, Biotechnologies d'aujourd'hui, 1993; inventor genes for desaturase and oxalate oxidase. Recipient Rhône-Poulenc innovation prize, 1995. Mem. Soc. French Physiologie Végétale, Internat. Soc. Plant Molecular Biology, Am. Soc. Plant Physiology. Home: 21 rue de Nervieux, 69450 Saint Cyr au Mt D'or Rhône, France Office: Aventis CropScience, BP9613, 69263 Cedex France

FREYTAG, RICHARD ARTHUR, banker; b. Chgo., Oct. 26, 1933; s. Elmer Walter and Mary Louise (Mayo) F.; m. Pamela Burge, Feb. 11, 1989; children: Richard Christopher Hughes Freytag, Bliss Louise Mayo Smith. AB, Trinity Coll., Hartford, Conn., 1955; MBA, Harvard U., 1961; MS, MIT, 1971. Map salesman Rand McNally & Co., Chgo., 1955-56; internat. salesman Diversey Corp., Chgo., 1959-60; with Citibank, Japan, Taiwan, Korea, 1962-70; v.p., sr. credit officer Citibank, 1971-73; sr. officer Citibank, Hong Kong, China, Vietnam, 1973-76; investor rels. and problem loan recovery mgmt. Citibank, N.Y.C., 1977-84; pres. Citicorp Holdings, Inc., Citibank Overseas Investment Corp., 1984-96, vice chmn., dir., 1996-98; pres., CEO Citicorp Banking Corp., New Castle, Del., 1984-96, vice chmn., dir., 1996-98; pres. Citibank Del., 1989-96, vice chmn., dir., 1996-98; vice chmn. Far East Bank, Ltd., Hong Kong, 1973-76, sr. ptnr. Washington Capital Ptnrs., 1999—; bd. dirs. Citicorp Capital Investors Europe Ltd., The Thomas Group, Inc., Irving, Tex.; mem. expanded sr. panel on N.E. Asian Ltd. Nuclear Arms Agreement. Trustee Med. Ctr. of Del.; bd. visitors Nat. Def. U., 1988-93; chmn. Nat. Def. U. Found., 1993-99, chmn. emeritus, 1999—; mem. Gov.'s Coun. on Banking, 1994-97. 1st lt. USAF, 1956-59, maj. gen. USAFR, 1959-93. Decorated D.S.M.; recipient Brooks prize MIT, 1971; Alfred Sloan fellow The Nat. City Found., N.Y.C., 1969. Mem. Nat. Air Force Salute Found. (pres. 1988-90, chmn. 1990-92), Air Force Assn. (Iron Gate chpt. pres. 1988-90, chmn. 1990-92, Ira Eaker fellow 1991, Medal of Merit 1990, Exceptional Svc. award 1989), Coun. on Fgn. Rels., Falcon Found. (trustee), Del. Bankers Assn. (dir., pres. 1992-97), Del. Bus. Roundtable (vice chmn. 1994-96). Episcopalian. Office: PO Box 921 Montchanin DE 19710-0921

FREYTAG, SHARON NELSON, lawyer; b. May 11, 1943; d. John Seldon and Ruth Marie (Herbel) Nelson; children: Kurt David, Hillary Lee. BS with highest distinction, U. Kans., Lawrence, 1965; MA, U. Mich., 1966; JD cum laude, So. Meth. U., 1981. Bar: Tex. 1981, U.S. Dist. Ct. (no. dist.) Tex. 1981, U.S. Ct. Appeals (5th cir.) 1982, U.S. Supreme Ct. 1993. Tchr. English Gaithersburg (Md.) H.S., 1966-70; instr. English Eastfield Coll., 1974-78; law clk. U.S. Dist. Ct. (no. dist.) Tex., 1981-82, U.S. Ct. Appeals (5th cir.), 1982; ptnr., chair appellate sect. Haynes and Boone, Dallas, 1983—; vis. prof. law Southern Meth. U., 1985-86; faculty Appellate Adv. program NITA. Editor-in-chief Southwestern Law Jour., 1980-81; contbr. articles to law jours. Woodrow Wilson fellow; recipient John Marshall Constl. Law award, Baird Cmty. Spirit award, 1995. Mem. ABA (litigation sect., chair subcom. on local rules), Fed. Bar Assn. (co-chmn. appellate practice and adv. sect. 1990-91), Tex Bar Assn. (appellate coun. 1995-98), State Bar Tex. (bd. dirs., exec. com.), Dallas Bar Assn. (appellate coun.), Higginbotham Inn of Ct., Barristers, Order of Coif, Phi Beta Kappa. Lutheran. Office: Haynes & Boone 3100 NationsBank Plz Dallas TX 75202

FREZZOTTI, RENATO, ophthalmologist; b. Imperia, Italy, Dec. 19, 1924; s. Giuseppe and Rosa (Pirani) F.; m. Angela Tabanelli, Feb. 6, 1961; children: Maria Luce, Paolo, Guido. Laureate in Medicine and Surgery, U. Perugia, 1949. Asst. and clin. oculist U. siena, 1950-67, full prof. ophthalmology, 1967—. Author: Oftalmologia Essenziale, 1982, Patologia, Clinica e Terapia delle Malattie dell'Orbita, 1985; contbr. 450 articles to sci. jours. Decorated grande ufficiale della Rep. Italiana; recipient Mangia d'Oro prize, Gold medal Italian Ministry Edn. and Culture, Gold medal Maestri della Oftalmologia. Mem. Italian Soc. Ophthalmology (pres. 1994-97), Yacht Club. Home: Viale XXIV Maggio 23, 53100 Siena Italy Office: U Siena, Dept Sci Oftalmologiche e Neurochir, 53100 Siena Italy

FRIAS, JAIME LUIS, pediatrician, educator; b. Concepcion, Chile, Mar. 20, 1933; came to U.S., 1970; s. Luis Humberto and Olga Ana (Fernandez) F.; m. Jacqueline May Steel, Apr. 8, 1961; children: Jaime Arturo, Juan Pablo, Patricio Andres, Maria Josefina. MD, U. Chile, 1959. Diplomate Am. Bd. Pediatrics, Am. Bd. Human Genetics. Intern Hospital Regional, Concepcion, 1958-59; resident in pediatrics Calvo Mackenna Hosp., Santiago, Chile, 1960-62; clin. genetics and dysmorphology fellow U. Wis., Madison, 1965-66, U. Wash., Seattle, 1966-67; asst. prof. pediatrics U. Concepcion, 1967-69; asst. prof. pediatrics U. Fla. Coll. Medicine, Gainesville, 1970-74, assoc. prof., 1974-77, prof., 1977-86, chief divsn. genetics, 1977-86, chmn. med. sch. admissions com., 1983-86; prof. pediatrics U. South Fla. Coll. Medicine, Tampa, 1991—, chmn. dept. pediatrics, 1991-99, dir. Birth Defects Ctr., 1999—; chmn. Com. for Protection of Human Subjects, 1975-78; chmn. Fla. Com. on Prevention Devel. Disabilities, 1979-82, chmn. infant hearing screening adv. coun., 1982-86; cons. Spanish Collaborative Project on Congenital Malformation, Madrid, 1983—. Contbr. chpts. to books, articles to profl. jours. Trustee All Children's Hosp., 1991-99, Ronald McDonald Charities of Tampa Bay, 1999—; mem. exec. com. Assn. Med. Sch. Pediatric Dept. Chmn., 1991-99; mem. steering com. Nat. Folic Acid Coun., 1999—. Named Tchr. of Yr., U. Fla. Coll. Medicine, 1978-79, Lewis A. Barness Endowed Chair Pediatrics, 1994-99. Mem. ACP (affiliate; W.K. Kellogg fellow 1965-67), Am. Acad. Pediatrics (com. genetics 1995—), Am. Pediatric Soc., Am. Soc. Human Genetics, Assn. Clin. Scientists, Tampa Yacht and Country Club. Democrat. Roman Catholic. Office: U South Fla Dept Pediat 17 Davis Blvd Ste 200 Tampa FL 33606-3438

FRICK, BENJAMIN CHARLES, lawyer; b. Overbrook, Pa., Feb. 23, 1960; s. Sidney Wanning and Marie Pauline Frick; m. Stephanie Ann Sears, June 1, 1991; children: Sarah Marie, Anna Elizabeth, Charles Andrew. BA, Cornell U., 1982; JD, U. Richmond, 1985; LLM in Taxation, Villanova U., 1994. Bar: Pa. 1985. Clerk to Hon. John B. Hannum U.S. dist. court, 1984; trust officer Provident Nat. Bank, Phila., 1985-89; sole practice Bryn Mawr, Pa., 1989—. Deacon Ardmore (Pa.) Presbyn. Ch. Mem. ABA, S.R. (bd. dirs. Pa. Soc. 1987—, sec. 1991-95, treas. 1995-97, v.p. 1997—), Pa. Bar Assn., Phila. Bar Assn., Soc. Mayflower Descs., Colonial Soc. Pa. (treas. 2000—), Soc. Colonial Wars (bd. dirs. Pa. chpt. 1999—), St. Andrew's Soc. Phila., Mil. Order Loyal Legion U.S. (sec. 1993-95, v.p. 1995-97, comdr. 1997-99, judge adv.-in-chief 1997—), The Racquet Club, The Union League of Phila., Athenaeum of Phila., The Phila. Club, Phi Alpha Delta (pres. local chpt. 1984-85), Alpha Delta Phi. Republican. Presbyterian. Office: Bldg 1 Ste 303 919 Conestoga Rd Bryn Mawr PA 19010-1352

FRICK, MARIO, head of government of Liechtenstein; b. May 8, 1965; m. Andrea Haberlander, 1992; 3 children. Dr.iur., St. Gall, Switzerland, 1992. Legal svc. mem. Nat. Adminstrn. Liechtenstein, 1991-93; mem. Communal Coun. Balzers, 1991-93; dep. head govt. Principality of Liechtenstein, 1993—, head govt., 1993—, Min. for Gen. Govtl. Affairs, Min. for Fins. and Constrn., 1993—. Office: Head of the Government, Regierungsgebaude, FL-9490 Vaduz Liechtenstein

FRICK, ROBERT HATHAWAY, lawyer; b. Cleve., June 28, 1924; s. Claude Oates and Urshal May (Hathaway) F.; m. Lenore M. Maurin, Aug. 16, 1947 (dec. Sept. 1993); children: Elaine D. Frick , Barbara A. Frick Bundick, Catherine L. Frick Cayer. BBA, U. Mich., 1948, JD, 1950; postgrad. Harvard Bus. Sch., 1965. Bar: Mich. 1951, Ill. 1951, Ohio 1952, N.Y. 1962, U.S. Supreme Ct. 1981. Atty., Amoco Corp. (formerly Standard Oil Co. Ind.), Chgo., 1950, 52-60, Paris, 1960-62, N.Y.C., 1962-68, Chgo., 1968-71, assoc. gen. counsel, Chgo., 1972-87; pvt. practice, Cleve., 1951-52. Served with USAAF, 1943-46. Mem. ABA, Am. Soc. Internat. Law, Assn. of Bar of City of N.Y., Ill. Bar Assn., Chgo. Bar Assn., Order of Coif, Westmoreland Country Club, Meadows Country Club, Univ. Club Chgo., Mid Am. Club, Sigma Phi Epsilon. Republican. Home: 921 Westerfield Dr Wilmette IL 60091-1810

FRICKE, RICHARD JOHN, lawyer; b. Ithaca, N.Y., Apr. 17, 1945; s. Richard I. and Jeanne L. (Hines) F.; m. Carol A. Borelli, June 17, 1967 (div. 1990); children: Laura, Richard, Amanda; m. Penny Yrizarry, Dec. 29, 1990 (div. 1999); children: Stephanie, Matthew, Tyler. BA, Cornell U., 1967, JD, 1970. Bar: Conn. 1970. Assoc. Gregory & Adams, Wilton, Conn., 1970-73; ptnr. Crehan & Fricke, Ridgefield, Conn., 1973-90; gen. counsel Connex Internat. Inc.; corp. counsel, pres. Safe Alternatives Corp. of Am., Inc.; pres., gen. counsel, dir. T.F.I. Industries, Inc.; gen. counsel Gold Mustache Pub. Corp., Inc.; sec., dir. DXTC.COM, Inc.; dir. Village Bank & Trust Co.; town atty. Town of Ridgefield, 1973-81. Co-patentee low reactive pressure foam, polyurethane foam for cellulostic products. Bd. dirs. Ridgefield Community Ctr., Ridgefield Montessori, Ridgefield Community Kindergarten; founder, pres. Ridgefield Lacross League; constable Town of Wilton, Conn.; mem. Conn. Bar Commn. on Women, 1976. Mem. ABA, Conn. Bar Assn., Danbury Bar Assn. Democrat. Roman Catholic. Address: 440 Main St Ridgefield CT 06877-4525

FRICKER, JACQUES, physician, nutrition specialist, researcher, consultant; b. Neuilly-sur-Seine, France, Dec. 8, 1955; s. Jacques and Micheline (Frere) F.; m. Corinne Gausseres, Feb. 2, 1984; children: Alexandra, Marie, Geoffroy, Claire, Hortense. MD, U. Paris, 1984, D in Physiology, 1990. Asst. prof. Bichat Hosp., Paris, 1986-90. Author: La Cuisine du Bien Maigrir, 1994, Traite de L'Alimentation et du Corps, 1994, Abrégé d'Obésite, 1995, Le Nouveau Guide du Bien Maigrir, 1996, Le Grand Livre de la Forme, 1997, Maigrir Vite et Bien, 2000, Le Regime Cretois, 2000. Mem. SNDLF, AFERO, N.Y. Acad. Scis. Home: 16 Sq Léon Blum, 92800 Puteaux France Office: Bichat Hosp Human Nutrition, rue Henri Huchard, 75018 Paris France also: 7 rue Marbeuf, 75008 Paris France

FRICKS, ERNEST EUGENE, engineering company official; b. Knoxville, Tenn., Jan. 16, 1948; s. Ernest E. Fricks and Barbara (Clark) Griffey; m. Dorothy Stanton; children: Natalie, Karen. AB, BSME, Rutgers U., 1970; MS, Pa. State U., 1974; graduate, Air War Coll., 1986, U. Pa. Wharton Sch. exec. mgmt, 1988. Lead engr. Pub. Svc. Electric & Gas Co., Newark, 1972-76; lead engr. Stone & Webster Engring. Corp., Cherry Hill, N.J., 1976-78, mgr. licensing, 1978-79, bus. developer, 1979-85, mgr. govt. mktg., 1985-90, project mgr. constrn. dept., 1990—; cons. Office Sec. of Navy, 1975. Author: The Thermodynamic Effect in Developer Cavitation in Freon 113, 1974. Trustee Camden County (N.J.) Hist. Soc., 1988-92. Lt. col. USAFR, 1970-92. Named Outstanding Augmentee Officer, Mil. Airlift Command, 1977. Fellow ASME (chmn. tech. and society divsn. 1996-98, Tech. Interests Activities award 1998), Soc. Am. Mil. Engrs. (life, pres. Phila. chpt. 1994-95), Royal Philatelic Soc. (London); mem. Royal Aero. Soc. U.K., Am. Philatelic Soc. (v.p. 1977-80), Rutgers Alumni Assn. (chmn. budget and audit coms. 1999), Rutgers U. Alumni Fedn. (treas. 1985-86, univ. sen. 1986-88), Rutgers Engring. Soc. (pres. 1976-77, sec. 1998-99), Newcomen Soc. (vice chmn. N.J. 1992-94, 96—), Collectors Club (N.Y.C.), Masons (past master, state grand sec., 33). Democrat. Baptist. Office: 3 Executive Campus Cherry Hill NJ 08002-4103

FRIDER, BERNARDO, physician, consultant; b. Montevideo, Uruguay, Sept. 27, 1942; s. Bernardo and Sara (Menkus) F.; m. Clara Silvia Kauf, Aug. 14, 1967; children: Nadina, Hernan. MD, U. Buenos Aires, 1965. Med. asst. in internal medicine Argerich Hosp.-U. Buenos Aires, 1966-69, attending in internal medicine sect. gastroenterology, 1970-80, cons. in ultrasonography, 1980—, chief Internal Medicine Unit, 1980-93, chief Hepatology Unit, 1989—, chief divsn. internal medicine, 1993—. Co-author: Library of Medicine, 1995, Michans Surgery, 1997; contbr. articles to med. jours. Advisor sec. of pub. health Ministry of Health, Buenos Aires province, 1986. Recipient Zavaleta award Nat. Acad. Medicine, Argentina, 1984. Mem. Argentine Gastroenterology Soc., Argentine Soc. Study of Liver Disease, Argentine Med. Assn., Internat. Assn. Study of Liver. Jewish. Fax: 54-1-801-0502. E-mail: frider@bigfoot.com. Office: Larrea 1231 PB1, 1117 Buenos Aires Argentina

FRIDJONSSON, THORDUR, economist, economic institute administrator; b. Reykjavik, Iceland, Jan. 2, 1952; s. Fridjon Thordarson and Kristin Sigurdardottir; m. Thrudur Gudrun Haraldsdottir, Apr. 8, 1971; children: Sigridur, Steinunn, Fridjon, Haraldur. Candidate in econs., U. Iceland, Reykjavik, 1977; MA, Queen's U., Kingston, Ont., Can., 1978. Chief economist Fed. Icelandic Industries, Reykjavik, 1978-80; econ. advisor Prime Min. Iceland, Reykjavik, 1980-86; part-time adj. instr. U. Iceland, 1979-87; mng. dir. Nat. Econ. Inst., Reykjavik, 1987—; sec. gen. Ministry Industry and Commerce, 1998-99; bd. dirs. Nordic Project Fund, Helsinki, Finland, 1982—; mem. econ. polic com. Orgn. Econ. Coop. and Devel. (OECD), Paris, 1987—; chmn. Agrl. Rsch. Inst., Hvanneyri, Iceland, 1993—; Iceland rep. Econ. and Devel. Rev. Com., OECD, Paris, 1987—; alternate gov. IMF, 1998-99, EBRD, 1998-99; chmn. coordinating com. aluminium project Iceland-North-Hydro, 1998—. Editor, author book on Icelandic economy. John Hicks fellow, Queen's U., 1977. Fellow Rotary-Reykjavik-Austurbaer (v.p. 1991); mem. Assn. Icelandic Economists (chmn. 1982-85), Icelandic Mgmt. Assn. (chmn. 1986-87). Avocations: outdoor activities, sports. Home: Engjasel 9, 109 Reykjavik Iceland Office: Nat Economic Inst, Kalkfnsvegur 1, 150 Reykjavik Iceland

FRIDMAN, BORIS EMMANUILOVICH, electromechanical engineer, mathematician; b. Magadan, USSR, Nov. 16, 1942; s. Emmanuel Moiseevich and Freda Grigor'evna (Breydo) F.; m. Margaret Vladimirovna Epshteyn, Apr. 4, 1942; children: Marina, Leonid. MSc in Electromechanics, Mech. Inst., Leningrad, USSR, 1966; MSc in Math., U. Leningrad, 1973; PhD in Elec. Pulsed Power Engring., N.W. Poly. Inst., Leningrad, 1975; DSc Inst. Problems in Electrophysics, Russian Acad. Scis., St. Petersburg (formerly Leningrad), 1999. Engr. VPTI Electro, Leningrad, 1963-87; sr. rsch. assoc. Inst. Problems in Electrophysics, Russian Acad. Scis., 1987—. Contbr. articles to profl. jours. Home: Mechnikov pr. 18, ap. 81, 195271 St Petersburg Russia Office: IPE, Russian Acad Scis, Dvortsovaya Nab, 18, 191186 St Petersburg Russia

FRIE, MICHAEL CARL, advocate; b. Kalmar, Sweden, Jan. 29, 1953; s. Sören Lennart and Barbro (Karlström) F.; m. Charlotte Gunilla Bagge, July 21, 1979; children: Mikaela, Amelie, Gabriella. LLM, U. Stockholm, 1978. Mem. Swedish Bar Assn., 1984. Rschr. Gothenburg (Sweden) U., 1978-79; lawyer Advokatfirman Tisell & Co., Stockholm, 1979-85; ptnr. Advokatbyran Frie, Stockholm, 1986-97, Gedda & Ekdahl Advokatbyraa, Stockholm, 1997—. Co-author: International Charitable Giving, Laws and Taxation, 1995. Hon. consul gen. to New Zealand in Sweden, 1994. Mem. SHT, IBA, IPBA, UIA, Nya Sallskapet. Avocations: sailing, golfing, tennis, skiing. Home: Erstaviks Kvarnväg 8, S-13336 Saltsjobaden Sweden Office: Gedda & Ekdahl, PO Box 5348, S-10247 Stockholm Sweden

FRIEBE, MICHAEL HORST, biomedical engineer; b. Nuremberg, Germany, Dec. 26, 1964; s. Horst W. and Hannelore (Basel) F.; m. Margaret Cannon, Apr. 7, 1994; children: Patrick Michael, Daniel Willem. BSc, Berufsakademie, Stuttgart, Germany, 1987, MSc, 1988; MSc, Golden Gate U., San Francisco, 1992; PhD, U. Witten, Germany, 1995. Rsch. engr. IBM, Germany, 1988; support engr. Diasonics Inc., South San Francisco, Calif., 1988-89; support engr. Toshiba MRI Inc., South San Francisco, 1989-90, systems engr., 1990-92, engring. group leader, 1992-93; R&D mgr. GIT, Germany, 1993-94; pres., CEO Neuromed, Castrop-Rauxel, Germany, 1994—. Contbr. articles to profl. jours. Mem. IEEE, Internat. Soc. Magnetic Resonance in Medicine. Achievements include interventional MRI sequence design patents, MRI system design patent. Office: Neuromed GmbH, Westring 170, 44575 Castrop-Rauxel Germany

FRIED, DANIEL, ambassador; b. Sept. 19, 1952; m. Olga Karpiw; children: Hannah, Sophie. BA in History magna cum laude, Cornell U., 1974; MA, Columbia U., 1977. Fgn. svc. officer, 1977—; jr. officer East-West Trade office Econ. Bus. Bur. State Dept., 1977-79; with Consulate Gen. Office, Leningrad, 1980-81; polit. officer U.S. Embassy, Belgrade, 1982-85; reg. affairs officer Soviet Desk State Dept., Washington, 1985-87; Polish desk officer State Dept., Washington, 1987-89; polit. counselor U.S. Embassy, Warsaw, 1990-93; dir. European affairs NSC, Washington, 1993-95, spl. asst. to pres., sr. dir. ctrl. and Ea. Europe, 1995—; amb. to Poland Warsaw, 1997—. Office: Am Embassy Warsaw Poland Dept Of State Washington DC 20521-0001

FRIED, ELAINE JUNE, insurance company executive; b. L.A., Oct. 19, 1943; m. Howard I. Fried, Aug. 7, 1966; children: Donnoven Michael, Randall Jay. Grad., Pasadena (Calif.) H.S.; various coll. courses. Agt., office mgr. Howard I. Fried Agy., Alhambra, Calif., 1975—; v.p. Sea Hill, Inc., Pasadena, 1973-95; spkr. on psycho-social aspects of diabetes, insurance, diabetes, ins. medicine. Contbr. articles to profl. jours. Publicity chmn., unit telephone chmn. San Gabriel Valley unit Am. Diabetes Assn., past chmn., vol. lobbyist, mem. patient edn. com. region II Calif. chpt., 1998; past publicity chmn. San Gabriel Valley region Women's Am. Orgn. for Rehab. Tng. (ORT); chmn. spl. events publicity, Temple Beth Torah Sisterhood, Alhambra, membership chmn., 1991-92, v.p. membership, 1991-93; former mem. bd. dirs., pub. rels. com., pers. com. Vis. Nurses Assn., Pasadena and San Gabriel Valley; chmn. outside Sisterhood publicity Congregation Shaarei Torah, 1993—, pub. rels. chmn., 1993—, membership v.p., 1999—. Recipient Vol. award So. Calif. affiliate Am. Diabetes Assn., 1974-77, 25 Yr. Vol. Svc. award, 1996, cert. of appreciation, 1987; co-recipient Ner Tamid Temple Beth Torah. Mem. ORT, Hadassah, Greater Pasadena Assn. Life Underwriters (co-v.p. cmty. affairs 1998—). Home: 404 N Hidalgo Ave Alhambra CA 91801-2640

FRIED, JOEL ROBERT, chemical engineering educator; b. Memphis, Dec. 9, 1946; s. Samuel J. and Mathilda (Kleinman) F.; m. Ava S. Krinick, June 8, 1969; children: Marc S., Aaron M. BS, Rensselaer Poly. Inst., 1968, 71, ME, 1972; MS, U. Mass., 1975, PhD, 1976. Mem. assoc. rsch. staff GE, Schenectady, N.Y., 1972-73; sr. rsch. engr. Monsanto Co., St. Louis, 1976-78; asst. prof. chem. engring. U. Cin., 1978-83, assoc. prof. chem. engring., 1983-90, dir. grad. studies, 1986-90, dir. polymer rsch. ctr., 1989-92, prof. chem. engring., 1990—, acting dir. membrane ctr., 1994, dir. Ohio Molecular Computation and Simulation Network, 1995—, interim head dept. chem. engring., 1998-99, head dept. chem. engring., 2000—; pres. Polymer Rsch. Assocs., Inc., Cin., 1984—. Author: Polymer Science and Technology, 1995; contbr. articles to sci. jours. Recipient Faculty Achievement award, 1994, Outstanding Prof., 96; Jr. Morr ow rsch. chair U. Cin., 1980; USAF summer faculty rsch. fellow, 1981, 93, 94. Mem. Am. Chem. Soc., Am. Inst. Chem. Engrs., Soc. Plastics Engrs. Achievements include patents in permeation modified separation membranes. Office: U Cin Dept Chemical Engineering Cincinnati OH 45221-0001

FRIED, MARVIN PETER, physician; b. N.Y.C., June 10, 1945; s. Otto and Leonore (Schwartz) F.; m. Rita Beth Hyfer, Jan. 25, 1970; children: Jaimie Lisa, Karen Lynn. BS, CUNY, 1961-65; MD, Tufts U. Sch. of Med., Boston, Mass., 1965-69. Diplomate, Am. Bd of Otolaryngology, 1975. Chief of otolaryngology Boston (Mass.) City Hosp., 1977-79; otolaryngolist Beth Israel Hosp., Boston, 1979-92; chief of otolaryngology Beth Israel Deaconess Med. Ctr., 1993-98; otolaryngologist Brigham & Womens Hosp., Boston, 1979-92; chief otolaryngology Brigham & Womens Hosp., 1993-98; otolaryngologist Childrens Hosp., Boston, 1979-98, Mass. Eye and Ear Infirmary, Boston, 1979; prof. otology and laryngology Harvard Med. Sch., Boston, 1997-99; prof., chmn. dept. otolaryngology Montefiore Med. Ctr., Albert Einstein Coll. Medicine, Bronx, N.Y., 1999—; co-dir. Head and Neck

Oncology program Dana Farber Cancer Ctr., 1996-98; prof. Otolaryngology Albut Emiten Coll. Medicine; chmn. Dept. Otolaryngology, Montifore Hosp., N.Y., 1999—. Editor: Complications Of Laser Surgery Of The Head And Neck, 1986, Manual of Otolaryngology, 1992, The Larynx, 1995; mem. editl. bd. Ear, Nose & Throat Jour., 1988, Laryngoscope, 1992, Archives of Otolaryngology, 1998. Surgeon (CDR), U.S. Public Health Svc., Norfolk, Va., 1975. Recipient Fowler award, 1984, Mark award, 1994. Fellow Am. Acad. of Otolaryngology, Am. Coll. of Surgeons, Triologic Soc., Am. Laryngological Soc., Am. Bronchoesophagological Soc., Am Soc. for Laser Med. and Surgery (v.p. 1994, pres.-elect 1998), Soc. Univ. Otolaryngology (pres-elect 1998), Phi Beta Kappa, Alpha Omega Alpha. Avocations: travel, music, tennis. Fax: (718) 405-9014. Office: Albert Einstein Coll Medicine Montefiore Med Ctr 3400 Bainbridge Ave Bronx NY 10467-2404

FRIED, MORRIS LOUIS, retired humanities educator; b. N.Y.C., Jan. 26, 1925; s. Abraham and Tillie (Marrus) F.; m. Helen Gorson, Feb. 26, 1949; children: Stephanie Fried, Pamela Crawford. BA, U. Buffalo, 1951; MA, New Sch. for Social Rsch., N.Y.C., 1958; PhD, New Sch. for Social Rsch., 1964. Verbatim reporter UN Security Coun./U.S. Dist. Cts., N.Y.C., 1958-62; lectr. in Sociology Fairleigh Dickinson U., Teaneck, N.J., 1962-64; lectr. in Labor Rels. Cornell U./Western N.Y. Dist. Internat. Labor Rels. Sch., Buffalo, 1972-78; vis. prof. Leicester (Eng.) U., 1970-71; asst., assoc. prof. Sociology SUNY, Buffalo, 1964-78; prof. Labor Studies & Sociology Ga. State U., Atlanta, 1978-81; ext. prof. continuing edn., adj. prof. sociology U. Conn., Storrs, 1981-92; ext. prof. emeritus U. Conn., 1992—; dir. Office of Pub. Svc. & Applied Rsch., U. Conn., 1988-92. Contbr. articles to profl. jours. Bd. dirs. Conn. Joint Coun. on Economic Edn., Storrs, 1987-91, Indsl. Rels. Rsch. Assn., Hartford, Conn. (pres. 1983-85); nat. chair Am. Hist. and Cultural Inst., N.Y.C., 1982-84; cons. Conn. State Dept. Labor, Hartford, 1987-89. Active in educating seniors and retired persons Shepherd's Ctr., Columbia, S.C., 1998—, Emory U., Atlanta, 1997, U. Conn., 1988-91. Named prin. investigator constrn. industry OSHA, 1978-81, mining industry Mine Safety & Health Adminstrn., 1982-88. Mem. Ctr. for Learning in Retirement (life). Avocations: computers, teaching, writing, developing new ideas for seniors. E-mail: MLFLCTR@aol.com. Home: 147 Old Hampton Ln Columbia SC 29209-1981

FRIED, ROBERT, psychology educator; b. Linz, Austria, July 27, 1935; s. Georg and Alice (Schwartz) F.; m. Virginia Lynn Cutchin, Nov. 16, 1991; children: Paul M., Steven G., Dennis A. AB, CCNY, 1959; PhD, Rutgers U., 1964. Lic. psychologist, N.Y.; cert. psychotherapy. Prof. CUNY, N.Y.C., 1964—; dir. biofeedback clinic Albert Ellis Inst., N.Y.C., 1985—; dir. rehab. rsch. Internat. Ctr. for the Disabled, N.Y.C., 1981-84. Author: The Hyperventilation Syndrome, 1987, The Breath Connection, 1990, The Psychology and Physiology of Breathing in Behavioral Medicine, 1993, The Arginine Solution, 1999, Breathe Well, Be Well, 1999; contbr. over 50 articles to profl. jours. Cpl. U.S. Army, 1953-55. Recipient Superior Accomplishment award USN, 1965, Citation for Outstanding Contbn. to Profession, N.Y. State Biofeedback Soc., 1988. Fellow N.Y. Acad. Scis.; mem. APA, Assn. for Applied Psychophysiology and Biofeedback, Am. Physiol. Assn. Achievements include patents for Cardiac Computer, Muscle Activity Recorder and Brain Wave Computer. Home: 1040 Park Ave New York NY 10028-1032 Office: Hunter Coll 695 Park Ave New York NY 10021-5024

FRIED, VANCE HOYT, educator; b. Mangum, Okla., Apr. 17, 1952; s. David Daniel and Elsie Elizabeth (Moreau) F.; m. Nancy Jane Petree, oct. 3, 1982; children: Regan, David. BS in Fin., Okla. State U., 1973, postgrad., 1986-87; JD, U. Mich., 1976. Atty. Stillwater, Okla., 1976-79, Wheatley & Fried, Stillwater, 1979-81; v.p., dir. and founding shareholder Red Eagle Exploration, Oklahoma City, 1981-84; v.p., corp. fin. Houchin, Adamson & Co., Oklahoma City, 1984-86; asst. to assoc. prof. Okla. State U., Stillwater, 1987-94, dir. Entrepreneurship Ctr., 1994-99; fin. and strategic cons. Vance H. Fried, Ltd., Stillwater, 1987—; mem. applied sci. and tech. com. Okla. Futures, Oklahoma City, 1996. Editl. bd.: Entrepreneurship Theory and Practice, Waco, Tex., 1991—; contbr. articles to academic and profl. jours. Sec., dir. Sheltered Workshop, Stillwater, Okla., 1996-99. Grantee Coleman Found., Chgo., 1998, Okla. Capital Investments Bd., 1988, 91, 98. Mem. Acad. mgmt., Okla. Investment Forum, Okla. Venture Forum (edn. com. 1991-98), Okla. Acad. (task force chair 1994). Republican. Achievements include rsch. on venture capital industry and mgmt. of venture capital-backed companies; design of university-based programs to promote technol. entrepreneurship. Office: Okla State Univ Coll Of Bus Adminstrn Stillwater OK 74078-0001

FRIEDA, ELAINA MARY, psychology educator; b. Ronkonkoma, N.Y., Sept. 8, 1969; d. Vincent Michael and Adeline Josephine Frieda. Bachelor's degree, SUNY, Stony Brook, 1992; PhD, MA, U. Ala., 1998. Lic. psychologist. Rsch. asst. U. Ala., Birmingham, 1993-98; asst. prof. U. Md. at Schwaebisch Gmuend, Germany, 1999-2000; postdoctoral fellow Ohio State U., 2000—. Contbr. articles to scholarly jours. Mem. Acoustical Soc. Am. Avocations: sculpting, writing, hiking. E-mail: efrieda@admin1.sg.umuc.edu. Office: U Md at Schwaebisch Gmuend, Universitaetspark, 73525 Schwaebisch Gmuend Germany

FRIEDBERG, ERROL CLIVE, pathology educator, researcher; b. Johannesburg, South Africa, Oct. 2, 1937; s. Edward and Rena (Berman) F.; children: Malcolm, Andrew, Jonathan, Lawrence. BSc, Witwatersrand U., Johannesburg, 1957, MB BCh, 1961. Intern King Edward VIII Hosp./U. Natal, Durban, South Africa, 1962; resident pathologist Witwatersrand U., 1963-64, Cleve. Met. Gen. Hosp., 1965; postdoctoral fellow dept. biochemistry Case Western Res. U., Cleve., 1966-68; rsch. investigator divsn. nuclear medicine Walter Reed Army Inst. Rsch., Washington, 1969-70; asst. prof. pathology Stanford (Calif.) U., 1971-77, assoc. prof. pathology, 1977-84, prof. pathology, 1984-90; prof., chair dept. pathology U. Tex. Southwestern Med. Ctr., Dallas, 1990—, Senator Betty and Dr. Andy Andujar chair pathology, 1990-93, Senator Betty and Dr. Andy Andujar disting. chair pathology, 1993—; co-organizer symposia and confs. in field. Author: DNA Repair, 1984, Cancer Answers: Encouraging Answers to 25 Questions You Were Always Afraid to Ask, 1992, 93, (with others) DNA Repair and Mutagenesis, 1995, Correcting the Blueprint of Life, 1997, (with others) Sydney Brenner: A Life in Science, 2000; editor or co-editor: DNA Repair Mechanisms, 1978, DNA Repair: A Laboratory Manual of Research Procedures, Vol. 1, 1981, Vol. 2, 1983, Vol. 3, 1988, Cellular Responses to DNA Damage, 1983, Scientific American Reader: Cancer Biology, 1985, Mechanisms and Consequences of DNA Damage Processing, 1988; contbr. numerous articles to profl. publs. Recipient Rsch. Career Devel. award USPHS, 1974-79, Merit award USPHS, 1988—, Rous-Whipple award Am. Soc. Investigative Pathology, 2000; Andrew W. Mellon Found. rsch. fellow, 1973-76; Joshua Macy Jr. Found. faculty scholar, 1978-79. Fellow Royal Coll. Pathology. Office: U Tex Southwestern Med Ctr Dept Path 5323 Harry Hines Blvd Dallas TX 75390-7208

FRIEDBURG, DIETER, ophthalmologist; b. Hamburg, Germany, Sept. 17, 1935; s. Rudolf and Erna (Windrath) F.; m. Susanne Zeller; children: Christoph, Julia. Physician, U. Munich, 1960, approved physician, 1963; specialist of ophthalmology, U. Kiel, 1966; prof. ophthalmology, U. Dusseldorf, 1971. Sr. resident dept. ophthalmology U. Dusseldorf, 1968-71, prof. ophthalmology, sr. resident, 1971-81; prof. ophthalmology, head of dept. Klinikum Krefeld, 1981—, mng. physician, dir., 1995-97. Author book chpts. in field; contbr. articles to profl. jours. Fellow Internat. Strabismol. Assn., German Ophthalmol. Assn. Office: Klinikum Krefeld, Augenklinik Luther Pl 40, 47805 Krefeld Germany

FRIEDE, PETER MAURICE, small business owner; b. Johannesburg, South Africa, Mar. 15, 1939; arrived in U.S., 1992; s. Harold George and Vera Welcome (Herman) F.; m. Maureen Ethylle Isenberg, Sept. 3, 1961; children: Giora, Jodi Cohen. Univ. Natal, Durban, South Africa, 1957, 58, Tech. Coll., Durban, South Africa, 1962. Tech. dir. Advanx Tire Co., Johannesburg, 1967-72; adminstr. dir. Pang Group of Cos., Johannesburg, 1973-80, CEO, 1981-92; prodn. mgr. Butler Tire Co., Atlanta, Ga., 1993; pres. Mr. Transmission, Marietta, Ga., 1994—. Mem. Hebrew Order of David (master of cermonies, 1999, 2000, brother). Avocations: video editing, conversions, computers. E-mail: petefriede@mindspring.com. Office: Mr Transmission 1000 Cobb Pkwy S Marietta GA 30060-9231

FRIEDEL, JACQUES, physics educator; b. Paris, Feb. 11, 1921; s. Edmond and Jeanne (Bersier) F.; m. Mary Horder, June 2, 1952; children: Jean, Paul. Degree in engring., Ecole Polytechnique, Paris, 1946; post grad., Ecole des Mines, 1948; doctorate, U. Paris., 1954; PhD in Physics., U. Bristol, Eng., 1952; doctorat (hon.), Ecole Polytechnique, Lausanne, Bristol U., Geneva U., Zagreb U., Cambridge U. Engr. Ecole des Mines, Paris, 1948-56; prof. physics U. Paris, 1956-89; ret.; pres. Com. Scientifique France Telecom Paris, 1991-98, Obs. Nat. la Lectr., 1994—; pres. Comite Consultatif de la Rechereche Scientifique et Technique, 1979-81. Author: Dislocations, 1956, 64, Graine de Mandarin, 1994; contbr. articles to profl. jours. With French Cavalry, 1944. Decorated grand officer Legion of Honor, comdr. Order Nat. Merit; recipient Gold medals CNRS, Ste. Française Metallurgie Paris, Acta Metallurgica, , prize Holweck French Soc. Physics and Inst. of Physics, Dannie Heineman prize Acad. Göttingen, von Hippel and Italgas awards. Mem. Acad. des Scis. (past pres.), Swedish Royal Acad. Scis. (hon.), Royal Soc. London (hon.), Am. Acad. Arts and Scis. (hon.), Leopoldina (hon.), Inst. Physics London (hon.), Am. Phys. Soc. (hon.), Nat. Acad. Sci. (hon.), Royal Belgian Acad. Sci. (hon.), Brazilian Acad. Sci. (hon.), European Phys. Soc. (hon.), Max Planck Gesellschaft (hon.). Avocation: gardening. Home: 2 rue Jean-Francois Gerbillon, 75006 Paris France Office: Physique des Solides U, Paris Sud, 91405 Orsay France

FRIEDEL, PAUL EDMOND, electronics company executive; b. Paris, Apr. 27, 1955; s. Jacques and Mary Winifred (Horder) F.; m. Brigitte Camille Fontès, Sept. 2, 1977; children: Marie, Guillaume, Vincent. Engr. degree, Ecole Poly., Palaiseau, France, 1979; diploma, U. d'Orsay, France, 1980, D Scs., 1987. Researcher Laboratoires PHILIPS (LEP), Limeil, France, 1980-87; postdoctorate Bell Labs., Murray Hill, N.J., 1987-88; rsch. coord. PHILIPS Netherlands, Eindhoven, 1988-90; group leader Lab d'Electron Philips, Limeil, 1990-94; devel. mgr. Philips Videocommunications, 1994-96; mng. dir. Labs. d'Electionique Philips, Limeil-Brevannes, France, 1997—; physics teacher Institut Supérieur d'Electronique de Paris, Paris, 1983-86; cons. Institut Supérieur d'Electronique du Nord, Lille, France, 1990-92. Author: Atomic and Electronic Structure of Surfaces, 1990. Lt. Arme Blindée, 1976-79. Mem. French Physical Soc. (coun. 1992—), Soc. des Electicien et Electioniedens. Avocations: violin, sailing, skiing. Home: 7 rue G Bizet, 78530 Buc France Office: Labs d'Electionique Philips, 22 ave Descartes BP15, 94453 Limeil Brevannes France

FRIEDEN, JANE HELLER, art educator; b. Norfolk, Va., Aug. 25, 1926; d. Samuel Ries and Saida (Seligman) Heller; m. Joseph Lee Frieden, Dec. 23, 1950 (dec. 1990); children: Nancy Frieden Crowe, Robert M., Andrew M. AA, Coll. of William and Mary, Norfolk, Va., 1945; BA, Coll. of William and Mary, Williamsburg, Va., 1947; MA, Columbia U., 1950. Lic. pvt. pilot. Tchr. art City of Norfolk Pub. Schs., 1947-48, Hudson Day Sch., New Rochelle, N.Y., 1948-49, Mt. Vernon (N.Y.) Pub. Schs., 1949-50, City of Norfolk Pub. Schs., 1950-51; prof. art Coll. William and Mary Extension, Williamsburg, 1957-72, U. Va. Extension, Norfolk, 1972-78, Community Colls. State of Va., Chesapeake and Hampton, 1978-82, St. Leo Coll., Norfolk, 1982-95; travel agt., 1977-89. Author: (dictionary) A is For Art, 1978-82; artist water color paintings and ink drawings at several shows. Asst. Gen. Douglas MacArthur Meml. Archives, Norfolk, 1945-95; vol. Chrysler Mus. Art, Norfolk, 1991—, Va. Symphony Aux., 1992—, Norfolk Little Theatre Box Office, 1991—, Meals on Wheels, 1962-66, Make a Wish Found., 1996, ARC, 1953-95, Grey Lady project, 1956-62, bloodmobile project, 1966-80, Va. Zool. Soc., 1996; tchr. drawing Ghent Venture, 1993; reader for the visually handicapped Intouch Network WHRO-TV, 1991—; mem. archives com. Ohef Sholom Temple; bd. dirs. Norfolk Little Theatre, 1996; vol. career svcs. Coll. William and Mary, 1992—, drawing tchr. Norfolk Sr. Ctr., 1998, 99. Mem. Ninety-Nines (treas. 1978-85), Tidewater Artists Assn. (bd. dirs. 1975-80, 91—, treas. membership coun.), Tidewater Orchid Soc., Am. Orchid Soc., Norfolk Soc. Arts, United Daus. Confederacy, Hermitage Soc., Norfolk Ex Libris Soc. Coll. William & Mary (mem. steering com. 1993—), Va. Belles (reunion com. 1993—), Chesapeake Watercolor Soc. Republican. Jewish. Avocations: drawing and water color painting, raising orchids, travel. Home: 221 Oxford St Norfolk VA 23505-4354

FRIEDENBERG, DANIEL MEYER, financial investor, writer; b. Mt. Vernon, N.Y., Feb. 24, 1923; s. Samuel and Rose Abravanel (Klein) F.; BS, U. Pa., 1943; m. Maria del Carmen Joy, May 1, 1956 (div. June 1964); children: Samuel Clark, Danielle Joy; m. June Meredith Daniels, Apr. 12, 1965 (div. May 1986); children: Jay Daniels, Bertrand Russell. With John-Platt Enterprises, Inc., N.Y.C., 1947—, pres., 1957—; curator coins and medals Jewish Mus., N.Y.C., 1962-82; emeritus, 1982—; guest lectr. Columbia U., Yale U., Swarthmore Coll., Hebrew U., Jerusalem. Sec. Young Democrats N.Y.C., 1952; exec. dir. N.Y. County Liberal Party, 1945. Served with AUS, 1943-44. Recipient Spl. Achievement award Loeb mag., 1962, Spl. Achievement award Loeb Newspaper, 1965; Heath Literary award distinguished numismatic achievement, 1969; Nat. Jewish Book award, 1988, 3rd Prize Nat. Libr. of Poetry, 1997. Fellow Am. Numismatic Soc. (life); mem. Am. Numismatic Assn. Author: Great Jewish Portraits in Metal, 1963; Jewish Medals from the Renaissance to the Fall of Napoleon, 1970, Jewish Mint Masters & Medalists, 1976, Medieval Jewish Seals from Europe, 1987, Life, Liberty and the Pursuit of Land, 1992; contbr. articles to newspapers and mags. Home: 79 Byram Shore Rd Greenwich CT 06830-6906 Office: 55 Central Park W New York NY 10023-6003

FRIEDERICHS, MICHELLE MAACK, English educator; b. Bemidji, Minn., June 16, 1969; d. Paul Allen and Mary Lou Maack; m. Charles B. Friederichs, Nov. 16, 1991. BA, Coll. St. Benedict, 1994; MA, Minn. State U., 1996; student, St. Mary's U. Dean instrnl. programs Rasmussen Coll., Mankato, Minn., 1996-98; asst. adj. program prof. St. Mary's U. Minn., Mpls., 1998—; adj. instr. Minn. State U., Mankato, 1996, 99—; judge 1998 STC Region 6 Tech. Publs. Soc. Tech. Comm., 1998. Sponberg scholar Minn. State U., 1995. Mem. Coll. Reading Assn. Roman Catholic. Avocations: running, hiking. Home: 124 Cayuga St Storm Lake IA 50588-2521

FRIEDL, PETER, biochemist; b. Cologne, Germany, Mar. 28, 1951; s. Ernst and Sophie (Hintzen) F.; m. Christina Sigel, Aug. 1, 1977; children: Paul, Hannah. Diploma in Biology, U. Cologne, 1975; PhD, U. Tbingen, Germany, 1978. Scientist GBF/Nat. Inst. for Biotechnol. Rsch., Braunschweig, Germany, 1978-88; prof. TH Berlin/Polytech. U., Berlin, 1988-91, Tech. U., Darmstadt, Germany; dir. Inst. of Biochemistry, Darmstadt, 1992-95. Avocations: chess, sports. Office: TU Darmstadt, Inst.f.Biochemie/Petersenstr, Darmstadt D-64287, Germany

FRIEDL, RANDALL RAYMOND, environmental scientist; b. San Fernando, Calif., Jan. 18, 1957; s. Raymond Joseph and Ione Louise (Anderson) F.; m. Myrna Wijmer, Dec. 20, 1980. BS, UCLA, 1978; MA, Harvard U., 1980, PhD, 1984. From rsch. assoc. to group supr. JPL, Pasadena, Calif., 1984-94, rsch. scientist, 1997—; lead scientist Jet Propulsion Lab., 1998—; project scientist NASA, Washington, 1994-96; co-mission scientist NASA/NOAA/Air Force sponsored field experiment, Atmospheric Chemistry of Combustion Emissions Near the Tropopause, 1999. Assessment chairperson (NASA publ.) Atmospheric Effects of Subsonic Aircraft, 1997; coord. lead author: Intergovernmental Panel on Climate Change Special Report on Aviation and the Global Environment, 1999; contbr. over 30 articles to profl. jours., chpts. to books. Mem. ACS, Am. Geophys. Union, Sigma Xi. Achievements include research on chemistry of importance to understanding anthropogenic impacts on earth's atmosphere. Office: Jet Propulsion Lab Mailstop 183-901 4800 Oak Grove Dr Pasadena CA 91109-8001

FRIEDL, RICHARD ANTON, international holding company executive; b. Meran, Italy, Feb. 11, 1949; arrived in Switzerland, 1995; s. Joseph and Frieda (Enderle) F.; m. Sandra Uribe; children: Rene, Brunella. Grad., Alexander von Homboldt Inst., Lima, Peru, 1968; PhD in Econs., U. Mayor de San Marcos, Lima, Peru, 1976; Dr. Engring., U. Karlsruhe, Germany, 1976. Mktg. and sales mgr. BBC, Mannheim, Germany, 1976-79; CEO, tng. mgr. for Pos. Ctr. BBC, Baden, Switzerland, 1984; country mgr. BBC, Bogota, Colombia, 1984-87; tech. sales dir. Ferrostaal/GHH Man, Lima, Peru, 1980-84; country mgr., CEO ABB, Lima Peru, 1988-90; regional mgr. ABB-Sace, Bergamo, Italy, 1990-95; sr. v.p. ABB, Baden, Switzerland, 1996—; CEO Rafe, Bergamo, Italy, 1990—, Cia Exportacion Esparragos SA, Lima, Peru, 1990—; exec. v.p. Guardian Trade Sales Co., Panama City, Panama, 1993—. Mem. Several C. of C.s (bd. dirs.). Mem. Latin Am. C. of C. (bd. dirs.), Spanish C. of C. (bd. dirs.), Arabic C. of C. (bd. dirs.), Italian C. of C., German C. of C. Avocations: flying, swimming, sailing, tennis. Office: Asea Brown Boveri Ltd, Haselstr 16, 5401 Baden Switzerland

FRIEDLAENDER, JONATHAN SCOTT, anthropology educator; b. New Orleans, La., Aug. 24, 1940; s. Marc and Clara May (Beer) F.; m. Bilge Civelekoglu, Apr. 3, 1971 (div. 1984); 1 child, Mira Asli; m. Rebecca Elizabeth Lewis, June 5, 1986 (div. 2000); 1 child, Benjamin Lewis. BA, Harvard Coll., 1962; MA, Harvard U., 1964, PhD, 1969. Postdoctoral fellow U. Wis., Madison, 1969-70, asst. prof., 1970-71; asst. prof. Harvard U., Cambridge, 1971-74, assoc. prof., 1974-76; assoc. prof. Temple U., Phila., 1976-81, prof. of anthropology, 1981—, chmn. anthropology dept., 1988-91; cons. VA, Boston, 1973-76; panelist Nat. Acad. Scis., Washington, 1972-74; mem. adv. bd. to trustees Wenner-Gren Found., N.Y.C., 1990-92; dir. anthropology program NSF, Washington, 1992-95. Author: Patterns of Human Variation, 1975, The Solomon Islands Project, 1985; editor Yearbook of Physical Anthropology, 1991-92; contbr. articles to profl. jours. Pres. Phila. Anthropol. Soc., 1990-93, Schuylkill River Park Cmty. Garden; mem. Center City Residents Assn., Phila., 1990—. Postdoctoral rsch. grant NSF, 1976, 85; writing grant Commonwealth Book Fund, 1975. Fellow AAAS; mem. Am. Assn. of Phys. Anthropologists (exec. com., chmn. publs. com.), Am. Assn. Human Biologists, Assn. of Social Anthropologists in Oceania, Am. Anthropological Soc. Avocations: flutist, bicyclist, windsurfer. Home: 201 S 25th St Apt 622 Phila PA 19103-6008 Office: Anthropology Dept Temple U Broad and Berks Philadelphia PA 19122

FRIEDLAND, KLAUS DIETRICH EBERHARD, historian, researcher; b. Erfurt, Germany, June 28, 1920; s. Max and Margarete (Duffing) F.; m. Eva Stelling von Wolffersdorff, Aug. 9, 1952; children: Kathrin, Tilman. PhD, U. Kiel, Germany, 1952. Cert. historian, tchr., archivist, libr., univ. rschr. Tchr. secondary sch. Gymnasium, Nether Saxony, Germany, 1953-61; archivist Lübeck (Germany) Archives, 1962-70; libr. Schleswigholstein Main Libr., Kiel, 1970-85; prof. U. Kiel, 1970—; sec. Hansischer Geschichtsverein, 1962-72; councillor Deutsche Seefahrtsgeschichtliche Kommission, 1975—; pres. Internat. Commn. Maritime History, 1985-90. Author: (books) Der Kampf der Stadt Lüneburg, 1953, Die Hanse, 1954, 91, 95, Mensch und Seefahrt zur Hansezeit, 1995; editor: (books) Hanserezesse, 1970, Bergen, Handelszentrum, 1971, Hansische-Geschichtsblatter, 1976-93, Frühformen Englisch-Deutschen Handels, Der Ostseeraum, 1980, Maritime Aspects of Migration, 1989, Maritime Food Transport, 1994; contbr. numerous articles to profl. jours. With German Navy, 1938-45. Recipient Hon. medal Town of Tallinn, 1990, Hon. award Inst. of History and Naval Culture, Spanish Armada, 1990. Mem. Deutsche Seefahrtsgeschichte Kommn. (hon.), Rotary Internat. (sr.). Avocations: painting. Home: Kreienholt 1, D 24226 Heikendorf Germany Office: Kiel U Historisches Sem, Olshausenstr 40, D 24098 Kiel Germany

FRIEDLANDER, EDWARD JAY, journalism educator; b. Portland, Maine, Apr. 24, 1945; s. Otto and Marguerite Evelyn (Smith) F.; m. Roberta Kay Burford, July 12, 1975; 1 child, Erika Anne. BS, U. Wyo., 1967; MA, U. Denver, 1970; EdD, U. No. Colo., Greeley, 1973. Reporter The Denver Post, 1967-68, U.S. Info. Agy., Washington, 1968-69; publicist Universal Pictures, N.Y.C., 1969-70; mag. editor Daily Times-Call, Longmont, Colo., 1970-71; media coord. Centaurus High Sch., Lafayette, Colo., 1972-73; asst. prof. mass communication Cen. Mo. State U., Warrensburg, 1973-75; asst. prof. dept. journalism U. Ark., Little Rock, 1975-77, assoc. prof. dept. journalism, 1977-81, prof. dept. journalism, 1981-95, chairperson dept. journalism, 1988-95; dir., prof. U. South Fla. Sch. Mass Comms., Tampa, 1995—; cons. Bur. Indian Affairs, Washington, 1972, The White House, Washington, 1979, Ark. Press Assn., Little Rock, 1980-95; cons., editor FCC, Washington, 1979-81. Author: Excellence in Reporting, 1987, Feature Writing for Newspapers and Magazines, 1988, 4th rev. edit., 2000, Modern Mass Media, 1990, 2nd rev. edit., 1994, Medios de Comunicación Social, 1992. William Robertson Coe fellow U. Wyo., 1973, German Acad. Exch. Svc. fellow, Bonn, 1982, European Acad. fellow, Berlin, 1984. Mem. Assn. Edn. in Journalism and Mass Comm., Assn. Schs. Journalism and Mass Comm. (exec. com. 1997-98, 98-2000), Soc. Profl. Journalists (officer exec. bd. Ark. profl. chpt. 1986-89, 92-94, v.p. 1989-91, pres. 1991-92), Kappa Tau Alpha. Office: U South Fla Sch Mass Comms CIS # 1040 4202 E Fowler Ave Tampa FL 33620-8000

FRIEDLANDER, EDWARD ROBERT, pathologist; b. Evanston, Ill., Jan. 9, 1952; s. Robert and Joanne (Hiscox) F. AB, Brown U., 1973; MD, Northwestern U., Chgo., 1977. Diplomate Am. Bd. Pathology. Pathologist Kansas City, 1988—; chmn. dept. pathology Univ. of Health Scis.; lectr. in field; operator free disease info. svcs. online. Author: (booklets) Christian Perspectives on Evolution, 1985, William Blake's Visions, 1986. Foster parent Juvenile Corrections, Johnson City, Tenn., 1984-85; bd. dirs. Tenn. Assn. Vols. Criminal Justice, 1983-86; prison vol. Yoke Fellow, Winston Salem, 1982-83. Fellow Coll. Am. Pathologists, Am. Soc. Clin. Pathologists, Lambda Chi Alpha. Home: 7909 Tauromee Ave Kansas City KS 66112-2639 Office: 1750 Independence Ave Kansas City MO 64106-1453

FRIEDLANDER, PAUL ALAN, government tax programs advisor; b. Miami, Fla., Oct. 1, 1947; s. Benjamin and Florence (Berman) F.; m. Faye Chernowsky, Sept. 1, 1969 (div. Nov. 1982); children: Howard, Janice; m. Katerina Kafati, Nov. 21, 1982. BBA, U. Miami, Coral Gables, Fla., 1970. Exec. v.p. Charles Friedlander Advt., Miami, 1971-73; pres., CEO, Advt. and Mktg. Cons., Miami, 1973-82; chmn., CEO, Immark, Ltd., Kingston, Jamaica and Miami, 1982-88; exec. v.p., COO, Bodner Advt., Miami, 1988-89; chmn. bd. Dynamic Comm., Inc. Pub. Rels., 1989; pres. Mktg. Dynamics Group Inc., 1990-94; with Fed. and State Corp. Advisors Inc., 1994—; lectr. U. W.I., Kingston, 1983-85. Author: (with others) Power Marketing, 1988, (novel) The Document, 1999; inventor Scotti Muffler System. Bd. dirs. Pros for Kids, Miami, 1988; bd. dirs. Temple Samuel, Miami, 1981-82; mktg. exec. All Am. Rodeo, Helsinki, Moscow, Paris, 1990. Avocations: golf, racquetball, water sports, created 1st extended payment program for cruise industry with Am. Express Sign & Sail program.

FRIEDLANDER, TRACEY KLINE, lawyer; b. Balt., May 4, 1966; d. Robert and Margo Kline; m. Andrew Scott Friedlander, June 16, 1990; children: Alexis, Jeremy, Kayla. BA, Lat. Am. Cert. magna cum laude, Dickinson Coll., 1988; JD with honors, Am. U., 1991. Legal asst. Nissan Motors Co., Tokyo, 1989; legal asst. high commn., refugees UN, Washington, 1990; clk., summer assoc. Stroock, Stroock & Lavar, Washington, 1990; assoc. Arnold & Porter, Washington, 1991-93, 94-98; sr. atty. LCC Internat., Vienna, Va., 1993-94; v.p., assoc. gen. counsel Teligent, Inc., Vienna, Va., 1998—. Paralegal, mem. adv. bd. AYUDA, Washington, 1994; bd. dirs. Discovery Creek Children's Mus., Washington, 1998—; mem. adv. bd. William F. Degan Scholarship Fund, Washington, 1997—; vol. Make-A-Wish Found., Md., 1999—, CASA, Md. Internat. fellow Rotary Club, 1987. Mem. ABA (mem. steering com. Ea. European law 1995), Md. Bar Assn., DC Bar Assn., Hispanic Bar Assn. (mentor 1995-97).

FRIEDMAN, BART, lawyer; b. N.Y.C., Dec. 5, 1944; s. Philip and Florence (Beckerman) F.; m. Wendy Alpern Stein, Jan. 11, 1986; children: Benjamin Alpern, Jacob Stein. AB, L.I. U., 1966; JD, Harvard U., 1969. Bar: N.Y. 1970, Mass. 1972. Rsch. fellow Harvard U. Bus. Sch., Cambridge, Mass., 1969-70; assoc. Cahill, Gordon & Reindel, N.Y.C., 1970-72, 77-80, ptnr., 1980—; spl. counsel SEC, Washington, 1974-75, asst. dir., 1975-77; lectr. internat. tax program, Harvard U. Sch. Law, 1971, 85. Mem. vis. com. Harvard U. Grad. Sch. Edn., 1995—, com. on univ. resources, 1996—; trustee Julliard Sch., 1988—, vice chmn., 1994—; trustee Brookings Inst., 1997—, chmn. N.Y. adv. com., 1997—, coun. fgn. rels., 1995—, jt. task force on resources for fgn. affairs; mem. ind. task force on non-lethal weapons; mem., del. to NATO Hdqrs. and Field, 1998; mem. adv. bd. Remarque Inst. NYU, 1997—, Internat. Inst. for Strategic Studies, 2000. Mem. Assn. Bar City of N.Y., Coun. Fgn. Rels., Explorers Club, Down Town Assn. (N.Y.C.), The River Club, City Tavern Club (Washington), The Tuxedo Club, Century Assn. Home: 1172 Park Ave Apt 5B New York NY 10128-1213 Office: Cahill Gordon & Reindel 80 Pine St Fl 17 New York NY 10005-1790

FRIEDMAN, ELAINE FLORENCE, lawyer; b. N.Y.C., Aug. 22, 1924; d. Henry J. and Charlotte Leah (Youdelman) F.; m. Louis Schwartz, Apr. 10, 1949; 1 child, James Evan. BA, Hunter Coll., 1944; JD, Columbia U., 1946.

Bar: N.Y. 1947, U.S. Dist. Ct. (so. and ea. dists.) N.Y., U.S. Ct. Appeals (2d cir.), U.S. Supreme Ct. 1954. Assoc. Oseas, Pepper & Siegel, N.Y.C., 1947-48, Bernstein & Benton, N.Y.C., 1948-51, Copeland & Elkins, N.Y.C., 1951-53; sole practice N.Y.C., 1953—; bd. dirs. Health Ins. Plan of Greater N.Y. Mem. Fedn. Internat. des Femmes Juristes (v.p. U.S. chpt. 1993-95), N.Y. State Bar Assn., Hunter Coll. Alumni Assn., Columbia Law Sch. Assn. Jewish. Avocation: poetry. Home: 2 Agnes Cir Ardsley NY 10502-1709 Office: 60 E 42nd St New York NY 10165-0006

FRIEDMAN, GERALD MANFRED, geologist, educator; b. Berlin, July 23, 1921; came to U.S., 1946, naturalized, 1950; s. Martin and Frieda (Cohn) F.; m. Sue Tyler Theilheimer, June 27, 1948; children: Judith Fay Friedman Rosen, Sharon Mira Friedman Azaria, Devorah Paula Friedman Zweibach, Eva Jane Friedman Scholle, Wendy Tamar Friedman Spanier. Student, U. Cambridge, Eng., 1938-39; BSc, U. London, Eng., 1945, DSc, 1977; student, U. Wyo., 1949; MA, Columbia U., 1950, PhD, 1952; Dr rer nat (hon.), U. Heidelberg, Fed. Republic Germany, 1986. Agrl. laborer Eng., 1938-39, baker, 1940-42; internee Brit. Army, 1940; lectr. Chelsea Coll., London, 1944-45; analytical chemist E.R. Squibb & Sons, New Brunswick, N.J., also J. Lyons & Co., London, 1945-49; asst. geology Columbia U., 1950; temporary geologist N.Y. State Geol. Survey, 1950; instr., then asst. prof. geology U. Cin., 1950-54; cons. geologist Sault Ste. Marie, Ont., Can., 1954-56; mem. rsch. dept. Pan Am. Petroleum Corp. (Amoco), Tulsa, 1956-64; sr. rsch. scientist Pan Am. Petroleum Corp. (Amoco), 1956-60, rsch. assoc., 1960-62, supr. sedimentary geology rsch., 1962-64; Fulbright vis. prof. geology Hebrew U., Jerusalem, Israel, 1964; prof. geology Rensselaer Poly. Inst., 1964-84, prof. emeritus, 1984—; prof. geology Bklyn. Coll., 1985-88, Disting. prof. geology, 1988—; prof. earth and environ. scis. Grad. Sch. CUNY, 1985-88, disting. prof. earth and environ. scis., 1988—, dep. exec. officer, 1992-94; pres. Gerry Exploration Inc., 1982-88; rsch. scientist Hudson Labs., Columbia, 1965, 66-69, rsch. assoc. dept. geology, 1968-73; vis. prof. U. Heidelberg, 1967; cons. scientist Inst. Petroleum Rsch. and Geophysics, Israel, 1967-71; lectr. Oil & Gas Cons. Internat., 1968-98; pres. Northeastern Sci. Found. Inc., 1979—; vis. scientist Geol. Survey of Israel, 1970-73, 78; mem. Com. Sci. Soc. Pres., 1974-76; Gerald M. Friedman post-doctoral fellow Inst. Earth Scis., Hebrew U., Israel, 1990—; vis. prof. Martin-Luther-Univ., Halle-Wittenberg, Germany, 1998. Co-author: Principles of Sedimentology (Outstanding Acad. Books, Choice, 1978/79), 1978, Exploration for Carbonate Petroleum Reservoirs, 1982, Exercises in Sedimentology, 1982, Principles of Sedimentary Deposits: Stratigraphy and Sedimentology, 1992; pub. Northeastern Environ. Sci., 1982-90; editor: Jour. Sedimentary Petrology, 1964-70 (Best Paper award 1961, hon. mention 1964, 66), Northeastern Geology (now Northeastern Geology and Environ. Scis.), 1979—, Earth Scis. History, 1982-93, Carbonates and Evaporites, 1986—, 10th Internat. Congress on Sedimentology, 1978, Oil Industry History, 1999—; sect. co-editor: Chem. Abstracts (Mineralogical and Geol. Chemistry), 1962-69, abstractor, 1952-69; editl. bd. Jour. Geol. Edn., 1951-55, Sedimentary Geology, 1967-95, Israel Jour. Earth Scis., 1971-76, Coral Reef Newsletter, 1973-75, Jour. Geology, 1977—, GeoJour., 1977-83, Facies, 1987—; mng. editor Sedimentology for Earth Sci. Revs., 1992—; contbg. co-editor: Carbonate Sedimentology in Central Europe, 1968, Hypersaline Ecosystems: The Gavish Sabkha, 1985, editor, contbr.: Depositional Environments in Carbonate Rocks, 1969; co-editor: Modern Carbonate Environments, 1983, Lecture Notes in Earth Scis., 1985—; founding editor: Earth Scis. History, 1982; contbr. articles to profl. jours.; patentee in field. Mem. phys. edn. com., judo instr. Tulsa YMCA, 1958-64, chmn. awards com., 1962-64; adviser, instr. Judo Club, Rensselaer Poly. Inst., 1964-84; bd. dirs. Troy Jewish Community Coun., 1966-72, 74-77; v.p. Temple Beth El, 1986-89, pres., 1989-91, bd. dirs., 1965-76; bd. dirs. Leo Baeck Inst., N.Y.C., 1986—; bd. dirs., chmn. pub. com. Drake Well Found., 1998—. Recipient award for devoted svc. Tulsa YMCA, 1963, Hon. W.Va. award, 1998; named hon. alumnus dept. geology Bklyn. Coll., 1989; grantee Office Naval Rsch., AEC, Dept. Energy, Petroleum Rsch. Fund, N.Y. Gas Assn., N.Y. State Energy Rsch. and Devel. Authority. Fellow AAAS (chmn. geology and geography 1978-79, councillor 1979-80, soc. rep. in geology and geography sect. 1989-97), Mineral. Soc. Am. (mem. nominating com. for fellows 1967-69, awards com. 1977-78), Mineral Soc. Gt. Brit. (abstractor mineralogical abstracts 1963-64), Geol. Soc. Am. (sr., chmn. sect. program com. 1969, candidate sect. chmn. 1969, publs. com. 1980-82, chmn. overseas pub. rels. com. internat. divsn., 1996-97, vice chair history geology divsn. 1997-99, chair 2000—, awards nom. com. sedimentary geol. divsn. 1999-2000), Geol. Soc. London (life, chartered geologist, hon. fellow, 1996), Geol. Assn. Can., Soc. Econ. Geologists (sr.) Explorers Club N.Y., N.Y. Acad. Scis. (vice chair geol. scis. sect., 1993-94, 96-97, chmn. 1994-96, 97—); mem. Russian Acad. Nat. Scis. - U.S. sect. (Kapitsa Gold medal of honor, 1996), Am. Inst. Profl. Geologists (cert.), Am. Chem. Soc. (group leader 1962-63), Am. Assn. Petroleum Geologists (nat. hon. mem. 1990, Nat. Disting. Svc. award 1988, Disting. Educator award 1996, Sidney Powers Meml. award 2000, chmn. carbonate rock com. 1965-69, mem. rsch. com. 1965-71, 76-82, lectr. continuing edn. program 1967—, chmn. Persian Gulf liaison com. 1968-70, mem. marine geology com. 1970-74, adv. coun. 1974-75, Disting. lectr. 1972-73, mem. disting. lectr. com. 1975-78, mem. vis. geologists program com. 1982-85, membership com. 1982-87, ho. of dels. 1977-80, 84-87, 91-93, alt. del. 1980-83, 87-90, 93—, sect. sec. 1979-80, sect. treas. 1980-81, sect. v.p. 1981-82, sect. pres 1982-83, div. profl. affairs rep. from Eastern sect. 1983-84, com. on convs. 1984-85, vice chair standing com. hist. petroleum geology 1997-2000, chair 2000—, nat. v.p. 1984-85, mem. select com. on future petroleum geologist 1985-86, cert. petroleum geologist, hon. mem. Eastern sect. 1984, chmn. sect. awards com., 1989-92, John T. Galey Meml. award Medal, 1993, sect. chmn. tech. program com. 1994-95, sect. cert of merit 1995), Soc. for Sedimentary Geology (nat. v.p. 1970-71, pres. 1974-75, sect. pres. pro tem 1966-67, sect. pres. 1967-68, chmn. Shepard award selection com. 1966-67, nat. hon. mem. 1984, Best Paper award Gulf Coast sect. 1974, Twenhofel medalist, 1997), Paleontological Soc. (hon. mention to Outstanding Paper award Jour. Paleontology 1971), History of the Earth Scis. Soc. (co-founder 1981), Hudson-Mohawk Profl. Geologists Assn. (bd. dirs. 1995—, program com. 1996-97, chmn. program com. 1997—), Capital Dist. Geologists Assn. (chmn. program 1966-73), New Eng. Intercollegiate Geol. Conf. (convenor, editor 1979), Am. Geol. Inst. (governing bd. 1971-72, 74-75), Geologists' Assn. (life), Internat. Assn. Sedimentologists (v.p. 1971-75, pres. 1975-78, past pres. 1978-82, nat. corr. U.S.A. 1971-73, hon. mem. 1986, program com. Internat. Sedimentological Congress 1978, excursion com. Internat. Sedimentological Congress 1982), Geol. Soc. Israel (hon.), Indian Assn. Sedimentologists (mem. governing coun. 1978-82), Geol. Vereinigung, Deutsche Geol. Gesellschaft, Soc. Venezolana Historia Geociencias (internat. corr. mem.), Nat. Assn. Geosci. Tchrs. (nat. treas. 1951-55, chmn. organizing and nominating com. establish east-ctrl. sect. 1952-53, pres. Okla. 1962-63, pres. Ea. sect. 1983-84), subscription and circulation mgr., Jour. of Geosci. Edn., 1953-55. Assn. Earth Sci. Editors (v.p. 1970-71, pres. 1971-72, host 1991, Outstanding Editorial Pub. Contributions award 1993), Geosci. Info. Soc. (mem. membership com. 1983-85, ad hoc com. to develop criteria for reviewing geosci. jours. 1985-86), N.Y. State Geol. Assn. (pres. 1978-79, bd. dirs. 1979-84), N.Y. State Mus.-N.Y. State Geol. Survey (James Hall medal 1997), Cin. Mineral Soc. (v.p., program chmn. 1953-54), U.S. Judo Fedn. (San Dan, cert. judo tchr.), Okla. Judo Fedn. (pres. 1959-60, v.p. 1961-64), Amateur Athletic Union (Okla., judo com. 1963), Empire State Judo Assn. (v.p. 1975-77, dir. coll. devel. 1972-82), Kodokan (Japan), Sigma Gamma Epsilon (nat. v.p. 1978-82, nat. pres 1982-86, nat. hon. mem. 1986), Sigma Xi (v.p. Rensselaer chpt. 1969-70). Home: 32 24th St Troy NY 12180-1915 Office: Bklyn Coll/Grad Sch CUNY Dept Geology Brooklyn NY 11210

FRIEDMAN, HUGH ROBERT, land developer, soccer coach, lacrosse referee; b. Boston, Apr. 22, 1966; s. Orrie Max and Laurel Ethel (Leeder) F. BA, Wittenberg U., 1988; Spl. Cert. in Bus. Adminstrn., Harvard U., 1995. Race ops. Taos Ski Valley (N.Mex.), Inc., 1988-90; sales Am. Ski Assn., Denver, 1990-91; ops. Sail Boston, Boston, 1992, Conventures, 1992-93; mktg./ops. Boston Host Com. for World Cup '94, 1993-94; pres. Full Moon Devel. Co., Taos, N.Mex., 1995—. Soccer coach Taos H.S. Boys Varsity Soccer, 1995—; trustee Orrie Friedman Scholarship, Taos, 1998—. E-mail: friedman@newmex.com. Home: HC 74 Box 21850 El Prado NM 87529-9542

FRIEDMAN, JAMES DENNIS, lawyer; b. Dubuque, Iowa, Jan. 11, 1947; s. Elmer J. and Rosemary Catherine (Stillmunkes) F.; m. Kathleen Marie Maersch, Aug. 16, 1969; children: Scott, Ryan, Andrea, Sean. AB in Polit. Sci., Marquette U., 1969; JD, U. Notre Dame, 1972. Bar: Wis. 1972, U.S. Supreme Ct. 1978, U.S. Ct. Appeals (D.C. cir.) 1973, U.S. Ct. Appeals (7th cir.) 1976, U.S. Ct. Appeals (6th cir.) 1989, Ill. 1996, U.S. Tax Ct. 1997. Pvt. practice Milw., 1972-81; ptnr. Quarles & Brady, Milw., 1981—; presenter in field; mem. legis. coun. spl. study com. on regulation of fin. instns. State of Wis., 1986-87; bd. dirs. Am. Paper and Packaging Corp., Concours Motors, Inc., Equal Justice Coalition, Inc.; mem. dept. fin. instns. task force on fin. competitiveness 2005, State of Wis., 2000. Mng. Editor: Notre Dame Law Review, 1971-72; contbr. articles to profl. jours. Alderman 4th and 7th dists. Mequon, Wis., 1979-85, pres. common coun., 1980-82, bd. ethics 1996-98, 2000—, chair blue ribbon visioning com. 1998-99; bd. dirs. Weyenrg, Pub. Libr. Found. Inc., 1983—, pres., 1984—; bd. dirs. Ptnrs. Advancing Values in Edn. Inc., 1987—, Wis. Law Found., 1998—; bd. visitors Marquette U. Ctr. for Study of Entrepreneurship, Milw., 1987-95; bd. dirs. Ozaukee Family Svcs., 1983-99, sec., 1993-98; bd. dirs. Notre Dame Club of Milw., 1984-88, sec., 1978, v.p., 1986-88; bd. dirs. Marquette Club of Milw., 1987-88; chair attys. unit United Way Fund Dr. Greater Milw., 1987; mem. St. James Ch., Mequon. Named Outstanding Sr., Coll. of Liberal Arts, Marquette U. Mem. ABA (banking law com. sect. bus. law), State Bar Wis. (chair bd. govs. 1999-2000, chair exec. com. 1999-2000, fin. com. 1997-98, strategic planning task force 1997-98, bd. govs. 1996-2000, exec. com. 1998-2000, internat. transactions sect. bd. dirs. 1984-99, sec. and chair-elect 1988-89, chair 1989-90, del. to ABA Ho. of Dels. 1980-82, standing com. on adminstrn. justice and judiciary 1979-81, legal edn. and bar admissions com. 1984-89, com. on minority lawyers 1992-99, chmn. 1997-1999, bd. dirs. young lawyers divsn. 1978-82, chmn. bar admission stds. and requirements com. 1979, So. Regional chair capital fund campaign 1998-99), Milw. Bar Assn., Wis. Acad. Trial Lawyers (bd. dirs. 1980-82), Wis. Bankers Assn., Milw. Country Club, Sigma Phi Epsilon. Roman Catholic. Avocations: tennis, golf. Office: Quarles & Brady 411 E Wisconsin Ave Ste 2550 Milwaukee WI 53202-4497

FRIEDMAN, JEROME ISAAC, physics educator, researcher; b. Chgo., Mar. 28, 1930; married, 1956; 4 children. A.B., U. Chgo., 1950, M.S., 1953, Ph.D. in Physics, 1956. Research assoc. in physics U. Chgo., 1956-57; research assoc. in physics Stanford U., Calif., 1957-60; from asst. prof. to assoc. prof. MIT, Cambridge, 1960-67, prof. physics, 1967—, dir. lab. nuclear sci., 1980-83, head dept. physics, 1983-88, William A. Collidge prof., 1988-90, instr. prof., 1990—. Recipient Nobel prize in physics, 1990. Fellow AAAS, Am. Phys. Soc. (co-recipient W.H.K. Panofsky prize 1989); mem. NAS, Am. Acad. Arts and Scis. Office: MIT Room 24-512/Dept Physics 77 Massachusetts Ave Cambridge MA 02139-4307

FRIEDMAN, MARIA ANDRE, public relations executive; b. Jackson, Mich., June 12, 1950; m. Stanley N. Friedman; children: Alexandra, Adam. BA cum laude, U. Md., 1972, MA, 1979; DBA, Nova U., 1993. Writer U.S. Bur. Mines, Washington, 1973-78; head writer Nat. Ctr. Health Svc. Rsch./Healthcare Tech. DHHS, Rockville, Md., 1978-85; chief publs. and info. br. Agy. for Healthcare Policy and Rsch., 1986-89; dir. office pub. affairs Healthcare Fin. Adminstrn., Washington, 1990—, acting assoc. adminstr. for comm., 1992-93; sr. rsch. advisor Healthcare Fin. Adminstrn., Balt., 1994-95, dir. dissemination staff ORB, 1995-96, sr. advisor for ins. reform, 1997-99, Y2K outreach coord. for medicaid program, 1999—. Mem. Assn. Health Svcs. Rsch., Acad. of Mgmt. Home: 713 Brandon Green Dr Silver Spring MD 20904-3564 Office: Health Care Fin Adminstrn 7500 Security Blvd Baltimore MD 21244-1849

FRIEDMAN, MARION, internist, family physician, medical administrator, medical editor; b. Onley, Va., Aug. 15, 1918; s. Jacob and Bertha (Bernstein) F.; m. Esther Lerner, May 29, 1941; 1 son, Barry Howard. BS, U. Md., 1938, MD, 1942. Diplomate Am. Bd. Family Practice (charter). Rotating intern U.S. Marine Hosp., Norfolk, Va., 1942-43; asst. health officer Montgomery County, Kans., 1943-44; health officer Cherokee County, Kans., 1944-45; asst. health commr. St. Louis County, Mo., 1945-46; resident internal medicine U.S. Marine Hosp., Balt., 1946-49; fellow medicine Johns Hopkins Sch. Medicine, Balt., 1948-49; pvt. practice in internal medicine and family medicine Balt., 1949-84; asst. medicine U. Md., Balt., 1954-72; chief dept. gen. practice Doctors Hosp., 1952-54; chief dept. family practice N. Charles Gen. Hosp., Balt., 1972-75, med. dir. ambulatory svcs., 1972-86, assoc. chief medicine, 1975-88; pres. med. staff, 1964, 68, chmn. med. exec. com. 1984-85, trustee, 1984-85, physician advisor 1984-91; physician advisor Delmarva Found. for Med. Care, 1984-90, 92-95; instr. Ctr. for Health Edn., 1985; lectr. Md. affiliate Am. Heart Assn., 1986-87; med. dir. Chesapeake Health Plan, 1991-92; task force on improving access to primary care Md.-DC AFL-CIO, 1993-94, consumer-managed care rels. task force, 1996. Mem. profl. adv. bd. Patient Care, 1994-96; chmn. cultural com. Liberty Jewish Ctr., 1960-62; mem. Md. High Blood Pressure Coordinating Coun., 1980-82; mem. task force on family physicians Md. Health Resources Planning Commn., Md. State Legislature, 1983-84; trustee Jimmie Swartz Found., 1982-95. With USPHS, 1942-49; lt. col. Md. Def. Force, 1995—. Fellow Am. Acad. Family Physicians (charter), Md. Acad. Family Physicians (chmn. comm. on health care svcs. 1978-83, 84-92, pres. 1983-84, mem. rsch. panel influenza surveillance network 1983, prodn. editor 1984-86, editor 1986—, bd. dirs. Found. 1998—, Chpt. Publ. award 1991, chmn. manpower adv. com. 1992-95, award superb compiling, writing and editing spl. 50th ann. history edit. Md. Family Doctor 1998); mem. AMA, AAAS, Am. Acad. Family Physicians, Md. Acad. Family Physicians Found. (bd. dirs. 1998—), Balt. City Med. Soc. (alt. del. 1978-82, 93-94, del. 1982-88, profl. edn. com. 1985-87, chmn. 1987-90, nominating com. 1992), Med. and Chirurg. Faculty Md. (lectr. 1983, legis. com. 1985-87, 90-93, pro com. 1989-94, std. benefits tech. adv. com. 1993-94, mem. editl. bd. Md. Med. Jour. 1994-96, co-editor Nov. 1995, editor 1996-2000, scientific activities com. 1995-2000, Dr. Henry P. & M. Page Laughlin Dist. Editl. award 1997), World Med. Assn., Pan-Am. Med. Assn., Md. Heart Assn., Am. Lung Assn. (mem. planning com. 1994—), Am. Thoracic Soc., Am. Heart Assn., Md. Taxpayers Assn. (bd. dirs. 1994-99, sec. 1996-97, mem. exec. com. 1996-99), Am. Lung Assn., Phi Kappa Phi. Democrat. Achievements include contbr. over 60 sci. articles and notes including first to suggest use of steroid in subacute deltoid bursis in world lit., 1952. Home: 7906 Terrapin Ct Baltimore MD 21208-3126

FRIEDMAN, MARLA LEE, media and investor relations coordinator; b. Chgo., May 26, 1953; d. Martin P. and Charlotte K. (Beilenson) F. BSC in Commerce, DePaul U., Chgo., 1977; MBA wih honors, Roosevelt U., Chgo., 1985. Gen. mgr., adminstr. Chgo. Ctr. for Devel. Learning, Inc., 1975-77; dist. health claims adminstrn. analyst Washington Nat. Ins. Co., Evanston, Ill., 1977-80; unit coord. computer resource liaison Luth. Gen. Hosp., Park Ridge, Ill., 1980-99; author fiction and nonfiction Glenview, Ill., 1990—; pres., owner Dancing By Candlelight, 1995-2000; media and investor rels. coord. IPA, Buffalo Grove, Ill., 2000—; mem. associated writing programs George Mason U. Contbr. prose poem Chips Off the Writer's Block, 1992, columnist, 1994; contbr. poem Guided By Voices Anthology, 1998, Best Poets of the 20th Century, 2000; author short stories, children's stories, novels and articles. Recipient Editors Choice award N.Am. Poetry Open Competition, 1998, awards for nonfiction articles. Fellow Life Mgmt. Soc. (cert. fin. scis.); mem. NAFE, Acad. Am. Poets. Avocations: drama, music, creative cookery. E-mail: dancingbc@cs.com.

FRIEDMAN, MARVIN ROSS, lawyer; b. Mpls., July 13, 1941; s. H. W. and Katherine F.; widowed; children: Natasha E., Chloe J. BBA, U. Miami, 1966, JD, 1969. Bar: Fla. 1969. Pvt. practice, Coral Gables, Fla., 1970—. Hon. trustee Mus. Contemporary Art, Miami, 1997—, Diabetes Rsch. Found., Miami, 1997—, Mus. Modern Art, Miami, 1997—. Mem. ATLA, Fla. Acad. Trial Lawyers, Dade County Trial Lawyers Assn. Office: Friedman & Friedman 2600 S Douglas Rd Ste 1011 Coral Gables FL 33134-6142

FRIEDMAN, MILES, trade association executive, financial services company executive, university lecturer; b. N.Y.C., Apr. 18, 1950; s. Sol and Rose (Schenkerman) F.; m. Susan Liles, Apr. 26, 1975; children: David Andrew, Diana Leigh. BA in Pub. Affairs, George Washington U., 1971, MA in Polit. Sci., 1972, PhD candidate in Polit. Sci., 1976. Dep. commr. pub. works Town of Ramapo, Suffern, N.Y., 1971; grad. teaching fellow George Washington U., Washington, 1972-75; sr. assoc. Lazar Mgmt. Group, Washington, 1976-77; dir. legis. and policy Nat. Council Urban Econ. Devel., Washington, 1977-80; pres., CEO Nat. Assn. State Devel. Agys., Washington, 1980—; founder, instr. trade specialist tng. program, Phoenix, 1980—, founder, instr. fgn. investment tng. program, 1988-96; instr. Fgn. Svc. Inst., U.S. and Fgn. Comml. Svc. Inst., Georgetown U., Washington, 1991, U. N.C. Basic Econ. Devel. Inst., Chapel Hill, 1984-85; cons. Pres.' Drug Abuse Prevention Office, Washington, 1972; lectr. George Washington U., Washington, 1975-77. Mem. editl. bd., contbg. editor Econ. Devel. Rev., 1991—; contbg. author to several books, directory; contbr. articles to profl. jours. including Wall St. Jour, Area Devel. mag., Export Today mag., others. Mem bd. dirs., sec./treas. Pub. Sector Devel. Found., Washington, 1983—; pres. Am. Devel. Fin., Inc., 1986-95, also bd. dirs.; liaison subcom. Pres.'s Export Council, Washington, 1981-82; Pinewood Forest Council Owners, 1977-78; chmn. Washington Symposium Higher Edn., 1970-71; pres. Coles Little League, 1997-98; chmn. Prince William County Econ. Devel. Coun., 1998—; bd. dirs. Friends of Brentsville Courthouse Hist. Ctr., 1998—. Recipient Pres.'s E award for Excellence in Export Svc., NASDA, 1993. S. C. of C., Am. Soc. Assn. Execs., Nat. Assn. Execs., Tau Kappa Epsilon, Delta Phi Epsilon, Lambda Alpha. Office: Nat Assn State Devel Agys 750 1st St NE Ste 710 Washington DC 20002-8004

FRIEDMAN, MILTON, economist, educator, writer; b. Brooklyn, N.Y., July 31, 1912; s. Jeno Saul and Sarah Ethel (Landau) F.; m. Rose Director, June 25, 1938; children: Janet, David. AB, Rutgers U., 1932, LLD (hon.), 1968; AM, U. Chgo., 1933; PhD, Columbia U., 1946; LLD (hon.), St. Paul's (Rikkyo) U., 1963, Loyola U., 1971, U. N.H., 1975, Harvard U., 1979, Brigham Young U., 1980, Dartmouth Coll., 1980, Gonzaga U., 1981; DSc (hon.), Rochester U., 1971; LHD (hon.), Rockford Coll., 1969, Roosevelt U., 1975, Hebrew Union Coll., L.A., 1981, Jacksonville U., 1993; LittD (hon.), Bethany Coll., 1971; PhD (hon.), Hebrew U., Jerusalem, 1977; DCS (hon.), Francisco Marroquin U., Guatemala, 1978; D honoris causa, Econ. U. Prague, 1997. Assoc. economist Nat. Resources Com., Washington, 1935-37; mem. research staff Nat. Bur. Econ. Research, N.Y.C., 1937-45, 1948-81; vis. prof. econs. U. Wis., Madison, 1940-41; prin. economist, tax research div. U.S. Treasury Dept., Washington, 1941-43; assoc. dir. research, statis. research group, War Research div. Columbia U., N.Y.C., 1943-45; assoc. prof. econs. and statistics U. Minn., Mpls., 1945-46; assoc. prof. econs. U. Chgo., 1946-48, prof. econs., 1948-62, Paul Snowden Russell disting. service prof. econs., 1962-82, prof. emeritus, 1983—; Fulbright lectr. Cambridge U., 1953-54; vis. Wesley Clair Mitchell research prof. econs. Columbia U., N.Y.C., 1964-65; fellow Ctr. for Advanced Study in Behavioral Sci., 1957-58; sr. research fellow Hoover Inst., Stanford U., 1977—; mem. Pres.'s Commn. All-Vol. Army, 1969-70, Pres.'s Commn. on White House Fellows, 1971-74, Pres.'s Econ. Policy Adv. Bd., 1981-88; vis. scholar Fed. Res. Bank, San Francisco, 1977. Author: (with Carl Shoup and Ruth P. Mack) Taxing to Prevent Inflation, 1943, (with Simon S. Kuznets) Income from Independent Professional Practice, 1946, (with Harold A. Freeman, Frederic Mosteller, W. Allen Wallis) Sampling Inspection, 1948, Essays in Positive Economics, 1953, A Theory of the Consumption Function, 1957, A Program for Monetary Stability, 1960, Price Theory: A Provisional Text, 1962, (with Rose D. Friedman) Capitalism and Freedom, 1962, (with R.D. Friedman) Free to Choose, 1980, Tyranny of the Status Quo, 1984, Two Lucky People: Memoirs, 1998, (with Anna J. Schwartz) A Monetary History of the United States, 1867-1960, 1963, (with Schwartz) Monetary Statistics of the United States, 1970, Monetary Trends in the U.S. and the United Kingdom, 1982, Inflation: Causes and Consequences, 1963, (with Robert Roosa) The Balance of Payments: Free vs. Fixed Exchange Rates, 1967, Dollars and Deficits, 1968, the Optimum Quantity of Money and Other Essays, 1969, (with Walter W. Heller) Monetary vs. Fiscal Policy, 1969, A Theoretical Framework for Monetary Analysis, 1972, (with Wilbur J. Cohen) Social Security, 1972, An Economist's Protest, 1972, There's No Such Thing as a Free Lunch, 1975, Price Theory, 1976, (with Robert J. Gordon et al) Milton Friedman's Monetary Framework, 1974, Tax Limitation, Inflation and the Role of Government, 1978, Bright Promises, Dismal Performan, 1983, Monetarist Economics, 1991, Money Mischief, 1992, (with Thomas S. Szasz) Friedman & Szasz on Drugs: Essays on the Free Market and Prohibition, 1992; editor: Studies in the Quantity Theory of Money. Chmn. bd. dirs. Milton and Rose D. Friedman Found.; mem. adv. bd. Calif. Parents for Ednl. Choice, 1999—. Decorated Grand Cordon of the 1st Class Order of the Sacred Treasure (Japan); recipient Nobel prize in econs., 1976, Pvt. Enterprise Exemplar medal Freedoms Found., 1978, Presdl. medal of Freedom, 1988, Nat. Medal of Sci., 1988, Prize in Moral-Cultural Affairs, Instn. World Capitalism, 1993; named Chicagoan of Yr., Chgo. Press Club, 1972, Educator of Yr., Chgo. Jewish United Fund, 1973, Source award for lifetime achievement The Primary Source, Tufts U., 1997, Robert Maynard Hutchins History Maker award for distinction in edn. Chgo. Hist. Soc., 1997, Templeton Honor Rolls Lifetime Achievement award, 1997, Goldwater award, 1997. Fellow Inst. Math. Stats., Am. Statis. Assn., Econometric Soc.; mem. NAS, Am. Econ. Assn. (exec. com. 1955-57, pres. 1967; John Bates Clark medal 1951), Am. Enterprise Inst. (adv. bd. 1956-79), Western Econ. Assn. (pres. 1984-85), Royal Economic Soc., Am. Philos. Soc., Mont Pelerin Soc. (bd. dirs. 1958-61, pres. 1970-72), Quadrangle Club. Office: Stanford U Hoover Instn Stanford CA 94305-6010

FRIEDMAN, RICHARD ALAN, psychiatrist; b. N.Y.C., Sept. 11, 1956; s. Jerome G. and Frances B. F. BA, Duke U., Durham, N.C., 1978; MD, Robert Wood Johnson Med. Sch., N.J., 1982. Assoc. prof. psychiatry Cornell U. Med. Coll., N.Y.C., 1987—. Fellow Am. Psychiatric Assn. Avocations: pianist, swimming, chamber music. E-mail address: rafriedm@mail.med.cornell.edu. Office: The New York Hosp Payne Whitney Clinic 535 E 68th St New York NY 10021-4870

FRIEDMAN, RICHARD I(RWIN), public defender; b. Newark, Oct. 2, 1947; s. Irving R. and Esther Friedman; m. Harriet Bronfeld, Sept. 23, 1982; children: Rebecca Friedman, Natasha Murphy. BA in Polit. Sci., Rutgers U., Newark, 1969; MSW in Cmty. Practice, U. Mich., 1971; JD, Rutgers U., Newark, 1980. Bar: N.J. 1980, U.S. Dist. Ct. N.J. 1980, N.Y. 1989, U.S. Supreme Ct. 1991, U.S. Ct. Appeals (3rd cir.) 1996; cert. in staff tng., behavior modification, school social worker, N.J. Caseworker Essex County (N.J.) Welfare Bd., 1969; cmty. organizer N.W. Interfaith Ctrs. for Racial Justice, Detroit, 1969-70; rschr., analyst legal svcs. bail project N.J. Adminstrv. Office of Cts., 1970; rschr. cmty. action program UAW, Mich., 1970-71; tchr. secondary sch., Newark, 1971-72; social worker South Orange-Maplewood Bd. Edn., 1972; program coord. North Essex (N.J.) Drug Abuse Coun., Inc., 1973-74; field rep. div. mental health advocacy N.J. Dept. Pub. Adv., 1971-81, asst. dep. pub. adv., 1981-94; atty. divsn. mental health and guardianship advocacy N.J. Office Pub. Defender, Newark, 1994-95, spl. counsel, 1995-96, asst. dep. pub. defender, 1996-98; deputy pub. defender, mng. atty. Newark, 1998—; prodr., host Sta. WFMU, East Orange, N.J., 1971-72; rschr. N.J. ACLU, 1971-72, cons. to dir. N.J. Coun. Chs., 1973; Krol coord., 1992-98; mem. adj. prof. Rutgers U. Law Sch., Newark, 1994, 97; adj. prof. Seton Hall Law Sch., 1996. Mem. N.J. State com. SANE, 1972-80, legal advisor, 1980-85; pres. Orange Tenants Assn., 1976; bd. govs. N.J. Fedn. YM-YWCA's Camps, 1981-97; mem. state wide task force outpatient civil commitment, 1999; mem. blue ribbon com. transfer Essex County Hosp. Ctr., 1999. Mem. ABA (ethics com. divsn. govt. and pub. sector lawyers 1994-96), ATLA, N.J. Bar Assn., N.Y. Bar Assn., Essex County Bar Assn. Home: 43 Green Pl North Caldwell NJ 07006-4545

FRIEDMAN, RICK ADAM, otologist; b. Sacramento, Feb. 16, 1962; s. Stuart Stanley and Sonia Kamhi Friedman; m. Rachel Collins Friedman, Feb. 26, 1994; children: Andrew Collin, Joshua Tyler. BA, UCLA, 1984; MD, U. Calif. San Diego, La Jolla, 1988, PhD, 1994. Asst. prof. U. Cin., 1996-98; assoc. House Ear Clin., L.A., 1998—; sci. reviewer DRF, N.Y.C. Contbr. articles to med. jours. Mem. Am. Acad. Otolaryngology-Head and Neck Surgery (sci. reviewer), Am. Neurotological Soc. Avocation: running. E-mail: rfriedman@hei.org.

FRIEDMAN, ROBERT BARRY, physician; b. Bklyn., Dec. 28, 1953; s. Roy and Bernice (Berger) F. BA, SUNY, Stony Brook, N.Y., 1975; MD, SUNY Health Sci. Ctr., Bklyn., 1980. Bd. Cert. Diplomate Am. Bd. Neurol. Surgery. Gen. med. officer USPHS Indian Health Svc., Sacaton, Ariz., 1981-82; neurosurgeon USAF, Wright Patterson AFB, Ohio, 1989-91, South Broward Neurosurg. Assn., Pembroke Pines, Fla., 1991-95, Cleve. Clinic Fla., Ft. Lauderdale, 1995-97, Spectrum Neurosurg. Specialists, Marietta, Ga., 1997-98, Henry Neurosurg. Specialists, P.C., Stockbridge, Ga., 1998—; med. staff fellow Nat. Inst. Health, Bethesda, Md., 1986-88. Contbr. articles to profl. jours. Maj. U.S.A.F., 1988-91. Recipient Neuroscience award U. Pitts., 1989. Fellow Am. Coll. Surgeons; mem. Am. Assn. Neurol. Surgeons, Congress of Neurol. Surgeons, Southern Med. Assn., Fla. Med. Assn., AMA. Avocation: private pilot. Home: 100 Ivy Mnr Stockbridge GA

30281-6433 Office: c/o Henry Neurosurg Specialists PC 297 Country Club Dr Stockbridge GA 30281-7350

FRIEDMAN, ROBERT ELLIOT, equity analyst; b. Newark, Feb. 18, 1962; s. Alfred and Sheila Ruth (Prussack) F. BA, Muhlenberg Coll., 1984; MBA, Fordham U., 1988, MS, 1990, advanced cert. in fin., 1996. CPA, N.J. Sr. assoc. Deloitte & Touche, Parsippany, N.J., 1990-92; pvt. practice acctg. Livingston, N.J., 1992-95; equity analyst Standard & Poor's Corp., N.Y.C., 1995—. Mem. AICPA, N.J. Soc. CPAs. Home: 6C Nobhill Roseland NJ 07068-1829 Office: Standard & Poors Corp 55 Water St Fl 44 New York NY 10041-0001

FRIEDMAN, SAMUEL SELIG, lawyer; b. N.Y.C., July 25, 1935; s. Nathan and Anne M. (Sobel) F.; m. Maxine E. Goldfarb, Jan. 7, 1961; 1 child, Alison J. BS, MIT, 1956; MBA, U. Pa., 1959; LLB, Columbia U., 1965. Bar: N.Y. 1965, U.S. Dist. Ct. (so. and ea. dists.) N.Y. 1967, U.S. Supreme Ct. 1984. Assoc. Lord, Day & Lord, N.Y.C., 1965-72; ptnr., mem. exec. com. Lord Day & Lord, Barrett Smith and predecessor firm, N.Y.C., 1972-94; ptnr. Morgan, Lewis & Bockius, N.Y.C., 1994—. Vice chmn., dir., mem. exec. com. Times Square Bus. Improvement Dist., 1992-95. 1st lt. U.S. Army, 1959-62. Mem. ABA, N.Y. State Bar Assn., Assn. of Bar of City of N.Y., MIT Club N.Y., The Penn Club, Phi Delta Phi. Avocations: travel, wine, sports. Office: Morgan Lewis & Bockius 101 Park Ave New York NY 10178-0060

FRIEDMAN, TREVOR, psychiatrist; b. London, May 1, 1958; s. Norman and Muriel F.; m. Stacey; children: Timothy, Benjamin, Samuel. BS with honors, London U., 1979, MB BS, 1982. Jr. dr. London, 1982-83, casualty dr., 1983; registrar pwychiatry, 1983-87; lectr. psychiatry U. Nottingham (England), 1987-90; cons. psychiatrist Leicester, England, 1990—. Mem. Royal Coll. Psychiatrists. Avocations: tennis, walking. Ofice: Leicester Gen Hosp Dept Psychiatry, Leicester Gen Hosp/Psychiat, Gwendolen Rd, Leicester LE5 4PW, England

FRIEDMAN, YONA, architect; b. Budapest, Hungary, June 5, 1923; arrived in France, 1957; s. Simon and Aurora (Vajda) F.; m. Erella Ur, 1949; 1 child, Anat; m. Denise Charvein, 1960; 1 child, Marianne. Degree, Technion U., 1949. Prof. UCLA, 1964-74; dir. Comm. Ctr., Paris, 1982-92. Author: L'architecture mobile, 1958, Towards a Scientific Architeture, 1975, Utopies réalisibles, 1975, L'Univers erratique, 1994. Recipient Architecture award Acad. of Berlin, 1972, Prime Minister's prize, Osaka, Japan, 1991, Habitat Scroll of Honors, UN, 1992. Fellow World Acad. Scis., Royal Acad. (The Hague, Netherlands), World Fedn. Sci. of Future. Home: 33 BD Garibaldi, 75015 Paris France

FRIEDMANN, BERNHARD, educator; b. Ottersweier, Germany, Apr. 8, 1932; married; three children. D in Econs., U. Freiburg, prof. h.c.; Dr h.c., U. Sibiu, Romania. Mem. German Parliament, 1976-90, mem. budget com., chair com. on budgetary control; apptd. mem. European Ct. Auditors, 1989, pres., 1996. Mem. European Ct. Auditors (pres. 1996-98). Office: 12 Rue Alcide de Gasperi, L-1615 Luxembourg Luxembourg*

FRIEDMANN, JULIAN, literary agent, writer, educator; b. Johannesburg, South Africa, Jan. 24, 1944; s. Alah Isadore and Marion Valerie (Bernstein) F. BA with honors, U. York, Eng., 1967; MA, U. London, 1971. Editor Irish Univ. Press, London, 1970-74, Angus & Robertson, London, 1974-75; mng. dir. Julian Friedmann Pubs., London, 1975-82; joint mng. dir. Blake Friedmann Lit. Agy., London, 1982—; head of studies MA in TV script-writing DeMonfort U. Author: Jomo Kenyatta, 1970, How to Make Money Scriptwriting, 1995, 2nd edit., 2000; editor: Writing Long-Running Television Series, vol. 1, 1996, vol. 2, 1995. Mem. European Union Media Programme (head studies pilots 1990-95, U.K. coord. Eave 1989-92), Assn. Ind. Producers (treas. 1983). Avocations: reading, gardening, cooking. Office: Blake Friedmann Lit Agy, 122 Arlington Rd, London NW1 7HP, England

FRIEDMANN, PATRICIA ANN, writer; b. New Orleans, La., Oct. 29, 1946; d. Werner and Marjorie Sybil (Cahn) F.; m. Robert E. Skinner, Mar. 17, 1979 (div. Nov. 1996); children: Esme Friedmann, Werner Skinner; m. Edward G. Muchmore, Nov. 11, 1999. AB, Smith Coll., 1968; MEd, Temple Univ., 1970; ABD, Univ. Denver, 1975. fiction workshop facilitator, New Orleans, 1994—; reviewer Publishers Weekly Brightleaf, Times-Picayune, 1993—; spkr. in field. Author: Too Smart to Be Rich, 1988, The Exact Image of Mother, 1991, Eleanor Rushing, 1999 (Barnes & Noble Discover Great Writers selection, Borders Original Voices selection), (play) The Accidental Jew as part of Native Tongues, 1994, Lovely Rita as Part of Native Tongues, 2000; short stories. Mem. Authors Guild. Home: 8330 Sycamore Pl New Orleans LA 70118-2941

FRIEDMANN, YOHANAN, Islamic studies educator; b. Zakamenné, Czechoslovakia, Mar. 28, 1936; arrived in Israel, 1949; s. Moshe and Jolana (Klein) F.; m. Zafrira Schmidt; children: Yasmin, Tamar. BA, Hebrew U., Jerusalem, 1959, MA, 1962; PhD, McGill U., Montreal, Can., 1966. Prof. Islamic studies Hebrew U., Jerusalem, 1966—, dean Faculty of Humanities, 1985-88, chair Sch. Grad. Studies, 1980-83, chair Inst. Asian and African Studies, 1975-78. Author: Shaykh Ahmad Sirhindi, 1971, Prophecy Continuous, 1989; translator: The History of Tabari, vol. 12, 1992; editor: Islam in Asia, 1984. Mem. Israel Acad. Scis. and Humanities. Home: 115 Uziel St, Jerusalem 96431, Israel Office: Hebrew U, Jerusalem 91905, Israel

FRIEDRICH, CHRISTOPH JOHANNES, pharmacist; b. Salzwedel, Germany, Feb. 18, 1954; s. Barbara (Hill) F.; m. Constanze Reinhold, Dec. 14, 1959. Grad. H.S., Salzwedel. Asst. U. Greifswald, Germany, 1979-83, dr., 1983-92, prof., 1992—; dir. Inst. Pharmacy, Greifswald, 1996-97. Author: Apotheke von Innen gesehen, 1995; co-author: Geschichte der Arzneimitteltherapie, 1996. Mem. German Soc. History Pharmacy (v.p. 1990-97, editor 1993).ú. Home: Gartenweg 29, D-17493 Greifswald Germany Office: Inst for Pharmacy, F-L-Jahn-Str 17, D-17487 Greifswald Germany

FRIEDRICH, FABIAN, biochemist; b. Blumenau, Brazil, May 2, 1965; s. Klaus and Maria Elgin (Wachholz) F. BSc, U. Fed. Santa Catarina, Florianopolis, Brazil, 1989; MSc, Inst. Oswaldo Cruz, Rio de Janeiro, 1993, PhD, 1996. Rschr. Inst. Oswaldo Cruz, Rio de Janeiro, 1996-2000; molecular virologist Inst. Oswaldo Cruz, 1990-2000. Contbr. articles to profl. jours. 2d lt. Brazilian Mil., 1984-85. Mem. Brazilian Soc. Virology. Avocations: exobiology, ufology, arqueology, parapsicology, music. Home: Rua Icara 122, 89030-170 Blumenau Brazil Office: Inst Oswaldo Cruz Dept Viro, Av Brasil 4365, 21040360 Rio de Janeiro Brazil

FRIEDRICH, INGO, member of European parliament; b. Kutno-Wartheland, Germany, Jan. 24, 1942. Mem. European Parliament, Germany, 1999—; mem. Group of the European People's Party (Christian Democrats) and European Democrats, mem. of bur.; v.p. European Parliament, vice-chmn. bur.; mem. com. on fgn. affairs, human rights, common security and def. policy; substitute mem. com. on econ. and monetary affairs; mem. delegation to the EU-Hungary Joint Parliamentary Com.; vice chmn. CSU.

FRIEDRICH, JEAN-JACQUES, accounting educator; b. Barr, France, Nov. 17, 1959; s. Jean-Pierre and Marguerite (Aubry) F.; children: Laura, Pauline. M.Acctg. and Fin. Scis., Grenoble (France) U., 1982; Diploma in Mgmt. Scis., U. Lyon III, France, 1987. CPA, France. Prof. econs. and mgmt. High Sch., Annecy, France, 1983-85; CPA trainee Guérard-Viala Internat. Auditing Office, Lyon, 1985-87; prof. acctg. U. Lyon III, 1985—, dir. Master's of Acctg. and Fin. Sci., 1988—; lectr. U. Lodz, Poland, 1992—, U. Budapest, Hungary, 1995—, U. Sun Yat-Sen, China, 1999—; cons. in field; mem. Bd. Univ. Studies U. Lyon III, 1993—; disciplinary com. U. Lyon III, 1993—. Author: Financial Accounting and Firm's Management, 2d edit., 1999, Financial Accounting-Training Exercises with Solutions, 1995, co-author: (dictionary) Lexicon of Management, 1996. With French Army, 1982-83. Mem. French Soc. Acctg., Assn. of Dirs. French Masters of Acctg. and Fin. Scis. (gen. sec. 1994—). Avocations: skiing, cinematographic arts. Home: 7 Allee de Valombre, 69300 Caluire France Office: U Lyon Inst Enterprise Admn, 15 Quai Claude Bernard, 69239 Lyon France

FRIEL, BRIAN (BERNARD PATRICK FRIEL), author; b. Omagh, County Tyrone, No. Ireland, Jan. 9, 1929; s. Patrick and Christina (MacLoone) F.; m. Anne Morrison, Dec. 27, 1955; children: Paddy, Mary, Judy, Sally, David. Student, St. Columb's Coll., 1941-46; BA, St. Patrick's Coll., Maynooth, Ireland, 1948; postgrad., St. Joseph's Tchrs. Tng. Coll., Belfast, Ireland, 1949-50; Litt.D. (hon.), Dominican Coll., Chgo., Nat. U. Ireland, New U. Ulster, Trinity Coll., Dublin, Ireland, Georgetown U. Tchr. various schs. Derry City, No. Ireland, 1950-60; freelance writer, 1960—; with Tyrone Guthrie Theatre, 1963; co-founder Field Day Theatre Co., Derry, No. Ireland, 1980. Author: (short stories) A Saucer of Larks, 1964, The Gold in the Sea, 1966, The Diviner: Brian Friel's Best Short Stories, 1983, (plays) This Doubtful Paradise, 1960, The Enemy Within, 1962, The Blind Mice, 1963, Philadelphia, Here I Come!, 1964, The Loves of Cass McGuire, 1966, Lovers, 1967, Crystal and Fox, 1968, The Mundy Scheme, 1969, The Gentle Island, 1971, The Freedom of the City, 1972, Volunteers, 1975, Living Quarters, 1977, Faith Healer, 1979, Aristocrats, 1979 (London Evening Standard Best Play award 1988, Best Fgn. Play award N.Y. Drama Critics Circle 1989), Translations, 1980 (Christopher Ewart-Biggs Meml. prize Brit. Theatre Assn. 1981, Plays and Players Best New Play award 1981), American Welcome, 1980, The Communication Cord, 1982, Making History, 1988, Dancing at Lughnasa, 1990 (Tony Best Play award 1992), Wonderful Tennessee, 1993, Molly Sweeney, 1994, Give Me Your Answer, Do!, 1997; (translator) Three Sisters (Anton Chekhov), 1981, Uncle Vanya, 1998; (adaptation) Fathers and Sons (Ivan Turgenev); (screenplay) Philadelphia, Here I Come!, 1970; (version) A Month in the Country; editor: The Last of the Name; contbr. short stories to New Yorker. Mem. Irish Senate, 1987. Recipient Macauley fellow Irish Arts Coun., 1963; hon. fellow U. Coll., Dublin. Fellow Royal Soc. Literature; mem. Nat. Assn. Irish Artists, Am. Acad. Arts and Letters. Office: Drumaweir House, Greencastle, Donegal Ireland

FRIEND, HAROLD CHARLES, neurologist; b. Chgo., Nov. 28, 1946; s. Leonard Nathan and Sharlee (Friedman) F.; m. Joyce Friend; children: Reed, Chad. BA, U. Tex., 1968, MD, 1972. Diplomate Am. Bd. Neurology. Resident Upstate Med. Ctr., Syracuse, N.Y., 1972-73, Albert Einstein Coll. Medicine, Bronx, N.Y., 1973-75; mem. staff Boca Raton (Fla.) Community Hosp., 1975—; pres. Neurosci. Ctr., Boca Raton, 1984—; spl. expert witness Fla. Agy. for Health Care Adminstrn.; mem. panel Statewide provider and Subscriber Assistance Program (Fla.); expert med. advisor divsn. workers compensation Fla. Dept. Labor and Employment Security; bd. dirs. So. Security Bankcorp., Mankrech Transp.; pres. Puget Sound Yellow Taxi, Inc., 1994-95. Author: Territorial Marking, 1968, Bell's Palsy, 1975, Transient Global Amnesia, 1987. Bd. dirs. Boca Raton Children's Mus., 1989-92; dist. chmn., assoc. lodge advisor Boy Scouts Am., 1980-89, mem. exec. bd., v.p. Gulfstream coun., 1988-93, pres. coun., 1993-95, area I v.p., 1990-92, area IV v.p., 1993-95, area IV pres., 1995-98, mem. so. region exec. bd., 1993—, mem. internat. scouting com., 1998—, chmn. direct svc. coun. exec. bd., 1999—, nat. adv. bd., 2000—; exec. bd. United Way, Palm Beach County Agy. Rels. Com., 1992-95, mem. allocation com., 1990-92; mem. nat. adv. coun. Boy Scouts Am., 2000—. Recipient Order of Arrow Vigil Honor award Boy Scouts Am., 1983, Dist. Merit award, 1987, Silver Beaver award, 1990, Wood Badge, 1990, Disting. Commr. award, 1991, Disting. Eagle Scout, 1997, Silver Antelope award, 1997; James West fellow, 1993, 1910 Soc., 1998, Baden Powell fellow, 2000. Fellow Am. Acad. Disability Evaluating Physicians, Am. Acad. Neurology; mem. Am. Soc. Neuroimaging (cert.), So. Clin. Neurol. Soc., Fla. Soc. Neurology, N.Y. Acad. Scis. (life), Sierra Club (life), Palm Beach Med. Svc. (vice chmn. med./legal com.), Rotary (bd. dirs., pres. Boca Raton chpt., dist. world fellowship chmn. 1992-94, 96-97, dist. found. chmn. 1994, chmn. dist. conf. 1995, gov.'s rep. 1994-95, 96-97, dist. gov. 1998-99, chmn. coll. govs. 1999-2000, zone coord. Children at Risk, 2000—, Paul Harris fellow, Dist. Found. Svc. award 1992, 95, Pres. Salute Commendation 1993, Internat. Fellowship Running and Fitness Rotarians (internat. chmn. 1992-98, internat. treas. 1998-99, internat. sec. 1999—), Internat. Fellowship Scouting Rotarians (N.Am. sect. chmn. 1995-96, internat. sec. 1996-98, internat. vice chair 1998-99, internat. chair 1999—), Boca Raton Road Runners Club (pres. 1992-93), Phi Beta Kappa, Phi Kappa Phi, Theta Xi, Alpha Phi Omega. Avocation: marathons. Office: 1500 NW 10th Ave Ste 105 Boca Raton FL 33486-1344

FRIENDLY, ED, television producer; b. N.Y.C., Apr. 8, 1922; s. Edwin S. and Henrietta (Steinmeier) F.; m. Natalie Coulson Brooks, Jan. 31, 1952; children: Brooke Friendly, Edwin S. III. Grad., Manlius Sch., 1941. Radio exec., dir. BBD&O, N.Y.C., 1946-49; sales exec. ABC-TV, N.Y.C., 1949-53; ind. producer and packager N.Y.C., 1953-56; producer, program exec. CBS-TV, N.Y.C., 1956-59; v.p. spl. programs NBC-TV, N.Y.C., 1959-67; pres., founding mem. Ed Friendly Prodns., Los Angeles, 1967—; co-chmn. steering com. Caucus for Producers, Writers and Dirs. Exec. producer: film Little House on the Prairie; Laugh-In; producer: film Peter Lundy and the Medicine Hat Stallion (Emmy nomination); Young Pioneers; mini-series Backstairs at the White House (11 Emmy nominations); also producer motion pictures and TV spls.; exec. producer/producer: Barbara Cartland's The Flame Is Love. Served to capt., U.S. Army, 1942-45, PTO. Recipient Spl. award Internat. Film and TV Festival N.Y., 1967; Emmy award for Laugh-In, 1968; Producer of Yr. award Producers Guild of Am., 1968; Golden Globe award Hollywood Fgn. Press, 1968; Gold medal of honor Internat. Radio and TV Soc., 1970; Christopher award for motion picture, 1975; Western Heritage award Nat. Cowboy Hall of Fame and Western Heritage Center, for Little House on the Prairie, 1975, for Peter Lundy and the Medicine Hat Stallion, 1978; Scout awards for best weekly series and show of yr. for Laugh-In, 1969. Mem. Calif. Horsemen's Benevolent and Protective Assn. (pres. 1994, former mem. bd. dirs.), Thoroughbred Owners Calif. (founder, pres., chmn. 1993-96, chmn. 1996-97, bd. dirs. 1993-2000), Nat. Thoroughbred Assn. (vice chmn., bd. dirs. 1996-98, founding mem.), Nat. Thoroughbred Racing Assn. (bd. dirs. 1997-99). Office: 9100 Wilshire Blvd Ste 455 E Tower Beverly Hills CA 92012-3420

FRIES, RAYMOND SEBASTIAN, manufacturing company executive; b. St. Paul, June 19, 1919; s. Jacob H. and Christine Fries; children: Raymond B., John A., Christine. B.S., U. Minn., 1948. Vice pres. Honeywell, Mpls., Los Angeles and Phila., 1944-65; v.p. Varian Assos., Palo Alto, Calif., 1965-67; pres. Esterline Angus, Indpls., 1967-71; v.p. Esterline Corp., N.Y.C., 1969-71; pres. Dietzgen Corp., Chgo., 1971-73; v.p. Allegheny Ludlum Industries, Pitts., 1973-80; exec. v.p. Allegheny Internat., Pitts., 1980-86; also dir. Allegheny Internat.; pres., mgmt. consulting assoc. Chematron Corp., Chgo.; dir. Phila. Corp. Contbg. author: Industrial Engineering Handbook. Mem. ASME, Fries Engring. Assn., Fossiville Yacht Club (commodore). Clubs: Duquesne, Pitts. Athletic Assn.

FRIES, THOMAS, company executive, physicist; b. Neunkirchen, Germany, July 24, 1961; s. Karl Dieter and Theresia (Krämer) F. Diploma, U. Saarbrücken, Germany, 1989; PhD, U. Bonn, Germany, 1993. Dept. head Günther GmbH, Königswinter, Germany, 1993-95; pres. Fries Rsch. & Tech. GmbH, Bergisch Gladbach, Germany, 1995—, FRT of Am., LLC, Wallingford, Ct., 1998—; bd. dirs. Interessengemeinschaft zur Verbreitung von Anwendungen der Mikrostrukturtechniken e.V., Interessengemeinschaft Neue Materialien eV., Deutsche Akkreditier und Prufdienst. Contbr. over 50 articles to profl. jours. Mem. Deutsche Vakuum-Gesellschaft, Deutsche Akkreditier und Prufdienst, Deutsche Physikalische Gesellschaft, Am. Vacuum Soc., Verein Deutscher Ingenieure, Interessengemeinschaft Neue Materialien e.V., Interessengemeinschaft Oberflachenanalytik. Avocations: motorbike, sports, marketing. Office: FRT GmbH, Friedrich-Ebert-Strasse, 51429 Bergisch Gladbach Germany

FRIESEL, EVYATAR, historian; b. Germany, July 25, 1930; arrived in Israel, 1953; s. Joseph Beer and Bluma (Bloner) F. PhD, Hebrew U., 1970. Prof. Ben Gurion U. of the Negev, Israel, 1965-76; prof. history Hebrew U. of Jerusalem, 1977—; archivist State of Israel, 1992—. Author: Atlas on Modern Jewish History, 1990, The Zionist Movement in the U.S., 1878-1914, 1970, Zionism After the Balfour Declaration, 1977, The Days and the Seasons - Memoirs, 1996. Home: Klausner St 7 Apt 6, 93388 Jerusalem Israel Office: Israel State Archives, Prime Ministers Office, 91-919 Jerusalem Israel

FRIESEN, ORIS DEWAYNE, software engineer, historian; b. York, Nebr., Jan. 4, 1940; s. Harry H. and Malita Wanda (Ratzlaff) F.; m. Carey Lea Burbank, May 28, 1964; children: Isabelle Anne, Aric Alan. BS, U. Ariz., 1964, MA, 1966; PhD, Ariz. State U., 1982. Computer sys. analyst Computer Scis. Corp., Richland, Wash., 1967-69; computer sys. designer GE, Phoenix, 1969-70; database sys. designer Honeywell Info. Systems, Phoenix, 1970-84, engring. fellow, database mgmt., 1984-90; engring. fellow, database mgmt. Bull Worldwide Info. Sys., Phoenix, 1990-99; adj. prof. engring. Ariz. State U., Tempe, 1984—; vice chmn. database stds. Am. Nat. Stds. Inst., Washington, 1980-85; rapporteur, database stds. Internat. Stds. Orgn., Geneva, 1984-85; gen. chmn. Internat. Conf. on Deductive and Object-Oriented Databases, Scottsdale, Ariz., 1991-94; treas. Steering Com. for Internat. Conf. on Deductive and Object-Oriented Databases, 1997—; mem. steering com. Advanced Info. and Comms. Infrastructure Found. Group of Ariz. Gov.'s Strategic Partnership for Econ. Devel., 1994-95; mem. indsl. coun. Coll. Engring., No. Ariz. U., Flagstaff, 1995-99; charter mem. Ariz. Telecomms. Info. Coun., Adv. Bd. to Ariz. Telecomms. Policy Office, Found. Group of Ariz. Gov.'s Strategic Partnership for Econ. Devel., 1995—; Ariz. rep. for N.Am. Free Trade Assn., Telecomms. Stds. Subcom. of Office of U.S. Trade Reps., 1994-96; charter mem., vice chair Ariz. Learning Tech. Partnership, 1996—; mem. bd. dirs. ACTC Technologies, Inc., Calgary, Alta., Can., 1996-98; chmn. Ariz. Telecomms. and Info. Coun., 1999—. Author: China Reporting: An Oral History of American Journalism in the 1930s-1940s, 1987; editor Procs. of Phoenix Conf. on Computers and Comms., 1987; contbr. articles to profl. jours. Mem. Phoenix Futures Forum, 1988-91; mem., officer North Tatum Cmty. Homeowners Assn., Phoenix, 1985-88; mem. steering com. for advanced info. comm. Infrastructure Found. of Ariz. Gov.'s Strategic Partnership for Econ. Devel., 1994-96. Mem. IEEE (sr., gen. chmn. Phoenix Conf. on Computers and Communications 1990-91, vice-chmn. Globecom 97 Conf., 1995-97), Assn. for Computing Machinery, Assn. Asian Studies, Am. Hist. Assn., Orgn. Am. Historians. Democrat. Avocation: Chinese language. Office: Friesen Info Tech 5136 E Le Marche Ave Scottsdale AZ 85254-1667

FRIESS, DONNA LEWIS, children's rights advocate, writer; b. L.A., Jan. 16, 1943; d. Raymond W. Lewis, Jr. and Dorothy Gertrude (Borwick) McIntyre; m. Kenneth E. Friess, June 20, 1964; children: Erik, Julina, Daniel. BA in Comm., U. So. Calif., 1964; MA in Comm., Calif. State U., Long Beach, 1966; PhD in Psychology, U.S. Internat. U., San Diego, 1993. Cert. tchr., Calif. Prof. human comm. Cypress (Calif.) Coll., 1966—; lectr. survivors of abuse, 1990—, mental health profls., 1990—; presenter and keynote presenter in field of child abuse, cmty. and lawmakers' groups; guest expert (TV shows) Sally Jessy Raphael, 1993, Leeza Gibbons Talk Show, 1994, Sonja: Live, 1994, Oprah Winfrey Show, 1991, many others. Author: Relationships, 1995, Just Between Us: A Guidebook for Survivors of Childhood Trauma, 1995, Cry the Darkness, 1993, European edits. 1995, Danish edit., 1999, Korean edit., 1995, Norwegian edits., 1998, Circle of Love: Secrets to Successful Relationships, 1996, Whispering Waters: The Story of Historic Weesha, 1998; contbr. articles to mags. Recipient Author's award U. Calif. Friends of Libr., 1996, recognition from U.S. Justice Dept. for outstanding efforts to stop child abuse, 1995, Lee Steelmon award, Recognition cert. for work to prevent child abuse Calif. State Senate, 2000, Orange County (Calif.) Bd. Suprs.' Resolution for Outstanding Efforts for Children, 2000; nominee for Pres.'s Am. Svc. award, 1996. Mem. Am. Coalition Against Child Abuse (founder), Task Force for ACCA to Educate American Judges on Issues of Sexual Abuse, One Voice, Calif. Psychol. Assn., Western Social Sci. Assn., Child Abuse Listening and Mediating (bd. dirs.), Am. Profl. Soc. on Abuse of Children, Mother Against Sexual Abuse (bd. dirs.), Laura's House for Battered Women (bd. dirs.), Calif. Tchrs. Assn., Faculty Assn. Calif. C.Cs., Speech Communication Assn. of Am., U.S. Internat. U. Alumni Assn. (bd. dirs.). Avocation: painting on porcelain. Office: Cypress College Dept Human Communications Cypress CA 90630

FRIESZ, MARY LEE, poet; b. Little Rock, Ark., Apr. 13, 1940; d. E. Lee and Lala Maurine (Bain) Franklin; m. David Wilson Dubbell, Jan. 28, 1961 (div. Aug. 1982); children: Cheryl Blaine Dubbell Knight, Paul Fremont Dubbell; m. Donald Stuart Friesz; July 5, 1985; children: Mark Allan Friesz, Carol Ann Friesz Leslie. BA in Psychology, U. Ark., 1962. Sec. Stanford U., Palo Alto, Calif., 1962-63; tchr. aide Pedregal Sch., Palos Verdes, Calif., 1974-78; corp. sec. Pel-Freez Biols., Inc., Palos Verdes, Calif., 1978-81; asst. mgr. May Co., Rolling Hills Estates, Calif., 1981-82; investment counselor Am. Savs. & Loan, Redondo Beach, Calif., 1982-84; founder, editor Mustard Seed Poetry, Palos Verdes, 1995—. Author books of poetry. Dir; Poetry By The Sea, Serenos de Point Vicente (televised, 1997-99). Mem. membership com. Assistance League San Pedro/South Bay, 1994-95. Recipient Cmty. Svc. award South Bay Panhellenic Coun., 1996. Mem. Palos Verdes Woman's Club (first v.p.), S.W. Manuscripters, So. Calif. Fedn. Zeta Tau Alpha (pres. 1994-95, pres. local chpt. 1990-91, cert. merit Nat. coun. 1994), Surfwriters (treas. 1994-99), Arts Coun. Torrance (sec.), Phi Beta Kappa. Home: 2725 Palos Verdes Dr W Palos Verdes Estates CA 90274-2837 Office: Mustard Seed Poetry PO Box 3842 Palos Verdes Estates CA 90274-9535

FRIGO, JAMES PETER PAUL, industrial hardware company executive; b. Iron Mountain, Mich., Jan. 11, 1942; s. Louis and Giustina (Carollo) F.; m. Patricia Mary Nellen, June 21, 1969; children: Christine, Catherine, P.J. Ortiz, Pamela, Steven, Sandy. BBA, U. Miami, 1966. Sales rep. Great Dane Trailers, Miami, 1966-67, Foster Inc., Miami, 1968, Lawson Products Inc., Miami, 1968—; pres. Jim Frigo Inc., Miami, 1972—. Asst. scoutmaster Troop 314, Boy Scouts Am. Mem. Nat. Speakers Assn., Fla. Speakers Assn., Internat. Platform Assn., Knights of Columbus. Republican. Roman Catholic. Office: Jim Frigo Inc 7420 SW 175th St Miami FL 33157-6313

FRIGOUT-BAUSSART, MARIJAN RENEE MONIQUE, physician; b. Roubaix, France, Aug. 4, 1951; d. Jean Desablin and Jacqueline Baussart; m. Fabien Frigout, July 9, 1977; 1 child, Laury. Medical Degree, Faculté de Lille, France, 1981. Practice medicine Wasquehal, France, 1981—. Home: Ave du Roi Albert 1er 52, 59290 Wasquehal France Office: Ave de Jovenaux 3, 59290 Wasquehal France

FRIIS, LYKKE, economist; b. Virum, Denmark, Oct. 27, 1969; d. Hans and Frauke (Hitzing) F.; m. Peter Warming, Aug. 9, 1997. BSc in Econs., London Sch. Econs., 1992; MA in Polit. Sci., U. Copenhagen, 1993, PhD in Internat. Rels., 1997. Sect. head. Min. Bus., Denmark, 1993-94; rschr. U. Copenhagen, 1994-96; rsch. fellow, sr. rsch. fellow Danish Inst. Internat. Affairs, Copenhagen, 1996—; lectr. Danish Internat. Study Program, 1996-97, Danish Sch. Pub. Adminstrn., 1997—. Co-author: Enlarging Europe, 2000; contbr. articles to profl. jours. Robert Schuman scholar European Parliament, Luxembourg, 1994; named Wise Women for Nordic Affairs, 1999—. Mem. Coun. European Policy. Avocations: tennis, soccer, arts. Office: Danish Inst Internat Affair, Nytorv 5, 1450 Copenhagen K, Denmark

FRIIS, SVEIN, research director, educator; b. Oslo, Mar. 24, 1945; s. Johan S.C. and Agga (Bang) F.; m. Tove Teigen, June 23, 1970; children: Eva, Hilde. MD, U. Oslo, 1969. Intern in surgery, internal medicine and gen. practice County Hosp., Alesund, Namsos, Norway, 1969-70; psychiat. resident Namdal Hosp., Namsos, Norway, 1971-72, Neevengaarden Univ. Hosp., Bergen, Norway, 1972-75; clin. instr. U. Bergen, 1972-75, asst. prof., 1975-79; rsch. fellow Norwegian Rsch. Coun., 1975, rsch. supr., 1984-90; dep. asst. prof. U. Oslo, 1979-80, rsch. asst., 1980-81, dep. prof. psychiatry, 1986-90, dir. tchg. dept. psychiatry, 1990-93, prof. psychiatry, 1990—, chmn. dept. psychiatry, 1994-99; rsch. dir. psychiat. dept. B Ulleval U. Hosp., Oslo, 1982-90, rsch. dir., head dept. rsch. and edn. divsn. of psychiatry, 1990—; sec. Norwegian Nat. Com. for Psychiat. Tng., 1981-85; chmn. joint com. Norwegian Rsch. Coun. and Norwegian Nat. Com., 1982-83. Mem. Norwegian Med. Assn., Norwegian Psychiat. Assn. (mem. minimal data set com.), Soc. Psychotherapy Rsch., Internat. Soc. Study of Personality Disorders, Internat. Soc. Psychol. Treatments Schizophrenia, World Assn. Psychosocial Rehab., Assn. European Psychiatrists, Norwegian Psychoanalytical Assn. (assoc. mem.1994—, bd. dirs. 1995-97, tchg. coord. 1995, sec. 1996), European Network for Mental Health Svc. Evaluation, Norwegian Nat. Adv. Group for Psychiatry, Acta Psychiatric Scandivaian, Internat. Early Psychosis Assn. Avocations: skiing, hiking, chess. Fax: 47-22-117848. E-mail: svein.frü@psykiatri.uio.no. Home: Vallertunet 14, N-1346 Gjettum Norway Office: Ulleval U Hosp, Dept Rsch & Edn Divns Psych, N-0407 Oslo Norway

FRIMMEL, HARTWIG EGBERT, geologist, educator, researcher; b. Linz, Austria, Oct. 1, 1960; s. Günther and Edith (Kontrus) F. PhD, U. Vienna,

1987. Rsch. fellow U. Vienna, 1987-89; from lectr. to assoc. prof. U. Cape Town, South Africa, 1989—; guest lectr. U. Vienna, 1994-95. Assoc. editor Mineralogy & Petrology, 1996—, Mineralium Deposita, 1999—; mem. editl. bd. Africa Geosci. Rev., 1994-95, 99—, South African Jour. Geology, 1996—; contbr. over 80 articles to profl. publs.; reviewer numerous profl. publs. Recipient Pres.'s award Found. Rsch. Devel., 1995. Mem. Coun. Geol. Soc. South Africa, Mineral Assn. South Africa, Soc. Geology Applied to Mineral Deposits (regional v.p. 1995—, Daume prize 1991), Deutsche Mineralogische Gesellschaft. Avocations: hiking, music, canoeing, photography. Home: 23 Upper Thistle St, 7700 Newlands South Africa Office: U Cape Town, Dept Geol Scis, Rondebosch 7701, South Africa

FRIMMER, ELLIOT M., fluid mechanics engineer; b. N.Y.C., Sept. 24, 1928; s. Isioore and Minnie (Lulov) F.; m. Marilyn; children: Rick, Linda, Cynthia. BS, MIT, 1955. Registered profl. engr., N.Y. Supr. Forsay Bros., N.Y.C; gen. mgr. Lee Myles Corp., N.Y.C, Queens Hydramatic, N.Y.C, Merlin Tool Corp., N.Y.C; R&D GM-Ford-Chrysler, N.Y.C. Bd. dirs. South Fla. Dem. Party, Davie; dir. water adv. bd. Town of Davie, Fla. Mem. Invention Soc. South Fla. (bd. dirs.). Achievements include development of two automatic transmissions. Avocations: inventions, biking, walking, swimming, travel. E-mail: emfwiz@aol.com. Home and Office: Wizard Techs Inc 1749 SW 81st Ter Davie FL 33324-4605

FRINERMAN, EFIM, physiologist; b. Chepetovka, Ukraine, Oct. 20, 1936; arrived in Israel, 1990; s. Alexander and Perel (Shluger) F.; m. Margaret Komarnitzki, Mar. 12, 1966. Physician, High Med. Sch., Czernovitz, Ukraine, 1961; PhD in Cardio-Respiratory Monitoring, Kiev, Ukraine, 1971. Cert. specialist in internal medicine and clin. physiology. Physician Kazan, USSR, 1961-66; dir. Dept. Internal Medicine, Zhitomir, Ukraine, 1966-86; dir., chief cons. Diagnosis Ctr., Zhitomir, 1986-88; vice-dir. Ukraine Ctr. Med. Rsch., Kiev, 1988-90; rschr. vascular physiology Holon, Israel, 1991—; med. dir. NIM Ltd. Co., Tel Aviv, 1991—. Author: (book) Basis of Clinical Rheography of the Lung, 1976 (prize Physiat. Assn. Ukraine 1977); inventor in field. Named Hon. Inventor of Ukraine, 1985, Excellent Physician of Ukraine, 1981, 83, 86, 88; recipient Vet. of Labor medal, 1984. Mem. Mediterranean Assn. Cardiology and Cardiac Surgery, N.Y. Acad. Scis. Avocation: playing chess. Home: Arlozorov Str 3/2, 59307 Bat-Yam Israel

FRINK, EUGENE HUDSON, JR., business and real estate consultant; b. Denver, Feb. 6, 1927; s. Eugene Hudson and Maxine Louella (Ingle) F.; m. Catherine Claire Heath, Dec. 27, 1947; children: Douglas Martin, Bryan Clifford, Daniel Neal. BA, Denver U., 1947. Mgr. Frink Creamery Co., Ft. Collins, Colo., 1948-64; co-founder, mgr. ops Aqua-Tec Corp. (Water Pik), Ft. Collins, 1964-66; archtl. designer Gene Frink Designers, Ft. Collins, 1967-84; ptnr. Wakaya Island, Ltd., Fiji, 1968-71; chmn. Beehive Internat., Salt Lake City, 1969-85; prin. Architecture Plus, P.C., Ft. Collins, 1985-88; ptnr. Naindi Plantation, Fiji, 1969—; pres. Ft. Collins Children's Clinic, 1993-99. Councilman, City of Ft. Collins, 1959-63, mayor, 1961-63; mem. Ft. Collins Regional Planning Bd., 1962-64. Mem. Rotary Club. Republican. Episcopalian. Avocations: industrial design, painting, swimming, hiking. Home: 1212 Morgan St Fort Collins CO 80524-3836

FRISHMAN, SCOTT P., lawyer; b. Pitts., Feb. 20, 1971; s. Ernest I. and Janet M. (DeBona) F. BSBA in Fin., Duquesne U., 1993; LLM in Taxation, Capital U., 1996, JD, 1996. Atty. Pa. Bar Assn., 1996—, ABA, 1996—. E-mail: sfrishman@dttus.com. Office: Deloitte & Touche LLP 2500 One PPG Pl Pittsburgh PA 15222

FRISINA, ROBERT DANA, sensory neuroscientist, educator; b. Evanston, Ill., Sept. 11, 1955; s. D. Robert and Louise (Boaz) F.; m. Susan Taylor Frisina, July 31, 1982; children: Laurin Taylor, Taylor Robert. AB in Exptl. Psychology summa cum laude, Hamilton Coll., 1977; PhD in Neurosci., Syracuse U., 1983. Rsch. asst. Hamilton Coll., Clinton, N.Y., 1977; Root fellow in sci. Inst. Sensory Rsch., Syracuse (N.Y.) U., 1977-78, NSF grad. fellow, 1978-81, grad. rsch. assoc., 1981-83; NIH rsch. fellow Ctr. Brain Rsch. U. Rochester, N.Y., 1983-85; asst. prof. physiology and otolaryngology U. Rochester, 1985-91, assoc. prof. surgery, neurobiology and anatomy, 1991-99, prof. surgery, neurobiology, anatomy, and biomed. engring., 1999—, dir. rsch. otolaryngology, 1988-92, assoc. chmn. otolaryngology, 1992—; v.p. and founder Auditory System Technologies, Inc., Pittsford, N.Y., 1989-98, adj. assoc. prof. comm. scis. Rochester Inst. Tech., 1993—; adj. clin. instr. comm. scis. U. Buffalo, 1998—; staff mem. Nat. Tech. Inst. for Deaf, Rochester, 1975; charter mem. adv. bd. Internat. Ctr. for Hearing and Speech Rsch., 1988—; assoc. editor, Jour. Acoustical Soc. Am., 1996-99. Author: Hearing, 1989; mem. editl. bd. Hearing Rsch. Jour., 1997—; contbr. articles to profl. jours. Dir. Vols. Hamilton Coll. Aspect of Marcy (N.Y.) Psychiat. Ctr., 1974-77. Recipient 1st Award in Communicative Disorders, NIH, 1988-94. Fellow Am. Acad. Otolaryngology-Head and Neck Surgery, Acoustical Soc. Am.; mem. Assn. Rsch. in Otolaryngology, Soc. Neurosci., Am. Speech-Hearing-Lang. Assn., Animal Behavior Soc., Acoustical Soc. Found. (charter, bd. dirs. 1996—, gen. sec. and chief fin. officer 1998—), Phi Beta Kappa, Sigma Xi, Psi Chi. Roman Catholic. Achievements include patents for a noise suppression electronic circuit for enhancing speech in the presence of background noise; a hearing aid circuit which can be custom fit to a patient's hearing loss using laser trimming. Office: U Rochester Med Ctr Otolaryngology Divsn Rochester NY 14642-0001

FRISTACKY, NORBERT, computer engineering educator, researcher; b. Puchov, Czechoslovakia, Nov. 8, 1931; s. Eduard and Anna (Janasova) F.; m. Hilda Matejcikova, June 6, 1957; 1 child, Tomas. Dipl.-Ing., Slovak Tech. U., Bratislava, Czechoslovakia, 1954, PhD, 1964. Asst. prof. Slovak Tech. U., 1955-62, 63-70, assoc. prof., 1971-85, full prof., 1985—, head dept. computer engring., 1978-90, mem. sci. coun., 1988-92; researcher Krizik Rsch. Inst., Prague, Czechoslovakia, 1962; vis. lectr. Salford (Eng.) U., 1970-71; vis. prof. Tech. U., Dresden, Germany, 1986; mem. supervisory com. R&D Inst., VUVT Engring., Zilina, Czechoslovakia, 1990-91. Author: (books) Programmable Logic Controllers, 1981 (Czechoslovakia Tech. Nat. Soc. prize 1981), Logic Circuits, 1986, 90 (Slovak Lit. Fund prize 1986), Digital Computers, 1993; editor-in-chief Elec. Engring. Jour., 1991—; mem. editorial bd. Jour. Computers and Artificial Intelligence, 1981—. Rector Slovak Tech. U., 1990-91. Mem. IEEE (chmn. Slovak com., Computer Soc. IEEE award Computer Pioneer 1997), Slovak Acad. Scis. (mem. sci. com. electronics and cybernetics 1988-96), N.Y. Acad. Scis., Slovak Soc. Cybernetics and Informatics (v.p. 1991), Am. Czechoslovak Soc. (hon.), Czechoslovak Elec. Engring. Soc. (chmn. spl. interest group in informatics sci. and engring. 1977-92), Slovak Informatics Soc., Internat. Fedn. Info. Processing (Slovak nat. com.). E-mail: fristacky@dcs.elf.stuba.sk. Home: JC Hronskeho 14, Bratislava Slovak Republic Office: Slovenska Tech U, Ilkovicova 3, 81219 Bratislava Slovak Republic

FRITHZ, GÖRAN M., cardiologist, educator; b. Strängnäs, Sweden, May 14, 1938; s. Malcolm and Margaretha Frithz; m. Lillemor Angantyr, Mar. 25, 1940; 1 child, Gustaf. Cert. physician, Univ. Uppsala, Uppsala, Sweden, 1963, MD, 1974. Head physician dept. internal medicine Mälarsjukhuset, Eskilstuna, Sweden, 1975—; asst. prof. medicine Univ. Uppsala, 1975—. Contbr. articles to profl. jours. With Royal Swedish Navy Med. Corps, 1964—. Mem. Internat. Soc. Hypertension, Europe Soc. Cardiology, Rotary. Avocations: skiing, photography. Office: Mälarsjukhuset dept internal medicine, S 631 88 Eskilstuna Sweden

FRITSCH, ALBERT JOSEPH, director environmental demonstration center; b. Maysville, Ky., Sept. 30, 1933; s. Albert Anthony and Mary Elizabeth (Schumacher) F. BS in Chemistry, Xavier U., 1955, MS in Chemistry, 1956; PhD in Chemistry, Fordham U., 1964; S.T.L. in Theology, Loyola U., Chgo., 1968. Ordained priest Roman Cath. Ch., 1967. Postdoctorate rsch. assoc. U. Tex., Austin, 1969-70; sci. cons. Ctr. for Study of Responsive Law, Washington, 1970-71; co-dir. Ctr. for Sci. in the Pub. Interest, Washington, 1971-77; dir. Appalachia--Sci. in the Pub. Interest, Lexington, Ky., 1977—; mem. A.S.P.I.; adv. coun. Ky. Appalachian Regional Commn.; Ky Outlook 2000, Sci. cons. Ctr. for Study of Commericalism, U.S. C.C. Environmental Justice Program, D.C.; bd. dirs. Nat. Cath. Rural Life Conf., 1994, U.S. Cath. Conf. Environ. Taskforce, Washington, 1994—. Author: A Theology of Earth, 1972, The Contrasumers: A Citizens Guide to Resource Conservation, 1974, 99 Ways to a Simple Lifestyle, 1976, Special Topics in Hetereocyclic Chemistry Vol. 30, Interscience, 1977, Household Pollutants Guide, 1978, Environmental Ethics, 1980, Green Space, 1982, Appalachia: A Meditation, 1987, Communities at Risk, Renew America, 1989, Eco-Church, 1991, Down to Earth Spirituality, 1992, Waste Minimization: Widening the Perspectives, 1993, Earth Healing, 1994; chpts. in Embracing the Earth, 1994, Ecological Prospects, 1994, The Greening of Faith, 1996, Ecology and Religion, 1998, The Spirituality of Gardening, 2000. Wade chair of Philosophy, Marquette U., 1998. Named Gamaliel Chair Lectr. Lutheran Ministry, U. Wis.. Milw., 1991; Bannon Chair lectr. U. Santa Clara, Calif., 1994; recipient St. Francis Xavier medal, Xavier U., Cin., 1993. Mem. Soc. of Jesus, Sigma Xi, Phi Lambda. Roman Catholic. Avocation: jogging. Fax #: (606) 256-2779. E-mail: aspi@kih.net. Home: 50 Lair St Mount Vernon KY 40456-2930

FRITSCH, FRITZ RUDOLF, mathematics educator; b. Johannisburg, Germany, Sept. 30, 1939; s. Gustav and Elfriede Else (Gollub) F.; m. Gerda Helene Leonore Schmidt, Aug. 27, 1966; children: Ursula Dorothee, Ute Veronika, Rudolf Bernhard. D. in Natural Scis., U. Saarland, Saarbrücken, Fed. Republic Germany, 1968; Habilitation, U. Konstanz, Fed. Republic Germany, 1973; D in Math Scis. (hon.), U. Sv. Kliment Ohridski, Sofia, Bulgaria, 1999. Asst. U. Saarland, Saarbrücken, 1964-67; high sch. tchr. Saarland, Fed. Republic Germany, 1967-69; lectr. U. Konstanz, 1969-73, assoc. prof., 1973-81; prof. U. Munich, 1981—, dean, 1987-89, 97-99. Author: Cellular Structures in Topology, 1990, Der Vierfarbensatz, 1994, The Four Color Theorem, 1998; editor Didaktik der Mathematik, 1985-95, Praxis der Mathematik, 1996—, Forum Geometricorum, 2000—, (book series) Symposia Gaussiana, 1990—, 25 Jahre Fakultät für Mathematik-Das Mathematische Institut 1971-96, 1996, Die Entwicklung der Region Königsberg Kaliningrad, 1997; contbr. articles to profl. jours. Fellow Altpreussische Gesellschaft für Wissenschaft, Kunst und Literatur, Sudetendeutsche Akadamie der Wissenschaften und Künste; mem. Deutsche Mathematiker-Vereinigung, Am. Math. Soc., Deutscher Verein zur Förderung des mathematischen und naturwissenschaftlichen Unterrichts, Deutsche Gesellschaft für Geschichte der Medizin, Naturwissenschaften und Technik. Lutheran. Home: Friedemann Bach Strasse 61, 82166 Gräfelfing Germany Office: Ludwig Maximilians U Math Inst, Theresienstrasse 39, 80333 Munich Germany

FRITSCHE, CLAUDIA, diplomat. Personal sec. Liechtenstein Head Gov., 1970-74, Dep. Head Gov., Liechtenstein, 1974-78; diplomatic collaborator Office of Fgn. Affairs, Liechtenstein, 1978-90; dep. Permanent Rep. to Coun. of Europe, Strasbourg, France, 1983-90; first sec. Liechtenstein Embassy, Berne, Switzerland, 1987-89; first sec., chargée d'affaires Liechtenstein Embassy, Vienna, Austria, 1989; now permanent rep. of Liechtenstein UN, New York; head Liechtenstein Nat. Com. on Equality between Women and Men, 1987-90; sec. Liechtenstein parliamentary del. to the Coun. of Europe, parliamentary del. to the European Free Trade Assn. Office: Perm Mission Liechtenstein to UN Fl 27 633 3rd Ave Fl 27 New York NY 10017-6706

FRITZ, EDWARD LANE, dentist; b. Evansville, Ind., Dec. 15, 1932; s. Edward E. and Virginia B. (Lane) F.; m. Bettye J. Samples, July 31, 1954; children: Mary Ann, Sarah Jane. AB, Ind. U., 1954, DDS, 1957; BS, U. Evansville, 1975, MBA, 1978. Pvt. practice dentistry Evansville, 1959-99; ret.; pres., chmn. bd. Health Resources, Inc., 1986—; corp. bd. dirs. Va. Corp., Evansville, 1962-72, Dynatron, Inc., 1980-87. Editor: The Bulletin of the Am. Assn. of Dental Examiners, 1981-85. Capt. U.S. Army, 1957-59. Named Disting. Alumnus Ind. U. Sch. Dentistry, 1991. Fellow Am. Coll. Dentists, Acad. Gen. Dentistry, Acad. Dentistry Internat., Internat. Coll. Dentists; mem. ADA (continuing edn. com. 1981-83, cons./evaluator 1980), Ind. Dental Assn. (trustee 1983-91, Disting. Svc. award 1996), Vanderburgh County Dental Soc. (pres. 1967, various offices), First Dist. Dental Soc. (pres. 1976-77, various offices), Am. Assn. Dental Examiners (pres. 1989, various offices), Ind. Bd. Dental Examiners (pres. 1982-83, sec. 1980-82), Acad. Operative Dentistry, Internat./Am. Assn. Dental Rsch., Am. Assn. Dental Editors, Acad. Gen. Dentistry, Pierre Fauchard Acad., Sagamores of the Wabash, Phi Kappa Phi. Home: 12200 Edgewater Dr Evansville IN 47720-8169

FRITZ, JACK, government official; b. Chuuk, Federated States Micronesia, Mar. 23, 1950; s. Songo and Anita (Dinney) F.; m. Francy Bossy; children: Frita, Jamie, Alinda, Jake, Jacklyn. BA, U. Hawaii, 1973, JD, 1979; diploma in Community Health, Medicine, and Surgery, John A. Sch. Medicine, Pohnpei, Federated States Micronesia, 1992. Legis. counsel Truk Legislature, Chuuk, 1979-81; senator Congress Federated States Micronesia, 1981-94, vice-chmn. commn. future polit. status and transition, 1981-83, chmn. J & CO Com., 1985-87, speaker, 1987—; advisor del. Federated States Micronesia Law of Sea, 1981-82. Pres. Appu Nat. Group, Federated States Micronesia, 1987-94. Office: Congress Federated State Micronesia Palikir Pohnpei FM 96941*

FRITZ, JUDITH ANN, special education administrator, educator; b. Topeka, Kans., Feb. 9, 1938; d. John Conrad Meister and Ann Elizabeth (Meek) Jackson; m. Charles Vincent Ijams, Oct. 19, 1957 (div. 1966); children: Wendy Garrett, Roy Ijams; m. Walter Neil Fritz, July 1, 1967 (div. 1991); stepchildren: Howard, Russell, Laura Fritz Ogle; adopted child, Kenton. BEd, Washburn U., 1962; MEd, U. Kans., 1971; PhD, Kans. State U., 1982. Cert. adminstr. spl. edn. Elem. tchr. Rochester Sch., Shawnee County, Kans., 1962-63, Tecumseh (Kans.) Sch., 1963-65; spl. edn. tchr. USD #501, Topeka, 1965-68, Family Svc. Guidance Ctr., Topeka, 1968-71; jr. high sch. tchr. Wabaunsee East USD #330, Eskridge, Kans., 1972-74, spl. edn. tchr., 1974-81, program coord., 1981-88; asst. dir. spl. edn. Flint Hills Spel. Edn. Coop., Emporia, Kans., 1988-99; dir. spl. edn. Coffey County Edn. Coop., Burlington, Kans., 1999—; spkr. in field. Editor Rural Spl. Edn. Quarterly, 1980-2000; contbr. Kans. Record, 1983. Pres. Kiwanis, Emporia, 1997; pres. bd. dirs. Mental Health Ctr. East Ctrl. Kans., Emporia, 1985-2000. Kans. Dept. Edn. grantee, 1981-97, Artist in Edn. grantee Kans Arts Commn., 1982-88. Mem. Kans. Assn. Spl. Edn. Adminstrs. (membership chair), Coun. Exceptional Children, Phi Delta Kappa. Democrat. Avocations: duplicate bridge, bowling, camping, reading, hiking. Home: 820 Weaver St Emporia KS 66801-3451 Office: Coffey County 200 S 6th St Burlington KS 66839-1700

FRITZ, MARTIN, occupational biomechanics researcher; b. Hamm, Germany, Apr. 17, 1949; m. Christa Fritz-Schwarzer, Mar. 25, 1975; children: Egmont, Antigone. D Engring., U. Bochum, Germany, 1979; Habilitation, U. Münster, Germany, 1999. Mem. sci. staff U. Bochum, 1974-82, IfADo, Dortmund, Germany, 1984—; lectr. U. Münster, 1999—. Mem. Internat. Soc. Biomechanics, Soc. for Tech. Biology and Bionics. Avocations: family, literature, theater. Home: Soldnerstrasse 10, D-44801 Bochum Germany Office: IfADo, Ardeystrasse 67, D-44139 Dortmund Germany

FRITZ, TERRENCE LEE, investment banker, strategic consultant; b. Ft. Dodge, Iowa, Mar. 10, 1943; s. George and Julia Evelyn (Katnik) F.; m. Pam Fritz; children: Erich, Kevin, Tanya. BS in Indsl. Engring., Iowa State U., 1967. Registered profl. engr., Colo. Mfg. system analyst Martin-Marietta, Denver, 1967-68; system fin. analyst N.Am. Philips, Denver, 1968-69; mgmt. cons. Denver, 1970-74; exec. dir. Met. Transit Authority-Iowa Dept. Transp., Des Moines, 1974-78; sr. v.p. mktg., strategic planning Holiday Inns, Trailways, Dallas, 1978-80; pres. Strategic Actions, Dallas, 1984-88; regional dir. capital markets group Grant Thornton, Dallas, 1988-90; pres. Capital Mkts. Group, Inc., Dallas, 1990—; mem. adv. bd. So. Meth. U., 1981-84, local adv. bd. Dallas Fed. Res., 1982-84; advisor transp. rsch. bd. NAS, 1980. Bd. dirs. Dallas-Ft. Worth Adv. bd., 1980-84; cons. Dallas-Ft. Worth Transp. Authority, 1980; mem. Gov.'s Com. on Tech., Austin, 1982-83; Dallas rep. U.S. President's Carribean Initiatives Program to Jamaica, Costa Rica, 1981-83; exec. dir. Japan-Tex. Conf., 1981-84; mem. adv. bd. So. Meth. U. Cox Sch. Bus., 1981-84. Mem. Dallas C. of C. (pres., chief exec. officer 1980-84). Avocations: skiing, sailing, wine collecting. Home: 9347 Briarhurst Dr Dallas TX 75243-6139 Office: Ste 300 2911 Turtle Creek Blvd Dallas TX 75219-6243

FRITZ, THOMAS VINCENT, association and business executive; b. Pitts., July 6, 1934; s. Zeno and Mary M. (Briley) F.; m. Barbara L. Jacob, Jan. 31, 1959; children: William T., James Z., Juliann W. BBA in Acctg. cum laude, U. Pitts., 1960; JD, Duquesne U., 1964; LLM, NYU, 1966; Advanced Mgmt. Program, Harvard Bus. Sch., 1975. Bar: Pa. 1964, U.S. Supreme Ct. 1969; CPA, Pa. 1962, other states. Ptnr. Ernst & Young (formerly Arthur Young & Co.), Pitts./N.Y.C./Washington, 1970, regional mng. ptnr., vice chmn., 1977-89, vice chmn., 1989-92; pres., CEO Pvt. Sector Coun., Inc., Washington, 1992—; adj. prof. Sch. Law Duquesne U., Pitts., 1966-79; bd. dirs. Pvt. Sector Coun., Washington, Innovative Sys., Inc.; chmn. Alliance for Free Enterprise, Washington. Editor Duquesne U. Law Rev., 1963-64. Active Century Club, Duquesne U.; bd. dirs. Evermay Comty. Assn., pres., 1994-96; bd. dirs. McLean Citizens Assn., 1994-97; co-chmn. U. Pitts. Katz Campaign 3d Century, 1988-91. With U.S. Army, 1955-57. Recipient Gorley award, 1964, Disting. Alumni award U. Pitts., 1981, Advancement Info. Tech. award, 1988, Federal 100 award, 1997. Mem. AICPA, ACBA, D.C. Inst. CPAs, Pa. Inst. CPAs, Harvard Bus. Sch. Assn., Duquesne Club, Met. Club, Rolling Rock Club, Avenel Club, Beta Gamma Sigma, Beta Alpha Psi. Home: 6303 Long Meadow Rd Mc Lean VA 22101-2314 Office: 1101 16th St NW Washington DC 20036-4803

FRITZE, JAMES NAPIER, automotive executive; b. Fostoria, Ohio, Aug. 8, 1925; s. George M. and Aileen Frances (Napier) F.; m. Claudia Elizabeth Hawkins; children: Claudia Elizabeth Fritze Oliver, George Patton Fritze, Mary Frances Fritze Swift. Student, Wagner Coll., 1943, Union Coll., 1943-44, Columbia U., 1945, Miami U., Oxford, Ohio, 1947-48, Tex. A&I U., 1952-53. With Red River Motor Co., 1953—, Centenary, 1955, La. State U., Shreveport, 1990-95. Deacon, elder First Presbyn. Ch. Lt. USN, 1943-53. Home: 6700 E Ridge Dr Shreveport LA 71106-2440

FRITZE, WALTER, physician, researcher; b. Wittmannsdorf, Styria, Austria, July 19, 1944; s. Paul and Therese (Wagner) F.; m.Hella M.D. Lücker, Aug. 29, 1969; children: Peter, Robert, Ewald. MD, Med. Sch., Vienna, 1969, Prof., 1991. Spls. ear, nose and throat U. Hosp., Vienna, 1970—; audiologist ENT-DEP, Vienna. Contbr. articles to profl. jours. Avocations: chaos theory, quantum mechanics, philosophy, art. Home: Aichholzgasse 15/7, A-1120 Vienna Austria Office: HNO-Klinik Wien, Währinger Gürtel 18, A-1090 Vienna Austria

FRITZSCHE, HARTMUT, biophysical chemist, educator; b. Weissenfels, Germany, Feb. 13, 1935; s. Martin and Gertrud (Wollny) F.; m. Bettina Wiangke, Apr. 10, 1959; children: Gisela, Wolfgang, Albrecht. PhD, Friedrich-Schiller U., Jena, Germany, 1963. Sci. coworker Inst. Microbiology, Jena, 1959-66, head of lab., 1967-89, head of dept., 1990-92; prof. biophys. chemistry U. Jena, 1993—; guest prof. U. Paris-Nord, 1993. Editor, author: Structural Investigations on Biopolymers, 1976. Mem. German Soc. Chemists, German Soc. Biophysics. Office: Fr-Schiller U Inst Mol Biology, Winzerlaer Str 10, D-07708 Jena Germany

FRIVALDSZKY, SANDOR, mathematician, civil servant; b. Budapest, Hungary, Dec. 29, 1938; s. Janos and Erzsebet (Landesz) F.; m. Emilia Huszar, Apr. 25, 1970. MSc, Eötvös U., Budapest, 1962, Doctor Dipl, 1962; PhD, Hungarian Acad. Sci., Budapest, 1971. Rsch. fellow Computer Ctr./ Ministry of Bldg. Industry, Budapest, 1969-70, Inst. of Ministry of Heavy Industry, Budapest, 1970-72, Inst. of Ministry of Machinery, Budapest, 1972-75; sci. rsch. fellow Computer Ctr. of Univ., Budapest, 1975-87; sr. sci. rsch. fellow U. of Econs., Budapest, 1987-92; sr. councillor Ministry of Transport, Budapest, 1992-99; tchr. Luth. Fasori Gimnázium, 1999-2000, Ref. Lónyai Gimnázium, 2000—. Mem. com. edn. Christian Dem. People's Party, Budapest, 1992; founding mem. Ind. Soc. Hungarian Creators and Thinkers, 1994; mem. Soc. Common Purpose, 1993—. Conservative. Roman Catholic. Avocations: corresponding chess, skating, music.

FRIZELL, SAMUEL, law educator; b. Buena Vista, Colo., Aug. 30, 1933; s. Franklin Guy and Ruth Wilma (Noel) F.; m. Donna Mae Knowlton, Dec. 26, 1955 (div. June 1973); children: Franklin Guy III, LaVerne Anne; m. Linda Moncure, Jul. 3, 1973 (div. June 1996); m. Jeannette Graham, Jan. 1997. AA cum laude, Ft. Lewis Coll., 1957; BA cum laude, Adams State Coll., 1959, EdM, 1960; JD, Hastings U. Calif., 1964. Bar: Calif. 1965. Assoc. atty. McCutcheon, Black, Verleger & Shea, L.A., L.A., 1964-67; atty. Law Offices Samuel Frizell, Santa Ana, Calif., 1967-82; adj. prof. Cerritos Coll., Norwalk, Calif., 1977-81; adj. prof. Western State U., Fullerton, Calif., 1982-84, assoc. prof., 1984-90, prof., 1990-98; prof. emeritus Western State U., Fullerton, 1998—; cons. Law Offices Samuel Frizell, Mira Loma, Calif., 1982—. Author: Frizell's Torts Tips, 1992; contbr. articles to profl. jours.; editor law jour. Mem. Main St. Adv. Panel, Garden Grove, Calif., 1975-76; judge pro-tem Orange County Superior Ct., Santa Ana, 1979-80; chair, com. atty. advertising Orange County Bar Assn., 1975; bd. dirs. Orange County Trial Lawyers Assn., 1972-75; adv. panel to legal assts. Cerritos Coll., Norwalk, 1982-86. Fellow Soc. Antiquaries; mem. Order of the Coif. Avocations: polo, history, horse breeding & training, saddle making. Office: Western State U 1111 N State College Blvd Fullerton CA 92831-3000

FRODON, JEAN-MICHEL, journalist, film critic, cinema historian; b. Paris, Sept. 29, 1953; s. Pierre and Ginette Billard; 1 child, Charlotte Billard. PhD in History, U. Paris VII, 1975. Social worker, Fontenay, France, 1971-81; photographer, Paris, 1981-84; journalist Le Point, Paris, 1984-90, Le Monde, Paris, 1990—. Author: L'Age Moderne du Cinema Francais, 1995, Le Projection Nationale, 1998; author, editor: Hoo Hsiao-Hsien, 1999. Decorated chevalier des arts et lettres French Ministry Culture, 1990. Office: 21 Bis Rue Claude Bernard, 75005 Paris France

FROEHLICH, WOJCIECH ANTONI, geomorphologist, researcher; b. Nowy Sacz, Poland, Mar. 25, 1943; s. Eugeniusz Jan and Zofia Maria (Pawlikowska) F.; m. Jolanta Michalina Lis, Sept. 29, 1964; children: Katarzyna, Dominika. MS, N. Copernikus U., Torun, Poland, 1965; D Geography, Polish Acad. Sci., D Hab. in Geography. From asst. to asst. prof. Polish Acad. Sci. Inst. Geography, Cracow, 1971-82; assoc. prof. Polish Acad. Sci., Cracow, 1982-95, prof., 1995—, head rsch. sta. Inst. Geography, 1992—; prof. Inst. Geography, 1995—; Com. mem. on Spatial Orgn. Mountain Areas, Cracow, 1992. Author: The Dynamics of Fluvial Processes in the Kamienica Nawojowska River, 1975 (award Sec. of Polish Acad. Scis.), The Dynamics and Typology of Slope and Channel Processess (award Sec. of Polish Acad. Scis. 1978), The Mechanism of Fluvial Processes and Sediment Supply Into the Stream Channel in a Mountainous Flysch Catchment, 1982 (E. Romer award Polish Acad. Sci.); co-editor: Landform Analysis. Grantee Com. Sci. Rsch., 1992, 96, Internat. Atomic Energy Agy., 1996. Mem. N.Y. Acad. Scis., Internat. Assn. Hydrological Scis., Internat. Commn. on Continental Erosion (v.p. 1991-99, pres. 1999—), Am. Geophys. Union, Internat. Assn. for Sediment Water Scis., Brit. Geomorphol. Rsch. Grp., Polish Assn. of Geomorphologists, Am. Bibl. Inst. (rsch. bd. advisors). Avocations: skiing, rafting, angling. Home: Kr Jadwigi 33/22, PO Box 72, PL33-303 Nowy Sacz Poland Office: Polish Acad Scis Inst Geography, Frycowa 113, PL33-335 Nawojowa Poland

FROESCHER, WALTER EBERHARD, neurologist; b. Biberach/Riss, Germany, Mar. 14, 1941; s. Julius Karl Georg and Emma Emilie (Wanner) F.; m. Mathilde Gertraud Huerkamp, Aug. 25, 1967; children: Rolf, Hans-Joerg, Felix. MD, U. Tuebingen, Germany, 1967; Habilitation, U. Bonn, Germany, 1978. Lic. neurologist and psychiatrist. Intern dept. internal medicine U. Tuebigen, Gen. Hosp., Laupheim, 1967-69; resident, asst. med. dir., prof. dept. neurology, epileptology and psychiatry U. Bonn, 1969-85; med. supt. dept. neurology and epileptology Ravensburg-Weissenau U. Ulm, Germany, 1985—; vis. assoc. prof. dept. neurology Johns Hopkins Hosp., Balt., 1984. Author: Treatment of Status Epilepticus, 1979, The Medical Treatment of Epilepsy, 3d edit., 2000; editor: Tolerance to Beneficial and Adverse Effects of Antiepileptic Drugs, 1986, Neurology, 1991, Mental Disturbance in Epilepsy, 1992, The Epilepsies, 1993; editor-in-chief Epilepsy-Reports, 1994—. With German Army, 1960-61. Grantee Fed. Sec. for Youth, Family and Health, 1975, Deutsche Forschungsgemeinschaft, 1977, 94. Mem. Polish League Against Epilepsy (hon.), N.Y. Acad. Scis., Royal Soc. Medicine. Office: U Ulm Dept Neurology & Epileptology, Weissenau Weingartshofer Str 2, D-88214 Ravensburg Germany

FROESHAUG, JAN OSCAR, media company executive; b. Oslo, Norway, Aug. 6, 1943; arrived in Denmark, 1966; s. Bjoern H. and Ruth (Bergli) F.; m. Dorthe Arnoldi; children: Christina, Johan. Degree in econs., U. Erlangen-Nurnberg, Germany, 1966; MS, Copenhagen Sch. Econs., 1969; MBA, Insead, Fontainebleau, France, 1972. Mng. dir. Norsk Hydro Olie A/S, Copenhagen, 1973-83; COO Great Nordic Group, Copenhagen, 1983-86; pres., CEO Egmont Group, Copenhagen, 1987—; chmn. Scandinavian Internat. Mgmt. Inst., Denmark, 1992—, Sophus Berendsen A/S, Denmark,

1999—, Ratin A/S, Denmark, 1999—, Ctr. Brain Injury, Denmark, 1993-99. Non-exec. dir. Rentokil Initial plc., England, 1999—, Ringier AG, Switzerland, 1998—, Royal Scandinavia, Denmark, 1998—, Danish Rsch. Found., 1997, Wittenborg, Denmark, 1985-93, Louis Poulsen, Denmark, 1988-90, Norsk Data, Norway, 1990-93, NTR Holding, Denmark, 1993-99, CARE Internat., Brussels, 1989-99. Mem. Denmark Am. Found., 1994—, Royal Danish Ballet Found., 1998—, INSEAD Internat. Coun., Fontainebleu, 1988—, World Pres. Orgn., 1993—, European Publisher's Coun., 1998—, Fgn. Policy Assn. (internat. adv. coun. 2000—), Knight of the Order of Dannebrog. Avocations: skiing, hunting, running. Fax: 45 33 32 45 08. Office: Egmont Group, Vognmagergade 11, DK-1148 Copenhagen Denmark

FROESSL, HORST WALDEMAR, business executive, data processing developer; b. Mannheim, Baden-Württemberg, Germany, Apr. 12, 1929; s. Otto and Friederike (Wieder) F.; m. Waltraut Kühnreich, Apr. 26, 1963 (div. Sept. 1971); m. Monika Morgener, Nov. 3, 1972. Student, pvt. schl., Shanghai, People's Republic China, 1945-50, pvt. schl., Mannheim, 1958-60. Interpreter, sect. chief Ordnance Procurement Ctr. U.S. Army, Mannheim, 1951-57; system analyst, mgr. data processing U.S. Army Indsl. Ctr. Europe, Mannheim, 1961-65; systems deliverer AEG-Telefunken, Konstanz, Fed. Republic Germany, 1966-68; mgr. orgn. and data processing Pakistan Machine Tool Factory, Karachi, 1969-71; researcher, inventor Hemsbach, Fed. Republic Germany, 1972-78; inventor, mgr., co-owner Froessl GmbH, Hemsbach, 1979—. Author 23 patents various data processing systems. Avocations: chess, writing poetry. Home and Office: Froessl GmbH, Gutenberg Strasse 2-4, D 69502 Hemsbach Germany

FROGGE, BEVERLY ANN, nurse, consultant; b. Wichita, Kans., Jan. 1, 1943; d. Owen Elba Frogge and Maudie Frances (Gillette) Surber; m. Jake C. Saubers (sept. 5, 1967 (div. May 1989); 1 child, Jeff Lee. Student, So. Meth. U., 1960-61, St. Mary of Plains Coll., 1961-62; diploma in nursing, Wichita-St. Joseph Hosp., 1964; student, UCLA, 1965. RN, Kans.; cert. health facility surveyor. Instr. LPN Program Neosho C.C., 1970-73; pub. health nurse Woodson Co., Yates Ctr., Kans., 1973-75; health facility surveyor Kans. Dept. Health and Environ., Topeka, 1975-77; nursing dir. Neosho Meml. Hosp., Chanute, Kans., 1977-84, Regency Health Care Ctr., Yates Ctr., 1985-89; psychiatric nurse VA Med. Ctr., Topeka, 1989-98; ret., 1998; dir. Neosho Meml. Hosp. Home Health Agy., Chanute, 1977-84; instr. Disaster Preparedness, Yates Ctr., 1973-75; cons. in field, 1975-77. Author: (textbook) Anatomy & Physiology Medical Treatment, 1965-67; contbg. author: (poetry) National Anthology of College Poetry, 1961; radio presenter weekly broadcast, 1978-84. Founder, dir., instr. Dresser Sch. U.S. Peace Corps, Makele, Ethiopia, 1965-67, spkr., 1967; adv. com. mem. Vocat. Edn. State Kans., Neosho C.C., Chanute, 1980-81. Avocations: music, writing, hiking, canoeing, painting. Home: 910 SW High Ave Topeka KS 66606-1827

FROHLICH, ANTHONY WILLIAM, lawyer, master commissioner; b. Covington, Ky., Dec. 8, 1954; s. Kenneth Raymond and Joan Jude (Laake) F.; m. Candace Powell Robbins, May 31, 1975; children: Kenneth Zane, Matthew Andrew. BS, No. Ky. U., 1976, JD, 1980. Bar: Ky. 1980, U.S. Dist. Ct. (ea. dist.) Ky. 1981. Staff atty. Boone County (Ky.) Child Support Program, 1980-97; city atty. City of Walton, 1980-89; master commr. Boone County Cir. Ct., Burlington, Ky., 1989—; asst. commonwealth atty. 54th Jud. Dist., Burlington, Ky., 1984-89; ptnr. Mathis, Dallas & Frohlich, Florence, Ky., 1980-96, Law Office of Anthony W. Frohlich, Florence, Ky., 1996—; pres. Soccer Tech., Union, Ky., 1994. Bd. dirs. No. Ky. Soccer Club, Florence, 1994; state coach Ky. Youth Soccer, 1994-96; coaching dir. Ky. Olympic Devel. Program Dist. One, Florence, 1992-94; active Union Town Plan Steering Com., 1999; bd. dirs. Greater Cin. Consumer Credit Counseling, 1999—; nominating chmn. Boy Scout Am., 1999—; mem. steering com. Boone County Parks & Recreation, 2000—. Named Coach of Yr., No. Ky. Soccer Club, 1992. Mem. ABA, ATLA, Ky. Bar Assn., Boone County Bar Assn. (treas. 1980), Ky. Acad. Trial Lawyers. Roman Catholic. Avocations: coaching soccer, basketball. Home: 9253 Us Highway 42 Union KY 41091-9470 Office: Law Office Anthony Frohlich PO Box 396 Florence KY 41022-0396

FROJDH, PER ANDERS, theoretical physics educator; b. Gothenburg, Sweden, Mar. 23, 1965; s. Rune A. and Margareta K.A. (Stromberg) Andersson. MS, Chalmers U., Gothenburg, 1988, PhD, 1993. Postdoctoral staff U. Wash., Seattle, 1993-96, Nordita, Copenhagen, 1996-97; asst. prof. Stockholm U., 1998-99, assoc. prof., 1999—. Office: Stockholm Univ Dept Physics, Box 6730, S-113 85 Stockholm Sweden

FROKJAER, SVEN, pharmaceutical scientist; b. Kolding, Denmark, Apr. 7, 1947; s. Asger Anders and Ella (Lund) F.; 1 child, Iben Hoelgaard Frokjaer; m. Jonna Merete Hindkaer, Aug. 17, 1994. MSc in Pharmacy, Royal Danish Sch. Pharmacy, Copenhagen, 1970, PhD, 1973. Asst. prof. Royal Danish Sch. Pharmacy, 1973-74; rsch. scientist Novo Nordisk, Bagsvaerd, Denmark, 1974-81, mgr. R&D, 1981-90, 92-93; dir. R&D Ferrosan, Søborg, Denmark, 1990-92; prof. Royal Danish Sch. Pharmacy, 1993—; mem. com. on chemistry Danish Rsch. Coun. for Tech. Scis., Copenhagen, 1994—; mem. Danish Pharmacopoeia Commn., Copenhagen, 1996—; mem. drug registration com. Danish Drug Agy., Copenhagen, 1996—; mem. Danish Med. Rsch. Coun., 2000; bd. mem. Alf Benzon Found. Contbr. articles to profl. jours.; patentee nutritionally complete enteral diet product, additives for energy supplement. Recipient H.C. Orsted award Royal Danish Sch. Pharmacy, 1970. Mem. Danish Pharm. Soc. (chmn. biopharm. sect. 1993—), Controlled Release Soc., Am. Assn. Pharm. Scientists. Lutheran. Avocations: contemporary art, skiing, sailing. E-mail: sf@clfh.dk. Office: Royal Danish Sch Pharmacy, Universitetsparken 2, DK-2100 Copenhagen Denmark

FROLANDER, LARS, olympic athlete; b. Boden, Sweden, May 26, 1974. Degree in Mgmt. Info. Sys., So. Meth. U., Dallas, 1999. Mem. swim team Sweden; winner silver in 4x200 meter freestyle relay Olympics, 1992, 96; winner gold in 100 meter butterfly Olympics, Sydney, Australia, 2000, European Championship, 1997, 99, 2000; winner silver in 100 meter butterfly World Championship, 1998, winner bronze in 100 meter freestyle, 1998. Office: Swedish Swimming Fedn, Idrottens Hus, S-123 87 Farsta Sweden*

FRÖLANDER, ULF, manufacturing company executive; b. Stockholm, Sweden, July 13, 1939; s. Ragnar and Gurli (Carlsson) F.; children: Mikael, Anne, Anders, Karin; m. Suzanne Tolstoy, 1995. MSChemE, Royal Inst. Tech., Stockholm, 1964, PhD, 1968. Staff STORA, Falun, Sweden, 1968-69; tech. service man STORA, Gävle, Sweden, 1969-70; salesman STORA, Falun, Sweden, 1970-73; prodn. man STORA, Ställdalen, Sweden, 1973-76, mill man, 1976-78; pres. Svenska Rayon, Karlstad, Sweden, 1978-82; dir. KF Ind., Stockholm, Sweden, 1982-83; pres. Boliden Kem., Helsingborg, Sweden, 1983-88, SCA Paper, Sundsvall, Sweden, 1988-90, SCA Graphic Paper AB, Sundsvall, 1990-96, SCA Raw Materials and Logistics, Brussels, 1997—. Mem. Swedish Pulp and Paper Engrs. Assn., Skogsindustrierna, Inst. Surface Chemistry, CEPI. Avocations: golf, skiing. Office: SCA RML Europe, Excelsiorlaan 79, 1930 Zaventem Belgium

FROLICK, PATRICIA MARY, retired elementary education educator; b. Portland, Oreg., May 17, 1923; d. Fred Anthony and Clara Cecelia (Riverman) F. BS in Edn., Marylhurst Coll., 1960; MS in Edn., Portland State U., 1970; student, U. Oreg., 1975; MA in Theology, St. Mary's Coll., Moraga, Calif., 1977. Joined Roman Cath. Order Sisters of Holy Names of Jesus and Mary, 1943. Left order in 1974. Elem. sch. tchr. Catholic Sch. System, Oreg., 1943-69; tchr., libr. Hood River Pub. Schs., 1970-74, Bend-La Pine (Oreg.) Pub. Schs., 1981-93; ret., 1993; part-time tchr's. asst., Portland, 1993—. Mem. NEA, Oreg. Edn. Assn., Met. Mus. Art (assoc.), Nat. Mus. Women in Arts (charter). Democrat. Roman Catholic. Avocations: watercolor painting, assisting local schools. Home: 3465 SE 153rd Ave Portland OR 97236-2265

FROLOV, SERGEI VLADIMIROVICH, physicist, educator, researcher; b. Leningrad, Russia, Aug. 14, 1967; s. Vladimir Fiodorovich Frolov and Valentina Yeremejevna Koutsakova. MS in Physics, U. Leningrad, 1989, PhD in Physics, 1993. Sci. rschr. U. St. Petersburg, Russia, 1994—; assoc. prof. Inst. of Refrigeration, St. Petersburg, 1995—. Contbr. articles to profl. jours. Home: Apraxin Str 9 Flat 26, 191023 Saint Petersburg Russia Office: Inst of Refrigeration, Lomonosova 9, 191002 Saint Petersburg Russia

FROLOV, VLADIMIR ALEXANDROVICH, physicist; b. Perm, Russia, Apr. 30, 1935; s. Alexandr and Lubov (Tikhonova) F.; m. Irina Sujetova, Mar. 9, 1935; two children: Elena, Alexandr. MSc, Perm U., 1958; PhD, Moscow Inst. Steel and Alloys, 1966, prof., 1992. Sr. rschr. Natural Scientific Inst. Perm U., 1958-60, Tula Br. Ctrl. Iron & Steel Inst., Russia, 1960-85; head plasma metallugrical lab. Tulachermet Corp., Tula, 1985-97, sr. engr., 1997-98, head energy efficient environ. and sources saving bur., 1999—. Mem. N.Y. Acad. Sci. Home: Metallurgov 43 A Fl 69, 300 027 Tula Russia

FROMBERG, KURT CHRISTIAN, retired company executive; b. Copenhagen, July 19, 1934. Various pub. rels., advt. and mktg. positions, 1952-79; dir. Gyldendalske Boghandel, Nordisk Forlag, Denmark, 1979-82, mng. dir., 1982-99; ret., 1999.

FROMENT, MICHEL LEON, research scientist; b. Choisy le Roi, France, Aug. 22, 1931; s. Roger Rene and Maria Josephine (Dupuy) F.; m. Therese Francoise Macquaire, June 29, 1961; children: Pascale, Denis, Agnes, Claire, Marie-Noelle. Degree in sci., U. Paris, 1953, DSc, 1958. Stagiaire de recherche Centre Nat. de la Recherche Scientifique (CNRS), Paris, 1954-56, attaché de recherche, 1956-58, chargé de recherche, 1958-62, maitre de recherche, 1962-69, dir. de recherche, 1969—, lab. dir., 1980-94. Editor: Passivity of Metals and Semiconductors, 1983, Surfaces, Interfaces and Couches Minces, 1990; assoc. editor Electrochimica Acta, 1985; editor Jour. de Microscopy and Spectrocopy Electron, 1976-88. Lt. French mil., 1959-68. Fellow: Electrochem. Soc. (bd. dirs., Electrodeposition divsn. award 1994); mem. Soc. Francaise de Microscopie Electronique (pres. 1982-83, Pres. award 1983), Soc. Internat. d'Electrochimie (pres. 1991-92). Roman Catholic. Avocations: cinema, gardening. Home: 5BIS Sentier du Parc, 91290 La Norville France Office: U Pierre et Marie Curie, 4 Place Jussieu, 75252 Paris France

FROMLET, K. HUBERT, banking economist; b. Stuttgart, Germany, May 22, 1947; arrived in Sweden, 1975; s. Kurt and Marianne (Schnitzler) F.; m. Cristina Lindqvist, June 1, 1979; children: Camilla, Pia. Diploma in bus., U. Würzburg, Fed. Republic Germany, 1971, D. in Polit. Sci., 1975. Researcher Saab-Scania, Södertälje, Sweden, 1975-81; researcher Swedish Coop. Banks, Stockholm, 1981-83, chief economist, 1983-84; chief economist Swed Bank, Stockholm, 1984—; lectr. various univs. Author: Das schwedische Bankensystem, 1975; contbr. articles to profl. jours. Avocations: sports, art.

FROMM, JEFFERY BERNARD, lawyer; b. Washington, Oct. 9, 1947; s. Seymour Morris and Frances Sylvia (Goldstein) F.; m. Mary Ellen Sommer, Sept. 11, 1971; children: Aaron M., David P. BS in Elec. Engring., BA in Physics, U. Pa., 1970; JD, Widener U., 1981. Bar: Pa. 1982, Calif. 1982, U.S. Ct. Appeals (9th and fed. cirs.) 1982, Colo. 1988. Patent atty. Hewlett-Packard Co., Palo Alto, Calif., 1981-83; sr. patent atty. Hewlett-Packard Co., Palo Alto, 1983-85; mng. patent counsel Hewlett-Packard Co., Andover, Mass., 1985-87; sr. mng. counsel intellectual property Hewlett-Packard Co., Ft. Collins, Colo., 1987—. Asst. scout master Boy Scouts Am., Ft. Collins, 1988-96; asst. coach-umpire Little League, Andover and San Jose, Calif., 1983-87. Mem. ABA, Pa. Bar Assn., Calif. Bar Assn., Colo. Bar Assn., IEEE, Am. Corp. Counsel Assn. Avocations: skiing, golf. E-mail: jeff fromm@hp.com. Office: Hewlett-Packard Co 3404 E Harmony Rd Fort Collins CO 80528-9599

FROMONT, MICHEL PIERRE, law educator; b. Rennes, France, Dec. 7, 1933; s. Pierre and Thérèse (Barbotte) F.; m. Marie-France Brachin, Sept. 18, 1963; children: Jean-Pierre, Pascale, Anne-Chantal, Héléne, Vincent, Sébastien. BA in Law, U. Paris, 1954, PhD, 1958; Dr. honoris causa, U. Saarbrücken, Germany, 1984. cert. prof. law. Univ. prof. U. Saarbrücken, 1962-66, U. Dijon, France, 1966-75, 76-88, U. Freiburg, Germany, 1975-76, U. Paris I Pantheon-Sorbonne, 1988—; dean Faculty Law, Dijon, 1971-74; dir. Inst. Comparative Law, Dijon, 1976-88, Inst. German Law, Paris, 1990—. author: Les recours contre l'administration en Europe, 1971, Grands Systemes de droit étrangers, 3d edit., 1998, La justice constitutionnelle dans le monde, 1996; author, editor: Introduction au droit allemand, 3 vols., 1977, 84, 91. Lt. French Air Force, 1958-60. Decorated Chevalier Legion d'Honneur, France, 1983, Grosses Verdienstkreuz, Germany, 1984-99; recipient Humboldt-Forschungspreis, Alexander von Humboldt Stiftung, 1992. Mem. Assn. Constitutionnalistes Françaises, Soc. Legislation Comparée, Deutsche Staatsrechtslehrervereinigung. Office: U Paris Panthéon-Sorbonne, 12 Pl du Panthéon, F-75005 Paris France

FRONZO, VICTOR JONATHAN, manufacturing engineer; b. Elizabeth, N.J., June 16, 1956; s. Vito Joseph and Florence June (Haefner) F.; m. Joanne C. Surgens, July 17, 1982; children: Jonathan, Joseph. AAS in Electronics Tech., Union County Tech. Inst., 1977; BS in Mgmt. Sci. and Indsl. Engring., Kean Coll. N.J., 1979. Technician supr. Sci. Atlanta, Randolph, N.J., 1980-83; sr. supr. Syntrex Inc., Eatontown, N.J., 1983-87; contract mfg. supr. Electronics Assoc. Inc., N.J., 1987-88; mfg. engring. mgr. Wheelock, Inc., N.J., 1988—. Mem. Soc. Mfg. Engrs., Surface Mt. Tech. Assn., Inst. Indsl. Engrs. (sr.), Omicron Delta Epsilon, AMC-Rambler Club, Titanic Hist. Soc., B&O R.R. Hist. Soc. Office: Wheelock Inc 273 Branchport Ave Long Branch NJ 07740-6899

FROOZANI, MINODOKHT, nutritionist, educator; b. Shiraz, Iran, Feb. 7, 1934; d. Aliakbar Froozani and Habibeh Ghatrifi; m. Asghar Shojamanesh, Oct. 30, 1961; 1 child, Homayoun. BS in Food and Nutrition, Utah State U., 1966, MS in Food and Nutrition, 1968; PhD in Food and Nutrition, Pa. State U., 1972. Tchr. and rsch. asst. Pa. State U., University Park, 1968-72; asst. prof. Sch. pub. Health, Med. Scis. U. Tehran, Iran, 1972-85; assoc. prof. Sch. pub. Health, Med. Scis. U. Tehran, 1985-93, prof., 1993—; vis. scholar UCLA, 1986-87, Harvard Sch. Pub. Health, Boston, 1996; lactation educator UCLA, 1986; breast-feeding counselor WHO, Tehran, 1994; workshop presenter in field. Author: Nutrition Education, 1984, Nutrition During Pregnancy, Lactation, Infancy and Childhood, 1993; co-author: Breast-Feeding and Nutrition of Infant, 1992, A Training Package on Promotion of Breast-Feeding, 1993, Infant Nutrition From 6-12 Months, 1998, What We Know About Infant Feeding, 1998; translator: The Management of Nutritional Emergencies in Large Population, 1978, Introductory Nutrition, 1985; contbr. articles to profl. jours. Recipient Letter of Thanks, Mins. of Health and Med. Edn., Tehran, 1988, 94; scholar Iranian Oil Co., Logan, Utah, 1966-68. Mem. Iranian Pub. Health Assn., Iranian Nutrition Soc. (founder), Soc. for Internat. Nutrition Rsch., Am. Inst. Nutrition, Nat. Com. on Promotion of Breast Feeding (founder). Avocations: reading, writing, traveling, ping pong, volleyball. Office: PO Box 14155/4487, Tehran Iran

FRÖROTH, RUNE INGVAR, publisher, academic writer; b. Delsbo, Sweden, Apr. 16, 1927; s. Bernhard and Anna (Bergen) F.; m. Marianne Palmqvist, Apr. 1, 1954; children: Anna-Karin (dec.), Ingvar, Gunnar. MA, Stockholm U., 1955. Tchr. Stockholm, 1950-75; ednl. cons. Bd. of Edn., Sweden, 1960-70; mng. dir. Libelli AB, Stockholm, 1965—. Author: Writers and Scribblers, 1963, Swedish for college Students, 1965, Factual Prose Anthology, 1970, Learn Swedish, 1976, Wide World, 1982, A Swedish History of Literature, 1984, First Word List, 1985; contbr. articles to profl. jours., to mags. and newspapers. Mem. Rotary. Avocations: books, concerts, theater, exhibitions, fishing. Home: Box 2027, 128 21 Stockholm Sweden

FROSCH, MATTHIAS, microbiologist, consultant, educator; b. Mainz, Germany, Feb. 24, 1960; s. Franz and Katharina (Schnitzlein) F.; m. Petra Sauter, May 6, 1988; children: Maximilian, Sebastian, Fabian. MD, U. Mainz, Germany, 1986; habilitation, Med. Sch., Hannover, Germany, 1992. Rsch. fellow Max-Planck-Inst., Tuebingen, Germany, 1986-87; rsch. group leader Med. Sch., Hannover, Germany, 1987-92, prof., 1993—; chair inst. hygiene and microbiology U. Würzburg, Germany, 1996—. Contbr. articles to profl. jours. Mem. German Soc. for Hygiene and Microbiology (sec. 1999—). Home: Gertraud-Rostosky St 41, 97082 Würzburg Germany Office: Inst Hygiene & Microbiology, Univ Wuerzburg, 97080 Würzburg Germany

FROSSARD, PHILIPPE MARCEL, science educator; b. Toulon, Var, France, Nov. 8, 1954; arrived in UAE, 1993; s. Marcel René and Anne-Marie (Koffel) F.; m. Sylvie Louise Joerger, Feb. 14, 1991; children: Philippe Jr., Sebastien, Alexandra. BSc, U. Louis Pasteur, Strasbourg, France, 1976, DEA, 1977, PhD, 1979, DSc, 1996. Med. fellow U. Mich., Ann Arbor, 1981-83; scientist Cal Bio, Inc., Mountain View, Calif., 1983-84, staff scientist, 1984-86, sr. scientist, 1986-88; cons. U.S. and Japan, 1989-92; prof. Faculty Medicine & Health Sci., Al Ain, United Arab Emirates, 1993—. Author: (book) The Lottery of Life, 1991; contbr. sci. articles to profl. publs. and conf. procs.; patentee in field. Named World's Young Scientist, UNESCO, 1971. Mem. Am Soc. Human Genetics. Avocations: martial arts, Eastern philosophies, writing. Office: Faculty Medicine & Health, PO Box 17666, Al Ain United Arab Emirates

FROST, DARREL RICHMOND, biologist, administrator; b. Mesa, Ariz., June 12, 1951; s. David Richmond and Lea Charlotte (Caldwell) F.; m. Lynne Celeste, May 27, 1951. PhD, U. Kans., 1988. Asst. curator Am. Mus. Natural History, N.Y.C., 1990-95, assoc. curator, 1995—, assoc. dean sci., 1997—, chair divsn. vertebrate zoology, 1999—; mem. scientific adv. bd. Edmund Niles Huych Preserve, Resselaeville, N.Y., 1998-2000. Editor: Amphibian Species of the World, 1985, Herpetol. Monographs, 1994-98. Grantee NSF, 1995-98, NASA, 1998-00. Fellow Willi Hennig Soc.; mem. Soc. Study Amphibians and Reptiles (pres. 1998), Assn. Systematics Collection (v.p. 1999—), Soc. Systematic Bilogists, Herpetologists' League (councilor 1998-00). Avocations: history. Office: Am Mus Natural History Central Park W at 79th St New York NY 10024

FROST, SIR DAVID (PARADINE), author, producer, columnist; b. Tenderden, Eng., Apr. 7, 1939; s. Wilfrid John Paradine and Mona Eveline (Aldrich) F.; m. Lynn Frederick, 1981 (div. 1982); m. Carina Fitzalan Howard, 1983; 3 sons. MA, Gonville and Caius Coll., U. Cambridge (Eng.). Chmn. The David Paradine Group of Cos., 1966—; joint founder London Weekend TV; joint founder, dir. TV-am plc, 1981-92. TV appearances include: That Was the Week That Was, 1962-63, A Degree of Frost, 1963-73, Not So Much a Programme, More a Way of Life, 1964-65, The Frost Report, 1966-67, Frost Over England, 1967, Frost over America, 1970, Frost's Weekly, 1973, David Frost at the Phonograph, 1966, The Frost Programme, 1966-68, David Frost's Night Out in London, 1966-67, The Nixon Interviews, 1977; series Headliners with David Frost, 1978, The Kissinger Interviews, 1979, The Shah Speaks, 1980, The Am. Movie Awards, 1980, David Frost Presents the International Guinness Book of World Records, ann., 1981—, Frost on Sunday (TV am) 1981-92, Spitting Image: Down and Out in the Whitehouse, 1986, The Spitting Image Movie Awards, 1987, The Next President with David Frost, 1987-88, Through the Keyhole, 1987-95, (PBS TV series) The President and Mrs. Bush Talking with David Frost, 1989, The Nobel Debate, 1991, (PBS TV series) Talking with David Frost, 1991—, The Frost Programme, 1993—, (BBC) Breakfast with Frost, 1993—, (NBC superchannel) Frosts Century, 1995—; theatrical appearances include: An Evening with David Frost (Edinburgh Festival), 1966; producer films The Rise and Rise of Michael Rimmer, 1970, Charley One-Eye, 1972, Leadbelly, 1974, The Slipper and The Rose, 1975, James A. Michener's Dynasty, 1975, The Ordeal of Patty Hearst, 1978, The Remarkable Mrs. Sanger, 1979; author: That Was the Week that Was, 1963, How to Live Under Labour; Or, At Least Have as Much a Chance as Anybody Else, 1964, Talking with Frost, 1967, To England with Love, 1967, The Presidential Debate, 1968, The Americans, 1970, Whitlam and Frost, 1974, I Gave Them a Sword: Behind the Scenes of the Nixon Interviews, 1978, (with Michael Deakin) I Could Have Kicked Myself, 1982, (with Deakin) Who Wants to Be a Millionaire?, 1983, (with Deakin) If You'll Believe That You'll Believe Anything, 1986, (with Michael Shea) The Mid-Atlantic Companion, 1986, (with Michael Shea) The Rich Tide, 1986, The World's Shortest Books, 1987, David Frost: An Autobiography-Part One, 1993. British/USA Bicentennial Liaison Com., 1973-76. Decorated Order Brit. Empire; recipient Golden Rose of Montreux, 1967; Silver medal Royal TV Soc., 1967; Richard Dimbleby award, 1967; Emmy award, 1970, 71; Guild of TV Producers award; named TV Personaltiy of Yr.; Religious Heritage Am. award, 1971; Albert Einstein award, 1971.

FROST, ELLEN LOUISE, political economist; b. Boston, MA, Apr. 26, 1945; d. Horace Wier and Mildred (Kip) F.; m. William F. Pedersen, Jr., Feb. 2, 1974; 1 son by previous marriage, Jai Kumar Ojha; children: Mark Francis Pedersen, Claire Ellen Pedersen. B.A. magna cum laude, Radcliffe Coll., 1966; M.A., Fletcher Sch. Law and Diplomacy, 1967; Ph.D., Harvard U., 1972. Teaching fellow, instr. Harvard U., Wellesley Coll., 1969-71; legis. asst. Office of Senator Alan Cranston, Washington, 1972-74; fgn. affairs officer Dept. Treasury, Washington, 1974-77; dep. dir. Office of Internat. Trade Policy and Negotiations, 1977; dep. asst. sec. of def. for internat. econ. and tech. affairs Dept. Def., Washington, 1977-81; dir. govt. programs Westinghouse Electric Corp., Washington, 1981-88; corp. dir., internat. affairs United Techs. Corp., Washington, 1988-91; sr. fellow Inst. for Internat. Econs., Washington, 1992-93, 95-98; vis. fellow Inst. for Internat. Econs., Washington, 1998—; counselor to U.S. Trade Rep., Washington, 1993-95. Author: For Richer, For Poorer: The New U.S.-Japan Relationship, 1987, Transatlantic Trade: A Strategic Agenda, 1997. Trustee Aspen Inst. Berlin, 1990-92. NSF trainee, 1967-69. Mem. Internat. Inst. Strategic Studies, Coun. Fgn. Rels., Phi Beta Kappa.

FROST, HELEN MARIE, writer; b. Brookings, S.D., Mar. 4, 1949; d. Reuben Bernhard and Jean Elizabeth (Timmons) F.; m. Chad Lawrence Thompson, July 23, 1983; 1 child, Glen Andrew Thompson; 1 stepchild, Lloyd Samuel Thompson. BS, Syracuse U., 1971; MAT, Ind. U., 1994. Cert. in elem. edn., Alaska, Ind., Mass. Tchr. Kilquhanity House Sch., Castle Douglas, Scotland, 1976-78; prin., tchr. Telida (Alaska) Sch., 1981-84; tchr. White Cliff Sch., Ketchikan, Alaska, 1990-91; tchr. English, dir. Writing Ctr. Ind. U./Purdue U., Ft. Wayne, 1996-97; cons. numerous schs. and orgns., 1990—; mem. Lane Literary Guild, Eugene, Oreg., 1986-89, pres. 1988-89. Author: (book) Skin of a Fish, Bones of a Bird, 1993 (Women Poets Series award 1993); co-author (play) Why Darkness Seems So Light, 1999; editor: (books) Why Darkness Seems So Light: Young People Speak Out About Violence, 1998, Season of Dead Water, 1990; also 52 nonfiction books for children. Poetry tchr. program for at-risk youth Arts United, Ft. Wayne, 1995—. Mem. Soc. Children's Book Writers and Illustrators, Tchrs. and Writers Collaborative, Poetry Soc. Am. (Robert Winner award 1992, Mary Carolyn Davies award 1993), Acad. Am. poets, Writers Ctr. Indpls. Avocations: crosscountry skiing, gardening, reading. E-mail: frost-thompson@worldnet.att.net. Home and Office: 6108 Old Brook Dr Fort Wayne IN 46835-2438

FROST, JAMES ARTHUR, former university president; b. Manchester, Eng., May 15, 1918; came to U.S., 1926, naturalized, 1942; s. Harry Arthur and Janet (Wilson) F.; m. Elsie Mae Lorenz, Sept. 14, 1942; children: Roger Arthur (dec.), Janet Linda Frost Naleski, Elise Anita Frost Alair. BA, Columbia U., 1940, MA, 1941, PhD, 1949; LLD, So. Conn. State U., 1993. Tchr. Am. history high sch., Nutley, N.J., 1946-47; instr. SUNY Coll.-Oneonta, 1947-49, asst. to pres., 1949-52, dean, 1952-64; assoc. provost acad. planning Cen. Adminstrn., SUNY, 1964-65, exec. dean for four year colls., 1965-68, vice chancellor for univ. colls., 1968-72; exec. dir. Conn. State Colls., New Britain, 1972-83; pres. Conn. State U., 1983-85, pres. emeritus, 1985—; instr. Am. history Columbia U., summers, 1947-48; Smith-Mundt prof. Am. history U. Ceylon, 1959-60; mem. com. on research and devel. Coll. Entrance Exam Bd., 1973-76; mem. adv. bd. Conn. Rev., 1972-76; mem. commn. on higher edn. Middle States Assn. Colls. and Secondary Schs., 1966-72; mem. Nat. Coun. Heads of Systems of Pub. Higher Edn., 1976-85, pres., 1979-80, now hon. mem. Author: Life on the Upper Susquehanna, 1783-1860, 1951; (with David M. Ellis, Harold Syrett, Harry J. Carman) A Short History of New York State, 1957, 2d edit., 1967; (with David M. Ellis and William B. Fink) New York: The Empire State, 1961, 5th edit., 1980; (with R.A. Brown, D.M. Ellis, William B. Fink) A History of the United States: The Evolution of a Free People, 1967, 2d edit., 1969, The Establishment of the Connecticut State University, 1965-85; Notes and Reminiscences, 1991, The Country Club of Farmington, Connecticut, 1892-1995, 1996; mem. editl. bd. SUNY Press, 1964-72; contbr. articles on history and edn. to mags. Trustee Robinson Sch., Hartford, 1973-77; bd. dirs. Conn. State U. Found., Inc., 1983— , treas., 1986-95, pres., 1995-98, investment com. 1995—, treas., 1999—; sponsor Soc. of Columbia Scholars, 1997—. Maj. AUS, 1941-46, lt. col. USAFR. Rockefeller grantee, 1959. Fellow N.Y. State Hist. Assn.; mem. Country Club of Farmington, Conn. Congregationalist. Home: 17 Neal Dr Simsbury CT 06070-2801 Office: Conn State U 39 Woodland St Hartford CT 06105-2337

FROST, JOHN ELLIOTT, minerals company executive; b. Winchester, Mass., May 20, 1924; s. Elliott Putnam and Hazel Lavera (Carley) F.; m. Carolyn Catlin, July 12, 1945 (div. 1969); children: John Crocker, Jeffrey Putnam, Teresa Baird, Virginia Nicholl; m. Martha Hicks, June 6, 1969 (div. 1984); m. Catherine Kearns, July 27, 1985 (dec. Jan. 1997); m. Betty Nelson, Sept. 12, 1997. BS, Stanford U., 1949, MS, 1950, PhD, 1965. Geologist Asarco, Salt Lake City, 1951-54; chief geologist, surface mines supt., gen. mgr. Philippine Iron Mines Inc., Larap, Camarines Norte, 1954-60; chief geologist Duval Corp. (Pennzoil Corp.), Tucson, 1961-67; minerals exploration mgr. Exxon Corp., Houston, 1967-71; divsn. minerals mgr. Esso Eastern Inc., 1971-80; sr. v.p. div. Exxon Minerals Co., Houston, 1980-86; pres. Exxon Minerals Internat., Houston, 1980-86, Frost Minerals Internat., Houston, 1986—; v.p. Kalahari Resources, 1996—; bd. dirs. Abitibi Mining Corp., Sedex Mining Corp., UnitedEngring. Trustees, N.Y.C., chmn. real estate com., 1986-89, v.p., 1989-91, pres., 1991-93. Mem. adv. bd. Earth Scis., Stanford (Calif.) U., 1983-85; pres. SEG Found., 1984, bd. dirs., 1981-84, 94-98. Served to 1st lt. USAAF, 1943-45, PTO. Fellow Geol. Soc. Am., Soc. Econ. Geologists (pres. 1989-90, councilor 1982-84, program com., chmn. nominating com. 1982); mem. AIME (chmn. edn. com. Soc. Mining Engrs. 1971; Charles F. Rand medal 1984, disting. mem. award 1984, Disting. Svc. award 1991), Australian Inst. Mining and Metallurgy, Am. Inst. Profl. Geologists, Sigma Xi. Republican. Methodist. Home and Office: 602 Sandy Port St Houston TX 77079-2419

FROST, LINDA GAIL, clergyman, hospital chaplain; b. Louisville, Feb. 26, 1950; d. Halqua Mildon and Christena (Crisp) F. BA, Georgetown (Ky.) Coll., 1972; MDiv, So. Bapt. Sem., Louisville, 1978, DMin, 1982. Ordained to ministry Bapt. Ch., 1978; bd. cert. chaplain. Social worker Dept. Pub. Welfare, Corpus Christi, 1972-76; assoc. to pastor Walnut St. Bapt. Ch., Louisville, 1979-89; chaplain, clin. supr. Koala Hosp., Columbus, Ind., 1989-92; dir. chaplain svcs. Caritas Med. Ctr., Louisville, 1993—; advisor pastoral svcs. Hospice of S.E. Ind., Jeffersonville, 1993—. Author, A Legacy in Missions and Ministry, 1993. Bd. dirs., pres. Neighborhood Devel. Corp., Louisville, 1979-89; mem., sec. Old Louisville Neighborhood Coun., 1979-87; active ARC Disaster Svcs., 1999—.

FROST, MOLLY SPITZER, Chinese culture educator; b. Washington, Nov. 30, 1944; d. John Brumback and Lucy Ohlinger Spitzer; m. Edmund Bowen Frost, June 18, 1966; children: Julia, Elizabeth, Edmund, Luette. BA in English, Wellesley Coll., 1966; PhD in Chinese Linguistics, Georgetown U., 1982. Rsch. assoc., grant proposal writer George Washington U., 1975-93, asst. adj. prof., 1989-90, 93—. Trustee Cleveland Park Club, Washington, 1980-84, 93-99; trustee, sec. Internat. Student House, Washington, 1991—; trustee,, pres. Parents Assn. Maret Sch., 1985-87; bd. dirs. Nat. Child Rsch. Ctr., 1982-84. Avocations: aerobics, swimming, travel. E-mail: msf@gwu.edu. Home: 3309 35th St NW Washington DC 20016-3141 Office: East Asian Langs Dept Rome Hall 462 George Washington U Washington DC 20052-0001

FROST, WINSTON LYLE, lawyer, educator; b. Washington, June 26, 1958; s. Lyle Gooden and Elizabeth Caddell (McLennan) F. BA in Social Sci., U. Calif., Irvine, 1979; JD, O.W. Coburn Sch. of Law, 1982; MBA, Pepperdine U., 1989; LLM in Taxation, Washington U., 1993; MA in Internat. Human Rights, Simon Greenleaf U., 1994; Diplomé Internat. Human Rights, Internat. Human Rights Inst., Strasbourg, France, 1995; MA in Faith and Culture, Trinity Internat. U., 1998; postgrad., Claremont Grad. Schs., 1998—. Bar: Ill. 1982, Calif. 1986, U.S. Dist. Ct. (cen. dist.) Calif. 1987, U.S. Supreme Ct. 1987, D.C. 1989. Pvt. practice Carthage, Ill., 1982-84; adjunct faculty Carl Sandburg Coll., Carthage, Ill., 1982-84; legal editor James Pub. Co., Costa Mesa, Calif., 1985-86; assoc. Law Offices of John Ford, Irvine, Calif., 1986-89, Hunt and Colaw, Inc., Santa Ana, Calif., 1989, Cassidy, Warner, Brown, Combs and Thurber, Santa Ana, Calif., 1989-90; ptnr. Harbin and Frost, Santa Ana, 1990-99; prof. Simon Greenleaf U., Anaheim, Calif., 1987-97, asst. dean Sch. Internat. Human Rights, 1994-96; acad. dean Trinity Sch. Law, 1996-97, dean 1998—; arbitrator Orange County Superior Ct., 1992—; judge pro tem Orange County Mcpl. Ct., 1992—; mediator Christian Conciliation Svc., 1995—; columnist Brokers and Agents mag., 1997—. Editor Jour. Christian Juris, 1980-81; editorial staff Athletes in Action mag., 1986-87; columnist Orange County Reporter, 1989-91; editor Orange County Bar Jour., 1991-93. Mem. campaign staff Reagan for Pres., 1980. Recipient Outstanding Achievement award The Travelers, 1987, 88. Mem. ABA, Orange County Bar Assn. (bd. dir. 1988-90, 92-95), Orange County Bar Found. (bd. dirs. 1992-95), Orange County Trial Lawyers Assn., Orange County Barristers (bd. dirs. 1989, pres. 1990), Orange County Ins. Def. Assn. (pres. 1991), Christian Legal Soc., Calif. Trial Lawyers Assn., Peter M. Elliot Inn of Ct., Kiwanis, Toastmasters. Republican. Avocations: collecting books, poetry, community theater, travel. Office: Trinity Law Sch 2200 N Grand Ave Santa Ana CA 92705-7016

FROSTEGÅRD, JOHAN ERIK, medical researcher, physician; b. Malmö, Skåne, Sweden, Oct. 2, 1959; s. Rolf Björn and Gerd Elisabeth (Ericsson) F.; m. Susanna Eva William, Apr. 19, 1990; children: Eleonor, Joakim. MD, Karolinska Inst., Stockholm, 1987, PhD, 1992. Physician in rheumatology and internal medicine Karolinska Inst., Stockholm, 1987—, rsch. fellow, 1992—, also bd. dirs. Author: (novels) Salomos Vikarie, 1991, Älgarnas Vinter, 1994; vis. scientist U. Calif. San Diego, 1997-98. Avocations: literature, music. Home: Törnrosavägen 9, 131 47 Stockholm Nacka, Sweden Office: Karolinska Inst, Dept Medicine, 171 76 Stockholm Sweden

FROSTIC, GWEN, paper company executive; b. Sandusky, Mich., Apr. 26, 1906; d. Fred Watson and Sara (Alexander) F. A in Teaching, Eastern Mich. U., 1965; BA, Western Mich. U., 1971; LLD (hon.), Ea. Mich. U., 1965; HHD (hon.), Western Mich. U., 1971; DFA (hon.), Mich. State U., 1973; DLitt (hon.), Alma Coll., 1977. Art tchr. Deabron (Mich.) Pub. Schs., 1927-39; tool designer Ford Motor Co., Dearborn, 1940-90; pres. Presscraft Papers, Benzonia, Mich., 1991—; mem. state bd. Bus. and Profl. Women, Wyandotte, 1930-60. Author: My Michigan, 1957, A Walk With Me, 1958, These Things are Ours, 1960, A Place of Earth, 1962, To Those Who See, 1965, Wingborne, 1967, Wisps of Mist, 1969, Beyond Time, 1971, Contemplate, 1973, The Enduring Cosmos, 1976, The Infinite Destiny, 1978, The Evolving Omnity, 1981, The Caprice Immensity, 1983, Multiversality, 1985, Heuristic, 1987, Chaotic Harmony, 1989, Abysmal Acuman, 1991, Aggrandize, 1993, Synthesis, 1995, Ruminate, 1997, Lilies of the Fields, 1999. Recipient Southwest Mich. Mensa award, 1981, Franfort C. of C. award, 1981, Ohio Gov.'s Youth Art Exhbn. award, 1981, Huron Valley Mich. Botanical Club award, 1982, Crooked Tree Girl Scout Coun. award, 1982, Mich. Outdoor Edn. Assn. award, 1983, Internat. Assn. Printing House Craftsmen award, 1984, Mich. Capitol Girl Scout Coun. award, 1985, Women's Nat. Farm and Garden Club award, 1986; named to Mich. Womens Hall of Fame, 1986, Jr. Achievment Bus. Hall of Fame, 1991. Mem. Nat. Fedn. Garden Club, PEO, Order Ea. Star, Alpha Delta Kappa, Delta Kappa Gamma, Omicron Nu, Alpha Sigma Tau. Republican. Home and Office: 5140 River Rd Benzonia MI 49616

FROST-SMITH, BRIAN MCLEAN, editor, writer, translator, consultant; b. Farnborough, Eng., June 8, 1946; arrived in France, 1974; arrived in Belgium, 1987; s. Edward Hilary and Pauline Patricia (Browne) F.-S. BA with honors, U. Keele, U.K., 1968; higher nat. diploma comml. translation, Acad. Strasbourg, France, 1976. Editl. asst. Internat. Pub. Corp., London, 1968-70; press and publicity officer Lambeth Coun., London, 1970-74; exec. officer Internat. Assn. Univs., Paris, 1977-79; asst. editor European Inst. Edn. and Social Policy, Paris, 1980-87; adminstrv. officer (info. and publs.) ERASMUS Bur., Brussels, 1987-95; rschr. European Commn., Brussels, 1996; cons. Brian Frost-Smith sprl, 1997—; cons. editor, translator EURYDICE, the info. network on edn. in Europe, Brussels, 1998—; cons. Orgn. Econ. Coop. and Devel., Paris, 1979; cons., editor and translator EURYDICE, info. network edn. in Europe, Brussels, 1998—. Cons. editor UNESCO (UN Conf. on Sci. and Tech. for Devel.), Paris, 1979; asst. to editors European Jour. Edn., 1980-87; editor ERASMUS Newsletter, 1987-93; cons. editor, translator EURYDICE, Brussels, 1998—. Vol. coord., French sect. Amnesty Internat., Paris, 1981-87; sec., Brussels br., Nat. Union Journalists, 1994-96. Mem. N.Y. Acad. Scis., Internat. Fedn. Journalists. Avocations: piano, outdoor walking and wildlife, European history, the Welsh language, cookery. Home and Office: av de Mai 206, B-1200 Brussels Belgium

FROWEN, STEPHEN FRANCIS, economist, educator; b. Remscheid, Germany, May 22, 1923; arrived in Eng., 1949; naturalized, 1956; s. Adolf and Anne (Bauer) Frowein; m. Irina Minskers, Mar. 21, 1949; children: Michael Bernard James (dec. 1989), Tatiana Mary Anne Hosburn. Student, U. Cologne, Germany, 1943-44, U. Würzburg, Germany, 1944-45; Diplom-Vokslwirt, U. Bonn, Germany, 1948. Editor The Bankers' Mag. (now Fin. World), London, 1954-60; econ. advisor Indsl. and Comml. Fin. Corp. Ltd. (now 3i), London, 1959-60; rsch. officer Nat. Inst. Econ. and Social Rsch., London, 1960-62; sr. lectr. U. Greenwich, London, 1962-67; sr. lectr. in monetary econs. U. Surrey, Eng., 1967-87; prof. econs. Johann Wolfgang Goethe-U., Frankfurt, 1987; Bundesbank prof. monetary econs. Free U. Berlin, 1987-89; hon. rsch. fellow Univ. Coll. London, 1989—; sr. rsch. assoc. Von Hügel Inst. St. Edmund's Coll., U Cambridge, 1991—; hon. prof. Inst. for German Studies, U. Birmingham, Eng., 1995—; fellow commoner St. Edmond's Coll., U. Cambridge, 1999—; vis. prof. various European univs.; spl. adv. UNIDO, Vienna, Austria, 1980-81; contbg. editor Ctrl. Banking, 2000. Editor Woolwich Economic Papers, 1963-67, Surrey Papers in Economics, 1967-87; editor: (with others) Enzyklopädisches Lexikon für das Geld, Bank- und Börsenwesen, 2 vols., 1957, (with H.C. Hillmann) Economic Issues, 1957, (with others) Monetary Policy and Economic Activity in West Germany, 1977, A Framework of International Banking, 1979, Controlling Industrial Economies: Essays in Honour of Christopher Thomas Saunders, 1983, Business, Time and Thought: Selected Papers of G.L.S. Shackle, 1988, Unknowledge and Choice in Economics, 1990, (with D. Kath) Monetary Policy and Financial Innovations in Five Industrial Countries: The UK, the USA, West Germany, France and Japan, 1992, Monetary Theory and Monetary Policy: New Tracks for the 1990s, 1993, 2d edit. 1994, (with F.P. McHugh) Financial Decision-Making and Moral Responsibility, 1995, (with J. Hölscher) The German Currency Union of 1990: A Critical Assessment, 1997 (with P. Askonas) Welfare and Values: Challenging the Culture of Unconcern, 1997, Hayek: Economist and Social Philosopher-A Critical Retrospect, 1997, (with R. Pringle) Inside the Bundesbank, 1998, (with F.P. McHugh) Financial Competition, Risk and Accountability: British and German Experiences, 2000, (with P.E. Earl) Economics as an Art of Thought, 2000; translator Value, Capital and Rent (Knut Wicksell) 1954, 2d edit., 1970, The Role of The Economist as Official Adviser (W.A. Jöhr and H.W. Singer), 1955; Die Wurzeln des Antikapitalismus (von Mises), 1958, 2d edit. 1979; (edited by Philip Arestis) Essays in Honor of Stephen Frowen: Contemporary Issues in Money and Banking 1988; 2d edit. Money and Banking: Issues for the Twenty-First Century, 1993; contbr. articles to profl. jours. Decorated comdrs. cross Order of Merit (Fed. Republic of Germany), 1993; knighthood Pontifical Order St. Gregory the Great (KSG), 1996. Mem. Internat. PEN Club, Reform Club. Roman Catholic. Avocations: numismatics, painting, music, reading. Office: Univ Coll London Dept Econs, Gower St, London WC1E 6BT, England

FROYEN, LUDO L.P., educator; b. Hasselt, Belgium, July 15, 1954; s. Hubert and Maria (Erna) F.; m. Ludwina H.F.K. van Hemelryck, Sept. 4, 1978; children: Lisenka, Heidi, Vroni. M of Engring., K.U. Leuven (Belgium), 1977, PhD, 1983. Rschr. K.U. Leuven, 1977-83, jr. staff rschr., 1983-91, asst. prof., 1991-93, assoc. prof., 1993—, prof., 2000—; cons. European Space Agy., 1993-96. Editor: Metal Matrix Composites, 1990. Recipient Belgian Aluminum prize, 1994. Mem. Materials Info. Soc., Internat. Metallographic Soc., Am. Powder Metall. Industries, European Powder Metall. Assn. Fax: 16321992. Home: Dutselhoek 13, B-3220 Holsbeek Belgium Office: KU Leuven Dept MTM, De Croylaan 2, B-3001 Leuven Belgium

FRUE, WILLIAM CALHOUN, lawyer; b. Pontiac, Mich., Dec. 29, 1934; s. William Calhoun and Evelyn Laura Frue; m. Eloise Saunders, June 22, 1956 (div. Dec. 1989); m. Jane Torres Fletcher, Dec. 30, 1989; children: William C. III, John C., Michael C., Victoria. BA, Washington & Lee U., 1956; LLB, U. N.C., 1960. Bar: N.C. 1960, U.S. Dist. Ct. (we. dist.) N.C. 1961, U.S. Tax Ct. 1968, U.S. Ct. Appeals (4th cir.) 1988. Rsch. asst. Inst. of Govt., Chapel Hill, N.C., 1958-60; assoc. Wright & Shuford, Asheville, N.C., 1961-69; ptnr. Shuford, Frue & Sluder, Asheville, 1969-72, Shuford, Frue & Best, Asheville, 1973-84, The Frue Law Firm, Asheville, 1984—. Editor Popular Govt. mag., 1958-60. Chmn. Asheville Police Retirement Fund, 1973-83, Morehead Scholarship Selectincom., 1965-90, Asheville Planning and Zoning Commn., 1982-92. Mem. N.C. Bar Assn., Burcombe County Bar Assn., (sec., v.p. 1978-92), Trout Unltd. (N.C. coun. 1965). Democrat. Episcopalian. Avocations: fishing, camping. Office: PO Box 7627 Asheville NC 28802-7627

FRUEHAUF, STEFAN, physician, researcher; b. Herborn, Hessen, Germany, Aug. 9, 1964; s. Peter and Marianne (Mohr) F.; m. Esther Willmann, May 8, 1992; children: Maximilian, Leopold. MD summa cum laude, U. Heidelberg, Germany, 1992, PhD Habilitation in Internal Medicine, 1999. Cert. internal medicine specialist, hematologist/medical oncologist. Clin. asst. Med. U. Hosp., Heidelberg, 1990-94, 95-99; attending physician Oberarzt Med. U. Hosp., Heidelberg, 1999—; rsch. fellow U. Leiden, The Netherlands, 1994-95; cons. German Cancer Rsch. Ctr., Heidelberg, 1992—. Contbr. articles to books and profl. jours. Scholar Studienstiftung des Deutschen Volkes, Bonn, Germany, 1985-90; recipient Scientific award for medical rsch. of Otto-Weber-Found., U. Heidelberg, 2000. Mem. Internat. Soc. Hematotherapy and Graft Engring., European Working Group Gene Therapy, Deutsche Arbeitsgemeinschaft Fuer Gentherapie, Deutsche Gesellschaft fuer Haematologie und Onkologie. Avocation: genealogical research. E-mail: stefan fruehauf@med.uni-heidelberg.de. Office: Med Univ Hosp Dept V, Hospitalstrasse 3, 69115 Heidelberg Germany

FRUEHWALD-SCHULTES, BERND, internist, researcher; b. Tries, Germany, Dec. 9, 1969; s. Horst Bert and Margarete (Baas) Schultes; m. Marion Fruehwald, Oct. 9, 1996; 1 child, Selina. MD, U. Mainz, 1997, PhD (hon.), 1998. Resident Med. U. Luebech, Germany, 1997—. Contbr. articles to profl. jours. Avocations: sports. Home: Behrningstrasse 12, 23562 Luebeck Germany Office: Med U Luebeck Internal Med, Ratzeburger Allee 160, 23538 Luebeck Germany

FRÜHAUF, WOLFGANG, librarian; b. Fuchshain, Germany, Oct. 4, 1945; s. Erich and Frieda Frühauf; m. Beate Lange, July 6, 1950; children: Matthias, Katja. Staatsexamen, Paedag. Hochschule, Dresden, Germany, 1968; promotion, Humboldt U., Berlin, 1982, PhD Habilitation, 1990. Asst. dir. Verlag Volk und Wissen, Berlin, 1968-71; head of libr. Paedagog Hochschule, 1971-77, libr. dir., 1979-88; dep. dir. libr. Sachsische Landesbibliothek, Dresden, 1989-90, dir., 1990-96. Mem. Lions. Avocations: music, gardening. Home: Duelferstrasse 3, 01069 Dresden Germany Office: Sachsische Landesbibliothek, Staats-und Univ Bibliothek, D-01054 Dresden Germany

FRÜHBECK DE BURGOS, RAFAEL, conductor; b. Burgos, Spain, Sept. 15, 1933; s. Guillermo and Estefania (Ochs) F.; m. Maria Carmen Martinez, Dec. 21, 1959; children: Rafael, Gema. Attended, Bilbao Conservatory, Madrid Conservatory, High Sch. for Music, Munich, Germany, U. Munich, Richard Strauss Price, 1958, U. Madrid; dr. honoris causa, U. Navarra, Pamplona, Spain, 1994, U. Burgos, Spain, 1998. Chief condr. Mcpl. Orch., Bilbao, Spain, 1958-62; chief condr. Nat. Orch., Madrid, 1962-78, hon. condr., 1998; gen. musik dir. Düsseldorfer Symphony, Germany, 1966-71; music dir. Montreal Symphony, Can., 1974-76, Vienna Symphony, Vienna, Austria, 1991-96, Deutsche Oper, Berlin, 1992-97, Rundfunk Symphony Orch., Berlin, 1994—; prin. guest condr. Nat. Symphony, Washington, 1980-90, Yomiuri Nippon Symphony Orch., Tokyo, 1980-90, hon. condr. 1991. Decorated Encomienda de la Orden de Alfonso X, El Sabio, 1966, Gran Cruz de la Orden del Mérito Civil (Spain), 1966; Ehrenmedaille in Gold Bürgermeister, Vienna, 1995, gold medal to the Civil Merit of Austria, 1996; recipient prize of mus. interpretation Larios-CEOE Found., 1992, gold medal Internat. Gustav Mahler Soc., Vienna, 1996, Fundacion Guerrero prize of Spanish Music, Madrid, 1996. Mem. Real Acad. de Bellas Artes de San Fernando (Madrid). Office: care Vitoria, Sagasta 3, 28004 Madrid Spain also: Shaw Concerts Inc 1900 Broadway New York NY 10023-7004 also: care Harold Holt Ltd, 122 Wigmore St, London W1H ODJ, England

FRUITMAN, FREDERICK HOWARD, investment banker; b. Toronto, Oct. 8, 1950; s. Herbert Lance and Libby (Kamin) F.; m. Marlin Sue Potash, Nov. 21, 1981 (div. Dec. 1996); children: Laura, Hilary, Charles; m. Susan Beth Levinsohn, Apr. 19, 1998. SB, MIT, 1972; BA, Oxford (Eng.) U., 1974, MA, 1981; LLB, U. Toronto, 1976; MBA, Harvard U., 1981. Assoc. Davies, Ward & Beck, Toronto, 1976-77, Merrill Lynch White Weld Capital Markets Group, N.Y.C., 1978-79; cons. Bain & Co., Boston, 1981-82; v.p. Investors in Industry Corp., Boston, 1982-84; assoc. E.M. Warburg, Pincus & Co. Inc., N.Y.C., 1984-86; sr. v.p. The Stuart James Co. Inc., N.Y.C., 1986-89; mng. dir. Loeb Ptnrs. Corp., N.Y.C., 1990—; bd. dirs. FIND/SVP, Inc. Mem. Law Soc. Upper Can., Can. Soc. of N.Y., Harvard Club (N.Y.C), Tuxedo Club. Office: Loeb Ptnrs Corp 61 Broadway New York NY 10006-2701

FRUMKIN, AMOS ALEXANDER, geomorphologist, educator; b. Tel Aviv, Feb. 20, 1953; s. Haim Jacob and Ruth (Ellern) F.; m. Ayala Harary, Aug. 23, 1978; children: Yaara, Rachel, Ariel, Shlomit, Ofer. PhD, Hebrew U., Jerusalem, 1992. Cert. in geology. Dir. Israel Cave Rsch. Ctr., Jerusalem, 1980—; lectr. Hebrew U., Jerusalem, 1995—; sr. lectr. Hebrew U. Jerusalem, 1998—. Capt. Israeli Def. Forces, 1971-75. Recipient Robert Lewin award Soc. for Protection of Nature, 1991. Mem. Internat. Speleol. Union (del. of Israel 1993—). Home: DN Mizrach Binyamin, 90627 Ofra Israel Office: Hebrew U, Geography Dept, 91905 Jerusalem Israel

FRUMKIN, LYN ROBERT, scientist; b. Oakland, Calif., Oct. 24, 1953; s. Perry and Gerda Frumkin. BS, U. Wash., 1975, MD, 1984, PhD, 1984. Intern internal medicine Stanford U., Palo Alto, Calif., 1984-85; resident neurology UCLA, 1985-89; sr. fellow infectious diseases U. Wash., Seattle, 1990-93, sr. rsch. assoc. dept. medicine, 1993-95; clin. scientist Amgen, Inc., Thousand Oaks, Calif., 1996-98, ICOS Corp., Bothell, Wash., 1998—. Author: Questions and Answers on AIDS, 1987, 94, 97 (Nat. Book award Health Info. Divsn. 1998); contbr. articles to profl. jours. Fellow Infectious Diseases Soc. Am.; mem. Internat. AIDS Soc., Am. Med. Writers Assn., Phi Beta Kappa, Alpha Omega Alpha. E-mail: lfrumkin@worldnet.att.net and lfrumkin@icos.com. Fax: 425-398-5986. Home: 1225 Evergreen Point Rd Medina WA 98039-3136 Office: ICOS Corp 22021 20th Ave SE Bothell WA 98021-4406

FRUMKINA, REVEKKA MARKOVNA, linguist, essayist; b. Moscow, Dec. 28, 1931; d. Mark Romanovitch and Nina Borisovna (Lokshina) Frumkin; m. Youri Arcadjevitch Rakovshtchik, Mar. 15, 1955. BA, MA in Philology, Moscow U., 1955; PhD, Inst. Russian Lang., Moscow Acad. Scis., 1963; LLD, Leningrad U., 1980. Cert. prof. State Certification Com. Rschr. Fundamental State Libr. in Humanities, Moscow, 1956-58; rschr. Inst. Linguistics, Moscow, 1958-80, head rschr., prof., 1980—. Author 7 books in Russian, 2 in English: Exact Methods in Linguistic Research, 1963, Meaning and Categorization, 1996; essayist Knowledge Itself is Power, 1989; (author of yr. 1990). Mem. Assn. for Computational Linguistics. Avocations: gardening, cooking. Home: Rv 135, Leningradski Prospekt 60-A, 125167 Moscow Russia Office: Acad Sci Inst Linguistics, Bolshoy Kislovsky 1/12, 103009 Moscow Russia

FRUSCELLA, PASQUALE, plastic surgeon; b. Campobasso, Molise, Italy, Jan. 25, 1953; s. Riccardo Fruscella and Rita Falcone. MD, 1977. Asst. surgeon Cardarelli Hosp., Campobasso, Italy. Author: Aesthetic Plastic Surgery, 1997, Gazzetta Medica Italiana, 1996, Realta' Nuova - Ist. Cultur. Rotariano, 1994, Riv.Ital.Chir.Plast., 1985. Office: Via Mazzini 38, 86100 Campobasso Italy

FRUSTACI, ANDREA, cardiologist; b. Sant Andrea Ionio, Catanzaro, Italy, Apr. 8, 1952; s. Domenico and Maria (Seminaroti) F.; m. Marina Caldarulo, Jan. 4, 1986; children: Maria Cristina, Fabiola, Emanuela. Degree, Cath. U. Rome, 1977. Inter Med. Clinic, Cath. U., Rome, 1979-82; vis. rsch. fellow King's Coll. Hosp., London, 1982, Nat. Heart Hosp., London, 1982-86; lectr. in cardiology Cath. U., Rome, 1983-91, asst. prof. Inst. Cardiology, 1991—. Reviewer Chest jour., 1996—. Nat. Italian Rsch. Coun. grantee, 1984. Fellow am. Coll. Chest Physicians (Young Scholar award 1987); mem. Internat. Soc. and Fedn. of Cardiology (mem. coun. on cardiomyopathies 1989-93). Office: Inst Cardiology/Cath Univ, Largo A Gemelli 8, 00168 Rome Italy

FRUTEAU, JEAN-CLAUDE, foreign diplomat; b. Saint-Benoît, France, June 6, 1947. Mem. European Parliament, 1999—, mem. com. on devel. and coop., substitute com. on regional policy, transport and tourism; mem. Group of the Party of European Socialists; mem. delegation for relations with the countries of South Asia and the South Asia Assn. for Regional Coop; vice chmn. Mems. from the European Parliament to the Joint Assembly of the Agreement between the African, Caribbean and Pacific States and the European Union. Socialist Party. Office: Parlement europé3n, Rue Wiertz ASP 14G253, B-1047 Brussels Belgium

FRY, BENJAMIN NICHOLAS, science educator; b. Ankara, Turkey, Dec. 4, 1968; s. Maxwell John Fry and Janny Klaaske Blaauw. MSc, Utrecht (The Netherlands) U., 1992, PhD, 1997. Postdoctoral fellow Royal Melbourne (Australia) Inst. Tech. U., 1997-99, lectr., 1999—. Faculty grantee Royal Melbourne Inst. Tech. U., 1999. Mem. Australian Soc. Microbiology, Am. Soc. Microbiology. Fax: 61-3-9662-3421. Home: 325 B Moreland Rd, Coburg VIC 3058, Australia Office: RMIT U Dept App Biol/Biotec, 124 LaTrobe St, Melbourne 3000, Australia

FRY, CHRISTOPHER, playwright; b. Bristol, Eng., Dec. 18, 1907; s. Charles John and Emma Marguerite Fry (Hammond) Harris; m. Phyllis Marjorie Hart, Dec. 3, 1936; 1 child. ArtsD, Manchester (Eng.) Met. U., 1966; DLitt, Lambeth and Oxford U., 1987; DLitt (hon.), De Monfort U., Eng., 1994, U. Sussex, Eng., 1994. Tchr. Bedford Froebel Kindergarten, 1926-27; actor, office worker Citizen House, Bath, Eng., 1927; schoolmaster Hazelwood Prep. Sch., Limpsfield, Surrey, Eng., 1928-31; sec. to H. Rodney Bennett, 1931-32; founding dir. Tunbridge Wells Repertory Players, 1932-35; lectr., editor sch. mag. Dr. Barnardo's Homes, 1935-40; dir. Oxford (Eng.) Playhouse, 1940, vis. dir., 1945-46; dir. Arts Theatre Club, London, 1945, staff dramatist, 1947; hon. fellow Manchester (Eng.) Polytechnic, 1988. Writings include: (plays) She Shall Have Music, 1934, Open Door, 1936, The Boy with a Cart: Cuthman, Saint of Sussex, 1938, The Tower, 1939, Thursday's Child: a Pageant, 1939, A Phoenix to Frequent, 1946, The Firstborn, 1947, The Lady's Not for Burning, 1948 (Shaw Prize Fund award 1948, N.Y. Drama Critics Cir. award 1951), Thor, with Angels, 1948, Venus Observed, 1950 (N.Y. Drama Critics Cir. award 1952), A Sleep of Prisoners, 1951, The Dark Is Light Enough, 1954, Curtmantle, 1961 (Heinemann award Royal Soc. Lit. 1962), A Yard of Sun, 1970, One Thing More, or Caedmon Construed, 1986; (librettos) Robert of Sicily: Opera for Children, 1938, Seven at a Stroke, 1939, Crown of the Year, 1958; (revue) The Canary, 1950; (teleplays) The Tenant of Wildfell Hall, 1968 (Best Brit. TV Dramatization award nominee Writers Guild 1971), The Brontes of Haworth, 1973, The Best of Enemies, 1976, Sister Dora, 1977, Star Over Bethlehem, 1981; (documentary) The Queen is Crowned, 1953; (screenplays) The Beggar's Opera, 1953, Ben Hur, 1959, Barabbas, 1961, (with Jonathan Griffin, Ivo Perilli and Vittorio Bonicelli) The Bible: In the Beginning, 1966; (radio plays) Children's Hour series, 1939-40, Rhineland Journey, 1948; (other writings) The Boat that Mooed, 1965, The Brontes of Haworth, 1975, Can You Find Me: A Family History, 1978, Death Is a Kind of Love, 1979, Charlie Hammond's Sketch Book, 1980, Genius, Talent and Failure, 1987, Looking for a Language, 1992; (translator) The Boy and the Magic (Sidonie Gabrielle Colette), 1964; (translator, adaptor) Ring Round the Moon: A Charade with Music (Jean Anouilh), 1950, Tiger at the Gates (Jean Giraudoux), 1955 (N.Y. Drama Critics Cir. award 1956), The Lark (Anouilh), 1955, Duel of Angels (from Pour Lucrece by Giraudoux), 1958, Judith (Giraudoux), 1962, Peer Gynt (Henrik Ibsen), 1970, Cyrano de Bergerac (Edmond Rostand), 1975; (opera librettist) Paradise Lost (Penderecki), 1978. Served Pioneer Corps, 1940-44. Recipient Queen's Gold medal for poetry, 1962. Fellow Royal Soc. Lit. (Benson Silver medal, 2000). Office: The Toft, East Dean West Sussex PO18 0JA, England

FRY, DOUGLAS POTTENGER, anthropologist, conflict resolution specialist; b. Boston, Sept. 20, 1953; s. C. Brooks and Carol P. Fry; m. Kathy M. Johnson, Aug. 23, 1980 (div. Apr. 1994); m. Sirpa-Raija Korpela, July 31, 1998. BA in Anthropology and Psychology, U. Calif., Santa Barbara, 1976; MA in Anthropology, Ind. U., 1980, PhD in Anthropology, 1986. Assoc. instr. Ind. U., Bloomington, 1977-85; rsch. assoc. U. Ariz., 1986-90; asst. prof. Eckerd Coll., Fla., 1990-96; docent of cross-cultural

psychology Åbo Akademi U., Finland, 1996—; Donner prof. Åbo Akademi U., 1999—; vis. assoc. prof. Åbo Akademi U., 1995-96; adj. rsch. scientist U. Ariz., 1996—; cons. Tucson Unified Sch. Dist., 1989. Co-editor: Cultural Variation in Conflict Resolution, 1997; contbr. articles to profl. jours. Pres. Tucson chpt. World Federalist Assn., 1989-90. Recipient rsch. award NSF, 1981; grantee Wenner-Gren Found., 1981, NSF, 1997, U.S. Inst. Peace, 2000. Fellow Soc. for Applied Anthropology; mem. Am. Anthropol. Assn., Internat. Soc. for Rsch. on Aggression (steering com. 1995), Sigma Xi. Avocations: running, travel, nature, cooking, reading. Office: Åbo Akademi U, Devel Psychology, FIN65100 Vaasa Finland

FRY, JAMES WILSON, retired state librarian; b. Canton, Ohio, May 8, 1939; s. Oris Wilson and Cora (Harmon) F.; m. Mary Kociban, June 21, 1986; children: Christine Lee, Mary Elizabeth. B.A., Milligan Coll., 1966; M.L.S., Ind. U., 1969; M.A., Ohio State U., 1971, postgrad., 1971-75. Reference libr. Ohio State U., Columbus, 1969-70; head regional campuses, tech. services div. Ohio State U., 1970-75; dep. asst. state libr. State Libr. of Ohio, 1975-83, dep. state libr., 1983-84; state libr. Libr. of Mich., Lansing, 1984-95; ret., 1995; cons. Columbus Pub. Schs., 1977; editorial cons. Mags. for Libraries, Columbus, 1978; sec. bd. OHIONET, Columbus, 1978-79; exec. council Mich. Library Consortium, Lansing, 1984. Author historic guide: Ohio State U. Library, 1972; contbr. articles to profl. jours. Bd. dirs. Mich. Ctr. for the Book, 1986-95; exec. dir. Libr. of Mich. Found., 1986-88, bd. dirs. 1991-95; mem. Mich. Martin Luther King Jr. Holiday Commn., 1987-91. Mem. Chief Officers of State Library Agencies (mem. legis. com.), ALA (resources and tech. services div.), Assn. Specialized and Coop. Library Agys., Mich. Library Assn. Home: 440 Delaneys Cir Powell OH 43065-7544

FRY, LOUIS EDWIN, JR., architect; b. Prairie View, Tex., Sept. 11, 1928; s. Louis Edwin and Obelia (Swearingen) F.; m. Genelle Wiley, Nov. 7, 1955; children—Jo Nisa, Louis Edwin, Vicki-Lynn, A'lexa. A.B., Howard U., 1949; B.Arch., Harvard U., 1953, M.Arch., 1954, M.Arch. in Urban Design, 1962. Registered profl. architect, D.C., Va., Md., Mass., Mich., Ala., Ga., Pa., Calif. Architect McGowan & Johnson, Washington, 1955-59; architect Fry & Welch Assoc. PC, Washington, 1959—; vis. critic Harvard U., Cambridge, Mass., 1970-74; bd. dirs. Mid Atlantic NCARB, Washington, 1979-81; pres. D.C. Arch. Regulation Bd., 1979-84; mem. Redevel. Land Agy., 1978—; mem. design com. Harvard U., 1980—, vis. mem. Grad. Sch. Design. mem. Shepherd Park Community Assn., Washington, Georgia Ave. Profl. and Civic Assn., Washington. Fulbright fellow, Holland, 1954-55. Fellow AIA; mem. Nat. Orgn. for Minority Architects, Omega Psi Phi. Democrat. Avocation: breeding salt-water fish. Office: Fry and Welch Assocs PC 7100 Alaska Ave NW Washington DC 20012-1544

FRY, LOWELL LAWRENCE, JR., minister; b. Wichita, Kans., July 13, 1956; s. Lowell Lawrence and Dorothy May (Baum) F.; m. Lucinda Marie Howrey, June 5, 1976; children: Jason Matthew, Lynelle Renee, Travis Tyler. Student, Butler Community Coll., El Dorado, Kans., 1974-75; BSL, Ozark Bible Coll., Joplin, Mo., 1979; MA, Cin. Bible Sem., 1997. Ordained to ministry, Christian Chs./Chs. of Christ, 1978. Min. Rose Hill (Kans.) Christian Ch., 1976-83; assoc. min. Western Hills Christian Ch., Lawton, Okla., 1983-86, sr. min., 1986-94; sr. min. O'Fallon (Mo.) Christian Ch., 1994-97; min. Foristell (Mo.) Christian Ch., 1999; bd. dirs. S.W. Evangelizing Assn., Lawton, 1986-94; co-dir. Shepherd's Voice Ministries, Lawton, 1989-94; supervisory com. Okla. Christian Conv., Stillwater, 1988-90; area registration chmn. N. Am. Christian Conv., Cin., 1989-90. Recipient Pentecost Speech award, Ozark Bible Coll., 1976; named Outstanding Young Minister, N. Am. Christian Coun., 1989. Mem. Am. Bus. Club (bd. dirs. 1989-90). Republican. Home and Office: 1821 Queen Anne Ct Wentzville MO 63385-2753

FRY, RANDY DALE, emergency medical technician, paramedic; b. Houston, Feb. 3, 1957; s. LeRoy D. Fry and Ardria Faye (Stegall) Boyd; m. Robbie Ruth Rippy, June 4, 1982. Paramedic Panola County Ambulance, Carthage, Tex., 1979-87; cardiac monitor tech. Bossier Med. Ctr., Bossier City, La., 1991—; instr. CPR, PALS Bossier Med. Ctr.; instr. EMS, coord. Panola Jr. Coll., Carthage. Home: 770 CR 3341 Joaquin TX 75954-4962 Office: Bossier Med Ctr Bossier City LA 75954

FRY, ROY H(ENRY), librarian, educator; b. Seattle, June 16, 1931; s. Ray Edward and Fern Mildred (Harmon) F.; m. Joanne Mae Van de Guchte, Sept. 12, 1970; 1 child, Andrea Joy. BA in Asian Studies, U. Wash., 1959, BA in Anthropology, 1959; MA in Libr. Sci., Western Mich. U., 1965; MA in Polit. Sci., Northeastern Ill. U., 1977; archives cert., U. Dever, 1970; advanced studies program cert., Moody Bible Inst., 1990. Cert. tchr., Wash.; cert. pub. libr., N.Y.; cert. Med. Libr. Assn. Libr. and audio-visual coord. Aillah (Wash.) Pub. Schs., 1960-61; libr. Mark Morris H.S., Longview, Wash., 1961-64; evening reference libr. Loyola U. of Chgo., 1965-67, head reference libr., 1967-73, bibliog. svcs. libr., 1973-74, head circulation libr., 1974-76, coord. pub. svcs., 1976-85, gov. documents libr., 1985-91; ind. libr. cons., 1991-94; ref. libr. Trinity Evang. Divinity Sch., Deerfield, Ill., 1994—; tchg. asst. in anthropology Loyola U. of Chgo., 1966-67, instr. libr. sci. program for disadvantaged students, 1967, 68, univ. archivist, 1976-78, bibliographer for polit. sci., 1973-91, instr. corr. study div., 1975-85. Mem. Niles Twp. Regular Rep. Orgn., Skokie, Ill., 1982-98, sec. 1986-98; mem. Skokie Caucus Party, 1981-98; vol. Dep. Registration Officer, 1986—; mem. Skokie Traffic Safety Commn., 1984—, Skokie 4th July Parade com., 1986—; election judge Niles Twp., 1983-98, Avon Twp., 1999—. With USNR, 1951-52. Mem. Nat. Librs. Assn. (founding mem., bd. dirs. 1975-76), Asian/Pacific Am. Librs. Assn. (founding mem.), Chgo. Area Theol. Librs. Assn., Pacific N.W. Libr. Assn., Chgo. Area Archivists (founding mem.), Midwest Archives Conf. (founding mem.), ALA, Assn. Coll. and Rsch. Librs., Ill. Prairie Path Assn., Royal Can. Geog. Soc., Skokie Hist. Soc. (recording sec. 1986—), Ballard Hist. Soc. (Seattle), Macon County Hist. Soc. (Decatur, Ill.), Nat. Right to Life Com., Ill. Fedn. for Right to Life, Am. Legion, VFW, Korean War Vets. Assn., Pi Sigma Alpha. Republican. Evangelical Free. Office: Trinity Evang Divinity Sch Rolfing Meml Libr 2065 Half Day Rd Deerfield IL 60015-1241 address: 335 S Arrowhead Ct Round Lake IL 60073-4209

FRY, SIRPA-RAIJA, psychoanalyst, researcher; b. Helsinki, Finland, May 19, 1946; d. Jalmari and Aili (Lipsonen) Raatikainen; m. Pekka Juhani Korpela, June 13, 1970 (div. Apr. 1996); 1 child, Hanna Marjaana; m. Douglas Pottenger Fry, July 31, 1998. BA in Psychology, Helsinki U., 1972, MA in Psychology, 1974; licentiate in psychology, Åbo (Finland) Akademi U., 1997. Vocat. psychologist State Employment Agy., Helsinki and Vantaa, Finland, 1975-81; psychologist Kellokoski Psychiat. Hosp., Tuusula, Finland, 1981-85; pvt. practice psychotherapist, psychoanalyst Helsinki, 1986—; rschr. dept. psychology Åbo Akademi U., 1991—; supr. mental health dist. Päijät Häme Ctrl. Hosp., Lahti, 1986-91, mental health offices, Helsinki, 1987-91. Contbr. articles to profl. jours., including Aggressive Behavior Jour. Rsch. grantee State Edn. Bd., 1991-96. Mem. Therapeia Found. (cofounder artistic theater group 1987, bd. dirs. 1992-95), Internat. Fedn. Psychoanalytic Socs. (diploma), Internat. Soc. Rsch. on Agression. Avocations: music, visual arts, dancing, travel, languages. Office: Lantinen Brahenkatu 10 B 78, 00510 Helsinki Finland

FRYDMAN, JAN ERIC, lawyer, executive; b. Stockholm, Sept. 9, 1958; s. Pawel and Maria Janina F. BBA with honors, U. Oreg., 1980; diploma in civil law, U. Stockholm Law Sch., 1982, diploma in tax and fin. law, 1982; cert., U. Paris-Sorbonne, 1984; LLM cum laude, U. Stockholm Law Sch., 1989; cert., U. Nice, 1991; PIL, Harvard Law Sch., 1998. Group comdr. Royal Swedish Air Force, Stockholm, 1981-82; mktg. mgmt. The Procter & Gamble Co., Stockholm, 1982-84; corp. officer, head internat. fin. instns. The First Nat. Bank of Chgo., Stockholm, 1984-87; v.p., dep. CEO Am. Profls. Ins. Co., Indpls., 1987-88; atty. at law Carl Swartling Advokatbyra, Stockholm, 1989-91; atty. at law Mannheimer Swartling, N.Y.C., 1991-92, Stockholm, 1992-95; head of info. Stockholm, 1995-96; legal advisor European Commn., Brussels, 1996-99, prin. adminstr., 1999—; dir. Interbrands Co., Stockholm, 1989—; country corr. Internat. Banking Law Jour., Oxford, Eng., 1990-94, Internat. Co. and Comml. Law Rev., Oxford, 1990-94. Author: Japanese Tort Law, 1989; contbr. articles to profl. jours. Recipient Superior Acad. Achievement award U. Oreg., 1979, Internat. Student of Yr. award U. Oreg., 1979; Sweden-Am. Found. scholar, 1978, Inst. Internat. Edn. scholar, 1978, U. Oreg. scholar, 1978-80. Mem. ABA, N.Y. State Bar Assn., Swedish Bar Assn., Internat. Bar Assn., Sweden-Am. Found., Am. Club Sweden, Am. Club Brussels, Swedish Club of Brussels, Am. C. of C., Alpha Kappa Psi, Beta Gamma Sigma. Avocations: travel, photography, music, reading, swimming. Office: European Commn, Rue de la Loi 200, B-1049 Brussels Belgium

FRYE, BERNHARD J., nephrologist; b. Herzebrock, Germany, Aug. 17, 1960; s. Bernhard and Elisabeth (Van Loon) F.; m. Jacqueline Schatorje, May 14, 1993; 1 child, Marcel. Postgrad., U. Lille, 1985, U. Zurich, 1986; MD, U. Muenster, Germany, 1987. Asst. physician St. Franziskus Hosp., Bielefeld, Germany, 1987-89, 90-92, U. Freiburg, Germany, 1989-90, U. Med. Sch., Muenster, Germany, 1992-95; head dialysis dept. Marien Hosp., Osnabrueck, Germany, 1995-96; dir. dialysis ctr. Haus Sentmaring, Germany, 1996—. Mem. Internat. Soc. Nephrology, German Soc. Nephrology, Am. Soc. Nephrology. Office: Haus Sentmaring, Sentmaringer weg 55, 48151 Münster Germany

FRYE, CLAYTON WESLEY, JR., finance company executive; b. L.A., May 18, 1930; s. Clayton Wesley Sr. and Mary Virginia (Briggs) F.; m. Dorothy Rumsfeld, Jan. 14, 1957; children: Carolyn Frye Halloran,, Diane Frye Tanner. AB, Stanford U., 1953, MBA, 1959. Pres. Sutter Hill Devel. Co., Palo Alto, Calif., 1962-69; gen. ptnr. Johnson & Frye Investment Co., San Antonio, 1970-73; sr. assoc. Laurance S. Rockefeller, N.Y.C., 1973—; ptnr. Rockefeller & Assocs. Realty, L.P., San Francisco, 1990-99, Pacific Property Svcs., San Francisco, 1984-98; bd. dirs. Col. Williamsburg (Va.) Hotel Properties, Inc., Woodstock Resort Corp., Vt., chmn. Trustee Hist. Hudson Valley, Tarrytown, N.Y.; trustee, chmn. Jackson Hole Preserve, Inc., Woodstock Found., White House Hist. Assn., bd. dirs.; vice-chmn., trustee South St. Seaport Mus., N.Y.C.; vice-chmn., bd. dirs. Rockresorts, Inc., N.Y.C., 1973-87. Office: 30 Rockefeller Plz Rm 5600 New York NY 10112-0002

FRYE, RICHARD ARTHUR, lawyer; b. Akron, Ohio, Sept. 3, 1948; s. Virgil Arthur and Margaret (Mullen) F.; children: Kathleen, Emily, Abigail. BA, Wittenberg U., 1970; JD, Ohio State U., 1973. Bar: Ohio 1973, U.S. Dist. Ct. (so. dist.) Ohio 1974, U.S. Ct. Appeals (6th cir.) 1978, U.S. Supreme Ct. 1980, U.S. Ct. Appeals (fed. cir.) 1987, U.S. Ct. Appeals (9th cir.) 1998. Ptnr. Chester, Willcox & Saxbe LLP, Columbus, 1996—. Coauthor: Ohio Eminent Domain Practice, 1977, Personal Injury Litigation in Ohio, 1985. Bd. dirs. Am. Heart Assn., Franklin County, Ohio, 1985-87, Legal Aid Soc. Columbus, 1996—, J. Ashburn Youth Ctr., 1996—; chmn. adv. com. on local rules U.S. Dist. Ct. for So. Dist. Ohio, 1990—; chmn. com. to rev. reporting of opinions Supreme Ct. of Ohio, 2000—; reporter adv. group Civil Justice Reform Act, 1992-97, mem. adv. group 1991-95; life mem. 6th Cir. Jud. Conf., ctrl. com. Franklin Co. Democratic Party, 2000—. Fellow Columbus Bar Found., Ohio State Bar Found.; mem. Fed. Bar assn. (pres. Columbus chpt. 1991), Ohio State Bar Assn. (chmn. fed. cts. and practice com. 1988-90), Columbus Bar Assn. (chmn. fed. ct. com. 1988-91). Methodist. Office: Chester Willcox & Saxbe LLP 17 S High St Ste 900 Columbus OH 43215-3442

FRYE, ROLAND MUSHAT, literary historian, theologian; b. Birmingham, Ala., July 3, 1921; s. John and Helen Elizabeth (Mushat) F.; m. Jean Elbert Steiner, Jan. 11, 1947; 1 child, Roland Mushat. AB, Princeton U., 1943, MA, 1950, PhD, 1952; postgrad., Princeton Theol. Sem., 1950-52. Instr. English Samford U., 1947-48; from asst. prof. to prof. Emory U., 1952-61; rsch. prof. Folger Shakespeare Libr., Washington, 1961-65; L.P. Stone Found. lectr. Princeton Theol. Sem., 1959, vis. prof., 1963; prof. U. Pa., Phila., 1965-83; emeritus prof. U. Pa., 1983—; trustee, vice-chmn., adv. com. Ctr. Theol. Inquiry, 1979—, chmn., 1989-91. Author: God, Man and Satan: Patterns of Christian Thought and Life in "Paradise Lost," "Pilgrim's Progress" and the Great Theologians, 1960, Perspective on Man: Literature and the Christian Tradition, 1961, Shakespeare and Christian Doctrine, 1963, Shakespeare's Life and Times: A Pictorial Record, 1967, Shakespeare: The Art of the Dramatist, 1970, Milton's Imagery and the Visual Arts: Iconographic Tradition in the Epic Poems, 1978, Is God a Creationist?: The Religious Case Against Creation-Science, 1983, The Renaissance Hamlet: Issues and Responses in 1600, 1984, Language for God and Feminist Language: Problems and Principles, 1988; editor: The Reader's Bible A Narrative: Selections from the King James Version, 1978; contbr. articles to profl. jours. Served to maj. AUS, 1943-46. Decorated Bronze Star; Guggenheim fellow, 1956-57, 73-74; mem. Inst. Advanced Study Princeton, N.J., 1973-74, 79; grantee NEH, 1973-74, Am. Coun. Learned Socs., 1966, 71, 78, Am. Philos. Soc., 1968, 71, 78; vis. scholar Am. Acad. in Rome, 1971; NEH-Huntington Libr. fellow, 1980-81. Mem. Am. Acad. Arts and Scis., Milton Soc. Am. (pres. 1977-78, James Holly Hanford award 1979), Am. Philos. Soc. (sec. 1978-81, John Frederick Lewis prize 1979, Henry Allen Moe prize 1988, Thomas Jefferson medal 1997), Rennaissance Soc. Am. (pres. 1984-85), Cosmos Club (Washington), Merion Cricket Club. Presbyterian. Home: 226 W Valley Rd Wayne PA 19087-2451

FRYE, STEVEN WAYNE, publishing consultant, software programmer; b. Rockford, Ill., July 25, 1954; s. Richard Vernon and Colleen Rae (O'Brien) F.; m. Debra Kay Wickliff, May 16, 1981 (div. Nov. 1991); 1 child, Jessalyn Marie; m. Patricia Gail Woodbury, Sept. 10, 1994; children: Hunter Steven, Joseph David. BSBA, Nat. Coll. Bus., 1978. Art dir. The Sat. Evening Post, Indpls., 1978-81; dir. art and prodn. The Country Gentlemen, Indpls., 1978-81; prodn. dir. Denver Mag., 1981; dir. art and prodn. Colo. Homes and Lifestyles, Denver, 1981; dir. mfg. CommTek Pub., Hailey, Idaho, 1982-85; cons. Frye & Assocs., Hailey, Idaho, 1985—; cons. Inc. Mag., Boston, 1986 , Inside Sports, Chgo., 1987 , AAAS/Sci., 1989 , Time Venture Publs., San Francisco, N.Y., 1991 , TV Guide, Toronto, 1990 , John Deere, Moline, Ill., 1989 , Nat. Wildlife Fedn., Vienna, Va., 1990 , AARP/Modern Maturity, Lakewood, Calif., 1990 , Walt Disney Publs., Burbank, Calif., 1992 , The Lions Club Internat., 1996 , Word Perfect, 1996 , Consumers Digest, 1997 , Warren Miller Entertainment, 1997 ; speaker numerous pub. confs., 1989 . Designer: (software) MFG.PRO, 1986; co-designer (software) PICA, 1994; contbr. articles to profl. jours. Recipient Excellence award Communication Arts Mag., 1985. Mem. Pub. Prodn. Group, Prodn. Club of So. Calif., Denver Prodn. Club. Avocations: hiking, fishing, skiing, camping. Home: 280 Melrose St Bellevue ID 83313-5152

FRYE-MOQUIN, MARSHA MARIE, social worker; b. Tecumseh, Mich., Aug. 1, 1950; d. Jesse Roberts Gray and Evelyn Marie Binns Wade; m. Paul Raymond Moquin, Apr. 20, 1990; children: Dawn M. Savidge, James M. Savidge Jr., David R. Frye. AS, Monroe County C.C., Monroe, Mich., 1976; ADN, U. Vt., 1988; BA in Sociology, North Adams (Mass.) State Coll, 1992; MSW, SUNY, Albany, 1994; cert. case mgmt., New Eng. Healthcare Assembly, 1997. Cert. social worker, Mass.; lic. ind. cert. social worker, Mass., clin. hypnotherapist. Sales clk./cashier Woolworth's dept. Store, Burlington, Vt.; clk./typist New Eng. Telephone, Burlington, 1978-80; unit sec. Prince Georges Hosp., Cheverly, Md., 1969-72, Fairfax Hosp., Falls Church, Va., 1972-73; nurses aide Burlington Convalescent Ctr., 1976-77; EEG technician Med. Ctr. of Vt., Burlington, 1980-88; lab. technician U. Vt., Burlington, 1987-88; staff nurse Berkshire Med. Ctr., Pittsfield, Mass., 1988-90, charge nurse, 1989-90; intern Women's Svcs. Ctr./Battered Women's Shelter, Pittsfield, Mass., 1991, No. Berkshire Health and Human Svcs. Coalition, North Adams, 1992, Hillcrest Ednl. Ctr., Lenox, Mass., 1992-93, Dept. Vet. Affairs Med. Ctr., Northampton, Mass., 1993-94; med. social worker Fairview Hosp., Great Barrington, Mass., 1994—; dir. social svcs., 1995—; nurse, med. social worker Vis. Nurses Assn. No. Berkshire, Williamstown, Mass., 1991-95. Vol. Am. Cancer Soc., 1995—; bd. dirs. United Cerebral Palsy Assn. Berkshire County, Inc. Recipient Clin. Excellence award The Vt. State Nurses Assn., Cert. of Honor for vol. svc. Women's Svc. Ctr., 1991, Cert. of Appreciation, No. Berkshire Health and Human Svcs. Coalition, 1991. Mem. NASW, New England Sociological Assn., Alpha Chi. Avocations: concerts, theater, movies. Home: 136 Ingalls Rd Cheshire MA 01225-9731

FRYT, MONTE STANISLAUS, petroleum company executive, speaker, advisor; b. Jackson, Mich., Aug. 3, 1949; s. Marion S. and Dorothy A. (Fischman) F.; m. Pollyanna Hayes, May 26, 1990. BS in Aerospace Engring., U. Colo., Boulder, 1971; MBA in Mgmt., U. Colo., Denver, 1988. Field engr. Schlumberger Well Svcs., Bakersfield, Calif., 1971-75; computer R & D engr. Schlumberger Well Svcs., Houston, 1975-77; account devel. engr. Schlumberger Well Svcs., L.A., 1977-78; dist. mgr. Schlumberger Well Svcs., Abilene, Tex., 1978-80, Williston, N.D., 1980-81; v.p. ops. Logmate Svcs. Inc., Calgary, Alta., Can., 1981-84; pres. Fryt Petroleum Inc., Denver, 1984-91; mgr. petrophysics Am. Hunter Exploration, Ltd., Denver, 1991-92; prin. Reservoir Evaluations Group, Denver, 1992-99; ptnr., mgr. Monteray Energy LLC, Denver, 1994-98; mgr. tech. Anschutz Exploration Corp., 1995—. Mem. Colo. Rep. Com., 1990—, Rep. Nat. Com., Colo. Rep. Leadership Program, 1992-93; mem. exec. com. Colo. Rep. Bus. Coalition, 1993—, vice-chmn., 1996-97, chmn., 1997-99. Mem. Am. Assn. Petroleum Geologists, Rocky Mountain Assn. Geologists, Elks, Rockies Venture Club, Independence Inst. Roman Catholic. Avocations: mountain climbing, skiing, running, biking, cultural and political reading. Home: 7400 S Curtice Ct Littleton CO 80120-3951 Office: Ste 2400 555 17th St Denver CO 80202-3941

FU, ADA WAI CHEE, computer science educator; b. Hong Kong, Nov. 2, 1959; arrived in Can., 1993; d. Hoi-Chow and Suet-Ngar (Ho) Foo; m. Steven Foo-Loy Yap, Feb. 20, 1985; children: Ava, Chwan-Lee, Kenrick, Chwan-Chi. BSc, Chinese U. of Hong Kong, 1983; MSc, Simon Fraser U., 1985, PhD, 1990. Mem. scientific staff Bell No. Rsch., Ottawa, Can., 1989-93; asst. prof. Chinese U. of Hong Kong, 1993-98, assoc. prof., 1999—; prin. investigator Database Rsch. Group, Chinese U. of Hong Kong, 1995—. Contbr. articles to profl. jours. Grantee Rsch. Grants Coun., 1995-98, 99—, Chinese U. Hong Kong Rsch. Com. Funding, 1993-95, 96-97. Mem. Assn. Computing Machinery (exec. com. Hong Kong 1995-97), IEEE. Avocations: painting, drawing. Office: Dept of Computer Sci & Engring, Chinese U of Hong Kong, Shatin Hong Kong

FU, BAOPU, meteorology educator, researcher; b. Xinyu, China, Feb. 24, 1927; s. Fu Quiqing and Hu Quiying; m. Ying L.Y. Lou, July 13, 1954; children: Yuquang, Yuming, Yulin. BS, Nanjing (China) U., 1952. Asst. Nanjing U., 1952-55, lectr. meteorology, 1956-77, assoc. prof., 1978-80, prof., 1981—, chmn. Climatol. Tchg. and Rsch. Office, 1983-89, vice chmn. Natural Resources Ctr., 1988—. Author: The Influence of Orography on Temperature, 1977 (agrl. sci. award State Sci. Comm. 1982), Mountain Climate, 1983 (sci. progress award State Edn. Commn. 1988), Microclimatology, 1994, Climatic Resources and Exploitation in Mountainous Areas, 1996. Com. mem. People's Polit. Consultative Conf., Jiangsu Province, China, 1983-92. Recipient 4 awards of significant achievement in sci. rsch. Govt. of Jiangsu, Shanxi and Hunan Provinces, 1981, 83. Mem. Chinese Meteorol. Soc. (vice chmn. climatology and long-range forecast commn. 1983-94), Chinese Geog. Soc. (vice chmn. climatology commn. 1986-95), Jiangsu Meteorol. Soc. (chmn. climatology and long-range forecast commn. 1978--92). Avocation: watching television and opera. Home: No 103 Bldg 9, 2 Beijing West Rd, Nanjing 210008, China Office: Nanjing U, Dept Atmospheric Scis, Nanjing 210093, China

FU, KUEN CHEN, law educator, arbitrator, government official; b. Pingtong, Taiwan, Nov. 14; s. Jian-wu Fu and Si-mong Lee; m. Li-hwa Doong, Sept. 3; children: Tzung-lin, Tzung-may. BA in Law, Nat. U. Taiwan, 1974, MA in Law, 1980; LLM, U. Va., 1983, SJD, 1986. Journalist China Times, Taipei, Taiwan, 1976-89; correspondent China Times, N.Y.C., 1983-85; law professor Nat. Taiwan U., Taipei, 1988-96; legislator Legis. Yuan, Taipei, 1996-99; dir. Chinese Soc. Human Rights, Taipei, 1987—; dir. Overseas Fishery Cooperation Coun., Taipei, 1989—; Sec. Gen. Chinese Soc. Internat. Law, Taipei, 1990-99. Author: Equitable Ocean Boundary Delimitation, 1987, The Legal Status of the South China Sea, 1996, International Law of the Sea and Fishing Disputes, 2d edit., 1997; dep. chief editor Chinese Yearbook of International Law and Affairs, 1999—. Recipient fellowship AsianPacific Culture Ctr., Seoul, Korea, 1980. E-mail: kcfu@tpts1.seed.net.tw. Home: PO Box 13-23 Mucha, Taipei 116, Taiwan

FU, SHAO-YUN, scientist, educator; b. Nanchang, Jiangxi, China, July 26, 1964; s. Ke-Hua Fu and Shui-Heng Zou; m. Sheng-Nan Li, Apr. 5, 1989; 1 child, Liao-Jiang. BS, Jiangxi U., 1986; MS, Chinese Acad. Scis., Shenyang, China, 1989, PhD, 1993. Rsch. staff Chinese Acad. of Scis., Shenyang, 1993-94; AvH rsch. fellow Humboldt Found., Bonn, Germany, 1995-97; rsch. fellow Nanyang Technol. U., Singapore, 1997—; vis. scholar Inst. Polymer Rsch., Dresden, 1997. Contbr. articles to profl. jours. Mem. Internat. Ctr. for Materials Physics, Chinese Soc. of Materials. Avocations: Bridge, Chinese Chess, badminton. Office: Advanced Materials Rsch Ctr, Nanyang Technol Univ, Singapore Singapore

FU, SHOU-CHENG JOSEPH, biomedicine educator; b. Peking, China, Mar. 19, 1924; s. W.C. Joseph and W.C. (Tsai) F.; m. Susan B. Guthrie, June 21, 1951; children: Robert W.G., Joseph H.G., James B.G. BS, MS, Cath. U., Peking, 1944; PhD, Johns Hopkins U., 1949. Postdoctoral fellow Nat. Insts. Health, Bethesda, Md., 1949-51, scientist, 1951-55; Gustav Bissing fellow Johns Hopkins U. at Univ. Coll. London, 1955-56; chief enzyme and bioorganic chemistry lab. Children's Cancer Rsch Found (now Dana Farber Cancer Inst.), 1956-65; rsch. assoc. Harvard U. Med. Sch., Boston, 1956-65; prof., chmn. bd. chemistry Chinese U., Hong Kong, 1966-70, dean sci. faculty, 1967-69; vis. prof. Coll. Physicians and Surgeons Columbia U., N.Y.C., 1970-71; prof. biochemistry and molecular biology U. Medicine and Dentistry of N.J., Newark, 1971—, asst. dean, 1974-77; acting dean Grad. Sch. Biomed. Scis., 1977-78, prof. ophthalmology, 1989—. Contbr. articles to profl. jours. Capt. USPHS Res., 1959—. Named Hon. Disting. Prof. and Acad. Advisor Inner Mongolia Med. U., Huthot, Peoples Republic of China, 1988—. Fellow AAAS, Royal Soc. Chemistry (U.K.); mem. Royal Hong Kong Jockey Club, Am. Club Hong Kong, Sigma Xi (chpt. pres. 1976-80, sec. 1974-76, 81-82). Home: 693 Prospect St Maplewood NJ 07040-3105 Office: U of Medicine and Dentistry NJ Med Sch Med Sci Bldg 185 S Orange Ave Newark NJ 07103-2757

FU, SHOUKUAN, polymer chemist, educator; b. Shanghai, China, July 15, 1940; s. PinLing Fu and Beiheng Li; m. Qingyu Yan, Jan. 1, 1967; children: Yuqinq Fu, Yulei Fu. Grad., Fudan U., Shanghai, 1962; Sch. of Fudan, 1966. Cert. prof. Lectr. Fudan U., 1978-87, assoc. prof. polymer chemistry, 1987-93, prof. polymer chemistry, 1993—, head dept. macromol sci., 1995-99; vis. scholar, Poly. U., N.Y.C., 1983-85; vis. prof. chemistry, Coatings Rsch. Inst., Eastern Mich. U., Ypsilanti, 1993-94. Mem. editl. com. Jour. Functional Polymers, (Shanghai) 1988—, Polymer Bull. (China), 1989—, Prgress in Polymer Sci., 1999—, Polymer Chemistry, 1999—, Chinese Jour. Polymer Sci., 1999—, Jour. Macromolecular Sci. (in Chinese)-Pure and Applied Chemistry, 1999—; co-author: Polymer Chemistry, (in Chinese) 1995, Recent topics on Polymer Science (in Chinese), 1998; inventor, patentee in field; contbr. articles to scientific jours. Recipient prize for Progress of Sci. and Tech., Nat. Commn. Edn., Beijing, 1988, Govt. Shanghai City, 1987. Mem. Chinese Chem. Soc. Avocations: music, reading, go chess, travel. Office: Fudan U Dept Macromol Sci, 220 Han Dan Rd, Shanghai 200433, China

FU, XIAO YUAN, chemistry educator, researcher; b. Da Lian, Liaoning, China, Feb. 17, 1928; d. Li Yu and Yu Yun (Zhang) Fu; m. Ruo Zhuang Liu, Aug. 15, 1965; 1 child, Kai Liu. BSc, Fu Jen U., Beijing, 1950. Asst. Fu Jen U., 1950-52; lectr. Beijing Normal U., 1956-77, asst. prof., 1978-82, prof., 1983—, PhD advisor, 1990—. Contbr. 172 articles to profl. jours. Recipient 4 nat. awards for articles and rsch. Mem. World Assn. Theoretical Oriented Chemists (bd. dirs. 1996—), Chinese Chem. Soc., Beijing Chem. Soc. (bd. dirs. 1984-88, 91-94). Achievements include finding a new reaction mechanism of cycloaddition reaction. Office: Beijing Normal U Dept Chemistry, Xin Wei St, 100875 Beijing China

FU, YING, scientist, educator; b. Wuxi, Jiangsu, China, May 9, 1964; arrived in Sweden, 1987; s. Yongsheng Fu and Xialian Cang; m. Yun Chen, Aug. 19, 1989; children: Stefan Xueyan, Lukas Chenyang. BS, Xiaman (China) U., 1984; MS, Shanghai Inst. Tech. Physics, 1986; PhD, U. Linköping, Sweden, 1990. Postdoctdoctoral rschr. U. Linköping, 1990-93, asst. prof., 1993-96; asst. prof. U. Gothenburg, Chalmers U. Tech., Sweden, 1996, sr. rsch. engr., 1997-99, assoc. prof., 1999—; reviewer Jour. Applied Physics, Applied Phys. Letters, 1995—, Solid State Electronics, 1999—. Author: Physical Model of Semiconductor Quantum Devices, 1999; contbr. articles to profl. jours. Avocation: water color painting. Office: BU/CTH Dept Physics, Fysikgrand 3, 412 96 Gothenburg Sweden

FU, YUHUA, researcher, editor; b. Chongqing, China, July 9, 1945; s. Juntao Fu and Chuanqin Guo; m. Guozhen An, Sept. 30, 1979; 1 child, Anjie. BS, Tangshan (China) Railway Inst., 1968; MS in Engring., Aviation

Rsch. Inst., Beijing, 1981. Technician Qiqihar (China) Railway Bur., 1968-74; engr. No. 1 Railway Design Inst., Lanzhou, China, 1975-78, No. 625 Aviation Rsch. Inst., Beijing, 1978-84, China Nat. Offshore Oil Corp., Beijing, 1984-88; sr. engr. China Offshore Oil Devel. and Engring. Corp., Beijing, 1990—; dep. chief editor China Offshore Oil and Gas Engring., Beijing, 1997—; vis. scholar ocean engring. and hydrology Trondheim (Norway) U., 1985-86; sci. and tech. export advisor Hong Kong New Time Internat. Culture and Publ. Ltd., 1997, Hong Kong Internat. Enterprise Publ., 1998. Contbr. more than 80 articles to profl. jours. Avocations: table tennis, fractals, forecasting economic data, tracking typhoons. Office: Jing Xin Mansion 26/F Jia 2, North Dong San Huan Rd, Beijing 100027, China

FUAD, KHUTU TEKIN, judge. Pres. Ct. Appeal Brunei Darussalam. Office: Supreme Ct, 2056 PO Box 2231, Bandar Seri Begawan 1922, Brunei*

FUCHIGAMI, YASUNORI, orthopedic surgeon; b. Masuda-shi, Shimane, Japan, Feb. 12, 1959; s. Katsumi and Shigeko (Yasuno) F.; m. Yuko Nagashima, Apr. 29, 1986; children: Kanako, Mikihiro, Tomohiro. MS, Yamaguchi U., 1984, MD, 1989. Asst. orthop. surgeon Yanaguchi Univ. Hosps. and Clinics, Ube-shi, 1992—. Author: Recent Advances in Human Neurophysiology, 1998, Mechanical Loading of Bones and Joints, 1999.

FUCHS, ANDREAS, marketing manager; b. Heidelberg, Germany, Sept. 30, 1966; arrived in Belgium, 1999; s. Heinz and Alise (Braun) F.; ptnr. Julie Elizabeth Gronlund. Diplom-Kaufman, U. Mannheim, Germany, 1993. Asst. to mktg. dir. VW Mex., Puebla, 1990, 92-93, VW Am., Detroit, 1991; trainee Audi AG, Ingolstadt, Germany, 1993-94; sales mgr. Audi AG, Ingolstadt, 1994-95, mktg. mgr., 1995-97; mktg. mgr. Audi Argentina, Buenos Aires, 1997-98, Toyota, Brussels, 1999—. Avocations: golf, skiing, traveling.

FUCHS, GREGORY OSKAR, marketing communications executive; b. Rochester, N.Y., May 29, 1965; arrived in The Netherlands, 1992; s. Otto and Edeltraud (Mayer) F.; m. Yvonne Odilia Janssen, Nov. 21, 1995; children: Frederique, Maximilian. BA, SUNY, Buffalo, 1988; MIM, Thunderbird AGSIM, Phoenix, 1989. Asst. account exec. ABC/Eurocom, Dusseldorf, Germany, 1990-91, account exec., 1991-92; project mgr. sponsorship Philips Internat., Eindhoven, The Netherlands, 1992-95, sponsorship mgr., 1995-97; mktg. comms. mgr. Philips Consumer Electronics, Amsterdam, The Netherlands, 1997—. Mem. Am. C. of C. in The Netherlands. Roman Catholic. Avocations: sports, family, reading, travel. Office: Philips Consumer Electronic, PO Box 77900, 1070 MX Amsterdam The Netherlands

FUCHS, LEO L., motion picture producer; b. Vienna, Austria, June 14, 1929; s. Osias and Mina (Hasenfratz) F.; m. Sylviane Anne Therese, Mar. 7, 1960; 1 child, Alexandre. Free-lance mag. photographer, 1946-64; producer Universal Pictures, 1964-67, CBS Cinema Ctr. Films, 1967-69; founder, producer Viaduc Prodns. S.A., Paris, 1971—. With U.S. Army, 1951-53. Home: 16 Rue de Sevres, Paris France 75007

FUCHS, MANFRED, lubricant company executive; b. Mannheim, Germany, Jan. 19, 1939; m. Lieselotte Werle; children: Susi, Stefan. Student, Mannheim U., 1958-62; Doctorate, 1965. Joined Fuchs Mineralölwerke GmbH, 1963; chmn. exec. bd. Fuchs Petrolub AG Oel & Chemie, Mannheim, 1984—. Mem. Union Européenne des Indépendants en Lubrifiants (pres.), Assn. Lubricants Industry (mem. exec. bd.), Chamber of Industry and Commerce Rhine-Neckar in Mannheim (v.p.). Avocations: painting, riding, skiing. Office: Fuchs Petrolub Oel & Chemie, Friesenheimer St 17, D-68169 Mannheim Germany*

FUCHS, MICHAEL, physician, hepatology/gastroenterology researcher; b. Ulm, Germany, Dec. 9, 1964; s. Karl Heinz and Ursula (Maier) F. MD, Albert Einstein U., Ulm, 1992, PhD, 1993. Resident Med. U. Luebeck, Germany, 1992-93; sr. rsch. fellow Brigham and Women's Hosp., Boston, 1993-96; instr. medicine Med. U. Luebeck, Germany, 1996—; instr. microbiology Albert Einstein U. Med. Sch., Ulm, 1986-88, tutor in physiology, 1989-91, instr. med. terminology, 1988-89, instr. medicine, 1990-92; instr. medicine U. Luebeck Sch. Nursing, 1992-93. Author numerous papers and book chpt. Grantee German Sci. Found., Bonn, 1993-95, 97-99, 2000—, Young Investigator award 4th UEGW, Berlin, 1995, 7th UEGW, Rom, 1999; Falk Found. fellow, 1995-96; Astra Merck Inc. sr. fellow, 1995-96. Mem. AAAS, German Assn. Physicians, German Gastroenterology Assn., Gastroenterology Rsch. Group, Am. Assn. for the Study of Liver Disease, European Assn. for the Study of the Liver, N.Y. Acad. Scis., Am. Soc. Cell Biology, Am. Physiol. Soc. Avocations: tennis, golf, music, photography, travel. Office: Med U Luebeck Divsn Gastroenterology, Ratzeburger Allee 160, D-23538 Lübeck Germany

FUCHS, OWEN GEORGE, chemist; b. Austin, Tex., June 22, 1951; s. Emil George and Hazel June (Johnson) F.; children from previous marriage: Ginny Lynn, William Oberholz, Owen George; m. Caroline S. Crook, Dec. 15, 1990; children: Evan Ashbey, Lindsey Nicole, Allison Mae. AA, Lee Jr. Coll., 1970, AS, 1973; BS, U. Houston, 1972. Chemist, Merichem Co., Houston, 1972-73; lab. mgr. Superintendence Co., Inc., Houston, 1973-78; dir. labs. and hydrocarbon research Chas. Martin Internat., Pasadena, Tex., 1978-79; pres., chief exec. officer Alpha-Omega Labs., Inc., Houston, Tex., 1979-88; bd. dirs. A.O.L. Inc., Houston, 1988—; pres., chief exec. officer Owen G. Fuchs & Assocs., Houston, 1988—, Texas City Testing Inc., 1989—, Environ. Testing Enterprises, Inc., 1991—, La. Testing Labs., Inc., 1992—. Mem. ASTM, NRA, Am. Chem. Soc., Nat. Space Soc. Home: PO Box 613 Highlands TX 77562-0613 Office: PO Box 3921 Texas City TX 77592-3921

FUCHS, PATRICK EUGENE, perfume company executive; b. Paris, Apr. 14, 1930; s. Georges and Florence Simone (Campbell) F.; m. Edina Maria de Marffy-Mantuano, June 23, 1960; children: Stephanie, Frederic, Sandrine. BS, U. Paris, 1946; postgrad. in chem. engring., E.N.S.C.P. (Paris), 1951; MS, Stevens Inst. Tech., 1952; MA, Harvard U., 1954, PhD, 1956. Tech. dir. S.A. Parfumerie Fragonard, Grasse, France, 1958-74, pres., 1974-96; pres. S.A. T.P.L.T., Grasse, 1974-96; pres. S.A. Societé Meridionale des Confiseries Florian, 1996—. Contbr. articles to profl. jours. Served with French Navy, 1956-58. Fulbright grantee, 1952-53. Mem. Am. Chem. Soc. Roman Catholic. Clubs: Harvard (N.Y.); M.B.C. (France). Avocations: skiing; tennis; golf. Home: La Petite Campagne, Les Quatre Chemins, 06130 Grasse France Office: SA SMC Florian, 14 Quai Papacino, 06300 Nice France

FUCHS, ROBERT F., lawyer; b. Milw., Feb. 25, 1924; s. Edgar and Josephine (Herzberg) F.; m. Lorraine C. Laserson, Nov. 29, 1949 (div. May 1974); children: Robin, James, Alison; m. Helene C. Dorfman. BS, U. Wis., 1946; LLB, Harvard U., 1948, JD, 1951. Bar: Ill. 1951, U.S. Dist. Ct. (no. dist.) Ill. 1951, U.S. Ct. Appeals (7th cir.) 1951, U.S. Tax Ct. 1958, U.S. Ct. Appeals (5th cir.) 1960, U.S. Supreme Ct. 1981. Assoc. Johnston, Thompson, Raymond & Mayer, Chgo., 1948-57, Schapiro & Schiff, Chgo., 1957-59; ptnr. Schapiro & Fuchs, Chgo., 1959-61, Schapiro, Fuchs & Temple, Chgo., 1961-65, Vihon, Fuchs, Temple & Berman, Chgo., 1965-77; pres. Fuchs, Temple & Berman, Ltd., Chgo., 1977-89; chmn. Fuchs & Roselli Ltd., Chgo., 1989-99; bd. dirs. Philip Lochman & Co., Evanston, Ill., Beacon, Berndt & Assocs., Arlington Heights, Ill. Author: Communism and the Constitution, 1949; contbr. articles to profl. jours. V.p., mem. exec. bd. Am. Jewish Com., Chgo., 1955-81; pres. Freedom Agenda, Chgo., 1957; mem. exec. bd. Thresholds, Chgo., 1987—; trustee North Shore Congregation Israel, Glencoe, Ill., 1989-95. Capt. USAAF, 1943-45, ETO. Decorated Disting. Flying Cross. Mem. ABA, Ill. State Bar Assn., Chgo. Bar Assn. (chmn. civil rights com. 1955-56), Standard Club, Bannockburn Bath and Tennis Club. Jewish. Avocations: tennis, Civil War, reading. Office: Fuchs & Roselli Ltd 440 W Randolph St # 500 Chicago IL 60606-1507 also: 11 Linden Ave Lake Forest IL 60045-2932

FUCHS, WALTER STEFAN, pharmacist, researcher, consultant; b. Mallersdorf, Germany, July 10, 1963; S. Karl and Dorothea (Bruckl) F.; m. Mechthild Lubbers, May 14, 1996. Pharmacist cert., U. Regensburg, Germany, 1987, PhD, 1992. Pharm. developer Bristol-Meyers Squibb, Regensburg, 1987-88; pharmacist Theresien-Pharmacy, Regensburg, 1988; rsch. asst. Inst. Physiology, Regensburg, 1989-92; pharmacokineticist Klinge Pharma, Munich, 1992-96; owner Bavaria-Pharmacy, Bad Abbach, Germany, 1996—; tchr. Bavarian Chamber Pharmacists, Munich, 1995—; cons. in field. Contbr. articles to profl. jours. Wtih German Air Force, 1983-84. Avocations: jogging, show jumping, antique furniture. Office phone: 9405-953515. Office: Bavaria Apotheke, Raiffeisenstr 19, 93077 Bad Abbach Germany

FUCHS, WOLFGANG EGMONT, primary care physician; b. Stuttgart, Germany, June 12, 1941; s. Rudolf Gustav and Gisela (Hennig) F. MD, U. Tuebingen, Germany, 1968. Intern Meml. Hosp., Worcester, Mass., 1971-72; resident Bexar County Hosp., San Antonio, 1972-74; fellow TxSA Health Sci. Ctr., 1974-75; resident Bürgerhosp., Stuttgart, Germany, 1975-78; primary care internist Stuttgart, 1978—. Office: Flamingoweg 14, 70378 Stuttgart Germany

FUCHS-BUDER, THOMAS, anesthetist, researcher; b. Neunkirchen, Germany, Mar. 23, 1961; s. Ernst and Evi (Mohr) Fuchs; m. Martine Buder, May 22, 1990; m. Max, Tim, Felix. MD, Justus-Liebig-U., Giessen, 1989. Intern Geneva Med. Sch., 1989-93; specialist anaesthetist Geneva U. Hosp., 1993-96, rsch. cons. dept. anesthesiology, 1997—; specialist anaesthetist U. Saarland, Homburg, Germany, 1997—. Contbr. articles to profl. jours. Grantee Swiss Nat. Rsch. Found., 1995—. Mem. European Soc. Anesthetists. Avocations: skiing, bicycling. Home: Pasteurpromenade 8, D-66119 Saarbrücken Germany Office: U Saarland, Dept Anesthesiology, D-66421 Homburg Germany

FUECHSEL, GLENN, gynecologist-obstetrician; b. Oberhausen, Germany, Feb. 14, 1961; s. Horst Robert Otto and Ilona (Jilek) F. MD, U. Freiburg, Germany, 1987. Asst. dr. Evangelical Hosp., Muelheim, Germany, 1987-90, Marienhospital, Wesel, Germany, 1990-93; head oncologist Univ. Hosp., Halle, Germany, 1993-2000, Policlinic Reil, Halle, 2000; chief physician gyn. dept. Hosp. Friedvichroda, 2000—. Contbr. articles to profl. jours. Chmn. Junge Union Party, Oberhausen, 1978. Mem. German Soc. Ob-Gyn., German Soc. Senology. Evangelical. Avocations: reading, tennis, arts, history. Home and Office: Marsstrasse 10, 06118 Halle Germany

FUEGER, GERHARD FRANZ, radiologist educator; b. Vienna, Austria, June 24, 1933; came to U.S., 1958; s. Franz F. and Hertha (Gerlach) F.; m. Isolde E. Eberstaller, Mar. 6, 1958. MD, U. Vienna, 1958. Diplomate Am. Bd. Radiology; diplomate Am. Bd. Nuclear Medicine. Assoc. prof. radiology Johns Hopkins Hosp. & Med. Sch., Balt., 1964-66; radiologist-in-charge nuclear medicine Karl-Franzens U., Graz, Austria, 1966-72, lectr., 1972, prof., 1975; chief div. nuclear medicine Univ. Hosp., Graz, Austria, 1972—. Author: Dosimetrie Offener Radionuclide, 1982. Office: Univ Hosp, Auenbruggerplatz 9, Graz A8036, Austria

FUENTE-DEL-CAMPO, ANTONIO, plastic and reconstructive surgeon, educator, researcher; b. Mexico City, Apr. 27, 1945; s. Antonio and Guadalupe Fuente-Del-Campo; m. Carmen Maria Procuna Chamorro, Aug. 2, 1975; children: Paloma, Daniela. MD, Nat. U. Autonoma de Mex., 1974. Cert. plastic surgery bd. Intern, resident Hosp. Gen. de Mex., 1969-73; plastic surgeon Hosp. Gen., Mexico City, 1974-78; assoc. prof. Hosp. Gea Gonzalez, Mexico City, 1978-99, chmn. Craniofacial Clinic, 1978—; instr. plastic surgery Ednl. Found., 1988—; prof. craniofacial fellowship U. Nat. Autonoma de Mex., 1996—; mem. Craniofacial Clinic Hosp. Infantil de Mex., Mexico City, 1997—; plastic surgery "B" rschr. Hosp. Gea Gonzalez, 1996—; rschr. plastic surgery level II Nat. Rsch. Sys., 1999—. Co-editor: Libro Texto Cirugia Plastica Latino Americana, 1994; editor Revista Assn. Mexicana Cir Plastica, 1979-80; mem. editl. bd. Rev. Latino Americana Cirugia Plastica, 1980-84, Rev. Anales Medicos, 1982-99, Revista Colombiana Cirugia Plastica, 1994, Aesthetic Plastic Surgery; instr. aesthetic surgery video jour. Recipient award for outstanding svcs. and contbns. in advancement of aesthetic surgery Am. Assn. Aesthetic Plastic Surgery, 1997. Mem. Internat. Soc. Aesthetic Surgery (v.p. 1995—), Am. Coll. Surgeons (Mex. chpt. pres. 1985-86), Assn. Mexicana Labio Paladar Hendido (pres. 1987-90), Am. Soc. Plastic and Reconstructive Surgeons (corr. 1982), Assn. Mex. Cirugia Plastica (chmn. sci. com. 1998—), Assn. Mexicana Cirugia Craneofacial (pres. 2000—), Academia Mexicana de Cirugia, Acad. Nacional Medicina, Am. Soc. Aesthetic Plastic Surgery (Best Paper of Yr. award), Am. Soc. Maxillofacial Surgeons, Am. Cleft Palate-Craniofacial Assn., Internat. Soc. Craniofacial Surgery. Roman Catholic. Avocations: art, tennis, skiing, swimming. Fax: (525)-652-6765. E-mail: AFDELC@IBM.NET. Home: CAP Interlomas #26, 52786 Mexico City DF, Mexico Office: Clinica de Cirugia Plastica, Camino Sta Teresa 1055-239, 10700 Mexico City DF, Mexico

FUENTES, ANGEL, health organization coordinator; b. Aquadilla, P.R., Aug. 2, 1961; s. Pablo Fuentes and Luz Maria Caban; m. Ana Celia (Sepulveda), June 4, 1988; children: Josuel, Angel, Mariangelis. BA in Philosophy, St. John Vianney Coll., 1985. Cert. social worker N.J. Religion tchr. San Carlos Colegio, Aquadillo, P.R., 1987; youth counselor Youth Adv. Program, Camden, N.J., 1987-93; rehab. counselor Goodwill Southern Industries, Camden, 1987-88; case mgr. The Steininger Ctr., Cherry Hill, N.J., 1988-90; family therapist Family Counselling Svc., Camden, 1990-96; with Cooper Health System, Camden, 1996—; cons. Senior Care, Camden, 1996; author of legislation, Camden Neighborhood Renaissance, 1996—, Mcpl. Aids/HIV Adv. Bd., 1999, Camden City Public Safety Council, 1999. Author: Se Salvo Por Un Sueno, 1985 (1st place award 1985). Pres., founder Youth Summit, Camden, 1999-00; sec. St. John the Baptist Parade, Camden, 1995; mem. planning com. U.S. Hispanic Leadership Inst., Chgo., 1995, 98; v.p. 4th Ward City Council, Camden, 1994—; founder Nonprofit City Volleyball C. Recipient Family Therapy award Family Inst., Philla., 1990, Whitney M. Young Jr. award Urban Emphasis, Boy Scouts Am., Cherry Hill, 1996, Prominent Hispanic Leader award Office Hispanic Affairs, Camden, 1996, Good Neighbor award, ARC, Cherry Hill, 1999, Healthy Mothers and Healthy Babies Coalition of N.J. Mem. Cramer Hill Lion's Club (chmn., recruiter award, 1999), ARC Camden chpt. (recognition award, 1999). Democrat. Catholic. Avocation: tennis, volleyball, spending time with friends, family, facilitator, mediator. Home: 1169 Bergen Ave Camden NJ 08105-4207

FUENTES, CARLOS, writer, former ambassador; b. Mexico City, Mexico, Nov. 11, 1928; s. Rafael Fuentes Boettiger and Berta Macias Rivas; m. Rita Macedo, 1959 (div. 1969); 1 dau., Cecilia; m. Sylvia Lemus, 1973; children: Carlos, Natasha. Ed., U. Mex., Institut des Hautes Etudes Internationales, Geneva; hon. degrees, Columbia Coll., Chgo. State U., Cambridge U., Essex U., Harvard U., Dartmouth Coll., Bard Coll., New Sch., Georgetown U., Washington U., St. Louis, Borwn U. Mem. Mexican del. ILO, Geneva, 1950-52; asst. chief press sect. Mexican Ministry Fgn. Affairs, 1954; asst. dir. cultural dissemination U. Mex., 1955-56; head dept. cultural relations Mexican Ministry Fgn. Affairs, 1957-59; fellow Woodrow Wilson Internat. Center for Scholars, Washington, 1974; Mexican ambassador to France, 1975-77; prof. English and romance langs. U. Pa., 1978-83; prof. comparative lit. Harvard U., 1984-86, Robert F. Kennedy prof., 1987-89; prof.-at-large Brown U., Providence, 1995—; Norman Maccoll lectr. Cambridge U., 1977, Simon Bolivar prof., 1986-87; Virgina Gildersleeve prof. Barnard Coll., 1977; Henry L. Tinker lectr. Columbia U., 1978; pres. Modern Humanities Rsch. Assn., 1989—; prof. at large Brown U., 1995—. Author: Los días enmascarados, 1954, La región más transparente, 1958 (ub. as Where the Air Is Clear, 1960), Las buenas conciencias, 1959 (pub. as The Good Conscience, 1961), Aura, 1962, La muerte del Artemio Cruz, 1962 (pub. as The Death of Artemio Cruz, 1964), The Argument of Latin America: Words for North Americans, 1963, Cantar de ciegos, 1964, Zona sagrada, 1967 (pub. as Holy Places, 1972), Cambio de piel, 1967 (pub. as A Change of Skin, 1968; Biblioteca Breve prize Barcelona 1967), Paris: la revolución de mayo, 1968, La nueva novela hispanoamericana, 1969, Cumpleaños, 1969, El mundo de Jose Luis Cuevas, 1969, Casa con dos puertas, 1970, Tiempo mexicano, 1971, Poemas de amor: cuentos del alma, 1971, Cuerpos y ofrendas, 1972, Chac Mool y otros cuentos, 1973, Terra Nostra, 1975 (Rómulo Gallegos prize Venezuela 1977), Cervantes: o, La critica de la lectura, 1976 (pub. as Don Quixote: or, The Critique of Reading, 1976), La cabeza de la hidra, 1978 (pub. as The Hydra Head, 1978), Una familia lejana, 1980 (pub. as Distant Relations, 1982), Agua quemada, 1981 (pub. as Burnt Water, 1981), High Noon in Latin America, 1983, Juan Soriano y su obra, 1984, Of Human Rights: A Speech, 1984, El gringo viejo, 1985 (pub. as The Old Gringo, 1986; L.A. Times Book award nomination 1986, Rubén Darío prize 1988, Italo-Latino Americano Instituto prize 1988), Latin America: At War with the Past, 1985, Palacio Nacional, 1986, Cristóbal Nonato, 1987 (pub. as Christopher Unborn, 1989), Gabriel García Marquez and the Invention of America, 1987, Myself with Others: Selected Essays, 1988, Constancia, y otras novelas para virgenes, 1989 (pub. as Constancia and Other Stories for Virgins, 1990), La campaña, 1990 (pub. as The Campaign, 1991), Valiente Mundo Nuevo, 1991, The Buried Mirror: Reflections on Spain and on the New World, 1992, Witnesses of Time, 1992, Return to Mexico: Journeys Beyond the Mask, 1992, El Naranjo, 1993 (pub. as The Orange Tree, 1993), Geografia de la Novela, 1993, Diana the Goddess Who Hunts Alone, 1995, The Crystal Frontier, 1995, La Edad del Tiempo, 1994—, A New Time for Mexico, 1994, Por un Progreso Incluyente, 1997, Retratos en el Tiempo, 1998, Los Anos con Laura Diaz, 1999; (plays) Todos los gatos son pardos, 1970, El tuerto es rey, 1970, Los reinos originarios, 1971, Orquídeas a la luz de la luna, 1982 (pub. as Orchids in the Moonlight, 1982; Mexican Nat. award for lit. 1984); screenwriter: (films) Pedro Paramo, 1966, Tiempo de morir, 1966, Los Caifanes, 1967, (TV series) The Buried Mirror, 1991; contbr. to mags. and newspapers including Los Angeles Times, N.Y. Times, Newsweek; editor: Revista Mexicana de Literatura, 1954-58, El Espectador, 1959-61, Siempre, 1960—, Politica, 1960—, Los signos en rotación y otra ensayos, 1971. Trustee N.Y. Pub. Library, mem. Mexican Nat. Commn. Human Rights, 1991—. Recipient Centro Mexicano de Escritores fellowship, 1956-57, Xavier Villaurrutia prize (Mex.), 1975, Alfonso Reyes prize (Mex.), 1979, Miguel de Cervantes Lit. prize Spanish Ministry of Culture, 1987, Medal of Honor for Lit., Nat. Arts Club, N.Y.C., 1988, Rector's medal U. Chile, 1991, Casita Maria medal, 1991, UCLA medal, 1993, Order of Merit (Chile), 1992, French Legion of Honor, 1992, Menèndez Pelayo Internat. award U. Santander, 1992, Picasso medal UNESCO, 1994, Principe de Asturias prize, 1994, Premio Grinzane-Cavour, 1994; named hon. citizen Santiago de Chile, 1993, Buenos Aires, 1993, Veracruz, 1993, Order of the So. Cross (Brazil), 1997, French Order of Merit, 1998, Latin Civilization prize French and Brazilian Acads., 1999. Mem. Am. Acad. and Inst. Arts and Letters, Nat. Coll. Mex., Inst. Nat. Strategy (bd. dirs.).

FUENTES, NESTOR OSVALDO, physicist, researcher; b. San Fernando, Argentina, Apr. 26, 1955; s. Martin Lorenzo and Ilia Azucena (Mastache) F.; m. Hebe Olga Gavarini, Nov. 18, 1987; 1 child, Natalia Celeste. BS in Physics, U. Buenos Aires, 1982, PhD, 1989. Tchg. asst. U. Buenos Aires, 1981-89; fellow Argentine CONICET, Buenos Aires, 1982-84; fellow Nat. Commn. on Atomic Energy, Buenos Aires, 1985-86, rschr., 1987—; vis. fellow Internat. Ctr. for Theoretical Physics, Trieste, Italy, 1987; sci. sec. IV Latin Am. Workshop on Plasma Physics, Buenos Aires, 1990; rsch. fellow ICTP-Istituto Gas Ionizzati, Padua, Italy, 1991-92; mem. organizing com. Sch. on Materials Surfaces, Buenos Aires, 1997; mem. Inst. of Tech. Prof. J.A. Sabato, Buenos Aires, 1998—; mem. organizing com. I Latin Am. Meeting on Acoustic Emission, Buenos Aires, 1999. Author articles and conf. presentations. Served with Argentine Army Res., 1976. Roman Catholic. Achievements include stochastic simulations of simultaneous erosion-redeposition processes on materials surfaces; use of SEM-digital images and fractal theory to determine materials surface roughness; characterization of surface morphology using Fourier and Wavelet processing of digitized images. Fax: (54) 11-4754-7362; email: fuentes@cnea.gov.ar. Office: Nat Commn Atomic Energy CAC-UA Materiales, Av del Libertador 8250, 1429 Buenos Aires Argentina

FUERST, ALBERT ALAN, remote sensing engineer; b. Steubenville, Ohio, Sept. 20, 1949; s. Albert Joseph and Helen Marie Fuerst; m. Ann Marie S. Fuerst, June 12, 1971; children: Alexander S., Berin A. Student, U. Vienna, 1969, U. Saarbruekan, Germany, 1979; BA, St. Loe Coll., 1970; MA, Troy State U., 1980. Staff dir. Govt. Applications Task Force, Washington, 1970, 1994-96; pres. Ukraine Land & Resource Mgmt. Ctr., Kyiv, 1999, pres. emeritus, 1999—. Contbr. articles to profl. publs. Coord. Boy Scouts Am. projects Nat. Park Svc., Fort Washington, 1996—. With U.S. Army, 1970-92. Decorated Bronze Star; grantee USIA, 1998. Mem. Ukraine Nat. Assn., Greenpeace. Avocation: collecting 19th century folk art. Home: 6830 Camus Pl Springfield VA 22152-3112

FUERSTENAU, DOUGLAS WINSTON, mineral engineering educator; b. Hazel, S.D., Dec. 6, 1928; s. Erwin Arnold and Hazel Pauline (Karterud) F.; m. Margaret Ann Pellett, Aug. 29, 1953; children: Linda (dec.), Lucy, Sarah, Stephen. BS, S.D. Sch. Mines and Tech., 1949; MS, Mont. Sch. Mines, 1950; ScD, MIT, 1953; Mineral Engr., Mont. Coll. Mineral Sci. and Tech., 1968; hon. doctorate degree, U. Liege, Belgium, 1989. Asst. prof. mineral engring. MIT, 1953-56; sect. leader, metals research lab. Union Carbide Metals Co., Niagara Falls, N.Y., 1956-58; mgr. mineral engring. lab Kaiser Aluminum & Chem. Corp., Permanente, Calif., 1958-59; assoc. prof. metallurgy U. Calif., Berkeley, 1959-62, prof. metallurgy, 1962-86, P. Malozemoff prof. of mineral engring., 1987-93, prof. grad. sch., 1994—; Miller research prof. U. Calif.-Berkeley, 1969-70, chmn. dept. materials sci. and mineral engring., 1970-78; bd. dirs. Homestake Mining Co.; mem. Nat. Mineral Bd., 1975-78; Am. rep. Internat. Mineral Processing Congress Com., 1979-97. Editor: Froth Flotation-50th Anniversary Vol., 1962; co-editor-in-chief: Internat. Jour. of Mineral Processing, 1974—; contbr. articles to profl. jours. Recipient Alexander von Humboldt Sr. Am. Scientist award, Germany, 1984, Frank F. Aplan award The Engring. Found., 1990, Internat. Mineral Processing Congress Lifetime Achievement award, 1995; Rsch. fellow Japan Soc. Promotion Sci., 1993; Douglas W. Fuerstenau professorship established at S.D. Sch. of Mines and Tech., 1998. Mem. NAE, AIChE, Am. Inst. Mining and Metall. Engrs. (chmn. mineral processing divsn. 1967, Robert Lansing Hardy gold medal 1957, Rossiter W. Raymond award 1961, Robert H. Richards award 1975, Antoine M. Gaudin award 1978, Mineral Industry Edn. award 1983, Henry Krumb disting. lectr. 1989, hon. 1989), Soc. Mining Engrs. (bd. dirs. 1968-71, Disting. mem.), Am. Chem. Soc., Russian Fedn. Acad. Natural Scis. (fgn. mem.), Sigma Xi, Theta Tau. Congregationalist. Home: 1440 Le Roy Ave Berkeley CA 94708-1912

FUES, WOLFRAM MALTE, German literature and culture educator; b. Bremen, Germany, Apr. 4, 1944; arrived in Switzerland, 1980; s. Willi and Doris (Stroux) F.; m. Suzanne Reichen, June 18, 1974. PhD, U. Zurich, 1978; Habilitation, U. Basel, Switzerland, 1987. Fellow U. Basel, 1978-83, assoc. prof. German literature, 1994—. Author: Mystik als Erkenntnis? Kritische Studien zur Meister-Eckhart-Forschung, 1981, Poesie der Prosa, Prosa als Poesie, Zur Geschichte der Gesellschaftlichkeit bürgerl. Lit., 1990, Text als Intertext, Zur Moderne in der dt. Lit. des 20 Jhdts, 1995, (poems) Verletzte Systeme, 1994. mem. N.Y. Acad. Scis., Deutsche Gesellschaft zur Erforschung des 18 Jahrhunderts, Goethe-Gesellschaft in Weimar, Grimmelshausen-Gesellschaft. Home: Brunaustr 161, CH-8951 Fahrweid Zurich, Switzerland Office: U Basel Deutsches Seminar, Nadelberg 4, CH-4051 Basel Switzerland

FUESS, BILLINGS SIBLEY, JR., advertising executive; b. N.Y.C., Mar. 11, 1928; s. Billings Sibley and Lucile (McNeill) F.; m. Doris Vannoy, July 19, 1952; children: Billings Sibley III, Doris Jr., Frederick, Lucile. AB in Journalism, U. N.C., 1949. Analyst Gallup & Robinson, Princeton, N.J., 1952-53; writer Kenyon & Eckhardt, N.Y.C., 1953-59, Batten, Barton, Durstine & Osborn, N.Y.C., 1959-65; creative dir. Ogilvy & Mather, N.Y.C., 1965-89; pres. Billings S. Fuess Advt., Summit, N.J., 1989—; mem. selection com. N.C. Advt. Hall of Fame award. Author, editor: How to Use the Power of the Printed Word, 1985. Mem. N.Y. Philharmonic Vol. Coun., 1976—. Recipient Grand award Internat. Film and Television Festival N.Y., 1984, Stephen E. Kelly award Mag. Pubs. Assn., N.Y.C., 1983, Gold award Art Dirs. Club N.J., numerous top industry awards; elected to N.C. Advt. Hall of Fame, U. N.C., Chapel Hill, 1995. Mem. Art Dirs. Club of N.J. (bd. trustees 1995—, treas. 1996—). Home: 19 Highland Dr Summit NJ 07901-3108

FUEST, CLEMENS, educator; b. Munster, Germany, Aug. 23, 1968; s. Franz and Francoise Marie (Bideau) F.; m. Ana-Maria Saldarriaga, Aug. 6, 1994; 1 child, Johannes. Diplom.volkswirt, U. Manheim, Germany, 1991; PhD, U. Koln, Germany, 1994. Lectr. U. Cologne, Germany, 1991-95; asst. prof. U. Munich, Germany, 1995—. Recipient Knut Wicksell prize European Pub. Choice Soc., 1998. Mem. Cesifo. Office: U Munich, Ludwigstr 28, D-80539 Munich Germany

FUGATE, CHARLES ROYCE, SR., civil engineer; b. Pomona, Mo., Aug. 13, 1935; s. Charles and Margaret Norene Fugate; m. Rita Sharon Fugate,

July 10, 1965; 1 child, Charles Royce Jr. BS in Civil Engring., U. Kans., 1958. Registered profl. engr., Mo. Various positions Mo. Dept. Transp., Jefferson City, Kansas City, Macon, 1959-90; dist. engr. Mo. Dept. Transp., Willow Springs, 1990-96; divsn. engr. rsch. devel. tech. Mo. Dept. Transp., Jefferson City, 1996—; city adminstr., engr. City of West Plains, Mo., 1996—. Fellow ASCE (sect. pres.); mem. NSPE (past nat. dir.), Mo. Soc. Profl. Engrs. (pres.), Rotary (Macon pres.-elect 1971, Jefferson City West charter sec. 1974, Willow Spring pres. 1994). Republican. Roman Catholic. Avocations: quail hunting, golf. E-mail: fugatr@townsqr.com. Office: City of West Plains 1910 N Holiday Ln West Plains MO 65775-8000

FUGATE, IVAN DEE, banker, lawyer; b. Blackwell, Okla., Dec. 9, 1928; s. Hugh D. and Iva (Holmes) F.; m. Lois Unita Rossow, June 3, 1966; children: Vickie Michelle, Roberta Jeanne, Douglas B., Thomas P. AB, Pittsburg (Kans.) State U., 1949; LLB, U. Denver, 1952, JD, 1970. Bar: Colo. 1952. Exec. sec., mgr. Jr. C. of C. of Denver, 1950-52; also sec. Colo. Jr. C. of C.; individual practice law Denver, 1954—; chmn. bd., pres. Green Mountain Bank, Lakewood, Colo., 1975-82; chmn., pres. Western Nat. Bank Denver (now Vectra Bank of Colorado); chmn. exec. com. North Valley Bank, Thornton, Colo., 1962—, chmn., pres., 1981-2000, chmn., 2000—; founder, chmn. emeritus Ind. State Bank of Colo. (now Bankers Bank of West), 1978—, Ind. Bankers of Colo., 1973—; former bd. dirs. Kit Carson State Bank, Colo.; sec. First Nat. Bank, Burlington, Colo.; owner, farms, ranches, Kans., Colo.; instr. U. Denver Coll. Law, 1955-60; mem. Colo. Treas's. Com. Investment State Funds, 1975—. Treas. to Rep. Assos., Colo., 1959-61, trustee, 1959-64. Maj. USAR, 1952-54. Mem. ABA, Colo. Bar Assn., Denver Bar Assn. (trustee 1962-65), Colo. Bankers Assn. (bd. dirs.), Colo. Cattlemen's Assn., Ind. Bankers Assn. Am. (pres. 1978, adminstrv. com., exec. coun. 1976—, bd. dirs. fed. legis. com., chmn. spl. tax com., instr. One Bank Holding Co. seminars 1976—), Denver Law Club, Petroleum Club, Denver Athletic Club, Lakewood Country Club, Phi Alpha Delta. Methodist. Home: 12015 W 26th Ave Lakewood CO 80215-1110 Office: North Valley Bank Bldg PO Box 29429 9001 Washington St Denver CO 80229-4363

FUGAZY, WILLIAM DENIS, transportation company executive. Grad., Fordham U., Cornell U. Chmn. Fugazy Franchise Internat. Corp., N.Y.C., 1947—. Founder, master-host All-Am. Collegiate Golf Found., chmn. ann. tournament A Day with the All-Ams., Palm Springs, Calif.; founder John V. Mara Meml. Fund for Cancer Rsch. St. Vincent's Hosp., N.Y.C., Cath. Youth Orgn. Summer Camps Program, Silver Shield Found. Scholarship Fund; chmn. Nat. Ethnic Coalition Orgns., N.Y. Yankee Homecoming Dinner, N.Y. Giants Football Luncheon, N.Y. Statue of Liberty Centennial Commn., Ellis Island Medals of Honor Selection Com.; pres. Coalition Italo-Am. Assns.; active Columbus Citizens Com.; apptd. to Westway Commn., Nat. Svcs. Bd. City of N.Y., Mayor's Immigration Coalition, 1997, Westway Commn., Nat Svcs. Bd.; bd. dirs., mem. exec. com. Police Athletic League, Cath. Youth Assn.; bd. instrnl. TV Archdiocese of N.Y.; chmn. The Forum Club, N.Y. State Trooper Found., N.Y. Statue of Liberty Centennial Commn.; named hon. fire commr., N.Y.C.; vice-chmn. U.S. Holocaust Meml. Coun.; hon. chmn. Dr. Martin Luther King Jr. Nat. Holiday Celebration Ambassadorial Reception and Program. Lt. USN, WWII. Decorated knight Equestrian Order Holy Sepulchre, Knight of the Grand Cross; recipient Meritorious award Pres. of Italy; co-recipient Congl. Gold Medal of Honor U.S. Congress, Gold medal Armenian Ch. U.S., 1986, Honor medal; named Sportsman of Yr. Cath. Youth Orgn. of Archdiocese N.Y., N.Y. Athletic Club, B'nai B'rith, 1983, Man of Yr. ITV-TV of Archdiocese N.Y., N.Y.C. Police Dept., 1984, Westchester County, 1985, Archbishop of N.Y., 1986, Angel Guardians, 1988, Italian Welfare League, N.Y. Baseball Fedn., St. Jude's Children's Rsch. Hosp., Disting. Citizen of Yr., N.Y. Conf. Italian-Am. Legislators, 1992, New Yorker of Yr. award Bowling Green Assn., 1993; recipient Congl. Ellis Island Medal of Honor, B'nai B'rith Sportsman of Yr. Citizen's award N.Y. State Br. Sons of Italy, 1983, Man of Yr. award Angel Guardians, 1988, Most Outstanding Role Model award Italian Am. Student Assn., 1989, Humanitarian award Coun. for Unity, N.Y. Industry award St. Mary's Hosp. for Children, 1990, Lifeline award Cooley's Anemia Found., 1991, Edward Corsi award LaGuardia Meml. House, 1992, Tree of Life award Jewish Nat. Fund, 1993, Donald C. Platten award We Care About N.Y., 1994, Humanitarian medal of honor Tara Cir., Inc., 1995; honored Italian Am. Club of No. Westchester, 1988, Cerebral Palsy of Westchester, 1988, Grand Lodge of State of N.Y., 1988, Columbian Lawyers Assn. Nassau County, 1989, Columbus Day Soc. of Harrison (Grand Master Parade), 1989, Ancient Order of Hibernians, 1995, Cath. Mus. Am., 1995, Order of Sons of Italy in Am., 1997, Am. Inst. Stress, 1997; others. Mem. Sons of Italy (co-recipient Citizen's award N.Y. State br. 1983), Coalition of Italo-Am. Assn., Golf Coaches Assn. Am. (hon.), The Forum Club (founder). Office: Fugazy Internat 555 Madison Ave New York NY 10022-3301

FUGGI, GRETCHEN MILLER, education educator; b. Westerly, R.I., Aug. 26, 1938; d. John Louis and Harriet (Scheid) M.; m. William Joseph Fuggi, Aug. 15, 1960; children: Gretchen, Juliann, John, Kristen. BS, So. Conn. State U., 1960, MS, 1969, 6th yr. diploma, 1991, 6th yr. Ednl. Leadership diploma, 1994. Reading cons. Washington Magnet Sch., West Haven, Conn., 1974—; adj. prof. So. Conn. State U., New Haven, 1988—. Pres. Cath. Charity League of Greater New Haven, 1989-90; bd. dirs. New Haven Symphony Aux., 1992—. Named Tchr. of Yr., West Haven Fedn. Tchrs., 1998-99. Mem. AAUP, Internat. Reading Assn., Conn. Reading Assn., Stonington Hist. Soc. of Conn., Delta Kappa Gamma Soc. Internat., Grad. Club New Haven. Roman Catholic. Home: 19 Westview Rd North Haven CT 06473-2013

FUGIEL, FRANK PAUL, insurance company executive; b. Chgo., Aug. 23, 1950; s. Richard A. and Sally (McKinney) F.; m. Nancy Campbell, Sept. 15, 1973; children: Michele, Rachelle. Student, SUNY, Albany. CLU; cert. managed healthcare profl. Individual underwriter Prudential Ins. Co., Merrillville, Ind., 1971-80, group claims mgr., 1980-82, underwriting mgr., 1982-84; group claims officer Employers Health Ins. Co., Green Bay, Wis., 1984-86, underwriting officer, 1986-88, managed care officer, 1988; 2d v.p. individual health ins. Washington Nat. Ins. Co., 1988-90, v.p. ops., 1990; exec. v.p. Oak Brook (Ill.) group divsn. Aegon U.S.A., 1990-94; exec. v.p. TPA divsn. Centennial Life Ins. Co., Merriam, Kans., 1994-95; v.p. managed care adminstrn. United Chambers HealthCare Corp., Naperville, Ill., 1995-96; v.p. bus. devel. Insurers Adminstrv. Corp., Phoenix, 1996—. Councilman Hobart, Ind. C. of C., 1981. Served as sgt. USMC, 1970-76. Fellow Life Office Mgmt. Inst., Acad. Life Underwriting; mem. Internat. Claims Assn. (assoc. life and health claims), Life Underwriting Edn. Com., Inst. Home Office Underwriters. Home: 22255 N 51st St Phoenix AZ 85054-7126 Office: Insurers Adminstrv Corp VP Bus Devel 2101 W Peoria Ave Phoenix AZ 85029-4925

FUGLSANG-FREDERIKSEN, ANDERS, neurophysiologist; b. Lemvig, Denmark, Apr. 4, 1946; s. Victor and Henriette (Petersen) F.-F.; m. Hanne Buch, Jan. 4, 1969; children: Christine, Joachim. MD, U. Copenhagen, 1972, D Med. Scis., 1981. Co-dir. dept. clin. neurophysiology Hvidovre Hosp., U. Copenhagen, 1985-92; dir. dept. clin. neurophysiology Gentofte Hosp., U. Copenhagen, 1992-2000; prof., dir. dept. clin. neurophysiology Århus (Denmark) U. Hosp., 2000—. Author: Electrical Activity and Force During Voluntary Contraction of Normal and Diseased Muscle, 1981; editor jour. Methods in Clin. Neurophysiology, 1990-94; bd. cons. editors Electroenceph. Clin. Neurophysiology, 1993—; mem. editl. bd. Acta Neurological Scandinavica, 1993—; contbr. articles to profl. jours. Recipient award Danish Soc. Against Poliomyelitis, 1982. Mem. Danish Soc. Clin. Neurophysiology (pres. 1988-96).

FUGMANN, NICOLE ELISABETH, English studies scholar; b. Munich, Jan. 26, 1968; arrived in Eng., 1991; BA in English Lit., U. Munich, 1992; MA in English and Comparative Lit., U. East Anglia, Norwich, Eng., 1993; M Studies, Oxford (Eng.) U., 1995. leader rsch. seminar Oxford U., 1996-97, mem. libr. com. Faculty of English, 1997. Mem. Oxford Civil Liberties Soc. Scholar German Acad. Exch. Svc., 1991—, doctoral scholar Oxford (Eng.) U., 1994—, scholar Brit. Acad., 1994—. Mem. MLA. Office: St Hugh's Coll MCR, Oxford OX2 6LE, England

FUGMANN, ROBERT, information scientist, lecturer; b. Moehrenbach, Germany, Jan. 11, 1927; s. Alfred and Elly (Thomas) F.; m. Brigitte Kirchhoff; children: Burkhard, Winfried, Patrizia. PhD in Chemistry, Hamburg (Germany) U., 1951. Rsch. chemist Hoechst AG, Frankfurt am Main, Germany, 1952-59; head scientific info. dept. Hoechstag, Frankfurt am Main, Germany, 1960-87; v.p. Internat. Soc. Knowledge Orgn., Frankfurt am Main, Germany, 1989-98. Author 5 books, including Subject Analysis and Indexing, 1993; contbr. numerous articles to profl. jours. (Best Paper Jour. Am. Soc. Info. Sci., 1985, Herman Skolnik award Am. Chem. Soc., Gmelin-Beilstein-Denkmünze Assn. German Chemists, Ranganathan award Internat. Fedn. Documentation). Mem. Am. Soc. Indexers, Soc. Indexers, Internat. Soc. Knowledge Orgn. Mem. New Apostolic Ch. Avocations: sports, chess. Fax: 49 6126 4366.

FUHLRODT, NORMAN THEODORE, retired insurance executive; b. Wisner, Nebr., Apr. 24, 1910; s. Albert F. and Lena (Schafersman) F.; student Midland Coll., 1926-28; A.B., U. Nebr., 1930; M.A., U. Mich., 1936; m. Clarice W. Livermore, Aug. 23, 1933; 1 son, Douglas B. Tchr., athletic coach high schs., Sargent, Nebr., 1930-32, West Point, Nebr., 1932-35; with Central Life Assurance Co., Des Moines, 1936-74, pres., chief exec. officer, 1964-72, chmn. bd., chief exec. officer, 1972-74, also dir. Named Monroe St. Jour. Alumnus of Month, U. Mich. Grad Sch. Bus. Adminstrn. Gen. chmn. Greater Des Moines United campaign United Community Service, 1969-70. Former bd. dirs. Des Moines Center Sci. and Industry. Fellow Soc. Actuaries. Home: 760 E Bobier Dr # 116B Vista CA 92084-3806

FUHRER, ARTHUR K., lawyer; b. N.Y.C., Oct. 19, 1926; s. Isidore and Toby (Schorr) Fuhrer; m. Lenore R. Lewis; children: Laura A., Robert A., David A. LL.B., Bklyn. Law Sch., 1949; postgrad. NYU Sch. Law, 1951, 52. Bar: N.Y. 1950, U.S. Dist Ct. (so. dist.) N.Y. 1951, U.S. Supreme Ct. 1977. Assoc. firm Sargoy and Stein, N.Y.C., 1951-52, firm Andrew D. Weinberger, N.Y.C., 1952-54; lawyer William Morris Agy., Inc., N.Y.C., 1954-75, v.p., 1975-95; of counsel Frankfurt, Garbus, Klein and Selz, 1995—; co-chmn. Television and Motion Picture Seminar Practicing Law Inst., 1973. Contbr.: Lindey on Entertainment and the Law. Office: Frankfurt Garbus Klein and Selz 488 Madison Ave Fl 9 New York NY 10022-5754

FUHRER, THOMAS, chemist, educator; b. Bern, Switzerland, Aug. 11, 1952; s. Hans and Rosa (Walther) F.; m. Kaethi Rosa Waelti; children: Samuel, Christina, Vera, Bettina. BS, NTA, Burgdorf, Switzerland, 1977. Scientist GRD, Bern, 1977-80; tchr. Gibb, Bern, 1980—. Pres. Ch. Coun., Bern, 1986-94. Home: Marzilistrasse 20, 3005 Bern Switzerland Office: Gibb, Seftigenstr 14, 3007 Bern Switzerland

FUHRER, URS, psychology educator; b. Belp, Switzerland, Dec. 18, 1950; s. Hans and Frieda (Gebhart) F.; m. Therese Schneeberger, Mar. 28, 1981. MD, U. Berne, Switzerland, 1979, PhD, 1982, Pvt. Dozent, 1989. Asst. U. Basel, Switzerland, 1978-81, 82-85; rsch. fellow U. Tuebingen, Germany, 1981-82, U. Calif., Irvine, 1985-86, U. Pitts., 1986-87, U. Freiburg, Germany, 1987-88; asst. prof. U. Berne, 1988-94; prof. U. Magdeburg, Germany, 1994—; sport psychologist Swiss Nat. Ski Team, 1978-82. Author books in field. Avocations: Alphorn and French horn performance. Office: U Magdeburg, Dept Psychology PF 4120, D-39016 Magdeburg Germany

FUHRMAN, DONALD C., systems engineer; b. Northridge, Calif., Aug. 9, 1953; s. John Elmer and Marguerite Louise Fuhrman; m. Linda Sophie Robeck, Mar. 30, 1997. BA, UCLA, 1975; MBA, Pepperdine U., 1998. Designer Spectrolab, Inc., Sylmar, Calif., 1977-82; system mgr. Cadds Svcs., Van Nuys, Calif., 1980-82; engr. Jet Propulsion Lab., Pasadena, 1982-84, system engr., 1988—; pres., owner Bushido Corp., Northridge, 1984-88. Avocations: music, basketball, flying. Home: PO Box 1046 Newburyport MA 01950-6046

FUHRMAN, KENDALL NELSON, software engineer; b. Evansville, Ind., Aug. 1, 1962; s. Ronald Charles and Mildred Elaine (Gulley) F.; m. Susan Ann Bagstad. BS in Computer Sci. and Math., U. Denver, 1984; postgrad., Colo. State U., 1988. Assoc. engr. Am. TV & Communications, Englewood, Colo., 1982-84; mem. tech. staff Hughes Aircraft Corp., Englewood, 1984-85; software engr. Ampex Corp., Golden, Colo., 1985-87, sr. software engr., 1987-88, project leader, 1988-92; project leader Ohmeda, Louisville, Colo., 1992-94; pres. founder Evolving Video Techs., 1994-99; dir. broadcast graphics RTSET, 1999-2000; pres., founder Interact-TVIncorp., 2000—; cons. in field, Arvada, Colo., 1990—. Contbr. articles to profl. jours.; patentee antialising algorithm, graphics rendering. Mem. Assn. for Computing Machinery, IEEE, Spl. Interest Group Graphics, Spl. Interest Group Computer Human Interaction, Phi Beta Kappa. Avocations: skiing, hiking, reading. Office: Evolving Video Tech Corp 8417 Pierson Ct Arvada CO 80005-5238

FUHRMANN, HORST, science administrator; b. Kreuzburg, Germany, June 22, 1926; s. Karl and Susanna F.; m. Ingrid Winkler-Lippoldt, 1954; 2 children. Dr.jur. h.c., U. Tübingen; Dr.phil. h.c., Bologna, Columbia, New York. Collaborator Monumenta Germaniae Historica, 1954-56; asst. Monumenta Germaniae Historica, Rome, 1957, asst., lectr., 1957-62; pres. Monumenta Germaniae Historica, Munich, 1971-94; prof. U. Tübingen, 1962-71, U. Regensburg, 1971-94; pres. Bavarian Acad. Humanities and Sci., Munich, 1992-97. Author: The Donation of Constantine, 1968, Influence and Circulation of the Pseudoisidorian Forgeries (3 vols.), 1972-74, Germany in the High Middle Ages, 1978, From Petrus to John Paul II: The Papacy, 1980, Invitation to the Middle Ages, 1987, Far from Cultured People: An Upper Silesian Town around 1870, 1989, Pour le Mérite: On Making Merit Visible, 1992, Überall ist Mittelalter, 1996, Scholarly Lives, 1996, The Popes, 1998. Recipient Premio Spoleto, 1962, Cultore di Roma, 1981, Upper Silesian Culture prize, 1989, Premio Ascoli Piceno, 1990, Order Pour le Mérite, Grosses Bundesverdienstkreuz mit Stern, Bayerischer Verdienstorden Maximilians Orden. Office: Bavarian Academy of Sciences, Marstallplatz 8, 80539 Munich Germany

FUHS, G(EORG) WOLFGANG, environmental research manager; b. Cologne, Germany, May 19, 1932; came to U.S., 1964; s. Friedrich Karl and Lisette I. (Stayen) F.; children: Lisette Fuhs Mallary, H. Georg, Dagmar Ariane Serota. Diploma in biology, D in Nat. Scis., U. Bonn, Germany, 1956; postdoctoral, Tech. U. Delft, The Netherlands, 1956-57. Sci. employee dept. botany U. Frankfurt, Germany, 1957-58; research assoc. dept. hygiene U. Bonn Sch. Medicine, 1958-63; fellow dept. genetics U. Cologne, 1963-64; sr., prin. research scientist div. labs. and research N.Y. State Dept. Health, Albany, 1964-72, dir. environ. health labs., 1973-85; chief div. labs. Calif. Dept. Health Services, Berkeley, 1985-89; rsch. scientist Calif./EPA Dept. Toxic Substances Control Lab., Berkeley, 1989-93, mgr. technology evaluation, 1993—; vis. prof. U. Wis., Milw., 1973; rsch. assoc. U. Minn. Sch. Pub. Health, Mpls., 1970-74; adj. prof. dept. biology SUNY, Albany, 1984-86; mem. explt. com. on human health effects of Great Lakes water quality U.S./Can. Internat. Joint Commn., 1978-88; tech. adv. com. San Francisco Estuary Project, 1987-92; mem. Calif. Environ. Technol. Partnership, Calif. Comparative Risk Project, 1993-94. Contbr. articles to profl. jours. (Inst. Sci. Info. award 1969); mem. editorial bd. Jour. Phycology, 1972-74, Limnology and Oceanography, 1973-76, Microbial Ecology, 1974-89. Mem. AAAS, Am. Soc. Microbiol. (past chmn. Eastern N.Y. br.), Internat. Assn. Theoretical Applied Limnology. Office: Calif EPA Dept Toxic Substances Control Lab 2151 Berkeley Way Berkeley CA 94704-1011

FUIA, STELIAN, business executive; b. Bucharest, Romania, Jan. 1, 1968; s. Gheorghe and Vasilica Fuia. Degree in agrl. scis., U. Bucharest, 1993; PhD in Mktg. and Mgmt. in Agr., U. Agrl. Scis., Bucharest, 1999; EMBA, Princeton U., 1999. Mktg. supr. AgrEvo GmbH, Bucharest, 1994-95; salesperson Monsanto Romania SRL, Bucharest, 1995-96; bus. mgr. for Ctrl. Europe Monsanto Europe SA, Brussels, 1996-99; comml. dir. Monsanto Romania SRL, Bucharest, 1999—. E-mail: stelian.fuia@monsanto.com. Office: Monsanto Romania SRL, Pictor Barbu Iscovescu 13, Bucharest Romania

FUJIEDA, KENJI, pediatrician, educator; b. Sapporo, Hokkaido, Japan, Mar. 29, 1947; s. Tadashi and Fumi (Iiyama) F.; m. Mihoko Koike, June 13, 1976; children: Yuichiro, Satoko, Michiko. MD, Hokkaido U., 1971, PhD, 1976. Clin. fellow Hokkaido U. Hosp., Sapporo, Japan, 1971-72, 76-77; rsch. fellow Children's Hosp. Winnipeg, Man., Can., 1977-80; vis. fellow NIH, Bethesda, Md., 1980-81; lectr. Hokkaido U., Sapporo, 1983-91, asst. prof., 1991—; dir. pediat. and endocrinology dept. Hokkaido U. Hosp., 1983—; bd. dirs. Japanese Pediat. Endocrine Soc.; internat. cons. endocrinologist, 1996. Editor-in-chief Clin. Pediat. Endocrinology, 1998. Recipient Novo Nordisk Growth award Novo Nordisk Pharm., 1996. Mem. Endocrine Soc., Am. Diabetes Soc. Avocations: golf, tennis, skiing, photography. Home: S-8 W-13 Chuo-ku, Hokkaido Sapporo 064-0808, Japan Office: Dept Pediatrics, Hokkaido Univ N-15 W-7, Hokkaido Sapporo 060-8638, Japan

FUJII, HIDEAKI, economist; b. Toyokawa, Japan, July 16, 1961; s. Akira and Kochiyo F.; m. Yuko Muramatsu, Nov. 8, 1987; children: Harunori, Momoko, Hisako, Hiromichi. BA, Waseda U., 1985; MA, Aoyamagakuin U., 1995; postgrad., Kyoto U., 1996-98. Economist Mitsubishi Bank, Tokyo, 1985-89, Japan Rsch. Inst., Ltd., Tokyo, 1989-93; sr. economist Inst. Energy Econs., Tokyo, 1993-97, Mitsubishi Rsch. Inst., Tokyo, 1997—; economist Japan Ctr. Econ. Rsch., Tokyo, 1990-91; lectr. Meikai U., Urayasu, Japan, 1997—, Daito Bunka U., Tokyo, 2000—. Author: Energy Watchers, 1997; contbr. articles to profl. jours. Home: 1-6-13-608 Tate, 353-0006 Shiki Saitama, Japan Office: Mitsubishi Rsch Inst Inc, 3-6 Otemachi 2-chome, Chiyoda-ku Tokyo 100-8141, Japan

FUJII, HIRONORI ALIGA, aerospace engineer, educator; b. Himeji, Hyogo, Japan, Apr. 6, 1944; s. Tokuichi and Chizuko (Ariga) F.; m. Naomi Matsumoto, Dec. 24, 1985; 1 child, Tomonori Fujii. M Engring., Kyoto (Japan) U., 1969, D Engring., 1975. Asst. prof., assoc., then prof. Tokyo Met. Coll. Tech., 1972-86; prof., chmn. dept. aero. engring. Tokyo Met. Inst. Tech., 1986—; adv. bd. Tokyo Met. Govt., 1991—; chmn. Japan Rsch. Group on Control of Space Structures, 1985—, Working Group for Space Robot Forum, Tokyo, 1988-90; mem. Com. for Utilization of Tokyo Area, 1991—. Author: Handbook of Aerospace Engineering, 1992; contbr. articles to profl. publs. Recipient Best Paper award Japan Soc. for Aero. and Space Scis., 1994. Mem. Japan Soc. Japanese Chess. Achievements include research on mechanics in control analysis with application to aerospace engineering. Home: 1-24-9, Lamiere Fussa 409, Musashinodai, Fussa, Tokyo 197-0013, Japan Office: Tokyo Met Inst Tech, 6-6 Asahigaoka, Hino Tokyo 191-0065, Japan

FUJII, MINORU, physicist, researcher; b. Kobe, Japan, Mar. 29, 1965; s. Tadashi and Kayoko (Syundo) F.; m. Shima Imayanagida, Aug. 1, 1989; children: Ayako, Hiroshi. BEng, Kobe (Japan) U., 1987, MEng, 1989, DSc, 1992. With Matsushita Elec. Indsl. Corp., Kadoma, Japan, 1992-94; rsch. assoc. Grad. Sch. Sci. and Tech. Kobe U., 1995-97, rsch. assoc. Faculty of Engring.,, 1997—. Contbr. articles to sci. jours. Recipient Young Author Best Paper award 20th Internat. Conf. on Physics of Semiconductors, Greece, 1990. Avocations: gardening, tennis, speed skating. Fax: 81-78-803-6081. Home: Katsuragi 1-8-45, Hyogo Kobe 651-1223, Japan Office: Kobe U Dept EE Engring, Rokkodai Nada, Kobe 657-8501, Japan

FUJII, SATOSHI, cardiology educator, researcher; b. Kitami, Hokkaido, Japan, Apr. 27, 1956; s. Tokuji and Etsuko (Shimizu) F.; m. Hitomi Fukushima, Oct. 3, 1981; children: Satomi, Michiko, Mariko. MD, Hokkaido U., Sapporo, 1981, PhD, 1987. Cert. cardiologist, Japan. Physician Hokkaido U. Hosp., 1981-87; asst. prof. Washington U., St. Louis, 1988-94; assoc. prof., dir. vascular biology U. Vt., Burlington, 1994-96; asst. prof. cardiology Hokkaido U., 1996-99, assoc. prof., 1999—, dir. rsch. in cariology, 1996—. Grantee Naito Found., Tokyo, 1987, Internat. Soc. Fibrinolysis, Denmark, 1992. Fellow Am. Coll. Cardiology; mem. Am. Heart Assn. (fellow coun. circulation). Mem. Sapporo Ch. of Nazarene. Avocations: skiing, swimming, foreign languages. Office: Hokkaido U Cardiol Dept, N15 W7 Kitaku, Sapporo 060-8638, Japan

FUJII, SHINGO, obstetrician, gynecologist, medical educator; b. Fukuyama, Hiroshima, Japan, Oct. 4, 1944; s. Yoshio and Takako (Kodama) F.; m. Yuko Kamoi, Feb. 28, 1976; children: Hiroko, Teruko. MD, Kyoto (Japan) U., 1971, PhD, 1981. Dir. dept. ob-gyn. Ise (Japan) Gen. Hosp., 1974-77; assoc. dept. ob-gyn. Kyoto U., 1978-80, asst. prof. dept. ob-gyn., 1980-85, assoc. prof. dept. ob-gyn., 1985-91; prof., chmn. dept. ob-gyn. Shinshu U., Matsumoto, Japan, 1991-97; prof. chmn. dept. ob-gyn. Kyoto U., Japan, 1997—, dir. dept. ob-gyn., 1997—; dir. divsn. gynecol. oncology, Kyoto U. Hosp., 1981-91, 97—; dir. dept. ob-gyn. Shinshu U. Hosp., Matsumoto, 1991-97. Author: Textbook of Uncommon Cancer, 1988; contbr. rsch. articles to profl. jours. Johns Hopkins U. fellow, Balt., 1986; Japan Ministry of Edn. grantee, 1987, 90, 93. Mem. Japan Soc. Ob-Gyn. (councilor), Internat. Gynecol. Cancer Soc., The Howard A. Kelly Gynecol. and Obstet. Soc. Fax: 81-75-751-3247. Office: Kyoto U Dept Gyn-Ob Faculty Medicine, 54 Kawahara-cho Shogoin Sakyo-ku, Kyoto 606-8507, Japan

FUJII, TAKASHI, neurosurgeon; b. Numata, Japan, July 23, 1947; s. Sumio and Tokie F.; m. Yuko Hayakawa; three children. MD, Shinsyu U., 1973; DSc, Gunma U., 1982. Resident Gunma U., Maebashi, Japan, 1973-75; neurosurgeon Kumagaya Gen. Hosp., Japan, 1975-76; asst. Gunma U., 1976-77; neurosurgeon Saitama Cancer Ctr., Inamachi, Japan, 1977-80; asst., lectr. Gunma U., 1980-89; chief exec. Fujii Neurosurg. Hosp., Kawachimachi, Japan, 1989—. Office: Fujii Neurosurg Hosp, 461 Nakaokamoto, Kawachi 329-1105, Japan

FUJII, TOSHIHIRO, chemistry educator, researcher; b. Kamakura, Kanagawa, Japan, Jan. 6, 1942; s. Inaho and Sadako (Tominaga) F.; m. Machiko Ishikawa, Dec. 15, 1969; children: Yoko Isao, Keiko, Masayoshi. BSc, Kyoto (Japan) U., 1964, MSc, 1966, PhD, 1974. Rsch. scientist JEOL, Japan, 1966-74; rsch. scientist NIES, Japan, 1974-89, leader, 1989-95, dep. dir., 1995—; invited prof. Ecole Normale Superieure, France, 1996; vis. prof. Tsukuba (Japan) U., 1990—. Author books, articles, procs.; patentee in field. Recipient award for remarkable invention Sci. and Tech. Agy., Japanese Govt., 1988. Mem. Mass Spectrometry Soc. Japan (exec.). Zen. Home: Gonokami 1-10-12, Hamura, Tokyo 205-0011, Japan Office: Nat Inst Environ Studies, Onogawa 16-2, Tsukuba, Ibaraki 305-0053, Japan

FUJII, TOSHIO, electrical engineering educator; b. Tokyo, Apr. 6, 1920; s. Takao and Yoshiko (Katsura) F.; m. Noriko Ohnuma, May 21, 1950; children: Soichi, Yasuko. BEng, Tokyo U., 1944, DEng, 1977. Design engr. Hitachi (Japan), 1944-60, sect. chief, 1960-68, div. mgr., 1968-72; asst. prof. elec. engring. Kyushu-Sangyo U., Fukuoka, Japan, 1972-77, prof., 1977-94; prof. emeritus, 1995—; cons. Ryobi, Fuchu, Japan, 1973-87, 94-99, Hitachi Koki, Katta, Japan, 1989—; vis. prof. Ehime U., Matsuyama, Japan, 1979-86. Patentee in noise suppression field; rsch. in universal motors. Mem. IEEE (life sr.), Inst. Elec. Engrs., Mito Golf Club (Ibaragi, Japan), Makalei Hawaii Country Club, Hatano Country Club (Kanagawa, Japan). Avocations: golf, classical music.

FUJIKI, NORIO, medical educator; b. Kobe, Hyogo, Japan, Nov. 17, 1928; s. Tokichi and Makiko (Kato) F.; m. Kazuko Tanaka, Oct. 30, 1955; children: Hidenori, Kuninori, Masanori. MD, Kyoto Prefectural U. Medicine, Japan, 1952, PhD, 1956. Lic., Nat. Bd. Med. Exam. Instr. dept. internal medicine Kyoto Prefectural U. Medicine, 1953-67, asst. prof., 1967-70, head divsn. hematology-genetics and genetic counseling unit, 1967-70, assoc. prof., 1970-72; head dept. genetics Inst. for Devel. Rsch., Aichi Prefectural Colony for Mentally-Physically Handicapped, Nagoya, Japan, 1972-81; prof. dept. internal medicine and med. genetics Fukui Med. Sch., Matsuokacho, Japan, 1981-94; prof., head dept. internal medicine and med. genetics Univ Hosp., Matsuokacho, Japan, 1983-94; med. advisor Gene Analysis Lab. TOYOBO, Tsuruga, Japan, 1994—; prof. emeritus Fukui Med. Sch., 1994—; clin. fellow M.D. Anderson Hosp. and Tumor Inst., U. Tex. Houston, 1956; rsch. assoc. dept. human genetics U. Mich., Ann Arbor, 1957; mem. expert adv. panel on human genetics WHO, Geneva, 1978—; v.p. internat. bioethics com. UNESCO, Paris, 1993-98; pres. Internat. Bioethics Seminar, Fukui, 1987, 90, 92, 93, 95, 97, 2000; advisor on med. genetics Japan Internat. Coop. Agy., Tokyo, 1988—; sec. gen. UNESCO Asian Bioethics Conf., 1997; vis. prof. U. of the Air, 1998—. Contbg. editor Bull. New Hematology, 1978, 90, Introduction to Medical Genetics, 1988, Human Dignity and Medicine, 1988, Isolation, Migration and Health, 1991, Medical Genetics and Society, 1991, Human Genome Research and Society, 1993, Intractable Neurol. Disorders, Human Genome Research and Society, 1994, Illustrated Medical Genetics, 1995, Protection of the Human Genome and Scientific Responsibility, 1996, UNESCO Asian Bioethics, 1998. Counsellor Fukui Prefectural Life Acad.,

1983-85; v.p. Fukui Prefectural Com. on Internat. Exch., 1985-88; chmn. Indo-Japanese Workshop on Med. Genetics, Lucknow, India, 1992. Grantee USPHS, Nat. Inst. Gen. Med. Sci., 1962-67; recipient Nat. Order of Merit, Pres. of France, 1982, Order of Arts and Lit., French Minister of Culture, 1993; named Man of the Yr. Am. Biog. Inst., 1995. Mem. Internat. Human Genome Orgn., Nat. Acad. Medicine (Paris, fgn. corr.), Japanese Soc. Human Genetics (bd. dirs., pres. mem. subcom. on genetic counselling 1974, 84, 94, 96, 98, hon. mem.), Internat. Assn. Human Biologists (pres. 1988-93), Mouvement Universale de la Responabilite Scientifique (sec. gen. Japan br.), Japan Paper Acad. (bd. dirs.), Order of Internat. Fellowship, ABIRA (dep. gov.). Avocations: handmade paper, Japanese Haiku, Noh, Utai. Home: 1009 Nakano 2 Chome, Fukui 918-8186, Japan Office: Fukui Med Univ Sch Medicine, Shimoaizuki, Matsuokacho Fukui 910-1193, Japan also: Gene Analysis Lab, Toyobo, Tsuruga 914-0047, Japan

FUJIMORI, KATSUYA, physician, researcher; b. Kanai-Machi, Japan, Aug. 18, 1960; s. Katsutoshi and Kazue (Yasuda) F.; m. Junko Sugawara, Dec. 4, 1988; children: Hiroki, Daichi, Shoya, Tomoya. MD, Jichi Med. Sch., Tochigi, Japan, 1985; PhD, Niigata (Japan) U., 1996. Clin. fellow Niigata U. Sch. Medicine, 1986—. Contbr. articles to med. jours., including Neurology, Endocrine Jour., Internat. Jour. Radiation Oncology, Chest, Respiratory Medicine, Allergology Internat., others. Mem. Japanese Soc. Internal Medicine, Japanese Soc. Allergology, Japanese Soc. Chest Diseases. Avocations: skiing, playing tennis. Office: Niigata Prefectural Shibata, Hosp, Ohte-cho 4-5-48, Shibata 957, Japan

FUJIMORI FUJIMORI, ALBERTO KENYO, president of Peru; b. Lima, Peru, July 28, 1938; s. Naochi and Matsue Fujimori; m. Susana Higuchi, 1974; children: Keiko Sofia, Hiro Alberto, Sachi Marcela, Kenji Gerardo. Grad. engr. in agronomy, La Molina, 1961; MA in Math., U. Wis., 1969; D honoris causa, U. Glebloux, Belgium, U. San Martin de Porres, Lima. Instr. math., later chmn. dept. La Molina (Agrarian Nat. U.), from 1962, dean Faculty Scis., 1984, prin., 1984-89; pres. Nat. Coun. Prins. of Peruvian U., 1987-89; co-founder Ind. Polit. Movement Cambio 90, 1988; pres. Govt. of Peru, Lima, 1990—. Roman Catholic. Address: Office of the Pres, Palacio de Gobernio Plaza de Armas s/n, Lima 1, Peru*

FUJIMOTO, JUNICHIRO, pathologist; b. Osaka, Japan, May 25, 1951. MD in Medicine, Gifu (Japan) U., 1977; PhD in Medicine, Sapporo U., Hokkaido, Japan, 1984. Sr. investigator dept. pathology Nat. Children's Med. Rsch. Ctr., Tokyo, 1985-89, dir. dept. pathology, 1989—. Avocation: driving. Fax: 81-3-3487-9669. E-mail: jfujimoto@nch.go.jp. Office: Nat Children's Med Rsch Ctr, 3-35-31 Taishido, Setagaya Tokyo 154-8509, Japan

FUJIMOTO, KOJI, linguistic researcher, educator; b. Osaka City, Japan, Aug. 20, 1969; s. Kaoru and Yukiko (Hashimoto) F.; m. Yasuko Higashi, May 11, 1996. BA, Kyoto U. Fgn. Studies, 1992, MA, 1995. Cert. in tchg. English. Instr. Nishiyamato Gakuen H.S., Nara, Japan, 1996-98, Hakuho Women's Coll., Nara, 1998—. Co-author: A Comprehensive Guide to Contemporary English Usage and Abusage, 1997, Studies in English Linguistics, 1997, A Dictionary of Technical Terms of English Linguistics, 1999, Nishiyamato English Studies, 1999, Introduction to International Human Studies, 2000, All Japan Universities' English Entrance Examinations Analysis, 2000. Morita scholar, 1993. Mem. English Lit. Soc. Japan, English Linguistics Soc. Japan, Linguistics Soc. Japan, Soc. English Grammar and Usage. Avocations: swimming, driving, gym-training. Home: 925-36 Shimomaki, Kanmaki-cho, Kitakatsuragi, 639-0205 Nara Japan Office: Hakuho Women's Coll, 1-7-17 Katsushimo, Oji-cho, Kitakatsuragi, Nara 636-0011, Japan

FUJIMOTO, MASATOSHI, physicist, researcher; b. Hirao Town, Yamaguchi, Japan, Mar. 17, 1973; s. Masanori and Aoi (Nishioka) F. BS, Kyoto (Japan) U., 1995, MS, 1997. Physicist Hamamatsu Photonics K.K., Hamakita City, Japan, 1997—. Contbr. article to Optics Letters. Avocations: glassmaking, motorcycling, table tennis, physics. Office: Hamamatsu Photonics KK Ctrl, Rsch Lab, 5000 Hirakuchi, Shizuoka Hamakita City 434-8601, Japan

FUJINO, KAZUO, marine geneticist; b. Tokyo, Sept. 22, 1925; s. Gen-ichi and Yaeko (Kunogi) F.; m. Junko Suzuki, Nov. 28, 1955; children: Tetsuya, Yoko. Bachelor's degree, U. Tokyo, 1950, PhD, 1962. Rsch. worker The Whales Rsch. Inst., Tokyo, 1950-64; program chief U.S. Dept. of Interior, Dept. Commerce, Honolulu, 1964-71; affiliate faculty U. Hawaii, Honolulu, 1965-71; prof. Kitasato U., Sanriku, Japan, 1972-91; dean Kitasato U., Sanriku, 1982-86; prof. emeritus Kitasato U., Tokyo, 1991—; coun. mem. Sci. Coun. of Japan, Tokyo, 1976-88. Contbr.: Population Genetic Studies on Marine Fish - Seeking Way to Explore New Order in International Fisheries, 1999; contbr. over 100 scientific articles to rsch. jours. and conf. procs. Councilor for revitalizing regional activities City of Minamata, Kumamoto, Japan, 1996—. Mem. Japanese Soc. Fisheries Sci. (regional dir. 1980-82), Soc. Fish Genetics and Breeding Sci. (hon. mem., pres. 1980-90), Japanese Soc. for Marine Biotech (coun. mem.). Avocations: Go. Home: 2-28-22 Shakujiidai Nerima, 177-0045 Tokyo Japan Office: Japanese Soc Marine Biotech, 3-18-6 Toranomon Minato, 105 Tokyo Japan

FUJINO, MASAKO, pharmacologist; b. Sapporo, Hokkaido, Japan, Aug. 6, 1958; d. Masahiro and Sumiko) F. MD, Hokkaido U., 1989; PhD, Sapporo Med. U., 1999. Postgrad. fellow Sapporo Med. U., 1989-97; rschr. Sapporo Rsch. Inst., 1997—; lectr. in field. Contbr. articles to profl. jours. Mem. Japan Pharmacol. Soc., Am. Fedn. Astrologers (life), Astron. Soc. Japan (spl. mem.), Youth Hostel (life), Smithsonian Assoc., Planetary Soc. Avocations: astronomy, astrology, travel. Phone: 81-11-588-2082. Home: Izumi-cho 1-1-6 Makomanai, Minami-ku Sapporo 005, Japan Office: Sapporo Rsch Inst Muscle Sc, 1-1-6 Izumi-cho Makamanai, Sapporo 005, Japan

FUJINO, MASAYUKI ALOIS, gastroenterologist; b. Tokyo, Nov. 28, 1937; s. Taketaro and Haru (Ohki) F.; m. Kazuko F. Kobayashi, Apr. 22, 1967; children: Marie A., Takayuki G., Toshiyuki S., Megumi T. MD, U. Tokyo, 1963, PhD, 1979. Med. diploma, Min. of Health and Welfare, Japan. Intern Tokyo U. Hosp., 1963-64; rsch. assoc. gastrointestinal unit 1st dept. medicine U. Tokyo Faculty Medicine, 1964-80; assoc. prof. Yamanashi (Japan) Med. U., 1980-92, prof. medicine, chmn. 1st dept. medicine, 1992—; vis. prof. faculty of medicine U. Tokyo, 1980-92; vis. prof. UCLA Sch. Medicine, 1998; trustee Found. for Promotion and Rsch. in Endoscopy, Tokyo, 1985—; chmn. com. colorectal cancer Coun. for Mass Screening in Yamanashi Prefecture, Kofu, 1989—. Editor: Illustrated Medical Pathophysiology, Vols. 4 and 5: Alimentary Tract, 1995, Stomach & Intestine Handbook, 1993, (periodical) Digestive Endoscopy, 1989—; editor-in-chief: (periodical) Endoscopic Forum for Digestive Disease, 1985—. Named 3d Francisco J. Roman Meml. lectr. Philippine Soc. of Gastrointestinal Endoscopy, Manila, 1987. Mem. Japan Gastroenterol. Endoscopy Soc. (councillor 1977—), Japanese Soc. Gastroenterology (councilor 1986—), Italian Soc. Gastroenterology, Am. Soc. for Gastrointestinal Endoscopy, Am. Gastroenterol. Assn., Yamanashi Acad. Scis. Roman Catholic. Avocations: classical music, swimming, ice skating, wine tasting. Home: 3-27-A-301 Nakadai, Itabashi Tokyo 174-0064, Japan Office: Yamanashi Med U 1st Dpt Med, 1110 Shimokato Tamaho, Yamanashi Nakakoma 409-3898, Japan

FUJINO, TAKEO, solid state chemistry educator; b. Fukuoka, Japan, Apr. 11, 1937; s. Takenori and Mieko (Saigusa) F.; m. Kiyoi Naruse, Oct. 29, 1967; 2 children. BS, U. Tokyo, 1960, D Sci., 1975. Rschr. Japan Atomic Energy Rsch. Inst., 1960-75, vice chief rschr., 1975-80, head nuclear fuel chemistry lab., 1979-89, chief rschr., 1980-89; vis. scientist Argonne Nat. Lab., 1982-83; prof. Inst. Adv. Materials Processing, Tohoku U., 1990—; adv. editl. bd. Jour. Nuclear Materials, Amsterdam, 1987—. Avocations: the game of go, walkng, painting. Office: Inst Adv Materials Proc, Tohoku U 2-1-1 Katahira, 980-8577 Sendai Japan

FUJINOKI, AKIRA, chemist, laboratory manager; b. Sumida-ku, Tokyo, Nov. 29, 1955; s. Nenomatsu and Miyoko (Ishii) F.; m. Fusako Kubota, Oct. 4, 1981; 2 children. BS, Tokyo U., 1979. Rschr. Shin-Etsu Chem., Isobe, Japan, 1979-80; engr. Shin-Etsu Quartz Hdqrs., Tokyo, 1981-82, Shin-Etsu Takefu (Japan) Plant, 1983-86; lab. mgr. Shin-Etsu Quartz Lab., Fukushima, Japan, 1987—. Contbr. articles to profl. jours. Mem. Japan Soc. Applied Physics. Avocations: fishing, painting. Home: 1-6-12 Midorigaoka-Nishi, Koriyama Fukushima 963-0701, Japan Office: Shin-Etsu Quarz Products, 88 Kanaya Kawakubo Tamura, Koriyama Fukushima 963-0725, Japan

FUJIO, HIRONOBU, internist, philosophy researcher; b. Fukuoka, Japan, Aug. 15, 1959; s. Kazuo Fujio and Shizuko (Tajiri) F.; m. Mayumi Yoshimoto, May 6, 1985; children: Tetsuya, Haruka. MB, Yamaguchi U., Ube, Japan, 1985; Cert. of Space Sci., Internat. Space U., Kitakyushu, Japan, 1992; PhD, U. Occupational/Environ Health, Kitakyushu, 1993. Extern Kyushu U. Hosp., Fukuoka, Japan, 1985-87; rschr. Inst. Oriental Philosophy, Tokyo, 1987-89; chief of medicine Kokura Nakai Hosp., Kitakyushu, 1993-96; pres. Inst. Human Cosmology, Kitakyushu, 1996—; cons. physician Soka Gakkai, Tokyo, 1990-96, Kawachi Mental Hosp., Kitakyushu, 1990-96; lectr. Nishinippon Nurses Sch., Kitakyushu, 1990—, Japan HIV Ctr., Kyushu, 1994; organizer Symposia on Brain Death, Fukuoka, 1991; vol. physician Hanshin earthquake disaster area, 1995. Co-author: Space Solar Program, 1992; author articles. Recipient Kin-Ho prize Soka Gakkai Internat., 1994. Mem. Japanese Soc. Psychosomatic Medicine, Kitakyushi Young Drs. Assn. (exec.), Japan Rescue Support Bike Network (exec.). Buddhist. Avocations: playing the horn in amateur orchestra, swimming. Home: 1-13-27 Izumigaura, Kitakyushu 807-0854, Japan Office: Inst Human Cosmology, 11-2-102 Kinkeicho, Kitakyushu 803-0843, Japan

FUJIOKA, MANABU, nuclear physics researcher and educator; b. Tokyo, June 4, 1936; s. Masataka and Fuji (Aoki) F.; m. Rutsuko Ohno (dec. Apr. 1990); children: Junko, Reiko, Aiko. BSc, U. Tokyo, 1960, MSc, 1962, DSc, 1971. Rsch. assoc. Tokyo Inst. Tech., 1962-73; assoc. prof. Tohoku U., Sendai, Japan, 1973-77, prof., 1977-2000; prof. emeritus Tohoku U., Sendai, 2000—; head accelerator divsn. in charge of a cyclotron Tohoku U., Sendai, Japan, 1977-2000; lectr. Hirosaki (Japan) U., 1982-99; mem. steering com. Kyoto U. Reactor Inst., Osaka, 1985-87; chmn., editor procs. 12th Internat. Conf. on Electromagnetic Isotope Separators, 1991; chmn. 5th Internat. Workshop on Ion Guide Isotope Separators On-Line, 1994. Mem. Phys. Soc. Japan, Inst. Phys. and Chem. Rsch. (mem. non-nuc. program adv. com. 1987-2000). Home: Yagiyama Kasumi-cho 10-10, Taihaku-ku Sendai 982-0831, Japan Office: Tohoku U Cyclotron & RI Ctr, Aramaki-Aoba, Sendai 980-8578, Japan

FUJIOKA, MASAKI, plastic surgeon; b. Shimonoseki City, Yamaguchi, Japan, Jan. 5, 1961; s. Kazuo and Mieko (Kameoka) F.; m. Ruriko Fujioka, May 20, 1980. MD, Nagasaki (Japan) U., 1997. Gen. physician Nishiki (Japan) Ctrl. Hosp., 1987-90; staff surgeon Yamaguchi Ctrl. Hosp., Houfu, Japan, 1990-91, 94-95; chief med. office Mishima Med. Office, Hagi, Japan, 1991-94; assoc. prof. Nagasaki U. Medicine, 1995-98; chief dept. plastic surgery Miyazaki (Japan) Social Ins. Hosp., 1998—. Contbr. articles to profl. jours. Recipient awards of rsch. encouragement Japan Cmty. Medicine Promotion Assn., 1989, 95. Mem. Japan Soc. Plastic and Reconstructive Surgery, Japanese Soc. for Burn Injuries, Hagi Rugby Football Club. Avocations: rugby football, jogging, drawing, reading. Office: Miyazaki Social Ins Hosp, Ohtsubo Nisi 1-2-1, Miyazaki City Japan

FUJIOKA, MASAYUKI, neurosurgeon, neuroscientist; b. Toyonaka, Japan, Nov. 9, 1963; s. Susumu and Toshiko F. Physician dept. neurosurgery Nara (Japan) Med. U., 1990-92, Osaka (Japan) Minami Hosp., 1992-93; chief dr. Nara Med. U., 1993-94; physician Osaka Police Hosp., 1994-95; assoc. dir. NaraPrefectural Hosp., 1995-96, Nara Emergency and Critical Med. Ctr., 1996-99, Neurosci. Inst., The Queen's Med. Ctr., Honolulu, 1999—. Contbr. articles to profl. jours. Mem. AAAS, Am. Heart Assn., N.Y. Acad. Scis., Internat. Soc. Neuroemergency, Internat. Stroke Soc. Avocations: travel, reading, movies, baseball, guitar. Office: Queen's Med Ctr UH Twr 8th Fl 1356 Lusitana St Honolulu HI 96813-2421

FUJIOKA, TOMOAKI, urologist; b. Morioka, Iwate, Japan, Nov. 12, 1948; s. Shinpei and Kimi (Murai) F.; m. Naoko Murata; children: Yasuko, Yoko, Yuko. MD, Iwate Med. U., Morioka, 1974. Resident St. Luke's Internat. Hosp., Tokyo, 1974-80; rsch. fellow UCLA Med. Ctr., L.A., 1980-81; with Fukushima Workmen's Hosp., Iwaki, Japan, 1982-84; asst. prof. Sch. Medicine Urology Iwate Med. U., 1986-88, assoc. prof. Sch. Medicine Urology, 1989-96, prof. Sch. Medicine Urology, 1996—. Mem. Am. Urol. Assn. (corr.), Am. Assn. Cancer Rsch. (corr.), Internat. Coll. Surgeons, Internat. Soc. Urology. Avocations: fishing, hunting, golf. Home: 11-11 Atago Cho, Morioka 020, Japan Office: Iwate Med U Sch Medicine, Dept Urology 19-1 Uchimaru, Morioka 020, Japan

FUJIOKA, YUICHI, chemical engineer; b. Kitakyushu, Fukuoka, Japan, Oct. 30, 1953; s. Mitsuo and Shigeko (Youda) F.; m. Toshiko Takimoto, Jan. 17, 1955; children: Kanako, Machiko. BA, U. Tokyo, 1976, M.Engring., 1978, Dr.Engring., 1997. Rschr. Mitsubishi Heavy Industries Ltd., Nagasaki, 1978-96; mgr. chem. lab. Nagasaki R&D Ctr., 1996—. Author: Fluidization, 1995. Avocation: golf. Office: Mitsubishi Heavy Ind Ltd, Nagasak R&D Ctr 5-717-1, Nagasaki 851-0392, Japan

FUJISAKI, HARUO, physicist; b. Kochi, Japan, Jan. 19, 1941. BS in Physics, U. Tokyo, 1965, MS in Physics, 1967, PhD in Physics, 1970. Lectr. in Physics Rikkyo U., Tokyo, Japan, 1970-72; assoc. prof. in Physics Rikkyo U., 1973-82, prof., 1983—; chmn. Dept. Physics, Rikkyo U., 1979; chmn. Grad. Sch. Physics, Rikkyo U., 1993, 95. Contbr. articles to profl. jours. Mem. Nature Conservation Soc. Japan. Recipient Matsunaga Sci. Found. fellowship, 1975. Mem. Physical Soc. Japan, U. Alumni Japan. Office: Rikkyo U, Nishi Ikebukuro 3 34 1, Toshima ku Tokyo 1718501, Japan

FUJISAKI, HIROYA, communications educator; b. Narita, Chiba, Japan, Oct. 18, 1930; s. Kohbun and Hoh (Sekigawa) F.; m. Nobuko Kajikawa, May 28, 1972; children: Kimisato, Toyokatsu. BS, U. Tokyo, 1954, Dr.Eng., 1962; SM, MIT, 1959, EE, 1961. Fulbright scholar MIT, Cambridge, 1958-61; prof. U. Tokyo, 1962-91, prof. emeritus, 1991—; prof. Sci. U. of Tokyo, 1991—; vis. prof. U. Tex., Austin, 1980, Royal Inst. Tech., Stockholm, 1981, U. Goettingen, 1981, Nanjing U., 1985, 86; guest prof. U. Sci. and Tech. of China, Hefei Anhui, China, 1987—; mem. permanent coun. Orgn. of Internat. Congresses of Phonetic Scis., 1979—; gen. chmn. Internat. Conf. on Acoustics, Speech and Signal Processing, Tokyo, 1986; founder chmn. Internat. Conf. on Spoken Lang. Processing, Kobe, Japan, 1990; chmn. joint meeting Acoustical Soc. Am. and Acoustical Soc. Japan, Honolulu, 1988; chmn. Internat. Symposium on Spoken Dialogue, Phila., 1996, Sydney, 1998, Beijing, 2000; co-chmn. Internat. Conf. on Signal Processing, Beijing, 1990, 93, 96, 98, 2000. Author: Speech Science, 1972, Speech Information Processing, 1973, Structure and Process in Speech Perception, 1975, The Production of Speech, 1983, Speech Science and Technology, 1992, Recent Research Towards Advanced Man-Machine Interface Through Spoken Language, 1996; contbr. over 500 articles to sci. jours. Recipient Design. Paper award Inst. Elec. Comm. Engrs. Japan, 1968, Inst. of Elec. Engrs. of Japan, 1967, Disting. Achievement award Inst. Electronics and Comm. Engrs. of Japan, 1973; named Person of Merit in Sci. and Tech., Mayor of Tokyo, 1989. Fellow Acoustical Soc. Am. (Spl. Disting. svc. award 1988), Inst. Electronics, Info. and Comm. Engrs.; mem. IEEE (life, Meritorious Svc. award 1987, 3d Millennium medal 2000), Acoustical Soc. Japan (hon.), Orgn. of Internat. Conf. on Spoken Lang. Processing (hon. life mem.), Orgn. Internat. Congresses of Phonetic Scis. (permanent coun. 1979—), MIT Alumni Assn. of Japan (pres. 1982-90, Meritorious Svc. award 1991, 99), Boston Assn. Japan (pres. 1996-98), Sigma Xi, Tau Beta Pi. Home: 3-31-12 Ebisu, Shibuya-ku Tokyo 150-0013, Japan Office: Science U of Tokyo Dept Applied Electronics, 2641 Yamazaki, Noda Chiba 278-8510, Japan

FUJISAWA, AKIHIDE, physicist; b. Matsumae, Japan, Jan. 28, 1961; s. Koushiro and Ryoko (Uebayashi) F.; m. Yuko Sagawa, Nov. 19, 1988; children: Rihoko, Kako, Kyoko. BS, U. Tokyo, 1985, MS, 1987, PhD, 1990. Rsch. assoc. Nat. Inst. Fusion Sci., Nagoyu, Japan, 1990-98; asst. prof. Nat. Inst. Fusion Sci., Toki, Japan, 1998—. Contbr. articles to profl. jours. Mem. The Physical Soc. Japan, The Japan Soc. of Plasma Sci. and Nuclear Fusion Rsch. Avocations: classical music, guitar. Office: Nat Inst Fusion Sci, Oroshi-cho, 509-5292 Toki Japan

FUJISAWA, SEIICHIRO, dentist, educator; b. Fukushima, Japan, Mar. 4, 1941; m. Hotta Fujisawa. DDS, Tokyo Med. and Dental U., 1967, D in Dental Sci., 1971. Sci. asst. Tokyo Med. and Dental U., 1971-93, lectr., 1994, assoc. prof. dentistry, 1995; prof. Meikai U., Sakado, Japan, 1995—. Contbr. articles to profl. jours. Mem. N.Y. Acad. Scis. Office: Meikai Univ Sch Dentistry, Dpt Orl Diag, 1-1-Keyakidai, Sakado Japan

FUJISAWA, YOSHIHARU, electronic distributing company executive; b. Tokyo, Apr. 21, 1939; s. Haruji Tanaka and Fukuko Fujisawa; m. Chikako Sakurai, Nov. 27, 1967; children: Natsuko, Kayo, Kaoru. BA, Columbia Coll., 1963. Product mktg. mgr. New Japan Radio Co., Tokyo, 1963-70; pres., CEO Internix Inc., Tokyo, 1970—, Tesmic Corp., Tokyo, 1982—. Author: (book) Studying Abroad, 1965. Scholar Am. Field Svc., 1956-57, Columbia Scholastic Press Assn., 1959-63. Mem. Japan Electronic Products Importers Assn. (vice chmn. 1985—), Keizai Doyukai. Shinto. Avocation: fishing. Home: 137-60 Yamaguchi, Tokorozawashi 359-1145, Japan Office: Internix Inc, 7-4-7 Nishi-Shinjuku, Tokyo 160-8388, Japan

FUJISE, KIYOTAKA, internist, researcher; b. Fukui, Japan, May 29, 1947; m. Kumiko Tango; 2 children. MB, Jikei U., Tokyo, 1972; MD, Jikei U., 1977. Lic. med. dr. Asst. dept. microbiology Jikei U. Sch. Medicine, Tokyo, 1972-77, asst. dept. internal medicine, 1977-81, 83-87; rsch. assoc. Cancer Inst., Columbia U., N.Y.C., 1981-83; lectr. dept. internal medicine Jikei U. Sch. Medicine, Tokyo, 1987-95, asst. prof. dept. internal medicine, 1995—. Mem. World Soc. Gastroenterology, Japanese Soc. Hepatology (councilor 1993—), Japanese Soc. Gastroenterology (councilor 1993—). Office: Jikei U Sch Med Dpt Int Med, 163-1 Kashiwashita, Kashiwa Chiba 277-8567, Japan

FUJITA, HIDEKI, electrical research engineer; b. Okazaki City, Japan, Mar. 28, 1951; s. Mitsuo and Satomi (Fukase) F.; m. Tomiko Mizutani, Oct. 12, 1978; children: Kentaro, Misato. BS, Nagoya U., 1973, DSc in Engring., 1995. Elec. engr. Chubu Elec. Power Co., Inc., Nagoya, Japan, 1973—. Achievements include research on superconducting magnetic energy storage system and power electronics application technology to power system. Home: 31 Hohbenno Kamisobami-cho, 444-3504 Okazaki Aichi, Japan Office: Chubu Elec Power Co, 20-1 Kitasekiyama Ohdakacho, Midori-ku 459 Nagoya 459-8522, Japan

FUJITA, HIROKO, clinical cytogenetist; b. Osaka, Japan, July 13, 1930; s. Suketaro Tanida and Chiyoko Murotani; m. Sei Fujita, Mar. 20, 1962; 1 child, Reo. BA, Osaka Women's Coll., 1953; M of Medicine, Osaka City U., 1959; MD, Osaka U., 1969. Med. intern Evangelical Deaconess Hosp., Cleve., 1959-60; asst. pediatrics Kyoto U. Hosp., Japan, 1961; asst. child health Osaka City U., 1961-66, instr. child health, 1966-74, assoc. prof. child health, 1974-89, prof. child health, 1989-90, prof. social welfare, 1990-94; counselor Mitsubishi Kagaku Bio-Clin. Labs. Inc., Osaka, 1994—; counselor Mitsubishi Kagaku Bioclin. Labs. Inc., Tokyo, 1994—; with Clinic for babies with down syndrome Hyogo Prefectural Tsukaguchi Hosp., 1970—. Author: Fitness Exercises for the Down Syndrom Baby, 1984 (in Japanese), 1986 (in English); co-editor, author: Atlas of Chromosomal Syndromes, 1981 (in Japanese), revised edition, 1997; contbr. articles to profl. jours. Del. from Osaka City UN Decade for Women, Kenia, 1985; mem. Japan Overseas Christian Cooperative Svc., Tokyo, 1990—; foster parent Plan Internat. Japan, Tokyo, 1992—. Mem. Japan Down Syndrome Assn., The Pediatrician Assn. for Handicapped (dir. 1985—), Japan Soc. of Human Genetics (councilor 1975—), Japanese Soc. of Pediatrics, Japanese Soc. of Child Health, Am. Soc. of Human Genetics. Buddhist. Avocations: gardening, recitation of a classical poem. Home: 4-5-11 Mukogaoka Uenoshiba, Sakaishi 593-8303, Japan

FUJITA, HIROMICHI, printing company executive; b. Mar. 21, 1928; m. Yoko Fujita. Student, Tokyo U., 1953. With Toppan Printing Co. Ltd., 1953, vice dir., 1976, dir., 1988, former v.p., now pres. Office: Toppan Printing Co Ltd, 1 Kanda-Izumicho, Chiyoda-ku Tokyo 101-0024, Japan*

FUJITA, MIHO, chemistry educator, researcher; b. Tajimi City, Gifu, Japan, Feb. 4, 1946; s. Yoneo and Kiriko (Tatai) F.; m. Yoko Kayaki, Apr. 23, 1972; children: Mariko, Akane. BSc, Nagoya (Japan) U., 1968, MSc, 1970, DSc, 1978. Rsch. assoc. Nagoya City U., 1973-76, lectr. chemistry, 1976-78, assoc. prof., 1978-93, prof., 1993—, head dept., 1994—. Contbr. articles to sci. jours. Dep. chmn. Kanie (Aichi, Japan) Internat. Friendship Assn., 1993—. Mem. Chem. Soc. Japan, N.Y. Acad. Scis. Avocations: plant growing, tennis, jogging, classical and jazz music. Office: Nagoya City U Inst Natural, Scis, Yamanohata, Mizuho, Nagoya 467-8501, Japan

FUJITA, SEI, political economist, educator; b. Kyoto, Japan, Mar. 20, 1928; s. Keizo and Hisa (Matsuzaki) F.; m. Hiroko Murotani, Mar. 20, 1962; 1 child, Reo. MS in Sociology, Hitotsubashi U., Tokyo, 1957, PhD in Sociology, 1961. Instr. in econs. Osaka (Japan) City U., 1963-66, assoc. prof. econs., 1966-75, prof. econs., 1975-91, prof. emeritus, 1991—; prof. econs. Osaka U. Econs. and the Law, Yao, Japan, 1991—; co-dir. Assn. Ann. Scientific Exch. with Scholars of the Far-East Region of the Russian Fedn., Osaka, 1984-95; dean faculty of econs. Osaka City U., 1981-82, Osaka U. Econs. and the Law, 1993-97. Author: Socialist Economy and the Law of Value, (in Japanese) 1967, Soviet Commodity Production: Its Semi-permanent Continuation, (in Japanese) 1991, The Soviet Economy as a Social Experiment: Lessons from the 20th Century, 1999; contbr. articles to profl. jours. Chmn. Movement Against Comml. Advt. through Loudspkr. in the Mcpl. Subway, Osaka, 1976-77. Recipient 3d Niigata prize, Prefectural Office of Niigata, Japan, 1997. Mem. Japan Assn. Comparative Econ. Studies (pres. 1993-95), Assn. Sci. of Thought, Assn. Evolutionary Econs., Internat. Ho. of Japan, Inc., Amnesty Internat., Japan Braille Libr. Buddhist. Avocations: go, gardening, art appreciation. Home: 4-5-11 Mukogaoka Uenoshiba, Sakai 593-8303, Japan

FUJITA, TOSHIO, chemist, researcher; b. Kyoto, Japan, Jan. 26, 1929; s. Shinzaburo and Hideko Fujita; m. Tetsuko Kurokawa, May 3, 1957; children: Yoshihiko, Tomoko, Naruhiko. BSc, Kyoto U., Japan, 1951, DSc, 1962; postdoctoral fellow, Pomona Coll., 1961-63, U. Ill., 1963-64. Asst. prof. Kyoto Univ., 1951-64, lectr., 1964-66, assoc. prof., 1966-81, prof., 1981-92, prof. emeritus, 1992—; cons. Kansai Systems Lab., Fujitsu Ltd., Osaka, 1992-98; dir. Japan Rsch. Assn. Quantitative Structure Activity Relationship, 1975-93. Co-editor: Rational Approaches to Structure Activity and Ecotoxicology of Agrochemicals, 1992, Classical and Three-Dimensional QSAR in Agrochemistry, 1995; editor: QSAR and Drug Design: New Developments and Applications, 1995; contbr. articles to profl. jours. Pres. Pesticide Sci. Soc. Japan, 1985-87; dir. Agri. Chemical Soc. Japan, Kansai sect., 1989-91. Mem. Japan Soc. Biosci, Biotech. Agrochem. (Rsch. Performance award 1989), Pharmaceutical Soc. Japan, Chem. Soc. Japan, Am. Chem. Soc. (Internat. Award Rsch., 1994), Pesticide Sci. Soc. Japan (Rsch. Performance award 1979). Avocations: listening to classical music, collecting CD records of non-famous good classical music. Home: 38-1 Iwakura-Miyakecho, Sakyoku, Kyoto 606-0022, Japan Office: EMIL Project #305 Hts Kyogosho, Fuyacho-Nishikikoji-Agaru, Nakagyoku Kyoto 604-8057, Japan

FUJITA, YOSHIO, astronomer; b. Fukui City, Japan, Sept. 28, 1908; s. Teizo Fujita; m. Kazuko Nezu, 1941; 3 children. Attended, Tokyo U. Asst. prof. U. Tokyo, 1931, prof., 1951-69, prof. emeritus, 1969—; vis. prof. Pa. State U., 1971; guest investigator Dominion Astrophysical Obs., 1960, Mt. Wilson and Palomar Obs., 1972, 74. Author: Interpretation of Spectra and Atmospheric Structure in Cool Stars, 1970. Decorated 2nd class Order of Sacred Treasure; recipient Cultural Merit award Fukui City, 1971; named Hon. Citizen, Fukui City, 1979; recognized as Person of Cultural Merit, 1996. Mem. Japan Acad. (pres. 1994—, Imperial prize 1955), Royal Soc. Scis. Liége (fgn. mem.). Office: Nippon Gakushiin, 7-32 Ueno Park, Taito-ku Tokyo 110-0007, Japan*

FUJITA, YOSHITAKA, economist, consultant; b. Tokyo, Nov. 27, 1929; s. Takeo and Nobu (Suzuki) F.; m. Tamie Hirano Fujita, Apr. 4, 1964; children: Marina, Erina, Yoshikazu. BA, Keio U., Japan, 1955, MA, U. Ill., 1963. Economist Bank of Am., Tokyo, 1955-60, Japan Fedn. Employer's Assn., Tokyo, 1960-72; prof. social security Asia U., Tokyo, 1972-98, Heisei Internat. U., Kazo, 1998—; adv. ILO, Geneve, Switzerland, 1987, Japan Fedn. Employer's Assn., Tokyo, 1992—. Author: Management and labor, 1965, Guidepost Wage Policy, 1967, Employee Benefits and Industrial Relations, 1984; author, editor: Employee Benefits and Social Security, 1997.

Mem. Govt. Adv. Com. on Social Ins., Tokyo, 1984; vice chmn. Govt. Adv. Coun. on Med. Ins., Tokyo, 1994. Japan Economic Policy Acad., Japan Personnel Mgmt. Acad., Japan Seamen Social Ins. Assn. Avocations: golf, world travel. Home: 7-5-31 Ohizumigakuen, Tokyo 178-0061, Japan Office: Heisei Internat U, Mizubuka, Kazo 347-0022, Japan

FUJIWARA, KIICHI, political science educator; b. Tokyo, June 16, 1956; s. Takaharu and Elko (Adachi) F.; m. Chiharu Takenaka, July 25, 1984; children: Megumi, Izumi. BA, U. Tokyo, 1979, MA, 1981. Assoc. prof. Chiba U., Japan, 1988-92; assoc. prof. Inst. Social Sci. U. Tokyo, 1992-99, prof. sch. law & politics, 1999—. Editor/author: (book) The 20th Century Global System (6 vols.) 1998. Mem. Japan Assn. Internat. Studies (coun. mem. 1998—), Japan Assn. Comparative Politics (coun. mem. 1996—). Office: U Tokyo/Faculty of Law, Hongo 7-3 1 Bunkyoku, 1130033 Tokyo Japan

FUJIWARA, MASAAKI, neurosurgeon; b. Osaka, Osaka, Japan, May 9, 1950; s. Kohmei Sugimori and Toshiko F.; m. Yasue Fujiwara, Nov. 13, 1975; children: Satoe, Kazue, Yukie. MD, Okayama (Japan) U., 1976, D in Med. Scis., 1980. Cert. neurosurgeon Japan Neurol. Soc. Neurosurgeon resident Osaka (Japan) Kohsei Nenkin Hosp., 1978-82; chief resident neurosurgery Osaka (Japan) U. Hosp., 1983; med. staff Toyonaka (Japan) Mcpl. Hosp., 1984-85; chief dept. neurosurgery Yukioka Hosp., Osaka, 1986—, Iseikai Hosp., Osaka, 1998—. Mem. Japan Asian Soc. and Asian Friendship Soc. Osaka (founding mem.), Assn. for Annapurna Neurol. Inst. Hiroshima, Goi Peace Found. Avocation: tennis. Fax: 06-6379-1211. Home: 3 chome, 32-4 Shinsenri minamimachi, Toyonaka, Osaka 560-0084, Japan Office: Iseikai Hosp, 2-25 Sugawara 6-chome, Osaka 533-0022, Japan

FUJIY, HERLEY, physician; b. Tokyo, Mar. 3, 1930; s. Rintaro and Tsuya Fujiy; m. Motoko Minagawa, Mar. 3, 1961; children: Rika, Yuka. MD, Keio Med. Sch., Tokyo, 1953, PhD, 1960. Straight med. intern Jersey City Med. Ctr., 1954-55; resident in medicine N.Y. Med. Coll., N.Y.C., 1955-57; asst. in medicine Keio Med. Sch., 1957-67, asst. chief in collagen diseases, 1967-76; chief of health care ctr. Suruga Bank, Tokyo, 1966-76; chief of infirmary Unitika Co., Tokyo, 1968—; chief Fujiy Med. Clinic, Tokyo, 1976-98; attending physician, cons. physician in collagen diseases Tokyo Saiseikai Chuo Hosp., 1976-94; cons. physician in collagen diseases Tokyo Musashino Hosp., Tokyo, 1976-80, Nerima Gen. Hosp., 1998—; clin. instr. Keio Nursing Sch., 1958-63; instr. Tokyo Saiseikai Nursing Sch., 1995-97; com. mem. postgrad. edn. Keio U. Med. Sch. Author and innovator in field. Mem. Health and San. Com., Shinagawa, Tokyo, 1960. Fulbright grantee, 1954. Mem. Japan Med. Assn., Japanese Soc. Internal Medicine, Japan Diabetic Assn., Japan Rheumatism Assn., N.Y. Acad. Scis. Home: 4-18-20-514, Mita Minatoku, Tokyo 108-0073, Japan

FUKADA, EIICHI, physicist, researcher; b. Kokura, Japan, Mar. 28, 1922; s. Nobunosuke and Hideko (Yamauchi) F.; m. Tomoko Uraki, Oct. 23, 1952 (dec. Feb. 1995); 1 child, Yoko. BSc, U. Tokyo, 1944, DSc, 1960. Rsch. mem. Kobayasi Inst. Phys. Rsch., Tokyo, 1944-63; rsch. dir. Biopolymer Physics Lab., Inst. Phys. and Chem. Rsch., Tokyo, 1963-80, exec. dir., 1980-84, emeritus scientist, 1981—; prof. Gakushuin U., Tokyo, 1961-80; vis. prof. NYU, 1965-66, U. São Paulo, Brazil, 1974, Tech. U. of Darmstadt, Germany, 1986, U. Konstance, Germany, 1986, Tech. U. Aachen, Germany, 1987; guest scientist Eisenhauer Med. Ctr., Rancho Mirage, Calif., 1988; chmn. 4th Internat. Congress of Biorheology, Tokyo, 1981; hon. chmn. 8th Internat. Congress Biorheology, Yokohama, 1992; rsch. advisor Inst. for Super Materials, ULVAC Japan Ltd., Tsukuba, 1987-98; exec. dir. Kobayasi Inst. Phys. Rsch., Tokyo, 1992—. Editor Jour. Biorheology, 1977-91. British Coun. scholar, U. London, 1956-58; recipient Natural Sci. award Yamaji Sci. Found., Tokyo, 1970, Achievement prize, Inst. of Electrostatics Japan, 1979, Sci. Achievement award Soc. Polymer Sci., 1984, Japanese Soc. Biomaterials, 1988, Galvani award Internat. Symposium Electro Biology, 1989, Third Order Sacred Treas., Japan, 1993, Poiseuille Gold medal Internat. Soc. Biorheology, 1995. Fellow Internat. Acad. Wood Sci. Home: Izumi 2-8-1-902 Kokubunji, Tokyo 185-0024, Japan

FUKADA, NAOHIKO, psychology educator, researcher; b. Osaka, Japan, June 4, 1923; s. Naokichi and Miyo F.; m. Kazu Umeuchi, Oct. 10, 1952; children: Maki, Naoaki. Attended, Tennoji Normal Coll., 1938-43, Osaka Coll., 1946-47; BA, Doshisha U., 1948-50, PhD, 1980. Tchr. Enami Primary Sch., Osaka, 1943-45; tchr. math. Tamagawa Girl's H.S., Osaka, 1947-49; clin. psychologist Kyoto Pref. Child Guidance Clinic, 1950-61; lectr. Doshisha Women's Coll., Kyoto, 1961-64, asst. prof., 1964-70, prof. psychology, 1970-89, emeritus prof., 1989—; prof. psychology Osaka U. Arts, 1989—, prof. grad. course, 1993—; pres. Osaka U. Arts and Osaka U. Arts Jr. Coll., 1995—; mem. Kyoto Prefecture Child Welfare Com., 1979-95. Author: Experimental Studies of Drawing Behavior, 1989, Women in Japan, 1991, Exploration on Drawings, 1992; contbr. articles to profl. jours. Children's drawing contest judge Kyoto Press, 1979—. 1st lt. Army, 1944-45, Japan. Mem. Japanese Psychol. Assn., Am. Psychol. Assn., British Soc. Aesthetics. Avocations: reading, music. Home: 37-12 Shimootani Kuze, Jyoyo-shi 610-0102, Japan Office: Doshisha Women's Coll, Imadegawadori Teramachi Nishiiru, Kyoto 602, Japan

FUKAMACHI, MASANOBU, chancellor, chaplain; b. Shizuoka City, Japan, July 25, 1936; s. Masakatsu and Teruko (Fukuda) F.; m. Yoriko Fukamachi; children: Masatoshi, Kazuya, Nobuyuki. BD, Tokyo Union Theol. Sem., 1959, MA, 1961; grad., Duke U., 1964; LHD, Am. U., Washington, 1994. Chaplain Shimuzu (Japan) Girls' H.S., 1961-63; asst. pastor Kamitomisaka Ch., Tokyo, 1964, Ginza Ch., Tokyo, 1966-70; pastor Kyodomidorigaoka Ch., 1970, Toriizaka Ch., Tokyo, 1976-84; chaplain, prof. internat. polit., econ. and bus. dept. Aoyama Gakuin U., Tokyo, 1984—, head chaplain, 1987, head chaplain Rsch. Inst., 1988, 12th chancellor, 1990—; chmn. of bd. trustees social welfare Christian Children's Welfare Program, 1989—; bd. trustees Shimizu Girls' H.S., 1972—, Shizuoka Eiwa Girls' Sch., 1991—, Soen Coll., 1989, Izumi Women's Coll., 1983—, councilor, 1976-77, regent, 1977-83; lectr. Aoyama Gakuin U., 1972-84, Tokyo Union Theol Sem. Grad. Sch., 1984—. Author: The List of Bibliography of John Wesley, 1973, The Concept of Salvation of John Wesley, 1985, The Doctorine of Christian Perfection, 1986, The Concept of Holy Spirit, 1987, Japanese Mission of Canadian Methodist Church, 1990, Exegesis of the Gospel According to Luke, 1990; translator: The Life of John Wesley, 1988; Invisible Education, 1996, The Faith of John Wesley and Methodist Church, 1996; contbr. articles to profl. jours. Councilor YMCA, 1992—. Democrat. Mem. United Church of Christ in Japan. Avocation: tennis. Office: Aoyama Gakuin Univ, 4-4-25 Shibuya, Tokyo Shibuya-ku 150-8366, Japan*

FUKATSU, EIICHI, law educator; b. Takahama, Japan, Dec. 4, 1923; s. Renpei and Yoshi (Kamiya) F.; m. Yoshiko Ogawa, Mar. 27, 1952. LLB, Nihon U., 1951, LLM, 1953; LLM, U. Toronto, 1963; LLD, Nihon U., 1988. Asst. Nihon U., Tokyo, 1951, lectr., 1956, asst. prof., 1965, prof., 1970-93, prof. emeritus, 1994—; lectr. Sofia U., Tokyo, 1976, Hitotsubashi U., Tokyo, 1987. Author: Enforcement of International Judicial Decision, 1969, Legal Structure of International Society, 1961, Economic Sanctions in International Legal Order, 1982, General Theory of International Law, 1984. V.p. YUAI Youth Assn., Tokyo, 1974—. Recipient Adachi Meml. award, 1970. Mem. Japanese Soc. Internat. Law (dir. 1973-91, emeritus). Avocations: music, painting, gardening. Home: Hakusan 4-26-15, Bunkyo-ku, Tokyo 112-0001, Japan Office: Nihon U Faculty Law, 21-3-1 Misaki-cho, Tokyo 112-0001, Japan

FUKATSU, TANEFUSA, retired Chinese classics educator; b. Toyota, Aichi, Japan, Apr. 23, 1923; s. Kingo and Shizu (Noba) F.; m. Michiko Kato, Jan. 17, 1954 (dec. 1981); children: Tomonao, Arikata. BA, Tokyo U., 1951. Tchr. Chinese classics Musashi High Sch., Tokyo, 1957-89; asst. prof. Chinese classics Musashi U., Tokyo, 1971-74, prof. Chinese classics, 1974-85; retired, 1989—; lectr. Chinese classics Nisho-Gakusha U., Tokyo, 1967-93, guest prof., 1993—. Author: Juzi Tongbian Jingdianshiwen, 1978, Lunyu Xidu, 1990, Laozi Xidu, 1994, Thought and Life of the Ancient Chinese-Mirror-, 1996, Japanese Culture and Chinese Culture-White Chrysanthemum and Yellow Chrysanthemum, 1997, Studies on the Latent Thought in Chinese Characters and Poetry, 1997, Chinese Thought and Culture, 1998, Studies of the Book of Laozi, 1999, Thought and Life of the Ancient Chinese Cock, 1999, Thought and Life of the Ancient Chinese—The Source and Course of the Thought of "The Book of Laozi", 2000. Mem. Nippon-Chugoku-Gakkai, Shibunkai (dir. 1990-93, councilor 1993—). Avocation: hiking. Home: 86-1-501 Konya-Cho, Saiwai-Ku Kawasaki-Shi, Kanagawa-ken 212-0026, Japan

FUKAZAWA, HAJIME, oral maxillofacial surgeon, educator; b. Mito-Shi, Ibaragi, Japan, May 25, 1947; s. Izumi Kudoh and Chizuko Fukazawa; m. Noriko Nitanai, May 2, 1975; children: Hanae, Yuhshi. DDS, Iwate Med. U., Morioka, Japan, 1975; D Med. Sci., Iwate Med. U., 1980. Chmn. Hachinohe (Japan) Red Cross Hosp., 1982-83; asst. prof. Iwate Med. U., 1981-92; vice chmn. Niigata Rohsai Hosp., Johetsu, Japan, 1993-94; asst. prof. Niigata U., 1992—; chmn. Yuri Nokyo Gen. Hosp., Honjoh, Japan, 1994-2000, Ookubo Hosp., Mito, Japan, 2000—; dir. dept. Iwate Med. U., 1980-82, 83-88, 89-92; lectr. Akita Ministry of Welfare, 1994. Contbr. articles to profl. jours. Recipient spl. award of invention Iwate Med. U., 1991, Thanksgiving award Japan Soc. for Cancer Therapy Sapporo, 1995, Ranking award Japan Cancer Hosp. by Media Works: Best Doctor of head and neck cancer, N. Japan, 1999. Fellow Am. Soc. for Head and Neck Surgery (corr.); mem. Internat. Physicians for the Prevention of Nuclear War, Japan Soc. Oral Tumors (coun.). Avocations: golf, skiing, baseball, travel. E-mail: hajimefu@ma3.justnet. Home: Morioka-shi, Yamagishi 6-39-12, Morioka-shi Iwate ken, Japan Office: 4-4040-32 Ishikawa Mito-shi, Honjoh-shi Ibaraki-ken 310-0905, Japan

FUKS, ROBERT, chemistry educator; b. Brussels, Jan. 8, 1936; s. Slama Fuks and Ester Dyner; m. Viviane Lambert, Aug. 26, 1983; children: Muriel, Laurent. M in Chemistry, U. Libre Brussels, 1957, PhD in Chemistry, 1963. Sr. staff scientist Union Carbide, Brussels, 1962-72; prof. U. Libre Brussels, 1977—. Editor: University Research, Industrial Research and Government Administration, a Feasible Cooperation; contbr. articles to profl. jours. Recipient Stas-Spring award Scis. Acad., 1963. Mem. Soc. Royale de Chimie (sec. gen. 1985—). Achievements include 5 patents. Office: U Libre Brussels, Bd du Triomphe, B-1050 Brussels Belgium

FUKSMAN, IRMA LUDVIGOVNA, chemist; b. Sortavala, USSR; d. Ludvig Georgievich and Helena Josifovna (Syarki) Haponen; m. Lev Lvovich Fuksman, Oct. 16, 1971; children: Dennis Lvovich, Natalya Lvovna. BEngring., Poly. Inst., Leningrad, USSR, 1972; MS, Inst. Wood Chem./Acad. Scis., Riga, Latvia, USSR, 1984; D in Biol. Sci., Forest Tech. Acad., St. Petersburg, Russia, 1999. Rschr. Inst. Forestry Karelian Sci. Ctr., Petrozavodsk, Russia, 1968—; team leader Inst. Forestry, Petrozavodsk, 1984—. Contbr. articles to profl. jours. Mem. Soc. Physiologists. Avocations: gardening, aerobics, travel, reading. E-mail: vitali.krutov@post.krc.karelia.ru. Home: Zeljonaja 3-53, 185007 Petrozavodsk Russia Office: Inst Forestry Karelian Sci, Pushkinskaja 11, 185610 Petrozavodsk Russia

FUKUDA, ATSUO, physicist, materials science researcher; b. Tokyo, Feb. 5, 1937; s. Katsuyuki and Kimiko (Maekawa) F.; m. Kyoko Omachi, Mar. 30, 1965; children: Mitsuhiro, Mitsunori. BSc, Tokyo Kyoiku U., 1960, MSc, 1962, DSc, 1965. Rsch. asst. U. Tokyo Inst. for Solid State Physics, Tokyo, 1965-69; vis. scientist Argonne Nat. Lab. Solid State Sci. Divsn., Argonne, Ill., U.S., 1969-71, U. Stuttgart (Germany) II Physikalisches Inst., 1971-72; assoc. prof. Nagasaki (Japan) U. Faculty Liberal Arts, 1973-75; assoc. prof. Tokyo Inst. Tech. Faculty of Engring., 1975-85, prof., 1985-97; prof. faculty textile sci. and tech. Shinshu U., Nagano, Japan, 1997—; pub. mgr. Japanese Jour. Applied Physics, Tokyo, 1987-89; dir. Ctr. for Rsch. Coop. and Info. Exch., Tokyo Inst. Tech., 1992-94. Co-author: (with Hideo Takezoe) Structure and Properties of Ferroelectric Liquid Crystals, 1990; editor, author: Future Liquid Crystal Display and Its Materials--Ferroelectric and Antiferroelectric Liquid Crystals, 1992; guest editor (with others) Conf. Procs. Ferroelectrics, 1993. Recipient Outstanding Paper award 9th Internat. Display Rsch. Conf., Kyoto, 1989, spl. recognition award Soc. Info. Display, 1997. Mem. Japan Soc. Applied Physics (mng. dir. 1985-87, A award Tokyo br. 1990), Phys. Soc. Japan, Internat. Liquid Crystal Soc. (pres. 1996-2000, mem. non-exec. bd. 1990-94). Avocation: hiking. Office: Shinshu U Dept Kansei Engr, Ueda-shi, Nagano-ken 386-8567, Japan

FUKUDA, CHISEKO, lawyer; b. Japan, Jan. 10, 1946; d. Toshiko Fukuda. LLB, Keio U., Tokyo, 1969; LLM, NYU, 1977; postgrad., Legal Tng. & Rsch. Inst. of Supreme Ct. of Japan, 1970-72. Cert. lawyer. Ptnr. Braun Moriya Hoashi & Kubota, Tokyo, 1972—, Lovejoy, Wasson, Lundgren & Ashton, N.Y.C., 1977, Merrill Lynch Internat. & Co., N.Y.C., 1978; mem. com. customs and tariffs Bur. of Ministry of Fin. of Japan, 1994—. Mem. First Tokyo Bar Assn. Avocation: travel. Office: Tokyo Sakurada Bldg Rm 505, 1-3 Nishi-shinbashi 1-chome, Minato-ku, Tokyo 105-0003, Japan

FUKUDA, ICHIZO, physician, researcher; b. Osaka, Japan, Feb. 5, 1932; s. Ritsutaro and Yoshiko (Nohama) F.; m. Hanako Sekita, July 10, 1965; children: Kazuhiro, Hideaki. MD, Osaka Med. Coll., 1956, PhD, 1963. Diplomate in medicine. Resident dept. medicine Osaka Med. Coll., 1957-60, asst. dept. medicine, 1960-67; rsch. fellow Inst. for Cardiovascular Diseases Scripps Clinic and Rsch. Found., La Jolla, Calif., 1964-66; fellow dept. cardiology City of Hope Med. Ctr., Duarte, Calif., 1966-67; asst. prof. dept. medicine Osaka Med. Coll., 1967-95; mem. com. exercise test standard Health Svc. Bur., Ministry of Health, 1972-79; vis. hon. lectr. dept. cardiology Sch. Medicine, Okayama U., 1992-2000; assoc. prof. Osaka Med. Coll., 1995-96, prof., 1997-2000; vis. prof. dept. cardiology Sch. Medicine, Fujita Gakuen U., 1995-2000. Co-editor: Cardiovascular Exercise Testing, 1978, 3d edit., 1991, Cardiology, 1981, Manual of Sports Medicine, 1995. Recipient Pub. Health Edn. award Mayor of Osaka, 1979, awards Mayor of Hirakata, 1987, 92, 97. Fellow ACP, Am. Coll. Chest Physicians, Am. Coll. Cardiology, Internat. Coll. Angiology, European Soc. Cardiology, Japanese Soc. Internal Medicine, Japanese Soc. Neurology, Japanese Circulation Soc., Royal Soc. Medicine, European Soc. Cardiology. Avocations: ancient Chinese paintings, Chinese calligraphy, ceramics, birds. Home: 36-1-101 Teratani-cho, Takatsuki, 569-1024 Osaka Japan Office: Osaka Med Coll/Int Medicine, 2-7 Daigaky-cho, Osaka Takatsuki 569-0801, Japan

FUKUDA, KANJI, orthopaedic surgeon; b. Kyoto, Japan, Sept. 6, 1956; s. Ryoji and Eiko Fukuda; m. Hikari Yada, Dec. 9, 1984; children: Megumi, Shota. MD, Kinki U., Osaka, Japan, 1980, PhD, 1986. Asst. prof. Kinki U. Sch. Medicine, Osaka, 1986—. Contbr. articles to profl. jours. Mem. Am. Physiol. Soc., Japanese Orthopaedic Soc., Orthopaedic Rsch. Soc. Avocations: tennis, golf. Office: Kinki U Sch Med Ortho Surg, Ohnohigashi 377-2, Osaka Sayama 589, Japan

FUKUDA, MITSUO, electronic engineering researcher; b. Imaichi, Tochigi, Japan, June 4, 1953; s. Tomokichi and Mitsuko (Tezuka) F.; m. Yumiko Numata, June 5, 1983; children: Kazutaka, Ayumi. BE, Ibaraki U., Hitachi, Japan, 1977; PhD, Tokyo Inst. Tech., 1985. Registered profl. engr. Rschr. Nippon Telegraph and Tel. Corp. Labs., Mitaka, Japan, 1977-82; rsch. engr. NTT Labs., Mitaka, Japan, 1982-86; sr. rsch. engr. NTT Opto-Electronics Labs., Atsugi, Japan, 1986—; supr. NTT Electronics Co., Atsugi, Japan, 1994—; sec. Japanese nat. com. Internat. Electrotechnical Commn./Tech. Com. 47/Sub-Com. 47C, Tokyo, 1993—; mem. program com. Inst. Europe, 1991—. Author: Reliability and Degradation of Semiconductor Lasers and Leds, Artech House, 1991 Optical Semiconductor Devices, JW&S, 1999. Mem. IEEE (instr. 1993-96), Optoelectronic Industry and Tech. Devel. Assn. (chmn. com. active device standardization 1995—), Applied Physics Soc. Japan, Inst. Comm., Info. and Electronic Engring. Avocations: oil painting, motor sports, instrument playing. Home: 287-171 Nishi-koiso, Ooiso-machi Nakagun, Kanagawa 255-0005, Japan Office: NTT Opto-Electronics Labs, 3-1 Morinosato Wakamiya, Atsugi 243-0198, Japan

FUKUDA, SETSUKO, translator; b. Higashi-matsuyama, Saitama, Japan, Dec. 27, 1940; d. Yasuhiro and Hatsu (Yamazaki) F.; m. Yasuo Kurata (div.); 1 child, Yujin. D in Am. Lit., Rissho U., Tokyo, 1972. Cert. secondary tchr., Japanese lang. tchr. With sales dept. Japan Trading Publ. Co. Ltd., Tokyo, 1980-83; receptionist Cuba Embassy in Japan, Tokyo, 1984-85; rep. Internat. Lang. Sys., Tokyo, 1986—; with Big Hotels, Tokyo, 1995-2000; translator, interpreter City Hotels, Tokyo, 1992-98, ACCJ, Tokyo, 1993-98, Big Hotels, Tokyo, 1995-98; translator N.G.O. in Japan, Tokyo, 1993, Ward Office of Tokyo, 1993-97, The Ministry of Justice, Tokyo, 1995. Appearance Nikkei Newspapers Co., Ltd., 1993-98, Japan Press Co., Ltd., 1993-2000; performer Nippon TV, 1996, author: Affiliates and Offices of Foreign Corps. in Japan, Translations of General Motor Co., Ltd., Documents translation of Toppan Printing Co., Ltd., Interpretation of Avery Dennison Co. Ltd., Translation of Hainbuch Spannende Technik, Singapore, Translation of International Beauty Show, Long Beach, Calif.; contbr. articles to profl. jours., chpts. to books. Mem. ACCJ (mem. program com.). Avocations: poetry, art, movies, golf, outdoor sports. E-mail: fwkp6089@nifty.com. Home: 325-1 Oaza-minowa, Osato-mura Osato-gun, Osato-mura Saitama Prefecture Saitama-ken, Japan Office: Internat Lang Sys 3-15-2, higashi-ikebukuro Rm 1111, Toshima-ku Tokyo Japan

FUKUDA, SHIGERU, business consultant; b. Osaka, Japan, Dec. 15, 1933; s. Shoichi and Misao Fukuda; m. Keiko Fukuda; children: Hatsumi, Emi. BBA, Kansai U., Osaka, 1955. Lab. tech. Anderson, Clayton & Co., Osaka, 1952-61; import/export mgr. Nanri Trading Co., Ltd., Kobe, Japan, 1961-68; export mgr. Yamazaki-Mazak Co. Ltd., Aichi, Japan, 1968-72; trade mgr. Refac Internat. Co., Ltd., Tokyo, 1972-74; export mgr. Roku-Roku Sangyo Co., Ltd., Tokyo, 1974-76; dir. Kai Tak Electric Co., Ltd., Hong Kong, 1976-79, Kai Tak Electric Pte. Ltd., Singapore, 1987-89; export mgr. Tokyo Parts Indsl. Co. Ltd., 1976-89; mgr. overseas div. Seiwa Techno Systems Corp., Tokyo, 1989-92, ret., 1992; bus. cons. Japan Travel Bur. Foresta, Tokyo, 1994-99; Japan liaison Sillner Industries GmbH & Co. KG, Regensburg, Germany, 1999—. Mem. Japan Automotive Fedn. Buddhist. Avocations: global intermediation, Internet, Soho, travel, photography. Home: 3-3-15-104 Nagayama, Tama 206-0025, Japan

FUKUDA, YOSHIHIRO, advertising company executive; b. Nagoya, Aichi, Japan, Oct. 24, 1959; s. Ichiro and Takako (Okoshi) F.; m. Yayoi Suzuki, Mar. 3, 1986. Mktg. degree, Waseda U., Tokyo, 1982. Acct. Tokyo Sowa Bank, 1982-83; prodr. ABI Promotion, Tokyo, 1984-85; dir. Kyodosenden Advt. Agy., Tokyo, 1986-96; CEO Ad Vanguard, Tokyo, 1996—. Recipient Yomiuri Advt. award Yomiuri Shinbun, 1994, 95, Indsl. Advt. award Nihon Kogyo Shinbun, 1995, JAA Consumer Advt. award Japan Advertiser Assn., 1995. Mem. Japan Ctrl. Polit. Inst. Avocations: travel, tennis, listening to music, painting, movies. Home: 1-8-13-302 Miyamae-ku, Miyamaedaira, Kawasaki-Shi 213-0006, Japan Office: Ad Vanguard Co Ltd, 2-14-5-202 Ebisu Shibuya-ku, Tokyo 150-0013, Japan

FUKUDO, SHIN, medical educator; b. Yuzawa, Akita, Japan, Dec. 8, 1958; s. Yusuke and Yuko (Tate) F. MD, Tohoku U., Aoba, Sendai, Japan, 198, PhD, 1990. Resident Towada City Hosp., Japan, 1983-84; fellow Tohoku U. Hosp., 1984-86; rsch. assoc. Duke U. Med. Ctr., 1987-88; asst. prof. Tohoku U., Aoba, 1987-97, lectr., 1997-98, assoc. prof., 1998-99; prof. behavioral medicine Tohoku U., 1999—; head med. office dept. psychosomatic medicine Tohoku U., 1993-97, vice dir., 1997—. Contbr. articles to med. jours. Sec.-treas. Kendo Club, Tohoku U., 1985—; coach Jr. Kendo Club, Nakayama, Sendai, 1995—. Recipient Travel award Internat. Symposium on Brain-Gut Interactions, 1995. Mem. Am. Psychosomatic Soc. (mem. program com. 1997-98, Early Career award 1994), Japanese Soc. Psychosomatic Medicine (mem. future programming com. 1994—, Ishikawa prize for best psychosomatic rsch. 1987), Functional Brain-Gut Rsch. Group (mem. membership com. 1995—). Buddhist. Avocations: Kendo, hiking, reading books, movies, Bob Dylan's music. Office: Tohoku U Sch Medicine, 2-1- Seiryo, Aoba Sendai 980-8575, Japan

FUKUHARA, HENRY, artist, educator; b. L.A., Apr. 25, 1913; s. Ichisuke and Ume (Sakamoto) F.; m. Fujiko Yasutake, Aug. 18, 1938; children: Joyce, Grace, Rackham, Helen. Student with Edgar A. Whitney, Jackson Heights, N.Y., 1972; student with Rex Brandt, Corona del Mar, Calif., 1974; student with Robert E. Wood, 1975; student with Carl Molno, Woodside, N.Y., 1976; student with Kero Antoyam, 1988. instr. Watercolor Venice (Calif.) Adult Sch., 1991-92, tchr. watercolor; instr. watercolor Parris Art Mus., N.Y., East Islip Mus., N.Y., Huntington Twp. Art League, N.Y., Oakdale Atum, N.Y. Exhibited in group shows at Friends World Coll., Lloyds Neck, N.Y., 1980, Elaine Benson Gallery, Bridgehampton, N.Y., 1979, 83, Nat. Invitational Watercolor, Zaner Gallery, Rochestr, N.Y., 1981, Fire House Gallery, 1982, Parrish Art Mus., 1982, Japan-R.I. Exch. Exhibit, Provincetown, R.I., 1986, Kawakami Gallery, Tokyo, 1986, Setagaya Mus. Art, Tokyo, 1988-91, 5th Ann. Rosoh Kai Watercolor Exhbn., Meguro Mus. Art, Tokyo, 1991, 6th Ann. Rosoh Kai Watercolor Exhbn. Meguro Mus. Art, 1992, 11th ann., 1999, Shinju ku Bunka Ctr., Tokyo, 1993-96, 10th ann., 1997, Stary Sheets Galleries Exhbn., Irvine, Calif., 1992-94, Laguna Beach, 1996—, Living Legends, Mira Mesa Colls., 1994, Miracosta, Coll., 1997, Japanese Am. Nat. Mus., 2000; represented in permanent collections at Heckscher Mus., Huntington, N.Y., Abilene Mus. Fine Art, Nassau C.C., Garden City, N.Y., SUNY-Stony Brook, L.A. County Mus. Art, Blaine County Mus., Chinook, Mont., Ralston Mus., Sydney, Mont., San Bernardino County Mus., Redlands, Calif., 1984, Riverside Mus. Art, Calif., 1985, Gonzaga U., Spokane, Wash., 1986, Nagano Mus. Art, Japan, 1986, Contemporary Mus. of Art, Hiroshima, 1988, Santa Monica (Calif.) Coll., 1988, City Hall, Culver City, Calif., 1999; subject of profl. publs. includin g Water Media Focus, Watercolor Magic. Recipient Purchase award Nassau C.C., 1976; Best in Show, Hidden Pond, Town of Islip, N.Y., 1978, Strathmore Paper Co., 1979, Creative Connections Gallery award Foothills Art Ctr., Golden, Colo., 1984, Judges Choice, Mont. Miniature Art Soc. 7th Ann. Internat. Show, Working with Abandoned Control, Am. Artist mag., 1994, Learn Watercolor Edgar Whitney Way, 1994, Splash 3 and 4 1995/96 in watercolor series, 1996, The Best of Watercolor 2, 1997, The Artistic Touch 3, 1999, others. Mem. Nat. Watercolor Soc., Ala. Watercolor Soc., Pitts. Watercolor Soc., Nat. Drawing Assn., Valley Water Color Soc. (hon.). Address: 1214 Marine St Santa Monica CA 90405-5815

FUKUHARA, MACHIKO, psychology educator, researcher; b. Kobe, Japan, Aug. 19, 1931; d. Eiji and Sadako (Takai) F. BA, Tsuda Coll., Japan, 1954, Iowa Wesleyan Coll., 1961; MEd, Springfield Coll., 1962; PhD, U. Tokyo, 1981. Cert. clin. psychologist, Japanese Assn. Clin. Psychology. Assoc. prof. Musashino Art U., Tokyo, 1962-70; lectr., counselor Chuo U., Tokyo, 1970-78; assoc. prof. Jissen Women's U., Tokyo, 1976-83, prof., 1983-90; prof. Tokiwa U., Mito, Japan, 1990-99, Bukkyo U., Kyoto, Japan, 1999—; dir.-at-large Internat. Coun. Psychologists, 1985-88, treas., 1990-93; mem. exec. bd. Japanese Assn. Student Counseling, Tokyo, 1970-95, Internat. Applied Psychology, Spain, 1994—. Author: (in Japanese) Factors Affecting Student Counseling, 1986; contbr. articles to profl. jours.; patentee in psycho-physiological behavior analyzer. Chair social welfare com. Japanese Assn. Univ. Women, Tokyo, 1990-92. Recipient Contbn. and Leadership award Internat. Coun. Psychologists, 1993. Mem. Japanese Assn. Applied Psychology (exec. bd. 1990—), Japanese Psychol. Assn., Japanese Microcounseling Inst. (dir.). Avocation: listening to classical music. E-mail: fmachiko@iijnet.or.jp. FAX: 81-3-3338-2983. Office: Bukkyo Univ, 96 Kitahananobo-cho, Murasakino Kyoto 603-8301, Japan

FUKUHARA, MIKIO, materials engineer, physicist; b. Wake-cho, Okayama, Japan, Mar. 23, 1948; s. Toshio and Chie (Tokumitsu) F.; m. Nobuko Nakatsukasa, May 22, 1982; children: Sanae, Kei, Teru. B in Engring., Ibaraki U., Japan, 1971; M in Engring., Osaka U., 1973, D in Engring., 1979. Rsch. engr. Toshiba Tungaloy, Yokohama, Japan, 1980-84; sr. engr. Toshiba Tungaloy, Yokohama, 1984-87, mgr., 1990-96, gen. mgr., 1996—; rsch. assoc. Pa. State U., 1987-89. Co-author: Nitride Ceramics, 1998; contbr. articles to profl. jours. Mem. Phys. Soc. Japan. Avocations: oil painting, gardening, Japanese folk song, table tennis. E-mail: a80010@ungaloy.co.jp. Fax: 81-45-503-9030. Office: Toshiba Tungaloy Tech Ctr, 2-7 Sugasawa-Cho Tsurumi, Yokohama 230-0027, Japan

FUKUI, YUKIO, engineering educator. B in Engring., Kyoto, Japan, 1973; M in Engring., Tokyo, 1980, D in Engring., 1993. Engr. Hitachi Co. Ltd., Mobara, Japan, 1973-76; rschr. Industrial Products Rsch. Inst., Tsukuba, Japan, 1980-92, Nat. Inst. Biosci. and Human Tech., Tsukuba, Japan, 1993—; lectr. Tsukuba U., 1990-94, prof., 1998—. Inventor: CAD, 1988, Applied Optics, 1993—. Mem. Assn. for Computing Machinery. Avocation: religion. Office: Inst Info Scis & Electronic, U Tsukuba, 1-1-1 Tennoudai, Tsukuba Ibaraki 305-8573, Japan

FUKUMOTO, BRIAN MICHAEL, mechanical engineer; b. Offutt AFB, Nebr., June 13, 1967; s. Malcolm Tatsumi and Lorraine Sachiko (Noguchi) F. BSME, U. Calif., Berkeley, 1989; MBA, Santa Clara U., 1998. Cable engr. INMAC, San Jose, 1989-91; mfg. engr. SOLECTRON Corp., Milpitas, Calif., 1991-93, sr. program mgr., 1993-95, mgr. spl. projects, 1996-97,

global bus. mgr., mgr. corp. ops., 1997-99; dir. bus. transformation SOLECTRON Corp., Milpitas, 1999—. Sustaining mem. Rep. Nat. Com., Washington, 1990. Mem. ASME, Calif. Alumni Soc., Berkeley Engring. Alumni Soc. (bd. dirs.). Avocations: tennis, classical piano, music, video, computers. Office: Solectron Corp 847 Gibraltar Dr Milpitas CA 95035-6332

FUKUMOTO, HIROAKI, pharmacologist, researcher; b. Kagoshima, Japan, Aug. 5, 1962; s. Nobuhiro and Kazuko (Nagai) F.; m. Misako Takakura, May 14, 1995; 1 child, Katsuaki. BA, Tokyo U., 1986, MS, 1988, PhD, 1995. Cert. h.s. tchr. Rschr. Takeda Chem. Industries Ltd., Osaka, Japan, 1988-94; rschr., assoc. rsch. head Takeda Chem. Industries Ltd., Osaka, 1995—; rschr., vis. scientist Tokyo U., 1994-95. Contbr. articles to profl. jours. Mem. Japanese Biochem. Soc., Japanese Pharmacol. Soc. Avocations: singing, playing tennis, listening to music. Office: Takeda Chem Industries, 2-17-85 Jusohnmachi, Yodogawa-ku, Osaka 532-8686, Japan

FUKUMOTO, MASAHIRO, engineering educator; b. Anan, Tokushima, Japan, Nov. 10, 1954; s. Tsuneji and Shigeru (Shimizu) F.; m. Kinuko Kakimoto, Aug. 18, 1980; children: Megumi, Satoshi. B of Engring., Keio U., 1978, M of Engring., 1980, D of Engring., 1983. Asst. prof. Toyohashi (Japan) U. of Tech., 1984-90, lectr., 1990-93, assoc. prof., 1993—. Contbr. articles to profl. jours. Mem. Japan Welding Soc., Japan Soc. of Mech. Engrs., Japan Inst. of Metals. Office: Toyohashi U of Tech, 1-1 Tempaku-cho, Toyohashi 441-8580, Japan

FUKUMOTO, YOHEI, medical educator, physician; b. Kuga, Yamaguchi, Japan, June 29, 1946; s. Itsuo Wakabayashi and Hisako F.; m. Kayomi Suenaga, Oct. 10, 1974; children Akiko, Hiroko, Yasuyuki. MB, Yamaguchi U., Ube, Japan, 1972, MD, 1974, PhD, 1978. Lectr. Yamaguchi U., Ube, 1988-90, assoc. prof., 1990-92, prof., 1995—. Mem. World Soc. Gastroenterology, World Orgn. Family Drs. Office: Yamaguchi U., Minami-Kogushi, Ube 755-8505, Japan

FUKUNAMI, MASATAKE, cardiologist, educator; b. Osaka, Minami, Japan, Sept. 30, 1949; s. Takao and Miyoko (Maekawa) F.; m. Mine Yoshimura, Nov. 9, 1980; children: Yasutaka, Ayuko, Naoko. MD, Osaka U., 1974, PhD, 1983. Registrar Osaka (Japan) U. Med. Sch., 1974-75, Sakurabashi Watanabe Hosp., Osaka, 1975-76; rsch. fellow Osaka U. Med. Sch., 1976-79; cons. Osaka Med. Ctr. for Cancer and Cardiovascular Diseases, Osaka, 1979-83; rsch. fellow St. Thomas' Hosp., London, 1983-84; chief divsn. cardiology Osaka Prefectural Gen. Hosp., 1984—, head clin. labs., 1999—; lectr. Osaka U. Med. Sch., 1993—. Author: Signal Averaged Electrocardiogram, 1993, Cardiac Adaptation and Failure, 1994, Advances in Body Surface Mapping and High Resolution ECG, 1995, Support for ECK Interpretation, 2000; inventor in field. Recipient Invention award Sci. and Tech. Agy., 1993. Avocations: golf, painting, cooking, Go, gardening. Fax: 81-6-6606-7031.

FUKUOKA, YUTAKA, biomedical engineer, researcher; b. Tokyo, Sept. 28, 1964; s. Toshihiko and Sumiko (Tsubono) F.; m. Naoko Seita, Oct. 22, 1995; 1 child, Rei. PhD, Keio U., Yokohama, 1992. Assoc. prof. Inst. Biomaterials and Bioengring., Tokyo, 1992—. Office: Inst Biomaterials & Bioengring, Kandasurugadai 2-3-10, Chiyoda-ku Tokyo 101-0062, Japan

FUKUSHIMA, JUN, microbiologist, researcher; b. Tokyo, Mar. 19, 1957; s. Hideo and Michiko (Ishida) F.; m. Satoko Niihori, Oct. 1, 1988; 2 children. BSc, Tokyo U. Agr. Tech., 1980, MSc, 1982; PhD, U. Tokyo, 1988. Asst. rschr. Yokohama City U., Japan, 1985-99; assoc. prof. Akita Prefectural U., Japan, 1999—. Author: Molecular Biology of Pseudomonads, 1996; contbr. articles to profl. jours. Mem. Am. Soc. for Microbiology. Home: 452-1 Iijima-Mizushiri, Akita 011-0911, Japan Office: Dept Biotech, Akita Prefectural U, Akita 010-0195, Japan

FUKUSHIMA, MASAKAZU, electronic engineering executive; b. Kanazawa, Japan, Mar. 3, 1937; m. Yoko Saito, Apr. 25, 1965; children: Masamitsu, Shin, Mayu. B Engring., Tohoku U., Sendai, Japan, 1959, M Engring., 1961. Rschr. Ctrl. Rsch. Lab. Hitachi, Tokyo, 1964-70, sr. rschr., 1971-86, sr. chief tech. advisor, 1987-89; sr. chief engr. Hitachi Device Engring. Co., Mobara, Chiba, Japan, 1990-95; technical advisor display R&D Ctr. Samsung Display Devices Co., Ltd., Suwon, Korea, 1996—. Editor: Image Engineering Handbook, 1990; contbr. chpt. to book; patentee in field. Fellow Soc. for Info. Display (chpt. chmn. 1991-92, bd. dirs. 1992-93, Spl. Recognition award 1986, Beatrice Winner award 1992); mem. IEEE, Inst. Electronic Info. Comm. Engring., Inst. TV Engrs. Japan. Avocations: contract bridge, tennis, Go. Office: Samsung Display Devices Co Ltd, 575 Shin-Dong, Paldal-Gu, Suwon 442-390, Republic of Korea

FUKUYAMA, TAKAYA, cardiologist; b. Saga, Japan, Dec. 20, 1945. MD, Kyushu U., Fukuoka, Japan, 1970, DMS, 1977. Diplomate Japanese Bd. Internal Medicine, Japanese Bd. Cardiology, Japanese Bd. Nuclear Medicine. Resident Kyushu U. Hosp., 1970-77, instr., 1980-82, asst. prof., 1982-83; fellow Washington U., St. Louis, 1977-80; head cardiology Matsuyama (Japan) Red Cross Hosp., 1983—, dir. Cardiovasc. Ctr., 1984—; guest instr. Ehime U. Sch. Medicine, Matsuyama, 1984-99, clin. prof., 1999—. Mem. editl. adv. bd. Japanese Jour. Interventional Cardiology; contbr. articles to Circulation, Heart, Jour. Am. Coll. Cardiology, Am. Jour. Physiology. Grantee Japanese Heart Found., 1981, Japanese Ministry Edn., 1982. Mem. Japanese Soc. Internal Medicine, Japanese Circulation Soc., Japanese Soc. Nuc. Medicine, Japanese Coronary Assn. (coun. 1995—), Am. Soc. Nuc. Cardiology. Avocation: classical music. Home: Anjoji Cho 1-110, Matsuyama 791-8006, Japan Office: Matsuyama Red Cross Hosp., Bunkyo-cho 1, Matsuyama 790-8524, Japan

FUKUYAMA, YUKIO, child neurologist, pediatrics educator; b. Takachiho-machi, Miyazaki, Japan, May 28, 1928; s. Masaharu and Kiku Fukuyama; m. Ayako Arai, Nov. 6, 1954. MD, U. Tokyo, 1952, postgrad., 1953-56, PhD, 1959. Intern U. Tokyo Hosp., 1952-53; asst. prof. pediatrics U. Tokyo Faculty Medicine, 1960-64, assoc. prof., 1964-65; dir. div. neurology Nat. Children's Hosp., Tokyo, 1965-67; prof. pediatrics Tokyo Women's Med. Coll, 1967-94, chmn. dept., 1967-94, prof. emeritus, 1994—; prof. pediatrics Saitama Med. Sch., 1994-99; dir. Child Neurology Inst., 1994—. Editor: (monographs) Epilepsy Bibliography, 7th edit., 1998, Child Neurology Atlas, 1986, EEG and Evoked Potentials in Children, 1990, Modern Perspectives of Child Neurology, 1991, Fetal and Neonatal Neurology, 1992, Crossroads of Child Neurology, 1995, Congenital Muscular Dystrophies, 1997; editor-in-chief No To Hattatsu, 1969-87, Brain and Devel., 1979-96. Recipient Hughling Jackson's prize Japan Found. Epilepsy Rsch., 1993, Grand award Japan Med. Assn., 1999, Duchenne-Erb prize Gesellschaft für Muskelkranke, 1999. Mem. Internat. Child Neurology Assn. (pres. 1982-86, v.p. 1986-90, Frank Ford Lectr. award 1992), Asian and Oceanian Child Neurology Assn. (pres. 1983-90, pres. hon. 1993—), Japanese Soc. Child Neurology (chmn. bd. trustees 1968-93, chmn. hon. 1993—), Am. Neurol. Assn. (corr.), Child Neurology Soc. (hon.), Am. Acad. Neurology (hon.), Can. Child Neurology Soc. (hon.), Czechoslovakian Neurol. Soc. (hon.), Royal Soc. Medicine, Japan Pediat. Soc. (hon.), Japan Epilepsy Soc. (hon.), Japan Teratology Soc. (hon.), Japan Soc. Clin. Neurophysiology (hon.), Japanese Soc. Human Genetics (hon., Grand award 1999). Avocation: philately. Home: 6-12-16 Minami-Shinagawa, Shinagawa-ku, Tokyo 140-0004, Japan Office: Child Neurology Inst, Sambancho TY Plz 5F 24 Sambancho, Chiyoda-ku Tokyo 102-0075, Japan

FUKUZAKO, HIROSHI, neuropsychiatrist; b. Kagoshima, Japan, July 25, 1957; s. Sigeo and Ayako (Higashi) F.; m. Kumiko Ikeda, Dec. 1, 1986; children: Hiroki, Tadayuki, Satoshi. Med. licensure, Nagasaki U., Japan, 1983; PhD, Kagoshima U., 1989. Nat. cert. psychiatrist; bd. cert. mem. Japanese Psychosomatic Medicine. Resident Kagoshima U. Hosp., 1983-84; rsch. assoc. Kagoshima U., 1990-96, asst. prof., 1997—; rsch. fellow McLean Hosp.--Harvard Med. Sch., Belmont, 1991-92; cons. Nat. Found. for Depressive Illness, N.Y., 1997—, Regional Com. in Mental Health, Kagoshima, 1998—; reviewer in field. Contbr. articles to profl. jours. Fellow Min. Edn., Sci. and Culture, 1991-92; grantee Min. Health and Welfare, 1992-95; grantee Min. Edn., Sci. and Culture, 1998—. Mem. Internat. Soc. Neuroimaging in Psychiatry, Internat. Behavioural and Neural Genetics Soc., Soc. Biol. Psychiatry. Avocations: baseball, golf. Office: Kagoshima U Dept Neuropsy, 8-35-1 Sakuragaoka, Kagoshima 890-8520 Kagoshima Japan

FUKUZAWA, KENJI, physicist; b. Komagane, Nagano, Japan, Jan. 10, 1962. BS, Nagoya (Japan) U., 1985, M Engring., 1987, PhD, 1997. Sr. rschr. Nippon Telegraph and Telegram Corp., Musashino, Japan, 1987—. Co-author: Handbook on Near-Field Optics, 1997. Mem. Japan Soc. Applied Physics, Inst. Electronics, Info. and Comm. Engrs.

FUKUZUMI, KAZUO, fats chemist; b. Nagoya, Japan, Dec. 14, 1915; s. Hideichi and Mitsuru (Yoshikawa) F.; m. Keiko Yoshimura, Nov. 30, 1943; children: Michiko, Shun-ichi. B of Engring., Tohoku Imperial U., Sendai, Japan, 1940; PhD, Nagoya (Japan) U., 1958. Asst. Tohoku Imperial U., Sendai, Japan, 1940-41, asst. prof., 1941-44; rsch. officer Govt. Indsl. Rsch. Inst., Tokyo, 1944-51; assoc. prof. Nagoya (Japan) U., 1951-66, prof., 1966-79, emeritus prof., 1981—; dir. Japan Oil Chemists' Soc., 1964-68, Tokyo, chief of branch, 1965-66, Nagoya, Japan; councilor Japan Vascular Soc., Tokyo, 1968-79. Author: Lipid Peroxides, Aging, and Diseases, 1992, 2d edit., 1998. Introductor Nagoya (Japan) Civic U. Chair, 1987—. Recipient Medal from Emperor, Prime Minister, Tokyo, 1989. Fellow Am. Oil Chemists' Soc.; mem. Japan Oil Chemists' Soc., Chem. Soc. Japan. Achievements also include the studies on the autoxidation, the hydrolysis, and the hydrogenation of fatty oils; besides originations and establishments of lipid peroxide theories mentioned above. Home: 2-6-41 Aoi Higashi-ku, Nagoya 461-0004, Japan

FULACHER, PASCAL MAURICE, journalist, publisher; b. Macon, France, Feb. 19, 1959; s. Jean and Marie-Thérèse (Devillard) F.; m. Sylvaine Lenell, Oct. 31, 1980; children: Capucine, Marjolaine, Angeline. Lic. Lettres, Sorbonne U., Paris, 1983; Maitrise, Inst. Hautes Etudes, Paris, 1984. Journalist, reporter Art & Metiers du Livre, Paris, 1985—; chief editor Art & Metiers du Livre/Edits., Paris, 1990—, pub., 1994. Author: Papiers & Moulins, 1989, 2d edit., 1997; contbr. articles to profl. jours. Office: Art & Metiers Du Livre/Edit, 4 rue des Hauchiettes, 75003 Paris France

FULCI, FRANCESCO PAOLO, diplomat; b. Messina, Italy, Mar. 19, 1931; s. Sebastiano and Enza (Sciascia) F.; m. Claris Glathar, 1965; children: Sebastiano, Marie Sol, William. LLD, U. Messina, Italy, 1953; M in Comparative Law, Columbia U., 1955; diploma, Acad. Internat. Law, The Hague, The Netherlands, 1956; LLD (hon.), U. Windsor, Ont., Can., 1981, St. Thomas Aquinas Coll., 1996, St. John's U., 1998. Joined Italian Fgn. Svc., 1956, attache directorate gen. for econ. affairs N.Am. desk, 1956-58, 1st sec. directorate gen. for polit. affairs Soviet and Ea. European desk, 1963-65, liaison officer with Parliament in Cabinet, 1965-68; 1st vice consul Consulate Gen. Italy, N.Y.C., 1958-61; 2nd sec. Italian Embassy, Moscow, 1961-63; counsellor, 1st counsellor Italian Embassy, Paris, 1968-74; min. counsellor Italian Embassy, Tokyo, 1974-76; mem. Italian del. UN Gen. Assembly, N.Y.C., 1965; chief of cabinet to Hon. Amintore Fanfani Italian Senate, Rome, 1976-80; amb. to Can. Ottawa, 1980-85; amb. and permanent rep. of Italy NATO, Brussels, 1985-91; sec. gen. of exec. com. for intelligence and security CESIS, 1991-93; permanent rep. of Italy UN, N.Y.C., 1993-99; head, Italian del. UN Security Coun., New York, 1995-96; first v.p. ECOSOC, New York, 1998-99, pres., 1999-2000; v.p. Ferrero Internat., Rome, 2000—. Decorated Cross of Merit (Germany), officer Legion of Honor (France), comdr. Imperial Order of Rising Sun (Japan), knight Gt. Cross of Order of Merit (Italy), knight Mil. Order of Malta, Grand Cross Portuguese Rep., Knight Grand Cross of Italian Rep.; Fulbright scholar Columbia U., 1954-55. Office: Salita S Nicolo, da Tolentino 1b, 00187 Rome Italy

FULCO, ARMAND JOHN, biochemist; b. L.A., Apr. 3, 1932; s. Herman J. and Clelia Marie (DeFeo) F.; m. Virginia Loy Hungerford, June 18, 1955 (div. July 1985); children: William James, Lisa Marie, Linda Susan, Suzanne Yvonne; m. Doris V.N. Goodman, Nov. 29, 1987. B.S. in Chemistry, UCLA, 1957, Ph.D. in Physiol. Chemistry, 1960. NIH postdoctoral fellow Lipid Labs. UCLA, 1960-61; NIH research fellow dept. chemistry Harvard U., Cambridge, Mass., 1961-63; biochemist, prin. investigator Lab. Nuclear Medicine and Radiation Biology, UCLA, 1963-80; asst. prof. dept. biol. chemistry UCLA (Med. Sch.), 1965-70, assoc. prof., 1970-76, prof., 1976—, prin. investigator lab. biomed. and environ. scis., 1981-93; prin. investigator lab. structural biology/molecular med. UCLA-Dept. of Energy, 1993-95; cons. biochemist VA, Los Angeles, 1968-79; mem. UCLA Molecular Biology Inst., 1991—; co-dir. Lipid-Hormone Core Lab., UCLA, 1989-96; mem. Jonsson Comprehensive Cancer Ctr. UCLA, 1994—. Author: (with J.F. Mead) The Unsaturated and Polyunsaturated Fatty Acids in Health and Disease, 1976; contbr. over 90 articles to sci. jours. Served with U.S. Army, 1952-54. Mem. AAAS, Am. Chem. Soc., Am. Soc. Biochem. and Molecular Biology, Am. Soc. Microbiology, Internat. Soc. for Study of Xenobiotics, Harvard Chemists Assn., Sigma Xi. Office: UCLA Sch Medicine Dept Biol Chemistry PO Box 951737 Los Angeles CA 90095-1737

FULD, RICHARD SEVERIN, JR., investment banker; b. N.Y.C., Apr. 26, 1946; s. Richard Severin and Elizabeth (Schwab) F.; m. Kathleen Ann Bailey, Sept. 24, 1978; children: Jacqueline, Christine, Richard S. III. BS, U. Colo., 1969; MBA, NYU, 1973. Mng. dir. Lehman Bros., N.Y.C., 1969-84; vice chmn. Shearson Lehman (merger Shearson and Lehman Bros.), N.Y.C., 1984-90; past CEO, pres. Lehman Bros., N.Y.C., now chmn. bd., CEO, pres.; bd. dirs. Shearson Lehman Mortgage Co.; vice chmn. Shearson Lehman Bros., N.Y.C., 1984—; chmn. Lehman Comml. Paper, N.Y.C., 1984—; mem. PSA Govt. and Fed. Agy. Securities Com. Assoc. trustee Mt. Sinai Hosp., N.Y.C.; trustee Wilbraham (Mass.) & Monson Acad., Mt. Sinai Med. Ctr., Ethical Culture Schs.; chmn. Mt. Sinai Children's Ctr. Found.; bd. dirs. Ronald McDonald House. Avocations: squash, photography.

FULDA, MICHAEL, political science educator, space policy researcher; b. Liverpool, Eng., Apr. 21, 1939; came to U.S., 1962, naturalized, 1966; s. Boris and Catherine (Von Dehn) F.; m. Rosa Bongiorno, July 19, 1970; children: Robert, George. Student, Polytechnique, Grenoble, France, 1956-57, Tech. U., West Berlin, Germany, 1957-58, Karl Eberhardt U., Tubingen, Germany, 1963-66; MA, Am. U., 1968, PhD in Internat. Studies, 1970. Prof. polit. sci. Fairmont State Coll., W.Va., 1971—; internat. rels. specialist NASA, Washington, 1979. Author: Oil and International Relations, 1979; (with other) United State Space Policy, 1985; contbr. articles to profl. jours. Bd. dirs. Fairmont Chamber Music Soc., 1983—; W.Va. state com. chmn., dir. space policy Nat. Unity Campaign for John Anderson, 1980; mem. nat. adv. com. John Glenn Presdl. Com., 1984, space policy group Dukakis/Bentsen Com., 1988; merit badge councilor Boy Scouts Am.; active psychol ops. Vets. Assn. With U.S. Army, 1962-66. Fellow NASA Marshall Ctr., Huntsville, Ala., summer 1977, Langley Ctr., Hampton, Va., 1976; Woodrow Wilson Found. fellow, 1969-70; Humanities Found. W.Va. grantee, 1978-80, NASA W.Va. Space Grant Consortium grantee, 1991—; named alt. del. to Aerospace States Assn. by the Gov. of W.Va., 1998. Fellow AIAA (assoc.), Brit. Interplanetary Soc.; mem. Am. Astronautical Soc., Nat. Space Soc. (dir. 1991-93), German Assn. for Luft and Raumfamrt, Soc. Espacial Mexicana, Nat. Space Club, Assn. Argentina Tech. Space, Inst. for Social Sci. Study of Space (pres. 1988—), Fairmont Elks Lodge (edn. com.). Avocations: physical fitness, weightlifting, tango, triathlons. Home: 1 Timothy Ln Fairmont WV 26554-1331

FULDER, STEPHEN JOHN, author, educator; b. London, Nov. 16, 1946; s. Max and Marie Louise (Orgler) F.; m. Rachel Ariel, Aug. 12, 1976; children: Yasmin, Tamarin, Aurielle. MA in Biochemistry with honors, Oxford (Eng.) U., 1969, Diploma in Human Biology, 1970; PhD, Nat. Inst. Med. Rsch., London, 1975. Staff mem. Nat. Inst. Med. Rsch., London, 1975-76; lectr. Chelsea Coll., London U., 1976-77, Hadassah Hosp., Jerusalem, 1977-80; dir., CEO Consultancy and Rsch. on Biomedicine, Israel, 1979—; lectr., acad. advisor Western Galilee (Israel) Coll., 1994—; founder Rsch. Coun. for Complementary Medicine, London, 1981; founder, chief rschr. Arabic Indigenous Medicine Resources Project, Israel, 1995—. Author: The Handbook of Complementary Medicine, 3d edit., 1996, How to Survive Medical Treatment, 1995, The Tao of Medicine, 1990; co-author: Towards a New Science of Health, 1993, others; contbr. articles to profl. jours. Chmn. bd. Citizens for the Environment, Galilee, 1994—; founder Insight Soc., Israel, 1995; mem. Reapproachment Facilitators for Israeli-Palestinian Dialogue, Jerusalem, 1995-96. Mem. Sci. and Med. Network. Avocations: meditation, gardening, stone-building.

FULKER, EDMUND NORMAN, management consultant; b. Pittsfield, Mass., June 14, 1927; s. Herbert Ernest Creal Fulker and Albina Archambault; m. Jeanette Ruth Fletcher, July 31, 1948; children: Pamela J. Fulker Leonard, Glenn Herbert. BS, Purdue U., 1950, MS in Psychology, 1951; EdD in Adult Edn., Am. U., 1970. Lic. psychologist, D.C. Instr. Purdue U., Indpls., 1952-54; tng. officer Hdqrs. USAF Pentagon, Washington, 1954-57, Hdqrs. USDA, Washington, 1957-59; asst. dir. USDA Grad. Sch., Washington, 1959-80, dir., 1980-85; cons. The World Bank, Washington, 1987-99; adj. faculty Am. U., 1955-56, Washington, George Washington U., Ctrl. Mich. U., Nat. Cheng Chi U., Taiwan; pres. Washington chpt. ASPA, 1977-78, nat. coun. mem., 1979-81. Contbr. articles to profl. jours. Mgmt. cons. U. Mich., Taipei, Taiwan, 1963, Ford Found., New Delhi, India, Nepal, 1970-71, Ohio State U., Ankara, Turkey, 1993, Egypt Gen. Petroleum Co., Cairo, 1996—. With USNR, 1945-47. Recipient Outstanding Pub. Adminstrn. award ASPA, Washington, 1984. Mem. ASTD (pres. chpt. 1964-65, Outstanding Trainer award 1963), APA, Internat. Club Washington. Avocations: boating, golfing, traveling. E-mail: edfulker@aol.com. Home: 15240 Sam Snead Ln Fort Myers FL 33917-3260

FULLENWIDER, NANCY VRANA, music composer, dance educator, pianist; b. Sheridan, Wyo., May 9, 1940; d. Jacob Allen and Edith Martha (Tripp) Fullenwider; m. Linsfred Leroy Vrana, Apr. 26, 1980. BA summa cum laude, U. Denver, 1962, MA, 1971, postgrad., 1974. Prin. dancer, instr. Colo. Ballet and Colo. Ballet Ctr., Denver, 1958-80; owner, instr. Idaho Springs (Colo.) Sch. Ballet, 1962-67, Sch. Ballet, Parker, Colo., 1974-79; curriculum developer Career Edn. Ctr., Denver Pub. Schs., 1973; grad. asst. U. Denver, 1974; guest artist, choreographer, composer Young Audiences, Denver, 1975-80; instr. ballet Ballet Arts Ctr., Denver, 1992-98, Colo. Dance Ctr., Littleton, 1992—; music dir., accompanist for Western Chamber Ballet, Denver, 1994-98, Colo. Ballet, 1999, Arvada Ctr., 1998, Ballet Arts, 1998. Composer (CD's) To the Pointe, 1997, Brava!, 1999, Curtain Call, 2000; commissioned ballet works performed at Arvada Ctr. for Performing Arts, Colo., 1991, Aurora (Colo.) Fox Arts Ctr., 1989-92, Buell Theatre, Colo., 1993, Cleo Parker Robinson Dance Theatre, Colo., 1992, Colo. Springs Fine Arts Ctr., 1991, Houston Fine Arts Ctr., Colo., 1971, San Luis Arts Festival, Colo., 1990, Bonfils Theatre, Colo., 1971, Denver Civic Theatre, 2000. Grantee Douglas County Schs., Colo., 1998. Mem. Phi Beta Kappa, Alpha Lambda Delta. Avocations: hiking, fly fishing, theatre, concerts.

FULLER, DAVID OTIS, JR., lawyer; b. Grand Rapids, Mich., May 28, 1939; s. David Otis and Virginia Chapin (Emery) F.; m. Isabelle Patrice Gigout, July 5, 1968; children: Thomas Andrew, Christian Scott, Pierre Emery, Margaret Isabelle. BA, Wheaton Coll., 1961; JD, Harvard U., 1964; postgrad. George Washington U., 1963, U. Paris, 1966. Bar: Mich 1964, N.Y. 1967, U.S. Sup. Ct. 1968. Law clk. U.S. Ho. of Reps. Judiciary Com., 1963; assoc. Amberg, Law & Fallon, Grand Rapids, 1964-65; asst. dist. atty. N.Y. County, 1966-72, law sec. to justice, 1972-73; corp. atty. Pan Am. World Airways, Inc., 1973-74; dep. gen. counsel Reader's Digest Assn., Inc., 1974-84; pvt. practice, N.Y.C., 1984-87; ptnr. Baker, Nelson & Williams, N.Y.C., 1987-94, Bosworth, Gray & Fuller, Bronxville, N.Y., 1994—; justice Tuckahoe Village, N.Y., 1986—; lectr. Am. Bar Assn., Practicing Law Inst., Bronx C.C. Warden Episc. Ch., 1991-97. Editor Harvard Jour. on Legislation, 1962-64; contbr. articles to profl. jours. Mem. ABA, Internat. Bar Assn., N.Y. State Bar Assn. (chmn. privacy com. 1982-84), Assn. Bar City N.Y. (communications law com. 1984-87), Am. Arbitration Assn. (arbitrator 1983-96), N.Y. State Magistrates Assn. (dir. 1998—), Westchester County Bar Assn., Westchester County Magistrates Assn. (pres. 1993-94). Republican. Club: Harvard (N.Y.C.). Avocations: fishing, skiing, coins, racquet sports, French. Office: Bosworth Gray & Fuller 116 Kraft Ave Bronxville NY 10708-3810

FULLER, EDWIN DANIEL, hotel executive; b. Richmond, Va., Mar. 15, 1945; s. Ben Swint and Evelyn (Beal) F. Student, Wake Forest U., 1965; BSBA, Boston U., 1968; postgrad., Harvard Sch. Bus., 1987. Security officer Pinkerton Inc., Boston, 1965-68; with sales dept. Twin Bridges Marriott Hotel, Arlington, Va., 1972-73; nat. sales mgr. Marriott Hotels & Resorts, N.Y.C., 1973-76; dir. nat. and internat. sales Marriott Hotels & Resorts, Washington, 1976-78; v.p. mktg. Marriott Hotels & Resorts, 1978-82; gen. mgr. Marriott Hotels & Resorts, Hempstead, N.Y., 1982-83, Marriott Copley Place, Boston, 1983-85; v.p. ops. Midwest region Marriott Corp., Rosemont, Ill., 1985-89; v.p. ops. Western and Pacific regions Marriott Corp., Santa Ana, Calif., 1989-90; sr. v.p., mng. dir. Marriott Hotels & Resorts-Internat., Washington, 1990-93; exec. v.p., mng. dir. internat. lodging Marriott Lodging Internat., Washington, 1994-97, pres., mng. dir., 1997—; chmn. bd. dirs. SNR Reservation Sys., Zurich, Switzerland, 1979-81; bd. dirs. Boston U. Hotel Sch., 1984—, Mgmt. Engrs. Inc., Reston, Va., Barnby Books, Barnaby Books, Honolulu, 1997—; treas. MEI Pacific Honolulu, 1985—; chmn. Fuller Properties, Laguna Hills, Calif., 1990—. Pres. Boston U. Gen. Alumni Assn., 1993—, v.p., 1990-93; v.p. Boston U. Sch. Mgmt. Alumni Bd., 1985—; mem. adv. bd. Boston U. Hospitality Mgmt. Sch., 1985—; trustee Boston U., mem. exec. com. bd. trustees, 1994—. Capt. U.S. Army, 1968-72, Vietnam. Decorated Bronze Star. Mem. Boston U. Alumni Coun. (v.p.), Harvard Sch. Bus. Advanced Mgmt. Program (fund agt.), Sigma Alpha Epsilon, Delta Sigma Pi. Republican. Avocations: real estate, travel, golf, history. Home: 25362 Derbyhill Dr Laguna Hills CA 92653-7835 Office: Marriott Hotels & Resorts 1 Marriott Dr Washington DC 20058-0001

FULLER, HARRY LAURANCE, oil company executive; b. Moline, Ill., Nov. 8, 1938; s. Marlin and Mary Helen (Ilsley) F.; m. Nancy Lawrence, Dec. 27, 1961; children: Kathleen, Laura, Randall. BSChemE, Cornell U., 1961; JD, DePaul U., 1965. Bar: Ill. 1965. With Standard Oil Co. (and affiliates), 1961-2000, sales mgr., 1972-74, gen. mgr. supply, 1974-77; exec. v.p. Standard Oil Co. (Amoco Oil Co. div.), Chgo., 1977-78; pres. Amoco Oil Co., Chgo., 1978-81; exec. v.p. Standard Oil Co. of Ind., Chgo., 1981-83; pres. Amoco Corp., Chgo., 1983-91, chmn., CEO, 1991-2000, also dir., 1999-2000; co-chair BP Amoco p.l.c., Chgo., 1999-2000; ret., 2000; bd. dirs. Chase Manhattan Corp., Chase Manhattan Bank N.A., Abbott Labs., Motorola, Inc. Bd. dirs. Chgo. Rehab. Inst.; trustee Orchestral Assn. Mem. Am. Petroleum Inst. (bd. dirs.). Republican. Presbyterian. Clubs: Mid-Am, Chgo. Golf, Chicago.

FULLER, JACK WILLIAM, writer, publishing executive; b. Chgo., Oct. 12, 1946; s. Ernest Brady and Dorothy Voss (Tegge) F.; m. Alyce Sue Tuttle, June 2, 1973; children: Timothy, Katherine. BS, Northwestern U., 1968; JD, Yale U., 1973. Bar: Ill. 1974. Reporter Chgo. Tribune, 1973-75, Washington corr., 1977-78, editorial writer, 1978-79, dep. editorial page editor, 1979-82, editorial page editor, 1982-87, exec. editor, 1987-89, v.p. and editor, 1989-93, pres., CEO, 1993-97, pub., 1994-97; pres. Tribune Pub. Co., 1997—; spl. asst. to atty. gen. U.S. Dept. Justice, Washington, 1975-77. Author: Convergence, 1982 (Cliff Dwellers award 1983), Fragments, 1984 (Friends of Am. Writers award 1985), Mass, 1985, Our Fathers' Shadows, 1987, Legends' End, 1990, News Values, 1996, The Best of Jackson Payne, 2000. Bd. dirs. McCormick Tribune Found., Field Mus.; mem. Pulitzer Prize Bd., 1991-2000; trustee U. Chgo. With U.S. Army, 1969-70. Recipient Gavel award ABA, 1979, Pulitzer prize for editl. writing, 1986. Fellow Am. Acad. Arts and Scis.; mem. Am. Soc. Newspaper Editors, Newspaper Assn. Am., Inter-Am. Dialogue, Inter-Am. Press Assn. (sec.), Comml. Club of Chgo. Office: Chgo Tribune Co 435 N Michigan Ave Chicago IL 60611-4066

FULLER, JOHN (LEOPOLD), poet; b. Ashford, Kent, Eng., Jan. 1, 1937; s. Roy Broadbent and Kathleen (Smith) F.; m. Cicely Prudence Martin, July 20, 1960; children: Sophie Claire, Louisa Charlotte, Emily Renira Alice. BA, New College, Oxford (Eng.) U., 1960, MA, 1964, BLitt, 1965. Asst. lectr. U. Manchester, Eng., 1963-66; fellow, tutor in English Magdalen Coll., Oxford (Eng.) U., 1966—; vis. lectr. in English SUNY, Buffalo, 1962-63. Writings include: (poetry) Fairground Music, 1961, The Tree That Walked, 1967, The Art of Love, 1968, The Labors of Hercules: A Sonnet Sequence, 1970, The Wreck, 1970, Cannibals and Missionaries, 1972 (Newdigate prize 1960, Richard Hillary award 1961, E.C. Gregory award 1965, Geoffrey Faber Meml. prize 1974), Boys in a Pie, 1972, Hut Groups, 1973, (with Adrian Mitchell and Peter Levi) Penguin Modern Poets 22, 1973, Epistles to Several Persons, 1973, Poems and Epistles, 1974, Squeaking Crust, 1974, A Bestiary, 1974, The Mountain in the Sea, 1975, Lies and Secrets, 1979, The Illusionists, 1980, Waiting for the Music, 1982, The Beau-

tiful Inventions, 1983, Selected Poems 1954-1982, 1985, (with James Fenton) Partingtime Hall, 1987, The Grey among the Green, 1988, The Mechanical Body, 1991, Stones and Fires, 1996, Collected Poems, 1996; (libretti with Bryan Kelly) Herod Do Your Worst: A Nativity Opera, 1967, Three London Songs, 1969, Half a Fortnight, 1970, The Spider Monkey Uncle King, 1971, Fox-Trot, 1972, The Queen in the Golden Tree, 1974, How Did You Get Here, Jonno?, 1975, The Ship of Sounds, 1975, Adam's Apple, 1975, Linda, 1977, St. Francis of Assisi, 1981; (criticism) A Reader's Guide to W.H. Auden, 1970, The Sonnet, 1972, W.H. Auden: A Commentary, 1998; (fiction) Flying to Nowhere, 1983, The Adventures of Speedfall, 1985, Tell It Me Again, 1988, The Burning Boys, 1989, Look Twice, 1991, The Worm and the Star, 1993, A Skin Diary, 1997; (children's lit.) The Last Bid, 1975, The Extraordinary Wool Mill and Other Stories, 1980, Come Aboard and Sail Away, 1983, Poets in Hand, 1985; editor: (with J. Mitchell and others) Light Blue Dark Blue, 1960, Oxford Poetry, 1960, Poetry Supplement, 1962, (with Harold Pinter and Peter Redgrove) New Poems 1967: A PEN Anthology of Contemporary Poetry, 1968, Poetry Supplement, 1970, Dramatic Works of John Gay, 1982, New Poetry 8, 1982, Nemo's Almanac, Chatto Book of Love Poetry, 1990, The Oxford Book of Sonnets, 2000. Recipient So. Arts Lit. prize, 1980, Whitbread prize, 1983, Forward prize, 1996. Address: 4 Benson Pl, Oxford OX2 6QH, England

FULLER, MARGARET JANE, medical technologist; b. Park Rapids, Minn., Jan. 29, 1947; d. Rudolph Kenneth and Jean Ellen (Klenk) Haas; m. Phillip Fuller, Aug. 7, 1970; 1 child, Sharon Dawn. BS in Chemistry, Muhlenberg Coll., 1969; diploma in med. tech., Allentown (Pa.) Hosp., 1972; MPA, Angelo State U., 1988; MS in Microbiology, Tex. Tech. U., 1992. Lab. dir. San Angelo-Tom Green County Health Dept., 1984-89; outpatient lab. supr. Meth. Hosp., Plainview, Tex., 1995-96; lab. mgr. Highland Med. Ctr., Lubbock, Tex., 1996-98; mem. med. adv. bd. Planned Parenthood West Tex., San Angelo, 1987-89; scientist-by-mail, assoc. Children's Mus. Houston, 1991-92; direct patient vol. Hospice of Lubbock, 1993-98. Bd. dirs. El Camino coun. Girl Scouts U.S.A. Recipient Thanks Badge, El Camino coun. Girl Scouts U.S.A., 1986. Mem. Am. Soc. Microbiology, Am. Soc. Clin. Lab. Sci., Am. Soc. Clin. Pathologists (assoc., cert. med. technologist), Tex. Soc. Clin. Lab. Tech. (regional sec. 1985-87), Tex. Pub. Health Assn., Clin. Lab. Mgmt. Assn., Mensa, Beta Beta Beta, Sigma Theta Tau. Episcopalian.

FULLER, PAMELA DORR, software engineer; b. Monrovia, Calif., July 23, 1956; d. Jack Glendon and Nancy (Tatnall) F.; m. Timothy Seth Daniel, July 5, 1985 (div. Dec. 1999). BS in Computer Sci., Coll. William and Mary, 1978; MS in Computer Sci., Va. Poly. Inst. and State U., 1989. Programmer/analyst United Info. Svcs., Falls Church, Va., 1978-83; software engr. Hadron, Inc., Fairfax, Va., 1983-88, Wollongong Group, McLean, Va., 1988-96, Attachmate Corp., McLean, 1996-99, DataSage, Inc., Gaithersburg, Md., 1999—. Avocations: sailing, scuba diving, travel, weaving. E-mail: pfuller@vignette.com.

FULLER, RAY GUY CYRIL, psychology educator; b. Bridlington, Yorkshire, Eng., Apr. 17, 1943; arrived in Ireland, 1968; s. Guy Henry and Ruth Thelma (Megginson) F.; m. Barbara Sheila Murray, July 15, 1966 (sep. 1991); children: Rupert, Robin. MA, U. St. Andrews, Scotland, 1965; PhD, U. Dundee, Scotland, 1970; MA de juri officii, Trinity Coll., Dublin, 1974. Cert. psychologist. Jr. rsch. lectr. Trinity Coll., Dublin, 1968-71, rsch. lectr., 1971-72, lectr. in psychology, 1972-80, sr. lectr. in psychology, 1980—, head dept. psychology, 1988-94; mem. CRM com. on toxic and psychol. factors in road traffic accidents, Commn. of the EU, Brussels, 1974-77; mem. European Transport Safety Coun. Working Party, Brussels, 1993—; cons. Brit. Airways, London, 1995—. Co-editor, co-author: Aviation Psychology in Practice, 1994; editor Seven Pioneers of Psychology, 1995; co-editor: Application of Psychology to the Aviation System, 1995, Human Factors in Aviation Operations, 1995, A Century of Psychology, 1997. Fellow Trinity Coll., Dublin, 1992; grantee Army Rsch. Inst. U.S. Dept. Def., 1976-82, Eolas-Dublin Bus., 1991-93. Fellow Psychol. Soc. Ireland (pres. 1977-78), Ergonomics Soc. Ireland; mem. Dublin Rd. Safety Coun. Avocations: running, opera, theatre, cinema, video direction and editing. Office: Dept Psychology, Trinity Coll, Dublin 2, Ireland

FULLER, RENEE NUNI, psychologist, educational publisher; b. Mannheim, Germany, Apr. 14, 1929; came to U.S., 1938; d. Eric Woldemar and Fridel Gronau (Henning) Stoetzner; widowed. Student, Swarthmore (Pa.) Coll., 1947-49; BA, Hunter Coll., 1951; MA, Columbia U., 1953; PhD, NYU, 1963. Research scientist Letchworth Village N.Y. State Dept. Mental Hygiene, Thiells, 1961-67; project dir. Staten Island (N.Y.) Soc. Mental Health, 1967-68; chief psychol. services Rosewood Hosp. Ctr., Owings Mills, Md., 1968-75; pres. Ball-Stick-Bird Publs. Inc., Colebrook, Conn., 1975—. Author: In Search of the IQ Correlation, 1977, (reading series) Ball-Stick-Bird; contbr. articles to profl. jours. Recipient Disting. Achievement award Fairleigh-Dickinson U., N.J., 1979. Fellow Am. Psychol. Soc.; mem. APA, Soc. for Rsch. in Child Devel. E-mail: bsbpub@snet.net. Office: Ball-Stick-Bird Publs Inc PO Box 13 Colebrook CT 06021-0013

FULLER, ROBERT KENNETH, architect, urban designer; b. Denver, Oct. 6, 1942; s. Kenneth Roller and Gertrude Ailene (Heid) F.; m. Virginia Louise Elkin, Aug. 23, 1969; children: Kimberly Kirsten, Kelsey Christa. BArch, U. Colo., 1967; MArch and Urban Design, Washington U., St. Louis, 1974. Registered profl. architect, Colo. Archtl. designer Fuller & Fuller, Denver, Marvin Hatami Assocs., 1968-69; architect, planner Urban Research and Design Ctr., St. Louis, 1970-72; urban designer Victor Gruen & Assocs., 1973-75; prin. Fuller & Fuller Assocs., Denver, 1975—. Past pres. Denver East Ctrl. Civic Assn., Country Club Hist. Dist.; bd. dirs. Cherry Creek Steering Com.; pres. Horizon Adventures, Inc.; permanent sec.-treas. Ednl. Fund, Colo. Soc. Archs. Sgt. USMCR, 1964-70. Mem. AIA (past pres. Denver chpt.), Colo. Arlberg Club (past pres.), Rocky Mountain Vintage Racing Assn., Phi Gamma Delta, Delta Phi Delta. Home: 2244 E 4th Ave Denver CO 80206-4107 Office: 3320 E 2nd Ave Denver CO 80206-5302

FULLERTON, DOROTHY MALLAN, artist, modeling agency executive; b. Ancon, C.Z., May 6, 1938; d. Daniel Harrington and Dorothy (Heintzelman) Mallan; m. George Latimer Fullerton, May 31, 1957 (div. 1979); children: Daphne, Stuart, Nicholas. Student, Women's Christian Coll., Madras, India, 1956, Corcoran Art Sch., 1960; Cours de Civilization certificate, Sorbonne, Paris, 1971, Ecole du Louvre, 1972. RN, Calif. Antique dealer, Paris, 1970-73, antique sales rep., Heritage Place, San Francisco, 1979-81; fashion model Model Mgmt., Ford, N.Y., Brebner, San Francisco, 1980-85, talent dir., model mgmt., San Francisco, 1983-85, Grimmé Agy, San Francisco, 1987. One man shows include Rehobeth Art League, Del., 1965, Boston Visual Artists, Union, Mass., 1976, Artist Co-op, 1984, Castlebury Gallery, Arlington, Tex.; group shows include Leahy Hosp., Boston, 1976, Chez Henri, Warren, Vt., 1977, Artist Co-op of San Francisco, 1980-85; represented in permanent collections Schueler, Boston, Latham, France, Frapier, France, McNally, Zena Jones, Ruth Assawa, Bea Kribs, San Francisco; also pvt. collections. Mem. Artist Cooperative Gallery (mem. bd.), San Francisco Women Artist Gallery, Artist Cooperative Gallery (pres. 1982), Jr. League San Francisco, Nat. Mus. Women in Arts. Republican. Episcopalian. Avocations: music; fishing; hiking; traveling. Home: 145 Connecticut St San Francisco CA 94107-2414 Office: 45 Castro St Ste 100 San Francisco CA 94114-1010

FULLERTON, SUSANNAH CHRISTINE, actress, freelance lecturer; b. Edmonton, Alberta, Can., July 14, 1960; arrived in New Zealand, 1964.; d. Ashley Francis and Jenny Elinor (Arnold) Wilson; m. Ian George Fullerton, Sept. 4, 1982; children: Kenneth, Carrick, Elinor. Diploma in Speech and Drama, U. Trinity, Belfast, Ireland, 1977; BA, U. Auckland, New Zealand, 1979; MSc in Arts, U. Edinburgh, Scotland, 1981; diploma in Speech and Drama, U. Trinity, Belfast, Ireland. Free lance lectr. clubs, schs. etc., various cities, Australia, 1992—. Contbr. articles to literary mags. Recipient scholarship U. Auckland, New Zealand, 1987. Mem. Jane Austen Soc. Australia (pres. 1996—), Bronte Soc. (spkr. 1992—), Dylan Thomas Soc. Australia (spkr. 1996—). Home and Office: 26 MacDonald St Paddington, Sydney NSW 2021, Australia

FULLERTON, THOMAS MANKIN, JR., economist; b. Ft. Worth, Aug. 31, 1959; s. Thomas Mankin and Katherine Jane (Copeland) F.; 1 child, Kristina Marie. BBA, U. Tex., El Paso, 1981; MS, Iowa Stata U., 1984; MA, U. Penn., 1988; PhD, U. Fla., 1996. Jr. economist El Paso (Tex.) Electric Co., El Paso, 1981-83; economist Exec. Office of the Gov., Boise, Idaho, 1984-87; internat. economist Wharton Econometrics, The WEFA Group, Bala Cynwyd, Pa., 1988-91; sr. economist U. Fla., Gainesville, 1991-96; rsch. assoc. U. Fla. Ctr. for Latin Am. Studies, Gainesville, 1991-96; asst. prof. U. Tex. El Paso, 1996—, coord. border region modeling project, 1996—; alternate, Nat. Gov.'s Assn. Energy Com., Boise, 1985-86; Idaho state expert, Wharton Econometrics Regional Network, Boise, 1986-87; Idaho coord., Fed. Program Population Estimates, Boise, 1985-87; broadcaster, Radio YSKL, San Salvador, El Salvador, 1976-77. Sponsor Save the children, Bogota, Colombia, 1985—; commr. U. Tex. Student Election Bd., El Paso, 1978-79, mortar bd. U. Tex., El Paso, 1981. Dean's fellow, Wharton Sch., 1987-88. em. Nat. Assn. Bus. Economists (policy panel 1989—, forecast panel 1984-88), Ri o Grande Econs. Assn., Wharton Alumni Assn., Beta Gamma Sigma, Phi Kappa Phi, Alpha Chi. Presbyterian. Office: U Tex Dept Econs And Fin El Paso TX 79968-0001

FULOP, ANDRAS KRISTOF, biologist, educator; b. Celldomolk, Hungary, Feb. 14, 1958; s. Jozsef and Margit (Almasi) F. MSc, Eotvos Lorand U., 1982, Dr, 1992, PhD, 1995. Lab. biologist Phylaxia Veterinary Co., Budapest, 1982-84; instr. Semmelweiss U., Budapest, 1984-95; postdoctoral fellow Roswell Park Cancer Inst., Buffalo, 1995-96; asst. prof. Semmelweis U., Budapest, 1995—. Mem. Hungarian Biol. Soc., Hungarian Soc. Microscopy, European Cell Biology Orgn., Hungarian Lab. Animal Scientists Soc. Avocations: hiking, playing tennis. Office: Semmelweis U Dept Genetics, POB 370, H-1445 Budapest Hungary

FULSCHER, MITCH R., accountant; b. Chgo., Aug. 18, 1941; s. Harry and Lillian F.; m. Sandra L Sandfor, Dec. 23, 1961 (div.); children: Debra, David, Michael; m. Tomoko Kano, Dec. 21, 1994. BBA, U. Wis., 1963. Ptnr. Arthur Anderson, Chgo., 1963-86, Tokyo, 1986—. Author: Finalcial Futures, 1989. Mem. Futures Industry Assn. (pres.), U. Club Chgo., Wilshire Country Club. Office: Arthur Andersen, Asahi Ctr Bldg 1-2 Tsukudo, Tokyo Japan

FULSHER, ALLAN ARTHUR, lawyer; b. Portland, Oreg., July 5, 1952; s. Rémy Walter and Barbara Lee (French) F.; m. Karen Louise Schmid, Dec. 28, 1974 (dec. Sept. 1990); children: Brian Rémy, Louise Katherine, Elizabeth Alane. BA in Biology, U. Oreg., 1974, BA in Econs., 1976; JD, U. of Pacific, 1979. Bar: Oreg. 1979, Calif. 1980, U.S. Dist. Ct. Oreg. 1980, U.S. Dist. Ct. (ea. dist.) Calif. 1981, U.S. Ct. Appeals (9th cir.) 1982, U.S. Dist. Ct. (no. dist.) Calif. 1985, U.S. Dist. Ct. (so. dist.) Calif. 1986. Assoc. Law Offices of Jacques B. Nichols PC, Portland, 1979-82, Ragen, Roberts, O'Scannlain, Robertson & Neill, Portland, 1982-83; shareholder Bauer, Hermann, Fountain & Rhoades PC, Portland, 1983-87, v.p., 1984-87; shareholder, v.p. Fulsher and Weatherhead PC, Portland, 1987-88, pres., 1988—; gen. counsel Peregrine Holdings, Ltd., Beaverton, Oreg., 1993-97, Peregrine Capital, Inc., Beaverton, 1993—; mgr. Stamford Bridge, LLC, 1995—; pres., mgr. Portland Profl. Soccer, L.L.C., Tigard, Oreg., 1998—; gen. counsel Premier Soccer Alliance, L.L.C., Dallas, 1998—. Mem. Audi Quattro Club U.S.A. Republican. Roman Catholic. Avocations: basketball, automobile racing and restoration, coaching youth and adult sports. Home: 16399 SE Sager Rd Portland OR 97236-5509 Office: Peregrine Capital Inc 9725 SW Beaverton Hillsdale Hw Beaverton OR 97005-3305

FULTON, GUY CHARLES, company executive; b. London, Dec. 9, 1970. Grad. in Chinese,, Oxford (Eng.) U., 1993. Mng. dir. FPDSAvills, Shanghai, 1994—. Mem. Brit. C. of C. (com. mem. Shanghai 1997—), Shanghai Cricket Club (pres. 1999), Waigaoqiao FTZ Club. Office: FPDSAvills Shanghai 2d Fl, 381 Huai Hai Middle Rd, Shanghai 200021, China

FULTON, NORMAN ROBERT, credit manager; b. L.A., Dec. 16, 1935; s. Robert John and Fritzi Marie (Wacker) F.; m. Nancy Butler, July 6, 1966; children: Robert B., Patricia M. AA, Santa Monica Coll., 1958; BS, U. So. Calif., 1960. Asst. v.p. Raphael Glass Co., L.A., 1960-65; credit adminstr. Zellerbach Paper Co., L.A., 1966-68; gen. credit mgr. Carrier Transicold Co., Montebello, Calif., 1968-70, Virco Mfg. Co., L.A., 1970-72, Superscope, Inc., Chatsworth, Calif., 1972-79; asst. v.p. credit and adminstrn. Inkel Corp., Carson, Calif., 1980-82; corp. credit mgr. Gen. Consumer Electronics, Santa Monica, Calif., 1982-83; br. credit mgr. Sharp Electronics Corp., Carson, Calif., 1983-96; credit mgr. Rocheux Internat., Inc., Carson, 1997-99; with Barron Chestney, Internat., 2000—. With AUS, 1955-57. Fellow Nat. Inst. Credit (cert. credit exec.); mem. Credit Mgrs. So. Calif., Nat. Notary Assn. Home: 6437 Kanan Dume Rd Malibu CA 90265-4037

FULTON-QUINDOZA, DEBRA ANN, nurse practitioner; b. Anne Arundel, Md., Dec. 16, 1961; d. William D. and Patricia A. (Rensel) Fulton; m. Stephen S. Quindoza, Nov. 17, 1998; children: William Benjamin Quindoza, Allison Marie Quindoza; 1 stepchild, Costas Quindoza. BSN, U. Tex., Galveston, 1983, MSN, 1986. Advanced RN practitioner, Fla.; cert. profl. nurse practitioner. Clin. nurse specialist Arnold Palmer Hosp. for Childen and Women, Orlando, Fla., 1988; pediatric and internal medicine nurse practitioner Office of Dr. Shirley Nagel, Mt. Dora, Fla., 1990-91; project leader in med. policy-med. rev.-fraud and abuse Medicare of Fla., Jacksonville, 1991-93; med. cons., outreach educator, project mgr. Medicare Fraud Br., Jacksonville, Fla., 1993-98; advanced RN practitioner part time Dr. Perry G. Carlos, 1996—; sr. healthcare analyst statis./med. data analysis dept. benefits/program integrity divsn. Medicare Fla., 1998—; med. cons. in field. Home: 12638 Point Park Dr Jacksonville FL 32225-5508 Office: Medicare Fraud Br 532 Riverside Ave Ste 11 T Jacksonville FL 32202-4914

FULTZ, JOHN HOWARD, middle school educator; b. East Liverpool, Ohio, Mar. 4, 1949; s. John C. and Irene (Christy) F.; m. Sandra Liebhart, 1975. BS in Edn., Kent State U., 1971, MEd, 1976. Cert. tchr., Ohio. Laborer Union Labor Local 809, Steubenville, Ohio, 1967-71; clk. Montgomery Ward, East Liverpool, 1967-71; tchr., tutor Wellsville (Ohio) Schs., 1968-70; tchr. Kent (Ohio) City Schs., 1971—; chmn. curriculum adv. com. Kent City Schs., 1982. Editor monthly publ. for pub. speakers Phantastic Phunnies, 1978-91. Active Make-A-Wish Found., Cleve., 1989—, Rails to Trails Conservation, Washington, 1992—, Spl. Olympics Ohio, Columbus, 1991—, No. Ohio chpt. Leukemia Soc. Am., 1995—; vol. Meml. Sloan Kettering Cancer Found., N.Y.C., 1991—; rep. to South Africa in Citizen Amb. Program, 1997. Martha Holden Jennings Found. scholar, Cleve., 1972; recipient Coast to Coast marathon award Mercedes-Benz Co., 1991, Vol. award Meml. Sloan Kettering Cancer Found., 1991-93, Leukemia Soc. Am., 1995. Mem. ASCD, Fraternal Order of Police, Masons (brother), Kent State Alumni and Blue and Gold Club, U.S. Athletics Congress, Ohio Athletics Congress, N.Y.C. Road Runners Club, Erie (Pa.) Road Runners Club, Summit Athletic Club, Scotish Rite, Phi Delta Kappa, Kappa Sigma. Avocations: marathon running, intramural sports, cooking, writing, reading, traveling. Home: 1450 Loop Rd Kent OH 44240-4619 Office: Stanton Middle Sch 6662 Cleveland Canton Rd Kent OH 44240

FULTZ, ROBERT EDWARD, lawyer; b. Columbus, Ohio, May 24, 1941; s. Clair Ervin and Isabelle (Eichelberger) F.; m. Judith Ann McClannan, June 15, 1963; children: Cynthia, Jennifer, Stephen. BA cum laude, Ohio State U., 1963; JD with distinction, U. Mich., 1965. Ohio 1966, U.S. Supreme Ct. 1970. Assoc. Porter, Wright, Morris & Arthur, Columbus, 1966-70, ptnr., 1971—. Past trustee Columbus Symphony Orch. and Ballet; past trustee, sec. United Cerebral Palsy of Columbus; past trustee, treas. Goodwill Industries; past trustee, pres. Cen. Community House; former advisor, bd. dirs. United Negro Coll. Fund; trustee Columbus Assn. for Performing Arts, Columbus Law Libr. Assn. Mem. Columbus Bar Assn., Phi Beta Kappa, Delta Upsilon (treas.). Home: 4630 Burbank Dr Columbus OH 43220-2806

FULZELE, RATNAKAR HARIBHAU, pharmacist, management consultant; b. Naspur, India, Apr. 25, 1957; s. Haribhau and Kamla Fulzele; m. Ratnaprabha Ratnakar Ratnaprabha, Dec. 5, 1980; children: Kumari Nilima, Master Punit. B of Pharmacy, Nagpur U., India, 1978, diploma in Bus. Mgmt., 1982, MBA, 1990, PhD, 1998. Mfg. pharmacist Ralli's India Ltd., Bombay, 1978-79; pharmacist ESIS Hosp., Bombay, 1979-82; incharge pharmacist Mahatma sandhi Inst. of Med. Scis., Sevagram, India, 1982—; dir. Gallop Pharma, Nagpur, 1977-80. Mem. Bhavsar Mandal, Wardh, India, 1980—, pres., 1996. Mem. Indian Pharm. Assn. (life), Indian Hosp. Pharmacist Assn. (life). Avocations: reading, music, painting. Home: 72 Ratnakunj Wardha Rd, Sevagram 442102, India Office: Mahatma Gandhi Inst, Med Scis, Sevagram 442102, India

FUMANAL, IGNACIO, telecommunications professional; b. Rabat, Morocco, Sept. 19, 1963; arrived in Spain, 1963; s. Francisco and Virtudes (Andres) F.; m. Paloma Galdon, June 18, 1994. English cert., U. So. Calif., Madrid, 1990; Microprocessors cert., F.C.S., Madrid, 1985; BS in Gen. Engring., Calif. Coast U. Programmer APL Informatica, Madrid, 1987-88; systems engr. Fujitsu Spain, Madrid, 1988-91, Fujitsu Ltd., Tokyo, 1991-92, Fujitsu Spain, Madrid, 1992-93, Synoptics Comms., Madrid, 1993-94, Bay Networks, Madrid, 1994-98; sys. engring. mgr. Nortel Networks, 1998—; tng. dir. APL Informatica, Madrid, 1988; tchr. seminars on computer sci. Philippines, Thailand, Japan, Singapore, 1992. Contbr. articles to profl. jours. Roman Catholic. Avocations: gardening, swimming, photography. Office: Edificio 4, Avda Dos Castillas 33, Madrid 28224, Spain

FUMARONI, DANIEL ANGEL, accountant, tax consultant; b. Mar Del Plaita, Buenos Aires, Argentina, Jan. 16, 1950. Degree pub. acctg., U. Nat. Mar del Plata, Argentina, 1972. Prof. tax dept. of capatization Direction Thxes Govt., 1977-78; prof. economy U. Nat. Mar Del Plata, 1970-87, prof. technique and legis. taxes, 1986-93; dir. Tourism Ctr., Mar del Plata, 1996—, mem. com. 1991. Author: Farms Cooperatives, 1972; contbr. articles to profl. jours. Hon. pres. Del Plata Conv. Bur., 1997—. Mem. Nat. Assn. of Pub. Accts.

FUNAHASHI, KEN-ICHI, mathematician, educator, computer scientist; b. Nagoya, Japan, Feb. 25, 1952; s. Hirotsugu and Tsutaye (Yamada) F.; m. Nobuko Harada, May 2, 1984; 1 child, Kunio. BS, Nagoya U., 1975, MS, 1977, DSc, 1980. Sr. engr. Sharp Corp., Tenri, Japan, 1980-89; asst. prof. math. Toyohashi (Japan) U. Tech., 1989-93; assoc. prof. math. U. Aizu, Aizu-Wakamatsu, Japan, 1993—; sr. rschr., ATR, Kyoto, Japan, 1987-89; engring. cons. Sharp Corp., 1990-95. Mem. Math. Soc. Japan, Japanese Neural Network Soc., Inst. Electronics, Info. and Comm. Engrs. Avocations: art appreciation, reading. Office: U Aizu Ctr Math Sci, Ikki-machi, Aizu-Wakamatsu 965, Japan

FUNAKAWA, ATSUSHI, management consultant; b. Tokyo; m. Debbie Funakawa; children: Keita, Kai. BA in Law, Keio U., Tokyo, 1980; M.Internat. Mgmt., Am. Grad. Sch. Internat. Mgmt., Glendale, Ariz., 1991. Corp. mktg. coord. Toshiba Corp., Tokyo, 1980-82; sect. chief corp. strategic planning Am. Life Ins. Co., Tokyo, 1983-99; intercultural bus. specialist, project leader Clarke Cons. Group, Inc., Redwood City, Calif., 1992-94; dir. intercultural bus. mgmt. Geonexus Comm., Palo Alto, Calif., 1994-95; sr. mgr. global learning and orgn. devel. Globis Corp., Tokyo, 1995-99; mng. ptnr. Global Impact Inc., Tokyo, 1999—; condr. numerous seminars in field; vis. prof. Am. grad. Sch. Internat. Mgmt., Japan Ctr.; lectr. in field. Author: Transcultural Management - A New Approach for Global Organizations, 1997; editor/translator: Global Management in the Era of Multicultural Environment, 1998, The Individualized Corporation, 1999. Fax: 81-3-5532-7373. Home: Mitaka-shi Hibiya Ctrl Bldg, 3-13-11-101 Inokashra, Tokyo 181, Japan Office: Global Impact Inc, 1-2-9 Nishi-shinnbashi, Minato-ku Tokyo 105-0003, Japan

FUNAMI, YUTAKA, surgeon; b. Yokohama, Japan, May 24, 1959; s. Taizan and Midori (Sawada) F.; m. Miyuki Sato, Apr. 8, 1989; children: Eureka, Ray. MD, Chiba U., 1986, PhD, 1995. Surgeon Chiba Univ. Hosp., Japan, 1986-95; from dep. dir. surgery to dir. surgery Labour Welfare Corp. Kashima Indsl. Injury Hosp., Hasaki, Japan, 1995—; surgeon Chiba U. Hosp., Japan, 1998—. Mem. Internat. Soc. for Diseases of the Esophagus, Internat. Coll. Surgeons, Japanese Surg. Soc., Japanese Assn. Thoracic Surgery. Office: Chiba U 2nd Dept Surgery, 1-8-1 Inohana Chuoku, 260 Chiba Japan

FUNAYAMA, SHINJI, chemist, educator; b. Sendai, Japan, May 31, 1951; s. Eiichi and Toshie (Ito) F.; m. Noriko Saito, Mar. 29, 1980; 1 child, Akiko. BPharm, Tohoku U., 1975, MS, 1977, PhD, 1980. Rsch. assoc. U. Ill., Chgo., 1980-83; rsch. fellow Tohoku U., Sendai, 1983-84; rsch. head Kitasato Inst., Tokyo, 1984-90; from instr. to asst. prof. Tohoku U., 1990-96; assoc. prof. Aomori U., Japan, 1996—. Author: The Alkaloids-A Treasure House of Poisons and Medicines, 1998; cons. editor Jour. Rsch. & Edn. Indian Medicine; editl. reviewer Pharm. Biology; contbr. articles to profl. jours. Mem. Japan Assn. Herbs (bd. dirs. 1991—), Am. Soc. Pharmacognosy, Japanese Soc. Pharmacognosy, Pharm. Soc. Japan. Avocations: gardening, reading. Office: Aomori U, 2-3-1 Kohbata, Aomori 030-0943, Japan

FUNCK-BRENTANO, CHRISTIAN JACQUES, physician, researcher; b. Neuilly-sur-Seine, France, May 30, 1955; s. Jean-Louis and Monique (Duhamel) F.-B.; m. Isabelle Camille Guénot, Dec. 15, 1978; children: Thomas, Charlotte. MD, Pitie-Salpetriere Sch. Med., Paris, 1982; PhD, U. Paris 6, 1990, postgrad., 1991. Diplomate French Bd. Cardiology. Intern Hosp. de Paris, 1979-86; clin. pharmacology rsch. fellow Vanderbilt U., Nashville, 1986-88; asst. prof. clin. pharmacology Assistance Publique Hopitaux de Paris/Paris VI U., 1988-92; assoc. prof. clin. pharmacology Assistance Publique Hopitaux de Paris/St.-Antoine, Paris, 1992-96, prof. clin. pharmacology, 1996—; vice head clin. investigation ctr. INSERM/Assistance Publique Hopitaux de Paris, 1995—; mem. clin. investigation coun. INSERM, Paris, 1991-95, mem. clin. rsch. bd., 1999—; mem. core group conceptors Nat. Clin. Investigation Ctrs. Program, France, 1989—. Contbr. over 70 articles to profl. jours., chpts. to books. External cons. French Min. Health, Min. Rsch., French Medicine Agy. Recipient Paul Neumann prize in pharmacology Hoechst, 1992; Merck-Sharp-Dohme internat. fellow in clin. pharmacology Vanderbilt U., 1986. Mem. French Soc. Pharmacology. Avocation: skiing. Office: Hosp St-Antoine Dept Pharm, 184 Rue Faubourg St Antoine, 75012 Paris France

FUNES, PABLO JOSE, computer science researcher; b. Cordoba, Argentina, Apr. 18, 1966; came to U.S., 1995; s. Everest Santiago Funes and Maria Del Carmen Arguello; m. Karina Judith Baum, July 20, 1995. Degree in math., U. Buenos Aires, 1994; PhD in Computer Sci., Brandeis U., 2000. Cons. in sys. FAO (UN), Mex., 1983-95; sys. mgr. UAPE, Buenos Aires, 1986-93; CTO MAPA Sys., Buenos Aires, 1991-93; cons. in modeling Ministry of Economy, Argentina, 1995. Inventor in field. E-mail: pablo@brandeis.edu. Office: Brandeis U MS 018 415 South St Waltham MA 02453-2700

FUNG, EVANDA KAM HA, insurance executive; b. Hong Kong, Aug. 5, 1958; d. Yung Yau and Sam Mui (Kwok) F. Grad., Wellington Coll., Hong Kong, 1976. Brokerage mgr. Transamerica Occidental Life, 1985—; counselor Hong Kong Chamber of Ins. Intermediaries, 1994-95; chmn. The Putonghua Soc. of the Sch. Profl. and Continue Edn., U. Hong Kong. Charter chmn. Inc. OWners Kam Fung Bldg., Hong Kong, 1996—. Mem. Y's Men's Club of Victoria (pres.). Avocations: scuba diving, skiing, trekking. Office: Rm 106 St Georges Bldg, 2 Ice House St, Hong Kong Hong Kong

FUNG, KWOK WING SHERMAN, chemist; b. Hong Kong, Aug. 17, 1963; m. Senny Wai King Cheung, 1997. BSc with 1st class honours, U. London, 1990; DPhil, Oxford (Eng.) U., 1993. Chartered chemist, U.K. Deptl. mgr. SGS Hong Kong Ltd., 1994-96, divsnl. gen. mgr., founder biosics. divsn., 1997—. Author: Biotechnology in Hong Kong, 1998; contbr. articles to sci. jours., including Hong Kong Chem. Soc., Asian Sustainable Devel. Prospects, Hong Kong Econ. Times, China Textiles and Apparel. Mem. Royal Soc. Chemistry (registered analytical chemist), Hong Kong Chem. Soc. (editor 1997—), Am. Oil Chemists Soc. (approved chemist), Hong Kong Inst. Engrs. (affil.), Practising Pharmacists Assn. Hong Kong, Pharm. Group, Royal Pharm. Soc. U.K., Lions (bd. dirs. Hong Kong, 1996—, svc. award 1996-98). Email: sherman fung@sgsgroup.com. Office: SGS Hong Kong Ltd Bio-Scis, 301 HKIB/12 Miles Tai Po Rd, Hong Kong China

FUNG, KWOK-KING VICTOR, merchant banker; b. Hong Kong, Oct. 16, 1945; s. Hon-Chu and Pui-Yui (Li) F.; m. Julia Nai-Kee Shen, June 14, 1969; children: Sabrina, Spencer, Stephen. BS, MS, MIT, 1966; PhD, Harvard U.,

1971. Planning officer Citibank, N.Y.C., 1970-72; asst. prof. Harvard Bus. Sch., Boston, 1972-74, 76; mgr. Li & Fung (Trading) Ltd., Hong Kong, 1974-76; mng. dir. Li & Fung (Trading) Ltd., 1976-80; group mng. dir. Li & Fung Ltd., Hong Kong, 1980-86; dep. chmn. Li & Fung Group, Hong Kong, 1986-89, chmn., 1989—; chmn., chief exec. officer Prudential Asia Capital Ltd., Hong Kong, 1986—. with Boston Cons. Group, Harbridge House, Boston, Mgmt. Analysis Ctr., Mass., Citibank, N.Y.C. Mem. Hong Kong-U.S. Econ. Cooperation Com., 1988—. Mem. Pub. Svc. Commn., Hong Kong, 1980—, Securities & Futures Commn., Hong Kong, 1989—. Mem. Order of the Brit. Empire, Sigma Xi, Eta Kappa Nu. Home: 11 Magazine Gap Rd, 10A Harbour View Mansions, Hong Kong China Office: Hong Kong Trade Development Coun, 1 Harbour Road 38th Fl Ofc Tower, Wanchai Hong Kong Address: Li and Fung Ltd, 888 Cheung Sha Wan Rd 11th Fl, Kowloon Hong Kong*

FUNG, ROSALINE LEE, educator; b. China, May 14, 1944; came to U.S., 1963; d. Frank Kwok-Wai and Teresa Wai-Hing (Cheung) Lee; m. Stephen Ying-Chung Fung, Aug. 23, 1968. BA, Briar Cliff Coll., 1966; MA, Idaho State U., 1968. Instr. Highland C.C., Freeport, Ill., 1968-69, Merced (Calif.) Coll., 1969-70; tchr. Linden (Calif.) High Sch., 1970-84; prof. San Joaquin Delta Coll., Stockton, Calif., 1984—; cons. in field. Author: (textbooks) ESL Writing Manual, 1992, Patterns for Success, 4 vols., 1997, Basic Composition, 1997, Writing Essays, 1998, Writing Paragraphs, 1999. Coord. cultural exch. San Joaquin Delta Coll., 1995, 96, 98. Mem. NEA, Calif. Tchrs. Assn. Avocations: reading, writing, concerts, theater, surfing the net. E-mail: rfung@sjdccd.cc.ca.us. Office: San Joaquin Delta Coll 5151 Pacific Ave Stockton CA 95207-6304

FUNG, STANISLAUS, architecture educator; b. Hong Kong, Nov. 13, 1961; arrived in Australia, 1979, naturalized, 1989; s. Patrick Kim-Ping Fung and Hing-Ming Chan. BS in Architecture with honors, U. NSW, Sydney, Australia, 1984. Lectr. in architecture U. NSW, Sydney, 1989; lectr. in history and theories of architecture U. Adelaide, Australia, 1989-96; sr. lectr. in history and theories of architecture U. Adelaide, 1997-99, dep. dir. Centre Asian & Mid. Eastern Architecture, 97-99; vis. lectr. Grad. Sch. Fine Arts, U. Pa., 1997-98; sr. lectr. in history and theory of architecture, U. NSW, 1999—; dir., Ctr. for Asian Environments, U. NSW, 1999—. Author: Australian Architectural Serials: A Preliminary list, 1985, The Salon (1912-1917): Studies and Indexes, 1996; editor: Australian Studies in Architectural History, 1990; founding editor Fabrications: Jour. of the Soc. of Archtl. Historians, Australia and New Zealand, 1988-92; cons. editor Penn Studies in Landscape Architecture, 1996—;. Fgn./Interdisciplinary Travel grantee Coll. Art Assn., 1997. Mem. Soc. Archtl. Historians Australia and New Zealand, Chinese Studies Assn. Australia. Office: Fac of Built Environment, Univ New South Wales, Sydney NSW 2052, Australia

FUNG, WING KAM, statistician, researcher; b. Hong Kong, Hong Kong, May 10, 1958; s. Kwong Yiu and Yau Yung (Chiu) F.; m. Yuet Siu Ma; children: Ka Chung, Ka Wing. BSocSc, U. Hong Kong, 1982; MSc, U. London, 1984; DIC, Imperial Coll., London, 1984; PhD, U. Hong Kong, 1987. Lectr. U. Hong Kong, 1988—, prof., assoc. dean, 1999—. Assoc. editor Computing Statis. and Data Analysis, Jour. Applied Statis. Sci. Exec. mem. Concerned Staff Tertiary Ednl. Instns. Bldg. Daya Bay Nuclear Plant, Hong Kong, 1986, Concerned Staff of Tertiary Ednl. Instns. Constnl. Devel., Hong Kong, 1987; chmn. Hong Kong Statistical Scoiety: Public Commentary Com., Hong Kong, 1989-91. Hon. rsch. fellow S.E. U. Fellow Royal Statistical Soc.; mem. Am. Statistical Assn., Internat. Statis. Inst. Avocations: table tennis, soccer, concerned political development in Hong Kong. Office: Dept Statistics U Hong Kong, Pokfulam Rd, Hong Kong China

FUNG, WYE POH, gastroenterologist, consultant, physician; b. Telok-Anson, Perak, Malaysia, Jan. 9, 1937; s. Kwok Chan and Swee Lin (Man) F.; m. Saw Lin Ong, Nov. 1961; children: Li-May, Chee-Ming. MBBS, U. Malaya, Singapore, 1961; MD, U. Singapore, 1972. Diplomate Med. Bd. West Australia, New South Wales, South Australia. Sr. lectr. in medicine U. Singapore, 1965-74, assoc. prof. medicine, 1975; sr. lectr. in medicine U. Western Australia, Perth, 1976-85; cons. physician Royal Perth Hosp., 1976-85; vis. assoc. prof. U. Calif. at San Francisco Med. Ctr., 1981-82; gastroenterologist St. John of God Hosp., Perth, 1985—; pvt. practice West Perth, 1985—; gastroenterologist Swan Dist. Hosp., Perth, 1985—, Osborne Pk. Hosp., Perth, 1986—, Armadale Kelmscott Hosp., Perth, 1987—; cons. physician Royal Perth Hosp., 1976-85. Contbr. articles to profl. jours. Fellow Royal Australasian Coll. Physicians, Am. Coll. Gastroenterology, Acad. Medicine Singapore; mem. Gastroent. Soc. Singapore (co-founder, sec. treas. 1967-75). Avocation: golf. Office: 1331 Hay St, 6005 West Perth Western Australia, Australia

FUNK, CHRISTIANE, biochemistry educator, researcher; b. Herford, Nordthein, Germany, Jan. 26, 1967; d. Albert Friedrich and Renate (Thiemann) F.; m. Wolfgang Schröder, July 30, 1999. Diplom, Georg-August U., Göttingen, Germany, 1991; PhD, Tech. U., Berlin, 1995. Rsch. asst. Tech. U., Berlin, 1992-95; vis. rschr. Stockholm U., Sweden, 1994, rsch. asst., 1998—; postdoctoral rschr. Ariz. State U., Tempe, 1996, Australian Nat. U., Canberra, 1997; bd. dirs. Dept. Biochemistry, Stockholm. Contbr. articles to profl. jours. Mem., vol. various environtl. orgns. Fellowship Studienstiftund d. dt Volkes, 1989-94, ARC, Australia, 1997; grantee Govtl. Rsch. Orgn., 1996-99. Mem. Internat. Soc. of Photosynthesis Rsch. Avocations: scuba-diving, skiing. Home: Torphagsvägen 16, 10405 Stockholm Sweden Office: Stockholm U Dept Biochem, Arrhenius Lab, 10691 Stockholm Sweden

FUNK, SHERMAN MAXWELL, former government official, writer, consultant; b. N.Y.C., Nov. 13, 1925; s. Bernard and Dorothy (Arkin) F.; m. Elaine Myrl Bayer, Mar. 6, 1953 (dec. 1977); children: Katherine Sara, Bernard Eugene; m. Sylvia Grunbaum Straka, June 3, 1978; children Eric, Marc, Paul. A.B., Harvard U., 1950; postgrad., Columbia U., 1956; U. Ariz., 1958. Salesman, sales exec. Bernard Funk Co., N.Y.C., 1950-54; history tchr. Catskill (N.Y.) High Sch., 1954-57; polit. sci. teaching asst. U. Ariz., Tucson, 1957-58; mgmt. intern USAF Hdqrs., Washington, 1958, war planning officer, mgmt. analyst, 1958-63, chief Air Force Mgmt. Improvement Programs Office, 1963-67, chief Air Force Cost Reduction Office, 1967-70; successively asst. dir. adminstrn. and program devel., dir. rsch. and program devel., asst. dir. planning and evaluation Office Minority Bus. Enterprise, Dept. Commerce, 1970-79; spl. asst. for small bus. Dept. Energy, 1979-81; insp. gen. Dept. Commerce, 1981-87; insp. gen. Dept. State, 1987-94, adviser to fgn. govts. on anti-corruption efforts, 1994—; vice chmn. Pres.'s Coun. on Integrity and Efficiency, 1989-90; TV commentator. Contbr. articles to profl. jours., major newspapers. Mem. Bowie City Council, (Md.), 1963-65, chmn. human relations com., 1964-65, chmn. charter rev. com., 1968; pres. Bethesda Jewish Congregation, 1986. Served with inf. AUS, 1943-46. Decorated Purple Heart; recipient Presdl. Unit Citation, spl. award Sec. Air Force, 1968, prizes Washington-Md.-Del Press Assn., 1970, 71, 73, 75, Silver medal Commerce Dept., 1972, Disting. honor award State Dept., 1992. Mem. Fed. Investigators Assn. Office: 5000 Battery Ln Ste 504 Bethesda MD 20814-2658

FUNKE, ENRIQUE, telecommunications industry executive, writer; b. Madrid, Dec. 13, 1958; s. Enrique Martin and Blanca Funke; m. Arantxa Prieto; children: Ignacio, Daniel, Mireya. B in Engring., Polytechnic U., Madrid, 1981; DEng in Telecom., Polytechnic U., 1990. Cert. engr. in telecom., Madrid. Rsch. engr. CETME, Madrid, 1981-84; mgr. ALCATEL, Madrid, 1984-87; project mgr. IBM, Madrid, 1988; mktg. mgr. INTEL, Madrid, 1988-96; comml. dir. BICC-CORNING, Madrid, 1996-97; gen. dep. dir. TELEFONICA, Madrid, 1997—; prof. Polytechnic U., 1986-88. Author: Microprocesadores Avanzados, 1992, 15 Horas con Amipro Windows, 1994; translator: Internet Para Dummies, 1997. 2nd lt. Spanish Army, 1978-80. Avocations: golf, jogging, tennis, computers. Office: TELEFONICA, Infanta Mercedes 90, E-28020 Madrid Spain

FUNKE, GRAYDON NEIL, retired pediatrician; b. Pasadena, Calif., May 23, 1930; s. Arthur Paul and Dorothy Mann (Smith) F.; m. Esther Chapman Funke, Dec. 3, 1966; children: Michael, Dan, Sheri. AA, John Muir, Pasadena, Calif., 1950; BA, UCLA, Westwood, Calif., 1954, MD, 1958. Cert. physician and surgeon, Calif. Staff pediatrics Southern Calif. Permenente Med. Group, 1966-95; clin. prof. pediatrics Harbor UCLA, Torrance, Calif., 1985—, clin. facility, 1966—; bd. Drug and Alcohol Commn., San Luis, Calif., 1995—, Sexual Abuse Victim Edn., San Luis, Calif., 1996—. Chair, chair rsch. com. Harbor-UCLA Rsch. and Edn. Inst.; chair Drug and Alcohol Commn., San Luis, Obispo County. Mem. AMA, Calif. Med. Assn., L.A. Med. Assn., San Luisobisbo Med. Assn., Amateur Radio Relay League. Avocations: amateur radio, travel. Home: 5465 Mira Estrella Ln San Luis Obispo CA 93401-7901

FUNKE, KARL-HEINZ, government official. Former agriculture min. Lower Saxony, Germany; now min. of agriculture Govt. of Germany. Office: Ministry of Agriculture, Rochusstr 1, 53123 Bonn Germany*

FUNKHOUSER, ARTHUR TAYLOR, psychotherapist; b. Evansville, Ind., Sept. 3, 1940; arrived in Switzerland, 1973; s. Arthur Taylor and Edwina Grace (Conry) F.; m. Meret Johanna Fluckiger, Apr. 5, 1975 (div. July 1986); children: David Andrew, Evelyn Christina, Jeannine Elisabeth. BS, MIT, 1962; MS, U. Mich., 1967; D of Tech. Sci., Fed. Inst. of Tech., Zürich, Switzerland, 1979; diploma, C.G. Jung Inst., Kusnacht, Switzerland, 1981. Lic. psychotherapist. Rsch. asst. RLE (MIT), Cambridge, 1960-62; rsch. assoc. U. Mich., Ann Arbor, 1962-67; physicist Nat. Bur. of Stds., Gaithersburg, Md., 1967-71; physicist U. Bern, 1981-93, rsch. assoc., 1998; pvt. practice, 1981—; cons. Inst. for Biomed. Tech., Zürich, 1973, Dept. of Chemistry, F.I.T., Zurich, 1974, programmer, 1979-81; lectr. C.G. Jung Inst., Kusnacht, 1989-98. Co-author: (chpt.) Computerized Visual Fields, 1985; contbr. articles to profl. publs. Recipient Albert Vogt prize Swiss Ophthalmol. Soc., 1991. Mem. Internat. Assn. for Analytical Psychology, Assn. of Grad. Analytical Psychology, Assn. for the Study of Dreams. Anglican. Avocations: Déjà Vu research, squash, Tai Chi, hiking, E-mail corresponding. Home and Office: Altenbergstr 126, 3013 Bern Switzerland

FUNNELL, CHRISTINA MARY, non-profit consultant; b. Wakefield, Eng., Aug. 24, 1947; d. Norman and Joanna Christina (Lenes) Beaumont; m. Ivan Neil Funnell (div. May 1994); children: Laura Jane, Thomas William. Student, Southgate, London, 1968-71; BA with spl. honors, Hull U., Yorkshire, Eng., 1968. Adminstrv. sec. Meth. Assn. Youth Clubs, London, 1965-68; organiser Orgn. for Vol. Youth Orgns., London, 1971-74; CEO Nat. Eczema Soc., London, 1982-96; feasibility cons. The Meth. North Bank Estate, London, 1999—; exec. mem. Assn. Chief Execs. Nat. Vol. Orgns., London, 1992-95; founder Long Term Med. Conditions Alliance, London, 1993, chmn., 1995-96; patient advisor All Party Parliamentery Group on Skin, 1994-97; CEO Skin Care Campaign, London, 1995-97. Mem. NHS Exec. Patient Partnership Strategy Working Group, London, 1994-97, Standing Adv. Group on Consumer Involvement in the NHS R&D Programme, 1996-98; exec. mem. Christian Socialist Movement; assoc. mem. The Iona Cmty.; steward Wesleys Chapel, London; chmn. Consumer Health Info. Centre; interim dir. Tchr. Support Svcs. TBF: the tchr. support network, 1999—. Mem. Labour Party. Methodist. Avocations: travel, human rights, history, current affairs, gardening. Home: 28 Queensbury St, London N1 3AD, England

FUQUA, JUDY See **FOUQUET, ANNE**

FURCHGOTT, ROBERT FRANCIS, pharmacologist, educator; b. Charleston, S.C., June 4, 1916; married, 1941; 3 children. BS, U. N.C., 1937; PhD in Biochemistry, Northwestern U., 1940; DM (hon.), Autonomous U., Madrid, 1984, U. Lund, 1984; DSc (hon.), U. N.C., 1989, U. Ghent, 1995; postgrad., Mt. Sinai Med. Sch., 1995, Ohio State U., 1996, Med. U. S.C., 1997, Med. Coll. Ohio, 1997, Northwestern U., 1998, U. Coll. London, 1998, Northwe. U., 1998. Rsch. fellow medicine Med. Coll. Cornell U., 1940-43, rsch. assoc., 1943-47, instr. physiology, 1943-48, asst. prof. med. biochemistry, 1947-49; from asst. prof. to assoc. prof. pharmacology Med. Sch. Wash. U., 1949-56; chmn. dept. pharmacology SUNY Health Sci. Ctr., Bklyn., 1956-83, prof., 1956-88, Univ. Disting. prof., 1988—, emeritus prof. pharmacology, 1990—; mem. pharmacol. tng. com. USPHS, 1961-64, mem. pharmacoltoxicol rev. com., 1965-68; Commonwealth fellow, 1962-63; vis. prof. U. Geneva, 1962-63, U. Calif., San Diego, 1971-72, Med. U. S.C., 1980, UCLA, 1980; adj. prof. pharmacology Sch. Medicine, U. Miami, 1989—. Recipient rsch. achievement award Am. Heart Assn., 1990, Bristol-Myers Squibb award for achievement in cariovasc. rsch., 1991, Gairdner Fund Internat. award, 1991, medal N.Y. Acad. Medicine, 1992, Roussel Uclaf prize for rsch. in cell communication and signalling, 1994, Wellcome Gold medal Brit. Pharmacology Soc., 1995, ASPET award for exptl. therapeutics, 1996, Gregory Pincus award for rsch., 1996, Lasker award for med. rsch., 1996, Lucian award, 1997, Nobel prize for medicine, 1998. Mem. AAAS, NAS, Am. Chem. Soc., Am. Soc. Biochemistry, Am. Soc. Pharmacology and Exptl. Therapeutics (pres. 1971-72, Goodman and Gilman award 1984), Harvey Soc., Polish Physiol. Soc. (hon.), Sigma Xi. Office: SUNY Health Sci Ctr Dept of Pharmacology 450 Clarkson Ave # 29 Brooklyn NY 11203-2056

FURCON, JOHN EDWARD, management and organizational consultant; b. Chgo., Mar. 17, 1942; s. John F. and Lottie (Janik) F.; children: Juliana, Annalisa, Diana; m. Orisha Agatha Kulick, Oct. 28, 1995. BA, DePaul U., 1963, MA, 1965; MBA, U. Chgo., 1970. With Human Resources Ctr. (name formerly Indsl. Relations Ctr.), U. Chgo., 1963-81, project dir., 1966-70, research psychologist, div. dir., 1970-81; with orgn. change practice Harbridge House, Inc., Northbrook, Ill., 1981—, v.p., 1987-93, ptnr., human resource adv. group Coopers & Lybrand, 1993-98; ptnr. Global Human Resource Solutions, PricewaterhouseCoopers, LLP, 1998—; mem. faculty Traffic Inst., Northwestern U., 1969-84, DePaul U. Sch. for New Learning, 1974-82; cons. bus., ednl. and govt. orgns.; bd. dirs. Bur. of Testing Svcs., 1975-77, Harbridge House, Inc., 1991-97; lectr. in field. Contbr. articles on personnel mgmt. and human resources planning to profl. jours. Active parents bd. Marquette U., 1988-89. Served to lt. AUS, 1963-65. Mem. Soc. Indsl. and Orgnl. Psychology, Indsl. Psychology Assn. Chgo. (chmn. 1973-75), Internat. Assn. Chiefs of Police, Chgo. Coun. Fgn. Rels., World Future Soc., Human Resource Mgmt. Assn. Chgo. Office: Global Human Resource Solutions PricewaterhouseCoopers LLP 203 N La Salle St Chicago IL 60601-1210 Address: PO Box 309 Westmont IL 60559-0309

FURDA, IVAN, chemist, consultant; b. Trnava, Czechoslovakia, Apr. 29, 1938; came to U.S., 1971; s. Juraj and Petronila (Didolicova) F.; m. Jana Stuchlikova, June 20, 1964; children: Peter Mark, Thomas Ronald. MS in Analytical Chemistry, Tech. U. Chem. Faculty, Bratislava, Czechoslovakia, 1960; PhD in Organic Chemistry, Czechoslovak Acad. Scis., Bratislava, Czechoslovakia, 1967. Post doctorate fellow Nat. Rsch. Coun. Canada, Ottawa, Ont., 1968-69, Trent U., Peterborough, Ont., Canada, 1969-70; project specialist Gen. Foods Corp., Tarrytown, N.Y., 1971-78; prin. scientist Gen. Mills Inc., Mpls., 1978-94; pres. Furda & Assocs. Inc. Internat. Consulting, Wayzata, Minn., 1994—; adv. bd. CRC Press Inc. Handbook of Dietary Fiber in Human Nutrition, Boca Raton, Fla., 1984-1986. Author, editor: Unconventional Sources of Dietary Fiber, 1983, New Developments in Dietary Fiber, 1990; patentee in field; inventor of fat-binding dietary fiber. Mem. Am. Chem. Soc., Am. Chitoscience Soc., Czechoslovak Soc. Arts and Scis. Avocations: swimming, tennis, music, economics. Home and Office: 16664 Meadowbrook Ln Wayzata MN 55391-2960

FÜREDI, MIHÁLY, librarian, researcher; b. Budapest, Hungary, July 30, 1947; s. László and Ilona (Jávorka) F.; m. Larisa Petrovna Popova, Feb. 8, 1970 (div. 1980); children: Anna, Maria. Math. Linguist, Leningrad (USSR) State U., 1970; D in gen. Linguistics, U. Eötvös Loránd, Budapest, Hungary, 1974. Rschr. Inst. Linguistics, Budapest, Hungary, 1970-86; dept. head Libr. of Hungarian Acad. Scis., Budapest, 1986-91; libr. documentation and info. ctr. Inst. Transp. Scis., Budapest, 1991—. Author, editor: (book) A Frequency Dictionary of Modern Hungarian Fiction, 1989. Mem. John von Neumann Soc., European Soc. Linguistics, Soc. Hungarian Linguistics, Hungarnet Assn, Hungarian Library Assn. Calvinist. Avocations: reading, travel, computers. Home: Szigony u 5 X 39, H-1083 Budapest Hungary Office: Inst Transport Scis Ltd, Than Károly u 3-5, H-1119 Budapest Hungary

FURER, VICTOR LVOVICH, physicist, educator, researcher; b. Kazan, Tatarstan, Russia, Aug. 20, 1949; s. Lev Naumovich and Lucia Victorovna (Pozhilova) F.; m. Tatyana Arcadievna Panteleeva, Nov. 30, 1972; 1 child, Sophia. Grad., U. Kazan, 1971. Asst. Kazan Civil Engring. Inst., 1971-78, sr. tchr., 1978-84, docent, 1984-93; prof. Kazan State Archtl. and Civil Engring. Acad., 1993—. Avocations: reading, basketball, chess. Home: Zorge 113-126, Kazan, Tatarstan Russia Office: Kazan State Civil Engr Acad, Zelenaya 1, Kazan, Tatarstan Russia 420034

FUREY, KEITH W., mechanical engineer; b. N.Y.C., Feb. 2, 1963; s. James M. and Virginia A. (D'Auria) F.; m. Deanna D. Schepisi, Oct. 22, 1994; children: Dominique Carpenito, Frank Carpenito, James K. Furey, Michael T. Furey. BE, Manhattan Coll., 1985. Profl. engr., N.Y. With Henry Smith, Inc./Brudon Constn. Co., Monsey, N.Y., 1983-85; project mgr. Cert. Tile & Marble, Inc., Elmsford, N.Y., 1985-87; dep. village engr. Village of Mamaroneck, N.Y., 1987-88; from sr. constrn. engr. to assoc. Blasland, Bouck & Lee, Inc., White Plains, N.Y., 1988-97; pres. York Svcs. Corp., Stamford, Conn., 1997-99; pres., CEO KW Furey Engring. P.C., New City, N.Y., 1999—, Reliance Telecom, Inc., New City, N.Y. Mem. Nat. Soc. Profl. Engrs., Water Environ. Fedn., N.Y. Water Environ. Assn. (bd. dirs. Lower Hudson chpt. 1990-96). Roman Catholic. Avocations: golf, skiing, weight lifting, automobile restoration, home improvements. Home: 1 Virginia St New City NY 10956-3015 Office: KW Furey Engring PC/ Reliance Telecom Inc New City NY

FURIC, MIROSLAV, physics educator; b. Davor, Croatia, Jan. 31, 1941; s. Ivan and Marija (Flegar) F.; m. Elizabeta Horvatic, July 26, 1969; children: Ivan Krešimir, Vesna. BSc, U. Zagreb, Croatia, 1964, MSc, 1968, PhD, 1970. Asst. Inst. R. Boskovic, Zagreb, 1965-71; rsch. assoc. U. So. Calif., L.A., 1971-72; rsch. assoc. Rice U., Houston, 1972-74, higher rsch. assoc., 1977-79; sci. assoc. CERN, Geneva, 1975-76; prof. faculty scis. U. Zagreb, 1980—, chmn. physics dept., 1986-92; prin. investigator several grants, Zagreb and Houston, 1985—; mem. Nat. Sci. Coun., Zagreb, 1994-98. Author: Modern Experimental Methods, Techniques and Measurements in Physics, 1992 (J. J. Strossmayer award 1993); co-author: (with Ivan Supek) Beginnings of Physics, 1994. Bd. govs. U. Zagreb, 1996—. Recipient R. Boskovic, Coun. Sci. Awards Croatia, Zagreb, 1987, Sci. medal Danica Hrvatska S Likom Rudera Boskovica, Pres. Croatia, Zagreb, 1996. Mem. Croatian Phys. Soc. (pres. 1993-97). Avocation: music. Home: LJ Sram 16, HR-10000 Zagreb Croatia Office: Physics/Faculty Scis, U Zagreb, Bijenicka 32, HR-10000 Zagreb Croatia

FURLEY, PETER A., university educator, researcher; b. Gravesend, Eng., Aug. 5, 1935; s. L.T. and M.E. (White) F.; m. Margaret B. Dunlop Furley, Mar. 23, 1963; children: Nicola, Andrew, Sara, Kirsten. BA, Oxford (Eng.) U., 1959; MA, 1962, PhD, 1966. Lectr., tutor Oxford (Eng.) U., 1959-62; lectr. Edinburgh (Scotland) U., 1962-76; prof. Brasilia U., Brazil, 1976-79; sr. lectr. Edinburgh (Scotland) U., 1979-89, reader, 1989-98; prof. tropical biogeography, 1998—; chmn. Brit. Biogeography Rsch. Group, 1987-91. Author: Geography of the Biosphere, 1983; author, editor: Nature and Dynamics of Forest-Savanna Boundaries, 1992, The Forest Frontier, 1994, Biogeography and Development in the Humid Tropics, 1989, Ecological and Environmental Research in Belize, Vol. 1, 2000. Flying officer, RAF, 1954-56, Germany. Pres.'s award Royal Scottish Geog. Soc., 1992. Mem. Royal Geog. Soc. Avocations: travel, literature. Home: Hawthorn Villa Main St, Aberlady, East Lothian EH32 ORB, Scotland Office: Univ Edinburgh, Drummond St, Edinburgh EH8 9XP, Scotland

FURLEY, WILLIAM DAVID, classics educator; b. London, July 6, 1953; arrived in Germany, 1979; s. David John and Diana Dill (Armstrong) F.; m. Alexandra Mechthildis Horowski, Sept. 24, 1977; children: Bettina, Philip. BA in Classics, U. Coll., London, 1975; PhD, Trinity Coll., Cambridge, Eng., 1979; Habilitation, U. Heidelberg, Germany, 1989. Rsch. asst. U. Tübingen, Germany, 1979-80; asst. prof. classics U. Heidelberg, 1980-89, assoc. prof., 1989—, coord. Erasmus program student mobility in ancient studies, 1996—; vis. prof. U. Tübingen, 1986-87, U. Mannheim, Germany, 1991, U. Saarbrücken, Germany, 1995. Author: Fire in Greek Religion, 1981, Andokides and the Herms, 1996. Recipient prize for Greek, U. London, 1975, Poetry prize New Poetry, London, 1979, Open Poetry Competition Heidelberg, 1996. Mem. Hellenic Soc., Mommsen Gesellschaft. Avocations: poetry, sailing. Office: U Heidelberg Dept Classics, Marstallhof, D-69117 Heidelberg Germany

FURLOTTI, ALEXANDER AMATO, real estate development company executive; b. Milan, Italy, Apr. 21, 1948; came to U.S., 1957; s. Amato and Polonia Concepcion (Lopez) F.; m. Nancy Elizabeth Swift, June 27, 1976; children: Michael Alexander, Patrick Swift, Allison Nicole. BA in Econs., U. Calif. Berkeley, Berkeley, 1970; JD, UCLA, 1973. Bar: Calif. 1973, U.S. Dist. Ct. (9th cir.) 1973. Assoc. Alexander, Inman, Kravetz & Tanzer, Beverly Hills, Calif., 1973-77, ptnr., 1978-80; ptnr. Kravetz & Furlotti, Century City, Calif., 1981-83; pres. Quorum Properties, L.A., 1984—; dir., CEO Transmar N.V., Netherland Antilles, 1984—. Trustee Harvard-Westlake Sch., L.A., 1989-97, Yosemite Nat. Inst., San Francisco, 1990-92. Recipient Grand award Pacific Coast Bldrs. Conf., 1993, 98, Golden Nugget award, 1993, 98, Grand award Nat. Assn. Home Builders, 1993, Platinum award, 1997, Best Attached Housing award, 1998, Residential Project of Yr., 1998. Mem. Am. Bar Assn., Urban Land Inst., The Beach Club, Calif. Club. Republican. Episcopalian. Office: Quorum Properties 1875 Century Park E Los Angeles CA 90067-2501

FURLOW, THOMAS WILLIAM, JR., neurologist; b. Orange, Calif., Sept. 11, 1946; s. Thomas William and Tweet Fentress Furlow; m. Leslie Anna Levitt; children: Christopher Thomas, Elisabeth Fentress, Gregory Scott. BA, George Washington U., 1968, MD, 1971. Diplomate Am. Bd. Psychiatry and Neurology. Intern Vanderbilt U. Hosp., Nashville, 1971-72; resident in neurology U. Va. Hosp., Charlottesville, 1972-75; prof. neurology U. Ala., Birmingham, 1978-83; dir. opers. Neurotechnics, Inc., Arnold, Md., 1985-95; clin. prof. neurology U. Md. Sch. Medicine, Balt., 1991—; col. U.S. Army/Walter Reed Army Med. Ctr., Washington, 1984—; rsch. officer Navy Med. Rsch. Inst., Bethesda, Md., 1977-78.. Co-designer intraoperative monitoring electrodes and prosthetic vertebral device; contbr. numerous articles to profl. jours. Col. USAR, 1975-78, 84-89, 94—. Mem. Phi Beta Kappa, Alpha Omega Alpha. Episcopalian. Avocations: photography, digital imaging, precision metalworking, classic motorcycles. E-mail: tfurlow@erols.com.

FURMAN, GREGORY BORISOVICH, physicist, educator, researcher; b. Slavuta, Ukraine, Apr. 25, 1954; s. Boris Moiseevich and Bazya Duvidovna (Ranish) F.; m. Milana Abramovna Zilberman, Mar. 31, 1972; children: Evgeniy, Larisa, Dmitry. MS in Physics, Perm (Russia) U., 1977; PhD in Physics, Acad. Scis., Tbilisi, Georgia, 1984. Sr. rsch. assoc. Perm U., 1977-86, head phys. chemistry lab., 1986-93, assoc. prof. physics, 1990-93; sr. rsch. assoc. Ben-Gurion U., Beer-Sheva, Israel, 1994—. Contbr. articles to profl. jours. Israel Sci. Found. grantee, 1996. Mem. Israel Phys. Soc., Inst. for Quantenlektronik. Home: PO Box 4879, Str Sion 59, 12900 Katzrin Israel

FURMAN, MARK EVAN, human performance scientist; b. Bronx, Mar. 14, 1962; s. Edward and Charlotte F.; m. Beth Ann Schad, Aug. 9, 1987; children: Lauren Ashley, Jonathan Cyle. BA in Behavioral Scis./Psychology, Coll. of S.I., 1984. Cert. practitioner of neuro-linguistic programming. Dir. edn. and rsch. Assoc. Schs. Music, Inc., Cooper City, Fla., 1988-97; spkr., author, human performance cons., 1990—; founder, exec. dir. Furman Rsch. Assocs., Pompano Beach, Fla., 1987—; dir. edn. and rsch. The Keys to Success, Inc., Coral Springs, Fla., 1992—, Ozone Park, N.Y., 1992—; lectr. in field of neurosci.; founder, exec. dir. Furman Rsch. Assocs.; designer comm. program Jewish Ednl. Found. of Am., theoretical tng. model Syntonics Ednls., Switzerland; cons. Keys to Success Music Sch., N.Y., Century 21, Fla.; founder Internat. Soc. for Edn. Neurosci.; developer Intelligent Learning Systems, neuroprint, Human Performance Modeling & Engineering; numerous others application models. Author: (book) Mind in Motion, The Human Performance Technology for the Next Millenum, 1996; author: Jour. for the Soc. of Neuro-Linguistic Programming, 1995-97, The Neurophysics of Human Behavior: Explorations at the Interface of Brain, Mind, Behavior and Information, 1999; contbr. articles to profl. jours. Mem. AAAS, APA (affiliate, divsn. 48, divsn. peace psychology), Internat. Soc. for Epistemiol. Neurophysics (founder), Soc. for Study of Peace, Conflict and Violence. Achievements include developing intelligent learning systems (ILS); currently pioneering coordinated research and development efforts in the field of education neuroscience, studying the neurophysics of human information processing and its application to the field of human education and psychotherapy; advanced standard theory: Pattern-Entropy

dynamics of matter and energy interaction; formerly established the interdisciplinary branch of science known as cognitive neurophysics. Home: 3370 Beau Rivage Dr Pompano Beach FL 33064-2057 Office: The Keys to Success Inc 10758 Wiles Rd Coral Springs FL 33076-2009

FURNAS, DAVID WILLIAM, plastic surgeon; b. Caldwell, Idaho, Apr. 1, 1931; s. John Doan and Esther Bradbury (Hare) F.; m. Mary Lou Heatherly, Feb. 11, 1956; children: Heather Jean, Brent David, Craig Jonathan. AB, U. Calif.-Berkeley, 1952, MS, 1957, MD, 1955. Diplomate Am. Bd. Surgery, Am. Bd. Plastic Surgery (dir. 1979-85, sr. examiner 1986—), Royal Coll. Surgeons Found. (trustee 1995—). Intern U. Calif. Hosp., San Francisco, 1955-56, asst. resident in surgery, 1956-57; asst. resident in psychiatry, NIMH fellow Langley Porter Neuropsychiat. Inst. U. Calif., San Francisco, 1959-60; resident in gen. surgery Gorgas Hosp., C.Z., 1960-61; asst. resident in plastic surgery N.Y. Hosp., Cornell Med. Center, N.Y.C., 1961-62; chief resident in plastic surgery Cornell U. Svc., VA Hosp., Bronx, N.Y., 1962-63; registrar Royal Infirmary and Affiliated Hosps., Glasgow, Scotland, 1963-64; assoc. in hand surgery U. Iowa, 1964-68, sr. resident, faculty assoc. in surgery, 1964-65, asst. prof. surgery, 1966-68, assoc. prof., 1968-69; assoc. prof. surgery, chief div. plastic surgery U. Calif., Irvine, 1969-74, prof., chief div. plastic surgery, 1974-80, clin. prof., chief div. plastic surgery, 1980-99, clin. prof. plastic surgery, 1999—; surgeon East Africa Flying Drs. Svc., African Med. and Rsch. Found., Nairobi, Kenya, 1972-73; plastic surgeon S.S. Hope, Nicaragua, 1966, Sri Lanka, 1968; mem. Balakbayan med. mission Mindanao and Sulu, The Philippines, 1980, 81, 82; overseas vis. prof. plastic surgery Ednl. Found., 1994. Contbr. chpts. to textbooks, articles to med. jours.; author, editor 6 textbooks; assoc. editor Jour. Hand Surgery, Annals of Plastic Surgery, Jour. Craniofacial Surgery. Expedition leader Explorer's Club Flag 171 Skull Surgeons of the Kisii Tribe, Kenya, Flag 44 Skull Surgeons of the Marakwet Tribe, Kenya, 1987; mem. bd. govs. Bowers Mus. Cultural Art, 2000—. Capt. Med. Corps, USAF, 1957-59; col. Med. Corps., USAR, 1989-92, ret. Recipient Golden Apple award for tcgg. excellence U. Calif.-Irvine Sch. Medicine, 1980, Kaiser-Permanente award U. Calif.-Irvine Sch. Medicine, 1981, Humanitarian Service award Black Med. Students, U. Calif. Irvine, 1987, Sr. Rsch. award (Basic Sci.) Plastic Surgery Ednl. Found., 1987, Cert. of Spl. Recognition, U.S. Congress, 1998; named Orange County Press Club Headliner of Yr., 1982, Physician of the Year, Orange County Med. Assn., 1998. Fellow ACS, Royal Coll. Surgeons Can., Royal Soc. Medicine, Explorers Club, Royal Geog. Soc.; mem. AMA, Calif. Med. Assn., Orange County Med. Assn. (Physician of Yr. 1998), Am. Soc. Plastic Surgery (bd. dirs. 1970-73), Am. Soc. Reconstructive Microsurgery, Soc. Head and Neck Surgery, Am. Cleft Palate Assn., Am. Soc. Surgery of Hand, Soc. Univ. Surgeons, Am. Assn. Plastic Surgeons (trustee 1983-86, treas. 1988-91, v.p. 1993-94, pres.-elect 1994, pres. 1995), Am. Soc. Craniofacial Surgery, Am. Soc. Aesthetic Plastic Surgery, Am. Soc. Maxillofacial Surgeons, Assn. Acad. Chairmen Plastic Surgery (bd. dirs. 1986-89), Assn. Surgeons East Africa, Assn. Plastic & Reconstructive Surgeons So. Africa (hon.), Pacific Coast Surg. Assn., Internat. Soc. Aesthetic Plastic Surgery, Internat. Soc. Reconstructive Microsurgery, Internat. Soc. Craniomaxillofacial Surgery, Pan African Assn. Neurol. Sci., African Med. and Rsch. Found. (bd. dirs. U.S.A. 1987—, team leader "Reconstruct!" mission for victims of Am. Embassy bombing, Nairobi, Kenya, 1999), Muthaiga Club, Ctr. Club, Club 33, Univ. Club, Phi Beta Kappa, Alpha Omega Alpha. Office: 1310 W Stewart Dr Ste 610 Orange CA 92868-3857

FURNHAM, ADRIAN FRANK, psychology educator; b. Port Shepstone, Natal, South Africa, Feb. 3, 1953; s. Leslie Frank and Lorna (Audrey) F.; m. Alison Clare Green, Oct. 8, 1990; 1 child, Benedict. MA, U. Natal, 1975, DLitt, 1997; MSc, U. London, 1976, DSc, 1991; DPhil, U. Oxford, 1981; MSc, U. Strathclyde, 1976. Rsch. officer Oxford U., 1978-81; lectr. London U., 1981-87, reader, 1988-91, prof., 1992—; dir. Applied Behavioral Rsch. Assocs., London, 1985—, Social Affairs Unit, London, 1995—. Author 32 books including Personality at Work, 1994, Compementary Medicine, 1997, Psychology of Behavior at Work, 1997, Psychology of Money, 1998, Personality and Social Behavior, 1999; contbr. over 400 articles to profl. publs. Named Most Published European Psychologist, 1985—; recipient numerous rsch. grants. Fellow British Psychol. Soc. Avocations: theatre, foreign travel, arguing. E-mail: ucjtsaf@ucl.ac.uk. Home: 45 Thornhill Sq, London N1 1BE, England Office: Dept Psychology U Coll, 26 Bedford Way, London WC1 OAP, England

FURNO, CARLO CARDINAL, archbishop; b. Bairo Canavese, Dec. 2, 1921. Tchr. Pontifical Ecclesiastical Acad., 1966-73; ordained titular bishop Abari, 1973; nuncio Peru, 1973-78, Lebanon, 1978-82, Brazil, 1982-92; nuncio Italy, 1992-94, archbishop and apostolic nuncio; created and proclaimed cardinal, 1994—; grand master Equestrian Order of the Holy Sepulchre of Jerusalem, 1995—; archpriest S. Maria Maggiore, 1997—.

FUROMOTO, ATSUKO, literature educator; b. Tokyo, Mar. 12, 1939; d. Tatsuo and Harumi (Saeki) Inoue; m. Taketoshi Furomoto, Dec. 11, 1965; children: Takenori, Kanae. BA, Tokyo Women's Christian U., 1961; MA, Tokyo Met. U., 1963. Full time lectr. Kobe (Japan) Women's U., 1976-81, assoc. prof., 1981-83; prof. Tokushima-Bunri U., Shido, Japan, 1983-91; assoc. W.E.B. DuBois Inst., Harvard U., Cambridge, Mass., 1988-89; prof. Kobe Coll., Nishimiya, Japan, 1991-99; dir. Women's Studies Inst. Kobe Coll., Nishimiya, 1996-99; prof. Nara (Japan) Women's U., 1999—. Author: African-American Literature and Folklore, 1986; editor, author: Women's Literature of the World, 1991; co-author: The River and American Literature, 1992, Literature and American Dream, 1997, American Studies and Gender, 1997. Mem. Kansai Am. Lit. Soc. (v.p. 1997—), Japan Black Studies Assn. (vice rep. 1995—). Home: 5-16 Mondo Okada-cho, Nishinomiya-shi, Hyogo-ken 662-0826, Japan

FURRER, ALBERT FRIDOLIN, physicist, researcher, educator; b. Zürich, Switzerland, Nov. 17, 1939; s. Albert Sebastian and Elisa (Aegerter) F.; m. Carla Maffioli, June 7, 1974; 1 child, Raffael. Diploma in Physics, ETH, Zürich, 1964, Dr.sc.nat., 1970. Postdoctoral fellow Risø Nat. Lab., Roskilde, Denmark, 1970-71; guest scientist Oak Ridge (Tenn.) Nat. Lab., 1972-73; sr. scientist ETH, Zürich, 1974-83; head of lab., prof. ETH and Paul Scherrer Inst., Zürich, 1984—; chmn. 1st European Conf. on Neutron Scattering, 1996. Editor: Crystal Fields in Metals and Alloys, 1976, Neutron Scattering from Hydrogen in Materials, 1994, Magnetic Neutron Scattering, 1995, Complementarity Between Neutron and Hydrogen X-Ray Scattering, 1998, Neutron Scattering in Layered Copper-Oxide Conductor, 1998, Frontiers of Neutron Scattering, 2000. Col. Swiss Army, 1990-94. Grantee Swiss Nat. Sci. Found., 1974-98, ETH, 1982-95, INTAS, Brussels, 1993, 2000. Mem. Swiss Soc. for Neutron Scattering (chmn. 1991—), European Neutron Scattering Assn. (chmn. 1997—), Swiss Phys. Soc., Swiss Crystallographic Soc., European Phys. Soc. Avocations: tennis, skiing, music. Home: Rehbalde 13, CH-8166 Nieder weningen Zurich, Switzerland Office: ETH/Paul Scherrer Inst, Lab Neutron Scattering, 5232 Villigen PSI Switzerland

FURRER, JOHN RUDOLF, retired manufacturing business executive; b. Milw., Dec. 2, 1927; s. Rudolph and Leona (Peters) F.; m. Annie Louise Waldo, Apr. 24, 1954; children: Blake Waldo, Kimberly Louise. BA, Harvard U., 1949. Spl. rep. ACF Industries, Madrid, 1949-51; asst. supr. thermonuclear devel. and test Los Alamos, Eniwetok Atoll, 1952-53; dir. product devel. ACF Industries, N.Y.C., 1954-59; dir. machinery, systems group, central engring. labs. FMC Corp., San Jose, Calif., 1959-68, gen. mgr. engineered systems div., 1968-70; v.p. in charge planning dept., cen. engring. labs. and engineered systems div. FMC Corp., Chgo., 1970-71; v.p. material handling group FMC Corp., Chgo., 1971-77, v.p. corp. devel., 1977-88, sr. v.p., 1988-90. Patentee in field. Trustee Ravinia Festival, 1986-90. Served with USN, 1945-46. Mem. ASME, Coun. Planning Execs. (chmn. conf. bd. 1986-87), Harvard Club N.Y.C., Riomar Bay Yacht Club, Mid-Am. Club, Ocean Reef Club. Home: PO Box 10849 Jackson WY 83002-0849 also: 203 Spinnaker Dr Vero Beach FL 32963-2953

FURRER, PATRICK BERNARD, biophysicist, consultant; b. Lausanne, Switzerland, Jan. 8, 1964; s. Albert Furrer and Yvette Hélène Abram; m. Sylvie Marianne Magnollay, Oct. 24, 1992; children: Céline, Etienne, Julien. M in Physics, U. Geneva, Switzerland, 1990; PhD in Natural Scis., U. Lausanne, 1995. Postdoctoral staff U. Calif., San Francisco, 1996-97; sci. collaborator Swiss Fed. Inst. Tech., Lausanne, 1998—; instr. sci. State Engring Sch. VAUD, Lausanne, Switzerland, 2000—; cons. R. Rossier S.A., Sierre, Switzerland, 1999. Young Scientist grantee Swiss NSF, 1995. Avocations: badminton, guitar, guiding ski excursions. E-mail: patrickb.Furrer@epfl.ch. Fax: 4121 6935530. Office: Dept Math, Swiss Fed Inst Tech, 1015 Lausanne Switzerland

FURSOV, VLADIMIR ALEXYEVICH, engineer, researcher; b. Veryovka, USSR, May 9, 1945; s. Alexey Grigoryevich and Anna Andreyevna (Shevshenko) F.; m. Julia Kirillovna Povkh, July 22, 1972; children: Dmitry, Alexey. Degree in engring., Moscow Aviation Inst., 1973, postgrad., 1980. Dep. chief mill factory, Orenburg, USSR, 1964; lectr. faculty Voskhod Moscow Aviation Inst., 1974-77, sr. lectr. Voskhod, 1980-92, dean faculty, 1985-92, head automated control sys. dept., 1990-92; sci. rschr. Image Processing Sys. Inst., Samara, Russia, 1992—; prof. Airspace U., Samara, 1999—. Contbr. articles to profl. jours. With Soviet Army. Recipient title On Excellence of Higher Sch., Ministry of Edn., 1984. Avocations: music, drawing. Office: Imaging Processing Sys Inst, 151 Moldogvardejskaya, 443001 Samara Russia

FURST, ALEX JULIAN, thoracic and cardiovascular surgeon; b. Augusta, Ga., Aug. 21, 1938; m. George Alex and Ann (Segall) F.; m. Elayne Kobrin, Aug. 11, 1962; children: James Andrew, Jeffrey Michael, Joseph Robert. Student, U. Fla., 1963; M.D., U. Miami, 1967. Intern U. Miami Hosp., 1967-68, resident, 1968-72, clin. instr. dept. surgery, 1974-91; chief resident in thoracic and cardiovascular surgery Emory U. Hosp., Atlanta, 1972-73, sr. surg. registrar of thoracic unit, 1972-73; sr. surg. registrar of thoracic unit Hosp. for Sick Children, London, 1973-74; practice medicine specializing in thoracic and cardiovascular surgery Miami, Fla.; assoc. prof. surgery and cardiology, chief surg. svc. Miami VA Med. Ctr., 1991—, prof., surgery and medicine; chief surg. West Palm Beach Med. Ctr., Va., 2000—; chief thoracic surgery, pres. med. staff Mercy Hosp.; mem. staff Bapt. Hosp., South Miami Hosp., Doctor's Hosp. (all Miami), North Ridge Gen. Hosp., Ft. Lauderdale; program dir. cardiothoracic surgery U. Miami Sch. of Medicine. Served with U.S. Army, 1958-60. Fellow Am. Coll. Cardiology, Am. Coll. Chest Physicians, A.C.S.; mem. Dade County Med. Assn., Fla. Med. Assn., Heart Assn. Greater Miami, Soc. Thoracic Surgeons, So. Thoracic Surg. Assn. Home: 8802 Arvida Dr Miami FL 33156-2302

FURST, ARTHUR, toxicologist, educator; b. Mpls., Dec. 25, 1914; s. Samuel and Doris (Kolochinsky) F.; m. Florence Wolovitch, May 24, 1940; children: Carolyn, Adrianne, David Michael, Timothy Daniel. AA, L.A. City Coll., 1935; AB, UCLA, 1937, AM, 1940; PhD, Stanford U., 1948; ScD, U. San Francisco, 1983. Mem. faculty, dept. chemistry San Francisco City Coll., 1940-47; asst. prof. chemistry U. San Francisco, 1947-49, assoc. prof. chemistry, 1949-52; assoc. prof. medicinal chemistry Stanford Sch. Medicine, 1952-57, prof., 1957-61; with U. Calif. War Tng., 1943-45, San Francisco State Coll., 1945; rsch. assoc. Mt. Zion Hosp., 1952-82; clin. prof. pathology Columbia Coll. Physicians and Surgeons, 1969-70; dir. Inst. Chem. Biology; prof. chemistry U. San Francisco, 1961-80, prof. emeritus, 1980—, dean grad. div., 1976-79; vis. fellow Battelle Seattle Research Center, 1974; Michael vis. prof. Weizmann Inst. Sci., Israel, 1982; cons. toxicology, 1980—; cons. on cancer WHO; mem. com., bd. mineral resources NRC; sr. mem. scientific advisory bd. Golden Neo Life Diamite Internat., Fremont, Calif. Author: Toxicologist as Expert Witness, 1997; contbr. over 300 articles to profl. and ednl. jours. Recipient Klaus Schwartz Commemorative medal Internat. Toxological Congress, Tokyo, 1986, Profl. Achievement award UCLA Alumni Assn., 1992, Henry Hall Clay award U. San Francisco, 1977. Fellow Acad. Toxicological Scis. (diplomate), AAAS, Am. Coll. Nutrition, Am. Coll. Toxicology (nat. sec., pres. 1985), N.Y. Acad. Scis., Am. Inst. Chemists; mem. Am. Soc. Pharmacology and Exptl. Therapeutics, Am. Chem. Soc., Am. Assn. Cancer Research, Soc. Toxicology, Sigma Xi, Phi Lambda Upsilon. Achievements include research activities on organic synthesis, chemotherapy cancer, carcinogenesis of metals and hydrocarbons. Fax: 650-967-4488. Home: 23500 Cristo Rey Dr Unit 211D Cupertino CA 95014-6524 Office: U San Francisco Inst Chem Biology San Francisco CA 94117-1080

FURST, DANIEL ERIC, rheumatologist, researcher, clinical pharmacologist; b. Tel Aviv, Israel, Dec. 28, 1942; came to U.S., 1947; s. Theodore Moses and Jeannette Furst; m. Elaine Anne Furst, Aug. 20, 1966; children: Marc, Shawn. AB cum laude, Johns Hopkins U., 1964, MD, 1968. Diplomate Am. Bd. Internal Medicine, Am. Bd. Rheumatology. Intern Johns Hopkins U., Balt., 1968-69, resident, 1969-70; fellow in rheumatology UCLA Med. Ctr., 1973-75, asst. prof. medicine/rheumatology, 1977-82; fellow in clin. pharmacology U. Calif. San Francisco Med. Ctr. (Moffitt Hosp.), 1975-77; assoc. prof. medicine/rheumatology U. Iowa Coll. Medicine, Iowa City, 1982-87; clin. prof. medicine/rheumatology U. Medicine and Dentistry N.J./Robert Wood Johnson Med. Sch., New Brunswick, 1987-92; dir. anti-inflammatory and pulmmary clin. rsch. Ciba-Geigy Pharms., Summit, N.J., 1987-92; dir. clin. rsch. programs Virginia Mason Med. Ctr., Seattle, 1992-93, 94, med. dir., 1993—, dir. arthritis clin. rsch. unit sect. immunology and rheumatology, 1994—; clin. prof. medicine U. Wash., Seattle, 1992—; chmn. subcom. on formulating guidelines for slow-acting anti-rheumatic drugs FDA, 1978-81; mem. WHO/Internat. League Against Rheumatism Guidelines on Rheumatic Drug Devel.; v.p. Scleroderma Clin. Trials Consortium, 19997-99; clin. attending physician U. Iowa Rheumatology Clinic, 1982-87, VA Rheumatology Clinic, 1982-87, U. Medicine and Dentistry N.J. Rheumatology Clinic, 1987-92, U. Wash. Clinics, 1992—, Harborview Med. Ctr., 1995—. Mem. editl. bd. Clin. Drug Investigation, 1989—, Inflammopharmacology, 1990—, Inpharma, 1992—, ADIS Publs., 1997—, Jour. Clin. Rheumatology, 1998—. Chmn. med. and sci. com. Wash. State Arthritis Found., 1993-97; bd. dirs., 1993—; chmn. Wash./Alaska chpt. Arthritis Found., 1997—. Maj. USAF Med. Corps, 1970-73. Recipient Clifford M. Clark award, 1997. Fellow ACP; mem. Am. Fedn. Clin. Rsch., Am. Coll. Rheumatology (clin. outcomes subcom. 1992-94, indsl. rels. com. 1996—), Am. Soc. Clin. Pharmacology and Therapeutics (com. for revision of guidelines for non-steroidal anti-inflammatory drugs 1984-86, long-term planning com. 1989—, bd. dirs. 1991-94), N.Y. Acad. Scis., King County Med. Soc., Wash. State Med. Soc., N.W. Rheumatism Soc. Avocations: travel, sailing, skiing, white water rafting. Office: Virginia Mason Rsch Ctr 1201 9th Ave Seattle WA 98101-2795

FURST, ERHARD, economist; b. Vienna, Austria, Jan. 30, 1942; s. Franz and Herta (Laminger) F. Cert. in econs., Inst. for Advanced Studies, 1966; JD, U. Vienna, 1964. Asst. prof. Inst. for Advanced Studies, Vienna, 1966-69; economist IMF, Washington, 1969-71, Inst. for Econ. Rsch., Vienna, 1971-73; dep. dir. Inst. for Advanced Studies, Vienna, 1973-83; chief economist Creditanstalt, Vienna, 1983-92; head econ. policy div. Fed. Austrian Industry, 1993—. Home: Lichtenauergasse 5-9, A-1020 Vienna Austria

FÜRST, SUSANNA, clinical pharmacologist; b. Budapest, Pest, Hungary, Mar. 18, 1939; d. Andor Fürst and Jolán Feldmann; m. József Solyom; children: János, Ádám. MD, Semmelweis U. Medicine, Budapest, 1963. Asst. prof. Semmelweis U. Medicine, Budapest, 1963-80, assoc. prof., 1981-91, prof., 1991-93, head dept. pharmacology, 1994—. Co-editor: Opiate Receptors and the Neurochemical Correlates of Pain, Vol. V, 1980 (award Hungarian Acad. Scis.), Adv. in Pharm. Res. and Practice, Vol. 2, Receptors and Centrally Acting Drugs, 1986, Compendium of Pain Semantics, Algological Dictionary, 1991. Mem. Hungarian Pharm. Soc. (bd. dirs.), Hungarian Neurosci. Assn. (bd. dirs.), Hungarian Soc. for Anesthesiology and Intensive Therapy (bd. dirs.), Hungarian Physiol. Soc., Internat. Narcotic Rsch. Club, Collegium Internat. Neuropsychopharmacologicum. Avocations: classical music, swimming, gardening. Office: Semmelweis U Medicine, Dept Pharmacology POB 370, Nagyvárad tér 4, 1445 Budapest Hungary

FURSTE, WESLEY LEONARD, II, surgeon, educator; b. Cin., Apr. 19, 1915; s. Wesley Leonard and Alma (Deckebach) F.; m. Leone James, Mar. 28, 1942; children: Nancy Dianne, Susan Deanne, Wesley Leonard III. A.B. cum laude (Julius Dexter scholar 1933-34); Harvard Club scholar 1934-35), Harvard U., 1937, M.D., 1941. Diplomate: Am. Bd. Surgery. Intern Ohio State U. Hosp., Columbus, 1941-42; fellow surgery U. Cin., 1945-46; asst. surg. resident Cin. Gen. Hosp., 1946-49; sr. asst. surg. resident Ohio State U. Hosps., 1949-50, chief surg. resident, 1950-51; limited practice medicine specializing in surgery Columbus, 1951—; instr. Ohio State U., 1951-54, clin. asst. prof. surgery, 1954-66, clin. assoc. prof., 1966-74, clin. prof. surgery, 1974-85, clin. prof. emeritus, 1985—; mem. surg. staff Mt. Carmel Med. Center, chmn. dept. surgery, 1981-85, dir. surgery program, 1981-82; mem. surg. staff Children's, Grant Med. Ctr., Univ., Riverside, Meth. Hosps., St. Anthony Med. Ctr., Park Med. Ctr. (all Columbus); surg. cons. Dayton (Ohio) VA Hosp., Columbus State Sch., Ohio State Penitentiary, Mercy Hosp., Benjamin Franklin Hosp., Columbus, Columbus Cmty. Hosp.; regional adv. com. nat. blood program ARC, 1951-68, chmn., 1958-68; invited participant 2d Internat. Conf. on Tetanus, WHO, Bern, Switzerland, 1966, 3d, São, Paulo, Brazil, 1970, 4th, Dakar, Sénégal, 1975, 5th, Ronneby Brunn, Sweden, 1978, 6th, Lyon, France, 1981, 7th, Copanello, Italy, 1984, 8th, Leningrad, USSR, 1987, 9th, Granada, Spain, 1991; invited rapporteur 4th Internat. Conf. on Tetanus, Dakar, Sénégal, 1975; mem. med. adv. com. Medic Alert Found. Internat., 1971-73, 76-80, bd. dirs., 1973-76; Douglas lectr. Med. Coll. of Ohio, Toledo; founder Digestive Disease Found; lectr. U.S. Army M.C. on WWII Chinese activities during 1943-46; invited orator for new citizens at naturalization ceremonies U.S. Dist. Ct. (so. dist.) Ohio. Prime author: Tétanos; Tetanus: A Team Disease; contbg. author: Advances in Military Medicine, 1948, Management of the Injured Patient, Immediate Care of the Acutely Ill and Injured, 1978, Anaerobic Infections, 1989, Procs. of Internat. Tetans Confs. in Switzerland, Brazil, Sweden, Sénégal, France, Italy, USSR, Current Therapy in Emergency Medicine, Surgical Infectious Diseases (3 edits.), Currenty Emergency Therapy, Surgical Infections, Current Diagnosis (multiple edits.), Current Therapy (multiple edits.), Surgical Infections, 5 Minute Clinical Consult, 8 edits. (4 and 5 CD-Rom, Internet), Medical Microbiology and Infectious Diseases, editor Surgical Monthly Review; contbr. articles to profl. jours. Mem. Ohio Motor Vehicle Med. Rev. Bd., 1965-67, Pres. Club, Ohio State Univ.; bd. dirs. Am. Cancer Soc. Franklin County, pres., 1964-66; adv. coun. Upper Arlington Sr. Ctr., 2000. Served to maj., M.C. AUS, 1942-46, CBI, 1951-53. Recipient China Liberation medal, 2 commendations for surg. service in China U.S. Army; cert. of merit Am. Cancer Soc.; award for outstanding achievement in field clostridial infection dept. surgery Ohio State U. Coll. Medicine, 1984, Outstanding Service award, 1985; award for outstanding and dedicated service Mt. Carmel Med. Ctr., 1985; award for over 25 yrs. service St. Anthony Med. Ctr., U.S.A. Nat. Softball Squash Champion for age group, (75+), Houston, 1992, (80+), Denver, 96. Mem. AMA, AAAS, APHA, Cen. Surg. Assn., Surgical Infection Soc., Internat. Biliary Assn., Shock Soc., Soc. Am. Gastrointestinal Endoscopic Surgeons (com. on stds. of practice, resident and fellow edn., com. legis. review), Soc. Surgery of Alimentary Tract, A.C.S. (gov.-at-large, chmn. Ohio com. trauma; nat. subcom. prophylaxis against tetanus in wound mgmt., Ohio chapter Disting. Service award 1987; regional credentials com.), Am. Assn. Surgery of Trauma, Ohio Surg. Assn., Columbus Surg. Assn. (hon. mem.; pres. 1983), Am. Trauma Soc. (founding mem., dir.), Ohio Med. Assn., Acad. Medicine Columbus and Franklin County (Award of Merit for 17 yrs. service, chmn. blood transfusion com., 50 Year Svc. award), Acad. Medicine Cin., Am. Med. Writers Assn., Grad. Surg. Soc. U. Cin., Robert M. Zollinger Surg. Ohio State U. Surg. Soc., Mont Reid Grad. Surg. Soc., Am. Geriatrics Soc., N.Y. Acad. Scis., Assn. Program Dirs. in Surgery, Assn. Physicians State of Ohio, Collegium Internationale Chirurgiae Digestivae, Assn. Am. Med. Colls., Internat. Soc. Colon and Rectal Surgeons, Soc. Internat. de Chirurgie, Am. Assn. Sr. Physicians, Société Internationale sur le Tētanos, Am. Physicians Art Assn., Am. Assn. Retired Persons (bd. dirs. Franklin County Unit), China-Burma-India Vets., Assn. Columbus Basha (vice comdr. 1992-93, comdr. 1993-94, V-J Day coord., surgeon gen. 1994—), Am. Legion NW Post # 443, Am. Med. Golfing Assn., Internat. Brotherhood Magicians, Soc. Am. Magicians, N.Y. Cen. System Hist. Soc., U.S. Squash Racquets Assn. (mem. ranking com., med. adv. com.), Am. Platform Tennis Assn., Columbus Squash Racquets Assn. (bd. dirs.), VFW of U.S. (lectr.), Pres.'s Club (Ohio State U.). Presbyterian. Fax: 614-457-5119. E-mail: wfursteii@aol.com. Home and Office: Ohio State Univ 3125 Bembridge Rd Columbus OH 43221-2203

FURTADO, HELOISA CUNHA, power company metallurgical and materials engineer; b. Rio de Janeiro, Oct. 6, 1961; d. Lauro and Dulce (Cunha) F. MS, COPPE/UFRJ, Rio de Janeiro, 1987. Rschr. CEPEL, Rio de Janeiro, 1986—. Author: ASM International, 1992; contbr. articles to profl. jours. Home: Av Lineu de Paula Machado, 117/502, 22470040 Rio de Janeiro Brazil Office: CEPEL, Av um S/N Cidade Universit, 68007 Rio de Janeiro Brazil

FURTH, JOHN JACOB, molecular biologist, pathologist, educator; b. Phila., Jan. 25, 1929; s. Jacob and Olga (Berthauer) F.; m. Mary Autry, June 24, 1959; children: Karen, Susan, Robin. BA, Cornell U., 1950; student, Yale Law Sch., 1950-51; MD, Duke U., 1958; MA (hon.), U. Pa., 1972. Intern Bellevue Hosp., N.Y.C., 1958-59; resident in pathology NYU Sch. Medicine, N.Y.C., 1959-60, postdoctoral fellow dept. microbiology, 1960-62; mem. faculty dept. pathology U. Pa. Med. Sch., Phila., 1962—, prof., 1978—. Contbr. articles to profl. jours. Bd. dirs., chmn. hist. sites com. Darby Creek Valley Assn., 1984-96, 1st v.p. 1997—; bd. dirs., founder Friends of the Swedish Cabin (constructed circa 1654), Upper Darby, Pa., 1987; bd. dirs. Fair Housing Coun. of Suburban Phila., 1995-97, 2d dist. leader Upper Darby Democratic Party, 1994—. 2d lt. Q.M.C., U.S. Army, 1951-53. Recipient Hoffman LaRoche award, 1958; Eleanor Roosevelt fellow, 1977-78. Mem. AAAS, Am. Soc. Biol. Chemists and Molecular Biologists, Am. Assn. Cancer Rsch., Am. Assn. Pathologists. Democrat. Mem. Soc. of Friends. Achievements include codiscovery of RNA polymerase. Home: 43 Roselawn Ave Lansdowne PA 19050-2317 Office: U Pa Sch Medicine Dept Pathology and Lab Med Philadelphia PA 19104-6082

FURUKAWA, MUTSUHISA, engineering educator, researcher; b. Fukuoka, Japan, Jan. 21, 1944; s. Shyunpei and Tiyo F.; m. Hideko; children: Tomoko, Eiko. B in Engring., Kagoshima (Japan) U., 1967; M in Engring., Kyushu U., Fukuoka, Japan, 1970, PhD in Engring., 1987. Rschr. Idemitsu Petroleum Chemistry Co Ltd., Tokyo, 1970-72; assoc. rschr. Nagasaki (Japan) U., 1972-82, asst. prof., 1982-87, assoc. prof., 1988-92, prof., 1993-94, 1998-2000; head of dept. Materials Sci. and Engring., Nagasaki U., 1995, 98. Contbr. artticles to profl. jours. Officer Soc. of Rubber Industry, Japan. Mem. Soc. Polymer Sci. (officer 1992—), Am. Chem. Soc., Soc. Rubber Industry. Home: 3-35-19 Yokoo, Nagasaki 852-8065, Japan Office: Nagasaki U, 1-14 Bunko-Machi, Nagasaki 852-8521, Japan

FURUKUBO-TOKUNAGA, KATSUO, biology educator; b. Nagoya, Aichi, Japan, Sept. 24, 1954; s. Kanjiro and Kiyoko (Hijikata) Tokunaga; m. Midori Furukubo, Sept. 24, 1979; 1 child, Mizuho. BSc, Kyoto (Japan) U., 1978; MSc, Nagoya (Japan) U., 1980, DSc, 1984. Rsch. fellow Nat. Inst. Basic Biology, Okazaki, Japan, 1983; sr. rsch. staff Chiba (Japan) Cancer Ctr., 1983-88; sr. rsch. assoc. U. Basel, Switzerland, 1988-92; ass.t prof. U. Basel, 1992-95; assoc. prof. U. Tsukuba, Japan, 1995—; project leader Tsukuba Adv. Rsch. Alliances. Contbr. articles to profl. jours. Rsch. grantee Roche Rsch. Found., Switzerland, 1993-95, Swiss NSF, 1994-97, Yamada Sci. Found., Japan, 1996-97. Mem. The Genetical Soc. (U.K.), The Genetics Soc. Am., Soc. for Neurosci. Avocations; mountain walking, traveling. Office: Inst Biol Scis, Univ Tsukuba, Tsukuba 305-8572, Japan

FURUSE, MITSUHIRO, nutritionist; b. Suzuka, Mie, Japan, Aug. 4, 1956; s. Minoru and Yasuko (Kamei) F.; m. Akemi Takamura, Oct. 11, 1980; children: Kana, Yukika, Koh. B in Agriculture, Nihon U., Tokyo, 1980; MAgr, Nagoya (Japan) U., 1982, PhD in Agriculture, 1985. Asst. prof. Nagoya U., 1988-97; assoc. prof. Kyushu U., 1997-2000, prof., 2000—. Contbr. articles to profl. jours. Recipient award for Young Animal Scientist, Japan Zootech. Sci. Soc., 1986, Japan Poultry Sci. Assn. award, 1995, award Pres. Faculty Agrl. and Vet. Sci., Nihon U., 1996, Goto Poultry Sci. Found. award, 1996. Mem. AAAS, Am. Diabetes Assn., Am. Soc. of Nutrition Scis., Nutrition Soc., Am. Physiol. Soc., Endocrine Soc., Soc. Endocrinology, Soc. Neurosci., N.Y. Acad. Scis. Home: 4-15-16 Mainosato Koga-shi, Fukuoka-ken 811-3114, Japan Office: Kyushu U Fac Agr, Lab of Animal Feed Scis, Fukuoka 812-8581, Japan

FURUTA, KATSUHISA, educator; b. Nerima-ku, Tokyo, Japan, Jan. 3, 1940; s. Yoshio and Chie (Fujioka) F.; m. Kumiko Watanabe, Mar. 26, 1967; children: Takehisa, Atsuhisa. BA, Tokyo Inst. Tech., 1962, MA, 1964, PhD, 1967. Rsch. assoc. Tokyo Inst. Tech., 1967-70, assoc. prof., 1970-82, prof., 1982-2000; prof. Tokyo Denki U., 2000—; postdoctoral fellow Laval U., Que., Can., 1967-69, vis. prof., 1973; vis. prof. U. Calif., Berkeley, 1997. Author: (all in Japanese) Linear Control Systems, 1973, Identification and Estimation,1975, Introduction to State Space, 1979. Fellow Soc. Instrument

and Control Engrs. (paper award 1973), IEEE; mem. Sci. Coun. Japan. Office: Tokyo Denki U, Hatoyama Hikigum, Saitama 350-0394, Japan

FURUTANI, KATSUSHI, technology educator. B of Engring., U. Tokyo, 1989, M of Engring., 1991, D of Engring., 1994. Cert. in engring. Rsch. assoc. Tokyo Inst. Tech., Yokohama, Japan, 1991-92; rsch. assoc. Toyota Technol. Inst., Nagoya, Japan, 1992-95, lectr., 1995-98, assoc. prof., 1998—. Fax: 81-52-809-1721. E-mail: furutani@toyota-ti.ac.jp. Office: Toyota Technol Inst, 12-1 Hisakata 2-chome, Nagoya 468-8511, Japan

FURUYA, KENICHI, reproductive endocrinologist, gynecologic surgeon; b. Tokyo, Sept. 18, 1953; s. Hiroshi and Setsue F. MD, Juntendo U., Tokyo, 1979, PhD, 1986. Clin. asst. Nat. Def. Med. Coll., Saitama, Japan, 1979-88, asst. prof., 1992—; post-doctoral fellow Inst. Hormone and Fertility Rsch. Hamburg U., Germany, 1988-90. Patentee in field. Mem. Japan Soc. Endocrinology (councillor 1992—), Japan Soc. Fertility and Sterility (councillor 1996—), Japan Soc. Gynecologic Endoscopic Surgery (councillor 1995—), Japan Soc. Gynecologic Microsurgery (councillor 1990—), N.Y. Acad. Scis. (Charles Darwin assocs. 1998—). Avocations: classical music, tennis, photography, Judo, Japanese Chess. Fax: 81-42-996-5213. Office: NDMC Dept Ob-gyn 3-2 Namiki, Tokorozawa, Saitama 359-8513, Japan

FURYK, JAMES MICHAEL, professional golfer; b. West Chester, Pa., May 12, 1970. Grad. in Gen. Bus., U. Ariz., 1992. Profl. golfer PGA, 1992—; mem. Ryder Cup team, 1997, President's Cup team, 1998. Winner Nike Miss. Gulf Coast Classic, 1993, Las Vegas Internat., 1995, United Airlines Hawaiian Open, 1996, Argentine Open, 1997, Las Vegas Invitational, 1998, Doral-Ryder Open, 2000; 2d pl. Meml. Tournament, 1997, The Tour Championship, 1997. Avocation: sports. Office: c/o PGA America Box 109601 100 Ave of Champions Palm Beach Gardens FL 33410

FUSAYAMA, TAKAO, dental educator; b. Mino City, Japan, Aug. 7, 1916; s. Hideo and Shin (Yamaghuchi) F.; m. Setsuko Mori; 3 children. DDS, Tokyo Med. and Dental U., 1938; PhD, Tokyo U., 1955. Lic. dentist, Japan. Lectr. Toyo Woman's Dental Coll., Tokyo, 1946-47, prof., 1947-50; lectr. Tokyo Med. and Dental U., 1950-53, asst. prof., 1953-60, prof., 1960-82, prof. emeritus, 1982—; guest prof. Showa U., Tokyo, 1982—; chmn. Nat. Bd. Dental Licensure Exam., 1970-71, Nat. Bd. Govtl. Rsch. Grants, 1974-80, Nat. Bd. Dental Sch. Insps., 1987-90. Author: New Concept in Operative Dentistry, 1980, Simple Pain-Free Adhesive Restorative System, 1993. Capt. signal corps Japanese Army, 1938-46. Recipient Wilmer Souder award Internat. Assn. for Dental Rsch., 1982, Hollenback Meml. prize Acad. Operative Dentistry, 1999. Mem. ADA (hon.; Gold medal award for excellence in dental rsch. 1997), Japan Dental Assn. (chmn. internat. rels. com. 1968-81), Japan Acad., Fed. Dentaire Internat. Avocations: judo (5-Dan), tennis, golf, pencil drawing. Home: 4-16-23 Kamiigusa, Suginamiku, Tokyo 167-0023, Japan

FUSELLA, JOSEPH PETER, physician; b. Amsterdam, N.Y., June 23, 1961; s. Joseph Peter and Joan F.; m. Loretta Giuliani, July 23, 1983; children: Nicholas, Michael. BS, Siena Coll., Loudenville, N.Y., 1983; DO, N.Y. Coll. Osteo. Medicine, Old Westbury, N.Y., 1987. Diplomate Am. Bd. Family Practice, Am. Bd. Osteopathic Family Physicians. Intern Suncoast Hosp., Largo, Fla., 1987-88; resident St. Clares Hosp., Schenectady, N.Y., 1988-91; pvt. practice Niskayuna Family Practice, Niskayuna, N.Y., 1991-93, The Primary Care Ctr., Schenectady, N.Y., 1993-98, Capital Care Med. Group, Schenectady, 1998—; dir. ostepathic internship program St. Clares Hosp. Mem. Am. Acad. Family Physicians, Am. Osteo. Assn., Am. Acad. Osteopathy, Am. Osteo. Dirs. Med. Edn., Med. Soc. State N.Y. Office: 624 Mcclellan St Ste G01 Schenectady NY 12304-1020

FUSTER, VALENTIN, cardiologist, educator; b. Barcelona, Spain, Jan. 20, 1943; s. Joaquin and Pilar Fuster; m. Angela-Maria Guals, Sept. 3, 1968; children: Pablo, Silvia. Baccaluarate, Colegio Jesuitas, Barcelona, 1961; MD, Barcelona U., 1967. Diplomate Am. Bd. Internal Medicine (mem. com. subspity. bd. cardiovas. disease), Am. Bd. Cardiology. Intern Hosp. Clinico, Barcelona, 1967-68; rsch. fellow U. Edinburgh, Scotland, 1968-71; fellow in medicine and cardiovasc. diseases Mayo Grad. Sch. Medicine, Rochester, Minn., 1971-74; asst. prof. medicine Mayo Med. Sch., Rochester, 1974-77, assoc. prof. medicine, 1978-81, assoc. prof. pediat., 1980—, prof. medicine and cardiovasc. diseases, 1981-82; Arthur A. and Hilda M. Master prof. medicine Mt. Sinai Sch. Medicine, N.Y.C., 1982-91, chief divsn. cardiology, 1982-91; head cardiology unit Mass. Gen. Hosp., 1991-93; Mallinckrodt prof. medicine Harvard Med. Sch., Boston, 1991-93; dir. Cardiovasc. Inst. Mt. Sinai Med. Ctr., N.Y.C., 1993—; mem. cardiology adv. com. NIH; mem. com. Am. Bd. Cardiology; hon. lectr. numerous orgns.; mem. adv. coun. Nat. Heart, Lung and Blood Insts., 1997. Mem. editl. bd. Am. Jour. Cardiology, 1982, Arteriosclerosis, 1982, Jour. The Am. Coll. Cardiology, 1987, Circulation, 1988, consulting editor, 1992, circulation rsch. consulting editor, 1997; contbr. over 400 articles to profl. jours. Recipient 30 rsch. and tchg. awards including Gruntzig award European Soc. Cardiology, 1992, Disting. Sci. award Am. Coll. Cardiology, 1993, Disting. Conner Lectr. award Am. Heart Assn., 1993, Principe de Asturias award for sci. and tech. Found. Principe de Asturias, Oviedo, Spain, Principe de Asturias award for sci. and tech. U. Asturias in conjunction with Royal Family of Spain, 1996. Fellow Am. Coll. Cardiology (chair tng. dirs. com. 1997, Disting. Bishop Lectr. award 1994, Disting. Svc. award 2000), Royal Coll. Physicians; mem. Am. Heart Assn. (chmn. pub. com., bd. dirs. 1994, pres.-elect 1997, pres. 1998—, Disting. Achievement award 1997), Am. Soc. Clin. Investigations, Assn. Am. Physicians, European Soc. Clin. Investigation, Brit. Cardiac Soc. (corr.). Office: Mt Sinai Med Ctr 1 Gustave L Levy Pl # 1030 New York NY 10029-6500

FUTCH, LYNN, lawyer; b. St. Petersburg, Fla., Apr. 22, 1961; d. M. Daniel Jr. and Florence Corrine (Coe) Futch. Student, Broward C.C., 1978-79; BS in Mktg. cum laude, Fla. State U., 1982, JD with honors, 1984. Bar: Fla. 1985, U.D. Dist. Ct. (so. dist.) Fla. 1985. Intern Broward County State's Atty., Ft. Lauderdale, Fla., 1984; with Pyszka, Kessler, Massey, Weldon, Catri, Holton, & Douberley, P.A., Ft. Lauderdale, 1985-89; assoc. Conrad, Scherer & Jenne, Ft. Lauderdale, 1989-95; ptnr. Conrad, Scherer & Jenne, P.A., Ft. Lauderdale, 1995-98; dir. dept. legal affairs Broward Sheriff's Office, Ft. Lauderdale, 1998—. Bd. dirs. Friends of Ft. Lauderdale Librs., 1987-94, Jr. League Ft. Lauderdale, 1988-93, Legal Aid Svcs., Broward, 1996-98; mem jud. selection, adminstrn. and tenure com. Fla. Bar, 1990-93, joint presdl. advt. task force, 1995-97, bd. govs. young lawyers divsn., 1993-99, 17th Jud. Cir. Grievence com., 1996-98, chair 1998. Mem. Broward County Bar Assn. (bd. dirs. 1990-99, sec.. treas. 1995-96, pres.-elect 1996-97, pres. 1998-99, young lawyers sect., exec. com., sec.-treas. 1989-90, pres.-elect 1990-91, pres. 1991-92), Fed. Bar Assn. (Broward County chpt., exec. com. 1988-90, sec. 1990-91, pres.-elect 1991-92, pres. 1992-93, 17th Jud. cir. professionalism com. 1998-99), Broward Lawyers Care (adv. com.), Zeta Tau Alpha. Republican. Roman Catholic. Office: Broward Sheriff's Office 2601 W Broward Blvd Fort Lauderdale FL 33312-1308

FUTRELL, JEAN H., research scientist, administrator, educator; b. Grant Parish, La., Oct. 20, 1933; s. Homer E. and Ellen Catherine (Padgett) Futrell; m. Earlene Welch, June 3, 1955 (div. Oct. 1976); children: Craig Forrest, Alison Renee; m. Nancy Nielson Futrell, Oct. 30, 1976 (div. Nov. 1987); m. Anne Krohn Graham, June 26, 1988. BSChemE, La. Tech. U., 1955; PhD in Chemistry, U. Calif., Berkeley, 1958. Rsch. scientist Exxon Rsch. Labs., Baytown, Tex., 1958-59; sect. chief high energy chemistry Aeropace Rsch. Labs., Dayton, Ohio, 1961-66; assoc. prof. of chemistry U. Utah, Salt Lake City, 1967-68, prof. chemistry, 1967-68; chair chemistry and biochemistry U. Del., Newark, 1986-97, Willis F. Harrington prof., 1989-99, Willis F. Harrington prof. emeritus, 1999—; dir. W.H. Wiley Environ. Molecular Scis. Lab., U.S. Dept. Energy, Richland, Wash., 1999—; adj. prof. U. Utah, 1999—, Wash. State U., 1999—. Alexander Von Humboldt fellow Hahn-Meitner Inst., Berlin, 1984-85, Fullbright fellow U. Innsbruck, Austria, 1978-79; numerous grants NSF, NIH, DOE, Petroleum Rsch. Fund of the Am. Chem. Soc., Air Force Office of Scientific Rsch., EPA,. Mem. AAAS, CCR (governing bd. of coun. for chem. rsch., 1995—, exec. com., 1995-2000, chair govt. rels. com., 1994-97, program chair 1998, chair 1999), Am. Soc. for Mass Spectrometry (founding mem. 1967, pres. 1976-78), Am. Chem. Soc., Am. Phys. Soc., Am. Inst. of Physics, Indian Soc. for Mass Spectrometry, Hungarian Soc. for Mass Spectrometry, Sigma Xi, Tau Beta Pi, Sigma Phi. Home: 2802 Appaloosa Way Richland WA 99352-9646 Office: Wiley Environ Molec Scis Labmistry Pacific NW Nat Lab Office of Dir Richland WA 99352

FUZES, ENDRE, ethnologist, museum director; b. Dobrokoz, Hungary, Apr. 27, 1932; s. Janos and Irma (Kovacs) F.; m. Julianna Hudak, Dec. 18, 1972; children: Gergely, Marton, Andras. Grad., Eotvos Lorand U., Budapest, Hungary, 1955. Asst. Mus. of City of Pecs, Hungary, 1955-63; counselor Hungarian Ministry Culture, Budapest, 1964-79; sci. researcher Ethnographical Inst., Hungarian Acad. Sci., Budapest, 1980-86; gen. dir. Open Air Mus. of Szentendre, Hungary, 1986—; ret. Author: A gabona tarolasa a magyar parasztgazdasagokban, 1984. Mem. Hungarian Ethnographical Assn. (treas.), Council Hungarian Mus., Council Hungarian Folk Art. Home: 4 Tornalja, 1124 Budapest Hungary Office: Open Air Mus Szentendre, PO Box 63, 2001 Szentendre Hungary

FÜZES, IVÁN, biophysicist, researcher; b. Budapest, Hungary, Apr. 25, 1948; s. Rezsö and Magdolna (Nébel) Schiffer; m. Éva Hrabéczy, July 15, 1972; children: Ádám, Fruzsina. MSEE, Tech. U. Budapest, 1975, PhD in Sci. of Modeling, 1981. Measuring technicist Budapest, 1966-68; designer VBKM Electronic Power Current Trust, Budapest, 1968-74, FOK-GYEM Electronic Instrument Mfg. Co., Budapest, 1974-75; rschr. dept. exptl. physiology Nat. Inst. Occupl. Health, Budapest, 1975-83; head dept. biophysics Nat. Inst. Neurosurgery, Budapest, 1983—. Contbr. articles to profl. jours.; patentee on high frequency precision surg. generator, 1995. Mem. Hungarian Measuring Technique and Automation Soc., Hungarian Physiol. Soc., Austrian Soc. for Tech. Biomedicine. Office: Nat Inst Neurosurgery, Amerikai ut 57, 1145 Budapest Hungary

FYDLER, CHRIS, Olympic athlete; b. Sydney, NSW, Australia, Aug. 11, 1972. Recipient Gold medal in 4 x 100m freestyle Sydney Olympics, 2000, Bronze medal in 100m freestyle, Sydney Triple Silver medal in 100m freestyle Commonwealth Games, 1990, 94, 98; 2d fastest swimmer 100m freestyle, Australia; anchor swimmer world championship-winning 4 x 100m medley relay World Champs Perth, 1998, World SC, Hong Kong, 1999, 2d 50 and 100m freestyle Telstra Selection Trials, 2000. Mem. Sydney Univ. Club. Avocations: family, surfing. Office: Australian Swimming Inc, PO Box 940, Dickson ACT 2602, Australia*

FYLER, CARL JOHN, dentist; b. Spearville, Kans., May 14, 1921; s. John Henry and Helen Elsie (Parthie) F.; m. Marguerite E. Burris, Feb. 14, 1946. DDS, U. Mo., Kansas City, 1950. Practice dentistry Topeka, Kans., 1950-92; ret., 1992. Author: Staying Alive. Served to maj. USAF, 1942-46, ETO. Decorated Purple Heart, 5 Air Medals, Distinguished Flying Cross, E.T.O medal with 3 battle stars, Prisoner of War medal. Mem. ADA (life), Kans. Dental Assn., Shawnee County Dental Assn., Internat. Fedn. Dentists, Am. Ex-Prisoners of War (nat. dir. 1974-85, nat. jr. vice comdr. 1984-85), Kans. Ex-Prisoners of War (Gov.'s adv. com. 1978-86), 303d H.B.G. Assn. (pres. 1987-89), Eighth Air Force Hist. Soc. (bd. dirs. 1989-92, heavy bomb group), Mil. Order of World Wars (pres. Topeka chpt. 1996—), Distinguished Flying Cross Soc., Am. Legion, D.A.V., Am. Vets. Republican. Presbyterian. Avocations: flying, lapidary, rock hunting. Home: 300 SW Yorkshire Rd Topeka KS 66606-2260

FYNES, SAVETHEDA, Olympic athlete. Winner Gold medal 4x100 meter relays Sydney, 2000. Office: Bahamas Amateur Athletic Assn, PO Box 55, Nassau 5517, Bahamas*

FYNTANIDIS, S., publishing executive. Dir. Eleftherotypia, Athens. Office: Eleftherotypia, 10-16 Myoos St, Athens 14743, Greece*

FYODOROV, ANATOLY ANDREEWICH, chemist; b. Riga, Latvia, Jan. 24, 1948; s. Andrew Fyodorovich and Evdokia Grigorievna (Golovkova) F.; m. Irina Victorovna Sigle, June 30, 1972; 1 child, Andrew. PhD, State U. Perm, Russia, 1972; cand. in Chemistry, State U. Perm, 1973; DSc in Chemistry, Higher Attestation Com., Moscow, 1994. Lab. asst., lectr. Pharm. Inst., Perm, USSR, 1966-76; sr. lectr., asst. prof., chmn. chemistry dept. Polytech Inst., Perm, 1976-86; lab. head Republic Ctr. Powder Metallurgy, Perm, 1986-90; leading sci. fellow, sci. sec. Inst. Tech. Chemistry Russian Acad. Sci., Perm, 1995—; prof. Chemistry State Tech. U., Perm, 1996—. Author: (book) High-permeable Cellular Catalyste, 1993; contbr. over 150 articles to profl. jours. With Army of USSR, 1973-74. Mem. Inst. Tech. Chemistry, Russian Acad. Scis. (sci. sec. dissertation coun.). Avocations: photography, fishing, boating. Home: K Cetkin Str 23a-34, 614010 Perm Russia Office: Inst Tech Chemistry, Ural Br Russian Acad Scis, 614000 Perm Russia

FYODOROV, YAN V., theoretical and mathematical physicist, educator; b. Leningrad, Russia, Feb. 4, 1962; s. Valerij P. and Inna S. (Tublin) F.; m. Olga L. Soudakova, Nov. 11, 1983; 1 child, Miron. M degree, Polytech. Inst., Leningrad, 1984; PhD, Nuclear Physics Inst., Leningrad, 1988; DSc, Nuclear Physics Inst., St. Petersburg, 1994. Rschr. Nuclear Physics Inst., St. Petersburg, 1989-94, sr. rschr., 1994—; rsch. assoc. Essen (Germany) U., 1994-2000; prof. math., physics Brunel U., London, 2000—. Contbr. articles to profl. jours. Fellow Alexander von Humboldt, Av. H. Stiftung (Germany), 1991, Sir Charles Clore, Weizmann Inst. Sci. (Israel), 1993; recipient Inst. Henri Poincare/Gauthier-Villars prize, 1999. Office: Brunel U, Dept Math Scis, Uxbridge UB8 3PH, England

GAADT, SUZANNE DEMOTT, graphic designer; b. Phila., Apr. 13, 1965; d. Evard O. and Anne (Stevens) DeMott; m. John Michael Gaadt, Apr. 4, 1992. BFA cum laude, Temple U., 1987. Graphic designer Bailey/Spiker Inc., Phila., 1987-89; art dir. Ardmoor Corp., Chadds Ford, Pa., 1989-90; publ. designer Brandywine River Mus., Chadds Ford, 1990-93; ptnr. Gaadt Perspectives, LLC, Chadds Ford, Pa., 1993—. Designer publs. and materials Winterthur Mus., Garden and Libr., Swarthmore Coll., Chester County Tourist Bur., Chester County Hist. Soc. Mem. Am. Inst. Graphic Artists, Am. Assn. Mus., Greater West Chester C. of C., Found. for Shamanic Studies. Democrat. Roman Catholic. Avocations: reading, writing, travel, music, arts. Home and Studio: 251 Fairville Rd Chadds Ford PA 19317-9438

GAARDHOJE, JENS JORGEN, physics educator, researcher; b. Copenhagen, Denmark, Nov. 7, 1954; s. Borge and Aase (Petersen) G.; m. Janne Lis Wardil Gaardhoje; children: Jacob, Johan, Jesper. DSc, U. Copenhagen, Denmark, 1993. Rsch. assoc. U. Copenhagen, Denmark, 1981-83; sr. rsch. assoc. Danish Nat. Sci. Found., Denmark, 1984-86; assoc. prof. rsch. Carlsberg Found., Denmark, 1987-93; assoc. prof Niels Bohr Inst. U. Copenhagen, Denmark, 1994—; mem. program adv. com. SARA Accelerator Facility Grenoble, France, 1987-93; deputy spokesman BRAHMS Exp. at RHIC:USA, 1997—; chmn. int. "Hector Collab., DK-I-PL-NL, 1986-96; heavy ion group leader U. Copenhagen, Denmark, 1995—; chmn. UNESCO Niels Bohr medal award com.; mem. exec. bd., chmn. sci. com. Danish Nat. Commn. for UNESCO; chmn. PhD Sch. Physics, Niels Bohr Inst. Author approximately 120 articles in internat. refereed scientific literature; editor of 3 books. Grantee Carlsberg Found. and Danish Natural Sci. Rsch. Coun. Mem. European Phys. Soc., Denmark Acad. Natural Sci., Danish Phys. Soc. Avocations: squash, skiing, windsurfing. Home: Kastebjergvej 22, 2750 Ballerup Denmark Office: Niels Bohr Inst, Blegdamsvej 17, 2100 København Denmark

GABANT, PHILIPPE, molecular biologist, researcher; b. Watermael-Boitsfort, Brussels, Belgium, Jan. 7, 1965; s. Gaston and Nicole (Demesmaeker) G. Grad. in Biology, U. Brussels, 1988, PhD in Biology, 1993; Grad. in Mgmt., ISC St. Louis, Brussels, 1995. Scientist, rschr. Ctr. for Genome Rsch., Edinburgh, 1996-97; scientist, rschr. Lab. Devel. Biology, Brussels, 1994-96, rsch. assoc., 1997—. Contbr. articles to profl. jours.; patentee positive selection vectors. Mem. Belgian Soc. Biochemistry, Belgian Soc. Cellular Biology. E-mail: gabant@dbm.ulb.ac.be Fax: 32-2-6509700. Office: Dept Molecular Biology, Rue Prof Jeneer et Brachet 12, B-6041 Gosselies Belgium

GABARD, DONALD LEONARD, medical educator; b. Winston-Salem, Sept. 3, 1946; s. Clarence W. and Clara (Pardue) G. MS, U. So. Calif., L.A., 1978, MPA, 1988, PhD, 1990. Staff therapist Calif. Children Svcs., L.A., 1976-78; co-owner Spl. Arrangements, L.A., 1982-87; phys. therapist Spl. Children's Ctr., Pasadena, 1978-86; dir. phys. therapy Univ. Affiliated Program, L.A., 1986-87, adminstr., 1987-90; assoc. prof. Children's Hosp., L.A., 1990-93; assoc. prof., chair dept. phys. therapy Chapman U., Orange, Calif., 1993—. Contbr. articles to profl. jours. Cons. Caring for Babies with AIDS, Culver City, Calif., 1985-95; vol. to help homeless All Saints Episc. Ch., Pasadena, 1994—. Recipient Samuel C. May Rsch. award Western Govt. Rsch. Assn., 1988. Mem. APHA (chair Lesbian and Gay Caucus 1995-97), L.A. Conservancy, L.A. Great Outdoors, So. Calif. Hort. Soc., U. So. Calif. Lambda Alumni Assn. (founder 1990, chair 1992-94, Outstanding Svc. award 1995). Democrat. Avocations: horticulture, travel. Home: 2341 Hidalgo Ave Los Angeles CA 90039-3633 Office: Chapman Univ Divsn Phys Therapy Orange CA 92666

GABBAY, MARCEL, management consultant; b. Istanbul, Turkey, June 25, 1923; arrived in Eng., 1944; s. Albert M. and Elise (Roditi) G.; m. Vera Beck, Dec. 23, 1948; children: John, Mark. BA in Commerce, Robert Coll., Istanbul, 1943; BSc in Tech., U. Manchester, Eng., 1948. Chartered textile technologist Textile Inst. Eng. Mgr. mill Makaracilik Tas & Kadiotti, Istanbul, 1950-56, Kraftcord Ltd., Radcliffe, Eng., 1956-58; cons. Assoc. Indsl. Cons./Inbucon Ltd., London, 1958-63; sr. exec. Friedland, Doggart Ltd., Stockport, Eng., 1963-67; mng. dir. Bias (Mgmt. Cons. Ltd.), Chorley, Eng., 1967-80; indsl. devel. cons. expert UN Indsl. Devel. Orgn., ILO and various countries, France, 1970—; non-exec. dir. Gabbay Group Ltd., Southampton, England. Decorated officier Palmes Academiques (France); recipient Disting. Svc. medal Servicio Nacional de Aprendizaje Nat. Coun., Bogota, Colombia, 1976; Paul Harris fellow, 1992. Fellow Brit. Inst. Mgmt.; mem. Inst. Mgmt. Cons. (mem. coun. 1971), Rotary (pres. St. Maxime/St. Tropez, France club), Assn. Des Anciens Fonctionnaires Des Nations Unies Resident En France (pres. 1995). Avocations: photography, music. Home: 5 Ave F Mistral, 83120 La Nartelle, Sainte Maxime Var France

GABBERT, ULRICH, engineering educator; b. Magdeburg, Germany, Apr. 11, 1947; s. Hans and Elfriede (Trebst) G.; m. Heidrun Kopietz, Jan. 8, 1972; children: Jens, Bettina. Engr., U. Magdeburg, 1971, D, 1974. Asst. U. Magdeburg, 1973-76, 79-91; engr. Pump & Impeller Co., Halle, Germany, 1976-79; prof. U. Magdeburg, 1992—. Mem. Internat. Union Theoretical and Applied Mechanics, Gesellschaft für Angewandte Math. and Mechanik, Verein Deûtscher Ingenieure. Avocations: literature, history, sports. Home: Goethe Strasse 36, D-39108 Magdeburg Germany Office: Univ Magdeburg, Universitäts Platz 2, D-39106 Magdeburg Germany

GABE, JONATHAN PETER, medical sociologist; b. Cardiff, Wales, Mar. 7, 1950; s. Peter Seymour and Claire Winsome (Wrigley) G.; m. Elizabeth Hardiman, Apr. 6, 1975; children: Claire, Rachel, Jonathan. B Social Sci. in Sociology with honors, U. Birmingham (Eng.), 1971, PhD in Sociology, 1989. Rsch. officer Bedford Coll. U. London, 1979-82; rsch. sociologist Inst. Psychiatry, London, 1983-86, lectr. in sociology, 1986-90; lectr. in sociology Royal Holloway U. London, 1990-91; sr. lectr. in sociology South Bank U., London, 1991-93; sr. rsch. fellow Royal Holloway U. London, 1993-2000; cons. Broadcasting Support Svcs., London, 1989—, Open U., Milton Keynes, Eng., 1995; external examiner Leeds (Eng.) Metro. U., 1993-96, U. Kent, Canterbury, Eng., 1996-99; editor Sociology of Health and Illness, Oxford, Eng., 1994-2000; sr. lectr. in sociology Royal Holloway U., London, 2000—. Author: Going Private. Why People Pay for Their Health Care, 1993; editor: Tranquilisers: Social, Psychological and Clinical Perspectives, 1986, Understanding Tranquiliser Use, 1991, Sociology of the Health Service, 1991, Challenging Medicine, 1994, Medicine, Health and Risk, 1995, Health and the Sociology of Emotions, 1996, Sociological Perspectives on the New Genetics, 1999, Health, Medicine and Society. Key Theories, Future Agendas, 2000. Grantee Econ. and Social Rsch. Coun., 1988, 98, Dept. Health, 1995, 99, Health Edn. Authority, 1995. Mem. British Sociol. Assn. (fin. com. 1994-99), Soc. for Study of Social Problems. Achievements include research on the social meaning of tranquiliser use and on tranquilisers as a social problem, research on why people pay for private health care and on violence against general medical practitioners in the community. E-mail: j.gabe@rhbnc.ac.uk. Office: Royal Holloway U London, Dept Social & Polit Sci, Egham TW20 OEX, England

GABEL, CONNIE, chemistry educator; b. Green Bank, W.Va.; d. William Ashby and Marie Lowry; m. Richard Gabel; children: Greg, Keith, Debbie. BS in Chemistry magna cum laude, James Madison U.; MA in Ednl. Adminstrn. summa cum laude, U. Colo., 1984; postgrad., 1997—. Teaching asst. U. Wis., Madison, 1969-70, specialist endocrinology, 1970-71; tchr. Dept. Defense Schs., Tokyo, 1972-74, Poudre R-1 Schs., Ft. Collins, Colo., 1975-78; tchr. Boulder (Colo.) Valley Schs., 1985-87, 96-98, intern asst. prin., 1984-85; intern supt. Jefferson County Schs., Golden, Colo., 1992; tchr. Mapleton Pub. Schs., Thornton, Colo., 1992-95; internat. studies Egyptian program Regis U., Denver, 1994; instr. chemistry Colo. Sch. Mines, 1995-98; dean of students Horizon H. S., Thornton, Colo., 1995-96; project 2061 coord. dept. chemistry/edn. U. Colo., Denver, 1998—; rechr. AMC Cancer Rsch. Ctr., Denver, 1993, rschr. Colo. U. Med. Ctr., Denver, 1994; cons. sch. fin. Colo. Dept. Edn., Denver, 1984; display tech Boulder-chemistry rsch., 1995. Charter mem., pres. Friends Louisville (Colo.) Libr., 1985—; charter mem., pres., v.p. Coal Creek Rep. Women, Louisville, 1987—; sec., mem. Boulder County Reps., 1988—, precinct chair; mem. Nat. Rep. Women, Washington, 1987—; sec. dist. 17 Colo. Senate, sec. Colo. Ho. Dist. 13; mem. Colo. Fedn. Rep. Women, 1987—, Colo. Rep. Ctrl. Com. Mem. ASCD, AAAS, AAUW, Am. Ednl. Rsch. Assn., Nat. Assn. Sci. Tchrs., Am. Chem. Soc., Nat. Assn. for Rsch. in Sci. Tchg., Colo. Assn. Sci. Tchrs., Colo.-Wyo. Acad. Sci., Colo. Chemistry Tchrs. Assn., Math, Engring. and Sci. Achievement (dir., advisor 1992-97, mem. state level adv. bd. 1992-96), N.Y. Acad. Scis., Phi Delta Kappa. Avocations: reading, hiking, gardening. Office: U Colo Campus Box 106 PO Box 173364 Denver CO 80217-3364

GABELGAARD, BENT, telecommunications executive; b. Gram, Denmark, Aug. 13, 1964; s. Alfred and Else (Jensen) G.; m. Pia Luciw; 1 child, Mads Emil Luciw Gabelgaard. BSc in Physics, U. Aarhus, Denmark, 1986, BSc in Computer Sci., 1986, MSc in Computer Sci., 1989. Educator U. Aarhus; rschr. European Orgn. Nuclear Rsch., Switzerland, 1986-87, Jutland Telecom Corp., Denmark, 1990-91; head fixed network planning Sonofon, Aalborg, Denmark, 1991—, mgr. network strategy and integration, 1997—; exec. advisor Tele Danmark, Copenhagen, 1998—; cons. Bell South, Spain, fall 1994, U.S.A., spring 1995; mem. GSM MoU Internat. Roaming Expert Group, 1992-98, European Telecomm. Standards Inst. Spl. Mobile Group, 1994-98; presenter profl. confs. Co-author: Object-Oriented Environments, 1993. Mem. IEEE. Danish Conservative. E-mail: bent.gabelgaard@tellabs.com. Home: Mosebakken 7, 2830 Virum Denmark Office: Tellabs Danmark A/S, Lautrupbjerg 7-11, DK-2750 Ballerup Denmark

GABER, AHMED OSAMA, surgeon; m. Lillian W. Gaber, 1980; children: Sherief, Nadia, Yousef. B Medicine B Surgery, Ainshams U., Cairo, 1976; postgrad., Ainshams U., 1977-80. Diplomate Am. Bd. Surgeons. Intern Ainshams U. Hosp., Cairo, 1977-78, jr. resident gen. and pediat. surgery, 1978-79, resident gen. and pediat. surgery, 1979-80; intern gen. surgery Washington Hosp. Ctr., 1980-81; jr. resident gen. surgery boston U. Med. Ctr., 1981-82, resident gen. surgery, 1982-83, sr. resident gen. surgery, 1983-84, chief resident gen. surgery, 1984-85; clin. transplant fellow U. Chgo., 1985-86, transplant rsch. fellow, 1986-87; asst. prof. dept. surgery U. Tenn., Memphis, 1987-91, assoc. prof. surgery, 1991-96, assoc. prof. Coll. Nursing, 1991—, prof. dept. surgery, 1996—, prof. nursing, prof. pharmacy, 2000—; mem. staff U. Tenn. Bowld Hosp., acting med. dir., 1999—; mem. staff Regional Med. Ctr.; cons. mem. staff Bapt. Meml. Hosp., Meth. Hosp., St. Francis Hosp.; mem. courtesy staff LeBonheur Children's Med. Ctr.; affiliate mem. staff St. Joseph Hosp.; endowed prof. transplantation Bapt. Meml. Health Care Found., 1995; lectr., presenter in field. Mem. editl. bd. Cancer Molecular Biology, 1996—; contbr. numerous articles to profl. jours. Founder, exec. dir. Nora's Life Gift Found. Recipient 2 Gift of Life awards Nat. Kidney Found., Disting. Svc. award Bould Hosp., Memphis, Resident Tchr. award Boston U., Am. Cancer Soc. award; grantee U. Tenn. Med. Group Found., 1999—, Fujisawa Pharm., Assissi Found., 2000—, NIH, Nat. Inst. Allergy and Immunology, 2000—, Juvenile Diabetes Found., 2000—. Fellow ACS; mem. AMA, AAAS, Assn. Acad. Surgery, Harwell Wilson Surg. Soc., Am. Diabetes Assn., Am. Soc. Transplant Surgeons, Am. Soc. Transplant Physicians, Memphis and Shelby County Med. Soc., Am. Fedn. Clin. Rsch., Southeastern Surg. Congress, Internat. Transplantation Soc., Tenn. Transplant Soc. E-mail: agaber@utmem.edu. Home: 220

Meadowgrove Ln Memphis TN 38120-2611 Office: U Tenn-Memphis 956 Court Ave A 202 Memphis TN 38163-0001

GABER, ROBERT, psychologist; b. N.Y.C., Nov. 5, 1923; s. William and Freda (Harris) G.; m. Heidi Walters, Apr. 3, 1967 (div. Jan. 5, 1976); 1 child, Nathan. BA, NYU, 1949, MA, 1951; PhD, Columbia Pacific U., San Rafael, Calif., 1982. Psychotherapist Nat. Hosp. for Speech Disorders, N.Y.C., 1954-57; psychologist Indsl. Home for the Blind, N.Y.C., 1957-58; sch. psychologist Roosevelt Sch., Stamford, Conn., 1958-60; sr. clin. psychologist N.Y. State Dept. Mental Hygiene, Thiells, 1960-64; staff psychologist N.Y. Med. Coll., N.Y.C., 1965-66; cons. psychologist The Salvation Army, Phila., 1971-72; psychologist Md. Dept. Mental Hygiene, 1975-76, Dept. Corrections, Balt., 1979-80; CEO Axxiom De-Stress Ctrs., Balt., 1980—; dir. Ctr. for Stress Rsch., Norristown, Pa., 1994—; cons. Family Crisis Ctr. of Balt., 1973-74, Gov., Pa. Dept. Corrections, 1971; dir. mental health, nursery div. Dept. Welfare, N.Y.C., 1953-56. Author: The Experience of Enlightenment, 1980, Federal Prisoners' Attitudes Toward Crime and Confinement, 1982, Personality Traits and Behaviorisms of a Well-Adjusted Person, 1993, What Kind of Person is the Drug Addict?, 1996, The Psychodynamics of Self-Hypnosis, 1998; author booklet: Comprehensive Therapy Questionnaire, 1978; author articles, pamphlets on crime, human behavior and higher states of consciousness. With USAAF, 1942-46; PTO. Mem. Am. Psychol. Assn. Democrat. Avocations: golf, horseback riding, snow and water skiing, tennis. Office: Axxiom De-Stress Ctrs PO Box 22115 Baltimore MD 21203-4115 also: Ctr for Stress Rsch 207 Swede St Ste 102 Norristown PA 19401-4955 also: Ctr for Stress Rsch 11 W Lafayette St Norristown PA 19401-4709

GABERINO, JOHN ANTHONY, JR., lawyer; b. Tulsa, Aug. 6, 1941; s. John A. Sr. and Elizabeth (McCafferty) G.; m. Marjory Ann Diamond, Aug. 21, 1965; children: Christina M., Megan E., Courtney L., John A. III, Kathleen A. AB cum laude, Georgetown U., 1963, JD, 1966. Bar: Okla. 1966, U.S. Dist. Co. (no. and we. dists.) Okla. 1968, U.S. Ct. Appeals (10th cir.) 1968, U.S. Tax Ct. 1968, U.S. Supreme Ct. 1994. Assoc. Huffman, Arrington & Kihle, Tulsa, 1968-75; ptnr. Arrington, Kihle, Gaberino & Dunn, Tulsa, 1975-87, also bd. dirs., 1987-97; sr. v.p., gen. counsel ONEOK, Inc., 1998—; counsel, bd. dirs. St. Francis Health Sys., Inc., Tulsa, 1989-97. Chmn. Georgetown U. Law Ctr. Alumni Bd., 1990-92; bd. govs. Georgetown U., 1990—, chair, 2000-01; pres. Georgetown U. Club Okla.; chmn. Georgetown U. AAP for Okla.; past chmn. Christ the King Bd. Edn.; past pres. bd. trustees Monte Cassino Sch.; chmn. bd. trustees Monte Cassino Sch. Endowment Fund; bd. dirs. W.K. Warren Found., Tulsa Area United Way; chmn. bd. dirs. Operation Aware, Inc., 1991. Capt. U.S. Army, 1966-68. Recipient John Carroll medal Georgetown U., Okla., 1993. Fellow Am. Bar Found. (chair 2000—); mem. NCCJ (bd. dirs. Tulsa chpt., pres. 1993-95), Okla. Bar Assn. (mem. bd. govs. 1990-92, 95, 97-99, v.p. 1995, pres. 1998), Tulsa Bar Assn. (chmn. constrn. and bylaws com., bd. dirs. 1989, 91-94, sec. 1988, pres. 1993), Tulsa County Bar Found. (bd. dirs. 1993-99, pres. 1994), Knights Holy Sepulchre (hon. soc. Cath. ch.), So. Hills Country Club (mem. bd. govs. 1990-95, 1st v.p. 1991-93, pres. 1994), Met. Tulsa C. of C. (bd. dirs. 1996—, chair 2001), Phi Beta Kappa. Democrat. Roman Catholic. Avocations: golf, tennis. Office: ONEOK Inc 100 W 5th St Tulsa OK 74103-4240

GABILONDO, FRANCISCO JAVIER, plastic surgeon; b. San Sebas Tian, Spain, Oct. 22, 1948; s. Ventura Gabilondo and Maria Zubizarreta. BS, San Ignacio Coll., San Sebastian, Spain, 1964; MD. Physician La Paz Hosp., Madrid, 1973-76; pvt. practice plastic and reconstructive surgery Spain; cons. Insalud, Spain, 1978; head burns and plastic surgery dept. Bilbao, 1988; pres. 10th congress Spanish Soc. Burns, 1990; pres. SVURNA of Plastic Surgery, 1995-97. Mem. SECPRE, EBA, Soc. Bilbiana. Office: Osakidetza Hosp de Cruces, Pza de Cruces, 48903 Baracaldo Vizcaya Spain

GABLE, EDWARD BRENNAN, JR., lawyer; b. Shamokin, Pa., Mar. 15, 1929; s. Edward Brennan and Kathleen (Welsh) G. B.S., Villanova U., 1953; J.D., Georgetown U., 1957; m. Judy Lipshy July 17, 1981; children by previous marriage: Karen Lynn, Kimberly Ann, Katherine Rebel; stepchildren: Steven H., Karen Sue, Scott Michael. Bar: D.C. 1957, U.S. Dist. Ct. D.C. 1957, U.S. Ct. Appeals (D.C. cir.) 1957, U.S. Ct. Customs and Patent Appeals, 1959, U.S. Customs Ct. , 1961, U.S. Ct. Mil. Appeals, 1966, U.S. Supreme Ct., 1967, U.S. Ct. Appeals (fed. cir.) 1982. With U.S. Customs Svc., Treasury Dept., Washington, 1958-88, chief documentation br., 1965-66, chief carrier rulings br., 1966-76, chief penalties br., 1976-78, spl. asst. to asst. commr. Office of Regulations and Rulings, 1978-82, dir. carriers, drawback and bonds div., 1983-88, legal cons. in martime law, Washington, 1988—; mem. U.S. del. Intergovtl. Maritime Cons. Orgn., London, 1972-75, U.S. rep., inter-sessional meeting, Hamburg, Fed. Republic Germany, 1973. Pres., Customs Fed. Credit Union, 1967-69. Recipient Superior Performance award Treasury Dept., 1962, commendation letter from asst. sec. treasury, 1964, Customs Outstanding Performance award, 1983, Customs Cash Performance award, 1984, 85. Mem. Customs Lawyers Assn. (pres. 1965-66), Fed. Bar Assn., Propeller Club U.S., United Seamen's Svc. (council of trustees 1986-88), Nat. Lawyers Club, Elks, Delta Pi Epsilon, Delta Theta Phi. Roman Catholic. Home and Office: 955 26th St NW Washington DC 20037-2009

GÁBOR, RÉVÉSZ, economist; b. Baja, Hungary, Apr. 14, 1924; s. Bela and Julia (Abonyi) R.; married; children: Gábor, Magda. MS in Econs., Karl Marx U., Budapest, Hungary, 1952; PhD, Hungarian Acad. Sci., Budapest, 1970, D of Acad., 1990. Sr. research worker Hungarian Planning Office, Budapest, 1961-67; head dept. research Inst. Econs., Hungarian Acad. Sci., Budapest, 1967-94; lectr. econs. Karl Marx U., Budapest, 1971—, Budapest Polit. Acad., 1968-89. Author: Problems of Collective Interest in Hungarian Firms, 1971, (with others) The Origins and Development of the Model of Social Economy and Economic Policy, 1985, Hungary's Economic Transformation (1945-1988), 1990; co-author: The Hungarian Economy (1850-1998), 2000. Mem. European Econ. Assn. Avocation: classical music. Home: Felsozoldmali ut 17, 1025 Budapest Hungary Office: Hungarian Acad Scis Inst Econs, Budaorsi ut 45, 1112 Budapest Hungary

GABORIT, ARIANE, media professional; b. Talence, Gironde, France, Dec. 20, 1970; d. Daniel Gaborit and Marie-Celine Lachaud. Baccalaureat, Victor Louis, Talenci, France, 1988; MA in Bus., ISC, Paris, 1993. With market rsch. Philips, Paris, 1992; account asst. Wunderman Cato Johnson, Paris, 1992; mktg. mgr. Objectiv Lune, Paris, 1994-95; sales exec. Silvedart, London, 1996; internat. sales mgr. Motive, London, 1996—. Recipient Best Campaign of the Yr. Media and Mktg. Europe, 1999, Best Internat. TV, 1999, Best Internet campaign, 1999, Best Fashion campaign, 1999. Avocations: theatre, cinema. Home: Flat 2 43 Centra Pk, London SE19 2LQ, England Office: Motive, 24 27 Great Pulteney St, London W1R 3DB, England

GABOVICH, ALEXANDER MARKOVICH, physicist, researcher; b. Kiev, Ukraine; s. Mark Davidovich Gabovich and Mira Borisovna Kaganskaya; m. Minna Goratsievna Bukhman, Oct. 5, 1977 (div. Jan. 1981); 1 child, Mary; m. Nadezhda Afanas'evna Malyovannaya, Apr. 23, 1987; 1 child, Vladimir. MSc, Kiev State U., 1969; PhD, Inst. Physics, Kiev, 1976; D in Physics, Inst. Low Temperature Physics, Kharkov, Ukraine, 1990. Sr. rsch. assoc. diplomate. Engr. Inst. Physics, Kiev, 1971-75, jr. rschr., 1975-82, sr. rschr., 1982-90, leading rschr., 1990—; prof. Internat. Solomon U., Kiev, 1993-94; sci. reviewer Russian Physics Abstracts Jour., All Russian Inst. for Sci. and Tech. Info., Moscow, 1976-98. Contbr. articles to profl. jours. Sr. lt. Soviet Army, 1969-71. Grantee INTAS, Brussels, 1994, NATO, Brussels, 1997. Mem. Ukrainian Phys. Soc., Am. Phys. Soc. (grantee 1992). Avocations: mountain tourism, history of science. E-mail: GABOVICH@MARION.IOP.KIEV.UA. Fax: 38 (044) 265-15-89. Home: Apt 26, Gorkogo St 162, 03150 Kiev Ukraine Office: Inst Physics, Prospekt Nauki 46, 03650-22 Kiev Ukraine

GABOVITCH, STEVEN ALAN, lawyer, accountant; b. Newton, Mass., Feb. 7, 1953; s. William and Annette (Richman) G.; m. Rhonda Merle Kitover, Aug. 6, 1978; childre: Daniel J., Lindsey D. BS in Acctg., Boston Coll., 1975, JD, 1978; LLM in Taxation, Boston U., 1982. Bar: Mass. 1978, R.I. 1979, U.S. Dist. Ct. R.I. 1979, U.S. Tax Ct. 1980, U.S. Ct. Appeals (1st cir.) 1980, U.S. Dist. Ct. Mass. 1981, U.S. Ct. Appeals (fed. cir.) 1982, U.S. Supreme Ct. 1983; CPA, Mass. Tax specialist Peat, Marwick, Mitchell & Co., Providence, 1978-80; prin. William Gabovitch & Co., Boston, 1980-97; pvt. practice Stoughton, Mass., 1998—; lectr. on bankruptcy taxation. Contbr. articles to profl. jours. Mem. Am. Bankruptcy Inst., Nat. Soc. Tax Profls., R.I. Bar Assn., Mass. Bar Assn., Boston Bar Assn., Beta Gamma Sigma. Office: 378 Page St 3 Deerfield Corp Ctr Stoughton MA 02072

GABR, YOUSRY AHMED, biochemistry educator, consultant; b. Alexandria, Egypt, May 18, 1929; s. El Sayed Ahmed and Zhira Mohamed (Metwali) G.; m. Laila Mahmoud El Sheik; 1 child, Manal. BSc 1st hons., Fouad 1st U., Cairo, 1949; PhD in Biochemistry, London (Eng.) U., 1954. Demonstrator dept. biochemistry Ain Shams Faculty of Medicine, Cairo, Egypt, 1949-50; Lister Inst. fellow U. London, 1950-54; head blood products unit Serum & Vaccine Inst., Cairo, Egypt, 1954-63; asst. rsch. prof. Alexandria (Egypt) Med. Rsch. Inst., 1963-68; prof. and chmn. biochemistry dept. Med. Rsch. Unit Alexandria U., 1968-89, prof. of biochemistry, 1989—; sec. High Sci. Coun., Cairo, 1956-63; session chmn. Fedn. European Biochem. Socs. 4th meeting, Oslo, 1967; mem. com. for promoting Profs. of Biochemistry, U. Alexandria. Editor Egyptian Jour. Biochemsitry, Jour. of the Med. Rsch. Inst., Alexandria. Mem. Egyptian Orgn. for Biolog. and Vaccine Prodn. (bd. mem. Cairo 1972). Achievements include Discovery of "G" acid a smooth muscle contracting substance isolated from human blood plasma; development of stable gelatin solutions as plasma protein substitutes. Home: El Misaha St 28, Dokky Cairo Egypt Office: Med Rsch Inst, 165 Tarik El Horreya, Alexandria Egypt

GABRIEL, JEANETTE HANISEE, curator, art historian; b. Long Beach, Calif., Jan. 12, 1940; d. William Edward and Lorena (Mansell) Lester; m. Robert Maxwell Hanisee, Sept. 28, 1973 (div. 1986); children: Robb Andrew Hanisee, Michele Alpoente Hanisee, Leigh Mathilde Hanisee, Caleb Joseph Hanisee, Patricia Lorena Hanisee, Molly Beverly Hanisee; m. Angelo Julius Gabriel, Oct. 1, 1992. BS, Calif. State U., Northridge, 1978, MS, 1978; MA, U. Calif., Santa Barbara, 1988. Instr. Ventura (Calif.) Coll., 1979-81; dir., founder Adoptions Unltd., Ontario, Calif., 1981-83; curator L.A. County Mus. Art, 1988-92, Gilbert Collection aka Gilbert Collection at Somerset House, L.A. and London, 1994—. Author: The Gilbert Collection of Mosaics, 2000; co-author: By Judgement of the Eye: The Varya and Hans Cohn Collection at the Los Angeles County Museum of Art, 1991, The World of Jade, 1992. Mem. Internat. Churchill Soc., The Churchill Ctr. (founding mem., Clementine Churchill assoc. 1998), Reform Club London. Avocations: antique collecting, movie memorabilia and autographs, gardening. Fax: 310-271-1854. Office: Arthur and Rosalinde Gilbert Collection 9536 Wilshire Blvd Ste 420 Beverly Hills CA 90212-2434

GABRIEL, RONALD SAMUEL, child neurologist; b. Monterey, Calif., Mar. 19, 1937; s. Philip Louis and Theresa Shaheen Gabriel; children: Philip Louis III, Paula Shaheen, Matthew William. BA with honors, Yale U., 1959; MD, Boston U., 1963. Diplomate Am. Bd. Psychiatry and Neurology (examiner 1978-88), Am. Bd. Pediatrics. Intern, resident in pediatrics Los Angeles County Gen. Hosp., 1963-66; fellow in neurology and pediatric neurology UCLA med. ctr., 1966-68, 70-71; head physician, cons. Calif. Children's Svcs., 1970—; clin. prof. neurology/pediatrics UCLA Sch. Medicine, 1971—, dir. pediat. neurology/outpatient, 1971-76; cons. Regional Ctr.-Calif., 1971—; vis. prof. Prince of Wales, Royal Children's Hosp., Sydney and Melbourne, Australia, 1978; mem. expert panel L.A. Superior Ct., 1992—; founding and mng. gen. ptnr. Med. Imaging of So. Calif., L.A., 1980-94; mng. dir. GFA Cattle and Farm Co. Author: The 410 Shotgun, 2000, Diary of a Mountain Hunter, 2000; contbr.: Textbook of Child Neurology, 1974, 4 edits., 1990, Difficult Diagnoses in Pediatrics, 1990, Founders of Child Neurology, 1990. Mng. dir. GFF Natural History Mus. Maj. U.S. Army, 1968-70. Spl. fellow Nat. Inst. Neurol. Disease/Stroke, 1966-68, 70-71. Fellow Am. Acad. Pediatrics, Am. Acad. Neurology; mem. Calif. Med. Assn. (mem. sci. adv. panel 1987-94, chmn. sci. adv. com. 1989-90). Roman Catholic. Avocations: writing, mountaineering, hunting. Fax: (310) 277-9285. Office: Neurology-Pediat Neurology Assocs 2080 Century Park E Ste 203 Los Angeles CA 90067-2005

GACICHIEVICI, MIHAELA, internist; b. Urziceni, Romania, May 6, 1950; d. Vasile and Maria (Proca) G.; m. Gheorghe Pintea. MD, U. Medicine & Pharmacy, Bucharest, Romania, 1975, PhD in Internal Medicine, 1994. Intern Fundeni Hosp., Bucharest, 1975-78; resident in internal medicine U. Hosp., Bucharest, 1978-81, asst. prof., 1981—; cons., presenter in field. Mem. Romanian Med. Assn., Romanian Internal Medicine Assn. Home: Parter Sector 2, Str Dumbrava Rosie 30A, Bucharest Romania Office: Univ Hosp, 169 Splaiul Independentei, Bucharest Romania

GACNIK, DARJA, travel agency executive, tourism administrator; b. Trbovlje, Slovenia, July 27, 1954; came to US, 1990; d. Zdranko and Angela G. Student, high sch., Trbovlye, Slovenia, 1973. Ground staff Airport Ljubljana (Slovenia), 1974-78; sales mgr. Kompas Yugoslavia, Ljubljana, 1978-90; office mgr. U.S., Can. Kompas Internat., N.Y.C., 1990-91; mgr. pub. rels. Yogoslav Nat. Tourism Office, N.Y.C., 1991; v.p. Double A Internat., N.Y.C., 1991-93; pres. Slovenia Travel Inc., N.Y.C., 1993—; dir. Slovenia Tourist Office, N.Y.C., 1991—. Vice chmn. E.T.C.U.S.A., N.Y.C., 1999—. Avocations: music, skiing, rollerblading, photography. Office: Slovenian Tourist Office 345 E 12th St New York NY 10003-7238

GAD, EMAD FAKHRY, engineering educator, researcher; b. Cairo, Jan. 15, 1970; arrived in Australia, 1988; s. Fakrhy Gad and Soria Elkomos. B Engrng. with honors, Monash U., Melbourne, Australia, 1993; PhD, Melbourne U., 1997. Civil engr. City of Yarra, Melbourne, 1992-94; rsch. fellow Melbourne U., 1996-97, lectr., rschr., 1998—; rsch. scientist CSIRO, Melbourne, 1998; cons. engr. Melbourne Enterprise Internat., 1995—; sr. tutor Pro Tng., Melbourne, 1994-98. Contbr. articles to profl. jours. Mentor Monash U., 1999. Postdoctoral fellow Australia Rsch. Coun., 1998. Mem. Instn. Engrs. Australia, Standards Australia. Avocations: sports, reading, theater. Office: U Melbourne, Dept Civil & Environ Engr, 3052 Parkville Victoria, Australia

GADDIS, EDWARD SHAFIK, engineering educator, researcher; b. Atbara, Sudan, Apr. 16, 1933; s. Shafik and Wadia (Fakhoury) G.; m. Ute Genders Gaddis, Feb. 14, 1963; children: Alexandra, Shafik, Isis. Advanced diploma Nuclear Engring., U. Manchester, Eng., 1965, PhD in Engrng, 1968; BS in Mech. Engring., U. Cairo, Egypt, 1953. Engr. Power Station, Cairo, Egypt, 1953-54; asst. Cairo (Egypt) U., 1954-57; engr. Min. Industry, Cairo, Egypt, 1957-63; rschr., asst. prof. Atomic Establishment, Cairo, Egypt, 1963-74; rschr. U. Karlsruhe, Germany, 1974-78; chief engr., sr. rschr. U. Clausthal, Germany, 1978-98; ret., 1998—. Author: (5 chpts.) German handbook VDI-Warmeatlas, 1994-97, (chpt.) International Handbook Heat Exchanger Design Handbook, 1986; inventor: Processes and apparatuses for intensive mixing of fluids, 1989, 96, Process and apparatus for wastewater treatment, 1993. Avocations: reading, walking. Home: Fingerhutweg 16, 38678 Clausthal-Zellerfeld Germany

GADEA, RAUL, cultural foundation administrator; b. Montevideo, Uruguay, Feb. 12, 1937; s. Pedro Gadea and Ena Iglesias; m. Carmen Tornaria, Dec. 16, 1968; children: Ximena, Santiago, Martina, Ramiro. B of Sci. and Letters, Inst. Alfredo Vázquez Acevedo, Montevideo, 1955; post-grad., U. de la Rep., Montevideo, 1956-59. Tech. sec. to pub. prosecutor 3d Dist., Uruguay, 1959-80; gen. coord. Found. J. Barrios Amorim, Uruguay, 1992-97, retired, 1997; writer, 1997—. Founder, co-editor: Cuadernos de Cine Club, 1962-66; cultural editor: Marcha, 1967-73; editor-in-chief La Democracia, 1980-85; founder, dir. Propuesta, 1982-83; editl. coun. Graffiti; Modernizacion e identidad en el Mercosur (Nat. Prize of Essay, Min. of Culture, Uruguay, 1998). Home: Aconcagua 5177, CP 11400 Montevideo Uruguay

GAD-EL-HAK, MOHAMED, aerospace and mechanical engineering educator, scientist; b. Tanta, El-Gharbia, Egypt, Feb. 11, 1945; came to U.S., 1968; s. Mohamed Gadelhak and Samira (Hosni) Ibrahim; m. Dilek Karaca, July 19, 1976; children: Kamal, Yasemin. BSc in Mech. Engrng. summa cum laude, Ain Shams U., Cairo, 1966; PhD in Fluid Mechanics, Johns Hopkins U., 1973. Instr. Ain Shams U., Cairo, 1966-68; postdoctoral fellow Johns Hopkins U., Balt., 1973, U. So. Calif., L.A., 1973-74; asst. prof. engrng. sci. & systems U. Va., Charlottesville, 1974-76; program mgr. Flow Rsch. Co., Seattle, 1976-86; prof. aerospace & mech. engrng. U. Notre Dame, Ind., 1986—; cons. USN, Washington, 1990-91, UN, N.Y.C., 1991, many others; lectr. in field. Author: Flow Control, 2000; assoc. tech. editor AIAA Jour., 1988-91; assoc. editor Applied Mechanics Revs., 1988—; contbg. editor: Springer Verlag's Lecture Notes in Engineering, 1988—; reviewer Jour. Fluid Mechanics, Physics of Fluids, AIAA Jour., Jour. of Aircraft, many others; editor: Advances in Fluid Mechanics Measurements, 1989, Frontiers in Experimental Fluid Mechanics, 1989, Flow Control: Fundamentals and Practices, 1998; contbr. numerous articles to profl. jours. Recipient Alexander von Humboldt prize, 1999; Whitehead fellow Johns Hopkins U., Balt, 1968-73; professeur invité Univ. de Grenoble, France, 1991-92; sr. guest NATO, Paris, 1991, USN Disting. Faculty fellow, 1993; professeur exceptionnel univ. de Poitiers, France, 1994; rsch. grantee USN, 1976-80, USCG, 1976-78, NASA-Ames, 1981, NASA-Langley, 1985-87, 86, ONR, 1981-85, AFOSR, 1982-85, 85, Boeing Co., 1984, NSF, 1986, 95, Flow Industries, Inc., 1986-88, Cortana Corp., 1989-90, ONR, 1991, DARPA, 1991, Bourse de Haut Niveau Ministere de la Recherche et de la Technologie, Paris, 1991-92, NATO, 1991-92, others. Fellow AIAA (assoc.), ASME (Freeman scholar 1998); mem. AAAS, Am. Phys. Soc. (life). Achievements include patents on method and apparatus for controlling bound vortices in the vicinity of lifting surfaces, for reducing turbulent skin friction, for controlling turbulent boundary layers, for micropumping. Office: U Notre Dame 379 Fitzpatrick Dept Aero & Mech Engring Notre Dame IN 46556

GADIT, AMIN ALI MUHAMMAD, psychiatrist, researcher; b. Karachi, Pakistan, Aug. 21, 1956; s. Ali Muhammad and Hanifa Gadit; m. Najma Billoo, Sept. 30, 1993; 2 children. MBBS, Dow Med. Coll., Karachi, 1984; PhD, Anglia U., Essex, Eng., 1997. Med. diplomate. Lectr. Sind Med. Coll., Karachi, 1986-87; registrar various psychiat. hosps., Ireland, 1988-93; asst. prof. Baqai U., Karachi, 1994-97; assoc. prof. Hamdard U., Karachi, 1997—; cons. psychiatrist I.Q. Hosp., Karachi, 1997—; rschr. Knoll Pharm., Karachi, 1995—. Editor The Med. Spectrum, 1997—; contbr. chpt. to book, articles to profl. jours. Recipient Gold medal Y. Trading Co., 1985. Mem. Coll. Physicians and Surgeons Pakistan, Royal Coll. Surgeons Ireland, Pakistan Med. Assn. (exec. mem.), World Psychiat. ASsn. Avocations: riding, sightseeing, reading, music, writing fiction. Home: KMCHS, Hillview Apt, Hill Park, Karachi, Sind Pakistan Office: Hamdard U, Muhammad Bin Qasim Ave, Karachi, Sind Pakistan

GADIYAK, GRIGORII V., physicist; b. Ust-Katav, Russia, Dec. 9, 1946; s. Vasilii E. and Nina I. (Kozlova) G.; m. Irina I. Mityukhina, Apr. 26, 1974; 1 child, Valeria. MS, Novosibirsk State U., 1970; PhD, Computer Ctr. Russian Acad.Sci, 1976; ScD, St. Petersberg State U., 1984. Probationer/investigator Computer Ctr. of Russian Acad. Scis., Novosibirsk, 1970-72, jr. scientist, 1972-76; sr. scientist Inst. Pure and Applied Mechanics/Russian Acad. Scis., Novosibirsk, 1976-79, head of lab., 1979-93; head of lab. Inst. Computational Technologies, Novosibirsk, 1993-98, prin. scientist, 1998—; prof. Novosibirsk Tech. State U., 1994—, Novosibirsk State U., 1986-95. Author: Nonlinear Mechanics, Chaos, 1974, Computational Physics, 1980, Atoms, Molecules and Equation of States in Superstrong Magnetic Fields, 1983, Phase Transitions in 2d Systems, 1985, Device and Technologies Simulation, 1990. Grantee Internat. Sci. Found., 1995, Russian Found. of Fundamental Rsch., 1994, 96. Avocations: reading, music, horses. Home: Tereshkova 8-57, 630090 Novosibirsk Russia Office: Inst Comp Tech, Lavrentjeva 6, 630090 Novosibirsk Russia

GADJIEVA, RIZA MAGOMEDOVNA, physicist, researcher; b. Sergokala, Daghestan, Russia, Mar. 8, 1938; d. Gadji Magomedovich and Sariyat Magomedovna (Gadaeva) G.; m. Magomed Rasulovich Sharapudinov, June 7, 1964; children: Sharapudin, Gadji. Master Degree, Daghestan U., Makhachkala, Russia, 1963. Rschr. Inst. Physics, Russian Acad. Scis., Makhachkala, 1964—. Contbr. articles to profl. jours. Moslem. Avocations: reading, cooking. Office: Russian Acad Scis Inst Phys, 26 Bakinskikh Komissarov 94, 367003 Makhachkala Russia

GADOR, DEBORAH ANN, lawyer; b. N.Y.C., May 6, 1953; arrived in Israel, 1981; d. Max and Esther Reva (Kaplan) Brandstater; m. Ardon Yehuda, 1985; children: Shai, Dan, Shlomo, Leora. BA, Wellesley Coll., 1975; JD, Cornell U., 1978. Bar: N.Y. 1979, U.S. Patent Office 1980, Israel 1982, Israel Patent Office 1982. Atty. Davis Hoxie Faithfull & Hapgood, N.Y.C., 1978-80; patent atty. Sanford T. Colb, Rehovot, Israel, 1980-83; patent atty. Seligsohn & Gabrieli, Tel Aviv, Israel, 1983-93, sr. patent atty., 1995—; pvt. practice Ganei Tikva, Israel, 1994-95. Mem. Assn. Americans and Canadians in Israel, Tel Aviv, 1983—; treas. Emunah Day Creche, Ganei Tikva, 1991-92, 96-97. Mem. Assn. Internat. Patent Practitioners, Assn. Israeli Patent Attys., Wellesley Coll. Club in Israel (co-organizer 1992—). Avocations: dancing, playing piano, ice skating, singing. Home: 19 Emek Zvulun St, 55900 Ganet Ganei Tikva Israel

GADRE, ANIRUDDHA DATTATRAYA, research engineer; b. Solapur, India, July 20, 1969; came to the U.S., 1993; s. Dattatraya S. and Arundhati D. Gadre; m. Anjali A. Sahasrabudhe, Apr. 21, 1999. B of Engring., U. Bombay, 1990; M of Tech., Indian Inst. Tech., Bombay, 1992; PhD, Rensselaer Poly. Inst., 1997. Project engr. Nat. Ctr. Geotech. Centrifuge Studies, Bombay, 1992-93; mech. engr. GE Corp. R&D Ctr., Niskayuna, N.Y., 1997—. Contbr. articles to profl. jours. Recipient Founders' award of excellence Rensselaer Poly. Inst. Mem. ASCE, Sigma Xi. Avocation: cricket. E-mail: gadre@crd.ge.com. Office: GE Corp R&D Ctr 1 Research Cir Niskayuna NY 12309-1027

GADSBY, ROGER, physician; b. Coventry, Eng., Feb. 3, 1950; s. Frank William and Nellie Irene (Faulconbridge) G.; m. Pamela Joy Gadsby, Oct. 1974; children: Emma Elizabeth, Andrew David. BSc, Birmingham U., Eng., 1971, MBChB, 1974. Sr. house officer in chest medicine East Birmingham Hosp., 1975-76; rotating sr. house officer in medicine Stoke on Trent, 1976-77, sr. house officer in ob-gyn., 1977-78, sr. house officer in pediatrics, 1978, gen. preactice trainee, 1978-79; gen. practice prin. Redroofs Surgery, Nuneaton, Eng., 1979—; course tutor for cert. in primary diabetics care, sr. lectr. in primary care U. Warwick. Contbr. articles to profl. jours. Mem. Royal Coll. Gen. Practice, Brit. Med. Assn., Brit. Diabetic Assn. Baptist. Avocations: jogging, gardening. Home: Rivendell School Ln, Coventry CV7 9GF, England Office: Redroofs Surgery, 31 Coton Rd, Nuneaton CU11 5TW, United Kingdom

GADSDEN, CHRISTOPHER HENRY, lawyer; b. Bryn Mawr, Pa., Aug. 7, 1946; s. Henry White and Patricia (Parker) G.; m. Eleanore R.B. Hoeffel, July 27, 1968; children: William C., Eleanore P., Patricia C. BS, Yale U., 1968, JD, 1973. Bar: Pa. 1973, U.S. Dist. Ct. (ea. dist.) Pa. 1973. Assoc. Drinker Biddle & Reath, Phila., 1973-80, ptnr., 1980-98; mng. ptnr. Drinker Biddle & Reath, 1998—; lectr. law U. Pa. Law Sch., Phila., 1986-89, 93. Author: Pennsylvania Estate Planning, 1996; contbg. author: Local Public Finance and the Fiscal Squeeze, 1977; co-editor: Administration of Estates, 1983. Mem. vestry St. Thomas Ch., Whitemarsh, Ft. Washington, Pa., 1980-82; trustee Abington (Pa.) Meml. Hosp., 1980—, chair bd. trustees, 1994-98; pres. bd. trustees Germantown Acad., Ft. Washington, 1987-90. With U.S. Army, 1968-70. Fellow Am. Coll. Trust and Estate Counsel; mem. Phila. Bar Assn. (probate and trust law sect., chair 1994), Phila. Cricket Club. Democrat. Avocations: squash, tennis, gardening. Home: 140 W Chestnut Hill Ave Philadelphia PA 19118-3702 Office: Drinker Biddle & Reath 1000 Westlakes Dr Ste 300 Berwyn PA 19312-2409

GAEHTGENS, PETER ARNOLD LUDWIG, physiology educator; b. Dresden, Germany, Sept. 1, 1937; m. Marianne, 1966; 1 child, Florian. MD, U. Cologne, 1964. Internship U. Cologne, U. Berlin, 1964-66; rsch. fellow Calif. Inst. Tech., Pasadena, 1967-69; from sr. lectr. to assoc. prof. U. Cologne, 1972-83; prof. Freie U., 1983—; vice dir. dept. physiology Freie U., 1984-86, vice dean faculty medicine, 1985-89, head dept. Inst. Physiology, 1987-91, commn. for rsch., 1990-91, v.p. medicine, 1992-95, dean faculty medicine, 1995-97, 1st v.p., 1997-99, pres., 1999 . Edtl. bd. Biorheology, 1986 , News in Physiol. Scis., 1987-89, Internat. Jour. Microcirculation: Clin. & Exptl., 1987 , Revista Portuguesa de Hemorreologia, 1988 , Pflugers Archiv European Jour. Physiology, 1989 , European Jour. Vascular Surgery, 1992 , Microvascular Rsch., 1992 . Served in German armed forces, 1957-58. Recipient Abbott microcirculation award, 1986, Malpighi award, 1990. Mem. German Physiol. Soc., Internat. Soc. Biorheology (sec. gen. 1986-92, v.p. 1992), German Soc. Microcirculation (sec. gen. 1975-80, chmn. exec. com., Malpighi award 1990), European Soc. Microcirculation, Microcircu-

latory Soc. U.S., European Soc. Clin. Haemorheology, European Soc. Cardiology (working group on angiology), Royal Soc. Medicine (chmn. internat. working group on red cell deformability), Internat. Union Physiol. Scis. (chmn. commn. on microcirculation and capillary transport 1986-97), Internat. Liaison Com., Berlin Physiol. Soc., Berlin Med. Soc., German Soc. Cardiac and Circulatory Rsch., Soc. Biomed. Rsch., Ernst Reuter Soc., Berlin Sci. Soc., Berlin-Brandenburg Soc. Cardiac and Circulatory Diseases, Berlin-Brandenburg Acad. Sci. Tech. Office: Free U Berlin Office Pres, Kaiserswertherstr 16-18, 14195 Berlin Germany

GAENGLER, PETER WOLFGANG, dentist, researcher; b. Meissen, Saxony, Germany, Oct. 30, 1941; s. Wolfgang Ernst-Otto and Dorothea Friedericke (Moebius) G.; m. Sabine Gertrud Ahlborn, Nov. 6, 1970; children: Felix Peter, Beate Petra. Stomatology Diploma, Faculty of Dental Medicine, Leningrad, Russia, 1965; DrMedDent, Sch. Dental Medicine, Dresden, Germany, 1967, PhD, 1974. Diplomate in dentistry. Dentistry Community Hosp., Wittenberge, Germany, 1965-66; asst. prof. Sch. Dental Medicine, Dresden, 1966-75; prof., chmn. Sch. Dental Medicine, Erfurt, Germany, 1975-92; dean Faculty of Dental Medicine, Witten, Germany, 1992è; mem. FDI/WHO Joint Working Group 1/10, Geneva, 1979; mem. IADR Com. on Membership and Recruitment, Washington, 1989-93. Author: Lehrbuch der Konservierenden Zahnheilkunde, 3d edit., 1995; editor Medizin aktuell, 1975-90. Recipient Humboldt medal Ministry Higher Edn., Berlin, 1978; grantee in field. Mem. Assn. Conservative Dentistry (pres. 1978-87), Assn. Stomatology (v.p. 1988-90, Philip-Pfaff medal 1988), Polish Assn. Dentistry (hon.), Hungarian Assn. Dentistry (hon.; Semmelweis medal 1993), Assn. Dental Edn. Europe (exec. com. 1997—, bd. dirs. 1997—), European Jour. Dental Edn. (bd. mem. 2000—). Avocations: literature, sailing, skiing. Home: Waldweg 9, D-58313 Herdecke Germany Office: U Witten/Herdecke, Faculty Dental Medicine, D-58448 Witten Germany

GAERTNER, WULF CHRISTIAN, economics educator; b. Berlin, Dec. 11, 1942; s. Herbert Carl and Ursula Helene (Liebald) G.; m. Antje Theresia Hartweg; 1 child, Sabine. PhD in Econs., U. Bonn., Germany, 1973. Asst. U. Bielefeld, Germany, 1973-78, dozent, 1978-80; prof. econs. U. Osnabrück, Germany, 1980—; vis. fellow All Souls Coll., Oxford, Eng., 1984, Harvard U., Cambridge, Mass., 1990-91, 95-96; Murphy Inst. Disting. vis. prof. Tulane U., New Orleans, 1987. Author: Social Choice and Bargaining, 1992; editor: The Economics of the Underground Economy, 1985; mng. editor Social Choice and Welfare jour., 1984—; contbr. articles to profl. jours. Mem. Osnabrücker Friedensgespräche, 1994—; mem. exec. com., chmn. com. for econs. and ethics in Verein Socialpolitik, Hamburg, Germany, 1994—. Fellow Wissenschaftskolleg, Berlin, 1985-86. Mem. Econometric Soc., European Econ. Assn., Gesellschaft Wirtschafts und Sozialwissenschaften. Avocations: music, theatre, tennis. Office: U Osnabrück Dept Econs, Rolandstr 8, D-49069 Osnabrück Germany

GAETE, ROLANDO EDUARDO, lawyer, political and social science lecturer; b. Santiago, Chile, Apr. 27, 1943; s. Rolando and Marta (Briseno) G.; m. Maria Elena Hurtado, Feb. 2, 1972; children: Sebastian, Alejandro. Grad. in law, U. Chile, Santiago, 1970; Diplome d'Etudes Francaises, U. Paris, 1970; cert. edn., Garnett Coll., London, 1985; PhD, London Sch. Econs., 1987. Lawyer in pvt. practice, Santiago, 1971; head legal dept. Ministry of Agr., Santiago, 1971-73; lawyer Com. Pro Peace, Santiago, 1974-76; lectr. South Bank U., London, 1982—, head law sch., head legal rsch., 1990-95, reader in socio-legal studies, 1997—; external examiner U. Kent, Canterbury, Eng., 1994—. Author: Human Rights and the Limits of Critical Reason, 1993; mem. editl. bd. Jour. Semiotics of Law, 1995—; contbr. articles to Jour. Law and Critique, Jour. Social and Legal Studies, Millenium: Jour. Internat. Rels., others. Mem. lawyers group Amnesty Internat., London, 1990—; mem. World Devel. Movement, London, 1995—. Mem. Assn. for Legal and Social Philosophy, Internat. Assn. for the Semiotics of law (sec.-gen. 1993-94). Avocations: bridge, reading, jazz, golf.

GAFFIN, STEPHEN LESLIE, physiologist, immunologist, biophysics researcher; b. Pontiac, Mich., Dec. 7, 1941; m. Rina Ginai; 1 child, Guy. BS, Rensselaer Poly. Inst., 1962, MS, 1964, PhD, 1967. Postdoctoral rschr. U. Calif., San Francisco, 1967-71, Weizmann Inst., Rehovot, Israel, 1971-73; sr. lectr. Tech. Med. Sch., Haifa, Israel, 1973-80; prof. physiology U. Natal Med. Sch., Durban, South Africa, 1980-90; vis. prof. San Diego State U., 1990-91; rsch. physiologist U.S. Army Rsch. Inst. Environ. Medicine, Natick, Mass., 1991—; lectr. U. Parma (Italy) Vet. Sch., 1995. Contbr. numerous articles, revs. to profl. publs.; patentee in field. Recipient Cohanim prize for med. rsch. Tel Aviv U., 1979; Rosenbach Family Sabbatical grantee U. Natal, 1987. Mem. Wildness Med. Soc., Soc. Gen. Physiology, Am. Physiological Soc. E-mail: stephen.gaffin@na.amedd.army.mil. Office: USARIEM/NBD 1000 Kansas St Natick MA 01760-5007

GAFFNEY, THOMAS FRANCIS, investment company executive; b. Rockford, Ill., Aug. 29, 1945; s. Francis William and Catherine Zeta (Haeberle) G.; m. Donna Lee Gottfried, Apr. 17, 1971; 1 child, Cory. BA, Brown U., 1967; MBA, U. Chgo., 1969. CPA, Ill. Fin. cons. Duff and Phelps, Inc., Chgo., 1969-70; dir. adminstrn. Masury-Columbia Co. subs. Alberto-Culver Co., Melrose Park, Ill., 1970-75; exec. v.p., dir. Guardian Industries Corp., Northville, Mich., 1975-87; chmn. bd. The Oxford Investment Group, Bloomfield Hills, Mich., 1985-90; chmn. bd., CEO Automotive Plastic Techs., Inc., Sterling Heights, Mich., 1990-92; chmn. Ashland Products, Inc., Chgo., 1992-95; mng. dir. Raymond James Captial, Inc., St. Petersburg, FL, 1997—; bd. dirs. Am. Life Holdings, Inc. Decorated Chevalier de L'Orde Grand Ducal de le Couronne de Chene Grand Duchy Luxembourg, 1983. Mem. AICPA. Home: 2091 Oceanview Dr Tierra Verde FL 33715-2512

GAGE, BEAU, artist; b. Rye, N.Y., Dec. 3, 1945; d. John Alden and Frances (Johnston) G.; m. Glenn A. Ousterhout, May 24,1980. BA, St. John's Coll., Santa Fe and Annapolis, Md., 1971; student, Internat. Ctr. Photography, N.Y.C., 1981-82, 82-83, Art Students League N.Y., 1983-87, The Sculpture Ctr. Sch., N.Y.C., 1985-87, Nat. Acad. Design, 1988-89. Staff asst. to the pres. The White House, Washington, 1972-73; key accounts mgr. Sterling Drug, Inc., Montvale, N.J., 1975-79. Works exhibited at Internat. Ctr. Photography, 1981-83, Art Students League, 1984-87, The Sculpture Ctr., 1985-87, Westbeth Gallery, N.Y.C., 1984, 86, Sotheby's Auction House, 1990, others; permanent pub. sculpture Jacksonville (Fla.) Jaguars, Inc.; permanent exhbn. Jacksonville Mus. Sci. & History. Supporter, guild mem. Martha Graham Dance Co., N.Y.C., 1989—; garden patron N.Y. Botanical Gardens, Bronx, 1999—. Fellow Mus. Modern Art; mem. Met. Mus. Art, Internat. Ctr. Photography, Orgn. Ind. Artists, The Nature Conservancy, Mass. Soc. Mayflower Descendants, Poets House (N.Y.C.). Avocations: astronomy, sailing, yoga. Home: 320 E 46th St Apt 34E New York NY 10017-3039

GAGE, GASTON HEMPHILL, lawyer; b. Charlotte, N.C., June 16, 1930; s. Lucius Gaston and Margaret (White) G.; m. Jane Basinger, July 11, 1959; children: Gaston Hemphill Jr., John Robert, Stephen Matheson. BA, Duke U., 1953; LLB, U. N.C., 1958. Bar: N.C. 1958, U.S. Ct. Appeals (4th cir.) 1964, U.S. Ct. Appeals (7th and fed. cirs.) 1983, U.S. Supreme Ct. 1965, U.S. Ct. Fed. Claims. Ptnr. Grier, Parker, Poe, Thompson, Bernstein, Gage & Preston, Charlotte, 1964-84, Parker, Poe, Thompson, Bernstein, Gage & Preston, Charlotte, 1984-90, Parker, Poe, Adams & Bernstein, Charlotte, 1990—. Dir. Elon Homes for Children, Elon Coll., N.C., 1986—, vice chair, 1995-96, chair, 1996-97; pres. Boys Town of N.C., Charlotte, 1974-78, A.G. Jr. High PTA, Charlotte, 1974-75, Mecklenburg Kiwanis, Charlotte, 1968; sec., ofcl. bd. Myers Park United Meth. Ch., Charlotte, 1970-72. Mem. ABA, N.C. Bar Assn., N.C. State Bar Assn., Mecklenburg County Bar Assn., Kiwanis (lt. gov. Carolinas dist. 1995-96). Methodist. Home: 324 Lockley Dr Charlotte NC 28207-2330 Office: Parker Poe Adams & Bernstein 201 S College St Ste 2500 Charlotte NC 28244-4468

GAGLIANO, ALFONSO, Canadian government official; b. Siculiana, Italy, Jan. 25, 1942; s. Vincenzo and Maria (Augello) G.; m. Ersilia Gidaro, July 3, 1965; children: Vincenzo, Maria, Immacolata. Cert. gen. acctg., George Williams U., Montreal. Sch. commr. Jérôme LeRoyer Sch. Bd., Montreal, Quebec, Can., 1977-83; pres. Jérôme-LeRoyer Sch. Commn., Montreal, 1983-84; MP St. Leonard Anjou Riding Can. Parliament, Ottawa, 1984-88, MP St. Leonard Riding, 1988-94; sec. state parliamentary affairs, dep. leader of govt. Can. Parliament House of Commons, Ottawa, 1994-96; min. of labour and dep. govt. house leader Can. Govt. House of Commons, Ottawa, 1996-97, min. pub. works and govt. svcs., 1997—; official opposition critic for small bus., rev. Canada and Canada Post Corp., 1984-91; opposition critic for industry dept., mem. permanent com. on fin. Can. House of Commons, 1988-91; opposition critic for immigration 1990-91; chair Quebec Liberal Caucus, 1988-91; chief govt. whip, 1993-94; chair electoral commn. Liberal Party of Canad (Quebec), 1994—. Office: Office Pub Works/Govt Svcs, Place Portage Phase 3 11 Laurier St, Hull, PQ Canada K1A OS5

GAGLIANO, MAURO ANTONIO, medical assistant; b. Bagheria, Palmermo, Italy, Jan. 17, 1958; s. Ignazio and Giuseppina (Carollo) G. Vol. med. asst. U. Palermo, 1984-89; med. asst. Policlinico P. Giaccone, Palermo, 1989—. Mem. AAAS, Italian Soc. Pharmacology, N.Y. Acad. Scis. Roman Catholic. Avocations: science fiction books and movies, horror and weird science stories, parapsychology. Office: Istituto di Farmacologia, Vespri 129, 90127 Palermo Italy

GAGLIARDI, RAYMOND ALFRED, physician; b. New Haven, Nov. 20, 1922; s. Carl Albert and Carmela (Esposito) G.; m. Patricia DeTuncq, Apr. 6, 1946; children: Laura E. Quigley, John Bell. BS, Yale U., 1943, MD, 1945. Pvt. practice radiology Pontiac, Mich., 1951-92; chmn. dept. radiology St. Joseph Mercy Hosp., Pontiac, 1976-91, chmn. emeritus, 1991—. Author: The Golf Story: An Anecdotal History of Golf, 1999, Reflections and Recollections, 2000; editor-in-chief History of the Radiological Sciences, 1995; contbr. articles to profl. jours. Capt. U.S. Army, 1946-48; PTO. Fellow Am. Coll Radiology; mem. Am. Roentgen Ray Soc. (pres. 1987-88, Gold Medal award 1989, Hartman medal 1995, Centennial lectr. 2000), Mich. Radiol. Soc. (pres. 1972), Mich. Med. Soc. (Disting. Svc. award 1988), Oakland Hills Country Club, Royal Palm Yacht and Country Club (past commodore 1994), Loch Lomond Golf Club, Heathers Club. Republican. Avocation: golf. Home: 2100 Queen Palm Rd Boca Raton FL 33432-7932 also: 789 Uper Scotsborough Way Boca Raton FL 33432

GAGLIARDI, UGO OSCAR, systems software architect, educator; b. Naples, Italy, July 23, 1931; came to U.S., 1956; s. Edgardo and Lina (Valenzuela) G.; m. Anna Josephine Italiano, July 7, 1954 (div. May 1972); children: Oscar Marco, Alex Piero. Diploma in Math. and Physics, U. Naples, Italy, 1951; DEng in Elec. Engring., U. Naples, 1954. Chief scientist U.S. Air Force, Hanscom AFB, Mass., 1965-66; rsch. fellow Harvard U., Cambridge, Mass., 1965-66; v.p. tech. ops. Interactive Scis., Inc., Braintree, Mass., 1968-70; dir. engring. Honeywell Info. Systems, Waltham, Mass., 1970-75; lectr. Harvard U., Cambridge, Mass., 1966-74, prof. practice computer engring., 1974-83, Gordon McKay prof. practice computer engring., 1983—; pres. Gen. Systems Group, Salem, N.H., 1975—; chmn. Ctr. for Software Tech., Inc., 1982-99; mem. NAS rsch. coun. panel Nat. Computer Systems Lab. (formerly Inst. Computer Scis. and Tech.), Nat. Inst. Standards and Tech. (formerly Nat. Bur. Standards), 1985-91, chmn., 1988-91. Fulbright scholar Columbia U., 1955-56. Office: Harvard U 33 Oxford St Bldg 139 Cambridge MA 02138-2901

GAGNE, ARMAND JOSEPH, JR., business administration and computer science educator, consultant; b. Lowell, Mass., July 21, 1936; s. Armand J. and Lillian J. (Clermont) G.; m. Beverly Ward, Dec. 19, 1970; children: Dana Andrea, Donna Angela, Deborah Ann, Denise Ann, Armand Joseph III, Charles Kenneth, Delannie Almeta. BBA, U. S.C., 1968, MBA, 1973, PhD, 1992; PhD in Religious Studies, Christian Bible Coll., 1992; MA, U. S.C., 1996. Mgr. systems procedures Gifford-Hill Inc., Charlotte, N.C., 1970-74; contr. Automation Internat., Charlotte, 1974-75; v.p. fin. Vanply of Liberia, Monrovia, N.C., 1975-76; pres. SMS Assocs., Pink Hill, N.C., 1976-80; assoc. prof. U. S.C., Sumter, 1980—; pres., cons. Systems People Inc., Sumter, 1982—; seminar cons. U. Miami, Fla., 1983-84; webmaster Sumter on Line, 1997-98. With USN, 1954-60, Africa. Recipient S.C. Gov.'s Prof. of yr. award, 1997-98, Outstanding Achievement award Greater Sumter C. of C., 1998, Internat. Vocat. Svc. award Sunrise Rotatary, 1998. Mem. Beta Gamma Sigma, Omicron Delta Epsilon. Republican. Mem. Assoc. Reformed Presbyn. Ch. Home: 1797 Wardland Rd Sumter SC 29154-7231 Office: U SC Miller Rd Sumter SC 29150-2403

GAGNÉ, ROBERT MILLS, educator; b. North Andover, Mass., Aug. 21, 1916; s. Alphonse F. and Alice E. (Mills) Gagne; m. Harriet N. Towle, Nov. 26, 1942; children: Samuel T., Ellen D. A.B., Yale, 1937; Ph.D., Brown U., 1940. Instr. psychology Conn. Coll., for Women, 1940-41, asst., then asso. prof. psychology, 1946-49; asst. prof. psychology Pa. State U., 1945-46; research dir. perceptual and motor skills lab. Air Force Personnel and Tng. Research Center, Air Research and Devel. Command, 1949-53, tech. dir. maintenance lab., 1953-58; prof. psychology Princeton, 1958-62; cons. Dept. Def., 1958-61; dir. research Am. Inst. Research, Pitts., 1962-65; prof. edni. psychology U. Calif., Berkeley, 1966-69; prof. dept. ednl. research Fla. State U., Tallahassee, 1969—; Fellow Center for Advanced Study in Behavioral Scis., 1972. Author: (with E.A. Fleishman) Psychology and Human Performance, 1959, The Conditions of Learning, 1965, 3d edit., 1977, 4th edit., 1985, (with L.J. Briggs) Principles of Instructional Design, 1974, 2d edit., 1979, 3d edit. (with L.J. Briggs & W.W. Wager), 1988, Essentials of Learning for Instruction, 1974, 2d. edit. (with M.P. Driscoll), 1987; editor: Psychological Principles in System Development, 1962, Learning and Individual Differences, 1966, (with W.P. Gephart) Learning Research and School Subjects, 1968, Instructional Technology: Foundations, 1987 . Served from pvt. to 1st lt. USAAF, 1941-45. Mem. Am. Psychol. Assn. (fellow div. 3, 15 and 19), Nat. Acad. Edn., Am. Ednl. Research Assn. Home: 100 James Blvd # Bu53 Signal Mountain TN 37377-1860

GAGNET, GRACE, safety consultant, translator; b. Cleve., Jan. 6, 1952; d. Robert Adrian and Dorothy Carter Drennan; m. Alan John Gagnet (div. Apr. 1989); children: Corinne, Louis. B in Tech., Fla. Internat. U., 1975; postgrad. cert., U. Miami, 1979. Cert. Bd. Cert. Safety Profls. Safety adminstr. Fla. Power & Light Co., Miami, 1972-80; safety analyst Gulf Power Co., Pensacola, Fla., 1987-91; safety svcs. supr. NJ & Assocs., Dallas, 1991-93; pres. AFA Safety Svcs., Dallas, 1994—; bd. mem. N.W. Fla. Safety Coun., Pensacola, 1990-91; cons. South Tex. Safety Coun., San Antonio, 1996-99. Author: Fall Protection & Scaffolding Safety, 2000. Mem. Am. Soc. Safety Engrs. (various offices). Republican. Roman Catholic. Avocations: diving, gardening, choir. E-mail: gagnet@flash.net. Fax: 972-620-0509. Home: 1843 Chevy Chase Dr Carrollton TX 75006-7524 Office: AFA Safety Svcs Inc 2995 Lbj Fwy Ste 200 Dallas TX 75234-7600

GAGNON, EDOUARD CARDINAL, ecclesiastic; b. Port Daniel, Que., Can., Jan. 15, 1918. Ordained priest Roman Catholic Ch., 1940, consecrated bishop, 1969. Bishop St. Paul, Alberta, Can., 1969-72; rector Can. Coll., Rome, 1972-77; v.p., sec. Vatican Com. for Family, 1973-80; titular archbishop of Guistiniana Prima, 1983; pro-pres. Pontifical Council for the Family, 1983-85, pres., 1985-90; pres. Pontifical Com. Internat. Eucharistic Congresses, 1991—; elevated to Sacred Coll. of Cardinals, 1985. Office: Pontifical Com Internat Eucharistic Congr, Piazza San Calisto 16, 00153 Rome Italy

GAGNON, JOHN HARVEY, psychotherapist, educator; b. Derby, Conn., Dec. 16, 1946; s. Ernest John and Pauline Stella (Dziedulonis) G.; m. Eleanor Moser, Apr. 22, 1995; 1 child, Isabelle Eleanor. BS, Fairfield U., 1969; MS, Western Conn. State Coll., 1976; PhD, Union Inst., 1982. Diplomate Am. Bd. Psychotherapy (fellow); lic. marriage and family therapist, EMT, Conn.; cert. family life educator; bd. cert. in med. hypnosis, clin. hypnotherpy and hynoanesthesiology. Counselor in tng. Conn. Valley Hosp., 1972-73; counselor Whiting Forensic Inst., 1973; coord., dir. Danbury Hosp. Day Treatment Program, 1973-77; pvt. practice, 1977-80; psychotherapy intern Counseling Ctr. and N.Y. Inst. for Gestalt Therapy, 1981-83; pvt. practice, 1983—; rsch. cons. Newtown Counseling Ctr., 1987-89; instr. N.Y. Inst. for Gestalt Therapy, 1983-89; lectr. Yale U., 1983; adj. prof. Western Conn. State U., 1983-86, U. Bridgeport, 1988-90; adj. lectr. U. Conn., 1990-93; cons. dept. psychology Fairfield U., 1994-95. Author: Gagnon's Directory, 1986, Wounded Healer, 1993; contbr. articles to profl. jours. Ofcl. emergency sta. Am. Radio Relay League, 1992—; chmn. adult program Unitarian-Universalist Soc. North Fairfield County, West Redding, Conn., 1990-91, tchr. religious edn., 1984-86; judge sr. divsn. Conn. State Fair, 1986—; bd. trustees Unitarian-Universalist Ch. of Stamford, 1996-98. Fellow Internat. Coun. for Sex Edn. and Parenthood; mem. ACA, AAUP, Assn. for Counselor Edn. and Supervision, Am. Soc. for Group Psychotherapy and Psychodrama, Am. Acad. Psychotherapists, Am. Assn. for Marriage and Family Therapy, Am. Bd. Hypnotherapy & Hypnotic Anesthesiology, Assn. for Humanistic Psychology, Internat. Assn. Marriage and Family Counselors, Nat. Coun. Family Rels., Phi Delta Kappa. Democrat. Office: 270 Greenwich Ave Ste 26 Greenwich CT 06830

GAGRAT, RUSTAM JEHANGIR, lawyer; b. Bombay; s. Jehangir Rustam and Maneck (Jehangir) G.; m. Lia Gagrat, July 10, 1994; 1 child, Jeh. BA with honors in Politics, Bombay U., 1979; BA with honors in Law, Cambridge (Eng.) U., 1981, MA, 1985; Program Instrn. for Lawyers, Harvard U., 1993. Advocate, India; solicitor, Eng. and Wales, Bombay. Ptnr. Gagrat & Co., Advocates and Solicitors, Bombay, 1981—, Gagrat & Co., Supreme Ct. Advocates, New Delhi, 1990—; trustee pub. and pvt. trusts; mem. coms. of C. of C.; presenter papers at internat. and domestic law confs. Tata scholar Cambridge JN Tata Trust, Bombay, 1979-81; recipient Rustomji Mulla prize Bombay Law Soc., 1984. Mem. Supreme Ct. of India Bar Assn., Law Soc. Eng. and Wales, Internat. Bar Assn., Internat. Law Assn., Bombay Law Soc., Bombay Bar Assn., Delhi Bar Assn., Oxford and Cambridge Soc., Willingdon Club, Cricket Club India, Bombay Gymkhana, Royal Western India Turf Club. Avocations: literature, music, history, art. Home: 9 Om Ratan, New Worli, Bombay 400 025, India Office: Gagrat & Co Alli Chambers, Nagindas Master Rd, Fort Mumbai Bombay 400 001, India

GAGZOW, WOLFGANG, economist; b. Wismar, Germany, May 7, 1953; s. Ronald Wermann and Hannelore (Gagzow) Stupnick; m. Dörte Hansen, Aug. 16, 1974 (div. Sept. 1987); children: Christoph, Tobias, Martin; m. Christina Ritter, July 28, 1989; children: Anja, Jürgen. Diploma in econ. engring., U. Rostock, Germany, 1977. Departmental mgr. Luth. Ch., Schwerin, Germany, 1977-81; chief mgr. hosp. Schwerin, 1981-91; chief mgr. Soc. of Hosps., Schwerin, 1991—; chmn. Soc. of Hosps., Schwerin, 1990-91, Soc. Hosp. Leading Orgns., Schwerin. Contbr. articles to mags. Mem. Local Coun., Boltenhagen, 1991-94, Dist. Assembly, Grevesmühlen, 1991-94. With Nat. People's Army, 1971-73. Mem. German Soc. Hosps. (mem. exec. com. 1991—), Protestant Hosp. Mgr. Soc. (chmn. 1985-91), Assn. Hosp. Dirs. (mem. exec. com. 1990—), Rotary. Social Democrat. Lutheran. Avocation: magic tricks. Home: Schelfstr 10, D-19055 Schwerin Germany Office: Soc of Hosps, Lankower Strasse 6, 19057 Schwerin Germany

GAHLER, MICHAEL, member of European parliament; b. Frankfurt, Fed. Republic Germany, Apr. 22, 1960. Mem. European Parliament, Germany, 1999—; mem. Group of the European People's Party (Christian Democrats) and European Democrats; mem. com. on fgn. affairs human rights, common security and def. policy; substitute mem. com. on devel. and cooperation; vice-chmn. delegation to the EU-Lithuania Joint Parliamentary Com. Office: 28 avenue J R Collon, B-1200 Bruxelles Belgium*

GAHRTON, GÖSTA CARL ARNOLD, internist, hematologist, educator; b. Malmö, Sweden, Dec. 20, 1932; s. Arnold Harald Valdemar and Asta Jula Rosette (de Shàrengrad) G.; m. Birgitta Irene Nilsson, Apr. 1959 (div. 1976); children: Måns, Charlotte; m. Astrid Elisabet Toresson, Sept. 27, 1976; children: Elisabeth, Caroline. MD, U. Lund, Sweden, 1959; PhD, Karolinska Inst., Stockholm, 1966. Cert. specialist in internal medicine and hematology. Resident dept. medicine U. Lund, 1959-61; rsch. assoc. Inst. Med. Cell Rsch., Karolinska Inst., 1961-67, mem. Nobel com., 1988-97, vice chmn. Nobel com., 1994-96, chmn., 1997; resident dept. medicine Karolinska Hosp., 1967-73; assoc. prof. Huddinge (Sweden) Hosp., 1973-85, prof., 1985-97, head dept. medicine, 1985-97; vis. rsch. assoc. Children's Cancer Rsch. Found., Harvard U. Med. Sch., Boston, 1963-64, 68-69. Editor: Blood Diseases, 1983, 2d edit., 1994, 3d edit., 1997, Multiple Myeloma, 1996; chmn. editl. bd. Jour. Internal Medicine, 1993; mem. editl. or adv. bd. 7 sci. jours.; contbr. over 350 articles on hematology and oncology to internat. sci. jours. Recipient Trafvenfelt diploma Swedish Soc. Med. Scis. 1976, A.F. Regnells prize 1990; Malthes Legat award Norwegian Med. Soc., 1981. Mem. Swedish Soc. Hematology (pres. 1985-86), European Group for Blood and Marrow Transplantation (pres. 1988-90), Internat. Soc. Hematology (councillor 1985—, v.p. 1995—), Austrian Soc. for Transplantation, Transfusion and Genetics (hon.), also others. Avocations: classical music, tennis, mountain climbing, hunting, skating. Home: Hallingsbacken 8, 16767 Bromma Sweden Office: Huddinge U Hosp, Dept Medicine, 14186 Huddinge Sweden

GAIDAU, CARMEN CORNELIA, chemical engineer, researcher; b. Braila, Romania, Mar. 8, 1958; d. Vasile and Paraschiva (Gheorghita) Rugina; m. Viorel Gaidau, July 26, 1982; children: Catalina-Gabriela, Raluca Mihaela. Degree in Chem. Engring., Tech. U., Jassy, Romania, 1982, PhD, 1998. Registered profl. engr. Engr. S.C. Rovex S.A., Oradea, Romania, 1982-84; engr. Leather and Footwear Rsch. Inst., Bucharest, Romania, 1984-88, sr. rschr., 1990—; cons. Technological Ednl. Inst., Kozani, Greece, 1997, Greek Fur Ctr. SA, Kastoria, Greece, 1998. Contbr. articles to profl. jours.; patentee in field. Mem. Romanian Soc. Chemists and Technologists in Leather Industry, Romanian Gen. Assn. Engrs., Romanian Soc. Chemists. Mem. Orthodox Ch. Avocations: literature, travel, art, philately, sport, music. Home: Papiu Ilarian, no 6 bl 42 ap 53, 74538 Bucharest 3 Romania Office: Leather Footwear Rsch Inst, 93 Ion Minulescu St, 74259 Bucharest 3 Romania

GAIG, PERE, allergist, immunologist; b. Barcelona, Spain, June 19, 1955; s. Pere Gaig and Concepcion Jane; m. Ester Ferrer; children: Ferran, Laura. Med. Diplomate, Autonoma U., Barcelona, 1981. Allergology fellow Hosp. Vall d'Hebron, Barcelona, 1987-91; allergist Clinica Dexeus, Barcelona, 1992-94, Hosp. Gen., Manresa, Spain, 1994-95, Hosp. Joan XXII, Tarragona, Spain, 1995—; assoc. prof. medicine U. Rovira i Virgili, Tarragona, 1997-99. Author: Manual de Alergologia, 1995. Mem. Soc. Catalana Allergia i Immunologia Clinica, Soc. Española de Allergia e Immunologia Clinica, Spanish Allergy Soc. (skin allergy com. 1999). Home: Avenida Madrid 7 7o-1a, 08028 Barcelona Spain Office: Hosp Joan XXIII, C/Dr Mallafre Guasch 4, 43007 Tarragona Spain

GAILLARD, JEAN-PAUL, consumer products company executive; b. Ardon, Valais, Switzerland, Apr. 24, 1954; s. Paul Marcel and Marilène (Fildermann) G.; m. Laurence Jacqueline Fonjallaz; children: Leonore, Candice, Virginia. BBA, UCLA, 1976; grad. in Bus. Langs., Lemania, Lausanne, Switzerland, 1981; grad. in Indsl. Mktg., European Coll. Mktg., Birmingham, Eng., 1981; grad., IMD, Lausanne, 1995. Sales mgr. Switzerland, country mgr. USA, Queval S.A., Roven, France and N.Y., 1978-81; bus. devel. analyst Warner Elec., Lausanne, Switzerland; European brand mgr. Marlboro Classics, Philip Morris, Lausanne, 1984-88; pres. Nespresso S.A., Pully, Switzerland, 1988-97; pres. ice cream divsn. Nestle USA, Solon, Ohio, 1997-98; CEO Möevenpick Foods Ltd., Cham and Lausanne, Switzerland, 1998—; bd. dirs. CIPAG, Switzerland, Bioring Ltd., Switzerland. With Swiss Army, 1977-95. Avocations: skiing, tennis, aviation. E-mail: jpg341@aol.com. Home: Ave de Villardin 4, 1009 Pully Switzerland Office: Movenpick Foods Ltd, Ave De Rhodanie 60, 1007 Lausanne Switzerland

GAINES, IRVING DAVID, lawyer; b. Milw., Oct. 14, 1923; s. Harry and Anna (Finkelman) Ginsburg; m. Ruth Rudolph, May 22, 1947 (dec. Apr. 5, 1979); children: Jeffrey S., Howard R., Mindy S. Gaines Pearce; m. Lois Shier, Nov. 25, 1979. BA, U. Wis., Madison, 1943; JD, 1947; postgrad., U. Pa., 1943-44. Bar: Wis. 1947, Fla. 1971, U.S. Dist. Ct. (ea. dist.) Wis. 1947, U.S. Dist. Ct. (we. dist.) Wis. 1970, U.S. Dist. Ct. (so. dist.) Fla. 1972, U.S. Dist. Ct. (mid. dist.) Fla. 1976, U.S. Ct. Appeals (7th cir.) 1954, U.S. Ct. Appeals (11th cir.) 1981, U.S. Supreme Ct. 1954. Sole practice Milw., 1947-72; ptnr. Gaines & Saichek, S.C. (and predecessor firm), Milw., 1972-78; sr. ptnr. Gaines Law Offices, S.C., Milw., 1979—; arbitrator N.Y. Stock Exchange, Nat. Assn. Securities Dealers, Am. Stock Exchange, Am. Arbitration Assn. 1988—. Mem. bd. visitor U. Wis. Law Sch., 1987-96, Cir. Ct. Commn., 1997—. Served with AUS, 1943-46. Mem. ABA (various coms.), Fla. Bar Assn. (past mem. exec. com., cts. com., econs. law com., past chn. unauthorized practice of law com., past chmn. negligence sect., lectr. programs, seminars), State Bar Assn. Wis. (bd. govs. 1982-85, comms. com. 1981-85, 88-91), 7th Fed. Cir. Bar Assn., Wis. Acad. Trial Lawyers (pres. 1958-59, 70-71). Home: 7821 N Mohawk Rd Milwaukee WI 53217-3123 Office: 312 E Wisconsin Ave Ste 208 Milwaukee WI 53202-4305

GAINES, ROBERT MARTIN, lawyer; b. Hartford, Conn., Nov. 27, 1931; s. Charles Edward and Ellen Marie (Hammerstrom) G.; m. Joan Isabel

Sanderson, May 20, 1961 (div. Oct. 1983); children: Todd, Dayna; m. Julie Ann Ramsdell, May 11, 1985. AB, U. Conn., 1953, JD, 1956. Bar: Conn. 1956, U.S. Ct. Mil. Appeals 1959, U.S. Dist. Ct. Conn. 1961, U.S. Tax Ct., 1994. Assoc. Regnier & Moller, Hartford, 1960-62; asst. counsel Pratt & Whitney, East Hartford, Conn., 1962—. Mem. Somers (Conn.) Bd. Edn., 1968-70. With USAF, 1957-60. Mem. Am. Corp. Counsel Assn. Republican. Roman Catholic. Avocations: sports, music. Home: 44163 S Main St Manchester CT 06040

GAINET, MICHEL EUGENE, physician; b. Hericourt, Haute Saone, France, Nov. 19, 1940; s. André and Mariette (Menetrez) G.; m. Annie Pautot, Oct. 29, 1965; children: Isabelle, Christine, Anne Valerie. MD, U. Besancon, France, 1969. Extern St. Jacques Hosp., Besancon, 1964-67; faculty asst. Faculty of Medicine, Besancon, 1966-69; sole practice Pierrefontaine Les Varans, France, 1969—. Co-author therapy test, film on pollution of water; contbr. articles to med. and sci. jours. Councillor Municipality of Pierrefontaine Les Varans, 1977—. Served to capt. Mil. Health Service of France, 1968-69. Decorated chevalier Ordre Nat. du Merite, chevalier Palmes Academiques. Mem. French Assn. Gen. Practice. Roman Catholic. Lodge: Lions. Avocation: judo.

GAINSBURG, ROY ELLIS, publishing executive; b. Bklyn., May 1, 1932; s. Herbert Harry Gainsburg and Etta (Stein) Kornfeld; m. Vicki Bloye, July 12, 1957; children: Julie, Jeanne. AB, Brown U., 1954; LLB, Harvard U., 1957. Bar: N.Y. 1957. From assoc. to ptnr. Szold & Brandwen, N.Y.C., 1957-87; exec. v.p. St. Martin's Press Inc., N.Y.C., 1987, pres., 1987-97, part-time v.p. adminstrn., 1997—; v.p. adminstrn. Holtzbrinck Publ.; bd. dirs. Grove's Dictionaries, Inc. Treas., bd. dirs. The Partnership for the Homeless, N.Y.C. Democrat. Home: 157 Ralston Ave South Orange NJ 07079-2344 Office: St Martin's Press Inc 175 5th Ave New York NY 10010-7848

GAINUTDINOV, KHALIL LATYPOVICH, physicist, researcher; b. Village Tukai, Tomsk, Russia, June 1, 1947; s. Latyp Shamsutdinovich and Shamsedukha Idiatulovna (Gatialullina) G.; m. Svetlana Stanislovovna Putugir, Oct. 12, 1973; children: Tatiana, Aliya. Student, State U., Novosibirsk, Russia, 1971; postgrad., Russian Acad. Scis., Novosibirsk, 1974-77, DSc, 1994; PhD in Biology (Physiology), Russian Acad. Med. Scis., Leningrad, 1979. Jr. rschr. Med. Inst., Novosibirsk, 1971-74; jr. rschr., rschr., sr. rschr. Inst. Aut. and Electronics, Russian Acad. Scis., Novosibirsk, 1977-89; sr. rschr. Kazan Phys.-Tech. Inst. Russian Acad. Scis., 1989-95, dep. lab. head, 1992-95, sci. sec., 1995-99, head lab., 2000—; seminar reader State U., 1979-89, lectr., 1982-89; kectr., seminar reader State U., Kazan, 1989-2000. Author: Biophysics of Macromolecules, 1999; contbr. articles to sci. jours., including Annals N.Y. Acad. Scis., Neuroreport, Procs. Russian Acad. Scis. Grantee Russian Found. for Basic Rsch., 1995-97, 1998-2002. Mem. Russian Soc. Neuroscis. (head Kazan regional dept. 2000). Avocation: dancing. Fax: (8432) 765075. E-mail: gainut.kfti.knc.ru. Home: Chischmale, 420140 Kazan Tatars, Russia Office: Kazan Phys Tech Inst, Sybirsky tract 10/7, 420029 Kazan Tatars, Russia

GAIROLA, SURESH CHANDRA, physics educator, researcher; b. India, May 10, 1967; s. Vachaspati and Shanti (Dobhal) G. BSc, B.G. R. Constituent Coll., Pauri, India, 1986; MSc, H.N.B. Garhwal U., Srinagar, India, 1988; PhD, Avadh U., Faizabad, India, 1992. Lectr. H.N.B. Garhwal U. Campus, Pauri, 1991-96, sr. lectr., 1996—; participant orientation course Punjab U., Chandigarh, India, 1996; participant nat. workshop H.N.B. Garhwal U. Campus, Tehri, India, 1997; presenter in field. Contbr. articles to profl. jours. Expert Sci. Exhbn. Dist. Level, Pauri, 1995, Sardotswa Sammittee, Pauri, 1998. Mem. IAPT (life), NTSI (life), Indian Phys. Soc. (life). Avocations: motivating people for good works, helping poor people, playing hockey, playing table tennis, writing. Office: HNB Garhwal U Dept Physics, HNB Garhwal U Campus, Pauri Garhwal 246001, India

GAISER, WOLFGANG BERNHARD, sociologist, researcher; b. Ansbach, Germany, Oct. 31, 1946; s. Klaiber Gaiser; m. Isabelle Weissmann; 1 child, Julie. Diploma in Sociology, Ludwig Maxmilians U., Munich, 1972; PhD, U. Bielefeld, 1987. Rschr., sr. rschr., editor Deutsches Jugendinstitut e.V., Munich, 1972—; part-time lectr. Fachhochschule Munich. Editor Sociol. Jour. of German Youth Inst., 1990-96; co-editor: Immerdiese Jugend, Ein Zeitgeschichtliches Mosaik von 1945 bis Heute, 1985. Mem. works coun. German Youth Inst. Mem. Soc. for Analytical Group Dynamics (supr. groups and instns.), UNESCO Network. Avocations: sports, gardening. Office: Deutsches Jugendinstitut, Nockherstr 2, 81541 Munich Germany also: Postfach 90 03 52, 81503 Munich Germany

GAIT, MICHAEL JOHN, biochemist; b. Calcutta, India, Dec. 23, 1948; s. John Erroll Holmes and Dorothy Vincent (Cooke) G.; m. Rachel Irma Factor, June 19, 1975 (dec. 1986); 1 child, Jane; m. Anna Cleaves, Apr. 10, 1994; children: Etala, Simmon. BSc, U. Birmingham (Eng.), 1970, PhD, 1973. Rsch. assoc. MIT, Cambridge, Mass., 1973-75; staff scientist Med. Rsch. Coun., Cambridge, Eng., sr. staff scientist, 1987-94, spl. appt., 1994—; cons. Collaborative Rsch. Inc., Waltham, Mass., 1979-85, British Biotech. Ltd., Oxford, Eng., 1986-92, Glaxo Group Rsch., Greenford, Eng., 1994-95; sci. adv. bd. Gilead Scis., Foster City, Calif., 1989—, RiboTargets, Cambridge, England, 1997—. Editor: Oligonucleotide Synthesis: A Practical Approach, 1984; sr. editor: Nucleic Acids Research; co-editor: Nucleic Acids in Chemistry and Biology, 1990, 96; contbr. more than 100 articles to profl. jours. Govt. of Australia Commonwealth vis. fellow, 1982. Mem. Biochem. Soc. (sec./treas. nucleic acids and molecular biology group 1988-92, chmn. 2000—). Avocations: singing, amateur operatics, hill walking. Home: 16 Forest Rd, Cambridge CB1 9JB, England Office: Med Rsch Coun Lab Molecular Biology, Hills Rd, Cambridge CB2 2OH, England

GAITHER, GEORGE MANNEY, marketing consultant; b. Mineola, N.Y., Sept. 21, 1930; s. Roscoe Bradley and Frances Bullitt (Williams) G.; m. Dorothy Wineman Streater, Apr. 4, 1953; children: Neal, George, Anne, Emee, Bruce. B in Journalism, U. Mo., 1952. From gen. mgr. to pres. Internat. Rsch. Assocs., Inc., N.Y.C., 1955-71; pres., founder Gaither Internat., Inc., Stamford, Conn., 1971-96; cons. GMG Cons., Winchester, Va., 1997—. Lt. U.S. Army, 1952-55, Korea. Mem. Market Rsch. Coun. Republican. Avocation: writing. Home: 2628 Windwood Dr Winchester VA 22601-6418

GAJIC, RANKA PEJOVIC, educator; b. Mostar, Bosnia-Herzegovina, Apr. 30, 1928; came to U.S., 1953; d. Radovan Ilija and Darinka Ducic Pejovic; m. Sreten Gajic, Sept. 26, 1954 (dec. Apr. 1991). Student, Belgrade (Yugoslavia) U., 1947-52; B Art Edn., Northeastern Ill. U., 1973; M Slavic Langs. and Lit., U. Ill., Chgo., 1979, ABD, 1990; MLS, Chgo. State U., 1987; PhD in Edn., Century U., 1995. Acct. Field Enterprises Ednl. Corp., Chgo., 1955-59; ins. policy writer Alexander & Co. Ins., Chgo., 1959-64; fgn. ind. travel agt. Am. Express, Chgo., 1964-69; tchr. Chgo. Pub. Schs., 1974-84, 85—; tchg. asst. U. Ill., Chgo., 1984-85. Exhibited paintings in group shows at Northeastern Ill. U., Chgo., 1976 (3d prize) Mus. Sci. and Industry, Chgo., 1976 (Hon. Mention), North River Gallery, Chgo., 1977, 79 (2d prize 1977, Hon. Mention 1979). Chgo. State U. scholar, 1986; recipient Nat. Collegiate award U.S. Achievement Acad., 1987. Mem. Am. Assn. for Advancement of Slavic Studies, U. Ill. Alumni Assn. (life), Mus. Contemporary Art (comm. chair North Side Affiliates chpt. 1999—), Golden Key Nat. Honor Soc. (U. Ill.). Avocations: art, literature, languages, travel. Home: 5901 N Sheridan Rd Apt 12J Chicago IL 60660-3638

GAJOVIC, SRECKO, medical educator, scientist; b. Zagreb, Croatia, Nov. 29, 1964; s. Djordje and Katarina Zagar; m. Andreja Sekulic, Apr. 25, 1998; 1 child, Lovorka. MD, U. Zagreb, 1988, MSc, 1990, PhD, 1993. From rsch. asst. to sr. asst. histology & embryology U. Zagreb Sch. Medicine, 1988-99, assoc. prof., 1999—; postdoctoral fellow Max-Planck Inst. Biophysical Chemistry, Goettingen, Germany, 1993-95, Internat. Ctr. Genetic Engrng. & Biotechnology, Trieste, Italy, 1995-97. Mem. Croatian Soc. Electron Microscopy. Office: U Zagreb Sch Med Histology, Embryology Salata 3, Zagreb Croatia

GAJOVIĆ, VILIMAN GAVRILO, information scientist; b. Kovaćica, Srbija, Yugoslavia, Mar. 28, 1939; arrived in Malta, 1994; s. Gavrilo Viliman and Jelisaveta Gotfrid (Wilner) G.; m. Julija Miroslav Stefanović, Feb. 19, 1971; two children. Diploma in elec. engring., U. Belgrade, Yugoslavia, 1962; govt. cert., Belgrade, 1964; PhD in Tech. Scis., U. Belgrade, 1989; BSEE, ECACS, Pretoria, South Africa, 1993, MB in Tech. Sci., 1993. Engr. Cmty. of Yugoslav Post, Telegraph, Telephone, Belgrade, 1962-76, dir., 1976-80, chief engr., 1980-86; head Post, Telegraph, Telephone Info. Sys., Belgrade, 1986-93; mgr. cons. Briltl/Sinesonics, South Africa, 1993-94; mgr. MITTS, Malta, 1994—; mem. YANA/EAN Mgmt. Bd., Yugoslavia, 1989-93, Mgmt. Bd. Yugoslav Engrs., 1989-93, ETIS Mgmt. Bd., Brussels, 1991-93; chmn. EDIFACT-EANCOM Working Group, Yugoslavia, 1990-92. Contbr. articles to profl. jours. Soldier Yugoslav Army, 1963-64. Avocations: walking, reading, collecting rarities, classic music. Office: MITTS Gattard House, National Rd, HMR02 Blata L Bajda Malta

GAKH, ANDREI ALEXANDROVICH, research scientist; b. Lipetsk, Russia, Mar. 21, 1957; came to U.S., 1991; s. Alexandr Abramovich and Galina N. (Likhachova) G.; m. Elena G. Cherepanova, Apr. 11, 1981; 1 child, Darja Andreevna. MS summa cum laude, Moscow State U., 1979; PhD in Chemistry, N.D. Zelinsky Inst. Org. Chem., Moscow, 1983. Rsch. scientist N.D. Zelinsky Inst. Organic Chemistry, Moscow, 1983-88, sr. rsch. sci. group leader, mem. sci. coun., 1988-91; postdoctoral rsch. assoc. U. Tenn., Knoxville, 1991-93; postdoctoral rsch. assoc. Oak Ridge (Tenn.) Nat. Lab., 1993-97, staff scientist, 1997—; cons. Molten Salts Technologies, Knoxville, Tenn., 1994. Contbr. more than 50 articles to profl. jours. including Jour. Am. Chem. Soc., Jour. Organic Chemistry, Angew Chem. Internat. and Tetrahedron. Patentee in field. Grantee USIC, NIS-IPP, 1994-2000; recipient Young Investigator award Russian Acad. Scis., 1990. Mem. Am. Chem. Soc. Office: Oak Ridge Nat Lab PO Box 2008 Oak Ridge TN 37831-2008

GÁL, DEZSÖ, science educator; b. Budapest, Hungary, July 25, 1926; s. Lajos Grauman and Szidi Glasel; m. Maria Ördögh, July 25, 1953. Diploma, Eötvoös Loránd U., Budapest, Hungary, 1948; PhD, Kossutca L. U., Debrecen, Hungary, 1951; candidate, József A. U., Szeged, Hungary, 1955; DSc, Acad. Scis., Budapest, 1963. Jr. asst. Kossuth L. U., 1948-51; asst. prof. József A. U., 1957-63, prof., 1963-70; head dept. Rsch. Inst. Chemistry, Budapest, 1971—; postdoctoral fellow Nat. Rsch. Coun. Can., 1962-63; vis. prof. Inst. Chem. Physics, Russia, 1966-67; assoc. prof. U. Paris VI, 1989, U. Naples, Italy, 1990, 91. Hon. and founding editor internat. jour. Oxidation Comms., 1985—; co-author: (monographs) The Kinetic Isotope Method, 1976, Modelling of Oxidation Processes, 1986; contbr. over 300 sci. articles to internat. jours. Recipient Officers Cross of Honors, Pres. of Parliament, Hungary, 1996. Mem. European Photochem. Assn. (standing com. 1980—, chmn. Hungarian sect. 1985—), Combustion Inst. Avocations: theater, books, internet. Home: Bérc utca 19/21, 1016 Budapest Hungary Office: Chem Rsch Inst Chemistry, Pusztaszeri ut 59-67, 1025 Budapest Hungary

GAL, RICHARD JOHN, industrial engineer; b. Youngstown, Ohio, Oct. 30, 1957; s. John and Maria (Hesch) G.; m. Connie Marie Norton, 1996; children: Stephanie, Kristin, Richard John Jr. B in Engring., Youngstown State U., 1979; MBA, Ea. Mich. U., 1981. Indsl. engr. trainee Nat. Steel, Ecorse, Mich., 1979-81; indsl. engr. Republic Steel, Massillon, Ohio, 1981-84; div. indsl. engr. Avery, Painesville, Ohio, 1984-87; assoc. prin. engr. Sverdrup Tech., Niceville, Fla., 1987-94; quality dir. Sverdrup Tech., Elgin AFB, Fla., 1995-98; quality officer Sverdrup Tech., Cape Canaveral, Fla., 1998—; examiner Malcolm Baldrige Nat. Quality award, 1998, 99, 2000; sr. examiner F.L. Sterling Award, 1995, 96, 97, 98, 99; chmn. Fla. Sch. to Work Program, 1998. Contbr. articles to profl. jours. Advisor Jr. Achievement, Canton, Ohio, 1981-82; rep. United Way, 1998, 99, 2000. Mem. Am. Soc. Quality Engrs. Home: 1180 Grand Cayman Dr Merritt Island FL 32952-7224 Office: 1613 Sab Rd Rm 18 Patrick A F B FL 32925

GAL, YEONG SOON, chemistry educator; b. Hapchon, Korea, Dec. 22, 1961; s. Si Bong and Yeong Ja (Cha) G.; m. Eun Sook Choi, Nov. 29, 1987; children: Jun-Sik, Su-Jeong. BS, Kyungpook Nat. U., 1983; MS, Korea Advanced Inst. Sci., 1985; PhD, Korea Adv. Inst. Sci. & Tech., 1988. Tchg. asst. Korea Advanced Inst. Sci. & Tech., Seoul, 1985-88; sr. researcher Agy. for Def. Devel., Taejon, Korea, 1988-95; asst. prof. Kyungil U., Korea, 1995—; program mgr. Agy. for Def. Devel., 1990-95; cons. Hankook Fiberglass Co., Milyang, Korea, 1993—.

GALACTÉROS-DE BOISSIER, LUCIE, art historian, educator; b. Marseille, France, Feb. 8, 1932; d. Louis-Alexis and Andrée-Clémence (Robert) de B.; m. Emmanuel Galactéros, Sept. 15, 1966; 1 child, Caroline. LittD in Art History, U. Lyon II, 1982; LittD, Agrégé des Universités. Chef de travaux U. Fribourg, 1978-82; titular prof. U. Neuchâtel, 1982-93; titular prof. art historian chair U. Sorbonne, Paris, 1993-97, emeritus prof., 1997—; sci. hist. counsel art Acad. Suisse des Scis. Humaines et Sociales, Berne, 1990; dir. rsch. classes Ctr. Nicolas-Ledoux, U. Paris I, Panthéon-Sorbonne. Author: Thomas Blanchet, Arthena, Paris, 1991; contbg. aughor L'Hotel de Ville de Lyon, Imprimerie Nationale, 1998. Home: 2 rue Antoine de St Exupery, 69002 Lyon France Office: UFR U Paris I, 3 rue Michelet, 75006 Paris France

GALALY, ENAN, corporate executive; b. Cairo, Jan. 1, 1947; s. Raouf and Ihsan El Galaly. Diploma, Aalborg Denmark, 1970. From dishwasher to maitre d'hotel Odense (Denmark) Kongresshus, 1967-69; exec. asst. mgr. Hotel Hvide Hus, Aalborg, Denmark, 1970-75, gen. mgr., 1975-78; mng. dir. Hvide Hus Hotel Chain, Denmark, 1978-82; chmn. Helnan Internat. A/S, Denmark, Egypt, Saudi Arabia and U.S.A., 1982—; chmn., travel agy., tour operator Scandinavian Tours A/S, Denmark, 1982-95; cons. numerous internat. and nat. hotel and tourist projects, tourism rep. Danish ofcl. dels., lectr. in field. Named Hon. Citizen numerous cities; recipient Cordon Bleu award Helwan Cairo U., 1984. Mem. Internat. Assn. U. Pres. (sr. advisor), Chaine Des Rotisseurs, Cordon Bleu Du Saint Esprit, numerous other hotel and tourist orgns. Avocations: swimming, lecturing. E-mail: hotel@helnan phonix hotel.dk. Office: Helnan Internat A/S, Vesterbro 77, 9000 Alborg Denmark

GALANAKIS, EMMANOUIL, pediatrician, educator; b. Heraklion, Crete, Greece, Sept. 21, 1957; s. Georgios and Maria Kanoupaki; m. Styliani Stavela, Mar. 9, 1991; children: Odysseus, Georgios. MB, Athens U., 1981, postgrad., 1982-86; BA in Philosophy, Ioannina (Greece) U., 1992, MD, 1993, PhD in Philosophy, 1996. Med. diplomate. Physician Ministry of Health, Crete, 1984-86; sr. house officer pediat. U. Hosp., Ioannina, 1986-90, specialist in pediat., 1990-97; specialist in pediat. U. Hosp., Heraklion, 1997-99; lectr. U. Ioannina, 1999-2000; asst. prof. U. Crete, 2000—; clin. fellow Great Ormond Street Hosp., London, 1993, 98, St. Mary's Hosp., London, 1994, 97. Contbr. articles to profl. jours. Served with Hellenic Army, 1982-84. Mem. AAAS, Hellenic Pediat. Soc., Hellenic Soc. Med. Ethics, European Soc. Pediat. Infectious Diseases. Christian Orthodox. Avocation: trekking. Office: Dept Pediatrics U Crete, POB 1393, 71500 Heralkiou Greece

GALANOS, DIMITRIS SPYROS, food chemistry educator; b. Athens, Greece, Aug. 28, 1927; s. Spyridon and Anna (Totomi) G.; m. Rebecca Sophia Turcovassili, Sept. 30, 1972; 1 child, Anna Amerimmi Papalexopoulos. Diploma in Chemistry, Nat. U. Athens, 1951, PhD in Chemistry, 1954; postgrad., Deutsche Forschungsanstalt Für Lebensmittelchemie, Munich, 1952-54. Tchg. asst. Lab. Food Chemistry, Nat. U. Athens, 1951-52, rsch. asst., 1956-58, lectr. food chemistry, 1958, sr. rsch. investigator, 1959, prof. food chemistry, 1963—, chmn. divsn. chemistry, 1985-90; rschr. divsn. biochemistry U. Ill., Urbana, 1954-56, rsch. assoc. chemistry, 1958-59; internat. lectr. Served Royal Hellenic Navy, 1948-50. Mem. Am. Chem. Soc., N.Y. Acad. Scis., Am. Oil Chemists Soc., Internat. Soc. Neurochemistry, Syrian Acad. Scis., Alpha Chi Sigma. Home: 73 Anagnostopulu St, 106-72 Athens Greece

GALANTE, ANN MURIEL, town official; b. N.Y.C., May 20, 1929; d. Johnson D. and Anna Francis (Donavan) Boyd; m. James Vincent Galante, June 25, 1949; children: Patricia, Ann, James, Margaret, Joseph. BS in Pub. Adminstrn., SUNY, Old Westbury, 1986, postgrad., 1996. Trustee Village of Mineola, N.Y., 1982-85, mayor, 1985-91; receiver of taxes Town of North Hempstead, Manhasset, N.Y., 1992—; mem. N.Y. State Gov.'s Task Force on State Mandates, N.Y.C., 1989-90, N.Y. State Gov.'s Task Force on Sexual Harassment, N.Y.C., 1993-94. Active numerous cmty., ednl., religious, sr. citizen, youth and women's orgns.; past pres. Mineola Welcome Wagon (now Friends and Neighbors); former mem. bd. dirs. Am. Heart Assn.; mem. citizenship com. Nassau County 4-H Clubs, Plainview, N.Y., 1983-87; com. mem. Nassau County Dem. Com., Carle Place, N.Y., 1991—; del. 19th Dist. Jud. Conv., Hauppauge, N.Y., 1992—; Presdl. elector N.Y. State Electoral Coll., Albany, 1996; mem.-at large bd. dirs. Shelter Rock dist. Boy Scouts Am., 1996-97; co-founder Mineola Homebound Svc.; eucharistic min. Corpus Christi Ch., Mineola, 1981—, also past chmn. justice and peace com., renew 1000 com., renew 2000 com., 100th anniversary com.; trustee Mineola Hist. Soc., 1990—; active Mineola Mustang Run Com., Mineola Bicentennial of Constn. Com.; charter mem. Circle of Friends Soc., Girl Scouts U.S.A., Nassau County; co-founder Mineola Friends of A. Holly Patterson Nursing Home, Mineola Homebound Svc.; mem. master plan and planning com. Village of Mineola, Pres.'s Coun. L.I. Womens Agenda; co-chair N.H. com. against domestic violence; del. Dem. Nat. Conv., 2000. Named hon. fire chief Mineola Fire Dept., 1985, Outstanding Friend, Corpus Christi Sch., 1996, Disting. Grad., Empire State Coll., 1996, Woman of Yr., Mineola Welcome Wagon; recipient numerous awards for cmty. svc., including Mother of Yr. award Southeastern Dist. Elks Club, Humanitarian award Nassau County Dem. Com. Mem. Tax Receivers and Collectors Assn., N.Y. State Assn. Towns, Soroptimists (past pres. Nassau County, Woman of Distinction award Nassau County 1995), Am. Assn. Ret. Persons, Rotary. Roman Catholic. Avocations: travel, theatre, women's history research, walking, swimming. Office: Town of North Hempstead PO Box 3000 Manhasset NY 11030-3000

GALATENKO, NATALIYA, chemist; b. Ivanovo, Russia, Aug. 21, 1948; d. Andrey and Mariya (Schogoleva) Spilnichenko; m. Anatoliy Galatenko, Apr. 22, 1969 (div. Dept. 1980); 3 child; m. Alexandr Snegirev, Mar. 28, 1986. Degree, U. Shevchenko, Kiev, Ukraine, 1974; Dandidate of Biology, Med. Inst., Kiev, 1984; D Biology, Bioorganic Chemistry, U. Kiev, 1997; hon. diploma, Nat. Acad. Sci. Ukraine, Kiev, 1998. Engr. Inst. Macromolecular Chemistry, Kiev, 1973-78, jr. sci. collaborator, 1978-85, sr. sci. collaborator, 1985-86, leading sci. collaborator, 1986-92, chief lab., 1992-95, chief dept., 1995—; dep. chief Com. New Med. Tech., Kiev, 1997-99, chief, 1999. Author: Glue Compounds in Maxilla-face Surgery, 1983, Morfological and Biochemical Aspects of Biodegradation of Polymers, 1986; patentee composition for aiding in regeneration of tissue, method of treatment of bone defects after removal of tumor. Recipient hon. diploma Ministry of Affairs of Sci. and Tech., Kiev, 1999; named Hon. Inventor, State Com. USSR on Bus. of Invention and Discovery, 1990. Mem. European Soc. Biomaterials. Avocations: reading, gardening. Fax: 552-4064. E-mail: polytox@ukrpack.net. Office: Inst Macromolecular Chem, Kharkovskoye shose 48, 253160 Kiev Ukraine

GALAZ, GASPAR ANTONIO, astronomer; b. Santiago, Chile, Sept. 7, 1967; s. Gaspar G. and María Teresa Lladser. BS in Physics, U. Chile, Santiago, 1991, MS in Astronomy, 1993; PhD in Astronomy, U. Paris, 1997. Postdoct. Carnegie Instn. Washington, Pasadena, Calif., 1997—.

GALBRAITH, JOHN KENNETH, retired economist; b. Iona Station, Ont., Can., Oct. 15, 1908; s. William Archibald and Catherine (Kendall) G.; m. Catherine Atwater, Sept. 17, 1937; children: Alan, Peter, James. BS, U. Guelph, 1931, LLD (hon.); MS, U. Calif., 1933, PhD, 1934; postgrad., Cambridge (Eng.) U., 1937-38; LLD (hon.), Bard Coll., U. Calif., Miami U., U. Mass., U. Mysore, Brandeis U., U. Toronto, U. Sask., U. Mich., U. Durham, R.I. Coll., Boston Coll., Hobart and William Smith Colls., Albion Coll., Tufts U., Adelphi Suffolk Coll., Mich. State U., Louvain U., Oxford U., U. Paris, Carleton Coll., U. Vt., Queens U., Moscow State U., Harvard U., Smith Coll. London Sch. Economics, others. Research fellow U. Calif., 1931-34; instr. and tutor Harvard U., 1934-39; asst. prof. econs. Princeton U., 1939-42; econ. adviser Nat. Def. Adv. Commn., 1940-41; asst. adminstr. in charge price div. OPA, 1941-42, dep. adminstr., 1942-43; mem. bd. of editors Fortune Mag., 1943-48; lectr. Harvard U., 1948-49, prof. econs., 1949-75, Paul M. Warburg prof. econs., 1959-75, ret., 1975; hon. fellow Trinity Coll., Cambridge U.; hon. prof. U. Geneva; U.S. ambassador to India, 1961-63. Author: numerous books including American Capitalism, 1952, A Theory of Price Control, 1952, The Great Crash, 1955, The Affluent Society, 1958, The Liberal Hour, 1960, Economic Development, 1963, The Scotch, 1964, The New Industrial State, 1967, Indian Painting, 1968, Ambassador's Journal, 1969, Economics, Peace and Laughter, 1971, A China Passage, 1973, Economics and the Public Purpose, 1973, Money: Whence It Came, Where It Went, 1975, The Age of Uncertainty, 1977, (with Nicole Salinger) Almost Everyone's Guide to Economics, 1978, Annals of an Abiding Liberal, 1979, The Nature of Mass Poverty, 1979, A Life in Our Times, 1981, The Anatomy of Power, 1983, The Voice of the Poor: Essays in Economic and Political Persuasion, 1983, A View From the Stands, 1986, Economics in Perspective: A Critical History, 1987, (with Stanislav Menshikov) Capitalism, Communism and Coexistence, 1988, (novel) The Triumph, 1968, (novel) A Tenured Professor, 1990, The Culture of Contentment, 1992, A Journey Through Economic Time, 1994, A Short History of Financial Euphoria, 1993, The Good Society, 1996, Name-Dropping From F.D.R. On, 1999; contbr. to econ. and sci. jours. Dir. U.S. Strategic Bombing Survey, 1945; dir. Office of Econ. Security Policy, State Dept., 1946. Fellow Social Sci. Research Council, 1937-38; Recipient Medal Freedom, 1946. Fellow Am. Acad. Arts and Letters (pres. 1984-87); mem. AAAS, Am. Econ. Assn. (pres. 1972), Am. Agrl. Econ. Assn., Ams. for Dem. Action (chmn. 1967-68). Clubs: Century, Saturday. Home: 30 Francis Ave Cambridge MA 02138-2010 Office: Harvard U 206 Littauer Ctr Cambridge MA 02138

GALBRAITH, NANETTE ELAINE GERKS, forensic and management sciences company executive; b. Chgo., June 15, 1928; d. Harold William and Maybelle Ellen (Little) Gerks; m. Oliver Galbraith III, Dec. 18, 1948; children: Craig Scott, Diane Frances. BS with high honors with distinction, San Diego State U., 1978. Diplomate Am. Bd. Forensic Document Examiners. Examiner of questioned documents San Diego County Sheriff's Dept. Crime Lab., San Diego, 1975-80; sole prop. Nanette G. Galbraith, Examiner of Questioned Documents, San Diego, 1980-82; pres., examiner of questioned documents Galbraith Forensic & Mgmt. Scis., Ltd., San Diego, 1982-97; cons., 1997—; one of keynote speakers Internat. Assn Forensic Scis., Adelaide, South Australia, 1990. Contbr. articles to profl. jours. including Jour. Forensic Scis., Forensic Sci. Internat., Internat. Jour. Forensic Document Examiners. Fellow Am. Acad. Forensic Scis. (questioned documents section, del. to Peoples Rep. of China 1986, USSR, 1988); mem. Am. Soc. Questioned Document Examiners (jour. editl. bd. 2000—), Southwestern Assn. Forensic Document Examiners (charter), U. Club Atop Symphony Towers, Phi Kappa Phi. Republican. Episcopalian.

GALBUT, MARTIN RICHARD, lawyer; b. Miami Beach, Fla., June 27, 1946; s. Paul A. and Ethel (Kolnick) G.; m. Cynthia Ann Slaughter, June 4, 1972; children: Keith Richard, Lindsay Anne. BS in Speech, Northwestern U., 1968, JD cum laude, 1971. Bar: Ariz. 1972, U.S. Dist. Ct. Ariz. 1972, U.S. Ct. Appeals (9th cir.) 1972. Assoc. Brown, Vlassis & Bain PA, Phoenix, 1971-75; founder, ptnr. McLoone, Theobald & Galbut PC, Phoenix, 1975-86; of counsel Furth, Fahrner, Bluemle & Mason, 1986-89; founder Galbut & Conant, PC, Phoenix, 1989—; presenter guest Law Talk cable TV; judge pro tem Maricopa County Superior Ct.; lectr. comml. real estate litigation, arbitration, mediation and intellectual property law Lorman Bus. Seminars. Contbr. articles to profl. jours. Chmn., law rev. Ariz. State Air Pollution Control Hearing Bd., 1984-89; mem. Govs. Task Force on Urban Air Quality, 1986, City Phoenix Environ. Quality Comm., 1987-88; bd. dirs. Men's Art Council Phoenix Art Mus.; bd. dirs., founder Ariz. Asthma Found. Clarion de Witt Hardy scholar, Kosmerl scholar; Russel Sage grantee. Mem. ABA, Ariz. State Bar Assn. (lectr., securities law and litigation com. and sect.), Am. Arbitration Assn. (arbitrator), Nat. Assn. Securities Dealers (arbitrator, trainer and lectr.). Democrat. Jewish. Avocations: painting, collecting antiques and fine art, international travel, go. Office: Galbut & Conant PC 2425 E Camelback Rd Ste 1020 Phoenix AZ 85016-4216

GALDAMEZ, RICARDO, internist; b. Suchitoto, Cuzcatlan, El Salvador, June 29, 1952; came to U.S., 1984; s. Santiago Galdamez and Maria Angela Monge; m. Elsa Ramos, Dec. 17, 1977; children: Emma, Ana, Martha. MD, U. El Salvador, 1982. Diplomate Am. Bd. Internal Medicine, Am. Bd. Forensic Medicine. Rotating intern (surgery, internal medicine, pediat., etc.) various hosps., El Salvador, 1979-81; pub. health dir. Ahuachapan, El

Salvador, 1981-82; dir. health care Self-Help Group, El Salvador, 1982-84; resident in internal medicine Woodhull Hosp., Bklyn., 1987-91, physician, 1991—; physician Montefiore Rickers Island Health Svcs., Queens, 1993-96; internist Elmhurst Hosp., Queens, 1997-98. Union del. Doctors Coun., N.Y., 1995—. Fellow AMA, Interam. Coll. Physician, Surgeon; mem. ACP, Am. Soc. Internal Medicine, Rosicrucian Order. Avocations: parapsychology, mystic work. Home: 5602 137th St Flushing NY 11355-5034 Office: North Bklyn Med Office 1155 Broadway Brooklyn NY 11221-3025

GALDI, VINCENZO, electrical engineer, researcher; b. Salerno, Italy, July 28, 1970; s. Isidoro and Gerarda (Romei) G. Degree in Computer Science, Istituto Tecnico Industriale, Salerno, 1989; BEE (laureate), U. Salerno, 1995, PhD in Applied Electromagnetics, 1999. Registered engr., Italy. Rsch. asst. U. Salerno, 1996-99; vis. rschr. European Space Agy., Noordwijk, The Netherlands, 1997; postdoctoral rschr. U. Sannio, Benevento, Italy, 1999, Boston (Mass.) U., 1999—; Reviewer sci. papers Optical Soc. Am., Washington, 1999. Soldier with cav., 1995-96. Italian Ministery U. and Sci. Rsch. PhD fellow Salerno, Italy, 1996-98, European Union postdoctoral fellow U. Sannio, Benevento, Italy, 1999. Mem. IEEE, Italian Nat. Inst. Nuc. Physics, Sigma Xi. Roman Catholic. Avocations: reading, traveling, music, soccer. Fax: 617-353-6440. E-mail: vgaldi@bu.edu. Home: 9 Summit Ave Apt 1A Brookline MA 02446-2718 Office: Boston U ECE Dept 8 Saint Marys St Boston MA 02215-2421

GALE, EDDIE, musician, composer, consultant; b. Bklyn., Aug. 15, 1941; s. Edward and Daisy Gale Stevens; m. Phyllis Marlene Manning (div. 1982); children: Donna, Mark, Patrice, D'Juana, Teyonda, Gwilu; m. Georgette D. Farley, Sept. 29, 1985. Student, San Jose State U., 1974-76. Founder, organizer Music in the Schs., N.Y.C., San Jose, 1968—; composer, rec. artist Blue Note Records, N.Y.C., 1968-70, Mapleshade Records, Upper Marlboro, Md., 1993; founder, organizer Evergreen Youth/Adult Jazz Soc., Inc., San Jose, Calif., 1985—, Students for World Peace, San Jose, 1996—. Author: (music rec.) Ghetto Music, 1968, Black Rhythm Happening, 1969, Live at the Knitting Factory, 1989. Recipient Best Jazz Record award N.Y. Village Voice, 1993; named San Jose's Ambassador of Jazz, City of San Jose, 1974, Music Ambassador, Assn. of World Citizens, 1995—. Mem. ASCAP. Achievements include appearance in Smithsonian Collection of Classic Jazz with Cecil Taylor. Avocations: camping, travel, videography. Office: PO Box 1551 San Jose CA 95109-1551

GALE, LEWIS RAYMOND, IV, economics educator; b. Fresno, Calif., Dec. 13, 1965; s. Lewis Raymond III and Beverly Ann Gale; m. Candice Lorraine Corrington, Aug. 18, 1990; 1 child, Madeline. BA in Econs., Calif. State U., Fresno, 1989; MS in Econs., Ariz. State U., 1994, PhD in Econs., 1994. Asst. prof. econs. U. La., Lafayette, 1994—; dir. Lafayette Trade Devel. Group, 1997—. Contbr. articles to profl. jours. Libertarian. Episcopalian. Avocations: Guitar, golf. Fax: 337-482-6675. E-mail: lrg3948.louisiana. Office: U La at Lafayette PO Box 44570 Lafayette LA 70504-0001

GALE, MICHAEL JONATHAN, entrepreneur; b. Adelaide, Australia, Oct. 27, 1962; s. Milton Ewart and Gwendoline Fay (Gilding) G.; m. Annette Francis Carr; 1 child, Kirsty Ellen; m. Allison Diane Owens; children: Matthew Jonathan, Cameron David. Prin. The Harbor Book Shop, Adelaide, 1982-86; bus. devel. mgr. Computer Power Group, Melbourne and Sydney, Australia, 1986-90; mng. dir. Macromedia Pacific, San Francisco and Sydney, 1990-93; CEO Double Impact, San Francisco, 1993—; bd. dirs. Double Impact Capital, Melbourne, Haht Asia, San Francisco, Voteglobal.com, San Francisco, Toggle Entertainment, N.Y. Office: Double Impact 10th Fl 785 Market St Fl 10 San Francisco CA 94103-2017

GALE, ROBERT L., educational association administrator, consultant; b. St. Cloud, Minn., Jan. 13, 1927; s. John Henry and Helen (Andrews) G.; m. Barbara Carr Davis, Oct. 19, 1951; children: Jennifer Gale Dunkin, Robert L. Gale, Jr., Morgan Andrews. Midshipman, U.S. Naval Acad., 1945-46; BA, Carleton Coll., 1948; DHL, U. N.C., Asheville, 1989. Editor-in-chief Maco Mag. Corp., N.Y.C., 1954-57; v.p. Carleton Coll., Northfield, Minn., 1957-63; dir. recruiting Peace Corps, Washington, 1963-65; dir. pub. affairs EEOC, Washington, 1965-66; chmn., ceo Gale Assocs., Washington, 1966-74; pres. Assn. Governing Bds. Univs. and Colls., Washington, 1974-92, pres. emeritus, 1992—; bd. trustees Carleton Coll., Northfield, 1972—; bd. dirs. Nat. Peace Corps Assn., Washington, Nat. Ctr. Nonprofit Bds., Washington, Nat. Exec. Svcs. Corps, N.Y.C., CARE, Inc., Atlanta, 1982-96, U. Pretoria Fund. Chmn. bd. Nat. Peace Garden Monument, Washington, 1995—. With U.S. Navy, 1944-45. Democrat. Episcopalian. Avocations: tennis, travel, volunteering. Home: Rte 1 Bethany Beach DE 19930-9801

GALEANA-SANCHEZ, HORTENSIA, mathematician, educator, researcher; b. Mexico City, Nov. 6, 1956; d. Bernardo and Amalia Galeana-Sanchez; children: Hugo Rincon-Galeana, Alberto Rincon-Galeana. MS, UNAM, Mexico City, 1982, PhD, 1985. Rsch. Inst. Math., Mexico City, 1985-86, rschr. "A", 1986-89, rschr. "B", 1989—; prof. A, Faculty of scis., Mexico City, 1985—. Home: Avenida Acueducto 5098 C-14, 16030 Mexico City Mexico Office: Univ Nat Autonoma Mexico, Inst Math, 04510 Mexico City Mexico

GALEEV, ALBERT ABUBAKIR, academic director, educator; b. Ufa, Bashkortstan, Russia, Oct. 19, 1940; s. Abubakir Akhmet Galeev and Gulyandam Rizvan Urmanova; m. Liudmila Dmitrii Shpak, Jan. 13, 1966; children: Rustam, Albert. Student, Novosibirsk State U., 1963; D in Sci., Nuclear Physics Inst., Novosibirsk, USSR, 1967; D (hon.), Paris South U. Sr. scientist Nuclear Physics Inst. Siberian Br. USSR Acad. Scis., Novosibirsk, 1965-70, Inst. High Temperature USSR Acad. Scis., Moscow, 1971-73; head dept. Space Rsch. Inst. USSR Acad. Scis., Moscow, 1973-88, dir., 1988—; prof. Moscow Inst. Physics and Tech., 1971—. Co-author: Nonlinear Plasma Theory, 1969; editor: Basic Plasma Physics, 1983. Recipient Lenin prize Lenin Prize Com., 1984. Mem. Russian Acad. Scis., Acad. Astronautics, Academia Europa, Max-Plank Soc. (fgn.). Office: Space Rsch Inst, Profsoyuznaya 84/32, 117810 GSP-7 Moscow Russia*

GALEMBO, ALEXANDER, acoustician; b. Dnepropetrovsk, USSR, Feb. 4, 1941; s. Semion and Maria G.; m. Tatiana Koshevaya, 1989; 1 child, Ilona. MS, Leningrad State U., 1965; PhD, Inst. Cinema and TV, St. Petersburg, Russia, 1995. Engr.-physicist Acoustics R&D Lab Leningrad Piano Factory, USSR, 1966-75, head of the engring. group Acoustics R&D Lab., 1975-79; head of Acoustics R&D Lab. Leningrad Piano Factory, 1979-82; head Acoustical R&D, Lab Leningrad Musical Instrument Indsl. Corp., 1982-87; guest rschr. dept. speech, music and hearing Royal Inst. Technology, Stockholm, 1993, 94, 98, 2000; NATO sci. fellow dept. psychology Queen's U., Kingston, Can., 1996-98; acoustics cons. Barmaley Movie Studio, St. Petersburg, 1998—; vis. rschr. Setchenov Inst. Evolutionary Physiology and Biochemistry, St. Petersburg, 1995—; cons. and lectr. in field, including lectr. Leningrad Piano Factory, 1979-82, Musical Instrument Indsl. Corp., Leningrad, 1982-86. Author: (books) Quality of Piano Sound, 1987, Birth of the Orchestra, 1987, Peterburg-Petrograd-Leningrad Ency. entries, 1993. Sci. fellow NATO, Can., 1996; rsch. grantee Wenner Gren Found., Sweden, 1994, Swedish Inst., Stockholm, 1993. Mem. Acoustical Soc. Am. Avocations: music, poetry. E-mail: galembo@galembo.mail.iephb.ru. Home: 47 Furstadtskaya St # 17, Saint Petersburg 191123, Russia Office: Setchenov Inst Evol Physiol, 44 Thoreza Pr Lab 32, Saint Petersburg 194223, Russia

GALEOTE QUECEDO, GERARDO, foreign diplomat; b. São Paulo, Brasil, Jan. 27, 1957. Degree in Law, U. Complutense, Madrid; postgrad., UNED. Mem. European Parliament, 1999—, mem. com. fgn. affairs, human rights, common security, mem. com. on legal affairs and the internal mkt.; mem. of bur. Group of the European People's Party (Christian Democrats) and European Democrats; chmn. delegation for relations with Israel. Mem. exec. com., mem. polit. bd. European Popular Party; mem. exec. com. Commn. for the European Union, Inst. European-Latin Am. Rels.; v.p. Found. European Studies; patron Found. of Humanism and Democracy; patron com. of assessment Popular Latim-Am. Found.; mem. Commn. of External Affairs, of Human Rights, of Pub. Safety, of Polit. Def., of Internal Market. Decorated Nat. Order Cruzeiro do Sul (Brazil), Ofcl. Order of San Carlos (Colombia), Order of Francisco de Miranda 1st class (Venezuela), comdr. Order Bernardino O'Higgins (Chile). Mem. People's Party (Spain).

GALES, SAMUEL JOEL, retired civilian military employee, counselor; b. Dublin, Miss., June 14, 1930; s. James McNary McNeil and Alice Francis (Smith) Broadus-Gales; m. Martha Ann Jackson (div. Jan. 1978); children: Samuel II (dec.), Martha Diane Townsend, Katherine Roselein, Karlmann Von, Carolyn B., Elizabeth Angelica McCain. BA, Chapman Univ., 1981, MS, 1987. Ordained Eucharist minister, Episcopal Ch., 1985; cert. tchr., Calif. Enlisted U.S. Army, 1948, advanced through grades to master 1st sgt., 1969, ret., 1976; tchr. Monterey (Calif.) Unified Sch. Dist., 1981-82; civilian U.S. Army Directorate of Logistics, Ft. Ord, Calif., 1982-93; collateral EEOC counselor Dept. Def., U.S. Army, 1987-93; peer counselor, 1982-84. Active Family Svc. Agy., Monterey, 1979-85; rep. Episc. Soc. for Ministry on Aging, Carmel, Calif., 1980-86, Task Force on Aging, Carmel, 1983-87, vestryman, 1982-85, 91-94; ombudsman Monterey County Long-Term Care Program, Calif. Dept. for the Aging, 1993-97; vol. guide Monterey Bay Aquarium Found., 1994—, vol. docent Bay Net, Ctr. for Marine Conservation, Monterey Bay Nat. Marine Sanctuary, 1997—. Decorated Air medal. Mem. Nat. Assn. Ret. Fed. Employees (pres. chpt. 579 1999—), Nat. Assn. Parliamentarians (pres. 2000—, pres. Pi Gamma unit Calif. State Assn. 2000—), Am. Legion (post comdr. 1973-74), Forty and Eight (chef-de-gare 1979, 80), Monterey Chess Club, Comdr.'s Club Calif. (pres. Outpost 28 1981-82). Republican. Avocation: classical music. Home: PO Box 919 1617 Lowell St Seaside CA 93955-3811

GALGUT, PETER NEIL, periodontist; b. Pretoria, Transvaal, South Africa, Dec. 30, 1946; s. Harry and Pondy (Kusner) G.; m. Harriet Batami Sher, Aug. 19, 1971; children: Resa, Saul. BDS, U. Witwatersrand, South Africa, 1971; MSc, U. London, 1982, MPhil, 1993. Gen. practice dental surgeon London, 1971-81; dir. Sch. Dental Hygiene Univ. Coll. Hosp., London, 1983-90, rsch. fellow, 1992-93; sr. rsch. fellow Eastmans Dental Inst., London, 1993—; lectr. U. London, 1993—; pvt. practice periodontist London, 1993—; del. to nat. coun. Gen. Dental Practitioners Assn., U.K., 1974-82; European coord. clin. trials, cons. in trial validation for clin. trials in oral hygiene products and regulatory approval for internat. pharm. cos., 1994-97. Contbr. numerous articles to profl. publs. Mem. coun., hon. sec., chmn. NWRS, London, 1988-96. Mem. Royal Coll. Surgeons, Brit. Dental Assn. (meetings sec. Middlesex and Hertfordshire br. 1986-90, chmn. Hendon sect. 1992-93), Brit. Soc. Periodontology, Am. Acad. Periodontology, Internat. Acad. Periodontology, Western Soc. Periodontology. Jewish. Avocations: photography, music, walking. Office: 28 Rundell Crescent, London NW4 3BP, England

GALIATSATOS, CHRISTOS G., bottling company executive; b. Athens, Greece, Aug. 25, 1961; s. Gerassimos V. and Paraskevi C. (Lenoutsos) G.; m. Georgia Dara, Apr. 20, 1991. BSc, U. Athens, 1984; MSc, U. Cin., 1986, PhD in Analytical Chemistry, 1988. Sr. chemist Miles Inc., Elkhart, Ind., 1988-90; logistics mgr. Procter & Gamble, Hellas, Greece, 1991-94; mgr. logistics and customer svc. Atlantic Super Mkts., Greece, 1995-97; logistics mgr. Elgeka S.A., Athens, 1997-98; mgr. logistics and distbn. Greece Hellenic Bottling Co., Athens, 1999—. Co-author: Chemical Sensors and Microinstrumentation, 1989, Efficient Unit Loads, 1996. Mem. Efficient Consumer Response (founding), Soc. Logistics Engrs. Avocations: internet surfing, hot air ballooning, soccer. Home: 370 Pattision St, 111 41 Athens Greece Office: Hellenic Bottling Co SA, 44 Kifissias Ave, 151 25 Maroussi Greece

GALIE, LOUIS MICHAEL, electronics company executive; b. Phila., Aug. 10, 1945; s. Adam Michael and Phyllis Anne (Bowers) G.; m. Elizabeth D. Viviano, June 23, 1969 (div. 1980); 1 child, Kathryn Louise; m. Martha Bancroft Campbell, May, 1990; 1 child, Grace F. BS, U. Chgo., 1967, MS, 1968. Prin. researcher System Devel. Corp., Santa Monica, Calif., 1975-80; dir. devel. Burroughs Corp., Danbury, Conn., 1980-82; dir. engring. Timex Corp., Waterbury, Conn., 1982-86, v.p. research and devel., 1986—. Author: Means for Database Search, 1980, Electronic Spelling Correction, 1981; patentee in field. Warden Trinity Episcopal Ch., Newtown, Conn., 1985-89. Comdr. USN, 1969-75. Mem. IEEE, Soc. for the History of Tech. Republican. Avocations: flying, racquetball, chess. Home: 141 Brushy Hill Rd Newtown CT 06470-2514 Office: Timex Corp PO Box 0310 Middlebury CT 06762-0310

GALIEV, SHAMIL USMANOVISH, mechanical engineer, researcher; b. Kazan, Tartar Republic, Apr. 18, 1942; s. Usman Zakirovich and Assar Hairutdinovna (Valitova) G.; m. Tamara Gatovna Valliulina, Nov. 21, 1972; children: Timur, Murat. BSc, MSc, Kazan U., 1964; PhD, Leningrad U., 1971; DSc (hon.), Kiev U., 1978. Rschr. Acad. Scis. of SSSR, Kazan, 1965-72; rschr. Acad. Scis. Ukraine, Kiev, 1972-81, head dept., 1981-95; prof. Kiev Politech. U., 1986-89; vis. prof. Brown U., Providence, 1992, Auckland U., N.Z., 1996—. Author: Dynamics of Hydroelastoplastic Systems, 1981 (Award of Acad. Sci. Ukraine 1985), Non-Linear Waves in Bounded Media, 1988; contbr. articles on structural dynamics and nonlinear wave theory to sci. jours. Office: Univ of Auckland, 20 Symonds St Pvt Bag 92019, Auckland New Zealand

GALIMA, LORETA VIVIAN B. RAMEL, educator; b. Cubao, The Philippines, Oct. 15, 1954; d. Arsenio Taberna and Marita (Beltran) Ramel; m. Lay Ciriaco Danguilan Galima, Dec. 10, 1977; children: Lay Kingston, Lay Voltaire. BA, U. of the Philippines, 1974, MA in Asian Studies, 1988, PhD, 1997. Grad. asst. U. of the Philippines, 1975-76, rsch. asst., 1976-77; instr. Nueva Vizcaya State Inst. Tech., Bayombong, The Philippines, 1980-89; asst. prof. Nueva Vizcaya State Inst. Tech., Bayombong, 1989-92, assoc. prof., 1992—; Editl. cons. Solano Pioneer Press, Inc., The Philippines, 1977-95, cons., 1995-99; bd. dirs. Nueva Vizcaya State Inst. Tech. Faculty Assn., 1998-2000. Columnist Vizcaya Advocate, 1978-91. Officer Asian Ctr. Alumni Assn., Up Diziman, 1997-98; founding mem. Vizcaya chpt. Zonta, 1997; treas. Assn. Philippines Coll. Arts and Scis., 1999. Mem. Women's Studies Assn. of the Philippines. Avocations: cross stitching, gardening, surfing the net, writing poetry, reading. Home: 166 Magsaysay St, Solano 3709, The Philippines Office: Nueva Vizcaya State Inst, Bayombong 3700, The Philippines

GALINA, SHEETIKOFF, plastic artist, watercolor painter; b. Tashauz, Turkestan, Russia, Apr. 8, 1933; arrived in Brazil, 1949; d. Vadim and Galina (Onischenko) Elman; m. George Nicolas Sheetikoff, May 18, 1958; children: Helena, Marina. Ed., Espade, Sao Paulo, Brazil, 1968, Panam. Paulista Belas Artes, Sao Paulo, 1969-73; ed. in painting and art history, U.S., Can., Brazil, 1973-96. Registered autonomous profl. art. Artist, tchr., condr. workshops Sao Paulo, 1972—; artist guest of honor Brazil Watercolor Show, Mexico City, 1996; invited artist for Brazil, Internat. Watercolor II Biennial, Mex. Nat. Mus. of Watercolor, Mexico City, 1996. Exhibited in over 220 art shows including Brazil Watercolor Show, Mexico City, 1996, Nat. Mus. Watercolor, 1996, 2000, Ctr. Culturel Jacques Brel, Thionville, France, 1998; group shows in Europe, U.S., Mex., Brazil. Recipient over 50 awards including: 15 Grand prizes and Gold medals Brazil Internat. Art Shows, 1976—, 9 Silver medals Brazil Art Shows, 1976—, numerous pvt. and pub. awards. Mem. Smithsonian Instn., UNESCO Assn. Profl. Artists, Nat. Geographic Soc. Avocation: gardening. Fax: 55-11-535-5037. E-mail: galina@amcham.com.br. Home: Av Cotovia 335, 04517001 São Paulo Brazil

GALINDO-SANCHEZ, ANGEL, engineering company executive, educator; b. Valladolid, Spain, Apr. 2, 1969; s. Angel Galindo-Garrote and Maria Isabel Sanchez-Rodriguez. MS in Indsl. Engring., U. Valladolid, 1996, M in Total Quality Mgmt., 1997, M in Occupl. Safety, 1999, postgrad., 1999—. Ast. tchr. EAFIT U., Medellin, Colombia, 1995; indsl. engr. Madrid, 1996-97; gen. mgr. Ascensores Galindo, Valladolid, 1997—; tchr. ESCAL-European Bus. Sch., Valladolid, 1999—, prodn. tech. tchr., 1999—; freelance safety cons., Valladolid, 1998—; bus. mgmt. rschr. U. Valladolid, 1997—. Contbr. articles to profl. jours. Mem. Engrs. Without Borders, Valladolid, 1996, Drs. Without Borders, Barcelona, 1997, Amnesty Internat., Madrid, 1998. Mem. N.Y. Acad. Scis., Sys. Dynamics Soc., Spanish Assn. Artificial Intelligence. Avocations: travel, literature, music, sports. Home: Camino Del Rio 6, 47270 Cigales, Valladolid Spain Office: Ascensores Galindo SL, Nueva de Diez Metros 9, 47008 Valladolid Spain

GALINOWSKI, ANDRE JEAN, psychiatrist; b. Paris, Apr. 12, 1951; s. Jan Galinowski and Krystyna Leliwa Ptaszynska; m. Laurence Madeleine Ruf, Sept. 7, 1979; children: Jean, Anne-Charlotte, Alexandra. MA, Sorbonne U., 1976; MD, U. Paris XII, 1979, diploma in psychiatry, 1988; MSc, U. Paris VI, 1986. Resident in psychiatry Ottawa (Ont., Can.) U., 1979-81; physician European Parliament, Luxembourg, 1984-85; chief clinic Cochin Med. Sch. U. Paris VI, 1986-90; rsch. psychiatrist St. Anne Hosp., Paris, 1990—; cons. to drug cos., France, 1990—. Co-author: Encyclopedia: Dictionnaire Larousse de Psychologie, 1991, Etudes sur la Dépression, 1991, Encyclopedie Medico-Chirurgicale, 1992, 2d edit., 1995; contbr. numerous articoes to profl. jours. Officer French Med. Svc., 1977-79. Mem. Assn. Française de Psychiatrie Biologique. Office: Hôpital Sainte-Anne, 1 rue Cabanis, 75014 Paris France

GALINSKY, DEBORAH JEAN, county official; b. Oakland, Calif., Jan. 22, 1951; d. Jerome James and Barbara Ann (Ball) G.; m. William H. Furr III, Sept. 27, 1997; 1 child by previous marriage, Lauren Rachel Lipscomb. BSW, Bowie State U., 1978. Cert. housing counselor. Substitute tchr. Anne Arundel County Schs., Ft. Meade, Md., 1972-74; addictions counselor Dept. of Health, Ellicott City, Md., 1977-78; coord. dept. Citizens Svcs., housing program specialist Housing and Cmty. Devel., Ellicott City, 1979; coord. youth teen devel. County of Howard, Ellicott City, 1978—; tchr. Rapides Parish Sch. Bd., Pineville, La., 1996—, arts and crafts youth tchr., 1997; rep. Inter-Agy. Com., Ellicott City, 1990-93; computer instr. Aerie; tchr. Cabrini Sch., Alexandria, La. Author homeownership programs. Vol. Bethany United Meth. Ch., Ellicott City, 1987; tchr. Woodland Presbyn. Ch., Pineville. Fellow Nat. Assn. Housing and Revel. Ofcls.; mem. Nat. Fedn. Housing Counselors, Assn. Cmty. Svcs. (counselors rep.). Democrat. Avocations: dance choreographing, creative art crafts, water aerobics, bicycling, camping. Home: 2228 Marye St Alexandria LA 71301-5241 Office: County of Howard Housing & Comm Devel Dept 3450 Court House Dr Ellicott City MD 21043-4330

GALIS, ZORINA SIMONA, medical researcher, biology educator,; b. Cluj-Napoca, Romania, Nov. 1, 1958; came to the U.S., 1992; d. Ilie and Maria Zorina Zdroba; div.; 1 child, Victor Horia. MSc in Biophysics, U. Bucharest, Romania, 1982; PhD in Pathology, McGill U., Montreal, Can., 1992. Rsch. fellow Inst. Cellular Biology and Pathology, Bucharest, 1984-87, sr. investigator, 1987-88; rsch. fellow vascular medicine Harvard U. Sch. Medicine, Boston, 1992-93, rsch. assoc., 1993-95; asst. prof. medicine Emory U. Sch. Medicine, Atlanta, 1995—; adj. asst. prof. biology Ga. Inst. Tech., Atlanta, 1996—; asst. prof. biomed. engring. Emory-Ga. Tech., Atlanta, 1999—; mem. peer rev. com. NIH. Reviewer Circulation, Circulation Rsch., Am. Jour. Pub. Health; contbr. chpts. to books and articles to profl. jours. Recipient Young Investigator award Can. Atherosclerosis Soc., 1993. Mem. Am. Heart Assn. (mem. peer rev. com., established investigator 2000), Am. Soc. for Cell Biology, N.Am. Vascular Biology Orgn. Avocations: rowing, water sports, arts, gourmet cooking, traveling. E-mail: zgalis@emory.edu. Office: Emory U Sch Medicine 1639 Pierce Dr Atlanta GA 30322-0001

GALITZINE, GEORGES PIERRE, company executive; b. Paris, Dec. 20, 1931; s. Alexandre and Olga Galitzine; m. Catherine de Schulthess Rechberg; children: Pierre, Cyril. H.E.C., Insead-Stanford advanced mgmt. program. Mgr. Au Printemps, Paris, 1955-75; pres. bd. AAF La Providence, Paris, 1976—. Lodge: Rotary. Home: 12 rue d'Angigné, 75116 Paris France Office: AAF La Providence SAS, 167 Blvd de la Villette, 75010 Paris France

GALKIN, NICKOLAY GENNADIY, physicist, educator, researcher; b. Vladivostok, Russia, Dec. 1, 1953; s. Gennadiy Nickolay and Elena Kouzma (Golovacheva) G.; m. Natalia Stepan Fomina, June 7, 1980; children: Anna, Konctantin. Degree in engring./physics, Moscow Inst. Elec. Technique, 1977; PhD in Physics and Math., Russian Acad. Scis., Vladivostok, 1990. Jr. rschr. Inst. Automation and Control Processes-Russian Acad. Scis., Vladivostok, 1977-85, rschr., 1985-90, sr. rschr., 1990-95, head lab., 1995—; sr. tchr. Far Ea. State U., Vladivostok, 1989-97; reader, 1997—; head joint lab. Far Ea. State Tech. U., Vladivostok, 1995—. Contbr. articles to profl. jours. Avocations: photography, joiner's works, walking tours. E-mail: galkin@iacp.vl.zu. Office: Inst Auto Control Process, Radio Str 5, 690041 Vladivostok Primorie, Russia

GALKIN, SAMUEL BERNARD, orthodontist; b. Newark, Feb. 9, 1933; s. Saul J. and Mollie (Kleinberg) G.; children from previous marriage: Jamie Michelle, Richard Stewart; m. Gail Beth Elkin, Feb. 26, 1972; children: Scott David, Seth Paul. Student, U. Conn., 1951-54; DDS, Temple U., 1958; MS in Histology, U. Ill., 1963, cert. grad. orthodontics, 1963; cert. in craniomandibular disorders, U. Medicine and Dentistry of N.J., 1989. Diplomate Am. Bd. Orthodontics. Group practice orthodontics Woodbridge, N.J., 1963—; staff orthodontist J.F.K. Community Hosp., Edison, N.J., 1966—, with cleft palate com., 1971—, dir. dental dept., 1979—; staff Woodbridge Health Ctr., 1967—, with dental adv. com., 1971—; dir. dept. dentistry John F. Kennedy Med. Ctr., Edison, 1979-81; staff orthodontist Perth Amboy (N.J.) Gen. Hosp., 1986—, dir. dept. dentistry, 1990—; staff orthodontist Rahway Hosp., N.J., 1986—; asst. prof. orthodontics N.J. Coll. Medicine and Dentistry, Jersey City, 1963-73; mem. panel physicians N.J. Crippled Children Program, 1971—; dentist Woodbridge Twp. Sch., 1989—. Chmn., Woodbridge Twp. Debutante Ball, 1970; bd. dirs. Woodbridge Twp. YMCA. Lt. Dental Corps, USN, 1958-61. Mem. ADA, Mid. Atlantic Soc. Orthodontists (chmn. clinics 1969-72), N.J. Dental Soc., Middlesex County Dental Soc., Am. Soc. Dentistry for Children, Am. Assn. Orthodontists, Am. Lingual Orthodontic Assn. (charter), Am. Assn. Dental Schs., Am. Acad. Head, Neck, Facial Pain and TMJ Orthopedics, N.E. Craniomandibular Soc., N.J. Craniomandibular soc. (charter), Am. Acad. Orofacial Pain, Am. Acad. Oral Medicine, Alpha Omega (chpt. v.p. 1969—), Omicron Kappa Upsilon. Home: 3 Dorset Rd Colonia NJ 07067-3101 Office: 711 Amboy Ave Woodbridge NJ 07095-3139 also: 233 Madison Ave Perth Amboy NJ 08861-4306

GALKIN, VSEVOLOD ALEXANDROVICH, internist, medical facility administrator; b. Moscow, Feb. 8, 1928; s. Alexander Petrovich and Elizaveta Petrovna (Erpylyova) G.; m. Olga Lipotova, Mar., 1954 (div. 1969); 1 child, Tatiana; m. Galina Dmitrievna Doukhovlinova, Apr. 29, 1971; children: Elizaveta, Pyotr. Gen. practitioner, 1st Moscow Med. Inst., 1949, MD, 1966, prof., 1969; academician, Russian Acad. Natural Scis., Moscow, 1991; scientist (hon.), Russian Fedn., Moscow, 1979; prof. (hon.), Moscow Med. Acad., 1999. Gen. practitioner Yakutsk Marine Clinic, Irkutsk, USSR, 1949-50; mil. physician Mil. Forces, Moscow, 1950-52; asst. prof. therapy 1st Moscow Med. Inst., 1952-65; chief gen. pracititoner mil. svc. Com. State Security, Moscow, 1965-67, chief dep. scientific coun., chmn. healthcare ministry, 1967-73; prof., chief therapy dept. Moscow Med. Acad., Russia, 1980—; chief therapeutical clin. dept. Royal Army of Yemen, Sana, 1960-61; leading gen. practitioner Anticholera Hosp., Gouriyev, Kazakhstan, 1970; cons. prof., constrn. Baikal-Amourskaya R.R., 1975-80; cons. prof. Ctrl. Mil. Hosp., Afghanistan, 1986; participant numerous internat. scientific events, including Switzerland, India, Sweden, Japan; invited lectr. univs. Poland, Cuba, Tunisia, Israel, U.K.; med. cons. China, Vietnam, Bulgaria. Author: Doctor in the Way, 1980, (textbook) Internal Diseases (silver medal 1989), (monograph) Chronic Cholecystitis, 1986 (gold medal 1988). Rector Pub. U. Med. Knowledge, Moscow, 1967-73. Col., Med. Mil. Svc., Moscow, 1980—. Decorated Def. of Moscow medal, Labor Valor Order (USSR), 50 Yrs. of Victory medal (Russia). Mem. Internat. Gastroenterologists Soc., Soc. Friendship Union (v.p. 1971-98), Russian Orthodox Palestinian Soc., Journalists Union Russia. Russian Orthodox. Avocations: documentary journalism, prose, travel. E-mail: egalkina@cityline.ru. Home: 2-90 Novodevichy St, 119435 Moscow Russia Office: Moscow Med Sechenov Acad, 2/6 B Pirogovskaya, 119881 Moscow Russia

GALL, ERIC PAPINEAU, physician, educator; b. Boston, May 24, 1940; s. Edward Alfred and Phyllis Hortense (Rivard) G.; m. Katherine Theiss, Apr. 20, 1968; children: Gretchen Theiss Gall, Michael Edward. AB, U. Pa., 1962, MD, 1966. Asst. instr. U. Pa., Phila., 1970-71, post doctoral trainee, fellow, 1971-73; asst. prof. U. Ariz., Tucscon, 1973-78, assoc. prof., 1978-83, prof. internal medicine, 1983-94, prof. surgery, 1983-94, prof. family/community medicine, 1983-94, chief rheumatology allergy and immunology, 1983-93, dir. arthritis ctr., 1986-94; Herman Finch Univ. of Health Scis. prof. of medicine The Chgo. Med. Sch., North Chicago, Ill., 1994—, prof. microbiology and immunology, 1994—, chmn. dept. medicine, 1994—, chief rheumatology sect., 1994-98, assoc. dean clin. affairs, 1996-97; dir. metabolic bone unit The Chgo. Med. Sch., North Chicago, 1998—. Author, editor: Rheumatoid Arthritis: Illustrated Guide to Path DX and Management of

Rheumatoid Arthritis, 1988, Rheumatic Disease: Rehabilitation and Management, 1984, Primary Care, 1984; editor Clin. Care in The Rhematic Diseases, 1996; contbr. numerous articles to profl. jours. Chmn. med. and scientific com. Arthritis Found., Tucson, 1979-81. Maj. M.C., U.S. Army; Vietnam. Decorated Bronze Star; recipient Addie Thomas Nat. Svc. award Arthritis Found., 1988. Fellow ACP (coun. Ill. chpt. 1995—), Am. Coll. Rheumatology (founding chair ednl. materials com. 1986-89, bd. dirs. 1992-95, chmn. rehab. sect. 1992-95), Chgo. Inst. Medicine; mem. AMA (rep. sect. on med. schs. 1995—), Arthritis Health Professions Assn. (nat. pres. 1982-83), Am. Assn. Med. Colls., Am. Fedn. Clin. Rsch., Inst. Medicine of Chgo., Ctrl. Soc. Clin. Investigation, Arthritis Found. (nat. vice chmn. 1982-83, chmn. profl. edn. com. 1996—, chmn. ednl. materials com. 1991-96, blue ribbon com. on qualty of life, bd. trustees Greater Chgo. chpt. 1997—, exec. com. 1998—), Assn. Profs. Medicine (bd. dirs.), Ill. Med. Soc., Lake County Med. Soc. (treas. 1998-99, sec. 2000—), Sigma Xi, Alpha Omega Alpha (regional counselor 1998—), Alpha Epsilon Delta. Avocations: photography, fishing. Office: The Chgo Med Sch Dept Medicine 3333 Green Bay Rd North Chicago IL 60064-3037

GALL, FRANCOIS, television executive producer; b. St. Germain, Ile de France, France, Nov. 9, 1922; s. Adolphe and Hemon (Suzan) G. Correspondent French Press, Indochina, 1948-50; correspondent freelance, 1951-56; reporter France Soir newspaper, Paris, 1956-68; TV producer French TV, Paris, 1968—; author free lance, 1954—. Author: numerous novels. Served in French Resistance Movement 1942-44, 2nd lt. First French Army, 1944-45, ETO. Roman Catholic. Home: 43 rue St Merri, 75004 Paris France Office: France 2TV Channel, Esplanade Henri de France, 75907 Paris Cedex 15 France

GALL, JEAN-CLAUDE, education educator; b. Hoenheim, Alsace, France, May 19, 1936; s. Alphonse and Therese (Wetzel) G.; m. Elfriede Stephanie Weber, Aug. 17, 1968. M Natural History, U. Strasbourg, France, 1959; Agregation Natural History, France, 1961; D Geology, U. Strasbourg, France, 1971; D Hon. Causa, U. Cluj, Rumania, 1993. Asst. prof. U. Strasbourg, France, 1960-67, miatre-asst., 1968-78, prof., 1978—; pres. Acad. of Alsace, France, 1996—. Author: (books) Paleoecology, 1976 (Soc. Geologique France award 1977), Fauna and Environments of Buntsandstein, 1971 (Acad. des Scs. Paris award 1973), Paleoecology, 1995, 98. Decorated Palmes Acad. Ministere Nat. Edn., 1981. Mem. Soc. Geologique de France, Geologische Vereinigung, European Palaeontol. Assn. (pres. 1991-95). Roman Catholic. Avocation: photography. Office: Univ Louis Pasteur, Inst Geologie/ 1 Rue Blessg, 67084 Strasbourg France

GALL, LENORE ROSALIE, educational administrator; b. Bklyn., Aug. 9, 1943; d. George W. Gall and Olive Rosalie (Weekes) Gall Bryant. AAS, NYU, 1970, cert. tng. and devel., 1975, BS in Mgmt., 1973, MA in Counselor Edn., 1977; EdM, EdD, Columbia U., 1988. Various positions Ford Found., N.Y.C., 1967-75; dep. dir. career devel. Grad. Sch. Bus., NYU, N.Y.C., 1976-79; dir. career devel. Pace Lubin Sch. Bus., N.Y.C., 1979-82, Sch. Mgmt., Yale U., New Haven, 1982-85; asst. to assoc. provost Bklyn. Coll., 1985-88, asst. to provost, 1988-91; asst. to v.p. acad. affairs Fashion Inst. Tech., 1991-94; asst. provost curriculum and instrn. N.Y.C. Tech. Coll., 1994-2000, dean students and acad. svcs., 2000—; adj. asst. prof. LaGuardia C.C., L.I. City, N.Y., 1981—, Sch. Continuing Edn. NYU, 1983-84; dir., sec. devel. workshop Coll. Placement Svcs., Bethlehem, Pa., 1978-81. Bd. dirs. Langston Hughes Cmty. Libr., Corona, N.Y., 1975-83, 86-92, chair, 1975-79, 82-83, 89-92, 2d v.p., 1986, 1st v.p., 1987-88, chair awards com. Dollars for Scholars, Corona, 1976-99, pres., 1999; active audience devel. task force Dance Theatre of Harlem, 1992-98, hon. co-chmn., 1994-95; active alumni coun. Tchrs. Coll., Columbia U. Recipient Concerned Women of Bklyn., Inc., 1994; grantee Jewish Fedn. for the Edn. of Women, 1986-87. Mem. AAUW, Assn. Black Women in Higher Edn. (exec. bd., membership chair, pres.-elect 1988, pres. 1989-93), Am. Assn. Univ. Adminstrs., Nat. Assn. Univ. Women (chaplain 1987-88, 2d v.p. 1988, 1st v.p. 1988-92, dir. N.E. sect. 1993-96, nat. 2d v.p. 1996-98, nat. first v.p. 2000), Nat. Assn. Women in Edn., Black Faculty and Staff Assn. Bklyn. Coll. (1st vice-chair 1986-87, chair 1987-88), New Haven C. of C. (chmn. women bus. and industry conf. 1984), Nat. Coun. Negro Women Inc. (life, 1st v.p. North Queens sect. 1986-89, pres. 1989-93), Nat. Assn. Negro Bus. & Profl. Women's Club (Sojourner Truth award 1991), Phi Delta Kappa, Kappa Delta Pi, Pi Lambda Theta, Delta Sigma Theta. Mem. A.M.E. Ch. Office: NYC Tech Coll 300 Jay St Brooklyn NY 11201-1909

GALLAGHER, BRIAN JOHN, lawyer; b. Bklyn., Oct. 24, 1939; s. John Joseph and Margaret R. Gallagher; m. Mary Loughney, Sept. 10, 1966; children: Amanda, Ian. BSS, Fairfield U., 1961; JD, Fordham U., 1964; postgrad., NYU Law Sch., 1969-70. Bar: N.Y. 1965, U.S. Dist. Ct. (so. dist.) N.Y. 1967, U.S. Ct. Appeals (2d cir.) 1971, U.S. Dist. Ct. (ea. dist.) N.Y. 1974, U.S. Ct. Appeals (11th cir.) 1982, U.S. Ct. Appeals (D.C. cir.) 1986. Asst. U.S. Atty. So. Dist. N.Y., 1967-71; ptnr. Kronish, Lieb, Weiner & Hellman, LLP, N.Y.C., 1976—. Mayor Village of Pelham Manor, N.Y., 1995-97, trustee, 1989-95. Mem. ABA, N.Y. State Bar Assn., Assn. Bar City N.Y., Fed. Bar Coun., Larchmont (N.Y.) Yacht Club, Williams Club, N.Y. Athletic Club. Office: 1114 Avenue Of The Americas New York NY 10036-7703

GALLAGHER, BYRON PATRICK, JR., lawyer; b. Bay City, Mich., Feb. 29, 1964; s. Byron Patrick and Ethel Jean (Gebowski) G.; m. Michelle Francis Burdick, May 21, 1994; 1 child, Byron Patrick III. AB, Kenyon Coll., Gambier, Ohio, 1986; JD, Washington U., St. Louis, 1989. Bar: Mich. 1989, U.S. Dist. Ct. (we. dist.) Mich. 1990, U.S. Dist. Ct. (ea. dist.) Mich. 1995. Ptnr. Gallagher Duby, PLC, Lansing, 1998—. Bd. dirs. Ingham County Social Svc. Bd., Mason, Mich., 1991-92, Ingham County Commn., Mason, 1993-97, Mich. Underground Storage Tank Fin. Assurance Authority, 1996—; Rep. cand. Mich. State Senate, 1998. Mem. Ingham County Bar Assn. (bd. dirs. 1996-99), County Club of Lansing, Mich. Athletic Club. Republican. Avocations: flying, golf. Home: 1203 Hillgate Way Lansing MI 48912-5014 Office: Gallagher Duby PLC 2510 Kerry St Ste 210 Lansing MI 48912-3671

GALLAGHER, DERMOT A., Irish diplomat; b. County Leitrim, Ireland, 1945. 1st sec. Irish Embassy, London, 1973-77; counsellor fgn. dept. Dublin, 1977-81; dep. chief of cabinet Commn. European Cmtys., 1981-82; counsellor Fgn. Dept., Dublin, 1983-85; amb. to Nigeria, 1985-87; asst. sec. for Anglo-Irish affairs Fgn. Dept., 1987-91; amb. to U.S. Washington, 1991-97; also amb. to Mex., 1991-97; 2d sec. Anglo Irish, press and info. divsn. Dept. Fgn. Affairs, Dublin, 1997—. Office: Dept Fgn Affairs, 80 St Stephens Green, Dublin 2, Ireland*

GALLAGHER, GERARD JAMES, maritime legal practitioner, educator, researcher; b. Glasgow, Scotland, Oct. 16, 1954; s. James and Mary (Hilferty) G.; m. Maria Esperanza Caro; children: Andrew Robert, Allyson Marie. Student, L.A. Trade Tech., 1972, L.A. City Coll., 1973-74, Immaculate Heart Coll., 1974-76, UCLA, 1976-78. Accredited to practice maritime law as legal practitioner before Fed. Maritime Commn. From practitioner to sr. ptnr. maritime law Maritime Consultants Internat., Washington, L.A., London,, Scotland, 1975—; cons. in transport and arbitration. Contbr. over 300 articles to profl. jours. Mem. Internat. Bar Assn., The Law Soc., London Maritime Arbitration Assn., Fed. Maritime Commn. (practitioner), and other maritime law assns. Avocations: golf, travelling, soccer, sailing. Office: Maritime Consultants Inter, PO Box 1497, Largs Ayrshire KA30 9NN, Scotland

GALLAGHER, JEROME FRANCIS, JR., lawyer; b. Passaic, N.J., Sept. 16, 1958; s. Jerome F. and Iris (Torres) G.; m. Deirdre O. Stewart, Sept. 27, 1992; children: Nicholas, Colin, Caroline. BS in Man and Tech. with distinction, N.J. Inst. Tech., Newark, 1980; JD, Rutgers U., Newark, 1983. Bar: N.J. 1983, U.S. Dist. Ct. N.J. 1983, U.S. Ct. Appeals (3d cir.) 1994. Assoc. Shanley & Fisher, P.C., Morristown, N.J., 1983-84, Dunn, Pashman, Sponzilli, Swick & Finnerty, Esq., Hackensack, N.J., 1984-90; ptnr. Baron, Gallagher & Perzley, Esq., Parsippany, N.J., 1990-99, Greiner Gallagher & Cavanaugh LLC, Parsippany, N.J., 1999—; mem. adv. coun. civil and environ. engrng. dept. N.J. Inst. Tech., 1999—. Adv. bd. mem. N.J. Inst. Tech. Civil and Environ. Engrng. dept.; panelist Lorman N.J. Collections Practice Seminar, 2000; mem. St. Mary's H.S. Assn., Wharton, N.J., 1993-95, 2000—. Mem. N.J. State Bar Assn., Bergen County Bar Assn., Comml. Law League Am. E-mail: jerrygal@grienergallagbrlaw.com. Office: Greiner Gallagher & Cavanaugh LLC 2001 Route 46 Ste 202 Parsippany NJ 07054-1315

GALLAGHER, KEVIN MICHAEL, writer, lyricist; b. Chgo., Feb. 27, 1956; s. William Joseph and Eileen Mary Gallagher. Assocs., Milw. Area Tech., 1995. Office temp Talent Tree, Chgo., 1986-89; mgr. Amoco Gas, Libertyville, Ill., 1978-86; lyricist Plato Zen, Chgo., 1989-99; writer D. Publs., Elgin, Ill., 1999—. With U.S. Army, 1975-78. Avocations: poetry, music, acting, working with the elderly. Home and Office: 1102 Wheeler Woodstock IL 60098

GALLAGHER, LINDY ALLYN, banker, financial consultant; b. Kalamazoo, Sept. 27, 1954; d. Karl P. Joslow and Audrey S. Phillips; m. Thomas J. Gallagher, Nov. 29, 1975; children: James Allyn Buckley, Phillip Graham, Charles Bedloe. BS, U. Pa., 1975; MBA, Columbia U., 1982. Mem. faculty, rschr. U. Pa., Phila., 1976-80; corp. banking officer Bank of Montreal, N.Y.C., 1982-84; v.p. Citibank NA, N.Y.C., 1984-89; v.p., mgr. Chase Manhattan Bank, N.Y.C., 1989-90; pres. The Allyn Co., New Canaan, Conn., 1990-99; prin. State Street Global Advs., 1999; pvt. fin. cons., 2000—; treas., dir. 957 Lexington Corp., 1981-87. Editor Columbia Jour. World Bus., 1980-82. Mem. Women's Nat. Rep. Club, 1986—; commr. Town of New Canaan, 1991-99; treas., sec. Young Women's League New Canaan, Inc., 1992-94. Mem. Stanwich Club, The Penn Club (N.Y.C.). Republican. Episcopalian.

GALLAGHER, THOMAS FRENCH, career officer, strategist; b. Centralia, Ill., July 23, 1939; s. Edgar French and Mary Maxine (Holmes) G.; m. Rebecca Agnes Belle Isle, June 6, 1963; children: Cheryl Ann Gallagher Lobb, Thomas French Jr. BS, U.S. Mil. Acad., 1963; MA, U. S.C., 1978. Commissioned U.S. Army, 1963, advanced through grades to col., 1985; facility engr. and readiness officer Safeguard Ballistic Missile Def. Complex, Nakoma, N.D., 1975-76; analyst Def. Intelligence Agy., Washington, 1978-81; sr. air def. advisor U.S. Mil. Tng. Mission to Saudi Arabia, Riyadh, 1981-82; staff officer Strategic Plans and Policy Div. U.S. Army, The Pentagon, Washington, 1982-85; dep. dir. Inst. for Nat. Strategic Studies Nat. Def. Univ., Washington, 1985-86, 88-90; dep. chief U.S. Mil. Tng. Mission to Saudi Arabia, Riyadh, 1986-88; acting dir. Inst. for Nat. Stragetic Studies Nat. Def. Univ., Washington, 1990; exec. dir. Nat. Def. Univ. Found., Washington, 1990—. Author: The Structure of Foreign Policy and Trade Relationships within North Africa, 1978; contbr. articles to profl. jours. Den leader Boy Scouts Am., Riyadh, 1986-87. Mem. Internat. Inst. for Strategic Studies, Internat. Studies Assn., Soc. of Gulf Arab Studies, Mid. East Studies Assn., Assn. of U.S. Mil. Acad. Grads. Republican. Episcopalian. Avocations: painting, woodworking, swimming, gardening. Home: 25 Misty Morning Dr Hilton Head Island SC 29926-2520 Office: Nat Def Univ Found Nat Def Univ Ft Mcnair Washington DC 20319-0001

GALLAHER, WILLIAM MARSHALL, dental laboratory technician; b. Philipsburg, Pa., June 10, 1952; s. Marshall William and Florence Marie (Millner) G. Degree in Dental Tech., Hiram G. Andrews Ctr., 1971; BS, Rutgers U., 1979. Cert. dental technician in full dentures. Dental lab. technician to pvt. practice dentist Osceola Mill, Pa., 1971-72; dental lab. technician Profl. Dental Lab., South Amboy, N.J., 1972-79; instr. dental lab. tech. Union Tech. Inst., Neptune, N.J., 1979-84, Hiram G. Andrews Ctr., Johnstown, Pa., 1980-91; owner Gallaher's Dental Lab., Asbury Park, N.J., 1982-90; sr. dental lab. technician Denture Walk-In Ctr., Harrisburg, Pa., 1991—; adv. bd. Union Tech. Inst., 1984-90, Hiram G. Andrews Ctr., 1991-92; founder, pres. Person Enjoying New and Innovative Software User Group, Asbury Park, 1985-90. Author instrnl. manuals. Vol. deaf svcs. Monmouth County Deaf Group, Asbury Park, 1976-77; publicity chmn. Neighbor Preservation Program, Asbury Park, 1979-82. Mem. Nat. Dental Lab. Assn., Nat. Denturist Soc., N.J. Denturist Soc., Pa. Denturist Assn., Indian Tribal Denturity Assn., Internat. Brotherhood Magicians, Internat. Magicians Soc. (life), Masons (sr. master of ceremonies 1982—). Achievements include research on low-cost denture procedures, cleft palate and post cancerous intra-oral appliances. Home: 1912 N 3rd St Harrisburg PA 17102-1855 Office: Denture Walk In Ctr 2023 N 2nd St Harrisburg PA 17102-2103

GALLANT, MAVIS, author; b. Montreal, Que., Can., Aug. 11, 1922. Hon. doctoral degree, U. St. Anne, N.S., Can., 1984, York U., Toronto, 1984, U. Western Ont., 1990; hon. doctoral degree, Queen's U., 1992, U. Montreal, 1995, Bishop's U., 1995. Writer-in-residence U. Toronto, 1983-84. Author: Green Water, Green Sky, 1959, 60, A Fairly Good Time, 1970; short stories The Other Paris, My Heart Is Broken: 8 Stories and a Short Novel (Brit. title An Unmarried Man's Summer), 1964, The Affair of Gabrielle Russier; introductory essay, 1971; The Pegnitz Junction, a Novella and Five Short Stories, 1973, The End of the World and Other Stories, 1974; short stories From the Fifteenth District, 1979, Home Truths, 1981, Overhead in a Balloon, 1985; play What Is To Be Done? (produced Toronto 1982), 1984, Paris Notebooks: Essays and Reviews, 1986, (short stories) In Transit, 1989, (short stories) Across the Bridge, 1993; The Moslem Wife and other stories, 1994, Collected Stories, 1996; contbr. to New Yorker, 1951—. Decorated Order of Can.; recipient Gov.-Gen.'s Lit. award, 1982, Molson award, 1997, Medaille de la Ville de Paris, 1999. Fellow Royal Soc. Lit.; fgn. hon. mem. Am. Acad. and Inst. Arts and Letters. Home: 14 rue Jean Ferrandi, Paris 75006, France

GALLARDO, HUGO SEGUNDO, oil company executive; b. Cordoba, Argentina, Oct. 9, 1956; s. Hugo Santos and Nelly Edith (Luque) G.; children: Rosario, Guadalupe, Pilar, Camila. Engr., Buenos Aires U., 1980; PhD in Bus. Adminstrn., Belgrano Univ., 1986. Maintenance supr. Esso Sapa, Campana, Argentina, 1980-81, planning analyst, 1981-87, system coord., 1987-88; internal auditor Exxon Corp., Buenos Aires, 1988-91; process and control advisor Esso Sapa, Buenos Aires, 1991-92, asst. controller, 1992-96, projects mgr., 1997—, adminstrn. and control mgr., 1997—; pres. bd. OSDIPP/Health Care Co., 2000—; pres. bd. dirs. OSDIPP/Health Care Co., 2000. Roman Catholic. Avocations: sports, reading, climbing. Home: 11 de Septiembre 2145, 5 Piso B, 1428 Buenos Aires Argentina Office: ExxonMobil Esso Sapa, Della Paolera 297, 1001 Buenos Aires Argentina

GALLARDO, ROBERTO BALTAZAR, shipping industry executive, consultant; b. Manila, June 2, 1956; arrived in Taiwan, 1987.; s. Bartolome L. Gallardo and Felicitas T. Baltazar; m. Mercedes Arevalo Ang, May 1974 (div. Apr. 1985); children: Rommer, Aloha, Cherryl; m. Mo Hua Wang, June 27, 1987; children: Jolly, Julian. Student, Adamson U., Manila, 1973-75. H.D. driver Arabian Bechtel Co., Ltd., Saudi Arabia, 1979-82; data entry specialist Internat. Airport Projects, Jeddah, Saudi Arabia, 1982-87; dir. R.B.G. Mining Co., Ltd., The Philippines, 1988-91; owner J. Wang Shipchandlers Co., Ltd., Hualien City, Republic of China, 1991—; cons. Meii Chi Indsl. Co., Hualien, 1991-93. Roman Catholic. Avocations: guitar, chess, tennis, swimming, reading. Home: 21-1 Chung IH 2d St, Hualien Taiwan Office: J Wang Shipchandlers Co Ltd, 21-1 Chung Ih 2d St, Hualien Taiwan

GALLARDO LANCHO, JUAN FERNANDO, biogeochemist, soil science educator, ecologist; b. Caceres, Spain, Apr. 18, 1945; s. Fernando Gallardo Alvarez and Julia Lancho Moreno; m. Isabel Mercedes González Hernández, Mar. 15, 1975; children: Juan-Fernando, Alvaro-Federico, Isabel-Mercedes, Pablo Miguel. Degree in chemistry, U. Salamanca, 1969; DSc, U. Salamanca, Spain, 1973; D in Pedagogy, U. Nancy I, France, 1974; specialist in humic substances, Denver Geol. Survey, 1976. Rsch. fellow Spanish Ministry Edn., Salamanca, Nancy, 1969-75; prof. soil science U. Salamanca, 1970-78; scientist Higher Coun. Sci. Rsch., Salamanca, 1975—; Nat. Inst. Scientific Rsch. (I.N.I.C.) fellow, Portugal, 1988, 89; fellow Royal Soc. London, 1980, 91, Swedish Instn., Uppsala, 1989, Nat. Coun. Rschs. (C.N.R.), Italy, 1991, Nat. Coun. Scientific & Tech. Rschs., Argentina, 1989, 95, 96; Fulbright fellow U.S.-Spain Cultural Agreement, Denver, 1976, Polish Acad. Sci., 1990, 96; vice dir. Inst. Terrestrial Ecology (IET), Salamanca, 1991, dir. Inst. Natural Resources and Agrobiology (I.R.N.A.), Salamanca, 1987-90 ; rschr. in 6 scientific projects and 2 COST actions, European Union, Brussels; prof. U. Salamanca. Co-editor spl. issue of Arid Soil Research and Rehabilitation, 1995; editor: Soil and Soil Degradation in Relation to Desertification, 1993; co-author: Vegetal Biology, 1988 (selected by Scientific American), The Chestnut, 1998; contbr. over 170 articles to scientific jours. mem. social coun. U. Salamanca, 1985-90. Recipient awards Spanish Ministry Agr., 1981, Agrarian Assn., Salamanca, 1986, Fertiberia, 1998; recipient acad. honor Argentinian Acad. Environment, Buenos Aires, 1995. Mem. Internat. Symposium Environ. Biogeochemistry (ISEB), Internat. Humic Substance Soc., Internat. Soc. Soil Sci., L.Am. Soil Sci. Soc., Ibero Am. Soc. Chem. Environ. Avocation: music. Fax: 34 923219609. E-mail: jgallard@gugu.usal.es. Office: CSIC Aptado #257, Cordel de Merinas 40, 37071 Salamanca Spain

GALLEGO, STEPHANE, scientist, consultant; b. Lyon, France, Oct. 21, 1971; s. Jacques and Danielle (Brissaud) G. MS, Biomedical, Lyon, 1993, student, 1994, PhD, 1998. Cert. engr. Clin. rsch. mgr. MXM, Vallauris, 1998—; rsch. cons. CNRS Lab., Lyon, 1998—; scientist mgr. GAM Surdite. Home: 11 rue du printemps, 06160 Juan Les Pins France Office: CNRS Labs, 3 Pl d'Arsonval Hosp Ed, 69437 Lyon France

GALLEGOS, IGNACIO, international lawyer, educator; b. San José, Costa Rica, Dec. 31, 1963; s. Alvaro and Muriel Gallegos; m. Astrid Guier, Aug. 24, 1990. JD, U. Costa Rica, 1985; MA in Law and Diplomacy, Tufts U., Medford, Mass., 1990; Candidate PhD, U. Oxford (Eng.), 1990—. Assoc., legal asst. Zürcher, Montoya & Zürcher, San José, 1984-88; spl. counselor internat. legal and econ. affairs Embassy of Costa Rica to U.K., London, 1990-94; vis. lectr., rschr. Facultad Latinoamericana de Ciencias Sociales, Mexico City, 1992-93; prof. pub. internat. law, internat. econ. law Fgn. Svc. Inst., Ministry Fgn. Rels., San José, 1995—; lawyer, internat. polit. economy cons. Bufete, Odio & Raven, San José, 1995-98, ptnr., 1999—; cons. presidency of Ams. free trade area working group on investment Ministry Fng. Trade, San José, 995-97. Recipient Registrar's acad. scholarship, 1986, Fulbright scholarship, 1988-90, Falconer scholarship, 1990-93. Mem Costa Rican Bar Assn., Colegio de Abogados. Home: PO Box 1994-1000, San José Costa Rica Office: Bufete Odio & Raven, PO Box 5069-1000, San José Costa Rica

GALLEGOS, MARIA BENNINE, artist; b. July 30, 1960. BFA, U. Mont., 1998. Freelance illustrator Missoula, Mont., 1996—; spl. edn. aide Arlee (Mont.) Elem. Sch., 1996, Charlo (Mont.) Elem. Sch., 1998; resource aide Dixon (Mont.) Elem. Sch., 1998-99.

GALLENGA, PIER ENRICO, medical educator, researcher; b. Parma, Italy, May 13, 1943; s. Riccardo and Fernanda (Gioccani) G.; m. Maria Antonietta Salme, Sept. 18, 1996; children: Paolo Antonio, Pierfrancesco, Carla Enrica. MD, U. Turin, Italy, 1967. Tng. in ophthalmology, 1970; rschr. U. Ferrara, Italy, 1970-79; prof. U. Chieti, Italy, 1984—, dir. Inst. of Ophthalmology, 1979—; councillor Bank of Italy, Chieti, 1996—. Author: Ecografia Clinica dell'occhio e dell'orbita, 1971; editor-in-chief Internet Jour. Ophthalmology, 1995. Chmn. Nat. Fedn. Ethics Coms., 1995—. Decorated grand ufficiale Italian Republic; recipient Controcampo Culturale, Rome, 1984. Mem. Italian Intraocular Implant Club (pres. 1982-93), Internat. Club Biomaterials in Ophthalmology (v.p. 1991-94), Ultrasound Soc. in Ophthalmology (pres. 1984-88), Italian Soc. Ophthalmology (coun. 1997—), Am. Acad. Ophthalmology, Rotary (pres. 1992-93, 2000-2001). Avocations: skiing, chess, paintings. Office: Piazza Templi Romani, 66100 Chieti Italy

GALLETTI, GIOVANNI, medical educator, medical institute administrator; b. Ozzano Emilia, Bologna, Italy, Aug. 16, 1926; s. Cleto and Bianca (Martelli) G.; m. Anna Maria Recchioni; children: Paola Emilia, Marco Edoardo, Carla. Sci. maturity, Liceum Righi, Bologna, 1946; MD, U. Bologna, 1953. Intern Buffalo Gen. Hosp., 1953-54, resident in surgery, 1954-57; resident in pediat. surgery Buffalo Children's Hosp., 1957-58, fellow in pediat. surgery, 1958-59; fellow in cardiac surgery St. Michael Hosp., Newark, 1959-60; asst. prof. U. Bologna Med. Sch., 1960-69, clin. prof. surgery, 1969—, dir. Inst. Exptl. Surgery, 1972—. Author: Principles of Experimental Surgery, 1976, Lectures of Surgical Pathophysiology, 1993, 2nd revised edit., 1997, Lectures of Vascular Microsurgery, 1993; editor: (procs.) Laser, 1986, Laser in Medicine and Surgery, 1992. Recipient Gold medal Italian Automobile Club, Gold medal Italian Red Cross. Fellow ACS; mem. Societo Italiana di Chirurgia (counselor), World Soc. Laser, Russian Acad. Scis., N.Y. Acad. Scis. Avocations: human history, tennis, skiing. Home: Via S Stefano 82, 40125 Bologna Italy Office: Univ of Bologna Inst Exptl Surg, Via Massarenti 9, 40138 Bologna Italy

GALLIER, WILLIAM THOMAS, JR., water utility executive; b. Beaumont, Tex., Aug. 7, 1954; s. William Thomas Sr. and Marjorie Katherine G.; m. Linda Genine Young, Oct. 1979 (div. Jan. 1999); children: Juli Heather, Katarine Genine. BS, Lamar U., 1977, M in Pub. Adminstrn., 1983. Water prodn. mgr. City of Beaumont, Tex., 1979-84; pub. utilities dir. City of Castle Rock, Colo., 1984-86; wastewater reclamation mgr. City of Ft. Collins, Colo., 1986-94; wastewater divsn. mgr. City of Fresno, Calif., 1994-95; dep. pub. works dir./water City of Tempe, Az., 1995—. Contbr. author: (book) Yearbook of Science and Technology, 1996; contbr. articles to profl. jours. Fax: 480-350-8336. E-mail: tom gallier@tempe.gov. Office: City of Tempe PO Box 5002 Tempe AZ 85280-5002

GALLIERS, ROBERT DAVID, information scientist, educator; b. London, Feb. 21, 1947; s. William Hadland and Kathleen Ellen Mary (Stevens) G. AB cum laude, Harvard U., 1970; MA with distinction, Lancaster (Eng.) U., 1978; PhD, London (Eng.) Sch. Econs., 1987; DSc in Info. Mgmt. (hon.), Turku Sch. Econs., Bus. Admin., Finland, 1995. Adminstr. social svcs. London Boroughs' Tng. Com., 1970-74, London Borough of Wangsworth, 1974-77; mgmt. cons. Internat. Sys. Corp. of Lancaster (Eng.), Ltd., U. Lancaster, 1978-82; sr. vis. fellow Western Australian Inst. Tech. now Curtin Univ., Perth, Australia, 1982; head Sch. Info. Sys. Western Australian Inst. Tech. now Curtin Univ., Perth, 1983-89; Lucas prof. bus. sys. engring. Warwick (Coventry, Eng.) Bus. Sch., U. Warwick, 1989-00; dean, 1994-98; vis. prof. information systems INSEAD, France, 1998-99; prof. info. systems London Sch. of Econs., 2000—; vis. prof. knowledge mgmt. U. St. Gallen, Switzerland, 2000—. Author: Information Analysis, 1987, Information Systems Research: Issues, Methods & Practical Guidelines, 1992; co-author: Strategic Information Management: Challenges and Strategies in Managing Information Systems, 1994, 2nd edit., 1999, IT and Organizational Transformation, 1998, Re-Thinking Management Information Systems, 1999; editor-in-chief Jour. Strategic Infor. Sys., 1991—. Recipient Best Paper award Australian Computer Jour., Australian Computer Soc., 1987; Harvard Coll. scholar Harvard Coll., 1966-70. Fellow Brit. Computer Soc., Royal Soc. Arts, European Inst. Advanced Mgmt. Studies; mem. Watford Football Club (v.p. 1981-95), Brit. Acad. Mgmt. (mem. coun. 1997—), pres., Assn. for Information Systems, 1999. Avocations: French, Italian and Indian cuisine, sports, music, travel, photography. Office: Dept Info Sys LSE, Houghton St, London WC2A 2AE, England

GALLIMORE, MARGARET MARTIN, poet; b. Winston Salem, Mar. 20, 1947; d. Holland Henry and Dallas Cornell (Robbins) Martin; m. Elmer Harold Holden Jr., Feb. 14, 1965; children: Andrew Harold, Amy Darlene, John Alan; m. Timothy Milton Gallimore, May 9, 1986. Student, High Point (N.C.) Coll., 1988. With AT&T Network Sys., Winston-Salem, 1965-69, 73-75, prodn. operator, 1979-89; real estate salesperson Lambe-Young Real Estate Co., Kernersville, N.C., 1975-79; leasing cons. Vinyard Gardens Apts./S.E. Atlantic Properties, Winston-Salem, 1994-95; comm. assoc. AT&T Phone Ctr., Winston-Salem, 1995-96; real estate salesperson Triad Piedmont Properties, Kernersville, 1996; real estate broker Winston-Salem, 1996—; asst. cmty. mgr. Lindsey Manor Apts./Steven D. Bell & Co., Kernersville, 1997; ret., 1997. Author poetry. Recipient Editors Choice awards (2) Nat. Libr. of Poetry, 1995, 97; named to Internat. Poetry Hall of Fame, Nat. Libr. Poetry, 1996. Mem. Internat. Soc. Poets (Disting. mem.). Home: 2534 Union Cross Rd Winston Salem NC 27107-4420

GALLINA, PASQUALE, physician; b. Corigliano, Italy, Aug. 29, 1959; s. Francesco and Giuseppina (Garofalo) G.; m. Cristina Marinelli, Sept. 30, 19991; children: Francesco, Luciana. Diploma in Medicine/Surgery, U. Florence, Italy, 1984; Specialization in Neurosurgery, U. Florence, 1992. Medical diplomate. Resident vis. Espedale Hosp. S. Anne Hosp., Paris, 1990-91; scholarship vis. Neurosurgery Clin., Grenoble, France, 1992; asst. neurosurgeon Ospedale Salpetriere Hosp., France, 1993-94; asst. Neurosurgery Clin./U. Hosp., Florence, 1994—. Contbr. articles to profl. jours. Recipient scholarship Erasmus, Paris, 1990. Mem. European Stereo-

tactic Neurosurgery. Avocations: reading, fencing. Office: CTO, Largo B Palagi 1, 50139 Florence Italy

GALLIS, KOSTAS JOHN, archaeology educator; b. Volos, Magnesia, Greece, Feb. 18, 1938; s. John Kostas and Ann John (Vlacchoutsos) G.; m. Katerina Zervou; children: Jane, Irene, Eugenia. 1st degree in archaeology, Athens (Greece) U., 1961; postgrad., Inst. Archaeology, London, 1963-65; Doctoral degree, Athens U., 1980. Cert. in prehistoric archaeology. Sci. asst. Archaeol. Svc., Rhodes, Greece, 1965-66; tchr. h.s. Skopelos and Volos, Greece, 1967-70; curator of antiquities Archaeol. Svc., Larisa, Greece, 1970-80; ephor of antiquities, dir. mus. Archaeol. Svc., Larisa, 1980-95; prof. prehistoric archaeology Dem. U. of Thrace, Komotini, Greece, 1995—; participant archaeol. confs. Author: Neolithic Cremation Burials in Thessaly, 1982, Atlas of Prehistoric Sites in the Eastern Thessalian Plain, 1992; contbr. numerous articles to profl. jours. Fellow St. John's Coll., Cambridge, Eng., 1986, Inst. for Advanced Study, Ind. U., 1991; Schliemann rsch. grant scholar German Govt. on 100th anniversary, 1991. Mem. Archaeol. Soc. Athens, Greek Archaeologists's Assn. (v.p. of coun. 1981-83), German Archaeol. Inst. Greek Orthodox. Office: Democriteian U of Thrace Faculty of History & Ethnology, Panepistimioupolis, 69100 Komotini Greece

GALLIX, FRANÇCOIS, English literature educator; b. Paris, Mar. 1, 1939; s. Pierre and Andrée (Mouchard) Vincent; children: Andrew, Sophie, Delphine. Agrégation, Sorbonne U., Paris, 1972, D d'État, 1984. Asst. Paris-Sorbonne, 1977-85, sr. lectr., 1985-88, prof., 1988—; dir. studies Europalangues, Paris, 1984—. Editor: Letters to a Friend, 1981, 84, Saki: The Seven Cream Jugs and Other Stories, 1989, Ghost Stories, 1991, Kazuo Ishiguro. The Remains of the Day, 1999; author: T.H. White: An Annotated Bibliography, 1986, Pratique de la Traduction, 1991, Dictionnaire de é'analyse litteraire, 1999; translator: Contes étranges et Histoires fantastiques de T.H. White, 1987, The Loneliness of the Long Distance Runner by Alan Sillikoe, 1999. Home: 9 Rue de Douai, 75009 Paris France

GALLO, ANTHONY ERNEST, economist, playwright; b. Vandergrift, Pa., Feb. 3, 1939; s. Dominic and Sara (Raso) G.; divorced; 1 child, Thomas Augustus. BA, Coll. William and Mary, 1961; MBA, U. Pa., 1963; postgrad., U. Pitts., 1966-70. Investment analyst Pitts. Nat. Bank, 1963-66; instr. mktg. and stats. Duquesne U., Pitts., 1964-69; instr. mktg. U. Pitts., 1965-69; instr. money and banking St. Vincent Coll., Latrobe, Pa., 1966-69; asst. prof. econs. Allegheny C.C., Pitts., 1966-70; econ. cons. SBA, Washington, 1967—; bus. economist Bur. Econ. Analysis/U.S. Dept. Commerce, Washington, 1970-71; sr. economist Econ. Rsch. Svc./USDA, Washington, 1971—; propr. Capitol Hill Victorian Restorations, Washington, 1970-90. Econs. editor U.S. Food Mktg. Rev., 1984—; contbr. more than 400 articles to profl. and govt. jours. include Food Mktg. Sys., Impact of Race on Consumer Food Expenditures, Sr. Citizens, Food Expenditures and Assistance, Couponings Growth in Food Marketing. Mem. Capitol Hill Restoration Soc., Washington, 1972—, mem. endowment bd., 1999; mem Capitol Hill Garden Club, Washington, 1972—; commr. Vandergrift Mcpl. Authority, 1965-67; pres. Civic League, Vandergrift, 1965-70; mem. governing coun., endowment bd. Holy Rosary Ch. With U.S. Army, 1963. Named Outstanding Civic Leader, Jaycees, Vandergrift, 1967. Mem. Am. Agrl. Econs. Assn., Cosmos Club (endowment advisor 1996—), Arts Club Washington (endowment bd. 1996-99), Cheverly Swim and Racquet Club, John Carroll Soc., Thomas Merton Soc., Red Circle, U.S. Food Distbn. Rsch. Soc. (bd. dirs. 1994-97), Wharton Sch. Club (bd. dirs. 1991—), Italian Cultural Soc. (bd. dirs. 1994-97), Playwright's Forum, Writers Ctr., Washington Ind. Writers, Washington Screenwriter's Group. Roman Catholic. Avocations: reading, gardening, soccer-volleyball, historic preservation, bridge. Home: PO Box 15414 Washington DC 20003-0414

GALLO, FAUSTA MARIA, retired biologist, researcher; b. Rome, Nov. 11, 1931; d. Alfonso and Maria (Iten) G. BSc, Rome U., 1953. Asst. to chair zoology U. Rome, 1954-57; dep. dir. Ctrl. Book Pathology Inst., Rome, 1973-75, dir. biology lab., 1972-96; lectr. in field, 1968-96; mem. interministerial commn. termite control, 1952-75, UNESCO commn. advise treatment books and documents damaged in flood in Florence, 1966, advise on measures to preserve libr. materials in Italian pub. librs., 1977-80. Contbr. more than 90 articles to profl. jours. Nat. coun. mem. Cultural Heritage, 1976-80. Recipient Silver Medal Ministry Edn., 1966. Home: Viale Giulio Cesare 47, 00192 Rome Italy

GALLO, ROBERT CHARLES, research scientist; b. Waterbury, Conn., Mar. 23, 1937; s. Francis Anton and Louise Mary (Ciancuilli) G.; m. Mary Jane Hayes, July 1, 1961; children: Robert Charles, Marcus. BA, Providence Coll., 1959, DSc (hon.), 1974; MD, Jefferson Med. Coll., 1963; 13 hon. degrees from univs. in U.S., Belgium, Italy, Israel, Sweden. Intern, resident medicine U. Chgo., 1963-65; clin. assoc. med. br. Nat. Cancer Inst. NIH, Bethesda, Md., 1965-68, sr. investigator human tumor cell biology br., 1968-69, head sect. cellular control mechanisms, 1969-72, chief lab. tumor cell biology, 1972-93; dir., prof. medicine and microbiology Inst. Human Virology U. Md., Balt., 1993—; adj. prof. genetics George Washington U.; adj. prof. biology Johns Hopkins U., Balt., hon. prof. biology, 1985—; hon. prof. medicine Karolinska Inst., Stockholm, 1998—, hon. prof. Karolinska Inst., Stockholm, 1998—; Hon. prof. Karolinska Inst., Stockholm, 1998—, U.S. rep. to world com. Internat Comparative Leukemia and Lymphoma Assn., 1981—; mem. bd. govs. Franco Am. AIDS Found., 1987, world AIDS Found., 1987. Author: Virus Hunting, 1991, author or co-author of more than 1,100 scientific papers. With USPHS, 1965-68. Recipient Dameshek award Am. Hematol. Soc., 1974, CIBA-GEIGY award in biomed. sci., 1977, 88, Superior Svc. award USPHS, 1979, Meritorious Svc. medal, 1983, Stitt award, 1983, Disting. Svc. medal, 1984, First F. Stohlman of Am. Soc. Hem lecture award, 1979, Lasker award for basic biomed. rsch., 1982, 86, Abraham White award in biochemistry George Washington U., 1983, 1st Otto Herz award for cancer rsch. Tel Aviv U., 1982, Griffuel prize Assn. for Cancer Rsch., France, 1983, GM award in cancer rsch., 1984, Gruber prize Am. Soc. Investigative Dermatology, 1984, Lucy Wortham prize in cancer rsch. Soc. for Surg. Oncology, 1984, Gold medal Am. Cancer Soc., 1984, Birla Internat. Sci. prize, India, 1985, Hammer prize for Cancer Rsch., 1985, Gairdner prize for Biomed. Rsch., Can., 1987, spl. award Am. Soc. Infectious Disease, 1986, Gold Plate award Am. Acad. Achievement, Lions Humanitarian award, 1987, Japan prize in Sci. and Tech., 1988, Ciba Corning award, 1993, 1st Dale McFarlin award for rsch. Internat. Soc. Human Retrovrology, 1994, 1st Gustav Embden award U. Frankfurt, 1996, Pomesa award, 1996, 1st award Internat. Soc. of Blood Transfusion, 1997, Nomura prize Japan for AIDS and Cancer Rsch., 1998, Warren Alpert prize Harvard U., 1998, Paul Erlich award, Germany, 1999. Mem. NAS, Inst. Medicine, Internat. Soc. Hematology, Am. Soc. Clin. Investigation, Am. Soc. Biol. Chemists, Am. Microbiology Soc., Biochem. Soc., Am. Assn. Cancer Rsch. (Rosenthal award 1993), Am. Soc. Microbiology, Am. Fedn. Clin. Rsch., Fedn. for Advanced Edn. in Scis., Royal Soc. Physicians of Scotland (hon.), Royal Soc. Medicine (hon.), Royal Soc. of Medicine (Belgium), Alpha Omega Alpha (hon.). Achievements include research on viruses, AIDS, and Leukemia; co-discoverer of AIDS virus; discovery of first and second human retroviruses. Office: 725 W Lombard St Ste S307 Baltimore MD 21201-1009

GALLOWAY, DANIEL LEE, investment executive; b. Columbia, Mo., Apr. 16, 1958; s. Robert Eugene and Lilie Ann (Riechard) G.; m. Wanda Sue Wegener, June 22, 1979; 1 child, Rob. BA, William Jewell Coll., Liberty, Mo., 1979; postgrad., Wolfson Coll., Cambridge, Eng., 1979-80. Asst. to pres. Galloway Limestone Co., Inc., Bowling Green, Mo., 1980-81; v.p. Galloway Limestone Co., Inc., 1981-90; pres., investment adviser Galloway & Galloway, Inc., 1989—; treas., chair fin. com. bd. dirs. Hannibal Regional Healthcare Sys., 1994-97, vice chair, 1997-99, chair, 1999—; cons. Cecil C. Daffron & Assocs., Bowling Green, 1987-96; mem. adv. bd., bd. dirs. Kids' Wall Street News, Inc., 1997—. Bd. dirs. Mo. State Sch. Bds. Assn. Region 6, 1989, 90; sec. Bowling Green R-1 Sch. Bd., 1989-92, First Presbyn. Ch. Bd. of Session, 1983-86; diaconate First Christian Ch., Hannibal, 1995-96; mem. South Side Christian Ch.; mem. steering com. Hannibal Accelerated Mid. Sch. Program, 1995-98, mem. tech. adv. com., 1996-97. Mem. Mo. Limestone Producers Assn. (bd. dirs. 1982-85), Mo. State Sch. Bd. Assn. (edn. com. 1989-90), British Caribbean Philatelic Study Group, Mo. Postal History Soc. Avocation: reading. Home: 15 Riverpoint Rd Hannibal MO 63401-2019 Office: Galloway & Galloway Inc PO Box 1256 Hannibal MO 63401-1256

GALLOWAY, DAVID MALCOLM, education educator; b. Marlow, England, July 5, 1942; s. Malcolm Ashby and Joan Dorah (Slater) G.; m. Christina Mary King, Dec. 29, 1971; children: Patrick, Sam, Catherine. BA, U. Oxford, 1970; MSc, London U., 1972; PhD, CNAA, 1980. Chartered psychologist. Sr. ednl. psychologist Sheffield (Eng.) Local Edn. Authority, 1974-79; sr. lectr. Victoria U., Wellington, New Zealand, 1980-83; lectr. Univ. Coll., Cardiff, Wales, 1983-87; lectr., reader Lancaster U., England, 1987-91; prof. primary edn. Durham U., England, 1991—. Author: Schools and Persistent Absentees, 1985; co-author: Schools and Disruptive Pupils, 1982, Primary School Teaching and Educational Psychology, 1991, The Assessment of Special Educational Needs: Whose Problem?, 1994, Motivating the Difficult to Teach, 1998. Mem. Fell Search and Mtn. Rescue Team. Fellow Br. Psychol. Soc.; mem. Assn. Child Psychology & Psychiatry (chmn. 1999—). Avocation: beekeeping. Home: Leases, Smardale, Kirkby Stephen, Cumbria CA17 4HQ, England Office: U Durham Sch Edn, Leazes Rd, Durham DH1 1TA, England

GALLOWAY, EILENE MARIE, space and astronautics consultant; b. Kansas City, Mo., May 4, 1906; d. Joseph Locke and Lottie Rose (Harris) Slack; m. George Barnes Galloway, Dec. 23, 1924; children: David Barnes, Jonathan Fuller. Student, Washington U., St. Louis, 1923-25; AB, Swarthmore Coll., 1928; postgrad., Am. U., 1937-38, 43; LLD (hon.), Lake Forest Coll., 1990, Swarthmore Coll., 1992. Tchr. polit. sci. Swarthmore Coll., 1928-30; editor Student Svc., Washington, 1931; staff mem. edn. div. Fed. Emergency Relief Adminstrn., 1934-35; asst. chief info. sect. div. spl. info Library of Congress, 1941-43; editor abstracts Legis. Reference Svc., 1943-51, nat. def. analyst, 1951-57, specialist in nat. def., 1957-66; sr. specialist internat. rels. (nat. security) Congl. Rsch. Svc., 1966-75, cons. internat. space activities, 1975—; staff mem. Senate Fgn. Rels. Com., 1947; profl. staff mem. U.S. group Interparliamentary Union, 1958-66; cons. Senate Armed Svcs. Com., 1953-74, Ford Found., 1958; spl. cons. Spl. Senate Com. on Space and Astronautics, 1958; spl. cons. to Senate Con. on Aero. and Space Sci., 1958-77; cons. to Senate Com. on Commerce, Sci. and Transp., 1977-82; chmn. com. edn. and recreation Washington, 1937-38; forum leader, 1976-79; guest Soviet Acad. Sci., 1982, adult edn. U.S. Office Edn., 1938; mem. Internat. Inst. Space Law of Internat. Astronautical Fedn., 1958—, U.S. bd. dirs., v.p., 1967-79, hon. dir., 1979—, Fedn. ofcl. observer at sessions UN Com. on Peaceful Uses Outer Space and legal sub-com., 1970-94, mem. com. for rels. with internat. orgns., 1979—; mem. Am. Rocket Soc.'s Space Law and Sociology Com., 1959-62; mem. adv. panel Office Gen. Counsel, NASA, 1971; adviser outer space del. U.S. Mission to UN Working Group on Direct Broadcast Satellites, 1973-75; observer UN Conf. Exploration and Peaceful Uses of Outer Space, Vienna, 1982; lectr. NAS, 1972, U.S. CSC, Exec. Seminar Ctr., Oak Ridge, 1973-77, 78; ednl. counselor Purdue U., 1974; lectr. Inst. Air and Space Law McGill U., 1975, Inter Am. Def. Coll., 1977, 78, U. Akron, 1984, 91; mem. panel on solar power for satellites and U.S. space policy Office Tech. Assessment, 1979-80, 82-86, cons., 1982; cons. COMSAT, 1983, FCC Commn. on U.S. Telecomm. Policy, 1983-87; spkr. internat. space law UN, N.Y.C., 1995; mem. NASA Nat. Adv. Com. on Internat. Space Sta., 1996-99, NASA Spaceflight Adv. com., 2000—, UN seminar Space Futures and Human Security, Alpbach, Austria, 1997, chmn. Session in Internat. Astronautical Fed. Congress Concepts of Space Law, 1997; active European Space Agy. Internat. Lunar Workshop, 1994, 1997; chair UN Workshop UNISPACE III Space Treaties: Strengths and Needs, Vienna, Austria, 1999. Author: Atomic Power: Issues Before Congress, 1946; (with Bernard Brodie) The Atomic Bomb and the Armed Services, 1947; History of United States Military Policy on Reserve Forces, 1775-57, 1957; The Community of Law and Science, 1958; United Nations Ad hoc Committee on Peaceful Uses of Outer Space, 1959;. Pres. Theodore Von Karman Meml. Found., 1973-84; mem. alumni council Swarthmore Coll., 1976-79; mem. organizing com., author symposium on Conditions Essential For Maintaining Outer Space for Peaceful Uses, Peace Palace, Netherlands, 1984; bd. advisers Student for Exploration and Devel. of Space, 1984—. Rockefeller Found. scholar-in-residence, Bellagio, Italy, 1976; elected to Coun. of Advanced Internat. Studies, Argentina, 1985, Uruguyan Centro de Investigacion y Difusion Aeronautica-Expacial, 1985; recipient Andrew G. Haley gold medal Internat. Inst. Space Law, 1968, Disting. Svc. award Libr. Congress, 1975, NASA Gold Medal for Pub. Svc., 1984, USAF Space Command plaque, 1984, Internat. Acad. Astronautics' Theodore Von. Karman award, 1986, Women in Aerospace Lifetime Achievment award Internat. Inst. Space Law, 1989, Leadership award NASA Johnson Space Ctr., 1997; Wilton Park fellow, Eng., 1968, NASA award for contbns. to internat. space sta., 1999. Fellow AIAA (tech. com. on legal aspects of aeros. and astronautics 1980-84, internat. activities com. 1985—, European space agy. internat. lunar workshop 1994), Am. Astronautical Soc. (John F. Kennedy Astronautics award 1999, Internat. Acad. Astronautics (Social Scis. award 1999); mem. LWV (chmn. study groups housing, welfare in D.C. 1937-38, mem. tech. com. on law and sociology task force on legal aspects 1979—), World Peace Through Law Ctr., Am. Soc. Internat. Law, Lamar Soc. Internat. Law, Internat. Law Assn., Phi Beta Kappa, Delta Sigma Rho, Kappa Alpha Theta. Episcopalian. Home: 4612 29th Pl NW Washington DC 20008-2105

GALLOWAY, JOSEPH LEE, JR., writer, journalist; b. Bryan, Tex., Nov. 13, 1941; s. Joseph L. and Marian D. (Dewvall) G.; m. Theresa Magdalene Null, Sept. 9, 1966 (dec. Jan. 1996); children: Lee T., Joshua J.; m. Karen Metsker McCray, Oct. 24, 1998; children: Alison, Abigail, Thomas. Grad., Refugio, Tex., 1959. Reporter Victoria (Tex.) Advocate, 1959-61, United Press Internat., Kansas City, Mo., 1961; bureau chief United Press Internat., Topeka, Kans., 1962-64; war correspondent United Press Internat., South Vietnam, 1965-66; correspondent United Press Internat., Tokyo, 1966-68; bureau chief United Press Internat., Jakarta, Indonesia, 1968-73; mgr. south Asia United Press Internat., New Delhi, India, 1973-74; mgr. southeast Asia United Press Internat., Singapore, 1974-75; bureau chief United Press Internat., Moscow, 1976-80, L.A., 1980-82; west coast editor U.S.News & World Report, L.A., 1982-84; assoc. editor U.S. News, Washington, 1984-86, sr. editor, 1986-90, sr. writer, 1990—. Co-author: Triumph Without Victory, 1992, We Were Soldiers Once... and Young, 1992. Dir. No Greater Love, Washington, 1990—; bd. adv. Vietnam Vets. Meml. Fund,. Decorated Bronze Star with V device; Recipient Nat Mag. award Am. Soc. Mag. Editors, 1991, Nat. News Media award Vet. of Fgn. Wars of U.S.A., 1992, Excellence in Arts award Vietnam Vets. Am., 1999. Mem. Soc. Profl. Journalists, Overseas Press Club, 7th Cavalry Assn., 1st Cavalry Divsn. Assn. Avocations: travel, gardening. Home: PO Box 6222 Falls Church VA 22040-6222 Office: U S News & World Report 1050 Thomas Jefferson St NW Washington DC 20007-3817

GALLOWAY, LILLIAN CARROLL, modeling agency executive, consultant; b. Hazard, Ky., Sept. 23, 1934; d. William Zion and Clemma (Lewis) Carroll; m. Thomas Roddy Galloway, Dec. 21, 1957; children: David Junkin, Scott Thomas, Donald Lewis. Student, Cumberland Coll., 1955, Ea. U., Richmond, Ky., 1956, U. Cin., 1958, John Robert Powers Sch., Cin., 1958. Tchr. Vandalia (Ohio) Elem. Sch., 1954-56, Kenwood Elem. Sch., Louisville, 1956-57, Cin. Pub. Schs., 1957-64; founder, pres. Fairfax Model Agy., Washington, 1964-67, Cin. Model Agy. Internat., 1967—, Lillian Galloway Modeling Acad., Cin., 1971—, Children Model Agy. Internat., Cin., 1985—, Lillian Galloway Fashion Show Prodn. Co., 1999—; cons., co-owner John Robert Powers Modeling Sch., Cin., 1957-64; pres. Student Model Bds., Cin., 1984—; dir. Career Day, Cin., 1967—. Mem. Cin. Better Bus. Bur., 1967—; trustee Knox Presbyn. Ch., Cin. Named Cin.'s Outstanding Bus. Woman, Sta. WCPO-TV, 1985, Outstanding Alumni, Cumberland Coll., 1988. Mem. DAR, Modeling Assn. Am. (chmn. convs. 1975-77), Am. Modeling Assn. Internat. (pres. 1976-77), Cin. Advertisers Club (membership and program coms., Outstanding Bus. Woman award 1985), Exec. Women Internat. (program com., chmn. bd. dirs. 1986, Woman of Achievement award 1986), Cin. C. of C., Cumberland Coll. Alumni Assn. (pres. 1982), English Speaking Union, Order Ky. Cols., Cin. Woman's Club (bd. dirs. 1992—, lecture/entertainment chmn. 1992-95), Town Club (bd. dirs. 1988—), Order Ea. Star (organist 1953—). Republican. Avocations: art, French antiques, gardening, music, travel. Home: 6027 Stirrup Rd Cincinnati OH 45244-3917 Office: 6047 Montgomery Rd Cincinnati OH 45213-1611

GALLUP, DONALD CLIFFORD, bibliographer, educator; b. Sterling, Conn., May 12, 1913; s. Carl Daniel and Lottie Elizabeth (Stanton) G. AB, Yale U., 1934, PhD, 1939; LittD, Colby Coll., 1971. Instr. English So. Meth. U., Dallas, 1937-40, 41-42; cataloguer library Yale U., 1940-41; asst. prof. bibliography, curator collection Am. lit., editor Library Gazette; fellow Jonathan Edwards Coll., 1947-80. Author: Ezra Pound Bibliography, 1983, T.S. Eliot Bibliography, 1969, T. S. Eliot & Ezra Pound, 1970, On Contemporary Bibliography, 1970, A Curator's Responsibilities, 1976, Pigeons on the Granite, Memories, 1988, What Mad Pursuits! More Memories, 1998, Eugene O'Neill and His Eleven-Play Cycle, 1998; editor: The Flowers of Friendship, 1953, Eugene O'Neill, Inscriptions, 1960, Eugene O'Neill, More Stately Mansions, 1964, Gertrude Stein, Fernhurst, Q.E.D., and Other Early Writings, 1971, Thornton Wilder, The Alcestiad, 1977, Eugene O'Neill, Poems, 1979, Thornton Wilder, American Characteristics, 1979, Eugene O'Neill, Work Diary, 1981, Eugene O'Neill, The Calms of Capricorn, 1981, Kathryn Hulme, Of Chickens and Plums, 1982, Thornton Wilder, The Journals, 1985, Ezra Pound, At the Circulo de Recreo, 1985, Ezra Pound, Plays Modelled on the Noh, 1987, Thornton Wilder, The Collected Short Plays, 1997-98. Served as lt. col. AUS, 1941-46. Decorated Bronze Star medal; Croix de Guerre avec étoile de vermeil (France); recipient Tao House award for svcs. to Am. theater Eugene O'Neill Found., 1994, Eugene O'Neill Soc. medal, 1995; Guggenheim fellow, 1961, 68. Mem. Bibliog. Soc. Am., Elizabethan Club (New Haven), Grolier Club (N.Y.C.), Grad. Club (New Haven), Phi Beta Kappa. Home: 216 Bishop St Apt 201 New Haven CT 06511-3742

GALLUPS, ORDICE ALTON, diaconal minister; b. Bessemer, Ala., June 17, 1954; s. Ordice Alton Gallups Sr. and Margaret Emma Fleming; m. Vivian Lylay Bess, July 12, 1975. BS, U. Ala., 1975; MA in Religion, Luth. Theol. So. Sem., 1992; M of Theol. Studies, Spring Hill Coll., 1997. Ordained to ministry Evang. Luth. Ch.; consecrated to sacred diaconte, 1999. Tech. aid So. Co. Svcs., Inc., Birmingham, Ala., 1976; verger Cathedral Ch. of the Advent, Birmingham, 1981-92; diaconal asst. Shades Valley Evang. Luth. Ch., Birmingham, 1992-94; social ins. specialist Social Security Adminstn., Birmingham, 1979-94; program analyst Social Security Adminstn., Balt., 1994-2000; diaconal min. All Saints Luth. Ch., Bowie, Md., 1999-2000; Evang. Luth. Ch. Am. diaconal ministry adv. panel, Chgo., 1998—; mem. worship office Evang. Luth. Ch. Am. Met. Washington, 1996—. Mem. interfaith action communities Price George's County, Md., 1998—. Named Hon. admiral Gov. of the State of Ala., 1999; recipient Nat. Performance Rev. Hammer award, 1997. Mem. N.Am. Assn. for the Diaconate, Assn. of Luth. Ch. Musicians, Liturgy Network, Vergers' Guild of the Episcopal Ch. Avocations: liturgical studies, music. Fax: 202-318-0267. E-mail: gallups@sprintmail.com. Home: 14144 Reverend Rainsford Ct Upper Marlboro MD 20772-5986

GALNOOR, ITZHAK, political scientist, retired Israeli government official; b. Sao Paulo, Brazil, Dec. 5, 1940; arrived in Israel, 1949; s. Abraham and Pnina (Sheinbaum) Goldendrut; m. Doron Rashkes, Aug. 21, 1966; children: Efrat, Shahar, Netta. BA, Hebrew U., Jerusalem, 1962; MPA, Syracuse U., 1966, PhD, 1969. From lectr. to prof. polit. sci. Hebrew U., 1969—, dir. pub. adminstrn. grad. program, 1975-78, chmn. polit. sci. dept., 1979-81, dir. L. Eshkol Rsch. Inst., 1982-86; civil svc. commr., head adminstrv. reforms Govt. of Israel, Jerusalem, 1994-96; editor Am Oved Book Series, Tel Aviv, 1985-93, Cambridge (Eng.) U. Press, 1991-93; head polit. reform project Israel Democracy Inst., 1991-93; dir. James Shasha Inst. Author, editor: Government Secrecy in Democracies, 1977; author: Steering the Polity, 1982, (with S. Lukes) No Laughing Matter, 1985, The Partition of Palestine, 1995; columnist Yediot Aharonot, 1990-93. Founder Peace Now, Israel, 1978—; v.p. New Israel Fund, U.S. and Israel, 1984-91; cons. Knesset Com. on Electoral Reforms, 1989-90. Maj. Israel Def. Forces, 1962-65. Recipient Peretz Nafali prize Tel Aviv Mcpl. Coun., 1987, civil rights honor Israel Assn. Civil Rights, 1996. Mem. Internat. Polit. Sci. Assn. (exec. com. 1985-91, editor book series 1991-93). Avocations: collecting political jokes, Don Quixote memorabilia. Office: Hebrew U, Dept Polit Sci, 91905 Jerusalem Israel

GALOFRE, GONZALO, physician, surgeon, educator; b. Barcelona, Spain, Oct. 16, 1963; s. Manuel Galofre and Ana Pujol; m. Minona Recasens, June 21, 1991; children: Maria, Patricia, Carla. Student, U. Autonoma Barcelona, 1982-89, MD, 1989. Diplomate Am. Bd. Surgery; cert. BCLS, ACLS, ATLS, ATLS instr. Intern La Crosse (Wis.) Luth. Hosp., Gunderson Clinic, 1990-91; resident gen. surgery divsn. gen. surgery U. Ala., Birmingham, 1991-96, adminstrv. chief resident, 1995-96; pvt. practice Quirón Clinic, Barcelona, 1996—, Teknon Clinic, Barcelona, 1996—; asst. prof. Red Cross Hosp., Barcelona, 1996—. Mem. Alpha Omega Alpha. Office: Gonzalo Galofre, Virgen de la Salud 78, 08024 Barcelona Spain

GALPER, ALEXANDER REM, physicist, researcher; b. Leningrad, Russia, Sept. 12, 1953; arrived in Israel, 1990; s. Rem Rachmiel Galper and Lubov Nikolay Zaluzkaya; m. Marina Semeon Kheifez, Sept. 13, 1989; 1 child, Daniel. PhD, Tel Aviv U., 1997. Sr. rschr. Oil State Inst., St. Petersburg, Russia, 1977-88; rschr. Tel Aviv U., 1990-95, sr. rschr., 1996—. Contbr. chpts. to books and articles to profl. jours. Home: Herzog St 36-8, 53587 Gevatayim Israel

GALPERIN, YURI ILICH, physics educator; b. Moscow, Sept. 24, 1932; s. Ilya Romanovich and Nadejda Michailovna (Goldman) G.; m. Natalia Gennadievna Fish, May 5, 1956; 1 child, Michael. PhD in Physics, Inst. Atmospheric Physics, Moscow, 1958; D of Phys. Sci., Moscow U., 1968. Cert. physicist. Rschr. Geophysical Inst. (name now Inst. Atmospheric Physics), Moscow, 1955-57, sr. rschr., 1957-67; chief of lab. Space Rsch. Inst., Moscow, 1967—, prof. physics, 1983. Co-author: Radiation Measurements in Space, 1972, Electromagnetic Compatibility of Scientific Space Complex ARCAD-3, 1984, Subauroral Upper Ionosphere, 1990; contbr. more than 200 articles to profl. jours. Recipient state prize USSR State Com., Moscow, 1986. Mem. Internat. Astron. Union, European Astron. Soc. (founding mem.), Am. Geophys. Union. Office: Space Rsch Inst, Profsouznaya St 84/32, 117810 Moscow Russia

GALT, JOHN WILLIAM, actor, writer; b. Jackson, Miss., Apr. 4, 1940; s. William Neal and Lyndel Janes (Fortenberry) G.; m. Anna Marie Kolenovsky, Dec. 14, 1965 (div. 1973); children: Joseph William, Edward Wayne; m. 2d Diane Renee Wallace, June 6, 1981; children: Christopher Wallace, Geoffrey Warren. Student, U. Md. at Munich (Germany), 1960-61; BA, Univ. Scis. Am., L.A., 1992. Owner Vox Omnia Prodns., 1999—; toured as folksinger U.S.A. and Europe, 1960-62; voice talent on numerous radio and TV commls., Dallas, 1965-78, 80—, L.A., 1978-80; 31 film appearances as actor; looped characters in 4 movies; voice of Lyndon B. Johnson in Oliver Stone's JFK, 1992, Forrest Gump, 1994; writer film script Iceman, 1976; contbg. writer For The Love of Benji, 1977; writer screenplay Step Back From Anger, 1986, The Guardians, 1987; contbg. writer The Internal Affair, 1988; v.p. Tex. Ind. Feature Prodns., Inc., 1981—, Jackson Galt Creative Enterprise Inc, 1991-99. Co-author numerous short fictions. With USAF, 1957-62. Recipient Dallas Citizen's Cert. Merit, 1973, Clios (28), Tellys (31), N.Y. Film Festival Silver, Addys (43), CHA Gold Spirit award; several Tops in advt. awards. Mem. NATAS (Heartland chpt.), Actor's Equity Assn., Screen Actor's Guild, AFTRA, Writers Guild of Am., Acad. for Preservation of Talking Pictures. Avocations: martial arts (2d degree black belt Tae Guek Kwan Kung Fu 1993, advanced oriental broad sword combat forms, brown belt Hapkiko OHTC 1989). Office: care Sylvia Gill Kim Dawson Agy 7210 Stemmons Twp N Dallas TX 75200

GALTUNG, JOHAN VINCENT, peace studies educator, administrator; b. Oslo, Oct. 24, 1930; s. August Andreas and Helga (Holmboe) G.; m. Ingrid Eide, Jan. 16, 1956 (div. Dec. 1968); children: Andreas, Harald; m. Fumiko Nishimura, Mar. 29, 1969; children: Fredrik, Irene. PhD in Math., U. Oslo, 1956, postgrad. in sociology, 1957; Dr.h.c., U. Tampere, Finland, 1975, U. cluj, Romania, 1976, U. Uppsala, Sweden, 1987, U. Soka, Japan, 1990, U. Osnabrück, Germany, 1995, U. Turin, Italy, 1998, Fern U., Hagen, Germany, 2000. Awarded hon. professorships Spain, China, and Germany. Asst. prof. Columbia U., N.Y.C., 1957-60; dir. Internat. Peace Rsch. Inst., Oslo, 1959-70; prof. peace rsch. U. Oslo, 1969-77, U. Geneva, Switzerland, 1977-82; dir. TRANSCEND: A Network for Conflict Transformation, Princeton, N.J., 1993—; vis. prof. various univs., including Princeton U., Berlin, Tokyo, Kyoto, Granada, others, 1982—; cons. UN, 1962—. Author: Theory and Methods of Social Research, vols. I-IV, 1977-88, Human Rights in Another Way, 1994, Peace by Peaceful Means, 1996; contbr. essays on peace rsch. to books, 1975-88. Recipient Right Livelihood award, Stockholm, 1987. Avocations: travel, languages, history. Home: 51 Bois Chatton, F-01210 Versonnex Ain, France

GALUN, MARGALITH, biologist, educator; b. Vienna, Austria, Feb. 21, 1927; arrived in Israel, 1939; d. Arie Katz and Amalia Katz-Teitelbaum; m. Esra Galun, May 3, 1953; children: Eithan, Ehud. MS, Hebrew U., 1954, PhD, 1960. Prof. Tel Aviv U., 1977-96, dean students, 1977-80, 89-92, mem. bd. govs., prof. emeritus, 1996—; pres. 6th Internat. Mycological Congress, 1998. Editor: Handbook of Lichenology, 3 vols., 1988; author: The Lichens of Israel, 1970; contbr. articles and revs. to profl. jours. and chpts. to books; co-author: The Lichens of the Holy Land, 1979; editor-in-chief: Symbiosis, 1985—; mem. editl. bd. several scientific jours. Grantee numerous orgns; recipient Alexander von Humboldt award, 1996, Disting. Scientist award Internat. Symbiosis Soc., 2000. Mem. Internat. Mycol. Assn. (exec. com. 1983-90, 94-98, pres. 1998), Internat. Assn. Lichenology (v.p. 1987-93), Israel Nat. Collections of Natural History (exec. com., Acharius Medal for outstanding contbn. to lichenology, Meitner-Humboldt award 1996). Office: Tel Aviv U Dept Botany, Ramat Aviv, Tel Aviv 69978, Israel

GALUSKA, VLADIMIR, diplomat. Student, Charles U., Prague, Czech Republic, 1970-75, JD, 1981. Corp. lawyer Skoda Praha, 1975-90; ministry fgn. affairs Czech Republic, 1990—; consul, dep. chief of mission Czech Embassy, Washington, D.C., 1990-94; dir. Dept. Pers., MFA, Prague, 1994-97; Czech Republic rep. UN, N.Y.C., 1997—; pres. ECOSOC UN, 1999—, chmn. IIIrd com. of Gen. Assembly, 1999—; pres. exec. bd. UN Devel. Programme/UN Population Fund —, 2000; consul, dep. chief mission Czech Republic Embassy, Washington, 1990-94; dir. Dep. Pers., MFA, Prague, 1994-97; permanent rep. to UN, 1997—. Office: UN 1109 Madison Ave New York NY 10028-0405

GALUSKE, MICHAEL ALFONS, social worker, educator; b. Bochum, Germany, Dec. 28, 1959. Doctorate. Rschr. U. Bochum, 1988-90; tchr. Elisabeth-Lüders-Schule, Hamm, Germany, 1991-93; scientist of social work U. Dortmund, Germany, 1993—. Author: Das Orientierungsdilemma (The Problem of Orientation), 1993, (with T. Rauschenbach) Jugendhilfe Ost (Child and Youth Care in East Germany), 1994, Methoden der Sozialen Arbeit (Methods of Social Work), 1998, (with W. Thole and H. Gaengler) KlassikerInnen der Sozialen Arbeit (Classic Authors of Social Work), 1998. Home: Ricarda-Huch-Str 9, 44807 Bochum Germany Office: Univ Dortmund, FB 12 ISEP Emil Figge St 50, 44221 Dortmund Germany

GALVAN, CESARE GIUSEPPE, social sciences educator; b. Borgo Valsugana, Italy, Sept. 10, 1930; immigrated to Brazil; Lic. in Philosophy, Aloisianum, Gallarate, Italy, 1955; MA in Econs., So. Meth. U., 1967; D of Social Scis., Gregorian U., Rome, 1976. Univ. tchr. U. Fed. da Bahia, Salvador, Bahia, Brazil, 1968-75; rschr. Inst. Nac. de Pesquisas Espaciais, Sao Paulo, Brazil, 1975-76; univ. tchr. U. Fed. de Pernambuco, Recife, Brazil, 1976-79, U. Nac. Autonoma de Mex., Mexico City, 1980-81, 90-91; vis. prof. U. Fed. de Santa Catarina, Florianspolis, Brazil, 1991-93; univ. tchr. U. Fed. do Ceara, Fortaleza, Brazil, 1993-95, U. Fed. da Paraiba, Joao Pessoa, Brazil, 1982-87, 95-97; rschr. Centro Josue de Castro, Recife, 1987-90, 97—; mem. editl. coun. REvista de Economia Politica, 1990—, Revista de Ciencia e tecnologia, Recife, 1997. Author: Per Capita Income in Brazil, 1967, German Nuclear Expansion: State, Capital, World Market, 1987, Questions on Capital and Technology, 1988, also articles. Avocation: music. E-mail: dugalvan@elogica.com.br. Home: Avenida Beira Rio 1065/401, 50610100 Recife Brazil Ofifce: Centro Josue de Castro, Rua Sao Goncalo 118-Coelhos, 50070600 Recife Brazil

GALVANI, CHRISTIANE MESCH, English as a second language educator, translator; b. Kiel, Fed. Republic Germany, Jan. 19, 1954; came to U.S., 1977; d. Edgar and Elisabeth (Depken) Mesch; m. Paul Andrew Galvani, Dec. 19, 1979; 1 child, Jacqueline. BA, U. London, 1977; MA, Rice U., 1986. Freelance translator Houston, 1979—; instr. English, German, French Berlitz Sch. Langs., Houston, 1981-82, interpreter, translator, 1981-84, prodn. coord., 1982-84; lead ESL instr. Tex. So. U., Houston, 1989—; instr. Rice U., Houston, 1990 (summer). Translator: The Flowing Light of the Divinity, 1991. Named to Outstanding Young Women of Am., 1986. Mem. MLA, TESOL, Am. Translators Assn., Am. Lit. Translators Assn., Houston Profl. Translators Forum (dir. 1982-83), Houston Interpreter's and Translator's Assn. Avocations: music, playing the recorder, reading. Home: 2926 Fairway Dr Sugarland TX 77478-4023 Office: Tex So Univ 3100 Cleburne St Houston TX 77004-4501

GALVEZ-DURAND, FEDERICO HUMBERTO ARTURO, electronic engineering educator, researcher; b. Chiclayo, Peru, Nov. 25, 1961; s. Luis Humberto and Gladys Hilda (Besnard) Galvez-D.; m. Lusmarina Campos Garcia, Dec. 15, 1991. B in Indsl. Engring., UDEP, Piura, Peru, 1984; MS in Electronics Engring., U. Fed. Rio de Janeiro, 1989, DSc, 1994. Engr. UDEP, Piura, 1983-85, Cibertec, Lima, Peru, 1985-87; rschr. PPE/CERN, Geneva, 1995-96, PEE/COPPE/UFRJ, Rio de Janeiro, 1996-98; assoc. prof. electronics engring. DEL/EE/UFRJ, Rio de Janeiro, 1998—. Avocation: long-distance running.

GALVEZ-JIMENEZ, NESTOR, neurologist; b. Panama City, Aug. 28, 1957. MD, U. San Carlos, Guatamala City, 1983. Diplomate Am. Bd. Neurology, Am. Bd. Internal Medicine. From intern to resident in internal medicine Booth Meml. Hosp., N.Y., 1986-90; resident in neurology Cleve. Clin. Found., 1991-94; fellow U. Toronto, 1994-96; dir. movement disorders program, cons. neurology Cleveland Clin. Fla., Ft. Lauderdale. Mem. Am. Acad. Neurology, Movement Disorder Soc. Office: Cleve Clin Fla Hosp Dept Neur Move Disord Prgm 3000 W Cypress Creek Rd Fort Lauderdale FL 33309-1710

GALVIN, CHRISTOPHER B., electronics company executive; b. 1951. BA, Northwestern U., MBA, 1977. With Motorola, Inc., 1973—; sr. exec. v.p., asst. COO Motorola, Inc., Schaumberg, Ill., 1989-95, pres., COO, 1995—, now CEO. Office: Motorola Inc 1303 E Algonquin Rd Schaumburg IL 60196-1079

GALVIN, JOHN ROGERS, educator, retired army officer; b. Wakefield, Mass., May 13, 1929; s. John James and Mary Josephine (Logan) G.; m. Virginia Lee Brennan, June 5, 1961; children: Mary Jo, Elizabeth Ann, Kathleen Mary, Erin Elizabeth. BS, U.S. Mil. Acad., 1954; MA, Columbia U., 1962; postgrad., U. Pa., 1964-65; grad., Command and Gen. Staff Coll., 1966. Commd. 2d lt. U.S. Army, 1954, advanced through grades to gen.; mil. asst. to Supreme Allied Comdr. Europe, 1974-75; comdr. DISCOM, chief of staff 3d Infantry div., Germany, 1975-78; asst. div. comdr. 8th Infantry div., 1978-80; comdg. gen. 24th Infantry div., Ft. Stewart, Ga., 1981-83, also post comdr.; comdg. gen. VII U.S. Corps, Stuttgart, Fed. Republic Germany, 1983-85; comdr. in chief U.S. So. Command, Quarry Heights, Panama, 1985-87; supreme allied comdr. Europe, comdr.-in-chief U.S. European Command, 1987-92; ret., 1992; Olin disting. prof. nat. security studies U.S. Mil. Acad., West Point, N.Y., 1992-93; disting. vis. policy analyst The Mershon Ctr., Ohio State U., 1994-95; dean Fletcher Sch. Law and Diplomacy, Tufts U., Boston, 1995-2000; dean emeritus, 2000—; bd. dirs. Raytheon. Author: The Minute Men, 1967, Air Assault, 1969, Three Men of Boston, 1976. Former bd. dirs. Wesleyan Coll. Fletcher Sch. of Law and Diplomacy fellow, 1972-73; decorated Silver Star, Legion of Merit, DFC, Bronze Star. Mem. Coun. Fgn. Rels., Ctr. for Creative Leadership (bd. govs.), Seligman (bd. dirs.), Am. Coun. on Germany (chmn. emeritus bd. dirs.), Inst. for Def. Analyses (trustee). Roman Catholic. Home: 2714 Jodeco Cir Jonesboro GA 30236-5329

GALYANOV, ALEXANDER PAVLOVITCH, academic administrator; b. Borovitchi, Russia, Nov. 6, 1931; s. Pavel and Zinaida (Yevdokimova) G.; m. Serafima Chudinova, June 9, 1954; children: Elena, Pavel. Grad. in marine engring., Murmansk Higher Marine Engring. Coll., 1955. Marine engr. Murmansk Trawl Fleet, Russia, 1956-60; dir. Ship-Repairing Plant, Murmansk, 1960-63; vice dir.-gen. Murmansk Shipyard, 1963-64; tech. dir. North Basin Fish Industry Adminstrn., Murmansk, 1964-72; vice-rector Murmansk Higher Marine Engring. Coll., 1972-90; rector Murmansk State Tech. U., 1990—. Author: Ship Repairs, 1986; contbr. articles to profl. jours. Home: Lenin Ave 70-73, 183038 Murmansk Russia

GALZERANO, GIUSEPPE, journalist, educator; b. Castelnuovo, Cilento, Italy, Mar. 22, 1953; s. Francesco Galzerano and Carmela Gentile; m. Caterina Di Rienzo, Oct. 29, 1983; children: Carmen, Alessandro. Laurea pedagogia, U. Salerno, 1977, laurea lettere, 1984. Editor Galzerano Editore, Casalvelino Scalo, Italy, 1975—; tchr. Scuola Elementare, Casalvelino Scalo, 1995—, Scuola Media, 1998—; tchr. Inst. Magistrale, Piaggine, 1985, Vallo della Lucania, 1988, Inst. Commerciale, Sapri, 1990; freelance journalist. Author: I Ricchi e Gli Oppressori Non Moriranno Piu, 1970, Grammatica Lingua Esperanto, 1970, Carlo Pisacane un Dirottatore di Cent'anni Fa, 1975, Gaetano Bresci La vita L'attentato il Processo E la morte del Regicida Anarchico, 1988, Giovanni Passannante La Vita L'attentato il Processo la condanna a Morte la grazia regale e gli anni di galera del cuoco lucano che nel 1878 ruppe l'incantesimo monarchico, 1997, Le Memorie di Antonio Galotti e la rivolta del Cilento del 1828, 1998, Vincenzo Perrone, la Vita e le Lotte, L'esilio e la Morte Dell'Anarchico Salernitano Volontario Della Liberta in Spagna, 1999. Home and Office: Casavelino Scalo, 84040 Salerno Italy

GAMAAN, HUSSEIN, graphic designer, educator, illustrator, artist; b. Kassala, Sudan, Nov. 28, 1949; arrived in Saudi Arabia, 1985; s. Gamaanomer Ahmed Omer and Nafeesa Ali (El Mahi) G.; m. Khalda El Mahadi Abd El Rahman; children: Nada, Reem, Sara, Mohamed. BA, Khartoum Coll. of Art, 1966; M degree, Royal Coll. of Art, London, 1973, cert., 1974. Mem. graphics staff Coll. of Art, Khartoum, 1966-70, head of graphic dept., 1974-76, head of printmaking and visual rsch., 1976-80, head of printing and bookbinding, 1980-84; art dir. Sudan Cultural Mag. Ministry of Culture, Khartoum, 1978-82; mem. art panel meeting Brit. Coun., Omdurman, 1980-81; art dir. Khartoum Mag. Nat. Coun. for Art and Letters, Khartoum, 1982-84; lectr. Dept. Edn. King Faisal U., Al-Hofuf, Saudi Arabia, 1985—; external examiner Inst. Music and Drama, Khartoum, 1980; mem. art and arch. com. Nat. Coun. of Art and Letters, Khartoum, 1979-81; mem. art panel meeting Ministry of Culture, Khartoum, 1980-82; chmn. refereeing com. Fifth Periodic Exhbn. for the Plastic Exhbn. and Arabic Caligraphy of the Gulf States, Dawha, 1999. Author: Omar Khayyam, 1974, Song of Songs, 1987, The Khatmeya Mountain, 1992; contbr. Al-Ayyam Newspaper, Khartoum Newspaper; illustrator: The Magic Bead, 1997; one-person show Gallery Space Pause, Tokyo, 1999, Koadansha Ltd. Bldg., Tokyo, 1999. Recipient Golden Sail award Arab Artists Assn. of Kuwait, 1976, Outstanding Achievement medal Sudan Govt., 1979, The Golden Shield, Sharjah 2d Biennial; 1995—, Grand Prix award Internat. Jury Asia/Pacific Cultural Ctr. UNESCO, Tokyo, 1998. Mem. Sudanses Art Assn., Sudan Film Assn., Coun. of Arts and Letters. Office: King Faisal U-Coll Edn, PO Box 1759, Al-Hofuf 31982, Saudi Arabia

GAMALEYA, NATALIA BORISOVNA, immunologist, narcologist; b. Moscow, May 23, 1951; d. Boris and Natalia (Rossichina) G.; m. Alexandre Hzmalyan, Nov. 11, 1979 (div. Mar. 1988); 1 child; m. Vladimir Naumov, Dec. 19, 1999. MD, 2d Med. Inst. Moscow, 1974, PhD, 1977; DSc, Ctr. of Addiction Moscow, 1992. Rsch. scientist Inst. Forensic Psychiatry, Moscow, 1977-88; chief lab. immunochemistry Ctr. Addiction Moscow, 1988—. Fellow Soc. Narcologists, Soc. Immunologists. Office: Rsch Inst on Addiction, Malyi Mogiltzevskii per 3, 121921 Moscow Russia

GAMARNIK, MOISEY YANKELEVICH, solid state physicist; b. Khmelnizky, Ukraine, USSR, Nov. 3, 1936; s. Yankel Khaymovich and Polya Iserovna (Gendelman) G.; m. Yevgeniya Adolfovna Lubomirskaya, Nov. 3, 1965; children: Yan, Alexander. Candidate of Scis. Phys.-Math., U. Kharkov, USSR, 1984, DSc Phys.-Math., 1992. Tchr. Pilyava (USSR) secondary sch., 1959-60, Kiev (USSR) Secondary Sch. N96, 1960-62; rschr., engr. Inst. Geol. Scis. Acad. Sci., Kiev, 1962-69, sr. rschr. Inst. Geochemistry and Physics Minerals, 1969-85, scientist, 1985-89, sr. scientist, 1989-93; crystallophysicist Instrumentation Tech. Assocs., Exton, Pa., 1994-98; assoc. prof. dept. materials engring. Drexel U., Phila., 1995—; x-ray crystallographer DuPont Pharms. Exptl. Sta., Wilmington, Del., 1999-2000; crystallophysicist Nanoscale Phases Rsch., Bensalem, Pa., 2000—. Contbr. articles to Phys. State Sollids. Grantee Internat. Sci. Found., 1995, NSF, 1997. Mem. Internat. Union Crystallography, Assn. for Aerosol Rsch. Achievements include research in problem of structure and properties of small crystal particles and nanophase substances and research in problem of crystallization and structure of proteins. Home: 2500 Knights Rd Apt 79-3 Bensalem PA 19020-3410 Office: Drexel Univ Dept of Materials Engring 32nd and Chestnut Sts Philadelphia PA 19104

GAMBA, ZULEMA BEATRIZ, chemical physics researcher, educator; b. Rosario, Santa Fe, Argentina, Aug. 1, 1947; d. Dante Walter and Maria Teresa (Moreira) G.; m. Jorge Andres Hernando, Dec. 27, 1971; children: Leticia Guadalupe, Irene Raquel. Lic. in phys. scis., U. Buenos Aires, 1971, D in Physics, 1984. Rsch. and tchg. asst. dept. physics U. Buenos Aires Faculty Exact Scis., 1970-74; rschr. Tecnitron Latinoamericana S.A., Buenos Aires, Argentina, 1974-76; rschr. dept. physics Nat. Commn. Atomic Energy, Buenos Aires, 1978—; part-time Inst. Tech., U. Gen. San Martin, Buenos Aires, 1994—; Natural Scis. and Engring. Rsch. Coun. Can. rsch. assoc. Chalk River Labs., Atomic Energy Commn. Can. Ltd., 1993; presenter in field at internat. meetings, including L.Am. Meeting on Solid State Physics, Mar del Plata, Argentina, 1985, XVI Internat. Workshop on Condensed Matter Theories, San Juan, P.R., 1992; vis. scholar dept. chemistry U. Pa., Phila., 1987, 89, 91, 92, U. Lille, France, 1996. Contbr. articles to sci. jours. Mem. Am. Phys. Soc. Avocations: walking, reading, music, ancient history, painting. E-mail: gamba@cnea.gov.ar. Office: CNEA Dept Physics, Ave Libertador 8250, 1429 Buenos Aires Argentina

GAMBARDELLA, PAUL CHARLES, veterinary surgeon; b. New Haven, Mar. 16, 1946; s. John Matthew and Nina Ardito G.; m. Susan Crawford, Aug. 10, 1968; children: Peter, Philip, Jeffrey. VMD, U. Pa., 1972; MS, U. Minn., 1975. Diplomate Am. Coll. Veterinary Surgeons. Staff surgeon Angell Meml. Animal Hosp., Boston, 1975-80; assoc. prof. surgery Tufts U. Sch. Veterinary Medicine, Boston, 1981-85; head dept. surgery, chief staff Angell Mem. Animal Hosp., 1985—. Mem. Am. Veterinary Med. Assn., Am. Animal Hosp. Assn. (outstanding svc. award 1986), Am. Coll. Veterinary Surgeons (pres. 1995), New Eng. Veterinary Med. Assn. (pres. 1995-96), Mass. Veterinary Med. Assn. Office: Angell Meml Animal Hosp 350 S Huntington Ave Boston MA 02130-4803

GAMBILL, JAN-MICHAEL, professional tennis player; b. Spokane, Wash., June 3, 1977. Professional tennis player, 1996—; team player Davis Cup, 1997. Office: c/o USTA 70 W Red Oak Ln White Plains NY 10604-3602*

GAMBLE, (GEORGE) ALVAN, retired marketing consultant, former Canadian government official; b. Guelph, Ont., Can., Jan. 10, 1916; s. Hugh Miskelly and Margaret (Quarrell) G.; m. Jean Christeen Melrose, Aug. 3, 1940; children: Stephen John, Timothy Clifford (dec.), Lois Rebekah. Mgr., cons., co./union negotiations conciliator Toronto, Ont., 1945-52; dir. merit employment project Am. Friends Svc. Com., Indpls., 1952-55; exec. asst. to gen. dir., dir. info. Can. Mental Health Assn., Toronto, 1955-62; dir. health svcs. Smith Kline & French (Can.), 1962-68; mktg. analyst Paul Maney Labs. (Can.) Ltd., Toronto, 1968-71; chief market rsch. and immigration fgn. svc. info. adviser Govt. of Can. Employment and Immigration Commn., Ottawa, Ont., 1971-81, cons. mktg. and pub. rels., 1981-90, ret., 1990. Mem. Markham Twp. (Ont.) Planning Bd., 1959; provincial health minister's rep. Bd. of Health Regional Municipality of York, 1965-71; bd. dirs. Union Villa Sr. Citizens Residence, Markham, 1965-71; vol. feature writer columnist Can. evang. chs. periodicals. Served with RCAF, 1940-45. Decorated Order of Can.; recipient Silver Jubilee medal, 1977, Assoc. Ch. Press award Atlantic Bapt., Canadian Ch. Press awards (2). Fellow Am. Pub. Health Assn.; mem. Profl. Mktg. Rsch. Soc. (life). Baptist. Club: Nat. Press (Ottawa). Home: # 2208, 1140 Fisher Ave, Ottawa, ON Canada K1Z 8M5

GAMBLE, THEODORE ROBERT, JR., investment banker; b. St. Louis, Sept. 18, 1953; s. Theodore Robert and Rispah Adele (Dowse) G.; m. Susan Lee Stupin, Mar. 3, 1984. AB, Princeton U., 1975; MArch, Harvard U., 1977, MBA, 1979. Assoc. Morgan Stanley & Co., Inc., N.Y.C., 1979-84, v.p., 1984-86, prin., 1986-87; pres. The Prescott Group Inc., N.Y.C., 1987—; mng. dir. Transwestern Commercial Svcs., LLC, N.Y.C., 1999—. Co-chmn. adv. com. real estate devel.; chmn. vis. com. Grad. Sch. Design Harvard U.; mem. bus. and vis. coms. Met. Mus. Art; mem. vestry St. Thomas Ch., N.Y.C.; bd. dirs., exec. v.p. Greater N.Y. coun. Boy Scouts Am.; bd. dirs. N.Y. Hist. Soc., Coll. of Arms Found.; vice chancellor, bd. govs. Am. Soc., Order St. John of Jerusalem.; mem. visiting com. Mary Inst. St. Louis Country Day Sch. Mem. Internat. Coun. Shopping Ctrs., Urban Land Inst. (comml. and retail devel. coun., internat. com.), Nat. Assn. of Real Estate Investment Trusts, Assn. Fgn. Investors in Real Estate, Internat. Assn. Corp. Real Estate Execs., Real Estate Bd. N.Y., Young Mortgage Bankers Assn., River Club, Racquet and Tennis Club, Univ. Club, Knickerbocker Club, Links Club, Brook Club, Doubles Club, Met. Opera Club, Princeton Club (bd. govs., exec. com., v.p. fin.), Harvard Club (N.Y.C. and Boston), City Club (Miami), Coral Beach and Tennis Club (Bermuda). Republican. Episcopalian. Home: 860 UN Pla New York NY 10017 Office: Transwestern Commercial Svcs LLC The Prescott Group Inc 535 Madison Ave Fl 17 New York NY 10022-4212

GAMBLING, WILLIAM ALEXANDER, electrical engineering educator, administrator; b. Port Talbot, Glamorgan, U.K., Oct. 11, 1926; s. George Alexander and Muriel Clara (Bray) G.; m. Margaret Pooley, July 26, 1952 (div. June 1994); children: Paul Maitland, Alison Jill, Vivien Ruth; m. Barbara Colleen O'Neil, July 21, 1994. BSc in Engring., U. Bristol, Eng., 1947, DSc, 1968, DEng (hon.), 1999; PhD, U. Liverpool, Eng., 1956; DUniv (hon.), U. Madrid, 1994; DSc (hon.), Aston U., Birmingham, Eng., 1995. Chartered engr. Lectr. U. Liverpool, 1950-55; NRC fellow U. B.C., Vancouver, Can., 1955-57; lectr., reader Southampton (Eng.) U., 1957-64, prof. electronics, 1964-89, dir. optoelectronics rsch. ctr., 1989-95; dir. optoelectronics rsch. ctr. City U. Hong Kong, 1996—; non-exec. dir. York Tech. Ltd., London, 1980-97; cons. Pirelli Gen. Ltd., Southampton, 1970-95; mem. internat. adv. ctr. Hong Kong U., 1995—; hon. prof. Beijing U. Posts and Telecomm., Shanghai, Shandung and Huazhung univs., China; mem. Engring. Coun., London, 1983-88; chmn. Commn. D, Internat. Union of Radio Sci., 1984-87 (vice chmn. 1981-84), chmn. Nat. Optoelectronics Com., London, 1988-91. Mem. editl. bd. Current Chemistry Ltd. for Solid State and Materials Sci., London, 1996—; contbr. articles to profl. jours. Freeman, City of London, 1988. Staff sgt. Royal Elec. and Mech. Engrs., U.K., 1947-49. Recipient Internat. Micro-Optics award, Japan, 1989, Dennis Gabor award Internat. Soc. for Optical Engring., 1990, medal and prize Found. for Computer and Comms. Promotion, Japan, 1993, Rank prize for optoelectronics Rank Found., London, 1991, others; liveryman Worshipful Co. of Engrs., City of London, 1988—. Fellow Royal Soc. London, Royal Acad. Engring., Instn. Elec. Engrs. (hon.); mem. Polish Acad. Scis. (fgn.), Instn. Elec. Engrs. London (past pres.). Avocations: reading, music, travel. Office: City U Hong Kong Optoelec Res Ctr, Tat Chee Ave, Kowloon Hong Kong China

GAMBOA, GEORGE CHARLES, oral surgeon, educator; b. King City, Calif., Dec. 17, 1923; s. George Angel and Martha Ann (Baker) G.; m. Winona Mae Collins, July 16, 1946; children: Cheryl Jan Gamboa Granger, Jon Charles, Judith Merlene Gamboa Hiscox. Pre-dental cert., Pacific Union Coll., 1943; DDS, U. Pacific, 1946; MS, U. Minn., 1953; AB, U. So. Calif., 1958, EdD, 1976. Diplomate Am. Bd. Oral and Maxillofacial Surgery. Fellow oral surgery Mayo Found., 1950-53; clin. prof. grad. program oral and maxillofacial surgery U. So. Calif., L.A., 1954-99; assoc. prof. Loma Linda (Calif) U., 1958-99, chmn. dept. oral surgery, 1960-63; pvt. practice oral and maxillofacial surgery San Gabriel, Calif., 1955-93; dir. So. Calif. Acad. Oral Pathology, 1995—. Mem., past chmn. first aid com. West San Gabriel chpt. ARC. Fellow Am. Coll. Dentists, Am. Coll. Oral and Maxillofacial Surgeons (founding fellow), Pierre Fauchard Acad., Am. Inst. Oral Biology, Internat. Coll. Dentists, So. Calif. Acad. Oral Pathology; mem. Am. Assn. Oral and Maxillofacial Surgeons, Internat. Assn. Oral Surgeons, So. Calif. Soc. Oral and Maxillofacial Surgeons, Western Soc. Oral and Maxillofacial Surgeons, Am. Acad. Oral and Maxillofacial Radiology, Marsh Robinson Acad. Oral Surgeons, Profl. Staff Assn. L.A. County-U. So. Calif. Med. Ctr. (exec. com. 1976-99), Am. Cancer Soc. (Calif. div., profl. edn. subcom. 1977-90, pres. San Gabriel-Pomona Valley unit 1989-90), Am. Dental Assn. (sci. session chmn. sect. on anesthesiology, 1970), Calif. Dental Soc. Anesthesiology (pres. 1989-94), Calif. Dental Found. (pres. 1991-93), Calif. Dental Assn. (jud. coun. 1990-96), San Gabriel Valley Dental Soc. (past pres.), Xi Psi Phi, Omicron Kappa Upsilon, Delta Epsilon. Seventh-Day Adventist. Home: 1102 Loganrita Ave Arcadia CA 91006-4535

GAMBOA, LUCITO G., physician; b. Pampanga, The Philippines, Jan. 7, 1929; came to U.S., 1952; s. Serapion M. and Jacinta L. Gamboa; m. Sylvia V. Roque, Sept. 18, 1953; children: Richard, Virginia Majer, Debra Jorgensen. MS, U. Colo., 1955; MD, U. Santo Tomas, Manila, The Philippines, 1952. Diplomate Am. Bd. Pathology. Dir. pathology and clin. labs. Edgewater Hosp., Chgo., 1958-69, 80-90; dir. blood bank and sr. pathologist Little Co. of Mary Hosp., Evergreen Park, Ill., 1969-80; mem. staff Ctrl. Valley Gen. Hosp., Hanford, Calif., 1990—. Contbr. numerous articles to profl. jours. Bd. dirs. Chgo. Dist. Tennis Assn., 1973-76. Recipient Disting. Physician award Philippine Med. Soc. Chgo., 1966. Mem. Assn. Philippine Physicians in Am. (pres., founder 1972-74, Disting. Svc. award 1975), Assn. Philippine Pathologists in Am. (pres., founder 1970-72), Dove Canyon Country Club. Avocations: golf, tennis, photography, travel. Home: 18 Golf View Dr Dove Canyon CA 92679-3802 Office: Ctrl Valley Gen Hosp 1025 N Douty St Hanford CA 93230-3722

GAMBONI, DARIO LIBERO, art historian, educator; b. Yverdon, Vaud, Switzerland, Dec. 26, 1954; arrived in France, 1991.; s. Pierre and Nadia (Beati) G.; m. Michèle Cusinay Conscience, Apr. 2, 1976 (div. Dec. 1983); children: Laura, Aurélien; m. Johanna Luise Weis, Mar. 26, 1990; 1 child, Vasco Rubén. MA, U. Lausanne, Switzerland, 1977, PhD, 1989. Tchg. asst. U. Lausanne, 1977-83; guest curator Mus. Fine Arts, Lausanne, 1983-85; fellow, rschr. FNSRS, Paris, 1986-89; editor Hist. Mus., Berne, Switzerland, 1989-91; prof. U. Lyon II, France, 1991-98, Case Western Res. U., Cleve., 1998—; vis. prof. U. Strasbourg, France, 1991; co-curator exhbn. Mus. Fine Arts, Lucerne, Switzerland, 1983-85; mem. editl. com. Pro Helvetia, Zurich, 1985-92. Author: Un iconoclasme moderne, 1983, La géographie artistique, 1987, La plume et le pinceau, 1989, The Destruction of Art, 1997; mem. editl. bd. Revue de l'Art, 1997—. Recipient prize Faculté of Lettres, U. Lausanne, 1989; CASVA sr. fellow, 1996. Mem. Institut Universitaire de France. Office: Case Western Reserve U Dept Art History and Art 10900 Euclid Ave Cleveland OH 44106-4901

GAMBRELL, SARAH BELK, retail executive; b. Charlotte, N.C., Apr. 12, 1918; d. William Henry and Mary (Irwin) Belk; m. Charles Glenn Gambrell (dec.); 1 child, Sarah Belk Gambrell Knight. BA, Sweet Briar Coll., 1939; D in Humanities (hon.), Erskine Coll., 1970, U. N.C., Asheville, 1986, Furman U., 1997. Dir. Belk Inc., 1947—. Hon. trustee emeritus Princeton (N.J.) Theol. Sem.; trustee Johnson C. Smith U., Charlotte, N.C., Warren Wilson Coll., Swannanoa, N.C., Hezekiah Alexander Found., Charlotte; hon. trustee Cancer Rsch. Inst.; trustee nat. bd. YWCA; bd. dirs. Parkinson's Disease Found., N.Y.C., N.C. Cmty. Found., Raleigh, (hon.) bd. dirs. YWCA, N.Y.C.; bd. dirs. Charlotte Philharmonic Orch., Cmty. Sch. Arts. Mem. Fashion Group, Inc. (N.Y.C.), Jr. League Charlotte, Nat. Soc. Colonial Dames, DAR. Home: 300 Cherokee Rd Charlotte NC 28207-1908 Office: Belk Inc 2801 W Tyvola Rd Charlotte NC 28217-4500

GAMBRELL, THOMAS ROSS, investor, retired physician, surgeon; b. Lockhart, Tex., Mar. 17, 1934; s. Sidney Spivey and Nora Katherine (Rheinlander) G.; m. Louise Evans, Feb. 23, 1960. Student summa cum laude, U. Tex., 1953, MD, 1957. Intern Kings County Hosp., Bklyn., 1957-58; company physician Hughes Aircraft, Fullerton, Calif., 1958-65, Chrysler Corp., Anaheim, Calif., 1962-65, L.A. Angels Baseball Team, Fullerton, 1962-64; pvt. practice medicine Fullerton, 1958-91; with St. Jude Hosp., Anaheim Meml. Hosp., Fullerton Cmty. Hosp., Martin Luther Hosp.; mem. utilization rev. com. St. Mary's Convalescent Hosp., Fullerton Convalescent Hosp., Sunhaven and Fairway Convalescent Hosp.; owner Ranching (Citrus) & Comml. Devel., Ariz., Tex., N.Y., 1962-94. Contbr. articles to profl. jours. Organizer of care for needy elderly, North Orange County, 1962-65; sponsor numerous charity events. Fellow Am. Acad. Family Physicians; mem. AMA, Am. Geriats. Soc., Calif. Med. Assn., Tex. Med. Assn., Tex. Alumni Assn., Orange County Med. Assn., Mayflower Soc., Plantagenet Soc., Sons of Confederacy, SAR, Order Royal Descendants Living in Am. (col., listed in Living Descendants of Blood Royal), Order Crown (col.), Baronial Order Magna Carta, Order of Aesculaepius, Phi Eta Sigma, Delta Kappa Epsilon, Phi Chi. Avocations: collecting, travel, history. Office: PO Box 6067 Beverly Hills CA 90212-1067

GAMBRO, MICHAEL S., lawyer; b. N.Y.C., July 15, 1954; s. A. John and Rose A. (Grandinetti) G.; m. Joan L. Thurneyssen, Aug. 9, 1980; children:

Dana E., Merrill R., Christopher J. BS summa cum laude, Tufts U., 1976; JD, Columbia U., 1980. Bar: N.Y. 1981, U.S. Dist. Ct. (so. dist.) N.Y. 1981, U.S. Dist. Ct. N.J. 1981, N.J. 1983, Calif. 1988. Assoc. Cadwalader, Wickersham & Taft, N.Y.C., 1980-86, ptnr., 1987-88; ptnr. Cadwalader, Wickersham & Taft, L.A., 1988-94, N.Y.C., 1994—. Harlan Fiske Stone scholar, 1978-79, 1979-80. Mem. ABA, Phi Beta Kappa, Psi Chi. Office: Cadwalader Wickersham & Taft 100 Maiden Ln New York NY 10038-4818

GAME, DAVID AYLWARD, physician; b. Adelaide, Australia, Mar. 31, 1926; s. Tasman Aylward and Clarice Mary (Turner) G.; m. Patricia Jean Hamilton, Dec. 8, 1949; children: Ann, Philip, Timothy, Ruth. MB, BS, U. Adelaide, 1949. Resident Royal Adelaide Hosp., 1950, Outpatient Registrar, 1951; gen. practice medicine Adelaide, 1953-96; officer Order of Australia, 1983; chmn. Eastern Region Geriatric and Rehab. Adv. Com., 1976-83; chmn. Cen. Ea. Health Adv. Com., 1983-86. Mem., chmn. social welfare coun. Diocese of Adelaide; chmn. Anglican Cmty. Svcs. Coun., 1989-95; mem. standing com. Synod Diocese Adelaide, Ch. of Eng., 1966-79, 81-84. Fellow Royal Australian Coll. Gen. Practitioners (chmn. fed. coun. 1969-72, pres. elec. 1972-74, pres. 1974-76, censor in chief, 1976-80), Royal Coll. Gen. Practitioners (hon., fellow ad eudem), Hong Kong Coll. Gen. Practitioners, Australian Postgrad. Fedn. in Medicine; mem. Coll. Family Physicians of Can. (life, gov., patron), World Orgn. Nat. Colls. and Acads. and Academic Assns. Gen. Practitioners/Family Physicians (hon. sec. treas. 1972-80, pres. 1983-86), Australian Postgrad. Fedn. Medicine (coun.), Australian Med. Assn., Australian Geriatric Soc., Lorna Laffer Med. Dir. of South Australian, Postgrad. Mech. Edn. Assn., Adelaide Club. Home and Office: 50 Lambert Rd, Royston Park 5070, Australia

GAMEA, AHMED MOAWAD, otorhinolaryngology educator; b. Tanta, Gharbia, Egypt, July 9, 1951; s. Moawad Mohamed and Fatma (Ahmed) G.; m. Faika Ahmed El-Tatawi, May 31, 1981; children: Mohamed, Ghada, Sarah. MB, Bch, Tanta U., 1975, MSc, 1979, MD, 1984. House officer Tanta U. Hosp., 1975-77, registrar in otolaryngology, 1977-79; asst. lectr. otolaryngology Tanta U. Faculty Medicine, 1979-84, lectr., 1984-89, asst. prof., 1989-94, prof., 1994—; cons. on health ins., Tanta, 1982—, Red Cescent Hosp., Tanta, 1983—. Editor Jour. Laryngology and Otology, 1988—. Named Best Physician, Egyptian Ministry Health, 1981. Mem. Egyptian Soc. Otorhinolaryngology. Avocations: tennis, football, music, chess, reading. Home: Omar Ben Abdel-Aziz St, Tanta 31111, Egypt Office: Tanta U Faculty Medicine, Osman Mohamed St, Tanta 31111, Egypt

GAMEIRA, ANTONIA CUNHA, banker, educator; b. Lisbon, Portugal, Mar. 22, 1936; s. Antonio David and Etelvina Oliveira (Cunha) G.; m. Marilia Figueiredo Martins, Aug. 29, 1959; 4 children. Lic. in Econ., ISCEF, Lisbon, 1959, MA in Mgmt., 1964. Gen. inspector Banco Comml., Angola, 1960-63; gen. mgr. BPA, Lisbon, 1964-75, exec. dir., 1976-86; chmn. SFP, Lisbon, 1986-89; vice chmn. Banco Itau, Sao Paulo, Brazil, 1986-89; CEO BFP, Paris, 1994—; vis. prof. Lisbon U. Cons. APM, Lisbon, 1970-94; pres. IPEF, Lisbon, 1987-93; dir. ITAU Found., Sao Paulo, 1988-89; cons. mem. CMVM, Lisbon, 1992-95. Mem. Gremio Literario. Avocation, art collecting. Home: AV EUA 114-9D, 1700 Lisbon Portugal Office: Banque Franco Portugaise, 8 Rue du Helder, 75009 Paris France

GAMET, DONALD MAX, appliance company executive; b. Mapleton, Kans., Feb. 21, 1916; s. Carl Adolph and Pearl May (McClanahan) G.; m. L. Pauline Fleming, Apr. 14, 1938 (dec. Dec. 1981); children: Merilyn Kay Gamet Paris, Carleton Lenoir, Kathy Lynn Gamet Stephenson; m. Marilyn Lang, Jan. 15, 1983. BBA, Ft. Hays State Coll., 1938; MBA, U. Kans., 1939, JD, 1942. CPA, Mo. Staff acct. Arthur Andersen & Co., Kansas City, Mo., 1942-46, mgr., 1946-54, ptnr., 1954-78, mng. ptnr. Kansas City office, 1956-70; vice chmn. tax practices Arthur Andersen & Co., Chgo., 1970-77, sr. ptnr., 1977-78; cons. Kansas City, 1978-84; v.p.-treas. Chgo. Pacific Corp. (merged with Maytag 1989), 1984-85, exec. v.p. fin., 1985-87, spl. cons. to chief exec. officer, 1987-89, ret., 1989. Pres., chmn. bd. dirs. Heart Am. United Funds, Met. Kansas City, 1967-68, chmn. spl. reorgn. study com., 1980-84; mem. adv. bd. Salvation Army Kansas City, 1982-84; mem. personnel com. Village United Presbyn. Ch., 1982-84; pres., bd. dirs. Estate Planning Council Kans., 1962-63, Minority Supplier's Devel. Council Kansas City, 1983-84; bd. dirs., mem. exec. com., treas. Civic Council Kansas City, 1967-70; bd. dirs., chmn. long range planning com. Geriatic Resources Corp. Kansas City, 1982-84; bd. dirs. Metro Kansas City C. of C., 1962-70, pres., 1969-70; bd. dirs. Kansas City Indsl. Found., 1968-70, Jr. Achievement Kansas City, 1960-65. Named Boss of Yr., Met. Kansas City Jaycees, 1962; recipient Alumni Achievement award Ft. Hays State Coll., 1969. Mem. AICPA, Kansas City Club. Republican. Home: 5220 W 121st St Shawnee Mission KS 66209-3501

GAMKRELIDZE, THOMAS VALERIAN, linguist, educator; b. Kutaisi, Georgia, USSR, Oct. 23, 1929; s. Valerian and Olimpiada G.; m. Nino Djavakhishvili, 1968; children: Eka, Sandro. Researcher Inst. Linguistics Georgian Acad. Scis., Tbilisi, Georgia, 1953-60, researcher Oriental Inst., 1960-73, dir. Oriental Inst., 1973—; prof. linguistics Tbilisi State U., 1960—; People's dep. of the USSR, 1989; mem. Parliament of Georgia, 1992-95, 95-99, 99—. Recipient Lenin prize in sci. and technology USSR, 1998, Alexander von Humboldt prize, Djavakhishvili prize, George. Fellow Brit. Acad.; mem. Georgian Acad. Scis., Russian Acad. Scis., Am. Acad. Arts and Scis. (fgn. hon. mem.), Austrian Acad. Scis., Sächsische Akademie der Wissenschaften (fgn. mem.), Soc. Linguistica Europaea (pres. 1987), Indogermanische Gesellschaft (hon.), Linguistic Soc. Am. (hon.). Office: Oriental Inst Parliament Ga, Rustaveli ave 8, 380018 Tbilisi Georgia

GAMM, ALEXANDER ZELMANOVICH, electric power researcher, educator; b. Stalingrad, Russia, Oct. 9, 1938; s. Zelman Abramovich and Revekka Izrailevna (Buchbinder) G.; m. Svetlana Nikolaevna Sazonova, June 19, 1963; children: Alexander, Tatjana. Engr., Novosibirsk Electrotech. Inst., Russia, 1967, Prof., 1982; DSc, Moscow Power Inst. Jr. rschr. Siberian Energy Inst., Irkutsk, Russia, 1962-67, sr. rschr., 1967-76, head of lab., 1976-97, chief rschr., 1997—; tchr. Irkutsk Tech. U., 1966—; cons. Amur U., Blagoveshchensk, Russia, 1995—, Angarsk (Russia) Tech. Inst., 1997—. Author: State Estimation in Electric Power Systems, 1983, Probability Models of EPS, 1993, Sensors and Weak Points in EPS, 1996; author, editor: Real Time Problem in EPS, 1990. Recipient Krzhizhanovsky prize Russian Acad. Scis., 1967, State Premium of USSR, 1986; named Honored Scientist of RF, 1997. Mem. IEEE (sr.), Acad. Electrotech. Sics. of Russia, Internat. Energy Acad. Scis. Avocations: reading, drawing. Office: Energy Sys Inst, Lermontov Str 130, 664033 Irkutsk Russia

GAMMAL, ROBERT MAURICE, dentist; b. Sydney, NSW, Australia, Sept. 26, 1951; s. Alex and Ilse (Kiefer) G. B in Dental Surgery, Sydney U., 1974; DRM, Natural Care Coll., Sydney, 1984. Pvt. practice dentist, 1975-98, pvt. practice biocompatible dentistry, 1991. Fellow Australian Coll. Nutritional and Environ. Medicine; mem. ASOMAT (founder, past pres. 1994-97, sec. 1997-98), ADA, IAOMT. Avocations: music, shakuhachi, cycling.

GAMMON, JONATHAN ROBERT ARTHUR, civil engineer; b. London, July 20, 1952; s. Robert Howard and Jean (Prentice) G.; m. Jennifer Mary Jones, Aug. 2, 1974; children: Bryony Mary Anne, Helena Mary Lyn. BSc, U. Surrey, 1974; MSc, U. London, 1975. Chartered engr. and geologist, Europe; registered profl. engr., New Zealand, China. Engr. site sect. Marti AG Bern, Switzerland, 1972-73; geotech. engr., sr. then chief engr. W.S. Atkins & Ptnrs., Epsom, U.K., 1975-80, 88-90; sr. geotech. engr., then assoc. Fugro Ltd., Hong Kong, 1980-84; sr. assoc., dept. head Murray-North Ltd., Auckland, New Zealand, 1984-88; sr. project engr., dept. head Trafalgar House Tech., London, 1990-91; sr. geotech. engr. Dar Al-Handasah Cons., London, 1991-93; assoc. Butler Pullet Ptnrs., Sevenoaks, Kent, U.K., 1993-95; tech. adviser engring. Inst. Civil Engrs., London, 1995-96; prin. engr. then assoc. dir. Atkins China Ltd., Hong Kong, China, 1996—. Contbr. chpts. in books and articles to profl. jours. Hon. pres. Horsham Round Table No. 40. Fellow Geol. Soc. London; mem. ASCE, Instn. Civil Engrs. (vice chmn. S.Ea. Local Assn. 1994-96, Hong Kong Instn. Engrs., Coun. on Tall Bldgs. and Urban Habitat 1992—, chmn. Piling and Ground Treatment Panel 1990-95), Instn. Profl. Engrs. New Zealand (fellow), Brit. Geotech. Soc., Concrete Soc. U.K., Internat. Geosynthetics Soc., Assn. Geotech. Specialists (mem. exec. com. 1998—), New Zealand Nat. Soc. for Earthquake Engring. Avocations: travel, foreign languages, bridge engineering, rugby, architecture. Home: 2 Coleridge Close, Horsham RH12 5PB, England Office: Atkins China Ltd, 16/F World Trade Ctr 280 Gloucester Rd, Causeway Bay Hong Kong Hong Kong

GAMMON, MALCOLM ERNEST, SR., surveying and engineering executive; b. Chattanooga, Tenn., Sept. 7, 1947; s. George A. and Frances Helen (Conway) G.; m. Glenna Dee Shirk, June 5, 1971; children: Malcolm Ernest Jr., Christopher Brian. BS, Miss. State U., 1970. Ops. mgr. Pyburn & Odom, Inc., Baton Rouge, 1970-84; chief exec. officer, prin. owner Hydro Cons., Inc., Baton Rouge, 1984—. Tech. contbr. (textbook) 4567 Review Questions for Surveyors, 11th edit., 1985, Elementary Surveying, 8th edit., 1989. State chmn. La. Trig Star Program, Baton Rouge, 1988-89; mem. adv. bd. La. Math. Coalition. Mem. La. Soc. Profl. Surveyors (registered, pres. 1990), Miss. Assn. Profl. Surveyors (registered), Nat. Soc. Profl. Surveyors (profl. mem., bd. govs.), Am. Congress on Surveying and Mapping (dir., profl. mem., cert. hydrographer), Ark. Soc. Profl. Surveyors (registered), Ala. Profl. Land Surveyors (registered). Home: 19021 Saint Clare Dr Baton Rouge LA 70810-7979 Office: Hydro Cons Inc 10275 Siegen Ln Baton Rouge LA 70810-4926

GAMORAN, SAMUEL HENRY, computer engineer, consultant; b. N.Y., Jan. 10, 1956; arrived in Israel, 1984; s. Abraham Carmi and Edith (Fetter) G.; m. Roxane Ginzberg Gamoran, July 31, 1977; children: Nathan Menachem, Ita Sarah, Avraham Carmi. BSEE, Cornell U., Ithaca, N.Y., 1977; MS in Computer Engring., U. Calif. Berkeley, 1978; MBA, Rutgers U., Newark, N.J., 1984. Registered engr., Israel. Co-op student GE, Syracuse, N.Y., 1975-76; tech. staff Bell Telephone Labs., Bell Comms. Rsch., N.J., 1977-84; vis. scientist Weizmann Inst. Sci., Rehovot, Israel, 1984-87; computer engr. Decision Sys. Israel, Givatayim, 1988-92; cons. Bell Comms. Rsch., Piscataway, N.J., 1992-93; project mgr. Motorola Israel, Tel Aviv, 1993—; cons. Tekmark Computer Svcs., N.Y.C., 1985-92; lectr. Jerusalem Coll. Mgmt., 1991. Gabbai Yad Moshe Synagogue, Hashmonaim, Israel, 1991-92. Recipient merit scholarship N.Y. State, 1973, Rutgers U., 1981, 84. Mem. IEEE (sr.), Assn. for Computing Machinery, Am. Radio Relay League. Jewish. Avocations: amateur radio electronics model rocketry. Home: Ramat Modiin PO Box 1521, 73123 Hashmonaim Israel Office: Motorola Israel, 3 Kreminetski St, 67899 Tel Aviv Israel

GAMST, FREDERICK CHARLES, anthropology educator; b. N.Y.C., May 24, 1936; s. Rangvald Julius and Aida (Durante) G.; m. Marilou Swanson, Jan. 28, 1961; 1 child, Nicole Christina. AA, Pasadena City Coll., 1959; AB, UCLA, 1961; PhD, U. Calif., Berkeley, 1967. Instr. anthropology Rice U., Houston, 1966-67, asst. prof., 1967-71, assoc. prof., 1971-75; prof. dept. anthropology U. Mass., Boston, 1975—, chmn. dept. anthropology, 1975-78, assoc. provost for grad. studies, 1978-83; cons. in social rels., human factors and ops. to R.R. industry, 1970—; acting dir. Houston Inter-Univ. African Studies Program, 1969-71, Behavioral Sci. Grad. Program, Rice U., 1974-75; mem. Joint Internat. Observer Group (for observation of Ethiopian elections), 1992; mem. com. on human factors for railroads and other fixed guideway transp. sys. Transp. Rsch. Bd., 1999—. Author: Travel and Research in Northwestern Ethiopia, 1965, The Qemant: A Pagan-Hebraic Peasantry of Ethiopia, 1969, Peasants in Complex Society, 1974, The Hoghead: An Industrial Ethnology of the Locomotive Engineer, 1980, Highballing with Flimsies: Working under Train Orders, 1990; editor: Studies in Cultural Anthropology, 1975, Letters from the United States of North America on Internal Improvements, Steam Navigation, Banking, Etc., 1990, Anthropology Quar., Golden Anniversary Spl. Issue on Indsl. Ethnology, 1977, (with Edward Norbeck) Ideas of Culture: Sources and Uses, 1976, Meanings of Work: Consideration for the Twenty-First Century, 1995, Early American Railroads: Franz Anton Ritter von Gerstner's Die Innern Communicationen (1842-1843), 2 vols., 1997, (video documentary) T-Time: The History of Mass Transit in Boston, 1984; contbr. articles and revs. to profl. publs., chpts. to books. Mem. adv. com. Quincy Quarries Hist. Site, Met. Dist. Commn. Mass., 1987—. N.Y. State Regents scholar 1954-58, UCLA scholar 1959-60, Haynes Found. scholar 1960-61; Woodrow Wilson Nat. fellow 1961-62, Ford Found. Fgn. Area fellow 1962-63, Social Sci. Research Council & Am. Council of Learned Socs. Fgn. Area fellow 1963-66; Rice U. research grantee 1967, NSF grantee 1970-72, NIMH grantee 1972-74, others. Fellow AAAS, Am. Anthrop. Assn. (Conrad Arensberg award 1995), Soc. Applied Anthropology, Royal Anthrop. Inst. Gt. Britain and Ireland; mem. Sci. Rsch. Soc., Ry. and Locomotive Hist. Soc. (dir., editor 4 vol. Franz Anton Ritter von Gerstner project 1988—), Indsl. Rels. Rsch. Assn., Soc. for History Tech., Lexington Group in Transp. History, Brotherhood Locomotive Engrs., Ry. Fuel and Operating Officers Assn., Am. Assn. R.R. Supts., Transp. Rsch. Bd., Soc. Anthrop. Work (pres. 1984-87, bd. dirs. 1987-90), Internat. Union Anthrop. and Ethnol. Scis. (chmn. curriculum com. Commn. Study of Peace 1983-86), Assn. for Study Lang. in Prehistory (bd. dirs. 1988—), Mass. Tchrs. Assn. (mem. exec. com. Faculty Staff Union 1996—). Office: U Mass Dept Anthropology Harbor Campus Boston MA 02125-3393

GAMUNDÍ, IRMA JOSEFA, mycologist, researcher; b. Buenos Aires, Argentina, Jan. 13, 1927; d. Andrés Oscar and Virginia (Bona) G.; m. Arturo Jorge Amos, May 15, 1953; children: Victoria, Cristina, Arturo Andrés. Lic. in Exact and Natural Scis., U. Buenos Aires, Argentina, 1953, D in Nat. Scis., 1959. Asst. prof. U. Buenos Aires, 1954-66; assoc. prof. U. La Plata, Argentina, 1966-71, prof., 1971-88; hon. prof. U. La Plata, 1988—, U. Comahue, Bariloche, Argentina, 1994—; jr. rschr. Nat. Rsch. Coun., Buenos Aires, 1961-73, sr. rschr., 1974—; dir. Inst. Botánica Spegazzini, La Plata, 1975-91; acad. guest EIDG Tech. Hochschul, Zürich, 1982; advisor CONICET, Buenos Aires, 1990-91, 96; invited prof. The Royal Soc., London, 1990, IMS link scientist, 1997. Editor: (book series) Flora Criptogamica Tierra Del Fuego Argentina, 1975-94; co-author: Fungi of the Andean-Patagonian Forest, 1993; author: Darwiniana 1962, 64 (Cristobal Hicken prize 1969). Mem. Brit. Mycol. Soc., Soc. Argentina Botanica (hon.), Mycol. Soc. Am., Latin American Mycol. Assn. (hon. mem.). Roman Catholic. Avocations: gardening, fishing, cooking. Office: Centro Regl U Bariloche, 8400 San Carlos Bariloche Rio Negro, Argentina

GAN, CHAYING, chemicals company executive; b. Manila, The Philippines, Apr. 3, 1949; s. Lian Chiao Gan an dKuan Tan; m. Linda Loo, Dec. 13, 1981; children: Ariane, Lennard, Gerrard, Howard. BSc in Chem. Engring., U. Philippines, Quezon City, 1971; MSc in Chem. Engring., U. Va., 1973; MBA, Lehigh U., 1977. Comml. devel. mgr. Air Products, Allentown, Pa., 1973-78; area mgr. Lubrizol Far East Ink, Manila, 1978-83; mng. dir. Lubrizol Sea Pte Ltd, Singapore, 1984-99; entrepreneur Petroleum Products, 2000—. Mem. Rotary (officer Jurong, Singapore chpt. 1985). Avocations: golf, arts.

GAN, SHIJUN, science and technology educator; b. Hanyang, Hubei, People's Republic of China, Nov. 27, 1939; s. Ying Liu; m. Ling Gao; children: Song, Bai. BS, Xian Transp. U., Shanxi, 1962. Engr., dir. Sci.-Tech. Forecast Bur. State Sci. & Tech. Commn., 1982-85, head divsn. sys. analysis dept. policy, 1985-87, exec. dep. dir., rschr. Rsch. Ctr. Sci. and Tech., 1987-90, dep. dir., 1990-91, dir. dept. sci. and tech. for social devel., 1991-98; chmn., CEO China Nat. Publs. Import & Export Co., 1998—; hon. prof. Qinhua U., 1993—; dir. project Water Resources Rsch., North China, 1991, China Info. Sys., 1985, Innovative Strategic Rsch. on Chinese Medicine-Tech., 1996; dir., implementer Stratetgic Guidelines on Sustainable Devel. of China, 1994; dir. Guideline on Development the Marine Economy in China, 1994. Author: The Science & Technology of China in the Year 2000, 1987 (1st prize for State Sci. and Tech. Progress, 1987), Science & Technology Progress & Social Development, 1993, Sustainable Development: The Choice at the Turn of the Century (award Pub. Industry China, 1998). Organizer Min.'s Conf. on Environ. and Devel. in Developing Countries, Beijing, 1991. Recipient prize State Sci. and Tech. Commn., 1996. Mem. N.Y. Acad. Scis. Home and Office: China Nat Pubs Imp & Exp Co, 16 Gongti E Rd/PO Box 88, Beijing 100020, Peoples Republic of China

GAN, VIVIEN HWEE-YONG, small business owner; b. Singapore, Republic of Singapore, June 13, 1962; d. Paul Boon-Peng and Hiro Mutsui Gan. BA in Econs., Boston U., 1985. Dep. mng. dir. Gan Teng Siew Investment Pte., Ltd., Singapore, 1985—, Good Old Days (Vintages and Antiques) Pte. Ltd., Singapore, 1986—, Good Old Days Food and Entertainment Pte. Ltd., Singapore, 1997—; v.p., CFO, CAO Food and Entertainment Pte Ltd. The Big Apple Coffee, Singapore, 1997—; exec. dir. Luxen Internat. Constrn. and Realty Pte., Ltd., Singapore, 1992. Mem. Nat. Assn. Watch and Clock Chpt., The Highlander, Oxford Club. Avocations: correspondence, rifle shooting, travel, reading. Home: 21-08 Katong Park Towers, 114A Arthur Rd S Tower, Singapore 439826, Singapore Office: Good Old Days Pte Ltd, c/o The Big Apple Coffee No 6 Dukes Rd, Singapore 268886, Republic of Singapore

GAN, WEI-QUN, physicist; b. Nanjing, Jiangsu, China, Dec. 17, 1960; s. Chen Gan and Lichun Wan; m. Jinlan Zhu, Apr. 18, 1987; 1 child, Di. BS, Nanjing U., 1983, MS, 1986, PhD, 1989. Asst. rschr. Purple Mountain Obs., Nanjing, 1989-91, assoc. prof., 1993-95, prof., 1996—; postdoctoral rschr. Max-Planck-Inst., Munich, 1991-93. Contbr. articles to profl. publs. Recipient 1st pl. Young Scientist award Chinese Acad. Scis., 1995, 2d pl. award for natural sci. Chinese Acad. Scis., 1995. Mem. Internat. Astron. Union. Office: Purple Mountain Obs, West Beijing Rd 2, Nanjing Jiangsu 210008, China

GAN, WOON SIONG, acoustician; b. Republic of Singapore, Mar. 6, 1943; s. Eng Hwa and Chai Luan (Tan) G.; m. Madam Chiong Siu Hui, Mar. 4, 1973; children: Gan Cheong Kiat, Judy Gan, Gan Cheong Toh. BSc in Physics, Imperial Coll., London, 1965, DIC in Acoustics and Vibration Sci., 1967, PhD in Acoustics, 1969. Assoc. prof. dept. physics Nanyang U., Singapore, 1970-79; dir. Acoustical Svcs. Pte Ltd., Singapore, 1976—; dir. WS Gan Realty & Devel. Pte Ltd., Galaxy Internat. Pte Ltd.; cons. in field. Assoc. editor Internat. Jour. Acoustical Holography and Imaging; contbr. articles to profl. jours. Internat. Centre for Theoretical Physics fellow Trieste, Italy. Fellow Inst. Acoustics U.K., Inst. Elec. Engrs. (U.K.), South African Acoustics Inst.; mem. AAAS (internat. mem.), Acoustical Soc. U.S., Acoustical Soc. France, Acoustical Soc. Japan, Acoustical Soc. Italy, Acoustical Soc. India, Acoustical Soc., IEEE (sr.), Am. Inst. Ultrasound in Medicine (sr.), N.Y. Acad. Sci. Office: 209-212 Innovation Ctr NTU, 16 Nanyang Dr, Singapore 637722, Singapore

GANAN-CALVO, ALFONSO MIGUEL, fluid mechanics educator, mechanical engineer; b. Cordoba, Spain, Aug. 11, 1962; s. Alfonso Ganan Torralbo and Avelina Calvo (Diaz) G.; m. Maria Pilar Riesco-Chueca, May 6, 1989; children: Braulio, Fabio, Dario. D in Mechanical Engring., U. Sevilla, Spain, 1989. Asst. prof. U. Sevilla, Spain, 1987-94; cons. engr. Office of Naval Rsch./U. Calif., San Diego, 1991-93; rsch. assoc. U. Southern Calif., L.A., 1989-90; adv. bd. The Aerosol Soc., U.K., 1997-98; cons. Aradigm Corp., Hayward, Calif., 1997-2000; bd. dirs. Flow Focusing Inc., Flowgenics, S.L. Inventor: A new liquid atomization procedure, 1997, a new procedure to produce compound micropellets, 1997. Recipient Annual Award for Doctoral Thesis, U. Sevilla, Spain, 1994, Smoluchowski award on aerosol sci., 1998. Mem. Am. Phys. Soc., Gesellschaft fur Aerosolforschung e. V. (GAeF). Roman Catholic. Avocations: catamaran sailing, cycling, artistical drawing, literature, philosophy. E-mail: alfonso@alfonso.us.es. Fax: (34) 5-448-7224. Home: c/Camilo Jose Cela 4 B8 3A, 41018 Sevilla Spain Office: ESI U Sevilla, Camino los Descubrimientos, 41092 Sevilla Spain

GANAPATHY, KOLLA RANGIAHSETTY, retired editor, educator; b. Chitradurga, India, Jan. 9, 1931; s. Arsikere Kolla Rangiahsetty and Rangiahsetty Kolla Sathyabhammamma; m. Kolla Ganapathy Chandramma, Feb. 23, 1958; children: Bhamamani, Suma, Mukund. BS, U. Mysore, 1951; MSc, U. Wis., 1968. From agrl. extension officer to agrl. demonstrator Dept. Agriculture, Bangalore, India, 1954-63; from tech. asst. to editor, prof. U. Agrl. Sci., Bangalore, 1963-91. Author: Writing for Low Level Literates, 1971, Dairy Farming in Bangalore Milk Shed Area, 1976, Potato in Diet (Kann ada), 1986; contbr. articles to profl. jours. Avocations: acting, social service, editing. Home: 228 I Cross II Block, III Phase III Stage, Banashankari Bangalore, India 560 085

GANCHERENOK, IGOR IVANOVICH, physicist, educator, researcher; b. Minsk, Belarus, Apr. 15, 1962; s. Ivan Ivanovich and Sofiya Alexandrovna (Yakubovskaya) G.; m. Tat'yana Grigor'evna Grachyova, Aug. 24, 1984; children: Natasha, Tina. Diploma in Physics, Belarusian State U., Minsk, 1984, PhD in Physics, 1987; DSc, Acad. Scis. of Belarus, Minsk, 1997. Cert. physicist. Instr. Belarusian State U., Minsk, 1984-85, rsch. asst., 1985-89, assoc. prof., 1989-94; vis. prof. Osaka Nat. U., Japan, 1992; dean Rep. Inst. Higher Edn., Minsk, 1994-96, dept. head, 1996—; dir. internat. program European Union, Minsk, Belarus, 1993—; referee Jour. Applied Spectrose, Minsk, Belarus, 1995—; mem. internat. adv. bd. Internat. Inst. on Higher Edn. Adminstrn., Md., U.S., 1995—; vis. prof. Tohoku U., Japan, 1996. Author: Bulletin of Inventions, Russia, 1989-96; mem. editl. bd. Jour. Management in Education, 1995—; author over 150 papers; contbr. articles to profl. jours. Grantee USIS, 1995, NATO, 1996, Am. Phys. Soc., 1995; Fulbright scholar U. Pitts., 1999. Mem. Russian Optical Soc., European Assn. Internat. Edn. Mem. Orthodox Ch. Avocations: swimming, volleyball. E-mail: gancher@nihe.unibel.by. Home: Voronyanskogo St 3-1-93, Minsk 220039, Belarus Office: Rep Inst Higher Edn, Moskovskaya St 15, Minsk 220001, Belarus

GANDHI, MANEKA, government official; b. New Delhi, India, Aug. 26, 1956; widowed; 1 child. Grad., Jawaharlal U., New Delhi, India. Founder Rashtriya Sanjay Manch Party, India, 1983; min. Ministry Environ. & Forests, India, 1989-91, Ministry Welfare, India, 1998—; min. state for small scale agro/rural industries. Office: Min Welfare, Dr Rajendra Prasad Rd, New Delhi 110 001, India*

GANDHI, RAVINDER SINGH, dairy research scientist; b. Tarin, India, Apr. 4, 1960; s. Piara Singh and Shanti Gandhi; m. Virinder Bhatia, June 21, 1987; children: Gurnoor S., Simran. BSc, Guru Nanak Dev U., 1979; MSc in Dairying, Nat. Dairy Rsch. Inst., 1982, PhD in Animal Genetics Breeding, 1987. Scientist Nat. Dairy Rsch. Inst., Karnal, India, 1986-91, sr. scientist, 1991—. Contbr. articles to profl. jours. Nat. scholarship Govt. of India, 1975, Merit scholarship Khalsa Coll., 1978, Outstanding Young Indian award Karnal Jr. Chamber, 1997, Outstanding Young Person awrad Indian Jr. Chamber, 1997; jr. rsch. fellowship Nat. Dairy Rsch. Inst., 1979, sr. rsch. fellowship, 1982. Mem. Indian Dairy Assn. (life), Indian Soc. of Animal Prodn. and Mgmt. (life), Agrl. Rsch. Svcs. Scientists Forum (life), Genetic Soc. of India, Indian Soc. of Life Scis., N.Y. Acad. Scis. Avocations: walking, reading, listening to classical music, gardening. Home: 28 Officers Colony, Behind DC's Residence, Karnal 132001, India Office: Nat Dairy Rsch Inst, Karnal 132 001, India

GANDHI, SONIA, government official; m. Rajiv Gandhi (former Prime Minister of India, dec.); children: Priyanka, Rahul. Pres. Rajiv Gandhi Found.; mem. Congress (I) Party; now pres. Congress Party; leader of opposition in Parliament. Office: 10 Janpath, New Delhi 110001, India*

GANDILHON, PHILIPPE ALBERT, nuclear medicine physician, researcher; b. Boulogne, France, Apr. 11, 1953; s. Jean Albert and Alice Juliette (Pinquier) G.; m. Francoise Anne Marie Royer, Aug. 4, 1974; children: Pachamma, Neltie. MD, Poitiers, France, 1980, PhD, 1982; nuclear medicine, Clermont Ferrand, France, 1987. Rschr. Inst. Nat. de la Santé et de la Rsch. Med., Marseille, France, 1983; MD Svc. de Médecine Nucléaire, Clermont-Ferrand, France, 1980-89; MD Centre de Médecine Isotopique, Vannes, France, 1989-94, Béziers, France, 1995—; pres. Nucleaire Med. S.A. Mem. Action Concertée en Médecine Nucléaire, European Assn. Nuclear Medicine, Soc. Medecine Nucleaire de L'ouest (v.p. 1989), Soc. Francaise Biophysique Medecine Nucleaire, Soc. Francaise Cancérologie Privé, Am. Soc. Privée, Soc. Nuclear Medicine, Am. Soc. Nuclear Cardiology, Radiol. Soc. N.Am. Home: 12 rue de Montmorency, 34500 Béziers France Office: Centre Liberal de Medecine Nucleaire, 2 rue Valentin Hauy, 34500 Béziers France

GANDINI, UMBERTO, organization director; b. Varese, Italy, Apr. 11, 1960; s. Enea and Annamaria (Gandini) Vedvrelli; m. Lorella Campi, June 27, 1992; children: Alessandro, Ludovica. Grad., State U. Milan, 1989. TV commentator RTI, Italy, 1988-89, acquisition exec., sports programs, 1989-98; organizing dir. AC Milan, 1993—, team mgr., 1998—; com. mem. Italian League Football, 1996—. Office: AC Milan, via Turati 3, 20121 Milan Italy

GANDOIS, JEAN GUY, steel company executive; b. Nieul, France, May 7, 1930; s. Eugène and Marguerite (Teillet) G.; children: Thierry, Philippe. Student, Poly. Coll., Paris, 1952, Ponts and Chaussées Coll., Paris, 1954. Engr. Dion Travaux Publics, Conakry, Guinea, 1954-58, road expert, 1959-60; mgr. mktg. Wendel, Paris, 1961-72; managing dir. Sacilor, Paris, 1972-76; chmn., chief exec. officer Sollac, Paris, 1975-76; pres., CEO Rhone-Poulenc, Paris, 1976-79, chmn., chief exec. officer, 1979-82; internat. cons., chmn., chief exec. officer Industrie Conseil S.A., Paris, 1983-86; chief exec. officer, chmn. bd. Pechiney, Paris, 1986-94; pres. Nat. Coun. French Employers, 1994-97; chmn. Cockerill Sambre, 1987; bd. dirs. Danone, France, Banque Nat. de Paris, Eurafrance, France, Soc. Gen. de Belgique,; mem. supervisory bd. Paribas, France, Suez-Lyonnaise de Eaux, France, Vallourec, France, Peugeot, France; mem. supervisory coun. Akzo Nobel, The Netherlands, Siemens AG, Germany. Author: Mission Acier, 1986. Decorated Grand Croix de L'Ordre de la Couronne (Belgium); grand officer Ordre du Chêne (Luxembourg); commdr. Legion of Honor (France). Office: rue du Faubourg St-Honoré 72, F-75008 Paris France

GANDOLFI, GIUSEPPE DOMENICO ANTONIO, lawyer; b. Salsomaggiore, Parma, Italy, Sept. 18, 1927; s. Gino and Graziella (Caviglia) G.; m. Letizia Ruffini, Sept. 16, 1970. LLD, U. Milan, Italy, 1949, Qualified Lectr., 1958; hon. doctor, U. Lausanne, Switzerland, 1996, U. Extremadura, Spain, 1999. Counsellor-at-law Ct. of Cassation. Lectr. U. Milan, 1960-67; prof. U. Camerino, Italy, 1967-70, U. Trieste, Italy, 1970-72, U. Padova, Italy, 1972-74, U. Pavia, Italy, 1974—; coord. Working Group for Drafting European Contract Code, Pavia, 1990—. Author: Studî sull'interpretazione degli atti negoziali, 1966, La conversione dell'atto invalido - 1. Il modello germanico, 1984, La conversione dell'atto invalido - 2. Il problema in proiezione europea, 1988, 90, Studi di diritto privato, 1994, Code European des Contrats, 1999; contbr. articles to profl. jours. Named Grand Officer Order of Merit of Italian Republic, 1984, gold medal for merits to sch., culture and arts Pres. of Italian Republic, 1988; fellow Istituto Lombardo-Accademia di Scienze e Lettere, Milan, 1982. Mem. Gesellschaft für Rechtsvergleichung, Acad. European Pvt. Lawyers (promoting mem., sec. 1992—, co-pres.). Home: Piazza Velasca 6, 6 20122 Milan Italy Office: Istituto di Studi Politico-Giuridici, Univ/Strada Nuova 65, I-27100 Pavia Italy

GANDOLFI, WALDIR, veterinary surgery educator; b. São Paulo, Brazil, Mar. 4, 1941; s. Sidney and Sylvia (Brunhare) G.; m. Dirce Nassif, Oct. 6, 1966; children: Sandra Cristina, Silvia Maria Gandolfi Chiarello. MS, U. São Paulo, 1969, PhD, 1972. Postdoctoral staff Hannover, Germany, 1975-76; prof. U. São Paulo, 1980; full prof. UNESP, 1982. Avocations: soccer, diving, biking. Home and Office: Francisco Lira Brandao 121, 18607000 Botucatu Brazil

GANDOLFO, ROBIN RAGSDALE, management analyst; b. Astoria, Oreg., Jan. 28, 1955; d. John O'Neill and JoAnn Lindsay Ragsdale; m. David Kevin Gandolfo, Apr. 16, 1983 (div. May 1996); children: Ashley Brooke, Gia Marie. BBA, U. Tex., 1978; MS, Naval Postgrad. Sch., 1987. Commd. ens. USN, 1980, advanced through grades to comdr.; occupl. analyst Navy Occupl. Devel. and Analysis Ctr., Washington, 1987-90; adminstrv. officer Nuclear Field A Sch., Orlando, Fla., 1990-93; exec. officer Navy Recruiting Dist., Memphis, 1993-95; mgmt. analyst Naval Edn. and Tng. Profl. Devel. Devel. and Tech. Ctr., Pensacola, Fla., 1995-98; ret. USN, 1998; mgmt. analyst Alpha Solutions Corp., Pensacola, 1998-99, Disney World, Orlando, 2000—; sales rep. Rexall Showcase Internat., Pensacola and Orlando, 1999—. Mem. Ret. Officer's Assn. Republican. Avocations: aerobics, quilting. Home: 6088 Raleigh St Apt 1705 Orlando FL 32835-2232

GANDRILLE, FABIEN M., reinsurance company executive; b. Paris, July 25, 1953; s. Philippe M. and Claude B. (de Lengaigne) G.; m. Christine E. de Monteville, Feb. 12, 1983; children: Hiérôme, Adélaïde. MS in Law, Paris II-Assas U., 1977. Attaché legal dept. Caisse Industrielle d'Assurance Mutuelle, Paris, 1982-87; mgr. gen. liability and fin. lines claims Am. Internat. Group, Paris, 1987-91; asst. claims mgr. Comml. Union Assurances, Paris, 1991-95; claims mgr. SOREMA, Paris, 1996—. Contbr. articles to Sci. Historique. Trustee Inst. Maison de Bourbon, 1978—, Assn. Ins. and Reins. Jurists, 1994—. Mem. Internat. Assn. Ins. Law, Racing Club France. Roman Catholic. Avocations: cross country skiing, fine arts history, genealogy. Home: 15 rue Marie Laurencin, F-75012 Paris France Office: SOREMA, 20 rue Washington, F-75008 Paris France

GANDY, GERALD LARMON, rehabilitation counseling educator, psychologist, writer; b. Thomasville, Ga., Feb. 9, 1941; s. Larmon Brinkley and Ruby Wylene (Vickers) G.; m. Patricia Kay Haltiwanger, Jan. 22, 1966. BA, Fla. State U., 1963; MA, U. S.C., 1968, PhD, 1971. Lic. profl. counselor, Va.; lic. clin. psychologist, Va.; nat. cert. rehab. counselor; nat. cert. counselor; nat. registered psychologist; cert. profl. qualification in psychology Assn. of State and Provincial Psychology Bds. Profl. counselor U. S.C. Counseling Ctr., Columbia, 1968-70; counseling psychologist VA Regional Office, Columbia, 1970-75, chief counseling psychologist, 1974-75; prof. emeritus Med. Coll. Va., Va. Commonwealth U., Richmond, 1996—, prof., program dir., 1975-95; chair nat. com. on undergrad. rehab. edn. Nat. Coun. on Rehab. Edn., 1984-89; mem. numerous state and govt. adv. coms., 1970—. Author: Mental Health Rehabilitation, 1995; co-author: Rehabilitation and Disability, 1990; co-author/editor: Rehabilitation Counseling and Services, 1987, Counseling in the Rehabilitation Process, 1999; co-editor: International Rehabilitation, 1980, 89; contbr. numerous articles to profl. jours. Faculty pres. Sch. of Community and Pub. Affairs, VA Commonwealth U., 1989-93. Capt. U.S. Army, 1963-66. Recipient Disting. Svc. award Sch. of Community and Pub. Affairs, 1988, School and U. Leadership award, 1993. Fellow Internat. Acad. of Behavioral Medicine, Counseling and Psychotherapy (diplomate); mem. APA, ACA, World Fedn. for Mental Health, Phi Kappa Phi. Home: Highland Springs 300 Southern Ct Richmond VA 23075-1519 Office: Va Commonwealth Univ Med Coll Va PO Box 980330 1112 E Clay St Richmond VA 23298-5007

GANDY, H. CONWAY, retired judge, state official; b. Washington, Nov. 3, 1934; s. Hoke and Anne B. (Conway) G.; m. Carol Anderson, Aug. 29, 1965; children: Jennifer, Constance, Margaret. BA, Colo. State U., 1962; JD, U. Denver, 1968. Bar: Colo. 1969, U.S. Dist. Ct. Colo. 1969. Pvt. practice Ft. Collins, Colo., 1969-81; adminstrv. law judge divsn. adminstrv. hearings State of Colo., Denver, 1981-99. Bd. dirs. Foothills-Gateway Rehab. Ctr., 1970-80, Colo. State Bd. Dental Examiners, 1976-81; Dem. candidate for Colo. Senate, 1974, dist. atty., 1976; trustee Internat. Bluegrass Music Assn. Trust Fund, 1990—. With USN, 1954-58. Mem. Nat. Assn. Adminstrv. Law Judges (pres. Colo. chpt. 1985-86), Sertoma (Centurion award 1973, Tribune award 1975, Senator award 1977, 79, sec. Honor club 1977-78, pres. Ft. Collins club 1978-79, pres. Front Range club 1988-89). Home: 724 Winchester Dr Fort Collins CO 80526-2636

GANDY, JAMES THOMAS, meteorologist, entrepreneur; b. Memphis, Tenn., Nov. 25, 1952; s. Thomas Marion and Sible Christaline (McBride) G.; m. Ann Cuppia, Apr. 12, 1986. BS, Fla. State U., 1974; postgrad., U. S.C. Meteorologist Sta. WREG-TV (CBS affiliate), Memphis, 1975-77; staff meteorologist Sta. KTVY-TV (NBC affiliate), Oklahoma City, 1977-82; dir. ops. Weather Data, Inc., Wichita, Kans., 1982-84; meteorologist Kans. State Network (NBC affiliate), Wichita, 1982-84; chief meteorologist Sta. WIS-TV (NBC affiliate), Columbia, S.C., 1984-98; pres. JAG Corp. of S.C. dba Cartoon Connection, 1997—; cons. meteorologist Gannett TV, Arlington, Va., 1998—; writer, cons. The State Newspaper, Columbia, S.C., 1999—; guest lectr. U. S.C., Columbia, 1991, 95, 98; writer, cons. The State Newspaper, Columbia, S.C., 1999—. Named Best TV Weather Forecaster, The State Newspaper, Columbia, S.C., 1993, Best TV Weather Personality, Columbia Met. Mag., 1994, 95, 96, 97, 98. Mem. AAAS, Am. Meteorol. Soc. (TV Seal of Approval 1985, Memphis chpt. sec. 1976-77, chmn. 1977, Ctrl. Okla. chpt. sec.-treas. 1979, 82, pres. 1980, Palmetto chpt. v.p. 1988-89, 97-98, pres. 1989-90, 98-99), Nat. Weather Assn., Planetry Soc. (charter mem.), N.Y. Acad. Scis., Order Internat. Fellowship (charter). Home and Office: 101 W Ashford Way Irmo SC 29063-8325

GANDY, PAUL DWAYNE, lawyer; b. Castle AFB, Calif., June 10, 1956; s. Lynell Wesley and Alice Marquette (Cross) G. BA, Harvard U., 1978; JD, U. Tex., 1984. Bar: Iowa 1987, U.S. Dist. Ct. (so. dist.) Iowa 1991, U.S. Ct. Appeals (8th cir.) 1995, U.S. Supreme Ct. 1997; cert. in consumer bankruptcy. Pvt. practice Fairfield, Iowa, 1991—. Mem. ABA, Am. Bankruptcy Inst., Iowa State Bar Assn., Nat. Assn. Consumer Bankruptcy Attys. Office: 104 1/2 N Main St Ste 2 Fairfield IA 52556-2802

GANE, MICHAEL, sociology educator, writer; b. Woking, Surrey, Eng., Nov. 21, 1943; s. John Roy and Winifred Edith (Allen) G. BA, Leicester (Eng.) U., 1968; PhD, London U., 1973. Tchg. asst. Leicester (Eng.) U., 1971-72; lectr. sociology Loughborough U., 1972-90, sr. lectr. sociology, 1990-98, reader sociology, 1998-2000, prof. sociology, 2000—. Author: On Durkheim's Rules of Sociological Method, 1988, Baudrillard: Critical and Fatal Theory, 1991, Baudrillard's Bestiary: Baudrillard and Culture, 1991, Harmless Lovers? Gender, Theory, and Personal Relationships, 1993, Jean Baudrillard: In Radical Uncertainty, 2000; co-author: Ideological Dilemmas, 1988; editor: Economy and Society, 1981—, Durkheimian Studies, Towards a Critique of Foucault, 1986, Ideological Representation and Power in Social Relations, 1989, The Radical Sociology of Durkheim and Mauss, 1992, Baudrillard Live: Selected Interviews, 1993, Foucault's New Domains, 1993. Mem. Brit. Sociol. Assn., Assn. Internat. Sociologues de Langue Française. Avocations: woodwind instruments, gardening, archery, marquetry, photography. Office: Loughborough Univ, Dept Social Scis, Loughborough LE11 3TU, England

GANESH GANI, GANI GANESH See KANNUSAMY, GANESH GANI

GANESHPURE, PRALHAD AMBADAS, science administrator, chemistry researcher; b. Kanshivani, India, May 24, 1954; s. Ambadas L. and Maina A. (Waghmare) G.; m. Madhavi T. Sawke, May 13, 1982; 1 child, Kunal. BSc, Nagpur (India) U., 1972, MSc, 1974, PhD, 1979. Postdoctoral fellow Brandeis U., Waltham, Mass., 1979-81; lectr. chemistry Nagpur U., 1981-83; mgr. R&D Indian Petrochemicals Corp. Ltd., Vadodara, India, 1983—; convenor of seminars Indian Petrochemicals Corp., Ltd., Vadodara, 1984-86, convenor of com. to evolve a manpower policy, 1990; rsch. guide Maharaja Sayajirao U. Vadodara, 1988—; A.V. Humboldt fellow U. Würzburg, Germany, 1991-93. Contbr. articles to profl. jours. Fellow Instn. Chemists India (life), Indian Chem. Soc. (life); mem. Am. Chem. Soc., Catalysis Soc. India (life), Marathi Vidnyan Parishad (life), Mem. Indian Soc. Analytical Scientists. Hindu. Avocations: music, reading, travel, table tennis. Home: B-21 Kinnery Duplex, Ellora Park, Vadodara Gujarat 390 007, India Office: Rsch Ctr, Indian Petrochem Corp Ltd, Vadodara Gujarat 391 346, India

GANG, RAJKUMAR, medical educator, consultant; b. Jodhpur, India, Jan. 27, 1950; s. Bastimal and Dhankanwar G.; children: Sudhir, Nirmit. MBBS, U. Rajasthan, Jodhpur, India, 1972; MS, 1976. Civil asst. surgeon SJ Hosp., Jaisalmer, India, 1976; sr. registrar Safdurjung Hosp., Delhi, India, 1976-77; Ministry of Health, Benghai, Libya, 1977-79; plastic surgeon Akademiska Sjukhuset, Uppsala, Sweden, 1979-80; lectr. U. Garyounis, Benghazi, Libya, 1980-84; asst. prof., 1984-86, assoc. prof., 1986-89; plastic surgeon Ministry of Health, Kuwait, 1989—. Contbr. numerous papers and research in field. Fellow ACS, RCS, Internat. Coll. Surgeons. Avocations: swimming, photography, writing, table tennis. Office: Dept of Plastic Surgery, PO Box 366, Salmiya Kuwait

GANGADHAR, BANGALORE NANJUNDAIAH, psychiatrist, consultant; b. Bangalore, Karnataka, India, Oct. 3, 1955; s. B.K. Nanjundaiah and N. Mukthikantha; m. Piriyapattana Seetharamaiah Lokeswary, Dec. 2, 1984; 1 child, B.G. Kalyani. MBBS, Bangalore U., 1977; MD, NIMH & Neuro Scis., 1981. Jr. resident in psychiatry NIMH & Neuro Scis., Bangalore, 1978-81, sr. resident in psychiatry, 1981-82, lectr. in psychiatry, 1987-92, assoc. prof. psychiatry, 1992—. Editor: Proceedings of the National Workshop on ECT: Priorities for Research and Practice in India, 1992; sci. reviewer Indian Jour. Psychiatry, Convulsive Therapy, Biol. Psychiatry; assoc. editor Acta Psychiat. Scandinavica, 1998; contbd. over 100 rsch. articles to profl. jours. Mem. Rastreeya Swayamsevak Sangh, Bangalore, 1970, sec., 1993, pub. rels. officer, 1995—. Mem. Internat. Brain Rsch. Orgn., Indian Psychiat. Soc. (co-recipient Bhagawat award 1989, Kala award 1992, Marfatia award 1993, 96, C.V. Roman award 1999). Hindu. Avocation: photography. Office: NIMH Neuro Scis Dept Psych, PO Box 2900 Hosur Rd, Bangalore 560 029, India

GANGADHARAN, NAGENDRA, engineer, educator; b. Jaffna, Eelam, Ceylon, Dec. 14, 1963; arrived in Singapore, 1994; p. Gangadharan and Sithadevi; m. Ranjani Sithamparanathan, June 21, 1989; children: Ganesh, Arun, Sivakami. BE in Electronics and Comm., U. Madras, India, 1989; ME in Elec. and Electronics, U. Auckland, New Zealand, 1995. Cert. engr. Med. technician Van-West Clinic and Nursing Home, Jaffna, 1983-85; design engr. Elec. Project Ltd., Auckland, 1990-91; biomed. engr. U. Auckland, 1992-94; lectr. Singapore Poly., 1994—; cons. Elec. Projects, Ltd., Auckland. Editor TxRx Newsletter, Commex & Projex, 1995—. Mem. IEEE. Hindu. Avocations: playing flute in Carnatic music, tennis, handyman. E-mail: Nagendra@pacific.net.sg and Nagendra@sp.ac.sg. Fax: 65 7721974. Home: Blk 202 Clmenti Rd #04-208, Singapore 129783, Singapore Office: Singapore Poly, 500 Dover Rd, Singapore 139651, Singapore

GANGOPADHYAY, SRIJIB, agricultural sciences educator, researcher; b. Calcutta, India, Jan. 8, 1941; s. Smarojit and Kamal Gangopadhyay; m. Yuthika Gangopadhyay; children: Banerjee, Shashwat. BSc in Agr., Kalyani U., West Bengal, India, 1962, MSc in Agr., 1964, PhD in Agr., 1968; DSc in Botany, Utkal U., Bhubaneswar, Orissa, India, 1998. Vegetable pathologist Indian Coun. Agrl. Rsch./Indian Agrl. Rsch. Inst., Katrain, India, 1971-77; head divsn. plant pathology Indian Coun. Agrl. Rsch./Ctrl. Rice Rsch. Inst., Cuttack, India, 1977-85; prin. scientist Indian Coun. Agrl. Rsch./Ctrl. Rice Rsch. Inst., Cuttack, 1986—. Author: Breeding for Disease Resistance in Rice, Farmers Friendly Diversified Plant Protection, Advances in Vegetable Diseases, Clinical Plant Pathology, Recent Advances in Fungal Diseases of Rice. Recipient Best Citizen award India, 1991. Fellow Phytopathol. Soc. India; mem. Indian Sci. Congress Assn. (life, pres.-agr. sec. 1993), Indian Phytopathology Soc. (life, East Zonal pres.), Indian Vegetable Rsch. (life). Home: Qrt T V/3 CRRI Campus, Cuttack 753006, India Office: Ctrl Rice Rsch Inst, Cuttack India

GANGRIWALA, HUNED AHMEDI, engineering executive; b. Bhopal, India, Oct. 16, 1953; came to U.S., 1977; s. Ahmedi Abdulla and Ateka Ebrahim (Muchala) G.; m. Elizabeth Katherine Thorpe, Sept. 16, 1982; children: John, Stephen, Adam, Amy. B Tech., Laxminarayan Inst. Tech., Nagpur, India, 1976; MS, Okla. State U., Stillwater, 1978. Mgr., process engr. Eickmeyer & Assocs., Overland Park, Kans., 1978-85; mgr. process engring. Glitsch, Inc., Dallas, 1985-89, mktg. mgr., 1989-92; mng. dir. Glitsch (U.K.) Ltd., Dorking, Eng., 1992-96; pres., CEO Glitsch Process Sys., Inc., Parsippany, N.J., 1996-98; pres. Sulzer Chemtech USA, Inc., Deer Park, Tex., 1998—; pres. Glitsch France, Arles, 1994-96; dir. Glitsch B.V., Amsterdam, The Netherlands, 1993-96, Otto York N.V., Antwerp, Belgium, 1995-96. Contbr. articles to profl. jours., chpt. to book. Mem. AIChE. Avocations: reading, racquetball, billiards, travel.

GANGULY, ANANDA ROOP, business management educator; b. Calcutta, India, Oct. 19, 1963; came to U.S., 1988; s. Purna Nanda and Kalyani Ganguly. B Comm. with honors, U. Calcutta, 1985; PhD, U. Pitts., 1995. Part-time lectr. U. Pitts., 1991-95; lectr. U. Ill., Champaign/Urbana, 1995, asst. prof., 1995—; assurance rsch. fellow Assurance and Adv. Svcs. Ctr., KPMG LLP, 1999-2000; mem., cons. Round Table Group, 1997—; session chair, conf. organizer in field; ad-hoc reviewer Am. Acct. Assn., Acctg. Rev., Contemporary Acctg. Rsch., Mgmt. Sci., 1996—; faculty advisor undergrad. case-study competitions Deloitte and Touche, 1995—. Mem. focus groups Deloitte Touche Tohmatsu, Pitts., 1994; faculty mentor summer rsch. opportunities program for minority students U. Ill., 1997. Grantee/fellow Case Devel., 1993, Arthur Andersen & Co. Found., 1994, U. Pitts., 1996, U. Ill., 1997, Caterpillar Inc., 1998. Mem. Am. Acctg. Assn. (doctoral consortium fellow 1994), Am. Econ. Assn., Soc. for Computational Econs., Soc. for Judgment and Decision Making, Mensa. Avocations: creative writing, computers, chess, photography, target shooting. Fax: (217) 244-0902. E-mail: aganguly@uiuc.edu. Office: U Ill Dept Accountancy MC-706 Champaign IL 61820

GANGULY, ASHIT KUMAR, organic chemist; b. New Delhi, Aug. 9, 1934; came to U.S., 1967; s. Apurba Kumar and Protiva (Chatterji) G.; m. Jean Currie Gowans, Sept. 10, 1966; 1 child, Nomita. PhD, U. Delhi, India, 1959, Imperial Coll., London, 1962. From sr. scientist to v.p. Schering-Plough Corp., Bloomfield, N.J., sr. v.p., 1998—; medicinal chemistry study sect. NIH, Bethesda, Md., 1986—; Khaira Disting. profl. Indian Assn. Cultivation Scis., Calcutta, 1975; Charles Sabat lectr. Rutgers U., N.J., 1987. Contbr. articles to profl. jours. Recipient Seshadri Meml. award Delhi U., 1982, Outstanding Scientist award Assn. Scientists Indian Origins in Am., 1991, Ranbaxy award, 1997; named 3rd Herman S. Bloch Meml. lectr., U. Chgo. Fellow Royal Soc. Chemistry; mem. ACS, N.Y. Acad. Scis. Achievements include patents on Oligosaccharide Antibiotics, Penems, Macrolide Antibiotics, PAF Antagonists, 5-Lipoxygenase Inhibitors. Office: Schering Plough Rsch Inst 2015 Galloping Hill Rd Kenilworth NJ 07033-1300

GANGULY, GAUTAM, materials scientist, research administrator; b. Calcutta, India, Oct. 25, 1960; s. Dilip Kumar and Manju Ganguly; m. Piyali Chakraborty, Dec. 12, 1990; 1 child, Koustav. BSc, U. Delhi, India, 1981; MSc, Indian Inst. Tech., 1983; PhD, Jadavpur U., Calcutta, 1989. Lectr. Indian Assn. Cultivation Sci., Calcutta, 1988-91; rschr. Electrotech. Lab., Tsukuba, Japan, 1991-93, sr. rschr., 1993-96, group leader, 1996-97; sr. scientist Solarex Corp., Newtown, Pa., 1997-99; scientist BP Solarex, Toano, Va., 1999—; referee Internat. Conf. Amorphous & Microcrystalline Semiconductors, 1997—, Solar Energy Materials & Solar Cells, Denver, 1995—, Jour. Applied Physics, N.Y.C., 1996—, Japanese Jour. Applied Physics, Tokyo, 1996—, Materials Rsch. Soc. Symp. Process, Pitts., 1994—. Contbr. articles to profl. jours. Recipient 5 star award Amateur Athletic Assn., Brit., 1972, 73. Mem. Japan Soc. Applied Physics, Materials Rsch. Soc. Home: 4781 Bristol Cir Williamsburg VA 23185-2477 Office: BP Solarex 3601 La Grange Pkwy Toano VA 23168-9348

GANI, OSMAN, publishing executive; m. Kamrumnessa Nargis; three children. BA in Edn., 1978. Mng. dir. Agamee Prakashani, Dhaka, Bangladesh. Exec. editor (Jour.) The Pustak. Mem. Nat. Book Cen. Mng. Bd., Yr. Bengali Nat. Com., Mng. Bd. Bangabandhu Coll., Dhaka, Book Selection Com. Cen. Pub. Libr.; dir. Bangladesh Publs. Coun.; v.p. Joy Bangla Cultural Forum; mem. FBCCI Gen. Body. Recipient Best Publishers award, Nat. Book Cen., 1995, Best Publ., Bnagladesh Publs. and Book Sellers Assn., 1995. Mem. Bangladesh Pubs. and Book Sellers Assn. (joint sec. gen.). Office: 36 Bangla Bazar, Dhaka 1100, Bangladesh

GANIC, EJUP, Bosnia-Herzegovina government official; b. Novi Pazar, Mar. 3, 1946. Student, Belgrade U., MIT. Rschr., cons., prof. mech. engring. U. Ill., Chgo., 1975-82; exec. dir. UNIS Co., 1982; prof. Sarajevo U.; advisor tech. devel. Govt. of Bosnia-Herzegovina, Sarajevo; v.p. Fedn. Govt. Bosnia and Herzegovina, Sarajevo; pres. Muslim-Croat Fedn. Govt., Sarajevo, 1994—; chair Fedn. Bosnians and Croats. Mem. Stranka Demokratske Akcije. Office: Office of President, Alipasina 41, 71000 Sarajevo Bosnia-Herzegovina*

GANN, LAURA VERA, educator; b. Flagstaff, Ariz., Mar. 18, 1971; d. William Edward and Catherine (Devere) Jenkins; m. Chris Shipley, May 23, 1992 (div. Dec. 1997); m. Clay Edward Gann, Dec. 28, 1998. BS, U. North Texas, Denton, 1993, MEd, 1994. Cert. tchr., Tex. Educator Grapevine Colleyville (Tex.) Ind. Sch. Dist., 1994—; mem. excellence in tchg. program Meadows Found., 1991-94. Recipient Robert and Martha Carter scholarship U. North Tex., 1992-93. Mem. United Educators Assn. E-mail: ljgann@ednet10.net.

GANNAM, MICHAEL JOSEPH, lawyer; b. Savannah, Ga., Nov. 10, 1922; s. Karam George and Annie (Abraham) G.; m. Marion Collins DeFrank, June 11, 1949; children: James, Ann, Elizabeth, Joseph. JD, U. Ga., 1948; MA, U. N.C., 1950. Bar: Ga. 1948, U.S. Dist. Ct. (so. dist.) Ga. 1950, U.S. Supreme Ct. 1971, U.S. Ct. Appeals (11th cir.) 1971. Assoc. Bouhan, Lawrence, Williams & Levy, Savannah, Ga., 1950-59; ptnr. Findley, Shea, Friedman, Gannam, Head & Buchsbaum, Savannah, Ga., 1959-70, atty. pvt. practice, 1970-81; sr. ptnr. Gannam and Gnann, Savannah, Ga., 1981—; instr. bus. law polit. sci. and history Armstrong State coll., 1951-62. Bd. dirs. Historic Savannah Found.; bd. dirs., legal counsel Telfair Acad. Arts & Scis.; past pres. Legal Aid Soc. Savannah; mem. Savannah-Chatham Bd. Zoning Appeals, 1961-63, Savannah Arts Com., 1982-85; chmn. Gilmer Lectr. Series Fund, 1980—; bd. dirs. Savannah Coun. World Affairs, 1983-87; pres. Savannah Bar Assn.; bd. govs. State Bar Ga., 1968-99. With USAAF, PTO, 1943-46. Home: 235 E Gordon St Savannah GA 31401-5003 Office: Gannam & Gnann 130 W Bay St Savannah GA 31401-1109

GANOE, BOB, model, actor; b. Louisville, Dec. 16, 1946; s. Harry Dubree and Dorothy (Clark) G. Student, U. Chgo., 1965-68. Photographer's model Bardshaw Models, Chgo., 1966-67; actor Film Inst. Amsterdam, 1968; photographer's model E.M. Jones Models Inc., Oracle, Ariz., 1980; fashion model Cosmo Model & Talent Agy., Louisville, 1998—. Appeared in (movie) American in Amsterdam, 1968; translator: Viva Surrealism (Salvador Dali). Social worker Bur. Pub. Assistance, Louisville, 1973. Grantee Carnegie Found., 1964; scholar U. Chgo., 1965-68. Avocations: collecting art, antiques, jewelry, vintage clothing. Home: Ste 203 1204 Bardstown Rd Apt 203 Louisville KY 40204-1361 Office: Cosmo Model & Talent Agy 7410 New Lagrange Rd Louisville KY 40222-4871

GANS, ERNA IRENE, printing company executive; b. Bielsko, Poland; d. Adolf and Rosa (Pelzman) Reicher; came to U.S., 1948, naturalized, 1953; BA, Roosevelt U., 1971; MA, Loyola U., Chgo., 1974; m. Henry Gans, Apr. 16, 1947 (dec. Oct. 1987); children: Alan, Howard. Asst. prof. dept. sociology Loyola U., Chgo., 1976; pres. Internat. Label & Printing Co., Bensenville, Ill., 1972-93. Chmn., Skokie (Ill.) Youth Commn., 1968-88; bd. govs. Israel Bond Orgn.; founder, chmn. Holocaust Meml. Found. Ill.; mem. U.S. Holocaust Meml. Council. Recipient Edward S. Sparling award Roosevelt U., 1987, 3d Ann. Humanitarian award Holocaust Meml. Found. Ill., 1988. Mem. Am. Sociol. Assn., Nat. Fedn. Ind. Bus., Am. Acad. Polit. and Social Sci. Republican. Jewish. Clubs: B'nai B'rith (pres. 1976-81). Office: 537 N Edgewood Ave Wood Dale IL 60191-2600 Address: PO Box 5155 Buffalo Grove IL 60089-5155

GANS, SAMUEL MYER, temporary employment service executive; b. Phila., June 10, 1925; s. Arthur and Goldie (Goldhirsh) G.; grad. in acctg. Peirce Jr. Coll., 1946-49; m. Ada S. Zuckerman, Aug. 1, 1948; children: Gary M., Jeffrey R. Public acct., 1949-55; sales exec., 1955-58; franchise owner, pres., chief exec. officer Manpower, Inc. Delaware Valley, Pennsauken, N.J., 1958-86; owner Micrographic Services Inc., Pennsauken, 1975—; with All-state Services Inc., County Maintenance Corp., Affiliated Personnel Svc.; owner Antique & Classic Cars Storage Garage Inc., Voorhees, N.J. ; franchise cons.; instr. motivation courses. v.p., exec. bd. United Fund Camden County; v.p., bd. dirs. So. N.J. Devel. Coun., ARC Camden County, Nat. Conf. of Christian and Jews; bd. mgrs. Am. Cancer Soc. Camden County; active Boy Scouts Am., Employer Legis. Com., Camden County Bicentennial Com., Score and Ace programs, Camden, YMCA, Allied Jewish Appeal, World Affairs Coun.; mem. N.J. Gov.'s Mgmt. Commn., 1971; trustee Camden County Heart Assn., Camden County Mental Health Assn.; exec. bd., founder Big Bros. Assn. Camden County; pub. rels. com. U.S. Savs. Bonds, Camden and Trenton. Served with USNR, 1943-46. Mem. Nat. Assn. Temp. Services (chpt. relations com. 1973), Nat. Soc. Public Accts., Camden County C. of C., S. Jersey Public Relations Assn. (pres. 1967), S. Jersey Mfg. Assn. (exec. bd., treas.), S. Jersey Personnel Assn. (treas.), Cherry Hill C. of C. (bd. dirs., v.p.), Better Bus. Bur. Camden County, Adminstrv. Mgmt. Soc., N.J. Assn. Temp. Services (pres. 1970-72, bd. dirs.), South Jersey Purchasing Agts. Assn., Assn. of Manpower Franchise Owners, Jewish War Veterans; Jewish (exec. bd. dirs. congregation). Club: Dolphin Beach Condo. Lodges: Masons, Lions (pres. Camden 1972-73, Lion of Year 1977), Shriners, B'Nai B'Rith, Home: 4 N Derby Ave Ventnor City NJ 08406-2356 Office: 3801 Marlton Pike Camden NJ 08105-3312

GANSBACHER, BERND, physician, educator; b. Sarnthein, Bolzano, Italy, Mar. 5, 1948; s. Franz and Irma Gansbacher; m. Karen Zier. MD, U. Innsbruck, Austria, 1974. Diplomate Am. Bd. Internal Medicine, Am. Bd. Oncology, Am. Bd. Allergy/Immunology. Resident U. Pa., Phila., 1980-83, fellow, 1983-85; fellow Meml. Sloan Kettering Cancer Ctr., N.Y.C., 1986-88; assoc. prof. MSKCC, N.Y.C., 1986-96; dir. Inst. Expertl. Oncology U.

Munich. Office: I Fuer Exp Onkologie, Ismanningerstr 22, 81675 Munich Germany

GANSKOPP, WILLIAM FREDRICK, oil company executive; b. Nanticoke, Pa., July 24, 1915; s. Herman and Ida Helene (Hecht) G.; m. Neale Irene Crosby, July 9, 1942; children: Jennifer Winell, Daryl Stephen. AB in Physics, Lafayette Coll., 1938; diploma in advanced mgmt., Northwestern U., Caracas, Venezuela, 1960. Engr. Standard Oil Co. of N.J., Elizabeth, 1938-42; capt. 703d engrs., Africa, Italy, 1942-45; gas engr. Creole Petroleum Corp., Caracas, Venezuela, 1946-51, mgr. gas sect., 1954-62; drilling engr. Creole Petroleum Corp., Jusepin, Venezuela, 1952-54; natural gas dept. head Esso Nederland, Hague, The Netherlands, 1962-65; natural gas exec. Esso Ea., Sydney, Australia, 1965-68; pres. Gan-Ed, Inc., Columbus, N.C., 1970-78, chief exec. officer, 1978-81; dir., cons. Owosso Gan, Inc., Gainesville, Fla., 1981—. Author: Despite The Odds, 1998; patentee self-propelled golf cart; patentee in Can., Japan and Mex. Recipient Barge Math. award Lafayette Coll., Easton, Pa., 1936, citation MTO, Livorno, Italy. Mem. Ret. Officers Assn. (life, program chmn. 1981-82), Gainesville Golf and Country Club, Masons. Republican. Lutheran. Avocations: golf, tennis, bridge, chess. Home and Office: 2803 B 108 NW 83rd St Gainesville FL 32606

GANT, VANYA ALASDAIR, infection and immunity physician; b. London, Oct. 16, 1956; s. Roland Frederick G. and Nadia Marie Louise (Warchawsky) Legrand; m. Susan Caroline Rodway, Apr. 23, 1994; children: Alexander, Zoe, Natasha, Gilles. PhD, London U., 1989. Physician various hosps., 1980-84; resident Guy's Hosp., London, 1989-90; microbiologist St. Thomas Hosp., London, 1990-94; cons. United Med. Dental Schs., London, 1994-99; clin. dir. infection divsn. and hosp. dir. Hosp. for Tropical Diseases, U. Coll. Hosp., London, 1999—; adviser and prin. investigator various rsch. clin. trials. Contbr. chpts. to books, articles to profl. jours. related to infection and immunity. Mem. Garrick Club. Avocations: paragliding, sports motorcycling, jazz piano. E-mail: vanya.gant@uclh.org. Office: Divsn Infection, Univ Coll Hosp, London WC1E 6DB, England

GANTAR, KAJETAN, classicist, educator; b. Ljubljana, Slovenia, Oct. 11, 1930; s. Kajetan and Frančiška (Rejc) G.; m. Roža Debevec, Sept. 5, 1959; children: Celina, Damjan, Marijana. Diploma in philosophy, Ljubljana (Slovenia) U., 1954, PhD in Philosophy, 1958. Instr. Ptuj (Slovenia) Gymnasium, 1955-57; referent Sec. of Culture, Ljubljana, 1958-62; asst. dept. philosophy Ljubljana U., 1962-67, asst. prof. philosophy, 1967-78, prof. philosophy, 1978-98, subdean dept. philosophy, 1983-85; vis. prof. U. Graz. (Austria), 1981-96; v.p. Slovenian Acad. of Scis. and Arts, 1999—. Author: Ancient Poetics, 1985; author, translator: Roman Lyrics, 1968 (Sovre's prize 1968), Studies to Horace, 1993; co-editor Živa antika--L'antiquité vivant, 1974—. Recipient Prize of Prešeren's Found., 1972. Mem. Soc. Ancient Studies of Slovenia (pres. 1974-80), Assn. Socs. Ancient Studies of Jugoslavia (pres. 1980-83), Soc. Slovenian Lit. Translators (pres. 1983-85), Slovenian Acad. Scis. and Arts, Acad. Latinitati Fovendae, Accademia Properziana, Istituto per gli Incontri Culturali Mitteleuropei. Roman Catholic. Avocations: skiing, hiking. Home: Rusjanov trg 6, SLO-1000 Ljubljana Slovenia Office: Faculty Philosophy, Slovenian Acad Scis/Art, Novi trg 3, Ljubljana Slovenia

GANTIN, BERNARDIN CARDINAL, archbishop, dean; b. Toffo, Dahomey (now Benin), May 8, 1922. Ordained priest Roman Catholic Ch., 1951; titular bishop of Tipasa di Mauritania, also aux. bishop of Cotonou, 1953; archbishop of Cotonou, 1960-71; asst. sec., then sec. Sacred Congregation for Evangelization of Peoples, 1971-75; pres. Pontifical Commn. Justice and Peace, 1975-76; elevated to Sacred Coll. Cardinals, 1977; deacon Sacred Heart of Christ the King; dean Coll. Cardinals, 1993; prefect Congregation for Bishops, 1984; pres. Pontifical Commn. for Latin Am., 1994; mem. Congregation Oriental Chs., Secretariat of Non-Christians; mem. Commn. Revision Code of Canon Law; pres. Commn. Revision of Oriental Code of Canon Law. Address: 00120 Vatican City State Vatican City State

GANTLA, VIDYASAGAR REDDY, chemist; b. Ogode, India, May 18, 1966; s. Ram Reddy and Chilkamma (Gaggenapally) G.; m. Madhavi Reddy Pannala, Nov. 27, 1997. MSc, Osmania U., 1990; MPhil, U. Hyderabad, 1991; PhD, Osmania U., 1998. Rsch. fellow Indian Inst. Chem. Technology, Hyderabad, 1992-96, rsch. assoc., 1996-98; postdoctoral assoc. N.Mex. State U., Las Cruces, 1999—. Avocations: music, TV, gardening, cricket.

GANTT, ELISABETH, plant biology educator, researcher; b. Gakovo, Yugoslavia, Nov. 26, 1934; m. R. Raymond, 1958; 1 child. BA, Blackburn Coll., 1958; MSc, Northwestern U., 1960; PhD in Biology, 1963. NIH rsch. assoc. microbiology Dartmouth Coll. Med. Sch., 1963-66, Smithsonian Inst. Radiation Biology Lab., 1966-88; prof. plant biology U. Md., 1988—; co-dir. MOCB; mem. bd. fellows and assocs. Nat. Rsch. Coun., 1973-76. Recipient Darbaker prize Botany Soc., 1981, G.M. Smith medal NAS, 1994. Fellow AAAS, Am. Inst. Biological Sci., Am. Soc. Photobiology, Am. Soc. Plant Physiologists (v.p. 1988, pres. 1989), Phycol. Soc. Am. (v.p. 1977, pres. 1978), Japan Soc. Plant Physiologists, Nat. Acad. Sci. Achievements include research in structure of photosynthetic apparatus; characterization of carotenoids and photosynthetic membrane structure. Office: U Md Dept Cell Biol and Molecular Genetics College Park MD 20742-0001

GANTZ, NANCY ROLLINS, nursing administrator, consultant; b. Buffalo Center, Iowa, Mar. 7, 1949; d. Troy Gaylord and Mary (Emerson) Rollins. Diploma in nursing, Good Samaritan Hosp. and Med. Ctr., Portland, Oreg., 1973; BSBA, City U., 1986; MBA, Kennedy-Western U., 1987, PhD, 1991. Nurse ICU Good Samaritan Hosp., 1973-75; charge nurse Crestview Convalescent Hosp., Portland, 1975; dir. nursing svcs. Roderick Enterprises, Inc., Portland, 1976-78; dir. nursing svcs. Holgate Ctr., Portland, 1978-80, nursing cons. in field of adminstrn., 1980-84, coord. CCU; mgr. ICU/CCU Tuality Cmty. Hosp., Hillsboro, Oreg., 1984-86; head nurse ICU, cardiac surgery unit, coronary care unit Good Samaritan Hosp. & Med. Ctr., Portland, 1986-88, mgr. critical care units, 1988-92, asst. v.p. patient care svcs., 1992-93; dir. heart ctr. Deaconess Med. Ctr., Spokane, Wash., 1992-93; asst. exec. dir. Children's Cancer Ctr. King Faisal Specialist Hosp. and Rsch. Ctr., Riyadh, Saudi Arabia, 1994—; asst. adminstr. King Fahad Nat. Children's Cancer and Rsch. Ctr., Riyadh, 1996-99; dir. pediatric intensive svcs. St. Louis Children's Hosp., 1999—; mem. spkrs. bur. Nurses of Am.; mem. task force Oreg. State Health Divsn. Rules and Regulations Revisions for Long Term Health Facilities and Hosp., 1978-79; numerous internat. and nat. speaking presentations. Contbr. chpts. to books and articles to profl. jours. Mem. ANA (cert.), AACN (chpt. cons. region 18 1978-89, mgmt. SIC region 18 1990-92, pres. elect greater Portland chpt. 1985-86, pres. 1986-87, bd. dirs. 1985—), AONE Coun. Nurse Mgrs. (bd. dirs. region 9 1991-92), Am. Heart Assn., Geriatric Nurses Assn. Oreg. (founder, charter pres.), Sigma Theta Tau. Home: 4605 Lindell Blvd Apt 1603 Saint Louis MO 63108-3714

GANTZ, SUZI GRAHN, special education educator; b. Chgo., May 17, 1954; d. Robert Donald and Barbara Edna (Ascher) Grahn; m. Louis Estes Gantz, July 11, 1976; children: Christopher, Joshua. BS in Edn. of Deaf and Hard of Hearing, U. Ill., 1976. Tchr. A.G. Bell Sch., Chgo., 1976-80, 88—; sales asst. Bob Grahn & Assocs., Chgo., 1982-84; with sales dept. Isis/My Sisters Circus, Chgo., 1984-86; interpreter Glenbrook North High Sch., Northbrook, Ill., 1986-87; interpreter, aide Lake Forest (Ill.) Dist. 67, 1987-88. Mem. Northbrook Citizens for Drug and Alcohol Alliance, 1988—; cubmaster Boy Scouts Am., Northbrook, 1990-93. Mem. Ill. Tchrs. of the Hearing Impaired, A.G. Bell Soc., Coun. on Exceptional Children. Avocations: dancing, swimming. Home: 485 Laburnum Dr Northbrook IL 60062-2259 Office: AG Bell Sch 3730 N Oakley Ave Chicago IL 60618-4813

GANUGAPATI, SUBBA RAO SREE RAMA, organic chemist educator, researcher; b. Kolavennu Andhra Pradesh, India, Aug. 21, 1937; s. Satyanarayana and Lakshmi (Narasamma) G.; m. Lakshmi Sita Valluri, Apr. 25, 1962; children: Rama, Krishna. BS with honors, Andhra U., Visakha Patnam, India, 1957, MS, 1958, DSc, 1962; PhD, U. Manchester, Eng., 1966. Asst. prof. Indian Inst. Sci., Bangalore, India, 1971-75, assoc. prof. organic chemistry, 1975-80, chmn. dept. organic chemistry, 1982-89, prof. organic chemistry, 1980—, dean Faculty Sci., 1995—. Recipient S. S. Bhatnagar award Coun. Sci. and Indsl. Rsch., New Delhi, 1982, Nat. Lectr. award U. Grants Commn., New Delhi, 1986, Sir C.V. Raman award U. Grants Commn., New Delhi, 1992, Prof. Seshadri 70th Birthday Commemoration medal Indian Nat. Sci. Acad., 1997, Indian Inst. Sci. Alumni award for excellence in rsch., 1998. Fellow Indian Acad. Scis., Indian Nat. Sci. Acad. Hindu. Office: Indian Inst Sci, Dept Organic Chemistry, Karnataka Bangalore 560012, India

GANZ, DAVID L., lawyer; b. N.Y.C., July 28, 1951; s. Daniel M. and Beverlee (Kaufman) G.; m. Barbara Bondanza, Nov. 3, 1974 (div. 1978); m. Sharon Ruth Lamnin, Oct. 30, 1981 (div. 1996); children: Scott Harry, Elyse Toby, Pamela Rebecca; m. Kathleen Ann Gotsch, Dec. 28, 1996. BS in Fgn. Svc., Georgetown U., 1973; JD, St. John's U., 1976. Bar: N.Y. 1977, D.C. 1980, N.J. 1985. Assoc. Regan, Dorsey & De Riso, Flushing, N.Y., 1977-79; ptnr. Durst & Ganz, N.Y.C., 1979-80; mng. ptnr. Ganz, Hollinger & Towe, N.Y.C., 1981-98, Ganz & Hollinger, N.Y.C., 1999—; exec. com. Industry Coun. Tangible Assets, Washington, 1983—, bd. dirs.; cons. in field. Author: A Critical Guide to the Anthologies of African Literature, 1973, A Legal and Legislative History of 31 USC Sec 342d-324i, 1976, The World of Coin Collecting, 1980, 3d edit., 1998, The 90 Second Lawyer, 1996, The 90 Second Lawyer's Guide to Selling Real Estate, 1997, How to Get an Instant Mortgage, 1997, Planning Your Rare Coin Retirement, 1998, Guide Commemorative Coin Values, 1999, Official Guide to America's State Quarters, 2000; corr. Numis. News Weekly, 1969-73, asst. editor, 1973-74, spl. corr., 1974-75, columnist, 1969-76, 96—; contbg. editor, columnist COINage Mag., 1974—; columnist Coin World, 1974-96, COINS Mag., 1973-83; contbr. articles to profl. jours. Mem. U.S. Assay Commn., 1974; bd. dirs. Georgetown Libr. Assocs., Washington, 1982—; mem. N.Y. County Draft Bd., 1984, Bergen County, N.J., 1985—, vice chair, 1996—; sec., mem. Zoning and Adjustment Bd., Fair Lawn, N.J., 1988-92, chmn., 1993-97; elected mem. Dem. County Com. Bergen County, 1988-96, borough coun. Borough of Fair Lawn, 1998—, mayor, 1999—. Decorated Order of St. Agatha (Republic of San Marino). Fellow Am. Numis. Soc. (life); mem. Am. Numis. Assn. (life, legis. coun. 1978-81, 83-95, elected bd. govs. 1985-95, v.p. 1991-93, pres. 1993-95), Assn. of Bar of City of N.Y. (com. on state legis. 1987-90), N.Y. State Bar Assn. (mem. civil practice com., chmn. subcom. 1978-84), Profl. Numis. Guild Inc. affiliated mem. 1989—, gen. coun. 1981-92), Am. Soc. Internat. Law, Nat. Assn. Coin and Precious Metals Dealers (asoc. mem., gen. coun. 1981-85), Flushing Lawyers Club (pres. 1982-83). Democrat. Jewish. Avocation: numismatic. Office: Ganz & Hollinger 1394 3rd Ave New York NY 10021-0404

GANZ, LEONARD IRA, cardiologist; b. Bklyn., May 4, 1962. BA, Harvard U., 1984, MD, 1989. Diplomate Am. Bd. Internal Medicine. Intern Brigham and Women's Hosp., Boston, 1989-90, resident, 1990-92, fellow, 1992-95, staff physician, 1995-97; staff physician Allegheny Gen. Hosp., Pitts., 1997-2000; dir. cardiac electrophysiology U. Pitts. Med. Ctr., 2000—. Editor: Management of Cardiac Arrhythmias, 2000; contbr. chpt. to book, articles to profl. jours. Mem. AMA, ACP, Am. Coll. Cardiology, N.Am. Soc. Pacing and Electrophysiology, Am. Heart Assn. Office: UPMC-CVI 200 Lothrop St Pittsburgh PA 15213-2546

GANZ, MARY KEOHAN, lawyer; b. Weymouth, Mass., Nov. 17, 1954; d. Francis and Margaret (Quinn) Keohan; m. Alan H. Ganz, Sept. 7, 1980. BA magna cum laude, Emmanuel Coll., 1976; JD, Suffolk U., 1979. Bar: Mass. 1979, U.S. Dist. Ct. Mass. 1979, N.H. 1981, U.S. Dist. Ct. N.H. 1981. Pvt. practice, Seabrook, N.H., 1981—. Bd. dirs. My Greatest Dream Inc., Seabrook, 1985—. Mem. ABA, N.H. Bar Assn., Rockingham County Bar Assn., Seabrook Bus. and Profl. Assn. (pres. 1986-87), Seacoast Vis. Nurses Assn. (bd. dirs. 1994—, sec. 1997-98, v.p. 1998-99, pres. 1999—), Phi Delta Phi, Kappa Gamma Pi. Roman Catholic. Office: 779 Lafayette Rd Seabrook NH 03874-4215

GANZ, PETER JOEL, lawyer; b. Charlotte, N.C., Feb. 12, 1962; s. Erwin M. and Rosalee Ganz; m. Toby Ganz, Sept. 20, 1990; children: Rebecca, Noah. AB, Duke U., 1984; JD, Harvard U., 1987. Bar: N.Y., N.J. Law clk. Hon. Annee Thompson, U.S. Dist. Ct., Trenton, N.J., 1987-89; assoc. Kramer Levin, N.Y.C., 1989-91; sr. assoc. Mc Carter & English, Newark, N.J., 1991-95; v.p. legal affairs and deputy gen. coun. GAF Corp./Internat. Splty. Products Inc., Wayne, N.J., 1995—. Mem. N.J. Assn. Corp. Counsel (bd. dirs. 1998—), Internat. Policyholders Assn. (bd. dirs. 1997—).

GANZARAIN, RAMON CAJIAO, psychoanalyst; b. Iquique, Chile, Apr. 18, 1923; s. Eusebio Ganzarain and Maria Cajiao; m. Matilde Vidal Soto, Oct. 10, 1953; children: Ramon, Mirentxu, Alejandro. BS, St. Ignacio Coll., Santiago, Chile, 1939; MD, U. Chile, Santiago, 1947; postgrad., Chilean Psychoanalytic Inst., 1947-50, cert. tng. analyst, 1953. Assoc. prof. psychiatry U. Chile, Santiago, 1955-68, dir. dept. med. edn., 1962-68; prof. depth psychology, sch. psychology Cath. U., Santiago, 1962-68; dir. Chilean Psychoanalytic Inst., Santiago, 1967-68; tng. analyst Topeka Inst. Psychoanalysis, 1968-87; dir. group psychotherapy services The Menninger Found., Topeka, 1978-87; geog. tng. analyst Columbia U. Ctr. for Psychoanalytic Tng. and Research, Atlanta, 1987; assoc. prof. psychiatry Emory U., Atlanta, 1988—; tng. analyst Emory U. Psychoanalytic Inst., 1988—. Author: Fugitives of Incest, 1988, Objects Relations Group Psychotherapy, 1989; contbr. articles to profl. jours., chpts. to books. Fellow Am. Group Psychotherapy Assn.; mem. AMA, Internat. Assn. Group Psychotherapy (bd. dirs., exec. counselor 1986), Am. Group Psychotherapy Assn. (bd. dirs. 1984-87, 93-96), Internat. Psychoanalytic Assn., Am. Psychoanalytic Assn., Kans. Med. Soc., Topeka Psychoanalytic Soc. (pres. 1985-87). Roman Catholic. Avocations: music, swimming, photography, writing, collecting Antarctic stamps. Office: Emory U Psychoanalytic Inst Dept Psychiatry PO Box AF Atlanta GA 30337-0503

GAO, CHANGLI, federal official. Vice-gov. Shandong Province People's Republic China, 1989—, min. of justice, 1998—; standing com. Shandong Province CP, 1986—. Office: Ministry Justice, 11 Xiaguangli Sanyuanqiao, Beijing 100016, China*

GAO, DACHAO, research scientist; b. Changchun, China, Jan. 30, 1950; arrived in Australia, 1988; s. Changqing and Jingzhao (Wang) G.; m. Guiqin Liu, Feb. 14, 1977; 1 child, Lulu. BS, Jilin U., China, 1975; PhD, Royal Melbourne Inst. Tech., Australia, 1993. Rsch. assoc. Academia Sinica, China, 1976-86; vis. scientist U. Manchester, Eng., 1987-88; guest scientist Commonwealth Sci. and Indsl. Rsch. Orgn., Clayton, Australia, 1988-92, rsch. scientist, 1993-98, sr. rsch. scientist, 1999—. Contbr. more than 40 articles to profl. jours. Recipient Merit citation RSNA, 1997, CSIRO medal, 1998, others. Office: CSIRO Divsn Mfg Sci & Tech, Normandy Rd, Clayton Vic 3168, Australia

GAO, DAMING, science educator; b. Luan, Anhui, China, Aug. 20, 1938; parents Daguan Gao and Lanqing Pan; m. Shuwen Zhong, Jan. 20, 1965; children: Hong, Feng. Student, Xian (China) Power Inst.; B of Engring., Sparetime U., Qiqihar, China, 1964. Technician, engr. China 1st Heavy Industries, Qiqihar, 1957-78; engr. Inst. Plasma Physics, Hefei, China, 1978-83, sr. engr., 1983-87, prof., 1988—. Contbr. rsch. articles to profl. jours. Named Advanced Scis. and Tech. Rschr., Anhui, 1995, Chinese Acad. Scis., 1997. Fax: 86 551 5591310. E-mail: dmgao@mail.ipp.ac.cn. Office: Inst Plasma Physics, PO Box 1126, Hefei Anhui 230031, China

GAO, HONGSHENG, data analyst; b. Changchun, Jilin, China; m. Zhao Ying; 1 child, Hannah H. BSc, Jilin U., Changchun, 1982, MSc, 1985; PhD, Victoria U. Wellington, New Zealand, 1997. From asst. lectr. to lectr. Changchun Post and Telecomm. Inst., 1985-93, assoc. prof., 1993. Contbr. articles to profl. jours. E-mail: gao@datamine.co.nz. Home: F2/43 Burrow Ave, Wellington New Zealand Office: Datamine Ltd, 36 Taranaki St, Wellington New Zealand

GAO, HUA, materials science researcher, educator; b. Hang-Zhou, Zhe-Jiang, China, Oct. 26, 1937; d. Yuan Chun Gao and Pu Dai; m. Zhi Guang Ling, Aug. 15, 1963; 1 child, Wei Ling. Student, Jiao-Tong U., Xian, China, 1960. Cert. engr. Lectr. Jiao-Tong U., Xian, 1960-72; assoc. rsch. prof. Chinese Acad. Scis., Beijing, 1972-86; prof. Shanghai U. Engring. Scis., 1986—; sr. rsch. fellow Sheffield (Eng.) U., 1981-83; vis. prof. Cambridge (Eng.) U., 1993-94; acad. com. mem. State Key Lab. of Fatigue and Fracture of Materials, Shenyang, China, 1988—. Contbr. articles to profl. jours. Recipient Sci. Progress award Academica Sinica, 1984, Nature Sci. award, 1994, Sci. Progress award Nat. Ednl. Com., 1993. Mem. C-MRS Fatigue (acad. com. 1994—). Avocations: music, traveling, sports. Home: Mao-Tai Rd Ln 300 #9 Rm 201, 200336 Shanghai China

GAO, LINGBIAO, physics educator, researcher; b. Shantou, Guangdong, China, Oct. 4, 1944; s. Chengqing G. and Wenjing Huang; m. Wenling Hong, Oct. 1, 1970; children: Xiaodan, Xiaohan. BA, Zhongshan U., Guangzhou, China, 1967; PhD, U. Hong Kong, 1998. Edn. diplomate. Lectr. S. China Normal U., Guangzhou, 1981-90, assoc. prof., 1991-98, prof., 1998—. Author: Developing Students' Abilities by Senior School Physics Course-Objectives and Exercises, 1993, School Physics Curriculum, 1995; co-author: Curriculum Studies and School Curriculum Design, 1991; chief editor: The Standardization of School Tests and Examinations-Theoretical Studies and Practical Experiences, 1988, On the Types and Functions of Test Items in National University Entrance Examination, 1992; co-editor: The Design of the Physics Exam in the National University Entrance Examination and an Analysis of Student Performances, 1994, On the Cultivation of Student Science Literacy and Ability, 1996; chief translator: Doing Your Research Project, 1990, The Principles of Objective Testing in Physics, 1994; co-translator: Physics at Work (Chinese version), 1996. Office: S China Normal U, Inst Curriculum Study and Tchg Material, 510631 Guangzhou Guangdong, China

GAO, MING, structures engineer; b. Hangzhou, China, Sept. 18, 1926; s. Sian and Bao G.; m. Yufang Qin, Feb. 1, 1959; three children. B in Engring., Shanghai Jiatung U., 1947; M in Engring., Okla. State U., 1956. Asst. engr. Keelung Harbor Bur., China, 1947-54; designer Jackson & Mooreland, Inc., Boston, 1956-58; engr. Transp. Engring. Rsch. Inst., Fuzhou, China, 1958-59; assoc. prof. Fuzhou U., 1959-63; sr. engr. Nanjing Hydraulic Rsch. Inst., China, 1963-81; prof., dept. dir. Materials & Structural Engring. Dept., Nanjing, 1981-93. Office: NHRI, 34 Hujuguan, 210024 Nanjing China

GAO, VINCENT CHUN XIN, chemist, researcher; b. Chongqin, SiChuan, China, May 18, 1956; came to U.S. 1984; s. Shi Do and SiJin (Zhang) G. BS, Chengdu U., China, 1982; MS, Northeastern U., Boston, 1986; PhD, Northeastern U., 1989. Asst. engr. Rsch. Inst. for Coal Ind., Xian, China, 1982-84; rsch. assoc. The Barnett Inst., Boston, 1985-89; teaching asst. Dept. Chemistry, Northeastern U., Boston, 1985-89; rsch. cons. The Barnett Inst., Boston, 1988-89; postdoctoral fellow Hemagen/PFC, St. Louis, 1989-90; sr. rsch. chemist Hemagen/PFC, 1990-93, Zeneca Pharm. Inc., Wilmington, Del., 1993-97; sr. LC/MS specialist PE Biosystems, Foster City, Calif., 1997-99, mktg. & application mgr., 2000—. Patents of chiral and achiral solid phase reagents for improved detectabilities of pharms. and bioorganics; contbr. numerous articles to profl. jours. Mem. Am. Chem. Soc., Am. Mass Spectroscopy Soc. Avocations: music, sports, fine arts, photography.

GAO, XINGJIAN, writer; b. Ganzhou, Jiangxi, China, Jan. 4, 1940; Arrived in France, 1988.; Diploma French language, Dept. of Foreign Languages, Beijing, 1962. Author: A Preliminary Discussion of the Art of Modern Fiction, 1981, A Pigeon Called Red Beak, 1985, Collected Plays, 1985, In Search of a Modern Form of Dramatic Representation, 1987, Fugitives, The Voice of the Individual, Without Isms, One Man's Bible, Soul Mountain, 1999 (Prix du Nouvel An Chinois, 1997, Nobel Prize, 2000); plays include Signal Alarm, 1982, Bus Stop, 1983, Wild Man, 1985, The Other Shore, 1986. Chevalier de l'Ordre des Arts et des Lettres, 1992, Prix Communauté française de Belgique, 1994.

GAO, YINGJUN, physicist; b. Jia County, Shaanxi, China, Sept. 18, 1946; s. Jingxu and Huilan (Yan) G.; m. Hailin Jiang; 1 child, Zhixuan. MSc, Chinese Acad. Scis., Xian, 1982. Prof. Xian Inst. Optics and Precision Mechanics, 1982-87, prof., dir., 1988—; vis. scientist Inst. Optics, U. Rochester, N.Y., 1984-85, Strathclyde U., Scotland, 1993-94, Brunel U., Eng., 1994-98, Nat. Phys. Lab., Eng., 1994—; sec. gen. Specialty Com. Fiber Optics and Integrated Optics, 1996—. Co-author: Fundamentals of Gradient Index Materials, 1991. Recipient Nat. Scis. award Chinese Acad. Scis. Avocations: swimming, racing, driving, chessing. Home: 121 W Youyi Rd, Xian 710068, China Office: Xian Inst Optics &, Precision Mechanics, Xian 710068, China

GAO, ZHIQIANG, chemistry educator; b. Kaifeng, Henan, China, Mar. 25, 1964; arrived in Singapore, 1994; s. Jiyie and Guilan (Sun) G.; m. Pin Li, Jan. 23, 1987; children: Shen, Yi, Xin. BSc, Wuhan (China) U., 1985, MSc, 1987, PhD, 1990. Lectr. dept. chemistry Henan U., Kaifeng, China, 1990-91; rsch. assoc. Åbo Akademi U., Turku, Finland, 1991-93; Feinberg postdoctoral rsch. fellow Weizmann Inst. Sci., Rehovot, Israel, 1993-94; Lee Kuan Yew rsch. fellow Nat. U. Singapore, 1994-97, lectr., 1997-99; sr. scientist TheraSense Inc., Alameda, Calif., 2000—. Reviewer Electroanalysis, 1994—, Electrochimica Acta, 1994—, Analytica Chimica Acta; contbr. articles to profl. jours.; inventor in field. Trainer Singapore Chemistry Olympiad Team, 1994-98. Recipient Lee Kuan Yew fellowship Nat. U. Singapore, 1994, Feinberg postdoctoral fellowship Weizmann Inst. Sci., Rehovot, Israel, 1993. Mem. AAAS, Internat. Union Pure and Applied Chemistry, Internat. Soc. Electrochemistry. Avocations: swimming, table tennis, chess, photography. Home: 07-03, 111 Clementi Rd, Singapore 129792, Republic of Singapore Office: TheraSense Inc 1360 S Loop Rd Alameda CA 94502-7000

GAONKAR, GOPAL HOSABU, mechanical engineer, educator; b. Hanehalli, Karnatak, India, June 12, 1937; came to U.S., 1964; s. Hosabu Krishna and Shivamma H. Gaonkar; m. Ana Gopal, Sept. 6, 1968; children: Mala, Gauri. BE, Karnatak U., India, 1960; ME, Bombay U., India, 1963; DSc, Washington U., St. Louis, 1967. Registered profl. engr., Fla. Asst. engr. M.M. Bilaney and Co., Bombay, 1960-61; lectr. V.J. Tech. Inst., Bombay, 1962-64; from rsch. asst. to asst. prof. Washington U., St. Louis, 1964-70; rsch. prof. Southern Ill. U., Edwardsville, 1970-78; Hal chair prof. Indian Inst. Sci., Bangalore, India, 1978-84; prof. Fla. Atlantic U., Baca Raton, 1984—; cons. Hindustan Aero., Bangalore, 1978-84, Nat. Aero. Lab., Bangalore, 1978-84. Contbr. articles to profl. jours. Senator Fla. Atlantic U. Senate, Boca Raton, 1987—. Assoc. fellow AIAA, 1976; grantee NASA, 1991-92. Fellow Indian Aero. Soc.; mem. ASME (sec. 1985-86), Am. Helicopter Soc. (assoc. editor 1990—). Office: Fla Atlantic U 500 NW 20th St # 3091 Boca Raton FL 33431-6415

GAPES, JAMES RICHARD, bioprocess engineer; b. Thames, New Zealand, Oct. 2, 1959; s. Robert Francis and Margaret Ann (Mac Farlane) G. B of Engring., Auckland U., 1980; M of Tech., Massey U., 1983; Diplomingenieur, Tech. U. Vienna, 1989, D of Tech., 1993. Supr. New Zealand Coop. Dairy Co. Ltd., Reporoa, 1983-84; plant design Mining & Process Engring. Svcs., Brisbane, Australia, 1984-85; engr. Gapes & Co. Cons., Auckland, New Zealand, 1982-86, 87-86; engr., founder BIUTEC, Vienna, Austria, 1988-89; head bioprocessing engring. sect. Tech. U. Vienna, 1987—. Contbr. articles to profl. jours. Avocations: travel, badminton, squash, cycling, scuba diving. Office: PO Box 9166, Newmarket Auckland New Zealand

GAPONENKO, SERGEI VASILEVICH, physicist, researcher; b. Minsk, Belarus, June 5, 1958; s. Vasilii Ivanovich and Alina Ivanovna (Adamik) G.; m. Olga Anatolevna Platonova, July 7, 1979; 1 child, Maxim. MS, Acad. Scis. Belarus, Minsk, 1980, PhD, 1984, DSc, 1996. Jr. rschr. Inst. Physics Acad. Scis. Belarus, 1983-85, rschr., 1985-88, sr. rschr., 1988-97; assoc. dir. Inst. Molecular and Atomic Physics Nat. Acad. Scis., Minsk, Belarus, 1997—. Author: Optical Properties of Semiconductor Nanocrystals, 1998; contbr. articles to sci. jours. Mem. Belorussian Phys. Soc. (bd. dirs.). Home: Odoerskogo 81 app 48, 220015 Minsk Belarus Office: Nat Acad Scis Inst Physics, F Skaryna Prosp 70, 220072 Minsk Belarus

GAPONOV, SERGEY PETROVICH, biology educator, researcher; b. Voronezh, Russia, Dec. 3, 1964; s. Petr Mikhailovich and Elizabetha Petrovna (Artiomenko) G. D of Biology, Voronezh (Russia) State U., 1990. Educator Voronezh State U., 1990-95, docent, 1995—. Contbr. articles to profl. jours. Recipient award Russian Acad. Natural Scis., 1995, award European Acad. Scis., 1996, Docent, Soros Found., 1997, 98, 99. Mem. Entomol. Soc. Russia, Parasitology Soc. Russia, N.Y. Acad. Scis. Avocations: sports, literature, classical music, ballet, arts. Home: Fl 98, Revolution Ave House 26/28, 394000 Voronezh Russia Office: Voronezh State Univ, University Sq 1, 394000 Voronezh Russia

GARAB, GYÖZÖ, biophysicist; b. Szomód, Hungary, Jan. 1, 1948; s. Imre Garab and Ilona Varga Garabnè; m. Katalin Puskás (div. 1978); children: Ildikó, Szabolcs; m. Anikó Bogdány, Oct. 27, 1979; 1 child, Ábel; stepdaughter: Zsófia Agoston. Diploma in Physics, Szeged U., Hungary, 1971, PhD, 1975; DSc, Hungarian Acad. of Scis., Budapest, 1993. Rsch. assoc. Biol. Rsch. Ctr./Hungarian Acad. Scis., Szeged, 1971-84; sr. rsch. worker Biol. Rsch. Ctr., Szeged, 1987-92, head of lab., 1987—, rsch. advisor, 1993—, dep. dir., 1999—; vis. scientist Brookhaven Nat. Lab., Upton, 1985-86, vis. prof. U. N.Mex., Albuquerque, 1986; chmn., sec./gen. organizing com. conf. in field, Budapest, 1992-93, 95-98; mem. steering com. European Sci. Found., 1993-99, dir. summer sch., 1993; area rep. Internat. Soc. Photsynthesis Rsch., 1998—. Editor: Photosynthesis: Mechanisms and Effects, 1998, Vols. I-V; contbr. numerous articles to profl. jours. and publs. pres. Trade Union of Scientific Workers Biol. Rsch. Ctr., Szeged, 1989-93, Assn. of Trade Unions of Univs. and Rsch. Insts., Csongrad County, 1993-95; sec. Soc. Eötvös Coll., Szeged, 1995. Recipient J. Ernst award Hungarian Biophys. Soc., 1994. Avocations: sports (soccer and skiing), classical music. Home: Dózsa György u 7, H-6720 Szeged Hungary Office: Biol Rsch Ctr, Temesvari Krt 62/Box 521, H-6701 Szeged Hungary

GARABIOL, DOMINIQUE YVES, banker, economist; b. Porto-Novo, Benin, Aug. 11, 1956; s. Robert and Genevieve (Kessler) G.; m. Anne-Christine Macherey; children: Alison, Sixtine, Philémon. MBA, Ecole Superieure des Scis. Economiques et Commerciales, Paris, 1979; M in Econs., Ecole des Hautes Etudes en Scis. Sociales, Paris, 1983; PhD in Econs., Paris U., 1992. Jr. mgr. Banque de France, Paris, 1981-82; fin. analyst Ministry of Industry, Paris, 1982-86; sr. mgr. Commn. Bancaire, Paris, 1986-91; v.p. Banque Indosuez, Paris, 1991-95, 1st v.p., 1995-97; head inspection Conseil des Marchés Financiers, 1997—; econ. analyst, Delegation a l'Amenagement du Territore et a l'Action Regionale, Paris, 1978-81; asst. prof. Paris U., 1987—, Inst. d'Etudes Politiques, 1989-91. Advisor to State Sec., Social Affairs Ministry, Paris, 1981-82; mem. rep. IIF, Washington, 1992-95. Fellow Assn. Francaise des Tresoriers de Banque. Home: 16 Rue Madeleine, 92160 Antony France Office: Conseil des Marches Finance, 31 Rue Saint Augustin, 75002 Paris France

GARAEV, KAVAS GARAEVICH, mathematician, educator, researcher; b. Bolshaya Atnya, Tatarstan, Russia, Aug. 29, 1944; s. Garay Shangaraevich Mubarakshin and Sara Gumerovna Gumerova; m. Svetlana Leonidovna Gorbacheva, Apr. 5, 1965 (div. May 1973); 1 child, Oleg; m. Ljudmila Mikhaylovna Nenakhova, Apr. 5, 1975; children: Timur, Alina. Degree in mech. engring., Aviation Inst., Kazan, Russia, 1967, PhD in Math., 1970, DSc in Math., 1991. Asst. prof. math. Aviation Inst., Kazan, 1970-72, prof. math., 1972-73, assoc. prof. math., 1973-91, full prof. math., 1991—, chair dept. math., 1984—, chair physics math. faculty, 2000—. Author: Mathematics for University Entrants, 1996; contbr. articles to profl. jours. Grantee St. Petersburg (Russia) State U., 1993, 95; J. Soros Found. Prof.'s grantee, Moscow, 1997. Grantee St. Ptersburg (Russia) State U., 1993, 95, 97, Scis. Acad. Tartarstan Republic, 2000; J. Soros Found. Prof.'s grantee Moscow, 1997. Mem. Am. Math. Soc. (award 1997), Math. Soc. Kazan (award 1997). Avocation: gardening. Home: Chekhova 8/2, Apt 52, 420012 Kazan Russia Office: Kazan State Tech U, K Marks, 10, 420111 Kazan Russia

GARANA, MARIA LUISA, communications company executive; b. Madrid, Spain, Mar. 4, 1968; d. Jose and Maria (Corces) G.; m. John Benjamin Reuter. BSBA, U. San Pablo, 1991; MBA, Harvard U., 1998. Market analyst City Bank, Madrid, 1991-93; from analyst cons. to sr. cons. Andersen Cons., Madrid, 1993-96; assoc. telecomms. Merrill Lynch Internat., London, 1997; strategy cons. Bain & Co., Inc., Mexico City, 1998-99; revenue mgmt. dir. TU Azteca, Mexico City, 1999—. Mem. Nat. Assn. Broadcasters, Harvard Club. Avocations: Spanish history, movies, sports. Home: Carretera Mexico, Toluca #5256 Apt 002, Mexico City Mexico Office: TU Azteca, Periterico Sur #4121, 14141 Mexico City Mexico

GARANCE, DOMINICK (D. G. GARAN), lawyer, author; b. Varaklani, Latvia, Oct. 14, 1912; came to U.S., 1950, naturalized, 1955; s. John and Virginia (Cakuls) Garans. LL.M., U. Riga, Latvia, 1935; J.U.D., U. Freiburg, Germany, 1945; LL.D., U. Paris, France, 1947; Ph.D., U. London, Eng., 1949. Bar: N.Y. 1958. Atty.-at-law, legal counsel Ministry of Welfare, Riga, 1936-42; law sec. French Mil. Govt. in Germany, Freiburg, 1945-46; documentary officer Harvard Law Sch. Internat. Program of Taxation, 1952-57; pvt. practice law N.Y.C., 1958—. Author: The Paradox of Pleasure and Relativity, 1963, Relativity for Psychology, A Causal Law for the Modern Alchemy, 1968, The Key to the Sciences of Man, 1975, Against Ourselves: Disorders from Improvements under the Organic Limitedness of Man, 1979, Our Sciences Ruled by Human Prejudice, 1987. Mem. ABA, N.Y. State Bar Assn., N.Y. State Trial Lawyers Assn., N.Y. Acad. Sci., Philosophy of Sci. Assn., Am. Assn. Advancement Sci., Lacuania. Address: 2926 E 196th St Bronx NY 10461-3804

GARASCIA, CHRISTIAN JOSEPH, lawyer; b. Mt. Clemens, Mich., Mar. 19, 1969; s. David Carl and Carol Ann Garascia; m. Christine Marie Garascia, July 9, 1994; 1 child, Joseph Ryan. BSME, GM Engring. and Mgmt. Inst., Flint, Mich., 1992; JD, U. Detroit, 1996. Bar: Mich. 1996. Project engr. Aero Detroit Inc., Troy, Mich., 1992-93; assoc. Young & Basile, P.C., Troy, 1996—. Assoc. editor U. Detroit Law Rev., 1995-96. Mem. ABA, Mich. Bar Assn., Mich. Patent Law Assn., Oakland County Bar Assn., GM Inst. Alumni Assn. (pres. 1999-00), Pi Kappa Alpha (v.p. alumni 1993-95, Alumni of Yr. award 1994). Republican. Avocations: woodworking, scuba diving, running. E-mail: garascia@ybpc.com. Home: 517 River Ridge Dr Waterford MI 48327-2888 Office: Young & Basile PC 3001 W Big Beaver Rd Ste 624 Troy MI 48084-3107

GARATTINI, SILVIO, science administrator; b. Bergamo, Italy, Nov. 12, 1928; s. Aristotele and Anita (Viaro) G. BS in Chemistry, U. Bergamo, 1948; MD with honors, U. Turin, Italy, 1954; Dr. Honoris Causa, Autonomous U. Barcelona, Spain, 1983, U. Bialystock, Poland, 1984. Asst. Inst. Pharmacology U. Milan, 1954-58, dep. dir., 1959-62; dir. Mario Negri Inst. Pharmacological Rsch., Milan, 1963—; adj. prof. biochemistry CUNY, 1971-75; lectr. in chemotherapy and pharmacology, 1955, 58; mem. com. on cancer chemotherapy Internat. Union Against Cancer, 1966; com. med. biology NRC, 1977; various coms. Ministry of Sci. Rsch., Rome, 1983-88; mem. Italian Drug Com., 1993-97, Com. for Proprietary Medicinal Products; spkr., mem. internat. med. and sci. coms., symposia and univs.; rschr. in field. Mem. editl. bd. Bioengring. in Exptl. Medicine, Bull. of Molecular Biology and Medicine, Cancer Metastasis Revs., Clin. and Exptl. Pharmacology and Physiology, Core Jours., Drug Metabolism Revs., European Jour. Cancer, European Jour. Pharmacology, many other med. jours. and revs.; contbr. to numerous med. jours. Recipient Marzotto prize for medicine for study of antitubercular drugs, 1954, prize Vittorio Emanuele Found., 1956, Pope John XXIII prize for cancer chemotherapy, 1970, Pitagora prize Port of Milan, 1988; named Hon. Citizen of Tex., 1974; Adriano Valenti scholar, 1951-52; scholar Nat. Italian Rsch. Coun., 1955, fellow, 1957, 60; hon. fellow Faculty Pharm. Medicine, Royal Colls. Physicians, 1998. Fellow AAAS, N.Y. Acad. Scis., Faculty Pharm. Medicine Royal Colls. Physicians; mem. WHO (expert adv. panel on cancer 1973—, sci. and tech. adv. com. World Bank spl. program for rsch. and tng. in tropical diseases Geneva chpt. 1988), Mario Negri South Soc. (pres. 1981—), Italian Soc. Biol. Psychiatry, Italian Soc. Cancerology, Italian Soc. Chemotheraphy (sec. 1955-60), Italian Soc. Applied Pharmacol. Scis., European Assn. Cancer Rsch., European Soc. Biochem. Pharmacology, Am. Chem. Soc., Brit. Pharmacological Soc., Polish Soc. Pharmacology (Cavaliere Legion d'Onore Francese 1984), Royal Coll. Biol. Psychiatry, many others. Office: Mario Negri Inst Pharmacological Rsch, Via Eritrea 62, 20157 Milan Italy

GARAUD, MARIE-FRANÇOISE, European parliament official. Mem. European Parliament, 1999—, mem. com. on legal affairs and the internal mkt.; substitute com. on regional policy, transport and tourism; mem. delegation to the European Econ. Area Joint Parliamentary Com. *

GARAVELLI, EDUARDO NORBERTO, mechanical engineer, consultant; b. Rosario, Santa Fe, Argentina, Sept. 10, 1945; s. Eduardo Cecilio and Aracelis Gallardo; m. Herminia Facciuto, Mar. 11, 1972. Mech. Engr., Nat. U. Rosario, Argentina, 1969; Indsl. Designer, Indsl. Design Inst., Rosario, 1969. Project engr. Somisa Corp., San Nicolás, Argentina, 1970-76; engring. mgr. Siderúrgica Integrada Inc., Buenos Aires, 1976-87; devel. officer N.L. Inc., Buenos Aires, 1987—; dir. Bouygues Argentina Inc., Buenos Aires, 1994—; project dir. Marina Punta del Este, Chihuahua Club Inc., Uruguay, 1990—; dir. Bautista Buriasco Inc., María Juana, Argentina, 1990-92; dir. S.A.B.B., Inc., Buenos Aires, 1992-93; apptd. agt. Bouygues, Inc., Saint-Quentin-en-Yvelines, France, 1994—; asst. mechanics dept. Faculty Scis., Engring. and Architecture, Nat. U. Rosario, 1970. Editor: General, Technical, Materials and Detailed Specifications, 1973-74; author: Prices and Costs of Money, 1981. Engring. dept. del. Somisa Hierarchical Pers. Assn., San Nicolás, 1975. Recipient Nat. U. Rosario Engring. Faculty Profs. Assn. award, 1971. Mem. Argentine Assn. Nuclear Tech. (founder 1972), Argentine Inst. Siderurgy, Newell's Old Boys. Roman Catholic. Avocation: horses.

GARAVELLI, PIETRO LUIGI, physician; b. Alessandria, Italy, June 17, 1961; s. Giovanni Garavelli and Angela Notte. MD, U. Pavia, Italy, 1985, Spl. in Infectious Diseases, 1989, Spl. in Pediatrics, 1993; postgrad. in Tropical Medicine, Brescia U., Italy, 1993. Asst. dept. infectious diseases Alessandria Gen. Hosp., Italy, 1987-90; assoc. chief dept. infectious diseases Piacenza Civil Hosp., Italy, 1990, Alessandria Gen. Hosp., Italy, 1990-2000; prof. infectious diseases and parasitology, faculty medicine Novara U., Italy, 1998—; dir. dept. infectious diseases Novara U. Hosp., Italy, 2000—. Contbr. articles to profl. publs. Mem. Am. Soc. Microbiology, N.Y. Acad. Sci., Soc. Francaise Parasitologie, European Soc. Clin. Microbiology Infectious Diseases, Italian Soc. Infectious Diseases. Home: Via Comunale 75, Valmadonna Alessandria Italy Office: U Hosp Dept Infectious Diseases, corso Mazzini 18, Novara Italy

GARAY, JESÚS DE, philosopher, educator; b. Madrid, Oct. 4, 1954; s. Jesús de Garay and María Isabel Suárez-Llanos; m. Rosa Maña, Oct. 24, 1997. Bachillerato, Sagrado Corazón, Madrid, 1970; PhD, U. Navarra, Pamplona, Spain, 1983. Ayudante, U. Navarra, 1976-80, adj., 1984-87; prof. U. Sevilla, Spain, 1987-91; dir. dept. U. Europea de Madrid, 1996—; mem. cons. com. rev. Themata, Seville, 1995-98; editl. cons. newspaper Gaceta de los Negocios, Madrid, 1997-98. Author: The Senses of the Form in Aristotle, 1987, Difference and Freedom, 1992, The Game: Ethics for Markets, 1994; co-author: Aristotle's Metaphysics. Annotated Bibliography of the Twentieth-Century Literature, 1997. With Spanish Inf., 1976-78. Recipient Beca Formación Personal Investigator, Ministry of Edn., Spain, 1978, Programa Gen. Becas en el Extranjero, Ministry of Edn., Spain, 1988. Avocations: cinema, painting, soccer, tennis. Office: U Europea Madrid Tajo S/N, Villaviciosa de Odón, 28670 Madrid Spain

GARBA, SAMUEL ALIMI, microbiologist; b. Okene, Nigeria, Aug. 25, 1944; s. Elijah and Ayi G.; m. Joan Mosugu, Mar. 2, 1974; children: Adinoyi, Oiza, Eneyamire, Itopa. BSc, Ga. State U., 1978; MSc, Brunel U., Uxbridge, Eng., 1981, PhD, 1983; assoc. cert., Nigerian Inst. Sci. Tech., 1972. Lab. technologist Nat. Vet. Rsch. Inst., Nigeria, 1973-87; from sr. lectr. to assoc. prof. Fed. U. Tech., Minna, Nigeria, 1988-91, prof., 1992—; head dept. microiology Fed. U. Tech., Minna, 1988-89, , head dept. biol. scis., 1992-93, agrl. dean post grad. sch., 1992, dep. vice-chancellor, 1993-97, acting vice-chancellor, 1997. Editor Nigerian Livestock Farmer, 1983-87, Bulletin Sci. Tech., 1986-88, Nigerian Jour. Tech. Rsch., 1988-90. Nigerian Inst. Sci. Tech. fellow, 1979; Unipetrol Nigeria Plc. grantee, 1994-98; recipient MAN Nat. Sci. prize Nigerian Acad. Sci., 1989, Disting. Svc. award Raw Materials R & D Coun., 1991. Fellow Nigerian Inst. Sci. Tech. (pres.), Biotech. Soc. Nigeria (nat. pres.); mem. Ebira People Assn., Nigerian Soc. for Microbiology (nat. v.p.). Avocations: ludo, badminton, preaching, walking, basketball. Home: Shiroro Hotel Rd, Minna Nigeria Office: Fed Univ Tech Dept Biol Scis, PMB 65, Minna Niger State, Nigeria

GARBAR, ISAAC JOSEPH, physicist, researcher, educator; b. Minsk, USSR, Jan. 20, 1939; arrived in Israel, 1991; s. Joseph Isaac and Bella (Lein) G.; m. Larisa Rakhlin, Oct. 2, 1962; 1 child, Alla. BSc, Inst. Phys. Culture, Minsk, 1960; MSc, U. Minsk, 1966; PhD in Engring. Tribology, Inst. Aircraft, Kiev, USSR, 1978; DSc in Engring. Tribology and Mat. Sci., Inst. Rlwy. Transport, Moscow, 1988. Rschr., sr. engr. Rsch. Inst., Minsk, 1966-78, sr. rschr., 1978-89, leading rschr., 1989-90, head rsch. group, 1990-91; sr. rschr., invited lectr. Ben-Gurion U. of the Negev, Beer-Sheva, Israel, 1992—; vis. prof. Tohoky U., Sendai, Japan, 1996. Contbr. articles to profl. jours. and conf. procs.; inventor in field. Grantee Israel Ministry of Sci. and Tech., 1995-97. Fellow Israel Tribology Soc.; mem. internat. coordination com. tribology divsn., ASME. Avocations: fencing, swimming. Home: Bialic 31/6, 84340 Beer Sheva Israel Office: Ben-Gurion U of Negev, PO Box 653, 84105 Beer Sheva Israel

GARBATOV, YORDAN IVANOV, marine engineer, educator, researcher; b. Pirgovo, Rousse, Bulgaria, July 26, 1960; s. Ivan Atanassov and Elenka Ilieva (Netsova) G.; m. Nadejda Stoyanova Russeva, Mar. 31, 1984; 1 child, Stoyan Yordanov. Engr., Tech. U., Varna, Bulgaria, 1986; DEng, Tech. U., Lisbon, Portugal, 1998. Designer Machine Bldg. Plant, Dobrich, Bulgaria, 1986-89; rschr. Tech. U., Varna, 1989-92; mgr. shipyard, Varna, 1992-95; rschr. Tech. U., Lisbon, 1995-98, asst. prof. marine tech. and engring., 1998-99; prof. marine tech. and engring., 1999—. Mem. Soc. of Naval Architects and marine Engrs. Office: Inst Higher Tech Unit Mar, Tech-Eng, Av Rovisco Pais, 1049-001 Lisbon Portugal

GARBATY, THOMAS JAY, retired English language educator; b. Jan. 10, 1930. BA, Haverford Coll., 1951; MA, U. Pa., 1954, PhD, 1957. Asst. prof. English Dept. Clemson U., 1957-60; mem. faculty dept. English, U. Mich., Ann Arbor, 1960-93, prof., 1971-1993, prof. emeritus, 1993—; vis. prof. U. Bern, Switzerland, 1970-80; TV commentator, PBS. Contbg. author Variorum Chaucer, 1970-90; asst. editor: Middle English Dictionary, 1960-61; mem. editl. bd. Genre, Envoi; editor Medieval English Lit., 1984—; contbr. to Medieval England, an Encyclopedia and Modern Language Assn. Approaches to Teaching the Canterbury Tales; reviewer, contbr. articles to profl. jours. Recipient Amoco Tchg. award, 1968, State of Mich. Tchg. Excellence award, 1990, First Biennial award U. Mich. Students with Disabilities, 1991. Mem. MLA (life, chmn. divsn. on Chaucer 1976), Medieval Acad., New Chaucer Soc., Phi Beta Kappa. E-mail: tgarbaty@umich.edu. Home: 2981 Hickory Ln Ann Arbor MI 48104-2840 Office: U Mich Dept English Ann Arbor MI 48109

GARBAYO, INES, chemist; b. Tudela, Spain, June 25, 1967; d. Francisco Javier Garbayo and Maria Carmen Nores. Grad. in pharmacy, U. Seville, Spain, 1991; PhD in Chemistry, U. Huelva, Spain, 1999. Prof. in chemistry secondary schs., Spain, 1992-98; rsch. scientist U. Huelva, Spain, 1994—, rsch. cons., 1998—. Contbr. articles to profl. jours., chpts. to books. Mem. Bioencapsulation Rsch. Group, Pharmacists' Spanish Assn. Home: Alameda Sundheim 10 7A, 21003 Huelva Spain Office: U Huelva Dept Chemistry, EPS La Rabida, 21819 Palos de la Frontera Huelva, Spain

GARBER, NICHOLAS JACK, civil engineer, educator; b. Freetown, Sierra Leone, Apr. 13, 1936; came to U.S., 1980; s. Nicholas Abisodun and Rosamond Marian (John) G.; m. Ada Mary Smith, Mar. 31, 1962; children: Alison, Valerie, Elaine. BSc in Civil Engring., U. London, 1961; MS, Carnegie-Mellon U., 1969, PhD, 1971. Chartered engr., Eng.; reg. profl. engr., Va. Engr. Jenkins, Porter & Bingham Consulting Engrs., London, 1961-62, Rendall, Palmer & Tritton consulting Engrs., London, 1962-63, Scott & Wilson Kirkpatrick Consulting Engrs., London, 1963-64; exec. engr. Min. Work, Freetown, Sierra Leone, 1964-67; asst. prof. SUNY, Buffalo, 1970-72; lectr. to sr. lectr. U. Sierra Leone, Freetown, 1972-74, 74-76; assoc. prof., dean faculty of engring. U. Sierra Leone, 1976-80; vis. assoc. prof. U. Va., Charlottesville, 1980-81, assoc. prof., 1981-91, prof., 1991—, chmn. dept. civil engring., 1996—; design engr. Consulting Engr., London, 1961-62; ptnr., dir. Techsult & Co., Freetown, 1972—; chmn. com. Transp. Rsch. Bd., Washington, 1989-95. Co-author: Traffic & Highway ENgineering, 2d rev. edit., 1999; contbr. articles to Transp. Rsch. Record. Mem. bd. dirs. Workshop V, Charlottesville, 1985-89. Recipient TRB D. Grant Mickle award, 1996. Mem. Sojourner Kilwinning Lodge (founding, Master's award 1996). Episcopalian. Achievements include development of a statistical sampling method for traffic counts, procedure for controlling speeds at highway work zones. Home: 104 Woodhurst Ct Charlottesville VA 22901-2236 Office: Thornton Hall Univ Va Charlottesville VA 22903

GARBERS, CHRISTOPH FRIEDRICH, science advisor, chemist, researcher; b. Piet Retief, Transvaal, Republic of South Africa, Aug. 21, 1929; s. Andris Wilhelm Friedrich and Lucy Sophia Carolina (Wolhuter) G.; m. Barbara Zacharia Gertruida Viljoen, Dec. 14, 1957; children: Andris Wilhelm Friedrich, H. Viljoen, Christoph Johan, Barbara H. BSc cum laude, U. Pretoria, 1949, MSc cum laude, 1951; DPhil cum laude, U. Zürich, Switzerland, 1954; DSc (hon.), U. South Africa, Pretoria, 1989, U. Cape Town, 1990, U. Stellenbosch, 1991, U. Pretoria, 1994. Rsch. worker Klipfontein Organic Products, Transvaal; rsch. officer then sr. rsch. officer Coun. for Sci. and Ind. Rsch., Pretoria, 1954-58; sr. lectr. U. Stellenbosch, Cape Province, 1958-65, prof. organic chemistry, 1966-78; vice dep. pres. Coun. of Sci. and Indsl. Rsch., Pretoria, 1979-80, pres., 1980-90; chancellor U. South Africa, Pretoria, 1990-2000; mem. coun. U. South Africa, Pretoria, 1980-90; mem. Adv. Coun. for Tech., Pretoria, 1987-89, Nat. Commn. for higher edn., 1995-96; bd. dirs. Tech. Fin. Corp., Johannesburg, 1987-89; chmn. cert. bd. Technikons, Pretoria, 1988-95; chmn. Found. Rsch. Devel., 1990-92; chmn. Sci. Adv. Coun., Pretoria, 1991-94; mem. Productivity Adv. Coun., Pretoria, 1991-92; bd. dirs. Allied Technologies, Ltd., 1991-96, v.p. Hans Merensky Found.; mem. IUPAC-UNESCO Internat. Chemistry Coun., 1995-99; trustee Trust for Health Sys. Planning and Rsch., 1992-94. Contbr. 68 articles to sci. publs. Recipient State Pres.'s Order for Meritorious Svc., 1989, Council medal Pretoria Technikon, 1999. Mem. South Africa Chem. Inst. (coun. 1970-79, pres. 1973-74, gold medal 1980, Van Eck medal 1991), South Africa Acad. Sci. and Arts (chmn. 1983, coun., Havenga prize for chemistry 1977, MT Steyn medal 1990), South Africa Assn. Advancement Sci. (South Africa medal 1990), Percy Fox Found. (award of merit 1991). Mem. Dutch Reformed Ch. Home: 443 Sussex St Domein 5, Lynnwood, Pretoria 0081, South Africa Office: Menlo Park, PO Box 36716, Pretoria 0102, South Africa

GARBINO, JORGE, physician, researcher, consultant; b. Montevideo, Uruguay, June 10, 1947; s. Carlos Garbino and Maria Julia Bonomi; m. Jenny Pronczuk, Jan. 18, 1974; children: Jorge, Nicolas, Alejandro. MD, Med. Sch. Uruguay, Montevideo, 1977. Asst. U. Hosp., Montevideo, 1977-81; chief clinique Hosp. Claude Bernard, Paris, 1979-80; mem. med. staff Coronary Mobile Unit, Montevideo, 1979-91, Casmu, Montevideo, 1982-91; clin. rsch. coord. U. Hosp. Geneva, 1993—; physician Hosp. St. Luc, Brussels, 1985; med. dir. Pan Am. Hosp., Montevideo, 1989-91. Contbr. articles to profl. jours. Mem. Infectious Diseases Soc. Am., Am. Soc. Microbiology, European Soc. Microbiology. Avocations: tennis, music, cars, antiques, water sports. Office: U Hosp Geneva, 24 Rue Micheli du Crest, 1211 Geneva Switzerland

GARCEA, NICOLA ANTONIO ALFREDO, obstetrician, gynecologist, educator; b. Catanzaro, Italy, Nov. 22, 1941; s. Salvatore Garcea and Giuseppina Bruno; m. Carla Vernini, July 25, 1971; children: Riccardo, Francesca. Grad. in medicine and surgery, La Sapienza U., Rome, 1966. Tng. in ob. and gynec. La Sapienza U., 1966-70; asst. prof. Cath. U. Sacred Heart, Rome, 1967-85; pvt. practice, 1975—; tng. in urology Cath. U. Sacred Heart, Rome, 1970-73, assoc. prof. gynecol. endocrinology, 1980—, chief of residents, 1975-89, head physician, 1989-99, assoc. prof. postgrad. sch. ob-gyn., 1979—, assoc. prof. postgrad. sch. endocrinology, 1991—, assoc. prof. postgrad. sch. genetics, 1993—, dir. cons. svc. ob-gyn., 1980; head physician S. Giovanni-Addolorata Hosp., Rome, 1999—. Author: Technique of Assisted Reproduction: da Louise Brown ad oggi, 1999; editor: Argomenti di sterilità—Irsutismo, infertilità, Sterilità di origine endocrina, 1979, Attualità in endoscopia ginecologica, 1983, Le malformazioni fetali: implicazioni mediche, psicosociali, etiche, 1986, Ambiente e fertilità, 1997. Mem. Italian Soc. Fertility and Sterility (sec. 1978-83, exec. 1983—), Italian Soc. Physiopathology of Reprodn. (exec. 1991—), Italian Soc. Endoscopy and Laser Therapy (exec. 1991-99), European Soc. Ob-Gyn., Roman Group Endoscopy (v.p. 1998—). Office: Via Ugo de Carolis 74, 00136 Rome Italy

GARCES, JUAN E., political scientist, lawyer; b. Lliria, Valencia, Spain, Aug. 15, 1944; s. Juan E. Garces and Carmen Ramon; m. Francisca Duran, July 2, 1974; children: Alexandra, Joan, Rodrigo, Hernan. Degree in polit. and econ. scis., U. Madrid, 1966, degree in law, 1967; M Polit. Scis., Fondation Scis. Politiques, Paris, 1967; PhD in Polit. Scis., Sorbonne, Paris, 1970. Vis. prof. U. Leuven, Belgium, 1969; prof. Autonomous U. Madrid, 1969-70; pers. advisor Pres. Allende, Chile, 1970-73; pers. advisor to gen. dir. UNESCO, Paris, 1974-75; rschr. Fondation Nationale des Scis. Politiques, Paris, 1974-77; pvt. practice law Madrid, 1982—; vis. fellow Inst. for Policy Studies, Washington, 1988-90; expert UN Devel. Program, 1970-73; social scis. expert UNESCO, Paris, 1968. Author 10 books in polit. scis. and internat. rels.; contbr. articles to profl. jours. Recipient Alternative Nobel award Right Livelihood Found., Stockholm, 1999, Letelier-Moffit award Inst. Policy Studies, Washington, 1999, Openness to Mass Media award Internat. Press Club, Madrid, 1999. Mem. Madrid Bar Assn. Avocation: music. Office: Calle Alfonso XII No 18, 28014 Madrid Spain

GARCIA, ALPHONSE, biologist; b. Lyon, France, Jan. 15, 1952; s. Antonio and Maria Angeles (Araujo) G.; m. Marie José Gomez-Sadaba, June 25, 1999. PhD, U. Lyon, France. Rsch. asst. Inst. Pasteur, Paris, 1983-90, charge rschr., 1990—. Contbr. articles to profl. jours.; inventor in field. Home: 22 rue Cauchy, 75015 Paris France Office: Inst Pasteur, 25 Rue D Roux, 75015 Paris France

GARCIA, ANDREW B., chemical engineer; b. Las Cruces, N.Mex., Apr. 22, 1949; s. Rudolf A. and Margaret (Rivera) G.; m. Katherine D. Montano, July 5, 1974 (dec. Aug. 1996); children: Lauren, Alexandra. BS in Chem. Engring. with honors, N.Mex. State U., Las Cruces, 1972; MBA, St. Mary's Coll., Moraga, Calif., 1979; postgrad., U. Calif., Berkeley, 1994. Registered environ. assessor; cert. hazardous materials mgr. Design engr. Gen. Electric Co., San Jose, Calif., 1972-75; chem. engr. Chevron Chem. Co., Richmond, Calif., 1975-78; supr. Chevron Corp., San Francisco, 1978-80; supply product mgr. Chevron USA Inc., Walnut Creek, Calif., 1980-89; project mgr. Chevron Land & Devel. Co., San Francisco, 1989-93; environ. project mgr. Alameda County, Oakland, Calif., 1993-95; environ. support mgr. Computer Scis. Corp., Edwards AFB, Calif., 1995-99; due diligence coordinator Greenberg Farrow Architecture, Inc., 2000—. Park and recreation commr. City of Martinez, Calif., 1984-89; mem. citizens adv. bd. City of Martinez, 1989-91. Mem. AIChE, Project Mgmt. Inst. Roman Catholic. Achievements include reputation for being expert on the site cleanup and remediation of rural, industrial and urban properties; successful management of multimillion dollar projects. Home: 28420 N Rock Canyon Pl Santa Clarita CA 91350-5227

GARCIA, ANIER, Olympic athlete. Winner Gold medal 110 meter hurdles Sydney, 2000. Office: Fedn Cuban Atletismo, 13 y C Vedado 1001, Ciudad Habana ZP 4, Cuba*

GARCÍA, CELSO-RAMÓN, obstetrician and gynecologist; b. N.Y.C., Oct. 31, 1921; s. Celso García y Ondina and Oliva Menéndez (del Valle) G.; m. Shirley Jean Stoddard, Oct. 14, 1950; children: Celso-Ramón, Sarita Stoddard. BS, Queens Coll., 1942; MD, SUNY Downstate Med. Ctr., 1945; MA (hon.), U. Pa. Intern Norwegian Hosp., Bklyn., 1945-46; resident, rsch. fellow in gynecology Cumberland Hosp., Bklyn., 1949-50; assoc. in ob-gyn. U. P.R., San Juan, 1953-54; asst. prof. ob-gyn. Sch. Medicine and Tropical Medicine, San Juan, 1954-55; co-dir. Rock Reproductive Study Ctr.; asst. obstetrician and gynecologist Boston Lying-In Hosp.; assoc. surgeon Free Hosp. for Women, Brookline, Mass., 1955-65; sr. scientist, dir. tng. program in physiology reprodn. Worcester Found. for Exptl. Biology, Shrewsbury, Mass., 1960-62; asst. surgeon, chief Infertility Clinic, Mass. Gen. Hosp.; from asst., instr. to clin. assoc. ob-gyn. Harvard Med. Sch., 1962-65; prof. obstetrics and gynecology U. Pa., Phila., 1965-92; William Shippen, Jr. prof. human reprodn. U. Pa., 1970-92, William Shippen, Jr. prof emeritus, 1992—, dir. infertility and reproductive endocrinology and surgery, 1987-95; extraordinary prof. U. San Luis Potosi, Mex., 1974; rapporteur com. of experts on clin. aspects oral gestogens WHO, Geneva, 1965; mem. ad hoc adv. com. contraceptive devel., contract program Nat. Inst. Child Health and Human Devel., 1971-75; mem. original team which developed clin. application of 1st FDA approved progestagen-estrogen combinations for oral contraception (the Pill); developer, dir. first formal tng. program in physiology of reprodn.

in U.S.; innovator surg. approach to infertility of women; cons. Pa. Hosp., 1973-94; asst. staff Faulkner Hosp., Jamaica Plain, Boston; courtesy staff Glover Meml. Hosp., Needham, Mass.; adv. bd. Global Alliance for Women's Health, 1995—. Chmn. nat. med. adv. com. Planned Parenthood World Population, 1971-74; mem. nat. adv. child and human devel. coun. Nat. Inst. Child Health and Human Devel., 1981-84. With AUS, 1943-48. Recipient Carl G. Hartman award Am. Soc. Study of Sterility, 1961, Sesquicentennial award U. Mich., 1967, MD Master Tchg. award Alumni Assn. SUNY, 1989, Recognition award APGO Wyeth-Ayerst, 1993, Frank L. Babbott award SUNY, 1995, Sci. Leadership award Global Alliance Women's Health, 2000; Sidney Graves fellow in gynecology Harvard Med. Sch., 1955. Fellow ACS, ACOG, Coll. Physicians Phila.; mem. AMA, Global Alliance Women's Health (adv. bd. 1994—, rep. to U.N. Economic and Social Coun. 1998), Am. Soc. Gynecol. Surgeons, Am. Gynecol. and Obstet. Soc., Am. Physiol. Soc., Assn. Planned Parenthood Physicians (past pres.), Soc. Reproductive Surgeons (founding pres.), Am. Soc. Reprodn. Medicine (bd. dirs., past pres.), Phila. Obstet. Soc., Boston Obstet. Soc. (emeritus), Fedn. Columbian Socs. Ob-Gyn. (hon.), Cuban Soc. Ob-Gyn. (in exile, hon.), Masons, Sigma Xi. Republican. Presbyterian. Home: 109 Merion Rd Merion Station PA 19066-1734 Office: 3400 Spruce St Philadelphia PA 19104-4206

GARCIA, CRÍSTÍNA, writer; b. Havana, Cuba, July 4, 1959; d. Frank M. and Hope Lois G.; 1 child, Pilar. BA, Barnard Coll., 1979; MA, Johns Hopkins U., 1981. Rschr., reporter Time mag., 1983-85, corr., 1985-87, Miami bur. chief, 1987-88, with, 1988-90. Author: Dreaming in Cuban, 1992 (nominated for Nat. Book award), The Aguero Sisters, 1997; co-author: (pictorial guide) Cars of Cuba, 1995. Recipient Whiting Writers award; Guggenheim fellow; Cintas fellow; Princeton U. Hodder fellow. Avocations: music, contemporary dance, travel, foreign languages. Office: care Random House Inc 1540 Broadway 11th Fl New York NY 10036*

GARCIA, DOMINGO, economics, finance and transport consultant; b. Buenos Aires, Dec. 15, 1935; s. Miguel and Julia (Garcia) G.; m. Elsa Matilde Massacane, Dec. 14, 1977. Lic. in Economy, U. Buenos Aires, 1970, D in Economy, 1977; Diploma in Adminstrn., U. Manchester, Eng., 1967; Spl. Cert. in Econs., London Sch. Econs., 1976. Auditor Price, Waterhouse, Peat & Co., Buenos Aires, 1960-65; acct. Compania de comercio Exterior S.A., Buenos Aires, 1965-67; mgr. adminstrn. and fin. Johnson Line, Buenos Aires, 1967-74; mgr. for S.Am. area Rotterdam Zuid Amerika Lijn, Buenos Aires, 1974-78; bd. dirs. Nat. Devel. Bank, Buenos Aires, 1978-82; v.p. Naviera Internacional S.A., Buenos Aires, 1982-84; advisor to the min. Ministry Transport and Pub. Works, Buenos Aires, 1984-87; v.p. Latin Am. Shipping Commn., Caracas, Venezuela, 1987-89; cons. in shipping and internat. trade Buenos Aires, 1989—; advisor in transport to Pres. of nation, 1995-96; mem. shipping confs. commn. U.N.C.T.A.D., Geneva, 1987-89; mem. grains transport commn. Argentine Govt., Buenos Aires, 1984-89, mem. port privatisation bd., 1991-93; prof. econs. and econ. history U. Buenos Aires, 1974—; dir. of studies for a land bridge between Atlantic and Pacific oceans, linking Brazil, Argentina and Chile, 1997—; prof. econ. history and econs. of transport in UADE U., 1988—; prof. econ. internat. rels. in U. La Matanza, 1997—; advisor to River Plate Bridge Commn., 1999. Author: Argentine Port Development, 1977 (Univ. prize 1977), Argentine Shipping Issues, 1982 (Seim prize 1982), World Economic History, 1983, Economic Geography, 1997, Latin America: Globalisation and Economic Growth, 1998, Mercosur Corridors and Multimodal Transport, 2000; contbr. numerous articles to profl. jours. Bd. dirs. Argentine Navy League, Buenos Aires, 1980-93. Mem. Profl. Coun. of Econ. Scis., Club de Gimnasia y Esgrima. Roman Catholic. Avocations: collecting photographs of ships, tennis, chess. Home and Office: San Jose de Calasanz 150, Piso 4 Dpto. 9, Buenos Aires 1424, Argentina

GARCIA, GARCIA ERNESTO LUIS, physician, researcher; b. Cogolludo, Spain, Aug. 23, 1946; s. Dominguez Casto and De Rivas Josefa Garcia; m. Maria Soledad Vicente Lopez, Oct. 5, 1971; children: Ernesto, Maria Soledad, Fernando Santiago. B, Sagrada Familia, Sigüenza, 1963; degree in law, medicine, and surgery, Med. Faculty Zaragoza, Spain, 1970, rehab. specialist, 1977, D in Medicine and Surgery, 1991. Gen. physician Gen. Health Mgmt., Spain, 1970-73, Royal and Provincial Hosp., Zaragoza, 1973-88; resident in rehab., specialist Miguel Servet Hosp., Zaragoza, 1974-77; rehabilitative physician Cerebral Palsy Ctr., Aspace-Aragon, 1980-92; rehab. specialist INSALUD/Miguel Servet Hosp., Zaragoza, 1977—; chmn. Spanish Med. Soc. Phoniatry, 1992-97; directing mgr. DERFONIA S.L. Dir., founding mgr. Madrid Spanish Phoniatry Mag., 1987-92; editor book chpts. and mags.; contbr. articles to profl. jours. Vol. Action Aid Spain, Zaragoza, UNICEF, Zaragoza, Diocesan Charity, Zaragoza, Coop. Nongovtl. Orgn for Health and Devel. Sgt. Spanish Infantry, 1973. Mem. Spanish Soc. Med. Physicians and Rehab., Aragon Soc. Med. Physicians and Rehab., Aragon Soc. Med. Otorinolarnigology, Spanish Rehab. Soc. Phys. Medicine (chmn. div. Soc. Phoniatry), Acad. Ciencis Medicas Aragon. Roman Catholic. Avocations: skiing, swimming, walking, tennis. E-mail: elgarcia23@airtel.net. Fax: 34 976 551046. Office: Miguel Servet Hosp, Isabel la Catolica 1-3, 50007 Zaragoza Spain

GARCIA, JOSÉ EMILIO, psychology educator; b. Asuncion, Paraguay, May 22, 1964; s. José Arnulfo and Mercedes Danelia (Noce) G. Lic., Cath. U., Asuncion, Paraguay, 1988. Cert. ednl. psychologist. Prof. U. of the North, Caaguazu, Paraguay, 1995-97; prof. Cath. U., Ciudad Del Este, Paraguay, 1995—, chair dept., 1998; prof. Cath. U., Villarrica, Paraguay, 1996—, Nat. U., Villarrica, Paraguay, 1998—; tutor student's thesis rsch. Cath. U., Villarrica, 1998—; mem. editl. bd. Revista Latinoamericana de Psicología. Author: (with others) School Psychology, 1993; contbr. articles to profl. jours. Mem. APA (fgn. affiliate), AAAS, Interam. Soc. Psychology, Internat. Soc. Comparative Psychology, Internat. Sch. Psychology Assn. (mem. ethics com.), Internat. Coun. Psychologists, N.Y. Acad. Scis. Avocations: reading science books and novels, watching films, listening to jazz and blues, writing essays on computer.

GARCIA, JOSE RODRIGUEZ, physician, researcher; b. Lugo, Spain, July 21, 1951; s. Jose Rodriguez Veiga and Joaquina Garcia Novo; m. Maria Teresa Lastra, July 4, 1976; 1 child, Maria. Licenciado, U. Santander, Spain, 1981, Dr, 1987; Prof., U. Oviedo, Spain, 1989. Sch. tchr. MEC, Oviedo, 19770-73; rschr. ETH, Zurich, 1986-87; rschr. in physics U. Santander, 1981-87; prof., rschr. U. Oviedo, 1988—. Author 5 books and 84 articles. Mem. SPIE, AAAS, N.Y. Acad. Scis., Optical Sci. Assn. Home: Pena Santa de Enol 13 3 B, Oviedo 33012, Spain Office: U Oviedo Fac Sci/Dept Phys, Calvo Sotelo s/n, 33007 Oviedo Spain

GARCIA, JOVENCIA TAROJA, librarian; b. Ubay, Bohol, The Philippines, June 1, 1946; d. Gabino Boaquin and Cecelia (Panganoron) Taroja. BSc in Edn., U. Bohol, Tagbilaran City, Bohol, 1970; diploma in librarianship, Philippine Normal U., Manila, 1990. Lic. profl. libr. Sci. rsch. asst. I, Nat. Inst. Sci. and Tech., Manila, 1979-80, sci. rsch. asst. II, 1980-82; sci. rsch. asst. II Materials Sci. Rsch. Inst., Manila, 1983-87, mem. com. on rev. evaluationa nd accreditation tech. papers, 1983-85; supervising libr. Indsl. Tech. Devel. Inst., Manila, 1988-89, libr. III, 1990—; mem. ad hoc thesaurus study com. Nat. Sci. and Tech. Authority, Manila, 1982-86; mem. dept. sci. and tech. Consortium Librs., Manila, 1982-86; facilitator creation databases for in-house tech. papers, serial collections and article indices, linkages with worldwide info. networks. Editor Current Awareness Svc., 1997—. Sec. Citihomes Homeowners Assn., Molino Bacoor, Cavite, The Philippines, 1997—, v.p., 1999; founder Ladies' Club of Citihomes, 1999. Recipient 3d prize essay writing contest Japan Internat. Cooperation Agy., 1981. Mem. Sci. Info. Network, Assn. Employees in Sci. Endeavor. Avocations: reading, swimming, joy riding, cooking. Home: Citihome, Phase IV, Block 11, Lot 67, Bacoor Cavite, The Philippines Office: Indsl Tech Devel Inst, Dost Compound Gen Santos Av, Bicutan Tagig MM 1604, The Philippines.

GARCIA, LOPEZ RODOLFO, construction executive; b. Guadalajara, Mex., Dec. 16, 1953; s. Rivas Raul and Martha (Castro) G.; m. Elba Ivonne Gonzalez Ascencio, July 28, 1979; children: Rodolfo, Paula. Diploma in arch., U. Guadalajara, 1979. Supr. Learner Familiar Constrn. Co., Guadalajara, 1969-70; freelance designer, contractor Guadalajara, 1971-73, 77-79; constrn. supr. Soltero Co., Cuernavaca, Mex., 1974-76, Indeco, Guadalajara, 1979-80, Elias-Aldana Aculfra Sys., Guadalajara, 1980-81; mgr. Garcia Lopez Arquitectos Constrn. Co., Guadalajara, 1982-99. Pres. Kinder Garden Sch. Father's Soc., 1986, Elem. Sch. Father's Soc., 1992, Jr. Sch. Father's Soc., 1996. Roman Catholic. Avocations: traveling, music, reading, swimming, rafting. Home: Privada Jacarandas # 5, 45160 Guadalajara Mexico

GARCIA, LOURDES GUERRA, manufacturing company executive, chemical engineer; b. Rosario, The Philippines, Apr. 4, 1952; d. Nicomedes Palinis and Rosita (Maranan) Guerra; m. Jesus Aguas Garcia, Dec. 10, 1978; children: Julius, Jun, Lorie Lou, James. BS in Chem. Engring., Mapua Inst. Tech., Intramuros, Manila, 1985; MBA, Ateneo Profl. Sch. Bus., Makati, Manila, 1985. From technician to tech. mgr. Muller & Phipps Mfg. Corp., Manila, Philippines, 1974-83, tech. mgr., 1983-84; from prodn. mgr. to plant mgr. Bayer Philippines, Inc., Pasig City, Philippines, 1984-86, plant mgr., 1986-95; plant dir. van Melle (Phils.), Inc., Calambra Laguna, Philippines, 1996-97, v.p. mfg., 1998—. Mem. Internat. Soc. Pharmaceutical Engrs., Internat. Assn. Analytical Scientists, Asian Productivity Orgn., Prodn. Assn. Philippines, Philippine Cultural Assn. Returned Overseas Scholars, Philippine Soc. Chem. Engrs., Philippine Soc. Cosmetic Scientists, Inc. Home: Blk 1 Lot 27 Phase 3, Mutual Homes Putatan, Muntinlupa Metro Manila Office: van Melle (Phils) Inc, Bgy Paciano Rizal, 4027 Calamba Laguna The Philippines

GARCIA, MERCEDES, pharmaceutical company executive; b. Madrid, Sept. 14, 1969; d. Eloy and Fuencisla Garcia; m. Jose-Luis Casado, July 6, 1996. Pharmacist, Complutense U., Madrid, 1985. Sales rep. Expancience, Madrid, 1986-87, area mgr., 1987-88; product mgr. Schering-Plough, Madrid, 1989-91, group product mgr., 1991-92; mktg. dir. I.M.S., Madrid, 1992-94; gen. mgr. Nexstar/Gilead, Madrid, 1994—. Avocations: gardening, reading, travel. Home: Luna 18 Ciudad Sto Domingo, 28120 Madrid Spain Office: Nexstar Farmaceutica SA, Agustin de Foxa 27 11o, 28036 Madrid Spain

GARCIA, OSCAR PABLO, forester; b. Viña del Mar, Chile, Aug. 26, 1945; s. Faustino G. and Maria Vidal; m. Hosliany Vargas; 1 child, Pablo Jose. MS in Math. Statis., U. Chile, Santiago, 1972; PhD in Forest Resources, U. Ga., 1976. Scientist Inst. Forestal, Santiago, Chile, 1969-72, head forest mgmt., 1972-74; scientist Forest Rsch. Inst., Rotorua, New Zealand, 1976-92; chair forest mansuration U. Austral, Valdivia, Chile, 1993-96; rschr. U. Santiago, Pontevedra, Spain, 1998-99; vis. prof. E.N.G.R.E.F., Nancy, France, 1995-96, KVL, Copenhagen, 1996-97, I. Politech. Madrid, 1997-98. Contbr. articles to profl. jours. Mem. IUFRO (chmn.). Home: Avda del Uruguay 11 5A, 36002 Pontevedra Spain Office: Forestry Ctr Investigation, Apartado 127, 36080 Pontevedra Spain

GARCIA, RAFAEL JORGE, retired chemical engineer; b. Havana, Cuba, July 2, 1933; came to U.S., 1962; s. Rafael and Martha Teresa (Suarez) G.; m. Amelia Fernandez, Feb. 23, 1958; children: Amelia Maria, Rafael Jorge Jr. BA, Columbia Coll., 1954; BS in Chem. Engring., La. State U., 1957; MS in Environ. Engring., Johns Hopkins U., 1975. Registered profl. engr., Ind., Ky., La., Md.; registered environ. mgr. Chem. engr. Freeport Sulphur Co., New Orleans, 1957-58; prodn. supt. Litografia Garcia Muniz, Havana, 1958-62; chem. engr. The Am. Sugar Refining Co., Balt., 1962-63, The House of Seagram, Balt., 1963-80; chief ecology engr. The House of Seagram, Louisville, 1981-97; cons. environ. regulatory affairs, 1998—; pres. Garcia Environ. Mem. Am. Inst. Chem. Engrs., Instrument Soc. Am., St. Matthews Lions (pres. 1986-87). Republican. Roman Catholic. Home: 912 Lake Forest Pkwy Louisville KY 40245-5126

GARCIA, SERGIO, professional athlete; b. Castellon, Spain, Jan. 9, 1980. Winner 19 events as amateur, winner Catalonian Open; joined PGA, 1999; winner Murphy's Irish Open, 1999, winner Linde German Masters, 1999, co-winner Dunhill Cup title; finished 2nd Casio Open Japan. Record holder as youngest Ryder Cup participant, youngest player to make cut Turespana Open Mediterranea, 1995, youngest winner European Amateur Championship, 1995. Avocations: soccer, computer games. Office: PGA Tour Box 109601 100 Ave of Champions Palm Beach Gardens FL 33410*

GARCIA-ARIETA, ALFREDO, pharmacist, drug assessment consultant; b. Madrid, Spain, Sept. 5, 1970; s. Santiago Garcia and Ana Maria Arieta. Degree in Pharmacy, U. Complutense of Madrid, 1993, M in Indsl. Pharmacy and Pharmaceutics, 1996, Dr in Pharmacy, 1999. Rschr. U. Complutense, 1993-99; cons. in drug assessment Spanish Med., Ministry Health and Consumer Affairs of Spain, Madrid, 1997—; expert European Agy. for the Evaluation of Medicinal Products.European Medicine Evaluation Agy., 1998—. Contbr. articles to profl. jours. Active Farmaceuticos Mundi, Madrid, 1996-97. Mem. Assn. Espanola de Farmaceuticos de la Industria. Home: Donoso Cortes, 6-3 DCHA, E-28015 Madrid Spain Office: Spanish Medicines Agy, Dept Pharmacy Huertas 75, E 28014 Madrid Spain

GARCIA-BACH, MARIA ÀNGELS, physicist, educator, researcher; b. Sant Vicens de Castellet, Catalunya, Spain, June 18, 1944; d. Silvestre Garcia and Ignàsia Bach; m. Santiago Olivella, Aug. 10, 1971; 1 child, Mireia. BS in Physics, U. Barcelona, 1969, MS, 1971, PhD, 1979. Tchg. asst. U. Barcelona, 1971-74, 77-78; rsch. asst. U. Tex., Austin, 1974-76; asst. prof. physics U. Barcelona, 1979-81, assoc. prof. physics, 1982—. Contbr. articles to profl. jours., chpt. to book. Mem. Catalonian Soc. Physics. Avocations: hiking, listening to music, reading, swimming. Office: U Barcelona Fac Física, Av Diagonal 647, E-08192 Barcelona Spain

GARCIA BARRON, RAMIRO, lawyer; b. H. Matamoros, Mexico, Aug. 18, 1966; s. Ramiro Garcia Jimenez and Lourdes Barron Schoellkopf; m. Cecilia Garcia Moreno, Mar. 5, 1994; 1 child, Ramiro A. Garcia. BBA, U. Monterrey, Mexico, 1989; MBA, U. Dallas, 1992; JD, So. Meth. U., 1993; grad. program of instrn. for lawyers, Harvard Law Sch., 2000. Bar: U.S. Dist. Ct. (no. dist.) Tex. 1995, U.S. Ct. Internat. Trade 1997, U.S. Ct. Appeals (5th cir.) 1997, U.S. Supreme Ct. 1998. Accts. aide investigational divsn. edn. dept. U. Monterrey, 1988-89; rsch. asst. Banco Nacional de Comercio Exterior, Dallas, 1993, Trade Commn. Mexico, Dallas, 1993; assoc. Roberts Cunninham, 1993-99; pvt. practice Law Offices of Ramiro Garcia, P.C., Dallas, 1999—; cons. in field; spkr. in field. Mem. ABA, Am. Soc. Internat. Law, Dallas Bar Assn. Avocations: swimming, cycling, hunting, fishing, triathlons.

GARCIA-BUÑUEL, LUIS, neurologist; b. Madrid, Feb. 24, 1931; came to U.S., 1955; s. Pedro Garcia and Concepcion Buñuel; m. Virginia May Hile, June 30, 1960. BA, BS, U. Zaragoza, Spain, 1949; MD, U. Zaragoza, 1955. Diplomate Am. Bd. Psychiatry and Neurology. Resident neurology Georgetown U., Washington, 1955-59; postdoctoral fellow Washington U., St. Louis, 1959-61; asst. prof. neurology Thomas Jefferson U., Phila., 1961-67; assoc. prof. U. N.Mex., Albuquerque, 1967-72, U. Oreg. Health Scis. Ctr., Portland, 1972-84; chief neurology svc. Portland VA Med. Ctr., 1972-84; pvt. practice, Phoenix, 1984—; chief staff Carl T. Hayden VA Med. Ctr., Phoenix, 1984-96. Contbr. articles to sci. jours., including Nature, Sci., Neurology, Jour. Neurol. Sci. Lt. Spanish Air Force, 1952-55. Fellow Am. Acad. Neurology (sr. mem.), Sigma Xi. Unitarian. Avocations: painting, computer art, steel-welded sculpture. Home and Office: 5939 E Orange Blossom Ln Phoenix AZ 85018-6732

GARCIA-CANO, PEDRO M., advertising agency executive; b. Madrid, Nov. 5, 1959; s. Manuel and Cecilia (Salgado) G.; m. Rocto Escondrillas, Apr. 8, 1989; children: Angela, Teresa, Beatriz, Lucia. BS, Columbia U., N.Y.C., 1981, MS, 1982. Cert. civil engr. Sr. cons. Arthur Andersen, Madrid, 1984-86; CFO Bates, Madrid, 1986-98, Grupo Solucian, Madrid, 1988-94; CEO MPA, Madrid, 1994—, Solucion, Madrid, 1994—, Grupo Solucion, Madrid, 1994—. Office: Grupo Solution, Viriato #20, 28010 Madrid Spain

GARCIA-CIMBRELO, EDUARDO, orthopaedic surgeon, researcher; b. Madrid, Nov. 9, 1946; s. Joaquin Garcia-Gallo and Amparo Cimbrelo-Baonza; m. Pilar Rey-Cuesta, Sept. 25, 1971; children: Eduardo, Pilar. BS, Sch. Medicine, Madrid, 1970, MD, 1970; PhD, Sch. Medicine Alcala Henares, Madrid, 1987. Resident La Paz Hosp., Madrid, 1971-75, staff physician, 1975-92, chief of sect., 1992—; hon. prof. U. Autonoma Madrid, 1992—; adviser to residents La Paz Hosp., 1991—, mem. rsch. commn., 1991-95. Reviewer jour. Hip Internat., 1996—; contbr. articles to profl. jours. Nat. Health Svc. Rsch. Fund, Madrid, 1985, 93. Mem. European Hip Soc. (founding), Spanish Orthopaedic Soc. Avocations: reading, poetry, music. Home: Pez Austral 13a 5o A, 28007 Madrid Spain Office: Hosp La Paz Orthopaedic Dept, Paseo de la Castellana 261, 28046 Madrid Spain

GARCÍA DE LEÓN, ROSA RAQUEL, telecommunications industry executive; b. Mexico City, Mex., Jan. 8, 1965; d. Manuel García de León and Rosa María Peniche; m. Juan Roberto Valenzuela, Mar. 31, 1959; children: Jorge Roberto, Fernando Rodrigo. Grad., UPIICSA, Mexico City, 1986; M in Mktg., Tech. Monterrey, Mexico City, 1995. Assoc. sys. engr. IBM, Mexico City, 1986-87, sys. engr., 1987-90, benchmark coord., 1989-90, advisor sys. engr., 1990-94; mktg. dir. Soluciones Integrales en Au, Mexico City, 1994—; gen. dir. Recursos Humanos en Informática, Mexico City, 1998. Author: Computers Architecture, 1992. Avocations: reading, puzzle assembly, aerobics. Home: Paseo de los Jardines 298, Col Paseos Taxqueña, 04250 Mexico City Mexico Office: Soluciones Integrales Mainf, Ave de Naciones #1 Fl 6-33, 03810 Ciudad de Mexico Mexico

GARCIA-FANTINI, MATIAS, obstetrician-gynecologist; b. Madrid, Aug. 22, 1962; s. Matias Pardo Garcia-Alba and Maria Teresa Garcia Fantini; m. Maria Carmen Rodriguez Miguez, Oct. 5, 1986 (div. 1992); 1 child; m. Begoña Tejero Miguez, Oct. 14, 1995; 2 children. MD cum laude, Monforte (Spain) Med. Sch., 1986; diploma in ecography, Barcelona (Spain) Med. Sch., 1988. Res. Porto (Portugal) Med. Sch., 1987-93; gynecologist Virgen la Luz Hosp., Monforte, 1993—, Sergas Hosp., Monforte, 1993—; dir. Virgen la Luz Hosp., 1993—; tchr. Porto Med. Sch., 1990-93; cons. Santiago (Spain) Med. Sch., 1986-87, 93—, Organon Lab., The Netherlands, 1993—; tchr. Santiago Med. Sch., 1999. Author: Menopause, (in Spanish) 1992; author, editor: Hypertension and Menopause, (in Spanish) 1998, Osteoporosis and Menopause, (in Spanish) 1999; author, editor: Alzheimer Disease and Menopause, 2000, Cerebral Blood Perfusion in the Postmenopausal Woman, 2000; editor, founder Menopause Jour., 1997—; participant TV program, Lugo, Spain, 1997—, radio program, Coruña, Spain, 1997—; contbr. articles to profl. jours. Recipient 1st Internat. Menopause award European Menopause Soc., Madrid, 1997; Almirall Lab. fellow, 1999—, Lilly Lab. fellow, 1999—. Fellow Menopause Group of Spain (1st Nat. Anticonception award 1993); mem. AAAS, European Reprodn. Soc., N.Y. Acad. Scis., Am. Soc. Andrology, Portuguese Soc. Pediatric Andrology (co-founder). Roman Catholic. Avocations: internet, literature, tennis, basket. Fax: 34-82-400865. E-mail: mgfantini@wanadoo.es. Home and Office: C/ Orense n 85, E-27400 Monforte Spain

GARCIA-FRUCTUOSO, GEMMA, neurosurgeon; b. Barcelona, Spain, Nov. 6, 1963; d. Joaquin Garcia-Martos and Maria Fructuoso. PhD in Skull Base Fractures, U. Barcelona, 1995. Med. licenciate U. Barcelona, 1987, resident in family medicine, 1988, resident in neurosurgery, 1988-94, specialist in neurosurgery, 1994; staff neurosurgeon Pediat. Hosp., Barcelona, 1994-95, Hosp. Del Mar, Barcelona, 1995—; prof. Neurosurgery for Nurses, Barcelona, 1993—. Contbr. chpt. to book. Rsch. post-residency grantee Hosp. Clinic, Barcelona, 1993. Mem. European and Spanish Skull Base Soc., Am. Assn. Neurol. Surgeons, Spanish Soc. Neurosurgery. Avocations: playing tennis, singing in chorus. Home: Josep Tarradellas 128, 08029 Barcelona Spain Office: Hosp del Mar Dept Neurosurg, Passeig Maritim 25-29, 08003 Barcelona Spain

GARCIA-GIMENO, ROSA MARIA, food science educator; b. Manizales, Colombia, Jan. 18, 1966; d. Casimiro and Maria (Rosa) G.; m. Blas Roca-Viana, May 18, 1996; children: Blas, Miguel. Veterinary, U. Cordoba, Spain, 1989; Food Sci. and Tech., U. Cordoba, 1993. Asst. prof. U. Cordoba, Spain, 1996—. Mem. Spanish Soc. Microbiology. Avocations: music, reading, travel, crochet. Home: Buenos Aires 8 p2 1-1, 14006 Cordoba Spain Office: U Cordoba Dept Bromatologia, Campus Rabanales Edif C-1, 14014 Cordoba Spain

GARCÍA GÓMEZ, ANTONIO, oceanographer; b. Madrid, Feb. 28, 1961; s. Antonio and Elena (Gómez Izquierdo) García Velasco; m. María Del Valle Díaz Díaz, June 12, 1986; 1 child, Antonio. Lic. in Biol. Sci., U. Autónoma, Madrid, 1985. Specialist in aquaculture Instituto de Cooperación Iberoamericana, Port-au-Prince, Haiti, 1986-87; expert in aquaculture Instituto de Cooperación Iberoamericana, Panama City, Panama, 1988-89; expert R&D pub. functionary Spanish Inst. Oceanography, Puerto de Mazarrón, 1990—; cons. Interam. Inst. for Coop. in Agr., Dominican Republic, 1986-87, Costa Rica, 1988-89. Contbr. articles to profl. jours., chpts. to books. Mem. exec. com. Union de Consumidores de España, Murcia, 1991. Mem. Colegio Oficial de Biólogos. Avocations: reading, music, swimming. Home: Av Magisterio Nacional, Parc 208 #2, 30860 Puerto de Mazarron Murcia, Spain Office: Spanish Inst Oceanography, Ctra de la Azohía S/N, 30860 Puerto de Mazarron Murcia, Spain

GARCIA-GONZALEZ, FRANCISCO, polymers company executive; b. Tampico, Mexico, Feb. 2, 1953; s. Francisco Garcia-Martinez and Minerva Gonzalez-De Garcia; m. Nora Eugenia Montemayor Trevino; children: Nora Iliana, Francisco Jose, Maria Lorena. M Engring, Manhattan Coll., 1976; Chem. and Adminstrn. Engr., Monterrey (Mex.) Tech., 1975. Cert. chem. and adminstrn. engr. Tech., fin. and sales profl. Alfa Group, Mexico, 1976-81; planning and devel. mgr. Protexa, Mexico, 1981-83; foreing trade reg. del. Fed. Govt., Mexico, 1983-85; pvt. cons. Mexico, 1985-89; product mgr. Indelpro, Mexico, 1990-93, comml. v.p., 1993-99; pres., CEO Colombin Bel, S.A. de C.V., San Nicolas, Mex., 1999—. Mem. Rotary. Roman Catholic. Avocations: tennis, fishing, camping, board games, gunsmithing. Office: Colombin Bel SA de CV, Av Munich 101, San Nicolas NL 66452, Mexico

GARCÍA-HERAS, MANUEL, archeologist, researcher; b. Madrid, Jan. 22, 1967; s. Manuel García and María Luisa Heras. BA, Complutense U., Madrid, 1990, MPhil, 1993, PhD, 1997. Rsch. assoc. Complutense U., 1993-96, postdoctoral fellow, 1997-98; Fulbright postdoctoral scholar Smithsonian Inst., Washington, 1999—. Author: Archaeometric Characterization of Numantian Pottery Production, 1998; contbr. articles to profl. jours. Mem. Spanish Soc. Archaeometry (bd. dirs. 1997—). Avocation: choral music. Office: Smithsonian Ctr Materials Rsch & Edn Mus Support Ctr Silver Hill Rd Suitland MD 20746-2863

GARCÍA LANDA, JOSÉ ÁNGEL, English educator; b. Biescas, Huesca, Spain, June 1, 1961; s. Angel García and Felisa Landa; m. María José Arán (div. 1996); m. Beatriz Penas, Nov. 9, 1996; children: Álvaro, Ivo. Lic., U. de Zaragoza, Spain, 1984, PhD, 1988; MA, Brown U., 1989. Asst. lectr. U. de Zaragoza, 1987-90, acting sr. lectr., 1991, sr. lectr., 1992—. Author: Samuel Beckett y la Narración Reflexiva, 1992, Acción, Relato, Discurso: Estructura de la ficcion narrativa, 1998; co-editor: Narratology, 1996, Gender, I-deology, 1996; editor Miscelánea-A Jour. of English and Am. Studies, 1991-99, A Bibliography of Literary Theory and Criticism. Grantee USA-Spanish Joint Com., 1988-89. Mem. Aedean (sect. convenor 1994-95, award 1993). Avocations: book collecting, guitar, drawing. E-mail: garciala@posta.unizar.es. Office: U de Zaragoza, Facultad de Filosofía, 50009 Zaragoza Spain

GARCIA-LARREA, LUIS JOSE, neurophysiologist, researcher; b. Madrid, Aug. 28, 1956; s. Luis José and Maria Eugenia (Larrea-Sanz) Garcia de Erenas; m. Héléne Bastuji, Sept. 7, 1988; children: Ana, Michel. Diplomate in Medicine, U. Barcelona, 1980, MD-PhD, 1988. Resident in clin. neurophysiology Univ. Hosp., Barcelona, 1980-84; fgn. resident Neurological Hosp., Lyon, France, 1984-85; rsch. fellow INSERM, Lyon, 1986-87, full rschr., 1988-92, rschr.-in-chg., 1992-99, dir. rsch., 2000—. Contbr. articles to profl. jours.; editor-in-chief Neurophysiol. Clin., 1997—; asst. editor The EEG Jour., 1990-95. Sous-lt. Spanish Inf., 1977-79. Recipient Mus. of Scis. award for best paper, 1981, 84. Mem. French Soc. Clin. Neurophysiology (sci. com.). Office: CERMEP Hosp Neurol, 59 Bd Pinel, 69003 Lyon France

GARCIA-MARGALLO Y MARFIL, JOSÉ MANUEL, foreign diplomat; b. Madrid, Aug. 13, 1944. Mem. European Parliament, 1999—, vice-chmn. com. on econ. and monetary affairs, substitute com. fgn. affairs, human rights, common security; mem. Group of the European People's Party (Christian Democrats) and European Democrats; vice-chmn. delegation for relations with the countries of Ctrl. Am. and Mex. Mem. People's Party. *

GARCÍA MÁRQUEZ, GABRIEL JOSÉ, author; b. Aracataca, Magdalena, Colombia, Mar. 6, 1928; s. Gabriel Eligio García and Luisa Santiaga Márquez; m. Mercedes Barcha, 1958; children: Rodrigo, Gonzalo. Ed., U. Bogotá; LLD (hon.), Colombia U., 1971. Journalist El Espectador, 1947-50, 54; fgn. corr. El Espectador, Paris, 1955; journalist El Heraldo, Barranquilla, 1950-54; film critic, reporter El Espectador, Bogotá, also European corr., Rome and Paris; with various periodicals in Venezuela, 1957-59; established Bogotá office Prensa Latina, 1959, later worked in Havana, asst. bur. chief, N.Y.C., 1961; editor, screenwriter, copywriter, Mexico City; founder, pres., Fundacion Habeas, 1979—. Author: La hojarasca, 1955, El coronel no tiene quien le escriba, 1957, La mala hora, 1962 (pub. as In Evil Hour, 1979; Premio Literario Esso Colombia 1961), Los funerales de la Mamá Grande, 1962, Isabel viendo llover en Macondo, 1967, Cien años de soledad, 1967 (pub. as One Hundred Years of Solitude, 1970; Chianciano award Italy 1969, Prix de Meilleur Livre Etranger France 1969, Romulo Gallegos prize Venezuela 1971), (with Mario Vargas Llosa) La novela en América Latina: diálogo, 1968, No One Writes to the Colonel and Other Stories, 1968, Relato de un náufrago, 1970 (pub. as The Story of a Shipwrecked Sailor, 1986), No One Writes to the Colonel/Big Mama's Funeral, 1971, Leaf Storm and Other Stories, 1972, La increíble y triste de la cándida Eréndira y de su abuela desalmada: siete cuentos, 1972 (pub. as Innocent Erendira and Other Stories, 1978), El negro qui hizo esperar a los ángeles, 1972, Ojos de perro azul: nueve cuentos desconocidos, 1972, Cuando era feliz e indocumentado, 1973, Cuatro cuentos, 1974, Todos los cuentos 1947-1972, 1975, El otoño del patriarca, 1975 (pub. as the Autumn of the Patriarch, 1976), El último viaje del buque fantasma, 1976, De viaje por los países socialistes: 90 días en la "Cortina de Hierro", 1978, Crónicas y reportajes, 1978, Periodismo militante, 1978, La batalla de Nicaragua, 1979, García Márquez habla de García Márquez, 1979, Obra periodística Vol. I: Textos constenos, 1981, Crónica de una muerte anunciada, 1981 (pub. as Chronicle of a Death Foretold, 1982; L.A. Times Book prize nomination 1983), El rastro de tu sangre en la nieve: el verano feliz de la señora Forbes, 1982, El olor de la guayaba, 1982 (pub. as The Fragrance of Guava, 1983), Obra periodística Vols. II-III: Entre cachacos, 1982, Obra periodística Vol. IV: De Europa y América 1955-1960, 1983, La soledad de América Latina: Brindis por la poesia, 1983, Collected Stories, 1984, Persecución y muerte de minorías, 1984, El amor en los tiempos del cólera, 1985 (pub. as Love in the Time of Cholera, 1988; L.A. Times Book prize for fiction 1988), La aventura de Miquel Littín, clandestino en Chile: un reportaje, 1986 (pub. as Clandestine in Chile: The Adventures of Miguel Littín, 1987), El cataclismo de Damocles = The Doom of Damocles, 1986, Textos costeños, 1987, (with Vargas Llosa) Dialogo sobre la novela latinoamericana, 1988, El general en su laberinto, 1989 (pub. as The General in His Labyrinth, 1990), Collected Novellas, 1990, Strange Pilgrims, 1993, Ultimo Viaje de Buque Fantasma, 1993, Of Love and Other Demons, 1995, News of a Kidnapping, 1997; (plays) Viva Sandino, 1982 (pub. as El asalto: el operativo con que el FSLN se lanzo al mundo, 1983), Diatribe of Love Against a Seated Man, 1988; screenwriter: El secuestro, 1982, María de mi corazón, 1983, Erendira, 1983. Recipient Colombian Association of Writers and Artists award, 1954 for story "Un dia despues del sabado", Neustadt Internat. prize for lit., 1972, Nobel prize for lit., 1982, Serfin prize, 1989. Fellow (hon.) Am. Acad. of Arts and Letters. Office: c/o Agy Lit Carmen Balcells, Diagonal 580, 08021 Barcelona Spain*

GARCIA-MARTINEZ, REINALDO, engineering educator; b. Havana, Cuba, Nov. 5, 1954; arrived in Venezuela, 1961; s. Francisco Garcia-Lopez and Bruna Marta Martinez; m. Marina Clara Ribbi, July 30, 1980; children: Arturo, Claudia. Civil engr., U. Cen. Venezuela, Caracas, 1980; DSc, U. Cen. Venezuela, 1999; MSc, Ecole Poly. Montreal, Can., 1984. Cert. in engring. From asst. prof. to aggregate prof. to assoc. prof. U. Cen. Venezeula, Caracas, 1984-98, prof., 1998—; rsch. fellow Wessex Inst. Tech., Southampton, Eng., 1997-98; cons. PDVSA, Caracas, Ministry of Environment, Caracas. Author: (computer model) HydroTrack/OilTrack, 1996; editor, author: (book) Oil and Hydrocarbon Spills, 1998; contbr. sci. papers to profl. jours. Recipient PPI Level I award CONICIT, 1997, Rsch. award Profs. Assn., 1988. Mem. ASCE, Internat. Assn. for Hydraulic Rsch., Assn. Venezuelan Engrs. Avocations: photography, walking, traveling, movies. Home: AP 47762, Caracas 1041-A, Venezuela Office: U Cen de Venezuela, Faculty Engring, Caracas Venezuela

GARCIA-MORAN, MANUEL, surgeon; b. Oviedo, Asturias, Spain, Feb. 17, 1935; s. Joaquin and Cecilia (Lopez) G.; m. Beatriz Bezares, Aug. 30, 1962; children: Beatriz, Alfredo, Elvira, Fernando. Lic. Med. Surgery, Med. Complutense U., Madrid, Spain, 1959. Intern Jimenez Diaz Found., Madrid, Spain, 1955-60; fgn. asst., resident Paris U., 1960-64; fellow in surgery NYU Med. Ctr., N.Y.C., 1968-70; asst. chief surgery Hosp. Gen. de Asturias, Oviedo, Asturias, Spain, 1964-68, 70-74, chief surgery, 1974—, head surgery, 1975-78; full prof. Oviedo U. Faculty of Medicine, Oviedo, Asturias, Spain, 1984—; pres. Asturias Fedn. U. Sports, Oviedo, 1973-74; pres. Acad. Med. Quirurgica, Asturias, Oviedo, 1981-84. Author: Liver Transplantation, 1973; contbr. articles to profl. jours. Competitor Spanish Olympic Ski Team, Squaw Valley, Calif., 1960; mem. Medicus Mundo, Asturias, 1975—. Recipient Scholarship Colegio de Espana, 1961-63, Premio San Nicolas, Real Acad. Nac. Medicine, 1974. Mem. Acad. Medico Quirurgica Asturiana, Soc. Espanola de Patologia Digestiva, Assn. Espanola de Cirujanos, Assn. Française de Chirurgie, AAAS, N.Y. Acad. Scis. Roman Catholic. Avocations: ski, tennis, golf, bridge. Home: Cervantes 4, 33004 Oviedo Asturias, Spain Office: Uria 18, 33003 Oviedo Asturias, Spain

GARCIA MORIYON, FELIX, philosophy educator; b. Madrid, Apr. 4, 1950; s. Jesus Garcia and Asuncion Moriyon; m. Pilar Pedraza-Moreno, Aug. 31, 1974; children: Ignacio, Paula, Guillermo. B, U. Complutense, Madrid, 1974, PhD, 1979. Tchr. pvt. sch., Madrid, 1970-79; head dept. Pub. H.S., Ocana, Spain, 1979-80, Coca, Spain, 1980-81, Allcorcon, Spain, 1981-91, Madrid, 1991—; assoc. prof. U. Atonoma, Madrid, 1994—; prin. H.S., Alcorcon, 1983-85. Author: Pensamiento Anarquista Español, 1982, De La Escuela y la Familia, 1984, Derechos Humandos y Educacion, 1999; dir. Aprender a Pensar, 1990-94. Sec. Tchrs. Trade Union, Madrid, 1990; treas. C.G.T. Madrid Castilla la Mancha, 1998. Grantee Ministry of Edn., Madrid, 1975-78, Joint Com. U.S.A.-Spain, Montclair State Coll., 1986-87. Mem. S.E.P.F.I. (pres. 1985-88), C.E.F.P.N. (pres. 1991-93), P.E.S.G.B. Anarcho Syndicalism. Roman Catholic. Avocation: photography. Home: Fernan Gonzalez 23 2o-A, 28009 Madrid Spain Office: IES, Avenida de los Toreros 57, 28028 Madrid Spain

GARCIA-ORCOYEN TORMO, CRISTINA, foreign diplomat; b. Madrid, Jan. 2, 1948. Mem. European Parliament, 1999—, mem. com. on environment, pub. health and consumer policy, substitute com. on women's rights and equal opportunities, substitute com. fgn. affairs/human rights/common security; mem. Group of the European People's Party (Christian Democrats) and European Democrats; mem. delegation for relations with S.E. Europe; substitute delegation for the EU-Hungary Joint Parliamentary Com. Mem. People's Party. Office: Parlamento Europeo, Rue Wiertz ASP 11E217, B-1047 Brussels Belgium*

GARCIA-PRADA, HENRY, urologist; b. Piedecuesta, Santander, Colombia, Oct. 5, 1929; s. Alejandro and Lola (Prada) Garcia; m. Josefina Alarcon; children: Jose, Luis, Martha, Claudia, Victor. MD, Nat. U., Bogota, Colombia, 1954. Med. diplomate in urol. surgery. Intern Hosp. Militar, Bogota, 1953-54; rotating intern at hosps. in, St. Louis, 1955-56; resident in surgery Bradford, Pa., 1956-57; resident in urology Buffalo Gen. Hosp., 1957-59, Roswell Park Meml. Inst., Buffalo, 1959-60; prof., instr. in urology U. Del Valle, Cali, Colombia, 1961—; cons. urologist Seguro Social, Cali, 1963-83, Clinica de Occidente, Cali, 1991—. Author: Mental Control, Its physiology, its practice, and its benefits, 1999; contbr. articles to profl. jours. Mem. Colombian Urol. Soc. (emeritus; v.p. 1986-88), N.Y. Acad. Scis., Colombia Social Club, Am. Urol. Assn. (corr.). Avocations: golf, swimming, billiards, music, reading. Home: Calle 13 Oeste No 2-17, Cali Colombia Office: Centro Medico Clinica Occidente, Calle 19 Norte No 5N-35, Cali Colombia

GARCIA-SALGADO, TOMAS, architect; b. Toluca, Mexico, Dec. 7, 1944; s. Lemuel and Maria De Los Angeles (Salgado) Garcia; m. Maria Del Carmen Aguirre, Sept. 24, 1969 (div. 1974); 1 child, Alejandra; m. Margarita Carlota Nicolín-Fischer, Dec. 16, 1977; children: Margarita, Tomás. BS faculty archtl., Nat. Autonomus U. of Mex., Mexico City, 1968, MArch. faculty archtl., 1981, PhD in Architecture, 1987. Instr. faculty of architecture Nat. Autonomus U. of Mex., Mexico City, 1967-78, prof. faculty of architecture, 1977-93, rschr. faculty of architecture, 1971-97; head TGS Architect, Toluca City, Mexico, 1969-97; rschr. Faculty of Architecture UNAM, 1971-97; head Archtl. Rsch. Ctr. Nat. Autonomus U. of Mex., Mexico City, 1982-85; cons. Inst. for the Urban and Social Integration, Toluca, 1973-74, Sec. of Human Settlement and Public Bldg., Mexico City, 1977-79, City Hall, Toluca, 1992-93; designer Social Security Fund for Housing, Mexico City, 1974-76. Author: Introducción a La Perspectiva Modular, 1st edit. 1973, rev. edit. 1989, Perspectiva Modular, Aplicada al Diseño Arquitectóninco, 1st edit. 1981, rev. edit. 1992, A Modular Perspective Handbook, 1st edit. 1988, rev. edit. 1991; designer two illusionistic murals, one sculpture in bronze, seven stained glass windows and about 300 artistic drawings. Nat. rschr. Sec. of Public Edn., 1985, Nat. Coun. for Sci. and Tech., 1991, 1997. Mem. Internat. Soc. for the Arts, Scis. and Tech. Presbyterian. Avocations: piano, swimming, painting. Office: TGS Architect, Constituyentes PTE # 814, 50080 Toluca Mexico

GARCIA-SANCHEZ, FRANCISCO ALBERTO, psychologist, educator, researcher; b. Cartagena, Spain, Sept. 18, 1961; s. Pedro Garcia-Hernandez and Natividad Sanchez-Sevilla; m. Pilar Castellanos; children: Francisco Alberto, Alejandro. BS, Faculty of Edn., Murcia, Spain, 1985; Dr, Faculty of Psychology, Murcia, Spain, 1989. Rsch. grantee Ministry of Edn., Murcia, 1987-90; asst. prof. U. Murcia, 1990-95, prof. psychology, 1995—; dir. rsch. team on early intervention Fedn. Assns. for Persons with Mental Retardation, Murcia, 1996—; coord. rsch. dept. Assn. for Treatment of Children with Cerebral Palsy, Murcia, 1994—. Author: Handbook of the Individual Following Record for Early Intervention, 1998; contbr. chpts. to books, articles to profl. jours. Fellow Profl. Assn. Early Intervention Murcia (v.p.); mem. Spanish Assn. on Spl. Edn., Internat. Soc. on Early Intervention. Office: Fac Edn U de Murcia, Campus de Espinardo, 30100 Murcia Spain

GARCÍA-VALDECASAS Y FERNÁNDEZ, RAFAEL, judge; b. Granada, Spain, Jan. 9, 1946; m. Rosario Castaña Parraga, 1975. Grad., U. Granada. Lawyer Office Atty.-Gen., 1976; mem. tax and judicial affairs office Office Atty.-Gen., Jaén, Spain, 1976-85, mem. econ. and adminstrv. ct., 1979-85; mem. econ. and adminstrv. ct. Office Atty.-Gen., Córdoba, Spain, 1983-85; mem. Tax and Judicial Affairs Office, Granada, 1986-87; head Spanish State Legal Svc. for cases before EC Ct. Justice, 1987-89; judge Ct. 1st Instance European Communities, Luxembourg, 1989—. Author: Comentarios al Tratado de Adhesión de España a la C.E.: La Agricultura, 1985, El 'acquis' comunitario, 1986, El medio ambiente: conservación de espacios protegidos en la legislación de la C.E., 1992, La Jurisprudencia del Tribunal de Justicia C.E. sobre la libertad de establecimiento y libre prestación de servicios por los abogados, 1993, El Tribunal de Primera Instancia de las Communidades Europeas, 1993, European Ct. of Justice case law on freddopm of establishment and the provision of services concerning lawyers, 1993,The Court of First Instance of the European Communities, 1993, Rights of Defense in the European Courts, 1995, Protection of Rights of Defense in Competition Law, 1997, El derecho de defensa en la jurisprudencia de los Tribunales comunitarios-Perspectivas juridicas actuales, 1995, El Respeto delDerecho de Defensa en Materia de Competencia, 1997. Avocations: swimming, cycling, fishing. Office: Ct 1st Instance European Cmtys, Bur 4051, Blvd Konrad Adenauer, 2925 Luxembourg Luxembourg

GARCIA Y CARRILLO, MARTHA XOCHITL, pharmacist; b. Austin, Tex., Dec. 7, 1919; d. Alberto Gonzalo and Guadalupe Eva (Carrillo) Garcia; m. Jerjes Jose Rodriguez, Oct. 9, 1943 (dec. 1987); children: Marie Eugenia, Jerjes Alberto, Nicanor Francisco. BS in Pharmacy, U. Tex., 1944. RPh, Tex. Retail pharmacist Ward Drug Store, Austin, Tex., 1952-57, Sommer's Drug Store, San Antonio, 1957-62, Skillern's Drug Store, Dallas, 1962-66; hosp. pharmacist Brackenridge Hosp., Austin, 1968-75; retail pharmacist Thorp Lane Pharmacy, San Marcos, Tex., 1975-77, The Pharmacy, San Marcos, 1975-79, MHMR Pharmacy, Austin, 1975-78, Ace Drug Co., Austin, 1979-82; ret. Contbg. author: The New Handbook of Texas, 1996. Recipient Citation of Achievement Tex. State Bd. Pharmacy, 1996. Mem. Am. Pharm. Assn., Tex. Pharmacy Assn., Capitol Area Pharmacy Assn., Tex. State Hist. Assn., Ex-Students Assn. U. Tex. (life, Golden Anniversary cert. 1994). Republican. Avocations: reading, playing piano, current events, pharmacy medicine. Home: 21107 Ridgeview Rd Lago Vista TX 78645-4617

GARDBERG, MIKAEL KLAS, obstetrician, gynecologist; b. Turku, Finland, Mar. 26, 1948; s. Klas Erik and Anita Margit (Thilén) G.; div.; children: Richard, Maria, Peter. MD, U. Basel, Switzerland, 1973; PhD, U. Tampere, Finland, 1996. Resident Turku U. Ctrl. Hosp., 1974-78; pvt. practice Bottenhavets Kretssjukhus, Finland, 1979-82; ob-gyn specialist Vaasa (Finland) Ctrl. Hosp., 1983—. With Finnish Mil., 1973-74. E-mail: mikael.gardberg@vshp.fi. Office: Vaasa Ctrl Hosp, 65100 Vaasa Finland

GARDENIER, JOHN STARK, II, statistician, management scientist; b. Portland, Maine, Apr. 10, 1937; s. John Stark and Lucia Esther (Christensen) G.; m. Margaret Elizabeth Mann, Jan. 26, 1962 (dec. 1976); children: Brenda Anne Marshall, Patricia Suzanne Depew, Linda Marie Sievering-Albrecht, Pamela Lee Antoun; m. Turkan Emine Kumbaraci, June 18, 1977; children: George Halil Bonneval, Jason Celal Stark. BA, Yale U., 1959; MS, George Washington U., 1968, DBA, 1973. Tech. staff Computer Scis. Corp., Falls Church, Va., 1968-69; sr. analyst CONSULTEC, Rockville, Md., 1969-71; ops. rsch. analyst USCG, Washington, 1971-90; survey statistician Nat. Ctr. Health Stats., Hyattsville, Md., 1990—; cons. in field, Washington, 1971-90; adj. assoc. prof. George Washington U., 1980-81; prof. lectr. Am. U., Washington, 1982-84. Comdr. USN, ret. Recipient Silver medal U.S. Dept. Transp., 1983. Mem. AAAS (profl. soc. ethics group), Am. Statis. Assn. (com. profl. ethics 1994-96, chair com. profl. ethics 1996-99), Soc. for Computer Simulation (sr.; bd. dirs. 1978-82, rep. to AAAS 1996—), Naval Res. Assn., Navy League, Assn. Practical and Profl. Etnics, Internat. Assn. Official Statistics. Avocations: music, jogging. Home: 1000 Salt Meadow Ln Mc Lean VA 22101-2027

GÄRDIN, KARL OLOV, customer service executive; b. Borås, Toarp, Sweden, Mar. 6, 1952; s. Karl Olov and Linnéa Cecilia (Engqvist) G.; m. Kerstin Elisabeth Jansson, June 1, 1974; children: Marcus, Martin, Annika. Mgmt. diploma, MGruppen, Stockholm, 1994. Police officer Sweden Police Force, Stockholm, Alingsås, 1974-88; cons. Data-Car AB, Stockholm, Herrljunga, 1987-90; dir. State of Sweden for Immigrants, Vårgårda, 1990-95; chief of customer svc. Newspaperiery AB, Alingsas, 1996—; owner Canvass Telemarketing HB, Herrljunga, 1994—. Author: Oats-Bread and Treacle-Water (Local Cultural prize 1986). Inst. Sr. Civilian Force, Herrljunga, 1996-99. Office Sweden AF, 1971-73. Fellowship Am. Bapt. Musicians. Lutheran. Avocations: choir-singing, genealogy, mountain tours, reading. E-mail: kalle.gerdin@telia.com. Fax: 513-35775. Home: Bangatan 27, SE-52431 Herrljunga Sweden

GARDINER, HOBART CLIVE, petroleum company executive; b. Boston, Jan. 12, 1929; m. Patricia Williams, Oct. 14, 1950. BA, Yale U., 1950; postgrad., U. Central Caracas, Venezuela. Various mgmt. positions Esso Standard Oil Co. S.A., Havana, Cuba, 1954, Panama City, Panama, 1954, San Salvador, El Salvador, 1954-56, Guatemala City, Guatemala, 1956; country mgr. Esso Standard Oil Co. S.A., San Jose, Costa Rica, 1956-57, Tegucigalpa, Honduras, Brit. Honduras, 1957-60; asst. employee rels. mgr. Esso Interamerica Inc., Coral Gables, Fla., 1960; pres., gen. mgr. Esso Standard Oil Co., S.A., San Juan, P.R., 1960-62; v.p. Internat. Petroleum Co. Ltd., Bogota, Colombia, 1962-64; ops. mgr. Internat. Petroleum Co. Ltd., Talara, Peru, 1964-66; pres. Esso Std. Oil (Chile), Santiago, 1966-69; L.Am. area advisor Standard Oil Co. N.J., N.Y.C., 1969-71; v.p. Esso Standard Oil Co. C.Am., Panama, San Salvador, El Salvador, 1971-74; also Standard Oil Co. N.J., N.Y.C.; gen. mgr. Esso Chile, Uruguay and Paraguay, Montevideo, Uruguay, 1974-77; pub. affairs program mgr. Exxon Corp., N.Y.C., 1977-79; asst. gen. mgr. Esso Caribbean, Coral Gables, Fla., 1979-81; v.p. fin. and adminstrn. Internat. Exec. Svc. Corps., Stamford, Conn., 1982-84, v.p. L.Am. and Caribbean, 1984-90, exec. v.p., 1990-93, pres., CEO, 1993—; trustee Internat. Devel. Conf. Adv. coun. Save the Children. With U.S. Marine Corps., 1950-52. Mem. Country Club of Fairfield, Met. Club Washington, D.C. Episcopalian. Office: IESC PO Box 10005 333 Ludlow St Stamford CT 06904-2005

GARDINER, JOHN GRAHAM, university dean, consultant, educator; b. Birmingham, Eng., May 24, 1939; s. William Clement and Ellen (Adey) G.; m. Sheila Joyce Andrews, Dec. 29, 1962; children: Tabitha Jane, Benjamin John, Emily Josephine. BSEE with honors, U. Birmingham, Eng., 1961, PhD in Elect. Engring., 1964. Sr. engr. Racal (Slough) Ltd., Eng., 1966-68; lectr. U. Bradford, Eng., 1968-72, reader, 1972-86, prof. elec. engring., 1986—, head elec. engring. dept., 1984—, dean engring., 1996—; dir. Aerial Group Ltd., Chesham, U.K., 1970-97, Nortel (Comms.) Ltd., Eng., 1976-96, Compec Ltd., Eng., 1996—, VCB Ltd., Bradford, U.K., 1995—. Author: Mobile Communication Systems, 1989; editor: Personal Communication Systesm and Technologies, 1995; contbr. over 200 articles to profl. jours. Chief examiner Engring. Coun., London, 1970-85; chmn. Univs. Mobile Radio Rsch. Consortium, U.K., 1986-89; nat. coord. LINK Programme, U.K., 1988-93; cons. European Commn., Brussels, 1989-91, 94. Fellow Royal Acad. Engring. London, Instn. Elec. Engrs., Royal Soc. Arts; mem. IEEE (sr.). Avocation: music (violin). Home: 1 Queens Drive Ln, Ilkley LS29 9QS, England

GARDINER, WILLIAM RALPH, electrical engineer, consultant; b. Washington, July 26, 1931; s. William Ralph and Mary Imogene (Perrie) G.; m. Eloise Lee, Dec. 24, 1959; children: Robin Claire, Melissa Elise; m. Susan Alice Dodson. BSEE, Thomas U., 1977; PhD, Am. State U., 1998. Enlisted man USAF, 1950, advanced through grades to tech. sgt., 1961, resigned, 1963; owner Electronic Comm. Co., Perry, Fla., 1963-75; enlisted USN, 1975, advanced through grades to master chief petty officer, 1985, ret., 1989; aerospace cons. E.I. Dupont, Wilmington, Del., 1989-92; tchr. Charles County C.C., La Plata, Md., 1992-93; drug and alcohol counselor Va. Dept. Corrections, Haynesville, Va., 1993-96. Mem. Royal Soc. St. George, SAR, VFW, Am. Legion (post comdr. 1998-2000), Assn. Naval Aviation, Fleet Res. Assn., Air Force Assn. Republican. Anglican. Achievements include contbn. to the development of USN FA-18 aircraft; assisted in the inauguration of wire/cable maintenance training for NASA space shuttle program; produced video for aircraft electricians use for armed forces and industry. Avocation: aviation. Home and Office: 314 Chilton Rd Zacata VA 22581-9999

GARDINO, VINCENT ANTHONY, broadcasting executive; b. N.Y.C., Sept. 19, 1953; s. Anthony John and Carmelina Mary (Boglia) G. BA magna cum laude in History, St. Francis Coll. V.p. N.Y. sales mgr., dir. spl. programming and sales Metro Radio Sales, N.Y.C., 1976-79; acct. exec. WABC Radio, N.Y.C., 1979-81; dir. ABC Radio Network, N.Y.C., 1981-85, ABC Direction and Entertainment Radio Networks, 1981-85; pres., COO Selcom Radio, N.Y.C., 1985—; v.p., gen. sales mgr. Sta. WOR-AM, N.Y.C., 1985-95; v.p. ea. sales CNBC, 1995-98; exec. dir., dir. corp. underwriting sales Sta. WNYC-FM, Sta. WNYC-AM, 1998—. Mem. Mus. Broadcasting, Internat. Radio and TV Soc., Famija Piemonteisa (bd. dirs.) NYU Med. Ctr. (Kaplan Cancer Ctr., bd. dirs.), St. Francis Coll. Alumni Assn. (bd. dirs.), N.Y. Athletic Club, Columbus Citizens Found., Inc. Roman Catholic. Avocations: tennis, golf, skiing, historical autograph collecting. Office: WNYC AM/FM 1 Centre St New York NY 10007-1602

GARDISSAT, JEAN-LOUIS, physical engineer; b. Aurillac, France, Mar. 17, 1949; s. Marcel and Jeanne Eugenie (Laroussinie) G.; m. Mireille Pretet; children: Jean, Marc. Student, Conservatoire National des Arts et Métiers, Paris, 1976. Trainee Office de Radio Television Francaise, Paris, 1969, Compagnie Generale du Duralumin, 1970, Ets Michelin, 1970-71, Cohérent Radiation France, 1976; engr. CNRS, various cities, 1976—; pres. CLAS CNRS, Villetaneuse, France, 1994—. Contbr. articles to profl. jours. Mem. Assn. Isabela (v.p. 1980—), Rugby Club (pres. Taverny chpt. 1992-93). Avocations: sports, computers. Home: 84 rue de Paris, 95150 Taverny France Office: CNRS Labo PMTM, 99 Av J B Clément, 93430 Villetaneuse France

GARDNER, ALEC SYDNEY, engineering training manager; b. Sydney, Kograh, Australia, July 28, 1953; s. Lawrence Paul and Loris Jean (Anderson) G.; m. Linda Anne Allen, Aug. 30, 1970; 1 child, Elizabeth Anne. BEE, U. NSW, Australia, 1976; BEd, Sydney Coll. Advanced Edn., Australia, 1986; Grad. Diploma in Mgmt., Charles Sturt U., Australia, 1992, Grad. Cert. in Human Resource Mgmt., 1993. Mgr. computer based tng. State Rail Authority, NSW, 1986-87, mgr. devel. tng., 1988-89, project officer state rail tng., 1989-90; nat. tng. mgr. Schindler Lifts Australia, NSW, 1990-92, Schneider Australia, Regents Park, 1993-97, NHP Elec. Engring. Products, Silverwater, NSW, 1998—; mng. dir. ASG Cons. Svcs., Sydney, 1986—. Mem. ASTD, IEEE, N.Y. Acad. Scis., Australian Inst. Tng. and Devel., Nat. Soc. Performance Instruction. Office: NHP Elec Engring Products, Day Street, Silverwater NSW 2128, Australia

GARDNER, ANTHONY LAURENCE, lawyer; b. Washington, May 16, 1963; s. Richard Newton and Danielle Almeida (Luzzatto) G. BA, Harvard U., 1985; MPhil with honors, Oxford (Eng.) U. (Balliol), 1987; JD, Columbia U., 1990. Bar: N.Y. 1991, D.C. 1993, Paris 1994. Asst. European Commn., Brussels, 1990, Commn. des Ops. de Bourse, Paris, 1991; atty. Treuhandanstalt, Berlin, 1991; assoc. Coudert Bros., Brussels, 1991-4; dir. European directorate Nat. Security Coun., The White House, Washington, 1994-5; assoc. Hogan & Hartson, Brussels, 1996-97, Coudert Bros., N.Y.C., Paris, 1997-2000, Weil, Gotshal & Manges, London, 2000—. Contbr. articles to Wall Street Journal, profl. jours.; patentee in watch face design. Stone scholar Columbia U. Law Sch., 1990. Mem. Coun. Fgn. Rels., Phi Beta Kappa. Avocation: travel. Office: Weil Gotshal & Manges, One South Pl, 75008 London EC2M ZW6, United Kingdom

GARDNER, BRIAN PATRICK, physician, surgeon; b. Chipato, Zambia, July 17, 1948; s. Trevelyn Codrington and Briege Therese (Feehan) G.; m. Stephanie Catherine Faller, Oct. 18, 1980; children: Catherine, Paul, Laura, Martin, Annabelle, Edel, Benedict, Liam, Felicity. BA, Oxford (Eng.) U., 1970, MB BS, 1973, MA, 1976. House physician/surgeon The London Hosp. Group, 1974; sr. house officer accident and emergency Whipps Cross Hosp., 1975; sr. house officer neurosurgery/neurology New Addenbrooke's, Cambridge, 1976-77, surg. registrar, 1978-79; sr. house officer gen. surgery Bedford Dist. Gen. Hosp., 1977-78; registrar in spinal injuries Stoke Mandeville Hosp., 1980; registrar in neurosurgery Royal Victoria Hosp., Belfast, No. Ireland, 1980; sr. registrar in spinal injuries Southport, 1982-85; cons. in spinal injuries Stoke Mandeville Hosp., Aylesbury, Eng., 1985—. Fellow Royal Coll. Surgeons, Royal Coll. Physicians (London), Royal Coll. Physicians (Edinburgh); mem. Brit. Med. Assn., Internat. Med. Soc. of Paraplegia. Avocations: church, family activities. Home: 2 Northumberland Ave, Bucks Aylesbury HP21 7HG, England Office: Stoke Mandeville Hosp, Nat Spinal Injuries Ctr, Bucks Aylesbury HP21 8AL, England

GARDNER, CLYDE EDWARD, healthcare executive, consultant, educator; b. Steubenville, Ohio, Oct. 8, 1931; s. Peter D. and Louella Mary (Gillespie) G.; m. Patricia Jackson, Oct. 4, 1953 (div. Dec. 1977); 1 child, Bruce Stephen. BA, San Francisco State U., 1969, MS, 1971. Adminstr. Gardner Convalescent Hosp., Napa, Calif., 1955-68; exec. dir. Haight Ashbury Free Med. Clinic, San Francisco, 1970-71; lectr. San Francisco State U., 1969-71; dir. planning and rsch. divsn. N. Country Com. on Area Wide Health Planning, Canton, N.Y., 1971-77; prof. Gov.'s State U., University Park, Ill., 1977-83; sr. ptnr. Health Care Cons., Park Forest, Ill., 1983-86; exec. dir. Mahoning Shenango Area Health Edn. Network, Youngstown, Ohio, 1986-90; pres., CEO Mahoning Edn. and Tng. Network, Youngstown, Ohio, 1990-92, Health Sci. Assocs., Tucson, 1992—; adj. prof. SUNY, Canton, 1975-76, Youngstown State U., 1987-90; bus. rep. Apollo Coll., 1994-95; rschr. FMR Rsch., 1996-97; lectr. San Francisco State U., 1969-71. Author: Data Book for Health and Institutional Planning, 1981; author of numerous pub. health planning, health edn. studies and funded pvt., state and fed. health care grants, 1971-90. Pres. Found. I Ctr. for Human Devel., Harvey, Ill., 1978-83, U. Profls. of Ill., Chgo., 1982-83; bd. dirs. Blue Cross/Blue Shield Drug and Alcohol Benefit Study, Chgo., 1980-83; coord. pub. rels. and resource devel. VISTA; vol. Habitat for Humanity, Vista Leadership Corp, Tucson, 1997-98. Recipient Recognition award Ill. Dangerous Drugs Commn., 1980, 81, Outstanding Svc. award U. Profls. Ill., 1983-84, Outstanding Svc. award Ill. Fedn. Tchrs., 1983. Mem. Disabled Artist Assn. (bd. dirs., chair resource devel. com. 1992-93). Democrat. Avocations: painting, writing.

GARDNER, DONALD ANGUS, architect; b. Portchester, N.Y., June 3, 1944; s. Angus John and Mercedes (Speedie) G.; m. Gloria Orr, Dec. 27,

1966; children: Angela Renee, Donald Angus, Sonia Dale. BArch., Clemson U., 1968. Draftsman J.B. Lindsay, Clemson, S.C., 1970-74; project architect Vickery Allen Bashor, Greenville, S.C., 1974-75; ptnr. Gardner, Edelbut & Assocs., Seneca, S.C., 1975-76; project architect Daniel Internat./Daniel Engrs., Greenville, 1976-79, Lockwood Greene Engrs., inc., Spartanburg, S.C., 1979-82; project mgr. Enwright Assocs., Inc., Greenville, 1982-84; pres., dir. Donald A. Gardner Architects, Inc., Greenville, 1978—, Donald A. Gardner Builders, Inc., Greenville, 1994—, Donald A. Gardner, Inc., Greenville, 1998—, Donald A. Gardner Interactive LLC; draftsman J.B. Lindsay, Clemson, S.C., 1970-74. Served to 1st lt. C.E., U.S. Army, 1968-70. Decorated Army Commendation medal. Mem. AIA, Nat. Assn. Home Builders, Urban Land Inst. Methodist. Home: 9 Rocky Creek Ln Greenville SC 29615-5819 Office: PO Box 26178 Greenville SC 29616-1178

GARDNER, ERIC RAYMOND, lawyer; b. Derry, N.H., Nov. 13, 1946; s. William Rudolph and Lois Brooks (Wilson) G.; m. Kathleen Linda Chertok, June 14, 1969 (div. Mar. 1985); children: Matthew Eric, Thomas Martin; m. Melissa Rae Hastings, Oct. 21, 1988. BA in Polit. Sci., U. N.H., 1969; JD, Boston U., 1972. Bar: N.H. 1972, Mass. 1972, U.S. Dist. Ct. Vt., 1987, U.S. Supreme Ct. 1979. Law clk. N.H. Supreme Ct., Concord, 1972-73; assoc. Goodnow, Arwe, Ayer & Prigge, Keene, N.H., 1973-76; ptnr. Goodnow, Arwe, Ayer, Prigge & Gardner, Keene, 1977-81; pvt. practice Keene, 1981—; appointee N.H. Supreme Ct. Profl. Conduct Com., Concord, 1984-93. Editor Boston U. Law Rev., 1971-72. Clk., dir. Monodnock United Way, Keene, 1975-80; dir. Keene Family YMCA, 1974-82; chair Cheshire County Crimestoppers, Inc., 1997-98. Fellow N.H. Bar Found.; mem. ABA, ATLA, Am. Bd. Trial Advocates, Nat. Bd. Trial Advocacy, N.H. Trial Lawyers Assn., Greater Keene C. of C. (clk./dir. 1975-80). Avocations: flying, golf, tennis, skiing, travel. Office: PO Box C 222 West St Keene NH 03431-2455

GARDNER, EVERETTE SHAW, JR., information sciences educator, consultant, author; b. Osceola, Ark., Oct. 3, 1944; s. Everette Shaw and Evelyn (Fletcher) G.; m. Mary Ann Sihelnik, May 28, 1966; children: Cynthia Anne, Stacey Diane. BBA, Memphis State U., 1966; MBA, U. N.C., 1974, PhD, 1978. Commd. ensign USN, 1966, advanced through grades to comdr., 1980, ret., 1986; assoc. prof. U. Houston, 1987-88, chmn. dept. of decision and info. scis., 1988-95, prof., 1989—, dir. Ctr. Global Mfg., 1991—; bd. dirs., pres. Gardner Rsch., Inc., Sugar Land, Tex., 1987—; cons. NASA Johnson Space Ctr., Houston, 1988-89, Shell Oil Co., Houston, Continental Airlines, Houston, 1993—, Continental Micronesia, Guam, Delta Airlines, Atlanta, 1997—, Hawaiian Airlines, Honolulu, 2000—, Texaco, Houston, Pennzoil, Houston, Arthur Andersen, Houston, Exxon Co. USA, Houston, Compaq Computers, Houston, Frito-Lay, Dallas, Southwestern Bell, Houston, Centel Comm., Houston, Sys. Evolution, Houston, Tenneco, Houston, Spring Comm., L.A., Alamo Water Refiners, San Antonio, Houston Livestock Show and Rodeo, 1992—, APS Holding Corp., Houston, Oil and Gas Consultants Inc., Tulsa, 1996-99, Telecheck Svcs. Inc., Houston, 1997-99, Randalls Food Markets, Inc., Houston, 1997-99, Trees Inc., Houston, 1999—. Co-author: Quantitative Approaches to Management, 1993; author: (software) Autocast: Business Forecasting System, 1992, The Spreadsheet Forecaster, 1994, The Spreadsheet Quality Manager, 1993; assoc. editor Internat. Jour. of Forecasting, 1985-87, Mgmt. Sci., 1987-91, Interfaces, 1987-92; contbr. articles to profl. jours.; columnist Lotus mag., 1986-92. Bd. dirs. Women's Home Houston, 1992-97; mem. Republican Nat. Com. Mem. NRA, La. Shooting Assn., Tex. State Rifle Assn., Internat. Inst. Forecasters (pres. 1990-92, dir. 1987-94), Inst. for Ops. Rsch. and Mgmt. Scis., Operational Rsch. Soc., U.S. Naval Inst., Am. Prodn. and Inventory Control Soc. (bd. dirs. Houston chpt. 1997-98), La. Hist. Assn., Ret. Officers Assn., Sons. of Confederate Vets., 100 Club of Houston. Presbyterian. Avocations: competitive pistol shooting, tennis, gardening, Civil War history. Office: U Houston 4800 Calhoun Rd Houston TX 77204-0001

GARDNER, FREDERICK BOYCE, library director; b. Hopkinsville, Ky., Mar. 12, 1942; s. Boyce and Alleen Louise (Brown) G. BA, U. Ky., 1964; MA, Ind. U., Bloomington, 1966. Head librarian U. Ky. Hopkinsville Community Coll., Hopkinsville, 1966-69; head, readers service CUNY, Manhattan Community Coll., N.Y.C., 1969-71; reference librarian Calif. Inst. of the Arts, Valencia, Calif., 1971-84; head, pub. svcs. Calif. Inst. of the Arts, Valencia, 1974-87, dir. computer svcs., 1984-87, acting dir., 1987-88, dean of the library, 1988—; del. Calif. Conf. on Networking, Pomona, 1985; mem. Calif. Networking Task Force, 1990-95. Sec. Sequoia String Quartet Found., L.A., 1977-87. Capt. USAF, 1968-69. Mem. ALA, Assn. Coll. and Rsch. Librs., Santa Clarita Interlibr. Network (pres. 1989-91), Calif. Pvt. Acad. Librs. (exec. bd. 1988-91, 96—, chmn. 1990), Total Interlibr. Exch. (v.p. 1980-81, pres. 1981-82, chmn. 1983-86, cons. 1983-85), Calif. Libr. Assn., Performing Arts Librs. Network (chmn. 1991), West Hollywood Chorale (exec. com. 1997—). Avocations: music, computers, hiking. Office: Calif Inst Arts 24700 McBean Pky Santa Clarita CA 91355-2397

GARDNER, GARY EDWARD, lawyer; b. Windsor, Ont., Can., Oct. 21, 1952; s. Edward Thomas and Antonionette Ursla (Urbanski) G.; m. Sheila Mary Hand, Oct. 5, 1984. BA, Mich. State U., 1975; JD, U. Detroit, 1981. Mktg. officer Ford Motor Co. Australia, Melbourne, 1975-77; analyst Ford Motor Co., Dearborn, Mich., 1977-79; asst. to gen. counsel Ford Motor Co. Australia, Melbourne, 1979-80; assoc. James R. Shively, P.C., Detroit, 1980-82; instr. law Detroit Coll. of Bus., Dearborn, Mich., 1982-84; ptnr. Shively, McCloskey, Corriveau & Gardner, Mich., 1984-86; pvt. practice Dearborn, 1986-90; ptnr. Gardner & Doyle, 1990-94, Gary Edward Gardner, P.C., Dearborn, Mich., 1995—; atty. pvt. practice, Dearborn, Mich., 1995—. Candidate Judge of Ct. of Appeals S.E. Mich., 1988; candidate Judge 19th Dist. Ct., 1992, 94, Judge Wayne County Cir. Ct., 1998; bench-bar liaison com. Wayne County Cir. Ct., 1999; mem. Wayne County Rep. Com., 1999-2000; chmn. Dearborn-Dearborn Heights Rep. Club, 2000. Mem. ABA, Mich. Bar Assn. (com. domestic violence 1993-99), Dearborn Bar Assn. (pres. 1996-97), Wayne County Family Law Bar Assn. (founding mem., pres. 1997-99), Fairlane Club, Detroit Coll. Rugby Club, Kiwanis Club Dearborn. Republican. Roman Catholic. Home: 246 River Ln Dearborn MI 48124-1047 Office: 25121 Ford Rd Dearborn MI 48128-1058

GARDNER, JAMES RICHARD, pharmaceutical company executive; b. Wellsville, N.Y., Nov. 18, 1944; s. James Myers and Adelaide (Stockman) G.; m. Linda Marie Cuomo, Oct. 14, 1967; children: Alexandra K., Mindy M. BS in Engring., U.S. Mil. Acad., 1966; M in Pub. Adminstrn., Princeton U., 1968, PhD, 1977; MBA, L.I. U., 1977; grad., U.S. Army War Coll., 1989. Commd. 2d lt. U.S. Army, 1966, advanced through grades to maj., 1976, resigned,, 1977; staff asst. Office of U.S. Atty. Gen., 1973; asst. prof. U.S. Mil. Acad., West Point, N.Y., 1974-77; dir. agrl. planning Pfizer, Inc., N.Y.C., 1977-81, dir. corp. strategic planning, 1981-89, sr. dir. corp. strategic planning, 1989-94, v.p. corp. investor rels., 1994—; v.p. Pfizer Found., N.Y.C., 1985-99; mem. faculty U.S. Army Command Gen. Staff Coll., 1986-92; mem. adv. coun. Ctr. Internat. Studies, Princeton U., 1987—; mem. adv. coun. Dept. Astrophysical Scis. Princeton U., 1992-99; head USAR polit. and mil. affairs div. Dept. Army, 1989-92; mem. adv. coun. Coll. Sci. Pa. State U., 1999—. Author: (with others) American National Security, 1981, Business Competitor Intelligence, 1984; editor: Handbook of Strategic Planning, 1986; contbr. articles to profl. jours. Strategic planning com. United Way of Tri-State, N.Y.C., 1984-87; dir. adminstrn. Pfizer Inc. United Way campaign, N.Y.C., 1985-87; bd. dirs. Greater N.Y. couns. Boy Scouts Am., 1988-2000; N.Y.C. chmn. Nat. Eagle Scout Assn., 1989-92. Col. USAR, 1988-93. Decorated Bronze Stars (3), Air medals, Rep. Vietnam Gallantry Cross with Silver Star, Army Ranger; Recipient George Washington medal The Freedoms Found., Valley Forge, Pa., 1970; recipient Silver Beaver award Boy Scouts Am., 1991, Disting. Eagle award, 1992. Mem. Planning Forum (pres. N.Y.C. chpt. 1985-86), N.Am. Soc. Corp. Planning (nat. v.p. 1984-85), West Point Soc. N.Y. (bd. dirs. 1984-91, v.p. 1986-88, pres. 1988-90), Nat. Investor Rels. Inst. (bd. dirs. N.Y.C. chpt. 1995-97), U.S. Mil. Acad. Assn. Grads. (strategic planning com. 1992-96), Phi Kappa Phi. Republican. Roman Catholic. Avocations: youth activities, woodworking, astronomy, outdoor sports. Home: 40 Brundige Dr Goldens Bridge NY 10526-1416 Office: Pfizer Inc 235 E 42nd St New York NY 10017-5755

GARDNER, JULIAN WILLIAM, electronic engineering educator; b. Oxford, Eng., May 8, 1958; s. William Edward and Rosemarie (Summers) G.; m. Shauna Margaret Kelham, Mar. 22, 1986; children: Ruth, Ethan. BS, Birmingham (Eng.) U., 1979; PhD, Cambridge (Eng.) U., 1983. Prof. officer AEA Tech., Eng., 1983-85; R & D engr. Molins Plc, Coventry, Eng., 1985-87; lectr. electronic engring. Warwick U., Coventry, 1987-93, sr. lectr., 1993-95, reader, 1996-98, prof., 1998—; dir. sensors rsch. lab. Warwick U., 1990—, dir. nanotech. ctr., 1996—; cons. Alpha Mos, Toulouse, France, 1994-96, Hewlett-Packer, 1997-98, Electronic Noses, 1999. Author: Microsensors, 1994. Alexander von-Humboldt scholar, 1994. Avocations: badminton, bridge. Office: Warwick U, Sch Engring, Coventry CV4 7AL, England

GARDNER, MARY JOSEPHINE, management development consultant; b. Lebanon, Pa., Sept. 10, 1943; d. John Edward and Gertrude Marie (Scanlon) G.; divorced; children: Susan Lupack, Joyce Lupack. BA magna cum laude, Fordham U., 1971; MA, Columbia U., 1983. Tchr. Cardinal Spellman H.S., Bronx, N.Y., 1971-77; asst. tng. specialist Prudential Ins. Co., Newark, 1977-79; mgr. tng. and devel. Am. Express Co., N.Y.C., 1979-82; v.p. Chase Manhattan Bank, N.Y.C., 1982-84; pres. Gardner Enterprises, N.Y.C., 1984—, Marblehead, Mass., 1991—; pres. WorkVision, Marblehead, 1999; mem. faculty Am. Women's Econ. Devel. Corp., 1985-89; adj. instr. Grad. Sch. Mgmt., New Sch. for Social Rsch., N.Y.C., 1986-89; bd. dirs. Consortium for Breakthroughs in Women's Leadership. Mem. Culver Lake (N.J.) Water Quality Com., 1985-90; vol. Marblehead Eco-Farm, 1995-96; vol. coord. Me and Thee Coffee House, Marblehead, 1995—, Marblehead Arts Festival, 1991—; vol. cons. Boston Mgmt. Consortium, 1996—; vol. Boston Mayor's Leadership Devel. Program; vol. cons. on performance mgmt. to Boston Pub. Schs.; vol. Boston Police Dept.; active Murder Victims Families for Reconciliation; mem., pastoral assoc. Unitarian Universalist Ch. of Marblehead, 1997—. Avocation: gardening. E-mail: mgardner@workvision.com. Home: 22 Circle St Marblehead MA 01945-3502 Office: WorkVision 22 School St Marblehead MA 01945-3327

GARDNER, NORD ARLING, management consultant administrator; b. Afton, Wyo., Aug. 10, 1923; s. Arling A. and Ruth (Lee) G.; m. Thora Marie Stephen, Mar. 24, 1945; children: Randall Nord, Scott Stephen, Craig Robert, Laurie Lee. BA, U. Wyo., 1945; MS, Calif. State U., Hayward, 1972, MPA, 1975; postgrad., U. Chgo., U. Mich., U. Calif., Berkeley. With U.S. Army, 1941, commd. 2nd lt., 1945, advanced through grades to lt. col., 1964, ret., 1966; pers. analyst Univ. Hosp., U. Calif., San Diego, 1966-68; coord. manpower devel. U. Calif., Berkeley, 1968-75; univ. tng. officer San Francisco State U., 1975-80, pers. mgr., 1976-80; exec. dir. CRDC Maintenance Tng. Corp., non-profit cmty. effort, San Francisco, 1980-85; pres., dir. Sandor Assocs. Mgmt. Cons., Pleasant Hill, Calif., 1974-86, 91-96; gen. mgr. Vericlean Janitorial Svc., Inc.; in-charge bus. devel. East Bay Local Devel. Corp., Oakland, Calif., 1980-85; incorporateor, pres. Indochinese Cmty. Enterprises, USA, Ltd., Pleasant Hill, 1985-87; freelance writer, grantsmanship cons., 1987—; ptnr. Oi Kit Bldg. Maint. Svc., 1988-91; dir. univ. rels. Internat. Pacific U., San Ramon, Calif., 1990—, exec. dir., bd. dirs. Internat. Pacific Inst., 1994—; cons. Phimmasone Internat. Import-Export, Richmond, Calif., Lao Lanx-Xang Assn., Oakland Refugee Assn., 1988-90; instr. Japanese, psychology, supervisory courses, 1977-78; bd. dirs. New Ideas New Impacts, Inc. Author: To Gather Stones, 1978. Adv. coun. San Francisco C.C. Dist. Decorated Commendation medal. Mem. ASTD, Ret. Officers Assn., No. Calif. Human Resources Coun., Am. Assn. Univ. Adminstrs., Intenrat. Personnel Mgrs. Asn., Coll. and Univ. Pers. Assn., Commonwealth Club Calif., U. Calif.-Berkeley Faculty Club, San Francisco State U. FAculty Club, Army Counter Intelligence Corps Vets., Inc. Republican. Office: Internat Pacific Inst 2995 Bonnie Ln Pleasant Hill CA 94523-4547

GARDNER, PAUL LESLIE, education educator, educational researcher; b. Melbourne, Australia, Dec. 21, 1939; s. Lothar and Irma (Badrian) G.; m. Isabel Helen Feld, Jan. 13, 1963; children: Naomi, Rachel, Steven, Anthony. BSc, U. Melbourne, 1959, BEd, 1963, MEd, 1970; PhD, Monash U., Melbourne, 1972. Tchr. Edn. Dept. of Victoria, Australia, 1961-66; lectr. Monash U., 1967-72, sr. lectr., 1972-75, reader in edn., 1975—, dir. rsch. degrees, 1999—; cons. Road Traffic Authority of Victoria, 1984-86. Editor: The Structure of Science Education, 1975; editor Rsch. in Sci. Edn., 1989-94; co-editor conf. procs.; contbr. numerous articles to profl. jours. Chmn. B'nai B'rith Anti-Defamation Commn., 1982-88; pres. B'nai B'rith Hillel found., Melbourne, 1976-78; chmn. bd. trustees Bernard Lustig Meml. Scholarship, Melbourne, 1981—. Recipient Freda Cohen prize U. Melbourne, 1970. Mem. Am. Edn. Rsch. Assn., Australian Sci. Edn. Rsch. Assn., Monash U. Edn. Alumni (founder 1988), B'nai B'rith (nat. v.p. Australia-New Zealand 1994-2000). Jewish. Avocations: international travel, philately. Office: Monash U, Faculty of Edn, Clayton Vic 3800, Australia

GARDNER, ROBERT JOSEPH, general and thoracic surgeon; b. Barrington, Ill., Dec. 26, 1924; s. Anthony Joseph and Elizabeth Caroline (Jurs) G.; m. Mary Anne Rickley, June 26, 1948 (dec. Nov. 1997); children: Susan Elizabeth, Nancy Gardner Hargrave, Julie Gardner Withrow. Student, Ill. Inst. Tech., Chgo., 1942-44; BS, Wash. State U., 1947; MD, Northwestern U., Chgo., 1951. Intern Cook County Hosp., Chgo., 1951-52; pvt. gen. med. practice Menomonie (Wis.) Clinic, 1952-58; surg. resident Northwestern U. Hosps., Chgo., 1958-62; staff surgeon Fairmont (W.Va.) Clinic, 1962-68; fellow thoracic surgery W.Va. Med. Ctr., Morgantown, 1968-69, instr. surgery, 1969-70, asst. prof. surgery, 1970-72, assoc. prof. surgery, 1972-75, prof. surgery, 1975-78; staff surgeon St. Joseph's Community Hosp., West Bend, Wis., 1978-95; ret., retired, 1995. Contbr. articles to profl. jours., chpts. to books. Ensign, USNR, 1944-46; PTO. W.Va. Heart Assn. grantee, 1968-73. Fellow ACS; mem. AMA, Wis. Med. Soc., Wis. Surg. Soc., Cen. Surg. Assn., Soc. Thoracic Surgeons, Am. Assn. Thoracic Surgeons. Avocations: golf, swimming, softball, money management. Home: PO Box 1980 West Bend WI 53095-7980 Office: First National Bank 321 N Main St West Bend WI 53095-3319

GARDNER, ROBERTA JOAN, retired library director; b. N.Y.C., Apr. 12, 1932; d. Philip R. and Rae (Spiegel) Beller; m. Edgar Talmus, Apr. 19, 1951 (div.); children: Evie Talmus, Laura Talmus. BA in Econs., Queens Coll., Flushing, N.Y., 1962; MLS, Pratt Inst., 1964. Dir. libr. svcs. Bus. Internat., Inc., 1965-70; mgr. bus. libr. Dun & Bradstreet Corp., 1970-78, mgr. info. svcs., 1978-80, dir. info. svcs., 1980-81; dir. commn./info. svcs. Moran, Stahl & Boyer, Inc., 1981-82; dir. info. svcs. Bernard Hodes Advt., 1983-84; cons. Pub. Rels. Soc. of Am., 1984—; mgr. records ctr. Real Estate dept. Met. Trans. Authority, 1986; libr. dir. Parade Publs., Inc., 1987-2000; cons. World Trade Inst. Libr. Author: (with others) Information Management, 1984; contbr. articles to profl. jours. Mem. Spl. Librs. Assn. Avocations: theater, reading, crossword puzzles, gardening. Office: Parade Publs Inc 711 3rd Ave New York NY 10017-4014

GARECKI, JANUSZ, mathematical and theoretical physics educator; b. Tomaszów Mazowiecki, Poland, Oct. 26, 1942; s. Franciszek and Krystyna (Andryszczak) G.; m. Małgorzata Wrotna, Jan. 12, 1980; children: Krzysztof, Patrycja-Monika, Damian-Kamil. MSc in Astrophysics, Jagellonian U., 1965, MSc in Theoretical and Math. Physics, 1969, PhD in Phys. Sci., 1974. Rschr. Jagellonian U., 1965-73; lectr. Pedagogical U., Szczecin, Poland, 1974-84; lectr. math. and theoretical physics U. Szczecin, 1985—, leader gen. relativity and cosmology group, 1990—. Contbr. articles to sci. jours., including Classical and Quantum Gravity, Gen. Relativity and Gravitation, Internat. Jour. Theoretical Physics, Reports on Math. Physics, Jour. Mathemat. Physics, Annals of Physics, Acta Phys. Pol. Recipient award Ministry Sci. and Technics, 1975, 79, hon. mention Gravity Rsch. Found., 1995, 99. Mem. Gen. Relativity and Gravitation Soc., Polish Phys. Soc., Einstein Found. Internat., Nat. Geographic Soc. E-mail: gareck-i@wmf.univ.szczecin.pl. Office: U Szczecin Inst Physics, Wielkopolska 15, 70-451 Szczecin Poland

GAREL, PASCAL, hospital administrator, consultant; b. Antony, France, Mar. 6, 1966; s. Henri and Monique (Desrieux) G. Diplome, Institut Etudes Politiques, Paris, 1986, Ecole Sante Publique, Rennes, France, 1989, Faculty de Droit, Rennes, 1990. Attache Univ. Hosp., Nantes, France, 1990-93; charge de mission Ministry of Health, Paris, 1994-95; mgr. Univ. Hosp., Rouen, France, 1996—; now dir. internat. affairs The French Hosp. Fedn., Paris; cons. European Union, Brussels, 1991-96; tchr. U. Nantes, 1991-93, U. Lille, France, 1994-95. Se.c-gen. Centre Democrates Sociaux, Paris, 1993-95. Mem. Young Health Mgrs.-Europe (pres. 1996). Home: 4 Passage Champ Marie, 75018 Paris France Office: French Hosp Fedn, 33 Ave D'Italie, 75013 Paris France

GAREY, DONALD LEE, pipeline and oil company executive; b. Ft. Worth, Sept. 9, 1931; s. Leo James and Jessie (McNatt) G.; m. Elizabeth Patricia Martin, Aug. 1, 1953; children: Deborah Anne, Elizabeth Laird. BS in Geol. Engring., Tex. A&M U., 1953. Registered profl. engr., Tex. Reservoir geologist Gulf Oil Corp., 1953-54, sr. geologist, 1956-65; v.p., mng. dir. Indsl. Devel. Corp. Lea County, Hobbs, N.Mex., 1965-72, dir., 1972-86, pres., 1978-86; v.p., dir. Minerals, Inc., Hobbs, N.Mex., 1966-72; pres., dir. Minerals, Inc., Hobbs, 1972-86, CEO, 1978-82; mng. dir. Hobbs Indsl. Found. Corp., 1965-72, dir., 1965-76; v.p. Llano, Inc., 1972-74, exec. v.p., COO, 1974-75, pres., 1975-86, CEO, also dir., 1978-82; pres., CEO Pollution Control, Inc., 1969-81; pres. NMESCO Fuels, Inc., 1982-86; chmn., pres., CEO Estacado, Inc., 1986—, Natgas Inc., 1987—; pres. Llano Co2, Inc., 1984-86; cons. geologist, geol. engr., Hobbs, 1965-72. Chmn. Hobbs Manpower Devel. Tng. Adv. Com., 1965-72; mem. Hobbs Adv. Com. for Mental Health, 1965-67; chmn. N.Mex. Mapping Adv. Com., 1968-69; mem. Hobbs adv. bd. Salvation Army, 1967-78, chmn., 1970-72; mem. exec. bd. Conquistador coun. Boy Scouts Am., Hobbs, 1965-75; vice chmn. N.Mex. Gov's Com. for Econ. Devel., 1968-70; bd. regents Coll. Southwest, 1982-85. Capt. USAF, 1954-56. Mem. AIPG, AAPG, SPE of AIME. Home: 315 E Alto Dr Hobbs NM 88240-3905 Office: Broadmoor Tower PO Box 5587 Hobbs NM 88241-5587

GAREY, PATRICIA MARTIN, artist; b. State College, Miss., Nov. 11, 1932; d. Verey G. Martin and Eva Myrtle Jones; m. Donald L. Garey, Aug. 1, 1953; children: Deborah Anne Garey Furst, Elizabeth Laird Garey Jones. BS in Costume Design, Tex. Women's U., 1953; MFA, Tex. Tech. U., 1973; postgrad. in art history, Two-Dimensional Studio Art, 1970-73. Prodn. mgr. Cox Advt. Agy., Roswell, N.Mex., 1958-63; art instr. Coll. of Southwest, Hobbs, N.Mex., 1967-69, 72-73; prof. art history, art appreciation Coll. of Southwest, Santa Fe and Hobbs, N.Mex., 1974-76; studio artist Hobbs, 1976—; prof. art/painting and drawing N.Mex. Jr. Coll., 1997-98; instr. Cloudcroft (N.Mex.) Artists Sch., 1991, prof. drawing, painting N.Mex. Jr. Coll., prof. art hist. Coll. of Southwest, 1999-2000; rep., drawing instr. Villa Maria Ctr. for the Arts, Perugia, Italy, 1996; apptd. to N.Mex. Arts Commn., 1999; artist-in-residence N.Mex. Art Commn., 1975-76. One-woman shows include N.Mex. Jr. Coll., Hobbs, 1969, Coll. of SW, 1974, 79, Sangre de Cristo Arts Ctr., Pueblo, 1979, U. Tex. of Permian Basin, Odessa, 1980, N.Mex. Jr. Coll.; represented by Beverly Gordon Gallery, Dallas, Sylvia Ullman Am. Crafts, Cleve., Design Today, Lubbock Tex., El-Dor Galleries Old-Town, Albuquerque, Galeria de la Paloma, Santa Fe; work exhibited at Roswell Mus. Art, Southeastern N.Mex. Small Painting Exhibit (2d pl., 1966, 2d pl. Graphics), 2d pl. Sculpture, 2d pl. Acrylics), 75 (1st pl. Ceramics), 76 (1st pl. Drawing, 2d pl. Painting), Americas Gallery, Taos, 1974, Blair Gallery, Santa Fe, 1974, Mus. Fine Arts, Santa Fe, 1976, Tex. Tech. U., 1977, Little Rock Art Ctr., Ark., 1978, Hills Gallery, Santa Fe, 1979, Dallas Mus. Fine Art, 1986, 87, 88, 90, Beaux Arts Ball Art Auction, 1990, Okla. City Mus. Art, Little Rock Art Ctr., El Paso (Tex.) Sun Carnival, Govs. Gallery, State Capitol, Santa Fe, 1997, L.E.A.A., Hobbs, N.Mex., 1999 (Best of Show); represented in collections Beverly Gordon Gallery, Dallas, Tex. Tech. U., The Round House/State Capitol, Santa Fe, Villa Maria Ctr. for the Arts, Perugia, Italy; docent Meadows Mus. of Art So. Meth. U., Dallas, 1990, Govs. Invitational, Govs. Gallery, 1996, 35 Clay Workers of N.Mex. Bd. dirs. The Bridge Breast Ctr., Dallas, 1992—, Llano Estacado Art Assn.; art assoc. S.W. Symphony, Hobbs, 1987-99; mem. artistic bd. Southwest Symphony; arts commr. State of N.Mex., 1999—. Recipient Best of Show award for mixed media Llano Estacado Art Assn. Regional Show, Hobbs, N.Mex., 1996, Best of Show award for ceramics, 1998, 1st pl. award for watercolor, 1996. Mem. Delta Phi Delta, Chi Omega. Democrat. Methodist. Avocations: swimming (mem. Sr. Olympics N.Mex. Nat. Swim Team 1997), southern cooking, piano, classical music, book collecting. Studio: 315 E Alto Dr Hobbs NM 88240-3905 also: Piney Woods Cloudcroft NM 88350

GARFIELD, MARTIN RICHARD, lawyer; b. N.Y.C., Feb. 19, 1935; s. Harry and Sarah (Spielman) G.; m. Susan Scher, July 20, 1978 (div. Oct. 1990); 1 child, Robin. BA, Hunter Coll., 1957; JD, Bklyn. Law Sch., 1964. Bar: N.Y. 1965, U.S. Dist. Ct. (ea. and so. dists.) N.Y. 1979, U.S. Supreme Ct. 1996. Assoc. Figueroa & Madow, N.Y.C., 1965-68, Schneider Kleinick & Weitz, N.Y.C., 1968-70; ptnr. Breadbar Garfield & Solomon, N.Y.C., 1970-86; sr. ptnr. Breadbar Garfield & Schmelkin, N.Y.C., 1986—; arbitrator Civil Ct. N.Y. County, 1986—; mgr. N.Y. State Athletic Commn., 1996—. Mem. Am. Trial Lawyers Assn., N.Y. State Bar Assn. (torts, ins. sect.), N.Y. Trials Lawyers Assn. Avocations: tennis, basketball, boxing analysis, body building. Office: Breadbar Garfield & Schmelkin 11 Park Pl Fl 10 New York NY 10007-2895

GARFINKEL, LAWRENCE SAUL, academic administrator, educator, television producer; b. N.Y.C., Mar. 9, 1932; s. Benjamin and Rose (Rochkind) G.; m. Adrienne Rederer, June 26, 1960; children: Andrew, Rodger, Craig. BS in Art Edn., NYU, 1953, MA in Higher Edn., 1955, postgrad. in Edn. Comm., 1975. Tchr., supr. art, prin. high schs. West Hempstead Pub. Schs., N.Y., 1954-56, dir. related arts, 1957-69, dir. cmty. rels., 1961-71; prof. edn. adminstrn. and comm., dir. instrnl. comm. program Hofstra U., Hempstead, N.Y., 1969-76; dir. gifted programs Sachem Pub. Schs., Lake Ronkonkoma, N.Y., 1978-79; dir. ednl. comm. Coll. Dentistry, Kriser Dental Ctr., NYU, 1979-91, ret.; adj. prof. dept. speech Baruch Coll., CUNY, 1980-91, Adelphi U., Stern Coll.-Yeshiva U., St. Johns U., Temple U., N.Y. Inst. Tech.; adj. prof. dept. media arts C.W. Post-L.I. U., 1991—; adj. assoc. prof. art dept. Nassau C.C.; cons. bd. regents N.Y. State Edn. Dept., Ctr. Urban Edn., N.Y.C. Editor: Restorative Dentistry, 1985; illustrator: Classroom Television, 1970; illustrator N.Y. Times, John Huston Prodns., Century Theatres, Nat. Audio Visual Assn., and numerous publs.; editl. cartoonist Merrick Life; asst. prodr. WPIX-TV, programming Dumont Network; pub. Garson Assocs.; contbr. articles to profl. jours. Coord. youth edn. Mothers Against Drunk Driving, Long Island Area, 1997-99; bd. dirs. Hist. Soc. Merricks, 1983—, Higher Edn. Assn. TV, 1972; v.p. Health Equities, N.Y.C.; oral historian Bi Centennial Commn., 1975. Recipient Grad. Arch award medal NYU, scholarship masters NYU, numerous awards Nat. Com. Sch. Pub. Rels.; grad. fellow NYU. Mem. N.Y. Acad. Scis., L.I. Art Tchrs. Assn. (pres. 1967-68), Nat. Com. Art Edn. (co-pres. 1967). Avocations: illustrating, lecturing on communications theory, arts, visual literacy, teaching. Home and Office: Garson Assocs 172 Babylon Tpke Merrick NY 11566-4407

GARFUNKEL, ADI ADRIAN, educator in oral medicine, researcher; b. Bucharest, Romania, Aug. 15, 1939; s. Moritz and Milly (Finkelstein) G.; m. Maya Farkas, Aug. 15, 1962; children: Roy, Keren. DMD, Hebrew U., Jerusalem, Israel, 1963; Cert., Acad. Oral Medicine, U.S., 1970; Oral Medicine Specialist, Sch. Dental Medicine, Jerusalem, Israel, 1980; D honoris causa, Carol Davilla U. Asst. Sch. Dental Medicine, Jerusalem, Israel, 1963; lectr. Sch. Dental Medicine, Jerusalem, 1971-75, sr. tchr., 1975-80, dean faculty dental medicine, 1986; prof. dental medicine Hebrew U., Jerusalem, Israel, 1986-90; dir. The DW Cohen Middle East Ctr. for Adv. Dental Edn.; tchg. assoc. Einstein Med. Ctr., Phila., 1973-74; vis. assoc. prof. Pahlavi U., Shiraz, Iran, 1977; prof., chmn. Oral Medicine dept., Hadassa Hosp., Jerusalem, 1984; vis. assoc. prof. Sch. of Dental Medicine, Phila., 1990, adj. prof. U. Pa., Phila., 1994, Hanneman Sch. of Dentistry, Phila, 1996. Co-author: (with others) Microbial Diseases in Internal Medicine for Dentistry, 1983, Burket's Oral Medicine, 1985; mem. editl. bd. Compendium, 1990—. Maj. Israeli Def. Forces, 1966-69. Recipient Hon. Diploma and Medal of City of Bucharest; grantee Grüenthal Co., 1996. Fellow Acad. Internat. Dental Studies (hon.); mem. ADA (hon.), Israeli Dental Assn., Internat. Assn. Dental Rsch., Alpha Omega. Home: Diskin St 5 Apt 13, Jerusalem Israel Office: Hadassa U Hosp, Eyn-Karem PO Box 12000, 91120 Jerusalem Israel

GARG, PRADEEP, surgical consultant, researcher; b. Bahraich, India, Oct. 26, 1957; s. Dinesh Chandra (dec.) and Nirmla (Govil) G.; m. Anita Tilak Garg, mar. 12, 1986; children: Richa, Tania. MBBS, MLB Med. Coll., Jhansi, India, 1982, MS in Surgery, 1985; DNB in Surgery, Nat. Bd. Examination, New Delhi, India, 1991. Sr. resident MCKR Hosp., New Delhi, India, 1985, N. Mohan Hosp., Ghaziabad, India, 1985-86, Willingdon Hosp., New Delhi, India, 1986-89; sr. specialist Steel Auth. of India Ltd., Bokaro, India, 1989-90; cons. Post Grad. Inst. Med. Scis., Rohtak, India, 1990—. Contbr. articles to profl. jours. Recipient Gold Medals, 1976-85, Merit scholarship, 1976-81, Dir. Med. Edn. MLB Med. Coll., Jhansi, Best Rsch. award Internat. Coll. Surgeons, Mumbai, 1997. Fellow Internat. Coll.

Surgeons; mem. Indian Assn. Surg. Gastroenterology, Assn. Surgeons India, Northern Chpt. Assn. Surgeons of India, Assn. Surgeons of Haryana, North Zone Chpt. Urological Soc. India. Home: 46/9J Medical Enclave, Rohtak 124001, India Office: Postgrad Inst Med Scis, Rohtak 124001, India

GARG, RAVINDRA KUMAR, neurologist; b. Sultanpur, India, Feb. 12, 1960; p. Deep Chandra and Sumat Gupta; m. Hema Chawla, Feb. 20, 1988; children: Shantanu, Chinkey. MB, BChir, Maharani Laxmi Bai Med. Coll., Jhansi, India, 1982, MD, 1987; DM in Neurology, King George's Med. Coll., Lucknow, India, 1991. Resident in internal medicine Maharani Laxmi Bai Med. Coll., Jhansi, 1983-88; sr. resident King George's Med. Coll., Lucknow, 1989-91, chief resident, 1992-94, sr. pool officer, 1995-97, asst. prof., 1999—; lectr. Inst. Med. Scis. Banares Hindu U., Varanasi, India, 1997-99; head lipid rsch. lab. Maharani Laxmi Bai Med. Coll., Jhansi, 1984-87. Editor: (book) Epilepsy, 1993, 2d edit., 95, Epilepsy Bulletin, 1994-95; contbr. articles to profl. jours. Dist. sec. Leo Club, Sultanpur, 1976. Recipient Late TD Shukla medal Jhansi U., 1986, Late PL Ghai medal, 1987, Late KB Kunwar award, 1995. Mem. Internat. Med. Paraplegia Soc., Indian Acad. Neurology, Neurolog. Soc. India, Indian Epilepsy Assn., Indian Epilepsy Soc. Hindu. Avocations: sports, stamp collecting. Email garg50@yahoo.com. Home: Deep Bhawan, Behind Bank of Baroda, 228001 Sultanpur India Office: King Georges Med Coll, Dept Neurology, 226003 Lucknow India

GARG, VIJAY KUMAR, telecommunications engineer; b. Jahangirabad, India, July 7, 1938; came to U.S., 1965; s. Reoti S. and Prem V. (Mittal) G.; m. Pushpa Bansal, May 11, 1961; children: Nina Taneja, Meena Dorr, Ravi K. Garg. BS, Banaras U., Varanasi, India, 1960; MS, U. Calif., Berkeley, 1966; PhD, Ill. Inst. Tech., 1973. Registered profl. structral engr., Ill., profl. engr., Ill. Asst. prof. engrng. U. Jodhpur, India, 1960-65; structural engr. Chgo. Bridge, Oakbrook, Ill., 1967-69; devel. engr. GMC, Lagrange, Ill., 1969-76; mgr. dynamic rsch. AAR, Chgo., 1976-84; assoc. prof. engrng. U. Maine, Orono, 1984-85; dist. mem. tech. staff Bell Labs Lucent Techs., Naperville, Ill., 1985—, Motorola Inc., Arlington Heights, Ill., 1997; vis. prof. elec. and comm. engrng. U. Ill., Urbana, 1996-97; adj. prof. engrng. Ill. Inst. Tech., Chgo., 1976-84. Author: Wireless and Personal Communications System, 1996, Applications of CDMA in Wireless Communications, 1997, Dynamics of Railway Vehicle System, 1984, Advanced Dynamics, 1984, Principles and Applications of GSM, 1999, CDMA IS-95 and CDMA 2000, 2000. Recipient NSF travel grants India, 1984, China, 1985. Fellow ASME, ASCE; mem. IEEE (sr.). Democrat. Hindu. Avocations: gardening, travel, reading, music. Home: 146 Somerset Rd Hinsdale IL 60521-5429 Office: Lucent Tech Inc Bell Labs 263 Shuman Blvd Naperville IL 60563-1255

GARGAN, THOMAS JOSEPH, plastic surgeon; b. Denver, Sept. 28, 1952; s. Thomas Joseph and Maria Augusta (Casagranda) G.; m. Nancy Lee Hall, Jan. 20, 1979; children: Daniel Thomas, John William. BA summa cum laude, Colo. Coll., 1974; MD, U. Colo., 1978. Diplomate Am. Bd. Plastic Surgery. Intern Presbyn. Med. Ctr., Denver, 1978-79, resident in surgery, 1978-79; resident in surgery Beth Israel Hosp., Boston, 1979-81, instr. gen. surgery, 1979-82, sr. resident in surgery, 1981-82, chief resident in plastic surgery, 1983-84; sr. resident in plastic surgery Cambridge (Mass.) City Hosp., 1982-83; resident in plastic surgery Children's Hosp. and Brigham and Women's Hosp., Boston, 1983, Newton-Wellesley Hosp., Mass., 1983; clin. fellow in surgery Harvard U. Med. Sch., Boston, 1979-84; clin. instr. plastic surgery U. Colo. Sch. Med., Denver, 1984; chief plastic surgery divsn. Rose Med. Ctr., 1987—; instr. plastic surgery Cambridge Hosp., Children's Hosp., and Beth Israel Hosp., Boston, 1982-84, Harvard Med. Sch., Boston, 1984. Contbr. articles to profl. jours. Bd. dirs. Rocky Mt. Adoption Exch., Lupis Found., Outward Bound Colo.; founder Plasticare for Kids Found. Recipient George B. Packard award for excellence in surgery U. Colo. Med. Ctr., 1978; Eagle Scout; Barnes Chemistry scholar Colo. Coll. Fellow ACS; mem. AMA, Denver Med. Soc. (pres. Gold Star award), Colo. Med. Soc., Am. Soc. Plastic and Reconstructive Surgeons, Rocky Mountain Hand Surgery Soc., Rocky Mountain Soc., Reconstructive Plastic Surgeons, Am. Soc. Aesthetic Plastic Surgeons, Order Hibernians in Am. Avocations: skiing, fly fishing, mountaineering, golf, tennis. Home: 6900 E Prentice Ave Englewood CO 80111

GARGANAS, NICHOLAS C(HRISTOS), economist; b. Soufli, Evros, Greece, Jan. 20, 1937; s. Christos N. and Eugenia C. (Hadjinicolaou) G.; m. Maria N. Kokka, Sept. 21, 1966; 1 child. BSc in Econs., Athens Sch. Econ./Bus. Studies, 1959; MSc in Econs., London Sch. Econs./Polit. Sci., 1963; PhD, Univ. Coll. London, 1971. Head econ. rsch. unit Agrl. Bank of Greece, Athens, 1964-66; rsch. officer Nat. Inst. Econ. and Social Rsch., London, 1968-75; sr. economist, dir./advisor Bank of Greece, Athens, 1975-93, econ. advisor, chief economist, 1993-96, dep. gov., 1996—; mem. EU Monetary Com., 1994-98; mem. EU EFC, 1999—; alt. gov. for Greece, IMF, 1996—. Contbg. author: Poverty and Progress in Britain 1953-1973, 1977; author: The Bank of Greece Econometric Model of the Greek Economy, 1992; joint mng. editor Greek Econ. Rev., 1979-85; contbr. articles to profl. jours. 2d lt. Greek Navy, 1959-61. LSE Hon. fellow, 1998. Mem. Am. Econ. Assn., Royal Econ. Soc., European Econ. Assn., EU (European Union) EFC, (Econ. and Fin. Com.), EU (monetary com. 1994-98). Fax: 001-908-771-8645. Home: 15 Vassileos Georgiou B St, Philothei Athens 152-37, Greece Office: Bank of Greece, 21 El Venizelos, 102-50 Athens Greece

GARGANO, GIULIO, oncologist, educator; b. Bari, Italy, Aug. 14, 1958; s. Giacomo and Giuseppina (Fiore) G. Degree in medicine, U. Bari, 1983, postgrad. degree in gynaecotokology, 1983; postgrad. degree in human cytogenetics, U. Favia, 1990; postgrad. degree in oncology, U. Bari, 1995. Med. sub-lt. Mil. Hosp., Bari, 1984-85; med. vol. svc. Gen. Hosp., Bari, 1986; rschr. Dept. Genetics, Basel, Switzerland, 1986-87; gynecologist Gynaecotokology Hosp., Bari, 1987; gynecologist Oncology Inst., Bari, 1989-94, prof.'s asst., 1994—. Avocations: riding, skiing, skindiving, motorcycling, shooting. Home: Via Giuseppe Capruzzi, 70124 Bari Italy Office: Oncology Inst, Via Amendola 209, 70126 Bari Italy

GARGIULO, ANDREA W., lawyer; b. Hartford, Conn., Apr. 26, 1946; d. Charles M. and Irma S. (Rubin) Weiner; m. Richard A. Gargiulo, Nov. 26, 1975; 1 child, John K. BA, Smith Coll., 1968; JD cum laude, Suffolk U., 1972. Bar: Mass. 1972, U.S. Dist. Ct. Mass. 1975, U.S. Ct. Appeals (11th cir.) 1981, U.S. Supreme Ct. 1983. Asst. dist. atty. Middlesex County, Mass., 1972-75; chmn. Boston Fin. Commn., 1975-77; counsel Gargiulo, Rudnick, & Gargiulo, Boston, 1976—; chmn. Boston Licensing Bd., 1977-89; lectr. Northeastern U. Coll. Criminal Justice, Boston, 1978, 80; bd. dirs. Arbella Mut. Ins. Co.; host (TV show) Women Today, 1994-96. Mem. Mass. Ethics Commn., 1985-88; mem. bd. overseers Children's Hosp., Boston, 1983-99; chmn. Mass. Bd. Overseers, 1996. Mem. Bay Club, Beacon Hill Garden Club, Harvard Mus. Assn., Wianno Yacht Club, Univ. Club. Democrat. Avocation: sailing, acting. Home: 13 W Cedar St Boston MA 02108-1211 Office: Gargiulo Rudnick & Gargiulo 66 Long Wharf Boston MA 02110-3605

GARGOUR, ALLENBY TOUFIC, automotive company executive; b. Jaffa, Palestine, Mar. 16, 1918; s. Toufic Nicolas and Adele (Finan) G.; m. Charlotte Gellad (dec. 1987); children: Denise, Samir, Adela, Ramzi. DSc, Freresla Salle, Jaffa, Palestine; postgrad., Saccre Coeur, Beirut. Dep. Ministry of Food, Egypt, 1946-49; pres. Modern Food Co., Alexandria, Egypt, 1956-62; dir. ptnr. T. Gargour & Fils, Libya, 1962-69; ptnr. T. Gargour & Fils, Beirut, 1970; pres. Societe Gargour Fonciere/Financiere, Beirut, 1980; gen. mgr. Lecico Sal., Kfarchima, Lebanon, 1980-97; pres. T. Gargour & Fils, 1997—; bd. dirs. Uniceramic Sal, Beirut, Lecico-Egypt Sae., Alexandria, Egypt, 1980-97, Mercedes-Benz Gen. Agy., Dora, Beirut, 1997. Mem. Lion's Club, Alumni Club of Am. Univ. Roman Catholic. Avocations: photography, gardening, swimming, rowing. Home: Warrenmere Lane, Weybridge Surrey KT130LH, United Kingdom Office: T Gargour & Fils, Mercedes Benz Gen Agy, Dora Beirut Lebanon

GARINGALAO, CARLOS VICTOR, JR., glass and aluminum dealer; b. Binalbagan Town, The Philippines, July 28, 1964; s. Carlos Gerona Sr. and Theresa (Gomilla) G.; m. Lily Tan, May 25, 1995; 1 child, Carlos III. BS in Agrl. Bus. Mgmt., La Salle Coll., Bacolod City, The Philippines, 1985. Human devel. officer First Farmers Human Devel. Found. Inc., Bacolod City, 1986-87; farm mgr. Singapore and Palay Prodn., Kaban Kalan City, The Philippines, 1987-92; mgr. Shell Svc. Sta., Kaban Kalan City, 1992-95; restaurant owner Balcolod City, 1995-96; glass and aluminum dealer, owner Carly Enterprises Glass Aluminum and Steelworks, Kaban Kalan City, 1996—; fin. cons. John Hancock Life Ins., Bacolod City, 1998-99, PruLife of U.K., Bacolod City, 1999—. Home: 5C-22 Sinulog St, Fiesta Homes Brgy Sum AG, 6100 Bacolod City Negros, The Philippines

GARISHIN, OLEG CONSTANTINOVICH, research scientist; b. Perm, Russia, May 20, 1958; s. Constantin Vasil'evich and Maya Fedorovna (Garina) G.; m. Helena Valentinovna Gordeeva, July 24, 1981 (div. Oct. 1987); 1 child, Ann; m. Marina Vladimirovna Subbotina, Feb. 11, 1994; 1 child, Denis. MSc, Perm Poly. Inst., 1980; PhD in Mech. Engring., Riga (Latvia) Polu. Inst., 1988. Engr. Inst. Continuous Media Mechanics, Perm, 1980-85, jr. rsch. scientist, 1985-86, rsch. scientist, 1986-90, sr. rsch. scientist, 1990—. Co-author: Structural Mechanisms of Mechanical Properties Formation in Patriculate Polymer Composites, 1997; contbr. articles to sci. jours., including Internat. Jour. Solids and Structures, Jour. Adhesion, Jour. Theoretical and Applied Fracture Mechanics. Grantee Russian Found. Basic Rsch., 1994-96, 98-99. Russian Orthodox. Avocations: ski racing, sports, travel. Home: 94/56 Komsomolsky Ave, 614010 Perm Russia Office: Inst Cont Media Mechanics, 1 Korolyov Str, 614 Perm Russia

GARISON, BRENDA MAE, forensic nurse; b. Birmingham, Ala., Mar. 13, 1953; d. Roland L. and Dovie J. McMurrey; m. L.C. Garison, July 13, 1985; children: Syrena Young, Tony Loggins. RN, Lamar U., 1991. RN, Tex.; cert. sexual assault nurse examiner, Tex., forensic nurse, expert witness in sexual assault in civil, criminal and fed. cts. Computer operator Conn Appliance, Beaumont, Tex., 1980-85; nurse extern St. Elizabeth Hosp., Beaumont, 1988-91, RN, sexual assault nurse, 1991-95; founder, dir. Child Abuse and Beyond, Inc., Beaumont, 1996—; bd. mem. Rodgers Cmty. Health Clinic, Beaumont, Rape & Suicide Crisis Ctr., Beaumont, Garth House, Child Adv. Ctr., Beaumont, Police Activities League, Beaumont, Tex. Assn. Against Sexual Assault, Austin, Commn. for Prevention of Child Abuse and Neglect, Beaumont. Recipient Child Adv. of Yr. award Ct. Appointed Spl. Adv., 1997. Mem. Internat. Assn. Forensic Nursing, Nat. Orgn. for Victim Assistance, Forensic Nursing Assn., Children's Advocacy Ctr. Tex., Tex. Assn. Against Sexual Assault (Edith Rust award 1995, bd. mem. 1996—), Jefferson County Cmty. Planning Com., Hardin County Cmty. Planning Com. Home: PO Box 13 Vidor TX 77670-0013 Office: Child Abuse and Beyond Inc 810 Hospital Dr Ste 105 Beaumont TX 77701-4633

GARKAVI, LJUBOV KHAIMOVNA, physiologist, researcher; b. Rostov-na-Donu, Russia, Jan. 25, 1936; d. Khaim Iosiph Garkavi and Sophia Abramovna Ginsburg. M in Medicine, Med. Inst., Rostov, Russia, 1958; PhD Inst. Normal & Path. Physiol., Acad. Med. Sci., Moscow, 1963; MD Med. Inst., Ministry Health USSR, Donetsk, Ukraine, 1970. Lab. asst. Cancer Rsch. Inst., Rostov, 1957-61, jr. rschr., 1962-64, sr. rschr., 1964-72, head lab., 1973—; academician Internat. Acad. Natural Sci., Moscow, 1995. Author: (with E. Kvakina and M. Ukolova) Adaptational Reactions and Body Resistance, 1975, 2nd edit., 1979, 3rd edit., 1990, (with E. Kvakina and T. Kuzmenko) Antistress Reactions and Activation Therapy, 1998; inventor in field. Avocations: poetry, art. Home: Flat 103, 197 Pushkinskaya St, 344022 Rostov-na-Donu Russia Office: Cancer Rsch Inst, 14 Line 63, 344037 Rostov-na-Donu Russia

GARLAND, JAMES H., bishop; b. Wilmington, Ohio, Dec. 13, 1931. Attended, Wilmington (Ohio) Coll.; B.A. Edn., Ohio State U., 1953; M.A. Philosophy, Mt. St. Mary's Sem., Cin., 1960; M.S. Soc. Work, Cath. U., Washington, 1965. Ordained priest Aug. 15, 1959; appointed to the Episcopacy, July 25, 1984. Titular bishop of Garriana; aux. bishop Archdiocese of Cincinnati, 1984-92; bishop Diocese of Marquette, 1992—; chmn. U.S. Catholic Conf. Comm. for the Campaign for Human Devel.; mem. admin. com. & bd. U.S. Catholic Conf./Nat. Conf. of Catholic Bishops. Address: Pastoral Office 300 Rock St PO Box 550 Marquette MI 49855-0550

GARLETTE, WILLIAM HENRY LEE, army officer; b. S. Charleston, W.Va., June 3, 1951; s. William Arthur Jr. and Margret Mary (Birmingham) G.; m. Janeth Mae Hintz, June 17, 1986; 1 child, Marlena Kristen. BS, William Paterson Coll., 1973; M. Music, SUNY, Stony Brook, 1974; bandmastercourse, U.S. Army Element SOM, 1984; M. in Music, Northwestern Univ., 1988. Cert. tchr., N.J., N.Y., Va. Music dir winds and vocal Essex Catholic High Sch., Newark, N.J., 1972-73; instr. instrumental music SUNY, Stony Brook, 1973-74; band dir., chmn. dept. music Woodrow Wilson H.S., Portsmouth, Va., 1974-77; rehearsal condr., instr. instrumental music U.S. Army Element Sch. Music, Norfolk, Va., 1977-78, chief, concert band br., 1978-79; assoc. condr., sr. instrumentalist 26th Army Band, N.Y.C., 1979-81; assoc. condr., clinician, sr. instrumentalist U.S. Continental Army Band, Hampton, Va., 1981-83; asst. officer in charge advance course U.S. Army Element Sch. of Music, Norfolk, 1984-85; commd. 2nd lt. U.S. Army, 1985, advanced through grades to maj., 1996; Midwest region staff bands officer 4th U.S. Army, Chgo., 1985-88; exec. officer, assoc. condr. U.S. Continental Army Band, Hampton, 1988-90, comdr., prin. condr., 1990-92; asst. comdt., dir. evaluations and standardization, staff and faculty comdr., dir. army band officer course U.S. Army Element Sch. Music, Norfolk, 1992-98; dep. comdr., assoc. condr. U.S. Mil. Acad. Band, West Point, N.Y., 1998—; guest condr. Northshore Concert Band, Glenview, Ill., 1988; adj. prof. grad. music studies Old Dominion U., Norfolk, 1995—, Cath. U. Am., Washington, 1995—. Named Jr. Officer of Yr., Assn. U.S. Army, Ft. Monroe, 1991. Mem. Nat. Band Assn., Percy Grainger Soc., Coll. Band Dirs. Nat. Assn., World Assn. Symphonic Bands and Ensembles, Internat. Mil. Musicians Soc. Anishnabe. Avocations: martial arts, numismatics, running, biking. Home: 3110 Paterson Loop Apt F West Point NY 10996-1863 Office: US Mil Acad Band West Point NY 10996

GARLIAUSKAS, ALGIS, neurocomputer scientist, researcher; b. Vilnius, Lithuania, Jan. 10, 1932; s. Juozas and Monika (Sukaravichiute) G.; m. Aurelija Grishkevichiute, Aug. 18, 1983; 1 child, Egle. Diploma, Vilnius Pedagogical U., 1955; D Tech. Scis., Russian Acad. Scis., Novosibirsk, 1978; Prof., Acad. Mgmt., Vilnius, 1986. Cert. Moscow Energetic Inst. Sr. scientist Rsch. Inst. Gas, Moscow, 1962-68; head lab. Rsch. Inst. Econs. Gas Industry, Moscow, 1968-78; sr. scientist Computer Ctr. Russian Acad. Scis., Moscow, 1978-82; head lab. Inst. Math. and Informatics, Vilnius, Lithuania, 1982—; chmn. Lithuanian Scientist Soc. Dept. Informatics, Vilnius. Author: Mathematical Modelling of Effective and Perspective Planning of Gas Transportation Systems, 1975, Systems Analysis and Optimization of Complex Networks; co-author of extra 3 monograph, over 160 papers. Recipient prize of Laureate, Lithuanian Ministry Coun., Vilnius, 1987; grantee Soros Internat. Sci. Program Fund, Washington, 1993, Natural Sci. and Engring. Rsch. Coun., Can., 1995, Tokyo Sci. U., 1989, North Country Coun. Fund, Vilnius, 1993, Collaborative rsch. award Riken BSI, Tokyo, 1999. Mem. Lithuanian Scientist Soc. (mem. coun.). Avocations: running, basketball. Home: Laisves prospect 99a-52, Vilnius 2022, Lithuania Office: Inst Math and Informatics, Akademijos 4, Vilnius Lithuania

GARLICK, STEPHEN EDWIN, advertising executive; b. Cardiff, England, Jan. 15, 1957; s. Edwin and Pamela Anne (Ogus) G.; m. Lynne Charrison, Sept. 28, 1985; children: Emily, Olivia. Exec. AK, London, 1978-84; gen. mgr. MacMillan Davies, London, 1984-86; dir. LBW, London, 1986-92; mng. dir. GMBM, London, 1992—. Mem. Ch. of England. Avocations: gardening, physical fitness. Office: Landseer House, 19 Charing Cross Rd, London WC2H 0ES, England

GARLOT, JOEL JEAN, consulting firm executive; b. Paris, France, May 20, 1944; s. Jacques J. and Gilberte M. (Kasper) G.; divorced: Camille; m. Annie Madec Sept 17, 1976; two children: David, Stephane. Diploma in Engring., Ecole Centrale, Paris, 1969. Cons. Andersen Consulting, France, 1970-80, ptnr., 1980-87, sr. ptnr., 1987091; pres. Price Waterhouse Consulting, France, 1991—; sr. ptnr. Europe, Mid. East, Africa Pricewaterhouse Coopers, France, 1998. Avocations: opera, cycling, golf. Office: Pricewaterhouse Coopers, Tour AIG 34 Pl Des Corolles, 92908 Paris La Defense France

GARLY, MAY-LILL, epidemiologist, researcher, physician; b. Rødovre, Denmark, Sept. 21, 1963; d. Sigurd Frede and Inge (Hansen) G.; m. Palle Valentiner-Branth, Sept. 23, 1964; 1 child, Rose. DTM & H, London Sch. Tropical Medicine, 1994; PhD, U. Copenhagen, 1999. Resident Frederiksberg (Denmark) Hosp., 1992-1993, Hvidovre (Denmark) Hosp., 1993-1994; rsch. fellow Statens Serum Inst., Copenhagen, 1994-1999, sr. rschr., 1999—. Office: Statens Serums Rsch Inst, Dept Epidemiology Artillerivej 5, 2300 Copenhagen Denmark

GARMANOV, MAKSIM EVGENIEVICH, electrochemist; b. Moscow, May 29, 1961; s. Evgenii Nikolaevich and Kira Aleksandrovna (Vozhik) G. Highest Degree with honors, Moscow State U., 1983; postgrad., Karpov's Physico-Chem. Rsch. Inst., Moscow, 1990. Jr. scientist Karpov's Physico-Chem. Rsch. Inst., Moscow, 1986-87; jr. scientistInst. Phys. Chemistry Russian Acad. Scis., Moscow, 1990-92; scientist Inst. Phys. Chemistry of Acad. Scis., Moscow, 1992—, spl. rschr., 1983-86; supernumerary mgr. on mktg. and prodn. JPHCAN Ltd., Moscow, 1992—; supernumerary computer programmist Inst. Phys. Chemistry of Russian Acad. Sci., 1990—, engr., designer on rsch. equipment and methods, 1990—. Contbr. articles to profl. jours. Mem. Komsomol, Moscow, 1977-89, Trade Union of Sci. Workers, Moscow, 1979—. With Russian Army Res., 1983—. Mem. N.Y. Acad. Scis. Avocations: yachting, photography, English language, IBM computer programming. Home: Apt 133, Leningradskoe shosse 35, 125212 Moscow Russia Office: Inst Phys Chemistry, Leninskii Prospect 31, 117915 Moscow Russia

GARN, SUSAN LYNN, secondary education educator; b. Astoria, Oreg., July 12, 1948; d. Everett Leslie and Jeanne Esther (Linquist) G. BA in Art, U. Nev., Reno, 1970; MEd in Ednl. Adminstrn. and Higher Edn., U. Nev., Las Vegas, 1990. Registered mem. Chinook Indian tribe. Tchr. art Desert Sands Unified Sch. Dist., Indio, Calif., 1973-74; art. resource tchr. Trinity County Schs., Weaverville, Calif., 1974-75; multi-subject tchr., primarily in visual arts, digital art edn. Clark County Sch. Dist., Las Vegas, 1975-80, 87—; tchr. English, reading Jordan Sch. Dist., Sandy, Utah, 1982-84; lead community sch coord. Lincoln County Sch. Dist., Newport, Oreg., 1984-87; sole propr. Sue Garn and Kids Art, Las Vegas, 1988-98; presenter at profl. confs.; long term substitute tchr. Chemawa Indian Sch., Salem, Oreg., 1984. Work displayed at Educators as Artists exhibit, 1990, 92, 93. Bd. dirs. Las Vegas Indian Ctr., 1996-99. Named Tchr. of Yr. Nev. State PTA, 1990; Excellence in Edn., CCSD, 1991. Mem. Nat. Art Edn. Assn. (mid. level liaison 1993-94, past pres. cadre, Nev. Art Educator of Yr. award 1993, v.p. pacific region 1997-2000), Art Educators So. Nev., Art Educators Nev. (pres. 1990-92), Am. Indian C. of C. Avocations: German short haired pointer and Weimaraner dogs, travel, movies, art. Home: 3709 El Jardin Ave Las Vegas NV 89102-3821 Office: Advanced Techs Acad 2501 Vegas Dr Las Vegas NV 89106-1643

GARNAEV, ANDREY YURYEVICH, mathematics educator, software developer; b. St. Petersburg, Russia, May 17, 1960; s. Yuriy Sergeyevich and Margarita Semyonovna (Baykova-Yakerson) G. MS, St. Petersburg State U., Russia, 1982, PhD, 1987, D of Math., 1997. Asst. prof. St. Petersburg State U. Arch. & Civil Engring., Russia, 1982-92, assoc. prof., 1992-97, prof., 1997—. Author Visual Basics 6.0, 2000, Microsoft Excel 2000, Search Games and Other Applications of Game Theory, 2000; co-author: Search Games, 1992, Microsoft Office 2000, 2000; contbr. articles to profl. jours. Postdoctoral fellow London Royal Soc., 1993. Avocations: reading, gardening. E-mail: Garnaev@AG2784.spb.edu. Office: St Petersburg State U Arch & Civ Engrg, 2-ya Krasnoarmejskaya 4, 198005 Saint Petersburg Russia

GARNAUT, MICHELLE ANNE, restaurateur; b. Melbourne, Australia, Jan. 31, 1957; arrived in Hong Kong, May 1, 1984; d. Louis A. Garnaut and Angela H. (Garnaut) Elliot. Cert. of catering. Trainee cook Wentworth Hotel, Melbourne, 1981-82; head cook Orient Express, London, 1983; free-lance cook Melbourne, 1983-84; restaurant mgr. 1997, Hong Kong, 1984-86; mng. dir. M.G. CCC, Hong Kong, 1986-89; owner, operator M at the Fringe, Hong Kong, 1989—, M on the Bund, Shanghai, China, 1999—. Editor: (book) Hong Kong Cooks, 1996. Organizer, founder Anti-Nuclear Action, Hong Kong, 1995—; chairperson Gt. Chefs of Hong Kong Heep Hong Soc., 1996, Com. Bela Vista Ball Worldwide Party Program. Recipient Australian Entrepreneur award, 1999. Avocations: hiking, traveling, environmental awareness, community and charity work, food. Office: M at the Fringe, 2 Lower Albert Rd, Hong Kong China

GARNAVOS, CHRISTOS, orthopedic surgeon; b. Piraeus, Greece, Apr. 28, 1959; s. Spiridon Thomas and Fotini (Marouda) G.; m. Satmatia Tina Xirou, Feb. 17, 1985; 1 child, Christina. MD, U. Patras, Greece, 1983. Gen. practice medicine Greece, 1984-86; sr. house officer gen. surgery Kavala (Greece) Gen. Hosp., 1986-87; trainee in orthopedic surgery Asklipiion Gen. Hosp., Athens, 1987-91, Derbyshire Royal Infirmary NHS Trust, Derby, Eng., 1991-94; staff orthopedic surgeon Telford, Eng., 1994-97; cons. orthopedic surgeon Evangelismos Gen. Hosp., Athens, 1997-99, Princess Royal Hosp., Telford, 1999—; tchr. nursing sch., Kavala, 1986-87; rep. non-cons. career grade drs., Telford, 1996-97. Patentee orthopedic implant intramedullary nail; contbr. articles to profl. jours. Fellow Greek Orthopedic Assn., Brit. Orthopedic Assn. Avocations: computing, stamp collecting, photography. Home: 8 Londou, 16675 Glyfada Greece Office: Evangelismos Hosp, Athens Greece

GARNER, CHARLES LARRY, retired military officer, human resources educator; b. Clinton, S.C., Feb. 2, 1941; s. Vernon Walter Garner and Susie Dominick Thomas; m. Frances King; children: Lynn G. Purkiss, Charles Philip. BS, Ga. Inst. of Tech., 1963; MS in Human Resources Mgmt., Houston Bapt. U., 1988; PhD, U. Tex., 1998. Commd. 2d lt. USAF, 1963, advanced through grades to maj., 1975, ret., 1984; mem. faculty Austin (Tex.) C.C., 1984-2000; mem. faculty, dir. orgn. learning Concordia U., Austin, 1997-99; cons. Core Cons., Austin, 1992—; asst. prof. mgmt. Tarleton State U., 1999—. Mem. adv. bd. Austin Ind. Sch. Dist., 1994-96; mem. city planning task force, City of Austin, 1985-87; dist. commr. Capital Area coun. Boy Scouts Am., 1984-88. Decorated Disting. Flying Cross. Mem. Phi Kappa Phi. Republican. Home: 1001 Wisteria Trl Austin TX 78753-5858 Office: Concordia U at Austin 1901 S Clear Creek Rd Killeen TX 76549-4111

GARNER, DORIS TRAGANZA, educator; b. Phila., Oct. 13, 1934; d. Charles Thomas and Elizabeth Marie (Blatteau) Traganza; m. Joseph Anthony DeMatteo, Apr. 12, 1958 (dec. Aug. 1968); children: Maria Louise, Carol Ann, Nicholas Joseph, Elizabeth Joan, Charles Traganza, Ann Seton; m. Doyle Daniel Garner, July 11, 1970 (div. Feb. 1989); 1 child: Jean Estelle. BA in Psychology cum laude, U. Pa., 1955; postgrad., Temple U., 1955-59; MS in Ednl. Adminstrn., SUNY, Albany, 1978, EdD in Ednl. Adminstrn. and Higher Edn., 1983. Cert. tchr., N.Y. Elem. tchr. Phila. Sch. Dist., 1955-59; asst. to asst. dean grad. studies SUNY, Albany, 1977-78, asst. to asst. v.p. acad. affairs, 1979; curriculum rsch. assoc. John Jay Coll., CUNY, N.Y.C., 1979; asst. in higher edn. doctoral office N.Y. State Edn. Dept., Albany, 1979-84, coord. program rev. master's programs, 1985-87, assoc. in higher edn. coll./univ. evaluation, 1987-89, asst. to dep. commr. higher edn. and professions, 1989-95, divsn. dir. coll./univ. evaluation, 1995-96; staff dir. N.Y. State Regents Task Force on Tchg. N.Y. State Edn. Dept., 1996-98, supr. acad. program rev., 1998—; featured spkr. CUNY conf. on tchr. edn. reform, 2000; expert witness for plaintiffs, Campaign for Fiscal Equity v. N.Y. State, 1999; invited participant Inaugural Portfolio Conf., Annenberg Inst. for Sch. Reform, Boston, 1998; chair session on state policy Am. Assn. Colls. for Tchr. Edn., New Orleans, 1988; plenary session panelist on tchg. reform Edn. Conf. of Empire State Reports, 1998; presenter in field. Editor (manuscripts) Regents College: The Early Years by D.J. Nolan, 1998. Mem. Shaker H.S. Theater Support, Latham, N.Y., 1988-89; pianist at non-profit functions, Albany, N.Y., 1992-94; cmty. theater actor Stagecrafters, Phila., 1951. Avocations: grandchildren and children, reading on social and political issues, piano, plays, concerts, nature. Home: 27 Henkes Ln Latham NY 12110-5013 Office: NY State Edn Dept Ed Bldg Fifth Fl Mezzanin Albany NY 12234-0001

GARNER, FRADLEY HAMILTON, writer, editor, narrator; b. Potsdam, N.Y., June 20, 1926; s. L. Hamilton and Geneva Van Bergen Garner; children: Luke, Glen, Nicholas. Pregrad, 24th Corps U., Seoul Korea, 1946; BS in Psychology, St. Lawrence U., Canton, N.Y., 1950; MA in Cultural Anthropology, Colgate U., Hamilton, N.Y., 1970; postgrad., 24th Corps Univ., Seoul, Korea, 1946, SUNY, Potsdam, 1950, Northwestern U., Evanston, Ill., 1951. Divsnl. pub. rels. mgr. Pfizer, Inc., N.Y.C., 1955-60. Author:

Environment Denmark, 1972, Donald Duck's Fritidsbok, 1976, Greenland: Arctic Denmark, 1977, Jakobshavn/Ilulissat: A Town in Greenland, 1977, The Haunted Hotel, 1978; co-founder, editor Scoot mag., 1955; assoc. editor Family Health mag., 1969; internat. editor, columnist Ecology Today, 1971-72, Environment mag., 1973-77; editor: TMI World, 1988; chief translator, copy editor: Danish Music Rev., 1994-95, Katalog, the Danish Jour. Photography and Video; covered Denmark's dogsled patro Sirius in No. Greenland for internat. edn. Reader's Digest; Nordic-Tanganyika rject in Dar es Salaam, Tanzania for Scanorama mag.; contbr. numerous articles to profl. jours. and gen. mags.; narrator over 500 indsl., sci. and gen. documentary films and videos. Bd. dirs. HOF Internat. Edn. Program, 2000—. Named Denmark amateur Runner of Yr., Aarets Eremitageløber, 1995. Mem. Fgn. Press Assn. in Denmark. E-mail: fradgar@apple.agora.dk. Home: Ordruphojvej 32, DK-2920 Charlottenlund Denmark

GARNETT, HELEN MARGARET, professional organization executive; b. Sydney, Australia, Sept. 23, 1946; d. Leonard William and Ilma Beatrice (Hayman) Bowden; m. David Livingstone Garnett, Sept. 12, 1970. BS with honors, U. Sydney, 1969; PhD, U. Wales, 1974. Rsch. officer Poliomyelitis Found. U. Witwatersrand, Johannesburg, South Africa, 1972-74, lectr./sr. lectr., 1974-79; found. prof. and head dept. microbiology U. Witwatersrand, Johannesburg, 1979-86; prof., head dept. biology U. Wollongong, N.S.W., 1987-92; dep. exec. dir. Australian Nuclear Sci. & Tech. Orgn., Menai, 1992-94, acting exec. dir., 1994-95, exec. dir., 1995—; dir. Integral Energy, N.S.W., 1996-2000; chmn. adv. bd. Key Ctr. for Biodiversity and Bioresources, Macquarie U., N.S.W., 1995—; chmn. Tracerco Bd. Mgmt., Australia, 1994-98; Australian alt. to bd. govs. Internat. Atomic Energy Agy., Vienna, Austria, 1994—; bd. dirs. Australian Acad. and Rsch. Network, Australia, 1995-98; mem. Coord. Com. Sci. and Tech., ACT, Australia, 1994—, Internat. Sci. and Tech. Adv. Com., 1994-98; dep. chair Australian Rsch. Coun. Instnl. Grants Com., Australia, 1996, mem. planning and rev. com., 1996; prof. emeritus U. Wollongong, 1995. Contbr. numerous articles and abstracts to profl. jours. Mem. Coun. U. Technology, Sydney, 1988, NSW Innovation Coun., 1998; mem. adv. coun. Australian Grad. Sch., 1998; mem. Bus./Higher Edn. Round Table, 1997. Recipient Hamilton Maynard award South African Med. Soc., 1992, Women in Engring. award Australian Inst. Refrigeration, Air Conditioning and Heating, 1991. Avocations: wine tasting, tennis, bridge. Office: Australian Nucl Sci/Tech, Pvt Mail Bag 1, Menai 2234 NSW, Australia

GARNETT, KEVIN, professional basketball player. Profl. basketball player Minnesota Timberwolves, 1995—. Named to All-NBA Third Team, 1998-99, NBA Player of Week, USA Basketball Sr. Nat. Team, 1999, All-Rookie Second Team, 1995-96. Office: Minnestoa Timberwolves 600 1st Ave N Minneapolis MN 55403-1400

GARNETT, LINDA KOPEC, nurse, researcher; b. Springfield, Mass.; d. Frank J. and Anna (Paul) Kopec; m. Thomas R. Garnett, Oct. 6, 1990. BSN cum laude, Fitchburg (Mass.) State Coll., 1983; MS in Health Svcs. Adminstrn., Ctrl. Mich. U., 1996. RN, Va. Nurse intern Med. Coll. Va. Hosps., Richmond, 1983, nurse clinician in neurosci. ICU, 1984-86; terr. mgr., patient care specialist Kinetic Concepts Therapeutic Svcs., Richmond, 1986-89; rsch. coord. dept. neurology Med. Coll. Va./Va. Commonwealth U., Richmond, 1989—. Mem. Sigma Theta Tau.

GARNHAM, ALAN, psychology educator; b. Harrogate, Eng., Sept. 15, 1954; s. Philip Henry and Mabel (Sulman) G.; m. Jane Oakhill, Dec. 22, 1990; children Robin Oakhill, Thomas Edward Oakhill; m. Wendy Clements, July 31, 1999. BA with honors, Oxford U., 1977, MA, 1996; DPhil, Sussex U., Brighton, Eng., 1981. Lectr. Reading (Eng.) U., 1983-85; lectr. psychology Sussex U., 1981, 85-94, rsch. fellow, 1981-83, reader, 1994, head of dept., 1994-98, prof., 1999—; vis. fellow Max-Planck Inst. für Psycholinguistik, Nijmegen, The Netherlands, 1986, Cath. U. Brabant, Tilburg, The Netherlands, 1987, U. Paris V, 1990; mem. working party horizons and opportunities in social scis. Econ. and Social Rsch. Coun. U.K., 1986-87, Biotech. and Biol. Rsch. Coun., Animal Scis. and Psychology Com., 1995-97. Author: Psycholinguistics: Central Topics, 1985, Mental Models as Representations of Discourse and Text, 1987, Artificial Intelligence: An Introduction, 1988, Becoming a Skilled Reader, 1988, The Mind in Action, 1991, Thinking and Reasoning, 1994; editor: Disourse Representation and Text Processing, 1992, Mental Models in Cognitive Science, 1996; contbr. articles to profl. jours. Grantee Econ. and Social Rsch. Coun. U.K., 1988-92, NATO, 1989-92, Joint Rsch. Coun. Cognitive Sci./HCI Initiative, 1990-93, Med. Rsch. Coun., 1993-94, Econ. and Soc. Rsch. Coun., 1996-99. Mem. Exptl. Psychology Soc., Behavioral and Brain Scis. Soc. (assoc.). Office: Sussex U, Lab Exptl Psychology, Brighton BN1 9QG, England

GARNIER, PHILIPPE-PIERRE, psychiatrist, psychoanalyst, educator; b. Montreuil, France, May 20, 1935; s. Jacques Jean and Pauline Adrienne (Bourgeois) G.; m. Marie-Chantal Singer, Nov. 20, 1964 (div. Apr. 1978); children: Catherine, Veronique, Karin, Brice, Violaine, Raphaele; m. Carinais Appavoupoulle, Jan. 2, 1984; 1 child, Mohini. BS in Math. and Philosophy, Paris, 1952; MD, Univ. Med. Sch., Paris, 1966. Resident various hosps., Paris, 1958-64; lectr. psychiatry, psychoanalysis Broussais Medical Sch., Paris, 1981-87; practice medicine specializing in psychiatry Paris. Contbr. Analyse Psychodrama, 1980, articles to profl. jours. Hon. pres. Centre Paul Lemoine, Palermo, Italy. Served to capt. French Air Force, 1962-64. Mem. Soc. d'Etudes Psychodrame Freudien (pres. 1993-97, 2000), Cartels Constituants de l'Analyse Freudienne. Club: Soc. Hippique du Hurepoix (pres. 1986—). Avocations: horseback riding, horse breeding, horse therapy, archeology, music. Home: 2 Grand St-Villeconin, 91-580 Etrechy France Office: 205 Blvd Vincent Auriol, 75013 Paris France

GARNOT, BENOÎT, history educator; b. Fontenay-le-Conte, France, Nov. 11, 1951; s. Marc-Jean Garnot and Odile Branchard; m. Françoise Chazeau, Oct. 8, 1976. Agrégation, U. Nantes, France, 1976; PhD, Rennes (France) U., 1979, Dr. d'Etat, 1985. Univ. prof. 2d class Burgundy U., Dijon, France, 1988-95, univ. prof. 1st class, 1995—; dir. Ctr. for Hist. Study, Dijon, 1990—, Collection Synthèse-Histoire, Paris, 1988—. Author: Un déclin: Chartres au XVIII siecle, 1991, Le peuple au siècle des Lumières, 1990, Societé, cultures et genres de vie dans la France moderne, 1991, La justice en France de l'An Mil à 1914, 1993, Vivre en prison au XVIIIe siecle, 1994, La culture materielle en France aux XVIe, XVIIe et XVIIIe siecles, 1995, Vivre en Bourgogne au XVIIIe siecle, 1996, Un crime conjugalau XVIII siècle, 1993, Le diable au couvent, 1995, Les campagnes en France aux XVIe, XVIIe et XVIIIe siècles, 1998, Crime et justice aux XVIIe et XVIIIe siècles, 2000, Justice et société en France aux XVIC, XVIIC, et XVIII siècles, 2000. Avocations: wine, walking. Home: 21 rue Vauban, 21000 Dijon France Office: Burgundy U, 2 Blvd Gabriel, 21000 Dijon France

GARNOVSKII, ALEXANDER DMITRIEVICH, chemist, academic administrator; b. Rostov-on-Don, USSR, Aug. 30, 1932; s. Dmitrii Ivanovich and Elena Veniaminovna (Turok) G.; m. Gaarik Raffievna Agabab'yants, Feb. 22, 1958; children: Dmitrii, Tat'yana. Diploma in chemistry, Sch. No. 51, Rosto-on-Don, 1956. Engr. Yuvenergochermet, Rostov-on-Don, 1957-58; aspirant Rostov State U., Rostov-on-Don, 1958-61, cons., 1961-63, asst. prof., 1963-73, prof. dept. phys. and colloid chemistry, 1974-79, prof., 1974-79, head dept. chemistry, 1983—; head dept. chemistry Agrl. Inst. Rostov, Rostov-on-Don, 1979-83. Author: Hard and Soft Interactions in Coordination Chemistry, 1986; author, editor: Direct Synthesis of Coordination and Organometallic Compounds, 1999. Head sect. com. connection sci. and industry, Rostov-on-Don, 1957-58; head komsomol com. chem. dept. State U. Rostov, 1958-59, head. chem. dept. com. trade union, 1963-64; head. com. chem. dept. Communist party Rostov State U., 1970-77. Mem. Acad. Natural Scis. Moscow. Avocations: music, football, tennis, athletics. Home: pr. Voroshilovskii, 8-5, 344006 Rostov-on-Don Russia Office: Inst Phys and Organic Chem, Stachki ave. 194/2, 344090 Rostov-on-Don Russia

GARONG, RIXON MAGNO, lawyer; b. Gapan, Nueva Ecija, Philippines, Nov. 5, 1968; s. Geronimo Timkang and Perlita (Magno) G. BA, Philippine Christian U., Dasmarinas, Cavite, 1989; LLB, Manuel L. Quezon U., Quiapo, Manila, Philippines, 1995; postgrad.', U. Philippines, Diliman, Quezon City, 1998—. Bar: Philippines 1997. Legal officer IV Philippine Export and Fgn. Loan Guarantee Corp., Makati City, 1997; divsn. chief litigation Trade and Investment Devel. Corp. Philippines, Makati City, 1998-99; head legal dept. Philippine Brit. Assurance Co., Inc., Makati City, 1999—; assoc. Puno and Assocs. Law Offices, Quezon City, 2000—; retained counsel Benton Packaging, Manila, Philippines, 1998—; instr. part-time Ctrl. Coll. Philippines, Manila, 1999. Mcpl. coord. Movement for Principled Politics, Gapan, Nueva Ecija, 1992; bus. mgr. United Meth. Pastors' Children, Manila, 1999—; pres. United Meth. Young Adult Fellowship, Philippine Ann. Conf.-East, 2000—. Recipient Plaque of Appreciation Middle Philippines Annual Conf. United Meth. Youth Fellowship in the Philippines, 1990. Mem. Integrated Bar Philippines (Nueva Ecija chpt.), Mu Kappa Phi. Methodist. Avocations: basketball, tennis, chess, reading, surfing the Internet. Home: Unit 2D10 Bldg 7 GSIS, City Metrohomes Anonas St, Sta Mesa Manila The Philippines Office: Puno and Assocs Law Office, 2d Fl 336 Roosevelt Ave, Quezon City 1200, The Philippines

GAROT, GEORGES, foreign diplomat; b. St. Berthevin, France, Apr. 7, 1936. Mem. European Parliament, 1999—, mem. com. on agr. and rural devel., substitute com. fgn. affairs/human rights/common security; mem. Group of the Party of European Socialists; mem. delegation for relations with the Maghreb countries and the Arab Maghreb Union. Socialist Party. *

GAROTTA, GIANNI, research scientist; b. Luino, Italy, July 8, 1943; s. Filippo and Erminia (Leoni) G.; m. Donata Cantoni, Feb. 1, 1973; children: Francesca, Marta, Paolo. D in Physiology, U. Milan, 1968, diploma biometry med. statis., 1970. Postdoctoral Physiology Inst., Milan, 1968-70, Immunology Inst., Milan, 1970-73; fellowship The Wistar Inst., Phila., 1973-74; asst. prof. immunology The Nat. Cancer Inst., Milan, 1974-77, 80-82; staff mem. The Basel Inst. of Immunology, Basel, Switzerland, 1977-80; staff project leader of interferon rsch. Hoffman-LaRoche, Basel, Switzerland, 1982-94; staff dir. biology Human Genome Sci., Rockville, Md., 1995-98; corp. dir. extramural rsch. and innovative tech. Ares Serono Internat., Geneva, 1998—. Patentee in field; contbr. articles to profl. jours. Mem. Am. Soc. of Clin. Immunology, Am. Soc. Microbiology, British Soc. for Immunology, Internat. Soc. for Interferon Rsch., Internat. Cytoking Soc., Italian Soc. for Immunology. Avocation: history. Office: Ares-Serono SA, 12 Chemin des Aulx, 1228 Plan les Ouates Geneva Switzerland

GARR, CHERYL DENISE, research chemist; b. Idaho Falls, Idaho, May 2, 1960; d. Jerry Lee and Jane Ellen (Wise) Gross; m. Westley Dean Garr, June 27, 1987; children: Taylor Kristen, Jamie Lynn. BS in Chemistry, Evergreen State Coll., Olympia, Wash., 1986; PhD in Chemistry, U. Oreg., 1992. Postdoctoral fellow Panlabs Inc., Bothell, Wash., 1992, scientist, 1993-95, group leader, 1995-96, project mgr. synthetic and combinatorial chemistry, 1996-97, dir. combinatorial chemistry, 1997-99; dir. synthetic discovery chemistry New Chem. Entities Inc., Bothell, 1999—. Contbr. articles to Jour. Am. Chem. Soc., Jour. Inorganic Chemistry, Bio-organic Med. Chemistry, Jour. Biomolecular Screening, Med. Chem. Letters. Mem. Am. Soc. Mass Spectrometry, Am. Chem. Soc., Soc. for Biomolecular Screening, Soc. for Indsl. Microbiologists, Wash. Biotech Bus. Assn. Home: 22717 NE 195th St Woodinville WA 98072-7538 Office: New Chem Entities Inc 18804 N Creek Pkwy Bothell WA 98011-8012

GARRAHAN-MASTERS, MARY PATRICIA, retired social worker, volunteer; b. Phila., June 6, 1951; d. Francis Edward and Mary Patricia McElduff Garrahan; m. Thomas Anthony Masters Mastrangelo, June 5, 1995 (div. Feb. 2000). Student, Georgetown U., 1971-72; Facultad Filosofía y Letras, Madrid; BA in Sociology with honors, Villanova (Pa.) U., 1973; M in Social Sci., M in Law and Social Policy, Bryn Mawr (Pa.) Coll., 1983. Geriat. case worker Schuylkill County Area Agy. on Aging, Pottsville, Pa., 1974-79; social svc. dir. Dowden Nursing Home, Newtown Sq., Pa., 1980-84; dir. admissions St. Francis County Ho., Darby, Pa., summer 1981; tchr. Delaware County Coll., Media, Pa., 1984; med. social worker VA Med. Ctr., Lebanon, Pa., 1985-88; part-time staff coord. Garrahan Equipment Inc., Havertown, Pa., 1973-92; parti-time social worker DeltaT Home Health Agy., Bryn Mawr, 1992-97. Contbr. poetry to mag. Assoc. mem. Rep. Nat. Com., Washington, 1993—; vol. Orrin Hatch for Pres., Salt Lake City, McCain 2000, Reform Party-Buchanan, 2000; eucharistic minister St. Richard's Roman Cath. Ch., Barnesville, Pa., 1974-79. Mem. Internat. Hypnosis Hall Fame Guild Inc., Nat. Assn. Ret. Employees, Alpha Zeta Delta. Home: 2707 Stoneham Dr West Chester PA 19382-6649

GARRELS, SHERRY ANN, lawyer; b. Chgo., Feb. 5, 1956; d. William Henry and Jacqueline Ann G.; m. Timothy Anthony Marion, Aug. 1, 1987 (div. June 1988); 1 child, William Garrels-Marion; 1 child, Georgianna Garrels-Rogers. BA, Barat Coll., 1980; certificate, Trinity Coll., 1989; JD, Western State U., 1990. Bar: Calif. 1992, U.S. Dist. Ct. (ctrl. dist.) Calif. 1992, U.S. Dist. Ct. (no. dist.) Calif. 1993, U.S. Dist. Ct. (so. dist.) Calif. 1996, U.S. Ct. Appeals (9th cir.) 1994, U.S. Tax Ct. 1996. Pvt. practice Huntington Beach, Calif., 1992—; arbitrator Nat. Panel Consumer Arbitrators, Huntington Beach, 1996, State Panel Consumer Arbitrators, Huntington Beach, 1996, Better Bus. Bureau, 1996—, U.S. C. of C., 1996, Huntington Beach C. of C., 1996. Editor The Dictum, 1989. Active 4th of July Exec. Bd., Huntington Beach, 1996—. Mem. Assn. Trial Lawyers, L.A. Trial Assn., Orange County Bar Assn., St. Bonny Golf Classic (dir. 1991-97), Delta Theta Phi. Republican. Presbyterian. Avocations: swimming, golf, scuba diving. Fax: 714-374-0104. Office: 5942 Edinger Ave Ste 113-702 Huntington Beach CA 92649-1763

GARRETSON, OWEN LOREN, mechanical and chemical engineer; b. Salem, Iowa, Feb. 24, 1912; s. Sumner Dilts and Florence (White) G.; m. Erma Mary Smith, Jan. 23, 1932; children: John Albert, Owen Don, Susan Marie, Leon Todd. Student, Iowa Wesleyan Coll., 1930-32; BSME, Iowa State U., 1937. Registered profl. engr., Okla., N.Mex., Iowa, Mo. Engr. Bailey Meter Co., Cleve., 1937, St. Louis, 1937-38; engr., dist. mgr. Phillips Petroleum Co., Bartlesville, Okla., 1938-39, Amarillo, Tex., 1939-40; engr., dist. mgr. Phillips Petroleum Co., Detroit, 1940-41, wholesale mgr. liquefied petroleum gas sales divsn., 1941-42; mgr. product supply and transp. divsn. Phillips Petroleum Co., Bartlesville, 1942-44, mgr. engring. devel. divsn., 1944-46, mgr. spl. products engring. devel. divsn., 1946-47; pres. Gen. Tank & Steel Corp., Roswell, N.Mex., United Farm Chem. Co.; pres., dir. Garretson Equipment Co., Mt. Pleasant, Iowa; v.p., dir. Valley Industries, Inc., Mt. Pleasant; pres., dir. Garretson Carburetion of Tex., Inc., Lubbock; v.p., dir. Sacra Gas Co. Roswell, 1957-58; exec. v.p., dir. Arrow Gas. Co. & Affiliated Corps., Roswell, N.Mex., Tex., Utah, 1958-60; asst. to pres. Nat. Propane Corp., Hyde Park, N.Y.; pres., chmn. bd. Plateau, Inc. Oil Refining, Farmington, N.Mex., 1960-82, also bd. dirs.; chmn. bd. S.W. Motels, Inc., Farmington; organizing dir. Farmington Nat. Bank, 1964; cons. Suburban Propane Gas Corp. Whippany, N.J. Contbr. articles to profl. jours.; 44 patents issued in several fields; inventor WWII aircraft engine power boost sys., 1942. Mem., past pres. Farmington Indsl. Devel. Svc., N.Mex. Lidquefied Petroleum Gas Commn., 1955-76, chmn., 1956-58; mem. Iowa Gov.'s Trade Commn. to No. Europe, 1970, Iowa Trade Mission to Europe, 1979; mem. com. natural gas/liquefied natural gas Internat. Petroleum Expn. and Congress, 1970-71; mem. Nat. Coun. Crime and Delinquency; bd. dirs. Suburban Propane Gase Corp., Whippany, N.J., 1974-84. Recipient Merit award Iowa Wesleyan Coll. Alumni Assn., 1968, Profl. Achievement Engring. citation Iowa State U., 1986. Mem. ASME, NSPE, Nat. Liquefied Petroleum Gas Assn. (bd. dirs., Disting. Svc. award 1979), Am. Petroleum Inst., Nat. Petroleum Refiner's Assn. (bd. dirs., pres.), Ind. Refiners Assn. Am., Agrl. Ammonia Inst. Memphis (bd. dirs.), N.Mex. Liquefied Petroleum Gas. Assn. (pres., bd. dirs.), Ind. Petroleum Assn. Am., N.Mex. Acad. Sci., Am. Soc. Agrl. Engrs., Am. Soc. Automotive Engrs., N.Mex. Amigos., Am. Inst. Chem. Engrs., Newcomen Soc. N.Am., Soc. Indsl. Archeology, Ancient Gassers (sec., pres.), 25 Yr. Club Petroleum Industry, Masons, Rotary, Phi Delta Theta, Tau Beta Pi. Home: 500 E La Plata St Farmington NM 87401-6940 Office: PO Box 108 Farmington NM 87499-0108

GARRETT, CHARLES GEOFFREY BLYTHE, physicist; b. Ashford, Kent, Eng., Sept. 15, 1925; came to U.S., 1950, naturalized, 1989; s. Charles Alfred Blythe and Laura Mary (Lotinga) G. B.A. in Natural Scis., Trinity Coll., Cambridge U., Eng., 1946; M.A. in Natural Scis., Ph.D. in Physics, Cambridge U., 1950. Instr. physics Harvard U., 1950-52; mem. tech. staff Bell Labs., Murray Hill, N.J., 1952-54; supr. Bell Labs., 1955-56, dept. head, 1960-69; dir. AT&T Bell Labs., Murray Hill-Morristown, N.J., 1969-87; chmn. Gordon Conf. on non-linear optics, 1964. Author: Magnetic Cooling, 1954, Gas Lasers, 1963; contbr. articles to profl. jours.; patentee in field. Named knight of Sovereign Order St. John of Jerusalem (Orthodox). Fellow Am. Phys. Soc., IEEE; mem. Guild of Carillonneurs in N.Am. Episcopalian. Avocations: piano, harpsichord, carillon, restoring 18th century houses and older Rolls-Royce cars. Home: 7 Fithian Ln East Hampton NY 11937-2605

GARRETT, EMANUEL, radio announcer; b. Birmingham, Ala., Oct. 20, 1951; s. Ernest and Katie (Cockrell) G.; m. Mildred Gay; children: Vincent, Michelle, Michael. Student, Ala. A&M U., 1970-73; diploma, Huntsville Vocat. Tech., 1970; student (corr. course), Cleve. Inst. Electronics. Announcer Sta. WFLI, Chattanooga, 1973; technician Sta. WAHR-FM, Huntsville, 1979-80; chief engr., announcer Sta. WEUP-Garrett Broadcasting Service, Huntsville, 1968-87; engr. Sta. WLRH-FM, Huntsville, 1988-89, Ga. Pub. TV, 1990—. Mem. NAACP (Huntsville chpt.). Named one of Outstanding Young Men of Am., U.S. Jaycees, 1977, 1982; recipient Black Achievement award, Unlimited Gospel Singers, 1983, Gospel M.C. award, Lighthouse Gospel Singers, 1987. Mem. Soc. Broadcast Engrs. (cert.), Nat. Assn. Radio and Telecommunications Engrs. Inc. (cert). Democrat. Methodist. Avocations: long-distance medium wave radio listing, music, reading, video cassette rec. E-mail: computing.emangarr@msn.com. Home: 1920 Cherwell Dr Riverdale GA 30296-1965

GARRETT, JOHN RAYMOND, pathologist, physiologist, educator, researcher; b. Winchester, Eng., Mar. 28, 1928; s. Charles Raymond and Irene Lily (Rogers) G.; m. Daphne Anne Parr, Apr. 28, 1958; children: Claire, Malcolm. LDS, King's Coll. Hosp. Dental Sch., London, 1949; BSc, King's Coll., London, 1956; MB BS with honors, King's Coll. Hosp. Med. Sch., London, 1959, PhD, 1965; MD, U. Lund, Sweden, 1985. Rsch. fellow Nuffield, London, 1961-64; sr. lectr. King's Coll. Hosp. Med. Sch., London, 1964-68, reader, 1968-71, prof., head oral pathology, 1971-93, prof. emeritus, 1993—. Author: Glandular Mechanisms of Salivary Secretion, 1998, Neural Mechanisms of Salivary Gland Secretion, 1999; contbr. articles to profl. jours. Capt. Royal Army Dental Corps, 1950-52. Fellow Royal Coll. Pathologists; mem. Royal Microscopical Soc. (pres. 1980-82), Royal Coll. Pathology, Internat. Fedn. Socs. Histochemistry and Cytochemistry (treas. 1980-84, sec. 1984-88, pres. 1988-92), Internat. Assn. Dental Rsch. (pres. salivary rsch. group 1977-78), Brit. Soc. Oral Pathology (pres. 1983-84). Avocations: medical history, photography. Home: 15 Deepdene Rd, London SE5 8EG, England Office: Rayne Inst KCSMD, 123 Coldharbour Ln, London SE5 9NU, England

GARRETT, JOSEPH EDWARD, aerospace engineer; b. Hendersonville, N.C., Mar. 4, 1943; s. Kenneth Pace and Anna Lou (Lytle) G.; m. Aurelia Jane Pryor, Aug. 7, 1971. BS in Aerospace Engring., N.C. State U., 1966; MS in Aerospace Engring., Ga. Inst. Tech., 1978. Registered profl. engr., Ga. Basic and fatigue loads assoc. aircraft engr. LASC-Ga. (formerly Lockheed-Ga.), Marietta, 1966-67, basic and fatigue loads structures engr., 1967-75, fatigue and fracture mechanics sr. structures engr., 1975-80, company planning, 1980-82, fracture mechanics structures engr., 1982-91, advanced structures sr. engr., 1991-96; fatigue and fracture mechanics sr. structures engr., 1996—. Loaned exec. United Way, Atlanta, 1984, Cobb County chmn. for Individual Gifts, Marietta, 1985, chmn. Cobb County Adv. Com., Marietta, 1987-88, bd. dirs., Atlanta, 1987-88. Fellow AIAA (assoc., dir. Region II 1990-96, Mem. of Yr. Atlanta sect. 1986, Booster of Yr. 1988, 92, 94, 95, Sustained Svc. award 1999); mem. Inst. Cert. Mgrs. Lockheed Ga. Mgmt. Assn. (v.p. mem. achievement 1988-89, v.p. adminstrn. 1989-90, Booster of Month 1980, 1st Cert. Mgr. of Yr. 1989). Republican. Baptist. Avocations: landscaping, woodworking. Home: 2291 Goodrum Ln Marietta GA 30066-5200 Office: LASC-Ga Dept 73-25 Zone 0160 86 S Cobb Dr Marietta GA 30063-0001

GARRETT, PAUL EDGAR, insurance executive, writer, poet; b. Timpas, Colo., Nov. 18, 1909; s. Charles Calvin and Ida Pauline (Guire) G.; m. Vera Griggs, Sept. 21, 1927 (dec. 1941); children: Donald (dec.), Gerald (dec.); m. Muriel Gladys Goodroad, Mar. 10, 1945 (dec. Aug. 1983); m. Ornetta Gardner, Oct. 27, 1984. BS in Biol. Scis., U. Wyo., 1935; CLU, Am. Coll., 1978. Pub. sch. adminstrn. Wyo., Alaska, 1932-36; gen. agt. Ohio Nat. Life, Billings, Mont., 1937-50; mem., chmn. field adv. bd. Ohio Nat. Life, Spokane, 1946-66, gen. agt. Idaho and Wash., 1950-66; mem., chmn. Ins. Examining Bd., Olympia, Wash., 1962-70. Author: (poems) Song of the North, 1936, Down By The Sea, 1994; author hunting and fishing stories, short stories, historical stories. Lt. USN, 1942-46, PTO. Mem. Wash. State Life Underwriters, Elks, Ret. Officers Assn., Sigma Chi. Avocations: short story writing. Home: Waterford Ste 240 2929 S Waterford Dr Spokane WA 99203-4400

GARRETT, SINEAD KATHERINE, research organization executive; b. Waterford, Ireland, July 7, 1971; arrived in Australia, 1971; d. Peter Alfred and Eileen Frances (Hanrahan) G.; m. Simon John Whitaker, Feb. 20, 1999. B Applied Sci., Latrobe U., 1992; MPH, Monash U., Australia, 1998. Cert. Orthoptic Bd. Australia. Rsch. asst. U. Melbourne, Australia, 1992-94; rsch. coord. Monash U., 1994-98; mgr. Health Rsch. Solutions, Fairfield, Victoria, Australia, 1998-2000; sr. med. info. assoc. Schering-Plough, 2000—. Contbr. articles to profl. jours. Assoc. investigator Nat. Health and Med. Rsch. Coun., 1999. Mem. Pub. Health Assn. Australia, Assn. Regulatory and Clin. Scientists. Avocations: Australian music, fiction, urban history.

GARRETT, THOMAS MONROE, chemist; b. San Francisco, Mar. 10, 1961; s. Walter Norman and Sally Ann (Sharpless) G.; m. Karen Lynn Garcia, June 7, 1987; children: Andrew Henry, Alexander Monroe. BS with hons., Stanford U., 1983; PhD, U. Calif., Berkeley, 1988. Postdoctoral fellow U. Louis Pasteur, Strasbourg, France, 1988-90; part owner, dir. of rsch. MCP Industries, Inc., Corona, Calif., 1990—. Contbr. articles to profl. jours.; patentee in field. Chmn. scholarship Rotary, Corona. Recipient Bourse Chateubriand, France. Fellow Am. Inst. Chemists; mem. Am. Chem. Soc., N.Am. Soc. Trenchless Tech., L.A. Soc. Coatings Technology, Phi Lambda Upsilon, Sigma Xi. Republican. Episcopalian. Achievements include co-discovery of first perfect trigonal prismatic iron (III) complex; strongest bidentate iron chelating agts.; self-assembling pentameric silver (I) complex; a process to make sand bounce like a superball; co-developer first U.S.-made clay microtunneling pipe; invented smart materials for redistribution of .5 kiloton construction forces. Office: MCP Industries Inc 1660 Leeson Ln Corona CA 92879-2061

GARRIDO, MIGUEL-ÁNGEL, philologist, researcher; b. Lubrín, Spain, Sept. 7, 1945; s. Miguel Garrido and Antonia Gallardo. Bachelor Degree, U. Complutense, Madrid, 1968, PhD in Romance Philology, 1971. Rsch. fellow Consejo Superior Investigaciones Cientificas, Madrid and Paris, 1968-78; full prof. Seville (Spain) U., 1979-81; rschr. Inst. Philology CSIC, Madrid, 1981—; rsch. prof. Dept. Linguistic and Literary Theory, Madrid, 1988—; pres. Assn. Española de Semiótica, Madrid, 1984-86; dir. Revista de Literatura, Madrid, 1988—. Author: Crítica literaria: L. Goldmann, 1971, Introducción a la Teoría de la Literatura, 1975, Teoría de los géneros literarios, 1988, La Musa de la Retórica, 1994, La Moderna Crítica Literaria Hispanica, 1997, Neura Introducción a la Teoná de la Literatura, 2000. Mem. Internat. Assn. for Semiotic Studies (mem. exec. com. 1984-99). Roman Catholic. Office: CSIC, Duque de Medinaceli 6, 28014 Madrid Spain

GARRIGA POLLEDO, SALVADOR, foreign diplomat; b. Gijon, Spain, Aug. 6, 1957. Mem. European Parliament, 1999—, mem. com. on budgets, substitute com. on budgetary control; mem. Group of the European People's Party (Christian Democrats) and European Democrats; mem. delegation for relations with the mem. states of ASEAN, S.E. Asia and Republic of Korea. Mem. Peole's Party. *

GARRIGUS, CHARLES BYFORD, retired literature educator; b. Benton, Ill., June 13, 1914; s. Charles Byford and Ailene Marie (Fowler) G.; m. Ferne Marie Fetters, Dec. 28, 1936 (dec.); children: Marmarie (dec.), Charles, Richmond, Karis, Rose Ann. AB, U. Ill., 1936, MA, 1937. Prof. humanities King's River Coll., Reedley, Calif., 1949-73; poet laureate for life of Calif., 1966—. Author: California Poems, 1955, (poems) Echoes of Being, 1975, Soundings, 1999, (novels) Brief Candel, 1987, Chas and The Summer of '26, 1994; editor: Modern Hamlet, 1950, An Evangel, 1998. Mem. Calif. Assembly, 1958-66. Democrat. Methodist. Avocations: lecturing, poetry readings. Home: 1623 Morgan Dr Kingsburg CA 93631-2619

GARRIONE, ROBERT MICHAEL, clergy member; b. Salina, Kans., Feb. 24, 1950; s. Alfonso Jacob and Josephine Patricia (Mason) G. B in Humanities, Holy Apostles Coll. Sem., Cromwell, Conn., 1985; BTh, Pontifical U. St. Thomas, Rome, 1987-88; MDiv, St. Joseph Seminary, Yonkers, N.Y., 1985-89. Assoc. pastor Our Lady of Guadalupe Parish, Holbrook, Ariz., 1989-91, St. Mary of The Angels Parish, Pinetop, Ariz., 1991; pastor St. Bonaventure Parish, Thoreau, N.Mex., 1991-93, St. Thomas Parish, Garden City, Kans., 1995-98; chaplain St. Francis Acad., Salina and Ellsworth, Kans., 1998-99; clergy staff St. Benedict's Abbey, Bartonville, Ill., 1999—; mem. adj. faculty Garden City C.C., 1997-98. Mem. Charles F. Menninger Soc. Episcopalian. Avocations: bike riding, reading, photography. Office: St Benedict's Abbey 7561 W Lancaster Rd Peoria IL 61607-9513

GARRIS, CHARLES ALEXANDER, mechanical engineer, educator; b. Pomona, Calif., Feb. 2, 1944; s. Charles Alexander and Kathleen Ann (White) G.; m. Eugenia Dolores Cardenas, Sept. 11, 1971; children: Charles Alexander, Eugenia Catalina. B Engring., SUNY, N.Y.C., 1965; MS, SUNY, Stony Brook, 1968, PhD, 1971. Registered profl. engr.; registered patent agt. Va. Rsch. chief mech. engr. dept. Venezuela Inst. Sci. Rsch., Caracas, 1971-73, chief mech. engring., 1976-78; rsch. assoc. MIT, Cambridge, 1973-76; prof. engring. George Washington U., Washington, 1978—; program dir. NSF; cons. in field. Contbr. articles to engring. publs.; patentee in field. Grantee Maritime Adminstrn., 1985, NASA, 1985. Fellow ASME; mem. AIAA (sr.), Am. Soc. Engring. Edn., Pi Tau Sigma, Sigma Xi. Roman Catholic. Avocations: bicycling, boating, swimming, racquetball, tennis. Home: 9616 Darrow Ct Vienna VA 22181-3255 Office: George Washington U Dept Civil Mech And Env Engr Washington DC 20052-0001

GARRISON, DAVID LACEY, JR., oil company executive; b. Houston, July 12, 1945; s. David Lacey and Marie Bel (Gardiner) G.; m. Pamela Jean Reid Adger, Mar. 7, 1970 (div. July 1975); 1 child, James Gardiner; m. Robin Childers, Apr. 2, 1977; children: Robert Adam, Susan Alexandra. LLD, La Academia Mexicana, Mexico City, 1991. Landman Chapman Oil Co., Houston, 1978; ptnr. J.A. Bel et al, Lake Charles, La., 1964—; pres. Garrison Oil Co., Houston, 1979-84, Lakeside Exploration Corp., Houston, 1984—; v.p., bd. mem. Lacassane Co., Inc., Lake Charles, 1990—. La. commr. of Indian Affairs, Baton Rouge, 1972-75; vice chmn. Sam Houston Area coun. Boy Scouts Am., 1995—; mem. exec. bd. Nat. Cath. Com. on Scouting, 1997—; bd. mem. So. Region Boy Scouts Am., 1999—. Decorated knight comdr. Pontifical Order St. Gregory the Gt. (Vatican City); knight comdr. Equestrian Order Holy Sepulchre,; knight grand cross with gold star Sacred Mil. Constantinian Order St. George, knight Sovereign Mil. Order of Malta (Rome),. Roman Catholic. Avocations: hunting, fishing. Home: 3731 Olympia Dr Houston TX 77019-3029 Office: Garrison Properties 3939 Essex Ln Houston TX 77027-5190

GARRISON, JOHN RAYMOND, organization executive; b. Bridgeton, N.J., Jan. 30, 1938; s. Raymond Wilson and Clara Ella (Moore) G.; m. Sally Anne Woodruff, Sept. 10, 1960; children: Glenn Thomas Wilson, Matthew Moore. AB, Harvard U., 1960; MPA (scholastic award), NYU, 1964. Adminstrv. asst. N.Y. State Banking Dept., 1962-63; planner N.J. Dept. Econ. Devel. and Conservation, 1963-64; sr. planner N.Y. State Office Regional Devel., 1964-66; mem. staff Gov. N.Y. State Exec. Chamber, 1966-71; program sec. Office of Lt. Gov., N.Y. State, 1971-73; dep. commr. adminstrn. N.Y. State Health Dept., 1973-75; exec. v.p. Hosp. Assn. N.Y. State, 1975-78; chief exec. officer Nat. Easter Seal Soc., 1978-90, Am. Lung Assn., N.Y.C., 1990—. Bd. dirs. Internat. Union Against TB and Lung Disease, 1996—. Mem. Harvard Club (N.Y.C.). Office: Am Lung Assn 1740 Broadway New York NY 10019-4315

GARRISON, SUSAN KAY, lawyer; b. Renton, Wash., Sept. 6, 1952; d. Walter Raymond and Rose Faye (Wilson) G.; m. William W. Mayer Jr., Aug. 4, 1973 (div. July 1988); 1 child, Jonathan William Mayer; m. Michael J.J. Campbell, Oct. 22, 1993; 2 stepchildren: Michael Sean and Andrew Jack Campbell. BA in Sociology cum laude, Gettysburg Coll., 1974; JD, Villanova U., 1980, LLM in Taxation, 1988. Assoc. Dechert Price and Rhoads, Phila., 1980-83, Surrick and Gollatz, Media, Pa., 1983-86; pvt. practice Media, 1986—; exec. trustee Garrison Family Found., Media, 1990—; pres., bd. mem. Nat. Abortion Rights Action League Pa., Phila., 1986-94. Mem. com. Middletown Twp. (Pa.) Open Space Commn., 1984-86; bd. dirs. Clara Bell Duvall Edn. Fund, Phila., 1987-90, NARAL-Pa. Found.,1994—; nat. coord. Nat. Evang. Women's Caucus, Chgo., 1990-91; commr. Delaware County Women's Commn., Media, 1989-92; pres. Friends of Delaware County Women's Commn., Media, 1990-96; trustee Media-Providence Friends Sch., 1988-99; dir. The Ctr. Found., 1995—; chair Reps. Choice Pa., 1995—; mem. Delaware County Planning Commn., 1997—; mem. adv. bd. Women's Assn. Women's Alternatives, Inc., 1997—; commr. Pa. Commn. for Women, 1998—; bd. dirs. Pa. Ct. Apptd. Spl. Advocates Assn., 1998—. Mem. ABA, Nat. Assn. Women and Law, Nat. Women History Network, Nat. Assn. Commn. for Women (bd. dirs. 1998—), Delaware County Estate Planning Coun., Pa. Bar Assn., Delco Bar Assn. Republican. Office: 220 N Jackson St Media PA 19063-2807

GARRISON-FINDERUP, IVADELLE DALTON, writer; b. San Pedro, Calif., Oct. 4, 1915; d. William Douglas and Olive May (Covington) Dalton; m. Fred Marion Garrison, Aug. 8, 1932 (dec. Nov. 1984); children: Douglas Lee, Vernon Russell, Nancy Jane; m. Elmer Pedersen Finderup, Apr. 8, 1994. BA, Calif. State U., Fresno, 1964; postgrad., U. Oreg., 1965, U. San Francisco, 1968. Cert. secondary tchr., Calif. Tchr. Tranquillity (Calif.) H.S., 1964-78, West Hills Coll., Coalinga, Calif., 1970-74; lectr. in field. Author: Roots and Branches of Our Garrison Family Tree, 1988, Roots and Branches of Our Dalton Family Tree, 1989, The History of James' Fresno Ranch, 1990, 3d edit., 1993, There is a Peacock on the Roof, 1993; (with Vernon R.) William Douglas Dalton, a Biography, 1995, Sam (The Cat That Thought He Was a Boy), 1997, Amanda and Her Feathered Friends, 1997, Freddy Goes on a Trailer Outing, 1998, David Learns to Count, 1998. Mem. DAR (sec. 1987-89, regent 1989-91, regent Fresno chpt. 1999—), Nat. Trust for Hist. Preservation, Archaeology Inst. Am., Frazier Clan N.Am., Fresno City and County Hist. Soc. (life), Fresno Archaeology Soc. (sec. 1994), Children of the Am. Revolution (life patriot, sr. pres. 1991-97), Westerners Internat., Fresno Gem and Mineral Soc., Thora # 11 Dannebrog, Friends of the Libr. (Fresno), Chaffee Zoolog. Gardens of Fresno, Archaeological Inst. Am. (San Joaquin Valley chpt., charter mem.), Fresno County Archaeological Soc, Fresno Met. Mus., Baker Hist. Mus. (life). Republican. Lutheran. Avocations: quilting, knitting. Office: Garrison Libr 3427 Circle Ct E Fresno CA 93703-2403

GARRITY, RODMAN FOX, psychologist, educator; b. Los Angeles, June 10, 1922; s. Lawrence Hitchcock and Margery Fox (Pugh) G.; m. Juanita Daphne Mullan, Mar. 5, 1948; children—Diana Daphne, Ronald Fox. Student, Los Angeles City Coll., 1946-47; B.A., Calif. State U., Los Angeles, 1950; M.A., So. Meth. U., Dallas, 1955; Ed.D., U. So. Calif., 1963. Tchr. elem. sch. Palmdale (Calif.) Sch. Dist., 1952-54; psychologist, prin. Redondo Beach (Calif.) City Schs., 1954-60; asst. dir. ednl. placement lectr., ednl. adviser U. So. Calif., 1960-62; asso. prof., coordinator credentials programs Calif. State Poly. U., Pomona, 1962-66; chmn. social sci. dept. Calif. State Poly. U., 1966-68, dir. tchr. preparation center, 1968-71, coordinator grad. program, 1971-73, prof. tchr. preparation center, 1968—, coordinator spl. edn. programs, 1979—; cons. psychologist, lectr. in field. Pres. Redondo Beach Coordinating Council, 1958-60; mem. univ. rep. Calif. Faculty Assns., 1974-76. Served with Engr. Combat Bn. AUS, 1942-45. Mem. Prins. Assn. Redondo Beach (chmn. 1958-60), Nat. Congress Parents and Tchrs. (hon. life), Am. Psychol. Assn., Calif. Tchrs. Assn. Democrat. Office: Calif State U Dept Special Edn Pomona CA 91768

GARSIEL, MOSHE, archaeology and biblical educator; b. Tel Aviv, Israel, Jan. 6, 1936; s. Jonah and Lea G.; m. Batsheva Amitai, Aug. 25, 1959; children: Adi, Galit, Nili. BA, Tel Aviv U., Israel, 1965, MA, 1968, PhD, 1974. Instr. dept. of Bible, Bar-Ilan U., Ramat Gan, Israel, 1968-73; lectr dept of Bible, Bar-Ilan U., Ramat Gan, 1974-77; chmn. dept. The Land of Israel Studies, Bar Ilan U., Ramat Gan, 1975-77; sr. lectr. dept. of Bible, Bar Ilan U., Ramat Gan, 1978-80, chmn., 1981-84, assoc. prof., 1984-92, prof., 1992-2000; coord. field rsch. team Bar Ilan U., Ramat Gan, 1968-84; participant in excavation at Tel Apheq, summer 1975; coord. excavation Izbet-Sarta, 1976-77; vis. prof. Bible and Biblical Archaeology The Hebrew Theol. Coll., Skokie, Ill., 1977-78, 81, grad. summer rsch., 1989, 91; vis. prof. of Bible and Bible Archaeology U. Wis., Milw., 1985-86, The Jews Coll. U. London, 1992-93; dean fac. Jewish Studies, Bar-Ilan U., 1997-2000. Author: The Kingdom of David: Studies in History and Inquiries in Historiography, 1975, The Beginning of the Kingdom in Israel, 1982, The First Book of Samuel: A Literary Study of Comparative Structures, Analogies and Parallels, 1983, English Translation, 1985, Midrashic Name Derivations in the Bible, 1987, Biblical Names: A Literary Study of Midrashic Derivations and Puns, 1991; co-author (with S. Abramski) The Book of 1 Samuel, Encyclopedia The World of the Bible, 1985, The Book of 2 Samuel, Encyclopedia The World of the Bible, 1989, (with others) The First Book of Chronicles, The World of the Bible, 1995. Avocations: walking, swimming, travel. Home: 110 Rothschild St, Retach-Tiqva 49333, Israel Office: Bar-Ilan U, Dept of Bible, Ramat Gan Israel

GART, HERBERT STEVEN, communications executive, producer; b. Phila., June 11, 1937; s. Jack and Celia (Miller) G.; m. Lillian Allen Jay, Aug. 12, 1969; 1 child, Heather Joy. Student, Temple U., 1955-59. Pres. BSM Prodns., Inc., N.Y.C., 1965-70, Herbert S. Gart Mgmt., Inc., N.Y.C., 1963-84, Whitfeld Music, Inc., N.Y.C., 1965-90, The Rainbow Collection, Ltd., N.Y.C., 1971—. Personal mgr.: (1963—) Bill Cosby, Buffy Sainte-Marie, Jose Feliciano, Jesse Colin Young, The Youngbloods (Gold Record award Rec. Industry Assn. Am. and RCA Records 1968), Don McLean (5 Platinum Record awards Rec. Industry Assn. Am. and United Artists 1972), Andy Breckman (3 Emmy awards 1982, 85), Peter Tork (The Monkees), Ed Begley Jr. (several Emmy nominations), Jack Bruce (Cream), Felix Pappalardi (Mountain), Tim Hauser (Manhattan Transfer), Tommy West, Jim Croce, The Persuasions, Headsoup, Roger Davidson, Roxy Dawn, Ashley Cleveland, (record prodn.) (1965—) Janis Ian (Gold Record award Rec. Industry Assn. Am. and Columbia Records 1975, 2 Grammy awards Nat. Acad. Rec. Arts and Scis. 1975), Dick Feller, Roy Buchanan, Charlie Daniels, Mississippi John Hurt, Felix Pappalardi, Headsoup, Roger Davidson. Office: The Rainbow Collection Ltd PO Box 300 Solebury PA 18963-0300

GART, JASON H., historian; b. Phila., Dec. 13, 1971; s. Stephen M. Gart and Paula A. Narin. BS, Drexel U., 1994; MA, Ariz. State U., 1996, PhD, 2000. Rsch. analyst Ctr. Forensic Econ. Studies, Phila.; 1993; v.p. Pub. History Ctr., Mesa, Ariz., 1994-98; pres., sr. historian History Internat., Inc., Mesa, Ariz., 1998—; pres. Askahistorian.com, Inc., Tempe, Ariz., 2000—; chair Cons. Working Group, 1998—. Author: Papago Park: A History of Hole-in-the-Rock, 1948-1995, 1996. Mem. Nat. Coun. Pub. History. E-mail: jason.gart@askahistorian.com. Office: History Internat Inc PO Box 331 Mesa AZ 85211-0331

GARTENBERG, SEYMOUR LEE, retired recording company executive; b. N.Y.C., May 27, 1931; s. Morris and Anna (Banner) G.; m. Anna Stassi, Feb. 18, 1956 (dec. Feb. 3, 1998); children: Leslie, Karen, Mark; m. Phyllis H. Hecker, Mar. 14, 1999. BBA cum laude, CCNY, 1952, LHD (hon.), 1996. Asst. contr. Finlay Straus, Inc., N.Y.C., 1950-56; contr. Tappin's Inc., Newark, 1956; sr. v.p. Columbia House divsn. CBS, N.Y.C., 1956-65; v.p. fin. Columbia Records divsn. CBS, N.Y.C., 1965-67; exec. v.p. Columbia House divsn. CBS, N.Y.C., 1967-73; pres. CBS Toys Divsn., Cranbury, N.J., 1973-78; v.p. CBS/Columbia Group, N.Y.C., 1978—; sr. group v.p. CBS Records Group, 1979-87; exec. v.p. CBS Records Inc., 1987-91; ret., 1991; dir. C-Phone Corp., Wilmington, N.C. Mem. Inst. of Mgmt. Accts., Am. Mgmt. Assn., Mill Island Civic Assn.

GARTMAN, MAX DILLON, language educator; b. Mobile, Ala., May 3, 1938; s. Noah Christopher and Edna Olga (Schwartzauer) G.; m. Marcia Ann Hubbard, Aug. 31, 1962; children: Noel Don, Polly Antoinette, Paul Dillon. AB in French and History, Samford U., Birmingham, Ala., 1960; MA in French, U. Ala., Tuscaloosa, 1962, PhD in Romance Langs., 1974; cert., U. Nice, France, 1985. NDEA fellow U. Ala., Tuscaloosa, 1960-65; prof. Romance langs. Samford U., 1965-82, head dept. fgn. langs., 1975-82; chmn. dept. fgn. langs., prof. romance langs. U. North Ala., Florence, 1982-99, dir. Ctr. for Critical Langs., 1999—; pres. Internat. Edn. Travel, Florence, 1982—. Editor SU Faculty Forum Ann., 1967-72; performer rec. The Holy City, 1976. Chmn. Ala. Assn. Fgn. Lang. Tchrs., 1973-74, So. Conf. Lang. Tchg., 1976; bd. dirs. Ala. Humanities Found., 1992-96. Mem. Ala. Assn. Tchrs. of French (chairperson 1995-97), Ala. Consortium for Fgn. Langs. (chairperson 1995-97), Rotary (sec. Oxmoor club 1981-82, music dir. 1982—). Baptist. Avocations: tennis, music, European travel. Home: 122 Lambeth St Florence AL 35633-1550 Office: U North Ala PO Box 5074 Florence AL 35632-0001

GARTNER, IAN RICHARD, librarian; b. Manchester, Eng., Feb. 8, 1962; s. Leopold and Greta (Grupman) G. BA with honours, King's Coll., Cambridge U., 1983, MA, 1987; Postgrad. Diploma, Coll. Librarianship, Wales, 1986. Pub. svc. support libr. Oxfordshire County Librs., Oxford, Eng., 1986-88; info. tech. libr. Oxford Poly., 1988-89; compuer officer Oxfam, Oxford, 1989-90; Pearson new media libr. Bodleian Libr., Oxford, 1991—; advisor Refugee Studies Program Documentation Com., Oxford, 1993—; guest lectr. symposium on new media Guangzhou (China) U. Libr., 1993, symposium on digital conversion of manuscripts, Kelo U., Tokyo, 1998; Brit. Coun. visitor to U. Dhaka, Bangladesh, 2000. Co-editor: On Internet '94, 1994; contbr./author: The Internet Library, 1994; editor Info. Networking News, 1992-93; contbr. articles to profl. jours. Chair Amnesty Internat., Oxford, 1987-92. Recipient Barbara Pym award, 1992. Avocations: cinema, classical music, travel, human rights work. Office: Bodleian Libr, Broad St, Oxford OX1 3BG, England

GARTNER, JOSEPH CHARLES, business systems administrator; b. Detroit, Feb. 3, 1945; s. Joseph Owen and Frances Alice (Harrington) G.; m. Marilyn Jean Kern, June 26, 1971; children: Stephanie, Jonathan, Jamie Lynn. Student, U. Mich., 1963-66; BSE, Marquette U., 1968; MBA, U. Rochester, 1979. Cert. systems profl. Constrn. engr. B.A.S.F., Wyandotte, Mich., 1966-67; systems engr. IBM Corp., Milw., 1968-70; mgr. mgmt. info. systems Borg Warner Corp., Toledo, Ohio, 1970-73; dir. info. systems Donnelly Corp., Holland, Mich., 1973-75; mgr. fin. systems Bausch & Lomb, Rochester, N.Y., 1975-82, mgr. EDP audit, 1982-85; mgr. bus. systems Wegmans Food Markets Inc., Rochester, 1985-97; group mgr. bus. sys. The Penn Traffic Co., Syracuse, N.Y., 1997—. Trustee Fairport (N.Y.) Pub. Libr., 1992—. Mem. Assn. for Systems Mgmt. (internat. dir. 1984-87, Disting. Svc. award 1988), KC (grand knight 1985-87), Genesee Valley Dist. PTA (legis. chmn. 1985—). Home: 3139 Fox Rd Syracuse NY 13215-9744 Office: The Penn Traffic Co PO Box 4737 1200 State Fair Blvd Syracuse NY 13221-4737

GARTZ, JOCHEN ERNST FRIEDRICH, chemist, mycologist; b. Mansfeld, Harz, Germany, Oct. 1, 1953; s. Harry and Margot (Göbecke) G. Diploma, Tech. U. Merseburg, Germany, 1976, PhD, 1980; DrScNat, Acad. Scis., Leipzig, Germany, 1989. Rschr. U. Merseburg, 1976-80, pharm. industry, Leipzig, 1980-83; chemist, rschr. Acad. of Scis., Leipzig, 1983-91; chemist, mycologist U. Leipzig, 1991—; mem. sci. bd. SISSC, Rovereto, Italy, 1994—; cons. to mushroom industry, Germany and Holland, 1996—. Author: Narrenschwamme, 1993, Magic Mushrooms Around the World, 1996; editor Integration, 1996—; contbr. about 60 articles to profl. jours. Mem. Europaisches Collecium fuer Bewusstseinstudien, Multidisciplinary Assn. for Psychedelic Studies. Avocations: mushroom cultivation, biotransformations. Home: Georg-Schumann-Str 1, D-04105 Leipzig Germany Office: U Leipzig, Permoserstr 15, D-04318 Leipzig Germany

GARTZ, ROLF FRITZ, foundation administrator; b. Bonn, Germany, Dec. 23, 1940; s. Fritz and Hildegard (Rhein) G.; m. Christel Anneliese Overgahr gen. Willebrand, Aug. 7, 1970; 1 child, Stephan. DSc in Cell Biology, Bonn U., 1969. Civil servant, govt. dir. Germany, 1970-90; mng. chmn. Eduard Rhein Found., Hamburg, Germany, 1990—; bd. dirs. Prof. Rhein Found., Koenigswinter, Germany, 1987—. Recipient Cross of the Order of Merit Fed. Republic of Germany, 1998. Mem. AAAS, N.Y. Acad. Scis., Assn. German Natural Scientists and Physicians, German Soc. Cell Biology, European Cell Biology Orgn., Max Planck Soc. for Advancement of Sci., Fedn. Biochemical Soc., Internat. Union Biochemistry and Molecular Biology. Avocations: hunting, riding. Home and Office: Eduard Rhein Found, Alexander-von-Humboldtstr 6, D-56727 Mayen Germany

GARVAN, STEPHEN BOND, artist manager; b. Hartford, Conn., Mar. 29, 1952; s. Joseph Bond Garvan and Catherine (Wheeler) Jones; m. Frances Jurga, Sept. 6, 1979 (div. 1984); m. Priscilla Lombard Lewis, 1994. BA, Clark U., 1974, postgrad., 1975; postgrad., Stanford U., 1998. Agt. Supreme Artists, N.Y.C., 1974-75, It's a Hit Prodns., Acton, Mass., 1975-79; artist mgr., chief exec. officer Bullet Mgmt., N.Y.C. and Harvard (Mass.), 1979-91, Boulder, Colo., 1991; artist mgr., CEO, Garvan Mktg. and Garvan Mgmt., Niwot, Colo., 1997—. Exec. producer records: Are You Afraid of Falling, Estes Boys, 1978, Save the Whales, Allen Estes Band, 1981, others. Treas., then chmn. Harvard Dem. Town Com., 1979-85; treas. 53 W. 87th St Coop. Corp., 1986-92, 97-99; bd. dirs. Swallow Hill Music Assn., 1994—, pres., 1998—. Mem. NARAS, Am. Music Assn. (founding mem., steering com. 1999—), Pubs. Assn. of the South, Mountains and Plains Booksellers Assn., New Eng. Booksellers Assn., Southeastern Booksellers Assn., Upper Midwest Booksellers Assn., Country Music Assn., Earth Comm. Office, Assn. Am. Pubs. (chair telemktg. com. 1986-88), Rocky Mountain Book Pubs. Assn. (bd. dirs. 1992-94), Young Dems., Warner Free Lectr. Series (bd. 1978-84, treas. 1979-84). Avocations: reading, tennis, travel, collecting books, music. Fax: 303-652-3610; e-mail: steve@garvanmanagement.com. Home and Office: 7919 Fairfax Ct Niwot CO 80503-7626

GARVENS, ELLEN JO, art educator, artist; b. Omro, Wis., Aug. 15, 1955; d. Leonard Kenneth and Eugenia Mary (Wetter) G.; m. James Patrick Phalen, Oct. 18, 1988; 1 child, Cole Garvens Phalen. BS in Art, U. Wis., 1979; MA, U. N. Mex., 1982, MFA, 1987. Asst. prof. of art Oberlin (Ohio) Coll., 1990-94, U. Wash., Seattle, 1994—. Artist: one person shows include: Jayne H. Baum Gallery, N.Y.C., 1986, 89, 93, Wooster (Ohio) Mus. of Art, U. R.I., Kingston. Recipient Wis. Women in Arts award Madison, 1978, Fullbright Hays scholarship Internat. Comm. Agy., Washington, 1979-80; grantee, NEA, Washington, 1986, HC Powers grant, Oberlin Coll., 1991, Royalty Rsch. Fund grant, U. Wash., 1996. Home: 19518 67th Ave NE Kenmore WA 98028-3447 Office: U Wash Sch of Art PO Box 353440 Seattle WA 98195-3440*

GARVEY, RICHARD ANTHONY, lawyer; b. N.Y.C., Jan. 10, 1950; s. James Joseph Garvey and Janet Mary (Mooney) Rowse. AB, Boston Coll., 1972; JD, Harvard U., 1975. Bar: N.Y. 1976. Assoc. Simpson Thacher & Bartlett, N.Y.C., 1975-82, ptnr., 1982-93, 97—. Mem. ABA, N.Y. State Bar Assn., Assn. Bar City N.Y., Phi Beta Kappa. Home: 330 E 38th St Apt 44N New York NY 10016-2783 Office: Simpson Thacher & Bartlett 425 Lexington Ave Fl 15 New York NY 10017-3954

GARVEY, RICHARD CONRAD, journalist; b. Northampton, Mass., May 23, 1923; s. Michael Edward and Lucy Lillian (Bradford) G.; m. Anne Elizabeth Vanasse, May 18, 1957 (dec. Jan. 1988); children: Philip, John, Mary, Margaret; m. Allison McCrillis Lockwood, Dec. 29, 1990. Student, U. Mass., 1941-43, LHD (hon.), 1974; D of Humanics (hon.), Springfield Coll., 1982; LLD (hon.), Our Lady of Elms Coll., 1982. Reporter Daily Hampshire Gazette, Northampton, 1943-44; reporter Springfield (Mass.) Daily News, 1944-50, asst. mng. editor, 1950-66, editor, 1966-87; assoc. pub. Springfield Union-News, Sunday Rep., 1987—. Author: Oliver Smith, Esq., 1948, (with others) The Northampton Book, 1954, St. Mary's of Haydenville, 1968, History of Springfield College, 1985, Bringing Home the News: 175 Years of the Springfield Newspapers, 1999; contbr. articles to World Book Ency., 1977—. Trustee Forbes Libr., Northampton, 1952-57, 2000—; chmn. bd. dirs. Springfield Coll., 1979-81, Mercy Hosp., Springfield, 1980-82. Decorated Knight-Comdr. of Holy Sepulchre; recipient Grenville Clark award World Federalists, 1962, Humanitarian award NCCJ, 1989. Mem. Rotary (pres. 1984-85, Paul Harris award 1985). Roman Catholic. Home: 19 Washington Ave Northampton MA 01060-2822 Office: Union-News and Sunday Rep 1860 Main St Springfield MA 01103-1073

GARVICK, KENNETH RYAN, broadcast engineer, announcer, educator; b. Akron, Ohio, Apr. 11, 1945; s. Kenneth Rodger and Dorothy Lillian (Lincks) G. Diploma, DeVry Inst. Tech., Chgo., 1966, Cleve. Inst., 1970, 81. Cert. electronic technician. Electronic repairman RCA Consumer Electronics, Indpls., 1966-70; compilation technician Howard W. Sams & Co., Indpls., 1970-73; broadcast engr. Sta. WIBC/WNAP Fairbanks Broadcasting, Indpls., 1973; announcer, engr. Stas. WHYT-AM, WNON-FM, 1974-76; transmitter engr. Sta. WISH-TV, Indpls., 1976-79; electronics instr. Arsenal Tech. High Sch., Indpls., 1979-82; announcer, engr. Stas. WSVL AM/FM, 1979-81; instr. various schs., Ohio, 1987—; announcer, engr. Sta. WMAN-AM, 1994-95. Author: Gerberich Descendants from York, PA, 1987; contbr. articles to profl. jours. With Signal Corps U.S. Army, 1966-72, Vietnam. Mem. Soc. Broadcast Engrs., Arsenal Tech., Radio Club (sec. 1979-82). Republican. Avocations: film history, amateur radio, bicycling. Address: PO Box 88 Shauck OH 43349-0088

GARVIE, ALEXANDER FEMISTER, classics educator; b. Edinburgh, Jan. 29, 1934; s. Alexander and Edith Florence (Tyson) G.; m. Jane Wallace Johnstone, Aug. 4, 1966; children: Margaret Jane, David Alexander. MA, U. Edinburgh, 1955; BA, U. Cambridge, Eng., 1959, MA, 1964. Asst. U. Glasgow, 1960-61, lectr., 1961-72, sr. lectr., 1972-88, reader in classics, 1988-98, prof. Greek, 1998-99, hon. profl. rsch. fellow, 1999—. Author: Aeschylus' Supplices, Play and Trilogy, 1969, Aeschylus Choephori, 1986, Homer Odyssey, VI-VIII, 1994, Sophocles Ajax, 1998; contbr. articles to profl. jours. Fellow Royal Soc. of Edinburgh; mem. Classical Assn. Scotland (pres. Glasgow and West Cen. 1984-86, 93-96), Hellenic Soc., Classical Assn., Scottish Hellenic Soc. Mem. Ch. of Scotland. Avocations: music, walking, travel. Home: 93 Stirling Dr Bishopbriggs, Glasgow G64 3PG, Scotland

GARVIN, FLORENCE WARD, management consultant; b. Ft. Sam Houston, Tex., Oct. 6, 1928; d. Edward Joseph and Florence Emily (Bock) Ward; m. Sheldon R. Rappaport, Mar. 2, 1950 (div. July 1969); children: Bruce Ward, Lisa Lynn; m. Stefan J. Garvin, Oct. 3, 1981. BA, Our Lady of Lake U., San Antonio, 1949; postgrad., Trinity U., San Antonio, 1949-50. Co-founder, asst. to pres. Pathway Sch., Norristown, Pa., 1961-68; adminstrv. dir. Neurosurg. Clinic for Children, Media, Pa., 1968-70; v.p. for devel. Vanguard Schs., Haverford, Pa., 1970-72; asst. to pres. Elwyn (Pa.) Inst., 1972-75; pvt. practice Media, 1976-78; cons. employee rels. dept. E.I. DuPont de Nemours & Co., Inc., Wilmington, Del., 1978-85; sr. bus. assoc. internat. dept. E.I. DuPont de Nemours & Co., Inc., Wilmington, 1985-89, mgr. bus. rels. devel., 1989-90, mgr. internat. human resources devel. human resources dept., 1990-94; ; pres. bd. dirs. AIDS Task Force/Phila. Community Health Alternatives, 1994-96; bd. dirs. Pacific Rim Bus. Coun., 1994-96, Nationalities Svc. Ctr., 1996-98, Green Cir. Program, 1996-98; bd. dirs. East Side Charter Sch., Wilmington, Del., 1996-98; mem. Phila. Com. AmFar, 1996-98; dir. spl. projects Gabriella and Paul Rosenbaum Found., 1997—. Charter mem. and bd. dirs. Montgomery County Mental Health Clinics, 1956-72; bd. dirs. Phila. United Fund, 1969-72; bd. mgrs., sec. Garrett-Williamson Found., 1973-81; bd. dirs. Mary Campbell Ctr., Wilmington, 1978-81; trustee Wilmington Coll., 1979—, Curtis Inst. Music, 1985-92; mem. devel. com. Mercy Haverford Hosp., 1994-95; mem. policy coun. Del. County Head Start, 1994-96; pres. bd. dirs. AIDS Task Force/Phila. Cmty. Health Alternatives, 1994-96; bd. dirs. Pacific Rim Bus. Coun., 1994-96, Nationalities Svc. Ctr., 1996-98, Green Cir. Program, 1996-98; bd. dirs. East Side Charter Sch., Wilmington, Del., 1996-98; pres. bd. dirs. Delaware County AIDS Network, 1999—. Home: 2 Yarmouth Ln Media PA 19063-4327

GARWOOD, ROBERT ASHLEY, JR., network communications analyst; b. Cordele, Ga., Sept. 11, 1955; s. Robert Ashley Sr. and Mary Ann (Meng) G.; m. Christine Allison Haire, Aug. 31, 1981. BA, LaGrange Coll., 1978. Rep. sales Met. Life Ins. Co., Atlanta, 1978-79; assoc. ptnr. Stephen D. Jones & Assocs., Roswell, Ga., 1979-80; supr. Six Flags Over Ga., Atlanta, 1979-86; asst. mgr. Wolf Camera, Kennesaw, Ga., 1986; asst. mgr. data base Days Inn Corp., Atlanta, 1986-92; comm. analyst The Emory Clinic, Atlanta, 1992-97; owner So. Visions-Comm. Cons., Norcross, Ga., 1997—; supr. U.S. Advanced Networks, Inc. Network Mgmt. Ctr., Norcross. Pastor United Meth. Ch., West Ga., 1975-79. Mem. Pi Tau Chi. Democrat. Avocations: writing, sports, philosophy. Home and Office: 3276 Harmon Ridge Ct Buford GA 30519-6986

GARY, C. CECI, primary school educator; b. Jackson, Miss., Mar. 24; d. Jesse and Ora Christine G. BS, Jackson State U., 1977, MS, 1984. Cert.

real estate broker. Claims examiner Miss. Employment Security Commn., Jackson, 1976-87; sales assoc., broker NuWorld Realty, Jackson, 1985-87; tchr. DeKalb County Schs., Decatur, Ga., 1987—. Author: The Iconoclast, 1993. Mentor tchr./student mentor program, 1991-93; bd. dirs. DeKalb County Exec. Bd. Vols., 1993; team leader Walk-Am., March of Dimes; dir. after sch. program Robert Shaw Theme Sch.; eucharistic min. Corpus Christi Cath. Ch. Recipient Dedication to Edn. in Sci. and Prestige award NAACP, 1993; named to 1993 Honor Roll of Tchrs. Fernback Sci. Ctr.; named Sci. Tchr. of the Year DeKalb County, 1993. Mem. Nat. Sci. Assn. Avocations: writing poetry, reading, tutoring "high risk" students, volunteering, tennis. Home: 4510 Hunters Way Stone Mountain GA 30083-2553

GARY, GERARD ELIE, mechanical engineer, educator; b. Perigueux, Dordogne, France, Feb. 15, 1945; s. Jean and Marthe (Chassagny) G. Diploma in engring., Ecole Polytechnique, Paris, 1966; diploma in civil engring., Ecole Nat des Ponts Chaussees, France, 1971; DSc, Paris VI U., 1980. Cert. solids dynamics-modeling and testing. Engr. Entreprise Industrielle, Paris, 1971-73; rschr. Ecole Polytechnique, Paris, 1973—. Avocation: trumpet jazz. Email: gary@athera.polytechnique.fr. Office: Ecole Polytechnique, Lab Mecanique des Solides, 91128 Palaiseau France

GARY, JAMES FREDERICK, business and energy advising company executive; b. Chgo., Dec. 28, 1920; s. Rex Inglis and Mary Naomi (Roller) G.; m. Helen Elizabeth Gellert, Sept. 3, 1947; children: David Frederick, John William, James Scott, Mary Anne. BS, Haverford (Pa.) Coll., 1942. With Wash. Energy Co. and predecessors, Seattle, 1947-67; v.p. Wash. Energy Co., 1956-67; pres., CEO Pacific Resources Inc., Honolulu, 1967-79, chmn., CEO, 1979-84, chmn., 1985, chmn. emeritus, 1986—, internat. bus. and energy advisor, 1987—; bd. dirs. Dole Food Co., Inc., Kennedy Assocs., Inc., Seattle; chmn. bd. dirs. Inter Island Petroleum, Inc.; bd. dirs. Episcopal Homes Hawaii, The Salk Inst. Coun., La Jolla; adv. bd. Harris-Manchester Coll. U. Oxford (Eng.), 1997—. Mem. Pacific Coast Gas Assn., 1965-75, pres., 1974-75; pres. Chief Seattle coun. Boy Scouts Am., 1966-67, Aloha coun., 1973-74, mem. nat. coun., 1964—, v.p. Western region, 1978-85, pres., 1985-91, also bd. dirs.; chmn. Aloha United Way, 1978, pres., 1979-80, chmn., 1980; mem. bd. regents U. Hawaii, 1981-89; trustee Hawaii Loa Coll., 1968-85, Linfield Coll., McMinnville, Oreg., 1983-89; mem. bd. mgrs. Haverford Coll., 1983-92; bd. dirs. Rsch. Corp. of U. Hawaii, 1971-77, chmn., 1974-77, Hawaii Ednl. Coun.; bd. dirs., officer, trustee Oahu Devel. Conf., Hawaii Employers Coun., Friends of East-West Ctr., Honolulu Symphony Soc., East-West Ctr. Internat. Found.; chmn. Hawaii Comty. Found., 1987-92, mem. bd. govs., 1987-94; mem. bd. regents Chaminade U., 1991-93. Capt. AUS, 1942-46. Recipient Pres.' trophy Pacific Gas Assn., 1960, Disting. Eagle award Boy Scouts Am., 1972, Silver Beaver award, 1966, Silver Antelope award, 1976, Silver Buffalo award, 1988. Mem. Am. Gas Assn. (bd. dirs. 1970-74), Nat. LP-Gas Assn. (bd. dirs. 1967-70), Am. Petroleum Inst., Inst. Gas Tech. (trustee 1975-86), Hawaii Econ. Coun., Nat. Petroleum Coun., Hawaii Dist. Export Coun., Japan-Hawaii Econ. Coun., U.S Nat. Com. for Pacific Econ. Cooperation, Pacific Basin Econ. Coun. (chmn. U.S. com. 1985-86), Japan-Am. Soc. Honolulu, Ctr. for Strategic and Internat. Studies-Pacific Forum, Honolulu Commn. on Fgn. Rels., Hawaii C. of C. (chmn. 1979). Episcopalian. Clubs: Pacific Union (San Francisco); Oahu Country, Waialae Country, Outrigger Canoe, Pacific, Plaza (Honolulu); Seattle Tennis, Wash. Athletic Rainier (Seattle). Office: 130 Merchant St Ste 1080 Honolulu HI 96813-4426

GARZA, GUSTAVO, economics and urban planning educator; b. Monterrey, Mex., Jan. 12, 1945; s. Gustavo and Alicia (Villarreal) G.; m. Aida Cervantes, June 2, 1970 (div. 1972); 1 child, Adolfo; m. Brigida Garcia, Dec. 17, 1973; children: Alicia, Ernesto. BA in Econs., U. Autonoma de Nuevo Leon, Mex., 1967; MA in Econs., El Colegio de Mex., 1970; MA in Planning, U. Cambridge, Eng., 1973; PhD in Econs., U. Nacional Autonoma de Mex., 1983. Prof., rschr. El Colegio de Mex., Mexico City, 1970—, coord. urban studies area, 1974-77, dir. Ctr. Demographic and Urban Studies, 1986-88, dir. demographic and urban studies rev., 1986-88; mgmt. advisor Nacional Financiera, S.A., Mexico City, 1974-75; sci. advisor Departamento del Distrito Federal, Mexico City, 1985-87; gen. dir. Inst. Urban Studies of Nuevo Leon, Mex., 1993-95, sci. advisor, 1995; vis. rsch. fellow U. Calif., 1984, U. Tex., 1989, U. Cambridge, 1991; mem. panel on urban population dynamics, U.S. Nat. Acad. Scis., 1999—. Author: The Urban Development of Mexico, 1976, Industrialization Process of Mexico City, 1985, Macroeconomic Dynamics of Mexican Cities, 1994, Municipal Management in the Metropolitan Area of Monterrey, 1998, Urban Regulations in the Main Mexican Metropolis, 1998, Demographic Atlas of Mexico, 1999, México City at the End of the Second Millennium, 2000, others; contbr. more than 170 articles on urban econ. and planning issues in Mex. to profl. jours. Orgn. sec. Prof.-Rschr. Fellow Union, 1983-84, gen. sec., 1984-85. Recipient Nat. award for econs. Nat. Bank of Mex., 1976, Gabino Barreda medal, 1985; Guggenheim fellow, 1990. Avocations: yoga, swimming, music, reading. E-mail: ggarza@colmex.mx. Office: Camino al Ajusco 20, Col Pedregal de Sta Teresa, 10740 Mexico City DF, Mexico

GARZANITI, LAURENT JOSÉ HENRI FRANÇOIS, lawyer; b. Liège, Belgium, Aug. 27, 1966; s. Agazio and Josette (Joannes) G.; m. Clare Janet Roberts, June 29, 1996. LLM magna cum laude, Columbia U., 1991; LLM in EEC Law magna cum laude, Cambridge (Eng.) U., 1990; lic. jur. summa cum laude, U. Liège, 1989. Bar: N.Y., Brussels, 1992. Assoc. Cleary, Gottlieb, Steen & Hamilton, Brussels, N.Y.C., 1991-99, Freshfields Bruckhaus Deringer, Brussels, 1999—. Author: Telecommunications, Broadcasting and the Internet: E.U. Competition Law and Regulation, 2000; contbr. articles to profl. jours. Belgian-Am. Ednl. Found. fellow, 1990-91, Province of Liège scholar, 1985-89, Acad. Internat. Law fellow, The Hague, The Netherlands, 1987. Mem. ABA, Assn. pour l'Étude du Droit de la Concurrence, Internat. League Competition Law, Cambridge Soc. Brussels, Columbia Club Brussels. Avocations: theater, tennis, soccer, jogging, cycling. Home: Ave Herbert Hoover 110, 1200 Brussels Belgium Office: Freshfields Bruckhaus Et Al, Place du Champ de Mars 5, 1050 Brussels Belgium

GASCOIGNE, JOHN, history educator; b. Liverpool, Eng., Jan. 20, 1951; arrived in Australia, 1951; s. Robert Mortimer and Elizabeth Mary (Meehan) G.; m. Kathleen May Bock; children: Robert, Catherine. BA with honors, Sydney (Australia) U., 1972; MA with distinction, Princeton U., 1976; PhD, Cambridge U., 1981. Lectr. St. Paul's Teachers' Coll., Rabaul, Papua, New Guinea, 1973; lectr. U. Papua, 1977-78; tutor, lectr., sr. lectr., assoc. prof. U. NSW, Sydney, 1980—. Author: Cambridge in the Age of Enlightenment, 1989, Joseph Banks and the English Enlightenment, 1991; contbr.: Reappraisals of the Scientific Revolution, 1990, Telling Lives. Scientific Biography, 1996, Science in the Service of Empire. Joseph Banks, the British State and the Uses of Science in the Age of Revolution, 1998, Science, Politics and Universities of Europe, 1999. Recipient Hancock prize Australian Hist. Assn., 1990. Home: 58 Bellevue Ave, Denistone NSW 2114, Australia Office: U New South Wales, Sch History, Sydney NSW 2052, Australia

GASCOIGNE, PAUL (GAZZA), professional soccer player; b. Wallsend, Eng., May 25, 1967. Formerly with Newcastle Utd, Spurs, Lazio, Rangers, 1984-88; with Tottenham Hotspur, 1988-92, Lazio Roma, 1992-95, Glaserow Ranger, 1995-97; midfielder Middlesbrough (Eng.) Football Club, 1997—. Office: Middlesbrough FC, Cellnet Riverside Stadium, Middlesbrough TS3 6RS, England*

GASIC, SLOBODAN, physician, researcher, educator; b. Prijedor, Bosnia, Yugoslavia, Jan. 1, 1942; s. Slavko and Elsa (Reiss) G.; m. Anna Chuman, Oct. 22, 1952; children: Georgina, Slavko, Bodo. Student, U. Vienna, Austria, 1961-62; MD, U. Vienna, 1968. U. asst. U. Vienna Clinic, 1968-1975, specialist internal med., 1984, specialist clin. pharmacology, 1981, specialist cardiology, 1984, universitatsdozent internal med., 1988, prof. internal med., 1992—; staff mem. 1. Medizinische Universitatsklinik, Vienna, 1977-91, Klinik Für Innere Medizin, dept. endocrinology and metabolism, 1992—. Author: Erregugsleitungsstörungen Des Herzens, 1976; contbr. articles to profl. jours. Mem. Europ Soc. Cardiology, Deutsche Pharm Gesellschaft, Am. Soc. Hypertension. Avocations: accordion, wood carver, foreign languages. Office: Klinik Fur Innere Medizin 3, Endokrinologie, 1090 Vienna Austria

GASICH, WELKO ELTON, retired aerospace executive, management consultant; b. Cupertino, Calif., Mar. 28, 1922; s. Elija J. and Catherine (Paviso) G.; m. Patricia Ann Gudgel, Dec. 28, 1973; 1 child, Mark David. A.B. cum laude in Mech. Engring. (Bacon scholar), Stanford U., 1943, M.S. in Mech. Engring., 1947, cert. in fin. and econs. (Sloan exec. fellow), 1967; Aero. Engr., Calif. Inst. Tech., 1948. Aerodynamicist Douglas Aircraft Co., 1943-44, supr. aeroelastics, 1947-51; chief aero design Rand Corp., 1951-53; chief preliminary design aircraft divsn. Northrop Corp., Los Angeles, 1953-56; dir. advanced systems Northrop Corp., 1956-61, v.p., asst. gen. mgr. tech., 1961-66, corp. v.p., gen. mgr. Northrop Ventura divsn., 1967-71, corp. v.p., gen. mgr. aircraft divsn., 1971-76, corp. v.p., group exec. aircraft group, 1976-79, sr. v.p. advanced projects, 1979-85, exec. v.p. programs, 1985-88, ret., 1988; aerospace cons. Encino, Calif., 1988—. Author: 40 Years of Ferrari V-12 Engines, 1990; patentee in field. Chmn. adv. council Stanford Sch. Engring., 1981-83; past mem. adv. council Stanford Grad. Sch. Bus.; chmn. United Way, 1964; chmn. Scout-O-Rama, Los Angeles council Boy Scouts Am., 1964; chmn. explorer scout exec. com., 1963-64. Served to lt. USN, 1944-46. Fellow AIAA, Soc. Automotive Engrs.; mem. NAE, Navy League, Stanford Grad. Sch. Bus. Alumni Assn. (pres. 1971), Conquistadores del Cielo Club, Bel Air Country Club. Republican. Office: 3517 Caribeth Dr Encino CA 91436-4103

GASIŃSKA, ANNA JANINA, radiobiologist, researcher; b. Craców, Poland, July 25, 1949; d. Jan Polewka and Zofia Matuch; m. Adam Marian Gasiński, Sept. 15, 1973; 1 child, Gabriela. MSc, Jagiellonian U., Craców, Poland, 1974, PhD, 1982; habilitation, Oncology Ctr., Warsaw, 1996. Radiobiologist Oncology Ctr., Craców, 1974—, sci. asst., 1974-78, sr. scientist, 1979-82, head radiation biology lab., 1983—, sr. lectr., 1983—. Contbr. over 97 articles in profl. jours., proceedings and abstracts for sci. meetings and confs. Contbr. articles to Internat. Jour. Radiation Biology, Brit. Jour. Radiology, Radiotherapy Oncology. Recipient Major of Craców award, 1980, fellowship Internat. Union Against Cancer 1985-86; grantee Internat. Atomic Energy Agy., Vienna, 1993-98. Mem. European Soc. for Therapeutic Radiology and Oncology, European Soc. for Radiation Biology, Polish Soc. Radiation Rsch. (pres. Cracow br., award 1989), European Tissue Culture Soc., Polish Oncological Soc. Roman Catholic. Avocations: opera music, cross country skiing. Home: Rozrywka 24/21, 31-419 Cracow Poland Office: Ctr of Oncology, Garncarska 11, 31-115 Cracow Poland

GASOLIBA I BÖHM, CARLES-ALFRED, foreign diplomat; b. Barcelona, Spain, Nov. 22, 1945. Mem. European Parliament, 1999—, mem. com. on econ. and monetary affairs, substitue com. on industry, external trade, rsch. and energy; treas. Group of the European Liberal, Dem. and Reform Party; mem. delegation for relations with the countries of Ctrl. Am. and Mex. Mem. Catalan Dem. Convergence.

GĄSOWSKI, WŁODZIMIERZ, mechanical engineering educator; b. Żyrardów, Poland, Mar. 23, 1933; s. Teofil and Kazimiera (Lazarczyk) G.; m. Nina Moszczyńska, Jan. 18, 1958; children: Igor, Piotr. MSc, Aviation Inst., Russia, 1958; DSc, Tech. U., Poland, 1970, DHabSc, 1982. Designer WSK Plant, Mielec, Poland, 1958-60, chief designer, 1960-62, dept. mgr., 1962-66; mng. dir. H. Cegielski Plants, Poznań, Poland, 1966-70; tech. dir. bd. Polish Railway Rolling Stock Industry, Poznań, Poland, 1970-73; pres. Inst. Heat Engring. and Combustion Engines U. Poznań, Poznań, Poland, 1973-93, prof., 1991—; academician Acad. Transportation of the Russian Fedn., 1993—. Author: Automatic Couplers, 1976, Railway Coaches and Wagons, 1988, Testing the Railway Vehicles, 1989, Electric Driven Railway Rolling Stock, 1995, Aerodynamics of Train 1998. Recipient Academic Edn. and Tech. award Polish Ministry of Sci., 1979, Academic Edn. award Polish Ministry of Sci., Didactic and Ednl. Achievements award Polish Ministry of Edn., 1989. Mem. Polish Soc. Metallography, Gesellschaft fur Angewandte Mathematik und Mechanik, Polish Acad. Sci. (com. mem. mech. and bldg. engring. 1972-92, sect. com. mem. com. on transport 1990-93, v.p. 1993—, chmn. editl. archives com. on transport 1994—), Transport Acad. of Russia. Home: Ostroroga 3 m 3, 60-349 Poznań Poland Office: Politechnika Poznańska, ul Piotrowo 3, 60-965 Poznań Poland

GASPA, LEONARDO, biomedical educator; b. Sassari, Sardegna, Italy, Sept. 13, 1944; s. Gaspa Francesco and Pinna Nicolosa; m. Sanna Gaspa maria Luisa, Dec. 8, 1971; children: Francesco, Giovanni. Maturita Classica, Liceo Glassico Azuni, Sassari, 1963; Laurea, Medicine Chirurgia, Sassari, 1969; Specialization, Morbia Anatomy/Lab. Techs., Parka, Italy, 1974, Oncology Pavia (Italy), 1978. Asst. U. Pavia, Italy, 1970-80; prof. U. Sassari, 1980-88; chief Chair Biophysic, Sassari, 1988-93; dir. Nat. Lab. of INBB, Sassari, 1993—; cons. histopathology Gen. Hosp., Sassari, 1983-93. Contbr. papers to internat. jours. and publs. Named Cavaliere di Malta, Ordine del Tempio Gran Pridrato, Scozia, 1986, Templare, Ordine del Tempio, Scozia, 1986. Mem. AAAS, Italian Assn. Pathology, Italian Assn. Biophysics, Internat. Acad. Pathology, Italian Soc. Pure and Applied Biophysics, N.Y. Acad. Scis., Sporting Club LeQuerce, others. Avocations: swimming, career, gardening. Office: Luna E Sole 70, 07100 Sassari Sardegna, Italy

GASPAR, VILMOS ZOLTAN, chemistry educator; b. Salgotarjan, Nograd, Hungary, May 25, 1953; s. Vilmos and Eleonora (Herczeg) G.; m. Iren Szaniszlo, Nov. 1, 1975; children: Judit, Andras. MS, Kossuth L. U., Debrecen, Hungary, 1977, PhD, 1980; candidate chemistry, Hungarian Acad. Scis., Budapest, 1990; habilitation, Kossuth L. U., 1999. Jr. rsch. fellow Kossuth L. U., 1981-85, asst. rsch. prof., 1988-90, assoc. rsch. prof., 1993—; postdoctoral fellow W.Va. U., Morgantown, 1986-87, vis. rsch. prof., 1991-93; sec. chemistry sect. Hungarian Acad. Scis., Debrecen, 1993-96. Hungarian Sci. Found. grantee, 1994; Szechenyi Prof. fellow, 1998—. Office: U Debrecen Inst Phys Chem, PO Box 7, H 4010 Debrecen Hungary

GÁSPÁR, ZSOLT, civil engineer; b. Budapest, Hungary, Dec. 13, 1944; s. László and Judit (Vargha) G.; m. Katalin Kutasy, Aug. 17, 1969; children: Szabolcs, Melinda. MSCE, Tech. U. Budapest, 1967; MS in Math., Eötvös Lorand U., Budapest, 1970; D in Tech. Sci., Hungarian Acad. Sci., Budapest, 1985. Registered profl. engr. Trainee Hungarian Acad. Sci., 1967-69, jr. rschr., 1969-70, rschr., 1970-79, sr. rschr., 1979-87, rsch. adviser, 1987-91; prof. Tech. U. Budapest, 1991—, dep. dean, 1991-94, head dept., 1993-96; vis. prof. Chalmers U. Tech., Sweden, 1988. Co-author: Imperfection-Sensitivity of Elastic Structures, 1987, Structural Stability in Engineering Practice, 1999; co-editor: Post-Bulking of Elastic Structures, 1986; contbr. articles to profl. jours. Mem. Hungarian Acad. Sci., Hungarian Acad. Engring. (chmn. com. theoretical and applied mechanics 1996—), Assn. U. Mechanics, Sigma Xi. Avocations: bridge, stamps. Home: Felso Zoldmali 3/B, H 1025 Budapest Hungary Office: Tech U Budapest Dept Civil Engring Mech, Müegyetem rkp 3, H 1521 Budapest Hungary

GASPARINI, GIAMPIETRO, clinical oncologist; b. Ancona, Marche, Italy, Feb. 5, 1955; s. Mario Gasparini and Franca Folco-Gasparini; m. Daniela Mazzocco, June 18, 1989; 1 child, Gabriella. MD, U. Padua, 1980. Fellow Nat. Cancer Inst., Milan, 1981-84; med. asst. Centro di Riferimento Oncologico, Aviano, Italy, 1984-86; assoc. dir. Clin. Oncology/St. Bortolo Vicenza Hosp., Italy, 1987-97; chief divsn. med. oncology Azienda Ospedaliera Di Reggio Calabria, Italy, 1997—, dir. dept. oncology, 2000—; specialist in oncology U. Padua, 1980-83, clin. pharmacology, 1984-87, oncol. radiotherapy/U. Brescia, Italy, 1988-91; lectr. U. Tor Vergata, Rome, 1993—. Contbr. 165 articles to profl. jours. and publs.; mem. editl. bd. 11 internat. oncological jours.; reviewer oncology articles for several internat. med. jours.; pioneer on clin. applications of rsch. on angiogenesis for mgmt. of cancer patients. Recipient L. Momigliano Sacerdote award Fondazione Italiana per la Ricerca Sul Cancro, Milan, 1993, grantee for projects on breast cancer, 1993—. Mem. Am. Soc. Clin. Oncol., Am. Assn. Cancer Rsch., European Soc. Med. Oncology, European Soc. Mastology, Assn. Italiana Oncol. Med. (Matilde Scalzi award 1987), Coll. Ital. Oncologi Medici. Office: Divsn Med Oncology, Azienda Ospedali Riuniti, Reggio Calabria 89100, Italy

GASPAROVIC, VLADIMIR JOSIP, internist, researcher; b. Bjelovar, Croatia, Jan. 1, 1948; s. Ivan and Ana (Skrtich) G.; m. Stojanka Drakulic, Sept. 6, 1971, (div.); children: Hrvoje, Maja; m. Vesna Elvegy, Apr. 23, 1993; 1 child, Luka. Diploma, Zagreb, Croatia, 1971, Zagreb, Croatia, 1980; Masters, Med. Faculty, Zagreb, Croatia, 1984, PhD, 1988. Med. diplomate. Head of Haemodialysis Interna Clinic, Zagreb, 1985—; vice head postdiploma study Emergency and Intensive Care Med. Faculty, Zagreb; cons. Surgical Intensive Care, Zagreb, General Hosp., Zabok, Croatia. Mem. European Soc. Intensive Care Medicine, Croation Soc. Intensive Care Medicine, Mem. Soc. Croatian Nephrology. Democrat. Roman Catholic. Home: Torbarova 10, 10000 Zagreb Croatia Office: Intensive Care Unit, Rebro Zagreb, 10000 Zagreb Croatia

GASPER, RICHARED JOSEPH, printing company executive; b. Fond Du Lac, Wis., Oct. 11, 1943; s. Harry M. and Valeria M. Gasper; m. Susan A., Nov. 6, 1965; children: Gregory, Rochelle. BBA, U. Wis., 1970. Gen. sales, mktg. mgr., opers. mgr. W.H. Brady Co., Milw., 1963-86; gen. mgr. Sonoco Products Co., Hartsville, S.C., 1986-92; v.p., gen. mgr. Label Products & Design, Green Bay, Wis., 1993-95; pres., CEO Northstar Print Group, Milw., 1996—; prin. Competitive Advantage Inc., Florence, S.C., 1992—; bd. dirs. Raabe Corp., Milw., Jour. Comms., Milw., Perry Printing Corp., Waterloo, Wis. Adv. N.E. Wis. Tech. Coll., Green Bay, Wis., 1993-95; state v.p. Wis. Jaycees, 1975-76, pres. Cudahy (Wis.) Jaycees, 1974-75. Mem. Am. Prodn. and Inventory Control Soc., Milw. World Trade Orgn., Label Pack Converting Inst. (bd. dirs. 1996—), The Exec. Com., Inst. Packaging Profls., Tag and Label Mfrs. Inst. (mem. com. 1993—). Avocations: autoracing, golf, reading, travel. Home: N18 W29856 Crooked Creek Rd Pewaukee WI 53072 Office: Northstar Print Group 5100 W Brown Deer Rd Milwaukee WI 53223-2322

GASPER, RUTH EILEEN, real estate executive; b. Valparaiso, Ind., July 16, 1934; d. Reuben John and Effie (Wesner) Tenpas; m. Ralph L. Gasper, May 25, 1957. Student, Purdue U., 1952-56; BA, Govs. State U., 1982. Analyst computer sys. Leo Burnett Advt., Chgo., 1958-69; nat. adminstr. registrars Sports Car Club Am., Denver, 1977-79; pres. Ainslie Inc., Chgo., 1982—; mem. North River Commn. Housing Com., Chgo., 1982-83, fin. com. Mayor's Task Force on Homelessness City of Chgo. Area coord. Concerned Action party, Lansing, Ill., 1977; chief race registrar Ind. N.W. Region Sports Car Club Am., 1969-80; co-founder, Single Rm. Operators Assn., 1987-98. Mem. Condo. Assn. Dolphin Beach Club (sec. Fantasy Island II). Avocations: sports car racing, classical music.

GASPERINI, MAURIZIO, physicist; b. Cesena, Italy, Mar. 25, 1952; s. Gino and Lilia (Bartolini) G.; m. Patrizia Bolognesi, Sept. 20, 1980; 1 child, Daniela. Diploma, U. Bologna, Italy, 1975, specialization, 1977; PhD in Physics, Ministry of Edn., Rome, 1987. Rschr. U. Turin, Italy, 1983-98; assoc. prof. theoretical physics U. Bari, Italy, 1998—; sci. assoc. European Ctr. Nuclear Rsch., Geneva, 1993, 96-97. Co-author: (with V. de Sabbata) Introduction to Gravitation, 1985; contbr. articles to sci. publs. Recipient awards Gravity Rsch. Found., Mass., 1996, 98. Roman Catholic.

GASPERONI, EMIL, SR., realtor, developer; b. Hillsville, Pa., Nov. 13, 1926; s. Attico and Rose Mary (Sarnicola) G.; m. Ellen Jean Lias, May 28, 1955; children: Samuel Dale, Emil Attico, Jean Ellen. Diploma in real estate, U. Pitts., 1957. Owner, pres. Gasperoni Real Estate, New Castle, Pa., 1956-63, Ft. Lauderdale, Fla., 1965-86; owner, pres. Gasperoni Internat. Group, Longwood, Fla., 1986—; founder, chmn. bd. Fill-R-Up Auto Wash Systems Inc., Ft. Lauderdale, 1967-72. With U.S. Army, 1945-46, ETO. Mem. Nat. Inst. Real Estate Brokers, Fla. Assn. Mortgage Brokers, Sweetwater Country Club, Lake Toxaway Country Club (N.C.). Home: 92 Cold Mountain Rd Lake Toxaway NC 28747-9630 Office: 931 Wekiva Springs Rd Longwood FL 32779-2501

GASPERONI, GIANCARLO, social researcher; b. Detroit, May 6, 1962; s. Giuseppe and Pierina (Pensierini) G. Degree in Polit. Sci., U. Bologna, Italy, 1987; Diploma in Internat. Studies, Johns Hopkins U., Bologna Ctr., 1988; D in Methodology of Social and Polit. Scis., U. Rome, 1992. Rschr. and rsch. dir. Econstat s.r.l., Bologna, 1988-92; cons. dept. Social Policy and Traffic City Adminstrn. of Bologna, 1992—; rschr. and rsch. dir. Istituto Carlo Cattaneo Rsch. Found., Bologna, 1992—; contract prof. U. Urbino Faculty of Edn. Sci., Urbino, Italy, 1995-97; rschr. U. Trento Faculty Sociology, Trento, Italy, 1997-98; faculty U. Bologna, Italy, 1998—; mem. Ministry Pub. Edn. Commn. Experts for the Devel. of Quality and Effectiveness of Schooling and Tng., Rome, 1998. Editor-in-chief: Polis jour., 1995—; author: (books) Scholastic Performance, 1997, Possessors of Diplomas and Educated, 1996, Itanes 1990-96: Italian National Election Studies, 1997, (ency. article) Method and Techniques in the Social Sciences, 1996. Recipient scholarship Johns Hopkins U., Bologna, 1987-88, postdoctorate scholarship U. Bologna, 1993-94. Mem. Assn. Italiana di Sociologia (sec. methodology sect. 1996-00), Internat. Sociol. Assn. (mem. com. on conceptual and terminological analysis 1994—). E-mail: gasperoni@iname.com. Office: Istituto Carlo Cattaneo, Via Santo Stefano 11, 40125 Bologna Italy

GASS, AILEEN, retired accountant; b. Beattock, Scotland, Jan. 15, 1935; d. Hugh and Sarah Montgomery Fergusson (Morrison) Anderson; m. Neil Kenneth Elphick, July 12, 1957 (div. Apr. 1969); 1 child, Vincent Neil; m. Irving Gass, Nov. 5, 1983. Ed., Charles Keen Coll., Leicester, Eng., 1971. Property mgr. London, 1963-68; clerical officer Dept. Employment, Leicester, Eng., 1968-69; tax officer Her Majesty's Insp. of Taxes, Dumfries, Scotland, 1969-73; tax mgr. S. Easton Summers C.A., Lochgilphead, Scotland, 1973-77, T. Alan Pratt & Co., Leicester, Eng., 1977-86; tax acct. Leicester and Lockerbie, Scotland, 1986-98; retired, 1998; cons. Conlon-Williams, C.A., Leicester, Eng., 1988-93. Contbg. poet Contemporary Verse, 1992, His Master's Voice, 1992, Visions in Verse, 1993, Quiet Moments, 1996. Served with Women's Royal Air Force, 1952-57. Recipient Gen. Svc. medal and cross Royal Air Force, Singapore, 1957. Mem. Internat. Soc. Poets (disting.). Avocations: breeding and showing German Shepherd dogs, writing poetry, travel, dancing. Home: 27 Tregarthen, Treverbyn Rd, St Ives Cornwall TR26 1HA, England

GASS, GERTRUDE ZEMON, psychologist, researcher; b. Detroit; d. David Solomon and Mary (Goldman) Zemon; m. H. Harvey Gass, June 19, 1938; children: Susan, Roger. BA, U. Mich., 1937, MSW, 1943, PhD, 1957. Lic. clin. psychologist, Mich. Mem. faculty Merrill-Palmer Inst., Detroit, 1958-69, lectr., 1967; mem. faculty Advanced Behavioral Sci. Ctr., Grosse Pointe, Mich., 1969-72; pvt. practice clin. psychology Birmingham, Mich., 1972—; adj. prof. psychology U. Detroit, 1969-75; cons. Continuum Ctr. Oakland U., Rochester, Mich., 1961-77, Traveler's Aid, Detroit, 1959-75; pres. Shapero Sch. Nursing, Detroit, 1967-72, cons. 1958-78; psychol. cons. Physician's Ins. Co. of Mich., 1988—, mgmt. Mich. Bell Telephone, 1979-82. Mem. Adv. Com Sch. Needs, 1954-56; trustee Sinai Hosp. Detroit, 1972-99; bd. dirs. Tribute Fund United Cmty. Svcs., 1955-67. Fellow Am. Assn. Marriage-Family, Am. Orthopsychiatric Assn. (v.p. 1975-76), Mich. Psychol. Assn.; mem. Am. Psychol. Assn., Psychologists Task Force (v.p. 1977-84), Mich. Inter-Profl. Assn. (pres. 1976-78), Mich. Assn. Marriage Counselors (1979-80, pres. 1979-80), Mental Health Adv. Svc., Blue Cross and Blue Shield of Mich., Phi Kappa Phi, Pi Lambda Theta. Office: 30200 Telegraph Rd Bingham Farms MI 48025-4502

GASSAN-ZADE, SALIM GULERZAEVICH, physicist, researcher; b. Kiev, Ukraine, July 13, 1945; s. Gulerza Rahimovich Gassan-zade and Vera Nikolayevna Hoshtaria; m. Elena Alexeyevna Karetnikova, Nov. 23, 1974; 1 child, Olga. Student, Kiev State U., 1970; PhD in Physics, Inst. Semiconductor Physics, Kiev, 1979. From sr. engr. to jr. rschr. Inst. Semiconductor Physics Ukrainian Nat. Acad. Scis., Kiev, 1972-86, sr. rschr., 1986—; postdoctoral fellow Inst. Semiconductor Physics, Kiev, 1996-98; project dir. Nat. Fundamental Rsch. Found., Kiev, 1996—, dep. dir. SONAR Rsch. Ctr. for Biotechnol. Systems, Ukrainian Nat. Acad. Sci., Kiev, 1997-98. Contbr. articles to profl. jours. Grantee Internat. Sci. Found., 1993, Am. Phys. Soc., 1993, Project grantee Nat. Fundamental Rsch. Found., Kiev, 1996. Mem. N.Y. Acad. Scis., Nat. Geog. Soc., Ukrainian Phys. Soc. Avocations: family weekends, tennis, boat-racing, hunting. Home: Pr Radianskoy Ukrainy 7, Apt 11, 04208 Kiev Ukraine Office: Inst Semiconductor Physics, Pr Nauki 45, 03650 Kiev Ukraine

GASSER, HERNAN JORGE, orthopaedic surgeon; b. Santa Cruz, Bolivia, Oct. 5, 1925; s. Gebhard and Juana (Sanz) G.; m. Franziska Monika Kessler, July 7, 1965; children: Eva Claudia Gasser-Sanz. MD, Med. Faculty U., Basel, Switzerland, 1954. Rsch. fellow pathology von Humboldt Found., Bonn, Germany, 1955-56; gen. intern Mount Sinai Hosp., Chgo., 1956-57; surg. resident Cantonal Hosp. Basel L., Liestal, Switzerland, 1958-63;

orthopaedic resident Children's University Hosp., Basel, 1963-64, N.Y.U. Hosp., 1964-66; head orthopaedic dept. Clinica Caurimare, Caracas, 1967-98; ret., 1998; v.p. Clinica Caurimare, 1977-80. Inventor in field; contbr. numerous articles to sci. jours. Pres. Swiss Benevolent Soc., 1970-97; v.p. Fundacion Benefica Campo Alegre, 1990-96; head adv. bd. Assn. Venezolana-Alemana De Socorro, 1970-97. Recipient Disting. Svc. medal Fed. Republic Germany, 1997. Fellow Internat. Coll. Surgeons; mem. Soc. Venezolana de Ortopedia y Traumatologia, Sociedad Latinoamericana de Ortopedia y Traumatologia. Avocations: neurology, numismatics, history, swimming. Home: 1631 W Mount Vernon Ln Naples FL 34110-8322

GASSER, ROBERT NIKOLAUS ANTONIUS, internist; b. Lienz, Tirol, Austria, Oct. 31, 1959; s. Robert Walter and Sonihild Auguste (Sassarak) G. MD, U. Innsbruck, 1985; PhD, U. Oxford, 1991. Diplomate internal medicine and cardiology. Rschr. U. Innsbruck, 1983-85, intern dept. medicine, 1987-88; rschr. U. Freiburg, Germany, 1985-87; rschr. dept. physiology U. Oxford, U.K., 1988-90; cons. dept. medicine U. Graz, Graz, Styria, Austria, 1990—, head divsn. exptl. cardiology, 1993, prof. internal medicine, 1997—. Author: Compendium of Clinical Electrocardiography, 1987, Antiarteriosclerotic Effect of Calcium Antagonists, 1990, Ionic and Electrical Changes in Early Myocardial Ischaemia, 1990, Die Krete Diat, 1998 (Best Seller); editor: Internat. Jour. Angiology, 1992; founder Jour. Clin. Bas. Cardiology, 1998. Recipient Young Investigator's award Internat. Coll. Angiology, N.Y.C., 1988, Erwin Schroedinger fellowship Austrian Rsch. Found., Vienna, 1986, ORS award Univs. of U.K., Oxford, 1988, Royal Soc. fellowship Royal Soc. London, 1989. Fellow Internat. Coll. Angiology; mem. Oxford and Cambridge Univ. Club, Am. Heart Assn., N.Y. Acad. Scis., Biochem. Soc. Avocations: foster parenting, fine arts, Buddhist art. Home: Gaussgasse 4, Styria Graz A-8010, Austria Office: Medizinische Uni-Klinik, Auenbruggerplatz 15, Styria Styria-Graz A-8036, Austria

GASSER, THOMAS PETER, economist; b. Zurich, Switzerland, July 16, 1933. Licentiate, U. of St. Gallen, Switzerland, 1957; D Nat. Econs., U. Zurich, 1959. Mktg. mgr. Procter & Gamble AG, Geneva, 1959-62; cons. McKinsey & Co., Inc., 1962-69, ptnr. France and Switzerland, 1969-74; sr. v.p., gen. mgr. Alusuisse, Zurich, 1974-82; exec. v.p., mem. BBC Corp. Mgmt., 1982—, CEO, 1987—; dep. CEO ABB Asea Brown Boveri Ltd., Zurich, 1988-96; chmn. bd. Keramik Holding Ltd., Laufen, 1998—, also bd. dirs.; chmn. bd. Asea Brown Bovery Ltd., Zurich. Office: ABB Ltd, PO Box 8131 Affolternstrasse 14, CH 8050 Zurich Switzerland*

GASSMANN, BERTHOLD JOHANNES, food chemist; b. Lutter, Germany, Jan. 3, 1927; s. Karl and Elisabeth (Guempel) G.; m. Renate Gisela Wegner, Sept. 28, 1957 (dec. June 1994); chldren: Christina Maria, Roland Christoph. Degree in Food Chemistry, U. Jena, Germany, 1951; Dr.rer.nat., U. Berlin, 1957, Dr.rer.nat. habilitation, 1967. Sci. asst. U. Jena, 1951-52, Inst. Vitamin Rsch., Potsdam-Rehbruecke, Germany, 1952-64; head dept. Ctrl. Inst. Nutrition, Potsdam-Rehbruecke, 1964-69, head divsn., 1969-82, dep. dir., 1982-88; cons. scientist German Inst. for Nutrition Rsch., Potsdam-Rehbruecke, 1988-94; prof. food chemistry and food tech., 1971—; cons. in field. Editor Ernaehrung's Umschau, 1991—; contbr. articles to profl. jours.; patentee in field. Soldier Germany Mil., 1944-45. Fellow German Soc. Nutrition (mem. presidency 1991—). Roman Catholic. Home: Jean-Paul St 12, D-14558 Bergholz-Rehbruecke Germany

GASTMANS, CHRIS ALBERT ELISABETH, medical ethics educator; b. Herentals, Antwerp, Belgium, Feb. 20, 1966; s. Stefaan Leon and Maria Van Olmen. B in Philosophy, Cath. U., Leuven, Belgium, 1988, D in Theology, 1995. Rschr. Cath. U., 1990-98, asst. prof., 1998—; ethical adviser Caritas Belgium, Brussels, 1995—. Author: Ethisch Zorg Verlenen, rev. edit. 1998; editor: Verpleegkundige Excellentie 2000 Book; editl. bd. Nursing Ethics, 1993—. Roman Catholic. Avocations: traveling, walking. Office: Centre Biomed Ethics & Law, Kapucynenvoer 35, 3000 Leuven Brabant Belgium

GASTON, BONNIE FAYE JAMES, elementary education educator; b. Littlefield, Tex., Apr. 17, 1931; d. John William and Kittie (Drake) James; m. Milburn Fenton Gaston, May 26, 1954; children: Terry Lynn, Dale Weldon, Randy Lee. BS in Edn., Tex. Tech U., 1952, postgrad. Tchr. Plainview, Tex., 1952-54, 55-58, San Angelo, Tex., 1954-55, Hale Ctr., Tex., 1968-72, 74-76, Olton, Tex., 1977-93; condr. elem. tchrs. workshops, mem. sch. evaluating vis. team, elem. math. and reading cons. Author, pub.: Gaston Enrichment Skills, 1979. Dist. sec. PTA. Recipient Outstanding Young Homemaker award State Senator Andy Rogers, Notable Women of Tex. award, 1984-85. Mem. Tex. Assn. for Improvement Reading (cons. West Tex. U.), Assn. Tex. Profl. Educators (local pres., sec. dist. 17), AAUW, Smithsonian Assocs., Nat. Mus. Women in Arts, Delta Kappa Gamma. Baptist. Avocations: art, reading, developing children's materials. Home: 1119 Holiday St Plainview TX 79072-6045

GASTON, MARGARET ANNE, retired business educator; b. Regina, Sask., Can., Aug. 28, 1930; Came to U.S., 1948.; d. William Julius and Mary Josephine (Collins) Grogan; m. Robert F. Gaston, 1955 (dec. Mar. 1970); 1 child, Robert. BA in Bus. Edn., Cen. Wash. U., 1959; MEd, Western Wash. U., 1972; postgrad., Boston U., 1984. Cert. tchr. K-12, cert. vocat. tchr., Wash. Bus. educator Manson (Wash.) Sch. Dist., 1956-59; instr. K-12 Eastmont Sch. Dist., East Wenatchee, Wash., 1959-63; instr. Shoreline Community Coll., Seattle, 1969-70; instr., chmn. dept. bus. Skagit Valley Coll. Whidbey Campus, Oak Harbor, Wash., 1970-90; part-time instr. bus. edn. Wenatchee Valley Coll., 1959-65. Contbr. articles to profl. jours. Fellow Western Wash. U., Bellingham, 1968-69. Mem. AAUW, NEA, Wash. Edn. Assn., Bus. and Profl. Women, Delta Pi Epsilon, Beta Sigma Phi. Home: # 20 2610 Little Mountain Rd # 20 Mount Vernon WA 98274-8315

GASZTOWTT, GUILLAUME PIERRE, finance company executive; b. Boulogne, France, June 11, 1949; s. Thadée and Marie Therese (de Marcellus) G.; m. Yolaine de Sinçay, Sept. 28, 1978; children: Ladislas, Lara, Alexis, Raphael, Priscilla. BA in Math. and Philosophy, Ecole St Louis Gonzague, Paris, 1967; student in engring., Ecole Poly., Paris, 1971; postgrad., Ecole Nat. Adminstrn., Paris, 1977. Sous-prefet French State, Nancy, France, 1977-78; sous-prefet, sec. gen. French State, Chaumont, France, 1978-80; inspector fin. French State, Paris, 1981-83; dir. Worms Bank, Paris, 1984-88; mem. mng. bd., CFO Promodes, Paris, 1993—. Served with French army, 1971-74. Mem. Circle du Bois de Boulogne, Club des Trente. Roman Catholic. Avocations: tennis, skiing, equitation. Office: Promodes, 123 Rue Jules Guesde, 92309 Levallois France

GAT, AZAR, history educator; b. Haifa, Isreal, June 24, 1959; s. Eli and Josepha (Ram) G.; m. Ruth Reich, Oct. 11, 1983; children: Tamara, Jonathan. BA, Haifa (Isreal) U., 1978; MA, Tel-Aviv U., 1983; PhD, Oxford U., Eng., 1986. Asst. prof. Tel-Aviv U., 1987-91, assoc. prof., 1991—; chmn. dept. polit. sci. Tel-Aviv U., 1999. Author: The Origins of Military Thought, 1989, The Development of Military Thought, 1992, Fascist and Liberal Visions of War, 1998, British Armour Theory and the Rese of the Panzer Arm, 2000. Maj. Israeli Army Res. Brit. Coun. scholar Britain, 1993, Alexander Von Humboldt scholar Germany, 1993, Fulbright scholar Yale U., 1994. Home: 9 Ha'eshel Street, 52435 Ramat Gan Israel Office: Tel Aviv U, Dept Pol Sci, 69978 Tel Aviv Israel

GATEAU, JEAN-CHARLES, literature educator; b. Tunis, Tunisia, Dec. 4, 1932; s. Albert Charles and Jeanne Marie (Besancon) G.; m. Claude Dominique Balsollier, Apr. 11, 1956 (div. 1968); children: Alain, Gilles; m. Marie-Christine Brachard, Oct. 14, 1968; children: Arielle, Sibylle. BA, Rabat, Morokko, 1950; Lic. de Lettres Classiques, Sorbonne, Paris, 1954; Agregation de Lettres Classiques, France, 1960, PhD, 1980. Tchr. Coll. Aurillac, France, 1960-61, Coll. Poitiers, France, 1961-67, Coll. Evian, France, 1967-71, Coll. St. Julien-en-Genevois, France, 1971-73; asst. Stendhal U., Grenoble, France, 1973-85, prof., 1985—; dean of arts Stendhal U., 1989-92. Author: Paul Eluard et la peinture surrealiste, 1982, Paul Eluard, Picasso et la peinture, 1983, Abecedaire critique, 1987, Eluard ou le Frere Voyant, 1988, Capitale de la douleur d' Eluard, 1991, Le parti pris des choses de Francis Ponge, 1997, La Representation Picturale, 1999. V.p. L.A.C., Douvaine, France, 1991-2000. Cpl. French infantry, 1958-60. Mem. Rsch. Ctr. on Representation Crisis. Avocation: journalism. Home: Route de la Marianne, 74140 Chens-sur-Leman France

GATES, BILL (III WILLIAM HENRY GATES), software company executive; b. Seattle, Wash., Oct. 28, 1955; s. William H. and Mary M. (Maxwell) G.; m. Melinda French, January 1, 1994. Grad. high sch., Seattle, 1973; student, Harvard U., 1973-75. With MITS, from 1975; founder, chmn. bd. Microsoft Corp., Redmond, Wash., 1976-99, now also chief exec. officer, 1999—, chief creative officer, 1999—. Author: The Future, 1994, The Road Ahead, 1995, Business at the Speed of Thought, 1999. Recipient Howard Vollum award, Reed Coll., Portland, Oreg., 1984, Nat. medal Tech. U.S. Dept. Commerce Tech. Adminstrn., 1992; named CEO of Yr., Chief Executive mag., 1994. Office: Microsoft Corp 1 Microsoft Way Redmond WA 98052-8300

GATES, BRIAN EDWARD, religious studies educator; b. Morecambe, Eng., Oct. 23, 1942; s. Edward and Dorothy (Taylor) G.; m. Brenda Fox, Aug. 8, 1967; children: Christopher, Jonathan. BA in Theology with honors, St. Johns Coll., Oxford U., 1964; STM, Yale U., 1966; PGCE, Cambridge U., 1967; PhD, Lancaster U., 1975. Lectr. Goldsmiths' Coll., U. London, 1967-69, sr. lectr., 1969-73; prin. lectr. Goldsmith's Coll., U. London, 1973-75; prof, head dept. religion and ethics U. Coll. of St. Martin, Lancaster, U.K., 1975—; cons. in field; external examiner Higher Edn. Instn., 1982—; dir. Electronic Media and Religions Project, UCSM, 1995—; rsch. cons. Nat. Rev. of Collective Worship in Schs., 1996—. Editor: Afro-Caribbean Religions, 1980, Freedom and Authority in Religions and Religious Education, 1996; editor, author: Religious Education Directory of England and Wales, 1982; author: Time for RE and Teachers to Match, 1994; chair editl. bd. Jour. of Moral Edn., 1983—. Fulbright Travel scholarship, 1964-66; Hockerill lectr., 1989. Mem. Religious Edn. Coun. of England and Wales (chmn. 1984-90), SHAP Working Party on World Religions in Education. Avocations: skiing, walking, archeology. Home: Keer Grange Capernway, LA6 1AD, Carnforth England Office: Univ Coll St Martin, Lancaster LA13JD, England

GATES, LAURA DAIGNAULT, museum executive; b. Hartford, Conn., May 29, 1950; d. Alfred P. and Jeane Lacine Daignault; m. Stephen F. Gates. AB in Econs., Wellesley Coll., 1972; MBA, Harvard U., 1976. Investment mgr. Harvard Mgmt. Co., Boston, 1976-77; dir. strategic planning Maremont Corp., Chgo., 1977-80; cons. McKinsey & Co., Chgo., 1980-88, ptnr., 1988-94; v.p. mus. affairs Field Mus. of Natural History, Chgo., 1994-98, v.p. internat., 1999-2000; dir. AML Residential Properties Trust, Chgo., 1996—. Mem. Chgo. Wellesley Club (pres. 1995-96), Wellesley Bus. Leadership Coun. (co-chair 1998-00).

GATES, RONALD CECIL, retired beef cattle breeder; b. Melbourne, Victoria, Australia, Jan. 8, 1923; s. Earle Nelson Gates and Elsie Edith Tucker; m. Barbara Mann, Dec. 19, 1953; children: Christopher (dec.), Felicity, Angela, Jeremy. B of Commerce, U. Tasmania, Hobart, Australia, 1946; BA, Oxford U., Eng., 1948, MA, 1952; D Econs., U. Queensland, Australia, 1978; DLitt, U. New England, 1986. Clk. Australia Taxation Office, Hobart, Tasmania, 1941-42; historian Australia Taxation Office, Canberra, Australia, 1949-52; sr. lectr. in econs. U. Sydney, N.S.W., Australia, 1952-64, assoc. prof. in econs., 1964-65; prof. econs. U. Queensland, Brisbane, 1966-77, pres. profl. bd., 1975-77, dean of faculty of commerce and econs., 1966-69, 71-74; vice-chancellor U. New Eng., Armidale, N.S.W., Australia, 1977-85; cons. City of South Melbourne, 1969-71, Papua New Guinea Adminstrn., Port Moresby, 1970-72, City of Subiaco, Perth, Western Australia, 1972-73, Media Coun. of Australia, Melbourne, 1976; sr. econ. adviser UN Econ. Commn. for Asia and the Far East, Bangkok, 1970-73. Author: La Septaga Murdenigmo, 1991, Sep Krimnoveloj, 1993, Kolera Afero, 1993, Refoje Krimnoveloj Sep, 1994, Morto de Sciencisto, 1994, Tria Kolekto da Krimnoveloj, 1996, La Vidvino kaj la Profesoro, 1997; co-author: Survey of Consumer Finances, Sydney, 1963-65, 7 vols., 1965-67, Simulation, Uncertainty and Public Investment Analysis, 1977; editor Econ. Papers, 1963-65, Econ. Analysis and Policy, 1970-74. Pres. Indsl. Rels. Soc. of Queensland, 1967-73, Australian Esperanto Assn., 1998-2001; chmn. Statutory Consumer Affairs Coun. of Queensland, 1971-73; commr. Commonwealth Commn. of Inquiry into Poverty, Canberra, 1973-77; chair Australian Inst. of Urban Studies, 1975-77, Adv. Coun. for Inter-Govt. Rels., Hobart, 1979-85; mem. Advt. Standards Coun., Sydney, 1974-79, Commonwealth Govt. Econ. Adv. Group, Canberra, 1976-83, others; dep. leader Australian delegation to extraordinary session of UNESCO Gen. Conf., Paris, 1982, 83, others. Rhodes scholar Rhodes Trust, Oxford U., 1946, Rockefeller fellow in the Social Scis. Rockefeller Found., Britain and Europe, 1955, Carnegie Travel grantee Carnegie Corp. of N.Y., 1960, Officer in the Order of Australia, 1978, others. Fellow Acad. Social Scis. in Australia, Royal Australian Planning Inst., Australian Inst. Urban Studies; mem. Econ. Soc. Australia and New Zealand (pres. 1969-72). Avocations: beef cattle breeding, music, Esperanto, bridge. Home: Wangarang MSF 2001, Armidale NSW 2350, Australia

GATEVA, PAVLINA ANGELOVA, biochemist, educator, researcher; b. Dalgodelci, Montana, Bulgaria, Aug. 8, 1937; d. Angel Todorov and Galunka Georgieva (Simeonova) P.; m. Geo Ivanov Gatev, Jan. 3, 1968; children: Geo Geov, Ivan Geov. MD, Med. U., Sofia, Bulgaria, 1961; PhD, Rsch. Inst. Pediatrics Med. U., 1971, DMS, 1987. Physician Ministry of Health, Ardino, Bulgaria, 1962-64; rsch. fellow Ctr. Gerontology Med. U., 1964-72, rsch. fellow Rsch. Inst. Pediatrics, 1972-87, sr. rsch. fellow Rsch. Inst. Endocrinology and Gerontology, 1987—, head clin. chem. lab., 1998—. Co-author: Textbook of Toxicology, 1985, Endocrinology, 1993; contbr. over 100 articles to profl. jours.; 4 inventions. Mem. Bulgarian Union of Scientists, N.Y. Acad. Sci. Eastern Orthodox. Avocations: painting, literature, music, traveling. Home: ZK Buckstone bl 10 Apt 57, 1618 Sofia Bulgaria Office: Clin Ctr Endocrinology Gero, Blvd Dame Gruev #6 Med U, 1303 Sofia Bulgaria

GATEWOOD, ROBERT PAYNE, financial planning executive; b. Nebr., Mar. 4, 1923; s. Robert Harvey and Bess (Payne) G.; m. Marilyn Wengert, June 6, 1946; children: Robert, Lottie, Traber, Cy, Marilyn, Bess, John, Anthony, Judemarie, Anne, Tressa, Joseph, Ruth. BS, U.S. Naval Acad., 1946; postgrad., La. State U., 1974. CLU. Estate planner J.D. Marsh & Assocs., 1950-56; pres. estate planning Fin. Corp. Am., 1956-61; pres. Robert P. Gatewood & Co., 1961-99; owner, operator Early Cellular Telephone Co.; internat. lectr. Contbr. articles to profl. jours. With USN, 1946-50. Recipient Bernard L. Wilner Meml. award. Mem. D.C. Assn. Life Underwriters (pres. 1965-66), Assn. Advanced Life Underwriting Million Dollar Round Table, Am. Soc. CLUs & Chartered Fin. Cons. (pres. 1975-76), Washington D.C. Estate Planning Coun., East Coast Estate Planning Coun., Fla. Assn. CLUs and ChFCs, Palm Beach Assn. Life Underwriters, 25 Million Dollar Internat. Dorum (founder), Knights Malta. Republican. Home: 6 Loggerhead Ln Manalapan FL 33462

GATEWOOD, TELA LYNNE, lawyer; b. Cedar Rapids, Iowa, Mar. 23; d. Chester Russell and Cecilia Mae (McFarland) Weber. BA with distinction, Cornell Coll., Mt. Vernon, Iowa, 1970; JD with distinction, U. Iowa, 1972. Bar: Iowa 1973, Calif. 1974, U.S. Supreme Ct. 1984. Instr. LaVerne Coll., Pt. Mugu, Calif., 1973; asst. city atty. City of Des Moines, 1973-78; sr. trial atty. and supervisory atty. EEOC, Dallas, Phila., 1978-91, acting regional atty. Dallas Dist., 1987-89; adminstrv. judge EEOC, Dallas, 1991-94; adminstrv. law judge Social Security Adminstrn., Oklahoma City, 1994—. Bd. dirs. Day Care Inc., Des Moines, 1975-78, sec., 1977, pres., 1978. Mem. ABA (labor law, litigation, govt. svc., judiciary sects.), NAFE, Nat. Assn. Female Judges, Fed. Bar Assn., U.S. Supreme Ct. Bar Assn., Calif. Bar Assn. Office: Social Security Adminstrn Office of Hearings and Appeals 420 W Main St Ste 400 Oklahoma City OK 73102-4435*

GATHEN, JOACHIM VON ZUR, information science educator; b. Solingen, Germany, Feb. 14, 1950; m. Dorothea von zur Gathen; children: Rafaela, Désirée. Diploma, ETH, Zürich, Switzerland, 1973; PhD, U. Zürich, 1980. Prof. U. Toronto, Ont., Can., 1981-94, U. Paderborn, Germany, 1994—; vis. prof. U. Zürich, 1984-85, U. Catolica, Santiago, Chile, 1988, Australian Nat. U., Canberra, 1989, ETH Zürich, 1993, Macquarie U., Sydney, 1997; vis. rschr. Internat. Computer Sci. Inst., Berkeley, Calif., 1996; cons. IBM Rsch. Lab., Yorktown Heights, N.Y., 1986, U. Witswatersrand, Johannesburg, 2000. Editor-in-chief Computational Complexity, 1991—; editor procs. Internat. Symposium on Symbolic and Algebraic Computation, 1994, SIAM Jour. on Computing, 1995—, Finite Fields and Their Applications, 1995—, Jour. Symbolic Computation, 1996—. Recipient Disting. Svc. award Assn. Computing Machinery, 1994, tchg. award CSSU, U. Toronto, 1992. Mem. Assn. Computing Machinery Spl. Interest Group for Symbolic and Algebraic Maniputation, Spl. Interest Group for Automata and Computation Theory. Avocations: languages, hiking, travel. Office: Fachbereich Math-Info, U Paderborn, 33095 Paderborn Germany

GATINSKY, YURY GEORGE, geologist, researcher; b. Moscow, Aug. 3, 1934; s. George and Helena Peter (Yakovleva) G.; m. Gertrude Joan Spiryakova, June 9, 1959 (div. Apr. 1985); children: Helena, Catherine; m. Nina Valentine Usova, Aug. 10, 1990. Geologist, Lomonosov State U., Moscow, 1958, M of Geology, 1972; DSc in Geology, Russian Acad. Scis., 1983. Cert. in geol. surveying and prospecting. Geologist, chief of group N.E. Geol. Bd., Magadan, Russia, 1958-65; from jr. to sr. to leading rschr. All-Russian Inst. Fgn. Country Geology, Moscow, 1965-94; leading rschr. Vernadsky State Geol. Mus., Russian Acad. Scis., Moscow, 1994—; cons. on stratigraphy Group of Russian Geologists, Bamako, Mali, 1963-65; cons. on stratigraphy and tectonics Group of Russian Geologists, Hanoi, Vietnam, 1968-69, 83-85, 89-91; cons. on geology Ministry of Economy, Vientiane, Laos, 1975; cons. on geol. mapping Ministry of Economy, Pnom Penh, Cambodia, 1988; mem. acad. bd. Geol. Inst., Russian Acad. Scis., 1986—, People Friendship U., Moscow, 1991—. Author: Lateral Structural-Stratigraphic Analyses, 1986 (3d degree diploma 1989); co-author: Global Correlation of Tectonic Movements, 1987; contbr. articles to profl. jours. Sci. sec. 27th Internat. Geol. Congress, Colloquium 05, Moscow, 1984. Recipient Friendship medal Govt. Vietnam, 1969, Gold diploma Organizing Com. 27th Internat. Geol. Congress, Moscow, 1984, Labour-Vet. medal Municipality of Moscow, 1988. Mem. Moscow Soc. Nature Rschrs. (3d degree diploma). Democrat. Orthodox. Avocations: classical music, jazz, Russian poetry of the Silvery Age, skiing, running. Home: 7-72 Lev Tolstoy str, 140007 Lyubertzy Moscow, Russia Office: Vernadsky State Geol Mus, 11 bld 2 Mokhovaya str, 103009 Moscow Russia

GATLIN, DANIEL GARETH, artist, psychologist, psychotherapist; b. Phoenix, Ariz., Apr. 11, 1957. BA in Anthropology summa cum laude, Chapman U., 1979, BA in Art, 1979; MA in Psychology, U.S. Internat. U., San Diego, 1990; PhD in Psychology, U.S. Internat. U., 1995. Planner Phelps Dodge Corp., Morenci, 1979-80; ceramic sculptor/designer Stoneware Unltd., Inc., Santa Ana, Calif., 1980-86; dir. adminstrn. Alternative Ways Inc., Long Beach, Calif., 1986-87; video editor, videographer Belmont Prodns., Long Beach, 1988-90; instr. Loyola Marymount U., L.A., 1990; case mgr. St. John's Hosp., Santa Monica, Calif., 1990-93; clin. supr. Jefferson Alcohol and Drug Abuse Program, Louisville, 1994-96; clin. mgr. chem. dependency unit Bapt. East Hosp., Louisville, 1996-98; unit mgr., psychologist Ctr. Supported Living, Louisville, 1998—; dir. edn. Fellowship of Pachamama, 1989—. Editor, art dir. For Love and For Life, 1988; dir., prodr.: (video documentary) A Shaman's World, 1989. Mem. APA, Nat. Assn. Alcohol and Drug Abuse Counselors, Ky. Psychol. Assn. Avocations: painting, medieval and celtic harp, writing.

GATON, DAN DINU, ophthalmologist, researcher; b. Bucharest, Romania, May 30, 1958; arrived in Israel, 1961; s. Radu and Edith (Merdinger) G.; m. Danna Gold, Oct. 22, 1962; 1 child, Dor. MD, Tel Aviv U., 1987, M in Ophthalmology with distinction, 1993. Intern Hillel Yaffe Med. Ctr., Hedera, Israel, 1986-87; intern Beilinson campus Rabin Med. Ctr., Petah Tikva, Israel, 1987; resident in ophthalmology Beilinson Med. Ctr., Petah Tikva, Israel, 1988-92; sr. ophthalmologist Shiba Med. Ctr., Tel Hashomer, Israel, 1993-94, Beilinson Med. Ctr., 1994—; clin., rsch. fellowship in glaucoma U. Calif., San Diego, Calif., 1997-98; rsch. fellow in histopathology Sackler Sch. Medicine, Tel Aviv U., 1990, lectr., 1991—, assoc. dir. pre-clin. studies N.Y. State/Am. program, 1992—; head ophthalmology outpatient clinic, dir. ambulatory svc. Beilinson campus Rabin Med. Ctr., 1995—. Co-author: General Pathology, 1984, 2d edit., 1987, Systemic Pathology I, 1994, Systemic Pathology II, 1997, Abbreviations in Medicine, 1997, 2d edit., 1999; contbr. articles to profl. and sci. jours. Mem. Israel Med. Assn., Israel Ophthalmol. Soc., Soc. for Medicine and Law in Israel (bd. dirs. 1995—), Am. Soc. Cataract and Refractive Surgery, Am. Acad. Opthalmology, Assn. for Rsch. in Vision and Ophthalmology, N.Y. Acad. Scis. Avocations: music, travel, philately. Home: Sokolov Str 39, 62485 Tel Aviv Israel Office: Rabin Med Ctr, Beilinson Campus, 49100 Petah Tikva Israel

GATOPOULOS, DENIS G., computer science and electrical engineer; b. Patra, Greece, Oct. 3, 1952; s. George D. and Amalia G. (Androutselli) G.; m. Angeliki C. Bakanaki, Sept. 22, 1984; children: George, Helena. Grad. Maitrise d'Informatique, U. Grenoble, 1975, degree in bus. adminstrn., 1976; MSEE, Wichita State U., 1978. Rsch. asst. Wichita State U., 1977; rschr. Rsch. Ctr. Nat. Def., Athens, 1979-80; systems programmer Peiraiki-Patraiki Mfg. Co., Athens, 1980-82; cons. info. tech. specialist IBM Hellas S.A., Athens, 1982—. Mem. Tech. Chamber of Greece, IEEE, Greek Computer Soc. Avocations: travel, photography, music, gardening, tennis. Home: G Lyra 94, 145 64 Kifisia Greece Office: IBM Hellas SA, Kifisias Ave 284, 152 32 Halandri Greece

GATT, SHIMON, biochemistry educator; b. Lublin, Poland, Sept. 29, 1926; s. Zadok and Bathsheva (Horowitz) Greenwald; m. Hanna Grreenwald; children: Orna, Lihi, Moshe. MS, Hebrew U., Jerusalem, 1950; PhD, Columbia U., 1956. From lectr. to prof. Hebrew U., Jerusalem, 1958-71, prof. emeritus, 1994—; vis. scientist Albert Einstein Coll. Medicine, N.Y.C., 1963-64, U. Calif., San Diego, 1968-69, Mt. Sinai Med. Sch., N.Y.C., 1980-81, 81-99. Contbr. 225 articles to profl. jours. Lt. Israeli Defense Forces, 1948-49, 50. Postdoctoral fellow Pub. Health Rsch. Inst., N.Y.C., 1955-57. Home: 11 Bartanura St, 92104 Jerusalem Israel Office: Hebrew U Hadassah Sch Med, Dept Biochemistry, 91120 Jerusalem Israel

GATT, SUZANNA, physics educator; b. Attard, Malta, Apr. 3, 1967; d. Ernest and Alice (Cachia) Balzan; m. Kevin Gatt, July 11, 1992. BEd with honors, U. Malta, 1990, postgrad., 1995—; MA in Sci. Edn., U. London, 1993. Tchr. Edn. Divsn., Malta, 1990-94; lab. demonstator physics U. Malta, 1993-95, paper setter, marker intermediate physics, 1997—, chairperson physics nat. exams, paper setter, examiner physics sch. leaving nat exams; examiner practical work-A level physics U. London, Malta, 1990-92; coord. conf. in sci. edn. U . Malta/Malta Coun. for Sci. and Tech., 1997; coord. Working Project in Distance Learning in Sci. for Elem. Tchrs., 1998. Mem. Inst. Physics (grad.). Roman Catholic. Avocations: crafts, English literature, antiques, home decorating. E-mail: sgat1@educ.um.edu.mt. Fax: 356 317938. Home: triq il-linja, Attard BZN 05, Malta Office: Faculty Edn Univ Malta, Tal-Qroqq, Msida MSD 06, Malta

GATTI, GABRIELE, San Marinese government official; b. Domagnano, Mar. 27, 1953. Sec. state for fgn. and polit. affairs San Marino, 1986—. Office: Min Foreign & Political Affairs, Palazzo Begni Contrada Omerelli, 47890 San Marino San Marino

GATT-RUTTER, JOHN ARTHUR, Italian studies educator, literary translator; b. Malta, July 3, 1941; arrived in Australia, 1987; s. Tancred Edward and Teresa (Caruana Galizia) G.-R.; m. Esther Onajite Oberia, June 4, 1986; children: Nkemfuni Angelo, Roseanne Ifeanyi, Tessa Uche. BA, Cambridge (Eng.) U., 1962, MA, 1983; Cert. Applied Linguistics and Teaching English, U. Essex, Eng., 1983. Asst. lectr. Univ. Coll. Wales, Aberystwyth, 1963-64; asst. lectr. U. Hull, Eng., 1964-66, lectr., 1966-76, sr. lectr., 1976-83; lectr. Griffith U., Brisbane, Australia, 1987-89, sr. lectr., 1990; prof. Italian, La Trobe U., Melbourne, Australia, 1991—. Author: Writers and Politics in Modern Italy, 1978, Italo Svevo—A Double Life, 1988, Alias Italo Svevo, 1991, Oriana Fallaci-The Rhetoric of Freedom, 1996; editor: Novel Turns--Critical Perspectives on Recent Narrative Writing from Western Europe. Office: La Trobe U, Melbourne, Bundoora 3083, Australia

GATTULLO, FRANCESCA ELENA, language educator, trainer, consultant; b. Bologna, Italy, Oct. 25, 1964; d. Mario Cattullo and Rosalia Mustacchia. Degree in philosophy, U. Bologna, Italy, 1990; MA in Applied Linguistics, U. Reading, Eng., 1992; DEd, U. Rome La Sapienze, 1998. Lang. asst. U. Reading, 1992-94, U. Warwick, Coventry, Eng., 1994-95; cons. Comune Di Bologna, Italy, 1997; lectr. U. Bologna, 1998-99; fellow U. Trieste, 1999—. Contbr. articles to profl. jours. Fundraiser Amnesty Internat., Reading, 1993-94. Postgrad. grantee U. Bologna, 1991-92; TMR scholar European Union, 1997-98. Avocations: cello player in Baroque

ensemble, hiking, cycling. Home: via M De' Maria 2, I-40129 Bologna Italy Office: U Bologna SSLIT, Via Repubblica, Forli Italy

GATTUPALLI, NARESHKUMAR, biochemistry educator; b. Guntur, Andhra Pradesh, India, Dec. 20, 1956; s. Krishnamurthy Mannara and Anjanee (Murthy) G.; m. Archana Gayatri, Dec. 28, 1988; 1 child, Srujana. MS in Chemistry with honors, Birla Inst. Tech. and Sci., India, 1980; PhD in Molecular Biology, Tata Inst. Fundamental Rsch., Bombay, 1989. Postdoct. fellow dept. biology Rice U., Houston, 1987-88; scientific officer Bhabha Atomic Rsch. Ctr., Bombay, 1989-90; lectr. dept. biochemistry M.S. U. Baroda, Vadodera, India, 1990-96; reader dept. biochemistry M.S. U. Barode, Vadodera, 1996—. Recipient Nat. Sci. Talent Search award Nat. Coun. Ednl. Rsch. Tng., 1974. Office: MS U Baroda Faculty Sci, Dept Biochemistry, 390 002 Vadodara India

GATZOULIS, KOSTAS ATHANDSIOUS, physician; b. Drama, Macedonia, Greece, Oct. 14, 1956; s. Athanasios K. and Soteria M. (Papadopoulos) G.; m. Lila H. Sklavi, Feb. 12, 1956; children: Nasos, Rozita. MD, U. Thessaloniki, Greece, 1980; PhD, U. Athens, Greece, 1993. Diplomate Am. Bd. Internal Medicine, Am. Bd. Cardiology. Dir. Med. Cmty. Ctr., Paranesti, Greece, 1983-84; resident Couvahoga County Hosp., Cleve., 1984-87; resident in cardiology Univ. Hosps. Cleve., 1987-89, fellow in electrophysiology, 1989-91; cardiology cons. Univ. Hippokration Hosp., Athens, 1991—; asst. prof. cardiology Univ. Thessalia, Larissa, Greece, 1995-97. Contbr. articles to profl. jours. Sgt. Air Force, 1981-83, Athens. Mem. Hellenic Cardiology Soc., Athens Mem. Soc., N.Y. Acad. Sci. Greek Orthodox. Avocations: tennis, music, sailing. Home: Fragoyiani 34, 15669 Papagos Greece Office: Skoufa 77, Kolonaki 106-80, Greece

GAUCHER, DONALD HOLMAN, public opinion research company executive; b. Port Arthur, Tex., Aug. 2, 1931; s. Leon Phillip and Hattie Lu (Holman) G.; m. Jane Peel Heyck, June 15, 1957; children: Susan Heyck, Beverly Jane. BA, The Rice Inst., Houston, 1953, BSChemE, 1954; grad., Sch. of Reactor Tech., Oak Ridge, Tenn., 1955; JD cum laude, U. Houston, 1962. With Humble Oil and Refining Co., Houston, 1957-64, Std. Oil (N.J.), N.Y.C., 1964-68, Exxon Co. USA, Houston, 1968-91; pres. Gaucher Rsch. Assoc., Houston, 1991—; mem. pub. opinion task force Am. Petroleum Inst., Washington, 1986-91, Chem. Mfrs. Assn., Washington, 1991-96; cons. Exxon Chem. Co., Houston, 1991-97. Pres. Mus. So. History, Sugar Land, Tex., 1997-99. Mem. Am. Nuc. Soc., Am. Inst. Mining, Metall. and Petroleum Engrs., Am. Assn. Pub. Opinion Rsch., Tex. Bar Assn., Kiwanis, Sons of Confederate Vets. (past comdr. Albert Sidney Johnston Camp), Mil. Order of Stars and Bars (past comdr.), Sons of the Republic of Tex., Terry's Tex. Rangers Assn., Order of Barons, Phi Delta Phi. Avocations: tennis, bird photography, golf. E-mail: texasdhg@aol.com. Home: 1905B Potomac Dr Houston TX 77057-2921

GAUCHER, ELISABETH MARIE, French language and literature educator; b. Maubeuge, France, Nov. 19, 1964; d. René and Madeleine (Monateri) G. Grad., Ecole Normale Supérieure, Paris, 1985; Maîtrise in Greek Lit., U. Paris IV, Sorbonne, 1986, Agrégation in Classical Lit., 1987, Lic. in History, 1988; D in Medieval French Lit., U. Paris III, 1993. With U. Paris XII, Créteil, 1987-89, U. Paris III, Sorbonne, 1989-92, U. Orléans, 1992-93, U. Lille III, France, 1993—; asst. in Latin, U. Paris XII, 1987-89; asst. in French lit. U. Paris III, 1989-92; asst. in French lit. and lang. U. Orléans, 1992-93; maître de conf. in French lit. and lang. U. Lille III, 1993. Author: La Biographie Chevaleresque, 1994; (with L. Mathey) Le Chevalier de la Charrette, 1996; (with J. Dufournet) L'Hagiographie, 1998; (with F. Lestringant) Topiques Romanesques: Réécriture des romans médiévaux, 1999. Mem. Soc. Medieval Lang. and Lit., Ctr. Medieval Study and Dialect, U. Lille, Ctr. Burgundian Lit. and Soc. XIVth-XVth Century. Home: 11 rue Emile Desmet, 59800 Lille France Office: Univ Lille III, B P 149, 59653 Villeneuve d'Ascq France

GAUCI-MAISTRE, JOHN A., finance company executive; b. Sliema, Malta, Dec. 27, 1947; s. Agostino and Winnifred (Mifsud) G-M.; m. Ann Marie Pace; m. Rebecca, Sarah, Jean Pie, Greta. Articled clerk Turquand, Young & Co., London; sr. auditor Southwell & Tyrell, London; chmn. Economicard Worldwide Ltd., Valletta, Malta, 1973—, GM Internat. Svcs. Ltd., Valletta, 1974—; dir. Datavision Ltd., Valletta, 1984—; mng. dir. G.M. Nominee Ltd., Valetta, 1990—; hon. consul gen. Panama in Malta Consulate of Panama, Valletta, 1994—; dir. GM Corporate & Fiduciary Svcs. Ltd., 1998—; dir. Fiars and Exhibitions Ltd., Internat. Confs. and Exhbns. Ltd.; coun. mem. Malta Trade Corp. Mem. Assn. Hon. Consuls (pres.), Fedn. des Unions des Consuls Honoraires en Europe (pres.), Maltese-Italian C. of C. (hon. sec.). Avocation: sailing. Fax: 356 220101, 244821. E-mail: jagm@gmint.com. Office: Economicard Group of Cos, 147/1 St Lucia Street, VLT 04 Valletta Malta

GAUDART, HYACINTH MARIE, educator; b. Malacca, Malaysia, Apr. 8, 1946; d. Stennard William and Josephine Theresa (Gomes) Bell. BA, Univ. Malaya, 1969; MA, Univ. Leeds, 1977; diploma, Univ. Malaya, 1970; EdD, Univ. Hawaii, 1984. Tchr. Sultan Abu Bakar Sec. Sch., Muar Johor, Malaysia, 1979-72, Tun Fatimah Sec. Sch., Johor Baru, Malaysia, 1973-75; lectr. Univ. Malaya, Kuala Lumpur, Malaysia, 1978-88, assoc. prof., 1988-95, prof., 1995—. Author: Reaching Out to Learners, 1997, Bilingual Education in Malaysia, 1992; editor: The English Teacher, 1986-92; composer collection songs for language learning, 1993. Recipient EWC Makana award East West Ctr., 1983, Newman Ctr. award Newman Ctr., 1982. Mem. Malaysian English Lang. Teaching Assn. (pres. 1992-96, 98—, v.p. 1996-98), East West Ctr. Alumni Assn. of Malaysia (com. mem. 1996—). Avocation: writing. Office: U Malaya, 50603 Kuala Lumpur Malaysia

GAUDEAU, CLAUDE JULES MICHEL, biomedical engineer; b. Tours, Centre, France, Nov. 12, 1930; s. Daniel and Olga Cathinka (de Gerlicz) G.; m. Marianne Bosma, Oct. 15, 1975; children: Danielle, Christian, Gerard. Dipl., Sch. Transp. Paris, 1956; grades, Minn. Inst. Tech., 1963; DEA in Math. Stats., ISUP Paris, 1967; PhD of Human Biology, Sch. Medicine Tours, 1975. Physicist Ctr. d'Etudes Geophysics Nat. Ctr. Sci. Rsch., Paris, 1958; rsch. asst. Minn. Inst. Tech., Mpls., 1961-63, MIT, Cambridge, 1963; rsch. attache Inst. Blaise Pascal Nat. Ctr. Sci. Rsch., Paris, 1965-70; prof. Ecole Superieure d'Informatique-Electronique Automalique, Paris, 1969—; rsch. engr. Lab. de Recherches Avancees en Moyens Informatiques, Paris, 1970-71, Lab. de Physiologie et Bio Informatiques, Tours, France, 1971—; prof. Conservatoire des Arts et Metiers Tours, 1983—; sci. dir. Ste de Bio-Informatique et de Bio-Technologie, 1996—; mem. nat. com. physcology sect. Nat. Ctr. Sci. Rsch., 1977; cons. Harvard U., Cambridge, 1967-68, Ste de Bio Informatique et de Bio Tech., 1981-95, sci. dir., 1996—; mem. conseil superieur de la meteorologie nationale Bioclimatologie; leader topical team on simulator of space motion sickness adaption syndrome European Space Agy., 1999. Co-editor: Bio Mecanique et Informatique dans les Explorations Fonctionnelles en Cardiologie, 1979; patentee in field. With French infantry, 1949-51. Mem. IEEE, Planetary Soc., French Nat. Superior Coun. of Meteorology, Institut Europeen de Formation des Aductes et de Conseil (mem. adminstrn. coun.), Institut de Recherches et d'Applications de Methodes Psycho-Educatives (pres.). Avocation: research on extraterrestrial life. Home: 32 rue Emile Zola, 37000 Tours France Office: Ste Bio Informatique & Bio Tech, 45 rue Emile Zola, 37000 Tours France

GAUDEFROY, ALAIN LOUIS, retired mathematician; b. Marseille, Provence, France, Mar. 25, 1946; s. Gauthier Pierre and Francine Aimee (Arnaud) G. D of Acoustics, U. Aix-Marseille, 1985. Oenologist expert Faculty Pharmacy, Montpellier, 1968; head Oenology Lab, Marseille, 1968—; prof. math. U. Marseille-Aix, 1978. Contbr. articles to profl. jours. Mem. Am. Math. Soc., Math. Soc. France, London Math. Soc., Edinburgh Math. Soc., Math. Soc. Glasgow, Math. Soc. Japan, Math. Soc. Poland, Math. Soc. Australia, Math. Soc. Punja, Math. Soc. India, Fencing Circle Contre de Quarte Club, Cercle des Phoceens Club. Home: 165 rue de Rome, 13001 Marseille France

GAUDEMET, YVES HENRI JEAN MARIE, law educator; b. Paris, Apr. 4, 1946; s. Jean Charles Paul Eugène Gaudemet and Marie Christiane Percerou; m. Agnès Meyer-Lucet, May 15, 1971; children: Mathieu, Sophie, Antoine. Diplome, Inst. Etudes Politiques, 1968; LLD, Faculté Droit Paris, 1972. Prof. law Faculté Droit Rabat, Morocco, 1971-74, U. Paris, 1974—; tech. counselor Cabinet du Ministre du Université, 1975-77, 85-87;. Author: Les Méthodes du Juge Administratif, 1971, Traité de Droit Administratif, 1992, others. Mem. Gen. Counsel Mines, Lomité Lontentitus Title Paris. Named Chevalier des Palmes Academiques, 1983, Chevalier l'Ordre Nat. Mèrite, 1987, Chevalier de la Legion d'honneur, 1994. Home: 9 rue de Thann, 75017 Paris France Office: Faculté de Droit Paris, 12 Place de Panthéon, 75005 Paris France

GAUL, HANS MÍCHAEL, diversified services company executive. Chief fin. officer Veba AG, Dusseldorf, Germany; mem. bd. mgmt. VEBA AG. Office: VEBA-AG, Alexander-von-Humboldt Str, 45896 Gelsenkirchen Germany*

GAUL, LOTHAR, educator, mechanical systems consultant; b. Wilhelmshaven, Germany, Nov. 17, 1946; s. Adolf and Erna (Maier) G.; m. Ulrike Reiners, Aug. 1, 1975; children: Jan Hendrik, Claas Christoffer. Degree in welding engring., SLV, Berlin, 1969; degree in mech. engring., Fachhochschule Wilhelmshaven, 1969; M of Engring., U. Hannover, Germany, 1973, D of Engring., 1976. Rsch. asst. U. Hannover, 1973-78, chief engr., lectr., 1978-81; prof., head Inst. Mechanics U. Fed. Armed Forces Hamburg, Germany, 1981-93, dean engring., 1991-93; dir. Inst. Mechs. U. Stuttgart, Germany, 1993—; dean U. Stuttgart Sch. Process Engr. and Engring. Cybernetics, 1999—; vis. prof. Fla. Atlantic U., 1991—, offer chair A of Mechs. T.U., Muenchen reject, 1996; VDI bd. Vibration Analysis and Measurement, 1990—. Mem. editl. bd. Mech. Systems and Signal Processing, Boundary Element Comms., Mech. Rsch. Comm.; patentee seal with polygon profile, active control of structural joint connections. Recipient Hon. Ring, German Engring. Soc., 1985. Mem. Soc. Applied Math. and Mechanics (vice-sec. 1995). Avocations: jogging, tennis, table tennis, golf, guitar. E-mail: gaul@mecha.uni-stuttgart.de. Home: Stresemannstrasse 5, Ludwigsburg, 71634 Baden Wuerttemberg Germany Office: U Stuttgart Inst Mechanics, Pfaffenwaldring 9, 70550 Stuttgart Germany

GAULT, THOMAS EMERSON, healthcare business executive, accountant; b. Cin., June 25, 1941; s. Emerson and Helen (Romer) G.; m. Patricia Ann Taylor, Sept. 25, 1965; children: Jeff, Sherri, Greg. BBA, U. Cin., 1965. CPA, Ohio. Supr. Coopers & Lybrand, Cin., 1965-72; contr. Garden Manor Extended Care Ctr., Middletown, Ohio, 1972-73; contr.-v.p. fin. Hyde Park Villa, Inc., Cin., 1973-80, pres., CEO, 1980-86; contr.-v.p. fin. Harrison House, Inc., Cin., 1970-80, pres., CEO, 1980—; pres., CEO Trine Technic, Inc., Cin., 1980—; CEO Day Share Ltd., Cin., 1993—; lectr. in field. Trustee St. Theresa Home for Aged, Cin., 1983—; mem. Nursing Home Ombudsman Steering com., Cin., 1983—; instr. Referee Clinics, 1983-84; spkr. IBM Exec. Health Seminar, 1982; coach, mem. nominating com. Delhi Athletic Assn., Cin., 1979-84; mem. nat. referee com. U.S. Soccer Fedn., Chgo., 1991—; dir. instrn. Ohio South Soccer Assn., Dayton, Ohio, 1992-96; mem. Soccer Assn. Youth Nat. Referee Coun., Cin., 1983-84, chmn., chief referee, coord. Westside Soccer Club, Cin., 1983-84; pres. Western Area Soccer Assn., Cin., 1983; bd. dirs., coach, soccer coord. St. Dominic Athletic Assn., Cin., 1978-84; chmn. fin. com. St. Dominic Ch., 1994—. Recipient Silver Ball award Soccer Assn. Youth, 1986; named to Hall of Fame St. Dominic Athletic Assn., 1989. Fellow Am. Coll. Health Care Adminstrn. (pres. Ohio chpt. 1994-96, pub. svc. award 1989); mem. Nat. Health Lawyers Assn. (assoc.), Nat. Fire Protection Assn. (health sect. 1994—), Ohio Health Care Assn. (chmn. dist. I 1980—, state bd. dirs./sec. 1984-85, chmn. reimbursement com. 1984, pres. 1987-89, v.p. ednl. found. 1994—, pres.'s award 1984), Hosp. Fin. Mgmt. Assn. (advanced mem.), Am. Inst. CPAs, Ohio Soc. CPAs (dir. Cin. chpt. 1967—), Am. Health Care Assn. (conv. del. 1983—, bd. dirs. 1987-89, chmn. data com. 1996—, region IV vice chmn. 1998—), Great Cin. Nursing Home Assn., St. Dominic Men's Soc. (Cin., pres. 1982-83). Republican. Roman Catholic. Office: Trine Technic Inc 2171 Harrison Ave Cincinnati OH 45211-8159

GAULTIER, JEAN-PAUL, fashion designer; b. Paris, Apr. 24, 1952. Launched 1st collection with ptnr., 1976, 1st jr. collection, 1988. Designed costumes for (film) The Cook, the Thief, His Wife, and Her Lover, 1989, Kika, 1993, La Cité des Enfants Perdus, 1995, The Fifth Element, 1997, (ballet) le Défile de Règime Chopinot, 1985, (music) Madonna's World Tour, 1990; rec. How to Do That, 1989 (Progetto Leonardo award 1989). Recipient Fashion Oscar award 1987. Office: 30 Faubourg St Antoine, 75012 Paris France*

GAUNT, BOBBIE, automotive executive. B in Bus., U. Pitts. Car merchandising mgr., bus. mgmt. mgr., field mgr. Pitts. Ford Motor Co., 1972-79; dist. sales mgr. Lincoln-Mercury divsn. Ford Motor Co., Cleve., Detroit, 1979-86; exec. asst. dealer affairs, we. regional sales mgr. Ford Motor Co., 1986; dir. mktg. rsch. N.Am. oper., 1986-92; gen. sales mgr. Lincoln-Mercury divsn., mgr. gen. mktg. Ford Motor Co., 1992-97; pres., CEO Ford Motor Co. Can., Ltd., 1997—. Recipient Profl. Achievement award Women's Automotive Assn. Internat., 1998, Disting. Svc. citation Automotive Hall of Fame, 1999; named CEO of Yr., Can. Pub. Rels. Soc., 1998. Mem. Can. Vehicle Mfrs. Assn. (chairperson 1998-99). Office: Ford Motor Co Can Ltd, Canadian Rd PO Box 2000, Oakville, ON Canada

GAUR, AMAR CHAND, microbiologist; b. Azamgarh, India, July 20, 1933; s. D. N. and Dhanpati G.; m. Chhaya, Feb. 20, 1943; children: Anupam, Amitabh. BS, Agra U., India, 1952, MS, 1954; DPhil, U. Allahabad, India, 1957; DS, U. Paris, 1962. Soil microbiologist I.A.R.I., New Delhi, 1964-70, sr. microbiologist, 1971-78, prof., 1978-82, prin. scientist, 1983-85, prof. head, 1986-93; prof. A.M.U., Aligarh, India, 1995-96; emeritus scientist Dept. Sci. and Tech., New Delhi, 1998-2000; vis. scientist Inst. Agrl. Microbiology, St. Petersburg, Russia, 1976; cons. biofertilizers, improved compost techs. and biopesticides; rschr. in field. Author: A Practical Manual of Rural Composting, 1982, Organic Manures, 1984, Phosphorus Solubilising Microorganisms as Biofertilizers, 1990, Microbial Technology for Composting of Agricultural Residues By Improved Methods, 1999. Fellow Nat. Acad. Agrl. Sci.; mem. Nat. Acad. Scis., Assn. Microbiologist India. Avocations: photography, stamp collecting, gardening. Home: Sector XV, Pusa Apts E-7 Rohini, Delhi 110085, India

GAUR, JOGI RAM, biologist; b. Karnal, Haryana, India, Aug. 15, 1954; d. M. C. and S.D. (Sharma) Gaur; m. Raj Bala Gaur, May 10, 1980; children: Kapil, Kanika, Kashish. BSc, Panjab U., Chandigarh, India, 1974, MSc in Phys. Anthropology, 1976, PhD in Sci., 1990. Jr. rsch. fellow Panjab U., Chandigarh, 1976-77; sci. asst. Forensic Lab., Haryana, India, 1978-79, sr. sci. asst., 1979-80, sr. sci. officer, 1980-90; asst. dir. Forensic Lab., Himachal, India, 1990-94, dep. dir., 1994-97, dir., 1998—; examiner Panjab U., 1985-97; tchr. Haryana Police, Karnal, 1978-90, Himachal Police, Shimla, 1990-97; lectr. in field. Editor: Him Police Patrika, 1995-96; mem. adv. bd. Internat. Jour. Human Ecology; mem. editl. bd. Internat. Jour. The Authropologist; contbr. articles to profl. jours.; inventor in field. Recipient Home Monister's award Union India, 1998. Mem. Indian Acad. Forensic Scis. (life), Forensic Sci. Soc. India (life), Brit. Acad. Forensic Scis., Electron Microscope Soc. India (life). Avocations: gardening, Yoga, motorbiking, music. Home: Village Brass, Karnal 132037, India Office: State Forensic Sci Lab, Himachal Pradesh, Junga 173216, India

GAUSCH, KURT, retired prosthodontics educator, physician; b. July 25, 1932. MD, U. Innsbruck, 1956, DDS, 1958. Prof. prosthodontics U. Innsbruck, Austria, 1974-98, dean Dental Sch. and clinic, 1978-98; ret., 1998. Home: Schiessstandgasse 11A, A-6020 Innsbruck Austria

GAUSMAN, THOMAS ANTON, economics educator; b. Morris, Minn., July 24, 1963; s. Sidney Anton Jr. and Donna Mae Gausman; m. Nancy Kay South, Nov. 7, 1992; 1 child, Eric Wicklund. BA in Econs., U. Minn., 1987; MA in Econs., No. Ill. U., 1990, MS in Fin., 1991. Acct. West Ctrl. Minn. Cmtys. Action, Elbow Lake, 1991-93; prof. econs. Fergus Falls (Minn.) C.C., 1993—; advisor Students in Free Enterprise, Phi Theta Kappa, Fergus Falls. With USAR, 1992-00. Sam M. Walton Students in Free Enterprise grantee, 1997, 98. Avocations: camping, reading, travel. Fax: 218-739-7475. E-mail: tgausman@mail.ff.cc.mn.us. Office: Fergus Falls CC 1414 College Way Fergus Falls MN 56537-1009

GAUSTER, CHRISTIAN BELRUPT, business administration educator, consultant; b. St. Gilgen, Salzburg, Austria, Dec. 30, 1945; s. Wilhelm Friedrich and Marietta (Belrupt-Tissac) G.; m. Fay Ann Sullivan, May 5, 1984; children: Maria Victoria, Sophie Elisabeth. BA, U. Tenn., 1966, MA, 1972; MS in Indsl. Mgmt., Ga. Inst. Tech., 1977; Magister, U. Vienna, Austria, 1993. Lectr. Ga. Inst. Tech., Atlanta, 1968-76; cons. tng., 1976-79; meeting adminstr., prof. devel. adminstr. Tech. Assn. Pulp and Paper Industry, Atlanta, 1979-81; cons. Peachtree Assocs., Atlanta, 1981-83; engring. editor Gen. Dynamics Corp., Atlanta, 1981-83; mktg. svcs. mgr. Novo Industri GesmbH, Vienna, 1984-86; lectr. Vienna U. Econs. and Bus. Adminstrn., 1987-93; prof. U. Vienna, 1992—; sec. Am. Assn. Tchrs. German, Atlanta, 1970-75; assoc. Integrated Fin. Planning Svcs., Vienna, 1992—; cons. Creditanstalt-Bankverein, Vienna, 1992-94. Home: Neuwaldegger Strasse 16/2/4, A-1170 Vienna Austria Office: U Vienna BWL, Bruenner Strasse 72-74, A-1210 Vienna Austria

GAUT, BERYS NIGEL, philosophy educator; b. Griffithstown, Wales, Feb. 17, 1958; s. Desmond and Barbara Myfanwy (Thomas) G.; m. Morag Macaulay Crawford, July 22, 1996. BA in History with honors, Oxford U., Eng., 1979; MA in Philosophy, Princeton U., 1988, PhD in Philosophy, 1991. Lectr. moral philosophy U. St. Andrews, Scotland, 1990—. Book rev., editor: Philos. Quar., 1994-98; co-editor: Ethics and Practical Reason, 1997; co-editor: Routledge Companion to Aesthetics, 2000; contbr. articles to profl. jours. Grantee Mind Assn., 1995, Brit. Acad., 1995, Aristotelian Soc., 1995, Scott Philos. Club, 1995. Mem. Brit. Soc. Aesthetics in Scotland (sec. 1994—), Am. Soc. for Aesthetics, Aristotelian Soc. Avocations: music, walking, swimming.

GAUTHIER, ANDRE PIERRE, gastroenterologist, educator; b. Brioude, France, Aug. 4, 1933; s. Marcel Antoine and Odette (Soulier) G.; m. Claude Marie Caire, Sept. 22, 1962; children: Pascale Michele, Pierre-Andre. MD, Med. Sch. Marseilles, 1960, Prof. Medicine, 1966. Intern, resident Marseilles Pub. Assistance, 1956-60, hosp. asst., 1960-62; chief of clinic Med. Sch. Marseilles, 1962-66, aggregation, 1966-76, prof., 1976-80, prof. 1st class, 1980—; chief of dept. Sainte Marguerite Hosp., Marseilles, 1973-82; chief of dept. La Conception Hosp., Marseilles, 1982-98, med. cons., 1998—; adminstr. Marseilles Hosp., 1984-88, Observatoire Regional de la Sante, Marseilles, 1985—. Author: Digestive Allergy, 1960, Intensive Care in Hepatology, 1984; contbr. numerous articles to profl. jours. Regional councillor Provence, France, 1992-98; city councillor, Marseilles; mil. affairs and vets. attaché. With French Army, 1957-58. Named Knight Ordre Nat. du Merite. Roman Catholic. Home: 302 Rue Paradis, Marseilles France 13008 Office: Hopital la Conception, 147 Bd Baille, Marseilles France 13005 also: City Hall, Hotel de Ville, 13233 Marseilles Cedex 01, France

GAUTIER, MAURICE PAUL, educator; b. Marseille, France, June 30, 1922; s. Maurice Pierre and Josephine (Natali) G.; m. Renee Suzanne Gillot, July 21, 1947; children: Philip, Michele, Christine. MD, Sorbonne, Paris, 1945, D, 1972. Prof. Lycee, Cognac, France, 1949-54, Lycee Voltaire, Paris, 1954-57, Lycee Henri IV, Paris, 1957-60; sr. lectr. Univ., Caen, 1966-68; prof. Paris IX Dauphine U., 1968-79, Sorbonne, Paris, 1979-91; vis. prof. Marquette U., Milw., 1967. Author: Regards sur les pays de langue anglaise, 1965, Captalm Frederick Marryat, 1972, Le Middle West, 1995. Comdr. French Navy. Mem. Internat. Assn. Am. Univs., French Am. Found. (bd. dirs. 1979—), French Assn. Can. Studies (bd. dirs. 1982—), European Assn. Tchrs. (bd. dirs. 1990—). Avocations: tennis, skiing. Home: 15 Rue Auguste Vitu, 75015 Paris France

GAVA, GIACOMO MARIO, philosophy educator; b. San Giorgio della Richinvelda(Aurava), Pordenone, Italy, Feb. 2, 1934. BA, Don Bosco Coll., Newton, N.J., 1956; degree, U. Bologna, Italy, 1964. Tchr. h.s., Ramsey, N.J., 1956-57; tchr. English Berlitz Sch., Padua, Italy, 1958-63; tchr. secondary sch. Venice, Italy, 1961-67; grad. technician U. Padua, 1967-82, assoc. prof., 1982—; vol. asst. lectr. U. Padua, 1964-65. Author: Science and Philosophy of Consciousness, 1991, Brain-Mind: 20th Century Thinkers, 1994, The Reductionism of Science, 1996, others; contbr. articles to jours. in field. Mem. State Examining Bd. Logic and Philosophy of Sci., 1984, 90. Served with Italian mil., 1960-61. Mem. Italian Soc. Logic and Philosophy of Sci. Office: Dept Gen Psychology, Via Venezia 8, 35131 Padua Italy

GAVEAU, DOMINIQUE ERIC, lawyer; b. Neuilly, France, Apr. 9, 1955; s. Michel Etienne and Anne Marie (Villiers) G.; m. Sylviane Larivain, June 20, 1987; 1 child, Pierre. MBA, U. Paris, 1976, Degree in Law, Bus. Adminstrn., 1977. CPA; Bar: Nanterre 1991. Auditor Horwarth and Horwarth, Paris, 1977-79; auditor Ernst and Young, Paris, 1979-88, legal and tax ptnr., 1989—; cons. UN for Devel. Co-author: Corporate Tax Strategy, 1989; contbr. articles to profl. jours. Treas. Pvt. Coll., Courbevoie, France, 1993. Mem. Bar of Nanterre. Home: 19 Rue Cernuschi, 75017 Paris Cedex, France Office: Ernst & Young, 14 Ave de l' Arche, 92067 Paris La Defense Cedex, France

GAVELLA, MIRJANA, biochemist, researcher; b. Zagreb, Croatia, Dec. 16, 1946; d. Milan and Ljudmila (Žun) Wolheim; m. Nikola Gavella, May 16, 1970. BS, U. Zagreb, 1970, MS, 1975, PhD, 1983. Rsch. asst. Croatia Joing program NIH, U.S., 1971-76; sci. rschr. Ministry of Sci. and Tech., Zagreb, 1975-88; rsch. scientist Vuk Vrhovac Inst. Med. Faculty Univ. Zagreb, Zagreb, 1983-86, sr. rsch. scientist, 1986—; prin. sci. rschr. Min. Sci. and Tech., Zagreb, 1990—; lectr. in continuing med. edn. Sch. Medicine, Zagreb, 1985—. Exec. editor jour. Diabetologia Croatica, 1971—; contbr. articles to sci. jours. Mem. Pagwash Orgn., 1976—. Recipient award Internat. Soc. for Andrology, 1993. Mem. Croatian Biochem. Soc., Croatian Soc. Med. Biochemists. Roman Catholic. Avocation: painting. Home: Varšavska 2, 10 000 Zagreb Croatia Office: U Zagreb Sch Medicine, Vuk Vrhovac Inst Diabetes & Endocrinolog, 4 A Dugi Dol 10 000 Zagreb Croatia

GAVIAN, PETER WOOD, investment banker; b. Brewster, Mass., Dec. 8, 1932; s. Sarkis Peter and Ruth Millicent (Wood) G.; m. Natalie Greenough, Sept. 10, 1955 (div. 1966); children: Sarah, Deborah Gavian Costolloe; m. Kathleen Byrne Covert, Aug. 30, 1975; 1 child, Margaret Elizabeth. BA, Yale U., 1954; MBA, Harvard U., 1959. Chartered fin. analyst; USCG master's lic. Assoc. McKinsey & Co., N.Y.C., 1959-61; sec./treas. Greater Washington Investors, 1961-64, 70-71; v.p. fin. NUS Corp., Washington, 1965-66; asst. to group v.p. internat. Carborundum Co., Niagara Falls, N.Y., 1966-68; pvt. investment banker Washington, 1968-70, 71-76; pres. Corp. Fin. of Washington, Inc., 1976—; expert witness in bus. valuation, 1980—; lectr. Am. U., Washington, 1978-80; trustee Calvert Group Funds, Bethesda, Md., 1980—; dir. Am. Civil Liberties Union Va., 1993-95. Contbr. articles to profl. jours. Vol. varsity sailing coach U.S. Naval Acad., 1981-88. Lt. USN, 1954-57. Mem. Washington Soc. Investment Analysts (pres. 1978-79), Am. Soc. Appraisers (pres. Washington chpt. 1998-99), Assn. Investment Mgmt. and Rsch. Avocation: sailboat racing. Home: 3005 N Franklin Rd Arlington VA 22201-3917

GAVILAN, JAVIER, physician, surgeon; b. Valladolid, Spain, May 8, 1956; s. Cesar Gavilan and Maria del Carmen Bouzas; m. Mercedes Cabello, Sept. 25, 1979; children: Cristina, Jaime. MD, U. Autonoma Madrid, 1979. Otorhinolaryngology cert. Resident La Paz Hosp., Madrid, 1980-84, mem. staff, 1985-89, prof. otolaryngology, 1989—, chmn. dept. otolaryngology, 1997—. Author: Cirugia de Tiroides y Paratiroides, 1987, Fonoaudiologia Para Educadores, 1988, Fisiologia del S.O.M., 1987. Recipient Best Otology Video award Pulitzer Soc., 1997, Silver Medal profl. video IFOS World Congress, 1997. Mem. Am. Acad. Otolaryngolgy-Head and Neck Surgery (corr., honor award 1997), Sir Charles Bell Soc. (founding), European Group for Functional Surgery following Laryngectomy. Avocations: ski, paragliding, sailplanes. Home: Iliada 17, 28220 Majadahonda Madrid, Spain

GAVIN, MARY JANE, medical and surgical nurse; b. Prairie Du Chien, Wis., Sept. 1, 1941; d. Frank Grant and Mary Elizabeth Wolf; m. Alfred William Gavin, Nov. 9, 1963; children: Catherine Heidi Elizabeth, Carl Alfred Eric. Student, North Cen. Coll., Naperville, Ill., 1959-61; BS, RN, U. Wis., 1964; postgrad., Deepmuscle Tng. Ltd., 1980; postgrad. in deep muscle therapy. RN, Wis. Staff nurse U. Wis. Hosps., Madison; RN home response VA, Milw. Unit chair Badger Girls State, 1991—; mem. Wis. Am. Legion Aux.; mem. task force for handicapped Eastside Wis. Evang. Luth. Ch., Madison, 1993. U. Wis. scholar. Mem. Monona Grove Am. Legion Aux. (pres. Unit 429 1990—). Home: 702 Fairmont Ave Madison WI 53714-1424

GAVIRIA TRUJILLO, CESAR, international organization administrator, former president of Colombia, economist; b. Pereira, Colombia, Mar. 31, 1947; m. Ana Milena Muñoz Gómez; children: Simón, María Paz. BA, economics, U. de Los Andes, Bogota; JD (hon.), U. Libre de Colombia, 1990. Chief of planning Dept. of Risaralda, 1969; mem. council Pereira, 1970-74; asst. to chief Nat. Planning Dept., 1971-72; dir. Transformadores T.P.L., SA, 1972-73; mem. Ho. of Reps., 1974-90; mayor Pereira, 1975-76; dep. min. of devel. Republic of Colombia, Bogota, 1978-79; pres., third commn. Ho. of Reps., 1980-81, pres., 1983-84; adj. dir. Liberal Party, 1986; min. of fin. and pub. credit Republic of Colombia, Bogota, 1986-87, min. of interior, 1987-89, pres., 1990-94; sec. gen. Orgn. Am. States, 1994—. La Intervención del Estado en la Economía, Aspectos Políticos del Plan de Integración Nacional, Deuda Pública Latinoamericana; columnist El Tiempo. Office: OAS Office of Secretary General 17th St and Constitution Ave NW Washington DC 20006

GAVISH, MOTTI, electronic systems engineer, researcher; b. Bucharest, Romania, Dec. 5, 1954; s. Leib and Maria (Abramovici) Grimberg; m. Vira Gerstenhaber, Jul. 13, 1978; 1 child, Lior. BSEE, Technion Israel Inst. of Tech., Haifa, Israel, 1978; MSEE, Tel-Aviv Univ., Tel-Aviv, 1984, PhD, 1995. Elec. engr. Israel Def. Forces, 1978-81; devel. engr. Tadiran Ltd. Communication Divsn., Holon, Israel, 1981-82; lectr. of elec. engring. Ctr. for Tech. Edn., Holon, Israel, 1985-86; signal processing engr. Elta Ltd. Radar Divsn., Ashdod, Israel, 1982-86; expert engr. Tadiran Ltd. Systems Divsn., Holon, 1986-90; sr. scientist Elta Ltd. Comm. Sys. Divsn., Ashdod, 1990-98, chief engr., 1998—. Contbr. numerous articles to profl. jours. Mem. IEEE (sr., sec. 1995-97). Home: 1/13 Ben Yosef St, 69125 Tel Aviv Israel Office: Elta Elec Industries Ltd, PO Box 330, 77102 Ashdod Israel

GAVRAS, KONSTANINOS See COSTA-GAVRAS

GAVRIISKY, SVETOSLAV VELESLAVOV, bank executive; b. Svishtov, Dec. 18, 1948. Student fgn. trade econs., Inst. Econs., Sofia, Bulgaria, 1972. Economist fgn. trade fin. divsn. Min. Fin., Sofia, 1972-77, economist Forex dept., 1977-87; sr. economist nat. currency balance dept. Min. Econs., Sofia, 1987-88; chief expert internat. fin. rels. dept. Min. Fin., Sofia, 1990-91, head dept. external fin. dept., 1991-92, dep. min., min. fin. care taker cabinet, 1997; chmn., gov. Bulgarska Narodna Banka, Sofia, 1997—. Office: Bulgarska Narodna Banka, 1 Alexander Battenberg Sq, 1000 Sofia Bulgaria*

GAVRIK, VITALI VITALEVICH, research scientist; b. Bobrovy Kut, Kherson, Ukraine, Jan. 1, 1942; s. Vitali Yakovlevich and Maria Sergeyevna (Chernenko) G.; m. Alla Yakovlevna. PhD, S.I. Vavilov Optics Inst., St. Petersburg, Russia, 1974, DSc, 1996. Cert. engr.-technologist Inst. Cinematographic Engring. Engr. S.I. Vavilov Optics Inst., 1966-68, rschr., 1972-76, leading rschr., 1977—, dir. rsch. lab., 1977-96; cons. Inst. Internat. Standard Orgn., Geneva, 1990-97; expert Commn. for Photographic Chemistry, Acad. Scis. USSR, Moscow, 1973-75. Contbr. articles to profl. jours. IS&T Conf. grantee G. Soros Internat. Sci. Found., 1994, 95. Mem. Sos. Imaging Sci. and Tech., Rozhdestvenski Optical Soc., N.Y. Acad. Scis., Mendeleev Chemical Soc. Avocations: home library, walking tours, ancient history, languages. E-mail: gavrik@metronet.de. Home: Ludwig-Gies-Str 18, 50769 Cologne Germany

GAVRILOVA, MARIA KUZMINICHNA, geographer, climatologist, geocryologist, educator; b. Yakutsk, Sakha, Russia, Dec. 7, 1928; d. Kuzma Osipovich and Maria Fedorovna (Kharitonova) G.; m. Vasili Afanasievich Bosikov, Apr. 7, 1962. Grad. in Climatology, Lomonosov Moscow State U., 1954; postgrad., Voyeikov Main Geophys. Obs., Leningrad, 1954-58; DSc in Geography, Russian High Cert. Com. Jr. rsch. assoc. Permafrost Inst., Yakutsk, 1958-62, sci. sec., 1962-63, sr. rsch. assoc., 1963-83, head of lab., 1984-94, prin. rsch. assoc., 1994—; prof. Ammosov Yakut State U., Yakutsk, 1994—; rsch. mgr. Acad. Scis. of Republic of Sakha, Yakutsk, 1994-99, advisor, 1999—; advisor Pub. Cons. Coun. for Pres. of Republic of Sakha, Yakutsk, 1994-96. Author: Radiation Climate of the Arctic, 1963, Climate and Perennially Frozen Ground, 1978, Modern Climate and Permafrost on Continents, 1981 (Litke Gold medal of USSR Geog. Soc. 1985), Climate of Cold Regions of the Earth, 1998. Pub. assessor Mcpl. Ct. of Justice, Yakutsk, 1963-65; presidium mem. Edn. and Sci. Trade-Union Com. of Yakutia, Yakutsk, 1962-64, Moscow, 1972-74; dep. Mcpl. Soviet, Yakutsk, 1965-67. Recipient Erdem medal Mongolian Acad. Scis., 1985, Kapitsa medal Russian Acad. Natural Scis., 1995, Silver medal Acad. Scis. for Republic of Sakha, 1998. Mem. Russian Geog. Soc. (hon.), Russian Acad. Nat. Scis., Acad. Scis. Republic of Sakha, North Forum Acad., N.Y. Acad. Scis. Avocations: autobiographical writing, collecting dolls in ethnic clothing. Office: Acad of Scis, Lenina Ave 33, Yakutsk Republic of Sakha Russia 677007

GAVRILYUK, VLADIMIR ILLICH, physicist, electronics educator, researcher; b. Dnepropetrovsk, Ukraine, Feb. 24, 1948; s. Illja Mackarovich and Nina Vasilevna (Ogolihina) G.; children: Tatjana, Yuri. Diploma in physics, State U., Dnepropetrovsk, Ukraine, 1971; Candidate in Physics and Math., Inst. Physics Nat. Acad. Sci., Riga, Latvia, 1983; D Physics and Math., Nat. Acad. Sci., Kiev, Ukraine, 1995. Instr. State Tech. Transport U., Dnepropetrovsk, 1981-84, assoc. prof., 1984-95, prof., 1995-96, 1997—, head dept., 1886—, rschr., 1981—. Contbr. articles to profl. publs. Mem. Ukraine Transport Acad. (corr.). Russian Orthodox. Avocations: sports, football, volleyball, swimming. Home: Zhukovskogo St 21 # 70, Dnepropetrovsk Ukraine Office: State Tech Transport U, 2 Acad Lazaryan St, 49010 Dnepropetrovsk Ukraine

GAW, ROBERT BRUCE, sales executive; b. Fall River, Mass., Oct. 5, 1957; s. Robert E. and Jean S. Gaw; m. Catherine M. Quintial; children: Robert M., Megan K., Kyle M. BS in Mgmt., U. Mass., Dartmouth, 1979. Recognition products cons. L.G. Balfour Co., Attleboro, Mass., 1979-83; med. equipment sales cons. Brentwood Instruments, Torrance, Calif., 1983—; also adv. bd. Brentwood Instruments, Torrance; pres. Physicians Resource Network, 1989—. Chmn. St. Elizabeth's Cath. Charity Appeal, Fall River, 1987. Mem. Pres.' Club, Million Dollar Club, 100,000 Dollar Club. Avocations: fishing, boating, travel. Home and Office: 199 Lepes Rd Tiverton RI 02878-1303

GAWALEK, WOLFGANG, physicist; b. Schwarzheide, Germany, Oct. 2, 1948; s. Gerhard and Helene (Frotscher) G.; m. Ulrike Schneider, May 26, 1973; 1 child, Heide. Diploma, Tech. U., Dresden, Germany, 1972, D of Natural Scis., 1977; D, GDR Acad. Scis., 1986; D (hon.), Moscow State Aviation Inst., 1999. Rschr. Zentralinstitut füer Festköerphysik Werkstoffforschung, Jena, Germany, 1972-77; sr. rschr. Zentralinstitut füer Festköerphysik Werkstoffforschung, Jena, 1977-82; sr. rschr. Physikalisch-Techniches-Inst., Jena, 1982-87, head of dept., 1987-93; head of dept. Inst. füer Physikalische Hochtechnologie, Jena, 1993—; guest prof. Zhongshan U., Guangzhou, China, 1999; head German High Temperature Superconductors Std. Group, 1993—; head European SCENET Group, 1998—; spkr. in field. Contbr. articles to profl. jours.; patentee in field. Recipient sci. award Inst. for Superconductor Tech., Tokyo and Materials Rsch. Soc., Honolulu, 1994, Product award Russian Fedn. Ministry of Sci. and Tech., Moscow, 1995, Product Performance award Materials Rsch. Soc. (U.S.), Morioka, Japan, 1999. Home: Am Burggarten 7, 07749 Jena Germany Office: Inst Physikalische Hochtechnologie, Winzerlaer Str 10, 07745 Jena Germany

GAWKRODGER, DAVID JOHN, dermatologist; b. Bristol, England, Nov. 14, 1953; s. Walter and Elma (Chalmers) G. MB ChB, U. Birmingham, 1976, MD, 1988. House physician Queen Elizabeth Hosp., Birmingham, England, 1976-77; sr. house officer, registrar North Staffs Hosps., Stoke on Trent, England, 1978-81; registrar, sr. registrar Royal Infirmary, Edinburgh, Scotland, 1981-85; lectr. U. Edinburgh, 1985-88; cons. Ctrl. Sheffield U. Hosps., England, 1988—. Editor British Jour. of Dermatology, 1996-99. Fellow Royal Coll. Physicians London and Edinburgh. Office: Royal Hallamshire Hosp, Sheffield S10 2JF, England

GAWLER, ROSS ANDREW, consulting company director; b. Melbourne, Victoria, Australia, July 13, 1950; s. Philip Harold and Winifred Maud (Dunsford) G.; m. Margaret Begg Robertson McDonald, Dec. 23, 1974; children: Catherine, Geoffrey. B in Engring., Monash U., Melbourne, 1972, PhD, 1979; grad. diploma in mgmt., Deakin U., Geelong, Australia, 1991. Sr. engr. State Electricity Commn. Victoria, Melbourne, 1981-86, mgr. power sys. devel., 1986-89, project mgr., 1989-92; mktg. mgr. EDS Australia Pty. Ltd., Melbourne, 1992-93, mng. cons., 1993-96, bus. devel. mgr., 1996-98; dir. McLennan Magasanik Assocs., Melbourne, 1998—. Contbr. articles to profl. jours. and conf. procs. Trustee Australian Fellowship Evang. Students, Melbourne, 1972-96. Recipient Wilson Electric Transformer Co. prize, Melbourne, 1971. Mem. IEEE (sr.), Inst. Engrs. Australia, Assn. Profl. Engrs. and Sr. Mgrs. Australia. Anglican. Avocation: tennis. Office: McLennan Magasanik Assocs, 242 Ferrars St, South Melbourne Vic 3205, Australia

GAWRECKI, LECHOSŁAW KAZIMIERZ, education management educator; b. Poznań, Poland, Dec. 26, 1942; s. Julian and Zofia (Hakowska) G.; m. Gertruda Szefler, Dec. 26, 1964; 1 child, Krzysztof. PhD, Adam Mickiewicz U., Poznń, 1976. Tchr. Primary Sch. #84, Poznń, 1964-66, Pedagogic Secondary Sch., Rogozno, 1966-69, Tchr.'s Study, Kalisz, 1969-75; lectr., studies mgr., dep. mgr. Tchr.'s Edn. Inst., Kalisz, 1975-90; sr. lectr. Pedagogy Inst. Adam Mickiewicz U., Kalisz, 1990—; founder, dir. Sch. for Edn. Mgrs., Kalisz, 1993—; ednl. journalist Głos Nauczycielski weekly, 1972—; cons. Polish TV and radio, 1972-90. Author: (books) TV as Integrator in Teaching Primary Classes, 1988, Manager at School, 1995, Activities of School Manager, 1997, Application of Radio and TV Programs, 1976, others; contbr. numerous articles to sci. publs. Assessor Regional Ct., Kalisz, 1983-94. Recipient awards Ministry of Edn., 1979, 85, 90, Golden and Silver Orders ofMerit, Medal of Edn. Mem. Kalisz Assn. Scis. Roman Catholic. Avocations: sports, radio, modern history. Office: Sch for Edn Mgrs, Aleja Wolmosci 5, 62-800 Kalisz Poland

GAWROŃSKA, GRAŻYNA TERESA, astronomer, researcher; b. Sztum, Poland, Dec. 14, 1949; d. Kazimierz and Urszula (Mania) G. MS, Nicolaus Copernicus U., Toruń, Poland, 1977. Tchr. primary sch. Boręty, Poland, 1968-69, Międzyłęże, Poland, 1969-70; tchr. planetarium Grudzi—dz, Poland, 1977-79; tech. asst. Ctr. for Astronomy Nicolaus Copernicus U., Toruń, 1979—. Contbr. articles to profl. jours. Mem. Solidarity, Toruń, 1980—, mem. univ. commn., 1995—. Mem. Polish Astron. Soc., Polish Amateur Astron. Assn. Roman Catholic. Avocations: music, bicycling, touring, psychology, theatre. Home: Słowackiego 99C/62, 87-100 Toruń Poland Office: Toruń Ctr for Astronomy, Piwnice, 87-148 Łysomice Poland

GAWRONSKI, ELIZABETH ANN, retired army officer; b. Panama City, Fla., Oct. 11, 1943; d. Myron Harvey Belyeu Sr. and Irene (Sewell) Belyeu Coates; m. Kenneth E. Gawronski Sr., Sept. 16, 1972; 1 child, Kenneth Edward Jr. BS in Edn., Fla. State U., 1965; MA in Edn., U. Ala., 1974, EdS, 1975. Commd. 2d lt. USAR, 1965, advanced through grades to lt. col., 1986; comdr. Women's Army Corps, Aberdeen Proving Ground, Md.; asst. to chief-of-staff U.S. Army Missile Command, Redstone Arsenal, Ala.; officer-in-charge, instr. Women's Army Corps Sch., Ft. McClellan, Ala.; ops. officer 3392d USAR Sch., Huntsville, Ala.; occupl. specialty instr. 1163d USAR Sch., Bronx, N.Y.; pers. mgmt. staff Adjutant Gen. Corps; staff officer LOGEX, Ft. Lee, Va.; pers. staff officer LOGEX, Camp Pickett, Va.; postal staff officer Mil. Postal Svc. Agy., Alexandria, Va.; inspector gen. U.S. Army Missile Sch., Redstone Arsenal, sr. staff officer, various positions, 1988-94; comdg. officer 184th IMA Detachment, Redstone Arsenal, 1994-96; ret., 1996. Vol. Huntsville City Schs., 1988-96, Boy Scouts Am., Huntsville, 1993-95, Huntsville Art League, 1997. Decorated Meritorious Svc. medal. Mem. Res. Officers' Assn. (life). Methodist. Home: 8044 Lauderdale Rd SW Huntsville AL 35802-2916

GAWRONSKI, JAS, journalist, politician; b. Vienna, Feb. 7, 1936; s. Jan and Luciana (Frassati) G.; children: Jan, Carolina. LLM, U. Rome, 1958. Corr. on ea. Europe Daily Il Giorno, Warsaw, 1959-62; prodr. programs RAI Italian TV, various cities, 1962-66; corr. RAI Italian TV, N.Y.C., 1966-77, Paris, 1977-80, Moscow and Warsaw, 1980-81; mem. European Parliament, Brussels, 1981-94, 1999—; spokesman for prime min. Beilusconi, 1994—. Editor: Primi Piani, 1989, Il Mondo di Giovanni Paolo III, 1994. Recipient Highest award of merit Pres. of the Republic of Poland, Warsaw, 1993. Roman Catholic. Avocations: swimming, tennis. Office: Largo Fontanella Borghese 19, I-00186 Rome Italy*

GAWTHROP, PETER JOHN, engineering educator; b. Seascale, Cumbria, Eng., Mar. 10, 1952; s. John and Freda (Johnson) G. BA, Oxford (Eng.) U., 1973, PhD, 1977. Chartered engr., U.K.; registered European engr., EU. Rsch. asst. Oxford U., 1976-80; rsch. fellow New Coll., Oxford, 1980-81; lectr. Sussex (Eng.) U., Brighton, 1981-87; Wylie prof. control engring. Glasgow (Scotland) U., 1987—. Author: Metamodelling, 1996. Recipient Honeywell medal Inst. Measurement and Control, London, 1994. Fellow Inst. Mech. Engring., Instn. Elec. Engring., RSA; mem. IEEE (sr.). Avocations: hiking, windsurfing. Office: U Glasgow Dept Mech Eng, James Watt Bldg, Glasgow G12 8QQ, Scotland

GAXER, WALTER PETER, academic director, educator; b. Basle, Switzerland, June 10, 1945; s. Walter and Hortense (Brand) Boehler. Degree in polit. sci., U. Lausanne (Switzerland), 1974, degree in ednl. sci., 1975; degree in ednl. planning, U. Geneva, 1976. Mng. dir. Imano Ltd., Lausanne, 1983—, IMECO, Lausanne, 1988—, ASIMO Corp., Lausanne, 1989—, Linguaco Ltd., Lausanne, 1989—, Sophros Ltd., Lausanne, 1996—; pres., chmn. AFA Corp., Lausanne, 1992—; lectr. Fed. Inst. Tech., Lausanne, 1989—, U. Lausanne, 1995—; pres. Interdisciplinary Acad., Lausanne, 1995. Editor, funder (periodical) Le Plurilogue, 1985—, (jour.) Les Actualites, 1994—. Funding pres. Swiss Life-long Learning Assn., Lausanne, 1992. Mem. Interdisciplinary Synergical Acad. Ventures Club, Dem. Circle. Avocations: reading, writing. Office: ASI-ISA, Rue Grand Port 18, CH-1001 Lausanne Switzerland

GAXIOLA, ENRIQUE HUMBERTO, electrical engineer, researcher; b. Villa Obregon, Mex., May 1969; s. Jose Gaxiola and Margriet Vocks. MSc, Eindhoven U. Tech., The Netherlands, 1988, PhD, 1999. Cert. in elec. engring. Sci. asst. Eindhoven U. Tech., Eindhoven/Noord-Brabant, 1994-99; devel. engr. Philips Lighting B.V., Eindhoven/Noord-Brabant, 1999—. Mem. IEEE, Dutch Royal Inst. Engrs., Dutch Electronics and Radio Engring. Assn., Dutch Nat. Student Sailing and Windsurfing Assn. (bd. dirs. 1997-99), Eindhoven Student Windsurfing Assn. (chmn. 1996-98). Avocations: windsurfing, soccer. Office: Philips Lighting BV, Mathildelaan 1, Eindhoven The Netherlands

GAY, DAVID HOLDEN, project technician; b. Boston, Jan. 5, 1954; s. Ernest and Mary (Holden) G.; divorced; 1 child, David C. Student, Northeastern U., Boston, 1972, 75, 80, 81, 83, 84, Lowell U., 1987-92; BS in Mgmt., Lesley Coll., 1994. Cert. tutor. Floor mgr. Harvard Coop. Soc., Cambridge, Mass., 1972-76; R&D tech. Polaroid Corp., Cambridge, 1976-85; project tech. Draper Lab., Cambridge, 1985—. Pres. R&D and Tech. Employee's Union, Belmont, Mass., 1990 ; legis. agt. State of Mass., 1991 , legis agt. federal, 1991 ; mem. pers. bd. Town of Tewksbury, Mass. Roman Catholic. Avocations: karate, baseball, basketball, skiing, swimming. Home: 5 Decarolis Dr Tewksbury MA 01876-3361 Office: Draper Lab 555 Technology Dr Waltham MA 02453-8905

GAY, ELISABETH FEITLER, actress; b. Vienna, Dec. 16, 1916; d. Paul and Loni (Rosenbaum) Feitler; m. Joseph Gay (dec.); children: Cathy, Paul, Jill. BA, Sarah Lawrence Coll., 1974, MFA, 1977; PhD, NYU, 1986. Head of acting co. Sara Lawrence Players, Bronxville, N.Y., 1974-79; artist in residence Westchester Schs., 1974-79; acting tchr. U. Bridgeport, Conn., 1977-79; drama therapist, acting tchr. Bellevue Hosp., N.Y.C., 1984-86; acting tchr. Sarah Lawrence Coll., 1986. Author short stories. Brownie leader Stephenson Sch., New Rochelle, 1951-53; actress Guidance Ctr., New Rochelle, 1950. Mem. AFTRA, Am. Sr. Profls. at Eckerd Coll., Actors Equity, Assn. Sr. Profls., Kappa Delta Pi. Democrat. Jewish. Avocations: play directing, theatre, movies, gardening, reading. Home: 65 Seaview Ave New Rochelle NY 10801-5329 also: 4801 Osprey Dr S Apt 106E Saint Petersburg FL 33711-4699

GAY, JOHN MARION, federal agency administrator, organization-personnel analyst; b. Houston, Sept. 23, 1936; s. John Henry and LolaBell (Collins) G.; m. Rebecca Jane Gay; children—John Marion II, Dierdre, Michael, Michelle (dec.), Steven, Christina. B.A., Tex. So. U., 1956; MSW, U. Richmond, 1968, B.S., Fla. Meml. Coll., 1976, MBA, Nova U., 1977. Cert. tchr., Fla. Compensation analyst SE Banks, N.A., Miami, Fla., 1976-78; personnel job analyst Kaiser Transit Group, Miami, 1978-80; tribal adminstr. Miccosukee Indians, Everglades Nat. Park, Fla., 1980-81; tchr. Broward County Schs., Fort Lauderdale, Fla., 1981-83, Dade County Schs., Miami, 1983-84; postal employee U.S. Postal Service, North Miami Beach, Fla., 1984—, consumer affairs officer, 1985-87, supt. Sta. Br. OONS, 1987—, supr. Mails/Delivery, 1988—, coord. for on-line computerized mail forwarding system, 1989, div. rte. insp., 1992—; inspection team leader S. Fla. Postal Ops., 1993—, detailed: Postal Inspection Svc. DHQ, 1996—. Corp. coord. United Negro Coll. Fund, Dade County, 1977. Served with USAF, 1956-59. Max Fleischmann scholar United Negro Coll. Fund, 1975; recipient mems. award of honor Alpha Kappa Mu, 1974; award Fla. Meml. Coll. Alumni Assn., 1978. Fellow NEA; mem. Nat. Assn. Postal Suprs., Tuskegee Airmen, Inc. Democrat. Avocations: tennis, bowling, writing. Home: 9700 NW 70th St Tamarac FL 33321-1902

GAY, SUSAN MATTHEWS, publishing professional; b. Atlanta, Dec. 14, 1954; d. Brinton Bizzelle, Jr. and Evelyn (Ward) G.; m. Jonathan P. Andrews, Dec. 14, 1991; children: Katherine Rose Andrews, Paul Brinton Andrews. BS, Presbyn. Coll., 1976; MA, Emory U., 1980. Continuing edn. coord. Emory U. Sch. of Medicine, Atlanta, 1976-79; editor Ctrs. for Disease Control, Atlanta, 1979; editor, sr. editor Butterworth Pubs., Inc., Boston, 1979-82; sr. editor to exec. editor Grune & Stratton, Inc., N.Y.C., 1982-85; exec. editor J.B. Lippincott, Inc., Phila., 1986-88; exec. editor to editor-in-chief Mosby, Inc., Phila., 1988-95; v.p., pub. Williams and Wilkins (Waverly, Inc.), Balt. and Phila., 1995-99; pres., CEO InfoBrand Pub. Inc., Phila., 1999—; spkr. Thomas Jefferson Med. Coll., Phila., 1997, others. Co-author: (book) Clinical Methods Learning System, 1979. Sec. Presbyn. Coll. Alumni Assn., Clinton, S.C., 1980-81; bd. dirs. New Gulph Children's Ctr., Villanova, Pa., 1996-98, Found. for Architecture, Phila., 1989-91. Mem. Am. Med. Writers Assn. (bd. dirs., chmn. audiovisual sect. 1978-85), Am. Med. Publishers Assn. (pres. 2000—). Avocations: hist. architecture, design, gourmet cooking.

GAYLOR, BARBARA GAIL DAVIS, geriatric nurse; b. Tampa, Fla., Sept. 26, 1956; d. Roscoe and Audrey Iris (Knowles) Davis; m. Frank Hogan Gaylor, Apr. 12, 1980; children: Cassandra Michelle, Jennifer Lynn, Catherine Ann. AA, St. Petersburg Jr. Coll., 1976, AS, 1978. RN, Fla.; cert. gerontol. nurse, ANCC. Nurse Bay Pines VA Hosp., St. Petersburg, Fla., 1995—. Leader, co-leader Girl Scouts Am., Va., Fla., 1992-98. Republican. Lutheran. Avocations: sailing, swimming, camping.

GAYMARD, ROBERT, petroleum engineer, retired; b. Honfleur, Normandy, France, Dec. 29, 1923; s. Ludovic and Jeanne (Bréhier) G. Grad., Ecole Poly., France, 1944, French Petroleum Sch., France, 1949. Engr. S.N. Repal, Algeria, 1949-51; divsn. mgr. Schlumberger, 1951-72; pres. SEAL France, France, 1973-74; sales mgr. Europe and Africa COFLEXIP, France, 1975-83; sales mgr. indsl. divsn. Inst. Français du Pétrole, France, 1984-88; mgr. petroleum divsn. PCM Pompes, France, 1989-91; ret., 1991; tech. adv. Kudu Industries, Inc., Calgary, Canada, 1992. Mem. Soc. Petroleum Engrs. Home: 124 Blvd de la Republique, 92210 Saint Cloud France

GAYOOM, MAUMOON ABDUL, president of Maldives; b. Dec. 29, 1937; m. Nasreena Ibrahim; 4 children. Degree, Al-Azhar U., Cairo; D.Letters (hon.), Aligarh Muslim U. India, 1983, Pondicherry U. India, 1994, Jamia Millia Islamia of India, 1990; PhD in Polit. Sci. (hon.), Internat. U. Found., 1988. Rsch. asst. in Islamic history Am. U., Cairo, 1967-69; lectr. in Islamic studies and Philosophy Abdullahi Bayero Coll., Ahmadu Bello U., Nigeria, 1969-71; tchr. Aminiya Sch., 1971-72; mgr. govt. shipping dept. Govt. of Maldives, 1972-73, under sec. telecoms. dept., 1974, dir. telephone dept., 1974, spl. under sec. office of the prime min., 1974-75, dept. amb. to Sri Lanka, 1975-76, under sec. dept. external affairs, 1976, permanent rep. to UN, 1976-77, dep. min. of transport, 1976, min. of transport, 1977-78, pres., comdr. in chief of the armed forces, 1978—, min. of def. and nat. security, 1982—, min. of fin., 1989-93, min. of fin. and treasury, 1993—; gov. Maldives Monetary Authority, 1981—; mem. Constituent Coun. of Rabitat Al-Alam Al-Islami. Author: The Maldives: A Nation in Peril, 1998. Recipient The Grand Order of Mugunghawa, Rep. of Korea, 1984, Global 500 Honour Roll award UN Environ. Programme, 1988, Man of the Sea 1990 award, 1991, Knight Grand Cross St. Michael & St. George, 1997, WHO Health-for-All Gold medal, 1998, DRV Internat. Environment award, 1998. Avocations: astronomy, calligraphy, photography, badminton, cricket.

GAYOSO, ANA MARIA, botanist; b. La Plata, Argentina, Aug. 20, 1948; d. Pedro Ramon and Manuela (Garcia Diaz) G.; m. Vicente Horacio Muglia, Sept. 17, 1971; children: Ana Gabriela, Cecilia, Beatriz, Juan. Lic. botany, Facultad de Ciencias, 1972; DS, Facultad Ciencias Naturales, 1981. Asst. researcher Consejo Nacional, Buenos Aires, Argentina, 1977-81; independent. researcher Conicet, Bahía Blanca, Argentina, 1991-93; prof. U. Nacional del Sur, Bahía Blanca, Argentina, 1981-94; independent researcher Conicet, Puerto Madryn, Argentina, 1994—; adj. researcher Conicet, Bahia Blanca, 1981-91. Contbr. articles to profl. jours. Achievements include discovery of two new species for the science: Thalassiosira solitaria gayoso and Thalassiosira hibernalis gayoso. Home: Thomas 2222, 9120 Puerto Madryn Argentina Office: Centro Nacional Patagonico, B Brown S/N, 9120 Puerto Madryn Argentina

GAYSSOT, JEAN-CLAUDE, government official; b. Beziers, France, Sept. 6, 1944; married; 3 children. Student, Tech. Coll.; cert. d'aptitude professionnelle. Mem. Confedn. Gen. Travail, 1976; councilor Bobigne Mcpl., 1977; nat. assembly deputy Seine-Saint Denis, France, 1986—, mayor, 1997; min. Ministry Pub. Works, Transport & Housing, Paris, 1997—. Mem. French Community Party, 1963—, nat. sec. Party's Nat. Directorate, 1985. Office: Ministry Pub Works Transp & Housing, 246 Blvd Saint Germain, 75007 Paris France

GAZARIAN, IRINA GEORGIEVNA, biochemist; b. Baku, USSR, Mar. 20, 1957; d. Georgi T. Gazarian and Valentina D. Kandalova; m. Mikhail M. Hushpulian, Feb. 6, 1980 (div. Jan. 2000); 1 child, Dmitry. MS, Moscow State U., 1979, PhD, 1984, DSc, 1996. Lic. chemist. Jr. rschr. Moscow State U., 1984-88, rsch. scientist, 1988-91, sr. scientist, 1991-96, leader scientist, 1996—. Contbr. numerous rsch. papers to sci. jours.; patentee in field. INCO-Copernicus grantee, 1997-2000, INTAS grantee, 2000-2002. Mem. ACS.

GAZAY, HENRY G., company executive; b. Paris, Sept. 12, 1967; s. Frangois and Marie Bourdon; m. Elisabeth Hasdenteufel, Mar. 26, 1995; children: Clementine, Laetitia. Engr., Ecole Centrale, Lyon, France, 1991. CEO Tekmark, Paris, 1991—; expert. European Cmty., Brussels, 1997—. Contbr. reports to profl. publs. Mem. World Assn. for Pub. Opinion Rsch., European Soc. Mktg. Rsch., Brit. Std. Athletic Club. Avocations: tennis, sailing, astronomy. Office: Tekmark, 263 bis bd Pereire, 75017 Paris France

GAZDA, GRZEGORZ JÓZEF, humanities educator; b. Srock, Piotrkow, Poland, Oct. 13, 1943; s. Józef and Genowefa (Grochulska) G.; m. Irena Barbara Grundniewska, Aug. 30, 1969; children: Michat, Tomasz. MA, U. Łódź, Poland, 1966, qualifying cert. asst. prof., 1986; PhD, Polish Acad. Scis., Warsaw, 1972. Vice-mgr. Inst. Theory Lit., Theatre and Film U. Łódź, 1978-81, vice-dean faculty philology, 1987-90, prof., chief dept. film, 1987-91, prof., chief dept. theory of lit., 1991—; prof., chief dept. theory of lit. H.S. of Towics, Poland, 1994—; sec. Com. Poetics, Internat. Com. Slavists, 1970—. Author: Futurism in Poland, 1974 (Ministry of Higher Edn. award 1974), The Avant-Garde Tradition and Modernity, 1987 (Ministry of Higher Edn. award 1987); editor: (book series vol. 1-5) The Problems of the Avant Garde, 1982-95; editor-in-chief Les Problèmes des Genres Littéraires, 1995—; chief lit. sect. Weekly Mag. Odgtosy, 1984-87; co-editor bimonthly Film in the World, 1991-93. Recipient Gold Cross of Merit of Polish Republic, 1988, medal Nat. Edn. Com., 1989. Mem. Acad. Soc. Łódź, Polish Writers Union. Avocations: books, mushrooming party, voyages. Home: Lermontowa 1/67, 92-512 Lodz Poland Office: Katedra Teorii Literatury, Sienkiewicza 21, 90-114 Lodz Poland

GAZE, NIGEL RAYMOND, plastic surgeon; b. Leamington Spa, Warwick, Eng., Nov. 2, 1943; s. Raymond Ernest and Beatrice Maud (Caswell) G.; m.

Heather Winifred Richardson, Aug. 6, 1966; children: Julia, Celia, Richard, Thomas, Mary, Harry. MB, ChB, Liverpool U., 1966; BMus, London U., 1986. House officer Whiston Hosp., Prescot, Lancashire, Eng., 1966-67, sr. house officer orthopaedics, 1967-68; sr. casualty officer Royal So. Hosp., Liverpool, Eng., 1969-70; surg. registrar Liverpool Regional Hosp. Bd., 1970-72; gen. surgery registrar Chester (Eng.) Royal Infirmary, 1972-73; registrar in plastic surgery Wordsley Hosp., Stourbridge, Worcs, Eng., 1973-75; sr. registrar plastic surgery Yorks Region Health Authority, Leeds, 1975-79; cons. plastic surgery Royal Preston (Lancashire) Hosp., 1980—. Contbr. med. articles to profl. jours.; composer choirs, organs, and solos. Condr. Elizabethan Singers, Preston; accompanist County Hall Singers, Preston, 1980—, Clitheroe Assn. Ch. Choirs, Preston, 1984—; organist Fishergate Bapt. Ch., Preston, 1994—. Fellow Trinity Coll. Music, Royal Coll. Organists. Fellow Royal Soc. Medicine, Royal Coll. Surgeons Edinburgh, Royal Coll. Surgeons; mem. Royal Acad. Music (licentiate), Brit. Acad. Experts, Brit. Inst. Organ Studies, Brit. Assn. Plastic Surgeons, Brit. Assn. Aesthetic Plastic Surgeons, Brit. Assn. Head and Neck Oncologists, B.M.A. (chmn., Preston Div. 1997) Victorian Soc., Select Vestry Club, Assn. Brit. Choral Condrs. Mem. Conservative party; mem. Ch. of Eng. Avocations: collecting books and antiques, walking. Home: 11 Norbreck Ct, Norcliffe Rd, Blackpool Lancs FY2 9BN, England Office: Fulwood Hall Hosp, Midgery Ln, Preston Lancashire PR1 OAR, England

GAZICKA, DOROTA KRYSTYNE, geographer, librarian; b. Warsaw, Poland, Oct. 13, 1958; d. Mieczyslaw and Zofia Zembrzuski; children: Anna, Leszek. MA, Warsaw U., 1982. Bibliographer Inst. Geography and Spatial Orgn., Polish Acad. Sci., Warsaw, 1982-92; chief libr. Ctrl. Libr. Geography and Environ. Protection, Warsaw, 1992—. Author/editor: Bibliography of Polish Geography, 1979-80, 85—. Roman Catholic. Avocations: photography, reading, travel. Office: Ctrl Lib geography, ul Twarda 51/55, 00-818 Warsaw Poland

GAZSO, FERENC, sociologist, educator; b. Bekesszentandras, Hungary, Oct. 8, 1932; s. Ferenc Gazso and Ilona Borbely; m. Ferencné Dudas Aliz, Dec. 12, 1959; 1 child, Tibor, Ferenc. MA, Eötvcs Lorand Tudomauyegyeten, Budapest, 1954; PhD, Hungarian Acad. Scis., Budapest, 1978. Prof. sociology Budapest Közgazdasagtudonanyi Egyetem, Budapest, 1980—. Author: Choice of Profession, 1970, Students' Life in Budapest, 1971, Education System and Social Mobility, 1976, Reproduction of Inequalities, 1988.

GAZZETTA, MORENO AUGUSTO, engineer; b. Zurich, Switzerland, July 7, 1962; s. Giobatta and Velia Anna Gazzetta; divorced; children: Timo, Nadine, Ramon, Dominic. Diploma in elec. engring., ETH, Zurich, 1985. Engr. RCA, Zurich, 1986-89, Oerlikon-Contraves, Zurich, 1990—. Mem. IEEE, Sportfischer Verein Rumlang (treas. 1992—), Handharmonika Club Zurich Albisrieden (mem. elite orch., musician, Silver medal). Avocations: family, fly fishing, fly tying, playing accordion, composing and arranging music. Office: Oerlikon-Contraves AG, Birchstr 155, 8050 Zurich Switzerland

GAZZOLI, RUBEN NESTOR, urban planner, researcher; b. Buenos Aires, Argentina, Apr. 16, 1935; s. Guido and Micaela Zulema (Massa) G.; children: Silvina, Virginia, Guido. Grad., Indsl. Sch. Ing. Luis A Huergo, Capital Federal, Argentina, 1953; Degree in Architecture, U. Buenos Aires, 1965. External rschr. CEUR Ctr. for Urban and Regional Studies, Buenos Aires, 1971-76, prin. rschr., 1976-81; external rschr. Ctr. for Demographic Studies, Buenos Aires, 1985-86; dir. Marcos Winograd Habitat Ctr., Buenos Aires, 1984-85, Habitat Program, Buenos Aires, 1986-96; dir. social housing devel. unit Sch. Architecture and Urbanism, U. Buenos Aires, 1998—; coord. urbanpolicies work group Latin Am. Coun. Social Sci., 1976-77; lectr. postgrad. course urban and regional planning U. Buenos Aires, 1985—; exec. sec. Habitat Exch., Buenos Aires, 1994-96. Advisor, Shanty Towns Movement, Buenos Aires, 1991-92, Mcpl. Legislators from the Popular Socialist Party, 1993-95, Nat. Legislators from the Popular Socialist Party, 1996—; apptd. advisor Buenos Aires Environ. Urban Plan. Ford Found. fellow, 1976-77. Mem. Ctrl. Soc. Architects (steering com. 1998—), N.Y. Acad. Sci., Internat. HIC. Mem. Popular Socialist Party. Avocations: painting, drawing, literature, drama. E-mail: rgazzoli@yahoo.com. Office: FADU-UBA, Ciudad Univ Pabellon 4to, Capital Federal 1428, Argentina

GBADEGESIN, ADENIYI SULAIMAN, geographer, researcher; b. Oyo, Nigeria, Apr. 6, 1955; s. Alade Kareem and Ayoka Sabitiyu (Akanbi) G.; m. Abimbola Olanrewaju Coker, Dec. 10, 1983; children: Opeyemi, Tolulope, Ayodamope. BSc in Geography, U. Ibadan, Nigeria, 1979, MSc in Geography, 1981, PhD in Geography, 1984. Cert. in soil data base mgmt., 1989. Assoc. prof. U. Ibadan, Nigeria, 1996—; assoc. lectr. Ogun State U., Nigeria, 1995-96; warden Obafemi Awolowo Hall, Ibadan, Nigeria, 1996-99; cons. RIM, London, 1992, Chevron, Ibadan, 1993, Shell, Nigeria, Warri, 1995-96. Author: (book) Physical Geography for School, 1989; contbr. articles to jours. Recipient fellowship Social Sci. Rsch. Coun. N.Y., 1990, Social Sci. Acad. Nigeria, Nigeria, 1993, Third World Acad. Sci. (Chinese), 1991. Mem. Internat. Soil Sci. Soc., Internat. Geog. Union, Nigerian Geog. Assn. Avocations: reading, watching soccer, dancing. Home: Rd D, Tinuoye Estate, Ibadan Nigeria Office: Dept Geography, U Ibadan, Ibadan Nigeria

GBOLADE, BABATUNDE ABIODUN, gynecologist; b. Jos, Plateau, Nigeria; s. A. A. and E. I. Gbolade; m. Linda Ibidunni Gbolade; children: Taiwo, Kehinde, Oluwaseun. M.B.B.S., U. Ibadan, 1978. Registrar in obgyn. Queen's Park Hosp., Blackburn, Eng., 1989-90, St. Mary's Hosp., Manchester, Eng., 1990-91, North Manchester Gen. Hosp., 1991-92; registrar in genito-urinary medicine Manchester Royal Infirmary, 1992-93; clin. lectr. U. Manchester, 1994-97; cons. gynecologist, dir. fertility control unit St. James' Univ. Hosp., Leeds, Eng., 1997—. Contbr. articles to profl. jours. Recipient Decree of Merit, Internat. Biog. Ctr., Cambridge, Eng., 1995, Best Poster prize Faculty of Family Planning, London, 1997; Ogun State Govt. of Nigeria scholar, 1979. Fellow Royal Soc. Health, Royal Coll. Physicians Ireland; mem. Royal Coll. Obstetricians and Gynecologists, N.Y. Acad. Scis. Avocations: classical music, travel, reading, swimming, medical computing. Office: St James U Hosp, Fertility Contl/Beckett St, Leeds LS9 7TF, England

GBONEY, WILLIAM KWASI, mechanical engineer; b. Accra, Ghana, Feb. 28, 1960; s. Peter Mensah and Rhoda Ama (Ababio) G.; m. Florence Afua Kofi, Aug. 7, 1993. BSME, U. Sci. and Tech., Kumasi-Ghana, 1987; MBA in Fin., U. Ghana, Legon, 1998. Cert. in maintenance and retrofitting of hydro-electric turbines and generators. Asst. mech. engr. Volta River Authority, Akosombo, Ghana, 1987-91; mech. maintenance engr. Volta River Authority, Akuse, 1992-94, sr. mech. engr., 1994-2000; with Pub. Utilities Regulatory Commn., Accra, 2000—; mech. constrn. engr. Acres Internat. Consulting Firm, Akosombo, 1992-93, commissioning engr., 1992-93, pre-commissioning engr., Linz, Austria, 1993; gen. engr. Volta River Authority and Toshiba Corp., Akuse, 1993-94. Mem. ASME, Ghana Inst. Engrs. Roman Catholic. Avocations: soccer, reading, watching Am. football, films, music.

GE, LI-FENG, engineer, physics educator, researcher; b. Chuzhou, Anhui, China, Mar. 18, 1947; s. Tian-Min and Ji-Hua (Fan) G.; m. Jing-Ping Shao, Mar. 24, 1982; 1 child, Zhong-Qi. BS, Hefei (China) U. Tech., 1970; MS, U. Sci. and Tech. China, Beijing, 1980; postgrad., Nat. Inst. Metrology, Beijing, 1980-81. Registered profl. engr., China. Engr. Wuhu (China) Diesel Engine Factory, 1970-77, Wuhu Bur. of Standards and Metrology, 1978, Nat. Inst. Metrology, Beijing, 1981-82; rsch. engr. Anhui Bur. of Standards and Metrology, Hefei, 1982-86, sr. rsch. engr., 1988—, chmn. Acoustic Lab., 1988-92; dep. dir. Anhui Inst. Metrology and Measurement, Anhui Bur. Tech. Supervision, Hefei, 1992-97, rsch. prof., 1994—; prof. dept. physics Anhui U., 1997-99, prof. dept. automation Sch. Electronics Engring.-Info. Sci., 1999—; vis. scholar PCB Piezotronics Inc., Buffalo, 1986; hon. sr. vis. fellow Royal Soc. U.K., City U., London, 1995; guest scientist Nat. Inst. Standards & Tech., Gaithersburg, Md., 1986-88. Inventor piezoelectric reciprocity method and apparatus for absolute calibration of high-frequency primary vibration standards. Mem. Acoustical Soc. China, Acoustical Soc. Am. Achievements include contribution to the understanding of the operation mechanism of electrostatic ultrasonic transducers; inventor piezoelectric reciprocity method and appratus for absolute calibration of high-frequency primary vibration standards. Office: Anhui U Dept Automation, 3 Feixi Rd, Hefei 230039, China

GE, SHUZHI SAM, electrical engineering educator; b. Anqiu, Shandong, China, Sept. 20, 1963; s. Fushun Ge and Yanying Wang; m. Jinlan Cui, Nov. 30, 1988; children: Yaowei Jasmine, Yaolong George, Yaohong Lorraine. BSc, Beijing U. Aeros. and Astrons., 1986; PhD, diploma Imperial Coll., U. London, 1993. Post-doctoral rsch. assoc. U. Leicester, U.K., 1992-93; lectr. Nat. U. Singapore, 1993-98, sr. lectr., 1998-2000, assoc. prof., 2000—; tech. cons. Grumman Internat. Nanyang Tech. Inst. CAD/CAM Ctr. Inst. Mfg. Tech., Singapore, 1996—, Ordnance Devel. and Engring., Singapore, 1999-2000. Author: Adaptive Neural Network Control of Robotic Manipulators; assoc. editor IEEE Trans. on Control Sys. Tech., 1999. Recipient French Acad. Exch. award Ministry Fgn. Affairs, Grenoble, France, 1996, Internat. Exch. Agreements Collaborative Rsch. award U. Melbourne, Australia, 1998, Nat. Tech. award Nat. Sci. and Tech. Bd., Singapore, 1999; Sino-Brit. Friendship scholar Brit. Coun., London, 1989. Mem. IEEE (sr.), Singapore Robotic Games. Achievements include patent for structural network modelling and adapitve control of dynamical systems. Avocations: travel, reading, chess, fishing. E-mail: elegesz@nus.edu.sg. Fax: 65-779 1103.

GE, ZHENCHANG, retired engineering educator; b. Jilin, China, May 24, 1933; m. Xiangsheng Ni, May 31, 1966; children: Ping, Ding. B, Hehai U., Nanjing, China, 1961. Technician Xinjiang Water Resource Office, Urumqi, China, 1961-79; lectr. Xinjiang U., Urumqi, 1980-87, prof., 1988-93; ret., 1993. Home: Sheng Li Lu 14 #, 830046 Urumqi Xinjiang, China Office: Xinjiang U, Shng Li Lu 14 #, 830046 Urumqi Xinjiang, China

GEAGEA, TOMMY, surgeon; b. Becharry, Lebanon, Oct. 11, 1956; s. Emile and Nohad (Lahoud) G.; m. Helene Abtour, Nov. 9, 1982; children: Anna, Laura, Katia, Emile. MD, St. Joseph, Beirut, Lebanon, 1982. Cert. specialist of province of Quebec. Surgeon Gen. Hosp., Galce Bay, Can., 1987-91, Lebanese Hosp., Beirut, 1991—. Contbr. numerous articles to profl. jours. First surgeon to perform a repair of a hiatal hernia by laparoscopy, 1991. Fellow Royal Coll. Surgeons Can., Am. Coll. Surgeons; mem. Soc. Am. Gastrointestinal Endoscopic Surgeons. Avocations: skiing, tennis, jogging. Home: Rzk Tower, PO Box 166285, Beirut Lebanon Office: Lebanese Hosp, Geitawi, Beirut Lebanon

GEANTĂ, VICTOR, engineering educator; b. Bogati, Arges, Romania, Oct. 24, 1956; s. Gheorghe and Lucretia (Dima) G.; m. Marinela Lucia Iancu, Aug. 31, 1980; children: Irina Mihaela, Simona Daniela. Engr., U. Poly. Bucharest, Romania, 1981, D Engring., 1998. Engr. ICNPTO, Oltenita, Calarasi, Romania, 1981-83; engr. U. Poly. Bucharest, 1983-84, asst. prof., 1984-90, lectr. prof., 1990-99, reader, 1999, prof. engring., 2000—; cons. Relansin, Bucharest, 1999. Author: (with I. Butnariu) Special Technologies of Steel Manufacturing and Refining, 1993, (with others) Applications in Steel Metallurgy, 1993, Unconventional Technologies of Ferrous Ores Reduction, 1994, Technological Design in Steel Metallurgy, 1997, The Mathematical Modeling and the Management of the Processes from the Ferrous Metallurgy, 1997, Alternative Processes and Technologies in Ferrous Metallurgy, 1997, The Continuous Casting of the Steel Semis, 1999, The Manufacturing of Ferrous Metallic Materials, 2000, The Steel Refining, 2000; inventor in field. 1st lt. Romanian mil., 1975-76. Mem. ASM Internat., Soc. Romania Metalurgie, The Mineral, Metals and Materials Soc., Associazione Italiana di Mettallurgia. Mem. Orthodox Ch. Avocations: music, soccer, travel. Home: Iani Buzoiani, Bucharest Romania Office: U Politehnica Bucharest, Splaiul Independenti 313, 77206 Bucharest Romania

GEARHART, MARVIN, oil company executive; b. Erie, Kans., May 13, 1927; s. Charles Herman and Marjorie Catherine (Hudson) G.; m. Jan Olson, Feb. 14, 1947; children: Dee Ann Gearhart Stenberg, Dale Alan, Jill Sue Gearhart Johnston, Janice Kay Parys. B.S. in Mech. Engring., Kans. State U., 1949. Logging engr. Welex, 1949-53; chief field engr. Security Engr. div. Dresser, 1953-55; co-founder, chmn., pres. Gearhart Industries Inc., Ft. Worth, 1955-89; bd. dirs. Halliburton Logging Svcs., Ft. Worth, 1989-90; bd. dirs. subs. Go Oil Well Services (now Gearhart Industries Inc.); bd. dirs. Justin Industries Inc., Ft. Worth; chmn. Rock Bit Industries, Inc., Ft. Worth. Contbr. tech. papers in field. Trustee Tex. Christian U., Ft. Worth, 1978—. Served with USAF, 1944-46. Recipient Ike Harrison award Tex. Christian U. Mgmt. Alumni Assn., 1979; named Hon. Alumnus Tex. Christian U. Mgmt. Alumni Assn., 1982, Bus. Exec. of Yr. Tex. Wesleyan Coll., Ft. Worth C. of C., 1982. Mem. Soc. Petroleum Engrs. (disting. lectr. 1981-82), Soc. Profl. Well Log Analysts (pres. Dallas-Ft. Worth chpt. 1969), Am. Petroleum Inst., Nomads Club (bd. regents 1971-72), Petroleum Club (bd. dirs. 1990—), Ft. Worth Wildcatters Club (chmn. exec. com. 1983), Ft. Worth Petroleum Club (pres. 1992-93). Office: Rock Bit Industries Inc 7601 Will Rogers Blvd Fort Worth TX 76140-6023

GEARING, JOHN WILLIAM, polymer testing consultant; b. Malvern, Eng., Jan. 20, 1947; s. Harold W.G. and Florence Grace Gearing; m. Heather May Gearing, June 1979; children: Tom, Oliver, Louis, Charlotte. MA in Engring. Sci., Oxford (Eng.) U., 1968. Grad. trainee BICC Ltd., Helsby, Eng., 1968-70; sales engr. Brookdeal/ORTEC, Bracknell, Eng., 1970-75; sales exec. DuPont Ltd., Hitchin, Eng., 1976-81; sales dir. Polymer Labs. Ltd., Loughborough, Eng., 1981-94; cons. partner Gearing Sci., Ashwell, Eng., 1995—. Contbg. editor and author: Handbook of Polymer Testing, 1999. Warden St. Mary's Ch., Ashwell, 1991-94. Recipient Queen's award to Industry, 1985, 86. Mem. Brit. Soc. Rheology (com.), Am. Chem. Soc., Inst. Materials. Anglican. Avocations: tennis, music, foreign languages. Fax: (44) 1462 742 565. Please give your wife's maiden name and give your home address (not for publication). Office: Gearing Sci, 1 Ashwell St, Herts Ashwell SG7 5QF, England

GEARY, DAVID CYRIL, psychology educator; b. Providence, June 7, 1957; s. Cyril Geary and Shirley Irene Files; m. Leslie Lynne Reller, Aug. 21, 1982; children: Corie, Nicholas. BS, U. Santa Clara, 1979; MS, Calif. State U., Hayward, 1981; PhD, U. Calif., Riverside, 1986. Vis. asst. prof. U. Tex., El Paso, 1986-87; asst. prof. psychology U. Mo., Rolla, 1987-89; prof. psychology U. Mo., Columbia, 1989—. Author: Children's Mathematical Development, 1994; Male, Female: The Evolution of Human Sex Differences, 1998; contbr. articles to profl. jours. guest Voice of Am., NPR, 1992, 95, 97; contbr. Math. Framework for Calif. Pub. Schs., Calif. Dept. Edn., 1999. Recipent Excellence in Rsch. in Intelligence award MENSA Edn. and Rsch. Found., 1992; grantee NIH, 1994-98. Mem. AAAS, Am. Psychol. Soc., Psychonomic Soc., Human Behavior and Evolution Soc. Avocation: black belt karate. E-mail: GearyD@Missouri.edu. Fax: 573-882-7710. Office: U Mo Dept Psychology 210 Mcalester Hall Columbia MO 65211-2500

GEARY, DAVID LESLIE, communications executive, educator, consultant; b. Connellsville, Pa., Sept. 30, 1947; s. Harry and Edith Marie (Halterman) G. BA, Otterbein Coll., 1969; MSJ, W.Va. U., 1971; postgrad., U. Denver, 1974-75; diploma, Def. Info. Sch., 1971, exec. communications curriculum, U. Okla., 1978, Def. Dept. Sr. Pub. Affairs Officers Course, 1984, Fgn. Svc. Inst., U.S. Dept. State, 1984, Nat. Def. U., 1986; postgrad., U. Sarasota, 1992-95, U. N.Mex., 1998, U. San Jose, 1998 ; D Lit. (hon.), Fairfax U., 1998. Admissions counselor Otterbein Coll., 1968-69; instr. English, staff counselor Office of Student Ednl. Svcs. W.Va. U., Morgantown, 1969-71; dir. info. Luke AFB, Ariz., 1971-72; course dir. English and comm. U.S. Air Force Acad., Colo., 1972-76; dir. pub. affairs Loring AFB, Maine, 1976-79; spl. asst. pub. affairs Seymour Johnson AFB, N.C., 1980; dir. pub. affairs USAF Engring. and Svcs., Tyndall AFB, Fla., 1980-84, UN and US Air Forces, Korea, 1984-85; asst. prof., asst. dept. chmn., mem. coun. of assoc. and asst. deans U. Ala., 1985-88; dir., nat. cmty. rels. dir., acting dir. pub. affairs USAFR, 1988-92; prin. Leadership Comm. Counsel, 1992-95; comm. program mgr., dir. pub. affairs U.S. Dept. Energy, Albuquerque, 1995-99; dir. comms. Lockheed Martin Corp., 1999—; adj. prof. pub. rels. Ga. State U., Atlanta, 1993-95; guest lectr. U. Maine, 1976-79, USAF Inst. Tech., 1981-82, Fla. State U., 1982-83, U. Md., 1984-85, U.So. Calif., 1984-85, Seoul (Korea) Nat. U., 1985, U. Ala., 1988, Ga. State U., 1991, U. Ga., 1991, U. N.Mex., 1997 ; profl. advisor Pub. Rels. Student Soc. Am. Contbr. articles to profl. jours.; mem. bd. profls. Pub. Rels. Rev.: A Jour. of Rsch. and Comment, 1996 ; mem. editl. bd. Jour. of Employee Comm. Mgmt., 1996 . Decorated 4 U.S. Meritorious Svc. medals, 2 Air Force Commendation medals, Air Force Achievement medal, Armed Forces Res. medal, Humanitarian Svc. medal, 2 Nat. Def. Svc. medals, Pres.'s Extraodinary Svc. award Otterbein Coll., 1969, Hon. Citizen of Ariz. award, 1971, Mayor's Community Svc. medallion, Songtan, Korea, 1985, Nat. Disting. Svc. medal Arnold Air Soc., 1986, Nat. citation Angel Flight, 1986, George Washington Honor medal from Freedom's Found., 1988, Outstanding Faculty Advisor award U. Ala. Student Govt. Assn., 1988, Exemplary Svc. award Nat. Com. for Employer Support of Guard and Res., 1991, U.S. Dept. Energy Quality award, 1995, U.S. Dept. Energy Spl. Orgnl. Achievement Recognition, 1995, 96, 97, 98; Readers Digest Found. grantee, 1970. Mem. NATAS, VFW, Assn. for Edn. in Journalism and Mass Commn., Internat. Comm. Assn., Pub. Rels. Soc. Am. (profl. advisor U.N.Mex.), Internat. Assn. Bus. Communicators (bd. dirs. N.Mex. chpt. 1998), SAR, Am. Legion, N.Mex. Pub. Affairs Roundtable (founding), Air Force Pub. Affairs Alumni Assn. Republican. Episcopalian. Office: 6224 Rio Hondo Dr NE Albuquerque NM 87109-3835

GEARY, PATRICK JOSEPH, naval security administrator; b. Milw., Mar. 6, 1957; s. David Patrick and Mary Ann (Delavan) G. BS, Va. Commonwealth U., 1984; MA, U. Richmond, 1987, U.S. Naval War Coll., 2000. Tech. publs. writer Dept. Def. Security Inst., Richmond, Va., 1987-88; ops. security officer David Taylor Naval Rsch. Ctr., Bethesda, Md., 1988-91, Space and Naval Warfare Sys. Command, Arlington, Va., 1991-92; divsn. head office of security Naval Sea Sys. Command, Arlington, 1992—. Pres. Ybor City Jaycees, Tampa, Fla., 1979, Reno Jaycees, 1980-81; regional/dist. dir. Nev. Jaycees, Reno, 1981-83; co-campaign mgr. state assembly Rep. Party of Nev., Reno, 1982; senator Jaycees Internat., Coral Gables, Fla., 1983, life mem.; active West End Jaycees Richmond, 1983-98. Decorated superior civilian svc. medal Dept. Navy, 1995; recipient Charles Kulp meml. award U.S. Jaycees, 1981, Nat. Interagy. award for individual achievment in ops., 1998; Albright grad. fellow U. Richmond, 1985. Mem. NRA, KC, Nat. Def. Indsl. Assn. (life), Ops. Security Profls. Soc. (life, charter, nat. bd. dirs. 1995—, pres. 2000—), Nat. Assn. Parliamentarians, Am. Inst. Parliamentarians, Nat. Mil. Intelligence Assn. (life), U.S. Naval War Coll. found. (alumni life), Va. Commonwealth U. Alumni Assn. (life), Pi Sigma Alpha, Alpha Phi Sigma. Roman Catholic. Avocations: water skiing, basketball, football, parliamentary procedure, pistol shooting. Home: 816 Cresthill Rd Fredericksburg VA 22405-1614

GEBART-EAGLEMONT, JACK EDMUND, psychologist; b. Warsaw, Poland, Mar. 30, 1946; s. Jan and Maria (Winska) G. M of Psychology, U. Warsaw, 1975; PhD, La Trobe U., 1990. Registered psychologist. Clin. psychologist Neuropsychiat. Ctr., Poland, 1975-76, Mother & Child Inst., Poland, 1977-78; counsellor Inst. of Music Edn., Poland, 1979-80; clin. psychologist Ctr. for Therapy, 1980-81; counsellor Social Guidance Svc., Wels, Austria, 1982; rschr. U. Melbourne, 1988-91; lectr. Victoria U. of Tech., 1991-92, Royal Melbourne Inst. of Tech., 1993-94, Swinburne U. of Tech., 1995—. Contbr. articles to profl. jours. Rsch. scholarship Commonwealth of Australia, 1984-87. Mem. Australian Psychol. Soc., Internat. Soc. Philos. Enquiry, N.Y. Acad. Scis. Avocations: philosophy, anthropology, behavioral genetics. Home: 42 Gabonia Ave, Watsonia VIC 3087, Australia Office: Swinburne U of Tech, Psychology Dept, Hawthorn VIC 3122, Australia

GEBCZYNSKI, MAREK, biologist, educator, researcher; b. Slemien, Poland, Jan. 9, 1938; s. Stanislaw Bebczynski and Julia Gach; m. Zofia Augusta Nowicka, May 15, 1961; children: Peter, Andrew. MSc, Jagiellonian U., Krakow, Poland, 1961, PhD, 1966, DSc, 1975. Rsch. asst. Mammals Rsch. Inst., Bialowieza, Poland, 1961-76, assoc. prof., 1976-83; assoc. prof. U. Bialystok, Poland, 1984-93, prof., 1994—, dean faculty, 1984-90, 94-99, vice-rector, 1999—. Co-author, co-editor: Ecology of the Bank Vole, 1983 (Polish Acad. Scis. award 1985); asst. editor Acta Theriologica, 1963-70, editor, 1971-84. Fellow Polish Soc. Zoologists, Polish Soc. Ecologists (standing com. 1990—); mem. Am. Soc. Mammalogists. Roman Catholic. Avocations: international literature, sightseeing. Home: Radzymniska St, 15-863 Bialystok Poland Office: U Bialystok, Swierkowa 20B, 15-950 Bialystok Poland

GEBHARDT, EVELYNE, member of European parliament; b. Montreuil-sous-Bois, France, Jan. 19, 1954. Mem. European Parliament, Germany, 1999—; mem. Group of the Party of European Socialsts; mem. com. on legal affairs and the internal market; substitute mem. com. on citizen's freedoms and rights, justice and home affairs. Mem. Social Democratic Party. Office: Europa-Buro, Lehmgrubengasse 1, D-74653 Kunzelsau Germany*

GEBRE SELASSIE, GETACHEW TADESSE, epidemiologist; b. Addis Ababa, Ethiopia, June 21, 1938; s. Tadesse Gebre Selassie and Tsedek (Banjaw); m. Elizabeth Mengistu Amete, May 4, 1956; children: Betelihem, Esete. BS, Gondar Coll., 1959; MD, Belgrade U., 1973, MS, 1981, degree in epidemiology, 1981. Asst. dir. hosp. Harar, Ethiopia, 1973-76; joint coord. med. svcs. Armed Forces, Asmara, Ethiopia, 1976-78, 2d comdr., 1980-82; permanent sec. Ministry of Health, Addis Ababa, 1982-83, vice min., 1984-91; mgr. ABCD in Health, Addis Ababa, 1992—; prin. Pvt. Health Mgmt. Consultancy Svc. and Clin. Practice, 1996—; advisor UN, Zaire, 1960-61; cons. WHO, New Delhi, 1984, WHO/UNICEF, Jamaica, 1984, chmn. exec. bd., Genea, 1984-86. Active Red Cross, Harar, 1973-76, M.O. Sport & Culture, Addis Ababa, 1985-91. Mem. Ethiopian Med. Assn., Ethiopian Pub. Health Assn. Avocations: football, swimming, walking. Home: PO Box 1151, Addis Ababa Ethiopia

GEBRSELASSIE, HAILE, long distance runner; b. Arassi, Ethiopia, Apr. 18, 1973. Recipient Gold medal for 10,000 meters, 1996 Summer Olympics; broke 15 world records for 3,000 meter, 5,000 meter, 10,000 meter, and 2 mile races; World champion for 10,000 meters, 1993, 95, 97, 99; winner Golden League, 1998. Address: Snelliusstraat 10, 6533 NV Nymeyen The Netherlands Address: Ethiopian Athletic Fedn, PO Box 3241, Addis Adaba Stadium Eehiopee Ethiopia

GEDAI, ISTVÁN, retired museum administrator, numismatist; b. Szentmártonkáta, Pest, Hungary, Sept. 17, 1934; s. István and Istvánné Etel (Rada) G.; m. Istvánné Edit Németh, Sept. 25, 1958; 1 child, Csaba. Grad., U. Lórand Eötvös, Budapest, Hungary, 11957, MA, 1963, PhD, 1964. Curator Hungarian Nat. Mus., Budapest, 1966-75, keeper, 1975-89, dep. dir., 1989-93, dir., 1993-99; ret., 1999; dep. pres. Internat. Numismatic Commn., 1979-92, hon. mem., 1992; sec. Numismatic Commn., Acad. Scis., 1974-85. Author books; contbr. over 350 articles to profl. jours. Mem. Hungarian Numismatic Soc. (pres. 1980-92, hon. pres.), Archaeol. Soc., Hist. Soc., Am. Numismatic Soc. (corr.), Austrian Numismatic Soc. (hon.), Croation Numismatic Soc. (hon.). Home: Galagonya utca 23, H-2112 Budapest Hungary

GEDDIE, ROWLAND HILL, III, lawyer; b. Tuscaloosa, Ala., Jan. 7, 1954; s. Rowland Hill Jr. and Mary Martha (McGaughy) G.; m. Peggy O'Neal Emmons, Aug. 13, 1977; children: Mary Catherine, Virginia Jane. BA, U. Miss., 1976, JD, 1978. Bar: Miss. 1978, U.S. Dist. Ct. (no. dist.) Miss. 1978, Tex. 1979, Mo. 1995. Assoc. Baker & Botts, Houston, 1978-87; assoc. gen. counsel Lower Colo. River Authority, Austin, Tex., 1987-88; sr. counsel Houston Industries Inc./Houston Lighting & Power Co., 1988-92; contract atty. Tandy Corp./TE Electronics Inc., Ft. Worth, 1993; v.p., gen. counsel, sec. O'Sullivan Industries Holdings Inc., Lamar, Mo., 1993—. Treas. Southgate Civic Club, Houston, 1991-92. Presdl. scholar U.S. Govt., Washington, 1972. Mem. ABA, Am. Corp. Counsel Assn. (co-chair EDGAR issues practice group of corp. and securities law com. 1997-98, chair ann. meeting shareholders and proxy statement issues practice group corp. and securities, 1999, co-chair litigation 2000), Rotary. Methodist. Avocations: personal computers, cycling, scuba diving, swimming. Home: 1503 Gulf St Lamar MO 64759-1830 Office: O'Sullivan Industries Inc 1900 Gulf St Lamar MO 64759-1899

GEDIN, PER, publisher; b. Berlin, July 23, 1928; s. Georg Israel and Lena Gedin; m. Birgitta Atmer, Mar. 19, 1954 (div. 1983); m. Ann Katrin Pihl Atmer, July 28, 1989; children: Marika, Andreas, David. D of History of Art, Uppsala U., Sweden, 1953; PhD (hon.), Stockholm U., 1999. Mng. dir. Bokklubben Svalan, Bonniers, Stockholm, 1953-60, Bokförlaget Aldus, Stockholm, 1960-62, Wahlström & Widstrand, Stockholm, 1962-86, Gedins Förlag, Stockholm, 1987—; bd. dirs. Manadens Bok, Stockholm, Pocket Shop, Stockholm. Author: Den Nya Boken (The New Book), 1966, Literature In The Market Place, 1977, Förläggarliv, 1999. Mem. Swedish Pubs.

Assn. (bd. dirs. 1967-79, 88-93, chmn. 1990-93). Office: Gedins Förlag, Tysta Gatan 10, 11520 Stockholm Sweden

GEE, CHUCK YIM, dean; b. San Francisco, Aug. 28, 1933; s. Don Yow Elsie (Lee) G. AA, City Coll. of San Francisco, 1953; BSBA, U. Denver, 1957; MA, Mich. State U., 1958; PhD (hon.), China Acad. Chin. Cultural U., 1972; D of Pub. Svc. (hon.), U. Denver, 1991. Assoc. dir. Sch. of Hotel and Restaurant Adminstn. U. Denver, 1958-68; cons. East West Ctr., Honolulu, 1968-74; assoc. dean and prof. Sch. of Travel Industry Mgmt. U. Hawaii, 1968-75, dean and prof. Sch. Travel Industry Mgmt., 1976-99, interim dean Coll. Bus. Adminstrn., 1998-99, dean emeritus, 2000—; vis. prof. Sch Bus. and Commerce, Oreg. State U., 1975; hon. prof. Nankai U., Tianjin, China, 1987—, Shanghai Inst. Tourism, 1994—, Dept. Tourism Huaqiao U., Xiamen, China, 1995—; cons. Internat. Sci. and Tech. Inst., Washington, 1986-90; trustee Pacific Asia Travel Assn. Found., San Francisco; chmn. Govs. Tourism Tng. Coun., Honolulu, 1989-92, chmn., 1992-96, chmn. industry coun. PATA, 1994-96, PATA Human Resource Devel. Coun., 1996-99, chmn. PATA Coun. on Ednl. Devel. and Certification, 2000—; mem. State Workforce Devel. Coun., 1997-98, Pacific Asia Travel Assn. Human Resource Devel. Coun, 1996-98; acad. Inst. Cert. Travel Agts., Wellesley, Mass., 1989—; mem. Coun. on Hotel, Restaurant and Edn., Honolulu Commn. on Fgn. Rels., Pacific Asian Affairs Coun.; sr. acad. adv. China Tourism Assn. Cons., Inc., 1993—; adv. World Tourism Orgn. Internat. Tourism Edn. and Tng. Ctr., 1991—; external examiner sch. accountancy and bus. Nanyang Tech. U., Singapore, 1996-98; bd. dirs. ProjectonNet.com. Author: Resort Development and Management, 1988, 2d edit.; co-author: The Travel Industry, 1988, 3d edit., 1997, Professional Travel Agency Management, 1990, International Hotels: Development and Management, 1994; editor: International Tourism: A Global Perspective, 1997; mem. adv. bd. Asian Hotelier mag., 1997-99. Bd. dirs. Hawaii Visitors Bur., 1993-95, Kaukini Med. Ctr., Honolulu, 1986-95, KMC, 1996—, Travel and Tourism Adv. Bd., U.S. Dept. Commerce, Washington, 1982-90, Pacific Rim Found., Honolulu, 1987-93; vice-chmn. Tourism Policy Adv. Coun., Dept. Bus. and Econ. Devel., Honolulu, 1978-92; chmn. Kaukini Geriatric Care, Inc., bd. dirs., 1992-95; trustee Pata Found., 1984-95, Kuakini Health System, 1988—; consulting com. Beijing Inst. Tourism, 1992—; v.p. Hawaii Vision 2020, 1992-93; mem. Mayor's Task Force on Waikiki Master Plan, 1992-93; mem. workforce devel. coun. Hawaii Dept. of Labor and Indsl. Rels., 1996-98; bd. dirs. Cyberspace Enterprises, Hawaii Dept. Edn., 1997—. With U.S. Army, 1953-55. Recipient NOAH award Acad. Tourism Orgns., 1987, Gov.'s Proclamation honors State of Hawaii, 1998; named State Mgr. of Yr., State of Hawaii, 1995; named to list of 100 Who Made a Difference in Hawaii during 20th Century, Star Bull., 1999. Fellow Internat. Acad. Hospitality Rsch.; mem. Pacific Asia Travel Assn. (bd. dirs. 1993-96, 99—, chmn. industry coun. 1994-96, Grand award for individual edn. 1991, Life award 1990, Presdl. award 1986), Travel Industry Am. (Travel Industry Hall of Leaders award 1988), China Tourism Assn. (award of excellence in tourism edn. 1992), C. of C. of Hawaii, Soc. for Advancement of Food Svc. Rsch., Chaine des Rotisseurs, Golden Key. Office: U Hawaii Sch Travel Industry Mgmt 2560 Campus Rd Honolulu HI 96822-2217

GEENEN, VINCENT GASTON MARCEL JEAN, internist; b. Verviers, Liege, Belgium, Feb. 6, 1958; s. Marcel and Claire (Fontaine) G.; children: Jerome, Pierre-François. MD, U. Liege, 1982, PhD, 1987; degree in internal medicine, Liege Med. Sch., 1988; biotech. cert., U. Paris VII, 1988. Intern U. Hosp. Liege, Belgium, 1982-89, sr. clin. head in endocrinology and internal medicine, 1989—; rsch. fellow Nat. Fund Sci. Rsch., Liege, 1982-86, rsch. asst., 1986-88, rsch. assoc., 1988-96, sr. rsch. assoc., 1997—; mem. rsch. coun. U. Liege, 1989-93, assoc. prof. in embryology and devel. biology, 1994—; adminstrv. bd. U. Hosp., Liege, 1991-97; mem. Rsch. Coun. French Cmty., Belgium, 1993; chmn. 3d Gordon Conf. on Neuroendocrine-Immunology; rschr. thymus physiology and tolerogenic therapy. Editor: Regulatory Peptides, 1993; co-editor: Horizons in Endocrinology, 1991, Thymus, 1993, In Vivo Immunology, 1994; author: Cryptocrine Signaling in the Thymus and the Central T-Cell Self Tolerance of Neuroendocrine Principles, 1995; contbr. Encycl. Neurosci. on CD-ROM, 2d edit., 1997; contbr. more than 100 articles to profl. jours. in field of thymus physiology and tolerogenic therapy. Travel grantee State of Belgium, Brussels, 1984; recipient Masius prize Medico-Surg. Soc., Liege, 1985, Semper prize Nat. Fund Sci. Rsch., Brussels, 1988, Smith Kline-Beecham prize Royal Acad. Medicine, Brussels, 1992, Alumni prize Belgium U. Found., 1993. Mem. Endocrine Soc., Internat. Soc. Neuroimmuno modulation (charter mem.), Internat. Soc. Molecular Evolution, N.Y. Acad. Scis., European Found. Immunogenetics, Molecular Medicine Soc., Juvenile Diabetes Found., Am. Diabetes Assn., European Assn. for the Study of Diabetes, Eurosci., Am. Assn. Immunologists, 2000. Roman Catholic. Address: Inst Pathology, CHU-B23, B-4000 Liège 1, Belgium

GEERDES, BASTIAAN PETRUS, surgeon; b. Heerlen, Limburg, The Netherlands, Jan. 18, 1965; s. Antonius Theodorus and Theresia (Zwaard) G. MD, Erasmus U., 1992; PhD, U. Maastricht, 1997. Rsch. fellow U. Md., Balt., 1992-93; sho surgery NHS, U.K., 1993; rsch. fellow U. Maastricht, The Netherlands, 1993-96; resident surgery Diaconessenhuis Eindhoven, The Netherlands, 1996—. Author: Dynamic Graciloplasty, 1997. Avocations: literature, music, repairing old clocks.

GEERLINGS, PETER JOHANNES, psychiatrist, psychoanalyst; b. Jakarta, Indonesia, Nov. 13, 1939; arrived in Netherlands, 1951; s. Johannes J. and Anna W. (Bauer) G.; m. Eugenie A. Oosterhuis, Feb. 24, 1965 (div. May 1985); children: Suzanne, Mirjam, Paulien; m. Adelaide M. Katz, Mar. 25, 1997. MD, U. Amsterdam, Netherlands, 1965. Chmn. dept. psychiatry U. Amsterdam, 1984-91, assoc. prof. dept. psychiatry, 1984—; med. dir. Jellinek for Addictions, Amsterdam, 1991—; coord. ednl. program, U. Amsterdam; sec. addiction psychiatry sect. World Psychiat. Assn. Contbr. numerous articles to med. jours. Chmn. com. on addictions, Nat. Coun. Health in the Netherlands, 1988-90; mem. com WHO, Div. Mental Health, Geneva, 1989. Mem. Dutch Assn. for Group Psychotherapy (supr.), Dutch Assn. for Psychoanalytic Psychotherapy (training analyst), Dutch Psychoanalytic Assn. Home: C Krusemanstraat 8, 1075 NL Amsterdam The Netherlands Office: Jellinek Clinic, Jacob Obrechtstraat 92, 1071 KR Amsterdam The Netherlands

GEERLINGS, SUZANNE EUGENIE, internist, researcher; b. Amsterdam, The Netherlands, Nov. 30, 1965; d. Peter Johannes Geerlings and Eugenie Antoinetta-Maria Helena Oosterhuis; m. Edward Ferdinand Klungers, June 7, 1999. MD, U. Amsterdam, 1993. Trainee internal medicine, 1993-96, 99—, rschr. infectious diseases, 1996-99. Author: Urologische Infehticnser Manhlingen, 1997; contbr. articles to profl. jours. Mem. Dutch Physicians Soc. (chair 1999). Home: Kinheimweg 91, 2061 TM Bloemendcal The Netherlands Office: Utrecht Med Ctr, PO Box 85500 For 126, Utrecht 3508 GA, The Netherlands

GEESEMAN, ROBERT GEORGE, lawyer; b. Shreveport, La., Oct. 23, 1944; s. George Robert and Cora (Hamilton) Glasgow; m. Rosemary Monahan, Aug. 19, 1967; 1 child, Regan Glasgow. BA, Yale U., 1966; JD, U. Mich., 1969. Bar: Pa. 1969, U.S. Dist. Ct. (we. dist.) Pa. 1969, U.S. Tax Ct. 1979, U.S. Supreme Ct. 1973. Assoc. Blaxter, O'Neill, Houston & Nash, Pitts., 1969-75; ptnr. Lynch, Lynch, Carr & Kabala, Pitts., 1975-81, Lynch, Kabala & Geeseman, Pitts., 1981, Kabala & Geeseman, Pitts., 1981—; lectr. on tax law and employee benefits; legal adv. bd. Small Bus. Coun. Am. Mem. ABA (mem. profl. svc. corps. com. sect. on taxation, chmn. prof. corp. com. sect. on econs., bd. editors Withdrawal Retirement and Disputes, What You and Your Firm Should Know), Pa. Bar Assn., Allegheny County Bar Assn., Pitts. Inst. Legal Medicine, Phi Delta Phi. Clubs: Rosslyn Farms Country, Rivers, Chartiers Country, Mory's (New Haven, Conn.), John's Island Country (Vero Beach, Fla.). Address: Kabala & Geeseman 2900 CNG Tower 625 Liberty Ave Pittsburgh PA 15222-3110

GEFFEN, AMY, education executive; b. N.Y.C., Apr. 24, 1949; d. Julius Dan and Rose Geffen; m. George Lawrence Shapiro, June 21, 1980; children: Andrew, Douglas. BA, Bklyn. Coll., 1970; MA, Harvard U., 1971; PhD, NYU, 1980. V.p., dean, dir. Coll. of Ins., N.Y.C., 1987-91; nat. dir. tng. Nat. Multiple Sclerosis Soc., N.Y.C., 1991-93; asst. dean continuing edn. Westchester C.C., Valhalla, N.Y., 1993-97; dir., profl. developer Risk and Ins. Mgmt. Soc., Valhalla, 1997—; acting dir. tng. N.Y.C. Dept. Personnel, 1985-89; dir. corp. edn. L.I. Univ., Bklyn., 1980-85; tchr. ESL N.Y.C. Bd. Edn., Bklyn., 1972-86; bd. mem. SUNY adv. bd. for workforce tng., 1994-98. Author: Training Resource Compendium, 1993, Quality Toolkit, 1998; contbr. articles to profl. mags. Recipient James C. Hall Exemplary Program award Continuing Edn. Assn. of N.Y., 1995-96, Muriel Neiman Outstanding Program award Westchester Assn. Continuing Edn., 1995-96. Mem. Am. Soc. Assn. Execs., Am. Coun. on Edn. Nat. Identity Program for Women, Nat. Assn. for Women Deans, Adminstrs. and Counselors, Phi Beta Kappa (assoc. mem.). E-mail: ageffen@rims.org. Home: 69-10 108 St Apt 8F Forest Hills NY 11375

GEGELIYA, DMITRIY ILICH, chemist, researcher; b. Tbilisi, Republic of Georgia, May 24, 1933; came to U.S., 1993; s. Ilia Gegeliya and Ketevan Dahulabishvili; 1 child, Ketevan; m. Tamara Boguslavskaya, April 21, 1987. Engr., Tech. U., Tbilisi, 1958; PhD, Postgrad. Cours, Moscow, 1974. Engr. Road Project Inst., Tbilisi, 1958-61; sr. engr. Phys. Chem. Inst., Moscow, 1961-63; sr. rschr. Road Rsch. Inst., Moscow, 1963-80, lab. chief, 1980-83; dep. dir. Road Rsch. Inst., Tbilisi, 1983-93; prof. Peninsula Inst., Mountain View, Calif., 1995. Author: Asphalt Concrete Pavement for Roads, Bridges and Airports, 1978 (Gold medal 1981), Directions for Optimal Regime of Asphalt Concrete Production, Storage and Transportation, 1989. Mem. Ho. of Scientists (pres. 1996), Internat. Acad. Scis., Edn. Industry & Arts (pres. 1997). Roman Catholic. Avocations: wood decoration, inlay. Home: 1120 Hyde St Apt 102 San Francisco CA 94109-3990

GEGIOU, CONSTANTINA PANAGOS, food scientist, researcher; b. Athens, Greece, Nov. 17, 1931; d. Panagos Leonidas and Anastasia Theodoros (Angelopoulos) G.; m. Eugene Kleanthis Hadjoudis, July 4, 1968. Diploma in Chemistry, Athens U., 1955; PhD in Phys. Chemistry, Weizmann Inst. Sci., Rehovot, Israel, 1967; diploma (hon.), Uppsala U., 1973. Chemist Gen. State's Lab., Athens, 1957-68, dir. rsch. divsn., 1969-89, dir. food divsn., 1989-92; rsch. advisor N.C.S.R., Athens, 1992—; v.p. Supreme Chem. Bd. Greece, 1987-92; mem. Greek Ctrl. Coun. Health, 1990-92; evaluator sci. programs EU, Brussels, 1995; assoc. prof. food chemistry Athens U., 1984. Contbr. numerous articles to profl. jours. Recipient Rsch. Assoc. award Northeastern U., 1968-69. Mem. European Photochemistry Assn., Greek Soc. Nutrition and Food, Greek Union of Chemists (elected mem. gov. body 1994—). Home: Alexandrou Soutsou 15, 10671 Athens Greece Office: Inst Physical Chemistry NCSR, Demokritos Aghia Paraskevi-Attiki, 15310 Athens Greece

GEGUS, ERNÖ, retired chemical engineer, researcher; b. Budapest, Hungary, Dec. 24, 1921; s. Imre and Julianna (Kovats) G.; m. Sara Regeczy-Nagy, Sept. 4, 1953; children: Gabor, Marta, Sara. Chem. Engr. Diploma, Jozsef Nador Tech. U., Budapest, 1944; Univ Dr, Tech. U. Budapest, 1974; Dr Chem. Sci., Hungarian Acad. Scis., 1989. Asst. electrochem. dept. Tech. U. Budapest, 1944-50, rsch. fellow dept. gen. chemistry, 1951-58; rsch. fellow Iron and Steel Rsch. Inst., Budapest, 1959-74; sr. rsch. worker dept. analytical chemistry U. Veszprem, Hungary, 1974-96; Titul. prof. U. Veszprem, 1989. Co-author: Emission Spectrochemical Analysis, 1978, Die Roem. Orgel von Aquincum, 1976, Der Kultgegenstand von Balkakra, 1994; mem. adv. bd. ICP Inf. Newsletter, 1983-94, Can. Jour. Spectroscopy, 1984-95; contbr. articles to profl. jours. Recipient medal Soc. Mech. Engrs. Budapest, 1978, Pattantyus Abraham award Soc. Mech. Engrs., 1988; Silver medal of labour Ministry of Edn., Budapest, 1981. Mem. Hungarian Spectrochem. Soc. (hon. v.p. 1994—). Mem. Hungarian Reformed Ch. Achievements include patents on spectrometric standard probe production, steel and cast iron samples. Home: Lupeny u 12, H-1026 Budapest Hungary Office: U Veszprem, U Veszprem, PO Box 158, H-8201 Veszprem Hungary

GEH, HANS-PETER, retired library director, consultant; b. Frankfurt am Main, Germany, Feb. 11, 1934; s. Peter and Maria Geh; m. Roswitha Dieterich, Aug. 31, 1968. MA, U. Bristol, Eng., 1963; PhD, U. Frankfurt am Main, 1963. Subject specialist City and Univ. Libr., Frankfurt am Main, 1962-69; dir. Libr. Sch., Frankfurt am Main, 1967-69, Stuttgart, Germany, 1970-80; dir. Württemberg State Libr., Stuttgart, 1970-97; cons. UNESCO, 1971—; chmn. libr. assns. and lit. socs., Germany, 1965—. Author: Insular Policy in England before the Tudors, 1964; co-editor jours., 1965—; also articles. Decorated Order of Merit (Germany). Mem. Internat. Fedn. Libr. Assns. and Instns. (pres. 1985-91); European Found. for Literary Coop. (pres. 1991-95); hon. mem. numerous internat. libr. assns. Avocation: travel. Home: Hebbergstrasse 76/1, 70794 Filderstadt Germany Office: Württemberg State Libr, Konrad-Adenauer-Strasse 8, 70049 Stuttgart Germany

GÉHER, KÁROLY, electrical engineering educator; b. Derecske, Hungary, Aug. 13, 1929; s. Lajos and Vilma (Vajsz) G.; m. Judit Glücklich, July 19, 1958. Diploma, Tech. U., Budapest, Hungary, 1952, D Engring., 1963; DSc, Acad. Scis., Budapest, 1973. Asst. lectr. Tech. U., Budapest, 1952-59, asst. prof., 1959-64, assoc. prof., 1964-74, prof. elec. engring., 1974-99, prof. emeritus, 2000—; rsch. fellow Telecomm. Rsch. Inst., Budapest, 1958-67. Author: (in Hungarian) Linear Networks, 1968, 4th edit., 1979, Theory of Network Tolerances, 1971, (with others) Design of Linear Circuits, 1992; editor-in-chief: (in Hungarian) Telecommunications, 1993. Recipient Best Tech. Book award Tech. Pub. Co., 1969, award Acad. Scis. Hungarian Acad. Scis., 1985, Szent-Gyorgyi award, 1998, Szechenyi award 1998. Mem. IEEE, Sci. Soc. Telecomm. (Best Paper award), N.Y. Acad. Scis. Avocations: collecting postcards, classical music. Home: Jászai M tér 5, H-1137 Budapest Hungary Office: Tech U, Stoczek u 2, H-1111 Budapest Hungary

GEHLAUT, BALBIR SINGH, veterinarian medicine educator; b. Sonepat, Haryana, India, May 10, 1950; s. Shri Chand Singh and Gyanwati Kaur (Hooda) G.; m. Krishna Singh Gupta-Kashyap, Dec. 7, 1976; children: Nidhi, Varun Singh. BSc, Panjab U., Chandigarh, India, 1970; MSc, Haryana Agrl. U., Hisar, India, 1973; PhD, J.N. Argl. U., Jabalpur, India, 1986. Sr. rsch. fellow J.N. Agrl. U. Coll. Vet. Sci. and Animal Husbandry, 1974-75, asst. prof., 1975-83, sr. asst. prof., 1983-88, assoc. prof., 1988—; biochemist MIC-Union Carbide, Bhopal, India, 1984, MIC-Indian Coun. Med. Rsch., Bhopal, 1985. Contbr. over 20 articles to profl. jours. Jt. sec. SAI com., Napier, Jabalpur, 1998, pres., 1999. Haryana Fed. Bd. fellow, Hau-Hisar, 1971-72; Nat. Merit scholar Panjab U., 1966-70. Mem. Soc. Vet. Physiol. Pharmacologists and Biochemists India (life), Animal Nutritionists of India (life), Officers' Club J.N. Agrl. U. (jt. sec.). Avocations: reading, gardening, music. Home: Veterinary Coll Campus, Jabalpur 482 001, India Office: Dept Animal Biochem, JN Agrl U Coll Vet Sci, Jabalpur 482 001, India

GEHLAWAT, JAGDISH KUMAR, chemical engineering educator, researcher; b. Nizampur Majra Sonepat, Haryana, India, Sept. 11, 1937; s. Maya Chand and Biran Vati (Malik) G.; m. Vimal Kumari Pawar, May 4, 1963; children: Rajnish, Ritu, Seema. B Chem. Engring., Bombay U., 1962, MS Tech., 1965, PhD, 1969. Chem. engr. Sr. chem. engr. Gharda Chems., Bombay, 1969, R & D mgr., 1972; works mgr. Laxmi Starch Ltd., Hyderabad, India, 1969-71; tech. dir. U. Starch Ltd., Bombay, 1973-74; asst. prof. Indian Inst. Tech., Kanpur, India, 1975-77, prof., 1977-98; cons. Universal Starch Ltd., Bombay, 1976-78, Navin Engring. Co. (P) Ltd., Mathura, India, 1980-87, Amaravathi Chems. Ltd., Madras, India, 1985-90, Radhanagri Coop. Starch Ltd., Kolhapur, India, 1991-95, Invertex India, Ltd., Dhampur, India, 1996-98; mem. adv. bd. Nat. Sugar Inst., Kanpur, India, 1991-96. Editor: Strategies for Rural Development, 1987, Modernisation of Indian Sugar Industry, 1990; author: Monograph on Jaggery and Khandsari, 1994. Recipient Nat. Organic Chems. Industries Ltd. award, 1983. Fellow Inst. Engrs. India (Chem. Engring. award 1997); mem. Technology Info. Forecasting and Assessment Coun., Indian Inst. Chem. Engrs., People Oriental Sci. and Tech. Soc. (founder, pres.). Hindu. Avocations: reading and writing popular articles on science and technology. Home: 248 RK Vihar 29 IP Extn, 110-092 New Delhi India

GEHLER, MICHAEL KARL MILON, historian, educator; b. Innsbruck, Austria, Jan. 15, 1962; s. Horst Karl and Eva-Maria (Unterkircher) G.; m. Angeglika Luise Mayr, Feb. 26, 1994; children: Maximilian, Stefan. D in History, U. Innsbruck, 1987, M in History, 1988, univ. asst., 1996. Univ. lectr. in history U. Innsbruck, 1989-96, asst. prof. history, 1996-99, univ. prof., 1999—. Author: Students and Politics at the University of Innsbruck, 1918-1938, 1990; co-author (with Dietrich Heither): Blut und Paukboden, History of the Burschenschaften, 1997; editor: Karl Gruber: Speeches and Documents, 1945-1993, 1994, Verspielte Selbstbestimmung? South Tyrol Question, 1945/46, 1996, (with Rolf Steininger) Austria and European Integration 1945-1953, 1993, (with Hubert Sickinger) Political Scandals and Affairs in Austria, 2d edit., 1996, (with Rainer F. Schmidt) Unequal Partners? Austria and Germany in the 19th and 20th Century, 1996, (with Thomas Albrich) Austria in the Nineteen Fifties, 1995, (with Rolf Steininger) Austria in the 20th Century, 2 vols., 1997; editor: Tirol Land im Gebirge Zwischen Tradition und Moderne, 1999, (with Rolf Steininger) The Neutrals and the European Integration 1945-1995, 2000. Vol. Red Cross, Innsbruck, 1982-92. Rsch. fellow Fonds zur Foerderung der Wissenschaftlichen Forschung, 1992-96, sr. fellow Ctr. for European Integration Studies, U. Bonn, 2000; recipient various rsch. grants, Ludwig Jedlicka Memory prize, 1987, Dr. Wilfried Haslauer prize, 1994, Theodor Koerner Found. prize, 1994, Kardinal Innitzer prize, 1996. Mem. Leopold von Ranke-Gesellschaft Kiel-Hamburg (bd. dirs.). Avocations: biking, soccer, music, reading, playing with children. Office: U Innsbruck Inst Cont Hist, Innrain 52, A-6020 Innsbruck Austria

GEHLMANN, SHEILA CATHLEEN, psychologist, research analyst; b. Lorain, Ohio, Mar. 25, 1958; d. Donald Eugene and Barbara Ann Gehlmann. BSBA and Psychology, Aquinas Coll., 1986; MS in Applied Indsl./Orgnl. Psychology, Stevens Inst. Tech., 1991. Grad. intern selection and testing divsn. AT&T, Morristown, N.J., 1989-90; projects mgr. Stevens Inst. Tech., Hoboken, N.J., 1988-90; test and measurement specialist Dept. Pers. City of New York, 1990-91; rsch. analyst APA, Washington, 1991-97; rsch. cons. Denver, 1997—; pvt. practice Highlands Ranch, Colo., 1998—. Author: (with others) Stress and Well Being at Work: Assessments and Interventions for Occupational Mental Health, 1992; assoc. editor Jour. Psychol. Practice, 1995—. Vol. Sta. WCTC Cable Channel 9, Wyoming, Mich., 1980-85; participant K-9 walk, Muscular Dystrophy Assn., Fairfax, Va., 1993-94. Named one of Outstanding Women of Am., 1988. Mem. APA (assoc.), NAFE, Soc. Indsl. Orgnl. Psychology, N.Am. Assn. Masters in Psychology, Am. Psychol. Soc., Mid-Atlantic Camaro Club, Colo. Camaro Club. Avocations: photography, camping, cross-country skiing, needlepoint, tennis. Home and Office: Apt 201 600 W County Line Rd Bldg 14 Hghlnds Ranch CO 80129-6512 Address: 10 Lowell Dr Castle Rock CO 80104-2084

GEHRELS, TOM, astronomer; b. The Netherlands, Feb. 21, 1925; married; children: Neil, George, Jo-Ann. BS, Leiden U., 1951; PhD, U. Chgo., 1956. Rsch. assoc. Ind. U., Bloomington, 1956-61; assoc. prof. U. Ariz., Tucson, 1961-67, prof., 1967—; Contbr. to books and papers to profl. publs. With Spl. Airborne Svcs., 1944-48. Mem. Am. Astron. Soc., Am. Astron Union. Achievements include wavelength dependence of polarization; discovery of asteroids. Avocations: hiking, yoga. Office: U Ariz Space Sci Bldg Tucson AZ 85721-0001

GEHRER, ELISABETH, government official; b. Vienna, Austria, May 11, 1942; married. Tchr. Zillertal, 1961-64; elected Vosarlberg State Parliament, 1984, caucus leader, 1989; fed. min. Ministry Edn. & Cultural Affairs, 1995—. Office: Fed Ministry Edn, Minoritenplatz 5, A-1014 Vienna Austria*

GEHRINGER, PETER, chemist; b. Stockerau, Austria, Nov. 21, 1939; s. Franz and Franziska G.; m. Lieselotte Waldbauer, May 30, 1970. Diploma in engring., Tech. U. Vienna, 1966, PhD, 1971. From scientist to sr. scientist Austrian Rsch. Ctr., Seibersdorf, 1967—. Co-author: Environmental Applications of Ionizing Radiation, 1998, Physical, Chemical & Thermal Technologies, 1998; contbr. articles to profl. jours. Mem. Internat. Water Assn., Internat. Ozone Assn., European Soc. New Methods in Agriculture. Office: Austrian Rsch Ctr, Seibersdorf Ltd, A-2444 Seibersdorf Austria

GEHRKE, HANS-JOACHIM, historian; b. Salzgitter, Germany, Oct. 28, 1945; s. Hans and Grete (Jürgens) G.; m. Gudrun Hascher, Aug. 29, 1969; children: Katja, Christina, Silvia. PhD, U. Göttingen, Germany, 1973. Asst. U. Göttingen, 1974-82; prof. U. Würzburg, Germany, 1982-84, Free U., Berlin, 1984-87, U. Freiburg, Germany, 1987—. Author: Phokion, 1976, Stasis, 1985, Jenseits von Athen und Sparta, 1986, Geschichte des Hellenismus, 1995, Alexander der Grosse, 1996, Kleine Geschichte der Antike, 1999; editor-in-chief Klio, 1991—; co-editor Gnomon, 1996—. Lt. German Army, 1965-67. Mem. German Archeol. Inst., Acad. Scis. Erfurt, Acad. Scis. Heidelberg. Mem. Evangelian Ch. Office: Seminar Alte Geschichte, Werthmannplatz, D-79098 Freiburg Germany

GEHRY, FRANK OWEN, architect; b. Toronto, Ont., Can., Feb. 28, 1929; came to U.S., 1947; s. Irving and Thelma (Caplan) G.; children: Leslie, Brina; m. Berta Aguilera, Sept. 11, 1975; children: Alejandro, Samuel. B. in Architecture, U. So. Calif., 1954; postgrad., Harvard U., 1956-57. Registered profl. architect, Calif. Designer Victor Gruen Assocs., L.A., 1953-54, planning, design and project dir., 1958-61; project designer, planner Pereira & Luckman, L.A., 1957-58; prin. Frank O. Gehry & Assocs., Santa Monica, Calif., 1962—. Architect Loyola Law Sch., L.A., 1978-92, Temporary Contemporary Mus., L.A., 1983, Calif. Aerospace Mus., L.A., 1984, Frances Goldwyn Regional Br. Libr., Hollywood, Calif., 1986, U.C.I. Info. and Computer Sci./Engring. Rsch. Lab. and Engring. Ctr., Irvine, Calif., 1986-88, Vitra Internat. Mfg. Facility and Design Mus., Weil am Rhein, Germany, 1989, Chiat/Day Hdqs., Venice, Calif., 1991, Am. Ctr., Paris, 1994, Advanced Tech. Labs. Bldg., Iowa City, 1992, U. Toledo Ctr. for Visual Arts, 1992, Walt Disney Concert Hall, L.A., Frederick R. Weisman Art Mus., Mpls., 1993, Vitra Internat. Hdqs., Basel, Switzerland, 1994, Disney Ice, Anaheim, Calif., 1995, EMR Communication and Tech. Ctr., Bad Oeynhausen, Germany, 1995, Team Disneyland Adminstrn. Bldg., Anaheim, 1996, Nationale-Nederlanden Bldg., Prague, Czech Republic, 1996, Guggenheim Mus., Bilbao, Spain, 1997, Experience Music Project, Seattle, 2000. Trustee Hereditary Disease Found., Santa Monica, Calif., 1970—. Recipient Arnold W. Brunner Meml. prize in architecture, 1983, Eliot Noyes Design chair Harvard U., 1983, Charlotte Davenport Professorship in architecture Yale U., 1982, 85, 87-89, Pritzker Architecture prize, 1989, Wolf prize in art, 1992, Praemium Imperiale, 1992, Dorothy and Lilian Gish award, 1994, Nat. Medal of Arts, 1998. Office: Frank O Gehry & Assocs 1520B Cloverfield Blvd Santa Monica CA 90404-3502

GEIBERGER, BRENT ANDREW, professional golfer; b. Santa Barbara, Calif., May 22, 1968; s. Al G. Student, Pepperdine U. Profl. golfer, 1993—; finished top 10 NIKE San Jose Open, 1996, NIKE Ala. Classic, 1995, 1996; finished top 10 NIKE Dakota Dunes Open, 1996; finished 7th pl. PGA Tour Qualifying Tournament, 1996; runner-up LaCantera Tex. Open, 1997; tied for 11th pl. Buick Open, 1998; tied for 12th pl. Greater Vancouver Open, 1998; tied for 14th pl. Las Vegas Invitational, 1998; runner-up Phoenix Open, 1998; finished top 10 Nat. Car Rental Golf Classic at Walt Disney World Resort, 1998, Buick Invitational, 1998, Honda Classic, 1998; mem. PGA Tour charity team Buick Challenge, 1999. Winner Canon Greater Hartford Open, 1999. Avocations: computers, basketball, computers. Office: PGA So Calif Sect 601 Valencia Ave Ste 200 Brea CA 92823-6300*

GEIGER, BRENDA, criminology and education educator, philospher; b. Cairo; arrived in Israel, 1969; cane to U.S., 1978 (naturalized U.S. and Israeli citizen); d. Franz Haidu-Geiger and Esther Sabbah; m. Michael Fischer; children: Adina, Danielle, Arielle, Avital, Eliana. BA in French Lang., Lit. and Philosophy, Haifa (Israel) U., 1974, tchg. diploma, 1974, MA in Philosophy, 1977; MA in Clin. Criminology, Tel Aviv U., 1980; MSc in Ednl. Psychology and Stats., SUNY, Albany, 1989, PhD in Philosophy, 1986, PhD in Ednl. Psychol. and Stats., 1995. Cert. high sch. French tchr., N.Y.; lic. psychologist, Israel. Tchr. philosophy Re'ally H.S., Haifa, 1973-75; tchr. delinquents and marginal youth Ministry Edn., Haifa, 1975-78; tchg. asst. dept. philosophy SUNY, 1978-86, hon. asst. prof. dept. edn. psychology and stats., 1995-97; asst. prof. social and behavioral scis. Richard Stockton Coll., N.J., 1996-97; assoc. prof. criminology, head tchr. union Safed (Israel) Regional Coll., 1997-2000; assoc. prof. criminology and edn. Bar Ilan U. Western Galilee Coll., Acco, Israel, 1997—, Jordan Valley Coll., Israel, 1999—; paper presenter at sci. confs.. 1090—, latest being Internat. Conf. on Immigration, Culture, and Crime, Jerusalem, 1999; expert testifier N.Y. State Assembly, 1997, Glens Falls (N.Y.) Ct., 1997.; head tchr. union Western Galilee Coll., 1998-2000. Author: (with M. Fischer) Reform through Community: Resocializing Offenders in the Kibbutz, 1991, Family, Justice, and Delinquency, 1995; Fathers as Primary Caregivers, 1996; contbr. articles to profl. jours., including Jour. Offender Rehab., Aggression and

Villent Behavior: Rev. Jour., Jour. Directions in Mental Health Counseling, Internat. Jour. Offender Therapy and Comparative Criminology, Am. Secondary Edn., High Sch. Jour. Vol. Ministry Edn., Haifa, 1975-78, Manof Instn. for Marginal Youth, Acco, 1998-2000; mem. edn. com. Temple Israel, Albany, 1995-97; vol. bridging gap unit Haifa U., 1973-78. Jewish. Achievements include research on phenomenological interview with Israeli prisoners, verbal and emotional abuse in family and school, emancipation of Arab Israel battered women, date rape among high school students, custody disputes and importance of children in life of fathers. Avocations: swimming, hiking, talking to her children, friends, solving social problems. E-mail: geigerb@netvision.net.il. Office: Bar Ilan U We Galilee Coll, Dept Behav Sci, PO Box 2125, 24121 Acco Israel also: SUNY Dept Ednl Psychology Albany NY 12222-0001

GEIGER, HARALD, optoelectronics researcher; b. Sinsheim, Germany, June 10, 1965; s. Hermann Heinrich and Hilde (Esenwein) G. Diploma in electronic engring., Fachhoschule Heilbronn, 1990; MS in Comm., U. Manchester, Eng., 1991; PhD in Optoelectronics, U. Southampton, Eng., 1995. Trainee in electronic engring. Deutsche Telekom, Heilbronn, Germany, 1985-86; asst. electronic engr. Honeywell, Mpls., 1988-89; electronic design engr. Transferzentrum Heilbronn, 1990; rsch. asst. U. Southampton, 1991-93, rsch. fellow, 1994-97, sr. rsch. fellow, 1998; R&D group leader Siemens AG, Munich, Germany, 1998-2000; head hardware design Siemens AG, Munich, 2000—. Contbr. articles to profl. jours. and confs. Scholar Rotary Club Heilbronn, 1988, VDE prize, 1990. Mem. IEEE. Achievements include patents pending for optical fiber sensors and communications. E-mail: h.geiger@ieee.org. Office: Siemens AG, Hofmannstr 51, 81359 Munich Germany

GEIGER, JAMES NORMAN, lawyer; b. Mansfield, Ohio, Apr. 5, 1932; s. Ernest R. and Margaret L. (Bauman) G.; m. Paula Hunt, May 11, 1957; children: Nancy G., John W. Student Wabash Coll., Crawfordsville, Ind., 1950-51; BA, Ohio Wesleyan U., 1954; JD, Emory U., 1962, LLD, 1970. Bar: Ga. 1961, U.. Dist. Ct. (mid. dist.) Ga. 1966, U.S. Ct. Appeals (5th and 11th cirs.) 1980, U.S. Dist. Ct. (so. dist.) Ga. 1983. Ptnr. Henderson, Kaley, Geiger and Thurmond, Marietta, Ga., 1962-64, Nunn, Geiger and Hunt, Perry, Ga., 1964-72, Geiger & Geiger, P.C. and predecessors, 1972—. T-rustee Westfield (Ga.) Schs., 1970-74; mem. civilian adv. bd. Warner Robins AFB, 1976; chmn. coun. ministries Perry United Meth. Ch., 1970-71, mem. adminstrv. bd., 1968—. Capt. USAF, 1954-57. Mem. ABA, Ga. Bar Assn., Houston County Bar Assn., South Ga. C. of C. (bd. dirs.) Perry C. of C. (pres. 1976, 90), Perry Kiwanis (pres. 1968, Man of Yr. 1968), Perry Club Coun. (pres. 1967), Phi Delta Phi, Pi Sigma Alpha. Methodist. Home: 1910 Northside Rd Perry GA 31069-2223 Office: Geiger & Geiger 1007 Jernigan St Perry GA 31069-3325

GEIGER, JOHN GRIGSBY, editor, newswriter, reporter; b. Ithaca, N.Y., Jan. 20, 1960; s. Kenneth Warren and Shirley Frances (Gilchrist) G.; m. Marina Jimenez, Oct. 15, 1999. BA, U. Alberta. Weekly columnist Edmonton Sun, 1981-83, reporter, 1983-86; reporter Edmonton Jour., 1986-87, columnist, 1987-95, edtl. writer, 1995-98; dep. nat. editor Nat. Post, 1998-99, acting nat. editor, 1999-2000, fgn. editor-UN, 2000. Co-author: Frozen in Time: The Fate of the Franklin Expedition, 1987 (best seller in U.K., Germany, Canada), Dead Silence, 1993 (best seller Canada), (children's book) Buried in Ice, 1992; editor: Empire of the Bay, 1989. Recipient Edward Dunlop Excellence award Edward Dunlop Found., 1984. Episcopalian. Fax: 416-442-2212. E-mail: jgeiger@nationalpost.com. Office: Nat Post, 300-1450 Don Mills Rd, Toronto, ON Canada M3B 3R5

GEINGOB, HAGE GOTTFRIED, prime minister of Namibia; b. Grootfontein Dist., Namibia, Aug. 3, 1941; m. Loine Kandume. BA, Fordham U.; MA, New Sch. U. for Social Rsch.; LLD (honoris causa), Columbia Coll., Ill., Delhi U., U. Namibia, 1997; DHL (honoris causa), Am. U., Rome, 1998. Joined SW Africa People's Orgn. Namibia (SWAPO),, 1962, mem. Politburo; asst. SWAPO rep. to Botswana, 1963-64, SWAPO rep. to UN and Americas, 1964-71; orgn. sec, mem. cen. com. Tanga Consultative Congress, 1969; polit. affairs officer UN Secretariat, 1972-75; dir. UN Inst. for Namibia, 1975-89, dir. of elections for SWAPO, 1989, chmn. Constitnent Assembly, 1989-90; chmn. 14th meeting of experts UN Programme in Pub. Adminstrn. and Fin. Decorated Swapo Ongulumbashe medal for bravery and long svc., 1987, Palmes Academiques, French Govt., 1980, Carlos Manuel de Cespedes order, Cuba, 1994, Order of the Sun 1st Class, Govt. of Namibia for outstanding polit. leadership, 1994. Address: Office of Prime Min, Robert Mugabe Ave, Private Bag 13338, Windhoek Namibia

GEIPEL-FABER, UTE MAJA, banker; b. Regensburg, Germany, Oct. 14, 1950; d. Heinz and Irma Wally (Barth) G.; 1 child, Nicolas Philipp August. Dipl., U. Regensburg, Germany, 1975; BA, London Sch. Econs., 1973; PhD, U. Regensburg, 1979. Asst. tchr. U. Regensburg, 1976-80; staff mem. Coun. of Econ. Advisors, Wiesbaden, 1981-84; chief economist Citibank Germany, Frankfurt, 1984-86, head investment mgmt. and rsch., 1987-91; head investor rels. Bayerische Vereinsbank, Munich, 1991-93, head of fin. instns., 1993-97, real estate asset mgr., 1997—; lectr. in field of econs. Contbr. articles to profl. jours. Mem. Verein Fuer Socialpolitik, Profl. Women's Club. Avocations: skiing, swimming, dancing. Office: Bayerische Hypo-und, Vereinsbank, 80311 Munich Germany

GEIRSSON, REYNIR TOMAS, obstetrics and gynecology educator; b. Reykjavik, Iceland, May 13, 1946; s. Geir Reynir and Elfriede Maria (Bell) Tomasson; m. Steinunn Jona Sveinsdottir, Mar. 21, 1971; children: Asta Kristin, Maria. Cand. Med. et Chir., U. Iceland, 1973, MD, 1986. Practice gen. medicine Iceland, 1973-75; resident, 1973-75; registrar, lectr. Nat. Univ. Hosp. Iceland, 1975-85, Univ. Hosps. in, Glasgow, Dundee, London, 1975-84; cons. obstetrician Nat. Univ. Hosp., Reykjavik, 1984-93; sr. lectr. U. Iceland, 1986-93, chmn. prof. dept. ob-gyn., 1994—; sr. lectr. U. Edinburgh, 1989-90; dean faculty medicine U. Iceland, 2000. Contbr. numerous articles to profl. jours. NATO fellow, 1981; European Coun. fellow, 1986; Sci. Fund of Iceland grantee, 1984, Nat. Univ. Hosp. Rsch. Fund grantee, 1987, Icelandic Sci. fund grantee, 1990, numerous others. Fellow Royal Coll. Ob-Gyn. (U.K.); Icelandic Cancer Assn., Icelandic Sci. Soc., Icelandic Med. Assn., Am. Inst. Ultrasound Medicine, others. Home: Safamyri 91, 108 Reykjavik Iceland Office: Dept Ob-Gyn, Nat U Hosp, 101 Reykjavik Iceland

GEISEL, HAROLD WALTER, diplomat; b. Chgo., May 11, 1947; s. Gustav and Stefi Geisel; m. Susan L. Gordon, Oct. 2, 1983; children: Jacqueline Julie, Katherine Louise. BA in History, Johns Hopkins U., 1968; MBA, U. Va., 1970. Commd. fgn. service officer Dept. State, 1970; adminstrv. officer Dept. State, Washington, 1973-75; 1st sec. Am. embassy, Bern, Switzerland, 1975-78, Bamako, Mali, 1978-80; adminstrv. officer Dept. State, Washington, 1980-82; consul gen. U.S. consulate gen., Durban, South Africa, 1982-85; mem. NATO Def. Coll., Rome, 1985-86; adminstrv. counsellor Am. embassy, Rome, 1986-88; adminstrv. minister-counsellor Am. embassy, Bonn, 1988-92; adminstrv. minister-counselor Am. Embassy, Moscow, 1992-93; exec. asst. to under-sec. Dept. State, Washington, 1993-94, deputy inspector gen., 1994-95, dep. asst. sec. for info. mgmt., 1995-96, amb. to Mauritius, Seychelles, and Comoros, 1996-99, sr. negotiator, 1999—. Jewish. Office: Dept State PM Washington DC 20520-0001

GEISENDORFER, JAMES VERNON, religious writer, researcher; b. Brewster, Minn., Apr. 22, 1929; s. Victor H. and Anne B. (Johnson) G.; m. Esther Lillian Walker, Sept. 23, 1949; children: Jane, Karen, Lois. Student, Augustana Coll., 1950-51, Augsburg Coll., 1951-54, Orthodox Luth. Sem., 1954-55; BA, U. Minn., 1960; LLD, Burton Coll. and Sem., 1961. Grain buyer Pillsbury Mills, Inc., Worthington, Minn., 1947-48; acct. Boote Hatcheries, Worthington, 1949-50; night supr. Strutwear, Inc., Mpls., 1951-52; dispatcher Chgo. and North Western Ry., 1953-54; office mgr. Froedtert Malt Corp., Mpls., 1955-56, Nat. Automotive Parts Assn., 1957-60; sr. creative writer Brown & Bigelow, St. Paul, 1960-72; religious rschr., writer, 1972—; rsch. cons. Inst. for the Study of Am. Religion; mem. panel of reference Chelston Bible Coll., New Milton, Eng. Author: (with J. Gordon Melton) A Directory of Religious Bodies in the United States, 1977, Religion in America, 1983, Religion USA, 1989; mem. editl. bd. Biog. Dictionary Am. Cult and Sect Leaders; contbr. articles to books and jours.; cons. editor Directory of Religious Organizations in the United States, 1977. Recipient Amicus Poloniae medal Polish Ministry of Culture and Edn., 1969. Mem. AAAS, Am. Acad. Religion, Philos. Soc. Eng., Acad. Ind. Scholars, Wis. Evang. Luth. Synod Hist. Inst., Augustana Hist. Soc., Royal Anthropological Inst., Ea. Territorial Hist. Soc. (charter), Medieval Acad. Am., Renaissance Soc. Am., George Eliot Fellowship, Wis. Acad. Scis., Arts and Letters, N.Y. Acad. Scis., Aristotelian Soc., Hegel Soc. Am., Sixteenth Century Studies Conf., Am. Cath. Philosophical Assn., Internat. Soc. for Comparative Study of Civilizations, Collingwood Soc., Internat. Assn. Greek Philosophy, Boethius Soc., Brit. Soc. Philosophy Religion, Inst. Interdisciplinary Rsch. Lutheran. Address: 1001 Shawano Ave Green Bay WI 54303-3020

GEISER, FRITZ, zoology educator; b. Heidelberg, Germany, Jan. 8, 1953; m. Bronwyn Marie McAllan, May 1985; 1 child, Tom. Diploma in biology, U. Hohenheim, Stuttgart, Fed. Republic Germany, 1980; PhD, Flinders U., Adelaide, Australia, 1985. Demonstrator in zoology U. Hohenheim, 1978-81; demonstrator in biology Flinders U., 1983-85; rsch. assoc. in biology Macquarie U., Sydney, New South Wales, Australia, 1981-83; postdoctoral fellow in zoology U. Wash., Seattle, 1985-87, Adelaide U., 1987-88; lectr., then assoc. prof. in zoology U. New Eng., Armidale, New South Wales, 1988—. Contbr. over 100 articles to profl. publs. Australian Rsch. Coun. grantee, 1989—. Avocations: planting trees, music, reading. Office: U New Eng, Dept Zoology, Armidale NSW 2351, Australia

GEISLER, JOHANNES ANDREAS, hospitality service professional; b. Roermond, Limburg, The Netherlands, May 18, 1954; s. Ferdinand Gerard and Susanne Maria (Beukkers) G. Grad., Hotel Mgmt. Sch., Maastricht, The Netherlands, 1975; cert. of mgmt., McGill U., Montreal, Can., 1980. Cert. higher food and svc. mgmt. for instns. and comml. hotels. Restaurant mgr. Tott Resorts, Aruba, 1975-77; asst. restaurant mgr. WIH Hotel Group, Montreal, 1977-79; asst. controller Airport Schiphol Catering, Amsterdam, The Netherlands, 1982-85; cons. H&G Hospitality Industry Svcs., Maastricht, 1986-89; co-owner Restaurant de Passory, Cadier Keer, The Netherlands, 1989-92; owner, cons. H&S Assocs., Maastricht, 1992—. Fellow Castle Site Botanic Garden Soc. Mem. Dutch Liberal Party. Roman Catholic. Avocations: tennis, art collecting, land site protection. Office: H&G Assocs, Pr Margrietstr 103-A, NL6101XG Beek Limburg, The Netherlands

GEISLER, THOMAS MILTON, JR., lawyer; b. Orange, N.J., Jan. 16, 1943; s. Thomas M. and Helen K. (Thomas) G.; m. Sarah Ann Farrell Geisler, Aug. 6, 1977; children: Sarah C., Ann. C. AB in Math. (cum laude), Harvard Coll., Cambridge, Mass., 1965; JD, Harvard Law Sch., Cambridge, Mass., 1968. Bar: N.J., N.Y., Conn., U.S. Dist. Cts. (2nd cir.), U.S. Supreme Ct. Asst., base legal officer U.S. Naval Submarine Base, New London, Conn., 1969-71; appellate def. counsel Naval Appellate Review Activity, Washington, 1971-72; assoc. Shearman & Sterling, N.Y.C., 1973-80, ptnr., 1980-91; pvt. practice N.Y.C., 1991-96, New Haven, Conn., 1994—; dir., bd. dirs. Friends of Harvard Law Record, Cambridge, Mass., 1997—. Author: Am. Jur. Proof of Facts 3d, 1995, 96, 98, 99; editor: Trial Practice Newsletter, 1986—. Lt., USNR, 1969-72. Recipient Litigation Star ABA Litigation Sect., 1997, Navy Achievement award USN, Washington, 1971. Mem. ABA (trial practice com.), Conn. Bar Assn., Harvard Club of So. Conn., Harvard Club of N.Y.C., Quinnipiack Club, Madison Beach Club. Presbyterian. Avocations: tennis, squash, theater, concerts. Office: 205 Church St Ste 508 New Haven CT 06510-1805

GEISSER, JOHN EDWARD, legislative representative; b. Worcester, Mass., Oct. 5, 1970; s. John M. and Phyllis E. G. BA in Politics, St. Anselm Coll., Manchester, N.H., 1992; MA in Polit. Sci., U. R.I., Kingston, 1993. Legis. analyst Williams & Jensen, P.C., Washington, 1995-97; legis. asst. Congressional Cons., Washington, 1997-98; legis. analyst Acad. Managed Care Pharmacy, Alexandria, Va., 1998-00, dir govt. rels., 2000—. Mem. ASAE. Avocations: political campaign, reading, hiking, skiing. E-mail address: jgeisser@amcp.org. Home: 1204 Q St NW Washington DC 20009-4360

GEISSLER, ERIK, physics researcher, educator; b. Edinburgh, Scotland, July 12, 1938; s. William Hastie and Alison Cornwall (McDonald) G.; m. Judith Margery Elliott, July 13, 1968; children: Beatrice, Stephen, Leonie. BS, Edinburgh U., 1960; DPhil, Oxford (Eng.) U., 1965. Chargé de recherche Ctr. Nat. Sci. Rsch., France, 1971-90, dir. rsch., 1990—. Contbr. numerous articles to sci. jours. Mem. Inst. Physics, Royal Soc. Chemistry. Office: U J Fourier de Grenoble, Lab Phys Spectrometry, 38402 Martin d'Hères France

GEISSLER, HEINER, political leader; b. Oberndorf/Neckar, B.-W., Germany, Mar. 3, 1930; m. Susanne Thunack, 1962; children: Dominik, Michael, Nikolai. Student philosophy and law, U. Munich and U. Tübingen, Germany, 1st State Law Exam., 1957; 2d State Law Exam., Stuttgart, Germany, 1960; Dr iur. Judge; head office Ministry Labor and Social Affairs, Baden-Württemberg, Germany, 1961-65; mem. Bundestag (German parliament), Bonn, then Berlin, 1965-67, 80—; mem. Rheinland-Pfalz State Parliament, 1971-79; minister social affairs, health and sport Rheinland-Pfalz, 1967-77; minister of youth, family and health Fed. Republic Germany, 1982-85. Mem. fed. bd. Christian Democratic Union, 1967-77, gen. sec., 1977-89, vice chmn., 1989-90, mem. presiding bd., 1990-94, mem. Fed. Bd., 1994—; vice chmn. parliamentary group CDU/CSU. Author: Die Neuer Soziale Frage, 1976, Abschied von der Männergesellschaft, 1986, Zugluft-Politik in stürmischer Zeit, 1990, Heiner Geissler im Gespräch mit Gunter Hofmann and Werner A. Perger, 1993, Gefährlicher Sieg-Die Bundestagswahl 1994 und ihe Folgen, 1995, Der Irrweg des Nationalismus, 1995. Decorated Grand Fed. Cross of Merit. Roman Catholic. Avocations: paragliding, mountaineering and climbing. Office: German Bundestag Pl der, Rep 1 Unter den Linden 71, 11011 Berlin Germany

GEISSNER, EDGAR, psychology educator; b. Frankfurt, Germany, July 5, 1952; s. Rolf and Martha (Lintl) G. BA in Edn., U. Frankfurt, 1974; diploma in psychology, U. Trier, Germany, 1981, PhD in Psychology, 1988; habilitation, U. Münster, 1997. Scientific employee Beltz Testing Svc., Weinheim, Germany, 1988-91; head psychologist Clinic Roseneck, Ctr. Behavioral Medicine, Prien, Germany, 1991-94; prof. psychology Cath. Coll. Northrhine-Westphalia Sch. Social Work, U. Applied Sci., Münster, 1994—; Extraordinary Prof. U. Münster, 1997—. Home: Schillerstrasse 19, D-06114 Halle Germany Office: U Applied Sci Kath Fachhochschule, Piusallee 89, D-48147 Münster Germany

GEIST, KARIN R., secondary education educator, realtor, musician; b. Urbana, Ill., Nov. 23, 1938; d. Wilber Harold and Bertha Amanda Sofia (Helander) Tammeus; m. David Pendleton McPhail, Sept. 7, 1958 (div. 1972); children: Julia Elizabeth, Mark Andrew; m. John Charles Geist, June 4, 1989 (div. 1995). BS, Juilliard Sch. Music, 1962; postgrad., Stanford U., 1983-84, L'Academia, Florence and Pistoia, Italy, 1984-85, Calif. State U., 1986-87, U. Calif., Berkeley, 1991, 92. Cert. tchr., Calif.; lic. real estate agt., Calif. Tchr. Woodstock Sch., Musoorie, India, 1957, Canadian, Tex., 1962-66; tchr. Head Royce Sch., Oakland, Calif., 1975-79, 87—, Sleepy Hollow Sch., Orinda, Calif., 1985—; realtor Freeholders, Berkeley, Calif., 1971-85, Northbrae, Berkeley, Calif., 1985-92, Templeton Co., Berkeley, 1992—; organist Kellogg Meml., Musoorie, 1956-57, Mills Coll. Chapel, Oakland, 1972—; cashier Trinity U., San Antonio, 1957-58; cen. records sec. Riverside Ch., N.Y.C., 1958-60; sec. Dr. Rollo May, N.Y.C., 1959-62, United Presbyn. Nat. Missions, N.Y.C., 1960, United Presbyn. Ecumenical Mission, N.Y.C., 1961, Nat. Coun. Chs., N.Y.C., 1962; choral dir. First Presbyn. Ch., Canadian, Tex., 1962-66; assoc. in music Montclair Presbyn. Ch., Oakland, 1972-88; site coord., artist, collaborator Calif. Arts Coun. Artist; cons. music edn. videos and CD Roms Clearvue EAV, Chgo., 1993—. Artist: produced and performed major choral and orchestral works, 1972-88; prodr. Paradiso, Kronos Quartet, 1985, Magdalena, 1991, 92, Children's Quest, 1993—. Grantee Orinda Union Sch. Dist., 1988. Mem. Berkeley Bd. Realtors, East Bay Regional Multiple Listing Svc., Calif. Tchrs. Assn., Commonwealth Club (San Francisco). Democrat. Home: 7360 Claremont Ave Berkeley CA 94705-1429

GEISTFELD, JAMES GORDON, veterinarian; b. St. James, Minn., Oct. 11, 1947; s. Victor Edgar and Viola Otille (Becker) G.; m. Barbara Jean Lane, July 22, 1972; children: Matthew James, Erin Michal. BA, St. Olaf Coll., Northfield, Minn., 1969; DVM, U. Minn., 1973; MBA, U. Evansville, 1983. Diplomate Am. Coll. Lab. Animal Medicine. Epidemiologist Ctrs. for Disease Control, Atlanta, 1973-75; postdoctoral fellow Bowman Gray Sch. Medicine, Winston-Salem, N.C., 1976-77; staff veterinarian Mead Johnson Rsch. Ctr., Evansville, Ind., 1977-82; sr. rsch. scientist Bristol-Myers Co., Evansville, Ind., 1982-87; dir. lab. animal medicine and surgery Rorer Pharm. Co., Ft. Washington, Pa., 1988-90; v.p. TNT Genetics Svcs., Albany, N.Y., 1995-97; dir. lab. animal medicine, v.p. Taconic Ventures, Inc., Germantown, N.Y., 1990—; cons. Ind. State U., Terre Haute, 1982-87, U. Evansville, 1983-87, OrienTreich Found., Cold Spring-on-Hudson, N.Y., 1992—, SUNY, Albany, 1997—; adj. prof. U. Pa., Phila., 1989-90; mem. expert coms. NIH/ILAR; dir. Mutant Mouse Regional Resource Ctr., NIH; bd. dirs. La Mesa Group, McKinney, Tex. Contbr. articles to profl. jours. Mem. ch. coun. 3d Luth. Ch., Rhinebeck, N.Y., 1992-96; trustee Friends of Clermont, Germantown, 1994-96; mem. C.L. Davis Found. Recipient Hole-In-The-Shoe award USPHS, 1975; NIH fellow, 1975-77. Mem. AVMA, Am. Soc. Lab. Animal Practitioners, Am. Coll. Lab. Animal Medicine, Am. Assn. for Lab. Animal Sci., Am. Assn. Ind. Vets., Am. Gnotobiotic Soc., Internat. Soc. for Gnotobiology, Global Alliance Lab. Animal Standardization Coun., Am. Soc. Microbiology, Rip Van Winkle Hiking Club (leader 1991-94), Catskill 3500 Hiking Club, Sigma Xi. Lutheran. Achievements include design of a new dog run, new animal research facilities; first to report a new mouse bacterial pathogen-group B type V streptococcus; discovery of several new animal models for human disease research. Avocations: gardening, hiking (climbed and hiked on all continents). Home: 288 Linden Ave Red Hook NY 12571-1032 Office: Taconic Inc 273 Hover Ave Germantown NY 12526-5320

GEISTHÖVEL, FRANZ WERNER, gynecologist; b. Hildesheim, Germany, Jan. 24, 1950; s. Werner Theodor and Maria (Eisenhardt) G.; m. Gisela Scharpe, Apr. 10, 1976; children: Katrin, Moritz. MD, U. Freiburg (Germany). Resident in gynecol. endocrinology and reproductive medicine U. Freiburg, Germany, 1980-85, asst. prof., 1985-87, 88-91; fellow in gynecol. endocrinology and reproductive medicine U. Calif., Irvine, 1987-88; pvt. practice Inst. Gynecol. Endocrinology and Reproductive Medicine, Freiburg, 1991—; lectr. U. Freiburg, 1991—. Mem. editl. bd. Human Reprodn., 1992-98. Spkr. Angell-Förderverein of Angell-Sch., Freiburg. Mem. German Soc. Ob-Gyn. (bd. dirs. 1994-96, bd. dirs. sect. gynecol. endocrinology and reproductive medicine 1993—, v.p. 1999—). Social Democrat. Avocations: music, art, travel. E-mail: jeisthoevel@t-online.de. Home: Stahlenhofgasse, D-79279 Vörstetten Baden-W, Germany Office: Inst Gyn Endocr/Reprod Med, Kaiser Joseph Str 168, D-79098 Freiburg Baden-W, Germany

GEITUNG, JONN TERJE, radiologist; b. Bergen, Norway, Apr. 19, 1958; s. Godtfred Bernard and Brita Monsine (Hevrøy) G.; m. Daghild Irene Dencker, Aug. 15, 1998; 1 child, Anne-Grete. MD, U. Bergen, Norway, 1984; PhD, U. Gothenburg, Sweden, 1996; M of Health Adminstrn., U. Oslo, Norway, 1999. Cert. specialist in radiology. Intern Voss Hosp., Øygarden Munic., Norway, 1985-86, resident, 1986-87; resident Haukeland Hosp./U. Bergen, Norway, 1987-90; fellow Östra Hosp./U. Gothenburg, Sweden, 1990-92, cons., 1992-95; chief gastrointestinal/genitourinary radiology Ullevål Hosp./U. Oslo, 1995—. Contbr. sci. articles to profl. jours. Mem. Municipality Coun., Askøy, Norway, 1983-85; active various student poli. orgn. U. Bergen, 1978-84, Conservative Party, 1974-84. Lt. comdr. Res. of Royal Norwegian Navy. Mem. several profl. radiol. socs. Avocations: music, history, chess. Office: Ullevål Hosp Dept Radiol, Kirkevn 166, 0407 Oslo Norway

GELA, GEORGE, electrical engineering researcher; b. Przemysl, Poland, Jan. 24, 1950; came to Can., 1965, came to U.S., 1984; s. Bogdan and Stefania (Olejnik) G.; m. Joanne Lillian Babyn, June 19, 1976; children: Natalka, Oksana. BASc, U. Toronto, Ont., Can., 1973; MASc, U. Toronto, 1975, PhD, 1980. Registered profl. engr., Ont. Rsch., teaching asst. U. Toronto, 1973-80; project leader Trench Electric Co., Toronto, 1980-83; asst. prof. elec. engring. Ohio State U., Columbus, 1984-90; sr. rsch. engr. EPRI-Lenox, 1990—; cons. Trench Electric, Toronto, 1978-79, Panex, Newark, Ohio, 1987-88, Edison Welding Inst., Columbus, 1988-90, Ont. Hydro, Toronto, 1988. Contbr. numerous articles to sci. jours. Nat. Rsch. Coun. Can. fellow, 1980-82, 82-83. Mem. IEEE (sr., officer exec. com., chmn. corona and field effects subcom., chmn. tech. working group of ESMOL), Power Engring. Soc., Conf. Internat. Grands Reseaux a Haute Tension, Internat. Chmn. IEC/TC78 Live Working. Ukrainian Catholic. Avocations: sports, chess, stamp collecting, photography. E-mail: geogela@epri.com. Office: EPRI-Lenox 115 E New Lenox Rd Lenox MA 01240-2245

GELB, BRUCE STUART, city commissioner, consultant; b. N.Y.C., Feb. 24, 1927; s. Lawrence M. and Joan Friedman (Hewett) G.; m. Lueza Denise Thirkield, June 6, 1953; children: John T., Joan H., Richard E., M. Constance. BA, Yale U., 1950; MBA, Harvard U., 1953. With Clairol Inc., 1950-51, 1959-61, v.p. mktg., 1961-65, exec. v.p., pres., 1965-76; brand mgr. Procter & Gamble, 1953-57; brand mgr. Bristol-Myers Co., N.Y.C., 1957-77, sr. v.p., 1977-85, exec. v. p., 1981-84, pres. consumer products group, 1985-89; dir., vice-chmn. Bristol-Myers Squibb, 1985-88, sr. cons.; dir. USIA, Washington, 1989-91; amb. to Belgium Brussels, 1991-93; N.Y.C. commr. UN Consular Corps and Internat. Bus., N.Y.C., 1994-97. sr. cons. Bristol Myers, 1997. Life trustee Choate Rosemary Hall Sch.; mem. Pres.'s Arts and Humanities Com., 1989-91; trustee John F. Kennedy Ctr. for Performing Arts, 1989-91, Howard U., 1987-89. Office: 150 E 52nd St Fl 12 New York NY 10022-6017

GELB, JUDITH ANNE, lawyer; b. N.Y.C., Apr. 5, 1935; d. Joseph and Sarah (Stein) G.; m. Howard S. Vogel, June 30, 1962; 1 child, Michael S. B.A., Bklyn. Coll., 1955; J.D., Columbia U., 1958. Bar: N.Y. 1959, U.S. Dist. Ct. (so. dist. and ea. dist.) N.Y. 1960, U.S. Ct. Appeals (2d cir.) 1960, U.S. Ct. Mil. Appeals 1962. Asst. to editor N.Y. Law Jour., N.Y.C., 1958-59; confidential asst. to U.S. atty. ea. dist. N.Y., Bklyn., 1959-61; assoc. Whitman & Ransom, N.Y.C., 1961-70, ptnr., 1971-93; ptnr. Whitman Breed Abbott & Morgan LLP, N.Y.C., 1993—. Mem. ABA (individual rights sect., real property & trust law sect.), Fed. Bar Counsel, N.Y. State Bar Assn. (trusts and estates com.), N.Y. State Dist. Attys. Assn., Assn. of Bar of City of N.Y., Columbia Law Sch. Alumni Assn. (bd. dirs.), Girls, Inc. (resources com.), Princeton Club. Home: 169 E 69th St New York NY 10021-5163 Office: Whitman Breed Abbott & Morgan LLP 200 Park Ave New York NY 10166-0005

GELB, NORMAN, writer; b. N.Y.C., Nov. 9, 1929; s. Samuel and Minnie (Friedman) G.; m. Barbara Levine; children: Mallary, Amos. Degree, U. Vienna, 1956, Bklyn. Coll., 1951, Columbia U., 1954. Correspondent Mut. Broadcasting Sys., Berlin, 1960-62, London, 1962-75; correspondent New Leader Mag., London, 1975—; Author: Ike and Monty: Generals at War, Jonathan Carver's Travels Through America 1766-1768, Desperate Venture, Dunkirk, The Berlin Wall, Scramble, Less Than Glory, The British. Mem. Soc. Authors London, Fgn. Press Assn. Office: c/o Fgn Press Assn, c/o Fgn Press Assn, 11 Carlton House Terrace, London SW1Y5AJ, England

GELBARD, ROBERT SIDNEY, ambassador; b. N.Y.C., Mar. 6, 1944; s. Charles and Ruth (Fisher) G.; m. Alene Marie Hanola, July 27, 1968; 1 child, Alexandra Pauline. AB, Colby Coll., 1964; MPA, Harvard U., 1979; JD (hon.), Villanova U., 1998. Vol. Peace Corps, Bolivia, 1964-66; joined Fgn. Svc., Dept. State, 1967; staff asst. sr. seminar in Fgn. Policy, Fgn. Svc. Fgn. Svcs., Dept. State, 1967-68; assoc. dir. Peace Corps, The Philippines, 1968-70; vice consul U.S. Consulate, Porto Alegre, Brazil, 1970-71, prin. officer, 1971-72; internat. economist Office Devel. Fin., Bur. Econ. and Bus. Affairs, Washington, 1973-75, Office Regional Polit. Econ. Affairs, Bur. European Can. Affairs, Dept. State, Washington, 1976-78; first sec. Am. Embassy, Paris, 1978-82; dep. dir. Office Western European Affairs, Bur. European and Can. Affairs, Washington, 1982-84; dir. Office So. African Affairs, Bur. African Affairs, Washington, 1984-85; dep. asst. sec. Bur. Inter-Am. Affairs, Dept. State, Washington, 1985-88; amb. to Bolivia La Paz, 1988-91; prin. dep. asst. sec. Bur. Inter-Am. Affairs, Dept. State, 1991-93; asst. sec. of state Internat. Narcotics and Law Enforcement Affairs, Washington, 1993-97; special rep. of pres. and sec. state for implementation of Dayton Peace Accords, 1997-99; U.S. amb. to Indonesia Jakarta, 1999—. Mem. internat. adv. coun. Mus. Am. Folk Art, N.Y.C., 1989. Mem. Am. Fgn. Svc. Assn. Office: US Embassy Indonesia Jakarta APO AP 96520 Office: Dept Of State Washington DC 20520-0001

GELDART, DEREK, retired chemical engineering educator; b. Stockton-on-Tees, England, Sept. 4, 1931; s. Alfred Redvers and Ivy Lillian (Hilton) G.; m. Margaret Wright, Aug. 11, 1956; children: Jonathan Redvers, Andrew Hilton. BSc, U. Newcastle, Eng., 1952, MSc, 1954; PhD, U. Bradford, Eng., 1971. Chem. engr. UK Atomic Energy Authority, 1954-60; lectr. chem. engring. U. Bradford, 1960-68, sr. lectr., 1968-79, reader chem. engring., 1979-88, prof. powder tech., 1988-97, emeritus prof., 1997—; hon. prof. chem. engring. Heriot-Watt U., 2000—; dir. Powder Rsch. Ltd., Harrogate, 1993—. Author: (book) Gas Fluidization Technology, 1986. Recipient Fluidization award AIChE, 1988, Fluidization medal Engring. Found., 1995. Methodist. Office: Dept Chemical Engring, U Bradford, BD7 1DP Bradford England

GELDER, MICHAEL GRAHAM, psychiatry educator; b. Ilkley, Yorkshire, Eng., July 2, 1929; s. Philip Graham and Alice Margaret (Graham) G.; m. Margaret Constance Anderson, Aug. 21, 1954; children: Colin, Fiona, Nicola. MA, Oxford (Eng.) U., 1952, MB, 1953, MD, 1962; diploma in psychological medicine, London U., 1961. House physician, sr. house physician U. Coll. Hosp., London, 1955-57; registrar, sr. registrar Mandsley Hosp., London, 1958-62; fellow in clin. rsch. Med. Rsch. Coun. U.K., 1962-64; sr. lectr. Inst. Psychiatry, 1965-67; physician Bethlem Royal & Mandsley Hosps., 1968-69; prof., chmn. dept. psychiatry U. Oxford, Eng., 1969-96; prof. emeritus U. Oxford, Oxford, Eng., 1996—; chmn. Assn. Univ. Tchrs. Psychiatry of U.K., 1979-82, Joint Com. on Higher Psychiat. Tng. U.K., 1981-85, Wellcome Trust, Neurosci. Com., 1990-95; Mayne guest prof. U. Queensland, 1990; lectr. in field; fellow Merton Coll., Oxford, 1969—; spl. advisor to World Health Orgn., 1995—. Author: Agoraphobia: Nature and Treatment, 1981, The Oxford Textbook of Psychiatry, 1983, 3d edit., 1996, Concise Oxford Textbook of Psychiatry, 1994 (Brit. Med. Assn. prize for best textbook of psychiatry 1995), 2d edit., 1998; joint editor: 2000 New Oxford Textbook of Psychiatry; contbr. chpts. to books and articles to profl. jours. Recipient Gold medal Royal Medico-Psychol. Assn., 1962; grantee in field. Fellow Royal Coll. Physicians London, Royal Coll. Psychiatrists (mem. coun. 1981-90, v.p. 1982-83, sr. v.p. 1983-84, chmn. rsch. com. 1986—), Acad. Med. Scis.; mem. Med. Rsch. Coun. U.K. Avocations: photography, gardening, travel. Office: Univ Dept Psychiatry, Warneford Hosp, Oxford OX3 7JX, England

GELFAND, ANDREW, design consultant; b. N.Y.C., Jan. 7, 1947; s. Alex and Shirley (Press) G.; m. Lynne Gelfand; 1 child, Christoph Eli. BA, SUNY, Stony Brook, 1969; MFA, Rochester Inst. Tech., 1974; MS summa cum laude, N.Y. Inst. Tech., 1991. Cert. limited broker rep. Nat. Assn. Securities Dealers. Applications mgr. Scitex Am. Corp., Bedford, Mass., 1982-84; sr. product mgr. Eastman Kodak/Atex Inc., Burlington, Mass., 1984-86; mktg. mgr. Xyvision Inc., Wakefield, Mass., 1986-88; mgr. curriculum devel. Linotype Hell Co., Hauppauge, N.Y., 1988-93; dir. electronic performance support sys. Mellon Bank/Dreyfus Corp., N.Y.C., 1993-95; pres. Stillwater Media, LLC, Northport, N.Y., 1995-99; tng. and instnl. design cons., 1999—; chmn. vocat. tng. subcom. Assn. Graphic Arts, 1992-93. Mem. working com. The Edn. Network, N.Y. chpt., 1990; gen. mgr. Ctr. for the Study of Zen Martial Arts, Newburyport, Mass., 1979; regional support team Werner Erhard & Assocs., N.Y. chpt., 1989; bd. trustees, membership chmn. Newburyport Arts Coun., 1979. Recipient Devel. grant City Redevel. Office, 1979, Ct. of honor N.Y. State Craftsmen Fair, 1976, Outstanding Achievement award Rochester Craftsmen Guild, 1975, graphic design award 55th Ann. Graphic Arts Exhbn., N.Y.C., 1997, L.I. Software award Listnet, 1998. Mem. ASTD (mem. nat. exec. com. profl. practice area 1993-95), Nat. Soc. Performance and Instrn., Soc. Applied Learning Tech. (instrnl. design excellence award 1992). Avocations: textile arts, folk guitar, zen sword, multi-media development. Home: 368 Half Hollow Rd Dix Hills NY 11746-5866 Office: Stillwater Media LLC PO Box 789 Northport NY 11768-0789

GELFENBEIN, MIKHAIL, neurosurgeon; b. Moscow, Sept. 6, 1955; s. Semen and Narina G.; m. Maya Myagkova; children: Boris, Kirill. MD, Semashko Med. Inst., Moscow, 1978, PhD, 1991. Gen. surgeon State Hosp. 81, Moscow, 1978-81; neurosurgeon Sklifosovsky Inst. for Emergency Medicine, Moscow, 1981-95, head dept. neurosurgery, 1995—. Co-author: XIth International Congress of Neurological Surgery, 1997, XIth European Congress of Neurosurgery, 1999. Recipient Moscow award Major of Moscow, 1995. Mem. N.Y. Acad. Scis. E-mail: gelfen@aha.ru. Home: Osenniy Blvd 12-4-515, 121614 Moscow Russia Office: Sklifosovsky Inst Emerg Med, 3 B Sukharevskaya sq, Moscow 129090, Russia

GELHAUS, ROBERT JOSEPH, lawyer, publisher; b. Missoula, Mont., Oct. 17, 1941; s. Francis Joseph and Bonnie Una (Mundhenk) G. A.B. magna cum laude, Harvard Coll., 1963; LL.B., Stanford U., 1968. Bar: Calif. 1970, U.S. Dist. Ct., U.S. Ct. Appeals 1970. Assoc. firm Howard, Prim, Rice, Nemerovski, Canady & Pollak, San Francisco, 1970-74; sole practice, San Francisco, 1974—; editor in chief Harcourt Brace Jovanovich Legal & Profl. Publs., Inc., 1974-78; pres. Robert J. Gelhaus, A Profl. Corp., 1978—; instr. econs. U. Wash., 1964-65; instr. law Stanford Law Sch., 1968-69; cons. FCC, 1968-69; asst. Calif. Law Revision Commn., 1967-68. Mem. Calif. Bar Assn., Omicron Delta Epsilon, Order Coif. Club: Harvard of San Francisco. Author: (with James C. Oldham) Summary of Labor Law, 11th edit., 1972. Home: 1756 Broadway San Francisco CA 94109-2458

GÉLINEAU, ALAIN-RENÉ, publisher; b. Ceaux, France, May 21, 1952; s. Henri and Marie-Thérèse (Dillot) G.; m. Geneviève Grelier, June 25, 1983 (div. Nov. 1986). Lic., Faculté de Poitiers, France, 1975; MA in French Lit., U. Iowa, 1979, PhD in French Lit., 1982. Tchg. asst. U. Iowa, Iowa City, 1977-83; prof. Faculté de Poitiers, France, 1983-85; founder, mgr., pub. ARGEL, Paris, 1985-90; founder A.L.T.E.S.S., Paris, 1990—; founder Espace Harmonie, Paris, 1998. Author: The Poetry of Transcendence, 1984, Victor Hugo and the Experience of Transcendence, 1985. Avocations: yoga, singing, piano. Fax: 01.47.70.78.77. Office: ALTESS, 4 rue des Petits Hôtels, 75010 Paris France

GELISEN, MEHMET ILKER, medical administrator; b. Mar. 11, 1953; married; 1 child. Student, Izmir (Turkey) Coll., Hacettepe U., Ankara, Turkey, Wuppertal, Germany. Asst. in anaesthesiology Wuppertal, 1978-84; med. dir. Ciba-Geigy, Turkey, 1985-90, Hoechst, Turkey, 1990-91; asst. med. dir., responsible for registration Pfizer, Turkey, 1991-92; asst. med. dir., product scientist Pfizer, 1992-94; med. dir. Bristol-Myers Squibb, Turkey, 1995—; presenter in field. Contbr. articles to profl. jours. With Turkish Mil., 1984-85. Mem. Turkish Med. Assn., Turkish Hypertension and Atherosclerosis Assn., Turkish Infectious Diseases Assn., Turkish Clin. Pharmacology Assn. (steering com.), Turkish Pharm. Technologists Assn., Turkish Pharmacology Assn., Turkish Pharm. Mfrs. Assn. (standby com. auditing com.), Bornova Anadolu Lisesi Edn. Found. (steering com.), Grads. Izmir Coll. (class rep.), Grads. Hacettepe Univ. Faculty Medicine (v.p.). Avocations: reading, traveling, history, medical anthropology, collecting photos of old Istanbul, Ankara and Izmir. Fax: 212 286 2478. Home: Sayhan Sitesi F Blok #8, 80840 Ortaköy Istanbul, Turkey

GELL, GUNTHER, medical educator; b. Leoben, Austria, Sept. 10, 1941; s. Karl and Herma (Kolitsch) G.; m. Ingrid Stengg, Dec. 22, 1967; children: Georg, Barbara. PhD, U. Graz, Austria, 1967. Scientific asst. dept. theoretical physics U. Graz, 1966-67, asst. dept. applied math., 1968-70, asst. dept. radiology, 1970-84, assoc. prof., 1984-89, prof., chmn. dept. med. informatics, 1989—. Fax: 43 316 385-3590. E-mail: guenther.gell@kfunigraz.ac.at. Office: U Graz Dept Medical Informatics, Engelgasse 13, 8010 Graz Austria

GELLER, BUNNY ZELDA, poet, author, publisher, sculptor, artist; b. N.Y.C., May 21, 1926; d. Herman and Shirley (Shoenfeld) Juster; m. Lester Roy Geller; children: Judy Lynn, Robert Douglas, Sheryl Sue, Wayne Mitchell. Student, UCLA, 1944-46, Fla. Internat. U., 1989-97. invited artist Pegasus Internat. Corp., N.J., 1981-85, Internat. Art Expo., N.Y., 1982-83; invited guest artist Broward County Main Lib., Ft. Lauderdale, Fla., 1988; pres. BZG Enterprises. Author: Bunny Geller Original Poetry, 1995, Destiny, 1995, Choices (poetry), 1996, The Monkey and the Parakeet (A Poetic Tale for Children), 1997, Kaleidoscope (poetry), 1997, Impressions (poetry), 1999, Bunny Geller Original Sculpture, 1985; one woman sculpture shows include Bowery Savings Bank, N.Y.C., 1978, Lynn Kottler Galleries, N.Y.C, 1978, Hollywood (Fla.) Art Mus., 1978-79, Broward County Main Libr., Fla., Hallandale Cultural Ctr., 1996; group exhbns. include All Broward Exhibit 78, Ft. Lauderdale, Fla., 1978, Old Westbury Hebrew Congregation, Westbury, N.Y., 1978, De Ligny Galleries, Ft. Lauderdale, Fla., 1979, 1983-84, Internat. Treas. Fine Art, Plainview, N.Y., 1978, 79, 80, 81, Artists Equity Assn. Hollywood (Fla.) Art Mus., 1979, Limited Edition Galleries, Bal Harbour, Fla., 1979, Temple Beth-El, Boca Raton, Fla., 1979, Expo 79, Pompano, Fla., 1979, Hilda Rindom Galleries, Hallendale, Fla, 1980, Jockey Club Art Gallery, Miami, 1980, 81, 83, 84, Gallery SO-HO 7, Ltd., Great Neck, N.Y., 1979-80, Exhibition of Fine Art Nassau Mus. of Fine Art Assn., 1985, Gallery at Turnberry, Turnberry Isle, Fla., 1980-81, Galleria Martin, Palm Beach, Fla., 1981, Contextual Fine Arts, Ft. Lauderdale, Fla., 1980-81, Art and Culture Ctr. of Hollywood (Fla.), 1981, Miami Convention Ctr., 1981, Anita Gordon Gallery, Inc., North Miami Beach, 1981, Collier Art Internat., Ltd., Westbury, N.Y., 1981, Tavistock Country Club, Haddonfield, N.J., 1982, Internat. Art Expo, N.Y.C., 1982, 83, Ohio All Arabian Show and Buckeye Sweepstakes, Columbus, 1982, West Elec. Co., Hopewell, N.J., 1982, Devon (Pa.) Arabian Horse Show, 1982, Bondstreet Art Gallery, Pitts., 1982, Blumka II Gallery, N.Y.C., 1982, Korby Gallery, Cedar Grove, N.J., 1982, Washington Internat. Horse Show, Gaithersburg, Md., 1982, Pegasus Internat. Corp., Pennington, N.J., 1981, 82, 83, 84, 85, Patricia Judith Art Gallery, Boca Raton, Fla., 1983-84, Panache Gallery, Ft. Lauderdale, Fla., 1983, The Nelson Rockefeller Collection, Inc., N.Y.C., 1983, Shorr Goodwin Gallery, N.Y.C., 1983, Carrier Found. Auxiliary, Belle Meade, N.J., 1983, First Annual Internat. Wildlife Exposition, Atlantic City, N.J., 1983, Amann Gallery, Inc., Palm Beach, Fla., 1984-85, Robert's One-of-a-Kind, Bal Harbour, Fla., 1984, Hallandale (Fla.) Pub. Lib., 1984-85, Galleria Camhi, Bar Harbor Is., Fla., 1984-85, Tatem Galleries, Ft. Lauderdale, Fla., 1984-85, Westbury (N.Y.) Meml. Lib., 1984, Trenton Country Club, 1984, Designers' Showcase 1985 Cashelmara, Glen Cove, N.Y., 1985, UN Conf., Nairobi, 1985, Hallandale Cultural Ctr., Fla., 1998; sculptures on permanent exhibits; featured in (book) Artists/USA, 1979-80, The Am. Album, Nat. Mus. Women Arts permanent collection, Washington, 1985, Art Expo N.Y. catalogue, 1982, 83, 92, Limited Collectors Edition, 1982, Town and Country mag., 1982, Gold Coast Life mag., 1983, Art in America mag., 1983-84, Sunstorm Arts Mag., 1984; represented in permanent collection Kushi Found.; Wrote words, music to song One World, 1989. Pres. Sisterhood Westbury Hebrew Congregation, Westbury, N.Y., 1967-69; judge Fine Art and Craft Show, Ft. Lauderdale, Fla., 1979-81; art adv. coun. Westbury Meml. Libr., 1990-94. Recipient 1st prize Carrier Found. Aux. 2d Ann. Arts Festival, 1983; named to Internat. Poetry Hall Fame, 1996. Mem. Nat. Mus. Women in the Arts (assoc.), Nat. Libr. Poetry (Editor's Choice award 1995, published in Best Poems of the 90s 1996), Internat. Soc. Poets (disting. mem. 1995, Poet of Merit 1995, semi-finalist symposium 1995, inducted into Internat. Poetry Hall of Fame 1996). Avocations: tennis, all sports, cultural events, national events, art shows. Home: 400 Diplomat Pkwy Apt 711 Hallandale FL 33009

GELLER, JEFFREY LAWRENCE, financier; b. N.Y.C., Sept. 23, 1953; s. Jerome Charles Geller and Harriet (Rogers) Blum; m. Karina Musheli, Nov. 22, 1990. BA, Columbia U., 1975, MBA, 1979. Sr. fin. analyst W.R. Grace & Co., N.Y.C., 1979-83, asst. to the pres., 1983; v.p. Bank of Am., N.Y.C., 1984-86; exec. v.p. Union Holdings, Inc., N.Y.C., 1986-91; pres., CEO Geller Ptnrs., Inc., N.Y.C., 1991—, also bd. dirs.; pres. Std. Capital Holdings L.L.C., N.Y.C., 1996—; v.p. Idle Wild Foods, Inc., Liberal, Kans., 1986-91, ZG Holding Corp., N.Y.C., 1986-91, also bd. dirs., Acorn Internat. Ltd., N.Y.C., 1993-94, pres. 1995-96; bd. dirs. Deran Holding Co., Inc., Nicola Corp., Soprigest Corp. Fin. Ltd., The Silverstone Corp. Co-author: President's Private Sector Survey on Cost Control, 1983. Mem. com. Am. Cancer Soc., N.Y.C., 1982-86, Friends of Lenox Hosp., N.Y.C., 1985—, Children's Village, Dobbs Ferry, N.Y., 1985-87, Save Venice, Inc., N.Y.C., 1987—. Mem. Columbia Club, Rockefeller Club, Le Club. Avocations: tennis, riding, skiing. Office: Geller Partners Inc 750 Lexington Ave 30th Fl New York NY 10022*

GELLER, NORMAN HARVEY, music arranger, conductor; b. Pitts., Dec. 30, 1934; s. Jack and Rose (Block) G. Student, John Carroll U., 1953-55, Cleve. Conservatory Music, 1952-53. Music dir., pianist RCA Records, N.Y.C. and Los Angeles; arranger, condr., orchestrator NBC-TV, N.Y.C.; music dir. The Great Radio City Spectacular, Las Vegas, 1995-2000. Music dir., arranger numerous performers including Lena Horne, 1990-93, Vic Damone 1977-96, Diahann Carroll, 1985-96, Ed Ames, 1967-73, Ed McMahon, 1976-77, John Gary, 1968-69, Phil Ford and Mimi Hines, 1972-77, Joe Williams, 1973, Ethel Merman, 1964, Peter Nero, 1965-66, Paul Lynde, 1976-77, Monty Hall, 1976, Ray Bolger, 1962-63, Kay Armen, 1963-68, Allen and Rossi, Dick Haymes, 1971-72, Rip Taylor, 1972, Susan Anton, 1995—; music dir. Playboy Clubs, 1961-62, Thunderbird Hotel, 1973, Sands Hotel, 1981-82, (TV series) The New Original Amateur Hour, 1992-93; condr. natl. co. "I Do, I Do," 1969-70, Gene Kelly's Salute to Broadway nat. tour, 1976. Mem. Nat. Acad. Rec. Arts and Scis. Club: Friars (N.Y.C.).

GELLER, ROBERT JAMES, advertising agency executive; b. N.Y.C., May 5, 1937; s. Jerome and Pearl (Klein) G.; m. Lois Dee Fromkin, June 9, 1968; children: Richard Evan, Stephen Laurence. BS, CCNY, 1958. Account exec. Furman, Feiner & Co., N.Y.C., 1958-62; media supr. Interpublic Group of Cos., N.Y.C., 1962-64; asst. media dir. Foote, Cone & Belding, N.Y.C., 1964-69; pres. Adforce, Inc., N.Y.C., 1970-92, Robert J. Geller & Assocs., Inc., N.Y.C., 1993—; pres., CEO Reel Am., Inc., N.Y.C., 2000—. Contbr. numerous articles to profl. jours. Mem. Assn. Nat. Advertisers (mem. mgmt. policy com. 1980-92, corp. membership com. 1990-92), Am. Advt. Fedn. (bd. dirs. 1988—, mem. corp. membership com. 1989—, plans rev. com. 1990—, asst. sec. 1992—), Advt. Club N.Y.C. Republican. Home: 155 E 76th St New York NY 10021-2810 also: Parsonage Ln Sagaponack NY 11962 Office: Robert J Geller & Assocs Inc 122 E 42nd St Rm 1017 New York NY 10168-1017

GELLER-BERNSTEIN, CARMI, allergist; b. Suceava, Romania, Nov. 20, 1934; arrived in Israel, 1958; d. Imanuel and Henriette Roxane (Sternberg) Geller; m. Dinu Vlad Bernstein, Nov. 20, 1958; children: Alina, Alon. MD, U. Bucharest, 1958; degree in pediatrics, U. Jerusalem, 1965; degree in allergy, immunology, U. Tel Aviv, 1976. Head pediat. allergy clinic Kaplan Hosp., Jerusalem U., Rehovot, Israel, 1965—; dir. allergy clinic Gen. Sick Fund Zamenhoff, Tel Aviv, 1983—; cons. Weizmann Inst., Rehovot, 1972—, Tel Aviv U., 1980—. Contbr. articles to sci. and profl. jours. Mem. European Acad. Allergy Clin. Immunology, European Soc. Pediatric Allergy Clin. Immunology. Avocations: classical music, theater, travel, sports, gardening. Home: 68 Herzl Str, 59454 Bat Yam Israel Office: Kaplan Hosp, Rehovot Israel

GELLERT, EDWARD BRADFORD, advertising agency executive; b. Meadowbrook, Pa., Sept. 8, 1924; s. N. Henry and Edna Louise (Smith) G.; m. Audrey Marie Bethilde Freese, Dec. 18, 1948; children: Audrey M.F. Gellert Taylor, E. Bradford III, Christina M.H.E. BA, Yale U., 1945W, PBK, 1946-48; student Law, NYU, 1950-51, studies in advt. effectiveness, 1949-50; French, Berlitz Sch., 1967; student, N.Y. Inst. Fin., N.Y.C., 1972; student creative writing course, U. Conn., 1960, real estate broker's lic., 1971. From trainee to new product mgr. Vick Chem. Co., N.Y.C., 1948-55; account exec. Compton Advt., N.Y.C., 1956-60; v.p., acct supr. Young and Rubican Advt. Agy., N.Y.C., 1960-67; pres. Gellert & Jackson Acquisitons and Mergers, N.Y.C., 1969-74; sales and mktg. dir. The Gellert Co., Boise, Idaho, 1975-79; pres., owner CIPRA Advt., Boise, 1979—; bd. dirs. Healthwise, Boise, Idaho, 1993—. Author, illustrator, publisher: You're Not Too Old to Win at Tennis, 1984 (1988 selected by U.S. Dept. Info. 1 of 200 Sports Books for exhibit in 100 internat. cities). 2d lt. Army Air Corps, 1943-45. Recipient Harvard Club award, 1941; Bronze award Am. Legion, 1939. Mem. Boise C. of C., Nat. Fedn. Ind. Bus., Nat. Eagle Scout Assn. (life), U.S. Tennis Assn. (life), Yale Club N.Y.C., Boise Racquet and Swim Club. Republican. Episcopalian. Avocations: tennis, creative writing, art, yard work. Home and Office: Cipra Advt 314 E Curling Dr Boise ID 83702-1629

GELLES, ROMY SUSAN, psychologist; b. Phila., Aug. 25, 1965; d. Herman Theodore and Renee (Miller) G. BA, NYU, 1987; MS, Stevens Inst. Tech., Hoboken, N.J., 1992; PhD, U.S. Internat. U., San Diego, 1995. Mgmt. trainee Thomson McKinnon Securities, Inc., N.Y.C., 1987-89; program mgr. Pvt. Industry Coun., N.Y.C., 1989-91; cons. R.S. Global Resources, N.Y.C., 1991-98; dir. global tng. Red Planet Solutions GmbH, Frankfurt, Germany, 1998—. Rsch. test developer leadership devel. survey: Who Should Lead?, 1994; co-developer manual: Women in Leadership Roles Women's Work, 1995. Big sister Big Sisters/Big Bros., N.Y.C., 1988-92. Mem. APA, European Women's Mgmt. Devel. Network, Internat. Women's Club. Avocations: rollerskating, tennis, baking, yoga. Office: Red Planet Solutions GmbH, Nordendstrasse 32, 60318 Frankfurt Germany

GELLMAN, ROBERT, psychiatrist; b. Paris, Nov. 10, 1935; s. Georges and Dora (Limiski) G.; m. Claire Barroux, Sept. 23, 1969; children: Emmanuel, Antoine, Eve, Sophie. MD, U. Paris, 1962, psychiatrist specialist, 1964, neurologist specialist, 1967, pedo-psychiatrist specialist, 1999. Asst. dept. psychiatry Marseilles U., 1966, U. Paris, 1967-69; mgr. dept. psychiatry Hosp. Gireugne, 1970; psychiatrist dept. mgr. Hosp. Gonesse, 1971-81, Hosp. Maison Blanche, Paris, 1981-2000; prof. Valencia U., Spain, 1996—; lectr. Casablanca U., Morocco, 1997—; pres. French Sch. Sexology, 1996-2000; bd. dirs. Alhus. Author: Actuality Sexologious T1, 1979, Actualities Sexologious T2, 1981, Psycho-Sexology, 1994, Integrative Sexo-Therapies, 1997, Complexes, Myths of Sexuality, 1998. With Mil. Health Svc., 2000. Mem. French Soc. Sexology (bd. dirs., pres.), Medico-Psychologist Soc., Myths and Psychotherapy Soc. Avocations: opera, theatre, cinema, painting, arts. Home: 3 Rue Copernic, 75116 Paris France Office: Hopital Maison Blanche, 20 Rue de la Tour DAuvergne, 75009 Paris France

GELL-MANN, MURRAY, theoretical physicist, educator; b. N.Y.C., Sept. 15, 1929; s. Arthur and Pauline (Reichstein) Gell-M.; m. J. Margaret Dow, Apr. 19, 1955 (dec. 1981); children: Elizabeth, Nicholas; m. Marcia Southwick, June 20, 1992; 1 stepson, Nicholas Levis. BS, Yale U., 1948; PhD, Mass. Inst. Tech., 1951; ScD (hon.), Yale U., 1959, U. Chgo., 1967, U. Ill., 1968, Wesleyan U., 1968, U. Turin, Italy, 1969, U. Utah, 1970, Columbia U., 1977, Cambridge U., 1980; D (hon.), Oxford (Eng.) U., 1992, So. Ill. U., 1993, U. Fla., 1994, So. Meth. U., 1999. Mem. Inst. for Advanced Study, 1951, 55, 67-68; instr. U. Chgo., 1952-53, asst. prof., 1953-54, assoc. prof., 1954; assoc. prof. Calif. Inst. Tech., Pasadena, 1955-56; prof. Calif. Inst. Tech., 1956-67, R.A. Millikan prof. physics, 1967-93, R.A. Millikan prof. emeritus, 1993—; disting. fellow Santa Fe Inst., 1993—, co-chmn. sci. bd., 1985-2000; vis. prof. MIT, spring 1963, CERN, Geneva, 1971-72, 79-80, U. N.Mex., 1995—; vis. assoc. prof. Columbia U., 1954; overseas fellow Churchill Coll., 1966; mem. Pres.'s Sci. Adv. Com., 1969-72, Pres.'s Com. of Advisors on Sci. and Tech., 1994—; mem. sci. and grants com., Leakey Found., 1977-80; chmn. bd. trustees Aspen Ctr. for Physics, 1973-79; founding trustee Santa Fe Inst., 1982, chmn. bd. trustees, 1982-85, co-chmn. sci. bd. 1993-2000, prof., disting. fellow, 1993—; cons. Inst. Def. Analysis, Arlington, Va., 1961-70, Rand Corp., Santa Monica, Calif., 1956; mem. physics panel NASA, 1964, Coun. Fgn. Rels., 1975—, Los Alamos (N.Mex.) Sci. Lab., 1956—, Lab. fellow, 1982—; mem. adv. bd. Network Physics, 1999—. Author: (with Y. Ne'eman) Eightfold Way. Citizen regent Smithsonian Instn., 1974-88; trustee Wildlife Conservation Soc., 1994—; bd. dirs. J.D. and C.T. MacArthur Found., 1979—, Calif. Nature Conservancy, 1984-93; bd. dirs. AeroVironment, Inc., 1971—; chmn. Lovelace Insts., 1993-95. NSF post doctoral fellow, vis. prof. Coll. de France and U. Paris, 1959-60; recipient Dannie Heineman prize Am. Phys. Soc., 1959; E.O. Lawrence Meml. award AEC, 1966; Franklin medal, 1967; Carty medal Nat. Acad. Scis., 1968; Rsch. Corp. award, 1969; named to UN Environ. Program Roll of Honor for Environ. Achievement, 1988; Nobel prize in physics, 1969, Erice prize, 1990. Fellow Am. Phys. Soc.; mem. NAS, AAAS, Am. Acad. Arts and Scis. (v.p., chmn. Western ctr. 1970-76), Council on Fgn. Relations, French Phys. Soc. (hon.), Am. Philos. Soc., Conservation Internat. (sci. adv. com. 1993), Royal Soc. London (fgn.), Pakistan Acad. Scis. (fgn.), Indian Acad. Scis. (fgn.), Russian Acad. Scis. (fgn.). Clubs: Cosmos (Washington); Century Assn., Explorers (N.Y.C.); Athenaeum (Pasadena). Address: Santa Fe Institute 1399 Hyde Park Rd Santa Fe NM 87501-8943

GELMAN, LEONID MOISEEVICH, scientist, vibroacoustician, educator; b. Kiev, Ukraine, Apr. 15, 1949; s. Moisey Morduh-Leybovich and Mariya Grigorevna (Dubinskaya) G.; 1 child, Anna. MS with honors, Nat. Tech. U. Ukraine, 1972; PhD, Acoustical Inst., Moscow, 1987, DSc, 1993. Prof. dept. nondestructive testing, dept. orientation, navigation Nat. Tech. U. Ukraine; prof. dept. mech. engring. Zhitomir Inst. Engring. Tech.; academician Russian Acad. Natural Scis., Ukrainian Acad. Scis. of Nat. Progress, Acad. Scis. of Applied Radioelectronics of Belarus, Russia, Ukraine; head dept. vibroacoustical diagnostics sci. prodn. union Slavutich; vis. lectr. Cleve. U., 1996, Boston U., 1997, Wayne U., Detroit, 1997, U. Mich., Ann Arbor, 1997, NYU, 1998; vis. prof. U. Le Mans, France, 1998, Technion, Israel, 1999, U. S.C., 2000; mem. coun. conferment DSc, PhD, Nat. Tech. U. Ukraine, prin. investigator, chief designer grants contracts, mil. oriented rsch. developer, 1972-92. Contbr. more than 100 articles to profl. jours.; holder 17 patents. Recipient award U.S. Internat. Sci. Found., award U.S. Civilian R&D Found., award U.S. MacArthur Found., award Israel Lady Davis Fellowship Trust; Italian Landau-Volta fellowship. Mem. Acoustical Soc. Am. (award), Acoustical Soc. Japan, Russian Acoustical Soc., Ukrainian Soc. Nondestructive Testing, London Inst. EE, Internat. Inst. Acoustics Vibration. Avocations: modern literature, sports, dancing. Fax: (38044) 296 58 82. E-mail: ania@gelman.pp.kiev.ua. Home: PO Box 794/6, 103 Kiev 01103, Ukraine Office: Nat Tech U Ukraine Dept, Nondestructive Testing, Kiev-103 252103, Ukraine

GELZER, DAVID GEORG, English educator, missionary; b. Vevey, Vaud, Switzerland, Oct. 7, 1919; came to U.S., 1937; s. Heinrich Gelzer and Charlotte Elisabeth Lüdecke; m. Elisabeth Genilla Bennett, June 12, 1949; children: Charlotte, Rebekah, Miriam, Christian, Stuart. BA, U. Dubuque, 1941, B. in Div., 1943; PhD, Yale U., 1952; D. Humane Letters (hon.), Wilson Coll., Chambsburg, Pa., 1972; D. Div. (hon.), Tainan (Taiwan) Theol. Sem., 1994. Ordained to ministry Presbyn, Ch., 1943. Prof. religion, German Albertson Coll., Caldwell, Idaho, 1946-50; prof. religion, German, Coll. Evangélique de Libamba, Makak, Cameroon, 1952-61; prof. history theology and ecumenics Faculté Théologie Protestante, Yaoundé, Cameroon, 1960-75, dean, 1960-69; prof. theology, ch. history Tainan Theol. Sem., 1975-84; lectr., ecumenics Yale Div. Sch., New Haven, Conn., 1982; lectr. ecumenics McCormick Theol. Sem., Chgo., 1984; prof. theology, ecumenics Talua Ministry Training Ctr., Luganville, Vanuatu, 1985-88; acting prin. Talua Ministry Training Ctr., Luganville, 1985-87. English lang. editor Taiwan Ch. News, 1980-84. Canterbury Cleric (pres. 1992-95, sec. 1995-99), Phila., governing bd. Stony Point, N.Y.; election judge Swarthmore (Pa.) We. Dist., 1994—; treas., bd. dirs. Swarthmore Sr. Citizen Assoc., Swarthmore, 1997-2000. Recipient Alumnus Distinction award U. Dubuque, 1949, 20th Century Achievement award Internat. Biog. Ctr.; decorated Chevalier de la Légion d'Honneur, Republic of Cameroon, 1971. Internat. Assn. Mission Studies. Democrat. Presbyn. Avocations: classical music, reading, swimming. Home and Office: 912 Harvard Ave Swarthmore PA 19081-2208

GEMAYEL, (EDMOND) BOUTROS, archbishop; b. Ain el Khar, Metn, Lebanon, June 29, 1932; s. Fares Bargis and Mathilde (Amin) G. MA in Theology, St. Joseph U., Beirut; PhD in Oriental Scis., Pontifical Oriental Inst., Rome. Archbishop of Cyprus Maronite Cath. Ch., Nicosia. Author several books. Office: Maronite Archbishop's House, 8 Ayios Maronas St PO Box 22249, Nicosia Cyprus

GEMBITSKY, DMITRY S., peptide biologist, pharmacologist; b. Minsk, Belarus, Aug. 10, 1967; came to U.S., 1996; s. Sergei Alexandrovich and Regina Iosifovna (Bobrovich) G. MD summa cum laude, 2d Moscow Pirogov Med. Inst., 1990; PhD, Russian State Med. U., 1994. Asst. dir. medico-biol. sch. Russian State Med. U., Moscow, 1990-92, instr. biology, 1990-94, postgrad. rschr., 1991-94; rsch. fellow Nat. Hosp., Oslo U., 1995-96; rsch. scientist Creighton U., Omaha, 1996—; Author: (chpt.) Progress in Molecular and Subcellular Biology, vol. 20, Inhibitors of Cell Growth, 1998; contbr. articles to profl. jours. Rsch. fellow Medinnova Found., 1995-96; grantee Dept. Health Nebr., 1997—, travel grantee Bachem Chem. Co., 1998, 2000, travel grantee Am. Peptide Soc., 1999. Mem. AAAS, Am. Assn. for Cancer Rsch., Am. Peptide Soc., Fedn. Am. Socs. Experimental Biology, European Peptide Soc., Am. Antivivisection Soc. Avocations: music, opera, languages, travelling.

GEMÜNDEN, HANS GEORG, economist, educator, marketing educator; b. Ingelheim, Germany, July 16, 1949; s. Karl Julius Ernst and Anna Louise Eugenie (Willms) G.; children: Claudia, Cornelia, Christian. PhD in Bus. Adminstrn., U. Saarland, Saarbrücken, Germany, 1979; degree, U. Kiel,

Germany, 1986. Head of Inst. for Applied Mgmt. Sci. and Corp. Strategy U. Karlsruhe (Germany), 1988—, dean faculty of econs., 1990-92. Author: Interaction, Relationships and Networks, 1996, Relationships and Networks in International Markets, 1997; contbr. articles to profl. jours. Home: Klostergasse 3, 76275 Ettlingen Germany Office: Univ Karlsruhe, Waldhornstr 27, 76131 Karlsruhe Germany

GENA, ANGELIKI CONSTANTINE, psychologist, educator; b. Mandraki, Rhodes, Greece, June 3, 1964; d. Constantine G. and Maria C. (Contoveros) G.; m. Emmanuel N. Tsihlis. BA, CUNY, 1985, MA, 1987, PhD, 1995. Coord. Kinesthetic After Effect Lab., N.Y., 1985-87; asst. rschr. Infant Lab. Queens Coll.-CUNY, 1988-92; fellow Princeton (N.J.) Child Devel. Inst., 1992-94; dir. ednl. programming Alpine Learning Group, N.J., 1994-95; pvt. practice with Autistic children Athens, Greece, 1995—; cons. Elpides-Greek Women's Assn., N.Y., 1994-95; adj. prof. Queens Coll.-CUNY, 1994-95; fellow Inst. Behavioral Rsch. and Therapy, Athens, 1995-96; prof. U. Thessaly, Volos, Greece, 1996-99; prof. U. Athens, 1998—. Author: Alpine Learning Group Staff Training Manual, 1993, Therapeutic Issues in Cognitive and Behavioral Therapy, 1996, Co-Education of Children With and Without Learning and Behavioral Problems, 1997; inventor in field. Recipient Katsimatidis award Gnomagoras-Non-For-Profit Orgn., N.Y., 1982; grad. fellow Queens Coll. CUNY, 1986, Doctoral Rsch. fellow Princeton Child Devel. Inst., 1992. Mem. APA, Assn. Behavior Analysis, Greek Assn. for Behavioral Rsch. (bd. dirs. 1997—). Avocations: playing piano, poetry, theater, traveling, religion. Home: Aigaiou 50, NEA SMYRNI 17124 Athens Greece Office: U Athens, Sch of Philosophy, 15784 Panepistimiopolis Athens, Greece

GENAIN, MARC P., engineering consultant. Grad. in Engring., Ecole Nat. Superieure de l'Aéronautique et de l'Espace, France, 1973; MS in Aeronautics and Astronautics, MIT, 1975; Profl. Engr. in Mech. Engring., 1989. CPA, France; cert. proficiency in English. Rsch. asst. Charles Stark Draper Lab., MIT, Cambridge, 1973-74; project engr. SNECMA, France, 1975-76; rsch. computer engr. EDF, France, 1975; project engr. Paris Transp. Authority, 1976-78; project engr. SOFRETU, Caracas, Venezuela, 1978-81, Busan, Republic of Korea, 1981-82; project engr. SOFRETU, Singapore, 1982-83, proposal mgr., 1983-86; mgr. systems engring. LSTS, Bloomfield, N.J., 1984-88; sr. cons., ops. and design mgr. Trans Manche Link, Folkstone, Kent, Eng., 1989-94; project dir., bus. devel. mgr. Hong Kong, Singapore, NY, 1994-98; project dir. Channel Tunnel High Speed Rail Link, 1996-98; assoc. dir. SYSTRA, 1998—. Mem. Assn. SUP-AERO, Assn. CPA, MIT Club Paris, Sci. Rsch. Soc. N.Am., Sigma Xi. E-mail: mgenain@systra.com. Home: 35 rue du Marechal Joffre, 78100 Saint Germain en Laye Paris, France Office: SYSTRA, 5-7 Ave du Coq, 75009 Paris France

GENDEL, LEONID YAKOVLEVICH, biophysicist, researcher; b. Moscow, June 29, 1944; s. Yakov Savelievich Gendel and Maria Abramovna Sonkina; m. Elena Evgenievna Fadeeva, Dec. 12, 1975; 1 child, Ekaterina. Ms, Lomonosov Moscow State U., 1966; PhD, Russian Acad. Scis., Moscow, 1973, DSc in Biology, 1988. Rsch. scientist Semenov Chem. Physics Inst., Russian Acad. Scis., Moscow, 1971-73, sr. rsch. scientist, 1973-80, head rsch. group, 1980-96; head rsch. group Biochem. Physics Inst., Russian Acad. Scis., Moscow, 1996—; vis. prof. Lomonosov Moscow State U., 1990—. Contbr. articles to profl. jours. Recipient medal in memory of 850 years of Moscow, The Pres. Russian Fedn., 1999. Mem. Internat. Electron Paramagnetic Resonance (Electron Spin Resonance) Soc., N.Y. Acad. Sci. Office: RAS Biochem Physics Inst, u Kosygina 4, 117977 Moscow Russia

GENDEN, TSERENDULAM, museum director, physician; b. Taragt Somon, Mongolia, May 31, 1927; d. P. Genden and D. Donjid; m. Namsrain Sodnom, Aug. 25, 1945; children: Sarna, Hongorzul, Zambaga, Enhbat, Behbat, Dulma. Diploma, Mongolian State U., Ulaanbaatar, Mongolia, 1948; cert., 1st Moscow Med. Inst., 1957, Cardiol. Inst., Praha, Czechoslovakia, 1965, Cardiol. Inst., Beograd and Zagreb, Yugoslavia, 1966. Physician City Clinic, Ulaanbaatar, 1948-59; assoc. prof. Med. Inst., Ulaanbaatar, 1956-59; with City Clinic, Dubna, USSR, 1967-73; dir. Meml. Mus. for Victims of Polit. Persecution, Ulaanbaatar, 1993—; cons. 1st and 3d City Clinics, Ulaanbaatar, 1959—. Contbr. articles to profl. jours. Mem. Mongolian Trade Union, 1948—, Mongolian Repressed Women, 1996, Mongolian Red Cross Soc. Recipient Mother's Glory Order Govt. Mongolia, 1961, Polar Star Order, 1977, Leading Health Worker, 1973, 80, prize Govt. Agy. for Polit. Rehab., 1996. Buddhist. Home: PO Box 46/16, Ulaanbaatar Mongolia Office: Meml Mus Victims Polit Pers, 1 Genden St, Ulaanbaatar Mongolia

GENDERS, KEITH DUNCAN, winery proprietor, viticulturist; b. Adelaide, Australia, May 23, 1927; s. Eustace Alexander Genders and Edith Lillian Laurie; m. Rosemary Bowen Pridmore, Nov. 22, 1950; children: Duncan Forbes (dec.), Nigel Forbes, Diana Bowen Heinrich. Degree, St. Peter's Coll. Owner Genders Wines, McLaren Vale. Creator classic table wines and vintage port wines. Recipient medals Australian wine shows, 1970—. Mem. Adelaide Club, Rolls Royce Owners Club, Bentley Club. Liberal. Anglican. Avocations: motor sport, music, history. Office: Genders McLaren Park Wines, Park Ave, McLaren Vale SA 5171, Australia

GENDI, NAGUI SAFWAT TAWFIK, consultant rheumatologist; b. Cairo, Oct. 21, 1954; arrived in Eng., 1985; s. Safwat Tawfik and Mounira Ayoub (Farag) G.; m. Naira Nessim Asaad, Nov. 12, 1978; children: Bishoy, George, Michael. MBChB, Alexandria (Egypt) U., 1978, MSc in Internal Medicine, 1984; MRCP, Eng., 1986. Cert. specialist in rheumatology and rehab. House officer Alexandria U. Hosp., 1978-79; resident internal medicine Ras, Elteen Hosp. & Univ. Hosp., Alexandria, 1982-85; sr. house officer in rheumatology Robert Jones and Agnes Hunt Orthop. Hosp., Oswestry, Eng.; registrar in gen. medicine Macclesfield (Eng.) Gen. Hosp., 1987-88; registrar in rheumatology Royal Free Hosp., London, 1988-90; sr. registrar in rheumatology and rehab. Nuffield Orthop. Ctr., Oxford, Eng., 1990-95; cons. rheumatologist Basildon (Eng.) & Thurrock NHS Trust, 1995—. Contbr. articles to profl. jours., chpts. to books. With Egyptian mil., 1979-82. Mem. Royal Coll. Physicians, Brit. Soc. Rheumatology, Brit. Soc. Rehab. Medicine, Nat. Back Pain Assn., N.Y. Acad. Scis. Coptic Orthodox. Avocations: chess playing, cycling. Home: 24 Hall Green Ln, Hutton/Brentwood CM13 2QX, England Office: Basildon Hosp, Nether Mayne, Basildon SS16 5NL, England

GENDRE, PIERRE EMILE, airline passengers consultant; b. Quimper, France, Apr. 7, 1929; s. Ernest Leonard and Mary Anne (Forlay) G.; m. Jacqueline Yvonne Le Garrois, Mar. 1954 (div. Dec. 1974); children: Christian, Alain, Laurent. Degree, U. Bordeaux. Electronic engr. French Army, 1949-50, Am. Machine and Foundry, N.Y.C., 1952-53, U.S. Signal Corp., 1957-61; v.p., account exec. AMPCO, Seattle, 1972-74; v.p. Am. French Food Corp., 1978-87, Gendre Assocs., U.S. and France, 1978—. Patentee in field. Activist Freedom Internat. With U.S. Signal Corps, 1957-61. Republican. Roman Catholic. Home and Office: Gendre & Assocs, 18 Rte d'Arsac, 33480 Avensan France

GENEL, MYRON, pediatrician, educator; b. York, Pa., Jan. 6, 1936; s. Victor and Florence (Mowitz) G.; m. Phyllis Norma Berkman, Aug. 25, 1968; children: Elizabeth, Jennifer, Abby. Grad., Moravian Coll., 1957; MD, U. Pa., 1961; MA (hon.), Yale U., 1983; DSc (hon.), Moravian Coll., 1995. Diplomate Am. Bd. Pediat. Intern Mt. Sinai Hosp., N.Y.C., 1961-62; resident in pediat. Children's Hosp. Phila., 1962-64; trainee pediat. endocrinology Johns Hopkins Hosp., Balt., 1966-67; instr. pediat. U. Pa. Sch. Medicine, 1967-69, assoc. in pediat., 1969-71; trainee in genetics, inherited metabolic diseases Children's Hosp. Phila., 1967-69, assoc. physician, 1969-71; attending physician Yale-New Haven Hosp., 1971—; faculty Yale U. Sch. Medicine, New Haven, 1971—, dir. pediat. endocrinology, 1971-85, program dir. Children's Clin. Rsch. Ctr., 1971-86, prof., 1981—, assoc. dean, 1985—, dir. Office Govt. and Cmty. Affairs, 1985-2000; genetic adv. bd. State of Conn., 1979-82, 94—; cons. subcom. investigations, oversight com. sci. and tech. U.S. Ho. of Reps., 1982-84; mem. adv. bd. New Eng. Congenital Hypothyroidism Collaborative; cons. Hosp. St. Raphael, Milford Hosp., Norwalk Hosp., Stamford Hosp., Danbury Hosp., Greenwich Hosp.; chmn. transplant adv. com. Office of Commr., Conn. Dept. Income Maintenance, 1984-92; health policy fellowhsip bd. Inst. Medicine, 1989-95; clin. rsch. roundtable Inst. Medicine Nat. Rsch. Coun., 2000—; bd. dirs. Rsch. America!. Contbr. articles to profl. jours. Capt. U.S. Army, 1964-66. Robert Wood Johnson Health Policy fellow Inst. Medicine NAS, Washington, 1982-83; recipient ann. award Conn. Campaign Against Cooley's Anemia, 1979, Ann. Comenius Alumni award Moravian Coll., 1990, Abraham Jacobi Meml. award Am. Acad. Pediat. and AMA, 1999. Fellow AAAS; mem. APHA, AMA (med. schs. sec. 1985—, alt. del. governing coun., med. schs. sec. 1995-98, del. 1998—, coun. on sci. affairs, 1994—, Task force on fin. grad. med. edn. 1995, mem. task force on privacy and confidentiality 1998-99), Am. Acad. Pediatrics (task force organ transplants, coun. on govt. affairs), Am. Assn. Clin. Endocrinologists, Am. Coll. Nutrition, Am. Coll. Preventive Medicine, Am. Diabetes Assn. (co-recipient Jonathan May award 1979), Am. Fedn. Med. Rsch., Am. Pediatric Soc., Am. Soc. Bone and Mineral Rsch. Assn. Am. Med. Colls. (mem. adminstrv. bd. coun. acad. socs. 1987-92, chmn.-elect coun. acad. socs., 1989-91, mem. exec. coun. 1989-92, mem. advisory panel on rsch. 1999—), Assn. Health Svcs. Rsch., New Haven County Med. Assn. (bd. govs. 1990—), Assn. Program Dirs. (pres.-elect 1980-81, pres. 1981-82), Nat. Assn. Biomed. Rsch. (bd. dirs. 1990-93, exec. com. 1991-93), Conn. Endocrine Soc., Conn. United for Rsch. Excellence (chmn. steering com. 1989-90, pres. 1990-93, chmn. bd. dirs. 1993-94), Endocrine Soc. rsch. initiative com., 1995-99), Soc. Pediat. Rsch., Conn. Acad. Sci. and Engring. (council 2000—), N.Y. Acad. Medicine, N.Y. Acad. Scis., Assn. Patient Oriented Rsch., Sigma Xi. Jewish. Home: 30 Richard Sweet Dr Woodbridge CT 06525-1126 Office: PO Box 3333 New Haven CT 06510-0333

GENERAL, JAIME MEDINA, insurance broker; b. Manila, Aug. 13, 1952; s. Honesto Castro General and Fermina Medina; m. Maria Elena Dabao, June 26, 1982; children: Miguel, Carlos, Rafael, Maria Isabel, Alfonso. BS in Mgmt., Ateneo Manila U., 1974. Cert. ins. broker. Mem. mgmt. staff Dept. Agr., Manila, 1974-76; fleet sales exec. No. Motors Sales Corp., Manila, 1976-78; sales mgr. Commart Philippines, Inc., Manila, 1978-80; v.p. Tech. Ins. Brokers, Inc., Manila, 1980—; pres. Aguq Azul, Inc., Naga City, The Philippines, 1996—, Bald Spot Barbershop, Paranaque City, The Philippines, 1999—, Fire Tree Ventures, Inc., Paranaque City, 1999—; ins. cons. Social Security Sys., Manila, 2000—, Dole Asia Ltd., Manila, 2000—. Mem. Alabang Country Club (chmn. caddies com. 1999—, mem. membership com. 1999—). Roman Catholic. Avocations: golf, fishing. Fax: 815-2933. Office: Tech Ins Brokers Inc 5th Fl, Prudential Bk Bl, Ayala Ave, Luzon 1703, The Philippines

GENESI, SUSAN PETROVICH, educator; b. Philipsburg, Pa., Mar. 24, 1957; d. Richard and Margaret (Ohs) Petrovich; 1 child, Lindsay Margaret. BS in Elem. Edn., Pa. State U., 1981, cert. ednl. adminstrn., 1998, MA in Edn. Adminstrn., 1999. Cert. elem. tchr., Pa.; cert. kindergarten tchr., Pa. Tchr. Philipsburg-Osceola Area Sch. Dist., Pa., 1981—; prin. Philipsburg-Osceola Area Sch. Dist.; commr. Pa. Profl. Stds. and Practices Commn., Harrisburg, Pa., 1995—; mem. content validation panel for early adolescence English Nat. Bd. for Profl. Tchg. Stds., Atlanta, 1997; workshop presenter on topics of coop. learning; presenter Keystone State Reading Assn., Hershey, Pa., 1995, 96; coop. tchr. Pa. State U., State College, 1994—; mem. various coms. throughout the sch. dist. Contbr. articles to profl. jours. Mem. Philipsburg Bicentennial Com., 1996-97; organizer Philipsburg Elem. Philipsburg Days, 1994. Mem. ASCD, NEA, Pa. State Edn. Assn., Philipsburg-Osceola Area Edn. Assn. (com. 1981—), Phi Delta Kappa. Republican. Presbyterian. Avocations: traveling and shopping with daughter, computer technology, exploring new trends in education and technology, relaxing at the beach. E-mail: sxg23@psu.edu. Office: North Lincoln Elem Sch/ Wallaceton Boggs Elem Sch 200 Short St Philipsburg PA 16866-2640

GENESOVE, DAVID, economics educator, editor; b. Regina, Sask., Can., Jan. 1, 1963; arrived in Israel, 1998; s. Louis Jack and Belle (Schacter) G.; m. Dina Herz, Mar. 27, 1996; children: Michal, Nadav. BA, U. Toronto, Can., 1986; PhD, Princeton U., 1991. Asst. prof. MIT, Cambridge, 1991-96, assoc. prof., 1996-98; sr. lectr. Hebrew U. Jerusalem, 1998—. Editor Jour. Indsl. Econs.; contbr. articles to profl. jours. Mem. Am. Econ. Assn., Econ. Soc. Home: Disraeli 3 Apt 6, 92222 Jerusalem Israel Office: Hebrew U Jerusalem, Dept Econs, 92222 Jerusalem Israel

GENG, SHU, agronomy educator; b. Sichung, China, Sept. 3, 1942; s. Mei-Chang and S.Q. (Ho) G.; m. Hai-Yen Wong, June 29, 1968; children: Elvin H., Joy J. BS, Nat. Taiwan U., Taipei, 1964; MS, Kans. State U., 1969, PhD, 1972. Biostatistician The Upjohn Co., Kalamazoo, 1972-76; asst. prof. U. Calif., Davis, 1976-78, assoc. prof., 1978-84, prof., 1984—; assoc. dean Coll. Agrl. and Environ. scis., 1988-92. Contbr. articles to profl. jours. Fellow AAAS, Am. Soc. Agronomy. Home: 425 Grande Ave Davis CA 95616-0213 Office: U Calif Dept Agronomy And Rang Davis CA 95616

GENGOR, VIRGINIA ANDERSON, financial planning executive, educator; b. Lyons, N.Y., May 2, 1927; d. Axel Jennings and Marie Margaret (Mack) Anderson; m. Peter Gengor, Mar. 2, 1952 (dec.); children: Peter Randall, Daniel Neal, Susan Leigh. AB, Wheaton Coll., 1949; MA, U. No. Colo., Greeley, 1975, 77. Chief hosp. intake service County of San Diego, 1966-77, chief Kearny Mesa Dist. Office, 1977-79, chief Dependent Children of Ct., 1979-81, chief child protection services, 1981-82; registered rep. Am. Pacific Securities, San Diego, 1982-85; registered tax preparer State of Calif., 1982—, registered rep. (prin.) Sentra Securities, 1985—; assoc. Pollock & Assocs., San Diego, 1985-86; pres. Gengor Fin. Advisors, 1986—; cons. instr. Nat. Ctr. for Fin. Edn., San Diego, 1986-88; instr. San Diego Community Coll., 1985-88. Mem. allocations panel United Way, San Diego, 1976-79, children's circle Child Abuse Prevention Found., 1989—; chmn. com. Child Abuse Coordinating Council, San Diego, 1979-83; pres. Friends of Casa de la Esperanza, San Diego, 1980-85, bd. dirs., 1980—; 1st v.p. The Big Sister League, San Diego, 1985-86, pres., 1987-89. Mem. NAFE, Inst. Cert. Fin. Planners, Internat. Assn. Fin. Planning, Inland Soc. Tax Cons., AAUW (bd. dirs.), Nat. Assn. Securities Dealers (registered prin.), Nat. Ctr. Fin. Edn., Am. Bus. Women's Assn., Navy League, Freedoms Found. Valley Forge, Internat. Platform Assn. Presbyterian. Avocations: community service, travel, reading. Home: 6462 Spear St San Diego CA 92120-2929 Office: Gengor Fin Advisors 4950 Waring Rd Ste 7 San Diego CA 92120-2700

GENIESER, LARS HERBERT, chemical engineer; b. Phila.. BSChemE, Princeton U., 1989; PhD in Chem. Engring., MIT, 1994, DSChemE, 1997. Engr. in tng., Mass. Postdoctoral rschr. Eindhoven U. Tech., The Netherlands, 1997-98. Contbr. articles to profl. jours. NSF-NATO postdoctoral fellow NSF, 1996, German Acad. Exch. Svc. fellow, 1989. Mem. AIChE (recipient Ctrl. Jersey Sect. award excellence in chem. engring. 1989), Sci. Rsch. Soc. of Sigma Xi. Avocations: foreign travel, classical music, running.

GENIN, JEAN-CLAUDE, history and legal educator; b. Auxerre, Yonne, France, May 18, 1937; s. Lucien Genin and Francine Duriez; m. Régine Mercier, June 4, 1963; children: Eric, Sophie. Cert. secondary sch. in Roman law. Lectr. U. St. Etienne, 1971-73; lectr. U. Lyon III, 1973-81, prof., 1981—; dir. Faculty of Juridical Scis., U. St. Etienne, 1971-73; dean law faculty U. Lyon III, 1976-79, mem. adminstrv. coun., 1993—. With Adminstrn., 1964-66. Decorated knight Order Acad. Palms, knight Order of Merit. Barriste. Roman Catholic. Avocations: rugby, track, gardening. Home: 45 Cours A Briand, 69300 Rhône France Office: U Lyon III, Ave Pierre Mendes, 69676 Rhône France

GENINI, RONALD WALTER, history educator, historian; b. Oakland, Calif., Dec. 5, 1946; s. William Angelo and Irma Lea (Gays) G.; m. Roberta Mae Tucker, Dec. 20, 1969; children: Thomas, Justin, Nicholas. BA, U. San Francisco, 1968, MA, 1969. Cert. secondary edn. tchr., Calif.; adminstrv. svcs. credential. Tchr. Ctrl. Unified Sch. Dist., Fresno, Calif., 1970—; judge State History Day, Sacramento, 1986-94; mem. U.S. history exam. devel. team Golden State, San Diego, 1989-93; securer placement of state-registered landmarks. Author: Romualdo Pacheco, 1985, Darn Right It's Butch, 1994, Theda Bara, 1996; contbr. articles to profl. jours.; cited as authority on Theda Bara by Ency. Brit. Online Am. Women in History, 1999, also on Romualdo Pacheco by Biog. Directory of Am. Congress. Bd. dirs. Fresno Area 6 Neighborhood Coun., 1973-74, Fresno City and County Hist. Soc., 1975-78, St. Anthony's sch. bd., Fresno, 1980-84; mem. Good Company Players, Fresno, 2000—. Named one of Outstanding Young Educators Am., Fresno Jaycees, 1978; recipient recognition for Tchr. Cares award Calif. State Assembly and Fresno City Coun., 1996. Mem. Calif. Hist. Soc. Democrat. Avocations: writing history 19th century Calif. and early Hollywood, motion picture scriptwriter, commercial acting. E-mail: rgenini@hotmail.com. Home: 1486 W Menlo Ave Fresno CA 93711-1305 Office: Ctrl HS 2045 N Dickenson Ave Fresno CA 93722-9643

GENIS, ALICE SINGER, psychologist; b. Vilnius, Lithuania, June 8, 1926; d. Nahum Signer and Miriam Singer (Smith) Galerkin; widowed; children: naomi Genis-Mazin, Robert Genis. Esq., Ludwig Maximillian U., Munich, 1950; BA, Pace U., 1974; MA, Mercy Coll., Dobbs Ferry, N.Y., 1978, Coll. of New Rochelle, 1983. Cert. sch. psychologist. Lab. tech. Queens Gen. Hosp., N.Y.C., 1952-55; with Daycare Ctr. Presbyn. Ch., Peekskill, N.Y., 1972-73; psychologist Mental Health Clinic, Peekskill, 1978-80; asst. sch. psychology Pines Bridge Sch., Yorktown, N.Y., 1980-82; biofeedback therapist Med. Cmty. Ctr., Cortland, N.Y., 1985-94; sch. psychologist BOCES, Yorktown, N.Y., 1983-85; presenter in field. Contbr. articles to profl. jours. Vol. Hosp. Aux., Peekskill, 1962-98; com. Heart Fund Ball, Westchester, 1970s, 80s; pres. Norchester Hadassam, Peekskill, 1983-85, 88-91; mem. The Field Libr., Peekskill. Named Woman of Merit, Westchester Hadassh, White Plaines, N.Y., 1996; recipient New Life award Israel Bonds, Peekskill, 1979, Presl. awards Norchester Hadassah, 1985, 91. Mem. Nat. Assn. Sch. Psychologists, Biofeedback and Psychophysiology Performing Ctr. for the Arts. Avocations: music, piano, swimming, gardening, travel. Home: 1 Birchwood Ln Cortlandt Mnr NY 10567-6709

GENIUŠAS, RIMAS JUOZAS, conductor, educator; b. St. Petersburg, Russia, Aug. 28, 1920; arrived in Lithuania, 1921; s. Juozas and Stasė (Blaževičiute) G.; m. Irena Žemaitytė, Oct. 4, 1959; children: Petras, Julius. Grad. piano, State Conservatory, Kaunas, Lithuania, 1945, grad. conducting with honors, 1948. Pianist, coach Opera House, Kaunas, 1942-44, condr., 1945-47; condr. Opera House, Vilnius, Lithuania, 1952-96, chief condr., 1958-75, 91-94; tchr. Lithuanian Conservatory, Vilnius, 1949-75, docent, 1975-81, head dept., 1975-90; prof. Lithuanian Acad. Music,Vilnius, 1981-99. Pianist soloist, condr. Symphony Orch.; author: Conducting and the Lithuanian Conductors, 1973, Exercises of Opera Singer, 1986; (with others) Balys Dvarionas, 1982, Kipras Petrauskas, 1988; recs. Not Only Love opera, fragments of opera The Astrayds Birds, fragments of ballet On the Sea Shore, others; guest condr., Moscow, St. Petersburg, Poland, Bulgaria, Germany, Italy, Latvia; pianist Spain; contbr. articles to profl. jours. Recipient State Prize of Lithuania Govt. of State Lithuania, 1960; named People's Artist of Lithuania Govt. of State Lithuania, 1964, Order of Grand Duke of Lithuania Gediminas, 1996. Avocations: yoga, jogging, bell collecting, history, psychology.

GENNETT, TIMOTHY, academic administrator; b. Richmond, Ind., July 25, 1951; s. Henry and Barbara Milda (Collignon) G.; m. Sharon Gail Cox, Mar. 5, 1976. BS in Chemistry, Purdue U., 1973, MS in Indsl. Adminstrn., 1974, MSEd, 1984. Lic. amateur radio operator. Sales engr. Gulf Oil Corp., San Antonio, 1975-77; asst. mgr. residence halls Purdue U., West Lafayette, Ind., 1977-82, mgr. residence halls, 1982-90, asst. dir. residence halls, 1990-95, dir. facilities housing and food svcs., 1995—; dir. Gennett Graphics, Lafayette, Ind., 1992—; presenter Assn. Coll. and Univ. Housing Officers, 1994, 96, 2000. Contbr. articles to profl. jours. Damage assessement coord. ARC, Tippecanoe County, Ind., 1998—. Named Vol. of Yr. Disaster Svsc. ARC, 1996. Mem. Assn. Higher Edn. Cable TV Adminstrs. (presenter 2000, bd. dirs. 2000—), Tippecanoe Amateur Radio Assn. (sec. 1995-97), Soc. Cable TV Engrs. Office: Purdue U 105 Smalley Ctr West Lafayette IN 47906-4205

GENSCHER, HANS-DIETRICH, German politician; b. Reideburg, Mar. 21, 1927; s. Kurt G. and Hilde (Kreime) G.; m. Barbara Schmidt; 1 dau., Martina. Ed., Leipzig U., Halle U. Lawyer, then parliamentarian, 1965—; fgn. min. Govt. Germany; minister interior Fed. Republic of Germany, Bonn, 1969-74, vice chancellor, minister fgn. affairs, 1974-92. Vice chmn. Free Dem. Party, 1968-74, chmn., 1974-85. Address: Persönliches Buro, Postfech 200 655, D-53136 Bonn Germany

GENS DE MOURA RAMOS, RUI MANUEL, judge; b. 1950. Prof., law faculty Coimbra; law faculty Cath. U., Oporto, Jean Monnet chair; course dir. Acad. Internat. Law, The Hague, 1984; vis. prof. Paris I Law U., 1995; Portuguese Govt. del. UN Commn. on Internat. Trade Law, 1980-89, Hague Conf. Pvt. Internat. Law, 1982-95; judge Ct. of First Instance of European Communities, Luxembourg, 1995—, Coun. Europe, 1992-95, Internat. commn. on Civil Status, 1986-95. Mem. Inst. Internat. Law. Office: Ct of First Instance EC, Bl Konrad Adenauer, L-2925 Luxembourg Luxembourg

GENTILCORE, EILEEN MARIE BELSITO, elementary school principal; b. Glen Cove, N.Y.; d. Samuel Francis and Nellie Theresa (McKenna) Belsito; m. James Matthew Gentilcore, Aug. 4, 1951; children: Kevin, John, Scott. BS in Edn., SUNY, Potsdam; MS in Edn., Hofstra U., 1968, profl. diploma, 1976, EdD, 1979. Tchr., first grade Sea Cliff, N.Y., 1951-52; founder, pre-K Germany Officers Sch., Munich, 1952-53; tchr., first grade Peekskill (N.Y.) Schs., 1953-54; tchr., second grade Syosset, N.Y., 1954-55, reading cons., 1970-84, head tchr., 1974-84; prin. Syosset, 1985-96; ret., 1996; bicentennial adv. bd. Syosset Community, 1976; adv. bd. mem. Telicare, Uniondale, N.Y., 1978-80; cons. in field. Author: Developmental Learning, 1979. Mem. Nassau County Graffiti Task Force, 1994—; organizer med. team to Honduras, 1998. N.Y. State PTA fellow, 1971, 72, 73, Hofstra fellow, 1971; recipient Jenkins award N.Y. State PTA, 1968, Hon. Life, 1976, Pius X award Rockville Ctr. Diocese, 1985, Disting. Svc. award, N.Y. State PTA Dist., 1996, UP Abe Gordon award UP RD; named Woman of Distinction, N.Y. State Senate, 1998, Woman of Distinction, Syosset-Woodbury Rep. Club and Senator Carl Marcellino, 1999, Teddy Roosevelt Achievement award, 1999, R.I. Internat. achievement award, grant Karla Project; honoree Gift of Life Inc., 1999, Internat. Task Force for Children at Risk. Mem. Syosset Prins. (pres. 1992), Rotary (pres. Syosset-Woodbury 1993-95, Gift of Life pres. 1996-97, med. mission to Russia 1995 dist. 7250, gov. aide, 1995, vocat. dir. dist. 7250 1996-97, med. mission to Honduras 1997, 1st woman dist. gov. dist. 7250 1998-99, Children at Risk Task Force 2000—, conf. chair Zone 32 2000—, launched Operation Mitch, Paul Harris fellow, N.Y. State Senate Woman of Distinction 1998, Achievement award, coord. Children at Risk Task Force), Phi Beta Kappa, Alpha Sigma Omicron, Kappa Delta Pi. Roman Catholic. Avocations: swimming, writing, reading, gardening. Fax: 516-921-0206.

GENTILE, MELANIE MARIE, record producer, marketing and public relations consultant, writer; b. N.Y.C., Apr. 27, 1944; d. Frank Joseph and Jean Ferreri; m. R.P. Gentile, Apr. 4, 1964 (div. 1982); children: Robert, Jessica. Student, Calif. State U., 1967-70. Pres. U.S. venture Yasu Corp. of Tokyo, 1971-86; cons. in mktg., 1986-89; exec. prodr. and pres. Schrimshaw Prodn. Co. and Record Co., Nashville, 1975—; owner Triad Music, 1996—; account exec., creative cons. Erwin Wasey Advt. Corp.; freelance creative cons. Jacques Yves Cousteau, 1968—. Author: Look Back But Don't Stare, Out of the Mouths of Babes; co-author: Essays of the Heart-What Our Youngest Really Think of the World We've Given Them. Mem. ASCAP (CMA award Acad. of Country Music, Billboard mag.). Home and Office: PO Box 588 Beakes Rd Cornwall NY 12518

GENTILE, ROBERT DALE, optometrist, consultant; b. Pottsville, Pa., Oct. 24, 1946; s. Joseph and Evelyn Marie (Warfield) Gentile; m. Patricia Diane Fernsler, June 20, 1969; 1 child, Heather Ly Luxon. BA in Sci., Pa. State U., 1968; BS in Optometry, Pa. Coll. of Optometry, Phila., 1974, OD, 1977; MA in Human Resources, Webster U., 1985. Bd. cert. Am. Acad. Optometry. Advanced through ranks to lt. col. AUS, 1968-94; chief optometry 9th Gen. Dispensary, Aschaffenburg, Germany, 1977-80; optometrist Brook Army Med. Ctr., Ft. Sam Houston, Tex., 1980-82; chief eye sect., medicine and surgery divsn. Acad. Health Scis., Ft. Sam Houston, 1982-84; chief optometry Dunham Army Health Clinic, Carlisle Barracks, Pa., 1984-88, Med. Dept. Activity, Berlin, 1988-91, 121st Evacuation Hosp., Seoul, Republic of Korea, 1991-93; optometry cons. 18th Med. Command, Seoul, 1991-93; chief optometry Raymond W. Bliss Army Cmty. Hosp., Ft. Huachuca, Ariz., 1993-94; optometrist Naval Hosp., Camp Pendleton, Calif., 1994-96; cons. New Vision Internat., Escondido, Calif., 1996—; adj. prof. U. Houston Coll. Optometry, 1980-84, Pa. Coll. Optometry, 1980-84, New England Coll. Optometry, Boston, 1980-84. Decorated Legion of Merit, Meritorious Svc. medal with 3 Oak Leaf Clusters, Army Commendation medal with 4 Oak Leaf Clusters. Fellow Am. Acad. Optometry; mem. Am.

Optometric Assn., Armed Forces Optometric Assn., Calif. Optometric Assn., Berlin Internat. Med. Soc., 38th Parallel Med. Soc., Silver Caduceus Soc. of Korea. Avocations: golf, gymnastics, table tennis, nutrition, exercise. Home and Office: 2241 Canyon View Gln Escondido CA 92026-5020

GENTRY, JAMES WALTER, chemical engineer, educator; b. Hobart, Okla., Nov. 27, 1939; s. J. Bryan and Juanita F. (Davis) Gentry. BSChemE, Okla. State U., 1961; MSChemE, U. Birmingham, U.K., 1963; PhDChemE, U. Tex., 1969. Asst. prof. U. Md., Coll. Pk., 1969-72; assoc. prof. U. Md., 1972-78, prof., 1978—; ofcl. rep. GAeF at founding meeting Aerosol Soc. U.K.; cons. Bur. Comml. Fisheries, Asphalt Inst., 1975, Fraunhofer Gesellschaft, 1977, Health and Safety Exec., London, others; vis. scientist Institut fur Aerobiologie, Schmallenberg, West Germany, 1976-77, 1979, 1977-85, Kernforschung Zentrum, Karlsruhe, West Germany, 1986, Forschungszentrum fur Umwelt und Gesundheit, Frankfurt, 1993. Mem. edit. bd. Jour. Aerosol Rsch., 1982-86; contbr. numerous chpts. to books and articles to profl. jours. Fulbright fellow, 1961-62; grantee NSF, 1970-71, 77-78, 78-79, 80-84, Am. Standard Corp., 1972, EPA, 1979-81, 3M Corp., 1985, others. Fellow AIChE, Washington Acad. Sci. (Engring. Scis. award 1983); mem. Am. Chem. Soc., Gesellschaft fur Aerobiologie, Fine Particle Soc., N.Y. Acad. Scis., Phi Kappa Phi, Phi Lambda Upsilon, Omega Chi Epsilon, Pi Mu Epsilon (Alexander von Humboldt Sr. Scientist award 1993, Internat. Aerosol fellow 1996). Achievements include research in aerosol science and serosol mechanics with particular emphasis on non-spherical particles and electrical charging. Office: U Md Dept Chem Engring College Park MD 20742-0001

GENTRY, JAMES WILLIAM, retired state official; b. Danville, Ill., Aug. 14, 1926; s. Carl Lloyd and Leone (Isham) G.; m. Dorothie Shirley Hechtlinger, Mar. 18, 1967; 1 stepdau., Susan Mushkin. AB, Fresno State Coll., 1948; MJ, U. Calif., Berkeley, 1956. Field rep. Congressman B.W. Gearhart, Fresno, Calif., 1948; field rep. Assemblyman Wm. W. Hansen, Fresno, 1950, sec., 1953-56; exec. asst. Calif. Pharm. Assn., L.A., 1956-69; asst. adminstr., dir. pub. info. So. Calif. Comprehensive Health Planning Coun., 1969-71, acting adminstr., 1971-72, exec. sec., 1972-73; exec. sec. Calif. Adv. Health Coun., 1973-85, fed. cons., 1986-88; editor, pub. Calif. Pharmacy Jour., L.A., 1956-69; pub. rels. dir. PAID Prescriptions, 1963-64; dir. pub. info. Comprehensive Health Planning coun., L.A. County, 1969; fed. cons. Calif. Health Care Commn., 1973-75; acting pub. info. officer Calif. Office Statewide Health Planning and Devel., 1978-79, interim dir., 1983; mem. L.A. Civil Svc. Police Interview Bd., 1967-72, Calif. Health Planning Law Revision Commn.; asst. sgt.-at-arms Calif. State Assembly, 1950; exec. sec. Calif. Assembly Interim Com. on Livestock and Dairies, 1954-56; mem. adv. bd. Am. Security Coun.; former mem. Calif. Bldg. Safety Bd. Editor: Better Health, 1963-67, Orientation Conf. Comprehensive Health Planning, 1969, commentary, 1969-71, Program and Funding, 1972, Substance Abuse, 1972; editl. adv. Pharm. Svcs. for Nursing Homes: A Procedural manual, 1966. Mem. Fresno County Rep. Ctrl. Com., 1950; charter mem. Rep. Presdl. Task Force. Served to col. AUS, 1949-85, Korea, 1950-53. Decorated Legion of Merit, Bronze Star medal, Commendation Ribon with metal Pendant; recipient pub. awards Western Soc. Bus. Publs. Assn., 1964-67. Mem. Am. Assn. Comprehensive Health Planning, Pub. Rels. Soc. Am., Allied Drug Travelers So. Calif., L.A. Press Club, Mil. Police Assn., Ret. Officers Assn. (life), Res. Officers Assn. (life), Assn. U.S. Army, U.S. Senatorial Club, The Victory Svcs. Club of London, Pi Gamma Mu, Phi Alpha Delta, Sigma Delta Chi. Home: 1603 Patriots Colony Dr Williamsburg VA 23188-1341

GENTZ, MANFRED, automotive company executive; b. Riga, Latvia, Jan. 22, 1942. Studied law, U. Berlin and U. Lausanne; LLB, 1965, LLD. Jr. mgmt. trainee, sr. dir.'s asst. pers. sector Daimler-Benz A.G., 1970—, various positions to sr. dir. pers. and soc. welfare sectors, 1978-82, mgr. comml. vehicle divsn., 1982-83, dep. mem. bd. mgmt., 1983-85, mem. bd. mgmt., mem. bd. mgmt. holding co., 1985—; pres., CEO Daimler-Benz Intersvcs. AG Daimler-Benz A.G., Berlin, 1990-95; also bd. dirs. Daimler-Benz A.G.; mem. bd. mgmt. Daimler-Benz AG, 1995-97, CFO, 1997—; CFO Daimler-Chrysler AG; mem. supervisory and adv. bd. Hannoversche Leben A.G., Deutsche Hypothekenbank, DWS Deutsche Gesellschaft für Wertpapersparen mbH; hon. judge Fed. Labour Ct. Active sci. edn. instns. Mem. Confederation German Employers' Assns. (mem. exec. bd. dirs., mem. presiding com.), Metal Industry Assn. Baden-Württemberg (mem. exec. bd. dirs.), Chamber Industry and Commerce in Berlin (mem. presiding bd.). Office: Daimler-Chrysler AG, Epplestrasse 225, Stuttgart 70546, Germany*

GENZ, MICHAEL ANDREW, lawyer; b. N.Y.C., Jan. 24, 1947; s. Leonard Francis and Martha Virginia (Tidwell) G.; m. Patricia Ann Hayes, July 8, 1972; children: Andrew, Daniel. BS in Fgn. Svc., Georgetown U., 1969; MA in Tchg., Yale U., 1970; JD, Cath. U., 1980. Police officer New Haven Police Dept., 1971-73; program analyst Nat. Planning Assn., Washington, 1974-76; staff atty. Client Centered Legal Svcs. S.W. Va., Inc., Castlewood, 1980-83; chief atty. So. Md. office Legal Aid Bur., Inc., Hughesville, 1983-95; program officer Legal Svcs. Corp., Washington, 1995-98, dir. office of program performance, 1999—; atty. mem. Md. Trial Ct. Jud. Selection Com. Dist. 12, Charles County, Md., 1986-95; mem. bd. govs. ACLU of Md., Balt., 1986-91. Contbr. articles to profl. jours. Bd. mem. Campaign for Human Devel., Washington, 1986-91; pres. Charles County Human Svcs. Coun., La Plata, Md., 1987-88. Mem. ABA, Va. State Bar Assn., Md. State Bar Assn., Charles County Bar Assn. Home: 7706 Spring Oak Dr La Plata MD 20646-3984 Office: Legal Svcs Corp 750 1st St NE Washington DC 20002-4241

GEOFFREY, IQBAL (MOHAMMED JAWAID IQBAL JAFREE), art educator; b. Chiniot, Pakistan, Jan. 1, 1939; s. Syed Iqbal Hussain and Shahzadi Mumtazjehan Shah; m. Regina Wai-ling Cheng, 1967 (div. 1978); children: Syed Hussain Haider, Shahzadi Zohra Elinoi Cheng-Jafree; m. Ceyyeda Ferzawna Nuccwe, Mar. 3, 1988. BA with distinction, Govt. Coll., Lahore, 1957; LLB summa cum laude, Punjab U., Lahore, 1959; trained under Chief Justice of Pakistan, Malik Mohammed Akram, 1959-60; LLM with honors, Harvard U., 1966; A.I.C.E.A., London, 1961, A.M.B.I.M., 1969; PhD, Read U., 1970; also LLD; MA with highest honors, U. Ill., Springfield, 1973; cert. in postgrad. bus. adminstrn., Bradford U., 1976. Bar: Pakistan 1959, U.S. Supreme Ct. 1975, Pakistan Supreme Ct., 1996. Ptnr., chair firm Geoffrey & Khitran (internat. lawyers), 1960—; gen. counsel Pakistan Inst. Human Rights, 1960—; human rights officer UN, 1966-67; chief acct. Brit. Lion Films, London, 1968-69; asst. atty. gen. State of Ill., 1972-73; gen. counsel The Shahzadi Mumtaz Jehan Trust, 1972—; chief acct. Embassy of Kuwait, London, 1974-75; Mem. bd. govs. Hunerkada Coll. of Art, Islamabad, 1991—; drafted Art. 164 of the Pakistan Law of Evidence, Establishment of Office of Ombudsman Order, Pakistan, 1983; spl. advisor to the Pres. of Pakistan, 1980-84; examiner Pub. Internat. Law Punjab U., 1969-70; prof. St. Mary's Coll., 1967-68, CWS U., 1970-71, Cleve. State U., 1971-72; disting. univ. vis. prof. Hunerkada Coll. Art, Lahore Law Coll. and Silver Jubilee U. prof. Read U. Law Ctr.; presenter, lectr., art critic, conceptual art, fine arts, urban affairs and aesthetics; founder Am. U. Pakistan, 1990. Author: Qose-Qizah, 1957, Justice is the Absence of Dictatorial Prerogative, 1965, Human Rights in Pakistan, Harvard 1966, A Critical Study of Moral Dilemmas, Iconographical Confusions and Complicated Politics of XX Century Art Harvard U., 1967, The Concept of Human Rights in Islam (foreword by ICJ Mr. Justice Richard R. Baxter), 1980 Art Embodies Cerebral Legerdemain of Accelerated Communal Soul; co-author: ABA: BLI Recognition and Enforcement of Money Judgments, 1994, International Agency and Distribution Law, 1996; editor: Law Rev., 1958-59; grad. editor: Harvard Art Rev., 1965-66; one-man shows include Hyde Park, London, 1960-62, Galerie de Seine, Alfred Brod Galleries, 1962, New Vision Centre, 1963, Drian Gallery, 1965, London, Ward-Nasse, Boston, Hull (Eng.) U., Birmingham (Eng.) U., Queens U., Arts Coun. No. Ireland, Los Angeles Mcpl. Art Gallery, Pakistan Arts Council, Lahore, Grand Central Moderns, N.Y.C., Henri Gallery, Washington, St. Mary's Coll., Ind., Franklin Coll., Miami Mus. Modern Art, Herbert Johnson Art Mus. Cornell U., Everson Art Mus., Syracuse, N.Y., Indus Gallery, Karachi, 1988, Hayward Gallery, London, 1989-90, The Embassy of France, Islamabad, 1992, 2000, Victoria Miro Gallery, 1992-93, Royal Coll. Art, 1993, The Lavatory, NI, 1993—, The Southall Graveyards, Middlesex, 1993—, The Highbury Cemetery, London, 1994—, Nat. Art Gallery, Pakistan, 1994, H.W. Janson Gallery Modern Art, 1994, 2000, Lahore Art Gallery, 1993, 95, 98-99, 2000, Shakir Ali Mus. Art, Lahore, 1996, Golden Jubilee, Sua Sponte Artfest, Tate Gallery, Britain, 2000—, Nat. Gallery, London, 1998—; Durriya Kazi/AN Gallery, Karachi, 1998, Sadiq Pub. Sch., 1999, Croweaters Gallery, Lahore, 1999—, Canvas Gallery, Karachi, 2000, Alliance Francaise Gallery, Islamabad, 2000, Lahore Art Gallery, 2000, Tate Modern Sua Sponte show, 2000—; group shows include bicentennials, Paris, Sao Paolo, Brazil, N.Y.C., Montreal, Tokyo World Fairs, Ljubljana, Yugoslavia, Arts Council Gt. Britain touring exhibits, Hayward Gallery, London, The Asia House, London, 2000—, others include six sculptures, 3-D paintings, 18 constitute primal, ethereal art works Brunei Gallery U. London SOAS, 2000, other 60 art work pieces; represented in permanent collections Herbert Johnson Mus. Cornell U., Philips Collection, Washington, Boston Mus. Fine Arts, Pasadena Mus. Art, Arts Council Gt. Britain, Tate Gallery, London, Eng., Brit. Mus., London, Chase Manhattan Bank, N.Y.C., Boston Safe Deposit and Trust Co., St. James's Palace, Worcester Art Mus., U. Mass., Smith Coll., Lord Baden-Powell House, London, U. London, also pvt. collections; pioneer Conceptual Art. Recipient The Albairuni Prize, Central Model High Sch., Lahore, 1953, Paris Biennial award, 1965, pub. radio tribute by Pakistan Pres., Sir Ayub Khan, 1964, Lauréat de la Biennale de Paris award André Malraux Min. Culture, Sir Philip Hendy and Lord Goodman Bursary award Arts Coun. Gt. Britain, 1968, Disting. Comty. Svc. award L.A.W., 1970, Outstanding Citizenship award Citizenship Coun. Met. Chgo., 1979, Sir Herbert Read medal, 1992, State of Wash. Cen. Wash. State U. award for creativity, 1970; Aug. 14 designated Syed Iqbal Jafree Day by Gov. Thompson, Ill., 1977, Iqbal Geoffrey Day-Jan. 20 Gov. Edgar, Ill., 1992; Huntington Hartford II and John D. Rockefeller III fellow, 1962-65, Queen Elizabeth II fellow Bradford U. Mgmt. Ctr., 1975-76, Fay B. Kent fellow Alpha Chi Omega, 1963, 65; named as Arts Coun. Great Britain by Her Majesty Queen Elizabeth II, Young Virtuoso Time Mag., Disting. Lord William Gaunt, Much More Than a Genius Sir Jeffrey Jowell; designated a living legend Govt. Pakistan, 1994; featured in Oxford Companion to the Twentieth Century Art Mag. Fellow Royal Soc. Arts, London, 1961. Fax: 92-42-636-9430. E-mail: iqbaljafree@hotmail.com. Home: 416 S Warson Rd Saint Louis MO 63124-1212 Office: Geoffrey & Khitran, 1 Mozang Rd, I Geoffrey Sq, Lahore 54000, Pakistan

GEOGHEGAN, WILLIAM DAVIDSON, religion educator, minister; b. Wilmington, Del., July 16, 1922; s. Presley Downs and Mildred Alphaeus (Davidson) G.; m. Sarah Elizabeth Phelps, Oct. 5, 1946; children: Grace, Andrew, Emily, William Davidson II. BA, Yale U., 1943; postgrad., Harvard U., 1943-44; MDiv, Drew U., 1945; PhD, Columbia U., 1951. Ordained to ministry United Meth. Ch. as deacon, 1947, as elder, 1948. Pastor United Meth. Ch., Christiana, Del., 1947-50; chaplain, asst. prof. religion U. Rochester, N.Y., 1950-54; asst. prof. religion Bowdoin Coll., Brunswick, Maine, 1954-62, assoc. prof., 1962-66, prof., 1966-90, prof. emeritus, 1991—, chmn. dept. religion, 1954-79, 81-85, spring 1988; vis. scholar Columbia U. and Union Theol. Sem., 1964-65; founder, chair Bowdoin Coll. Jung Seminar, 1980—. Author: Platonism in Recent Religious Thought, 1958. Recipient Alumni award Bowdoin Coll. Alumni Assn., 1981. Mem. AAUP, Am. Acad. Religion, Hegel Soc. Am., Internat. Soc. for Neoplatonic Studies, Soc. Christian Philosophers, Town and Coll. Club, Phi Beta Kappa, Zeta Psi. Address: Bowdoin Coll 8400 College Sta Brunswick ME 04011-8484 also (summer): PO Box 336 10 Burroughs Ln Wolfeboro NH 03894-4917

GEORGAKIS, KYRIAKOS, furniture company executive; b. Athens, Greece, Apr. 10, 1959; s. Spyros and Maria (Stassi) G.; m. Anastasia Kondyli, July 28, 1994; children: Myrto, Nefeli. Diploma in chem. engring., Nat. Tech. U., Greece, 1983; M Applied Scis., U. Toronto, Ont., Can., 1986; cert. advanced mktg., Hellenic Ctr. Productivity, Greece, 1988, cert. fin. mgmt., 1989. Registered profl. engr., Greece. Cons. Chem. Engring. Cons., Inc., Toronto, 1983-86; asst. product mgr. P.N. Gerolymatos S.A., Athens, 1988, product mgr., 1989-92; product mgr. Neoset S.A., Athens, 1992-96, group product mgr., mktg. mgr., 1996—. Contbr. articles to profl. jours. Mem. Hellenic Mktg. Assn., U. Toronto Alumni Assn. Avocations: chess, basketball, computing. Home: Meteoron 18, 165-61 Glyfada Greece

GEORGAKOPOULOS, ANASTASIOS, molecular biology; b. Athens, Greece, Jan. 31, 1965; s. Elias and Aikaterinh (Anagnostopoulou) G. BS, U. Athens, Greece, 1988, PhD, 1997. Lab. asst. U. Athens, Greece, 1983-84, 84-85; rsch. coord. Greek Ministry Health, Athens, 1984; asst. rschr. Greek Anticancer Inst., Athens, 1985-86; lab. rschr. Nat. Hellenic Rsch. Found., Athens, 1989-90, postdoctoral fellow, 1997; postdoctoral fellow dept neurobiology and psychiatry Mount Sinai Sch. Medicine, N.Y.C., 1997—; computer specialist NHRE/IBRB, Athens, 1990—; cons. in field of computer graphics, Athens, 1989—. Co-author: Study for the Greek Ministry of Health, 1984. With Greek Med. Corps, 1994-96. Mem. AAAS, N.Y. Acad. Scis., Mensa. Avocations: music, drawing, photography, exercising. Office: Mt Sinai Sch Medicine Dept Psychiatry One Gustave L Levy Pl New York NY 10029

GEORGE, ARTHUR CHARLES, lawyer; b. Boston, Dec. 9, 1954; s. Charles Arthur and Diana Kanavos George; m. Soteria Liousas, May 22, 1983; children: Charles Arthur, Peter Arthur, Elizabeth Diana. BS in Bus. Adminstrn., New Eng. Sch. Law, 1976, JD, 1979. Bar: Mass. 1980, U.S. Dist. Ct. Mass. 1981, U.S. Ct. Appeals (1st cir.) 1981. Lawyer Arthur C. George, Esq., Randolph, Mass., 1980-86; ptnr. George & George, Stoughton, 1987—. Town counsel Town of Holbrook, Mass., 1986—; mem. Rep. Town Com., Holbrook, 1988-2000, chmn., 1990-2000; co-leader Adventurer's 4-H Club, Holbrook, 1988—; trustee Bridgewater State Coll., 1999—. Recipient Cert. of Appreciation, Mass. Chpt. Black Rep. Coun., citation Mass. State Senate, 1995, Salute to Excellence award U. Mass. Ext. and Mass. 4-H Found., 1998. Mem. Mass. Bar Assn., Bar Assn. Norfolk County (former coun. mem.), Ripon Soc. (nat. sec. 1992-94). Avocations: research and policy, political speechwriting, chess, baseball. Office: 1st Fl 10 Cabot Pl Fl 1 Stoughton MA 02072-4600

GEORGE, CEDRIC MATTHEW, artist, art educator; b. Castries, W.I., Sept. 21, 1954; s. Edwin McDonald and Marie Elizabeth (Edward) G.; m. Mathilda Gustave, June 22, 1985. Cert. with distinction, diploma honors, Edna Manley Sch. Fine Arts, Jamaica, 1988. Printing technician Govt. of St. Lucia, 1972-85; art officer Ministry of Edn. and Culture, St. Lucia, 1989—. Exhibited in group shows Carifesta (Caribbean Festival of Arts), 1976, 81, 92, U. of W.I., St. Augustine Campus, Trinidad, 1981, Benson and Hedges Caribbean World of Art Competition, 1986, Artist Mag. Dream Studio Competition, U.S., 1996, Ea. Caribbean Cen. Bank, St. Kitts, 1994, Ptnrs. of the Ams., U.S., 1996, 3d Biennial of Latin and Am. Art, 1996, C'MAC ART, Martinique, W.I., 1989, Inter-Caribbean Art Exhbn., Dominican Republic, 1999; prin. works include paintings, portraits, calendars, logos. Founder Nat. Portrait Gallery, Nat. Archives, 1981. Recipient Fine Arts award Minvielle & Chastanet, 1981, 94; scholar UNESCO, 1985. Fellow St. Lucia Girl Guides, St. Lucia Nat. Archives. Avocations: gardening, swimming, yoga, meeting people, writing. Home: PO Box GM 938, Castries Saint Lucia Office: Dept Culture, Barnard's Hill, Castries Saint Lucia

GEORGE, SIR CHARLES FREDERICK, health facility administrator; b. Birmingham, England, Apr. 3, 1941; s. William Hubert and Evelyn Margaret (Pryce) G.; m. Rosemary Moore, May 1969 (div. 1973). BSc, U. Birmingham, England, 1962, MB, BChir, 1965, MD, 1974. Med. registrar United Birmingham Hosps., England, 1967-69; med. registrar Hammersmith Hosp., London, 1969-71, sr. registrarr, 1971-73; sr. lectr. U. Southampton, Eng., 1973-75; prof. clin. pharmacology U. Soton, Eng., 1975-99; med. dir. British Heart Found., London, England, 2000—; dean medicine, health & biol. scis., U. Soton, 1993-98. Author: Drug Therapy in Old Age, 1998, Presystemic Drug Metabolism, 1982. Fellow Royal Soc. Encouragement Arts; mem. British Pharm. Soc., Med. Rsch. Soc., British Cardiac Soc. Home: 15 Westgate St, Southampton SO14 2AY, England Office: U Southampton Biomed Bldg, British Heart Found, 14 Fitzhardinge St, London WOH 4DH, England

GEORGE, CHARLES RAYMOND PAX, renal physician, consultant; b. Killara, Australia, Nov. 26, 1940; s. Charles Raymond and Dorothy (Dibb) G.; m. Elizabeth Gordon Smith, Dec. 27, 1967; children: Alexandra Elizabeth, Charles Raymond Robert, Andrew Gordon Anschütz, Sophia Emelie Dibb George. MB, BS, U. Sydney, Australia, 1966, BA with hons., 1995, MSc, 1997. Sr. specialist Renal Medicine Concord Hosp., Sydney, Australia, 1975—; clin. lectr., sr. lectr. in medicine U. Sydney, Australia, 1975—. Author over 105 articles and chpts. to profl. publs. Anglican. Office: Renal Unit, Concord Hospital, Concord 2139, Australia

GEORGE, DAVID, technology company executive; b. Bryn Mawr, Pa., Apr. 1, 1942; s. Charles Wendell David and Margaret Simpson; m. Barbara Osborn, 1965; 3 children. Degree, Harvard U.; MBA, U. Va. Asst. prof. U. Va., Charlottesville, 1967-68; sr. v.p. Boston Cons. Group, 1968-75; sr. v.p. corp. planning and devel. Otis Elevator Co., N.Y., 1975-77; sr. v.p., gen. mgr. L.Am. Ops. Otis Elevator Co., West Palm Beach, Fla., 1977-81; pres. N.Am. ops. Otis Elevator Co., Farmington, Conn., 1981-85, pres., CEO, 1985-89, chair, CEO, 1989—; exec. v.p., pres. United Techs. Corp., Hartford, Conn., 1989-94, pres., CEO, COO, 1994—. Office: United Techs Corp 1 Financial Plz Ste 22 Hartford CT 06103-2607*

GEORGE, EDWARD ALAN JOHN, banker; b. Sept. 11, 1938; s. Alan and Olive Elizabeth George; m. Clarice Vanessa Williams, 1962; 3 children. Student, Dulwich Coll.; grad. econs., Emmanuel Coll., 1962; DS in Econs. (hon.), Hull Univ., 1993; LittD (hon.), Loughborough U., 1994; DSc (hon.), City Univ., 1995; PhD (hon.), London Guildhall U., 1996; DSc (hon.), Cranfield U., 1997; LLD (hon.), U. Exeter, 1997; DSc, UMIST, 1998; LLD (hon.), U. Bristol, 1999, U. Hertfordshire, 1999, U. Sheffield, 1999, U. Cambridge, 2000; DSc (hon.), U. Buckingham, 2000. With Bank of Eng., London, 1962—; asst. to chair deps. of Com. of 20 internat. monetary reform IMF, 1972-74; adviser internat. monetary questions Bank of Eng., 1974-77, dep. chief cashier, 1977-80, asst. adviser dir. gilt-edged divsn., 1980-82, exec. dir., 1982-90, dep. gov., 1990-93, gov., 1993—, chmn. of the govs., 1999—; apptd. mem. privy coun., 1999. Apptd. Knight Grand Cross of Order of Brit. Empire, 2000. Avocations: sailing, bridge. Office: Bank of Eng, Threadneedle St, London EC2R 8AH, England

GEORGE, ERNEST THORNTON, III, financial consultant; b. Charleston, S.C., Dec. 29, 1950; s. Ernest Thornton and Betty (Long) T.; m. Frances Thomson, Sept. 30, 1977; children: Ernest Thornton IV, Andrew Neal, Katherine Frances. Student, U. Miss., 1969-71; BS in Mktg., Miss. State U., 1973. CFP; CLU; registered investment advisor. Product cons. Mfrs. Life Ins. Co.; prin. N.Y. Stock Exch., 1977—; rep., br. mgr. Raymond James Fin. Svcs., Starkville, Miss., 1989—; owner, prin. Investment Mgmt. Group Inc., Starkville, 1982—, Wealth Mgmt. Group, Inc.; founding mem. bd. dirs. First Citizens Nat. Bank of Starkville; guest lectr. Miss. State U.; Dalbar rated adv. Contbg. author: Business Strategies; mem. editl. bd. Fin. Svcs. Advisor; contbr. articles to profl. jours. Bd. dirs. exec. bd. Pushmataha area coun. Boy Scouts Am., Republican party; past pres. Men of Ch., Presbyn. Ch., chmn. bd. deacons, elder, men's Sunday Sch. tchr.; bd. dirs. Oktibbeha County Libr., past pres.; bd. dirs. Oktibbeha Devel. Coun., Starkville Acad.; mem. stds. com. Miss. Pub. Libr.; bd. dirs. Miss. chpt. Nat. Com. on Planned Giving. Recipient Silver Beaver award. Mem. Nat. Assn. Christian Fin. Advisors, Nat. Assn. Life Underwriters (nat. committeeman nat. mtg.), Nat. Assn. Securities Dealers, East Miss. Life Underwriters Assn. (past pres.), Soc. Fin. Svcs. Profls. (bd. dirs. Miss. chpt.), Miss. Estate Planning Coun., Inst. for Investment Mgmt. Cons., Internat. Assn. for Fin. Planning (bd. dirs. Miss. chpt.), Million Dollar Round Table (life, qualifying), Ct. Round Table, Oktibbeha County C. of C. (exec. bd.), Rotary (bd. dirs. Starkville, Paul Harris fellow), Sigma Chi, Pi Sigma Epsilon. Home: 1672 Valley Hill Cir Starkville MS 39759-9748 Office: Raymond James Fin Svcs 102 S Jackson St PO Box 963 Starkville MS 39760-0963

GEORGE, FRANCIS CARDINAL, archbishop; b. Chgo., Jan. 16, 1937. Ordained priest Roman Cath. Ch., 1963. Provincial ctrl. region Oblates of Mary Immaculate, 1973-74, vicar gen., 1974-86; bishop Diocese of Yakima, Wash., 1990-96; archbishop Archdiocese of Portland, Oreg., 1996-97, Archdiocese of Chgo., 1997—; chancellor Cath. Ch. Extension Soc., U. St. Mary of the Lake, 1997; mem. Congregation Divine Worship and the Discipline of the Sacraments, Congregation Insts. Consecrated Life and Socs. of Apostolic Life, and Pontifical Coun. "Cor Unum", 1998, Congregation Evangelization of Peoples. Mem. Coll. Cardinals. Office: Archdiocese of Chicago Pastoral Ctr PO Box 1979 Chicago IL 60690-1979

GEORGE, JOHNSON, biology educator; b. Adoor, Kerala, India, Mar. 9, 1965; s. Chantukavil Abraham and Aliyamma G.; m. Shiny Mathew, Feb. 25, 1993; children: Jeslin, Joel. BS, Ravishankar U., India, 1984; MS in Zoology, Ravishankai U., India, 1986, PhD in Entomology, 1991. Jrs. rsch. fellow Govt. Coll., Durg, India, 1987-90; hon. asst. prof. in zoology Govt. Coll., Jagdalpur, India, 1990-91; lectr. in biology Govt. Girls H.S. Sch., Sambalpur, India, 1992-99. Contbr. articles to profl. jours. Office: Govt Girls HS Sch, Sambalpur PO 494635, Dist Kanker MP India

GEORGE, NELSON RAJ, electrical engineer, engineering executive; b. Palliyadi, Tamil Nadu, India, May 23, 1948; s. George Pakyanathan and Nesamal Eliyas; m. Sonia Ramalingan Nadar, Oct. 24, 1977; 1 child, Bejoy Nelson. BE in Elec. Engring., U. Madras (India), 1970; MS in Engring., U. Kerala (India), 1975; MBA in Engring. Mgmt., Century U., Calif., 1986. Profl. engr., India; lic. elec. engr. Bahrain Electricity Dept. Lectr. in elec. engring. TKM Coll. Engring., Kollam, India, 1974-76; asst. exec. engr. Govt. India, New Delhi, 1976-77; head elec. and electronics dept. Premier Cable Co., Ltd., 1977-83; elec. engr. Gulf Cable Co., Kuwait, 1983-86; chief engr. Peace Shield project Al Harbi Co., Saudi Arabia, 1988-90; sr. elec. engr. Airmech W.L.L., Bahrain, 1991-94; project mgr. Esmaely Svcs., Bahrain, 1998-99; cons. engr. Engeel Electrotech Ltd., India, 1995-96, dir., 1996-99, exec. dir., 1999—. Contbr. over 22 articles to profl. jours. Fellow Instn. Engrs. India, Bahrain Soc. Engrs.; mem. IEEE (Outstanding chpt. award 1997, chmn. Kerala chpt. Industry Applications Soc.). Mem. C.S.I. Cong. Avocations: photography, technical writing, travel, driving, music. Home: TC 50/1643(1) Dream Land, Kalady, Karamana Trivandrum Kerala, India 695002 Office: Engeel Electrotech (P) Ltd, Karamana, 695002 Trivandrum Kerala, India

GEORGE, NICHOLAS, lawyer, entrepreneur; b. Seattle, July 11, 1952; s. Harry and Mary (Courounes) G.; children: Harry Nicholas, James Michael. BA in Polit. Sci. cum laude, Whitman Coll., 1974; MBA in Mktg. and Corp. Planning, U. Chgo., 1979; JD, U. Puget Sound, 1989. Bar: Wash. 1991, U.S. Dist. Ct. (we. dist.) Wash. 1991, U.S. Ct. Appeals (9th cir.) 1991, U.S. Tax Ct. 1992, U.S. Dist. Ct. (ea. dist.) Wash. 1994, U.S. Supreme Ct. 1994. Fin. cons. Pacific Western Investment Co., Lynnwood, Wash., 1975-77; planning dir. Clinton Capital Ventures, Seattle, 1979-81; corp. planning mgr. Tacoma Boatbldg., 1981-83; pres. MegaProf Investors, Bellevue, Wash., 1983-89; practice trial-settlement law bus., Seattle, 1989—; free-lance coll. counselor, Seattle, 1980—. Author: Legitimacy in Government: Ideal, Goal, or Myth? 1974. Bd. auditor St. Demetrios Greek Orthodox Ch., Seattle, 1982-83; bd. dirs. Hellenic Golfers Assn., Seattle, 1981-83. Mem. ABA, Assn. Trial Lawyers Am., Wash. State Bar Assn., Wash. Assn. Criminal Def. Lawyers, Wash. State Trial Lawyers Assn., Fed. Bar Assn., Nat. Assn. Criminal Def. Lawyers, Tacoma-Pierce County Bar Assn., Seattle-King County Bar Assn., Wash. Defender Assn., Wash. State Hist. Soc., Am. Inst. Archeol., Phi Alpha Delta. Greek Orthodox. Avocations: weightlifting, travel, family history, football coaching, writing. Home: 5007 80th St SW Lakewood WA 98499-4077 Office: 1201 Pacific Ave Ste 1502 Tacoma WA 98402-4322

GEORGE, RICHARD NEILL, lawyer; b. Watertown, N.Y., Apr. 6, 1933; s. Wendell Dow and Frances Laura (Small) G.; m. Patricia Harman Jackson, June 21, 1958; children—Frances Harman, Richard Neill, Mary Elizabeth. A.B., Yale U., 1955; J.D., Cornell U., 1962. Bar: N.Y. 1962. Assoc. Nixon Peabody, LLP (formerly Nixon, Hargave, Devans & Doyle), Rochester, N.Y., 1962-70, ptnr., 1970—. Committeeman, Brighton Town Republican Com., Rochester, 1966-78; ruling elder Twelve Corners Presbyn. Ch., Rochester, 1977-79, 84-87; mem. permanent jud. commn. Presbytery of Genesee Valley, 1988-94, also moderator. Capt. USAF, 1956-59. Mem. ABA, N.Y. State Bar Assn., Monroe County Bar Assn., Fed. Energy Bar Assn., Exeter Alumni Assn. of Rochester (pres. 1970—). Republican. Clubs: Country of Rochester, Yale of N.Y.C., Amelia Island. Avocations: golf; reading. Home: 14 Oakfield Way Pittsford NY 14534-1888 Office: Nixon Peabody LLP PO Box 1051 Clinton Sq Rochester NY 14604-1729

GEORGES, MARI ELIZABETH KLEIN, software engineer; b. Stamford, Conn., Nov. 22, 1949; arrived in France, 1972; d. Norman Edward and Helen Louise (Shell) Klein; m. Patrick Jacques, Dec. 9, 1972; children:

Romain, Pascal, Christine. BS, Carnegie-Mellon Univ., 1971; postgrad., McGill Univ., Montreal, Can., 1971-72. Programmer L'Oreal, Paris, 1972; programmer analyst Centre de Recherche d'Urbanisme, Paris, 1973-74; software engr. Gamma Informatique, Paris, 1974-76, SESA, Paris, 1976-89; tech. mgr. Cap Gemini Innovation, Paris, 1989-95; asst. dir. R&D ILOG, Paris, 1995-98, sr. dir. engring., 1998—; expert adv. svcs. Commn. of the European Union, Brussels, 1991—. Contbr. articles to profl. jours. Mem. IEEE, Internat. Conf. on Software Maintenance (program co-chair, gen. chair). Office: ILOG, 9 rue de Verdun BP 85, 94253 Gentilly Cedex France

GEORGES, PETER JOHN, lawyer; b. Wilmington, Del., Sept. 8, 1940; s. John Peter and Olga Demetrius (Kazitoris) G. BS in Chemistry, U. Del., 1962; JD, John Marshall Law Sch., 1967; LLM in Patent and Trade Regulations, George Washington U., 1973. Bar: Ill. 1970, U.S. Ct. Appeals (fed. cir.) 1972, D.C. 1973, U.S. Supreme Ct. 1973, Del. 1977. Chemist engring. labs Bell & Howell Co., Chgo., 1966; patent coordinator Armour & Co., Chgo., 1967; patent agt., atty. UOP Inc., Chgo., 1968-71; Washington counsel UOP Inc., Arlington, Va., 1972-77; ptnr. Kile, Gholz, Bernstein & Georges, Arlington, 1977-78; assoc., then ptnr. Law Office Sidney W. Russell, Arlington, 1978-83; mng. officer Breneman & Georges (and predecessor law firms), Alexandria, 1983—; founding ptnr. Lenastri Properties and Joanastri Properties, Alexandria, Va. Served to 1st lt. USMC, 1963-65, Vietnam. Mem. ABA, Ill. Bar Assn., D.C. Bar Assn., Del. Bar Assn., Fed. Cir. Bar Assn., Assn. Trial Lawyers Am., Am. Intellectual Property Law Assn., Am. Hellenic Lawyers Soc. Home: 1637 13th St NW Washington DC 20009-4302 Office: Breneman & Georges 3150 Commonwealth Ave Alexandria VA 22305-2712

GEORGESCU, EMILIAN ION, chemist, researcher; b. Goicea, Dolj, Romania, Dec. 15, 1946; s. Ion Constantin and Gheorghita (Geanta) G.; m. Florentina Frunzescu, Aug. 20, 1969; 1 child, Emil. MSc in Chemistry, U. A.I. Cuza, Iasi, Romania, 1970; D Chemistry, Poly. Inst. G. Asachi, Iasi, 1981. Chemist Chem. Plant, Rm. Vâlcea, Romania, 1970-74; rschr. Rsch. Ctr., Ramnicu Vâlcea, 1974-80, head rsch. lab., 1980-90; rsch. dir. Inst. for Chem. Rsch., INCERCHIM, Ramnicu Vâlcea, 1990-95; head rsch. lab. S.C. OLTCHIM-S.A., Ramnicu Vâlcea, 1995-99, head rsch. ctr., 1999—; lectr. organic chemistry chem. tech. dept. Bucharest Poly. Inst., Rm. Vâlcea, 1981-92. Contbr. articles on heterocyclic chemistry to sci. jours.; over 50 patents in field. Mem. Romanian Chem. Soc. Orthodox. Home: Calea lui Traian 115, Bl3, ScB, Ap4, 1000 Ramnicu Vâlcea Romania Office: OLTCHIM SA, Uzinei nr 1, 1000 Ramnicu Vâlcea Romania

GEORGESCU, GEORGE, mathematician, educator; b. Căpreni, Gorj, Romania, Apr. 4, 1946; s. Constantin and Elena (Becheanu) G.; m. Iulica Bădele, June 2, 1969; 1 child, Irina-Alexandra. PhD, Inst. Math., Bucharest, Romania, 1972. Cert. rsch. scientist. Rschr. Inst. Math., Bucharest, 1969-75, Inst. Computer Sci., Bucharest, 1975-76; prof. Mil. Tech. Acad., Bucharest, 1976-96, U. Bucharest, 1996—. Author: (with others) Lukasiewicz-Moisil Algebras, 1991, also chpts. in books; contbr. papers to profl. jours. Avocations: music, philosophy. Office: U Bucharest, Str Academie i 14, Bucharest Romania

GEORGESCU, HORIA DAN, physician, consultant physicist; b. Bucharest, Romania, May 2; arrived in France, 1990; s. Nicolae and Sofia (Secareany) G.; m. Maria Cristiana Baranga, June 24, 1978; children: Emanuela, Irina-Ingrid, Christophe. MD, Faculty of Medicine, Bucharest, 1976, Anesthesiologist, 1982; PhD, U. Bucharest, 1984. Med. diplomate; diplomate European Acad. Anesthesiology; bd. cert. in France. Intern Univ. Hosp. Fundeni, Bucharest, 1975-78; resident sect. anesthesia Univ. Hosp. Urgentza, Bucharest, 1978-82, prin. anesthesiologist, 1982-90, first class anesthesiologist, 1990; anesthesiologist CHU Pitie-Salpetriere, Paris, 1990-96, Clinique Lambert, Lagarenne-Colombes, France, 1996—. Author: Cardiopulmonary and Cerebral Resuscitation, 1982, also articles; patentee in field. Mem. AAAS, N.Y. Acad. Sci., Soc. Tech. Anesthesiology, SFAR. Avocations: computer-generated holograms, philosophy, humanitarian medicine, swimming. Home: 2 Rue Antonio Vivaldo, 78100 St-Germain-en-Laye France

GEORGI, STEFAN, venture strategist; b. Sofia, Bulgaria, Feb. 23, 1968; s. George and Nina Gueorguiev; m. Rosita Georgi. BA, Stockholm Sch. Econs., 1991. Strategy cons. various cos., Stockholm, 1988-89; ptnr. G & H AB, Stockholm, 1989-93; exec. ptnr. Trout & Ptnrs. Co., Stockholm, 1994-99; ptnr. The Odin Group, Stockholm, 1999—. Author: The Most Important Positioning Principles, 1995; contbr. articles to various publs., including Svenska Dagbladet, Resumé. Avocations: tennis, music, modern art. Office: The Odin Group, Master Samuelsgatan 4, S-111 44 Stockholm Sweden

GEORGIEV, DIMITER BORISSOV, gynecologist, consultant; b. Sofia, Bulgaria, Mar. 19, 1962; s. Boris Dimitrov and Genka Assenova (Usheva) G. MD, Sofia, 1988; PhD, 1996. Cert. physician, gynecologist. Gynecologist Dist. Hosp., Targoviste, Bulgaria, 1989-91, II Ob-Gyn. Hosp., Sofia, 1991—; cons. Internat. Planned Parenthood Fedn., Sofia, 1995—; sec./treas. Bulgarian Menopause Soc.; mem. adv. panel FIGO on Menopause. Author: HELLP-Syndrome-10 Years of Research, 1992, To Remain Young, 1994; contbr. articles to profl. jours. Mem. Internat. Menopause Soc. Christian Orthodox. Home: 16 Vladajska Str, 1606 Sofia Bulgaria Office: II Ob-Gyn Hosp, 19 Sheinovo Str, 1504 Sofia Bulgaria

GEORGIEV, PAVEL STEFANOV, history educator; b. Ruse, Bulgaria, Dec. 23, 1948; s. Stefan Georgiev Kanchev and Zhechka Pencheva Kancheva. BTh, Theol. Acad., Sofia, Bulgaria, 1975; M in History, Ctrl. European U., Budapest, Hungary, 1997; PhD, Inst. Philosophy, Sofia, 1997. Cert. theologian and historian-cleric. Sec. Metropolia, Lovech, Bulgaria, 1976-79; parish priest Ruse, 1979-82; sr. rschr. Church History Inst., Sofia, 1983-86; asst. prof., assoc. prof. ch. history U. Shumen, Bulgaria, 1993—. Translator: Ancient Paterikon, 1992, Under the Balkans (R.J. More), 1993, The Lost Ship of Noah (C. Berlitz), 1997, History of the Russian Orthodox Church in the 20th Century, 1997, The Jewish Heritage (D. Kohn-Sherbok), 1999; host Shoumen Radio; editor Episkop-Konstantinovi chetenya, 1994—, Troudove, Shumen U., 1997—. Tempus scholar, Wolverhampton, Eng., 1995, Open Soc. scholar, Budapest, 1997, Keble Coll. scholar, Oxford, Eng., 1999, Ostkirchliches Inst., Regensburg, Germany, 2000. Mem. N.Y. Acad. Scis., Union Bulgarian Scientists, Bulgarian Hist. Soc., Orthodox Students Union (hon. pres. 1992—). Mem. Orthodox Ch. Avocations: music, fine art, hatha yoga, internet. Office: Rm 301, Shumen University, 9712 Shumen Bulgaria

GEORGIEVA, VESSELINA, marketing executive, consultant; b. Sofia, Bulgaria, Nov. 23, 1970; d. George Petrov and Krassimira Dimitrova (Kocheva) G. Cert., Econ. Inst. Comm., Bulgaria, 1990; MB in Agr., Sofia U. Nat. & World Economy, 1995; cert., Washington and Lee U., 1996, Am. U., Bulgaria, 1996. Cert. economist. Tech. asst. Montaji Inc., Sofia, Bulgaria, 1989-90; mgr. asst. Alma Drug, Sofia, 1993; client svc. dir. Iksi Ltd., Sofia, 1994; sales person Berkeley (N.J.) Sweet Shop, 1994; account exec. Ogilvy & Mather, Sofia, 1995—. Avocations: Music, golf, polo, skating. Home: Apt 63, JK Mladost 1 Bl 49 VHG, 1784 Sofia Bulgaria Office: Ogilvy & Mather, Expo 2000 Vaptzarov Blvd, 1407 Sofia Bulgaria also: PO Box 141, Sofia 1784, Bulgaria

GEORGIEVSKY, VICTOR PETROVICH, pharmacologist, research institute director; b. Artyomovsk, Dddonetsk, USSR, June 23, 1937; s. Pyotr Alexandrovoch and Anastasya Sergeyevna (Pasechna) G.; m. Alexandra Ivanovna Kharchenko, Feb. 14, 1968; 1 child, Gennadiy. Pharmacist, 1st Moscow Inst. Medicine, 1959; Candidate Pharm. Scis., State Sci. Ctr. Drugs, Kharkov, Ukraine, 1964, D Pharm. Scis., 1981. Lab. asst., sci. collaborator, lab. chief All-Union Rsch. Inst. Pharm. Chemistry and Tech. (now State Sci. Ctr. Drugs), 1958-88, dir., 1988—; chmn. Pharmacopoeial Com. Ukraine, 1992—. Author: Biologically Active Substances of Medicinal Plants, 1992, New Natural and Semi-Synthetic Substances of Medicinal Plants, 1995, Drug Standardization and Technology, 1996; contbr. over 300 articles to sci. jours., including USSR Med. Industry, Pharmacy, Chem. and Pharm. Jour., Pharm Jour., Jour. Analytical Chemistry, Jour. Phys. Chemistry, Lectures USSR Acad. Scis., Chemistry Natural Compounds; numerous patents in field. Decorated 3 medals of USSR, Order for the Deserts 3d degree (Ukraine); named Honored Worker Sci. and Engring. Ukraine, 1991. Mem. Internat. Engring. Acad., Internat. Assn. Chromatographists, Engring. Acad. Ukraine, N.Y. Acad. Scis. Avocations: fishing, hunting, touring, paintings. Fax: 38 0572 44 11 18. E-mail: georgiev@phukr.kharkov.ua. Office: State Sci Ctr Drugs, 33 Astronomicheskaya St, Kharkov Ukraine

GEORGII, ROBERT HEINRICH, physicist, researcher; b. Munich, Apr. 3, 1965; s. Peter and Margot (Herrmann) G.; m. Martina Pflitsch, July 25, 1998. Diploma, Tech. U. Munich, 1989, D in Natural Scis., 1994. Postdoctoral Tech. U. Munich, 1994; postdoctoral fellow European Cmtys., Frascati, Italy, 1995; postdoctoral U. Oxford, Eng., 1995; rsch. fellow Max Planck Assn., Germany, 1995—; co-investigator Integral SPI rsch./gamma ray astronomy Max Plank Assn., Germany, 1998—, co-investigator GBM Glast, 2000—. Mem. German Physics Assn. Avocations: mountaineering, theatre, cooking, history. Office: Max Planck Assn, Giessenbachstr, D-85740 Garching Bavaria, Germany

GEORGIN, MICHEL HUBERT, information technology company executive; b. Paris, Jan. 17, 1947; s. Rene M. and Marguerite (Bonnard) G.; m. Fanny Marie Cambier, Sept. 4, 1951; children: Raphael, Sophie, Gabriel, Marie-Ange. Degree in polytechnics, Econ. and Stats. Sch., Paris, 1971. Adminstr. Ministry of Fin. and Equip., Paris, 1971-79; del. dir. CIT-ALCATEL, Paris, 1979-82, CGE Hdqrs., Paris, 1982-88; dir. fin. CIMSA SINTRA, Paris, 1988-90; v.p. software engring. Thomson-CSF, Paris, 1991-95; sr. exec. v.p. strategy/DUT SYSECA, 1996—. E-mail: mickel.georgin@syseca.thomson-csf.com. Home: 7 rue Emile Dubois, 75074 Paris France Office: SYSECA, SYSECA, 66-68 av Pierre Brossdette, 92140 Malakoff France

GEORGIOU, CHRISTOS DIMOS, biochemistry educator, researcher; b. Patra, Greece, July 7, 1951; s. Dimos Stefanos and Kyriakoula (Photakopoulou) G. Diploma, U. Thessaloniki, Greece, 1975; MSc in Biochemistry with honors, U. Roosevelt, 1979; PhD in Biology-Biochemistry, Ill. Inst. of Tech., 1985; postdoctoral in molecular biology, U. Ill., 1987; MSc with honors, Roosevelt U., 1979. Asst. prof. U. Thessaloniki, 1991-92; asst. prof. biochemistry U. Patra, 1992-2000, assoc. prof., 2000—. Author: Experimental Biochemistry, 1993, Research and Experiments in Biochemistry, 1994, Applications of Biocatalysts in Biotechnology, 1996; translator: The Lives to Come (Philip Kitcher), 1997, The Clone (Gina Kolata), 1997; contbr. articles to sci. jours.; holder 2 diplomas for inventions. Fellow Am. Heart Assn., Am. Chem. Soc., European Soc. for Free Radical Rsch. (Greek sect.), Internat. Soc. for Free Radical Rsch.; mem. AAAS. Avocations: painting, music. Office: Univ Patra, Biology Dept, 26100 Patra Greece

GEORGIOU, CONSTANTINOS ANDREAS, chemist, educator; b. Athens, Dec. 7, 1961; s. Andreas and Maria (Kardara) G. BS in Chemistry, U. Athens, 1984, PhD, 1990. Biochemist Chief Agia Eleni Hosp., Athens, 1991-95; asst. prof. Agrl. U. Athens, 1992—; cons. in analytical chemistry, Athens, 1987—. Contbr. articles to profl. jours. Sgt. Greek Air Force, 1985-86. Scholar Greek Scholarship Found., 1986, Secretariat of Rsch. and Technology, 1987, Greek Drug Orgn., 1989. Mem. Am. Chem. Soc., Am. Assn. Clin. Chemistry, Greek Chemistry Soc., Greek Clin. Chemistry Soc. Greek Orthodox. Home: 17 Matrozou St, GR11741 Athens Greece Office: Agrl U Athens, 75 Iera Odos, 11855 Athens Greece

GEORGIOU, DIMITRIOS, mathematics educator; b. Thessaloniki, Greece, Mar. 20, 1948; s. Antonios and Beatrice (Spengos) G.; m. Helen Karoni, Dec. 26, 1975; children: Antonios-Alexandros, Vasilios. Bachelor, U. Thessaloniki, 1974; PhD, Democritus U. of Thrace, Xanthi, Greece, 1980. Asst. Aristoteles U. of Thessaloniki, 1974-75; lectr. in math. Democritus U. of Thrace, 1975-85, asst. prof., 1986-91, assoc. prof., 1991—; vis. prof. U. Calif.-Davis, 1981-82; prof. Postgrad. Sch. in Teaching, Kavala, Greece, 1983-87; vis. prof. U. R.I., Kingston, 1989-91. Author 5 books in Greek; also articles. Served to lt. inf. Greek Army, 1970-72. Mem. Am. Math. Soc., Greek Math. Soc. Office: Democritus U of Thrace, 67100 Xanthi Greece

GEORGIOU, VASSILIS ANDREAS, cardiologist; b. Patrae, Greece, May 5, 1931; s. Andreas Vassilis and Effrossini Vassilis (Arvanitis) G.; m. Maria N. Diradaki, June 5, 1960; children: Andreas, Effrossini. Med. Doctor, U. Athens, Greece, 1957. MD. Intern Evagelismos Hosp., Athens, Greece, 1959-60; resident Spiliopoulion Hosp., Athens, Greece, 1963-65, chief resident, 1965-67; fellow in cardiology Hippokrateon Hosp., Athens, Greece, 1966-72; rsch. fellow Postgrad. Med. Sch. Hammersmith Hosp., London, 1972-73; asst. prof. cardiology Hippokrateon Hosp., Athens, 1975-80, assoc. prof. cardiology, 1980-90, prof. cardiology, 1990—; cardiologist pvt. practice Athens, 1972—; Inventor in field. Mem. Hellenic Soc. Cardiology, Hellenic Soc. Study and Application of Ultrasound in Medicine and Biology, Soc. Med. Studies, Rotary Club (Athens-North), Club of Athens, Club Yaht of Greece. Avocation: golf. Office: 26 Karneadou St, 10675 Athens Greece

GEORGOUSSIS, GEORGE EUSTATHIOS, cardiologist, writer; b. Polydrosson, Fokidos, Greece, May 3, 1941; s. Eustathios George and Titsa Eustathios (Sakellariou) G.; m. Filio Porpodias, July, 8, 1982; 1 child, Eustathios. Diploma, Athens Coll., Greece, 1959, Athens U., Greece, 1966; D (hon.), Athens U., Greece, 1980. Med. Diplomate. Ensign med. officer Greek Navy Hosp., Athens, Greece, 1967-69; med. house officer Hosp. Broussais, Paris, 1969; sr. house officer N.H.S. Hosps., London, 1969-72; registrar Sismanogleio Hosp., Athens, Greece, 1973-75, sr. registrar, 1975—; dir. intensive coronary unit Sismanogleio Hosp., Athens, 1997—. Author: Noctilique, 1966, (medical book) The Lown-Ganong-Levine Syndrome, 1980, The Returns, 1984, Diaries of Abscence, 1985, Rocky Walls, 1986, Double Sentry, 1987, Note-Books of the South, 1988, Palinody, 1989, 90, Stigmata, 1999. Mem. Hellenic British Med. Soc. (v.p. 1982-94), Internat. Union Doctor's and Writer's, Greek Writer's Soc. Mem. Greek Orthodox Ch. Avocation: literature. Home: Maurommateon 6, 106 82 Athens Greece Office: Sismanogleion Hosp, 15126 Maroussi Attiki, Greece

GEORGY, MICHEL SALIB, obstetrician and gynecologist; b. Cairo, Egypt, 1946; arrived in U.K., 1974; s. Salib and Thoria (Giurgis) G.; m. Samia Fayek, Feb. 14, 1980; children: Vivian, Mark. MB BCh, Ain Shams U., Cairo, 1970. Registrar Newcastle (Eng.) Gen. Hosp., 1978-80, Bellshill Hosp., Scotland, 1980-82; sr. registrar NGKH Hosp., Jeddah, Saudi Arabia, 1982-84; cons. Nat. Guard King Khalid Hosp., Saudi Arabia, 1984-94, Royal Shrewsbury Hosp., Eng., 1994-96, Grantham Hosp., Eng., 1996—; sr. house officer Royal Victoria Infirmary, 1976-78. Contbr. articles to profl. jours. Fellow Royal Coll. Ob-Gyn.; mem. Saudi Ob-Gyn. Soc., Internat. Continence Soc., Birmingham Ob-Gyn. Soc., Brit. Soc. Colposcopy and Cervical Pathology. Home: 36 Rollswood Dr, Solihall W Midlands B91 1NL, England Office: Ormskirk and Dist Hosp, Wigan Rd, Ormskirk, Lancashire L39 2AZ, England

GEPFORD, WILLIAM GEORGE, minister; b. Kansas City, Mo., Jan. 12, 1927; s. Herbert John and Anna Ruth (Minckemeyer) G.; m. Barbara Joan Beebe, Dec. 28, 1952; children: David Proctor, Scott Allen, Joanna Lynn, Andrea Laine. BS in Elec. Engring., Colo. State U., 1949; MDiv., McCormick Sem., 1953; MEd, U. Colo., 1957; DSc in Theology, San Francisco Sem., 1973. Ordained to ministry Presbyn. Ch. (U.S.A.), 1953. Edn. missionary Presbyn. Ch., Lebanon, 1953-63; dean students Am. U., Beirut, 1961-63; asst. min. First Presbyn. Ch., Boulder, Colo., 1963-65; missionary, student min. Presbyn. Ch., Hong Kong, 1965-71; chaplain, student life dir. Muskingum Coll., New Concord, Ohio, 1972-79; dir. Am./Arab Ministry Presbytery of Detroit, Mich., 1979—; dean of students Am. Univ. Beirut, Lebanon, 1961-63; dir. student ctr. YMCA (Chinese), Hong Kong, 1965-71; acting assoc. dean of students, Muskingum Coll., New Concord, 1977-78; mem. gen. assembly, adv. study com. on Islam, N.Y., 1983-86; bd. dirs. Interfaith Activities, Presbytery of Detroit; founder Muslim/Christian Dialogue Group, 1985; adv. bd. Arab Community Ctr. of Econ. and Social Svcs., Dearborn, 1983—; mem. Am. Arab Anti-Discrimination com., adv. com., Detroit, 1984—, others; cons. Interfaith Ministries, Presbytery of Detroit, 1992—. Mem. adv. bd. ACCESS, Dearborn, Mich., 1985—; clergy participant Interfaith Round Table of Detroit, 1985—; bd. dirs. Human Svcs., Inc., Dearborn; mem. citizens adv. bd. WTVS Ch. 56 PBS, Detroit, 1986-89; bd. dirs. Freedom House, Detroit; mem. Mich. Coalition Human Rights, 1999—, Met. Christian Coun., 1996—; mem. planning com. Detroit 300 Celebration. With USN, 1945-46. Mem. McCormick Sem. Alumni Assn. (pres.-elect 1991-93), Kiwanis (pres. Dearborn 1986-87), Phi Delta Kappa. Democrat. Home: 9421 Westwind Dr Livonia MI 48150-4530

GEPP, DAVID, photographer, lecturer; b. Belfast, No. Ireland, May 27, 1948; s. Samuel and Josephine Gepp; m. Merlyn Hancock, July 27, 1985. Lectr. photography Hereford Coll. Art, 1993—; lectr. U. Nottingham Trent, U. Staffordshire, 1997, Swansea Coll., 1998, U. Wales, 1999, also workshops for Brunel U. and Photographers at Duckspool; subject of BBC Documentary An Italian Dream, 1997. One-man shows Brewery Arts Ctr., Kendal, 1994, Oriel 31, Powys, 1994, 96, Aberystwyth (Wales) Arts Ctr., 1994, 98, Clotworthy Arts Ctr., Antrim, 1994, 97, St. David's Hall, Cardiff, Wales, 1995, The Gallery, Telford, 1995, OMAC, Belfast, 1995, Harmony Hill Arts Ctr., Belfast, 1995, 97, Mus. Modern Art, Wales, 1995, Sperrin Heritage Ctr., 1997, Ardhowen Theatre, Enniskillen, 1997, Newry Arts Ctr., 1997, Flowerfield Arts Ctr., Portstewart, 1997, Ruthin Craft Ctr., 1997, Ulster Mus., Belfast, 1997, Glynn Vivian Art Gallery, Swansea, Wales, 1998, Ruskin Gallery, Sheffield, Eng., 1998, Nat. Bot. Garden Wales, 2000; represented in permanent collections Nat. Libr., Paris, Nat. Libr. Wales, BT Irish New Media Collection, 2000. Travel grantee 92, Arts Coun. Wales, 1991-93, 94-95, Arts Coun. Wales, Visual Artists' Bursary, 1999. Avocations: reading, walking, drinking. Home and Studio: Ger Yr Ywen, Llanerfyl, Powys SY21 0EG, Wales

GER, GÜLIZ, marketing/consumer research educator, researcher; b. Ankara, Turkey, Aug. 14, 1952; d. Erdogan Mustafa and Sencan Saliha (Hisim) Mestci; m. Ahmet Metin Ger, Aug. 6, 1970; children: Baris, Ali. BS cum laude, U. Ill., 1974; MS, Mid. East Tech. U., Ankara, 1977; PhD, Northwestern U., 1985. Asst. Mid. East Tech. U., 1975-77, instr., 1977-80; lectr. Northwestern U., Evanston, Ill., 1983-84; asst. prof. U. Ill., Chgo., 1984-85; asst. prof. Bilkent U., Ankara, 1986-90, assoc. prof., 1990-98, prof., 1999—; vis. prof. INSEAD, Fontainbleau, France, 1986—, Odense (Denmark) U., fall 1994, London Bus. Schs., fall 1994, Theseus, France, 1998, CEIBS, China, 1999, Northwestern U., summer 1989. Co-editor: Consumption in Marketizing Economies, 1994; contbr. articles to profl. jours. Recipient Fulbright-Hays grant, 1980-84. Mem. Internat. Soc. Mktg. and Devel. (bd. dirs. 1990—), Internat. Jour. Rsch. Mktg. (mem. editl. bd. 1990—), Assn. for Consumer Rsch. Avocations: drawing, reading, bicycling, swimming, hiking. Office: Bilkent Univ, Faculty Bus Adminstrn, 06533 Ankara Turkey

GERA, DINESH, mechanical engineer; b. New Delhi. MSME, W.Va. U., 1992, PhD, 1994. Rsch. asst. prof. W.Va. U., Morgantown, 1994-97, Brigham Young U., Provo, Utah, 1997-98; consulting engr. Fluent, Inc., Morgantown, 1998—. Mem. ASME. Office: Fluent Inc 3647 Collins Ferry Rd Morgantown WV 26505-2352

GERA, DOV, ancient historian; b. Jerusalem, Mar. 2, 1948; s. Nathan and Rebecca (Wistanietcky) Grossowicz; m. Deborah H. Levine, Apr. 5, 1979; children: Avital, Chaim-Itzhac, Ariel. BA, Hebrew U., 1972, MA, 1977, PhD, 1986. Instr. Hebrew U., Jerusalem, 1980-81, 83-86, lectr., 1986-88; instr., lectr. Tchrs. Ctrl. Inst. for Exterior Studies, Tel-Aviv, Israel, 1985-94; outside lectr. Ben Gurion U., Be'er Sheva, Israel, 1988-89, lectr., 1989-99, sr. lectr., 1999—; scientific advisor Open U., Israel, 1988-89; vis. scholar Wolfson Coll., Oxford, 1995-96, Oxford Ctr. for Hebrew and Jewish Studies, Oxford U., 1995-96. Author: Judaea and Mediterranean Politics, 1998; contbr. articles to profl. jours. Sgt. Israel Def. Forces, 1966-69. Warburg scholar Hebrew U., 1978-80, Meml. Found. for Jewish Culture scholar, 1981; Rothschild Found. publ. grantee, 1994. Mem. Israel Hist. Soc. Jewish. Home: 87 Bar-Kochva St, 97892 Jerusalem Israel Office: Dept History, Ben Gurion U of the Negev, 84105 Beer Sheva Israel

GERACI, GIUSEPPE FEDERICO ELIO, molecular biologist, educator; b. Naples, Italy, Mar. 18, 1933; s. Arturo and Pia (Spezzaferro) G.; m. Rosa Alberti, Mar. 27, 1960. D in Chemistry, U. Naples, Italy, 1956. Rschr. Pharm. Industry, Naples, Italy, 1958-62, Italian Nat. Rsch. Coun., Naples, Italy, 1962-71; assoc. rschr. Cornell U., Ithaca, N.Y., 1966-67; assoc. rschr. Harvard Med. Sch., Boston, 1967-68, assoc. staff in medicine, 1968-69; dir. rsch. Lab. of Molecular Embryology, Naples, 1971—; prof. molecular biology U. Naples, 1981—; vis. prof. Harvard Med. Sch., Boston, 1991; sci. adv. bd. CNR Ctr. for Molecular Biology, Rome, 1971-80, Ctr. for Genetic Engring., Naples, 1985—; dir. Inst. Gen. Biology and Genetics, U. Naples, 1981-85, pres. U. Coun. on Biol. Sci., dir. dept. gen. and molecular biology, 1996-98. Editor, author: (book) Le Nuove Frontiere della Biologia, 1991; contbr. papers to Jour. Biol. Chemistry, Biochemistry, Jour. Molecular Biology and other profl. jours. Recipient award Italian Soc. Biochemistry, 1988. Mem. Italian Soc. Biophys. and Molecular Biology (cons. 1966-68), Italian Soc. Biochemistry, Italian Nat. Acad. Letters, Scis. and Arts (pres. 1997-99), Internat. Lions Club. Roman Catholic. Achievements include the distinction of being the first to demonstrate Allosteric Regulation in mammalian enzyme; first to prepare human hemoglobin chains with different functional properties; demonstration of evidence of pre-determinative events in sea urchin embryo development. E-mail: geraci@dgbm.unina.it. Home: Via Botteghelle 212, 80046 S Giorgio a Cremano Italy Office: U Naples, Dept Genetics, Via Mezzocannone 8, 80134 Naples Italy

GERALDSON, RAYMOND I., JR., lawyer; b. Racine, Wis., Oct. 19, 1940; s. Raymond I. Sr. and Evelyn (Thorpe) G.; m. Melinda Paine, June 13, 1964; children: Amy Geraldson-Bhote, Raymond I. III. BA, DePauw U., 1962; JD, Northwestern U., 1965. Bar: Ill. 1965, D.C. 1966, U.S. Dist. Ct. (no. dist.) Ill. 1967. Ptnr. Pattishall, McAuliffe, Newbury, Hilliard & Geraldson, Washington, 1965-67, Chgo., 1967—; adj. prof. John Marshall Law Sch. 1978—; lectr. in field. Contbr. articles on trademark law to profl. jours. Trustee Kendall Coll., 1985—, chmn., 1990—. Mem. ABA, Ill. State Bar Assn. (coun. sect. intellectual property law 1978-82, chmn. 1980-81), Chgo. Bar Assn., 7th Crct. Intellectual Property Law Assn. Chgo. (bd. dirs. 1984-86, 92-93, pres. 1991-92), Internat. Trademark Assn. (bd. dirs. 1985-87), Am. Intellectual Property Law Assn., Lawyers for Creative Arts (hons. coun. 1994—, bd. dirs. 1974-94, pres. 1976-78), Legal Club Chgo., Law Club Chgo., Econ. Club Chgo., Sunset Ridge Country Club, Union League Club of Chgo., Sigma Chi. Office: Pattishall McAuliffe Newbury Hilliard & Geraldson 311 S Wacker Dr Ste 5000 Chicago IL 60606-6631

GERAMANI, KONSTANTINA, biomedical engineer, researcher; b. Athens, Greece, May 25, 1968; d. Nikolaos and Areti (Benetou) G. MSc, Nat. Tech. U., Athens, 1991; postgrad., U. Heidelberg, Germany, 1998; PhD, Nat. Tech. U., 1999; diploma in mgmt. studies, Buckinghamshire Chilterns U., London, 2000. Rschr. Nat. Tech. U., Athens, 1991-93; cons. elec. engr., 1993-96; biomed. engr. State Hosp. Offenbach, Germany, 1996—. Contbg. author: New Developments in Interstitial Brachytherapy, 1997. Leonardo grantee European Commn., Germany, 1996. Mem. IEEE (student), Am. Assn. of Physicists in Medicine (assoc.), German Assn. Med. Physics. Home and Office: Am Koppenberg 3, D-28239 Bremen Germany

GERANIOS, ATHANASSIOS, nuclear physicist, educator; b. Athens, Greece, Mar. 25, 1944; s. Konstantinos and Maria (Michalopoulou) G.; m. Zoi Psarrou, May 21, 1973; children: Maria, Kostis. Diploma in physics, Athens U., 1967, PhD, 1970, habilitation, 1980. Scientific collaborator Athens U., 1969-71, sr. asst., 1973-79, permanently employed asst., 1979-80, docent, 1980-83, docent, prof. nuc. physics, 1984—. Author (univ. textbooks): Nuclear Technology, 1982, Nuclear Energy Society, 1985; contbr. numerous articles to profl. jours. and internat. conf. procs., including Jour. Geophys. Rsch., Solar Physics, Planetary and Space Sci., others. Recipient several bilateral rsch. grants, Max-Planck, Greek-Czech Ministries Tech., Munich, Heidelberg, Lindau, Rome, Prague, 1978—. Office: Athens U Nuc Particle Phys, Panepistimioupoli, 15557 Athens Greece

GERARD, GARY, neurologist; b. N.Y.C., Apr. 16, 1949; s. Victor and Sylvia G.; m. Pauline Judd; 1 child, Michael. BA, NYU, 1971; MD, Hahnemann U., 1975. Diplomate Am. Bd. Neurology and Psychiatry. Intern medicine Brookdale Med. Ctr., Bklyn., N.Y., 1975-76; resident in diagnostic radiology Mt. Sinai Med. Ctr., N.Y.C., 1976-78; resident in neurology L.I. Jewish Med. Ctr., New Hyde Park, N.Y., 1978-81; chief of neurology Winthrop U. Hosp., Mineola, N.Y., 1984-89; assoc. prof. neurology and radiology, dir. cerebrovascular lab. Med. Coll. Ohio, Toledo, 1990-94, vice chmn. neurology, 1991-94; med. dir. Neurology Ctr. Ohio, Toledo, 1994—, dir., 1994-96. Contbr. chpts. to books; guest editor jour. Seminars in Neurology, 1986. Bd. dirs. Ohio Rsch. Ctr., Toledo, 1994-97. Recipient Robert J. Tidrick award Med. Coll. Ohio, 1991. Fellow Am. Heart Assn. (stroke coun.); mem. Am. Acad. Neurology (neuroimaging com.

1985-90), Am. Pain Soc., Am. Acad. Pain Mgmt., Am. Assn. Study of Headache, Am. Soc. Neurorehab., Nat. Headache Found., Am. Soc. Neuroimaging (bd. dirs. 1984-90).

GERARD, MANJU, physicist, researcher; b. Kheiri Nagar, Rajasthan, India, Sept. 11, 1969; d. Kalingal Raphael and Sosamma (Abraham) Verghese; m. Gerard Abraham, Dec. 29, 1996; children: Gerard, Rebecca, Ann. BS with honors, Rajasthan U., 1988, MS, 1990; PhD, Jama Millia Islamia, India, 1997. Asst. tchr. Ceeri Vidya Mandir, Palani, India, 1991-92; guest researcher Nat. Phys. Labs., New Delhi, India, 1992-93; scientist fellow Nat. Phys. Labs., New Delhi, 1993-95, sr. rsch. fellow, 1995-97, rsch. assoc., 1997—. Mem. Indian Women Scientist Assn. (life), Chem. Rsch. Soc. India. Avocations: sketching, music, table tennis. Office: Nat Phys Lab BECPRG, Dr KS Krishnan Rd, 110 012 New Delhi Pusa, India

GERARD, PAUL, oral surgeon; b. Sydney, Australia, Sept. 30, 1927; s. Allen Willie and Abigail G.; m. Margaret Helen Patton, Sept. 23, 1950 (div. 1980); children: Alistair, Robert (dec.), David, Pauline, Andrew; m. Kathleen Barrett, Mar. 21, 1998. B Dental Surgery, U. Sydney, 1949, M Dental Surgery, 1974, FRACDS, 1974; postgrad., Brisbane Coll. Theology, 1. Resident in dental surgery Royal Prince Alfred Hosp., Sydney, 1949-51; pvt. practice, Australia, U.K., Can., 1952-80; asst. prof. U. B.C., Vancouver, Can., 1976-80; assoc. prof. King Saud U. Coll. of Dentistry, Riyadh, Saudi Arabia, 1981-87; con. oral and maxillofacial surgeon Ministry of Def. and Aviation, Saudi Arabia, 1988-93; clin. head Tasmanian Govt. Dental Ctr., Launceston, Tasmania, 1995—. Mem. Brit. Soc. Oral and Maxillofacial Surgeons. Anglican. Home: 1/1 Beverley Hills Rd, Newstead/Tasmania 7250, Australia Office: Nthn Dental Ctr, Kelham St, 7250 Launceston/Tasmania Australia

GERARDIN, BERNARD, international banking consultant; b. Nancy, France, Apr. 28, 1953; s. Jean and Simone (Arnould) G.; m. Marie Colette Jacquin, June 19, 1976; children: Aurelie, Delphine. Degree in engring., Ecole Centrale de Lyon, 1974, MS in Polit. Scis., 1979, PhD in Econs., 1980. Cons. Inst. Econ. Studies, Lyons, France, 1976-77; researcher CNRS, Lyons, 1977-81; lectr. U. Lyons, 1976-81; tech. adviser Ministry of Transport, Govt. of France, Paris, 1981-86; dir. programs INRETS, Paris, 1986-91; tech. adviser European Investment Bank, Luxembourg, 1991-93; ind. cons. France, 1993-2000; expert European conf. of Ministers of Transport, Paris, 1975-99; cons. European Investment Bank, 1993-99; assoc. prof. U. Lyons, 1981-91; part-time prof. ENPC-UTC, 1993-97; mem. Cabinet of Minister of Transport, 1981-86. Author: Evaluer les politiques des transports, 1977, Le transport-employeur, 1981; editor: Travel Behaviour Research, 1988. Mem. Internat. Assn. Travel Behaviour (chmn. 1991-93), PTRC Internat. Assn. (bd. dirs. 1983-97). E-mail: bgerardin2@aol.com. Home and Office: 76 quai de Tounis, 31000 Toulouse France

GERARDOT, MARK STEVEN, construction executive; b. Ft. Wayne, Ind., July 12, 1955; s. Roger Anthony and Jocile Click Gerardot; m. Julia Anne Pegram, May 12, 1979; children: Jarrod Pegram, Luke Anthony. Student, Ill. State U., 1973-75. Carpenter Hassebrock Constrn., Mt. Pulaski, Ill., 1972-76; carpenter, foreman Hassebrock Constrn., Mt. Pulaski, 1976-79; owner M. Gerardot Carpenter/Builder, Lincoln, Ill., 1979-85; project mgr. Capitol Devel. Bd., Springfield, Ill., 1985—; performance rev. com. Capital Devel. Bd., Springfield, 1999—. Author: Procedures and Forms, 1990. Mem. Am. Correctional Assn., Door and Hardware Inst. Republican. Avocations: woodworking, golfing, camping. E-mail: mgerardo@cdb.state.il.us. Office: Capital Devel Bd 3rd Fl Stratton 401 S Spring St Springfield IL 62706-4050

GERASIMCHUK, VICTOR SEMENOVICH, physics educator, mathematician; b. Perm, Russia, Nov. 8, 1950; s. Semen Stepanovich and Katerina Vladimirovna (Albrekht) G.; m. Natalia Ivanovna Maljutina Gerasimchuk, Aug. 25, 1973; children: Igor, Sergey. PhD, Donetsk State U., Ukraine, 1980; DSc, Donetsk Physico-Tech. Inst., Ukraine, 1996. Cert. theoretical and mathematical physicist. Rschr. Donetsk State U., Ukraine, 1976-79; asst. prof. Donbass Civil Engring. Inst., Ukraine, 1979-83, assoc. prof., 1983-95; prof., head of chair Donbass State Acad. Civil Engring. and Arch., Ukraine, 1996—; head of works Donbass Civil Engring. Inst., Ukraine, 1987-88; cons. Donetsk Physico-Technical Inst., Ukraine, 1991—. Author: (textbook) Classical Problems of Mathematical Physics, Par 1, Donetsk, 1999; contbr. articles to profl. jours. Recipient Internat. Soros Sci. Edn. Programme award, 1996. Mem. N.Y. Acad. Scis. Avocations: books, volleyball, swimming. E-mail: vsg@donace.dn.ua. Office: Donbass State Acad Civ Engr, Derzhavin str, Makeyevka 86123, Ukraine

GERASIMOV, OLEG IVANOVICH, physicist, theorist, researcher; b. Odessa, Ukraine, Jan. 23, 1955. DS, Odessa State Hydrometeor. Inst. Rsch. assoc. Odessa State U., 1980-83, sr. rsch. assoc., 1983-84, assoc. prof., 1984-90, head Lab. Theoretical Physics, 1984-90; prof. dept. solid state physics Nat. Ukrainian Acad. Scis. Bogolyubov Inst. Theoretical Physics, Kiev, 1994, sr. rsch. assoc., 1990-94, sr. rsch. doctorate, 1994; prof., head gen. and theoretical physics dept. Odessa State Hydrometerol. Inst., 1994—; guest prof. dept molecular physics Leuven Katolic U., Belgium, 1987, dept. chem. physics Free U. Brussels, 1989, Centrum of Nonlinear Phenomena and Complex Systems, 1993, 96, dept. gen. physics and structure of matter U. Messina, Italy, 1994, 95, dept. applied physics nd transport processes Tech. U. Eindhoven, The Netherlands, 1995; contract prof. dept. gen. physics and structure of matter U. Messina, 1992, dept. applied physics and transport processes Tech. U. Eindhoven, 1997; team leader INTAS Project, 1997. Author monographs: Line shape in EELS of simple disordered systems, 1989, quantum mechanics in two Dimension: theory of surfaces and interfaces, 1995, Scattering of external radiations in statistical systems, 1999; contbr. articles to profl. jours. Mem. Am. Phys. Soc., N.Y. Acad. Scis. E-mail: ogerasimov@paco.net. Home: Shevchenko Av 11 Ap 27, 270044 Odessa Ukraine

GERASIMOV, VICTOR GRIGORIEVICH, engineering educator; b. Novaya Village, Russia, Mar. 22, 1928; s. Grigory Kalinovich and Uliana Ivanovna (Naumova) G.; m. Nona Ivanovna Bahanova-Golenberg, Sept. 29, 1950; children: Vjacheslav Victorovich, TAtiana Victorovna Galkina. MSC, Moscow Power Engring. Inst., 1951, PhD, 1956, DSc, 1970. Rschr. Moscow Power Engring. Inst., 1951-53, asst. prof., 1953-58, assoc. prof., 1959-67, head dept. gen. elec. engring., 1972-93, prof. dept. elec. engring. and introscopy, 1993—; head divsn. univs. Ministry Higher Edn., Moscow, 1967-72. Author: Electromagnetic Testing of Single and Multilayer Objects, 1972, Non-destructive Electromagnetic Quality Testing of Objects, 1978, Methods and Devices for Electromagnetic Testing of Industrial Objects, 1983; author, editor: Electrical Engineering and Electronics, 3 vols., 1996-98; mem. editl. bd. Defectoscopy Jour., 1972—. Mem. dist. com. CPSU, Moscow, 1961-63, 78-90; mem. ctrl. com. Higher Sch. Trade Union, Moscow, 1968-76; chmn. dist. orgn. bd. Znanie Soc., 1978-90, electrotech. edn. coun. USSR Ministry Edn., 1974-91; v.p. World Conf. on Non-Destructive Testing, Moscow, 1982; bd. dirs. Russian Soc. Non-Destructive Testing, 1992—. Recipient Badge of Honor, USSR, 1971, State prize, Russia, 1997; named Honored Sci. Worker, Russia, 1982. Mem. Internat. Acad. Electrotech. Scis. (v.p. 1994—), Russian Acad. Electrotech. Scis. (pres. 1993—). Avocations: tennis, travel, walking. Home: Energeticheskaja 16-1-144, 111116 Moscow Russia Office: Moscow Power Enring Inst, Krasnokazarmennaja 14, 111250 Moscow Russia

GERBER, EDWARD F., lawyer, educator; b. Houston, Oct. 10, 1932; s. Edward F. and Lucille (Beaver) G.; m. Eileen Healy, Sept. 1, 1956; children: Gretchen, Eric, Nils. BS, Syracuse U., 1957, LLB, 1960, JD, 1968. Bar: N.Y. 1960, U.S. Dist. Ct. (no. dist.) N.Y. 1960. Pvt. practice law Syracuse, N.Y., 1960-64; first asst. dist. atty. Onandaga County, Syracuse, N.Y., 1964-67, spl. prosecutor, 1976; pvt. practice law Syracuse, N.Y., 1977—; lectr. Coll. of Law Syracuse U., 1968—; counsel Onondaga County Sheriff, 1978-94, N.Y. State Police Benevolent Assn., 1983—, N.Y. State Police Investigators Assn.; faculty Criminal Law Services Syracuse U. Trial Practice Sessions. Bd. dirs. Onandaga County Young Rep. Club, 1964-66. With USN, 1951-54. Named one of Best Lawyers in Am., 1989. Fellow Am. Coll. Trial Lawyers; mem. Upstate Trial Lawyers Assn. (pres. 1978-79), Onandaga County Bar Assn. (dir. 1969-71), Onandaga Bar Found. (pres. 1983). Home: 21 Drumlins Ter Syracuse NY 13224-2217 Office: 224 Harrison St Ste 500 Syracuse NY 13202-3060

GERBER, FRITZ, pharmaceutical company executive, insurance company executive, diversified financial services company executive; b. Berne, Switzerland, Mar. 22, 1929. LLM, U. Berne, 1956; Dr. h.c. phil II, U. Basel, 1995. Bar: Switzerland, 1956. With Fed. Dept. Econ. Affairs, Berne, 1956-57; with Zürich Ins. Co., 1958, gen. mgr., 1969-74, chmn. mgmt. bd., 1974-75, chmn. bd. dirs., 1977-95; chmn. bd. dirs. Roche Holding Ltd., Basel, 1978—; CEO F. Hoffman-La Roche Ltd., Basel, 1978-97; hon. chmn. Zürich Ins. Co., 1995—; mem. internat. adv. coun. Chase Manhattan Bank; chmn. bd. dirs. Alpina Ins. Co., Agrippina Ins. Co., Zurich Kosmos, Genevoise Ins. Co.; bd. dirs. Nestlé, Union Rück, Zurich Holding Co. Am., Inc., Zurich Internat. Comania de Seguros y Reaseguros S.A., Zurich-Agrippina Beteilgungs AG, Bank Sal. Oppenheim Jr. & Cie. Col. artillery Swiss Army. Named CEO of Yr. Europe, Fin. World mag., 1994. Mem. European Round Table. Avocations: belletristic literature, military and economic history. Office: F Hoffman-LaRoche Inc, Grenzacherstresse 124, CH-4070 Basel Switzerland

GERBER, JEFFREY ROBERT, pastor; b. Zanesville, Ohio, May 23, 1953; s. Robert Eugene and Ruth Yvonne Gerber; m. Beverly Davis, Feb. 5, 1953; 1 child, Larissa Michelle. BA, Ohio U., 1975; MDiv, Meth. Theol. Sem. Sch. Ohio, Delaware, 1978. Pastor South High St. United Meth. Ch., Columbus, Ohio, 1977-79, Cmty. United Meth. Ch., Frederiksted, 1979-84; assoc. pastor United Meth. Ch., Doylestown, Pa., 1984-88; pastor St. Peter's United Ch. of Christ, Perkasie, Pa., 1988-90; sr. pastor St. Paul's United Ch. of Christ, New Bremen, Ohio, 1990-99, First United Ch. of Christ, New Philadelphia, Ohio, 1999—; dir. Ohio Conf. Confirmation Camp, Brinkhaven, Ohio, 1998—. Bd. dirs. Sharing Am.'s Resources Abroad-United Ch. of Christ, Columbus, Ohio, 1999—. Mem. Rotary (New Philadelphia chpt.). Avocations: aviation, foreign languages, hiking, Turkic studies, amateur radio. Office: First United Ch of Christ 201 Fair Ave NW New Philadelphia OH 44663-3728

GERBER, RICHARD, physicist, educator, researcher; b. Kolin, Czech Republic, Mar. 21, 1935; arrived in U.K., 1969; s. Vitezslav and Hermina (Calkova) G.; m. Eva Vohnoutova, Jan. 24, 1961; children: Richard, Robert, Barbara. Dipl.-Phys. with 1st class honors, Charles U., Prague, 1958, RNDr, 1967; CSc, Czech Acad. Scis., Prague, 1966; DSc, Salford (U.K.) U., 1990. Sr. scientist, rsch. group leader Inst. Physics, Prague, 1958-69; Royal Soc. rsch. fellow Oxford (Eng.) U., 1969-70; SRC fellow Essex U., Colchester, 1970-72; lectr. Salford U., 1972-80, sr. lectr., reader, 1980-95, prof., 1995—; vis. prof. Purdue U., West Lafayette, Ind., 1982-83, Nagoya (Japan) U., 1990-91; dir. NATO ASI Internat. Sch., Erice, Italy, 1992. Author: High gradient Magnetic Separation, 1983; editor, author: Applied Magnetism, 1993; contbr. over 100 articles to profl. jours.; patentee in field. Exec. com. Tripol Resistance Group, Czech Republic, 1956. Recipient Medal of Merit, Union of Czech Mathematicians and Physicists, 1992, Disting. Paper award IUMRS-ICAM, 1993; European Union fellow, 1993. Fellow of IEEE, Magnetic Soc. (chpt. treas. 1987—). Avocations: thinking, walking. Office: U Salford Dept Physic, The Crescent, Salford M5 4WT, England

GERBERDING, WILLIAM PASSAVANT, retired university president; b. Fargo, N.D., Sept. 9, 1929; s. William Passavant and Esther Elizabeth Ann (Habighorst) G.; m. Ruth Alice Albrecht, Mar. 25, 1952; children: David Michael, Steven Henry, Elizabeth Ann, John Martin. B.A., Macalester Coll., 1951; M.A., U. Chgo., 1956, Ph.D., 1959. Congl. fellow Am. Polit. Sci. Assn., Washington, 1958-59; instr. Colgate U., Hamilton, N.Y., 1959-60; research asst. Senator E.J. McCarthy, Washington, 1960-61; staff Rep. Frank Thompson, Jr., Washington, 1961; faculty UCLA, 1961-72, prof., chmn. dept. polit. sci., 1970-72; dean faculty, v.p. for acad. affairs Occidental Coll., Los Angeles, 1972-75; exec. vice chancellor UCLA, 1975-77; chancellor U. Ill., Urbana-Champaign, 1978-79; pres. U. Wash., Seattle, 1979-95; bd. dirs. Wash. Mut. Bank, Safeco Corp., Seattle; cons. Dept. Def., 1962, Calif. Assembly, 1965. Author: United States Foreign Policy: Perspectives and Analysis, 1966; co-editor, contbg. author: The Radical Left: The Abuse of Discontent, 1970. Trustee Macalester Coll., 1980-83, 96—. With USN, 1951-55. Recipient Distinguished Teaching award U. Calif., Los Angeles, 1966; Ford Found. grantee, 1967-68. Office: Univ Wash PO Box 352800 Seattle WA 98195-2800

GERBERICH, SUSAN GOODWIN, education educator; b. Cortland, N.Y.; d. Arthur George and Elizabeth Pratt Goodwin; m. William Warren Gerberich; children: Bradley Kent, Brian Keith, Beth Clarice. BS summa cum laude, U. Minn., 1975, MS, 1978, PhD, 1980. Prof. U. Minn., Mpls., 1983—; dir. Regional Injury Prevention Rsch. Ctr., Mpls., 1987—, Ctr. for Violence Prevention and Control, Mpls., 1994—; pres. Gerberich, Inc., Shorewood, Minn., 1985—; cons. Injury Prevention/Epidemiology, 1985—; cons. Nat. Inst. for Occupl. Safety and Health and Ctrs. for Disease Control. Contbr. articles to profl. jours. Trauma adv. com. Minn. Dept. of Health, Mpls., 1999—, mem. Brain and Spinal Cord adv. com., 1993—. Named to Blue Ribbon Panel Nat. Inst. for Occpl. Safety and Health, Washington, 1990-93, 96, Ctr. for Disease Control, Atlanta, 1986-91. Mem. APHA (gov. coun. 1994-2000), Injury Control and Emergency Health Svcs., Soc. for Epidemiol. Rsch. Avocations: tennis, golf, sailing, rollerblading. Office: EOH/SPH/U Minn/MMC 807 420 Delaware St SE Rm 1156 Minneapolis MN 55455-0374

GERBOUD, GILBERT, mathematician, educator, researcher; b. Marseille, France, Nov. 26, 1959; s. René and Juliette (Vecco) G.; m. Marie-Ange Lepeltier, June 24, 2000; 1 child, Natalia Gerboud-Lepeltier. D in Maths., U. Provence, Marseille, 1986, DSc, 1989. Cert. tchr., France. Tchr. math. Marseille H.S., 1987-88, Maisons-Alfort (France) H.S., 1988; rschr. U. d'Aix-Marseille, 1988-91; maitre de confs., mem. edn. and sci. bds. Inst. U. Formation des Maitres de l'Acad. d'Amiens, France, 1991—, bd. govs., 1991-95, dir. dept. math., 1998—. Contbr. articles to profl. jours. Avocation: water polo. Jr. French Champion, 1979, French Champion, 1981; participated in World Masters Swimming Championships, 2000. Home: 134 rue Jeanne d'Arc, 80000 Amiens France Office: Inst U Formation des Maitres de l'Acad d'Amiens, 51 Blvd de Chateaudun, 80000 Amiens France

GERDES, NEIL WAYNE, library director; b. Moline, Ill., Oct. 19, 1943; s. John Edward and Della Marie (Ferguson) G. AB, U. Ill., 1965; BD, Harvard U., 1968; MA, Columbia U., 1971; MA in Libr. Sci., U. Chgo., 1975; DMin, U. St. Mary of the Lake, 1994. Ordained to ministry Unitarian Universalist Assn., 1975. Copy chief Little, Brown, 1968-69; instr. Tuskegee Inst., 1969-71; libr. asst. Augustana Coll., 1972-73; editl. asst. Library Quar., 1973-74; libr., prof. Meadville Theol. Sch., Chgo., 1973—; libr. program dir. Chgo. Cluster Theol. Schs., 1977-80; dir. Hammond Libr., 1980—; prof. Chgo. Theol Sem., 1980—. Mem. exec. bd. Sem. Coop. Bookstore, Chgo., 1982—, Ctr. for Religion and Psychotherapy, Chgo., 1984-97, Ind. Voters of Ill., 1986-89, Hyde Park-Kenwood Cmty. Orgn., Chgo., 1988-89; pres. Hyde Park-Kenwood Interfaith Coun., 1986-90; chair libr. coun. Assn. Chgo. Theol. Sch., 1984-88, 96-98; trustee Civitas Dei Found., 1994—; mem. alumni coun. Harvard Divinity Sch., 1999—. Mem. ALA, Am. Theol. Library Assn., Chgo. Area Theol. Library Assn., Unitarian Universalist Mins. Assn. (sec., treas. nat. body 1990-94), Assn. Liberal Religious Scholars (sec., treas. 1975—), Phi Beta Kappa. Office: Chgo Theol Sem Hammond Libr 5757 S University Ave Chicago IL 60637-1507

GERDNER, LINDA ANN, nursing researcher; b. Burlington, Iowa, Sept. 17, 1955; d. Richard Paul and Edna Marie Gerdner. AA, Southeastern C.C., 1975, ADN, 1977; BSN, Iowa Wesleyan Coll., 1980; MA, U. Iowa, 1992, PhD, 1998. RN, Iowa, Ark. Staff devel. coord. Elm View Care Ctr., Burlington, Iowa, 1985-88, DON, 1988-89; tchg./rsch. asst. U. Iowa Coll. Nursing, Iowa City, 1989-92; nursing faculty Grand View Coll., Des Moines, Iowa, 1992-93; project dir. Nat. Caregiver Tng. Project, U. Iowa Coll. Nursing, 1992-97, predoctoral fellow, 1996-98; postdoctoral fellow/faculty dept. psychiatry U. Ark. Med. Scis., VA Med. Ctr., Little Rock, 1999—; cons. Alverno Health Care Facility, Clinton, Iowa, 1997—; presenter in field. Mem. referee panel Clin. Nursing Rsch., 1997, Western Jour. Nursing Rsch., 1998, Jour. Gerontol. Nursing, 1999; contbr. chpts. to books and articles to profl. jours. Recipient AARP Andrus Found. grad. fellowship in gerontology Assn. Gerontology in Higher Edn., 1996-97, Rsch. award Am. Soc. Aging, 1999. Mem. ANA, Internat. Psychogeriatric Assn. (task force on behavioral and psychol. symptoms of dementia 1999—, IPA/Bayer Rsch. award 1999), Am. Geriatric Soc., Mid-Am. Congress on Aging (Best Grad. Paper award 1994), Midwest Nursing Rsch. Soc. (Outstanding Poster award 1993), Sigma Theta Tau (Best of Image award 1997). Avocations: reading, traveling, walking, music, photography. E-mail: gerdnerlindaa@exchange.uams.edu. Home: 2420 Riverfront Dr Apt 406 Little Rock AR 72202-2272 Office: Little Rock VA Med Ctr VA HSR&D CeMHOR 152/NLR 2200 Fort Roots Dr Bldg 58 North Little Rock AR 72114-1709

GERE, TIBOR, agriculturalist; b. Ozd, Hungary, July 22, 1937; s. Sandor and Sandorne (Nagybali Emma) G.; m. Gizella Tiborne, July 22, 1961; children: Tunde, Zsolt. MSc, U. Agrl. Scis., Godollo, Hungary, 1960; PhD, Hungarian Acad. Scis., Budapest, 1970, DSc, 1988. Asst. prof. U. Agrl. Scis., 1960-80; dir. Rsch. Inst. Animal Breeding, Godollo, 1980-90; prof. U. Agrl. Scis., 1991—. Author: Animal Breeding, 1995, Artificial Insemination, 1996. Mem. N.Y. Acad. Scis., Hungarian Acad. Scis. (Dr.), Russian Acad. Scis., Slovikian Acad. Scis. Avocations: tourism, fishing, horseback riding. Office: Coll Agriculture, Matrai str 36, H-3200 Gyongyos Hungary

GEREDE, R. SELCUK, medical director; b. Istanbul, Turkey, Mar. 19, 1927; s. Hüsrev Zülfikar and Lamia Fatma (Söylemezoglu) Canan Vafi, Apr. 18, 1968; children: Shiva, Bennû. BA, Robert Coll., Istanbul, 1946; MD, U. Lausanne, 1954; MD in Hematology, U. Freiburg, Germany, 1958; cert. epidemiology, Inst. Pasteur, Paris, 1977. Med. officer Airfoce Gen. Hosp., Eskisehir, 1962; med. officer U.N.O., N.Y.C., 1972-76, dep. med. dir., 1976-87, ret., 1987; specialist in internal med. Istanbul Med. Faculty; dep. med. dir. UN Med. Svc., N.Y.C., 1976-87. Author: Eponymic Hematology, 1979; contbr. articles to profl. jours. Mem. Deutsche Gesellschaft F. Innere Medizin, European Soc. of Haematology, N.Y. Acad. Scis., Turkish Med. Soc. Avocations: methodology, archeology, ficology, astrology, mythology. Home: Tesvikiye Husrev, Gerede Cad 104/1, Istanbul 80200, Turkey

GEREMEK, BRONISLAW, government official; b. Warsaw, Poland, Mar. 3, 1932; s. Stefan and Maria Geremek; m. Hanna Geremek, 1952; 2 children. Student, Warsaw U., Ecole des Hautes Etudes, Paris; Dr. h.c., U. Tours, 1982, U. Utrecht, 1986, Columbia U., 1989, U. Bologna, 1989, Oberlin Coll., 1990, U. Paris-Sorbonne, 1990, U. Libre, Brussels, 1991, U. Leicester, 1992, Brown U., 1994, U. Sofia, 1998, Freie U., Berlin, 1999, Brandeis U., 1999. Sci. worker History Inst. Polish Acad. Scis., Warsaw, 1954-60, staff mem. History Inst., 1965-85, asst. prof., 1972, head rsch. unit history of medieval culture, 1965-80, prof., 1989—; lectr. Sorbonne, Paris, 1962-65; minister fgn. affairs Poland; dep. to Sejm (legislature), 1989—; mem. Polish United Workers Party, 1950-68; co-founder, lectr. Sci. Courses Soc., 1978-81; adviser to Interfactory Strike Com., Gdańsk Shipyard, 1980; founding com. Solidarity Ind. Self-Governing Trade Union, Gdańsk, Nat. Understanding Com. of Solidarity Trade Union, 1980; chair program coun. Social and Labour Study Ctr., Nat. Com. of Solidarity, 1980-81; chair program com. 1st Nat. Congress of Solidarity Trade Union, 1981, adviser to provisional coord. com., 1983-87, adviser to nat. exec. com., 1987-90, mem. civic com. to Lech Walesa, 1988-91; prof. Coll. de France, 1992—; chair parliamentary Caucus Solidarity, Dem. Union for Freedom, 1989-97. Coauthor: numerous books in field; contbr. numerous articles to profl. jours. Decorated officer Legion of Honor; recipient Alfred Jurzykowski Found. award, 1986, Prix Louise de Culture prize, 1993, Heroler prize, Vienna, 1990, Karl prize, Aachen, 1998, Disting. Leaders award UCLA, 1999. Mem. Polish Hist. Soc., Soc. Européenne de Culture (award 1993), Assn. Authors of Sci. Works, Academia Europaea, European Medieval Acad., Acad. Universelle des Cultures, PEN Club. Fax: 623-0500. Office: Al Zucha 23, 00-580 Warsaw Poland

GERERSDORFER, HANS KARL, steel company executive, consultant; b. Tru bau, Austria, Aug. 2, 1944; s. Hanns-Karl and Johanna (Zimprich) G.; m. Waltraud Maria Izl, Feb. 2, 1973. D of Econs., U. Linz, Austria, 1974, M of Econs., 1972. Expert advisor Pub. Svc., Linz, Austria, 1966-74; sales mgr. Chem. Industry, Linz, Austria, 1974-78; personal adviser Mgmt. Consultation, Linz, Austria, 1978-79; project mgr. Steel Industry, Linz, Austria, 1979—; cons. Econ. Acad. League, Vienna, Linz, Austro-Brit. Soc., Linz, Officers Assn., Linz. Lt. col. Austrian Mil. Avocations: skiing, shooting, travel. Home: Kaisergasse 11, A-4010 Linz Austria Office: Postfach 2, Turmstr 44, A-4013 Linz Austria

GEREY, TAMAS, mechanical and environmental engineering educator; b. Budapest, Hungary, Mar. 16, 1924; s. Gyula and Melanie (Lorberer of Lorbersberg) G.; m. Magdolna Dezsenyi, July 1, 1967; children: Tamas, Agnes, Balazs, Agoston. MS in Engring., U. Engring. of Budapest, 1947, Postgrad. Economist, 1948; Specialist-Engr., U. Veszprem, Hungary, 1977. Diplomate in mech. engring., envin. engring. Assoc. prof. U. Engring. of Budapest, 1945-62; prin. rsch. engr. Ganz Works, Budapest, 1962-63; assoc. prof. Pannon U., Keszthely, Hungary, 1963-64; prin. engr. for standardization Ctr. for Machines in Chem. Industries, Budapest, 1964-65; prin. structural engr. as polit. prisoner Budapest, 1964-66; various positions factories, Budapest, 1966-67; chief prodn. engr. Works of Equipment for Water Purification, Tatabanya, Hungary, 1967-77; mem. office of chief exec., 1968-69; advanced rsch. engr. Mavag Works, Budapest, 1969-70; tech. and econ. mgr. Planning Office in Water Industries, Budapest, 1977-78; tech. and econ. advisor Regional Water Works at the Danube, Vac, Hungary, 1978-91; prof. Pannon U., Keszthely, 1964—. Co-author: Pattantyus: Practical Fluid Flow Mechanics, 1959; contbr. articles to profl. jours.; inventor. Recipient Jubilee award ASME, 1972, prize for tech. lit. work Hungarian Acad. Scis., 1974, Anniversary award ASME, 1976, Golden Jubilee diploma U. Engring. Budapest, 1997. Mem. Sci. Soc. Mech. Engrs. (past v.p.), Hungarian Hydrol. Soc., Hungarian Soc. for Agrl. Machinery (past pres.), N.Y. Acad. Scis. Roman Catholic. Avocations: history of art and architecture, philately, concerts, photography. Home: XI Budafoki-ut 17, H-1111 Budapest Hungary

GERG, HILDE, skier; b. Bad Tolz, Bavaria, Germany, Oct. 19, 1975. Mem. Ski Club Lenggries, 1982—, German Nat. Women's Ski Team, 1992—. Recipient Gold medal women's Alpine skiing slalom, Olympic Games, Nagano, Japan, 1998, bronze medal women's Alpine skiing combined event, 1998, winner World Championship, 1997, Bronze medal SG & Kombind, World Cup, 1996-97, 1997-98, 1998-99. Avocations: reading, tennis. Office: Nat Olympic Com for Germany, Postfach 71 02 63 Otto-Fleck-Schneise 12, 60528 Frankfurt am Main Germany*

GERGELY, ANIKÓ EVA, editor-in-chief, translator; b. Budapest, Hungary, Jan. 31, 1938; d. János Gergely and Margit Förstner; m. Illes Dési, Aug. 5, 1962; children: János, András. MA, U. Eötvös Loránd, Budapest, 1963. Editor Kossuth Pub. House, Budapest, 1963-80; editor in chief Nök Magazinja, Budapest, 1980-88; mng. editor Budapest Pub., Budapest, 1989-92; editor in chief Vince Books (Kulturtrade Pub.), Budapest, 1993—. Author: Culinaria Ungarische Spezalitäten; editor: Library of Nök Magazinja, Ladies' Magazine, Ladies' Yearbook, 1980-88; translator of numerous books. Recipient award for Socialist Culture, Hungarian Govt., 1985. Mem. Assn. Hungarian Journalists. Home: Lágymányosi 13, 1111 Budapest Hungary Office: Vince Books, Margit Krt 64 B, 1027 Budapest Hungary

GERGELY, MIHÁLY, surgery educator, retired; b. Kassa, Slovakia, Mar. 1, 1933; s. Mihály Gergely and Jolán Schalkház; m. Ildikó Adorján, Mar. 31, 1958; children: Mihály, Ildiké, Péter, András, György. MD, Med. Sch. Debrecen, Hungary, 1958, M in Surgery, 1963; PhD, Med. Sch., Szeged, Hungary, 1973. House officer various small hosps., 1958-63, registrar, 1963-67; sr. registrar Szeged (Hungary) Med. Sch., 1967-75; head dept. Dist. Hosp., Szentes, Hungary, 1975-83, Hetényi Gé Hosp., Szolnok, Hungary, 1983-90, Magyar Imre Hosp., Ajka, Hungary, 1990-93; ret., 1993; surg. supr. County Szolnok, 1983-90. Contbr. numerous articles to sci. and profl. jours. Mem. town coun. Town of Szolnok, 1990. Fellowship Hungarian Acad. Sci. Mem. South Hungarian Surg. Assn. (chmn. 1976-80), Internat. Hepato-Pancreato-Billiary Assn., others. Roman Catholic. Avocations: driving, gardening, reading, swimming. Home: Farm PO Box 8433, H-5002 Szolnok Szoropuszta, Hungary

GERHARD, HARRY E., JR., counter trader, management and trade consultant; b. Phila., Aug. 7, 1925; s. Harry E. and Frances Jane (Edwards) G.; children: Susan Jillson, John, Barbara Thomas. Student, Muhlenberg Coll., 1943-44; AB, George Washington U., 1968, MA, 1969. Commd. ensign USN, 1943, advanced through grades to rear adm., 1971, exptl. test pilot, 1955-57; ret., 1976; exec. v.p., COO Costa Line Cargo Svcs., Inc., N.Y.C., 1976-80; gen. mgr. Olayan Transp. Group, Dammam, Saudi Arabia, 1980-

82; pres., owner Domestic & Overseas Countertrade & Cons. Svcs., Ltd., Washington, Pa., N.Y., 1983—. Decorated Silver Star, D.F.C. (2), Meritorious Svc. medal (2), Air medals (16), Navy Commendation medal with combat v (2). Mem. Assn. Naval Aviation, Air Force Assn., Am. Def. Preparedness Assn., U.S., Navy League U.S., Nat. Aero. Assn., Ret. Officers Assn., Order of Daedalians, Tailhook Assn., Cousteau Soc., Fleet Res. Assn., Maritime and Aviation Cons., Mil. Order World Wars, Nat. War Coll. Alumni Assn., U.S. Def. Com., Am. Security Coun., Internat. Platform Assn., Greater Pitts. C. of C., Smaller Mfrs. Coun., Wings Club, N.Y. Yacht Club, Army Navy Club, Masons, Shriners. Republican. Address: 320 Fort Duquesne Blvd Ste 20F Pittsburgh PA 15222-1133

GERHARDSSON, LARS GERHARD, environmental scientist; b. Stockholm, May 21, 1952; s. Gideon and Runa Margareta (Rönnmark) G. MD, Med. U., Stockholm, 1979; cert., Ednl. Commn. Fgn. Med. Grad., Stockholm, 1979; PhD, U. Umeå, Sweden, 1986; postgrad., Northwestern U., Chgo., 1991-92. Registrar physician Hosp. Skellefteå, Sweden, 1977-79; resident dept. medicine U. Hosp., Umeå, 1979-84, resident dept. occupl. medicine, 1984-85, specialist dept. occupl. medicine, 1985-89, assoc. prof., cons. dept. occupl. medicine, 1989-90; assoc. prof., cons. dept. occupl. and environ. medicine U. Hosp., Lund, Sweden, 1990—. Contbr. sci. handbooks and articles to profl. jours. Active Amnesty Internat., Lund, 1992—; choir mem. All Saints Ch., Lund, 1992—. Capt. Swedish Army Svc. Corps. Mem. Swedish Soc. Medicine, Swedish Med. Assn., Swedish Soc. Occupl. and Environ. Medicine, Internat. Soc. for Trace Element Rsch. in Humans. Avocations: classical reading, music, folk dancing, golf, athletics. Home: Kulgränden 15A, SE 22649 Lund Sweden Office: Univ Hosp, Dept Occupl and Environl Medicine, SE 22185 Lund Sweden

GERHART, CHARLES JAMES, art director, illustrator; b. Reading, Pa., Dec. 22, 1919; s. Clarence Arthur and Laura Ann (Deeter) G. Cert. in illustration, Pratt Inst., Bklyn., 1949; BFA, Yale U., 1952. Designer, illustrator various orgns., N.Y.C., 1952-71; instr. watercolor painting workshops. Solo exhbns. include Bklyn. Botanic Gardens, 1984 (award Chase Manhattan Bank), Reading Mus., 1940 (Purchase award); commns. include Bklyn. Union Gas Co., 1980s. With U.S. Army Corps Engrs., 1941-46, PTO. Featured American Artist mag., 1990. Fellow Am. Artist Profl. League (nat. bd. mem. 1974—), Hudson Valley Art Assn., Bklyn. Watercolor Soc. (membership sec. 1975). Home: 52 Clark St Apt 8E Brooklyn NY 11201-2402

GERHART, EUGENE CLIFTON, lawyer; b. Bklyn., Apr. 7, 1912; s. Herman Eugene and Mary Elizabeth (Hamilton) G.; m. Mary Richardson Schreiber, Mar. 30, 1939; children: Catherine Gerhart Landon, Virginia Gerhart Mason. AB, Princeton U., 1934; LLB, Harvard U., 1937. Bar: N.J. 1938, N.Y. 1945. Practiced in Newark, 1938-43, Binghamton, N.Y., 1946—; counsel firm Coughlin & Gerhart, Binghamton; sec. to Judge Manley O. Hudson, Secretariat/League of Nations, Geneva, 1934; lectr. bus. law U. Newark, 1942-43, Triple Cities Coll., 1946-48, Harpur Coll., Endicott, N.Y., 1953-55; lectr. indsl. and labor relations Cornell U., Ithaca, N.Y., 1946; dir., gen. counsel Columbian Mut. Life Ins. Co., 1949-83, acting pres., 1969-70, chmn. bd., 1970-82; mem. coun. SUNY, Cortland, 1967-77, chmn., 1971-77; mem. Select Task Force on Ct. Reorgn. N.Y. State Senate; mem. jud. nominating com. 3d Jud. Dept., State of N.Y.; mem. N.Y. Unified Ct. Sys. Judicial Records Disposition and Archives Devel. Com. Author: American Liberty and Natural Law, America's Advocate: Robert H. Jackson, Robert H. Jackson: Lawyer's Judge, Arthur T. Vanderbilt: The Compleat Counsellor, Quote It!, Quote It II, The Lawyer's Treasury, Quote It Completely!, 1998, World Reference Guide to more than 5500 Memorable Quotations from Law and Literature, 1998; spl. contbg. author: Law Office Econs. and Mgmt, 1962—; mem. editl. bd. Quar. Report of Conf. on Personal Fin. Law, 1965; contbr. articles to legal, other publs. Chmn. Harpur Forum SUNY, Binghamton, 1983-84. Lt. USNR, 1943-46. Fellow Am. Bar Found., Am. Coll. Probate Counsel, N.Y. State Bar Found.; mem. ABA (editor Jour. 1946-67, Ross Essay award 1946), Internat. Assn. Ins. Counsel, Assn. Life Ins. Counsel, Am. Judicature Soc., Am. Law Inst., N.Y. State Bar Assn. (editor-in-chief jour. 1961-97, editor-in-chief emeritus 1997—, Disting. Svc. award 1998), Assn. Bar City N.Y., Broome County Bar Assn. (pres. 1961-62, Lifetime Achievement award 1995), Selden Soc., Broome County Princeton Alumni Assn., Harvard Law Sch. Assn. Upstate N.Y. (pres. 1955-57), Scribes (pres., dir. 1966-67), St. Andrew's Soc. Republican. Clubs: Rotary (pres. 1969-70), Cosmos, Oteyokwa Lake (pres. 1971-73), Nassau, Harvard of N.Y., Princeton of N.Y. Home: 34 W End Ave Binghamton NY 13905-4026 Office: 20 Hawley St Binghamton NY 13901-3216

GERHARTZ, STEVEN LEWIS, artist; b. Sheboygan, Wis.; s. Gary Francis and Mary Jane (Justina) G.; m. Sherry Lynn Gerhartz, Oct. 9, 1999. A, Lyme Acad. Fine Arts, Old Lyme, Conn., 1990-92. Artist Two Rivers, Wis., 1992—. Exhibited in group shows at G.C. Lucas Gallery, Indpls., Gallery 3916, Mpls., Edgewood Orchard Gallery, Fish Creek, Wis., others; prin. works include bronze war meml. sculpture, 1997. Sculptor Am. Legion, West Bend, Wis., 1997. John Stobart outdoor painting fellow Lyme Acad. Fine Arts, 1992. Avocations: hunting, fishing, skiing, hiking. Office: E River Ctr 2117 E River St Two Rivers WI 54241-2616

GERHOLD, REINHARD KARL FRIEDRICH, economist; b. Wolfhagen, Germany, Oct. 24, 1967; s. Hermann and Anna (Rittberg) G.; m. Sabine Gerhold. Diploma, U. Kassel, 1994. Rsch. assoc. Gesamthochschule, Kassel, Germany, 1994—. Home: Baerenbergstrasse 48, 34466 Wolfhagen Hessen, Germany

GERHOLM, TOR RAGNAR, physics educator; b. Bklyn., Dec. 21, 1925; arrived in Sweden, 1926; s. Tor Vilhelm and Rakel (Lind) G.; m. Lena Backlin, Apr. 29, 1948 (div. 1967); children: Jonas, Maria, Mikael; m. Maud Birgitta Ellemo, Oct. 3, 1970; 1 child, Niklas. PhD, Uppsala (Sweden) U., 1956. Asst. prof. U. Uppsala, 1956-62; prof. physics U. Stockholm, 1962-90, prof. emeritus, 1990—; cons. Kreab, Stockholm, 1991—; adv. coun. SE-Banken, Stockholm, 1969—, chmn., 1993-96; mem. commn. World Energy Coun., London, 1975-80, Internat. C. of C., Paris, 1980—; vice-chmn. Swedish Indsl. Devel. Fund, Stockholm, 1979-92; sci. adv. coun. Incentive AB, Stockholm, 1963-92; bd. dirs. Swedish Inst. Fgn. Affairs, Stockholm, 1975-97; chmn. Internat. Conf. Unity Sci., 1993—. Author: Physics and Man, 1962, Futurum Exactum, 1972, Idé och Samhälle, 1966, Futurum Exactum Facit, 2000, Climate Policy after Kyoto, 2000. With Swedish army, 1945-60. Recipient Litt prize Swedish Authors' Assn., 1962, Nordstjerneorden, 1975, Cultural prize Natur och Kultur, Stockholm, 1978, Cultural prize Langmanska Kulturfonden, 1999. Fellow Swedish Phys. Assn., Am. Phys. Assn., European Phys. Assn.; mem. Royal Acad. of Scis., Royal Acad. Engring. Scis. Avocation: cooking. Fax: 46 8 723 4225. Home: Svartmangatan 21, S 111 29 Stockholm Sweden Office: U Stockholm, Fysikum Box 6730, S 113 85 Stockholm Sweden

GÉRIN, VINCENT, civil engineer; b. Brussels, May 9, 1970; s. Yves and Conception (Simo-Canto) G. Degree in civil engring., U. Libre, Brussels, 1994. Computer aided facility mgmt. cons. DB Assocs., Brussels, 1994-95, quality mgr., 1995-96; computer aided facility mgmt. dir. DB Assocs., Luxembourg, 1996-97, gen. mgr., 1996-98; dir. gen. DB Assocs., Spain, 1998-99; mgr. PriceWaterhouseCoopers, Woluwe St Stevens, Belgium, 1999—. Mem. Internat. Facility Mgmt. Assn., Orde des Ingenieurs-Conseils, Assn. Royale des Civil Engrs. de U. Libre de Brussels. Avocations: informatics, golf, travel. Fax: 32 2 710 7999. E-mail: vincent.gerin@be.pwcglobal.com. Home: 124 Ave De Broqueville, B-1200 Brussels Belgium Office: PriceWaterhouseCoopers, Wolvwe Garden Woluwedal 18, B-1932 Woluwe St Stevens Belgium

GERKE, JORG, chemist; b. Rahden, Westfalen, Germany, Sept. 30, 1958; s. Ernst-August and Luise (Buck) G.; m. Regina Genelauszus, Aug. 6, 1981; children: Johannes, Thomas. Diploma in Engring., Georg-August-U., Gottingen, 1984, Dr. Agr., 1988, Privatdozent, 1995. Scientist Lehrgebiet Chemie, Gottingen, 1985-88; asst. prof. Inst. Agrikulturchemie, Gottingen, 1989-95, privatdozent, 1995—; farmer Mecklenburg/Güstrow, Germany, 1994—. Contbr. articles to profl. jours. Office: Inst Agrikulturchemie, Von Siebold Str 6, 37075 Göttingen Germany

GERKEN, MANFRED, chemist; b. Bremerhaven, Bremen, Germany, Mar. 1, 1955; s. Walter and Emma (Gehrking) G.; m. Birgit Elsbeth Garrels, Nov. 27, 1992; children: Henrik, Christian. Diploma in Chemistry, U. Hamburg (Germany), 1980, PhD in Chemistry, 1983. Tchg. asst. U. Hamburg, 1982-83; rsch. assoc. Nat. Rsch. Coun. Can., Ottawa, 1983-85; Nuclear Magnetic Resonance application chemist Varian GmbH, Darmstadt, Germany, 1985; rsch. chemist Behringwerke AG, Marburg, Germany, 1985-96; sr. scientist Hoechst AG, Marburg, 1996-99, Hoechst Marion Roussel, Frankfurt, Germany, 1999, Aventis Pharma, Frankfurt, 2000—. Contbr. more than 20 articles to profl. jours.; patentee in field. Mem. Gesellschaft deutscher Chemiker. Avocations: family, sailing. Office: Aventis Pharma, Bldg D 729, D-65926 Frankfurt Hessen, Germany

GERLACH, DIETER, biologist; b. Magdeburg, Germany, Sept. 19, 1939; s. Martin and Margarete (Andert) G.; m. Doris Cruse, Jan. 31, 1969; children: Brigitte, Gabriele. D in Natural Scis., U. Erlangen, Germany, 1965. Acad. dir. U. Erlangen, 1975—. Author: Anatomie der Blütenlosen Pflanzen, 1982, Botanische Mikrotechnik, 1984, Das Lichtmikroskop, 1985, Taschenatlas zur Pflanzenanatomie, 1986, Mikroskopieren-ganz einfach, 1987, Lichtmikroskopie, 1995, Die Anfänge der histologischen Färbung und der Mikrophotographie-Josef von Gerlach als Wegbereiter, 1998. Fellow Royal Micros. Soc., Mitglied Mikroskopische Gesellschaft Zürich. Avocation: history. Office: Univ Erlangen, Bot Inst, Staudtstr 5, D-91058 Erlangen Germany

GERLACH, THURLO THOMPSON, electrical engineer; b. Sparta, Ill., Oct. 30, 1916; s. Kenneth Frederick and Golda M. (Thompson) G.; m. Ellen Marie Kuhn, July 14, 1946. BEE, Tri-State U., 1937; grad., Air Force Command and Staff, 1952. Registered profl. engr., Ill., Mont. Dist. engr. Ill. Power Co., Centralia, 1937-40; area engr. Ill. Power Co., Sparta, 1940-41, Granite City, Ill., 1946-48; engr. U.S. Bur. Standards, Washington, 1948-50, Fed. Power Commn., Washington, 1953-56, Bur. of Reclamation, Billings, Mont., 1950-51, 56-77; cons. Billings, 1977—; del. heavy engr. constrn. program Citizen Amb. Program, Peoples Republic of China, 1990, USSR, 1991, Panama, 1996. Active People to People Internat., Kansas City, Mo., 1989—. Major USAF, 1941-46, 51-53. Mem. NSPE, IEEE, U.S. Com. Large Dams, Elks, Masons. Methodist. Achievements include participation in development, construction and operation of Missouri River Basin power system. Home and Office: 533 Park Ln Billings MT 59102-1018

GERLOTTO, FRANÇOIS MICHEL, research director, marine biologist; b. Limoges, Haute-Vienne, France, Jan. 2, 1948; s. Maurice Francois and Anne Camille (Villemonteix) G.; m. Marcelle Marie Telliez, Aug. 2, 1972; children: Marie, Veronique. Master, U. Paris, 1972; DEA, U. Bretagne, Brest, France, 1973, PhD, 1993. Eleve French Inst., Abidjan, Ivory Coast, 1973-74, charge de recherches, 1975-80; maitre de recherches French Inst., Margarita, Venezuela, 1980-85, Fort-de-France, Martinique, 1985-91; dir. rsch. French Inst., Montpellier, France, 1991-98; dir. rsch. Institut de Recherche Pour Le Developpement, Montpellier, 1998—, rsch. unit head, 1994—; dept. head Flasa, Margarita, 1980-83; dir. Project European Commn., Brussels, 1997—; chmn. working group Internat. Coun. for the Exploration of the Sea, Copenhagen, 1996—. Co-author: Acoustic Survey Design, 1993; editor, author Aquatic Living Resources, 1993; contbr. articles to profl. publs. Mem. Caribbean Acoustic Network (pres. 1990-95, v.p. 1996—). Roman Catholic. Avocations: scuba diving, chess, model making. Office: IRD, BP 5045, 34032 Montpellier Herault, France

GERMAN, JUNE RESNICK, lawyer; b. N.Y.C., Feb. 24, 1946; d. Irving and Stella (Weintraub) Resnick; m. Harold Jacob German, May 31, 1974; children: Beth Melissa, Heather Alice, Bret. BA, U. Pa., 1965; JD, NYU, 1968. Bar: N.Y. 1968, U.S. Dist. Ct. (ea. and so. dists.) N.Y. 1974, U.S. Ct. Appeals (2d cir.) 1973, U.S. Supreme Ct. 1973. Atty., sr. atty., supervising atty. Mental Health Info. Svc., N.Y.C., 1968-77; atty./advisor Course in Human Behavior Mems. of N.Y. State Judiciary, Nassau and Suffolk County, 1980; pvt. practice, Huntington, N.Y., 1985—. Contbg. author: Bioethics and Human Rights, 1978, Mental Illness, Due Process and the Acquitted Defendant, 1979; contbr. chpts. to books, articles to profl. jours. Chmn. Citizen's Ad Hoc Com. Constrn. of the Dix Hills Water Adminstrn. Bldg., Huntington, N.Y., 1985-90; mem. Citizens Adv. Com. for Dix Hills Water Dist., Huntington, 1992—; dir. House Beautiful Assn. at Dix Hills, 1986—; dir. Citizens for a Livable Environment and Recycling, Huntington, 1989-93; mem. Suffolk County (N.Y.) Dem. Com., 1986—; mem. Deer Park Avenue Task Force, Town of Huntington, 1997-98; mem. Dix Hills Revitalization Com., 1999-00. Mem. Suffolk County Bar Assn. Jewish. Avocations: tennis, hiking, travel. Office: 150 Main St Huntington NY 11743-6908

GERMINARIO, LOUIS THOMAS, materials scientist; b. Molfetta, Apuglia, Italy, Sept. 27, 1947; came to U.S., 1956; s. Diego and Angela Germinario; m. Violet Joan Maas, May 19, 1984; children: Stephanie, Victoria. BA, Gettysburg (Pa.) Coll., 1970; MS, Cath. U. Am., 1972, PhD, 1973. Staff scientist, cons. EMV Assocs. Microanalysis Lab., Rockville, Md., 1972-73; postdoctoral rsch. assoc. Ariz. State U., Tempe, 1973-75; NIH fellow Johns Hopkins U., Balt., 1975-78; sr. rsch. assoc. Case Western Res. U., Cleve., 1978-81; rsch. chemist Eastman Chem. Co., Kingsport, Tenn., 1981-86, sr. rsch. chemist, 1986-91, prin. rsch. chemist, 1991-95; rsch. assoc., 1995—; session chmn. IUPAC Internat. Symposium on Macromolecules, Akron, 1995. Contbr. articles to profl. jours. Grantee Sigma Xi, 1972, Biophys. Soc., 1978. Mem. Am. Chem. Soc., Electron Microscopy Soc. Am. (session chmn. 1975), N.Y. Acad. Sci., Microscopy Soc. Am. (session chmn. 1995), Sigma Xi, Beta Beta Beta. Achievements include new concepts in catalysis design via mixed metal oxide polyester catalysis, polymer structure-property behavior; heterogeneous catalyst characterization; patents on improved photostability and weatherability of polyesters, methods for reducing peel defects on adhesive bonded plastics, nanostructured coatings for improved gas barrier properties of shaped plastic articles. Office: Eastman Chemical Co Eastman Rd Kingsport TN 37662-5150

GERMISHUIZEN, GERRIT, botanist, researcher, editor; b. Pretoria, S. Africa, Feb. 25, 1950; s. Willem Andreas and Jacoba Katherina (Potgieter) G.; m. Elizabeth Maria Burger (div. 1979); children: Willem Andreas, Charl-Louis. BSc in Botany, U. Pretoria, 1972, BSc with honors, 1973, MSc in Taxonomy, 1983. Profl. officer Bot. Rsch. Inst., Pretoria, 1975-76, sr. profl. officer, 1976-96; asst. curator herbarium Nat. Bot. Inst., Pretoria, 1994-95, asst. dir. pubs., 1997—. Author: (with Anita Fabian) Transvaal Wild Flowers, 1982, Wild Flowers of Nothern South Africa, 1997; Editor: Succulents of the Transvaal, 1992; editor Bothalia, 1998, 99, Flora of So. Africa, 1999, Flowering Plants of Africa, 1999; contbr. articles to profl. jours. Recipient Allan Dyer bookprize, 1989. Mem. S. African Assn. Botanists (treas. no. Transvaal br. 1984-85), Deondrological Soc. (mem. ctrl. com. 1980-88, assoc. editor 1980—). Home: 195 Beckett St, Pretoria 0083, South Africa Office: Nat Bot Inst, Private Bag X101, Pretoria 0001, South Africa

GERMROTH, PETER, private school educator; b. Frankfurt, Hessen, Germany, Dec. 15, 1958; came to US, 1998; m. Jennifer R. Langford, Aug. 7, 1998. Dr. phil. nat., Johann Wolfgang U., Frankfurt, 1990. Tchg. cert. Hessen, Germany. Researcher Max Planck Inst. Brain Rsch., Frankfurt, 1987-90; tchr. Goethe Sch., Frankfurt, 1993-98; tchr. biology North Shore Country Day Sch., Winnetka, Ill., 1999—; adj. lectr. Pensacola (Fla.) Jr. Coll., 1999, Okaloosa Walton C.C., Niceville, Fla., 1999. Editor, translator: Spectrum Akademischer Verlag, 1988-98, The Forebrain in Non-Mammals, 1990; mem. editl. bd., contbr. Neuropsychology, German edit., 1993; contbr. articles to profl. jours. Bd. dirs., pub. rels. officer Hessischer Philologen Verband, Wiesbaden, Germany, 1992-98. Mem. Soc. German Physicians and Scientists. Avocations: reading, writing, SCUBA diving. Office: North Shore Country Day Sch 310 Green Bay Rd Winnetka IL 60093-4094

GERNIK, VLADISLAV VALERIANOVICH, geophysicist, researcher; b. Moscow, Jan. 27, 1932; s. Valerian Victorovich and Zinaida Vladimirovna (Vasil'eva) G.; m. Machikhina, May 22, 1973 (div. Mar. 3, 1994); children: Marina, Tatjana. Diploma in Mining Engr.-Geologist, Ural Mining Coll., Ekaterinburg, Russia, 1956, diploma in Mining Engr.-Geophysicist, 1960; student in Geol.-Mining Sci., All-Russian Geol. Rsch., 1970; d of Geol.-Min. Sci., St. Petersburg State U., Russia, 1991. Geologist Ural Geol. Dept., Ekaterinburg, Russia, 1956-57; tech. info. editor Ural Factory of Chem. Machinery Constrn., Ekaterinburg, Russia, 1957-58; technician, engr., head of a party Pechora Geophys. Expedition, Vorkuta, Russia, 1958-67; sr. scientist worker All-Russian Inst. Exploration Geophysics, St. Petersburg, Russia, 1967-68, 76-77; head of a party Western Geophys. Trust, St. Petersburg, Russia, 1968-74; head of paleomagnetic lab. Kamchatka Geol. Dept., Petropavlovsk, Russia, 1977-83; team head, leading scientist worker All-Russian Geol. Rsch. Inst., St. Petersburg, Russia, 1984—. Author: Magnetic Methods of Geology, 1993; co-author: (with A.N. Khramov) Magnetistratigraphic Correlation of the Sedimentary Formations, 1997; contbr. articles to profl. jours. Mem. Am. Geophys. Union. Avocations: volleyball, mushrooming, inventiveness. E-mail: gernik@mail.dux.ru. Home: Box 29, 195298 Saint Petersburg Russia Office: All-Russian Geol Rsch Inst, 74 Szedny pZ, Saint Petersburg 199106, Russia

GERONZI, CESARE, bank executive. Pres. Savs. Bank of Rome; chmn. Banca di Roma, Rome. Office: Banca di Roma, Via Marco Minghetti 17, 00187 Rome Italy

GEROSTERGIOS, ASTERIOS NICHOLAS, priest, writer, translator; b. Kallipefki, Greece, Dec. 8, 1936; came to U.S., 1968; s. Nicholas Gerostergios and Panagio Drogogias. Degree in Theology, U. Athens, 1965; ThD, Boston U., 1974. Ordained priest Greek Orthodox Ch., 1972. Priest Greek Orthodox Ch., Cambridge, Mass., 1972—; sec. Inst. Byzantine and Modern Greek Studies, Belmont, Mass. 1978—. Author: Saint Photios the Great, 1980, Justinian the Great, 1982, Great Vesper Service in Honor of Saints Constantine and Helen, 1998, 80th Anniversary of the Greek Orthodox Community of Saints Constantine and Helen in Cambridge, Massacusetts, 1997; translator: On the Divine Liturgy, Orthodox Homilies, 1986, Follow Me, 1989, Sparks From the Apostles, Orthodox Homilies on the Sunday Apostolic Readings, 1992, A Letter of Consolation to the Bereaved, 1993, Orthodox House of Worship, Informative and Interpretive Homilies on Liturgical Themes, 1994, Orthodox Faith and Life in Christ, 1994, Miracles, Orthodox Homilies on Miracles in Nature, Man, Holy Scripture, the History of Nations, and the Church,The Greek Nation, 1998; editor: Transmission of the Text of the Holy Bible, 1997,. Recipient Golden Medal award Greek Orthodox Patriarch Benedictos I of Jerusalem, 1979, Golden Key, City of Cambridge, 2000. Avocation: travel. Office: Inst for Byzantine 41 Harding Ave Belmont MA 02478-4412

GEROULAKOS, GEORGE, vascular surgeon; b. Athens, Greece, Apr. 7, 1956; s. Constantine and Dora (Coumidou) G.; m. Viki Christopoulos, May 22, 1993; 1 child, Constantine. MD, Athens Med. Sch., 1981; FRCS, Imperial Coll. Sci. Tech., 1989; PhD, Imperial Coll. Sci. Tech., London, 1994, DIC (hon.), 1995. Diplomate in gen. and vascular surgery. Sr. house officer in surgery Univ. Hosp., Nottingham, Eng., 1984-86; registrar in surgery Royal London Hosp., 1988-90; Eastcott rsch. fellow St. Mary's Hosp., London, 1991-93; lectr. surgery St. Bartholomew's Hosp., London, 1994-95; clin. fellow in vascular surgery Ohio State U., Columbus, 1995-96; cons. and sr. lectr. Charing Cross Hosp., London, 1997—, sr. lectr. vascular surgery, 1997—; dir., cons. vascular surgery Ealing Hosp., London, 1997—. Author chpts. in books; contbr. articles to medical jours. Fellow Royal Soc. Medicine, Royal Coll. Surgeons; mem. Hellenic Med. Soc. Gt. Britain (pres. 1999-00), European Soc. Vascular Surgery, Peripheral Vascular Soc., Zollinger Surg. Soc. Avocations: skiing, rafting. Office: Ealing Hosp NHS Trust, Uxbridge Rd Southall, Middlesex UB1 3HW, England

GERRISH, CATHERINE RUGGLES, retired food company executive; b. Winona, Minn., July 10, 1911; d. Clyde O. and Frances (Holmes) Ruggles; m. Hollis G. Gerrish, Sept. 10, 1946. AB, Radcliffe Coll., 1932, AM, 1934; PhD, Harvard U., 1937. Instr., asst. prof. econs. U. Ill., 1939-42, assoc. prof., 1946; economist Bur. Budget, Exec. Office President, 1943-45; asst. editor Quar. Jour. Econs., 1951-69; treas., v.p. Squirrel Brand Co., Cambridge, Mass., 1966-97, pres., 1998, ret., 1999; Corporater The Cambridge Homes, pres., 1990-91. Mem. Am. Econ. Assn., Nat. Tax Assn., Coll. Club of Boston (pres. 1953-55). Home: 207 Grove St Cambridge MA 02138-1013

GERS, JUAN MANUEL, electrical engineer, consultant, educator; b. Cali, Valle, Colombia, Jan. 6, 1954; s. Jose and Mara (Ospina) G.; m. Pilar Hernandez, Nov. 5, 1988; children: Angela Maria, Juan Felipe, Juan Jose. BSc, U. Valle, Cali, Colombia, 1977; MSc, U. Salford, Eng., 1981; PhD, U. Strathclyde, Scotland, 1998. Constrn. engr. CVC (now EPSA), Cali, Colombia, 1977-79; prof. U. Valle, Cali, 1981—; gen mgr. GERS Ltda., Cali, 1981—. Co-author: Protection of Electricity Distribution Networks, 1998. Mem. IEEE, IEE (London, charter), CIGRE. Avocations: volley ball, cycling, jogging, guitar. Office: Gers USA 2645 Executive Park Dr Ste 111 Weston FL 33331-3624

GERSCHMAN, JACK ALLEN, oral medicine-pain specialist, oral pathologist; b. Windsheim, Germany, June 3, 1947; s. Josef and Renia (Frochter) G.; m. Tania Manowicz, Dec. 19, 1976; children: Joel, Elliot. BDSc, Melbourne U., Australia, 1971, PhD, 1983, diploma in mental health sci., 1997. Diplomate Am. Acad. Pain Mgmt. Dir. Melbourne Med. Ctr. Pain Clinic, $Dstralia, 1973—; rsch. assoc. dept. psychology U. Melbourne, Australia, 1972—; sr. assoc. sch. dental sci. U. Melbourne, 1992—; specialist clin. assoc. dentistry U. Sydney, Australia, 1995—; assoc. prof. Sch. Dental Sci. U. Melbourne, 1999—; postgrad. lectr. Austlian Dental Assn., 1972—; coord. oro-facial pain clinic Royal Dental Hosp. Melbourne, 1974—; fellow faculty pain mgmt. Australian and New Zealand Coll. Anesthesiologists; cons. in field. Author: Hypnosis in Dentistry, 1980, Diagnosis and Management of Oro-facial Pain, 1986. Mem. Oral Medicine Soc. Australia and New Zealand (sec.-treas. 1995-97, pres. 1997—). Avocations: classical music, tennis, philosophy. Home: 15 Snowdon Ave, Melbourne 3162, Australia Office: Melbourne Med Ctr Pain Clinic, 517 St Kilda Rd Ste 5, Melbourne 3004, Australia

GERSH, BERNARD J., cardiologist, researcher, educator; b. Johannesburg, South Africa, Oct. 2, 1941; came to U.S., 1978; s. Maurice and Revee Gersh; m. Alison D. Brunette, 1967 (div. 1973); children: Brunette, Jonathan, Amanda; m. Ann Gersh, Oct. 28, 1977; children: Kate and Sarah (twins); 1 stepchild, Brione. MB BChir,, U. Cape Town, South Africa, 1965; DPhil, Oxford (Eng.) U., 1970. Cons. Mayo Clinic, Rochester, Minn., 1978-93, 98—; prof. medicine Mayo Med. Sch., Rochester, 1985-93, 93-98, 98—; W. Proctor Harvey tchr. Georgetown U. Med. Ctr., Washington, 1993-98, chief divsn. cardiology, 1993-98, prof. medicine; sr. specialist, sr. lectr. Groote Schuur Hosp. and U. Cape Town, 1973-78. Editor/author 8 books; contbr. 400 articles to profl. jours. Past chmn. coun. clin. cardiology Am. Heart Assn., 1995-98. Rhodes scholar, 1965. Fellow Royal Coll. Physicians; mem. Am. Coll. Cardiology (bd. trustees, 1995-2000), Cosmos Club (Washington), Vincent's Club (Oxford U.), Western Province Cricket Club. E-mail: gersh bernard@mayo.edu. Home: 2501 Institute Rd SW Rochester MN 55902-1156 Office: Mayo Clinic Cardiovasc Diseases 200 1st St SW Rochester MN 55905-0002

GERSHMAN, ALEXEI, electrical engineer, researcher; b. Nizhny Novgorod, Russia, Oct. 10, 1962; arrived in Germany, 1995, Can., 1999; s. Boris N. Gershman and Emma F. Krupnova; m. Olga L. Jarakhtina, Nov. 24, 1990; 1 child, Ekatherina. Diploma in elec. engring., Gorky (Russia) State U., 1984, PhD in Elec. Engring., 1990. Cert. in radiophysics and electronics. Jr. rschr. Inst. Radiotechnics, Gorky, 1984-87; rsch. scientist Inst. Radiophysics, Gorky, 1987-89; rsch. scientist Inst. Applied Physics, Nizhny Novgorod, 1989-95, sr. rsch. scientist, 1995-99; guest scientist Swiss Fed. Inst. Tech. (EPFL), Lausanne, 1994-95, Ruhr U., Bochum, Germany, 1995-97, scientific rschr., 1997-99; assoc. prof. McMaster U., 1999—. Contbr. over 120 articles to profl. jours. Multiple grantee Internat. Sci. Found., N.Y.C., Internat. Assn. (INTAS), Brussels, Russian Found. Basic Rsch., Moscow, 1993—, German Rsch. Found., Nat. Scis. and Engring. Rsch. Coun. Can.; recipient Young Scientist award Union Radio Sci. Internat., Kyoto, 1993, Branco Weiss Found.; Disting. Young Scientist fellow, Pres. Russia, 1994, Swiss Acad. Tech. Sci. fellow, 1994, Alexander von Humboldt Found. fellow, 1995. Mem. IEEE (sr., assoc. editor IEEE Transactions on Signal Processing 1999—, mem. sensor array and mutichannel processing tech. com. IEEE signal processing soc., 1999—). Avocations: history of science, table tennis, travel. Office: McMaster U Comm Rsch Lab, Dept Elec and Computer Engring, Hamilton, ON Canada L8S 4K1

GERSHTEIN, ELENA SERGEYEVNA, biochemist, researcher; b. Moscow, Jan. 4, 1954; d. Sergey Borisovitch and Lidiya Mikhailovna (Tyurina) G. Diploma in chemistry, Moscow State U., 1976; PhD in Biology, Russian Acad. Med Sci., Moscow, 1980; D of Biol. Scis., Russian Acad. Med. Sci., Moscow, 1996. Jr. rschr. Cancer Rsch. Ctr.-Russian Acad. Med.

Sci., 1979-87, sr. rschr., 1987-90, leading rschr., head sci. group, 1995—. Co-author: Steroid Hormone Receptors in Human Tumors, 1987, Clinical and Endocrinological Investigations in Benign Breast Disease and Breast Cancer, 1998; contbr. over 60 articles to profl. jours. Fellowship for prominent scientists Pres. Russian Fedn., 1997; grantee Soros Found., N.Y.C., 1993. mem. Russian Soc. Oncology. Avocations: downhill skiing, literature, tourism. Home: Leningradskoye shosse 31-14, 125212 Moscow Russia Office: Cancer Rsch Ctr RAMS, Kashirskoye shosse 24, 115478 Moscow Russia

GERSIN, KEITH STEVEN, surgeon; b. Boston, Oct. 14, 1964; s. Alvin and Joyce Saundra Gersin. BA cum laude, Boston U., 1986; MD, Georgetown U., 1991. Diplomate Am. Bd. Surgery. Resident in gen. surgery Berkshire Md. Ctr., Pittsfield, Mass., 1991-97; gen. surgeon Berkshire Med. Ctr., Pittsfield, Mass., 1998-2000; endoscopic surgery fellow The Cleve. Clinic Found., 1997-98. Contbr. articles to profl. jours. Recipient Disting. Leadership award Internat. Directory Disting. Leadership, 1998. Fellow ACS (assoc.); mem. Am. Soc. Gastrointestinal Endoscopy, Soc. Am. Gastrointestinal Endoscopic Surgeons. Office: U Cin Med Ctr Dept Surgery 231 Bethesda Ave Dept S Cincinnati OH 45267-0001

GERSON, DONALD JEROME, computer scientist, consultant; b. N.Y.C., Apr. 26, 1934; s. Irwin I. Gerson and Helen Sacks; m. Barbara A. Jaques, Aug. 21, 1960 (dec. Oct. 1998); 1 child, Laura Melissa; m. Emma Sue Gaines, June 24, 2000. BA in Meteorology, N.Y.U., 1956; MS in Computer Sci., U. Md., 1975. Oceanographer Naval Oceanographic Office, Suitland, Md., 1956-78; physical scientist Defense Mapping Agy., Bethesda, Md., 1978-83; imagery scientist CIA, Langley, Va., 1983-97; prin., owner Gerson Imaging Solutions, LLC, Silver Spring, Md., 1997—; instr. George Washington U., Washington, 1983-88; mem. working group on sea ice World Meteorological Org., Geneva, 1975-77. Author: (with others) Processes in Marine Remote Sensing, 1982, Radius, Image Understanding for Imagery Intelligence, 1997; contbr. articles to profl. jours. Recipient Goldsborough award for best tech. paper of yr., 1983, Intelligence Commendation medal CIA, 1997. Fellow The Explorers Club (Wash. chpt. chmn. 1986-88); mem. IEEE Computer Soc., Applied Imagery Pattern Recognition Com. (chmn. 1975—), Am. Soc. Media Photographers, The Cosmos Club, Sigma Xi. Avocations: photography, racewalking, recreational vehicle camping, hiking, book collecting. E-mail: dgerson@GersonImagingSolutions.com.

GERSON, STANTON L., physician, educator; b. Cambridge, Mass., Apr. 8, 1951; m. Deborah Levitan Gerson, 1978; children: Ruth, James, David. AB magna cum laude, Harvard Coll., 1973, MD cum laude, 1977. Intern, resident dept. medicine U. Pa.; asst. prof. medicine and oncology Case Western Res. U. Sch. Medicine, Cleve., 1983-88, assoc. prof. medicine dept. medicine, 1988—, assoc. prof. environ. health scis., 1991—, prof. medicine, oncology and environ. health scis., 1994—, mem. Cancer Rsch. Ctr., 1985—, chief divsn. hematology/oncology, 1995—, assoc. dir. for clin. rsch. Ireland Cancer Ctr., 1995—; sci. adv. bd. Osiris Therapeutics, Balt., 1994-99, Edison Biotech. Ohio, 1994—. Author: (with E. Lattime) Gene Therapy of Cancer, 1998. Chmn. pilot rev. com. Am. Cancer Soc., Ohio, 1985—. Recipient Edward Mallinckrodt scholar award E. Mallinckrodt Found., St. Louis, 1987-92. Mem. Am. Soc. Clin. Investigation, Am. Assn. Physicians, Am. Assn. for Cancer Rsch., Am. Soc. Hematology. Democrat. Achievements include inventor of gene therapy using Mesenchymal stem cells and bone marrow transplantation of Mesenchymal stem cells. Avocations: flute, golf, tennis. E-mail: slg5@po.cwru.edu. Home: 37995 Fairmount Blvd Chagrin Falls OH 44022-6617 Office: Case Western Res Univ BRB 3 West 10900 Euclid Ave Cleveland OH 44106-4901

GERSONI-EDELMAN, DIANE CLAIRE, author, editor; b. Bklyn., Apr. 16, 1947; d. James Arthur and Edna Bernice (Krinski) Gersoni; B.A. cum laude, Vassar Coll., 1967; m. James Neil Edelman, Oct. 5, 1975; children—Michael Lawrence, Sara Anne. Asst. editor, then assoc. editor Sch. Library Jour. Book Rev., 1968-72; free lance writer, 1972-74, 77—; writer, editor Scholastic Mags., Inc., N.Y.C., 1974-77; author: Sexism and Youth, 1974; Work-Wise: Learning About the World of Work from Books, 1980; cons., speaker in field. Club: Vassar (N.Y.C.). Contbr. articles, book revs. to anthologies, newspapers, mags. Home: care Edelman 301 E 78th St New York NY 10021-1322

GERSTEIN, DAVID BROWN, hardware manufacturing company executive, professional basketball team executive; b. N.Y.C., Jan. 30, 1936; s. Frank and May G.; m. Jane Ellen Bender, May 4, 1963; children: Mark, James. Student, Columbia U., 1951-54, postgrad., 1954-58; B.S., Seton Hall U., 1959. With Thermwell Products Co., Paterson, N.J., 1958—; sales mgr. Thermwell Products Co., 1965-68, v.p., 1968-74, pres., 1974—; prin. owner N. J. Nets NBA franchise, 1978—; v.p. Lever Mfg. Co., Paterson; pres. Woodlowe Realty, Paterson, Wait Assocs., Paterson, Dim Assocs., Mahwah, N.J. Chmn. adv. council energy and conservation State of N.J.; co-chmn. athletic program Seton Hall U. Office: NJ Nets Meadowlands Arena East Rutherford NJ 07073

GERSTEL, BIRGIT, biologist; b. Wolfsburg, Lr. Saxony, Germany, July 12, 1963; d. Benedykt and Olga (Seiler) G.; m. Andreas Wehran, Mar. 21, 1997; children: Philip, Meret. Abitur, Gymnasium Fallersleben, Wolfsburg, 1982; Diploma, Tech. U., Braunschweig, Germany, 1988; PhD, Gesellschaft für Biotech., Forschung, Braunschweig, 1992. Postdoctoral fellow Gesellschaft für Biotechnologische Forschung, Braunschweig, 1993—. Contbr. articles to profl. jours. Avocations: horseback riding, reading, traveling. Office: GBF ZIB/ZB, Mascheroder Weg 1, 38124 Braunschweig Germany

GERSTER, RICHARD, economist; b. Winterthur, Switzerland, May 29, 1946; s. Karl and Emilie (Mattmann) G.; m. Doris Frischknecht, Oct. 9, 1971; children: Dominique, Rahel, Sarah. PhD in Econs., U. St. Gall, Switzerland, 1973. Univ. asst. U. St. Gall, 1970-71; program coord. Helvetas, Zurich, 1972-73; program dir. Helvetas, Buea, Cameroon, 1973-74; program coord. Helvetas, Zurich, 1975-79, dep. dir., 1979-81; coord. devel. policy Swiss Coalition, Berne, 1982-92, exec. dir., 1992-98; dir. Gerster Devel. Cons., Richterswil, 1998—; bd. dirs. State Bank Zurich. Contbr. articles to profl. jours.; author books on North-South relations. Mem. Parliament, Canton, Zurich, 1987-92; mem. adv. com. to Swiss Govt. in devel. policy, 1978-94. Recipient Media award Christoph Eckenstein Found., 1986. Mem. Green Party. Roman Catholic. Office: Gerster Devel Cons, Goeldistr 1, CH-8805 Richterswil Switzerland

GERSTMEIER, ROLAND, zoologist, educator; b. Lindau, Bavaria, Germany, Sept. 3, 1953; s. Klemens and Erika (Urban) G. Dr.rer.nat., U. Munich, Bavaria, Germany, 1985. Univ. asst. Tech. U. Munich, 1988-95, univ. dozent, 1995—, prof., 2000—. Author: Welcher Schmetterling ist das?, 1988, Marokko-Landschaften, Tiere, Pflanzen, 1990, Käfer, 1992, The Checkered Beetles of the Western Palaearctis, 1997. E-mail: n.gerstmeier@lrz.tum.de. Office: Tech Univ Munich, Tech Univ Munich, Angewandte Zoologie, D-85350 Freising Germany

GERSTNER, LONISE, internet company executive; b. Porto Alegre, Brazil, July 15, 1962; d. Cylon Lothario and Varise Terezinha (Iserhard) G.; m. Mauro Pippi De Rosa, June 9, 1990; children: Pedro, Luisa. B Informatic, UFRGS, Porto Alegre, Brazil, 1982, B Psychology, 1984; German Translator, Goethe Inst., Karlsruhe, German, 1988; English Translator, Mich., Porto Alegre, 1983. Trainee UFRGS, Porto Alegre, 1981; mgr. Alta. Wheat Pool, Calgary, Can., 1982, Olvebra, Porto Alegre, 1983, Novadata Computer Sys. AG, Karlsruhe, 1984-90; dir. Terra Networks S.A., Porto Alegre, 1990—; dir. Seprors, Porto Alegre, 1999, Assespro, Porto Alegre, 1998-99. Inventor remote job entry. Mem. Interactive Media Assn. Avocations: tennis, farming, travel. Home: Rua Santo Inacio 188/21, 90570150 Porto Alegre Brazil Office: Terra Networks SA, Rua Joao Manoel 90-10 Andar, 90010030 Porto Alegre Brazil

GERSTNER, LOUIS VINCENT, JR., diversified company executive; b. Mineola, N.Y., Mar. 1, 1942; s. Louis Vincent and Marjorie (Rutan) G.; m. Elizabeth Robins Link, Nov. 30, 1968; children: Louis, Elizabeth. BA in Engring., Dartmouth Coll., 1963; MBA, Harvard U., 1965; DBA (hon.), Boston Coll., 1994; LLD (hon.), Wake Forest U., 1997, Brown U., 1997. Dir. McKinsey & Co., N.Y.C., 1965-78; exec. v.p. Am. Express Co., N.Y.C., 1978-81; vice-chmn. bd. Am. Express Co., 1981-83, chmn. exec. com., 1983-85, pres., 1985-89, chmn., CEO travel related svcs., 1985-89; chmn., CEO RJR Nabisco Inc., N.Y.C., 1989-93; chmn. bd., CEO IBM, Armonk, NY, 1993—, also dir.; bd. dirs. Bristol-Meyers Squibb Co.; mem. Pres.'s Nat. Security Telecom. Adv. Com., 1994-97, Adv. Com. for Trade Policy and Negotiations, 1995—. Co-author: Reinventing Education: Entrepreneurship in America's Public School, 1994. Bd. dirs. Meml. Sloan Kettering Hosp., 1978-89, 98—, vice-chmn., 2000—, United Negro Coll. Fund, 1987-91, Lincoln Ctr. for Performing Arts, 1984—, Am.-China Soc., 1987—, N.Y. Times, 1986-97, AT&T, 1987-93, Caterpillar, 1984-89; trustee Joint Coun. on Econ. Edn., 1975-87, chmn. 1983-85; active Bus. Roundtable, 1991-98, The Bus. Coun., 1992; vice-chmn., bd. dirs. New Am. Schs. Devel. Corp., 1991-98; adv. bd. Ctr. for Strategic and Internat. Studies, 1987—; trustee N.Y. Pub. Libr., 1991-96; bd. regents Smithsonian Instn., 1996-99. Recipient Cleveland E. Dodge Medal for disting. svc. to edn. Tchrs. Coll., Columbia U., Disting. Svc. to Sci. and Edn. award Am. Mus. Natural History, Award for Excellence in Bus., Engring. and Tech., Washington U., 1999. Fellow Am. Acad. Arts and Scis.; mem. Coun. Fgn. Rels., N.Y. City Partnership, Japan Soc. (bd. dirs. 1992-97), Nat. Acad. Engring. Office: IBM Corp New Orchard Rd Armonk NY 10504-1709

GERT, HEATHER J., philosophy educator; b. Hanover, N.H., Feb. 8, 1962; d. Bernard and Esther L. Gert. BA, Kenyon Coll., 1984; PhD, Brown U., 1991. Asst. prof. Tex. A&M U., Coll. Sta., 1991-97, assoc. prof., 1997—; vis. asst. prof. Hamilton Coll., Clinton, N.Y., 1990-91. Contbr. articles to profl. jours. Mem. Amnesty Internat., Austin, 1998-99; reader Reading for the Blind, Austin, 1998-99. Summer Sem. fellow NEH, 1991, 96, Summer Inst. fellow, 1993. Mem. AAUP, Am. Philos. Assn. Avocations: contra dancing, dancing, reading, travel, outdoor activities. Office: Tex A&M U Philosophy Dept College Station TX 77843-0001

GERTIS, NEILL ALLAN, writer; b. Buffalo, Mar. 24, 1943; s. Alfred Charles and Gertrude Charlotte (Hurst) G.; m. Gail C. Morgan, Oct. 3, 1966 (div. Aug. 1982); m. Alma Ann Sullivan, Sept. 15, 1984; children: Charlotte Ann, Joseph Alfred, Daniel Andrew, Martin Alexander. Community planner Alaska State Housing Authority, Anchorage, 1968-72, libr. dir., 1968-72; real estate appraiser Gertis Assocs., Buffalo, 1972-76; ops. mgr. Chem. Equipment Labs., Phila., 1979-83; tech. writer Gen. Dynamics, Groton, Conn., 1983-84; sr. tech. writer communication products MTS Systems Corp., Mpls., 1984-94, mgr. tech. tng., 1994-97; supr. tech. publs. Rockwell Automation, Mpls., 1997—. Author: Student Housing Demand in Anchorage, 1972; editor: Guide to Periodical Holdings in the Anchorage Area, 1970, Storm Drainage for Chester Creek, Anchorage, 1969; editor Engring. Graphics, Anchorage, 1968-72. Served with U.S. Army, 1965-69. Mem. Alaska Library Assn. Republican. Avocations: computers, antiques, restoration, writing, reading. Home: 1157 Tyler St S Shakopee MN 55379-2070 Office: Rockwell Automation GMC Eden Prairie Facility 6950 Washington Ave S Eden Prairie MN 55344-3450

GERTLER, MENARD M., physician, educator; b. Saskatoon, Sask., Can., May 19, 1921; came to U.S., 1947, naturalized, 1953; s. Frank and Clara (Handelman) G.; m. Anna Paull, Sept. 4, 1943; children—Barbara Lynn, Stephanie Jocelyn, Jonathan Paull. BA, U. Sask., Saskatoon, 1940; MD, McGill U., Montreal, Que., Can., 1943, MS, 1946, DS (honoris causa), 1999; DSc, NYU, 1960. Intern Royal Victoria Hosp., Montreal, Que., Can., 1943-44; resident Mass. Gen. Hosp., Boston, 1947-50; also research fellow in medicine Mass. Gen. Hosp., Harvard Med. Sch., 1947-50; dir. cardiology Francis Delafield divsn. Columbia Presbyn. Med. Ctr., N.Y.C., 1950-54; spl. research fellow NIH, NYU Dept. Biochemistry, 1954-56; prof. Sch. Medicine, dir. cardiovascular research Rusk Inst. NYU Med. Ctr., 1958-71; sr. med. examiner FAA, 1975; dir. Washington Fed. Savs. & Loan Assn., 1972-83; adj. prof. medicine McGill U., 1996—; clin. prof. medicine N.Y. Hosp.-Cornell Med. Ctr., attending physician; prof. medicine Weill Med. Sch., Cornell U.; attending physician N.Y. Hosp./Presbyn. Hosp., 1998—; med. dir. Sinclair Oil Corp., 1958-68; internat. cons. cardiovascular diseases, social and rehab. svcs. HEW, Washington, 1968-92. Author: Coronary Heart Disease in Young Adults, 1954, Coronary Heart Disease, 1974; Contbr. articles to profl. jours. Pres. Friends of McGill U.; mem. dean's com. McGill U. Med. Sch. With M.C., Royal Can. Army, 1940-43. Recipient Founders Day award NYU, 1959, medal of honor McGill U., 1993, award of merit McGill U., 1993. Mem. Gallatin Assocs. NYU, Cosmos Club (Washington), Harvard Club (Boston), Univ. Club. Home: 1000 Park Ave Apt 2C New York NY 10028-0934 Office: 1000 Park Ave # 2C New York NY 10028-0934

GERTZ, DAVID LEE, homebuilding company executive; b. Denver, July 30, 1950; s. Ben Harry and Clara (Cohen) G.; m. Bonnie Lee Schulein, June 2, 1973; children: Joshua, Eva. BS, U. Colo., 1972; MBA, U. Colo., Denver, 1993. Real estate broker Crown Realty, Denver, 1972-73; pres. Sunshine Plumbing Co., Lakewood, Colo., 1974-76, Sunshine Diversified, Inc., Lakewood, 1976—, Sunshine Master Builders, Ltd., Lakewood, 1990—; sec.-treas. Wight Lateral Ditch Co., Lakewood, 1987-91. Builder of custom and semi-custom homes. Cub master Boy Scouts Am., Lakewood, 1989-91, asst. scout master, 1991-94; co-chair bldg. com. Hebrew Ednl. Alliance, bd. dirs., Denver, 1991-94; mem. Anti-Defamation League, Denver, 1989—; chmn. Parade of Homes com., 1999. Scholar, Evans Scholars, U. Colo., 1968-72. Mem. Home Builders Assn. of Denver (bd. dirs., legis. com.), Colo. Assn. Home Builders (alt. dir.). Avocations: skiing, golf, softball. Office: Sunshine Master Builders 8125 W Belleview Ave Littleton CO 80123-1203

GERVAIS, JEAN-MARIE KACOU, ambassador. Amb. Cote d'Ivoire UN, Paris, France. Office: Amb Cote d'Ivoire, 102 Ave Raymond Poincare, 75016 Paris France

GERVAIS, MICHEL, theology educator, hospital executive; b. Levis, Que., Can., May 27, 1944; s. Paul and Ghislaine (Gosselin) G. BA, Coll. Levis, 1962; LTh, U. Laval, Can., 1966, LPh, 1968; DTh, Pontifical U. of St. Thomas Aquinas, Rome, 1973; D Civil Law (hon.), Bishop U., 1993; DDiv (hon.), McGill U., 1993; LLD (hon.), U. Man., 1994; D (hon.), U. Montreal, 1996. Mem. faculty theology, now assoc. prof. U. Laval, also rector, 1987-97; exec. dir. Robert Giffard Hosp. Ctr., Beauport, Que., 2000—; chmn. Quebec Commn. on Univ. Programs, 1998-2000; vice chmn. Can. Found. Innovat ion, 1997—. Office: Centre Hosp Robert Giffard, 2601 de la Canardière, Beauport, PQ Canada G1J 2G3

GERVAIS, PAUL NELSON, foundation administrator, psychotherapist, public relations executive, writer; b. Augusta, Maine, June 28, 1947; s. Adrien and Phyllis (Sullivan) G. B in Bible and Doctrine/Ministerial Studies, Berean Coll., 1975; M, U. Maine, 1987; M in Marriage and Family Therapy, Coll. Clin. Family Sci., 1988; cert. in Constl. Law, U. Maine, 1969; Dr., N.Am. Biblical Sem., Buffalo, 1987; M. in Marriage and Family, San Antonio Theol. Sem., 1988; PhD in Psychology, San Antonio Theol. Sem., St. Paul, 1989; PhD in Marriage and Family Therapy, Minn. Grad. Sch., 1990. Cert. behavioral analyst, clin. supr.; registered clin. therapist; lic. marriage and family therapist, Tex.; lic. marriage and family therapist, clin. profl. counselor, profl. counselor, pastoral counselor, Maine. Reporter No. New Eng. divsn. News dept. NBC Radio divsn., N.Y.C., 1966-70; dir. pub. rels. Kennebec Valley Med. Ctr., Augusta, 1970-73, Penobscot Bay Med. Ctr., Rockport, Maine, 1973-74; pres., chmn. bd. dirs. Ministry of Miracles Evangelistic Assn., Maine, 1975—; news dir. Maine Broadcasting System, Augusta, 1966-70; advisor, assoc. dir. pub. rels. state VA svcs., Maine, 1969-70; family counselor Gracelawn Meml. Pk., Auburn, Maine, assoc. dir., 1987; pres., CEO Motivational Resources. Pioneered one of first radio and TV health edn. programs from which proceeded other nat. and internat. programs in field; mental health columnist Maine Sunday Paper. Active Rep. Nat. Com., Washington, 1987, Dole for Pres. exploratory Com., 1987—, also adv. com., 1987, steering com. Campaign Am., 1987-88; mem. Presdl. Task Force, Washington, 1989, Rep. Senatorial Inner Circle, 1989—, U.S. Senatorial Club, Washington, 1989-90, Nat. Rep. Senatorial Com., Washington, 1990; CEO Gracelawn Meml. Park, Auburn, Maine, 1988—; spl. advisor, dep. Kennebec County Sheriff's Office, also dep. sheriff. Recipient vice-presdl. Citation Office of U.S. V.P. Hubert Humphrey, 1968, Malcolm T. MacEachern Citation Am. Health Congress, 1973; cert. in pub. rels. Chgo. chpt. Am. Hosp. Assn.; Presdl. Medal of Merit Pres. George Bush, 1989. Fellow Profl. Assn. Christian Counselors and Therapists; mem. AACD, Am. Acad. Family Therapists (exec. dir.), Acad. for Eating Disorders, Nat. Assn. Anorexia Nervosa and Associated Disorders, Publicity Club Boston (disting. bell ringer award 1974), Nat. Christian Counselors Assn. (mem. licensing bd., chmn. legal com.), Am. Mental Health Counselors Assn., Maine Network Associated Profl. Practitioners, Maine Assn. for Counseling and Devel., Mensa. Baptist. Home and Office: Am Acad Profl Family Therapists 16 Julianne Ln Augusta ME 04330-6251

GERVASIO, SUSANA GRACIELA, chemical engineer; b. Rosario, Santa Fe, Argentina, Sept. 3, 1951; d. Roberto and Ana (Iglesias) G.; m. Gerardo Daniel Lopez; children: Javier A., Mariana B., Diego J. BS in Econs., Escuela Superior Comercio Sch., Rosario, Argentin, 1969. Chem. engr. Beca John Deere Arg., Argentina, 1973-76; engr. Min. de Hacienda & Economia, Rosario, 1977-79; prof. C.O.N.E.T., Rosario, 1977-79; profl. asst. Intec/Conicet, Santa Fe, Argentina, 1980—; prof. prin. Ceride/Conicet, Santa Fe. Mem. Argentine Corrosion Assn., Argentine Chem. Engrs. Assn. Office: Ceride, Guenes 3450, 3000 Santa Fe Argentina

GERVAZIEV, VICTOR BORISOVICH, surgery educator, researcher; b. Constantinovka, Ukraine, Aug. 15, 1929; s. Boris Alexandrovich and Taisija Nikanorovna Gervaziev; m. Irina Dmitrievna Lovlja, July 10, 1955 (div. 1962); 1 child, Dmitrij; m. Nelli Ivanovna Leontjeva, July 15, 1965; 1 child, Jury. Higher med. edn., Med. Inst., Chernovtsy, 1946-51; DMS, Russian Acad. Med. Scis., Moscow, Russia, 1970. Specialty in surgery; surgeon of highest category. Clin. sub-intern Med. Inst., Chernovtsy, 1951-54, asst., 1954-60; asst. Med. Inst., Barnaul, 1960-62, asst. prof., 1962-68, prof., 1968-71, head of chair hosp. surgery, 1971-99, honorary prof., 1999—; pro-rector sci. Med. Inst., Barnaul, 1970-74, rector, 1979-88; merited sci. worker Russian Federation, 1996. Inventor in field. Decorated Order Sign of Honorary, 1976, Order October Revolution, 1981. Mem. Acad. Natural Sci. Avocations: tourism, photos, chess. Home: Proletarskaya st 67-11, 656056 Barnaul Altai, Russia Office: Med U, Lenin prospect 40, 656099 Barnaul Altai, Russia

GERVEREAU, LAURENT, curator; b. Neuilly Sur Seine, France, Jan. 19, 1956; s. Louis and Annie (Bost) G.; children: Antoine, Pauline. BA, Ecole Des Hautes Etudes. Adj. bibliothecaire Musee d'histoire contemporaine, Paris, 1978-91, conservateur, 1991—; pres. Internat. Assn. Mus. of History, Paris, 1991—; dir. L'Image, Paris, 1995—. Author: La propagande par l'affiche, 1991, Voir, comprendre, analyser les images, 1995, Terroriser, manipuler, convaincre-Histoire mondiale de l'affiche politique, 1996, Guernica, Autopsie d'un chef d'oeuvre, 1996, Les Images qui Mentent, Histoire du Visuel au XX Siecle. Mem. Coll. Pataphysique. Avocation: creation plastique. Office: Musee d'Histoire Contemporaine, Hotel Des Invalides, 75007 Paris France

GERVITS, LEONID, artist, art educator; b. Odessa, Ukraine, USSR, Apr. 12, 1946; came to U.S., 1991; s. Vladimir Mikhailovich Gervits and Polina Abramovna Gurevich; m. Irina Tatarinova; 1 child, Mikhail. BFA, Art Coll., Odessa, 1966; MFA in Painting and Drawing, Nat. Acad. Art Repin Inst., Russia, 1973. From asst. to assoc. prof. Nat. Acad. Art Repin Inst., St. Petersburg, Russia, 1975-91; instr. painting and drawing N.Y. Acad. Art, N.Y.C., 1992—; represented by Portrait South, Inc., Raleigh, N.C., The Portrait Co., Seattle; instr. painting Art Student's League, N.Y.C., 1998—; vis. prof. Korean Nat. U. Art, Seoul, Korea, 1998; leader workshops Acad. der Bildende Künste, Stuttgart, Germany, 1998, Seattle Acad. Realist Art, 1995, 99, 2000. One-man shows include Art Union, St. Petersburg, Russia, 1984, Gallery Pushkin Preservation, Russia, 1985, Gallery Knüphausen, Nekarrems, Germany, 1990, Gallery Boursheid, Luxemburg, 1991, Gallery Künstlergruppe Experiment, Stuttgart, Germany, 1991, Princeton (N.J.) U., 1992, Dow Jones Gallery, Princeton, 1992, 1100 Madison Gallery, N.Y.C., 1999, 2000; exhibited in group shows at Leningrad Sch. Art, Helsinki, Finland, 1988, Carnegie Hall, N.Y.C., 1993, Endy Gallery, N.Y.C., 1993, Kergima Gallery, Ridgewood, N.J., 1994, Case Mus., Jersey City, N.J., 1995, Polo Gallery, Edgewater, N.J., 1995, Grant Gallery, Soho, N.Y., 1999, Chrysalis Gallery, Southampton, N.Y., 1999; art dir. Internat. Pushkin Soc. Mag. Arzamas, 1998-99. Office: 286 Barron St Jersey City NJ 07302

GERWARD, LEIF INGEMAR, physicist; b. Lund, Sweden, May 2, 1939; m. Gullan I. Jacobsson. MSc, Chalmers U. Tech., Gothenborg, Sweden, 1963, PhD, 1970, DSc, 1974. Lectr. Chalmers U. Tech., Gothenburg, Sweden, 1963-64, 66-70; stipendiary Max Planck Inst., Stuttgart, Germany, 1964-66; amanuensis Tech. U. Denmark, Lyngby, 1970-72, lectr., 1972-89, assoc. prof. docent, 1989—. Contbr. numerous articles to sci. jours.; pioneer energy-dispersive method and synchrotron radiation x-ray diffraction. Sgt. Swedish Army, 1958-59. Mem. Internat. Radiation Physics Soc. (exec. coun. 1994—), Internat. Ctr. Diffraction Data, Danish Nat. Com. Crystallography, Danish Phys. Soc. Avocations: old roses, history of physics. E-mail: Leif.Gerward@fysik.dtu.dk. Office: Tech U Denmark, Dept Physics Bldg 307, DK-2800 Kings Lyngby Denmark

GERZABEK, MARTIN HUBERT, research scientist; b. Vienna, Austria, June 9, 1961; s. Hubert Heinrich Gerzabek and Elisabeth Maria Lindermann; m. Andrea Maria Kopelent, Mar. 3, 1989; children: Sophie, Maria, Severin, Helene. Diploma in engring., U. Agrl. Scis., Vienna, 1985, D of Tech. Scis., 1987, assoc. prof. soil sci., 1993. Cert. civil engr. for agr. Fed. Ministry Economy. Rsch. scientist Austrian Rsch. Ctr. Seibersdorf, 1984-92, head agrl. rsch. unit, 1993-96, head dept. environ. rsch., 1997—; cons. EMBRAPA, Rio de Janeiro, 1996; expert Internat. Atomic Energy Agy., Vienna, 1995—; univ. lectr. U. Agrl. Scis., Vienna, 1991—; guest prof. Agrl. Acad. Gorki, Belarus, 1997. Contbr. articles to profl. jours. Mem. Austrian Soil Sci. Soc. (treas. 1994—), European Soc. for New Methods in Agrl. Rsch. (chmn. working group soil-plant relationships 1993). Avocation: sailing.

GESCH, CARL BERNARD, research charity director; b. Oxford, Eng., Oct. 6, 1958; s. Karl Dietrich and Magdalena Berta Elsa (Beer) G. Cert. of qualification in social work, Suffolk (Eng.) Coll., 1982. Criminal justice officer Social Svcs. Dept., Northampton, Eng., 1982-84; rsch. project dep. S. Cumbria Alternative Sentencing Options, Cumbria, Eng., 1984-86; project dir. South Cumbria Alternative Sentencing Options, Cumbria, 1986-91; dir. Natural Justice, Cumbria, 1991—; rsch. fellow U. Surrey, Guildford, Eng., 1996-2000, sr. rsch. fellow Sch. Biol. Scis., 2000—; assoc. lectr. Inst. Optimum Nutrition, London, 1996—; assoc. lectr. nutritional medicine U. Surrey, 1998—. Contbr. articles to profl. jours. Chmn. World Peace Found., TASHI, Ulverston Cumbria, 1995-96. U. Surrey fellow, 1996—; recipient New Century award The Barons 500. Mem. AAAS, N.Y. Acad. Sci. Buddhist. Avocations: walking, cycling, reading, music. Office: U Surrey, Dept Psychology, Guildford England

GETOVA-SPASSOVA, DAMIANKA PETEVA, pharmacology educator; b. Lovetch, Bulgaria, Feb. 25, 1950; d. Petyo and Paraskeva Petkova (LUkanova) Getov; m. Vassil Alexandrov Spassov, Aug. 9, 1987. MD, Med. U., Sofia, Bulgaria, 1977, degree in pharmacology, 1983; PhD in Pharmacology, Bulgarian Acad. Sci., Sofia, 1986. Physician Regional Hosp., Lovetch, 1978-79; rschr. Inst. Physiology Bulgarian Acad. Sci., Sofia, 1979-93; assoc. prof. dept. pharmacology Med. U., Plovdiv, Bulgaria, 1994—; assoc. prof. dept. pharmacology Med. U., Sofia, 1983-89. Author textbooks in field. Recipient 6th prize ECNP Congress, 1993; rsch. grantee Wellcome Trust, 1995, 96—. Mem. Internat. Brain Rsch. Orgn., Bulgarian Pharm. Soc., European Neuropeptide Club. Avocation: music. Home: Evlogi Georgiev Str 155, 1504 Sofia Bulgaria Office: Med U Dept Pharmacology, Vassil Aprilov Str 15A, 4002 Plovdiv Bulgaria

GETTLER, BENJAMIN, lawyer, manufacturing company executive; b. Louisville, Ky., Sept. 16, 1925; s. Herbert and Gertrude (Cohen) G.; m. Deliaan Angel, Mar. 1972; children: Jorian, Thomas, Gail, John, Benjamin. BA in Econs. with high honors, U. Cin., 1945; JD (Frankfurter scholar), Harvard U., 1948. Bar: Ohio 1949, U.S. Supreme Ct. 1955. Ptnr. Brown & Gettler, Cin., 1951-73, Gettler, Katz & Buckley, Cin., 1973-87, Gettler & Buckley, 1987—; chmn. bd. Am. Controlled Industries Inc., Cin., 1973-86; chmn. bd. dirs., pres. Colorpac Inc., Franklin, Ohio, 1973-86; chmn. bd., pres. Vulcan Internat. Corp., Wilmington, Del., 1988—, Vulcan Corp., Clarksville, Tenn., 1988—; chmn. exec. com. Valley Industries, Inc., Cin., 1973-86; vice chmn. bd. Cin. Southern R.R., 1987-91; chmn. bd. Trusthouse, Inc., Cin., 1987—; chmn. bd. dirs. ACI Internat., Inc., Cin., 1990—; spl. counsel U. Cin., 1975-77, trustee, 1994—, vice chmn. bd., 1999-2000, chmn., 2000—; bd. dirs. PNC Bank, Ohio, 1988-96. Chmn. bd. Jewish Inst. Nat. Security Affairs, 1994-98, chmn. policy com., 1998—; chmn. Cin. Bonds

for Israel, 1969; chmn. Nat. Israel Commn., Nat. Jewish Cmty. Rels. Adv. Coun., 1981-82; mem. Ohio, Ky. and Ind. Mass Transit Policy Com., 1970-75; pres. Cin. Jewish Cmty. Rels. Coun., 1978-80; trustee Jewish Hosp. Cin., 1978-92, chmn., 1991-92; trustee U. Cin., 1994—; chmn. Midwest Hosp. Sys., Inc., 1987-90, 92-93; pres. Jewish Found. Cin., 1995-99, chmn., 1999—; trustee Health Alliance Greater Cin., 1995-96, 2000—; chmn. Cin. Coalition for Reagan, 1980; co-chmn. Hamilton County Reagan Bush Campaign Ohio, 1984; chmn. Rep. Fin. Com., Hamilton County, 1991-92; mem. Hamilton County Rep. Policy Com., 1990—; trustee Rockwern Found., 1998—. Capt. U.S. Army, 1955-56. Mem. ABA, Cin. Bar Assn., Shoe Last Mfrs. Assn. (pres. 1984-85), Footwear Industries Am. (bd. dirs. 1989—), Phi Beta Kappa, Omicron Delta Kappa. Clubs: Coldstream Country, Harvard. Office: Vulcan Corp 30 Garfield Pl Ste 1040 Cincinnati OH 45202-4322

GETZ, MORTON ERNEST, medical facility director, gastroenterologist; b. Bklyn., May 22, 1930; s. Jacob Michael and Regina (Kohn) G.; m. Carol Washer, Aug. 12, 1956; children: Jacob Michael, Deborah Etta. AB, Emory U., 1950; MS, Purdue U., 1952; MD, Wake Forest U., 1956. Intern Jackson Meml. Hosp., Miami, Fla., 1956-57; resident in medicine Jackson Meml. Hosp., 1957-58; sr. surgeon NIH, Atlanta and Bethesda, Md., 1958-60; chief resident in medicine Jackson Meml. Hosp., 1960; NIH fellow in gastroenterology U. Miami, 1960-61; pvt. practice internal medicine and gastroenterology Coral Gables, Fla.; mem. courtesy staff South Miami Hosp., Bapt. Hosp., Drs. Hosp., Coral Gables Hosp., Larkin Comty. Hosp.; attending physician Cedars Med. Ctr. Contbr. articles to profl. jours. With USPHS, 1958-60. Mem. AMA, Am. Soc. Internal Medicine, Internat. Hospice Physicians, Am. Assn. Hospice and Palliative Medicine, Nat. Coun. Hospice Profls., Miami Fla. Gastroenterologic Soc., Dade County Soc. Internal Medicine, So. Med. Assn., Fla. Med. Assn., Dade County Med. Assn., Ind. Acad. Scis., N.C. Acad. Sci., Phi Rho Sigma. Democrat. Jewish. Avocations: art collecting, fishing. Office: Ste 300 14100 Palmetto Frontage Rd Miami Lakes FL 33016-1557

GEURTS, THEODORUS BERNARDUS, pharmaceutical executive; b. Cuijk, The Netherlands, Dec. 20, 1961; s. Wilhelmus Theodorus and Maria (Arntz) G. BSc, Hogeschool Gelderland, Nymegen, The Netherlands, 1983. Product specialist NV Organon, Oss, The Netherlands, 1985-91, internat. publ. mgr., 1994-98, internat. product mgr., 1998—; med. writer Organon Inc., West Orange, N.J., 1992-93; presenter in field. Author: Summary of Drug Interactions with Oral Contraceptives, 1993; contbr. articles to profl. jours. With Royal Dutch Army, 1984-85. Mem. Internat. Soc. for Studies in the Aging Male. Avocations: field hockey, cycling, mountaineering, reading, music. Office: NV Organon, PO Box 20, 5340 BH Oss The Netherlands

GEUS, ARMIN, biology educator, publisher; b. Staffelstein, Bavaria, Germany, Apr. 10, 1937; s. Ludwig and Elisabeth (Schmidt) G. D in Natural Sci., Friedrich-Alexander U., Erlangen, Germany, 1963. Asst. prof. U. Erlangen, 1963-70, U. Marburg, Germany, 1970-72; prof. U. Marburg, 1972—; pres. Gesellschaft zur Gründung und Förderung eines Museums für die Geschichte der Biologie e.V., 1982—; dir., founder Biohistoricum, Museum und Forschungsarchiv für die Geschichte der Biologie, Neuburg an der Donau, Germany. Author, editor, pub. numerous books and articles in field. Mem. Deutsche Gesellschaft für Geschichte und Theorie der Biologie (pres.). Home: Hirschberg 5, 35037 Marburg Germany Office: Philipps U Marburg, Bahnhofstr 7, 35037 Marburg Germany

GEVA, TAL, cardiology educator; b. Beer Sheba, Israel, July 8, 1956; s. Nimrod and Malka (Koren) Graiver; m. Judith Geva, Aug. 15, 1978; children: Alon, Omri. MD, Tel-Aviv (Israel) U., 1983. Asst. prof. Baylor Coll. Medicine, Houston, 1993-94; asst. prof. Harvard U., Boston, 1994-99, assoc. prof., 1999—; dir. cardiac MRI Children's Hosp., Boston, 1999—; N. Weiner Meml. lectr. N.Y. Acad. Medicine, 1998. Guest editor: Progress in Pediat. Cardiology, 2000; mem. editl. bd. Pediat. Cardiology, 1998—, guest editor, 2000. Lt. Israel Def. Svc., 1974-77. Fellow Am. Coll. Cardiology (assoc., Travel award 1992); mem. AHA, , Am. Soc. Echocardiography, N.Am. Soc. Cardiac Imaging, Mass. Med. Soc., Physicians for Human Rights.

GEVERS, ROLF DIETER, insurance executive; b. Tsumeb, Nambia, Jan. 14, 1963; arrived in South Africa; s. Rainer and Hildegard Beate (Buchholtz) G.; m. Marlene Van Der Spek, Dec. 8, 1990; children: Marelise, Rainer Dieter. Diploma police adminstrn. Commd. officer South African Police Svc., Pretoria, 1980, advanced through grades to capt., resigned, 1994; mem. CC Bateleur Assessors and Loss Adjusters, Pretoria, 1995—. Avocations: airplanes, woodworking. Home: Tooks Corner 7, Pierre Van Ryneveld Pk, Centurion South Africa

GEVGILILI, ALI, journalist, writer; b. Izmir, Turkey, Jan. 14, 1938; s. Halil and Munevver (Ege) G.; m. Emel Hurbas, Mar. 7, 1962; children: Elif, Asli, Halil. Degree in journalism, Istanbul U., 1960. Journalist Ege Ekspres, Izmir, 1954-55; editor Yeni Istanbul, 1955-56; editor, writer Vatan, Istanbul, 1956-62; econs. editor, columnist, editor-in-chief Milliyet, Istanbul, 1963-80; lectr. comms. Istanbul U., 1973—. Author: Ataturk's Foreign Policy, NATO and Turkey, 1968, The Growth of Capitalism and Social Classes in Turkey, 1973, 1971 Military Regime in Turkey, 1973, The Rise and Fall—A History of Multi-party Democracy in Turkey 1944-73, 1981, Films that Inquire Their Times, 1989, Modernisation of Turkey, Civic Society, Press and Ataturk, 1990, Discussions on Turkey with Idris Kucukomer, 1994. Mem. Internat. Journalists Fedn. (bd. dirs. 1973-74), Turkish Journalists Assn., Internat. Press Inst. Avocations: arts and cinema.

GEWEILY, SAID M.H., police officer; b. Cairo, Nov. 13, 1938; s. Mahmoud Hammad Geweily and Ahssan Mahmed Amaira; 2 daus. Grad. secondary sch., Cairo. Police officer Alexandria, Egypt, 1961-86, Cairo, 1986—. Club: El Trsana. Home: PO Box 2433 El Horria, Heliopohs, Cairo Arab Republic of Egypt

GEWERTZ, BRUCE LABE, surgeon, educator; b. Phila., Aug. 27, 1949; s. Milton and Shirley (Charen) G.; children: Samantha, Barton, Alexis; m. Diane Weiss, Aug. 31, 1997. BS, Pa. State U., State Coll., 1968; MD, Jefferson Med. Coll., Phila., 1972. Diplomate Am. Bd. Surgery. Surg. resident U. Mich., Ann Arbor, 1972-77; asst. prof. U. Tex., Dallas, 1977-81; assoc. prof. U. Chgo., 1981-87, prof. surgery, 1988—, faculty dean med. edn., 1989-92, Dallas Phemister prof., chmn. dept. surgery, 1992—; teaching scholar Am. Heart Assn., Dallas, 1980-83; pres. Assn. Surg. Edn., 1983-84. Author: Atlas of Vascular Surgery, 1989, Surgery of the Aerta and its Branches, 2000; editor Jour. Surg. Rsch., 1987—; patentee removable vascular filter. Recipient Jobst award Coller Surg. Soc., 1975, Coller award Mich. chpt. Am. Coll. Surgeons, 1975. Mem. Soc. Vascular Surgery, Midwestern Vascular Soc. (pres. 1993, 94-95), Soc. Clin. Surgery, Soc. Univ. Surgeons, Chgo. Surg. Soc. (treas. 1989-92), Am. Surg. Assn., Point O'Woods Club (Benton Harbor, Mich.). Office: U Chgo MC 5029 5841 S Maryland Ave Chicago IL 60637-1463

GEWIRTZMAN, GARRY BRUCE, dermatologist; b. Albany, N.Y., Mar. 26, 1947; s. Benjamin Joseph and Mary (Leibowitz) G.; m. Sheila Ellen Cuba, July 4, 1971; children: Beth Lauren, Aron Jeffrey. BA, Rutgers U., 1969; MD, Albany Med. Coll., 1973. Diplomate Am. Bd. Dermatology. Intern U. Miami (Fla.), 1973-74; resident in dermatology SUNY-Buffalo, 1974-77; practice medicine specializing in dermatology; attending staff Humana Hosp., Plantation (Fla.) Gen. Hosp.; pres. Arbet Enterprises Inc. Author: Smooth as a Baby's Bottom, Skin Care Tips and Skin Sense; contbr. articles to profl. jours. Fellow Am. Acad. Dermatology; mem. AMA, Fla. Med. Assn., Broward County Med. Assn., Fla. Soc. Dermatology, Soc. Dermatol. Genetics, Broward Bus. and Profl. Assn. (pres.), Broward County Dermatol. Soc. Office: Bennett Med Park 201 NW 82nd Ave Plantation FL 33324-7808

GEWITZ, MICHAEL HAROLD, pediatrician; b. Jan. 20, 1949; m. Judith Lipshutz, May 12, 1973; children: Emily, Andrew. BA, Yale U., 1970; MD, Hahnemann U., 1974. Intern Children's Hosp. Phila., Phila., 1974-75, resident, 1975-76; resident Hosp. Sick Children, London, England, 1976-77; fellow Yale New Haven Hosp., 1977-79; dir. noninvasive cardiology Children's Hosp. Phila., 1979-83; asst. prof. pediat. Sch. Medicine U. Pa., Phila., 1979-83; dir. dept. pediat., chief pediat. cardiology Children's Hosp. Westchester, Valhalla, N.Y., 1991—; prof., vice chair dept. pediat. N.Y. Med. Coll., Valhalla, N.Y., 1992—; mem. exec. com. Coun. on Cardiovasc. Disease in the Young, Am. Heart Assn. Editor: (book) Primary Pediatric Cardiology, 1995; assoc. editor: (journal) Heart Diseases, 1999—. Fellow Am. Acad. Pediatrics, Am. Coll. Cardiology, N.Y. Acad. Medicine; mem. Pediat. Acad. Soc.

GEX, NORBERT PAUL, export sales manager; b. New Rochelle, N.Y., May 18, 1960; s. Jean Paul and Marie Françoise (Bureau du Colombier) Gex. Maitrise Bus. Law, Sorbonne, Paris, 1985, Dess Econs., 1986; grad., Institut D'interpretation et Traduction, Paris, 1984. Sales engr. Soc. Gen. de Belgique, Paris, 1987-90; area sales mgr. Rhone Poulenc Systems, Noisy, France, 1990-93; supplies bus. mgr. Lexmark Europe, Orleans, France, 1993-95; export sales mgr. Lexmark Internat., Paris, 1996—. Lt., French Navy, 1984-85. Mem. Reserve Navy Officers Assn., ISIT Alumni Assn. (sec. gen. 1990-92). Avocations: canyoning, skiing. Home: 11 Ave Gambetta, 94160 Saint Mande France

GEYER, DENNIS LYNN, university administrator and registrar; b. Bay City, Mich., Feb. 17, 1950; s. Walter R. and Bettie Jane (Powers) G.; m. Karen Sue Bickel, Sept. 5, 1970; children: Sarah Denise, Zachary Dennis. Student, Northwestern Luth. Coll., 1967-68; BA, Mich. State U., 1971, MA, 1976. Tchr., coach Aurora (Colo.) Jr. High Sch., 1972-74; asst. to the registrar Lansing (Mich.) C.C., 1974-77; counselor Adams County Sch. Dist. # 14, Commerce City, Colo., 1977-78; registrar, asst. dir. student svcs. U. Colo. Health Sci. Ctr., Denver, 1978-88; univ. registrar, NCAA compliance officer, instnl. rsch. rep. Humboldt State U., Arcata, Calif., 1988-98; dir. admissions and records Humboldt State U., Arcata, 1996-98; univ. registrar SUNY, Stony Brook, 1998—. Co-author: A Guidebook for Student Services, 1977. Mem. Jaycees, Bay City, 1971-73; mem. Luth. Ch. of Arcata, pres., 1993-96, chair edn. com., 1990-93, mem. campus ministry bd., 1993-98, cochair pastoral search com., 1996-97; mem. Messiah Evang. Ch., campus ministry bd., 1999—; mem. Lord of Life Luth. Ch., sec., 1983-87, pres., 1987-88; mem. Promise Keepers, 1994-98; active Messiah Luth. Ch.; v.p. Ch. COun., Campus Min. Bd. Mem. Am. Assn. Collegiate Registrars and Admissions Officers (chair distance edn. com. 1999—), Nat. Collegiate Athletic Assn. (instn. compliance officer 1990-98, oversight com., student info. lead), Calif. Assn. Instl. Rsch., SUNY Registrar's Assn. Avocation: traveling. Home: 79 Quaker Path Stony Brook NY 11790-1334 Office: SUNY PO Box 584 Stony Brook NY 11790-0584

GEYER, GERD, paleontologist; b. Wlrzburg, Germany, Feb. 23, 1956; s. Otto and Elvira (Schipper) G.; m. Marion Kranitzer Geyer, Feb. 4, 1984; children: Florian, Stefan. Grantee Deutsche Forschungsgemeinschaft, Würzburg, Germany, 1984-85; asst. prof. U. Würzburg, Germany, 1985-90; Heisenberg fellowship Deutsche Forschungsgemeinschaft, Würzburg, Germany, 1990-96; rschr. U. Würzburg, Germany, 1996—, prof., 1998—; sec. Internat. Subcommission on Cambrian Stratigraphy, 1996-00; rsch. assoc. N.Y. State Mus., 1999—. Author: Geologie von Unterfranken und den angrenzenden Gebieten; contbr. articles to profl. jours. Mem. Päldontologische Gesellschaft, Paleontological Soc., Deutsche Stratigraphische Commn. Avocations: botany, stamps. E-mail address: palo001@rzbox.uniwuerzburg.de. Fax: 49-931-312504. Home: Madrider Ring 49, 97084 Wurzburg Germany Office: Inst of Paleontology, Pleicherwall 1, 97070 Wurzburg Germany

GEYSER, LYNNE M., lawyer, writer; b. Queens, N.Y., Mar. 28, 1938; d. Henry and Shirley Dannenberg; m. Lewis P. Geyser, 1956 (div. 1974); 1 child, Russell B. Geyser. BA, Queens Coll., 1960; JD, UCLA, 1968. Bar: Calif. 1969. Atty. Zagon, Schiff, Hirsch & Levine, Beverly Hills, Calif., 1969-70; atty., registered legis. advocate Beverly Hills, Malibu, Calif., 1973-75; atty. Freshman, Marantz, Comsky & Deutsch, Beverly Hills, Malibu, Calif., 1971-74; prof. law Glendale (Calif.) U. Law, 1974-76, U. Iowa Sch. Law, Iowa City, 1976-77, Pepperdine U., Malibu, 1977-78; pvt. practice Newport Beach, Calif., 1978-81, San Clemente, 1978—; part-time prof. law Western State Law Sch., Fullerton, Calif., 1978; cons. atty. The Irvine Co., Newport Beach, 1981-86, Std. Mgmt. Co., L.A., 1987-88; instr. Saddleback Coll., Mission Viejo, Calif., early 1990's; lectr., instr. Calif. Assn. Realtors Grad. Realty Inst., 1972-78, U. So. Calif. brokers tng. courses, L.A., 1978-80, UCLA real estate and corp. courses for paralegals, 1973-76; creator and lectr. course on disclosure for licensees, L.A., San Diego and Orange Counties, Calif., 1978-81; faculty advisor, rev. advisor Glendale U. Coll. Law, 1975-76. Chief articles editor UCLA Law Rev., 1967; adv. bd. The Rsch. Jour., 1976; contbr. poetry and short stories to jours. Mem. exec. bd. L.A. County Art Mus. Contemporary Art Coun., L.A., 1971-73; bd. trustees Westwood (L.A.) Art Assn., 1974; bd. govs. La Costa Beach Homeowners Assn., Malibu, 1975; pres. Dana Point (Calif.) Coastal Arts Coun., 1989-90; teaching participant Jr. Achievement, Newport Beach, 1985. Recipient 6 Am. Jurisprudence awards, 1966-68, 2 West Hornbook awards, 1967; nom. Douglas Law Clk. UCLA Law Sch., 1967. Fellow The Legal Inst.; mem. AALS (chair-elect environ. law sect. 1977), San Clemente Sunrise Rotary, Order of Coif. Avocations: world travel, fine arts, writing, computers, performing arts, graphics. Office: PO Box 4715 San Clemente CA 92674-4715

GHAFFAR, MOHAMMAD ASIF, food service executive; b. Karachi, Sind, Pakistan, Mar. 27, 1970; s. Shaikh Abdul and Shaikh Suriay (Idress) G. BComm, U. Karachi, 1991; BBA, Intercoll., Larnaca, Cyprus, 1994; MBA, Maastrict Sch. Mgmt., The Netherlands, 1996. Mgr. front office Arion Hotel, Larnaca, 1993-95; mgr. food and beverage Kition Hotel, Larnaca, 1996; restaurant mgr. MacDonald Corp. Pakistan, Karachi, 1997-98, supr. opers., 1999—. Avocations: cricket, football, swimming, gym activities. Home: C-18 Block 4A, Gulsham-I-Igbal, Karachi Sind, Pakistan Office: MacDonald's Pakistan, Lakson Sq Bldg 2 Sarwar Shaheed Rd, Karachi Sing, Pakistan

GHAFFAR, MUHAMMAD ABDUL, ambassador; b. Manamah, Bahrain, Jan. 15, 1949; married; 5 children. BA, Poona U., India, 1974; MA, New Sch. for Social Rsch., N.Y.C., 1981; PhD, SUNY, Binghamton, 1991. Tchr. Bahrain, 1967-69; polit. editor Sada al-Usbou, 1974; joined as attache Fgn. Ministry, 1975, 2d sec. liaison officer, 1975-76, sr. 1st sec. Econ. Directorate, 1984-86, sr. 1st sec. internat. affairs and internat. orgns., 1987-88, counsellor, sr. counsellor, 1988-90; 2nd sec. Bahraini Embassy, Amman, Jordan, 1977-78; 1st sec. Permanent Mission to UN, N.Y.C., 1979-84, permanent rep., 1990-94; amb. to U.S. Washington, 1994—; non-resident amb. to Can., 1996—, Argentina, 1998—. Office: Embassy of Bahrain 3502 International Dr NW Washington DC 20008-3035*

GHAFOOR, ABDUL, civil engineer; b. Mansehra, Pakistan, Feb. 10, 1928; s. Mohammad and Jannat (Nissa) Ismail, m. Tahera Ghafoor, Oct. 7, 1955; 1 child, Tariq Nadeem. Degree in Urdu lang. and lit. with honor, Punjab U., Lahore, Pakistan, 1948, BA, 1955; BSCE, Mil Coll. Engring., Risalpur, Pakistan, 1966; PhD in Civil Engring. with honors, LaSalle U., 1996. Lt. col. Pakistan Army, 1952-77; project engr. Punjab Govt., Lahore, 1977-79; dir. works, chief engr. Constrn. Co., Islamabad, Pakistan, 1979-81; gen. mgr., chief engr. Saudi Devel. Co., Jeddah, Saudi Arabia, 1981-82; chief resident engr. Cons. Engrs. Co., Islamabad, 1982-85; project dir. UK Cons. Engrs. Co., Riyadh, Saudi Arabia, 1985-87; dir. works Tarmac Constrn. Ltd., Islamabad, 1987-98; Constrn. Co., Islamabad; chief engr. Al Beruni Group for Edn., Islamabad, 1998—. Fellow Instn. Engrs.; mem. ASCE, Pakistan Engring. Coun. Home: House 36 St 5 F-8/3, Islamabad Pakistan Office: Tarmac Constrn Ltd, Block 18/1 Markaz F-7, Jinnah Super Islamabad Pakistan

GHAFOURIFAR, PEDRAM, pharmacologist; b. Tehran, Iran, Dec. 23, 1965; s. Ahmad and Sorour (Ghashghai) G.; m. Zahra Ramezani, Feb. 17, 1987; children: Parnian, Parham. PharmD, U. Tehran, 1990, PhD, 1995. Postdoctoral fellow Swiss Fed. Inst. of Tech., Zurich, Switzerland, 1996—; hon. rsch. fellow Wolfson Inst. for Biomed. Rsch., U. Coll. London, 1999-2000; prin. rsch. fellow Univ. Coll. London, 1999-2000; invited vis. scientist Dana-Farber Cancer Inst., Harvard Med. Sch., Boston, 1999-2000. Author: Methods in Enzymology, 1998, Endocytobiology, 1999, Mitocondrial Ubiquinone, 2000; contbr. articles to profl. jours. Recipient The New Century award of the Europe 500, 2000. Mem. AAAS, N.Y. Acad. Sci., Soc. Physiology and Pharmacology, Swiss Tissue Culture Soc., Iranian Pharm. Soc., Oxygen Soc., The Cell Death Soc., Nat. Orgn. for Outstanding Talents. Home: Bachlerstrasse 51, 8046 Zurich Switzerland Office: Swiss Fed Inst Tech, Universitatstr 16, 8092 Zurich Switzerland

GHAI, SURINDER KUMAR, publishing company executive; b. Jalandhar, Panjab, India, Aug. 18, 1945; s. Om Parkash and Vimla Ghai; m. Geeta Ghai, Apr. 16, 1968; children: Vikas, Gaurav. BA, Dayanand Ayuedic Coll., Jalandhar, 1965. Mng. dir. Sterling Pubs. (P) Ltd., New Delhi, India, 1965-92, chmn. and mng. dir., 1992—; Exec. mem. 2000 Chimmaya Mission, New Delhi. Co-editor: Afro Asian Publishing: Contemporary Trends, 1992; editor: Directory of Indian Publishers, 1995, 97, Keys to Success: Traits of Leadership, 1999, Optimum Output, 1999, Business Ethics, 1999, Organizational Ability, 1999, Aspiring to Excel, 1999, Attitudinal Behaviour, 1999, Professional Commitment, 1999. Mem. Asian Assn. Scholarly Pubs. (pres. 1992—), Fedn. Indian Pubs. (hon. gen. sec. 1994-96, exec. mem., v.p. 1998—, chmn. World Book Day 1999—), Internat. Assn. Scholarly Pubs. (regional rep. 1992—), Inst. Book Publishing (vice chmn.), Acad. Fine Art & Literature (dir. 1995—), Rotary Club Delhi Southend (pres. 1994-95, chmn. Delhi book fair 1997). Office: Sterling Publishers (P) Ltd, L-10 Green Park Ext, New Delhi 110016, India

GHAITH, HISHAM AHMAD, management professional, mechanical engineer; b. Beirut, Lebanon, May 24, 1965; s. Ahmad Souleiman and Ihtidal (Mezher) G. BSME, So. Meth. U., 1986, MSME, 1988. Mech. engr. Al Jaber Est, Abu Dhabi, 1989-91, engring. dir., 1993-97; dir. Italian Tech. Co. LLC, Abu Dhabi, 1997—. Mem. ASME, Soc. Automotive Engrs., Am. Soc. Profl. Engrs. Avocations: volleyball, car racing, shooting. Home: Main St, Niha El Shouf Lebanon

GHALI, ANWAR YOUSSEF, psychiatrist, educator; b. Cairo, May 30, 1944; came to U.S., 1974, naturalized, 1980; s. Youssef and Insaf Wahba (Soliman) G.; m. Violette Fouad Saleh, May 23, 1968; 1 child, Susie. MD, Cairo U., 1966, DPM, 1970, DM, 1971; MPA, NYU, 1999. Diplomate Am. Bd. Psychiatry and Neurology; cert. adminstrv. psychiatry. Registrar in psychiatry Woodilee Hosp., Glasgow, Scotland, 1973-74; resident in psychiatry N.J. Med. Sch., Newark, 1974-77, instr., 1977-78, clin. asst. prof., 1978-79, asst. prof., 1979-83, clin. assoc. prof., 1983—; chief Outpatient Dept.-Community Mental Health Ctr., N.J. Med. Sch., Newark, 1978-86; dir. Emergency Psychiat. Svcs. Univ. Hosp., U. Medicine and Dentistry of N.J., Newark, 1986-87; med. dir. Profl. Counsel Ctr., Westfield, N.J., 1984-87; med. chief ambulatory psychiat. svcs. Elizabeth (N.J.) Gen. Hosp., 1987-89; dir. psychiat. tng. VA Med. Ctr., East Orange, N.J., 1989—, asst. chief psychiatry, 1990-91, assoc. chief psychiatry, 1991—. Contbr. articles to profl. jours. Recipient Exceptional Merit award Coll. Medicine & Dentistry, Newark, 1981. Mem. AMA, Christian Med. Soc., Am. Psychiat. Assn., N.J. Psychiat. Assn., N.Y. Acad. Scis. Republican. Presbyterian. Home: 22 Benvenue Ave West Orange NJ 07052-3202

GHALY, EVONE SHEHATA, pharmaceutics and industrial pharmacy educator; b. Cairo; d. Shehata Ghaly Shenouda and Amalia Elias Tadros; m. Nagdy Roshdy Mehany; children: Maichel Nagdy Roshdy, Mary Nagdy Roshdy. B in Pharm. Scis., Assiut U., Egypt, 1970; M in Pharm. Sci., Cairo U., 1979, PhD of Pharmaceutics, 1984; postdoctoral fellow, Phila. Coll. Pharm., 1986-88. Specialist and pharmacist in R&D Arab Drug Co., Cairo, 1970-75, sr. pharmacist in R&D, mgr. rsch. devel., 1975-86; assoc. rschr. Phila. Coll. Pharm., 1988-89; vis. prof., asst. prof. Sch. Pharmacy U. P.R., San Juan, 1989-92, assoc. prof., 1992-97, prof., 1997—; cons. Smith Kline & Beecham, Inc., P.R., 1990—, Eli Lilly found., P.R., 1993—, Merck Sharp and Dohme Inc., P.R., 1994; instr., lectr. FDA, 1991, Warmer Lambert Inc., P.R., 1993-94, Ciba Geigy Inc., P.R., 1995. Contbr. articles to profl. jours. Grantee Colorcon Pharm. Inc., 1993-94, Baker Norton Pharm. Inc., 1993, INDUNIV Rsch. Ctr., 1990-92, 92-93, IBM, NIH-BRSG, 1991-92, Knoll AG Co., 1983, others. Mem. AAAS, Fed. Internat. Pharmaceutics, Am. Assn. Pharm. Scientists, Am. Pharm. Assn., Am. Assn. Coll. Pharmacy, Controlled Release and Bioactive Material, Sigma Xi, Rho Chi. Avocations: chess, piano, photography, sports, travel. Home: Condominio Puerta Sol 2000 San Juan PR 00926 Office: Univ PR Sch Pharmacy PO Box 5067 San Juan PR 00936-5067

GHAMBIR, RAMESH CHANDER, gynecologist; b. Campbellpur, Pakistan, Aug. 28, 1938; s. Gobind Ram and Savitri Devi (Kasturi) G.; m. Michele Renee Gintz, May 15, 1964; children: Christophe, Anne-Marie. BS, U. Delhi, India, 1959; MD, U. Heidelberg, Fed. Republic Germany, 1967; specialist diploma, U. Stuttgart, Fed. Republic of Germany, 1973; MD, U. Angers, France, 1975. Intern various hosps., Stuttgart, Cologne, Fed. Republic Germany, 1967-69; fgn. asst. Maternity of Port Royal, Paris, 1969-71; med. asst. Maternity of Margariten Hosp., Gmuhd, Fed. Republic Germany, 1972-74; med. officer Ob-Gyn dept. 2d Gen. U.S. Army Hosp., Landstuhl, Fed. Republic Germany, 1974-75; practice medicine specializing in ob-gyn. Laval, France, 1975—. Contbr. articles to profl. jours., various case studies. Mem. France-German Soc. Gynecology, German Soc. Ob-Gyn, French Soc. Gynecology, French Nat. Soc. Ob-Gyn, Bombay's Gynecol. and Obstet. Soc. Hindu. Avocations: jogging, reading, travel. Home: #19 Carrefour aux Toiles, 53000 Laval France Office: Cabinet Med, #20 Carrefour aux Toiles, 53000 Laval France

GHANASHEV, IVAN PETROV, physicist, educator, engineer; b. Sofia, Bulgaria, May 28, 1960; s. Peter and Hélène (Colmar) G.; m. Vania Petkova Georgieva, Dec. 24, 1988; children: Petko, Elena. MSc in Physics, Sofia U., 1986, PhD in Physics, 1992; DEng, Nagoya U., 1999. Rschr. Telecom. Inst., Sofia, 1988; asst. prof. physics Sofia U., 1989—, sr. asst. prof., 1992-94, main asst. prof. physics, 1994—; vis. rschr. Ruhr U., Bochum, Germany, 1994, Nagoya (Japan) U., 1995—. Contbr. articles to profl. jours. Recipient 1st prize Internat. Physics Olympiad, Moscow, 1979, 2d prize Nat. Physics Olympiad, Sofia, 1979, 1st prize Nat. Students Software Design contest Bulgarian Acad. Scis., 1981. Fellow Japan Soc. Promotion of Sci.; mem. IEEE, Microwave Theory and Techniques Soc., Nuclear and Plasma Sci. Soc., Japan Soc. Applied Physics, Am. Vacuum Soc., Am. Inst. Physics, Bulgarian Union of Physicists, Nat. Geog. Soc. Eastern Orthodox Ch. Avocations: foreign languages, motorcycles, piano, collecting maps. Office: Nagoya U Dept Elec Engring, Furo-cho Chikusa-ku, Nagoya 464-8603, Japan

GHANEM, JOSEPH DIB, mill executive; b. Bkassine, Lebanon, Mar. 23, 1943; s. Dib Sassine and Afifeh (Harfouche) G.; m. Fadia Michel Zabbal, June 6, 1975; children: Michele, Marc-Karl. BSc in Indsl. Engring., Loughborough (Eng.) U., 1967; BSc with honours, London U., 1967, grad. mgmt. course, 1969. Mgr. Tiger Mills Co., Beirut, 1969-73, CEO, 1973—; gen. mgr. Provimi M.E., Beirut, 1979-86; bd. dirs. J. Printing, Jordan, Provimi Jordan; cons. J.T.C., Jordan, 1984-89, Cicoda, France, 1984-89; legal and gen. couns., Lebanon, 1972-89,. Mem. S.O.S. Handicap, Lebanon, 1984. Fellow Brit. Inst. Engrs. Avocations: tennis, swimming, diving, volleyball. Office: TMC, PO Box 11-2278, Beirut Lebanon

GHANEM, SHIHAB MUHAMMAD ABDUH, engineering and economics educator; b. Oct. 1940; m. Jihad A. Lugman; children: Wiaam, Waddah, Wajd.; BSME, BSEE, U. Aberdeen, 1964; ME, U. Roorkee, 1975; PhD in Industrialization, Cardiff U., 1989. Chief engr. Eterno Supplies, Lebanon, 1972-74; plant mgr. Gulf Eternit Industries, Dubai, United Arab Emirates, 1974-85; dir. engring. Dubai Ports Authority, 1988—, Jebel Ali Free Zone Authority, 1988—; permanent dep. sec. Ministry of Pub. Works and Comms., 1966-72. Author: Industrialization in the United Arab Emirates, 1992, The Eternal Miracle and Other Articles, 1999. (collections of poems) Bayna Shatten Wa Akher, 1982, Nanwyat, 1982, Basamat Ala Al-Rimal, 1983, Shiwath Fil Atamah, 1986, Saheel Wa Tarteel, 1987, Hwa Al-Hob, 1991, Qabdan Ala Al-Jamr, 1993, Shades of Love, 1995, Pearls and Shells, 1996, Poetry from the Land of Sheba, 1999, The Eternal Miracle, 1999, Al-Zaman Al-Suriali, 1999, In the Valley of the Muses, 2000. Fellow Instn. Mech. Engrs. U.K. (chartered engr.), Inst. of Mgmt. of the U.K.; mem. United Arab Emirates Soc. (chief editor tech. mag.), Assn. of Yemeni Engrs. (sec.). Office: Dubai Port Authority, PO Box 17000, Dubai United Arab Emirates

GHANEM, SHOKRI, oil organization administrator; b. Tripoli, Libya, Oct. 9, 1942; s. Mohamed G. and Zohra El Majresi; m. Nagat Elhadi Ben Kura, Aug. 2, 1952; children: Mohamed, Ghada, Nahla, Aiya. BA in Econs., U.

Libya, Benghazi, 1963; MA in Econs., Fletcher Sch. Law & Diplomacy, Boston, 1972, MA in Law and Diplomacy, 1973, PhD in Internat. Econs., 1975. Dep. dir., dir. fgn. trade Ministry of Economy, Tripoli, Libya, 1963-68; dir. mktg., undersec., chief adv. Ministry of Petroleum, Tripoli, Libya, 1968-77; chief economist Arab Devel. Inst., Tripoli, Libya, 1977-88; prof. internat. econs. Al-Fateh U., Tripoli, Libya, 1988-93; dir. rsch. divsn. OPEC, Vienna, 1993—; academic visitor Sch. Oriental and African Studies U. London, 1982-84. Contbr. articles to profl. jours. Office: OPEC, Obere Donaustrasse 93, 1020 Vienna Austria

GHANNAM, ADEL NABIH, computer software company executive; b. Egypt, June 10, 1946; s. Mohamed Nabih G.; m. Enas Refaat, Sept. 8, 1978; children: Nihal, Cherif. BSc in Elec. Engring., Cairo U., 1966, MSc in Elec. Engring., 1970, PhD in Computer Sci., 1975. Rsch. engr. Nat. Rsch. ctr., Egypt, 1966-72, Italy, 1972-74; prin. researcher Nat. Rsch. ctr., Egypt, 1974-78; devel. mgr. Egypt br. Internat. Computers Ltd., 1978-81, tng. mgr., 1981-86, mktg. mgr., 1986-88; gen.mgr. Integrated Systems Group, Cairo, 1989—; tchr. computer sci., Cairo U., Ain Shams U., Cairo, 1975-79; cons. UN, Bagdad, Iraq, 1986-89, Enppi, Cairo, 1986-87. Contbr. tech. papers to profl. publs. Mem. IEEE, Computer Soc. Home: Gaza St 39, 12411 El-Mohandisin Cairo Egypt Office: Integrated Systems Group, PO Box 182, 12411 Cairo Egypt

GHANNAM, MAMDOUH TAHA, chemical engineering educator; b. Cairo, Dec. 2, 1957; arrived in United Arab Emirates, 1998; s. Taha Ghannam and Awatef Mohammed Ali Shehata; 1 child, Nourhan. BS, Cairo U., 1981, MS, 1985; PhD, U. Sask., Can., 1991. Asst. prof. Cairo U., 1991-93; postdoctoral rsch. engr. U. Sask., Saskatoon, Can., 1993-98; asst. prof. United Arab Emirates U., Ali-Ain, 1998—. Contbr. articles to profl. jours. Undergraduate scholar Cairo U., 1978-81; scholar No. Telecom Ltd., 1988-89, U. Sask., 1990-91. Mem. Egyptian Profl. Engrs. Assn. Avocations: squash, tennis, running, reading, music. Office: United Arab Emirates U, Chem & Petroleum Engr Dept, Al-Ain 17555, United Arab Emirates

GHANNOUCHI, MOHAMED, government official; b. Sousse, Tunisia, Aug. 18, 1941; m. Nehra Ayachi, Dec. 7, 1970; children: Mehdi, Salma. M Economy, U Tunis, Tunisia, 1966. Min. internat. cooperation fgn. investment Govt of Tunisia, Tunis, prime min. Mem. Ctrl. Com. R.C.D.,Tunisia. Avocations: chess, swimming. Office: Ministry Internat Cooperation, 149 Ave of Liberty, 1002 Tunis Tunisia also: Embassy of Tunisia 1515 Massachusetts Ave NW Washington DC 20005-1801 Address: Place du Gouvernement, La Kasbah, 1001 Tunis Tunisia*

GHAREEB, GHAREEB ABDEL-FATTAH, social sciences educator; b. Cairo, June 23, 1943; s. Abdel-Fattah Ghareeb Ahmed and Hayat Abrahim Hasanan; widower; children: Haytham, Hany, Basim, Heba. BA in Psychology, Ain-Shams U., Egypt, 1966; diploma in sociology, Cairo U., 1968, diploma in applied psychology, 1972; MS in Ednl. Psychology, Al-Azhar U., Egypt, 1976; PhD in counseling edn. & edn. rsch., Pitts. U., 1983. Psychologist, head dept. psychology Ministry Social Affairs, Egypt, 1966-73; asst. tchr. to assoc. prof. Coll. Edn., Al-Azhar U., Cairo, 1973-94, chmn. mental health, 1992—, prof., 1994—. Author: Criminal Psychology, 1987, Selected Topics in Social Psychology, 1993, Psychological Research in United Arab Emirates and Egypt, 1995, Mental Hygiene, 1999; presentor in field; contbr. articles to profl. jours. With Egypt Army, 1968-73. Mem. ACA, APA, Egyptian Assn. Psychol. Studies, Internat. Coun. Psychologists., Egyptian Assn. Mental Health, Egyptian Psychologists' Assn. Home: 9 Adnan El-Madany St, 12411 Giza Egypt Office: Coll Edn, Al Azhar U, Cairo Egypt

GHAREIB, MOHAMED, microbiologist, researcher; b. Mansura, Dakahlia, Egypt, Mar. 2, 1950; s. Ghareib I. Emaish and Momena Abdalla El-Nadi; m. Magda Hassan Sakr, Jan. 30, 1979; children: Nermine, Hani, Hesham. BS in Edn., Ain Shams U., Cairo, 1972, BS, 1975, MS, 1978, PhD, 1982. Ednl. diplomate. Demonstrator botany Ain Shams U., Cairo, 1972-78, asst. lectr. microbiology, 1978-82, lectr. microbiology, 1982-87, asst. prof. microbiology, 1987-93, prof. microbiology, 1993-96, chmn. botany dept. faculty edn., 1996-99, chmn. biol. and geol. scis. dept., 1999—; chmn. sci. dept. Tchrs. Tng. Coll., Muscat, Oman, 1987-89. Contbr. articles to profl. jours. Mem. Egyptian Botan. Soc., Egyptian Mycol. Soc. Muslim. Avocations: reading, swimming, table tennis. Office: Ain Shams U Faculty of Edn, Biology Dept, ROXY 11757 Cairo Egypt

GHASSEMLOOY, ZABIH, engineering educator; b. Tekab, Iran, Sept. 22, 1958; came to the U.K., 1975; s. Eskandar Ghassemlooy and Fatemeh Youseafzadeh. BSc with honors, Manchester (Eng.) Met. U., 1981; MSc, U. Manchester Inst. Sci. Engring., 1984, PhD, 1987. Sys. engr. Dobear Ltd., Manchester, 1981-82, Gaurdian Alarm, Manchester, 1982-83; demonstrator UMIST, Manchester, 1986-87; post-doctoral rschr. The City Univ., London, 1987-88; lectr. Sheffield (Eng.) Hallam U., 1988-96, reader, 1996-97, prof. comm. engring., 1997—. Editor: Analogue Optical Fibre Communications, 1995; guest editor IEE Procs. J9, 1994; editor First Internat. Workshop on Materials for Optoelectronics, 1995; editor Procs. 1st Internat. Symposium on Communication Systems and Digital Signal Processing v. 1 & 2, 1998. Mem. IEEE (transaction on consumer electronics reviewing com., sec. Internat. Symposium on Communication Systems, Networks and Digital Processing), IEE, Inst. Engring. (chartered engr.). Avocations: jazz music, walking, reading current affairs. Office: Sheffield Hallam U, Sch Engring Pond St, Sheffield S1 1WB, England

GHASSEMZADEH, HABIBOLLAH, psychologist, researcher; b. Shaut, Iran, 1944; s. Ghanbar Ghassemzadeh and Khanim Taghizadeh; m. Akram Khamseh, June 21, 1979; 1 child, Maral. BA, Tehran (Iran) U., 1968; MA, Vanderbilt U., 1972, PhD, 1976. Clin. psychologist Tehran U. Med. Scis., 1976—, head Ctr. Clin. Psychology, 1997—; mem. com. libr. Tehran U., 1990-97, sec. com. rsch., 1997-99, dir. clinic, 1998—. Author: Behavior Therapy, 1985, Metaphor and Cognition, 2000; translator: Languate 78 Thought, 1990; editor Baztab, 1979-81; contbr articles and papers to jours. Avocations: stamp collecting, reading poetry or philosophical works. Home: Phelestin, Helali Ave #29 13167, 96311 Tehran Iran Office: Roozbeh Hosp, Kargar Ave, 13185 Tehran Iran

GHATALIA, KIM SHAH, management consultant; b. Ridley Park, Pa., May 16, 1968; arrived in Hong Kong, 1995; d. Dinesh S. and Hansa D. Shah; m. Rajiv Arvind Ghatalia, Nov. 23, 1995. BA in Psychology, BS in Fin., U. Pa., 1990; MBA, Harvard U., 1995. Loan officer Sumitomo Trust and Banking, N.Y.C., 1990-93; analyst PepsiCo, Purchase, N.Y., 1993; assoc. Mercer Consulting, N.Y.C., 1994; mgr. AT Kearney, Hong Kong, 1995—. Mem. Harvard Bus. Sch. Alumni Club (sec.), Psi Chi. Avocations: traveling, reading, tennis. E-mail: kshah@mab1995. Fax: 85225301545. Office: AT Kearney, 88 Queensway Level 31, Admiralty Hong Kong

GHAURI, PERVEZ NASIM, finance educator, consultant; b. Lahore, Pakistan, Mar. 19, 1948; arrived in Sweden, 1975; s. Nasim Mahmood and Iftikhar Khanum G.; m. Tyaba Sadiqa Salahuddin, April 29, 1987; 1 child, Saad Pervez. B in Commerce (hons), U. Punjab, Lahore, Pakistan, 1968; M in Bus., Uppsala U., Sweden, 1976, cert. in internat. rels., 1977, PhD in Mktg. and Internat. Bus., 1983. With head office United Bank Ltd., Karachi, Pakistan, 1969-72; br. mgr. United Bank Ltd., Gujranwala, Pakistan, 1972-75; coord. undergrad. studies final yr. courses dept. bus. study Uppsala U., 1979-80, coord. grad. studies dept. bus. studies, 1980-81, asst. prof. bus. studies dept. bus. studies, 1981-83, elected mem. bd. higher edn. postgrad. studies, 1981-83, assoc. prof. mktg. and internat. bus. dept. bus. studies, 1984-89; dean acad. affairs Oslo Bus. Sch., 1989-93; prof. mktg. Norwegian Sch. Mgmt., Oslo, 1992-93; prof. bus. to bus. mktg. faculty econs. and bus. adminstrn. Maastricht U., The Netherlands, 1991-95; prof. mktg. and internat. bus. faculty mgmt. and orgn. U. Groningen, The Netherlands, 1993—, dean acad. affairs faculty mgmt. and orgn., 1997—, dir. internat. bus. program faculty mgmt. and orgn., 1994—; vis. lectr. exec. edn. program mktg. for engrs. dept. bus. adminstrn. U. Aarhus, Denmark, 1985; vis. prof. internat. bus. Copenhagen Bus. Sch., 1995, 96; vis. prof. Heinrich Heine U., Düsseldorf, Germany, 1994, 97, 98, Robert Schuman U., Strasbourg, France, 1994, 97; vis. prof. Copenhagen Internat. Mgmt. Inst., 1993-95, acad. advisor for curriculum devel. in mktg. and internat. bus., 1993-95; vis. prof. for curriculum and faculty devel. for MBA program Lahore Grad. Sch. Bus. Lahore U. Mgmt. Scis., 1986; coord. for eastern Europe Oslo Bus. Sch., 1991-93; acad. advisor for curriculum devel. in internat. bus. Open U., Milton Keynes, England, 1994-96; bd. dirs. Clear Water Holding AS, Oslo and Edinburgh; cons. to attract fgn. investment Netherlands Fgn. Investment Agy. Min. Econ. Affairs, 1994; cons. for curriculum devel. and tchrs. tng. EUROSAS, Blagnac, France, 1992-94; cons. Internat. Trade Ctr., Geneva, 1989—; mem. indsl. mktg. and purchasing group Dept. Bus. Studies Uppsala U., 1978—, and numerous others. Author: International Business Negotiations, 1996, International Marketing, 1999; editor: (book) International ization of the Firm, 1994, 99, (jours.) Internat. Bus. Rev. Jour.; mem. editl. bd. Jour. Euromarketing, Jour. Market Focused Mgmt., Jour. Tchg. Internat. Bus., Jour. Internat. Consumer Mktg., Advances in Internat. Mktg., European Jour. Mktg.; editor in chief Internat. Bus. and Mgmt., 1996—; founding editor: Internat. Bus. Rev.; contbr. articles to profl. jours., chpts. to books. Mem. European internat. Bus. Assn., Acad. Internat. Bus., European Mktg. Acad., Am. Mktg. Assn. (bd. dirs. steering com. for global mktg.), Acad. Mktg. Sci. (country rep.), European Found. Mgmt. Devel., European Network for Project Mktg. and Sys. Selling. Avocations: traveling, golf, gardening. Fax: 31-50 363 2174. E-mail: p.n.ghauri@bdk.rug.nl. Address: Ruitersteeg 14, 9752 VB Haren-Groningen The Netherlands Office: U Groningen, Landleven 5, 9700 AV Groningen The Netherlands

GHAZAL, MICHEL, process negotiation consultant, mediator; b. Beirut, Sept. 1, 1950; arrived in France, 1973; s. Joseph and Mathilde (Abu-Mrad) G.; m. Danielle Rossi, Dec. 28, 1982; children: Laura, Remy. BA, U. Lebanon, 1973; DBA, U. Paris IX, 1981. Dir. mktg. studies Inst. de Developpement de Entreprises, Paris, 1974-77; cons. Orgatec, Paris, 1977-80; dir., founder Ctr. Europeen de la Negociation, Paris, 1980—; pres. Dialogue Mediation, Mediateurs Sans Frontières. Author: Mange Ta Soupe et Tais Toi!, 1992; editor: D'une Bonne Relation a une Negociation Reussie, 1991, Negocier avec les Gens Difficiles, 1993; contbr. articles to profl. jours.; co-author: Circuley Y A Rien A...Negocier!. Avocations: tennis, skiing, writing. Home: 60 Av de la Bourdonnais, 75007 Paris France Office: Ctr Européen Negociation, 77 Ave des Champs-Elysees, 75008 Paris France

GHAZAL, SAMIR SAADUDDIN, human resources professional; b. Tripoli, Lebanon, Mar. 21, 1952; s. Saaduddin Mohammed Ghazal and Monawar Khaleel Taleb; m. Hajr Buckley, June 5, 1972; Khalid, Ahmed, Nadia, Sara, Fatima. AA, Miami Dade C.C., 1979; postgrad., Fla. Internat. U., 1980. Adminstr. Ghazal Workshops, Dammam, Saudi Arabia, 1973-77; mgr. Ghazal Enterprises, Dammam, 1981-84; advisor Saudi Yanbu Petrochem. Co., Yanbu, Saudi Arabia, 1984-86; indsl. rels. mgr. Saudi Aramco Mobil Refinery Co., Yanbu, 1986—. Author: Indigenous Manpower in the Private Sector of the Arabian Peninsula, 1997. Mem. Arabian Soc. Human Resources Mgmt., Am. Mgmt. Assn. Avocations: fishing, swimming, reading, writing, traveling. Office: Saudi Aramco Mobil Refinery, PO Box 30078, Yanbu Al Sinaiyah Saudi Arabia

GHEBREBRHAN, OGUBAZGHI M., geophysicist; b. Aykebetsu, Eritrea, Oct. 26, 1942; s. Medhanie M. Ogubazghi and Mengistu T. Abrhet; m. Hadgu A. Abeba, Sept. 16, 1973; children: Bereket, Medhanie, Asmayt, Selamawit. BS, Addis Ababa U., 1977; MS, U. Nice, 1982; PhD, U. Toulon, 1987. Rsch. asst. U. Addis Ababa, Ethiopia, 1977-87, asst. prof., 1987-89, assoc. prof., 1989-92; dir. Inst. R&D U., Asmara, Eritrea, 1992-94; dean coll. sci. U. Asmara, 1994—. Editor: Ethiopian Jour. Sci., 1987-90, editor-in-chief, 1990-92. Mem. Internat. Ctr. Theoretical Physics, Eritrean Tech. Profl. Assn. (bd. dirs. 1993—), Am. Phys. Soc. Achievements include development of method for full decoding of truncated ranges in meteorological radars; research in optimizing performances of meteorological radars. Home: PO Box 5604, Asmara Eritrea Office: U Asmara, PO Box 1220, Asmara Eritrea

GHEBREHIWET, BERHANE, immunologist, educator; b. Asmara, Eritrea, Sept. 28, 1946. D.V.M., Sch. Vet. Medicine, Warsaw, Poland, 1971; MVSc, Ecole Nationale Vétérinaire D'Alfort, France, 1973; DSc, U. Paris VII, 1974. Rsch. assoc. dept. molecular immunology Scripps Clinic and Rsch. Found., La Jolla, Calif., 1974-79; asst. prof. medicine SUNY, Stony Brook, 1979-85, asst. prof. pathology, 1983-85, assoc. prof. medicine and pathology, 1985-92, prof. medicine and pathology, 1992—; vis. scientist Green Coll., U. Oxford, 1991-92, 95; mem. immunology, virology, pathology study sect. NIH, 1992-96. Contbr. articles to profl. jours. Fogarty Internat. sr. fellow MRC immunochemistry unit U. Oxford, Eng., 1991-92, Burroughs Wellcome Rsch. fellow, 1995. Mem. Am. Assn. Immunology, Am. Fedn. Clin. Rsch., N.Y. Acad. Sci., Am. Chem. Soc., Am. Assn. Vet. Immunology, Clin. Immunology Soc., Soc. Leukocyte Biology, The Planetary Soc., Sigma Xi. Coptic Orthodox. Office: SUNY Stony Brook HSC T-16 Rm 040 New York NY 11794-8161

GHELMEZ, MIHAELA DIMITRU, physics educator, lecturer; b. Giurgiu, Romania, July 21, 1952; d. Anghel Tudor and Alice-Jeni Tânase (Tânăsescu) Ghelmez; m. Gabriel-Marius Alexandru Dumitru, July 23, 1977; 1 child, Bogdan. PhD in Lasers Physics, Atomic Inst. Physics, Bucharest, Romania, 1990. Diplomate physicist. Prof. Lyceum, Bucharest, 1976-80; univ. asst. Politehnica U., Bucharest, 1980-90, univ. lectr., 1990—; form master Lyceum, 1976-80; lab. responsible Politehnica U., 1980; optoelectronics jour. referee Optoelectronics Inst., Bucharest, 1994—. Author: (textbook) Lasers Physics and Applications, 1993; (booklet and slides) New Discoveries in Physics - Academy of Theatre and Film - Romania, 1993; (proceedings) Flexible Learning in Physics, 1994; contbr. articles to profl. jours. Mem. Internat. Soc. for Optical Engring., European Phys. Soc., European Soc. for Formation Engrs. (working group in physics). Romanian Phys. Soc., Romanian Soc. Optoelectronics. Avocations: writing, painting, computer graphics, Internet resources user. Home: Str Vlădeasa 11, Bucharest Romania Office: Politehnica U Physics Dept, Splaiul Indepentei 313, Bucharest 77206 1, Romania

GHELMEZ, MIHAELA (DUMITRU), physics educator; b. Giurgiu, Romania; d. Anghel and Alice-Jeni (Tanase) Ghelmez; divorced; 1 child, Bogdan. Degree in Physics, Craiova U., Romania, 1976; PhD in Laser Physics, Atomic Physics Inst., Bucharest, Romania, 1990. Cert. physicist. Tchr., master secondary schs., Bucharest, Romania, 1976-80; asst. Politehnica U., Bucharest, Romania, 1980-90, lectr. physics, 1990-98, sr. lectr. and reader physics, 1998—; lab. head Politehnica U., Bucharest, 1980. Author: Lasers Physics and Applications, 1993, Nonlinear Optics, 1998, Optical Bistable Systems, 1999; editor proceedings; contbr. numerous articles, proceedings to profl. jours. Recipient Gold Record of Achievement award ABI Inst., 1997, Gold medal of year 2000, 1997; rsch. grantee Swedish Inst., Stockholm, 1995, 2 month individual mobility grantee TEMPUS Phare, Romania, 1996, 3 month mobility grantee TEMPUS, Stockholm, 1996. Mem. Internat. Soc. for Optical Engring. (free membership award), Women in Optics Working Group, European Physics Soc., European Soc. for Formation Engrs., Romanian Physics Soc. Avocations: writing, painting, computer graphics, internet. E-mail: dem@physics2.physics.pub.ro. Home: Vladeasa 11, Bucharest Romania Office: Politehnica U Physics Dept, Splaiul Independentei 313, 77 206 Bucharest Romania

GHERMAN, IONEL, general and vascular surgeon, educator; b. Cluj-Napoca, romania, Feb. 13, 1950; s. Ioan and Elisabeta Gherman; m. Madeleine Nica Negrut, June 25, 1977; 1 child, Rares Ioan. MD, Cluj U., 1975, PhD in Surgery, 1992. Resident in gen. surgery 2d Surg. Clinic, Cluj-Napoca, 1980-83; asst. Faculty of Medicine, Cluj-Napoca, 1980-92; sr. surgeon in gen. surgery 2d Surg. Clinic, Cluj-Napoca, 1990—, sr. surgeon in vascular surgery, 1991—; asst. prof. U. Medicine and Pharmacy, Cluj-Napoca, 1993; assoc. prof. Faculty of Medicine, Cluj-Napoca, 1994—. Author: Das Polytrauma, 1993, others; contbr. articles to profl. jours. Mem. Romanian Soc. Angiology and Vascular Surgery (gen. sec. 1990—), Balkan Soc. Angiology and Vascular Surgery (treas. 1992), Romanian Surg. Assn., Internat. Union Angiology, N.Y. Acad. Scis. Home: Andrei Muresanu 33, 3400 Napoca Romania Office: 2d Surg Clinic, Clinicilor Str 4-5, 3400 Napoca Romania

GHETTI, ROBERTA, physicist, educator; b. Alfonsine, Italy, May 19, 1964; arrived in Sweden, 1990; d. Merano and Lucia (Boldrin) G.; m. Johan Peter Ulf Helgesson, June 26, 1994. Degree in physics, U. Bologna, Italy, 1990; Lic. of Physics, U. Lund, Sweden, 1993, PhD in Physics, 1997. H.s. tchr. Lugo, Italy, 1993-94; vis. scholar Lawrence Berkeley (Calif.) Nat. Lab., 1994-95, European Ctr. for Theoretical Studies in Nuclear Physics, Trento, Italy, 1997; postdoctoral fellow U. Bari, Italy, 1998, U. Lund, 1998—. Avocations: travel, cooking. Office: U Lund Dept Physics, Box 118, 221 00 Lund Sweden

GHIACY, SABOUR, radiologist; b. Kabul, Afghanistan, Aug. 14, 1952; s. Raouf and Fatima Zahra (Dastagir) G.; m. Lynne Teresa Goodall, June 13, 1987 (div.); children: Alexandra, Andrew. MBBS, Bangalore Med. Coll., 1978; MBA, Henley Mgmt. Coll., Eng.; DBA, Open U., Milton Keynes, Eng. Diplomate in medicine. Sr. house officer in gen. surgery Torbay (Eng.) Hosp., 1981-82; registrar in radiology Plymouth (Eng.) Gen. Hosp., 1982-85; sr. registrar in radiology North Manchester (Eng.) Gen. Hosp., 1985-86, Hope Hosp., Salford, Eng., 1986-87, Manchester Royal Infirmary, 1987-88; cons. radiologist Cmty. Health NHS Trust, Berkshire, Eng., 1988—; head dept. back pain svc. King Edward VII Hosp., Windsor, Eng., 1996—, head dept. radiology, 1995—; head dept. radiology Upton Hosp., Slough,Eng., 1995—. Contbr. articles to profl. jours. Am. Field Svcs. scholar, 1969-70; Indian Coun. for Cultural Rels. scholar, 1971-78. Fellow Royal Coll. Surgeons Edinburgh, Royal Coll. Radiologists. Avocations: travel, history. Office: Kin Edward VII Hosp/Radiol, Frances Rd, Windsor Berkshire, England

GHINEA DUMITRO, LUCIAN, microbiologist; b. Malovat, Mehedinti, Romania, June 22, 1936; s. Dumitru and Virginia (Stuparu) G.; m. Elena Bleoanca, Mar. 3, 1959; children: Tugulea, Anca-Maria. Degree in biology, U. Biol. Faculty, Bucharest, Romania, 1958, PhD, 1966. From rschr. to sr rschr. 3rd class Rsch. Inst. for Cereals & Indsl. Crops., Fundulea, Romania, 1960-90, sr. rschr. 1st class, chief lab., 1990-97; prof. Ecological U., Bucharest, 1990-93, U. of Agrl. and Vet. Scis. of the Banat, Timisoara, Romania, 1993—; pres. Sci. Acad. for Commn. for Pesticides Agrl. & Registration, 1996-2000; counciller Min. of Sci. & Tech., Bucharest, 1997. Author: Soil Microbiology, 1975; contbr. articles to profl. jours. Active Interministerial Commn. for Pesticies, Bucharest, 1993-2000; com. for food security Romanian Acad. for Medicine, Bucharest, 1990-97. Mem. Romanian Acad. for Agrl. and Forestry (dep. 1993-97), Romanian Soc. for Herbology (v.p. 1990-2000), European Weed Rsch. Soc., Soil Sci. Soc. Home: Soseaua Cotroceni #27 Apt 1, Bucharest Romania Office: Rsch Inst for Cereals Indsl, 8264 Distr, Calarasi Fundulea Romania

GHITA, RODICA, engineer-physicist, researcher; b. Bucharest, Romania, Sept. 9, 1957; d. Virgil and Maria (Gramada) Dima; m. Petre Ghita. M in Physics, Faculty of Physics, Bucharest, 1981; Dr in Physics, Inst. Atomic Physics, Bucharest, 1999. Scientist Nat. Inst. for Material Rsch. in Physics, 1987-90; sr. scientist Nat. Inst. for Material Physics, 1990—; cons. Romanian Soc. Optoelectronics, Bucharest, 1992. Contbr. articles to profl. jours. Fellow Romanian Soc. Physics. Orthodox Christian. Avocation: clothes design. Office: Nat Inst Materials Physics, PO Box MG7, Bucharest Romania

GHIZAWI, NIDAL AWNI, aerospace engineer, researcher; b. Jenin Camp, West Bank, Palestine, Sept. 25, 1968; came to U.S., 1993; s. Awni Abdel-Kareem and Aysheh Eisa Ghizawi; m. Aidah Khaled Elokour, Feb. 15, 1998. BSc in Mech. Engring., U. Baghdad, Iraq, 1990; MSc in Mech. Engring., U. Jordan, Amman, 1992; PhD in Aerospace Engring., U. Cin., 1997. Rsch. asst. U. Cin., Ohio, 1994-97; aerodynamicist Garrett Engine Booshing Systems-Honeywell, Torrance, Calif., 1997—. Contbr. to profl. jours. Recipient R.T. Davis award for excellence in computational sci. and engring., 1997. Mem. AIAA. Avocations: reading science fiction stories, solving puzzles, soccer, volleyball. Office: Garrett Engine Booshing Systems Honeywell 3201 Lomita Blvd Torrance CA 90505-5015

GHOHESTANI, REZA F., immunologist, dermatologist; b. Tehran, Iran, 1967; s. A. A. Ghohestani and S. B. Amirsalam. MD, Shiraz U., Iran, 1993; MS in Immunology, Claude Bernard U., Lyon, France, 1994; PhD, Claude Bernard U., 1998; MS in Cutaneous Biology, Paris VII, 1996. Fellow, resident E. Herriot Hosp., Lyon, 1993-96, resident, 1995-96, asst. prof., 1996-98; fellow Thomas Jefferson U., Phila., 1997; prof. Jefferson Med. Coll., Thomas Jefferson U., 1998—; rschr. Inserm, Lyon, 1996-98. Contbr. articles to profl. jours. Recipient Rene Touraine award St. Louis Hosp., Paris, 1996, Soc. Rsch. Dermatology award, 1996, Leo prize Journee Dermatology, Paris, 1996, Found. France award, Paris, 1997, Rsch. award European Acad. Dermatology, Dublin, 1997, Kharazmi Internat., Tehran, 1998, Albert Kligman award, Chgo., 1999. Mem. Am. Assn. Immunologists, N.Y. Acad. Scis., European Soc. Dermatol. Rsch., Soc. Cutaneous Ultra Structural Rsch., Soc. Rsch. Dermatol., Soc. France Dermatology (immunodermatology), Soc. France Immunology. Office: Thomas Jefferson U Jefferson Med Coll Dept Dermatology & Cutaneous Biology 233 S 10th St # 450 Philadelphia PA 19107-5541

GHOJEL, JAMIL IBRAHIM, mechanical engineering educator, researcher; b. Kuneitra, Syria, Mar. 19, 1944; arrived in Australia, 1988; s. Ibrahim Hajmet and Zeineb (Samkough) G.; m. Alia Kachaeva, June 20, 1976; 1 child, Alan. BSc in Mech. Engring., Leeds (Eng.) U., 1968; PhD in Mech. Engring., Moscow Automotive & Road Engring. Inst., Russia, 1974. Chartered profl. engr. Mech. engr. Petroleum Transp. Co., Homs, Rmeilan, Syria, 1968-69; asst. prof. U. Damascus, Syria, 1975-80; assoc. prof. U. Damascus, 1981-86; rsch. engr. CFR, Inc., Ann Arbor, Mich., 1986-87; rsch. fellow U. Melbourne, Australia, 1988-89; sr. lectr. U. Melbourne, 1989-94, Monash U., 1995—; cons. Kassioun Constrn. Co., Damascus, 1983-86; Russian-English tech. translator Hemisphere Pub. Corp., N.Y.C., 1986-88, ASME, N.Y.C., 1987-88. Author: (textbook) Internal Compustion Engines, 1981 plus 12 tech. books in mech. engring. translated from Russian into English; contbr. articles to profl. jours. and internat. confs. Recipient Undergrad. scholarship Syrian Govt., Eng., 1963-68, Postgrad. scholarship, Syrian Govt., Russia, 1969-74, Fulbright scholarship USA Govt., Mich., 1981-82. Mem. ASME, Instn. Engrs. Australia (corp. mem., mentor). Avocations: reading, gardening, tennis, cooking. Office: Monash U Caulfield Campus Mech Engring, 900 Dandenong Rd, Caulfield East VIC 3145, Australia

GHOMASHCHI, REZA, materials scientist; b. Rasht, Gilan, Iran, Nov. 20, 1955; s. Rahim Ghomashchi and Monavar Shekarian; m. Gisso Mirzadeh, Feb. 18, 1994; children: Mazdak, Kimia. B Engring. in Metallurgy, U. Sci. and Tech., Tehran, Iran, 1978; MPhil in Materials Engring., Cambridge (Eng.) U., 1979; PhD in Metallurgy, Sheffield (Eng.) U., 1983. Quality control engr. Iran-Abzar, Tehran, 1977-78; rsch. metallurgist GKN, Wolverhampton, Eng., 1979; sr. rsch. fellow U. Southampton, Eng., 1983-86, U. Bradford, Eng., 1987-88; materials scientist BHP Steels, Whyalla, Australia, 1988-90; sr. lectr. U. South Australia, Adelaide, Australia, 1990—; vis. prof. MIT, Cambridge, Mass., 1994; cons. UNDP, Tehran, 1995. Contbr. numerous articles to profl. pubs. Grantee Australian Rsch. Coun., BHP Steel, 1990, 91, U. South Australia, 1992, 97, Govt. Rsch. Insts., others. Achievements include research in cleanliness of steel, ingot and continuous casting, application of novel coatings productd by PVD, solidification, powder metallurgy, composites, metal and intermetallic matrix. Office: U South Australia, The Levels, Adelaide SA 5095, Australia

GHONIEM, NIHAD AHMED METWALLY, microbiology educator, consultant; b. Cairo, Jan. 5, 1932; s. Ahmed Metwally and Wahiba Omar (Osman) G.; m. Hanifa Mourst Sayed-Alj, Mar. 7, 1957 (div. Sept. 1998); children: Nancy, Nesrin. B Vet. Sci. and Surgery, Cairo U., Giza, Egypt, 1954, M in Microbiology, 1957, PhD in Bacteriology, 1963; PhD in Microbiology, Faculty Vet. Medicine, Hanover, Germany, 1965. Vet. officer microbiology dept. Mil. Vet. Lab. Svc., 1954-63; dir. Mil. Vet. Labs., 1963-69; prof. microbiology faculty vet. medicine Zagazig (Egypt) U., 1969-74, dean faculty, head microbiology, path. & parasitology depts., 1974-76, prof. microbiology, faculty vet. medicine, 1984-88; expert FAO, 1976-81, 81-83, 1988-94; hygiene cons. Isis Tourist Co. for Nile Cruises, 1995—. Col. Egyptian mil., 1955-69. Mem. Am. Soc. Microbiology, Egptian Soc. Microbiology, Egyptian Vet. Syndicate. Avocations: tennis, volleyball, billiards, baggamon, cards, chess. Home: 10 El-Biblawy St, Giza 12111, Egypt

GHORAYEB, FAY ELIZABETH, nurse educator; b. Sydney, Australia, 1936; d. Claude Ernest and Doris Venezia (Shannon) Seabrook; m. Ibrahim Anis Ghorayeb, July 20; children: Anthony, Mark. RN, Royal Prince Alfred Hosp., Sydney, 1959; Postgrad. Diploma, St. Luke's Hosp., N.Y.C.,

1961; BA, Rutgers U., 1992. Jr. sister and sr. sister Royal Prince Alfred Hosp., Sydney, 1959-60; vis. nurse Vis. Nurse Assn., N.Y.C., 1960-61; pub. health instr. Beirut Coll. for Women, Lebanon, 1967-71, instr. sport and pub. health, 1974-75; coord. Women's Wellness Ctr. U. Medicine and Dentistry N.J., New Brunswick, 1991-98. Mem. Theatre Guild, Naples Comty. Hosp. Aux. Mem. Douglass Alumni Club, PEO, Naples Women's Club (bd. dirs.), Internat. Club. Mem. Ch. England. Avocations: travel, walking, swimming, reading, family, cooking. Home: 137 2d Ave N Naples FL 34102

GHOSH, ASOKE KUMAR, publisher; b. Calcutta, W. Bengal, India, Oct. 31, 1942; s. Bhupendra Krishna and Suniti G.; m. Sagarika Chowdhury, Mar. 6, 1972; 1 child, Pushpita. Degree in printing tech., Jadavpur U., Calcutta, 1959; BA, Calcutta U., India, 1961; postgrad. diploma in Mktgl, Mgmt., Delhi (India) U., 1971. Supr. Times of India, New Delhi, India, 1961-65; prodn. mgr. Prentice Hall of India, New Delhi, 1965, dep. mng. dir., 1971-72, mng. dir., 1972-78, chmn. and mng. dir., 1978—. Mem. Indian Soc. Mass Comm. (exec. com.), Nat. Book Devel. Coun. of India, Fedn. of Indian Publishers (pres., Gold medal 1988, Most Disting. Publisher 1996), Internat. Publishers Assn. (mem. exec. com., v.p. 2000, Decorated for Outstanding Leadership and Freedom to Publish), Book Export Promotion Coun. (chmn.) India Internat. Ctr., Rotary (dist. gov. 2000—). Avocations: literacy campaign, environ. protection. E-mail: akghosh@giasdl01.vsnl.net.in. Home: 8/10 Kalkaji Extension, New Delhi 110 001, India Office: Prentice-Hall India Pvt Ltd, M-97 Connaught Circus, New Delhi 110 001, India

GHOSH, BIMAL, international consultant economic development; b. Barisal, India; settled in Switzerland, 1979; s. Akshoy Kumar and Nalinibala (Bose) G.; m. Manjula Guha, June 7, 1956; children: Swati Reina, Atish Rex. Student, Calcutta (India) U., Oxford (Eng.) U. Prof., dept. head City Coll., Calcutta, 1947-50; chief workers' edn. Internat. Labour Orgn., Geneva, 1952-54; dir. West Africa ILO, Lagos, Nigeria, 1962-66; chief rural devel. ILO, Geneva, 1966-70; resident rep. UN, Colombia, 1970-73; dir. South Asia ILO, New Delhi, India, 1974-79; dir., spl. advisor ILO, Geneva, 1983-86; coord., sr. dir. UN, Geneva, N.Y.C., 1986-87; prin. cons., mission leader UN/World Bank, N.Y.C., Geneva, 1988, 92-94; sr. cons. Internat. Orgn. for Migration, Geneva, 1991—; project dir. New Internat. Regime for Orderly Movements of People, Geneva, 1997—; sec.-gen. Conf. on Sedantarisation of Nomads in the Sahel, Niamey, Niger, 1968, Latin Am. Conf. on Role of Agrl. Orgns. in Econ. and Social Devel., Santiago de Chile, Chile, 1969; sci. coord. West African Conf. Migration and Devel., Dakar, 2000; prof. emeritus Grad. Sch. of Pub. Adminstrn., Bogota, Colombia, 1974—; leader various UN agys., 1962—; vis. fellow Sussex U. (Eng.), 1977; vis. scholar Johns Hopkins U., 1981; vis. lectr., spkr. Inst. Mgmt. Devel., Lausanne, Switzerland, 1988, U. S.C., 1993, Grad. Inst. Internat. Studies, Geneva, 1994, U. Antwerp, 1994, Inst. Internat. Studies U. Pitts., 1995, U. Lausanne, 1996, U. Notre Dame, Ind., 1998, U. Inst. Devel. Studies, Geneva, 1999—, U. Nijmegen, The Netherlands, 2000; cons. Coun. on Europe, 1991-92, UN, 1992-94, 97—, Commn. on Global Governance, 1994-95, German Tech. Coop. Agy., 1995; mem. working group human rights of migrants UN Human Rights Commn., 1998-99; mem. adv. coun. Nigerian Ctr. for Human Resources Devel., Lagos, 2000—. Author, coord. various econ. assistance plans, worldwide; contbr. articles to profl. jours.; author books including Gains from Global Linkages, 1997, Huddled Masses and Uncertain Shores, 1997, Managing Migration: Time for a New International Regime?, 2000. Keynote spkr. various civic and acad. confs. including The Coun. Europe, Helsinki, 1991, The Royal Inst. Internat. Affairs, London, 1992, Aspen Inst., Berlin, 1992, The Initiative for Human Rights in Kurdistan, Bremen, Germany, Acad. of the Kingdom of Morocco, Rabat, 1993, German Soc. for Fgn. Affairs, Berlin, 1995, Adenauer Found., Tunis, 1995, European Am./ACP Secretariat, Brussels, 1996, World Employment Svc. Congress, Nuremberg, Germany, 1997; participant UN Tech. Symposium Internat. Migration and Devel. The Hague, Netherlands, 1998, Nanovic Inst. for European Studies, U. Notre Dame, 1998, Georgetown U., 1998, Internat. Conf. on Migration, Vienna, Austria, 1998, Conf. on Globalization, German Employment Inst., Frankfort, 1999, Italian Sen. Com., Naples, 1999, Internat. Migration, European Ctr./Min. Soc. Affairs, Tel-Aviv, 1999, Migration and Devel., Swedish Min. Fgn. Affairs, Stockholm, 1999, World Conf. on Globalization and Social Security, Byatislava, Slovakia, 1999. Recipient Grand Cross of San Carlos, Colombia, 1973; hon. fellow Sch. of Internat. Policy and Diplomacy U. Tadeo Lozano, Bogota, 1973. Mem. India International Ctr. New Delhi, Geneva Ctr. for European Polit. & Econ. Analysis. Avocations: reading, antiques, music, swimming. Home: Villa Riant Lac 4 Ch, 1295 Mies/Vaud Switzerland Office: Internat Orgn Migration, 17 Rte Morillons PO Box 71, 1211 Geneva Switzerland

GHOSH, JAGABANDHU, physician, researcher; b. West Bengal, India, Nov. 19, 1950; s. Parimal Kumar and Bhakti Rani Ghosh; m. Dipti Ghosh, Feb. 24, 1980; children: Basabadatta, Sri Joydeep. MBBS, Med. Coll., Calcutta, 1975; MD, U. Calcutta, 1980. Clin. tutr R.G. Kar Med. Coll., Calcutta, 1981-85; pediatrician Dist. Hosp., Berhampur, India, 1985-89; lectr. B.S. Med. Coll., Bankura, India, 1989-92, asst. prof., 1992-95, reader, assoc. prof., 1995-99; prof. Inst. Postgrad. Med. Edn. and Rsch., Calcutta, 1999—. Contbg. author: Nelson Textbook of Pediatrics, 14th edit., 1995; contbr. articles to profl. jours. Mem. Indian Acad. Pediatrics, Internat. Coll. Pediatrics, N.Y. Acad. Scis. Avocations: listening to Tagore songs, reading journals, magazines and fiction. Home: North Pratapbagan, Bankura West Bengal 722101, India

GHOSH, KANJAKSHA, hematologist, researcher; b. Bhagalpur, India, Dec. 3, 1952; s. Kartikchandra and Nilimarani (Sinha) G.; m. Uma Sarkar, June 29, 1983; children: Kinjalka, Kinanka. B Medicine B Surgery, Calcutta Med. Coll., 1976; MD, All India Inst. Med. Scis., New Delhi, 1980. Diplomate Nat. Bd. Examination, India. Rsch. officer Postgrad. Inst. Med. Edn. and Rsch., Chandigarh, India, 1980-83, lectr. in hematology, 1983-85, asst. prof. hematology, 1985-87; sr. specialist in hematology MPH, Kuwait, 1987-91; overseas visitor, bone marrow transplant coord. Leicester (Eng.) Royal Infirmary, 1991-94; asst. dir. Indian Coun. Med. Rsch., Mumbai, 1994—; vis. cons. in hematology Sultan Qaboos U., Muscat, Oman, 1998, dir. BMT program, 1998-99; sr. rsch. fellow Indian Coun. Med. Rsch., 1977-80; assoc. prof. Sultan Qaboos U., Muscat. Editor: Venoms and Toxins, 1996; author: Current Problems in Pediatrics, 1997, Geriatric Medicine in India, 1999; contbr. over 125 articles to profl. jours. Talent search fellow Indian Coun. Med. Rsch., 1977-80; recipient award Ctr. for Cryopreservation Technique, 1995-98, Ctr. for Diagnosis of Genetic Disorders, 1995—. Fellow ACP; mem. Indian Soc. Hematology (life), N.Y. Acad. Scis., Assn. Physicians India (life), Nat. Acad. Med. Scis., Royal Coll. Physicians London, Royal Coll. Physicians Ireland, Royal Coll. Pathologists. Hindu. Avocations: study, gardening, comparative religion. Office: Inst Immunohematology, KEM Hosp 13th Fl, Mumbai 400012, India

GHOSH, SOMNATH, engineering educator; b. Calcutta, India, Aug. 21, 1958; p. Debi Prasanna and Lalita Ghosh; m. Chandreyee Majumder, Dec. 14, 1985; 1 child, Anirban. B in Tech., Indian Inst. Tech., West Bengal, 1980; MS, Cornell U., 1983; PhD, U. Mich., 1988. Asst. prof. U. Ala., Tuscaloosa, 1988-91; asst. prof. Ohio State U., Columbus, 1991-95, assoc. prof., 1995-99, prof., 1999—. Editor: The Integration of Materials, Process and Product Design, 1999; contbr. articles to profl. jours. Recipient Rsch. Initiation award NSF, Washington, 1990, ALCOA Found. award, 1990; named Nat. Young Investigator, NSF, Washington, 1994. Fellow ASME; mem. Am. Acad. Mechanics, Internat. Assn. Computational Mechanics, U.S. Assn. Computational Mechanics. Avocations: music, reading, sketching. E-mail: ghosh.5@osu.edu. Fax: 614-292-3163. Office: 2021 D Robinson Lab 206 W 18th Ave Columbus OH 43210-1189

GHOSH, SOUMITRA, research center director; b. Calcutta, India, Oct. 30, 1958; came to U.S., 1992; s. Dhrubabrata and Jharna Ghosh; m. Indrani Ghosh, Nov. 21, 1984; children: Vivekananda, Sharmila. BSc in Biochemistry, St. Thomas's Hosp., London, 1980, MB BChir, 1983; DPhil, Oxford (Eng.) U., 1992. Sr. house officer Cen. Middlesex Hosp., London, 1985-86; registrar St. Charles and St. Mary's Hosp., London, 1987-89; Wellcome rsch. fellow Oxford U., 1989-92; rsch. investigator U. Mich., Ann Arbor, 1992-94; vis. scientist NIH, Bethesda, Md., 1994-99; dir. Max McGee Nat. Rsch. Inst. for Juvenile Diabetes Med. Coll. Wis., Milw., 1999—; ad hoc reviewer for study sect. Nat. Inst. Allergy and Infectious Disease, Nat. Inst. for Dental and Craniofacial Rsch.,. Contbr. articles to profl. jours. Plimmer scholar London U., St. Thomas's Hosp., 1979; rsch. grantee Children's Hosp. of Wis., 1999. Mem. Royal Coll. Physicians London. Hindu. Avocations: running, jazz music. E-mail: sghosh@mcw.edu. Home: 8430 N Fielding Rd Milwaukee WI 53217-2423

GHOSH, SOUMITRA KUMAR, electrical engineer; b. Calcutta, Bengal, India, Aug. 15, 1959; came to U.S., 1991; s. Kali P. and Suparna (Mitra) G.; m. Sumona Dutt, June 30, 1989; 1 child, Semanti. B in Engring. with hons., Jadavpur U., Calcutta, 1981; M in Engring., So. Ill.U., Edwardsville, 1993. Registered profl. engr., Ill. Asst. engr. Brown Boveri Co., Baroda, India, 1981-83, Engrs. India Ltd., New Delhi, 1983-85; sr. engr. Al Jizzi Electricals, Muscat, Oman, 1985-91, Magnum Techs., Belleville, Ill., 1993-94; sys. engr. Sverdrup Facilities, St. Louis, Mo., 1994—; standard advisor Inst. Soc. Am., Raleigh, N.C., 1993—; examiner Nat. Coun., Clemson, S.C., 1996—. Contbr. articles to IEEE Jour., IEEE Mag. Nat. Merit scholar Govt. India, 1976. Mem. IEEE. Avocations: journalism, soccer, teaching, internet. Home: 219-4A Enchanted Ct Manchester MO 63021 Office: Sverdrup Facilities 400 S 4th St Saint Louis MO 63102-1815

GHOSH, SUBRATA, gastroenterology consultant, educator; b. Calcutta, India, June 13, 1956; arrived in Eng., 1990; s. Sailesh Ranjan and Kamala (Basu) G.; m. Chhanda Roy, Dec. 9, 1985; 1 child, Abhisek. MB, BS, Med. Coll., Calcutta, 1982, MD, 1986; MD, U. Edinburgh, Scotland, 1996. Diplomate Nat. Med. Bd., India. Rsch. fellow U. Edinburgh, 1992-95; cons. gastroenterologist Western Gen. Hosp., Edinburgh, 1995—; part-time sr. lectr. U. Edinburgh, 1995—; overseas postgrad. dir. Royal Coll. of Physicians of Edinburgh; mem. specialty questions group MRCP (UK). Contbr. articles to profl. jours. Internat. fellow Royal Coll. Physicians, London, 1987, fellow Japanese Coun. Med. Tng. Program, 1988. Fellow Royal Coll. Physicians (Edinburgh); mem. Brit. Soc. Gastroenterology, European Fedn. Internal Medicine (sci. adv. com.). Home: 107 Craigleith Hill Ave, Edinburgh EH4 2NB, Scotland Office: Western Gen Hosp, Crewe Rd S, Edinburgh EH4 2XU, Scotland

GHOSH, SUCHITA, physicist; b. Bihar, India, Sept. 30, 1957; d. Harihar Chandra and Pranati Sinha G. BS, Patna U., India, 1980, MS, 1983; PhD, U. Delhi, India, 1995. Rsch. fellow Coun. of Scientific and Indsl. Rsch., India, 1990-95, rsch. assoc., 1995-96; lectr. J.P. Univ., 1996—. Contbr. articles to profl. jours. Recipient Gold medal Bihar Sch. Exam. Bd., India, 1974. Mem. Am. Geophys. Union. Avocations: travel, star-watching. Office: Physics Dept/Rajendra Coll, JP Univ, 841301 Chapra/Bihar India

GHOSHAL, UDAY CHAND, gastroenterologist; b. Oltora, Bankura, India, Jan. 3, 1962; s. Nalini Ranjan and Shanti Sudha Ghoshal; m. Ujjala Mukherjee, Feb. 7, 1993; 1 children: Udit, Utsav. MB BChir, Burdwan Med. Coll., West Bengal, India, 1986; MD in Medicine, Postgrad. Inst. Med. Edn. & Rsch., Chandigarh, India, 1991; DM in Gastroenterology, Sanjay Gandhi Postgrad. Inst. Med. Scis., Lucknow, Uttar Pradesh, India. DNB in medicine Bd. Exam., New Delhi. Intern Burdwan Med. Coll., 1986-87, housestaffship, 1987-88; jr. resident Postgrad. Inst. Med. Edn. & Rsch., Chandigarh, 1988-91; sr. resident Sanjay Gandhi Postgrad. Inst. Med. Scis., Lucknow, 1992-95; sr. rsch. assoc. Inst. Postgrad. Med. Edn. and Rsch., Calcutta, 1995-96, gastroenterologist, 1996-2000; asst. prof. dept. gastroenterology Sanjay Gandhi Postgrad. Inst. Med. Scis., Lucknow, 2000—. Inventor in field; contbr. articles to nat. and internat. jours. Participant in HBV and HCV screening Thalassemia Welfare Soc., Burdwan, 1999. Recipient Prepulsid Motility award Indian Soc. Gastroenterology, 1996, Best Paper award Indian Soc. Gastroenterology, 1997, J Mitra Meml. award for best sci. contbn. of yr., 1998, Best Paper award Soc. Gastrointestinal Endoscopy of India, 1999. Mem. Lions Club Internat. Avocations: painting, writing Bengali poetry. Fax: 0091-9522-440017. Home: Rajganj PO Nutanganj, Burdwan 713102, India Office: Sanjay Gandhi Post Grad Inst Med Scis, Dept Gastroenterology Raebareli Rd, Lucknow 226014, India

GHOSH MOULIC, SANDIPAN, mechanical engineering educator, researcher; b. Asansol, India, Nov. 2, 1962; s. Kapali Krishna and Kalpana (Sinha) Ghosh Moulic; m. Sutapa Debray, June 18, 1997. B Tech., Indian Inst. Tech., Kharagpur, 1985; MS, Ariz. State U., 1988, PhD, 1993. Rsch. scholar Indian Inst. Tech., Kharagpur, 1985-86, vis. lect., 1994; rsch. asst. Ariz. State U., Tempe, 1986-88, rsch. assoc., 1988-93, faculty assoc., 1993-94; asst. prof. mech. engring. Indian Inst. Tech., Bombay, 1994—; vis. lectr. Indian Inst. Tech., Kharagpur, 1994. Contbr. articles to profl. jours. Scholar Govt. of India, 1979, J.C. Ghose scholar Indian Inst. Tech., Kharagpur, 1985, Regents scholar Ariz. State U., 1987. Mem. Phi Kappa Phi. Office: Indian Inst Tech, Mech Engring Dept, Bombay 400076, India

GHOSN, MARWANE GEORGES, oncologist; b. Zouk Mosbeh, Lebanon, Feb. 10, 1959; s. Georges Eshaya and Josephine (Alwane) G.; m. Karine Antoine Doummar, Aug. 8, 1992; children: Georges, Marie. MD, Saint Joseph U., 1983, med. oncology, 1987. Lic. bd. med. oncology. Head of dept. hematology and oncology Hotel Dieu de France Hosp., Beirut, 1991-95. Contbr. articles to profl. jours. including Jour. d'Urologie, Jour. of Clin. Oncology, European Jour. of Cancer and Clin. Oncology, Cancer Comms., Med. and Pediatric Oncology and many others. Mem. Lebanese Cancer Soc. (treas. 1994—), Lebanese Cancer Soc. (gen. sec. 1992-94), Am. Soc. of Clin. Oncology, Am. Assn. for Cancer Rsch., European Soc. for Med. Oncology, Multinatal Assn. of Supportive Care in Cancer, N.Y. Acad. Scis., Euro. Hematology Assn. Office: Hotel Dieu France Hosp, A Naccache Blvd POB 166830, Beirut Lebanon

GHOUSE, MOHAMMED, chemical engineering educator, researcher; b. Hyderabad, India, Aug. 15, 1949; came to Saudi Arabia, 1989; s. Shaikh Mohammad and Bali Bee; m. Sabera Begum, May 12, 1972; children: Nussrat, Waheeda, M.I. Hassan, M.A. Hussain, Massarat, M. Zakariah, M. Ilyas. BTech, Osmania U., Hyderabad, 1972, MTech, 1975; PhD, Indian Inst. Tech., Madras, India, 1980; diploma in basic computer programming, Internat. Corr. Sch., 1996. Sr. engr. Bharat Heavy Elecs. Ltd. R&D, Hyderabad, 1980-84, dep. mgr., 1984-87, mgr., 1987-89; asst. prof. King Saud U., Riyadh, Saudi Arabia, 1989-90; sci. specialist King Abdulaziz City for Sci. and Tech., Riyadh, Saudi Arabia, 1991-93, assoc. rsch. prof., 1994-2000, rsch. prof., 2000—. Contbr. tech. papers to internat. jours.; patentee in field. Recipient Nat. R&D Corp. award, 1991. Mem. Internat. Assn. Hydrogen Energy, Soc. Advancement Electrochem. Sci. and Tech. India. Avocation: reading religious books. Fax: 009661 481 3880. Office: King Abdulaziz City for Sci and Tech, PO Box 6086, Riyadh 11442, Saudi Arabia

GHULGHULE, JAYANT RAMCHANDRA, physics educator; b. Nagpur, Maharashtra, India, July 17, 1962; s. Ramchandra Shankarrao and Shailaja Ramchandra (Mahajan) G.; m. Shraddha Jayant Deshpande, Dec. 27, 1991; children: Minakshi, Madhav. BSc, M.M. Coll. Sci., Nagpur, India, 1982; MSc, Nagpur U., 1984, PhD, 1996; diploma in Digital Electronics, Visvesvaraya Regl. Coll. Eng., Nagpur, 1985. Lectr. Yeshwantrao Chavan Coll. Engring., Nagpur, 1984-93, sr. lectr., 1993-98, lectr. selection grade, 1998—. Mem. Indian Assn. Crystal Growth (life). Avocations: yoga, music, sitting in silence. Home: Bilwadal Rahate Colony, No 2 Jail Rd, Nagpur 440022, India Office: YCCE Wanadongri, Dept Physics, Nagpur 441110, India

GHUYSEN, JEAN-MARIE, microbiologist; b. Trembleur, Belgium, Jan. 26, 1925; s. Julien and Berthe (Woyave) G.; m. Jeanne-Marie Defourny, July 13, 1950; children: Véronique, Collette, Vincent. Diploma in Pharmacy, U. Liège, Belgium, 1947, PhD in Phys. Chemistry, 1951; D (hon.), U. Nancy (France), 1975, U. Debrecen, Hungary, 1990, U. Montreal, Que., Can., 1993. Head biochemistry and microbiology unit Labaz Pharm. Co., Brussels, 1957-58; asst., assoc. prof. dept. gen. and med. microbiology U. Liège, 1958-69, head dept. microbiology applied to pharm. scis., 1969-90, dir. Ctr. for Protein Engring., 1990-95, sci. advisor, 1995—; sr. scientist NSF, U.S., 1965-66; vis. prof. NYU, 1971, U. Los Andes, Venezuela, 1973, Temple U., 1975, 86, Francqui chairperson Free U. Brussels, 1983-84; mem. tchg. staff Pasteur Inst., Paris, 1973-83. Contbr. over 340 papers to profl. jours. Named Grand Officier de l'Ordre de la Couronne, Royaume de Belgique, 1987, Grand Officer de l'Ordre de Léopold, 1993; recipient Citation Classic award, 1989, Quinquennal J. Maisin prize Found. Nat. Sci. Rsch., 1980, Tech. Innovation award Walloon Region Govt., 1984, Gairdner Found. Internat. award in med. sci., 1989, Carlos J. Finlay award in microbiology UNESCO, 1991, Albert Einstein World Sci. award, World Cultural Coun., 1997. Mem. AAAS, U.K. Biochem. Soc., U.K. Gen. Soc. for Microbiology, Am. Soc. Microbiology, European Molecular Biology Orgn., N.Y. Acad. Scis., Acad. Royale Médecine Belgique, Acad. Royale Scis., Lettres et Beaux-Arts Belgique, Academia Europaea. Office: Ctr Protein Engring U Liege, Sart Tilman, 4000 Liege Belgium

GHWANMEH, SAMEH HUSSEIN, engineering educator; b. Irbid, Jordan, July 2, 1963; s. Hussein Salameh and Fatmeh Ahmad G.; m. Suhad Ahmad Tawalbeh Ghwanmeh, July 2, 1988; children: Assil, Rawan. BS, Yarmouk U., Jordan, 1985; MS, Liverpool John Moores U., Eng., 1993; PhD, 1996. Elec. engr. Jordan Army, 1985-87; sys. mgr. Yarmouk U., Jordan, 1987-92; rsch. asst. Liverpool John Moores U., Eng., 1992-96; asst. prof. Yarmouk U., Jordan, 1996—, dir. computer ctr., 1998—. Recipient Prize of the 5th Computerization Essay Contest CICC, Japan, 1991. Mem. IEEE, Jordan Engring. Assn., Lebanese Assn. for Advanced Scis. Avocations: swimming, soccer, driving. Office: Tech Engineering Faculty, Yarmouk University, 211-63 Irbid Jordan

GHYMN, ESTHER MIKYUNG, English educator, writer; b. Seoul; d. Yong Shik and Kyung hee (Park) Kim; m. Kyung-Il Ed Ghymn; children: Jennifer, Eugene. MA, U. Hawaii; MAT, U. Pitts.; PhD, U. Nev., Reno, 1990. Lectr. English, U. Nev., Reno, 1993—, ESL coord., 1996—, mem. ethnic studies bd., 1998—. Author: The Shapes and Styles of Asian American Prose Fiction, 1990, Images of Asian American Women Writers, 1995; editor APANN News, Asian Am. Studies, 2000. Bd. dirs. Asian Americans N. Nev., 1992-95, Multicultural Office, Truckee Meadows C.C., Reno, 1994-96, mem. steering com. Access to Success, 1996; mem. affirmative action adv. bd. U. Nev., Reno, 1998, ethnic studies bd., 1997—, women's studies bd., 1998—, chair liaison com., 1998—, chair lang. com., 1999—; series editor Peter Lang Pub. Mem. Phi Beta Delta (sec.). Avocations: teaching, writing, reading, travel.

GIACCONI, RICCARDO, astrophysicist, educator; b. Genoa, Italy, Oct. 6, 1931; came to U.S., 1956, naturalized, 1967; s. Antonio and Elsa (Canni) G.; m. Mirella Manaira, Feb. 15, 1957; children: Guia Giacconi Trutter, Anna Lee, Marc A. Ph.D., U. Milan, Italy, 1954; Sc.D. (hon.), U. Chgo., 1983; laurea honoris causa in astronomy, U. Padua, 1984; ScD (hon.), Warsaw U., 1996; laurea honoris causa in physics, U. Rome, 1996; Dr Tech. and Sci. (hon.), U. Uppsala, 2000. Asst. prof. physics U. Milan, 1954-56; research assoc. Ind. U., 1956-58, Princeton U., 1958-59; exec. v.p., dir. Am. Sci. & Engring. Co., Cambridge, Mass., 1959-73; prof. astronomy Harvard U.; also assoc. dir. high energy astrophysics divsn. Center Astrophysics, Smithsonian Astrophys. Obs./Harvard Coll. Obs., Cambridge, 1973-81; dir. Space Telescope Sci. Inst., Balt., 1981-92; prof. astrophysics Johns Hopkins U., 1981-99, U. Milan, Italy, 1991-99; dir.-gen. European So. Obs., Garching, Germany, 1993-99; pres. Assoc. Univs., Inc., Washington, 1999—; rsch. prof. Johns Hopkins U., 1999—; Richtmyer meml. lectr. Am. Assn. Physics Tchrs., 1975; mem. space sci. adv. com. NASA, 1978-79, mem. adv. com. innovation study, 1979—; mem. NASA Astrophysics Council; mem. adv. com. innovation study astronomy adv. com., 1979—; mem. high energy astronomy survey panel Nat. Acad. Scis., 1979-80, mem. Space Sci. Bd., 1980-84, 89—; mem. adv. com. Max-Planck Inst. für Physik und Astrophysik; chmn. bd. dirs. Instituto Guido Donegani, Gruppo Montedison, 1987-89; mem. vis. com. to divsn. of phys. scis. U. Chgo., U. Padua; chmn. ISC E-1 (galactic and extragalactic astrophysics) Com. on Space Rsch. (COSPAR), 1982-93. Co-editor: X-ray Astronomy, 1974, The X-Ray Universe, 1985; author numerous articles and papers in field; inventor x-ray telescope, discovered x-ray stars. Decorated Targhe d'Oro della Regione Puglia; Fulbright fellow, 1956-58; recipient Röntgen prize astrophysics Physikalish-Medizinische Gesellschaft, Wurzburg, Germany, 1971; Exceptional Sci. Achievement medal NASA, 1971, 80; Disting. Public Service award, 1972; Space Sci. award AIAA, 1976; Elliott Cresson medal Franklin Inst., 1980; Gold medal Royal Astron. Soc., 1982; A. Cressy Morrison award N.Y. Acad. Sci., 1982; Bruce medal; Heinneman award, Wolf Prize in Physics, 1987; Russell lectr. Mem. Am. Astron. Soc. (Helen B. Warner award 1966, chmn. hign energy astrophysics divsn., NASA Disting. Pub. Svc. award 1992, Henry Norris Russel lectr. 1981, Darwin lectr. Royal Soc. 1993), Italian Phys. Soc. (Como prize 1967), AAAS, Internat. Astron. Union (nat. Acad. Scis. rep. 1979-82), Nat. Acad. Scis., Am. Acad. Arts and Scis., Md. Acad. Sci. (sci. coun. 1982—), Accademia Nazionale dei Lincei (fgn.), Max-Planck Soc. (ext. mem.), Royal Astron. Soc., Am. Phys. Soc., Cosmos Club (Washington). Office: Associated Univs Inc 1400 16th St NW Ste 730 Washington DC 20036-2252

GIACOMELLI, GIORGIO MARIA, physics educator; b. Cagli, Italy, May 30, 1931; s. Giuseppe and Elda (Marinelli) G.; m. Maltoni Giuseppina, Aug. 8, 1958; children: Paolo, Roberto. Laurea in Fisica, U. Bologna, Italy, 1954; PhD in Physics, U. Rochester, 1958. Prof. incaricato U. Bologna, Italy, 1958-63, asst. ordinario, 1964-71, prof., 1974—; dir. dept. physics U. Bologna, 1983-88; rsch. assoc. CERN, Geneva, 1959-61; vis. assoc. physicist Brookhaven Nat. Lab., Upton, N.Y., 1964-66; vis. physicist Fermilab, Batavia, Ill., 1973-75, 87; prof. U. Padua, Italy, 1971-74; dir. Inst. Physics, Bologna, 1975-82; amb. drug control program UN, Vienna. Contbr. articles to profl. jours. Recipient Premio Operosità Scientifica, U. Bologne, 1967, Premio a della Riccia, 1970. Mem. Italian Phys. Soc. (Premio Citta di Bari award 1963), European Phys. Soc., Am. Phys. Soc. Home: Via Ranzani 13/5, 40127 Bologna Italy Office: U Bologna Dept Physics, Via Irnerio 46, 40126 Bologna Italy*

GIACOMELLI, LUIZ ROBERTO BIGCO, biochemical researcher; b. Mandaguari, Brazil, Dec. 4, 1967; s. Pedro Giacomelli Sobrinho and Abigail Guimarces Bigco Giacomelli; m. Flavia Roseli Baptista, June 6, 1992. Pharmacist and biochem. degree, State U. Maringa, Brazil, 1993; specialization in healthy scis., State U. Maringa, 1999; specialist in clin. analysis, Brazilian Soc. Clin. Analysis, Recife, Brazil, 1995. Leader divsn. tchg. pharmacy State U. Maringa, 1993, tchr. clin. pathology, 1999—; biochemist Lab. Clin. Analysis Sco Camilo, Maringa, 1994-99; biochemist lab. U. Hosp. Maringa, 1995-98, lab. mgr., 1998-99; sci. dir. Pharmacists Assn. Maringa, 1995-97; coord. biochem. students courses U. Hosp. Maringa, 1998-99. Lt. Brazilian Army, 1986-88. Fellow Brazilian Soc. Clin. Analysis; mem. Am. Soc. for Microbiology. Avocations: soccer, diving, traveling, movies. E-mail: betofla@teracom.com.br and humbiblioteca@wnet.com.br. Fax: 55 44 225 8484. Home: Dr Luiz Teixeira Mendes, Ave N 680 Ap 302, 87015250 Maringa PR, Brazil Office: Univ Hosp Maringa, Mandacarz Ave, 87080000 Maringa Brazil

GIACONA, CORRADO ANTHONY II, container company executive; b. New Orleans, Dec. 14, 1942; s. Louis Joseph and Claire (LaRocca) G.; m. Patricia Ellen Nunez, July 25, 1964; children: Gina Lisa, Corrado Anthony, Louis. BA, U. New Orleans, 1965. Plant mgr. Amos C. Harris Can Co., New Orleans, 1962-64; ter. mgr. Ross Labs., New Orleans, 1964-72; pres. Giacona Container divsn. Giacona Group, New Orleans, 1972—. Mem. U. New Orleans Bus./Higher Edn. Coun.; bd. dirs. La. Maritime Mus., Sci. Ctr., La. Sci. Ctr., Family Svcs. of La., New Orleans Conv. and Vis. Bur.; pres. La. Maritime Mus.; officer Krewe of Alla; bd. dirs. World Trade Ctr., New Orleans; mem. adv. bd. Tulane Med. Sch. Mem. K.C., (bd. dirs.) N.O. Convention and Vis. Bureau, Timberlane Country Club, Phi Kappa Theta. Republican. Roman Catholic. E-mail: giacona@giacona.com. Office: Giacona Container 121 Industrial Ave New Orleans LA 70121-2908

GIACOPELLO, SERGIO, chemist; b. Buenos Aires, Dec. 14, 1964; s. Duilio and Lidya H. (Gentili) G.; m. Marcela E.C. Gimenez, June 12, 1993. Lic. in Chemistry, U. Buenos Aires, 1989, Health and Safety Specialist, 1994, PhD in Chemistry, 1995. Tchg. asst. U. Buenos Aires, 1993-94, tchg. asst. in chief, 1994-96; rsch. asst. Fla. State U., Tallahassee, 1995-96; rsch. asst. Gador SA, Pilar, Argentina, 1996-98, pilot plant chief, 1998—. Contbr. articles to profl. jours. Home: Cabildo 2982 PB #C, 1429 Buenos Aires Argentina

GIAEVER, IVAR, physicist; b. Bergen, Norway, Apr. 5, 1929; came to U.S., 1957, naturalized, 1963; s. John A. and Gudrun (Skaarud) G.; m. Inger Skramstad, Nov. 8, 1952; children: John, Anne Kari, Guri, Trine. Siv. Ing., Norwegian Inst. Tech., Trondheim, 1952; Ph.D., Rensselaer Poly. Inst., 1964. Patent examiner Norwegian Patent Office, Oslo, 1953-54; mech. engr. Can. Gen. Electric Co., Peterborough, Ont., 1954-56; applied mathematician Gen. Electric Co., Schenectady, 1956-58, physicist Research and Devel. Ctr., 1958-88; Inst. prof. Rensselaer Poly. Inst., Troy, N.Y., 1988—; also prof. U.

Oslo, 1988—. Served with Norwegian Army, 1952-53. Recipient Nobel Prize for Physics, 1973; Guggenheim fellow, 1970. Fellow Am. Phys. Soc. (Oliver E. Buckley prize 1965); mem. IEEE, Norwegian Profl. Engrs., Nat. Acad. Sci., Nat. Acad. Engring. (V.K. Zworykin award 1974), Am. Acad. Arts and Scis., Norwegian Acad. Sci., Norwegian Acad. Tech. Office: Rensselaer Poly Ins Physics Dept 110 8th St Troy NY 12180-3522

GIAKAS, GIANNIS, health services educator; b. Karditsa, Thessalia, Greece, Jan. 1, 1971; arrived in Eng., 1994; s. Kimon Giakas and Vasiliki (Yiota) Giaka. BSc, U. Thessaloniki, Greece, 1993; PhD, M.M. U., Eng., 1997. Lectr. Staffordshire U., Stoke, Eng., 1997—. Contbr. articles to profl. jours. Holt rsch. fellow U. Manchesterm, 1999. Mem. Internat. Soc. Biomechs., Brit. Assn. Sport and Exercise Scis., European Soc. Biomechs., European Coll. Sport Scis., European Soc. Movement Analysis in Children. Avocations: music, sports, movies. Office: Hope Hosp Clin Sci Bldg, Eccles Old Rd, Salford M6 8HD, England

GIAMBENE, GIOVANNI, research associate; b. Florence, Italy, Aug. 16, 1966; s. Gianfranco and Marisa (Breschi) G. DEng, U. Florence, Italy, 1993, PhD in Telecomm. and Informatics, 1997. With electronic engring. dept U. Florence, 1994-97; GSM sys. engr. OTE, Florence, 1997-98; rsch. assoc. U. Siena, Italy, 1999—; rsch. asst. U. Florence, 1997—. Contbr. articles to profl. jours. Mem. IEEE (travel grantee 1995). Avocations: football, model-making. Home: Via Pratese No 297, 51030 Chiazzano Italy

GIAMMARCO, MARIO J., investment manager; b. Bklyn., Mar. 31, 1950; s. Antonio Giammarco and Antoinette Verde; m. Barbara Sommers, Sept. 22, 1982; children: Christopher, Mario, Maryann. BSEE, N.Y. Inst. Tech., 1973. Registered options prin. N.Y. Stock Exch., investment advisor. Investment mgr., pres. Bernard Herold & Co., Inc., S.I., N.Y. Pres. Alice Austin Mus., 1992-93. Capt. U.S. Army, 1971-84. Mem. S.I. C. of C. (chmn. 1997-98), S.I. Rotary (pres. 1997-99), Italy-Am. C. of C. (bd. dirs. 1999—). Avocations: boating, golf, poker. Office: 1190 Hylan Blvd Staten Island NY 10305-1920

GIAMMETTI, LUCA, fashion company marketing professional; b. Parma, Italy, Sept. 6, 1969; s. Fulvio and Lucia (Fiaccavento) G. Grad. in Bus. Adminstrn., Bocconi U., Italy, 1988-96. Cons. Valentino Couture Inc., N.Y.C., 1996; mktg. asst. Valentino SpA, Rome, 1996—.

GIAMPIETRO, WAYNE BRUCE, lawyer; b. Chgo., Jan. 20, 1942; s. Joseph Anthony and Jeannette Marie (Zeller) G.; B.A., Purdue U., 1963; J.D., Northwestern U., 1966; m. Mary E. Fordeck, June 15, 1963; children—Joseph, Anthony, Marcus. Bar: Ill. 1966, U.S. Dist. (no. dist.) Ill. 1966, U.S. Tax Ct. 1977, U.S. Ct. Appeals (7th cir.) 1967, U.S. Supreme Ct. 1971. Assoc. Elmer Gertz, Chgo., 1966-73; mem. firm Gertz & Giampietro, Chgo., 1974-75; sole practice, 1975-76; ptnr. Poltrock & Giampietro, 1976-87, ptnr. Witwer, Burlage, Poltrock and Giampietro, 1987-94, Witwer, Poltrock & Giampietro, 1995—. Former cons. atty. Looking Glass div. Traveler's Aid Soc. Contbr. articles to profl. jours. Pres. Chgo. 47th Ward Young Republicans, 1968. Bd. dirs. Ravenswood Conservation Commn. Mem. Ill. Bar Assn. (chmn. sect. on Individual Rights and Responsibilities, 1986-87, 2d pl. Lincoln award 1975), Chgo. Bar Assn., Ill. Bar Assn., First Amendment Lawyers Assn. (sec. 1982, treas. 1983, pres. 1986, nat. chmn. 1987), Chgo. Coun. of Lawyers (mem. ethics com. 1992—), Order of Coif, Phi Alpha Delta. Lutheran. Avocation: stamp collecting. Home: 23 Windsor Dr Lincolnshire IL 60069-3410 Office: Witwer Poltrock & Giampietro 125 S Wacker Dr Ste 2700 Chicago IL 60606-4401

GIANAKOS, PATRICIA ANN, social programs administrator; b. Warren, Ohio, Oct. 14, 1948; d. Jimmie Lambros and Julie (Mougianis) G. BA in Pre-Profl. Social Work, Kent State U., 1970; MSSA (Master of Sci. in Social Administration), Case Western Res. U., 1998. Lic. social worker, diplomate, Amer. Psychotherapy Assn. Aid for aged workers Trumbull County Human Svcs. Dept., Warren, 1970-71, social svc. worker, 1971-88, adult svcs. worker, 1988—, excellence com., 1991, 93, contbg. editor County Line newsletter, 1991-98, mem. awards com., 1991-93, chmn. awards com., 1993-98; mem. Trumbull County Task Force on Wellness in Later Yrs., Warren, 1991-92. Vol. St. Demetrios Festival, Warren, 1979—; mem. Dem. Nat. Com., Warren, 1992—, Ladies Philoptochos Soc., Warren, 1979—; co-founder, adviser Sr. Citizens Orgn. St. Demetrios Ch., Warren, 1979—. Mem. ACA, NASW, Am. Bus. Women's Assn., Assn. for Adult Devel. and Aging, Nat. Com. for Prevention of Elder Abuse, Tri-County Social Workers Assn., Sr. Svcs. Network, Early Intervention County Collaborative Grp.; Mentoring Mom's Oversight Com. Greek Orthodox. Avocations: reading, crafts, decorating, movies. Home: 1786 Dodge Dr NW Warren OH 44485-1823 Office: Trumbull Cou Human Svcs 150 S Park Ave Warren OH 44481-1018

GIANI, SIMONE, software projects manager; b. Florence, Italy, Nov. 27, 1964; s. Vittorio and Enrica (Stopani) G.; m. Cristina Peroni, Sept. 8, 1990; 1 child, Leonardo. D of Phys., U. Florence, Italy, 1991. Staff mem. CERN, Geneva, 1992-94, simulation sect. leader, 1994-98, staff indefinite contract, 1995—; LHCC/RD44 spokesman, A World Wide Collaboration of High Energy Physics Labs.; internat. adv. com. Centro Studi A.Volta; software domains and subdetectors coord. CMS Experiment at the Large Hadron Collider, 1999-2000; mem. sci. com. EUROSIM; project mgr. on-line and off-line software CERN, 2000. With Italian Mil., 1986-87. Office: CERN, 1211 Geneva Switzerland

GIANITSOS, ANESTIS NICHOLAS, surgeon; b. Chios, Greece, Aug. 31, 1961; came to U.S., 1966; s. Dimitrios and Soultani (Zannikos) G.; m. Laurie S. Hallmark, 1 child, Alexia Soultani. BA summa cum laude, Boston U., 1983, MD, 1987. Physician U. Wis. Hosp., Madison, 1987-92; pres. Tricorp Informational Svcs., Williams Bay, Wis., 1989-93; staff urologist Riverview Clinic, Janesville, Wis., 1992-98; pres. Geneva Mktg. Sys., Lake Geneva, Wis., 1996—; med. dir. Men's Health Ctr. Mercy Health Sys., So. Wis., No. Ill., 1998—; staff urologist Mercy Health Sys., Janesville, 1998—; cons. Rural Wis. Hosp. Coop., Sauk City, 1989-93; staff urology Mercy Health Sys., Janesville, 1998—; med. dir. So. Wis. chpt. US TOO, 1993—. Contbr. articles to profl. jours. Commonwealth scholar, Augustus Howe Buck scholar. Fellow Internat. Coll. Surgeons; mem. Am. Assn. Clin. Urologists, Am. Urologic Assn., Wis. Med. Soc. Republican. Greek Orthodox. Avocations: photography, travel, baseball, investing, rare wine. Home: 1237 Geneva National Ave W Lake Geneva WI 53147-5009 Office: Mercy Men's Health Ctr 1000 Mineral Point Ave Janesville WI 53545-2940

GIANNAKIS, IOANNIS STAVROU, information systems specialist, educator; b. Patras, Greece, Mar. 17, 1971; s. Stavros Giannakis and Eleni Kerasioti. Diploma in mech. engring., Tech. Ednl. Inst., Patras, 1994; BME, U. Brighton, Eng., 1995; MSc in Computer Tech. Manufacture, U. Sussex, Brighton, 1996. Pvt. computer instr. Patras, 1990—; adminstr. Fluid Dynamics Computer Ctr. Tech. Ednl. Inst., Patras, 1992-94, 97—, mech. engr. Computer Numerical Control Lab., 1994, 96, 97—, lectr., 1997—; external cons., mem. purchases com. Tech. Ednl. Inst., Patras, 1997—. Advisor, revisor: Principles of Fluid Dynamics, 1995, Turbomachinery, 1996, Basic of Machine Elements, 1996, Fluid Dynamics Exercises & Introduction to Computational Fluid Dynamics, 1999. Vol. cons. U. Sussex, Brighton, 1998—. Scholar Nat. Greek Found., 1994; grantee U. Cranfield, 1996. mem. ASME, AAAS, Inst. Elec. Engrs., N.Y. Acad. Scis. Avocations: swimming, cycling, reading, music. Office: Tech Ednl Inst, Megalou Alexandrou 1, 26334 Patras Greece

GIANNAKOPOULOS, GABRIEL BASIL, educator; b. Volos, Greece, Oct. 23, 1950; s. Basil Constantine and Sofia (George) G.; m. Zoh Zerdeva, Jan. 6, 1980; children: Sofia, Basil, Angel. Diploma, U. Patras, Greece, 1975, PhD, 1978. Asst. prof. U. Patras, Greece, 1985-90, assoc. prof., 1990-97, prof., 1997—. Author: Power System Analysis, 1986, Computer Techniques in Power System Analysis, 1991. Mem. IEEE (sr.). Home: Koran 31, 26222 Patras Greece Office: U Patras, 26500 Patras Greece

GIANNAKOU-KOUTSIKOU, MARIETTA, member European Parliament; b. Gerakion, Lakonias, Greece, June 5, 1951. Mem. European Parliament, Brussels; mem. com. on fgn. affairs, human rights, common security and def. policy, com. on citizens' freedoms and rights, justice and home affairs, mem. substitute del. to European Union-Turkey Joint Parliamentary Com. Mem. Bur., Group of European People's Party (Christian Dems.) and European Dems. Mem. New Democracy Party. *

GIANNAMORE, DAVID MICHAEL, electronics engineer; b. Steubenville, Ohio, May 25, 1956; s. Robert Anthony and Marjorie Irene (Smith) G.; m. Tracy Lynn Rayburn, Apr. 3, 1982; children: Cynthia Marie, Robert Joseph. AAS in Electronic Engring., Jefferson County Tech. Inst., 1977. Video tech. Sta. WSTV-TV, Steubenville, 1977; svc. tech. TCI of Ohio, Steubenville, 1978-80; cable splicer Gen. Telephone Ohio, Cadiz, 1980-81; customer svc. rep. Ohio Power Co., Steubenville, 1981-84; svc. engr. Warner Amex, Columbus, Ohio, 1985-86; tng. instr. Liebert Global Svcs., Worthington, Ohio, 1986-90, tng. instr., supr., 1990-93, project mgr., 1993-95, quality mgr., 1995—. Mem. Am. Soc. for Quality (cert. quality mgr., cert. quality auditor), Assn. for Svc. Mgmt. Internat. Avocations: family activities, karate, sports, music. Office: Liebert Global Svcs 610 Executive Campus Dr Westerville OH 43082-8871

GIANNETTI, CLAUDIA, art historian, educator; b. Belo Horizonte, Brazil, Oct. 21, 1961; d. Murillo and Laura Virginia F. Giannetti; m. Thomas Dietrich Nölle, Sept. 21, 1982. Degree in art history, U. Barcelona, Spain, 1993. Dir. Galerie Raue, Bonn, Germany, 1989-92, Assn. de Cultura Contemporania l'Angelot, Barcelona, 1993-97; prof. art history U. Barcelona, 1997—. Editor: Media Culture, 1995, Arte en la Era Electrónica, 1997. Home: Plz Mercadal, 39-40 1-1, 08030 Barcelona Spain Office: Asn Cultura Cntmp l'Angelot, Correu Vell, 10 bxs 3, 08002 Barcelona Spain

GIANNI, WALTER, physician, researcher; b. Rome, July 8, 1967; s. Domenico and Wanda (Sette) G.; m. Paola Gazzaniga, Oct. 12, 1994; 1 child, Irene. MD, U. La Sapienza, Rome, 1992, grad. in Geriatrics, 1996; PhD in Immunology, U. Aquila, Italy, 1999. Intern in geriatrics, 1988-92, intern in immunology, 1988-90; asst. geriatric divsn. U. Rome Med. Clinic, 1992-96; asst. Nat. Inst. Rsch. and Cure, 1996-98; rschr. U. La Sapienza, 1999—; dir. Italian Group Geriatric Oncology, 1997—. Author: Comprehensive Geriatric Oncology; editor sect. Gedestria. Sci. dir. Home Care Assn., 1997-99. Mem. AAAS, Italian Soc. Internal Medicine, Italian Soc. Geriatric Oncologists, Italian Soc. Gerontology and Geriatry, Charles Darwin Assn., N.Y. Acad. Sci. Avocations: tennis, soccer, jogging. Home: Via Appennini 38, 00198 Rome Italy Office: Univ La Sapienza Rome, Viale Del Policlinico, 00161 Rome Italy also: INRCA, Via Cassia, 1167 Rome 1167, Italy

GIANNINI, VALERIO LOUIS, investment banker; b. N.Y.C., Feb. 7, 1938; s. Gabriel M. and Luisa M. (Casazza) G.; m. Linda Martin, Oct. 6, 1979; children: Martin Louis, Alexander Elliot, Charles Gabriel. BSE, Princeton U., 1959. With Kidder Peabody & Co., N.Y.C., 1961-64; sr. cons. IIT Research Inst., Chgo., 1964-66; sec. Giannini-Voltex, L.A., 1966-68; pres. V.L. Giannini & Co., L.A., 1968-76; chmn. Namco Chems., Inc., 1975; dir. White House ops., Washington, 1977-78; dep. spl. asst. to Pres. for adminstrn. White House, 1979-80; dep. asst. sec. Dept. Commerce, Washington, 1980-81; prin. Cumberland Investment Group, N.Y.C., 1981-87; pres. Numex Corp., 1986-87; CEO, Geneva Bus. Network, Inc., Irvine, Calif., 1987-90; founder Eurosearch Ptnrs., Newport Beach, Calif., 1990; prin. Newcap Ptnrs., 1995; bd. dirs. Meridian Health, Inc., Aqua Ventures 2000, Dudek & Assocs., iMet Technologies, Inc. Lt. USNR, 1959-61. Mem. N.Y. Yacht Club, Newport Harbor Yacht Club.

GIANNITSIS, ANASTASIOS CONSTANTINE, economics educator; b. Athens, Greece, May 4, 1944; s. Constantin and Terpsichori (Papadopoulou) G.; m. Anna-Irene Stefanopoulou, July 18, 1968; children: Constantin, Andreas. MA in Law, U. Athens, 1967, MA in Econs., Polit. Sci., 1969; PhD in Econs., Free U. Berlin, 1973. Councillor to minister Greek Ministry Nat. Economy, Athens, 1982-86; asst. prof. U. Athens, 1985-87, prof. econs., 1989—; min. labor and social ins. Govt. of Greece, 2000—; v.p. Ctr. Planning and Rsch., Athens, 1983-86; pres. Greek Productivity Ctr., Athens, 1986-88; v.p., bd. dirs. Bank of Investment, Athens, 1987—; reseracher Greek Ministry Industry/Tech., Athens, 1986-89, Commn. European Community, Brussels, 1987-88; mem. sci. coun. Greek Ctr. European Studies, Athens, 1989; pres. Coun. Econ. Advisors, 1989-90, 93-94; econ. adv. to prime min., 1994-2000. Author books, articles; co-editor, Economy and Soc., 1979, Rev. of European Community, 1988. Grantee, Japan Found., 1988; rsch. fellow, Deutscher Akademischer Austauschdienst, Fed. Republic Germany, 1989. Mem. Royal Econ. Soc., Am. Econ. Assn. Christian Orthodox. Avocations: travel, music. Home: Koritsas 9, 14561 Kifissia Greece Office: U Athens, Pesmazoglou 8, 10559 Athens Greece

GIANNOPOULOS, GEORGE ANASTASIOS, transportation engineer, educator, consultant; b. Megara, Attika, Greece, Nov. 26, 1946; s. Anastasios George and Irene (Kiousi) G.; m. Artemis Vadoka, Nov. 20, 1962; children: Anastasios, Thanos. Diploma in Civil Engring., Athens Tech. U., 1968; Diploma, Imperial Coll., London, 1969; MS in Engring., U. London, 1970, PhD in Transportation, 1973. Transp. cons. Athens, 1973-75; counsellor Ministry of Transport, Athens, 1975-81, dep. min. transport European conf., 1977-81; assoc. prof. engring. U. Thessaloniki, Salonika, Greece, 1979-81, prof., 1981—, dir. transport engring. lab., 1981—, chmn. dept. civil engring., 1991-93; prin. advisor Truth S.A., Thessaloniki, 1992—, TRD Internat. S.A., Thessaloniki, 1992—; vis. lectr. U. Patras, Greece, 1977-79; mem. mgmt. com. Advanced Transport Telematics, 1989-96; chmn. S.E. European Transport Rsch. Forum. Author 7 books; mem. editl. bd. Jour. Transport Revs., 1987—; contbr. articles to profl. jours. Founding mem. Greece 21st Century, Athens, 1994. Fulbright Found. scholar, 1985-86. Mem. Hellenic Inst. Transport Engrs. (founding mem., chmn. 1984-86, various coms.), World Conf. Transport Rsch., U.S. Transp. Research Bd. (com.), Tech. Chamber of Greece. Greek Orthodox. Avocations: tennis, yachting, travel. Office: Aristotle U Thessaloniki, Transport Sect, 54006 Thessaloniki Greece

GIANNOTTI, CHARLES, researcher; b. Contes, France, Feb. 20, 1937; s. Oreste and Maria (Barcacci) G.; m. Monique Cohen, July 18, 1963; children: Odile, Dominique, Anne. D, U. Paris, 1963, Univ., Orsay, France, 1969. Attache rsch. CNRS, Gif-Sur-Yvette, France, 1964-68, charge rsch., 1968-74, dir. rsch., 1974—. Contbr. articles to profl. jours. Mem. French Soc. Chem. Avocations: tennis, mountain hiking. Home: 14 Allee J Guesde, 91300 Massy France Office: CNRS, Ave De La Terasse, 91198 Gif-Sur-Yvette France

GIANNUZZI-SAVELLI, RICCARDO VITTORIO, antiquarian bookseller; b. Palermo, Italy, Feb. 12, 1945; s. Luigi and Margherita (Martinez) G.-S.; m. Marika C. Salerno, July 11, 1973; children: Eleonora, Floriana. Degree in natural scis., U. Palermo, 1967. Sr. official Provincia Regionale, Palermo, 1973-97; antiquarian bookseller Palermo; malacological cons. Mus. Zoology, U. Palermo, 1983, Mus. Paleontology, 1986, Acquario Civico, Milan, Italy, 1988, Istitazione Culturale Federico II, Menfi, Fondazione Mandralinea, Cefalú. Author: Atlas of Mediterranean Nudibranchs, 1990, Annotated Check List of Mediterranean Mollusks, 1992, 94, Atlas of Mediterranean Seashells, 1995, 2000; contbr. articles to profl. publs. Mem. Soc. Siciliana Natural Sci., Soc. Italiana Malacologia (pres. 1997), Associazione Naturama (pres. 1992), Ray Soc. Avocations: bridge, trips, book collecting. Home: Via Mater Dolorosa 54, 90146 Palermo Italy

GIARDINA, GIANCARLO, classics educator; b. Bologna, Italy, Sept. 8, 1939; s. Baldassare and Viranda (Bergonzoni) G.; m. Giulia Alampi, Nov. 14, 1973; 1 child, Federico. Grad., Faculty of Arts, Bologna, 1961. Fellow Faculty Arts, Bologna, 1962-72, full prof. Latin lit., 1973—; dir. Dept. Classics, Bologna, 1989-94. Editor: Seneca's Tragedies, 1966, Propertius Book Two, 1977, Petronius, 1995; contbr. articles to profl. jours. Roman Catholic. Home: Via Gandino 3, 40137 Bologna Italy Office: Dept Classics, Via Zamboni 32, 40126 Bologna Italy

GIARDINI, FABIO, theologian, educator; b. Forte dei Marmi, Italy, Aug. 7, 1929; s. Tosca and Lupi (Aroldo) G. B in Philosophy, U. St. Thomas, 1949, B in Theology, 1951, D in Theology, 1955. Prof. moral and spiritual theology P. U. St. Thomas, Rome, 1956—; vis. prof. Catholic U., Washington, 1974, St. John's U., N.Y.C., 1980, U. Dallas, Irving, Tex., 1975-81, U. Santo Tomas, Manila, Philippines, 1981, Georgetown U., Washington, 1983, Providence Coll., 1995, 97, 99. Home: Pust Largo Angelicum 1, 00184 Rome Italy

GIBB, ALAN GEORGE, otorhinolaryngologist, educator; b. Aberdeen, Scotland, June 2, 1919; s. George and Elizabeth Latto (Ewan) G.; m. Elisabeth Anne Addison, Sept. 6, 1966; children: Andrew George, Susan Elisabeth Catriona. MB, ChB, U. Aberdeen, 1941. Intern Aberdeen Royal Infirmary, Scotland, 1941-42, Stracathro Hosp., Angus, Scotland, 1942-44; resident City Gen. Hosp, Carlisle, Eng., 1948-50; cons. otolaryngologist Dundee & Tayside region, Scotland, 1950-84; head dept. otolaryngology U. Dundee, 1960-84; vis. prof. otolaryngology U. Kebangsaan, Malaysia, 1985-87; vis. prof. otolargynology Chinese U., Hong Kong, 1988-89, Nat. U., Singapore, 1992-97; Li Dak Sum vis. prof. surgery Chinese U., Hong Kong, 1992. Co-editor: Otology, 1982; co-editor, author: Nasopharyngeal Carcinoma, 1991, 2d edit., 1999; author: The ORL Club, 1991; guest editor, author Ear Nose and Throat Jour., 1990. Maj. Royal Army M.C., 1944-48. Recipient Lawrence Abel Cup, Brit. Med. Assn., 1969, Walter Jobson Horne prize, 1981, Michael Cook Found. fellowship, U.K., 1983. Fellow Royal Soc. Medicine (pres. sect. otology 1975-76), Royal Coll. Surgeons (Edinburgh), Coll. Surgeons Hong Kong; mem. Brit. Assn. Otolaryngologists (hon. life, pres. 1981-84), Scottish Otolaryngol. Soc. (hon. life, pres. 1979-80). Presbyterian. Avocations: choir, golf, angling, snow skiing.

GIBB, ROBERT M., real estate company executive; b. Dodge City, Kans., Dec. 24, 1944; s. Edward O. and Wilda C. G.; m. Noel L. Bowen, Mar. 16, 1974 (div. May 1980); m. Wheatley H., June 25, 1983; 1 child, Mary McReynolds. Degree in bus., Kans. U., 1968. V.p., head trader 1st Nat. City Bank, N.Y.C., 1968-74; trader sales Ernlich-Bober, N.Y.C., 1974-78; sales Smith Barney, N.Y.C., 1978-80; nat. sales mgr. Paine Webber, N.Y.C., 1981-89; sales, owner Johns Island Real Estate Co., Vero Beach, Fla., 1989—. Republican. Episcopal. Avocations: golf, tennis, travel.

GIBBES, WILLIAM HOLMAN, lawyer; b. Hartsville, S.C., Feb. 25, 1930; s. Ernest Lawrence and Nancy (Watson) G.; m. Frances Hagood, May 1, 1954; children: Richard H., William H. Jr., Lynn. BS, U. S.C., 1952, LLB, 1953. Bar: S.C. 1953, U.S. Ct. Mil. Appeals 1954, U.S. Dist. Ct. S.C. 1956, U.S. Supreme Ct. 1959, U.S. Ct. Appeals (4th cir.) 1965. Asst. atty. gen. Columbia, S.C., 1957-62; ptnr. Berry & Gibbes, Columbia, 1962-68, Berry, Lightsey, Gibbes, Columbia, 1968-72; mem. Gibbes Law Firm, P.A., Columbia, 1972—; house of dels. S.C. Bar, 1994-96; chief judge U.S. Army Legal Svcs. Agy., 1980-83. Author: Control of Highway Access - Its Prospects and Problems, Legal Dimensions of Community Health Planning, 1969, Manual for Fee Appraisors, 1960; contbr. articles to S.C. Law Review, Law Rev. Digest, 1960. Chmn. bd. dirs. U. S.C. YMCA, 1956-60. Brig. gen. JAGC, USAR 1980-83. Recipient Legion of Merit, U.S. Army, 1983. Mem. ABA (mil. laws com. 1984-90, meml. com.), S.C. Bar Assn. (exec. com. 1961-62), Am. Bd. Trial Advocates (sec.-treas. 1994-95, pres.-elect 1995-96, pres. 1996-97), Judge Advs. Assn. (pres. 1982-83), Richland County Bar Assn., S.C. Credit Ins. Assn. (gen. counsel 1963-94), Tarantella Club, Caprician Club, Summit Club, Forest Lake Country Club, Kiawah Island Club, Kappa Sigma Kappa, Omicron Delta Kappa. Episcopalian. Home: 4925 Forest Lake Pl Columbia SC 29206-4965

GIBBINS, BOB, lawyer; b. Seminole, Okla., Feb. 27, 1936; s. Robert Lee and La-Ceile Rene (Shackelford) G.; m. Suzanne K. Gibbins (div. Oct. 1975); children: Bob Jr., Steven, Jenny Durbin, Kyndall Krebs; m. Pam Reed, Feb. 26, 1982. BBA, U. Tex., 1958, LLB, 1961. Bar: Tex. 1961, U.S. Dist. Ct. (no. dist.) Tex. 1961, U.S. Ct. Appeals (5th cir.) 1971, U.S. Supreme Ct. 1974, Colo. 1991; diplomate Am. Bd. Trial Advs., Am. Bd. Profl. Liability Attys. Assoc. Morehead, Sharpe, Tisdale & Gibbins, Plainview, Tex., 1961-71; ptnr. Gibbins & Spivey, Austin, Tex., 1971-76; pvt. practice, Austin, 1976-78; sr. ptnr. Gibbins, Wash and Bratton, Austin, 1978-79, Gibbins, Burrow, Wash & Bratton, Austin, 1979-81, Gibbins, Burrow & Bratton, Austin, 1981-86, Gibbins & Bratton, Austin, 1986-89, Gibbins, Winckler & Bayer, Austin, 1989-91, Gibbins, Winckler & Harvey, Austin, 1991-97; pvt. practice law Austin, 1997—. Co-author: Texas Practical Guide: Personal Injury, 1988, Products Liability Litigation: Trial Strategy, 1988. Recipient War Horse award So. Trial Lawyers Assn., 1991, Faculty Svc. award, Univ. Tex. Sch. of Law, 1992; Bob Gibbins endowed presdl. scholarship named in his honor U. Tex. Sch. of Law, Austin, 1991. Fellow Internat. Acad. Trial Lawyers (bd. dirs. 1993-97), Internat. Soc. Barristers, State Bar Tex., Coll. of the State Bar Tex.; mem. Assn. Trial Lawyers Am. (pres. 1991-92, Lifetime Achievement award 1998, Champion of Justice award 1999), Nat. Bd. Trial Advocacy (civil trial adv.), Am. Bd. Trial Advocates (pres. Austin chpt. 1981), Trial Lawyers for Pub. Justice (bd. dir.s 1993), Tex. Trial Lawyers Assn. (dir. emeritus). Office: 500 W 13th St Austin TX 78701-1827

GIBBONS, ALLEN RAY, production engineer, tooling consultant; b. Holland, Mich., Apr. 28, 1955; s. Frank Roy and Charlotte Jean (Folkert) G.; m. Lois Jean Vander Ploeg, June 30, 1975 (div. Sept. 1984); m. Kay Ann Koch, Aug. 24, 1985; children: Greg, Eric. Diploma in drafting, La Salle U., Chgo., 1977; cert. in supr., Mgmt. Inst., Grand Rapids, Mich., 1984, cert. in comms., 1984. Mitre saw operator Howard Miller Clock Co., Zeeland, Mich., 1973; mem. customer svc. staff Zeeland Lumber Co., Zeeland, Mich., 1973-78; bldg. contractor Knopper Constrn., Zeeland, Mich., 1978-80; prodn. engr. S2 Yachts, Holland, Mich., 1980-95; tooling cons. Maverick Boats, Ft. Pierce, Fla., 1995-96, 97-99, Rio Mar Yachts, Vero Beach, Fla., 1996-97, Garlington/Landeweer, Stuart, Fla., 1997-99; composites technician The New Piper Aircraft Inc., 1999—. Mem. Am. Boat and Yacht Coun., Soc. Naval Arch. and Marine Engrs. Avocations: sailing, golf, theater, restorations, parenting. Home: 4465 62nd Ct Vero Beach FL 32967-7815 Office: Piper Aircraft 2926 Piper Dr Vero Beach FL 32960-1964

GIBBONS, CINDY LOUISE, molecular parasitologist; b. Oxford, UK, May 3, 1972; d. Michael and Ann (Cleary) G. BSc, King's Coll., 1994; MSc, London Sch. Hygeine Trop. Med., 1995. Scientific officer Internat. Inst. Parasitology, St. Albans, 1995-96; rsch. asst. Imperial Coll. Sci., Technology & Medicine, London, 1996—. Mem. Br. Soc. Parasitology.

GIBBONS, LARRY ROLAND, civil engineer; b. Vancouver, Wash., Apr. 23, 1943; s. John Roland and Hazel Gibbons; m. Mary Anne Gibbons, Aug. 8, 1944; children: Karen Sue Gibbons Brown, Jerrod Roland, Mary Cameron. BS in Civil Engring., U. Wash., 1966. Registered profl. engr., Wash. Civil engr. GSII U.S. Army C.E., Seattle, 1966-70; assoc. engr. flood control divsn. King County, Seattle, 1970-72, sr. engr. surface water mgmt. divsn., 1973-79, mgr. surface water mgmt. divsn., 1979—. Mem. Am. Soc. Engring. Mgmt. (pres. bd. dirs. 1994-96, Most Inspirational award 1994), Am. Pub. Works Assn. Avocations: golf, fly fishing, gardening. Home: 19812 108th Ave NE Bothell WA 98011-2414

GIBBONS, MARY PEYSER, civic volunteer; b. N.Y.C., Dec. 15, 1936; d. Frederick Maurice and Catherine Mary (McKelvey) Peyser; m. John Martin Gibbons, Dec. 26, 1955; children: Catherine Way, Mary Sloan, John, Fredericka Kerr, Myles. Trustee Wadsworth Atheneum, 1978-99, hon. trustee, 2000; trustee Hartford Art Sch., 1985-95; regent U. Hartford, 1988-95—; bd. dirs. Hartford Ballet, 1981-95, Conn. Valley Girl Scouts, 1994-95, U.S. Found. World Fedn., Friends of Museums, 1990—; vol. Com. Art Mus., U.S. and Can., 1982-91; pres. Am. Assn. Mus. Vols., 1983-91, adv. bd. mem., 1991—; corporator St. Francis Hosp., 1990—, Hartford Ballet, 1995-97, Conn. Inst. for the Blind; mem. alumnae bd. divs. Convent of the Sacred Heart, 91th St., N.Y.C. Mem. Hartford Golf Club, Town and County Club. Office: Sefton & Sheil Ltd 1130 Prospect Ave Hartford CT 06105-1124

GIBBONS, MICHAEL LAWRENCE, software engineer; b. New Haven, Conn., May 15, 1969; s. Robert Joseph and Kathryn Antoinette (Sheldon) G. Student, Villanova U., 1986-88; AS, Ohlone Coll., Fremont, Calif., 1990-92; BS in Computer Sci. Engring., U. Tex., Arlington, 1994. Systems engr. Tandy Corp., Phila., 1986-87; systems engring. mgr. Tandy Corp., Orange, Conn., 1988; systems engr. Grid Systems, Stamford, Conn., 1989; mktg. mgr. Grid Systems, Fremont, Calif., 1990-92, Fort Worth, 1992-93; instr. U. Tex., Arlington, 1994; software engr. Digital Print, Inc., Ft. Worth, 1995-96; systems engr. Telxon Corp., Dallas, 1996-98; dir. info. systems The Great Train Store Ptnrs., L.P., Dallas, 1998-99, chief info. officer, 1999-2000; dir. info. sys. Tex. Pacific Group, Ft. Worth, 2000—. Mem. Aircraft Owners and Pilots Assn., Alpha Gamma Sigma. Home: 1814 Hunters Ridge Dr Grapevine TX 76051-7923

GIBBONS, ROBERT EBBERT, university official; b. Sharon, Pa., Nov. 15, 1940; s. Thomas Michael and Mary Jane (Ebbert) G.; m. Patricia Arlene Fox, Aug. 18, 1962; children: Patrick, Timothy, Roberta, Aaron. B.S., John Carroll U., 1962; M.A., Bowling Green State U., 1963, Ph.D., 1967. Pres. Viterbo Coll., La Crosse, Wis., 1980-91; asst. prof. English Our Lady of the Lake U., San Antonio, 1969-72, chmn. English dept., 1972-74, dir. humanities div., 1974-77, exec. asst. to pres., 1977-80, exec. v.p., 1991-99, prof. English, 1999—. Bd. dirs. Wis. Found. of Ind. Colls., Milw., 1980-91, pres., 1987-88; mem. USCC Com. on Cert. and Accreditation, 1988-94, vice chair, 1991-93. Mem. Phi Kappa Phi. Roman Catholic. Home: 3518 Hunters Gate St San Antonio TX 78230-2820 Office: Our Lady of the Lake U 411 SW 24th St San Antonio TX 78207-4666

GIBBONS, ROBERT PHILIP, management consultant; m. Mary Jane M. Jamieson, June 12, 1965; children: Laura Ann, Robert John. BSME, Stevens Inst. Tech., 1955; MS in Indsl. Mgmt., Purdue U., 1959. Ptnr., Touche Ross Co., N.Y.C., 1959-74; v.p., gen. mgr. Carborundum Co., Niagara Falls, N.Y., 1975-78; ptnr. Main Hurdman, N.Y.C., 1978-84, Zolfo, Cooper & Co., 1984-86, ptnr. Gibbons, Quintero & Co., N.Y.C., 1986-90, Gibbons & Co., 1990—; apptd. trustee U.S. Trustee and U.S. Bankruptcy Ct.; bd. dirs., chmn. audit com., compensation com. Weldotron Corp., 1974-91. Contbr. sect. to Am. Mgmt. Assn. Management Handbook, 1970. With U.S. Army, 1956-58. Mem. Am. Prodn. and Inventory Control Soc. (cert.), Inst. Mgmt. Cons. (cert.), Am. Bankruptcy Inst., Turnaround Mgmt. Assn. Office: Gibbons & Company 46 Knoll Rd Tenafly NJ 07670-1050

GIBBS, BARRY MARSHALL, acoustical engineer, educator, researcher; b. Sunderland, Eng., Mar. 20, 1946; s. Stanley and Harriet (Jollif) G.; m. Sally Irene Thurstan; children: George, Lily, Harry. BSc in Physics, Sheffield (Eng.) U., 1968, MA in Arch., 1970; PhD, Aston U., Birmingham, Eng., 1974. Chartered engr., Eng. Rsch. asst. Aston U., Birmingham, Eng., 1970-76, rsch. fellow, 1976-77; lectr. Liverpool (Eng.) U., 1977-90, sr. lectr., 1990-92, reader, 1992-97, prof., 1997—, cons., 1977—; Editor Bldg. Acoustics, 1993—. Fellow Inst. Acoustics (coun. 1998—), Internat. Inst. Acoustics and Vibration, Brit. Stds. Instn. Office: U Liverpool/Leverhaume Bldg, Abercromby Sq, Liverpool L69 3BX, England

GIBBS, BRIAN J., behavioral scientist, business researcher, educator, consultant; b. Vancouver, B.C., Can., July 28, 1959; came to U.S., 1985; s. Richard H. and Jean E. Gibbs. BSc in Biopsychology, U. B.C., 1982, MA in Psychology, 1985; PhD in Behavioral Sci. and Mktg., U. Chgo., 1992. Rschr. Psychophysics Lab., Vancouver, 1980-82, Attention Lab., Vancouver, 1982-85, Decision Rsch. Lab., Chgo., 1985-90; asst. prof. mktg. and behavioral sci. Grad. Sch. Bus. Stanford (Calif.) U., 1990-98; assoc. prof. mgmt. (mktg. and behavioral sci.) Owen Grad. Sch. Mgmt., Vanderbilt U., Nashville, 1998—; hon. bd. dirs. Round Table Group, Inc.; presenter rsch. seminars, U.S. and abroad. Contbr. sci. articles to profl. jours. Natural Scis. and Engring. Rsch. Coun. Can. postgrad. scholar, 1983-84, 85-86; Social Scis. and Humanities Rsch. Coun. Can. doctoral fellow, 1985-89. Mem. APA, Am. Mktg. Assn., Am. Psychological Soc., Assn. Consumer Rsch., Inst. for Ops. Rsch. and Mgmt. Sci., Soc. for Consumer Psychology, Soc. Judgment and Decision Making. Avocations: martial arts, photography, snorkeling, hiking, film. Office: Vanderbilt U Owen Grad Sch Mgmt 401 21st Ave S Nashville TN 37240-1104

GIBBS, CLYDE BAXTER, JR., medical examiner specialist; b. Belhaven, N.C., Dec. 3, 1970; s. Clyde Baxter and Connie Brown Gibbs. BS in Anthropology/Allied Health, Appalachian State U., 1993; AS in Mortuary Sci., Gupton-Jones Coll., 1994. Funeral svc. lic. Periodicals asst. Belk Libr., Appalachian State U., Boone, N.C., 1991-93; funeral svc. trainee H.M. Patterson & Son, Atlanta, 1993-94; funeral svc. apprentice Paul Funeral Home, Inc., Washington, N.C., 1994-95; funeral svc. licensee Cremation Soc. of the Carolinas, Durham, N.C., 1996-98; libr. page Durham County Libr., Durham, 1997-98; med. examiner specialist Office of the Chief Med. Examiner, Chapel Hill, N.C., 1997—. Mem. Population Comm. Intenrat., Am. Humanist Assn., Ams. United for Separation of Ch. and State, So. Poverty Law Ctr., World Wildlife Fund, Zero Population Growth, Pi Gamma Mu. Avocations: reading, darts, watching movies, disc golf. E-mail: cgibbs@ocme.unc.edu. Home: 5639 Chapel Hill Blvd Apt 608 Durham NC 27707-3320 Office: Office of the Chief Med Examiner PO Box 7580 Chapel Hill NC 27599-0001

GIBBS, DAVID LEE, microbiologist, executive; b. San Francisco, July 5, 1948; s. John O. and Ruth E. Gibbs; m. Barbara J. Gibbs, Dec. 17, 1987; 1 child, Carmen Mauck. BS, U. of Pacific, 1970; PhD in Microbiology, Cornell U., 1974. Diplomate Am. Bd. Med. Microbiology. Fellow Ctrs. for Disease Control, Atlanta, 1974-76; cons. WHO, Arrah, Bihar, India, 1977; asst. prof. microbiology Med. Coll. Cornell U., N.Y.C., 1977-80; dir. labs. Communicable Diseases Lab., Salvador, Brazil, 1977-80; dir. clin. microbiology Santa Clara Med. Ctr., San Jose, Calif., 1980-81; dir. clin. rsch. Pfizer Inc., N.Y.C., 1981-98; pres., founder Giles Sci. Inc., Santa Barbara, Calif., 1984—. Contbr. over 40 articles to sci. publs.; patentee microbiology instrumentation (6). Grantee, NIH, Washington, 1970-74, 74-76, 79, Rockefeller Found., N.Y.C., 1977-79. Mem. Am. Soc. Microbiology, Coral Casino Club. E-mail: giles@biomic.com. Office: Giles Sci Inc 331 N Milpas St Ste A Santa Barbara CA 93103-3299

GIBBS, NORMAN CHARLES WILLIAM, accounting and finance educator; b. Croydon, Eng., Mar. 21, 1923; s. Charles Alfred and Kathleen Florence (Reeve) G.; m. June Isabel Goldsack; children: Lyndall Anne, Vanessa Susan. MSc in Econs., London Sch. Econs., 1971. Dep. sec., chief acct. Ozalid Co. Ltd., London, 1954-63; prin. lectr. acctg. and fin. City Guild Hall U., London, 1963-74; assoc. prof. acctg. Nairobi (Kenya) U., 1974-76; chief tech. adviser, prof. fin. mgmt. UN Agy. Inst. Fin. Mgmt., Dar es Salaam, Tanzania, 1977-79; chief tech. adviser UN Agy., Lilongwe, Malawi, 1979-84; cons. fin. mgmt., 1991—; cons. acctg. edn. Asian Devel. Bank, Manila, 1985-90. Contbr. articles to profl. jours. With RAF, 1942-46; 322 Squadron Spitfire Pilot. Fellow Assn. Chartered Cert. Accts.; mem. Chartered Inst. Secs. and Adminstrs. (assoc.), Aero Club of Barcelona. Avocations: private pilot. Home and Office: Paseo 328 No 20, Castelldefels, Barcelona Spain

GIBBS, PATRICIA HELLMAN, physician; b. Boston, Oct. 22, 1958; d. Frederick Warren and Patricia Christina (Sander) H.; m. Richard D. Gibbs, Dec. 22, 1984; children: Ruth, Samuel, Matthew, Kate, Frank. BA summa cum laude, Williams Coll., 1982; MD, Yale U., 1987. Diplomate Am. Bd. Family Practice. Intern, resident in family practice U. Wash., Seattle, 1987-90; ptnr. Tricia Gibbs, MD and Richard Gibbs, MD, San Francisco, 1990-95; co-founder, med. dir. San Francisco Free Clinic, 1993—; supervising physician San Francisco Ballet, 1990-95. Co-author: Medical and Orthopedic Issues of Active and Athletic Women-Skiing, 1993, Spine Care-Dance, 1993. Founder Sugar Bowl Acad., 1999. Women's scholar Williams Coll., 1982, Class of '25 Athlete scholar, 1982; named Family Physician of Yr., Calif. Acad. Family Physicians, 1998. Mem. AMA, Am. Acad. Family Physicians, Phi Beta Kappa, Sigma Xi. Avocations: distance running, ski racing, computers. Office: San Francisco Free Clinic 4900 California St San Francisco CA 94118-1115

GIBBS, SYDNEY ROYSTON, health facility administrator; b. West Plains, Mo., June 15, 1934; s. Wallace Pemberton and Leila Mary (Royston) G.; m. Clarice Ellen Smith, Dec. 28, 1958; children: Sydney Royston Jr., Julie Gibbs Erwin. BS with honors, U. Ala., 1955; MD, U. Tenn., 1958. Diplomate Am. Bd. Surgery. Intern U. Tenn. Hosps., Knoxville, 1959; pvt. practice Roberta, Ga., 1960; jr. asst. surgery resident U. Ala. Hosps., Birmingham, 1961; ptnr. Drs. Clinic and Hosp., Bessemer, Ala., 1963-66; jr. surgery resident Lloyd Noland Hosp., Birmingham, 1967-68, sr. surgery resident, 1969; pvt. practice Bessemer, 1970-88; med. dir. ACIPCO Health Svcs., Birmingham, 1989—; pres. med. staff Bessemer Carraway Med. Ctr., 1982-83, mem. bd. trustees, 1982-83, chief of surgery, 1974-75. Contbr. articles to profl. jours. Witness on employer mandate/health security act U.S. Ho. of Reps., 1994; active deacon bd. Shades Mountain Bapt. Ch., 1980; med. missionary Antigua, West Indies, 1975, 78. Major U.S. Army, 1962. Fellow ACS, Southeastern Coll. Surgeons; mem. Am. Coll. Physician Execs., Birmingham Acad. Medicine. Avocations: woodworking, travel. E-mail: sydney@wwisp.com. Office: ACIPCO Health Svcs 2930 16th St N Birmingham AL 35207-4806

GIBBY, MABEL ENID KUNCE, psychologist; b. St. Louis, Mar. 30, 1926; d. Ralph Waldo and Mabel Enid (Warren) Kunce; student Washington U., St. Louis, 1943-44, postgrad., 1955-56; B.A., Park Coll., 1945; M.A., McCormick Theol. Sem., 1947; postgrad. Columbia U., 1948, U. Kansas City, 1949, George Washington U., 1953; M.Ed., U. Mo., 1951, Ed.D., 1952; m. John Francis Gibby, Aug. 27, 1948; children—Janet Marie (Mrs. Kim Williams), Harold Steven, Helen Elizabeth, Diane Louise (Mrs. Roderick Rohrich), John Andrew, Keith Sherridan, Daniel Jay. Dir. religious edn. Westport Presbyn. Ch. Kansas City, Mo., 1947-49; tchr. elementary schs., Kansas City, 1949-50; high sch. counselor Arlington (Va.) Pub. Schs., 1952-54; counselor adult counseling services Washington U., 1955-56; counseling psychologist Coral Gables (Fla.) VA Hosp., 1956—; counseling psychologist Miami (Fla.) VA Hosp., 1956—, chief counseling psychology sect., 1982-86; sr. psychologist Office Disability Determination Fla. Hdqrs., 1987-94. Sec. bd. dirs. Fla. Vocat. Rehab. Found. Recipient Meritorious Service citation Fla. C. of C., 1965, President's Com. on Employment of Handicapped, 1965; commendation for meritorious service Com. on Employment of Physically Handicapped Dade County, 1965, named Outstanding Rehab. Profl., 1966, 81; named Profl. Fed. Employee of Year, Greater Miami Fed. Exec. Council, 1966; Outstanding Fed. Service award Greater Miami Fed. Exec. Council, 1966; Fed. Woman's award U.S. Civil Service Commn., 1968, Community Headliner award Theta Sigma Phi, 1968, Outstanding Alumni award Park Coll., 1968, Freedom award The Chosen Few, Korean War Vets. Assn., 1986; certificate of appreciation Bur. Customs, U.S. Treasury Dept., 1969, Fla. Dept. Health and Rehab. Services, 1970. Mem. Am., Dade County (past sec.) psychol. assns., Nat., Fla. (past dir. Dade County chpt.) rehab. assns., Nat. Rehab. Counseling Assn. (past sec.). Patentee in field. Home: 7107 Aberdeen Ave Dallas TX 75230-5406

GIBELLINI, ROSINO, publishing executive, theologian; b. Gambara, Italy, July 22, 1926. PhD in Theology, Gregorian U., Rome, 1955; PhD in Philosophy, Cath. U. Milan, 1968. Literary dir. Editrice Queriniana, Brescia, Italy, 1965—. Author: Teilhard de Chardin: L'Opera e le Interpretazioni, 1992, La Teologia di Jürgen Moltmann, 1975, Teologia e Ragione, Itinerario e Opera di Wolfhart Panenberg, 1980, Il Dibattito Sulla Teologia Della Liberazione, 1986, La Teologia del XX Secolo, 1996. Roman Catholic. Avocations: reading, travel. Home: Via Cremona, 99, I-25124 Brescia Italy Office: Editrice Queriniana, Via Ferri, 75, I-25123 Brescia Italy

GIBELLO, BERNARD, psychopathologist of thinking, psychoanalyst, psychiatrist; b. Paris, May 6, 1932; s. Henri and Denise (Pradier) G.; m. Marie-Luce Verdier, June 11, 1971; children: Emmanuelle, Hélène. MD, U. Paris, 1969, PhD in Psychology, 1983. Resident Hosp., Bourges, France, 1957-62; resident Hosp. Salpétrière, Paris, 1962-66, founder, dir. Lab. Functional Exploration and Therapeutical Rsch. Applied to Cognitive and Intellectual Disorders; extraordinary prof. U. Paris, 1967-85; ordinary prof. U. Dijon, France, 1986-91; ordinary prof. psychopathology U. Paris, 1991—. Author: (with H. Beauchesnel) Traité de psychopathologie infantile, 1991, L'enfant A L'intelligence Troublée, 1984, La Pensée Décontenancée, 1995; editor: Pensée Sans Langage, 1995, Perspectives Psychiatriques, 1967-97. Mem. Group for Study Psychiatry, Psychology and Social Scis. (gen. sec. 1967-97), Soc. for Psychology. Home: Place St Georges, F-70310 Faucogney France Office: Hosp Salpétrière, Clin G Heuyer Cedex 13, F-75651 Paris France

GIBERT, THIERRY MICHEL, merger and acquisition specialist; b. Metz, France, July 9, 1963; s. Pierre Jean and Monique Marie (Briot) G. Degree in Engring., Ecole Centrale De Paris, 1986; MS, Fla. Atlantic U., Boca Raton, 1988. Cons. Bossard Consultants, Paris, 1988-90; sr. cons. Bossard Consultants, Warsaw, 1990-91, Co. Assistance Ltd., Warsaw, 1991-92; v.p. Econ. Innovation Internat., Boston, 1992-94; specialist Dirigeants & Investisseurs, Paris, 1994-98; investment banking Die Erste Bank, 1998—; cons., expert OECD, Paris, 1994-97; cons. Slovak Assn. for Reg. Devel., Bratislava, 1995. Mem. bd. dirs. ECP Alumni Orgn., Paris, 1989—, chmn. internat. affairs, 1996-98; mem. French-Austrian C. of C., Vienna, 1994—. Office: Die Erste Bank/CDI, Schellinggasse 7, 1010 Wien Austria

GIBLIN, MICHAEL ERIC, ophthalmic surgeon; b. Sydney, NSW, Australia, Aug. 3, 1953; s. Dexter Frederick and Marian Joyce (Niebling) G.; m. Elizabeth Ellen Hartigan, Apr. 15, 1978; twins: Damien, Stephanie. MB, BS, Sydney U., 1978. Intern, resident, registrar Sydney Hosp., Sydney Eye Hosp., 1978-84; fellow cataract surgery Hamburg (Germany) U. Eye Clinic, 1985; locum cons. Addenbrooke's Hosp., Cambridge (Eng.) U., 1986; fellow ocular oncology Wills Eye Hosp., Phila., 1986-87; vis. med. officer Royal Alexandra Hosp. for Children, Sydney, 1988—, Sydney Eye Hosp., 1990—; presenter in field. Asst. editor Australian and New Zealand Jour. Ophthalmology, 1990—; contbr. articles to profl. jours. Fellow Royal Australian Coll. Ophthalmologists (sec. NSW br. 1991-92, fed. sec. 1992-99), Royal Australasian Coll. Surgeons, Am. Acad. Ophthalmology; mem. Australian Med. Assn., Australian Club. Avocations: gliding, surfing, skiing, magic, music. Home: 18 Melbourne Rd, Lindfield NSW 2070, Australia Office: Ste 304, 7 Help St Chatswood, Sydney NSW 2067, Australia

GIBNEY, FRANK BRAY, publisher, editor, writer, foundation executive; b. Scranton, Pa., Sept. 21, 1924; s. Joseph James and Edna May (Wetter) G.; m. Harriet Harvey, Dec. 10, 1948 (div. 1957); children: Alex, Margot; m. Harriet C. Suydam, Dec. 14, 1957 (div. 1971); children: Frank, James, Thomas; m. Hiroko Doi, Oct. 5, 1972; children: Elise, Josephine. BA, Yale U., 1945; DLitt (hon.), Kyung Hee U., Seoul, Korea, 1974. Corr., assoc. editor Time mag., N.Y.C., Tokyo and London, 1947-54; sr. editor Newsweek, N.Y.C., 1954-57; staff writer, editorial writer Life mag., N.Y.C., 1957-61; pub., pres. SHOW mag., N.Y.C., 1961-64; pres. Ency. Brit. (Japan), Tokyo, 1965-69; pres. TBS-Brit., Tokyo, 1969-75, vice chmn., 1976-99; v.p. Ency. Brit., Inc., Chgo., 1975-79; vice chmn., bd. editors Ency. Brit., Chgo., 1978—; pres. Pacific Basin Inst., Pomona Coll., Claremont, Calif., 1979—; prof. Pomona Coll., 1997—; bd. dirs. U.S. Com. for Pacific Econ. Cooperation, 1988—, v.p., 1993-95; cons. com. on space and aeros. U.S. Ho. of Reps., Washington, 1957-59; vice chmn. Japan-U.S. Friendship Commn., 1984-90, U.S.-Japan Com. Edn. and Cultural Interchange, 1984-90. Author: Five Gentlemen of Japan, 1953, The Frozen Revolution, 1959, (with Peter Deriabin) The Secret World, 1960, The Operators, 1961, The Khrushchev Pattern, 1961, The Reluctant Space Farers, 1965, Japan: The Fragile Super-Power, 1975, 3rd edit., 1996, Miracle by Design, 1983, The Pacific Century, 1992, Korea's Quiet Revolution, 1993; co-author: The Battle for Okinawa, 1995; editor: The Penkovskiy Papers, 1965, Senso, 1995, Unlocking The Bureaucrats' Kingdom, 1998, The Nanjing Massacre, 1999. Served to lt. USNR, 1942-46. Decorated Order of the Rising Sun 3d Class Japan, Order of Sacred Treasure 2d Class Japan. Mem. Council on Fgn. Relations, Tokyo Fgn. Corr. Club, Am. C.of C. (Tokyo), Japan-Am. Soc., Japan Soc. Roman Catholic. Clubs: Century Assn., Yale (N.Y.C.); Tokyo; Tavern, The Arts (Chgo.). Home: 1901 E Las Tunas Rd Santa Barbara CA 93103-1745

GIBSON, CHARLES ANTHONY, archivist; b. Belize, June 8, 1953; s. Edward Bernard and Olive Cressy (Usher) G.; m. Karen Therese Tate, Dec. 15, 1985; children: Giselle Jolene, Kamille Patrice. BA in Libr. Scis., U. West Indies, 1980; MA in Archives Studies, U. London, 1982. Libr. asst. Nat. Libr. Svc., Belize City, Belize, 1973-80; libr. Nat. Archives, Belmopan, Belize, 1980-81, archivist, 1981-83; chief archivist Belize Archives Dept., Belmopan, 1983—; lectr. Belize Inst. Mgmt., 1990—; bd. dirs. Belizean Studies; sec. Belize Archives Adv. bd., 1986—. Mem. Assn. Pub. Svc. Sr. Mgrs. (sec. 1992-94), Caribbean Archives Assn. (immediate past pres.), Assn. Commonwealth Archivist and Record Mgrs. (chmn.), Internat. Coun. on Archives (sec. Commn. for Archival Devel.). Office: Belize Archives Dept, 26/28 Unity Blvd, Belmopan Belize*

GIBSON, DAVID MARK, biochemist, educator; b. Kokomo, Ind., Aug. 7, 1923; s. Carl Banta and Marie (Loop) G.; m. Margaret Lockhart, June 2, 1951 (dec. Apr. 1992); children: Carl L., John L., Shauna Gibson Kopp, Heather Gibson Garrison, Mark C. AB, Wabash Coll., 1944; MD, Harvard, 1948. Intern Northwestern U. Med. Sch., 1948-49; research assoc. biochemistry U. Ill., Urbana, 1950-53; research assoc., asst. prof. Inst. Enzyme Research, U. Wis., 1953-55, 55-58; assoc. prof. biochemistry Ind. U. Sch. Medicine, Indpls., 1958-61, prof. biochemistry, 1961—, Grace M. Showalter prof., 1974-92, prof. emeritus, 1992—, chmn., 1967-88; vis. prof. U. Padua, Italy, 1964-65, U. Utrecht, The Netherlands, 1975; established investigator Am. Heart Assn., 1957-62. Recipient NIH career devel. award, 1962-67. Mem. AAAS, Am. Soc. Cell Biology, Am. Soc. Biol. Chemists, Am. Diabetes Assn., Biochem. Soc. (Eng.), Sigma Xi. Achievements include rsch. of biochem. mechanisms and control fatty acid synthesis and cholesterol synthesis. Home: 3436 Brisbane Rd Indianapolis IN 46228-2715

GIBSON, DOUGLAS L., lawyer, state judge; b. Folkston, Ga., Mar. 17, 1955; s. Lamar and Betty (Jones) G.; m. Delores Taylor, Sept. 30, 1978; children: Taylor Lamar, Adrienne Jewell. BA cum laude, Mercer U., 1977; JD, U. Ga., 1980. Atty. Gibson, McGee & Jackson, Waycross, Ga., 1980-81, 84-87; pub. defender Ware County, Waycross, Ga., 1981-82; solicitor State Ct. of Ware County, Waycross, Ga., 1987-96; ptnr. Gibson & Jacksoon, PC, Waycross, Ga., 1987-93; pres. Gibson & Spivey, PC, Waycross, Ga., 1994—; judge State Ct. Ware County, Waycross, Ga., 1997—; bd. govs. State Bar Ga., Atlanta, 1996-98; bd. dirs. Atty.'s Title Guaranty Fund, Macon, Ga. Coach, h.s. mock trial team, Ware County Sch. Agrl. Forestry & Environ. Scis., Manor, Ga., 1994—. Methodist. Avocations: private pilot, scuba diving. E-mail: gibspi@accessetc.net. Office: Gibson & Spivey PC 117 Albany Ave Waycross GA 31501-3502

GIBSON, EDWARD WILLIAM, plastic surgeon, educator; b. Sydney, Australia, Apr. 24, 1920; s. Leslie James and Catherine May (Wall) G.; m. Barbara Hildegard Granowski, Jan. 9, 1949; children: Amanda Julia, Edwina Michelle. M.B., B.S., U. Sydney, 1942, M.S., 1947. Intern Royal Prince Alfred Hosp., Sydney, 1942, chmn. med. bd., 1971-75; resident in plastic and reconstructive surgery Queen Victoria Hosp., East Grinstead, End., 1949; sr. registrar in plastic and reconstructive surgery Queen Victoria Hosp., East Grinstead, 1950-51; practice medicine specializing in plastic and reconstructive Sydney, 1951—; sr. lectr. plastic surgery U. Sydney, 1960—. Co-author: Plastic Surgery-A Guide to Clinical Practice, 1968, 3d edit., 1979; contbr. articles to profl. jours. Served with Australian Air Force, 1943-46. Nuffield fellow, London, 1949-50. Fellow Royal Australian Coll. Surgeons (chmn. divsn. plastic surgery 1963-65, ct. examiner 1962-72), ACS; mem. Australian Soc. Plastic Surgeons (coun. 1966). Clubs: Royal Sydney Golf, Australian (Sydney). Avocations: aviation, golf, skiing, tennis, trout fishing. Home: 135 Victoria Rd, Bellevue Hill 2023, Australia Office: 193 Macquarie St,, 2000 Sydney New South Wales Australia

GIBSON, FLORENCE ANDERSON, talking book company executive, narrator; b. San Francisco, Feb. 7, 1924; m. V.H. Carlos Gibson, Aug. 30, 1947; children: Nancy Derwent, Christopher Carlos, Katherine Wayne Bolland, Diana Corona. Student, Finch Jr. Coll., N.Y.C., 1941-42; BA in Dramatic Lit., U. Calif., Berkeley, 1944; student, Neighborhood Playhouse, N.Y.C., 1944-45. Radio actress San Francisco, 1944, 46, 47; chmn. Washington com. Am. Field Svc., 1958-60, 62-65; founder, chmn. Peruvian Com. Am. Field Svc., Lima, 1960-62; treas., distbn. mgr. Living Garden and Concern 1975 calendars, 1971-75; sec. exec. com Fgn. Student Svc. Coun., 1973-76; narrator Talking Books Libr. of Congress div. for Blind and Physically Handicapped, 1975-96; narrator Recorded Books, Inc., 1979; founder, pres. Audio Book Contractors, Inc., 1982—; narrator numerous unabridged books on cassettes. Actress, appearing in Blithe Spirit, 1945, Ah, Wilderness, 1946, Traffic Ct. TV series, others, more than 914 books on cassettes. Bd. dirs. Fgn. Student Svc. Coun., Concern, Inc., Rec. for the Blind, Children's Theater of Washington; vol. in occupational therapy Children's Hosp., Washington, 1949-50; vol. lobbyist student exch. program Am. Field Svc. Recipient 3 Parents' Choice awards, 1983, 84, 86, Audiophile Earpone award, 2000; named Best Female Narrator, Book World, 1989; selected as A Notable Children's Recording, ALA, 1983, 87, 88, 89. Home: 4626 Garfield St NW Washington DC 20007-1025 Office: Audio Book Contractors Inc PO Box 40115 Washington DC 20016-0115

GIBSON, FRANCES, nurse; b. Junction, Tex., Sept. 28, 1936; d. August and Juanita (Corpus-Garcia) Rehwoldt; m. Richard Gibson, July 4, 1954 (dec. July 25, 1962); children; Kenneth, René, Allison. AA, East Los Angeles Coll. Lic. vocat. nurse, Calif.; RN, Calif.; cert. oper. rm. technician, Calif.; cert. adult edn. tchr.; paralegal. Instr., profl. expert East Los Angeles Coll., Monterey Park, Calif., 1971-74; hostess talk show (in Spanish) Sta. KMEX-TV, L.A., 1970-76; tchr. adult edn. Garvey Sch. Bd., Rosemead, Calif., 1976-77; case mgr. AIDS Healthcare Found., L.A., 1991-93; clin. nurse Los Angeles County/U. So. Calif. Med. Ctr., 1981-89, AIDS clinician, 1993; vol. nurse Lung Assn., L.A., 1970-76, ARC, L.A., 1969—; instr. health classes ARC, also instr. Spanish to ARC pers., mgr. info. booths at health fairs and convs., provider first aid at various gatherings, immunization clinics, chmn. adv. bd., 1971-72, bd. dirs., 1972-75, 79-82; med. editor, legal asst. Ivie & McNeill, L.A., 1986—. Author: Spanish for English-Speaking Personnel, 1972. Recipient Spotlight award ARC, 1972, Clara Barton award ARC, 1976, 30-Yr. Vol. award ARC, 1999, Associate Womens Students award East L.A. Coll., 1969; named one of Ten Prettiest Chicanas in East Los Angeles, East L.A. Merchants, 1970. Mem. Nat. Assn. Chicano Nurses, AFL-CIO, Alpha Gamma Sigma. Democrat. Baptist. Avocations: gardening, crafts. Home: 2241 Charlotte Ave Rosemead CA 91770-3624

GIBSON, GARY RICHARD, educator; b. Feb. 2, 1942. BS, Brigham Young U., 1974, MS, 1979. Personnel and labor rels. mgr. W.T.D. Corp., L.A., 1976-79; adminstrv. mgr. Wycoff Trucking, Salt Lake City, 1979-82; academic divsn. chair Lee Coll., Huntsville, Tex., 1982—. Home: 45 Elkins Lk Huntsville TX 77340-7301

GIBSON, IAN BENNETT, retired business executive; b. Leeds, Eng., June 10, 1936; s. Stanley Silvers and Florence Muriel (Blackie) G.; m. Jane Macvean Graham-Pole, June 3, 1961; children: David Antony, Robert Alan. Student pub. schs., Leeds. Master mariner. Cadet officer Ellerman's Wilson Line Ltd., Hull, Eng., 1952-56, navigating officer, 1956-58; navigating officer Lyle Shipping Co. Ltd., Glasgow, Scotland, 1958-59; navigating officer United Baltic Corp. Ltd., London, 1960-64, ship's master, 1964-65; sales dir. Carron Becander Ltd., Falkirk, Scotland, 1965-69; gen. mgr. for tractors Brit. Leyland (U.K.) Ltd., Bathgate, Scotland, 1969-74; mgmt. cons. Stirling, Scotland, 1974-78; mng. dir. United Baltic Corp GmbH, Kiel, Germany, 1978-96, Baltic Marine Svcs. GmbH, Kiel, 1988-96; ret., 1996; hon. Brit. consul, Kiel, 1988-96. Decorated Order Brit. Empire. Mem. Farmer's Club London, Libbaton Golf Club. Anglican. Home: 25 Fairways View, High Bickington, Devon EX37 9BZ, England

GIBSON, JAMES ELLIOTT, architect; b. McMinnville, Oreg., Aug. 14, 1922; s. James H. and Julia Etta (Cummins) G.; m. Clara June Bosson, Dec. 19, 1948 (dec. Sept. 1967); children: Graeme E.B., Randolph U., James B.P.; m. Suzan Bailliere Brand Brown, Jan. 1, 1980 (dec. June 1998); children: John W. Brown, Natalie T. Brown, Frank D. Brown, Susannah Brown Kavanaugh. BS in Music, U. Oreg., 1944; BArch, U. Mich., 1950. Registered architect, Mich., Fla., S.C., Ohio; cert. NCARB. Architect Harley, Ellington & Day, Inc., Detroit, 1950-69, James E. Gibson, Architects & Assocs., Inc., Vero Beach, Fla., 1969-83, Gibson & Silkworth, Architects & Assocs., Inc., Vero Beach, 1983-97, Gibson & Assocs., Architects, Inc., Vero Beach, 1997—. Pres. Vero Beach Concert Assn., 1971-79, 81-83, pres. Treasure Coast Opera Assn., Vero Beach, 1979-81; bd. dirs. Atlantic Classical Orch., Vero Beach, 1992—, pres., 1998—; bd. dirs., mem. adv. bd. Riverside Theatre, Vero Beach; mem. adv. bd. Ctr. for the Arts, Vero Beach. Staff sgt. U.S. Army, 1942-46, ETO. Recipient Bus. in the Arts award, 1986, Aurora Grand award Assoc. Gen. Contractors, 1985. Mem. AIA, John's Island Club (Vero Beach), Riomar Bay Yacht Club (Vero Beach), Carolina Yacht Club (Charleston, S.C.). Avocations: musical performance, antiques collecting, sculpture, historical preservation. Office: Gibson & Assocs Architects 606 Azalea Ln Vero Beach FL 32963-1832

GIBSON, JANNETTE POE, educator, consultant; b. Lubbock, Tex., Oct. 29, 1948; d. Hugh Miller and Norma Grace (Harrison) Poe; m. William Carroll Gibson, June 30, 1967; children: Darin L., Arminda L. Gibson Peery, Victoria L. Gibson Dixon. BS, East Tex. State U., 1971, MEd, 1981; postgrad., Tex. A&M U., Commerce, 1992—. Tchr. Como (Tex.)-Pickton Ind. Sch. Dist., 1971-77; tchr., cons. Diosese of Dallas, Diocese of Tyler, Tex., 1982-87; tchr., supr. Hyder Migrant Ctr., Dateland, Ariz., 1987-88; tchr., adult ESL edn. dir. Ariz. Western U., Hyder Campus, 1988-89; tchr. Sulphur Springs (Tex.) Ind. Sch. Dist., 1989-98; cons., presenter Multicultural/Migrant Edn., 1987—; edn. diagnostician Sulphur Springs ISD Spl. Edn. Dept., 1998—; cons. ESL edn. and early childhood edn. and child devel. U.S. Dept. Edn., 1988-89; profl. adv. com. Sulphur Springs Ind. Sch. Dist., 1990, 92, 96; doctoral adv. bd. East Tex. State U., 1993-96; regional

adv. com. migrant edn. Region V111 Svc., 1994-97, advisor Tex. Edn. Agy. assessments of ESL/LEP children, 1997-98; cons. for devel. of culture and lang. bias-free assessments to sch. dists. in Tex.; presenter in fields of migrant edn. and ESL; private cons. assessment in sch. dists., Tex. Mem. AAUW, NEA, Tex. State Tchrs. Assn., TAMU Doctoral Students Assn., TESOL, Classroom Tchrs. Assn. Tex., Tex. Ednl. Diagnosticians Assn., N.E. Tex. Assn. Ednl. Diagnosticians, Mensa, Alpha Chi, Phi Beta Kappa, Kappa Delta Pi. Democrat. Methodist. Avocations: reading, gardening. Home: 1707 Houston St Sulphur Springs TX 75482-2319 Office: 411 College St Sulphur Springs TX 75482-2809

GIBSON, JOHN FREDERICK, administrator; b. Darlington, England, Jan. 26, 1938; s. Frederick Roberts and Molly (Forrest) G. Degree in chem. engring., Imperial Coll., London, 1961, PhD, 1964. Sec. scientific affairs Royal Soc. Chemistry, London, 1966-80, gen. mgr. confs. & awards, 1980—. Fellow RSC (OBE 1998). Mem. Ch. of England. Avocations: sports, cricket, music, travel, bridge, mountain walking. Home: Ford House Eynsford, Kent DA4 0AA, England Office: Royal Soc Chemistry, Burlington House, London W1V 0BN, England

GIBSON, JOHN NICOLAS ALASTAIR, orthopaedic surgeon; b. Bellshill, Scotland, Oct. 21, 1954; s. John Alastair and Isabel Young (Gebbie) G.; m. Laurie-Ann Robb, June 28, 1986; Arran, Rory, Caitlin. MB, BS, London Hosp. Med. Coll., 1978; MD, London U., 1987. House surgeon London Hosp., 1978-79; surg. registrar Ninewells Hosp., Dundee, Scotland, 1981-83; clin. rsch. fellow U. Dundee, 1984-86; lectr. U. Edinburgh, 1986-91, sr. lectr., 1993-97; spinal fellow Royal North Shore Hosp, Sydney, 1992; cons. Royal Infirmary, Edinburgh, 1993—; part-time sr. lectr. U. Edinburgh, 1993—; orthop. cons. The Thistle Found., Edinburgh, 1995. Contbr. articles to profl. jours. Vice-chmn. Lothian Regional Coun. Sch. Bd., Edinburgh, 1995-99. Vis. scholar Sydney U., 1992. Fellow Brit. Orthop. Assn., Royal Coll. Surgeons Edinburgh, Intercollegiate Fellowship in Orthop. Surgery; mem. Internat. Soc. for Study Lumbar Spine, Med. Rsch. Soc., N.Y. Acad. Scis. Avocation: golf. E-mail: j.n.a.gibson@ed.ac.uk. Office: Princess Margaret Rose, Orthopaedic Hosp, Edinburgh EH10 7ED, Scotland

GIBSON, JOHN WILLIS, educator; b. Sydney, N.S.W., Australia, July 18, 1944; s. William Aubrey and Thelma (Willis) G.; m. Lesley Ailsa Moon, May 10, 1968; children: Peter John, Andrew Graham. BSc, U. N.S.W., Sydney, 1966; MA, U. Sydney, 1989. Chartered profl. engr., Australia. Asst. tchr. NSW Dept. Edn., Wellington, Australia, 1966, Sefton, Australia, 1966-68, Meadowbank, Australia, 1969-72; lectr. Sydney Tchrs. Coll., Newtown, Australia, 1973-81; lectr. Sydney Coll. Advanced Edn., Newtown, 1982-85, sr. lectr., 1986-89; sr. lectr. U. Sydney, 1990—; mem. Bd. Studies Syllabus writing team for Engring. Studies, 1999—. Co-author 4 books on materials sci.; contbr. articles to profl. jours. Bicentennial Community grantee Bathurst (Australia) City Coun., 1986-88. Fellow Inst. Tech. Edn. (fed. pres. 1982-89); mem. Inst. Engrs. Australia, Australian Coll. Edn. Anglican. Avocations: model engineering, vintage vehicles. Office: U Sydney Faculty of Edn, Manning Rd, New South Wales 2006, Australia

GIBSON, JOSEPH WHITTON, JR., retired chemical company executive; b. Norristown, Pa., Feb. 24, 1922; s. Joseph Whitton and Nellie (Dear) G.; m. Norma Jean Stewart, Sept. 21, 1946; children: Joseph Whitton, Winn S. Gobeil, Philip B. BS, Worcester Poly. Inst., 1944; postgrad., Princeton U., 1944, MIT, 1945. With E. I. duPont de Nemours & Co., Wilmington, Del., 1946-91; sr. research engr. E. I. duPont de Nemours & Co., 1961-79, sr. tech. specialist printing systems, imaging systems, 1979-91; mem. pantyhose sizing com. Nat. Assn. Hosiery Mfrs., 1969-71. Contbr. articles to profl. jours. Treas. Mayfield Civic Assn.; v.p. Brandywine Babe Ruth; treas. Shellcrest Swim Club; IRS VITA vol., 1995—; vol. LPGA/AJGA, 1997—, US Census 2000, 1999—. Served to lt. USNR, 1944-46. Recipient Joseph W. Gibson Jr. award tech. excellence established duPont, 1992, Internat. Man of Yr. award Internat. Biog. Centre, Cambridge, Eng., Dateline Recognition award Chem. Heritage Found., Phila., Dupont Lavoisier award, 2000. Mem. Am. Assn. Textile Chemists and Colorists (mem. history and archives com. 1994—, Olney medal 1979), Am. Chem. Soc., Fiber Soc. (hon.), Internat. Platform Assn., Planetary Soc., Sigma Xi, Tau Beta Pi. Republican. Episcopalian. Achievements include the invention of thermosol dyeing, sparkle hosiery, synthetic leather, fish swimway, printing plates. Home: 1215 Hillside Blvd Wilmington DE 19803-4211

GIBSON, LAWRENCE EDWARD, dermatologist; b. Rochester, Minn., Oct. 21, 1955; s. Smith Hison and Lucille (Holmes) G.; m. Rokea Adel El-Azhary, Apr. 5, 1995; children: Sarah Elizabeth, Dylan Sharif Myers, Matthew Edward. BA, Carson-Newman Coll., Jefferson City, Tenn., 1976; MD, U. Louisville, 1980. Diplomate Am. Bd. Dermatology; lic. physician Minn., Ariz., Fla. Internal medicine Mayo Clinic, Rochester, Minn., resident in determatology, 1982-85; staff St. Mary's Hosp., Rochester, Minn., 1986—, Meth. Hosp., Rochester, Minn., 1986—; fellow in dermatopathology Mayo Clinic/Mayo Grad. Sch., Rochester, Minn., 1985-86; cons., asst. prof. Mayo Clinic and Mayo Med. Sch., Rochester, 1986-98, prof. dermatology, 1998—. Contbr. chpts. to books. Vol., coach Rochester Youth Soccer, 1996, 99. Nancy Middleton Smith lectr. U. Louisville, 1997. Fellow Am. Acad. Dermatology, Am. Soc. Dermatopathology (head quality assurance program for dermatopathology 1992-94); mem. Internat. Soc. Dermatopathology (dir. dermatopathology internat. workshops 1997, 98, 99). Avocations: travel, fitness, woodworking, sailing. Office: Mayo Clinic 200 1st St SW Rochester MN 55905-0002

GIBSON, LEWIS FORT, microbiologist, educator; b. Edinburgh, Midlothian, Scotland, June 13, 1938; s. Lewis Fort and Helen Main Ferguson (Smith) G.; m. Moira Swanson Herkes, Aug. 5, 1960; children: Steven, Andrew, Amanda. BSc with hons., Edinburgh U., Scotland, 1960; PhD, Melbourne (Australia) U., 1972. Bacteriologist DSIR, Hull/Aberdeen, ž, Scotland, 1960-63, MDU (PHL), Melbourne, Australia, 1964-72; lectr./sr. lectr. U. Tech., Sydney, Australia, 1973—; cons. Insearch U. Tech., Sydney, 1986—. Contbr. articles to profl. jours. including Jour. Applied Microbiology, Jour. Applied Bacteriology, Letters in Applied Microbiology, Jour. Hygiene, Cambridge, Med. Jour. Australia, others; sub-editor, contbr. (parasitology slide sequence). Fellow Australian Soc. Microbiology (treas. 1977—); mem. Australian Inst. Biology, SGM, SAB. Fax: 61 0 2 9514 4026. E-mail: lewis.gibson@uts.edu.au. Office: U Tech Sydney Dept Cell &, Molecular Biology, Sydney NSW 2007, Australia

GIBSON, MEL, actor, film director; b. Peekskill, N.Y., Jan. 3, 1956; emigrated to Australia, 1968; s. Hutton and Anne Gibson. Grad., Nat. Inst. Dramatic Art, Sydney, Australia, 1977. Founder Icon Prodns. Works include: (films) Summer City, 1977, Mad Max, 1979, Tim, 1979, Attack Force Z, Gallipoli, 1981, The Road Warrior (Mad Max II), 1982, The Year of Living Dangerously, 1983, The Bounty, 1984, The River, 1984, Mrs. Soffel, 1984, Mad Max Beyond Thunderdome, 1985, Lethal Weapon, 1987, Tequila Sunrise, 1988, Lethal Weapon II, 1988, Bird on a Wire, 1989, Hamlet, 1990, Air America, 1990, Lethal Weapon III, 1992, Forever Young, 1992, Maverick, 1994, Pocahontas, 1995 (voice only), Father's Day, 1997, Conspiracy Theory, 1997, Lethal Weapon 4, 1998, The Million Dollar Hotel, 1999, Payback, 1999; actor, dir.: The Man Without a Face, 1993; actor, dir., prodr.: Braveheart, 1995 (Golden Globe award for best dir. of film 1996, Acad. award for best dir. 1996, Acad. award for best picture of yr. 1996, Outstanding Directorial Achievement in Motion Picture award nominee Dir. Guild Am. 1996, Oscar award for Best Dir.), Ransom, 1996, (voice) Chicken Run, 2000, The Patriot, 2000; performed with Nimrod Theatre Co. in plays including Death of a Salesman, Romeo and Juliet, with South Australian Theatre Co., from 1978, appeared in plays including Oedipus, Henry IV, Cedoona; work in TV series includes The Sullivans, The Oracle (Australia); exec. prodr. (TV) The Three Stooges, 2000. Favorite Movie Actor, People's Choice award, 1997. Roman Catholic. Office: ICONS Productions Producers Bldg # 3 4000 Warner Blvd Rm 17 Burbank CA 91522-0001

GIBSON, MELVIN ROY, pharmacology educator; b. St. Paul, Nebr., June 11, 1920; s. John and Jennie Irene (Harvey) G. BS, U. Nebr., 1942, MS, 1947, DSc (hon.), 1985; PhD, U. Ill., 1949. Asst. prof. pharmacognosy Wash. State U., Pullman, 1949-52, assoc. prof., 1952-55, prof., 1955-85, prof. emeritus, 1985—. Editor: Am. Jour. Pharm. Edn, 1956-61; editorial bd., co-author: Remington's Pharm. Sci, 1970, 75, 80, 85; editor, co-author: Studies of a Pharm. Curriculum, 1967; author over 100 articles. Served as arty. officer AUS, 1942-46. Decorated Bronze star, Purple Heart; sr. vis. fellow Orgn. for Econ. Cooperation and Devel., Royal Pharm. Inst. (now part of Uppsala U.), Stockholm, Sweden and U. Leiden (Holland), 1962; recipient Rufus A. Lyman award, 1972, Wash. State U. Faculty Library award, 1984, Disting. Alumnus award U. Nebr., 1999; named Wash. State U. Faculty Mem. of Yr., 1985. Fellow AAAS; assoc. fellow Am. Coll. Apothecaries; mem. AAUP, VFW (life), N.Y. Acad. Scis., Am. Pharm. Assn., Am. Soc. Pharmacognosy (pres. 1964-65), Am. Assn. Coll. Pharmacy (exec. com. 1961-63, bd. dirs. 1977-79, chmn. coun. faculties 1975-76, pres. 1979-80, Disting. Educator award 1984), U.S. Pharmacopeia (revision com. 1970-75), Am. Found. Pharm. Edn. (hon. life, bd. dirs. 1980-85, exec. com. 1981-85, vice chmn. 1982-85), Am. Inst. History of Pharmacy (sponsor), U. Nebr. Chancellor's Club, U. Nebr. Pres. Club, Sigma Xi, Phi Kappa Phi, Omicron Delta Kappa, Rho Chi, Spokane Club, Kappa Psi (Nat. Svc. citation 1961). Democrat. Presbyterian. Home: 707 W 6th Ave Apt 41 Spokane WA 99204-2813

GIBSON, MICHAEL FRANCIS, art critic, author; b. Brussels, Belgium, July 18, 1929; arrived in France, 1958; s. Hugh Simons and Ynès (Reyntiens) G.; m. Odile Geoffroy, Mar. 22, 1969 (div. 1976); children: Emmanuel, Marguerite; m. Monika Truszkowska, Apr. 23, 1977; children: Matthew, Olivia. MA, U. Louvain, Belgium, 1951; PhD, U. Paris, 1987. Founder, dir. Coll. Musical Trie, Trie-la-Ville, France, 1963-68; art critic Internat. Herald-Tribune, Paris, 1969—; lectr. Am. Ctr. Students Artists, Paris; producer Radio-Can., Paris, 1969-79, France-Culture, Paris, 1980—; pres. jury Aschberg Bursaries prize UNESCO, 1998—. Author: Pieter Bruegel, 1980, Les Symbolistes, 1984, Les Horizons du Possible, 1984, The Symbolists, 1988, Alexander Calder, 1988, Peter Bruegel, 1989, Gauguin, 1989, Duchamp - Dada, 1990 (Internat. Art Book award Vasari prize 1991), Tua Res Agitur, 1992, Adam Henein, Sculptor, 1993, The contextual abstraction of Dani Karavan, 1994, Odilon Redon, 1995, Zoran Music, 1995, Le Portement de croix de Pierre Bruegel l'Ainé, 1996, André Naggar, Images mentales, 1998, The Mill and the Cross, Peter Bruegel's Way to Calvary, 2000; editor: World Heritage Rev. UNESCO, 1998—; contbr. articles to profl. jours. Active UNESCO (program coordinator for project financed by Internat. Fund Devel. Culture, 1986—). With U.S. Army 1951-53. Mem. NAACP (life), Internat. Assn. Art Critics (program coord. 1986—). Democrat. Home: 34 Ave de Flandre, 75019 Paris France

GIBSON, MORGAN, writer, educator; b. Cleve., June 6, 1929; s. George Miles and Elizabeth (Leeper) G.; m. Barbara Ann Browne, Sept. 1, 1950 (div. 1972); children: Julia Mary, Lucy Alice; m. Keiko Matsui, Sept. 14, 1978; 1 child, Christopher So. BA, Oberlin (Ohio) Coll., 1950; MA, U. Iowa, 1952, PhD, 1959. Instr. English, humanities Shimer Coll., 1953-54; instr. Wayne State U., Detroit, 1954-58; asst. prof. English Am. Internat. Coll., Springfield, Mass., 1959-61; asst. prof., then assoc. prof. U. Wis., Milw., 1961-72; chmn. grad. faculty Goddard Coll., 1972-75; prof. English, Am. lit. Osaka (Japan) U., 1975-79; prof. English Chukyo U., Nagoya and Toyota, Japan, 1987-89; vis. disting. prof. English Knox Coll., Galesburg, Ill., 1989-91; lectr. in English Pa. State U., 1991-92; prof. English Japan Women's U., 1993-97, Kanda U. of Internat. Studies, 1997—; vis. prof. creative writing Mich. State U. Extension, Traverse City, 1979; vis. prof. comparative lit. U. Ill., 1982. Poetry editor Arts in Soc., 1965-72; pub. Great Lakes Books, Milw., 1967-68; author: (with Barbara Gibson) Our Bedroom's Underground, 1962; Mayors of Marble, 1966, Stones Glow Like Lovers' Eyes, 1970, Crystal Sunlake, 1971, Kenneth Rexroth, 1972, Dark Summer, 1977, Wakeup, 1978, Speaking of Light, 1979, (with Keiko Matsui Gibson) Kokoro: Heart-Mind, 1980, The Great Brook Book, 1981, (with Hiroshi Murakami) Tantric Poetry of Kukai (Kobo Daishi) Japan's Buddhist Saint, 1987, Revolutionary Rexroth: Poet of East-West Wisdom, 1986 (posted on internet 2000), Among Buddhas in Japan, 1988; contbg. editor, columnist Kyoto Jour., 1996—; contbr. poems, essays, articles, autobiographies, revs. and plays to anthologies, profl. jours. worldwide. Grantee U. Wis., 1967-69, U. Ill. Ctr. for Advanced Study, 1982. Mem. Am. Greens in Japan, Buddhist Peace Fellowship. Avocation: philosophy.

GIBSON, PETER RAYMOND, gastroenterologist, educator, researcher; b. Sydney, N.S.W., Australia, Sept. 23, 1952; s. Jack and Gweneth Elaine (Johnston) G.; m. Susan Mary Ryan, Dec. 8, 1975; children: Matthew, Christopher, Daisy. B in Medicine and Surgery with hons., Monash U., Melbourne, Australia, 1975, MD, 1985. Fellow Royal Australasian Coll. of Physicians, 1984. Intern Royal Hobart (Australia) Hosp., 1976-77; resident med. officer Alfred Hosp., Melbourne, 1977-79, registrar in gastroenterology, 1979-81; rsch. fellow Radcliffe Infirmary, Oxford, Eng., 1982-84, John Curtin Sch. of Med. Rsch. Australian U., Canberra, 1984-87; sr. lectr. U. Melbourne, Australia, 1992-94; assoc. prof. U. Melbourne, 1994—; gastroenterologist Royal Melbourne (Australia) Hosp., 1992-97, dep. dir. gastroenterology, 1997—. Mem. editl. bd. Clin. Sci., Inflammatory Bowel Diseases; contbr. numerous articles to profl. jours., scholarly revs. or chpts. to books. Grantee Nat. Health and Med. Rsch. Coun. Australia, Anti-Cancer Coun. Victoria. Fellow Royal Australian Coll. Physicians; mem. Gastroenterol. Soc. Australia, Am. Assn. for the Study of Liver Disease, Australian Soc. Med. Rsch., Internat. Orgn. Inflammatory Bowel Disease, Med. Rsch. Soc. Office: Royal Melbourne Hosp, Dept Medicine, Melbourne Victoria 3050, Australia

GIBSON, ROBERT JOHN, scientist, researcher; b. Bombay, Feb. 3, 1931; arrived in Can., 1958; s. Robert Boyce and Kathleen (Flood) G.; m. Judith Ann MacLellan, July 13, 1963; children: Caroline Flood, Mary Jane. BA, Dublin (Ireland) U., 1958, MA, 1961; BSc, U. Western Ont., London, Can., 1964, MSc, 1965; PhD, U. Waterloo, Can., 1973. Asst. scientist Fisheries Rsch. Bd. Can., St. Andrews, N.B., Can., 1958-62; fisheries biologist, profl. officer IV Govt. Man., Can., 1965-69; postdoctoral rschr. Woods Hole Oceanographic Instn., 1973-74, asst. scientist, 1974-78; sr. biologist MacLaren Marex Inc., St. John's, Can., 1978-80; rsch. scientist II Fisheries and Oceans Govt. Can., St. John's, 1980-91, rsch. scientist III Fisheries and Oceans, 1991-97, scientist emeritus Fisheries and Oceans, 1997—; dir. Matamek Rsch. Sta., Woods Hole Oceanographic Instn., Sept-Iles, Que., Can., 1973-78; assoc. faculty mem. faculty grad. studies U. Guelph, Can., 1978-80; adj. assoc. prof. dept. biology Meml. U. Nfld., St. John's, 1981—; dir., environ. scientist Environature Recovery Assocs., St. John's, 1997—; co-editor procs., chmn. organizing com. Prodn. Juvenile Atlantic Salmon, Salmo Salar, in Natural Waters, Fisheries and Aquatic Scis., 1993; designer Fluvarium, Nfld. Freshwater Resources Ctr., St. John's. Contbr. numerous articles, reports, and papers to profl. and popular publs. Exec. mem. Quidi Vidi Rennies River Devel. Found., St. John's; pres. Nfld. and Labrador Natural History Soc., St. John's, 1994. Recipient Tuck-Walters award Nfld. and Labrador Natural History Soc., 1986, Guenther-Behr Salmonid Conservation award Salmonid Assn. Ea. Nfld., 1996, Nfld. and Labrador Provincial Environ. award Provincial Govt. and Nfld. and Labrador Women's Insts., 1997. Mem. Am. Inst. Fishery Rsch. Biologists (scientist emeritus), Can. Soc. Environ. Biologists (chmn. Nfld. and Labrador chpts. 1997), Am. Fisheries Soc. (emeritus), Internat. Soc. Limnology (emeritus), Freshwater Biol. Assn. Avocations: angling, swimming, rowing, cycling, natural history. E-mail: gibby@iol.ie. Home: 29 North Ave, Mount Merrion Dublin, Ireland Office: Dept Fisheries and Oceans, PO Box 5667, Saint John's, NF Canada A1C 5X1

GIBSON, ROBERT VAN RENSSELAER, accountant, financial executive; b. Bridgeport, Conn., Aug. 16, 1942; s. Van Rensselaer and Josa Elizabeth (Marsh) G.; m. Joyce Ann Tasch; children: David, Jennifer. BBA, Iona Coll., 1964; postgrad., U. Hawaii, 1964-66, U. L.I., 1967-69. CPA, N.Y., N.J. Auditor Deloitte and Touche CPA's, N.Y.C., 1966-70; v.p. fin. Better Built Machinery Corp., Saddlebrook, N.J., 1970-76; firm adminstr. M. Sternlieb and Co., Hackensack, N.J., 1976-78; controller Publicker Chem. Corp., Greenwich, Conn., 1978-81; v.p., treas. Gunnebo Corp., Bristol, Conn., 1981-93; v.p. fin. Datron Inc., Windsor, Conn., 1993-99; v.p., CFO Advanced Products Co., North Haven, Conn., 1999—. Mem. Am. Inst. CPA's, N.Y. State Soc. CPA's, N.J. Soc. CPA's, Fin. Execs. Inst. Avocations: flying, boating. Office: Advanced Products Co 33 Defco Park Rd North Haven CT 06473-1141

GIBSON, WILLIAM LEE, financial consultant; b. Newark, Dec. 1, 1949; S. Joseph Wilton Gibson and Margaret (Reynolds) Gibson Leavens; stepson William Barry Leavens, Jr.; m. Lorraine Wrightson Besch, July 10, 1982. BA in chemistry, Bucknell U., 1972; postgrad., Harvard Bus. Sch., 1977; MBA, NYU, 1987; Sch. of Advanced Fin. Mgmt., 1995. With Bur. Solid Waste Mgmt EPA, Cin., 1970-71; chemist Dow Chem. Co., Midland, Mich., 1972-75; mktg. cons. Westvaco, Charleston, S.C., 1976; sales rep. Diamond Shamrock Co., Cleve., 19777-79; market devel. specialist strategic planing and ventures operation GE, Pittsfield, Mass., 1979-81; mktg. programs mgr. Allied-Signal Corp., Morristown, N.J., 1981-86, mgr. tech. and bus. devel., 1986-91, sr. sales mgr., 1991-93; v.p. Merrill Lynch, Short Hills, N.J., 1994—; Former pres., trustee Hartford Family Found; v.p. Leavens Found. Trustee Jr. Achievement No. N.J., N.J. Symphony Orch., Coun. N.J. Grantmakers, Wrightson Beach Found. Mem. Harvard Bus. Sch. Club N.Y., Harvard Club N.Y. Home: 8 Lone Oak Rd Basking Ridge NJ 07920-1613 Office: 51 John F Kennedy Pky Short Hills NJ 07078-2702

GIBSON, WILLIAM THOMAS, university administrator; b. Gloucester, U.K., June 22, 1959; s. Francis Edward Thomas and Eileen (Margarson) G. BA with Honors, U. Wales, 1980, MA, 1982; PhD, U. Middlesex, 1994. Lectr. Southampton City (U.K.) Coll., 1986-90; sr. lectr. Basingstoke (U.K.) Coll. Tech., 1990-92, prin. lectr., 1992-94, dir. student svcs., 1994—; hon. rsch. assoc. U. Wales, Lampeter, 1991; editl. dir. Icepick Mag., U.K., 1981-83. Author: Church, State and Society 1760-1850, 1994, The Anglican Achievement 1689-1800, 1995, A Social History of The Domestic Chaplain 1530-1840, 1997, Religion and Society 1689-1800, 1999, Two Church of England 1688-1832, 2000; contbr. articles to profl. jours. Recipient Thomas ellis Meml. award U. Wales, 1992; UCLA Disting. Vis. scholar, 1994; fellow Hartley Inst., Southampton U., 1999-2000. Fellow Royal Soc. Arts, Royal Hist. Soc.; mem. N.Y. Acad. Scis. Avocations: cinema and theatre, travel, archives. Home: 9 Honeysuckle Way, Chandlers Ford, Hampshire S053 4LR, England Office: Basingstoke Coll of Tech, Worting Rd, Basingstoke RG21 8TN, England

GICHAGA, FELIX KARIUKI, energy company executive; b. Nairobi, Kenya, July 18, 1975; s. Alfred Manyuira and Shiphrah (Nyakeru) G. BSBA, BS in Mktg. and Adminstrn., Daystar U., Nairobi, Kenya, 1999. Mng. dir. Worldnet Vehicles Supplies Kenya Ltd., 1995-99, Bus. Energy Solutions, Ltd., Nairobi, 1999—; dir. Get Smart Svcs., Ltd., Nairobi, 1998—, Pop Media, Nairobi, 1999—. Avocations: chess, golf, karate, swimming. E-mail: FKG1@hotmail.com. Office: Bus Energy Solutions Ltd, PO Box 53328, Nairobi Kenya

GICHON, MORDECHAI, archaeologist, historian, educator; b. Berlin, Aug. 16, 1922; arrived in Israel, 1934; s. Nahum and Charlotte (Salomon) Gichermann; m. Chava Renate Goldberg, June 27, 1948; children: Eran Zeev, Arion Ramit, Eyal Nahum. Grad., Ben Yehuda Coll., Tel Aviv, 1941; MA, Hebrew U., Jerusalem, 1956, PhD, 1967; grad., Israel Staff Command Coll., Gelilot, 1959. Asst. dir. intelligence, research Israeli Armed Forces, Jerusalem, 1949-55, dir. sch. strategic intelligence, 1955-57; head chair mil. history Tel Aviv U., 1962-65, sr. lectr. archaeology, 1965-71, assoc. prof., 1971-80, prof., 1980-90, emertus prof., 1990—; chmn. Israel Roman Milestone Com., Tel Aviv, 1970—; vis. fellow Archeology Inst. Oxford U., Wolfson Coll., Oxford, Eng., Birmingham U., Eng., Inst. Jewish Studies, Oxford, Annenberg Inst., Phila., 1968-87, others. Author: Carta's Atlas of the Military History of Israel, 1969, 2d rev. edit., 1975, (with H. Herzog) Battles of the Bible, 1978 (enlarged rev. edit. 1997), Excavations at En Bogeg I, 1993; contbr. articles to profl. jours. Served Jewish Brigade, Brit. Army, World War II, to lt. col. Israeli Armed Forces, 1947-62. Recipient Gold medal The Internat. Napoleonic Soc., Sukenik Prize for Archaeology, Hebrew U., 1956. Fellow Soc. Antiquaries, Royal Spanish Acad. for History (corr.), The Internat. Napoleonic Soc. (chmn. Israeli br., Gold medal); mem. Israel Exploration Soc. (council mem.), Israel Soc. Mil. History (bd. dirs. 1986—), Israel Assn. for Classical Studies, Deutsches Archaeologisches Inst., Israel Numismatic Soc., Israel-Deutschland Gesellschaft (bd. dirs. 1978-90), The Internat. Forum for a United Jerusalem (coun. mem. 1990—), Israeli War Vets. and Ret. Officers Assns. Club: Explorer. Lodge: Rotary (past pres. 1965-91). Avocations: travel, reading. Home: Zahala, Tel Aviv 69083, Israel Office: Tel Aviv U, Ramat Aviv, Tel Aviv Israel

GIDALI, JULIA, scientist, hematologist; b. Budapest, Hungary, Apr. 17, 1937; d. Mark and Ilona (Indig) G.; m. Imre Feher, July 27, 1963; 1 child, Tamas. Diploma summa cum laude, Med. Sch., Budapest, Hungary, 1961; PhD, Hungarian Acad. Scis., 1973, DSci, 1984. Jr. rsch. fellow Nat. Inst. Radiobiology, Budapest, 1961-63, rsch. fellow, 1963-70, sr. rsch. fellow, 1972-86; IAEA fellow Paterson Inst., Manchester, Eng., 1970-71; sr. rsch. fellow Nat. Inst. Hematology, Budapest, 1986-90, head dept. cytomorphology, 1991—. Contbr. articles to profl. jours. Recipient award Union Tech. and Sci. Socs., Budapest, 1986; named Doctor Laudetur, Ministry of Health, Budapest, 1983. Mem. European Stem Cell Club, European Study Group for Cell Proliferation, European Soc. Radiation Biology, Hungarian Biophysical Soc. (sec. gen.). Office: Nat Inst Hematology, PO Box 424, 1515 Budapest Hungary

GIDLEY, GUSTAVUS MICK, American literature educator; b. Southampton, Hampshire, Eng., Mar. 1, 1941; s. Gustavus and Doris Florence (Boulton) G.; m. Nancy Rebecca Gordon, Oct. 17, 1964; children: Ruth Mayen, Benjamin Peter. BA, U. Manchester, Eng., 1963; MA, U. Chgo., 1966; DPhil, U. Sussex, Brighton, Eng., 1976. Sr. tchr. English, Aggrey Meml. Coll., Vol. Svc. Overseas, Arochuku, Nigeria, 1963-65; fellow Am. studies U. Sussex, 1969-71; lectr. Am. lit. U. Exeter, Eng., 1971-78, sr. lectr., chmn. Am. and Commonwealth arts, 1978-93, reader Am. studies, 1993-95; prof. Am. lit. U. Leeds, Eng., 1995—; vis. prof. Am. lit. San Diego State U., 1985; U.K. rep. bd. European Assn. for Am. Studies, 1998—. Author: With One Sky Above Us: Life on an Indian Reservation, 1979, Kopet: A Documentary Narrative of Chief Joseph's Last Years, 1981, American Photography, 1983, Edward S. Curtis and The North American Indian, Incorporated, 1998; editor: The Vanishing Race, 1978, 87, Views of American Landscapes, 1989, Representing Others, 1992, Modern American Culture, 1993, American Photographs in Europe, 1994. Am. Coun. Learned Socs. fellow Burke Mus., Seattle, 1976-77, fellow Netherlands Inst. for Advanced Study, Wassenaar, 1991-92; grantee Nuffield Found., Am. Philos. Soc., Brit. Acad., Brit. Coun., also others. Mem. Brit. Assn. for Am. Studies (com. exec. 1981-91, 95—), Am. Studies Assn., Soc. Authors. Avocations: cinema, walking, swimming. Office: U Leeds, Sch English, Leeds LS2 9JT, England

GIDWITZ, TERI LYNNE, marketing professional; b. Chgo., Apr. 23, 1961; d. Ralph Wolff and Jane Audrey Gidwitz. BA, U. Mich., 1983; M in Mgmt., Northwestern U., 1985. Asst. account exec. DDB Needham, Chgo., 1985-86; account exec. Sampling Corp. Am., Glenview, Ill., 1987, Feldman Assocs., Chgo., 1987-88; promotion asst. Helene Curtis Industries, Chgo., 1988-90; dir. mktg. Sta. WXRT-FM, Chgo., 1990-97, Sta. WSCR-AM, Chgo., 1991-95, Tunes.com, Chgo., 1997-2000, Household Credit Svcs., 2000—; advisor Chgo. Beach LLC, 1995-98; dir. Ind. Label Festival, Chgo., 1995-97. Mem. Chgo. Interactive Mktg. Assn. Avocations: music, travel. Home: 1542 W School St Apt E Chicago IL 60657-2191 Office: Household Credit Svcs 200 W Adams St Chicago IL 60606-5208

GIEBEL, MIRIAM CATHERINE, librarian, genealogist; b. Williamsburg, Iowa, Oct. 10, 1934; d. John Timothy and Helen Gertrude (Wright) Donahoe; m. William Herbert Giebel, Sept. 30, 1967; 1 child, Sara Ann Giebel Ward. BS, Marquette U., Milw., 1956; MS in Library Science, Rosary Coll., River Forest, Ill., 1960; Cert. Paralegal, Roosevelt U., Chgo., 1992; Cert. in Family History Rsch., Brigham Young U., Provo, Utah, 1992. Asst. acquisitions dept. Marquette U. Libr., Milw., 1956-58; tech. svcs. librarian Chicago Heights (Ill.) Pub. Libr., 1959-63; librarian Little Company of Mary Nursing, Evergreen Park, Ill., 1963-64; asst. librarian hdqrs. ALA, Chgo., 1964-67; extension, reference librarian Chicago Heights (Ill.) Pub. Libr., 1974-99, vol. coord./webmaster, 1999-2000, webmaster, 2000—. Mem. Ill. Fedn. Bus. Profl. Women (state library chair 1994-96), U.S. Daughters of 1812 (Ill. state registrar 1994-97, Ill. state pres. 1997-99, hon. state pres. life, chpt. pres. 1991-97, nat. chair lineage and geneal. records 1997-2000, chpt. registrar 1997—), DAR (chpt. registrar 1994—), Ill. Cameo Soc. of DAR (state v.p. 1996-99, state pres. 1999—), Soc. Ind. Pioneers (life). Roman Catholic. Avocations: reading, personal genealogical research, surfing internet.

GIEBELMANN, ROLF WILHELM, forensic toxicologist, consultant; b. Magdeburg, Saxonia, Germany, Nov. 20, 1933; s. Wilhelm and Jenny

(Püschel) G.; m. Heidemarie Dudeck, July 6, 1979; children: Frank, Volker. Diploma in chemistry, U. Greifswald (Germany), 1959, D in Chemistry, 1962. Diplomate Assn. of Toxicol. and Forensic Chemistry. Asst. U. Greifswald, 1959-65, sr. asst., 1965-90, pvt. toxicologist, 1990—; mem. toxicology commn. Acad. Med. Postgrad., 1981-91. Co-author: Toxicological Analysis, 1991, Use of Ion-Pairs in Analysis, 1994, Kult und Kunst um Kräuter, 1996. Recipient Richard Kockel medal Assn. of Forensic Medicine, 1981. Mem. Helmholtz-Bund, Assn. of Toxicol. and Forensic Chemistry, The Internat. Assn. of Forensic Toxicologists. Avocations: culture history, philately. Home: Newtonstrasse 2B, D-17491 Greifswald Germany Office: Inst Legal Medicine, Kuhstrasse 30, D-17489 Greifswald Germany

GIEBELS, SHARON J., human services manager; b. Chgo., Aug. 21, 1946; d. George A. and Margaret C. (Hilgers) Joosten; m. Gary F. Giebels, Oct. 1, 1966; children: Marci Viola, Mindy Jean. BS, SUNY, Albany, 1996; MS in Health Svcs. Adminstrn., Nova Southeastern U., 1998. Cert. retirement housing profl. Am. Assn. Homes and Svcs. for the Aging. Dir. village svcs. Gulf Coast Village, Cape Coral, Fla., 1988-96; dir. rsch. and edn. Gulf Coast Village, Cape Coral, 1996-98; dir. resident svs. Cypress Cove, Ft. Myers, Fla., 1998—; team mem. Gerontology Process Mgmt., Ft. Myers, 1998—; bd. mem. Dr. Piper Ctr., Ft. Myers, 1999—, pers. com. chmn. 1999—; internat. spkr. in field; Alzheimer's rschr. Sec. Cape Coral Civic Assn., 1992. Mem. Am. Med. Dirs. Assn. (spkrs. bur.), Am. Geriatrics Soc. (spkrs. bur.), Sigma Beta Delta. Roman Catholic. Avocations: music, sailing, writing, traveling. E-mail: giebels@iline.com. Office: Cypress Cove 10200 Fort Myers FL 33908

GIEDEMAN, CHARLES P., horticulture coordinator; b. East St. Louis, Ill., Aug. 29, 1944; s. George F. and Lillian M. Giedeman; m. Julia Ann Wedel, Jan. 17, 1968; children: Teresa, Daniel, Ronald, Sara, Marc. BA in Zoology/Botany, So. Ill. U., Edwardsville, 1966, MSEd in Biol. Sci., 1970; PhD in Plan Biology, So. Ill. U., Carbondale, 1999. Instr. biology St. Mary's H.S., St. Louis, 1966-73; horticulture cons. Spl. Sch. Dist., St. Louis County, Mo., 1974; horticulture coord. Belleville (Ill.) Med. Coll., 1974—; field trip leader B.A.C. Hort. Club, Ont., Que., Can., 1980, 82, 85, 86, 88, Ill.-Mo. Greenhouse Grower, Iceland, Holland, Eng., 1997; fellow NSF, Redding, Calif., 1997. Author weekly gardening column Belleville News-Democrat, 1989—. Mem. Belleville Park Bd., 1991—, pres., 1996-99. Mem. Ill. Acad. Sci., Sigma Xi. Avocations: photography, hockey. E-Mail: giedemcp@SMTP.bacnet.edu. Home: 826 E Main St Belleville IL 62220-3944 Office: Belleville Area Coll 2500 Carlyle Ave Belleville IL 62221-5859

GIEDKE, GEZA KOLOMAN, physicist, consultant; b. Munich, Germany, Sept. 11, 1970; s. Henner Walter V. and Adelheid (Buetikofer) G. Diplom-Physiker, U. Tuebingen, Germany, 1996. Rsch. asst. Inst. for Theoretical Physics, Innsbruck, Austria, 1997—; acting ptnr. G&G Cons. GbR, Moessingen, Germany, 1996—. Friedrich-Naumann-Stiftung fellow. Mem. Deutsche Physikalische Gesellschaft, Landesverband Liberaler Hochschulgruppen Baden-Wuerttemberg (v.p. 1995-96). Avocations: literature, stocks/investing, politics, handball. E-mail: geza.giedke@uibk.ac.at. Office: Inst Theor Phys/U Innsbruck, Technikerstrasse 25, Innsbruck Austria 6020

GIELE, HENK, plastic surgeon; b. Singapore, Nov. 30, 1964; arrived in Australia, 1977; s. Henk and Ching (Looi) G. MB, BS, U. Western Australia, 1987. Trainee plastic surgery Perth, Australia, 1992-95; sr. registrar plastic surgery Radcliffe Infirmary, Oxford, Eng., 1995, cons. plastic surgeon, 1996—. Contbr. articles to profl. jours. Microsurgery fellow Bernard O'Brien Inst. Microsurgery, Melbourne, Australia, 1991, hand surgery fellow Inst. De La Main, Paris, 1996. Mem. Australian Med. Assn., British Soc. Surgery of the Hand. Office: Radcliffe Infirmary Dept Plastic Surgery, Woodstock Rd, Oxford OX2 6HE, England

GIELEN, MARCEL, chemist, educator; b. Etterbeek, Belgium, July 1, 1938; s. Robert Gielen and Alice Van Humbeek; m. Bernadette Marechal; children: Arnaud, Mathys. PhD, U. Libre, Brussels, 1963. Lectr. Vrije Univ., Brussels, 1966-71, prof., 1972—. Author: The Permutational Approach to Dynamic Stereochemistry, 1983; editor: Metal-Based Antitumour Drugs, 1992, Advanced Applications of NMR to Organometallic Chemistry, 1996; contbr. 277 articles to profl. jours. Mem. ACS. Avocation: classical music. Office: Vrije Universiteit Brussel, Pleinlaan 2 Rm 8G512, 5-1050 Brussels Belgium

GIELGUD, SIR JOHN (ARTHUR JOHN GIELGUD), actor, theater director; b. London, Apr. 14, 1904; s. Frank and Kate (Terry-Lewis) G. Student, Hillside Godalming, 1913-18, Westminster Sch., 1918-20, Lady Benson, 1920-21, Royal Acad. Dramatic Art, 1922-23; LLD (hon.), U. St. Andrews, 1950, U. London, 1977; LittD (hon.), Oxford (Eng.) U., 1953. Established repertory theater in London, 1938, Haymarket, 1943-44. Shakespearean roles include Hamlet, 1929, 30, 34, 36, 37, 39, 44, Richard II, 1929, 38, Macbeth, 1929, 42, Mark Antony in Julius Caesar, 1929, Hotspur in Henry IV, 1930, Malvolio in Twelfth Night, 1930, Shylock in The Merchant of Venice, 1938; achieved first London success as Lewis Dodd in The Constant Nymph, 1926, other stage appearances in The Good Companions, 1930, Musical Chairs, 1931, Richard of Bordeaux, 1932, School for Scandal, 1938, Dear Octopus, 1939, The Importance of Being Earnest, 1930, 39-40, 43, Love for Love, Eng. and U.S.A., 1942-44, 47, The Duchess of Malfi, 1944, Crime and Punishment, London, 1946, Medea, U.S.A., 1947-48, The Return of the Prodigal, 1948, Much Ado About Nothing, 1949, 50, 52, 55, N.Y.C. and Boston, 1959, Ages of Man, 1959, 63, Australia and New Zealand, 1963-64, Othello, 1961, as Gaev in Cherry Orchard, Broadway, 1961, Aldwych, London, 1962, as Julian in Tiny Alice, N.Y.C., 1964-65 (Della Austrian medal Drama League of N.Y. 1965), at Stratford-On-Avon Festival in Measure for Measure, Julius Ceasar, Much Ado About Nothing, King Lear, 1950, A Winter's Tale, 1951, The Best of Friends, 1988; also toured in King Lear with Stratford-On-Avon Co., London and other locations, 1955; dir., actor in Nude With a Violin, 1956-57, The Tempest, 1957, 58, Joseph Surface in School for Scandal, Broadway, 1963, Ages of Man, Lyceum Theater, N.Y.C., 1963, Australia and New Zealand, 1963-64, Julian in Tiny Alice, Broadway, 1964-65, Hamlet, Broadway, Boston and Can., 1974, The Best of Friends, 1988; dir. plays Lady Windemere's Fan, 1946, The Glass Menagerie starring Helen Hayes, 1948, Medea, 1948, The Heiress, 1949; producer, dir. Berlioz's The Trojans, Covent Garden, 1958, Britten's A Midsummer Nights Dream, Royal Opera House, Covent Garden, London, 1961, Big Fish, Little Fish, Broadway, 1961 (Tony award), Dazzling Prospect, 1961, The School for Scandal, Haymarket Theatre, 1962; film appearances include Diary for Timothy, The Good Companions, 1932, The Secret Agent, 1937, The Prime Minister, 1940, Julius Caesar, 1952, A Day By The Sea (also dir.), 1953, The Cherry Orchard (also dir.), 1954, Richard III, 1955, The Barretts of Wimpole Street, 1957, St. Joan, 1957, Becket, 1964, The Loved One, 1964, Chimes at Midnight, 1966, Mister Sebastian, 1967, The Charge of the Light Brigade, 1968, The Shoes of the Fisherman, 1968, Oh! What a Lovely War, 1968, Julius Caesar, 1970, Lost Horizon, 1972, Eagle in a Cage, 1973, Murder on the Orient Express, 1974, 11 Harrowhouse, 1974, Gold, 1974, Aces High, 1976, Joseph Andrews, 1977, Providence, 1977, Portrait of a Young Man, 1977, Caligula, 1977, The Elephant Man, 1979, The Human Factor, 1979, The Conductor, 1980, Murder by Decree, 1980, The Formula, 1980, Chariots of Fire, 1981, Arthur, 1981, (Academy award for best supporting actor) Sphinx, 1981, Lion of the Desert, 1981, Priest of Love, 1982, Gandhi, 1982, Wagner, 1983, Invitation to the Wedding, 1983, Scandalous, 1983, The Wicked Lady, 1983, Camille, 1984, The Shooting Party, 1985, Plenty, 1985, Leave All Fair, 1985, The Whistle Blower, 1987, Appointment With Death, 1988, Arthur 2, 1988, Getting It Right, Strike It Rich, Prospero's Books, 1991, Shining Through, 1992, Power of One; TV appearances include Probe, 1972, QB VII, 1973, Frankenstein: The True Story, 1973, Les Miserables, 1978, Richard II, 1979, Brideshead Revisited, 1981, Marco Polo, 1982, Inside the Third Reich, 1982, The Hunchback of Notre Dame, 1982, Neck, 1983, The Scarlet and the Black, 1983, The Master of Ballantrae, 1984, The Far Pavillions, 1984, War and Remembrance, 1988, Someday's Dream, Morse, Alleyn Mysteries, Lovejoy, Swansone, Quarmaines Ferms, Scarlett, Hand in Glove, 1994; author: (autobiography) Early Stages, 1938, Stage Directions, 1964, Distinguished Company, 1972, Gielgud: An Actor and His Time, 1980, Backward Glances, 1989. Decorated Knight Order Brit. Empire, Companion of Honor, chevalier Legion of Honor; recipient Antoinette Perry award Ages of Man, 1958, spl. award, 1959, Best Actor award Providence N.Y. Film Critics, 1977, Emmy award for Outstanding Lead Actor in a Miniseries or Special ("Summer's Lease," PBS) Nat. Acad. TV Arts and Scis., 1991; named Brandeis University Companion, 1960. Mem. Shakespeare Reading Soc. (pres. 1958—), Royal Acad. Dramatic Art (pres. 1977-89). Clubs: Garrick, Players (N.Y.C.). Office: Care Internat Famous Agy, Oxford House 76 Oxford SE, London W1R 1RB, England

GIELGUD, MAINA, ballerina; b. London, Jan. 14, 1945; d. Lewis and Elisabeth (Grussner) Gielgud.; Brevet d'Etudes du Premier Cycle. Dancer Ballet du Marquis de Cuevas, 1962-63, Ballet Classique de France, 1965-67, Ballet of the 20th Century, Maurice Bejart, Brussels, 1967-72, Royal Ballet London, 1977-78; guest dancer numerous cos. worldwide, 1978—; prodr., dir. show: Steps, Notes and Squeaks, 1978; rehearsal dir. London City Ballet; artistic dir. The Australian Ballet, 1983-96; artistic dir. Royal Danish Ballet, 1997-99; freelance prodr., dir., coach English Nat. Ballet, Béjart Ballet Lausanne, Tokyo Ballet, 1999-2000. Home: 1/9 Stirling Ct, 3 Marshall St, London W1 V1LQ, England

GIEM, ROSS NYE, JR., surgeon; b. Corvallis, Oreg., May 23, 1923; s. Ross Nye and Goldie Marie (Falk) G.; children: John, David, Paul, James, Ross N. III, Matthew John, Julie. Student, U. Redlands, Walla Walla Coll.; BA, Loma Linda U., MD. Diplomate Am. Bd. Surgery. Intern Sacramento Gen. Hosp., 1952-53; resident in ob-gyn Kern County Gen. Hosp., Bakersfield, 1956-57; resident in gen. surgery Kern County Gen. Hosp., Bakersfield, 1957-61; practice medicne specializing in gen. surgery Sullivan, Mo., 1961-70; staff emergency dept. Hollywood Presbyn. Med. Ctr., 1971-73, Meml. Hosp., Belleville, Ill., 1973-87, St. Elizabeth Hosp., Belleville, 1973-90, St. Luke Hosp., Pasadena, 1973-89, Doctors Hosp., Montclair, Calif., 1990-93, Harriman Jones Med. Group, Long Beach, Calif., 1993—; instr. nurses, physicians, paramedics, emergency med. technicians, 1973-91. Served with AUS, 1943-46. Fellow ACS, Am. Coll. Emergency Physicians; mem. AMA, Ill. Med. Assn., Pan Am. Med. Assn., Pan Pacific Surg. Assn., Royal Coll. Physicians (Eng.).

GIENAPP, HANS REINHARD, physicist, researcher, educator; b. Hamburg, Germany, Oct. 24, 1927; s. Richard Karl and Frieda Lucia (Muhme) G.; m. Marianne Sorber, Jan. 28, 1957; 1 child, Tonja. Diploma in physics, U. Hamburg, 1953, Dr.rer.nat., 1956. Group leader Forschungsinstitut fur Physik der Strahlantriebe e.v., Stuttgart, Germany, 1957-65, Deutsches Hydrogr Inst., 1965-90; lectr. Zoro Astrian Coll., Bombay, 1987—. Contbr. articles to profl. jours. Mem. Am. Geophys. Union, Deutsche Physikalische Gesellschaft, Zoroastrian Coll. (German sect.). Achievements include discovery of 48 hours-tides, discovery of synergetic sea waves; invention of a new system of oceanographic research; invention of metaphotography. Home and Office: Grönländerdamm 15, 22145 Hamburg Germany

GIERSCH, ANNE, medical researcher; b. Strasbourg, Alsace, France, Sept. 29, 1964; d. Pierre and Monique (Strauel) G. Masters, Strasbourg Sch. Medicine, 1988; PhD in Neurosci., Strasbourg U., 1997. Lic. psychiatrist. Intern Strasbourg (France) Hosp., 1990-93, laureat d'internat., 1993-94; poste d'accueil INSERM, Strasbourg, 1995-97, recruited in, 1998—. Contbr. articles to profl. jours. Grantee Roche Inst., 1994-95, INSERM Tubingen, Germany, 1998—. Mem. Soc. Neurosci., European Soc. Cognitive Psychology, Psychonomic Soc. Avocations: reading, painting, biking, diving. Office: INSERM U405, 1 place de l'hopital, 67091 Strasbourg France

GIERSCH, HERBERT HERMANN, economist, educator; b. Reichenbach, Germany, May 11, 1921; s. Hermann and Helene (Kleinert) G.; m. Friederike Koppelmann; 3 children. Dr. rer. pol., U. Munster; Dr. (hon.), U. Erlangen, F U. Basle, U. Saarbrucken. Asst. to prof. U. Munster, 1948, 50, Privatdozent, 1950-52; Brit. Council fellow London Sch. Econs., 1948-49; adminstr. econs. directorate OEEC, 1950-52, counsellor, head div. trade and fin. directorate, 1953-54; in charge econs. chair Technische Hochschule, Brunswick, W.Ger., 1954; prof. econs. U. Saarbrucken, Fed. Republic Germany, 1955-69, U. Kiel, Fed. Republic Germany, 1969-89, prof. emeritus, 1989—; pres. Inst. World Econs., 1969-89; ret., 1989; vis. prof. econs Yale U., 1962-63, 77-78; mem. German Econ. Expert Coun., 1964-70; chmn. Assn. German Econ. Rsch. Insts., 1970-82. Author: Acceleration Principle and Propensity to Import, 1953; The Trade Optimum, 1957; Allgemeine Wirtschafts politik, 1977; Growth, Cycles and Exchange Rates—The Experience of West Germany (Wicksell Lecture), 1970; Kontroverse Fragen der Wirtschaftspolitik, 1971; Indexation and the Fight against Inflation, 1973-74; The European Community and the World Economy (Spaak Lecture), 1976; Im Brennpunkt: Wirtschaftspolitik-kitische Beitrage von 1967-77, 1978; A European Look at the World Economy (MacInally Lecture), 1978; Deutsche Wirtschaft wohin, 1980; Aspects of Growth, Structural Change and Employment—A Schumpeterian Perspective, 1979; Die Rolle der reichen Länder in der wachsenden Weltwirtschaft, 1980; Problems of Adjustment to Imports from Less-Developed countries, 1981; Rationality in Political Economy, 1981; Wachstum durch dynamischen Wettbewerb, 1982; Schumpeter and the Current and Future Development of the World Economy, 1982; Arbeit, Lohn und Produktivität, 1983; The World Economy in Perspective: Essays on International Trade and European Integration, 1991; (with others) The Fading Miracle: Four Decades of Market Economy in Germany, 1992; Openness for Prosperity, 1993; Marktwirtschaftliche Perspektiven für Europa, 1993. Hon. fellow London Sch. Econs. Mem. Internat. Econ. Assn. (council 1971—, exec. com. 1971—, treas. 1974—, hon. pres. 1983—), Am. Econ. Assn. (hon.), Order Pour le Mérite für Wissenschaften and Künste, Paolo Baffi Intern prize, Prognos prize, The German Fed. Republic's Great cross of Merit including star and sash, Joachim Jungius medal, 1998. Office: Kiel Inst World Econs, Duesternbrooker Weg 120, D-24100 Kiel Germany

GIERZYŃSKA-DOLNA, MONIKA, engineering educator, science administrator; b. Myszków, Poland, June 29, 1935; d. Władysław and Marinna Pawłowska; m. Albin Dolny, 1977. MSc in Engring., Tech. U. Częstochowa, Poland, 1959; Doctorate, Poly. Śląska, Gliwice, Poland, 1964, Doctorate habilitation, 1974. Asst. Tech. U. Częstochowa, 1959-64, adj., 1964-74, prof., 1974—, dean machine bldg. dept., 1978-81, rector edn., 1982-84; dir. Inst. Metal Working and Plastics, Częstochowa, 1970. Author: Friction Wear and Lubrication in Metal Forming, 1983; co-author: Working Liquid for Machining; contbr. articles to profl. jours. Mem. Rada Główna Nauki Szkolnictwa Wyższego, Poland, 1984-88, Japan Soc. for Tech. Plasticity, Tokyo; sect. mem. Podstaw Eksploatacji Komitetu Budowy Maszyn PAN, Teorii Procesów Przeróbki Plastycznej Komitetu Metalurgii, PAN. Recipient award for a monography PAN, Poland, 1974, III and II-degree sci. award MNSzWiT, Poland, 1975, 83, II-degree sci. award MEN, Poland, 1989. Achievements include 11 patents in field. Office: Tech U Częstochowa, al Armii krajowej 21, 42-200 Częstochowa Poland

GIES, ROBERT JAY, mechanical engineer; b. Washington, July 27, 1967; s. Edward L. and Beatrice Y. Gies; m. Louisa Manalac, May 15, 1993. BS in Mech. Engring., Old Dominion U., 1990, M in Engring. Mgmt., 1994. Registered engr.-in-tng. Facilities analyst Old Dominion U., Norfolk, Va., 1987-90; assoc. engr. Newport News (Va.) Shipbuilding, 1990-94, engr., 1994-96, sr. engr., 1996, engring. supr., 1996—; instr. design apprenticeship program Newport News Shipbuilding, 1994—, instr. carrier engring., 1995—. Author articles, tech. papers, presentations, manuals and guides. Usher Aldersgate United Meth. Ch., Chesapeake, Va., 1994—; asst. scoutmaster Boy Scouts Am., Chesapeake, 1985—; asst. coach Little League Baseball, Poquoson, Va., 1989, 91-92. Recipient NNS Vol. Cmty. Svc. award, Pres. model of Excellence award, Young Engr. of Yr. award Peninsula Engrs., 2000. Mem. Old Dominion U. Alumni Assn. (co-v.p. univ. rels. com. 1996-98, bd. dirs. 1995—, v.p. alumni orgns. 1998-99, pres.-elect 1999-2000, pres. 2000—), ASME (assoc., chair egg drop com. 1995—, exec. com. 1995-99, program dir. 1997-98, treas., 1998-99, sec. 1999-2000, vice chair 2000—), Soc. Naval Architects and Marine Engrs. (assoc.), Navy League, Nat. Eagle Scout Assn., Am. Soc. of Naval Engrs., Progressive Club, Omicron Delta Kappa. Republican. Home: 2951 Bruce Sta Chesapeake VA 23321-4258 Office: Newport News Shipbldg Dept E54 4101 Washington Ave Bldg 86 Newport News VA 23607-9700

GIESBERT, FRANZ OLIVIER, journalist; b. Wilmington, Del., Jan. 18, 1949; s. Frederick and Marie (Allain) G.; children: Aurélien, Claire, Alexandre, Julien. Degree in Journalism, Centre de Formation des Journalistes, Paris. Journalist 6 Nouvel Observateur, France, 1971-85, editor in chief, 1985-88; editor in chief 6 Figaro, France, 1988-2000, pub., 1999-2000; dir. 6 Point, France, 2000—. Office: Le Point, 74 Avenue des Maine, 75 862 Paris Cedes, France

GIESE, WILLIAM HERBERT, tax accountant; b. Boston, Jan. 19, 1944; s. Robert Ewald and Harriet (Blaney) G.; m. Elaine Rabe, May 26, 1973; children: Amy Theiss, Katherine Clark, Lauren Stearns. BA, Amherst Coll., 1966; MBA, U. Pa., 1968. CPA. Staff acct. Price Waterhouse, Phila., 1968-70, sr. acct., 1970-73, mgr., 1973-79, ptnr., 1979-95; pres. William H. Giese, Ltd., Ardmore, Pa., 1995-97, Tax Counselors of Bryn Mawr, Inc., Pa., 1997—; spkr. Wharton Tax Conf. Phila., 1988; bd. dirs. Carewide, Inc., Valley Forge, Pa., Verion, Inc., Exton, Pa. Bd. dirs, treas. Dunwoody Home and Village, Newtown Square, Pa., 1988—; bd. dirs. Lankenau Found., Phila., 1990—; past pres. North Ardmore Civic Assn., Phila. Squash Racquets Assn., Bala Cynwyd; fin. chmn. U.S. Amateur Golf Tournament, 1989; past treas. U.S. Squash Racquets Assn., Bala Cynwyd. Mem. AICPA, Pa. Inst. CPA's, Merion Golf Club (Ardmore, Pa.), Merion Cricket Club (Haverford, Pa.), Phila. Racquet Club. Republican. Presbyterian. Avocations: squash, golf, tennis. Home: 133 Edgewood Rd Ardmore PA 19003-2507 Office: 801 W Lancaster Ave Bryn Mawr PA 19010-3305

GIESELMANN, MORITZ PETER, cinematographer; b. Karlsruhe, Fed. Republic Germany, May 20, 1956; arrived in Austria, 1969; s. Reinhard and Maria Verena (Fischer) G.; m. Gerda Hoscher Hoschek, Dec. 3, 1992; children: Josefine, Luise. Student, Hochschule für Musik und Darstellende Kunst, Vienna, 1974-79. 2d asst. cameraman, grip various TV shows, Austria, 1974-77; 1st asst. cameraman various TV shows, Vienna, 1977-82; cinematographer, 1982—. Recipient Prix Spl. Jury, Festival du Film d'Art, UNECO, Paris, 1990. Mem. Austrian Assn. Cinematographers, German Soc. Cinematographers. Home and Office: 4 Neubaugasse, 1070 Vienna Austria

GIESEMANN, GERHARD, Russian literature educator; b. Zwickau, Germany, July 14, 1937; s. Theodor and Berne (Lütgert) G.; m. Edith Dobeler, Apr. 1, 1966; children: Christine, Jens. PhD, U. Frankfurt, Germany, 1969. Asst. prof. U. Frankfurt, 1969-79; prof. U. Giessen, Germany, 1980—; dean philosophy dept. U. Giessen, 1982-83, 92-93; dir. Inst. Slavic Langs. and Lit., Giessen; chmn. partnership Lódz U., 1994—; expert Deutsche Forschungs Gemeinschaft, Bonn, Germany, 1996—. Author: Kotzebue in Russia, 1972, Slovene National Theatre, 1975, Satire and Parody in Soviet Literature, 1983, Russian Literary Romance, 1985, Slovene Litarature, 1997; editor: Kritikon Litterarum, 1972. Presbyter, synodalist Nat. Ch., 1984—. Recipient medal U. Lódz, 1987, 98, honor award Tatarstan Republic, 1999. Mem. Acad. Scis. Slovenia, Verband der Hochschullehrer für Slavistik (chmn. 1994—). Lutheran. Avocations: music, piano, vocal music. Home: Paul-Hutten-Ring 31, 35415 Pohlheim Germany Office: Inst Slavistik, Karl-Gloeckner-Str 21 G, 35394 Giessen Germany

GIESEN, KLAUS-GERD, political scientist, educator; b. Haldern, Germany, Mar. 5, 1958; s. Wilhelm and Liane (Seesing) G.; m. Solange Kunz, Aug. 25, 1988; 1 child, Gaëlle. PhD in Polit. Sci., U. Geneva, 1991. Asst. U. Geneva, 1984-88; lectr. U. Lausanne, Switzerland, 1991-94; prof. U. Louvain, Belgium, 1994-97; prof. polit. sci. U. Leipzig, Germany, 1997—; vis. scholar U. So. Calif., 1988-89; vis. prof. U. Reims, France, 1994, 96, Ecole des Hautes Etudes en Scis. Sociales, Paris, 2000. Author: L'Europe des Surrégénérateurs, 1989, L'éthique des Relations Internationales, 1992; editor: L'éthique de l'Espace Politique Mondial, 1997. Mem. Internat. Studies Assn., German Polit. Sci. Assn. Office: U Leipzig, Burgstr 21, D-04109 Leipzig Germany

GIESSAUF, ANDREAS, chemist; b. Wagna bei Leibnitz, Austria, May 19, 1969; s. Andreas and Mathilde G. DSc, Karl Franzens U., 1996. Postdoctoral rschr. Tech. U. Munich, 1999-2000; rsch. asst. Leopold Franzens U., 2000—. Mem. Austrian Chem. Soc., Austrian Biochem. Soc.

GIESSER, BARBARA SUSAN, neurologist, educator; b. Bronx, N.Y., Jan. 21, 1953; d. David and Evelyn (Cohen) G.; m. Philip D. Kanof, June 17, 1979; children: David, Marisa. BS, U. Miami, 1972; MS, U. Tex., Houston, 1974; MD, U. Tex., San Antonio, 1978. Diplomate Am. Bd. Psychiatry and Neurology. Intern Montefiore Hosp., Bronx, 1978-79; resident Bronx Mcpl. Hosp. Ctr. (Albert Einstein Coll. Medicine), 1979-82; asst. prof. neurology Albert Einstein Coll. Medicine, Bronx, 1983-91; med. dir. Gimbel MS Comprehensive Care Ctr., Teaneck, N.J., 1985-90, Rehab. Inst. of Tucson, 1991-95; assoc. prof. clin. neurology Ariz. Health Scis. Ctr., Tucson, 1993—. Author: Neurology Specialty Board Review, 3d edit., 1986, 4th edit., 1996; contbr. articles to profl. publs. Dean's Tchr. scholar Ariz. Health Scis. Ctr., 1995. Fellow Am. Acad. Neurology (undergrad. edn. subcom. 1999—); mem. Nat. Multiple Sclerosis Soc. (rsch. grant 1989, 97, mem. profl. adv. com. Desert S.W. chpt. 1994—, bd. dirs. 1994-2000, counselor Am. Acad. Neurology sect. on Multiple Sclerosis 1997-99, nat. chair client edn. com. 1999—, mem. med. adv. bd. 1999—). Office: Ariz Health Scis Ctr 1501 N Campbell Ave Tucson AZ 85724-0001

GIESZL, LOUIS ROGER, mathematician; b. Inglewood, Calif., Sept. 14, 1937; s. Clifford G. and Zelma R. (Thompson) G; m. Geraldine C. Cirigliano, Sept. 22, 1963; children: Louis G., Lisa M. BS in Math., U. Houston, 1958; MA in Math., Rice U., 1965; MS in Computer Sci., U. Md., 1976; MS in Tech. Mgmt., Johns Hopkins U., 1985. Designer large-scale simulations USN Ops. Analysis, 1967-80; cons. computer technology USAF, 1980-81; dir. info. sys. project Logistics Command/USAF, 1981-82; computer cons. Warfare Analysis Lab., Johns Hopkins U. Applied Physics Lab., Laurel, Md., 1982—, computer cons. advanced sys. devel. group, 1982—, expert systems devel., 1983-87, test and evaluation mgmt., 1988-90, instr. software engring., 1988—. Referee, mem. editl. bd. and contbr. articles to profl. jours. and publs.; developer computer software/warfare simulation models. Capt. USAF, 1963-67. Mem. IEEE, Am. Legion. Office: Johns Hopkins U Applied Physics Lab Johns Hopkins Rd Laurel MD 20723

GIFFIN, GORDON D., ambassador, lawyer; b. Springfield, Mass.; m. Patti Alfred; 1 child, Kelley. BA, Duke U., 1971; JD, Emory U., 1974. Bar: Ga. 1974, DC 1979. Dir. legis. affairs, chief counsel to Senator Sam Nunn U.S. Senate, 1974-79; assoc. Hansell and Post, Atlanta, 1979-86; sr. ptnr. Long, Aldridge & Norman, Atlanta and Washington, until 1997; amb. to Can., Am. Embassy, Ottawa, Ont., 1997—; former adj. prof. law Emory U. Sch. Law, Atlanta; bd. dirs. Overseas Pvt. Investment Corp., 1993-97. Treas. Senator Sam Nunn Campaign Com., 20 yrs.; with Senator Nunn and Gov. Clinton founder Dem. Leadership Coun., 1984, mem. bd., 1984-96; mem. com. to host Dem. Nat. Conv., Atlanta, 1988, chmn. site selection com., Chgo., 1996, gen. counsel, 1992, 96; presdl. elector, Ga., 1992, 96; chmn. Ga. Clinton primary campaign, 1992, Clinton-Gore Gen. Election Campaign, 1992; dep. dir. pers. White House Transition Team, 1992; sr. advisor on south, also chmn. Clinton-Gore effort in Ga., Clinton Reelection Campaign, 1996; active Atlanta Olympic Games Com., 1996; former mem. bd. dirs. Ga. C. of C., Trees Atlanta Found., Atlanta Hist. Soc., Atlanta Ballet. Named One of 100 Most Influential Georgians, Ga. Trend mag., 3 times. Office: Dept State Am Ambassador To Canada Washington DC 20521-0001

GIFFIN, MARGARET ETHEL (PEGGY GIFFIN), management consultant; b. Cleve., Aug. 27, 1949; d. Arch Kenneth and Jeanne (Eggleton) G.; m. Robert Alan Wyman, Aug. 20, 1988; 1 child, Samantha Jean. BA in Psychology, U. Pacific, Stockton, Calif., 1971; MA in Psychology, Calif. State U., Long Beach, 1973; PhD in Quantitative Psychology, U. So. Calif., 1984. Psychometrician Auto Club So. Calif., L.A., 1973-74; cons. Psychol. Svcs., Inc., Glendale, Calif., 1975-76; mgr. Psychol. Svcs., Inc., Glendale, 1977-78, dir., 1979-94; rschr. Social Sci. Rsch. Inst., U. So. Calif., L.A., 1981; dir. Giffin Consulting Svcs., L.A., 1994—; instr. Calif. State U., Long Beach, 1989-90; mem. tech. adv. com. on testing Calif. Fair Employment and Housing Comm., 1974-80, mem. steering com., 1978-80. Mem. APA, Soc. Indsl. Organizational Psychology, Pers. Testing Coun. So. Calif. (pres. 1980, exec. dir. 1982, 88, bd. dirs. 1980-92). Home and Office: 260 S Highland Ave Los Angeles CA 90036-3027

GIFFORD, CHARLES KILVERT, banker; b. Providence, Nov. 8, 1942; s. Clarence H. and Priscilla (Kilvert) G.; m. Anne Dewing, Oct. 3, 1964;

children—Ramsay, Charles, John, Jessica. B.A., Princeton U., 1964. With Chase Manhattan Bank, N.Y.C., 1964-66; with BankBoston, 1966—, loan officer, 1967, asst. v.p., 1970, v.p., 1973, first v.p., 1978, sr. v.p., 1979, exec. v.p., 1981; vice-chmn. BankBoston and First Nat. Bank of Boston, 1987, pres., 1989, chmn., CEO, 1995—; pres. & COO FleetBoston Fin. Corp., Boston; group exec. Corp. Banking Group, 1984; dir. Mass. Mut. Life Ins. Co., Boston Edison Co. Trustee New Eng. Aquarium, Boston, 1982, Dana Farber Cancer Ctr., Boston, 1982, Sta. WGBH, Make-A-Wish Found., Northeastern U., Junior Achievement; bd. dirs. Boston Pvt. Ind. Coun., Assn. Res. City Bankers; chmn. success by 6 leadership coun. United Way, mem. exec. com.; chmn. Boston Plan for Excellence in Pub. Schs. Mem. Greater Boston C. of C. (chmn.). Office: FleetBoston Financial Corp 1 Federal St Fl 8 Boston MA 02110-2003

GIFFORD, HEIDI, writer, editor; b. New Haven, Jan. 28, 1961; d. Prosser and Dee Dee (O'Sullivan) Gifford; m. George Melas, July 15, 1995; 1 child, Luke. BA in English Lit., Yale U., 1983; MPA in Internat. Econs., Columbia U., 1991. Editl. asst. Yale U. Press, New Haven, 1985; asst. to the dir. Gov.'s Office of Fed. Rels., Boston, 1987-89; asst. dir. internat. trade and econs. Coun. on Fgn. Rels., N.Y.C., 1991-94; elections analyst Nightly News with Tom Brokaw/NBC News, N.Y.C., 1995-96; writer and editor Comms. Devel., N.Y.C., 1997—; assoc. USIA Fgn. Press Ctr., N.Y.C., 1990-91. Mem. Inst. of World Affairs. Episcopalian. Avocations: crew, marathon running.

GIFFORD, JOHN IRVING, retired agricultural equipment company executive; b. Lockport, N.Y., July 23, 1930; s. John Jacob and Carrie (McAdam) G.; m. Sara Jane Bauer, Jan. 28, 1955; children: John Hutchins, James Scott. BS, Purdue U., 1952, MS, 1956. Sales trainee Am. Nat. Foods, Inc., L.A., 1956; economist Deere & Co., Moline, Ill., 1956-65; pers. adminstr. Deere & Co., Moline, 1965-70, mgr. data svcs., 1970-96; stats. cons. to cos. and trade assns., 1996—; mem. USDA Agrl. Stats. adv. com., 1997—. Bd. dirs., Rock Island (Ill.) sect. Easter Seal Found., 1981-87; v.p. coun., St. John Luth. Ch., Rock Island, 1981-82; pres., Rock Island Little League, 1981-82; v.p. Babe Ruth Baseball, Rock Island, 1983; mem. agrl. census adv. com. U.S. Dept. Commerce, 1997-98; mem. adv. com. stats. USDA, 1999—. 1st lt. U.S. Army, 1952-54, Korea. Recipient Leadership recognition Equipment Mfrs. Inst. Mem. Nat. Assn. Bus. Econs., Equipment Mfrs. Assn., Farm and Indsl. Equipment Inst., Constrn. Industry Mfrs. Assn., Outdoor Power Equipment Inst., Engine Mfrs. Assn., Internat. Farm Tractor Com., Internat. Harvesting Equipment Com. (chmn. statistics com. 1994-95). Avocations: reading, golf.

GIFFORD, ROGER MATTHEW, research scientist; b. Worcester, Eng., Mar. 13, 1944; s. Peter Walter and Betty Elaine (Pearson) G.; m. Jean Kathryn Grossman, July 25, 1970; children: Jamie Andrew, Toby Michael. BSc with honors, U. Nottingham, Eng., 1965; PhD, Cornell U., 1969. Rsch. scientist C.S.I.R.O. Australia, Canberra, 1970—; sect. head C.S.I.R.O. Divsn. of Plant Industry, Canberra, 1977-87, subprogram leader, 1988—. Editor of 3 books; contbr. over 140 rsch. papers to plant sci. and global change jours. and books. Recipient numerous grants in field. Avocations: recreational and display folk dancing, walking, cycling, music. Office: CSIRO Divsn Plant Industry, CSIRO Plant Industry, GPO Box 1600, Canberra 2601, Australia

GIGENA, SALVADOR DANIEL RAMÓN, mathematician; b. Cordoba, Argentina, Apr. 19, 1939; s. Salvador Israel Luján and Teresa Blanca (Santoro) G.; m. Haydée Brígida Villegas, Dec. 26, 1966; children: Daniel Edgardo, Adrián Horacio, César Gabriel, Oscar Fernando. B, Coll. Nat. Monserrat, Cordoba, 1958; Lic. Math., U. Nat. Cordoba, 1964; PhD in Maths., U. Pa., Phila., 1973. Ayudante U. Nat. Cordoba, 1961-63; jefe tra. prácticos U. Nat. La Plata, Argentina, 1965-68; teaching fellow U. Pa., 1968-73; prof. visitante U. Fed. Ceará, Fortaleza, Brazil, 1976-78, U. São Paulo, Brazil, 1978-81; prof. titular U. Nat. Rosario, Argentina, 1981—; vis. prof. Tech. U. Berlin, 1986, U. P.R., 1989-91; prof. titular U. Nat. Cordoba, 1986—. Contbr. articles to profl. jours. DAAD Rsch. fellow, 1985; Fulbright Found. grantee, 1968. Avocations: playing soccer, playing piano, singing. Home: Copacabana 854, 5008 Cordoba Argentina Office: U Nat Rosario Dept Math, Avda Pellegrini 250, 2000 Rosario Argentina Office: U Nat Cordoba Dept Math, Avda Velez Sarsfield 299, 5000 Cordoba Argentina

GIGLIOTTI, RICHARD JOSEPH, nuclear security executive; b. North Adams, Mass., June 15, 1945; s. Victor and Ida (Antenucci) G.; m. Diane Carol Gigliotti; children: Gina Bianca, Victoria Marie, Richard Joseph Jr. BA, Norwich U., 1968; postgrad., Mass. State Coll., 1968-70. Police officer North Adams Police Dept., 1966-70, Wethersfield (Conn.) Police Dept., 1973-77; security supr. UNC Naval Products, Montville, Conn., 1977-78, corp. security dir., 1984-92; mgr. security UNC Recovery Systems, Charlestown, R.I., 1978-80; dir. loss prevention Colt Firearms, Hartford, Conn., 1980-84; mgr. security RUST Geotech Inc., Grand Junction, Colo., 1992-96; cons. security, 1996—; adj. faculty Ea. Conn. State U., Willimantic, Mohegan C.C., Norwich, 1984-92; guest lectr. various colls., univs., and corps., 1978—. Author: Security Design for Maximum Protection, 1984, Emergency Planning for Maximum Protection, 1991; contbr. articles to profl. jours. Active Gov.'s and Gen. Assembly's Task Force on Pvt. Security in Conn., 1983. 1st lt. U.S. Army, 1970-73. Recipient Chief Samuel Luciano award Mcpl. Police Tng. Coun., 1974. Mem. Internat. Assn. Chiefs Police, Am. Soc. for Indsl. Security, Ret. Officers Assn., Blue Knights Law Enforcement Motorcycle Club. Roman Catholic. Avocations: fishing, hunting, writing, bicycling, motorcycling.

GIGLMAYR, JOSEF, electrical engineer, researcher; b. Weissbach/Lofer, Salzburg, Austria, Nov. 3, 1941; s. Josef and Bibiana (Haitzmann) G.; m. Sabine Eschment, Aug. 30, 1985 (div. Feb. 1996); 1 child, Fanny Elisa. Grad. in Engring., Eng. Sch., Furtwangen, Germany, 1970; diploma in Engring., Tech. U. Berlin, 1973, DEng, 1977, diploma in Math., 1981. Apprentice electrician O. Ganz Bergheim, Salzburg, 1956-60; electrician F. Mayerhofer, Lamprechtshausen, Austria, 1961, E. Werner Magasin, Drammen, Norway, 1962-63; ship electrician F. Olsen, Oslo, 1963; electrician Siemens Norge A/S, Oslo, 1963-64; ship electrician W. Wilhelmsen, Oslo, 1964; electrician Ing. V. Sachs, Salzburg, 1965, Schrack, Salzburg, 1965; ship electrician Lorentzen Co., Oslo, 1965-66; electrician S. Siedle, Furtwangen, Germany, 1969, 70; programmer Tech. U. Berlin, 1971; electrician Weri-Electronics, Furtwangen, 1972; tutor Tech. U. Berlin, 1972-74, asst., 1974-77; rsch. mem. Heinrich-Hertz Inst., Berlin, 1981-2000; prof. info. and comms. Kwangju Inst. Sci. and Tech., Korea, 2000—; vis. lectr. Stanford U., MIT, 1984, Phillips Industry, Nürnberg, Germany, 1985, Politechica Torino, U. Torino, U. Stuttgart. Contbr. over 80 articles to books and profl. jours. With Austrian Mil., 1961. Mem. IEEE, Optical Soc. Am., N.Y. Acad. Scis. Avocations: drawings, painting, walking, swimming, reading. E-mail: giglmayr@kjist.ac.kr.

GIJSBERS, ALAN JOHANNES, physician, counselor; b. Adeldoorn, Gelderland, The Netherlands, Apr. 10, 1949; arrived in Australia, 1958; s. Johannes Willem and Phyllis Ellen (Richards) G.; m. Lois Irene Wilson, Jan. 8, 1972; children: Kerryn Ruth, David John, Rachel Claire. MBBS, U. Melbourne (Australia), 1973; postgrad. diploma in epidemiology, 1994; diploma of tropical medicine and hygiene, London Sch. Tropical Medicine, 1980. Vis. physician Christian Med. Coll. and Hosp., Vellore, India, 1985-86, dep. dir. dept. cont. edn., 1986-88; gen. physician St. Vincent's Hosp. and Royal Victorian Eye and Ear Hosp., Melbourne, Australia, 1989-95; splst. physician dept. drug and alcohol studies St. Vincent's Hosp., Melbourne, Australia, 1990—; sr. lectr. clin. medicine dept. psychol. medicine Monash U., Melbourne, Australia, 1992—; cons. physician Epworth Hosp., Melbourne, Australia, 1995—; cons. physician Victorian Aborigine Health Svc., 1990-98; specialist phys. Turning Point Drug & Alcohol Ctr. 1998—; cons. Victorian Govt. Cervical Cancer Screening Program, 1995, Victorian Govt. Health Svcs. Commn., 1996; chief investigator study of drinic drivers in edn. course Victorian Health Promotion Found., 1992-94. Contbr. articles to med. jours. Chmn. Christian Med. and Dental Fellowship of Australia, Victoria, 1992-96, nat. chmn. 1999—. Fellow Royal Australasian Coll. Physicians, Inst. Study of Christianity in an Age of Sci. and Tech.; mem. Australian Med. Assn. Avocations: reading theology, gardening. Home: 20 Sassafras Dr, Victoria 3107, Australia Office: Epsorth Cons Stes 2-4A, 62 Erin St, Richmond 3121, Australia

GIJSEN, PAUL HUBERTUS, finance administrator; b. Nieuwenhagen, The Netherlands; m. Mariet Wlhelmina Rutten; children: Vincent, Paula, Lidwien. Grad. in Bus. Econs., U. Tilburg, 1978; grad. in Accountancy, U. Tilburg, The Netherlands, 1981; grad. in Bus. Econs., U. Filburg. Chartered acct., The Netherlands. Acct. Ernst & Young, 1978-81, Van Dien and Co., 1981-86; contr. Hendrix Noeders Nutreco, Boxmeer, The Netherlands, 1986—; fin. dir. Hendrix Feed Nutreco, Boxmeer, The Netherlands, 1997—. Mem. Rotary. Home: Provincialeweg 7, 5827AA Vortum Mullem The Netherlands Office: Hendrix Voeden, Veerweg 38, 5830MA Boxmeer The Netherlands

GIL, DAVID GEORG, social policy educator; b. Vienna, Austria, Mar. 16, 1924; came to U.S., 1953; s. Oskar and Helene (Weiss) Engel; m. Eva Aviva Breslauer, Aug. 2, 1947; children: Daniel W. and Gideon R. (twins). BA, Hebrew U., 1957; MSW, U. Pa., Phila., 1958, DSW, 1963. Lic. social worker, Mass.; lic. ind. clin. social worker. Farmworker, laborer Sweden and Palestine, 1939-43; counselor, tchr. Home for Dependent, Neglected and Delinquent Children, Tel-Mond, Palestine, 1943-45; probation officer Dept. Social Welfare, Palestine and Israel, 1945-53; fellow UN, Phila., 1953-54; asst. dir. Youth Probation Svc., Jerusalem, 1955-57; family counselor Jewish Family Svc., Phila., 1957-59; supr., rsch. assoc. Assn. Jewish Children, Phila., 1959-63; rsch. dir. Soc. to Prevent Cruelty to Children, Boston, 1963-64; from asst. to prof. social policy Brandeis U., Waltham, Mass., 1964—; dir. Ctr. for Social Change, Heller Grad. Sch., Brandeis U., Waltham, 1984-96, ret.; Kenneth L. Pray lectr. U. Pa., Phila., 1991; vis. prof. George Washington U. Sch. of Social Work, 1975—. Author: Violence Against Children, 1970, Unravelling Social Policy, 1973, 76, 81, 90, 92, The Challenge of Social Equality, 1976, Beyond the Jungle, 1979, Confronting Injustice and Oppression, 1998; editor: Child Abuse and Violence, 1979; co-editor: Toward Social and Economic Justice, 1985, The Future of Work, 1987; chair faculty senate Brandeis U., 1989-92. Rep. bd. trustees Brandeis U., 1990-94; co-chair Socialist Party, 1995-99; mem. exec. com. Nat. Jobs for All Coalition, 1997—. Rsch. grantee U.S. Children's Bur., Washington, 1965-73, project grantee Levinson Found., Boston, 1983, 85. Mem. NASW (del. assembly 1987-90, Social Worker of Yr. award 2000), NASW Mass., Assn. Humanist Sociology (pres. 1981), Am. Orthopsychiat. Assn. (bd. mem. 1990-93). Office: Heller Sch Brandeis U Waltham MA 02454-9110

GIL, FERNANDO MIGUEL, Catholic priest, historian; b. Montevideo, Uruguay, May 8, 1953; arrived in Argentina, 1967; s. Fernando Gil Zorrilla and Beatriz A. Eisner. Degree in theology, Cath. U., Buenos Aires, 1987; ThD, Gregorian U., Rome, 1989. Ordained Roman Catholic priest, Mar. 25, 1983. Assoc. prof. Cath. U., Buenos Aires, 1989-93, prof. Latin Am. Ch. History, 1993—. Author: Primeras Doctrinas del Nuevo Mundo, 1992, Discusiones en torno al uso del término "persona divina" en nahuatl en la evangelizacion mexicana del siglo XVII, 1998; contbr. articles to profl. jours. Mem. Junta Historia de la Iglesia (Argentina). Avocation: mountaineering. E-mail: pfernando@uca.edu.ar. Home: Repetto 1037, B1640EMO Martinez Argentina Office: Cath U Argentina, Concordia 4422, C1419AOH Buenos Aires Argentina

GIL, GUILLERMO EDUARDO, conservation biologist; b. Morón, Argentina, Nov. 19, 1966; s. Jesus and Marta Alicia (Musso) G.; m. Norma Inés Hilgert, Nov. 18, 1995. Grad. in Biol. Scis., Buenos Aires U., 1992. Fellowship Argentina Wildlife Found., Buenos Aires, 1985-86, natural areas helper, 1986-90; initiation fellowship Nat. Pks. Adminstrn., Buenos Aires, 1990-93, superior formation fellowship, 1993; superior formation fellowship Nat. Pks. Adminstrn., Salta, Argentina, 1994-98; tech. asst. Nat. Pks. Adminstrn., Iguazu, Argentina, 1998—; naturalist guide Argentina Wildlife Found., 1984-86. Contbr. articles to profl. jours. Vol. Argentina Wildlife Found., Buenos Aires, 1984-88; hon. wildlife nat. insp. Wildlife Nat. Direction, Buenos Aires, 1990-92. Recipient Claes Olrog fellowship, Misiones, Argentina, 1994, CYTED fellowship, Xalapa, Mex., 1997. Mem. Argentina Soc. for Mammals Study (del. 1997-98), Argentina Wildlife Found., Plata's Ornithol. Assn. (birdwatch guide 1988-94, del. 1997-98). Avocations: birdwatcher, photographer of nature. Home: JB Alberdi 1238, 1706 Haedo Buenos Aires Argentina Office: Admnstrn ParquesNacionales, Av Santa Fe 690, 1059 Buenos Aires Argentina

GIL, MICHAEL IOSIF, mathematician; b. Kharkov, Ukraine, Mar. 10, 1941; arrived in Israel, 1991; s. Iosif Moshe and Eugenia Avraham (Benzionov) G.; m. Lubov Lazar Shargorodski, Jan. 16, 1971; children: Alla, Lior, Alex. MS, Polytechnic Inst., Kharkov, 1967; PhD, State U. Voronezj, Russia, 1983; DSc, Inst. Sys. Rsch., Moscow, 1991. Sr. rschr. Design Office, Kharkov, 1967-71; sr. lectr. State U., Elysta, Russia, 1971-78; head lab. Inst. Acad. Sci., Khabanovsk, Russias, 1978-91; prof. math. Ben Gurion U., Beer Sheva, Israel, 1991—. Author: Operator Functions, 1984, The Operator-Functions Method in Theory of Differential Equations, 1990, Estimates for Norms of Operator-Valued Functions, 1995, Stability of Finite and Infinite Dimensional Systems, 1998. Israel Min. of Sci. grantee, 1992. Mem. Am. Math. Soc. Office: Ben Gurion Univ Dept Math, PO Box 653, 84105 Beer Sheva Israel

GILAD, GAD M., neuroscientist, educator; b. Nahalal, Israel, Jan. 5, 1948; s. Gershon Greenberg and Rivka (Habinsky) G.; m. Varda Hayman, Aug. 27, 1969; children: Ayelet, Iris, Yotam. BS in Biology, Tel Aviv U., 1971; spl. student in social scis., Brandeis U., 1971-72; PhD in Neurobiology and Behavior, Cornell U., 1977. Grad. rsch. asst. Cornell U. Med. Coll., N.Y.C., 1972-77; Fogarty vis. fellow Nat. Inst. Mental Health, Bethesda, Md., 1977-79; scientist Weizmann Inst., Rehovot, Israel, 1979-81, sr. scientist, 1981-87; sabbatical, spinal cord injury rsch. VA Med. Ctr., Harvard Med. Sch., West Roxbury, Mass., 1986-87; head dept. neurobiology Coriell Inst. Med. Rsch., Camden, N.J., 1987-88; Fogarty vis. scientist Nat. Inst. Mental Health Neurosci. Ctr. St. Elisabeths, Washington, 1988-92; vis. assoc. prof. The Bruce Rappaport Faculty Medicine Technion-Israel Inst. Tech., Haifa, Israel, 1992-94; head lab. neurosci. dept. neurology Tel Aviv-Sourasky Med. Ctr., Tel Aviv, 1995-96; dir. R & D, head lab. neurosci. Assaf Harofeh Med. Ctr., Zrifin, Israel, 1996—; incumbent Paul and Gabriella Rosenbaum Career Devel. chair Weizmann Inst. Sci., 1983-86; organizer and chmn. symposia and confs.; founder Israeli Forum of Med. Rsch. of Devel. Dirs., 1999—. Mem. editl. bd.: Internat. Jour. Devel. Neurosci., 1985—, Jour. Neurotrauma, 1988-94; reviewer: (jours.) Brain Rsch., Exptl. Neurology, Life Scis., Physiology and Behavior; contbr. numerous articles to profl. jours. including Annals Neurology, Brain Rsch., Life Sci. Mem. City Coun., Nes-Ziona, Israel, 1983-86; chmn. Movement for Nes-Ziona, 1982-86. Capt. Israel Def. Forces, 1965-68. Recipient Ben-Zvi award City of Givataim, 1970, 1st prize Med Johnson award for gen. excellence Am. Med. Student Rsch. Forum, 1976, 1st prize Roche Labs. award in neurosci., 1976, Curt. P. Richter prize Internat. Soc. Psychoneuroendocrinology, 1986, Travel award Am. Soc. for Pharmacology and Exptl. Therapeutics, 1978, Travel award Internat. Brain Rsch. Orgn., 1992. Mem. AAAS, Soc. for Neurosci., Israel Soc. Neurosci. Avocation: painting, public and community activity. Office: Assaf Harofeh Med Ctr, R & D Neuro Lab, Zrifin 70300, Israel

GILARDI, GIANFRANCO, biochemist, biomedical engineer, educator; b. Turin, Italy, Apr. 29, 1961; s. Giovanni and Olga (Giacosa) G. Lauream in Biol. Scis., U. Turin, 1986; diploma Imperial Coll., Royal Coll. Sci., London, 1991; PhD in Biotech., Imperial Coll., London, 1991. Rsch. in drug metabolism faculty pharmacy U. Turin, 1986-87; indsl. rsch. fellow in biotech. Montedison SpA, Milan, Italy, 1987-91; postdoctoral rsch. asst. dept. chemistry Leiden (The Netherlands) U., 1991-93; postdoctoral rsch. fellow dept. biochemistry Imperial Coll., London, 1993-95, lectr. in protein engring., 1990-99, sr. lectr. in protein and drug design, 2000—; mem. Sci. Adv. Bd. to Protein Arrays Ltd., London. Author editorials in protein engring. and design Current Biology, Ltd., 1993—; contbr. articles to profl. jours. Civil protection officer Ministry of Interior, Italy, 1986-87. Mem. Royal Soc. Chemistry London (chartered chemist), Inst. Biology London (chartered biologist), Italian Biochem. Soc. (medal 1993), Biochem. Soc. London. Roman Catholic. Avocations: interior design, naval modelling, skiing, archaeology, contemporary and modern art. Home: 77 Harefield Rd, London UB8 1PJ, England Office: Imperial Coll Sci Tech Med, Dept Biochemistry, London SW7 2AY, England

GILAT, AVRAHAM, defense company executive; b. Petah-Tikva, Israel, Nov. 17, 1949; s. Zvi Horowitz and Hanah (Verber) G.; m. Ayelet Dor, Sept. 25, 1974; children: Omri, Timna, Matan. BA, Tel-Aviv U., 1974; MBA, NYU, 1976. Economist IMI, Tel-Aviv, 1976-78, mktg. mgr., 1978-81; br. mgr. IMI, Washington, 1981-85; v.p. mktg. IMI, Ramat-Hasharon, Israel, 1986-93; dir. Mikal, Hertzlia, Israel, 1993—; chmn. Soltam, Yokneam, Israel, 1999—; bd. mem. Merhav, Ashdod, Israel, 1998—; chmn. BAT, Beit-Alfa, Israel, 1998—; bd. mem. Fresh-Cup Tel-Aviv, 1994—. Bd. mem. Israel Waterpolo Assn., 1996—. Maj. Israeli mil., 1968-71. Jewish. Avocations: swimming, waterpolo.

GILBAR, PETER JEFFREY, pharmacologist, pharmacist; b. Mt. Morgan, Queensland, Australia, Aug. 13, 1956; s. Kenneth and Evelyn Margaret (Nash) G.; m. Janelle Margaret Logan, Jan. 25, 1992; children: Erin Claire, Holly Renee. B in Pharmacy, U. Queensland, Brisbane, Australia, 1977; diploma in hosp. clin. pharmacy practice, SHPA, Melbourne, Australia, 1994; M in Palliative Care, Flinders U., Adelaide, Australia, 2000. Pharmacist Retail Pharmacy, Townsville, Australia, 1977-82, Toowoomba (Australia) Base Hosp., 1982-88, 1989-91; pharmacist Hillingdon Hosp., London, 1988; oncology and palliative care pharmacist Toowoomba Health Svc., 1991—; presenter in field. Contbr. articles to profl. jours. Dep. chmn. Toowoomba Police Youth Club, 1994—. Clin. Pharmacy Practice grantee SHPA, 1994, Allied Health Travel grant Queensland Cancer Fund, 1998. Mem. Soc. Hosp. Pharmacists Australia, Internat. Soc. Oncology Pharmacy Practitioners, Clin. Oncological Soc. Australia. Avocations: traveling, sports, reading, weight training. Office: Toowoomba Health Svc, Private Mail Bag 2, Toowoomba QLD 4350, Australia

GILBERT, ALAN D., university president. Grad., Australian Nat. U.; DPhil in Modern History, U. Oxford, 1973; DLitt (hon.), U. Tasmania, 1995. Prof. history various univs., Australia and Papua New Guinea; pro-vice-chancellor U. New South Wales, 1988-90; vice-chancellor U. Tasmania, Australia, 1991-95, U. Melbourne, 1996—; mem. Australian Higher Edn. Coun., 1991-95; chmn. Universitas 21. Author: Religion and Society in Industrial England, 1976, churches and Churchgoers, 1978, The making of Post-Christian Britain, 1980; jt. gen. editor: Australians: A Historical Library, 1988; contbr. articles to profl. jours. Chmn. bd. Melbourne Univ. Pvt. Ltd.

GILBERT, ANNA See LAZARUS, MARGUERITE

GILBERT, CREIGHTON EDDY, art historian; b. Durham, N.C., June 6, 1924; s. Allan H. and Katharine (Everett) G. BA, NYU, 1942, PhD, 1955; DHL (hon.), Adelphi U., 1990, U. Louisville, 1997. Assoc. prof. Brandeis U., 1961-65, Sidney and Ellen Wien prof. history of art, 1965-69; prof. Queens Coll. City U. N.Y., 1969-77; Jacob Gould Schurman prof. art history Cornell U., 1977-81; prof. Yale U., 1981-2000, prof. emeritus, 2000—; Fulbright sr. lectr. U. Rome, 1951-52; fellow Netherlands Inst. for Advanced Study, 1972-73; vis. prof. U. Leiden, 1974-75; Zacks Found. vis. prof. Hebrew U. Jerusalem, 1985. Author: Change in Piero della Francesca, 1968, History of Renaissance Art, 1972, The Works of Girolamo Savoldo, 1986, Poets Seeing Artists' Work: Instances from the Italian Renaissance, 1991, Michelangelo On and Off the Sistine Ceiling, 1994, Piero della Francesca et Giorgione: Problèmes d'Interpretation, 1994, Caravaggio and His Two Cardinals, 1995; editor: Italian Art 1400-1500, Sources and Documents, 1979, enlarged Italian edit., 1988; editor-in-chief: The Art Bull, 1980-85; translator: Complete Poems and Selected Letters of Michelangelo, 1963, 3d edit., 1979. Recipient Mather award Coll. Art Assn., 1964. Fellow Am. Acad. Arts and Scis., Ateneo Veneto (fgn.). Office: Yale U Dept Art History Box 208272 New Haven CT 06520-8272

GILBERT, DEBBIE ROSE, entrepreneur; b. Indpls., Jan. 18, 1961; d. James Taylor and Rosemary (Robinson) G. BA, Ind. U., 1984; diploma in computer literacy, St. Augustine Coll., Chgo., 1995. Student typing asst. Shortridge H.S./Indpls. Pub. Schs./Bd. Sch. Commrs., Indpls., 1978-79; substitute tchr. Indpls. Pub. Schs./Bd. Sch. Commrs., 1985-89, Washington Twp. Schs., Indpls., 1992; CHA housewatcher, clothes distbr. The Inner Voice, Inc., Chgo., 1994-95; vol. Lakefront Single Room Occupancy Employment Program, Chgo., 1997—. Dep. registrar O.N.E./Bd. Election Commrs., Chgo., 1996—; mem. People for the Am. Way, Chgo., 1995-96; mem. Access Living, Chgo., 1996—, mem. Southern Poverty Law Ctr., Tchg. Tolerance, Militia Task Force, Klanwatch Org., Montgomery, 1998—. Mem. ACLU, NOW, AAUW, NAACP, The Natl. Mus. of Women in the Arts Org., OWL (The Older Women's League), The Voice of Midlife & Older Women, Wash. D.C., Mental Health Consumer Edn. Consortium, Inc. Democrat. Baptist. Avocations: modeling, singing, race walking, bingo, reading. Home: 5012 N Winthrop Ave Apt 224 Chicago IL 60640-3124 Office: 4753 N Broadway St Ste 632808 Chicago IL 60640-4986

GILBERT, DOUGLAS WAYNE, environmental services administrator, inspector; b. London, Ky., Jan. 20, 1955; s. Lowell and Grace G.; m. Deborah Kay Clark, Aug. 16, 1974; 1 child: Kristopher Hayes. Grad., Sue Bennett Coll., London, Ky., 1973, Corbin Vocat. Sch., Ky., 1974, Career Devel. Ctr., Lexington, Ky., 1979. Cert. bldg. insp. level II, Ky, 1 & 2 family dwelling insp., Ky., 1 & 2 family mech. insp., Ky, mech. insp., Ky.; licensed real estate sales assoc. Apprentice carpenter Y & S Constrn., Corbin, Ky., 1971, Six Industries, Springfield, Ohio, 1972; labor foreman J.E. Crain Co., Nashville, 1973-75; bldg. contractor Lowell Gilbert Constrn., London, Ky., 1975-81; self-employed contractor London, 1981-88, 90; bldg. supt. Levi Jackson Constrn., London, 1989, London Devel. Inc., 1991-92, Chamber Inc., London, 1993; code enforcement, bldg. inspector City of London, 1994-99; dir. environ. svcs. Marymount Med. Ctr., London, 1999—; zoning officer London, Ky., 1994-99. adminstrv. aide London Bd. Zoning Adjustment, 1994-99; mem. London/Laurel County Planning Comm., 1999-2000, adminstrv. aide, 1999, plan reviewer, 1994-99; trustee Laurel River Bible Camp, London, exec. bd. mem., treas., 1993-2000. Mem. Nat. Fire Protection Assn., Bldg. Ofcls. and Code Adminstrs. Internat. (cert. bldg. insp., mech. insp., 1 & 2 family dwelling bldg. and mech. insp.), So. Bldg. Code Congress Internat. (cert. mech. and bldg. insp.), Code Adminstrs. Ky. Republican. Avocations: civil war collector, woodworking, blue print drafting, motorcycle touring. E-mail: dgilbert@marymount.com. Home: 225 Substation St London KY 40741-2205 Office: Marymount Med Ctr 310 E 9th St London KY 40741-1204

GILBERT, HAMLIN MILLER, JR., publishing executive; b. Bridgport, Conn., Mar. 12, 1940; s. Hamlin Miller and Charlotte E. (Munn) G.; m. Emmy Lou Chatterton, July 20, 1963; children: Bradley, Kim. BA, Cornell U., 1962. Fin. analyst Chem. Bank, N.Y.C., 1963-64; sales rep. Continental Can Co., Teterboro, N.J., 1964-65, Time, Inc., N.Y.C., 1965-70; package goods mgr. Time Mag., 1970-75, travel advt. mgr., 1975-80, divsn. mgr., 1980-83, assoc. N.Y. dir., 1983-85, U.S. dir. spl. sect., 1985-92; N.Y. advt. sales dir. Smithsonian Mag., N.Y.C., 1992-95, dir. bus. devel., 1995-97, mktg. exec. web site, advt. svcs. dir., 1997-2000, ret., 2000. Editor spl. advt. sect., Time-Am. Cup, 1987, Time-Winter Olympic Preview, 1987. V.p. comm. New Canaan H.S. Sports Council, Conn., 1987-89; instr. U.S. Power Squadron, Darien, Conn., 1986—. Mem. Travel Rsch. Assn. (dir. 1979-81), Cornell U. Alumni Assn. (area dir. 1980-95), Woodway Country Club (bd. dirs. 1980-86), Austin Healey Club Am. Republican. Episcopalian. Avocations: sailing, skiing, golf, tennis, gardening, scuba diving (cert.). Home: 774 Norton St Longboat Key FL 34228-1448 Office: Smithsonian Mag 420 Lexington Ave Rm 2335 New York NY 10170-1845

GILBERT, JAN WADE, dentist, marketing professional; b. Bklyn., June 19, 1945; s. Joseph and Sylvia (Gilbert) Hoffman; m. Sharon Mary Sikorski, Apr. 18, 1981; 1 child, Lynsey Grey. BS, Bklyn. Coll., 1967; DMD, U. Pitts., 1971. Gen. dentist Dentistry For Nice People, Lawrence, N.Y., 1973—, owner, founder, pres., 1990—; pres. The Dental Mktg. Study Club, Lawrence, 1990—. Author: The Traveler's Diet, 1999, Secrets of Toothbrushing, 1991. Chmn. DisneyDay, L.I., N.Y., 1999; developer Reading Aloud, L.I., 1999. Mem. Kiwanis Club. Avocations: writing, photography, chess. E-mail: janwg@lawrence.csnet.net. Office: Dentistry for Nice People 176 Broadway Lawrence NY 11559-1731

GILBERT, MARIE ROGERS, poet; b. Florence, S.C., Jan. 27, 1924; d. Frank Mandeville and Marie Barringer Rogers; m. Richard Austin Gilbert, Apr. 24, 1946; children: Richard Austin Jr., Laurie Gilbert Sanford. BA in Psychology and Theater Arts, Rollins Coll., 1945. read poetry at Spoleto Festival, Charleston, S.C., 1999. Contbr. poetry to anthologies including Word and Witness: 200 Years of North Carolina Poetry, 1999; author:

Brookgreen Oaks, 1999, Connexions, 1994, Myrtle Beach Back When, 1989, Forever New, 1987, The Song and the Seed, 1983, From Comfort, 1981. Driver ARC, Florence Army Air Base, summer 1943-44; bd. visitors St. Andrews Presbyn. Coll., Laurinburg, N.C., 1995-98. Recipient Poet Laureate Sam Ragan Fine Arts award St. Andrews Presbyn. Coll., 1994. Mem. Poetry Soc. N.C. (v.p., 1988-89, pres. 1990-92), Poetry Soc. S.C. (1st pl. for lyric poetry 1987, 90), N.C. Writers Conf., N.C. Writers Network, Colonial Dames of Am. in state of N.C. (sec. 1990-91, v.p. 1992-93), Jr. League. Avocation: poetry readings and seminars. Home: 2 Saint Simons Sq Greensboro NC 27408-3833

GILBERT, MICHAEL JOHN, barrister, solicitor; b. Milton, New Zealand, Mar. 29, 1953; s. John McEwan and Janette)Penny) G.; m. Lorna May Starling, Dec. 8, 1979; children: Matthew John, Olivia May. LLB, Otago U., Dunedin, New Zealand, 1978. Staff solicitor Tonkinson Wood & Adams, Dunedin, New Zealand; staff solicitor Pitt & Moore, Nelson, New Zealand, 1985-88, prin., 1989-94; prin. pvt. practice, Nelson, New Zealand, 1995—. Anglican. Avocations: running, mountain biking, snow boarding, scuba diving, windsurfing. Home: 44 Tasman St, Nelson New Zealand Office: 92 Collingwood St, Nelson New Zealand

GILBERT, PATRICK NIGEL GEOFFREY, organization executive; b. May 12, 1934; adopted s. Geoffrey and Evelyn (Miller) Devon. Ed. Cranleigh Sch., Merton Coll., Oxford; D.Litt. (hon.), Columbia Pacific U., 1982. Lectr. in further edn. South Berks Coll., 1959-62, personal asst. to Sir Edward Hulton, 1962-64; with Oxford U. Press, 1964-69; mng. dir. Westinghouse group, 1970; gen. sec. Soc. for Promoting Christian Knowledge, London, 1971-92; cons. Three Georges Devel. Co., 1994-97, Saga Travel, 1994-98; dir. Surrey Bldg. Soc., 1988-93. Chmn. Camden Arts Council, 1970-74, v.p., 1974-90; steward Artists' Gen. Benevolent Instn., 1971-93; trustee Richards Trust, 1971-92, Buxton Trust, 1973-92, chmn., 1983-92; trustee Overseas Bishoprics Fund, 1971-92, World Assn. Christian Communication, 1975-87; gov., vice chmn. St. Martin's in Fields Sch., 1971-92; fellow Corp. of Saints Mary and Nicholas (Woodard Schs.), 1972-92, trustee, corp. exec., 1981-92; chmn. bd. trustees, hon. treas. Art Workers Guild, 1976-86; chmn., founder Nat. Assn. Local Arts Councils, 1976-80, v.p., 1980-93; mem. governing body SPCK Australia, 1977-92, New Zealand, 1988-92, India, 1971-92; gov. Ellesmere Coll., Shropshire, 1978-87; gov. St. Michael's Sch., Petworth, 1978-88, Roehampton Inst. Higher Edn., 1978-92, Pusey House, Oxford; mem. All Saints Ednl. Trustee, chmn. fin. and investment com., 1978-92; mem. Partnership for World Mission, 1979-92, Church Pub. Com., 1980-84; chmn. Concord Multicultural Arts Trust, 1980-89; gov. Contemporary Dance Trust, 1981-90; mem. Exec. Anglican Centre, Rome, 1981-90; trustee Anglican Consultative Council Research Project, 1982-84; trustee Dancers Resettlement Fund, chmn. fin. com., 1982-90, Dancers Resettlement Trust, 1987-90; mem. Ct. of City Univ., 1987-93; bd. dirs. SPCK, U.S., 1983-92; chmn. acad. disciplinary appeals tribunal Roehampton Inst., 1983-89, chmn. audit com., 1989-92. Decorated Lord of Manor of Cantley Netherhall, Norfolk; Order of St. Vladimir; recipient numerous awards for civic and profl. service. Mem. Greater London Arts Assn. (hon. life mem.; chmn. 1980-84), Master Worshipful Co. of Woolmen, 1985-86, Pubs. Assn. (coun. mem. 1990-92). Clubs: Athenaeum (chmn. exec. com., 1985-89), Nikaean (chmn. 1984-92). Address: 3 The Mount Sq, London NW3 6SU, England

GILBERT, PAUL THOMAS, chemical development engineer; b. Chgo., July 29, 1914; s. Paul T. and Ilse (Forster) G.; m. Phyllis A. Simons, Oct. 17, 1942 (div. July 1955); children: Susan R. Sorensen, John (dec.), Brian (dec.), Wendy E. Levy; m. Hazel L. Dalton, July 9, 1955 (dec. Jan. 1999); children: Michael L. Pinizzotto, Michele L. Urquhart; m. Erlinda M. Rodriguez, Apr. 10, 1999; children: Desiree A. Milling, Vincent L. Ruiz, Stephanie D. Ruiz, Donald P. Ruiz. BS in Chemistry, Northwestern U., 1936; postgrad., U. Wis., 1936-38; MA in Math., U. Minn., 1940; postgrad., Calif. Inst. Tech., 1941, U. Calif., Santa Barbara, 1971-74. Tchg. asst. math. U. Minn., Mpls., 1939-41; instr. math. Utah State Agrl. Coll., Logan, 1941, 43-44, U. Minn., Mpls., 1943; rsch. chemist Metalloy Corp., Mpls., 1944-46; rsch. scientist Beckman Instruments, South Pasadena, Calif., 1946-52, N.Am. Aviation, Downey, Calif., 1952-55, Beckman Instruments, Fullerton, Palo Alto, Calif., 1955-71; devel. engr. Chemistry Dept. U. Calif., Santa Barbara, 1971-93; tchr. math. NW Mil. and Naval Prep. Sch., Mpls., 1939-41, 45; tech. translator, 1946—; cons. Atomics Internat., Canoga Park, Calif., 1956-59, lectr. Fullerton Youth Mus., 1963-65, bd. dirs. Co-author (translator) Chemical Analysis by Flame Photometry, 1963; translator: Fundamentals of Analytical Flame Spectroscopy, 1979; patentee in field; contbr. articles to profl. jours. Racecourse measurer Santa Barbara Athletic Assn., 1978—. Cadet USAF, 1941-43. Mem. AAAS, Am. Chem. Soc., Am. Math. Soc., Phi Beta Kappa, Sigma Xi, Phi Eta Sigma. Avocations: running, surfing, natural history, indexing, piano. Home: 715 Via Miguel Santa Barbara CA 93111-2743 Office: Univ Calif Dept Chemistry Santa Barbara CA 93106

GILBERT, RICHARD JOSEPH, economics educator; b. N.Y.C., Jan. 14, 1945; s. Michael N. and Esther (Dillon) G.; m. Sandra S. Waknitz, Sept. 7, 1974; children: Alison, David. BEE with honors, Cornell U., 1966, MEE, 1967; MA in Econs., Stanford U., 1976, PhD, 1976. Rsch. assoc. Stanford U., Calif., 1975-76; from assist. prof. to assoc. prof. econs. U. Calif., Berkeley, 1976-83; assoc. prof engring-econ. systems Stanford U., 1982-83; prof. econs. U. Calif., Berkeley, 1983—, dir. energy rsch. inst., 1983-93, prof. bus. adminstrn., 1990—; dep. asst. atty. gen. antitrust divsn. U.S. Dept. Justice, 1993-95; prin. Law & Econ. Cons. Group, Berkeley, 1989—. Contbr. numerous articles to profl. jours.; editor scholarly jours. Adv. U.S. Dept. Energy, Washington, 1983—, World Bank, Washington, 1980—, NSF, Washington, 1985—, Calif. Inst. Energy Efficiency, Berkeley, 1990—. Fulbright scholar Washington, 1989; vis. scholar Cambridge U., 1979, Oxford U., 1979. Mem. Tau Beta Pi, Eta Kappa Nu, Sigma Xi. Office: U Calif Dept Economics Berkeley CA 94720-0001

GILBERT, RICHARD KEITH, education educator, researcher; b. St. Louis, Apr. 23, 1958; s. William Ray and Janice Sylvia (Rephlo) G. BA, U. Calif., Santa Barbara, 1981, MA, 1990, postgrad., 1993; PhD, U. So. Calif., 1997. Secondary tchg. credential, Calif. Rschr. Marine Sci. Inst., Santa Barbara, 1979-82; rschr., coord. Catalina Island (Calif.) Marine Inst., 1983-85; tchr. sci. L.A. Unified Sch. Dist., 1985-87; sci. and calculus educator Am. Internat. Sch., Johannesburg, South Africa, 1987-89; rschr. psychotherapy U. Calif., Santa Barbara, 1990-92; cons. advanced tech. divsn. spl. projects Gen. Rsch. Corp., Santa Barbara, 1992-94; instr., rschr. U. So. Calif., L.A., 1993—; rschr., cons. Human Scis. Rsch. Coun., Pretoria, South Africa, 1995; cons. spl. project divsn. binary systems and geographic area specialist Akela Corp., 1994; team leader, cons. Tertiary Edn. Linkages Project USAID, Pretoria, 1996; profl. expert rsch. and evaluation dept. alternative edn. L.A. County Office Edn.; adj. prof., rschr. U. So. Calif., 1993—; con. tech. Capabilities, Assessment Geographic Info. Systems; peer evaluator SMET Projects, NSF, 1999. Active re-election campaign Hon. Robert Lagomarsino, Santa Barbara, 1992. Named Outstanding Tchr. Advanced Biol. Sci., NSF, Calif. State U., Northridge, 1986-87, Internat. Man of Yr. Sci. and Edn., 1996-97; Grad. fellow Calif. State U., U. So. Calif., 1993. Mem. AAAS, N.Y. Acad. Scis., Comparative Internat. Edn. Soc., Am. Ednl. Rsch. Assn., U.S. Naval Inst., Phoenix Soc. (outstanding mem. 1987), Order Internat. Ambs., Phi Beta Delta. Presbyterian. Avocations: climbing, scuba, photography, trekking, music. Home: 6285 Avenida Ganso Goleta CA 93117-2063 Office: 123 S Figueroa St Apt 202 Los Angeles CA 90012-5485

GILBERT, SAMUEL LAWRENCE, business owner; b. Chgo., Mar. 3, 1950; s. Robert Augustus and Ruby Elizabeth (Gammon) G.; m. Sharon Faye Warner, Nov. 3, 1972 (div. Oct. 1984); children: Shaundra, Shari, Sharita. AA in Health Care, Malcolm X Coll., Chgo., 1969; cert. in acctg., Bryant Stratton Coll., Chgo., 1989. Mail/shipping coord. Natural Gas Pipeline Co. Am., Chgo., 1970-82; mailroom asst. IBM Corp., Chgo., 1982-83; CEO Genesis Comics Group, Inc., Chgo., 1986-94; chmn., pub., CEO Genesis Pub., Ltd., Chgo., 1994—; pub. Gilben Comics, 2000—; sr. v.p. creative design Gilben Prodn. Ltd., 2000—; sr. v.p. creative design Gil Ben Comics. Editor: Gil Ben Prodns. Deacon Christ the King Temple Ch., Chgo., 1985-87; asst. pastor Greater Holy Rock MBC, Chgo., 1988-92, St. Titus MBC, Chgo., 1994—; assoc. min. Greater New Mt. Carmen, Chgo., 1992-94. Mem. Am. Mgmt. Assn., Rsch. Inst. Am. Democrat. Baptist. Avocation: building model aircraft.

GILBERT, STEVEN JEFFREY, venture capitalist, screenwriter, lawyer; b. N.Y.C., Apr. 6, 1947; s. Bernard and Ruth (Turner) G.; m. Anita Schneider, Apr. 25, 1987; children: Steven Turner, Anna Christina. BS in Econs., U. Pa., 1967; JD, Harvard U., 1970, MBA, 1972. Bar: Mass. 1970. Assoc. Morgan Stanley and Co., N.Y.C., 1972-76; v.p. Wertheim and Co., N.Y.C., 1976-78; mng. dir. E.F. Hutton, Internat., N.Y.C., 1978-80; pres., chief exec. officer Lion's Gate Films, Inc., Los Angeles, 1980-82; gen. ptnr. Cen. Devel. Ptnrs., N.Y.C., 1982-83; mng. gen. ptnr. Chem. Venture Ptnrs., N.Y.C., 1983-88; mng. dir. Commonwealth Capital Ptnrs., N.Y.C., 1988—; mng. gen. ptnr. Soros Capital, N.Y.C., 1992—; chmn. bd. Gilbert Global Equity Ptnrs., L.L.C., 1997—; bd. dirs., vice chmn. NFO Worldwide, Inc., A.C.X. Pacific, Inc.; bd. dirs. Vertias-DGC, Inc., Uromed, Inc., Syndney Harbour Casino Holdings, Ltd., Veritas, Inc., Terra Nova Ins. Co., Ltd., Bermuda, The Asian Infrastructure Fund, LCC Internat., Inc., OneTel Ltd.; trustee NYU Med. Ctr., Hosp. for Joint Diseases. Screenwriter Chapter XI, 1982. Mem. Writers Guild Am., Young Pres. Orgn., Coun. on Fgn. Rels. Office: Gilbert Global Equity Ptnrs LLC 785 Smith Ridge Rd New Canaan CT 06840-3228 also: NFO Rsch Inc 2 Pickwick Plz Ste 400 Greenwich CT 06830-5576

GILBERT, WALTER, molecular biologist, educator; b. Boston, Mar. 21, 1932; s. Richard V. and Emma (Cohen) G.; m. Celia Stone, Dec. 29, 1953; children: John Richard, Kate. AB, Harvard U., 1953, AM, 1954; PhD, Cambridge U., 1957; DSc (hon.), U. Chgo., 1978, Columbia U., 1978, U. Rochester, 1979, Yeshiva U., 1981. NSF postdoctoral fellow Harvard U., Cambridge, Mass., 1957-58, lectr. physics, 1958-59, asst. prof. physics, 1959-64, assoc. prof. biophysics, 1964-68, prof. biochemistry, 1968-72, Am. Cancer Soc. prof. molecular biology, 1972-81, prof. biology, 1985-86, H.H. Timken prof. sci., 1986-87, Carl M. Loeb Univ. prof., 1987—, chair dept. cellular and devel. biology, 1987-93; chmn. sci. bd. Biogen N.V., Dutch Antilles, 1978-83, co-chmn., supervisory bd., 1979-81, chmn. supervisory bd., chief exec. officer, 1981-84; vice chmn., bd. dirs. Myriad Genetics, Inc., 1992—; chmn. of bd. NetGenics, Inc., 1996—; V.D. Mattia lectr. Roche Inst. Molecular Biology, 1976. Recipient U.S. Steel Found. NAS, 1968, Ledlie prize Harvard U., 1969, Warren triennieal prize Mass. Gen. Hosp., 1977, Louis and Bert Freedman Found. N.Y. Acad. Scis., 1977, Prix Charles-Leopold Mayer Academie des Scis., Inst. de France, 1977, Nobel prize in chemistry, 1980, New Eng. Entrepreneur of Yr. award, 1991; co-winner Louisa Gross Horwitz prize Columbia U., 1979, Gairdner prize, 1979, Albert Lasker Basic Sci. award, 1979; Guggenheim fellow, 1968-69; hon. fellow Trinity Coll., Cambridge, U.K., 1991. Mem. Am. Phys. Soc., Nat. Acad. Scis., Am. Soc. Biol. Chemists, Am. Acad. Arts and Scis.; fgn. mem. Royal Soc. Office: The Biol Labs 16 Divinity Ave Cambridge MA 02138-2097

GILBERTSON, STEVEN E(DWARD) SATYAKI, real estate broker, guidance counselor; b. Winona, Minn., Nov. 5, 1951; s. Conrad Orville and Lorraine Kristina (Munson) G.; m. Jayne Ann Rock, June 13, 1992. BA, U. Minn., Morris, 1974; MS, Winona State U., 1982. Math tchr. Winona Pub. Schs., 1974-76, Owatonna (Minn.) Pub. Schs., 1976-77; tie gang laborer Milw. Railroad, Winona, 1978; spl. edn. tchr. Winona Heights Acad., 1978-79; math tchr. Rushford (Minn.) Pub. Schs., 1980-81, Gale Ettrick Trempealeau Sch., Galesville, Wis., 1981-82; salesperson Winona Realty, 1983-86, broker, 1987—; broker S.G. Realty, Winona, 1986-93; tchr. elem. phys. edn. St. Francis Sch., Rochester, Minn., 1993; spl. edn. tchr. Austin Pub. Schs., 1994-96, Racine Unified Sch. Dist., 1996-97; guidance counselor, dept. head Mpls. Pub. Schs., 1997—; mem. edn. com., multiple listing svc. com. Multiple Listing Svc., Winona, 1988-90, 93. Fundraiser YMCA, Winona, 1990; mem. focus group Winona County Chem. Abuse Prevention Task Force, 1991-93; facilitator Course in Miracles Study Group, Winona, 1991-93, Racine, Wis., 1996-97; creator Adult Children Anonymous, Emotions Anonymous (Winona chpt.), 12-Step Groups, 1990. Mem. Minn. Assn. Realtors, Sons of Norway, Westfield Golf Club (men's league champion 1987, 89), Minn. Sch. Counselors Assn., Minn. Fedn. of Tchrs. Avocations: sports and fitness, basketball, tennis, meeting people. E-mail: Steven.Gilbertson@mpls.k12.mn.us. Home: 3444 41st Ave S Minneapolis MN 55406 Office: Sanford Middle Sch 3524 42nd Ave S Minneapolis MN 55406-2813

GILBOA, DAVID, agricultural economist, consultant; b. Jerusalem, Sept. 5, 1933; s. Israel and Eva (Auerbach) Skvirsky; m. Chava Marokko, Oct. 10, 1958; children: Paz, Zohar. BSc in Agr., Hebrew U., Jerusalem, 1958; MSc in Econs., London Sch. Econs., 1962; MBA, Tel Aviv U., 1972. Asst. agrl. attache Israeli Embassy, London, 1959-62; head of office of min. of agr., econ. advisor Min. of Agr., Jerusalem, 1962-68; mng. dir. Israel Crop Ins. Co., Tel Aviv, 1968-79; dep. mng. dir. Yardenia Ins. Co., Tel Aviv, 1979-81; dir. rural devel. divsn. Degem Sys., Tel Aviv, 1981-85; cons. Bain Hogg Ins. Brokers (now Aon Group), London, 1985-2000; cons. FAO, Rome, 1978—, Hannover (Germany) RE, 1989-93, Agroasemex, Queretaro, Mexico, 1990-2000; ptnr. Reinsurance (Agr.), Switzerland, 1998—. Mem. DASH (Dem. Movement), Israel, 1977. Mem. N.Y. Acad. Sci. Mem. Labour Party. Jewish. Avocations: walking, basketball, bowling. Home and Office: 15 Komemiut, 46683 Herzliyya Israel

GILDAN, PHILLIP CLARKE, lawyer; b. West Palm Beach, Fla., July 17, 1959; s. Herbert Leonard and Kathleen (Yeager) G.; m. Laurie Beth Leinwand, Aug. 25,1985; children: Tyler Ross, Jacob Lee. AB magna cum laude, Dartmouth Coll., 1981; JD cum laude, Harvard U., 1984. Bar: Fla. 1984, U.S. Ct. Appeals (11th cir.) 1986, U.S. Supreme Ct. 1989. Assoc. Nason, Gildan, Yeager, Gerson & White, P.A., West Palm Beach, 1984-89, shareholder, 1989-96; shareholder Greenberg Traurig PA, West Palm Beach, 1997—; lectr. Reinventing Govt. Symposium, Hollywood, Fla., 1994, Risk Mgmt. State Conf., Deerfield Beach, Fla., 1995. Contbr. articles to profl. jours. Dir. Com. for Good Govt., Palm Beach, Fla., 1990-94. Mem. Fla. Bar Assn., Palm Beach County Bar Assn., Am. Inns of Ct. LIV (exec. com. 1991-94), Phi Beta Kappa. Office: Greenberg Traurig Hoffman Lipoff Rosen & Quentel PA 777 S Flagler Dr Ste 300 West Palm Beach FL 33401-6161

GILDBERG, ASBJORN, biochemist, writer; b. Steinkjer, Norway, July 21, 1947; s. Leif and Agnes (Vist) G.; m. Berit Saxi, Aug. 4, 1989; children: Hilde, Eva. B in Civil Engring., Tech. U. Trondheim, 1973; DSc, U. Tromso, 1982. Engr. U. Tromso, Norway, 1974-75; researcher Norwegian Inst. Fish Tech., Tromso, 1975-86; lab. mgr. Marine Biochems., Tromso, 1986-87; researcher Norwegian Inst. Fish Aquaculture, Tromso, 1987—; program bd. The Norwegian Rsch. Coun., 1996-2000. Author (children's books) Skiing in the Forest, 1996, A Fishing Trip to Blamyrtarn, 1998, Even and the Cowshed Nisse, 1999. Avocations: slalom skiing, jogging. Office: Norwegian Inst Fisheries & Aquaculture, Breivika, 9005 Tromsø Norway

GIL-DELGADO, JOSE MARIA GIL-ROBLES, retired parliamentary president; b. Madrid, June 17, 1935; s. José María Gil-Robles Quiñones; married; 4 children. D (hon.), State Inst. Internat. Rels., Moscow, 1998; hon. fellow, Cath. U. Chile, 1998; D honoris causa, U. Sofia, Bulgaria, 1999. Bar: Madrid, Barcelona, Bilbao, Salamanca. Atty., 1959—; mem. European Parliament, 1989—, v.p., 1994—, pres., 1997-99; mem. com. on petitions, com. on rules of proc. and verification of credentials, com. on social affairs and employment and com. on instl. affairs, European Parliament, 1989-94, group coord. for parliament com. on instl. affairs, vice chmn. group of European People's Party, mem. European Parliament Bur., 1990—. Author numerous works on law and restoration of democracy. Mem. Spanish Assn. for European Cooperation/European Movement, 1957; mem. Christian Social Dem. movement, 1962; mem. exec. bd. Christian Dem. Unit of Spanish State, Basque Nationalist Party, Dem. Union of Catalonia, Christian Dem. Left and Christian Social Dems., 1972, sec.-gen., mem. Bur. of European Union of Christian Dems., 1977; pres. Ctr. for Cmty. Studies, Spanish Christian Dems., 1984; v.p. Found. for Humanism and Democracy/Konrad Adenauer Found., 1985; pres. Spanish Coun. del. European Movement, 1996; mem. nat. exec. com. Spanish Partido Popular, 1990—; pres. European Movement Internat., 1999. Recipient Schuman medal, Cross of Order of Agrl. Merit, Order of Francisco Morazán, Ctrl. Am. Parliament, 1997, Grand Cross of Order of Merit, Chile, Grand Cross of Order of Liberator San Martín, Argentina, Medal of Rep., Uruguay, Grand Cross of Order of Antonio José de Irizarri, Guatemala, Medalla de Plata de Galice, 2000, Gran Cruz de la Orden de Isabel la Católica, 2000; named Adopted Son of City of Salamanca, Oficial de la Legión de Honor, Francia, 2000; hon. fellow Cath. U. Chile. Mem. Madrid Bar Assn., Barcelona Bar Assn., Bilbao Bar Assn., Salamanca Bar Assn. Fax: 437009. Office: European Parliament, Rue, B-1047 Wiertz Brussels

GILDENHORN, JOSEPH BERNARD, lawyer, businessman, former diplomat; b. Washington, Sept. 17, 1929; s. Oscar and Celia (Koval) G.; m. Alma Lee Gross, June 28, 1953; children: Carol Winer, Michael Saul. BS, U. Md., 1951; LLB, JD, Yale U., 1954. Bar: D.C. 1954, U.S. Ct. Appeals (D.C. cir.) 1954, U.S. Supreme Ct. 1954. Ptnr. Brown, Gildenhorn & Jacobs, 1955—; vice chmn. D.C. Nat. Sovran Bank, Washington, 1979-89; amb. to Switzerland Dept. State, Bern, 1989-93; ptnr. The JBG Cos.; adj. prof. George Washington U., D.C. Bar Assn.; pres. JBG Properties, Inc., 1956-88; chmn. adv. bd. BB&T; bd. dirs. The Mills Corp.; D.C. chmn. George W. Bush for Pres. Mem. editl. bd. Yale Law Jour., 1954. D.C. campaign chmn. Bush-Quayle, 1988; past pres., bd. dirs. Hebrew Home Greater Washington, 1975-77; bd. dirs. Washington Jewish Cmty. Found., Inst. for Study of Diplomacy, Georgetown U., Ctr. for Strategic and Internat. Studies, Internat. Inst. Strategic Studies; treas. Am. Joint Distbn. Com., 1999—; pres. bd. dirs. Jewish Fedn. Greater Washington, 1988-89; vice chmn. D.C. Sports Commn., mem. Woodrow Wilson Internat. Ctr. for Scholars; participant Nat. Prayer Breakfast, 2000. With AUS, 1954-56. Recipient David Ben Gurion award State of Israel, 1977, Hyman Goldman Humanitarian award, 1984, B'nai B'rith Humanitarian award, 1985, Ourisman Cmty. Svc. award, 1987, Ottenstein Cmty. Svc. award, 1991, B'nai B'rith Disting. Alumnus award, 1983, Jewish Inst. for Nat. Security Affairs Leadership award, 1993, U. Md. Disting. Alumnus award, 1996, Leadership award Washington Inst., 1999, Corp. Citizenship award Woodrow Wilson Internat. Ctr. for Scholars, 2000; named Washingtonian of Yr. Washingtonian mag., 1996. Mem. Order of Coif, Team 100, Presdl. Trust. Home: 2030 24th St NW Washington DC 20008-1608 Office: 1250 Connecticut Ave NW Washington DC 20036-2603

GILDER, RICHARD EARL, clinical information system administrator, data analyst; b. Dallas, July 21, 1951; s. Elbert Earl Jr. and Mary Francis G.; m. Mary Ann Meier, Apr. 26, 1975; children: Stephen Earl, David Andrew, Katherine Rose. AS in Nursing, El Centro Coll., Dallas, 1974; BS cum laude in Nursing, Tex. Woman's U., 1996. RN, Tex.; cert. oper. room nurse. Staff nurse emergency dept. Parkland Hosp., Dallas, 1974-81; chem. engrng. cons. Kool-X-Co., Dallas, 1981-82, Hon Mining Co., Laguna Hills, Calif., 1981-82; owner, pres. Gilder Co., Dallas, 1983—; staff nurse, clin. nurse III Presbyn. Hosp., Dallas, 1986-97; clin. info. sys. adminstr. dept. clin. outcomes/resource mt., sr. data analyst Presbyn. Healthcare Sys., Inc., 1998—; instr. rifle, pistol and shotgun, 1984. Sustaining mem. Rep. Nat. Com., 1980—; asst. scout master Boy Scouts Am., Dallas, 1985—; founder United Nurses Internat.; asst. moderator Microsoft Nursing Network Forum. Mem. AAAS, Assn. Oper. Rm. Nurses (Dallas chpt. rsch. com. chair 1992—, perioperative nursing informatics splty. assembly 1998—), Am. Soc. Ophthalmil Registered Nurses, Tex. Astron. Soc., Golden Key Nat. Honor Soc., Gamma Beta Phi, Sigma Theta Tau. Republican. Achievements include proposal for structure and name for the third elemental form of carbon. Fax: (214) 345-6436. E-mail: gilderr@wpmail.phscare.org. Home and Office: Gilder Co 13318 Mount Castle Dr Dallas TX 75234-5048 Office: Presbyn Healthcare Sys 8440 Walnut Hill Ln Dallas TX 75231-3833

GILES, ALLEN, pianist, composer, music educator; b. Cambridge, Mass., Dec. 26, 1924; s. Allen Lester and Clara Lillian (Collins) G.; m. Marilla Jane Roberts, May 26, 1950 (div. 1970); children: Marilyn, Andrea, Cynthia; m. Anne Watson Diener, Sept. 26, 1970 (div. 1996); 1 child, Katherine Anne. MusB in Piano, Boston U., 1946, MA in Music, 1949; EdD in Music Edn., Columbia U., N.Y.C., 1981. performing pianist, soloist and chamber musician, U.S., Europe, Japan, 1945—; adjudicator for competitions nationwide, 1956—. Pvt. piano tchr. Mass., N.Y., Calif., 1944—; head piano dept., assoc. dir. music dept. SUNY, Buffalo, N.Y., 1952-64; chair, music dept., dir. Inst. of Music Villa Maria Coll., Buffalo, 1964-68; prof. music, chair performing arts Golden West Coll., Huntington Beach, Calif., 1972-93, prof. emeritus, 1993-2000; exec. dir. South Bay Conservatory, Torrance, Calif., 1997-98; owner, pres. GME Piano Video, 1984—; artistic dir. Learning Ctr. for Arts Excellence, Torrance, Calif., 1999-2000; DVD annotator Media Hyperium/Pioneer Classics, 2000—. Author: (books) Beginning Piano-An Adult Approach Vol. 1, 1978, Vol. 2, 1988, Beginning Piano Telecourse Student Study Guide, 1979; Learning To Play The Piano By Television, 1982; course designer, tchr. on camera (video series) Beginning Piano-An Adult Approach, 1978-80; contbr. articles to profl. jours. Recipient Annual Piano Tchr. award SUNY, Fredonia, 1968; Radio and TV award for Noteworthy Achievement in Serious Music, Sigma Alpha Iota, 1980; named Master Tchr., Univ. Tex., Austin, 1986, Master Tchr. (piano), Music Tchrs. Nat. Assn., 1989. Mem. Music Tchrs. Nat. Assn., Calif. Assn. Profl. Music Tchrs. (v.p. 1990-91), Nat. Piano Found., Music Tchrs. Assn. Calif., Am. Fedn. Musicians. Home: 10 Beaver Pond Rd Lincoln MA 01773-3309 Office: GME Piano Video PO Box 6035 Lincoln MA 01773-6035

GILES, CONRAD LESLIE, ophthalmic surgeon; b. N.Y.C., July 14, 1934; s. Irving Samuel Giles and Victoria Ampole; m. Marilyn Toby Schwartz, June 20, 1955 (div. 1978); children: Keith Martin, Suzanne Speer, Kevin William, Brian Alan; m. Lynda Fern Schenk, Nov. 26, 1978; stepchildren: Jared Schenk, Jamie Schenk. MD, U. Mich., 1957, MS, 1961. Diplomate Am. Bd. Ophthalmology. Clin. assoc. NIH, Bethesda, Md., 1961-63; clin. asst. prof. Wayne State U. Sch. Medicine, Detroit, 1965-72, clin. assoc. prof. ophthalmology, 1973-89, clin. prof. ophthalmology, 1989—; chief ophthalmologist Children's Hosp. Mich., 1985-99, emeritus chief, 1999—, chief emeritus, 2000—. Contbr. articles to med. jours. Active Jewish Welfare Fedn., Detroit, 1981-86, pres., 1986-89; bd. govs. Jewish Agy. for Israel, 1995—; vice-chair United Jewish Communities, 2000—. Fellow Am. Acad. Ophthalmology; mem. AMA, USA Fedns. NA (co-pres. 1997-99), Mich. State Ophthal. Soc., Coun. Jewish Fedns. (v.p. 1992-95, treas. 1995-96, pres. 1996-99), United Jewish Appeal Fedns. N.Am. (pres. 1997-99), Mich. Jewish Conf. (pres. 1992-95), United Jewish Cmtys. (vice chair 2000—). Avocations: golf, tennis, skiing. Home: 6300 Westmoor Rd Bloomfield Hills MI 48301-1359 Office: 4400 Town Ctr Southfield MI 48075-1601

GILES, PATRICIA CECELIA PARKER, retired art educator, graphic designer; b. Chgo., Mar. 8, 1925; d. Frederick Louis and Bernice Clara (Kennedy) Parker; m. Lewis Wentworth Giles, June 20, 1946 (div. 1960); children: Alan Julian, Kay Celeste. BS in Fine Arts, U. Ill., Urbana, 1946; postgrad., Howard U., Washington D.C., 1947, U. Mass., Amherst, 1974-75, Washington Sch. Psychology, 1962. Reg. sec. tchr. art Ill., 1972. Sec. tchr. art Randall Jr. High, Washington, D.C., 1947-48; art cons. Elem. Sch., Washington, 1952-53; tchr., chmn. art dept. Theodore Roosevelt H.S., Washington, 1959-60, Boys Sr. H.S., Washington, 1961-63, Carter G. Woodson Jr. H.S., Washington, 1963-72, Howard D. Woodson Sr. H.S., Washington, 1973-85; mgr. Foreverl Living Products, Washington, 1985—; v.p. D.C. Art Assn., 1964-65; cons. art-math. with humanities Upward Bounders U. Md., College Park, 1966-67; potential supr. of student tchg. in art therapy Planning Program Staff George Washington U., Washington, 1972; visual arts coord. D.C. Congress PTA Cultural Arts, Washington, 1972; artist-in-residence Washington Srs. Wellness Ctr., 1987-88, 97-98, 98—; tennis instr. Tenn. Edn. Found.; calligraphy instr. D.C. Pk. & Recreation, 34th Smithsonian Folklife Festival. Painter: (oil painting) Mud and Roots, 1971 (award 1971), Mural: Infinite Joy, 1991 (Golden Dolphins Commendation award 1991), Kenkin, oils, 1992 (award 1992); author: (book of poetry) Mud and Roots, 1976; illustrator: (children's book) Short Fuzzy Hair, 1999. Taught art workshop in cmty. Fort DuPont Civic Assn., Washington, 1960, defining creative art Channel 14 WOOK-TV, Washington, 1963, comparing and interacting with cultures and govts. Am. Forum for Internat. Study, Senegal, Ghana, Ethiopia, Kenya, Tanzania, 1970; peer leader in tennis and yoga Washington Seniors Wellness Ctr., Washington, 1995, 96, 97, 98, 99, 2000; charter mem. Nat. Mus. Art Women. Recipient Commendation award Ft. DuPont Civic Assn., Washington, 1960, 1st prize for watercolor Arch.'s Wives Assn., 1962, Gold medal D.C. Sr. Olympics in Tennis, 1993, 95, 96, 97, Silver medal, 1998, 99, Gold medal in Swimming, 1993; 2 Gold medals Sr. Olympics in Tennis, 2000. Mem. Nat. Conf. of Artists, Am. Art League (D.C.), D.C. Nat. Tennis Assn., D.C. Social Club, Golden Dolphins (Outstanding Swimming Trophy 1993), Detakas Swim Club, Alpha Kappa Alpha, Delta Ka. Democrat. Seventh Day Adventist. Avocations: tennis, swimming, yoga, tai chi, silk screen. Home: 3942 Blaine St NE Washington DC 20019-3333

GILES, PHYLLIS LENORE WILLIAMS, retired elementary educator; b. Fowler, Colo., Oct. 11, 1912; d. Odin Neil and Lillian Valeria (Deutschman) Williams; m. Albert E. Giles, 1943 (dec.); children: Richard Brian, Tyler William. BA, U. No. Colo., 1939; MA, Northwestern U., 1964. Elem. sch. tchr. Delearbon, Colo., 1933-34; elem. sch. tchr. La Veta, Colo., 1934-35, Colorado Springs, Colo., 1934-38; exch. tchr Shaker Heights Sch. Dist., 1939-40; tchr. jr. high sch. Colorado Springs, 1940-43; elem. sch. tchr. Montgomery, Ala., 1943, Denver, 1947-48; tchr. Pocatello (Idaho) Jr. High, 1950-51; elem. sch. tchr. Salt Lake City, 1951-53, Park Ridge, Ill., 1953-78; mem. Cleve. Symphony Chorus, 1939-40, Utah Symphony Chorus, 1951-53; part-time instr. edn. music. Planner weekly classical music programs USO, Colorado Springs, 1941-42; mem. many ch. choirs. Mem. AAUW (chmn. daytime bridge 1988-90, internat. rels. N.W. Suburban br. 1988, 89, 2d v.p. N.W. program, chair 1991-93, networking com., program chmn. 1991-93, AAUW Edn. Found. Scholarship named in honor 1993, 50-Yr. Membership honor 1996), PEO (1st pres., charter mem. chpt. Denver 1947, selected charter mem. 1986—, chaplain N.W. Suburban Roundtable 1987-88, 2d v.p. 1990-91, mem. planning com., N.W. Roundtable activities, honored 66 yr. mem. 1999). Congregationalist. Avocations: opera, book review clubs, bridge, reading, foreign affairs.

GILES, WALTER EDMUND, alcohol and drug treatment executive; b. Omaha, Aug. 9, 1934; s. Walter Edmund and Julia Margaret (Shively) G.; m. Ellen M. Garton, June 13, 1953; m. Dona LaVonne Foster, Sept. 29, 1970 (dec. 1990); children: Sue, Stephen, Theresa, Marcy, Kim, Tim, Nadine, Charles; m. Yvonne Marie Fink, Nov. 29, 1991; children: Jessica Nicole Farr, Walter Edmund III, David Michael. BA, U. Nebr., Lincoln, 1972, MA, 1977. Counselor VA Hosp., Lincoln, Nebr., 1969-70; coord. alcohol programs Mcpl. Ct., Lincoln; dir. Orange County Employee Assistance, Santa Ana, Calif., 1977-79; adminstr. Advanced Health Ctr., Newport Beach, Calif., 1979-81; pres. Great West Health Svcs. Inc., Orange, Calif., 1982-86, Pine Ridge Treatment Ctr. Inc., Running Springs, Calif., 1986—. Author (book) The Workbook, 1985, Intervention, 1986; host (radio show) Addictions, 1984. Mem. Nat. Assn. Alcoholism Counselors, Calif. Assn. Alcoholism Counselors.

GILES, WARWICK BRUCE, obstetrician, gynecologist; b. Sydney, Australia, June 11, 1950; s. Bruce Payton and Dorothy Edna (Hammill) G.; m. Roslyn Joy Miller, Apr. 19, 1973; children: Katherine, Victoria, Edward. MB, BS in Biology, U. NSW (Australia), 1974; PhD, U. Sydney (Australia), 1987. Intern Wollongong and Port Kembla Hosps., NSW, 1975; resident gen. practice Kiama Hosp., NSW, 1976; registrar in obstetrics Wollongong Hosp., 1977; registrar in ob-gyn. Women's Hosp. Crown St., Sydney, 1977-79; postgrad. rsch. fellow ob-gyn. U. Sydney, 1982-85; registrar in ob-gyn. Westmead (Australia) Hosp., 1980-82, staff specialist ob-gyn., 1985, supr. tng., 1985-89, sec. med. staff coun., 1988-90; assoc. prof. reproductive medicine and health scis. John Hunter Hosp. U. Newcastle, Hunter Regional Mail Ctr., NSW, 1991—; vis. rsch. fellow ob-gyn. U. Lund, Malmo, Sweden, 1984; mem. faculty bd. Newcastle U., 1991—; mem. numerous coms. John Hunter Hosp., 1991—; mem. exec. com. NSW Perinatal Svcs. Network, 1995-2000; vis. rsch. scholar U. Utah, 1996-97; vis. prof. ob-gyn. U. Colo., 1997. Contbr. numerous articles to profl. jours. Fellow RANZCOG (maternal fetal medicine subcom. 1997—), Royal Soc. Medicine, Royal Australian Coll. Ob-gyn.; mem. Australian Soc. Ultrasound in Medicine, Australian Perinatal Soc., Am. Inst. Ultrasound in Medicine, Australian Soc. for Study of Hypertension in Pregnancy, Australian Teratology Soc., Australian Soc. HIV Medicine, Human Genetics Soc. Australia, Soc. Maternal Fetal Medicine, Swedish Ultrasound Soc. (hon.), Amnesty Internat., Med. Assn. Prevention of War, Australian Conservation Found., Greenpeace, Internat. Perinatal Doppler Soc. Avocations: swimming, skiing, bushwalking, longboard surfing, rock climbing.

GILES, WILLIAM JEFFERSON, III, lawyer; b. Manila, The Philippines, Apr. 10, 1936; came to U.S., 1938; s. William Jefferson and Gardner (Anderson) G.; m. Nancy Gifford Seff, May 9, 1957; children: William Jefferson IV, Gregory Gifford. BS, U. Calif., Berkeley, 1957; postgrad., Golden Gate Coll., 1958-59, Stanford U., 1960; JD, U. S.D., 1961. Bar: Iowa 1961, U.S. Dist. Ct. Iowa 1961, U.S. Ct. Appeals (8th cir.) 1971, U.S. Supreme Ct. 1971, Nebr. 1982, U.S. Ct. Appeals (9th cir.) 1988. Pvt. practice Sioux City, Iowa, 1961—; of counsel Whicher & Whicher, Sioux City, 1966-75, Whicher & Hart, Sioux City, 1975-77; lectr. in field. Contbr. articles to profl. jours. Bd. dirs. Sioux City Mus. and Hist. Soc., 1976-79, Sioux City Cmty. Theatre, 1974-76. Capt. USAR, 1957-68. Recipient Gold Seal award Phi Beta Kappa, 1953. Fellow Am. Acad. Matrimonial Lawyers (chmn. bankruptcy com. 1992-99), Internat. Acad. Matrimonial Lawyers; mem. ABA, ATLA, Iowa Bar Assn., Iowa Assn. Trial Lawyers, Comml. Law League Am., Sioux City Country Club, Phi Delta Phi, Phi Phi. Republican. Home: 3827 Country Club Blvd Sioux City IA 51104-1327 Office: 322 Frances Bldg 505 5th St Sioux City IA 51101 also: 3940 Hideaway Acres Crofton NE 68730-0088

GILHUS, NILS ERIK, neurologist, educator; b. Oslo, June 12, 1950; s. Kaare and Alette (Finne) G.; m. Ingvild Saelid, Mar. 11, 1972; children: Alette, Margrete, Kristoffer, Kaare, Ingjerd. MD, U. Oslo, 1975; DPhil, U. Bergen, Norway, 1984. Intern Kongsberg (Norway) Ctrl. Hosp., 1975-76; resident Haukeland Univ. Hosp., Bergen, 1977-81, 83-85, dep. chmn. dept. neurology, 1990—; rsch. fellow Broegelmann Rsch. Lab., Bergen, 1981-83; sr. lectr. U. Bergen, 1985-86; vis. scholar Inst. Molecular Medicine, Oxford, Eng., 1992-93; prof., cons. Haukeland Univ. Hosp. and U. Bergen, 1986—; vice dean Med. Faculty, Bergen, 1999—; chmn. Inst. Neurology, Bergen, 1990-98; bd. dirs. European Bd. Neurology. Contbr. over 170 articles to profl. publs. Lt. Royal Norwegian Navy, 1977. Recipient prize for neurology Dr. Ragnar Forsberg, 1981, prize for med. rsch. Soren Falch, 1985, prize for neurol. rsch. Monrad-Krohn, 1992. Mem. Nordic Neurol. Assn. (bd. dirs. 1994—), Norwegian Neurol. Assn. (chmn. 1994-97), Europfeder Neurol. Soc. (com. chmn. 1997—). Office: Haukeland U Hosp, Haukeland U Hosp, Dept Neurology, N-5021 Bergen Norway

GILIOMEE, JOHANNES HUMAN, entomologist, educator; b. Ugie, South Africa, Apr. 8, 1936; s. Gerhardus Adriaan and Catharina Gesa (Buhr) G.; m. Warnia Coba Lombard, Jan. 6, 1960; children: Gerhard, Adri, Johan. BSc, U. Stellenbosch, 1957, MSc in Agrl., 1961; PhD, U. London, 1964; BA, U. South Africa, 1969; M in Urban and Regional Planning, U. Stellenbosch, 1973. Rsch. officer Dept. Agrl., Stellenbosch, South Africa, 1957-60; lectr. U. Stellenbosch, 1961-64, sr. lectr., 1965-75, assoc. prof., 1976-86, prof., chmn., 1987-2000; prof. emeritus, 2000—; chmn. environtl. monitoring com. Saldanha Steel, 1996—. Author: Morphology and Taxonomy of Adult Males of the Family Coccidae, 1967; contbr. numerous articles to profl. jours. Mem. Ent. Soc. of So. Africa (pres. 1980-81). Avocation: tennis. Home: 1 Rowan St, Stellenbosch 7600, South Africa Office: U Stellenbosch Fac Agrl, Pvt Bag X1 Matieland, Stellenbosch 7602, South Africa

GILIS, CONSTANTINE, logistics administrator; b. Thessaloniki, Macedonia, Greece, May 30, 1971; s. Odysseas and Keratsoula (Hriti) G. BA in Econs., Aristoteleio U., Thessaloniki, 1993; MS in Computer Sci., Sheffield (U.K.) U., 1997; PhD candidate in Applied Informatics, U. Macedonia, Thessaloniki. On-line sys. mgr. Shelman S.A., Thessaloniki, 1991-93, logistics mgr., 1995—. Mem. Soc. Logistics Engrs. (Thessaloniki bd. dirs. 1997—), Econ. Chamber of Greece, Internat. Soc. Logistics. Avocations: computers, music, reading, photography, car driving. Office: Shelman SA, 4 k/m Thessaloniki-kalohori, Thessaloniki 54628, Greece

GILKEY, GORDON WAVERLY, curator, artist; b. Albany, Oreg., Mar. 10, 1912; s. Leonard Ernest and Edna Isabel (Smith) G.; m. Vivian Malone, Oct. 17, 1938 (dec. Sept. 1995); 1 son, Gordon Spencer. BS, Albany Coll., 1933; MFA, U. Oreg., 1936; ArtsD (hon.), Lewis and Clark Coll., 1957; D in Arts and Humanities (hon.), Oreg. State U., 2000. Mem. art staff Stephens Coll., Mo., 1939-42; prof. art, head dept. Oreg. State U., 1947-64; dean Oreg. State U. (Sch. Humanities and Social Scis.), 1963-73, Oreg. State U. (Coll. Liberal Arts), 1973-77; curator prints and drawings Portland (Oreg.) Art Mus., 1978—; prof. and printmaker-in-resident Pacific N.W. Coll. Art, 1978—; spl. asst. to exec. dir. Portland Art Mus., 1988-94; dir. Internat. Exc. Print Exhibits, 1956-78; U.S. adviser IV Bordighera Biennale, Italy, 1957; chmn. Gov.'s Planning Coun. for Arts and Humanities in, Oreg., 1965-67; mem. Gov.'s Commn. on Fgn. Lang. and Internat. Studies. Ofcl. etcher New York World's Fair, 1939, 1937-39; etcher Nat. Broadcasting Co., Radio City, N.Y.C., 1937-39; artist-author: Etchings: New York World's Fair, 1939; contbr. articles on art; major work in permanent collection, Met. Mus. Art, others. Trustee Oreg. State U. Found.; bd. govs. Pacific N.W. Coll. Art. Col. U.S. Army Air Corps, 1942-47, ret. Decorated Palmes Academiques (France), officer's cross and comdr.'s cross Order of Merit (Fed. Republic Germany), Order Star of Solidarity (Italy), comdr. Order of Merit (Italy), officer Order Acad. Palms (France), officer Legion of Honor (France), Grand Cross Order St. Gregory the Illuminator, comdr. Order Polonia Restituta, chevalier Order of Holy Sepulchre, chevalier mil. and hospitaller Order of St. Lazarus, chevalier mil. and hospitaller Order of Our Lady of Mt. Carmel, chevalier St. Dennis of Zante, knight Grand Cross Order of St. Basil the Great, knight Imperial Order of St. Eugene of Trebizond, Order of the Knights of Sinai, order of Temple of Jerusalem, comdr. Order St. Stephan the Martyr; recipient King Carl XVI Gustaf's Gold Commemorative medal in art Sweden, German Friendship award, Aubrey R. Watzek award Soc. Mayflower Descendants, Ellis F. Lawrence medal U. Oreg.; named AIA-Carnegie Corp. fellow, summers 1930, 32. Mem. Am. Print Alliance (bd. dirs.), Portland Art Mus. (founder), Soc. Am. Graphic Artists, Calif. Soc. Printmakers, Coll. Art Assn., UN Assn. Oreg. (past pres.), Oreg. Internat. Coun. (bd. dirs.), Print Coun. of Am., N.W. Print Coun. (trustee), NW Coll. Art (bd. govs.), Oreg. St. U. Fdn. (trustee), Phi Kappa Phi, Kappa Pi. Home: 1500 SW 5th Ave Apt 2401 Portland OR 97201-5437 Office: 1219 SW Park Ave Portland OR 97205-2430

GILL, BECKY LORETTE, psychiatrist; b. Phoenix, Mar. 16, 1947; d. David Franklin and Lorette (Cooper) Brinegar; m. Jim Shack Gill, Jr., Aug. 5, 1978. BA in Biology, Stanford U., 1968; MD, U. Ariz., 1973. Diplomate Am. Bd. Psychiatry and Neurology; cert. addiction counselor; substance abuse residential facility dir., addictions specialist, clin. supr. Clerk typist Ariz. Med. Ctr. Med. Libr., Tucson, Ariz., 1970; asst. ref. libr. Ariz. Med. Ctr. Med. Libr., Tucson, 1971; surg. extern Tucson Med. Ctr., summer 1970; med. extern Fed. Reformatory for Women, Alderson, W.Va., 1972-73; commd. lt. USN, 1974, advanced through grades to capt., 1992; intern in medicine USPHS Hosp., Balt., 1973-74; resident in psychiatry Nat. Naval Med. Ctr., Bethesda, Md., 1974-77; head alcohol rehab. svc./substance abuse dept., staff psychiatrist Naval Hosp., Camp Lejeune, N.C., 1977-85; head alcohol rehab. svc./substance abuse dept., head psych. Naval Hosp., Millington, Tenn., 1985-88; head alcohol rehab. dept. Naval Hosp., Long Beach, Calif., 1988-94; head Navy Addictions Rehab. and Edn. Dept., Camp Pendleton, Calif., 1994—; mem. tumor bd. Naval Hosp., Camp Lejeune, 1977-85, cons. Tri-Command Consolidated Drug and Alcohol Counseling Ctr. Agy., 1977-85, phys. fitness program com., 1980-85, med. liaison on substance abuse, 1982-85, drug/alcohol program advisor, 1983-85, Tri-Command Consolidated Drug and Alcohol Adv. Coun., 1983-85, controlled substance abuse review subcom. of pharmacy and therapeutics com., 1984-85; watch officer Acute Care Clinic, Naval Hosp., Millington, 1985-86, cons. Counseling and Assistance Ctr., 1985-88, mem. bioethics com., chmn. med. records, utilization review com., 1985-88, exec. com. med. staff, chmn., 1986-87, psychiatric cons. to NAS Brig, 1986-88, mem. quality assurance com., 1986, mem. credentials com., 1986-87, pharmacy and therapeutics com., 1986, pos. mgmt. com., 1986-87, dir. med. svcs., 1986-88, dir. surgical svcs., 1986, commd. duty watch officer, 1986-87, watch officer acute care clinic, 1987-88, mem. Navy Drug and Alcohol adv. coun., 1987-88, preceptor to social worker, 1987-88, pos. mgmt. com., 1988, mem. commd. retention coun., 1988; also, numerous coms. at Naval Hosp., Long Beach, Calif., Naval Hosp., Camp Pendleton, Calif. Capt. USN. Recipient Commendation medal USN, 1988, meritorious svc. medal, 1994. Mem. Am. Acad. of Psychiatrists in Alcoholism and Addictions (founding mem.), Am. Soc. of Addiction Medicine, Assn. Mil. Surgeons of U.S., Addiction Profls. of N.C. (chmn. pub. info. com. 1979-80, ea. regional v.p. 1981-82, chmn. fall meeting planning com. 1983, sec. 1984-85), Nat. Assn. of Alcoholism and Drug Abuse Counselors, Calif. Assn. Alcohol and Drug Abuse Counselors, Am. Legion, VFW Aux. U.S. Lawn Tennis Assn. (hon. life), Stanford Cap and Gown, Stanford Alumni Assn., U. Ariz. Alumni Assn., Stanford Cardinal Club. Democrat. Avocations: tennis, swimming, jogging. Home: 32155 Corte Florecita Temecula CA 92592-6319

GILL, ELIZABETH EATON, film director, writer; b. Dublin, Ireland, Apr. 5, 1966; d. Michael Gates and Mary Frances (Lyon) G. Student, Stella Adler Conservatory, N.Y.C., 1985, Columbia U., 1985-88, NYU, 1988-90; diploma cert. in film health and safety, Royal Acad. Dramatic Art, London, 1987. 1st asst. dir. various films, N.Y.C. and Dublin, 1990-93; writer, dir. Grand Illustions, N.Y.C., 1993-94; writer Mad Dog Films, N.Y.C., 1994-95, Ferndale Films, Dublin, 1995-99; dir. Wilde Films, Dublin and N.Y.C., 1995-96, Wildfire Films, Dublin, 1999; with Ardmore Studios, Bray, Ireland, 1999—. Writer, dir., prodr. (play) A Woman's Place, 1994, (feature film) Goldfish Memory, 1999-2000; writer feature film screenplay Lulu, 1995-99; dir. feature film Gold in the Streets, 1996. Grantee Irish Film Bd., 1996, Nat. Writers Workshop grantee Univ. Coll. Galway, Ireland, 1999. Mem. Irish Writers Union, SIP Tech. Union. Avocations: photography, travel. Home: 9A Merton Pk, South Circular Rd, Dublin 8, Ireland Office: Armore Studio, Herbert Rd, Bray Co Wick, Ireland

GILL, EVALYN PIERPOINT, writer, editor, publisher; b. Boulder, Colo.; d. Walter Lawrence and Lou Octavia Pierpoint; m. John Glanville Gill; children: Susan Pierpoint, Mary Louise Glanville. Student, Lindenwood Coll.; BA, U. Colo.; postgrad., U. Nebr., U. Alaska; MA, Ctrl. Mich. U., 1968. Lectr. humanities Saginaw Valley State Coll., University Ctr., Mich., 1968-72; mem. English faculty U. N.C., Greensboro, 1973-74; editor Internat. Poetry Rev., Greensboro, 1975-92; pres. TransVerse Press, Greensboro, 1981—. Author: Poetry by French Women, 1930-1980, 1980, Dialogue, 1985, Southeast of Here: Northwest of Now, 1986, Entrances, 1996; editor: O. Henry Festival Stories, 1985, 87, Women of the Piedmont Triad: Poetry and Prose, 1989, Edge of Our World, 1990, A Turn in Time: Piedmont Writers at the Millennium, 1999. Bd. dirs. Eastern Music Festival, Greensboro, 1981—, Greensboro Symphony, 1982—, Greensboro Opera Co., 1982—, Weatherspoon Assn.; chmn. O Henry Festival, 1985, 95. Recipient numerous poetry prizes, Fortner award St. Andrews Coll., 1995, Altrusa Internat. Cmty. Arts award, Greensboro, 1998. Mem. MLA, Amn. Lit. Translators Assn., N.C. Poetry Soc., Phi Beta Kappa. Home: 2900 Turner Grove Dr N Greensboro NC 27455-1977

GILL, GEORGE WILHELM, anthropologist; b. Sterling, Kans., June 28, 1941; s. George Laurance and Florence Louise (Jones) G.; BA in Zoology with honors (NSF grantee), U. Kans., 1963, M.Phil. Anthropology (NDEA fellow, NSF dissertation research grantee), 1970, PhD in Anthropology, 1971; m. Pamela Jo Mills, July 26, 1975 (div. 1988); children: George Scott, John Ashton, Jennifer Florence, Bryce Thomas. Mem. faculty U. Wyo., Laramie, 1971—, prof. anthropology, 1985—, chair dept. anthropology, 1993-96; forensic anthropologist law enforcement agys., 1972—; sci. leader Easter Island Anthrop. Expdn., 1981; chmn. Rapa Nui Rendezvous: Internat. Conf. Easter Island Rsch., U. Wyo., 1993. Served to capt. U.S. Army, 1963-67. Recipient J.P. Ellbogen meritorious classroom teaching award, 1983; research grantee U. Wyo., 1972, 78, 82, Nat. Geog. Soc., 1980, Center for Field Research, 1980, Kon-Tiki Mus., Oslo, 1987, 89, 94, 96, World Monuments Fund, 1989. Diplomate Am. Bd. Forensic Anthropology (bd. dirs. 1985-90). Fellow Am. Acad. Forensic Scis. (sec. phys. anthropology sect. 1985-87, chmn. 1987-88); mem. Am. Assn. Phys. Anthropologists, Plains Anthrop. Soc., Wyo. Archael. Soc. Republican. Presbyterian. Author articles, monographs; editor: (with S. Rhine) Skeletal Attribution of Race, 1990. Home: 649 Howe Rd Laramie WY 82070-6885 Office: U Wyo Dept Anthropology Laramie WY 82071

GILL, GERALD LAWSON, librarian; b. Montgomery, Ala., Nov. 13, 1947; s. George Ernest and Marjorie (Hackett) G.; m. Nancy Argroves, Mar. 5, 1977 (div. 1982). AB, U. Ga., 1971; MA, U. Wis., 1973. Cert. profl. libr., Va. Cataloger James Madison U., Harrisonburg, Va., 1974-76, reference libr., 1976-87, bus. reference libr., 1987-99, govt. documents libr., 1998—, instr., 1974-80, asst. prof., 1980-90, assoc. prof., 1990—; lectr., spkr. nat. and regional groups; cons. in field; mem. faculty senate James Madison U., 1975-79, 96-98, sec. curriculum and instrn. com., 1976-78, chair, 1978-79, univ. coun., 1996-98. Mem. editl. bd. James Madison Jour., 1977-80; reviewer Am. Reference Books Ann.; contbr. articles to profl. jours. Mem. libr. adv. com. State Coun. for Higher Edn. in Va., 1986-87; virtual Va. Coord. Mgmt. Bus. com. Mem. ALA (chmn. bus. reference svcs. com. 1984-86, sec. law and polit. sci. sect. 1982-85, chmn. bus. reference svcs. discussion group 1986-87, chmn. bus. reference in acad. librs. com. 1988-91, Gale Rsch. award 1991), AAAS, Am. Soc. for Info. Sci., Va. Libr. Assn. (coun. 1986-87, parliamentarian 1979, 81), Spl. Librs. Assn. (treas. Va. chpt. 1983-85, pres. 1986-87), Internat. Platform Assn., World Future Soc., Harrisonburg C. of C. Democrat. Roman Catholic. Avocations: art collecting, travel. Home: 326 Westfield Rd Charlottesville VA 22901-1660 Office: James Madison U Library Harrisonburg VA 22807-0001

GILL, GRAEME JOSEPH, government educator; b. Melbourne, Victoria, Australia, Dec. 10, 1947; s. Joseph Harold Francis and Gwyneth Florence Mary (Sherriff) G.; m. Heather Pomroy, Jan. 8, 1972; children: Fiona Jane, Lachlan David. BA with honors, Monash U., Australia, 1971, MA, 1973; PhD, London U., 1976. Tutor dept. polit. sci. U. Tasmania, Hobart, 1976-77, lectr., 1978-81; lectr. dept. govt. U. Sydney, Australia, 1981-83, sr. lectr., 1984-88, assoc. prof., 1988-90, prof., 1990—; dep. chair acad. bd. U. Sydney, 1991, chair acad. forum, 1997—; mem. internat. adv. bd. Europe-Asia Studies, 1995—; head Sch. Econ. and Polit. Sci., U. Sydney. Author: Stalinism, 1990, The Origins of the Stalinist Political System, 1990, The Politics of Transition, 1993, The Collapse of a Single Party System, 1994, Power in the Party, 1996; mem. editl. bd. Politics, 1982-87, Elites & Leadership in Russian Politics, 1998, Russia's Stillborn Democracy?, 2000, The Dynamics of Democratization, 2000; mem. internat. adv. bd. Jour. Communist Studies and Transition Politics, 1994—. Grantee Australian Rsch. Coun., 1989-93, 94-96, 97-99, 99-2000; fellow Acad. Social Scis. A ustralia, 1994. Mem. Am. Assn. Advancement of Slavic Studies, Australasian Assn. for Study of Socialist and Post-Socialist Countries, Australasian Polit. Studies Assn. Avocations: reading, music, sports. Home: 14 Werona St, Pennant Hills NSW 2120, Australia Office: Univ Sydney, Dept Govt, Sydney NSW 2006, Australia

GILL, HARDAYAL SINGH, electrical engineer; b. Amritsar, Punjab, India, Aug. 18, 1952; came to U.S., 1974; BSc with honors, Punjabi U., Patiala, 1971, MSc, 1973; PhD, U. Minn., Mpls., 1978. Sr. engr. Nat. Semiconductor, Santa Clara, Calif., 1978-81; mem. tech. staff Hewlett-Packard, Palo Alto, Calif., 1981-83, project leader, 1983-85, project mgr., 1985-90; sr. engr. IBM, San Jose, Calif., 1990-94, sr. tech. staff, 1994-97; IBM Disting. engr., 1997—. Contbr. articles to profl. jours. Fellow IEEE (chmn. Magnetics Soc. 1987-88, chmn. Santa Clara sect. 1992-93, adminstrv. com. Magnetics Soc. 1992-94); mem. Am. Phys. Soc. Achievements include 60 patents on computer storage/memory devices; avocations: tennis, bike riding. Office: IBM Corp MS N17/142 5600 Cottle Rd San Jose CA 95123-3696

GILL, JERRY WAYNE, publisher, writer; b. Amarillo, Tex.; s. Robert L. and Edith Cavell (Amos) G.; children: Jerianne, Daric. BS, SUNY, Albany, 1977; MA, N.Mex. State U., 1980. Learning specialist N.Mex. State U., Las Cruces, 1979-82; dir. staff devel. RE Thomason Gen. Hosp., El Paso, Tex., 1982-85; rehab. cons. IRA, San Jose, Calif., 1986-89; mgmt. devel. specialist Queens Med. Ctr., Honolulu, Hawaii, 1989-91; owner GLB Worldwide, Kaneohe, Hawaii, 1991—. Author: Staying Alive: Handbook of International Survival Tactics, 1999; editor: Cheat Sheet for ICD-9 Coding, 1990-99, There is Only One, 2000, UPIN Directory, 1998-99. With U.S. Army, 1970-78. Republican. Avocations: hiking, jogging, writing, travel. Fax: 888-326-3701. E-mail: jerry@glbworld.com. Office: GLB Worldwide PO Box 6495 Kaneohe HI 96744-9176

GILL, ROGER WILLIAM THOMAS, leadership specialist; b. Whitehaven, Eng., Oct. 3, 1945; came to U.S., 1978; s. Wilfred Henry and Marie Eleanor (Gilmore) G.; children: Victoria Louise, Julian Charles. BA, Oxford (Eng.) U., 1968, MA, 1971; BPhil, Liverpool (Eng.) U., 1969; PhD, U. Bradford, Eng., 1980. Chartered psychologist. Personnel asst. English Electric Co., Liverpool, 1965-66; personnel officer English Electric Computers/ICL, Winsford, 1968-69; mgmt. cons. Inbucon, Birmingham, Eng., 1969-71; personnel mgr. De La Rue Co., London, 1971-72; manpower mgr. Associated Weavers, Bradford, Eng., 1972-74; lectr. U. Bradford Mgmt. Centre, 1974-78; asst. prof. orgnizational behavior, human resources mgmt., dir. mgmt. programs Sch. Mgmt. SUNY, Binghamton, 1979-82; mng. dir., prin. cons. Roger Gill and Assocs. Pte, Ltd., 1982-90; regional mgr. HR Cons., PA Cons. Group, Singapore, 1990-91; prof. bus. adminstrn. Sch. Bus. U. Strathclyde, Scotland, 1992-96, vis. prof., 1997—; dir. Rsch. Ctr. for Leadership Studies Leadership Trust Found., Ross-on Wye, Eng., 1997—; cons. to industry, govt., U.K., U.S., Malaysia, Brunei, Hong Kong, Indonesia, UAE, Singapore; vis. prof. Queen's Sch. of Mgmt., Queen's U. Belfast, No. Ireland, 1999—. Fellow Found. for Mgmt. Edn., 1978; grantee Prodn. Mgmt., 1977-78, SUNY, 1979-80. Mem. Am. Soc. Tng. and Devel. (pres. So. Tier, N.Y., 1980-81), Am. Psychol. Assn., Acad. Mgmt., Internat. Assn. Applied Psychology, British Psychol. Assn., Singapore Nat. Productivity Assn. (1st v.p. 1985-87), Brit. Acad. Mgmt., Inst. Pers. and Devel., Inst. Mgmt., Royal Soc. Arts, Royal Over-Seas League, Tanglin Club. Home: Craigmarloch Cottage, Port Glasgow Rd, Kilmacolm PA13 4SE, Scotland

GILL, RONALD SCOTT, technology company executive; b. LaGrange, Tex., Feb. 25, 1966; s. Ben Gilmer Gill and Barbara Anne (Evans) Cluck; m. Erica Sasaki, May 26, 1996. BBA, Baylor U., 1988; M in Internat. Bus., U. S.C., 1991. Sr. fin. analyst Sony Corp., Tokyo, 1991-97; contr. tech. ops. Sap Japan, Tokyo, 1997-99, v.p. ops., 1999-2000; COO Softfront, Inc., San Jose, Calif., 2000—. Office: Softfront Inc Ste 650 1737 N First St San Jose CA 95112

GILL, SUKHDEV SINGH, governement agency technical director; b. Jullander, Punjab, India, Jan. 29, 1952; s. Gurmej Singh and Resham Kaur (Johal) G.; m. Amarjit Kaur Samra; children: Charn Kaur, Kiran Kaur, Aug. 15, 1982. BSc, U. Surrey, 1976, PhD, 1980; MBA, London Bus. Sch., 1995. Acad. staff U. Surrey, U.K., 1980-83; rschr. Def. Rsch. Agy., Malvern, U.K., 1983-87, project mgr., 1987-91, tech. mgr., 1991-95, project dir., 1995-96, tech. dir., 1996—; tech. mem. B.T. (U.K.), Birmingham, 1969-76. Contbr. articles to profl. jours.; patentee in field. Fellow Inst. of Elec. Engrs. (U.K.); mem. Inst. of Physics. Avocations: field hockey, photography, restoring furniture. Home: The Fountain, Malvern WR14 3PN, England Office: DERA, Court Rd, Malvern WR14 3PS, England

GILL, TERRY DOUGLAS, law educator; b. El Paso, Tex., June 19, 1952; arrived in The Netherlands, 1973; s. John Charles and Stacy Kathleen (Moore) G.; m. Annette Elizabeth Postma. LLB, U. Utrecht, The Netherlands, 1981, LLM, 1984, LLD cum laude, 1989. Civil servant Mcpl. Utrecht, The Netherlands, 1973-83, dpet. head, 1983-85; assoc. prof. internat. law U. Utrecht, The Netherlands, 1985—; vis. fellow Rsch. Ctr. for Internat. Law, U. Cambridge, Eng., 1997. Author: Litigation Strategy at the International Court, 1989; co-author: The World Court: What It Is and How It Works, 1989; mem. editl. bd. Netherlands Internat. LAw Rev., 1995—, Mil. Law Rev., The Netherlands, 1994—. Fulbright scholar, 1991. Mem. Netherlands Soc. Internat. Law, Am. Soc. Internat. Law, Soc. Mil. Law and the Law of War. Avocations: mil. history, political philosophy, long distance walking. Office: Inst Pub Internat Law, Achter St Pieter 200, 3512 HT Utrecht The Netherlands

GILLAM, IAN HERBERT, nutrition consultant; b. Melbourne, Australia, Feb. 4, 1951; s. Leon Roberts and Edna Charlotte (Clarke) G.; m. Robyn Joy Beniot, Dec. 11, 1976 (div. Feb. 1996); children: Melinda, Paul and Kirsty (twins); m. Maryanne Denbeigh Long. BS with honors, Melbourne U., Australia, 1976, MS, 1980, PhD, 1996. Lectr. Victoria Coll., Burwood, Australia, 1977-79, 82-83; hosp. scientist Royal Childrens Hosp., Melbourne, Australia, 1980-81; lectr., sr. lectr. Phillip Inst. Tech., Melbourne, Australia, 1983-89; sr. lectr. RMIT U., Melbourne, Australia, 1992-97; nutrition and exercise cons. Melbourne, Australia, 1998—. Rsch. fellow Australian Inst. Sport, Canberra, 1990-91. Fellow Sports Medicine Australia (v.p. 1990-91, 98—, dir. pub. health 1998—); mem. Australian Assn. Exercise and Sports Sci. (dir. 1991-93, 98—), Soc. Free Radical Rsch. Australia, Australian Nutrition Found. Avocations: skiing, surfing, sailboarding, swimming, running. Office: 738 Burke Rd Ste 23, Camberwell 3124, Australia

GILLAM, LINDA DAWN, cardiologist, researcher; b. Corner Brook, Nfld., Can., Sept. 23, 1952; d. Donald Samuel and Vera (Pieroway) G.; m. Vincent Charles DiCola, Aug. 30, 1985 (div. 1995); children: John William DiCola, Laura Ann DiCola. BS, McGill U., Montreal, Que., Can., 1972; MD, Queen's U., Kingston, Ont., Can., 1976. Diplomate Am. Bd. Internal

Medicine, Am. Bd. Cardiovascular Disease. Intern U. Toronto, 1976; resident in medicine St. Michaels Hosp., Toronto, 1977-79; fellow in cardiology U. Toronto, 1979-81, Mass. Gen. Hosp., Boston, 1981-83; instr. in medicine Harvard U. Med. Sch., Boston, 1983-86; clin. asst. prof. medicine U. Conn., Farmington, 1986-95, clin. assoc. prof., 1995—; dir. echocardiography U. Conn. Health Ctr., Farmington, 1986-90, Hartford (Conn.) Hosp., 1990—; spkr. in field. Contbr. articles to profl. jours. Active St. Thomas's Episcopal Ch., New Haven, 1993—. Rsch. grantee Can. Heart Assn. Fellow Am. Coll. Cardiology (gov. 1996-99, chpt. pres. 1996-99, govt. rels. com. 1997—, mem. steering com. bd. govs., chair task force on comm., mem. awards com., edtl. bd. website), Am. Heart Assn. (task force on guidelines for echocardiography, com. on women in cardiology, ARDMS adult echo exam task force); mem AMA, Conn. State Med. Soc., Am. Bd. Echo (bd. dirs. 1999—), Am. Soc. Echocard iography (legis. and regulatory affairs com. 1993—, bd. dirs. 1995-98, com. on sonographer tng. 1997—). Avocations: ballet, opera, classical music, aerobics, tennis. Office: Hartford Hosp 80 Seymour St Hartford CT 06102-8000

GILLAM, SIR PATRICK, oil company executive; b. London, Apr. 15, 1933; s. Cyril Bryant and Mary Josephine (Davis) G.; m. Diana Echlin, Nov. 23, 1963; children: Jane, Luke. BA in History with honors, London Sch. Econs., 1954. With Fgn. Office, London, 1956-57, Brit. petroleum Co. p.l.c., London, 1957-91; v.p. BP (N.Am.) Inc. subs., N.Y., 1971-74, gen. mgr. supply, 1974-78; dir. BP Internat. Ltd., 1978-81, mng. dir., 1981-91; non-exec. dir. Comml. Union, 1991-96; bd. dirs. Standard Chartered p.l.c., 1988-91, dep. chmn., 1991-93, chmn., 1993—; chmn. ICC U.K., 1989-98, Booker Tate Ltd., 1991-93, Asda p.l.c., 1991-96, Royal & Sun Alliance, 1997—; mem. exec. bd. dirs. ICC World Wide, 1991-98. Created knight, 1998; hon. fellow London Sch. Econs. & Polit. Sci. Fellow London Sch. Econs. (hon.). Avocation: gardening. Office: Std Chartered PLC, 1 Aldermanbury Sq, London EC2V 7SB, England

GILLAN, GARTH JACKSON, writer, former educator; b. Washington, Feb. 14, 1939; s. James Joseph and Lolita Jackson G.; m. Mary Elizabeth Marlene (McCormick), Dec. 29, 1965; children: Johanna, Rebecca, Daniel, Susannah, Jonathan, Miriam. PhD, Duquesne U., 1966; MA in Pastoral Theol., St. Mary in the Woods Coll., 1992; MS in Edu. Psychology, So. Ill. U., 1991. Asst. prof. Seton Hill Coll., Greensberg, Pa., 1965-66, Canisius Coll., Buffalo, 1966-69, So. Ill. U., Carbondale, Ill., 1969-73; assoc. prof. So. Ill. U., 1973-82, prof., 1982-99, prof. emeritus, 1999—. Author: Horizons of the Flesh, 1973, From Sign to Symbol, 1982, Michel Foucault, 1982, Rising From the Ruins, 1997. Mem. Soc. Advancement Am. Phil., Soc. Phenomenology. Home: 120 Cooper St Spring Mills PA 16875-8102

GIL LAVEDRA, RICARDO RODOLFO, minister of justice; b. July 24, 1949; married; 4 children. Degree in law, U. Buenos Aires, 1972. Ct. reporter Chief Justice of Supreme Ct., Buenos Aires, 1974-75, lawyer, examining magistrate, 1974-75; undermgr. legal affairs Pérez Companc group, 1979-83; judge Nat. Ct. Appeals, Buenos Aires, 1984-87; state sec. Ministry of Interior, 1988-89; min. of justice Argentina, 1999; dir. studies U. de La Plata Sch. of Law, 1975; prof. grad. dept. U. Buenos Aries Law Sch., 1986-88, also sr. lectr.; v.p. com. against torture UN, 1987-95. Contbr. articles to profl. publs. Mem. Internat. Assn. Penal Law, Permanent Assmebly on Human Rights, Ctr. Instnl. Studies, Argentine Assn. Telecomms. Law. Office: Minister of Justice, Sarmiento 329 5th Fl, Buenos Aires Argentina*

GILLELAND, JOHN ROGERS, technology company executive; b. Gadsden, Ala., Jan. 12, 1941; s. Earl Rogers and Margaret Eta Gilleland; m. Kim Denise Turos, Aug. 23, 1987. BS in Physics, Yale U., 1963; MS in Physics, U. Mich., 1964, PhD in Physics, 1969. Scientist Gulf Gen. Atomics, La Jolla, Calif., 1970-72, dir. Doublet III program, 1972-78, sr. v.p. fusion energy program, 1985-87; program dir. U.S.-Japan Fusion rsch. Collaboration, La Jolla, 1978-85; mng. dir. Internat. Thermonuclear Exptl. Reactor Project, Garching, Germany, 1987-91; v.p., chief scientist Bechtel Corp., San Francisco, 1991-98; pres., CEO Archimedes Tech. Group, San Diego, 1998—; advisor space def. initiative Dept. Def., Washington, 1985-86; advisor Nat. Acad. Scis., Washington, 1984-87; dir. Fusion Power Assocs., Washington, 1994-00. Named Young Engr. of the Yr. Am. Nuc. Soc., 1980; recipient Achievement award Am. Nuc. Soc., 1992. Avocations: cello, squash, art. Home: PO Box 9154 Rancho Santa Fe CA 92067-4154 Office: Archimedes Tech Group 5405 Oberlin Dr San Diego CA 92121-1700

GILLEN, HOWARD WILLIAM, neurologist, medical historian; b. Chgo., Nov. 25, 1923; s. John Howard and Emily Elizabeth (Bayley) G.; m. Corinne V. Neese, July 24, 1948. BS, U. Ill., 1947; MD, U. Ill., Chgo., 1949. Hon. active neurologist New Hanover Regional Med. Ctr., Wilmington, N.C., 1973-93, emeritus neurologist, 1993—; cons. neurologist Cape Fear Meml. Hosp., Wilmington, 1973-93; clin. prof. neurology U. N.C., Chapel Hill, 1973-93, clin. prof. emeritus, 1993—; adj. prof. biol. sci. U. N.C., Wilmington, 1986—; rsch. assoc. I.R.I.S.C., Wilmington, 1989-93, sr. investigator, 1993—. Capt. USNR, ret. Home: 500 Sand Castle Ct Wilmington NC 28405-8386

GILLEN, JAMES ROBERT, lawyer, insurance company executive; b. N.Y.C., Nov. 14, 1937; s. James Matthew and Katharine Isabel (Fritz) G.; m. Rita Marie Wahleithner, June 15, 1963 (div. 1992); children: Jennifer Elaine, Nancy Louise, Paula Anne; m. Edda Lya Pacheco, Dec. 10, 1994. AB magna cum laude, Harvard U., 1959, LLB cum laude, 1965. Bar: N.Y. 1966, N.J. 1975. Assoc. firm White & Case, N.Y.C., 1965-72; v.p., assoc. gen. counsel Prudential Ins. Co. Am., Newark, 1972-77, sr. v.p., assoc. gen. counsel, 1977-80, sr. v.p. pub. affairs, 1980-84, sr. v.p., gen. counsel, 1984-98; mem. bd. trustees Columbia Inst. Investor Project, 1991-97; legal adv. com. New York Stock Exch., 1986-89. Trustee United Way Essex and West Hudson Counties, 1981-90, pres., 1986-88; mem. Mendham Twp. (N.J.) Bd. Edn., 1981-82; trustee N.J. Shakespeare Festival, 1991-99, Mendham Twp. Libr., 1979-82; dir., chmn. Neurol. Inst. N.J., 1998—. Lt. (j.g.) USN, 1959-62. Mem. ABA, N.J. Bar Assn., Assn. Life Ins. Counsel, Harvard Club (N.Y.C.), Morris Country Golf Club. Home: 72 Washington Valley Rd Morristown NJ 07960-3332

GILLESPIE, THOMAS WILLIAM, theological seminary administrator, religion educator; b. L.A., July 18, 1928; s. William A. and Estella (Beers) G.; m. Barbara A. Lugenbill, July 31, 1953; children: Robyn C., William T., Dayle E. BA, George Pepperdine Coll., 1951; BD, Princeton Theol. Sem., 1954; PhD, Claremont Grad. Sch., 1971; DD (hon.), Grove City Coll., 1984; ThD (hon.), Theol. Acad. Debrecen, Hungary, 1988; DTh (hon.), Karoli Gaspar Reformed U., Budapest, Hungary, 1994; DPhil (hon.), Soong Sil U., Seoul, Korea, 1994; DD (hon.), U. St. Andrews, Scotland, 1996; LHD (hon.), King Coll., Bristol, Tenn., 1999. Ordained to ministry Presbyterian Ch., 1954. Pastor 1st Presbyn. Ch., Garden Grove, Calif., 1954-66, Burlingame, Calif., 1966-83; pres., prof. N.T. Princeton (N.J.) Theol. Sem., 1983—. Author: The First Theologians: A Study in Early Christian Prophecy, 1994. Chmn. bd. trustees Ctr. Theol. Inquiry, 1992—. With USMC, 1946-47. Recipient A.A. Hodge prize in systematic theology Princeton Theol. Sem., 1953; Disting. Alumnus award Claremont Grad. Sch., 1984; Disting. Alumnus award Pepperdine U., 1986. Mem. Soc. Bibl. Lit., Studiorum Novi Testamenti Societas, Rotary Internat. Republican. Home: Springdale 86 Mercer St Princeton NJ 08540-6819 Office: Princeton Theol Sem Office of Pres PO Box 552 Princeton NJ 08542-0552

GILLESPIE, WILLIAM HARRY, forestry executive, geology educator; b. Webster Springs, W.Va., Jan. 8, 1931; s. William Marston and Rosalie Casteel (Frazee) G.; m. Betty Jean Rasnick, Dec. 23, 1950; children: William A., Linda M., Clifton P., Laura L., James D. BS, W.Va. U., 1952, MS, 1954, postgrad., 1956-60. Forest biologist W.Va. Dept. Agr., Morgantown, 1956-66; asst. dir. plant pest control W.Va. Dept. Agr., Charleston, 1966-67, dir. plant pest control, 1967-69, asst. commr., 1969-80, dep. commr., 1980-85; instr. dept. geology W.Va. U., Morgantown, 1958-74, asst. prof., 1974-77, assoc. prof., 1979-80, prof., 1980-99; dir. W.Va. Dept. Forestry, Charleston, 1985-93; cons. forester-geologist, W.Va., 1993—; rsch. paleobotanist U.S. Geol. Survey, Reston, Va., 1974-95. Author: W.Va. Geology, Archaeology and Pedology, 1964, W.Va. Plant Fossils, 1978, Wild Foods of Appalachia, 1986; contbr. articles to profl. jours. Recipient Disting. Achievement in Earth Scis. award Am. Fedn. Mineral. Socs., 1982, Outstanding Contbn. to Forestry award W.Va. Forestry Assn., 1986; Outstanding Svc. award Nat. Assn. State Foresters, 1993, Nat. Assn. State Depts. Agr., 1994, W.Va. U. Dept. Geology, 1995; W.Va. Coll. Agr. and Forestry, 1999; fossil plant genus Gillespieisporites named in honor of by J. A. Clendening, 1969, fossil plant genus Gillespia named in honor of by Erwin and Rothwell, 1989; named to W.Va. Agr. and Forestry Hall of Fame, 1998. Fellow Soc. Am. Foresters; mem. W.Va. Assn. Soil Conservation Suprs. (hon. life mem.), Geol. Soc. Am., Am. Assn. Petroleum Geologists, Botanical Soc. Am., Internat. Assn. Plant Taxonomists, Internat. Assn. Paleobotanists, Soc. Am. Foresters, Lions. Democrat. Avocations: woodworking, fishing, photography. Home and Office: 916 Churchill Cir Charleston WV 25314-1747

GILLET, VINCENT PAUL, physicist, researcher, retired; b. Nice, France, June 13, 1931; s. Olga G.; m. Myriam Da Fano, Apr. 25, 1952; children: Philip, Daniel. Student, Lycée Condorcet, Paris, 1943-50; PhD, U. Paris, 1961. Physicist Commissariat L'Energie Atomique, Ctr. Nuc. Studies, Saclay, France, 1957-92; vice-head dept. nuclear physics Commissariat L'Energie Atomique, Ctr. Nuc. Studies, Saclay, 1972-78; head dept. nuclear physics Commissariat L'Energie Atomique, 1978-87, rsch. dir., 1987-92; prof. Ecole Poly. Palaiseau, France, 1977-85; ret., 1992; dir. Sch. Theoretical Physics, Les Houches, France, 1968; mem. nat. com. CNRS, France, 1971-75, 82-86; pres. scientific com. Accelerator Linac, Saclay, France, 1976-79, Accelerator Tandem, Saclay, 1989-91; mem. evaluation com. Swedish Nuclear Rsch., 1987; pres. dir. com. Nuclear Physics Inst. Orsay, France, 1989-91. Author: Methods in Relativistic Nuclear Physics, North-Holland edit., 1984, Angular Momentum Calculus in Quantum Physics, World Sci. edit., 1991; mem. editl. bd. Jour. Nuc. Physics, 1968-90; contbr. over 100 articles to profl. jours. Recipient Joliot-Curie prize French Soc. Physics, 1964, Doineau-Butuel prize French Acad. Scis., 1970, Great prize Jaffé, French Acad. Scis., 1971. Mem. Nat. Order Merit (officer), Order Les Palmes Acad. (chevalier). Avocations: music, literature, theatre. E-mail: vincent.gillet@wanadoo.fr. Home: 49 Rue De Chatenay E 4, 92160 Antony France

GILLETT, GROVER, author; b. Whitewright, Tex., June 22, 1927; s. Grover Cleveland and Gertrude (Holland) G.; m. Mary Margaret Landress, Oct. 2, 1941. BBA, Tex. Tech. U., 1949; MBA, U. Tex., 1951; postgrad., Columbia U., 1953. CPA, Tex. Auditor Lumberman's Mutual Casualty Co., Dallas, 1954-56; operational auditor Dept. of Def., Dallas, 1956-58; self-employed CPA Dallas, 1958-64; asst. prof. McMurry Coll., Abilene, Tex., 1964-66; sr. internal auditor Ling-Temco-Vought Aerospace Corp., Dallas, 1966-67; instr. El Centro Coll., Dallas, 1967-96. Author: Personnel Policies of Public Accounting Firms in Texas, 1951, 1988, (booklet) Marriage Quotables, 1999; author 39 other books and booklets. Bd. dirs. Twenty-One Turtle Creek Homeowners Assn., Dallas, 1996-98; mem. Dallas Coun. on World Affairs. Lt. (j.g.) USN, 1945-46. Mem. AICPAs, Tex. Soc. CPAs, World Future Soc., Dallas UN Assn., S.W. Social Sci. Assn., Lions. Democrat. Unitarian. Avocations: reading, collecting antiques. Home and Office: Apt 1103 3883 Turtle Creek Blvd Dallas TX 75219-4426

GILLETT, JAMES WALTER, minister, missionary; b. Waterloo, Iowa, Feb. 19, 1949; arrived in Ireland, 1970; s. James L. and Mabel M. (Hersey) G.; m. Jean Nancy Brewster, Mar. 29, 1969; children: Jonathan, Julie. Student, McPherson (Kans.) Coll., 1967-68, Missionary Tng. Ctr., 1968-69. Founder and dir. Aids for Bible Edn., Dublin, 1970—, Emmaus Corres. Sch., Ireland, 1972—, Overseas Assistance Teams, Dublin, 1980—; founder and pres. Ireland Outreach Internat., Dublin, 1972—, Waterloo, 1980—; dir. Source of Light Assoc. Sch., Dublin, 1978—; asst. leader Lit. Crusades Team, Lyon, France, 1969; regional dir. Emmaus Corr. Sch., Dublin, 1972—; mem. European Emmaus Com., 1993—; founder, dir. Emmaus Bible Ctr., Nigeria, 1994; founder, internat. coordinator Emmaus Bible Centres, Ghana, 1997; participant Congress for Itinerant Evangelists, Amsterdam, 1983. Actor screening for Pilgrims Progress, 1977; film rschr.; Patmos, 1981. Participant Lausanne Congress on Evangelism, 1974, Internat. Prayer Assembly, Seoul, 1984, Lausanne II Congress for World Evangelism, Manila, 1989. Mem. Christian European Visual Media Assn. Republican. Plymouth Brethren. Avocations: swimming, travel. Office: Ireland Outreach Internat, Charleville Harbour Rd, Dalkey County Dublin, Ireland

GILLETT, PAULA, humanities educator; b. N.Y.C., July 15, 1934; d. Ira and Sophie (Silvershein) Levy; m. Eric Gillett, June 23, 1956; children: Walter, Nadia, Noel. BA, Bklyn. Coll., 1955; MA, Yale U., 1956; PhD, U. Calif., Berkeley, 1979. Project dir. Grad. Sch. Edn., U. Calif., Berkeley, 1984-89; prof. San Jose (Calif.) State U., 1989—; co-chair Com. on History in the Classroom, 1992-96; vis. scholar Inst. for Rsch. on Women and Gender, Stanford U., 1996-97. Author: Worlds of Art: Painters in Victorian Society, 1990, Musical Women in England, 1870-1914: Encroaching on All Man's Privileges, 2000. Project dir. New Faces of Liberty, San Francisco, 1985-89. Summer fellow Am. Coun. Learned Socs., 1994; Mellon fellow Harry Ransom Humanities Rsch. Ctr., U. Tex., Austin, 1996. Mem. Am. Hist. Assn., Phi Beta Kappa. Avocation: choral singing. Office: Humanities Dept San Jose State Univ San Jose CA 95192-0001

GILLETT, RICHARD CLARK, JR., physician, educator, health facility administrator; b. Richmond, Va., Mar. 27, 1950; s. Richard Clark and Mary Caperton (Renshaw) G.; m. Barbara Jean Bolecek, Aug. 12, 1972; children: Douglas Clark, Ann Caperton. BA, U. Va., 1971, MD, 1977. Diplomate Am. Bd. Family Practice. Tchr. Prince William County Schs., Manassas, Va., 1971-72; resident Roanoke (Va.) Meml. Hosp., 1977-80; family physician Family Practice Clinic, Inc., Radford, Va., 1981-82; emergency physician Montgomery Regional Hosp., Blacksburg, Va., 1982-83; pvt. practice Radford, Va., 1983-85; asst. prof. family medicine, asst. dean continuing med. edn. East Tenn. State U., Johnson City, 1986-91; dir. med. edn. Columbus (Ga.) Regional Healthcare Sys., 1991-2000. Bd. dirs. Stewert Cmty. Home, Columbus, 1996-99, Human Experience Theater, Columbus, 1997, Springer Theater, Columbus, 1993-94, 99-00. Mem. AMA (rep. sect. on med. schs. Chgo., 1996-2000), Am. Assn. Family Physicians, Med. Assn. Ga. (mem. com. med. schs.), Muscogee County (Ga.) Med. Soc. Avocations: gardening, flying. Fax: 706-571-1604. Home e-mail: gillettrc@kndogy.net. Office e-mail: clark.gillett@crhs.net.

GILLETTE, P. ROGER, physicist, systems engineer; b. Mt. Vernon, Iowa, May 12, 1917; s. Clinton Edgar and Celia (Rogers) G.; m. Bettelaine Dunbar, April 26, 1947 (dec. Mar. 1986); children: Kenneth Lee, Sandra Jo. B.A., in Physics, Cornell Coll., 1937; B.S. in Engring. Physics, U. Ill., 1938, M.S. in Physics, 1939, Ph.D. in Physics, 1942. Staff mem. Radiation Lab. MIT, Cambridge, Mass., 1942-45; research engr. Sperry Gyroscope Co., Great Neck, N.Y., 1945-48; physicist Hanford Works Gen. Electric Co., Richland, Wash., 1948-50; sr. research physicist SRI Internat. Menlo Park, Calif., 1950-92. retired, SRI Internat., 1992. Co-author: Pulse Generators, 1948. Bd. dirs. West Bay Opera Assn., Palo Alto, Calif., 1959-64, 1977-79, Inst. for Continued Learning, Willamette U., Salem, Oreg., 1996-98. Mem. AAAS, IEEE (sr. life mem.), Am. Phys. Soc. (life), Am. Acad. Religion, Inst. on Religion in an Age of Sci., Sigma Xi, Phi Beta Kappa, Tau Beta Pi, Phi Kappa Phi. Achievements include development of pulse transformer theory, of system design concepts for command, control, communications, and intelligence systems, electronic combat systems, and air combat training systems. Home: 2385 Crestview Dr S Salem OR 97302-5373

GILLIAM, TERRY VANCE, film director, actor, illustrator, writer; b. Mpls., Nov. 22, 1940; s. James Hall and Beatrice (Vance) G.; m. Margaret Weston; children: Amy Rainbow, Holly du Bois, Harry Thunder. BA, Occidental Coll., 1962, DFA (hon.), 1988; hon. doctorate, Royal Coll. Art, London. Assoc. editor HELP! mag., 1962-64; free-lance illustrator, 1964-65, advt. copywriter, art dir., 1966-67; TV resident cartoonist We Have Ways of Making You Laugh, 1968; animator Do Not Adjust Your Set, 1968-69, The Marty Feldman Comedy Machine, 1971-72; with Monty Python's Flying Circus, 1969-76. Animator (film) And Now For Something Completely Different; illustrator (book) The Cocktail People, 1966; co-dir., actor (film) Monty Python and the Holy Grail, 1974, The Do It Yourself Animation Film, 1974, The Miracle of Flight, 1974; dir. (film) Jabberwocky, 1976; designer, actor, animator (film) Monty Python's Life of Brian, 1978; co-writer, producer, dir. (film) Time Bandits, 1980; actor, dir. (film) Monty Python Live at the Hollywood Bowl, 1982; dir., actor, animator, co-writer (film) Monty Python's Meaning of Life, 1983; dir., writer (film) Brazil, 1985; dir., co-writer (film) The Adventures of Baron Munchausen, 1988; dir. (film) The Fisher King, 1991, Twelve Monkeys, 1995; co-writer, dir. Fear and Loathing in Las Vegas, 1998; author: Gilliam on Gilliam, 1999, Dark Knights and Holy Fools, 19989 co-author: The Brand New Monty Python Book, 1973, Monty Python and the Holy Grail, 1977, Monty Python Life of Brian, 1979 Monty Python's Big Red Book, Monty Python's Papperbok, 1977, Monty Python's Scrapbook, 1979, Animations of Mortality, 1979, Time Bandits, 1981, Monty Python's The Meaning of Life, 1983, The Adventures of Baron Munchausen, 1989, Not the Screenplay of Fear and Loathing in Las Vegas, 1998; presenter TV series The Last Machine, 1995; exec. prodr. (CD ROM) Monty Python's Complete Waste of Time, 1995.

GILLICE, SONDRA JUPIN (MRS. GARDNER RUSSELL BROWN), sales and marketing executive; b. Urbana, Ill.; d. Earl Cranston and Laura Lorraine (Rose) Jupin; m. Gardner Russell Brown, Jan. 12, 1980; 1 child, Thomas Alan Gillice. BS, Lindenwood Coll.; MBA, Loyola Coll. Pers. officer N.Y. Citibank, 1968-70, 1st Nat. Bank Chgo., 1970-72; mgr. human resources Potomac Electric Power Co., Washington, 1973-81; dir. pers. U.S. Synthetic Fuels Corp., Washington, 1981-86; v.p. human resources Guest Svcs., Inc., 1987-90, v.p. sales and mktg., 1990-93; sr. v.p. govt. rels. Drake Beam Morin, Inc., 1994-98; pres. RusSon, Inc., 1998—; bd. govs. Nat. Coal Coun., exec. com. Bd. dirs. KHG Dance Theatre, Nat. Womens Econ. Alliance, Life With Cancer; chmn. Career & Life Learning Sys., Inc. Mem. AAUW (pres. Falls Church br. 1976-78), Edison Electric Inst. (chair tng. and mgmt. devel. com.), Soc. for Human Resource Mgmt., Greater Met. Washington Bd. Trade, Soroptimists (pres. Washington chpt. 1979-80), DAR, Army Navy Country Club, Army Navy Club, Soc. Magna Charta Dames, Edgartown Yacht Club, Georgetown Club. Republican.

GILLILAND, JOHN CAMPBELL, II, lawyer; b. Bellefonte, Pa., June 4, 1945; s. John Campbell and Miriam Ruth (Forsythe) G.; m. Karen Gardner, Nov. 2, 1997; children: Jennifer, John, David. BA, Pa. State U., 1967; JD, Georgetown U., 1971. Bar: Pa. 1971, Ind. 1979, Ky. 1991, Ohio 1992. Ptnr. McQuaide, Blasko & Brown, Inc., State College, Pa., 1974-79, DeFur, Voran, Hanley, Radcliff & Reed, Muncie, Ind., 1979-90; prin. Gilliland & Assocs., Covington, Ky., 1991-2000, Locke Reynolds LLP, Indpls., 2000—; lectr. econs. dept. Ball State U., Muncie. Bd. dirs. United Way Delaware County, v.p., 1983-85; bd. dirs. Vis. Nurses Assn.; v.p. Muncie chpt. ARC, 1983-85; bd. govs. Friends of Bracken Libr. Served to capt. U.S. Army, 1971-72. Fellow Rotary Found., Queens Coll., Belfast, Ireland, 1968-69. Mem. ABA, Ind. Bar Assn., Ky. Bar Assn., Ohio Bar Assn., Am. Health Lawyers Assn., Ind. Soc. Hosp. Attys. (chmn. 1989), Pa. Soc. Hosp. Attys. (pres. 1978-79), East Central Ind. Pers. Assn. (bd. dirs.). Republican. Presbyterian. Home: 38 Kathryn Ave Florence KY 41042-1536 Office: 201 N Illinois St Ste 1000 Indianapolis IN 46204-4227

GILLILAND-SWETLAND, ANNE JERVOIS, archivist, educator; b. Londonderry, Northern Ireland, Apr. 30, 1959; came to the U.S., 1983; d. David Jervois Thetford and Patricia Gilliland; m. Luke Jerome Swetland, Aug. 27, 1990; children: Tanner Samuel Jervois, Fionn Aidan Lee. MA, U. Dublin, Ireland, 1982; MS, cert. advanced studies, U. Ill., 1985; PhD, U. Mich., 1995. Archivist, records specialist U. Cin., 1985-90; assoc. archivist U. Mich., Ann Arbor, 1991-92, dir. Source LINK Project, 1993-95; asst. prof. U. Calif., L.A., 1995—. Contbr. articles to profl. jours. Fellow Soc. Am. Archivists (coun. mem. 1996-99, C.F.W. Coker award 1998), Midwest Archives Conf. (coun. mem. 1993-95, Margaret Cross Norton award 1997), Internat. Dendrology Soc., Assn. Libr. and Info. Sci. Educators, Beta Phi Mu. Avocations: gardening, hiking. E-mail: swetland@ucla.edu. Fax: 310-206-4460. Office: U Calif LA Dept Info Studies 212 Gse & Is Bldg Los Angeles CA 90095-0001

GILLILLAND, THOMAS, art gallery director; b. Bladen, Nebr., Feb. 14, 1932; s. Whitney and Virginia (Wegmann) G.; m. Cora Lee Critchfield, Aug. 23, 1956; children: Shaun, Ruth, Virginia. Grad., Wentworth Mil. Acad., 1952; BA, Am. U., 1963, MA, 1967. Dep. dir. congl. liaison AID, Washington, 1969-75; congl. liaison officer USDA, Washington, 1975-76, dir. legis. affairs Animal and Plant Health Inspection Svc., 1976-83; dir. external affairs Fin. Mgmt. Svc. U.S. Dept. Treasury, Washington, 1983-93; owner Art in the Hand Gallery, St. Augustine, Fla., 1994—. Contbr. mag. articles. Mem. Nat. Assn. Govt. Communicators (Blue Pencil award 1986), Soc. for Preservation and Encouragement of Barbershop Quartet Singing in Am., Nat. Press Club. Republican. Presbyterian. Home: 227 Mountain View Dr Willsboro NY 12996-3506

GILLINSON, CLIVE DANIEL, performing company executive, former musician; b. Bangalore, India, Mar. 7, 1946; arrived in Eng., 1948; s. Stanley and Regina Rebecca (Schein) G.; m. Susan Sheppard, 1980 (div. 1986); m. Penelope Sara Morsley, June 1, 1989; children: Sarah Helen, Miriam Catherine, David Michael. Student, Queen Mary Coll., London, 1963-64; diploma, recital, Royal Acad. Music, 1968; diploma in music (hon.), Guildhall Sch., London, 1992, City U., London, 1994; doctorate, City of London U., 1995. Cellist London Symphony Orch., 1970-84, mng. dir., 1984—; ptnr. Clive Daniel Antiques, London, 1980-86. Named Freeman of the City of London, Corp. of London, 1984, Comdr. British Empire, 1998. Fellow Royal Acad. Music; mem. Assn. Brit. Orchs. (chmn. 1982-85), Nat. Youth Orch. Avocations: theatre, reading, skiing, tennis, concerts. Office: London Symphony Orch, Barbican Centre Silk St, London EC2Y 8DS, England

GILLIS, JACK C., JR., energy executive; b. Dallas, Dec. 14, 1949; s. Jack C. Sr. and Billie R. Gillis; m. Jennifer N. Caillavet, Jan. 12, 1998; 1 child, Brittany L. BBA in Mgmt./Econ., U. Tex., Arlington, 1972; BBA in Real Estate, U. N. Tex., 1982, MBA in Fin., 1983; JD, Tex. A&M U., 1987. Bar: Tex. 1987. Regional mgr. AAMCO Industries, Inc., Phila., 1974-76; capt., asst. dir. Dallas Narcotics Task Force, 1976-81; v.p. Lomas & Nettleton, Dallas, 1981-82; pres., CEO Gillis Devel. Corp., Dallas, 1982-86; atty., ptnr. Burke & Wright, P.C., Dallas, 1986-94; atty. Gillis Law Firm, Dallas, 1994-98; pres., CEO Gillis Energy Corp., Dallas, 1998—; mem. adv. bd. BridgeBuilders, Plano, Tex. Republican. Baptist. Avocations: flying, scuba diving. Fax: 972-633-8787. Office: Gillis Energy Corp PMB 539 18352 Dallas Pkwy Ste 136 Dallas TX 75287-8209

GILLIS, LYNN SINCLAIR, psychiatrist; s. Julius and Ann (Lynn) G.; m. Shirley Emily Lurie, Aug. 20, 1950; children: Susan, Jennifer. MB BCh, U. Witwatersrand, 1948, DPM, 1952, MD, 1955. Resident Tara Hosp., Johannesburg, South Africa, 1949-53, psychiatrist, 1955-62; head, prof. psychiatry U. Capertown, 1962-89; registrar Maudsley Hosp., U. London, 1953-59; mem. Med. Rsch. Coun.; dir. MRC Clin. Psychiatry Rsch. Unit, 1981-89; prof. emeritus U. Capetown, 1989—; sr. psychiatrist UCT and Valkenberg Hosp., Capetown. Author: Human Behavior in Illness, 1961, Guidelines to Psychiatry, 1977; contbr. numerous articles to profl. jours. With S.A. Med. Corp., 1944-46. Recipient Salus award Govt. of South Africa Dept. Health, 1989, Merit award Med. Assn. of South Africa, 1990; fellowship in psychiatry WHO, 1961. Mem. Am. Psychiat. Assn. Avocations: mountaineering, sculptor. Home: 6 Eventide 24 Victoria Rd, Cape Town 8005, South Africa

GILLIS, MICHAEL KERBY, lawyer; b. Boston, Sept. 11, 1957; s. Joseph Leo and Eileen Rose (Fleming) G., m. Dec. 31, 1996, children: Michaela Margaret, Erin Fleming. BA, Boston Coll., 1979; JD, Suffolk U., 1982. Atty. Mut. Liability Ins. Co., Lynn, Mass., 1982-83, Travelers Ins. Co., Boston, 1983-84, Law Offices of Thomas J. Kelley, Wellesley, Mass., 1984-88; ptnr. Gillis & Bikofsky P.C., Newton, Mass., 1988—. Author: Massachusetts Motor Vehicle Torts, 1987, Liquor Liability-Primer for Winning Your Case, 1999. Chmn., trustee Milton Pub. Libr., Mass., 1988-94; bd. dirs. Cath. Lawyers Guild, Boston, 1992—; exec. bd. Mass. Acad. Trial Attys., Boston, 1995—; trustee Suffolk U., Boston, 1996-99. E-mail: mgillis@gillisand bikofsky.com. Office: Gillis & Bikofsky PC 1340 Centre St Newton MA 02459-2499

GILLIS, NELSON SCOTT, financial executive; b. Pitts., May 6, 1953; s. Nelson Williams and Elinor (Miller) G.; m. Vickie Sue Hall, Nov. 22, 1980; children: Michael David, Matthew Daniel, Nathan Alexander, Alexander Joshua, Artyom Jonathan, Kirill Stephen. BS in Acctg., Fla. State U., 1975; postgrad., AEA Exec. Inst., Stanford, 1984. CPA, Ga.; cert. fin. planner. Audit sr. Price Waterhouse & Co., Atlanta, 1975-78; sr. acct. Siemens Energy and Automation, Inc., Atlanta, 1978-80; divsn. contr. Siemens Energy and Automation, Inc., Portland, Oreg., 1980-83; v.p. fin. Integrated Circuits, Inc., Redmond, Wash., 1983-85; dir. Controls Evaluation and

Audit Kaufman & Broad, Inc., Atlanta, 1985-89; v.p., contr. SunAm. Life Ins. Co. Anchor Nat. Life Ins. Co., First Sun Am. Life Ins. Co., L.A., 1989-94, sr. v.p., contr., 1994-99; sr. v.p., contr. CalAm. Life Ins. Co., L.A., 1995-99, SunAm. Nat. Life Ins. Co., L.A., 1996-2000, John Alden Life Ins. Co., N.Y., 1997-98; v.p. SunAm., Inc., 1998—, v.p., contr., 2000—; exec. v.p. SunAmerica Financial, 2000—; sr. v.p., treas. SA Inv. Group, SAL Inv. Group, 2000—; bd. dirs. SunAm. Life, Anchor Nat. Life, First SunAm. Life, SA Investment Group Inc., SAM Holdings Corp., Saamsun Holdings Corp. Bd. dirs., treas. So. Calif. Ski Edn. Found., 1998—. Master fellow Life Inst.; mem. AICPA (life ins. and disability plans com. 1991-94, 98—, task force on disclosure of risks and uncertainties in the ins. industry 1992-95, rels. with actuaries com. 1993-96, ins. plans exec. com. 1995-98, chmn. personal lines ins. com. 1995-98), Inst. CFPs, Life Office Mgmt. Assn. (fin. controls and reports com. 1987-90), Ga. Soc. CPAs (ins. plans com. 1988-89), Ga. Soc. CPAs (ins. plans com. 1988-89), Calif. Soc. CPAs (L.A. mems. in industry, acctg. principles/auditing stds. and ins. industry coms. 1991-94), Ins. Acctg. and Sys. Assn., Internat. Assn. for Fin. Planning, Am. Assn. Individual Investors, Fla. State Alumni Assn., Nat. Assn. Securities Dealers (registered prin. 1989-98), Fin. Execs. Inst., Beta Gamma Sigma, Lambda Chi Alpha. Republican. Office: SunAmerica Inc/Century City 1 Sun Am Ctr MS 36-07 Los Angeles CA 90067-6022

GILLIS, RICHARD, solicitor; b. Dundee, Scotland, Apr. 22, 1950; s. Harold and Anne Gillis; m. Anna Burland, 1982 (div. 1993). Student, Coll. of Law, Guildford, Eng., 1970-73, Kenya Sch. Law, Nairobi, 1977. Lic. solicitor, Eng., 1975; advocate, Kenya, 1978. Solicitor Greater London Coun., 1975-77; advocate Archer & Wilcock, Nairobi, Kenya, 1977-80; solicitor Shoosmiths & Harrison, Northampton, Eng., 1980-81; asst. to sec. TI Group plc, Birmingham, Eng., 1981-85; co. sec. ABB Transp. Holdings Ltd., Derby, Eng., 1985-95; clk. to coun. and co. sec. U. Derby, 1995—; dir. Crewe (Eng.) Devel. Agy., 1992-95, vice-chmn. 1993-95; mem. CBI East Midlands Regional Coun., Eng., 1993-95; trustee ABB Transp. Pension Plan, Derby, 1991-95; mem. Stakeholders' Forum, Derby City Challenge, 1993-98. Chmn. property com. Coun. of Order of St. John for Derbyshire, 1994—, Officer of the Order, 1999; regional mem., coun. and chpt. chmn. audit com. and Priory Regulations Steering Group, Priory of England and Islands of the Order of St. John, 1999—; trustee St. John Ambulance, 1999—. Fellow Royal Soc. Arts (life); mem. Licensing Execs. Soc., Worshipful Co. of Basketmakers (liveryman), Nairobi Club (life, liveryman, steward 2000—), Reform Club, East India Club, City Livery Club (life), The Maccabaeans, Guild of Freemen of City of London (life). Avocation: music, historical films, watching tennis. Home: Thatched Cottage, Shirley, Ashbourne Derbyshire DE6 3AS, England Office: U Derby, Kedleston Rd, Derby DE22 1GB, England

GILLISPIE, HAROLD LEON, minister; b. Levant, Kans., May 11, 1933; s. Harold Leon and Agnes Anne (Dryden) G. BA in Bus. Adminstrn., Kans. Wesleyan U., 1955. Youth dir. Cen. YMCA, Des Moines, 1957-61; exec. dir. West Des Moines br. YMCA, 1961-65; exec. dir. Aurora Br. YMCA, Denver, 1965-69; exec. dir. YMCA, McCook, Nebr., 1969-75, Junction City, Kans., 1975-79; owner H & R Block Franchise, Manhattan, Kans., 1979-91; lay pastor Presbyn. Ch., Oak Hill, Kans., 1996—; vice moderator Presbyn. of Northern Kans., 1999-00, moderator, 2000—; proof-reader text H & R Block, Kansas City, Mo., 1986-92. Bd. dirs. Flint Hills Breadbasket, Manhattan, Kans., 1982-89, treas., 1987; bd. dirs. Big Bros. Big Sisters, Manhattan, 1981-85, pres., 1983-85; pres. Downtown Manhattan, Inc., 1986; bd. dirs. Manhattan Main Street, 1986-89; bd. dirs. Ecumenical Campus Ministry, Kans. State U., 1995-99, chmn., 1996-98. Republican. Presbyterian. Avocations: theology, tennis, baking, working with youth. Home: 710 Bertrand St Manhattan KS 66502-5156

GILLMAN, LEONARD, mathematician, educator; b. Cleve., Jan. 8, 1917; s. Joseph Moses and Etta Judith (Cohen) G.; m. Reba Parks Marcus, Dec. 24, 1938; children: Jonathan Webb, Michal Judith. Diploma (fellow in piano 1933-38), Juilliard Grad. Sch. Music, 1938; BS, Columbia U., 1941, MA (Carnegie fellow math. statistics 1942-43), 1945, PhD, 1953. Asst. in math. dept. Columbia U., 1941-42, lectr., 1942-43; ops. analyst Tufts Coll., MIT, 1943-51; from instr. to assoc. prof. math. Purdue U., 1952-60; prof. math., chmn. dept. U. Rochester, 1960-69; prof. math. U. Tex., Austin, 1969-87, prof. emeritus, 1987, chmn. dept., 1969-73; mem. Inst. Advanced Study, Princeton, 1958-60; cons. editor W.W. Norton Co., Inc., 1967-80. Author: (with Meyer Jerison) Rings of Continuous Functions, 1960, 76, You'll Need Math, 1967, (with Robert H. McDowell) Calculus, 1973, 78, Writing Mathematics Well, 1987; mem. editorial bd. Topology and Its Applications, 1971-94. Guggenheim fellow, 1958-59; NSF sr. post-doctoral fellow, 1959-60. Mem. Am. Math. Soc. (assoc. sec. 1969-71, mem. com. to monitor problems in commn. 1972-77), Nat. Coun. Tchrs. Math., Math. Assn. Am. (bd. govs. 1973-95, treas. 1973-86, pres.-elect 1986-87, pres. 1987-89, past pres. 1989-90, Lester R. Ford award for expository writing 1994, Yueh-Gin Gung and Dr. Charles Y. Hu award for disting. svc. to math. 1999). Home and Office: 1606 The High Rd Austin TX 78746-2236

GILLMAN, MARK ALFRED, medical research facility administrator, dentist; b. Johannesburg, Transvaal, South Africa, Nov. 18, 1943; s. Michael and Martha (Rosenthall) G.; m. Barbara Louise Solomon, Sept. 1, 1968; children: Michael, Luis, Sarah. B in Dental Sci., Wits U., Johannesburg, 1968; MSc, Potch U., Potchefstroom, South Africa, 1982, DSc, 1985. Pvt. practice dentistry Johannesburg, 1968-89; sr. lectr. dentistry Wits U., 1981-85; exec. dir. South African Brain Rsch. Inst., Johannesburg, 1981—; hon. clin. pharmacologist Rand Aid Soc., Johannesburg, 1982—; hon. clin. cons. Kwa Zulu (Natal, South Africa) Health Dept., 1987—; hon. rsch. assoc. Wits U., 1993-94; dir. addiction rsch. unit Rand Aid-South African Brain Rsch. Inst., 1984—; pharmacological advisor Coun. Sci. Indsl. Rsch., Pretoria, South Africa, 1982—; mem. com. Primary Health Care, Pretoria, 1993—. Author: Envy as a Retarding Force in Science, 1996; contbr. over 250 articles to local and internat. sci. jours. Recipient Elida Gibbs award, Johannesburg, 1981, 88; Sailor Malan fellow U. Wits, 1982, 83. Jewish. Avocations: music, aviation. Home: PO Box 1315, Highland North 2037, South Africa Office: S African Brain Rsch Inst, 6 Campbell St, Waverly 2090, Johannesburg South Africa

GILLMAN-WELLS, JAY, lawyer; b. Launceston, Tasmania, Australia, Apr. 2, 1965; d. Derek Carl and Beverly Jean (Kemp) H.; m. Jeremy Robert Gillman-Wells (div. Oct. 1999); children: Jamie Brooke, Christopher Charles. Diploma in law, U. Sydney, Australia, 1992; LLM, U. NSW, Sydney, Australia, 1995. Solicitor Abbot Tout, Sydney, 1992; dir. legal svcs. Internat. Mgmt. Group Am., Sydney, 1997-98; sr. legal counsel ISL TV Ltd. (U.K.), 1999—; ptnr. Nicholson Graham & Jones-Solicitors, London; bd. dirs. ISL TV (U.K.) Ltd., London. Author: Generic Drafting Clauses in Media-underworks. Mem. Soc. Sr. Execs. Avocations: writing, sports. Home: 51 St Nicholas Crescent, Pyrford Surrey GU22 8TD, England Office: Nicholson Graham & Jones, 110 Cannon Street, London EC4N6AR, England

GILLON, RAANAN EVELYN ZVI, medical ethicist, family physician, editor; b. Jerusalem, Apr. 15, 1941; arrived in Eng., 1947; s. Meir and Diana (Case) G.; m. Angela Spear, 1966; 1 child, Rachel. Med. journalist, editor Med. News Tribune, Med. Tribune, 1964-71; various hosp. positions U.K. Nat. Health Svc., London, 1971-74; part-time gen. med. practice London, 1974—; clin. asst. dermatology Univ. Coll. Hosp., London, 1975-82; part-time dir. Imperial Coll. Health Svc., London, 1982-95; vis. prof. med. ethics Kings Coll., London, 1988-91, Imperial Coll., 1989-95, full prof., 1995-99, prof. emeritus, 2000—, chmn. ethics com., 2000—; mem. governing body Inst. Med. Ethics, London, 1989—; mem. med. ethics Archbishop of Canterbury's Adv. Group, 1999—. Author: Philosophical Medical Ethics, 1985; contbg. author, sr. editor: Prins. Health Care Ethics, 1994; editor Jour. Med. Ethics, 1981-2001; contbr. numerous articles on med. ethics to profl. jours. Recipient Henry Knowles Beecher award for contbns. to ethics and life scis. Hastings Ctr., Garrison, N.Y., 1999. Fellow Royal Coll. Physicians, Royal Soc. Medicine; mem. Royal Coll. Music (hon.), Brit. Med. Assn. (mem. ethics com. 1998—), Internat. Assn. Bioethics (bd. mem. 1992-99), Soc. Applied Philosophy, European Soc. for Philosophy in Medicine and Health Care, U.K. Forum for Health Care Ethics and Law, Med. Journalists Assn. (founder), Brit. Sci. Writers Assn. Avocations: family activities, skiing, swimming, cooking, reading. Home: 42 Brynmaer Rd, London SW11 4EW, England Office: Imperial Coll Health Ctr, Southside Prince's Gardens, London SW7 1LU, England

GILLY, FRANÇOIS-NOEL, surgeon, educator, researcher; b. Lyon, France, May 1, 1955; s. Robert and Jacqueline (Rivoire) G. MD, Lyon (France) U., 1980; degree in general surgery, Lyon Hosp., 1995. Intern Lyon U. Hosp., 1980-84; assoc. prof. U. Lyon, 1989-95, prof., 1995—, dean faculty medicine, 1999—; rsch. dir. Oncologic Lab., Lyon, 1986—. Author: Intra Peritoneal Chest Hyperthermia, 1990, Surgical Gene Therapy in Oncology, 1995. Pres. Art Humanitaire, Lyon, 1994—. Recipient Rsch. prize A. Poncet, France, 1989. Mem. Internat. Soc. Clin. Hyperthermia (pres. 1992), Internat. Soc. Operative Radiation (treas. 1996), Internat. Gastro Surg. Club, French Soc. Surgery. Avocations: yachting, theatre. Office: Lyon Univ CHLS, Dept Surgery, 69495 Pierre Benite Cedex, France

GILMAN, ALFRED GOODMAN, pharmacologist, educator; b. New Haven, July 1, 1941; s. Alfred and Mabel (Schmidt) G.; m. Kathryn Hedlund, Sept. 21, 1963; children: Amy, Anne, Edward. BS, Yale U., 1962; MD, PhD, Case Western Res. U., 1969; DSc (hon.), U. Chgo., 1991, Case Western Res. U., 1995; DMS, Yale U., 1997; DSc (hon.), U. Miami, 1999. Pharmacology research assoc. NIH, Bethesda, Md., 1969-71; from asst. prof. to assoc. prof. pharmacology U. Va., Charlottesville, 1971-77, prof., 1977-81, dir. med. sci. tng. program, 1979-81; prof. pharmacology, chmn. dept. U. Tex. Southwestern Med. Ctr., Dallas, 1981—, Raymond and Ellen Willie disting. chmn. molecular neuropharmacology, 1987—, regental prof., 1994—; mem. pharmacology study sect. NIH, 1977-81, mem. nat. adv. gen. med. scis. coun., 1992-95; bd. sci. counselors Nat. Heart, Lung & Blood Inst. NIH, 1982-86; sci. adv. com. Am. Cancer Soc., N.Y.C., 1982-86; adv. com. Lucille P. Markey Charitable Trust, Miami, Fla., 1984-96; sci. rev. bd. Howard Hughes Med. Inst., Bethesda, 1986-93; dir. Regeneron Pharmaceutics, 1989—, Eli Lilly and Co., Inc., 1995—; mem. vis. com. Sch. Medicine Case Western Reserve U., 1995—; mem. sci. adv. bd. Huntsman Cancer Inst. U. Utah, 1995—, Ernest Gallo Clinic and Rsch. Ctr. U. Calif., San Francisco, 1996—. Editor: The Pharmacological Basis of Therapeutics, 1975, 80, 85, 90; consulting editor, 1996; contbr. over 225 articles to profl. jours. Recipient Poul Edvard Poulsson award Norwegian Pharmacology Soc., 1982, GairdnerFound. Internat. award, Can., 1984, Albert Lasker Basic Med. Rsch. award, 1989, Passano Sr. award Passano Found., 1990, Waterford Biomedical Sci. award Scripps Clinic and Rsch. Found. 1990, Basic Sci. Rsch. prize Am. Heart Assn., 1990, Steven C. Beering award Ind. U., 1990, City of Medicine award, Durham, N.C., 1991, CIBA-GEIGY Drew award, 1991, Nobel Prize in Physiology or Medicine, 1994, ACP award, 1995, Disting. Alumnus award Case Western Reserve U., 1995, Am. Acad. Achievement award, 1995, Med. Honor award Am. Cancer Soc., 1995. Mem. Am. Soc. Pharmacology & Exptl. Therapeutics (John J. Abel award in pharmacology 1975, Louis S. Goodman and Alfred Gilman award 1990, Torald Sollman award 1997), Am. Soc. Biol. Chemistry, Nat. Acad. Scis. (Richard Lounsbery award 1987), Am. Acad. Arts and Scis., Inst. Medicine of NAS. Office: U Tex Southwestern Med Ctr Dept Pharmacology 5323 Harry Hines Blvd Dallas TX 75390-7208

GILMAN, SHELDON GLENN, lawyer; b. Cleve., July 20, 1943. BBA, Ohio U., 1965; JD, Case Western Res. U., 1967. Bar: Ohio 1967, Ky. 1971, Ind. 1982, Fla. 1984, D.C. 1985, Tenn. 1985, U.S. Supreme Ct. 1987. Assoc./ptnr. Louisville law firms, 1972—; ptnr. Lynch, Cox, Gilman & Mahan, P.S.C., Louisville, 1987—; gen. counsel Louisville Assn. Life Underwriters, 1977, 78, 90; adj. prof. law U. of Louisville Sch. of Law. Bd. dirs., chmn. Louisville Minority Bus. Resource Ctr., 1975-80; pres. Congregation Adath Jeshurun, 1986-88; bd. dirs., v.p., sec. Louisville Orch., 1982-85; bd. dirs. City of Devondale, Ky., 1976, United Synagogue of Cons. Judaism, N.Y., 1989—, also pres. Ohio Valley region. With JAGC, AUS, 1968-71. Fellow Am. Coll. Trust and Estate Counsel, Am. Bar Found.; mem. ACLU (bd. dirs. 1998—), Ky. Bar Assn. (ethics com. 1982—, ethics hotline com. 1990), Louisville Employee Benefit Council (pres. 1980). Office: Lynch Cox Gilman & Mahan 400 W Market St Ste 2200 Louisville KY 40202-3354

GILMARTIN, CLARA T., volunteer; b. East Stroudsburg, Pa., Jan. 23, 1922; d. Harry and Clarissa (Snearley) Treible; m. John Gilmartin, Jan. 18, 1945 (dec. Feb. 1956); children: Ronald, Donald; m. William Gilmartin, Mar. 17, 1973 (dec., 1992). BA, Rutgers U., 1961, MA, 1966. Elem. sch. tchr. Union Beach (N.J.) Pub. Sch., 1956-61; lang. arts tchr. Holmdel Village (N.J.) Intermediate Sch., 1961-82. Chair bd. trustees Grace Meth. Ch., Union Beach, 1997—. Mem. Monmouth County Retired Educators Assn., Am. Legion (Post 321 Color Guard scholarship com., trustee). Democrat. Home: PO Box 143 Keyport NJ 07735-0143

GILMARTIN, RAYMOND V., health care products company executive; b. Washington, Mar. 6, 1941; m. Gladys Higham; 3 children. BS in Elect. Engring., Union Coll., 1963; MBA, Harvard U., 1968. Sr. cons. Arthur D. Little Inc., 1968-76; v.p. corp. planning Becton Dickinson & Co., Paramus, N.J., 1976-79, pres. Becton Dickinson divsn., 1979-87, group pres., 1982-83, sr. v.p., 1983-86, exec. v.p., 1986-87; pres. Becton Dickinson & Co., Franklin Lakes, N.J., 1987-94, CEO, 1989-94, also bd. dirs.; chmn., pres., CEO Merck, White House Station, NJ, 1994—; bd. dirs. Pub. Svc. Enterprise Group; dir. Gen. Mills, Inc.; chmn. Inter-faculty initative in Health Policy, adv. bd. Harvard U. Trustee Valley Health Systems, Inc., Ridgewood, N.J.; bd. dirs. Coll. Fund/United Negro Coll. Fund, Pharm. Rsch. and Mfrs. Am., Healthcare Leadership Coun.; vice-chmn. Healthcare Inst. of N.J. bd. dirs., bd. assocs. Harvard Bus. Sch.; mem. Bus. Coun., Bus. Roundtable, Com. Econ. Devel.; chmn. exec. com. Coun. on Competitiveness; mem. Alliance for Healthcare Reform. Office: Merck & Co 1 Merck Dr Whitehouse Station NJ 08889-3497

GILMORE, DAVID SCHNEITER, administrator; b. St. Louis, Nov. 27, 1951. BS in Psychology, S.E. Mo. U., 1974, MA in Psychology, 1981. Bd. cert. psychotherapist; cert. hypnotherapist. Chief psychologist State of Mo., Farmington, 1975-80; pvt. practice Farmington, 1978-80; prof. State of Mo., Flat River, 1978-80; rehab. cons. Ft. Myers, 1980-85; adminstr., dir. Ctr. for Pain Control, Ft. Myers, 1985-91; adminstr. Bayshore Workplaces, Ft. Myers, 1990-91, Vocat. and Rehab. Svcs., Ft. Myers, 1980—; prin. The Gilmore Clinic, Ft. Myers, Sarasota, St. Petersburg, Orlando, St. Louis, Miami, Fla., 1986—; rehab. cons. Walt Disney World, Orlando, Fla., 1998—; dir. rehab. AAR Svcs., 1990—. Mem. Am. Psychol. Assn., Fla. Rehab. Assn. (pres. S.E. chpt.).

GILMORE, DUNCAN BARTLETT, mechanical engineer; b. Townsville, Queensland, Australia, Nov. 29, 1951; s. George Harold and Nell (Philp) G.; m. Jennifer Lynne Voigt, Mar. 8, 1975; children: Benjamin James, Kate Lisa. BSME, U. Queensland, 1972, MS in Engring., 1974, PhD, 1978. Chartered profl. engr. Project engr. Queensland Elec. Commn., Brisbane, Australia, 1977-79; sr. rsch. fellow U. Queensland, Brisbane, 1979-85, sr. lectr., 1986-93; vis. prof. Mass. Inst. Tech., Boston, 1988, MITI Labs., Tsukuba, Japan, 1988; pres. Gilmore Engrs. Ltd., Brisbane, 1993—. Contbr. to profl. jours.; patentee in field. Recipient U. of Queensland medal, 1972. Fellow Inst. Engrs. Australia (nat. v.p. 1991, 92, chmn. mech. coll. 1989-93); mem. ASME, Soc. Auto. Engrs. Australia (RODDA award and medal, 1982). Mem. Australian Liberal Party. Anglican. Avocations: swimming, tennis, sailing, theatre. Home: 16 Corella Ave, Brisbane 4520, Australia Office: Gilmore Engrs Pty Ltd, QLD Clunies Ross Ctr, Miles Platting Rd, Eight Mile Plains 4113, Australia

GILMORE, FIONA CATHERINE, consultant; b. London, Nov. 7, 1956; d. Robin and Jean Margaret (Herring) Triefus; m. Richard J.M. Gilmore, May 5, 1979; children: Daniel, Alex, Edward. MA in Modern Langs., Cambridge (Eng.) U., 1977. With Ted Bates Advt. Agy., London, 1977-78, Benton & Bowles Advt. Agy., London, 1978-84; mktg. dir. Michael Peters & Ptnrs., London, 1985, devel. dir., 1986, mng. dir., 1987-90; mng. dir. Lewis Moberly, London, 1990-91; mng. dir., founding ptnr. Springpoint Ltd., London, 1991—, Springpoint Inc., N.Y.C., 1996—; coun. mem. Water Aid, London, 1997—. Editor: Brand Warriors, 1997, 99; contbr. CBI Growing Business Handbook, 1997. Fellow RSA. Mem. Ch. of Eng. Avocations: music, skiing, sailing, tennis. Office: Springpoint Ltd, 31 Corsica St, London N51JT, England

GILMORE, JAMES STANLEY, JR., broadcast executive; b. Kalamazoo, June 14, 1926; s. James Stanley and Ruth (McNair) G.; m. Diana Holdenreide Fell, May 21, 1949 (dec.); children: Bethany, Sydney, James III, Elizabeth, Ruth. Student, Culver Mil. Acad., Western Mich. U., Kalamazoo Coll., 1945; Litt.D. (hon.), Nazareth Coll. Owner, chmn. CEO Jim Gilmore Enterprises, Kalamazoo, 1960—; CEO Gilmore Broadcasting Corp.; chmn. Cole/Gilmore; chmn., dir. Continental Corp. Mich.; former asst. sec. dir. Fabri-Kal Plastics Corp., Kalamazoo; pres. Wings Stadium Mgmt. Co.; former dir. First Am. Bank-Mich. N.A., First Am. Bank Corp.; former mem. Pres.' Citizens Adv. Com. on Environ. Quality; former dir. Fed. Home Loan Bank Bd., Indpls.; mem. past chmn. Mich. Water Resources Commn.; past mem. Pres.'s Commn. Health Phys. Edn. Sports; Nat. Assn. Broadcasters' adv. com. to Corp. for Pub. Broadcasting; pres. Kalamazoo County Young Rep. Club, 1947-49; mayor Kalamazoo, 1959-61; past mem. Kalamazoo County Bd. Suprs.; past chmn. exec. com. Kalamazoo County Reps., del. Rep. Nat. Conv. Assoc. bd. dirs.; 1st 4-time Indy 500-mile race with AJ Foyt as driver (Gilmore/Foyt Team). Assoc. bd. dirs. Boys Clubs Am.; bd. dirs., past chmn. Kalamazoo County chpt. A.R.C.; former chmn. bd. trustees Nazareth Coll.; trustee, mem. finance com. Greater Mich. Devel. Found.; mem., chmn. bldg. com. fund dr. Constance Brown Speech and Hearing Center; past trustee Kalamazoo Coll.; mem. adv. group Center Urban Studies and Community Services; trustee past vice chmn. Kalamazoo Nature Center; mem. bldg. and exec. coms. Bronson Hosp., also chmn. ad hoc legis. com.; past trustee, past v.p. Mich. Found. for Arts, Detroit; founding chmn. Kalamazoo City High on Heroes; founder bd. dirs. Martin Luther King Meml. Fund; life dir. Family Service Center Kalamazoo; mem. Mich. bd. dirs. Radio Free Europe, Novi Motorsports Mus.; nat. sponsor Ducks Unltd.; life mem. March Dimes; chmn. spl. reorganizational com. United Fund; mem. fund raising com. Pres. Ford Library/Mus.; mem. Pres.'s Council Phys. Fitness and Sports; mem. Republican Nat. Adv. Bd.; hon. trustee Mich. Alvin Bentley Charitable Found.; trustee emeritus coun. Kalamazoo Found. Served with USAAF, 1943-46. Named Kalamazoo Young Man of 1960, One of Mich.'s 5 Young Men of 1960, hon. citizen of Houston and Indpls.; recipient Ann. Service to Mankind award Sertoma Club, Man of Yr. award Mich. Auto Racing Fan Club, Auto Racing Found. Frat., honors Hoosier Racing Assn., Auto Racing Frat. Found., Inc., Milw. Mem. Kalamazoo County C. of C. (past pres., dir., mem. exec. com., indsl. devel. com.), Mich. C. of C. (law and order com.), NAM, Mich. Acad. Sci., Arts and Letters, Capitol Hill Club, Nat. Captioning Inst. (bd. dirs.), Park Club (past dir.), Mid-Am. Club, Kalamazoo Country Club, Met. Club. Roman Catholic. Office: Jim Gilmore Enterprises 162 E Michigan Ave Kalamazoo MI 49007-3908

GILMORE, JENNIFER A.W., computer specialist, educator; b. San Fernando, Trinidad, Jan. 12, 1954; came to U.S., 1972; d. Fitzroy Grant and Zelma (Williams) Oudkerk; m. Frederick R. Gilmore, June 17, 1983. BA, MA, Bklyn. Coll., 1984; BBA, MS, Baruch Coll., 1993; MBA, L.I. U., 1994; postgrad., Walden U., 1994—. COBOL programmer MetLife, N.Y.C., 1972-86; computer specialist, sr. sys. analyst human resources adminstrn. mgmt. info. sys. City of N.Y., 1990—; adj. prof. N.Y.C. Tech. Coll., 1997—, Kingsborough C.C., 1998—, St. Francis Coll., Bklyn., 1998—, Medgar Evers Coll., 1998—, Borough of Manhattan C.C., 1998—, Touro Coll., 1999—, Baruch Coll., 1999—, Monroe Coll., 1999—. Home: 47 Mckeever Pl Apt 16J Brooklyn NY 11225-2537 Office: NYC-HRA-MIS 111 8th Ave New York NY 10011-5201

GILMORE, JUDITH MARIE, physician; b. Houston, Dec. 28, 1942; d. Howard Ray and Mary Gardner (Currier) G.; m. Richard E. Kelley, July 21, 1974 (div. 1981); 1 child, Lisa Kelley. BA, U. Maine, 1965; MA, NYU, 1968; MD, Woman's Med. Coll., 1972. Diplomate Am. Bd. Internal Medicine, Am. Bd. Endocrinology. Resident St. Vincent's Hosp., N.Y.C., 1972-74; fellow in endocrinology St. Raphael's Hosp., New Haven, 1974-75, West Haven VA-Yale Hosp., New Haven, 1975-76; pvt. practice Bridgeport, Conn., 1976-80, Cranston, R.I., 1986—; mem. staff St. Joseph's Hosp., Providence, 1986—; mem. cons. staff Newport (R.I.) Hosp., 1986—; mem. courtesy staff Roger Williams Hosp., Providence, 1994—, R.I. Hosp., Providence, 1995. Lt. comdr. USNR, 1980-86. Mem. ACP, AMA, Am. Assn. Endocrine, Am. Diabetes Assn., R.I. Endocrine Assn. Avocations: hiking, music, art. Office: 725 Reservoir Ave Ste 2 Providence RI 02910-4450

GILMOUR, THOMAS CALUM, publisher, priest; b. Auckland, New Zealand, Nov. 16, 1936; s. Walter Allison and Amy Barbara (Lilly) G.; m. Raewyn Joy Figg, May 9, 1961; children: Stephen, Phillip, Simon. LTh with honors, St. John's Coll., Auckland, 1959; BA, U. Auckland, 1974, MA, 1976, PhD, 1983. Ordained priest Anglican Ch., 1959. Vicar Anglican Diocese of Auckland, 1964-96, dir. No. Ministry Tng., 1993-98; sr. lectr. St. George's Coll., Jerusalem, 1998; mng. dir. Polygraphia Ltd., Auckland, 1998—; lectr. dept. classics U. Auckland, 1976-97; instr. Motor Cycle Riding Sch., Auckland, 1985-95. Author: A Guide to Mark's Gospel, 1996, Galilee and the Historical Jesus, 1999, The Sound of the Gospel, 1999; contbr. articles to profl. jours. Mem. Auckland Motorcycle Club Inc. (life mem., sec. 1980-89). Avocations: boating, motorcycling. Office: Polygraphia Ltd, PO Box 60-505, Titirangi Auckland 1007, New Zealand

GILMUTDINOV, ALBERT KHARISOVICH, physicist, educator; b. Kazan, Russia, July 27, 1956; s. Kharis and Sania Gilmutdinov; m. Guzel Gilmutdinova, 1955; children: Lilia, Alina. MS, Kazan State U., 1978, PhD, 1983, DSc, 1999. From sr. rschr. to asst. prof. State U., Kazan, 1983-88, assoc. prof., 1988-95, prof., 1997—; vis. prof. Carleton U., Ottawa, Ont., Can., 1991-92, Perkin-Elmer Co., Überlingen, Germany, 1995-97. Recipient Johanus Marcus Marci medal, 1998. Mem. Soc. Applied Spectroscopy, N.Y. Acad. Scis. Avocations: books, soccer, cross-country skiing. Home: Chekhova St 51-70, 4200043 Kazan Tatarst, Russia Office: State U Dept Physics, Kremlevskaja St, 420 008 Kazan Tatarst, Russia

GILOT, PHILIPPE JULES JEAN, molecular biologist, researcher; b. Namur, Belgium, May 11, 1961; s. Pol and Thérèse (Gilon) G. Graduat Degree in Clin. Chemistry, U. Louvain, Brussels, 1984, Licence Degree in Biomed. Tech., 1986, PhD in Biomed. Scis., 1993. Rschr. Internat. Inst. Cellular and Molecular Pathology, Brussels, 1986-93, Inst. Hygiene and Epidemiology, Brussels, 1994-97, Pasteur Inst., Brussels, 1997—. Contbr. articles to profl. jours. Specialization fellow Institut Pour L'Encouragement De La Recherche Scientifique Dans L'Industrie Et L'Agriculture, Brussels, 1989-91, Eugene Yourassowsky award, 2000. Mem. Am. Soc. Microbiology, Internat. Assn. for Paratuberculosis, Belgian Soc. Biochemistry, Belgian Soc. Microbiology. Avocation: classical guitar. Office: INRA Lab Path Infect Immun, Domaine de l'Orfrasiere, 37380 Nouzilly France

GILPATRIC, LAWRENCE, hospitality management educator; b. Bridgeport, Conn., Aug. 3, 1948; s. Ralph Edwin and Doris Rose (McCormack) G.; m. Suzanne Bronstein, Aug. 10, 1975; children: Rebecca Lynn, Jeremy Todd, Brendan Scott. AS, Manchester Community Coll., 1978; BS, Charter Oak Coll., 1990; MS, Cen. Conn. State U., 1991; sixth yr. cert., So. Conn. State U., 1994. Cert. hotel adminstr., foodsvc. mgmt. profl., exec. chef, culinary educator. Exec. chef Holiday Inns, Bridgeport and New London, Conn., 1971-73; chef mgr. Szabo Food Svc., Hartford, Conn., 1973-74; chef instr. Assoc. Restaurants of Conn., Hartford, Conn., 1974-77; exec. chef Burning Tree Country Club, Greenwich, Conn., 1977-79; pres. Stowe's Pilot House Restaurant, West Haven, Conn., 1979-81; exec. chef Coveleigh Club, Rye, N.Y., 1981-84; gen. mgr. H. B. Brownson Country Club, Huntington, Conn., 1984-88; asst. prof. Gateway Community-Tech. Coll., New Haven, 1987-95; assoc. prof., coord. hospitality mgmt. U. Akron, Ohio, 1995—; interim gen. mgr. Winged Foot Golf Club, Mamaroneck, N.Y., 1991; satirical columnist Naugatuck Daily News, 1993-94; mgr. Copper Valley Club, Cheshire, Conn., 1994-95. Lector St. Vincent Ferrer Ch., Naugatuck, Conn., 1990-95; cantor Holy Spirit Ch., Uniontown, Ohio, 1996—. With USMC, 1966-69. H. J. Heinz Grad. fellow The Edn. Found. of Nat. Restaurant Assn., 1991; recipient Silver Plate scholarship Nat. Inst. Foodservice Industry, 1977, Excellence in Edn. award, 1991. Home: 312 W Maple St Hartville OH 44632-9689 Office: U Akron 102 Gallucci Hl Akron OH 44325-0001

GILSINN, DAVID EDMUND, mathematician, researcher; b. Washington, Jan. 25, 1943; s. David Leo and Doris (Dyson) G.; m. Judith Helen Forward, Aug. 6, 1966; 1 child, James David. BS, Georgetown U., 1964, PhD, 1969; MS, Rutgers U., 1966. Mathematician Melpar, Inc., McLean, Va., 1969-70, Nat. Inst. Standards & Tech., Gaithersburg, Md., 1970—. Contbr. articles to profl. jours. Fundraiser, co-chair St. Rose Lima Cath. Ch.,

Gaithersburg, 1993-99. Recipient Bronze medal U.S. Dept. Commerce, Washington, 1994. Mem. ASME, Am. Soc. Precision Engring., Soc. Indsl. & Applied Math. Democrat. Office: Nat Inst Standards & Tech Rm B102 Bldg 223 Gaithersburg MD 20899-0001

GILSON, WARREN E., medical inventor; b. Seattle, Mar. 20, 1917; s. Lucian Ellsworth Gilson and Katherine Berto. BS, U. Wis., 1937, MD, 1940. Intern Milw. Hosp., 1940-41; post doctoral fellow U. Wis., Madison, 1941-45; special cons. USAF, Dayton, Ohio, 1943-45; founder Gilson, Inc., Middleton, Wis., 1945—; founder Gilson, Inc., 1945. Inventor in field. Mem. N.Y. Acad. Scis. Office: Gilson Inc 3000 W Beltline Hwy Middleton WI 53562-1617

GIMBEL, ALFRED ADOLF, employee benefits professional; b. Ladendorf, Austria, Nov. 5, 1944; came to U.S., 1969; s. Adolf and Olga (Hiltz) G.; m. Judy Mae Adams, Mar. 22, 1968; children: Heidi Lynn, Shannon Noel. BSc, U. Man., 1965. Mgmt. trainee GM, Winnipeg, Man., Can., 1965-66; group underwriter, rep. Gt. West Life, Winnipeg, 1966-69, mgr. underwriting, group mgr., 1972-75; group mgr., dir. group sales IDS Life Ins. Co., Detroit and Mpls., 1969-72; cons., exec. v.p., sec.-treas. Byerly & Co., Inc., Denver, 1975—, also bd. dirs.; mgr. Rocky Mountain Region Watson Wyatt Worldwide, 1994—. Bd. dirs. Perry Park Met. Dist., Larkspur, Colo., 1986-88. Mem. Denver Rustlers, Optimist Internat., Perry Park Country Club. Republican. Lutheran. Avocations: golf, skiing, cycling, reading. *

GIMBEL, HERVEY WILLIS, medical administrator; b. Calgary, Alta., Can., Nov. 25, 1926; s. Jacob Allen Gimbel and Ruth Helen Johnson; m. Ann Matterand Gimbel, Dec. 23, 1951; children: Shirley Tetz, Denise Ayoub, Kenneth, Marlin, Beverly Kramer. BA, Walla Walla Coll., 1950; MD, Loma Linda U., 1955, MPH, 1978. Diplomate Nat. Bd. Medicine; cert. Am. Bd. Preventive Medicine. Med. dir. North Hill Med. Clinic, Calgary, 1957-82; assoc. prof. Loma Linda (Calif.) U., 1982-84; med. dir. Parkview Ctr. for Occupl. Medicine, Riverside, Calif., 1985-91, Rancho Canyon Occupl. Medicine, Temecula, Calif., 1991—; cons. China Nat. Health Edn. Inst., Beijing, 1992—; dir. China-U.S.A. Health Project, Redlands, Calif., 1991—, Health Edn. Ctr., Calgary, 1969-82. Contbr. articles to periodicals. Flight lt. Royal Can. Air Force Res., 1958-60. Recipient China Tobacco Control award Chinese Assn. on Smoking and Health, 2000. Fellow Am. Coll. Preventive Medicine; mem. Am. Coll. Environ. and Occupl. Medicine, Med. Coll. Can. (licentiate), Delta Omega. Avocations: traveling, photography, history. Home: PO Box 1167 Redlands CA 92373-0383 Office: Prime Care Med Group 27699 Jefferson Ave Temecula CA 92590-2661

GIMELSTOB, JUSTIN, professional tennis player; b. Livingston, N.J., Jan. 26, 1977. Professional tennis player, 1996—. Office: c/o USTA 70 W Red Oak Ln White Plains NY 10604-3602*

GIMENEZ-DIXON, MARIANO, conservationist; b. Corrientes, Argentina, Oct. 9, 1955; s. Jorge Joaquin Gimenez-Dixon and Laura Gonzalez-Cazón. Licentiate in ecology, U. La Plata, Argentina, 1979, D of Natural Scis., 1991. Mem. profl. staff Dir. Natural Resources, Buenos Aires, 1980-84; mem. profl. staff Dir. Natural Resources and Ecology, Buenos Aires, 1984-87, chief dept. fauna and commercialization, 1986-88; mem. profl. staff Dir. Natural Environments Conservation, Buenos Aires, 1987-88, 89-91; ecology advisor to v.p. Natural Resources and Environ. Commn., Buenos Aires, 1988-89; program officer species survival program Internat. Union Conservation of Nature and Natural Resources, Gland, Switzerland, 1991—; mem. bd. dirs. Profl. Coun. Natural Scis., Buenos Aires, 1986-88, sec. bd. dirs., 1988-90, mem. Auditory Commn., 1990-91; mem. conservation policy and program com. World Pheasant Assn., 1996—. Contbr. articles to sci. jours., including Game Wildlife, Jour. Conchology, others. Mem. Argentine Ecol. Assn., Soc. Argentina Estudio de los Mamíferos, Soc. Zool. del Plata, Wildlife Soc., Nat. Geographic Soc. Office: IUCN World Conservation Un, Mauverney 28, CH 1196 Gland Switzerland

GIMENEZ LLORT, LYDIA, biologist, researcher; b. El Masnou, Spain, Sept. 13, 1966; d. Antonio and Merce (Llort Sender) G.; m. Thierry Pardo Chassel, Oct. 17, 1998. BA, U. Barcelona, Spain, 1989; MS in Biology, U. Barcelona, 1991, PhD in Biology, 1996. Postdoctoral student Karolinska Inst., Stockholm, Sweden, 1996-98; rschr. Autonomous U. Barcelona, 1999—. Vol. Coob Olympic Com. Barcelona, 1992; chief of assistants of Asian Delegations, Paralympic Games, 1992; sec. Friends of China Assn., 1993-96. Mem. Catalan Soc. Biology, N.Y. Acad. Scis., Spanish Soc. Neuroscience. Roman Catholic. Office: Univ Autonoma De Barcelona, Campus Bellaterra, 08193 Bellaterra Spain

GIMENO SANZ, ANA MARIA, philology lecturer, researcher; b. Narborough, U.K., Mar. 19, 1962; d. Salvador and Ana Maria Sanz; m. Juan Vicente Martinez Luciano, Feb. 3, 1989. Degree in English Philology, U. Valencia, 1985, PhD in English Lit., 1990. Prof. titular de escuela univerditaria U. Polytech. of Valencia, 1985-95, prof. titular de universidad, 1995—; multimedia devel. project mgr. U. Polytech. Valencia. Author: Multimedia Spanish Courseware on CD-ROM, 1997, 98, W.H. Auden: Edicion bilingue anotada de "In Time of War". Mem. European Assn. for Computer Assisted Lang. Learning. Avocations: travel, reading, theatre. E-mail address: agimeno@idm.upv.es. Office: U Polytech Valencia, Camino de Vera 14, 46022 Valencia Spain

GIMM, OLIVER, physician; b. Flensburg, Germany, Sept. 2, 1967; s. Gunther and Helgard (Schwind) G. MD, Med. Sch. Hannover, 1994. Resident U. Halle-Wittenberg, 1995-97; rsch. fellow Harvard U., Boston, 1997-98, Ohio State U., Columbus, 1999—. Contbr. articles to profl. jours. Mem. Red Cross Germany, 1986. Mem. Internat. Soc. Surgery, Internat. Assn. Endocrine Surgeons, European Thyroid Cancer Rsch. Network, German Soc. Surgery, German Soc. Endocrinology. Avocation: magic. Office: Univ Halle-Wittenberg, Ernst-Grube-Str 40, 06097 Halle Germany

GINETSINSKY, VLADISLAV J., educational psychology educator; b. Moscow, Dec. 30, 1940; s. Boris Nikhamkin and Tatanya Nikhamkina G.; m. Marina Zagrabina, Feb. 24, 1963; children: Maxim, Ksenya. Psychologist, State U, Leningrad, USSR, 1966, Candidate Pedagogical Scis., 1971, D. Pedagogical Scis., 1989. Asst. State U., Leningrad, 1969-77, asst. prof., 1977-90; prof. State U., St. Petersburg, 1990—. Author: (books) Knowledge as Category in Pedagogics, 1989, Principles of Theoretical Pedagogics, 1992, Subject of Psychology: Didactic Aspect, 1994, Propaedeutical Course of General Psychology, 1997. Mem. Acad. Acmeology Scis., N.Y. Acad. Scis. Home: 113 Apt Bl 23/1 Solidarnost, 193231 Saint Petersburg Russia Office: State Univ, Univesitetskya emb 7/9, 199034 Saint Petersburg Russia

GINGRICH, NEWTON (LEROY) (NEWT GINGRICH), former congressman; b. Harrisburg, Pa., June 17, 1943; s. Robert Bruce and Kathleen (Daugherty) G.; children: Linda Kathleen, Jacqueline Sue.; m. Marianne Ginther, Aug. 1981. B.A., Emory U., 1965; M.A., Tulane U., 1968, Ph.D. in European History, 1971. Faculty W. Ga. Coll., Carrollton, 1970-78; asst. prof. history W. Ga. Coll., until 1978; mem. 96th-105th Congresses from 6th Ga. dist. U.S. Ho. of Reps., Washington, 1979-99; speaker U.S. Ho. Reps., 104th-105th Congress, 1995-99; founder The Com. for New Am. Leadership, Washington; speaker, chmn. emeritus GOPAC; co-founder Conservative Opportunity Soc., congl. mil. caucus, space caucus; mem. joint com. on printing, house adminstrn. com.; co-chmn. Leader's Task Force on Health; adj. prof. Reinhardt Coll., Waleska, Ga., 1994-95. Author: (with Marianne Gingrich) Window of Opportunity, 1984, Renewing American Civilization, 1995, (with William Forschen) 1945, 95, To Renew America, 1995. Named Man of Yr., 1995. Mem. AAAS, Ga. Conservancy. Republican. Baptist. Lodges: Kiwanis, Moose. Office: The Com for New Am Leadership 1800 K St NW Ste 714 Washington DC 20006-2211

GINGU, OANA, mechanical engineer, educator; b. Bacau, Romania, July 11, 1968; d. Vasile and Georgeta Eugenia Hutu; m. Ion Cristian Gingu, Nov. 7, 1992; children: Ion Victor, Ionut Viorel. Degree in Mech. Engring., U. Craiova, Romania, 1991; elem. diploma for common French, U. Craiova, 1992. Univ. preparator faculty mechanics U. Craiova, 1991-95, univ. asst. faculty mechanics, 1995-99, univ. lectr. faculty mechanics, 1999—. Contbr. articles to profl. jours. Mem. Powder Metallurgy Soc. Romania, Romanian Assn. Nonconventional Techs., Tribology Romanian Assn., Welding Assn. Romania. Avocations: music, movies. E-mail: prorec@central.ucv.ro. Fax: 00 40 51 411688. Office: Univ Craiova, 13 A I Cuza, 1100 Craiova Dolj, Romania

GINKEL, JOHANNES AUGUSTE VAN, geographer, educator; b. Kota-Radjah, Indonesia, June 22, 1940; arrived in the Netherlands, 1950; s. Gysbert and Anna Sipkje W. (Westra) van G.; m. Anna Maria E. Teepen, Aug. 25, 1965; children: Auke Gysbert Heino, Mapje Ank Marit. MS in Geography and History cum laude, Utrecht (Netherlands) U., 1966, PhD in Social Scis. cum laude, 1979; Dr (hon.), Babes-Bolyai U., Cluj-Napoca, 1996. Prof. geography and history Thomas à Kempis Coll., Arnhem, Netherlands, 1965-68; assoc. prof. geography Utrecht U., 1968-80, full prof. human geography and planning, 1980—, dean of faculty, 1981-85, mem. bd. govs., 1985-97, rector magnificus, 1986-97; rector UN U., Tokyo, 1997—; chmn. Netherlands Trilateral Adv. Coun. Sci. Policy, 1991-97; bd. dirs. European Assn. Univs., 1989-98, v.p. 1994-98; mem. coun. UN U., 1992-97, v.p., 1995-97; bd. dirs. Internat. Assn. Univs., 1990-95, v.p., 1995-2000, pres., 2000—; mem. European Sci. and Tech. Assembly, 1994-97; mem. adv. group higher edn. UNESCO, 1995—; steering group World Conf. on Higher Edn., Paris, 1996-98; vice chair bd. trustees Asian Inst. Tech., 1997—; chmn. organizing com. 28th Internat. Geog. Congress, The Hague, The Netherlands, 1996. Author: a.o. Zicht op de Stad, 1977, Die Randstad Holland, 1979, Suburbanisatie en Recente Woonmilieus, 1979, Algemene Sociale Geografie, 1984, Nederland in Delen, 1989, University 2050: the Organization of Creativity and Innovation; editor: Geografisch Tijdschrift, 1970-79. Chmn. Regional Conf. of Municipalities, Utrecht, 1988-93; treas. Netherlands' Univs. Found. for Internat. Cooperation, Nuffic, 1986-97. Decorated Knight Netherlands LIon, 1994. Mem. Royal Netherlands Acad. Arts and Scis. (social scis. coun.), Academia Europea, Found. for Fundamental Rsch. in Geog. and Environ. Scis. (chmn. 1982-91), Netherlands Interdisciplinary Demographic Inst. (chmn. sci. com. 1986-95, chmn., bd. govs. 1996—), Internat. Tng. Ctr. for Aerospace Survey and Earth Scis. (bd. dirs. 1986-94, chmn. 1994-98), Internat. Geog. Union (chmn. Netherlands br. 1988-92), Royal Netherlands Geog. Soc., Internat. Geog. Cong. (pres. organizing com. 1996), Netherlands' Inst. for Urban and Regional Planning and Pub. Housing, Rotary, Sports Coun. Hoevelaken Municipality (chmn., 1969-73, The Netherlands), Hockey Club Amersfoort (mem. tech. com. 1970-75), Sports Club Kampong, Utrecht (chmn. youth divsn. 1976-82). Avocations: sports, travel. Home: Park Arenberg 63, De Bilt NL3731EP, The Netherlands Office: UN U 5-53-70, Jingumae Shibuya-ku Jingumae, Tokyo 150-8925, Japan

GINN, CONNIE MARDEAN, retired nurse; b. Nevada, Mo., July 22, 1951; d. Walter Jess and Marjorie Dean (Bowman) Andrews; 1 child, Justin Andrew Hutchinson; m. Robert Bob Ginn, Feb. 18, 1978; 1 child, Heather Diane. Student in residency assistance, Kansas City, Mo., 1997. LPN, Okla., Pa.; cert. gastrointestinal nurse clinician. Med./surgical nurse Jane Phillips Mem. Med. Ctr., Bartlesville, Okla., 1971-72, Baptist Med. Ctr., Oklahoma City, 1972-73; emergency rm. nurse Baptist Med. Ctr., 1973-75, with, 1975-77; with South Community Hosp., Oklahoma City, 1977-79; digestive disease nurse James L. Stammer, M.D. and area hosps., Oklahoma City, 1979-86; clin. coord. Regional Gastroenterology Assocs., Ben G. Lazarus, D.O., Lancaster, Pa., 1986-88; nurse Springer Clinic, Paul W. Hathaway, M.D., Tulsa, 1988-90; gastrointestinal clinician Hillcrest Med. Ctr., 1990-94; nurse coord. In His Image residency program Family Med. Care of Tulsa, 1994-98; ret.; dir. Okla. Ednl. Seminars, 1983-85, course coord., 1983-85; item writer Nat. Coun. State Bd. Nursing for LPN State Bd. exams. Presented articles on diseases and patient care to various confs. Pro rescuer and vol. ARC, first responder, vol. instr. health and safety, mem. disaster svcs., vol. health and safety. Mem. Soc. Gastroenterology Nurses and Assocs. (regional del. to nat. seminars 1982-85, dir. at large 1984-86, co-divsn. chmn. regional socs. 1984, mem. program com. 1985, mem. scholarship com. 1987-88), Regional Soc. Gastrointestinal Assts. (pres.-elect Okla. and Ark. 1981-82, pres. Okla. 1980-85, founder and first pres. Okla. 1982), Northeastern Okla. Soc. Gastrointestinal Nurses and Assocs. (founder, bd. advisors 1991—), Pa. Soc. Gastrointestinal Assts., Nat. Soc. Gastrointestinal Nurses and Assocs., Nat. Assn. LPNs, LPN Assn. Pa., Nat. Soc. Physicians Nurses, Nat. Coun. Nurses, Nat. Assn. Office Nurses, Assn. Family Practice Residency Nurses (membership com.), Tulsa Christian Women's Club, Nat. Multiple Sclerosis Soc. Republican. Avocations: needlecraft, healthcare lobbying, rubber stamping, painting. Home: 11386 S Date Ave Jenks OK 74037-3240

GINN, SAM L., telephone company executive; b. Saint Clair, Ala., Apr. 3, 1937; s. James Harold and Myra Ruby (Smith) G.; m. Meriann Lanford Vance, Feb. 2, 1963; children: Matthew, Michael, Samantha. B.S., Auburn U., 1959; postgrad., Stanford U. Grad. Sch. Bus., 1968. Various positions AT&T, 1960-78; with Pacific Tel. & Tel. Co., 1978—; exec. v.p. network Pacific Tel. & Tel. Co., San Francisco, 1979-81, exec. v.p. services, 1981-82, exec. v.p. network services, 1982, exec. v.p., strategic planning and adminstrn., 1983, vice chmn. bd., strategic planning and adminstrn., 1983-84; vice chmn. bd., group v.p. PacTel Cos. Pacific Telesis Group, San Francisco, 1984-86; pres. Air Touch Commn., San Francisco, 1984-87; vice chmn. bd., pres., chief exec. officer PacTel Corp. Pacific Telesis Group, San Francisco, 1986; pres., chief operating officer Pacific Telesis Group, San Francisco, 1987-88, former chmn., pres., chief exec. officer; chmn. Air Touch Commn., San Francisco, 1993—; now chmn. bd., CEO Air Touch Commn., San Francisco, Calif.; mem. adv. bd. Sloan program Stanford U. Grad. Sch. Bus., 1978-85, mem. internat. adv. council Inst. Internat. Studies; bd. dir. 1st Interstate Bank, Chevron Corp., Safeway, Inc. Trustee Mills Coll., 1982—. Served to capt. U.S. Army, 1959-60. Sloan fellow, 1968. Republican. Clubs: Blackhawk Country (Danville, Calif.); World Trade, Pacific-Union; Rams Hill Country (Borrego Springs, Calif.), Bankers. Office: Air Touch Commn 1 California St San Francisco CA 94111-5401

GINOCCHIO, GREG J., social services professional; b. Concord, Calif., Aug. 10, 1974; s. August John and Julie Ann Ginocchio. BA, U. Notre Dame, 1996. Active Americorps VISTA program Making Adequate Nutrition Accessible, Mission Dolores Sch., San Francisco, 1996-98; program dir. Making Adequate Nutrition Accessible, Kings Beach, Calif., 1998—; tchr. mid. sch. music, HIU educator/counselor Tahoe Truckee Unified Sch. Dist., Truckee, Calif., 1997—; ind. tchr. music Carnelian Bay, Calif., 1992—; coord. Mt. Prevention Coalition, Truckee, 1997—; co-coord. Interagy., Kings Beach, 1997—; treas. HIVCAN (Cmty. Action Network), Truckee, 1997—. Recipient Stan Baer III award Sierra Foothill AIDS Found., Nevada City, Calif., 1997, 98, Corp. for Nat. Svc. Edn. award U.S. Govt., 1997, 98. Roman Catholic. E-mail: mana@northtahoe.com. Office: Project MANA PO Box 3980 Incline Village NV 89450-3980

GINOS, JAMES ZISSIS, retired research chemist; b. Hillsboro, Ill., Feb. 1, 1923; s. Zissis and Nicoletta M. (Sakellaris) G.; m. Chrisilla Katsas, June 13, 1947; children: Geoffrey, Milton. BA, Columbia U., 1954; MS in Chem. Engring., Stevens Inst. Tech., 1962; PhD in Organic Chemistry, Stevens Inst. Tech., 1964. Chemist, Colgate Palmolive Co., Jersey City, 1953-57; chief chemist Diamond Shamrock Corp., Newark, 1957-58; project coordinator Nopco Chem. Co., Harrison, N.J., 1959-64; asst. scientist Brookhaven Nat. Labs., Upton, N.Y., 1964-68; research asst. prof. Mt. Sinai Sch. Medicine, N.Y.C., 1968-70; assoc. scientist Brookhaven Nat. Labs., 1970-74, scientist, 1974-75; research assoc. prof. Cornell U. Med. Coll., 1975-92, assoc. rsch. prof. neuroscience, 1989-92; ret., 1992; sr. research assoc. neuro-oncology Lab. Meml. Sloan-Kettering Cancer Center, N.Y.C., 1980-84, assoc. lab. mem., 1984-89, assoc. lab. mem. nuclear medicine cyclotron core, 1989-93. Contbr. articles to profl. jours. Mem. Am. Chem. Soc., AAAS, Harvey Soc., Am. Soc. Pharmacology and Exptl. Therapeutics, N.Y. Acad. Sci., Soc. Nuclear Medicine. Research on synthesis of radiopharmaceuticals labelled with shortlived positron emitting radioisotopes used in positron emission tomography. Patentee in field. Home: 200 Winston Dr Apt 3016 Cliffside Park NJ 07010-3234

GINOZA, WILLIAM, retired biophysics educator; b. L.A., Feb. 7, 1914; s. Shinkichi and Kame (Yamashiro) G.; m. Midori Sugita, Oct. 4, 1944 (dec. May 1987); children: Lillian, Donn. BA, U. Calif., Berkeley, 1937, MA, 1939; PhD, UCLA, 1952. Asst. rsch. biochemist dept. botany UCLA, 1952-55, rsch. scientist atomic energy commn., 1956-61; assoc. prof. dept. biophysics Pa. State U., University Park, 1961-67, prof., 1967-79, prof. emeritus, 1979—; invited speaker ednl. instns. and sci. confs., including Internat. Congress Biochemistry, Vienna, 1958, Faraday Soc. meeting on nucleic acids, Birmingham, Eng., 1958; vis. fellow Yale U., New Haven, 1958-60; vis. prof. U. Kyoto, Japan, 1974. Co-author: Methods in Virology, Vol IV, 1968.; contbr. reviews to Ann. Reviews Nuclear Sci., Ann. Reviews Microbiology; contbr. articles to profl. jours. Fellow AAAS; mem. Biophys. Soc., Sigma Xi, Phi Lambda Upsilon. Achievements include illucidation of molecular structure of Tobacco Mosaic Virus and its RNA, mechanisms by which heat or high energy radiations destroy the biological functions of nucleic acids of viruses and bacteria. Home: 962 E McCormick Ave State College PA 16801-6529

GINSBERG, BARRY GAVRILLE, psychologist, consultant, trainer; b. Bklyn., July 25, 1936; s. Elias Ginsberg and Lea Schwartz Epstein; m. Mindi Silverberg, Feb. 22, 1962; children: Joshua, Neil Daniel, Jeremy Marc. BS in Pharmacy, columbia U., 1958; MS in Edn./Clin. Sch. Psychology, CCNY, 1969; PhD in Human Devel. and Family Studies, Pa. State U., 1971. Lic. pharmacist, N.Y., N.J., Calif., Fla.; cert. tchr., N.Y.C.; lic. psychologist, Pa., Mass.; diplomate in family psychology Am. Bd. Profl. Psychology; cert. play therapist/supr., cert. marriage and family therapist; nat. cert. sch. psychologist. Pharmacist, mgr. Ginsberg Pharmacy, Bronx, N.Y., 1958-63; tchr. jr. and sr. h.s. N.Y.C. Bd. Edn., 1963-69; psychologist Bucks County Psychiat. Ctr., Chalfont, Pa., 1971-73; dir. child and family unit Lenape Valley Found., Chalfont, 1973-75, dir. cmty. svcs., 1975-78; psychologist dir. Ginsberg Assocs., Doylestown, Pa., 1978—; cons. and trainer, dir. Ctr. Relationship Enhancement, Doylestown, 1981—; adj. assoc. prof. Temple U., 1975-85; cons. Bucks County Area Coun. Aging, 1988—, Bucks County Children and Youth, Doylestown, 1989—, Bucks County Head Start, Bucks County Assn. Retarded Citizens, Doylestown, 1982—; adj. prof. psychology Phila. Coll. Osteopathic Medicine, 1997; bd. dirs. Am. Bd. Family Psychology, 1997. Author: Relationship Enhancement Family Therapy, 1997; columnist Parenting, 1988-89; co-host Cable TV program Parenting, 1994—. Bd. dirs. Big Bros./Big Sisters of Bucks County, 1972—, Bucks County Drug and Alcohol Commn., 1981-87, Network of Victims Asistance, 1990-95. Recipient Sterling Vol. award Ctrl. Bucks C. of C., 1996, Meritorious award Am. Bd. Profl. Psychology, 1992, Meritorious award Bucks County Drug and Alcohol Commn., 1987. Fellow APA (bd. dirs. divsn. family psychology, Meritorious awards divsn. family psychology 1986, 87, 88, 89), Pa. Psychol. Assn. (bd. dirs., pres. cmty. divsn.), Am. Assn. Marriage and Family Therapists (clin. mem., approved supr.), Ctrl. Bucks C. of C. (v.p., bd. dirs. 1975-89). Avocations: racquetball, folk dancing, Nutcracker Ballet. Office: Ctr Relationship Enhancement 17 W State St Doylestown PA 18901-4225

GINSBERG, JUDITH, foundation administrator; b. New Rochelle, N.Y., Aug. 7, 1946; d. Benedict Ginsberg and Adele Wall; m. Paul O. LeClerc, Oct. 26, 1980; 1 child, Adam Louis. BA, MA, Brown U., 1968; PhD, CUNY, 1976. Instr. CCNY, N.Y.C., 1970-75; asst. and assoc. prof. Union Coll., Schenectady, N.Y., 1975-84; program officer NEH, Washington, 1984-86; dir. rsch. Fordham U., Bronx, N.Y., 1986-88; dir. fgn. lang. programs MLA & Assn. of Depts. of Fgn. Langs., N.Y.C., 1988-90; exec. dir. Covenant Found., N.Y.C., 1990—; cons. Elie Wiesel Found. for Humanity, 1992—. Bd. mem. Resources for Children, Theatreworks USA, Jewish Funders Network. Jewish. Office: Covenant Found 215 Park Ave S New York NY 10003-1603

GINSBERG, MALCOLM, editor, air transportation consultant; b. London, Oct. 7, 1942; s. David and Anne (Woolfe) G.; m. Linda Press; children: Jackie, Sharon, Paul. Journalist, 1963-67; publicity mgr. Lotus Cars, 1967-71; aviation cons. Malcolm Ginsberg & Assocs., 1971—; cons. Belfast Internat. Airport, Brit. World Airlines, CSE-Oxford Air Tng. Sch., European Aviation Group, (Southend project), World Aviation Support; clients have included Air Atlantique, Air Belfast, Air Bristol, Globespan Travel group, Regional Airports, Ltd., AB Airlines, Brit. World Airlines, World Aviation Support, Home Improvement Bur., AB Shannon, Air Exel Belgium, All Nippon Airways, Am. Airlines, Australia's No. Ter., Belfast Internat. Airport, Birmingham European Airways, Brit. World Airlines, Brymon Airways, Clan Cars, Conti-Flug Internat. Airlines, Davis Estates, Effingham Park Hotel, Excalibur Airways, FLABEG GmbH, Garfield Glass Group, HeavyLift Cargo Airlines, The Home Improvement Bur. Ltd., KGB Computers, Lamborgini UK, Leaver Proprs., London European Airways, Lotus Cars, Luton Internat. Airport, MirrorWall, Moonraker Boats, Monarch Airlines, Orion Airways, Portman Garages/Lancia/Lamborgini, Ryanair, Siva Cars, Team Lotus, Templewood Aviation, Tempair Internat. Airlines, Thames Water Plc, Transavia Airlines, Trans European Airlines, World Aviation Svcs., among others. Editor Flight Directories, 1979—. Mem. Royal Aero. Soc., Aviation Club of Great Britain, Inst. Journalists, Airline Pub. Rels. Orgn., Guild Brit. Travel Writers (assoc.), Soc. Air Cargo Corr. (assoc.). Office: Aviation Directories LTD, PO Box 1315, Potters Bar EN6 1PU, England

GINSBERG, MARC C., former diplomat, investment company executive; b. N.Y.C., Oct. 18, 1950; m. Janet Louise Ginsberg; two children. BA, Am. U.; JD, Georgetown U. Legis. asst. to Sen. Edward Kennedy, 1973-76; spl. asst. to under sec. of mgmt. Dept. State, 1977-80; dep. sr. adviser to Pres. for Middle East affairs, 1980-81; atty. Surrey & Morse, D.C., 1981-87, Galland, Kharasch, Morse & Garfinkle, D.C., 1987-93; U.S. amb. to Morocco, 1993-98; pres. Georgetown Global Investments Corp., Washington, 1998-2000; CEO, mng. dir. Northstar Equity Group Inc, Washington, 2000—. Mem. ABA, D.C. Bar Assn. Office: Northstar Equity Group Inc 1615 L St NW Ste 900 Washington DC 20036-5623

GINSBURG, CHARLES DAVID, lawyer; b. N.Y.C., Apr. 20, 1912; s. Nathan and Rae (Lewis) G.; m. Marianne Laïs; children by previous marriage: Jonathan, Susan, Mark. AB, W.Va. U., 1932; LLB, Harvard U., 1935. Bar: W. Va. 1935, U.S. Supreme Ct. 1940, D.C. 1946, U.S. Ct. Appeals (2d, 3rd, 4th, 7th, and Fed. cirs.) 1946, U.S. Claims Ct. 1960, U.S. Tax Ct. 1961. Atty. for public utilities div. and office of gen. counsel SEC, 1935-39; law sec. to Justice William O. Douglas, 1939; asst. to commr. SEC, 1939-40; legal adviser Price Stblzn. Div., Nat. Def. Adv. Com., 1940-41; gen. counsel Office Price Adminstrn. and Civilian Supply, 1941-42, OPA, 1942-43; pvt. practice law Ginsburg, Feldman and Bress, Washington, 1946-98; founding ptnr. Ginsburg, Feldman & Bress, 1946-98; sr. counsel, firm Powell, Goldstein, Frazer & Murphy, LLP, 1998; adminstrv. asst. to Senator M.M. Neely, W.Va., 1950; adj. prof. internat. law Georgetown U. (Grad. Sch. Law), 1959-67; Dep. commr. U.S. del. Austrian Treaty Commn., Vienna, 1947; adviser U.S. del. Council Fgn. Ministers, London, 1947; Mem. Presdl. Emergency Bd. 166 (Airlines), 1966; mem. Pres.'s Commn. on Postal Orgn., 1967; chmn. Presdl. Emergency Bd. 169 (Railroads), 1969; exec. dir. Nat. Adv. Commn. Civil Disorders, 1967. Author: The Future of German Reparations; Contbr. to legal jours. Bd. mem., chmn. exec. com. Nat. Symphony Orch. Assn., 1960-69; bd. govs. Weizmann Inst., 1965 (hon. fellow 1972); mem. vis. com. Harvard-Mass. Inst. Tech. Joint Ctr. on Urban Studies, 1969; trustee St. John's Coll., 1969-76, chmn. bd., 1974-76; overseers com. Kennedy Sch. Govt. Harvard, 1971—; mem. coun. Nat. Harvard Law Sch. Assn., 1972—, gen. counsel Dem. Nat. Com., 1968-70. Served from pvt. to capt. AUS, 1942-46; dep. dir. econs. div. Office Mil. Govt., 1945-46, Germany. Decorated Bronze Star, Legion of Merit; recipient Presdl. Cert. of Merit. Mem. ABA, Fed. Bar Assn, Am. Law Inst., Coun. on Fgn. Rels., Met. Club, Army and Navy Club, Phi Beta Kappa. Democrat. Home: 619 S Lee St Alexandria VA 22314-3819 Office: 1001 Pennsylvania Ave NW Washington DC 20004-2505

GINSZTLER, JÁNOS, mechanical engineer, educator; b. Budapest, Hungary, May 23, 1943; s. Dezsö and Dezsöné (Ritter) G.; m. Jánosné Lers, Aug. 31, 1968; children: János, Christine. MSc in Mech. Engring., Tech. U. Budapest, 1966, diploma in welding engring., 1970, PhD, 1973; D of Tech. Scis., Hungarian Acad. Scis., Budapest, 1988; DSc (hon.), La Trobe U., Melbourne, Australia, 1996, Helsinki U. Tech., 1998. Assst. lectr., assoc. prof. Tech. U. Budapest, 1966-88, prof., dept. head Dept. Elec. Engring. Materials, 1988—, v.p. internat. affairs, 1991—. Contbr. 163 articles to profl. jours. Coun. mem. Nat. State Office Technol. Devel., Budapest, 1994—; mem. governing coun. UN Assn. Budapest, 1990—; pres. Found. Buda Mountains Reformed Ch. Named hon. mem. Tech. U. Munich, 1994, hon. sen. Tech. U. Karlsruhf, Germany, 1995, Dr. h.c. La Trobe U.,

Melbourne, 1996, Dr. h.c. Helsinki (Finland) U. Tech., 1998; recipient Pattantyus prize Sci. Soc. Mech. Engring., Budapest, 1986, Eötvös Loránd prize Min. Industry, Budapest, 1993, ASM Europe prize ASM Europe, Brussels, 1993, Prize Hungarian Acad. Scis., 1998. Mem. Internat. Soc. Engring. Edn. (hon), European Engring. Fedn. (v.p. 1992-95, pres. Hungarian nat. com. 1990—), Hungarian Acad. Engring. (sec. gen. 1990-96, pres. 1996—), Fedn. Tech. and Sci. Studies (v.p. 1990-99), Peregrinatio Found. (pres. 1991—), World Fedn. Engring. Orgns. (pres. com. edn. tng. 1998—, v.p. 1999—). Office: Tech U Budapest, Goldman Sq 3 I Fl Rm 153, 1111 Budapest Hungary

GINTER, CAROLYN AUGUSTA ROMTVEDT (CAROL AUGUSTA ROMTVEDT GINTER), retired bond underwriter; b. Toledo, Oreg., May 24, 1926; d. Fred and Mary Elizabeth (Whitney) Romtvedt; m. Paul Peter Ginter, June 2, 1951 (dec. Dec. 1995); children: Joan Paula, Teresa Ginter Ward, Philip M., Jeffrey G. Student, U. Oreg., 1945-46. Office and dispatch clk. Oregonian Newspaper, Portland, 1943-45; clk. typist USN Supt. of Ships, Portland, 1945; gen. ins. clk. Fidelity & Deposit Co., Portland, 1946-48; bond clk. Aetna Casualty & Surety Fireman's Fund, Transamerica, Portland, 1956-65; surety bond underwirter Cole, Clark & Cunningham/Rollins, Burdick Hunter, Portland, 1965-79; freelance publicity specialist Waldport, Oreg., 1986—. Pub., coord. family history: Fred Romtvedt, His Life and Loves, 1980. Publicity specialist ARC, 1991—; lay min. Sacred Heart Cath. Ch., Newport, 1990—. Mem. South County Women's Club (sec. 1984-94, 96, 98), Waldport C. of C. (vol. visitors ctr. 1995—), Lincoln County Hist. Soc., Alsi Hist. Soc. Republican. Avocations: family reunion organization, water exercise, travel, gardening. Home: 1802 NW Canal St Waldport OR 97394-9424

GINTER, VALERIAN ALEXIUS, urban historian, educator; b. Chgo., Nov. 4, 1939; s. Valerian Adalbert and Bernice (Podraza) G.; m. Linda Garner Tadlock, Feb. 24, 1968 (div. 1973). BS in Speech, Northwestern U., 1962; postgrad., L.I.U., 1979-81. Investigator Acme Secret Service Ltd., Chgo., 1960-62; producer, dir. Sta. WAAY-TV, Huntsville, Ala., 1965-68; comml. coordinator CBS TV, N.Y.C., 1968-70; buyer SSC&B Lintas Worldwide, Furman-Roth Inc., SFM Media Corp., N.Y.C., 1970-79; prin. Ginter-Gotham Urban History, N.Y.C., 1981—; adj. lectr. Kingsborough C.C., N.Y., 1990—, LaGuardia C.C., N.Y., 1998—. Author: Manhattan Trivia: The Ultimate Challenge, 1985; contbr. articles to profl. jours., The Ency. N.Y.C., 1995. Cons., lectr. Mcpl. Art Soc., N.Y., 1975—, dir. video tng., St. Bartholomew's Cmty. House, N.Y.C., 1974-77. With U.S. Army, 1962-65. Mem. Theatre Hist. Soc., Victorian Soc. Am., Nat. Trust Historic Preservation, Soc. Archtl. Historians. Roman Catholic. Avocation: jazz accordionist. Home and Office: 50 W 72nd St Ste 312 New York NY 10023-4132

GINZBURG, BORIS MOISEEVICH, research scientist; b. St. Petersburg, Russia, Mar. 13, 1937; s. Moses Borisovich Ginzburg and Ljubov' Lazarevna Potaschnikova; m. Kira Nikolajevna Pisareva (div. 1996); children: Michael, Phillip; m. Olga Artemievna Schyrjaeva, May 28, 1949. Magister, St. Petersburg Tech. U., 1960; PhD, Inst. High Molecular Compounds, 1967, DS, 1980; prof., 1990. Jr. rschr. Inst. Polymer Plastics, St. Petersburg, 1960-63; rschr. Inst. High Molecular Compounds, St. Petersburg, 1963-86; sr. rschr. Inst. Mech. Engring. Problems, St. Petersburg, 1986-96, lab. head, 1996—. Editor Russian Chem. Abstracts, 1983—; contbr. numerous articles to profl. jours. Grantee Internat. Sci. Found./Govt. Russian Fedn., 1995-96, Russian Sci.-Tech. Program, 1995-97. Mem. Inst. High Molecular Compounds (sci. coun.), Inst. Mech. Engring. Problems (sci. coun.), Club of Scientists. E-mail: ginzburg@tribol.ipme.ru. Office: Inst Mech Engring Problems, Bolshoi pr 61 VO, 199178 Saint Petersburg Russia

GINZBURG, LEV PAVLOVICH, physicist, educator; b. Moscow, Dec. 12, 1923; s. Pavel Lvovich and Civia Ruvimovna (Segal) G.; m. Nelli Arcadievna Ferdinand, Nov. 25, 1960 (dec. Sept. 1993); 1 child, Renata. Cand. physical and math. sci., Polytech. Inst., Leningrad, 1983. Sch. tchr. Moscow, 1951-53; scientific worker Coal Inst., Karaganda, 1953-56, Inst. of Sci. and Tech. Info., Moscow, 1957-60; asst. Inst. of Electrotech. Communications, Moscow, 1960-83; tchr. Inst. of Communications, Moscow, 1983-93; reader Tech. Univ. of Communications & Info., Moscow, 1993—. Contbr. articles to profl. jours. With Soviet Army, 1941-45. Recipient Rsch. grant Internat. Sci. Found., 1993. Avocations: classical music, football. Home: 41 Pokrovka St Apt 98, 103062 Moscow Russia Office: Tech Univ Communication, 8A Aviamotornaya, 111024 Moscow Russia

GINZBURG, VITALY LAZAREVICH, physicist; b. Moscow, Oct. 4, 1916; s. Lazar and Augusta G.; m. Nina Ginzburg, 1946; 1 child. PhD, Moscow U., 1940. With P.N. Lebedev Phys. Inst. Russian Acad. Scis., 1940—, dir. I.E. Tamm dept. theoretical physics, 1971-88, adv., head theoretical group in P.N. Lebedev Physical Inst., 1988—; prof. Gorky U., 1945-68, Moscow Tech. Inst. Physics, 1968—. Author: Theoretical Physics and Astrophysics, 1979, Waynflete Lectures of Physics, 1983, (with S.I. Syrovatskii) Origin of Cosmic Rays, 1964, Propagation of Electromagnetic Waves in Plasma, 1970, (with V.M. Agranovich and Springer-Verlag) Crystal Optics With Spatial Dispersion and Excitons, 1984, Physics and Astrophysics: A Selection of Key Problems, 1985, (with V.N. Tsytovich and Adam Hilger) Trasition Radiation and Transition Scattering, 1990, On Physics and Astrophysics (in Russian), 1992, About Science, Myself and Others, 1997; Contbr. articles to profl. jours. Decorated Order of Lenin; recipient Manelstam prize, 1947, Lomonosov prize, 1962, USSR State prize, 1953, Lenin prize, 1966, M. Smoluchovskii Medal Polish Physics Soc., 1987, Bardeen prize, 1991, Wolf Found. prize, 1994, 95, Vavilov Gold medal, 1995, Big Lomonosov Gold medal, 1995, UNESCO-Nils Bohr Gold medal, 1998, Nicholson Medal Am. Phys. Soc., 1998; Indian Acad. Sci. hon fellow, 1977, Indian Nat. Sci. Acad. fgn. fellow, 1981, NAS, 1981. Mem. AAAAS, Acad. Sci. USSR (elected people's dep. mem. of Soviet parliament 1989), Royal Soc. (London), Royal Astonomy Soc. London (assoc., Gold Medal 1991), Academia Europaea, Internat. Acad. Astronautics, Royal Danish Acad. Sci. (fgn.), Indian Acad. Sci. (hon. fellow), Indian Nat. Sci. Acad. (fgn. fellow). Fax: 095-135-85-33. E-mail: ginzburg@lpi.ru. Address: PN Lebedev Phys Inst RAN, Leninsky Prospect 53, 117924 Moscow Russia

GINZBURG, VLADIMIR B., metal products company executive; b. Moscow, June 6, 1935; came to U.S., 1974; s. Bencion Yakovlevich Ginzburg and Cecilya Vladimirovna Kotlyarova; m. Tatyana Veronica Kostomarova, Apr. 10, 1960; children: Ellen, Eugene. MSME, All-Union Machinery Eng. Inst., Moscow, 1961; PhD in Tech. Sci., Moscow Rail Transp. Inst., 1968. Project dir. All-Union Geol. Exploration Design Inst., Moscow, 1959-74; staff engr. Wean United, Inc., Pitts., 1975-80; v.p. R&D Tippins Machinery Co., Pitts., 1980-85; pres. Internat. Rolling Mill Cons., Inc., Pitts., 1985—; cons. Wean United, Inc., Pitts., 1985-87, United Engring., Inc., Pitts., 1987-94, Danieli United, Inc., Pitts., 1994—. Author: (books) Steel Rolling Technology, 1989, High-Quality Steel Rolling, 1993, Spiral Grain of the Universe, 1996; patentee in field. With Russian Air Force, 1954-57. Mem. Assn. Iron and Steel Engrs. Republican. Jewish. Avocation: studying physics. Office: Internat Rolling Mill Cons Inc 612 Driftwood Dr Pittsburgh PA 15238-2516

GIOFFRE, BRUNO JOSEPH, lawyer; b. June 27, 1934; s. Anthony B. and Louise (Giorno) G.; m. Kathleen M. Bartlik, Nov. 14, 1959; children: Kathleen, Lisa, Michael, Christopher, B. Scott, David, Kerry. BA, Cornell U., 1956, JD, 1958. Bar: N.Y. 1958, U.S. Dist. Ct. (so. dist.) N.Y. 1973. Counsel Gioffre & Gioffre, P.C., Purchase, N.Y., 1958-99, 2000—; justice Town of Rye (N.Y.), 1965-99. Chmn. bd. dirs. Sound Fed. Savs. & Loan Assn.; trustee United Hosp.; counsel Port Chester Pub. Library. Mem. ABA, N.Y. Bar Assn., N.Y. Magistrate's Assn., Westchester County Magistrate's Assn., Westchester Bar Assn., Port Chester-Rye Bar Assn., Elks, KC. Home and Office: 2900 Westchester Ave Purchase NY 10577-2552

GIOR, FINO (SERAFINO GIORDANO), electrology company executive; b. Hollywood, Calif., Sept. 8, 1936; s. Jack and Mary G.; m. Carole Chalupa, Sept. 23, 1961; children: John, Maryann, James, Matthew. Student, St. John's U., Queens, N.Y., 1955-57; cert., Kree Inst. Electrology, Manhattan, N.Y., 1958. Pres. N.Y. State Electrologists, Inc., N.Y.C., 1978-79; founder, pres. Internat. Guild Profl. Electrologists Inc., High Point, N.C., 1979-84; pres. Advanced Electrology Clinics Am., Great Neck, N.Y., 1958—; advisor Internat. Guild Profl. Electrologists, Inc., 1980—; cons. and presenter various electrology-related orgns. Author: Modern Electrology, 1987, 3rd edit., 2000, First Official Standards For Electrology and Laser Research; contbr. articles to numerous nat. mags. and profl. publs. Sgt. U.S. Army N.G., 1954-59. Recipient E. Michael, MD award 1984. Mem. Internat. Guild of Electrologist Inc. (3d v.p.). Roman Catholic. Avocations: sports, art, reading, gardening, photography. Office: Advanced Electrology 15 Bond St Great Neck NY 11021-2002

GIORDANO, MICHELE CARDINAL, archbishop; b. Sant'Arcangelo, Italy, Sept. 26, 1930. Ordained priest Roman Cath. Ch., 1953. Elected to titular Ch. of Lari Castello, 1971; consecrated bishop, 1972; prefect Matera e Irsina, 1974; transferred to Naples, Italy, 1987; created cardinal, 1988. Office: Largo Donnaregina 23, I-80138 Naples Italy*

GIORDANO, NICHOLAS ANTHONY, stock exchange executive; b. Phila., Mar. 7, 1943; s. Nicola and Aida (Gioioso) G.; m. Joanne M. Pizzuto, Oct. 21, 1967; children: Jeannine, Colette and Nicholas (triplets). BS, LaSalle Coll., 1965. CPA, Pa. Mem. staff Price Waterhouse & Co., Phila., 1965-68; with various brokerage cos. Phila., 1968-71; controller stock exchange and stock clearing corp PBW (later Phila.) Stock Exch., Inc., 1971-72, v.p. ops., 1972-75, sr. v.p., 1975-76, exec. v.p., 1976-81, pres., CEO, 1981-97, bd. dirs.; interim pres. LaSalle U., 1998-99; cons. to securities markets and fin. cos. Vice chmn. bd. trustees LaSalle U.; chmn. bd. dirs. Mt. St. Joseph Acad.; bd. dirs. Fotoball USA, Inc., Greater Phila. Urban Affairs Coalition, Ind. Blue Cross, Union League Phila.; trustee, bd. dirs. WT Mutual Fund. Fax: 610-834-0898. Home: 1755 Governors Way Blue Bell PA 19422-2554 Office: PO Box 984 Blue Bell PA 19422-0984

GIORDANO, RICHARD VINCENT, chemicals executive; b. N.Y.C., Mar. 24, 1934; s. Vincent and Cynthia (Cardetta) G.; m. Barbara Claire Beckett, June 16, 1956 (div.); children: Susan, Anita, Richard; m. Susan Mary Ware, May 6, 2000. BA, Harvard U., 1956; LLB, Columbia U., 1959; D in Comml. Sci., St. John's U., 1975; LLB (hon.), U. Bath, Eng., 1999. Bar: N.Y. 1961. Assoc. Shearman & Sterling, N.Y.C., 1959-63; asst. sec. Air Reduction Co. Inc., N.Y.C., 1963-64; v.p. distbr. products div. Air Reduction Co. Inc., 1964-65, exec. v.p., 1965-67; group v.p. Airco Inc. (now the BOC Group Inc.), 1967-71, pres., COO, 1971-78, CEO, 1978; mng. dir., CEO BOC Internat. Ltd., 1979-85; chmn., CEO, bd. dirs. BOC Group, Murray Hill, N.J., 1985-90, non-exec. dir., 1991-96, non-exec. chmn., 1994-96; dep. chmn. Grand Met. PLC, London, 1991-97; chmn. BG Group PLC, London, 1994—; bd. dirs. Ga. Pacific Corp. Decorated knight comdr. Order Brit. Empire, 1989. Mem. Assn. Bar City N.Y., Links Club (N.Y.C.).

GIORDANO, ROBERTO, chemist, researcher; b. Cuneo, Italy, Dec. 9, 1948; s. Walter Giordano and Fernanda Caprino; m. Naima Benali, Mar. 1, 1994. D Chemistry, U. Turin, Italy, 1980. Chartered chemist, Royal Soc. Chemistry, U.K. Asst. rschr. Ctr. Exploratory Organic Chemistry, Montedison S.P.A., Novara, Italy, 1973; postdoctoral fellow Inst. Phys. Chem., Ecole Polytech. Federale de Lausanne, Switzerland, 1980-81; rschr. dept. inorganic chemistry U. Turin, 1982-99; rschr. Ecole Nat. Superieure de Cimie de Toulouse, France, 1999—. Contbr. articles to sci. jours. Mem. Royal Soc. Chemistry (U.K.). Avocations: mountain climbing, biking, collecting antique ornaments, Egyptology.E-mail: rgiordano@ensct.fr. Home: 38 Viale Stazione, 12025 Dronero CN, Italy Office: INP - ENSCT Lab de Catalyse, 118 Route de Narbonne, 31077 Toulouse Cedex 04, France

GIORDANO, SERAFINO See GIOR, FINO

GIOT, CHRISTOPHE J., cardiologist; b. Etterbeek, Brabant, Belgium, Oct. 22, 1965; s. Henri E. and Marie A. (Walgraffe) G.; m. Denise J. Daems, Oct. 17, 1987 (div. 1995); children: Stéhanie, Thomas. MD, U. Brussels, 1991, specialty degree in cardiology, 1996. Fellow in cardiology Erasme Hosp., Brussels, 1991-96, resident, 1996; med. advisor Bristol Myers Squibb, Waterloo, Belgium, 1997-2000; therapeutic area leader Astrazeneca, Brussels, 2000—. Mem. Am. Heart Assn. (coun. on arteriosclerosis 1995—), Belgian Com. Against Hypertension, N.Y. Acad. of Scis. Avocation: golf. Home: 47 Ave Des Lilas, B-1410 Waterloo Belgium Office: Astrazeneca, Vanophemstraat 110, 1180 Brussels Belgium

GIOURELIS, STEFANOS N., computer company executive; b. Athens, Greece, July 5, 1964; s. Nikolaos S. and Despoina V. (Sakelariou) G.; m. Filio J. Gizori, Oct. 8, 1992. Degree in mining engring. and metallurgy, Nat. Tech. U. Athens, 1987. Software engr. CG-Soft Ltd., Athens, 1990-92; account mgr., distbr. Com-Quest SA, Athens, 1992-93; accounts mgr., major accounts Info-Quest SA, Athens, 1993-94, product mgr., 1994-95, group product mgr., 1995-96; channel sales mgr. Compaq Computer, Athens, 1996—. Contbr. articles to profl. jours. Sgt. Hellenic Air Force, 1987-89. Mem. Soc. Mining Engrs.-Metallurgists Greece, Tech. Chamber of Greece. Avocations: computers, Internet, literature, travel. Office: Compaq Computer, 90 Kifisias Ave Marousi, 15125 Athens Greece

GIOVANNINI, JEAN FRANÇOIS, federal agency administrator; b. Switzerland, June 7, 1936; s. Margret Ellinghaus, 1964; children: Christophe, Pascal. M in Econs., U. Fribourg, Switzerland, 1959. Amb., dep. dir. gen. Swiss Agy. Devel. Coop., Bern, Switzerland. Office: Fed Dept Fgn Affairs, 3003 Bern Switzerland

GIRALDO, ANTONIO, mathematician; b. Madrid, Sept. 22, 1965; s. Antonio Giraldo and Consolación Carbajo; m. Sonia Sastre, July 28, 1987; children: Tania, Ana. Bachelor's degree, Complutense U., Madrid, 1988, PhD, 1995. Asst. lectr. faculty computer sci. U. Poly. of Madrid, 1990-97, lectr. faculty computer sci., 1997—, chmn. math. applied dept., 1999—; vis. scholar U. Wash., 1996. Contbr. papers to sci. jours. Rsch. grantee Nat. Coun. Sci. Rsch., 1987-88, doctorate grantee U. Complutense, 1989. Mem. Am. Math. Soc., Real Soc. Mat. Esp. Avocations: billiards. Home: C/Los Arces 8 Portal 6 1B, 28922 Alcorcón Madrid, Spain Office: U Poly of Madrid Faculty Informática, Campus de Montegancedo, 28660 Boadilla Del Monte Madrid, Spain

GIRALDO, JESÚS, pharmacology researcher; b. Baena, Spain, Apr. 11, 1957; s. Juan Giraldo and Rafaela Arjonilla; m. Pilar Tejero, Sept. 5, 1987; children: Rafael, Alba. PhD in Chemistry, U. Autonoma Barcelona, Spain, 1992. Assoc. prof. secondary edn. Generalitat de Catalunya, Barcelona, 1983-87; asst. prof. U. Autónoma Barcelona, 1987-97, assoc. prof., 1997—; cons. Merck Farma y Química, S.A., Barcelona, 1988-95, Labs. Dr. Esteve, S.A., Barcelona, 1992—. Contbr. articles to profl. jours. Mem. Spanish Soc. Med. Chemistry. Office: U Autonoma Barcelona, lab Med Computacional, 08193 Bellaterra Spain

GIRARD, RENÉ MICHEL, psychiatrist; b. Paris, Nov. 20, 1935; s. André G.; m. Jeannine Brun, May 31, 1958; children: Fabienne, Pascale, Pierre-André. MD, Lyon, France, 1962; Neuropsychiatre, U. Caen, France, 1969. Intern Hosp. Psychiatriques Seine, Paris, 1960-64, asst., 1964-68; chief medicine Hosp. Psychiatrique, Caen, 1969—. Editor Jour. Confrontations Psychiatriques, 1968—. Home: 48 Haie Vigné, 14000 Caen France Office: Ctr Hosp Spécialisé, 93 rue Caponiè, 14000 Caen France

GIRARDI SCHOEN, ELIZABETH CATHERINE, chemical engineer; b. N.Y.C., Apr. 19, 1960; d. John Batista and Virginia Marie Girardi; m.l Robert Karl Schoen, Nov. 3, 1985; children: Matthew Robert, Catherine Elizabeth, William John, Robert Karl, Jr. B in Chem. Engring., CCNY, 1982; M in Chem. Engring., Manhattan Coll., 1988. From process engr. to dir. environ. health & safety Pfizer Inc., N.Y.C., 1982—. Office: Pfizer Inc 235 E 42d St New York NY 10017

GIRAUD, RENÉ ERNEST, academic administrator, economist, educator; b. Avlnay-De-Saintonge, Charente-Maritime, France, Mar. 28, 1925; s. Ernest and Marguerite (Geoffroy) G.; m. Madeleine Ferru, Aug. 9, 1948; children: Christine, Philippe, Bernard, Nathalie. Student, U. Poitiers; PhD in Statistics-Math., PhD in Economics. Dean of students, adj. tchr. Lycées de Châtellerault, Poitiers, La Rochelle, 1946-54; prof. math. Lycées Niort, Poitiers, 1954-68; lectr. dept. econ. U. Poitiers, 1968-84, prof., 1984, dean dept. econs., 1986-88, pres., 1988-93; mem. Comitè Èconomique et Social de la Règion Poitou-Charentes, 1989-93; prof. U. Clermont, 1984-87; mem. grad. faculty U. Paris, 1975-94, mem. adminstrv. coun., 1982-93; mem. grad. faculty Inst. Français de Pètrole, 1981-96; mem. Conseil de Circulation de l'Univ. de la Rochelle, 1992-98; pres. de Commn. des Etudies, 1998-98; administrateur des Lycie Comit. Cruerin de Poitier, 1997—. Author: Econométrie, 1989, 2d edit., 1994, Mathématique-Statistique-Probabilités, 1989, L'Économetrie Aue Seis-je, 1993, Poitias le 15 Msi, 1997. Decorated chevalier de L'Ordre Nat. Du Mérite, Commandeur des Palmes Académiques. Avocations: cycling, swimming, tennis, Romanesque art. Home: 30 Rte de Gencay, F 86000 Poitiers France

GIRAUD, XAVIER, mathematics educator, consultant; b. Rabat, Morroco, Oct. 10, 1963; s. Jean-Marie and Marie Claude (Guepin) G.; m. Sophie Boisseau, Sept. 23, 1989; children: Paul, Clotilde, Emmanuel. Diploma in engring., Ecole Nat. Superieure Telecomm, Paris, 1986, PhD in Electrical Engring., 1993; M in Math., U. Paris, 1986. Aggregation in math., France. Project engr. Sofrecom, Paris, 1989-91; math. educator Min. Edn., Paris, 1991—, Ecole Nat. Superior Telecomm., 1994—; cons. COMSIS, Paris, 1995—. Author: Algebre Lineair, 1994; contbr. articles to profl. jours. Mem. IEEE. Avocation: horseback riding. Home: 30 rue Vaugelas, 75015 Paris France

GIRDLER, RONALD WILLIAM, research geophysicist, educator; b. Reading, Berkshire, Eng., Aug. 2, 1930; s. George William and Annie Louisa (Sinkins) G. BSc, Reading U., 1955; PhD, Cambridge (Eng.) U., 1958. Rsch. assoc. Lamont-Doherty Geol. Obs., Columbia U., N.Y.C., 1958-60; Imperial Chemical Industries fellow in geophysics Durham (Eng.) U., 1960-63; lectr. physics Newcastle (Eng.) U., 1963-66, sr. rsch. fellow, 1966-70, reader in geophysics, 1970-94, prof. geophysics, 1994-95, prof. emeritus, 1995—; NRC sr. resident rsch. assoc. NASA/Goddard Space Flight Ctr., Greenbelt, Md., 1988-89; Conselho Nat. de Desenvolvimento Cientifico e Technológico vis. prof. Nat. Obs., Rio de Janeiro, 1990-91; vis. prof., Weeks lectr. dept. geology and geophysics U. Wis., Madison, 1995; hon. prof. dept. geol. scis. U. Durham, Eng., 1996—; Disting. vis. scholar U.S. Geol. Survey, Menlo Pk., Calif., 1996-97; mem. Inter-Union Commn. on Geodynamics, Internat. Upper Mantle Com., various sci. coms., Eng.; mem. Deep Sea Drilling Project, 1972; prin. scientist R/V Shackleton Rsch. Cruises, Gulf of Aden, Red Sea, 1975, 79; vis. scientist NASA/Goddard, 1998; vis. lectr. Warsaw Univ., Poland, 1998; vis. scholar U.S. Geol. Surv., Menlo Park, Calif., 1999, 2000. Editor: East African Rifts, 1972; author articles on geophys. Red Sea, Gulf of Aden, rifts of East Africa and their relevance to continental drift and evolution of ocean basins; continental satellite magnetic anomalies and meteorite impacts. Agy. Indsl. Sci. and Tech. fellow Geol. Surv., Japan, 2000. Mem. Fellow Royal Astron. Soc. (life); mem. AAAS, Am. Geophys. Union (life), Soc. Exploration Geophysics (life), Math. Assn. (life), Seismol. Soc. Am. Anglican. Episcopalian. Avocations: squash, music, Japan, gardening. Home: 33 South St, Durham DH1 4QP, England Office: Dept Physics, Newcastle U, Newcastle upon Tyne NE1 7RU, England

GIRES, JEAN-MICHEL, oil industry executive; b. Bourg-La-Reine, France, Dec. 23, 1957; s. François and Colette (Jauvain) G.; m. Marie-Helene Adrien; children: Pierre-Yves, Ghislaine, Cedric, Marc-Henri. Ingenieur, Ecole Poly., Paris, 1979; Ingenieur Corps des Mines, Ecole Mines, Paris, 1981. Dir. Bur. Controle Constrn. Nucleaire, Dijon, France, 1982-88; dir. econ. studies TOTAL Oil Great Britain, London, 1988-90; mng. dir. TOTAL Spain, Madrid, 1990-92; v.p. mktg. Petrogal, Lisbon, Portugal, 1992-94; v.p. strategy exploration prodn. TOTAL (France), 1994-98; v.p. North Sea opers. TOTALFINA (France), 1998—. Sous lt. French Air Force, 1976. Home: 111 Blvd de la Republique, 92420 Vaucresson France Office: TOTALFINA Exploration Prodn, 24 cours Michelett, 92069 La Defense Cedex, France

GIRGIS, ADEL YOUSSEF, food scientist, educator; b. Cairo, Mar. 28, 1959; s. Youssef Girgis and Aziza magar Shehalah; m. Mona Sobhy Nessim, May 28, 1996; 1 child, Goseph Adel. BSc in Food Scis., Ain Shams U., 1981; MSc in Food Scis., Zagazig U., 1989; PhD in Food Scis., 1995. Chemist El-Gahad Factory, Cairo, 1983-84; quality control engr. Cairo Oils and Soap Co., 1984-91, chmn. quality control lab., 1991-93, mgr. dept. quality control, 1993-94; assoc. researcher Food Tech. Rsch. Inst., Giza, Egypt, 1994-95, doctoral researcher, 1995—; cons. El-Gahad Soap Mfg. Factory, 1984—, Cairo Oils and Soap Co., 1995—; instr. Food Tech. Rsch. Inst., Giza, 1995—; trainer El-Baramos ministry, Wady El Natron City, Egypt, 1985—. Patentee in field. With Egyptian Army, 1981-82. Fellow Egyptian Soc. of Food Scis., Agrl. Orgn. Avocations: reading, music, sports. Home: 9 El-Hossany St, 11433 Cairo Egypt Office: Food Tech Rsch Inst, Oil/Fat Rsch 9 El Gamaa St, 12619 Giza Egypt

GIRI, GEORGE ANAND RURIK, surgeon, military officer; b. London, Apr. 28, 1923; s. D.V. Giri and Princess Kossatkine Rosstoffsky Marina; m. Karin Dora Francesca Margaretha Lewenhaupt, Jan. 26, 1957; children: Michael G.R., Christopher, Alexandra G.F. MA with honors, Cambridge, Eng., 1944; Lic. in Medicine and Surgery, Soc. Apothecaries, London, 1947; diploma in Pub. Health, London, 1962; mem., Faculty Cmty. Medicine, 1964; assoc., Faculty Occupational Medicine, 1980. Surgeon capt. Royal Navy, 1949-77, asst. dir. gen.; dir. studies Inst. Naval Medicine; chief staff officer Med. Ministry Defense, 1992-96; asst. sec. Brit. Med. Assn., 1977-82. Ch. warden St. Philip and St. James Palma Mallorca, 1990—. Recipient Order of Brit. Empire, 1970, silver medal World Masters Games, Portland, Oreg., 1998. Anglican. Avocations: sports, violin. Home: Can Quint, Mancor del Valle, 07312 Mallorca Spain

GIRIDHAR, RAJANI, pharmacy educator; b. Chennai, Tamilnadu, India, Mar. 3, 1953; d. Rathangapani and Mohana Pani Sampathkumar; m. Giridhar Sesha IYegar, July 1, 1979; children: Satish Giridhar Iyengar. B-Pharm, Madras (India) U., 1973; MPharm, B.I.T.S. Pilani, Rajasthan, India, 1975; PhD in Pharmacy, M.S. U. of Baroda, India, 1987. Tchg. asst. M.S. U. Baroda, 1975-76, lectr. in pharm. chemistry, 1976-84, reader in pharm. chemistry, 1984—, rsch. coord., 1981-91; chief coord. R&D project All India Coun. Tech. Edn., 1999—. Contbr. articles to profl. jours. Recipient Gold medal Indian Drugs Mfg. Assn., 1973. Mem. Assn. Pharm. Tchrs. India (life), Indian Women Scientists Assn. (life), Indian Pharm. Assn. (life). Avocations: internet, reading, music. Home: 104 Anand Bhavan, 390 001 Baroda Gujarat, India Office: MS U Baroda, Pharmacy Dept, 390 001 Baroda Gujarat, India

GIRIJAVALLABHAN, VIYYOOR M., research executive; b. Trichur, Kerala, India, May 31, 1942; came to U.S., 1975; s. Melangath Achyutha Menon and Moopil Meenakshi Amma; m. Shabari Girijavallabhan, Sept. 9, 1974; children: Vinay, Ajay Menon. BSc, St. Thomas Coll., Trichur, Kerala, India, 1963, MSc, 1965; PhD, Kerala U., Trivandrum, India, 1969; postgrad., Imperial Coll., London, 1970-74. Rsch. fellow Regional Rsch. Lab., Hyderabad, India, 1965-69; postdoctoral fellow Imperial Coll., London, 1970-74; rsch. scientist Schering-Plough Corp., Bloomfield, N.J., 1975-79, prin. scientist, 1979-82, sect. leader, asst. dir., 1982-87, dir. rsch., 1988-94; dir., disting. rsch. fellow Schering-Plough Corp., Kenilworth, N.J., 1994—. Holds 45 patents for drug substances; contbr. 75 articles to profl. jours. Mem. AAAS, Am. Chem. Soc., N.Y. Acad. Scis., Antiviral Rsch. Avocations: gardening, tennis, pingpong, cooking, music. E-mail: vallabhan@aol.com. Home: 10 Maplewood Dr Parsippany NJ 07054-1421 Office: Schering-Plough Corp 2015 Galloping Hill Rd Kenilworth NJ 07033-1310

GIRISH, KUDHUVALLI PURNAIAH, education and management trainer, educator; b. Mysore, India, May 20, 1960; s. Kudhuvalli Narasimhaiah Purnaiah and Chamarajnagar Subba Rama Annapurna; m. Kudhuvalli Suryanarayana Malini, Aug. 25, 1988; 1 child, Master Amith. Assoc. Degree, C. Perumalu Chetty Poly. U., India, 1980; B in Commerce, Mysore U., India, 1981; LLB, Bangalore U., India, 1986; MBA, Newport U., 1988; PhD, Harrington U., 1999. Vocat. instr. Vocat. Rehab. Ctr., Bangalore; asst. tng. officer Ministry of Labor, Bangalore, 1983-85; tng. officer Ministry of Labor, New Delhi, 1986-96; lectr. Jubail Industrial Coll., Jubail Industrial City, Saudi Arabia, 1996—; counselor physically handicapped NTTF, Bangalore, 1982; vol. trainer Vocat. Tng. Inst., Bangalore, 1983; fin. and legal cons. Trendy Fin., Investment and Leasing, Mumbai, 1996—; mgmt. and tng. cons. Sabic Group Cos., Jubail Industrial City, 1996—; consumer protectionist Consumer Protection Forum, Mumbai, 1992-96; spl. invitee UN U., Amman, Jordan, 1999. Contbr. articles to profl. jours. Co. quarter master Nat. Cadet Corps, 1976-80; active physically

handicapped Rehab. Ctr. for Physically Handicapped, Bangalore, 1982; active family planning Family Planning Assn. India, New Delhi, 1985; active women's edn. Nat. Vocat. Tng. Inst., New Delhi, 1986; active adult edn. Bombay Women's Assn., Mumbai, 1992. Mem. Nat. Geog. Soc., Lions Club Internat., Rotary Internat. Mem. Indian Nat. Congress. Avocations: cricket, soccer, tennis, travel, reading and writing books. E-mail: kengpgirish@yahoo.com. Office: Jubail Indsl Coll, PO Box 10099, Jubail Indsl City 31961, Saudi Arabia

GIRLING, DAVID JOHN, medical researcher; b. Eastbourne, Sussex, Eng., May 1, 1937; s. John Beecroft and Evelyn Maud (Roxby) G. BM BCh, Oxford (Eng.) U., 1964, MA, 1965. Mem. sci. staff Med. Rsch. Coun., London, 1971-90; hon. sr. lectr. Cardiothoracic Inst., London, 1982-90; clin. coord. MRC HIV Trials Ctr., London, 1988-90; mem. sci. staff cancer divsn. MRC Clin. Trials Unit, Cambridge, Eng., 1990—; sec., coord. MRC Lung Cancer Working Party, Cambridge, 1978—, Med. Rsch. Coun. Oesophageal Cancer Working Party, Cambridge, 1990—. Contbr. over 200 articles to sci. publs., chpts. to med. books, including Oxford Textbook of Medicine, 3d edit., 1995. Lic. lay reader Diocese of Ely, 1991—. Lt. Brit. army, 1956-58. Fellow Royal Coll. Physicians; mem. Internat. Assn. for Study of Lung Cancer, Brit. Thoracic Soc., Brit. Med. Assn. Mem. Ch. of England. Avocations: music, drama, magic, church, literature. Home: 11 Bateman Mews, Cambridge CB2 1NN, England Office: Cancer Div MRC Clin Trials, 222 Euston Rd, London NW1 2DA, England

GIRLING, JOHN (LAWRENCE SCOTT), writer; b. Farnborough, Eng., May 21, 1926; s. Lawrence H.G. and Mary M.A.M. (Scott) G.; m. Nina Ludmila Simansky, Apr. 12, 1953. BA, Queen's Coll., Oxford (Eng.) U., 1950; PhD, Australian Nat. U., 1983. Mem. rsch. staff Fgn. Office, London, 1951-57, 63-66, Thailand, 1958-63; sr. rsch. fellow Australian Nat. U., Canberra, 1966-69, fellow internat. rels., 1969-78, sr. fellow, 1978—, rschr. rsch. sch. Pacific studies, 1966-91. Author: People's War: Conditions and Consequences in China and Southeast Asia, 1969, America and the Third World: Revolution and Intervention, 1980, Thailand: Society and Politics, 1981, The Bureaucratic Polity in Modernizing Societies, 1981, Capital and Power, 1987, Myths and Politics in Western Societies, 1993, Interpreting Development, 1996, Corruption, Capitalism and Democracy, 1997, France, Political and Social Change, 1998. Coder Royal Navy, 1947-50. Mem. Assn. Asian Studies, Asian Studies Assn. Australia, Australian Inst. Internat. Affairs (pres. Canberra br. 1970-71). Social Democrat. Office: Australian Nat Univ Dept Internat Rels, RSPAS, Canberra ACT 0200, Australia

GIROD, CHRISTIAN ALPHONSE, educator; b. Bone, Algeria, Aug. 31, 1930; s. Lucien Alphonse and Ernestine (Guy) G.; m. Raymonde Vaille, Dec. 19, 1995; children: Michele, Monique, Anne-Marie, Genevieve, Isabelle. MD, Faculty Medicine, Algiers, 1957, PhD, 1961. Assoc. prof. Univ., Algiers, 1961-62; assoc. prof. Univ., Lyon, France, 1962-67, prof., 1967-95; biologist Hopitaux, Lyon, France, 1967-95. Author: Introduction a l'etude des glandes endocrines, 1980, Histochemistry of the Adenohypophysis, 1976, Immunocytochemistry of the Vertebrate Adenohypophysis, 1983; co-author: Biologie de la Reproduction, vol. 1, 1970, vol. 2, 1977. Mem. Acad. European Scis., N.Y. Acad. Scis. Avocations: painting, symphony music. Home: 51 Ave Rockefeller, 69003 Lyon France

GIROD, FRANK PAUL, retired surgeon; b. Orenco, Oreg., Aug. 13, 1908; s. Leon and Anna (Gerig) G.; m. Nadine Mae Cooper, Aug. 26, 1939; children: Judith Anne, Janet Carol, Franklin Paul, John Cooper. AB, Willamette U., Salem, Oreg., 1929; MD, U. Colo., 1938. Diplomate Am. Bd. Family Practice. Tchr. physics and chemistry, athletic coach Cortez High Sch., Colo., 1929-34; intern U. Colo., Denver, 1938-39; resident surgeon U.S. Marine Hosp., Balt., 1939-41; pvt. practice specializing in family practice and surgery Lebanon, Oreg., 1946-95; ret., 1995; bd. dirs. Lebanon Hosp., 1960-99, pres. med. staff. Trustee, sec. Blue Shield Ops., Oreg., 1950-60; grand marshal Lebanon Strawberry Festival, 1988; mem. bd. Coun. of Govts. Sr. Svcs., 1991, 92-97. Maj. Army Med. Corp, 1942-45. Decorated Bronze Star; recipient Disting. Svc. First Citizen award Lebanon, Oreg., 1989; Frank P. Girod Med. Scholarship named in his honor, 1995. Mem. AMA, Oreg. Med. Assn. (trustee), Am. Acad. Family Practice, Kiwanis (pres. 1947-48). Republican. Methodist. Avocation: travel. Home: 625 E Rose St Lebanon OR 97355-4544

GIRONDI, PATRIZIO F., investment company executive; b. Chgo., Nov. 24, 1957; s. Gerald F. Finley and Evelina Carmela Girondi; m. Ortensia Caputo, Dec. 13, 1969; children: Rocco, Francesco, Giancareo. Founder Robin Hood, U.S.A., 1983-99, Italy, 1995-99; pres. BPT Trading, Switzerland, 1991-99; dir. Bridgeport Securities Group, 1979-99, Bracon Pharm., 1995-99. Author: Diamond in The Rough, 1984. Treas. Valentine Boys Club, Chgo., 1983-88; del. Pres. conv., 1984. Airman USAF, 1975-77. Roman Catholic. Avocations: curing son of blood disease. Office: BPT Trading, Piazza Duomo 5, 70022 Altamura Bari Italy

GIROUD, JEAN-PAUL, pharmacology educator; b. Paris, Nov. 6, 1936; s. Paul Giroud and Maria Caselli. MD, U. Paris, 1964, DSc, 1970; PhD, U. London, 1968. Sr. lectr. pharmacology Paris, 1966; sr. lectr. in pharmacology Tours, France, 1967; prof. clin. pharmacology U. Benin, Togo, 1973-85; full prof. clin. pharmacology Hosp. Cochin, Paris, 1970—; rsch. fellow Ctr. Claude Bernard, Paris, 1960-62, St. Bartholomew's Hosp., London, 1968-69; dir. rsch. group Ctr. Nat. Rsch. Sci., Paris, 1974—. Coeditor Future Trends in Inflammation, 1974-75, Perspectives in Inflammation, 1979; chief editor Pharmacologie Clinique Base de la thérapeutique, 1978, 88; author 8 books in field of self-care and home medicine. Advisor Ministry of Health, Ministry of Rsch., French Sci. Coun. for Life Scis.; expert on drug evaluation and essential drugs WHO. Recipient Laureate Acad. Nat. Medicine, 1969, 76, 84, Acad. Scis., 1974, Officier de l'Ordre du Merite, 1993, Médaille de Vermeil de la Ville de Paris, 1993, Grand Prix Claude Bernard for Med. Rsch., 1992, Chevalier de la Legion d'Honneur, 1997. Mem. French Acad. Medicine, Academia Europaea (physiology and medicine). Fax: 01 44 41 25 57. E-mail: giroud@cochin.inserm.fr. Home: 66 Ave de Breteuil, 75007 Paris France Office: Hosp Cochin Dept Clin Pharmacol, 27 rue Faubourg St Jacques, 75679 Paris Cedex 14, France

GIROUX, PAUL HENRY, retired music educator, musician; b. Humboldt, Ariz., May 24, 1916; s. Frank William and Adda Jenny Mae (Gilbert) G.; m. Flo Annette Carroll, Dec. 26, 1945 (dec. June 1996); 1 child, Nicki Suzette Giroux de Navarro. Student, No. Ariz. U., 1934-39, BA in Music Edn., 1947; BS in Psychology, U. Wash., 1952, MA in Music Edn., 1952. Cert. secondary tchr., Wash. Undergrad. asst. dept. music No. Ariz. U., 1935-39; music dir. Radio KTAR, Phoenix, 1939-49; cantor Temple Beth Israel, Phoenix, 1939-49; organizer band for prisoners Ariz. State Prison, 1947—; grad. asst. music and psychology U. Wash., Seattle, 1950-52; music tchr. Jefferson Jr. H.S., Olympia, Wash., 1953-55; chmn. arts divsn. Everett (Wash.) C.C., 1955-78; ret.; organizer ongoing prisoners concert band, Ariz. State Prison, 1947. Flute soloist Everett Cmty. Band, 1960-78, Nat. Champion Shrine Band, Tucson, 1978—. Condr. Everett Symphony, 1955-65; choir master Trinity Episcopal Ch., Everett, 1963-69; band master of ceremonies Sabbar Shrine, Tucson, 1979—, band flute soloist, 1979—. Capt. U.S. Army Ordnance, 1942-45. Decorated Bronze star U.S. Army, Philippines, 1945; Contemporary Music grantee Ford Found., Eastman Sch., Rochester, N.Y., 1969; Theodore Presser fellow Theodore Presser Pub., U. Wash., Seattle, 1952-53. Mem. NEA (life), Am. Fedn. Musicians (life), Music Educators Nat. Conf. (life), VFW (life), Elks (life), Masons (life), Phi Delta Kappa (emeritus), Phi Mu Alpha Sinfonia (life). Episcopalian. Achievements include undergraduate assistant work in music for the first world-wide broadcast conducted, NBC-BBS Easter Sunrise Service, Grand Canyon, Arizona. Avocations: teaching bible class, studying child psychology, reading. Home: 1750 S Desert Vista Dr Tucson AZ 85748-7503

GISH, EDWARD RUTLEDGE, surgeon; b. St. Louis, Sept. 5, 1908; s. Edward C. and Bessie (Rutledge) G.; A.B., Westminster Coll., 1930; MD, St. Louis U., 1935, MS, 1939; m. Miriam Schlicker, July 8, 1938; children: Ann Rutledge, Mary Priscilla. Intern, St. Louis U. Hosps., 1935-36; resident in surgery St. Mary's Group Hosps., St. Louis, 1936-39; pvt. practice medicine specializing in surgery, Fulton, Mo., 1946—; former sr. instr. surgery St. Louis U. Med. Sch.; staff mem. Callaway Meml. Hosp., Fulton. Author: Plantagenet Portraits in Stone: Unique XII Century, 1989. Bd. dirs. Mo. Symphony Soc., pres., 1981; med. dir. Callaway County CD. Served from maj. to lt. col., AUS, 1943-46; lt. col. ret. Res. Hon. col. Gov.'s Staff Mo. Fellow ACS; mem. Royal Soc. London (affiliate), Internat. Coll. Surgeons, AMA, Mo. Med. Soc., Callaway County Med. Soc. (nat. bd. dirs.), Red Poll Breeders Assn., Am. Law Enforcement Officers Assn., Delta Tau Delta, Alpha Omega Alpha. Contbr. articles to profl. jours. Co-capt. U.S. team World Masters Cross-Country Ski Assn., 1985. Address: 7 W 10th St Fulton MO 65251-1937

GISIN, BORIS, physicist; b. Smolensk, Russia, Apr. 20, 1939; arrived Israel, 1992; s. Beniamin and Bassia (Eisenberg) G.; (dec. 1977); children: Natalia, Julia. MSc, State U., Alma-Ata, 1961; PhD, Inst. Crystallography, Moscow, 1972. Engr. Ctrl. Scientific Rsch. Inst. Comm., Moscow, 1965-67, rschr., 1967-70, sr. scientist, 1970-91; rschr. Tel-Aviv U., 1992-95, sr. scientist, 1995—; cons. Dialit Ltd., Holon, Israel, 1995-96. Contbr. articles to profl. jours.; patentee in field. Office: Tel Aviv U, 69978 Tel Aviv Israel

GISINGER, CHRISTOPH, medical educator; b. Vienna, Austria, Nov. 10, 1953; s. Ernst and Elfriede (Müller) G.; m. Jutta G. Schumacher, Apr. 25, 1991; children: Sophia, Teresa. MD, U. Vienna, 1980; MBA in Hosp. Adminstrn., Vienna Bus. Sch., 1993. Asst. prof. Vienna Med. Sch., 1981-86, assoc. prof., 1986-88; rsch. assoc. Med. U. S.C., Charleston, 1988-90; prof. medicine Vienna Med. Sch., U. Vienna, 1990—, head divsn. rheumatology, 1991-94; pres. Med. Info. Ctr., 1986—; med. dir. Haus Der Barmherziakeit, 1999—. Contbr. sci. papers to med. publs. Recipient Squibb award, 1989. Mem. European Soc. Clin. Investigations (v.p. 1993-96), Vienna Chamber of Physicians (chmn. rsch. task force 1997—). Avocations: theater, collecting expressionism paintings. Office: U Vienna Dept Medicine III, Haus Der Barmherziakeit, Vinzenzg 2-6, A-1180 Vienna Austria

GISLASON, GISLI MAR, limnology and entomology educator; b. Reykjavik, Iceland, Feb. 18, 1950; s. Gisli Kristjansson and Thorbjorg Magnusdottir; divorced; children: Gisli Jokull, Hersit, Hafsteinn, Thorbjorg. BS, U. Iceland, Reykjavik, 1973, diploma, 1973; PhD, Newcastle, U.K., 1978. Lectr. U. Iceland, Reykjavik, 1971-88, prof., 1988—, dean faculty of sci., 1999—; councillor Nature Conservation Coun., Reykjavik, 1987-2000; dir. Inst. of Biology U. Iceland, 1987-99; chmn. bd. Myvatnol (Iceland) Rsch. Sta., 1987—. Contbr. numerous articles to profl. publs. Advisor Internat. Whaling Commn., Iceland, 1988-90, Ministry for the Environ., Govt. of Iceland, 1987—. Fellow Royal Entomological Soc. E-mail: gmg@hi.is. Home: Heidarsel 6, IS-109 Reykjavik Iceland Office: Inst of Biology, U Iceland, 15-108 Reykjavik Iceland

GISONDI, JOHN THEODORE, theater and television designer; b. Tucson, Ariz., Apr. 7, 1949. BFA, So. Meth. U., 1975. Credits include (TV) Good Morning America, The Arab World with Bill Moyers, ABC Wide World of Sports, National Geographic Explorer, Mariah Carey Spl., Ghost Writer PBS, Buying a Landslide BBC, A Christmas Carol Live from Fords Theatre, ABC, CBS, NBC; prodr. A Texas State of Mind; designer (stage prodns.), N.Y.C.: Sound & Beauty (Drama Desk award), Fathers Day, Three Sisters, Julius Caesar, Dexter Creed, (regional theatres) Guthrie Theatre, Kennedy Ctr., Fords Theatre, (opera) Opera Metropolitana, Caracas, Venezuela, Va. Opera Co. Mem. United Scenic Artists, Dirs. Guild of Am. Home and Office: 21 Cornelia St Apt 1 New York NY 10014-4121

GISONNI, CORRADO, civil engineer, educator, researcher, consultant; b. Naples, Italy, Mar. 21, 1965; s. Vittorio and Nunzia (Manna) G.; m. Anna Rispoli. Hydraulic Engr., U. Naples, 1989; PhD in Hydraulic Engring., 1994. Fluid dynamics equipment engr. Aeritalia, Italy, 1989-90; rschr. engr. 2d U. Haples, Aversa, 1995—, sr. lectr. civil engring., 1995—; cons. in hydraulic engring., Naples, 1991—; specialist lectr. Italian Ministry Fgn. Affairs, Rome, 1995. Author: (with others) Sewer Systems Design, 1998; contbr. articles to sci. jours., including ASCE jours., Internat. Congresses in Hydraulic Engring. Mem. ASCE. Roman Catholic. Office: 2d U Naples Dept Civil Eng, via Roma 29, 81031 Aversa (Caserta) Italy

GISSMANN, LUTZ, research scientist; b. Kaufbeuren, Bavaria, Germany, Sept. 18, 1949; s. Hans and Jutta Gissmann; m. Gabriele Hoffmann, Aug. 15, 1986; 1 child, Julia. Diploma, U. Erlangen, Germany, 1974, PhD, 1977. Head divsn. German Cancer Rsch. Ctr., Heidelberg, 1983-93, 1997-98, 99—; dir. rsch. Loyola U. Med. Ctr.-Chgo., Maywood, Ill., 1993-96; v.p. rsch. MediGene AG, Martinsried, Germany, 1998-99. Avocation: classical music. E-mail: Lutz.Gissmann@t-online.de and L.Gissmann@dkfz-heidelberg.de. Fax: 49-6221 424932. Office: German Cancer Rsch Ctr, Im Neuenheimer Feld 242, 69120 Heidelberg Germany

GIST, JOHN MONTFORT, publishing executive; b. Denver, Oct. 26, 1963; s. Christopher Gist and Phyllis Ann (Angevine) Jozwik. BA, U. Wyo., 1992; MFA, U. Alaska, 1996. Editor, pub. Exegesis Writing Svcs., Laramie, Wyo., 1992-96; tchr. English U. Alaska, Fairbanks, 1994-96; owner All-Terrain Writing Cons., 2000—. Author: Crow Heart, 1999; editor: Plants for Profit, 1998, Perennial Plants for Profit, 1998; editor: The Greenhouse & Nursery Handbook, 1999, Illustrated Handbook of Landscape Plants, 2000, Make Money Growing Trees, 2000, Creation Through Evolution, 2000, The Voice of Creation, 2000. Tchr. Acad. Decathlon, Fairbanks, 1994-96, Upward Bound, Laramie, 1998—. Mem. Poets and Writers, U. Alaska Alumni Assn., U. Wyo. Alumni Assn. Avocations: hunting, fishing, reading, quantum theory.

GIST, WILLIAM CLAUDE, JR., dentist; b. Chattanooga, May 14, 1935; s. William Claude and Dorothy Virginia (Gibbs) G.; widower. BSc, U. Tenn., Knoxville, 1958; DMD, U. Louisville, 1967. Diplomate Am. Bd. Forensic Dentistry, Am. Bd. Forensic Medicine, Am. Bd. Forensic Examiners. Pvt. practice Louisville, 1967—. Chmn. celebrations Bicentennial of Pres. Zachary Taylor's Birth, Louisville, 1984; pres. Louisville Civil War Roundtable, 1990-91. Recipient Presdl. commendation Pres. Ronald Reagan, 1985, DAR medal of honor, 1996, DAR history award, 1985. Mem. ADA, Ky. Dental Assn., Louisville Dental Soc., Nat Soc. SAR (pres. gen. 1995-96, Ky. pres. 1985-86, nat. trustee 1986-87, v.p. gen. Ctrl. dist. 1989-90, historian gen. 1991-93, registrar gen. 1993-94, sec. gen. 1994-95, nat. chmn. centennial observances com. 1985, nat. chmn. hdqrs. com. 1989-94, nat. chmn. nominating com. 1996-97, nat. chmn. George Washington Fund Bd. 1997-98, nat. chmn. ethics com. 1999-2000, dir. mus. 1998-2000, Gold Good Citizenship award 1996, Minuteman award 1990, Disting. Svc. medal 1999), Continental Soc. Sons of Indian Wars (nat. gov. 1990-92), Nat. Order of the Blue and Gray (comdg. gen. 1996-98), Nat. Gavel Soc., Magna Charta Barons (Somerset chpt.), Order Ams. Armorial Ancestry, Jamestowne Soc., Gen. Soc. Colonial Wars, Colonial Order of Acorn, Nat. Soc. Sons and Daughters of Pilgrims (Ky. gov. 1990-93), Gen. Soc. Sons Revolution, Hereditary Order Descendants Loyalists-Patriots, Gen. Soc. War 1812 (Ky. pres. 1986-88, v.p. gen. 1990-93), Aztec Club, Mil. Order Stars-Bars (Ky. comdr. 1988-90), Fi. Republican. Avocations: history, genealogy, historic preservation. Home: Springfield Zachary Taylor House 5608 Apache Rd Louisville KY 40207 Office: 4229 Bardstown Rd Ste 309 Louisville KY 40218-3241

GITIS, VALERI GRIGORIEVICH, computer scientist, researcher; b. Briansk, USSR, Sept. 4, 1938; s. Grigoriy Isaevich and Inna Illinichna (Tamarina) G.; m. Vera Grigorievna Ivanova, Apr. 20, 1964 (dec. May 1995); 1 child, Julia; m. Vera Evgenievna Smirnova, Feb. 14, 1996. BA, Tech. U., Cheliabinsk, 1960; MA, Aviation U., Moscow, 1965; PhD in Info. Transmission, Acad. Scis. USSR, Moscow, 1971. Engr. Radioelectronic Inst., Cheliabinsk, 1960-63; rschr., head of dept. Inst. for Info. Transmission Problems Russian Acad. Scis., Moscow, 1965—. Author: Pattern Recognition, 1971; contbr. articles to profl. jours. Geog. Info. Sys., Natural Hazard, Artificial Intelligence in Engring., among others. Mem. Internat. Acad. Informatization (corr.). Avocations: wooden sculptures, sports. E-mail: gitis@iitp.ru. Fax: 007-095-2090579. Home: Apt 176, Savvinskaia Embankment 3, 119 121 Moscow Russia Office: Russian Acad Scis Inst Info, B Karetniy Ln 19, 101447 Moscow Russia

GITMAN, DMITRY MAXIMOVICH, physicist; b. Tashkent, Uzbekistan, Russia, July 2, 1944; s. Maxim Semenovich Gitman and Evgenia Jacovlevna (Telijatnikova) Shershevskaja; m. Vera Borisovna Levina (div. 1971); 1 child, Alexander. M in Physics, Tomsk State U., 1966, PhD, 1969; DSc, Novosibirsk U., 1979. Asst. prof. TIASUR, Tomsk, Russia, 1966-68, assoc. prof., 1968-75; full prof. Tomsk State Pedagogical U., Russia, 1975-85, Moscow Radio Ingineer U., Russia, 1985-92, U. São Paulo, 1992—. Contbr. to 5 books on relativistic quantum theory and quantum field theory; contbr. more than 180 articles to profl. jours. Home: Rua Souza Reis 120, Apt 84B, 05586080 São Paulo Brazil Office: Inst Fisica, U São Paulo CP 66318, 05315970 São Paulo Brazil

GIUBBILINI, PIERLUIGI VITTORIO, physics educator; b. Livorno, Tuscany, Italy, Apr. 28, 1945; s. Euro and Silvana (Cerri) G. Doctorate Degree, U. Pisa, Italy, 1970. tchrs. diploma exam in phys. scis. Tchr. physics H.S., Livorno, Italy, 1971-84; prof. physics Accademia Navale, Livorno, 1984—; headmaster Piero Calamandrei H.S., Firenze, Italy, 1998—. Reviewer Jour. Applied Physics, 1997—, Applied Physics Letters, 1997—; contbr. articles to profl. jours. Mem. N.Y. Acad. Scis. Avocations: history, poetry, fiction, movies, swimming. Office: Accad Navale Gruppo Fisica, Viale Italia 72, 57100 Livorno Italy

GIUDICE, CARLOS ALBERTO, research educator; b. La Plata, Argentina, Dec. 20, 1948; s. Domingo Luis Giudice and Elba Matilde Aiello; m. Irma Noemi Argondizzo, Feb. 13, 1975; children: Carlos Hernan, Carlos Fabian. Chem. technician, Albert Thomas, La Plata, 1967; chem. engr., Nat. U., La Plata, 1973, PhD, 1993. Engring. diplomate. Technician Lemit, La Plata, 1968-74; head of pilot plant Cidepint, La Plata, 1975—; rschr. Sci. Rsch. Commn., La Plata, 1980-83, Conicet, La Plata, 1983—; prof. Nat. U., La Plata, 1981-83, Nat. Technol. U., La Plata, 1995—; vice-head Cidepint, La Plata, 1991-94. Contbr. rsch. articles to profl. jours. Fin. grantee Conicet, 1985, 92, Sci. Rsch. Commn., 1993. Mem. Argentinian Corrosion Assn. (pres. 1996—), Chem. Engrs. Assn. Roman Catholic. Avocations: gymnastics, jogging, listening to classical music, reading detective stories. Home: Calle 71 n 485, 1900 La Plata Argentina Office: Cidepint, Calle 52 e/ 121 y 122, 1900 La Plata Buenos Aires

GIUDICE, GIOVANNI GIUSEPPE, biology educator; b. Palermo, Italy, Sept. 24, 1933; s. Vito and Eleonora (La Bua) G.; m. Anna Maria Amore, June 27, 1961; children: Silvia, Elisa. MD, U. Palermo, 1956. Prof. U. Palermo, 1971—, dean Faculty Sci., 1973-76, dir. dept. cell devel. biology, 1983-89, 93-99, dir. Inst. Devel. Biology, 1980-94, vice rector, 1993-96; pres. Inst. Gramsci Sicil, 1992—; mem. corp. Woods Hole, Mass., 1966—; mem. sci. coun. 1st Sup. Sanità, Rome, 1977-83. Author: Developmental Biology Sea Urchin Embryos, 1973, 86; mem. editl. bds. several sci. jours.; author novels; contbr. articles to profl. jours. Senator, Italian Republic, Rome, 1973-79; dep. Italian Chamber, Rome, 1974-83. Recipient prize Mondello, 1990, Dorso prize Nat. Rsch. Coun. Naples, 1988. Mem. Acad. Naz. Lincei (Feltrinelli prize 1996), Internat. Cell Rsch. Orgn., European Cellular Biol. Orgn., Italian Assn. Cell Biology (hon.; pres. 1986-90), Italian Soc. Reproductive Devel. (pres. 1973-83). Avocation: writing novels. Home: Via Pie di Paterno 172, 190145 Palermo Italy Office: Dept Biology, Viale delle Scienze, 90128 Palermo Italy

GIUFFRÉ, JOHN JOSEPH, lawyer; b. Bklyn., Nov. 30, 1963; s. John B. and Marilyn N. G.; m. Lauren P. Dippel, Sept. 1, 1990; 1 child, John Paul. BA, Columbia Coll., 1984; JD cum laude, U. Pa., 1987. Bar: N.J. 1987, N.Y. 1988, Conn. 1988, Pa. 1988, U.S. Dist. Ct. (so. and ea. dists.) N.Y. 1989. Assoc. labor and employment law sect. Morgan, Lewis & Bockius, N.Y.C., 1987-88; assoc. McLaughlin & McLaughlin, Bklyn., 1988-93; founding ptnr. Giuffré & Kaplan, PC, Hicksville, N.Y., 1994—. Editor: U. Pa. Jour. Comparative Bus. and Capital Market Law, 1985-86; sr. editor: U. Pa. Jour. Internat. Bus. Law, 1986-87. Vol. lawyer Bklyn. Bar Assn. Vol. Lawyer Project, 1992-93; trustee 1st Presbyn. Ch., Flushing, N.Y., 1991-92, pres. bd. trustees, 1993, elder, 1996—; bd. dirs. Flushing Christian Sch., 1994—. Mem. Nassau County Bar Assn., Phi Beta Kappa. Avocations: reading, studying history, ice hockey. Office: Giuffré & Kaplan PC 28 E Old Country Rd Hicksville NY 11801-4207

GIUFFRIDA, DARIO F., oncologist, consultant; b. Catania, Sicily, Italy, Aug. 25, 1957; s. Cesare P. Giuffrida and Giulia M. Campisi; m. Rosaria G. Catalfamo, July 28; children: Giulia, Paolo. MD, U. Catania, 1982. Fellow in endocrinology U. Catania, 1982-85, resident in oncology, 1985-89; cons. in endocrinology, Catania, 1989-95; vice chief med. oncolgy Hops. S. Luigi, Catania, 1995—; cons. in oncology, Catania, 1995—. FIRC Mayo Clinic, Rochester, Minn., 1994, 99. Mem. ATA, ESMO, ETA. Avocations: philately, music, reading, sports. Home: Via G Verga 43, 95030 S Agata li Battiati CT, Italy Office: Hosp S Luigi Onc Med Svc, Viale Fleming 24, 95125 Catania CT, Italy

GIULIO, LUDOVICO FILIPPO, veterinary physiology educator, neurophysiologist; b. Casale, Italy, Sept. 29, 1926; s. Francesco Paolo and Maria Vittoria (Callori) G.; m. Maria Marta Mongini, Dec. 18, 1954; children: Barbara, Alessandra. MD, U. Turin, Italy, 1949. Extraordinary prof. vet. physiology U. Perugia, Italy, 1965-68, prof. vet. physiology, 1968-72; prof. vet. physiology U. Turin, 1972-97, dir. Inst. Vet. Physiology, 1972-87. Author: Time's Molecules, 1991; co-author handbook: Physiology of Domestic Animals, 1992. Mem. N.Y. Acad. Scis., Accademia delle Scienze Torino, Rotary Internat. Home: Genovesi 15, 10128 Turin Italy Office: U Turin, viale Mattioli 25, 10125 Turin Italy

GIUNTI, MARCO, philosophy educator; b. Florence, Italy, Aug. 6, 1955; s. Mario and Pierina (Buffoni) G. Laurea in Filosofia, U. Florence, 1981; MA in History and Philosophy of Sci., Ind. U., 1988, PhD in History and Philosophy of Sci., 1992. Philosophy tchr. Liceo Rodolico, Florence, 1992-93, Liceo Copernico, Prato, Italy, 1995-96, Istituto Magistrale Rodari, Prato, 1996-97, Liceo Machiavelli-Capponi, Florence, 1998-99, Liceo Giotto Ulivi, Florence, 1999—; rsch. assoc. dept. history and philosophy of sci. Ind. U., Bloomington, 1993. Author: Computation, Dynamics and Cognition, 1997; contbr. articles to profl. jours. Mem. Am. Philos. Assn., Cognitive Sci. Soc., Philosophy of Sci. Assn., Società Italiana di Logica e Filosofia delle Scienze, Società Filosofica Italiana. Home: Borgo Ognissanti 94, I-50123 Florence Italy

GIVEN, DAVID ROGER, research scientist; b. Nelson, New Zealand, Nov. 8, 1943; s. Bruce and Brenda (Gower-Jones) G.; m. Karina Jansen, May 4, 1968; children: Bronwyn, Andrew, Craig. BS, Canterbury U. N.Z., 1965, PhD, 1970; theology cert., Moore U. Sydney, 1975. Scientist DSIR, New Zealand, 1965-92; prin. David Given & Assocs., Christchurch, New Zealand, 1992—; mgr., assoc. prof. Internat. Ctr. for Nature Conservation, Lincoln U., New Zealand; rsch. fellow Nat. Rsch. Coun. Can., 1973-74; contract lectr. Lincoln U., N.Z., 1996—; exec. IUCN Species Survival Commn., Switzerland, 1996—, chair plant program, 1996—; trustee Pacific Conservation and Devel. Trust, N.Z., 1993-99; mem. UNEP/STAP Roster of Experts, 1994—; cons. to Coun. Sarawak Biodiversity Ctr., Malaysia, 1998—. Author: Principles and Practice Plant Conservation, 1995, Rare and Endangered Plants of New Zealand, 1981; co-author: Red Data Book of New Zealand, 1981; contbr. numerous articles to profl. jour. Chair regional bd. New Zealand Bible Coll., Christchurch, 1996-98; mem. conservation bd. Riccarton Bush Trust, Christchurch, 1995-99. Recipient Loder Cup New Zealand Min. Conservation, 1995, Assoc. of Honor award Royal New Zealand Inst. Horticulture, 1993; named Artiste, Fed. Internat. d'Arte Photographique, 1990. Fellow Linnean Soc. London; mem. Soc. Conservation Biology, New Zealand Photographic Soc. (internat. judging panel). Avocations: exploring, photography, music, tourism guiding. Home and Office: 101 Jeffreys Rd, Christchurch 8005, New Zealand

GIVENCHY, HUBERT JAMES MARCEL TAFFIN DE, fashion designer; b. Beauvais, France, Feb. 20, 1927; s. Lucien and Béatrice (Badin) Taffin de G. Ed., École nationale supérieure des beaux-arts. Faculty of Law U. Paris; Apprenticeship fashion houses of Lelong, 1945-46; apprentice fashion houses of Piquet, 1946-48; Apprenticeship fashion houses of Fath, 1948-49, Schiaparelli, 1949-51; opened his own fashion house, Paris, 1952-56; pres., dir. gen. Givenchy-Couture, 1954—; pres. Christie's France, 1997—. Designer costumes for films Breakfast at Tiffany's, 1961, Charade, 1963, Paris When It Sizzles, 1964, How To Steal a Million, 1966. Decorated chevalier Legion of Honor. Avocations: tennis; swimming; skiing; horseback riding. Home: 3 Ave George V, F-75008 Paris France Office: 9 Ave Matignon, 75008 Paris France*

GIVHAN, ROBERT MARCUS, lawyer; b. Mineral Wells, Tex., May 10, 1959; s. Walter Houston Givhan and Marion Blackwell Callen Stothart; m. Janet Lee Dothard, May 6, 1989; children: Vivian Lee, Charlotte Ann, Virginia Mae. BA, U. Ala., Tuscaloosa, 1981; JD, Cumberland Sch. Law, Birmingham, Ala., 1986. Bar: Ala. 1987, D.C. 1989, U.S. Supreme Ct. 1989, U.S. Ct. Appeals (D.C. and 11th cirs.), U.S. Dist. Ct. (so., mid. and no. dists.) Ala. 1987. Assoc. Perry and Russell, Montgomery, Ala., 1987-88; dep. dist. atty. 15th Jud. Cir. of Ala., Montgomery, 1988-91; dep. atty. gen. Office of Atty. Gen. of Ala., Montgomery, 1991-95; ptnr. Johnston Barton Proctor & Powell LLP, Birmingham, 1995—. Fellow Am. Coll. Pros. Attys.; mem. ABA (vice chmn. antitrust competition and trade regulation com. of adminstrv. law sect. 1994—), Ala. State Bar Assn., Birmingham Bar Assn. (co-chmn. econs. of law practice com. 1998, 99), Am. Health Lawyers Assn. Episcopalian. Avocations: whitewater rafting, hiking, music collecting, book collecting. Home: 427 Cliff Pl Birmingham AL 35209-5201 Office: 2900 AmSouth/Harbert Plz 1901 6th Ave N Birmingham AL 35203-2618

GIVHAN, STEVEN ALLEN, engineering company executive; b. Chgo.; s. Claude Raymond and Christine E. (Jackson) G.; m. Octavia Walker, Jan. 3, 1982; children: Khaliah, Kevin. BS in Mech. Engring., U. Calif., Santa Barbara, 1974; MS, U. Hawaii, 1976; MBA (hon.) Oxford U., Eng., 1981. Registered profl. engr., Ill., Calif., D.C. Mech. designer Sonicraft Inc., Chgo., 1980-82; pres. NDT 1 Inc., Chgo., 1982—; dir. Auburn Park Engelwood Local Devel. Corp. Patentee in field. Bd. dirs. Kennedy King Coll., Chgo., 1984; mem. Congl. Task Force, Chgo., 1984—; indsl. task force Dawson Inst., Chgo.; mem. task force 1st Congl. Dist., 1989—, mem. Chgo. task force; mem. 1990 Presdl. Commn. on Minority Bus. Devel. Lt. comdr. USN, 1973-79. Mem. ASME, AAAS, Internat. Atomic Agy., Nat. Assn. Profl. Engrs., No. Def. Coun. for Small Bus., Am. Trial Lawyers Assn., Vietnam Vets. Roman Catholic. Avocations: golf, swimming, tennis, model railroading.

GIVOT, WINNIE, artist, educator; b. Mount Holly, N.J., Dec. 29, 1944; d. Richard H. and Mary E.G. Rhoads; m. Irv Givot, Aug. 24, 1968; children: Rima M., John A. BA in Econs., Wheaton Coll., 1967; postgrad. in Econs., Brown U., 1968-70. Artist Givot Studio and Gallery, Sisters, Oreg., 1992—; workshop asst. Art in the Mountains, Bend, Oreg., 1996—; interior design Two Rivers Farm, Aurora, Oreg., 1980-92, Metanoia Soc., Bend, Oreg., 1996-99; tchr. Givot Studio and Gallery, 1996—; juror art shows Mirror Pond Gallery, Bend, Oreg., 1996-98. Exhibited in numerous one-person and group shows; represented in numerous pub. and pvt. collections. Mem. Watercolor Soc. Oreg., Northwest Watercolor Soc., Ctrl. Oreg. Arts Assn. (exhibit com. 1993-95), Ga. Watercolor Soc., Ctrl. Oreg. Artist Assn., Tex. Watercolor Assn. E-mail: givots@outlawnet.com. Home and Office: Givot Studio and Gallery 69953 Holmes Rd Sisters OR 97759-9706

GJEDREM, SVEIN, banker. Gov. Ctrl. Bank of Norway. Office: Norges Bank, Bankplassen 2, 0107 Oslo Norway

GJERMANI, LINDA, educational researcher, consultant; b. Tirana, Albania, Feb. 9, 1962; d. Nos and Hafize (Abazi) Nosi; m. Mishel Gjermani, Sept. 27, 1984; children: Kejda, Milida. Univ. diploma, U. Tirana, 1984; MS, U. Twente, Enschede, The Netherlands, 1997. Tchg. diploma for h.s. physics. Tchr. h.s. Kruja, Albania, 1984-85; tchr. mid. sch. Tirana, 1985-87; editor-in-chief Inst. Pedagogical Rsch., Tirana, 1987-94, rschr., 1994—; cons. Children's Aid Direct, Tirana, 1998, Soros Found., Tirana, 1996-98, Cath. Relief Svcs., Tirana, 1996-98, mem. steering com., 1996-98; project dir. UNICEF, Tirana, 1994-97; cons. World Bank, 1998-99. Author: (books) Pedagogical Review, 1996, 97, Education in Albania, A National Dossier, 1997, The Parents and the School-Possible Friends, 1998, The Professional Ethics of Teachers, 1999; editor-in-chief: (book) Vocational Education, 1987-93; contbr. articles to mags. Rep. Property with Justice, Albania, 1993. Fellow Albanian Physicists Assn.; mem. Edn. Devel. Ctr. Avocations: reading, music, swimming. Home: Pall 39 Shk 4 Ap 46, RR Kongresi I Lushnjes, Tirana Albania Office: Inst Pedagogical Rsch, RR Naim Frasheri, NR 37 Tirana Albania

GJERRIS, FLEMMING OTT, neurosurgeon, educator; b. Copenhagen, Denmark, July 1, 1936; s. Jens Christian and Erna (Petersen) G.; m. Annette Jensen, Mar. 9, 1963; children: Christine, Helene, Casper. MD, U. Copenhagen, 1963, specialist in neurosurgery, 1973, DSc, 1979. Cons. neurosurgeon U. Clinic Neurosurgery, Rigshospitalet, Copenhagen, 1976-83, prof., dir., 1985—; dir. dept. neurosurgery Copenhagen County Hosp., Glostrup, 1983-85; pres. Danish Neurol. Soc., 1980-83; councillor Scandinavian Neurosurg. Soc., 1985-92; v.p., pres. Academia Eurasiana Neurochirurgica, 1990-94. Contbr. chpts. to books and articles to profl. jours. Mem. European Assn. Neurosurg. Socs. (v.p. 1987-91, pres. 1995-99). Avocations: sailing, fishing. E-mail: flemmingg@gjerris.dk. Home: Svanevaenget 3, DK-2100 Copenhagen Denmark Office: Univ Clin Neurosurgery, Rigshospitalet, DK-2100 Copenhagen Denmark

GJERSHAUG, JAN OVE, wildlife biologist; b. Verma, Norway, May 7, 1952; s. Magnar and Margit (Moen) G.; m. Gunn Elin Alsaker, May 21, 1976; children: Svanhild, Ane Marte. MSc, U. Trondheim, Norway, 1981. Wildlife biologist Norwegian Inst. for Nature Rsch., Trondheim, 1981—. Author: Dovrefjell, 1994; editor: Norsk Fugleatlas, 1994. Mem. World Working Group of Birds of Prey and Owls, Norwegian Ornithol. Soc., Raptor Rsch. Found. Avocations: bird watching. Office: Norwegian Inst Nature Rsch, Tungasletta 2, 7005 Trondheim Norway

GJØRTLER, PETER, lawyer; b. Copenhagen, Aug. 19, 1956; s. Erik and Kirsten (Mørkeberg) G.; m. Annette Midtgaard Madsen, Aug. 9, 1986; 1 child, Marie. MA in Law, U. Copenhagen, 1985, BA in Econs., 1989. Head sect. Ministry of Justice, Copenhagen, 1985-92; legal sec. European Ct. of Justice, Luxembourg, 1987-90; advocate Kammeradvokaten, Copenhagen, 1990-91, Dragsted & Helmer Nielsen, Copenhagen, 1995-99, DSPA Internat., Copenhagen, 1999-00; judge High Ct. of Appeals, Copenhagen, 2000—. Author: The Treaties of the European Union, 1996; contbr. articles to profl. jours. Mem. Danish Coun. European Policy, 1993—; mem., past pres. Danish Mil. Hist. Soc. Sr. rsch. fellow U. Copenhagen, 1992-95. Mem. Danish Soc. European Lawyers (bd. dirs. 1992—), Danish Bar Assn. (com. mem. 1995). Home: Skolebakken 13, DK-2820 Gentofte Denmark

GJURIĆ SMREVAR, IVA, deputy director; b. Zagreb, Croatia, May 15, 1971; d. Mihajlo and Gorjana (Pepcić) Gjurić Smrevar. BA, Faculty of Econs., Zagreb, Croatia, 1994, postgrad. in orgn. and mgmt. Rep. AMECO, Zagreb, Croatia, 1994-95; product mgr. Pliva, Zagreb, Croatia, 1995-97; dep. dir. Organochem doo, Zagreb, Croatia, 1997—. Home: Krizanceva 11A, 10000 Zagreb Croatia Office: Organochem doo, Mallinova 7, 10000 Zagreb Croatia

GLAAB, CHARLES NELSON, educator, historian; b. b Williston, N.D., Dec. 19, 1927; s. Reuben and Betty (Nelson) G.; m. Mary Ellen Anderson, Nov. 5, 1949; children—Martha Ann, John Reuben. BPh, U. N.D., 1951, MA, 1952; PhD, U. Mo., 1958. Rsch. assoc. history Kansas City project U. Chgo., 1956-58; from instr. to asst. prof. history Kans. State U., 1958-60; from assoc. prof. to prof. history U. Wis., Milw., 1960-68; dir. urban history sect. Wis. Hist. Soc., 1960-63; prof. history U. Toledo, 1968—; Dir. Fox Valley research project Wis. Hist. Soc., 1963-64; mem. Milw. Landmarks Commn., 1965-68, Toledo Landmark Com., 1968-70, Ohio Hist. Site Preservation Bd., 1979-81. Author: Kansas City and the Railroads, 1962, The American City: A Documentary History, 1963, (with A.T. Brown) A History of Urban America, 1967, (with L.H. Larsen) Factories in the Valley, 1969, (with Morgan A. Barclay) Toledo: Gateway to the Great Lakes, 1983; editor: Urban History Group Newsletter, 1962-68; co-editor, 1968-70, N.W. Ohio Quar., 1994-99; mem bd. editors Urban Affairs Quar, 1966-74, Soc. Press Wis, 1966-7 Jour. Urban History, 1973-88, Urban Affairs Ann. Rev, 1978-82, Frederick Law Olmsted Papers, 1985-90, Hayes Hist. Jour., 1987-91. Served with AUS, 1946-48. Mem. Orgn. Am. Historians, Am. Hist. Assn., Urban History Assn., Phi Beta Kappa. Home: 3021 Hopewell Pl Toledo OH 43606-3105

GLABINSKI, ANDRZEJ ROMAN, neurologist, educator, researcher; b. Myszkow, Poland, Aug. 20, 1961; came to U.S., 1993; s. Antoni and Ewa (Spiolek) G.; m. Ewa Maria Stankiewicz, Nov. 29, 1986; children: Piotr, Agata. BA, City Coll., Myszkow, Poland, 1980; MD, Silesian Med. Acad., Katowice, Poland, 1986; PhD, Med. Acad. Lodz, Poland, 1992. Jr. asst. Med. Acad. Lodz, Poland, 1987-88, asst. prof. dept. physiology, 1988-90, asst. prof. dept. neurology, 1990-98, assoc. prof. dept. neurology, 1998—; postdoctoral fellow Cleve. Clinic Found., 1993-96; asst. resident Silesian Cardiology Ctr., Katowice, Poland, 1986-87; resident in neurology Barlicki Hosp., Lodz, 1987—. Contbr. articles to profl. jours. Mem. Polish Neurol. Soc. Home: ul Gorkiego 83 m 27, 92-518 Lodz Poland Office: Med Univ Dept Neurology, ul Kopcinskiego 22, Lodz 90-153, Poland

GLACEL, BARBARA PATE, management consultant; b. Balt., Sept. 15, 1948; d. Jason Thomas Pate and Sarah Virginia (Forwood) Wetter; m. Robert Allan Glacel, Dec. 21, 1969; children: Jennifer Warren, Sarah Allane, Ashley Virginia. AB, Coll. William and Mary, 1970; MA, U. Okla., 1973, PhD, 1978. Tchr. Harford County (Md.) Schs., 1970-71; tchr. Dept. Def. Schs., W.Ger., 1971-73; ednl. counselor U.S. Army, Germany, 1973-74; mgmt. cons. Barbara Glacel & Assocs., Anchorage, 1980-86, Washington, 1986-88; ptnr. Pracel Prints, Williamsburg, Va., 1981-85; sr. mgmt. tng. specialist Arco Alaska, Inc., 1984-85; gen. mgr. mgmt. programs Hay Systems, Inc., Washington, 1986-88; CEO VIMA Internat., Burke, Va., 1988-99, chmn. emeritus, 2000; 2d v.p., bd. dirs. Chesapeake Broadcasting Corp. Md.; prin. Glacel Devel. Group, 2000—; adj. prof. U. Md., 1973-74, Suffolk U., Boston, 1974-77, C.W. Post Ctr., L.I. U., John Jay Coll. Criminal Justice, N.Y.C., 1979-80, St. Thomas Aquinas Coll., N.Y.C., 1981, St. Mary's Coll., Leavenworth, Kans., 1981, Anchorage C.C., 1982; acad. adviser Ctrl. Mich. U., 1981-82; asst. prof. U. Alaska, Anchorage, 1983-85; mem. adj. faculty Ctr. for Creative Leadership, 1986—; guest lectr. U.S. Mil. Acad.; mem. U.S. Army Sci. Bd., 1986-90; mem. U.S. Dept. Def. Sci. Bd. Quality of Life Panel, 1994-95, Def. Adv. Com. on Women in the Svcs., 2000—. Author: Regional Transit Authorities, 1983; (with others) 1000 Army Families, 1983, The Army Community and Their Families, 1989, Light Bulbs for Leaders, 1994, Coping With Cancer, 2000. Chmn. 172d Inf. Brigade Family Coun. Recipient Comdr.'s award for pub. svc. U.S. Dept. Army, 1984, U.S. Army Patriotic Civilian Svc. award 1991, U.S. Army Forscom Svc. award 1993, Dept. of Army Outstanding Civilian Svc. medal, 1999, Yellow Rose of Tex. award, 1999, Helping Hand Cmty. Svc. award, 1999; AAUW grantee, 1977-78. Mem. ASTD (bd. dirs. Anchorage chpt.), Am. Psychol. Assn., Soc. for Indsl. and Organizational Psychology, Instrnl. Systems Assn. (v.p. 1993-96), Soc. of Alumni Coll. of William and Mary (bd. dirs. 1992-98, v.p., 1997-98).

GLADDEN, GARNETT LEE, educator, psychologist; b. May 8, 1922. AB, U. Calif., 1943; MA, Claremont Coll., 1948; PhD, Honolulu U., 1989. Prof. emeritus Riverside (Calif.) City Coll., 1946-77; psychologist Anza Human Rels. Ctr., Riverside, 1948-78; v.p. Golden State U., L.A., 1978-82; dean Grad. Studies, provost Honolulu U., 1982-98; scientific cons. Japan LifeLtd., L.A. & Tokyo, 1986-98. Author: (with M. Vivianne Cervantes Gladden) How to Win the Aging Game, 1958. Home: 24414 University Ave # 17 Loma Linda CA 92354-2648

GLADFELTER, HARRY FOSTER, chemist, researcher; b. Audobon, N.J., Apr. 6, 1943; s. Harry A. and Marion A. (Stetler) G.; Marsha Rice, Jan. 28, 1967 (div. 1979); children: Christian F., Heather G., Harry A.; m. v. Jerene Abbett Gladfelter, June 20, 1992. Cert., Temple U., Phila., 1963; BS in Chemistry, Phila. Coll. Textile & Sci., Phila., 1973. Product devel. mgr. Asten Group, Charleston, S.C., 1974-81; product concept mgr. Federal Mogul Sys. Protection Group, Exton, Pa., 1981—. Inventor: Shielding Fabric, 1987, Protective Fabric Sleeve, 1990, Sound Absorbent Sleeve, 1991, Wraparound Device, 1993, Abrasion Resistance Sleeve, 1993, Wraparound Sleeve, 1994, Reflective Foam, 1998, Wrappable Sleeve, 1998. Dist. Commr. Boy Scouts of Am., Chester County Coun., Pa., 1995—. Staff sgt. USMC, 1964-70. Recipient Dist. Award of Merit, 1994, chmn.'s award, 1993, BSA Diamond Rock Dist., Chester County Coun., Pa. Mem. ACS., Order of the Arrow. Democrat. Lutheran. Avocations: camping, fishing, hiking, biking. Home: 103 Brian Way Kimberton PA 19442 Office: Federal Mogul Sys Protection Group 241 Welsh Pool Rd Exton PA 19341-1316

GLADFELTER, WILBERT EUGENE, physiology educator; b. York, Pa., Apr. 29, 1928; s. Paul John and Marea Bernadette (Miller) G.; m. Ruth Isabelle Ballantyne, Jan. 26, 1952; children: James W., Charles D., Mary A. AB magna cum laude, Gettysburg (Pa.) Coll., 1952; PhD, U. Pa., 1960. NSF fellow U. Pa., Phila., 1956-58, NIH fellow, 1958-59, asst. instr., 1954-56; instr. physiology W.Va. U., Morgantown, 1959-61, asst. prof., 1961-69, assoc. prof., 1969-96, prof. emeritus, 1996—. Contbr. articles to profl. jours. Treas., Monongalia County chpt. W. Va. Heart Assn., 1976-95. With USN, 1946-48. NSF fellow, 1956-58. Mem. Am. Physiol. Soc., Soc. Neurosci., Soc. for Integrative and Comparative Biology, Sigma Xi, Phi Beta Kappa, Beta Beta Beta. Lutheran. Home: 70 Pine Tree Ln Morgantown WV 26508-2929 Office: WVa U Health Sci Ctr Dept Physiology Morgantown WV 26506

GLADKI, HANNA ZOFIA, civil engineer, hydraulic mixer specialist; b. Krakow, Poland, Dec. 30, 1933; came to U.S., 1984; d. Stanislaw Wojtanowski and Maria (Ekiert) Wojtanowska; m. Jozef Gladki, July 2, 1955 (dec. 1982); 1 child, Ania. ScD, Tech. U., Warsaw, Poland, 1966; postgrad. degree, Agrl. U., Wroclaw, Poland, 1977. Asst. prof. Agrl. Acad. Krakow, 1966-70, assoc. prof., 1970-81, chair dept., 1973-83, dean of faculty, 1977-81, prof., 1981-85; hydraulic mixer specialist ITT Flygt Corp., Norwalk, Conn., 1985—; presenter at profl. confs. Contbr. articles to profl. publs. Mem. AIChE, N.Am. Mixing Forum, Internat. Assn. Hydraulic Rsch. Roman Catholic. Achievements include expertise in hydraulics, flow velocity, pressure, mixing slurry and viscous fluid in tanks, non-Newtonian fluids and slurry for industry; designing mixers in the process industry and for biological and sludge treatment; development of method for sizing mixers in oxidation ditches with clarifier, and method of determining power dissipation and thrust force in the mixing tank with Free Jet Flow Agitators (FJFA). Home: 10 Greenview Ln Milford CT 06460-2364 Office: ITT Flygt Corp PO Box 1004 Trumbull CT 06611-0943

GLADKOV, PETER STEFANOV, physicist, researcher; b. Plovdiv, Bulgaria, June 28, 1940; arrived in the Czech Republic, 1995; s. Stefan Petrov and Christina Angelova (Nikova) G.; m. Hana Gulova, Feb. 16, 1989; 1 child, Christina. Masters Degree, Sofia (Bulgaria) U., 1966; PhD, Lebedev's Inst. Acad. Scis., Moscow, 1973. Cert. physics of semiconductors. Asst. sci. rschr. Sofia U., 1966-68, asst. prof. faculty physics, 1973-75, assoc. prof. faculty physics, 1975-95, vice-dean faculty physics, 1978-82, vice-rector, 1987-89, dir. Inst. Semiconductor Physics and Tech., 1989-94; sci. rschr. Inst. Radioengring., Acad. Sci., Prague, Czech Republic, 1995—. Contbr. articles to profl. jours. Alexander von Humboldt fellow U. Stuttgart, Germany, 1977-78. Mem. Phys. Soc. Bulgaria. Mem. Orthodox Church. Avocations: classical music, photography, sports. E-mail: gladkov@ure.cas.cz. Home: ul Prava No 5, 147 00 Praha 4, Czech Republic Office: Inst Radioengring & Electr, Chaberska 57, 182 51 Praha 8, Czech Republic

GLADOVSKY, SERGEY ALEKSANDROVITCH, governmental manager; b. Priluky, Ukraine, Feb. 5, 1954; s. Ninel Viktorovna (Gladovskaya) Shershakova; m. Galina Virtorovna Rassolova, Aug. 1, 1979; children: Irina, Oksana. Navgator-engineere, High-Marine, Vladivostok, Russia, 1977. Chiefmate Prisco, Narhodka, Russia, 1977-94; mgr. Foreign Econ. Activity Dept., Narhodka, 1994—. Avocations: soccer fan, books, internet. Office: Promorsk Shipping Corp, Adminstrn Gorodok, 632900 Narhodka Russia

GLADYSHEV, GEORGI PAVLOVICH, research chemist; b. Alma-Ata, Kazakhstan, USSR, Sept. 19, 1936; s. Pavel Jakovlevich Gladyshev and Apollinariya Michaelovna Zaikova; children: Andrei, Ekaterina. Candidate of sci., Kazakhstan Acad. Scis., Alma-Ata, 1962, DSc, 1966; prof. phys. chemistry, USSR Acad. Scis., Uta, 1969; prof. biomed. systems, State Tech. U., Moscow, 1975. Sci. worker Kazakhstan Acad. Scis., 1962-68; chief of lab. USSR Acad. Scis. Inst. Organic Chemistry, Uta, 1968-69, USSR Acad. Scis. Inst. Chem. Physics, Moscow, 1970—; pres., founder Internat. Acad. Creative Endeavors, Moscow, 1989—, dir. Inst., 1990—; vis. lectr. State U. Alma-Ata, 1963-67; vis. adviser Indsl. Chem. Firm, Dzerjinsk, USSR, 1966-76; vis. prof. macromolecular chemistry State U. Uta, 1968-70; vis. prof. phys. chemistry State Tech. U., Moscow, 1975-85. Author: The Polymerisation of Vinyl Monomers, 1964 (Inst. of Chemistry award 1965), Thermodynamics and Macrokinetics of Natural Hierarchical Processes, 1988, Thermodynamic Theory of the Evolution of Living Beings, 1997; contbr. articles to profl. jours. Mem. Presidium br. USSR Acad. Sci., Uta, 1968-70; sec. Moscow br. Union Scientific and Engring. Soc. Moscow, 1987-94. Hon. mem. Internat. Order of Merit, Cambridge, Eng., 1994, Internat. Higher Edn. Acad. Scis., Moscow, 1995; recipient Willard Gibbs Gold medal, acad. com. under leadership of N.N. Bogolubov, Moscow, 1991. Mem. Moscow Acad. Natural Scis., Internat. Acad. Scis. (Munich). Avocations: science, medicine, music, mountaineering, travel. Office: Internat Acad Creative Endeavors, 36 Novy Arbat, 121205 Moscow Russia

GLADYSHEVA, INNA, biochemist, researcher; b. Kazakhstan, Russia, July 12, 1966; d. Pavel Pavlovich and Galina Pavlovana Gladyshev; m. Ilia Valterovich Fourman, Mar. 30, 1990; 1 child, Anastasiya. BSc, S.M. Kirov Kazakh State U., Alama-Ata, Kazakhstan, 1986; Msc in Chemistry, M.V. Lomonosov Moscow State U., 1989, PhD in Chemistry, 1994. Rschr. divsn. chem. enzymology dept. chemistry Moscow State U., 1992-94, sci. rschr., 1994—; buyer women's evening dresses Intercon. Devel. LLC, Moscow and N.Y.C., 1996-99. Contbr. articles to sci. jours., including Cancer Jour., FEBS Letters, Physiol. Plantarum. Recipient award Controlled Release Soc., 1999; sci. grantee Soros Internat. Found., 1995-96; travel grantee for meeting, Pisa, Italy, 1999. Mem. Biochem. Soc., N.Y. Acad. Scis. Avocations: travel, sports. Fax: 007-095-9395417. E-mail: gladysheva@enzyme.chem.msu.ru. Office: Moscow State U, Chemistry Dept, 1199889 Moscow Russia

GLADYSZ, ANTONI, sociology educator; b. Kluczbork, Poland, Nov. 18, 1915; s. Jan and Rosalia (Langhammer) G.; m. Luzia Szczurek, Mar. 6, 1945; children: Marzeli, Jan. BA, U Adam Mickiewicz, Poznan, Poland, 1938; PhD, U Wroclaw (Breslau), Wroclaw, Poland, 1966. Asst. Silesian Inst., Katowice, Poland, 1963-73; proctor Silesian U., Filia Cieszyn, Poland, 1974-77, dean, 1977-78, chmn. Cultural Animation Faculty, 1974-98. Author: A Book in Upper-Silesian Industry Region, 1970, Workmen and Books, 1972, Culture in Gross Industrial Societies, 1975, Education, Culture and Science in Poland, 1947-1969, 1981, 87. Mem. Polish Sociological Soc. Christian Dem. Roman Catholic. Avocation: classical music. Home: Paderewskiego 7, 43400 Cieszyn Poland

GLAENZER, CAMILLE HENRI, security consultant; b. Le Chesnay, France, June 20, 1932; s. Louis J. and Helene T. (Frey) G.; m. Francoise S. Danmanville, Sept. 18, 1956; children: Christian, Olivier, Laurent, Eric. Diploma in bus., Sch. Superieure Commerce, Paris, 1954. Asst. to European mgr. Bendix Aviation Corp., N.Y.C., then Paris, 1954-59; br. mgr. SKF, Paris, then Bordeaux, France, 1959-63; comml. mgr. Glaenzer & Spicer, Paris, 1963-71; security equipment export dir. Fichet Bauche, Paris, 1972—. City counsellor, City Town Hall, St. Germain-en-Laye, France, 1965-73. Lt. French armed forces, 1957-59. Mem. Am. Soc. Indsl. Security, Mktg. and Export Group Paris, Brit. C. of C. of Paris. Avocation: photography. Home: Ferney Voltaire, 78100 Saint-Germain-en-Laye France

GLAESER, WILLIAM A., materials scientist, consultant; b. Utica, N.Y., Aug. 25, 1923; s. Hugo W. and Irene G. G.; m. Betty G. Glaeser, May 6, 1951. BS in Mech. Engring., Cornell U., 1949; MSMetE, Ohio State U., 1959. Engr. Clark Brothers, Olean, N.Y., 1949-51; rsch. leader Battelle, Columbus, Ohio, 1951—; Mem. editl. bd. Wear Jour. Elsevier, 1960—, Elsevier Tribology Series, 1970—; chmn. Gordon Conf. Tribology, New London, N.H., 1982; mem. Erosion Control Adv., Nat. Acad. Scis., Washington, 1977. Author: (textbooks) Materials for Tribology, 1992, Characterization of Tribological Materials, 1993; contbr. more than 50 articles to profl. jours. Elder Overbrook Presbyn. Ch., Columbus, 1978—; vol. Pub. Broadcasting Sta. WOSU, Columbus; charter mem. Clintonville Arts Guild (pres. 1978-81). Fellow Soc. of Tribologists & Lubrication Engrs. (bd. dirs., chmn. Wear of Materials Confs. 1983); mem. Am. Soc. for Metals, Sigma Xi. Avocations: oil painting, fly fishing, swimming, piano. E-mail: glaeser@battelle.org. Home: 731 Lauraland Dr S Columbus OH 43214-2433 Office: Battelle Columbus OH

GLAESSNER, GERT-JOACHIM, science educator; b. Erfurt, Thuringia, Germany, Sept. 13, 1944. Univ. diploma, Free U., Berlin, 1971, PhD in Polit. Sci., 1976, Habilitation, 1982. Cert. in polit. sci. and social scis. From asst. prof. to assoc. prof. Free U., 1980-89, prof., 1990-91; prof. Humboldt U., Berlin, 1992—, chair German politics; vis. prof. U. Loughborough, U.K., 1989, U. Conn., 1989, London Sch. Econs., 1994, N.Y.U., 1997. Bd. dirs. Protestant Acad. Berlin, 1976-92. Mem. German Soc. (bd. dirs. 1990—), Am, Polit. Sci. Assn. (bd. dirs. 1991—). E-mail: gert=glaessner@sowi.hu-berlin.de. Office: Humboldt U Berlin, Unter den Linden 6, 10099 Berlin Germany

GLAHN, ESTHER, humanities educator; b. Copenhagen, Apr. 19, 1932. Cand.Mag., U. Copenhagen, 1960. H.S. tchr. Denmark, 1960-66; asst. prof. Odense (Denmark) U., 1966-71; assoc. prof. U. Copenhagen, 1971—. Editor: (in Danish) Foreign Language Pedagogy, 1977, (with Anne Holmen) Learner Discourse, 1985, Applied Linguistics, 1990. Mem. Nat. Com. for Rsch. Planning, Copenhagen, 1975-83, Nordic Counselling Com. for Rsch. Scandinavia, 1976-82. Mem. European Second Lang. Assn. (v.p. 1994-96, pres. 1996-98). Mem. Social Democratic Party. Office: U Copenhagen Inst Almen, Njalsgade 80, DK-2300 Copenhagen Denmark

GLAISE, JOYCE ELIZABETH, secondary education educator, city councilor; b. Danville, Va., June 3, 1950; d. William Felix and Sallie (Grave) G. BS, N.C. Agr. & Tech. State U., 1972, MS, 1975; EdS, U. Va., 1983. Tchr. Danville Pub. Schs., 1972-78, sch. social worker, 1978—. Mem. Danville Voters League, 1984-00, Southside Va. Bus. & Edn. Bd., 1991-95; mem. city coun., Danville, 1988—; bd. dirs. Va. Mus. Natural History, 1990-99; trustee Camp Grove Bapt. Ch., 1993—; v.p. Boys & Girls Clubs Am., 1996-99, Danville Dems.; mem. 5th Dist. Dem. Caucus. Named Outstanding Young Woman Am., 1985; recipient State Achievement award Mins. Wives & Widows, 1995, State Disting. Woman award NAACP. Mem. Rotary, Links (pres. Denville chpt. 1990—), Delta Sigma Theta (pres.). Avocations: sports events, traveling, writing. Home: 122 Tyler Ave Danville VA 24541-4552 Office: Danville City Coun PO Box 3300 Danville VA 24543-3300

GLANCY, DEBORAH A., instructional designer; b. Pawtucket, R.I., Aug. 9, 1966; d. Hugh H. Jr. and Elaine B. G.; m. Anthoula Kyriakou, Oct. 21, 1995 (dec. Feb. 1998). BS in Edn., Lesley Coll., 1990, MS in Tng. and Devel., 1999; cert. in biotech., Middlesex Coll., 1992. Tng. and audit specialist Biogen Inc., Cambridge, Mass., 1992-99; tng. mgr., instructional designer Alkermes Inc., Cambridge, Mass., 1999—. Democrat. Roman Catholic. Avocations: travel, dining, tennis, golf. Office: Alkermes Inc 64 Sidney St Cambridge MA 02139-4170

GLANCY, WALTER JOHN, lawyer; b. L.A., Mar. 8, 1942; s. Walter Perry and Elva Thomasin (Douglass) G.; m. Jane Whetstone Schroeder, Sept. 30, 1995; children by previous marriage: Jill Marie, Gregory Owens. AB, Princeton U., 1964; BA, Oxford U., Eng., 1966; LLB, Yale U., 1969. Bar: Tex. 1971. Law clk. to assoc. justice Byron R. White U.S. Supreme Ct., 1969-70; staff asst. Nat. Security Council, 1970-71; staff asst. to Peter M. Flanigan, The White House, 1971; assoc. then ptnr. Jackson, Walker, Winstead, Cantwell & Miller, Dallas, 1972-76; ptnr. Hughes & Luce and predecessor, Dallas, 1976-85, Baker & Botts, Dallas, 1985-88, Hughes & Luce, Dallas, 1988-90; pvt. practice law Dallas, 1991-95; cons. Meyer, Hendricks, Victor, Osborn & Maledon, Phoenix, 1991-95; ptnr. Weil, Gotshal & Manges LLP, Dallas, 1995-96; pvt. practice Dallas, 1997-99; sr. v.p., gen. counsel, dir. Holly Corp., 1999—; adj. lectr. corp. taxation So. Meth. U. Sch. Law, 1988. Note and comment editor Yale Law Jour., 1968-69. Mem. bd. dirs. Dallas YMCA Urban Svcs., 1975-84; bd. dirs. Dallas Family Guidance Ctr., 1982-96, pres. bd. dirs., 1985-86, Child & Family Guidance Ctrs., Dallas, 1996—; mem. adminstrv. bd. Lovers Ln. United Meth. Ch., Dallas, 1984-86, 88-89; bd. dirs. Dallas Opera, 1984-88, 96-97; trustee Hockaday Sch., Dallas, 1989-95; deacon Park Cities Bapt. Ch., Dallas, 1996—. Nat. Merit scholar, 1960-64; Marshall scholar, 1964-66. Mem. ABA, Dallas Bar Assn. (chmn. legal ethics com. 1980-81), Am. Law Inst., State Bar Tex. (profl. ethics com. 1982—, chmn. tax. sect. 1985-86, chmn. profl. ethics com. 1999—), Park Cities Rotary Club (dir. 1999—), Order of Coif, Phi Beta Kappa. Republican. Home: 9162 Clearlake Dr Dallas TX 75225-2001 Office: 100 Crescent Ct Ste 1600 Dallas TX 75201-6915

GLANTE, NORBERT, member of European parliament; b. Caputh, Germany, Aug. 8, 1952. Mem. European parliament, Germany, 1999—; mem. Group of the Party of European Socialists; mem. com. on industry, external trade, rsch. and energy; substitute com. on econ. and monetary affairs; mem. delegation to the EU-Slovak Republic Joint Parliamentary Com.; substitute mem. delegation to the EU-Poland Joint Parliamentary Com. Office: SPD-Europaburo, Friedrich Ebert-StraBe 61, D-14469 Potsdam Germany

GLANTZ, PER-OLOF JOHAN, dental researcher, dental educator, oral surgeon; b. Lund, Sweden, July 23, 1936; s. Johan Hartvig and Astrid Lilly (Grundström) G.; m. Margareta Anna Weman, Oct. 7, 1961 (dec. Apr. 1999); children: Johan, Charlotta, Eva. DDS, Royal Dental Sch., Malmö, Sweden, 1961; PhD, Odontology Dr., Lund (Sweden) U., 1969; Dr. odontology., U. Oslo, 1986. Bd. cert. specialist in prosthetic dentistry. With Swedish Army Dental Corp., 1961, advanced through grades to lt., ret., 1983; Cons. in prosthetic dentistry Malmö (Sweden) Gen. Hosp., 1967-73; assoc. prof. prosthetic dentistry Lund U., Malmö, 1969-73; prof. dental tech. U. Gothenburgh (Sweden), 1973-77; prof. prosthetic dentistry Lund U., Malmö, 1977—; pro vice chancellor Lund U., 1989-92; dean Faculty Odontology Lund U., Lund-Malmö, 1984-89, 93—; vice chancellor Malmö U., 1998—. Contbr. over 175 articles to dental jours. Recipient W.D. Miller award Swedish Dental Soc., 1979, G.V. Black award, 1990. Fellow Royal Coll. Surgeons Eng., Royal Coll. Surgeons Edinburgh (Scotland), Acad. Dental Materials (Chgo.); mem. Internat. Assn. Dental Rsch. (Washington, Rsch. in Prosthodontics award 1983, pres. 1997-98). Office: Fac Odontology, Carl Gustav 34, S-21421 Malmö Sweden

GLAROS, DIMITRIS, medical physicist, educator; b. Chalkis, Greece. Student, U. Athens, Greece, NRC Democritus, Athens; PhD, U. Strathclyde, Glasgow, Scotland; D (hon.), MIH, Marioupol, Ukraine. Rschr. Saclant Rsch. Ctr., La Spezia, Italy; med. physicist Greek Anticancer Inst., Athens; head med. physics dept. Pamakaristos Hosp., Athens; prof. med. physics U. Ioannin, Greece, rector, prorector; com. mem. European Rectors Conf., Geneva, 1994-99; mem. NRC, Greece, 1993-98; bd. dirs. Greek Atomic Energy Commn., 1987-99; pres. Aimos U. Network, 1996-99. Author books on med. physics; contbr. articles to profl. jours. Pres. Anargyrios Coll. Spetses, Greece, Nat. Repatriation Found., Athens, Greek Red Cross; Gen. Sec. Rsch. and Tech. Sub-lt. Greek Spl. Forces. Fellow I.P.S.M., London. Mem. Hellenic Biomed. Engring. Soc. (pres. 1986-96), N.Y. Acad. Scis.

GLASBERG, SCOT BRADLEY, plastic surgeon; b. N.Y.C., June 30, 1964; s. H. Mark and Paula (Drillman) G.; m. Alisa Goldman, Oct. 17, 1999. BA cum laude, Columbia U., 1986; MD with honors, NYU, 1990. Diplomate Am. Bd. Surgery, Nat. Bd. Med. Examiners, Am. Bd. Plastic Surgery. Resident in surgery U. Conn./Hartford Hosp., 1990-95, chief resident, 1995-96; craniofacial rsch. fellow Inst. of reconstructive Plastic Surgery, NYU Med. Ctr., N.Y.C., 1992-93; fellow SUNY Health Sci. Ctr., Bklyn., 1996-98, assoc. program dir., dir. plastic surg. edn., 1998—. Contbr. articles to profl. jours. Mem. young plastic surgeons com. Plastic Surgery Ednl. Found., Am. Soc. Plastic Surgery, 1996-97, 99—. N.Y. State Regents scholar, 1982-86. Fellow ACS (assoc.); mem. AMA (del. to resident physician sect. 1990-93, 96-98, 99—, plastic surgery caucus 1996-97, 99—, del. to young physicians sect. 1999—), Northeastern Soc. Plastic Surgery (resident/fellows award 1997), Med. Soc. State of N.Y. (del. to AMA resident physician sect. 1996-98, to young physician sect. 1999—, Outstanding Svc. award 1990), N.Y. County Med. Soc., N.Y. Reg. Soc. Plastic and Reconstructive Surgeons (winner clin. paper competition 1997). Avocations: tennis, golf, swimming, card collecting. Office: 42A E 74th St New York NY 10021-2735

GLASBY, MICHAEL ARTHUR, experimental neurology educator, researcher; b. Nottingham, Eng., Oct. 29, 1948; s. Fred and Margaret (Eyres) G.; m. Celia Mary Elizabeth Robinson, July 16, 1981. MA, Oxford (Eng.) U., 1975, MSc, 1975, MB, BChir, 1976; MA, Cambridge (Eng.) U., 1985. Cardiac surgeon Nat. Health Svc., U.K., 1980-83; fellow in anatomy New Hall U. Cambridge, 1983-87; lectr. in anatomy Royal Coll. Surgeons, London, 1984-87; lectr. in anatomy U. Edinburgh, Scotland, 1987-89, sr. lectr. in anatomy, 1989-92, reader in anatomy, 1992-97, reader in exptl. neurology, 1997—; cons. dept. clin. neuroscis. U. Edinburgh. Editor: Applied Physiology for Surgery and Critical Care, 1995; contbr. articles to profl. jours. Fellow Royal Coll. Surgeons of Eng., Internat. Coll. Surgeons, Royal Coll. Surgeons of Edinburgh; mem. Brit. Orthoped. Rsch. Assn., Inst. Biology, Brit. Soc. Surgery of the Hand (assoc.). Avocations: music, Latin and Greek languages, wine, golf. Office: U Edinburgh Clin Neuroscis, Western Gen Hosp Crewe Rd, Edinburgh EH4 2XU, Scotland

GLASCO, KIMBERLY, ballet dancer. Grad., Nat. Ballet Sch. With Nat. Ballet of Can., 1979-83, 84—, 2nd soloist, 1981-82, 84-85, 1st soloist, 1982-83, 85-87, prin. dancer, 1987—; with Am. Ballet Theatre, 1983-84; guest appearances at Australian Spoleto Festival, 1987, World Ballet Festival (Japan), Verona (Italy) Festival. Created roles of Alice in Alice (Glen Tetley), and the Parlormaid in La Ronde (Glen Tetley), Swan Lake, Queen/Black Swan, Sleeping Beauty, Aurora, Valantanes (Kliin Etudes), Transfigured Night, Elite Syncopations, Paquita, Merry Widow, Month in the Country (Kenneth MacMillan), Volantaires (Glen Tetley), Cruel World (Sames Hudelka), Don Q (Petipa), Les Sylphide, La Sylphide, Giselle, Romeo & Juliet, Manon (Kenneth MacMillan), 4 Temperaments (Balanchine), Mozartina (Balanchin), Episodes, among others; appeared also in Footnotes, Nutcracker, Desir, Musings, Symphony in C, Giselle, Onegin, Cinderella, Daphnis and Chloe. Recipient Silver medal Moscow Internat. Ballet Competition, 1981. Office: National Ballet of Canada, 470 Queens Quay W, Toronto, ON Canada M5V 3K4

GLASE, ANNE-KARIN, member European parliament; b. Neuruppin, Germany, July 24, 1954. Mem. European Parliament, Germany, 1999—; mem. Group of the European People's Party (Christian Democrats) and European Democrats; mem. com. on employment and social affairs, com. on devel. and cooperation; substitute mem. European Parliament to the Joint Assembly of the Agreement between the African, Caribbean and Pacific States and the European Union (ACP-EU). Office: H-Rau-StraBe 31, D-16816 Neuruppin Germany*

GLASER, ARTHUR HENRY, lawyer; b. Jersey City, May 1, 1947; s. Ned C. and Lorraine I. (Neil) G.; m. Waynelia Potter, Mar. 19, 1994; children: Kimberly N., Kevin M., Daniel J. BS, Hampden-Sydney Coll., 1968; JD, U. Va., 1973. Bar: Ga. 1973, U.S. Dist. Ct. (no. and mid. dists.) Ga., U.S. Ct. Appeals (11th cir.). Assoc. Swift, Currie, McGhee & Hiers, Atlanta, 1973-78, ptnr., 1978-83; ptnr. Drew, Eckl & Farnham, Atlanta, 1983-98, Self, Glaser & Davis, LLP, Atlanta, 1999—. Mem. ABA, Ga. Bar Assn., Atlanta Bar Assn. Presbyterian. Home: 1540 Burnt Hickory Rd NW Marietta GA 30064-1308 Office: Self Glaser & Davis LLP Ste 1650 400 Interstate North Pkwy SE Atlanta GA 30339-5029

GLASER, BRUNO JOSEF, chemist, researcher; b. Kemnath-Stadt, Bavaria, Germany, Dec. 12, 1966; s. Hermann and Hildegard Glaser. Grad., Fachoberschule, Bayreuth, Germany, 1984; PhD, U. Bayreuth, 1999, postdoctoral, 2000—. Technician U. Bayreuth, 1986-92, scientist, 1996—; lab. leader GTZ, Rwanda, 1990; leader, cons. UTC, Bayreuth, 1998—; web designer BG Cons., Bayreuth, 1999—; translator U. Bayreuth, 1986—. Patentee in field. Friedrich-Ebert-Stifting grantee, Wuppertal, 1992-95. Avocations: stocks, sports, guitar. Home: Hauptstr 29, D-95694 Mehlmeisel Germany Office: Inst of Soil Sci, Universitatsstr 30, 101251 Bayreuth Germany

GLASER, DAVID, painter, sculptor; b. Bklyn., Sept. 29, 1919; s. Samuel and Jennie (Oiffer) G.; m. Millie Sappol, Feb. 19, 1944; children: Susan, Sherry. Student, N.Y. Sch. Indsl. Art, 1937, N.Y. Sch. Contemporary Art, 1947-48, Bklyn. Mus. Art Sch., 1948-50. Illustrator, cartoonist comic books Popular Mechanics, Electronics Illustrated, Popular Sci., N.Y.C., 1939-42, 46-50; pres., designer, inventor Mosamics Co., Bklyn., 1948-50; art dir., advt. mgr. Univ. Loudspeakers, White Plains, N.Y., 1951-60; owner, mgr., graphic designer Studio Concepts, Wantagh, N.Y., 1957—; artist Civilian Conservation Corps, Adirondacks, 1936; tchr. art Ctr. Island Jewish Sch., Freeport, N.Y., 1959; newspaper artist Bering Breeze, Aleutian Islands, 1945-46; cofounder Northwest Pacific chpt. AVC Adak, 1945. Author: (poetry) My Mother Died Dancing, 1960; contbr. poetry to anthologies; three-man show Heckscher Mus., Huntington, N.Y., 1964; exhibited in group shows Mcpl. Gallery, Jackson, Miss., 1943, Allied Artists of Am., 1957-85, Nat. Art Club, N.Y.C., 1959, Art Directions, 1959, ACA Galleries, 1960, Hofstra U., Adelphi U., Nassau C.C., 1980, L.I. Art Dirs. Exhbn. Firehouse Gallery, 1980, Nassau County Art Mus., 1980, Hempstead Harbor Art Assn., Glen Cove, L.I., 1982, Knickerbocker Artists, Islip Mus., 1983, Wantagh Libr., 1975, Levittown Libr., 1986, Freeport Libr., 1987; illustrator: Planets (Willie Ley); author, creator: American Indian, Crime and Punishment, Superstition and Parapsychology, 1947-50; prodr. bicentennial pictorial chronological map of Entire Am. Revolution, Spirit of '76, 1975; inventor process for mass prodn. ceramic and transparent mosaics, silk screen sys. for printing inside compound curves; creator innovative 2 color graphics method; new age art: developer combining chemically colored copper (sculpture) plastic, resins and reflective integral elements with electronics, 1973—; prodr. crossover filming of painting, sculpture and poetry recitation as ongoing creative product of Bridges of Mind, 1993—, Career Forum, 1999—. Designer war posters visual aids for U.S. Army, 1942-44; creator comic character Giggy F. Useless, used in basic tng. and theatre dramatizations for Army newspaper, 1943-46. Sgt. AUS, 1942-46. Art Student's League scholar, 1936; recipient grand prize for redesign Levitt Home, 1967, Printing Industries, N.Y., 1973, numerous graphics awards, 1973-84, graphic excellence award Monadnock Mills, 1975, Desi grand award, 1980-82, poetry award Nassau County Fine Arts Mus., 1981, award of excellence IEEE, World Trade Ctr., N.Y.C., 1984, Vets. Soc. Am. Artists, 1984, award of excellence Long Beach Art League, 1989. Mem. Internat. Soc. Poets, Freeport Arts Coun., Allied Artists Am. (pres. 1985-86), Huntington Twp. Art League, DAV, Comic Artist Guild (treas.), Nature Conservancy, various environ. groups. Achievements include development of process for mass-producing mosaics, both traditional and current for architecture as well as home decor; transparent (per-stained glass) and opaque. Avocations: swimming, camping, hiking, mechanics. Home and Office: 33 Downhill Ln Wantagh NY 11793-1817

GLASER, DONALD ARTHUR, physicist; b. Cleveland, Ohio, Sept. 21, 1926; s. William Joseph Glaser. BS, Case Inst. Tech., 1946, ScD, 1959; PhD, Calif. Inst. Tech., 1949. Prof. physics U. Mich., 1949-59; prof. physics U. Calif., Berkeley, 1959—; prof. physics, molecular and cell biology, divsn. neurobiology U. Calif., 1964—. Recipient Henry Russel award U. Mich., 1955, Charles V. Boys prize Phys. Soc., London, 1958, Nobel prize in physics, 1960, Gold Medal award Case Inst. Tech., 1967, Golden Plate award Am. Acad. of Achievement, 1989; NSF fellow, 1961, Guggenheim fellow, 1961-62, fellow Smith-Kettlewell Inst. for Vision Rsch, 1983-84. Fellow AAAS, Fedn. Am. Scientists, The Exploratorium (bd. dirs.), Royal Soc. Sci., Royal Swedish Acad. Sci., Assn. Rsch. Vision and Ophthalmology, Neurosis. Inst., Am. Physics Soc. (prize 1959); mem. Nat. Acad. Scis., Am. Assn. Artificial Intelligence, N.Y. Acad. Sci., Internat. Acad. Sci., Am. Philos. Soc., Sigma Xi, Tau Kappa Alpha, Theta Tau. Home: 41 Hill Rd Berkeley CA 94708-2131 Office: U Calif Dept Molecular & Cell Biology 337 Stanley Hl Berkeley CA 94720-0001

GLASER, ROLAND, biophysicist, educator; b. Jena, Thuringia, Germany, Mar. 23, 1935; s. Paul and Erna (Jagemann) G.; m. Eva-Maria Bormann, May 6, 1962; 1 child, Mareike. Diploma in Biology, Friedrich-Schiller U., Jena, Germany, 1958, Dr.rer.nat., 1961, Dr.habil., 1965. Sci. co-worker Nat. Atomic Energy Agy., Berlin, 1958-62, Inst. Cardiology, Acad. Sci., Berlin, 1962-65; asst. prof. Friedrich-Schiller U., Jena, 1965-70; prof. biophysics Humboldt U., Berlin, 1970—; mem. Acad. Sci., Germany, 1979-90, Nat. Radiation Protection Commn., Bonn, 1993-98. Author:Biologie einmal anders., 1974, 2d edit., 1979, Umweltbiophysik, 1976, Grundriss der Biomechanik, 1983, 2d edit., 1988, Biophysics of the Cell Surface, 1990, Biophysics, 5th edit., 2000; contbr. articles to profl. jours. Fax: 49-30-2093-8520. Home: Waldsassener Str 54, D-12279 Berlin Germany Office: Humboldt U Inst Biology, Invalidenstr 42, D-10115 Berlin Germany

GLASER, STEFFEN JOHANNES, physicist, educator; b. Gochsheim, Baden, Germany, Aug. 10, 1958; s. Johann and Mina (Knötzele) G.; m. Astrid Lansing, Aug. 10, 1993; children: Clarissa, Niklas Johannes. Diploma in Physics, Ruprecht-Karls-U., Heidelberg, Germany, 1984, PhD, 1987; Habil., J.W. Goethe U., Frankfurt, 1994. Postdoctoral rsch. assoc. U. Wash., Seattle, 1987-90; habilitand J.W. Goethe U., Frankfurt, 1990-94, privatdozent, 1994-99; prof. Technical U., Munich, 1999—. Contbr. articles to profl. jours., chpts. to books. Mem. German Chem. Soc. Office: Inst Organic Chemistry & Biochemistry, Lichtenbergstrasse 4, D-85747 Garching Germany

GLASER, TRACY L., manufacturing engineer, executive; b. Canton, Ohio, Aug. 30, 1970; d. Thomas L. and Gladys J. Glaser. BSME, U. Akron, 1993. CAD drafting cons. Seifert Techs., Mssillon, Ohio, 1994-96; engr., environ. coord. Timken Co., Canton, 1996-98, corp. environ. affairs analyst, 1998—. Mem. Larg Industry Rep. (mem. Stark-Tusc-Wayne joint solid waste dist. policy com. 1999—), Canton C. of C. (mem. environ. quality steering com. 1999—), Psi Chi. Democrat. Avocations: hiking, biking, softball, golf, music. Fax: 330-471-3541. Home: 1420 18th St NW Canton OH 44703-1050 Office: Timken Co 1835 Dueber Ave SW Canton OH 44706-2798

GLASGOW, NORMAN MILTON, lawyer; b. Washington, Aug. 14, 1922; children—Norman M., Heather Glasgow Harris, Glenn. BS, U. Md., 1943; LLB, JD George Washington U., 1949. Bar: D.C. 1949, U.S. Supreme Ct. 1956, Md. 1960. Assoc. Wilkes, McGarraghy & Artis, Washington, 1949-55; ptnr. Wilkes & Artis, Washington, 1955-82; pres. Wilkes, Artis, Hedrick & Lane, Washington, 1982-86, sr. prin., 1988—. Bd. dirs., gen. counsel Greater Washington Bd. Trade, 1986, 87, 88; mem., chmn. Md. PAC, 1981-93; bd. govs. Washington Bldg. Congress; mem. Citizens Tech. Adv. Com. for Drafting Bldg. Code and Zoning Regulations, Washington, Commrs. Citizens Adv. Com. on Zoning, Washington, Balt. Conv. Ctr. Authority Transp. Revenue Com., Gov.'s Salary Commn., Gov.'s Special Com. on Vehicle Emissions Inspection Program, Gov.'s Adv. Redistricting Com.; chmn. Govs. Task Force Statewide Bldg. Performance Standards, Md. Stadium Authority, 1993-97, Md. Economic Growth, Resource Protection and Planning Commn., co-chair subcom. for updating state planning and zoning laws, 1993-97; chmn. Md. Econ. Growth Task Force; mem. Gov.'s Western. Md. Econ. Devel. Strategies Task Force, 1998—, co-chair Updating Md. Zoning and Planning Regulations (Article 66B). Served to 1st lt. U.S. Army, 1942-46, ETO. Recipient Outstanding Alumni award George Washington U., 1985, Outstanding Service award D.C. Real Estate, Greater Washington Bd. Trade, 1978, named Convenor Class of 1949 50th Reunion. Mem. Supreme Ct. Bar Assn., D.C. Bar Assn., Md. Bar Assn., Urban Land Inst., Am. Soc. Planning Ofcls., Washington Bldg. Congress, Nat. Assn. Bus. Economists, Nat. Conf. of States on Bldg. Codes and Standards, Lambda Alpha. Avocation: gardening. Home: 9012 Brickyard Rd Potomac MD 20854-1634 Office: Wilkes Artis Hedrick & Lane 1666 K St NW # 300 Washington DC 20006-2803

GLASHAN, CONSTANCE ELAINE, retired nurse, civic worker; b. San Pedro, Calif., Oct. 15, 1932; d. Clyde Frizzell and Winifred Anne (Todd) Lapier; widow; children: Marilyn, Susan, Nanci, Linda. Dental and med. degrees, Lux Coll., San Francisco, 1953; student, Bryman Coll., San Jose, Calif., 1973; grad., Pacific Regional Staff Coll., 1998. With Family Practice Physician, 1974-80; pvt. home caregiver Carson City, Nev., 1980-91. Noon supr. Santee Sch., Franklin-McKinley Sch. Dist., San Jose, 1969-71; former leader Oak Hill 4-H Club; sec. Valley Glen Homeowner's Assn., 1967-70; exec. sec. Greater East San Jose Homeowners's Coun., 1969-82, del. to Calif. Met. Transp. Commn., 1972-82l exec. sec. UN Cultural Festival, Santa Clara County, Calif., 1969-75, exec. v.p., 1974-76; mem. Citizen's Cmty. Improvement Com., San Jose, 1969-82; former del. and mem. coordinating coun. on narcotics San Jose Police Dept., recorder for exec. bd. Anti-Crime Commn., from 1970; charter mem., exec. sec. Tchr.'s Day Com., 1970; citizen's coord. human rels. subcom. narcotics and cmty. rels. units San Jose Police Athletics League, 1971-72; former mem. bd. dirs. Pacific Neighbor's: San Jose's Sister Cities Program; formerly active Robert Smith Meml. Cultural Found.; charter mem. Performing Arts League, 1971—; charter mem. Coun. of Arts, City of San Jose; mem. Transp. Study Task Force, from 1972; former leader Brownies and Cadettes, Girl Scouts U.S.A.; formerly active San Jose C.C. Dist.; formerly active San Jose Mus. and Youth Sci. Inst., San Jose Hist. Mus., San Jose Zool. Soc.; formre mem. San Jose Mayor's Adv. Bd. Health.; vol. No. Nev. Healthfair, Carson City, 1982—, Make A Wish Found., 1984—; foster parent Spl. Olympics, 1984; nen, Advs. for Domestic Violence; lt., adminstrv. officer Carson Composite Squadron, CAP, Douglas County Composite Squadron, CAP; foster parent. Named Lady of Day, Sta. KARA, 1973. Mem. AAUW, Nat. Trust for Hist. Preservation, Beta Sigma Phi. Republican. Roman Catholic. Avocations: horseback riding, swimming, fly fishing, camping, fishing.

GLASHOW, SHELDON LEE, physicist, educator; b. N.Y.C., Dec. 5, 1932; s. Lewis and Bella (Rubin) G.; m. Joan Glashow; children: Jason David, Jordan, Brian Lewis, Rebecca Lee. AB, Cornell U., 1954; AM, Harvard U., 1955, PhD, 1958; DSc (hon.), Yeshiva U., 1978, U. Marseille, 1982, Adelphi U., 1989, Bar Ilan U., 1989, Gustave Adolphus Coll., 1989. NSF fellow U. Copenhagen, Denmark, 1958-60; rsch. fellow Calif. Inst. Tech., 1960-61; asst. prof. Stanford U., 1961-62; asst. prof., assoc. prof. U. Calif. at Berkeley, 1962-66; mem. faculty Harvard U., 1966—, prof. physics, 1967-84, Higgins prof. physics, 1979—, Mellon prof. scis., 1988-93; univ. prof. Boston U., 1984—; cons. Brookhaven Nat. Lab., 1966-73, 75—; mem. sci. policy com. CERN, 1979-84; vis. prof. U. Marseille, 1971, MIT, 1974-80, Boston U., 1983; affiliated sr. scientist U. Houston, 1983-96; univ. scholar Tex. A&M U., 1983-86; hon. prof. U. Nanjing, 1998—. Author: (with Ben Bova) Interactions, 1988, Charm of Physics, 1990, From Alchemy to Quarks, 1994; contbr. articles to profl. jours. and popular mags.; founding editor Quantum mag., 1989—. Pres. Andrei Sakharov Inst., 1980-85, Nat. Com. for Excellence in Edn., 1985-88. Recipient J.R. Oppenheimer Meml. prize, 1977, George Ledlie prize, 1978, Nobel prize in physics, 1979, Castiglione di Sicilia prize, 1983, Erice Sci. for Peace prize, 1991; NSF fellow, 1955-60, Sloan fellow, 1962-66, CERN vis. fellow, 1968. Fellow Am. Phys. Soc., AAAS; mem. Am. Acad. Arts and Scis., Nat. Acad. Scis., Russian Acad. Sci. (fgn. mem.), Korean Acad. Sci. (fgn. mem.), Sigma Xi. E-mail: glashow@boyle.harvard.edu.

GLASNER, PETER EGON, economics and social science educator; b. Bairagarh, Bhopal, India, Nov. 9, 1944; s. Kurt Martin and Aloisia Maria (Stach) G.; m. Angela Mary (Hale) G., Nov. 2, 1968; children: Emma, Matthew, James, Tom. BSc in Sociology, U. London, 1968; PhD, London Sch. Econs., 1973. Tutor U. Kent, Canterbury, Eng., 1970-71; lectr. Australian Nat. U., Canberra, 1971-78; prin. lectr. Poly. of North London, 1978-85; head dept. Bristol (Eng.) Poly., 1985-92; exec. dean U. West of Eng., Bristol, 1992-97, rsch. prof. sociology, 1997—; vis. rsch. fellow U. Sussex, Brighton, Eng., 1977; Morris Ginsberg fellow London Sch. Econs., 1984; specialist adviser Coun. for Nat. Acad. Awards, London, 1989-92; auditor Higher Edn. Quality Coun., London, 1993-97; assessor Econs. and Social Rsch. Coun. Tng. Bd., Swindon, Eng., 1996—. Author: The Sociology of Secularisation, 1977; co-author: The Politics of Uncertainty, 1986; editor: The Contemporary Australian Parish and Ministry, 1975; co-editor: Practice and Belief, 1983, Genetic Imaginations, 1998, The Social Management of Genetic Engineering, 1998. Fellow Royal Soc. Arts; mem. Assn. Learned Socs. in Social Scis. (pres. 1992-95), Brit. Sociol. Assn. (hon. sec. 1985-87). Avocations: food, music, gardening. Office: U West of Eng, Coldharbour Ln, Frenchay Bristol BS16 12Y, England

GLASS, CHARLES FREDERIC, JR., editor; b. Nov. 24, 1972. BA in English, U. Colo., 1995. Asst. editor Skiing Trade News, N.Y.C., 1996-97, Skiing mag., Boulder, Colo., 1997—. Office: Skiing Mag 929 Pearl St Ste 200 Boulder CO 80302-5108

GLASS, DAVID D., department store company executive, professional baseball team executive; b. Liberty, Mo., 1935; married. Gen. mgr. Crank Drug Co., 1957-67; v.p. Consumers Markets Inc., 1967-76; exec. v.p. fin. Wal-Mart Stores Inc., Bentonville, Ark., to 1976, vice chmn., CFO, 1976-84, pres., 1984-2000, COO, 1984-88, CEO, 1988-2000, also bd. dirs., chmn. exec. commn., 2000—; CEO, chmn. bd. dirs. Kansas City Royals, 1993—. Office: Wal-Mart Stores Inc 702 SW 8th St Bentonville AR 72716-6299 also: Kansas City Royals PO Box 419969 Kansas City MO 64141-6969*

GLASS, ROBERTA JEAN, statistician; b. Boston, June 15, 1958; d. Walter R. and Alice D. Branagan; m. Peter S. Glass, June 20, 1988; 1 child, Jedidiah S. BA magna cum laude, Wheaton Coll., 1980; MS, Harvard Sch. Pub. Health, 1997. Sr. programmer/analyst Abt Assocs., Cambridge, Mass., 1984-95; statistician Harvard Ctr. for Risk Analysis, Boston, 1995-98; statistician/researcher Harvard Sch. Pub. Health, Boston, 1997-99; cons. Brown Univ., Providence, R.I., 1996, Sudbury, Mass., 1999—. Contbr. articles to profl. jours. Safety advocate Partnership for Child Passenger Safety, 1996—; automotive safety working group Harvard Ctr. for Risk Analysis, 1999—; children program coord. Sudbury Grange No 121, 1999—; bd. dirs., sec. Rodgers Peirce Children's Ctr., Arlington, Mass., 1992093, PTA rep. Arlington Pre-Sch., 1991-94. Mem. Mass. Publ. Health Assn., Phi Beta Kappa, Omicron Delta Epsilon. Avocations: hiking, gardening. E-mail: rglass@post.harvard.edu.

GLASSBURN, TRACY ANN, geochemist, researcher; b. St. Petersburg, Fla., Oct. 7, 1962; d. Paul Douglass and Sharon Lou (DeVore) Glassburn; m. Stefan Ryszard Witek, Nov. 26, 1986 (div. Apr. 1991); m. Paul Slusarewicz, May 7, 1995. BSc, Coll. William and Mary, 1984; MS, Lehigh U., Bethlehem, Pa., 1987; PhD, U. London, 1993; DIC, Imperial Coll. Sci., Tech., London, 1993. Grad. rsch. asst. Lehigh U., Bethlehem, 1984-85, grad. teaching asst. geology, 1985-86, rsch. asst. dept. materials sci., 1987; rsch. scientist Cookson Rsch. Group, plc, London, 1988; teaching asst. geology Imperial Coll. Sci., Tech. and Medicine, London, 1989-92, rsch. asst. geology, 1990-91, rsch. assoc. geology, 1993-94; geochem. cons. Enfield, N.H., 1995—. Author abstracts in profl. jours. Mem. Brit. Geol. Soc., Paleontological Soc., Sigma Xi, Phi Eta Sigma, Alpha Lambda Delta, Sigma Gamma Epsilon. Achievements include development of new statistical, morphometric technique to describe bivalve evolution; discovered method to solid state sinter SIC at lower temperatures with smaller grain sizes; designed experimental apparatus to simulate high temperature/pressure geological conditions. Avocations: travel, cooking, collecting/building automatons. Home: 358 Goldington Rd, Bedford MK41 9LS, England Office: Colworth House, Bedford MK44 1LQ, England

GLASSELL, ALFRED CURRY, JR., investor; b. Cuba Plantation, La., Mar. 31, 1913; s. Alfred Curry and Frances (Lane) G.; m. Clare Attwell; children: Jean Curry, Alfred Curry III. B.A., La. State U., 1934. Investor, 1936—; cons. Glassell Producing Co., 1938—; past bd. dirs. Transco Cos., El Paso Nat. Gas, First City Bancorp. Trustee Houston Mus. Natural Sci., Internat. Oceanographic Found., Houston Mus. Fine Arts, chmn. bd.; former trustee Kinkaid Sch., Tex. Children's Hosp., Smithsonian Nat. Bd. Recipient Marine Sci. ann. award Internat. Oceanographic Found., 1971, Soc. Grand Founders medallion U. Miami, 1984, James Smithson award, 1991. Mem. Am. Geog. Soc., Am. Mus. Natural History, Tex. Angus Assn., Can. Chianini Assn., Houston Horse Show Assn., Tex. Cattle Breeders Assn., Am. Nat. Cattlemen's Assn., Tex. and Southwestern Cattle Raisers Assn., Mil. and Hospitaller Order St. Lazarus of Jerusalem. Clubs: Atlantic Tuna (Providence), Boston (New Orleans), Cabo Blanco Fishing (Peru), Tex. Game Fishing (Dallas), Tex. Corinthian Yacht (Kemah), Bay of Islands Swordfish and Mako Shark (New Zealand), Anglers of N.Y., Houston, Petroleum, Ramada, Bayou, Houston Country, River Oaks Country. Achievements include being a holder of the record of world's largest fish, former holder of numerous world record salt water game fish. Office: 1021 Main St Ste 2300 Houston TX 77002-6606

GLASSER, ADRIAN, physiologist, researcher, scientist; b. Johannesburg, South Africa, June 19, 1964; came to U.S., 1985; s. Leslie and Peta (Jaentsch) G. BS, SUNY, Albany, 1989, MS, 1990; PhD, Cornell U., 1994. Postdoctoral fellow U. Waterloo, Ont., Can., 1994-96; asst. scientist U. Wis., Madison, 1996-98; asst. prof. U. Houston, 1998—; cons. numerous internat. pharm. cos.; expert in physiol. optics. Contbr. articles to profl. jours. and book chpts. Fellow Natural Scis. and Engring. Rsch. Coun. Can., 1994. Mem. Assn. for Rsch. in Vision and Ophthalmology, Sigma Xi. Avocation: tennis. Office: U Houston Coll Optometry 4901 Calhoun Rd Houston TX 77004-2612

GLASSMAN, ARMAND BARRY, physician, pathologist, scientist, educator, administrator; b. Paterson, N.J., Sept. 9, 1938; s. Paul and Rosa (Ackerman) G.; m. Alberta C. Macri, Aug. 30, 1958; children: Armand P.,

Steven B., Brian A. BA, Rutgers U., N.J., 1960; MD magna cum laude, Georgetown U., Washington, 1964. Diplomate Am. Bd. Pathology, Am. Bd. Nuclear Medicine. Intern Georgetown U. Hosp., Washington, 1964-65; resident Yale-New Haven Hosp., West Haven VA Hosp., 1965-69; asst. prof. pathology, Coll. Medicine U. Fla.; chief radioimmunoassary lab. Gainesville VA Hosp.; practice lab. and nuc. medicine, 1969-71; dir. clin. labs., assoc. prof., prof. pathology, cellular, molecular biology Med. Coll. Ga., Augusta, 1971-76; cons. physician in nuclear medicine Univ. Hosp., Augusta, 1973-76; med. dir. clin. labs. Med. U. S.C. Hosp., Charleston, 1976-87; attending physician in lab. and nuclear medicine Med. U. S.C., Charleston, 1976-87, assoc. med. dir. Med. U. Hosp. and Clinics, 1982-86; med. dir. clin. labs. Charleston Meml. Hosp., S.C., 1976-87; cons. VA Hosp., Charleston, 1976-87; prof., chmn. dept. lab. medicine Med. U. S.C., 1976-87, med. dir. MT and MLT programs, 1976-87, clin. prof. pathology, lab. medicine, and radiology, 1987—, acting chmn. dept. immunology and microbiology, 1985-87, assoc. dean Coll. Medicine, 1979-85, asst. and assoc. dean Coll. Allied Health Sci., 1984-87, chmn. hosp. exec. com., 1985-86, acting med. dir. Univ. Hosp. and Clinics, 1985-86; sr. v.p. med. affairs, prof. lab. medicine and nuclear medicine Montefiore Med. Ctr. and Albert Einstein Coll. Medicine, Bronx, N.Y., 1987-89; v.p., lab. dir. Nat. Reference Lab., Nashville, 1989-92; cons., 1992-95; clin. prof. dept. pathology Vanderbilt U., Nashville, 1990-92, prof. pathology, 1992-94; dir. Vanderbilt Pathology Lab. Svcs., 1992-94; dir. clin. labs. Vanderbilt U. Med. Ctr., 1993-94, O. Stribling chair, prof., 1994—; head and chair divsn./dept. lab. medicine U. Tex., M.D. Anderson Cancer Ctr., Houston, 1994-96, also med. dir. Med. Tech. & Cytogenic Tech. programs, 1994-96, also dir. sect. cytogenetics to mem. steering com. pathology and lab medicine, 1994-96, 98—, chair ops. & improvement mgmt. com. dept. hematopathology, 1998—; Mem. adv. coun. Trident Tech. Coll., 1976-87; bd. dirs. Fetter Family Health Ctr.; founding dir., bd. dirs. Sealite, Inc., 1987-99, chmn. bd. dirs., 1995-99; mem. med. adv. com. Nashville Red Cross Blood Ctr., 1991-94, acting med. dir., 1991-92; mem. bd. sci. advisors Nat. Health Labs./Nat. Reference Lab., 1992-94, cons., 1992-95; trustee, bd. dirs. Gulf Coast Cmty. Blood Ctr., 1994—. Editor, co-editor 4 books; contbr. more than 150 refereed articles to profl. jours., 30 chpts. to books. Trustee Coll. Prep. Sch., 1979-84, chmn. bd., 1983-84; trustee, bd. dirs., v.p. Mason Prep. Sch., 1984-87; bd. dirs. United Way, 1983-87, Am. Cancer Soc., 1984-87; co-founder, bd. dirs. Glassman Family Fund, 1998—. With USMCR, 1956-64. Johnson and Avalon Found. scholar Georgetown U., 1961-64; State scholar Rutgers U., 1956-60. Fellow Coll. Am. Pathologists (numerous coms.), ACP, Assn. Clin. Scientists (Diploma of Honor 1987, pres. 1990-91, exec. com. 1990-95, Clin. Scientist of Yr. 1993, C.P. Brown lectr. 1995), Am. Soc. Clin. Pathology (coun. immunohematology and blood banking 1983-89, coun. grad. med. edn. and rsch. 1998—, Commr.'s award for Commn. Continuing Edn. 1989), Am. Bd. Pathology (transfusion medicine/blood bank test com. 1984-88), Am. Coll. Nuc. Medicine, N.Y. Acad. Medicine; mem. Internat. Acad. Pathology, Am. Assn. Pathologists, Soc. Nuc. Medicine (chmn. edn. com. 1973-77, acad. coun. 1979-92), AMA (Physician's Recognition award, instnl. rep. to sect. on med. schs.), So. Med. Assn., Am. Geriat. Soc. (founding fellow So. divsn.), Am. Soc. Microbiology, Am. Assn. Blood Banks (chmn. cryobiology com. 1974-83, edn. com. 1978-85, sci. program com. 1981-84, autologous transfusion com. 1979-83, bd. dirs. 1984-87, transfusion practices com. 1992-96), Assn. Schs. Allied Health Professions (bd. editors jour. 1979-83), Soc. Cryobiology (treas., bd. dirs. 1978-80), AAAS, N.Y. Acad. Scis., Acad. Clin. Lab. Physicians and Scientists (exec. coun. 1978-85, pres. 1982-83), S.E. Area Blood Bankers (pres. 1979-81, exec. coun. 1980-85), Tenn. Assn. Blood Banks (treas. 1993-94), Am. Coll. Physician Execs., Sigma Xi, Alpha Eta, Alpha Omega Alpha. Avocations: jogging, tennis, community svc. Office: MD Anderson Cancer Ctr Lab Medicine Box 350 1515 Holcombe Blvd Houston TX 77030-4009

GLASSMAN, JON DAVID, business executive; b. N.Y.C., Jan. 8, 1944; s. J. and Dorothy (Witkin) G.; m. Francesca Regina Smoot, Dec. 31, 1986; 1 child, Amanda Louise; 1 stepchild, James Smoot Decherd. B in Fgn. Svc., U. So. Calif., 1965; MA, Columbia U., 1968, cert. Russian Inst., 1968, PhD, 1976. Joined Fgn. Svc. Dept. State, 1968; officer Am. Embassy, Madrid, 1968-70, Moscow, 1971-73, Havana, Cuba, 1977-79, Mexico City, 1979-81; officer Dept. State, Washington, 1974-77, 81-87; charge d'affaires Am. Embassy, Kabul, Afghanistan, 1987-89; dep. asst. for nat. security affairs to V.p. The White House, 1989-90, asst. to V.p. of U.S., 1990-91; amb. to Paraguay Asuncion, 1991-94; dept. state chair Indsl. Coll. of the Armed Forces, Washington, 1994-96; dep. for Balkan mil. stabilization Dept. State, Washington, 1996-97; v.p. internat. bus. devel. electronic sensors & sys. sector Northrop Grumman Corp., Balt., 1998—; mem. bd. Bus. Coun. for Internat. Understanding, 1999—. Author: Arms for the Arabs, 1976. Bd. dirs. Bus. Coun. for Internat. Understanding. Recipient Presdl. Meritorious Svc. award, 1991. Mem. City Tavern Club. Home: 3240 Q St NW Washington DC 20007-3032 Office: Northrop Grumman Corp Elec Sensors & Sys Sector PO Box 1897 Baltimore MD 21203-1897

GLATZEL, PETER MICHAEL, psychologist; b. Berlin, June 26, 1947; s. Oswald and Ilse (Kasper) G.; m. Margit Muck, 1972 (div. 1984); 1 child, Dina; m. Marylou Carrière, 1999. Diploma in psychology, U. Saarbrücken, Germany, 1976. Clin. psychologist Landeskrankenhaus, Merzig, Germany, 1977-97, asst. psychology dir., 1992-97; psychology dir. St. Nikolaus Hosp., Wallerfangen, Germany, 1997—. Contbr. articles to profl. jours. Fellow Commn. Devel. Psychotherapy; mem. German Soc. for Systemic Therapy (tng. therapist, cons., supr. 1990—, award 1994, fellow rsch. com.), German Psychol. Assn. (pres. 1993-95). Office: St Nikolaus Hosp, Hospitalstr 5, D 66798 Wallerfangen Germany

GLATZER, MICHAEL, editor, academic administrator; b. Dallas, Mar. 7, 1946; arrived in Israel, 1968; s. Fred and Miriam (Feder) G.; m. Shoshana Friedman, Jan. 7, 1973; children: Daniella, Nahum, Ilana, Daphna. BA, So. Meth. U., 1968; postgrad., Hebrew U., Jerusalem, 1968-73. Student advisor Hebrew U., 1970-73; tchg. asst. Haifa U., Israel, 1974-79; acad. sec. Ben Zvi Inst., Jerusalem, 1979—. Editl. sec. Peamim jour., 1979—. Cpl. artillery force Israel Def. Force, 1973-74. Office: Ben Zvi Inst, PO Box 7660, 91076 Jerusalem Israel

GLAVE, ADOLFO ENRIQUE, retired academic administrator; b. Buenos Aires, May 9, 1933; s. Ernesto and Emma Paulina (Kugler) G.; m. María José Charbonnier, Mar. 1, 1963; children: María Alicia, Sergio Adolfo, Luis Horacio, Maria Ines, Maria Jose. Grad., Agronomía U., Buenos Aires, 1959. Asst. dir. INTA Inst. Agriculture, Bordenave, Buenos Aires, 1970-76, dir., 1978-84, investigator, 1961-94; adviser in field; cons. IICA, Bazil, 1984, Chile, 1987, Bolivia, 1988; cons. FAO, Bolivia and Paraguay, 1990. Recipient Premium award Cargill Found., 1988. Roman Catholic. Home and Office: Libertad 767, Darregueira, 8183 Buenos Aires Argentina

GLAVIČ, PETER, chemical engineering and material science educator; b. Ljubljana, Slovenia, July 3, 1940; s. Henrik and Marija (Miklič) G.; m. Marija Zorec, Sept. 11, 1965; children: Marjana, Tomaž, Miha. BS in Chem. Tech., U. Ljubljana, 1964, BSBA, 1973, MS in Chemistry, 1967, PhD in Chemistry, 1968. Asst. rschr. Inst. J. Stephan, Ljubljana, 1965-68; prodn. mgr. Paloma, Sladki vrh, 1968-73; quality control and R&D mgr. Tovarna Dusika Ruse, Ruse, 1973-77; prof. U. Maribor, 1977—, vice rector, 1988-90, vice dean, 1999—. Contbr. articles to profl. jours.; mem. internat. bodies and editl. bds. in chem. engring. and environl. protection. Pres. Rsch. Coun., Maribor, 1975-89; pres. Sect. Chem. Engring., Maribor, 1992—; mem. Slovenian Parliament, Ljubljana, 1990-97. Mem. Slovenian Soc. Engrs. (chem. engring. sect. 1987), Slovenian Engring. Acad., Sports Club (pres. 1976—), Soc. Economists Maribor (pres. 1996—). Roman Catholic. Avocations: skiing, hiking, swimming, cycling. Home: Falska c 43, 2342 Ruse Slovenia Office: U Maribor Fac Chem/Engring, Smetanova 17, 2000 Maribor Slovenia

GLAVIN, KEVIN CHARLES, lawyer, educator; b. Providence, R.I., Aug. 1, 1949; s. Charles Francis and Lola Glavin; m. Donna Bettencourt, Aug. 23, 1980. AB, Providence Coll., 1971; JD, Suffolk Law Sch., 1974. Bar: R.I. 1975, Mass. 1984, U.S. Dist. Ct. R.I. 1975, U.S. Supreme Ct. 1979. Spl. asst. atty. gen. R.I. Dept. Atty. Gen., Providence, 1975-79; mng. atty. Kemper Ins. Co., Providence, 1979-94; arbitrator R.I. Superior Ct., Providence, 1989—; ptnr. Murray, Cutcliffe & Glavin, Providence, 1994—; adj. faculty Roger Williams U., Bristol, R.I., 1986—. V.P. Kent Heights PTA, East Providence, 1989; treas. Colt Andrews PTA, Bristol, 1993; judge Acad. Decathlon R.I., 1999-00. Recipient Order of the Gavel, Newport Ski Club, 1982. Mem. R.I. Superior Ct. (bench bar com. 1992—), Pawtucket Bar Assn. Avocations: tennis, skiing, sailing. Office: Murray Cutcliffe and Glavin 155 S Main St Providence RI 02903-2963

GLAZE, MICHAEL (JAMES), diplomat; b. Rochford, Essex, Eng., Jan. 15, 1935; s. Derek Newey and Shirley Winifred (Ramsay) G.; m. Rosemary Duff, May 21, 1965; children: Fiona, Deirdre. MA in Modern and Medieval Langs., Cambridge (Eng.) U., 1958; postgrad., Oxford (Eng.) U., 1958. Dist. officer Brit. Overseas Civil Svc., Lesotho, 1959-65; dep. permanent sec. Fin. Ministry, Lesotho, 1965-70; prin. Dept. of Trade, U.K., 1971-73; 1st sec. Brit. Diplomatic Svc., London, Abu Dhabi and Morocco, 1973-80; consul gen. Brit. Diplomatic Svc., Bordeaux, France, 1980-83; Brit. amb. to Cameroon, 1983-87, Brit. amb. to Angola, 1987-90, Brit. amb. to Ethiopia, 1990-94; dep. sec. gen. Most Venerable Order St. John, 1994—. Lt. Brit. Army, 1953-55. Decorated companion Order St. Michael and St. George (Eng.); officer Order of St. John. Mem. Athenaeum Club. Anglican. Avocations: golf, music, gardening.

GLAZEK, WLODZIMIERZ STANISLAW, computer scientist; b. Gdansk, Poland, Apr. 29, 1966; s. Tadeusz and Józefa (Pirsztuk) G.; m. Ewa Nowaczewska, Sept. 2, 1995; 1 child, Witold Tadeusz. MS, Tech. U., Gdansk, 1992, PhD, 1999. Software engr. Gtech Corp., Warsaw, Poland, 1993-96; faculty Tech. U., Gdansk, 1997-99, asst. prof., 1999—. Contbr. articles to profl. jours. Office: Tech U Gdansk Info Dept, Narvtowicza 11/12, 80-952 Gdansk Poland

GLAZEMAKER, ANTONIUS JAN, retired archbishop; b. Hilversum, The Netherlands, Apr. 19, 1931; m. G.G. de Groot; 2 children. Theol. degree, Old Cath. Sem. Ordained priest, 1956; consecrated bishop, 1979. Parish priest Old Cath. Ch. The Netherlands, Leiden, 1956-63, Ijmuiden, 1963-80; bishop Old Cath. Ch. The Netherlands, Arnhem, 1980-82; archbishop Old Cath. Ch. The Netherlands, Utrecht, 1982-00; ret., 2000; pres. Internat. Old Cath. Bishops' Conf.; dean of Harlem, 1976-80. Author: Communion and episcopacy: an Old Catholic Perspective, 1988; contbr. articles to profl. jours. Avocations: music, liturgy. Office: Kon Wilheminalaan 3, NL 3818 Amersfoort The Netherlands

GLAZER, GUILFORD, real estate developer; b. Knoxville, Tenn., July 17, 1921; s. Aaron Usher and Ida (Bressoff) G.; children: Emerson, Erika; m. Diane Pregerson, Jan. 29, 1967. Mech. Engr., George Wash. U., 1939; Metallurgy, U. Louisville, 1943. Bd. dirs. The Torrance (Calif.) Co., 1990, Del Amo Fashion Ctr., Torrance, Calif., 1990; owner operator Allegheny Ctr., Pitts; bd. dirs. Rand-UCLA Ctr. Study Soviet Internat. Behavior, L.A. developer various shopping ctrs. and office bldgs. in U.S. Pres. Reagan Libr. Found., Nixon Libr. Foun.; trustee L.A. Holocaust Meml., Jerusalem Found., Stop Cancer, Bell Shelter for Homeless; founder Ford's Theatre, Washington, Am. Friends of the Israel Def. Force; mem. Wilshire Blvd. Temple, L.A.County Mus. Art, Unified Fund Music Ctr. With USN, 1942-45. Recipient Hon. Fellow U. Tel Aviv. Mem. World Affairs Coun., Tamarisk Club, Hillcrest Country Club, Monterey Country Club, Palm Desert Club. Jewish. Avocation: golf. Office: Krasne & Mellon LLP 9440 Santa Monica Blvd Ste 610 Beverly Hills CA 90210-4619*

GLAZER, REA HELENE **See KIRK, REA HELENE**

GLAZER, TOM (THOMAS ZACARIAH GLAZER), folksinger, writer, composer; b. Phila., Sept. 2, 1914; s. Jacob and Sonia (Schochet) G.; m. Miriam Reed Eisenberg, June 25, 1944 (div.); children: John P.; m. Peter R. Student, CCNY, 1938-41. Rec. artist, 1946—; folksinger. Author: (songbooks) Tom Glazer's Treasury of Songs for Children, 1963, America the Beautiful, 1987, others, ltd. edit. selected poems, 1994; composer: Melody of Love (No. 1 song U.S. 1956), Till We Two Are One, A Worried Man, Skokiaan, On Top of Spaghetti; first artist to record Greensleaves and Twelve Days of Christmas, 1946; composer songs and score for film A Face in the Crowd. Recipient several Peabody awards for radio and TV shows. Mem. ASCAP, AFTRA, Am. Fedn. Musicians, Screen Actors Guild, Songwriters Guild Am. Club: The Coffee House (N.Y.C.). Avocations: tennis, literature, French, science, philosophy. Home and Office: 5500 Wissahickon Ave Apt 403A Philadelphia PA 19144-5638

GLAZIER, LYLE, writer, educator; b. Leverett, Mass., May 8, 1911; s. Harry Lee and Mertie Abby (Briggs) G.; m. Amy Louise Niles July 15, 1939 (dec. Mar. 1987); children: Laura, Susan, Alis. AB, Middlebury Coll., 1933, MA Bread Loaf Sch. of English, 1937; PhD, Harvard U., 1950; postgrad. in word processing, Vt. C.C., 1993-94. Prin. Northfield Mass. Ctr. Graded Sch., 1934-35; housemaster Mt. Hermon Sch. for Boys, Gill, Mass., 1935-37; instr. English, Bates Coll., Lewiston, Maine, 1937-42, Tufts Coll., Somerville, Mass., 1942-44; asst. in Shakespeare, Harvard U., Cambridge, Mass., 1944-45; tchg. fellow Harvard U. and Radcliffe Coll., Cambridge, Mass., 1945-47; asst. prof. English, U. Buffalo, 1947-52, assoc. prof., chmn. Am. studies, 1952-63; prof. English and Am. studies SUNY, Buffalo, 1965-72, prof. emeritus, 1972—; Fulbright chair Am. studies U. Istanbul, 1961-63, Fulbright Lectr. Hacettepe U., Ankara, Turkey, 1968-69, vis. prof., 1970, 71; lectr. U. Madras, India, 1970, 71; cons. thematic studies CUNY, 1973-75; vis. prof. Sana'a U., North Yemen, 1980; vol. adj. prof. So. Vt. Coll., Bennington, 1984-86; USIS vol. expert Am. lit., India, 1971; vol. prof. Miles Coll., Birmingham, 1967. Author: (novel) Summer for Joey, 1987, Stills from a Moving Picture, 1974, (poetry) Orchard Park and Istanbul, 1965, You Too, 1969, Voices of the Dead, 1971, The Dervishes, 1971, Two Continents, 1976, Azubah Nye, 1988, Recalls, 1986, Prefatory Lyrics, 1991, Searching for Amy, 1993, 2d edit. 2000 (criticism) American Decadence and Rebirth, 1971, Great Day Coming, 1988, Bennington Politics and Schools, 1986, Included in Reflections on a Gift of a Watermelon Pickle and Other Modern Verse (children's poetry anathology selected by children), 1966, 95, Contemporary Authors Autobiography Series, 1996; contbr. poems and articles to profl. and lit. jours.; contbr. to Festschrift for S.M. Pandeya, Banaras Hindu U., 1996. Exec. com. Friends of Bennington Free Libr., 1990-92; mem. sch. bd., vice chmn. Orchard Park (N.Y.) Sch. Dist., 1952-58; mem. Town Charter Commn., Bennington, 1987-89; mem. Gamaliel Painter's Cane Soc., Middlebury Coll., 1990—, mem. founders soc. Founders Soc., 1998—, mem. exec. com. Friends of Libr., Middlebury Coll., 1987-89, Abernathy Poetry/Rare Book Collection, Starr Libr., Middlebury, 2000; mem. Ret. Srs. Vol. Program, 1973—; mem. Bennington County Dem. Com., 1984-87; mem. exec. com. Bennington Area AIDS Project, 1990—; mem. nat. steering com. Clinton/Gore 1996, 1995-98, Gore 2000, 1999—; mem. Bennington Area Art Coun., 1990—; mem. Bennington Area Home Health Assn., 1990—, Bennington Counseling Svc., 1990; mem. Bennington County Chorus, 1973-79, patron, 1980—; mem. Grad. Students Middlebury Gay Lesbians, 1995, Vt. Mountain Pride Media, 1999; mem. Acad. of Am. Poets, ACLU, Bennington Mus. Found. Libr. of Congress Assocs., S.W. Vt. Regional Cancer Ctr., Rattlesnake Gutter Trust, Bread Loaf Writers' Conf. Fellow Am. Coun. Learned Socs., 1951-52. Mem. MLA, Bennington Robert Frost Soc., Vt. Coun. on Arts, League Vt. Writers, Poets and Writers, Am. Assn. Ret. Persons, Edmund Hayes Soc., North Bennington Artists Soc., Bennington County Humane Soc., Vt. Hist. Soc., Nat. Trust for Hist. Preservation. Avocation: music. Home: RR 3 Bennington VT 05201-9803

GLAZIER, STEPHEN DAVEY, anthropologist, theologian; b. New London, Conn., June 10, 1949; s. David Arthur and Betty (Davey) G.; m. Rosemary Custer, Sept. 24, 1977; 1 child, Catherine Marie. AB, Eastern Coll., 1971; MDiv, Princeton Theol. Sem., 1974; MA, U. Conn., 1976, PhD, 1981. Rschr. Yale U., New Haven, Conn., 1981-82; asst. prof. Trinity Coll., Hartford, Conn., 1982-83, Conn. Coll., New London, 1983-84; assoc. prof. Wayland Bapt. U., Plainview, Tex., 1984-86, Westmont Coll., Santa Barbara, Calif., 1986-88; dept. chmn. Kearney (Nebr.) State Coll., 1988-91; assoc. prof. U. Nebr., Kearney, 1991-94, prof., grad. faculty fellow, 1994—; vis. prof. U. Nebr., Lincoln, 2000—; vis. scholar Yale U. Divinity Sch., 1996. Author: Marchin' the Pilgrims Home, 1983; editor: Caribbean Ethnicity Revisited, 1985, Anthropology of Religion, 1997, Anthropology and Contemporary Religions, 1998, Encyclopedia of African and African American Religions, 2000; book rev. editor Anthropology of Consciousness, 1996—. Summer fellow U. Calif., Yale U., U. Hawaii, Princeton U., U. Colo., U. Mich., Haverford Coll., U. Tex., 1986, 88-93, 95-96, 2000, Mellon fellow Rice U., 1987, AAR/Lilly fellow, 1997-98; recipient Rsch. Svc. Coun. awards, 1990, 92. Fellow Am. Anthrop. Assn., Royal Anthrop. Inst.; mem. Am. Folklore Soc., Am. Acad. Religion, Mid-West Sociol. Assn. (endowment coun. 1991-96), V.I. Archaeol. Soc. (pubs. bd. 1976-92), Soc. for Sci. Study of Religion (exec. com. 1991-94, sec. 1998—), Soc. for Anthropology of Consciousness (pres. 2000—). Republican. Baptist. Avocations: classical guitar, antique maps, hiking. Office: U Nebr Dept Sociology Anthrop Kearney NE 68849-0001

GLAZUNOV, GENNADY PAVLOVICH, soil scientist; b. Lvov, Ukraine, July 2, 1948; s. Pavel Alexandrovich and Maria Stepanovna (Malykhina) G.; m. Natalia Vladimirovna Pimenova, Nov. 24, 1972; children: Alexei, Alexander. Diploma in biology, Moscow Lomonosov State U., 1972; CandSci, Moscow State U., 1976. Rsch. asst. Moscow State U., 1975-85, asst., 1981-85, sr. lectr., 1985—; dep. dir. Dept. Soil Erosion, Moscow, 1981—. Author: Soil Erosion and Conservation, 1996; mem. editl. bd. Vestnik MGU, 1981-98; contbr. articles to profl. jours. Travel grant MacArthur Found., Germany, 1996. Mem. European Soc. for Soil Conservation (exec. com. 1996-2000), Soil Sci. Soc. Russia (sec. commn. 1996—, Academician V.R. Williams 2d prize 1999). Avocation: swimming. Home: Viktorenko 8 28, 125167 Moscow Russia Office: Moscow State U, Faculty Soil Sci B-234, 119899 Moscow Russia

GLEASON, JOHN THOMAS, consultant software development planner; b. South Amboy, N.J., Jan. 14, 1936; s. John Thomas and Evelyn Patricia Gleason; m. Irene Theresa Wallace, June 8, 1957; children: Maureen Gleason Bryant, John Kevin, Diane. BS in Engring., U.S. Mil. Acad., 1957; M Bus., U. Conn., 1964. Cert. nat. security mgmt. Commd. 2d lt. USAF, 1957, advanced through grades to col., 1982; ret., 1982; ops. rsch. analyst USAF Sys. Command, Andrews AFB, 1969-70; chief aircraft maintenance 459th Airlift Wing, Andrews AFB, 1971-77; chief strategic mobility br. Dept. of Def., Joint Chiefs of Staff, Washington, 1978-82; logistics engr. C3 TRW, Washington, 1983-84; logistics engr. space sys. fed. sys. divsn. IBM, Gaithersburg, Md., 1984-87, new bus. coord., 1987-89, planner airport automation gen. systems divsn., 1989-91; lead planner, image and records Image Plus IBM, Bethesda, Md., 1991-93, project mgr., 1993-95; instr. program mgmt. Strategic Resources Inc., Falls Church, Va., 1996-97, ret., 1997; cons. Integrated Computer Engring., Campbell, Calif., 1998—; FAA comml. pilot Cloud Club II, Hyde Field, Md., 1992-94. Mem. coms. Boy Scouts Am., Ohio, Fla., Md., 1959-61, 64-65, 71-78; pres. Ft. Washington (Md.) Pool Assn., 1991-92; pres. So. Prince Georges' Reps. Club, Prince Georges' County, Md., 1990-92, treas., 1995-97; mem. Rep. Ctrl. Com., Prince George's County, 1997-99, 2nd vice-chmn., 1999; chmn. Tax Reform Initiative by Marylanders, Prince Georges' County, 1982-95; bd. dirs. Md. Taxpayers Assn., 1985-99, U.S. Mil. Acad. Class of 57, Washington Group, 1989-95; vol. canoe guide Jug Bay Park, Md., 1997-99. Mem. Aircraft Owners and Pilots Assn., Ret. Officers Assn., Nature Conservancy, Md. Res. Officers Assn. (pres. Dept. of Md. 1982-83), Exptl. Aircraft Assn., Mensa, Intertel, Beta Gamma Sigma. Republican. Roman Catholic. Avocations: scuba diving, hiking, travel, flying. Home and Office: 36 Sycamore Dr Lewes DE 19958-9750

GLEASON-JORDAN, IRENE, pathologist; b. Maui, Hawaii; d. Yong Woon Ow and Charng Hee Loo; children: Barbara Irene, Edward Donald, Colin Sean. AA, San Mateo Jr. Coll., 1952; AB, Stanford U., 1947; MD, U. Calif., San Francisco, 1951. Intern pathology Harbor Gen. Hosp./L.A. County, L.A., 1951-52; resident pathology Bellevue Hosp., N.Y.C., 1951-54, VA Hosp., 1954-56; pathologist chief grade VA Hosp., L.A., 1956-67, acting chief lab. svcs., 1958-65; chief grade pathologist surg. pathology VA Hosp., Long Beach, Calif., 1967-79; chief clin. pathology and quality control, Coll. Am. Pathologists inspector VA Hosp., Long Beach, 1967-79; lab. dir. Lancaster (Calif.) Cmty. Hosp., 1979-86, Temple U., L.A., 1987-91; pathologist, dir. histopathology, chemistry & spl. chemistry King/Drew Med. Ctr., L.A., 1991-94, pathologist, dir. hematology, ctrl. receiving & phlebotomy, 1994-96, acting chair dept. pathology, 1996—; rsch. asst. anatomy Sch. Biol. Scis., Stanford U., 1944-47; instr. dept. pathology NYU Sch. Medicine, 1952-54; dermatopathology cons., lectr. to med. students UCLA and U. Calif. Irvine Sch. Medicine, 1955—; clin. instr. VA Hosp., L.A., Long Beach, 1956-67; clin. instr. dept. pathology UCLA Sch. Medicine, 1957-61, asst. clin. prof., assoc. clin. prof. dept. pathology, 1961-73, assoc. clin. prof. dept. pathology, 1979-91; assoc. clin. prof. dept. pathology, lectr. U. Calif. Irvine Sch. Medicine, 1967-79; lectr. dept. pathology UCLA Sch. Dentistry, 1967- 68; commr. Calif. Med. Bd., 1974-92; assoc. prof. dept. pathology Charles R. Drew U. Medicine and Sci., 1991-97, prof. step I career acad. series, 1997—, UCLA Sch. Medicine, 1997—; chmn. cancer com. King/Drew Med. Ctr., L.A., 1999—; cons. in field. Editor Radioassay News, 1961-79; contbr. articles to profl. jours. Judge, trustee, chmn. rsch. Am. Orchid Soc., 1962—; sponsor Planetary Soc., Pasadena, 1991. Carson scholar Stanford U., 1945-46, Sara Hoyt scholar UCLA Sch. Medicine, 1948; grantee USPHS, 1958-60. Mem. AMA, Coll. Am. Pathologists (accreditation com. 1967-79), N.Y. Acad. Scis., Phi Beta Kappa (UCLA selection com. Eta chpt. 1957-67). Office: King/Drew Med Ctr Dept Pathology 12021 Wilmington Ave Los Angeles CA 90059-3019

GLEAVE, JOHN R. WALLACE, administrator neurosurgical service, educator; b. Coventry, Eng., Apr. 6, 1925; s. John Wallace and Dorothy Littlefair (Green) G.; m. Margaret Anne Newbolt, Sept. 6, 1952; children: Frances, John Mark, Humphry, Charity Anne, Arthur, Emily. MA in Natural Sci., Oxford U., 1947, BM BCh in Medicine, 1950; MA, Cambridge U., 1975. Reg. med. practitioner. Resident med. officer Radcliffe Infirmary, Oxford, Eng., 1950-52; registrar accident and orthopaedics Oxford U., 1954-56, sr. registrar neurosurgery, 1958-62; registrar gen. surgery U. Liverpool, Eng., 1956-58; cons. neurosurgeon Cambridge U., Eng., 1962-90, emeritus cons. neurosurgeon, 1990—; dir. neurosurgical and head injury svc. Cambridge and East Anglia, 1979-90; advisor, 1990—; lectr. U. Cambridge, 1970—; fellow and praelector St. Edmund's Coll., Cambridge, 1975—. Contbr. chpts. to profl. books and articles to profl. jours. Maj. M.C., Royal Army, 1952-54. Fellow Royal Coll. Surgeons, Royal Soc. Medicine; mem. European Soc. for Stereotactic and Functional Neurosurgery, Soc. Brit. Neurol. Surgeons, Vincents, Leander, United Oxford and Cambridge U. Club. Mem. Ch. of Eng. Avocations: rowing, gardening, classical langs. Home: Riversdale Great Shelford, Cambridge England CB2 5LW Office: Addenbrooke's Hosp, Hills Rd, Cambridge England CB2 2QQ

GLEESON, ANTHONY MURRAY, judge. Grad. in arts and law, U. Sydney. Bar: New South Wales, 1963, Queen's counsel, 1974. Chief justice Supreme Ct. New South Wales, 1988-98; lt. gov. New South Wales, 1989-98; chief justice High Ct. Australia, 1998—. Apptd. companion gen. divsn. Order of Australia, 1992. Mem. New South Wales Bar Assn. (pres. 1984-85). Office: PO Box E435, Kingston Canberra ACT 2604, Australia*

GLEESON, DERMOT JAMES, construction company executive; b. London, Sept. 5, 1949; s. Patrick Joseph and Margaret Mary (Higgins) G.; m. Rosalind Mary Moorhead, Sept. 6, 1980; children: Catherine, Patrick. MA, Fitzwilliam Coll., Cambridge, Eng., 1971. Desk officer Conservative Rsch. Dept., London, 1974-77; mem. Cabinet of C. Tugendhat European Commn., Brussels, 1977-79, asst. dir., cons. rsch. dept., 1979; EEC rep. Midland Bank, Brussels, 1979-81; dep. chmn. M.J. Gleeson Group Plc., Surrey, Eng., 1982-95, md. chief exec., 1988—, chmn., 1995—; dir. Housing Corp., 1991-96; bd. dirs. Constrn. Industry Tng. Bd. Trustee Tory Reform Group. Mem. Beefsteak Club, RAC Club. Home: Hook Farm White Hart Ln, Wood St Village, Surrey GU3 3EA, England Office: M J Gleeson Group Plc, Haredon House London Rd, Surrey SM3 9BS, England

GLEICH, CAROL S., health professions education executive; b. Kewanee, Ill., Jan. 18, 1935; d. Carl and Edna (Krause) Gleich. BA, U. Iowa, 1958, MS, 1967, PhD in Health Sci. Edn., 1972. Cert. clin. chemistry technologist, Nat. Registry Clin. Chemistry. From instr. to asst. prof. pathology U. Iowa Sch. Medicine, Iowa City, 1972-77, edn. specialist divsn. allied health, 1977-88, chief resource devel. sec., 1988-90, health manpower edn. officer, physician manpower and credentialing, chief spl. projects and data analysis br. divsn. medicine, 1991-95, exec. sec. coun. grad. med. edn., 1996-99; dir. area health edn. ctr. nat. program Bur. Health Professions, Health Resources & Svcs. Adminstrn., Rockville, Md., 1977—; allied health cons. to Egypt; gov. cons. in internat. health profl. ed., Russia, 1993-99; dir. Geriatric Edn. Ctrs. PHS; adj. assoc. prof. U. Md. Sch. Medicine; meme. Iowa Health Manpower Com., 1972—; cons. U. Wis. System Acad. Affairs, 1974; panelist and participant workshops; presenter and U.S. chief del. internat. congress. Assoc. editor Am. Jour. Med. Tech., 1974-83, Jour. Allied Health, 1982-85;

contbr. articles to profl. jours. Mem. Am. Soc. Clin. Pathologists (assoc., cert. med. technologist, sec. ASCP Bd. Registry 1975-77), Am. Soc. Clin. Lab. Sci., D.C. Soc. Med. Tech. (Outstanding Med. Technologist of Yr. 1975), Beta Beta Beta (Pub. Health Svc. award 1995), Alpha Mu Tau. Home: 14800 Rocking Spring Dr Rockville MD 20853-3635

GLEICHAUF, JOHN GEORGE, ophthalmologist; b. Rochester, N.Y., Mar. 21, 1933; s. George William and Cecelia Frieda (Lehner) G.; m. Barbara Helen Warm, Aug. 20, 1960 (div. 1980); children: Kurt John, Karin Marie; m. Jacqueline Kay Thompson, June 20, 1985 (div. Feb. 1997). AB, U. Rochester, 1955; MD, SUNY, Buffalo, 1962. Diplomate Nat. Bd. Med. Examiners, Am. Bd. Ophthalmology. Resident in ophthalmology Thomas Jefferson U., Phila., 1964-67; pvt. practice Santa Fe, N.Mex., 1967-79; ophthalmologist, chief of svc. Littleton Clinic, Denver, 1981-85; pres. Aiken (S.C.) Ophthalmology, 1985-95; cons. State of N.Mex., Santa Fe, 1973-77, Moonshot Program, Holloman AFB, N.Mex., 1968-69, Med-Tech. Inc., Aiken, 1986-87, Koirala Lion's Ctr. Ophthalmic Studies, Kathmandu, Nepal. Active Aiken Choral Soc., Aiken Arts Coun. 1st lt. USMC, 1955-58. Recipient Lion Club Nepal award, 1994. Fellow ACS, Internat. Coll. Surgery, Am. Acad. Ophthalmology; mem. AMA, N.Y. Acad. Scis., S.C. Med. Soc., Cataract and Refractive Surgery Soc. Republican. Roman Catholic. Avocations: skiing, travel, symphonic music, sailing. Home and Office: Cerro de Sao Miguel, 8300 003 Silves Portugal

GLEICHMAN, JOHN ALAN, safety and loss control executive; b. Anthoney, Kans., Feb. 11, 1944; s. Charles William and Caroline Elizabeth (Emch) G.; m. Martha Jean Cannon, July 1, 1966; 1 son, John Alan Jr. BS in Bus. Mgmt., Kans. State Tchrs. Coll., 1966. Cert. hazard control mgr.; cert. safety profl.; cert. safety exec. Office mgr. to asst. supt. Barton-Malow Co., Detroit, 1967-72, safety coord., 1972-76, corp. mgr. safety and security, 1976-89, dir. corp. safety and loss control, 1989—; instr. U. Mich., Wayne State U., 1977-81, Lawrence Technological U., 1994-96; mem. constrn. safety standards commn. adv. com. for concrete constrn. and steel erection Bur. of Safety and Regulations, Mich. Dept. Labor, 1977—; rep. constrn. standards com. Am. Nat. Standards Inst., 1984—. Author: (with others) You, The National Safety Council, and Voluntary Standards, 1981, Construction Accident Analysis: The Inductive Learning Approach, 1991; mem. editl. adv. bd. Safety and Health: The Internat. Safety, Health and Environ. Mag., 1989—. Instr. multi media first aid ARC, 1976-89; past trustee Apostolic Christian Ch., Livonia, Mich. Recipient Safety Achievement awards Mich. Mut. Ins. Co., 1979-83; Cameron award Constrn. sect. Indsl. div. Nat. Safety Coun., 1982, 1987. Mem. Mich. Safety Conf. (pres. 1984-85), Am. Soc. Safety Engrs. (pres. Detroit chpt. 1982, nat. adminstr. constrn div. 1988-89, bd. dirs. 1988-90, Safety Prof. of Yr. 1984) Nat. Safety Coun. (chmn. tech. rev. constrn. sect. indsl. div. 1980-84, chmn. standards com. indsl. div. 1983-85, chmn. assn. com. indsl. div. 1985-86, dir. tech. support com. indsl. div. 1986-87, dir. sects. group indsl. div. 1987-89, chmn. elect indsl. div. 1989-90, chmn. 1990-91, bd. dirs. 1987-92, Disting. Svcs. to Safety award, 1993), Am. Arbitration Assn. (panel arbitrators 1985). Office: Barton Malow Co 27777 Franklin Rd Ste 800 Southfield MI 48034-8258

GLEIJESES, MARIO, holding company executive; b. Italy, Feb. 27, 1955; came to U.S., 1985; s. Luigi Gleijeses and Rosalba Catanoso; m. Betsy L. Miller, Mar. 14, 1992; children: Rosalba, Caterina. Student, U. Naples, 1973-77. Chartering mgr. Itex subs. Italgrani, Zurich, 1977-82; asst. to pres. Italgrani Spa, Naples, Italy, 1982-85; exec. v.p., bd. dirs. Italgrani USA Inc. and Italgrani Elevator Co., St. Louis, 1985-89; v.p., bd. dirs. New Eng. Milling Co., Ayer, Mass., 1987-89; bd. dirs. Green Bay Elevator Co., Burlington, Iowa; v.p., bd. dirs. Mayco Export, Inc., Mpls., 1988-89; pres., bd. dirs. McLean Elevator Co., Benedict, N.D., 1989; founder, pres., bd. dirs. Agricorp Holding Inc., 1989-92; pres., bd. dirs. Granicorp Inc., 1989-92, Granicorp Export, Inc., U.S. Virgin Islands, 1989-92; chmn., CEO, bd. dirs. Granicorp France, S.A., Paris, 1991-92; founder, pres., bd. dirs. Gleijeses, Inc., 1993—; founder, chmn. bd. dirs. Lithoflex Corp., 1994—; pres. Hoky-Contico, LLC, 1995-96.

GLEISPACH, HELMUT, biochemist, educator; b. Tegernsee, Bayern, Germany, Mar. 22, 1937; s. Ernst Gottstein and Maria Gleispach; m. Barbara Kogl, Aug. 18, 1966 (dec. Mar. 1977); children: Friederike, Dietmar, Franziska, Harald; m. Waltraud Paar, June 1, 1982. PhD, U. Innsbruck, Austria, 1966. Asst. Chem. Inst., Innsbruck, 1964-66; indsl. chemist Berghofer-Peintings, Schwaz, Austria, 1966-67; asst., lectr. Children's Hosp., Innsbruck, 1967-73, Graz, 1973-89; sci. King Faisal Specialist Hosp., Riyadh, Saudi Arabia, 1989-91; asst. prof. Children's Hosp., Graz, Austria, 1991-97; ret., 1997; lectr. U. Graz, 1973, assoc. prof., 1989. Contbr. numerous articles to profl. jours. Mem. European Soc. Pediatric Endocrinology, Swiss Soc. Clin. Chemists, Osterreich Alpenklub, Osterreich Alpenverein. Avocations: sports climbing, mountaineering, riding, diving, music and arts. Home: Franck Str 10, A8010 Graz Austria

GLÉMET, FRANÇOIS JEAN, management consultant; b. Bergerac, Dordogne, France, Oct. 21, 1949; s. Roger J. and Jacqueline (Piteau) G.; m. Marie-Laure Thaumiaux, June 5, 1976; children: Emilie, Camille. Degree in civil engring., Ecole des Mines de Paris, 1972; MBA, Harvard U., 1974. Fin. analyst Nestle Alimentana, Vevey, Switzerland, 1974-75; divsn. contr. Nestle France, Courbevoie, 1975-77; cons. McKinsey & Co., Paris, 1977-82, ptnr., 1984-96; dir. McKinsey & Co., Paris, Madrid, 1996—. Author: El Futuro de la Distribucion Alimentaria en Espana, 1995; contbr. articles to profl. jours. Dir. Soc. Française de Bienfaisance, Madrid, 1971-94, v.p., 1994-95. Fulbright scholar, 1972-74. Mem. Harvard Bus. Sch. Club. Avocations: skiing, sailing, hiking, cycling, playing music. Office: McKinsey & Co, 79 Ave Des Champs Elysees, 75008 Paris France

GLEMP, JOZEF CARDINAL, archbishop; b. Inowroclaw, Poland, Dec. 18, 1929; s. Kazimierz and Salomea (Kosmicka) G.; grad. Priests Sem. Gniezno, 1956; D. Canon and Roman Law, Lateran U., Rome, 1964. Ordained priest Roman Catholic Ch., 1956; sec. to Cardinal Primate Stefan Wyszynski, 1967-79; bishop of Warmia, 1979-81; archbishop of Gniezno and Warsaw, 1981-92, archbishop of Warsaw, 1992—, primate of Poland, 1981—, elevated to cardinal, 1983; pres. Polish Episcopal Conf.; mem. Cong. for the Eastern Ch. Author: De conceptu fictionis iuris apud Romanos, 1974, Lexiculum iuris romani, 1974, Through Justice in Charity, 1982, Czlowiek wielkiej wiary, 1983, Kosciol na drogach Ojczyzny, 1985, Chcemy z tego sprawdzianu wyjsc prawdomowni i wiarygodni, 1985, Kosciol i Polonia, 1986, Umocnieni nadzieja, 1987, W teczy Frankow orzel i krzyz, 1987, O Eucharystii, 1987, Nauczanie Pasterskie vol. 1 1981, vol. 4 1982, vol. 6 1985, vol. 6 1987, vol. 7 1988, A wolanie moje niech do Ciebie przyjdzie, 1988, Let My Call Come to You, 1988, Boze cos Polske poslal nad Tamize, 1988, Nauczanie spoleczne, 1981-86, 89, Na dwóch wybrzezach, 1990, U przyjaciól Belgów, 1990, I uwierzyli uczniowie, 1990, Tysiaclecie wiary Swietego Wlodzimierza, 1991, Slowo Boże nad Łyna, 1991, Zamyslenia Maryji, 1991, Gniezno-ciagla odnowa, 1991, Niebo sciagaja na ziemie, 1991, Służyc Evangelii słowem, 1991, Poet-Priests Vis-a-Vis The New Evangelisation, 1991, Na skałce-na opoce, 1991, Miedzy ewangelia a konstytucja, 1991, Na wyspie Swietego Patryka, 1992, Idzmy do Betlejem, 1992, Wartosci chrzescijanskie nabywane pod Kalwaria, 1993 Bycznakiem milosci, 1994, W blaskach zmartwychwstania, 1994. Address: Rezydencja Prymasa Polski, ul Miodowa 17/19, 00-246 Warsaw Poland*

GLEN, ERIC STANGER, urologist, surgeon; b. Glasgow, Scotland, Oct. 20, 1934; s. William Kerr and Ann Pullar (Hughes) G.; m. Patricia Alexa Scott Nicholson, Apr. 7, 1965; children: Jeremy, Stephen, Paul. MB, BChir, Glasgow (Scotland) U., 1960. Sr. resident Western Infirmary, Glasgow, 1961; ship surgeon Royal Fleet Auxiliary, U.K., 1962; sr. registrar Victoria Infirmary, Glasgow; cons. urological surgeon So. Gen. Hosp., Glasgow, 1973-99; hon. sr. clin. lectr. U. Glasgow; past mem. panel of examiners Royal Coll. Physicians and Surgeons Glasgow; nat. panelist Scottish Home and Health Dept., Scotland, 1985-88, 91-93; chmn. area med. com. Greater Glasgow Health Bd., 1993-94; trustee Walton Found., 1991—, Coloplast Trust, 1991-93; vis. lectr. Caledonian U.; med. dir. Continence Resource Ctr. and Helpline, Scotland, 1989-99. Contbr. chpts. to books and articles to profl. jours. Gov. Belmont Preparatory Sch., Glasgow, 1978-84. Fellow Royal Coll. Physicians and Surgeons Glasgow, Royal Coll. Surgeons Edinburgh; mem. Brit. Assn. Urol. Surgeons, Scottish Urol. Soc. (pres. 1992-94), Internat. Soc. Urology, Internat. Continence Soc. (hon.; founder, sec. 1971-85), Urol. Computing Soc. (founder, coord.). Avocations: reading, sailing, travel, computers. Home: 9 St Johns Rd, Glasgow G41 5RJ, Scotland Office: Ross Hall Hosp, 221 Crookston Rd, Glasgow G52 3NQ, Scotland

GLEN, ROBERT ALEXANDER, state official; b. Phila., July 13, 1957; s. John Alexander and Natalie (Musser) G.; m. Lee Taylor Glen, Oct. 20, 1984; children: Elizabeth Anne, Catherine Lee. BA in Econs., Williams Coll., Williamstown, Mass., 1979; MS in Acctg., NYU, 1981; JD, U. Pa., 1986. Acct. Ernst & Whinney, N.Y.C., 1979-80; vol. Peace Corps, Fiji Islands, 1981-82; atty. Skadden Arps Slate Meagher & Flom, Washington, 1986-94; dep. atty. gen. State of Del., Wilmington, 1994; dep. bank commr. State of Del., Dover, 1994-98, bank commr., 1999—. Office: Office of the State Bank Commr 555 E Loockerman St Dover DE 19901-3779

GLENDENNING, DON MARK, lawyer; b. Dallas, Dec. 24, 1953; s. Don Thomas and Nancy (Malloy) G.; m. Carol Peterson, Dec. 30, 1979. BA, Rice U., 1976; JD, Stanford U., 1979. Bar: Tex. 1979. Assoc. Rain Harrell Emery Young & Doke, Dallas, 1979-85; ptnr. Rain, Harrell, Emery, Young & Doke, Dallas, 1985-87; shareholder Locke Liddell & Sapp (formerly Locke Purnell Rain Harrell, P.C.), Dallas, 1987-98; ptnr. Locke Liddell & Sapp LLP, Dallas, 1999—. bd. dirs. Nat. Tree Trust, Dallas Trees and Park Foound., Thanks-Giving Found., Scenic Tex., Human Rights Initiative N. Tex., Dallas Zool. Soc. Republican. Presbyterian. Office: Locke Liddell & Sapp LLP 2200 Ross Ave Ste 2200 Dallas TX 75201-6776

GLENN, CORNELIA JARMON, education educator; m. James H. Glenn; children: Kimberly L., James H. Glenn III. BS, Wis. State U., 1971; M of Spl. Edn., U. Wis., 1974; postgrad., U. Ky. Elem. tchr. Greendale (Wis.) Pub. Schs., 1971-72; primary tchr., spl. edn. Wauwatosa (Wis.) Pub. Schs., 1975-76, 1976-77; elem. tchr. Dist. 88, Bellwood, Ill., 1987-88; assoc. prof. Ky. Cmty. and Tech. Colls., Owensboro, 1988-94; mem. primary assessment task force Ky. Dept. Edn.; mem. adv. com. Commonwealth Ky. Goals 2000, Ky. Edn. Reform Act Regional Svc. Ctr. Vice-pres., state and local edn. chair LWV, Owensboro, 1988—; bd. dirs. Owensboro Dance Theatre, 1989-95, Girls Inc. Am., Owensboro, 1989-95; scholarship chmn. Owensboro Career Devel., 1990-94. Grantee Dept. Edn., Frankfort, 1992. Mem. ASCD, AAUW, Assn. Childhood Edn. Internat., Am. Assn. Women in C.C., O.H.R.C. (bd. dirs.), Ky. Blacks in Higher Edn. (conf. chair), Human Devel. Coun. (bd. dirs.), Ky. Assn. Devel. Edn., Laubach Internat. Avocations: painting, gardening, down hill skiing, reading. Home: 1001 Michaels Ct Owensboro KY 42303-6443 Office: Owensboro Community Coll 4800 New Hartford Rd Owensboro KY 42303-1800

GLENN, GUY CHARLES, pathologist; b. Parma, Ohio, May 13, 1930; s. Joseph Frank and Helen (Rupple) G.; m. Lucia Ann Howarth, June 13, 1953; children: Kathryn Holly, Carolyn Helen, Cynthia Marie. BS, Denison U., 1953; MD, U. Cin., 1957. Diplomate Am. Bd. Pathology, Am. Bd. Radioisotopic Pathology. Intern Walter Reed Army Med. Ctr., Washington, 1957-58; resident in pathology Fitzsimmons Army Med. Ctr., Denver, 1959-63; commd. 2d lt. U.S. Army, 1956; advanced through grades to col., 1977; demonstrator pathology Royal Army Med. Coll., London, 1970-72; chief dept. pathology Fitzsimmons Army Med. Ctr., Denver, 1972-77; past pres. med. staff St. Vincent Hosp., Billings, Mont.; past mem. governing bd. Mont. Health Systems Agy. Fellow Coll. Am. Pathologists (chmn. chemistry resources com., chmn. commn. sci. resources, mem. budget com., coun. on quality assurance, chmn. practice guidelines com., outcomes com., bd. govs., chmn. nominating com.), Am. Soc. Clin. Pathology, Am. Registry Pathology (bd. dirs.), Soc. Med. Cons. to Armed Forces, Midland Empire Health Assn. (past pres.), Rotary (bd. dirs. local chpt.). Home: 3225 Jack Burke Ln Billings MT 59106-1113

GLENN, HUGH VICTOR, educator; b. Belfast, No. Ireland, July 20, 1938; s. Hugh Victor Glenn Sr. and Annie McMillan. Tchg. cert. in art and gen. subjects, Stranmillis Coll., Belfast, 1961; student, Dublin (Ireland) U., 1971, MA, 1976; postgrad. cert. in cmty. work, Queen's U. Belfast, 1974, postgrad., 1997—. Tchr. Glastry Secondary Sch., Ballyhalbert, 1961-64, Kilcoan Pub. Sch., Island Magee, 1964-67, Boys Model Ballysillen, Belfast, 1971-74, Aylestone H.S., London, 1974-77, Five Miletown H.S., Fermanagh, Tyrone, No. Ireland, 1977-78, Parkhall H.S., Antrim, No. Ireland, 1979-80, East Antrim Inst., Newtownabbey, Belfast, 1980-90; part-time tutor Horizons Programme E. Antrim Inst. Further and Higher Edn., 1995-96, Ards Leisure Ctr., Newtownards, Northern Ireland, 1996-97. Compiler: (local history) History of Island Magee, 1967; author poetry. Comty. svcs. Fermanagh Dist. Coun., 1978-79; registrar No. Ireland Amateur Weight-lifting Assn., No. Ireland, 1980-85; coach Sunshine Hour, Belfast, 1979—; sport therapist Irish Football Assn/Milk Cup, No. Ireland, 1990—; sec. Action Concern Europe, No. Ireland, 1995—; swimming tchr. Irish Amateur Swimming Assn., 1977—. Mem. Assn. Swimming Therapy, Football Assn. Regional Med. Soc., Inst. Sports Therapists. Avocations: computers, environment, relief missions to Europe, swimming therapy, foreign languages. Home: 398 Beersbridge Rd, Belfast BT5 5EA, Northern Ireland

GLENNER, RICHARD ALLEN, dentist, dental historian; b. Chgo., Apr. 14, 1934; s. Robert Joseph and Vivian (Prosk) G.; m. Dorothy Chapman, July 13, 1957; children: Mark Steven, Alison, Scott Jay. BS, Roosevelt U., 1955; BS in Dentistry, U. Ill., 1958, DDS, 1959. Pvt. practice Chgo., 1962—; cons. on dental history to Smithsonian Instn., ADA, various corps., librs., univs., museums, dental jours, Dr. Samuel D. Harris Nat. Mus. Dentistry; dental and anthropol. rschr. Nat. Park Svc., Nat. Mus. Health and Medicine, 1993—; lectr. to various orgns. Author: The Dental Office: A Pictorial History, 1984, How it Evolved: Dentistry's Pursuit for Excellence, 1997; co-author: The American Dentist, 1990, A Visit to the Dentist: Then & Now, 1996; appeared in PBS video Sci. Am. Frontiers: The Wild West, 1995; cons. editor A Bicentennial Salute to Am. Dentistry, 1976; contbr. articles to profl. and popular jours.; film maker The Dental Office, 1994; reviewer Jour. ADA, 1999—. Served to capt. AUS, 1960-62. Mem. ADA (life), Ill. Dental Assn., Chgo. Dental Soc., Acad. Gen. Dentistry, Assn. Mil. surgeons U.S., Am. Acad. History of Dentistry (historian 1984, chmn. smithsonian Instn. adv. group 1987, Hayden-Harris award 1983, columnist Jour. History of Dentistry 1989—, mem. editl. bd. 1993—, hist. display com. 1993—, pub. com. 1993—, Hayden-Harris award com. 1995-99), Fed. Dentaire Internat., Lindsay Soc. G.B., Ill. Dental Soc. (history com.), The Pierre Fauchard Acad., Am. Med. Writers Assn., Sci. Instrument Soc., Jewish War Vets. U.S., Alpha Omega, Th Westerners, The Titanic Hist. Soc., Titanic Internat. Soc. Home: 6715 N Lawndale Ave Lincolnwood IL 60712-3711 Office: 3414 W Peterson Ave Chicago IL 60659-3447

GLENNY, ROBERT JOSEPH ERVINE, retired civil servant, consultant; b. Belfast, No. Ireland, May 14, 1923; s. Robert and Elizabeth Rachel (Ervine) G.; m. Joan Phillips Reid, Dec. 16, 1947; children: Helen Patricia, Michael. BSc in Chemistry, Queens U., Belfast, 1945; BSc in Metallurgy, London U., 1947, PhD in Metallurgy, 1962. Chartered engr. Rsch. metallurgist English Elec. Co., Stafford, Eng., 1943-47; sci./sr. sci. officer Nat. Gas Turbine Establishment, Leicester, Eng., 1947-55; prin./sr. prin. sci. officer Nat. Gas Turbine Establishment, Farnborough, Eng., 1955-70; supt. divsn. materials application Nat. Phys. Lab., Teddington, Eng., 1970-73; head materials dept. Royal Aircraft Establishment, Farnborough, 1973-79, group head aerodynamics, structures and materials depts., 1979-83; ret.; R&D cons. Commn. of European Communities, Brussels, 1986, 91; chmn. sci. recruiting bd. Cabinet Office, Basingstoke, 1983-88; program coord. Sci. and Engring. rsch. Coun., Swindon, 1986-88; program coord. and monitor Dept. of Trade and Industry, London, 1989—. Contbr. articles to profl. jours. Fellow Inst. of Materials. Avocations: walking, gardening, reading. Home: 77 Gallyhill Rd, Fleet Hants GU13 0RU, England

GLENTHOJ, BIRTE YDING, psychiatrist; b. Odder, Denmark, June 19, 1951; d. Frank Pedersen and Ulla Yding; m. Anders Glenthøj, Dec. 20, 1975; children: Rasmus, Andreas. MD, U. Copenhagen, 1977, DMSc, 1994. Jr. resident Inst. Medicine, Surgery, Pediat., Psychiatry, Neurology, Ålborg, Hillerod and Roskilde, Denmark, 1977-83, 85-86; sr. resident Univ. Hosps., Kommune Hosp. and Rigshosp., Copenhagen, 1984-85, 86-87; rsch. fellow State U. Hosp., Denmark, 1987-91; sr. resident, chief psychiatrist U. Hosp. Bispebjerg and Hillerod Hosp., Denmark, 1991-96; chief psychiatrist Univ. Hosp., Bispebjerg, 1996—; aassoc. prof. U. Copenhagen, 1996—; mem. rsch. team Bispebjerg Hosp., 1991—. Contbr. articles to profl. jours. Recipient The Rafaelsen award, Copenhagen, 1991. Mem. AAAS, Internat. Brain Rsch. Orgn., Scandinavian Socs. Psychopharmacology (Best Young Scientist paper award 1991), Danish Soc. Biol. Psychiatry (pres. 1993-97), N.Y. Acad. Scis., World Fedn. Socs. Biol. Psychiatry (v.p. 1997—), Collegium Internat. Neuropsychopharmacology, European Soc. Neuropsychopharmacology. Office: U Hosp Bispebjerg Dept Psychiatry E, Bispebjerg Bakke, DK-2400 Copenhagen Denmark

GLERUP, HENNING, endocrinologist; b. Randers, Jylland, Denmark, Feb. 22, 1957; s. Kristian and Erna (Rosenlund) G.; m. Inger Jorgensen; children: Lea, Ditte. MD, Aarhus (Denmark) U., 1987, PhD, 1999. Registrar Kjellerup Sygehus, Denmark, 1987-90; sr. registrar Horsens Sygehus, Denmark, 1990-92; sr. registrar dept. hepatology Aarhus Kommune Hosp., 1992-93; registrar dept. infectious diseases Marselisborg Hosp., Aarhus, 1994; rsch. fellow dept. endocrinology bone/mineral rsch. group Aarhus Amtssygehus, 1994-98, sr. registrar dept. endocrinology, 1998—; presenter in field. Author: Textbook on Vitamin D in Dermatology, 1999. Mem. Am. Soc. Bone and Mineral Rsch. Home: Gartnervaenget 24, DK-8680 Ry Denmark Office: Dept Endocrinology C, Tage Hansensgade 2, DK-8000 Århus Denmark

GLESK, IVAN, physicist, educator, researcher; b. Martin, Czechoslovakia, Sept. 1, 1957; came to U.S., 1990; s. Pavol and Elena (Orszaghova) G.; m. Helena Gleskova, Aug. 18, 1984; 1 child, Ivan. BS, MS in Physics, Comenius U., Bratislava, Slovak Republic, 1981, PhD in Physics, 1989; DS, Slovak Acad. Scis., 1998. Asst. prof. Comenius U., Bratislava, 1986-95, assoc. prof., 1996—; vis. fellow Princeton (N.J.) U., 1990-91, vis. rsch. staff mem., 1991-94, rsch. staff mem., 1994-2000, rsch. scientist in physics, 1995-2000, sr. rsch. scientist, 2000—; chmn. Slovak Com. for Optics, 1998—; presenter at numerous confs. Contbr. over 100 articles to profl. jours. IREX Bd. fellow, 1990. Mem. Optical Soc. Am., SPIE. Achievements include first demonstration of ultrafast all-optically controlled routing switch capable of Tb/s operation; first demonstration of all-optical address recognition and self-routing in a 250 Gb/s packet-switched network; first demonstration of all-optical demultiplexing of TDM data at 250 Gb/s; first demonstration of 100 Gb/s optical shuffle network; pioneering work in ultra fast all-optical switching; first demonstration of 100 Gb/s optical computer interconnect.

GLESMANN, SYLVIA-MARIA, artist; b. Spardorf/Erlangen, Germany, June 8, 1923; arrived in the U.S., 1925; d. Rolf-Joseph and Auguste (Schultheiss) Hoffmann; m. John Brainerd Glesmann, Apr. 30, 1948; children: Glenn M., Eric B., Jonathan M. Degree, Acad. Fine Arts, Nurnberg, Germany, 1940, Acad. Fine Arts, Munich, 1944. instr. Somerville Adult Edn. Classes. Paintings exhibited in group shows including Carrier Clinic, 1993, Bergen Mus., 1993, Morris Mus., 1993, Nabisco Brands, 1993, Tribute to Spring Cultural and Heritage Gallery, Somerville, N.J., 1993, 94, 95, Salmagundi Juried Mems. Show, 1994, Garden State Water Color Assn., Princeton, N.J., 1994, Barrons Art Ctr., 1993, Art on the Ave. Group Show of Flowers, 1991, Nat. Assn. Women Artists Show, N.Y.C., 1991, The "Big Picture" NAWA, N.Y., 1994, "105 Exhibition" SoHo, 1994, Bridgewater N.J. County Libr. Show, 1996, Nat. Assn. Women Artists 110th Ann. New World Art Ctr., Soho, N.Y., 1999; others; exhibited painting in more than 22 one woman shows including Childrens Specialized Hosp., Mountainside, N.J., N.U.I. Corp., Bridgewater, N.J., 1987, Salmagundi Club Juried Show, N.Y.C., 1995, Am. Artists Profl. League Juried Show, 1995, 96, 97, Somerset County Libr., Bridgewater, N.J., 1996, Barrons Art Ctr. 20th Anniversary Exhbn. Invitational, Woodbridge, N.J., 1997, Salmagundi Club, 2000, Barrons Art Ctr., Bridgewater (N.J.) Mcpl. Bldg, 1999-2000, Nat. Assn. Women Artists (N.Y.C.), Feminist Expo-Balt. Conv. Ctr., Balt., 2000, others; author: numerous poems. Recipient over 50 awards in water color, Editor's Choice award, 1998. Mem. Am. Artists Profl. League (pres. N.J. chpt. 1988-91), Nat. Assn. Woman Artists, Raritan Valley Arts Assn. (pres. 1976-78), Somerset Art Assn. (chairwoman 10th outdoor art show), Nat. Assn. Women Artists, Salmagundi Club, Nat. Mus. for Women in Arts (charter mem.). Lutheran. Avocations: sports, music, reading, poetry. Home and Office: 36 Twin Oaks Rd Bridgewater NJ 08807-2343

GLIBIN, EVGENII NIKOLAEVICH, chemist, researcher; b. Leningrad, Soviet Union, Mar. 17, 1937; s. Nikolai Fedorovich and Larisa Vyacheslavovna (Zubko) G.; m. Zinaida Ivanovna Korshunova, Sept. 1, 1972; children: Olga, Larisa. Degree in chemistry, Leningrad Lensoviet Tech., 1969, D in Chemistry, 1985. Jr. rschr. Leningrad Lensoviet Tech. Inst., 1967-70, sr. rschr., 1970-86; leading rschr. St. Petersburg State Tech. Inst., 1986—; cons. Indsl. Pharm. and Chem. Assn., St. Petersburg, 1995. Contbr. articles to profl. jours. including Chromatographia. Grantee Russian Found. Fundamental Investigations, 1994-97, 99-01, Internat. Assn. for Promotion of Cooperation with Scientists from New Ind. States of the Former Soviet Union, 1999-02. Mem. Mendeleev All-Union Chem. Soc. (award 1986), Mendeleev Russian Chem. Soc. (dep. head sect. organic chemistry 1986-95), Soc. Blockading Leningrad Residents. Avocations: gardening, mushroom picking, skiing. Home: Prospect Metallistov 118, Apt 17, 195197 Saint Petersburg Russia Office: St Petersburg State Tech In, Moskovskii Prospect 26, 198013 Saint Petersburg Russia

GLICK, JANE MILLS, biochemistry educator; b. Memphis, Nov. 26, 1943; d. Albert Axtell Jr. and Mary Louise (Baynes) Mills; m. John Harrison Glick, May 25, 1968; children: Katherine Anne, Sarah Stewart. AB, Randolph-Macon Woman's Coll., 1965; PhD, Columbia U., 1971. Postdoctoral trainee NIH, Bethesda, Md., 1971-73; postdoctoral fellow Sch. of Medicine Stanford (Calif.) U., 1973-74; rsch. asst. prof. biochemistry Sch. Dental Medicine U. Pa., Phila., 1974-77; asst. prof. biochemistry Med. Coll. Pa., Phila., 1977-82, assoc. prof. biochemistry, 1982-90, prof. biochemistry, 1990-94; sr. rsch. investigator Inst. Human Gene Therapy, U. Pa. Sch. Medicine, 1994—; mem. metabolism study sect. NIH, 1993-97; adj. assoc. prof. U. Pa. Sch. Medicine, 1996—. Assoc. editor: Jour. Lipid Rsch., 1985-86, mem. editorial bd., 1987-99; contbr. articles to profl. jours. Trustee Episcopal Acad., Merion, Pa., 1989-95, Swarthmore Presbyn. Ch., 1995-97, pres. 1997. Recipient Rsch. Svc. award NIH, 1975-77, Young Investigator award, 1980-83, Teaching award Lindback Found., 1985. Mem. AAAS, AAUP (sec. 1990-92), Arteriosclerosis Coun. Am. Heart Assn. (program com. 1990-93), Am. Soc. for Biochemistry and Molecular Biology, Am. Soc. for Human Genetics, Phi Beta Kappa, Sigma Xi. Presbyterian. Office: U Pa Med Coll Inst Human Gene Therapy 613 BRB II/III 421 Curie Blvd Philadelphia PA 19104

GLICK, SHIMON MICHAEL, medical educator; b. Paterson, N.J., June 30, 1932; arrived in Israel, 1974; m. Oct. 1956; six children. AB magna cum laude, NYU, 1951; MD, SUNY, Bklyn., 1955. Diplomate Nat. Bd. Med. Examiners, Am. Bd. Internal Medicine, Am. Bd. Internal Medicine Subspeciality Endocrinology Bd.; cert. specialist internal medicine, Israel, cert. specialist endocrinology, Israel; lic. N.Y., Conn., Pa., Israel. Intern Maimonides Hosp., Bklyn., 1955-56; asst. resident internal medicine Yale U., Grace New Haven (Conn.) Hosp., 1956-57; chief outpatient dept. and med. clinic USAR Army and Navy Hosp., Hot Springs, Ark., 1957-59; asst. resident internal medicine Mt. Sinai Hosp., N.Y.C., 1959-60; trainee in diabetes and metabolic disorders USPHS Jewish Chronic Disease Hosp., Bklyn., 1960-61; spl. rsch. fellowship USPHS VA Hosp., Bronx, 1961-63, clin. investigator, 1963-64; assoc. dir. divsn. metabolism and endocrinology Maimonides Med. Ctr., 1964-74; prof. medicine Ben-Gurion U. of the Negev, Faculty of Health Scis., Beer-Sheva, Israel, 1974-97; dean Ben-Gurion U. of the Negev, Faculty of Health Scis., Beer-Sheva, 1986-90; head internal medicine Soroka U. Hosp., 1974—; chief div. metabolism and endocrinology Coney Island Hosp. of Maimonides Med. Ctr., 1964-69, chief med. svcs., 1967-74, vis. physician, 1967-74; clin. asst. prof. medicine SUNY, Downstate Med. Ctr., 1965-68, clin. assoc. prof., 1968-72, clin. prof., 1972-74; attending physician Maimonides Med. Ctr., 1967-74; chmn. divsn. medicine Ben-Gurion U. of the Negev and Soroka U. Hosp., 1974-83; established investigator Israel Ministry of Health, 1978-81, mem. nat. health coun., 1996—, nat. ombudsman, 1998—; vis. scientist NIH, 1983-84; chmn. faculty of health scis. Ctr. for Med. Edn., Ben-Gurion U. of the Negev, 1990—. Editorial bd.: Jour. Clin. Endocrinology and Metabolism, 1971-74; assoc. editor: Israel Jour. Med. Scis., 1978-98. Mem. nat. adv. com. on human experimentation Ministry of Health, Israel, 1985—; head health svcs. Negev region, Kupat Holim (Sick Fund) of Gen. Fedn. of Labor, 1986-90, chmn. med. coun., 1986-90. Fellow ACP; mem. Israeli Soc. for Med. Ethics (coun. 1989—), Endocrine Soc., Assn. Orthodox Jewish Scientists (pres. 1965-67), Israel Soc.

Internal Medicine, Israel Diabetes Assn., Soc. Urban Physicians (pres. 1969), Am. Soc. for Clin. Investigation, Com. of Concerned Scientists (co-chmn. med. sci. sect. 1973-74), Israel Endocrine Soc. (pres. 1979-82), Phi Beta Kappa, Alpha Omega Alpha (pres. sch. chpt. 1954-55). Office: Ben Gurion U of the Negev, PO Box 653, 84105 Beersheva Israel

GLICKMAN, DANIEL ROBERT, federal official; b. Wichita, Kans., Nov. 24, 1944; s. Milton and Gladys Anne (Kopelman) G.; m. Rhoda Joyce Yura, Aug. 21, 1966; children: Jonathan, Amy. B.A., U. Mich., Ann Arbor, 1966; J.D., George Washington U., Washington, 1969. Bar: Kans. 1969, Mich. 1970. Trial atty. SEC, 1969-70; assoc., then ptnr. Sargent, Klenda & Glickman, Wichita, 1971-76; mem. 95th-103rd Congresses from 4th Kans. Dist., 1977-95; mem. agrl. com. 95th-10rd Congresses from 4th Kans. Dist., mem. judiciary, sci., space and tech. coms.; chmn. permanent select com. on intelligence 103d Congress; sec. U.S. Dept. Agriculture, Washington, 1995—, now chmn. Mem. Wichita Bd. Edn., 1973-76, pres., 1975-76. Mem. Order of Coif, Phi Delta Phi, Sigma Alpha Mu. Democrat. Jewish. Office: Office of the Secretary USDA Ste 200-A 1400 Independence Ave SW Washington DC 20250-0002

GLICKMAN, MARLENE, non-profit organization administrator; b. Evansville, Ind., May 13, 1936; d. Morris Jack and Sarah (Krawll) Foreman; m. Marshall Levi Glickman, Jan. 9, 1956; children: Cynthia Anne, Joseph Leonard. Student, Ohio State U., 1954-56. Area dir. Am. Jewish Com., Buffalo, 1981—. Pres. Human Rights Adv. Coun., Western N.Y., 1988-96; bd. dirs. YWCA, Buffalo and Erie County, 1990-96, Buffalo Fedn. Neighborhood Ctrs. Inc., 1994-98, Sheehan Meml. Hosp., Inc., 1994-98; pres., bd. dirs. Western N.Y. Martin Luther King Jr. Commn., 1991-97; mem. United Way Agy. Allocations Com.; chairwoman Towns and Villages divsn. United Way, 1981; pres. N.E. Lakes coun. Union Am. Hebrew Congregations, 1982-86, Meals on Wheels of Buffalo and Erie County, 1981-83, Coun. Congl. Pres. Erie County, 1979-81, Temple Beth Am, 1978-80, Sisterhood Temple Beth Am, 1969-71, 76-77; vice chair gen. campaign United Jewish Appeal, 1980, chair woman's divsn., 1979; mem. Western N.Y. Vision for Tomorrow 2000 C. of C./Buffalo Partnership. Recipient Abraham Pugash Cmty. Rels. award for establishing Kosher Meals on Wheels, Jewish Family Svc., Buffalo and Erie County, N.Y., 1975, NAACP Human Rels. award, 1997; Am.-Pol Eagle Citizen of Yr., 1995. Mem. Am. Hebrew Congregations (bd. dirs. 1982-99, exec. com.), Commn. on Synagogue Music, Joint Cantorial Placement Commn., Hadassah (life), Assn. Reform Zionists Am. (del. to Israel 1987), Brandeis Women's Com., Nat. Coun. Jewish Women (life, Hannah G. Solomon award 1985), Assn. Jewish Cmty. Rels. Workers, Jewish Communal Svc. Assn., Arza/World Union (bd. dirs. 1992—). Avocation: singing. Home: 94 Broadmoor Dr Tonawanda NY 14150-5532 Office: Am Jewish Com 3407 Delaware Ave Buffalo NY 14217-1421

GLICKSMAN, ARVIN S(IGMUND), radiation oncologist; b. Bklyn., Mar. 14, 1924; s. Charles and Myrtle (Fetner) G.; m. Bernice R. Grobstein, Jan. 30, 1956; children: Jonathan, Jane Ellen, Merrylee, Caroline, Jeanette. MB, MD, Chgo. Med. Sch., 1949. Intern Kings County Hosp., Bklyn., 1948-50; AEC postdoctoral research fellow Duke U., 1950-51; postgrad. rsch. fellow Brookhaven Nat. Labs., Upton, N.Y., 1951-52; resident in medicine Meml. Hosp., N.Y.C., 1952-54; clin. asst. physician in medicine Meml. Hosp., 1955-64, asst. attending radiation therapist, 1964-65; rsch. fellow Sloan-Kettering Inst., N.Y.C., 1954-60; assoc. Sloan-Kettering Inst., 1960-65; mem. med. rsch. inst. Michael Reese Hosp., Chgo., 1964-65; assoc. chmn. dept. radiation therapy Michael Reese Hosp., 1965-67; dep. dir. radiotherapy Mount Sinai Hosp., N.Y.C., 1967-73; prof. radiotherapy Mount Sinai Sch. Medicine, 1971-73; dir. radiation oncology R.I. Hosp., Providence, 1973-84, chmn. dept. radiol. medicine and biol. rsch., 1984-89; prof. med. scis. Brown U., 1973-95, prof. emeritus, 1995—; chmn. dept. radiation oncology Roger Williams Med. Ctr., 1989-95; practice medicine specializing in radiation oncology; hon. med. cons. NIH, Royal Marsden Hosp.; mem. cancer clinic, investigation rev. com. Nat. Cancer Inst., 1975-79, mem. radiation oncology com., 1976-86, mem. cancer intervention study sect., 1991-94. Editor: (with others) Computers in Radiotherapy, 1970, 73; contbr.: numerous articles to profl. jours. Mem. exec. com. Am. Cancer Soc., R.I., 1987-96—, pres., 1987-89, nat. bd. dirs., 190-93; chmn. radiotherapy com. Cancer and Leukemia Group B.; dir. Quality Assurance Rev. Ctr., R.I. Cancer Control Bd., 1980-98, chmn. task force info. sys., mem. exec. com.; co-chmn. exec. com. ASSIST Program Nat. Cancer Inst./Am. Cancer Soc., 1991-98; exec. dir. R.I. Cancer Coun., 1999—. Dillon fellow Royal Marsden Hosp., Surrey, Eng., 1961-62; Rsch. Career Devel. awardee NIH, 1962-64; Fulbright sr. scholar, 1986-87; recipient St. George medal Am. Cancer Soc., 1991. Fellow Am. Coll. Radiology; mem. New England Soc. Radiation Oncologists (pres. 1975-76), N.Y. Roentgen Ray Soc. (chmn. sect. therapeutic radiology 1972-73), Am. Soc. Clin. Oncology, Am. Assn. Cancer Edn., Am. Assn. Cancer Rsch., Am. Radium Soc., Am. Soc. Therapeutic Radiologists, Brit. Inst. Radiology. Fax: 401-728-4816. Home: Old Blackstone Rd AKA Brown Terrace Uxbridge MA 01569 Office: RI Cancer Coun Inc 249 Roosevelt Ave Ste 201 Pawtucket RI 02860-2134

GLIEGE, JOHN GERHARDT, lawyer; b. Chgo., Aug. 3, 1948; s. Gerhardt John Gliege and Jane Heidke; children: Gerhardt, Stephanie, Kristine. BA, Ariz. State U., 1969, MPA, 1970, JD, 1974. Bar: Ariz. 1974. Pvt. practice Scottsdale, Ariz., 1974-81, Flagstaff, Ariz., 1981-94, 98—, Sedona, Ariz., 1994-97, Williams, Ariz., 1997-98; prof. paralegal studies No. Ariz. U., Flagstaff, 1981-83, prof. urban planning and cmty. devel., 1984—; prof. paralegal studies Yavapai Cmty. Coll., Prescott, Ariz., 1995-97. Address: PO Box 1388 Flagstaff AZ 86002-1388

GLIESCHE, CHRISTIAN GEORG, microbiologist; b. Germany, May 26, 1955; m. Dagmar Annette Thiele, Dec. 30, 1987. Office: Inst for Okologie, Schwedenhagen 6, 18565 Kloster Germany

GLIKSBERG, ALEXANDER DAVID, engineering executive; b. Odessa, Ukraine, Feb. 24, 1936; came to U.S., 1978; s. David L. and Eneta S. Gliksberg; m. Sofia M. Heifetz, Dec. 3, 1959; 1 child, Inna A. MS in Mech. Engring., Odessa Inst. Tech., 1963; MS in Elec. Engring., Moscow Polytech. Inst., Moscow, 1971; postgrad., Harvard U., 1984. Lead program mgr. Rsch. and Design Inst., Odessa, Ukraine, 1967-78; dir. quality and reliability Wang Labs., Inc., Lowell, Mass., 1979-85, dir. mfg. engring., 1985-87, dir. engring., 1987-93; dir. engring. Waters Corp., Milford, Mass., 1993—. Patentee in fields of Automatic Control Systems and Automated Equipment; contbr. articles to profl. jours. Recipient Gold medal Nat. Econ. Exhbn., Moscow, 1975. Avocations: chess, collecting stamps, swimming. Office: Waters Corp 34 Maple St Milford MA 01757-3696

GLIKSMAN, DAVID, gynecologist-obstetrician; b. Johannesburg, South Africa, Feb. 12, 1946; s. Zenon and Edith (Talekinsky) G.; m. Marion Novick, 1973; 3 children. MB BChir, Witwatersrand U., Johannesburg, 1968. Cert. Am. Bd. Ob-Gyn. Cons. gynecologist JHB Gen. Hosp., 1974-75, Parklane Clinic, Johannesburg, 1974-99, Morningside Clinic, Johannesburg, 1999—. Fellow Royal Coll. Obstetricians-Gynecologists; mem. South African Med. and Dental Coun., South African Med. Assn. Avocations: antiques, silver, art, walking, traveling. Home: 73 Central Ave, Johannesburg 2196, South Africa Office: Block R Rochester Pl, 173 Rivonus Rd Pvt Bag X6, Johannesburg 2021, South Africa

GLINER, ERAST BORIS, theoretical physicist; b. Kiev, USSR, Feb. 3, 1923; came to U.S., 1980; s. Boris Moses Gliner and Bella Boris (Pauckman) Rubinstein; m. Galina Ilchenko, Dec. 12, 1944; children: Bella, Arkady. MS in Physics, Leningrad U., USSR, 1963; PhD in Physics, Tartu U., Estonia, 1972. Head theoretical dept. Spl. Design Office, Leningrad, 1954-63; sr. scientist A Ioffe Inst. for Physics and Tech. of Soviet Acad. Scis., Leningrad, 1963-80; vis. fellow Joint Inst. Lab. Astrophyiscs U. Colo., Boulder, 1982-83; rsch. assoc. McDonnel Ctr. Space Sci. Washington U., St. Louis, 1983-86; vis. scientist Stanford Linear Acceleration Ctr. Stanford U., Palo Alto, Calif., 1987—; guest nuc. physics divsn. Lawrence Berkeley Lab., 1987. Co-author: Differential Equation of Mathematical Physics (English, Russian, Japanese edits.), 1962-65; contbr. articles to profl. jours. Polit. prisoner USSR, 1945-54. Sgt. field arty. Soviet Army, 1942-44. Decorated Russian Orders Red Star and Patriotic War; recipient rsch. award USSR Govt., 1958-60, USSR Acad. Scis., 1977, 78. Mem. Am. Phys. Soc. Jewish. Achievements include patents in field (USSR); research in solar physics (combined effect of global and upper magnetic fields on solar atmosphere, coronal asymmetry as evidence of solar quadrupole magnetic field), and in Einstein gravitational theory (introduction of vacuumlike state of matter, covaiant energy description in general relativity, foundation of general relativity on the basis of Sakharov's concept of gravity; investigation of non-singular black hole geometry; general relativistic background of quantum non-locality). Office: Stanford U SLAC PO Box 4349 Palo Alto CA 94309-0450

GLINES, STEPHEN RAMEY, software industry executive; b. N.Y.C., Mar. 3, 1952; s. Earl Stanley and Catherine Van Arman (Stevenson) G.; m. Susan Leigh Collings; children: Elizabeth, Catherine. Pres. Brahman Publ., Cambridge, Mass., 1973-77; system designer Wakefield Software System, Woburn, Mass., 1973-74; sr. product mgr. Atex, Lexington, Mass., 1983; pres. S.R. Glines & Co., Belmont, Mass., 1983-91; rsch. assoc. J. Forrester, MIT, Cambridge, 1978-79; cons. Logistics Systems, Newton, Mass., 1979-82; fellow Ctr. for Advanced Profl. Studies, Cambridge, 1991-99; CEO NuCache Corp., 1999—. Author 5 books; columnist Altos World, 1988-90; contbr. articles to profl. jours. Mem. IEEE, IUSR group, Mt. Auburn Club (Watertown, Mass.). Avocation: sailing. Home: 62 Tobey Rd Belmont MA 02478-4226

GLINIANOWICZ, KRZYSZTOF, manufacturing executive; b. Pszczyna, Poland, Oct. 1, 1957; s. Franciszek and Jozefa (Gotdy) G.; m. Iwona Pasek, June 3, 1958. MS, Tech. U., Gliwice, Poland, 1981. Specialist Huta Silesia, Rybrik, Poland, 1981-84; mgr. maintenance dept. Huta Silesia, Rybrik, 1985-89, mgr. rsch. and devel., 1990-92, tech. dir., 1992-93; establishment mgr. Van Leer, Rybrik, 1993-95; mgr. bus. unit Van Leer, 1996—. Avocations: tourism, music, sports. Office: Van Leer Silesia, ul Przemystowa 3, 44 203 Rybnik Poland

GLINSEK, GERALD JOHN, lawyer; b. Akron, Ohio, Jan. 16, 1939; s. Rudolph Paul and Angela Louise (Stanger) G.; m. Karen Rosemary Mehen, Oct. 17, 1968 (div. Aug. 1990); children: Kelli, Daniel; m. Maureen Louise Nuosce, May 7, 1994 (dec. Aug. 1998); 1 child from previous marriage, Rebecca Ann. BA, U. Akron, 1963, JD, 1967. Bar: Ohio 1967, U.S. Dist. Ct. (no. dist.) Ohio 1969, U.S. Ct. Appeals (6th cir. 1986), U.S. Supreme Ct. 1986. Asst. pros. atty. Summit County Prosecutors Office, Akron, 1967-71; pvt. practice Akron, 1971—. With U.S. Army, 1957. Mem. ABA, Ohio Bar Assn., Akron Bar Assn. (treas. 1981), Summit County Legal Aid Soc. (pres. 1978-82), Phi Kappa Tau (advisor 1982—). Democrat. Roman Catholic. Avocations: travel, skiing. Home: 1861 Wiltshire Rd Akron OH 44313-6101 Office: 88 S Portage Path Akron OH 44303-1023

GLOBER, GEORGE EDWARD, JR., lawyer; b. Edwards AFB, Calif., Aug. 10, 1944; s George Edward and Catharine (Crain) G.; m. Deirdre Denman, May 22, 1971; children: Denman, Nancy King. AB, Cornell U., 1966; JD, Harvard U., 1969. Bar: Tex. 1969, U.S. Supreme Ct. 1976. Tchg. fellow natural scis. Harvard U., 1967-69; assoc. Vinson & Elkins, Houston, 1969-77; dir. Houston Dept. Pub. Svc., 1977-78; mem. law dept. Exxon Mobil Corp. and Affiliates, Irving, Tex., 1978—; counsel Exxon Mobil Corp., Irving, Tex., 1995—; asst. gen. counsel Exxon Chem. Co., 1991-94; chief atty. refining, environ. and health Exxon Co. USA, 1988-91; gen. counsel Exxon Prodn. Rsch. Co., 1982-88. With Air N.G., 1969-75. Office: Exxon Mobil Corp 5959 Las Colinas Blvd Irving TX 75039-2298

GLOBUS, RUDO STEVEN, behavioral and social scientist; b. N.Y.C., Oct. 15, 1923; s. Joseph Haim and Margareta (Gans) G.; m. Luci Turner, June 30, 1947 (div. 1969); children: Andrew, Daniel; m. Maria Luisa Costantino, Dec. 29, 1972; children: Jennifer, Amy, Susan. Student, Brown U., 1940-42, 43-44; BA, Rutgers U., 1943, U. Ill., 1943; MA; PhD, New Sch. Social Rsch., 1952, 54. Account exec. Inst. Pub. Rels., N.Y.C., 1945-48; v.p. creative dir. GreenBrodie Advt., N.Y.C., 1948-53; grad. faculty political and social sci. New Sch. Social Rsch., 1948-54; exec. v.p., CEO Abbot-Kimball Advt., N.Y.C., 1953-54; assoc. dir., chmn. bd. Simon & Schuster Pub., N.Y.C., 1954-58; pres., CEO Globus Co., N.Y.C., 1958-61; pres. Rudo S. Globus Pub., N.Y.C., 1959-62; sr. assoc. James O. Rice, Inc.; v.p., creative svcs. Mktg. & Mgmt. Cons., N.Y.C., 1963-67; exec. v.p., CEO Bliss Grunewald Advt., N.Y.C., 1967-69; pres., CEO The Adv. Inc., N.Y.C., 1969-72; pvt. practice N.Y.C., 1972—; pres., CEO Timeaus, Inc.; lectr. in field; cons. to pres. Brit. Bd. Trade, 1955; guest lectr. U. Ill., Western Reserve, U. Chgo., London Sch. Econs., Harvard U., Sorbonne, We. Res., Suffolk U. With Intelligence, U.S. Army, 1943-45, ETO.

GLOD, BRONISLAW KRZYSZTOF, research scientist; b. Ciechanow, Poland, Oct. 14, 1955; s. Wladyslaw and Franciszka (Lesniak) G.; m. Anna Krystyna Zloch; children: Karolina Agnieszka, Agnieszka Aleksandra. MSc, U. Warsaw, Poland, 1980, DSc, 1998; PhD, Polish Acad. Scis., Warsaw, 1988. Sr. asst., asst. prof. Inst. Phys. Chemistry Polish Acad. Scis., Warsaw, 1980-83; rsch. assoc. U. NSW, Sydney, Australia, 1990-91; sr. lectr. U. Warsaw, 1993-95; assoc. prof. Med. Rsch. Ctr., Polish Acad. Scis., Warsaw, 1996—; hon. sr. rsch. assoc. U. Tasmania, Hobart, Australia, 1999—; dealer, sci. cons. Varian-Candela, Warsaw, 1994-97; sci. cons. COMED/JSCO, Warsaw, 1994, Polygen/Dionex, Warsaw, 1998—; cons. Inst. Biocybernetics, Warsaw, 1992-93. Author, editor: Introduction to HPLC, 1992; author: Ion Exclusion Chromatography, 1997; patentee in field. Mem. region coun. Unia Pracy party, Warsaw, 1997-99. Fellow Polish Chem. Soc. Avocations: travel, music, philately, history, politics. Home: ul F Pancera 12/55, 03-187 Warsaw Poland Office: Med Rsch Ctr, Ul Piwinskiego 5, 02-106 Warsaw Poland

GLOMSKI, EDWARD EARL, electronic company executive, bookseller; b. Royal Oak, Mich., July 21, 1955; s. Edward James and Lorraine Anne Glomski; 1 child from previous marriage, Hannah Michelle; m. Shellee Anita. Grad. with honors, Nat. Inst. of Tech., 1983. Owner The Book Nook, Akron, Ohio, 1999; purchasing mgr. Stellar Pvt. Cable, Akron, 1997—. With USN, 1974-76. Mem. East Ctrl. Ohio Mensa (exec. bd. 1997-99), Intertel (jour. editor 1998—, area. coord. Ohio 1997—). Home: 300 Malacca St Akron OH 44305-3652

GLONTI, OMAR ALEKSANDRES, mathematician, researcher; b. Gori, Georgia, USSR, Oct. 12, 1939; s. Alexander and Rusudan (Suskiashvili) G.; m. Ketevan Goderzishvili, June 24, 1971; children: Rusudan, Khatuna. D in Physical and Math. Scis., Tbilisi (USSR) State Univs., 1962. Sci. rschr. Inst. Cybernetica, Tbilisi, 1962-65; postgrad. Tbilisi Math. Inst., 1965-68; sci. rschr. Inst. Applied Math., Tbilisi, 1968-73; dept. chief Inst. Econs. and Law, Tbilisi, 1973-83; sector chief Tbilisi Ramadze Math. Inst., 1983-90; lab. chief Tbilisi State U., 1990—; prof. in probability theory and math. stats., Tbilisi State U., 1968—. Author: Investigations in the Theory of Conditionally Gaussian Processes, 1985; contbr. over 50 articles to profl. jours. dealing with probability theory and math. stats., 1968—. Mem. Am. Math. Soc., Internat. Statis. Inst. Avocations: reading, painting. Home: 18 Kekelidze Str Apt 35, 380009 Tbilisi Georgia Office: Tbilisi State U, 17a I Chavchavadze Ave, 380079 Tbilisi Georgia

GLOSS, LAWRENCE ROBERT, fundraising executive; b. Colorado Springs, Colo., Oct. 31, 1948; s. Kenneth Edwin and Clara U. (Haeker) G.; divorced; children: Alexander Edwin, Carolyn Claire. BA, U. Denver, 1970. Dir. natl. congress on volunteerism and citizenship NCVA, Washington, 1975-76; dir. devel. Vis. Nurses Assn., Washington, 1976-77; devel. cons. Am. Lung Assn., Washington and N.Y.C., 1977-78; exec. dir. Colo. Conservation Fund, Denver, Colo., 1978-79; dir. devel. Rose Med. Ctr., Denver, 1985-86; exec. dir. Rose Found., Denver, 1979-86; sr. campaign dir. J. Panas, Young and Ptnrs., San Francisco, 1986-88; pres. Gloss and Co., Denver, 1988—; mem. adv. coun. non-profit mgmt. Metro State Coll., Denver, 1994; cons. Native Am. Rights Fund, Boulder, Colo., Arts at the Sta., Denver, 1994, Up With People, 1995, 96, Emily Griffith Ctr. Found., 1995, 96, Colo. CASA, 1998-99, Women of the West Mus., 1998, 2000, Sister Cities-Denver and Kumming, China, 1999. Vol. Peace Corps, Columbia, Peru, 1970-75; guest spkr. Tech. Assistance Ctr., Denver, 1992-94; bd. dirs. Alzeimer's and Related Disorders Assn., Denver, 1985-86; bd. dirs. Woman's Sch. Network, Denver, 1984-85, Colo. PTA, Englewood, 1991-92; active Emily Griffith Ctr. Found., 1997, U. Denver, Episcopal Ministries of U. Colo., Boulder, 1996—, Colo. Pub. Expenditure Coun., 1998—, Columbine H.S. Permanent Meml., Srs. Resource Ctr., 1998—, Am. Humane Assn., 1998—, BMH-BJ Congregation, 1999—. Mem. NSFRE (Colo. chpt. 1992-94, bd. dirs.), Arapahoe House, Englewood Hist. Soc., Am. Humane Assn., Women of the West Mus. Nat. Assn. of Mus. Exhibitors, Colo. Planning Giving Roundtable, Nat. Com. on Planned Giving, Am. Prospect Rsch. Assn., Am. Humane Assn., Assn. of Healthcare Philanthropy (regional XII 1993-94), Assn. Profl. Rschrs. Advancement, Rotary Club of Denver. Lutheran. Avocations: dressage, art, soccer. Office: Gloss Co 2755 S Locust St Ste 113 Denver CO 80222-7131

GLOUSCHENKOV, VLADIMIR ALEKSANDROVICH, metallurgy engineer, educator; b. Samara, Russia, Dec. 16, 1941; s. Aleksander Mikhailovich and Nadezhda Ivanovna (Ryzhikova) G.; m. Kaleriya Grigoryevna Shishkanova, Sept. 26, 1969; children: Oleg, Aleksandra. Engr. metallurgy, Kuibyshev Aviation Inst., 1964, cand. tech. scis., 1972. Rsch. engr. Kuibyshev (Russia) Aviation Inst., 1964-68, jr. prof., 1970-76, asst. prof., 1976—. Author: Advances and prospects for application of high pressures in science and technology. Part.2. Application of pulsed loads, 1987; contbr. more than 120 articles to profl. jours.; holder more than 90 patents. Trade union com. mem. Samara (Russia) State Aerospace U., 1972-84, 86—. Recipient USSR State prize, 1982, Gold and Bronze medals Russian Nat. Exhbn., Regional prize in field of sci. and tech. Mem. Am. Welding Soc. (Scandinavian sect.), State Com. Sci. and Tech. Russia (chmn. pulse-magnetic processing metals sect. 1980-91), N.Y. Acad. Scis., Soc. TMS, MNOM Internat. Assn. (pres.). Avocations: hiking, kayaking, skiing, bicycling, swimming. E-mail: gl@libl.ssau.ru. Home: App 59, 153 Molodogvardeyskaya St, 443001 Samara Russia Office: Samara State Aerospace Univ, 34 Moskovskoye Shosse, 443086 Samara Russia

GLOVER, ALBERT DOWNING, retired veterinarian; b. Newark, Mo., Dec. 4, 1907; s. Albert D. and Mattie O. (Downing) G.; m. Mildred Elva Haselwood; children: Allen, Gary, Janet. BS in Agr., U. Mo., 1932; DVM, Colo. State Coll., 1936. Former chmn. City Coun., Canton, Mo., other civic activities. Mem. Mo. VMA (pres. 1951, legis. commn.), AVMA (v.p. 1952), Mo. Vet. Examining Bd., Am. Legion (past comdr.), Shriners, others. Home: 806 Lewis St Canton MO 63435-1449

GLOVER, CLAIBORNE VAN CORTLANDT, III, biochemistry and molecular biology educator; b. Atlanta, July 8, 1947. BA, Duke U., 1969; MS, Ga. State U., Atlanta, 1974; PhD, U. Rochester, N.Y., 1979. Postdoctoral fellow Stanford (Calif.) U., 1979-83; asst. prof. U. Ga., Athens, 1983-88, assoc. prof., 1988-92, prof. biochemistry and molecular biology, 1992—; mem. biol. scis. study sect. NIH, Bethesda, Md., 1990-94. Mem. editl. bd. Jour. Biol. Chemistry, 1992-96; contbr. articles to profl. jours. Sgt. U.S. Army, 1970-71. Recipient Creative Rsch. medal U. Ga., 1993; Angier B. Duke Meml. scholar, 1965-69; NIH grantee, 1975-78, 79-82. Mem. AAAS, Am. Soc. for Biochemistry and Molecular Biology. Office: U Ga Dept Biochem/Molec Bio Life Scis Bldg Athens GA 30602

GLOVER, JOEL CLINTON, anatomy and embryology educator, neuroembryologist; b. Akron, Ohio, Dec. 11, 1956; arrived in Norway, 1984; s. Lynn Walter and June Robin (Mihalik) G.; m. Janet Dunlap, 1984 (div. 1986); 1 child, Kjersti Litleskare. BA, U. Calif., San Diego, 1978; PhD, U. Calif., Berkeley, 1984. Postdoctoral fellow U. Oslo, Norway, 1984-86; rsch. assoc. U. Oslo, 1987-94, assoc. prof., 1994-96, prof., 1996—; rsch. assoc. Washington U., St. Louis, 1986-87. Contbr. articles to profl. jours. Mem. Norwegian Physiol. Soc. (pres. 1991-93), Scandanavian Physiol. Soc., Soc. Neurosci. Avocations: skiing, Indonesian music, scuba diving, glacier trekking. Home: Nyborgasen 53, 1389 Heggedal Norway Office: U Oslo Dept Anatomy, PB-1105-Blindern, 0317 Oslo Norway

GLOVER, SIR VICTOR JOSEPH PATRICK, former chief justice; b. London, Nov. 5, 1932; arrived in Mauritius, 1937; s. Harold Joseph George and Mary Catherine (Reddy) G.; m. Marie Cecile Ginette Gauther, June 6, 1960; childrten: Gavin, Brian. BA with honors, Jesus Coll., Oxford, Eng., 1956; postgrad., Mid. Temple U., London, 1956-57. Bar: London. Dist. magistrate jud. dept. Supreme Ct., Mauritius, 1962-64, crown counsel atty. gen.'s office, 1964-66, sr. crown counsel, 1966-70, prin. crown counsel, 1970-72, parliamentary counsel, 1972-76, puisne judge jud. dept., 1976-82, sr. puisne judge, 1982-88, chief justice, 1988-94; sr. legal cons. Price Waterhouse, Mauritius, 1996—; hon. prof. law U. Mauritius, 1987—; chmn. Coun. Legal Edn., Mauritius, 1985-88; hon. bencher Mid. Temple, London, 1992. Editor: Abstracts of Decisions of Supreme Ct. of Mauritius, 1982, supplement, 1987. Acting gov.-gen., Govt. of Mauritius, 1988—; pres., English Speaking Union. Named Knight Her Majesty the Queen of Eng., 1988. Mem. Oxford Union Soc., Oxford U. Boat Club. Office: 309 Chancery House, L Geoffrey St, Port Louis Mauritius

GLOWINSKI, STANISLAW, surgeon, consultant; b. Szczuczyn, Poland, Jan. 31, 1932; s. Henryk and Czesława (Truszkowska) G.; m. Lidia Dubinska, July 1, 1967; children: Jerzy, Barbara. MD, U Bialystok, Poland, 1957, PhD, 1969. Asst. dept. surgery U. Bialystok, 1957-64, asst. dept. thoracic, cardiac and vascular surgery, 1964-82, asst. prof., 1982-87, head dept. vascular surgery and transplantology, 1987—; dist. cons. for vascular surgery, Poland, 1993—. Contbr. numerous articles to med. jours., including Jour. Cardiovasc. Surgery, Jour. Vascular Surgery, Jour. Haemostasis, Jour. Atherosclerosis. Mem. European Soc. for Surg. Rsch. (pres. 1988), European Soc. for Vascular Surgery (sec. 1993), Internat. Union Angiology (pres. 1994). Avocations: opera, sailing. Office: U Bialystok Dept Vasc Surg, 24A M Sklodowskiej-Curie St, 15-276 Bialystok Poland

GLUCKMAN, JACK LOUIS, otolaryngologist, educator, dean; b. Johannesburg, South Africa, Aug. 15, 1945; s. Samuel V.P. and Martha G.; children: Nick, Kate, Simon, Jonathan. MD, U Cape Town, 1967. Asst. prof. dept. otology U. Cin., Ohio, 1977, assoc. prof.dept. otology, 1981, prof. dept. otology, 1985; assoc. dean clin. affairs, chief staff U. Cin., Univ. Hosps., Ohio, 1987, chmn. dept. otology, 1991. Mem. Am. Acad. Otolaryngology (pres. 2000—). Home: 3 Grandin Ln Cincinnati OH 45208-3358 Office: U Cin Med Sci Bldg Cincinnati OH 45267-0001

GLUSCHENKOV, OLEG, electrical engineer; b. Samara, Russia, July 12, 1970; came to the U.S., 1992; s. Vladimir and Kaleria G. Diploma, Moscow Inst. Physics & Tech., 1992; MSEE, U. Ill., 1997, PhDEE, 2000. Rsch. fellow, asst. Dartmouth Coll., Hanover, N.H., 1992-94; rsch. asst. U. Ill., Champaign-Urbana, 1994-99; mem. devel. staff semiconductor rsch. and devel. ctr. IBM Microelectronics, Hopewell Junction, N.Y., 1999—. Contbr. articles to profl. jours. Mem. IEEE, Am. Vacuum Soc., Electrochem. Soc. Office: IBM 1580 Rte 52 Z/33A Hopewell Junction NY 12533

GLUSHIEN, MORRIS P., lawyer, arbitrator; b. Bklyn., Oct. 15, 1909; s. Isaac and Minnie (Hoffman) G.; m. Anne Williams, Nov. 18, 1945; children: Minna Taylor, Ruth Wedgwood. A.B. with honors, Cornell U., 1929, J.D. with honors, 1931. Bar: N.Y. 1932, U.S. Supreme Ct. 1940. Pvt. practice Bklyn., 1932-38; mem. faculty Cornell Law Sch., 1938-39, New Sch. for Social Rsch., 1977-78; chief U.S. Supreme Ct. sect., assoc. gen. counsel NLRB, 1939-47; gen. counsel Internat. Ladies Garment Workers Union, AFL-CIO, 1947-72; arbitrator, 1972—, spl. master fed. ct., 1976-78; mem. Nat. Acad. Arbitrators; mem. arbitration panels Am. Arbitration Assn., Fed. Mediation and Conciliation Service, various state and city agys. Editorial bd.: Cornell Law Quar, 1930-31; Contbr. legal periodicals. Bd. dirs. Nat. Legal Aid and Defender Assn., 1954-72. Served with AUS, as cryptanalyst, 1942-45. Mem. ABA (past chmn. labor law sect.), N.Y. State Bar Assn. (labor rels. com.), Assn. of Bar of City of N.Y. (past chmn. com. labor and social security legis.), Indsl. Rels. Rsch. Assn., Practicing Law Inst., Am. Jewish Congress (com. law and social action), Am. Judicature Soc., AFL-CIO (past mem. nat. legis. coun.), Civil Svc. Reform Assn. (exec. com.), N.Y. Com. for Modern Cts. (past v.p., bd. dirs.), Nat. and N.Y. State Against Discrimination in Housing Coms., ACLU (com. free speech and assn.), Ams. for Dem. Action, NYU Conf. on Labor, Curia, Phi Beta Kappa, Phi Kappa Phi. Home: 2228 Westwood Blvd Los Angeles CA 90064-2018

GLUSHKO, EUGENE YAKOVLEVICH, physics educator, researcher; b. Bolgrad, Odessa, Ukraine, Oct. 27, 1951; s. Yakov Dorofeevich and Maria Konstantinovna (Jel'askova) G.; m. Natalia Grigorievna Novikova, Aug. 24, 1974; children: Yuri, Alexander, Konstantin. PhD, Inst. for Spectroscopy, Troitsk, USSR, 1985; DS, Inst. for Physics, Kiev, Ukraine, 1996. Asst. Pedagog. Inst., Krivoi Rog, Ukraine, 1979-85, assoc. prof. physics, 1983-96, prof. physics, head physics dept., 1996—. Patentee in field; contbr. articles

to profl. jours. Sci. grant J. Soros Found., 1994. Mem. N.Y. Acad. Scis., Five O'Clock Regional Philosophic Club (chief 1996). Fax: 715521. E-mail: eyagl@kpi.dp.ua. Home: Korneichuk Str 13/87, 50076 Krivoi Rog Ukraine Office: Pedagog Inst, Gagarin Str 54, 50086 Krivoi Rog Ukraine

GLUSHKOV, ANDREI NIKOLAEVICH, immunologist, researcher; b. Tomsk, Russia, Apr. 24, 1956; s. Nikolai Efimovich Glushkov and Valentina Mikhailovna (Kalinin) G.; m. Tatjana Alexeevna Svischova, May 31, 1977 (div. 1985); children: Maria Andreevna, Olga Andreevna; m. Stella Andreevna Mun, Oct. 28, 1995; 1 child, Anton Andreevich. MD, Med. Inst., Kemerovo, Russia, 1979, CandMed Scis, 1985, DMed Scis, 1996. Jr. scientist Med. Inst., Kemerovo, 1979-85; elder scientist, chief of group Inst. Bioorganic Chemistry, Novosibirsk, Russia, 1986-92; prin. scientist Kemerovo Ctr. Russian Acad. Scis., 1992-99, chief of lab., 1992-99, chief dept. cancer immunology, 1999—. Contbr. articles to profl. jours.; patentee in field. Mem. Russian Acad. Natural Scis. Office: Kemerovo Sci Ctr, Rukavishnikov 21, 650025 Kemerovo Russia

GLUSKIN, EMANUEL, physicist, engineer, researcher; b. Leningrad, Russia, Dec. 2, 1949; arrived in Israel, 1975; s. Leib Vilsker and Gita Gluskin; m. Shlomit Shalom; children: Reuth-Esther, Eithan-Haim, Gili-Hemda, Shira-Rachel. BSc, MSc, Leningrad Poly. Inst., 1974; PhD, U. Ben-Gurion, 1991. Lab. asst. Inst. Semiconductor Study, Leningrad, 1967-68; elec. engr. Leningrad Factory of Polygraph Machines, 1974-75; electronics engr. Telrad Co., Rehovot, Israel, 1976; rschr. Applied Rsch. Inst., Beer-Sheva, Israel, 1978-86; rsch. asst. Ben Gurion U. of the Negev, Beer-Sheva, 1987-90, lectr. elec. engring., 1991—; lectr. elec. engring. dept. Ctr. Ctr. Technol. Edn., Holon, 1998—. Contbr. numerous articles to profl. jours. Avocations: reading, painting, song writing. Home: Hertzel str 79/8, Kfar-Saba Israel Office: Ben Gurion Univ Negev, Dept Elec Engring Box 653, 84105 Beer Sheva Israel

GLUZMAN, DANIIL FISHELEVICH, oncohematologist; b. Kiev, Ukraine, June 4, 1936; s. Fishel Abramovich Gluzman and Maria Izrailevna Factorovich; m. Ludmila Ivanovna Komarova, Mar. 23, 1963; 1 child, Dimitri. Candidate Med. Sci., Inst. Exptl. Pathology, Oncol., Kiev, 1967, D Med. Sci., 1976. Jr. rschr. Inst. Exptl. Pathology, Oncology and Radiobiology, Kiev, 1962-71, sr. rschr., 1971-76, head lab., 1976-81; head dept. Inst. Exptl. Pathology, Oncology and Radiobiology, 1981—, prof., 1985—; cons. in field; dep. editor Jour. Eksperimentalnaya Oncologia, 1985-96. Author: Diagnostic Cytochemistry of Hemoblastoses, 1978, Embryonal Haemopoiesis and Hemoblastoses in Children, 1988, Immunocytochemistry and Monoclonal Antibodies in Oncohematology, 1990, Laboratory Diagnosis of Oncohematological Diseases, 1998. Chmn. All-Ukrainian Non-Profit Found. Haemophathologists for Patients with Haemotol. Malignancies, Kiev, 1995—. Mem. Internat. Assn. Hematologists of the World to Children, Ukrainian Soc. Hematologists, Ukrainian Soc. Oncologists. Fax: 380-44 2671656. E-mail: espera@onconet.kiev.ua. Home: Kolomyevski Str 12 Ap 17, 03127 Kiev Ukraine Office: Inst Exptl Pathology, Vasilkovskaya 45, 03022 Kiev Ukraine

GLUZMAN, PAULA, human resources administrator, orgnization consultant; b. Medellin, Colombia, Sept. 29, 1942; arrived in Israel, 1968; d. Jacobo and Victoria Rose (Ades) Cohen; m. Isaias Gluzman, May 31, 1968; children: Yoel, Shai, Eldad. MA in History, U. Tel-Aviv, Israel, 1996; LLB, U. Medellin, 1966. Cert. tchr., human resources mgr. Sec.-gen. Kibbutz Ein Dor, 1986-88; amb. WZO, L.A., 1988-91; dir. social affairs dept. Kibbutz Artzi, Israel, 1991-96; human resources mgr. Teldor, Israel, 1996-99; chair Hashomer Hatzaer Internat., Israel, 1998—; dir. Tzavta Cultural Orgn., Israel, 1995-99; dir. mental health Kibbutz Dept., Israel, 1993-97; dir. Civil Rights Orgn., Israel, 1994-98. Office: Teldor, Kibbutz Ein Dor, 19355 Yzreel Israel

GLYNN, GARY ALLEN, pension fund executive; b. Springfield, Vt., July 13, 1946; s. Allen Joseph and Josephine (Patnode) G.; m. Beth Wade Nelson, May 28, 1983. BS, U. Vt., 1968; MBA, U. Pa., 1970. Chartered fin. analyst. Fin. analyst U.S. Steel Corp., Pitts., 1970-71; investment analyst U.S. Steel and Carnegie Pension Fund, N.Y.C., 1971-84, v.p. investments, 1984-85, pres., 1985—; v.p. investments USX Found., Pitts., 1985—. Nonmem. trustee, chmn. bd. Gen. Svcs. Bd. Alcoholics Anonymous. Mem. Fin. Exec. Inst., N.Y. Soc. Security Analysts, Assn. Investment Mgmt. and Rsch., Econ. Club of N.Y., Tuxedo Club, Met. Opera Club, Drones Club, Met. Club. Episcopalian. Home: 1112 Park Ave New York NY 10128-1235 also: West Lake Rd Tuxedo Park NY 10987 Office: 350 Park Ave New York NY 10022-6022

GLYNN, IAN MICHAEL, retired physiology educator; b. London, June 3, 1928; s. Hyman and Charlotte Glynn; m. Jenifer Muriel Franklin, Dec. 9, 1958; children: Sarah, Judith, Simon. BA with honors, Cambridge (Eng.) U., 1949, MB, BChir, 1952, PhD, 1956, MD, 1970; MD (hon.), Aarhus (Denmark) U., 1988. House physician Ctrl. Middlesex Hosp., London, 1952-53; asst. lectr., lectr. in physiology U. Cambridge, 1958-70, reader in physiology, 1970-75, prof. membrane physiology, 1975-86, prof., chmn. physiology, 1986-95, emeritus prof. physiology, 1995—; mem. Brit. Med. Rsch. Coun., 1976-80, Coun. of the Royal Soc., 1979-81, 91-92, Brit. Agrl. Rsch. Coun., 1981-86; vice-master Trinity Coll., Cambridge, 1980-86. Author: An Anatomy of Thought: The Origin and Machinery of the Mind, 1999; editor: (with J.C. Ellory) The Sodium Pump, 1985; chmn. editl. bd. Jour. Physiology, 1968-70; contbr. articles to profl. jours. Flight lt. Royal Air Force, 1956-57. Fellow Royal Coll. Physicians; mem. AAAS (fgn. hon. mem.). Home: Daylesford, Conduit Head Rd, Cambridge CB3 0EY, England Office: Trinity Coll, Cambridge CB2 1TQ, England

GLYNN, KATHLEEN DEARY, museum director; b. Boston, Feb. 22, 1948; d. John Bernard and Marie T. (Giffels) D.; m. Henry R. Martin, July 6, 1969 (div. Dec. 1998); children: Joshua H., Christopher J. AB, Emmanuel Coll., Boston, 1969; MAT, Manhattanville Coll., 1986. Dir. fine arts Litchfield (Conn.) Auction House, 1989-90; asst. v.p. Am. paintings Sotheby's, N.Y.C., 1990-93, dir. Am. arts course, 1993-98, v.p., dir. Sotheby's Inst., 1996-98; exec. dir. Richmond (Ind.) Art Mus., 1999—; mem. art adv. bd. Lehigh U., Bethlehem, Pa., 1994, Ind. U. East, Richmond, 1999—. Editor-in-chief: Great Estates: Greenwich 1880-1930, 1986 (Excellence award 1986). Mem. Assn. Am. Museums, Assn. Midwest Museums.

GMACHOWSKI, LECH ZBIGNIEW, chemical physicist, researcher; b. Warsaw, Poland, Apr. 10, 1948; s. Jerzy and Helena (Stępień) G.; m. Urszula Wanda Bojar, May 5, 1973; children: Agata, Katarzyna. MSc, Warsaw Tech. U., 1971, DSc, 1994; PhD, Polish Acad. Scis. Inst., Warsaw, 1980. Rsch. asst., asst. prof. Inst. Phys. Chemistry Polish Acad. Scis., 1980—. Contbr. articles to profl. jours. Recipient award Japan Soc. for Promotion of Sci., 1987, Com. of Sci. Rsch., 1992. Avocation: touring. Home: Klaudyny 16 m 148, 01-684 Warsaw Poland Office: Polish Acad Scis Inst Phys Chemistry, Kasprzaka 44/52, 01-224 Warsaw Poland

GMEINER, FRANZ, accountant; b. Oberosterreich, Austria, Mar. 10, 1958; s. Franz and Johanna (Russmann) G.; m. Antoinette Christine De Villiers, Dec. 15, 1990; children: Nadia, Ingrid, Franz. BCom with honors, Rand Afrikans U., Johannesburg, South Africa, 1981, Rand Afrikans U., Johannesburg, South Africa, 1983. Chartered acct., South Africa. Trainee acct. MWM, Johannesburg, 1979-83; bus. analyst Sentrachem, Johannesburg, 1983-85; audit ptnr. Cohen & Gmeiner, Johannesburg, 1985-98; bd. dirs. Salger Investments. Ltd., Johannesburg, Primrose Mall, Johannesburg, St. 19 Northcliff, Johannesburg, Eseza Property Holding Ltd., Johannesburg, Devonshire Hotel Ltd., Orion Hotels & Resorts Ltd., Erf 600 Wendywood Ltd., Orion Real Estate Ltd. Mem. Pub. Accts. Bd., Johannesburg Country Club, Rand Club JHB. Roman Catholic. Avocations: travel, squash, business. Office: 16th Fl Devonshire House, 49 Jorissen St Braamfontein, Johannesburg 2000, South Africa

GMEL, GERHARD, psychologist, researcher; b. Berlin, Germany, Oct. 18, 1960; arrived in Switzerland, 1994; s. Eduard and Edda Boettcher (Beblik) G.; m. Christiane Doll, July 24, 1988; children: Gerrit, Annik. PhD, Tech. U. Berlin, 1991; MS in Stats., U. Neuchatel, Switzerland, 1999. Asst. prof. Tech. U. Berlin, 1987-92; prin. investigator telescopie media analysis, Berlin, 1992-94; dep. of rsch. dept. Swiss Inst. Prevention, Lausanne, 1994—. Contbr. articles to profl. jours. Office: SIPA, Ave de Ruchonnel 14, 1001 Lausanne Switzerland

GNAEDINGER, JOHN PHILLIP, structural engineer, consultant; b. Oak Park, Ill., Jan. 11, 1926; s. Robert Joseph and Edna Mary (Metz) G.; m. Elizabeth Williams, Mar. 15, 1956; children: John Phillip Jr., Sarah Gnaedinger Booras. BCE, Cornell U., 1946; MCE, Northwestern U., 1947. Registered profl. engr., Ariz., Calif., Conn., Ga., Ill., Ind., Iowa, Kans., Ky., Mich., Minn., Mo., Nev., N.J., N.Y., N.C., N.D., Ohio, S.D., Vt., Va., Wash., Wis.; registered structural engr., Ill. Structural engr. Shaw Metz-Dolio, Chgo., 1946-49; founder, pres. Soil Testing Svcs., Inc., Evanston and Vernon Hills, Chgo., 1948-91, J.P. Gnaedinger Rsch. Corp., Glenview, Ill., 1991—; chmn. emeritus STS Cons., Ltd., Vernon Hills, Ill., 1991—; lectr. China Coal Mine Design Inst., 1984; past chmn. bldg. rsch. adv. bd. NRC-Nat. Acad. Sci. Contbr. articles to profl. jours.; patentee in field. Creator Careers for Youth; mediation, arbitration Sys. Resolving Disputes. Recipient Merit award Northwestern U., 1966, Quarter Century award BRAB, 1977, John F. Parmer award Structural Engrs. Assn. Ill., 1978. Fellow ASCE (chmn. std. com. on shore protection systems, std. com. on ind. project peer rev., std. com. on design and analysis nuclear safety-related earth structures, Chgo. Civil Engr. of Yr. award 1979), Assn. Soil and Found. Engrs. (founder, past pres.); mem. ASTM (past sec., hon. mem. D-18), Western Soc. Engrs. (past pres., hon.), Chgo. Assn. Technol. Socs. (past pres.), Ill. Soc. Profl. Engrs., Ill. Engring. Coun., Econ. Club Chgo., Chief Execs. Orgn. Republican. Avocations: tennis, bassoonist, golf. Home: 2020 Chestnut Ave Apt 501 Glenview IL 60025-1651 Office: STS Cons Ltd 750 Corporate Woods Pkwy Vernon Hills IL 60061-3153

GNANADESIKAN, RAMANATHAN, retired statistics educator, researcher; b. Madras, India, Nov. 2, 1932; came to U.S., 1953; s. Ambalavanan and Jegathambal Ramanathan; m. Mrudulla G., Feb. 18, 1965; children: Anand, Mukund. BSc with honors, U. Madras, 1952, MA, 1953; PhD, U. N.C., 1957. Sr. rsch. statistician Procter & Gamble Co., Cin., 1957-59; tech. staff Bell Telephone Labs., Murray Hill, N.J., 1959-68, dept. head, 1968-83; divsn. mgr. Bellcore, Morristown, N.J., 1983-86, asst. v.p., 1986-91; prof. stats. Rutgers U., Piscataway, N.J., 1991-98; prof. emeritus, 1998—; adv. com. U.S. Bur. Census, Washington; math. scis. edn. bd. NAS, Washington; adv. com. NSF, Washington; panel chmn., NRC; various other coms. Author: Methods for Statistical Data Analysis of Multivariate Observations, 1977, 2d edit., 1997. Vol. Mended Hearts, N.J., 195-99, Northwest Interfaith Ctr., Tucson, 1999—; v.p. Down Harbor Assn., Martha's Vineyard, Mass., 1979-81, pres., 1999—. Recipient Ann. Recognition award Asian Indian Assn., 1989, Founders award, Am. Statis. Assn., 1997; cited for contbns. to State of N.J., N.J. State Legis., Trenton, 1989. Mem. Internat. Statis. Inst. (v.p. 1997—). Avocations: world travel, gourmet foods, boating, fishing, photography. E-mail: RG@stat.rutgers.edu.

GNANAHARAN, RAJAMONEY, research administrator; b. Sivakasi, Tamilnadu, India, Oct. 28, 1949; s. Thankappan and Manonmani (Senthiappan) Rajamoney; m. Santhy Anie Henry, Aug. 28, 1980; children: Irene, John, Charis. B Tech., U. Madras, 1971; ME, Indian Inst. Sci., Bangalore, 1973; PhD, U. Minn., 1978. Chem. engr. Indian Plywood Mfg. Co., Dandeli, India, 1973-75; scientist Kerala Forest Rsch. Inst., Peechi, India, 1979-81; head, Wood Sci. Divsn. Kerala Forest Rsch. Inst., 1981-99, rsch. coord., 1999—; cons. M/S. Poabs Timber Products, Tiruvalla, India, 1995—; working group coord. Internat. Union of Forestry Rsch. Orgns., Vienna, 1995—. Author: Handbook of Kerala Timbers, 1981; editor: (book) Ecodevelopment of Western Ghats, 1984, Bamboos: Current Research, 1988; inventor prediction model for strength of bamboo, 1993. Recipient Ron Cockcroft award Internat. Rsch. Group on Wood Preservation, Stockholm, 1993, Internat. Tropical Timber Orgn. award, Yokohama, Japan, 1995. Fellow Internat. Acad. Wood Sci., Indian Acad. Wood Sci.; mem. Bur. Indian Stds. (sectional com. 1986—), Internat. Network for Bamboo and Rattan (working group 1994—). Office: Kerala Forest Rsch Inst, 680 653 Peechi India

GNANALINGHAM, KANNA KIRUPALINGHAM, neurosurgeon, researcher; b. Colombo, Sri Lanka, Nov. 25, 1968; arrived in Eng., 1982; s. Sivagururnathar and Rajeshwari (Kandiah) G. BSc in Anatomy with honors, U. Manchester, 1990; PhD in Neuropharmacology, King's Coll., London, 1993; MBChB (honors), U. Manchester, 1996; MRCS, London, 1999; AFRCS, Edinburgh, 1999. Specialist registrar neurosurgery London. Contbr. articles to profl. jours. Recipient Dickinson Trust prize Anatomy, Preiskel elective prize in surgery Royal Coll. Surgeons England, 1995, Case award Sci. and Engring. Rsch. Coun., England, 1990-93, Welcome Trust Elective prize, 1995. Fellow Royal Coll. Surgery (Edinburgh); mem. Royal Coll. Surgery (Eng.), Br. Med. Assn., Assn. Surgeons in Tng. Hindu. Avocations: cricket, badminton, chess, current affairs, spirituality. E-mail: kannagnana@hotmail.com.

GNASPINI, PEDRO, biologist, researcher, educator; b. Lins, Sao Paulo, Brasil, Apr. 2, 1961; s. Pedro Jr. and Solange (do Prado) G.; m. Sonia Maria Marques Hoenen, July 10, 1997. BS in Biology, U. Sao Paulo, 1987, MS in Zoology, 1991, PhD in Scis., 1993. Asst. prof. Inst. Bioscis., U. Sao Paulo, 1991-98, assoc. prof., 1998—. Contbr. numerous articles to profl. jours. Rsch. grantee FAPESP Found., 1991-93, 94-95, Nat. Coun. Sci. Devel., Brazil, 1994—. Mem. Brazilian Soc. Entomology (sec. 1990-98, pres. 1998—), Brazilian Soc. Speleology (sec. 1987-89), Brazilian Soc. Zoology, Soc. Biospeleology (France). Avocations: caving, cooking, hiking, climbing. Office: USP Dept Zoology Bioscis, Caixa Postal 11461, 05422-970 São Paulo Brazil

GNATCHENKO, SERGIY LEONIDOVYCH, physicist, researcher; b. Kupyansk, Ukraine, Mar. 20, 1947; s. Leonid Mykolaiovych and Antonina Andriiovna (Kozyr) G.; m. Olena Vasylivna Kryvoshyi, Apr. 30, 1969. MS, Kharkov State U., 1971; PhD, Inst. Low Temperature Physics, Kharkov, 1977, D of Scis., 1991, prof., 1998. Engr. Inst. Low Temperature Physics & Engring., Kharkov, 1971-74, rschr., 1977-80, sr. rschr., 1980-93, head of lab., 1993-94, head of dept., 1994-98, dep. dir., 1999—. Contbr. articles to profl. jours. Recipient Acad. Scis. prize USSR and Poland, 1987. Mem. Phys. Soc. Ukraine. Home: 32 Apt. 63 Chernyshevskogo, 310002 Kharkov Ukraine Office: Inst Low Temp Physics, 47 Lenin Ave, 61002 Kharkov Ukraine

GNIAZDOWSKI, MAREK ANDRZEJ, biochemistry educator; b. Poznań, Poland, June 18, 1935; s. Włodzimierz and Zofia (Szałkowska) G.; m. Maria Gusta, Aug. 1, 1959; 1 child, Paweł. M in Chemistry, U. Łódź (Poland), 1957, DSc, 1966, PhD, 1974. Asst. Dept. Physiol. Chemistry, Łódź, 1954-70; postdoctoral fellow Inst. Neurochemistry, Strasbourg, France, 1969; head dept. gen. chemistry Inst. Physiology and Biochemistry Med. U., Łódź, 1970—, asst. prof., 1974-88, prof. biochemistry, 1988—; dep. dir. Inst. Physiology and Biochemistry Med. U. Łódz, 1975-88; mem. com. biochemistry and biophysics Polish Acad. Scis., 1981-84, 93-96; cons. Com. of Admission Exams for Faculties of Medicine at Ministry Health and Social Welfare, Warsaw, 1982-91, 95—. Co-author, editor exptl. biochemistry and chemistry manuals; contbr. numerous exptl. papers on drug-DNA interactions to profl. jours. Mem. Solidarity Trade Union, Łódź, 1980—. Recipient awards for sci. activity Ministry Health and Social Welfare, Warsaw, 1975, 80, 90. Mem. Polish Biochemical Soc. (chmn. Łódź br. 1971-77), Klub Inteligencji Katolickiej Łódź (com. mem. 1990—), Sci. Soc. Łódź, Sci. Soc.Tóolz. Roman Catholic. E-mail: magn@psk2.am.lodz.pl. Office: Med U Łódz Dept Gen Chem, Lindleya 6, 90-131 Łódź Poland

GO, GRACE GLORY, publisher, newspaper executive; b. Manila, Mar. 20; d. Puan Seng and Felisa Chua (Velasco) G.; 1 child, Vernon. BA in English/Journalism, U. The Philippines, 1967. Exec. v.p. The Philippine Star, Ang Pilipino Star Ngayon, Manila, 1994—; pres., pub. The Fookien Times Philippines Yearbook, Manila, 1994—; bd. dirs. The Philippine STAR, Filipino STAR Ngayon; v.p. mktg. The Philippine STAR, The Philippines Yearbook, 1988-94; pub. PULP mag., 1999—; bd. dirs. Alliance Francaise and Museo Pambata. Office: Star Group Publs PO Box 747, 13th St cor Railroad St, Manila The Philippines

GOASGUEN, JEAN ETIENNE, hematologist, immunologist; b. Saint Segal, France, Jan. 11, 1945; s. Jean Guillaume and Aline (Morvan) G.; m. Marie-France Creignou, Aug. 4, 1967; children: Fabienne, Sabine, Sebastien. MD, U. Rennes, France, 1971; PhD, U. Rennes, 1978, habilitation, 1991. Maitre de conf. des univ. Biologiste Des Hopitaux, U. Rennes, 1971—; cons. in oncology U. Rochester, N.Y., 1989-91; cons. in immunology Dhahran Med. Complex, Saudi Arabia, 1994—; elected mem. bd. govs. Faculte De Medecine, Rennes, 1993-94; elected mem. Nat. Bd. Univ., 1982—; elected Dep. Dean Faculté de Medicine, 1999—. Contbr. more than 250 articles to profl. jours. Elected 2d mayor Saint Gilles, France, 1983-89. Recipient grant Nat. Inst. Med. Rsch., France, 1971-73, grant French Nat. Assn. Cancer Rsch., France, 1987, 89. Mem. Am. Soc. Hematology, N.Y. Acad. Scis., European Soc. Pediat. Haematology and Immunology. Avocation: photography. Office: Hospital SUD, 16 Boulevard de Bulgarie, 35056 Rennes France

GOBBA, MOSTAFA ABDELHAKIM MAMDOUH, marketing professional; b. Damascus, Syria, July 14, 1969; s. Abdelhakim Mamdouh and Mervat Kamel (Aly) G.; m. Nayera Mokhless, Aug. 4, 1995; 1 child, Mokhless. Higher Edn. Cert., Orman, Egypt, 1986; BA in Commerce, Ainshams U., Egypt, 1990; MBA, Washington U., 2000. Profl. mktg. planner. Product mgr. Intertec Internat. Group Investment, Egypt, 1991-92; group brand mgr. Ismail Aly Abudawood Establishment, Saudi Arabia, 1992-95, mktg. mgr., 1995-96; gen. mgr. Amacom Advt., Saudi Arabia, 1996-97; mktg. mgr. Koki-Americana, Egypt, 1998-2000, FarmFrites.Egypt. Avocations: sports, music, reading. Home: 46 Mossadak St, Dokki Giza, Egypt Office: Cairo Poultry Processing Co, Koki-Americana, 10th of Ramadan City Egypt

GOBELI, VIRGINIA C., national program leader; b. Providence, R.I., July 14, 1942; d. Albert and Claire Estelle (Plante) Ouellette; m. Garrett Frederick Gobeli, Aug. 17, 1974; children: Gayla Elizabeth, Gregory Alfred. BA, Salve Regina U., 1964; MA, U. R.I., 1972; EdD, Boston U., 1989. Dietetic internship N.Y. Hosp. - Cornell Med. Ctr.; adminstrv. dietitian N.Y. Hosp. - Med. Ctr., 1965-67; ext. home economist Cooperative Ext. U. of R.I., Kingston, 1967-69; dairy food publicist Am. Dairy Assn., Springfield, Mass., 1969-72; state 4-H leader, home economics Cooperative Ext./U. Mass., Amherst, 1972-73; 4-H youth devel. specialist Cooperative Ext./U. Nev., Reno, 1973-81, Cooperative Ext./U. Nebr., Lindoln, 1981-90; youth devel. cons. Cooperative Ext., U. Mass., 1987; cons. FAO/UN, Rome, 1995; amb. tng. Nat. 4-H Conf., Washington, 1981-84. Contbr. articles to profl. jours. Mem. Fine Arts Bd., U. Nev., Reno, 1978-90, Glucester Hist. Soc., R.I., 1981-83; bd. dirs. Cajir/Consejo Asesor Internat. de la Juventud Rural. Mem. Nat. Assn. Ext. 4-H Agts. (Disting. Svc. award 1978, 25 Yr. Svc. award 1998), Assn. Leadership Educators, Soc. for Internat. Devel., Epsilom Sigma Phi (team award 1986). Avocations: handcrafts, needlecrafts, cooking, travel, reading. Office: Families 4-H Nutrition/USDA Stop 2225 1400 Independence Ave SW Washington DC 20250-0002

GOBER, HERSHEL W., government official; b. Monticello, Ark., Dec. 21, 1936; m. Mary Lou Keener. With USMC, 1956-59; with U.S. Army, 1961, advanced through grades to maj., 1978, ret., 1978; supr., dir. N.W. Alaska Pipeline Corp., 1978-83; instr. Jr. Reserve Officers Tng. Corps., Ark.; dir. Ark. Vets. Child Welfare Svc., Ark. Dept. Vets. Affairs, 1988-93; dep. sec. Dept. Vets. Affairs, Washington, 1993-99, acting sec., 2000—. Decorated numerous military awards. Mem. Am. Legion (adj.). Office: Dept of Veterans Affairs Office of Dep Sec 810 Vermont Ave NW Washington DC 20420-0002

GOBLE, ALAN REGINALD STANLEY, compiler; b. Brighton, East Sussex, Eng., Jan. 21, 1938; s. Reginald and Cynthia (Cope) G.; m. Valerie Anne Edis, Sept. 14, 1963. Examiner Dept. of Trade, Brighton, Eng., 1975-93, asst. offcl. receiver, 1994-95; self-employed compiler, 1995—. Editor: Complete Index to British Sound Film Since 1928, 1999, Complete Index to Literary Sources in Film, 1999, International Film Index, 1991, 2 vols.; compiler (CD-ROM) Complete Index to World Film Since 1895, 1998. Avocations: book collecting, sports. Home: Bookends, 7 Raphael Rd, Hove BN3 5QP, England

GÖBLYÖS, PÉTER KORNÉL, radiologist; b. Györ, Hungary, Nov. 21, 1936; s. Michael and Barbara (Fölsey) G. MD, Med. U. Budapest, Hungary, 1961; PhD, Hungarian Acad. Scis., Budapest, 1977; habilitation, Semmelweis Med. U., Budapest, 1995. Resident Town Hosp. Miskolc, Hungary, 1961-64; asst. 2nd Clinic of Surgery, Semmelweis Med. U. Budapest, 1964-69; asst. Clinic of Radiology Postgrad. Med. Sch. Budapest, 1970-73, adj., 1973-82, assoc. prof., 1982-93; head radiologist Nat. Inst. Hematology and Immunology, Budapest, 1993—; hon. prof. U. Budapest, 1999; lectr. in field. Contbr. articles to profl. jours. Founder, sec. Hungarian Albert Schweitzer Soc., 1988. Recipient, Prof. Honor, Haynal Imre Med, Univ., Budapest, 1999. Fellow Hungarian Radiol. Soc., Hungarian Oncol. Soc. (founder, sec. Mammological sect. 1994), Hungarian Biophys. Soc., Hungarian Soc. Nuclear Medicine, Hungarian Thermogrammetrical Soc.; mem. Hungarian Senological Soc. (hon.), Hungarian Soc. Radiologists (mammograph. sect.). Roman Catholic. Avocations: classical music, organ playing, traveling, arts. Home: Bogdanfy u 5a, 1117 Budapest Hungary Office: Nat Inst Hematology & Immun, PO Box 424, H-1519 Budapest Hungary

GOC, JACEK PRZEMSLAW, physicist, researcher; b. Poznań, Poland, July 9, 1952; s. Boleslaw and Maria (Mazany) G.; m. Danuta Miezal, June 21, 1975; 1 child, Piotr. MSc, A. Mickiewicz U., Poznan, 1976; PhD in Phys. Sci. and Molecular Physics, Polish Acad. Sci., Poznan, 1985, Dr Habil. in Phys. Sci., 1999. Asst. lectr. Poznan U. Tech., 1976-86, asst. prof., 1986-95—; vice-dean faculty tech. physics Poznan U. Tech., 1999—; asst. rschr. Nat. Inst. for Advanced Interdisciplinary Rsch., Tsukuba, Japan, 1994-95. Contbr. articles to profl. jours. including Jour. Photochemistry and Photobiology, Biophys. Chemistry, others. Mem. Polish Phys. Soc., Polish Biophysics Soc., Japanese Chem. Soc. Home: OS B Crhobrego 40 m 27, 60-681 Poznań Poland Office: Poznań U Tech Inst Physics, ul Piotrowo 3, 60-965 Poznań Poland

GOCAN, SIMION GAVRIL, chemistry educator; b. Berind, Cluj, Romania, Dec. 26, 1930; s. Gavril Iacob and Lucretia Lica (Dragan) G.; m. Maria-Elena Ioan Ciupală, Oct. 1, 1960; children: Simona, Mircea. BSc, U. Babes-Bolyai, Cluj-Napoca, Romania, 1954, PhD, 1968. Chemist diplomate. Asst. Tech. U., Cluj-Napoca, 1954-64; lectr. Pedagogical Inst., Cluj-Napoca, 1964-72; assoc. prof. Babes-Bolyai, U. Cluj-Napoca, 1972-91, prof., 1991-96, cons. prof., 1996—. Author: Gradient Liquid Chromapography, 1974, Separatologia Analitica, 1981, Imunochimie Analitica, 1995, Cromatografia de gaze, 1998; contbr. articles to profl. jours. Mem. Chromatographic Soc., Chem. Soc. Romania, Analytical Soc. Romania. E-mail: sgocan@chem.ubbcluj.ro. Home: Tarnita No 7 Ap 30, 3400 Cluj-Napoca Romania Office: U Babes-Bolyai, Arany Janos 11, 3400 Cluj-Napoca Romania

GOCKLEY, BARBARA JEAN, business executive; b. Pitts., July 26, 1951; d. William Ervin and Dorothy Marie (Wolf) Cain; m. William Lee Gockley, Mar. 29, 1975 (div. Aug. 1989); children: Ervin Cain, Marianne Cain, William Cain, Malinda Cain. Student, Indiana U. Pa., 1969-70, Thomas Edison State Coll., 1986-88; BA in Bus. Mgmt. and Mktg. Mgmt., Alvernia Coll., 1993; MBA, Univ. Wis., 1997. Cert. in purchasing mgmt.; cert. prodn. and inventory mgmt. Asst. materials mgr. Redman Mobile Homes, Ephrata, Pa., 1972-75; mgr. inventory control Gym-Kin, Inc., Reading, Pa., 1975-77; supr. prodn./inventory control Wyomissing Converting, Reading, 1979-82; mgr. prodn./inventory control Dorma Door Controls, Inc., Reamstown, Pa., 1982-85, project mgr., 1985-86; materials mgr. Powder Coatings Group-Morton Internat., Reading, 1986-94; dir. purchasing Dexter Corp., Waukegan, Ill., 1994-99; dir. procurement Unisource, Berwyn, Pa., 1999—; v.p. global strategic sourcing Spectrum Brands, St. Louis, 1999—; dir. programs Congress for Progress Inc., 1984-88, vice chmn., 1988-89, 99-2000, chmn., 1989-90, 2000-2001; dir. programs PRMS User Group Internat. Conf., 1991, 92; instr. Berks Campus, Pa. State U., Reading, 1985-86. Dir. Reinholds (Pa.) PTA, 1978-81; bd. dirs. Cocalico Sch. Bd., Denver, Pa., 1985-89. Mem. Am. Prodn. and Inventory Control Soc. (cert. prodn. and inventory mgmt., treas. Schuylkill Valley chpt. 1981-82, pres. 1982-84, dir. membership region IX 1985-86, asst. v.p. 1987, v.p. 1988-89, Internat. Vol. Svc. award 1986), Nat. Assn. Purchasing Mgrs., Assn. Mfg. Excellence. Republican. Presbyterian. Office: Spectrum Brands Inc PO Box 15842 8825 Page Ave Saint Louis MO 63114-6105

GODAL, BJÖRN TORE, Norwegian government official; b. Skien, Norway, Jan. 20, 1945; s. Aksel Godal and Kari (Pettersen) Lia; m. Sissel Rönbeck, 1971 (div. 1982); 1 child, Anne Marit; m. Gro Balás, Nov. 18, 1988. Grad., Holly Royde Coll., U. Manchester, U.K., 1965; candidate in Sociology, Polit. Sci. and History, U. Oslo, 1969. Chmn. Norwegian Labor League of Youth, Oslo, 1971-73; sec.-gen. Nat. Com. for Internat. Youth Work, Oslo, 1973; policy rsch. officer Norwegian Labor Party, Oslo, 1973-80; sec., chmn. Oslo Labor Party, 1980-90; dep. rep. Storting, Oslo, 1986-89, M.P., 1989—; min. trade and shipping Govt. of Norway, Oslo, 1991-94, min. fgn. affairs, 1994-97, labor defence spokesman, 1997—; min. def. Govt. of Norway, 2000—; mem. Govtl. Com. to Evaluate Polit. Activities in Mil. Svc., 1970-72; mem. adv. bd. Study of Distbn. of Power in Norway, 1972-80; mem. ctrl. exec. com. Norwegian Labor Party, Oslo, 1983-90; mem. Parliamentary Com. on Fin. Affairs, Oslo, 1986-89; mem., chmn. Parliamentary Com. on Fgn. Affairs, Oslo, 1989-91, chmn., 1990-91. Pres. Coun. European Nat. Youth Coms., 1973-75. Lutheran. Avocations: music, reading. Office: Norwegian Min Def, PO Box 8126 Dep, 0032 Oslo Norway

GODARD, MICHEL PAUL, engineering educator; b. Bertrix, Luxembourg, Belgium, Mar. 14, 1949; s. Albert and Simone (Renaux) G.; m. Nadine Marie Collot, Oct. 13, 1972; children: Philippe, Bertrand. Ingenieur Civil Physicien, U. Liege, Belgium, 1972; postgrad., Von Karman Inst., Rhode-St-Genese, Belgium, 1977. Asst. U. Zaire, Kinshasa, 1972-76; rschr. Von Karman Inst., Rhode-St-Genese, 1976-77; prof. Ecole Mohammadia d'Ingenieurs, Rabat, Maroc, 1977-85; charge de cours U. Liege, 1985-87, chef de mission, 1992-94; vis. prof. U. Liege, Thies, Senegal, 1986; prof. engring. Inst. Gramme, Liege, 1987—, coord. unités énergie et mécanique, 1996—; coord. Erasmus/CEE, various locations, 1992—. Author/editor: Thermodynamique, 1996; contbr. articles to profl. jours. Administrateur-delegue Gramme sans Frontieres, Liege, 1988—. Erasmus/CEE grantee, 1992—. Avocations: travel, history, homemade engines. Home: Ave des Chevrefeuilles 23, 4121 Neuville-en-Condroz Belgium Office: Institut Gramme, Quai du Condroz 28, 4031 Liege Angleur, Belgium

GODBOUT, ARTHUR RICHARD, JR., lawyer; b. Hartford, Conn., Oct. 7, 1957; s. Arthur Richard and Elizabeth Anne (Desmond) G. BSBA, Georgetown U., 1979, JD, 1986. Bar: Conn. 1987. Pres. A.R. Godbout & Co., Avon, Conn., 1987—. Home: 8 Cheltenham Way Avon CT 06001-2444 Office: PO Box 1175 Avon CT 06001-1175

GODDARD, CLAUDE PHILIP, JR., lawyer; b. Long Beach, Calif., Oct. 31, 1952; s. Claude Philip and Doris Marian (Dow) G.; m. Ellen Kohn, May 23, 1981; children: Marian Laura, Nora Margaret. BS with distinction, U.S. Naval Acad., 1974; JD cum laude, U. Pa., 1979. Bar: N.H. 1979, D.C. 1985, Va. 1999, U.S. Dist. Ct. D.C. 1989, U.S. Ct. Appeals (9th cir.) 1985, U.S. Ct. Appeals (fed. cir.) 1991. Ensign U.S. Navy, 1974, advanced through grades to lt. comdr., 1987, atty., 1979-87, resigned, 1987; assoc. Keck, Mahin & Cate, Washington, 1987-89, ptnr., 1990; ptnr. Jenner & Block, Washington, 1990-95; shareholder Kilcullen, Wilson and Kilcullen, Chartered, Washington, 1995-99, Wickwire Gavin, P.C., Vienna, Va., 1999—.

GODDARD, EDWARD DEAN, stockbroker, accountant; b. Danville, Ill., Oct. 13, 1929; s. Oscar E. and Dorothea Goddard; m. Mary Lenny, Jan. 29, 1955; children: James, Daniel, Steven, Mark. BS in Acctg., U. Ill., 1955. CPA, Ill. Auditor Ernst & Ernst, Chgo., 1955-58; comptr., treas. various small/large corps., Chgo./Grand Rapids, Mich., 1958-69; stockbroker Kenower McArthur/The Ohio Co., Grand Rapids, 1969-80, Morgan Stanley Dean Witter, Orlando, Fla., 1980—. Writer, prodr. host TV shows: Relax It's Income Tax 13 Weeks, 1981, 89, Corporate Profile Weekly, 1982-87, Ballroom Dance Class, 13 weeks series, 1989. Candidate U.S. Congress, Dist. 7, 1994. With U.S. Army, 1946-48, Korea. Mem. Maitland Toastmasters Club (pres. 1997-98, gov. area 49 1998-99, Disting. Toastmaster 1999). Democrat. Episcopalian. Avocations: ballroom dance instructing, stamp collecting. E-Mail: edgoddard@aol.com. Home: 1316 Classic Dr Longwood FL 32779-5817

GODDARD, PHILLIP C., Barbadian government official; b. Barbados, 1939; divorced; 4 children. Student, Lodge Sch. With family bus. J.N. Goddard & Sons; with Harrison Dept. Store, 1974; dir. Barbados Adv., 1979-94; Sunday columnist, 1991-94; dir. Courtesy Garage Ltd., 1991-94; min. fgn. trade and internat. bus. Govt. of Barbados, min. of internat. trade and bus., min. health. Mem. Barbados C. of C. and Industry (pres. 1984-85), Barbados Dairy Industries (chmn. 1982-87). Mem. Labour Party. Office: Min Internat Trade and Bus, Upton, Saint Michael Barbados Office: Sr Frank Walcott Bldg, Culloden Rd 4th Fl, St Michael Barbados*

GODEAUX, JEAN EUGENE AUGUSTE, retired marine biology educator; b. Liège, Belgium, Mar. 6, 1920; s. Lucien Auguste and Maria Henriette (Luthers) G.; m. Rita Marie Berland, Oct. 27, 1945; children: Christiane Marie, Jean Claude. MS, U. Liège, 1941, PhD summa cum laude, 1948, DSc in Zoology, 1958. Belgian Nat. Rsch. Found. scholar U. Liège, 1942-48, chief practical works, supply tchr., 1948-59, Belgian Nat. Rsch. Found. assoc., 1955-59; head Zoology Lab. U. Belgian Congo (later U. Zaire), Elisabethville/Lubumbashi, 1959-68; dean faculty agronomy U. Liège, 1961-62, asst. prof., 1968-70, head. Marine Biology Lab., 1970-85, head Gen. Biology Lab., 1975-85, prof. emeritus, 1985—; mem. plankton com. Internat. Commn. for Sci. Exploration Mediterranean Sea, Monaco, 1958—, pres., 1989-96; convenor Colloquium Oceanographic Rsch. in Mediterranean, Liège, 1988, also editor; convenor Round Table on Comparative Study Levantine Basin, Suez Canal and Red Sea, Athens, Greece, 1988, also editor. Recipient Friends of U. prize U. Liège, 1954. Mem. Royal Acad. Belgium (hon., nat. com. oceanography 1972, sec. 1982-91, Agathon de Potter prize 1954, Edmond de Sélys-Longchamps prize 1971), Royal Soc. Scis. Liège (past pres., gen. sec. 1983-2000), Belgian Zool. Soc. (pres. 1980-81, exec. bd. 1980-2000), Inst. for Marine Rsch. (pres. 1985-89, 98-99, v.p. 1999—), Fifty One Club (hon. pres. 1982-84). Avocations: Middle East ancient history, philately. Home: Chemin du Carmel 22, B-4053 Chaudfontaine Belgium Office: U Liège Zool Inst, Quai Edouard Van Beneden 22, B-4020 Liège Belgium

GODEBERGE, PHILIPPE DOMINIQUE, gastroenterologist, proctologist, consultant; b. Paris, Aug. 20, 1956; s. Julien and Monique (Gros) G.; m. Beatrice Holik, Mar. 16, 1985; children: Camille, Charlotte, Celine, Alice. MD, U. Paris VI, 1982; MA in Pharmacy, U. Paris VII, 1984; degree in gastroenterology, U. Paris VI, 1986; Attestation d'Etudes Supezieures in proctology, U. Paris VII, 1986. Intern Paris hosps., 1982-86, resident, 1986-88; clin. head Faculty of Paris, 1986-88; hosp. fellow Paris, 1988—; dept. head proctology Centze Medico Chirurgical de Pa Porte de Chorsy, Paris, 1995—. Author: Maladie de P'Appareil Digestif, 1993; editor: (rev.) Actualites Bibliographiques en Colo Proctologie, 1993—; contbr. articles to profl. jours. Pres. Interns Union of Hosps. of Paris, 1984-85. Avocation: music. Office: 10 rue Jean Richepin, 75116 Paris France

GODEC, ZDENKO, electrical engineer, consultant, educator; b. Nis, Yugoslavia, Sept. 14, 1939; s. Franjo and Greta (Krahenfels) G.; m. Mirjana Urh, Sept. 24, 1965; children: Denko, Tihomir. Diplom Engr., Electrotech. U., Zagreb, Croatia, 1962, M.Sc., 1970, PhD, 1975. Devel. engr. Rade Koncar-Electrotech. Inst., Zagreb, 1962-72, R & D engr. elec. transformer dept., 1972-81, leader thermal group, 1981-90, cons., 1986-90; cons. Koncar Elec. Engring. Inst., Zagreb, 1990—; asst. prof. Electrotech. U., Osijek, Croatia, 1993-97, assoc. prof., 1997—; mem. Worker's Coun. Elec. Inst., Zagreb, 1977-80, 82-86, Republic Self-Mng. Community Interest, Zagreb, 1982-86, Scientist's Mcpl. Assembly, Zagreb, 1982—. Author Expressing Measurement Result, 1995, Measurements Basics, 1998; contbr. over 60 articles to sci. publs. Mem. Croatian Sys. Soc., Croatian Metrology Assn., CIGRE (nat. com. Croatia), Mountaineer's ZG Matica. Avocation: mountain climbing. Office: Koncar Elec Engring Inst, Bastijanova BB, HR-10000 Zagreb Croatia

GODEKE, RAYMOND DWIGHT COOK, insurance company executive, accountant; b. San Diego, Nov. 26, 1947; s. Robert Carroll and Julia Mae (Caeser) G.; m. Norma Dean Rhodes, Oct. 31, 1966(div. 1970); 1 child, Melyssa Dawn; m. Vicki Lorraine Coleman, Feb. 19, 1972; 1 child, Kristin Francine. AA, Fullerton Coll., 1976; BA, Calif. State U.-Fullerton, 1978; MBA, Pepperdine U., 1980. Cert. internal auditor, cert. mgmt. accountant. Acct. Robert Johnston & Assocs., Lynwood, Calif., 1974-75; mem. acctg. staff Denny's, Inc., La Mirada, Calif., 1975-82, div. controller, 1982-87; div. contr. Foster Farms, Livingston, Calif., 1987-90; indsl. healthcare exec. Tri-Care, Irvine, Calif., 1990-92; produce distbn. exec. J.C. Produce, L.A., 1992-94; contr. Zacky Farms, South El Monte, Calif., 1994-98, Word & Brown Ins. Adminstrs. Inc., Orange, Calif., 1998—. Chmn. Arrowhead dist. Boy Scouts Am., 1986. Mem. NRA (endowment), Nat. Assn. Accts. (bd. dirs. 1982-83), Inst. Internal Auditors (cert. internal auditor), Inst. Mgmt. Accts. (cert. mgmt. acct.), Masons (past master), Scottish Rite, York Rite, Shriners. Republican. Presbyterian. Avocations: golf, reading. Office: Word & Brown 721 S Parker St Ste 300 Orange CA 92868-4732

GODFRAIND, THEOPHILE JOSEPH, pharmacologist, educator; b. Bande, Belgium, Feb. 18, 1931; m. De Becker Anne, July 12, 1957; children: Pierre, Catherine. MB, U. Libre de Bruxelles, Belgium, 1951; MD, U. Catholique de Louvain, Belgium, 1955; Cert., Inst. de Med. Tropicale, Anvers, Belgium, 1958; PhD, U. Catholique de Louvain, Belgium, 1958. Prof. U. Lovanium, Leopoldville, Congo, 1958-65, Université Catholique de Louvain, Brussels, 1965—; fellow Royal Acad. Medicine, Brussels, 1974-88, v.p., 1988-91, pres., 1991—; sec. gen. Internat. Union Pharmacology, 1987-94, pres., 1994-99. Recipient Lauréat du Concours des Bourses de Voyage, 1955, Lauréat du Prix Spécia, 1955, Lauréat du Priz J.F. Heymans, 1967, Lauréat du prix Quinquennal des Sciences Thérapeutiques, 1973, Lauréat du Prix Smith Kline, 1982, Peter Debye prize U. Limburg, 1987, Lauréat du Prix de la Fondation de Physiopathologie Prof. Lucien Dautrebande, 1988, ASPET award, 1991, Europe and Medicine prize, 1997. Mem. Acad. Royale de Médecine de Belgique, Acad. Nat. de Médecine de France, Acad. Nat. de Pharmacie de France, Acad. Europaea, Assn. des Physiologist, Deutsche Pharmakologische Gesellschaft, Biochem. Soc., Brit. Pharmacol. Soc., Physiol. Soc., N.Y. Acad. Scis., Am. Soc. for Pharmacology and Exptl. Therapeutics, Brit. Pharmacol. Soc. (hon.), Italian Pharmacol. Soc. (hon.), Slovak Pharmacol. Soc. (hon.). Achievements include pioneering work in the phaarmacology of calcium channel blockers. Home: Rue du Bémel 19, B 1150 Brussels Belgium Office: Lab de Pharmacologie UCL 5410, Av Hippocrate 54, B-1200 Brussels Belgium

GODFREY, CARL FRANKLIN, JR., government affairs consultant; b. El Paso, Tex., Aug. 10, 1953; s. Carl Franklin and Anne (Gregory) G. BS, Va. Poly. Inst., 1975; MS, George Washington U., 1983. Legis. asst. Office of the Spkr. Thomas P. O'Neill, Jr., Washington, 1975-79, sr. legis. asst., 1979-80, exec. asst., 1980-83; assoc. Cassidy & Assocs., Washington, 1983—, exec. v.p. Office: Cassidy and Assocs 655 15th St NW Ste 1100 Washington DC 20005-5701

GODFREY, JOHN CARL, medicinal chemist; b. Cornelius, Oreg., Mar. 11, 1929; s. Carl H. and Ruth Emma (James) G.; m. Nancy Jane Williams, June 12, 1954; children: Laura Alexis, Helen Rebecca, Sabrina Lee. BA in Chemistry, Pomona Coll., Claremont, Calif., 1951; PhD in Organic Chemistry, U. Rochester, 1954. Rsch. chemist Shell Devel. Co., Emeryville, Calif., 1954-55; instr. chemistry Rutgers U., New Brunswick, N.J., 1955-59; asst. dir. clin. rsch. Bristol Labs., Syracuse, N.Y., 1959-79, Revlon Health Care, Tuckahoe, N.Y., 1979-86; assoc. dir. clin. rsch. Rorer Pharm. Corp., Horsham, Pa., 1986-90; pres. Godfrey Sci. & Design, Inc., Huntingdon Valley, Pa., 1979—; cons. Godfrey Sci. & Design, Inc., Huntingdon Valley, 1990—. Contbr. over 56 articles to profl. jours. NSF fellow, 1951; DuPont fellow, 1952-53. Fellow Am. Inst. Chemists; mem. AAAS, Am. Soc. Microbiology, Am. Chem. Soc. Achievements include patents for formulation to deliver active zinc in treatment of common cold (U.S., U.K., Can., Europe), 37 others; elucidation of mechanism of action of zinc against common cold in humans; development of major common cold intervention lozenges; invention of Godfrey Stereomodels which uniquely demonstrate mechanisms of formation, properties and reactions. Office: Godfrey Sci & Design 1649 Old Welsh Rd Huntingdon Valley PA 19006-5835

GODIN, CHRISTINE, physician; b. Paris, Jan. 12, 1958; d. Yves and Tatiana (Fredloff) G. Tropical Medicine Diploma, La Pitie Salpetriere U., Paris, 1984; Emergency Care Diploma, Bobigny U., France, 1985, MD, 1987; Diploma in Biostats./Epidemiology, U. Paris VI, 1989; MS in Pub. Health, Tulane U., New Orleans, 1991; Qualification in Exotic Medicine, Conseil Nat. del'Ordre des Medecins, Paris, 1997, Qualification in Pub. Health Medicine, 1997. Medical diplomate. Resident physician France, 1980-83; physician Doctors of World, Afghanistan, summer 1985; emergency care physician Paris, 1984-87; physician Medecins Sans Frontieres, Uganda, 1987; field med. coord. Medecins Sans Frontieres, Sri Lanka, winter 1988; physician Paris, 1988-89; field med. coord. Doctors without Borders, Malawi, 1989-90; program dir. River Blindness Found., Cameroon, 1992-95; country dir. River Blindness Found./Carter Ctr., Cameroon, 1995-96; dep. programs mgr., coord. Health Ocular Network in Africa, Paris, 1997—. Contbr. articles to profl. jours. Mem. Soc. Epidemiol. Rsch. Am. Public Health Assn., Delta Omega. Avocations: humanitarian activities, animal care, sports. Office: Org Prevent Cecite, 9 Rue Mathurin Regnier, 75015 Paris France

GODO, EINAR, computer engineer; b. Aalesund, Möre, Norway, May 31, 1926; came to U.S. 1953; s. Lars and Oline (Blindheim) G.; m. Betty Jane Graba, 1955; children: Kjell Einar, Greta Anne, Erik Lars. BS in Aero. Engring., U. Wash., 1956, BSEE, 1958, MS, 1964. Electronic designer Boeing Aerospace, Seattle, 1959-82; prime investigator Computer Devel., Bellevue, Wash., 1982-98, in computer hardware devel., 1998—. Achievements include patent for bating machine (Norway), Word Recognition System(USA, Can., Japan, Brit., France, Ger.); contributor engineering to most or all programs for putting man/hardware on the moon including lunar orbiter, lunar rover, Saturn 5 booster.

GODONE-MARESCA, LILLIAN, lawyer; b. Buenos Aires, June 9, 1958; came to the U.S., 1991; d. Armand C.E. Godone-Signanini and E. Nydia Soracco-Godone; m. Paul Alexander Maresca-Lowell (dec.); children: Catherine Victoria, Gerard Frank, Warren Paul. BA, Cath. U. Buenos Aires, 1975, MA, 1977, JD summa cum laude, 1979, advanced tchg. degree in jud. sci., 1981. Bar: Dist. Ct. Buenos Aires 1980, Calif. 1995, U.S. Dist. Ct. (ea. dist.) Calif. 1995, U.S. Dist. Ct. (so. dist.) Calif. 1998; lic. real estate broker, Calif. Advisor Sub-Sec. of State for Fgn. Trade, Buenos Aires, 1982; pvt. practice law Buenos Aires, 1982-86; therapist Ocean Pkwy. Developmental Ctr., N.Y., 1992; pvt. practice law Sacramento, 1995-96, San Diego, 1997—; asst. instr. Cath. U., Buenos Aires, 1983-86; adj. instr. U.S. Internat. U., San Diego, spring 1998. Contbr. articles to profl. jours.; author of poetry. Vol. San Diego Vol. Lawyer Program, 1993-94, Legal Svcs. No. Calif., Sacramento, 1995-96; catechist St. Ignatius, Sacramento, 1995-96, St. Michael's, Poway, Calif., 1997-98. Mem. Internat. Soc. Poets (disting.), State Bar Calif., Mothers Twins Club. Republican. Roman Catholic. Avocations: spending time with her children, the right to life, writing. Home: 11551 Avenida Sivrita San Diego CA 92128-4519

GODOSKY, ROBERT E., lawyer; b. N.Y.C., Jan. 1, 1963; s. Richard and Marcia Godosky; m. Laurie L. Pridgeon, Oct. 12, 1996; children: Jacob, Joshua. BA, Hamilton Coll., 1985; JD, Fordham U., 1988. Atty. Gair, Gair & Conason, N.Y.C., 1988-96, Godosky & Gentile, P.C., N.Y.C., 1996—. Mem. ABA, ATLA, N.Y. State Trial Lawyers (instr. 1997—), N.Y. County Lawyers Assn., N.Y. State Bar Assn. Democrat. Jewish. Avocations: golf, reading. Office: Godosky & Gentile PC 61 Broadway New York NY 10006-2701

GODOT, THIERRY, psychiatrist, consultant; b. Saint-Die, France, May 10, 1961; s. Michel and Monique (Laxenaire) G. BA, Lycee Jules-Ferry, Saint-Die, France, 1979; MD, U. Strasbourg, Besancon, France, 1992. Intern Hopitaux U. de Strasbourg, France, 1979-87; psychiatrist Gen. Hosp. Belfort, France, 1995—; cons. psychiatrist law cts., Belfort, 1997. Fellow APA. E-mail: thaa.godot@wanadoo.fr. Office: Hopital Pierre-Engel, F-90800 Bavilliers France

GODOY, ARNALDO JOSÉ, clinical neurologist, educator; b. São Carlos, Brazil, Feb. 28, 1963; s. Argemiro Apparecido and Maria José (Vidotti) G.; m. Lilian Yuri Suzuki, Sept. 3, 1988; children: Tiago Suzuki, Lucas Daniel Suzuki. MD, São Paulo (Brazil) U., 1987; PhD in Med. Scis., Kyushu U., Fukuoka, Japan, 1996. Resident in neurology São Paulo U., 1988-91; rsch. student Kyushu U., 1991-92, grad. student, 1992-96; univ. tchr. U. Ribeirão Preto, Brazil, 1996—. Recipient Kuroiwa-Goto prize, Kyushu U. Dept. Neurology, 1996. Mem. N.Y. Acad. Scis. Roman Catholic. Avocations: guitar, dancing, music, swimming. Home: Rua Garibaldi 411 Ap 44, 14010170 Ribeirão Prêto Brazil

GODOY, LUIS A., engineering researcher, educator; b. Cordoba, Argentina, May 8, 1950; s. Juan C. and Matilde F. (Rodriguez) G.; m. Nora Valeiras, Sept. 16, 1992; children: Gonzalo, Diego, Fernanda, Federico. BS in Engring., U. Cordoba, 1975; PhD, U. London, 1979. Prof. Nat. U. Cordoba, 1980—; rschr. Sci. Rsch. Coun., Argentina, 1981—; vis. prof. W.Va. U., Morgantown, 1992-93; prof. U. P.R., Mayaguez, 1994-96; prof. Nat. U. Cordoba, 1996-2000, dean engring. rsch., 1986-88. Author: Thin-Walled Structures with Imperfections, 1996, Theory of Elastic Stability, 2000; editor: Applied Mechanics in the Americas, 1995; editor Pan Am. conf. Applied Mechs., 1995—; contbr. over 70 articles to profl. jours. Named Outstanding Scientist, Govt. of Province of Cordoba, 1991, Outstanding Prof., Nat. U. Cordoba, 1992, 94, Outstanding Prof. U. P.R., 1996, Outstanding Rschr. U. P.R., 1997, 99. Mem. ASCE, N.Y. Acad. Scis., Am. Acad. Mechanics, Am. Soc. Engring. Edn., Sigma Xi. Avocation: collecting masks. Home: Av Richieri 2378, 5000 Cordoba Argentina

GODSOE, PETER COWPERTHWAITE, banker; b. Toronto, May 2, 1938; s. J. Gerald and Margaret (Cowperthwaite) G.; m. Shelagh Cathleen Reburn, Nov. 30, 1963; children: Craig, Cynthia, Eden. BSc, U. Toronto, 1961; MBA, Harvard U., 1966. Chartered acct., Can. Gen. mgr. The Bank of N.S., Toronto, 1971-78, sr. v.p., 1979-80, exec. v.p., 1980-82, vice chmn., dir., 1982-92, pres., COO, vice-chmn., 1982-92, dep. chmn., pres., CEO, 1993-95, chmn. bd., CEO, 1995—, also bd. dirs.; chmn., bd. dirs. The Bank of N.S. Internat. Ltd., 1995—; bd. dirs. BNS Internat. (Hong Kong) Ltd.; chmn. The Bank of N.S. Internat. Ltd., Scotiabank (Ireland) Ltd.; bd. dirs. Empire Co. Ltd., BNS Internat. (Panama) S.A., Bank N.S. Jamaica Ltd., Bank N.S. Trinidad and Tobago Ltd., Bank N.S. Trust Co., Bank N.S. Trust Co. (Bahamas) Ltd., Bank N.S. Trust Co. (Cayman) Ltd., N.S. Corp., Scotiabank Jamaica Trust and Mcht. Bank Ltd., West India Co. Mcht. Bankers Ltd., Bank of N.S. Trust Co. Trinidad and Tobago Ltd., Aon Reed Stenhouse; trustee Scotiabank Pension Plan, Scotia Mortgage Corp.; chancellor U. of Western Ont. Bd. dirs. Can. Coun. of Christians and Jews, Toronto, 1972—, Mt. Sinai Hosp., 1986; past pres. Bd. of Trade, Toronto, 1984-85; mem. adv. com. Western Bus. Sch., Richard Ivey Sch. Bus.; assoc. mem. bd. govs. Dalhousie U.; mem. chancellor's coun. Victoria U.; mem. Mayor's Econ. Partnership Coun.; mem. adv. bd. Ctr. Rsch. Neurodegenerative Diseases; dir. (hon.) Sheena's Pl. Mem. Can. Bankers Assn. (past chmn.), Jr. Achievement of Met. Toronto and York Region (bd. govs.), Can. Club (past pres. 1982-83). Office: Bank of Nova Scotia, Scotia Plz/44 King St W, Toronto, ON Canada M5H 1H1

GODT, PAUL JAY, political science educator; b. Rockville Centre, N.Y., Oct. 21, 1943; arrived in France, 1970; s. Albert and Rita (Weidenfeld) G.; m. Sonia Solange Baldoni, Aug. 6, 1965; children: Sandrine, Nicolas Robin. BA, Bowdoin Coll., 1965; MA, New Sch. for Social Research, 1967, PhD, 1972. Prof. U. Grenoble (France), 1970-74; prof. polit. sci. Am. U. of Paris, 1972—, dean acad. affairs, 1995-98. Co-author and editor: Policy-Making in France: from de Gaulle to Mitterrand, 1989; co-editor International Political Science Abstracts; contbr. articles to profl. jours. Recipient Disting. Tchr. award Am. U. of Paris, 1985; Fulbright scholar, Grenoble, 1970-71. Mem. Internat. Polit. Sci. Assn., Am. Polit. Sci. Assn., Assn. Française Sci. Politique. Avocations: guitar, computer, photography. Home: 32 rue d Yerres, 91800 Brunoy France Office: Am U, 31 Ave Bosquet, 6 rue du Col Combes, 75007 Paris France

GODUKHIN, OLEG VIKTOROVITCH, neuroscientist, researcher; b. Gorky, Russia, Sept. 10, 1947; s. Viktor Makarovitch Godukhin and Tamara Ivanovna Arkhiereeva; m. Valentina Fedorovna Victorova, May 8, 1970; 1 child, Marina Olegovna. Degree in biophysics, Gorky State U., 1970; PhD in Biol. Scis., Russian Acad. Scis., Pushchino, 1977, D of Biol. Scis., 1990. Rsch. scientist Ints. Biophysics-Russian Acad. Scis., Pushchino, 1970-86, sr. rsch. scientist, 1986-91; head rsch. group Inst. Theoretical and Exptl. Biophysics-Russian Acad. Scis., Pushchino, 1991—; prof. Pushchino State U., 1993—. Rsch. grantee, 1994, 96. Mem. Russian Physiol. Soc. Avocations: art, music, historical literature. Home: Microregion AB, 142292 Pushchino Moscow, Russia Office: Inst Theor & Exptl Biophys, Russian Acad Scis, Pushchino Moscow 142292, Russia

GODWIN, DENISE ANN, languages educator; b. Johannesburg, South Africa, May 3, 1941; d. Herbert William and Norah Kathleen (Siddle) Chalmers; m. John Robert Godwin; children: Stuart William, Andrew John, Janis Elizabeth. BA, U. Witwatersrand, 1961, U. South Africa, 1965; MA, Rand Afrikaans U., 1981; Doctorate, U. Provence, 1985. Tchr. various h.s., South Africa, 1964-79; from jr. lectr. to chair, full prof. Rand Afrikaans U., South Africa, 1980—. Mem. South African Folklore Soc., Assn. French Studies in So. Africa, Soc. Study Topos in French Prose Fiction Before 1800. Avocations: reading, embroidery, dollhouses and miniature making. Home: PO Box 566, Pinegowrie 2123, South Africa

GOEDINGS, EDUARD CLEMENS MARIA, sales professional; b. Amsterdam, The Netherlands, Sept. 22, 1938; s. Jan Albertus and Wilhelmina (van Dijk) G.; m. Martha Johanna Maria Molenaar, Mar. 18, 1961; children: Wilhelmina, Maria, Martha, Linda. Grad., Tomas Bata Tech. Sch., The Netherlands, 1958. Owner area shoe store, Scheveningen, The Hague, The Netherlands, 1961-63; rep. Clark, Amsterdam, 1963-69; owner, mediator Active Footwear and Ed Goedings, De Meern, The Netherlands, 1969-96. Designer leather shoes, sport-inspired city shoes and leather sport sandals. Vol. Red. Cross, Utrecht, The Netherlands, 1996—. 1st lt. mil. intelligence, The Netherlands, 1958-61. Mem. Two/Ten Nat. Found. (Boston, life). Liberty Democratic. Roman Catholic. Avocations: sailing, skiing, dancing, singing. Home: Meentweg N 81, 3454 AR De Meern Utrecht, The Netherlands

GOEDSCHALK, HENK OTMAR, banker, educator; b. Paramaribo, Suriname, Dec. 16, 1946; s. Hein Eduard Johan and Emmy Charlotte (Balinge) G.; children: Graciella, Ilana, Carlos, Janine, Yasser; m. Jenny Jamila Karamat-Ali. D in Econs., U. Groningen, The Netherlands. Economist Bur. for Regional Devel., Paramaribo, 1975-80, coordinator, 1980-81; dep. dir. Nat. Planning Office, Paramaribo, 1981-82, dir., 1982-83; advisor Minister of Trade and Industry, Paramaribo, 1983-84; pres. Fgn. Exchange Bd., Paramaribo, 1984-85; gov. Ctrl. Bank van Suriname, Paramaribo, 1985—, pres., 1985-94, 97—; bd. dirs. S.L.O.C.; extraordinary lectr. U. Suriname. Founder Found. for Suriname and Antillian, 1970. Named Commander Order of Palm, Republic Suriname, 1987. Mem. Com. Caribbean Economists. Democrat. Mem. Moravian Ch. Avocations: tennis, music. Home: Einsteinstraat 20, Paramaribo Suriname Office: Ctrl Bank van Suriname, 16-24 Waterkant 20 PO Box 1801, Paramaribo Suriname

GOEKJIAN, CHRISTOPHER ALLAN, investment banking executive; b. Nov. 17, 1961; s. Samuel Vahram and Jean Alison (MacLeod) G.; m. Rosalind Kim Dunn, July 20, 1991. BA summa cum laude, Hamilton Coll., 1982; MA, U. Mich., 1983. Assoc. derivatives Bankers Trust, N.Y.C., 1983-84; v.p. derivatives Bankers Trust, Tokyo, 1984-88; mng. dir. head equity derivatives Bankers Trust, London, 1988-90; mng. dir., head derivatives trading Credit Suisse Fin. Products, London, 1990-92; mng. dir., co-head global derivatives, head European fixed income CS Fin. Products, London, 1992-95; pres., CEO Credit Suisse Fin. Products, 1995-98; mem. exec. bd., Credit Suisse First Boston, 1997-2000, head fixed income and derivatives divsn., 1999-2000.

GOEL, ATUL, neurosurgeon, educator, consultant; b. Chandigarh, India, June 24, 1959; s. Harigopal and Swaraj Goel; m. Naina Kataria, Dec. 29, 1990; 1 child, Aimee. MB, BChir, Nagpur (India) U., 1982; CM in Neurosurgery, Bombay U., 1987. Med. diplomate. Lectr. neurosurgery King Edward Meml. Hosp., Bombay, 1986-95, assoc. prof., 1995-98, prof., chmn., 1998—; cons. neurosurgeon King Edward Meml. Hosp., Bombay, 1987—, Seth Gordhandas Sunderdas Med. Coll., Bombay, 1987—; hon. cons. prof. Shinshu U., Matsumoto, Japan, 1993; chief cons. neurosurgeon TATA Meml. Hosp. and Cancer Rsch. Inst. Author, editor: Neurosurgery of Complex Tumor and Vascular Lesions, 1997; contbr. chpts. to books and articles to profl. jours. Recipient Shakuntala Devi Amirchand award Govt. of India, New Delhi, 1995, Amrut Mody Unichem Prize Govt. of India,

1996. Mem. Neurol. Soc. India (life), Indian Soc. Neuroequilibrium (life), Asia-Oceanian Skull Base Soc. (coun. mem.). Home: Dept Neurosurgery, King Edward Meml Hosp, Parel Mumbai 400012, India

GOEL, RAJNISH KUMAR, geologist, mining engineer, consultant; b. Bulandshahr, India, June 15, 1960; s. Raghubir Singh and Prabha (Rani) G.; m. Meenu Rani, Mar. 7, 1988; 11 children. BSc, Lucknow (India) U., 1978; M of Tech., U. Roorkee (India), 1982; PhD, Nagpur (India) U., 1995. Sr. rsch. fellow Ctrl. Mining Rsch. Inst., Dhanbad, India, 1982-83, scientist B, 1983-88, scientist C, 1988-91, scientist EI, 1991-96, scientist EII, 1996—; vis. cons. U.S., Korea, Sweden, Singapore and Malaysia; examiner U. Roorkee, India. Co-author: Rock Mass Classification: A Practical Approach in Civil Engineering, 1999; editor: Jour. Rock Mechanics and Tunnelling Tech.; patantee in field. Recipient Srimatl Indira Joshi award Indian Geotech. Soc., 1986, Best Scientist award, CMRI Whitaker, 1996, 2nd best tech. paper award, 1998, 2d Khosla Ann. Rsch. prize U. Roorke, 1998, 1st Khosla Ann. Rsch. prize U. Roorkee, 1999. Mem. Bur. Indian Standards. Avocations: table tennis, cricket, organizing meetings. Home: 84/1 Nehru Nagar, Roorkee 247 667, India Office: Ctrl Mining Rsch Inst, Regional Ctr CBRI Campus, Roorkee 247 667, India

GOENKA, HARSH VARDHAN, diversified company executive; b. Calcutta, India, Dec. 10, 1957. Student, St. Xavier's Coll., Calcutta, Internat. Inst. Mgmt. Devel., Switzerland, 1980. Chmn., CEO RPG Enterprises Ltd., Bombay, 1986—; chmn. RPG Life Scis., Ltd., KEC Internat., RPG Cables Ltd., Fujitsu ICIM Ltd. Fax: 81-22-493-8933. Office: CEAT Mahal, 463 Dr Annie Besant Rd, Worli Mumbai India

GOEPEL, LUTZ, member of the European parliament; b. Gotha, Germany, Oct. 10, 1942. Mem. European Parliament, Germany, 1999—; mem. Group of the European People's Party (Christian Democrats) and European Democrats; mem. com. on agr. and rural devel., com. on budgets; substitute delegation to the EU-Slovenia Joint Parliamentary Com. Office: Gartenstraβe 12, D-04720 Mochau Germany*

GOERTTLER, KLAUS JUERGEN, pathologist, researcher; b. Munich, Bavaria, Germany, Mar. 24, 1925. Dir. exptl. pathology German Cancer Rsch. Ctr, Heidelberg, Germany, 1967-85; dir. exptl. pathology Inst. Pathology U. Heidelberg, 1967-93, prof. emeritus, 1993—. Office: U Heidelberg Dept Pathology, Im Neuenheimer Feld 220, D 69120 Heidelberg Baden-W., Germany

GOERTZ, ROGER LAMAR, retired education counselor; b. Freer, Tex., Apr. 24, 1938; s. Albert F. and Dorothy N. Goertz; m. Jean L. Humphrey, Mar. 29, 1980. BA, S.W. Tex. State U., 1964; MEd, Suh Ross State U., 1974. Cert. vocat. and spl. edn. counselor. Tchr., coach Knippa (Tex.) Schs., 1964-65, Sanderson (Tex.) Schs., 1965-69; tchr., coach Big Spring (Tex.) Schs., 1969-76, vocat. counselor, 1981-94, career svcs. coord., 1994-98; plan a counselor Plainview (Tex.) Schs., 1976-78; vocat. counselor Svc. Ctr. XV, San Angelo, Tex., 1978-81; ret., 1998. Mem. goals com. Future Goals City of Big Spring, 1995. Lutheran. Avocations: plays, jazz concerts, athletic events. Home: 4018 Vicky St Big Spring TX 79720-7020

GOES, KATHLEEN ANN, secondary education educator, choral director; b. New Bedford, Mass., Jan. 13, 1951; d. Filento Andrade and Lillian (Cabral) G. BA in Psychology, U. Mass., North Dartmouth, 1976; postgrad., Ctrl. Conn. State U., 1987-98. Cert. K-8 elem. tchr., K-12 music tchr., Mass. Social worker Dept. Social Svcs., Cambridge, Mass., 1980-85; pvt. tchr. voice and piano, New Bedford, 1985-88; tchr. vocal music New Bedford Pub. Sch., 1985-90; tchr. music, choral dir. Fairhaven (Mass.) H.S., 1991—; singer, actress, southeastern New Eng., 1974—; dir. music ministry St. Mary's Ch., South Dartmouth, Mass., 1988—; bd. dirs. , sec. New Bedford Festival Theatre, 1990-97, v.p., 1997-99, mem. adv. bd., 1999—. Dir. musicals Bye, Bye Birdie, You're a Good Man Charlie Brown, How to Succeed in Business Without Really Trying, Little Shop of Horrors, The Boyfriend, Godspell, Jesus Christ Superstar; performed the mother in Amahl and the Night Visitors; actress, singer in musicals Fiddler on the Roof, Godspell, Phantom. Bd. dirs. New Bedford Symphony Orch., 1994-96. Named Promising Young Artist, Crescendo Club, Boston, 1981; recipient outstanding leadership award Fairhaven Assn. for Music Edn., 1995. Mem. NEA, Am. Choral Dirs. Assn., Nat. Pastoral Musicians Assn., New Eng. Theatre Conf., Drama League, Music Educators Nat. Conf., Mass. Tchrs. Assn., Mass. Music Educators Assn., Whale Hist. League. Roman Catholic. Avocations: cooking, crafts, computers, boating, scenic design. Home: 61 Rockdale Ave New Bedford MA 02740-1075 Office: Fairhaven HS 12 Huttleston Ave Fairhaven MA 02719-3122

GOETSCHEL, WILLI, foreign literature educator; b. Zürich, Switzerland, Mar. 13, 1958; came to U.S., 1983; s. Robert and Charlotte (Hayum) G.; m. Samira Afrasiabi. MPhil, U. Zürich, 1982; PhD, Harvard U., 1989. Instr. Harvard U., Cambridge, Mass., 1988-89; vis. asst. prof. Bard Coll., N.Y., 1989-91; asst. prof. Columbia U., N.Y.C., 1991-97, assoc. prof. German, 1997-2000; exec. editor German Rev., 2000—. Author: Constituting Critique: Kant's Writing as Critical Praxis, 1994; editor: Wege des Widerspruchs, 1984, Werkausgabe Hermann Levin Goldschmidt, 9 vols., 1993 , Perspektiven der Dialogik, 1994; contbr. numerous articles to profl. jours.; book rev. editor Germanic Rev., 1996 . Pres. Dialogik Found., Zürich, 1998 . Humboldt Found. fellow, 1996-97, Andrew W. Mellon fellow, 2000 . Office: Stanford U Dept German Studies Bldg 260 Pigott Hall Stanford CA 94305-2030

GOETZ, THOMAS HALL, English educator; b. Milw., Mar. 21, 1961; s. George and Judith (Johnson) G.; m. Hideko Kamemaru, June 10, 1989; children: Asher, Heidi. BA, Lewis & Clark Coll., 1984; MDiv, Princeton (N.J.) Theol. Sem., 1989; MEd, Temple U., 1995. Asst. pastor Internat. Christian U., Tokyo, 1989-91; asst. prof. Kwansei Gakuin U., Nishinomiya, Japan, 1992-96, Hokusei Gakuen U., Sapporo, Japan, 1996—. Vol. Habitat for Humanity, Japan, 1992—. Presbyn. E-mail: thgoetz@hotmail.com. Office: Hokusei Gakuen U, Oyachinishi 2-3-1 Atsubetsu, Sapporo 004-8631, Japan

GOFF, CHRISTOPHER WALLICK, pediatrician; b. Phila., Jan. 24, 1948; s. Donald Heiserman and Jean Christman Wallick G.; m. Holly Lynn Housner, Aug. 1970; children: Heather Elizabeth, Rebecca Ann, Abigail Christine. BA in Psychology, Yale U., 1970; MD, U. Pa., 1974. Diplomate Am. Bd. Pediatrics, Pediatric Endocrinology, Nat. Bd. Med. Examiners. Intern, then resident in pediatrics Yale-New Haven (Conn.) Hosp., 1974-76, chief resident in pediatrics, 1977; pvt. practice specializing in pediatrics Wildwood Pediatrics, Essex, Conn., 1977—; alternate dir. Health Town of Essex, 1980-81, dir. Health, 1981—; co-dir. Child Diagnostic Assocs., Essex, 1983—; assoc. staff Yale-New Haven Hosp., 1977-80, attending staff, 1980—; clin. instr. Pediatrics Yale U. Sch. Med., 1977-79, clin. asst. prof., 1979-97, clin. assoc. prof., 1997—; bd. dirs. Wildwood Med. Ctr. Assn., 1986-89, treas. 1988—; co-med. adviser Mt. St. John Sch., Deep River, Conn., 1977—, Oxford Acad., Westbrook, Conn., 1990-95; acting med. adviser Essex Elem. Sch., 1981—; med. adviser Old Saybrook Sch. sys., 1992-97. Reviewer Clinical Pediatrics; clin. reactor Contemporary Pediatrics; contbr. articles to prof. jours. Chmn. prof. adv. com. Visiting Nurses Lower Valley, 1980—, med. dir., 1996—; devel. bd. Tri-Town Youth Svc. Bur., 1987-88; mem. Sexual Abuse Prevention Task Force, 1987-95, Tri-Town Substance Abuse Task Force, 1988-95, Westbrook Sexual Abuse Prevention Task Force, 1988-93, Shoreline Child Protection Team, 1988-93, Tri-Town Sexual Abuse Response Team, 1990-91; vestryman St. John's Episcopal Ch., Essex., 1978-79, sr. warden, 1979-83, coord. Youth Ministry program, 1986-90, treas. 1994-96; lector 1989-96; pres. Marlins Parents Club, 1989-91; bd. dirs. Lower Valley Cmty. Health Svcs., 1979-80, Essex Ambulance Assn., 1985-89, Cougar Aquatic Team, 1992-96, v.p. 1992-93, treas. 1993-94. Recipient Joel Gordon Miller award, 1974. Fellow Am. Acad. Pediatrics; mem. AMA, N. Am. Soc. Pediatric and Adolescent Gynecology, New England Soc. Clin. Hypnosis, Conn. State Med. Soc. (malpractice claims rev. bd., 1981-84), New Haven County Med. Soc., Lawson Wilkins Pediatric Endocrine Soc. Republican. Avocations: sailing, skiing, ballroom dancing, stamp collecting, golf. Office: Wildwood Pediatrics and Adol Med 1 Wildwood Medical Ctr Essex CT 06426-1190

GOFF, JAMES FRANKLIN, physicist, consultant; b. Louisville, Aug. 1, 1928; s. James Robert and Mary Louise (Kubaugh) G.; m. Barbara Louise Kral, June 20, 1959; children: Sidra Denise, Alexander Kral. BS in Physics, MIT, 1950; PhD in Physics, Purdue U., 1962. Rsch. physicist Naval Ordnance Lab., Silver Spring, Md., 1961-80; dir. materials applications office Naval Surface Weapons Ctr., Silver Spring, Md., 1980-90. Contbr. articles to profl. jours. With U.S. Army, 1953-55. Fellow Washington Acad. Scis. (pres. 1982); mem. Philos. Soc. Washington (pres. 1980), Cosmos Club (program chmn. 1986-90). Achievements include reformulation of thermoelectric figure-of-merit so that it could be computed from realistic band structure and scattering; research on electron-phonon interactions in GE at low temperatures, contributions of real density states to anomalous electronic transport properties of transition metals and alloys. Home: 3405 34th Pl NW Washington DC 20016-3135

GOFF, KIMBERLY, art dealer, writer; b. Phila., Apr. 6, 1955; d. Warren Goff and Elaine Benson; m. Kenneth Knollenberg, Apr. 6, 1985 (dec. July 1997). Owner Kimberly's E., Bridgehampton, N.Y., 1974-86; artist Baja Califonia, Mex., 1986-92; apprentice Elaine Benson Gallery, Bridgehampton, 1993-95, co-dir., 1996-98, owner, dir., 1999—; mem. adv. bd. Nature Art, N.Y.C., 1997—, Internat. Toy Bank, L.A., 2000. Columnist Dan's Papers, 1999-2000. Bd. dirs. CMEE Children's Mus. Art E. End, Bridgehampton, 1999—, John Steinbeck Com., Southampton, N.Y., 1999-2000, Southampton Cultural Ctr., 1999-2000, Robert Wilsons' Watermill Ctr. Cmty., 1999-2000, Fish Unlimited, Shelter Island, N.Y., 2000. Avocations: kayaking, fishing. Office: Elaine Benson Gallery 2317 Montawk Hwy Bridgehampton NY 11932-3034

GOFF, WILLIAM M., JR., art director, graphic designer; b. Tampa, Fla., June 21, 1959; s. Willam M. and Flora G. Goff. Degree in gen. aviation, Ala. Aviation Tech. Coll., 1983; BA, Spring Hill Coll., 1990; cert. in advanced graphic design, Chyron Corp., Melville, N.Y., 1993; cert. in animation design, Alias/Wavefront Animation, Santa Barbara, Calif., 1995. Cert. in advanced graphic design Chyron Corp. Disk jockey, mem. prodn. staff Sta. WABB-FM Radio, Mobile, Ala., 1975-78; photographer Palmer Photography, Mobile, Ala., 1978-79; mem. gen. maintenance staff Mobile Air Ctr., 1980-83; courier, mem. office svcs. staff Delchamps, Inc., Mobile, 1983-87; art dir., animator Sta. WKRG-TV 5, Inc., Mobile, 1988-98, dir. art internships, 1995-98; digital graphic cons., tech. dir., freelance animator/artist, 1998—. Art dir. (TV spl.) Someone You Know-AIDS, 1992 (AP award 1993); graphic design (documentary) Indian Blood, 1993 (award 1994). Troop leader Boy Scouts Am., Eagle Scouts, Mobile, 1977-79; past pres. Explorers Am., Mobile, 1977-78; prodr. dir. Jr. Achievement, Mobile, 1975-78. Recipient Excellence in Broadcasting award CBS, 1993, Best Sports Event award AP/Ala., 1995, 96, Best Scheduled Live Event award, 1995. Avocations: music, art, outdoor activities, writing, movies. Office: Global Village PO Box 91594 Mobile AL 36691-1594

GOGA, MARIAN PETER, economist, educator; b. Topolcany, Westslovakia, Czechoslovakia, Dec. 8, 1950; s. Gejza and Rozalia (Gero) G.; m. Anna Valkovic, Oct. 29, 1977; children: Monika, Lenka. Diploma in engring., Vysoka Sch. Econs., Bratislava, Czechoslovakia, 1976, postgrad., 1983. Asst. Vysoka Sch. Econs., 1976-79, spl. asst. optimal programming, 1979-89, lectr., 1989—, vice dean, 1995-99, vice dir., 2000—. Recipient Czechoslovakian Acad. Sci. Honor award, 1984, Slovak Acad. Sci. Honor award, 1986, 89. Mem. Czechoslovakian Sci. and Tech. Soc. Avocations: jogging, collecting stamps. Office: Univ Econs, Dolnozemska 1, 85235 Bratislava Slovakia

GÖGEN, SEDAT, physician, consultant; b. Izmir, Turkey, Oct. 8, 1969; s. Ali Riza and Feride (Golakoglu) G.; m. Füsun Isin, July 29, 1995. MD, Dokuz Eylûl U., Izmir, 1992. Rschr. Dokuz Eylûl U., Izmir, 1992-97; cons. Torbali Statement Hosp., Izmir, 1997-99. Contbr. articles to profl. jours. Lt. Turkish Med. Corps, 1999-2000. Mem. Turkish Soc. Orthopedic Surgery and Traumatology. Moslem. Avocations: football, bridge, reading, book, music. Home: 186/1 Sok. No. 1/13, 35040 Izmir Turkey

GOGGIN, MARGARET ENID (KNOX), librarian, educator; b. Nyack, N.Y., Feb. 24, 1919; d. Henry Julian and Eleanor (Green) Knox; m. John Mann Goggin, Nov. 22, 1962. A.B., Maryville Coll., 1940; B.S., Peabody Coll., 1942; M.S., U. Ill., 1948, Ph.D., 1957. Tchr., librarian Flintville (Tenn.) High Sch., 1940-42; reference asst. Joint U. Library, Nashville, 1942-43; acting reference librarian Joint U. Library, 1943-45; vis. instr. Peabody Library Sch., Nashville, 1943-45; readers adviser Youngstown (Ohio) Pub. Library, 1945-46; bibliographer, reference librarian Office Tech. Services Dept. Commerce, Washington, 1946-47; reference asst. U. Ill., 1948-49; asst. to dir. U. Fla. Libraries, asst. prof. library sci., 1949-50, head dept. reference and bibliography, asso. prof. library sci., 1950-62; asst. dir. U. Fla. Libraries (Readers Services), asso. prof. library sci., 1965-66, asst. dir. libraries, prof. library sci., 1966, acting dir. libraries, 1967-68; dean Grad. Sch. Librarianship, U. Denver, 1968-79, prof., 1979-84, prof. emeritus, 1984—; vis. lectr. U. Okla. Libr. Sch., summer 1959, Emory U. Sch. Librarianship, 1965; dir. Satellite Libr. Info. Network, 1974-76; prin. investigator Telefax Libr. Info. Network, 1978-79; cons. U.S. Office Edn. divsn. Libr. Programs, 1968-69, 87, Aims C.C., Greeley, Colo., 1973, Wash. State Libr., 1978-79, Loretto Heights Coll., Denver, 1981; co-owner Book Seminars, Inc., 1986-95; interim dir. Collection Mgmt., Emory U., 1986-88; owner Margaret K. Goggin Books, 1994—. Recipient Colo. Libr. of Yr. award, 1979, Outstanding Svc. award U. Denver, 1985, Alumni citation Maryville Coll., 1987, Disting. Alumnus award Peabody Coll., 1987; Rockefeller Found. grantee, Haiti and Paris, 1958, 61-62, Fulbright grantee, 1972, OAS grantee for multi-nat. libr. edn. program, 1974-75. Mem. ALA (past div. pres.), Colo. Libr. Assn. (dir. 1978-79), Mountain Plains Libr. Assn. (dir. 1978-79), Assn. For Library and Info. Sci. Edn. (pres. 1977), Nat. League Am. Pen Women, Fla. Ctr. for the Book (mem. exec. bd. 1988—), Delta Kappa Gamma, Beta Phi Mu (past dir.), PEO. Club: Altrusa (bd. dirs. Denver 1974-76, 80-82, pres. 1983-84). Home: 4024 NW 15th St Gainesville FL 32605-1912

GOGGINS, JEAN, biomedical engineer, foundation administrator. BS in Biology, Molloy Coll., 1969; MS in Biology, Fordham U., 1973; PhD in Biomed. Engring., Case Western Res. U., 1985. Tchr. N.Y. schs., 1969-71; rsch. technician GTE Labs., Inc., Bayside, N.Y., 1971; supr. ultrastructure lab. Fordham U., Bronx, N.Y., 1971-72; electron microscopist Yale U. Sch. Medicine, New Haven, 1972-74; rsch. asst. Mt. Sinai Sch. Medicine, N.Y.C., 1979-80; grad. fellow dept. biomed. engring. Case Western Res. U., Cleve., 1980-85; sr. rsch. scientist Meadox Meds., Inc., Oakland, N.J., 1985-86, mgr. R&D, 1986-90, mgr. med./tech. rels., 1990-93, dir. med./tech. rels., 1993-95; med. dir. Meadox, Boston Sci. Corp., Oakland, 1995-97; dir. stent devel. and clin. affairs Medtronic Interventional Vascular, San Diego, 1997-98, dir. coronary stent devel., 1998-99; exec. dir. tech. evaluation William J. von Liebig Found & Drax Group, 1999—; ind. cons. in med. devices, cardiovascular implants, vascular implants, endovascular devices, stents, implant materials, mechanical, chem. and physiol. interactions of implants; presenter, panelist in field; convenor internat. stds. working group, mem. editl. bd. Jour. Biomed. Materials Rsch., 1996—. Contbr. articles to profl. jours. N.Y. State Regents scholar, 1965; NSF grantee, 1978; Timken Honors fellow, 1980-84, Cross-Jones Med. Rsch. Found. fellow, 1984-85. Fellow Am. Inst. Med. and Biol. Engring.; mem. Am. Heart Assn., Internat. Soc. Applied Cardiovascular Biology, Internat. Soc. Endovascular Surgery, N.Y. Acad. Scis., Soc. Biomaterials, Sigma Xi.

GOGINENI, BABU RAJAJI RAMANADHA, association executive; b. Hyderabad, India, Apr. 14, 1968; arrived in U.K., 1997; s. Gurubabu and Aruna Kumari (Vegunta) G.; m. Sahana Kanjula, July 4, 1999. Diplôme de langue, Alliance Française de Paris, 1986; BSc, Nizam Coll., Hyderabad, 1988; postgrad. diploma in Internat. Trade, Bhavans Inst., Hyderabad, 1990. Tchr. French lang. Alliance Francaise, Hyderabad, 1986-89, coord. cultural activities, 1989-92, coor. Sci. Resource Ctr., 1993-96; exec. dir. Internat. Humanist and Ethical Union, London, 1997—; mem. internat. adv. coun. Oslo Coalition on Freedom of Religion or Belief, 1994—; trustee Indian Renaissance Inst., Delhi, 1992—; freelance translator lit. and tech. texts. Coeditor: Rationalist Essays, 1992, Humanist Essays, 1996; translator: Maupassant's Stories, 1999; mem. editl. bd. Revista Peruana Philosofila Applicada, Peru, 1997—. Joint sec. Indian Radical Humanist Assn., Bombay, 1988-96; v.p. Indian Rationalist Assn., Hyderabad, 1993-96; sec. gen. Rationalist Assn. India, Hyderabad, 1996-99, South Asian Humanist Network, Bombay, 1999. Avocations: debates, cinema, travel, reading, language. Office: Internat Humanist & Ethical, Union, 47 Theobalds Rd, London WC1X 8SP, England

GOGLIA, CHARLES A., JR., lawyer; b. Phila., Aug. 26, 1931; s. Charles and Marie A. (Beckman) G.; m. Patricia A. Morrissey, July 26, 1958; children: Philip L., Catherine A. BS, St. Joseph's U., Phila., 1953; LLB, Boston Coll., 1958. Bar: Mass. 1958, U.S. Dist. Ct. Mass. 1959, U.S. Ct. Appeals (1st cir.) 1964, U.S. Tax Ct. 1977, U.S. Supreme Ct. 1993. Atty. Sheff & Gens, Boston, 1958-61, Foley, Hoag & Eliot, Boston, 1961-68; ptnr. Foley, Hoag & Eliot, 1968-74; pvt. practice Wellesley, Mass., 1974—; corporator, trustee, mem. bd. investment, exec. com. Bank Five for Savings, Burlington, Mass., 1974-92; mem. hearing com. Bd. Bar Overseers, Boston, 1984-86. Counsel Town of Nantucket, Mass., 1970-82, spl. counsel, 1982-85, Town of Weston, Mass., 1974-85, town counsel, 1986-92, spl. counsel, 1992—, mem. zoning bd. appeals, 1964-66, 74-85, mem. planning bd., 1973-74; spl. counsel Mass. Cable TV Commn., Boston, 1973-74. With USNAR, 1951-59. Mem. Wellesley Country Club (past pres.). Avocations: golf, travel. Home: 1 Hopewell Farm Rd Natick MA 01760-5570 Office: Wellesley Office Pk 65 William St Wellesley MA 02481-3802

GOGNALONS, MARYVONNE NICOLET, scientist, educator; b. Algiers, Algeria, May 30, 1942; d. Paul and Yvonne (Francois) G.; m. Frederic Caillard (div. 1979); m. Albert Nicolet; children: Nicolet, Marion. MA, SUNY, 1970; PhD in Human Scis., Sorbon U., Paris, 1988. Researcher SUNY, 1968-71; researcher, tchr. Paris, 1971-80; researcher H.U.G., Geneva, 1980—; vis. prof. Lyon, France, 1995—; cons. for internat. orgns.; organizer internat. confs. Author: Genre et Sante Apres 40 Ans, 1998, Entre Sante et Maladie, 1993; La Maturescence, 1989; (with E.C. markson) Older Women, 1980. Ageing and Health Sci. Network, Paris, 1993; women rights, , Geneva, 1990—. Fullbright scholar, N.Y., 1968-70. Mem. Commn. on Women Rights. Avocation: painting. Home: 12 rue G Vallette, 1206 Geneva Switzerland

GOGOLASHVILI, EDWARD LAURENTYEVICH, chemist, researcher; b. Aznakaevo, Tatarstan, USSR, Feb. 17, 1951; s. Laurenty Arkhipovich and Lyubov Grigorievna (Susloparova) G.; m. Fahima Kiyamovna Mukhitova, Sept. 17, 1977; children: Bulat, Timur. Chemist, Kazan State U., USSR, 1973, PhD, 1984. Rsch. fellow Kazan State U., 1973-76, lectr., 1976-90; sr. rsch. scientist Tatar Oil Rsch. Inst., Kazan, 1990-94; head chem. lab. Kazan 1st Heating and Power Station, 1994-99; chief rsch. dept. Energoprogress Chem. Svc., Kazan, 1999—. Contbr. articles to profl. jours.; patentee in field. E-mail: Kitaevaly@eprog.tatenergo.ru. Home: PO Box 130, 420054 Kazan Tatarstan, Russia Office: Energoprogress Chem Svc, Bondarenko St 3, 420044 Kazan Tatarstan, Russia

GOGOTSI, YURY, materials science educator; b. Kiev, Ukraine, Dec. 16, 1961; s. George A. and Svetiana (Potarykina) G.; m. Larissa Ganzha, Mar. 18, 1989; children: Pavel, Nathalie. MS, Kiev Poly., 1984, PhD, 1986; DSc, Ukrainian Acad. Sci., Kiev, 1996. Rsch. assoc. Ukrainian Acad. Sci., 1986-90; Alexander von Humboldt fellow U. Karlsruhe, Germany, 1990-92; JSPS fellow Tokyo Inst. Tech., 1992-93; NATO rsch. fellow U. Oslo, 1993-95; rsch. assoc. U. Tÿbingen, Germany, 1995-96; asst. prof. U. Ill., Chgo., 1996-99, assoc. prof., asst. dir. Rsch. Resources Ctr., 1999-2000; prof. materials sci. Drexel U., Phila., 2000—. Author: Corrosion of Structural Ceramics, 1989, Corrosion of High-Performance Ceramics, 1992 (I.N. Frantsevich prize 1993); editor: Materials Science of Carbides, Nitrides and Borides, 1999; issue editor Jour. Materials Mfg. and Processing Sci., 1998. Lt. engr. USSR Army, 1984. Grantee NSF, 1999. Mem. Am. Ceramic Soc., Materials Rsch. Soc. (best poster award 1999), Electrochem. Soc., Inst. Materials (U.K.). Christian Orthodox. Avocations: travel, reading. Fax: 312-413-0447. E-mail: ygogotsi@uic.edu. Office: Drexel U Chestnut St Philadelphia PA 19104

GOGUS, FAHRETTIN, food engineer, educator; b. Gaziantep, Turkey, Mar. 5, 1964; s. Ozcan and Akgun (Kutlar) G.; m. Isil Tataroglu, Aug. 11, 1995; 1 child, Sinan. BSc, Middle East Tech. U., Ankara, Turkey, 1987, MSc, 1989; PhD, Leeds (Eng.) U., 1995. Refining unit engr. Akyag A.S., Gaziantep, Turkey, 1986-87; prodn. mgr. Portalin-R.C. Cola, Gaziantep, 1987-89; rsch. asst. Gaziantep U., 1989-91, asst. prof., 1995-98, assoc. prof., 1998—, asst. to chmn. food engring. dept., 1995—. Contbr. articles to profl. jours. Pvt. Turkish Army, 1990-91. Grantee Turkish Higher Ednl. Coun., 1991. Mem. Food Engrs. Chamber. Avocations: poem writing, jogging, natural history, music, traveling. Home: Ali Nadi Unler Cad Av, Nail Bilen Apt 109/4, 27090 Gaziantep Turkey Office: Gaziantep Univ, Food Engring Dept, 27310 Gaziantep Turkey

GOH, CHAN HON, ballerina; b. Beijing, Feb. 1, 1969; arrived in Can., 1977; d. Choo Chiat and Lin Yee (Zhang) G. Dancer Goh Ballet Tng. Co., Vancouver, B.C., Can., 1986-87; corp de ballet dancer Nat. Ballet of Can., Toronto, 1988-90, second soloist, 1990-92, first soloist, 1992-93, prin. dancer, 1993—; advisor in dance Met. Toronto Arts Coun., 1992-94; guest artist The Royal Danish Ballet, Hong Kong Ballet, Singapore Dance Theatre, Washington Ballet, Nat. Ballet of China. Prin. full length ballet roles in The Sleeping Beauty, La Fille Mal Gardée, Don Quixote, Romeo & Juliet, The Merry Widow, The Nutcracker, Taming of the Shrew, Onegin, Swan Lake, Giselle, Cinderella, La Boutique Fantasque, Tales of Arabian Night, La Sylphide, Swan Lake; other maj. roles include Sylvia Pas de deux, Paquita, Dream Dances, Divertimento No. 15, Les Sylphides, Theme and Variations, Désir, The Four Temperaments, La Ronde, Dahnis and Chloe, Mozartiana, Song of the Earth, LaBayadere Act II, Etudes, Napolie Act 3; Can. premieres include Jewels (George Balanchine), Concerto for Flute and Harp (John Cranko), 1990, The Leaves Are Fading (Antony Tudor), 1990, Pastorale (James Kudelka), 1990, Musings (Kudelka), 1991, The Actress (Kudelka), 1993, Now and Then (John Neumeier), 1993, The Four Seasons (Kudelka), 1997, Terra Firma, Forgotten Land (Kylian). Can. Coun. grantee, 1987; recipient Solo Seal award Royal Acad. Dancing, 1988, Prix de Lausanne, 1986, Silver medal Adelene Genee Comp., London, 1988. Avocations: reading, music, theatre. Office: Nat Ballet of Canada, 470 Queens Quay W, Toronto, ON Canada M5E 3K4

GOH, CHOK TONG, prime minister; b. Singapore, May 20, 1941; s. Goh Kah Khoon and Quah Kwee Hwa; m. Tan Choo Leng, 1965; 2 children (twins). B. Econ. with First Class Honours, U. Singapore; M in Devel. Economics, Williams Coll., USA. With econ. planning unit Singapore Adminstrv. Svc., 1964-69; with Neptune Orient Lines Ltd., 1969-77; man. dir. Neptune Orient Lines, 1973-76; mem. parliament Singapore, 1976—; 1st orgnl. sec. Peoples' Action Party, 1979, 2d asst. sec.-gen., 1979-84, asst. sec.-gen., 1984-89, 1st asst. sec.-gen., 1989-92, sec.-gen., 1992; sr. minister of state Ministry of Fin. Govt. Singapore, 1977-79, minister for trade and industry, 1979-81, minister for health, 2d minister for def., 1981-82, minister for def., dep. minister for health, 1982-85, 1st dep. prime minister, minister for def., 1985-90, prime minister, 1990—. Chair Singapore Labour Found.; bd. dirs. Nat. Trades Union Congress Fairprice and Income. Recipient medal of honor Nat. Trades Union Congress, 1987. Mem. Econs. Soc. Singapore. Avocations: tennis, golf. Office: Office of Prime Minister, Istana Annex Orchard Rd, Singapore 238823, Singapore*

GOH, KUANG HUAH, business consulting company administrator; b. Kajang, Selangor, Malaysia, Nov. 28, 1946; arrived in Singapore, 1964; s. Peng Khiang and Joo Lan (Ng) G.; m. Lim Siew Hiang, Dec. 6, 1973; children: Puay San, Teck Wee. MBA, Oklahoma City U., 1988; DipSm, 1986. Asst. co. sec. Lee Wah Bank, Singapore, 1971-73; corp. sec. Comml. & Indsl. Security Corp., Singapore, 1973-75; mgr. Harapan (Singapore) Co. Pte. Ltd., 1977-79; adminstrn. mgr. Marissco Pte. Ltd., Singapore, 1979-80; acct., co. sec. Ceilcote Pte. Ltd., Singapore, 1981-82; mgr. fin. and adminstrn. Singapore Island Country Club, 1982-90; br. mgr. Unbrako Inc., Singapore, 1990-91; gen. mgr. Adgrow Bus. Cons., 1991—. Founder, mem. com. Singapore Credit Club, 1973; asst. sec. 7th SEAP Games, Singapore, 1973; v.p. com Mgmt. Devel. Inst. of Singapore, 1988, 90-93; mem. exec. com. St. Andrews Parent-Tchr. Assn., 1990-93. Fellow Inst. Chartered Secs. and Adminstrs. (U.K.)); mem. Nat. Productivity Assn. (strategic mgmt. group com. 1989-91), Singapore Inst. Mgmt., Singapore Assn. Inst. Chartered Secs. and Adminstrs. (mgmt. com. 1972-74, 88-91), Oklahoma City U. MBA Alumni Assn. (hon. sec. 1988, com. 1990-93), Mktg. Inst. Singapore (membership com. 1994-95), Lion City Toastmasters (hon. treas. 1989-90,

hon. auditor 1990-91), Singapore Employers Group, Chartered Inst. Mgmt. Accts. Buddhist. Avocations: readinng, walking. Office: Adgrow Bus Cons 02-09 Shun Li Indsl Complex, Adgrow Bus Cons 02-09, Shun Li Indsl 705 Sims Dr, 1438 Singapore 387384, Singapore

GOH, KUN, mayor; b. Jan. 2, 1938; married; 3 children. BS in Pol. Sci., Seoul (South Korea) Nat. U., 1960, MS in City Planning, 1971; LLD (hon.), Won Kwang U., 1992. Asst. jr. ofcl. Ministry of Home Affairs, South Korea, 1962-65, asst. dir. planning office, 1965-68; dir. interior dept. Jeonbuk Province, South Korea, 1968-71; commr. New Village Movement, South Korea, 1971-73; vice gov. Kangwon Province, South Korea, 1973; dir. local adminstrn. bur. Ministry of Home Affairs, 1973-75; gov. Jeonnam Province, South Korea, 1975-79; chief sec. polit. affairs Chong Wa Dae (The Blue House), 1979-80; chief advisor Korea Rsch. Inst. for Human Settlement, 1980; min. transp. Govt. of South Korea, 1980-81, min. agr. and marine affairs, 1981-82; mem. 12th Nat. Assembly Min. of Home Affairs, 1987; mayor Seoul Met. Govt., 1988-90, 98—; pres. Myong Ji U., 1994-97; prime min. Republic of Korea, Seoul, 1997-98; co-pres. Korea Fedn. for Environ. Movement, 1996-97; vis. fellow Harvard U., 1983, MIT, 1984. Author: The Strategies of Administrative Reform in the Age of Localization, 1995, Prime Minister Goh Kun's Speeches, 1998, Speeches by Mayor Goh Kun of the Seoul Metropolitan Government, 1999. Co-chmn. 2002 FIFA World Cup Korea-Japan Hosting Local Govt.'s Coun. Recipient Red Stripes Order of Svc. Merit, 1972, Blue Stripes, 1982. Mem. Gov.'s Assn. (pres.), Met. Coun. Pub. Adminstrn. (pres.). Avocations: reading, tennis. Office: Seoul Met Govt, 31 Taepyong-no 1ga Chung-gu, Seoul 100-744, Korea

GOH, MARK KENG H., educator, researcher, consultant; b. Singapore, Singapore, Mar. 26, 1960; s. Chin Teck Goh and Sai Yoh Kan; m. Po Jan Chen, Feb. 28, 1988; children: Timothy, Lawrence, Reginald, Francis. BSc in Math., U. Adelaide, Australia, 1983, BSc in Math with honors, 1984, PhD, 1987; MBA, Deakin U., Australia, 1993. Assoc. prof. Nat. U. of Singapore, 1989—; lectr. U. South Australia, 1991; vis. prof. Chula Long Korn U., Thailand, 1999—; adj. prof. U. South Australia, 1996—; part-time lectr. U. Adelaide GSM, 1991; assoc. dir. edn. The Logistics Inst., Asia-Pacific, 1999—; cons. Lucent Technologies, Singapore, Perkins Parts, U.K., Unilever East Asia Pacific, Fuji-Xerox Singapore, MSAS, HP (APDO), others; prin. rschr. Ctr. for Transp. Rsch., Singapore, 1995—. Author: Strategic Business Opportunities, 1992; editor: OR Applications in Singapore, 1995; assoc. editor Asia Pacific Jour. of OR, 1995—; contbr. articles to profl. publs. Mil. officer Singapore Armed Forces, Singapore, 1987-89. Scholarship Colombo Plan, 1980, U. Adelaide, 1984; Commonwealth fellow ACU, 1998, Citibank Internat. fellow UNC, 1998. Mem. Chartered Inst. of Transport/Singapore (dir. edn. 1998—), OR Soc. Sinapore (v.p. 1996-97), SIPMM (acad. chmn. 1997—), Australian Alumni (v.p. 1996-98). Methodist. Avocations: badminton, fishing, swimming. Office: Nat U of Singapore, 15 Law Link, Singapore 117591, Singapore

GOH, RONALD, audioengineer, engineering executive; b. Singapore, Singapore, Nov. 18, 1944; s. Kiokchuan Goh and Siewboey Khoo; m. Dora Lee, Dec. 11, 1971; children: Vanessa, Gary, Jonathan. Grad., Singapore Poly., 1965. Cert. sound system engr. Sales mgr. Electronics & Engring. PTE Ltd., 1965-68, sales dir., 1968-92, mng. dir., 1992—. Mem. Audio Engring. Soc., Highlander Club, Oxford Club (life), Kiwanis of Singapore (charter). Avocations: golf, sailing, gardening, outdoor activities. Office: 285 Outram Rd, 169069 Singapore Singapore

GOH, ZENTON, researcher; b. Singapore, May 17, 1968; s. Heon-Seng and Mary G.; m. Siew-Choon Ting, Mar. 15, 1995; children: Joven, Joshaun. BS in Math. with honors, Nat. U. Singapore, 1992. Analyst DSO Nat. Labs., Singapore, 1993-96; project officer Ctr. for Signal Processing, Singapore, 1996-98, rsch. program mgr., 1998-2000; chief tech. officer Addest Technovation Pte. Ltd., Singapore, 2000—. Contbr. articles to profl. jours. Recipient Singapore Nat. Acad. Sci. award, 1991, Tan Siak Kew gold medal, Nat. U. Singapore, 1990, 1991, Toh Chin Chye book prize, Nat. U. Singapore, 1989, Lijen Indsl. Devel. medal, Nat. U. Singapore, 1992. Avocations: music, basketball, table tennis, pinball. E-mail: zgoh@addest.com. Office: Addest Technovation Pte Ltd, 20 Ayer Rajah Crescent, Singapore 139964, Singapore

GOIC, SRECKO, economics educator, consultant; b. Supetar, Croatia, Nov. 24, 1959; s. Mihovil and Jelica (Bakovic) G. BSc in Econs., Faculty Econs., Split, Croatia, 1981; MSc in Mgmt., Faculty Econs., Zagreb, Croatia, 1990, PhD in Econs., 1996. Tchg. asst. Faculty Econs., Split, Croatia, 1986-97, asst. prof., 1997—; head devel. dept. Split Polytechnic, 1998—. Mng. editor: Enterpirse in Transition 2, 1997, Enterprise in Transition 3, 1999. Office: Faculty Econs, Radovanova 13, 21000 Split Croatia

GOIKHMAN, OSCAR JAKOVLEVICH, institute director; b. Moscow, June 9, 1939; s. Meer Petrovich and Maria Grigorievna (Shpak) Shysterman; m. Erna Ahmetovna Muzafarova, July 24, 1964; 1 child, Koshlykova Maria. Journalist, Moscow U., 1967, PhD in Philology, 1975; hon. degree, Acad. Social Edn., Russia, 1997, Acad. Scis., N.Y.C., 1997. Tuner Plant, Moscow, 1958-65; chief reductional dept. U. Svc., Moscow, 1965-75, sr. lectr. lang. and lit. dept., vice dean faculty, 1980-89, dean faculty, 1989-96, prof., 1993—, dir. inst., 1996—; head dept. Russian New U., Moscow, 1996—. Author: (Russian text) Phrase-book, 1985; author, sci. editor: Fundamentals of Speech Communication, 1997, Theory End Practice Referentic Activity, 1999; contbr. chpt. to book. Asst. dep. State Dyta, 1995-99. Recipient Vet. of Labour award Suprim Soviet USSR, 1991, medal 850 yrs. Moscow, Moscow Govt., 1997; named Hon. Functionary Higher Edn. Minisry, 1998. Mem. Journalists Union. Jewish. Home: Petrovsko-Rasumovsky, pro 4a k9 kv6, 103220 Moscow Russia Office: Moscow U Sci, Glavnaya St, 141220 Posolok Cherkisovo Russia

GOILAV, BÉATRICE SARAH, physician, educator; b. Winterthur, Zurich, Switzerland, Aug. 28, 1972; d. Yoan and Florenza (Glück) G. Candidatus Medicus, U. Basel, Switzerland, 1994, MD, 1999. Intern Beilinson Med. Ctr., Petah Tiqva, Israel, 1996-97; resident dept. internal medicine B Kantonal Hosp. of Basel, 1999—; lectr. internal medicine Sch. Phys. Therapy Basel. Music critic: (newspaper) Jüdische Rundschau, 1992-94. Home: Hegenheimerstr 14, 4055 Basel Switzerland Office: Kantonsspital Basel, Petersgraben 4, 4031 Basel Switzerland

GOIN, MICHEL, physician; b. Aulnay-Sous-Bois, Seine St. Denis, France, May 30, 1951; s. Jean Etienne and Gisele (Baudrion) G.; m. Francoise Jeanne Gibiot, July 28, 1973; children: Vincent, Ludivine. D of medicine, Rene Descartes U., Paris, 1977; postgrad. diploma, U. Continuing Edn., 1999. Chief doctor clin. medicine "Les Sources" Nursing Home, Ville d'Avray, France, 1978-80; gen. practice medicine Saint-Cloud, France, 1980—. Mem. Saint-Cloud and Garches Gen. Practitioners Friendly Mtg. Avocations: exotic fish, cats, music, sports. Home and office: 8 Rue Lelégard, 92210 Saint-Cloud France

GOINES, LEONARD, music educator, consultant; b. Jacksonville, Fla., Apr. 22, 1934; s. Buford and Willie Mae (Lamar) G.; m. Margaretta Bobo (div.); 1 child, Lisan Lynette. BMus, Manhattan Sch. Music, 1955, MMus, 1956; MA, Columbia U., 1960, profl. diploma, 1961, EdD, 1963; BA, New Sch. Social Rsch., 1980; MA, NYU, 1980; CAS, Harvard U., 1984. Lectr. music Queens Coll. CUNY, 1969, York Coll. CUNY, 1969, NYU, 1970—; trumpeter Symphony New World, N.Y.C., 1965-76; assoc. prof. music Morgan State Coll., Balt., 1966-68, Howard U., Washington, 1970-72; prof. Manhattan C. C. CUNY, N.Y.C., 1970—; freelance musician Broadway shows, theatre, orchestras, recording ensembles, jazz groups, 1959—; vis. prof. Williams Coll., Williamstown, Mass., 1984, Vassar Coll., Poughkeepsie, N.Y., 1985; co-exec. prodr., Bklyn. Acad. Music Majestic Theatre, 1988-96; dist. vis. prof. Lafayette Coll., Easton, Pa., 1986; postdoctoral fellow Harvard U., Cambridge, Mass., 1982-85; ptnr. Shepard & Goines Organizational and Ednl Art. cons., Jazz rsch. cons. Nat. Endowment Arts, 1983; appointee U.S. Dept. Interior, Smithsonian Inst.; mem. Preservation Jazz Adv. Commn., 1992-93; cons. in field. Contbr. articles to profl. jours. Folklore cons., field rschr., African Diaspora, Smithsonian Instn., 1972-76; trustee Nat. Assn. Community Schs. of Arts, N.Y.C., 1982-85; chmn. spl. arts section panel N.Y. State Council on Arts, N.Y.C., 1982-85; music panelist Arts Connection, N.Y.C., 1985. Recipient Pub. Svc. award U.S. Dept. Labor, 1980, Scholar Incentive award CUNY, 1983-84; named Hon. Citizen City of Winnipeg, Can., 1958; Coll. Tchrs. fell NEH, 1982-83; Faculty Rsch. grantee Howard U., CUNY, NYU, 1971-73. Mem. Local 802 of Am. Fedn. Musicians, AAUP, Nat. Acad. Rec. Arts and Scis., Phi Delta Kappa, Phi Mu Alpha. Democrat. Episcopalian. Avocations: running, photography, travel. Home: 221 W 131st St New York NY 10027-2030 Office: CUNY Manhattan Community Coll 199 Chambers St New York NY 10007-1044

GOKEL, GEORGE WILLIAM, organic chemist, educator; b. June 27, 1946; s. George William and Ruth Mildred G.; m. Kathryn Smiegocki, June 2, 1978; children: Michael Robert, Matthew George, Mark Arlington. BS in Chemistry, Tulane U., 1968; PhD in Organic Chemistry, U. So. Calif., 1971. Postdoctoral fellow UCLA, 1972-74; chemist cen. rsch. dept. E.I. Du Pont de Nemours & Co., Wilmington, Del., summer 1974; asst. prof. chemistry Pa. State U., University, 1974-78; assoc. prof. chemistry U. Md., College Park, 1978-82, prof. chemistry, 1982-85; prof. chemistry U. Miami, Coral Gables, Fla., 1985-93, prof. dept. molecular biology and pharmacology Sch. Medicine, 1993—; dir. bioorganic chemistry program Washington U., 1993—; cons. W.R. Grace Co., 1977-86, Lion Detergent Co., Tokyo, 1985—, Seal Sands Chem. Co., Stockton-on-Tees, Eng., 1983-88, Monsanto Co., St. Louis, 1989-91, A.H. Marks, Eng., 1990-99; lectr. in field. Editor Supramolecular Chemistry jour., 1992-2000; author: Phase Transfer. Recipient Allan C. Davis medal Md. Acad. Sci., 1979; Leo Schubert award Washington Acad. Scis., 1980, Macrocycle Chemistry award Izatt-Christensen, 1996; Petroleum Rsch. Fund grantee, 1976-78; grantee NIH, 1979—, NSF, 1998—. Fellow AAAS; mem. Biophys. Soc., Protein Soc., Am. Chem. Soc., Chem. Soc. (London), Sigma Xi, Alpha Chi Sigma. Republican. Methodist. Home: 1817 Stenton Path Chesterfield MO 63005-4733 Office: Washington U Sch Medicine Dept Molecular Biology & Pharmacology Saint Louis MO 63110

GÖKER, MEHMET HAYRI, design engineer, research scientist; b. Istanbul, Turkey, Apr. 26, 1964; s. Yurdagün Hasan and Güler Göker. BSc in Aeronautcal Engring., Tech. U. Istanbul, Turkey, 1986; MSc in Computer Engring., Bogazici U., Istanbul, 1990; MS in Aerospace Engring., U. Mich., 1988; PhD in Mech. Engring., Tech Hochschule Darmstadt, Germany, 1996. Rsch. asst. Bogazici U., Istanbul, 1986-90; tchg. asst. Tech. Hochschule Darmstadt, Germany, 1990-96; rsch. scientist DaimlerChrysler R&T, 1997—. Scholar Turkish State, 1987-88, German State, 1990-93. Mem. AIAA, Assn. Computer Machinery, Am. Assn. Artificial Intelligence. Home: 2333 Eastridge Ave Apt 4 Menlo Park CA 94025-6741

GOKHALE, SRIKANT, operations manager, management consultant; b. New Delhi, Jan. 14, 1964; parents Maruti and Kamala Gokhale; m. Saloni Gokhale, Feb. 27, 1990; 1 child, Siddhant. B of Mech. Engring., Delhi Coll. Engring., 1985; MBA, Indian Inst. Mgmt., Ahmedabad, 1987. Mgr. purchasing Bajaj Auto Ltd., Pune, India, 1987-89; sr. mgr. strategic planning Kirloskar Oil Engines Ltd., Pune, 1989-92; mgr. fin. Alghanim Industries, Kuwait, 1992-98, head ops. (electronics group), 1998—; dir. Advantage India, Mumbai. Exhibited paintings in solo show, 1988. Avocations: collection of data economies, traveling, reading management-related books. E-mail: srikant@alghanim.com. Office: Alghanim Industries, PO Box 223, Safat Kuwait

GOKTAY, AHMET YIGIT, radiologist; b. Ankara, Turkey, Nov. 25, 1965; s. Lutfi and Bilge Goktay; m. Aylin Demir, Nov. 14, 1998. Diploma in medicine, Hacettepe U., Ankara, 1991. Resident in radiology Dokuz Eylul U. Sch. Medicine, Izmir, Turkey, 1992-96, specialist, 1996-97, clin. rsch. fellow, 1997-99, asst. prof., 2000—. Contbr. articles to sci. and profl. jours. With Turk. Med. Students Exch. Cmty. Program, Ankara, 1987-90. Fellow Cardiovasc. and Interventional Radiol. Soc. Europe, European Fedn. of Socs. for Ultrasound in Medicine and Biology, Turkish Soc. Med. Imaging and Interventional Radiology, Turkish Soc. Radiology (Radiology award 1998). Avocations: bridge, basketball, diving. Office: Dokuz Eylul U Med Sch Hosp, Inciralti, Izmir 35340, Turkey

GOKUL, BINDIGANAVILE NARASIMHAMURTHY, microbiologist; b. Bangalore, Karnataka, India, Nov. 8, 1949; s. Narasimhamurthy Bindiganavile and Shakunthala Acharya; m. Bharati Iyengar, May 10, 1985; children: Wyneth Keshav, Sridutt Pawan. MB, BS, Bangalore Med. Coll., 1975, MD in Microbiology, 1981. Intern Victoria, Vani Vilas, Minto Ophthalmic Hosps., 1974-75; Indian Coun. Med. Rsch. sr. rsch. fellow dept. microbiology St. John's Med. Coll., Bangalore, 1976-78, tutor, 1981; lectr. M.S. Ramaiah Med. Coll., Bangalore, 1981-83; asst. prof. Nat. Inst. Mental Health and Neuroscis., Bangalore, 1983-85, assoc. prof., 1986-89, adj. prof., 1989-90; specialist, chief, dir. lab. and blood bank, infection control officer Midhnab Gen. Hosp., Gassim, Saudi Arabia, 1990-2000. Contbr. articles to med. jours., including Neurology, Progress in Clin. Neuroscis., Indian Jour. Path. Microbiology, Indian Jour. Pediat., Indian Jour. Tuberculosis, Indian Jour. Med. Rsch., Saudi Med. Jour. Mem. Indian Med. Assn. (life), Indian Immunological Soc. (life), Acad. Med. Spltys., Indian Red Cross Soc. (life assoc.). Hindu. Avocations: reading, teaching children, meeting people, socializing, cricket. Home: Wyneth 1 2d Cross Kumaracot, Layout, High Grounds, Bangalore 560001, India Office: Midhnab Gen Hosp, Al Midhnab, PO Box 253, Gassim Saudi Arabia

GOLABEK, WIESLAW, surgeon; b. Baltow, Poland, May 16, 1940; s. Stanislaw and Stanislawa (Matraszek) G.; m. Joanna Ciezka, Aug. 21, 1966; children: Ewa, Anna. MD, Med. Acad., Lublin, 1971, PhD, 1980. Assoc. prof. Med. Acad., Lublin, 1980-90, prof., 1990—; vice-rector Med. Acad., Lublin, 1990-93; regional cons. otolaryngology. Recipient Sci. award Polish Minister Health, 1987. Mem. Polish Soc. Otolaryngology, German Soc. Head and Neck Surgeons. Office: Med Acad, Ul Jaczewskiego 8, 20-090 Lublin Poland

GOLAN, DAVID ERIC, biophysicist, pharmacologist, hematologist; b. Boston, Mar. 10, 1953; s. Harold Philip and Irene Judith (Soble) G.; m. Laura Carolyn Green, Nov. 29, 1981; children: Liza Green-Golan, Sarah Green-Golan. AB, Harvard Coll., 1975; MD, Yale U., 1979, PhD, 1982. Diplomate Am. Bd. Internal Medicine, Am. Bd. Hematology. Clin. and rsch. fellow Harvard Med. Sch., Brigham and Women's Hosp., Boston, 1979-83; intern Brigham & Woman's Hosp., Boston, 1979-80, resident in internal medicine, 1980-83, fellow in hematology/oncology, 1983-85; instr. Harvard Med. Sch., Brigham and Women's Hosp., Boston, 1983-87, asst. prof., 1987-94, assoc. prof., 1994—; assoc. physician Brigham and Women's Hosp., Boston, 1985-92, physician, 1992—; reviewer NIH study section, 1997—; mem. med./sci. adv. bd. Alza Corp., 1994—; Applied Pharm. Task Force and Test Material Devel. com. Nat. Bd. Med. Examiners, 1996-98, Pharm. Test Com. and Test Material Devel. Com. 1998—, Interdisciplinary Test Com., 1999—. Contbr. more than 65 articles to profl. jours.; author: (computer software) Pharm Aid, 1991. Med. Found. rsch. fellow, 1985-87, Faculty prize for excellence in teaching, 1996; recipient Merit award NIH, 1997—, Student award for Excellence in Tchg. Harvard Med. Sch., 1998, 99, 2000. Fellow Molecular Med. Soc.; mem. ACP, Biophys. Soc., Am. Soc. for Cell Biology, Am. Chem. Soc., Am. Soc. Hematology, Am. Soc. for Clin. Investigation. Achievements include demonstration of control of transmembrane protein diffusion by membrane skeletal proteins in human red blood cells, development of novel system for visualization of contact area between cell membrane and target membrane, and elucidation of molecular mechanisms by which cells respond to ac electric fields. Office: Harvard Med Sch 250 Longwood Ave Boston MA 02115-5731

GOLAN, JONATHAN SAMUEL, mathematics and computer science educator; b. Milw., May 29, 1942; arrived in Israel, 1967; s. Ezriel and Naomi Ruth (Bernstein) G.; m. Hemda Mousaieff, Sept. 10, 1968; children: Aharon, Elitsur, Yael. BA, U. Wis., 1964; MA, U. Calif., Berkeley, 1965; PhD, Hebrew U., Jerusalem, Israel, 1971. Vis. prof. math. U. Fla., Gainesville, 1971-72, McGill U., Montreal, Que., Can., 1972-73, Ind. U., Bloomington, 1978-79, George Mason U., Fairfax, Va., 1983-84, U. Idaho, 1997—; prof. math. U. Haifa, Israel, 1973—. Author: Localization of Noncommutative Rings, 1975, Decomposition and Dimension in Module Categories, 1977, Structure Sheaves over a Noncommutative Ring, 1980, Studies in Modern Algebra, Vol. 1, Group Theory and Ring Theory, 1981, Vol. II, Field Theory and Galois Theory, 1982, Torsion Theories, 1986, Linear Topologies on a Ring: an Overview, 1987, (with Harold Simmons) Derivatives, Nuclei, and Dimensions on the Frame of Torsion Theories, 1988, (with Tom Head) Modules and the Structure of Rings—A Primer, 1991, The Theory of Semirings, 1992, Foundations of Linear Algebra, 1992, Studies in Modern Algebra, revised and expanded edit., 1992, Solved Problems in Linear Algebra, 1993, Foundations of Linear Algebra, 1995, 2d edit., 1995, Semirings and Their Applications, 1999, Power Algebras Over Semirings, 1999; contbr. over 60 articles to internat. math. and computer sci. jours. Mem. Am. Math. Soc., Math. Assn. Am., Israel Math. Union. Jewish. Office: U Haifa, Dept Math, 31905 Haifa Israel

GOLAN, RACHEL, biochemistry educator; b. Tel Aviv, July 3, 1942; d. Jacob and Zvia (Lipovitz) Lurie; m. Amiram Golan; children: Dana, Roni. MSc in Microbiology with distinction, Tel Aviv U., 1967, PhD, 1976. With Inst. Chem. Pathology Chaim Sheba Med. Ctr., Tel Hashomer, Israel, 1967-83; asst. dept. chem. pathology Tel Aviv U., 1969-72, instr., 1972-76, lectr., then sr. lectr., 1976-81; coord. postgrad. clin. chemistry course Sackler Sch. Medicine, Tel Aviv U., 1989, 94-95; participant 6th Internat. Congress Human Genetics, Jerusalem, 1981, Internat. Congress Clin. Biochemistry, London, 1996, many profl. confs.; presenter, lectr. in field. Contbr. chpt., co-contbr. chpt. to: Metabolism in Health and Diseases, 1985; contbr. articles to profl. publs., conf. procs. Mem. Israel Soc. Clin. Biochemistry (sec., alt. pres. 1991-96, nat. rep. 1996—, Best Poster award 1985, 95, 2nd Best Poster award 1996), Israeli Fertility Assn. Avocation: bridge (nat. master). E-mail: rachelgo@post.tav.ac.is. Home: 5 Uziel St, 62333 Tel Aviv Israel Office: Tel Aviv U Dept Clin Chem, Sackler Med Sch, 69978 Tel Aviv Israel

GOLAN, ZIONA, cognitive psychologist; b. Jerusalem, July 19, 1926; d. Nahum and Shoshana (Reznik) Goldman; m. David Golan (Goldsberg), Sept. 14, 1948 (dec. Nov. 1988); children: Orna, Hemda, Nahum. BA in Philosophy, Pedagogy, Hebrew U., Jerusalem, 1961, BA in Psychology, 1966; MA in Cognitive Psychology, Tel Aviv U., 1984. Cons. psycological svcs. Jerusalem, 1967-68; cons. Seligsberg H.S., Jerusalem, 1969. Mem. Israel Psychol. Assn., Israel Assn. Grads. in Social Scis. and Humanities, Israel Friends of Tel Aviv U., Movement for Quality Govt. in Israel.

GOLANKA, STANLEY RICHARD, airline executive; b. Niagara Falls, N.Y., Feb. 2, 1931; m. Mary L. Lowe, Dec. 29, 1962 (div. Dec. 1987); children: Stan, Steve, Andrea; m. Elzbieta M. Skalska, June 12, 1993; children: Aleksandra, Karolina. BSME, Purdue U., 1953; MS in Mgmt., Navy Postgrad. Sch., Monterey, Calif., 1967. Commd. ens. USN, 1954, advanced through grades to comdr., ret., 1974; sales engr. Western Constrn. Co., Tonawanda, N.Y., 1975-76; asst. prof. Robert Morris Coll., Pitts., 1976-78; engr. Boeing Co., Seattle, 1978-82; field svc. engr. Boeing Co., Miami, Fla., 1982-86, Winston Salem, N.C., 1986-89; mgr. Boeing Co., Warsaw, Poland, 1989—. Mem. Polish Nat. Aviation Coun., Am. C. of C., Polish Sr. Aviators Club. Republican. Roman Catholic. Avocations: flying, golf, tennis, sailing. Home: Graniczna 5A, 05-501 Piaseczno Poland Office: Boeing-Lot Polish Airlines, 17 Stycznia 39, 00-906 Warsaw Poland

GOLAS, ASHOK, telecommunications engineer; b. Agra, India, June 15, 1950; s. Kailash Chandra and Kamla (Gupta) G.; m. Sarita Gupta, June 25, 1950; children: Abhishek, Avantika, Abhinav. B Tech. in Elec. Engring., Indian Inst. Tech., Kanpur, 1971; M Tech. in Comm. and Radar Engring., Indian Inst. Tech., New Delhi, 1979, M Tech. in Computer Sci. and Engring., 1995. Asst. dir. Telecomm. Rsch. Ctr., New Delhi, 1976-81, dep. dir., 1981-87; dir. microwave project task force Dept. Telecomm., Jorhat, India, 1987-89; dir. telecom. commn. Dept. Telecomm., New Delhi, 1989-93; gen. mgr. Mahanagar Telephone Nigam Ltd, Delhi Telephones, New Delhi, 1994-95; dep. dir. gen. radio Telecomm. Engring. Ctr., New Delhi, 1995—; cons. Internat. Telecomm. Union, Switzerland, 1991, 92. Contbr. article to profl. jours. Fellow Inst. Elec and Telecomm. Engrs. India; mem. IEEE (sr., sec., chmn. 1986-95), Soc. EMC Engrs., Computer Soc. India. Hindu. Avocation: chess. Home: 101-A Mount Kailash, New Delhi 110065, India Office: Telecom Engring Ctr, 656 Khurshid Lal Bhavan, Janpath New Delhi 110001, India

GOLBACH, RODOLFO LUIS PABLO, retired entomologist, foundation consultant; b. Leizig, Germany, June 8, 1916; arrived in Argentina, 1936; s. Federico Golbach and Ludmila Nedelka; m. Susana Rosa Zapata, July 31, 1954; children: María Isabel, Marta Susana, José Rodolfo, Guido Antonio. Caretaker insects Fundación Miguel Lillo, Argentina, 1944-48, prof. sugar entomology, 1948-58; researcher forest entomology U. Santiago del Estero, Argentina, 1958-92; ret. Decorated Crux of Merit Govt. Germany, 1993; named Hon. Citizen Province of Tucumán (Argentina). Fellow World Census Tropical Ecology Inst. Ecology; mem. AAAS, Rotary Internat. (Paul Harris fellow 1998). Office: U Santiago del Estero, Av Belgrano (S), 1912 Tucuman Argentina

GOLCZEWSKI, FRANK, history educator; b. Katowice, Poland, Oct. 8, 1948; s. Hans-Georg and Gertrud (Simon) G.; m. Mechthild Kohleick, Mar. 25, 1975. PhD, U. Cologne, Germany, 1973, Habilitation, 1979. Wissenschaflicher asst. Pädagogische Hochschule, Neuss, Fed. Republic Germany, 1974-80, U. Dusseldorf, Fed. Republic Germany, 1980-83; prof. modern and European history U. Fed. Armed Forces, Hamburg, Fed. Republic Germany, 1983-94; prof. East European history U. Hamburg, 1994—. Author: Polnisch-Jüdische Beziehungen 1881-1922, 1981, Kölner Universitaetslehrer und der Nationalsozialismus, 1988, Geschichte der Ukraine, 1993, Russischer Nationalismus, 1998, others; European editor Nationalities papers.

GOLD, ALLAN HAROLD, architect, structural engineer, educator; b. Chgo., Jan. 12, 1942; s. Melvin King and Estelle M. (Zucker) G.; m. Barbara Gail Edelstein, June 20, 1967 (div. Feb. 1989); children: Grant, Ross, Susan; m. Susan Carlucci, Dec. 30, 1989. BArch, U. Ill., Urbana, 1966, MS, 1967. Registered architect, Conn., Colo., Ill., Ind., La., Okla., Wis.; registered structural engr., Ill; registered profl. engr., Ind., La., Okla., Wis., Tex., Mich.; cert. Nat. Coun. Archtl. Registration Bds. (juor registration exam. 1985), Nat. Coun. Examiners Engrin. and Surveying Certification. Architect, project engr. various archtl., engring. cos., Chgo. area, 1963-68; project structural engr. Perkins & Will Architects, Chgo., 1968-70; structural engr. Chgo. Dept. Bldgs., 1970-73; owner, operator Allan H. Gold & Assocs., Architects/Cons. Structural Engrs., Hazel Crest, Ill., 1973-81; project mgr., sr. structural engr. HKS/Structures, Dallas, 1981-84; dir. architecture and structural engring. dept. URS Engrs., Dallas, 1984; owner, operator Allan H. Gold, Architect/Structural Engr., Dallas, 1985-88; project mgr. Hoffmann Architects, North Haven, Conn., 1988-90; prin. Allan H. Gold, Archt. & Structural Engr., Chgo., 1990-93; v.p. Salse Engrs., Northbrook, Ill., 1993-96; assoc. Thornton-Tomasetti Engrs./LZA Tech., Chgo., 1996—; asst. prof. archtl. tech. dept. constrn. tech. purdue U., Hammond, Ind., 1976-80; assoc. prof. architecture U. Okla., Norman, 1980-81; adj. assoc. prof. architecture U. Tex., Arlington, 1983-85; guest lectr. U. Wis. Ext., 1981. Structural engr. Century Shopping Ctr., Chgo., 1973, Phoenix Tower, Houston, 1983, Xerox II, Irving, Tex., 1984. Mem. Village of Hazel Crest Plan Commn., 1979-81. Fellow ASCE (mem. tall bldgs. com. 1983-86, std. com. design loads on structure during constrn. 1989—, std. com. design engineered wood constrn. 1989—, editl. bd. Jour. Archtl. Engring. 1995—); mem. Structural Engrs. Assn. Ill., AIA, Am. Arbitration Assn., Masons, Scottish Rite, Shriners (master Skokie, Ill. 1979). Jewish. Home: 360 E Randolph St # 4204 Chicago IL 60601-7341 Office: Thornton Tomasetti Engineers/LZA Tech 14 E Jackson Blvd Ste 1100 Chicago IL 60604-2209

GOLD, BELA, economist, educator; b. Kolozsvar, Hungary, Jan. 30, 1915; came to U.S., 1920, naturalized, 1927; s. Leo and Esther (Ludwig) G.; m. Sonia Steinman, July 5, 1938; 1 son, Robert. B.S. in Mech. Engring, NYU, 1934; Ph.D. (Univ. fellow 1936-37), Columbia U., 1948. Research cons. Life Ins. Sales Research Bur., Hartford, Conn., 1938-39; asst. head div. program surveys Bur. Agr. Econs., 1939-42; econ. cons. subcom. war mblzn. U.S. Senate, 1943-44; econ. adviser FEA and Dept. Commerce, 1944-46; prof. indsl. econs. U. Pitts. Grad. Sch. Bus., 1947-66; Timken prof. and William E. Umstattd prof. indsl. econs., dir. research program indsl. econs. Case Western Res. U., 1966-83, chmn. dept. econs., 1967-73; Fletcher Jones prof. tech. and mgmt. Claremont Grad. Sch. (Calif.), 1983-2000; pres. Indsl. Econs. and Mgmt. Assocs., 1980-2000; vis. professorial fellow Nuffield Coll., Oxford (Eng.) U., 1964; vis. prof. Imperial Coll. Scis. and Tech., London, 1967, 73; Disting. Internat. Sr. Rsch. fellow Centre Internat. Rsch. on Computer and Info. Tech., Melbourne, Australia, 1989, Adminstrv. Staff. Coll. India, Hyderabad, 1992, Rand Afrikaans U., South Africa, 1995; cons. to industry and ednl. instns., 1950—; mem. com. on steel industry Nat. Acad. Scis.-Nat.

Materials Adv. Bd., 1977-78; mem. assembly of engring. com. on computer-aided mfg. NRC, 1978-82, mem. mfg. studies bd., 1982-86, mem. com. on machine tool industry, 1982-84; mem. Interdepartmental Adv. Com. on Fed. Policy on Indsl. Innovation, 1978-79; mem. ferrous metals panel Nat. Acad. Engring., 1980-84, panel on improving the competitiveness of U.S. Industries, 1985. Author: Wartime Economic Planning in Agriculture, 2d edit., 1969, How is Higher Education Financed, 1959, Foundations of Productivity Analysis, 1955, Explorations in Managerial Economics, 1971, Japanese edit., 1977, Technological Change: Economics Management and Environment, 1975, 80, Applied Productivity Analysis for Industry, U.K. edit., 1976, Russian edit., 1981, Chinese edit., 1982, Research, Technological Change and Economic Analysis, 1977, Productivity, Technology and Capital, 1979, 2d edit., 1982, Evaluating the Effects of Technological Innovations, 1980, Appraising and Stimulating Technological Advances in Industry, 1980, Improving Managerial Evaluations of Computer-Aided Manufacturing, 1981, Technological Progress and Industrial Leadership, 1984, 85, On the Increasing Role of Technology in Corporate Policy, 1991, Strengthening Corporate and National Competitiveness Through Technology, 1992, New Technological Foundations of Strategic Management: Some International Perspectives, 1993, Needed Technological Responses to International Competition, 1994, Emerging Technological Frontiers in International Competition, 1995, Changing the Technological Determinants of International Competitiveness, 1996, Advancing the International Competitiveness of U.S. Manufacturing, 1999; mem. editl. bd. Acad. Mgmt. Jour., 1962-73, Omega: Internat. Jour. Mgmt. Scis., 1972-99, Jour. Product Innovation Mgmt., 1983-99, Internat. Jour. Tech. Mgmt., 1989-99; corr. mem. editl. bd. Revue d'Économie Industrielle, 1978-90; mem. adv. editl. bd. Jour. Computer Integrated Mfg., 1985—,Transactions in Engring. Mgmt., 1986—, Jour. Engring. and Tech. Mgmt., 1988—, Mfg. Rev., 1989—, Prodn. and Ops. Mgmt., 1991—, Mng. Tech. Today, 1992—; contbr. numerous articles to profl. jours., chpts. in books. Social Sci. Research Council fellow, 1937-38, 77, 83; Ford Found. fellow, 1961-62, 66-67, 72. Mem. Am. Econ. Assn., Inst. Mgmt. Scis. (chmn. Coll. on Mgmt. of Technol. Change 1970-85), Nat. Assn. Accts. (subcom. on productivity measurement 1977-79), AAUP. Home: The Classic 6380 Common Cir West Palm Beach FL 33417-4266

GOLD, BETTY VIRGINIA, artist; b. Austin, Tex., Feb. 15, 1935; d. Julius Ulisses and Jeffie Mae (Meek) Lee; 1 child, Laura Lee Gold Bousquet. Student, U. Tex. lectr. Gazi U., Ankara, Turkey, 1988, NAshida Gallery, Nara, Japan, 1989, Met. State Coll. Denver, 1992, Downey Mus., Calif., 1993, Foothills Art Ctr., Golden, Colo., 1994, Triskel Art Ctr., Cork, Ireland, 1994, ARmand Hammer Mus., L.A., 1994, Austin Art Mus., 1996. One-woman shows include Sol Del Rio Gallery, San Antonio, 1971, Parkcrest Gallery, Austin, 1972, Rubicon Gallery, L.A., 1973, Downtown Gallery, Honolulu, 1974, Esther Robles Gallery, L.A., 1975, Laguna Gloria Art Mus., Austin, 1976, Charles W. Bowers Meml. Mus., Santa Ana, Calif., 1977, Phoenix Art Mus., 1979, Baum-Silverman Gallery, L.A., 1988, Del. Art Mus., Wilmington, 1981, Univ. Art Mus., Austin, 1981, Decias Art, LaJolla, Calif., 1982, Patrick Gallery, Austin, 1983, Jan Baum Gallery, L.A., 1984, Boise State U., 1985, Purdue U., West Lafayette, Ind., 1986, Walker Hill Art Ctr., Seoul, Korea, 1987, Nishida Gallery, Nara, Japan, 1989, Armeson Fine Arts, Ltd., Vail, Colo., 1991, Downey Mus., Calif., 1993, ARt Mus. South Tex., Corpus Christi, 1995, Austin Art Mus., Austin, 1996, The Czech Mus. Fine Arts, Prague, 1998, Elite Gallery, Venice, 1998, others; group shows include Enhol Gallery, Dallas, 1971, Bestart Fallery, Houston, 1972, Gargoyle, Inc., Aspen, Colo., 1975, Aronson Gallery, Atlanta, 1976, Shidoni Gallery, Sante Fe, N.Mex., 1977, Elaine Horwich Gallery, Scottsdale, Ariz., 1981, Fordham U., Bronx, 1983, Nat. Mus. Contemporary Art, Seoul, 1987, John Thomas Gallery, Santa Monica, Calif., 1989, La Quinta Sculpture Park, Calif., 1994, Bova Gallery, L.A., 1995, Museo Nacional Centro de Arte Reina Sofia, Madrid, Spain, 1997, Threshold Gallery, Santa Monica, 1998, others; represented in permanent installations at RCA Bldg., Chgo., Cedars Sinai Hosp., L.A., Sinai Temple, L.A., Hawaii State Fond. Arts, Apollo Plastic Corp., Chgo., Houston First Savs., Pepperdine U., Malibu, Calif., No. Ill. U., Dekalb, Mus. Nacional-Centro de Arte Reina Sofia, Madrid, Texas U., Austin, City of Palma de Mallorca (1999), Spain, Duke U. Med. Ctr. (1999), others. Fax: 310-399-3745.

GOLD, DORE, diplomat. MA in Polit. Sci., Columbia U., 1976, cert. Mid. East Inst., 1978, PhD, 1984. Fgn. policy advisor to Prime Min. Netanyahu Israel, 1996-97; permanent rep. of Israel UN, 1997-99; dir. U.S. fgn. and devl. policy project Jaffe Ctr. for Strategic Defense Studies, Tel Aviv U., 1987-96; advisor to Israeli delegation to Madrid Peace Conf., 1991. Author: Arms Control in the Middle East, 1990, American Military Strategy in the Middle East, The Implications of the US Regional Command Structure (CENTCOM) for Israel, 1993, Israel as an American Non-NATO Ally: Parameters of Defense and Industrial Cooperation, 1992; contbr. articles to profl. pubs. Office: Jerusalem Ctr for Pub Affairs, 13 Tel Hai St, 92107 Israel Jerusalem

GOLD, HYMAN, cellist; b. Cleve., Aug. 26, 1914; s. Isaac and Fanny (Liebenson) g.; m. Ruth Olgin, Feb. 4, 1936; 1 child, Ronald Kenneth; m. Sue DiCicco, Oct. 2, 1982. Student, Cleve. Inst. Music, 1932-38; studies with Victor DeGomez, Cleve., 1938-40; studies with Leonard Rose, 1941-43. Cellist Gold Trio, Cleve., 1935-46, Paul Whiteman and Cleve. Orch., 1940; musician, actor 170 films numerous studios, Los Angeles and Las Vegas, Nev., 1947—, Jack Benny TV Show, L.A., 1953-70; cellist numerous symphonies and ballet cos., L.A., 1955-65; condr. Beverly Hills (Calif.) Ensemble, Las Vegas, 1965—; cellist TV commls., L.A., 1960-73; condr. Las Vegas Pops Orch., 1977—; prin. cellist/soloist Nat. Sr. Symphony, New London, Conn., 1990-95; prin. cellist, soloist Las Vegas Civic Symphony, 1994—; pres. Gold 'N' Cello Rec. Co., 1964—. Performer numerous recs. and club shows, Los Angeles and Las Vegas, 1947—. Grantee Cleve. Inst. Music, 1935, 36, Nev. State Council for Arts, 1977-80. Mem. SAG, Am. Fedn. Musicians, B'nai B'rith. Democrat. Jewish. Club: Scrabble (Las Vegas). Avocations: gardening, tennis, bowling, travel. Home and Office: 2416 Laurie Dr Las Vegas NV 89102-2104

GOLD, JEFFREY PHILIP, cardiothoracic surgeon; b. N.Y.C., Aug. 16, 1952. BSE in Theoretical & Applied Mechanics, Cornell U., 1974, MD, 1978. Intern in gen. surgey The N.Y. Hosp., N.Y.C., 1978-79, resident, 1979-82, adminstrv. chief resident, 1982-83, attending cardiothoracic surgeon, attending pediatrician, 1993-96; resident cardiothoracic surgery Brigham & Women's Hosp., Boston, 1983-84; resident pediatric cardiothoracic surgey Boston Children's Hosp., 1984-85; asst. prof. surgery cardiothoracic surgery Hosp. Spl. Surgery, 1983-91, asst. prof. pediatrics cardiothoracic surgery, 1983-91, assoc. prof., 1991-94; cardiothoracic surgeon-in-chief Albert Einstein Coll. Medicine, 1987—, Montefiore Med. Ctr., 1996—; prof. cardiothoracic surgery Med. Coll. Columbia U., 1993-96; prof., chmn. Unified Dept. Cardiothoracic Surgery Albert Einstein Coll. Medicine, 1996—, prof. pedicatrics cardiothoracic surgery; instr. surgery Cornell Med. Coll., biology Cornell Arts Coll., physics, grad. bioengring. Cornell Engring. Coll., undergrad. bioengring ; clin. fellow surgery Harvard Med. Sch.; clin. instr. Cornell U. Coll. Medicine Surgery; instr., prosecutor Cornell U. Coll. Medicine Anatomy; program lectr. Surgeon's Asst. Program Cornell U.; dir. Montefiore Thoracic Surgery Tng. Program; co-dir. Montefiore-Einstein Cardiovascular Ctr. Assn. Abstract editor Surgery Gynecology & Obs.; editor: Internat. Dictionary of Biology & Medicine in Pediatric & General Surgery; sr. dept. editor Infections in Surgery; contbr. articles to profl. jours. Com. advisor N.Y. State Cardiac Adv. Com. John T. Hirschl scholar; recipient Degenshein award Greater N.Y. Breast Cancer Group, 1983, Excellence in Profl. & Scholarly Pubs. award Assn. Am. Pub., 1993, Acad. Excellence in Medicine award Merck Sharp & Dohme, Med. Scholarship award Lange Pubs.; named The Best Drs. in Am. Am. Health Mag., Best Drs. in N.Y. N.Y. Mag.; #1 rated cardiac surgeon N.Y. State Dept. Health. 1991, 92, 93; ann. endowed lectureship Jeffrey P. Gold Professordhip in Cardiothoracic Surgery, 1996. Fellow AMA, NIH, Am. Assn. Thoracic Surgeons (young profs. com.), Am. Coll. Angiology, Am. Coll. Cardiology, Am. Coll. Chest Physicians (surg. liaison com., program com. 1995, 96, surg. forum chmn. 1995), Am. Coll. Surgeons, Am. Heart Assn. (bd. dirs. 1995—, devel. com. 1995—, gala planning com. 1995, 96, 97), Assn. Acad. Surgery, Assn. Advancement Med. Instrumentation, N.Y. Acad. Medicine (adv. com., bioengring. com.), Internat. Soc. Cardiac Transplantation, Mass. Med. Soc., Nat. Assn. Advancement Sci., N.Y. Cardiol. Soc., N.Y. Pediat. Soc., N.Y. Soc. Thoracic Surgery (pres. 1994-95, v.p. 1993-94, sec.-treas. 1988-93, chmn. post-grad. edn. 1999—), N.Y. Soc. Cardiology (bd. dirs.), N.Y. State Soc. Surgeons, Royal Soc. Medicine, Soc. Thoracic Surgeons, Soc. Univ. Surgeons, Tau Beta Pi (Eminent Engr. award 1983), Thoracic Surgery Dirs. Assn. (curriculum implementation task force, prerequisite edn. task force). Office: Montefiore Med Ctr 111 E 210th St Bronx NY 10467-2401

GOLD, MARK STEPHEN, psychopharmacologist, physician; b. N.Y.C., May 6, 1949; s. Meyer M. and Helene (Levy) G.; m. Janice Finn, June 19, 1971; 4 children. BA, Washington U., 1967; MD, U. Fla., 1975. Neurobehavior fellow Yale U. Sch. Medicine, 1975-78; dir. rsch. Fair Oaks Hosp., Summit, N.J., 1978-91; vis. prof. psychiatry and neurosci. Coll. Medicine U. Fla., 1991—, prof. dept. neurosci., psychiatry, cmty. health, family med., 1992—, disting. prof., 1999—; cons. substance abuse unit Yale U. Sch. Medicine, 1979-89; founder Nat. Cocaine Hotline 800-COCAINE, 1983; cons. Office Drug Abuse Policy White House, 1984-86; presdl. appointee White House Conf. for Drug Free Am., 1988, William Bennett Kitchen Cabinet, 1988-90; spl. cons. Office Nat. Drug Policy, 1995—; mem. adv. bd. Am. Coun. Drug Edn., DEA Mus.; bd. dirs. P.R.I.D.E., Physicians for Prevention, DARE, Child Welfare League, Nat. Families in Action, Mus. Sci. and History, Gateway Rehab. Svcs. Author: 800-Cocaine, 1984, Stop Drugs at Work, 1986, Wonder Drugs, 1987, The Good News About Depression, 1987, rev. edit., 1995, The Facts About Drugs and Alcohol, 1987, Marijuana, 1989, The Good News About Panic, Anxiety and Phobias, 1989, Alcohol, 1991, Dual Diagnosis in Substance Abuse, 1991, The Good News About Drugs and Alcohol, 1991, Cocaine, 1993, Pharmacological Therapies for Drug and Alcohol Addiction, 1995, Tobacco, 1995, Smoking and Illicit Drug Use, 1999; editor-in-chief Facts About Tobacco, Alcohol and other Drugs; co-editor Internat. Jour. Psychiatry in Medicine, Advances in Substance and Alcohol Abuse, Jour. Substance Abuse Treatment, ASAM Prins. Addiction Medicine, Am. Jour. Drug and Alcohol; editor drugs and alcohol lifescape.com; contbr. articles to profl. jours. and books; contbr. Internet content Koop.com, Lifescript.com, and uptodateinc.com. Recipient Seymour F. Lustman award for rsch. Yale U. Sch. Medicine, 1978, Founds Fund prize for rsch. in psychiatry Am. Psychiat. Assn. Found., 1981, Presdl. award for disting. leadership in psychiat. rsch. Nat. Assn. Pvt. Psychiat. Hosps., 1982, Silver Anvil award, Am. Coun. Drug Edn., 1984, Nat. Fedn. Parents award, 1986; named one of Today's Most Valuable Persons, USA Today, 1986, one of People of Yr., 1987, one of Best Psychiatrists in Am., Good Housekeeping, 1995, one of Best Doctors in Am., 1993—; NIMH grantee; named Disting. Alumni Washington U. Fellow Am. Coll. Clin. Pharmacology, Am. Psychiat. Assn., Am. Coll. Forensic Medicine; mem. AAAS, Am. Soc. Addiction Medicine, Soc. Neurosci., Biol. Psychiatry, Internat. Soc. Psychoneuroendocrinology. Achievements include patentee in field. Office: Brain Inst Depts Neurosci and Psychiatry PO Box 100246 Gainesville FL 32610-0246

GOLD, PHRADIE KLING See KLING, PHRADIE

GOLDAMMER, JOHANN GEORG ANDREAS, scientist; b. Marburg, Lahn, Germany, Aug. 23, 1949; s. Kurt and Inge (Rodewald) G.; m. Dorothea C. Knappe, Apr. 10, 1982; 1 child, Katharina. Diploma in forest sci., U. Freiburg, Germany, 1977, Dr.rer.nat., 1983, Dr.rer.nat. habilitation, 1994. Cert. state forester Hesse State Forest Svc., Wiesbaden, Germany, 1979. Asst. prof. Inst. Forest Zoology, Freiburg, 1979-84; rsch. scientist Freiburg U., 1985-90; sr. scientist Max Planck Inst. for Chemistry, Mainz and Freiburg, Germany, 1990—; tech., sci. adviser UN-ECE/FAO/GTZ, 1984—; co-convener IGBP-IGAC-BIBEX Steering Com., 1998—; v.p. German Soc. for Tropical Ecology, 1991-94; chmn. IUFRO Group Forest Fire Rsch., Vienna, Austria, 1992-95; head Global Fire Monitoring Ctr. Author: Feuer in Waldökosystemen der Tropen und Subtropen, 1993; editor: Fire in the Tropical Biota, 1990, Fire in the Environment, 1993; editor UN Internat. Forest Fire News, 1988—. Leader UN-FAO/ECE/ILO Team of Specialists on Forest Fire, Geneva, 1994—; mem. sci. coun. Siberian Ctr. for Ecology, Krasnoyarsk, Russian Fedn., 1995—; mem. German IDNDR Com., 1998-2000; mem. exec. bd. German Com. Disaster Reduction, 2000—. Comdr. German Navy Res., 1968-72. Decorated Silver Cross of Honour, German Armed Forces, Bonn, 1983, Govt. of Russia medal of honour for protecting forests Russia, Moscow, 1999. Mem. Soc. Am. Foresters (corr.), Assn. German Naval Officers. Office: Fire Ecology Rsch Group, Freiburg Univ, D-79085 Freiburg Germany

GOLDANIGA, ALESSANDRO EDOARDO, chemical engineer, researcher; b. Milan, Aug. 31, 1971; s. Gilberto Edoardo and Marcella Luisella (Cossali) G.; m. Anna Truzzi. Grad., Milan Poly., 1995, PhD in Chem. Engring., 2000. Engring., 1996. Chem. engr. Milan Poly., 1995—, cons. researcher, 1996—. Contbr. articles to profl. jours. Lt. Aeronautic, 1995—. Roman Catholic. Avocations: collecting stamps, reading, squash.

GOLDANSKII, VITALII IOSIFOVICH, chemist, physicist; b. Vitebsk, USSR, June 18, 1923; s. Iosif Efimovich and Yudif' Iosifovna (Melamed) G.; m. Lyudmila Nikolaevna Semenova; children: Dmitrii, Andrei. Grad. in Chemistry, Moscow U., 1944, M of Chemistry, 1947, DSc in Physics, 1954. Scientist Inst. Chem. Physics-USSR Acad. Scis., Moscow, 1942-52, 1961—, from div. head to dir., 1988—; sr. scientist P.N. Lebedev Phys. Inst.-USSR Acad. Scis., Moscow, 1952-61; asst. prof. Phys.-Tech. Inst., Moscow, 1947-51; asst. prof., then prof. Inst. Phys. Engring., Moscow, 1951—. Author: Kinematics of Nuclear Reactions, 1959, Mössbauer Effect and its Applications in Chemistry, 1963, Physical Chemistry of Positron and Positronium, 1968, Tunneling Phenomena in Chemical Physics, 1986, many others; contbr. numerous articles and revs. to profl. jours.; patentee (numerous) in field. Chmn. Russian Pugwash Com., Moscow, 1987—; people's dep. of USSR; mem. com. fgn. affairs Supreme Soviet of USSR, 1989-92. Decorated Lenin Order, Order of October Revolution, numerous other orders and medals; recipient Lenin prize, 1980; Golden Mendeleev medal USSR Acad. Scis., 1975, Karpinsky prize Friedrich von Schiller Found., Hamburg, Germany, 1983, Boris Pregel award N.Y. Acad. Scis., 1990, Alexander von Humboldt award, Germany, 1991, Golden Semenov medal Russian Acad. Scis., 1996. Fellow Am. Chem. Soc. (hon.), Am. Phys. Soc., Am. Acad. Arts and Scis., Am. Philos Soc., Acad. Scis. German Dem. Republic, Royal Swedish Acad. Scis., Royal Danish Acad. Scis. and Lettrs, Deutsche Akademie der Naturforscher Leopoldina, World Acad. Arts and Sci., Hungarian Eotvos Lorand Phys. Soc.; mem. NAS USA (fgn., assoc.), N.Y. Acad. Scis. (life.), Russian Acad. Scis., Finnish Acad. Scis. (fgn.), Acad. Europaea, Acad. Georgia. Avocations: writing humor and aphorisms, record collecting, movies, CDs, videos. Home: Bldg 8 Apt 66, Ulitsa Zelinskogo 38, Moscow 117334, Russia Office: Russian Acad of Scis, Inst Chem Phys Ulitsa Kosygina 4, Moscow 117334, Russia

GOLDBERG, ALAN JOEL, lawyer; b. Bklyn., Jan. 22, 1943; s. Ralph and Dorothy (Rolnick) G.; 1 child, Cary Adam. BA, U. Miami, 1965, JD, 1968. Bar: Fla. 1968, U.S. Supreme Ct., U.S. Ct. Appeals (4th cir.). Ptnr. Goldberg, Young, Goldberg & Borkson, P.A., Ft. Lauderdale, Fla., 1968-82; atty. City of Margate, Fla., 1969-70, City of Tamarac, Fla., 1970-71; pvt. practice Ft. Lauderdale, 1982—; pres. Diversified Oil Co., 1996—, Diversified Realty Holdings Co., 1996—. Mem. Citizen's Task Force on Transp., State of Fla.; mem. Broward County Planning Coun., 1984-92, chmn., 1988, 91; pres. Boys and Girls Clubs of Broward County, Inc., bd. dirs., 1995—, pres. bd. dirs., 1999-2000. Mem. ABA, Fla. Bar Assn. Republican. Office: PO Box 13111 Port Everglades Sta 999 Eller Dr Ste A8 Fort Lauderdale FL 33316

GOLDBERG, AVRAM JACOB, consulting and investing company executive, arbitrator; b. Boston, Jan. 26, 1930; s. Lewis and Mildred (Levine) G.; m. Carol Rabb, June 18, 1950; children: Deborah Beth, Joshua Rabb. AB magna cum laude, Harvard U., 1951, JD cum laude, 1954; LLD (hon.), Northeastern U., 1982. Bar: Mass. 1954, U.S. Supreme Ct 1954. Assoc. firm Hill Barlow Goodale & Wiswall, Boston, 1954-55; with The Stop & Shop Cos. Inc., Boston, 1958-89, exec. v.p., 1968-71, pres., 1971-85, chief exec. officer, 1979-89, chmn. bd., 1985-89; chmn. Avcar Group with Whole Food Markets, Austin, Tex.; vis. prof. mgmt. MBA program Babson Coll.; disting. vis. lectr. Boston U. Sch. Bus. Mgmt., 1990-91; bd. dirs. Boston Safe Deposit & Trust Co., Whole Foods Markets, Inc., Ekco Group, Inc.; chmn. The Avcar Group, Ltd., 1989—. Mem. class com. Harvard Class of 1951, past class sec.; trustee Mass. Eye and Ear Infirmary; past trustee Boston Coll.; overseer Beth Israel-Deaconess Med. Ctr., Boston; hon. life trustee Beth Israel Hosp.; hon. trustee, mem. exec. bd. Combined Jewish Philanthropies Greater Boston; past trustee Boston Plan for Excellence in the Pub. Schs.; past chmn. exec. com. Alden Seminars on Higher Edn. former mem. bd. dirs. Mass. Bus. Devel. Corp.; former chmn. Brookline Redevel. Authority; former mem. corp. Boston Mus. Sci.; past chmn., bd. overseers, trustee Boston Symphony Orch.; bd. dirs., Food Mktg. Inst.; past bd. dirs. Harvard Bus. Sch. Assocs., Mass. Bus. Roundtable; founder The Ireland Fund (co-chair Boston Dinner 1992), chmn., bd. dirs. Ctr. for Collaborative Edn. Metro Boston. Lt. j.g. USNR, 1955-58. Named Man of Yr. Boston Latin Sch. Alumni Assn., 1987; fellow Brandeis U. Fellow Am. Acad. Arts and Sci., Food Mktg. Inst. (S.R. Rabb award 1993); mem. Boston C. of C. (bd. dirs., v.p.), Confrerie des Chevaliers du Tastevin, Confrerie de la Chaine des Rotisseurs (comdr., bailli honoraire), Phi Beta Kappa (hon. Alpha chpt. Mass.). Jewish (trustee temple). Office: Avcar Group Ltd 225 Franklin St Ste 2700 Boston MA 02110-2804 Office: Whole Food Market Inc 601 N Lamar Ste 300 Austin TX 78703*

GOLDBERG, DAVID BRYAN, biomedical researcher; b. San Bernardino, Calif., Mar. 29, 1954; s. Gus and Rose (Goldrich) G.; m. Dianne Rae, Dec. 19, 1976; children: Jason, Mark, Eric, Ashley. BA, UCLA, 1976, PhD, 1987. Rsch. asst. Calif. State U., L.A., 1976-79; rsch. assoc. UCLA, 1979-82; sci. project mgr. Alpha Therapeutic Corp., L.A., 1989—; adj. prof. Chaffey Coll., Alta Loma, Calif., 1990—. Contbr. articles to N.Y. Acad. Scis., Jour. Clin. Apheresis, Proceedings of ASCO, FASEB Jour., Fedn. Preceedings, Nat. Hemophelia Found. Mem. PTA, Alta Loma, 1991. Basic Rsch. grantee, Cancer Rsch. Ctr., 1987, 88, Cancer Seed grantee 1989; Teaching fellow, UCLA, 1982-87, Rsch. fellow II, City of Hope, Duarte, Calif., 1987-89. Mem. Fedn. Am. Socs. Experimental Biology, N.Y. Acad. Sci. Achievements include patents; development of IL-2/LAK immunotherapy for the treatment of malignant melanoma; formulation chemistry; pharmaceutical product and device development. Office: Alpha Therapeutic Corp 1213 John Reed Ct La Puente CA 91745-2405

GOLDBERG, HERB, psychologist, educator; b. Berlin, Germany, July 14, 1937; came to U.S., 1941; s. Jacob and Ella (Nagler) G.; 1 child, Amy Elisabeth. BA cum laude, CUNY, 1958; PhD, Adelphi U., 1963. Lic. psychologist, Calif. Pvt. practice, L.A., 1965—; prof. Calif. State U., L.A. Author: Creative Aggression, 1972, The Hazards of Being Male, 1976, Money Madness, 1978, The New Male, 1979, The Inner Male, 1986, The New Male/Female Relationship, 1982, What Men Really Want, 1991. Mem. APA, Phi Beta Kappa. Office: 3739 Mayfair Dr Los Angeles CA 90065-3208

GOLDBERG, IVAN, ophthalmologist, surgeon; b. Johannesburg, South Africa, Apr. 25, 1947; arrived in Australia, 1962;; s. Ben and Zelda (Y-udelman) G.; m. Vera Katherina Winter, May 25, 1969; children: Daniel, Nicole, Tanya. MB, BS, U. Sydney, Australia, 1971. Intern Sydney Hosp., 1971-72, resident in internal medicine & intensive care, 1972-73; registrar in ophthalmology Prince of Wales Hosp., Sydney, 1973-75, sr. registrar in ophthalmology, 1976-78, dir. glaucoma svc., 1980—; ophthalmology rsch. fellow U. NSW, Sydney, 1975-76; from glaucoma fellow to instr. Washington U., St. Louis, 1978-80; grant reviewer Nat. Health and Med. Rsch. Coun., Australia, 1987—; jour. reviewer and presenter in field. Contbr. articles to profl. jours. V.p. Glaucoma Australia, 1987—; pres. Australasian Jewish Med. Fedn., 1991-94. Fight for Sight fellow, 1979; recipient Nat. Soc. for Prevention Blindness award, 1979; Rsch. grantee Ophthalmic Rsch. Inst. Australia. Fellow Royal Australian Coll. Ophthalmologists (censor-in-chief 1993-99, chmn. part I bd. examiners 1987-93, v.p. elect 199—), Royal Australasian Coll. Surgeons; mem. Cossom Assn. (chmn. 1990-98), Fellowship Jewish Drs. (pres. 1987-91), Am. Glaucoma Soc. (corres. mem.). Jewish. Avocations: music, movies, theatre, tennis, books. Office: Eye Assoc, 187 Macquarie St, 2000 Sydney Australia

GOLDBERG, JAY, lawyer; b. N.Y.C., Jan. 2, 1933; s. Joseph and Lillian (Adler) G.; m. Rema, Dec. 27, 1959; children: Justin, Julie. BA, Bklyn. Coll., 1954; JD, Harvard U., 1957. Bar: N.Y. 1957, U.S. Ct. Appeals (2d, 4th and 9th cirs.) 1971, U.S. Supreme Ct. 1961. Asst. dist. atty. N.Y. County Dist. Atty. Office, N.Y.C., 1957-61; spl. asst. to atty. gen. Washington, 1961-63; spl. asst. to U.S. Atty. no. dist. Hammond, Ind., 1961-67; lawyer, sole practice N.Y.C., 1963—; lectr. trial practice Harvard Law Sch., 1976-88; com. on grievances U.S. Dist. Ct. (so. dist.) N.Y., 1989—. Editorial mgr. White Collar Crime Law Reporter, 1989—; contbr. articles to profl. jours. Recipient Merit award for Advocacy of Individual Rights for Persons Advised, N.Y. Criminal Bar Assn., 1989. Mem. Friars Club (gov. 1988-92). Home: 200 E 65th St New York NY 10021-4451 Office: 250 Park Ave New York NY 10177-0001

GOLDBERG, JORGE, internist; b. Mexico City, Nov. 18, 1954; s. Lova Goldberg and Mina Dryjanski; m. Betty Shteremberg, June 17, 1977; children: Ricardo, Eduardo, Jack. MD, U. Autonoma Mex., Mex., 1977; post-grad., Johns Hopkins Hosp./Sinai Hosp, Balt., 1982. Diplomate Am. Bd. Internal Medicine, Mex. Bd. Internal Medicine, Mex. Bd. Gastroenterology and Endoscopy. Intern Am. Brit. Cowdray Hosp., Mex., 1977-79; resident Johns Hopkins Hosp./Sinai Hosp., Balt., 1979-82; pvt. practice ABC Hosp., Mexico City, 1982—, dir. dept. medicine, 1993; co-dir. Clinica Lomas Atlas, Mexico City, 1999—; dir. Internistas Asociados, Mexico City; mem. adv. bd. IMIFAP, Mex.; advisor Clinica Lomas Altas, Mex. Mem. editl. bd. Revista Anales Medicos, 1997—; contbr. articles to profl. publs. Mem. social com. Bet-El, Mex., 1997—. Jewish. Avocations: music, painting. Fax: 55407300. E-mail: jgold18@yahoo.com. Home: Av Lomas Encanto 32, Lomas Country Club, Mexico City DF 52779, Mexico Office: Internistas Asociados, Palmas 745 PB, Mexico City DF 11000, Mexico

GOLDBERG, LEE WINICKI, furniture company executive; b. Laredo, Tex., Nov. 20, 1932; d. Frank and Goldie (Ostrowiak) Winicki; m. Frank M. Goldberg, Aug. 17, 1952; children: Susan, Arlene, Edward Lewis, Anne Carri. Student, San Diego State U., 1951-52. With United Furniture Co., Inc., San Diego, 1953-83, corp. sec., dir., 1963-83, dir. environ. interiors, 1970-83; founder Drexel-Heritage store Edwards Interiors subs. United Furniture, 1975; founding ptnr., v.p. FLJB Corp., 1976-86; founding ptnr., sec., treas. Sea Fin., Inc., 1980; founding ptnr. First Nat. Bank San Diego, 1982. Den mother Boy Scouts Am., San Diego, 1965; vol. Am. Cancer Soc., San Diego, 1964-69; chmn. jr. matrons United Jewish Fedn., San Diego, 1958; del. So. Pacific Coast region Hadassah Conv., 1960, pres. Galilee group San Diego chpt., 1960-61; supporter Marc Chagall Nat. Mus., Nice France, U. Calif. at San Diego Cancer Ctr. Foun., Smithsonian Instn., Los Angeles County Mus., San Diego Mus. Contemporary Art, San Diego Mus. Art; pres. San Diego Opera, 1992-94. Recipient Hadassah Service award San Diego chpt., 1958-59; named Woman of Dedication by Salvation Army Women's Aux., 1992, Patron of Arts by Rancho Santa Fe Country Friends, 1993. Democrat. Jewish.

GOLDBERG, MARK JOEL, lawyer; b. Pitts., June 2, 1941; s. Charles J. and Eleanore (Letwin) G.; m. Wendy Witt, Dec. 23, 1988; children: Michael, Wendy, Josh, Jamie. BA, Washington and Jefferson Coll., 1963; JD, Case Western Res. U., 1966. Bar: Pa. 1966, Ohio 1966, U.S. Tax Ct. 1969, U.S. Supreme Ct. 1972. Assoc. Jerome Silver, Cleve., 1966-67; pvt. practice, Pitts., 1967-69; ptnr. Goldberg & Wedner, Pitts., 1969-80; ptnr., shareholder Gillotti Goldberg & Capristo, Pitts., 1981-91, Goldberg Gentile & Voelker, Pitts., 1991-92, Goldberg, Gruener, Gentile, Horoho & Avalli, P.C., Pitts., 1992—; mem. drafting com. Pa. Divorce Code, 1978-80, 88; frequent lectr. Pa. Bar Inst., Pa. Trial Lawyers Assn., Am. Acad. Matrimonial Lawyers. Contbr. articles to profl. jours. Committeeman Dem. Party, Pitts., 1970's; pres. bd. dirs. Parent and Child Guidance Ctr., Pitts., 1984-86. Fellow Am. Acad. Matrimonial Lawyers (pres. Pa. chpt. 1988-90, nat. bd. govs. 1991-95); mem. Am. Coll. Family Trial Lawyers (diplomate, officer), Allegheny County Bar Assn. (coun. mem. family law sect. 1972—, chmn. 1982-84), Pa. Bar Assn. (family law sect. chmn. 1986-88), Westmoreland Country Club, Rivers Club. Jewish. Avocations: golf, travel. Home: 14 Carmel Ct Pittsburgh PA 15221-3618 Office: Goldberg Gruener Et Al 230 Grant Bldg Pittsburgh PA 15219-2200

GOLDBERG, MARTIN, physician, educator; b. Phila., Sept. 15, 1930; s. Samuel and Esther (Shreibman) G.; m. Lynn Taksey, June 17, 1951 (dec. Aug. 31 1976); children: Meryl I., Karen L., Dara S.; m. Marion Lindblad, May 26, 1978; 1 child, David S. BA, Temple U., 1951, MD, 1955; MA (hon.), U. Pa., 1971. Diplomate: Am. Bd. Internal Medicine (chmn. nephrology com. 1976-79, bd. govs. 1976-79), Nat. Bd. Med. Examiners.

Intern Phila. Gen. Hosp., 1955-56, resident, 1957-59, sr. attending physician, 1970-76; resident Cleve. Clinic, 1956-57; fellow nephrology Hosp. U. Pa., Phila., 1959-61; sr. attending physician Hosp. U. Pa., 1962-79; mem. faculty U. Pa. Sch. Medicine, 1960-79, prof. medicine, 1970-79, chief renal electrolyte sect., 1966-79, acting chmn. dept. medicine, 1975-76; sr. attending physician Phila. VA Hosp., 1968-79; Gordon and Helen Hughes Taylor prof. medicine U. Cin., 1979-86; chmn. internal medicine U. Cin. Coll. Med. and Hosp., 1979-86; prof. medicine Temple U. Sch. Medicine, Phila., 1986-96, dean, vice pres., 1986-89, prof. emeritus, 1997—, asst. to dean for computer assisted instrn., 1997—; chmn. sci. adv. com. Gen. Clin. Rsch. Ctr. Temple U. Hosp., 1993—; mem. sci. adv. bd. Nat. Kidney Found., 1970-76; chmn. kidney council Am. Heart Assn., 1973-74; study cons. NIH, 1968-72, 82-85; bd. mgrs. St. Christopher's Hosp. Children, 1986-89. Mem. editl. com. Jour. Clin. Investigation, 1969-70, Kidney Internat., 1972-74, Jour. Mineral and Electrolyte Metabolism, 1977-91; mem. editl. bd. Am. Jour. Hypertension, 1990-97; physician-editor Nephrology MKSAP Am. Coll. Physicians, 1991-94; assoc. editor MKSAP 11, MKSAP 12, ACP, 1996—. Recipient Alumni prize Temple U. Sch. Medicine, 1955, Lindback award for distinguished teaching U. Pa., 1972; Disting. Med. Scientist of Yr. award Med. Alumni Temple U. Sch. Medicine, 1985; Research Career Devel. award NIH, 1963-70, Honoree of Yr. award Greater Del. Valley Kidney Found., 1997, A.N. Richards award for disting. contbns. to nephrology U. Pa., 1998; research grantee NIH, 1962-89; research grantee John Hartford Found., 1970-73, Centennial award Assn. Chmn. of Depts. Physiology, 1989. Fellow ACP (nat. sci. program com. 1976-81), Am. Coll. Clin. Pharmacology, Royal Soc. Medicine; mem. Assn. Am. Med. Colls. (coun. of deans 1986-89), Assn. Am. Physicians, Am. Soc. Clin. Investigation, Am. Physiol. Soc., Am. Fedn. Clin. Rsch. (chmn. ea. sect. 1967), Am. Soc. Nephrology (sec.-treas. 1975-78), Interurban Clin. Club, Internat. Soc. Nephrology (coun. 1975-84), Am. Med. Informatics Assn., Coll. Physicians Phila., Physicians for Social Responsibility (adv. bd. Phila. chpt.), Alpha Omega Alpha. Rsch. and publs. in renal physiology and disease; electrolyte and acid-base metabolism, computer-assisted instruction and diagnosis. Office: Temple U Health Scis Ctr Nephrology Parkinson Pavilion Philadelphia PA 19140

GOLDBERG, MARTIN STANFORD, lawyer; b. Youngstown, Ohio, July 11, 1924; s. George and Bee (Walker) G.; m. Donna Mae Lowry, Nov. 18, 1962; children: Jeffrey A., Jeralyn Goldberg Mercer. B.A., Ohio State U., 1952, J.D., 1952. Bar: Ohio 1952, Calif. 1981. Sole practice law Youngstown, Ohio, 1952—. Served with USAF, 1942-45, PTO. Decorated D.F.C. Mem. ABA, Calif. Bar Assn., Ohio Bar Assn., Mahoning County Bar Assn., Am. Trial Lawyers Assn. Republican. Jewish. Lodges: Masons, Friars Club. Avocations: reading, writing, music. Home: 74513 Old Prospector Trl Palm Desert CA 92260-5624 Office: 6600 Summit Dr Canfield OH 44406-9510

GOLDBERG, MARVIN ALLEN, lawyer, business consultant; b. Phila., Jan. 9, 1943; s. Daniel and Elizabeth (Katz) G.; m. Kathryn Elizabeth Balotsky, Apr. 27, 1974; children: Robert Andrew, MaryBeth Anne. BS, Temple U., 1964, JD, 1967. Bar: Pa. 1968, U.S. Dist. Ct. (ea. dist.) Pa. 1980, U.S. Supreme Ct. 1976. Estate tax atty. IRS, Phila., 1967-68; staff atty. Legal Aid Soc. Northampton County, Easton, Pa., 1969-70, Northampton County Pub. Defender, Easton, Pa., 1969-70; pvt. practice law Phila., 1970-76; tchr. Inst. for Paralegal Tng., Phila., 1973; staff atty. Legal Aid Soc. Phila., 1974-76; CEO Goldberg & Assocs., P.C., Phila., 1976—; cons. Butcher Trade Exchange, Ft. Washington, Pa., 1982-92; dir. North Am. Resources, Phila.; pres. MAGCO, Inc., Mt. Laurel, N.J., 1989-92. Mem. Chestnut St. Assn., Phila; dir. Sr. Citizen Judicare Project, Phila., 1977. With USAF, 1967-73. Mem. ABA, Phila. Bar Assn., Phila. Trial Lawyers Assn., Assn. Trial Lawyers Am., Pa. Trial Lawyers Assn., Attys. Across Am. (founding mem.), Jewish War Vets, Beta Gamma Sigma, Phi Alpha Delta. Avocations: running, sailing, chess, Algebra, 19th century physics. Office: Goldberg & Assocs PC 1334 Walnut St Fl 5 Philadelphia PA 19107-5311

GOLDBERG, MAXWELL HENRY, retired humanities educator; b. Malden, Mass., Oct. 22, 1907; s. Felix and Zelda Janet (Kushlansky) G.; m. Shirley Alberta Bliss, Sept. 2, 1937 (div. Nov. 1957); children: Naomi Jean, Deborah Martha, Rachel Elizabeth; m. Ethel Stella Zeidman, July 29, 1962. BS, U. Mass., 1928; MA, Yale U., 1932, PhD, 1933; LHD (hon.), U. Mass., 1988. From instr. to prof., dept. head U. Mass., Amherst, 1928-61, First Commonwealth prof. humanities, 1960-61, emeritus Commonwealth prof. humanities, 1962—; prof. & dir. humanities U. Fla., Tampa, 1960-61; prof. English & humanities, assoc. dir. Humanities Ctr. for Continuing Liberal Edn. Pa. State U., State College, 1962-72, emeritus prof. English & humanities, 1972—; Helmus Disting. prof. humanities & lit. Converse Coll., Spartanburg, S.C., 1972-77, emeritus prof. humanities & lit., 1977—; lectr., author Grad. Sem. for Fed. Execs., Washington, 1962-63; dir., editor humanities project on technol. change and human values CCLE-IBM, 1962-72; lectr. Danforth Disting. Lectr. Program Assn. Am. Colls., N.Y.C., 1968-72; field reader U.S. Office HEW, Washington, 1968-72; exec. dir. Humanities Ctr. for Liberal Edn. in an Indsl. Soc., 1951-62, pres., 1963-74; chief humanities cons. Morehouse Coll., 1972-87; feature writer Spartanburg Herald-Jour., 1990—. Author: Design in Liberal Learning, 1971, Thomas Carlyle's Relationships with The 'Edinburgh Review, 1971; contbr. The University Today, Its Role and Place in Society, An International Study, 1960; author, editor: Blindness Research--The Expanding Frontiers, 1969; editor, contbr. Telics and Holistic Edn. for the Technol. Age: Internat. Jour. Innovative Higher Edn., 1985; editor: Automation, Education and Human Values, 1966, Thomas Carlyle Family Letters, 1987. Pres. Caring Coalition of Spartanburg, 1992—; bd. dirs. Spartanburg Repertory Co., 1989-94, Bicentennial Forums of Greater Spartanburg, 1973-78; mem. ednl. adv. com. S.C. Appalachian Coun. Govts., Greenville, 1989-94; bd. dirs., pres. Shepherd's Ctr. of Spartanburg, 1983-89; pres. Friends of Pub. Libr. of Spartanburg, 1980-87. Ford Found. fellow, 1959-60; recipient David W. Reid award for achievement in arts Arts Coun. Spartanburg County, 1981, Judge Davenport disting. svc. award Mental Health Assn., Piedmont, 1991; scholar Yale U., 1932-33; named disting. alumnus U. Mass. Alumni Assn., 1963, Ann. Friend of Pub. Libr. of Spartanburg County, 1985, Outstanding Older S. Carolinian Appalachian Region, 1993; U. Mass. Hillel Living and Lng. Cmty. dedicated in his honor, 1998. Mem. MLA (life), Coll. English Assn. (past v.p., exec. dir., editor 1950-59, prof. of yr. 1989), Oak Ridge Assn. Univs. (lectr., author 1965), Phi Kappa Phi (chpt. pres. 1936-37), Alpha Epsilon Pi (Gitelson meml. medallion 1945). Jewish. Avocations: gardening, photography.

GOLDBERG, PAMELA WINER, business manager; b. Boston, Oct. 14, 1955; d. Arthur Leonard and Marilyn (Miller) Winer; children: Frederick Warren, Alyssa Rachel, Meredith Hayley. BA, Tufts U., 1977; MBA, Stanford U., 1981. Day care dir. Community Action Inc., Haverhill, Mass., 1977-79; lending assoc. Bankers Trust Co., N.Y.C., 1980-81; mgr., bank officer, corp. fin. dept. Citicorp, N.Y.C., 1981-82; assoc. dir., mergers and acquisitions group State Street Bank, Boston, 1983-85; ind. strategic cons. Wellesley, Mass., 1986-97; dir. bus. rels. Babson Coll., Wellesley, 1998—. Bd. Friends Beth Israel Hosp., Boston, 1987-96; mem. exec. bd. trustees Temple Beth Elohim, Wellesley, 1992-2000, treas., 1997-2000; trustee Recuperative Ctr., Boston, 1988-95; bd. dirs. Wellesley League Women Voters, 1995-98; mem. Hunnewell Sch. PTO Bd., 1991-96. Avocations: swimming, tennis, singing. Home: 34 Ivy Rd Wellesley MA 02482-4554 Office: Babson Coll Babson Park MA 02457

GOLDBERG, PAUL BERNARD, gastroenterologist, clinical researcher; b. Bklyn., Apr. 11, 1950; s. Samuel and Eva (Turkenitz) G.; m. Harriet Ruth Ferrer, July 8, 1973 (div. 1987); children: Deborah Lynn, Susan Michelle; m. Mary Alice Denaro, June 23, 1990; 1 child, Laura Alicia. BA in Chemistry summa cum laude, Cornell U., 1967-71, MD, 1971-75. Diplomate Am. Bd. Internal Medicine, Am. Bd. Gastroenterology. Intern in medicine Hosp. of U. of Pa., Phila., 1975-76, resident in medicine, 1976-78, fellow in gastroenterology, 1978-80, fellow in nutritional support svc., 1979-80; med. coord. and founder nutritional support svc. Lakeland (Fla.) Gen. Hosp., 1980-81; attending physician Halifax Med. Ctr., 1980—, Ormond Meml. Hosp., 1980—, Atlantic Med. Ctr., 1980—, Fish Meml. Hosp., New Smyrna Beach, Fla., 1989—, Peninsula Med. Ctr., 1989-94; pres. Sunshine Health Care Plan, Inc., 1983-86, v.p., 1986-87; chief staff Humana Hosp., Daytona Beach, 1986-88, trustee, 1986-89, mem. exec. com., 1984-91; mem. rev. bd. Coastal Instnl. Rev., 1990-93, chmn. rev. bd., 1993-96; expert reviewer Fla. Dept. Profl. Regulation, 1990—; pres. med. staff Halifax Hosp., 1996-97; clin. asst. prof. medicine dept. family medicine U. South Fla. Rschr. and author in field. Physician adv. Daytona chpt. Crohn's and Colitis Found., 1991-95. Recipient Nat. award Ford Future Scientists of Am., 1967, Westinghouse Sci. Talent Search finalist, 1967. Fellow ACP, Am. Coll. Gastroenterology; mem. Am. Gastroent. Soc., Am. Soc. Gastrointestinal Endoscopy, Am. Soc. for Parenteral and Enteral Nutrition (pres. Fla. chpt. 1991-92), Volusia County Med. Soc. (exec. com. 1991-94, co-chmn. mini internship program 1992-94), Fla. Gastrointestinal Soc., Fla. med. Assn. (alt. del. to ho. of dels. 1990-95), Fla. Assn. Nutritional Support (1st pres.), Rotary, Phi Beta Kappa, Alpha Omega Alpha. Office: Gastrointestinal Assocs 201 N Clyde Morris Blvd Ste 100 Daytona Beach FL 32114-2765

GOLDBERG, RAY ALLAN, agribusiness educator; b. Fargo, N.D., Oct. 19, 1926; s. Max and Anne G.; m. Thelma R. Englander, May 20, 1956; children: Marc E., Jennifer E., Jeffrey L. AB, Harvard U., 1948, MBA, 1950; PhD, U. Minn., 1952. Officer, dir. Moorhead (Minn.) Seed & Grain Co., 1952-62; dir. Experience, Inc., Mpls., 1963-78, Arbor Acres Farm, Inc., N.Y.C., H.K. Webster Co.; mem. faculty Harvard U. Grad. Bus. Sch., 1955—, Moffett prof. agr. and bus., 1970-97; Moffett prof. agr. and bus. emeritus, 1997—; also dir. continuing edn. programs, participant seminars Harvard U. Grad. Bus. Sch.; bd. dirs. All-Flow, Inc., RDO Equiptment, Daymon Assocs., Food One, Internet Commerce Sys., Inc., Veritec, Cyber Crop.com, Smithfield Foods; hon. prof. Royal Agrl. Coll., Cirencester, England, 1996; vis. prof. U. Minn. Grad. Sch., summer 1960; adv. coun. Foods Multinat., Inc., 1972-77; mem. agrl. investment com. John Hancock Ins. Co., 1971-95; cons. in field, 1955—; adviser Instituto Centroamericano de Administracion de Empresa, Managua, Nicaragua, 1973—, Instituto Panamericano de Alta Direccion de Empressa, Mexico City, 1973—, U.S. Comptroller of Currency, 1975—, Food and Agr. Policy Project, Ctr. Nat. Policy, 1984—; mem. study team, subgroup chmn. world food and nutrition study NRC, 1975—; mem. com. tech. factor contbg. to nation's fgn. trade positions Nat. Acad. Engring., 1976—; chmn. agribus. adv. com. on Caribbean Basin USDA, 1982—; mem. com. on indsl. policy for developing countries Commn. on Engring. and Tech. Systems, NRC, 1982—; mem. task force on agr. Fowler-McCracken Commn., 1984—; adv. bd. The First Mercantile Currency Fund Inc., 1985—; internat. adv. bd. Atlantic Exchange Program, 1987—; mem. V.I. Lenin All-Union Acad. of Agrl. Scis., 1988—; mem. U.S. Presdl. Econ. Del. to Poland, Nov., 1989; scientific advisory bd. Sepragen Corp., 1993—, Inst. Food Technologists, 1999—; chmn. joint bus. scientific pub. policy consumer policy tech. com. U.S. Food System and Seminar, 1994—; mem. internat. bd. visitors Zamorano, 1995—; mem. adv. com. Foodfit.com., 1999—, sci. adv. bd., IFT/FDA Rsch. Contract, 1999, chmn. adv. panel for World Bank Guide to Developing Agrl. Markets and Agro-Enterprises, 1999; dir. Genomic FX, LP, 2000—. Author numerous books, 1948— including Agribusiness Management for Developing Countries-Latin America, 1974, (with Lee F. Schrader) Farmers' Cooperative and Federal Income Taxes, 1974, (with John T. Dunlop et al) The Lessons of Wage and Price Controls-The Food Sector, 1977, (with Richard C. McGinity et al), Agribusiness Management for Devloping Countries-Southeast Asia Corn Study, 1979; editor: Research in Domestic and International Agribusiness Management, Vol. 1, 1980, Vol. 2, 1981, Vol. 3, 1982, Vol. 4, 1983, Vol. 5, 1984, Vol. 6, 1986, Vol. 7, 1987, Vol. 8, 1988, Vol. 9, 1989, Vol. 10, 1981, Vol. 11, 1995, Vol. 12, 1996; co-editor; (with Gerald E. Gaul) New Technologies and the Future of Food and Nutrition, 1991, The Emerging Global Food System: Public and Private Sector Issues, 1993; contbr. numerous articles to profl. jours.; chmn. editl. adv. bd. Agribus.: An Internat. Jour., 1983—. Bd. govs. Internat. Devel. Rsch. Ctr., Govt. of Can., 1978—; trustee Roxbury Latin Sch., Boston, 1973-76, Beth Israel Hosp., Boston, 1978—, mem. com. on patents and tech. transfer, 1982—, chmn. gerontology com., 1991—; mem. adv. com. to prep. sch. New Eng. Conservatory Music, 1974—, assoc. trustee, 1978—; vice chmn. bd. Spoleto Festival U.S.A., 1993; adv. mem. Polish Investment Fund, 1994—; chmn. adv. com. Sonoma Internat. Capital Assocs., 1994—. Recipient Outstanding Alumni award, Dept. Agrl. Econs. U. Minn., 1992. Mem. Royal Agrl. Coll. Eng. (hon. prof. 1996—), V.I. Lenin All-Union Acad. Agrl. Scis. (fgn.), Am. Agrl. Econs. Assn. (editl. coun. 1974-78, nat. agribus. edn. commn. 1988—), Internat. Agribus. Mgmt. Assn. (pres. 1990-92, bd. dirs. 1990—, chmn. Russian food mgmt. program sponsored rsch. project 1994—, coord. nonpartisan ednl.,vt., sci., med. and consumer group for food, safety, nutrition and environ. 1994—), Agribus. Inst. Cambridge (chmn. bd., treas. 1991-93), Am. Mktg. Assn., Am. Dairy Sci. Assn., Food Distbn. Rsch. Soc., Harvard Club (Boston and N.Y.C.), Bus. Coun. for Sustainable Devel. (adv. group for sustainable paper cycle project 1994—). Address: 975 Memorial Dr Apt 701 Cambridge MA 02138-5803

GOLDBERG, RON, plastics broker executive; b. N.Y., Dec. 1, 1954. BA, Queens (N.Y.) Coll., 1976. V.p. Standard Polymers Corp., Tenafly, N.J., 1975-91; pres. RSG Polymer Corp., Stony Brook, N.Y., 1991—. Office: RSG Polymers Corp PO Box 778 Stony Brook NY 11790-0778

GOLDBERG, SIDNEY, editor; b. N.Y.C., Mar. 1, 1931; s. Emanuel and Florence (Fischbein) G.; m. Lucianne S. Cummings, April 10, 1966; children: Joshua John, Jonah Jacob. BA, U. Mich., 1950, MA, 1952; postgrad., NYU, 1952-53. Editor North Am. Newspaper Alliance, N.Y.C., 1957-71; editor Bell-McClure Syndicate, N.Y.C., 1957-71, pres. N. Am. Newspaper Alliance, 1971-72; reporter clk. Washington Post, 1955; fgn. editor World Week Mag., N.Y.C., 1956-57; v.p., dir. internat. newspaper ops. United Media, N.Y.C., 1972-94, sr. v.p., gen. mgr., 1994—. Pres. Newspaper Features Coun., 1999—. With AUS, 1953-55. Mem. Nat. Cartoonists Soc., Internat. Press Inst., Interam. Press Assn. Soc. of Silurians, Dutch Treat Club, Sigma Delta Chi. Jewish. Home: 255 W 84th St New York NY 10024-4321 Office: United Media 200 Madison Ave Fl 4 New York NY 10016-3911

GOLDBERGER, GEORGE STEFAN, finance executive; b. Oradea, Romania, July 3, 1947; came to U.S., 1962; s. Ladislau and Margareta (Schwartz) G.; 1 child, David Michael. BS in Systems Engring., Bklyn. Polytechnic U., 1969; MBA in Fin., U. Pa., 1975. Systems analyst Grumman Corp., Bethpage, N.Y., 1969-73; ops. analyst Internat. Paper Co., N.Y.C., 1973-74; mgmt. cons. Booz, Allen & Hamilton, N.Y.C., 1975-77; asst. to chmn. W.R. Grace & Co., N.Y.C., 1977-85; pres. Citizens Against Govt. Waste, Washington, 1986-89; COO Pres.'s Pvt. Sector Survey on Cost Control (Grace Commn.), Washington, 1986-89; dir. mergers and acquisitions Figgie Internat., Inc., Willoughby, Ohio, 1989-90; pres. Goldberger & Assocs., Inc., N.Y.C., 1991-98; chief op. officer Progenitor Cell Therapy, LLC, Hackensack, N.J., 1999—. Contbr. articles to publs. Avocation: skiing.

GOLDBERGER, MARVIN LEONARD, physicist, educator; b. Chgo., Oct. 22, 1922; s. Joseph and Mildred (Sedwitz) G.; m. Mildred Ginsburg, Nov. 25, 1945; children: Samuel M., Joel S. B.S., Carnegie Inst. Tech., 1943; Ph.D., U. Chgo., 1948. Research assoc. Radiation Lab., U. Calif., 1948-49; research assoc. Mass. Inst. Tech., 1949-50; asst.-assoc. prof. U. Chgo., 1950-55, prof., 1955-57; Higgins prof. physics Princeton U., 1957-77, chmn. dept., 1970-76, Joseph Henry prof. physics, 1977-78; pres. Calif. Inst. Tech., Pasadena, 1978-87; dir. Inst. Advanced Study, Princeton, N.J., 1987-91; prof. physics UCLA, 1991-93; prof. physics U. Calif., San Diego, 1993-2000, dean divsn. natural scis., 1994-99, prof. emeritus, 2000—; mem. President's Sci. Adv. Com., 1965-69; chmn. Fedn. Am. Scientists, 1971-73. Fellow Am. Phys. Soc., Am. Acad. Arts and Scis.; mem. Nat. Acad. Scis., Am. Philos. Soc., Council on Fgn. Relations.

GOLDEN, EDWIN HAROLD, insurance company executive; b. Corsicana, Tex., Dec. 14, 1931; s. Mace Benjamin and Sarah (Alterman) G.; m. Dolly Moskowitz, Aug. 3, 1952; children: Jeffrey L., Beth Golden Marsh. BBA, U. Tex., 1953. Agt. N.Y. Life Ins. Co., Austin, Tex., 1955-80; ptnr. Hodges, Golden & Duckworth, Austin, 1967-77; owner Ed Golden & Assocs., Austin, Tex., 1977—; pres. Golden World Travel, Austin, 1993, CEO mem. Benefits Group, Inc., 1999, Tex. Package Stores Assn., Austin, 1985—, SupportmyAssociation.com, Inc., 1999; CEO Support My Association.com., Inc., 1999. Chmn. bd. trustees City of Austin Retirement Sys., 1975—; bd. dirs. James Dick Found. for Performing Arts, Round Top, Tex., 1979—. With U.S. Army, 1953-54. Mem. CLU (Austin chpt., certs. in pension planning and estate planning), Nat. Assn. Life Underwriters, Million Dollar Round Table (life), Top of the Table (charter), Am. Soc. Pension Actuaries, Internat. Found. Employee Benefit Plans, Shriners, Masons, Travelers' Century Club. Jewish. Avocation: travel. Office: Ed Golden and Assocs 5407 Parkcrest Dr Austin TX 78731-4911

GOLDEN, ELLIOTT, judge; b. Bklyn., June 28, 1926; s. Barnet David and Rose (Fistel) G.; m. Ana Valbuena, July 8, 1990; children: Jeffrey Stephen, Marjorie Ruth, Peter Michael (dec.); stepchildren: Robert, Elizabeth, William, John. Student, Maritime Acad., 1944-46, NYU, 1947-48; LLB, Bklyn. Law Sch., 1951. Bar: N.Y. 1952, U.S. Dist. Ct. (ea. dist.) N.Y. 1953, U.S. Tax Ct., U.S. Dist. Ct. (so. dist.) N.Y. 1953, U.S. Supreme Ct. 1961. Assoc. Golden & Golden, 1952-64; asst. dist. atty. Kings County, N.Y., 1956-64; chief asst. dist. atty. Kings County, 1964-76; acting dist. atty. Kings County, N.Y., 1968; judge Civil Ct. of City of N.Y., 1977-78; justice Supreme Ct. State of N.Y., 1979-98, jud. hearing officer, 1998—; adj. assoc. prof. N.Y.C. Tech. Coll., 1987-93; arbitrator, mediator Nat. Arbitration & Mediation, 1998—; cons. in field. Contbr. articles to profl. jours. Bd. trustees Greater N.Y. coun. Boy Scouts Am.; hon. vice chmn. March of Dimes; bd. dirs. Bklyn. Philharmonia; mem. adv. bd. Bklyn. PAL; chmn. Bklyn. Lawyers div. Fedn. Jewish Philanthropies; co-chmn. Bklyn. Lawyers div. State of Israel Bonds; assoc. trustee Temple Beth Emeth of Flatbush; mem. exec. com. Lawyers div. United Jewish Appeal; past pres. counsel Hosp. Relief Assn.; bd. dirs. Kings Bay YM-YMHA of Bklyn.; bd. dirs. Bklyn. ARC, Archway Sch. for Spl. Children, Bklyn. Sch. for Spl. Children. Recipient Cert. of Merit, Hosp. Relief Assn., numerous plaques, awards and certs. of appreciation various civic orgns. Mem. Nat. Dist. Attys. Assn. (dir. 1976-77, Disting. Svc. award), Combined Coun. Law Enforcement Ofcls. State N.Y., N.Y. State Dist. Attys. Assn. (sec. 1965-77), K.P. (supreme coun.). Avocations: golf, fishing, computers.

GOLDEN, HERBERT HERSHEL, retired Romance languages educator; b. Boston, Nov. 1, 1919; s. Max and Minnie (Turetzky) G.; m. Hilda Rachel Lazerow, June 13, 1943 (dec. May 1964); children: Robert Sherman, Barry Allen, Steven Eliot; m. Evelyn Pauline Sowa, Oct. 7, 1965. BA, Boston U., 1941, MA, 1942; MA, Harvard U., 1947, PhD, 1951. Lectr. Spanish and French, Boston U., 1945-49, instr. Romance langs., 1949-53, asst. prof., 1953-57, assoc. prof., 1957-63, prof., 1963-85, prof. emeritus, 1985—; cons. for NDEA lang. insts. U.S. Office Edn., HEW, Washington, 1955-56; asst. to mng. editor Modern Lang. Jour., Nat. Fedn. Modern Lang. Tchrs. Assns., Boston, 1955-58; instr. French and Italian, Harvard U. Ext., Cambridge, Mass, 1960-79; mem., editor, mem. adv. com. on fgn. langs. Mass. Dept. Edn., Boston, 1960-69; Fulbright lectr. U. Rome, 1962-63. Co-author: Modern French Literature and Language: A Bibliography of Homage Studies, 1953, reprinted 1971, Modern Iberian Language and Literature: A Bibliography of Homage Studies, 1958, reprinted 1971, Modern Italian Language and Literature: A Bibliography of Homage Studies, 1959, reprinted 1971, Histoire de France à Travers les Journaux du Temps Passé (1715-1789). Lumières et Lueurs du XVIII Siècle, 1986; editor: Studies in Honor of Samuel Montefiore Waxman, 1969, Giulio Bertoni and the Aesthetic Factor in Linguistics, 1969; contbr. articles and revs. to profl. jours. With U.S. Army, 1942-45, ETO. Decorated Purple Heart, Bronze Star, gold medal of cultural merit (Italy); recipient diploma of merit Internat. Assn. for Study Italian Lang. and Lit., 1973; rsch. fellow Marion and Jasper Whiting Found., 1979-80. Mem. MLA (steering com. fgn. lang. program 1956-59), Am. Soc. for 18th Century Studies (editor Festschriften: 18th Century Bibliography), Am. Assn. Tchrs. Italian (sec.-treas. 1959-64, pres. 1964-66), French Soc. 18th Century Studies, Masons, Phi Beta Kappa (pres. Mass. Epsilon chpt. 1970-72, cert. disting. merit 1985). Avocations: classical music, collecting French films on video, reading. Home: 29 Thorndike St Brookline MA 02446-2405

GOLDEN, JAMES LESLIE, information technology executive; b. Balt., Aug. 5, 1944; s. Leslie Logan and Gladys (Kinser) G.; m. Patsy Ann Creech, June 4, 1966; children: James Brett, Courtney Leigh. BA in Math. and Edn., U. Ky., 1966; MS in Tech. of Mgmt., Am. U., Washington, 1973. Bus. sys. planning staff U.S. Postal Svc. Hdqs., Washington, 1980-83, dir. planning and devel., 1983-86, dir. data mgmt., 1986-89, dir. info. svcs., 1989-92, mgr. office and exec. info., 1992-94, with, 1994-97, exec. program dir. Yr. 2000 initiative, 1997-2000, exec. dir. info. security and cyber assurance program, 2000—; adj. faculty math. No. Va. C.C., 1976-77; adj. faculty Nat. Cryptologic Sch., 1993-99. Coach Sterling (Va.) Youth Soccer Assn., 1980-86; pres. exec. exch. program Mobile Corp., 1979-80. Capt. USNR, 1990-99, ret. Recipient Fed. 100 awad, 2000; named Ky. col., 1995—; grantee NSF, 1968. Home: 117 Peyton Rd Potomac Falls VA 20165-5605 Office: US Postal Svc 475 Lenfant Plz SW Rm 2300 Washington DC 20260-0004

GOLDEN, JOSEPH AARON, lawyer; b. Detroit, MI, Oct. 27, 1940; s. Milton and Sally (Schweitzer) G.; m. Frances Miriam Rubenstein, Aug. 16, 1965 (div. Apr. 1973); children: Manine Rosa, Jay Dylan, Nicholas Michael Estuardo, Samuel Marcos, Jennifer Rose Mead, Natlaie Elizabeth Mead; m. Cynthia Sisson Mead, June 24, 1979. BBA, Wayne State U., 1962; JD, U. Detroit, 1967. Bar: Mich. 1968, U.S. Ct. Appeals (6th cir.) 1974, U.S. Ct. Appeals (3d cir.) 1995. Supervising atty. Wayne County Neighborhood Legal Services, Ecorse, Mich., 1968-70; ptnr. Craig, Fieger & Golden, Southfield, Mich., 1970-73, Fieger, Golden & Cousens, Southfield, 1973-78; pvt. practice, Southfield, 1978-85; prin. Sommers, Schwartz, Silver & Schwartz, P.C., Southfield, 1985—; adj. prof. labor law U. Detroit, 1987—. Co-author: Wrongful Termination Litigation in Mich., 1986; contbrg. author: Employee Dismissal Law: Forms and Procedures, 1986. Founder, pres. Coalition for Fairness in Workplace, 1993. Fellow Coll of Labor and Employment Lawyers; mem. ABA (pub. co-chmn. employee rights and responsibilities com. labor and employment law sect., sect. coun. 1988-92), ATLA, Mich. Trial Lawyers Assn., Nat. Employmenbt Lawyers Assn. (nat. exec. bd. 1984-95, pres. 1991-93), Mich. Employment Lawyers Assn. (founder, v.p.).

GOLDEN, KIMBERLY KAY, critical care, flight nurse; b. Munich, July 31, 1961; came to U.S., 1961; d. Henry Davis and Mary Walker G. AA, Hinds Jr. Coll., Raymond, Miss., 1980, ASN, 1984; BSN, U. Miss., Jackson, 1987, AS in EMT-Paramedic, 1990; postgrad., U. Health Scis., Antigua, W.I., 1997—. Cert. ACLS instr., PALS provider and instr.; emergency nurse, crit. care RN; cert. paramedic, Miss., Tenn. Staff nurse neuro ICU U. Miss. Med. Ctr., 1984-85, staff nurse surg. ICU, 1985-87; staff nurse emergency rm. Rankin Gen. Hosp., Brandon, Miss., 1987-88; flight nurse Lifestar Helicopter Flight Svc., 1988-91; staff nurse emergency rm., ICU Nightingale Nursing, Jackson, 1988-91, Riveroaks Hosp., Jackson, 1990-91; staff RN emergency rm., Aerovesta flight Midland Meml. Hosp., Tex., 1991-93; flight nurse Hosp. Wing BTLS, Memphis, Tenn., 1993-99, U. Health Sci. Med. Sch., Antigua, West Indies, 1997—; nurs Univ. Health Scis./Antigua Sch. Medicine, 1997—; examiner Nat. Registry EMT-P; advanced trauma life support station instr.; affiliate faculty paramedic program U. Miss. Faculty scholar Hinds Jr. Coll., 1983. Mem. AACN, Nat. Flight Assn., Emergency Nurses Assn. Baptist. Avocations: karate, skiing, horse back riding, camping. Office: PO Box 140466 Austin TX 78714-0466

GOLDEN, LEON, classicist, educator; b. Jersey City, Dec. 25, 1930; s. Nathan and Regina (Okun) G. BA, U. Chgo., 1950, MA, 1953, PhD, 1958. Instr. ancient langs. Coll. William and Mary, 1958-60, asst. prof. ancient langs., 1960-65; assoc. prof. classical langs. Fla. State U., Tallahassee, 1965-68, prof., 1968—, dir. program in humanities, 1976—, chmn. dept. classics, 1986-95; bd. dirs. Fla. Endowment for Humanities, 1983-87. Author: In Praise of Prometheus: Humanism and Rationalism in Aeschylean Thought, 1966, (with O.B. Hardison Jr.) Aristotle's Poetics, 1968, Aristotle: On Tragic and Comic Mimesis, 1992, Horace for Students of Literature, 1995. With AUS, 1953-55. Fellow coop. program humanities U.N.C. and Duke, 1964-65; fellow coop. program humanities Soc. for Religion in Higher Edn., 1971-72. Mem. Am. Philol. Assn., Archeol. Inst. Am., Classical Assn. Mid. West and South (pres. So. sect. 1972-74), Phi Beta Kappa. Office: Fla State U Dept Classics Tallahassee FL 32306

GOLDENBERG, DAVID, physician, computer/internet consultant; b. Hempstead, N.Y., May 18, 1962; s. Herbert and Sarah (Elbaum) G.; m. Renee Flax, Aug. 17, 1986; children: Michael, Ellie, Dana. BSc, Ben Gurion U. of the Negev, Beer-Sheva, Israel, 1992, MD, 1996. Tchr. human anatomy Ben Gurion U. of the Negev/Technion Med. Faculty, Israel, 1991-98; computer cons., advisor to hosp. dir. Soroka Med. Ctr., Beer-Sheva, Israel, 1995-96, webmaster, 1995-96; webmaster Faculty of Medicine/Technion-Israel Inst. Tech., Haifa, 1996—; webmaster Ramban Med. Ctr., Haifa, 1997—,

otolaryngologist, chief resident, 1999—; Tae Kwon Do instr., Beer-Sheva, 1989-96. Contbr. articles to profl. hours. Lt. Airborne Inf., Israeli Def. Forces, 1980-83. Recipient Close-up award Israel Magic Assn., 1984. Mem. Israel Tae Kwon Do Assn. (v.p. 1995—), Israel Soc. Otolaryngology-Head and Neck Surgery, Israel Soc. Head and Neck Oncology. Jewish. Avocations: magic, piano, Tae Kwon-Do, painting.

GOLDENBERG, GEORGE, retired pharmaceutical company executive; b. N.Y.C., Mar. 12, 1929; s. Gersh and Rose (Kolpacci) G.; m. Arlene Sandra Yudell, May 22, 1955; children: Steven Alan, Heidi Michele Goldenberg Handelsman, Jeffrey Evan Student, Bklyn. Coll., 1946-47; BS, Bklyn. Coll. Pharmacy of L.I. U., 1951. Pharmacist Dolcorts Pharmacy, N.Y.C., 1951-56; export mgr. Chem. Specialties Co., Inc., N.Y.C., 1956-58; sales mgr. Syntex Chem. Co., Inc., N.Y.C., 1958-60; asst. to pres. Syntex Labs., Inc., N.Y.C., 1960-61; gen. sales mgr. Panray-Parlam Corp., Englewood, N.J., 1961-63; v.p. Ormont Drug & Chem. Co., Inc., Englewood, 1963-64, exec. v.p., dir., 1964-66, pres., dir., 1966-81; sec., dir. Goldleaf Pharmacal Co., Inc., Englewood, N.J., 1966-81; pres., dir. Moleculon, Inc., 1982-88; pres., chief exec. officer, dir. Argus Pharmaceuticals Inc., The Woodlands, Tex., 1988-92; bd. dirs. Fed. Pharmacal Co., Ft. Lauderdale, Fla., Bedford Acme Surg. Co., Inc., Bklyn., Lawton Labs., Inc., Englewood, Ormont Diagnostics Ltd., London. Trustee L.I. U., Bklyn. Coll. Pharmacy. Mem. Bklyn. Coll. Pharmacy Alumni Assn. (pres.), Fedn. Alumni Assns. L.I. U. (pres.), Am. Pharm. Assn., Englewood Jr. C. of C., Young Pres. Orgn., Am. Mgmt. Assn., Drug and Allied Trades Assn., Delta Sigma Theta. Club: B'nai B'rith, The Polo Club of Boca Raton (pres. bd. govs.). Home: 16730 Colchester Ct Delray Beach FL 33484-6946

GOLDENBERG, SOLOMON MAURICE, family physician; b. Khartoum, Sudan, Mar. 16, 1940; arrived in U.K., 1963; s. Maurice and Rachel (Polon) G.; m. Annette Diane Spencer, July 7, 1941; 1 child, Lisa Natalie. M.B.B.S., U. Khartoum, 1963, MSc in Drug Addiction, 1997. Registered physician, U.K. Intern Khartoum Hosp., 1963-64; resident in haematology United Oxford (Eng.) Hosp., 1964-65; gen. practice tng. Clapham, Eng., 1966-67; resident in ob-gyn. King George Hosp., Ilford, Eng., 1967-68; prin. gen. practitioner Drs. Pollak and Ptnrs., Eng., 1968-79; dir. Raleigh Clinic, London, Eng., 1980-87; prin. gen. practitioner Prof. Freeling and Ptnrs., Eng., 1987-90; pvt. practice London, 1990—; cons. in drug addiction D.A.C.A.S./St. George's Hosp., London, 1992—; part-time prison med. officer Wandsworth Prison, London, 1992. Co-author: Babyshock, 1980. Fellow Royal Coll. Gen. Practice (sec. 1973-80) mem. Royal Coll. Obstetricians and Gynecologists. Conservative Party. Jewish. Achievements include study of long-term benzodiazepines in a South London practice. Home: 15011 Featherstone Way Davie FL 33331-2939 Office: 657 Garratt Ln, London SW17 0PB, England

GOLDER, HERBERT ALAN, classics educator; b. Oct. 29, 1952. BA, Boston U., 1975; MA, Yale U., 1977, MPhil, 1979, PhD, 1984; postgrad., Oxford U., 1982. Tchg. fellow, instr. in classics Yale U., New Haven, Conn., 1977-80; asst. prof. of classics Syracuse (N.Y.) U., 1982-85, Emory U., Atlanta, 1985-87; asst. prof. of classics Boston U., 1988-93, assoc. prof. of classics, 1993—; vis. asst. prof. classics Emory U., Atlanta, 1984-85. Asst. dir. (to Werner Herzog): (documentary film) Little Dieter Needs to Fly, 1997 (Emmy nomination 1999, Disting. Achievement award Internat. Documentary Assn. 1998, Spl. Jury prize Amsterdam Internat. Documentary Film Festival 1997), Wings of Hope, 1999, My Best Fiend, 1999, The Lord and the Laden, 2000; asst. dir. (to Werner Herzog), co-writer (feature film) Invincible, 2001; actor: (feature film) Invincible, 2001; editor-in-chief: Arion, A Jour. of Classics and the Humanities, 1990 (winner CELJ Phoenix award for Significant Editl. Achievement 1992); writer: (books) Sophocles' Aias, 1999 (nominated for PEN/Book of Month Club Translation prize 1999), Euripides' Bacchae, 1999. Office: 621 Commonwealth Ave Boston MA 02215

GOLDFARB, C. RICHARD, radiologist; b. N.Y.C., Feb. 22, 1946; s. Harold and Lenore (Goldenheim) G.; m. Linda Markovitz; children: Adina R., Akiva M., Aviva S., Aliza L., Atara C. AB, Columbia U., 1966; MD, N.Y. Med. Coll., 1970. Diplomate Am. Bd. Radiology, Am. Bd. Nuclear Medicine. Intern Met. Hosp. Ctr., N.Y.C., 1970-71; resident in diagnostic radiology St. Luke's Med. Ctr., N.Y.C., 1971-74, fellow in nuclear medicine and ultrasound, 1974-75; dir. nuclear medicine Nassau County Med. Ctr., East Meadow, N.Y., 1976-79; chief nuclear medicine Beth Israel Med. Ctr., N.Y.C., 1979—; assoc. prof. radiology Albert Einstein Coll. Medicine, N.Y.C., 1988—. Editor Practical Reviews in Nuclear Medicine, 1992—; contbr. articles to profl. jours. Maj. U.S. Army, 1971-84. Named Tchr. of the Yr. Radiology Dept., Nassau County Med. Ctr., 1979. Mem. N.Y. Acad. Sci., Radiol. Soc. N.Am., Soc. Nuclear Medicine, Am. Coll. Radiology. Jewish. Home: 490 W End Ave New York NY 10024-4329 Office: Beth Israel Med Ctr 1st Ave and 16th St New York NY 10003

GOLDFARB, MURIEL BERNICE, marketing and advertising consultant; b. Bklyn., Mar. 29, 1920; d. Barnett Goldfarb and May (Steinberg) Goldfarb Oshman; BA, U. Miami, Coral Gables, Fla., 1942; postgrad. CCNY, 1950. Pub. info. asst. UNESCO, Paris, 1946-47; advt. mgr. Majestic Specialties Co., N.Y.C., 1947-50; retail promotion mgr. Glamour Mag., 1955-61; advt. dir. Country Tweeds Co., N.Y.C., 1961-65; advt. dir. S. Augstein & Co., N.Y.C., 1966-72, Feature Ring Co., Inc., Gotham Ring Co., Inc., Fidco Inc., N.Y.C., 1972-77; dir. advt. and promotion Wasko Gold Products Corp., N.Y.C., 1977-81; advt. and mktg. cons. specializing in promotions and sale of vintage jewelry and Bric á Brac. Lt. WAVES, 1943-46. Mem. Fashion Group N.Y. Inc., Women's Jewelry Assn. (corr. sec. 1983-85). Jewish.

GOLDFELD, LEV NAUM, communication engineer; b. Tashkent, USSR, Jan. 3, 1943; s. Naum Abraham and Rivka Bary (Kychyc) G.; m. Asia Vsevolod Shkinev, Sept. 4, 1965 (div. 1973); 1 child, Andrea; m. Sofia Samuel Sysmam, May 16, 1973; children: Julia, Eugeny. BSc, MSc, U. Comms., Tashkent, USSR, 1964; PhD, U. Comms., Leningrad, USSR, 1970. Sr. lectr. U. Comms., Tashkent, 1970-74, asst. prof., 1974-90; sr. rschr. Ben-Gurion U., Beer-Sheva, Israel, 1992—; dir. MicroTag-Temed Ltd., Beer-Sheva, 1993—. Patentee in field. Grantee Israel Ministry of Sci., 1992, Israel Ministry of Def., 1996, 97. Mem. N.Y. Acad. Sci. Home: Israel Eshaygu 14/3, 84787 Beer Sheva Israel Office: Ben Gurion U of the Negev, POB 653, 84105 Beer Sheva Israel

GOLDFINCH, EDWARD PETER, physicist; b. Lydd, Kent, Eng., May 30, 1934; s. Edward William and Nora May (Bowen) G.; m. Gill Patricia Hurford, Apr. 4, 1959; children: Richard Edward, Clare Elisia. BSc, U. Birmingham, Eng., 1955, MSc, 1956. FInstP, CPhys, FSRP. Physicist Hobsons, Wolverhampton, Eng., 1956-58, tech. group leader, 1958-62; sta. health physicist CEGB, Dungeness, Eng., 1962-73; health physics svcs. mgr. Nuclear Electric, London, 1973-90; chief exec. Nuclear Technology Pub., Ashford, Eng., 1990—; cons. IAEA, Vienna, 1980—, ISO, Paris, 1980—; chmn. IEC, Geneva, 1980-85, 90—. Founder/editor: Applied Health Physics Abstracts and Notes jour. 1973, Radiation Protection Dosimetry jour. 1981, Internat. Jour. of Radioactive Materials Transport, 1990, Radiation Protection Abstracts, 1999; author numerous scientific publs. Sch. gov. KCC, Ashford, 1980-86. Winston Churchill fellow, 1970. Fellow Inst. Physics, Soc. for Radiol. Protection (pres. 1993-94). Avocations: gardening, tennis, reading. Office: Nuclr Tech Pub Royal Bank Chmbrs, 17 Drum Ln, Ashford Kent, England

GOLDIE, JULIAN DOMINIC, retired financial adviser, educator; b. London, Aug. 3, 1931; s. George Edward and Noemi Maria (de Normanville) G.; m. Adele Mae Rundlett, Oct. 10, 1953 (div. 1978); children: Peter John, Elizabeth Teresa, Mary Anne. CFP. Banker Lloyds Bank, London, 1961-71; mem. life ins. staff Target Life, 1971-75, Can. Life, 1975-85; ind. fin. adviser Lucas Fettes & Ptnrs., London, 1985-99; ret., 1998—. Parliamentary candidate Social Dem. Party, 1982, 87, chmn. Croydon dist., 1983; sch. gov. Croydon Edn. Authority, 1984-96. Nat. svc. with Royal Army Ordnance Corps, 1950-52, Korea. Mem. Life Ins. Assn.; mem. Amnesty Internat., Brit. Korean War Vet. Assn. Mem. Liberal Dem. Party. Home: 30 Quadrant Rd, Thornton Heath CR7 7DA, England

GOLDIE, RAY ROBERT, lawyer; b. Dayton, Ohio, Apr. 1, 1920; s. Albert S. and Lillian (Hayman) G.; m. Dorothy Roberta Zafman, Dec. 2, 1941; children: Marilyn, Deanne, Dayle, Ron R. Student, U. So. Calif., 1943-44, JD magna cum laude, 1957; student, San Bernardino Valley Coll., 1950-51. Bar: Calif. 1957; cert. specialist estate planning, trusts and probate law, Calif. Bd. Legal Specialization. Elec. appliance dealer various locations, 1944-54; dep. atty. gen. State Bar of Calif., L.A., 1957-58, 1957-58; pvt. practice San Bernardino, Calif., 1958-87, Rancho Mirage, Calif., 1987—; pres. Trinity Acceptance Corp., 1948-53. Mem. World Peace Through Law Ctr., 1962—; regional dir. Legion Lex U. So. Calif. Sch. Law 1959-75; chmn. San Bernardino United Jewish Appeal, 1963; v.p. United Jewish Welfare Fund, San Bernardino, 1964-66; Santa Anita Hosp., Lake Arrowhead, 1966-69; bd. dirs. San Bernardino Med. Arts Corp.; trustee McCallum Theater, Bob Hope Cultural Ctr., 1996-99, Friends of Cultural Ctr. Found.; bd. dirs. Palm Canyon Theater, 1998—; legal counsel Lake Arrowhead Skating Found., 1998. Fellow Internat. Acad. Law and Sci.; mem. ABA, Assn. Naval Aviation Desert Storm Sqdn. (adminstrv. officer, sec.), San Bernardino County Bar Assn., Riverside County Bar Assn., State Bar Calif. (cert. specialist estate planning, probate and trust law), Am. Judicature Soc., Am. Soc. Hosp. Attys., Calif. Trial Lawyers Assn. (v.p. chpt. 1965-67, pres. 1967-68), Am. Arbitration Assn. (nat. panel arbitrators), Coachella Valley Desert Bar Assn. (chmn. taxation and estate planning, trusts, wills and probate com. 1992-94), Order of the Coif, Lake Arrowhead Country Club (pres. 1972-73, 80-81), Lake Arrowhead Yacht Club, Club at Morningside (CFO 1992-93, sec. 1993-94), Nu Beta Epsilon (pres. 1956-57). Home and Office: 1 Hampton Ct Rancho Mirage CA 92270-2585

GOLDIN, CLAUDIA DALE, economics educator; b. N.Y.C., May 14, 1946; d. Leon and Lucille (Rosansky) G. BA magna cum laude with distinction, Cornell U., 1967; MA, U. Chgo., 1969, PhD, 1972; MA (hon.), U. Pa., 1985, Harvard U., 1990; DHL (hon.), U. Nebr., Lincoln, 1994. Asst. prof. econs. U. Wis., Madison, 1971-73; asst. prof. Princeton (N.J.) U., 1973-79, vis. fellow indsl. relations sec., 1987-88; vis. lectr. Harvard U., Cambridge, Mass., 1975-76, prof., 1990—; assoc. prof. U. Pa., Phila., 1979-85, prof., 1985-90; vis. fellow The Brookings Instn., 1993-94; mem. Inst. Advanced Study, Princeton, 1982-83; rsch. assoc., project dir. Nat. Bur. Econ. Rsch., Cambridge, 1979—. Author: Urban Slavery in the American South, 1976, Understanding the Gender Gap, 1990; editor: Strategic Factors in 19th Century American Economic History, 1992, The Regulated Economy, 1994, The Defining Moment: The Great Depression and the American Economy in the 20th Century, 1997, Jour. Econ. History, NBER Series on Long-Term Factors in Econ. Devel.; edtl. bd. Am. Econ. Rev., 1985-91, Quar. Jour. Econs., 1992—, Rev. Econs. & Statistics; contbr. articles to profl. pubis. Recipient NSF award, 1975-77, 79-81, 81-82, 84-86, 87-89, 92-93, 96-99, Spencer Found. rsch. award, 1996-99; Guggenheim fellow, 1987-88. Fellow Econometric Soc.; mem. Am. Acad. Arts and Scis., Am. Econ. Assn. (v.p. 1990-91), Econ. History Assn. (pres. 1999-00, trustee 1984—, v.p. 1988-89). Avocations: jogging, aerobics, hiking, bird watching. Office: Harvard U Nat Econs Rsch Dept Econs Cambridge MA 02138*

GOLDIN, DANIEL S., federal agency administrator; b. N.Y.C., July 23, 1940; m. Judith Linda Kramer; children: Ariel, Laura. BS in Mech. Engring., CCNY, 1962; PhD (hon.), Case Western Res. U., Cen. State U., CCNY, Fla. Inst. of Tech., Framingham State U., Poly. U. of N.Y., U. Ariz., U. Md., U. Mich. Rsch. scientist Lewis Rsch. Ctr., NASA, Cleve., 1962-67; with TRW, from 1967, mem. tech. staff, 1967; v.p., gen. mgr. Space & Tech. Group, TRW, Redondo, Calif., 1987-92; adminstr. NASA, Washington, 1992—. Recipient 1996 Chmn. award Am. Assn. Engring. Societies, 1997, Civilian Kitty Hawk Sands of Time award, Goddard Quality award, Heald award Ill. Inst. of Tech., Nelson P. Jackson Aerospace award Nat. Space Club, Internat. Von Karman Wings award Aerospace Hist. Soc., Meritorious award (2) Nat. Assn. of Small and Disadvantaged Businesses, President's medal N.Y. Inst. of Tech., Nat. award for Space Achievement, Rotary, Space Pioneer award Nat. Space Soc.; named one of 100 Most Influential in Govt. Nat. Jour., One of 40 Most Influential Def. Industry Leaders, Def. Bus. mag. Fellow AIAA (Piper Gen. Aviation award), Am. Astronom. Soc. (John F. Kennedy Astronautics award), Inst. for Advancement of Engring. Achievements during his tenure at TRW include the building of 13 spacecraft, the launch and operation of NASA tracking and Data Relay Satellite-5 and the Compton Gamma Ray Observatory. The group also has worked on other NASA programs including the successfull grinding and testing of the worlds two largest X-ray mirrors fot the Advanced X-ray Astrophysics Facility. Office: NASA Office of Adminstr 300 E St SW Washington DC 20546-0005

GOLDIN, IAN ANDREW, executive; b. Pretoria, South Africa, Mar. 3, 1955; s. Harry and Alice (Widrich) G.; m. Theresa Ruth Webber, Aug. 23, 1992; children: Olivia, Alexander. BS in Math., U. Cape Town, South Africa, 1976, BA in Econs. (hon.), 1977; MS in Econs., London Sch. Econs., 1979; D, Oxford U., England, 1983. Lectr. econs. Oxford U., England, 1981-83; dir. Landell Mills Com., London, 1984-88; dir. programs OECD, Paris, 1988-92; prin. economist World Bank, Washington, 1992-95; sr. economist EBRD, London, 1995-96; chief exec., mng. dir. DBSA, Johannesburg, South Africa, 1996—; dir. Nat. Housing Fin. Corp., 1996—, Lesotho Highlands/South Africa Water Corp., 1997—, Khula Small and Medium Enterprise Fin. Co., 1996—, Commonwealth Africa Investment Fund, 1996—, Africa Infrastructure Fund. Author: Trade Liberalization: Global Economic Implications, 1996, others; author, editor: Open Economics, 1992, The Economics of Sustainable Development, 1995; coauthor: Economic Reform, Trade and Agriculture Development, 1994; contbr. articles to profl. jours. Dir. Cape Town 2004 Olympic Bid Co., 1996—. Fellow Ctr. Econ. Policy Rsch. WEF Global Leader. Avocations: music, saxophone, skiing, scuba, cinema, hiking.

GOLDIN, JACOB ISAAK, software executive; b. Leningrad, Russia, Aug. 29, 1958; came to U.S., 1990; s. Isaak and Tamara (Rozhetsky) G.; m. Marina I. Vaynstein, May 17, 1983; children: Daniel, Simon. BS in Computer Sci., Leningrad Inst. Tech., 1978, MS in Chem. Engring., 1980; PhD in Chem. Engring., Leningrad Acad. Wood Chemistry, 1987. Programmer/analyst All-Union Hydrolysis Corp., Leningrad, 1979-83, chem. engr., 1983-84, sr. chem. engr., 1984-87, sr. rschr., 1987-90; pres., owner Jacob's Chem. Assoc., Livingston, N.J., 1993—; sr. programmer, analyst Givaudan-Roure Corp., Clifton, 1995-96; gen. project mgr. Reed-Elsevier, 1998—; cons. Atlas Refinery, 1993-96, ACIMI Corp., 1992-96; specialist in design and implementation of object-oriented multi-tier software architectures. Author software packages for analytical chemistry; contbr. articles to profl. jours. in phys. chemistry and software engineering. Mem. AIChE, Am. Oil Chem. Soc., NRA. Avocation: computer programming.

GOLDIN, MILTON, fund raising counsel, writer; b. Cleve., Jan. 8, 1927; s. Hyman and Ida (Felsher) G.; m. Aranka Nemcek, June 17, 1950; children: Karen Goldin Sriuttamayotin, David. BA, NYU, 1953, MA, 1955. Adminstrv. dir. Am. Choral Found., 1955-61; assoc. dir. devel. Brookdale Hosp. Ctr., 1963-66; fund raising campaign dir. Washington Sq. Coll. and Grad. Sch. Arts and Sci., NYU, 1966-67; v.p. Oram Assocs., Inc., 1967-72, exec. v.p., 1972-75; fund raising couns., 1975-78; pres. The Milton Goldin Co., 1978—; mgr. Amor Artis Chorale and Orch., 1961-78. Mem., N.Y.C. Symphony, 1944-45, Denver Symphony Orch., 1949-51; Author: The Music Merchants, 1969, Why They Give, 1976; contbg. editor: PS, 1996-99; contbr. articles to periodicals. Served with AUS, 1945-46. Recipient ASCAP Deems Taylor award, 1970. Mem. Nat. Coalition of Ind. Scholars (bd. dirs. 1997-99), Phi Beta Kappa, Psi Chi, Mu Sigma. Home and Office: 266 Crest Dr Tarrytown NY 10591-4328

GOLDING, GRAHAM LIONEL, broadcaster, writer; b. Wellington, New Zealand, Jan. 14, 1924; arrived in Australia, 1959; s. Lionel Arthur Golding and Elvra Jean McDonald; m. Audrey May Chetwynd Nevin, June 1953 (div. 1959); 1 child, Christopher Graham; m. Patricia Mary Bower Butt, 1971 (div.); children: Melissa, Gabrielle, Deanna. Woolbuying cert., Bradford, 1948; postgrad., Victoria U. and Leeds U., 1949. Wool buyer Prevost, New Zealand, 1949-50; announcer NZBS, New Zealand, 1950-58; journalist Sydney (Australia) Herald), 1959-60; broadcaster NQ Radio/TV, Townsville, 1960-78; writer Townsville, 1982-88; news reader ABC, Townsville, 1978-82; dir. greeting svcs. Brisbane (Australia) Airport Corp. Ltd., 2000—. Author: Memory, 1962, Speech, 1973, Pieces of Eight, 1994; songwriter: I'm in Love with You, 1956, Alphabetically, 1989; poet: Potpourri of 100. Charity coord. Multiple Sclerosis Soc. Queensland, GROW Australia, CARE, Townsville, 1978-89; speech therapist, Brisbane, 1989—, counselor Care, Townsville and Brisbane, 1978-89; pres. Yr. of the Disabled, Queensland, 1982; pres. AFL Townsville, 1968-72, Social Cricket Assn., Townsville, 972-75; v.p. Rowing Pine Rivers, 1989—. With Royal Navy ret. Recipient Livesaving award Royal Humane Soc. (3), Red medal, Bombay, Campaign medal (5); named Citizen of Townsville. Mem. LDS Ch. Avocations: yachting, rugby, tennis, swimming, athletics. Home: 328 Dayboro Rd, Brisbane 4503, Australia Office: Coord Parks, NPCP Dayboro Rd, Brisbane 4503, Australia

GOLDING, RAYMUND MARSHALL, university administrator, retired; b. Westport, New Zealand, June 17, 1935; arrived in Australia, 1968; s. Austin Everard and Marion (Marshall) G.; m. Ingeborg Anna Maria Carl, June 16, 1962; children: Tanya, Elke. BSc, Auckland U., 1957, MSc, 1958; PhD, U. Cambridge, U.K., 1963; DSc, U. N.S.W., Sydney, 1986. Rsch. scientist DSIR, New Zealand, 1957-63, sr. rsch. scientist, 1963-68; prof. theoretical and phys. chemistry U. N.S.W., Sydney, 1968-86, pro vice-chancellor, 1978-86; vice chancellor James Cook Univ., Townsville, Australia, 1986-96; retired, 1996; chmn. Australasian Marine Sci. Consortium; mem. edn. com. N.S.W. Chiropractic Registration Bd.; mem. The Chiropractors and Osteopaths Bd. of Queensland; chmn. nat. unit for multidisciplinary studies of spinal pain Townsville Gen. Hosp.; mem. adv. com. Australian Osteopathy Assn. Author: Wave Mechanics, 1969, Chemistry, Multistrand Senior Science for Hig School Students, 1975, The Goldings of Oakington, 1992; contbr. articles to profl. jours. Hon. chmn., dir. Australian chpt. PACON Internat. Recipient Officer of the Order of Australia Gen. Divsn. Commonwealth of Australia, 1994, Easterfield award New Zealand Royal Inst. of Chemistry, 1967. Fellow New Zealand Inst. of Chemistry (Easterfield award 1967), Royal Australian Chem. Inst., Inst. of Physics, Royal Soc. of Arts, Australian Acad. Technol. Scis. Engring., Korean Chem. Soc. (hon.). Home: 5 Tolson Rd Mooloolah, Queensland 4553, Australia

GOLDMAN, BARBARA DEREN, film and theatrical producer; b. Bridgeport, Conn., Dec. 22, 1949; m. James Goldman, Oct. 25, 1975. Pres. Barbara Deren Assocs., N.Y.C., 1975—, Raoulfilm Inc., N.Y.C., 1979—; v.p. Trans-Internat. Revisions, 1980—. Co-author: Where to Eat in America, 1987; contbr. to book Feast of Wine and Food, 1987; producer Tolstoy, London, 1996.

GOLDMAN, CHARLES, electromechanical engineer; b. N.Y.C., Sept. 19, 1968; s. Ira and Marilyn Goldman. BSME, Rutgers U., 1995; BSEE, Ariz. State U., 1999. Chem. coater Nat. Starch Corp., Bridgewater, N.J., 1992-93, engring. asst., 1994; engring. asst. Rsch. Devel. and Engring. Ctr., Dover, N.J., 1995. Tutor math and physics CCM Ambs., 1992-93, video mgr., 1992-93. Rsch. Coun. N.J. engring. scholar, 1993, Coll. Morris scholar, 1992. Mem. NSPE, ASME, AIAA, The Planetary Soc., Am. Phys. Soc., Phi Theta Kappa, Tau Alpha Pi. Avocations: travel, space science, astrophysics,. Home: PO Box 64371 Phoenix AZ 85082-4371

GOLDMAN, GARY CRAIG, lawyer; b. Dec. 28, 1951; s. Ronald Walter and Connie Sylvia (Stein) G.; m. Diane Rose Lane, Oct. 1, 1977; children: Justin Edward, Gregory David. BA magna cum laude, Temple U., 1973; JD, Villanova U., 1976. Bar: Pa. 1976, U.S. Dist. Ct. (ea. dist.) Pa. 1981. Jud. law clk. Common Pleas Ct., Northampton County, Pa., 1976-77; asst. atty. gen. office of legal counsel Pa. Dept. Pub. Welfare, Phila., 1977-81, asst. counsel, 1981-84; staff counsel CDI Corp., Phila., 1984-86, v.p., assoc. gen. counsel, 1986—; mem. faculty, planning chmn. Nationwide Comml. Real Estate Leasing Programs. Author: Drafting a Fair Office Lease, 1989, 2d edit., 2000; contbg. author: The Commercial Real Estate Tenant's Handbook, 1987, The Practical Real Estate Lawyer's Manual, 1987, Commercial Tenants' Leasing Transactions Guide, 1991, Office Planning and Design Desk Reference, 1992, Negotiating and Drafting Office Leases, 1995; assoc. editor: Villanova Law Rev., 1974-76; contbr. articles to legal jours. Mem. ABA, Am. Corp. Counsel Assn., Phila. Bar Assn. Republican. Jewish. Avocation: golf. Home: 210 Fox Hollow Dr Langhorne PA 19053-2477 Office: CDI Corp 1717 Arch St Fl 35 Philadelphia PA 19103-2713

GOLDMAN, IRA STEVEN, gastroenterologist; b. Bronx, N.Y., May 19, 1951; s. George David and Belle (Hans) G.; m. Niki Ellen Kantrowitz, Jan. 20, 1980; children: Zachary, Joshua. BA, U. Rochester, 1973; student, Oxford U., 1972; MD, Columbia U., 1977. Diplomate Am. Bd. Internal Medicine, Am. Bd. Gastroenterology. Intern Columbia Presbyn. Med. Ctr., N.Y.C., 1977-78, resident in internal medicine, 1978-80; fellow in gastroenterology and liver diseases U. Calif. Sch. Medicine, San Francisco, 1980-83; instr. in anatomy Columbia U., N.Y.C., 1978; asst. prof. medicine U. Calif., San Francisco, 1983-85, Cornell U. Med. Coll., N.Y.C., 1985-91; assoc. prof. clin. medicine Cornell U. Med. Coll., 1991-96; attending physician North Shore Univ. Hosp., Manhasset, N.Y., 1985—; assoc. prof. clin. medicine NYU Sch. Medicine, 1996—; attending physician St. Francis Hosp., Roslyn, N.Y.; physicians adv. bd. Am. Liver Found., Greater N.Y. chpt., 1985—; mem. sci. adv. commn. L.I. chpt. Nat. Found. for Ileitis and Colitis, 1985-91; vice chair clin. practice sec. Am. Gastroent. Assn., 1995-97, chmn., 1997-2000. Reviewer jours. Gastroenterology; contbr. articles, book chapts. to profl. jours. Rsch. fellow Am. Liver Found., 1982, Clin. Investigator award NIH, 1983. Fellow ACP, Am. Coll. Gastroenterology; mem. Am Fedn. for Clin. Rsch., Am. Assn. for Study of Liver Diseases, Med. Soc. State of N.Y., Nassau County Med. Soc., Nassau County. Acad. Medicine, N.Y. Soc. for Gastrointestinal Endoscopy (pres. 1996-97), Alpha Omega Alpha. Avocations: sailing, tennis. Office: 310 E Shore Rd Great Neck NY 11023-2432

GOLDMAN, JOEL J., retired lawyer; b. N.Y.C., Sept. 7, 1940; s. Myron and Pearl (Jacobs) G.; m. Jane I. Stalker, July 23, 1973; children: Elizabeth Ann, Rebecca Lynn. BS, U. Va., 1962, JD, Syracuse U., 1965. Bar: N.Y. 1966, U.S. Dist. Ct. (we. dist.) N.Y. 1966. Law clk. Myron Goldman, N.Y.C., 1965; staff atty., chief trial counsel Legal Aid Soc. Rochester, N.Y., 1966-73; ptnr. Kaman, Berlove, Marafioti, Jacobstein & Goldman, Rochester, 1973-97; ret., 1997; lectr. family law; spl. investigator N.Y. State Spl. Commn. on Attica, 1972; mem. panel arbitrators Am. Arbitration Assn.; mem. faculty Nat. Bus. Inst., 1985-97. Referee, Ea. Assn. Inter-Collegiate Football Ofcls., 1974-95, v.p. Empire chpt., 1988, pres. 1989, Observer, Ea. Coll. Athletic Conf., 1996—, Inductee Jewish Athletes Sports Hall of Fame, 1996. Fellow Am. Acad. Matrimonial Lawyers (ret.); mem. ABA, N.Y. State Bar Assn. (exec. com. family law sect. 1982, mem. exec. com. 1981-97), Monroe County Bar Assn. (chmn. family law sect. 1982, exec. com. 1981-86), Assn. Trial Lawyers Am. Jewish. Author continuing edn. materials. Contbg. editor Bender's Forms for Civil Practice, 1986, Medina's Bostwick, 1986. Home: 67 Mountain Rd Rochester NY 14625-1816 also: 21 Bluebill Ave Apt 1005B Naples FL 34108-1765

GOLDMAN, JOHN MICHAEL, physician, consultant hematologist, educator; b. London, Nov. 30, 1938; s. Carl Heinz and Bertha (Brandt) G. BM BCh, Oxford U., 1963, DM, 1981. Dir. LRF Centre for Adult Leukaemia Imperial Coll. Sch. Medicine Hammersmith Hosp., London, 1989—, chmn. dept. haematology, 1994—; med. dir. Anthony Nolan Bone Marrow Trust, London, 1989—. Editor Bone Marrow Transplantation, 1985—. Fellow Royal Coll. Physicians, Acad. Med. Scis., European Group for Bone Marrow Transplantation (pres. 1990-94); European Hematology Assn. (pres. 1996-98). Office: Imperial Coll Sch Medicine, Hammersmith Hosp Du Cane Rd, London W12 0NN, England

GOLDMAN, MINTON F., political science educator; b. June 3, 1933; s. Julius and Hessie F. Goldman; m. Maureen Goldman, June 15, 1962; 1 child, Joyce Ellen. MALD, Fletcher Sch. Law & Diplomacy, 1958, PhD, 1965. Prof. polit. sci. Northeastern U., Boston; USIA lectr. Belgrade U., 1996. Author: (books) Revolution and Change Central/Eastern Europe, 1997, Slovakia Since Independence, 1998, Russia, The Eurasian Republic and Central/East Europe, 2000. Nat. Woodrow Wilson fellow Princeton U., 1955-56. Mem. Am. Assn. for Advancement of Slavic Studies, So. Conf. on Slavic Studies. Home: 32 Avalon Rd Needham MA 02492-1602 Office: Northeastern U 350 Huntington Ave Boston MA 02115-5005

GOLDMAN, NATHAN CARLINER, lawyer, educator; b. Charleston, S.C., Mar. 19, 1950; s. Reuben and Hilda Alta (Carliner) G.; m. Judith Tova Feigon, Oct. 28, 1984; children: Michael Reuben, Miriam Esther. BA, U. S.C., 1972; JD, Duke U., 1975; MA, Johns Hopkins U., 1978, PhD, 1980. Bar: N.C. 1975, Tex. 1985, U.S. Dist. Ct. (mid. dist.) N.C. 1975. Paralegal

City Atty.'s Office, Durham, N.C., 1975-76; asst. prof. govt. dept. U. Tex., Austin, Tex., 1980-85; pvt. practice Houston, 1985-86; assoc. Liddell, Sapp, Zivley, Hill & LaBoon, Houston, 1986-88; pvt. practice Houston, 1988-2000; adj. prof. space law U. Houston, 1985-88; rsch. assoc. Rice U. Inst. Policy Analysis, 1986—; lectr. bus. law, 1988-95; mem. coordinating bd. Space Architecture, U. Houston, 1985—; v.p. Internat. Design in Extreme Environments Assn., U. Houston, 1991—; vis. asst. prof. U. Houston-Clear Lake, 1989-91, 99—; adj. prof. South Tex. Coll. Law, 1994-95; gen. counsel Internat. Space Enterprises, 1993—, Globus Ltd. Co., 1994—; info. officer Israel Consulate, 1996-97, atty. Judith G. Cooper, P.C. Author: Space Commerce, 1985, American Space Law, 1988, 2d edit., 1996, Space Policy: A Primer, 1992; editor: Space and Society, 1984; assoc. editor Jour. Space Commerce, 1990-91; exec. editor Space Governance, 1996-99; also articles. Mem. com. on governance of space U.S. Bicentennial Commn., 1986-88, Clear Lake (Tex.) Area Econ. Devel. Found., 1987, Space Collegium, Houston Area Rsch. Ctr., 1987; pres. Windermere Civic Assn., 1990-92; bd. dirs. Hebrew Acad., 1994-96, Men's Club United Orthodox Synagogues, 1994—, pres., 1999—. U.S. Dept. Justice grantee, 1979-80, U. Tex. Inst. for Constructive Capitalism U. grantee, 1983; E.D. Walker Centennial fellow, 1984; NASA Summer fellow U. Calif., 1984. Fellow Internat. Inst. Space Law; mem. ABA, Tex. Bar Assn., Nat. Space Soc. (v.p. 1989-91), Inst. for Social Sci. Study Space (mem. adv. bd. 1990, editor Space Humanization Jour. 1993—), Am. Astronautical Soc., Inst. for Design in Extreme Environment Assn. (v.p. 1991-96), Space Bus. Roundtable. Avocations: reading, hiking, baseball, softball. Home: 4419 Meyerwood Dr Houston TX 77096-3523 Office: Rice U 3040 Post Oak Blvd Ste 1450 Houston TX 77056-6544

GOLDMAN, RICHARD GRAYBELL, physicist, psychologist; b. Washington, Oct. 11, 1923; s. Marcus Isaac and Mary Lily Dove (Ware) G.; m. Sarah Ellen Lindsley, June 15, 1950 (div. Feb. 1971); children: David Todhunter, Paul Atkinson, Peter Graybell. BS, MIT, 1948; MS, Rensselaer Poly. Inst., 1956; PhD, U. Calif., Santa Barbara, 1981. Lic. psychologist, Calif. Engr. GE, Schenectady, N.Y., 1950-63; project mgr. NASA, Cleve., 1963-74; pvt. practice psychology Santa Barbara, 1984-96; ret.bs. Author: Ultrasonic Technology, 1962; editor: SERT II Design Manual, 1971; contbr.: STOL Tecyhnology, 1972; patentee in field. With U.S. Army, 1943-46; ETO; PTO. Mem. Sigma Xi, Alpine Club of Can. Avocations: hiking, skiing, sailing, mountaineering, research. Home: 6724 S Olympus Dr Evergreen CO 80439-5312

GOLDMAN, RICHARD MARTIN See GOULD, R(ICHARD) MARTIN

GOLDMAN, WILLIAM, writer; b. Chgo., Aug. 12, 1931; s. M. Clarence and Marion (Weil) G.; m. Ilene Jones, Apr. 15, 1961; children: Jenny, Susanna. BA, Oberlin Coll., 1952; MA, Columbia U., 1956. Author: (novels) The Temple of Gold, 1957, Your Turn to Curtsy, My Turn to Bow, 1958, Soldier in the Rain, 1960, Boys and Girls Together, 1964, No Way to Treat a Lady, 1964, The Thing of It Is, 1967, Father's Day, 1971, The Princess Bride, 1973, Marathon Man, 1974, Wigger, 1974, Magic, 1976, Tinsel, 1979, Control, 1982, The Silent Gondoliers, 1983, The Color of Light, 1984, Heat, 1985, Brothers, 1987; (non-fiction) The Season: A Candid Look At Broadway, 1969, Adventures in the Screen Trade, 1983; (with Mike Lupica) Wait Until Next Year, 1988, Hype and Glory, 1990, Four Screenplays, 1995, Five Screenplays, 1997, Which Lie Did I Tell, 2000; (essays) The Big Picture, 1999; (play, with James Goldman) Blood Sweat and Stanley Poole, 1961; (musical comedy, with James Goldman and John Kander) A Family Affair, 1962; (screenplay) Masquerade, 1965, Harper, 1966, Butch Cassidy and The Sundance Kid, 1969 (Acad. award best original screenplay 1970), The Hot Rock, 1972, The Stepford Wives, 1974, The Great Waldo Pepper, 1975, Marathon Man, 1976, All the President's Men, 1976 (Acad. award best screenplay adaptation 1977), A Bridge Too Far, 1977, Magic, 1978, The Princess Bride, 1987, Heat, 1987, Misery, 1990, The Year of the Comet, 1992, Memoirs of an Invisible Man, 1992, Chaplin, 1992, Maverick, 1994, Ghost and the Darkness, 1996, Absolute Power, 1997. Recipient Laurel Award for lifetime achievement in screenwriting, 1983. Office: c/o CAA 9830 Wilshire Blvd Beverly Hills CA 90212-1804

GOLDMAN, WILLIAM SCOTT, lawyer; b. Far Rockaway, N.Y., July 31, 1966; s. Elliot and Karen Goldman; m. Catharine Goldman. BA, Oberlin Coll., 1988; JD, Dickinson Sch. Law, 1991; LLM, George Washington U., 1993. Bar: Pa., U.S. Ct. Appeals (fed. cir.), Ct. Internat. Trade. Mng. atty. Litman Law Offices, Ltd., Arlington, Va., 1992—. Contbr. articles to profl. jours. Mem. ABA, Am. Intellectual Property Law Assn., Fed. Circuit Bar Assn. Jewish. Avocations: sports, music, reading. Office: Litman Law Offices Ltd 3717 Columbia Pike Arlington VA 22204-4255

GOLDMAN, YACOV, aerospace engineering researcher, educator; b. Klinsi, Briansk, Russia, Sept. 30, 1930; arrived in Israel, 1972; s. Avraham Adolf Goldman and Sofia Bogin; m. Ada Sirotkin, Dec. 1955 (div. 1963); 1 child, Ana; m. Sofia Bogdanov, Aug. 1963; children: Ella, Doron. Grad. in engring., Inst. Steel, Moscow, 1953; MSc in Math., U. Moscow, 1967; PhD, Inst. Aero. Tech., Moscow, 1968. Engr. Plant Indsl. Furnaces, Sverdlovsk, USSR, 1953-55; sr. engr. Inst. Energy, Moscow, 1955-66, head lab., 1967-72; vis. assoc. prof. Ohio State U., Columbus, 1979-80; sr. rsch. asst. Technion, Haifa, Israel, 1973-79, sr. rsch. fellow, 1981—, head lab., 1990-95; vis. sr. rsch. assoc. Yale U., New Haven, 1986-87. Contbr. articles to profl. jours., including Combustion Sci. and Tech., Jour. Aerosol Sci., Jour. Fuel. Mem. N.Y. Acad. Scis.. Home: 11 Biram Rd, 34986 Haifa Israel Office: Technion, Faculty Aerospace Engring, 32000 Haifa Israel

GOLDMANN, THOMAS, management consultant; b. Wiesbaden, Fed. Republic Germany, May 15, 1950; s. Horst and Anne Katrin (Immel) G.; m. Wilhelmine Lettner, Apr. 1976; children: Agnes, Bruno. M Econs., U. Vienna, Austria, 1976. Vol. Österreichische Länderbank AG, Vienna, 1976; head dept. Austrian Ministry Commerce and Industry, Vienna, 1976-80; expert advisor Österreichische Industrie Holding AG, Vienna, 1980-86; head dept. Elin Union AG, Vienna, 1986-89; dir., head fin. dept., treas. Elektro & Elektronik Industrie Holding AG, Vienna, 1989-90; ptnr., mng. dir. corp. fin. internat. Goldmann & Ptnr. GmbH, Vienna, 1991-92; sr. mgr. Price Waterhouse Corp. Fin., Vienna, 1992-97; dir. Austrian Securities Authority, Vienna, 1997—; adv. bd. Z-Beteiligungsfonds AG, Vienna, 1984-88, Horizonte Venture Mgmt. GmbH, Vienna, 1985-89, Kabel & Draht Werke AG, Vienna, 1989-90. Contbr. articles to profl. jours. Office: Austrian Securities Auth, Canovagasse 7, A-1010 Vienna Austria

GOLDNER, BRUCE GARY, physician; b. Bklyn., Aug. 1, 1961; s. Leonard and June Goldner. BA, Franklin & Marshall Coll., 1983; MD, Georgetown U., 1987. Attending physician North Shore U. Hosp., Manhasset, N.Y., 1994—. Fellow Am. Coll. Cardiology. E-mail: bgoldner1@msn.com1. Office: North Shore U Hosp 300 Community Dr Manhasset NY 11030-3801

GOLDREICH, YAIR, climatologist, geographer; b. Tel-Aviv, Oct. 28, 1937; s. Yoseph Ya'acov and Ada (Blechmann) G.; m. Avrille Sandra Fine, Aug. 14, 1962; children: Tovi, Motie, Dafna, Nurith, Moshe. BA, Hebrew Univ., 1961, MA, 1963; PhD, Univ. Witwatersrand, Johannesburg, 1970. Lectr. dept. geography Bar-Ilan Univ., Ramat-gan, Israel, 1970-73; lectr., sr. lectr. Tel Aviv Univ., 1972-76; head dept. geography BIU, 1971-78; sr. lectr. Bar Ilan Univ., Ramat-Gan, 1973-85, assoc. prof., 1985-95, prof., 1995—; cons. climatologist, Tel-Aviv, 1968—. Author: The Climate of Israel, 1998; contbr. articles to profl. jours.; mem. editorial adv. bd. Jour. Atmospheric Environment, 1991-2000. With Israeli Army, 1956-58. Recipient numerous rsch. grants. Mem. Elizur Sport Chess Club. Avocation: chess. Home: 50 Montefiori St, 49490 Petah Tiqwa Israel Office: Bar Ilan Univ dept geography, Dept Geography, 52900 Ramat Gan Israel

GOLDSCHMIDT, ERNST WALTER MATTHIAS, ophthalmology educator, ophthalmic surgeon; b. Frankfurt, Germany, Aug. 24, 1933; arrived in Denmark, 1937; s. Hans Hellmuth and Jeltje Hendrika (Jolles) G.; m. Vibeke Vejlsgaard Bakke; 5 children. MD, U. Copenhagen, 1958, D Med. Sci., 1968. Intern KAS, Genofte, 1958-59; resident various hosps., Copenhagen, 1959-71; head dept. ophthalmology Odense (Denmark) U., 1971-83, assoc. prof., 1971-79, prof., 1979-84; head dept. ophthalmology Hillerød (Denmark) Sygehus, 1983—; chmn. specialist bd. Danish Nat. Bd. Health, 1972-77; mem. bd. Adv. Com. on Med. Tng. of European Communities, 1975-85; cons. Danida, New Delhi, 1988-89; prof. ophthalmology U. Hong Kong, 1992-94. Editor Procs. 3rd Internat. Conf. on Myopia, 1980, Myopia Workshop, 1987. Officer Danish Navy, 1960-61. Office: Cent Sygehuset Hillerod, Dept Eye 00821 Helsevej 2, 3400 Hillerød Denmark

GOLDSCHMIDT, JOHN ANTHONY, film producer, film director; b. London, England, Aug. 1, 1943; s. Hans Eberhardt and Susan (Gilpin) G. MA, Royal Coll. Art, London, 1968. Prodr., dir. TV programs including World in Action. Recipient British Acad. award, Prix Italia Rai prize, The Golden Nymph, Monte CArlo, The Cine Del Luca award, Austrian Culture prize, Silver Hugo, Chicago, Royal TV Soc. award, Emmy Nomination, German Cinema Owner's prize, The Silver Bear, Berlin, Cableace award, Silver Nymph, Monte Carlo. Mem. British Acad. Film and TV Arts, Groucho Club, Dirs. Guild of Great Britain. Office: Viva Films c/o NLPAC, 76 St James Ln, London N10 3DF, England

GOLDSMITH, BARBARA CECILE, sculptor, curator; b. Chgo., June 8, 1938; m. Morton Goldsmith, Sept. 12, 1959; children: Marc Richard, Lesley Sue Nemzoff. BFA, U. Ill., 1960; cert., Sch. Art Inst. Chgo., 1990; student, Evanston (Ill.) Art Ctr., 1976-80, U. Minn., 1989. Cert. tchr., Ill. Art tchr. mid. and secondary schs., 1960-65; curator Noyes Cultural Art Ctr. Gallery, 1983—, Evanston Art Ctr., 1976; with Art Adventure, Inc., 1992; bd. dirs. Skokie (Ill.) Northshore Sculpture Park, 1993—; com. mem. Evanston Art Coun., 1983—; mem. exhbn. com. Evanston Arts Ctr., 1986—. One-woman shows include Northcare Ctr., Evanston, 1981, Loyd Shin Gallery, Wilmette, Ill., 1987; exhibited in group shows at Spertus Mus. Judaica, 1981-82, 88, 90, Dellora A. Norris Cultural Arts Ctr., St. Charles, Ill., 1982, Livertyville Art Ctr., 1982-83, Countryside Gallery, 1982, Peace Mus., Chgo., 1984, Grove St. Gallery, Evanston, 1984, Minn. Art Inst., 1984, U. Wis., 1984, Burpee Art Mus., Rockford, Ill., 1985, Triton Coll., River Grove, Ill., 1985, Alliance Gallery, Ft. Wayne, Ind., 1986, 87, 88, 89, 90, David Adler Cultural Ctr., 1988, 90, Noyes Cultural Arts Ctr. Gallery, Evanston, 1988, 93, 96, South Bend (Ind.) Art Ctr., 1988, 89, 90, Arc Gallery, Chgo., 1990, Spertus Mus., Chgo., 1990, Galesburg (Ill.) Art Ctr., 1990, Evanston Art Ctr., 1990, 94, Elgin (Ill.) Coll., 1991, Signature Gallery, Stoughton, Wis., 1991, 92, 93, 94, Uhlein Peters Gallery, Milw., 1992, Calumet City (Ill.) Gallery, 1993, Northwest Cultural Coun. Gallery, Rolling Meadows, Ill., 1994, Suburban Fine Arts Ctr., Highland Park, Ill., 1994, 96, Sch. Art Inst. Chgo., 1994, Friendship Village Corp. Gallery, Schaumberg, Ill., 1995, Norris Gallery, St. Charles, 1996, Noyes Cultural Art Ctr., Evanston, 1996, 97, Chgo. Cultural Ctr., 1998, The Three Arts Club, Chgo., 1998, Time-Life Bldg., Chgo., 1999, Gallery 510, Decatur, Ill, 1999, James R. Thompson Ctr., Chgo., 1999, others; commd. Stockholm, 1993, Lake Geneva, Wis., 1993, Skokie Northshore Sculpture Park, 1994; also pvt. and corp. collections. Recipient award for extraordinary dedication and profl. curatorial experties Evanston Arts Coun., 1997, Mayors Arts awards, Evanston. Home: 9055 Keystone Ave Skokie IL 60076-1723

GOLDSMITH, GERALD P., lawyer; b. N.Y.C., Feb. 28, 1930; s. Lazarus A. and Sylvia Lila (Goldfarb) G.; m. Leda Carroll, Aug. 2, 1957; children: Leslie Sara, Nicole. Student, Bradley U., 1948-52; LLB, N.Y. Law Sch., 1958. Bar: N.Y. 1959, U.S. Dist. Ct. (so. and ea. dists.) N.Y. 1963, U.S. Supreme Ct. 1970, U.S. Ct. Appeals (2d cir.) 1984. Pvt. practice, N.Y.C., 1959—. Author: Boatfixit, 1959. Pres. young men's divsn. Grand St. Boys Assn., 1954-59; group leader Univ. Settlement House, 1954-59; chmn. Anti-Defamation League, Bronx County, N.Y., 1962-64, co-chmn. met. coun., 1964-66; founder, former mem. exec. com., former chmn. legal and comty. affairs Benjamin Franklin Reform Dem. Club, Bronx County; founder Riverdale YM-YWHA, Bronx, 1967; chmn., v.p. bd. trustees, former sec., chmn. various coms., pro bono atty.; candidate for Bronx County Civil Ct., 1974, 75; campaign chmn., organizer, legal advisor to local, city, state and nat. elections; bd. dirs., pro bono legal advisor Children's Day Treatment Ctr. and Sch., 1980; com. chmn. Assn. Bronx Comty. Orgns. Mem. ATLA, Jewish Trial Lawyers Assn., N.Y. State Trial Lawyers Assn., Bronx County Bar Assn., Rotary Club of Chinatown (pres. 1995-96, exec. com., chmn. various coms., Paul Harris fellow). Democrat. Avocations: boating, jazz. Office: 299 Broadway Rm 1820 New York NY 10007-1901

GOLDSMITH, JOCELYN STONE, state employment professional; b. Columbus, Ohio, Aug. 26, 1933; d. Roy J. Stone and Lillian Stone Frazin Alterman Friedland; m. Daniel J. Goldsmith, Mar. 15, 1953 (div. Nov. 1972); children: Debra Ann Goldsmith Wilson, Jeffrey Robert (dec.), David Michael; m. Chester G. Bandman, Sept. 20, 1992 (dec. Jan. 1995). BS in Bus., Frankin U., 1980, BS in Employee Assistance Counseling, 1989. User svcs. coord. R.G. Barry Corp., Columbus, 1974-82; claims mgr. Ohio Bur. Employment Svcs., Columbus, 1983—; Adopt-A-Sch. coord. Columbus Pub. schs., Greater Columbus C. of C., 1979—. Mem. safe and drug-free schs. consortium Frnklin County Ednl. Coun. Recipient plaque Ohio Sch. Partnership, 1995. Mem. Internat. Assn. Personnel in Employment Security. Jewish. Avocations: reading, enjoying plays, concerts and ballet. Office: Ohio Dept Jobs & Family Svcs 145 S Front St Columbus OH 43215-4116

GOLDSMITH, LOWELL ALAN, medical educator; b. Bklyn., Mar. 29, 1938; s. Isidore Alexander and Ida (Kaplan) G.; m. Carol Amreich, June 11, 1960; children: Meredith, Eileen. AB, Columbia Coll., 1959; MD, SUNY, Bklyn., 1963. Diplomate Am. Bd. Dermatology. Intern, then resident in medicine UCLA Med. Ctr., 1963-65; resident in dermatology Harvard Med. Sch., Boston, 1967-69; asst. prof. dermatology Harvard U. Med. Sch., Boston, 1970-73; asst. in dermatology Mass. Gen. Hosp., Boston, 1970-71, asst. dermatologist, 1971-73; assoc. prof. medicine Duke U. Med. Ctr., Durham, N.C., 1973-78, prof., 1978-81; James H. Sterner prof. dermatology Sch. Medicine and Dentistry, U. Rochester, N.Y., 1981-96, chief dermatology unit, 1981-87, acting chmn. dept. medicine, 1985-87, chmn. dept. dermatology, 1987-96; dean Sch. Medicine and Dentistry U. Rochester, N.Y., 1996-2000; mem. dermatology adv. com. FDA, 1983-87; chmn. Gordon Rsch. Cong. on Epithelial Differentiation and Keratiniazation, 1987, AAD-CDC Conf. on skin cancer prevention and edn., Washington, 1995; mem. gen. medicine A study sect. USPHS, NIH, 1988-92, chmn., 1990-92; mem. coun. NIAMS, NIH, 1996-99; chmn. med. adv. bd. Nat. Alcopecia Areata Found., 1981-87, 90—, bd. dirs.; bd. dirs. Monroe Cmty. Hosp., Rochester, Ctr. for Alternatives in Animal Testing, Balt.; chmn. NIH Consensus Conf. on Diagnosis and Treatment of Early Melanoma, Bethesda, 1992. Author, editor: Biochemistry and Physiology of the Skin, 1983, 2d edit., 1991, Physiology, Biochemistry and Molecular Biology of the Skin, 1991, Differential Diagnosis of Skin Disease, 2d edit., 1996; mem. editl. bd. Archives Dermatology, 1981-92, Clinics in Dermatology, 1982-96, Jour. Investigative Dermatology, 1987-95, Seminars in Dermatology, 1991-96, Jour. Dermatological Sci., 1994—; also numerous articles. With USPHS, 1965-67. Recipient Rsch. Career Devel. award USPHS, 1975-80; Macy Found. fellow, 1978-79. Mem. Assn. Am. Physicians, Am. Soc. Clin. Investigation, Am. Acad. Dermatology (bd. dirs.), Soc. Investigative Dermatology (bd. dirs., pres. 1994-95), Nat. Ichthyosis Found. (chmn. adv. bd. 1981-85), Assn. Profs. Dermatology (bd. dirs. 1984-87, pres. 1992-94), Am. Bd. Dermatology (bd. dirs. 1993-96), N.Y. State Soc. Dermatology (pres. 1985-89), Buffalo-Rochester Dermatology Soc. (pres. 1987), Rochester Dermatology Soc., Rochester Acad. Medicine, Polish Dermatol. Assn. (hon.), Brit. Dermatology Assn. (hon.), Alpha Omega Alpha. Office: Univ Rochester Box 706 601 Elmwood Ave Rochester NY 14642-0001

GOLDSMITH, MICHAEL ALLEN, oncologist, educator; b. Bronx, N.Y., Jan. 28, 1946; s. Walter and Bertha (Tannenberg) G.; m. Judith Harriet Plaut, June 6, 1971; children: Sharon, Esther, Eva, Steven. BA, Yeshiva U., 1967; MD, Albert Einstein Coll. Medicine, 1971. Diplomate Am. Bd. Internal Medicine. Intern Bronx Mcpl. Hosp. Ctr., 1971-72; staff assoc. Nat. Cancer Inst., Bethesda, Md., 1972-74; resident in medicine Mt. Sinai Hosp., N.Y.C., 1974-75, fellow in neoplastic diseases, 1975-77, asst. clin. prof. medicine and neoplastic diseases, 1977—; attending physician Oncology Consultants, P.C., N.Y.C., 1977—; reviewer Jour. AMA, 1988-90, New Eng. Jour. Medicine, 1995—. Contbr. articles to med. jours. Vice-pres. Congregation Orach Chaim, N.Y.C., 1978-83. Lt. comdr. USPHS, 1972-74. Fellow ACP; mem. Am. Soc. Clin. Oncology, Am. Assn. Cancer Rsch. Achievements include research in new anticancer drugs. Office: Oncology Cons PC 1045 5th Ave New York NY 10028-0138

GOLDSMITH, PAUL FELIX, physics and astronomy educator; b. Washington, Nov. 5, 1948; s. Raymond William and Selma Evelyn (Fine) G.; m. Sheryl E. Reiss, June 5, 1988. AB, U. Calif., Berkeley, 1969, PhD., 1975. Mem. tech. staff AT&T Bell Labs., Holmdel, N.J., 1975-77; asst. prof. U. Mass., Amherst, 1977-82, assoc. prof., 1982-85, prof. physics and astronomy, 1985-92; prof. astronomy, dir. Nat. Astronomy and Ionosphere Ctr. Cornell U., Ithaca, N.Y., 1993—, James A. Weeks prof. phys. sci., 1999—; cons. MIT Lincoln Lab., Lexington, Mass., 1977-80; v.p. R & D Millitech Corp., South Deerfield, Mass., 1983-92. Author: Quasioptical Systems, 1998; editor: Instrumentation and Techniques for Radio Astronomy, 1988; contbr. articles on radio astronomy and millimeter and submillimeter wavelength tech. to profl. jours. Fellow IEEE; mem. Microwave Theory Tech. Soc. of IEEE (mem. spkr.'s bur. 1989-90, Disting. lectr. 1992-93), Am. Astron. Soc. Office: Nat Astronomy & Ionsphere Ctr Cornell University Space Sciences Building Ithaca NY 14853

GOLDSMITH, STUART ANDREW, corporate finance company executive; b. Ashford, Kent, England, Apr. 1, 1945. BA in Econs., U. Bristol, England, 1966. Investment dir. Britannia Arrow Holdings Plc, London, 1978-84; dep. chmn., CEO Fredericks Place plc, London, 1985-89; chmn. Ketton Securities Ltd., London, 1989—; dir. Savoy Asset Mgmt. plc, London, 1997-2000, AIM Distbn. Trust plc, London, 1996—, Refresh Ltd., London, 1995—, Paternoster Partnership Ltd., London, 1992-99. Chmn. Convocation U. Bristol, 1998—. Office: Ketton Securities Ltd, 27 Throgmorton St, London EC2N 2AQ, England

GOLDSMITH, WILLIS JAY, lawyer; b. Paris, Feb. 21, 1947; came to U.S., 1949; s. Irving and Alice (Rosenfeld) G.; m. Marilynn Jacobson, Aug. 12, 1973; children: Andrew Edward, Helene Sara. AB, Brown U., 1969; JD, NYU, 1972. Bar: N.Y. 1973, U.S. Ct. Appeals (2d cir.) 1975, D.C. 1978, U.S. Ct. Appeals (4th cir.) 1979, U.S. Ct. Appeals (D.C. cir.) 1979, U.S. Supreme Ct. 1980, U.S. Ct. Appeals (6th cir.) 1985, U.S. Ct. Appeals (7th cir.) 1989, U.S. Ct. Appeals (3d cir.) 1991, U.S. Ct. Appeals (5th cir.) 1998. Atty. Dept. Labor, Washington, 1972-74; assoc. Guggenheimer & Untermyer, N.Y.C., 1974-77; assoc. Seyfarth, Shaw, Fairweather & Geraldson, Washington, 1977-79, ptnr., 1979-83; ptnr. Jones, Day, Reavis & Pogue, Washington, 1983—, chmn. labor and employment law practice, 1991—; adj. prof. law Georgetown U., 1988-91; fellow Coll. Labor and Employment Law, 1997—. Contbg. editor Employee Rels. Law Jour., 1983-91; assoc. editor Occupl. Safety and Health Law; mem. editl. adv. bd. Benefits Law Jour., 1991—. Mem. ABA (sect. labor and employment law com. on employee benefits, com. on occupl. safety and health), NYU Ctr. for Labor and Employment Law (bd dirs. 1997—), D.C. Bar Assn., Met. Club (Washington), Kenwood Golf and Country Club (Bethesda, Md.). Democrat. Jewish. Home: 6409 Elmwood Rd Chevy Chase MD 20815-6621 Office: Jones Day Reavis & Pogue 51 Louisiana Ave NW Washington DC 20001-2113

GOLDSPINK, DAVID FRANK, cell and molecular biology educator; b. Hull, Yorkshire, Eng., Jan. 15, 1944; s. James Albert and Muriel (Gee) G.; m. Edith Miller, May 16, 1970; children: Wilkins Michelle Anwyn, Graham Jonathan. BSc in Physiology and Chemistry, U. Newcastle Upon Tyne, Eng., 1966, PhD in Clin. Biochemistry, 1969, DSc, 1986. Postdoctoral rsch. fellow Muscular Dystrophy Unit, U. Newcastle, 1969-71; rsch. fellow Harvard Med. Sch., Boston, 1971-73; lectr. in physiology Queen's U., Belfast, No. Ireland, 1974-82; reader in physiology Queen's U., Belfast, 1982-87; sr. lectr. cardiovascular studies U. Leeds, Eng., 1988-93, prof. cell biology Rsch. Sch. Medicine, 1993-98; emeritus prof. U. Leeds, 1998-2000; sr. rsch. fellow molecular medicine St. James' Hosp, Leeds, 1999; prof. cell and molecular sports sci. Liverpool John Moores U., Eng., 2000—; Grant application reviewer Med. Rsch. Coun., Brit. Heart Found. and NSF; external examiner of higher degrees for several univs., U.K. Editor: The Development and Specialization of Skeletal Muscle, 1981; referee for various sci. and med. jours.; contbr. chpts. to books and articles to profl. jours. Communicant, ch. warden, 1996-2000, mem. parochial ch. coun. Ch. of Eng., 1990-2000; appeals coord. Leeds Faith in Schs., 1994-97, St. George's Crypt for the Homeless, Leeds, 1997-98, trustee 1999-2000; mem. Yorkshire adv. panel Salvation Army, 1998-2000. Grantee various rsch. couns. and med. charities, 1974—. Mem. Brit. Soc. for Cardiovascular Rsch., Physiol. Soc., Biochem. Soc. (editl. advisor 1981-86). Avocations: sports, photography, church and charity related activities. Fax: 0151-231-4353. E-mail: d.goldspink@liv.jm.ac.uk.

GOLDSTEIN, BRENDA IRIS, retired elementary school educator; b. Bklyn., Mar. 18, 1940; d. Joseph and Gladys Gordon Goldstein. BA, Bklyn. Coll., 1960, MS, 1969. Ret. tchr. Bklyn., 1996; profl. reader, internet rschr. CIA, 1997—. Polit. writer, 1997—. Mem. Libr. of Congress Assocs. Congregationalist. Avocations: reading history and classic novels, listening to contemporary and classical music. Home: 73 Bay 22 St Brooklyn NY 11214-3854

GOLDSTEIN, DAVID, oncologist, educator; b. Melbourne, Victoria, Australia, May 22, 1952; s. Monasze and Ada (Ryzowy) G.; m. Jennifer Susan Shand; children: Michael Daniel, Adam Simon. MB, BChir, Monash U., Melbourne, Australia, 1975. Resident internal medicine Prince Henry Hosp., Melbourne, 1976-78; internal medicine physician Queen Victoria Hosp., Melbourne, 1979-80, Kings Coll. Hosp., London, 1980-81, St. Vincent's Hosp., Sydney, 1982-85; head clin. trials unit Nat. Ctr. in HIV Rsch. U. NSW, Sydney, Australia; dir. med. oncology Box Hill Hosp., Melbourne, 1994-96; sr. staff specialist Prince of Wales Hosp., Sydney, 1996—; rsch. fellow U. Wis. Clin. Cancer Ctr., 1986-89. Contbr. chpts. to books and articles to profl. jours. Fellow Coll. Physicians Australia; mem. Coll. Physicians U.K., Am. Soc. Clin. Oncology, Am. Assn. Cancer Rsch. Avocations: skiing, cinema. Home: 5 Warren Rd Bellevue Hill, Sydney NSW 2023, Australia Office: Prince Wales Hosp, High St Randwick, Sydney NSW 2031, Australia

GOLDSTEIN, DAVID ARTHUR, biophysicist, educator; b. Rochester, N.Y., Nov. 8, 1934; s. Jacob David and Elizabeth Maude (Brown) G.; m. Marie Elaine Nardone, May 25, 1969; 1 child, David James. AB in Physics, Harvard U., 1956, MD, 1960. Rsch. fellow biophys. lab Harvard Med. Sch., Cambridge, Mass., 1960-62; rsch. assoc. biophys. lab. Harvard Med. Sch., Cambridge, 1964-65; asst. prof. radiation biology and biophysics Rochester Sch. Med. and Dentistry, 1965-68, assoc. prof. biophysics, 1968-97, assoc. prof. biomath., 1969-74, assoc. prof. med. informatics, 1988-98, prof. emeritus med. informatics, 1999—; dir. Med. Ctr. Computing, U. Rochester Med. Sch., 1975-77, assoc. chmn. dept. radiation biology and biophysics, 1980-85, dir. divsn. med. informatics, 1988-98; cons. mathematician NIMH, Bethesda, Md., 1963-64. Contbr. articles to profl. jours. Treas. Stormers Soccer Club, Rochester, 1983-93; bd. dirs. Monroe County Girls Soccer League, Rochester, 1988-93. Surgeon, USPHS, 1963-64. Grantee AEC, NIH, NSF, ERDA, DOE, 1965-96. Mem. AAAS, Biophys. Soc., N.Y. Acad. Scis. Home: 75 Deer Creek Rd Pittsford NY 14534-4147

GOLDSTEIN, HARVEY, statistics educator, researcher; b. London, Oct. 30, 1939; s. Jack and Millicent (Belanoff) G.; m. Barbara Collinge, Aug. 1, 1970; 1 child, Thomas. BS in Math., Manchester U., Eng., 1961. Lectr. U. London, 1964-71; sr. lectr. Nat. Children's Bur., London, 1971-76; prof. U. London, 1977—. Author: Design and Analysis of Longitudinal Studies, 1979, Multilevel Statistical Models, 1995, Assessment, 1996. Fellow Royal Statis. Soc. (chartered statistician), Brit. Acad. Avocations: squash, playing flute, jogging. E-mail: h.goldstein@ioe.ac.uk. Office: Inst Edn, 20 Bedford Way, London WC1H 0AL, England

GOLDSTEIN, JEROME ERIC, emergency physician surgeon, lawyer; b. Bronx, Feb. 21, 1952; s. Stanley Irving and Hortense (Silverstein) G. BSc with honors, Tulane U., 1973; MD summa cum laude, U. Bologna, Italy, 1982; postgrad., U. Pitts., 2000—. Diplomate Am. Bd. Internal Medicine. Intern St. Orsula Hosp. U., Bologna, Italy, 1982; resident in gen. surgery Booth Meml. Med. Ctr., NYU Sch. Medicine, 1983; resident in pediatrics Morristown Meml. Hosp., Columbia U. Sch. Medicine, 1984; resident in gen. surgery Easton Hosp., Hahnaman U. Sch. Medicine, 1985-86, resident in internal medicine, 1987-88; emergency physician Albert Einstein Med. Ctr., Phila., 1989-94, Parkview Hosp., Phila., 1991-92, Chester (Pa.) Cmty. Hosp., 1992-94; med. dir. Holmsburg Prison, Phila., 1994-95; asst. emergency medicine dir. Clearfield (Pa.) Hosp., 1995-96; emergency physician Lewistown (Pa.) Hosp., 1996-98. Mem. ACP, Assn. Emergency Physicians. Republican. Jewish. Avocations: horology, gourmet cooking, international

travel, camping, photography. Home and Office: 3733 Rural Ct E Pittsburgh PA 15221-3915

GOLDSTEIN, JOSEPH LEONARD, physician, medical educator, molecular genetics scientist; b. Sumter, SC, Apr. 18, 1940; s. Isadore E. and Fannie A. Goldstein. BS, Washington and Lee U., Lexington, Va., 1962; MD, U. Tex., Dallas, 1966; DSc (hon.), U. Chgo., 1982, Rensselaer Poly. Inst., 1982, Washington and Lee U., 1986, U. Paris, 1988, U. Buenos Aires, 1990, So. Meth. U., 1993, U. Miami, 1996, U. Miami, 1006. Intern, then resident in medicine Mass. Gen. Hosp., Boston, 1966-68; clin. assoc. NIH, 1968-70; postdoctoral fellow U. Wash., Seattle, 1970-72; mem. faculty U. Tex. Southwestern Med. Ctr., Dallas, 1972—, Paul J. Thomas prof. medicine, chmn. dept. molecular genetics, 1977—, regental prof., 1985—; Harvey Soc. lectr., 1977; mem. sci. rev. bd. Howard Hughes Med. Inst., 1978-84, mem. med. adv. bd., 1985-90, chmn. med. adv. bd., 1995—; non-resident fellow Salk Inst., 1983-94; chmn. Albert Lasker Med. Rsch award jury, 1996—; mem. bd. sci. govs. Scripps Rsch. Inst., 1996—. Co-author: The Metabolic Basis of Inherited Disease, 5th edit., 1983; editorial bd. Jour. Biol. Chemistry, 1981-85, Cell, 1983—, Jour. Clin. Investigation, 1977-82, Ann. Rev. Genetics, 1980-85, Arteriosclerosis, 1981-87, Sci. 1985-98. Mem. bd. trustees Rockefeller U., 1994—; mem. sci. adv. bd. Welch Found., 1986—; bd. dirs. Passano Found., 1985—. Recipient Heinrich-Wieland prize, 1974, Pfizer award in enzyme chemistry Am. Chem. Soc., 1976; Passano award Johns Hopkins U., 1978; Gairdner Found. award, 1981; award in biol. and med. scis. N.Y. Acad. Scis., 1981, Lita Annenberg Hazen award, 1982; Rsch. Achievement reward Am. Heart Assn., 1984; Louisa Gross Horwitz award, 1984; 3M Life Scis. award, 1984, Albert Lasker award in Basic Med. Rsch., 1985; Nobel Prize in Physiology or Medicine, 1985, Trustees' medal Mass. Gen. Hosp., 1986, U.S. Nat. medal of Sci., 1988, prize Warren Alpert Found., 2000. Mem. NAS (Lounsbery award 1979, coun. 1991—), ACP (award 1986), Assn. Am. Physicians, Am. Soc. Clin. Investigation (pres. 1985-86), Am. Soc. Human Genetics (William Allan award 1985), Amer. Acad. Arts and Scis., Am. Soc. Biol. Chemists, Am. Fedn. Clin. Research, Am. Philos. Soc., Inst. Medicine, Royal Soc. London (fgn. mem.), Tex. Philos. Soc., Phi Beta Kappa, Alpha Omega Alpha. Home: 3831 Turtle Creek Blvd Apt 22B Dallas TX 75219-4538 Office: U Tex Southwestern Med Ctr 5323 Harry Hines Blvd Dallas TX 75390-7208

GOLDSTEIN, LEONARD BARRY, dentist, educator; b. Seaford, N.Y., Feb. 6, 1944; s. Jacob Martin and Adele (Pelzner) G.; m. Phyllis Lynn Kerwin, June 25, 1967; children: Marcie Ilene, Sherri Elysse. Student, Ind. U., 1961-63; DDS, Case Western Reserve U., 1967; Cert. in Orthodontics, Dewey Sch. Orthodontics, N.Y.C., 1969; PhD in Electro-Medicine, City U., Los Angeles, 1988. Diplomate Am. Acad. of Pain Mgmt., Am. Bd. Forensic Medicine, Am. Bd. Forensic Dentistry. Gen. practice dentistry Smithtown, N.Y., 1969—; attending orthodontist Abe Stark Philanthropies Dental Clinic, Bklyn., 1970-77; med. dir. TMJ Facial Pain Ctr. Southside Hosp., Bay Shore, N.Y., 1979—; guest prof. Dept. Phys. Edn. Queens Coll., N.Y., 1979—; guest lectr. Dept. Phys. Edn. Queensboro (N.Y.) Community Coll., 1980—; dir. dental services Good Samaritan Profl. Services, St. James, N.Y., 1979—, v.p. med. bd., 1979—; attending dental staff St. John's Episc. Hosp., 1980—, Community Hosp. Western Suffolk, 1980—; bd. dirs. L.I. Ctr. for Cranio-Facial Pain, Smithtown; med. dir. TMJ/Facial Pain Ctr., Southside Hosp. Contbr. articles to profl. jours. Served to capt. Dental Corps, U.S. Army, 1967-69. Recipient fellowship in removeable prosthetics U.S. Army Dental Corps, 1967. Fellow Acad. Stress and Chronic Disease, Acad. Gen. Dentistry, Am. Endodontic Soc., Internat. Coll. Dentists; mem. Am. Equilibration Soc., Am. Coll. Sports Medicine, Internat. Acad. Preventive Medicine, Cranial Acad. of Am. Osteopathic Soc., Am. Orthodontic Soc., Internat. Soc. Orthodontists, Am. Dental Soc., Cronio-Mandibular Study Club of N.Y., L.I. Gnathological Study Club, Northeastern Gnathological Soc. Office: 178 Alexander Ave Nesconset NY 11767-1602

GOLDSTEIN, MARGARET ANN, biologist; b. Sinton, Tex., Mar. 13, 1939; d. Daniel Archibald and Sarah Elizabeth (Tegg) McNeill; m. Alexander Goldstein, Jr., Feb. 14, 1959; 1 child, David William. BA magna cum laude, Rice U., Houston, 1965; PhD, Rice U., 1969. Lab instr. biology Rice U., 1965-69; instr. biology U. Tex./M.D. Anderson Hosp., Houston, 1969-70; asst. prof. biology U. Tex., Houston, 1969-77; instr. cell biophysics and medicine Baylor Coll. Medicine, Houston, 1970-73; asst. prof. cell biophysics and medicine Baylor Coll. Medicine, 1973-77, asst. prof. medicine and cell biology, 1977-79, assoc. prof. medicine and molecular and cellular biology, 1979-89, prof. medicine and molecular and cellular biology, 1989—; cons. NHLBI, NIH, 1986-94, NRC, 1996-2000; exec. com. basic scis. coun. Am. Heart Assn., Dallas, 1987-94, assembly del., 1995-98; biol. dir. Microscopy Soc. Am., 1990-92, chair internat. com., 1993-95, pres., 1995-96; liaison officer to AAAS/CAIP, 1990-95, resp. to AAAS bd., 1993-96. Contbr. articles to profl. jours. V.p., bd. dirs. Tex. Chamber Orch., Houston, 1982-86; bd. dirs. River Oaks Women's Breakfast Club, 1980-85, Houston Friends of Music, 1991—, Rice U. Shepherd Soc. Governing Coun., 1995—; mem. award com. YWCA Outstanding Houston Women, 1991-96; adv. bd. mem. Houston Grand Opera, 1995-96. Recipient Outstanding Houston Woman in Sci. and Tech. award YWCA, Houston, 1990, Order of Silver Thistle, Scottish Heritage Found., Houston, 1990, NASA Achievement award for Cosmos 2044, 1991, for Cosmos 2G, 1994; NIH grantee, 1974-98. Mem. AAAS (affiliate bd. consortium of affils. for internat. programs), Microscopy Soc. Am. (biol. dir. 1990-92, pres. 1995-96), Tex. Soc. for Electron Microscopy (pres. 1981-82, exec. coun. 1977-83), Am. Soc. Cell Biology, Assn. for Women in Sci. (v.p. 1979-80), Coun. Sci. Soc. Pres.'s (exec. bd. dirs. 1997). Avocations: music, gardening, physical fitness. Office: Baylor College Medicine Dept Medicine Houston TX 77030-3498

GOLDSTEIN, MARK KINGSTON LEVIN, high technology company executive, researcher; b. Burlington, Vt., Aug. 22, 1941; s. Harold Meyer Levin and Roberta (Butterfield) G.; m. Kyoko Matsubara, Mar. 8, 1984. BS in Chemistry, U. Vt., 1964; PhD, U. Miami, Coral Gables, 1971. Pres. IBR, Inc., Coral Gables, Fla., 1970-74; group leader Brookhaven Nat. Lab., Upton, N.Y., 1974-77; sr. rschr. East-West Ctr., Honolulu, 1977-79; sr. tech. advisor JGC Corp., Tokyo, 1979-81; pres., chmn. bd. Quantum Group, Inc., La Jolla, Calif., 1981—; exec. dir. Magnatek, Inc., Brotas, Brazil, 1982—; project leader proliferation and waste mgmt. policy study for Pres. Ford's sci. advisor. NSF fellow, 1964, 65. Mem. AAAS, Am. Chem. Soc., Hawaii Yacht Club (Honolulu). Patentee, inventor devices including biomimetic carbon monoxide sensor, thaser co-generators, supermitters, thermphotovoltaics self powered gas appliance, photon control systems, gas safety valve, eyesafe laser radar, photon wedding and superemissive light pipe. Home: 2248 Del Mar Heights Rd Del Mar CA 92014-3022 Office: Quantum Group Inc 11211 Sorrento Valley Rd San Diego CA 92121-1323

GOLDSTEIN, NORMAN RAY, international trading company executive, consultant; b. Chgo., Nov. 20, 1944; s. Max and Rose (Weiner) G.; m. Bonnie A. Brod, Aug. 31, 1969; children: Russell, Matthew, Jamie. AA, Wright Jr. Coll., 1965; BS in Fin., No. Ill. U., DeKalb, 1967; MS in Acctg. cum laude, Roosevelt U., 1986. Gen. bus. mgr. Greenstreet Corp., Whiting, Ind., 1967; wholesale credit mgr. Atlantic Richfield Co., Chgo., 1968-74; v.p. fin., treas. Barton Inc. (Barton Brands, Ltd.), Chgo., 1974-96; chmn., CEO Gold Internat., 1996—; spl. master U.S. Dist. Ct., 1998; chmn. ABC Fin. Communications Forum, Chgo., 1987-88; v.p., bd. dirs. Consort Corp., Chgo., 1971-80; spl. master U.S. Dist. Ct., 1998; adj. prof. fin. No. Ill. U., 2000—; speaker on treasury and fin. mgmt. Contbg. author: Handbook of Cash Flow and Treasury Management, 1987; contbr. articles to profl. publs. Bd. dirs. Maine Twp. Jewish Congregation Shaare Emet, Des Plaines, 1986—, pres. 1989-91. Named Outstanding Credit Exec. of Yr., Nat. Assn. Credit Mgmt., 1987, Disting. Alumnus Coll. of Bus. No. Ill. U., 1998. Fellow Nat. Inst. Credit; mem. Treasury Mgmt. Assn., Fin. Mgrs. Assn. Chgo. (treas. 1991-92), Treasury Mgmt. Assn. Chgo. (chmn. ednl. scholarship com. 1995-99, chmn. Windy City Summit Treasury Conf. 1999—), Distillers Imports and Vintners (chmn. 1980-82), N.Y. Credit and Fin. Mgmt. Assn., Chgo. Midwest Credit Mgmt. Assn. (bd. dirs. 1984-87).

GOLDSTERN, MARTIN, mathematician, educator; b. Vienna, Austria, May 7, 1963; s. Alexander and Christine (Hoser) G. MA in Computer Sci., Tech. U. of Vienna, 1985, D. Tech., 1986; postgrad., Bar Ilan U., Ramat Gan, Israel, 1990-92; PhD, U. Calif., Berkeley, 1991. Vis. rsch. asst. Hebrew U., Jerusalem, 1989; sci. asst. Free U., Berlin, 1992-93; univ. asst. Tech. U. Vienna, 1993-97, assoc. prof., 1997—. Author: The Incompleteness Phenomenon, 1994; contbr. articles to sci. publs. Recipient 1st prize Internat. Math. Olympiad, 1981. Mem. Am. Math. Soc., Austrian Math. Soc., Assn. for Symbolic Logic, Kurt-Gödel-Soc. Office: Tech U of Vienna, Wiedner Hauptstr 8/118.2, A-1040 Vienna Austria

GOLDSTONE, RICHARD JOSEPH, judge; b. Boksburg, Transvaal, South Africa, Oct. 26, 1938; s. Benjamin Harry and Catherine Rose (Jacobson) g.; m. Noleen Joy Behrman, Dec. 16, 1962; children: Glenda Brener, Nicole. BA, U. Witwatersrand, South Africa, 1959, LLB, 1962, LLD (hon.), 1994; LLD (hon.), U. Cape Town, South Africa, 1993, Hebrew U., Jerusalem, 1994, U. Natal, Durban, 1994, Wilfred Laurier U., Waterloo, Can., 1995, U. Glasgow, Scotland, 1997, Notre Dame U., 1997, Cath. U. Brabant, Tilburg, The Netherlands, 1997, U. Calgary, 1997; LHD (hon.), Maryland U. Coll., Mannheim, Germany, 1997. Bar: Johannesburg 1963. Sr. counsel, 1976; judge Transvaal Supreme Ct. South Africa, 1980-89; judge appellate divsn. Supreme Ct. South Africa, 1989-93; justice Constnl. Ct. South Africa, 1994—; nat. pres. Nat. Inst. for Crime Prevention and Rehab., 1982-99; chmn. Commn. Inquiry Regarding Pub. Violence and Intermediation, 1991-94; prosecutor Internat. Tribunal for the Former Yugoslavia and Rawanda, 1994-96; chancellor U. Witwatersrand, 1996—; fellow Ctr. for Internat. Affairs, Harvard U., 1989; hon. fellow St.John's Coll., Cambridge, 1995; hon. bencher Inner Temple, London, 1998; faculty mem. Salzburg Seminar, 1996, 98; chmn. Ind. Commn. on Kosovo. Chmn. Standing Adv. Com. on Co. Law, Johannesburg, 1991—, Bd. Human Right Inst. South Africa, 1996—. Recipient Internat. Human Rights award ABA, 1994; Paul Harris fellow Rotary Club Bloemfontedt, 1993. Mem. Am. Acad. Art and Scis. (fgn.), Assn. Bar N.Y. (hon.). Avocations: wine, reading, music, art, walking. Office: Constnl Ct, Pvt Bag X32, Braamfontein 2017, South Africa

GOLDSTON-MORRIS, MAURINE GERTRUDE, historian; b. Sydney, Australia, Nov. 2, 1923; d. Francis Morris-Dobbs and Mollie Goodwin; m. John Robert Goldston-Morris, Apr. 9, 1949 (dec. 1984); children: Neale Andrew, Anthony Clyde, Kathryn Lesley. Diploma in drama, Australian Acad., Sydney, 1945; MM, Coll. A.V.L., Sydney, 1990; DLitt, London Inst. Applied Rsch., 1992; PhD (hon.), Navigational Rsch., Melbourne, Australia, 1993; LLD (hon.), Applied Rsch., London, 1993. Grazier Wellington & Armidale, Wellington, 1947-64; mng. dir. M&J Morris, Sydney, 1969-82; presenter hist. exhbns.; Malaspina Exbhn. and lectr. Parliament House, Sydney; presenter Portuguesa Cartographia, 10,000 Years of Portuguese History; prof. history Oceania, Acad. Scis., Paris. Author: (monographs) Life of Admiral Arthur Phillip, Navigational Discoveries in the New World, Conquistadores of South America, others. Mem. Olympic Swimming Squad, 1938; pres. Women's Pioneer Soc. Australasia, 1982-84; pres. Capt. Arthur Phillip Bicentennial com., 1984-88, Scottish Australian Hritage Coun., Sydney, 1994, Australian Nat. Coun. 500th Anniversary Discover of Ams. by Christopher Colombus, 1992; patron Arthur Phillip H.S., Paramatta, Australia, 1994; preceptor Dame Companion Order St. Stanislas NSW, Australia, 1995; v.p. Fairlight br. Liberal Party, English Speaking Union; mem. Ibero-Am. Com. Australia; dep. mem. Internat. Parliament for Safety and Peace. Manly Lawn Tennis Champion, 1941; recipient Freedom of City of London award Guildhall, 1990, medal Order of Australia, 1991, Lazo Dama Order Isabel Catolica, 1993. Fellow Royal Geog. Soc.; mem. Royal Sydney Yacht Squadron, Internat. Coun. Women (life), NSW Coun. Women (life), Royal Commonwealth Soc. (past pres.), Hon. Co. Armigers Australia, Arthur Phillip Soc. Inc. (pres. 1989—), Women's Club (pres. 1991-94), Rotary. Avocations: sailing, historical pilgrimages, heraldry. Home: Unit 15 Mabuhay, 137 Sydney Rd, Fairlight 2094, Australia

GOLDSZAL, ALBERTO FIGUEIREDO, biomedical and electrical engineer; b. Rio de Janeiro, Sept. 26, 1964. BSEE, U. Brasilia, 1988; MSBE, Drexel U., 1992, PhD, 1994. Registered profl. engr. Systems analyst The House of Reps., Brasilia, Brazil, 1985-87, tchg. asst., 1987-88; elec. engr. Brasilia, Brazil, 1988-89; rsch. asst. U. Pa., Phila., 1992-94, Thomas Jefferson Hosp., Phila., 1993-94; rsch. faculty Drexel U., Phila., 1994-95; rsch. scientist NIH, Bethesda, 1995-97, chief info. officer Imaging Scis. Program, 1998—; cons. Johns Hopkins Hosp., Balt., 1997—. Contbr. articles to profl. jours. Recipient Shock award Nathan Shock Found., 1997; rsch. grantee Brazil Rsch. Coun., 1989-93. Fellow Nat. Inst. on Aging (rep. 1997-98); mem. IEEE, AAAS, Sigma Xi (Presdl. prize 1993, Coll. of Engring. prize 1992). Avocation: windsurfer. Office: NIH Dept Radiology Clin Ctr Bldg 10 Ste 2C20 Bethesda MD 20892

GOLDT, RAINER, Slavic studies educator; b. Marl-Huels, Germany, July 18, 1959; s. Heinrich Hubert and Helga (Gisse) G.; m. Malika Elise Ferhat, Aug. 11, 1984; children: Sebastian, Isabelle. PhD, U. Mainz, Germany, 1994. Author: Language and Myth in the Work of V. Chlebnikov, 1987 (German Assn. East European Studies award 1987), Thermodynamics as Textem, Entropy as a Poetological Cipher in the Writings of E. Zamyatin, 1995 (Mainz U. award 1994). Roman Catholic. Office: Johannes Gutenberg U, Welderweg 18, 55099 Mainz Germany

GOLDWURM, GIAN FRANCO, psychiatrist, psychologist, psychotherapist; b. Trento, Italy, June 17, 1929; s. Corrado and Olga (Casagranda) G.; m. Giovanna Negrin, Aug. 3, 1957 (div. 1988); children: Massimiliano, Andrea, Giuliano, Stefano; m. Concepción Monserrat Gomez Ocaña, July 7, 1991. MD, U. Milan, 1954; specialist in psychiatry, U. Psychiat. Sch. Milan, 1959. Med. rschr. Pharmacological Inst., U. Sch. Medicine, Milan, 1956-59; psychiat. asst. Psychiat. Clinic, U. Milan, 1959-68, psychiat. chief, 1968-72; psychiat. dir. Psychiat. Hosp. Trento, Italy, 1972-74, Psychiat. Hosp., Pavia, Italy, 1974-77, Psychiat. Hosp. (Paolo Pini) of Milan, 1977-81; psychiat. chief Psychiat. Oper. Unit 38 Niguarda Hosp., Milan, 1981-92; dir. Cognitive Behavioral Psychotherapy Sch. Milan, 1993—. Author: Psichiatria e Riforma Sanitaria, 1979; co-author: Dal Manicomio al Territorio, 1978, Le Tecniche di Rilassamento Nelle Terapie Comportamentali, 1986, I Disordini Schizofrenici, 1987; editor, co-author: Medicina Comportamentale, 1994; co-editor Terapia del Comportamento; co-worker Psicoterapia Cognitiva e Comportamentale. Lt. Italy Army Med. Svc., 1955-56. Mem. Italian Psychol. Assn., Italian Psychiat. Assn., Italian Assn. Anal. Modification of Behavior (pres. 1981-92, mem. dir. comm. 1992—), Collegium Internat. Activitatis Nervosae Superioris (pres. 1999—), European Assn. for Behavior Cognitive Therapy, N.Y. Acad. Scis. E-mail: gfgoldwurm@tiscalinet.it. Home: via Vanvitelli 50, 20129 Milan Lombardy, Italy Office: Cognitive Behav Psych Sch, via Settembrini 2, 20124 Milan Lombardy, Italy

GOLENETSKY, SERGUEI INNOKENTJEVITCH, seismologist, researcher; b. Irkutsk, RF, Mar. 15, 1926; s. Innokenty Fedorovitch and Valentina Ivanovna (Amvrosova) G.; m. Inna Gueorguievna Lukjanova, Sept. 24, 1960; children: Elena, Alexei. D in Physics and Math. with honors, State U. Irkutsk, 1948. Jr. rsch. worker Irkutsk U., 1948-49, Seismological Sta., Irkutsk, 1949-59; sr. rsch. worker East-Siberian Geol. Inst., Irkutsk, 1959-63; head lab. Inst. of the Earth's Crust, Irkutsk, 1963-92, leading rsch. worker, 1992—. Author: Earthquakes in Irkutsk, 1997; first author, mem. editl. bd.: Geology and Seismicity of the BAM Zone, 1985; author, editor Earthquakes of the Lake Baikal Region and East of Lake Baikal, 1970-97; contbr. articles to profl. jours. Recipient medal for the BAM (Rlwy.) Constrn., Supreme Soviet of the RSFSR, Moscow, 1983, prize Coun. of Mins. of the USSR, Moscow, 1988; Newton Honor grantee, Irkutsk U., 1947-48. Home: Apt 20, Lermontova St 313, 664033 Irkutsk Russia Office: Inst of the Earths Crust, Lermontova 128, 664033 Irkutsk Russia

GOLENKO-GINZBURG, DIMITRI, industrial engineering educator, researcher; b. Moscow, Nov. 24, 1932; arrived in Israel, 1985; s. Isaac Ginsburg and Anna Golenko; m. Tamar Milchenko, Jan. 23, 1960; 1 child, Ben-Yair Avner. MA in Econs., Inst. Nat. Economy, Moscow, 1954; MA in Math., Moscow State U., 1958; PhD in Computer Scis., Physico-Tech. Inst., Moscow, 1962; D in Tech. Scis., Chief Degree Awarding Coun., Moscow, 1966, prof. Computing Math. and Probability, 1968. Jr. rschr. Computing Ctr., Moscow, USSR, 1955-63; sr. rschr. Inst. Mgmt. Sci., Moscow, 1963-67; dept. head Inst. Control Machines, Moscow, 1967-69; prof. Economico-Statis. Inst., Moscow, 1969-77, Ben-Gurion U., Negev Beer Sheva, Israel, 1986—; v.p. Sci. Coun. on Network Planning for Defense Industries, USSR, 1964-70; mem. 8 Inst. sci. couns. in Leningrad, Moscow, Riga, Kiev, USSR, 1966-76; head Sci. area Inst. Standards in Machinery, Moscow, 1966-76; vis. rsch. prof. BHP, Melbourne Labs., Clayton, Australia, 1990; supr. 35 PhD Thesis and 150 MA Thesis, 1964-76, Moscow, 3 PhD Thesis and 8 MA Thesis, 1990-99, Ben-Gurion U., Israel. Author 14 books including Simulation and Statistical Analysis of Pseudo-Random Numbers on Computers, 1965, Statistical Methods in Network Planning and Control, 1968, Statistical Methods in Economical Systems, 1970, Statistical Methods in Production Control, 1973; (with S. Livshitz and S. Kesler) Statistical Modeling in Technico-Economical Systems, 1977; contbr. articles to profl. jours. Active Sci. Seminar of Soviet Jewish Refuseniks, Moscow, Tashkent, 1978-85. Recipient Hon. Citizenship, Israel, 1983; named to Rabby Gunther Plaut Chair in Project Mgmt., Ben Gurion U., of the Negev Beer Sheva, Israel, 1991. Mem. Paul Ivanier Ctr. Robotics, Ben Gurion U. Beer-Sheva. Avocations: swimming, travel, books. Home: St Shimoni 9/48, 84360 Beer Sheva Israel Office: Ben Gurion U of the Negev, Dept Indsl Engring Mgmt, 84105 Beer Sheva New Camp, Israel

GOLIC, JOVAN, electrical engineering educator; b. Belgrade, Serbia, Yugoslavia, Jan. 17, 1956; s. Djordje and Olga (Papic) G.; m. Kosa Radosavljevic, Dec. 8, 1985; 1 child, Djordje. BEE, Sch. Elec. Engring., Belgrade, Yugoslavia, 1979, MSc, 1981, PhD, 1985. Rsch. assoc. Inst. Applied Math. and Electronics, Belgrade, Yugoslavia, 1979-86; sr. rsch. fellow Inst. Applied Math. and Electronics, Belgrade, 1986-93, dept. head, 1986-93; rsch. scientist Info. Security Rsch. Ctr. Queensland U. Tech., Brisbane, Australia, 1993-97; assoc. prof. Sch. Elec. Engring. U. Belgrade, 1997—; adj. docent Faculty Tech. Scis., Novi Sad, Yugoslavia, 1986-97, Sch. Elec. Engring, Belgrade, 1988-97; adj. rsch. assoc. Math. Inst. Serbian Acad. Sci. and Arts, Belgrade, 1985—; Fulbright vis. scientist Cornell U., Ithaca, N.Y., 1987-88. lectr. at sci. confs. and symposiums; contbr. articles to internat. profl. jours. Named Best Student of Generation, Sch. of Elec. Engring, Belgrade, 1979; recipient Ann. October award City of Belgrade, 1979. Mem. Internat. Assn. Cryptol. Rsch. Serbian Orthodox Christian. Avocations: swimming, jogging, table tennis. Home: Kraljevačka 92, 11000 Belgrade Serbia, Yugoslavia Office: Sch Elec Engring U Belgrade, Blvd Revolucije 73, 11001 Belgrade Serbia, Yugoslavia

GOŁKIEWICZ, WŁADYSŁAW BOGDAN, chemist, educator; b. Kowel, Ukraine, Nov. 2, 1933; s. Michael and Łucja (Sobczak) G.; m. Barbara Krzywicka, July 29, 1960; children: Peter, Agnes, Monica. MSc, U. Mary Curie-Skiodowska, Lublin, Poland, 1955, D in Chemistry, 1971. Technologist Chem. Factory, Lublin, 1955-62; tchr. Med. Acad., Lublin, 1962-71, head of lab. of phys. chemistry, 1971-89, assoc. prof. chemistry, 1989-99, prof., 1999—, assoc. dean Faculty Pharmacy, 1993—, head dept. inorganic and analytical chemistry, 1998; mem. commn. of chromatography Polish Acad. Scis., Warsaw, 1984-97. Contbr. chpt. to: Handbook of Thin Layer Chromatography, 1990, 2nd edit., 1996; contbr. or co-contbr. over 70 articles to sci. jours.; patentee, co-patentee in field. Mem. Polish Chem. Assn. Avocations: classical music, recreational activities, tennis. Office: Med Acad, Staszica 6, Dept Inorganic Analyt Chem, 20-081 Lublin Poland

GOLLASCH, STEPHAN, marine biologist, researcher; b. Hamburg, Germany, Nov. 27, 1962. BS, U. Hamburg, 1988, MS, 1992, PhD, 1996. Asst. Biologische Anstalt Helgoland, Hamburg, 1990-91, U. Hamburg, 1991, Bundesforschungg. Fischer, Hamburg, 1994; scientist Inst. for Meerskunde, Kiel, Germany, 1992-96, 98—, Nederlands Inst. voor Onderzoek der Zee, Texel, The Netherlands, 1996, ABO Akademi U., Turku, Finland, 1997—; german Del. Internat. Maritime Orgn., 1997—; mem. Internat. Coun. for Exploration of the Sea Working Group on Introduction and Transfer of Marine Organisms, 1993—; mem. baltic Marine Biologists Working Group on Non-Indigenous Estuarine and Marine Organisms, 1995—; mem. Ices Study Group on Marine Biocontrol of Invasive Species; mem. Internat. Coun. for the Exploration of the Sea, Internat. Oceanographic Commn., Internat. Maritime Orgn. Study Group on Ballast Water and Sediments, 1995—. Contbr. articles to profl. jours. Collaborative Rsch. grantee, NATO, 1995. Mem. German Soc. Marine rsch., Protection Soc. German North Sea Coast, Soc. Genetics and Ethics Network. Home: Bahrenfelder Str 73a, 22765 Hamburg Germany Office: Inst for Meereskunde, Duesternbrooker Weg 20, 24105 Kiel Germany

GOLLEDGE, JONATHAN, surgeon; b. Cardiff, Great Britain, Jan. 20, 1965; s. Arthur and Colleen (Beryl) G. BA in Med. Scis. and Pathology, Cambridge U., 1987; BChir, Cambridge U.Med. Sch., 1989; MA, Cambridge U., 1990, MChir, 1997. Pre-registration dr. NHS, Cambridge/Great Yarmouth, 1990-91; sr. house surgeon NHS, London, 1991-94; surg. registrar NHS, Cardiff, 1994-95; specialist surg. registrar NHS, 1996—; lectr. in surgery Med. Sch. Chang Cross Hosp., London, 1995-96. Contbr. articles to profl. jours. Fellow Royal Coll. Surgeons. Avocations: running, cricket, computing. Home: 35 Sullivans Reach, Walton on Thames KT12 2QB, United Kingdom Office: Dept of Surgery, Charing Cross Hosp, London W6 8RF, United Kingdom

GOLLIN, SUSANNE MERLE, cytogeneticist, cell biologist; b. Chgo., Sept. 22, 1953; d. Harvey A. and Pearl (Reiffel) G.; m. Lazar M. Palnick; 1 child, Jacob Hillel. BA in Biology, Northwestern U., 1974, MS, 1975, PhD, 1980. Diplomate Am. Bd. Med. Genetics; cert. in clin. cytogenetics. Postdoctoral fellow U. Rochester (N.Y.) Med. Ctr., 1979-81; rsch. assoc. in cell biology Baylor Coll. Medicine, Houston, 1981-83, rsch. assoc. in genetics, 1983-84; asst. prof. dept. pathology and pediat. U. Ark. for Med. Scis., Little Rock, 1984-87; dir. cytogenetics lab. Ark. Children's Hosp., Little Rock, 1984-87; assoc. mem. Pitts. Cancer Inst., 1987-95, mem., 1995—; dir. U. Pitts. Cancer Inst. Cytogenetics Facility, 1989—; asst. prof. human genetics U. Pitts., 1987-95, dir. clin. cytogenetics lab., 1988-99, assoc. prof., 1995—, assoc. prof. pathology, 1997—, assoc. prof. otolaryngology, 1998—; dir. rsch., clin. cons. Pitts. Cytogenetics Lab., 1999—; mem. pediat. oncology grup, mem. exec. com. Ark. Genetics Program, 1984-87; mem. organizing com. Am. Cytogenetics Conf., 1990—; mem. Allegheny County Bd. Health, 1992—, vice chmn., 1997, 2000; mem. clin. lab. improvement adv. com. Ctrs. Disease Control and Prevention, HHS, 1994-2000, mem. genetic testing subcom., 1997-2000; vis. sci. German Cancer Rsch. Ctr., Heidelberg, 1995; cons. med. devices adv. com. FDA, 1996—; mem. oral biol. med. I study sect. NIH, 1997; master gardener trainee, 1999—. Contbr. articles to profl. jours. Mem. deans' adv. com. Pa. Sch. Excellence for Healthcare Profls., 1991-95; v.p. faculty senate U. Pitts. Grad. Sch. Pub. Health, 1994-95, mem. senate anti-discriminatory policies com., 1999—; vol. Lighthouse for Blind, Houston, 1983; chmn. med. ethics and civil liberties com. ACLU, Pitts., 1989-91; alt. del. Dem. Nat. Conv., 1992, 96, 2000. Fellow Am. Coll. Med. Genetics (founder); mem AAAS, Am. Assn. Cancer Rsch., Women in Cancer Rsch., Am. Soc. Human Genetics, Am. Soc. Cell Biology, Soc. Analytical Cytology, Pitts. Cancer Inst., S.W. Oncology Group (core com. on cytogenetics), Pitts. Cytogenetics Club (founder, coord. 1989-95), Pitts. Garden Place, Western Pa. Conservancy, Carnegie Museums, Pitts. Zoo, Sigma Xi. Avocations: mountain dulcimer, gardening, photography, pulled thread embroidery. Office: U Pitts Dept Human Genetics 130 Desoto St Pittsburgh PA 15213-2535

GOLLMANN, BIRGIT, biology and Russian educator, researcher, writer; b. Vienna, May 22, 1964; d. Gunter Stangl and Eva (Weissengruber) Jensen; m. Günter Gollmann, Mar. 28, 1990. M of Nat. Scis., U. Vienna, 1987, PhD, 1994. Demonstrator U. Melbourne, Australia, 1989; tchr. Fed. H.S., Vienna, 1989—; lectr. in ecology U. Vienna, 1995—. Author: Katzen, 1995, Prachtfinken, 1995; contbr. articles to profl. jours. Roman Catholic. Avocations: breeding of frogs, birds and small mammals, skiing, embroidery.

GOLOBIČ, AMALIJA, chemistry researcher, educator; b. Novo mesto, Dolenjska, Slovenia, Apr. 18, 1969; d. Franc and Marija (Jenko) Sinur; m. Anton Golobič, Aug. 19, 1995; 1 child, Jurij Golobic. Diploma in Chemistry, U. Ljubljana, Slovenia, 1992, PhD in Chemistry, 1996. Rsch. asst. faculty chemistry and chem. tech. U. Ljubljana, 1992-95, rsch. and tchg. asst., 1995—. Contbr. articles to profl. jours. Mem. Slovenian Chem. Soc., Slovenian Crystallographic Soc. Avocations: mountaineering, cycling. Home: Pod Trško goro 65, 8000 Novo Mesto Slovenia Office: U Ljubljana Faculty Chemistry and Chem Tech, Aškerčeva 5, 1000 Ljubljana Slovenia

GOLOBY, GEORGE WILLIAM, JR., environmental scientist, ornithologist, aviculturist; b. Franklin, Ky., Mar. 21, 1949; s. George William Sr. and Katherine Jacqueline (Panchot) G.; m. Diane Grayson, Dec. 29, 1974; children: Amy Vanessa, George William III. BS in Wildlife Sci., Tex. A&M U., 1971. Zookeeper of birds Houston Zool. Gardens, 1971-72; warehouseman, driver Houston Ind. Sch. Dist., 1972-76; lab. mgr. Empak Inc., Houston, 1976-80; asst. sect. chief City of Houston Dept. Pub. Works, 1980-90;

environ. quality specialist III City of Houston Dept. Pub. Works & Engring., 1990—; founder, owner Penfeathers Tours, Houston, 1984—; instr. Houston Arboretum and Nature Ctr., 1999; instr. Tex. birding cert. Armand Bayou Nature Ctr., U. Houston, 1999—. Editor (newsletters) Water Environment Assn. Tex. (WEAT) Pipeline, 1984—, Tex. Ornithol. Soc. Newsletter, 1989-99, Penfeathers Newsletter, 1986—, Panchot Paper, 1989-93, Houston Audubon Soc., 1977-80, The Naturalist, 1986-89; asst. editor (books) Houston, 1978, Encyclopedia of American Cities, 1979. Mem. Houston Proud, 1986, Cy-Fair Houston C. of C., 1986, Greater Houston Conv. and Vis. Bur., 1986-88. Mem. Water Environ. Assn. Tex. (com. chmn. 1984—), Tex. Water Utilites Assn., Houston Audubon Soc. (v.p. adminstrv. affairs 1986-89), Am. Birding Assn., Outdoor Nature Club, Parrot People Club (v.p. Houston chpt. 1985-86), Purple Martin Conservation Assn., Whooping Crane Conservation Assn., Tex. Nature Conservancy. Office: City Houston 4545 Groveway Dr Houston TX 77087-1122

GOLOMB, GERSHON, pharmaceutics educator, researcher; b. Tel Aviv, Jan. 5, 1952; s. Zeev and Pnina (Gantz) G.; m. Shimona Lindenbaum, Mar. 3, 1974; children: Motta, Assaf, Mattan. B of Pharm., Hebrew U., Jerusalem, 1978, MS, 1980, PhD, 1984. Asst. instr. sch. pharmacy Hebrew U., 1978-84, rsch. assoc. dept. pharmacy, 1986-87, lectr. dept. pharmacy, 1987-91, sr. lectr. dept. pharmacy, 1991-96, assoc. prof. dept. pharmaceutics, 1997—, head dept. pharmaceutics, 1997-2000, head Sch. Pharmacy, 2000—; vis. scientist Harvard Med. Sch./MIT, Boston, 1984-86, U. Mich., Ann Arbor, 1991-92; chmn. 3d Jerusalem Internat. Conf. Pharm. Sci. and Clin. Pharmacology, 1996; cons. in field. Maj. Israeli Defense Forces, 1971-74. Recipient Juludan prize for Excellence in Biomed. Rsch., Technion, Haifa, Israel, 1999; Am. Heart Assn. fellow, Mass., 1985. Fellow Am. Inst. Med. and Biol. Engring.; mem. Am. Assn. Pharm. Scientists, Controlled Release Soc., Profs. for a Strong Israel. Jewish. Avocation: theological philosophy. Home: 20 Tirosh St, 90435 Efrat Israel Office: Hebrew U, POB 12065, 91120 Jerusalem Israel

GOLOMB, JACOB S., urologist; b. Tel Aviv, Jan. 17, 1949; s. Zvi and Rachel (Malz) G.; m. Dalia Weiss, May 21, 1974; children: Shahar, Dor. MD with excellence, Tel Aviv U., 1975, M Urology, 1986. Resident in urology Tel Aviv Med. Ctr., 1979-85; attending urologist Wolfson Med. Ctr., Holon, Israel, 1986-87, 89-91; clin. fellow neurourology and female urology UCLA Sch. Medicine, 1987-89; attending urologist Sheba Med. Ctr., Tel Hashomer, Israel, 1991—, head female urology svc., 1991—; cons. in female urology Maccabi Health Orgn., Israel, 1991—. Contbr. chpts. to med. books. Maj. Israeli Def. Army, 1975-79. Mem. Israeli Med. Assn., Israeli Urol. Soc., Am. Urol. Assn. (corr.), Internat. Continence Soc., Urodynamics Soc. Avocations: jogging, physical fitness, classical music. Office: Tel Hashomer Med Ctr, Dept Urology, 52621 Tel Hashomer Israel

GOLOMBEK, MATTHEW PHILIP, planetary geologist; b. New Haven, Sept. 20, 1954; s. Martin I. and Sonia G.; m. Connie M. Morgan, Apr. 26, 1980; children: Sydney Morgan, Benjamin Clayton. AB in Geology with honors, Rutgers Coll., 1976; MS in Geology, U. Mass., 1978, PhD in Geology, 1981. Rsch. asst. in sedimentology Rutgers U., N.J., 1976; tchg. asst. U. Mass., 1979, rsch. asst. in structural and planetary geology, 1976-81; vis. postdoctoral fellow Lunar and Planetary Inst., Houston, 1981-82, vis. scientist, 1982-83; sr. scientist Jet Propulsion Lab. Calif. Inst. Tech., Pasadena, 1983-84, rsch. scientist Jet Propulsion Lab., prin. scientist, 1984—, Mars Pathfinder project scientist Jet Propulsion Lab., 1994-98; lectr. U. Houston, Clear Lake City, 1983, Calif. State Poly. U., Pomona, 1986; Viking guest investigator Jet Propulsion Lab., 1977, U.S. Geol. Survey, Astrogeology Br., Flagstaff, Ariz., 1978; mem. Mars Sci. Working Group, 1989-96, Mars Exploration Edn. Outreach Adv. Bd., 1994-98; chmn. Mars Pathfinder Project Sci. Group, 1994-98; mem. Am. Geophys. Union, Planetology Exec. Com., 1994-97; spkr., lectr. in field. Planetology editor EOS, Transactions Am. Geophy. Union; assoc. editor Tectonophysics, 1986; contbr. articles to profl. jours. Recipient Schlumberger scholarship Rutgers U., 1975-76, Vinton Gwinn Meml. prize Rutgers U., 1976, numerous grants, 1983—, Laurels award for Outstanding Achievement in Space, Aviation Week and Space Technology, 1997, award for excellence Jet Propulsion Lab./Project Scientist for Mars Pathfinder Mission, 1998, Disting. Alumni award for Profl. Svc. U. Mass., 1988, Hall of Disting. Alumni award Rutgers U. Alumni Fedn., 1998, NASA Exceptional Sci. Achievement medal, 1998, others; Dr. Matt Golombek Day named in his honor City of Hackensack, N.J., Feb. 12, 1998; asteroid named Golombek in his honor, 1992. Fellow Geol. Soc. Am.; mem. Am. Geophy. Union. Office: Jet Propulsion Lab MS 183-501 4800 Oak Grove Dr Pasadena CA 91109-8001

GOLOVANEVSKIY, VLADIMIR ARKADIEVICH, thermophysicist, researcher; b. Kharkov, Ukraine, USSR, June 2, 1963; arrived in Australia, 1994; s. Arkadiy Izraylevich and Zanna Illinichna (Gershanovich) G.; m. Marina Anatolievna Elperina, Nov. 17, 1989; children: Anna, Sophia Fayina. MSc, Poly. U., Ukraine, 1986; PhD in Engring., Ukrainian Acad. Scis., Ukraine, 1992. Sr. rsch. fellow Ukrainian Poly. U., Ukraine, 1988-94; rschr. Indsl. Plastics Svcs., Adelaide, Australia, 1995-96; materials scientist Advanced Technical Devel. for CRA, Perth, Australia, 1996—; lectr., councellor mech. engring. and materials Advanced Mfg. Technologies Ctr., Perth, Australia, 1998—.

GOLOVASHKIN, ALEKSANDER IVANOVICH, physicist, educator; b. Murom, Vladimir, Russia, Jan. 16, 1935; s. Ivan Prokop'evich and Elizaveta Ivanovna (Marova) G.; m. Emma Georgievna Bel'anina, Apr. 9, 1955; children: Vera, Maria. Degree, Moscow State U., 1958; Candidate of Sci., Phys. Inst., Moscow, 1965. Sci. rschr. Phys. Inst., 1958-70, sr. sci. rschr., 1970-73, head sector, 1973-85, head lab., 1985—, vice dir. divsn., 1995—; assoc. prof. Moscow Engr.-Physics Inst., 1982—. Author: Some Problems of Superconductivity, 1975, A15 Superconductors, 1984; editor: Metal Optics and Superconductivity, 1988; contbr. over 200 articles to profl. jours. Mem. Dist. Soviet of People's Deputies, Moscow, 1985-87. Named to Order of Red Banner, 1981; named Soros Assoc. Prof., 1995; grantee Russian Fundamental Sci. Found., 1991-97. Mem. Physics Soc. Moscow. Avocation: chess. Home: Oktober Str 91-2-24, 127521 Moscow Russia Office: PN Lebedev Phys Inst, Leninsky Prospect 53, 117924 Moscow Russia

GOLOVCHINER, GREGORY, cardiologist; b. Moscow, July 11, 1963; arrived in Israel, 1993; s. Nikolas and Galina (Chuvilenkov) G.; m. Kristina Zlochevsky, Jan. 23, 1986; children: Lev, David. MD, Moscow Med. U., 1986. Resident Transplantology Inst., Moscow, 1986-88, cardiologist, 1988-92; resident Soroka Med. Ctr., Beer Sheva, Israel, 1994-99; resident in cardiology Rabin Med. Ctr., Petakh-Tikva, Israel, 1999—. Contbr. articles to profl. jours. Lt. Israeli Res. Army, 1996. Mem. Israel Heart Soc. Avocations: hiking, travel, photography. Home: 6/5 Iris Kiryat, Ono 55453, Israel

GOLOVINSKI, PAVEL ABRAMOVICH, physics educator; b. Ulyanovsk, Russia, Sept. 30, 1955; s. Abram Isaakovich Golovinski and Galina Illarionovna Slepchenko; 1 child, Dmitri. PhD in Optics, Acad. Sci. USSR, 1982; DS in Theoretical Physics, St. Petersburg State U., 1995. Asst. VGASA, Voronezh, 1982-91, assoc. prof., 1991-95, prof., 1995-99, chmn. physics sect., 1999—; vis. prof. Laval U., Que., 1994. Author: Many-Body Processes in Atoms Under the Action of a Strong Light Field, 1994; contbr. articles to profl. jours. Soroc Assoc. Prof., Open Soc. Inst., N.Y., 1995. Mem. N.Y. Acad. Scis., Nat. Sci. Acad., Eurosci. Strasbourg. Avocation: tourism. Home: Semilukskaya St 46-35, 394027 Voronezh Russia Office: Physics Rsch Lab, 20-letiya Oktyabrya St 84, 394 680 Voronezh Russia

GOLOVIZNIN, VLADIMIR VASILJEVICH, physicist; b. Kirov, Russia, June 17, 1954; m. Svetlana Bogdanovna Krakhmalnik; children: Anton, Alexandra. MS, Moscow State U., 1977; PhD, Kurchatov Inst. Atomic Energy, Moscow, 1983. Jr. sci. fellow Kurchatov Inst. Atomic Energy, 1980-86, sr. sci. fellow, 1986—; sr. physicist Fundamenteel Onderzoek der Materie-Inst. Plasma Physics, Utrecht, The Netherlands, 1994—. Mem. Alexander von Humboldt Found. (Rsch. grant 1991). Office: FOM Inst Plasma Physics, PO Box 1207, 3430BE Nieuwegein The Netherlands

GOLOVKIN, BORIS GEORGIEVICH, chemist, researcher; b. Kotlas, Russia, Mar. 31, 1940; s. Georgi Flegontovich and Klavdiya Ivanovna (Popova) G.; m. Tatyana Vasilyevna Rijkova, Jan. 1965 (div. 1972); 1 child, Arthur; m. Larisa Nickolaevna Noskova, Feb. 6, 1982; children: Yegor, Catherine. Degree in chemistry, Moscow State U., 1964; degree in mechs., Railway's Sch. Sverdlovski, 1981. Tchr. Karaganda State U., Kazakhstan, 1972-73; rigger integrated Plant, Temir-Tay, Kazakhstan, 1977-79; mech. Russian Railway, Sverdlovsk, 1981-84; lab. asst. Inst. Chemistry, Sverdlovsk, 1984-86; sci. assoc. Inst. Solid State Chemistry, Ekaterinburg, Russia, 1986-97, sr. sci. assoc., 1997—. Patentee in field. Mem. Les Citoyens du Monde, Right of Man's Com., N.Y. Acad. Scis., Russian Acad. Scis. and Arts, Planetary Soc. Avocations: physics theories. Home: Cheluskinstsev 60 Art 173, 620027 Ekaterinburg Russia Office: InstSolid State Chemistry, Pervomayskaya 91, 620219 Ekaterinburg Russia

GOLOVKO, VITALI ANATOLIEVICH, physicist, educator; b. Vladivostok, Russia, Apr. 28, 1940; s. Anatoli Semenovich and Galina Mikhailovna (Zhdanova) G.; m. Gordana Leonidovna Linitskaya, Apr. 10, 1965 (div. Dec. 1986); 1 child, Leonid. Diploma in physics, State U., Moscow, 1963, PhD, 1967, DSc in Physics-Math., 1991. Cert. theoretical physics. Asst. prof. State Evening Metall. Inst., Moscow, 1966-70, docent, assoc. prof., 1970-90, prof., head chair of physics, 1991—; vis. prof. Inst. Nat. des Hydrocarbures et de la Chimie, Boumerdes, Algeria, 1970-75. Contbr. articles to profl. jours. Mem. Orthodox Ch. Avocations: literature, art, history, sports. Office: Moscow State Evening Metall, Inst Lefortovsky Val 26, 111250 Moscow Russia

GOLOVNEVA, ELENA IGOREVNA, theoretical physicist, researcher; b. Novosibirsk, Russia, Oct. 23, 1975; d. Igor Fedorovich and Valentina Vasiljevna (Malyisheva) G.; m. Artem Aleksandrovich Konev, July 11, 1997. B of Technics and Tech., Novosibirsk State Tech. U., 1996, MS, 1998. Lab. asst. Inst. Theoretical Applied Mechanics, Novosibirsk, 1994-97; jr. rsch. officer Inst. Theoretical and Applied Mechanics, Novosibirsk, 1997—. Contbr. articles to profl. jours. Grantee Russian Fundamental Rsch. Fund, 1996, Pres. of Russian Fedn., 1996, 97. Avocations: contemporary dance, tennis. Home: Arbuzova Str 1-47, 630117 Novosibirsk Russia Office: Inst Theoret Applied Mechs, Institutskaja Str 4/1, 630090 Novosibirsk Russia

GOLSHANI, ALIREZA, physicist, researcher; b. Shiraz, Iran, Sept. 21, 1966; s. Sadra Golshan and Robab Dastgheib; m. Parvin Hosseini, July 6, 1991; 1 child, Shayan. BSc, Shiraz U., 1990; MSc in Engring. Physics, Tech. U. Vienna, Austria, 1994, PhD in Tech. Scis., 1997. Rsch. engr. Fars Naval Rsch. Complex, Shiraz, 1990-91; rsch. asst. Tech. U. Vienna, 1994-97; rsch. assoc. Swiss Fed. Inst. Tech., Lausanne, 1997-98; mgr. product engr. JDS Uniphase Switzerland, Zurich, 1998—. Contbr. article to book, articles to profl. jours. Mem. IEEE, IEEE Lasers Electro Optics Soc., Optical Soc. Am., Am. Inst. Physics. Fax: 41-1-455-85-86. Avocations: soccer, swimming, hiking, biking. Home: Appisbergstrasse 4/1, CH-8708 Mannedorf Switzerland Office: JDS Uniphase Swizerland, Binzstrasse 17-19, CH-8045 Zurich Switzerland

GOLTSOV, ALEXEY NIKOLAEVICH, physicist, educator; b. Moscow, Feb. 9, 1961; s. Nikolay Alexeevich and Ekaterina Il'inichna Goltsov; m. Inna Petrovna Morozova, June 3, 1990; 1 child, Grisha. Masters Degree, Moscow State U., 1984, PhD, 1988. Rschr. Inst. Nuc. Physics, Moscow State U., 1984-87; sr. rschr. Inst. Physics and Tech., Moscow, 1987-95, head dept., 1995—; asst. prof. Moscow Inst. Radioelectronics and Automation, 1990—, asst. prof. dept. applied synergetics, 1999—; asst. prof. dept. applied math. Moscow Inst. Fine Chem. Tech., 1996-98; mgr. project Internat. Sci. and Technol. Ctr., Moscow, 1998—. Contbr. articles to profl. jours. Rsch. grantee Internat. Sci. Found., N.Y., 1993-95, Russian Found. for Basic Rsch., Moscow, 1999—, travel grantee Royal Soc., London, 1998. Home: Golubinskai St 25-2-138, 117463 Moscow Russia Office: Inst Physics & Tech, Prechistenka St 13/7, 119034 Moscow Russia

GOLTSOV, VICTOR ALEXEEVICH, physics educator, technology administrator; b. Siberia, Russia, Mar. 13, 1936; s. Alexei Alexeevich and Ekaterina Philippovna (Elizova) G.; m. Ludmila Feodorovna Kollegova, June 6, 1963; children: Alexei, Maria. Grad. in Engring., Ural Poly. Inst., Sverdlovsk, USSR, 1958, DSc (1st degree), 1964, DSc (2d degree), 1973. Engr. Indsl. Enterprise, Omsk, Russia, 1958-60; asst. prof. Ural Poly. Inst., 1963-67, assoc. prof., 1967-73; prof., chmn. dept. physics Donetsk (Ukraine) Poly. Inst., 1973—; lectr., cons. Carnegie-Mellon U., Champaign-Urbana, Ill., 1980, U. Sci. and Tech., Beijing, 1989-90, U. Jaen, Linares, Spain, 1995; cons. Johnson-Matthey Co., Reading, Eng., 1993. Author: Interaction of Hydrogen with Metals (in Russian), 1987; guest editor Internat. Jour. Hydrogen Energy, 1997; contbr. over 250 articles to profl. jours. Recipient grant Internat. Sci. Found., 1993, 95. Mem. Internat. Engring. Acad. (academician), Internat. Informatization Acad. (academician), Internat. Assn. Hydrogen Energy. Avocations: underwater swimming, gardening. Office: Donetsk State Tech U, 58 Artyom St, 83000 Donetsk Ukraine

GOLTZMAN, DAVID, endocrinologist, educator, researcher; b. Montreal, Que., Can., Sept. 22, 1944; s. Jack and Lily (Roth) G.; m. Naomi Lyon, Dec. 29, 1968; children: Jonathan, Rebecca, Daniel. BSc, McGill U., 1966, MD, 1968. Diplomate Am. Bd. Internal Medicine, Am. Bd. Endocrinology and Metabolism. Med. intern Royal Victoria Hosp., Montreal, 1968-69; med. resident Columbia U. Coll. Physicians and Surgeons, N.Y.C., 1969-71; clin. and rsch. fellow in endocrinology Mass. Gen. Hosp., Boston, 1971-75; instr. medicine Harvard Med. Sch., Boston, 1974-75; asst. prof. medicine McGill U., Montreal, 1976-78, assoc. prof., 1978-83, prof., 1983—, chmn. physiology, 1988-93, dir. calcium rsch. lab., 1981—, hosmer prof. physiology, 1992-93, Massabki prof. medicine, 1994—; chmn. medicine, 1994—; sr. physician dept. medicine Royal Victoria Hosp., 1987-94, physician-in-chief, 1994-98; physician-in chief, McGill U. Hlth. Ctr., 1998—; chmn. exptl. medicine com. Med. Rsch. Coun. Can., Ottawa, Ont., 1984-88; mem. gen. medicine B study sect., NIH, Bethesda, Md., 1987-91; active Exec. Med. Rsch. Coun. Can., 1993—. Author: (with others) Principles of Bone Biology, 1996, Primer of Metabolic Bone Disease and Disorders of Mineral Metabolism, 1996, 1989, Principles and Practice of Endocrinology and Metabolism, 1995; editl. bd. Endocrinology Jour., 1985-90, Jour. Bone Mineral rsch., 1985-90, Bone and Mineral, 1991-94, Osteoporosis Internat., 1991-94, Assoc. Edn. Bone, 1989-94; assoc. editor: Jur. Bone Mineral research, 1995—; contbr. numerous articles to profl. jours. Recipient Chercheur Boursier award Que. Med. Rsch. Coun., 1980-83, Scientist award Med. Rsch. Coun. Can., 1983-88, Andre Lichtwitz prize Nat. Inst. for Med. Rsch., France, 1987. Fellow Royal Coll. Physicians and Surgeons, Royal Soc. Canada; mem. Can. Soc. Endocrinology and Metabolism (pres. 1990-92), Am. Soc. for Bone and Mineral Rsch. (chmn. program com. 1989-90, pres. 1999-00), Am. Assn. Physicians, Endocrine Soc. (program com. 1989-91), Can. Soc. Clin. Investigation (councillor 1986-89, pres. 1998-99) Am. Soc. Clin. Investigation, Canadian Assn. Profs. of Medicine (pres. 1998-99). Avocations: classical music, gardening, tennis. Office: Royal Victoria Hosp, 687 Pine Ave W, Montreal, PQ Canada H3A 1A1

GOLU, MIHAI ION, psychologist, educator; b. Poienari, Romania, Mar. 4, 1934; s. Ion Petre and Gheorghita Ion (Burlan) G.; m. Elena Constantin Filip, May 14, 1957; children: Adrian, Felician-Cristinel. M in psychology, Lomonosov U., Moscow, 1958; PhD, U. Bucarest, Bucarest, Romania, 1968. Asst. prof. U. Bucharest, Bucharest, 1958-62, lectr., 1962-82, prof., 1990—; worker Vulcan Plant, Bucharest, 1982-90; bd. dirs. Res. Inst. of Psychology, Bucharest, Faculty of Soc. and Psychol., Bucharest, Inst. for Study of the Totalitarism, Bucharest. Author: General Cybernetics, 1970, Introduction to Psychology, 1971 (Price of Acad. of Soc. Sci., 1972), Handbook of Psychophisiology, 1978 (Price of Romanian Acad. 1980), Principles of Cybernetic Psychology, 1975 (Price of Romanian Acad. 1976), The Dynamics of Personality, 1993, Fundamentals of Psychology, 2000; co-author: Neuropsychology, 1983. Active Mins. of Edn., 1991-92, Min. of Culture, 1992-93. Fulbright fellow Carnegie-Mellon U., 1973-74; recipient Pablo Picasso medal UNESCO, 1992, Jan Amos Commehius medal Tcheh Acad., 1993. Mem. Psychology Assn., Ednl. Assn., Romanian Assn. of Psychologists (pres. 1990—), Romanian Nat. Assn. Edn. (pres. 1992—). Avocations: history, bibgraphees of prominent personalities, music, beletistic literature, excursions. Home: 22 Libertatii Bloc 102, Scara 5 Apt 89, 72200 Bucharest Romania Office: Facultatea Psihologie, 1 Armata Poporului Str, Bucharest Romania

GOLUB, HARVEY, financial services company executive; b. N.Y.C., Apr. 16, 1939. Student, Cornell U., 1956-58; BS, NYU, 1961. Jr. ptnr. McKinsey & Co. Inc., N.Y.C., 1967-74, sr. ptnr., 1977-83; pres. Shulman Air Freight, N.Y.C., 1974-77; chmn., pres. IDS Fin. Svc., Mpls., 1984-90; chmn., CEO IDS Fin. Svcs. (name changed to Am. Express Fin. Advisors), Mpls., 1990—; vice chmn., dir. Am. Express Co., N.Y.C., 1990-91, pres., 1991-93; CEO, chmn. bd. dirs. Am. Express Co., 1993—; chmn., CEO Am. Express Travel Related Svcs. Co. Inc., N.Y.C., 1991. Bd. dirs. Am. Enterprise Inst., Columbia Presbyn. Hosp., Carnegie Hall, N.Y.C. Partnership, N.Y. C. of C. and Industry, United Way of N.Y.C.; mem. Bus. Roundtable, Bretton Woods Com.; apptd. mem. Pres.'s Com. for Arts and Humanities, Pres.'s Adv. Trade and Policy Negotiations. Mem. World Travel and Tourism Coun. (exec. com., chmn.-elect). Office: Am Express Co Tower C 3 World Fin Ctr 200 Vesey St New York NY 10285-1000

GOLUB, MICHAEL ARONOVICH, optical company scientist, executive, educator; b. Samara, USSR, July 28, 1955; arrived in Israel, 1995; s. Aaron Issaakovich Golub and Fira Moiseevna Erenburg; m. Ariana Sudman, 1996. MS cum laude, Samara State Aerospace U., 1978; PhD in Laser Optics, Lebedev Phys. Inst., Moscow, 1988; Dr.Sc., Russian Acad. Scis., Moscow, 1991. Rsch. engr. Samara State Aerospace U., 1978-82, fellow rschr., 1982-86, assoc. prof., 1986-89, prof., 1992-95, head lab. Image Processing Sys. Inst., 1989-94; chief scientist Holo-Or, Ltd., Rehovot, Israel, 1995—; vis. sr. rschr. Friedrich-Schiller U, Jena Inst. Applied Optics and Physics, Germany, 1994, 95; invited prof. Nat. Sch. Physics, Strasbourg, France, 1994; cons. FIAT Co., Orbassano, Italy, 1992; patentee in field. Author: Laser Beam Mode Selection by Computer Generated Holograms, 1994; contbr. articles to profl. jours. Mem. Optical Soc. Am. Jewish. Avocations: travelling, swimming, bicycling, badminton, skating. Office: Holo-Or Ltd, Kiryat Weizmann PO Box 1051, 76114 Rehovot Israel

GOLUMBECK, CARL TIMOTHY, forensic psychiatrist; b. Chgo., Mar. 12, 1947; s. Carl A. and Ivy (Hannam) G.; m. Karyn Ingrid Kramer, Dec. 4, 1971; 1 child, Elizabeth. BA, Johns Hopkins U., 1968, MD, 1971. Diplomate Am. Bd. Psychiatry and Neurology, Am. Bd. Forensic Psychiatry; cert. mental health adminstr. APA. Asst. prof. psychiatry Emory U., Atlanta, 1977-80; supt. Ga. Regional Hosp., Savannah, 1977-80; dir. tng., asst. prof. SUNY, Buffalo, 1981-83; asst. prof. psychiatry and psychology Johns Hopkins U., Balt., 1983-85; chief psychiatry Wyman Park Health System, 1983-85; psychiatrist pvt. practice Kailua-Kona, Hawaii, 1985-87; asst. prof. psychiatry UCLA, 1987-93; dir. forensic psychiatry Alascadero (Calif.) Forensic Ctr., 1987-93; cons. psychiatrist Rosanna Forensic Psychiatry Ctr., Rosanna, Victoria, Australia, 1994-96; pvt. practice of psychiatry Delmont Pvt. Hosp., Burwood, Victoria, Australia, 1994-97; chmn. med. adv. bd. Delmont Pvt. Hosp., 1995-97. Maj. USAR-MC, 1975-77. Fellow Royal Australian and New Zealand Coll. Psychiatrists, Australian Coll. Legal Med., Am. Soc. for Psychical Rsch.; mem. Am. Psychiat. Assn., Australian Med. Assn. Avocations: fountain pen repair and collecting. Home: 3 Victoria Ave, Canterbury VIC 3126, Australia Office: 16 Walpole St, Kew VIC 3101, Australia

GOLUSIN, MILLARD R., obstetrician and gynecologist; b. Detroit, Feb. 14, 1947; s. Raddie and Joan (Lalich) G.; m. Yvonne Marie Cronovich, Sept. 29, 1974; children: Milan, Marko, Matthew. BS with honors, Wayne State U., 1968, MS, 1970, MD, 1975. Diplomate Am. Bd. Obstetrics and Gynecology. Intern, then resident William Beaumont Hosp., Royal Oak, Mich., 1975-78; practice medicine specializing in obstetrics and gynecology Village Gynecologic and Obstetric Assocs., P.C., Southfield and Troy, Mich., 1978-92; pvt. practice specializing in obstetrics and gynecology Troy, Mich., 1992-98; assoc. Wilshire Obstetrics-Gynecol. Assocs. PC, Troy, 1998—; mem. quality assurance com. William Beaumont Hosp., Royal Oak, Mich., 1979—, mem. gynecol. quality assurance com., 1993—; charter mem., pres. Preferred Ob-Gyn. Mgmt. Group L.L.C. Trustee, mem. credentials com. Preferred Provider Network, 2000; trustee United Beaumont Physicians Group, 1993—. Served with U.S. Army, 1969-71. Fellow ACOG; mem. Am. Soc. Reproductive Medicine, Mich. State Med. Soc., Am. Inst. Ultrasound Medicine, Serbian Singing Soc., Ravanica (musical dir. 1967—, pres. 1981-82). Republican. Serbian Eastern Orthodox. Avocations: music, golf. Office: Wilshire Obstetrics-Gynecol Assocs PC 4600 Investment Dr Ste 170 Troy MI 48098-6369

GOMANKOV, ALEXEY VLADIMIROVICH, paleontologist; b. Moscow, Russia, Jan. 9, 1953; s. Vladimir and Natalia (Kvitko) G. Grad., Moscow State U., 1975. From postgrad. rsch. fellow to sr. rschr. Geol. Inst. Russian Acad. Sci., Moscow, 1975—; guest tchr. Moscow State U., 1985—. Author: Tatarina Flora, 1986, Confidence Intervals for the Shares of Taxa in Misopore Assemblages, 1993; contbr. articles to profl. jours. Mem. Internat. Union Geol. Scis., Internat. Fedn. Palynological Socs. Avocations: Christian theology and philosophy, teaching Sunday school. Home: App 45, 31 Miklukho-Maklai St, 117485 Moscow Russia Office: Russian Acad Scis Geol Inst, 7 Pyzhevsky pereulok, 109017 Moscow Russia

GOMBER, DREW JOSEPH, historian, writer; b. N.Y.C., May 18, 1949; s. John Francis and Annamay (O'Neill) G.; m. Nancy Lynn Greene, Feb. 4, 1989 (div.); 1 child, Randi Lee. Paste-up artist St. Petersburg (Fla.) Times, 1974-78; proofreader Adams & Abbott, Boston, 1978-81; computer operator St. Petersburg Times, 1981-94; pressman Ruidoso (N.Mex.) News, 1994-97; historian Lincoln (N.Mex.) Heritage Trust, 1997-99; historian, Hubbard Mus. Am. West, Ruidoso. Author: Heroes & Villains, 1998, American Souls, 2000. Sgt., USAF, 1968-72. Home: PO Box 221 Lincoln NM 88338-0221 Office: Hubbard Mus Am West PO Box 40 Ruidoso Downs NM 88346-0040

GOMBERG, MIKHAIL ALEXANDROVITCH, laboratory administrator, science educator; b. Moscow, Oct. 25, 1954; s. Alexander Yefimovitch and Pasha S. (Bim) G.; m. Irina M. Yanovskaya; children: Andrei, Natalia. MD, Moscow Med. Stomat. U., 1977; PhD, Crtl. Rsch. Inst. for Skin and Venereal Diseases, Moscow, 1988. Dr. ambulance Moscow, 1978-81; dr. Skin Dispensary, Moscow, 1981-83; rschr. Moscow Med. Stomat. U., 1983-87, asst. prof., 1988—; head dept. Cen. Rsch. Inst. Skin and Venereal Disease, Moscow, 1997—. Mem. Lions Club. Office: Cen Rsch Inst Skin/Ven Dis, Korokemko 3, 107076 Moscow Russia

GOMBOCZ, ERICH ALFRED, biochemist; b. Vienna, Austria, Aug. 29, 1951; came to U.S., 1990; s. Erich and Maria (Mayer) G.; m. Gisela M. Dorner, June 12, 1973 (div. Apr. 1992); 1 child, Manfred Alexander (dec.). Cert., T.U., Vienna, 1970-75. With Fed. Inst. for Food Analysis and Rsch., Vienna, 1975-90, head of sect. dept. biochem. analysis, 1980-90, contbr. Cen. Lab. Info. Mgmt. System, 1987-90; chmn. scientific adv. bd. LabIntelligence, Inc., Menlo Park, Calif., 1989-99, COO, v.p. R & D, 1989-99; chief sci. officer NucleoTech Corp., San Mateo, Calif., 1999—; speaker and lectr. in field. Editor: Computers in Electrophoresis; contbr. articles to profl. jours.; patentee in field. Postdoctoral Rsch. award NIH, Bethesda, Md., 1985-86, 88. Mem. Internat. Assn. for Cereal Chemistry, Internat. Electrophoresis Soc., Am. Electrophoresis Soc., Am. Chem. Soc., N.Y. Acad. Scis. Roman Catholic. Office: NucleoTech Corp 1400 Fashion Island Blvd San Mateo CA 94404-2060

GOMBRICH, SIR ERNST (HANS JOSEF), art historian, educator; b. Mar. 30, 1909; s. Karl and Leonie (Hock) G.; m. Ilse Heller, 1936; 1 child, Richard Francis. Ed, Theresianum and Vienna U., Vienna; PhD, LittD (hon.), Queen's U., Belfast, No. Ireland, 1963; LLD (hon.), St. Andrews, 1965; LittD (hon.), Leeds U., 1965, Oxford U., 1969, Harvard U., London U., 1976, U. Cambridge, 1970, Manchester U., 1974, NYU, 1986, Emory U., Atlanta, 1991, Universitas Complutense, Madrid, 1992, U. Urbino, 1992, Amer. U. London, Richmond Coll., 1993, Vienna U., 1999. Rsch. asst. Warburg Inst., U. London, 1936-39; with BBC Monitoring Svc./WWII; sr. rsch. fellow Warburg Inst., U. London, 1946-48, lectr., 1948-54, reader, 1954-56, spl. lectr., 1956-59, dir., 1959-76; prof. history of classical tradition U. London, 1959-76, prof. emeritus, 1976—; Slade prof. fine art U. Oxford, 1950-53, 61-63; Durning-Lawrence prof. history of art Univ. Coll., London U., 1956-59; Lethaby prof. Royal Coll. Art, 1967-68; prof.-at-large Cornell U., 1970-76; vis. prof. Harvard U., 1959; trustee Brit. Mus., 1974-79; mem. Standing Commn. on Mus. and Galleries, 1976-82. Author: (with E. Kris) Caricature, 1940, The Story of Art, 1950 (16 edits.), Art and Illusion, 1959, Meditations on a Hobby Horse, 1963, Norm and Form, 1966, Aby Warburg, 1970, In Search of Cultural History, 1972, Symbolic Images, 1972, Illusion in Nature and Art, 1973, Art Perception and Reality, 1973, Art History and the Social Sciences, 1975, Means and Ends, 1976, The Heritage of Apelles, 1976, The Sense of Order, 1979, Ideals and Idols, 1979, The Image and the

Eye, 1982, Tributes, 1984, New Light on Old Masters, 1986, Oskar Kokoschka in His Time, 1986, Reflections on the History of Art, 1987, Topics of Our Time, 1991, (with D. Eribon) Ce que l'image nous dit, 1991, Styles of Art and Styles of Life, 1991, Gastspiele: zur Deutschen Sprache u. Germanistik, 1992, Künstler, Kenner, Kunden (Wiener Vorlesungen im Rathaus), 1993, Das Forschende Auge, 1994, Shadows, 1996; editor: (with R. Woodfield) The Essential Gombrich, 1996, On pride and Prejudice in the Arts, 1997, Speis der Malerknaben, 1997, The Uses of Images, 1999. Decorated comdr. Order Brit. Empire, 1966, knighted, 1972, Internat. Balzan prize, 1985, Cross of Honor 1st class (Austria), Pour le Merite, 1977, Ehrenzeichen, Austria, 1989, Order of Merit, 1988; recipient W.H. Smith and Son Ann. Lit. award, 1964, medal NYU, 1970, Erasmus prize, 1974, Hegel prize City of Stuttgart (W. Germany), 1977; Kulturpreis, Vienna, 1986, Ludwig Wittgenstein prize Osterrichische Forschungsgemeinschaft, 1988; Pergameno D'onore Faenza, 1991, Goethe prize City of Frankfurt, 1994; Ehren medaille ol Stadt Wien, 1994, The Mongan prize Villa i Tatti, 1996; hon. fellow Jesus Coll., Cambridge U., 1963, Gottingen Acad. Scis., 1986, Univ. Coll. London, 1992, FBA, FSA, FRSL, RIBA; corr. mem. Turin Acad., Uppsala Acad., Netherlands Acad., Bavarian Acad., Acad. dei Lincei, Swedish Acad., Belgian Acad.; hon. mem. Austrian Acad., Am. Acad. and Inst. Arts and Letters, Am. Acad. Arts and Scis., Deutsche Akademie fur Sprache und Dichtung, 1988, Hon. Citizen of Mantova, 1998; hon. fellow Vienna Acad. Fine Arts, 1999. Mem. Am. Philos. Soc. *

GOMES, JOSÉ ALBERTO, chemistry educator, university official; b. Bustelo-Penafiel, Portugal, July 14, 1947; s. Alberto Ferreira Gomes and Maria José T.M. Nunes; m. Maria do Pilar Figueroa Goncalves, Aug. 2, 1983; children: Luis, Filipe, Pilar. Degree in chem. engring., U. Porto, Portugal, 1972; MS in Math., U. Oxford, Eng., 1974, PhD in Theoretical Chemistry, 1976. Jr. prof. chemistry U. Porto, 1976-85, prof., 1985—, head theoretical chemistry rsch. group, 1985—, vice rector, 1998—; mem. CIQ rsch., 1976-92, CEQUP rsch., 1993—. Mem. Portuguese Chemistry Soc. (v.p. 1999-2000). E-mail: jfgomes@reit.up.pt. Office: U Porto Faculty Sci Quimica, Rua do Campo Alegre 687, 4150 Porto Portugal

GOMES, NORMAN VINCENT, retired industrial engineer; b. New Bedford, Mass., Nov. 7, 1914; s. John Vincent and Georgianna (Sylvia) G.; grad. U.S. Army Command and Gen. Staff Coll., 1944; BS in Indsl. Engring. and Mgmt., Okla. State U., 1950; MBA in Mgmt., Xavier U., 1955; m. Carolyn Moore, June 6, 1942 (dec. Apr. 1983); m. Helen Groesbeck Kurzawa, April 22, 1995. Asst. chief engr. Leschen divsn. H.K. Porter Co., St. Louis, 1950-52; staff mfg. cons. Gen. Electric Co., Cin., 1952-57: lectr. indsl. mgmt. U. Cin., 1955-56; vis. lectr. indsl. mgmt. Xavier U. Grad. Sch. Bus. Adminstrn., 1956-57; staff indsl. engr. Gen. Dynamics, Ft. Worth, 1957-60; chief ops. analysis Ryan Electronics, San Diego, 1960-64; sr. engr., jet propulsion lab. Calif. Inst. Tech., Pasadena, 1964-67, mem. tech. staff, 1967, mgr. mgmt. sys., 1967-71; industry rep. and cons. U.S. Commn. on Govt. Procurement, Washington, 1970-72; adminstrv. officer GSA, Washington, 1973-78, program dir., 1979; vis. lectr. mgmt. San Antonio Coll., 1982-85. Active Serra, Internat., v.p. membership San Antonio chpt., 1991-92, mem. Drug and Alcohol Adv. Coun. N.E. Ind. Sch. Dist., San Antonio, 1989-95. 2d lt. to maj. C.E., AUS, 1941-46; engring. adviser to War Manpower Bd., 1945. Decorated Army Commendation medal, Armed Svcs. Res. medal; recipient Apollo Achievement award, 1969; Outstanding Performance award GSA, 1974- 75, 76, 77, 79. Mem. Am. Inst. Indsl. Engrs. (nat. chmn. prodn. control research com., 1951-57; bd. dirs. Cin., Fort Worth, San Diego, Los Angeles, San Antonio chpts. 1954-84, pres. Cin. chpt. 1956-57, pres. Los Angeles 1970-71, nat. dir. community services 1969-73), Ret. Officers Assn. U.S. (chpt. pres. 1968-69, recipient Nat. Pres. certificate Merit 1969), Nat. Security Indsl. Assn. (mgmt. systems subcom. 1967-69), Vis. Nurse Assn. of San Antonio (mem. adv. coun. 1988-95), Freedoms Found. at Valley Forge (v.p. edn. and youth leadership programs San Antonio chpt. 1987-89), Pillars San Fernando Cathedral, Old Dartmouth Hist. Soc., Equestrian Order of the Holy Sepulchre of Jerusalem (knight comdr. with star). Republican. Roman Catholic. Club: K.C. (4th deg.). Home: 24834 Shining Arrow San Antonio TX 78258-2744

GOMES, ÓSCAR, judge. Pres. Supremo Tribunal da Justiça, São Tiago, Cape Verde. Office: Supremo Tribunal da Justica, Praça Plato Alexander de Alburquerque, CP 117 Praia Sao Tiago, Cape Verde*

GOMES, ROMEU, public health educator; b. São João de Meriti, Brazil, Apr. 10, 1946; s. Leonel Gomes and Claridade De Jesus; m. Orsinda de Oliveira, Jan. 6, 1966; children: Clarissa de Oliveira Gomes, Raquel de Oliveira Gomes. Grad. in edn., U. Fed. Fluminense, Niterói, Rio de Janeiro, 1970, MPhil in Edn., 1975; PhD in Pub. Health, Fundagco Oswaldo Cruz, Rio de Janeiro, 1994. Cert. sociology and psychology tchr. Elem. sch. tchr. Pub. Elem. Sch., Sã Joã de Merit, 1967-70; H.S. tchr. Pub. H.S., Sã Joã de Merit, 1970-72; univ. lectr. ednl. psychology U. do Estado do Rio de Janeiro, 1972-95; rschr. in pub. health Fundação Oswaldo Cruz, Rio de Janeiro, 1995—; coord. PhD program Fundação Oswaldo Cruz, Rio de Janeiro, 1996-99; head dept. U. do Rio de Janeiro, 1984-86. Author: O Corpo da Rua e O Corpo Na Rua, 1996, Saúde Escolar, 1997. Recipient Visitor Rsch. award Fundação Oswaldo Cruz, Rio de Janeiro, 1995; named Hon. Citizen, Corp. Seal of the City of Balt., 1982. Mem. Associaçãs Brasileira de Pós-Graduaças em Saúde. Avocations: theatre, reading, television, music. E-mail: romeu@iff.fiocruz.br. Fax: 0115521-5538094. Home: Rua Viuva Lacerda 249B3104, 22261050 Rio de Janeiro Brazil Office: Inst Fernandes Figueira/Fundacao Oswaldo Cruz, Av Rui Barbosa 716, 22250020 Rio de Janeiro Brazil

GOMES, VINCENT G., chemical engineering educator; b. Calcutta, Bengal, India, Feb. 19, 1955; s. Andrew and Cecilia Gomes; 1 child, Avanti. B Engring., Indian Inst. Tech., 1978; M Engring., McGill U., Montreal, Que., Can., 1986, PhD, 1990. Process engr. Engrs. India Ltd., 1977-83; rsch. and tchg. asst. McGill U., 1983-85; rsch. assoc. McGill U., Montreal, 1991-95; rsch. engr. Rheology Lab., Montreal, 1985-86; postdoctoral fellow U. Montreal, 1990; sr. lectr. chem. engring. U. Sydney, Australia, 1998—. Contbr. articles to profl. jours. Recipient Silver award UNESCO Internat. Ctr. for Engring. Edn., Sydney, 1999; major fellow McGill U., 1987-88. Fellow Rsch. Inst. for Asia and Pacific; mem. Chem. Inst. Can. Avocations: music, reading, bush walking. Office: U Sydney, Dept Chem Engring, Sydney NSW 2006, Australia

GOMEZ, ALBERTO, biomedical researcher; b. Bogota, Colombia, Jan. 17, 1958; s. Carlos Gomez-Vesga and Martha Gutierrez-Bessudo; m. Elena Garcia-Reyes Rothlisberger, July 3, 1982; children: Daniel, Cristina, Miguel. Biologist, U. de los Andes, Bogota, 1981, Microbiologist, 1982; MSc, Inst. Pasteur, U. Paris, 1985; PhD, U. Paris, 1989. Rschr. INSERM U-159, Paris, 1983-87; sci. dir. Laboratorios Gomez Vesga, Bogota, 1987—; rschr. Hosp. Militar, Bogota, 1987-89, Unidad de Inmunogenetica, Bogota, 1987—; dir. Unidad de Inmunogenetica Inst. de Genetica Humana U. Javeriana, Bogota, 1992—; project cons. Colciencias, Bogota, 1989—; bd. dirs. Banco Biologico Humano U. Javeriana, 1991—. Author: Scientific Expeditions in Colombia, 1998; editor Laboratorio & Medicina, 1993—; mem. editl. bd. Universitas Medica, 1995—; author sci. papers and sci. manuals. Assn. pour la Recherche du Cancer grantee, France, 1985-88; Colciencias rsch. grantee, Colombia, 1989—. Mem. Corp. para el avance de la Genetica (v.p. 1989-92), Colombian Assn. for Allergy and Immunology, Colombian Soc. for History Medicine, Club Los Lagartos, Club 74, Jockey Club. Avocations: golf, tennis, swimming, genealogy. E-mail: alberto@gomezvesga.com. Office: Unidad de Inmunogenetica, Inst de Genetica Human, Univ Javeriana Bogota Colombia

GOMEZ, FRANCIS D(EAN), corporate executive, former foreign service officer; b. Belle Fourche, S.D., July 24, 1941; s. Frank Garcia and Mae Elizabeth (Larive) G.; m. Severa Narino, Sept. 30, 1966; children: Frank T., Laura E. BA, U. Wash., 1964; MS in Adminstrn., George Washington U., 1982; cert. in translation, NYU, 1995. With U.S. Info. Agy, 1965; asst. cultural affairs officer Bogotá, Colombia, 1965-67, San José, Costa Rica, 1968-71; Caribbean desk officer, 1971-72; writer, editor West Hemisphere Newswire, 1972-73; mid-career fellow USIA, Princeton, N.J., 1973-74; pub. affairs officer Am. Embassy, Bamako, Mali, 1974-76; pub. affairs Am. Embassy, Haiti, 1976-78; chief fgn. service personnel USIA, Washington, 1978-80; dep. asst. sec. pub. affairs Dept. State, Washington, 1980-82; dir. fgn. press centers USIA, Washington, 1982-84; cons. pub. affairs Washington, 1984-86; pres. Pub. Affairs Resources Inc., 1986-88; dir. pub. affairs Philip Morris Mgmt. Corp., N.Y.C., 1988—; adj. faculty NYU, 1995—. Founder, pres. Hispanic Employees Coun., Dept. State, 1979-81; trustee WETA TV, Washington, 1983-86; bd. dirs. Nat. Hispanic Scholarship Fund, 1991-94, Pan Am. Devel. Found. Recipient Superior Honor award USIA, 1967, Meritorious Honor awards, 1976, 78, Annual Agy. EEO award, 1980; named Outstanding Young Men Am. U.S. Jaycees, 1968, NYU Outstanding Svc. award, 2000. Mem. Am. Fgn. Svc. Assn., Nat. Assn. Hispanic Journalists, Nat. Press Club, Hispanic Coun. Internat. Rels. (chmn., bd. dirs.), Global Pub. Affairs Inst. (bd. dirs.), Princeton Club N.Y., Pi Alpha Alpha. Office: Philip Morris Mgmt Corp 120 Park Ave New York NY 10017-5592

GOMEZ, GONZALO A., physician, consultant; b. Santiago, Chile, Nov. 29, 1938; s. Isidro and Catalina (Auger) G. Grad., Alianza Francesa, Santiago, 1956; MD, U. Chile, Santiago, 1963. Cons. Calvo Mackenna Hosp., Santiago, 1963-76, Clinica Servet, Santiago, 1976—; cons. respiratory diseases in children Conacem-Chile. Editor: Sinoptic Revition of Childhood Asthma, 1986. Mem. Am. Acad. Pediatrics, Internat. Assn. Allergology and Clin. Immunology, Soc. Chilena Enfermedades Respiratorias Chile. Avocations: music, piano playing, concerts, operas. Office: Clinica Servet Correo 9, Almirante Pastene 150, 16237 Providencie Santiago, Chile

GÓMEZ, LUIS CARLOS, engineer; b. San José, Costa Rica, July 24, 1915; s. Eduardo and Gertrudis (Portuguéz) G.; m. Virginia Diaz (div. Dec. 1959); children: Virginia, Carlos, Willy, Ana, Randall; m. Rosa Amalia Chinchilla, Aug. 10, 1959; children: Oscar, Carlos, Patricia, Doris, Catalina, David, Anna. Degree in engring., Universidad, San José, 1937; degree in electronics, Nat. Schs., Los Angeles, 1951. Maintenance engr. Tropical Radio and Telegraph Co., Golfito, Costa Rica, 1939-47; engr., installer Compañia de FuerzavLuz, San José, 1951-52, USA Bur. Pub. Roads Adminstrn., San José, 1952-55, Electronic Service Co., San Pedro Sula, Honduras, 1955—; cons. Audio Video S.A., Tegucigalpa, Honduras, 1957-70, Radio Cultura, 1962, Radio El Mundo, San Pedro Sula, 1960—, Radio Internat., 1986—. Recipient Spl. Services diploma Juntade Gobierno, 1979. Lodge: Mason. Avocation: electronics. Office: Electronic Service Co, PO Box 1175 2d St 9-10 Ave NO, San Pedro Sula Honduras

GOMEZ-ALBARRAN, MERCEDES, computer scientist, educator, researcher; b. Madrid, Aug. 26, 1970; d. Juan Vicente Gomez-Debora and Isabel Albarran-Garcia. BS, U. Complutense, Madrid, 1993, MSc, 1995. Tutor U. Complutense, Madrid, 1994-97, asst. prof. computer sci., 1997—. Contbr. articles to profl. jours., chpts. to books. Avocations: music, theater performances, ten pin bowling.

GOMEZ-ARBESU, JESUS, immunologist; b. Havana, Cuba, Aug. 17, 1956; s. Jesus and Carmen (Arbesu) G. MD, Inst. Med. Scis., Havana, 1980; Immunologist/1st degree, Pub. Health Ministry, Havana, 1983, Immunologist/2nd degree, 1990. Med. diplomate. Immunologist Inst. of Hematology and Immunology, Havana, 1981-84; head of immunology lab. J.L. Miranda Hosp., Sta. Clara, Cuba, 1984-86; immunologist Hnos. Ameijeiras Hosp., Havana, 1986—; instr. Inst. of Med. Scis., Havana, 1990. Collaborator: (book) Dengue Haemorrhagic Fever Hematology and Immunological Aspects, 1986 (Ann. award of Pub. Health 1983); contbr. articles to profl. jours. Mem. Cuban Immunology Soc. (bd. dirs. 1995—). Avocations: beach, movies, reading. Office: Hosp Hnos Ameijeiras, San Lazaro # 701, 10300 Habana Cuba

GÓMEZ-BEZARES, FERNANDO, business educator; b. Logrono, Spain, Jan. 15, 1956; s. Fernando Gómez and Carmen Bezares; m. Dolores Revuelta, July 6, 1979; children: Fernando, Ana-Maria. MBA, U. Deusto, Bilbao, Spain, 1978, PhD in Bus. and Econs., 1980. Asst. prof. statistics, bus. sch. U. Deusto, 1978-79, prof. statistics, 1979-83, prof. quantitative methods, 1980-86, prof. fin., 1983—, full prof., 1984—, dir. finance dept., 1984—, dir. masters program, doctorate program, 1987—, vice dean, 1988-90, dean, 1990-96; vice rector Deusto U., 1998—; vis. prof. numerous univs. in Spain, Europe, and Am.; bd. dirs. El Avion, S.A., Logrono, Spain, Boletin de Estudios Econs., Bilbao, BBVA Gestion, Madrid; collection dir. Desclée de Brouwer, Bilbao, 1986—; cons. in field. Author numerous books including Diagnostico en la Empresa, 1982, Estadistica, 1983, Metodos Cauntitativos, 1985, Decisiones Financieras, 1986, Direccion Financiera, 1989, Gestion De Carteras, 1993, Valoracion de Acciones, 1994, Finanzas y creacion de valor, 1998, Ejercicios de Teoria y Politica Financiera, 1999; contbr. articles to profl. jours. Mem. Assn. Comercial Deusto, Sociedad Española de Estadistica, Fin. Mgmt. Assn., Am. Fin. Assn., Inst. Analistas Financieros, Asociación Española de Finanzas (first pres.), Hipica Club (Logroño, Spain), Cantabria (Logroño). Roman Catholic. Avocations: reading history, music. Office: Univ Comercial de Deusto, Hnos Aguirre 2 Ap 20044, Bilbao 48080, Spain

GOMEZ C., DORA MARIA, chemist, physicist; b. Santa Ana, Venezuela, Apr. 1, 1954; d. Martin A. and Ana Luisa (Caraballo) Gómez; m. José Andérez; children: Ana Virginia, José Maria. Lic. in Chemistry, U. de Los Andes, Méida, Venezuela, 1980; PhD in Physics, U. York, Eng., 1990. Instr. in quantum mecanic and molecular spectroscopy U. de Los Andes Sci. Faculty, Dept. Chem., 1980-83, asst. prof., 1983-86, agregated prof., 1986-90, assoc. prof., 1990-96; vis. assoc. prof. U. Pierre et Marie Curie, 1994-95; vis. prof. Academia de Versalles U. Paris XI, 1995; titular prof. sci. faculty U. de Los Andes, 1996—; dir. crystallography group, sci. faculty U. de Los Andes, 1990-92, mem. rsch. commn. sci. faculty dept. chemistry, 1990-94, faculty coun. mem. sci. faculty, 1993-95, coun. mem. dept. chemistry, 1994-96, dir. rsch. commn. sci. faculty dept. chemistry, 1997—, faculty coun. mem. sci. faculty, 1993—. Author: Manual of Laboratory of General Chemistry, 1984, Study of the Synchrotron Laue Method for Quantitative Structure Determination, 1991; (chpt.) X-Ray Cristallography, 1993; contbr. articles on x-ray molecular structures determinations to profl. jours. Sci. attache Venezuelan Embassy, Paris, 1994-95. Fellow Venezuelan Assn. for Advance of Sci. (sec. fin. 1992-94, 97—); mem. Venezuelan Crystallographic Assn. (v.p. 1993—), Brit. Crystallographic Assn. Avocations: traditional Chinese phylosophy, art martial, swimming. Fax: 58-401286. E-mail: gomez@ciem-s.ula.ve. Office: Univ de Los Andes, Fac de Quimica La Hechicera, 5101 Merida Venezuela

GOMEZ-GONZALEZ, CARMEN, English as second language educator; b. Cosio, Spain, Oct. 9, 1964; d. Jesus Gomez and Marina Gonzalez; m. Juan Carlos Rodriguez-Alonso, June 14, 1997. BA in English Pathology, U. Valladolid, Spain, 1988; Cert. of English with distinction, Mt. Holyoke Coll., 1989; Rschr.'s Degree, U. Oviedo, Spain, 1995. Cert. ESL tchr. English as second language tchr. Ministry of Edn., Madrid, 1989-90; English as second language tchr. Ministry of Edn., Aviles, Spain, 1990-91, head of studies, 1991-92; Englsih as second language tchr. Ministry of Edn., Aviles, 1992—. Vol. worker Youth for Understanding, Spain, 1984-88. Mem. Emily Dickinson Intenrat. Soc., Internat. Spanish Soc. U.S. (hon.). Roman Catholic. Avocations: reading, music, nineteenth-century Anglo-Saxon literature, literary criticism, internet. Home: Avenida de Alemania 25 5-J, 33400 Aviles, Asturias Spain Oifce: Escuela Oficial de Idiomas, Prol de Jose Cueto, 33400 Aviles, Asturias Spain

GOMEZ LOPEZ-EGEA, JOSE LUIS, university president; b. Valencia, Spain, Feb. 6, 1933; arrived in Argentina, 1951; s. Sandalio and Maria Del Carmen (Lopez-Egea) Gomez. BA, Nuestra Señora Del Pilar, Spain, 1950. Acct. U. Del Litoral, Argentina, 1956, Samider SA, Buenos Aires, 1953-58; sr. auditor Price Waterhouse and Co., Buenos Aires, 1958-61; fin. cons. Buenos Aires, 1961-78; treas. Assn. Fumento Cultura, Buenos Aires, 1961-78; pres. U. Austral, Buenos Aires, 1994—; dean Inst. de Altos Estudios Empresariales, Buenos Aires, 1978-94; dir. Wagon-Lits Cook, 1984—. Contbr. articles to profl. jours. Office: Univ Austral, Juan de Garay 125, Buenos Aires 1063, Argentina

GOMEZ-LUCIA, E., veterinarian. DVM, Veterinaria, Madrid, 1980, PhD, 1985. Asst. prof. Sch. vet. Scis., Madrid, 1985-87, assoc. prof., 1987—. Patentee in field; contbr. articles to profl. jours. Fulbright grantee, 1983; U. Complutense fellow, 1989-90, Spanish Min. of Sci. and Edn. fellow, 1996. Mem. Am. Soc. Microbiology, Am. Soc. Virology, Spanish Soc. Microbiology, Spanish Soc. Immunology, Spanish Soc. Virology. Roman catholic. Achievements include discovery of a new human retrovirus. Avocations: travel, cross-stitch, reading, classical music, astronomy. Home: Cardenal Cisneros 52, 28010 Madrid Spain Office: Univ complutense de Madrid, Fac de Veterinaria, 28040 Madrid Spain

GÓMEZ-PINEDA, EDGARDO ALFONSO, chemist, researcher, educator; b. Valdivia, Chile, Dec. 30, 1956; arrived in Brazil, 1982; s. Alfonso Gómez García and Noelia Pineda Muñoz; m. Ana Adelina Winkler-Hechenleitner, Aug. 26, 1983; children: Gustavo Alfonso, Carolina Andrea, Manuel Edgardo. BSc, U. Concepción, Chile, 1982, lic. in chemistry, 1982; DS, UNICAMP, Brazil, 1987. Assoc. prof. UEM/DQI, Maringá, Brazil, 1987—. Fellow CAPES, CNPOJ (award 1983), FAPESP, CNPG-I-C. Office: UEM Dept Chemistry, Av Colombo 5790, 87020900 Maringá Brazil

GOMEZ-SKARMETA, ANTONIO F., technology educator; b. Santiago, Chile, Sept. 11, 1965; s. Antonio W. Gomez and Rebeca Skarmeta; m. Isabel Jimenez, June 30, 1994. BSc with honors, U. Murcia, Spain, 1989, PhD in Informatics with honors, 1995; MSc with honors, U. Granada, Spain, 1991. Asst. prof. U. Murcia, 1990-96, assoc. prof. informatics, 1997—, comms. cons., 1990-94, vice dean faculty informatics, 1991-93, 97-99; mem. steering com. Essimur Comms. Autonoma, Murcia, 1997-98. Contbr. articles to profl. jours. Recipient Nixdorf award, 1988. Office: U Murcia Dept Informatics, Apartado Correas 4021, 30001 Murcia Spain

GOMIDE, ALOYSIO MARÉS DIAS, diplomat; b. Rio de Janeiro, Brazil, Apr. 14, 1929; s. José and Erycina (Dias) G.; m. Maria-Apparecida Leal Penna, Nov. 22, 1930; children: Maria Dulce, Maria Beatrix, Maria Christina, José, Maria Carmen, Aloysio, Maria Apparecida. Student, Cath. U., Rio de Janeiro, 1951, 53; Diploma, Diplomatic Acad., Rio de Janeiro, 1952. Vice council of Brazil Consulate of Brazil, Miami, Fla., 1955-57; 3rd and 2d sec. Embassy of Brazil, San José, Costa Rica, 1957-61; with ministry external rels. Gov. Brazil, Rio de Janeiro, 1961-64; 2d and 1st sec. Embassy of Brazil, Rome, 1964-67; asst. consul Consulate Gen. Brazil, Montevideo, Uruguay, 1967-71; ministry external rels. Counsellor and Ministry 2d class, Rio de la Janeiro and Brazilia, 1971-75; consul gen. Consulate Gen. Brazil, Montreal, Can., 1975-84, Vancouver, Can., 1984-87; amb. Embassy of Brazil, Port-au-Prince, Haiti, 1987-89; amb., min. 1st class Ministry External Rels., Rio-de Janeiro, 1989-94; ret., 1994. Decorated Medal of Lauro Müller Ministry External Rels., 1964, Order of Rio Branco, 1971; Order of Merit (Haiti), 1989. Mem. Brazilian Soc. Cath. Philosophers, Clube das Nações-Brasilia, Mt. Stephen Club Montreal. Roman Catholic. Home: Rua Tonelero 180 Apt 102, Rio de Janeiro 22030-000, Brazil

GOMMERY, DOMINIQUE, palaeoanthropologist, researcher; b. Nogent-sur-Seine, France, May 23, 1966; s. Jacky and Laurette (Miret) G. Licence, U. Burgundy, Dijon, France, 1987, maîtrise, 1988; diplôme d'études approfondies, Inst Paléontologie Humaine, 1989; PhD, U. Paris 7, 1995. Attaché Mus. Nat. D'Histoire Naturelle, Paris, 1996-98; chargé de recherche Centre Nat. de la Recherche Scientifique. Author, editor: Stigny: Un Village du Tonnerrois, 1989, Les Primates une Fabuleuse Aventure de 70 Millions d'Années, 1990; contbr. articles to profl. jours. Recipient prize Found. Marcel Bleustein Blanchet pour La Vocation, Paris, 1992; grantee Found. Fyssen, Paris, 1996-97. Mem. European Anthropol. Assn., Soc. d'Anthropologie de Paris, Soc. Francophone de Primatologie, Soc. de Scis. Naturelles et de Préhistoire de La Vallée de l'Armançongon (sec. asst. 1993). Avocations: aquarium, nature, history, middle age period, customs. Home: 58 rue Villiers lIsle Adam, 75020 Paris France Office: UPR 2147 du CNRS, 44 rue de l'Amiral Mouchez, 75014 Paris France

GOMOLKA, ALFRED, member of European parliament; b. Breslau, Germany, July 21, 1942. Mem. European Parliament, Germany, 1999—; mem. Group of the European People's Party (Christian Democrats) and European Democrats, mem. of bur.; mem. com. on fgn. affairs, human rights, common security and def. policy, com. on industry, external trade, rsch. and energy; substitute mem. delegation to the EU-Latvia Joint Parliamentary Com.; chmn. delegation to the EU-Estonia Joint Parliamentary Com. Office: Am Markt 1, D-17489 Greifswald Germany*

GOMORY, FEDOR, electrical engineer, researcher; b. Bratislava, Slovakia, Dec. 26, 1952; s. Ivan and Antonia (Hladikova) G.; m. Anna Vojenciakova, Sept. 3, 1982; children: Veronika, Andrej. Grad. engring., Slovak Tech. U., Bratislava, 1976; PhD in Elec. Engring., Slovak Acad. Scis., Bratislava, 1985. Rsch. engr. Joint Inst. for Nuc. Rsch., Dubna, Russia, 1981; rsch. engr. Inst. Elec. Engring., Slovak Acad. Scis., Bratislava, 1982-85, rsch. scientist, 1986-95, 98—; rsch. scientist Pirelli Cavi e Sistemi, Milan, 1996-97; head sci. coun. Inst. Elec. Engring., Slovak Acad. Scis., Bratislava, 1992-96. Contbr. chpt. to book and articles to profl. jours. Fax: 4217-54775816. E-mail: elekgomo@savba.sk. Home: Sevcenkova 33, 85101 Bratislava Slovakia Office: Slovak Acad Sci Inst Elec, Dubravska 9, 84239 Bratislava Slovak Republic

GONCALVES, DANIEL MILSTEIN, aircraft maintenance engineer; b. São Paulo, Brazil, Dec. 18, 1966; s. Joao Guilherme and Alla (Milstein) G. Degree in Naval Engring., U. São Paulo, 1991. Cert. naval engr. Mgr. liaison heavy maintenance divsn. TAM Regional Airlines, São Paulo, structures engr., 1992-99, air safety cons., 1992—. Mem. São Paulo Air Club (tech. dir. 1995-96). Avocation: private pilot. Home: 294 Manoel de Gois, 05604020 São Paulo Brazil

GONÇALVES, ELISABETO RIBEIRO, physician, ophthalmology educator; b. Oeiras, Piaui, Brazil, June 6, 1942; d. Paulo de Tarso Ribeiro and Yolanda (Carvalho) G.; m. Marcia Maria Ribeiro Goncalves, Dec. 8, 1979; children: Paulo de Tarso, Anathalia, Mario Vinicius. MD, U. Pernambuco, Recife, Brazil, 1966; cert. in ophthalmology, Brazilian Coun. Ophthalmology, São Paulo, 1971; cert. in retinal and vitreous surgery, Fed. U. Minas Gerais, Belo Horizonte, Brazil, 1972. Resident Fed. U. Minas Gerais, Belo Horizonte, 1969; head Ocular Propaedeutic Svc., Belo Horizonte, 1969-72; head Ophthalmol. Clinic Armed Forces Hosp., Brasilia, 1974-79; ophthalmology instr. Dist. Hosp. Brasilia, 1973-76, Armed Forces Hosp., Brasilia, 1973-74; head electrophysiology svc. Hilton Rocha Inst., Belo Horizonte, 1979-92; head retinal and vitreous svc. Belo Horizonte Eye Inst., 1992—. Author: Problematica da Cegueira, 1986, Diabetes e Hipertensao Arterial, 1994; contbr. articles to profl. jours. With Brazilian Army Forces, 1961. Recipient Hilton Rocha award Fedn. U. Minas Gerais, 1994. Fellow Am. Acad. Ophthalmology, Soc. Francaise d'Ophthalmologie; mem. Ecuadorian Assn. Ophthalmology, Rotary. Roman Catholic. Avocations: reading, movies, music, table tennis, snooker. Home: Rua Dr Mario Pires 224, 30350660 Belo Horizonte Brazil Office: Inst de Olhos de Belo Horiz, Rua Padre Rolim 541, 30130090 Belo Horizonte Brazil

GONCALVES, PAULO ALEXANDRE DE JESUS, controller; b. Lisbon, Portugal, July 16, 1967; s. Emidio Jose Goncalves Alves and Maria Da Conceição De Jesus Gonçalves; m. Vanda Marisa Martins De Matos De Jesus, July 17, 1993; 1 child, Alexandre Matos de Jesus. Adminstrn., U. Internat. Lisbon, 1997. Mid. mgr. Cimpomovel-Veiculos Ligeiros, 1989-95, Prosegur, Lisbon, 1995-97, Unisys, 1996-97; dir. Comfort Hotel Oeiras, Queluz, 1997-98; credit risk analyst Optimus-Telecomm. SA, 1998—. Avocation: sports. Fax:; 351 93 102 3934. Home: Rua Tomas Da Anunciacao, 1-4o Esquerdo, 2675-455 Odivelas Portugal

GONCALVES DA SILVA, CYLON E.T., physicist; b. Ijui, Rio Grande, Brazil, Nov. 14, 1946; s. Solon Goncalves Da Silva and Jorgelina Tricot Da Silva; m. Jennifer Isabel Harris, Apr. 26, 1972; children: Anders, Per. B in Physics, Rio Grande do Sul Fed. U., Porto Alegre, Brazil, 1967; M in Physics, U. Calif., Berkeley, 1971, PhD in Physics, 1972. Prof. Campinas State U., 1982—; with IBM Rsch. Lab., Yorktown Heights, 1985-86; dir. gen. Brazilian Assn. Synchrotron Light Tech., Campinas, Brazil, 1997—. Editor: Solid State Comms., 1987—, numerous conf. proceedings; contbr. more than 80 articles to profl. jours. Fellow Guggenheim Found., 1978. Mem. Brazilian Acad. Sci. Avocations: Oriental art, classical music. Office: Lab Nac de Sincrotron, Caixa Postal 6192, 13083970 Campinas Brazil

GONCHAROV, ALEXANDER PAVLOVICH, mathematician, educator; b. Novoshakhtinsk, Rostov, Russia, Oct. 10, 1954; arrived in Turkey, 1994; s. Pavel Ivanovich and Zoja Alexandrovna (Kalashnikova) G.; m. Liudmila Alexandrovna Sumarokova, June 15, 1985; 1 child, Maria. Bachelor's degree, Rostov U., 1977, Master's degree, 1980, PhD, 1986. Instr. Higher

Tech. Sch., Rostov, 1980-81; from instr. to asst. prof. Rostov Civil Engring. U., 1982-94; asst. prof. Bilkent U., Ankara, Turkey, 1994—. Contbr. articles to profl. jours. Grantee Turkish Scientific & Tech. Rsch. Com., 1994. Avocation: volleyball. E-mail: goncha@fen.bilkent.edu.tr. Home: Bilkent East Campus C-9, 06533 Ankara Turkey Office: Bilkent U, Math Dept, 06533 Ankara Turkey

GONCHAROV, GERMAN ARSEN'EVICH, physicist; b. Tver', Russia, July 8, 1928; s. Arsenii Aleksandrovich and Serafima Vladimirovna (Shokina) G.; m. Vera Dmitrievna Zaitseva, Apr. 23, 1955; children: Irina Germanovna, Yurii Germanovich. Cert. engr., physicist, Moscow State U., 1952; DPh in Physics, All-Union Sci. Rsch. Inst., Sarov, Russia, 1964; DSc in Physics, USSR Higher Attestation Commn., Moscow, 1973, cert. prof. theoretical physics, 1995. Lab. asst. Inst. Theoretical & Experimental Physics-USSR Acad. Scis., 1951-52; rsch. engr. All-Union Sci. Rsch. Inst. Experimental Physics, 1952-55, scientist, 1955-60, head group, 1960-64, sr. scientist, 1964-67; head divsn. Russian Fed. Nuc. Ctr.-All Russian Sci. Rsch. Inst. Exptl. Physics, 1967—. Author 2 books on Soviet atomic project; contbr. over 20 articles to profl. jours. Recipient Lenin prize USSR Coun. of Mins., 1962, Order of Labor Red Banner, USSR Supreme Coun., 1956, Hero of Socialist Labor, 1971, Order of Lenin, 1971, others; named Honored Scientist Russian Fedn., 1999. Mem. Internat. Info. Acad., Russian Natural Scis. Acad. Avocation: nuclear history. Office: RFNC-VNIIEF, 37 Mir Ave, 607190 Sarov NizNovgo, Russia

GONCHAROV, NIKOLAI P., endocrinologist; b. Karayashnik Village, Voronezh, Russia, Jan. 1, 1935; s. Peter V. Goncharov and Ekaterina S. Rad'kova; m. Emilia A. Agievich; 1 child, Nikolai. DMS, Med. Sch., Leningrad, Russia, 1952; PhD in Medicine, Postgrad. Sch., Leningrad, 1961. Rsch. fellow Primate Ctr., Sukhumi, Georgia, USSR, 1961-68; sr. rsch. fellow Primate Ctr., Sukhumi, 1968-71, head endocrinology dept., 1972-88; scientist human reprodn. program WHO, Geneva, Switzerland, 1981-86; head dept. biochem. endocrinology and hormonal analysis Nat. Endocrinology Ctr., Moscow, 1988—; cons. matched reagents program WHO, Geneva, 1992-98; cons. Human Reprodn. Ctr., Moscow, 1995—. Contbr. numerous sci. papers to profl. jours. and conf. procs. Tng. grantee WHO, 1978, 80, rsch. grantee Internat. Assn. for Promotion of Cooperation with Scientists from New Ind. States of Former Soviet Union, Brussels, 1995. Mem. Internat. Assn. for Study of Cortisol and Anti-cortisols, Internat. Soc. for Study of the Aging Male, Nat. Soc. for Endocrinology, European Acad. Andrology (academician 1997). Avocations: Russian history, memory books, arts, mountaineering. Fax: 7-095 126 44 58. E-mail: endo@mail.sitek.net. Office: Endocrinology Rsch Ctr, Dm Ulyanova St 11, Moscow 117036, Russia

GONCZ, ARPAD, president of Hungary, writer; b. Budapest, Hungary, Feb. 10, 1922; s. Lajos and Ilona (Heimann) G.; m. Zsuzsanna Maria Gonter, Jan. 11, 1947; children: Kinga, Benedek, Annamaria, Daniel. JD, U. Pázmány Péter, Budapest, 1944. Journalist, editor, 1945-48, iron worker, agrl. engr., 1948-56, prisoner for involvement in revolution, 1957, released with amnesty, 1963, freelance writer, lit. transl., 1963—; pres. Govt. of Hungary, 1990—. Transl.: The Sound and the Fury (William Faulkner), Ragtime (E.L. Doctorow), World's Fair (Doctorow), The Centaur (John Updike), The Witches of Eastwick (Updike). Mem. exec. com. Assn. of Free Dems., Budapest, 1988-90; v.p. Com. for Hist. Justice, Budapest, 1986—; exec. pres. League for Human Rights Budapest chpt., 1989-90. Mem. Union of Writers (pres. 1988-89), Assn. Hungarian Writers (pres. 1989-90), Hungarian PEN Club (v.p. 1989-94, hon. pres. 1994—). Roman Catholic. Office: Parliament, Kossuth Lajos tér 1-3, H- 1357 Budapest Hungary

GÖNCZÖL, KATALIN, lawyer, sociologist; b. Nagykörös, Hungary, Apr. 17, 1944; d. Gyula and Maria (Fülep) Gönczöl; m. Laszlo Valki, Oct. 21, 1967. Diploma of Law, Eötvös U., Budapest, 1968; Diploma of Sociology, Budapest U., 1976, PhD in Criminology, 1978. Asst. prof. criminology Eötvos U., Budapest, 1968-78, assoc. prof., 1978-89, prof., 1989—, head dept. legal sociology, 1990-94; Parliamentary commr. for human rights (ombudsman) Republic of Hungary, 1995—; mem. directory Bd. Penal Reform Internat., London, 1989—; mem. sci. bd. Internat. Ctr. for Criminology, Montreal, 1995—. Author: Typology of Recidivists, 1980, Crime and Social Policy, 1987, The Poor Criminal, 1991; co-author: Violent Crime and Their Offenders, 1973. Mem. Hungarian Soc. Criminology (sec. gen.), Internat. Soc. Criminology (v.p.). Avocations: classical music, reading, fine art, travel, swimming. Office: Ombudsmans Office, Tüköry u 3, H-1054 Budapest Hungary

GONDER, ATILA, engineering executive; b. Antalya, Turkey, Jan. 1, 1949; s. Mehmet and Muserref Gonder; m. Ayse Fusun Ercelebi, Dec. 8, 1977. BSc, Middle East Tech. U., Ankara, Turkey, 1971, MSEE, 1973; PhD in Biophysics, Hacettepe U., Ankara, Turkey, 1977. Rsch. asst. Middle East Tech. U., Ankara, 1971-73, part-time instr., 1984-86; rsch., instr. Hacettepe U., Ankara, 1973-84; cons. Aselsan Inc., Ankara, 1984-85, mgr., 1985-92, dir. info. systems, 1992—. Contbr. articles to profl. jours. Recipient Rsch. Furthering prize Sci. and Tech. Rsch. Coun. Turkey, 1982. Mem. Computer Applications for Mfg. Users Soc., Chamber Elec. Engrs. Turkey, Mid. East Tech. U. Alumni Assn., Holliday Club. Avocations: playing tennis, swimming, gardening, bicycling, fishing. Office: Info Sys Dir Aselsan Inc, PO Box 101, 06172 Ankara Turkey

GONDRA, JOSÉ MARIA, psychologist, educator; b. Bilbao, Spain, Sept. 12, 1940; s. José M. Gondra and Josefina Rezola. Lic. in Philosophy, U. Complutense, Madrid, 1967, Lic. in Psychology, 1972, PhD in Psychology, 1974; Lic. in Theology, U. Comillas, Madrid, 1971. Diplomate in clin. psychology, Spain. Clin. psychologist Marañón Hosp., Madrid, 1971-73; asst. prof. U. Deusto, Bilbao, Spain, 1973-76; postdoctoral rsc. fellow Fordham U., N.Y.C., 1976-77; asst. prof. U. Complutense, Madrid, 1977-86; prof. psychology Basque Country U., San Sebastián, Spain, 1986—; dir. collection of psychology Desclée de Brouwer, Bilbao, 1974—. Author: La Psicoterapia de Carl Rogers, 1975, History of Psychology, vol. 1, 1997, vol. 2, 1998; editor: La Psicología Moderna, 1982. Mem. Spanish Soc. History of Psychology (v.p. 1992-95, pres. 1998—), European Soc. for History of Human Scis. Roman Catholic. Home: 50 Camino de Mundáiz, E-20012 San Sebastian Spain Office: Basque Country U, Avda de Tolosa 70, 20018 San Sebastian Spain

GONG, ZHENGQUAN, engineer; b. Kun shan, Jiangsu, China, June 5, 1937; parents Yushen Chen and Yingchu Gong; m. Guizhi Diao, Aug. 7, 1968; children: Gong, Xinyu. BS, Mil. Engring. Inst. Harbin, China, 1961; PhD, U. Miss., 1985. Lectr. Nat. U. Sci. & Tech., Changsa, China, 1978-82, assoc. prof., 1985-89; vis. rschr. U. Miss., University, 1982-85; sr. engr. Nanjing Telecomm. Tech. Rsch. Inst., 1989-96, rsch. fellow, 1997, sr. specialist, 1998—; vis. prof. North-East Normal U., Shanghai, 1989-92. Author: VHF Radiowave Propagation, 1962,, Radiowave Propagation, 1963; patentee in field. Mem. IEEE (sr.), Inst. Electronic (sr.), N.Y. Acad. Sci. Office: Nanjing Telecomm Tech Rsch, 18 Houbiaoying, 210016 Nanjing Jiangsu, China Address: Nanjing Telecomms Tech Rsch, 18 Hou Biao Ying, 210016 Nanjing Jiangsu, China

GONNERING, RUSSELL STEPHEN, ophthalmic plastic surgeon; b. Milw., Nov. 21, 1949; s. Russell Richard and Virginia Mary (Mlinar) G.; m. Sandra Lynne Brubaker, Aug. 6, 1971; children: Julie Kathleen, Stephen Russell, Scott Duncan. Student, U. Vienna, Austria, 1969-70; AB in History cum laude, Boston Coll., 1971; MD, Med. Coll. Wis., 1975. Diplomate Am. Bd. Ophthalmology; lic. physician, Wis. Intern St. Luke's Hosp., Milw., 1975-76; fellow in ophthalmic plastic and reconstructive surgery U. Wis., Madison, 1980-81, asst. clin. prof. dept. ophthalmology, 1981-92, assoc. clin. prof. dept. ophthalmology, 1992-96, clin. prof. dept. ophthalmology, 1996—, Kambara lectr., 1997; resident in ophthalmology Med. Coll. Wis., Milw., 1977-80, asst. clin. prof. dept. ophthalmology, 1985—; ophthalmologist Children's Hosp. Wis., Milw., St. Joseph's Hosp., Milw.; ophthalmologist St. Luke's Hosp., Milw., chief ophthalmologist, 1983-94, 97-99, vice chief staff, 2000—; pvt. practice Ophthalmic Plastic & Reconstructive Surgery, 1981—; rsch. assoc. in corneal physiology Med. Coll. Wis., 1976-77; rsch. advisor to fellowship in ophthalmic plastic and reconstructive surgery U. Wis. Madison, 1983—. Author: (with others) Infections of the Eye and Ocular Adnexa, 1986, Oculoplastic, Orbital and Reconstructive Surgery, 1988, Oculoplastic and Orbital Emergencies, 1990, Ophthalmic Plastic, Reconstructive and Orbital Surgery, 1997, Ophthalmic Surgery: Principles and Techniques, 1999; sect. editor: Principles and Practice of Ophthalmic Plastic and Reconstructive Surgery, 1995; contbr. numerous articles to profl. jours.; presenter in field. Recipient George K. Kambara award U. Wis., 1997, Wisdom Soc. Honor award, 1999. Fellow ACS (coun. Wis. chpt. 1996—), Am. Acad. Ophthalmology (basic and clin. sci. course com. 1986-92, chmn. 1988-92, Honor award 1990, Ruedemann lectr. 1994), Am. Soc. Ophthalmic Plastic and Reconstructive Surgery (editl. bd. 1987-99, edn. com. 1988—, vice chmn. edn. com. 1995-97, chmn. edn. com. 1997—, Marvin H. Quickert award 1982, Rsch. award 1982, Reeh Pathology award 1999); mem. Internat. Soc. Orbital Disorders, European Soc. Ophthalmic Plastic and Reconstructive Surgery, Internat. Dacryology Soc., Assn. for Rsch. in Vision and Ophthalmology, Med. Soc. Wis., Milw. County Med. Soc. (del. to state med. soc. 1987-90, bd. dirs. 1989-94, Dirs. citation 1994), Milw. Acad. Medicine, Milw. Ophthalmol. Soc. (treas. 1989-90, sec. 1990-91, v.p. 1991-92, pres. 1992-93), Am. Soc. Ocularists (med. adv. bd. 1987—), Nat. Soc. to Prevent Blindness (med. adv. bd. Wis. chpt. 1987-88). Avocations: sailing, skiing, Tai Kwon Do. Office: Oculoplastic & Orbital Cons 2600 N Mayfair Rd Ste 950 Milwaukee WI 53226-1307

GONSCHOREK, KARL HEINZ, science educator; b. Jeinsen, Germany, Sept. 26, 1946; s. Walter Heinrich and Helene Maria (Jagusch) G.; m. Marion Maria Müller, Mar. 29, 1973; children: Michael, Sonja. Diploma in engring., U. Hanover, Germany, 1975; D of Engring., U. of Armed Forces, Hamburg, Germany, 1980. Jr. clerk Privat Bank, Hanover, 1963-65; scientific co-worker U. Armed Forces, Hamburg, 1975-80; scientific employee Siemens, Erlangen, Germany, 1980-88; prof. Tech. U. Hamburg, 1988-95; prof., electromagnetic compatibility chair Tech. U., Dresden, Germany, 1995—, dean faculty electrotechnique, 2000—; mem. Mil. Standardization, Koblenz, Germany, 1980—, chmn., 1990—; cons. Shipyard, Emden, Germany, 1989—. Author, editor: Elektromagnetische Verträglichkeit, 1992; author: Die Elektromagnetische Umwelt des Kraftfahrzeugs, 1993; contbr. more than 100 articles to profl. jours. Lt. Reconnaissance artillery, 1968-70. Mem. IEEE (sr.), Verband Deutscher Elektrotechniker. Avocations: garden works, science fiction. Home: Gostritzer Strasse 106, D-01217 Dresden Germany Office: Dresden U of Tech, Helmholtzstrasse 9, D-01069 Dresden Germany

GONSON, S. DONALD, lawyer; b. Buffalo, June 13, 1936; s. Samuel and Laura Rose (Greenspan) G.; m. Dorothy Rose, Aug. 28, 1960; children: Julia, Claudia. A.B., Columbia U., 1958; J.D., Harvard U., 1961; postgrad., U. Bombay, India, 1961-62. Bar: Mass. 1962. With Hale and Dorr, Boston, 1962—, sr. ptnr., 1972—; co-chmn. Speech-Tech., N.Y.C., 1987; instr. in law Boston U., 1963-65, bd. trustees Boston Five Cents Savs. Bank, 1978-83, bd. advisors, 1983-88; adj. prof. internat. law Tufts U. Fletcher Sch. Law and Diplomacy, 1999—; lectr. Fin. Times (U.K.), Instnl. Investors, New Eng. Law Inst., Mass. Soc. CPA's. Chmn. Mass. Comty. Devel. Fin. Corp., 1976-82; pres. Cambridge Ctr. for Adult Edn., 1985-88; bd. dirs. Boston Psychoanalytic Soc. and Inst., 1994—, chair Internat. Law Sect. Boston Bar Assn., Fellow, Am. Bar. Found., 1998—. Fulbright scholar, 1961-62. Mem. ABA, Internat. Bar Assn., Mass. Bar Assn., Boston Bar Assn. (chmn. internat. law sect. 1998—), Harvard Club. E-mail: donald.gonson@haledorr.com. Home: 32 Hubbard Park Rd Cambridge MA 02138-4731 Office: Hale & Dorr LLP 60 State St Boston MA 02109-1816

GONTIER, JEAN ROGER, medicine and physiology educator; b. Lens, France, Mar. 8, 1927; s. Paul Maurice and Marie Jeanne (Tricoche) G.; m. Sylviane Prevost, Dec. 8, 1968; children: Sylviane, Yannick, Jean-Yves, Yann. BA magna cum laude, Arras Coll., France, 1944; BS summa cum laude, Etampes Coll., Paris, 1946; MS magna cum laude, Coll. Scis., Paris, 1948; MD summa cum laude, Sch. Medicine, Paris, 1965. Prof., chair dept. physiology UGSEL, Paris, 1957-62; instr. in medicine Sch. Medicine, Paris, 1960-65; resident Hop Cochin, Paris, 1964; assoc. prof. medicine Hop Bicetre, Paris, 1966; dir. physiology Sch. Medicine, Reims, 1966-68; prof. physiology U. Montreal, 1970-78; cons. in internal medicine Paris, 1979—; prof. physiology Bicetre U. Hosp., Paris, 1967-68; cons. editor various pubs., N.Y.C., 1975-78, Paris, 1969-73, Montreal, 1986-89; rsch. in diving physiology in man. Author: (textbooks) Hormones, Nervous System and Digestion, 1968, Respiration, 1971, 77, Digestion, 1969, 82, Textbook of Medical Physiology, 1980, Human Physiology, 1989, Biochemistry For Medical Students, 2000, Physiology for Medical Students, 2001. Recipient Silver medal Sch. Medicine, Paris, 1965. Mem. AAAS, Am. Physiol. Soc. (teaching physiology/respiration/cardiovascular/history sects.), Can. Physiol. Soc., N.Y. Acad. Scis., French Physiol. Soc., Cercle de l'Etrier Club, La Baule Country Club. Roman Catholic. Achievements include research in diving physiology in man. Avocation: sailing. Home and Office: 133 Rue Michel Ange, F75016 Paris France

GÖNÜL, BILGE, physiologist, educator; b. Ankara, Turkey, Oct. 20, 1949; d. Ismail Ismet and Saime (Yalkin) Uzalp; m. Hulusi Itri Gönül, Apr. 19, 1983; 1 child, Can. Student, Faculty of Pharmacy, Ankara, 1970. Cert. in pharmacy. Rsch. asst. Ankara U., 1970-74, PhD ast. faculty of pharmacy, 1974-79; rschr. Chiba (Japan) U. Pharm. Faculty, 1979-80; asst. prof. Ankara U., 1981-85; asst. prof. Gazi U. Med., Ankara, 1985-88, prof., 1988—; mem. Ankara U. Pharmacy F. Directory Com., 1983-85; dir. physiology Dept. Med. F., Ankara, 1985—; mem. Med. Faculty Com., Ankara, 1991-94, Gazi U. Health Scis. Inst., Ankara, 1993—. Contbr. rsch. articles to profl. jours. Recipient Profl. Accomplishment award Ankara Pharmacy Assn., 1981, Congratulation letter Pres. of Yök, 1997. Mem. Internat. Union Physiol. Scis., Fedn. European Physiol. Scs., Soc. Ankara Pharm. Scis. (mem. jour. editl. bd.), Nat. Geog. Soc., Fgn. Student Assn. Osaka Gaidai, Gazi Med. Faculty Soc., Atatürk Soc., Gazi U. Women Rsch. Inst., N.Y. Acad. Scis. Avocations: cats, decorating, cooking. Home: Beril Sitesi 421 Sok Apt 46, 06530 Ankara Turkey Office: Gazi U Faculty Medicine, Besevler, 06500 Ankara Turkey

GONZALES, DANIEL S., lawyer; b. San Antonio, Nov. 10, 1959; s. Sam and Mary Louise (Stewart) G.; m. Mary David McCauley, May 16, 1980 (div. 1983); m. Devon Elaine Cattell, Jan. 1, 1988. BA, U. Notre Dame, 1981; JD, Stanford U., 1984. Bar: Calif. 1986, U.S. Dist. Ct. (no. dist.) Calif. 1986, U.S. Tax Ct. 1987, U.S. Ct. Appeals (9th cir.) 1988, U.S. Dist. Ct. (ea. dist.) Calif. 1990. Trivia game writer Axlon Games, Sunnyvale, Calif., 1984; legal writer Matthew Bender & Co., San Francisco, 1984-86; assoc. Carey & Carey, Palo Alto, Calif., 1986-96, Ferrari, Olsen, Ottoboni & Bebb, San Jose, Calif., 1996-97, Bryant, Clohan, Eller, Maines & Baruh, San Jose, 1997—. Mng. editor Stanford Jour. Internat. Law, 1983-84. Candidate Menlo Park (Calif.) City Coun., 1988; bd. dirs. Page Mill YMCA, Palo Alto, 1993-99, YMCA of the Midpeninsula, 1999—, Project Match, San Jose, 1997—, pres., 1998-99; pres. Menlo Park Dispute Resolution Svc., 1994-95. U. Notre Dame scholar, 1977, Nat. Merit scholar, 1977, scholar Nat. Hispanic Scholarship Bd., 1980. Mem. ABA, San Mateo County La Raza Lawyers (pres. 1994), Santa Clara County Bar Assn. (chmn. minority access com. 1994, chmn. judiciary com. 1995), San Mateo County Bar Assn., Palo Alto Area Bar Assn. Democrat. Avocations: guitar, college football. Office: Bryant Clohan Eller Et Al 303 Almaden Blvd 5th Fl San Jose CA 95110-2721

GONZALES, FROILAN TAYAG, fashion designer; b. Manila, Mar. 23, 1944; s. Francisco and Josefina Paras (Tayag) G. Designer R.T. Paras, Manila, Pierre Cardin, Paris, 1964-70; asst. modeliste Cerruti, Paris, 1972-73; modelist Jean Patou, Paris, 1973-77, art dir., 1977-82; modeliste-styliste Dorothée Bis, Paris, 1982; modeliste-designer Lecoanet Hemant, Paris, 1984-98; co-mgr. family affairs Couture House R.P. Paras, Manila, 1998—; fashion cons. Bloch Pub. House, Brazil, 1968. Recipient 1st place award Chambre Syndicale de la Couture Parisienne, 1963-64. Roman Catholic.

GONZALES, RICHARD DANIEL, manufacturing executive; b. Heidleburg, Germany, July 10, 1958; came to the U.S., 1962; s. Lewis and Josephine (Lucia) G. Student, Cypress Coll., 1976-77, Fullerton Coll., 1976-77, Calif. State U., Fullerton, 1981. Leadman Steel Case, Tustin, Calif., 1981-84; project engr. Allied Signal, Garden Grove, Calif., 1984-87; pres. Advanced Composite Systems, Irvine, Calif., 1987-93, L.A.S. Composites, Perris, Calif., 1993—. Vol. Rep. Cen. Com., Irvine, 1992. Mem. AIA, Soc. for Advancement Process Engring., Am. Soc. Metals, Perris C. of C. (pres. 1996-97). Avocations: flying, jet skiing, snow skiing. Office: LAS Composites 871 Park Ave Bldg 01 Perris CA 92570-2339

GONZALES, RICHARD ROBERT, counselor; b. Palo Alto, Calif., Jan. 12, 1945; s. Pedro and Virginia (Ramos) G.; m. Jennifer Ayres; children: Lisa Dianne, Jeffrey Ayres. AA, Foothill Coll., 1966; BA, San Jose (Calif.) State U., 1969; MA, Calif. Poly. State U., San Luis Obispo, 1971; grad., Def. Info. Sch., Def. Equal Opportunity Mgmt. Inst. Lic. marriage family child counselor, Calif. Counselor student activities Calif. Poly. State U., San Luis Obispo, 1969-71, instr. ethnic studies, 1970-71; counselor Ohlone Coll., Fremont, Calif., 1971-72; coord. coll. readiness Ohlone Coll., Fremont, 1971; counselor De Anza Coll., Cupertino, Calif., 1972-78; mem. cmty. spkrs. bur. De Anza Coll., Cupertino, 1975-78; counselor Foothill Coll., Los Altos Hills, Calif., 1978—; mem. cmty. spkrs. bur. Foothill Coll., Los Altos Hills, 1978—; instr. Def. Equal Opportunity Mgmt. Inst., 1984-96. Mem. master plan com. Los Altos (Calif.) Sch. Dist., 1975-76; vol. worker, Chicano cmtys., Calif.; active mem. Woodside (Calif.) Recreation Commn. With Calif. Army N.G., now ret. Adj. Gen. Corps, USAR. Recipient Counselor of Yr. award Ohlone Coll., 1971-72; Masters and Johnson fellow. Mem. ACA, Am. Coll. Counseling Assn., Calif. Assn. Marriage and Family Therapists, Calif. C.C. Counselor Assn. (former pres.), Calif. Assn. Counseling and Devel. (former pres. Hispanic Caucus), Calif. Assn. for Humanistic Edn. and Devel., Calif. Assn. for Multi-Cultural Counseling, Res. Officers Assn., La Raza Faculty Assn. Calif. C.C., Nat. Career Devel. Assn., Phi Delta Kappa, Chi Sigma Iota. Republican.

GONZÁLES MARTÍN, MARCELO CARDINAL, archbishop; b. Villanubla, Spain, Jan. 16, 1918; ordained priest Roman Catholic Ch., 1941; formerly tchr. theology and sociology Valladolid Diocesan Sem.; founder orgn. for constrn. houses for poor; consecrated bishop of Astorga, 1961; titular archbishop of Case Medinae, also coadjutor of Barcelona, 1966; archbishop of Barcelona, 1967-71, archbishop of Toledo, Spain, 1971—, now archbishop emeritus; elevated to Sacred Coll. Cardinals, 1973; mem. Congregation of Evangelization of Peoples. Address: Residencia Madre Genoveva, Avda de Francia 6, 45005 Toledo Spain*

GONZALEZ, ANTONIO, academic administrator, mortgage company executive; b. Edinburg, Tex., Mar. 14, 1943; s. Manuel Gonzalez and Natalia Torres; m. Elma De Luna, Oct. 10, 1975; 1 child, Julissa Priscilla. BA, U. Md., Balt., 1971; MA, U. Tenn., 1973; JD, Miles Coll., 1979. Law clk. Crain Caton James & Oberwetter, Houston, 1979-81; instr. U. Houston, 1981-83, asst. dir., 1983-86; instr. Houston C.C., 1982-85, 95; assoc. dir. No. Ill. U., Dekalb, 1986-88; adminstr. Prairie View (Tex.) A&M U., 1988-95; instr. Houston Internat. U., 1988-89, pres., CEO, 1989-90; pres., CEO Am. Fidelity Mortgage & Title Co., Houston, 1992-95; instr. North Harris Coll., Houston, 1994-95, Wharton County Jr. Coll., 1996—; mem. adv. com. Houston C.C., 1994-95. Editor: Mexican-American Musicians, 1987; mem. editl. bd. Jour. Minority Issues, 1993-94. Chair tng. and devel. LULAC Dist. 18, Houston, 1994-96; dir. Inst. Chicano Culture, Houston, 1995; mem. SER Jobs for Progress, Houston, 1994-96; Dem. candidate Tex. Ho. Reps. Dist. 130, 1994; mem. Tejano Ctr. for Cmty. Concerns. With USAF, 1966-70, Vietnam. Named Man of Yr. LULAC, Ill., 1987. Mem. AAUP, ABA, VFW, Am. Hist. Assn., Tex. Assn. Chicanos in Higher Edn., Tex. Assn. Coll. Admissions Counselors, Tex. C.C. Tchrs. Assn., Tex. Assn. Mortgage Brokers, Tex. Fgn. Lang. Assn., Nat. Bar Assn., Tex. Assn. Coll. Univ. Student Pers. Adminstrs., Phi Delta Kappa, Delta Theta Phi. Roman Catholic. Avocations: writing, research. Home: 16614 Dounreay Dr Houston TX 77084-3410 Office: Wharton County Jr Coll 911 E Boling Hwy Wharton TX 77488-3252

GONZALEZ, ARTHUR PADILLA, artist, educator; b. Sacramento, July 22, 1954; s. John and Rita (Padilla) G.; m. Christine Carol Ciavarella, Feb. 11, 1988; stepchild, Nick Port. BA, Calif. State U., Sacramento, 1977, MA, 1979; MFA, U. Calif., Davis, 1981. Vis. artist La. State U., Baton Rouge, 1982-83, U. Ga., Athens, summer 1984, R.I. Sch. Design, Providence, 1985; asst. prof. U. Calif., Davis, 1985-86, Berkeley, 1987-88; vis. artist, instr. San Francisco Art Inst., 1990-91; assoc. prof. art Calif. Coll. Arts & Crafts, Oakland, 1991—; mem. adv. bd. Calif. Craft Mus., San Francisco, 1994-95; juror Sacramento Met. Arts Commn., 1994-95. One-person shows include Sharpe Gallery, N.Y.C., 1984, 85, 86, 88, Phyllis Kind Gallery, N.Y.C., 1995, Susan Cummins Gallery, Mill Valley, Calif., 1997. Recipient awards Nat. Endowment for Arts, 1982, 84, 86, 90, Virginia Groot award, 1997. Democrat. Avocation: Polynesian dance. Home: 1713 Versailles Ave Alameda CA 94501-1650 Office: Calif Coll Arts & Crafts 5212 Broadway Oakland CA 94618-1426

GONZÁLEZ, DOMINGO, neurosurgeon; b. Buenos Aires, Sept. 15, 1939; s. Salvador Gonzalez and Concepcion Moles; m. Beth Henry, Dec. 15, 1980; children: Gustavo, Paola, Aimee. MD, U. Buenos Aires, 1964. Diplomate Am. Bd. Neurol. Surgeons. Resident in neurosurgery Wayne State U., 1966-72; neurosurgeon Knud-Hansen Meml. Hosp., St. Thomas, U.S. V.I., 1972-73, Timiken Mercy Hosp., Canton, Ohio, 1973-80, Massillon Cmty. Hosp., Ohio, 1973-80, Doctor's Hosp., Massillon, Ohio, 1973-80; chief neurosurgery Sanatorio Guemes, Buenos Aires, 1981-89, Swiss Med. Group, Buenos Aires, 1981-2000; with biology dept. Kent State U., Canton, Ohio, 2000—. Mem. Am. Assn. Neurol. Surgeons, Ohio State Med. Soc., Colegio Argentino de Neurocirujanos. Avocation: woodworking. Home: 420 19th St NE Massillon OH 44646-4957

GONZALEZ, EDUARDO, telecommunications specialist; b. Balt., Apr. 15, 1958; s. Lincoyan Gonzalez and Anamarma Csaszar; m. Marma Pma Busta, Dec. 21, 1987; children: Barbara, Josefa, Antonia. Diploma in civil engring., U. Chile, Santiago, 1987; PhD in Electronic and Elec. Engring., U. London, 1997. Asst. tchr. U. Chile, Santiago, 1978-83; project engr. Air Force, Santiago, 1982-85; R&D engr. electronics divsn. ENAER, Santiago, 1985-88; telecom. engr. SISTECO, Santiago, 1988-89; head telecom. unit Banco A. Edwards, Santiago, 1989-91, telephony area vice mgr., 1996—; cons. Nat. Telecom. and Svcs., Santiago. Mem. IEEE, Microwave and Techniques, Laser and ElectroOptics Soc., Comm. Soc. Avocation: jogging. Fax: 56-2-388-4208. Office: Banco A Edwards, Huirfanos 740, 6760496 Santiago Chile

GONZÁLEZ, ENRIQUE, industrial engineer, consultant; b, Paris, July 15, 1905; s. Nicanor González and Tulia Meza; m. Maruja Rodriquez; children: Hernán, Cecilia, Ana, Javier, Marta, Lia, Silvia, Clara, Hilda, Ignacio, Gloria, Amparo. Civil Engring., Nat. U., Antioquia, 1927. Engr. Dir. Rds., Andes, Antioquia, 1927-28, Planta Guadalupe, Santa Rosa, Colombia, Brazil, 1928-32; metals control dir. House of Money, Medellin, Colombia, Brazil, 1932-35; engr., dir. Colombian Chem. Industry, Santa Rosa, 1935-36; engr., maintenance Colombian Textile Co., Medellin, 1937-62; engr., dir. Sec. Pub. Works, Antioquia, 1964-65; cons. engr. Solla S.A., Bello, Colombia, 1965-90; indls. cons. engr. Medellin, 1965-90. Recipient Shield award Colombian Constrn. Bd. Office, 1988, Antioquia Gov.'s Office, 1989, Colombian Soc. Architects and Engrs., 1990. Avocation: reading. Home: Carrera 65 No 48-72, Medellin Colombia

GONZALEZ, GUILLERMO ENRIQUE, diplomat; b. Córdoba, Argentina, Dec. 30, 1942; m. Adriana Posse; six children. Degree in Polit. and Social Scis. Joined Fgn. Svc. Argentine Republic, 1965, promoted to rank amb. extraordinary and plenipotentiary, 1993; mem. Office Dir. Gen. Policy Ministry Fgn. Affairs, Buenos Aires, 1965; with Embassy of Argentina Ministry Fgn. Affairs, Lima, Peru, 1970; with Ministry Fgn. Affairs, Buenos Aires, 1972; mem. Argentine permanent mission to Orgn. Am. States Ministry Fgn. Affairs, Washington, 1975; chief cabinet dep. asst. sec. fgn. affairs Ministry Fgn. Affairs, Buenos Aires, 1980, permanent rep. Argentine Republic Food & Agrl. Orgn., 1982-87, gov. Internat. Fund for Agrl. Devel., 1987, dir. gen. Internat. Agrl. Affairs, 1987, dir. gen. Internat. Econ. Rels., 1989, dep. asst. sec. internat. econ. negotiations, 1993, dep. asst. sec. fgn. policy, 1994; amb. extraordinary and plenipotentiary to Swiss Confedn. Ministry Fgn. Affairs, 1996, amb. extraordinary and plenipotentiary Liechtenstein, 1997; amb. to the United States Ministry of Fgn. Affairs, 1999—. Fax: 202-332-3171. E-mail: albertod@intr.net. Office: Embassy of the Argentine Republic 1600 New Hampshire Ave NW Washington DC 20009-2582

GONZALEZ, LUIS A., medical equipment company executive; b. Havana, Cuba, Oct. 23, 1963; came to U.S., 1965; s. Luis Gregorio Gonzalez and Georgina Jimonez; m. Cary, May 13, 1993; children: Luis, Ana, Jovanna, Nicole, Daniele. Degree, U. Calif., Fullerton, 1992. Police officer Maywood (Calif.) Police Dept., 1992—; pres. Unique Medical Diversity, Inc., Miami,

Fla., 1998—. E-mail: uniqmed@gateway.com. Office: Unique Medical Diversity Inc 12356 SW 117th Ct Miami FL 33186-3932

GONZALEZ, RICARDO, surgeon, educator; b. Buenos Aires, June 26, 1943; s. Salvador Maria and Clyde Alcira (Prevettoni) G.; children: Diego Andres, Carlos Ricardo. BA, Coll. Nat. San Isidro, Buenos Aires, 1959; MD, U. Buenos Aires, 1965. Diplomate Am. Bd. Urology. Resident in surgery Hosp. Militar Cen., Buenos Aires, 1966-68; intern in surgery U. Minn., 1969-70, resident (med. fellow) in urologic surgery, 1970-74; from instr. to prof. urology U. Minn., Mpls., 1974-85, prof. urology, 1985-94, prof. pediat., 1993-94; chief, pediat. urology Children's Hosp. of Mich., Detroit, 1994; prof. urology Wayne State U., Detroit, 1995-99; prof. urology and pediats., chief pediat. urology divsn. U. Miami (Fla.)/Jackson Meml. Hosp., 1999—; pres. Pediat. Urology P.C., Detroit, 1995-2000; vis. prof. Harvard U., Cambridge, Mass., 1994, Johns Hopkins U., Balt., 1995, U. Washington, Seattle, 1995, U. Calif., San Francisco, 1996, Cornell U., N.Y., 1998; presenter in field. Contbr. over 170 articles to profl. jours., over 50 chpts. to books; editor 2 books. Am. Acad. Pediat. fellow, 1981, Nat. Kidney Found. rsch. fellow 1974-76; co-prin. investigator USPHS cancer grant 1976-78. Fellow Am. Acad. Pediat. (mem. exec. sect. on urology com. 1995-98); mem. Am. Urologic Assn., Mex. Coll. Urology (hon.), Venezuelan Soc. for Spina Bifida, Argentine Confedn. Urology, Societé Internat. d'Urologie, Ibero-Am. Soc. Pediat. Urology (pres. 1995-98), Soc. for Pediatric Urol. Surgeons (by invitation). Avocations: opera, music, language, reading, writing. E-mail: rgonzal4@med.miami.edu. Office: U Miami Urology Dept PO Box 16960 Miami FL 33101-6960

GONZALEZ, RICHARD, quality performance professional; b. 1966. BA in Spanish with honors, U. Minn., 1991; BA in Polit. Sci., 1991; MPA, Fla. Atlantic U., 1998. Regulatory project officer, analyst USCG Hdqtrs., Washington, 1992-93; divsn. head, supply dept., deck watch officer CGC Courageous, Panama City, Fla., 1993-95; chief, uninspected vessel safety sect. (7th Dist.) USCG, Miami, 1995-98, quality performance cons., 1998—. With USCG, 19875. Decorated Nat. Def. Svc. medal, numerous commendation medals USCG, others. Mem. Am. Soc. for Quality, Am. Soc. Pub. Adminstrn., Phi Gamma Delta, Alpha Phi Omega, Alpha Mu Gamma, Pi Alpha Alpha, Pi Gamma Mu. Home: # 204 6920 SW 44th St Apt 204 Miami FL 33155-4773

GONZALEZ, RICHARD THEODORE, photographer; b. Trona, Calif., Nov. 9, 1939; s. Alfonso Contreras and Mary (Duarte) G.; m. Gerry Price, Oct. 30, 1958 (div. 1972); children: Richard K., Debra G., Maria E., Felicia F.; m. Yolanda Quijano, Apr. 18, 1991; 1 child, Andrea. Degree in profl. still photography, N.Y. Inst. Photography, 1962. Photographer Kerr McGee Chem. Corp., Trona, 1962-86, San Bernadino, Calif., 1987-89; founder Gonzalez's Modeling Agy., Midwest City, Okla., 1996—; newspaper photographer Trona Argonaut, 1962-86; freelance photographer, Trona, 1962-86. Democrat. Roman Catholic. Home: 769 NW 1st St Moore OK 73160-2329 Office: 700 S Air Depot Blvd Ste D-366 Midwest City OK 73110-4833

GONZALEZ, ROLANDO NOEL, secondary school educator, religion educator, photographer; b. Rio Grande City, Tex., Sept. 10, 1947; s. Ubaldo and Beulah (Gutierrez) G. BA, U. Tex., 1968; MA, Tex. A & I U., 1972. Cert. tchr. all scis., guidance and counseling. Tchr., head sci. dept. Roma (Tex.) Jr. High Sch., 1968-71; migrant/Title I counselor Roma Elem. and Roma Jr. High Sch., 1972-76; head sci. dept. Rio Grande High Sch., Rio Grande City, Tex., 1976-78; tchr., head sci. dept. Ringgold Jr. High Sch., Rio Grande City, 1982-83, Pharr-San Juan-Alamo High Sch., Pharr, Tex., 1986—; seminarian Diocese of Brownsville, San Antonio, 1979-82; pastoral asst. Our Lady, Queen of Angels Ch., La Joya, Tex., 1982-83; coord., lay ministries Brownsville Diocese, McAllen, Tex., 1983-85; lectr., tchr. on scripture Perpetual Help Ch., McAllen, 1986-88, Holy Spirit Ch., McAllen, 1989—; scripture tchr., lectr. St. Mary Margaret Ch., Pharr, 1988; instr. history of chemistry U. Tex.-Pan Am., Edinburg, 1990; wedding and portrait photographer, 1973—. Contbr. articles to profl. jours. tchr. scripture, lectr. Sts. Mary and Margaret Ch., Pharr, 1988, Sacred Heart Ch., Mercedes, Tex., 1990. Recipient Appreciation award Sacred Heart Ch., 1990, Tchr. of Yr. award Rio Grande Valley Sci. Assn., 1996-97. Home: 2800 W Iris Ave Mcallen TX 78501-6200

GONZALEZ, ROSE A-NAVARRO, artist; b. Granada, Nicaragua, May 22, 1936; d. Manuel Navarro and Candelaria (Guerrero) Martinez; m. Simeon Gonzalez, Oct. 15, 1959. Diploma, Nat. Inst. Orient, Granada, Nicaragua, 1956, Sch. Art and Design, N.Y.C., 1964, Abbey Sch. N.Y., 1972; postgrad., Art Student's League, N.Y.C., 1972-73. Group exhbns. include Empire Savs. Bank, N.Y.C., 1973, Mus. City of N.Y., 1977, 82, Cayman Gallery, 1977, New Rochelle Gallery, 1978, Los Sures Gallery, 1978, Bklyn. Mus. Gallery, 1979, Louis Aborns Arts for Living Ctr., 1979, Studio 54, 1983, Keanne Mason Gallery, N.Y.C., 1983, Queen's Coll., 1984, St. Sabastian Parish Ctr., 1991, Latino Open-Air and Cultural Festival, N.Y.C., 1992, SUNY, 1992, Agora Gallery, N.Y.C., 1993, Progress Gallery, N.Y.C., 1993-94, 98, Dist. Coun. 37, N.Y.C., 1994, 95, New Rochelle Pub. Libr., 1996, Goya Gallery, N.Y.C., 1997, Colombian Consulate, N.Y.C., 1997, Aguilar Libr., N.Y.C., 1997, Oller Campeche Gallery, 1997, N.Y.C., Taller Romano Gallery, Madrid, 1998, N.E. Hispanic Cath. Ctr., N.Y.C., 1999, Dic St. Coun. 37, N.Y.C., 1999. Mem. coun. Eisenhower Commn., Rep. Nat. Com., Washington, 1995. Recipient spl. prize Friends of Puerto Rico; Comision awarded Hispana Pro-Obra Ruben Dario, 1999; recipient Medal of Freedom, 1999, Outstanding Artist and Designer of the 20th Century medal, award Nicaraguan Consultate, N.Y.C. Mem. Lions Club Internat. (v.p. 1995—, Melvin Jones award 1993-94). Republican. Roman Catholic. Home: 1121 Morrison Ave Bronx NY 10472-4235

GONZALEZ, WENCESLAO JOSE, philosopher, educator; b. Ferrol, Spain, Sept. 21, 1957; s. Jose-Manuel and Maria-Paz (Fernandez) G. BA in Philosophy, U. Salamanca, Spain, 1979; PhD, U. Murcia, Spain, 1983. Lectr. U. Murcia, 1979-82, sr. lectr., 1983-87, mem. governing bd., 1985-87, titular prof. philosophy and logic, 1987-96; prof., chair U. La Coruna, 1996—; vis. fellow Ctr. Philosophy Sci., U. Pitts., 1993-94, 96, 99; vis. prof. U. La Coruña, 1994-96. Author: La Teoria de la Referencia. Strawson y la Filosofia Analitica, 1986, Jour. on Action Theory, 1991, Aspectos metodológicos de la investigación científica, 2d revised edit., 1990; editor Accion e Historia, 1996, Progreso científico e Innovación Tech., 1997, Pensamiento de L. Laudan, 1998, Ciencia y valores éticos, 1998, Philosophy and Metodology of Economics, 1998, Problemas filosóficos y metodológicos de la Economía en la Sociedad tecnológica actual, 2000; contbr. 50 articles to profl. jours. Mem. Am. Philos. Assn., Philosophy Sci. Assn., Brit. Soc. for the Philosophy of Sci., The Mind Assn., The Aristotelian Soc., Austrian L. Wittgenstein Soc., Sociedad española de Lógica Metodología y Filosofía de la Ciencia, Sociedad española de Historia de las Ciencias y las Técnicas. Avocations: soccer, jogging. Home: Calle Iglesia 184 2 B, 15402 Ferrol (La Coruna) La Coruna, Spain Office: Faculty Humanities U La Coruña, Dr Vazquez Cabrera St s/n, 15403 Ferrol Spain

GONZÁLEZ ALVAREZ, LAURA, foreign diplomat; b. Avilés (Asturias), Spain, July 9, 1941. Mem. European Parliament, 1999—, mem. com. on petitions, mem. com. on environment, pub. health and consumer policy, substitute com. on employment and social affairs; mem. Confederal Group of the European United Left/Nordic Green Left; mem. delegation for relations with the countries of Ctrl. Am. and Mex. Mem. United Left. Office: Plaza America 10-4, E-33005 Oviedo Spain*

GONZALEZ BLASCO, PEDRO, economics educator; b. Valdeavellano de Tera, Spain, Apr. 14, 1937; s. Gonzalo Gonzalez Gomez and Concepcion Blasco Las Heras. MS in Physics, U. Complutense, Madrid, 1962; PhD in Politics, MA in Sociology, U. Complutense, 1980; MA, PhD in Sociology, Yale U., 1977; MA in Econs., U. Autonoma, Madrid, 1994. Asst. prof. U. Autonoma, Madrid, 1972-77, prof. econs., 1991—; asst. prof. U. Alcala, Madrid, 1978-83; prof., head dept. econs. U. Zaragoza, Spain, 1984-90; prof. U. Autonoma de Madrid, 1991; mng. dir. Grupo SM; assessor evaluation CYCIT, Madrid, 1984-94; dir. rsch. unit U. Autonoma, Madrid, 191-93. Co-author: Modern Nationalism in Old Nations, 1974, España, Un Presente Para El Futuro, 1984; author: El Investigador Cientifico en España, 1980, Jovenes Españoles 89, 1990, 96, 99. Fellow Yale U., 1970-71, Salzburg Seminar, 1980. Fellow European Studies Found.; mem. N.Y. Acad. Scis., Scientometrics Rev., Reis Rev. Home: c Joaquin Turina 39, 28044 Madrid Spain Office: Univ Autonoma de Madrid, Ciudad Univ de Cantoblanco, 28049 Madrid Spain

GONZALEZ CALLEJA, EDUARDO, history educator, researcher; b. Madrid, Mar. 12, 1962; s. Eduardo and Begoña (Calleja) Gonzalez; m. Juana Maria Malca. Grad., U. Complutense, Madrid, 1988, PhD in History, 1990. Rschr. Consejo Superior de Investigaciones Cientificas, Madrid, 1990—; guest history educator U. Provence, France, 1991-93, 94-95; associated eductor U. Carlos III, Madrid, 1998-2000. Author: Hispanidad as a Weapon, 1988, Elections and Parliamentaries, 1993, The Armed Defense Against Revolution, 1995, The Reason of Force, 1998, The Mauser and The Vote, 1999, The Spanish Mediterranean, 2000. Office: Inst de Historia, Duque De Medinaceli 6 3o, 28014 Madrid Spain

GONZALEZ DE BULNES, ANTONIO, veteranian, researcher; b. Caceres, Spain, Oct. 6, 1967; s. Antonio and Isabel (Lopez) G.; m. Maria Angeles Herreros, Nov. 5, 1995. MVM, U. Complutense, 1991; DVM, U. Complutense, Madrid, 1997. Prof. U. Complutense, Madrid, 1993; postgrad. CIATA, Asturias, Spain, 1997-98; rschr. INIA, Madrid, 1998—; cons. U. Complutense, Madrid, 1996—. Contbr. articles to profl. jours. Mem. Vet. Collegue, Vet. Conseil. Avocations: hunting, fishing, camping, riding. Office: SGIT-INIA, Avda Puerta de Hierro s/n, 28040 Madrid Spain

GONZALEZ-ECHEVERRIA, FRANCISCO, pediatrician, researcher; b. Zaragoza, Spain, Oct. 5, 1956; s. Avrelio Gonzalez and Carmer Echeverria; m. Teresa Ancin, Sept. 5, 1981; children: Miguel, Raquel, Hector. MB, U. Zaragoza, 1979; MD, U. Salamanca, Spain, 1985. Med. diplomate, Spain. Resident C. Hosp. L.U., Salamanca, 1981-85; asst. pediatrician C. Hosp., Estella, Spain, 1985-86, Reina Sofia Hosp., Tudela, Spain, 1986—; cons. Michel Servet Inst., Hvesca, Spain, 1995—; rschr. Studies Ctr., Tudela, 1996. Author: The Biosynthesis of Immunogobulins in Cell Cultures of Lymphoproliferative Syndromes, 1985, Michael Servet, Dioscerides Editor, 1997, also articles to med. jours. Recipient Immunolab award Biopathology Soc., Madrid, 1989, award Pverículture Soc., Madrid, 1995. Mem. Spanish Pediat. Soc. (award 1991), Soc. Internat. History of Medicine (del.), EAACI, N.Y. Acad. Scis. Avocations: world history, languages, medical research, paleography. Home: Ximenez de Rada 23, 31500 Tudela Navarra, Spain Office: Reina Sofia Hosp, Ctra Tarazona, 31500 Tudela Navarra, Spain

GONZALEZ FERNANDEZ, JOSE ANTONIO, government official; b. Mexico City, Mex., Mar. 8, 1952. BA in Law, Free Sch. Law, 1975; MA in Pub. Adminstr. & Polit. Sci., U. Warwick, England, 1978. Dir. gen. jud. affairs, Sec. Health, 1982-83, sr. officer, 1983-85, undersec. health regulation, 1985; sr. ofcl. Fed. Chamber Deputies, 1985-87; ofcl. legal affairs Embassy Mex. in U.S., 1987-88; chief dir. spl. affairs, dir. gen. N.Am. Sec. Fgn. Affairs, 1989-90, sec. great commn., pres. fgn. affairs commn., govt. commn., 1991-94; rep. gen. N.Am. XI Electroal Dist., Assembly Reps., 1994; atty. gen. Fed. Dist., 1995-97; dir. gen. Inst. Security & Social Svcs., 1997-98; sec. Labor & Social Welfare, Tialpan, Mex., 1998—, Health, Tialpan. Office: Sec Labor & Social Welfare, Periferico Sur, Tailpan 14149, Mexico Office: Lieja Núm 7, Colonia Juárez i Piso, 06696 Mexico City Mexico*

GONZALEZ FRAGA, JAVIER ANTONIO, economist; b. Buenos Aires, May 12, 1948; s. Marcial Vicente and Maria Elvira (Fraga) Gonzalez; m. Patricia Domecq, Dec. 15, 1972 (div. Dec. 1988); children: Sol, Santiago, m. Barbara Maria Josè Morea, May 11, 1992; children: Rodrigo, Marcial. M Econs., Argentina Cath. U. Pres. J.A. González Fraga y Assocs., Argentina, 1974-89, G.F. Macroeconomia, Argentina, 1985-89; gov. Ctrl. Bank of Argentina, 1989-91; pres. La Salamandra S.A., 1992—; v.p. Buenos Aires Stock Exch., 1994-99; dir. Argentine Inst. Capital Markets, 1992-99. Office: La Salamandra Cramer 4457, 1429 Buenos Aires Argentina

GONZALEZ-GARZA, ANA MARIA, psychology educator, researcher; b. Mexico City, Mex., Mar. 28, 1936; d. Jorge Gonzalez Gazcon and Ana Garza de Gonzalez; m. René Desiderio Galindo, Oct. 12, 1955 (dec. Nov. 1971); children: Ana Maria, René Carlos, Jorge Rodrigo, Patricia Elisa, Maria Gabriela, Pedro Ignacio; m. Carlos Pulido Ballesteros, Oct. 13, 1973; 1 child, Carlos Rodrigo. BA in Ednl. Psychology, Iberoamericana U., Mexico City, Mex., 1980, MD in Human Devel., 1986, PhD in Human Devel., 1999; PhD (hon.), Internat. U. Alt. Medicines, Colombo, Sri Lanka, 1995. Head human devel. dept. Centro de Integracion Educativa, Mexico City, 1972-86; dir. Quenamican Human Devel. Inst., Mexico City, 1985-87; head postgrad. studies human devel. Iberamericana U., Mexico City, 1987-90, head edn. and human devel. dept., 1991—; cons. Hebraic U., Mexico City, 1992-94; advisor Centro de Integracion Educativa, Mexico City, 1988—. Author: Enfoque Centrado en la Persona: Aplicaciones a la Educacion, 1991, El Nino y la Educacion, 1991, El Nino y Su Mundo, 2nd edit., 1993, From Shadow to Light, 1995, (with others) La Conciencia Transpersonal, 1999. Mem. Internat. Acad. Scis., Sci. and Med. Network (London), Person-Centered Expressive Therapy Assn. (bd. advisors 1987—), Centro de Estudios de La Diversidad Religiosa. Roman Catholic. Avocations: classical music, classical and folklore dance, tai chi chuan, reading. Office: Iberamericana U, Prol Paseo de la Ref No 880, Mexico City 01210, Mexico

GONZALEZ-GONZALEZ, JESUS MARIA, dentist, stomatologist, researcher in medicine; b. Herreros de Suso, Spain, Jan. 25, 1961; s. Francisco Gonzalez-Martin and Maria-Jesus Gonzalez-Herraez. BM, State U., Salamanca, Spain, 1985; Specialist in Stomatology, State U., Murcia, Spain, 1992; MD, State U., Alicante, Spain, 1992. Cert. med. specialist in stomatology. Med. practitioner State Health Svc., San Pedro del Valle, Spain, 1987, Aldearubia, Spain, 1987, Salamanca, 1988, Fuenteguinaldo, Spain, 1988, Barbadillo, Spain, 1988, La Manga, Spain, 1990; dentist State Health Svc., Cartagena, Spain, 1990-91, Bejar and Ciudad Rodrigo, Spain, 1992; dentist pvt. clinic, Lorca, Spain, 1991; med. specialist in stomatology pvt. clinic, Salamanca, 1991—; speaker in field. Author: Estudio Morfologico y Funcional de la Articulacion Temporomandibular en el Hombre y Animales Mamiferos, 1993; contbr. numerous articles to profl. jours.; patentee in field. Mem. N.Y. Acad. Scis., Profl. Assn. Dentists in Spain, Ski Club of Salamanca. Avocations: the arts, reading science books and research journals, sports, travel, science fiction films. Office: Pvt Dental Clinic, c/ Avila 4 1 o A, 37004 Salamanca Spain

GONZALEZ-GUERRA, MIGUEL GERONIMO, medical educator; b. La Guaira, Venezuela, Sept. 30, 1936; s. Segundo and Eulalia (Guerra) G.; m. Angela Paula Rodriguez, Aug. 21, 1961; children: Cesar Alberto, Oscar Eduardo, Laura Beatriz. Grad., Salamanca U., Spain, 1961; MD, Ctr. U., Caracas, Venezuela, 1967. Physician Min. Pub. Health, Caracas, Venezuela, 1962-98; prof. pub. health Ctrl. U., Caracas, Venezuela, 1980-91, prof. history medicine, 1983—, head history medicine, 1991—. Author: Lorenzo Campins y Ballester, 1996, Medical Studies in U.C.V. From 1891, 1998. Fellow Venezuelan Soc. History Medicine, Latin Soc. History Medicine (pres., founder 1998—). Home: Av PAez Resid 2000, Caracas 1021, Venezuela Office: Ctrl U Venezuela, Caracas Venezuela

GONZALEZ-HERMOSILLO, BRENDA, economist, researcher; b. Mexico City, Oct. 28, 1955; d. Jesus and Emilia (Gonzalez Watkins) G. BA in Econs., Inst. Tech. Autonomo de Mexico, Mexico City, 1979; MA in Econs., U. Western Ont., London, 1980, PhD in Econs., 1983. Rsch. asst. Bank of Mex., Mexico City, 1977; economist Banco Nacional de Mex., Mexico City, 1978, Min. of Fin., Mexico City, 1979, Bank of Montreal, Toronto, Ont., 1983-84, Bank of N.S., Toronto, 1985-89; sr. economist Bank of Can., Ottawa, Ont., 1989-94, Internat. Monetary Fund, Washington, 1994—. Contbr. articles to profl. jours. Recipient Govt. of Can. award to fgn. nationals, 1980-83; Inst. of Tech. scholar, 1976-78, U. Western Ont. scholar, 1979-80. Mem. Can. and Am. Econ. Assn. Achievements include research on financial crises, financial markets, monetary policy, medicare. Avocations: sports, outdoors, pets. Home: 4332 Leland St Chevy Chase MD 20815-6064 Office: Internat Monetary Fund 700 19th St NW Washington DC 20431-0001

GONZALEZ-LAMA, ZOILO, microbiologist, educator; b. Cabra, Cordoba, Spain, Mar. 19, 1949; s. Bartolome Manuel Gonzalez and Maria de la Sierra Lama; m. Ana Maria Lamas, Sept. 28, 1975; children: Zoilo, Ana Maria. BSc in Biology, Fac. Cien. Biol., Sevilla, Spain, 1972; MSc in Biology, 1972; PhD in Scis., Fac. Ciencias, Granada, Spain, 1975. Cert. microbiologist. Rsch. fellow C.S.I.C., Granada, 1972-75; investigator assoc. Argonne (Ill.) Nat. Lab., 1975-76; prof. Medicine Sch. U. Las Palmas, Spain, 1976—; head dept. U. Las Palmas, 1989—. Contbr. articles to profl. jours. Grantee Ednl. Sci. Ministry 1972-75, 75-76, C. Gulbenkian Found. 1974, 75. Mem. AAAS, Am. Soc. Microbiologist, Am. Soc. Parasitologist, Soc. Gen. Microbiology, N.Y. Acad. Sci., Spanish Soc. Microbiologist, Spanish Soc. Biochemistry. Roman Catholic. Avocations: golf, music, reading, bullfighting. Home: Nestor Alamo 39, 35018 Santa Brigida Spain Office: U Las Palmas, Microbiology APDO 550, 35080 Las Palmas Spain

GONZALEZ-MENDOZA, JORGE E., infectious diseases physician, consultant; b. Lima, Peru, June 30, 1959; s. Jorge M. Gonzalez and Maria E. Mendoza; m. Flor N. Ponce, Dec. 19, 1990; 1 child, Flor de Maria Gonzalez-Ponce. Master, Tchg. Scis., Lima, 1975; MS, London Sch. Hygiene and Tropical Medicine, 1993, diploma, 1996. Diplomate infectious diseases. Intern in medicine Hosp. Cayetano Heredia, Lima, 1985-86, resident in infectious diseases, 1988-92; cons. infectious diseases Clinica San Camilo, Lima, 1990-95; cons. in internal medicine and infectious diseases Peruvian Social Security, Lima, 1995—; assoc. instr. infectious diseases U. Peru and Cayetano Heredia, Lima, 1996—; med. adviser Warner-Lambert Labs., Lima, 1997—; med. translator Roche, Bristol-Myers Squibb, Warner Lambert, Abbott, Lima, 1995—. Co-author: A Practical Manual of Antimicrobial Therapy, 1996, Medical Vademecum La Revista Medica, 1998; editor, chief med. writer La Revista Medica, 1994—. Mem. Am. Soc. Microbiology, Peruvian Coll. Physicians. Roman Catholic. Avocations: listening to adult contemporary and pop music, playing guitar and keyboards, reading, going to museums and art exhibits. Home: Manuel Vildoso 824, Urb Sta Catalina, Lima 13, Peru Office: Medex, Rep Panama 3065, San Isidro Lima, Peru

GONZALEZ NARBONA, JOSE CARLOS, lawyer; b. Madrid, Dec. 14, 1959; s. Jose Luis Gonzalez Calisalvo and Concepcion Narbona Bracho; m. Mar Gil Zapardiel, Nov. 30, 1996. LLB, Complutense U., Madrid, 1987; LLM, U. of Pacific, 1989. Bar: Madrid, 1989. Intern Attia, Bartel, Eng & Torngren, Sacramento, Calif., 1989; assoc. Sanchez-Bella & Aldama, Madrid, 1989-90, Rodriguez Molnar & Assocs., Madrid, 1990-91; legal advisor Stein Group, Mallorca, Spain, 1991-92; dir. legal confs. Inst. Internat. Rsch. Spain, Madrid, 1993-97; dir. internat. Bufete Diaz-Arias, Madrid, 1997-99; fir. internat. dept. Herus Estudio Legal, Madrid, 1994-97; bd. dirs. ATD Internat.; mng. ptnr. Levy Gee Espana. Mem. bd. dirs. Fedn. Madrileña Motociclismo, Madrid, 1993-97; pres. Moto Club Guadarrama, Madrid, 1996-97. Mem. Spanish Co. Lawyers Assn. (bd. dirs. 1996—), Internat. Bar Assn. Roman Catholic. Avocations: motorcross, archery, fencing, mountain biking. E-mail: josen@evygee.com. Office: Levy Gee Espana, Zurban 76, 28010 Madrid Spain

GONZALEZ-PRADAS, EMILIO FERNANDO, chemistry educator; b. Alhucemas, Melilla, Spain, Sept. 12, 1948; s. Emilio Gonzalez Cidron and Carmen Pradas Pelegrin; m. Matilde Villafranca, NOv. 10, 1973; children: Emilio Gonzalez Villafranca, Elena Gonzalez Villafranca; m. Carmen Senés-Motilla, Spe. 1, 1999. PhD in Chemistry, Granada (Spain) U., 1980. Assoc. prof. Granada U., 1973-75; asst. prof., 1975-86, prof. (titular), 1986-93, gen. sec., 1984-86; prof. (titular) Almeria (Spain) U., 1993-94; prof. (catedrático), 1994—, rsch. dir., 1992-93, dir. transfer tech., 1993-95, vice-chancellor rsch. and technol. devel., 1997-99; sci. cons. Nat. Vegetables Exporter Assn., Madrid, 1987-88; expert for evaluation of rsch. proposals European Commn., Brussels, 1999—. Contbr. articles to profl. jours. Head sci. office County Coun., Almería, 1988-91. Sgt. engr. Spanish Army, 1972. Recipient Duna award Mediterranean Ecol. Assn, 1993. Mem. Assn. Formulation Chemists, Internat. Soc. Soil Sci., Soil Sci. Soc. Am. Roman Catholic. Avocations: marathon running, writer, music, reading, athletics. Home: Nueva Alcazaba Ave 15, 04007 Almeria Andalucia Spain Office: U Almeria, Sacramento Rd n/n, 04120 Almeria Andalucia Almeria-Awoalucia, Spain

GONZALEZ-PRIETO, SERAFIN, biochemist; b. Ourense, Spain, July 30, 1961; s. Pablo Gonzalez and Felicia Prieto; m. Nelida Leite, Nov. 17, 1990. Biology Degree, Santiago de Compostela U., 1984, Santiago de Compostela U., 1984; PhD in Biology, Santiago de Compostela U., 1989. Tenured scientist Spanish Coun. for Sci. Rsch., 1995-2000, rschr., 1994-96; postdoctoral student CNRS, Lyon, France, 1993; dir. Et Brana, Ourense, 1989-92; cons. Consello Galego de Medio Ambiente, Santiago de Compostela, Spain, 1995-2000. Contbr. articles to profl. jours.; author: (book) Atlas de Vertebrados de Galicia, 1995. Mem. Sociedade Galega de Historia Natural, Sociedad Española para la Conservación y el Estudio de los Murcielagos, Sociedad Española de Ornitologia. Office: CSIC, Avda de Vigo s/n, E-15706 Santiago Compostela Spain

GONZALEZ-QUIJANO VAZQUEZ, GUSTAVO ERNESTO, trade association administrator; b. Stockholm, Mar. 26, 1960; s. Gonzalez-Quijano y Gonzalez de la Peña and Maria Luisa (Vazquez Huertas) G.; m. Katelyne Ghémar, Oct. 2, 1993 (div. Feb. 2000). Office: Cotance, Rue Belliard 3, 1040 Brussels Belgium

GONZÁLEZ-REY, GONZALO, engineering educator; b. Havana, Cuba, Sept. 27, 1958; s. Gonzalo González Pereira and Elida Rey Martinez; m. Norys Margarita Muñoz Maranje, July 30, 1983 (div. Aug. 1986); m. Ivis Maria Alfonso Arce, Aug. 12, 1986; children: Ivis Maria, Cyndi. Diploma in Mech. Engring., Higher Poly. Inst., Havana, 1982; D in Tech. Sci., ISPJAZ, 1997. Instr. ISPJAE, Havana, 1982-86, asst. prof., 1986-92, assoc. prof., 1992—, head machine elements divsn., 1992—, cons. of mech. design, 1984—, asst. ASME Caribbean corr., 1995—, vice-dean rsch. mech. faculty, 1998—; mem. ISOTC60/WG6, Germany, 1991—. Author: (software) Mechanical Transmission CAD, 1992, CAD-CAM for Bevel Gears, 1993; editor: jour. Ingenieria Mecanica, 1998—; contbr. articles to profl. jours. Mem. ASME (assoc.), AGMA (assoc., ofcl. rep. 1991—). Avocations: movies, tennis. Home: Calle 96 #717 e/ 7 y 9, Havana 16, Cuba Office: ISPJAE Faculty Mech Engring, Calle 116 s/n CUJAE, Marianac 15 Havana, Cuba

GONZALEZ-SANCHEZ, ENRIQUE, economist; b. Concepcion del Oro, Zacatecas, Mex., May 28, 1959; s. Pablo and M. de la Luz (Sanchez) Gonzalez. B in Econs., U. Nuevo Leon, Monterrey, Mex., 1981; MA in Econs., U. Chgo., 1986; diploma, Studien Centrum Gerzensee, Switzerland, 1991, Internat. Monetary Fund, Washington, 1992, EU-Rio Group, Montevideo, Uruguay, 1994. Analyst Bank of Mex., Mexico City, 1982-84, specialist, 1986-88, chief economist, 1988-93, vice mgr. internat. economy, 1993-98; asst. to exec. dir. Internat. Monetary Fund, Washington, 1998—. Contbr. articles to profl. publs. Recipient Disting. Pl. award Internat. Essay Contest Ludming von Mises, Mexico City, 1990. Fellow U. Chgo. Ex-Students in Mexico Soc. (founder). Avocation: swimming. Home: 2510 Virginia Ave NW Apt 412-n Washington DC 20037-1904 Office: International Monetary Fund 700 19th St NW Rm 13-718 Washington DC 20431-0002

GONZALEZ-SCARANO, FRANCISCO ANTONIO, neurologist, virologist; b. Ponce, P.R., Mar. 23, 1950; s. Francisco and Genoveva (Scarano) Gonzalez-Hernandez; m. Barbara Jean Turner, June 23, 1979; children: Genevieve Carre, Stephanie Katharine, Lisa Frances. BA, Yale U., 1971; MD, Northwestern U., Chgo., 1975; MA, U. Pa., Phila., 1988. Diplomate Am. Bd. Neurology. Intern Hosp. U. Pa., 1975-76, resident in neurology, 1976-79; fellow U. Pa., Phila., 1979-82, NIMR, London, 1981-82; asst. prof. depts. neurology and microbiology U. Pa., Phila., 1982-88, assoc. prof., 1988-94, prof., 1994—; vice-chair for rsch. neurology dept. U. Pa, 1998-99, chair 1999—; co-dir. Pa. Ctr. for HIV and AIDS, 1998—; chmn. bd. sci. counselors Nat. Inst. Neurol. Diseases and Stroke, Bethesda, Md., 1991-97. Assoc. editor Viral Pathogenesis, 1997; editl. bd. Jour. Neurovirology, 1996—, Virus Rsch., 1997—, AIDS, 1995—, Jour. Virology, 2000—. Bd. trustees Swarthmore Presbyn. Ch., 1997-2000. Harry Weaver scholar Multiple Sclerosis Soc., N.Y.C., 1982-87. Mem. Am. Neurol. Assn., Am. Acad. Neurology (mem. sci. issues com. 1985-89, profl. and pub. issues com. 1987-93), Am. Soc. Clin. Investigation, John Morgan Soc., Penn Club. Presbyterian. Avocations: photography, skiing. Office: U Pa Dept Neurology Hosp of Univ of Pa 3 W Gates Bldg Philadelphia PA 19104-4283

GONZÁLEZ VIDOSA, FERNANDO MANUEL, road bridge designer, civil engineer, educator; b. Valencia, Spain, Sept. 8, 1960; s. José León and Felisa Carmen (Vidosa Gallastegui) González Barrachina. BSc in Civil Engring., Tech. U. Valencia, 1984; PhD, U. London, 1989; diploma, Imperial Coll., London, 1989. Tchg. asst. U. Politécnica de Valencia, 1984-85, asst. prof., 1988-92; pvt. cons., bridge designer Postesa Ltd., Valencia, 1993—; rsch. concrete in the nineties program Imperial, U.K. Dept. Energy, 1986-87. Contbr. articles to profl. jours. Low lt. Spanish Army, 1983-84. Grantee Bank of Bilbao/Brit. Coun., 1985, Imperial Coll., 1986, Valencian Govt., 1986, Imperial Coll., 1987; recipient Armstrong medal, Imperial Coll., U. London, 1991. Mem. Spanish Concrete Soc., Spanish Soc. Computer Simulation. Avocations: volleyball, private piloting, parashooting, scuba diving. Home: Poeta Vicente Gaos 11, 46021 Valencia Spain Office: Paseo Facultades 10, 46021 Valencia Spain

GONZALEZ ZUMARRAGA, ANTONIO JOSE, archbishop; b. Pujili, Cotopaxi, Ecuador, Mar. 18, 1925; s. Luis González and Leonor Zumárraga. Seminario mayor, Quito, Ecuador; D in Derecho Canónico (hon.), U. Salamanca, Spain. Ordained priest Roman Cath. Ch., 1951. Bishop of Machala Ecuador, 1978; co-adjutor archbishop of Quito, 1980, archbishop of Quito, 1985—, pres. Episcopal Conf., 1987—; consejero Pontificia Comisión para América Latina, 1989—. Author: Mensaje Dominical, Vol. I, 1987, Vol. II, 1989. Mem. Junta Consultiva de Relaciones Exteriores del Ecuador. Office: Arzobispado, Calle Chile 1140 y Venezuela, Apdo 17-01-00106 Quito Ecuador

GONZALO, JOSÉ LUIS, lawyer; b. Toledo, Spain, May 10, 1965. JD, Complutense U., Madrid, 1989; LLM, U. Pacific, Sacramento, 1990. Atty. Maitland & Co., Luxembourg, 1990-93; assoc. Uria & Menéndez, Madrid, 1993-96; sr. mgr. Ernst & Young, Madrid, 1996—. Mem. Internat. Bar Assn., Internat. Fiscal Assn. Office: Ernst & Young, Torre Picasso Pza Ruiz Picasso S/N, 28020 Madrid Spain

GOOCH, ANTHONY CUSHING, lawyer; b. Amarillo, Tex., Dec. 3, 1937; s. Cornelius Skinner and Sidney Seale (Crawford) G.; m. Elizabeth Melissa Ivanoff, May 27, 1963 (div. Nov. 1983); children: Katherine C., Jennifer C. Gooch Avery, Melissa G., Andrew E.; m. Linda B. Klein, Nov. 7, 1987. BA, U. of South, 1959; diploma, Coll. of Europe, 1960; JD, NYU, 1963, M in Comparative Law, 1964. Bar: N.Y. 1963. Assoc. Cleary, Gottlieb, Steen & Hamilton, N.Y.C., Paris, Brussels, 1963-72; ptnr. Cleary, Gottlieb, Steen & Hamilton, Rio de Janeiro, 1973-78, N.Y.C., 1978-99; of counsel Cleary, Gottlieb, Steen & Hamilton, 2000—; gen. counsel Internat. Inst. Rural Reconstruction, 2000—. Co-author: Loan Agreement Documentation, 1982, 2d edit., 1991, Swap Apreement Documentation, 1987, 2d edit., 1988, Documentation for Derivatives, 1993, Credit Support Supplement, 1995, Cross-Product Risk Mgmt. Supplement, 2000, Documentation for Loans, Assignments and Participations, 1996; articles editor NYU Law Rev., 1962-63. Mem. ABA, N.Y. State Bar Assn., Assn. Bar City N.Y., New York County Lawyers Assn. Democrat. Episcopalian. Home: 7 Mine Hill Rd Redding CT 06896-2701 Office: 1 Liberty Plz New York NY 10006-1470

GOOCH, DON A., manufacturing executive; b. Lexington, Mo., Aug. 27, 1960; s. Clifford A. and Virginia F. G.; m. Elizabeth G., Aug. 3, 1985; 1 dau. BS, U. Mo., 1983. Mktg. splst. internat. mktg. program Mo. Dept. Agr., Jefferson City, 1987-89, coord. internat. mktg. program, 1989-90; internat. product mgr. Marley Pump Co., Mission, Kans., 1990-92; internat. mktg. mgr. Marley Pump Co., Mission, 1992-95; internat. sales mgr. Sioux Chief Mfg. Co. Inc., Peculiar, Mo., 1995-96; mgr. internat. bus. devel. Sioux Chief Mfg. Co. Inc., Peculiar, 1996—. Founding bd. mem. Make-A-Wish Found., Albuquerque, N.Mex., 1986; sec. Operation Good Neighbor, Peculiar, 1998; exch. student German Acad. Exch. Svc., Kirchdorf, Germany, 1979. Mem. Internat. Trade Club, Dist. Export Coun. Office: Sioux Chief Mfg Co Inc 24110 S Peculiar Dr Peculiar MO 64078

GOOD, IRVING JOHN, statistics educator, mathematician, philosopher of science; b. London, Dec. 9, 1916; came to U.S., 1967; s. Morris Edward and Sophia (Polikoff) G. ScD, Cambridge (Eng.) U., 1963; DSc, Oxford (Eng.) U., 1964. Scientific officer Fgn. Office, Bletchley, Eng., 1941-45; lectr. math. and electronic computing Manchester (Eng.) U., 1945-48; sr. prin. sci. officer Govt. Communications Hdqrs., Cheltenham, Eng., 1948-59; spl. merit dep. chief sci. officer Admiralty Rsch. Lab., Teddington, Middlesex, Eng., 1959-62; sr. rsch. fellow Trinity Coll., Oxford U. and Atlas Computer Lab., Didcot, Berkshire, Eng., 1964-67; Univ. disting. prof. stats, adj. prof. philosophy Va. Poly. Inst. and State U., Blacksburg, 1967—; prof. emeritus; adj. prof. Ctr. Study of Sci. in Society; mem. comm. theory com. Ministry Supply, London, 1953-56; mem. comm. com. electronics rsch. com. Ministry Aviation, London, 1960-62; mem. rsch. sect. com. Royal Statis. Soc., London, 1965-67. Author: Probability and the Weighing of Evidence, 1950, The Estimation of Probabilities, 1965, Good Thinking, 1983; gen. editor: The Scientist Speculates, 1962 (also French and German translations); chpt. in The Codebreakers, 1994; also 5 chpts. in Festschriften; contbr. 800 articles to profl. jours. Grantee NIH, 1970-89; recipient Smith's prize, Cambridge, Eng., 1940. Fellow Am. Acad. Arts and Scis., Va. Acad. Scis., Inst. Math. Stats., Am. Statis. Assn.; mem. IEEE Computer Soc. (Pioneer award 1998), Internat. Statis. Inst. (hon.), Internat. Order Merit. Home: 1309 Lynn Dr Blacksburg VA 24060-3001 Office: Va Poly Inst and State U Dept Stats Blacksburg VA 24061-0439

GOOD, ROBERT ALAN, physician, educator; b. Crosby, Minn., May 21, 1922; s. Roy Homer and Ethel Gay (Whitcomb) G.; m. Noorbibi K. Day, 1986; children from previous marriage: Robert Michael, Mark Thomas, Alan Maclyn, Margaret Eugenia, Mary Elizabeth. BA, U. Minn., 1944, MB, 1946, PhD, 1947, MD, 1947, DSc (hon.), 1989; MD (hon.), U. Uppsala, Sweden, 1966; DSc (hon.), N.Y. Med. Coll., 1973, Med. Coll. Ohio, 1973, Coll. Medicine and Dentistry N.J., 1974, Hahnemann Med. Coll., 1974, U. Chgo., 1974, St. John's U., 1977, U. Health Scis., Chgo. Med. Sch., 1978, Miami Children's Hosp., 1986, Med. Sch., U. Minn., 1989, U. Rome, Rome. Teaching asst. dept. anatomy U. Minn., Mpls., 1944-45; instr. pediatrics U. Minn. (Med. Sch.), 1950-51, asst. prof., 1951-53, asso. prof., 1953-54, Am. Legion Meml. research prof. pediatrics, 1954-73, prof. microbiology, 1962-72, Regents prof. pediatrics and microbiology, 1969-73, prof., head dept. pathology, 1970-72; intern U. Minn. Hosps., 1947, asst. resident pediatrics, 1948-49; pres., dir. Sloan-Kettering Inst. for Cancer Research, 1973-80, mem., 1973-81; prof. pathology Sloan-Kettering div. Grad. Sch. Med. Scis. Cornell U., 1973-81, dir., 1973-80; adj. prof., vis. physician Rockefeller U., 1973-81; prof. medicine, pediatrics and pathology Cornell U. Med. Coll., 1973-81; dir. research Meml. Sloan-Kettering Cancer Ctr., v.p., 1980-81; dir. research Meml. Hosp. for Cancer and Allied Diseases, 1973-80, also attending physician depts. medicine and pediatrics; attending pediatrician N.Y. Hosp., 1973-81; mem., head cancer research program Okla. Med. Research Found., 1982-85; prof. pediatrics, research prof. medicine, Okla. Med. Rsch. Found. prof. microbiology and immunology U. Okla. Health Scis. Ctr., 1982-85; attending physician, head div. immunology Okla. Children's Meml. Hosp., 1982-85; attending physician in internal medicine Okla. Meml. Hosp., 1983-85; physician-in-chief All Children's Hosp., St. Petersburg, Fla., 1985—; prof., chmn. dept. pediatrics U. South Fla., St. Petersburg, 1985-91, prof. depts. pediatrics, microbiology, immunology and medicine, 1985—; head allergy and clinical immunology, dept. pediatrics U. South Fla./All Childrens Hosp., St. Petersburg, 1985—; disting. univ. prof. U. South Fla., St. Petersburg, 1989—; vis. investigator Rockefeller Inst. for Med. Rsch., N.Y.C., 1949-50, asst. physician to Hosp., 1949-50; attending pediatrician Hennepin County Gen. Hosp., 1950-73, cons., 1960-73; mem. Unitarian Svc. Commn. Med. Exch. Team to France, Germany, Switzerland and Czechoslovakia, 1958; cons. VA Hosp., Mpls., 1959-60; cons., sci. adviser Nat. Jewish Hosp., Denver, Children's Asthma Rsch. Inst. and Hosp., Denver, 1964-69; mem. study sects. USPHS, 1952-69; mem. expert adv. panel on immunology WHO, 1967—; cons. Merck & Co., N.J., 1968-72, Nat. Cancer Inst., 1973-74; mem. ad hoc com. Pres.'s Sci. Adv. Coun. on Biol. and Med. Sci., 1970, Pres.'s Cancer Panel, 1972; mem. Lyndon B. Johnson Found. awards com., 1972; mem. adv. com. Bone Marrow Transplant Registry, 1973—; chmn. Internat. Bone Marrow Registry, 1977-79; bd. dirs. Nat. Marrow Donor Program, 1987-94; fgn. adv. Acad. Med. Scis., People's Republic of China, 1980—; chmn. Fla. Gov.'s Task Force on AIDS, 1985-87, mem., 1988-94. Author, editor numerous books; contbr. many articles to profl. jours. Mem. adv. council Childrens Hosp. Research Found., Cin., 1954-58; bd. dirs. Allergy Found. Am., 1973; bd. sci. advisers Jane Coffin Childs Meml. Fund Med. Research, 1972-74, Merck Inst. Therapeutic Research, 1972-76; trustee Eleanor Naylor Dana Charitable Trust, 1982—. Recipient Borden Undergrad. Research award U. Minn. Med. Sch., 1946, E. Mead Johnson First award, 1955, Theobald Smith award, 1955, Parke-Davis 6th Ann. award, 1962, Rectors medal U. Helsinki, 1963-64, Pemberton Lectureship award, 1966, Gordon Wilson Gold medal, 1967, R.E. Dyer Lectureship award, 1967, Clemens Von Pirquet Gold medal 9th Ann. Forum on Allergy, 1968, Presidents medal U. Padua, Italy, 1968, Robert A. Cooke Gold medal Am. Acad. Allergy, 1968, John Stewart Meml. award Dalhousie U., 1969, Borden award Assn. Am. Med. Colls., 1970, Howard Taylor Ricketts award U. Chgo., 1970, Gairdner Found. award, 1970, City of Hope award, 1970, Am. Acad. Achievement golden plate award, 1970, Albert Lasker award for clin. and med. research, 1970, ACP award, 1972, Am. Coll. Chest Physicians award, 1974, Lila Gruber award Am. Acad. Dermatology, 1974, award in cancer immunology Cancer Research Inst. N.Y., 1975, Outstanding Achievement award U. Minn., 1978, award Am. Dermatological Soc. Allergy and Immunology, 1978, 1st Sarasota Med. award, 1979, sect. on mil. pediatrics award Am. Acad. Pediatrics, 1980, recipient Univ. medal Hacettepe U., Ankara, Turkey, 1982, Pres. medal U. Lyon, France, 1986, Merieux Found. award Internat. Soc. Preventive Oncology, 1987, Claude Bernard prize World Med. Communications, Inc., 1987, Disting. Med. Sci. of Fla. award Fla. Soc. Pathologists, 1989, Gold-Headed Cane award Dept. Pediatrics U. Minn., 1990, Askounces-Ashford Disting. Scholar award, USF, 1990, Excellence award Ronald McDonald Children's Charities, 1991, Councill C. Rudolph award, All Children's Hosp., 1991, Merit award for outstanding and superior res., Dept. Health and Human Services, Md., 1992, Lifetime Achievement award Immune Deficiency Found., Md., 1992, Asthma and Allergy Found. Am. award 1993, Univ. Rsch. medallion award Disting. Rsch. Prof. U. South Fla., 1993, Immune Deficiency Found. award, 1993, Internat. Nutritional Immunology Group award, 1993, Paul Harris Fellow award Rotary Found. of Rotary Internat., 1994, Steven C. Beering award Indiana U., 1996, Internat. Bone Marrow Transplant Registry award, 1997, Gold and Silver Star The Order of the Sacred Treasure, 1998, Disting. Scientist award, Turkey Acad. Scis., 1999, numerous others; named one of top physicians in U.S., The Best Doctors in Am., 1992, 94-95; Endowment chair named in honor Children's Hosp. and U. South Fla., 1994; Fellow Nat. Found. for Infantile Paralysis, 1947, Helen Hay Whitney Found. fellow, 1948-50; Markle Found. scholar, 1950-55; award Miami Children's Hosp. Mary Ann Knight Internat. Inst. Pediat., Miami, 1999, Disting. Scientist awd. with hon., The Turkey Acad. of Scis., 1999, induction into The Ambassador David M. Walters Hall of Fame, Miami Chldrns. Hosp., The Mary Ann Knight Internat. Inst. of Pediatrics, 1999. Fellow AAAS, Am. Coll. Physicians (award 1993), Royal Soc. Medicine, Acad. Multidisciplinary Research, N.Y. Acad. Sci., Am. Acad. Arts and Scis., Am. Coll. of Allergy and Immunology (hon., John P. McGovern Lectureship award 1993, Schering Jaros Lecture award 1993), Am. Acad. Pediat. (1st hon. fellow sect. on allergy and immunology), The Philippine Pediat. Soc. (hon.); mem. NAS, Am. Soc. Transplant Surgeons (hon.), Am. Assn. History of Medicine, Am. Fedn. Clin. Research, Am. Assn. Anatomists, Am. Assn. Immunologists (past pres.), AAUP, Am. Pediatric Soc. (John Howland award 1987), Mpls. Pediatric Soc., Northwestern Pediatric Soc., Am. Rheumatism Assn., Am. Soc. Clin. Investigation (past pres.), Am. Soc. Exptl. Pathology (past pres.), Am. Soc. Microbiology, Assn. Am. Physicians, Central Soc. Clin. Research (past pres.), Harvey Soc., Infectious Disease Soc. Am. (Squibb award 1968), Internat. Soc. Nephrology, Internat. Acad. Pathology, Internat. Soc. for Transplantation Biology, Minn. State Med. Assn., NAS Inst. Medicine (charter), Reticuloendothelial Soc. (past pres.), Soc. for Exptl. Biology and Medicine (past pres.), Soc. for Pediatric Research, Am. Clin. and Climatol. Assn. (Gordon Wilson Gold medal 1967), Detroit Surg. Assn. (McGraw medal 1969), Internat. Soc. Blood, Transfusion, Practitioners' Soc., Am. Assn. Pathologists, Internat. Soc. Exptl. Hematology (award in pioneering leadership and accomplishments 1994), Transplant Soc., Western Assn. Immunologists, Internat. Soc. Immunopharmacology (founding mem.), Am. Soc. Transplant Surgeons, Pioneer, Internat. Bone Marrow Transplant Registry (charter), Phi Beta Kappa, Sigma Xi, Alpha Omega Alpha. Office: All Children's Hosp 801 6th St S Saint Petersburg FL 33701-4899

GOOD, SHELDON FRED, realtor; b. Chgo., June 4, 1933; s. Joseph and Sylvia (Schwartz) G.; children: Steven, Todd; m. Susan Forman, Dec. 22, 1990. BBA, U. Ill., 1955. Sales mgr. Baird & Warner Real Estate, Chgo., 1957-65; chmn. Sheldon F. Good & Co. Realtors, Chgo., 1965—; guest lectr. Northwestern U., U. Chgo., U. Calif., Wharton Grad. Sch., U. Pa., Stanford U., Vanderbilt U., U. Ill.; staff instr. Cen. YMCA City Coll., Chgo.; guest spkr. Wall St. Week UN, 1993; cons. in field. Chmn. United Settlement Appeal, Chgo., YMCA Edn. Libr. Drive, Chgo., Chgo. Jewish United Fund.; bd. dirs. Child, Inc.; pres. Gastrointestinal Rsch. Found., U. Chgo., 1979; chmn. Chgo. Assn. Realtors Hall of Fame, 1996-97; bd. dirs. U. Ill. Found., 1995-97. Served with AUS, 1955-57. Recipient Levi Eshkol Premier medal State Israel, 1967, Crown of a Good Name award Jewish Nat. Fund, 1972, Chgo. Realtor of Yr. award 1991; first recipient of Richard W. Dewees Meml. award 1998; named one of 10 outstanding young men Chgo., 1968, Chgo. Man of Yr., 1998, Illini of Yr. Chgo. Assn. Realtors, 1999, Achievement award U. Ill., 2000. Mem. Chgo. Real Estate Bd. (treas., pres. 1988-89), Nat. Assn. Real Estate Bds., Nat. Assn. Realtors (chmn. nat. auction com. 1990, RTC task force), State of Ill. Internat. Real Estate Assn. Home: 180 E Pearson St Chicago IL 60611-2130 Office: 333 W Wacker Dr Chicago IL 60606-1220

GOOD, VIRGINIA JOHNSON, real estate executive; b. Onancock, Va., Mar. 1, 1919; d. Obed Wilbur and Sallie Mildred (Deyerle) Johnson; m. William Dennis Good, Jan. 14, 1941 (dec. Apr. 1970). Bus. cert., Elon College, N.C., 1937; real estate cert., U. Miami, 1973; student, Montgomery County Jr. Coll., 1974. Acct. Carolina Biol. Supply Co., Elon College, N.C., 1935-39, Sears Roebuck, Richmond, Va., 1939-40, Ritchie Electric, Charlottesville, Va., 1940-41; mgmt. investor Dr. & Mrs. William D. Good Real Estate, Washington and Gaithersburg, Md., 1941-70, Good Properties, Washington and Miami Beach, Fla., 1970-94, Dennis Apts., Miami Beach, Fla., 1972-94; owner Good Properties, Orlando, Fla., 1994—; Mem. D.C. Apt. Owners/Mgmt. Assn., Washington, 1970-84, Miami Beach Apt. Owners Assn., 1970-86, North Shore Apt. Owners Assn., Miami Beach, 1986-88. Exec. com. Anti Rock Quarry, Dawsonville, Md., 1959, Save Our Coast, Miami Beach, 1982-86; mem. Montgomery County Hist. and Geneal. Soc., Rockville, Md., 1977—, Nat. Geneal. Soc., 1980-95, Greater Miami Geneal. Soc., Miami, 1982-96, Va. Hist./Geneal. Soc., Richmond, 1988—, Bradley Blvd. Civic Assn., Bethesda, Md., 1989. Mem. La Gorce Country Club, Miami Beach, Columbia Country Club (Chevy Chase, Md.), DAR, Nat. Soc. So. Dames, United Daus. of Confederacy, Nat. Soc. Colonial Dames of XVII Century, Nat. Huguenot Soc. Mem. United Church of Christ. Avocation: genealogy. Home & Office: 3607 Lake Sarah Dr Orlando FL 32804-3425

GOODACRE, JASON DEAN, informations system specialist; b. Sydney, NSW, Australia, Sept. 26, 1971; s. Gordon Edward and CArol Joy (McFarlene) G. Data coord. County Natwest, Sydney, 1989-92; with customer svc. Datastream, Sydney, 1992-94, mgr., 1994—. Named Young Achiever of Yr. Channel Ten, 1994. Avocations: golf, reading, skiing, motor sports. Home: 21 134-150 Bulwara Rd, Pyrmont Sydney NSW, Australia

GOODACRE, SELWYN HUGH, physician; b. Bradford, Yorkshire, Eng., Mar. 5, 1940; s. Norman William and Ruth Mary (Leighton) G.; m. Janet Patricia Hick, Apr. 10, 1964; children: Jonathan, Mark, Nicola. MBChB, Birmingham (Eng.) U., 1963, Diploma in Obstetrics Royal Coll. ObGyn., 1965. House officer Queen Elizabeth Hosp., Birmingham, 1963, Royal Hosp., Wolverhampton, Eng., 1963-64, Sorrento Maternity Hosp., Wolverhampton, 1964-65; prin. Swadlincote (Eng.) Surgery, 1965—; Editor Jour. Lewis Carroll Soc., 1982-97; contbr. articles to jours. Avocations: book collecting. Home: 69 Ashby Rd Woodville, Swadlincote DE11 7BZ, England Office: Swadlincote Surgery, Darklands Rd, Swadlincote DE11 0PP, England

GOODALE, RALPH E., Canadian government minister; b. Regina, Sask., Can., Oct. 5, 1949; s. Thomas Henry and Winnifred Claire (Myers) G.; m. Pamela Jean Kendel, Feb. 8, 1986. BA, U. Regina, 1971; LLB, U. Sask., 1972. M.P. from Assiniboia, Sask. Ho. of Commons, Ottawa, 1974-79; leader Sask. Liberal Party, 1981-88; mem. Legis. Assembly from provincial riding Assiniboia-Gravelbourg, Sask., 1986-88; corp. sec. Pioneer Life Ins. Co., 1989-90, Soveriegn Life Ins. Co., 1990-93; M.P. from Wascana Ho. of Commons, Ottawa, 1993—; min. Nat. Resources Can., Can. Wheat Bd., Ont., 1997—; also min. Agr. and Agri-Food Can., Ottawa, 1993-97; fed. interlocutor for Metis and Non-States Indians, 1997—; parliamentary sec. to Min. Transport, Min. Wheat Bd., Pres. Privy Coun., 1974-79. Active polit. coms. Mem. Law Soc. Sask. Lutheran. Office: Natural Resources Canada, 407 Confederation Bldg, Ottawa, ON Canada K1A 0A6

GOODALL, ARTHUR ALAN, accountant; b. Rhyl, Wales, Apr. 3, 1936; s. Douglas Bates and Mildred Frances (Harrison) G.; m. Kathleen Elizabeth Holmes, Aug. 23, 1962; children: Rosalind Elizabeth, Kevin Alan. Chartered acct. Founder, sr. ptnr. Alan Goodall Co., Prestatyn, Wales, 1964—. Treas. Prestatyn Parochial Ch. Coun., 1986—, Chatsworth House League of Friends, Prestatyn, 1988—; sch. gov. Prestatyn H.S., 1988—, St. Brigids Sch., Denbigh, 1992—; mem. coun. Tennis Wales, 1989—. Mem. Prestatyn Tennis Club (chmn., officer 1971—). Home: Four Gables, 68 Pendre Ave, Prestatyn LL19 9SL, Wales Office: 71 A 75 High St, Prestatyn LL19 9AH, Wales

GOODALL, DAVID WILLIAM, botanist; b. Edmonton, Middlesex, Eng., Apr. 4, 1914; arrived in Australia, 1948; s. Henry William and Isabel Blanche (Harlow) G.; m. Audrey Veronica Kirwin, Aug. 31, 1940 (div. 1948); 1 child, Patrick Thompson; m. Muriel Grace King, Sept. 20, 1949 (div. 1974); children: Peter Jan, Glyn, Karen; m. Ivy Nelms, Apr. 3, 1976. BSc, Imperial Coll., 1935, PhD, 1941; DSc, U. Melbourne, 1953; DSc (hon.), U. Trieste, 1990. Rsch. officer Rsch. Inst. Plant Physiology, London, 1939-46; plant physiologist W. African Cacao Rsch. Inst., Tafo, Ghana, 1946-47; sr. lectr. Melbourne U., Australia, 1948-52; reader U. Coll. Gold Coast, Achimota, Ghana, 1952-54; prof. agrl. botany U. Reading, Eng., 1954-56; dir. CSIRO Tobacco Rsch. Inst., Mareeba, Australia, 1956-61; sr. prin. rsch. scientist CSIRO Divsn. Math. Stats., Perth, Australia, 1961-67; prof. biol. sci. U. Calif., Irvine, 1967-68; prof. range sci. Utah State U., Logan, 1968-74; sr. prin. rsch. scientist CSIRO Divsn. Land Resources Mgmt., Canberra & Perth, Australia, 1974-79. Editor: Evolution of Desert Biota, 1976, Arid Land Ecosystems, 1979, 81, (series) Ecosystems of the World, 1977—; contbr. articles to profl. jours. Recipient Disting. Statis. Ecologist award Internat. Assn. Ecology, 1994. Fellow Linnean Soc. London, Inst. Biology; mem. Brit. Ecol. Soc., Ecol. Soc. Am., Ecol. Soc. Australia, Am. Rangeland Soc., Classification Soc., also others. Avocations: community theatre, bushwalking. Office: Ctr for Ecosys Mgmt, Edith Cowan U, Joondalup 6027, Australia

GOOD-BLACK, EDITH ELISSA (PEARL WILLIAMS), writer; b. Hollywood, Calif., Jan. 10, 1945; d. Jack Brian and Rose Marie (Miller) Good; m. Michael Lawrence Black, Dec. 18, 1986. Student, U. Calif., Berkeley, UCLA; BA in English, Calif. State U., Northridge, 1974; student, UCLA and U. Calif., Berkley, 1962-92. Author, pub. Gull Press, L.A., 1990-95; participant numerous dance, art, music, lit., math. and sci. classes; dancer Hajde Dance Troop, Berkeley, Calif., 1962-66; artist/one-woman shows in L.A., 1962-95; art and lit. collected in Libr. of Congress, Washington, 1990-99; singer coffee houses, cafe, night clubs, half-way houses, librs., others., L.A., 1986-96; contbr. poetry to numerous publs. and radio and internet broadcasts; author: (pseudonym Pearl Williams) The Trickster of Tarzana, 1992, Short Stories, 1995, Mad in Craft, 1995, Missives, 1995, others. Supporter Westside Women's Ctr., Venice, Calif., 1971-79; fundraiser, del. to local convs. Beverly Hills and Marina del Ray, Calif. Dem. Clubs, 1974-79. Mem. Mensa, Am. Soc. Composers, Authors, and Pubs., Plummer Park Writers, Westside Writers. Home: 335 N Stanley Ave Apt 220 Los Angeles CA 90036-6205

GOODE, BOBBY CLAUDE, retired secondary education educator, writer; b. Celeste, Tex., Dec. 10, 1940; s. Claude Elmer and Clarice Edna G.; m. Jean Helen Ames, June 9, 1963; children: James Lonnie, Joel Dietrich, John Shalom. BS, MIT, 1963; MA, Andover Newton Sem., Newton Centre, Mass., 1968; MS, Rensselaer Poly. Inst., 1972. Cert. tchr. sci. and math. Tchr. math. Lawrence D. Bell High Sch., Hurst, Tex., 1966-67; tchr. physics and chemistry Grapevine (Tex.) High Sch., 1967-70; tchr. advanced physics, advanced chemistry, advanced biology South Plainfield (N.J.) High Sch., 1970-96, ret., 1996; sci. tchr. Princeton (N.J.) U., 1983, Disting. Secondary Sch. Tchg. finalist, 1983. Author: (booklets) Lap Physics, 1973, Stars, Planets, People, 1980, Atoms and Molecules, 1980, Physics Problem Solutions, 1980. Mem. Civil Rights Commn., Piscataway, N.J., 1977, Sr. Citizens Housing Com., Piscataway, 1975; ch. sch. tchr. First Bapt. Ch. of New Market, 1970-96. Named Outstanding Sci. Tchr., Sigma Xi, 1986. Mem. NEA, N.J. Edn. Assn., Am. Assn. Physics Tchrs., Nat. Sci. Tchrs. Assn. (recipient Exemplary Secondary Sci. Tchr. Nat. award 1980). Democrat. Avocations: family, travel, writing, sports. Home: 129 Stonegate S Boerne TX 78006-3411

GOODE, CHARLES BARRINGTON, company director; b. Melbourne, Australia, Aug. 26, 1938; s. Charles Thomas and Jean Florence G.; m. Cornelia Baillieu; 1 stepchild, Robert; m. Cornelia Ladd, June 1, 1987. BCom with honors, Melbourne U., LLD (hon.); MBA, Columbia U. Assoc. Potter Ptnrs., Ltd., Melbourne, 1961-69; ptnr. Potter Ptnrs., Ltd., 1969-80, sr. ptnr., 1980-86; chmn. Potter Ptnrs. Group Ltd., Melbourne, 1986-89, Potter Warburg Asset Mgmt. Ltd., Melbourne, 1989-97; bd. dirs. CSR Ltd., Singapore Airlines Ltd., Australian Investment Ltd., Diversified United Investment Co. Ltd., Air New Zealand Ltd.; chmn. Australia and New Zealand Banking Group Ltd., Woodside Petroleum Ltd., Ian Potter Found., Howard Florey Inst. Physiology and Medicine. Mem. Melbourne Club, Australian Club, Royal Melbourne Golf Club. Avocations: tennis, golf. Home: 294 Walsh St, South Yarra Victoria 3141, Australia also: ANZ Bank 1177 Ave of Americas New York NY 10036

GOODELL, JOHN DEWITTE, electromechanical engineer; b. Omaha, Nebr., Sept. 20, 1909; s. Edwin Dewitte and Vera May (Watts) G.; m. Bernadette Michel, Apr. 27, 1943; children: Mary, Greg, Thomas, Caroline, Daniel. Cons. engr. N.Y.C., 1931-41; tech. dir. U.S. Army Detroit Signal Lab., 1941-43; dir. engring. Minn. Electronics, St. Paul, 1946-57; mgr. new product design CBS Lab., Stamford, Conn., 1957-60; dir. engring. Robodyne, U.S.Industries, Silver Spring, Md., 1960-61; corp. tech. dir. U.S. Industries, N.Y.C., 1962-63; producer Goodell Motion Pictures, St. Paul, 1964-75; cons. engr. New Product Design, St. Paul, 1976-90; exhibit prototyper Sci. Mus. of Minn., St. Paul, 1990-93; dir. engring. Tomorrow's World, St. Paul, 1993—. Author: The World of Ki, 1967; writer, dir. (motion picture) Always a New Beginning, 1973, (acad. nominated best documentary 1973), (TV documentary) Wisdom and Change, 1992; dir. Challenge for Tomorrow, 1964 (indsl. Oscar); inventor: automatic mail handler, automatic manipulator, magnetic pulse controlling device, conditioned reflex teaching machines and others, 1954—; editor Jour. of Computing Systems, 1965-70. With U.S. Navy, 1943-46, S. Pacific. Recipient Master Design award, Product Engring., 1962. Mem. IEEE (sr.), Soc. Motion Picture and TV Engrs. Avocations: Oriental Game of Go (capt. U.S team 2nd place winners Internat. Go Cong., 1964). Home: 1455 Almond Ave # 121 Saint Paul MN 55108-2514

GOODEN, ROBERT, chemist; b. Shreveport, La., Jan. 4, 1949; s. Arthur and Geneva (Knighten) G.; children: Nakida, Michele, Ashley; m. Althea G. Gooden. BS in Chemistry, So. U., 1974; PhD in Chemistry, Stanford U., 1979. Mem. tech. staff AT&T Bell Labs., Murray Hill, N.J., 1978-89; rsch. leader Dow Chem. Co., Plaquemine, La., 1989-91; assoc. prof. dept. chem. U. Baton Rouge, 1992—; vis. prof. dept. chemistry So. U., Baton Rouge, 1987-88. Contbr. over 20 articles to tech. jours., chpts. to books. With USMC, 1969-72. Mem. AAAS, Nat. Orgn. Profl. Advancement Black Chemists, Soc. Plastics Engrs., Am. Chem. Soc. Office: So U Dept Chemistry Baton Rouge LA 70813-0001 Home: 5905 Bennington Ave Baton Rouge LA 70808-3508

GOODENBERGER, MARY ELLEN, English educator; b. Trenton, Nebr., Aug. 4, 1923; d. George Andrew and Ida May (Stewart) Marshall; m. Marvin Eugene Goodenberger, Aug. 9, 1947; children: Daniel Marvin, Beverly Jane, Marshall Eric. BSEd, U. Nebr., 1947, MEd, 1963, PhD, 1976. Elem. tchr. Culbertson (Nebr.) Pub. Schs., 1940-41, 43-44; prin., tchr. English, libr. Trenton (Nebr.) Pub. Sch., 1957-58, 60-66; cons. in English Nebr. Dept. Edn., Lincoln, 1968-72; K-12 dir. instrn. McCook (Nebr.) Pub. Schs., 1973-80; coll. instr. U. Nebr. at Kearney, Lincoln, 1967-68, 80-85;

county supt. Hitchcock County Schs., Trenton, 1984-90. Author: (books) Ida May's Real People, 1985, Of Mice and Birds, 1986, Aedith's Fables, 1987, (curriculum) Breakthrough in English, I, II, III, 1969-71. County chair Rep. Party, Red Willow County, 1950-54; Sunday sch. tchr. Youth Fellowship, leader, choir mem. local ch., McCook, Trenton, 1950-66; 4-H leader, Trenton, 1956-66; mem. Women's Fellowship, Trenton, 1980-90, pres. 1988-90. Regents scholar U. Nebr., Lincoln, 1940, 42, grad. study scholar Delta Kappa Gamma, Nebr., 1968, Disting. Educator award U. Nebr. at Omaha, 1980. Mem. Nebr. State Edn. Assn. (pres.-elect McCook and Holdrege 1966), Nebr. Coun. Tchrs. of English (pres. 1973), Nebr. Assn. for Supervision and Curriculum Devel. (bd. dirs. 1973-78), Nebr. Schoolmasters Club (pres. 1977), Delta Kappa Gamma (various offices), Phi Beta Kappa, Pi Lambda Theta. Methodist. Home: HC 2 Box 123 Trenton NE 69044-9744

GOODENOUGH, BELINDA JANE, psychologist; b. Kidderminster, Eng., May 13, 1964; arrived in Australia, 1974; d. Michael M. and Diana J. (Seazell) G.; m. Mitchell G. Landrigan, July 23, 1988; 1 child, Emma. BA in Psychology with honors, U. New South Wales, Sydney, Australia, 1988, PhD in Psychology, 1992. Registered psychologist, NSW, Australia. Assoc. lectr. U. NSW, Sydney, 1988-92, sr. rsch. asst., 1992-94, sr. rsch. officer, 1994—, lectr., 1995—; rsch. cons. U. of Tech., Sydney, 1997—. Co-author: (book chpt.) Measurement of Pain in Infants and Children, 1998, Children's Understanding of Biology and Health, 1999; contbr. articles to profl. jours. Mem. Ch. Missionary Soc., Australia, 1988—. Rsch. grantee Australian Rsch. Coun., 1996, Nat. Health and Med. Rsch. Coun., 1997—; recipient Achiever award Queen's Trust, 1996, Clin. Initiative award Sydney Children's Hosp. Found., 1999. Mem. Internat. Assn. for Study of Pain, Australia Psychol. Soc., Internat. Assn. for Study of Humor, Australian Pain Soc., Australian Soc. Hypnosis (assoc.). Home: 485 Gardeners Rd, Rosebery NSW 2018, Australia Office: Sydney Children's Hosp, High St, Randwick NSW 2031, Australia

GOODHART, CHARLES BURFORD, zoology educator; b. London, Jan. 7, 1919; s. Burford Henryson and Nellie (Goodhart) G.; m. Diana Helen Downing Fullerton, Sept. 2, 1950; children: Peter Burford, Michael Patrick, Stephen Downing, Louisa Clare. BA, Cambridge U., England, 1940, MA, 1946, PhD, 1950. With Gonville & Caius Coll., Cambridge, England, 1946—. Mem. Soc. Protection Unborn Children, 1966—, coun. mem., 1967-76. Capt. English Mil., 1940-46. Fellow Gonville & Caius Coll., 1946. Fellow Linnean Soc. (v.p. 1974), Zool. Soc., Galton Inst. Mem. Ch. of England. Avocations: sailing, gardening. Home: 8 Burnt Close, Grantchester CB3 9NJ, England Office: Gonville & Caius Coll, Cambridge CB2 1TA, England

GOODHARTZ, GERALD, law librarian; b. N.Y.C., Oct. 23, 1938; s. Jack and Anna (Sperling) G.; m. Carol Scialli, Aug. 18, 1969; children: Joanna, Allison. BSCE, CCNY, 1961; MLS, U. So. Calif., 1970. Night reference asst. Assn. Bar of City of N.Y., 1956-61; libr. asst. Cravath, Swaine & Moore, N.Y.C., 1961-65; head libr. Rosenman, Colin, Freund, Lewis & Cohen, N.Y.C., 1965-69, Keatinge & Sterling, L.A., 1969-70, Kaye, Scholer, Fierman, Hays & Handler, N.Y.C., 1970-98; mgr. info. svcs. Broad and Cassel, Orlando, 1998-99; dir. libr. svcs. Brown Raysman Millstein Felder & Steiner LLP, N.Y.C., 1999—; libr. planning cons. Olympic Towers, N.Y.C., 1975; lectr. in field. Mem. ABA, ALA, Am. Assn. Law Librs. (cert.), Law Libr. Assn. Greater N.Y., Assn. Law Librs. of Upstate N.Y., Spl. Librs. Assn., Am. Soc. Info. Scientists, Am. Mgmt. Assn., Assn. Info. Mgrs., Nat. Micrographics Assn. Office: Brown Raysman Millstein Felder & Steiner LLP 120 W 45th St New York NY 10036-4041

GOODHEER, WIL CHARLES, academic administrator; b. Martinsville, N.J., May 2, 1932; arrived in Austria, 1987; s. Frederick Charles and Dorothy (Wilde) G.; m. Lee Albright, July 2, 1955; children: Thomas Clark, Jesse Philip, Janet Marye Goodheer Lamb. Student, Harding U., 1952-55; BA, David Lipscomb U., 1958; grad. cert., Leiden (The Netherlands) U., 1968; MA in Religion, Ea. Bapt. Theol. Sem., 1974; LLD (hon.), Lubbock Christian U., 1990; D in Econ., prof., Kiev State Econ. U., 1995; PhD in Bus. Adminstrn., Internat. Pers. Acad., 1997, Am. U. Cyprus. Ordained to ministry Ch. of Christ. 1953. Minister to deaf Ch. of Christ, Washington, 1955-57; missionary, educator Ch. of Christ, The Hague, The Netherlands, 1958-70; minister Ch. of Christ, West Chester, Pa., 1970-77, King of Prussia, Pa., 1977-81; prof. Abilene (Tex.) Christian U., 1981-87; v.p. Internat. Christian U., Vienna, Austria, 1982-87, pres., 1988—; founder, pres. Internat. Christian U., Prague, Czech Republic, 1992—, Kiev, Ukraine, 1993—; academician, prof. Internat. Pers. Acad., Kiev, Ukraine, 1997; founder, pres. Internat. U., Alicante, Spain, 1999—; founder. Children's Camp, Solwaster, Belgium, 1964-70; tchr. Children's Camp, Douglasville, Pa., 1971-76; tchr. Belgium Bible Coll., Verviers, 1967-68; prison chaplain, 1984-87; trustee SHILOH, Inc., N.Y.C., 1978-87, pres., 1979-87; bd. dirs., lectr. Internat. Campaigns, Europe, 1961—; adj. faculty Northeastern Christian Jr. Coll., Villanova, Pa., 1971-81; mem. Accrediting Coun. Bus. Colls., Russia, Ukraine, and other C.I.S. countries, 1996; founding pres. Internat. U., Moscow, 1997; established Palestinian Internat. U., Ramallah, 2000, coop. degree programs with Waynesburg (Pa.) Coll., 1997, Regent U, Va., 2000. Editor, pub. jour. Het Levende Woord, 1960-70; editor: The Man of the Messianic Reign; contbr. articles to profl. jours. Trustee Internat. Christian U., 1980—; bd. dirs. Blue Danube Lectureships, Vienna, 1984—, Valley Forge Family Encampment, Villanova, 1977-87, U. Kiev-Mohyla, Ukraine; leader 4-H Clubs, Pa., 1976-78. Recipient Cert. of Appreciation, State of Ala., 1994; named Ark. Traveler, Gov. of Ark., 1969, Honorable Prof. Moscow External U. of Humanities, 1996, Acad. World Star Internat. Acad. Authorized Edn., 1996. Mem. Assn. Christian Prison Workers, Am. Camping Assn., Evang. Missiology Soc., Evang. Theol. Soc., Acad. of Mgmt., Am. Assn. Univ. Adminstrs., Rotary, Knights of Malta, Optimist Club (v.p., bd. dirs. 1980-81). Republican. Office: Internat U, Rennweg 1, A-1030 Vienna Austria

GOODHUE, WILLIAM WALTER, JR., pathologist, military officer, medical educator; b. St. Louis, Feb. 5, 1945; s. William W. and Rose Marie (Vahousek) G. BS cum laude, Georgetown U., 1966; MD, Cornell U., 1970. Diplomate Am. Bd. Pathology. Intern N.Y. Hosp.-Cornell Med Ctr., N.Y.C., 1970-71, resident, 1971-74; chief resident Columbia-Presbyn. Med. Ctr., N.Y.C., 1974-75; resident Tripler Army Med. Ctr., Honolulu, 1976-78, chief resident, 1978; practice medicine specializing in pathology Honolulu, 1975—; chief dept. pathology U.S. Army Hosp., Ft. Campbell, Ky., 1978-80; chief dept. pathology, med. dir. Sch. Med. Tech., dir. pathology residency tng. Gorgas Army Hosp., C.Z. and assoc. prof. med. tech. Panama Canal Coll., 1980-82; resident officer U.S. Army Command and Gen. Staff Coll., Ft. Leavenworth, Kans., 1982-83. divsn. surgeon 2d Inf. Divsn., 1983-84; dep. comdr. clin. svcs., chief dept. primary care and cmty. medicine, staff pathologist, acting comdr. Bayne-Jones Army Hosp., Ft. Polk, La., 1984-85; chief dept. pathology and are lab. svcs., dir. pathology residency tng. Dwight David Eisenhower Army Med. Ctr., Ft. Gordon, Ga., 1985-94; clin. assoc. prof. pathology Med. Coll. Ga., Augusta, 1986-94; chief pathology grad. med. edn., dir. electron microscopy Tripler Army Med. Ctr., 1994-97, asst. chief dept. pathology and are lab. svcs., 1997—; clin. assoc. prof. pathology Sch. Medicine U. Hawaii, Honolulu, 1997—; cons. in pathology Eisenhower health svc. region go comdg. gen.; cons. ARC, 1978-80; rep. Alt. Army Med. Dept. Coll. Am. Pathologists Ho. of Dels., Am. Soc. Clin. Pathologist Adv. Coun., 1990—; mem. profl. adv. bd. Med. Lab. Observer, 1993-95; Army councillor-at-large Armed Forces Med. Lab. Scientists, 1993—; v.p., Land Bd., R.W. Meyer, Ltd. Contbr. articles to profl. jours. Col. M.C. U.S. Army, 1975—. Decorated Order Mil. Med. Merit; recipient Surgeon Gen.'s "A" designator med. splty. excellence, 1997; USPHS Rsch. fellow, 1971-74. Fellow Am. Soc. Clin. Pathologists (lab. accreditation insp. inspection and accreditation program 1988—), Am. Soc. Abdominal Surgeons; mem. Soc. Pediatric Pathology, Med. Assn. Isthmian C.A. (v.p. 1980-81), Assn. Mil. Surgeons U.S., Am. Assn. Blood Banks, Soc. Ultrastructural Pathology, Hawaii Soc. Pathologists, AAAS, N.Y. Acad. Scis., Soc. Armed Forces Med. Lab. Scientists, Assn. Practitioners in Infection Control, Clin. Lab. Mgrs. assn. (bd. dirs. 1989-92), Ctrl. Savannah River Area Assn. Med. Lab. Personnel, Assn. U.S. Army, AMA (Physician's Recognition award 1976, 78, 80, 82, 86 89, 92, 95, 98), Alliance Francaise, Cornell Club N.Y., Kauai Yacht Club. Republican. Roman Catholic. Home: 45-237 Kokokahi Pl Kaneohe HI 96744-2424 Office: TAMC DPALS Honolulu HI 96859-5000

GOODIN, LEONARD CHARLES, plumbing and drainage contractor; b. Ipswich, Queensland, Australia, Jan. 1, 1927; s. Eric and Edith Mary (Patterson) G.; m. Joan Olive Butler, Nov. 27, 1948; children—Peter, Barry, Wayne. Scholar, Brassall, Ipswich, Australia, 1939; Junior, Ipsich Tech. Coll., 1941. Lic. plumber and drainer, 1945. Plumber and drainer, Queensland, 1948-69, 1974—; mech. services supr. Dillingham Cons., Sydney, Australia, 1972-74; contracting ptnr. Fleetline Services, Nambour, Queensland, 1974—. Mem. Master Plumbers Assn. (pres. 1984—), Jaycees (sec. 1947). Church of England. Club: Nambour Cricket (life mem., pres. 1959-69). Lodges: Lions (pres. 1984, chmn. cabinet 1985, key mem. Internat. 1984); Masons. Avocations: oil painting, spectator motor sport, fishing. Home and office: 4 Blackall Terrace,, Nambour,, Queensland 4560, Australia

GOODISON, SIR NICHOLAS PROCTOR, banker; b. Radlett, Eng., May 16, 1934; s. Edmund Harold and Eileen Mary Carrington (Proctor) G.; m. Judith Abel Smith, 1960; children: Katharine, Adam, Rachel. Student, Marlborough Coll.; BA in Classics, King's Coll., 1958, MA; PhD in Arch., History of Art, Cambridge U., 1981; LittD (hon.), City U.; LLD (hon.), Exeter U.; DSc (hon.), Aston U.; DArt (hon.), De Montfort U.; DCL (hon.), Northumbria U.; FRIBA (hon.). Mem. stock exch. H.E. Goodison & Co. (name changed to Quilter Goodison Co. and now Quilter & Co. Ltd.), ptnr., 1962, chmn., 1975-88; elected to the Coun. of Stock Exch., 1968; chmn. of the Stock Exch. Internat. Stock Exchs. (FIBV), 1976-88; chmn. TSB Group plc, 1989-95, TSB Bank plc, 1989-99; dep. chmn. Lloyds TSB Group plc, 1995-2000, Brit. Steel plc, 1993-00; dir. Corus Group plc (formerly Brit. Steel plc), 1989—; dir. Gen. Accident plc, 1987-95, Burlington Mag., Ltd.; mem. Panel on Takeovers and Mergers, 1976-88, Coun. for Securities Industry, 1978-85, Securities Assn., 1986-88; mem. exec. com. Nat. Art Collections Fund, 1976—, chmn. 1986—; chmn. Courtauld Inst. of Art, 1982—; chmn. Crafts Coun., 1997—; dir. English Nat. Opera, 1977-98, vice-chmn., 1980; hon. keeper of furniture Fitzwilliam Mus., Cambridge; trustee Nat. Heritage Meml. Fund, 1988-97; gov. Marlborough Coll., 1981-97; mem. adv. bd. Judge Inst. Mgmt. Studies, Cambridge, 1999—; mem. Royal Commn. on Long-term Care for the Elderly, 1997-99. Author: English Barometers 1680-1860, 1968, rev. edit., 1977, Ormolu: The Work of Matthew Boulton, 1974; also articles and papers. Fellow Royal Acad. Arts in London, Royal Soc. of Arts, Antiquaries; mem. Furniture History Soc. (pres.), Brit. Bankers Assn. (pres. 1991-96), Arts Club, Atheneaum Club, Beefsteak Club. Avocations: study the history of furniture and decorative arts, opera, walking. Home and Office: PO box 2512, London W1A 5ZP, England

GOODLAD, ROBERT ANDREW, biologist; b. Banff, Scotland, Feb. 15, 1951; m. Paula Ruth Yallop; children: Anna, Adam, Duncan. BSc, London U., London, 1973; PhD, Aberdeen U., Aberdeen, Scotland. Rsch. scientist Rowet Rsch. Inst., Aberdeen, 1977-80; chief rsch. officer Royal Postgrad. Med. Sch., London, 1980-88; prin. scientific officer Imperial Cancer Rsch. Fund, London, 1988—. Contbr. articles to profl. jours. Office: Imperial Cancer Rsch Fund, 35-43 Lincolns Inn Fields, London WC2A 3PN, England

GOODLOE, JAMES EDWARD, protective services official, emergency manager; b. Clearwater, Fla., Oct. 26, 1951; s. Bessie Beatrice (Ivery) B.; m. Brenda Richella Payne, Mar. 29, 1986; children: Christopher Leon, Britt'ny Shae. AA, St. Petersburg Jr. Coll., 1978; BA, Eckerd Coll., 1984; postgrad., Nat. Fire Acad. Cert. contractor, Fla., cert. exec. fire officer. Camera specialist J.C. Penney Co., Clearwater, 1974-77; rodman City of Clearwater, 1975-77, fire fighter, 1977-79, fire inspector, 1979-90, fire marshal, 1990-98; bur. chief Fla. Divsn. State Fire Marshal, Bur. Fire Prevention, Fla., 1998—; adj. instr. St. Petersburg Jr. Coll., Criminal Justice Inst. Coord. Neighborhood Watch, Clearwater, 1988—. With USN, 1969-93, Res. ret. Recipient Grad. Leadership award Pinellas Community Leadership Program, Clearwater, 1988. Mem. Nat. Fire Protection Assn., Fla. Fire Marshal's Assn., Fla. Fire Sprinklers Assn., Tampa Bay Fire Marshal's Assn. (v.p. 1990-93, pres. 1993-94). Democrat. Methodist. Avocations: photograhy, sports. Home: 457 San Martin Dr Tallahassee FL 32312-4521 Office: Divsn State Fire Marshal 200 E Gaines St Tallahassee FL 32399-6502

GOODMAN, BARRY JOEL, lawyer; b. N.Y.C., May 28, 1953; s. Walter Louis and Shirley (Lenzer) G.; m. Nicole Goodman; children: Aaron, Rebecca. BA, Bradley U., 1974; JD with honors, Stetson U., 1977. Bar: Fla. 1977, U.S. Ct. Appeals 1978, Mich. 1979, U.S. Dist. Ct. (we. dist.) Fla., U.S. Dist. Ct. (ea. dist.) Mich. With Diecidue, Ferlita & Prieto, Tampa, Fla., 1977-78; assoc. Provizer, Eisenberg et al, Southfield, Mich., 1979-82; assoc. Thurswell, Chayet & Weiner, Southfield, 1982-87, ptnr., 1987-93; owner Gordon, Goodman & Acker, Southfield, 1993-98, Goodman Acker, Southfield, 1998—; lectr. Inst. Continuing Legal Edn., Ann Arbor, Mich., Mich. Trial Lawyer's Assn., State Bar of Mich. Pres., bd. dirs. West Bloomfield (Mich.) Woods Homeowners Assn., 1980-83; bd. dirs., v.p. Anti-Defamation League, Mich., 1983—; bd. dirs. B'nai B'rith Youth Orgn., Mich., 1995-97. Mem. ATLA, Mich. Trial Lawyers Assn. (bd. dirs. 1985—, treas. 1995, sec. 1996, v.p. 1997, pres.-elect 1998, pres. 1999—), Oakland County Bar Assn., Oakland County Trial Lawyers Assn. Democrat. Jewish. Avocations: tennis, golf, reading, theater. Office: Goodman Acker PC 17000 W 10 Mile Rd Ste 150 Southfield MI 48075-2945

GOODMAN, EDMUND NATHAN, surgeon, pain management consultant; b. N.Y.C., July 14, 1908; s. Benjamin Harry and Sophia (Schweisheimer) G.; m. Marian Powers, Mar. 9, 1950; children: Wendy, Tonne, Edmund Jr., Stacy. BS, CCNY, 1928; MD, Columbia U., 1933, MEd, DSc, 1942; postgrad. Cambridge U., 1935-36. Intern in surgery Columbia-Presbyn. Hosp., N.Y.C., 1936-38, asst. resident, then resident in surgery, 1938-41, instr. in surgery, 1941, asst. clin. prof. surgery, 1950-65, assoc. clin. prof., 1965-81; attending surgeon Mt. Sinai Hosp., N.Y.C., 1947-49; practice medicine specializing in pain mgmt., Roslyn, N.Y., 1982-96. Lt. comndr. USN, 1941-46. Mem. ACS, N.Y. Surg. Soc., N.Y. Acad. Med., Am. Bd. Surgery. Home and Office: 35 Sterling Ln Sands Point NY 11050-1239

GOODMAN, GERTRUDE AMELIA, civic worker; b. El Paso, Tex., Oct. 24, 1924; d. Karl Perry and Helen Sylvia (Pinkiert) G. BA, Mills Coll., 1945. Pres. El Paso chpt. Tex. Social Welfare Assn., 1963-65, bd. dirs. 1965-70, state bd. dirs., 1965-70; state bd. dirs. Pan-Am. Round Table, El Paso, 1966—, bd. dirs. 1970-71, sec., 1973-74, life mem.; founder, 1st chmn. El Paso Mus. Art Mem. Guild, 1962-68; bd. dirs. Mus. Art Assn., 1962-69, also v.p.; chmn. dir. El Paso C. of C. women's Dept., 1976-77; bd. dirs. Rio Grande Food Bank, 1988-94; bd. dirs. El Paso Pub. Libr., 1972-80, pres. bd. dirs., 1978-80; pres. El Paso County Hist. Soc., 1981-82, bd. dirs., 1986-92; mem. planning com. El Paso United Way, 1953—; mem. El Paso Mus. Art Bd. Coun.; pres. Las Comadres, 2000—. Recipient Hall of Honor award El Paso County Hist. Soc., Nat. Human Rels. award NCCJ, 1981, numerous awards for civic vol. work. Avocations: tennis, travel, art, books. Home: 905 Cincinnati Ave El Paso TX 79902-2435

GOODMAN, JACK, journalist; b. Bklyn., Oct. 23, 1913; s. Joseph and Anna (Birnbaum) G.; m. Marjorie, May 10, 1942; children: Nathaniel, Kathryn, Jean. BS, NYU, 1936, MA, 1937. News editor Radio Sta. WNYC, N.Y.C., 1938-45, Radio Sta. KALL, Salt Lake City, 1946-49; reporter, feature writer Salt Lake Tribune Telegram, Salt Lake City, 1949-51; news dir. KTVT-Channel 4, Salt Lake City, 1951-55, KUTA-Channel 2, Salt Lake City, 1955-60; writer Evans Advt. Agy., Salt Lake City, 1960-70; stringer corr. for Utah, N.Y. Times and Newsweek, Engring. and Mining Jour., 1947-75; interim dir. Utah State Travel Commn., 1960-61; columnist Salt Lake Tribune, 1980—. Author, illustrator: As You Pass By, 1996. Bd. dirs. Marriott Libr., Salt Lake City, 1980, Utah State Hist. Soc., 1992. Democrat. Jewish. Home: 6053 S 23rd E Salt Lake City UT 84121-1439

GOODMAN, JEFFREY ALLAN, poet, educator; b. Woonsocket, R.I., July 5, 1946; s. Martin Goodman and Gloria Medoff; m. Nancy J. Waddell, Aug. 27, 1972; children: John, Margaret, Anna. BA, U. Pa., 1968; MA, Stanford U., 1978, PhD, 1981. Instr. English Stanford U., Palo Alto, Calif., 1980; asst. prof. English U. Santa Clara, Calif., 1981-84; tutor St. John's Coll., Santa Fe, 1987-91; prof. English Ala. Sch. Math. and Sci., Mobile, 1991—. Author: After the War, 1998, A Strung Bow, 2000. Stanford Poetry fellow Stanford U., Palo Alto, 1972, Fulbright fellow U.S. Info. Agy., Washington, 1985. Democrat. Avocations: yoga, philosophy, walking. E-mail: jgood@asms.net. Home: 301 S Georgia Ave Mobile AL 36604-2315

GOODMAN, KENNETH JOEL, radiologist; b. N.Y.C., Oct. 3, 1946; s. Herman and Mina G.; m. Kathleen Christine Frappaolo, June 23, 1974; children: Eric, Laura. BA, CUNY, 1967; MD, U. Tex., San Antonio, 1972. Diplomate Am. Bd. Radiology. Intern in internal medicine Cornell Cooperating Hosp., N.Y.C., 1972-73, resident in internal medicine, 1973-74; resident in diagnostic radiology N.Y. Hosp.-Cornell U., N.Y.C., 1974-77, fellow in computered tomography and ultrasound, 1977-78; assoc. prof. radiology, chief divsn. diagnostic radiology SUNY, Stony Brook, 1979-87; dir. dept. radiology St. Francis Hosp., Roslyn, N.Y., 1988—; pres. Physicians Diagnostic Imaging, Roslyn, 1988—. Contbr. over 15 articles to med. jours.; manuscript reviewer Radiology, 1985. Bd. dirs. Pt. Washington Staff Orgn., 1988—; trustee Village of Matinecock, N.Y., 1998—, dep. mayor, 1998—. Fellow Am. Coll. Radiology (councilor); mem. N.Y. State Radiol. Soc. (del. 1996). Avocations: scuba diving, skiing, mountaineering, photography, cycling. Office: Phys Diag Imaging PC 100 Port Washington Blvd Roslyn NY 11576-1353

GOODMAN, MARVIN DAVID, architect; b. Paterson, N.J., Feb. 3, 1933; m. Rosalie Hart; children: Danielle, Marc. BArch, U. Fla., 1955. Registered architect, Fla. Asst. to chief engr. constr. of UNESCO bldg., Paris, 1958; pvt. practice Marvin D. Goodman & Assocs., Ltd., Kingston, Jamaica, 1960—; mem. Archtl. Registration Bd. Jamaica, 1987—; chmn. joint cons. com. Bldg. and Constrn. Industry Jamaica, 1986; chmn. adv. coun. Caribbean Sch. Arch. U. Technology, Kingston, 1987—. Prin. works include Petroleum Corp. of Jamaica Bldg., Goblin Hill Villas Resort Complex, Hillel Acad., Hedonism II Resort, Half Moon Hotel, French Embassy, Mex. Embassy, master plan for Port Royal, Bank of N.S., Ritz Carlton Golf Club House Rose Hall. Mem. town planning rev. com. Ministry of Devel.; mem. nat. adv. coun. on energy conservation Ministry of Mining and Energy; trustee, bd. dirs. Hillel Acad.; chmn. Jamaica House Basic Sch. Bd.; mem. energy code devel. com. Bur. Standards; mem. zoning devel. com. Office of Prime Minister. Lt. U.S. Army Corps Engrs., 1955-57. Recipient Gov. Gen.'s award, Disting. Alumnus award U. Fla., 1987, Silver Musgrave medal Inst. Jamaica, also others. Mem. AIA, Jamaican Inst. Architects (pres. 1984-86), Alliance Francaise Jamaica (pres. 1985-90). Office: Marvin D Goodman & Assocs, 11 East Ave, Kingston 10, Jamaica

GOODMAN, NEAL ROBERT, international management consultant and educator; b. Jersey City, May 13, 1947; s. Leo and Beatrice (Gering) G.; m. Varda Armoni, June 20, 1971; children: Jennifer, Laurie. BA, St. Peter's Coll., 1969; MA, CCNY, 1970; PhD, NYU, 1977. Faculty St. Peter's Coll., Jersey City, 1971—; prof. St. Peter's Coll., 1986—; pres. Global Dynamics, Inc., Randolph, N.J., 1984—. Author: Doing Business with China, 1998, Doing Business with India, 1998, Doing Business with Asia, 1998, Doing Business with Brazil, 1998, Intercultural training, 1987, Doing Business with Japan, 1998, Doing Business with Germany, 1998, Internationalizing the Curriculum, 1991. Mem. ASTD (field editor, internat. tng.), Soc. Intercultural Edn. Tng. and Rsch. (treas. 1988-92, exec. bd. 1988-92), Nat. Soc. for Performance Instrn., Am. Sociol. Assn., Nat. Assn. Foreign Student Affairs, Inst. for Internat. Edn., Soc. Human Resource Mgmt. Avocations: tennis, skiing, racketball, gardening, travel. Home: 19 Wilkinson Rd Randolph NJ 07869-3472 Office: St Peters Coll 2641 John F Kennedy Blvd Jersey City NJ 07306-5943

GOODMAN, SYLVIA KLUMOK, volunteer; b. Moorhead, Miss., June 19, 1940; d. Sol Harry and Fannie Ida (Davidson) Klumok; m. Carl Gerald Goodman, June 5, 1960; children: Lisa Wynne Goodman Stone, Gary Steven, Jeffrey David. BS in Zoology with honors, Newcomb Coll., 1962; M in Zoology, Tulane U., 1963; postgrad., Harvard U., summer 1990. Tchr. Midway Jr. H.S., Shreveport, La., 1963-68; instr. biology La. State U., Shreveport, 1967-68; instr. physiology, asst. coord. plans La. State U. Med. Ctr., Shreveport, 1970-74. Mem. Shreveport Mayor's Women's Commn., 1986-90; vice-chair La. State Mineral Bd., Baton Rouge, 1988-92; chmn. Food Project, Shreveport, 1990-92; chair beautification com. Shreveport Regional Airport, 1990-94; bd. dirs. Sci-Port Discovery Ctr., Shreveport, 1990—, pres., 1993-95; bd. dirs. La. Endowment Humanities, 1996-99; pres. Shreveport Jewish Fedn., 1982-83; trustee Shreveport-Bossier Cmty. Found., chmn., 1993—; bd. dirs. Meadows Art Mus., 1991-97, vice chmn., 1995; chancellor's adv. com. LSU-S, 1996—; mem. Red River Refuge Com., 1999; chair So. Jewish Inst., 2000—. Recipient Humanitarian award NCCJ, Humanitarian award Caddo Commn., 1991, Vol. Fundraiser award Nat. Fedn. Fundraising Execs., 1996, Angel award Blue Cross Blue Shield, 1998, Point of Light award, 1999; named Women Who Make a Difference Shreveport Celebration of Women Week, 1996, Best-Dressed Woman of No. La. Shreveport Times, 1998. Mem. Jr. League Shreveport (Sustainer of Yr. award 1995, Daily Point of Light 1999), Mensa, Phi Beta Kappa, Alpha Epsilon Phi. Jewish. Avocations: theater, piano, dance, taking courses, movies. Home: 409 Southfield Rd Shreveport LA 71106-2213

GOODMAN, TIMOTHY NICHOLAS TREWIN, mathematics educator; b. Redhill, Surrey, Eng., Apr. 29, 1947; s. Joseph Vincent and Eileen May (Sherwell) G.; m. Choo-Tin Soon, Dec. 1, 1973; children: Joy Ai-Leen, Kim Mei-Leen, Ruth Su-Leen. BA, St. John's Coll., Cambridge, Eng., 1969; MS, Warwick U., Eng., 1970; DPhil, Sussex U., Eng., 1972. Tchr. vol. svc. overseas K.E. VII Secondary Sch., Taiping, Malaysia, 1973; tchr. St. Andrews Secondary Sch., Singapore, 1974-75; lectr. U. Sains Malaysia, Penang, 1975-79; lectr. Dundee (Scotland) U., 1979-90, reader, 1992-94, prof., 1994—; prof. Tex. A&M U., College Station, 1990-91. Contbr. articles to profl. jours. Recipient open scholarship St. John's Coll., 1966. Fellow Royal Soc. Edinburgh; mem. Edinburgh Math. Soc. Mem. Ch. of Scotland. Avocations: Scottish country dancing, hillwalking, music. Office: U Dundee, Maths Dept, DD1 4HN Dundee Scotland

GOODMAN, WILLIAM RICHARD, insurance adjusting company executive; b. Staunton, Va., Sept. 19, 1930; s. Harry and Ruth (Meyer) G.; m. Alice Helene Katzenstein, June 13, 1954; children: Harvey, Laurie, Barry. BS, U. Md., 1952; JD, U. Balt., 1955. Cert. profl. pub. adjuster FPPA. Pub. ins. adjuster, lawyer Goodman-Gable-Gould Co., Balt., 1952-73, v.p., 1973-85, pres., 1985-97, CEO, 1985—, chmn. bd., 1989—. Chmn. Baltimore County Indsl. Devel. Commn., 1967-69; mem. Met. Transit Authority, Balt., 1969-71, bd. rev. Dept. Transp., Md., 1971-76, Md. Racing Commn., 1984. Mem. Nat. Assn. Pub. Ins. Adjusters (dir., v.p., pres., chmn. bd. dirs., Disting. Svc. award 1987, Man of Yr. 1995, fellow in profession of pub. adjusting), B'nai B'rith (v.p. Menorah Lodge 1992-94, pres. 1996-98). Democrat. Jewish. Avocation: collector of toy trains and antique cars. Home: 7811 Park Heights Ave Baltimore MD 21208-4322 Office: Goodman-Gable-Gould Co Adjusters Internat 6 Reservoir Cir Ste 202 Baltimore MD 21208-7310

GOODMANLOWE, GWEN DAVIES, biology educator; b. Livingston, N.J., Sept. 11, 1961; d. Rowland Davies II and Ruth Julia (Birnbaum) Goodman; m. Christopher Gale Lowe, June 22, 1991. BS, Fairleigh Dickinson U., 1983; MS, Calif. State U., Long Beach, 1991; PhD, U. Hawaii, 1998. Instr. Catalina Island Marine Inst., Avalon, Calif., 1985-87; tchg. asst. Calif. State U., Long Beach, 1987-91, lectr., 1999—; rsch. asst. U. Hawaii, Honolulu, 1991-98; cons. Chamber's Group, Santa Ana, Calif., 1990-91, Nat. Marine Fisheries Svc., Honolulu, 1993—. Contbr. articles to profl. jours. Sci. judge Hawaii State Sci. Fair, Honolulu, 1995-98, Hawaii Trivial Pursuits Ednl. Game Show, Honolulu, 1997. Grantee Waikaloa Marine Life Fund, 1995, 96, 97. Mem. Western Soc. Naturalists. Avocations: photography, scuba diving, running, hiking, skiing. Office: Calif State U Long Beach Dept Biology 1250 N Bellflower Blvd Long Beach CA 90840-0006

GOODPASTURE, PHILIP HENRY, lawyer; b. Lisbon, Portugal, Sept. 16, 1960; s. Henry McKennie and Ellen Ingabor (Moller) G.; m. Paige Everett Hargroves, June 25, 1994. BA with high distinction, U. Va., 1982, JD, 1985. Bar: Va. 1985, U.S. Dist. Ct. (ea. dist.) Va. 1985. Assoc. Christian & Barton and predecessor firm, Richmond, Va., 1985-92, ptnr., 1993—, vice-chmn. corp. team, 1994-97, mem. exec. com., 1998. Dir. Downtown Presents Inc., Richmond, 1993—, Va. League for Planned Parenthood, Richmond, 1989-95, Vol. Emergency Families for Children, Richmond, 1998-2000; dir. Parliament City of Richmond, 1997-98; mem. Leadership Metro Richmond, 1994; mem. leadership devel. coun. ARC, 1995. Mem. Va. Bar Assn., Richmond Bar Assn. Office: Christian & Barton 909 E Main St Ste 1200 Richmond VA 23219-3013

GOODRICH, ISAAC, neurosurgeon, educator; b. Milledgeville, Ga., Sept. 19, 1939; s. Ellis and Frieda (Bergman) G.; m. Dianne L. Brittain, Aug. 28, 1965; children: Mindy Anne, Scott David, Jennifer Gale. AA, Ga. Mil. Coll., 1959; BS, U. Ga., 1961; MD, Med. Coll. Ga., 1964. Cert. Am. Bd. Neurol. Surgery. Intern Columbia-Presbyn. Med. Ctr., N.Y.C., 1964-65; resident in neurosurgery Yale-New Haven Med. Ctr., 1967-71; practice medicine specializing in neurosurgery New Haven, 1971—; instr. neurosurgery, Yale U. Med. Sch., 1970-71, asst. clin. prof., 1978-86; assoc. clin. prof., 1986—; attending neurosurgeon Yale-New Haven Hosp., 1973—, Hosp. St. Raphael, 1971—; mem. courtesy staff Milford Hosp., 1986—; cons. staff Midstate Med. Ctr., 1986—, VA Hosp., West Haven, 1990—, Griffin Hosp., 1992-99, St. Mary's Hosp., 1995-99, courtesy staff, 1999—. Contbr. articles to profl. jours. Capt. U.S. Army, 1965-67. Decorated Bronze Star, Air Medal; recipient Disting. Alumni award Ga. Mil. Coll., 1980; named Hon. Citizen, Boys Town, Nebr., 1971. Fellow ACS, Internat. Coll. Surgeons, Royal Soc. Medicine; mem. AMA (Physicians Recognition award for Continuing Med. Edn. 1969, 72, 75, 78, 81, 85, 88, 91, 94, 97), AAAS, Congress Neurol. Surgeons, New Eng. Neurosurg. Soc. (pres. 1997-99), Pan Pacific Surg. Assn., Soc. Med. Cons. to Armed Forces, Soc. 1st Inf. Divsn., 28th Inf. Assn., Am. Assn. Neurol. Surgeons, Conn. State Neurol. Soc., Conn. State Med. Soc. (v.p. 2000-01), New Haven City (pres. 1989-90), New Haven County Med. Assn. (pres. 1998-99), N.Y. Acad. Scis. Jewish. Home: 264 Rimmon Rd Woodbridge CT 06525-1847 Office: 330 Orchard St Ste 316 New Haven CT 06511-4430

GOODRICH, NORMA LORRE (MRS. JOHN H. HOWARD), French and comparative literature educator; b. Huntington, Vt., May 10, 1917; d. Charles Edmund and Edyth (Riggs) Falby; m. J.M.A. Lorre, Dec. 10, 1943 (div. June 1946); 1 son, Jean-Joseph; m. John Hereford Howard, Jan. 20, 1964. BS cum laude, U. Vt., 1938; postgrad. (U. Vt. fellow), U. Grenoble, France, 1938-39; PhD (Ellis fellow), Columbia U., 1965; LittD, U. Vt., 1993. Tchr. high schs., Vt., 1939-43, Bentley Sch., N.Y.C., 1943-47; owner dir. Am. Villa in Normandy, Trouville, France, 1947-53; tchr. Fieldston Sch., N.Y.C., 1954-63; asst. prof. French U. So. Calif., 1964-66, assoc. prof., 1966-71; dean faculty Scripps Coll., Claremont, Calif., 1971-72; prof. French and comparative lit. Claremont Colls., 1972, prof. emeritus, 1982—; vis. scholar Calif. Luth. Coll., 1965, Isle of Man, U.K., 1986, Claremont McKenna Coll., 1986; vis. prof. John Carroll U., Cleve., 1987, Calif. State U., Long Beach, 1986, 87, 88, Cal Arts, Pasadena, 1989, Calif. Poly. U., Pomona, 1992, Southwestern Coll., 1993, Riverside Bapt. Coll., 1994, Scripps Coll., Claremont, 1994; lectr. Arthurian Soc., Carlisle, Cumbria, Eng., 1994, 96, 97, Santa Anita (Calif.) Ch., 1995, Trinity Episc. Ch., Redlands, Calif., 1996. Author: Ancient Myths, 1959, rev. edit., 1977, 94, Medieval Myths, 1960, rev. edit., 1977, 94, Doctor and Maria Theresa, 1961, Myths of the Hero, 1961, Ways of Love, 1963, Charles of Orleans: A Study of Themes in His French and English Poetry, 1967, Giono: Master of Fictional Modes, 1973, Afterword for the Man Who Planted Trees (Jean Giono), 1985 (New Eng. Book award), London edit., 1989, King Arthur, 1986, 2d edit., 1989, Merlin, 1987, 2d edit., 1989, Il Mito della Tavola Rotonda (transl. of King Arthur), 1989, Le Roi Arthur, 1989, Die Ritter von Camelot, 1994, 95 (transl. of King Arthur), Castle Epstein (transl. of Alexander Dumas), 1989, Priestesses, 1989, Guinevere, 1991, The Holy Grail, 1992, Il Mito di Merlino, 1992 (transl. of Merlin), Heroines, 1993, Il Mito di Ginevra (transl. Guinevere), 1995; editor: Bullfinch Mythology, The Age of Fable, 1995, Bullfinch Mythology, The Age of Chivalry, 1995, Il Santo Graal, 1997, (boxed edit.) Hors Commerce, 1997; contbr. articles to internat. profl. jours.; guest appearances various TV and radio shows, Eng., 1986, 94, U.S., 1986-90, 93, 94. Mem. pub. rels. staff Worthington Corp., N.Y.C., 1953-54; bd. dirs. patron West End Opera Assn., 1973-74, program dir., 1975-76; guest lectr. Flower Festival, Arthuret Ch., Longtown, Cumbria, Eng., 1991, guest preacher, 1992. Recipient Good Citizen medal SAR, 1989, Martha Washington medal, 1992, Wallace award Am. Scottish Found., 1990; invested as Dame Knights Templar, Commandery of Nova Scotia, in the Rosslyn Chapel, Scotland, 1990; reinvested as Knight Templar, Dame and Officer with the rank of comdr. in Teampull of Sion, Edinburgh, Scotland, 1990, St. Mary's Cath., Edinburgh, Order of St. George, 1993, Mil. Order Fgn. Wars, 1994, Calif. Commandery medal, 1997. Fellow Soc. Antiquarians, Nat. Inst. Social Scis.; mem. Assn. Study of Dada and Surrealism (sec. 1970-72), Philol. Assn. Pacific Coast (nominating com. 1971-72), MLA (mem. del. assembly's election com. 1975), The Prehistoric Soc., Am. Assn. Tchrs. French, Medieval Assn. Pacific, Medieval Acad. Am., Nat. Soc. DAR (vice-regent 1996-97), Columbia U. Alumni Assn., Dante Soc., Pierport Morgan Libr., Clan MacArthur, Clan MacKay (hon.), 78th Fraser's Highlanders 2d Bn. of Foot Am. (lt.), Tordarroch Trust (Scotland and U.S.), Met. Opera Guild, Order of the Crown of Charlemagne in the U.S.A. (life), Phi Kappa Phi. Avocations: gymnastics, gardening, dressmaking, traveling in South Pacific, studying U.S. battle sites and prisons in South Pacific. Home: 620 Diablo Dr Claremont CA 91711-1616

GOODROW, GERARD ANDREW, art historian, contemporary art specialist; b. South Amboy, N.J., Dec. 28, 1964; s. Joseph Harold and Carol Jane (Worswick) G. BA, Rutgers U., 1987; postgrad., CUNY, 1988-89, U. Cologne, Germany, 1989—. Asst. to dir. New Mus. of Contemporary Art, N.Y.C., 1985-87; guest curator Kunst-Sta. Sankt Peter, Cologne, 1987-88; registrar Rubell Collection, N.Y.C., 1988-89; art critic Artnews, N.Y.C., 1990-96; curator Mus. Ludwig, Cologne, 1992-96; assoc. dir., specialist for contemporary art Christie's, London and Cologne, 1996—. Author, editor: Fabrizio Plessi-Progetti del Mondo, 1997, Jack Pierson-The Lonely Life, 1997, Exotik Erotik, 1996, Ego Alter Ego, 1999, Painting Beyond Painting, 1998. Trustee Ursula Blicke Found., Kraichtal, Germany, 1994—. Named Henry Rutgers scholar Rutgers U., 1982; Fulbright fellow, 1987-88; grantee Carl Duisburg Soc., 1992. Mem. Modern Art Soc. Cologne, Soc. Friends of the Kunstsammlung NRW. Home: Forststr 84, D-50767 Cologne Germany Office: Christie's Contemporary, 8 King St St James, London SW1Y 6QT, England

GOODSELL, DAVID SCOTT, JR., molecular biologist; b. Honolulu, Oct. 25, 1961; s. David Scott and Cheryl Darlene (Dodge) G. BS in Chemistry, BS in Biology, U. Calif., Irvine, 1982; PhD in Biochemistry, U. Calif., L.A., 1987. Rsch. and teaching asst. dept. of Chemistry and Biochemistry U. Calif., L.A., 1982-87; rsch. assoc. dept. of Molecular Biology Rsch. Inst. Scripps Clinic, La Jolla, Calif., 1987-90, sci. assoc. dept. molecular biology, 1990-92; asst. rschr. Molecular Biology Inst. U. Calif., L.A., 1992-94; asst. prof. dept. molecular biology The Scripps Rsch. Inst., La Jolla, Calif., 1995—. Author: The Machinery of Life, 1992, Our Molecular Nature, 1996; contbr. articles to profl. jours., including Am. Scientist, Sci. Am., others. Mem. AAAS, Am. Crystallography Assn., Assn. Computing Machinery, Internat. Soc. for Arts Sci. and Tech., Molecular Graphics Soc. Avocations: watercolor, ceramics. Office: The Scripps Rsch Inst MB5 10550 N Torrey Pines Rd La Jolla CA 92037-1000

GOODSON, FREDERICK BRIAN, business consultant; b. Belfast, No. Ireland, May 21, 1938; s. Frederick Orlando and Edythe (Hamer) G.; m. Susan Mary Firmin, AUg. 25, 1965; children: Philippa, Simon, Hugo, Rebecca. Student, Campbell Coll., Belfast, 1952-54, Britannia Royal Naval Coll., Dartmouth, 1955-58; Royal Coll. Defense Studies, 1992. Commd. ensign Royal Navy, 1955, advanced through grades to rear adm., with coastal forces, 1958-74, supply officer HMS Invincible and fleet supply officer, 1980-82, dir. Naval Logistic Planning, Ministry of Defense,, 1985-87, commdr. HMS Centurion,, 1988-92, asst. chief of defense staff logistics Ministry of Defense,, 1993-96, ret., 1996; chmn. Trading Force Group of COS, 1999—; chmn. Eurolog Naval Group (NATO), 1985-87, Western European Union Logistics Group, 1993-96; chmn. Bath & West Cmty. NHS Trust, 1997—. Chmn. govs. St. Francis Spl. Sch., Fareham, 1988-91; chmn. St. John's Ambulance, Wiltshire, 1997—, mem. chpt. gen., 1998—. Mem. IOD, Royal Navy Sailing Assn., Bowood Golf & Country Club. Conservative. Anglican. Avocations: sailing, golf, squash, outdoors. Home: New Homestead Farm, Chppham North Wraxhall SN14 7AJ, United Kingdom

GOODSON, HARLAN WAYNE, state regulator, educator; b. Newhall, Calif., Mar. 9, 1947; s. Robert Thurman Goodson and Margeret Loraine Underwood; m. Darla Kay Hinderks, (div. Feb. 1987); children: Kimberly, Marc. BA, Golden Gate U., 1976; JD, John F. Kennedy U., 1995; MPA, Golden Gate U., 1999. Sgt. of police Oakland (Calif.) Police Dept., 1971-92; cons. to pres. pro tempore Calif. State Senate, Sacramento, 1994-99; dir. Divsn. of Gambling Control Office of the Atty. Gen., Sacramento; adj. prof. law John F. Kennedy U. Sch. Law, Orinda, Calif., 1996—; mem. gov.'s adv. panel Calif. Earthquake Authority, Sacramento, 1996, 97; mem. governing bd., 1996, 97. Del. Dem. Conv., Sacramento, 1997, L.A., 1998. With USN, 1967-71. Mem. ABA, Calif. State Bar, Oakland Police Activities League (founder, exec. dir. 1982-85, Wish Upon a Star Spl. Recognition 1988), Sigma Chi (charter Zeta Omicron chpt.). Democrat. Avocations: reading, golfing. E-mail: hgoodson@hdcdojnet.state.ca.us. Home: 1208 Grand River Dr Sacramento CA 95831-4420 Office: Office of the Atty Gen 1435 River Park Dr Fl 2D Sacramento CA 95815-4509

GOODWIN, ANDREW WIRT, II, radiologist; b. Oil City, Pa., Feb. 4, 1932; s. Frank Bert and Florence Bickford (Green) G.; m. Anita Faye Adkins, May 27, 1987; children: Andrew, Victoria, Mary Elizabeth, Mark H., Martha J., Lisa R. BA, Colgate U., 1953; MD, U. Mich., 1957. Intern Mary Hitchcock Meml. Hosp., Hanover, N.H., 1957-58; resident in radiology Mayo Clinic, Rochester, Minn., 1958-61, resident, 1958-61; radiologist Associated Radiologists, Inc., Charleston, W.Va., 1961-86, Radiol. Physicians Assn., Fairmont, W.Va., 1988—; pvt. practice. Republican. Episcopalian. Home: 205 Whispering Woods Rd Charleston WV 25304-2761 Office: Radiol Physicians Assocs Inc 700 Village Dr Fairmont WV 26554-2409

GOODWIN, BILLY WAYNE, chemical engineer; b. Memphis, Nov. 12, 1954; s. Jess W. and Florence (Adams) G.; m. Carole McCutcheon, July 25, 1992; children: Hayley M., Maura M. BSChemE, La. State U., 1992. Fin. cons. Goodwin & Assocs., Inc., Baton Rouge, 1976-86, mgr., investment broker, 1986-87; mgr. Cadgis Rsch. Lab., La. State U., Baton Rouge, 1987-89; student engr. Ethyl Corp. R & D, Baton Rouge, 1989-92; engr. Walk, Haydel & Assocs., Inc., New Orleans, 1992-95; prodn. mgr. vinyl chloride monomer Ga. Gulf Corp., Plaquemine, La., 1995-97; ops. mgr. UOP, LLC, Baton Rouge, 1997—. Grantee Air & Waste Mgmt. Assn., Baton Rouge chpt., 1991. Mem. AIChE, Am. Inst. Chemists (hon.), Air and Waste Mgmt. Assn. (hon.), Golden Key, Omega Chi Epsilon, Tau Beta Pi, Phi Eta Sigma. Republican. Episcopalian. E-mail: billigoodwin@uop.com. Home: 1540 Ridgeland Dr Baton Rouge LA 70810-3056 Office: UOP LLC PO Box 1031 1200 Airline Hwy Baton Rouge LA 70821

GOODWIN, BRIAN CAREY, biology educator, science writer, researcher; b. Montreal, Quebec, Can., Mar. 25, 1931; arrived in Eng., 1954; s. William Murray and Muriel Margaret (Forrest) G.; m. Hazel Ida Hutchinson, Sept. 19, 1971; children: Annette, Lynn, Esther, Ivan. BSc, McGill U., Montreal, Can., 1952, MSc, 1954; BA, Oxford U., Eng., 1957; PhD, Edinburgh U., Scotland, 1960. Cert. Biologist. Postdoctoral fellow McGill U., Montreal, Can., 1960-61, MIT, Cambridge, Mass., 1961-64; lectr. biology U. Edinburgh, Eng., 1964-65; reader in devel. biology U. Sussex, Brighton, Eng., 1965-84; prof. biology The Open U., Milton Keyner, Eng., 1984-97; dir. holistic sci. Schumacher Coll. Dartington, Devon, Eng., 1997—. Author: Temporal Organization in Cells, 1963, Analytical Physiology, 1976, How The Leopard Changed Its Spots, 1994, (with Gerry Webster) Form and Transformation, 1996. Rhodes scholar Oxford U., 1954-57. Mem. Sci. and Med. Network (v.p. 1995-97). Avocations: piano music, tennis, sailing. Office: Schumacher Coll, The Old Postern Dartington, TQ9 6EA Devon England

GOODWIN, FELIX LEE, retired educational administrator, retired army officer; b. Lawrence, Kans., Nov. 24, 1919; s. Felix and Lucille Marie (Lee) G.; m. Esther Brown, Nov. 1, 1941 (dec.); children: Cheryl Washington, Sylvia, Judith Barnes; m. Barbara Gilpin, Aug. 15, 1988. BS, U. Md., 1958; M of Pub. Adminstrn., U. Ariz., 1965, EdS, 1974, EdD, 1979. Enlisted U.S. Army, 1939, advanced through grades to lt. col., 1963; ret., 1969; asst. prof. army mil. sci. dept. U. Ariz., Tucson, 1968-69, asst. to pres., 1969-83. Chmn. Pima County Merit Sys. Commn., 1975-77, 79-82, Pima County Law Enforcement Merit Coun., 1973-82; mem. Ariz. Bicentennial Commn., 1974-77, chmn., 1976-77. Decorated Legion of Merit, Army Commendation medal with 2 oak leaf cluster, Meritorious Svc. medal; recipient Cert. of Appreciation, City of Tucson, 1967, 83, Man of Yr. award Una Noche Plateada, Tucson, 1976, Leadership award Tucson Urban League, 1975, IRS award, 1981; named Hon. Citizen, Sierra Vista, Ariz. Mem. NEA, NAACP (life), DAV (life), NRA, Nat. Alliance Black Sch. Educators (life), Soc. Ethnic and Spl. Studies Assn. U.S. Army, Am. Legion, Amvets, Ret. Officers Assn., Kiwanis (life), K.C., VFW, Phi Delta Kappa, Alpha Phi Alpha (life), Pi Lambda Theta, Alpha Delta Delta, Beta Gamma Sigma. Roman Catholic.

GOODWIN, GREGORY R., family physician with obstetrics subspecialty; b. Kansas City, Mo., Dec. 16, 1960; s. Roger M. and Barbara Joan Goodwin; m. LaDawn Sue Wood, Nov. 7, 1992; children: Katy Belinda, Clarissa LaDawn, Trent. BS, Park Coll., 1985; D in Chiropractic, Cleve. Chiropractic Coll., Kansas City, Mo., 1985; MS, U. Bridgeport, 1986; DO, U. Health Scis., COM, 1991. Diplomate Am. Bd. Family Practice; cert. Am. Bd. Hospice and Palliative Medicine. Osteopathic intern Phelps County Regional Med. Ctr., Rolla, Mo., 1991-92; resident in family practice U. Mo. Truman Med. Ctr., Kansas City, 1992-94; family practice obstetrics S.W. Mo. Family Health Care, Mountain Grove, Mo., 1994-95; med. dir. Providence Hospice, Salem, Mo., 1996-98; obstetrician, family practice physician Salem Family Health Care, 1995-98; med. dir. Hospice of Care, Houston, Mo., 1998—, Cmty. Hospice of Am., 1999—; family practice/obstetrics TCMH Family Clinic, Houston, Mo.; asst. clin. prof. Kirksville (Mo.) Coll. Osteo. Medicine, 1996—. Fellow Am. Acad. Family Physicians; mem. Am. Osteo. Assn., Am. Acad. Family Physicians, Christin Med. and Dental Soc., Mo. Assn. Osteo. Physicians (mem. young physicians sect.), Am. Coll. Osteo. Family Physicians. Baptist. Avocations: fishing, travel, reading, collecting antique medicine bottles, hunting. Office: TCMH Family Clinic 1335 S Sam Houston Blvd Houston MO 65483-2046

GOODWIN, IRWIN, magazine editor; b. Chgo., Aug. 19, 1929; s. Albert and Sarah Esther (Wallen) G.; m. Mary Margaret Revell, Apr. 21, 1966 (div. 1987). AB, Roosevelt U., Chgo., 1948; MA, U. Mich., 1949. Reporter City News Bur., Chgo., 1949-50; reporter, asst. editor Newsweek, Chgo. and N.Y.C., 1952-58; dir. pub. info. Sci. Rsch. Assocs., Chgo., 1958-60; corr. Newsweek, London, 1960-70; Caribbean corr. Washington Post, San Juan, P.R., 1970-72; spl. asst. to dir. Smithsonian Instn., Washington, 1972-73; sr. editor Nat. Acad. Scis., Washington, 1973-82; editor Washington bur. Physics Today, Washington, 1983-93, sr. editor Washington bur., 1993—. Co-author: Physics and Nuclear Arms Today, 1991; editor: Paying for America's Health Care, 1973, Energy and Environment: Collision of Crises, 1974; contbr. articles to profl. jours. Sgt. maj. U.S. Army, 1950-52. Recipient News Writing award Overseas Press Club, 1971, 72, Pub. Svc. Group Achievement award NASA, 1981. Mem. AAAS, Nat. Assn. Sci. Writers, Fedn. Am. Scientists, D.C. Sci. Writers Assn., Nat. Press Club, Phi Beta Kappa. Office: Physics Today 1050 National Press Bldg 529 14th St NW Washington DC 20045-1000

GOODWIN, JAMES E., air transportation executive. BBA, Salem Coll. With United Airlines, 1967, sr. v.p. internat., 1992, sr. v.p. N.Am., pres, COO, 1998; chmn., CEO UAL Corp., Chgo. Trustee Lewis U.; bd. dirs. Chgo. Coun. Fgn. Rels. Mem. Exec. Club Chgo. (bd. dirs.), Comml. Club Chgo. (civic com.). Office: UAL Corp 1200 E Algonquin Rd Elk Grove Village IL 60007*

GOODWIN, JEAN MCCLUNG, psychiatrist; b. Pueblo, Colo., Mar. 28, 1946; d. Paul Stanley and Geraldine (Smart) McClung; m. James Simeon Goodwin, Aug. 8, 1970; children: Laura (dec.), Amanda Harding Goodwin, Robert Caleb, Paul Joshua, Elizabeth Cronin Goodwin. BA in Anthropology summa cum laude, Radcliffe Coll., 1967; MD, Harvard U., 1971; MPH, UCLA, 1972. Diplomate Am. Bd. Psychiatry and Neurology, Am. Bd. Forensic Psychiatry; added qualifications in forensic psychiatry, psychoanalytic tng. Resident in psychiatry Georgetown U. Hosp., Washington, 1972-74; resident in psychiatry U. N.Mex. Sch. Medicine, 1974-76, asst. dir., dir. psychiat. residents tng., 1979-85; prof. Med. Coll. Wis., 1985-92; prof. U. Tex. Med. Br., Galveston, 1992-98, prof. clin. psychiatry, 1998—; pvt. practice in gen. & forensic psychiatry, psychoanalysis; from instr. to assoc. prof. dept. psychiatry U. N.Mex. Sch. Medicine, 1976-85; cons. protective services Dept. Human Services, N.Mex., 1976-84; lectr. profl. groups; faculty assoc. Houston-Galveston Psychoanalysis Inst., 1999—. Author: Effects of High Altitude on Human Birth, 1969, Sexual Abuse: Incest Victims and Their Families, 1982, 2d edit., 1989, Rediscovering Childhood Trauma: Historical Casebook and Clinical Applications, 1993, Mischief and Mercy, 1993; co-author (with Reina Attias) Splintered Reflections: Images of the Body in Trauma, 1999; mem. editl. bd. Jour. Traumatic Stress, 1985-93, Dissociation, 1988-98, Psychotherapy Rev., 1998—; contbr. numerous articles on child abuse to profl. jours. Chmn. work group on child sexual abuse Surgeon Gen.'s Conference on Violence and Pub. Health, Leesburg, Va., 1985; mem. adv. bd. Nat. Resource Ctr. on Child Sexual Abuse, 1989-96. Recipient Esther Haar award Am. Acad. Psychoanalysis, 1990, Cornelia Wilbur award Internat. Soc. for Study of Dissociation, 1994; Nat. Cen. Child Abuse and Neglect grantee, 1979-82, Nat. Inst. Aging grantee, 1980-85. Fellow Internat. Soc. Study Dissociation (exec. com. 1991-96), Am. Psychiat. Assn. (dist. br. treas., sec. N.Mex. br. 1980-82, exhibits and programs subcoms. 1985-91); mem. Am. Profl. Soc. on Sexual Abuse in Children (bd. dirs. 1986-90). Democrat. Roman Catholic. Fax: 409-762-1163. Office: 4925 Fort Crockett Blvd Apt 510 Galveston TX 77551-5949

GOODWIN, MARCY, architectural planner, consultant; b. San Diego, Mar. 11, 1948; d. Don and Beverly (Stern) G. BFA, Chouinard Art Sch., 1965-69; MFA in Painting, Claremont Grad. Sch., 1969-71. Exhibition coordinator Office of Charles & Ray Eames, Venice, Calif., 1977-79, curator Inventions exhibit, 1977-79; exhibition cons. IBM, Armonk, N.Y., 1980-81; mus. cons. R. Meier & Assocs. Architect, N.Y.C., 1982; bldg. project dir. Mus. Contemporary Art, Los Angeles, 1980-86, Tech. Ctr. Silicon Valley, San Jose, Calif., 1986-87, San Francisco Mus. Modern Art, 1987-89, Napa (Calif.) Valley Arts Found., 1988, Chgo. Mus. Contemporary Art, 1989-90, Wellesley (Mass.) Coll. Art Mus., 1989; bldg. program cons. Mus. Contemporary Art, Chgo., 1988, Craft and Folk Art Mus., L.A., Andy Warhol Mus., Pitts., 1990-92, Latino Mus., L.A., 1991-92, Santa Barbara Mus. Art, 1991-92, Scripps Coll., 1991, Bronx Acad. Arts, 1991, Hoover Dam Visitors Ctr., 1991, Tech. Ctr. Silicon Valley, 1991-92, L.A. County Mus. of Art, Calif., 1993, Walker Art Ctr., Mpls., 1994, Milw. Art M,us., Wis., 1994, Nelson Atkins Mus. of Art, Kansas City, Mo., 1994-95, Jewish Mus. of San Francisco, 1995, Meadows Mus. So. Meth. U., 1995, Ventura County Mus. History and Art, 1995-96, N.C. Mus. Art, 1996-97, Snite Mus. Art U. Notre Dame, 1997, Va. Mus. Fine Arts, 1998, Walker Art Ctr., 1998—, Miami Art Mus., 1998—, Berlinische Galerie, Berlin, 1998, The Tech San Jose Mus. Tech., 1995, Blairton Mus. U. Tex., Austin, 1998-99, Me Nay Mus. Art, 1998-99, RISD Art Mus., 1999, Yale U. Art Mus., 1988—, Seattle Art Mus., 1999, U. Iowa Art Mus., 1998, Duke U. Art Mus., 1999, U. N.Mex. Art Mus., 1996, Albuquerque Mus. History and Art, 1998; curator Automobile and Culture exhibit Mus. Contemporary Art, L.A., 1982-83; design cons. San Diego Arts Ctr., 1984-86, curator On the Drawing Bd. exhibit, 1984-85, J. Jerde exhibit, 1985-86; panelist, speaker Nat. Conf. on Arts and the Handicapped, Washington, 1975, West Week conf. Pacific Design Ctr., Los Angeles, 1984; panel moderator conf. on architecture and art AIA, Los Angeles, 1985; panel moderator annual meeting Am. Assn. Mus., Los Angles, 1986; spl. speaker, seminar dir. Am. Assn. Art Mus. Dirs., Ann. Conf., 1988, 97. Author: LA/ACCESS, 1980-81; contbr. articles to Los Angeles Mag. Calif. Arts Commn. grantee, 1974, 75. Office: M Goodwin Assocs Inc 7461 Beverly Blvd Ste 304 Los Angeles CA 90036-2773

GOODWIN, ROBERT CRONIN, lawyer; b. Cleve., Mar. 17, 1941; s. Robert Clifford and Marion (Schmadel) G.; m. Judith Mary Baxter, June 7, 1968; children: Anne, Helen, Sharon, Katherine. AB, Fordham U., 1963; JD, Georgetown U., 1969. Bar: D.C. 1970, Md. 1990. Vol. Peace Corps, Thailand, 1964-65; asst. cmty. devel. advisor AID, Thailand, 1965-66; atty. advisor Office Gen. Coun., Dept. Commerce, 1969-74; dep. asst. gen. coun. internat. & resouce devel. programs Fed. Energy Adminstrn., Washington, 1974-77, asst. gen. coun. internat. conservation & resource devel., 1977; asst. gen. coun. internat. trade & emergency preparedness Dept. Energy, Washington, 1977-79; ptnr. Thompson, Hine & Flory, 1979-82; v.p., gen. coun. China Energy Ventures, Washington, 1982-86; ptnr. Goodwin & Soble, 1986-90; pvt. practice, 1990-92; exec. v.p., gen. coun., dir. U.S.-China Indsl. Exch., Inc., 1992—; dir. Med. Adv. Sys., Inc., 1999—; guest lectr. internat. petroleum contracts East China Petroleum Inst. Beijing, 1985; frequent lectr. on internat. contracts and Chineses legal and bus. issues; adj. assoc. prof. internat. mgmt. progam, U. Md., 1990—. Editor-in-chief Law and Policy in International Business, 1968-69; co-editor Legal Environ. for Fgn. Direct Investment in U.S., 1994; contbr. articles to profl. jours. Mem. bd. sch. bd., 1980-83. Recipient cert. of Merit Fed. Energy Adminstrn., 1974, cert. Spl. Acheivement, 1974, 76. Mem. ABA, D.C. Bar Assn., Thai-Am. Assn. (chmn. bus. com. 1991, pres. 1995), Nat. Coun. U.S. China Trade (chmn. legal com. 1987), Am. Corp. Counsel Assn., Md.-China Bus. Coun. (bd. dirs., v.p. 1999—). Home: 3710 Bradley Ln Chevy Chase MD 20815-4257 Office: 7201 Wisconsin Ave Ste 703 Bethesda MD 20814-4850

GOODYEAR, JOHN L., artist; b. L.A., Oct. 22, 1930; s. Ronald R. and Lillian Lake G.; m. Anne Dixon, Dec. 12, 1953; children: Sarah Goodyear La Grange, Amy. B of Design, U. Mich., 1952, M of Design, 1954. Instr. U. Mich., Ann Arbor, 1956-62, U. Mass., Amherst, 1962-64; prof. Rutgers U., New Brunswick, N.J., 1964-97. One-man shows include Amel Gallery, N.Y.C., 1964-66, Inhibodress Gallery, Sydney, Australia, 1972, MIT, Cambridge, 1976, N.J. State Mus., Trenton, 1981, Princeton Gallery Fine Arts, N.J., 1987, Pyramid Gallery, N.Y.C., 1989, Snyder Fine Art, N.Y.C., 1992, Frank Martin Gallery, Allentown, Pa., 1995, Michener Mus., Doylestown, Pa., 2000, Ericson Gallery, Phila., 2000; exhibited in group shows at Mus. Modern Art, N.Y.C., 1965, 72, Whitney Mus. Am. Art, N.Y.C., 1966, 68, Milw. Art Ctr., 1968, Chgo. Mus. Contemporary Art, 1968, Albright-Knox Gallery, Buffalo, 1968, MIT, 1973, Neuberger Mus, Purchase, N.Y., 1980, Atrium Gallery, Schenectady, 1985, Macedonian Ctr. for Contemporary Art, Thessalonika, Greece, 1987, Kunsthalle, Karlsruhe, West Germany, 1988, Henri Gallery, Washington, 1989, Amerikahaus, Cologne, 1990, Horodner-Romley Gallery, N.Y.C., 1992, Art Gallery of Hamilton, Can., 1994, N.J. State Mus., Trenton, 1996, Snyder Fine Art, N.Y.C., 1997; represented in permanent collections Whitney Mus. Art, N.Y.C., Princeton U. Art Mus., Neuberger Mus., NYU, Nat. Mus. Am. Art, Smithsonian Instn., Mus. Modern Art, N.Y.C., Mus. des beaux arts de l'Ontario, Toronto, Met. Mus. Art, N.Y.C., Herbert F. Johnson Mus., Ithaca, N.Y., Solomon R. Guggenheim Mus., N.Y.C., British Mus., London, Biblioteque Nat., Paris, Biblioteca di Gallery Nat. Modern Art, Rome. Mem. Am. Abstract Artists. E-mail: goodyear@crusoe.net. Home: 167 Seabrook Rd Lambertville NJ 08530-2406

GOODYER, IAN MICHAEL, psychiatrist; b. London, Nov. 2, 1949; s. Mark Leonard and Belle (Warwick) G.; m. Jane Elizabeth Akister, May 24, 1979; children: Adam, Sarah. MB, BChir, London U., 1974, MD, 1985. Fellow Royal Coll. Psychiatrists, U.K. House officer in medicine, surgery, pediat. Oxford U., Eng., 1974-76, resident in psychiatry, 1976-79; rsch. fellow Brown U., Providence, N.J., 1979-80; sr. registrar Newcastle Health Authority, Eng., 1980-83; cons., sr. lectr. Manchester U., Eng., 1983-87; lectr., child psychiatry Cambridge U., 1987-91, prof. child and adolescent psychiatry, 1992—; v.p. Internat. Assn. of Child/Adolescent Psychiatry, 1994—. Author: Life Experiences, Development and Psychopathology, 1991; editor: The Depressed Child and Adolescent: Developmental and Clinical Perspectives, 1995. Fellow Wolfson Coll. Cambridge. Fellow Royal Coll. Psychiatrists, Acad. Med. Scis. Avocations: physical fitness, guitar. Office: Developmental Psychiatry, 18b Trumpington Rd, Cambridge CB2 2AH, England

GOOI, HOAY BENG, electrical engineer, educator; b. Georgetown, Penang, Malaysia, Aug. 14, 1954; arrived in Singapore, 1991; s. Kin Hai Gui and Mei Ying Chong; m. Lai Lai Siew, June 13, 1983; 1 child, Yi Hua. BEE, Nat. Taiwan U., Taipei, 1978; MEE, U. New Brunswick, Fredericton, Can., 1980; PhD in Elec. Engring., Ohio State U., 1983. Reg. profl. engr., Singapore, Pa. Asst. prof. dept. elec. engring. Lafayette Coll., Easton, Pa., 1983-85; sr. engr. Empros, Plymouth, Minn., 1985-91; assoc. prof. sch. elec. engring. Nanyang Technol. U., Singapore, 1991—; mem. advanced diploma rev. com. Singapore Poly., 1993; mem. adv. com. Exhbn. on Energy, Singapore Sci. Ctr., 1995; mem. com. Singapore Nat. Com. World Energy coun., 1996—. Contbr. articles to IEEE Transaction Power Apparatus Sys., Jour. Elec. Power Engy Sys., Elec. Power Sys. Rsch., Knowledge-Based Sys. Mem. IEEE (sr.). Achievements include design of a new algorithm for calculating ground fault currents, new ordering methods for sparse matrix inversion. Home: 45 Jurong E Ave 1 # 03-02, Singapore 609779, Singapore Office: Sch EEE S1 Block, Nanyang Technol U Nanyang Ave, Singapore 639798, Singapore

GOOKIN, THOMAS ALLEN JAUDON, civil engineer; b. Tulsa, Aug. 5, 1951; s. William Scudder and Mildred (Hartman) G.; m. Sandra Jean Andrews, July 23, 1983. BS with distinction, Ariz. State U., 1975. Registered profl. engr., Calif., Ariz., Nev., land surveyor Ariz., hydrologist. Civil engr., treas. Gookin Engrs. Ltd, Scottsdale, Ariz., 1968—. Chmn. adv. com. Ariz. State Bd. Tech. Registration Engring., 1984—. Recipient Spl. Recognition award Ariz. State Bd. Tech. Registration Engring., 1990. Mem. NSPE, Ariz. Soc. Profl. Engrs. (sec. Papago chpt. 1979-81, v.p. 1981-84, pres. 1984-85, named Young Engr. of Yr. 1979, Outstanding Engring. Project award 1988), Order Engr., Ariz. Congress on Surveying and Mapping, Am. Soc. Civil Engrs., Ariz. Water Works Assn., Tau Beta Pi, Delta Chi (Tempe chpt. treas. 1970-71, sec. 1970, v.p. 1971), Phi Kappa Delta (pres. 1971-73). Republican. Episcopalian. Avocations: Disneyana, science fiction, computer gaming. Home: 10760 E Becker Ln Scottsdale AZ 85259-3868 Office: Gookin Engrs Ltd 4203 N Brown Ave Ste A Scottsdale AZ 85251-3946

GOOLKASIAN, PAULA A., psychologist, educator; b. Methuen, Mass., Aug. 9, 1948; d. Paul K. and Sadie T. (Touma) G.; m. Francis C. Martin, July 29, 1978; 1 child, Christopher. BA, Emmanuel Coll., 1970; MS, Iowa State U., 1972, PhD, 1974. Asst. prof. U. N.C., Charlotte, 1974-79, assoc. prof., 1979-85, prof. psychology, 1985—, pres. faculty, 1989—; cons. in field. Contbr. articles to profl. jours. Nat. Def. Ednl. Act. fellow, 1971-74; grantee NSF, NIH, and numerous others. Mem. AAAS, APA, Am. Psychol. Soc., Psychonomics Soc., Soc. for Computers in Psychology (sec.-treas. 1989-91, pres. 1994), Sigma Xi, Phi Kappa Phi. Home: 20125 River Chase Dr Cornelius NC 28031-7175 Office: U NC Dept Psychology Charlotte NC 28223

GOON, ANTHONY TEIK JIN, dermatologist; b. Georgetown, Penang, Malaysia, July 26, 1967; s. Goon Cheng Huat and Siew Han Foong; m. Sylvia Tzu Li Teo, May 16, 1998; children: Rachel, Hui Zhen. MBBS, Nat. U. Singapore, 1995. Med. diplomate. House officer Ministry of Health, Singapore, 1992-93, med. officer, 1993-98; registrar Nat. Skin Ctr., Singapore, 1998—. Mem. Royal Coll. Physicians. Buddhist. E-mail: anthonygoon@nsc.gov.sg.

GOONETILLEKE, DEVAPRIYA CHITRA RANJAN ALWIS, English language educator; b. Colombo, Sri Lanka, Oct. 9, 1938; s. Richard Arthur Alwis and Tilothamawa (Amerasinghe) G.; m. Chitranganie Lalitha Dalpatadu, Nov. 23, 1967; children: Krishantha Surendra, Dilhan Virendra. BA, U. Ceylon, 1961; PhD, U. Lancaster, Eng., 1970. Asst. lectr. Vidyodaya U., Sri Lanka, 1962-70, lectr., 1970-73; lectr. Vidyalankara Campus, Sri Lanka, 1973-74, sr. lectr., 1974-79; assoc. prof. U. Kelaniya, Sri Lanka, 1979-80, prof., 1980—; dir. studies Buddhist and Pali U., Sri Lanka, 1982-87; DAAD guest prof. U. Tubingen, Germany, 1999-2000. Author: Introducing English Literature Vol. I: First Steps to Literary Criticism, 1975, Vol. II: A Study of Fiction, 1976, Vol. III: A Study of Poetry, 1977, Developing Countries in British Fiction, 1977, Between Cultures: Essays on Literature, Language, and Education, 1987, Images of the Raj: South Asia in the Literature of the Empire, 1988, (with Mona Gooneratne and Mirelle Jayawardena) Learning English: Book I, 1988, Joseph Conrad: Beyond Culture and Background, 1990, Salman Rushdie, 1998; editor: Modern Sri Lankan Stories, 1986, Modern Sri Lankan Poetry, 1987, Modern Sri Lankan Drama, 1991, The Penguin New Writing in Sri Lanka, 1992, Joseph Conrad: Heart of Darkness, 1995, 2d edit., 1999, The Penguin Book of Modern Sri Lanka Stories, 1996, Sri Lankan Literature in English 1948-1998: A 50th Independence Anniversary Anthology, 1998; editor (jour.): Navasilu, 1983, 84, 87, Phoenix, 1990-93; assoc. editor Jour. South Asian Lit., 1980—; regional rep. Jour. Commonwealth Lit., 1978-94; contbr. articles to profl. jours. Commoner Churchill Coll. fellow U. Cambridge, 1977-78, Found. Vis. fellow Clare Hall, U. Cambridge, 1987-88, Henry Charles Chapman Vis. fellow U. London, 1988-89. Mem. Assn. Commonwealth Lit. and Lang. Studies (regional rep. Sri Lanka 1978-92, chmn. 1993-97), Assn. Commonwealth Univs. (scholarship 1966-70), Internat. Fedn. Modern Langs. and Lits. (v.p. 1993-99). Home: 1 Kandawatta Rd, Nugegoda Sri Lanka Office: U Tubingen Sem Eng Philol, Wilhelmstrasse 50, 72074 Tubingen Germany

GOOSSENS, ARIE GERHARD, chemical engineering consultant; b. De Bilt, Utrecht, The Netherlands, May 14, 1939; s. Gerard Goossens and Antoinette Maria van Zuylen; m. Maria Aletta van Bruggen, June 28, 1966 (div. May 1983); 2 children. Ingenieur, MSChemE, Tech. U., Delft, The Netherlands, 1967. Cert. chem. engring. Process engr. Kinetics Tech. Internat., Zoetermeer, The Netherlands, 1967-73, mgr. licensing and tech., 1973-80; sr. devel. engr. Shell Internat. Chemie Maatschappij B.V., The Hague, The Netherlands, 1980-94; ethylene manufacture cons., Bilthoven, The Netherlands, 1994—. Contbr. articles to sci. jours., including Hydrocarbon Processing, Chemiker Zeitung, Nitrogen, AIChE Jour., Indsl. Engring. Chem. Rsch. Avocations: tennis, sailing. Home and Office: Bosuillaan 74, 3722 XP Bilthoven The Netherlands

GOOSSENS, PIERRE JACQUES, mining company executive; b. Brussels, Mar. 17, 1939; s. Jacques and Emilia (Triest) G.; m. Lydia Anne Kreilmann; children: Nathalie, Arnaud-Werner. MSc, U. Louvain, Belgium, 1962, PhD, 1965. Exploration geologist UN, Ecuador, 1965-69; chief geologist UN, Burkina Faso, 1969-70; project mgr. UN, Burma, 1974-77; chief tech. advisor UN, India, 1977-81; asst. prof. U. So. Miss., 1970-71; assoc. prof. Mich. Tech. U., 1971-74; CEO Bur. of Geol. Cons., Braine l'Alleud, Belgium, 1982—; cons. Union Miniere, Belgium, 1981-86; vis. prof. U. Liege, Belgium, 1984—. Author: Musee Royal Afrique Centrale, 1983, Société de L'Industrie Minerale, 1998; contbr. articles to profl. jours. Decorated King Leopold Officer, Govt. Belgium, 1990. Fellow Geol. Soc. Am., Soc. Econ. Geology; mem. Royal Acad. Scis. Belgium. Avocations: tennis, bridge. Home: 1 Ave du Longchamp, 1410 Waterloo Belgium Office: Bur of Geological Cons, 40 Rue de Bois-Seigneur-Isa, 1421 Briane l'Alleud Belgium

GOOVAERTS, PIERRE ETIENNE, agriculture engineering educator; b. Charleroi, Hainaut, Belgium, June 12, 1964; s. Jacques and Bernadette (Philippe) G.; m. Nathalie Marthe Vandecan, Jul. 26, 1988; children: Maxime, Xavier. Degree in agrl. engring., Cath. U. Louvain, 1987, PhD in Agr., 1992. Rsch. asst. Nat. Fund for Sci. Rsch., 1988-92, sr. rsch. scientist, 1994-97; postdoctoral fellow Stanford (Calif.) U., 1993-94; asst. prof. U. Mich., Ann Arbor, 1997—. Author: Geostatistics for Natural Resources Evaluation, 1997; contbr. articles to profl. jours. Lt. Belgian Air Force, 1987-88. Grantee Fulbright, 1993, NATO, 1994, Belgian Am. Ednl. Found., 1993; recipient Vistelius Rsch. award, 1999. Mem. Am. Coun. Geostatistics (mem. exec. com.), Internat. Assn. for Math. Geology, Internat. Assn. Soil Sci. (working group on pedometrics). Avocations: soccer, stamps. Home: 1346 Ravenwood St Ann Arbor MI 48103-2655 Office: U Mich Ewre Bldg Rm 117 Ann Arbor MI 48109-2125

GOPAL, BRIJ, ecologist; b. Muzaffarnagar, India, Mar. 7, 1944; s. Jagdish Pershad and Krishna Kanta (Agrawal) Mittal; m. Madhu Garg (div.); children: Sudha, Anjali, Rajeev. BS, Meerut Coll., India, 1961; MS in Botany, Christ Ch. Coll., Kanpur, India, 1964; PhD, Banaras Hindu U., Varanasi, India, 1968. Postdoctoral fellow Banaras Hindu U., Varanasi, 1969-70; lectr. in botany Agra Coll., 1970-71; asst. prof. botany Rajasthan U., Jaipur, India, 1972-85; assoc. prof. Jawaharlal Nehru U., New Delhi, 1986—, prof., 1998—; vis. prof. Geobotany Inst., Swiss Fed. Inst. Tech., Zurich, 1984. Author: (books) Water Hyacinth, 1987, Plant Ecology and Phytogeography, 1978; editor: (book) Ecology and Management of Aquatic Vegetation in the Indian Subcontinent, 1990, Biodiversity in Wetlands, 2000. Recipient Young Scientist's medal Indian Nat. Sci. Acad., New Delhi, 1974, Alexander von Humboldt fellowship Alexander von Humboldt Stiftung, Bonn, 1982, Internat. Fellow award Soc. Wetland Scientists, 1997. Fellow Nat. Inst. Ecology/India; mem. Internat. Assn. Limnology (chmn. comm. on limnology in developing countries 1989—). Office: Sch Environ Scis, Jawaharlal Nehru U, New Delhi 110067, India

GOPAL, NAKKA, university official, poet; b. Bhongir, Hyderabad, India, June 25, 1948; s. Nakka Chennaiah; m. A. Aruna; children: Chaithanya, Nakka. BA, Osmania U., Hyderabad, 1971, MA, 1973, PhD, 1979, post-grad. diploma in applied linguistics, 1990. 0. Head dept. Telugu, Osmania U., chmn. bd. studies; vice chancellor P.S. Telugu U., Hyderabad, 1999—. Author: (poetry collections) Yellow Flowers, 1976, Milestone, 1981, Colored Lights, 1989, The Bridge, 1993, I Will Not Let Time To Sleep, 1998, Naaneelu, 1998, (lit. essays) Niluvettu Telugu Santhakam-Cinare Vyakthithawam, 1992, Gavaksham, 9192, Vyasanavami, 1996, (prefaces collection) Saalochana, 1998. Recipient Krishna Sastri award Andhra Mahila Sabha, 1978, Dusarathi award Arundhathi Kala Samiti, 1999, Sugunamani Lit. awad Fyostina Kala Peetham, 1999. Home: Hno 13-1/5B Srini Vasapuram, Ramanthapur, AP Hyderabad 500 013, India Office: PS Telugu U, Public Gardens, AP Hyderabad 500 004, India

GOPAL, SARVEPALLI, history educator; b. Madras, India, Apr. 23, 1923; s. Sir Sarvepalli Radhakrishnan (former President of India). Ed. U. Madras, Oxford U.; M.A., D.Phil., D.Litt.; D.Litt. (hon.), Andhra U., 1975, Sri Venkateswere U., Tirupati, 1979, Banaras U., 1984, Hyderebed U., 1993. Lectr., reader in history Andhra U., Waltair, India, 1948-52; asst. dir. Nat. Archives, New Delhi, 1952-54; dir. hist. div. Ministry External Affairs, New Delhi, 1954-66; reader in South Asian history Oxford U. (Eng.), 1966-71, fellow St. Anthony's Coll., 1966-95, hon. fellow, 1996—; prof. contemporary history Jawaharlal Nehru U., New Delhi, 1971-83, prof. emeritus, 1983—; chmn. Nat. Book Trust of India, 1973-76; mem. exec. bd. UNESCO, 1976-80; chmn. Indian Inst. Advanced Study, 1993-98, Inst. Social Scis., 1995-98, Madras (India) Inst. Devel. Studies, 1995-97. Author: The Viceroyalty of Lord Ripon; The Viceroyalty of Lord Irwin; British Policy in India; Jawaharlal Nehru, 3 vols. Radhakrishnan; editor Selected Works of Jawahrlal Nehru, 1969-98, gen. editor, 1998—. Address: 97 Radhakrishna Salai, Mylapore, Madras 600004, India Office: St Antony's Coll, Oxford England*

GOPALA, VAIDYANATHAN, science educator; b. Palur, Tamil Nadu, India, June 17, 1945; s. Gopala Suryanarana Ramapuram and Alamelu Gopala; m. Banumathi Venkataramani, June 20, 1985; children: Vidya, Hari Harasubramanian. BSc, Madras Christian Coll., Tambaram, India, 1960, MSc, 1968, PhD, 1982. Lectr. Am. Coll., Madurai, India, 1970-72, Madur Srmvarts Coll., Coimbatore, India, 1972-73, Coll. Karaikudi, India, 1973-74, Anna U., Madras, 1976-85; from asst. prof. to prof. Pondicherry (India) Engring. Coll., 1985—. Contbr. articles to profl. jours. Mem. Indian Soc. Tech. Edn. (life), Indian Soc. Magnetic Fluid Rsch. Avocation: carnatic vocal music. Office: Pondicherry Engring Coll, Pillaichavady, 605014 Pondicherry India

GOPALAKRISHNAKONE, PONNAMPALAM, medical educator; b. Jaffna, Ceylon, Sept. 23, 1945; arrived in Singapore, 1982; s. Kana and Poniah (Pakiam) Ponnnampalam; m. Premala Balasingham, Aug. 29, 1976; children: Dharshini, Sasheendran. MBBS, U. Ceylon, 1971; PhD, U. London, 1979; DSc, Nat. U. Singapore, 1998. Physician Ministry of Health, Ceylon, 1971-73; demonstrator, anatomy U. Ceylon, 1973-74, lectr. anatomy, 1974-76; rsch. scholar U. London, 1976-79; sr. lectr. U. Ceylon, 1979-82; sr. lectr. Nat. U. Singapore, 1982-91, assoc. prof., 1991-98, prof. anatomy, 1998—; chmn. Venom & Toxin Rsch. Group, Singapore, 1986—; cons. Poison Info. Centre, Singapore, 1990—; founder pres. I.S.T. (Asia-Pacific), 1987-90; rsch. fellow Bio Sci. Centre, Singapore, 1995—. Mem. editl. bd. Toxicon, 1988—; author: A Field Guide to Dangerous Snakes, 1987, Snake Bites and Their Treatment, 1990; editor: Snakes of Medical Importance, 1990, Sea Snake Toxinology, 1994. Recipient Commonwealth Med. Scholarship, Eng., 1976-79, Brit. Coun. award, 1990, WHO fellowships. Fellow Acad. Medicine Singapore; mem. Internat. Soc. Toxinology (coun. mem. 1991—, outstanding univ. rschr. award 1998). Avocations: natural history, photography, computer graphics, exotic pets. Office: Nat U Singapore, Dept Anatomy Faculty Medicine, 119260 Singapore Singapore

GOPALAKRISHNAN, IYYANI KUNJAPPU, chemist, researcher; b. Edathiruthy, India, Oct. 2, 1948; s. Iyyani Gopalan Kunjappu and Munpuveetil Krishnan Subhadra; m. Charangath Ayyappan Suseela, Nov. 1, 1975; children: Mili, Lili. BSc, U. Bombay, 1968, MSc, 1975, PhD, 1989. Sci. asst. Bhabha Atomic Rsch. Ctr., India, 1968-1985, sci. officer, 1985—; vis. scientist Royal Inst. Tech., Sweden, 1991. E-mail: ikgopal@magnum.barc.ernet.in. Home: D6 Indraprastha Anushakti, Nagar Mumbai 400-094, India Office: Bhabha Atomic Rsch Ctr Div, Chemistry, Mumbai 400-085, India

GOPALAKRISHNAN, SRINIVASAN, civil engineer; b. Perundurai, Tamil Nadu, India, July 18, 1946; s. Sitaraman and Janaki Srinivasan; m. Ramamani Gopalakrishnan, Jan. 31, 1975; children: G. Rathipriya, G. Manjunathan. BSc in Civil Engring., U. Peradeniya, Sri Lanka, 1972. Resident engr. Malaysia Internat. Cons., Trengganu, 1973-76, Pahang, 1977-79; resident engr. Jurutera Konsultant (SEA), Kotakinabalu, Malaysia, 1980-83; project mgr. Pub. Wks., Bandar Seri Beghwan, Brunei, 1984-90, Rds. and Traffic Authority, Goulburn, N.S.W., Australia, 1991-97; contract devel. mgr. Rds. and Traffic Authority/ydney Rd. Svc., Yennora, N.S.W., Australia, 1997—. Contbr. articles to profl. jours. Mem. Lions Club. Avocation: chess. Home: 7/239 Marsden Rd, Carlingford NSW 2118, Australia

GOPALAN, MYSORE NARAYANA IYENGAR, engineering educator; b. Mysore, India, May 14, 1935; s. Mysore Narayana Iyengar and Mysore Narayana Iyengar Yeggamma; m. Mysore Narasi Odayar Yadugiri, Apr. 6, 1946. BSc with honors, U. Mysore, 1956, MSc, 1957; PhD, Indian Inst. Tech., Madras, 1973. Statis. asst. dept. stats. Govt. of Karnataka, India, 1958-60; tech. asst. Indian Inst. Tech., Bombay, 1960-62, assoc. lectr., 1962-63, lectr., 1963-73, asst. prof., 1973-81, prof., 1981-95, co-head reliability engring. group, 1984-87, head reliability engring. group, 1988-95; emeritus fellow All India Coun. Tech. Edn., 1995-97, Univ. Grants Commn., 1998-2000; prof. emeritus Sri Jayachamarajendra Coll. Engring., Mysore, India. Fellow The Instn. Engrs. (India), Instn. Electronics and Telecom. Engrs., Indian Instn. Indsl. Engring., Indian Instn. of Plant Engring., Indian Instn. of Prodn. Engring.; mem. Internat. Soc. Reliability Engrs. (founding pres. Indian chpt. 1989-92). Avocations: environmental protection, education, social work. Home: Model House 56 Maruthi Temple St, 4th Main Kuvempu Nagar, Mysore 570009, India Office: Dept Mech Engring, Sri Jayachamarajendra Coll Engring, Mysore 570006, India

GOPALAN, VAIDYANATHAN, physics educator; b. Palur, Tamilnadu, India; s. Ramapuram Suryanayana and Alamelu G.; m. Vaidyanathan Bhanumathy, June 20, 1985; children: Vidya, Hariharasubramanian. BSc in Physics, Madras Christian Coll., 1966, MSc in Physics, 1968; PhD, Madras U., 1982. Lectr. Am. Coll., Madhurai, India, 1970-72, SRMV Arts Coll., Coimbatore, India, 1972-73; demonstrator AC Coll. of Karaikudi, India, 1973-74; sr. instr. CN Poly., Madras, 1974-76; lectr. Anna U., Madras, 1976-85; asst. prof. Pondicherry Engring. Coll., 1985—, head dept. physics, 1985—, prof., 1999—. Contbr. articles to profl. jours. Mem. Indian Soc. Tech. Edn., Indian Soc. Mag. Fluid Res. Avocation: carnatic music (vocal). Office: Pondicherry Engring Coll, Pillaichavadi, Pondicherry 605014, India

GOPALASWAMY, SRINIVASAN, electrical engineer; b. Neyveli, India; s. V. and Jayalakshmi Gopalaswamy; m. Jayashree Gopalan, Dec. 4, 1997. B of Tech., Indian Inst. Tech., 1989; MS, Carnegie Mellon U., 1992, PhD, 1996. Grad. asst. Carnegie Mellon U., Pitts., 1990-96; sr. rsch. engr. Data Storage Inst. Nat. U. Singapore, 1996-98, prin. rsch. engr., 1998-99; design engr. Advanced Rec. Channels Group Quantum Corp., Milpitas, Calif., 2000—. Contbr. articles to profl. jours. Nat. Talent Search scholar Nat. Coun. Edn. Rsch. and Tng., 1985; Tchg. fellow Carnegie Mellon U., Pitts., 1993. Mem. IEEE.

GOPINATH, SUBASH CHANDRA BOSE S., botany researcher; b. May 17, 1971. BS in Botany, Madurai Kamaraj, India, 1991; MS in Botany, Madurai Kamaraj, 1993, PhD in Botany, 1998. Rsch. fellow U.G.C., 1994-96, sr. rsch. fellow, 1996-98; with U. Madras, Chennai. Contbr. articles to profl. jours. Home: Villapuram, Madurai Tamil Nadu 625 012, India Office: U Madras, Guindy Campus, Chennai Tamil Nadu 600 025, India

GOPINATHAN, MAMBULLY CHANDRASEKHARAN, research and development manager; b. Trichur, Kerala, India, Nov. 16, 1954; s. M.K. Chandrasekharan and N.K. Susheela; m. P.K. Prasanna; children: Hima, Greeshma. BS, St. Thomas Coll., India, 1976; MS, Govt. Victoria Coll., India, 1978; MPhil, U. Delhi, India, 1980, PhD, 1983. Doctorate in Botany. Scientist U. Delhi, 1983-86, project coord. All India, 1986-88; dep. mgr. EID Parry (India) Ltd., Madras, India, 1988-89; mgr. R&D EID Parry (India) Ltd., Madras, 1989-93, sr. mgr. R&D, 1993-95, dep. gen. mgr. R&D, 1995—. Contbr. rsch. papers to profl. jours. Mem. All India Biotech Orgn., N.Y. Acad. Sci., Bangalore Club. Avocations: reading scientific and general articles, trekking, table tennis. Home: Karianapalaya, 1187 Anugraha Muniswamappa Garden, Bangalore 560084, India Office: EID Parry (India) Ltd, Devanahalli Rd, 560049 Bangalore India

GOPYCH, PETRO MYKHAYLOVYCH, physics educator, researcher; b. Komarivtsi near Bar, Ukraine, Feb. 17, 1947; s. Mykhaylo Safronovych and Nataliya Mykhaylivna (Shmorgun) G.; m. Raisa Ivanivna Tabanova, Aug. 14, 1971; children: Mykhaylo, Ivan. MSc, Kharkiv (Ukraine) State U., 1971, PhD, 1974, DSc, 1992. Engr. Joint Inst. Nuc. Rsch., Dubna, Russia, 1970; sr. rschr. Kharkiv State U., 1974-79, sr. lectr. dept. physics and techniques, 1979-80, assoc. prof., 1980-90, leading rschr., 1992—; rschr. Tech. U. Dresden, Germany, 1983. Author: (textbook) Nuclear Spectroscopy, 1980; contbr. articles to profl. jours. Mem. Ukrainian Nuc. Soc. Home: PO Pokotilovka, 27 Pushkin St, 62458 Kharkiv Ukraine Office: Kharkiv Nat U, 4 Svoboda Sq, 61077 Kharkiv Ukraine

GORALSKI, DONALD JOHN, public relations executive, counselor; b. Buffalo, Apr. 21, 1957; s. John Bernard and Irene (Kazmierczak) G. BA, Canisius Coll., 1980. Cmty. svc. rep. western N.Y. chpt. March of Dimes Birth Defects Found., Buffalo, 1981-82, pub. rels. dir. western N.Y. chpt., 1982-83; pub. rels. dir. no. Jersey chpt. March of Dimes Birth Defects Found., Fairfield, N.J., 1983-84; pub. rels. dir. Ellis Singer, Greve, St. Paul, Minn., 1984-87, Buffalo, 1984-87; sr. pub. rels. officer Multidisciplinary Ctr. for Earthquake Engring. Rsch., Buffalo, 1987—; guest lectr. U. Buffalo, Buffalo State Coll., Medaille Coll., 1984-88, 95, Canisius Coll., 1990, 95, 97, 99, 2000. Mem. spl. events com. Am. Cancer Soc., Western N.Y. chpt., 1985-86; mem. mktg. subcom. St. Mary's Sch. for Deaf, 1987; mentor Pub. Rels. Student Soc. of Am., Buffalo, 1989-91; mem. Allied Comm. Talent for Literacy, Buffalo, 1990-91; mem. meeting and event planners coun. Univ. at Buffalo, 1992; mem. comm. com. World Assn. Vet. Athletes 1995 Games, 1994-95; mem. ad coun. we. N.Y., 1993 ; mem. comms. com. Buffalo Alliance for Edn., 1993 ; mem. Mayor's Advisory Com. for a City Vision, Buffalo, N.Y., 1994-95; trustee Turner/Carroll H.S., 1996-97; mem. Dr. Marilyn G.S. Watt scholarship com. Canisius Coll., 1997 , May C. Randazzo Meml. scholarship com., 1997 ; liaison State Employees Federated Appeal/United Way, 1998, 99. Mem. Pub. Rels. Soc. Am. (bd. dirs. Buffalo-Niagara chpt. 1987-91, pres.-elect 1992, pres. 1993, past pres. 1994-95, accredited, 1995, assembly del. 1997-99, N.E. dist. sec./treas. 1999, N.E. dist. chair elect 2000, Cert. Recognition 1993, Nat. Chpt. Banner award Buffalo/Niagara chpt. 1993), Pub. Rels. Assn. Western N.Y. (treas. 1986-87, v.p. 1987-88, pres. 1989), Western N.Y. Pub. Rels. and Comm. (exec. steering com. 1987-90, 92-94, chmn. 1994). Avocations: golf, football, reading, current events, on-line computer networks/services. E-mail: goralski@acsu.buffalo.edu. Home: 4284 Coventry Green Cir Williamsville NY 14221-7237 Office: Multidisciplinary Ctr Quake Engring Rsch U Buffalo Red Jacket Quad Buffalo NY 14261-0001

GORARD, DAVID A., gastroenterologist; b. London, Dec. 23, 1960; s. William J. and Antonia Gorard; m. Philippa M. Cooper, June 7, 1986; children: Lucy, Camilla, Henry. MB, BChir, St. Mary's Hosp. Med. Sch., London, 1984; MD, U. London, 1994. Registrar Westminster & Queen Mary's Hosp., London, 1987-89; rsch. fellow St. Bartholomew's Hosp., London, 1990-94; sr. registrar Royal London Hosp., 1994-96; cons. physician Wycombe Hosp., Bucks, England, 1996—. Contbr. articles to profl. jours. Mem. Royal Coll. Physicians, British Soc. Gastroent. Office: Wycombe Hosp, High Wycombe, Bucks HP11 2TT, England

GORAS, LIVIU, engineering educator; b. Iasi, Romania, Oct. 20, 1948; s. Teodor and Elena (Neagu) G.; m. Tecla Castelia Alexandrescu, Nov. 21, 1981; 1 child, Bogdan Tudor. Diploma in Elec. Engring., Tech U. Iasi, 1971, PhD in Fundamentals of Elec. Engring., 1978. Rschr. P. Poni Inst. Macromolecular Chemistry, Iasi, Romania, 1971-73; asst. prof. Tech U. Gh. Asachi, Iasi, 1973-78, lectr., 1978-91, assoc. prof., 1991-94, prof. engring., 1994—, vice dean faculty electronics and telecomm., 1990-92, vice rector, 1996-2000. Author: Signals, Circuits and Systems, 1994; contbr. articles to profl. jours. Mem. IEEE (chmn. circuits and systems chpt. 1996—), European Circuit Soc. Mem. Orthodox Ch. Avocations: music, literature. Home: sc Al, et 3, ap 10, Str St Lazar 53 Bl A1, 6600 Iasi Romania Office: Tech U Gh Asachi, Bd Copou 22, 6600 Iasi Romania

GORAY, GERALD ALLEN, real estate executive, lawyer; b. Detroit, Aug. 22, 1939; s. James A. and Lucille (Rankin) G.; m. Donna Marie Belian, Apr. 26, 1958; children: Brian M., Gregory D. BBA magna cum laude, U. Detroit, 1963; JD, U. Mich., 1965. Bar: Mich. Atty. Parsons, Tennant et al, Birmingham, Mich., 1966-70, U.S. Dept. of Housing, Detroit, 1970-71, Rodgers & Goray, Southfield, Mich., 1971-75; pres. Goray Devel. Co., Boca Raton, Fla., 1975—; bd. dirs. Monroe (Mich.) Bank & Trust, 1968-70; ptnr. Nat. Self-Storage Equities Fla., Tucson, 1984—; pres. Stonemark Devel. Co., Boca Raton, 1988—. Vice-chmn. Lathrup Village (Mich.) Zoning Bd. Appeals, 1981. Mem. Village Athletic Club (pres. 1975-76). Office: Goray Devel Co 621 NW 53rd St Ste 255 Boca Raton FL 33487-8281

GORBACHEV, MIKHAIL SERGEYEVICH, former president of the former Union of Soviet Socialist Republics; b. Stavropol, Krai, USSR, Mar. 2, 1931; m. Raisa Maximovna, 1953; 1 child, Irina. Grad., Faculty of Law, Moscow State U., 1955, Stavropol Agrl. Inst., 1967; D (hon.), U. Alaska, 1990, U. Bristol, Eng., 1993, U. Durnham, Eng., 1995. active Komsomol and Party work, 1955-91, 1st sec. Stavropol city Komsomol com., dept. head Propaganda dept., 2nd and 1st sec. Stavropol Krai Komsomol Com., 1955-62; party organizer Stavropol Territorial Prodn. Bd. Collective and State Farms, then head dept. party bodies Stavropol, Krai Party Com., 1962-66, 2nd sec., 1968-70, 1st sec., 1970-78; 1st sec. Stavropol city CPSU Com., 1966-68; mem. Ctrl. Com. Communist Party Soviet Union, 1971-91, sec., 1978-85, gen. sec., 1985-91, alt. mem. Ctrl. Com. Politburo, 1979-80, mem. 1980-91; dep. USSR Supreme Soviet, 1970-89, head fgn. affairs com., 1984-85; mem. Presidium, 1985-88, chair, 1988-89; dept. Congress People's Deputies USSR, 1989-90, chair Supreme Soviet, 1989-90; exec. pres. Soviet Union, 1990-91; head Internat. Found. for Social Econ. and Polit. Studies, Moscow, 1992—, Internat. Green Cross, 1993—. Author: Perestroika: New Thinking for Our Country and the World, 1987, The August Coup: Its Cause and Results, 1991, December 91, My Stand, 1992, The Years of Hard Decisions, 1993, Erinnerungen, 1995, Life and Reforms, 1995, Reflections on the Past and Future, 1998, Moscow, 1998. Decorated Order of Red Banner of Labour, 3 Orders of Lenin, Order of October Revolution, Order Badge of Honour, others; recipient Indira Gandhi award, 1987, Nobel peace prize, 1990, Peace award World Meth. Coun., 1990, Albert Schweitzer leadership award, 1992, Ronald Reagan freedom award, 1992, Hon. Citizen of Berlin, 1992, Freeman of Aberdeen, 1993, Urania-Medaille, Berlin, 1996, over 40 others. Office: Internat Found Socio-Econ and Polit Studies, Leningradsky Prospect 49, 125468 Moscow Russia*

GORBACHEV, VALERY NIKOLAEVICH, physics educator; b. St. Petersburg, Russia, Oct. 31, 1951; s. Nikolay Dmitrievich and Ludmila Evgenievna Gorbachev; m. Marina Vladimirovna Geracimova, Nov. 20, 1974; children: Ekaterina, Tatiana. MS in Physics, Radiophysics, State U., St. Petersburg, 1977. Rsch. engr. Inst. Physics of State U., St. Petersburg, 1973-89; asst. prof. physics Trade Econ. Inst., St. Petersburg, 1990-95; assoc. prof. physics Inst. Moscow State U. of Printing, St. Petersburg, 1995—; rschr. Inst. Physics of State U., St. Petersburg. Avocations: quantum computing, painting. Home: Babushkina 29-2-86, 193029 St Petersburg Russia Office: St Petersburg Inst, Moscow State U Printing Djambula 13, 191180 St Petersburg Russia

GORBUNOV, LEONID MIKHAILOVICH, physicist; b. Moscow, Russia, Aug. 4, 1934; s. Mikhail Petrovich and Ecaterina (Gavrilovna) G.; m. Galina Anatol'evna Sokolina; 1 child, Alexei. Grad., Moscow State U., 1956; Candidate of Sci. in Physics, Lebedev Phys. Inst., Moscow, Russia, 1965, DSc in Physics, 1974, Prof., 1991. Scientist Bur. Stds., Moscow Region, Russia, 1957-61; postgrad. student Lebedev Phys. Inst., Moscow, Russia, 1961-64, scientist, 1964-71, sr. scientist, 1971-85, prin. rsch. scientist, 1985—; prof. People's Friendship U., Moscow, 1978-91; sci. sec. attestational coun. for doctoral sci. conferment, 1980—; mem. sci. coun. Lebedev Phys. Inst., Moscow, 1990—; invited prof. U. Paris-Sud, Orsay, France, 1994-96. Author: (textbook) Instroduction in Plasma Electrodynamics, 1992; contbr. more than 140 articles to profl. jours. Mem. trade union coun. Lebedev Phys. Inst., 1968-74. Recipient prize Govt. Soviet Union, 1987; grant In-

ternat. Sci. Found., 1994, Russia Found. for Basic Rsch., 1993-99. Mem. U.S. Nat. Geog. Soc. Avocations: tourism (boat, bicycle, ski), drawing, classical music. Home: Michurinski pr 12/1, Ap 73, 117192 Moscow Russia Office: Lebedev Phys Inst, Leninski pr 53, 117924 Moscow Russia

GORBUNOV, MIKHAIL EVGENIEVICH, physicist; b. Moscow, Sept. 7, 1960; s. Evgeny Aleksandrovcih and Valentina Mikhailovna (Dubilt) G.; m. Natalia Sergeyevna Tikhonova, Jan. 24, 1987; children: Gleb, Marina. Phys. Diplomate, Moscow Physical-Tech. Inst., 1983; PhD, Inst. for Atmospheric Physics, Moscow, 1989. Cert. physicist. Minor scientist Inst. for Atmospheric Physics, Moscow, 1986-90, scientist, 1990-92, sr. scientist, 1992—; Author reports, contbr. articles to profl. jours. Avocation: music. Home: Znamenskie Sadki 7, 113628 Moscow Russia Office: Inst Atmospheric Physics, Pyzhevsky Per 3, 109017 Moscow Russia

GORBUNOVS, ANATOLIJS, engineer, construction specialist, politician; b. Ludza Distr., Republic of Latvia, 1942; married; 1 child. Diploma, Riga (Latvia) Poly. Inst., Latvia, 1970; grad., Acad. Social Scis., Moscow, 1978. Constructor on state farm Rural Design Inst., 1959-62; sec. Komsomol com. Riga Poly. Inst., 1969-70, sr. lectr., 1970-74; various offices Latvian Communist Party, 1974-88; presidium, chmn. presidium Supreme Coun. Latvia SSR, 1988-90, chmn., 1990-93; chmn. 5th Saeima Latvia, 1993-95; dep. 6th Saeima Latvia, 1995-96; min. environ. protection and regional devel. Ministry Environ. Protection, Riga, 1996-98, dep. prime min., chmn. Latvian-Russian Intergovtl. Commn., 1996-99; minister of transp. Ministry Transport, Riga, 1998—; chmn. European Affairs Com; mem. Com. of Nat. Economy and Agriculture; mem. land com. 6th Saeima Republic Latvia, 1995-96. Served with Soviet Mil. Forces, 1962-65.

GORCZYNSKA, ELEONORA, physiologist, researcher; b. Gniezno, Poland, July 1, 1955; arrived in Australia, 1988; d. Ryszard Ptak and Helena Gertruda (Smorgol) Biernacka; m. Jan Maciej, Feb. 10, 1979 (div. 1984). BSc, U. Szczecin, 1979, MSc, 1979; PhD, U. Nicholas Copernicus, Torun, Poland, 1983. Lic. molecular biologist. Rsch. asst. Pomeranian Med. U., Szczecin, 1979-83, postdoctoral fellow, 1984-85; sr. lectr. U. Agrl. Sci., Szczecin, 1985-87; rsch. fellow U. Nottingham, Eng., 1987-88, U. Sydney, Australia, 1988—; cons. Pharm. Co., Polfa, Poland, 1983-87. Contbr. articles to profl. jours. Recipient Primus Inter Pares, U. Szczecin, Poland, 1979, Silver medal of Nicholas Copernicus, U. Szczecin, 1979. Mem. Australian Physiol. and Pharmacol. Soc., Endocrine Soc. Australia. Avocations: art, surrealistic painting. Office: U Sydney, Dept Medicine, Sydney 2006 NSW, Australia

GORDEEV, ALEXANDER VASILIEVICH, physics researcher, editor; b. Dmitrov, Moscow Region, Russia, July 7, 1936; s. Vasilii Vasilievich and Maria Ivanovna (Guseva) G.; m. Nadezhda Alexandrovna Dobrovol'skaja, Apr. 28, 1973 (div. Jan. 1985); children: Ivan, Andrew. PhD, Kurchatov Inst., Moscow, 1978, DSc, 1988. Sr. lab. asst. Inst. Phys. Problems, Moscow, 1959; sr. lab. asst. Kurchatov Inst. Russian Rsch. Ctr., Moscow, 1959-66, jr. rschr., 1966-80, sr. rschr., 1980-90, leading rschr., 1990—; expert Russian Found. for Basic Rsch., Moscow, 1996-98. Author: Magnetic Self Insulation of Vacuum Coaxial Lines, 1978; co-author: Generation and Focusing of High-Current Relativistic Electron Beams, 1990; sci. editor Plasma Physics Reports; author poems; contbr. articles to profl. jours. Grantee Soros Fond., 1995. Avocations: poetry, drawing in pencil, tourism. Home: Ulitsa Marshala Meretskova, House 12 Apt 10, 123060 Moscow Russia Office: Russ Rsch Ctr Kurchatov Ins, Kurchatov Sq 1, 123182 Moscow Russia

GORDEEV, EVGENII ILJICH, physicist, science administrator; b. Orenburg, USSR, Nov. 25, 1948; s. Ilya A. and Antonina T. (Lapshina) G.; m. Lubov V. Kirnosenko, Apr. 22, 1972; children: Denis E., Antonina E. MS, U. Moscow, 1972, D in Physics and Maths., 1980. Researcher Inst. Volcanology, Petropavlovsk-Kamchatsky, USSR, 1972-79; chief lab. Inst. Volcanology, Petropavlovsk-Kamchatsky, 1979-80, chief dept., 1980-96; dir. Geophys. Svc. Kamchatkian dept. Russian Acad. Scis., Petropavlovsk-Kamchatsky, 1997—; prof. Hokkaido U. Contbr. articles to profl. jours. NATO-CNR grantee NATO, 1997. Mem. Am. Geophys. Union. E-mail: gord@emsd.iks.ru. Home: Abelya 27 apt 22, 683006 Petropavlovsk-Kamchatsky Russia Office: Geophys Svc, Bld Pijpa 9, 683006 Petropavlovsk-Kamchatsky Russia

GORDETSOV, ALEXANDER SERGEYEVICH, chemistry educator, researcher; b. Nizhnii Novgorod, Russia, May 11, 1946; s. Sergei Ivanovich and Nina Ivanovna (Antropova) G.; m. Olga Alexandrovna Gavriluk, May 27, 1968; children: Elena, Svetlana. Chemistry D., Tech. U. N. Novgorod, 1978; PhD, Technol. Inst. St. Petersburg, 1992. Jr. rschr. Inst. Nitric Industry, Dzerjinsk, 1969-78; sr. rschr. Med. Acad. N. Novgorod, 1978-79, lectr., 1979-86, assoc. prof., 1986-93, prof., 1993-95, head chem. chair, 1995—. Contbr. articles to profl. jours. Capt. Soviet Army, 1970-71. Soros Fund grantee, 1993. Mem. European-Asian Acad. Med. Sci. N. Novgorod (corr.)., N.Y. Acad. Scis. Baptist. Avocations: painting, reading. Home: 13-12 Politboitsov St, 603138 Nizhny Novgorod Russia Office: Med Acad N Novgorod, 10/1 Minin Sq, 603000 Nizhny Novgorod Russia

GORDIMER, NADINE, author; b. Republic of South Africa, Nov. 20, 1923; d. Isidore and Nan (Myers) Gordimer; m. Reinhold Cassirer, Jan. 29, 1954; children: Oriane, Hugo. Ed., Convent Sch., Springs, Republic of South Africa. Author: (story collections) Face to Face, 1949, The Soft Voice of the Serpent, 1952, Six Feet of the Country, 1956, Friday's Footprint, 1960 (W.H. Smith and Son Literary award 1961), Not for Publication, 1965, Livingstone's Companions, 1971, Selected Stories, 1975, Some Monday for Sure, 1976, A Soldier's Embrace, 1980, Something Out There, 1984, Crimes of Conscience, 1991, Jump, 1991, Why Haven't You Written?, 1992; (polit. and lit. essays) The Essential Gesture, 1988, Three in a Bed, 1991, Living in Hope and History: Notes From Our Century, 1999; (literary criticism) The Black Interpreters, 1973, Writing & Being: Charles Eliot Norton Lectures, 1995; (essays) Living in Hope and History: Notes from Our Century, 1999; (novels) The Lying Days, 1953, A World of Strangers, 1958, Occasion for Loving, 1963, The Late Bourgeois World, 1966, A Guest of Honour, 1970 (James Tait Black Meml. prize 1973), The Conservationist, 1974 (Booker prize for fiction Eng. 1974), Burger's Daughter, 1979, July's People, 1981, A Sport of Nature, 1987, My Son's Story, 1991, None to Accompany Me, 1994, The House Gun, 1998; (other) On the Mines, 1973, Lifetimes Under Apartheid, 1986; editor: (with Lionel Abrahams) Southern African Writing Today, 1967. Decorated comdr. de l'Ordre des Arts et des Lettres (France), 1986; recipient Thomas Pringle award English Acad. South Africa, 1969, CNA award, 1974, 79, 81, 91, Grand Aigle d'Or, 1975, Disting. Svc. in Lit. Commonwealth award, 1981, MLA award, 1982, Nelly Sachs prize (Germany), 1985, Malaparte award (Italy), 1986, Bennett award, 1986, Benson medal, 1990, Nobel Prize for Literature, 1991; Neil Gunn fellow Scottish Arts Coun., 1981. Fellow Royal Soc. Lit.; mem. AAAS, Com. European Authors, Am. Acad. (hon.), Inst. Arts and Letters (hon.), PEN (v.p.). *

GORDON, ANTHONY GRANT, psychologist, audiologist; b. Carmarthen, Wales, Oct. 15, 1942; s. Ian Grant and Mary Josephine (Miller) G.; m. Ann Diane Hitchings, May 28, 1966 (div. Mar. 1975); children: Neil Christopher, Lynn Margaret; m. Mavis Anne Frisby, Oct. 28, 1978. BSc in Psychology, London U., 1969. Cert. audiological scientist. Rsch. asst. Inst. Laryngology and Otology, London, 1970-71; audiology technician King's Coll. Hosp., London, 1973-84; audiologist Mayday Hosp., Croydon, 1985-86; sci. reader Oxford English Dictionary, Oxford U. Press, 1989—; ind. sci. rsch. London. Contbr. articles to med. and sci. jours. Mem. Cmty. Health Coun., Southwark, London, 1993—. Fellow Royal Soc. Medicine. Avocations: cricket, literary competitions, cycling, television. Home: 32 Love Walk, London SE5 8AD, England

GORDON, ARNOLD MARK, lawyer; b. Norwich, Conn., Oct. 2, 1937; s. Barney and Rose (Bilsky) G.; m. Carolyn. BSBA, Wayne State U., Detroit, 1959, JD, 1962. Bar: Mich. 1962. With Gordon & Gordon P.C. and predecessor firms, Southfield, Mich.; arbitrator Am. Arbitration Assn., 1969—; lectr. in field. Mem. Am. Coll. Trial Lawyers, State Bar Mich. (chmn. med.-legal com. 1976—, negligence sect. 1977-78, pub. negligence sect. bull.), Detroit Bar Assn. (co-chmn. trial advocacy program continguing legal edn. 1972—), Assn. Trial Lawyers Am. (exec. bd. Mich. 1967—), Mich., Detroit trial lawyers assns., Tau Epsilon Rho. Club: Masons. Office: Gordon & Gordon PC 18411 W 12 Mile Rd Ste 200 Southfield MI 48076-2663

GORDON, COREY LEE, lawyer; b. Mpls., Aug. 22, 1956; s. Jack I. and LaVerne (Shedlov) G.; m. Ciel Schaeffer, Aug. 29, 1982; children: Jared Isaac, Lian Miriam. BA, Macalester Coll., 1976; JD cum laude, U. Minn., 1980. Bar: Minn. 1980, U.S. Dist. Ct. Minn. 1981, U.S. Ct. Appeals (8th cir.) 1983, U.S. Supreme Ct. 1983, Wis. 1987, U.S. Dist. Ct. (ea. and we. dists.) Wis. 1987, N.Y. 1991, U.S. Dist. Ct. (so. dist.) N.Y. 1991, U.S. Ct. Appeals (3d cir.) 1992, Ill. 1993, U.S. Dist. Ct. (no. dist.) Ill. 1995, Fla. 1995, U.S. Dist. Ct. (we., ea., and no. dists.) N.Y. 1999, U.S. Ct. Appeals (11th cir.) 1999, U.S. Ct. Appeals (7th cir.) 1999, U.S. Dist. Ct. (so. and ctrl. dists.) Ill. 1999, U.S. Ct. Appeals (2d cir.) 1999, U.S. Dist. Ct. (so. and no. dists.) Fla. 2000. Assoc. Fried, Frank, Harris, Shriver & Jacobson, N.Y.C., 1980-81; ptnr. Shapiro, Lavintman & Gordon P.A., Mpls., 1982-85; assoc. Robins, Zelle, Larson & Kaplan, St. Paul, 1986-88; ptnr. Robins, Kaplan, Miller & Ciresi, Mpls., 1989—; bd. dirs. Jewish Family and Children's Svc. of Mpls., 1992-96, Mpls. Fedn. for Jewish Svc., 1994-99. Treas. The H.H.H. Fund, Minn., 1984-89; bd. dirs., sec.-treas. Minn. Humane Soc., 1985-86; active Dem. Farm Labor Party; trustee Bet Shalom Synagogue, 1992-93, v.p., 1993-97, pres., 1997-99. Mem. ABA, ATLA (co-chair inadequate security litigation group 1992-95). Jewish. Avocations: folk music, scuba diving, photography. Home: 2640 Glenhurst Pl Saint Louis Park MN 55416-3957 Office: Robins Kaplan Miller & Ciresi 2800 LaSalle Pla 800 Lasalle Ave Ste 2800 Minneapolis MN 55402-2015

GORDON, CYRUS HERZL, Orientalist, archaeologist, educator; b. Phila., June 29, 1908; s. Benjamin Lee and Dorothy (Cohen) G.; m. Joan Elizabeth Kendall, Sept. 22, 1946 (dec. 1985); children: Deborah J. Gordon Friedrich, Sarah Y. Gordon Krakauer, Rachel K. Gordon Bernstein, Noah D., Dan K; m. Constance Victoria Wallace, Oct. 18, 1986. AB, U. Pa., 1927, MA, 1928, PhD, 1930; D Hebrew Letters (hon.), Balt. Hebrew Coll., 1981; DHL (hon.), Hebrew Union Coll., 1985; LittD (hon.), Boston Hebrew Coll., 1995; D Hebrew Laws (hon.), Gratz Coll., 1996. Instr. semitics U. Pa., 1930-31; field archaeologist, fellow Am. Schs. Oriental Research, Near East, 1931-35; tchg. fellow Oriental Sem., Johns Hopkins U., 1935-38; lectr. Bible, Smith Coll., 1938-39, 40-41; mem. Inst. Advanced Study, Princeton, N.J., 1939-40, 41-42; prof. Assyriology and Egyptology, Dropsie U., Phila., 1946-56; prof. Near Eastern studies Brandeis U., Waltham, Mass., 1956-73, prof. emeritus, 1973—, also chmn. dept. Mediterranean studies, 1958-73, dir. Grad. Sch., 1957-58, assoc. dean faculty, 1957-58; Gottesman prof. Hebrew studies NYU, 1973-89, prof. emeritus, 1989—; dir. Ctr. Ebla Rsch., NYU, 1982—; vis. fellow humanities U. Colo., 1967; Gay lectr. Simmons Coll., 1970; vis. prof. NYU, 1970-73; vis. fellow Japan Found., 1974; vis. prof. history and anthropology U. N.Mex., 1976; vis. prof. humanities S.W. Mo. State U., 1977-79; Disting. vis. prof. N.Mex. State U., Las Cruces, 1979-80; vis. prof. Judaic studies SUNY, Albany, 1981-82, U. Hawaii, Honolulu, 1988; Del Grauer lectr. U. B.C., Vancouver, 1988; vis. Brownstone prof. Dartmouth Coll., 1990; vis. prof. Maritime Civilizations, U. Haifa, Israel, 1993; elected Soc. Scholars, Johns Hopkins U., 1990—; archeol. expdns.; lectr. Cornell U., 1992. Author: Ugaritic Grammar, 1940, Ugaritic Handbook, 1947, Ugaritic Manual, 1955, The Living Past, 1941, Adventures in the Nearest East, 1957, Ugaritic Literature, 1949, Smith College Tablets, 1952, Introduction to Old Testament Times, 1953, Hammurapi's Code, 1957, The World of the Old Testament, 1958, rev. as The Ancient Near East, 1965, rev., expanded edition (by C.H. Gordon and G.A. Rendsburg), 1997, Before the Bible, 1963, rev. as The Common Background of Greek and Hebrew Civilizations, 1965, Ugaritic Textbook, 1965, rev. with supplement, 1967, 2nd rev. printing, 1998, Ugarit and Minoan Crete, 1966, Forgotten Scripts, 1968, rev. edit., 1971, rev. and enlarged edits., 1982, 87, Before Columbus, 1971, Riddles in History, 1974, The Pennsylvania Tradition of Semitics, 1986, The Background to Jewish Studies in the Bible and in the Ancient East, 1994, A Scholar's Odyssey, 2000; contbg. author, editor Pub. Ctr. for Ebla Rsch., vol. 1, 1987, vol. 2, 1990, vol. 4, 2000; also numerous articles; contbg. editor Am. Jour. Archaeology, 1938-45; edtl. coun. Encounter, 1956; internat. adv. coun. Jewish Quar. Review, 1979-82. Trustee, Boston Hebrew Coll.; corr. mem. Inst. Antiquity and Christianity Claremont Grad. Sch. and Univ. Center; trustee Internat. Council Etruscan Studies of Order of Holy Cross; mem. mng. com. Am. Sch. Classical Studies, Athens, 1958-73. Served as officer U.S. Army, 1942-46; col. USAF Res., ret.; flight comdr. Boston Air Res. Center 1958-61; moblzn. assignee Hdqrs. U.S. Army, 1961-67. Harrison scholar U. Pa., 1928-29; Harrison fellow, 1929-30; Am. Council Learned Socs. fellow, 1932-33; Am. Scandinavian Found. fellow, 1939; recipient Alumni award Gratz Coll., Phila., 1961, cert. of merit Acad. for Jewish Religion, 1991; honored 4 Festschriften: Orient and Occident: Essays presented to Cyrus H. Gordon on the Occasion of his 65th Birthday, 1973, The Bible World: Essays in Honor of Cyrus H. Gordon, 1980, A Synthesis of Cultures: Essays on the Major Contributions of Cyrus Gordon, 1996, Boundaries of the Ancient Near Eastern World: A Tribute to Cyrus H. Gordon—Four Score and Ten, 1998. Fellow Am. Acad. Arts and Scis., Royal Asiatic Soc. (hon.), Am. Acad. Jewish Rsch., Explorers Club; mem. Am. Hist. Assn., Am. Oriental Soc. (exec. com. 1964-67), Am. Philol. Assn., Archaeol. Inst. Am., Soc. Bibl. Lit. and Exegesis, Soc. for Nr. Ea. Studies in Japan (hon.).

GORDON, EDWARD HARRISON, choral conductor, educator; b. N.Y.C., Aug. 24, 1946; s. James Sumter and Marguerite Catherine (Thomas) G.; m. Marilyn Clarke, Oct. 21, 1967; children: Harrison, Eva. BA, Bklyn. Coll., 1972; MA, Columbia U., 1977, MEd, 1983. Choir dir. various area jr. high schs., N.Y.C., 1972-84; choir dir., coord. music Boys and Girls H.S., Bklyn., 1984-88; choir dir., coord. Carnasie H.S., Bklyn., 1988-94; choir dir. Thomas Jefferson H.S., Bklyn., 1994-98, John Dewey H.S., Bklyn., 1998—; pres. Nubian Conservatory Music, Bklyn., 1977—, mem. chancellor's music com. Author: Black Classical Musicians, 1978; condr. A Collection of Afro-American Spirituals, 1978, also others. Treas. Winthrop St Block Assn., Bklyn., 1991; appt. chancellor Music Comm., 1998; apptd. cultural com. Cmty. Planning Bd., 1998. With U.S. Army, 1967-69, Vietnam. Mem. Assn. Supervision and Curriculum Devel., United Fedn. Tchrs., Kappa Delta Pi. Presbyterian. Avocations: archery, chess. Home: 233 Winthrop St Brooklyn NY 11225-3811 Office: John Dewey H S 50 Avenue X Brooklyn NY 11223-5799

GORDON, FLORENCE IRENE, graphic artist, illustrator; b. L.A., Oct. 22, 1928; d. Harry and Etta (Goldstein) Gronoff; widowed; 1 child. Student, Chounard Art Inst., L.A., Santa Monica City Coll.; BA, Art Ctr., L.A. Graphic artist Ned North Enterprises, L.A.; artist Hawaii Newspaper, Oahu; tech. illustrator Northrop-Aircraft, L.A., McDonnell Douglas, L.A. Exhibited in group shows. Art scholar Chounard Art Inst., 1950. Home: 5166 Sepulveda Blvd Apt 208 Culver City CA 90230-5235

GORDON, GILLIAN WENDY, company training and communication consultant; b. Enfield, Middlesex, Eng., Dec. 28, 1950; d. Thomas William and Gwendoline Arabella (Drake) Hollands; m. Thomas Gordon, Oct. 25, 1975; children: Isobel Shona, Peter David Thomas. Assoc. in Singing, Guildhall Sch. Music and Drama, London, 1972, Assoc. in Piano, 1973; grad. in Pers. and Devel., U. of West of Eng., Bristol, 1996. Lic. trainer quantum reading. Piano tchr. Inner London Edn. Authority, 1970-75; prof. piano Medina Sch. Music, Finchley, Eng., 1973-75; freelance musician Avon, Eng., 1976-87; advt. and comm. exec. Eng., 1987-89, freelance comm. and mktg. cons., 1989-91; tng. and devel. advisor Das Legal Expenses Ins. Co., Bristol, 1991-98, asst. human resources mgr.; mktg. dir. Novus 2000, London, 1990-94, tng. dir., 1997—; tng. dir. The Doorway Tngs. Ltd., London, 1990-94; chair Chartered Ins. Inst. Tng. and Devel. Forum, London, 1999—; mem. com. Ins. Industry/Edn. Group, Bristol, 1991-95; assoc. trainer Key Learning, London, 1998—. Appeared in numerous musical performances. Roller skating coach Stratfordpark Skating Club, Stroud Gloucestershire, Eng., 1992—, club sec., 1996; music adjudicator Music Festivals, Bristol, 1994, 95, 96, 98, 99. E-mail: g gordon@dos.co.uk. Office: Das Legal Expenses Ins Co, Quayside Temple Back, Bristol BS1 6NH, England

GORDON, HARRY, telecommunications consultant; b. N.Y.C., Dec. 10, 1954; s. Harry and Edith Gordon; m. Kathleen June Schatzel, Nov. 9, 1985; children: Kristin, Jessica. BS in Comms. and Leadership, Duquesne U., 1995, MA, 1997. Sales specialist AT&T Corp., Pitts., 1983-88, sys. cons., 1988-98; applications cons. Lucent Techs., Pitts., 1998—. Roman Catholic. Avocation: financial analysis. Office: Lucent Techs 5315 Campbells Run Rd Pittsburgh PA 15205-9019

GORDON, HELEN TATE, nurse assistant; b. Washington, Ga., Dec. 17, 1948; d. Geraldine Tate; m. Marvin Gordon (div. 1968); children: Stedric, Itanza. Grad. high sch., Atlanta; cert. acad. excellence, Atlanta Met. Coll., 1990. Cert. nurse asst. Data transcriber IRS, Chamblee, Ga., 1966-67; sec.-steno IRS, Atlanta, 1967-70, U.S. Dept. Labor, Atlanta, 1970-77; sec.-steno U.S. Dept. Transp., Atlanta, 1977-80, equal opportunity specialist, 1980-83, adminstrv. officer, safety officer, 1984-85; adminstrv. sec. Atlanta Job Corps/MTC, Atlanta, 1986-90; adminstrv. asst. Spelman Coll., Atlanta, 1990-93; cert. nurse asst. Imperial Health Care Ctr., Atlanta, 1995-97, Sun Rise Care & Rehab., Atlanta, 1997-98, IHS of Atlanta Buckhead, 1999—. Recipient Adminstr. Safety award Fed. Hwy. Adminstrn., 1985. Baptist. Avocation: sewing. Office: IHS of Atlanta Buckhead 54 Peachtree Park Dr NE Atlanta GA 30309-1304

GORDON, IAN LEWIS, history educator, academic administrator; b. Sydney, Australia, Oct. 16, 1954; s. Cameron Wallace and Helen (Orea) G.; m. Chaity Tan, June 12, 1998. BA with honours, U. Sydney, 1986; MA, U. Rochester, N.Y., 1989, PhD, 1993. Meatworker South Australian Meat Corp., Adelaide, 1976; libr. technician State Libr. of NSW, Sydney, 1977-79, systems team officer, 1980; judgments officer Law Cts. Libr., Sydney, 1981-83; rsch. assoc. Archives Centre Smithsonian Instn., Washington, 1992-93; head of faculty of visual comm. KvB Inst. Tech., Sydney, 1994-97; acting dir. residential colls., U. So. Queensland, Towoomba, Australia, 1998-99; asst. prof. Nat. U. of Singapore, 1999; cons. State Libr. of NSW Press, Sydney, 1994; mem. Libr. Technician Course adv. bd., Sydney, 1980. Author: Comic Strips and Consumer Culture, 1890-1945, 1998, (book chpt.) Bonzer: Australian Comics, 1900s-1990s, 1999; contbr. articles to profl. jours. Treas. Libr. Assn. of Australia, 1983-84; sec. Sydney U. Postgrad. Rep. Assn., 1987; editor H-AMSTDY Internet discussion list, 1999—; mem. editl. bd. Australasian Jour. Am. Studies, 1999—. H.J. Swinney rsch. intern Strong Mus., Rochester, 1988; Swann Found. fellow, Washington, 1990, predoctoral fellow Smithsonian Instn., 1991, Grad. Dean's Dissertation fellow in humanities U. Rochester, 1992. Mem. Am. Studies Assn., Orgn. Am. Historians, Australian and New Zealand Am. Studies Assn. Home E-mail: ilgordon@ozemail.com.au. Office E-mail: ascilg@nus.edu.sg. Home: Blk C 02-04 111 Clementi Rd, Singapore 129792, Singapore Office: Am Studies Ctr U Singapore, Shaw Found Bldg AS7 5 Arts, Singapore 117570, Singapore

GORDON, JAMES MAYNARD, marine and mechanical engineer, consultant; b. Ellsworth, Maine, Nov. 20, 1950; s. Cecil Everet and Martha (Gregory) G.; m. Christine Davis, Oct. 22, 1973. BS, Maine Maritime Acad., 1973. Marine engr. Seatrain Shipbuilding, Bklyn.; nuclear engr. Newport News (Va.) Shipbuilding, mech. engr., guarantee engr., sr. test engr., spl. project engr.; cons. engr. USN, 1974—. Contbr. articles to profl. jours. Lt. comdr. U.S. Power Squad, Mobjack Bay, Va., 1990—, treas., 1994—; trustee Susanna Wesley United Meth. Ch., Gloucester, Va., 1995, 98—. Recipient numerous awards USN, 1980—. Avocations: fishing, boating, woodworking, auto repair, golf. E-mail: jgordon@CCSINC.com. Home: 7262 Wellford Ln Gloucester VA 23061-5110

GORDON, JAMES S., lawyer; b. N.Y.C., Feb. 15, 1941; s. George S. and Sylvia A. (Wolfson) G.; m. Marcia G. Gordon, Dec. 22, 1968 (dec.); children: Daniel, Sarah; m. Debbie S. Pase, June 15, 1996. BA with high honors, U. Fla., 1962; LLB, Yale U., 1965. Bar: Ill. 1965, Fla. 1966, U.S. Supreme Ct. 1974. Asst. prof. Ind. U. Sch. Law, Bloomington, 1967-68, assoc. prof., 1969; ptnr. Feiwell, Galper & Gordon, Chgo., 1970-72; sole practice Chgo., 1972-80; pres. James S. Gordon, Ltd., Chgo., 1981-93; chmn. Gordon, Glickman, Flesch & Woody, 1994—. Editor Yale Law Jour., 1963-65; contbr. articles to profl. jours. Mem. Winnetka Caucus, 1981-82. Ford Found. grantee, 1965-66. Mem. Chgo. Bar Assn., Yale U. Law Alumni Assn. (exec. com. 1987-94), Order of Coif, Phi Beta Kappa, Phi Alpha Delta, Legal Club, Birchwood Club (Highland Park, Ill.). Office: 140 S Dearborn St Ste 404 Chicago IL 60603-5202

GORDON, JEFFREY (JACK) (JACK GORDON), lawyer; b. Boston, Sept. 6, 1964. BA, Tulane U., 1986, JD, 1989. Bar: Fla. 1990, U.S. Dist. Ct. (mid. dist.) Fla. 1995. Law clk. intern 1st dist. Ct. Appeal Fla., Tallahassee, 1989; spl. asst. pub. defender Dade County, Miami, Fla., 1990-92; cert. cir. ct. arbitrator Palm Beach County, West Palm Beach, Fla., 1990-92; ptnr. Maney & Gordon, P.A., Tampa, Fla., 1992—. Teen ct. judge pro bono Hillsborough County, Tampa, 1992-98. Mem. ATLA, Acad. Fla. Trial Attys., Animal Legal Def. Fund. Office: Maney & Gordon PA 101 E Kennedy Blvd Ste 3170 Tampa FL 33602-5151

GORDON, JUDITH, communications consultant, writer; b. Long Beach, Calif.; d. Irwin Ernest and Susan (Pearlman) G.; m. Lawrence Banka, May 1, 1977. BA, Oakland U., 1966; MS in Libr. Sci., Wayne State U., 1973. Researcher Detroit Inst. of Arts, 1968-69; libr. Detroit Pub. Libr., 1971-74; caseworker Wayne County Dept. Social Svcs., Detroit, 1974-77; advt. copywriter Hudson's Dept. Store, Detroit, 1979; mgr. The Poster Gallery, Detroit, 1980-81; mktg., corp. communications specialist Bank of Am., San Francisco, 1983-84; mgr., consumer pubs. Bank of Am., 1984-86; prin. ACTIVE VOICE, San Francisco, 1986—. Contbr. edit. The Artist's Mag., 1988-93; contbr. to book Flowers: Gary Bukovnik, Watercolors and Monotypes, Abrams, 1990. Vol. From the Heart, San Francisco, 1992, Bay Area Book Festival, San Francisco, 1990, 91, Aid & Comfort, San Francisco, 1987, Save Orch. Hall, Detroit, 1977-81, NOW sponsored abortion clinic project. Recipient Nat. award Merit. Soc. Consumer Affairs Profls. in Bus., 1986, Bay Area Best award Internat. Assn. Bus. Communicators, 1986, Internat. Galaxy awards, 1992, 95, 97, Internat. Mercury awards, 1995, Charles Schwab Excellence in Svc. award, 2000. Mem. AAUW, Internat. Assn. Bus. Communicators, Nat. Writers Union, Freelance Editl. Assn., Clarity, Achenbach Graphics Arts Coun., Women's Nat. Book Assn., Assn. for Women in Comms., FIMA West (bd. dirs.), ZYZZYVA (bd. dirs.). E-mail: activvduo@msn.com. Office: 899 Green St San Francisco CA 94133-3756

GORDON, KEVIN DELL, lawyer; b. Oklahoma City, June 23, 1958; s. James Dell and Mary Lurana (Tracewell) G.; m. Janice Linn Mathews, Aug. 4, 1979; children: Tracewell, Elise. BA cum laude, Westminster Coll., 1981; JD, Washington U., 1984. Bar: Okla. 1984, U.S. Dist. Ct. (we., no. and ea. dists.) Okla. 1984, U.S. Ct. Appeals (10th cir.) 1985, U.S. Supreme Ct. Shareholder, dir. Crowe & Dunlevy, Oklahoma City, 1984—; adj. prof. health law U. Okla. Law Sch., 1997—. Editor Washington U. Law Quarterly, 1982-84. Trustee, past pres. Youth Svcs. Oklahoma County, 1986—; chair adv. com. Okla. Assn. Youth Svcs., 1994-98. Mem. ABA (ins. coverage com. 1990—), Okla. Bar Assn. (uniform laws com. 1994-97, coord./moderator ann. ins. law update 1999—, mentorship com. 1999—, Outstanding CLE award 1999), Am. Health Lawyers Assn. (HMO and ins. coms. 1998—), Oklahoma County Bar Assn. (professional com. 2000—, legal aid com. 1990-98, comty. svc. com. 1997—), Ruth Bader Ginsberg Am. Inn of Ct. (chair mentoring com. 1996-99, chair membership com. 1999-2000, pres.-elect 2000—, Master of Yr. 1998), Order of Coif. Avocations: sports, gardening, guitar, reading. Home: 8309 Glenwood Ave Oklahoma City OK 73114-1111 Office: Crowe & Dunlevy 20 N Broadway Ave Ste 1800 Oklahoma City OK 73102-8273

GORDON, NEIL STUART IAN, urologist; b. U.K., June 15, 1952; s. Ian James and Pamela Nonette (Harris-Wright) G.; m. Deanna Felicity Louise Carbone, Apr. 6, 1985; children: Lachlan Andrew Neil, Felicia Siobhan Deannetta, Tasciana Tiffany Danielle, Ciara Kimberley Louise. MBBS, U. Melbourne, 1977. Vis. urologist Bendigo Nthn Dist Base Hosp, 1989-97, Mt. Alvernia Hosp., Bendigo, 1989-97; cons. urologist Anne Caudle Ctr., Bendigo, 1990-97; vis. urologist Cairns Base Hosp., 1997, Calvary Hosp., Cairns, 1997; prin. Cairns Urology, 1997—; cons. urologist Cairns Day Surgery, 1997. Contbr. articles to profl. jours. Fellow Royal Coll. Surgeons (Glasgow); mem. N.Y. Acad. Sci., Am. Inst. of Ultrasound in Medicine, Endourology Soc., Soc. Internat. Urologie, Am. Urol. Assn., Australian Ctr. for Med. Laser Tech. Inc., Soc. for Minimally Invasive Therapy, Australian Prostate Health Coun., Royal Australasian Coll. Surgeons, British Assn. of Urol. Surgeons, Australian and New Zealand Assn. of Urol. Surgeons, Internat. Coll. Surgeons, Royal Australasian Coll. Surgeons, Urol. Soc. of

Australasia, Royal Coll. Surgeons, Royal Coll. of Physicians and Surgeons, Australian Med. Assn., U. Melbourne Med. Grads. Assn., U. Melbourne Alumni Assn., Sandhurst Club, Bendigo Golf Club, Carlton Cricket and Football Social Club, Old Melburnians, Union of the Fleur de Lys. Avocations: skating, skiing, golfing, photography. Home: PO Box 6662, Cairns 4870, Australia Office: Cairns Urology, Level 2 19 Aplin St, Cairns 4870, Australia

GORDON, NEVE, social sciences educator; b. Magal, Israel, Mar. 18, 1965. BA, Hebrew U., Israel, 1991; MA, U. Notre Dame, 1997, PhD, 1999. Exec. dir. Physicians for Human Rights, Tel Aviv, 1992-94; lectr. polit. and govt. Ben-Gurion U., Israel, 1999. Co-author: Is the Struggle for Human Rights the Struggle for Emancipation?, 2000; co-editor: TORTURE: Human Rigths, Medical Ethics and the Case of Israel, 1995; contbr. articles to profl. jours. Bd. dirs. HaMoked Ctr. Right of the Individual, Jerusalem, 2000. E-mail: ngordon@bgumail.bgu.ac.il.

GORDON, PAMELA FELICITY, Bermuda government official; b. Bermuda, Sept. 4, 1955; d. E. F. Gordon. MBA, Queen's U.; LLD (hon.), U. New Brunswick. Sales acct. St. George's Club Timeshare Resort, 1983, asst. controller, 1987, membership dir., controller, 1989—; dep. chairperson United Bermuda Party, 1989—; senator, 1991—; mem. Ho. Assembly, 1993—; prime min. Gov. Bermuda, Hamilton, 1997-98; now leader United Bermuda Party, Hamilton. Mem. Coun. Women World Leaders, Global Leader for Tomorrow, World Econ. Forum Davos Switzerland. Mem. United Bermuda Party. Office: Leader of Opposition, 38 Front St, Hamilton HM 12, Bermuda*

GORDON, RICHARD DOUGLAS, physician, clinical researcher; b. Brisbane, Australia, Jan. 3, 1934; s. Eric Douglas and Violet Eleanor (Preston) G.; m. Margaret Ellen Holle, Apr. 26, 1960; children: Susan Jennifer, Michael Richard, Sara-Jane, Christina Helen. MB BS with honors, U. Queensland, Australia, 1957; MD, U. Queensland, 1966, PhD, 1981; MD, U. Adelaide, 1967. Intern, registrar Brisbane Teaching Hosps., 1958-62; rsch. fellow Alfred Hosp., Melbourne, 1963, Prince Henry's Hosp., Melbourne, 1964; endocrine fellow Vanderbilt U. Hosp., Nashville, 1964-66; Michell rsch. fellow, sr. lectr. in medicine U. Adelaide, 1966-69; reader in medicine U. Queensland-Greenslopes Hosp., Brisbane, 1970-82; prof. medicine U. Queensland, 1982-99, emeritus prof. medicine, 1999—; dir. hypertension unit Greenslopes Hosp., 1978—. Contbr. chpts. to textbooks on mineralocorticoid hypertension and Gordon's syndrome; author jour. articles. Decorated Officer The Order of Australia, Gen. Divisn. 1994. Mem. Queensland Hypertension Assn. (founder, vice-patron), Internat. Soc. Hypertension, Endocrine Soc. Australia, Endocrine Soc. U.S. Avocations: music, gardening, golf. Office: U Dept Medicine Hypertension Unit, Greenslopes Hosp, Brisbane 4120, Australia

GORDON, RICHARD LEWIS, mineral economics educator; b. Portland, Maine, June 19, 1934; s. Benjamin M. and Sara I. Gordon; m. Nancy Ellen Helfand, June 8, 1958; children: David William, Benjamin Mark. A.B., Dartmouth Coll., 1956; Ph.D., MIT, 1960. Econ. analyst Union Carbide Corp., 1960-64; asst. economist First Nat. City Bank, N.Y.C., 1964; mem. faculty Pa. State U., State College, 1964—, prof. mineral econs., 1970-96, prof. emeritus, 1996—; Shell lectr. on energy econs. Surrey (Eng.) U., 1981; bd. dirs. Ctr. for Energy and Mineral Policy, 1987-96; Micasu U. endowed fellow in mineral econs., 1990. Author: The Evolution of Energy Policy in Western Europe, 1970, U.S. Coal and Electric Power Industry, 1975, Coal in the U.S. Energy Market, 1978, An Economic Analysis of World Energy Problems, 1981, Reforming the Regulation of Electric Utilities, 1982, World Coal Economics, Policies and Prospects, 1987, Regulation and Economic Analysis: A Critique Over Two Centuries, 1994. Recipient Scholars medal The Pa. State U., 1989; decorated officer with honors 1st class Decoration of Andres Bello, Venezuela, 1989. Mem. AIME (chmn. coun. econs. 1973 Mineral Econs. award), Internat. Assn. Energy Economists (Outstanding Contbn. award 1992), Am. Econ. Assn., Econometric Soc., Royal Econ. Soc. Jewish. Home: 214 Horizon Dr State College PA 16801-8616 Office: Pa State U 2217 Earth Engring Sci Bldg University Park PA 16802-6813

GORDON, SANDY GALE COMBS, medical/surgical nurse, community health nurse; b. Lafollette, Tenn., Sept. 8, 1950; d. Wise and Edna Leona (Boshears) Combs; m. Ralph William Gordon, Aug. 30, 1975 (dec. Feb. 1998). Diploma, Middletown Hosp., 1971. RN, Ohio. Pub. health nurse Bur. Pub. Health, Middletown, Ohio, 1979-82; staff nurse Middletown Hosp., 1971-79. Named Internat. Women of Yr., 1994-95. Mem. Middletown Hosp. Alumni Assn. E-mail: sgordon@erinet.com. Home: 1107 Ellen Dr Middletown OH 45042-3341

GORDON, VALERY S., mathematician; b. Podolsk, Russia, Mar. 3, 1945; s. Sergei A. Gordon and Ljudmila V. Golovistikova; m. Natalia V. Bogush, Apr. 29, 1968; children: Ekaterina, Andrei. MS, Byelorussian State U., Minsk, 1967; PhD, Acad. of Scis. of BSSR, Minsk, 1974; DSc, Inst. Engring. Cybernetics, Minsk, 1995. Sr. rsch. fellow Acad. of Scis. of USSR, Moscow, 1981; assoc. prof. State Com. on Edn. of USSR, Moscow, 1990; engr. Designer Inst. of Engring. Cybernetics, Minsk, 1967-70; jr. rschr. Inst. of Engring. Cybernetics, Minsk, 1970-72, sr. rschr., 1972-88, leading rschr., 1988-95, prin. rschr., 1995—; head math and computer sci. dept. European Humanities U. Minsk, 2000—; lectr. Byelorussian State U., Minsk, 1979-84, assoc. prof., 1984-94; vis. rschr. U. Manitoba, Winnipeg, Can., 1991, Meml. U. Nfld., St. John's, Can., 1995, INRIA, Metz, France, 1998, U. Tech. Troyes, France, 1998. Author: (book) Scheduling Theory, Single-Stage Systems, 1994; contbr. articles, scientific pubs. on scheduling theory to profl. jours. Grantee Internat. Assn. INTAS, Brussels, 1995, 97; recipient Belarus State prize, 1998. Mem. N.Y. Acad. Scis., Byelorussian Operational Rsch. Soc. (v.p. 1996—), Math. Programming Soc. Avocations: hiking, mountaineering, biking, stamp collecting. Office: Inst of Engring Cybernetics, Surganova 6, 220012 Minsk Belarus

GORE, ALBERT, JR., Vice President of the United States; b. Washington, DC, Mar. 31, 1948; s. Albert and Pauline (LaFon) G.; m. Mary Elizabeth Aitcheson, May 19, 1970; children: Karenna, Kristin, Sarah, Albert III. BA cum laude (Univ. scholar), Harvard U., 1969; postgrad., Grad. Sch. of Religion, Vanderbilt U., 1971-72, Law Sch., 1974-76. Investigative reporter, editorial writer The Tennessean, 1971-76; mem. 95th-98th Congresses from Tenn., 1977-85; U.S. senator from Tenn., 1985-93; homebuilder and land developer Tanglewood Home Builders Co., 1971-76; livestock and tobacco farmer, from 1973, V.P. of U.S., 1993—. Author: Earth in the Balance: Ecology and the Human Spirit, 1992. Served with U.S. Army, 1969-71, Vietnam. Mem. Farm Bur., Tenn. Jaycees. Democrat. Baptist. Clubs: Am. Legion, VFW. Office: The White House Office of Vice President Old Executive Office Bldg NW Washington DC 20501-0001

GORE, DONALD RAY, orthopedic surgeon; b. Michigan City, Ind., Mar. 13, 1936; s. Clarence Bernard and Susan Leone (Fuller) G.; m. Jacqueline Marie Kraabel, Aug. 25, 1956; children: Donald, Daniel, Jennifer, Elizabeth. BS, U. Ill., 1958, MD, 1960; MS, Marquette U., 1967. Cert. Am. Bd. Orthopaedic Surgery. Intern Milw. County Gen Hosp., 1960-61; resident gen. surgery Marquette U. Sch. Medicine, Milw., 1961-64, resident orthopaedic surgery, 1964-67; fellow Biomechanics Lab U. Calif., San Francisco, 1967-68; practice medicine specializing in orthopaedic surgery Sheboygan (Wis.) Orthopaedic Assocs., S.C., 1968—; clin. prof. dept. orthopaedic surgery Med. Coll. Wis., Milw., 1980—; staff St. Nicholas Hosp., Sheboygan, Sheboygan Meml. Hosp.; cons. surgery Wood (Wis.) VA Hosp., 1970—; asst. instr. dept. surgery Med. Coll. Wis., 1964-68, clin. instr. dept. surgery, 1969-72, asst. clin. prof., 1972-73, assoc. clin. prof., 1973-80; research assoc. VA Med. Ctr., Milw., 1970—, co-investigator kinesiology research lab., 1970-84. Mem. bd. editors Jour. Orthopaedic Surg. Techniques, 1985—; contbr. articles to profl. jours. Served to capt. USAF, 1962-63. Fellow Am. Acad. Orthopaedic Surgeons (bd. councilors 1985—); mem. AMA, Mid-Am. Orthopaedic Soc., Clin. Orthopaedic Soc., Wis. Orthopaedic Soc. (pres. 1982-84), Milw. Orthopaedic Soc., Wis. Arthritis Found. (bd. dirs. 1974-82), Sierra Cascade Trauma Soc., Cervical Spine Research Soc. Republican. Lutheran. Avocations: skiing, fishing, tennis, golf, backpacking. Home: 2528 N 3rd St Sheboygan WI 53083-5007 Office: Sheboygan Orthopaedic Assocs SC 2920 Superior Ave Sheboygan WI 53081-1944

GORE, MADHAV SADASHIV, social work educator; b. Hubli, India, Aug. 15, 1921; s. Sadashiv Ramchandra and Venutai (Sadashiv) G.; m. Phyllis Madhav, May 2, 1949; children: Vikas, Anita. BA with honors, Bombay U., 1942, MA, 1948; Dip. S.S.A., Tata Inst. Social Sci., Bombay, India, 1945; PhD, Columbia U., 1960. Lectr. Delhi Sch. Social Work, New Delhi, 1948-53, prin., 1953-62; dir. Tata Inst. Social Sci., Bombay, 1962-82; vice chancellor Bombay U., 1983-86; chancellor Jawaharlal Nehru U. Author: Social Work and Social Work Education, 1964, Urbanization and Family Change, 1968, Immigrants and Neighborhoods, 1969, Some Aspects of Social Development, 1973, Indian Youth: Process es of Socialization, 1977, Education and Modernization in India, 1982; co-author: The Beggar Problem in Metropolitan Delhi, 1969, Field Studies in the Sociology of Education, 1970; editor: Problems of Rural Change, 1963, Indian Jour. Social Work, 1962-82; co-editor Papers in the Sociology of Education, 1967. Recipient award Govt. of India, 1975. Mem. Indian Sociol. Soc. (pres. 1981-82), Indian Soc. Criminology (pres. 1977-79), Indian Assn. Schs. Social Work (pres. 1962-66), Assn. Indian Univs. (pres. 1984-85), Internat. Assn. Schs. Social Work (v.p. 1962-66). Office: Jawaharlal Nehru Univ, New Mehrauli Rd, New Delhi 110067, India*

GORE, MICHAEL EDWARD JOHN, former governor, former ambassador, author; b. Kingston on Thames, Surrey, England, Sept. 20, 1935; s. John and Elsa (Dillon) G.; m. Monica Shellish, May 19, 1957; children: Marina Brownlow, Jacqueline Gore Russell, Michelle Boobier. Student, Xaverian Coll., 1948-52. Journalist Portsmouth & Sunderland Newspapers Ltd., 1952-55; with Ministry of Def., 1959-63; Brit. ambassador to Liberia, 1988-90, high commr. to the Bahamas, 1991-92; trustee Trust for Oriental Ornithology; gov. of Cayman Islands, 1992-95; chmn. Wider Caribbean working group U.K. Overseas Territories Conservation Forum, 1997—. Author: (with Won, Pyong-Oh) The Birds of Korea, 1971, (with A.R.M. Gepp) Las Aves del Uruquay, 1978, Birds of the Gambia, 1981, 90, On Safari in Kenya: A Pictoral Guide to the National Parks and Reserves, 1984; editor Jour. of the East African Natural History Soc., 1981-84. Recorder Cyprus Ornithol. Soc., 1960-63, The Gambia Ornithol. Soc., 1974-78; chmn. Malawi Wildlife Soc., 1985-87; v.p. Soc. for the Conservation of Nature in Liberia, 1989-90. Capt. Brit. Army, 1955-59. Fellow Royal Photographic Soc.; mem. Brit. Ornithologists Union, Army & Navy Club (London). Avocations: ornithology, wildlife photography, fishing. Address: 5 St Mary's Close Fetcham, Surrey KT22 9HE, United Kingdom

GORE, PRASANNA, management consultant; b. Bombay, India, Dec. 5, 1966; came to U.S., 1989; s. Rameschchandra Vinayak and Vandana Rameshchandra Gore. BPharm, U. Bombay, 1988; MS, W.Va. U., 1992, PhD, 1995. Pharm. sales staff Wockhardt, Bombay, 1988-89; rsch. asst. W.Va. U., Morgantown, 1989-95; asst. prof. U. Ill., Chgo., 1995-98; mgmt. cons. SRI Consulting, Boston, 1998-99; pres. Gore & Co., Brookline, Mass., 1999—; cons. W.Va. U., Morgantown, Ctrs. for Disease Control, Atlanta. Treas. Internat. Student Assn., Morgantown, 1990; fundraiser Am. Liver Found., Newton, Mass., 1998—. Recipient Boston Marathon Finisher's medal Boston Athletic Assn., 1999. Mem. Am. Assn. Pharm. Scientists (exec. com. mem. econ., mgmt. and mktg. sect., vice-chair 1999-2000), Rho Chi. Avocations: marathon running, photography, wine tasting, traveling. E-mail: pgore@goreconsulting.com. Fax: 617-689-2088. Office: Gore & Co 231 Freeman St Apt 1 Brookline MA 02446-6794

GORELIK, ALLA, piano educator; b. Chernobyl, Ukraine, Oct. 9, 1949; came to U.S., 1992; d. Simon and Eugena (Ben) Tsoiref; m. Roman Gorelik, June 16, 1971 (div. Apr. 1978); m. Valentin Stadnik, Dec. 26, 1979; children: Regina, Vladislav. BA, State Mus. Coll., Kiev, Ukraine, 1970. Piano and theory tchr. Music Sch. #5, Kiev, 1970-91; accompanist Fort Myers, Fla., 1992—; organist Temple Beth El, Fort Myers, 1993—; music instr. Learning Tree, Fort Myers, 1994—; piano and theory tchr. Fort Myers, 1992—; children musical program dir. North Shore Child Care, Fort Myers, 1993-95; youth art dir. Music Sch. #5, Kiev, 1986-90. Vol., performer Jewish Fedn., Fort Myers, 1992—, Hadassah, Fort Myers, 1993—; vol., accompanist Temples Beth-El and Judea, Fort Myers, 1992—. Recipient Labor Merit medal Ministry of Culture, 1990. Mem. Nat. Music Tchrs. Assn. Avocations: travel, cooking, reading. Home: 18257 Huckleberry Rd Fort Myers FL 33912-5234

GORELIK, VADIM SEMENOVICH, metallurgical engineering educator, consultant; b. Donetsk, Ukraine, Oct. 31, 1935; s. Symon Moiseyevich Gorelik and Genrietta Solomonovna Gantser; m. Tamara Alexandrovna Maltseva, Oct. 19, 1963; children: Irina, Eugenij. Grad., Tech. U. Donetsk, 1959; postgrad., Inst. Metallurg. Machine Bldg., Moscow, 1967, PhD, 1967; DSc, Metallurg. Acad., Dniepropetrovsk, Ukraine, 1980. Engr., designer Metallurg. Plant, Tcheliabinsk, Russia, 1959-62; with Inst. Metallurg. Machine Bldg., Moscow, 1962-67; sr. rschr. Tech. U., Donetsk, 1967-80, assoc. prof., 1980-82, prof., 1982—, chief of dept., 1985-97; cons. Metallurg. Plant, 1964-66, Zaporojie, 1966-72, Mariupol, 1972-80, Tcherepovec, Russia, 1980-85. Author: A Raise of Plate Milling Roll's Accuracy, 1969, A Technology of a Milling Roll's Manufacture, 1989, Technological and Power Abilities of Milling Rolls, 1976 (award Ministry of edn. 1980); numerous patents in field. Mem. Sci. and Didactic Coun. Ministry of Edn., Sci. Coun. Donetsk State Tech. U. Avocations: travel, history. Office: State Tech U, Artioma Str 58, 340000 Donetsk Ukraine

GORELOV, IGOR PAVLOVICH, chemist, educator; b. Leningrad, Russia, Apr. 22, 1938; s. Pavel Mikhailovich and Maria (Zhavoronkova) G.; m. Rimma Ivanovna, July 27, 1960; 1 child, Igor. BS in Chemistry, Tomsk State U., 1959, MSc in Chem. Scis., 1964; DSc, Kiev State U., 1981. Rsch. scientist Tomsk State U., Russia, 1959-63; head lab. phys.-chem. methods of analysis Chem. and Pharm. Instn., Novokuznetsk, Russia, 1963-65; from asst. prof. to head inorganic chemistry Tver Poly. Inst., Russia, 1965-72; asst. prof. dept. chemistry Tver Agrl. Inst., 1972-82; prof., head organic & analytical chemistry Tver State U., 1982—; dir. Inter-Univ. Lab. Instrumental Methods of Analysis, Tver, 1983-91; cons. Tver Electromech. Plant, 1970-75; hon. prof. Tver State U., 1997. Author: Physico-Chemical Methods of Analysis, 1972; editor: Chemistry of Surfactants, 1984, Chemistry of Complexones and Their Use, 1990; contbr. articles to profl. jours.; patentee in field. Party com. Communist Party Soviet Union, Tver, 1974-78. Honoured Scientist Russian Fedn., 1998. Mem. Russian Soc. Material Scis. (pres. Tver br. 1994—, bd. dirs. 1994—), All-Russian Chem. D.I. Mendeleev Soc., Sigma Xi. Avocations: ham radio, cars, photography. Home: Sportivny per dom 3 kv 14, Tver 2 Russia 170002 Office: Tver State U, ul Zhelyabova 33, Tver Russia 170000 Mailing: PO Box 0223, 170002 Tver 2 Russia

GORENBERG, CHARLES LLOYD, financial services executive; b. Phila., Mar. 1, 1938; s. Abraham and Esther (Freedman) G.; m. Roslyn Grobman, May 22, 1960; children: David M., Kenneth M. BA, Franklin & Marshall Coll., 1960; MS, The Am. Coll., Bryn Mawr, Pa., 1981. Cert. Employee Benefit Specialist, CLU, ChFC. Sales assoc. Landis & Co., Phila., 1960-62; agt. Phoenix Mut. Life, Phila., 1962-64, supr., 1964-67; dir. tng. Rittenhouse Assocs., Phila., 1967-75; exec. v.p. Corp. Pension Actuaries, Phila., 1975-91; pres. Delta Fin. Group, Phila., 1991-97, Chaslyn Fin. Group, Marlton, N.J., 1997—. Co-editor: (book) Planning for Business Owners and Professionals, 1988; contbr. over 35 articles to mags. Mem. Internat. Soc. Cert. Employee Benefit Specialists, Am. Soc. CLUs and ChFCs (various offices), Am. Soc. Pension Actuaries. Avocation: golf. Office: Chaslyn Fin Group 2001 Lincoln Dr W Ste B Marlton NJ 08053-1531

GORENFLO, RUDOLF, mathematics educator, researcher; b. Friedrichstal, Germany, July 31, 1930. Diploma in Math., Technische Hochschule, Karlsruhe, Fed. Republic Germany, 1956, Dr. rer. nat., 1960; Habilitation, Technische Hochschule, Aachen, Fed. Republic Germany, 1970. Scientific asst. Technische Hochschule, Karlsruhe, 1957-61; mathematician Standard-Elektrik Lorenz, Stuttgart, Fed. Republic Germany, 1961-62; rsch. mathematician Max-Planck-Inst. f. Plasmaphys., Garching, Fed. Republic Germany, 1962-70; prof. math. Technische Hochschule, Aachen, 1971-73, U. Heidelberg, Fed. Republic Germany, 1972; full prof. math. Free U., Berlin, 1973—; vis. prof. Univ. Tokyo, 1995. Co-author book on Abel integral equations; co-editor book reports on sci. confs.; contbr. rsch. papers to profl. publs. Mem. N.Y. Acad. Scis., Gesellsch. für Angew. Math. und Mechanik, Berliner Math. Gesellschaft (pres. 1980-84), Deutsche Math.-Vereinigung, Österreichische Math. Gesellschaft, Am. Math. Soc., Soc. Indsl. and Applied Math., Vereiningung Deutscher Wissenschaftler. Avocations: walking, swimming, bicycling, playing piano, skat. E-mail: gorenflo@math.fu-berlin.de. Fax: 49-30-838-75403. Office: Free U Berlin Dept Math Inf, Arnimallee 3, D-14195 Berlin 62, Germany

GORI, ROLAND CLAUDE, psychology educator, psychoanalyst; b. Marseilles, France, Nov. 22, 1943; s. Georges and Anna (Jorio) G.; m. Marie-José Del Volgo, Nov. 23, 1996; children: Régine, Hélène. Lic. Psychology, U. Aix en Provence, France, 1965; diploma in psychology, U. Paris Sorbonne, 1966; D of Psychology, U. Paris X, 1969, D of Humane Sci. and Letters, 1976. Clin. psychologist, 1967—; asst. U. Aix Marseille, 1970-71, asst. and asst. lectr., 1970-79; prof. U. Montpellier, 1979-83, U. Aix-Marseille, 1983—; psychoanalyst, 1978—; dir. Ctr. Inter-Regional de Recherches en Psychopathologie Clinique, 1983—; dir. rev. Cliniques Mediterraneenes, 1984—; pres. Groupe Mediterraneen d'Etudes Freudiennes, 1993—. Author: (books) Le corps et le signe dans l'acte de parole, 1978, La preuve parla parole Surla causalité en psychanalyse, 1996, La science au risque de la psychanalyze, 1999; contbr. numerous articles to profl. jours. Mem. European Found. for Psychoanalysis, Internat. Assn. History of Psychoanalysis. Home: 101 rue Sylvabelle, 13006 Marseille France Office: U Provence Ctr d'Aix, 23 Ave Robert Schuman, 13621 Aix-en-Provence Cedex 1, France

GORILOVICS, TIVADAR, literature educator; b. Ruttka, Czechoslovakia, Aug. 19, 1933; s. Tivadar and Ilona (Stulakovics) G.; m. Anna Szabo, July 3, 1974. BA, Eotvos Lorand U., 1955. Tchr. Högyes Endre Gimnazium, Hajduszoboszlo, Hungary, 1955-58; tchr., rschr. U Debrecen, Hungary, 1958—; teaching asst. Hungarian lang. The Sorbonne, Paris, 1962-64; invited prof. U. Stendhal, Grenoble (France) III, 1993; chmn. dept. French Kossuth Lajos U., 1970-91, vice dean faculty of arts, 1972-75, vice-rector, 1983-86, dean faculty of arts, 1986-89. Author: Recherches sur les origines et les sources de la pensée de R. Martin du Gard, 1962, La Légende de V. Hugo de Paul Lafargue, 1979, Correspondance de J.R. Bloch et André Monglond I (1913-1920), 1984, II (1921-1939), 1989, J.R. Bloch, Lettres du régiment (1902-1903), 1997; editor: Studia Romanica de Debrecen, 1978—. Named Officer of Order of Palmes academiques Govt. French Republic, 1980. Mem. Hungarian Acad. Scis. (sec. bd. Debrecen's com. 1993—), Soc. d'Hist. Litt. de la France (corr.), Assn. Etudes Jean-Richard Bloch (bd. dirs.). Home: Doczy u 1, H-4032 Debrecen Hungary Office: Debrecen U, Dept French BP 47, H-4010 Debrecen Hungary

GORITA, ION, ambassador. Perm. rep. of Romania UN, N.Y., 1994—. Office: Permanent Mission of Romania UN 573 3rd Ave New York NY 10016-3109

GORIUP, PAUL DAVID, ecologist, consultant; b. Reading, Berkshire, Eng., July 8, 1955; s. Marjan Paul and Beryl (Dormon) G.; m. Susan Joy Everett, Oct. 12, 1991 (div. Aug. 1994); children: David, Maria; m. Nataliya Sergeivna Panchenko, Jan. 4, 1995; stepchildren: Denis, Lydia, Alisa. BSc in Botany and Zoology, U. Reading, Eng., 1976; MSc in Conservation Sci., U. Coll. London, 1977. Asst. dir. Birdlife Internat., 1983-86; sr. ptnr. The Nature Conservation Bur., 1986-89, chmn., mng. dir., 1989—; vis. rsch. fellow Rutherford Coll., U. Kent; chmn. internat. adv. com. Nat. Avian Rsch. Ctr., Abu Dhabi, United Arab Emirates, 1990-96; exec. dir. Inst. Ecology and Environ. Mgmt., 1991-96; resident adviser Danube Delta Environ. Rsch. Program, Romania, 1993-95; convener European Workshop on Grassland Ecosys., 1996; mem. com. mgmt. plan for Mai Po/Inner Deep Bay Ramsar Site, Hong Kong, 1996; cons. numerous orgns. Editor Parks Jour., 1990—; contbr. articles to profl. jours. Recipient gold medal Duke of Edinburgh, 1975, Queen's Scout award, 1975, bronze medal St. John Ambulance Brigade, 1976. Fellow Zool. Soc. London (sci.), Inst. Ecology and Environ. Mgmt.; mem. Inst. Dirs., Brit. Ecol. Soc., Brit. Ornithol. Union, African Bird Club, Bombay Natural History Soc. (life), Brit. Assn. Nature Conservationists, Brit. Trust for Ornithology, Fauna and Flora Internat., Ornithol. Soc. of the Mid. East, Oriental Bird Club (founder, coun. 1985-88), Reading Orthnithol. Club, Royal Soc. for the Protection of Birds, Internat. Union for Conservation of Nature (chmn. Bustard Specialist Group 1990—, head secretariat of U.K. com. 1995-2000, project leader sustainable agr. and steppe biodiversity in Russian and Ukraine 1996-98). Avocations: birdwatching, nature photography, travel, chess, table tennis. Office: Nature Conservation Bur, 36 Kingfisher Ct Hambridge, Newbury Berkshire RG14 5SJ, England

GORLACH, WILLI, member of European parliament; b. Butzbach, Germany, Dec. 27, 1940. Mem. European Parliament, Germany, 1999—; mem. Group of the Party of European Socialists, mem. of bur.; mem. of com. on agr. and rural devel., com. on fisheries; substitute mem. com. on fgn. affairs, human rights, common security and def. policy, delegation for rels. with Can. Office: SPD-Europaburo, FischerfeldstraBe 7-11, D-60102 Frankfurt Germany*

GORLATCH, SERGEI, computer scientist; b. Kiev, Ukraine, Aug. 27, 1957; s. Maria G.; m. Galina Ugljarenko, June 19, 1986; 1 child, Alexey. MS, Kiev U., 1979; PhD, Inst. Cybernetics, Kiev, 1984; Dr. habil., U. Passau, Germany, 1998. Engr. Inst. of Cybernetics, Kiev, 1979-82, rsch. assoc., 1983-87, sr. rsch. assoc., 1987-91; asst. prof. U. Passau, Germany, 1992-2000. Contbr. articles to profl. jours.; editor conf. proceedings, 1997-2000. Recipient Young Rschr. award, Ukraine, 1988; fellow Alexander von Humboldt Found., Bonn, 1991-92. Office: Univ Passau, D-94030 Passau Germany

GORMAN, GERALD WARNER, lawyer; b. North Kansas City, Mo., May 30, 1933; s. William Shelton and Bessie (Warner) G.; m. Anita Belle McPike, June 26, 1954; children: Guinevere Eve, Victoria Rose. AB cum laude, Harvard U., 1954, LLB magna cum laude, 1956. Bar: Mo. 1956. Assoc. firm Dietrich, Tyler, Davis, Burrell & Dicus, Kansas City, 1956-62; ptnr. Dietrich, Davis, Dicus, Rowlands, Schmitt & Gorman, 1963-90; dir. Slagle, Bernard & Gorman, P.C., 1990—; bd.dirs. Musser-Davis Land Co., Curry Investment Co. Bd. govs. Citizens Assn. Kansas City, 1962—; trustee Harvard/Radcliffe Club Kansas City Endowment Fund, chmn. bd. trustees, 1977-83; trustee Kansas City Mus., 1967-82; chmn. bd. trustees Avondale Meth. Ch., 1969-92; mem. Citizens Bond Com. of Kansas City, 1973-2000, chmn. 7th jud. cir. citizens com., 1982-84; chmn. Downtown Coun. Allis Plaza Reconstrn., 1983-85; bd. dirs. Spofford Home for Children, 1972-77, Clay County Econ. Devel. Commn., 1989-94, mem. exec. com., 1991-93. With U.S. Army, 1956-58; capt. USAR, 1958-64. Mem. Lawyers Assn. Kansas City (exec. com. 1968-71), ABA, Mo. Bar Assn., Kansas City Bar Assn., Clay County Bar Assn., Harvard Law Sch. Assn. Mo. (pres. 1973), Harvard Club (pres. 1966), Univ. Club (bd. dirs. 1983-86, 88-93, pres. 1990-91), Kansas City Club (bd. dirs. 1993-97), 611 Club (bd. dirs. 1987-91, pres. 1990), Kansas City Country Club, Old Pike Country Club, River Club. Republican. Home: 917 NE Vivion Rd Kansas City MO 64118-5317 Office: 4600 Madison Ave Ste 600 Kansas City MO 64112-3031

GORMAN, JONATHAN LAMB, philosopher, educator; b. Middlesex, Eng., Jan. 14, 1946; s. Reginald and Flora May (Renwick) G.; m. Kyra Hodges, Sept. 6, 1969; children: Rupert Ivor Lamb, Claudia Rose Sarah, Aurelia Sylvie Kyra. MA, U. Edinburgh, Scotland, 1970; PhD, U. Cambridge, Eng., 1973. Rsch. fellow in philosophy U. Birmingham, Eng., 1973-75; lectr. in social philosophy Queen's U., Belfast, Northern Ireland, 1976-85; sr. lectr. Queen's U., Belfast, 1985-90, reader in philosophy, 1990-95, prof. moral philosophy, 1995—, head sch. philos. studies, 1998—; John Milton Scott vis. prof. philosophy Queen's U., Kingston, Can., 1981-82; vis. fellow Princeton (N.J.) U., 1982; head dept. philosophy Queen's U., Belfast, 1993-98. Author: The Expression of Historical Knowledge, 1982, Understanding History, 1992; mem. editl. com. History and Theory, 2000—; contbr. articles to profl. jours., chpts. to books; mem. adv. bds., referee various acad. jours. Sr. scholar Fulbright Found., 1982; Hamilton Philos. fellow Cambridge U., 1970-73. Mem. Soc. for Applied Philosophy (founder, exec. com.), Royal Irish Acad. (chmn. nat. com. for philosophy 2000—), World Congress of Philosophy (subject chmn. 1993), Irish Philos. Club (controlling sec. 1984-97), Mind Assn., Assn. Legal and Social Philosophy. Avocations: restoring old buildings, walking. Office: Sch Philos Studies, Queen's U, Belfast BT7 1NN, Northern Ireland

GORMAN, JOSEPH TOLLE, corporate executive; b. Rising Sun, Ind., 1937. BA, Kent State U., 1959; LLB, Yale U., 1962. Assoc. Baker, Hostetler & Patterson, Cleve., 1962-67; with legal dept. TRW Inc., Cleve., 1968-69, asst. sec., 1969-70, sec., 1970-72, v.p. sr. counsel automotive worldwide ops., 1972-73, v.p., asst. gen. counsel, 1973-76, v.p., gen. counsel, 1976-80, acting head communications function, 1978, exec. v.p. indsl. and energy sector, 1980-84, exec. v.p., asst. pres., 1984-85, pres., chief operating officer, 1985-88, chmn., CEO, 1988—, also bd. dirs. Aluminum Co. Am., Procter & Gamble Co.; mem. adv. bd. BP Am. Inc.; bd. dirs. U.S.-China Bus. Coun., bd. dirs.; mem. Bd. of The Prince of Wales Bus. Leaders Form; mem. hon. com. Fedn. Internat. des Soc. d'Ingenieurs des Tech. de l'Automobile; mem. Def. Industry Initiative Steering Com.; chmn. Internat. Trade and Investment Task Force; mem. strengthening of Am. Initiative Ctr. for Strategic and Internat. Studies; adv. com. Nat. Security Telecom.; mem. Conf. Bd., Bus. Coun., Trilateral Commn., Bus. Roundtable's Policy Com., Coun. on Fgn. Rels., Pres.'s Export Coun., Coun. on Competitiveness. Trustee New Ohio Inst., Cleve. Tomorrow, Mus. Arts Assn., Cleve. Inst. Art, United Way Svcs., Cleve. Clinic Found., Com. for Econ. Devel., com. for econ. devel. and the Malcolm Baldrige Nat. Quality Award Found.; mem. Ohio Gov.'s Edn. Mgmt. Coun., Kent State U. Found.; bd. mem. The New Am. Schs. Devel. Corp., The Bus.-Higher Edn. Forum, Civic Vision 2000 and Beyond. Recipient Japan Prime Minister's Trade award, 1994. Fax: (212) 334-2463. E-mail: nhgall@mindspring.com.

GORMAN, LYN, educator, editor; b. Tamworth, NSW, Australia, June 22, 1947; d. Thomas Max and Edna Merle (Mortimer) Chaffey; 1 child, Caroline Theresa Holmes. BA with honors, U. New Eng., Australia, 1967; DPhil, U. Sussex, Eng., 1972; grad. cert. mgmt., U. Western Sydney, 1999. Adminstr., asst. sec. Inst. Devel. Studies U. Sussex, 1974-80; freelance editor, indexer Eng., U.S., Australia, 1979—; faculty adminstr. Brighton (Eng.) Poly., 1981-83; external assessor Deakin U., Australia, 1985-91; lectr. European and internat. history, media history Charles Sturt U., Wagga Wagga, NSW, Australia, 1991-96, sr. lectr., 1996—; head Sch. Humanities and Social Scis. Charles Sturt U., Wagga Wagga, 1999—; coord. modern and ancient history NSW HSC Online Project, Australia, 1997—. Co-author: (with G. E. Gorman) Theological and Religious Reference Materials, 3 vols., 1984-86 (Am. Libr. Assn. Outstanding Reference Book of Yr. 1984, 85), (with R. Israeli) Islam in China, 1994, Modern and Ancient History, 1986; contbr. articles to profl. jours.; mem. bd. mgmt. NSW HSC Online Project. Office: Charles Sturt U, Locked Bag 678, Wagga Wagga 2678 NSW, Australia

GORMAN-GORDLEY, MARCIE SOTHERN, personal care industry franchise executive; b. Feb. 25, 1949; d. Jerry R. and Carole Edith (Frendel) Sothern; m. N. Scott Gorman, June 14, 1969 (div.); children: Michael Stephen, Mark Jason; m. Mark A. Gordley, June 26, 1994. AA, U. Fla., 1968; BS, Memphis State U., 1970. Tchr. Memphis City Sch. Sys., 1970-73; tng. dir. Weight Watchers Palm Beach County, Weight Watchers So. Ala., West Palm Beach, Fla., 1973-97; pres. Weight Watchers Franchise Assn., 1999—; pres. Markel Enterprises, LLC (formerly Markel Ads, Inc.). Cubmaster Boy Scouts Am. Hon. lt. col. a.d.c. Ala. Militia. Mem. NAFE, NOW, Women Am. ORT (program chmn. 1975), Weight Watchers Franchise Assn. (chair mktg. com., advt./mktg. coun., chairperson region IV bd. dirs., treas., 2d v.p. 1991, 1st v.p., region IV co-chair 1998-99, bd. dirs., nat. pres. 1999—), Exec. Women of Palm Beaches, Am. Bus. Women's Assn., Zonta. Home: 429 N Country Club Dr Lake Worth FL 33462-1003 Office: 2403 10th Ave N Lake Worth FL 33461-3128

GORMLEY, DAVID JOSEPH, broadcasting company executive; b. Birmingham, England, Jan. 8, 1963; s. Patrick Michael and Rosina Margaret (Lane) G.; m. Tricia Anne Dewyer, Aug. 3, 1991; 1 child, Emma Caitlin. Degree in co. adminstrn., Sheffield City Polytech., England, 1985, degree in fin. sector studies, 1984. Asst. co. sec. Guinness Plc, London, 1985-88; asst. co. sec. Albert Fisher Group Plc, Windsor, England, 1988-91, co. sec. continental Europe, 1991-94; co. sec. Brit. Sky Broadcasting Group Plc, Isleworth, England, 1995—. Fellow Inst. Chartered Secs. and Adminstrs. Avocations: football, tennis, badminton, squash, fell walking. Office: Brit Sky Broadcasting Group, Grant Way, Isleworth TW7 5QD, England Address: Brit Sky Broadcasting, 6 Centaurs Bus Ctr GrantWay, Isleworth TW7 5QD, England

GORMLEY, LAURENCE WILLIAM, law educator; b. Macclesfield, England, July 2, 1953; s. Eric William and Bridget (O'Connor) G. BA, Oxford U., 1975, MA, 1979; MSc, London U., 1976; LLD, Utrecht U., 1985. Barrister Middle Temple, London. Lectr. law U. Liverpool, England, 1980-83; adminstr. Commn. European Cmtys., Belgium, 1983-90; prof. European law U. Groningen, The Netherlands, 1990—; vis. prof. U. Coll., London, 1990—, U. Bremen, Germany, 1994—, Coll. Europe, Poland, 1993-99, Bonn, 1999-2000. Author: Prohibiting Restriction on Trade Within the EEC, 1985; author or editor numerous publs. Mem. Dutch Assn. Procurement Law (chmn.), Athenaeum Club. Avocations: food and wine, sailing, music. Office: Rijksuniversiteit Groningen, Dept European Law PBox 716, 9700 AS Groningen The Netherlands

GORNALL, ALASTAIR CHARLES, public relations executive; b. London, June 6, 1956; s. Ian and Liz (Leighton) C.; m. Sarah McCall, May 9, 1984; children: Sophie, Kakie, Isabella. Internat. acct. mgr. Bus. Week, 1979-81; dir. Shale Gornall, England, 1981-82; mng. dir. Scope Comm., England, 1982-90, Consolidated Comm., England, 1990—. Lt. Brit. Army, 1975-78. Royal Air Force Flying scholar, London, 1973. Office: Consolidated Comm, 1-5 Poland St, London W1V 3DG, England

GORNBEIN, HENRY SEIDEL, lawyer; b. Detroit, May 27, 1943; s. Abe Siedel and Lillian (Westerman) G.; m. Debra Marilyn Gornbein, June 13, 1993; children: Jonathan David and Laurie Beth. B Philosophy, Montieth Coll., Wayne State, 1965; JD, Univ. of Mich.-Ann Arbor, 1968. Bar: Mich. 1968. Law clk. Wayne County Cir. Ct., Detroit, 1968-69; assoc. Gage & Brukoff, Southfield, Mich., 1969-70, Coleman, Goodman & Schifman, Southfield, 1970-71; ptnr. Bayer, Goren, Gornbein, Gropman & Kaplan, P.C., Southfield, 1979-81; sole practice and ptnr. in various entities, 1971-81; assoc. Baskin, Feldstein & Gornbein, Birmingham, Mich., 1982-85; pvt. practice, Birmingham, 1985-95; ptnr. Bookholder, Bassett, Gornbein, Solomon & Cohen, PLLC, 1995-98; creator, host (cable TV show) Practical Law; pres. Am. Divorce Info. Network, Inc., pub. Divorce Online (internet). Home and Office: 4190 Telegraph Rd Ste 3000 Bloomfield Hills MI 48302-2082

GÓRNIAK-KOCIKOWSKA, KRYSTYNA STEFANIA, philosopher, educator; b. Potczyn Zdrój, Poland, Oct. 10, 1947; came to U.S., 1989; d. Kazimierz and Stefania Wiktoria (Jagielska) Górniak; m. Andrzej-Bogdan Kocikowska, Aug. 3, 1974; 1 child, Mikotaj. MA in German philology, Adam Mickiewicz U., Poznań, Poland, 1973, PhD in philosophy, 1981; MA in Religion, Temple U., 1992. Lectr. philosophy dept. Adam Mickiewicz U., 1976-81, sr. lectr., 1981-89; lectr. Internat. Ctr. for Postgrad. Studies, Dubrovnik, Yugoslavia, 1983; adj. prof. La Salle U., Phila., 1989-92; sr. lectr. U. R.I., Kingston, 1990-92, 92-97; asst. prof. philosophy dept. So. Conn. State U., New Haven, 1992—; assoc. prof. So. Conn. State Univ., New Haven, 1997—; sr. rsch. assoc. So. Conn. State Univ. Rsch. Ctr. on Computers and Society, 1997—. Co-author: On Selected Problems in Contemporary Ethics, 1979, From The History of German Mental Culture, 1985 (Minister Higher Edn. award 1986). Rsch. and Travel grantee Kosciuszko Found., 1990-91, Metaphilosophy Found., 1995; grantee NEH, 1992; scholar Temple U., 1989-92. Mem. Polish Philos. Soc., Am. Philos. Assn., Am. Acad. Religion (co-chair group on religion in Ea. Europe and former USSR 1996-99), Karl Jaspers Soc. N.Am., Internat. Hegel Soc., European Bus. Ethics Network, Internat. Soc. for the Study of European Ideas. E-mail: gorniak@scsu.ctstateu.edu. Office: So Conn State U 501 Crescent St New Haven CT 06515-1330

GÓRNY, RAFAL LONGIN, medical educator, researcher; b. Sosnowiec, Poland, Jan. 27, 1966; m. Joanna Katarzyna Watola, Oct. 21, 1995. MSc, Silesian Med. Acad., Katowice, Poland, 1992, PhD, 1999. Asst. Inst. Occupl. Medicine and Environ. Health, Sosnowiec, 1992-99, assoc. prof., 1999—; rsch. scholar U. Cin., 1999—. Home: Piekna 64/11, 40-591 Katowice Poland Office: Inst Occ Med & Environ Hlth, 13 Koscielna St, 41-200 Sosnowiec Poland

GORODISCHER, RAFAEL, pediatrician; b. Santiago, Chile, Apr. 26, 1939; arrived in Israel, 1969; s. Nathan and Berta (Rapaport) G.; m. Michal Skolnick, June 3, 1979; children: Anat, Yonathan, Na'ama. MD, U. Chile, Santiago, 1964. Intern U. Chile, 1963; resident Children's Hosp. Buffalo, 1964-66; fellow in pediatric pharmacology SUNY, Buffalo, 1966-69; dir. pediatric svc. A Soroka Med. Ctr., Beer-Sheva, Israel, 1979—; chmn. dept. pediatrics Soroka Med. Ctr., Beer-Sheva, 1984-91; prof. pediatrics Ben-Gurion U., Beer-Sheva, 1989—, Milada Ayrton prof. pediat., 1989; vis. scientist FDA, Washington, 1985-86; mem. exam. com. Israel Pediat. Bd., 1990-92; expert Internat. Pediat. Assn., 1990-95; vis. prof. Hosp. for Sick Children, U. Toronto, Ont., Can., 1992-93. Contbr. chpts. to books. Capt. Israel Def. Force Res. Fellow United Health Found., N.Y., 1968. Mem. European Soc. Pediat. Rsch., Soc. for Pediat. Rsch., Israel Pediat. Assn. (exec. com. 1991-95, 99—), European Soc. for Devel. Pharmacology (pres. 1998-2000). Home: 21 Hardoof St, 84965 Omer Israel Office: Soroka Med Ctr, PO Box 151, 84101 Beersheva Israel

GORODNIJ, MIKOLA MICHAILOVICH, chemist, ecologist, researcher; b. Topchiyvka, Ukraine, July 29, 1936; s. Michailo Gavrilovich and Varvara Jakivna (Bichinock) G.; m. Marija Jakivna Krivokhizha, Dec. 31, 1964. DSc, Ukrainian Agr. Acad., Kiyv, 1964. Docent Ukrainian Agr. Acad., Kiyv, 1967-72, prof., 1972—, dean agrochemisry faculty, 1972-76, 85-90, academician, 1992—; cons. Agr. Min., Havana, Cuba, 1978-80. Author: Agorecology, 1993, Bioconversion in Agroecosystems Management, 1995, Agrochemistry, 1995, Bioconversion of Organic Waste in Biodinamical Economy, 1990 (Ukrainian Govt. prize 1996); contbr. over 300 articles to profl. jours.; patentee in field. Recipient Pryanishnikow prize, 1987, Disting. Man Edn. award Govt. Ukraine, 1986, for Complex System of Organic Scrupe Biotech. Mem. Mendeleew Chem. Orgn., World Agroecology Orgn., USA Agronomy Orgn. Avocations: travel, autosports, reading, science fiction. Home: 40 Years Oct 88/49, 03040 Kiev Ukraine Office: Nat Agrl Univ, Geroev Oborony Str 15, 03041 Kiev Ukraine

GÖRÖG, SÁNDOR, analytical chemist, researcher; b. Szombathely, Hungary, Dec. 27, 1933; s. Dénes and Klára (Szemző) G.; m. Zsuzsanna Pászthory, May 27, 1958 (div. May 1987); children: Klára, Péter, Judit; m. Marianne Hajnóczy, Oct. 17, 1987. MS in Inorganic and Analytical Chemistry, U. Szeged, Hungary, 1957, PhD in Inorganic and Analytic Chemistry, 1959; CSc, Hungarian Acad. Scis., Budapest, 1968, DSc, 1973. Rsch. chemist Chem. Works Gedeon Richter Ltd., Budapest, 1959-76, head dept., 1976-86, dir. synthetic rsch., 1986-92, dir. analytical rsch., 1992—; hon. prof. Semmelweis Med. U. Sch. Pharmacy, Budapest, 1975—; mem. adv. bd. ACH Models in Chemistry. Author: Analysis of Steroid Hormone Drugs, 1978, Quantitative Analysis of Steroids, 1983 (Russian edit. 1985), Steroid Analysis in the Pharmaceutical Industry, 1989, Ultraviolet-Visible Spectrophotometry in Pharmaceutical Analysis, 1995 (Hungarian edit. 1994); editor: Advances in Steroid Analysis, 1982, 85, 88, 91, 94, Identification and Determination of Impurities in Drugs, 2000; editor-in-chief Acta Pharmaceutica Hungarica; mem. editl. bd. Magyar Kémiai Folyóirat, Kémiai Közlemények (Chem. Comm.); contbg. editor Trends in Analytical Chemistry; regional editor Jour. Pharm. and Biomed. Analysis; contbr. over 150 articles to sci. jours. Recipient Széchenyi award Pres. Hungarian Republic, 1997. Mem. Hungarian Acad. Scis. (chmn. working party for pharm. and organic analysis 1986-90, vice chmn. chem. divsn. 1989-96, chmn. chem. divsn. 1999—), Hungarian Chem. Soc. (vice chmn. analytical divsn. 1980-89, chmn. 1989-95, mem. presidium 1989-99, Than medal 1994), Hungarian Pharm. Soc. (chmn. analytical divsn. 1975-83, vice chmn. 1992-96, chmn. sci. com. 1995—, Schulek medal 1983, Szebelledy medal 1996, Kazay medal 1999), Fedn. European Chem. Socs. (coun. mem. divsn. analytical chemistry), European Fedn. for Pharm. Scis. Avocations: touring, hiking, classical music. Home: 3 Pitypang u, H-1025 Budapest Hungary Office: Chem Works G Richter Ltd, 21 Gyömroi u, PO Box 27, H-1475 Budapest Hungary

GÖRÖG, YVETTE, lawyer; b. Pecs, Hungary, Dec. 30, 1966; d. Miklós and Szabó Éva G.; m. Theodore Sebastian Boone, July 6, 1991. Student, U. Heidelberg, Germany, 1988, U. Helsinki, Finland, 1988, U. Riga, Latvia, 1989; JD summa cum laude, Eötvös Loránd U., Budapest, Hungary, 1991; LLM, Georgetown U., 1993. Assoc. Multijuris Law Firm, Budapest, 1990-91, Barkats & Assocs., Washington, 1993-94, Dewey Ballantine, Budapest, 1995—; legal advisor Estonian Govt., Washington and Tallin, Estonia, 1992; judicial intern Superior Ct. of Washington, 1994. Contbr. chpt. to book: Taxes in Hungary, 1990. Mem. Hungarian Bar Assn. Avocations: classic literature, swimming, theater. Office: Dewey Ballantine Law Firm, Andráassy öt 60, 1062 Budapest Hungary

GOROKHOV, IGOR M., isotope geochemist, researcher; b. Leningrad, Russia, Apr. 6, 1932; s. Mikhail P. Gorokhov and Nina A. Tikhomirova; m. Irina A. Ostrovskaya, May 18, 1957; 1 child, Svetlana. Cert. rsch. chemist with honors, Leningrad State U., 1954; PhD In Chem. Scis., Leningrad Tech. Inst., 1965; DSc in Geol. and Mineralog. Scis., Inst. Geochemistry, Kiev, Ukraine, 1981. Jr. rsch. fellow V.G. Khlopin Radium Inst., USSR Acad. Scis., Leningrad, 1954-61, jr. rsch. fellow Lab. of Precambrian Geology, 1961-67; jr. rsch. fellow Inst. Precambrian Geology and Geochronology USSR Acad. Scis., St. Petersburg, 1967-72, sr. rsch. fellow, 1972-86, leading rsch. fellow, 1986-93, prin. rsch. fellow, 1993—; bd. dirs. Coun. on Isotope Geology and Geochronology, USSR Acad. Scis., Moscow, 1973-91; mem. Ea. European Commn. on Earth Crust Investigation, Moscow, 1978-89, Upper Precambrian Stratigraphic Commn., 1988—; mem. coun. geochemistry Russian Acad. Scis., Moscow, 1992-93, 1999—. Author: Rubidium-Strontium Method of Isotope Geochronology, 1985, (with Shukolyukov and Levchenkov) Graphical Methods in Isotope Geology, 1974; contbr. over 100 articles to sci. publs.; mem. editl. bd. Chem. Geology, 1987-1999. Recipient medal for sci. svc. Geol. Survey Czechia, Prague, 1986, Geol. Survey Slovakia, Bratislava, 1986; grantee Presidium Russian Acad. Scis., Moscow, 1994, 97, 2000. Mem. N.Y. Acad. Scis. Avocations: chess, St. Bernard dogs. E-mail: gorokhov@ig1405.spb.edu. Fax: 812-3284801. Office: RAS Inst Precambrian Geol Geochron, nab Makarova 2, 199034 Saint Petersburg Russia

GOROSHKEVICH, SERGEJ, botanist, researcher; b. Tara, Omskaja Oblast, Russia, Oct. 9, 1960; s. Nikolaj and Nadegda (Pokroeva) G.; m. Irene Sladkova, Sept. 30, 1983; children: Margaret, Dmitrij. BSc, State Pedagogical U., Omsk, Russia, 1982; MSc, Inst. Forest and Wood, Krasnojarsk, Russia, 1986; PhD, Tomsk State U., Russia, 1989. Cert. botanist, sr. rsch. worker. Lab. asst. Inst. for Ecology of Natural Complexes, Tomsk, Russia, 1986-88, jr. rsch. worker, 1988-90, rsch. worker, 1990-92, sr. rsch. worker, 1992—. Author: (with V.N. Vorobjev, N.A. Vorobjeva) Growth and Sex in Siberian Cedar, 1989; contbr. articles to profl. jours. Mem. Russian Bot. Soc. Avocations: poetry, tennis. Home: Vavilova 2 94, 634055 Tomsk Russia Office: Inst Ecol & Nat Complexes, Akademicheskij 2, 634021 Tomsk Russia

GOROSTIAGA ATXALANDABASO, KOLDO, foreign diplomat; b. Bilbao, Spain, May 30, 1940. Mem. European Parliament, 1999—, mem. com. on employment and social affairs, mem. com. on women's rights and equal opportunities, substitute com. on environment, pub. health, consumer policy; mem. delegation for relations with the countries of Ctrl. Am. and Mex. *

GOROSTIZA LÓPEZ, JORGE, architect; b. Santa Cruz Tenerife, Canarias, Spain, Dec. 4, 1956; s. Fernando Gorostiza and Consuelo Lopez; m. Ana Perez, Dec. 10, 1992. BArch, Sch. Tech. Arch., Las Palmas, Spain, 1986. Arch. Palerm, Tabares, Gorostiza Arch., Santa Cruz Tenerife, 1986-93, Mcpl. Mgmt. Urbanism, Santa Cruz Tenerife, 1993—; spkr. in field. Author: Cinema and Architecture, 1990, Peter Greenaway, 1995, The Supposed Image. Architects in Cinema, 1996, Art Directors Of The Spanish Cinema, 1997, Casino/To Have and to Have Not, 1999, Builders of Chimeras, 1999. Mem. Acad. Artes y Ciencias Cinematográficas España, Asociación Española Historiadores Cinematográficos. Roman Catholic. Avocations: sailing. Office: Estudio Arch, Gaspar Fernandez 13, 38001 Santa Cruz Tenerife, Spain

GORRELL, MARK DOUGLAS, research biologist; b. Camden, Australia, July 1956; m. Anne Marie Cunningham, June 3, 1989; 1 child, Sarah. BS, Australian Nat. U., Canberra, 1978, PhD, 1982. Scientist Monoclonal Australia, Sydney, 1982-84; rsch. fellow U. Melbourne, 1984-88, Royal Prince Alfred Hosp., Sydney, 1988-89, 94—, Johns Hopkins U., Balt., 1989-94. Contbr. articles to profl. jours. Grantee Australian Wool Corp., 1986, Nat. Health and Med. Rsch. Coun. of Australia, 1994, 97. Mem. AAAS, Am. Soc. Virology, Australia New Zealand Soc. for Cell Biology (treas. 1994-96), Australian Soc. for Immunology, N.Y. Acad. Sci. Achievements include patent on vaccine composition; discovery that most lymphocytes in normal sheep liver are CD8lo CD5 neg discovery that liver GP110 is dipeptidyl peptidase IV, discovery of novel protective effect of Sindbis virus nonstructural proteins, delineation of structure-function relationships in dipeptidyl petidase IV. Office: Centenary Inst, Locked Bag 6, Newtown NSW 2042, Australia

GORSKI, TADEUSZ STANISLAW, climatologist, researcher; b. Orchow, Masovia, Poland, Feb. 18, 1930; s. Leon and Maria (Gabryanczyk) G.; m. Krystyna Irena Kutnik, Dec. 12, 1971. MS in Geography-Climatology, Wroclaw (Poland) U., 1959; PhD in Agr., Inst. Soil Sci. and Plant Cultivation, Pulawy, Poland, 1966, Habilitation in Agr., 1973. Navigator lic. Merchant Navy Sch., Poland. Deck officer Merchant Navy, Poland, 1949-51; instr. Navy, Poland, 1951-54; rsch. asst. Wroclaw U., 1956-60; meteorologist State Meteorol. and Hydrol. Inst., Klodzko, 1961-62; head agrometeorology dept. Inst. Soil Sci. and Plant Cultivation, Pulawy, 1962-95, prof., 1983—; leader working group Solar Radiation in the Atmosphere Commn. for Global Geophys. Processes Polish Acad. Scis., 1978-82, chmn. agrometeorology sect. com. meteorology and atmospheric physics, 1984-90. Co-author: (books and maps) Evaluation of Natural Capability of Agricultural Areas in Poland, 1977, Agroecological Foundations of Plant Cultivation, 1983; contbr. articles to profl. jours. Recipient State award in sci. and tech. Govt. of Poland, 1974, award Ministry of Agr., 1970, 78, W. Goetel award for environ. protection W. Goetel Found., 1989; decorated companion Polonia Restituta Cross Coun. of State, 1989. Mem. Polish Geophys. Soc., World Meteorol. Orgn. (mem. commn. agrl. meteorology 1977—), Lublin Scientific Soc., N.Y. Acad. Scis. Home: Kollataja 39/7, Pulawy 24-100, Poland Office: Inst Soil Sci & Plant Culti, Osada Palacowa, Pulawy 24-100, Poland

GORSKY, MEIR, clinical oral pathologist; b. Katovitz, Poland, Mar. 7, 1946; arrived in Israel, 1950; s. Leon Goldberger and Irene (Glicksman) G.; m. Hana Geisler, July 9, 1947; children: Mody, Sharon, Idan. DMD, Hebrew U., 1972; cert. in oral medicine, U. Calif., San Francisco, 1982. Dir. oral medicine clinic Tel Aviv U., 1977—, coord. sect. oral pathology & medicine sch. dental medicine, 1982-87, assoc. prof., 1995—; vis. prof. U. Calif., San Francisco, 1985, 88, 89, Cancer Agy., B.C. Vancouver, Can., 1997—; dir. retraining program Ministry Health and Tel Aviv U., 1976-77; cons. in oral medicine Tel Hashomar Hosp., Ramat Gan, Israel, 1977—; dir. dept. evaluation for splty. in oral medicine Israel Dental Assn., 1995, chmn. oral medicine com., 1990-95; bd. dirs. Sch. Dental Med. Tel-Aviv U. Contbr. chpts. to books and articles to profl. jours. Mem. bd. examinations Ministry Health, Israel, 1985—; mem. pub. rels. com. sch. dental medicine Tel Aviv U., 1985-88, mem. curriculum com. to upgrade profl. knowledge in dentistry, 1990, mem. coun. faculty medicine, 1996—. Capt. Israeli Med. Forces, 1972-95. Grantee Alpha Omega, 1981. Fellow Am. Acad. Oral Medicine, Am. Acad. Oral Pathology, Internat. Assn. Dental Rsch. Avocations: photography, music. Office: Tel Aviv U Sch Dental Medic, Sect Oral Pathology, Tel Aviv 69978, Israel

GORTNER, SUSAN REICHERT, nursing educator; b. San Francisco, Dec. 23, 1932; d. Frederick Leet and Erida Louise (Leuschner) R.; m. Willis Alway Gortner, Aug. 25, 1960 (dec. Sept. 1993); children: Catherine Willis, Frederick Aiken. AB, Stanford U., 1953; M Nursing, Western Res. U., 1957; PhD, U. Calif., Berkeley, 1964; postgrad., Stanford U., 1983. Staff nurse, instr., supr. Johns Hopkins Hosp. Sch. Nursing, Balt., 1957-58; instr. to asst. prof. Sch. Nursing U. Hawaii, Honolulu, 1958-64; staff scientist, rsch. adminstr. div. nursing USPHS, Bethesda, Md., 1966-78; assoc. dean rsch. Sch. Nursing U. Calif., San Francisco, 1978-86, acting chmn. dept. family health, 1982, prof. dept. family health care nursing, 1978-94; prof. emerita, 1994—; fellow, assoc. mem. faculty Inst. Health Policy U. Calif., San Francisco, 1979-94, mem. affiliated faculty Inst. for Aging and Health, 1981-94, adj. prof. internal medicine dept. gen. medicine, 1989-94, dir. cardiac recovery lab. Sch. Nursing, 1987-95, spl. asst. to dean, 1993-94; Fulbright lectr., rsch. scholar Norwegian Fulbright Commn., Oslo, 1988; invited prof. U. Montreal, 1991; vis. prof. U. Alta., Edmonton, Can., 1995. Contbr. articles, papers to profl. publs., chpts. to books. Health advisor N. Fork Assn., Soda Springs, Calif., 1981—. Disting. scholar Nat. Ctr. Nursing Rsch., 1990; named Disting. Alumna Frances Payne Bolton Sch. Nursing, 1983. Fellow Am. Acad. Nursing; mem. ANA (chair exec. com., coun. nurse rsch. com. 1976-80, cabinet on nursing rsch. 1984-86), Am. Heart Assn. (coun. cardiovasc. nursing exec. com. 1987-91, coun. epidemiology 1989—, Katharine Lembright award 1991, fellow cardiovasc. nursing coun. 1992), Sigma Theta Tau (Alpha Eta chpt., Margretta M. Styles award 1994). Office: U Calif 4th And Parnassus # N411Y San Francisco CA 94143-0001

GORUP, GREGORY JAMES, marketing executive; b. Kansas City, Kans., Mar. 27, 1948; s. Mike and Helen F. Gorup; m. Kathleen Susan Grogan, Apr. 12, 1986 (div.); children: Michael Thomas, Ryan Nicholas. BA in Econs., St. Benedict Coll., 1970; MBA, U. Pa., 1972. Market analyst product planning and devel. dept. Citibank, N.Y.C., 1972-73, market planning officer corp. product mgmt. divsn., 1973-74, product mgr. securities svcs., 1974-75; v.p., dir. product devel. Irving Trust Co., N.Y.C., 1975-80, mgr. product mgmt. dept., 1980-81; v.p. mktg. U.S. area Credit Suisse, 1981-84; sr. cons. Wesley, Brown and Bartle, N.Y.C., 1985-86; bank mktg. mgr. Digital Equipment Corp., N.Y.C., 1986-87; money mktg. mgr. Reuters N.Am., 1987-88; pres. Gorup Assocs., 1989-91; dist. v.p. Nat. Computer Sys., N.Y., 1991-94; regional mgr. Soc. Worldwide InterBank Fin. Telecomm., 1994-96, sr. regional mgr., 1996-98, mgr., 1998-2000, sr. mgr., 2000—. Mem. Rep. Nat. Com., Nat. Rep. Senatorial Com., U.S. Shooting Team. Mem. NRA (life), West Point Soc. N.Y., Wharton Bus. Sch. Club, Princeton Club N.Y., Orienta Beach Club, Willow Wood Gun Club, Army "A" Club, U.S. Naval Inst., Naval League of the U.S., Air Force Assn. Roman Catholic. Home: 910 Stuart Ave # 2-0 Mamaroneck NY 10543-4134 Office: 200 Park Ave Fl 38 New York NY 10166-3899

GORYACHEVA, IRINA GEORGIEVNA, mechanics educator, researcher; b. Sverdlovsk, Russia, May 30, 1947; d. Georgii Petrovich and Elena Vasilievna (Zmeeva) Mitkevich; m. Alexandre Petrovich Goryachev, Sept. 29, 1972; 1 child, Ekaterina. MSc, Moscow State U., 1970, PhD, 1974; DSc, Russian Acad. Scis., 1988. Jr. rschr. Inst. for Problems in Mechancis, Russian Acad. Scis., Moscow, 1973-87, sr. rschr., 1987-89, leading rschr., 1989-96, head lab. of tribology, 1996—; prof. Moscow Inst. Physics and Tech., 1979—; cons. Purdue U., West Lafayette, Ind., 1994, 95, 97, 98, 99, 2000. Author: Contact Problems in Tribology, 1988, Contact Mechanics in Tribology, 1998; contbr. articles on sci. and tech. to profl. jours. Recipient Lenin Komsomol prize USSR State Prizes, 1979, 850 Yrs. of Moscow medal Govt. of Moscow, 1997. Mem. Russian Acad. Scis. (corr. mem. 1997—), Gesellschaft Angewandte Mathematik und Mechanik, European Mechanics Soc. Avocations: music, cycling, skiing, dancing. Office: Inst Problems in Mechanics, prosp Vernadskogo 101, 117526 Moscow Russia

GORYAEV, MIKHAIL ALEXANDROVICH, physicist; b. Arkhangelsk, Russia, Apr. 16, 1949; s. Alexander Mikhailovich and Maria Andreevna (Gudkova) G.; m. Elena Mikhailovna Zinina, Mar. 19, 1976; 1 child, Olga. BS, St. Petersburg State U., Russia, 1972; PhD, Vavilov State Optical Inst., St. Petersburg, 1977. Tchr. Acad. Gymnazium, St. Petersburg, 1968-80; rsch. specialist Vavilov State Optical Inst., St. Petersburg, 1972-82, sr. leading rsch. specialist, 1988-94; dep. dir., dir. Br. of State Inst. of Photochem. Industry, St. Petersburg, 1982-87; head of lab. Cen. Design Bur. of Mech. Engring., St. Petersburg, 1994—; lectr. Herzen State Pedagogical U. of Russia, St. Petersburg, 1995-98; mem. Coun. of Inst. of Cinema Engrs., St. Petersburg, 1985-91; mem. sect. chmn. Imaging Processes Coun. of Russian Acad. Scis., Moscow, 1985-95; invited lectr. Minn. Mining and Mfg., St. Paul, 1993. Patentee in field; contbr. articles to profl. jours.; contbg. author: Spectroscopy of Phototransformations in Molecules, 1977. Named Internat. Man of Yr., Cambridge, 1999-2000. Mem. Rozhdestvensky Optical Soc., Soc. for Imaging Sci. and Technology, N.Y. Acad. Sci. Avocations: fishing, music, playing cards. Office: Ctrl Design Bur Mech Engrin, 3 Krasnogvardeyskaya Sq., 195112 Saint Petersburg Russia

GORYAEVA, ELENA MIKHAILOVNA, research scientist; b. Leningrad, Russia, Nov. 11, 1944; d. Mikhail Danilovitch and Nadezgda Vladimirovna (Milstein) Zinin; m. Stanislav Mikhailovitch Lifshitch, May 7, 1966 (div. Oct. 1972); m. Mikhail Alexandrovitch Goryaev, Mar. 19, 1976; 1 child, Olga. MS in Optico-Electronics, Leningrad Inst. Optics and Exact Mechanics, 1967. Engr. State Optical Inst., Leningrad, 1967-72, jr. rsch. specialist, 1972-82, rsch. specialist, 1982—; rsch. areas include photochemistry, liquid lasers, luminescence spectroscopy. Contbr. articles to profl. jours.; inventor in field. Tech. informator State Optical Inst., 1974-80, trade union organizer, 1972-76; recruiter Bibliophilic Soc., Leningrad, 1980-86. Recipient Labour Vet. medal Leningrad City Coun. of People's Deps., 1988. Avocations: swimming, cycling, museum visiting, classical music concerts. Home: Plekhanova 33/5 55, 190000 St Petersburg Russia Office: State Optical Inst, 199164 St Petersburg Russia

GORYNOV, YURI VLADIMIROVITCH, physicist, researcher; b. Panovka, USSR, Jan. 9, 1959; s. Vladimir Ivanovich Goryunov and Anna Pavlovna Shypkova Goryunova; m. Svetlana Mikhailovna Maximova, July 27, 1984 (div. Aug. 1998); 1 child, Alexandra; m. Tat'yana Vladimirovna Formanyuk, Jan. 29, 1999. Diploma, Kazan (USSR) State U., 1981, D in Physics and Math., 1995. Engr. Kazan Chem. Tech. Inst., 1981-84; engr. Kazan Phys.-Tech. Inst., 1984-92, jr. rsch. worker, 1992-97, sr. rsch. worker, 1997—. Contbr. articles to profl. jours. Home: Lesgafta, 28-6, 420043 Kazan Russia Office: Kazan Phys Tech Inst, Sibirskii trakt, 10/7, 420029 Kazan Russia

GOSA, NOLUTHANDO PRIMROSE, telecommunications commissioner; b. East London, South Africa, Feb. 9, 1963; d. Lizo an Elda Nontombi (Gosa) Jonas. BA in Comm. with honors, Ft. Hare U., Alice, South Africa, 1985, BA in Comm., 1987; MBA, U. N.B., Fredericton, Can., 1993; internat. cert. telecomm. regulation, City U., London; diploma in telecomm. regulation, Adams Inst., London; postgrad., Stellenbosch U., South Africa. Brand mgr. Protea Pharms., East London, South Africa, 1989-90; chairperson Sauteny Liquor Bd., Johannesburg, South Africa, 1996-97; mktg. mgr. Telkom S.A., Pretoria, South Africa, 1994-96; commr. Broadcasting Complaints Commn., Johannesburg, 1996-97, SATRA, Johannesburg, 1997—; grad. tchg. asst. comm. Ft. Hare U., Alice, 1986; councillor South African Nat. Def. Liaison Coun., Pretoria, 1997—. Mem. African Nat. Congress, Johannesburg, 1999; vol. People Opposed to Women Abuse, Johannesburg, 1999. Methodist. Avocations: reading, golf, chess, tennis, music, movies, travel. Home: PO Box 78761, Sandton, Sautens 2146, South Africa Office: SATRA Block B, Pinmill Farm, 164 Katherine St, Sandton, Johannesburg 2196, South Africa

GOSAIN, ARUN KUMAR, physician, surgeon; b. Jamshedpur, India, Sept. 1, 1955; s. Girdhari Lal and Urmil Kalia G.; m. Smita Tewari G., Sept. 2, 1983; children: Sankalp, Sidhi. AB in Biology, Princeton U., 1977; MD, UCLA, 1981. Asst. prof. of plastic surgery Med. Coll. Wis., Milw., 1992-96, assoc. prof. surgery, 1996—, assoc. program dir., plastic surgery residency, 1997—; invited referee Jour. of Plastic and Reconstructive Surgery, 1995—, Jour. of Cleft Palate: Craniofacial Jour., 1998—. Contbr. articles to profl. jours. Preceptor Minority Student Rsch. Tng. Program, Milw., 1995-96, Summer Program for Undergrad. Rsch., Milw., 1996-99, Summer Sci. Tchr. Program, Milw., 1997, others. Rsch. grantee in field; faculty fellow Am. Coll. Surgeons, 1993-95; acad. scholar Am. Assn. Plastic Surgeons, 1995-97; travelling fellow Royal Coll. of Surgeons, London, 1998. Mem. Plastic Surgery Rsch. Coun. (scientific program chair 1999-2000, 2000-01), Assn. Acad. Chmn. in Plastic Surgery, Am. Soc. Maxillofacial Surgeons (chmn. biomaterials com. 1998—), Alpha Omega Alpha. Avocation: running. E-mail: agosain@mcw.edu. Office: Dept PlsSurg/Med Coll Wisc 9200 W Wisconsin Ave Milwaukee WI 53226-3522

GOSALVEZ, MARIO, biochemist, biophysicist; b. Madrid, Sept. 11, 1940; s. Fernando and Concepcion Gosalvez; m. Mariflor Blanco, Oct. 2, 1964; children: Mario, David, Elena. MD, U. Madrid, Spain, 1963. Asst. prof. U. Madrid, 1964-66, assoc. prof., 1966-70; assoc. prof. Autonoma U. Medicine, 1971-74, full prof., 1974-77; titular prof. Dept. Edn., Spain, 1985—; chief of svc. Clinica Puerta De Hierro, Madrid, 1975—; cons. editor IMES, 1996; bd. dirs. Biomed. Ctr. Moscow, 1993—. Contbr. numerous articles to profl. jours.; patentee in field; editl. bd. Centro di Epistemologia, 1993—. Lt. Spanish Mil., 1960-62. Recipient Nat. Prize, Min. of Health, Madrid, 1977, 79, Rodriguez Pascual prize Banco Hispano Americano, 1979. Mem. Am. Assn. for Cancer Rsch. (emeritus), Spain Cancer Rsch. Assn. (v.p. 1982-84), Internat. Soc. of Oxygen Transport to Tissue (emeritus). Roman Catholic. Avocations: philosophy, painting, dancing. Office: Clinica Puerta de Hierro, San Martin de Porres 4, 28035 Madrid Spain

GOSE, RICHARD VERNIE, lawyer; b. Hot Springs, S.D., Aug. 3, 1927. MS in Engring., Northwestern U., 1955; LLB, George Washington U., 1967; JD, George Washington U., 1968. Bar: N.Mex. 1967, U.S. Supreme Ct. 1976, Wyo. 1979; registered prof. engr., Wyo.; children: Beverly Marie, Donald Paul, Celeste Marlene. Exec. asst. to U.S. Senator Hickey, Washington, 1960-62; mgr. E.G. & G., Inc., Washington, 1964-66; asst. atty. gen. State of N.Mex., Santa Fe, 1967-70; pvt. practice law, Santa Fe, 1967—, Santa Fe/Prescott, 1989—; assoc. prof. engring. U. Wyo., 1957-60; owner, mgr. Gose & Assocs., Santa Fe, 1967-78; pvt. practice law, Casper, Wyo., 1978-83; pres. Argosy Internat., Inc., 1994—; ranch mgr., foreman, 1945-49; mem. Phoenix com. on fgn. rels., 1980—; co-chmn. Henry Jackson for Pres., M.Mex., 1976, Wyo. Johnson for Pres., 1960. With U.S. Army, 1950-52. Mem. N.Mex. Bar Assn., Wyo. Bar Assn., Yavapai County Bar Assn., Masons, High Country Hounds, Phoenix Com. Foreign Rels., High Country Hounds, Phi Delta Theta, Pi Tau Sigma, Sigma Tau. Methodist. Home and Office: PO Box 3998 Prescott AZ 86302-3998

GOSE, WILLIAM CHRISTOPHER, retired chemist; b. Dante, Va., Oct. 8, 1940; s. Willie Gibson and Lillian Beatrice (Addington) G.; m. Mary Hildreth Gross, Dec. 31, 1974. BS in Chem. and Math., East Tenn. State U., 1976; MBA in Bus. Mgmt., U. Tenn., 1983. Chief lab. analyst Holston Def. Corp., Kingsport, Tenn., 1961-74; sr. technician Holston Def. Corp./Tenn. Eastman Co., Kingsport, 1974-78; rsch. chemist Tenn. Eastman Co., Kingsport, 1978-85; tech. rep. Eastman Chem. Products, Inc., Kingsport, 1985-94; prin. tech. rep. Eastman Chem. Co., Kingsport, 1994-98, ret., 1998. Contbr. papers to profl confs. including Scotland Conf., Houston, 1990, Polymer Conf., Lucerne, Switzerland, 1991. With USN, 1958-61. Mem. Soc. Plastics Engrs. (sr., author papers plastics recycle conf. Atlanta 1992, additives conf. Orlando, Fla. 1993), Am. Chem. Soc., Elks (exalted ruler 1991-93, state officer 1991-96, Merit award 1991-93), Optimist Internat. (pres. local chpt. 1993-94). Republican. Methodist. Achievements include 13 U.S. patents and multiple foreign patents for co-development of a methodology for preparation and application of polymer modifiers and additives to the surface of polymer substrates in aqueous medium. Address: PO Box 6604 Kingsport TN 37663-1604

GOSHIMA, KIYOTA, cell biologist, educator; b. Osaka, Japan, Mar. 3, 1943; s. Eiichi and Sadame (Muraki) G.; m. Fusako Nii, May 10, 1973; children: Gohta, Ryota. BS, Osaka (Japan) U., 1966, MS, 1968, DSc, 1972. Rschr. Takeda Chem. Industry, Osaka, 1972-77; assoc. prof. Nagoya (Japan) U., 1977-87; prof. cell biology Kobe Gakuin U., Kobe, Japan, 1987—. Contbr. articles to Jour. Cell Biology, Circulation Rsch. Home: 3-10-41 Uenonishi, Toyonaka, 560-0011 Osaka Japan Office: Kobe Gakuin U Lab Life Scis Dept Human Behavior, 518 Arise Ikawadani-cho, Nishi-ku Kobe 651-2180, Japan

GOSLIN, GERALD HUGH, concert pianist, educator; b. Detroit, Jan. 7, 1947; s. Hugh Jennings and Helen Margaret (Senauit) G. Student, Wayne State U., Detroit, 1966-69. Music tchr. Peralta Music, Farmington, Mich., 1965-80, Hammell Music, Livonia, Mich., 1980-83; prof. music Oakland C.C., Farmington Hills, Mich., 1983—; host The Piano Hour Sta. WHND-AM, Oak Park, Mich., 1995; recitalist Allen, Rodgers and Baldwin Organs, Detroit, 1975—; prof. voice, theory and piano Livonia (Mich.) Music Conservatory, 1998—; judge Leontyne Price Vocal Competition, 1986—, Verdi Opera Assn. Vocal Competition, 1995-96. Block capt. Rogers Park Residents Assn., Redford, 1995—; choirmaster-organist Littlefield Presbyn. Ch., Dearborn, Mich., 1997—. Mem. Detroit Fedn. of Musicians Local #5, Am. Choral Dir. Assn., Am. Guild of Organists. Home and Office: 19782 Olympia Redford MI 48240-1334

GOSLING, DAVID, architect, urban design educator; b. Manchester, Eng., Sept. 14, 1934; came to U.S., 1989; s. John Arthur and Clara Novello (Shaw) G.; m. Miriam Caetano De Deus Vieira, Mar. 10, 1965; children: Maria-Cristina, Ana-Lucia, Stephen. BA, U. Manchester, Eng., 1956; MArch, MIT, 1958; MCP, Yale U., 1960; PhD, Sheffield (Eng.) U., 1986. Registered architect, Ohio, U.K. Sr. asst. architect Manchester City Architect Dept., 1960-62; assoc. ptnr. Leach, Rhodes & Walker, Architects, Manchester, 1962-65; dep. chief architect Runcorn (Eng.) New Town Devel. Corp., 1965-68; chief architect Irvine (Scotland) New Town Devel. Corp., 1968-73; prof., dean architecture Sheffield (Eng.) U., 1973-89; prof. U. Cin., 1989—; eminent scholar in urban design State of Ohio, 1989—; dir. Ctr. for Urban Design, Coll. Design, Architecture and Planning, U. Cin., 1989-96; city planning commr. City of Cin., 1996; regional planning commr. Hamilton County, Ohio, 1996-2000; tech. expert Ministry of Overseas Devel., Rio De Janeiro, 1973, Ministry of the Interior, Brasilia, 1976-77; planning cons. Cent. Bank of Barbados, Bridgetown, 1977-78; ptnr. Saudi-European Assocs., Ministry of the Interior, Saudi Arabia, 1981-84; urban design cons. London Docklands Devel. Corp., London, 1980-88. Co-author: The Design and Planning of Retail Systems, 1976, 77, 79, 84, Concepts of Urban Design, 1984, 85; author: Gordon Cullen: Visions of Urban Design, 1996 ; chief editor: Irvine New Town Plan, 1971; assoc. editor 3rd World Planning Rev., 1979-89. Staff rep. Nat. Whitley Coun., London, 1966-68; chmn. Brit. New Towns Tech. Officers Com., London, 1968-70; chmn., trustee North Sheffield Housing Assn., 1975-89; regional planning commr. Hamilton County, 1996—; alt. mem. bd. trustees Ohio Ky. Ind. Regional Coun. Govt., 1998, exec. com. Recipient Pub. Realm Design award Progressive Architecture, 1992, DAAP award for outstanding rsch. U. Cin., 1993-94, Preservation award, Gov. of Ohio Proclomation for Retoration of Frank Lloyd Wright's Boulter House, 1999; Commonwealth (Harkness) fellow Harkness Found., 1957-59, Leverhulme sr. fellow Leverhulme Trust, 1980, Quantas Disting. scholar Australian U., 1984, State of Ohio eminent scholar in urban design, 1989—, Graham Found. (Chgo.) fellow for advanced studies, 1994. Fellow Royal Soc. Arts, Inst. Urban Design (N.Y.); mem. AIA (emeritus mem. 2000—, Honor award for archtl. advancement 1996), Royal Inst. Brit. Architects (chmn. accreditation bd. 1983-88, Rsch. award 1994, Preservation award 1999), Royal Town Planning Inst., Royal Incorp. Architects (Scotland). Roman Catholic. Avocations: photography, 20th century classical music, narrow gauge railroads, swimming. Home: 1 Rawson Woods Cir Cincinnati OH 45220-1130 Office: Coll DAAP Univ Cin Architecture Art-Planning PO Box 210016 Cincinnati OH 45221-0016

GOSLINGS, JOHAN CAREL, surgeon; b. Leiden, Zuid-Holland, The Netherlands, Sept. 13, 1968; s. Bernard and Antoinette (Mees) G.; m. Karin van Gilst; 1 child, Wessel Oege. MD, Acad. Med. Ctr. Amsterdam, The Netherlands, 1993, PhD, 1999. Rsch. fellow AO Rsch. Inst., Davos, Switzerland, 1991-92; surg. resident St. Lucas Andreas Hosp., Amsterdam, 1995-98, Acad. Med. Ctr., Amsterdam, 1998—; rsch. fellow U. Tex. Med. Br., Galveston, 1999. Editl. bd. mem. Netherlands Jour. Surgery, 1998—; contbr. articles to med. jours.; patentee in field. 1st med. lt. The Netherlands Army, 1995. Mem. Netherlands Soc. Traumatology, Netherlands Soc. Surgery. Avocations: running, skating, cycling. E-mail: goslings@knmg.nl.

GOSPER, BRETT, advertising agency executive; b. Melbourne, Australia, June 21, 1959; s. Richard Kevan and Jillian Mary (Galwey) G.; div. Oct. 1994; 1 child, Jonathan Kevan Thomas; m. Elizabeth Bernsen, May 9, 1998; 1 child, Ella Jillian. Grad. in econs. and politics, Monash U., Melbourne, 1981. Exec. Ogilvy & Mather, Melbourne, 1981-82; acct. supr. Ogilvy & Mather, Paris, 1982-86, acct. dir., 1986-89; dir. BDDP, Paris, 1989-91, dep. mng. dir., 1991-93; mng. dir., founder BDDP, Frankfurt, Germany, 1993-94; CEO Euro RSCG-Wnek-Gosper Advt., London, 1994—, bd. dirs. world wide; Rugby player rep. Victoria, Queensland, Australia, 1982, French Barbarians versus New Zealand All Blacks at Rugby, 1986; capt. Italian Zebras, Monaco Sevens, 1987. Recipient Best Player award Melbourne Rugby Club, 1978, 79, 80. Mem. Racing Club de France Rugby (Best Club Player award 1987), Marylebone Cricket Club, Melbourne Cricket Club. Home: 19 Inner Park Rd Wimbledon, London SW196ED, England Office: Euro-RSCG-Wnek-Gosper Advt, 11 Great Newport St, London WC2H 7JA, England

GOSS, COLLEEN FLYNN, lawyer; b. Youngstown, Ohio, Mar. 26, 1955; d. William John and Amanda Elizabeth Flynn; m. Richard Ingersoll Goss Jr., June 28, 1986 (div. July 1996); children: Geoffrey Ingersoll, Charles Flynn. BA in Econs., Tufts U., 1977; JD, Case Western Res. U., 1980. Assoc. Benesch, Friedlander, Coplan & Aronoff, Cleve., 1980-85; corp. atty. Midland Ross Corp., Cleve., 1985-87, Sudbury Inc., Cleve., 1987-89; asst. sec., corp. counsel The Lamson & Sessions Co., Cleve., 1990-94; assoc. Fay, Sharpe, Fagan, Minnich & McKee LLP, Cleve., 1995—. Mem. ABA, Am. Intellectual Property Law Assn., Ohio State Bar Assn., Cleve. Bar Assn., Cleve. Intellectual Property Lawyers Assn. Roman Catholic. Avocations: squash, snow skiing, genealogy. Office: Fay Sharpe Fagan Minnich & McKee 1100 Superior Ave E Fl 7 Cleveland OH 44114-2518

GOSS, JAMES WILLIAM, lawyer; b. London, Ont., Can., Mar. 10, 1941; s. Joseph Allen and Virginia Ruth (Farrah) G.; m. Rita Meyer, Aug. 2, 1969; children: Anne Candace, Jennette Courtney. BBA, West Mich. U., 1966; MS, U. Ill., 1972; JD, Georgetown U., 1974. Bar: Mich. 1974, U.S. Dist. Ct. (ea. dist.) Mich. 1974, U.S. Ct. Appeals (6th cir.) 1974. Sr. acct. Price Waterhouse & Co., Washington, 1969-71; assoc. Miller, Canfield, Paddock & Stone, Detroit, 1974-82, James W. Goss P.C., Southfield, Mich., 1982-88; ptnr. Dean & Fulkerson, Troy, Mich., 1988-95, James W. Goss P.C., Grosse Pointe Farms, Mich., 1995—; adj. lectr. U. Mich. Law, Ann Arbor, 1978-82. Bd. dirs. Old Newsboys Goodfellow Fund of Detroit, 1990-96, Adrian Coll., 1991-96; bd. dirs., v.p. Svc. to Older Citizens Soc., Grosse Pointe, Mich., 1997—; bd. govs. William L. Clements Libr., U. Mich., 1998—. Named Outstanding Goodfellow, Old Newsboys Goodfellows of Detroit, 1991; recipient Disting. Alumni award Western Mich. U., 1995. Mem. Georgetown U. Law Alumni Assn., Grosse Pointe Yacht Club, Georgetown Club of Mich., Commanderie de Bordeaux, Hundred Club, Rotary, Masons. Presbyterian. Avocations: philately, wine collecting, cartographic collecting. E-mail: jameswgosg@earthlink.net. Home: 398 Rivard Blvd Grosse Pointe MI 48230-1629 Office: 230 Punch and Judy Bldg 21 Kercheval Ave Grosse Pointe MI 48236-3698

GOSS, J.B., psychopharmacologist; b. Bklyn., June 1, 1956; s. Bernard David and Catherine (Marino) G.; m. Linda M. Goss, Dec. 28, 1979; children: Catherine, Jessica, Joseph S. B in Pharmacology, St. John's U., 1982; PhD in Psychology, LaSalle U., 1994. Diplomate Am. Bd. Psychopharmacology and Psychotherapy. Prof. Union U., Albany, 1985-96; dir. pharmacy O'Connor Hosp., Delhi, N.Y., 1985; v.p. for pharmacy svcs. Advanced Med. Cons., N.Y.C., 1987-93; psychiatric pharmacotherapeutics Stratton VA Med. Ctr., Albany, 1993-96; regional dir. Med. Pharmacology Rsch. Unit, Albany, 1993-96; pub. health dir. N.E. region Janssen Rsch. Found., 1996—; med. dir. A.E.C.H.O., Malta, N.Y., 1994-98; chair mental health N.Y. State Coun. of Hosp. Pharm., Albany, 1995—; mem. regional IRB Albany Med. Coll., 1993, others; mem. Freund's Scholarly Rsch. Group Think Tank, 1994—. Author: Hydroponic Workbook, 1985, Depression, the Secret War, 2000; adv. bd. mags., 1987-94. Avocation: patron of arts.

GOSS, JEFFERY ALAN, lawyer; b. Sydney, N.S.W., Australia, July 31, 1953; s. Henry George and Marjorie Edna (Gaughan) G.; m. Christine Joan Tebb, Feb. 22, 1975; children: Mathew Alan, Adam Eric. LLB, Sydney U., 1975. Articled clk. Dunhill, Morgan & Macready, Sydney, N.S.W., Australia, 1974-76; solicitor, 1976-77; solicitor Middletons, Moore & Bevins, Sydney, 1977-80, assoc. ptnr., 1980-82, ptnr., 1982-99; resident ptnr. Middletons, Moore & Bevins, Hong Kong, 1982-83; chmn. Sydney Partnership, 1996-99; hon. chmn. Australian Interest Rate Swap Terms Legal Com., 1985-86. Legal asst. Sydney U. Legal Aid Scheme, 1975; trustee Com. for Econ. Devel. of Australia; custodian State Libr. N.S.W. also: Level 29, 200 Queen St, Melbourne Victoria 3000, Australia also: 241 Adelaide St Level 14, Brisbane Queensland, Australia

GOSS, JOSEPHUS JOHANNES SYDNEY, geographer, consultant; b. Bletchley, Buckingham, Eng., Jan. 5, 1947; s. Sydney Harold and Johanna (Grassens) G. BA with honors, U. Leicester, Eng., 1969, MA, 1970. Asst. map rsch. officer Ministry of Def., London, 1970-76; editorial cons. Map Collector Pub., Tring, 1976-81, 90-97; cataloger, cons. Sotheby's, London, 1981-96; cons. Sanders of Oxford, 1997—; cons. Studio Editions, London, 1989-97, Batsford, London, 1989-95; cons. Atlas collation project British Libr., London, Ebury Press, 1996—, Bonhams Auctioneers, London, 1997—, Christie's Auctioneers, London, 1998, Bank of Cyprus Cultural Found., Nicosia, 1998—. Author: The Mapping of North America, 1989-90, Blaeu's The Grand Atlas, 1989-90, Braun & Hogenberg's City Maps of Europe, 1992, The Mapmakers Art, 1993 (Geog. Book of Yr. award Chgo. Geog. Soc. 1993); cons. editor Tooley's Dictionary of Mapmakers, 2d edit. Coord. local neighborhood watch activities, Milton Keynes, Eng., 1990—; mem. Bletchley Park Trust Com., 1993—. Fellow Royal Geog. Soc.; mem. Hist. Vereniging Roterodamum, Hist. Vereniging Holland. Avocations: gardening, filming, railways and tramways, Dutch lang. and culture, Australian history. Home: Bletchley, 16 Selbourne Ave, Milton Keynes MK3 5BX, England Office: Sanders of Oxford, 104 High St, Oxford OX1 4BW, England

GOSS, WILLIAM ALLAN, author, speaker; b. Summit, N.J., Apr. 23, 1955; S. Eugene Joseph and Barbara Tennyson (Dacey) G.; m. Margaret Mary Goss, Apr. 10, 1980; children: Brian William, Christina Marie. BA, Rutgers Coll., New Brunswick, N.J., 1980; MBA, N.H. Coll., 1988. Pilot USN, 1980-95; author, spkr. pvt. practice, Jacksonville, Fla., 1994—; cons. Goshawk Internat., Jacksonville, Fla., 1994-96. Author: The Luckiest Unlucky Man ALive, 1997; contbg. author: Chicken Soup for the Soul, 1997, Earth Angels, 1997. Vol. self def. instr. Battered Women Shelters, Jacksonville, Fla., 1994-97; contbr. HawkWatch, N.Mex., 1993-97, Jacksonville Zoo, 1992-97. Lt. Comdr. USN, 1980-97. Named Navy Officer of Yr., Navy League, Corpus Christi, tex., 1987, Writer of Yr., Navy Flying Mag., Washington, 1988. Mem. Nat. Spkrs. Assn., North Fla. Spkrs. Assn. Avocations: flying, writing, scuba diving, hiking, self-defense. Office: PO Box 7060 Orange Park FL 32073-5562

GOSSAGE, WAYNE, library director, management consultant, entrepreneur, executive recruiter; b. Bellingham, Wash., June 13, 1926; s. Coy Dell and Sadie Fay (Campbell) G.; m. Grace Villella, July 3, 1950; children: Leslie Anne, Gordon. BS, U. Wash., 1947; MS, Columbia U., 1951, MA, 1969. Asst. head adult svcs. East Orange (N.J.) Pub. Libr., 1951-54; head adult svcs. Levittown (N.Y.) Pub. Libr., 1954-55; dir. Warner Libr., Tarrytown, N.Y., 1956-63; asst. libr. Tchrs. Coll., Columbia U., N.Y.C., 1964-67; dir. Bank St. Coll. Edn. Libr., N.Y.C., 1967-80; pres. Gossage Regan Assocs., Inc., N.Y.C., 1980—; libr. cons. Gossage Regan Assocs., Inc., N.Y.C., 1980—; cons. to corp. librs., univs., assns., founds., chs., pubs., govt. agys. Contbr. articles to profl. jours. Vice pres. Hist. Soc. Tarrytown, 1960-61; trustee Harvard Libr., N.Y., 1978—; mem. alumni trustee nominating com. Columbia U., 1974-76; bd. advisors Pratt Inst. Sch. Info. and Libr. Sci., 1988—. With USNR, 1944-46. Coun. on Libr. Resources fellow, 1978-79; recipient Disting. Community Svc. award Tarrytown, 1962. Mem. ALA (notable books coun. 1961-62, ACRL bd. dirs. 1975-76, chmn. edn. and behavioral scis. sect. 1975-76, Ralph Shaw award for libr. lit. jury 1975-76, chmn. Wilson indexes com. 1978-81, Mudge citation com. 1985-87), N.Y. Libr. Assn. (v.p. resources and tech. svcs. sect. 1974-75, legis. com. 1974-75, pres. coll. and univ. librs. sect. 1978-79), N.Y. Libr. Club (pres. 1990-91), Spl. Libr. Assn. (chmn. div. social sci. 1975-76), Columbia U. Sch. Libr. Svcs. Alumni Assn. (sec.-treas. 1974-76, pres. 1977-78), Archons of Colophon (convenor 1989-90). Avocations: reading, writing, walking, travel. Home: 382 W Clinton Ave Irvington NY 10533-2132 Office: Gossage Regan Assocs Inc Ste 812 25 W 43d St New York NY 10036-7406

GOSSARD, WILLIAM H(ERBERT), JR., federal agency program administrator; b. Hickory, N.C., Dec. 2, 1945; s. William Herbert and Zelma Charlotte (Parnell) G.; m. Cara Stirling, Feb. 14, 1976; children: Jace Stirling, Michelle Reneé, Kathryn Jean-Marie. BA, Ottawa U., 1967; MPA, Ball State U., 1971. Mgmt. analyst U.S. Dept. Transp./Fed. R.R. Adminstrn., Washington, 1971-77; program mgr. U.S. Nat. Transp. Safety Bd., Washington, 1977—; pres. Med. Mktg. and Mgmt. Svcs., Centreville, Md., 1991—; cons. Am. Internat. Health Svcs., 1991—. Contbr. to nat. and internat. publs. Sr. exec. fellow Harvard U., 1985. Mem. Nat. Water Safety Congress (region 2 v.p. 2000), Nat. Safe Boating Coun. (sec.), Nat. Recreational Boating Coalition, Internat. Assn. Waterborne Emergency Response Activities (steering com.), U.S. Marine Safety Assn. (hon.), Nat. Rescue Soc. of Italy (hon.), Md. Ptnrs. for the Ams., Lions. Republican. Presbyterian. Avocations: tennis, skiing, reading, horseback riding, travel. Home and Office: Med Mktg and Mgmt Svcs 102 Fort Point Rd Centreville MD 21617-2652

GOSSELIN, CLAUDE A(LPHONSE) R(ENÉ), curator; b. Valleyfield, Que., Can., June 5, 1944; s. Sauveur and Georgette (Belair) G. D.E.S., U. Montreal, Que., 1969; Bacc. Spec., U. Que., 1969-71, postgrad. in history art, 1971. Tchr. Burundi, 1966-68; coordinator Que. Profl. Artists Soc., 1972-74; art critic Le Devoir newspaper, Montreal, 1974-75; visual arts officer Can. Council, Ottawa, Ont., 1975-79; curator, head exhbns. Musee d'Art Contemporain, Montreal, 1979-83; pres., founding dir. Montreal Internat. Ctr. Contemporary Art, 1983—; founding dir. La Giennale de Montreal, 1998—. Mem. Internat. Council Mus., Societe Des Musees Quebecois, Can. Mus. Assn. Office: CP 760 Succ Place du Parc, Montreal, PQ Canada H2W 2P3

GOSSELIN, DERRICK-PHILIPPE, business company executive; b. Menen, Belgium, Sept. 12, 1956; s. Joseph Arthur and Lea Genevieve (Van Assche) G.; m. Belinda Adelaide (de Saedeleer) G., Oct. 04, 1980; children: Anne-France, Marie-Charlotte. MSEE, U. of Ghent, Belgium, 1982; MS in Mgmt. and Indsl. Engring., U. of Ghent, 1984; MBA, INSEAD, Fontainebleau, France, 1995; doctoral student in Applied Econs., U. Ghent, Belgium, 1999—. Advisor to the prime minister Office of the Prime Minister, Brussels, 1982-84; sr. mgr. Arthur Andersen, Brussels, 1984-88; dir. of mktg. CSC, Brussels, 1989-90; v.p. Alcatel, Antwerp, Belgium, 1990—; advisor to Minister of Fgn. Trade, Belgium, 1997—, King Bauduin Found., Belgium, 1987-94, Prince Philippe Found, Belgium, 1998—; prof. U. Antwerpen, 1993—; adv. bd. Euroregio, 1999—. Hon. pres. Youth Club of the Cercle Chateau St. Anna, Brussels, 1996-99; pres. Ann. Price for Meriting Young People, Brussels, 1998-99; bd. dirs. Belgium Security and Control Inst., Brussels, 1996—, bus. sch. State U., Ghent, 1996—, Assn. Advisors Fgn. Trade, Brussels, 1997—; pres. Flanders Bus. Sch., 1999—. Decorated knight comdr. Order of Holy Sepulchre (Vatican), knight officer Leopold II Order (Belgium). Mem. UNICE (chmn. Asia commn. 1996—), Cercle Royal Gaulois litt. et Artistique, Country and Golf Club of Oudenaarde, Rotary Ghent-Zuid, Mensa, others. Avocations: golf, heraldry. Fax: 32 9 258 02 20. E-mail: Derrick.Gosselin@Advalvas.Be. Office: ALCATEL, F Wellesplein 1, Antwerp B-2018, Belgium

GOSSETT, PHILIP, musicologist; b. N.Y.C., Sept. 27, 1941; s. Harold and Pearl (Lenkowsky) G.; m. Suzanne Solomon, Aug. 4, 1963; children: David, Jeffrey. BA summa cum laude, Amherst Coll., 1963; student, Columbia U., 1961-62; MFA, Princeton U., 1965, PhD, 1970; LHD, Amherst Coll., 1993. Asst. prof. music and humanities U. Chgo., 1968-73, assoc. prof., 1973-77, prof., 1977-84, Robert W. Reneker Disting. Svc. prof. music, 1984—, dean divsn. humanities, 1989-99; vis. assoc. prof. Columbia U., 1975, Inst. de Musicologie Universite de Paris, 1988, Gauss seminars, Princeton U., 1991; cons. in field. Gen. editor: The Works of Giuseppe Verdi, Opera Omnia di Gioachino Rossini; mem. editorial bd. Am. Musicol. Soc., 1972-78; cons. editor: Critical Inquiry, 1974—, Ninteenth Century Music, 1976—, Cambridge Opera Jour., 1987—; translator Treatise on Harmony (Jean-Philippe Rameau), (with Charles Rosen) Early Romantic Opera, Anna Bolena and the Maturity of Gaetano Donizetti, 1985, Il Barbiere di Siviglia, 1993, Don Pasquale, 2000, also numerous critical edits.; prepared vocal ornamentation for operas in Milan, Rome, Bologna, Pesaro, Chgo., Miami, St. Louis, N.Y., Santa Fe. Trustee Chgo. Symphony Orch., 1991—, Ct. Theatre, Chgo., 1994—. Decorated Gold medal 1st class (Italy), 1985, Grande Ufficiale della Rep. (Italy), 1997, Order Rio Branca, Brazil, 1998, Cavaliere di gran Croce (Italy), 1998; Woodrow Wilson fellow, 1963-64, 66-67; Fulbright scholar Paris, 1965-66; Martha Baird Rockefeller fellow, 1967-68; Guggenheim fellow, 1971-72; NEH sr. scholar, 1982-83; Deems Taylor award of ASCAP, 1986. Fellow AAAS, Academia Filarmonica of Bologna (hon.); mem. Am. Musicol. Soc. (coun. 1972-74, bd. dirs. 1974-76, v.p. 1986-88, Albert Einstein award 1969, pres. 1994-96), Internat. Musicol. Soc., Am. Inst. Verdi Studies (bd. dirs.), Societa Italiana di Musicologia, Soc. Textual Scholarship (pres. 1993-95), Premio Paolo Borciani (pres. 1997). E-mail: phgs@midway.uchi-

cago.edu. Home: 5810 S Harper Ave Chicago IL 60637-1843 Office: U Chgo Dept Music Chicago IL 60637

GOSSETT, ROBERT FRANCIS, JR., merchant banker; b. San Antonio, Tex., Nov. 19, 1943; s. Robert Francis and Anne Elizabeth (Donnell) G.; m. Pauline Washington Gillespie, June 27, 1964; children: Robert Francis III, Frank Morgan Gillespie. BA, U. Tex., 1964; JD, Georgetown U., 1967; MBA, U. Pa., 1969. Assoc., investment bank div. Merrill Lynche, Pierce, Fenner & Smith, N.Y.C., 1969-74; v.p. Oppenheimer Properties, Inc., N.Y.C., 1974-78; exec. v.p., dir. Loeb Rhoades Hornblower Capital Corp., N.Y.C., 1978-81; chmn. bd., pres. Vance Capital Corp., N.Y.C., 1981—; gen. ptnr. First San Bernardio Assoc., Ltd., Long Beach, Calif., 1979—, First Riverside (Calif.) Assoc., 1980—, First Portland Assoc., Beaverton, Oreg., 1980—, Corp. Realty Income Fund I, Ltd., N.Y.C., 1986—, Vance, Teel & Co. Ltd., San Antonio, 1998—; chmn. bd. dirs. 1345 Realty Corp., N.Y.C., 1994—, Minn. Street Assoc., Inc., St. Paul, 1988—; gen. ptnr. Hoopes Assocs., Ltd., Rockport, Tex., 1989—, Teel Land and Cattle Co., LLC, Yancey, Tex., 1997—. Mem. bd. regents Georgetown U., 1993-99. Mem. Campfire Club, The Mashomack Preserve Club. Office: Vance Capital Corp 406 E 85th St New York NY 10028-6302

GOSSWEILER, ROBERT MARTIN, oil company executive; b. La Paz, Bolivia, July 13, 1949; s. Robert Fritz and Hildegard (Zewrkowsky) G.; m. Dawn Ann Phillips, Sept. 21, 1974 (div. Sept. 1990); m. Luz Elena Tena, June 28, 1991; children: Brant Robert; m. Georgina Lua Guizar, Dec. 3, 1997; children: Annemarie Hildegard, Brant Robert. BA in Lit., San Andres U., La Paz, 1967; BS in Econs., U. Pa., 1972, MBA, 1974. Purchasing agt. Samincorp Inc., N.Y.C., 1974-75; v.p. mktg. J. Mueller Corp., Zurich, 1976-78; v.p. Closomat USA Inc., Franklin Lakes, N.J., 1979-83; pres. Aquamatics Co., Tallman, N.Y., 1984-85, Sodiesa Petroleum, N.Y.C., 1986—; pres. Sodiesa Petroleum, Finamex Found. of Econ./Ecol. Studies, Mexico, Cosmana Found., Zurich-Switzerland, 1990—; dean bus. sch. and mktg. coord. LaSalle U., Tarimbaro, Mex., 1990—; developer magnet bus. schs. Contbr. articles to profl. jours. Pres. Cozmana Found., Zurich, Switzerland, 1998—; coord. ednl. programs for Mexican/Americans NMSU-DONA ANA chpt., Las Cruces, N.Mex., 1988. Recipient Spl. Mention, Phila. chpt. SBA, 1974. Mem. Wharton Alumni Club. Avocations: languages, music, tennis, tropical fish studies. Fax: 52-43-17-05-07. E-mail: magnetbiz@yahoo.com. Office: Cosmana & Finamex Founds AC, Colima 136 Molino De Parras, 58010 Morelia Michoacan, Mexico

GOSTIAUX, BERNARD, secondary education educator; b. Raimbeaucourt, France, Feb. 21, 1944; s. Henri Gostiaux and Louise Le Maire; m. Catherine Rousselle, Sept. 3, 1971; children: Michel, Louis. Degree in number theory and algebra, U. paris, 1965; student, Ecole Normale Supérieure de Saint Cloud, 1963-67. Cert. tchr. math. Asst. U. Paris, 1967-69; tchr. Lycée J.B. Say, Paris, 1969-73, Lycée St. Louis, Paris, 1973—. Author: Géometrie Différentielle, 1971, Cours de Mathématiques Spéciales, 1993, 95. Mem. Nautical Soc. Perreux. Roman Catholic. Home: 60 Rue Gilbert Méderic, 94170 Le Perreux France Office: Lycée St Louis, 44 Blvd St Michel, 75006 Paris France

GOSWAMI, AJANTA, psychiatrist; b. Guwahati, Assam, India, Dec. 3, 1960; came to U.S., 1993; d. Kamala and Nirvpama G.; m. Gautam Phookan, Jan. 26, 1987; 1 child, Sujoy. MBBS, Assam (India) Med. Coll., 1984; MD in Psychol. Medicine, Ctrl. Inst. Psychiatry, Ranchi, India, 1987; M in Med. Sci., U. Leeds, 1993. Diplomate Indian Bd. Psychiatry. Resident in psychiatry Ctrl. Inst. Psychiatry, Bihar, India, 1984-87; vis. registrar Nat. Health Svcs., Leicester, Leeds, Eng., 1989-93; resident, fellow Milton Hershey Med. Ctr., Pa. State U., Hershey, 1994-97, asst. dir. child inpatient unit, 1997-98, child and adolescent psychiatrist, 1997-98, dir. child psychiatry outpatient svcs., 1998-99; asst. prof. psychiatry Pa. STate U., 1997-99. Recipient Gold medal Govt. India, 1984; Rsch. fellow Christian Med. Coll., Vellore, India, 1987-88, Vis. fellow Cambridge Hosp., Harvard Med. Sch., 1988. Mem. Am. Psychiatry Assn., Am. Acad. Child Adolescent Psychiatry, Pa. Psychiat. Assn. Avocations: reading, gardening. Office: Ball Meml Hosp 2401 W University Ave Muncie IN 47303-3499

GOSWAMI, KANAN BIHARI, foreign language educator; b. Baghnapara, India, Nov. 14, 1939; s. Bon Bihari and Savitri (Banerjee) G.; m. Sipra Chakraborty, Feb. 9, 1966; 1 child, Swapnanjan. BA in Bengali with honors, Presidency Coll., Calcutta, 1958; MA in Bengali, Calcutta U., 1960, PhD in Bengali, 1977, LLB, 1979. Lectr. in Bengali Scottish Ch. Coll., Calcutta, 1961, Chandernagore (India) Coll., 1961-70, Jhargram (India) Raj Coll., 1970-75; asst. prof. Bengali, head lang. dept. Goenka Coll., Calcutta, 1975-79; asst. prof. Bengali A.B.N. Seal Coll., Cooch Behar, India, 1979-80; lectr. Bengali Rabindra Bharati U., Calcutta, 1980-85, reader Bengali, 1985—, head Bengali dept., 1995-97. Author: Bhasha Darpan, 1976, Bangabani, 1978, Baikuntherwill-Samiksha, 1979, Baghapara-Sampradaya O Vaisnav Sahitya, 1993; contbr. articles to profl. jours.; author of poetry. Programme officer Nat. Social Svc., Rabindra Bharati U., Calcutta, 1981-92, coord., 1993. Sr. grade govt. scholar D.P.I. Govt. West Bengal, Calcutta, 1956. Mem. All India Drama Judges Soc., Rabi Basar (life). Hindu. Avocation: tagore song and Bengali traditional songs. Home: Sector III, FE126 Salt Lake City, Calcutta 700091, India Office: Rabindra Bharati Univ, 56A Barrackpore Trunk Rd, Calcutta 700050, India

GOSZTONYI, GEORG, neuropathologist, educator; b. Budapest, Hungary, Mar. 30, 1932; s. Lajos and Terezia (Neuberger) G.; m. Eva Maria Kerpel-Fronius, Oct. 22, 1962; children: Kristof, Andras. MD, Semmelweis Med. U., Budapest, 1956; PhD, Hungarian Acad. Scis., Budapest, 1978. Med. diplomate. From resident to sr. lectr. neurology U. Pécs, Hungary, 1956-66, chief neuropathol. lab., 1966-68; rsch. fellow MRC Labs., Carshalton, Surrey, Eng., 1965-66; sr. lectr. psychiatry Semmelweis Med. U., Budapest, 1968-80; vis. prof. dept. neuropathology Freie U., Berlin, 1980-84, prof., 1984—, dep. dir. dept. neuropathology, 1985-98; cons. neurologist Nat. Inst. Vascular and Heart Surgery, Budapest, 1972-80. Editl. bd. Clin. Neurosci. Recipient Charles Schaffer Meml. award Hungarian Soc. Neurology and Psychiatry, 1976. Mem. Internat. Soc. Neuropathology (hon.), AAAS, Am. Assn. Neuropathologists, Brit. Neuropathol. Soc., French Soc. of Neuropathology, German Soc. for Neuropathology and Neuroanatomy, Hungarian Soc. Neuropathology. Home: Grenzburgstrasse 5, D-12165 Berlin Germany Office: Freie U Berlin Dept Neuropathology, Hindenburgdamm 30, D-12200 Berlin Germany

GOTH, CHRISTIAN, ethnologist, consultant; b. Paris, Nov. 5, 1945; s. Roland and Ginette (Massias) G.; m. Denise Moruzzi; children: Julia, Arthur. M in Sociology, U. Paris, 1981, M in Ethnology, 1982. Cons. Europsychologies, Paris, 1983—; pres. Interconsulting, Luxembourg, 1999—. Author: Ecrivains, Ecriture, 1984, Ethnologie de la vie Quotidienne, 1987; (software) Tests HK, 1989. Named Officer of Merite et Devoir, Paris, 1972. Mem. Soc. Cons. Luxembourg (pres. 1997), N.Y. Acad. Scis. Democrat. Roman Catholic. Avocations: golf, opera. Home: 33 rue Jean L'aveugle, 1148 Luxembourg Luxembourg Office: Interconsulting, BP 1932 Luxembourg-Gare Luxembourg

GOTH, LASZLO, chemistry educator; b. Keszthely, Hungary, Aug. 23, 1943; s. Janos and Margit (Renczes) G.; m. Hajnalka Nemeth, Aug. 2, 1971; 1 child, Julia. M, Chem. U., Yeszprem, Hungary, 1967, PhD, 1971. Head lab. dept. Hosp., Sumeg, Hungary, 1967-93; assoc. prof. dept. clin. chemistry Med. U., Debrecen, Hungary, 1994—. Fulbright scholar Stanford U., Calif., 1992-93. Mem. Am. Assn. Clin. Chemistry, N.Y. Acad. Scis., Internat. Soc. Clin. Enzimology. Avocations: soccer, swimming, gardening. Home: Sagi Janos 74, H-8360 Keszthely Hungary Office: Med U Dept Clin Chemistry, PO Box 40, H-4012 Debrecen Hungary

GÖTHERT, MANFRED, pharmacologist; b. Braunschweig, Germany, Dec. 12, 1939; s. Rudolf and Luise (Freise) G.; m. Irmgard Karin Scheiber, Aug. 31, 1966; children: Joachim, Wolfram, Martin. Abitur, Martino-Katharineum, Braunschweig, Germany, 1959; Med. State Examination, U. Göttingen (Germany), 1965, MD, 1965; PhD in Pharmacology, U. Hamburg (Germany), 1971. Rsch. asst. U. Hamburg (Germany), 1967-71, lectr., 1971-76, assoc. prof., 1976-78; prof. biochem. pharmacology U. Essen (Germany), 1978-85; prof. pharmacology and toxicology, dir. Inst. Pharmacology U. Bonn (Germany), 1985—, dean med. faculty, 1998—. Editor;. Mem. German Soc. Exptl. and Clin. Pharmacology and Toxicology (pres. 1997-99), Serotonin Club (v.p. 1995-98), N.Y. Acad. Scis., Soc. Neurosci., Polish Acad. Arts and Sci., German Acad. Arts and Sci., German Acad. Natural Scientists Leopoldina. Office: U Bonn Inst Pharmacol, Reuterstr 26, 53113 Bonn Germany

GOTLIB, VICTOR ABRAHAM, mathematician; b. Moscow, May 30, 1948; arrived in Israel, 1990; s. Abraham and Maria (Nabutovsky) G.; m. Alla Muller, Mar. 14, 1978; children: Yury, Vladimir. MS, State U., Nizhni Novgorod, 1971; PhD, Inst. Fine Chem. Tech., Moscow, 1984. Engr. Sci. Rsch. Inst. Wood Chemistry, Gorky, 1974, sr. engr., 1975-78, group leader, 1978-84, sr. rschr., 1984-90; assoc. rschr. Holon Acad. Inst. Tech. (formerly Ctr. Tech. Edn.), Israel, 1991-96, sr. rschr., 1996—; assoc. lectr. Ctr. Tech. Edn., Holon, Israel, 1991—; master thesis supr. State U., Gorky, 1979-90, Ctr. Tech. Edn., Holon. Editl. bd. mem.: Far East Jour. of Dynamical Systems, 2000—; contbr. articles to profl. jours. Mem. Israel Assn. Immigrant-Scientists (vice chmn. engring. mechanics sect. of acad. coun. 1996-99), Israel Math. Union, European Math. Soc. Jewish. Avocation: classical music. Home: 28/7 Dov Gur, Ashdod 77554, Israel Office: Holon Acad Inst of Tech, PO Box 305, Holon 58102, Israel

GOTO, FUMIO, anesthesiologist; b. Komochi Village, Japan, July 13, 1941; s. Shihei and Toshi (Hashizume) G.; m. Misuzu Goto, Apr. 8, 1970; 2 children. MD, Gunma U., 1968, PhD, 1976. Asst. prof. Gunma U., Maebashi, Japan, 1976-87, assoc. prof., 1987-91, prof., 1996—; prof. Kitasato U., Sagamihara, Japan, 1991-96. Editl. bd. Jour. of Anesthesia, 1992—. Mem. Japan Soc. of Anesthesiologists (elder, com. on bd. qualification 1996—, Yamamura award 1982, 85), Japan Clin. Soc. of Anesthesiologists (elder, Kosaka award 1991, 95), Japan Pain Clinic Soc. (elder). Home: 2-4-2 Motosoja-machi, Maebashi 371-0846, Japan Office: Gunma U Sch Medicine, 3-39-22 Showa-machi, Maebashi 371-8511, Japan

GOTO, IWAO, law educator; b. Matama, Oita, Japan, Mar. 8, 1930; s. Hidtaka and Tazu (Fujiwara) G. BA, Chuo U., Tokyo, 1953; MA, Hosei Grad. Sch. Law, Tokyo, 1958, D, 1961. Comml. law lectr. Yahata U., Kitakyusyushi, Japan, 1961-67, law assoc. prof., 1967-68, law prof., 1968-69; law prof. Kyusyu Internat. U., Kitakyusyushi, Japan, 1969—. Author: On the Study of Commerical Law, 1998; co-author: On Corporation, 1980; editor: Yahata U. Law Econ. Jour., 1968, Kyushu Internat. U. Law Jour., 1994. Mem. Internat. Bar Assn., London Ct. Internat. Arbitration, Japan Privet Law Assn. Avocations: journey to visit museum, painting, watching sports games, reading. Fax: 093-641-5067. Home: 3-14-2-408 Yahatanishi-ku, Kitakyusha-shi Fukuoka-Ken 806-0043, Japan Office: Kyushu Internat U, 1-6-1 Hirano Yahatahigashi, Fukuoka Kitakyushushi 805-8512, Japan

GOTO, JUNICHI, economics educator; b. Ube, Yamaguchi, Japan, July 22, 1951; s. Torao and Masako Goto; m. Yoshie Watakabe, Jan. 9, 1988; children: Yoichiro, Shinichi. BA, Yamaguchi U., 1975; MA, Yale U., 1981, PhD, 1986. Economist Ministry of Labor, Tokyo, 1975-87, The World Bank, Washington, 1987-90; dep. dir. Ministry of Labor, Tokyo, 1990-91; prof. econ. Kobe (Japan) U., 1991—; cons. The World Bank, 1986, 96-97, Inter-Am. Devel. Bank, 1998-99; vis. scholar MIT, Cambridge, 1993-94, Yale U., 1995-96. Author: International Labor Economics, 1988 (Nikkei Best Book award 1988), Economics of Migrant Workers, 1990 (Okinaga prize 1991), Labor in International Trade Theory, 1990, Migrant Workers and the Japanese Economy, 1993. Mem. Am. Econ. Assn., Japanese Econ. Assn. Avocations: travel, reading. Home: 3-3-16 Yamamoto-Dori, Chuo-ku Kobe 650-0003, Japan Office: Kobe Univ, Rsch Inst Econ and Bus, Nada Kobe 657, Japan

GOTO, MASAHIRO, chemist; b. Kumamoto, Japan, Aug. 10, 1961; s. Zenji and Noriko (Tominaga) G.; m. Yumiko Shimizu, Feb. 26, 1989; two children. BSc, Kyushu U., 1984, MSc, 1986, PhD, 1989. Rschr. JSPS, Fukuoka, Japan, 1989-90; assoc. prof. Kyushu U., Fukuoka, 1990—; vis. prof. MIT, 1994-95. Recipient young rschr. award Chem. Engrs. Soc. Japan. Avocations: gardening, travel. Office: Kyushu U Dept Chem Sys Engr, Hakozaki, Fukuoka 812-8581, Japan

GOTO, MASAYUKI, sociology researcher and educator; b. Sagamihara-shi, Kanagawa, Japan, June 14, 1957; s. Akira and Chiyo (Imanari) G.; m. Yumi Matsuo, June 4, 1989; 1 child, Yosuke. BA in Social Scis., U. Tokyo, 1981, MA in Sociology, 1983; PhD in Sociology, U. Calif., Santa Barbara, 1996. Rsch. assoc. U. Tokyo, 1985-90; assoc. prof. sociology Japan Ministry Edn., Tokyo, 1990-92, Seijo U., Tokyo, 1992—. Author: George Herbert Mead: His Theory of Communication and Social Psychology, 1988, A Theory of Communication: On Love and Distrust, 1999; translator: Symbolic Interactionism (Herbert Blumer), 1991. Recipient Japanese Nebula award Japan Writers Sci. Fiction, 1993. Mem. Japan Sociol. Assn., Am. Sociol. Assn., Japan Writers Assn. Avocations: writing fiction, marine diving. Home: 4-24-30-303 Haramachida, Machida, Tokyo 194-0013, Japan Office: Seijo U, 6-1-20 Seijo, Setagaya, Tokyo 157-8511, Japan

GOTO, NOBUYUKI, engineering educator; b. Yokohama, Kanagawa, Japan, Aug. 4, 1940; s. Katsuo and Sumie (Wada) G.; m. Nobuko Komori, May 17, 1967; children: Natsuko, Muneaki, Makiko. B Engring., Tokyo U., 1964, D Engring., 1986; MS, MIT, 1970. Rsch. scientist Toshiba Corp., Kawasaki, Japan, 1973-76, sr. rsch. scientist, 1977-86, chief rsch. scientist, 1987-88, sr. mgr., 1989-95; prof. Shonan Inst. Tech., Fujisawa, Japan, 1996—, dir. computer ctr., 1997—; instr. Saitama (Japan) Inst. Tech., 1995—. Author: Automation of Visual Inspection, 1984, Troubleshooting of Microprocessor-based Systems, 1987; contbr. articles to profl. jours. Mem. IEEE (sr.), Assn. for Computing Machinery, Sigma Xi. Avocations: music, photography, diy, personal computing, ballroom dancing. Home: 6-15-5 Saginomiya Nakano-ku, 165-0032 Tokyo Japan Office: Shonan Inst Tech, 1-1-25 Tsujido-Nishikaigan, 251-8511 Fujisawa Japan

GOTO, SHOHACHIRO, economics educator; b. Nobeoka, Miyazaki, Japan, Jan. 5, 1933; s. Chyuzaburo and Seki (Inada) G.; m. Takako Kikuchi, Nov. 19, 1964; children: Kaeko, Chizuko, Mikiko. B of Econs., Meiji U., Tokyo, Japan, 1961, M of Econs., 1963, PhD in Econs., 1976. Asst. Meiji U., Tokyo, Japan, 1963-67, lectr., 1967-70, asst. prof., 1970-75, prof., 1975—; vis. scholar UCLA, 1979-80;. Author: Fundamental Theory of Economic Policy, 1974, Analysis of Productivity and Economic Policy, 1993, AI-S Analysis and Economic Policy, 1993, A Study in the Principles of Economic Policy, 2000. Mem. Japan Econ. Policy Assn. (dir. 1983—). Liberal Democrat. Buddhism. Avocations: reading, fishing. Home: 2-6-29 Nishi-Kashiwadai, Kashiwa Chiba 277-0886, Japan Office: Meiji U Faculty Econs, 1-1- Kanda Surugadai, Chiyoda 101-8301, Japan

GOTO, TOSHIO, engineering educator; b. Inuyama, Aichi, Japan, Nov. 11, 1941; s. Motosaburo and Shigee (Kosaka) G.; m. Kazuyo Suzuta, Sept. 12, 1971; children: Yoichiro, Yuhko. B.Engring., Nagoya (Japan) U., 1964, M.Engring., 1966, Dr.Engring., 1969. Cert. electronic engr. Rsch. assoc. Nagoya U., 1969-73, asst. prof., 1974-77, assoc. prof., 1978-85, prof. engring., 1986—, vice dean Sch. Engring., 1993-94, dean Sch. Engring., 2000—; exec. dir. Nagoya Industry Sci. Inst., 1993—; com. mem. Min. of Internat. Trade and Industry, Tokyo, 1997—. Author: Handbook of Plasma Material Science, 1992; contbr. articles to profl. jours.; patentee in field. Japan Soc. for Promotion of Sci. fellow, 1974; Min. of Edn., Sci. and Culture grantee, 1987, 93. Mem. IEEE (sr.), AAAS, Japan Soc. Applied Physics (exec. dir. 1992-93), Sci. Coun. of Japan (com. mem. 1997—). Home: 3-2110 Goshikien, Nisshin 470-0105, Japan Office: Nagoya Univ, Furo-cho Chikusa-ku, Nagoya 464-8603, Japan

GOTOVSKA-HENZE, TEODORITCHKA ILIEVA, historian, educator; b. Sofia, Bulgaria, May 1, 1958; d. Ilia Sergeev Gotovsky and Maria Pencheva Ikonopissova; m. Dimiter Petrov Popov, July 28, 1983 (div. Dec. 1994); 1 child, Irina; m. Rolf Heinrich Henze, Apr. 30, 1995. BA, Sofia U., 1982; PhD, Charles U., Prague, Czech Republic, 1989. Specialist Sofia U., 1982-83; scientific rschr. Inst. History, Sofia, 1989—; fellow Bologna (Italy) Ctr. J.H. U., 1990-91, Ctrl. European U., Prague, 1993-94, Cath. U. Eichstatt, Germany, 1997; cons. Criteria Assn., Sofia, 1997—. Author: Toward the Lost Throne, 1996. Mem. Masaryk Found., Prague, 1994. Home: Schillerstr 42, D-37083 Göttingen Germany Office: Inst History Bl 17, Shipchenski Prochod 52, 1313 Sofia Bulgaria

GOTSDINER, MURRAY BENNETT, lawyer; b. Des Moines, Jan. 2, 1953; s. harold B. and Shirlee Ann (Gorshel) G.; m. Debora Zadina, Feb. 5, 1972; children: Alexander, Erik, Elizabeth. BA, Drake U., 1975, JD, 1979. Bar: Iowa 1980, Tex. 1989, U.S. Dist. Ct. Iowa, 1980, U.S. Ct. Appeals (8th cir.), 1982, U.S. Supreme Ct. 1983. Shareholder McEnroe, McCarthy & Gotsdiner, P.C., Des Moines, 1980—. Mem. Iowa Bar Assn., Tex. Bar Assn., Polk County (Iowa) Bar Assn., Des Moines Club. Republican. Jewish. Avocations: golf, deep sea fishing. Home: 13211 Sunset Cir Clive IA 50325-8805 Office: McEnroe McCarthy & Gotsdiner PC Westown Bus Ctr Ste 100 1701-48th St West Des Moines IA 50266-6723

GOTT, MARJORIE EDA CROSBY, conservationist, former educator; b. Louisville; d. Alva Baird and Nellie (Jones) Crosby; m. John Richard Gott, Jr., Mar. 12, 1946 (dec. Sept. 1993); 1 child, J. Richard III. AB in Math., U. Louisville, 1934; postgrad., U. Ky., 1938-42. Nationally accredited flower show judge, landscape design critic and judge. Underwriter Commonwealth Life Ins. Co., Louisville, 1934-37; tchr. English Hikes Sch., Buechel, Ky., 1937-43; civilian chief statis. control unit Materiel Command, Army Air Force, Dayton, Ohio, 1943-46; tchr. psychology Bapt. Hosp. and Gen. Hosp., Louisville, 1950-52; dedicated Ky.'s Floral Clock to All Kentuckians Who Take Pride in the Beauty of Their State Commonwealth of Ky.,1961. Author: (booklet) How a Garden Club Beautifies a City, 1967. Pres. Young Women's Rep. Club of Louisville and Jefferson County, 1938-40; pres. Beautification League Louisville and Jefferson County, 1963-64; co-chair Keep Ky. Cleaner-Greener, 1963-68; bd. dirs. Scenic Ky., Inc., 1989—, Nat. Coun. State Garden Clubs, 1961-83. Recipient Conservation award of merit Commonwealth of Ky., 1963, Landscape Design Critics award Nat. Coun. State Garden Clubs, 1979. Mem. Woman's Club of Louisville (pres. 1973-75, hon. 1991—), Garden Club of Ky. (pres. 1961-63), Nat. Assn. Parliamentarians (founder, pres. Louisville unit 1961-63), Louisville Astron. Soc. (hon.). Presbyterian. Avocations: travel, bridge, cooking. Home: 136 Indian Hills Trl Louisville KY 40207-1541

GOTT, YURI VLADIMIROVICH, physicist, researcher; b. Kharkov, Ukraine, Sept. 15, 1937; s. Vladimir Spiridonovich and Klaudia Nikolaevna (Lazareva) G.; m. Tatjana Mikhailovna Dmitrieva; children: Natalia, Maria. Diploma, U. Moscow, 1960; Cand. Sci., Russian Rsch. Ctr./Kurchatov, Moscow, 1967; ScD, U. Kharkov, 1976. Rschr. Russian Rsch. Ctr./Kurchatov Inst., Moscow, 1960-78, prin. rschr., 1978—. Author: Interaction of Slow Particles with a Matter and Plasma Diagnostics, 1973, Interactions of Particles with a Matter in Plasma Researches, 1978; contbr. articles to profl. jours. Fax: 007-095-943-00-73. E-mail: gott@qq.nfi.kiae.ru. Office: RRC Kurchatov Inst, Pl Kurchatova, 123182 Moscow Russia

GOTTA, ALEXANDER WALTER, anesthesiologist, educator; b. Bklyn., Apr. 10, 1935; s. A. Walter and Helen C. (Bruskewic) G.; m. Colleen A. Sullivan, July 17, 1965; 1 child, Nancy C. BS summa cum laude, St. John's U., 1956; MD, NYU, 1960. Diplomate Am. Bd. Anesthesiology, Am. Bd. Med. Examiners. Intern U. Chgo., 1960-61; resident Boston City Hosp., 1961-62, N.Y. Hosp.-Cornell U., N.Y.C., 1962-64; instr. anesthesiology Cornell U., 1965-66; asst. prof., 1978-79; dir. anesthesia St. Mary's Hosp., Bklyn., 1968-78; asst. prof. SUNY, Bklyn., 1968-78; assoc. prof. SUNY, 1978-85, prof., 1985-97; prof. emeritus, 1997—; dir. anesthesia L.I. Coll. Hosp., Bklyn., 1983-90; dir. anesthesia Kings County Hosp. Ctr., 1990-97; spkr. in field. Editor: Anesthesiology Clinics Trauma, 1996; contbr. articles to profl. jours. Capt. U.S. Army, 1966-68, Vietnam. Fellow N.Y. Acad. Medicine (chmn. anesthesia sect. 1990, recognition for svc. to urban medicine 1997), Am. Coll. Anesthesiologists, Am. Soc. Anesthesiologists (ho. dels. 1986-97, chmn. refresher course com. 1995); mem. N.Y. Soc. Anesthesiologists (bd. dirs. 1983-97, chmn. sci. program com. 1991-93, chmn. PGA 1994-96, v.p. 1994, pres.-elect 1995, pres. 1996), N.Y. Soc. Critical Care Medicine (pres. 1985), Assn. Univ. Anesthesiologists, Acad. Anesthesia. Republican. Roman Catholic. Home: 29 Ascot Ridge Rd Great Neck NY 11021-2912 Office: Kings County Hosp Ctr 451 Clarkson Ave Brooklyn NY 11203-2097

GOTTARDI, WALDEMAR ARTHUR, chemist, hygienist, researcher; b. Meran, Italy, June 1, 1935; s. Bruno and Waltraut (Hirn) G.; m. Barbara Riedl, Jan. 4, 1975; children: Roman, Elvira, Nora. PhD, U. Innsbruck, Austria, 1965. Asst. inst. inorganic chemistry U. Innsbruck, 1965-73, asst. inst. hygiene, 1974-79, asst. prof. inst. hygiene, 1979-92, assoc. prof. inst. hygiene, 1992—. Violinist, leader string quartet. Home: Hoher Weg 13, A 6020 Innsbruck Austria Office: Inst Hygiene U Innsbruck, Fritz Pregl Str 3, A 6010 Innsbruck Austria

GOTTESMAN, ROY TULLY, chemical company executive; b. Bayonne, N.J., Mar. 6, 1928; s. Harry and Sarah (Schneier) G.; m. Sandra Florence Cohen, Mar. 6, 1954; children: Lee Daniel, Cheryl Sue. BSc in Chemistry, Rutgers U., 1947, MS, 1950, PhD, 1951; postgrad., U. Minn., 1947-48. Chemist R & D Heyden Chem. Corp., Garfield, N.J., 1951-56; group leader R & D Heyden Newport Chem. Corp., Garfield, 1956-60; supr. R & D Tenneco Chems. Inc., Garfield, 1960-65, mgr. R & D, 1965-70; dir. chem. devel. Tenneco Chems. Inc., Piscataway, N.J., 1970-77; dir. environ. and regulatory affairs Tenneco Chems. Inc., Saddle Brook, N.J., 1977-79; v.p. Tenneco Chems. Inc., Saddle Brook, 1979-83; pres. Chem. Mgmt. Resources, Toms River, N.J., 1983-97; exec. dir. The Vinyl Inst., Wayne, N.J., 1983-92, founding dir., cons., 1992-98. Patentee in field. Pres. Glen Rock (N.J.) Bd. Edn., 1963-69; councilman Borough Glen Rock, 1973-85; mem. N.J. Hazardous Waste Facility Siting Commn., Trenton, 1982-94; bd. dirs. Plastics Recycling Found., Washington, 1987-90. Named Man of Yr., Glen Rock Jewish Ctr., 1969; recipient Negev award Israel Bond Orgn., 1982. Mem. Am. Chem. Soc., Soc. Plastics Engrs.(sr.), Chem. Industry Coun. N.J. (exec. bd. 1976-90), Phi Beta Kappa, Sigma Xi. Republican. Avocations: tennis, photography. Home and Office: 1619 Lacebark Rd Toms River NJ 08755-1811

GOTTFELD, GUNTHER MAX, retired urban mass transit official, consultant; b. Berlin, June 13, 1934; came to U.S., 1941; s. William James and Charlotte Jeanette (Less) G.; m. Linda Stratton Keene, Oct. 26, 1969 (div. Jan. 1976); children: Deborah Charlotte, David William; m. Ann Richmond, July 13, 1985. BS, Shepherd Coll., 1958; MA, Am. U., 1960. Transp. planner Nat. Capital Trnasp. Agy., Washington, 1961-63; cons. Stockholm Transit Authority, 1963-64; fed. liaison officer Mass. Bay Transp. Authority, Boston, 1965-70; sr. transp. planner Md. Mass Transit Adminstrn., Balt., 1970-74, intergovtl. coordinator, 1974-94. Mem. Am. Pub. Transit Assn. (mem. legis. com. 1981—), Md. Mass Transit Adminstrn., Am. Rd. and Transp. Builders Assn. (mem. pub. transit council 1986-94, mem. legis. watch com. 1986-94), Internat. Union Pub. Transport (rail transit new starts com. 1992—). Democrat. Jewish. Avocations: European travel, cross-country skiing, hiking, classical music. Home: 5301 Hesperus Dr Columbia MD 21044-1808

GOTTFRIED, MARK ELLIS, accountant, consultant; b. Toledo, Mar. 12, 1953; s. Max and Barbara Alice (Johnston) G.; m. Linda Jean Perkins, Aug. 7, 1976; children: Christopher Ellis, Katherine Powell. BA, Northwestern U., 1975; MBA, U. Chgo., 1980. CPA Ill., Ind. Sr. acct. Deloitte Haskins & Sells, Chgo., 1980-84; corp. mktg. mgr. Micro Data Base Systems, Lafayette, Ind., 1984-85; sr. cons. Deloitte Haskins & Sells, Indpls., 1985-86, mgr., 1986-88; owner Gottfried & Assocs., Indpls., 1988-91; v.p. fin., sec. Trilithic, Inc., Indpls., 1989-92; pres. TriVox Corp., 1990-92, Performance Ptnrs., Inc., 1991-93; prin., owner Gottfried Assocs., Va., 1995—; bd. dirs., treas. Ptnrs. in Mktg. Inc., 1992-93; bd. dirs. ReproComm. Inc., 1992-95. Editorial bd. Computers in Acctg., 1984-89. Bd. dirs. Chgo. Theatre Group, 1984; bd. dirs. Ind. Repertory Theatre, mem. fin. com., 1987—; cons. Jr. Achievement, Indpls., 1986-87. Mem. AICPA, Ind. Soc. CPAs, Indpls. C. of C. (govt. com. 1986-89), Ind. Electronics Mfrs. Assn. (v.p. fin. and legal 1989-91), Ind. Small Bus. Coun., U. Chgo. Grad. Sch. Bus. Alumni Assn. (pres. Ind. chpt. 1987-95), Columbia Club. Republican. Episcopalian. Home: 109 William Claiborne Williamsburg VA 23185-6536

GOTTFRIED, PAUL EDWARD, humanities educator, editor; b. N.Y.C., Nov. 21, 1941; s. Andrew Gottfried and Ruth Weiser; m. Diane Zelcer, June 15, 1969 (dec. Feb. 1994); children: Barbara Hollander, Joseph, Jonathan, Beth, Sara; m. Mary Zwir, May 12, 2000. BA, Yeshiva U., 1963; MS, Yale U., 1965, PhD, 1967. Grad. fellow Yale U., New Haven, 1965-66; asst. prof. history Case Western Res. U., Cleve., 1968-71; vis. asst. prof. history NYU, N.Y.C., 1971-72; chmn. history dept. Rockford (Ill.) Coll., 1974-86; sr.

editor The World and I, Washington, 1986-93; prof. humanities Elizabethtown (Pa.) Coll., 1989—; editor-in-chief This World, 1992—. Author: The Conservative Movement, 1993, After Liberalism, 1999; contbr. articles to profl. jours. Recipient award NEH, 1969; Earhart fellow, 1970, 73, 77, 83, 88, Guggenheim fellow, 1984; NEH tchg. fellow U.S. Naval Acad., 1993. Mem. Neoclassical Reform Jewish Movement (organizer), Società Libera (assoc.). Avocations: jogging, tennis, gardening. E-mail: gottfrpe@etown.edu. Home: 327 College Ave Elizabethtown PA 17022-2414

GÖTTIG, JOSÉ MARIA, engineering executive; b. Crespo, Argentina, Feb. 20, 1951; s. Ignacio Göttig and Yolanda Margarita Gignone; m. Margarita Susana Clotta, Jan. 15, 1977; children: Leticia Noelia, Mercedes Cecilia. BS, Coll. San Jose, Esperanza, Argentina, 1967. Registered profl. chem. engr. Process engr. PASA S.A., Santa Fe, Argentina, 1977-86, quality assurance and SPC chief, 1986-91, quality and tng. chief, 1991-94, quality assurance chief, 1994-2000; mgr. environ. quality Edejur SA, Buenos Aires, 2000—; prof. Secondary Sch., Rosario, Argentina, 1981-86, UTN, Rosario, 1995, UNL State, 1999—. Author: (handbook) SPC Manual-PASA, 1988. provincial com. del. UCR, Argentina, 1983-87; pres. Family Parents Union, Coll. Guadalupe, Rosario, 1991-95; mem. coun. Parroquia Perpetuo Socorro, Argentina, 1994; judge NQuality award, 1994-99. Mem. ASQ (cert.), IACC, IPACE. Roman Catholic. Avocations: playing soccer, taking pictures and movies, reading books, computers, chess. Office: Edesur SA, San Jose 140, Buenos Aires Argentina

GOTTLANDER, ROBERT JAN LARS, dental company executive; b. Bohuslan, Sweden, Sept. 5, 1956; came to U.S., 1986; s. Jan H. K. and Ragnhild S.E. (Rutgerson) G.; m. Eva L.M. Svenson, July 4, 1987; children: Daniel J.R., Magdalena A.E., Linnea E.R. Student, Kongahalla Coll., Sweden, 1975; candidate of odontology, U. Gothenburg, Sweden, 1976, DDS, 1980. Dentist Swedish Health Care, Trollhattan, Sweden, 1980-82; asst. prof. dept. orthodontics Community Dentistry, Trollhattan, 1982-84; mgr. tng. and edn. Nobelpharma AB, Gothenburg, 1984-85, product mgr., 1985; v.p., mgr. edn. and product Nobelpharma USA Inc., Waltham, Mass., 1986-87, v.p. profl. affairs, 1987-88; v.p., gen. mgr. Nobelpharma USA Inc., Chgo., 1988—; pres. V-Dal Union of Dentists, Trollhattan, Sweden, 1982-84; chmn. V-Dal Dental Soc., Sweden, 1983-84, sec. 1981-82. Lt. Swedish Royal Navy, 1976-79. Mem. AMA, Swedish Dental Soc., Swedish Orthodontic Soc.; affiliate mem. ADA, Acad. of Osseointegration. Lutheran. Avocations: sailing, skiing, tennis, reading.

GOTTLIEB, GILBERT, psychobiologist, educator; b. Bklyn., Oct. 22, 1929; s. Leo and Sylvia Sherman; m. Nora Lee Willis, Feb. 28, 1961; children: Jonathan Brian, David Herschel (dec.), Aaron Lee, Marc Sherman. AB, U. Miami, 1955, MS, 1956; PhD, Duke U., 1960. Clin. psychologist Dorothea Dix Hosp., Raleigh, N.C., 1959-61; rsch. scientist N.C. Divsn. Mental Health, Raleigh, 1961-82; head dept. psychology U. N.C., Greensboro, 1982-86, Excellence Found. prof., 1982-95; mem. faculty Carolina consortium human devel. U. N.C., Chapel Hill, 1988—; rsch. prof. psychology U. N.C. Ctr. Devel. Sci., Chapel Hill, 1995—; guest Czechoslovak Acad. Scis., 1967, USSR Acad. Scis., 1989; advisor German NSF, 1977; U.S. del. Internat. Ethological Congress com., 1977-83; mem. exec. com. Ctr. for Devel. Sci., U. N.C., 1993—; vis. lectr. Inst. Child Devel., U. Minn., 1975; vis. scholar Ctr. Interdisciplinary Rsch., U. Bielefeld, Germany, 1977; disting. vis. prof. psychology dept. U. Colo., Boulder, 1985; vis. fellow The Neuroscis. Inst., San Diego, 1996; disting. vis. lectr. dept. psychology U. Alta., 1996, Clark U., 1999. Author: Development of Species Identification in Birds, 1971, Individual Development and Evolution: The Genesis of Novel Behavior, 1992, Synthesizing Nature-Nurture: Prenatal Roots of Instinctive Behavior, 1997 (APA Book award 1998), Probabilistic Epigenesis and Evolution, 1999; editor: Behavioral Embryology, 1973, Aspects of Neurogenesis, 1974, Neural and Behavioral Specificity, 1976, Early Influences, 1978, Measurement of Audition and Vision in the First Year of Postnatal Life, 1985; assoc. editor Jour. Comparative and Physiol. Psychology, 1974-80; editl. cons. various sci. jours. and pub. houses. Recipient Disting. Sci. Contbn. award for child devel. Soc. Rsch. Child Devel., 1997; NSF grantee, 1963, 85-88; Nat. Inst. Child Health grantee, 1964-85; NIMH grantee, 1989—. Mem. Internat. Soc. Devel. Psychobiology (pres. 1986-87), Internat. Conf. Infant Studies. Home: 4908 Forestville Rd Raleigh NC 27616-9683 Office: U NC Ctr Devel Sci Chapel Hill NC 27599-0001

GOTTLIEB, HANS PETER WOLFRAM, mathematics educator; b. Sydney, July 2, 1944; s. Leon and Anny (Wolfram) G.; m. Nanette Rae Twine, Aug. 26, 1978; children: Susan Alison, Gregory Peter. BA with honors, U. Melbourne, 1965, BSc, 1966, MSc, 1968; PhD, U. Cambridge, 1971. Royal Soc. postdoctoral fellow U. Karlsruhe, Germany, 1971-72; SRC postdoctoral rsch. fellow Imperial Coll., London, 1972-73; URG postdoctoral rsch. fellow U. Adelaide, South Australia, 1973-75; lectr. Griffith U., Brisbane, Australia, 1975-80, sr. lectr., 1981-87, assoc. prof., 1987—. Contbr. over 100 articles to profl. jours.; patentee annular drum. Wyselaskie scholar U. Melbourne, 1965, Overseas scholar Royal Commn. for Exhbn. 1851, 1968-71. Fellow Inst. Physics, Australian Inst. Physics, Inst. Maths. and its Applications, Australian Math. Soc.; mem. Internat. Assn. Math. Physicists. Avocations: music, reading, films. Office: Griffith U Sch Sci, Kessels Rd, Qnsland Nathan 4111, Australia

GOTTLIEB, JONATHAN W., lawyer; b. Washington, June 24, 1959; s. Julius Judah and Charlotte (Papernick) G.; m. Deborah Jo Levine, June 28, 1987; children: Maya Lane, Seth Joseph. BA with honors, DePaul U., 1982; student, Am. U., 1984-85; JD, N.Y. Law Sch., 1985. Bar: Pa. 1986, D.C. 1989, U.S. Ct. Appeals (D.C. cir.) 1990. Trial atty. Fed. Energy Regulatory Commn., Washington, 1987-88; assoc. Wickwire, Gavin & Gibbs, Washington, 1988-89, Ballard Spahr Andrews & Ingersoll, Washington, 1990-92; assoc. Reid & Priest, Washington, 1992-94, ptnr., 1995-98; ptnr. Thelen Reid & Priest, Washington, 1998-99, Baker & McKenzie, Washington, 1999—; chmn. legal affairs task force Nat. Hydropower Assn., 1992-95; counsel Mid-Atlantic Ind. Power Producers; gen. counsel Power Markets Devel. Co. (PPL Global), 1995-96; adv. bd. Bradley Energy Internat., 1997—; acting gen. counsel Packard Bell NEC, Inc., 1998. Contbg. editor Project Fin. Monthly; editor Competitive Utility, 1993—. Donor mem. Corning Mus. Glass. Mem. Fed. Energy Bar Assn., Pa. Bar Assn., D.C. Bar Assn., Southeastern Energy Soc. Republican. Avocations: glass collecting, stained glass making, gardening. E-mail: jonathan.w.gottlieb@bakernet.com. Home: 9317 W Parkhill Dr Bethesda MD 20814-3966

GOTTLIEB, JULIUS JUDAH, podiatrist; b. Jersey City, May 27, 1919; s. Joseph Uziel and Gussie (Farber) G.; m. Charlotte Papernik, Oct. 18, 1942; children: Sheldon, Cynthia, Lorinda, David, Jonathan. Student, NYU, 1938-39, Ill. Coll. Podiatric Medicine, 1940-42; DPM, Ohio Coll. Podiatric Medicine, 1943. Diplomate Am. Podiatric Med. Specialties Bd. Pvt. practice podiatric medicine Washington, 1943-92; pres. Chevy Chase Profl. Cons., 1993-96; past cons. Army Footwear Clinic. Co-inventor fiberglass foot prosthetics and plastic shoe lasts. Podiatry dir. Greater Washington Hebrew Home for the Aged, 1963; pres. Franklin Knolls Citizens Assn., 1963, Ridgefield Citizens Inc., 1994-96, 97—; chmn. com. Nat. Capital Area coun. Boy Scouts Am., 1969-73; pres. Active Retirees of Kehilat Shalom, 1996-98. Recipient Shofar award Boy Scouts Am. Fellow Acad. Ambulatory Foot Surgeons (region 8 sci. chmn. 1987-88); mem. Am. Podiatric Med. Assn. (life), Am. Pub. Health Assn., Am. Podiatric Circulatory Soc., Am. Bd. Foot Surgeons (founding diplomate), D.C. Podiatric Med. Soc. (past pres.), Am. Assn. Foot Specialists (past pres., Foot Specialist of the Yr. 1973), Am. Assn. Individual Investors, Internat. Platform Assn., Am. Physicians Fellowship Inc. for Medicine in Israel, Columbia Heights Bus. Men's Assn. (past pres., Man of Yr. 1964), Parents Assn. U. Md. (co v.p. parents fund 1980-81, co-recipient Outstanding Svc. Award), B'nai B'rith. Republican. Jewish. Home: 15812 Ancient Oak Dr Darnestown MD 20878-2110

GOTTLIEB, LESTER M., entrepreneur; b. N.Y.C., May 3, 1932; s. Samuel and Eva (Schoenfeld) G.; children: Cynthia, Curtis, Mark, Alyssa, Adine. BA, CCNY, 1954; postgrad. NYU, 1956. With IBM, 1956-69, mgr. bus. planning for systems devel. div., 1967-69; pres. Data Dimensions, Inc. 1969-84, vice chmn., 1984-90; pres. CAMAC Securities, Ltd., Greenwich, Conn., 1981-91, also chmn. bd. dirs., 1991—; pres. CAMAC Equities, Ltd., 1981—; chmn. bd. dirs. Safe, Inc., Stamford, Conn., Elite Health, Peekskill, N.Y., Ripe and Ready Music, Inc., YPY Group, Stamford; adj. asst. prof. econs. U. Bridgeport; nat. lectr. Assn. Computing Machinery. bd. dirs. Ctr. for Internat. Mgmt. Studies. Nat. Bd. YMCA's 1972-90, Greater N.Y. YMCA; bd. dirs., treas. City Coll. Fund, 1990, v.p., 1996-99. With AUS, 1954-56. Recipient Leo Klauber award, Mark Asa Abbott award; named Vol. of Yr. Greater N.Y. YMCA, 1994. Mem. Am. Arbitration Assn. (comml. arbitrator 1981—), CCNY Alumni Assn. (bd. dirs. 1983, pres. alumni varsity assn. 1987-88, Alumni Svc. award, Athletic Hall of Fame), Land Mark Club (emeritus). Republican. Home: 1 Byram Dock St Greenwich CT 06830-6901

GOTTLIEB, PAUL, publishing company executive; b. N.Y.C., Jan. 16, 1935; s. Vitaly Matthew and Liza (Rabinowitz) G.; m. Linda Ellen Salzman, June 19, 1960 (div. Nov. 1989); children: Nicholas, Andrew; m. Elisabeth Lohman Scharlatt, Jan. 27, 1990; 1 stepchild Nicholas T. Scharlatt. BA, Swarthmore Coll., 1956; LHD (hon.), SUNY, Purchase, 1999. Lit. agt. William Morris Agy., N.Y.C., 1956-57, 59-60; asst. to pres. Omni Products Corp., N.Y.C., 1960-62; with Am. Heritage Pub. Co. Inc., N.Y.C., 1962-75; pres. Am. Heritage Pub. Co. Inc., 1970-75; chmn. bd. Fulfillment Corp. Am.; pres. Paul Gottlieb Assos., Inc., 1975—, Thames and Hudson Inc., 1976-79; vice-chmn, pub., editor-in-chief Harry N. Abrams, Inc., N.Y.C., 1980—; bd. dirs. Tanya Corp.; cons. in field. Guide U.S. exhbns., Moscow, 1959, 61; vice chmn. E. Harlem Coll. and Career Counseling Program, 1971-74; trustee Mus. Modern Art, Dalton Sch.; bd. dirs. Nat. Found. Depressive Illness, Pub. Ctr. for Cultural Resources, N.Y. Studio Sch. Drawing, Painting and Sculpture, Acad. Am. Poets. Mem. Assn. Am. Pubs., Chevalier des Artes et des Lettres, Coffee House Club (N.Y.C.), Century Assn. Club (N.Y.C.). Clubs: Coffee House (N.Y.C.), Century Assn. (N.Y.C.). Home: 1 Fifth Ave New York NY 10003 Office: Harry N Abrams Inc 100 5th Ave Fl 6 New York NY 10011-6999

GOTTRUP, FINN, gastroenterologist, surgeon; b. Billund, Denmark, Apr. 2, 1944; s. Kristian Henning and Agnete Skov (Frandsen) G.; m. Eva Stubkjaer Huttel (Feb. 3, 1971); children: Christian, Rikke. MD, U. Aarhus, 1971, D in Med. Sci., 1981, Specialist in Surgery, 1985; Specialist in Surg. Gastroenterology, U. Copenhagen, 1990. Physician U. Aarhus, Denmark, 1971; assoc. prof. of anatomy U. Aarhus, 1983-86; resident various hosps., Denmark, 1971-80; postdoctoral rsch. surgeon U. Calif. San Francisco, 1981-82; asst. prof. of surgery U. Hosps., Denmark, 1986; prof. Copenhagen Wound Healing Ctr., Denmark, 1991—, head, 1996—; mem. exec. bd. Wound Healing Consortium, 1998. Co-editor: Wound. Rep. Reg., 1995; author/editor: (textbook) Wounds - Background, Diagnosis and Treatment, 1996, General Surgery, 2000; contbr. numerous articles to profl. jours. and publs.; presenter in field. Recipient N.C. Nielsens Hon. award, 1992. Mem. European Tissue Repair Soc. (bd. dirs., pres. 1998-99), European Wound Mgmt. Assn. (bd. dirs., pres. 1997-99), Danish Wound Healing Soc. (pres. 1992). Office: Copenhagen Wound Healing Ct, Bispebjerg Univ Hosp, DK-2400 Copenhagen NV, Denmark

GOTTS, ILENE KNABLE, lawyer; b. Phila., Nov. 25, 1959; d. Harry Lee and Ethel Beatrice (Teitelman) Knable; m. Michael D. Gotts, May 25, 1986; children: Isaac, Samuel. BA magna cum laude with hon., U. Md., 1980; JD cum laude, Georgetown U., 1984. Bar: D.C. 1984, N.Y., 1997, U.S. Dist. Ct. D.C. 1986, U.S. Ct. Appeals (D.C. cir.) 1985, U.S. Dist. Ct. Md. 1987, U.S. Ct. Appeals (fed. cir.) 1989, U.S. Supreme Ct. 1988. Staff atty. FTC, 1984-86; assoc. Foley & Lardner, Washington, 1986-92, ptnr., head legis./adminstrv. group, antitrust practice group, 1992-96; ptnr. Wachtell, Lipton, Rosen & Katz, N.Y.C., 1996—; adj. prof. George Washington U. Law Ctr., 1995-96. Mem. editorial bd. The Practical Lawyer, 1994—; mem. editorial adv. bd. The Antitrust Counselor, 1995—; contbr. articles to profl. jours. Recipient Sklar award U. Md., 1980; Mary Elizabeth Robey scholar. Mem. ABA (health care com. antitrust sect. 1988—, vice chair intellectual property com. 1994-97, consumer protection com. 1994—, vice chair Clayton Act com. 1997-98, chmn. 1998—), FBA (chair health care com. of antitrust sect. 1991-95, chair antitrust and trade regulation sect. 1995-97), D.C. Bar (steering com., antitrust and trade regulation com. 1994-95), N.Y. Bar Assn. (task force of women and the law), Am. Law Inst., Washington Coun. Lawyers (exec. com. and bd. dirs. 1988-97, pres. 1994-95), N.Y. State Bar Assn. (exec. com. antitrust law sect. 2000—), N.Y. Women's Bar Assn., Internat. Bar Assn., Mortar Board, Phi Beta Kappa, Phi Kappa Phi, Pi Sigma Alpha, Phi Alpha Theta. Democrat. Jewish. Office: Wachtell Lipton Rosen & Katz 51 W 52d St New York NY 10019

GOTTSAUNER-WOLF, FLORIAN, orthopaedic surgeon, educator; b. Salzburg, Austria, Sept. 12, 1956; s. Andreas and Maria-Imogen (von Doderer) Gottsauner-Wolf; m. Caroline Eisenbach, Jan. 21, 1983; children: Moritz, Clara. MD, U. Vienna, Austria, 1981. Bd. cert. orthopaedic surgery. Resident Orthops. U., 1986-89; rsch. fellow Mayo Clinic, Rochester, Minn., 1989-91; cons. orthops. U. Vienna, 1991—, assoc. prof., 1993-97, prof., 1997—; dir. Orthop. Rsch. Lab., U. Vienna, 1991—. Contbr. articles to profl. jours. With Austrian Army, 1984. Recipient award Orthop. Soc. Austria, Vienna, 1993, Kardinal Innitzer award, Vienna, 1995. Mem. European Rsch. Soc. (mem. adv. bd. 1991—, mem. exec. com., 1999—), Mayo Alumnui. Home: Nikolaihofhasse 4, A-3400 Klosterneuburg Austria Office: Univ Orthop, Waehringer Guertel 18-20, A-1090 Vienna Austria

GOTTSCHALK, ALFRED, retired college chancellor, museum executive; b. Oberwesel, Germany, Mar. 7, 1930; came to U.S., 1939, naturalized, 1945; s. Max and Erna (Trum-Gerson) G.; m. Deanna Zeff, 1977; children by previous marriage: Marc Hillel, Rachel Lisa. AB, Bklyn. Coll., 1952; MA with honors, Hebrew Union Coll.-Jewish Inst. Religion, 1957; PhD, U. So. Calif., 1965, STD (hon.), 1968, LLD (hon.), 1976; LLD (hon.), U. Cin., 1976, Xavier U., 1981, Mt. St. Joseph Coll., 1995, No. Ky. U., 1996; DHL (hon.), U. Judaism, 1971, Jewish Theol. Sem., 1986, Bklyn. Coll., 1991, Trinity Coll., 1996; LittD (hon.), Dropsie U., 1974, St. Thomas Inst., 1982; D Religious Edn. (hon.), Loyola-Marymount U., 1977; DD (hon.), NYU, 1985. Ordained rabbi, 1957;. Dir. Hebrew Union Coll., Jewish Inst. Religion, L.A., 1957-59, dean, 1959-71, prof. Bible and Jewish intellectual history, 1965—, pres., 1971-95, chancellor, 1996-00, chancellor emeritus; pres. Mus. of Jewish Heritage, N.Y.C., 2000—; hon. fellow Hebrew U., Jerusalem, 1972, Oxford Ctr. for Hebrew and Jewish Studies, 1994. Author: Your Future as a Rabbi-A Calling that Counts, 1967, (translator) Hesed in the Bible, 1967, The Man Must be the Message, 1968, Jewish Ecumenism and Jewish Survival, 1968, Ahad Ha-Am, Maimonides and Spinoza, 1969, Ahad Ha-Am as Bible Critic, 1971, A Jubilee of the Spirit, 1972, Israel and the Diaspora: A New Look, 1974, Limits of Ecumenicity, 1979, Israel and Reform Judaism: A Zionist Perspective, 1979, Ahad Ha-Am and Leopold Zunz: Two Perspectives on the Wissenschaft Des Judentums, 1980, Hebrew Union College and Its Impact on World Progressive Judaism, 1980, Diaspora Zionism: Achievements and Problems, 1980, What Ecumenism Means to a Jew, 1981, Introduction: Religion in a Post-Holocaust World, 1982, Problematics in the Future of American Jewish Community, 1982, Introduction to the American Synagogue in the Nineteenth Century, 1982, A Strategy for Non-Orthodox Judaism in Israel, 1982, Our problems and Our Future: Jews and America, 1983, From the Kingdom of Night to the Kingdom of God: Jewish Christian Relations and the Search for Religious Authenticity after the Holocaust, 1983, The Making of a Contemporary Reform Rabbi, 1984, Is Yom Kippur Obsolete?, 1985, Ahad Ha-am: Confronting the Plight of Judaism, 1987, To Learn and To Teach, Your Future as a Rabbi, 1988, Preface to Gezer V: The Field I Caves, 1988, The American Reform Rabbinate Retrospect and Prospect, A Personal View, 1988, The German Pogrom of November 1938 and the Reaction of American Jewry, 1988, Building Unity in Diversity 1989, Ahad Ha'am and the Jewish National Spirit (Hebrew), 1992; contbr. to Studies in Jewish Bibliography, History, and Literature, 1971, The Yom Kippur War: Israel and the Jewish People, 1974, The Image of Man in Genesis and the Ancient Near East, 1976, The Public Function of the Jewish Scholar, 1978, The Reform Movement and Israel: A New Perspective, 1978, The Use of Reason in Maimonides--An Evaluation by Ahad Ha-Am, 1993; also numerous articles to profl. jours. Mem. Pres. Johnson's Com. on EEO, 1964-66, Gov.'s Poverty Support Corps Program, 1964-66, Pres.'s Commn. on Holocaust, 1979, U.S. Holocaust Meml. Coun., 1980-92, 96— (exec. com., 1980-87, 96—, chmn. edn. com., 1986-88, chmn. acad. com., 1988—, com. on conscience, 1996—); chmn. N.Am. Assocs. Internat. Ctr. Univ. Teaching of Jewish Civilization, 1982-93; bd. trustees Am. Sch. Oriental Rsch., Albright Inst. Archaeol. Rsch.; bd. govs. Oxford Ctr. for Hebrew and Jewish Studies, 1995; exec. com. Nat. Underground Railroad Freedom Ctr., 1997-2000, Nat. Adv. Bd., Nat. Underground Freedom Ctr., 1996—; mem. coun. World Union Jewish Studies, 1997. Recipient award for contbns. to edn. L.A. City Coun., 1971, Human Relations award Am. Jewish Com., 1971, Tower of David award for cultural contbn. to Israel and Am., 1972, Gold medallion Jewish Nat. Fund, 1972, Alumnus of Yr. award Bklyn. Coll., 1972, Myrtle Wreath award Hadassah, 1977, Brandeis award Z.O.A., 1977, Nat. Brotherhood award NCCJ, 1979, Alfred Gottschalk Chair in Communal Svc. HUC, 1979, Jerusalem City of Peace award 1988, Defender of Jerusalem award honoree, 1990, Isaac M. Wise award, 1991, Heritage award Jewish Club of 1933, 1991, Nat. award NCCJ, 1994, Shanghai Acad. Social Scis. award, 1994, others, Xavier Medallion, Xavier U., 1996; grantee State Dept./Smithsonian Instn., 1963, 67.; honoree Assn. Hebrew Union Coll., 1996. Mem. AAUP, NEA, Union Am. Hebrew Congregations and Ctrl. Conf. Am. Rabbis (exec. com., bd. govs. Hebrew Union Coll.), Soc. Study Religion, Am. Acad. Religion, Soc. Bibl. Lit. and Exegesis, Internat. Conf. Jewish Communal Svc., Israel Exploration Soc., So. Calif. Assn. Liberal Rabbis (past pres.), So. Calif. Jewish Hist. Soc. (hon. pres.), World Union Jewish Studies (internat. coun.), World Union Progressive Judaism (gov. bd.), Coun. for Initiatives in Jewish Edn. (bd. dirs.). Office: Mus of Jewish Heritage One Battery Park Plz New York NY 10004-1484

GOTTSCHALL, CARLOS ANTONIO MASCIA, cardiologist, medical researcher; b. Santa Maria, Brazil, Apr. 18, 1939; s. Carlos Henrique and Cecy Assumpta (Mascia) G.; m. Elisabete Maria Santos, July 30, 1963; children: Santiago, Cristina, Carlos. MD, U. Rio Grande do Sul, Porto Alegre, Brazil, 1963, M degree, 1975, PhD, 1977. Cardiologist Inst. Cardiology U. Found. Cardiology, Porto Alegre, 1966—, head rsch. unit, 1970-74, dir. lab. of hemodynamics and interventional cardiology, 1982—, prof. cardiology Postgrad. Med. Sch., 1988—, dir. Inst. Cardiology, 1993—; assoc. prof. U. Rio Grande do Sul, Porto Alegre, 1966-77, mem. postgrad. coord. bd., 1972-92; hon. vis. colleague U. London and Edinburg, 1978, Peninsula Cardiovasc. Med. Group, San Francisco, 1981; cons. Fed. Agys. for Postgrad. Edn., Nat. Coun. Sci. and Technologic Devel., Brasilia, 1993—; pioneer anti-smoking crusade. Author: Cardiac Function: From Normality to Failure, 1995; contbr. articles to profl. jours. including Jour. Invasive Cardiology. Recipient Acad. Excellence award State of Rio Grande do Sul, 1964. Fellow Soc. for Cardiac Angiography and Interventions, L.Am. Soc. for Interventional Cardiology (founder 1995); mem. Brazilian Soc. Hemodynamics and Interventional Cardiology (founder, pres. 1981-82, 30 Yrs. Coronariography in Brazil award 1996), Brazilian Soc. Cardiology (founder hemodynamics and angiocardiography sect. 1975, Merit award 1985), Internat. Andreas Grüntzig Soc. Roman Catholic. Avocations: jogging, growing birds, writing, poetry, chess. Home: Rua P Ulisses Cabral 1110, 91330520 Porto Alegre Brazil Office: Fund U de Cardiologia, Av Princesa Isabel 395, 90620001 Porto Alegre Brazil

GOTTWALD, FLOYD DEWEY, JR., chemical company executive; b. Richmond, Va., July 29, 1922; s. Floyd Dewey and Anne (Cobb) G.; m. Elisabeth Morris Shelton, Mar. 22, 1947; children: William M., James T., John D. BS, Va. Mil. Inst., 1943; MS, U. Richmond, 1951. With Albemarle Paper Co., Richmond, 1943-62, sec., 1956-57, v.p., sec., 1957-62, pres., 1962; exec. v.p. Ethyl Corp., Richmond, 1962-64, vice chmn., 1964-68, chmn., 1968-94, CEO, 1970-92, chmn. exec. com., 1970-94, vice chmn., 1994-96; bd. dirs. Tredegar Industries, Inc.; chmn., CEO Albemarle Corp. Past bd. dirs. Nat. Petroleum Coun.; trustee U. Richmond; mem. River Rd. Bapt. Ch.; past trustee V.M.I. Found., Inc.; mem. bd. visitors Coll. William and Mary, 1993-97; pres. bd. trustees Va. Mus. Fine Arts, 1994-96. Decorated Bronze Star, Purple Heart. Mem. NAM (former bd. dirs.), Am. Petroleum Inst. (bd. dirs.) Chem. Mfrs. Assn. (former bd. dirs.), Internat. Game Fish Assn. (trustee 1992—), Alfalfa Club, Country Club Va., Commonwealth Club. Office: Albemarle Corp PO Box 1335 Richmond VA 23218-1335

GOTZOYANNIS, STAVROS ELEUTHERIOS, cardiologist; b. Piraeus, Greece, June 18, 1933; s. Eleutherios G. and Irene Stavros (Nikitaki) G.; M.D. (Greek Govt. scholar), U. Salonica, 1957; Doctorate, U. Athens, 1968; m. Ourania Cavoulacou, Nov. 20, 1969. Intern, 401 Army Gen. Hosp., Athens, 1957-58; resident in internal medicine Army Pansion Share Hosp., Athens, 1960-63; fellow in cardiology Hellenic Red Cross Hosp., Athens, 1964-65; commd. 2d lt. M.C., Greek Army, 1957, advanced through grades to brig. gen., 1984; dir. internal medicine 403 Army Gen. Hosp., Kozani, 1963-64; research asso., div. cardiology Phila. Gen. Hosp., 1970-71; asst. attending physician Georgetown U. Hosp., Washington, 1971-72; asso. CCU, 401 Army Gen. Hosp., Athens, 1972-75, dir. cardiac catheterization lab., 1975-76; dir. cardiology dept. 409 Army Gen. Hosp., Patras, 1976-78; cardiology cons. to chief Hellenic Nat. Def. Gen. Staff, 1978-80; mem. staff cardiology dept. Army Pansion Share Hosp., Athens, 1980-81; dir. div. cardiology dept. 401st Army Gen. Hosp., Athens, 1981-83; cons. cardiology Hellenic Red Cross Hosp., Athens, 1965-69; instr. Army Nursing Sch., Athens, 1976. Fellow Fedn. Internat. Sport Medicine, Am. Coll. Cardiology; mem. Athens Med. Assn., Hellenic Cardiologic Soc., Greek Assn. Sports. Greek Orthodox. Contbr. papers, abstracts to med. books, jours. Home: 3 Evrou St, GR 115 28 Athens Greece

GØTZSCHE, PETER CHRISTIAN, internist, biologist; b. Copenhagen, Nov. 26, 1949; m. Helle K. Johansen. Fil. mag., U. Lund, Sweden, 1973; MSc, U. Copenhagen, 1974, MD, 1984, DrMed, 1990; Specialist in Internal Medicine, 1995. Intern, resident Bispebjerg Hosp., Copenhagen, 1984, Herlev Hosp., Copenhagen, 1984-85, 89-90, Rigshospitalet, Copenhagen, 86, 90-92, 93-5, Hvidovre Hosp., Copenhagen, 1986-87, 92-93, Nordic AIDS Trials Office, Copenhagen, 1987-89; with Astra Group, Denmark, 1975-77; physican various hosps., Copenhagen, 1984-85; dir. Nordic Cochrane Ctr., Copenhagen, 1993—. Author: På safari i Kenya, 1985; contbr. articles to profl. jours. Recipient En god start i livet 1997, Henrik R. Wulff prize, 1999. Office: Nordic Cochrane Ctr, Rigshosp 7112 18B Tagensvej, DK-2200 Copenhagen N, Denmark

GOUDA, ERIC JOHN, botanist, researcher, curator; b. Utrecht, The Netherlands, Feb. 10, 1957; s. Cornelis Serinus and Wijntje van der Zouw; m. Renate Verwer, Oct. 7, 1988; children: Imgard, Fastwin. Drs, Utrecht U., 1987. Software engr. CS Engring., Waddinxveen, The Netherlands, 1988-93; curator living collections Utrecht U. Botanic Gardens, 1993—. Author: Flora of The Guianas, Bromeliaceae (Tillandsioideae), 1987, Shaolin Ch'uan Fa, 1999; contbr. article to jour. Avocations: shaolin kempo, kung fu, growing Tillandsias, guitar, breeding poison arrow frogs. Office: Utrecht U Botanic Gardens, PO Box 80162, 3508 TD Utrecht The Netherlands

GOUDIS, CHRISTOS, astrophysicist; b. Pireaus, Greece, Apr. 15, 1947; s. Draculis and Ismini (Portocaloglou) G. BSc in Physics, U. Athens, 1969; MSc in Astronomy, U. Manchester, Eng., 1972, PhD in Astronomy, 1974. Rsch. assoc. dept. astronomy U. Manchester, 1974-79; rsch. scientist Max Planck Inst. für Astronomie, Heidelberg, Germany, 1979-81; prof. astronomy and astrophysics U. Patras, 1981—. Author: The Orion Complex: A Case Study of Interstellar Matter, 1982. Avocation: poetry. Office: U Patras, Astron Lab Dept Physics, 26500 Patras Greece

GOUDY, JOSEPHINE GRAY, social worker; b. Des Moines, Nov. 30, 1925; d. Gerald William and Myrtle Maria (Brooks) Gray; m. John Winston Goudy, June 5, 1948; children: Tracy Jean, Paula Rae. BA, State U. Iowa, 1954, MSW, 1966; cert. in gerontology, U. Ill. Cert. social worker, Iowa, Ill.; diplomate in clin. social work; lic. ind. social worker, Iowa. Child welfare supr. Iowa Dept. Social Svcs., 1960-68; psychiat. social worker Cmty. Mental Health Ctr., Scott County, Iowa, 1966-71; social work instr. Palmer Jr. Coll., Davenport, Iowa, 1967-70; psychiat. social worker, chief social svcs. Jacksonville (Ill.) State Mental Hosp., 1971-74; coord. cmty. mental health outpatient svcs. McFarland Mental Health Ctr., Springfield, Ill., 1974; exec. dir. Acoupin County Mental Health Ctr., Carlinville, Ill., 1974-98, Youth Attention Ctr., Jacksonville, Ill., 1998-99; pvt. practice, 1999—; chmn. Human Svcs. Edn. Coun., Springfield, 1979-81; bd. mem. Alzheimer's Disease and Related Disorders Assn., Springfield Ill. Area Chpt., past exec. Davenport Cmty. Welfare Coun.; adj. prof. dept. psychiatry So. Ill. U., Springfield. Mem. APA, Nat. Assn. Social Workers (Social Worker of Yr. Ctrl. Ill. area 1983), Acad. Cert. Social Workers, Am. Psychotherapy Assn., AAUW (br. pres. 1964-66, mem. state bar 1966-68, br. grantee 1975), Internat. Fedn. U. Women, U. Iowa Alumni Assn., Bus. and Profl. Women (Woman of Yr. 1983), Carlinville Women's Club (pres. 1975-77, 96-98), Delta Kappa Gamma, Kappa Delta Pi. Republican. Methodist. Home: 364 W Tremont St Waverly IL 62692-1073 Office: 100 N Side Sq Carlinville IL 62626-1748

GOUDY, KEN GORDON, graphic designer; b. Yakima, Wash., Sept. 15, 1936; s. Kenneth G. Sr. and Milinda Eileen Goudy; m. Elaine M. Goudy, Dec. 26, 1972. Grad. h.s., Yakima, Wash. Agt., sta. mgr. West Coast Airlines, Astoria, Oreg., 1962-68; terminal mgr. Oreg.-Nev.-Calif. Fast Freight, Ellensburg, Wash., 1968-70, Kennewick, Wash., 1970-75; owner, pres. Superior Signs, Walla Walla, Wash., 1975-97, Ken Goudy Graphics, Oregon City, Oreg., 1998—; mem. gen. adv. coun. Walla Walla Sch. Dist., 1996-97. Author: Overnight While You Sleep (Auto Freight Memories), 1992, Overnight While You Sleep (Western Trucking Pioneers), 1994. Named Rotarian of Yr., Walla Walla Rotary, 1983. Mem. Am. Truck Hist. Soc. (Oreg.-Wash. v.p. 1982-84, pres. Blue Mountain chpt. 1984-97, nat. treas. 1984-87, bd. dirs. 1987-2000, pres. Oreg. Trail chpt. 1998-2000). Republican. Avocations: pen and ink artist, trucking photos collecting, writing. E-mail: truckie1@home.com. Home and Office: 15140 S Burkstrom Rd Oregon City OR 97045-9408

GOUESBET, GERARD, systems and process engineering educator; b. Compiegne, France, Nov. 26, 1947; s. Maurice and Denise (Paillot) G.; m. Monique Levistre, July 26, 1969; children: Ludovic, Nicolas. Doctor, U. Rouen, France, 1973, D. of State, 1977. Lectr. Rouen U., 1974-75; researcher Nat. Ctr. Scientific Rsch., Rouen, 1975-83; prof. system and process engrng. Nat. Inst. Applied Scis., Rouen, 1983—; hon. prof. North Ea. U., Liaquning, China, Xidian (China) U.; cons. various French industries. Co-editor: Optical Particle Sizing; Theory and Practice, 1988, Instabilities in Multiphase Flows, 1993; contbr. over 350 papers to procs., profl. jours. Grantee Kyoto U., 1988. Mem. AIAA, Am. Physics Soc., Optical Soc. Am., French Soc. Physics, European Soc. Physics, Optical Soc. France, N.Y. Acad. Sci. Avocations: hiking, music, gymnastics. Office: LESP INSA-Rouen UA CNRS 230, BP-08, 76131 Mont-Saint-Aignan France

GOUGH, CAROLYN HARLEY, library director; b. Paterson, N.J., Sept. 23, 1922; d. Frank Ellsworth and Mabel (Harrison) Harley; m. George Harrison Gough, Sept. 21, 1944; children: Deborah Ann Gough Bornholdt, Douglas Alan. BA, Coll. William and Mary, 1943; MLS, Drexel U., 1966. Rsch. asst. Young and Rubicam, Inc., N.Y.C., 1943-44; libr. dir., asst. prof. Cabrini Coll.,, Radnor, Pa., 1966-81; chmn. Palm Beach County Libr. Bd., 1984-86; mem. resources study com. Tredyffrin Twp. Libr., 1964-65; docent Henry Morrison Flagler Mus., 1982-92. Mem. AAUP, DAR (Palm Beach chpt.), Tri-State Coll. Libr. Coop. (v.p. 1973-74, pres. 1974-75), Assn. Coll. and Rsch. Librs. (dir. 1978-81), Questers, Inc. (1st nat. v.p. 1964-66), Atlantis Golf Club, Atlantis Women's Club (co-pres. 1982-83), Sir Robert Boyle Soc., Beta Phi Mu, Kappa Delta. Republican. Episcopalian. Home: 458 S Country Club Dr Atlantis FL 33462-1238

GOUGH, IAN RONALD, surgeon; b. Brisbane, Queensland, Australia, Apr. 12, 1947; s. Ruth Gough, Dec. 11, 1972; children: Jenny, Helen. MB, BS, U. Queensland, Australia, 1970, MD, 1994. Cert. specialist gen. surgeon. Resident med. officer Princess Alexandra Hosp., Brisbane, Australia, 1971-72; surg. registrar NHS Hosps., 1973-75; lectr., sr. lectr. surgery U. Queensland, Brisbane, 1976-84, assoc. prof. surgery, 1984-91, clin. prof. surgery, 1991—; sr. cons. surgeon Royal Brisbane Hosp., 1991—; dep. dean U. Queensland Med. Sch., Brisbane, 1984-87; vis. prof. various univs., U.S.A., Sweden, Australia, 1984—. Mem. editl. bd. Australian and New Zealand Jour. Surgery, Current Surgery. Recipient travel grants, rsch. grants, 1971—. Fellow ACS, Royal Coll. Surgeons Edinburgh, Royal Australasian Coll. Surgeons (chmn.bd. gen. surgery 1988-97, chmn. sect. endocrine surgery 1993-96, sr. examiner in gen. surgery 1998-2000); mem. Royal Coll. Physicians U.K., Internat. Assn. Endocrine Surgeons, Societe Internat. de Chirurge. Office: Wesley Med Ctr, 40 Chasely St, Auchenflower 4066, Australia

GOUGH, JOHN BERNARD, former manufacturing company executive; b. Melbourne, Australia, Aug. 22, 1928; s. Leslie Stewart and Margaret Ellen (Bates) G.; m. Rosemary Olive Upjohn, June 15, 1955; children: Sara, Stewart, Anna. Ed. in Textile Industries, Leeds (Eng.) U., 1950; grad. Advanced Mgmt. Program, Harvard U., 1969. In various positions in advt., mfg. textile and footwear, 1950-69; gen. mgr., dir. Dunlop Footwear Group, Melbourne, 1969-73, mng. dir., 1973-76; mng. dir. Dunlop Clothing, Footwear & Textiles Group, Melbourne, 1976-79; gen. mgr. Dunlop Australia Ltd. (now Pacific Dunlop Ltd.), Melbourne, 1979-80, mng. dir., 1980-87, dep. chmn., 1987-90, chmn., 190-97; ret., 1997; dir. BHP Ltd., ret., 1998; dir. CSR Ltd., ret., 1999; participant Duke of Edinburgh Study Conf., Australia, 1968; exec. mem. Australian Mfg. Coun., 1980-83; chmn. Trade Devel. Coun. Australia, 1981-84, Australia Japan Bus. Forum, 1986-89; speaker Nat. Econ. Summit Conf., Canberra, Australia, 1983; chmn. Grad. Sch. Mgmt., Melbourne U., 1983-95; mem. adv. coun. GM, Holden, ret., 1998. Bd. dirs. Walter and Eliza Hall Inst. Med. Rsch., Australia, 1983—. Decorated Order Brit. Empire, Order of Australia. Fellow Inst. Mgmt., Melbourne Club. Office: Pacific Dunlop Ltd, 101 Collins St, Melbourne VIC 3000, Australia*

GOUGH, MARK ADRIAN, chemistry educator; b. Weymouth, Dorset, Eng., Mar. 12, 1963; s. John Richard and Elisabeth Eleanor (Ricer) G.; m. Julie Robson, Dec. 10, 1998. BSc, U. Southampton, Eng., 1984; postgrad. diploma, U. Liverpool, Eng., 1985; PhD, U. Plymouth, Eng., 1989. Rsch. asst. U. Plymouth, 1985-89; postdoctoral rschr. Plymouth Marine Lab., 1989-91; sect. head Nat. Rivers Authority, Portsmouth, Eng., 1991-94; sr. rsch. chemist Nalco/Exxon Energy Chems., Southampton, 1994-98, group leader, 1998—. Mem. Royal Soc. Chemistry (chartered), Nat. Assn. Corrosion Engrs., Soc. Petroleum Engrs. Avocations: travel, sailing, guitars, skiing.

GOUGH, MICHAEL PAUL, science educator; b. Sutton Coldfield, U.K., July 19, 1946; s. Sidney Walter and Cornelia Maria (Dicks) G.; m. Elizabeth Inez Fennel, Sept. 13, 1969; children: Mark Daniel, Alicia Claire, John Stuart, Corinna Louise. BS in Physics, U. Leicester, 1967, MS in Exptl. Space Physics, 1968; PhD of Space Physics, U. Southampton, 1972. Chartered engr. Royal Soc. fellowship São Paulo, Brazil, 1973-74; postdoctoral rsch. fellow Durham U., Smithsonian Astrophys. Obs., 1975-76; SERC rsch. fellow U. Sussex, U.K., 1976-85; lectr. engring. U. Sussex, 1986-97, prof. space sci., 1997—. Inventor in field; contbr. articles to profl. jours. Recipient Achievement award NASA, 1985, DFVLR/BMFT, 1985; grantee PPARC, 1987—. Fellow Inst. Elec. Engrs., Royal Astron. Soc.; mem. Am. Geophys. Union. Avocations: Scottish country dancing, travel, walking. Office: Univ Sussex Sch Engring, Falmer, Brighton BN1 9QT, England

GOUGHER, RONALD LEE, foreign language educator and administrator; b. Allentown, Pa., July 27, 1939; s. Samuel Franklin and Beatrice Dorothy (Shanaberger) G.; 1 child, Robert. BA, Muhlenberg Coll., 1961; MA, Lehigh U., 1964; postgrad., Albright Coll., 1962, Stanford U., 1963, Harvard U., 1964, U. Pa., 1964-75; advanced cert., Goethe Inst., Munich, 1969. Chmn. fgn. lang. dept. Parkland H.S., Allentown, Pa., 1961-65; tchr. German Moravian Sem. for Girls, 1965-69; instr. German Lehigh U., 1965-69; assoc. prof. German West Chester (Pa.) U., 196 -, dir. internat. edn., 1974-83, chmn. dept. fgn. langs., 1977-96, campus dir. Expt. in Internat. Living, 1972-92; treas. Pa. Consortium Internat. Edn., 1978-83, pres., 1983-86, World Learning Inc., 1992—; coord.-chairperson Assn. Depts. Fgn. Langs., State Sys. Higher Edn., Pa., 1984-88, del. First Joint Conf. Chinese and Am. Edn. Great Hall of People, Beijing, 1992; citizen amb. Linguistics del. to China, 1991, 92, lectr. in field, cons. Franklin Mint, 1992—; cons., program dir. Chester Conty Intermediate Unit; guest lectr. Ufa, Ivanova, Russia, 1993, Czestochowa, Poland, Ufa, Russia, Sendai, Japan, Jurmala, Riga, Valmiera, Latvia, 1994, 95, 96, Kaunus, Lithuania, 1995; participant Hungarian Parliament Sessions, Budapest, 1994; dir. Am.-European studies program, West Chester U. and Soros Found., Latvia, Lithuania, Czech Republic, Slovakia, Hungary, Romania, Yugoslavia, Bulgaria, Croatia, Slovenia, Macedonia, 1994, Moldova, 1995, Estonia, 1996, Albania, Bosnia, Kyrgystan, Mongolia, 1997—, Kazakhstan, 1998—, Azerbaijan, 1999; dir. Internat. Sch.-U. Partnership Program, West Chester U. and Chester County Intermediate Unit, 1988—. Co-editor, Individualization Fgn. Lang. Learning in Am., 1970-75; author numerous publs. in German lang. and lit., individualizing instrn. in fgn. langs. Bd. dirs. Peters Valley Crafts Ctr., U.S. Info. Agy., 1988-95; active Congress-Bundestag Youth Exch. Program, 1988-96, Citizen Amb. Program, China, 1991, 92. Fulbright travel grantee, 1963, 69, travel grantee Soros Found., 1990-94; travel and study grantee, Finland and Leningrad, USSR, 1990; travel grantee to Poland, Slovakia, Romania, 1991-92, Russia, 1993, 95, Bulgaria, Slovenia, 1994, Kagoshima, Japan and Taipei, Taiwan, 1996, Croatia, Latvia, Lithuania, Slovenia, 1996, Hungary, Bulgaria, Macedonia, 1999, Mongolia, 1999; Fed. Fgn. Lang. Assistance Act grantee, 1992-96, dir. Internat. Sch.-U. Ptnrs. program Chester County Intermediate Unit and West Chester U., 1991-97, Soros Found. grantee internat. program devel. Latvia, Lithuania, Czech Republic, Slovakia, Hungary, Slovenia, Yugoslavia, Romania, Bulgaria, Macedonia, Moldova, Estonia, Mongolia, Kyrgystan, Bosnia, Albania, 1994—; Open Soc. grantee, 1994-96, 97, 98, 99, 2000; recipient numerous grants for fgn. langs. and internat. studies programs, pub. and pvt. founds., NEH, Rockefeller Found.; recipient Chapel of Four Chaplins award, 1981. Mem. Am. Assn. Tchrs. German, Am. Coun. Tchg. Fgn. Langs., N.E. Conf. Tchg. Fgn. Langs., Internat. Platform Assn., Smithsonian Instn. Republican. Lutheran. Home: 3309 Windsor Ln Thorndale PA 19372-1038 Office: West Chester U Dept Fgn Langs West Chester PA 19380

GOUIRY, PIERRE LOUIS, anethesiologist; b. Narbonne, France, Mar. 9, 1924; s. Joseph and Antoinette (CapDeville) G.; m. Julienne Salles; children: Pierre-Jean, Jean-Claude, Anne, René. Degree, U. Montpellier, France, 1950. Anethesiologist Anesthesiologist Hosp., Narbonne, 1952-59, dir. blood transfusion div., 1959-63; chief of medicine Dept. of Service in Fire and Safety, Aude, France, 1963-74; chief of service Dept. Anesthesiology, Narbonne, 1974—; tech. cons. Dept. Civil Def., Aude, 1967, Narbonne Hosp., 1975; chief of service Secours D'Urcence, Narbonne, 1975. con. Sch. of Hygiene, Narbonne, 1977; asst. mayor Narbonne, 1983-89, 89-93. Mem. Fedn. French Studies of Underwater Sports. C.D.S. Roman Catholic. Avocations: scuba diving, philately. Home: 26 Blvd Frederie Mistral, 11100 Narbonne France

GOULAIT, JOHN JOSEPH, association professional; b. St. Clair, Mich., Nov. 16, 1944; s. John Lawrence and Elfrieda Elizabeth (Wenzel) G.; m. Dawn Marie Evans, June 26, 1970; children: Aimee Marie, Kathleen Elizabeth. BA, St. Leo Coll., 1968; MA, California U. Pa., 1991; postgrad., Nova Southeastern U., 1992—. Cert. coll. educator in mgmt. and geography, Tex. New Eng. rep. Diners Club Inc., N.Y.C., 1972-73; supr. Security Bur. Inc., Shippingport, Pa., 1973-74; millwright Jones & Laughlin Steel Corp., Aliquippa, Pa., 1974-81; aircraft maintenance specialist Pa. Air Nat. Guard, Pitts., 1981-2000; assoc. Tandy Corp., 1997-2000; nat. legis. coord. Assn. of Civilian Technicians, Lake Ridge, Va., 2000—; cons. career devel. Write On! Right On!, Rochester, Pa., 1991—; mem. strategic planning com. 171 Air Refueling Wing, Pitts., 1994—; logistics com. mem. Career Quest '95 of Allegheny County, Pitts., 1995; v.p. Pa. Assn. Civilian Technicians, 1996—. Eucharistic min. St. Cecelia's, Diocese of Pitts., Rochester, 1990—; referee U.S. Swimming, 1983-97. Mem. ASTD, Am. Indian Sci. and Engring. Soc., Rochester Boro Fire Dept. (med. officer 1985-86, Meritorious Svc. award 1983), Three Rivers Indian Coun. Roman Catholic. Avocations: computer technology, networking, swimming. Home: 457 Adams St Rochester PA 15074-0014

GOULART, JOSÉ ANTONIO MARTINS, applied mathematician, researcher; b. Horta, Azores, Portugal, June 7, 1948; s. António Sebastião and Maria Ester (Martins) G.; m. Maria Lusa Da Rosa. BSEE, Santa Clara U., 1969, MSEE, 1971; PhD in Applied Math., U. Calif., Davis, 1989. Registered prof. engr. Teaching/rsch. asst. Santa Clara (Calif.) U., 1969-71; asst. prof., rschr. Inst. Superior Técnico, Lisbon, Portugal, 1972-80; rschr. dept. oceanography and fisheries U. of the Azores, Horta, Portugal, 1980-90, auxiliary prof. math. dept., 1990—, chmn. math. dept., 1991-93, 97-98; tech. counselor, permanent delegation of Portugal to OECD, Paris, 1998, 2000; counselor sci., tech. and culture Embassy of Portugal, Washington, 2000—; presenter in field. Dep. Azores Regional Assembly, Horta-Azores, 1976-83, 88-93, 95-96, Portuguese Nat. Parliament, Lisbon, 1991-92, 94-95; pres. Partido Socialista, Azores, 1988-94; mem. fgn. affairs com. Portuguese Parliament, Lisbon, 1994-95. Recipient Outstanding Freshman Engr. award FMC Corp., San Jose, 1966; Fulbright-Hayes fellow Fulbright Found., 1978; Sea Grant Coll. Program scholar, 1986-88. Mem. Ordem dos Engenheiros, Tau Beta Pi (chpt. sec. 1968-69), Alpha Sigma Nu, Sporting Club Da Horta. Avocations: music, photography, fishing, sports, natural resources studies. Home: 4620 N Park Ave Apt Ph06W Chevy Chase MD 20815-4564 Office: Embassy of Portugal 2125 Kalorama Rd NW Washington DC 20008-1695

GOULD, ALVIN R., international business executive; b. Seattle, May 16, 1922; s. Charlie I. and Laura (Klos) G.; m. Ruth Nelson, May 25, 1946; children: Stephen Charles, Jon Patrick. Grad. pub. schs. Mem. engring. dept. Pacific Car & Foundry Co., Renton, Wash., 1943-45, asst. mgr. indsl. sales, 1945-48, mgr. indsl. sales, 1948-55, gen. sales mgr., 1956-60; gen. sales mgr. Peterbilt Motors Co., Newark, Calif., 1961-64; v.p., dir., gen. sales mgr. Honolulu Iron Works Co., 1964-66, exec. v.p., dir., chief operating officer, 1966, pres., dir., chief ec. officer, 1966-71; group pres. Food Equipment Group Ward Foods In , 1970-71; v.p. merchandising Dillingham Corp., Honolulu, 1972-75, v.p. mining and merchandising, 1973-75, group v.p., exec. mgmt. com. mining and merchandising; pres. Truck Center Corp., Seattle, 1976-90, co-owner, sec.-treas., 1991-95; pvt. practice in personal investments, 1995—. Mem. nat. export expansion Council Dept. Commerce, 1969-74, chmn. regional export expansion council, 1969-74; mem. Western Regional Export Council; chmn. Honolulu Export Council, 1975-77; Chmn. bd. trustees Hawaii Pacific Coll., 1973-77; bd. dirs. Center for Internat. Bus. Mem. Hawaii C. of C. (chmn. trade com. 1968-69), Hawaii World Trade Assn. (mem. exec. com. 1968-69), Hawaii Assn. Industries (v.p., dir. 1975-76), Navy League (dir.). Clubs: Rotary, Meridian Country, Outrigger Canoe, Rainier. Home: 8464 W Mercer Way Mercer Island WA 98040-5633

GOULD, D. JOY, social services administrator; b. Annapolis, Md., Oct. 30, 1951; d. Sidney and Portia (Greenblatt) G. BA in Psychology, Webster Coll., 1973; MPA, Calif. State U., Dominguez Hills, 1981. Cert. alcholism counselor. Adminstrv. mgr. Wayback Inn-Social Model Detox Ctr., 1978-81; dir. alcohol abuse program Hollywood Cmty. Svcs., 1981-85; dir. recovery svcs., acting exec. dir. People in Progress, Inc., 1985-86; program mgr. Pacifica Cmty. Hosp., 1986-88; dir. outpatient svcs. L.A. Ctrs. for Alcohol and Drug Abuse, 1988-89; dir. drug/alcohol studies program Pacific Oaks Coll., Pasadena, Calif., 1991-92; exec. dir. Helpline Youth Counseling, Inc., Norwalk, Calif., 1989—; founder and dir. Calif. Inst. for Counseling Studies, Pasadena, 1993—; prof. alcohol drug studies program Pacific Oaks Coll., 1989—; cons. youth residental program CLARE Found., Inc., 1986-87; treas. bd. dirs., chair fin. com. So. Calif. Women's Substance Abuse Task Force, Inc., 1987—; cons. chem. dependency rehab. program Redgate Meml. Hosp., 1988. Cons., contbr. chpts. to book: Coping With Sibling Rivalry, 1989. Office: Helpline Youth Counseling 12440 Firestone Blvd Ste 1000 Norwalk CA 90650-4366

GOULD, DANIEL ROBERT, health services information professional; b. Worcester, Mass., Sept. 15, 1957; s. Robert Daniel and Jeannette Marie Gould; m. Paula Estelle Brazeau, July 2, 1979 (div. May 1992); children: Melissa, Christopher; m. Alice June Yoder, Sept. 9, 1992; children: Kara Stearns, Kaci Stearns, Danielle. BS in Med. Tech., Nasson Coll., 1979. Med. technologist Worcester (Mass.) City Hosp., 1978-79; lab. supr. BioMed. Labs., Worcester, 1979-84, Burbank Hosp., Fitchburg, Mass., 1984-88; lab. mgr. Clini Tech Svcs., Worcester, 1988-90; lab. mgr. Path Lab., Inc., Portsmouth, N.H., 1990-98, dir. info. svcs., 1998—; mem. HEDIS collaboration com. N.H. Healthcare Assn.; clin. lab. inspector Am. Soc. Clin. Pathologists. Com. chair Boy Scouts Am., Leominster, Mass., 1990; bd. world svcs. United Ch. of Christ, Holden, Mass., 1998. Cert. med. technologist Am. Soc. Clin. Pathologists/Clin. Lab. Scientist, Health, Edn., and Welfare/Clin. Lab. Scientist, Nat. Certifying Agy. Avocations: skiing, golf. Home: 390 N Main St Mount Gilead OH 43338-9789 Office: Path Lab Inc 195 Hanover St Ste 44 Portsmouth NH 03801-3774

GOULD, HARRY EDWARD, JR., paper company executive; b. N.Y.C., Sept. 24, 1938; s. Harry Edward and Lucille (Quartucy) G.; m. Barbara Clement, Apr. 26, 1975; children: Harry Edward III, Katharine Elizabeth. Student, Oxford U., 1958; BA cum laude, Colgate U., 1960; postgrad., Harvard Bus. Sch., 1960-61; MBA, Columbia U., 1964. Assoc. in corp. fin. dept. Goldman, Sachs & Co., N.Y.C., 1961-62; exec. asst. to sr. v.p. ops. Universal Am., N.Y.C., 1964-65; sec., treas. Young Spring & Wire Corp., Detroit, 1965-67, exec. v.p., COO, 1967-69, also bd. dirs.; v.p. adminstrn. and fin. Universal Am. Corp., 1968-69; mem. exec. com., v.p., sec.-treas. Daybrook-Ottawa Corp., Bowling Green, Ohio, 1967-69; dir., mem. exec. com. Am. Med. Ins. Co., N.Y.C., 1966-74; chmn., pres., CEO Gould Paper Corp., N.Y.C., 1969—, also chmn. bd. dirs.; chmn. bd., dir. Vrisimo Mfg., Inc., Ceres, 1974—; chmn. bd. Lewis & Gould Paper Co., Inc., Northfield, Ill., 1975-78; chmn., pres., CEO, Signature Comm. Ltd., L.A. and N.Y.C., 1986—; chmn. bd. Legion Paper West Corp., Commerce, Calif., 1997—; chmn. bd. dirs. Samuel Porritt & Co., East Peria, Ill., Ingalls Mfg., Inc., Ceres, Calif., McNair Mfg., Inc., Chico, Calif., Hawthorne Paper Co., Kalamazoo, Weiss Mfg., Inc., Chico; bd. dirs. Reinhold Gould GmbH, Hamburg, Germany; ltd. ptnr. Hardy & Co., N.Y.C., 1973-78; chmn. exec. com., bd. dirs. Richard Lewis Paper Corp., Northfield, Ill., 1992-97; bd. dirs., mem. environ. and health and safety com. Domtar Inc., Montreal, 1995—. Co-chmn. Pacesetter's com. Boy Scouts Am., 1966-69; participant as U.S. Pres.'s rep. UN E-W Trade Devel. Commn., 1967; mem. N.Y. Gov.'s Task Force on N.Y. State Cultural Life and Arts, 1975—; pres. Harry E. Gould Found., N.Y.C., 1971—; mem. nat. coun. Colgate U., 1973-76, trustee, mem. budget, devel., fin. and student affairs com., 1976-82; mem. vis. com. Sch. Dramatic Arts of The New Sch., 1995—; mem. adv. bd. Columbia U. Grad. Sch. Bus., 1980—; bd. dirs. United Cerebral Palsy Rsch. and Ednl. Found., 1976—, Nat. Multiple Sclerosis Soc., 1977—, N.Y.C. Housing Devel. Corp., 1977—, USO of Met. N.Y., 1981—; bd. dirs. Housing N.Y. Corp., 1986—, vice chmn., 1987—; bd. dirs., chmn. exec. com. Cinema Group, Inc., L.A., 1979-86, chmn., pres., 1982-86; mem. Dem. Nat. Fin. Coun., 1974-78, also vice chmn. exec. com., chmn. budget and audit coms.; treas. N.Y. State Dem. Com., 1976-77; mem. mayor's citizens com. Dem. Nat. Conv., 1976; mem. U.S. Pres.'s Export Coun. (exec. com., chmn. export expansion subcom., mem. export promotion subcom.), 1979-82; mem. exec. br. Acad. Motion Picture Arts and Scis., 1985—; nat. trustee, mem. exec. com. Nat. Symphony Orch., Washington, 1978—; trustee Riverdale Country Sch., 1990—; bd. dirs. Residential Mortgage Ins. Corp., 1992—. Mem. Nat. Paper Trade Assn. (dir., mem. printing paper com. 1973—), Paper Mchts. Assn. N.Y. (dir. 1972—), Paper Distbn. Coun. (chmn. 1993—), Young Pres. Orgn., Am. Mgmt. Assn. (trustee, audit com. 1997—), Paper Club N.Y., Fin. Execs. Inst., Columbia U. Grad. Sch. Bus. Alumni Assn. (dir. 1980—), Phi Kappa Tau. Clubs: Pres.'s N.Y. (co-chmn. assocs. div. 1964-68), City Athletic, Harvard, Harvard Business, Friars, Marco Polo (N.Y.C.); Les Ambassadeurs (London); Rockrimmon Country (Stamford, Conn.). Office: Gould Paper Corp 11 Madison Ave Fl 14L New York NY 10010-3675

GOULD, LILIAN, writer; b. Phila., Apr. 19, 1920; d. Reuben Barr and Lilian Valentine (Scott) Seidel; m. Irving Gould, Nov. 16, 1944; children: Mark, Scott, Paul, John. Student, U. Pa., Charles Morris Price Sch. of Advt. and Journalism, Phila. Copywriter, mgr. advt. agys., Phila. Author: Our Living Past, 1969, Jeremy and the Gorillas, 1977 (award 1977); freelance journalist mags. and newspapers. Mem. Authors Guild, Phila. Children's Reading Roundtable, Phila. Writers Orgn. Home: 772 Newtown Rd Villanova PA 19085-1121

GOULD, R(ICHARD) MARTIN (RICHARD MARTIN GOLDMAN), marketing consultant, researcher; b. Auburn, N.Y., Aug. 19, 1941; s. Max and Lillian (Kanter) Goldman. Grad., Herman Ave. Sch., Auburn, N.Y., 1959; student, U. Buffalo, 1961; AB, Ohio No. U., 1963, JD, 1966; postgrad., U. Ariz., 1966. Tchr. Auburn (N.Y.) Pub. Schs., 1945-53, Auburn East H.S., 1953-59; athletic, pool staff Catskill (N.Y.) Resorts, 1960-63; legal dept. staff, welfare divsn. City of Auburn, 1963-66; dir. response mktg. Rep. Orgn., Tucson, 1966-67; legal rschr. ICC, Washington, 1967; asst. bank examiner Comptr. of the Currency, N.Y.C., 1967-68; pub. bond securities salesman Henry Harris & Sons, Inc., N.Y.C., 1968-69; pub. bond salesman Chester Harris & Co., Inc., N.Y.C., 1968—; land surveyor Interstate Gen. Corp., San Juan, P.R., 1969; with Gen. Devel. Corp., San Juan, 1969; marketer, new bus. rep. Canadaigua Enterprises, Inc., Farmington, N.Y.; assoc. Law Offices of Max Goldman, Auburn, N.Y., 1972-77; sales mktg. cons. G. Enterprises, Gould & Assocs., San Rafael, Calif., 1972—, pub. rels. exec., 1993-96, sales mktg. cons., 1996—. Mem. Internat. Platform Assn., Alpha Epsilon Pi, Phi Alpha Delta, Phi Beta Lambda. Humanist. Avocations: walking, table tennis, golf, reading, watching TV. Home and Office: Gould Consultants PO Box 6701 128 La Perdiz Ct San Rafael CA 94903-3541

GOULD, TAFFY, Internet company executive, real estate executive; b. Miami, Fla., Apr. 14, 1942; d. Emil J. and Estelle F. Gould; m. Bernard Arthur Beber, Apr. 5, 1964 (div. Jan. 1975); children: Karen B. Futernick, J. Gregory Beber. BA, Smith Coll., 1963. Cert. real estate broker, Fla. Exec. v.p. Housing Engrs. Fla., Inc., Miami, 1977—; COO Medix Software Sys. Ltd., Sydney, Australia, 1999—; lectr. Potomac Spkrs. Bur., Washington, 1993-98. Author: South Africa: Land of Hope, 1989, White Woman Witchdoctor, 1993 (Best Seller 1994); co-author: Create Your Own Future, 1996; newspaper columnist Miami Today, 1983-88; radio talk host WINZ, Miami, 1986-88. Mem. nat. com. Zionist Orgn. Am., N.Y., 1995—; bd. dirs. Alexander Muss H.S. in Israel, Miami, 1995—, Cen. Agy. for Jewish Edn.; dir. U. Miami, Miami Hot Glass, Coral Gables, Fla., 1998—; governing coun. Fla. Philharmonic Orch., 1998—. Recipient Humanitarian and Arts award Internat. Bolivarian Soc., Miami, 1994, City of the Future award City of Ariel, Israel, 1999, Louis Brandeis award Zionist Orgn. Am., N.Y., 2000. Avocations: classical music, reading, music. E-mail: taffyg@bellsouth.net. Fax: 305-668-3298. Home: 10 Edgewater Dr Apt 14F Coral Gables FL 33143-6968 Office: Australian Tech Park, 1 Central Ave, Eveleigh NSW 1430, Australia

GOULD, THOMAS DENTON, lawyer; b. Elmira, N.Y., Oct. 29, 1950. BS, Pa. State U., 1972; JD, Dickinson Coll., 1982. Bar: Pa., U.S. Supreme Ct. Pa. Mem. com. Shiremanstown Parks and Recreation, 1996—. Mem. ATLA, Pa. Bar Assn., D.C. Bar Assn., CCBA. Office: Law Offices of Thomas D Gould 2 E Main St Shiremanstown PA 17011-6309

GOULDEN, JOHN, diplomat, NATO official; b. U.K., Feb. 21, 1941; m. Diana Goulden; 2 children. Grad., Queens Coll., Oxford U., 1962; postgrad., London U. With Diplomatic Svc. of U.K., Ankara, 1963-67; 2d sec. Hungary/Romania/Czechoslovakia Desk, Fgn. Office Diplomatic Svc. of U.K., 1967-69; with Diplomatic Svc. of U.K., Manila, 1969-71; with Planning Staff, Fgn. Office Diplomatic Svc. of U.K., 1971-74, head recruitment program, Fgn. Office, 1974-76; head of chancery Diplomatic Svc. of U.K., Dublin, 1976-79; asst. head of dep. dept. for NATO affairs Diplomatic Svc. of U.K., 1979-81, head of personnel svcs., head of news dept., Fgn. and Commonwealth Office spokesman, 1982-84; head of chancery, U.K. REpresentation to European Cmtys. Brussels, 1984-87; asst. under sec. of State, Def., 1988-92; amb. Embassy of U.K., Ankara, 1992-95; permanent rep. of U.K. NATO and Western European Union, Brussels, 1995—. Office: NATO Hdqrs, Blvd Leopold III, 1110 Brussels Belgium*

GOULDER, GERALD POLSTER, retail executive, management consultant, lawyer; b. Columbus, Ohio, Apr. 30, 1953; s. Norman Ernest and Betty (Polster) G.; children: Gavrielle, Nathaniel. BA, Ohio State U., 1975; JD, Washington U., 1978. Bar: Ohio 1978, N.C. 1985; cert. mediator N.C. Superior Ct., N.C. Indsl. Commn. Spl. prosecutor office state atty. gen. Divsn. Medicaid Fraud Control, Columbus, 1979-80; spl. prosecutor Antitrust Divsn., Columbus, 1981-82; atty. James M. Schottenstein & Assocs., Columbus, 1982-84; chmn., CEO Carolina Drug Distbrs., Inc. and Emporium Stores, Ltd., Greensboro, N.C., 1984-96; mediator Mediation Practice N.C., Bus. Mediation Svc.; prin. Equine Dispute Resolution Svc., N.C. Bus. Mediation Coun. Assoc. editor Washington U. Urban Law Ann., 1977-78; contbr. articles to profl. jours. Trustee Wexner Heritage Village, Columbus, 1983-84, bd. dirs. Eastern Music Festival, Greensboro, 1991-94, U. N.C.-Greensboro Spartan Club, 1991-95; v.p. Beth David Synagogue, Greensboro, 1992-95, pres., 1996; participant Leadership Greensboro, 1985, Triad Leadership, 1991; mem. Crime Study Commn., Greensboro, 1992, Greensboro Devel. Corp., 1993-95. Mem. Am. Arbitration Assn., Am. Intellectual Property Lawyers Assn., N.C. Bar Assn., Greensboro Bar Assn., Columbus Bar Assn., Ohio Bar Assn., Leadership Greensboro Alumni Assn., Equestrian Dispute Resolution Assn. (bd. dirs. 1999—). E-mail: goulder@mediat8.net. Office: NC Bus Mediation Svc 1006 N Holden Rd Greensboro NC 27410-4826

GOULDEY, GLENN CHARLES, manufacturing company executive; b. N.Y.C., July 28, 1952; s. George Howard and Jeannette Ruth Williamson; m. Leslie Jeanne Ruth, Oct. 2, 1982; children: Jeremy Charles, Nicholas

Glenn, Alexander James George. BS in Bus., Coll. N.J., 1976; postgrad., Portland State U., 1980; MBA, Rider U., 1981; postgrad., Dartmouth Coll., 1994-95. Cert. in purchasing mgmt., cert. in prodn. and inventory control. Sr. planner Eaton Corp., Flemington, N.J., 1975-77, pricing mgr., distbn., 1977-79, inventory control mgr., 1979-80; materials mgr., purchasing Eaton Corp., Beaverton, Oreg., 1980-81, mfg. and materials mgr., 1981-83, mktg. and materials mgr., 1983-87, plant and gen. mgr., 1987-88; v.p. sales and mktg. Eaton Corp., Carol Stream, Ill., 1988-89, mgr. ops. divsn., 1989-93, gen. bus. mgr., 1993-95; pres., gen. mgr. Lectron Products divsn. Eaton, Rochester Hills, Mich., 1995-99; v.p., gen. mgr. Eaton Corp., Rochester Hills, Mich., 2000—. Patentee in field. Mem. bd. advisors Oakland U. Bus. Sch.; bd. dirs. Rochester Cmty. Schs. Found.; asst. coach lacrosse Rochester Hills United H.S. Mem. Am. Prodn. Inventory Control Soc., Nat. Youth Sports Coaches Assn. (cert.), Soc. Automotive Engrs. Internat. Republican. Lutheran. Office: Lectron Products Eaton Corp 1400 S Livernois Rd Rochester MI 48307-3362

GOULDING, MARRACK IRVINE, college administrator; b. Plymouth, Devon, Eng., Sept. 2, 1936; s. Ernest Irvine and Gladys Ethel (Sennett) G.; m. Susan Rhoda D'Albiac, Feb. 11, 1961 (div. 1996); children: Rachel Mary, James Marrack, Henry John; m. Catherine Pawlow, Dec. 14, 1996. BA with honors, Oxford (Eng.) U., 1959; DSc (hon.), Southampton (Eng.) U., 1997. Various posts with Brit. Diplomatic Svc., Lebanon, Kuwait, U.K., Libya, 1959-70; head of chancery Brit. Embassy, Cairo, 1970-72; pvt. sec. to minister of state Fgn. and Commonwealth Office, London, 1972-75; with cen policy rev. staff Cabinet Office, London, 1975-77; counselor Brit. Embassy, Lisbon, Portugal, 1977-79; head of chancery Brit. Mission to UN, N.Y.C., 1979-83; amb. Brit. Embassy, Luanda, Angola, 1983-85; under-sec.-gen. for spl. polit. affairs UN Secretariat, N.Y.C., 1986-91, under-sec.-gen for peacekeeping ops., 1992-93, under-sec.-gen. for polit. affairs, 1993-97; warden St. Antony's Coll., Oxford, Eng., 1997—. Dir. Internat. Peace Acad., N.Y.C., 1987-2000; trustee Stockholm Internat. Peace Rsch. Inst., 1997—. Named Knight Comdr. of Order of St. Michael and St. George, Queen of Eng., 1997. Mem. Royal Overseas League (London). Anglican. Avocations: bird watching, traveling. Office: St Antonys Coll, Oxford OX2 6JF, England

GOULKO, GENNADI, physicist, researcher; b. Kiev, Ukraine, Apr. 15, 1958; s. Michael Goulko and Anna Kanevskaya; m. Margarita Krisson; 1 child, Olga. MSc, Kiev State U., 1980, PhD in Radiation Biology, 1987. Cert. in radiation protection. Sr. engr. Inst. Radiology, Kiev, 1980-87; sci. worker Sci. Ctr. Radiation Medicine, Kiev, 1987-88, sr. sci. worker, 1988-91, head lab., 1991-94; scientist Sci. Ctr. for Environment and Health Rsch. Ctr., Munich, 1994-99, Inst. for Radiation Hygiene, Munich, 1999—. Contbr. articles to sci. jours., including Health Physics, Radiation and Environ. Biophysics. Office: Inst for Applied Radiation Protection, Ingolstädter-Landstr 1, 85764 Oberschleissheim Germany

GOUNARIS, BASIL, historian; b. Lausanne, Switzerland, Apr. 29, 1961; arrived in Greece, 1963; s. Konstantinos and Aikaterini (Asteriadis) G.; m. Helen Giannatsoulia, June 25, 1994; children: Konstantinos, Ioannis. BA, Aristotle U., Thessaloniki, Greece, 1983, MA, 1985; DPhil, Oxford U., England, 1988. Rsch. supr. Mus. of Macedonian Struggle, Thessaloniki, Greece, 1990—; cons. in field. Author: Steam Over Macedonia, 1993, Stis ochthes tou Ydragora, 2000; editor: Taftotites sti Makedonia, 1997. With Greek Mil., 1989-90. Saltzberg Sem. fellow, 1993; Found. State scholar, 1980-81, Ismene Fitch scholar, 1985-88; recipient Athens Acad. awards, 1995, 1998. Mem. Greek Hist. Assn., Assn. for Study of Ethnicity and Nationalism. Home: 17 Iatrou Zanna St, 54643 Thessaloniki Greece Office: Mus Macedonian Struggle, 23 Prox Koromila St, 54622 Thessaloniki Greece

GOURBESVILLE, PHILIPPE MARCEL, hydrology educator, consultant; b. Valognes, Normandy, France, Apr. 27, 1964; s. Bernard Maurice and Micheline Odette (Desfeux) G.; m. Florence Machecourt, Dec. 28, 1994; 1 child, Pierre. MSc, Caen U., France, 1987; D.E.A. (postgrad. degree), Caen U., 1988; PhD highest grade, Louis Pasteur U., Strasbourg, France, 1993. Project mgr., engring. cons. SOGETI, France, 1987-96; assoc. prof. U. Nice (France), 1997—; expert, cons. hydrol. projects, North area, France, 1996—, hydraulic vineyard optimization, Champagne area, France, 1996—, hydraulic mgmt., Senegal River, Senegal, 1997, marine environment mgmt., hydraulic projects, sustainable devel., Commores Islands, Indian Ocean, 1998—. Contbr. articles to profl. jours. Mem. Am. Geophys. Union, Internat. Assn. Hydraulic Rsch., Internat. Assn. Hydraulic Scis. Avocations: rowing, hiking, trekking. Home: Villa No 50, 240 Av Antony Fabre, 06270 Villeneuve-Loubet France Office: U Nice-Sophia Antipolis, 98 bd E Herriot, 06240 Nice France

GOURDINE, SIMON PETER, lawyer; b. Jersey City, July 30, 1940; s. Simon Samuel and Laura Emily (Rembert) G.; m. Patricia Campbell, Aug. 1, 1964; children: David Laurence, Peter Christopher, Laura Allison. B.A., City Coll. N.Y., 1962; J.D., Fordham U., 1965; P.M.D., Harvard Bus. Sch., 1979. Bar: N.Y. 1966, U.S. Dist. Ct. (so. dist.) N.Y. 1967, U.S. Supreme Ct. 1976. Asst. U.S. atty. So. Dist. N.Y., 1967-69; atty. Celanese Corp., 1969-70; asst. to commr. Nat. Basketball Assn., N.Y.C., 1970-72, v.p. adminstrn., 1973-74, dep. commr., 1974-81; commr. N.Y.C. Dept. Consumer Affairs, 1982-84; sec. The Rockefeller Found., 1984-86; dir. labor rels. Met. Transp. Authority, 1986-90; exec. dir., gen. counsel Nat. Basketball Players Assn., N.Y.C., 1990-96; gen. ptnr. TCS TV Ptnrs., LP, 1990-93; gen. counsel to chancellor N.Y.C. Bd. Edn., 1996-98; mem. N.Y. State Banking Bd., 1979-90; mem. N.Y.C. Charter Revision Commn., 1988-89. Bd. dirs. Police Athletic League, 1974—, Fresh Air Fund, 1985—, Fund for City of N.Y., 1990-94, Fleet Bank N.Y., 1993—; mem. N.Y.C. Civil Svc. Commn., 1981-82, Gov.'s Exec. Adv. Commn. on Adminstrn. Justice, 1981-82, Mayor's Com. on Taxi Regulatory Issues., 1981-82. Served to capt. U.S. Army, 1965-67. Decorated Army Commendation medal, South Vietnam, 1967. Mem. 100 Black Men Inc. Home: 5251 Fieldston Rd Bronx NY 10471-2911

GOURLAY, STEVEN GEOFFREY, physician, clinical pharmacologist, epidemiologist; b. Melbourne, Australia, Aug. 29, 1959; s. Geoffrey Downs and Deirdre Anne (Ellis) G. MBBS, Melbourne U., Australia, 1983; PhD, Monash U., Australia, 1995. Gen. practitioner Melbourne, 1986; sr. resident Austin Hosp., Australia, 1987-88; lectr. Monash U., 1989, Nat. Health/Med. Rsch. Coun. Australia pub. health fellow, 1990-93; cons. physician Monash Med. Ctr., 1990-94; Nat. Heart Found. Australia, Ralph Reader overseas fellow U. Calif., San Francisco, 1994-96; epidemiologist, clin. scientist Genentech, Inc., San Francisco, 1997—; mem. expert com. Nat. Drug and Alcohol Rsch. Ctr., 1991-92; adj. asst. prof. U. Calif., San Francisco, 1997—. Contbr. articles to profl. jours. Hon. treas. Movement Opposing the Promotion of Unhealthy Products, Australia, 1982—. PHS rsch. fellow Nat. Health and Med. Rsch. Coun. Australia, 1990. Fellow Royal Australasian Coll. Physicians; mem. Pub. Health Assn. Australia, Australian Soc. Clin. and Exptl. Pharmacology and Toxicology, Soc. for Rsch. on Nicotine and Tobacco, Am. Soc. for Clin. Pharmacology and Therapeutics. Avocations: restoration of Victorian houses, Asian and European languages, reading, swimming. Office: Genentech Inc 1 Dna Way South San Francisco CA 94080-4990

GOURLEY, J. LELAND, editor, publishing executive; b. Mounds, Okla., Jan. 29, 1919; s. Samuel O. and Lodema (Scott) G.; m. Vicki Graham Clark, Nov. 24, 1976; children: James Leland II, Janna Lynn Gourley, Kelly Clark, Brandon Clark. BA in Liberal Studies, U. Okla., 1963. Editor, pub., pres. Daily Free-Lance, Henryetta, Okla., 1946-73; editor-in-chief Oklahoma City Friday, 1974—; CEO Nichols Hills Pub. Co., 1974—; pres. Suburban Graphics, Inc., 1991-93; pres. Central Okla. Newspaper Group, 1987, 90, 93, 96, 98, 99, 2000; pres. Sta. KHEN, KHEN-FM, Henryetta, 1955-63; pres. Hugo (Okla.) Daily News, 1953-63; chief of staff gov. Okla., 1959-63; chmn., pres. State Capitol Bank, 1962-69; v.p. sta. KXOJ Sapulpa, 1972-75; treas. Sta. KJEM-FM, Oklahoma City, 1962-67. Mem. Pres. Nat. Pub. Advisory Com. to Sec. Commerce, 1963-66; exec. dir. Gov's Comm. Higher Edn., 1960-61; Dem. candidate for gov. Okla., 1966. Dist. chmn. Boy Scouts Am., 1963-65; bd. dirs. So. Regional Edn. Bd., 1959-67, Okla. Symphony Soc., 1976-88, Oklahoma City Crimestoppers, 1982—, Salvation Army, Oklahoma City, 1985-87, Okla. Goodwill Industries, 1989-91; mem. Gov.'s Reform Com., 1984; bd. trustees Okla. City Univ., 1993—; bd. dirs. Okla. City Edn. Round Table, 1992—. Maj. AUS, 1942-46, ETO. Recipient Best Okla. Small Daily newspaper awards, 1949-58, 69-72, Best Large City Weekly newspaper awards, 1977-80, 83-85, 87-91, 94-95, 97, 98; inducted into Okla. Journalism Hall of Fame, 1980. Mem. UP Internat. Editors Okla. (pres. 1958-59), Okla. Disciples of Christ Laymen (pres. 1964-65), Suburban Newspapers Am. (dir. 1980-89), Nat. Newspaper Assn., Okla. Press Assn. (pres. 1988-89, treas. 1991-93), Oklahoma City C. of C. (dir. 1975—), Henryetta C. of C. (pres. 1955), Oklahoma City Golf and Country Club (bd. dirs. 1991-95), Econ. Club Okla., Oklahoma City Com. of 100, Rotary (pres. Oklahoma City club 1992-93), Mil. Order of World Wars, The Ret. Officers Assn., Pi Kappa Alpha. Republican. Home: 6435 Grandmark Dr Oklahoma City OK 73116-6535 Office: 10801 Quail Plaza Dr Oklahoma City OK 73120-3123

GOURLEY, JAMES WALTER, III, airport executive; b. L.A., Jan. 8, 1941; s. James Walter and Eleanor Mae (Kanel) G.; children: Jennifer Lane, Matthew James; m. Dana C. Matthews, Dec. 20, 1986; stepchildren: Lance, Wendee. AA, Fullerton Coll., 1960; BS in Geology cum laude, U. Redlands, 1962; MS in Earth Scis., U. So. Calif., 1971; Exec. Mgmt. Program, Pa. State U., 1989. Cert. profl. geologist, Calif. Petroleum engr., geologist Standard Oil Calif., La Habra, 1964-72, devel. geologist, 1971-72; supr. energy planning, mgr. energy resources So. Calif. Gas Co., L.A., 1972-80, mgr. supply forecasting, 1980-82, mgr. underground storage, 1982-86, mgr. pub. affairs planning, 1986-89, mgr. West Valley divsn., 1989-92, mgr. Inland Empire Region, 1992-98; exec. dir. Inland Valley Devel. Agy./San Bernardino Airport Authority, 1998—. Exec. com. Inland Empire Econ. Partnership, 1992—, chmn., 1997. Mem. Soc. Petroleum Engrs. Republican. Fax: 909-382-4106. E-mail: jgourley@sbdairport.com. Home: PO Box 5301 Blue Jay CA 92317-5301 Office: 294 S Leland Norton Way Ste 1 San Bernardino CA 92408-0131

GOURLEY, JOHN TERRY, physicist, research administrator; b. Leongatha, Victoria, Australia, Nov. 12, 1944; s. John Norman and Ailsa Jean (Miles) G.; m. Jilliane Iris Rodger, Jan. 8, 1968; children: Belinda Mia, Tiffany Laura. BS with hons., U. Melbourne, Australia, 1966, diploma in Edn., 1967; PhD in Solid State Physics, Monash U., Melbourne, 1971. Student tchr. Dept Edn. of Victoria, Melbourne, 1962-66; tching. fellow dept. physics Monash U., Melbourne, 1967-70; postdoctoral fellow Rsch. Sch. of Phys. Scis., Canberra, Australia, 1971-73; rsch. scientist Rocla, Melbourne, Australia, 1974-86; rsch. mgr. Rocla, Melbourne, 1986—. Inventor Insulated Power Pole, patent, 1993, Composite Concrete Building Element patent, 1998; co-designer Cathodic Protection System for Pre-stressed Concrete Pipes, 1975; contbr. articles to profl. publs. Mem. Concrete Inst. Australia, Am. Concrete Inst., Nat. Assn. Corrosion Engrs., Victorian Standardbred Breeders Assn. Avocations: breeding harness racing horses, ornithology, fishing. Office: Rocla, PO Box 1564, Clayton South VIC 3169, Australia

GOUSOPOULOS, STAVROS, occupational health facility administrator; b. Naoussa, Greece, July 8, 1954; s. Epamidondas and Evagelia (Petsou) G.; m. Eleftheria Lolou, Nov. 22, 1986; children: Epaminondas, Evagelia. Student, U. Ferrara, Italy, 1974; MD, U. Thesaloniki, Greece, 1979; Doctorate, U. Thrace, 1995. Asst. 424 Mil. Hosp., Thesaloniki, 1981-82, Regional Gen. Hosp., Veria, Greece, 1982-84, St. Dimitrios Gen. Hosp., Thesaloniki, 1984-85; dir. occupl. health dept. Klonatex Co., Barbaressos SA, Varvaressos SA, Naoussa, Greece, 1986—; fellow Guy's Drug Rsch. Unit, London, 1993, Ahepa Gen. Hosp., Thesaloniki, 1994-95; sr. investigator dept. toxicology U. Thesaloniki, 1992-93, cons. dept. hygiene, 1994-97, cons. dept. internal medicine, 1994-97; cons. dept. toxicology U. Alexandroupolis, Greece, 1994—. Author: Textbook of Industrial Toxicology, 1995, Good Labor Practice, 1995; co-author: the Influence of EMF in Cardiac Rhythm, 1997. Gen. sec. Social Med. Help, Veria, 1999. Fellow Soc. Internal Medicine, Hypertension Soc.; mem. Internat. Commn. on Occupl. Health. Avocations: arborculture, wine-making. Office: 18 Stefanou Dragoumi St, 59200 Naoussa Greece

GOUTEUX, JEAN-PAUL, biomedical researcher; b. Paris, Aug. 24, 1948; s. Andre and Jeanne (Gaudet) G.; m. Mukashema Kabano; children: Bruno, Lionel, Davy, Ghislain, Olivier, Elodie. Diploma, Paris VI U., 1973; postgrad., Paris VII U., 1974; diploma, Paris XI U., 1977; PhD, Paris VII U., 1984. Med. asst. Paris VII U., Bobigny, 1970; rschr. IRSAC, Zaire, 1973-75, IRD, France, 1975-77; rschr. IRD-OCCGE, Burkina Faso, 1977-80, Ivory Coast, 1980-84; rschr. IRD, Brazzaville, Congo, 1984-88, 88-90, IRD-Ande, Centrafrican Republic, 1990-93, Pau U.-IRD, France, 1988-90, Pau U. (IPRA)-IRD, France, 1993—; med. asst. Paris VII U., Bobigny, 1970. Officer French Res. Mem. Soc. Entomologique de France, Soc. Francaise de Systematique, Soc. de Pathologie Exotique, Soc. des Amis du Mus. H.N., Soc. Archeologique du Gers. Home: A Caillaou, 32730 Villecomtal sur Arros France Office: IRD, La Fayette 213, 75010 Paris France

GOUVEIA-OLIVEIRA, ANTONIO MANUEL, physician, researcher; b. Lisbon, Portugal, Feb. 25, 1953; s. Alfredo and Cristina (Gouveia) Oliveira; m. Ana Cristina Mendes; 1 child, Miguel. MD, U. Lisbon, 1977, MSc, 1991, PhD in Biostats., Clin. Computing Sys., 1995. Resident U. Hosp., Lisbon, 1978-87; prof. biostats., clin. epidemiology and clin. computing U. Lisbon Med. Sch., 1988—, chmn. dept. biomath. and med. informatics, 1996—; vis. scientist Tech. U., Munich, 1992, U. Ulm, Germany, 1994; biostats. cons. Nat. Cancer Inst., Lisbon, 1991-98; dir. rsch. Datamedica Ltd., Lisbon, 1996—. Author: Computer-Based Clinical Reporting Systems, 1995; editor: Diseases of the Biliary System and Pancreas, 1996; patentee in Siscope, 1990, Coati, 1999, Cougar, 1999. Recipient Postgrad. grant French Govt., 1985, Rsch. grant Deutscher Akademischer Austauschedienst, 1992. Mem. Portuguese Statis. Soc., Am. Med. Informatics Assn. Avocation: photography. Office: Faculty Medicine Lisboa, Av Prof Egas Moniz, Biomath, 1700 Lisbon Portugal

GOUVERIS, JOHN GEORGE, internist, angiologist; b. Neapolis, Laconia, Greece, Apr. 19, 1953; s. George and Maria (Kolivodiakos) G.; m. Olga Bovopoulou, Dec. 26, 1980; children: Maria, George, Dimitris. Cert. in internal medicine, U. Athens, Greece, 1985, cert. in angiology, 1987, PhD, 1988, cert. in ultrasonography, 1993. Cert. in Diving Med., 1980, Cardiopulmonary Resuscitating (CPR), 1997, U. Athens. Chief med. officer Flotilla of Landing Ships, Salamina, Greece, 1980-82; registrar, lectr. Naval Hosp., Athens, 1983-85; dir. Sick-Bay, Poros, Pallaskas, Greece, 1986; dir. subsection staff security Hellenic Elec. Co., Nafplion, Greece, 1987—; pvt. practice Argos, Greece, 1987—. Contbr. articles to profl. jours. Lt. Greek Navy, 1984-86. Mem. N.Y. Acad. Scis., European Assn. Internal Medicine, others. Mem. Christian Orthodox Ch. Avocations: collecting stamps, swimming, diving. Home and Office: Nafplio 23, 21200 Argos Greece

GOUYON, PAUL CARDINAL, archbishop; b. Bordeaux, France, Oct. 24, 1910; s. Jean-Baptiste Louis and Jeanne (Chassaing) G.; ed. in France. Ordained priest Roman Catholic Ch., 1937, consecrated bishop, 1957; bishop of Bayonne, 1957, titular archbishop of Pessinonte, 1963, archbishop of Rennes, 1964-85, now archbishop emeritus of Rennes; elevated to Sacred Coll. Cardinals, 1969. Decorated Croix de Guerre, officer Legion of Honor, comdr. Nat. Order Merit. Mem. Pax Christi (past pres. French sect.). Author several books. Address: Ma Maison, 181 rue Judaique, 33081 Bordeaux Cedex, France*

GOVARE, PIERRE, marketing professional; b. Suresnes, France, Sept. 5, 1956; s. Claude and Brigitte (De Chollet) G.; m. Françoise Abraham, June 14, 1980; children: Maxime, Elodie, Constance, Agathe. MBA, HEC, Paris, 1979. Mktg. dir. RJ Reynolds France, Paris, 1985-89, mktg. sales dir., 1990-97; v.p. mktg. sales Eastern and Ctrl. Europe RJ Reynolds Inc., Geneva, 1992-95, sr. v.p. Ctrl. Europe and Africa, 1996-97, pres. Eastern and Ctrl. Europe, 1998, sr. v.p. strategic planning and bus. re-engring., 1999—; dir., bd. dirs. Tanzanian Tobacco Co., Dar es Salaam, Tanzania, 1996-97. Avocations: golf, sailing, squash, music. Home: 23 Chemin Prudent Balland, 1222 Vesenaz Switzerland Office: RJ Reynolds Internat, 12 Chemin Rieu, 1207 Geneve Switzerland

GOVATSOS, PANAGIOTIS ARISTIDIS, mechanical engineering consultant; b. Athens, Attiki, Greece, Sept. 19, 1969; s. Aristidis Panagiotis and Konstadine Theordore (Kripotov) G. Degree, Nat. Tech. U., 1992, PhD, 1996. Mech. engr. Public Power Corp. of Greece, Athens, 1993-94; rsch. engr. Lab. of Hydraulic Turbomachines, Nat. Tech. U. of Athens, 1992-97; cons. engr. Network Ltd., Athens, 1997-98; tech. head hydroelectric dept. construct group Elliniki Technodomiki A.E., Marousi, Greece, 1998—. Contbr. articles to profl. jours. Mem. Tech. Chamber of Greece, Greek Soc. of Elec. and Mech. Engrs., Soc. of Grads. of Nat. Tech. U. of Athens. Avocations: web-internet, swimming, traveling. Home: 6 Strojadon, 11362 Athens Greece Office: Elliniki Technodomiki AE, 39 Akakion & Monemvasias St, 151 25 Marousi Greece

GOVER, ALAN SHORE, lawyer; b. Lyons, N.Y., Sept. 5, 1948; s. Norman Marvin and Beatrice L. (Shore) G.; m. Ellen Rae Ross, Dec. 4, 1976; children: Maxwell Ross, Mary Trace. AB, Tufts U., 1970; JD, Georgetown U., 1973. Bar: Tex. 1973, D.C. 1980, U.S. Dist. Ct. (so. dist.) Tex. 1974, U.S. Dist. Ct. (we. dist.) Tex. 1976, U.S Dist. Ct. (no. dist.) Tex. 1988, U.S. Dist. Ct. (ea. dist.) Tex. 1990, U.S. Ct. Appeals (5th cir.) 1974, U.S. Ct. Appeals (D.C. cir.) 1977, U.S. Dist. Ct. (we. dist.) 1979, U.S. Ct. Appeals (2d cir.) 1979, D.C. 1980, U.S. Ct. Appeals (9th and 11th cirs.) 1981, U.S. Ct. Appeals (8th cir.) 1981, U.S. Supreme Ct. 1976. Assoc. Baker & Botts, Houston, 1973-80, ptnr., 1981-85; ptnr. Weil, Gotshal & Manges, Houston, 1985—. Co-author: The Texas Nonjudicial Foreclosure Process, 1990; editor, chmn. editorial bd. P.L.I. Oil and Gas and Bankruptcy Laws, 1985. Trustee Congregation Beth Israel, Houston, 1980-86, v.p., 1996—; trustee Houston Ballet, 1986—, v.p., 1993-96; chmn. ann. fund St. John's Sch., Houston, 1993-95, trustee 1996—; trustee Retina Rsch. Found., Houston, St. John's Sch., Houston, 1996—; chmn. East Downtown Mgmt. Dist., Houston, 2000—. Fellow Tex. Bar Found.; mem. ABA, Coronado Club, N.Y. Athletic Club, The Argyle (San Antonio). Jewish. Office: Weil Gotshal & Manges 700 Louisiana St Ste 1600 Houston TX 77002-2784

GOVIC, RUDOLF, structural engineer; b. Sibenik, Croatia, May 21, 1971; came to the U.S., 1976; s. Joso and Volga (Tanfara) G. B in Engring., Stevens Inst. Tech., 1994, M in Engring., 1996. Engr.-in-tng., N.J. Summer mgmt. intern Port Authority N.Y. and N.J., Newark, 1995; project engr. Paul Beck Assocs., P.A., Fairfield, N.J., 1996—. Engring. technician U.S. Army Corps Engrs., 1991. Mem. ASCE (assoc.), Am. Concrete Inst. Roman Catholic. Avocations: stamp collecting, swimming, coin collecting, aviation. Office: Paul Beck Assocs 12 Kulick Rd Fairfield NJ 07004-3308

GOVINDASAMY DASAMY, RAMU, marketing educator, assistant professor; b. Dharapuram, Tamilnadu, India; came to U.S., 1987; s. Palanisamy and Dhanalakshmi Govindasamy; m. Gnanasakthi Ramu, 1992; children: Anitha, Arthi. MS in Agrl. Econ., Tamilnadu Agrl. U., Coimbatore, 1987; MS in Econ., Iowa State U., 1992, PhD in Agrl. Econ., 1993. Rsch. asst. Iowa State U., Ames, 1987-92; rsch. assoc. U. Ark., Fayetteville, 1992-95; asst. prof. dept. agrl., food and resource econ. Rutgers U., New Brunswick, N.J., 1995—. Contbr. articles to profl. jours.; mem. editl. bd. Agrl. and Resource Econ. Rev., 1998-2000, Jour. Food Distbn. Rsch., 1999—. Mem. Am. Agrl. Econ. Assn., Food Distbn. Rsch. Soc., N.E. Agrl. Econ. Assn., So. Agrl. Econ. Assn. Fax: 732-932-8887. E-mail: govindasamy@aesop.rutgers.edu. Office: Rutgers U Dept Agrl Food Resource Econ 55 Dudley Rd New Brunswick NJ 08901-8520

GOVONI, ANTONIO FORTUNATO, radiologist; b. Ferrara, Italy, Apr. 8, 1920; came to U.S., 1955; s. Mario and Giselda Maria (Brunetta) G.; m. Ilse Louise Hayes, Dec. 4, 1954; children: Antonia C. Hayes, C. Graham Hayes. Cert. in Radiology, Royal Coll. Physicians and Surgeons, Can., 1963; MD, U. Modena (Italy), 1945, Cert. in Radiology, 1948. Instr. radiology U. Modena Med. Sch., 1950-55; asst. radiologist Reddy Meml. Hosp., Montreal, Que., Can., 1957-59; assoc. radiologist City and State Rita Hosps., Sydney, N.S., Can., 1959-61; chief radiologist St. Elizabeth Hosp., North Sydney, N.S., Can., 1961-64; cons. radiologist Gen. Hosp., Sault Ste Marie, Ont., Can., 1964-71; asst. radiologist N.Y. Hosp., N.Y.C., 1971-77, assoc. radiologist, 1977-89, attending radiologist, 1989-95; hon. attending radiologist N.Y. Presbyn. Hosp., N.Y.C., 1995—; asst. prof. radiology Cornell U. Med. Sch., N.Y.C., 1971-80, assoc. prof. radiology, 1980-90, prof. radiology, 1990-95, prof. emeritus radiology, 1995—. Contbr. articles to profl. jours. Recipient Medal of Med. Soc., Province of Ferrara. Fellow Royal Soc. Medicine Can.; mem. Am. Roentgen Ray Soc., Am. Coll. Radiology, Am. Soc. Breast Diseases, European Soc. Mastology, Can. Assn. Radiologists, Italian Soc. Radiology. Home: 234 Warner Ave Roslyn Heights NY 11577-1028

GOW, ALAN JAMES, automotive executive, consultant; b. Melbourne, Australia, June 23, 1955; s. William Cameron and Mary Corally (Barclay) G.; m. Leanne Joy Gow. Grad., Blackburn H.S., Melbourne. Mgr. Myer Ltd., Melbourne, 1975-78; automobile dealer Melbourne, 1978-86; investment mgr. Burlock Group, Melbourne, 1986-88; ptnr. Brock Racing, Melbourne, 1988-90; chief exec. Toca Ltd., Warwick, Eng., 1990—; dir. Natcc Inc., Tampa, Fla., 1995—, Toca Australia Ltd., Southport, 1994—, Motorsport Industry Assn., Eng., 1995—; cons. various motorsport cos., Europe, Asia, 1994—. Recipient Svc. Industry of Yr. award Motorsport Industry Assn., Eng., 1995, Outstanding Achievement award Assoc. of Mnging. Dirs. Inst., Australia, 1995. Avocations: private pilot license, motorsport. Office: Toca Ltd, Haseley Manor, Warwick CV35 7LS, England

GOW, NEIL MILNE, executive; b. Brisbane, Australia, Aug. 24, 1926; s. Stewart Neil and Nancye Muriel (Sack) G.; m. Jocelyn Rosemary Exon, July 30, 1955; children: Deborah Ann, David Neil, Stewart Andrew. BS, U. Queensland, Brisbane, Australia, 1950. Chemist R.M. Gow & Co., Brisbane, Australia, 1950-54, chief chemist, 1954-58, ops. mgr., 1958-65, CEO, 1965-69, chmn., 1969-86; chmn. Capita Fin. Group, Brisbane, 1986-91, Capita Village Group, Sydney, 1986-91; dir. Capita Group, Sydney, 1976-91, Jupiters Ltd., Gold Coast, Australia, 1987-98, Metway Credit Corp., Brisbane, 1986-90, Costian Ltd., Melbourne, Australia, 1985-90, Standard Chartered Bank Australia, Adelaide, 1986-88, Comsteel Vickers Ltd., Melbourne, 1984-86, Standard Chartered Fin. Ltd., Sydney, 1983-86, Pioneer Sugar Mills Ltd., Brisbane, 1973-86, Australian Interstate Pipeline Ltd., Sydney, 1984-86, Aquila Steel Ltd., Sydney, 1984-86, Vickers Aystralian Ltd., Melbourne, 1981-86, Australian Sugar Bd., Brisbane, 1988-91, Southeast Old Electricity Bd., Brisbane, 1977-88. Dir. Nat. Sci. & Tech. Ctr., Canberra, Australia, 1986-89; chmn. Australian Small Bus. Tng. Com., Canberra, 1979-84; mem. Nat. Tng. Coun., Canberra, 1977-84; mem. Industries Assistance Bd., Brisbane, 1977-86. Mem. Queensland Club, Indooroobilly Golf Club, Queensland Cricketers Club, Royal Queensland Yacht Squadron. Avocations: golf, boating, surfing. Home and Office: 59 O'Brien Rd, Pullenvale 4069, Australia

GOWA, ANDREW, real estate developer, lawyer; b. N.Y.C., Nov. 6, 1949; s. Everett M. and Louise (Friedman) G.; m. Robin P. Lincoln May 21, 1974; children: Catherine J., Jon T., Timothy M., Melissa Lincoln, Jennifer Lincoln. AB magna cum laude, Tufts U., 1971; JD, U. Pa., 1974. Bar: Pa. 1974, N.Y. 1982. From assoc. to ptnr. Blank, Rome, Comisky & McCauley, Phila., 1974-84; sr. v.p North Atlantic Investment Corp., Phila., 1984-85; pres., chief exec. officer First Equity Devel. Corp., West Chester, Pa., 1984-90; ptnr. Schnader Harrison Segal & Lewis LLP, Phila., 1990—; mem. adv. bd. Bell Savs. Bank, Phila., 1988-91; bd. dirs. Equitrust Real Estate Corp., West Chester; developer Brampton Chase, Malvern, Pa., 1988-89; faculty Grad. Builders Inst. Pa. State U., State Coll., 1987-90; faculty Pa. Bar Inst., 1991—; chmn. Allegheny Cardiovascular Inst., 1997, Likoff Cardiovascular Inst., 1995-97. Mem. Tufts U. Alumni Coun., Medford, Mass., 1982—; bd. overseers Tufts U., Medford, 1988-93; bd. dirs. Kaiserman Ctr. Jewish Community Ctrs. Phila, 1982-88. Recipient Disting. Service medal Tufts U., 1982. Mem. Pa. Bar Assn. (ho. dels. 1983-87), Phila. Bar Assn. (bd. govs. 1985, chmn. real estate sect. 1985, exec. com. real estate sect. 1983-89), Am. Coll. Real Estate Laywers, Internat. Coun. Shopping Ctrs. Avocations: amateur radio, cooking, philanthropy. E-mail: gowa@shsl.com. Fax: 215-972-7676. Office: Schnader Harrison Segal & Lewis 1600 Market St Ste 36 Philadelphia PA 19103-7240

GOWAL, DIPA, microbiologist, researcher; b. Calcutta, India, Nov. 22, 1951; d. Motilal and Namita (Dalal) Nath; m. Khagendra Gowal, May 5, 1979; 1 child. BSc in Med. Group, Guru Nanak Dev U., 1973; MA in English, Himachal Pradesh U., Simla, India, 1978, BSc in Microbiology, 1980, MSc in Microbiology, 1983, MPhil in Microbiology, 1989, PhD in Microbiology, 1994. Tech. supr. Ctrl. Rsch. Inst., Kasauli, India, 1977-84, asst. tech. officer, 1984—, officer in charge quality control of Japanese Encephalitis vaccine, 1984—. Contbr. articles to profl. jours. Fellow Japan Internat. Cooperation Agy., Tokyo, 1985, WHO, 1996, 97, 98. Mem. Indian

Assn. Vaccinology and Immunology, Indian Assn. Med. Microbiology. Avocations: reading, travel, scientific exchanges, nature, writing.

GOWARD, PRU, journalist. BA in Economics with honors, U. Adelaide. Juornalist, commentator Australian Broadcasting Commn.; first asst. sec. Office of the Status of Women, Commonwealth Govt., 1997-99; spokesperson Sydney 2000 games Australian Govt., 2000—. E-mail: pru.goward@pmc.gov.au. Home: PO Box 3540, Mansha ACT 2603, Australia Office: Office of the Status Women, 3-5 National Circuit, Barton ACT 2600, Australia

GOWENLOCK, BRIAN GLOVER, retired chemistry educator, researcher; b. Oldham, Lancashire, Eng., Feb. 9, 1926; s. Harry Hadfield and Hilda (Glover) G.; m. Margaret Lottie Davies, July 24, 1953; children: Stephen David, Cathren Elizabeth, Judith Margaret.; BSc, U. Manchester (Eng.ú, 1946, MSc, 1947, PhD, 1949; DSc, U. Birmingham (Eng.), 1962. Chartered chemist. Lectr. U. Wales, Swansea, 1948-55; lectr., sr. lectr. U. Birmingham (Eng.), 1955-66; prof. chemistry Heriot-Watt U., Edinburgh, 1966-90, Leverhulme emeritus fellow, 1990-92; hon. rsch. fellow U. Exeter (Eng.), 1992—. Co-author: First Year at the University, 1964, Experimental Methods in Gas Reactions, 1964, Chemistry in Heriot-Watt 1821-1991, 1998. Mem. Univ. Grants Commn. Gt. Britain, 1976-85; local preacher Meth. Ch. Decorated comdr. Order Brit. Empire. Fellow Royal Soc. Edinburgh, Royal Soc. Chemistry. Methodist. Avocations: genealogy. Home: 5 Roselands, EX10 8PB Sidmouth Devon, England Office: U Exeter, Dept Chemistry, EX4 4QD Exeter Devon, England

GOWENS, VERNEETA VIOLA, journalist; b. Mar. 19, 1913; d. William and Mary Cawthorne (Fowler) Gibson; m. Albert Gowens, July 17, 1936; children: Victoria Ann Goweks Utke, Mary Ann Gowens Buer. Student, Bryant and Stratton Bus. Coll. Clk., pub. rels. worker Chgo. and Riverdale Lumber Co., 1934-45; feature writer, women's editor Tribune Publs., Harvey, Ill., 1960-62, Star-Tribune, Williams Press, Chicago Heights, Ill., 1963-78; freelance writer; script writer variety shows Ship Ahoy, 1963, Fair 'n' Square, 1964. Contbr. to Internat. Altrusan, 1974, Ch. Herald, 1977. Sunday sch. tchr., youth leader 1st Ref. Ch., South Holland; mem. editl. coun. Ch. Herald, Ref. Ch. in Am., 1976-82; pres. Dist. 150 PTA, 1965-66; adv. com. program in ltd. occupation tng. Thornton H.S., 1963-69; mem. South Holland Indsl. Commn., 1965-68; bd. dirs. Family Svc. and Mental Health Ctr. of South Cook County, Ill., 1974-77; mem. South Holland unit Salvation Army, 1958—; judge Internat. Teen Pageant, 1969; mem. South Holland Cmty. Chest, 1978-87; adv. bd. Thornton C.C. nursing program, 1976-83; spl. events and publicity coms. South Holland Centennial, 1994; active South Holland Diamond Jubilee, 1969, South Holland Cable Commn., 1984—, South Holland Centennial Com., 1994. Recipient award South Holland C. of C., 1970, Genoa coun. K.C., 1974, Village of South Holland, 1969, 1st pl. in contest No. Ill. U., 1974, 75, award Suburban Press Found., 1969, 1st pl. award Ill. Press Assn., 1973, Sr. Medal of Honr. award Cook County Sheriff's Dept., 1997, 50 other awards in writing. Mem. Ill. Women's Press Assn. (Woman of Yr. 1974, award 1978), Nat. Fedn. Press Women (1st pl. Sweepstakes award 1976). Home: 16830 S Park Ave South Holland IL 60473-2961

GOWING, NIK, television news presenter; b. Jan. 13, 1951; s. Donald James Graham and Margaret Mary Elliott; m. Judith Wastall, July 10, 1982; children: Simon Donald Peter, Sarah Margaret. BSc, U. Bristol. Reporter Newcastle Chronicle, 1973-74; presenter, reporter Granada TV, 1974-78; Rome corr. ITN, 1979, Ea. Europe corr., 1980-83, fgn. affairs corr., 1983-87, diplomatic corr., 1987-89; diplomatic editor and newscaster Channel 4 News, 1989-96; co-presenter The World This Week, 1990-92; presenter BBC World TV, 1996—, BBC News, 2000—; cons. in media and conflict mgmt., cons. Carnegie Commn. on Prevention of Deadly Conflict, 1996-97; cons. EU Humanitarian Office, 1997-98; cons. European Commn. on Info. Mgmt. in Recent Wars, 1998; vis. fellow internat. rels. Keele U.; mem. adv. bd. Ctr. for Security and Diplomacy, Birmingham. U.; com. Rory Peck Trust, 1996—, Project on Justice in Times of Transition, 2000—. Author: The Wire, 1988, The Loop, 1993; mem. editl. bd. Jour. Press/Politico, 1996—. Vice chair bd. of govs. Westminster Found. for Democracy, 1996—. Fellowship Kennedy Sch. of Govt. Harvard U., 1994. Mem. Internat. Inst. for Strategic Studies, Royal Inst. Internat. Affairs (coun. mem. 1998—, exec. com. 1999—), Royal TV Soc., Brit. Assn. for Ctrl. and Ea. Europe (mem. governing body 1997—), Acad. Coun. Wilton Park. Avocations: cycling, skiing, authorship. E-mail: nik.gowing@bbc.is.uk. Office: BBC Rm 2524, BBC TV Centre, London W12 7RJ, England

GOWRA, SUGUNAKAR, export company executive; b. Bellary, India, Aug. 10, 1935; s. Sivaram and Sarojini Devi Gowra; m. Kasturi Venkatachalam, Oct. 24, 1956; children: Sumanth, Venkateswar, Naveenkrishna. B in Commerce, Madras U., Chennai, India, 1954. CEO Om Sri Sathya Sai Exports, Bangalore, India, 1954—. Dist. chmn. Lions Club Internat., 1998. Recipient Internat. Diabetes Awareness award Internat. Assn. Lions Clubs, 1998. Mem. Bangalore Club, Century Club, Karantaka Golf Assn. Avocations: tennis, golf. Home and Office: Om Sri Sathya Sai Exports, PO Box 8217, Jayanagar Bangalore 560082, India

GOYAL, ANAND NARAYAN, mathematician; b. Alwar, India, May 13, 1936; s. Ram Chandra and Savitri Devi Gupta; m. Shashi Prabha Goyal, Aug. 3, 1960; 1 child, Shikha. BS, Rajasthan U., Jaipur, India, 1954; MS, Rajasthan U., 1956, PhD, 1961; D Sci., Ranchi U., India, 1982. Sr. rsch. fellow Birla Coll., Pilani, India, 1956-60; rsch. assoc. Van Vleck, Middletown, Conn., 1960-61; asst. prof. Rajasthan U., Jaipur, 1961-79, assoc. prof., 1979-92, prof., 1992-96, ret. prof., 1996—. Contbr. articles to profl. jours. v.p. Sci. Assn., R.R. Coll., Alwar, 1953-54. Fellow Royal Astronomical Soc., Nat. Acad. Sci.; mem. Internat. Astron. Union. Home: B-133A, Rajendra Marg Bapu Nagar, 302015 Jaipur India

GOYAL, RAM TIRTH, mathematician, consultant; b. Faridkot, Punjab, India, Apr. 26, 1975; s. Rattan Lal and Swarn Lata (Gupta) G. Student, Aeronaut. Soc. India, Delhi, 1993; degree in aeronaut. engring., Soc. Aeronautics, Delhi, 1996. Planning engr. Direct Connection, Dehradun, India, 1994; course advisor Indian Inst. Aeronautics, Dehradun, 1994-95, instr., 1995; devel. exec. Software Option (P) Ltd., Bombay, 1995; airline mktg. exec. Khambat Aviation, Bombay, 1996; R & D engr. Bhullar Constrn. (P) Ltd., Bombay, 1996—; consulting engr. Bhullar Constrn. (P) Ltd., New Delhi, 1995-96; hon. cons. Gaytech Engring. (P) Ltd., Baroda, India, 1995-96; cons. B.C. Plastics, Dhuri, India, 1995-96; dir. WELL (World Econ. Lifetime Leaders)-TELL (Tree and Environ. Life Lovers)-CELL (Ctr. English Lang. Learning). Sec. Youth Congress, Bathinda, India, 1993; assoc. patron Indian Red Cross Soc., Bombay, 1996. Recipient Youth Leadership award Rotary, Bathinda, 1992. Mem. AIAA (Wash. chpt.), Western India Automotive Assn., Can. Aeronautics and Space Inst. (Ontario chpt.), Aeronaut. Soc. India, Marlborough Alumni Assn. USA., Sch. Online and Distance Studies India. Achievements include contributions to modernization of passenger flight. E-mail: vickygoyal@usa.net. Home: 716 Urban Estate, Bathinda 151001, India

GOYAL, RAMESHWAR PRASAD, physicist; b. Agra, India, July 2, 1947; s. Brijmohan Lal and Samoti Devi G.; m. Kusum Mittal, Apr. 15, 1968; children: Archana, Anoop. BSc, Agra (India) Coll., 1965, MSc, 1967, PhD, 1978. Reader in physics St. Johns Coll., Agra, 1967—; rsch. supr. Agra U., 1978—; gov. body St. Johns Coll., 1998. Author: Concise Physics, 1976, Higher Secondary Bhotiki, 1980, Unified Physics, 1985, Middle School Physics, 1995; contbr. articles to profl. jours. Exec. com. Maharaja Agrasen Sewa Sedan, 1996. Mem. Indian Assn. Physics Tchrs. (life). Avocation: researching. Home: D-38 Kamla Nagar, Agra 282 004, India Office: St Johns Coll, Dept Physics, Agra 282 002, India

GOYAL, VED PARKASH, soil science educator; b. Apr. 8, 1945. BSc in Agr., Punjab Agrl. U., MSc in Soil Sci.; PhD in Soil Sci., Haryana Agrl. U.; cert. in remote sensing, Indian Inst. Remote Sensing. Rsch. asst. CCS Haryana Agrl. U., Hisar, India, 1969-74, asst. prof., jr. pedologist, 1974-83, assoc. prof., pedologist, 1984-91, prof., sr. pedologist, 1990—; presenter, rschr. in field. Contbr. more than 65 articles to profl. jours. Fellow UN Devel. Programme, Coun. Agrl. Rsch., French Ministry Rsch. Home: 10/31 Old Campus, CCS Haryana Agrl U, Hisar Haryana 125 004, India Office: CSS Haryana Agrl U, Dept Soil Sci, Hisar 125 004, India

GOZALI, VICTOR KARTIKA, physician, surgeon, consultant; b. Jakarta, Indonesia, Nov. 2, 1957; s. Herman Gozali and Lily Kartika; m. Maria Lourdes Gomez, Dec. 20, 1989; children: Christine Marie Kara, Philip Armand, David Christopher, Kristina Francesca. BS, U. Santo Tomas, 1980, MD, 1984. Diplomate Philippine Bd. of Surgery. Fellow Philippine Soc. of Laparoscopic Surgeons, 1993—, Philippine Coll. of Surgeons, 1993—, Surg. Oncology Soc. of the Philippines, 1995—; faculty staff Coll. of Medicine, St. Luke's Med. Ctr., Philippine, 1996; dir. Maphilindo, Philippines, 1995—; v.p. Lemhai, Inc., Philippines, 1992. Fellow Am. Coll. Surgeons; mem. Asian Surg. Assn., Philippine Bd. Surgery Examiners, Philippine Assn. Tng. Officers in Surgery, K.C., Rotary. Avocations: reading, golf, travel, swimming. Office: St Lukes Med Ctr MC CHBC, 279 E Rodriguez Sr Blvd Ste 609, Quezon City 1700, The Philippines also: Makati Med Ctr, Ste 121, Makati The Philippines

GOZANI, TSAHI, nuclear physicist; b. Tel Aviv, Nov. 25, 1934; came to U.S., 1965; s. Arieh and Rivcca (Meiri) G.; m. Adit Soffer, Oct. 14, 1958; children: Mor, Shai Nachum, Or Pinchas, Tal. BSc, Technion-Israel Inst. Tech., Haifa, 1956, MSc, 1958; DSc, Swiss Fed. Inst. Tech. (ETH), Zurich, Switzerland, 1962. Registered profl. nuclear engr., Calif.; accredited nuclear material mgr. Rsch. physicist Israel Atomic Energy Commn., Beer-Sheva, 1962-65; rsch. assoc. nuclear engring. dept. Rensselaer Poly. Inst., Troy, N.Y., 1965-66; sr. staff scientist General-Atomic & IRT, San Diego, 1966-70, 71-75; prof. applied physics Tel Aviv U., 1971; chief scientist, divsn. mgr. Sci. Applications Internat. Corp., Palo Alto and Sunnyvale, Calif., 1975-84; v.p., chief scientist Sci. Applications Internat. Corp., Sunnyvale, 1984-87; corp. v.p. Sci. Applications Internat. Corp., Santa Clara, Calif., 1987-93, sr. v.p., 1993-97; pres., CEO Ancore Corp., Santa Clara, 1997—; Lady Davis vis. prof. Technion-Israel Inst. Tech., 1983-84; bd. dirs. Radiation Sci. Inst., San Jose State U. Author: Active Non-Destructive Assay of Nuclear Materials, 1981; co-author: Handbook of Nuclear Safeguards Measurement Methods, 1983; contbr. over 170 articles to profl. jours. Recipient 1989 Laurel award Aviation Week Jour., R&D 100 award, 1988, Most Innovative New Products. Fellow Am. Nuclear Soc.; mem. Am. Phys. Soc., Inst. Nuclear Materials. Achievements include patents for explosive detection system, explosive detection system using an artificial neural system, multi sensor explosive detection system, composite cavity structure for an explosive detection system, apparatus and method for detecting contraband using fast neutron activation, contraband detection system using direct imaging pulsed fast neutrons; invention of method to measure nuclear reactor's reactivity. Office: Ancore Corp 2950 Patrick Henry Dr Santa Clara CA 95054-1813

GÓŹDŹ, ANDRZEJ, physics educator, theoretical physics researcher; b. Olsztyn, Poland, Jan. 5, 1954; s. Czesław and Władysława (Broda) G.; m. Joanna Maria Janiszewska, Nov. 27, 1976; children: Marek, Agnieszka, Jacek. MSc, U. Marie Curie-Skłodowska, Lublin, Poland, 1976, PhD, 1980, D Habilitation, 1987. Asst. prof. U. Regensburg, Germany, 1983-85; asst. prof. physics U. Marie Curie-Skłodowska, 1976-82, 86-87, assoc. prof., 1987-91, prof., 1991—. Contbr. articles to sci. jours., including Nuclear Physics A, Physics Letters B, Jour. Physics. Mem. Polish Phys. Soc. (Sci. award II 1987), Polish Acad. Sci. (com. agrophysics), Inst. Agrophysics of Polish Acad. Sci. (sci. coun.). Avocations: jiu-jitsu, music, mountain climbing, sailing. E-mail: gozdz@neuron.umcs.lublin.pl. Home: Wiklinowa 6/39, 20-541 Lublin Poland Office: UMCS Inst Physics, pl M Curie-Sklodowskiej 1, 20-031 Lublin Poland

GOZDZ, ANTONI S., chemistry researcher; b. Klosowice, Poznan, Poland, June 2, 1949; came to U.S., 1981; s. Stanislaw M. and Aleksandra Gozdz; m. Ewa M. Gozdz, Nov. 15, 1975; 1 child, Anna A. MS in Chemistry, Wroclaw (Poland) U. Tech., 1972, PhD in Chemistry, 1976. Rsch. assoc. Wroclaw U. Tech., 1976-81; staff scientist TRI, Princeton, N.J., 1981-84; mem. tech. staff Bellcore, Red Bank, N.J., 1984-97; dir. Bellcore, Red Bank, 1997-98; chief scientist Telcordia Techs. (formerly Bellcore), Red Bank, 1998—. Contbr. articles to profl. jours.; patentee in field. Named to R & D 100, Rsch. and Devel. Mag., Chgo., 1995; recipient Tech. of Yr. award Industry Week Mag., 1994, Indsl. Design award Indsl. Design Mag., 1995. Republican. Home: 8 Wemrock Dr Ocean NJ 07712-3331 Office: Telcordia Techs 331 Newman Springs Rd Red Bank NJ 07701-5657

GOZES, ILLANA, neuroscientist, educator; b. Jerusalem, Mar. 1, 1949; d. Isac Berthold Fallenbaum and Esther Rachel (Haltovsky) Allon; m. Yehoshua Gozes, Sept. 18, 1973; 1 child, Adi. BSc, Tel Aviv U., 1972; PhD, Weizmann Inst. Sci., Rehovot, Israel, 1979. Postdoctoral fellow MIT, Cambridge, 1979-80; rsch. assoc. Salk Inst., San Diego, 1981-82; sr. scientist Weizmam Inst., Rehovot, Israel, 1982-87, assoc. prof., 1987-89; vis. scientist NIH/NICHD, Bethesda, Md., 1989-90; assoc. prof. Tel Aviv U., 1990-93, prof., 1993—, dept. chairperson, 1993-95, head internat. rels. Sackler Faculty of Medicine, 1998—; guest scientist NIH, Bethesda, 1990-2000. Editor Jour. Molecular Neurosci., 1998—; contbr. articles to profl. jours.; patentee in field. Pvt. Israeli Army, 1967-69. Recipient Bergmann prize, 1982, Juludau prize, 1992, Tera prize, 1993; Fogarty scholar, 1995-96; grantee U.S. Israel Binat. Sci. Found., 1992—, Ministry Sci. and Arts, 1992-95, Israel Cancer Rsch. Found., 1991-92, Israel Acad. Sci. and Humanities, 1999—, Inst. Study of Aging, 1999—. Mem. European Neuroendocrinology Assn., Soc. Clin. Biochemistry Israel, Soc. Neurosci. Jewish. Avocations: traveling, reading, computers. Home: 14 Hamal St, Ramat Hasharon Israel Office: Tel Aviv U Sackler Sch Medicine, Dept Clin Biochemistry, Tel Aviv Israel

GÖZÜBÜYÜK, IRFAN, otorhinolaryngologist; b. Kayseri, Centrum, Turkey, Mar. 13, 1965; s. Ahmet Ihsan and Gülümser (Kivanç) G. Med. faculty, Hacettepe U., Ankara, Turkey, 1983-89; otorhinolaryngologist, Haseki Hosp., Istanbul, 1993-96. Med. dr. diplomate; ear, nose, throat, head and neck surgery specialist diplomate. Resident in gen. surgery Istanbul U., 1989-93; resident in ear, nose and throat Haseki Hosp., Istanbul, 1993-96, fellow in ear, nose and throat, 1996—; cons. Istanbul Ear, Nose and Throat Ctr., 1994-96; observer Mt. Sinai Nasal Sinus Ctr., Cleve., 1996. Author: Antibiotic Use in Ear, Nose, Throat, Head and Neck Infections, 1995, (booklet) Follow-Up and Treatment Protocol in Ear, Nose and Throat, 1996; contbr. papers and articles to profl. publs. and confs. Mem. European Med. Laser Assn., Turkish Med. Assn., Turkish Orl, Head and Neck Surgery Assn. Muslim. Avocations: writing, playing tennis, computer, documentation. Home: Kamelya 1/15 # 7 Atasehir, 81120 Istanbul Turkey

GÖZÜKARA, ENGIN M., biochemistry educator; b. Malatya, Turkey, Mar. 12, 1942; s. Abdurrahman and Zeliha (Öner) G.; m. Yanina Leonidovna Fedorovskaya, Aug. 6, 1998; children: Harika Gözde, Gülen Kayra, Açelya. BS in Biology, Ankara (Turkey) U., 1963; PhD in Biology, Hacettepe U., Ankara, 1969. Rsch. asst. Hacettepe U. Med. Sch., Ankara, 1963-69; postdoctoral fellow dept. biology Ohio U., Athens, 1969-70; postdoctoral fellow dept. biochemistry U. Calif., Riverside, 1970-72; lectr. Hacettepe U., Ankara, 1972-74, assoc. prof., 1974-78, assoc. prof. molecular biology, 1982-84; Fulbright rschr. Nat. Cancer Inst., Bethesda, Md., 1978-79; vis. scientist Nat. Cancer Inst., NIH, Bethesda, 1979-82, 91-92; full prof. biochemistry Inönü U., Malatya, Turkey, 1984-85; dir. grad. studies sci. Inönü U., Malatya, 1985-86, v.p., 1986-91, pres., 1998-99, dir. grad. studies in health sci., 1999—. Author: Biochemistry I and II; contbr. articles to profl. jours. Lt. Turkish Army Air Force, 1975. Recipient Sci. Rsch. award Eczacibasi Pharm. Co., Istanbul, Turkey, 1985, Health Sci. award Sedat Simavi Found., Istanbul, 1994. Mem. Am. Assn. for Cancer Rsch., N.Y. Acad. Sci., Sigma Xi. Moslim. Avocations: fine arts, amateur oil painting. Office: Dept Biochemistry, Inönü U Med Sch, 44069 Malatya Turkey

GÖZÜKIRMIZI, NERMIN, geneticist, educator; b. Izmit, Kocaeli, Turkey, June 18, 1951; d. Sükrü and Refiye (Pekinoe) Eröktem; m. Erbil Gözükirmizi, Dec. 2, 1972; children: Basar, Cosar. BA, U. Istanbul, Turkey, 1972, Dr.rer., 1979. Rsch. asst. U. Istanbul, 1972-79, asst. prof. biology, 1979-87, assoc. prof. biology, 1987-93, prof. biology, 1993—; cons., head plant biotech. Tübitak, Gebze, Kocaeli, 1993; contact person Eureka Cereal Stresstol 1322, 1996. Editor: Biotechnology and Biotechnological Equipment, 1995; contbr. articles to scientific jours. Recipient NATO rsch. grants, 1987, 93, rsch. grant for biogenetic poplars, Paper and Pulp Industry of Turkey, 1995. Mem. Internat. Assn. Plant Tissue Culture. Moslem. Avocations: travel, reading. Home: Ahmet Cevdet Pasa sok Polat, Camlik Sitesi B Blok No9/12, Bostanci, Istanbul Turkey Office: Tübitak, Annibal, 41470 Gebze Kocaeli, Turkey also Office: U Istanbul, Dept Biology, Vezneciler-Istanbul Turkey

GOZZO, FRANCO, organic chemist, educator; b. S. Donà di Piave, Venice, Italy, Feb. 10, 1931; s. Massimiliano Gozzo and Teresa Vianello; m. Luciana Dal Bo, Oct. 1, 1960 (dec. 1985); children: Chiara, Andrea, Daniele. ChD, U. Padua, Italy, 1956; lectr. qualification, U. Rome, 1969. Rschr. Edison Group, Marghera, Italy, 1957-58; group leader Montedison, Bollate, Milan, Italy, 1960-70; dep. rsch. dir. Montedison, Linate, Milan, Italy, 1971-82; rsch. dir. Farmoplant, Linate, Milan, Italy, 1983-87; hon. cons. rschr. U. Milan, 1988—; lectr. U. Bologna, Italy, 1966-76; contract prof., Catholic U., Milan-Piacenza, 1992—. Contbr. over 70 sci. articles and congress reports; patentee in field of agrochemicals. G. Motta grantee Edison Co., 1959; scholar U. Birmingham, Eng., 1959-60. Home: via Pascoli 36-B, 20097 S Donato Milanese MIlan, Italy Office: U Milan Dept Sci Molec Agro, via Celoria 2, I 20133 Milan Italy

GRAACK, HANNS-ÜDIGER FRIEDRICH WILHELM, biochemist; b. Itzehoe, Germany, June 7, 1958; s. Hanns-Eberhard Karl and Thea Graack; m. Heidi Christiane Putter, Aug. 28, 1993; children: Johanna Dorothee, Julius Friedrich. Biochemistry diploma, Eberhard-Karls-U., 1986; PhD summa cum laude, U. Berlin, 1990. Rsch. asst. U. Fla., Gainesville, 1985-86; rschr. Max-Planck-Inst. for Molecular Genetics, Berlin, 1986-90; postdoctoral rschr. Ruhr-U., Bochum, Germany, 1990-91; rschr. Inst. for Neural Signal Recognition Ctr. for Molecular Neurobiology, Hamburg, Germany, 1991-94; non-tenured track asst. prof. Faculty Biology, Chemistry, Pharmacy, Genetics, Free U., Berlin, 1994-2000. Contbr. articles to profl. jours. Recipient multiple grants for basic rsch. in natural scis. Free U., Berlin, 1994, 97, 99. Mem. Soc. for Biochemistry and Molecular Biology, German Soc. for Cellular Biology, German. Soc. Scientists and Physicians, German-Am. Memmalian Mitochondrial Ribosomal Rsch. consortium (co-founder). Avocations: playing organ, singing in choir, hunting, politics/history. Fax: 49-30-838-53649. E-mail: graack@zedat.fu-berlin.de. Office: Free U Berlin Inst Biol-Gen, Arnimallee 7, D-14195 Berlin Germany

GRAAE, TAPANI CARL-GUSTAV, nuclear engineer, marketing consultant; b. Helsinki, Finland, June 4, 1942; s. Ulf and Kyllikki Aune (Huhtala) G.; m. Ritva Kaarina Herberz, Sept. 26, 1964; children: Jürgen, Christopher, Stephanie. MSc, Helsinki (Finland) U. Tech., 1968. Rsch. mgr. Finnatom, Helsinki, Finland, 1970-77; design mgr. ASEA, Helsinki, Finland, 1977-78; devel. ABB Atom, Vasteras, Sweden, 1978-84, info., 1984-90, devel. dir., 1990-94, mktg. and sales; asst. Helsinki U. Tech., 1966-68; steering com. mem. State Rsch. Ctr., Helsinki, 1974-77; mem Atomic Energy Commn., Helsinki, 1972-77. Contbr. articles to profl. jours. Lt. Navy, 1968-69, Helsinki. Mem. Finnish Nuclear Soc. Avocations: sailing, pistol shooting, farming, free masonry. Home: Bastugatan 3, 72921 Västerås Sweden Office: ABB Atom, Storagatan 3, 721 63 Västerås Sweden

GRAAF, JAN DE, engineering executive; b. Nieuw-Lekkerland, The Netherlands, Jan. 18, 1947; s. Arie de Graaf and Aagje Bakker; m. Dina Johanna Cornelia van Neutegem, July 7, 1972; children: Jan Arie, Daniel Cornelis, Magaretha Helena. MSc in Engring. & Physics, Delft Tech. U., The Netherlands, 1977. R&D engr. Pelgrim B.V., Gaanderen, The Netherlands, 1978-79; sys. engr. Thomassen Holland B.V., Rheden, The Netherlands, 1979-80; sr. project engr. Badger B.V., The Hague, The Netherlands, 1980-87, project mgr., 1987-92; mgr. projects JGC Dordtse Engring. B.V., Dordrecht, The Netherlands, 1992-95; sr. project mgr. AMEC Engring. Nederland B.V., Schiedam, The Netherlands, 1996-97, Washington Group Internat., The Hague, 1997—; lectr. practical physics Faculty Medicine, Erasmus U., Rotterdam, The Netherlands, 1974-78. 1st lt., weather officer Royal Dutch Air Force, 1967-69. Mem. Royal Inst. Engrs. in Netherlands. Avocations: swimming, cycling, canoeing, stamps. Fax: 3170-3494240. E-mail: jan.de.graaf@wxs.nl. Home: Boschpolderstraat 9, Gouda 2807 LJ, The Netherlands

GRAB, FREDERICK CHARLES, lawyer; b. N.Y.C., Aug. 1, 1946; s. Daniel Justin and Elizabeth (Kam) G. BS in Aerospace Engring., Polytech U. N.Y., 1967; JD, U. So. Calif., 1977. Bar: Calif. 1978, U.S. Dist. Ct. (cen. dist.) Calif. 1978, U.S. Supreme Ct. 1988, U.S. Ct. Appeals (9th cir.) 1989. Deputy atty. gen. Calif. Atty. Gen., L.A., 1977-2000. Contbr. articles to profl. jours. Avocations: playwright, author, composer, musician.

GRABACKI, JAN KAZIMIERZ, engineering educator; b. Cracow, Poland, Sept. 7, 1934; s. Józef Szymon and Jadwiga Antonina (Karcz) G.; m. Małgorzata Ewa Dolska; children: Agnieszka, Magdalena, Maja. MSc, Cracow U. Tech., 1959, DSc, 1973, PhD, 1992. Designer Biprostal Rsch. and Design Agy., Cracow, 1959-64, head designer, 1964-71; assoc. prof. Inst. Structural Mechanics, Cracow U. Tech., 1972-94, prof., 1992—; bd. dirs., proprietor Engring. and Consulting Agy., Cracow, 1994—. Author: Mechanics of Structured Materials, 1991 (award Polish Acad. Sci. 1994); co-author: Handbook of Computational Solid Mechanics, 1998 (award Min. Sci. and Edn. 1999). Active Solidarity, Cracow U. Tech., 1980. Mem. Assn. Theoretical and Applied Mechanics, Gesellschaft für Angew. Math. und Mech., N.Y. Acad. Scis. Avocations: music, drawings. Office: Cracow Univ Tech, Warszawska 24, 31-155 Cracow Poland

GRABAREVIĆ, ŽELJKO STJEPAN, veterinarian, educator; b. Mostar, Bosnia and Herzegovina, Feb. 17, 1956; s. Ivan and Julka (Krmpotić) G.; m. Sanja Marija Vasilj, Mar. 7, 1981; children: Lana, Dunja. DVM, Faculty Vet. Medicine, Zagreb, Croatia, 1980; MSc, Faculty Vet. Medicine, 1986, PhD, 1990. Diplomate Bd. Vet. Pathology. Asst. Vet. Faculty, Zagreb, 1983-92, asst. prof., 1992-97, assoc. prof., 1997—; sec. LJ. Jurak Meeting Comp. Pathology, Zagreb, 1989-96, pres., v.p., 1997—; cons. Pliva Pharm. Comp., Zagreb, 1992—. Co-author: General Veterinary Pathology, 1995; contbr. over 60 articles to profl. jours.; patentee in field. Recipient Meml. Homeland Gratitude award Republic of Croatia, 1995. Mem. European Soc. Vet. Pathology, Croatian Vet. Assn., Croatian Vet. Chamber. Avocations: music, chess. Office: Faculty Vet Medicine, Heinzelova 55, 1000 Zagreb Croatia

GRABCHEV, IVO KOTSEV, researcher; b. Bjala Slatina, Bulgaria, June 11, 1960; s. Kotse Petkov and Nikolina Dunova (Randashka) G.; m. Dessislava Staneva Topchieva, Jun. 11, 1995 1 child, Stanislav. MSc, Tech. Univ. Sofia, Sofia, Bulgaria, 1986, PhD, 1992. Researcher Inst. of Industrial Chemistry, Sofia, 1986-87; asst. prof. Tech. Univ., Sofia, 1991-94; researcher Inst. of Polymers Bulgaria Acad. Sci., 1994—. Contbr. articles to profl. jours. Mem. Bulgarian Chem. Soc., Bulgarian Polymer Soc. Avocations: jogging, tennis, chamber music. E-mail: grabchev@polymer.bas.bg. Home: Entr II, Dimitar Hazhikotsev 64, 1421 Sofia Bulgaria Office: Inst of Polymers Bulgarian Acad Scis, Acad Bonchev Str Bl 103A, 1113 Sofia Bulgaria

GRABER, WERNER KARL, atmosphere physicist, researcher; b. Basel, Switzerland, Dec. 14, 1951; s. Karl August and Lina (Schär) G.; m. Christine Regula Lienhard, Aug. 12, 1983; children: Adriel, Sereina. Diploma in Physics, Eidgenössisch Technische Hochschule, Zurich, Switzerland, 1977; D of Natural Scis., Eidgenössisch Technische, Zurich, Switzerland, 1985. Tchr. Freies Gymnasium, Zurich, 1985-86; tchr. Eidgenössisches Inst. Reaktorforschung Kantonsschule Oerlikon, Zurich, 1985-86; rschr. Eidgenössisches Inst. Reaktorforschung, Würenlingen, Switzerland, 1986-88; sect. head Paul Scherrer Inst., Villigen, Switzerland, 1988—. Contbg. author: Laser in Remote Sensing, 1993, Pollution Modeling, 1994; editor Phys. Review B, 1992. Home: Bergstrasse 7, CH-5417 Untersiggenthal AG, Switzerland Office: Paul Scherrer Inst, Abt 52, CH-5232 Villigen-PSI AG, Switzerland

GRABISCH, MICHEL JACQUES, electrical engineer, educator; b. Hayange, France, Sept. 30, 1956; s. Jean Charles and Solange Adeline (Speck) G.; m. Miwako Kinoshita, Aug. 28, 1982 (dec. June 1998); children: Francis, Raphaëlle, Rémi. Engring. degree, Sch. Elec. Engring., Grenoble, 1979; PhD, Ecole Ingenieurs Electriciens, Grenoble, 1982; Habil., U. Paris VI, 1997. Postdoctoral Tokyo Inst. of Tech., 1982-84; R&D engr. Thomson CSF, Cagnes/mer, France, 1984-89, 91-93, Ctrl. Rsch. Lab. of Thomson-CSF, Orsay, France, 1993-2000; prof. dept. computer sci. U. Paris VI, 2000—; educator Inst. Supérieur d'Optique, Orsay, 1995-2000, Ctr. Nat. Sci. Rsch., Gif/Yvette, France, 1992-96; invites rschr. Tokyo Inst. of Tech. and Lab. for Internat. Fuzzy Engring. Rsch., 1989-91. Author: Fundamentals of Uncertainty Calculi with Applications to Fuzzy Inference, 1995, Evaluation Subjective: Méthodes, Applications et Enjeux, 1997, Fuzzy Measures and Integrals - Theory and Applications, 2000; guest editor: Fuzzy Sets and

Systems, 1997, Internat. Jour. of Intelligent Sys., 1997; assoc. editor IEEE Theory on Fuzzy Systems. Mem. Internat. Fuzzy System Assn., Japan Soc. for Fuzzy Theory. Avocations: music, piano playing, Japanese calligraphy. Office: UPMC-Lip 6, 8 rue du Capitaine Scott, 75 015 Paris France

GRABNER, ERICH WALTER, physical chemistry educator; b. Grimma, Germany, Sept. 14, 1935; s. Georg and Helene (Morich) G.; m. Ursula Krauss, July 12, 1963; children: Constanze, Wolfgang. Diploma in chemistry, U. Leipzig, Germany, 1958; diploma in music, Musikhochschule, Freiburg, Germany, 1963; MD, U. Frankfurt, Germany, 1968, habilitation, 1977. Violoncellist Frankfurt Opera, 1963-66; sci. coworker Inst. Phys. Chemistry, Frankfurt, 1966-72, acad. councillor, 1972-90, prof., 1990-97; ret., 1997—. Home: Wenzel-Jaksch Str 6, D 61118 Bad Vilbel Germany Office: Inst Phys Chemistry, Marie Curie Str 11, D-60439 Frankfurt am Main, Germany

GRABOSCH, ALFONS, plastic surgeon; b. Wanne-Eickel, Germany, Dec. 2, 1951; s. Alfons and Sophie (Mroz) G.; m. Babette Thekla Bockmann, Aug. 25, 1989; children: Ralf, Friederike. Dr.med., Univ., Mainz, Germany, 1979. Sr. surgeon Hosp. Am Urban, Berlin, Germany, 1987-92; plastic surgeon pvt. practice, Berlin, Germamy, 1993—. Author: Die Pflege Des Brandverletzten. Mem. VDPC, DGAPC.

GRABOVAC, IVO, law educator; b. Split, Dalmatia, Croatia, Aug. 28, 1934; s. Milan and Wanda (Tocigl) G.; m. Milojka Dobronić, July 20, 1961; children: Irena, Inoslav. Jurist, Faculty of Law, Zagreb, Croatia, 1960, LLM, 1965; LLD, Faculty of Law, Split, 1967. Cert. lawyer, jurist, specialist for maritime law. Clk. Harbourmaster's Office, Split, 1955-61; asst. Faculty of Law, Split, 1961-65, asst. prof., 1965-71, assoc. prof., 1971-76, full prof., 1976—, dean, 1978-80, 94-96. Author: Analysis of the Bill of Lading Clauses, 1970, Liability of Carrier, 1989 (award of the City of Split 1991), Maritime Law, 1993, Croatian Maritime Law and International Convention, 1995 (award of the County of Split and Dalmatia 1996), Liability of Ship Operator, 1997, Transport Contract Law of the Republic of Croatia, 1999, The Basis of Liability in Transport Law, 2000; contbr. articles to profl. jours. Recipient State award of Croatia for Sci. Achievements, 1988, award for work County of Split and Dalmatia, 2000. Mem. Croatian Maritime Law Assn. (exec. bd.), Soc. for the Study and Devel. of the Maritime Economy of The Republic of Croatia, Com. Maritime Internat. Roman Catholic. Avocation: boat navigation. Home: Odeska 14, 21000 Split Dalmatia, Croatia Office: Pravni Fakultet, Domovinskog Rata 8, 21000 Split Dalmatia, Croatia

GRACE, JAMES MARTIN, JR., lawyer; b. Columbus, Ohio, Sept. 6, 1967; s. James Martin and Letitia Jean (Stively) G.; m. Michèle Lee Sirna, June 22, 1991. BA, U. Notre Dame, 1989; JD cum laude, U. Houston, 1992. Bar: Tex. Law clk. to Hon. Samuel B. Kent U.S. Dist. Ct. (so. dist.) Tex., Galveston, 1992-93; assoc. Baker Botts, LLP, Houston, 1993-2000; sr. counsel Enron N.Am. Corp., Houston, 2000—. Author tchr.'s guide: Copyright Law, 1992. Adv. coun. Local Initiatives Support Corp.; vol. R Club PAC, 1998-99; mem. Tex. Accts. and Lawyers for the Arts, 1998—. Mem. State Bar Tex., Houston Bar Assn., Houston Young Lawyers Assn., Houston Jaycees (dir. edn. 1993-94, legal counsel 1994, Outstanding Leadership award 1993, Silver Key award 1994), Notre Dame Alumni Assn. (treas. Class of '89), Notre Dame Club of Houston (bd. dirs.), Order of the Barons, Phi Delta Phi. Republican. Roman Catholic. Avocations: soccer, football, reading. Office: Baker & Botts LLP 910 Louisiana St Ste 3000 Houston TX 77002-4991

GRACE, THOMAS WILLIAM, JR., military officer, dentist; b. Niagara Falls, N.Y., Nov. 6, 1951; s. Thomas William Sr. and Thelma Louise Grace; m. Vaughn Marie Grace, Sept. 3, 1977; children: Thomas John, Jennifer Lee. BS in Chemistry, Hobart Coll., 1974; DDS, Temple U., 1982; student, Air War Coll., Air Command and Staff Coll. Diplomate Fed. Svcs. Bd. Gen. Dentristry; lic. dentist, Pa., Mass. Chemist PPG Industries, Pitts., 1974-78; dentist USPHS, Roxbury, Mass., 1982-86; dental officer 13 Med. Ctr., Clark Air Base, The Philippines, 1986-90; asst. base dental surgeon Aviano (Italy) Air Base, 1990-93; staff dentist Wilford Hall Med. Ctr., Lackland AFB, Tex., 1994, resident in comprehensive dentistry, 1995-96; dental officer 4 Med. Group, Seymour Johnson AFB, N.C., 1996-99; commd. capt. USAF, 1995, advanced through grades to lt. col.; comdr. 4 Aeromed. Dental Squadron, Seymour Johnson AFB, 1999—; clin. instr. dentistry U. N.C., 1997-99. Troop com. chmn. Boy Scouts Am., 1997—. Mem. Acad. Gen. Dentistry (peer lit. reviewer jour. 1998-99), Air Force Assn., KC. Avocations: woodworking, backpacking, fishing, photography, skeet shooting. E-mail: tom.grace@excite.com. Home: 107 Tracy Pl Goldsboro NC 27534-7600

GRACHOV, DIMITRY DIMITRIEVICH, foundation executive; b. Yakutsk, Russia, Oct. 7, 1954; s. Dimitry Ivanovich and Elizabeta Julievna (Kelle) G.; m. Nadezhda Sergejevna Kozyreva, Apr. 24, 1976; 1 child, Denys. MSc, Peoples Friendship U., Moscow, 1977, PhD in Physics, 1985; Expert, Moscow Bus. Sch., 1991. Head of group MIG Rsch. Ctr., Moscow, 1984-87, sr. scientist, 1987-89; sr. scientist Inst. Radioengring., Moscow, 1989-94; prin. scientist EPI Ctr., Moscow, 1994-98; pres. Fund for Entrepreneurship Support, Moscow, 1998—; project mgr. Ministry Higher Edn., Moscow, 1991-94, sci. sec., head coun. for optoelectronics, 1991-94; exec. dir. Inst. Info. Techs., Moscow, 1991-94; cons. Online Resource Ctr., Ltd., Moscow, 1997—. Contbr. articles to profl. jours. Head of staff Yabloko Party, Moscow, 1994-98; had of staff Entrepreneurship Devel. Movement, Moscow, 1998—. Mem. IEEE, Popov Radioengring. Soc., Acad. Natural Scis. (founder). Orthodox Christian. Avocations: travel, basketball, ancient history, deciphering of ancient scripts. Home: Filevsky blvd 17 app 416, 121601 Moscow Russia Office: Fund Engrepreneurship Suppt, Bolotnaja str 12 b3 app 517, 113035 Moscow Russia

GRACHYOV, ANDREY YURIEVICH, computer scientist, consultant; b. Moscow, Oct. 19, 1964; s. Yury Alexandrovich and Tamara Sergeevna (Shapkina) G.; m. Svetlana Vyacheslavovna Kuhtina, Oct. 11, 1985; children: Tatiana, Olga. Degreed specialist, Moscow State U., 1986, PhD, 1991. Cert. in applied math. Jr. sci. rschr. Moscow State U., 1989-92, software expert GV Dialogue,, 1992-93; database expert Tern Inc., Moscow, 1993-96; cons. Informix Software, Moscow, 1996-99; sr. sci. rshr. Moscow State U., 1999—; educator Mirea U., Moscow, 1997-98, Moscow State U., 1992-93; tchr. Exptl. H.S. # 710, Moscow, 1990-92; system analyst IBS, 1999—. Contbr. articles to profl. jours. Recipient Bronze medal USSR Exhbn. Econ. Achievements, 1986. Avocations: music, fishing. Home: Bestuzhevyh 9-15, 127566 Moscow Russia

GRACIA NUÑEZ, SABAS LUIS, electrical engineer, consultant; b. Gallur, Spain, Dec. 5, 1919; arrived in Argentina, 1920; s. Felipe and Anunciacion (Nuñez) Gracia; m. Olga Maria Costa Gracia Nunez; children: Luis Angel, Carlos Eduardo, Jose Luis. Degree in Mech. Tech., Otto Krause, Buenos Aires, 1938; degree in Mech. and Elec. Engring., LaPlata (Argentina) Nat. U., 1947. Pub. svc. dir. La Plata (Argentina) Muncipality, 1948-52; prof. LaPlata (Argentina) U., 1948-55, Army Tech. Superior Sch., Buenos Aires, Argentina, 1948-87, Buenos Aires U., Buenos Aires, 1952—; adviser State Sec. Energy, Argentina, 1952-62; nat. dir. Elec. Energy, 1962-87; under sec. Elec. Energy State Sec. Energy, Argentina, 1976; vice chmn. Com. for Regional Elec. Integration, Montevideo, Uruguay, 1976-77; cons. IADB, Washington, 1983; bd. dirs. EDESA. Author: Practice of Electrotechnics, 1960, Electrotechnics, 1984. Mem. Goberment Negotiation Team, Corpus Itaipu Treaty, 1979, Uruguay River Treaty, 1980. Named Comendador de la Orden de Cruceiro Do Sul, Govt. of Brazil, 1980; recipient 1st prize 4th World Electrotech. Fair and Congress, Buenos Aires., 1995. Mem. Argentine Engrs. Assn., Argentine Electrotechnics Assn., Argentine Scientific Assn. Roman Catholic. E-mail: edesa@datamarkets.com.ar. Home: Pueyrredon 1104, 1828 Banfield Buenos Aires, Argentina Office: EDESA SAC, Lavalle 437, 1047 Buenos Aires Argentina

GRACIN, DAVOR, physicist; b. Zagreb, Croatia, Nov. 22, 1951; s. Jure and Franka (Stambuk) G.; m. Dubravka Starcevic, July 10, 1976; children: Martina, Koraljka. BS, Physics/Fac. of Sci., Zagreb, 1979, MS, 1990, PhD, 1993. Asst. Rudjer Boskovic Inst., Zagreb, 1979-90, sr. asst., 1990-93, rschr., 1993-99, sci. assoc., 1999—. Contbr. articles to profl. jours. Mem. Croatian Phys. Soc., Croatian Vacuum Soc., Croatian Astron. Soc., Zagreb Astron. Soc. Roman Catholic. Avocations: art, cynology, astronomy, tennis. Office: Rudjer Boskovic Inst, Bijenicka 54, 10000 Zagreb Croatia

GRADIN, ANITA, former ambassador/European Commission member; b. Hörnefors, Vasterbotten, Sweden, Aug. 12, 1933; d. Ossian and Alfhild (Englund) G.; m. Bertil Kersfelt; 1 child, Cathrine. Degree in social work & pub. adminstrn., Coll. Social Work and Pub. Adminstrn., Stockholm, 1960. Journalist Västerbottens folkblad, 1950; with Swedish Union Forest Workers and Log Drivers, 1952; journalist Arbetarbladet, Gävle, Sweden, 1956-58, Cen. Orgn. of Salaried Employees, Sweden, 1960-63; mem. staff Social-Welfare Planning Com., Mcpl. Exec. Bd. Com. on Women, Stockholm, 1963-67; mem. Swedish Parliament, 1968-92; min. for migration and equality between men and women Govt. of Sweden, 1982-86, min. fgn. trade and European affairs, 1986-91, amb. to Austria, Slovenia and UN, 1993-94; commr. European Commn., Brussels, 1995-99; mem. Swedish Parliament, 1969-92, mem. standing coms. on edn. and fin., 1968-92; del. Coun. Europe, 1973-82, chair Coun. Europe's com. on migration, refugees, demography. Sec. com. women's affairs Stockholm Cen. Bd. Adminstrn., 1963-67; mem. Stockholm City Coun., 1966-68; chmn. dist. br. Fedn. Social Dem. Women, Stockholm, 1968-82, vice-chmn. Nat. Fedn. Social Dem. Women in Sweden, 1976-92; vice chmn. Socialist Internat., 1986-92; chmn. Socialist Internat. Women, 1986-92; chmn. migration, refugees and demographic questions com. Coun. of Europe, 1978-82; chmn. Swedish Assn. of Grads. from Schs. of Social Work and Pub. Adminstrn., 1978-82; chmn. Coun. Inter-Country Adoptions, 1973-80. Office: Svartviksslingan 27, 167 38 Bromma Sweden

GRĂDINARIU, LĂCRĂMIOARA, chemist; b. Galati, Romania, Mar. 21, 1968; d. Ioan and Virginica (Stoleru) Năstac; m. Dănut Grădinariu. B of Chemistry and Physics. Tchr. Galati, 1995-96; chemist Hosp.-Maternity, Galati, 1996—. Avocations: films, theatre, reading. Home: George Cojanc NR 25, 6200 Galati Romania Office: Hosp Maternity, Chicus, 6200 Galati Romania

GRADINAROVA, BOYKA ZHEKOVA, computer scientist, educator; b. Kiustendil, Bulgaria, Feb. 15, 1956; d. Zheko and Elena (Yaneva) Zhekov; m. Radosvet Gradinarov, May 3, 1981; two children. MSc, Tech. U. Varna, 1979, U. Sofia, 1989; DSc, Tech. U. Sofia, 1993. Constructor Radio Navigational Plant, Varna, Bulgaria, 1979-85; tchr. math. Varna H.S., 1985-87; lectr. Tech. U. Varna, 1987—; mem. working group Internat. Fedn. for Info. Processing. Author: Programming and Use of Computer Systems, 1993; contbr. articles to profl. jours. Mem. N.Y. Acad. Scis.

GRADOV, OLEG MIKHAELOVICH, physicist; b. Perm, Russia, Aug. 15, 1946; s. Mikhael Dmitrievich and Lidia Vasilyevna (Plotnikova) G.; m. Irina Victorovna Ulyanova, Jan. 6, 1971. MPhil, Moscow State U., 1970, PhD, 1973; PhD, Imea U., Sweden, 1985. Scientist Physical P.N. Lebedev Inst., Moscow, 1973-84; sr. scientist A.A. Baikov Inst., Moscow, 1984-89, Inst. Solid State Physics, Moscow, 1990-91, N.S. Kurnakov Inst., Moscow, 1992—; vis. lectr. Montreal U., Can., 1980, Umea U., Sweden, 1979, 81-83, 89, 92, 95, 97; dep. dir. lab. N.S. Kunrakov Inst., 1992—. Contbr. articles to profl. jours. Office: N S Kurnakov Inst RAS, Leninsky prosp 31, 117907 Moscow Russia

GRADO-WOLYNIES, EVELYN (EVELYN WOLYNIES), clinical nurse specialist, educator; b. N.Y.C., Apr. 2, 1944; d. Joseph Frederick and Evelyn Marie (Ronning) Grado; m. Jon Gordon Wolynies, July 12, 1964; children: Jon Andrew, Kristine Elisabeth. AAS, Burlington County Coll., 1990; AS, Camden C.C., 1990; BSN cum laude, Thomas Jefferson U., 1991, MSN summa cum laude, 1992; postgrad., Johns Hopkins U., 1993-95. RN, N.J., Pa., cert. clin. nurse specialist. Charge nurse Hampton Hosp., Westampton, N.J., 1990-92; adjunct clin. instr. psychiat. nursing Burlington County Coll., Pemberton, N.J., 1992-93; project leader Alzheimer's disease clin. drug study Olsten Health Care, Cherry Hill, N.J., 1992-95, psychiat. case mgr., 1992-94; CNS neuropsych in Huntingtons Disease Dr. Allen Rubin, Camden, N.J., 1992; psychiat. case mgr. Moorestown (N.J.) Vis. Nurses Assn., 1992; charge nurse, group therapist, rschr. Friends Hosp., Phila., 1994-99; clin. mgr. The Caring Link partial geriatric outpatient program Frankford Hosp., Phila., 1996-99; pvt. practice hypnotherapy/psychotherapy; cons. psychiat. care, Alzheimer's Disease, RN/home health aide instr. Olsten-Kimberly Home Care; clin. preceptor U. Pa. Sch. NSG, MSN, GNP and Adult Mental CS Programs. Contbr. articles to nursing jours. Mem. Burlington County Coll. Alumni Bd.; founder, dir. Support Group for Adult Children with Aging Parents; Developed music therapy/exercise program for Geriatric Psych patients. Recipient Juanita Wilson award, 1991, Farber fellowship, 1991-92.; Nurse in Washington intern, 1992; named to Burlington County Coll. Hall of Fame, 1994. Mem. Am. Assn. of Neuroscience Nurses, Am. Psychiat. Nurses Assn., N.J. State Nurses Assn., Sigma Theta Tau (Delta Rho chpt.), Phi Theta Kappa. Home: PO Box 3604 Cherry Hill NJ 08034-0550

GRADY, GREGORY, lawyer, banker; b. Takoma Park, Md., Oct. 10, 1945; s. Francis Joseph Grady and Deane (McGehee) Black; m. Carol Love Harrison, Feb. 25, 1978; children: Olivia Love, Blake McGregor, Harrison Edwards. BA in Econs., U. Va., 1969; JD, Tulane U., 1972. Bar: D.C. 1973, U.S. Ct. Appeals (D.C. cir.) 1973, U.S. Ct. Appeals (4th cir.) 1975, U.S. Supreme Ct. 1976, U.S. Ct. Appeals (5th cir.) 1977, U.S. Ct. Appeals (10th cir.) 1979, U.S. Ct. Appeals (11th cir.) 1981, U.S. Ct. Appeals (6th cir.) 1982, U.S. Dist. Ct. 1988. Staff atty., supervisory atty. FPC, Washington, 1972-74; assoc. Littman, Richter, Wright & Talisman, P.C., Washington, 1974-79; mem. Wright & Talisman, P.C., Washington, 1979—, pres., chmn. bd. dirs., chmn. exec. com., 1997-98, mng. mem., 1999—; bd. dirs. Bank of Franklin, Miss., D.R. McGehee Ins. Agy., Inc., Miss. Mem. Energy Bar Assn., D.C. Bar Assn., Congl. Country Club. Republican. Episcopalian. Home: 666 Live Oak Dr Mc Lean VA 22101-1569 Office: Wright & Talisman PC 1200 G St NW Ste 600 Washington DC 20005-3838

GRADY, SEAN MICHAEL, writer; b. Palo Alto, Calif., Oct. 3, 1965; s. Michael Wilmont and Naomi Jane (Gladstone) G. BA, U. So. Calif., 1988. Bus. writer Daily Press, Victorville, Calif., 1988-89; bus. editor The Olympian, Olympia, Wash., 1989-90; freelance writer, 1990-98; writer, asst. editor custom pub. group Reno Gazette-Jour., 1998—; instrnl. asst. Truckee Meadows C.C., Reno, 1992, part-time instr., 1993. Author: Plate Tectonics: Earth's Shifting Crust, 1991, Ships: Crossing the World's Oceans, 1992, The Importance of Marie Curie, 1992, Submarines: Probing the Ocean Depths, 1994, Illiteracy, 1994, Explosives: Devices of Controlled Destruction, 1995, Virtual Reality: Computers Mimic the Physical World, 1998. Mem. Soc. Profl. Journalists, Soc. Children's Book Writers and Illustrators (Sierra Nev. chpt.). Home and Office: 1555 Ridgeview Dr Apt 229 Reno NV 89509-6245 Office: 955 Kuenzli St PO Box 22000 Reno NV 89520-2000

GRAEFE ZU BARINGDORF, FRIEDRICH-WILHELM, member European parliament; b. Spenge, Germany, Nov. 29, 1942. Mem. European Parliament, Germany, 1984—; mem. Group of the Greens/European Free Alliance; mem. conf. of com. chmn., com. on agr. and rural devel., chmn. com. on budgets; substitute mem. delegation for rels. with South Africa. Office: Europaisches Parlament, Rue Wiertz ASP 8G301, Bruxelles Belgium

GRAELLS, FRANCISCO (PANCHO GRAELLS), painter, caricaturist; b. Caracas, Venezuela, Apr. 9, 1944; arrived in France, 1983; s. Pablo and Ethel (Piriz-Bascans) G.; m. Ingrid Tempel, May 9, 1969; 1 child, Andrea. Grad., U. Montevideo, Uruguay, 1971. Caricaturist, cartoonist Marcha, Montevideo, 1968-74, De Frente, Montevideo, 1969-70; co-dir. publ. La Balota, Montevideo, 1971-72, La Bocha, Montevideo, 1973; co-dir. Crisis, also Satiricon, Buenos Aires, 1973-75, El Nacional, Caracas, 1976-83; art dir. Caracas, 1979-83; cartoonist, caricaturist Cartoonists & Writers Syndicate, N.Y.C., 1983—, Le Monde, Paris, 1983—, Le Canard Enchaine, Paris, 1985—; cartoonist Il Sole 24 Ore, Milan, 1988—. Author: C'est Parti!, 1993. Office: Le Monde, 21 bis rue Claude-Bernard, 75005 Paris France

GRAESSMANN, ADOLF, physician, biomedical researcher; b. Bad Kissingen, Germany, Apr. 20, 1938; m. Monika Blohm, Dec. 18, 1968; 2 children. MD, Berlin, 1968, habilitation, 1975. Postdoctoral Weizmann Inst. Sci., Israel, 1969, Free U. Berlin, 1970-73, São Paulo (Brazil) U., 1971-72; full prof. U. Berlin, 1975—; vis. scientist Cold Spring Harbor, 1977-78, U. Calif. Berkeley, 1981, NIH, 1990; Fogarty scholar in residence, NIH, Bethesda, Md., 1993. Contbr. articles to profl. jours. (German Cancer Soc. award, 1994). Sec. gen. Internat. Wildlife Preservation Fund, France, 1999—. Mem. EMBO. Home: Am Hirschsprung 48b, D-14195 Berlin Germany Office: Free U Berlin, Arnimallee 22, D-14195 Berlin Germany

GRAEVE, PETER JOHN, county official; b. Bayshore, N.Y., June 15, 1962; s. George William and Marie Therese (Rizzo) G.; m. Heather Love Riedl, Oct. 5, 1991; children: Holland Love, Nicholas Ruger. BA in History, U. Fla., 1984; postgrad., Fla. Atlantic U., 1997—. Constrn. laborer family owned bus. U.S. and V.I., 1969-84; exec. v.p. Boynton Beach, Fla., 1994-95; mgr.-in-tng. Amoco Corp., Boca Raton, Fla., 1994; flatwork supr. Nat. Linen Svc., West Palm Beach, Fla., 1994-95; mgr. vet. svc. office Palm Beach Bd. County Commrs., West Palm Beach, Fla., 1995—. Co-author: Emergency Operations Center Deployment Plan for Operation Just Cause, 1989, Standard Operating Procedures for Light Tacfire, 1991. Mem. Cmty. Svcs. Adv. Bd., West Palm Beach, 1996-99. Maj. U.S. Army, 1984-93; maj. USAR. Mem. County Vet. Svc. Officer Assn. (area v.p. 1998). Lutheran. Avocations: traveling, military battle site tours.

GRAF, ENRIQUE, concert pianist, educator, academic administrator; b. Montevideo, Uruguay, July 18, 1953. MusB, Johns Hopkins U. Artist in residence Coll. Charleston, S.C., 1989—; artist lectr. Carnegie-Mellon U., Pitts., 1996—; chmn. piano dept. Peabody Prep. Johns Hopkins U., Balt.; dir. internat. piano series Coll. Charleston, 1990—. Artistic dir. young artist series Piccolo Spoleto Festival, Charleston; dir. Artists End Hunger, Balt., 1981-84. Recipient 1st prize nat. Ensemble Piano Competition, 1977, 1st prize William Kapell Internat. Piano Competition, 1978; named winner E. and W. Internat. Auditions, 1981. Mem. Music Tchrs. Nat. Assn. Democrat. Roman Catholic. Avocation: bridge. Fax: 843-853-6110.

GRAF, HANS, conductor; b. Austria, Feb. 15, 1949. Studied with Franco Ferrera and Arvid Jansons. Music dir. Mozarteum Orch., Salzburg, Austria, 1984-94, Calgary Philharm. Orch., 1995—; apptd. music dir. Orch. Nat. de Bordeaux-Aquitaine and Opera de Bordeaux, 1998—; guest condr. Vienna Symphony, Vienna Philharm., Orchestre Nat. de France, Leningrad Philharm., Pitts. Symphony, Boston Symphony. Office: Calgary Philharmonic Orchestra, 205 8th Ave SE, Calgary, AB Canada T2G 0K9

GRAF, STEFFI, retired professional tennis player; b. 1969; d. Peter and Heidi Graf. Winner numerous profl. women's tennis tournaments including Italian Open, 1987, French Open, 1987, The Golden Grand Slam (Australian Open, French Open, Wimbledon, U.S. Open, Olympics), 1988, Berlin Open, 1988, Wimbledon, 1989, 91, 93, 95, German Open, 1989, 91, 94, U.S. Open, 1989, 91, 92, 93, 95, 96, U.S. Hardcourt Championship, 1989, 91, Australian Open, 1990, 94, Players Challenge, 1990, French Open, 1993, 95, 96, 99; Paris Open, 1995, Lipton Open, 1995; State Farm Evert Cup, 1996, Chase Champ, 1996, WTA Tour Champ, 1995; ranked no. 1 in world for more consecutive weeks than any other player in tennis history; ret. from competition, 1999. Office: Steffi Fraf Sport GmBH, Mallaustrasse 75, 68219 Manheim Germany*

GRAFF, HENRY FRANKLIN, historian, educator; b. N.Y.C., Aug. 11, 1921; s. Samuel F. and Florence Babette (Morris) G.; m. Edith Krantz, June 16, 1946; children: Iris Joan (Mrs. Andrew R. Morse), Ellen Toby (Mrs. Martin A. Fox). BSS magna cum laude, Coll. City N.Y., 1941; MA, Columbia, 1942, PhD, 1949. Fellow history Coll. City N.Y., 1941-42, tutor history, 1946; lectr. history Columbia U., N.Y.C., 1946-47, instr. to asso. prof., 1946-61, prof. history, 1961-91, prof. emeritus, 1991—, chmn. dept. history, 1961-64; sr. fellow Freedom Forum Media Studies Ctr., N.Y.C., 1991-92; disting. lectr. Med. Sch. Columbia U., N.Y.C., 1992; lectr. Vassar Coll., 1953; chmn. advanced placement com. Am. History Coll. Entrance Exam. Bd., 1959-63; presdl. appointee Nat. Hist. Publs. Commn., 1965-71; mem. hist. adv. com. to sec. Air Force, 1972-80; acad. cons. Gen. Learning Corp., Time-Life Books; cons. editor Alfred A. Knopf, Inc.; hist. adviser to CBS for Bicentennial TV Series The American Parade, 1973-76, Presdl. Portraits, 1987-88; hist. adviser to ABC for TV series Our World, 1986-87, 20th Century Project, 1993-99; presdl. appointee J.F.K. Assassination Records Rev. Bd., 1993-98; humanities lectr. Med. Sch. Yale U., 1993; Richard W. Cooper lectr. Phi Beta Kappa Assocs., 1996. Author: Bluejackets with Perry in Japan, 1952, (with Jacques Barzun) The Modern Researcher, 1962, rev. edit., 1970, 3d edit., 1977, 4th edit., 1985, 5th edit., 1992, (with Clifford Lord) American Themes, 1963, (with John A. Krout) The Adventure of the American People, 3d edit., 1973, The Free and the Brave, 4th edit., 1980, Thomas Jefferson, 1968, American Imperialism and the Philippine Insurrection, 1969, The Tuesday Cabinet, 1970; (with Paul J. Bohannan) The Call of Freedom, 1978, The Promise of Democracy, 1978, This Great Nation, 1983, The Presidents: A Reference History, 1984, 2d edit., 1996, paperback, 1997, America: The Glorious Republic, 1985, rev. edit., 1990; cons. editor: Life's History of the United States, 1963-64; contbr. articles to profl. jours. 1st lt. AUS, 1942-46. Recipient citation War Dept., Townsend Harris medal CCNY, 1966, Mark Van Doren award Columbia U., 1981, Gt. Tchr. award Columbia U., 1982, Kidger award New Eng. History Tchrs. Assn., 1990; Am. Coun. Learned Socs. fellow, 1942, Presdl. medal George Washington U., 1997, James Madison award ALA, 1999, Disting. Author award Westchester C.C. Found., 2000. Mem. Orgn. Am. Historians, Am. Hist. Assn., Coun. Fgn. Rels., Author's Guild, P.E.N., Soc. Am. Historians, Soc. Historians Am. Fgn. Rels., Mass. Hist. Soc. (corr.), Century Assn. (N.Y.C.), Sunningdale Country Club, Phi Beta Kappa (former pres. Gamma chpt.), Phi Beta Assocs. (hon.). Home: 47 Andrea Ln Scarsdale NY 10583-3115

GRAFFEO, MARY THÉRÈSE, music educator, performer; b. Mineola, N.Y., Jan. 20, 1949; d. Michael Joseph and Florence Marie (Lonette) G. BA in Music Edn., Adelphi U., 1972; MusM in Vocal Performance, Kent State U., 1982. Cert. music tchr. N.Y. Tchr. music, therapist Nassau County Bd. Coop. Ednl. Svcs., Westbury, N.Y., 1972-85; tchr. music, developer curricula Great Neck (N.Y.) Pub. Schs., 1985-87; tchr. music Syosset (N.Y.) Pub. Schs., 1987-88, 89-90, Jericho (N.Y.) Pub. Schs., 1988-89; tchr. music, developer creative programs Lawrence (N.Y.) Pub. Schs., 1990-92; tchr. music Herricks Pub. Schs., New Hyde Park, N.Y., 1992-93, Hempstead (N.Y.) Pub. Schs., 1993—; music dir. summer programs Friends Acad., Locust Valley, N.Y., 1989-94. Author: (curriculum) Music for the Trainable Mentally Retarded, 1973, (book) Creative Enrichment Programs/America: The First 300 Years in Song, 1990; co-author: The Remediation of Learning Discrepancies Through Music, 1980; composer: (mus. play) Red Riding Hood's Day, 1993, The Bell of Atri, 1994, The Children's Song, 1995. Cultural adv. bd. Lawrence Pub. Schs., 1990-92, Hempstead Pub. Schs., 1993—; founding mem. United We Stand Am., Dallas, 1992—. Scholar Adelphi U., 1968-72, Blossom Festival Sch., Kent, Ohio, 1978-79. Mem. NEA, Music Educators Nat. Conf., N.Y. State United Tchrs., N.Y. State Sch. Music Assn., Nassau Music Educators Assn. Democrat. Roman Catholic. Avocations: aviculture, needlework, travel, photography, concerts. Home: 300 Edwards St Roslyn Heights NY 11577-1140 Office: Early Childhood Ctr 436 Front St Hempstead NY 11550-4212

GRAFFMAN, GARY, pianist, music educator; b. N.Y.C., Oct. 14, 1928; s. Vladimir and Nadia (Margolin) G.; m. Naomi Helfman, Dec. 5, 1952. Student, Curtis Inst. Music, 1936-46, Columbia U., 1947-48; studied with Vladimir Horowitz, Rudolf Serkin; MusD (hon.), Juilliard Sch., 1993, Moravian Coll., 1995. Dir. Curtis Inst. Music, Phila., 1986-95, pres., dir., 1995—. Soloist debut, Phila. Orch, 1947; first tours U.S., 1951, S.Am., 1955, Europe, 1956, Asia-Australia, 1958, South Africa, 1961; solo appearances with N.Y. Philharmonic, Boston, Chgo., Cleve., San Francisco, Los Angeles, London, Cape Town symphony orchs., Philharmonia London, Halle Orch. of Manchester, Royal Liverpool, Berlin, Lisbon, Oslo, Warsaw philharmonic orchs., Johannesburg, Sydney, Melbourne orchs., others; rec. artist with N.Y., Phila., Boston, Cleve., Chgo., San Francisco orchs., also solo recs.; author: I Really Should Be Practicing, 1981. Fulbright scholar, 1950; Ford Found. fellow, 1962; recipient Rachmaninoff Fund. spl. award, 1948, Leventritt award, 1949, Pa. Gov. Excellence in Arts award, 1991. Office: Curtis Inst Music Office of Director 1726 Locust St Philadelphia PA 19103-6187 also: ICM Artists Ltd 40 W 57th St Fl 16 New York NY 10019-4001

GRAFFY, ADRIAN JOSEPH, priest; b. Ilford, Essex, Eng., Mar. 2, 1950; s. Eric and Beatrice Imelda (Camilleri) G. Lic. in Philosophy, Urban U., Rome, 1970, B Theology, 1973; D in Sacred Scripture, Pontifical Biblical Inst., Rome, 1983. Priest Diocese of Brentwood, 1974—; lectr. in scripture St. John's Seminary, Wonersh, Guildford, England, 1983—; dir. of studies St. John's Seminary, Wonersh, Guilford, England, 1986-99; vice-rector St. John's Seminary, Wonersh, Guildford, England, 1995-99; chaplain St. Joseph's Sch., Cranleigh, 1985—; mem. Meth./Roman Cath. Com., Eng. and Wales, 1997—, co-sec., 1998—; mem. Ministry Adv. Group, Diocese of

Arundel, 1996—; dir. Programme for Former Anglican Clergy, St. John's Seminary, Wonersh, 1994-99; del. Bishops' Conf. Eng. and Wales to Cath. Bibl. Fedn., 1999—. Author: The Prophet Confronts His People, 1983 (award 1984), Alive and Active The Old Testament Beyond 2000, 1999, others; translator: Manual of Hebrew Poetics, 1988; contbr. articles to profl. jours. Mem. Soc. Old Testament Study, Clinical Theology Association. Avocations: writing, reading, swimming. Home: St Johns Seminary, GU5 OQX Wonersh Surrey, England

GRAFSTROM, NILS E.G., pulp and paper industry company executive; b. Madrid, Oct. 17, 1947; arrived in Sweden 1948; s. Gunnar T.E. and Lies Grafstrom; m. Wivi-Anne K. Bergman, Sept. 20, 1975; children: Anna, Mia. LLB, Uppsala (Sweden) U., 1971. Ct. clk. Dist. Ct., Falun, Sweden, 1971-74; lawyer Berglunds Law Firm, Stockholm, 1974-80, ptnr., 1979-80; gen. counsel STORA, Falun, 1981-98, exec. v.p., 1992-98; pres., CEO Veracel Celulose SA, São Paulo, Brazil, 1998—; chmn. Swedish-Brazilian C. of C.; bd. dirs. World Childhood Found., Brazil. Home: Dromstigen 24, S-167617 Bromma Sweden Office: Av Nacões Unidas 11.541, 04578-000 São Paulo Brazil

GRAHAM, ALAN MORRISON, surgeon; b. Perth, Scotland, Mar. 23, 1953; m. Michiko P. Graham; children: George A., Mie I, Fraser S. Queen's U., Kingston, Ont., 1973-75, MD, 1979. Diplomate Am. Bd. Surgery, Am. Bd. Gen. Surgery and Vascular Surgery. Internship Kingston Gen. Hosp. Queen's U., 1979-80; residency Royal Victoria Hosp. McGill U., 1980-84; fellowship U. Chgo., 1984-85; asst. prof. dept. surgery Montreal Children's Hosp., 1985-91, Royal Victoria Hosp., 1985-91; asst. prof. dept. surgery McGill U., 1985-91, assoc. prof., 1991-92; assoc. prof. dept. surgery Royal Victoria Hosp., 1991-92; assoc. prof., chief div. vascular surgery Robert Wood Johnson Medical Sch., 1992—, program dir. vascular fellowship program, 1992—. Author numerous book chapters; contbr. articles to profl. jours. Recipient Edgar Forrester scholarship, 1977, W.W. Near scholarship, 1977, Alice Pierce Waddington scholarship, 1977, Prof. prize in Surgery, 1979, Neil Currie Polson Meml. prize, 1979, Outstanding Tchr. award U. Chgo., 1985, E.J. Wylie Travelling fellowship, 1989, numerous grants. Fellow ACS, Royal Coll. Physicians and Surgeons; mem. Soc. Univ. Surgeons, Soc. Vascular Surgery, Ea. Vascular Soc., Can. Assn. Gen. Surgeons, Assn. Acad. Surgeons, Assn. Internat. Vascular Surgery, Can. Soc. Vascular Surgery, Peripheral Vascular Surgery Soc., Internat. Soc. Cardiovascular Surgery, Soc. Clin. Vascular Surgery, Phoenix Alliance, Inc., Vascular Soc. N.J. (pres.), Internat. Fedn. Surg. Colls., Soc. of Surgeons of N.J. Office: Robert Wood Johnson Med Sch 1 Robert Wood Johnson Pl New Brunswick NJ 08901-1928

GRAHAM, ALBERT CECIL, pediatrician, consultant; b. Bridgetown, Barbados, Jan. 22, 1928; s. George Washington and Cecille (Harding) G.; m. Lorraine Denise Reid, Oct. 1957 (div. Oct. 1974); children: Gillian, Leslie, Jennifer, Michael; m. Margaret Letitia Gale, Feb. 28, 1975; stepchildren: Alistair, Luisa. MBBS, London U., 1954; diploma in child health, U. London, 1955. Med. registrar Barbados Gen. Hosp., St. Michael, Barbados, 1959-62; cons. pediatrician Queen Elizabeth Hosp., St. Michael, 1962-90, Children's Devel. Ctr., 1982—, Delaware Med. Ctr., 1989—. Mem. coun. Barbados Mus., 1993-95, Barbados Assn. Mentally Retarded, 1975-95, NCH Action to Children, 1984—; pres. Parent Edn. for the Devel. of Barbados, 1985-95, advisor, 1995—; mem. garden com. Andromeda Botanical Gardens, 1990; advisor Caribbean Assn. Mental Retardation and Other Devel. Disabilities, 1994—. Recipient Gold Crown of Merit, Govt. of Barbados, 1978, G. Allan Roeher award Caribbean Assn. Mental Retardation and Other Devel. Disabilities, 1993. Fellow Royal Coll. Physicians U.K., Royal Coll. Pediatricians and Child Health (sr.); mem. Rotary. Anglican. Avocations: gardening, music, reading, travel. Home: 39 Prior Park, Saint James Barbados Office: Delaware Med Ctr, Jemmotts Ln, Saint Michael Barbados

GRAHAM, ALLISTER P., diversified company executive. Pres., COO The Oshawa Group Ltd., Toronto, Ont., Can., 1985—; now chmn. bd., CEO The Oshawa Group Ltd., Toronto; chmn. Nash Finch Co., Mpls. Office: 7600 France Ave S Minneapolis MN 55440-0355*

GRAHAM, ANNA REGINA, pathologist, educator; b. Phila., Nov. 1, 1947; d. Eugene Nelson and Anna Beatrice (McGovern) Chadwick; m. Larry L. Graham, June 29, 1973; 1 child, Jason. BS in Chemistry, Ariz. State U., 1969, BS in Zoology, 1970; MD, U. Ariz., 1974. Diplomate Am. Bd. Pathology. With Coll. Medicine U. Ariz., Tucson, 1974—, asst. prof. pathology, 1978-84, assoc. prof. pathology, 1984-90, prof. Pathology, 1990—. Fellow Am. Soc. Clin. Pathologists (bd. dirs. Chgo. chpt. 1993—, sec. 1995-99, v.p. 1999—), Internat. Acad. Pathology, Internat. Acad. Telemedicine, Coll. Am. Pathologists; mem. AMA (alt. del. Chgo. chpt. 1992-99, del. Chgo. chpt. 1999—), Ariz. Soc. Pathologists (pres. Phoenix chpt. 1989-91), Ariz. Med. Assn. (treas. Phoenix chpt. 1995-97). Republican. Baptist. Avocations: motorcycles, piano, choir. Office: Ariz Health Scis Ctr Dept Pathology Tucson AZ 85724-0001

GRAHAM, CHRISTOPHER FRANCIS, lawyer; b. Darby, Pa., June 21, 1957; s. Thomas Francis Graham and Margaret Veronica Kerr; m. Theresa Elizabeth Smith, Mar. 10, 1984 (dec. Apr. 1996); 1 child, Christopher F. Jr. Student, London U., 1978-79; BS in Bus. Adminstrn. magna cum laude, Georgetown U., 1979; JD, Pa. U., 1982. Bar: Hawaii 1997, U.S. Dist. Ct. (so. and ea. dist.) N.Y. 1983, U.S. Ct. Appeals (2d and 5th cirs.) 1991, U.S. Tax Ct. 1987, U.S. Supreme Ct. 1991. Assoc. Weil Gotshal & Manges, N.Y.C., 1982-84, Cadwalader Wickersham & Taft, N.Y.C., 1984-89; ptnr. Thacher Proffitt & Wood, N.Y.C., 1989—; mem. exec. com. Thacher Proffitt & Wood, 1997—; mem. bd. advisors, adj. prof. St. John's U. Sch. Law. Trustee Georgetown Dean's Coun., Washington, 1986-91; co-chmn. Save Our Aging Religious, N.Y.C., 1994—; head coach Eastchester (N.Y.) Youth Soccer, 1996—. Mem. ABA, Am. Bankruptcy Inst. (chmn. real estate com. 1996—, dir. law sch. medal program 1997—), Alpha Sigma Nu. Home: 3 Hillside Rd Bronxville NY 10708-5116 Office: Thacher Proffitt & Wood 2 World Trade Ctr New York NY 10048-0005

GRAHAM, DAVID MAXWELL, computer company executive; b. Melbourne, Australia, Sept. 24, 1959; s. Maxwell Norman and Jeanette Brook (Wilson) G.; m. Deborah Ann Wills. B of Bus. in Acctg. and Info. Tech., Darling Downs, Toowoomba, Australia, 1987; Dip Prog Tech, CDC, Melbourne, 1986. Sys. mgr. NZI Securities, Sydney, Australia, 1987-89; key account mgr. ITS, Sydney, 1989-92; gen. mgr. MFA, Sydney, 1989-92; bus. devel. mgr. Info. builders, Canberra, Australia, 1993-97; sr. account mgr. Computer Assocs., Canberra, 1997-98; bus. devel. mgr. Microhelp Pty. Ltd., 1998—; bd. dirs. Stromness Data Sys., Melbourne, Stromness Pty. Ltd., Melbourne. Campaign mgr. Liberal Party, Sydney, 1993; boating safety and nav. instr. Royal Vol. Coast Guard, Sydney, 1988-92. Lt. comdr. Royal Australian Navy, 1978-86. Mem. Inst. of Navigators, Naval and Mil. Club Victoria, Commonwealth Club (Canberra), Rotary (sec. Canberra East chpt.). Avocations: sailing, gardening, fine dining.

GRAHAM, DENIS DAVID, marriage and family therapist, educational consultant; b. Santa Rosa, Calif., Oct. 21, 1941; s. Elbert Eldon and Mildred Bethana (Dyson) G.; m. Margaret Katherine Coughlan, Aug. 31, 1968; children: Kathleen Ann, Todd Cameron (dec.). BS in Edn., U. Nev., 1964, MEd, 1973, MA, 1982. Cert. for ednl. pers.; lic. marriage and family therapist, Nev. Tchr. vocat. bus. edn. Earl Wooster H.S., Reno, 1964-66, chmn. dept. bus. edn., 1966-67; stare supr. bus. and office edn. Nev. Dept. Edn., Carson City, 1967-70, adminstr. vocat. edn. field svcs., 1970-74, asst. dir., 1974-78, vocat. edn. cons., 1978-85; edn. curriculum specialist Washoe County Sch. Dist., Reno, 1985-89, curriculum coord., 1989-94, ret., 1994; pres. Midpoint Inc., 1995—; marriage and family counselor Severance & Assocs., Carson City, 1983-85, Mountain Psychiat. Assocs., 1985-87; mem. tng. and youth employment coun. S.W. Regional Lab. for Ednl. R&D, Los Alamitos, Calif., 1982, mem. career edn. coun., 1980-81. Editor Coun. of Chief State Sch. Officers' Report: Staffing the Nation's Schools: A National Emergency, 1984; contbr. articles to profl. jours. Bd. dirs. U. Nev.-Reno Campus Christian Assn., 1988-90, 97-99; mem. adv. com. Truckee Meadows C.C., Reno, 1988-94; mem. Gov.'s Crime Prevention Com., Carson City, 1979-83, Atty. Gen.'s Anti-Shoplifting Com., Carson City, 1974-78, Gov.'s Devel. Disabilities Planning Coun., Carson City, 1977-79; bd. dirs. Jr. Achievement No. Nev., 1989-92, sec., mem. exec. com., 1990-91; bd. dirs. Friends of the Coll. of Edn., U. Nev., Reno, 1995-99. Recipient award for svc. Bus. Edn. Assn. No. Nev., 1973, Svc. award YMCA, 1962, 63, Helping Hand award Procter R. Hug H.S., 1993-94. Mem. ACA, Am. Vocat. Assn., Nat. Assn. Vocat. Edn. Spl. Needs Pers. (Outstanding Svc. award Region V 1982), Am. Assn. Marriage and Family Therapy, Nev. Vocat. Assn. (Outstanding Svc. award 1991, Bill Trabert Meml. award Excellence in Occup. Edn. 1994), Internat. Assn. Marriage and Family Counselors, U. Nev. Reno Alumni Assn. (exec. com. 1971-75), Phi Delta Kappa, Phi Kappa Phi. Democrat. Methodist. Home: 3056 Bramble Dr Reno NV 89509-6901 Office: PO Box 33034 Reno NV 89533-3034

GRAHAM, DIANE SHAFER, art and architectural history educator; b. N.Y.C., Nov. 19, 1942; d. Raymond Philip and Jane Harris (Davies) Shafer; m. Ian Charles Strachan, July 29, 1967 (div. Oct. 1987); 1 child, Shona Elizabeth Strachan; m. Larry Allan Graham, Dec. 27, 1987. BA, Allegheny Coll., Meadville, Pa., 1964; MA, Sophia U., Tokyo, 1983; postgrad., Binghamton U., 1990—. Apptd. lectr. U. Hong Kong, 1983-84; adj. faculty SUNY, Brockport, 1988-90, Binghamton, 1990-92; rsch. cons. Altfield Gallery, Hong Kong, 1982-83; U.S. rep. Orientations Mag., Hong Kong and N.Y.C., 1982-90; adj. faculty Nazareth Coll., Rochester, N.Y., 1989-95; owner, dir. The Gallery, Geneseo, N.Y., 1993—; curatorial cons. Asian collection Meml. Art Gallery, Rochester, 1993—, Asian collection The Univ. Mus., Binghamton (N.Y.) U., 1994—; English lang. libr. Nat. Mus. Art, Bangkok, 1976-77; lectr., tour leader Coll. Women's Assn. Japan, 1980-82; lectr., seminar leader Nat. Mus. Art Vols., Bangkok, 1974-77. Mem. preservation com. Assn. for Preservation of Geneseo, 1991—; sec. Republicans Abroad, Tokyo, 1980-82; campaign vol. Polit. Campaigns of Raymond P. Shafer, Pa., 1957-67. Binghamton U. fellow, 1993-94, Nat. Fgn. Lang. fellow U. Pa., 1986. Mem. Coll. Art Assn., Soc. Archtl. Historians, Am. Assn. for Asian Studies, Nat. Com. for U.S.-China Rels., Nat. Trust for Historic Preservation, Oriental Ceramic Soc. of Hong Kong, The Siam Soc. Republican. Avocations: reading, travel, photography, genealogy. Home: 61 2nd St Geneseo NY 14454-1227

GRAHAM, DOUGLAS ARTHUR MONTROSE, former New Zealand government official, consultant on indigenous people; b. Auckland, New Zealand, Jan. 12, 1942; m. Beverley V. Graham; 3 children. Student, U. Auckland, New Zealand, 1965; LHD (hon.), U. Waikato, 1999. Practicing lawyer, 1965-99, pvt. practice, 1968; barrister, solicitor High Ct. of New Zealand; lectr. in legal ethics U. Auckland, 1973-83; mem. Parliament Govt. of New Zealand, Wellington, 1984-99, min. cultural affairs, 1990-96, min. disarmament and arms control, 1990-96, min. in charge of Treaty of Waitangi Negotiations, 1991-99, min. of justice, 1990-98, min. for courts, 1996-97, atty. gen., 1997-99; ret. Govt. of New Zealand, 1999; cons. indigenous people, 1999—; apptd. to Her Majesty's Privy Coun., 1998. Recipient New Zealand Commemoration medal, 1990; named Knight Companion New Zealnd Order of Merit, 1999. Avocations: golf, music, rugby, football. Fax: 00-64-9-2948672. E-mail: douglas.graham@xta.co.nz.

GRAHAM, FRED PATTERSON, journalist, lawyer; b. Little Rock, Oct. 6, 1931; s. Otis Livingstone and Lois (Patterson) G.; m. Lucile McCrea, Dec. 28, 1961 (div. March 1982); children—Grier, David Silliman, Alyse; m. 2d Skila Harris, Sept. 11, 1982. B.A., Yale U., 1953; LL.B., Vanderbilt U., 1959; diploma in law, Oxford U., 1960. Bar: Tenn., 1959, D.C., 1974. Pvt. practice Nashville, 1960-63; chief counsel subcom. constl. amendments U.S. Senate, Washington, 1963; asst. to sec. labor Dept. Labor, Washington, 1964-65; Supreme Ct. corr. N.Y. Times, N.Y.C., 1965-72; law corr. CBS News, Washington, 1972-87; anchor, sr. editor Sta. WKRN-TV, Nashville, 1987-89; chief anchor, mng. editor Courtroom TV Network, N.Y.C., 1989—; Regents lectr. Boalt Sch. Law, U. Calif., Berkeley, 1982. Author: The Self Inflicted Wound, 1970, Press Freedom Under Pressure, 1972, The Alias Program, 1977, Happy Talk, 1990. Mem. bd. Boalt Hall Trust, 1985-90; bd. dirs. Nat. Constitution Ctr., 1987-90; trustee Reporters Com. for Freedom of Press, 1969-77, 87—. 1st lt. USMCR, 1953-56. Recipient George Foster Peabody award, 1975, 3 Emmy awards Am. Acad. TV Arts and Scis., 1974; Fulbright scholar, 1960. Home: 1733 19th St NW Apt 3 Washington DC 20009-1666*

GRAHAM, HOWARD LEE, SR., financial services company executive; b. Monroe, Mich., May 26, 1942; s. Carl Lee and Myrtle Leota (Manis) G.; m. Bobbie Jo Hamilton; children: Kimber Lee, Howard Lee Jr., Jacquelyn Leota, John-Nathan Howard. Grad., Dake Bible Sch., Atlanta, 1960-62; student, Cen. Bible Coll., Springfield, Mo., 1964-67; grad., Internat. Sem., 1993, DD, 1996. Debit agt. Met. Life Ins. Co., Colorado Springs, Colo., 1963-64; agt. Met. Life Ins. Co., Allen Park, Mich., 1964-67, 68; agy. mgr. Preferred Risk Life Ins. Co., Allen Park, 1968-72; agy. owner Howard Graham Ins. Agy., Taylor, Mich., 1972-85; spl. agt., rep. Prudential Ins. Co., Cleve., 1985-89; regional mgr. Primerica Fin. Svcs., Abingdon, Va., 1995—; pres. Graham & Graham Canvas Shoppe, Inc., 1976-95, CEO, 1995—; pres. Graham Enterprises, Cleve., 1985—; CEO Graham & Graham Canvas Shoppe, Inc., 1976; nat. and regional sales leader Preferred Risk Ins. Co., Des Moines, 1969-72. Life mem. Full Gospel Bus. Men's Fellow, Detroit, 1963-85, officer, 1974-80, officer, Cleve., 1985—; active Gideons Internat., Cleve., 1963—; pres. Truth Alive, Inc., 1988—; Bible tchr., missionary. Named Central Region Agt. of Yr., 1985; admitted to Million Dollar Round Table, 1985, Hall of Honor, 1986. Mem. Indsl. Fabrics Assn. Internat., Am. Coll., Nat. Assn. Life Underwriters, Internat. Platform Assn. Republican. Mem. Pentecostal Ch. Avocations: sports, Bible research. Home: 15178 Quail Ridge Way Abingdon VA 24210-1675 Office: PO Box 1805 Abingdon VA 24212-1805

GRAHAM, JAMES, mineralogist; b. Perth, Australia, Oct. 13, 1929; s. James Mitchell and Dorothea Isobel (Thrum) G.; m. Valerie Lois Elms, Mar. 22, 1958; children: Carolyn, Dorothy, Margaret. MSc in Physics, U. Western Australia, 1953; PhD in Phys. Metallurgy, U. Birmingham, U.K., 1956. Rsch. fellow U. Birmingham, 1955-56; rsch. officer, sr. rsch. officer CSIRO, Melbourne, Victoria, Australia, 1956-63; prin. rsch. scientist CSIRO, Perth, WA, Australia, 1964-94; hon. sr. rsch. fellow Rsch. Ctr. for Advanced Materials and Mineral Processing, U. Western Australia, Nedlands, Australia, 1994—; adv. bd. physics Curtin U., Perth, 1970—. Editor Australian Physicist, 1980-85; contbr. articles to profl. jours. Deacon Claremont Bapt. Ch., 1970—; mem. coun. West Australian Bapt. Theol. Coll., 1975—. Fellow Australian Inst. Physics; mem. Mineralogical Soc. Am. (v.p. internat. coun. for applied mineralogy 1993, pres. 1994-97). Achievements include development of technique for trace analysis by electron microprobe analyses; development pyrolysis method for recovery of refractory gold. Home: 24 Oban Rd, City Beach WA 6015, Australia Office: Rsch Ctr Advanced Materials and Mineral Processing, U Western Australia, Nedlands WA 6009, Australia

GRAHAM, JAMES HERBERT, dermatologist; b. Calexico, Calif., Apr. 25, 1921; s. August K. and Esther (Choudoin) G.; m. Anna Kathryn Luiken, June 30, 1950 (dec. May 1987); children: James Herbert, John A., Angela Joann; m. Gloria Boyd Flippin, July 29, 1989. Student, Brawley Jr. Coll., 1941-42; AB, Emory U., 1945; MD, Med. Coll. Ala., 1949. Diplomate: Am. Bd. Dermatology (dir. 1977-87, v.p. 1985-86, pres. 1986-87, Disting. Service medal 1987); diplomate in dermatopathology Am. Bd. Dermatology and Am. Bd. Pathology. Intern Jefferson-Hillman Hosp., Birmingham, Ala., 1949-50; resident in dermatology VA Center and UCLA Med. Center, 1953-56; clin. asst. instr. in medicine UCLA, 1954-56; Osborne fellow and NRC fellow in dermal pathology Armed Forces Inst. Pathology, Washington, 1956-58; vis. scientist Armed Forces Inst. Pathology, 1958-69, chmn. dept. dermatopathology, 1980-88; registrar Registry of Dermatopathology, Armed Forces Inst. Pathology, 1980-88, also program dir. dermatopathology, 1979-88; program dir. dermatopathology Walter Reed Army Med. Center, Washington, 1979-88; asst. prof. dermatology and pathology Temple U., 1958-61, assoc. prof., 1961-65, prof. dermatology, 1965-69, assoc. prof. pathology, 1965-67, prof. pathology, 1967-69; prof. medicine, chief div. dermatology, prof. pathology, dir. sect. dermal pathology and histochemistry U. Calif., Irvine, 1969-78; chief dermatology U. Calif. Med. Ctr., Irvine, 1977-78; prof. emeritus Coll. Medicine, U. Calif., 1978—; head sect. dermatology Orange County (Calif.) Med. Center, 1969-73; cons. dermatology VA Hosp., Long Beach, Calif., 1969-73; chief dermatology sect. VA Hosp., 1973-78, acting chief med. service, 1976; cons. dermatology, dermal pathology Regional Naval Med. Center, San Diego, 1969-82, Long Beach, 1969-78, Camp Pendleton, Calif., 1972-78; cons. dermatology, dermal pathology Meml. Hosp. Med. Center, Long Beach, 1972-86, Fairview State Hosp., Costa Mesa, Calif., 1969-78; cons. for career devel. for rev. clin. investigator applications VA Central Office, Washington, 1973-78; Disting. Eminent physician VA physician and dentist-in-residence program, 1980-88; mem. organizational com. Am. Registry Pathology, Armed Forces Inst. Pathology, Washington, 1976-77; mem. exec. com. Am. Registry Pathology, Armed Forces Inst. Pathology, 1977-78; prof. dermatology, clin. prof. pathology Uniformed Services U. of Health Scis., Bethesda, Md., 1979-88, prof. emeritus, 1989—; program dir. dermatopathology Naval Hosp. and Scripps Clin. and Rsch. Found., San Diego, 1991-94; head divsn. dermatopathology, dept. pathology Scripps Clinic and Rsch. Found., LaJolla, Calif., 1988-94, ret., 1994. Sr. author: Dermal Pathology, 1972; contbr. articles to profl. publs. Served with M.C. USNR, 1949-53. Named Disting. Alumnus, Med. Coll. Ala., 1994; recipient ASDP 3d ann. Walter R. Nickel Award for Excellence in Teaching of Dermatopathology, Hilton La Jolla (Calif.) Torrey Pines Hotel, 1999. Mem. AMA (accreditation coun. for grad. med. edn., 1977-87, residency rev. com. for dermatology 1977-87, chmn. 1984-87, cert. of merit 1960), Soc. Investigative Dermatology (life), U.S. and Can. Acad. Pathology (life), Am. Soc. Investigative Pathology (life, emeritus mem. 1995), Am. Dermatol. Assn. (essay award 1958, v.p. 1986-87), Am. Soc. Dermatopathology (pres. 1975-76, Founder's award 1990, rep. to bd. of mem. Am. Registry Pathology 1988-92), Dermatopathology Club (pres. 1980-81), Assn. Mil. Dermatologists (life), Am. Acad. Dermatology (life, dir. 1974-77, 82, v.p. 1980-81, rep. to bd. mems. Am. Registry Pathology 1977-78, hon. mem. San Francisco 2000), N.Am. Clin. Dermatologic Soc. (hon.), 1973, Pa. Acad. Dermatology, Pacific Dermatol. Assn. (dir. 1972-75, hon. mem. 1981), Dermatology Found. (Leader's Soc. and Annenberg Circle), Washington Dermatol. Soc. (spl. hon.), Phila. Dermatol. Soc. (pres. 1967-68, hon mem. 1994), San Diego Dermatol. Soc., Cutaneous Therapy Soc., Alpha Omega Alpha, Cosmos Club.

GRAHAM, JAMES MILLER, ecology researcher; b. St. Louis, Oct. 16, 1945; s. Alvin Rudd and Edrie (Miller) G.; m. Linda Kay Edwards, May 3, 1969; children: Michael Edwards, Melissa Edwards. MA, U. Mich., 1968, PhD, 1979. Postdoctoral scholar environ. engring. U. Mich., Ann Arbor, 1979-80; lectr. zoology U. Wis., Madison, 1981-82, rsch. assoc. physiology, 1983-88, lectr. botany, 1987-88, physiology researcher, 1988-99, microbial ecology researcher, 1999—; reviewer Phycological Soc. Am., Jour. Great Lakes Rsch., Microbial Ecology. Contbr. chpt. to Periphyton of Freshwater Ecosystems, 1983; contbr. articles to profl. jours. With U.S. Army, 1969-72. Mem. AAAS, Am. Soc. Limnology and Oceanography, Phycological Soc. Am., Phi Beta Kappa, Sigma Xi. Office: U Wis Dept Botany 430 Lincoln Dr Madison WI 53706-1313

GRAHAM, JOHN HAMILTON, II, airborne delivery service company official; b. Waynesboro, Va., Mar. 30, 1960; s. John Hamilton and Joan (Clay) G. BA in Polit. Sci., Christopher Newport Coll., 1983; DD, Am. Fellowship, 1986. Dir. pub. rels. Peninsula Pilots (minor league affiliate Phila. Phillies), Hampton, Va., 1977-79, dir. broadcasting and pub. rels., 1979-81, asst. gen. mgr., 1981-85; v.p., gen. mgr. Peninsula White Sox (minor league affiliate Chgo. White Sox), Hampton, 1985-87; gen. mgr. Auburn (N.Y.) Astros Baseball Club, 1988-92; pres. Sports of the Peninsula, Hampton, 1992-94; customer svc. specialist Airborne Express, Atlanta, 1994-96; sr. agt., night ops. mgr. Airborne Express Internat., College Park, Ga., 1996—. Vice-chmn. Rep. Nat. Com., 1981, Rep. Party Va., Hampton, 1982-92; election bd., election ofcl. Commonwealth of Va., Hampton, 1985-95; notary pub. Commonwealth of Va., Richmond, 1988—. Named Broadcaster of Yr. Carolina League, Hampton, Va., 1980, 81, 85, 87, Exec. of Yr. N.Y. Penn League, Auburn, 1991; named to Peninsula Pro Baseball Hall of Fame, Hampton Rds. Baseball Hall of Fame, Auburn Baseball Hall of Fame; recipient Bill Dancy award Phila. Phillies, 1987. Mem. Nat. Assn. Writers and Broadcasters, Assn. Profl. Ballplayers of Am., Probaseball Execs. Assn. (pres.), Moose, Am. Legion. Avocations: tennis, art. E-mail: john-graham1960@aol.com. Home: 105 Summer Glen Dr Union City GA 30291-2457

GRAHAM, LANIER, art historian, curator, cultural planner; b. Shawnee, Okla., Mar. 6, 1940; s. Floyd and Martha Graham; m. Gloria K. Smith; 1 child, Jennifer R. BA in Cultural Affairs, Am. U., 1963; MA in Art History, Columbia U., 1966; PhD in Art History, U. Berkley, 1968. Planner cultural instns., 1965—; assoc. curator architecture and design Mus. Modern Art, N.Y.C., 1965-70; curator of paintings and sculpture, renaissance to modern Fine Arts Mus., San Francisco, 1970-76; curator Cultural Resource Mgmt. Ctr., San Francisco, 1976-83; curator of prints and books Australian Nat. Gallery, Canberra, 1984-87; curator of paintings, sculpture and prints, renaissance to modern Norton Simon Mus. Art, Pasadena, Calif., 1987-91; dir., curator Art Info. Ctr. - An Info. Svc., Northbank, Calif., 1991-97, Univ. Art Gallery, Calif. State U., Hayward, 1997—; art history lectr., ethnics studies, religious studies, aesthetics, mus. studies and holistic studies educator NYU, Antioch U., U. San Francisco, U. Calif., Berkeley, John F. Kennedy U., Calif. Inst. Asian Studies, Calif. State U., Hayward, Naropa Inst., Boulder, Humboldt State U., Arcata. Author: Leonardo's Book Illustrations, 1961, Botticelli's Dante, 1963, Mies van der Rohe Drawings, 1966, The Architecture of Louis I. Kahn, 1966, Chess Sets, 1968, Hector Guimard, 1970, Three Centuries of American Painting, 1971, Three Centuries of French Art, vol. 1, 1973, vol. 2, 1976, Claude Monet, 1974, Flaming Waters: Books by William Blake, 1977, Brother Sun & Sister Moon: Alchemical Symbols in Traditional and Modern Art, 1979, Illustrated Books of Henri Matisse, 1979, Leonardo & the Androgyne: Nonduality in World Art, 1980, Decades of Light: Early Modern French Painting, 1980, Symbols of the Earth Spirit: Sacred Images of Shamanism, Taoism, Hinduism and Buddhism, 1982, Symbols of the Sky Spirit: Sacred Images of Judaism, Christianity and Islam, 1983, The Spontaneous Gesture: Prints and Books of the Abstract Expressionist Era, 1987, Vincent Van Gogh: Painter, Printmaker, Collector, 1990, The Prints of Willem de Kooning: A Catalogue Raisonne, vol. 1, 1991, Impossible Realities: Marcel Duchamp and the Surrealist Tradition, 1991, Sacred Visions: A Survey of World Art and Architecture, 1991, 92, The Tribal Culture of Our Ancestors: An Overview of Traditional Art from the Stone Age to the Iron Age, 1993, The Double Serpent: Symbol of Transformation in World Art, 1993, Rhythms and Reverberations: Multicultural Art in the United States and its Development from the Tribal World, 1993, Solidity and Infinity: The Symbolism of the Circle and Square in World Architecture, 1995, Goddesses in Art, 1997, Life, Death and Laughter: The Art of Masami Teraoka, 1998, The Art of the Book: The Modern Livre d'Artiste, 1999; collections of poetry include Nature Poems, 1958, The Sin of 100 Debts, 1967, Heavy Light: Haiku on the Theme of Modern Physics & Ancient Wisdom, 1978, Electro-Magnetism: Poems on the Theme of Complementarity, 1982, Fragments of Feelings: Selected Poems, 1994, Undulations of Eternity: Collected Poems, 1994; editor: The Rainbow Book: Color...from Ancient to Modern Times, 1975, 76, rev. edit., 1979, Rodin Graphics: A Catalogue Raisonne, 1975, Rodin Sculpture, 1977, American Paintings from the Collection of Mr. and Mrs. John D. Rockefeller 3d, 1976, Giorgione & the Experts: A Documentary Exhibition of the Three Ages of Man & the Process of Authentication, 1993, 94, Leonardo's Light in the Last Supper and Christ among the Doctors: The Story of an Unrecorded Canvas, With an Analysis of Its Style, Physical Properties, and Metaphysical Symbolism, 1995, Art & Technology: A Reader, 1997; contbg. co-author Codes of Ethics for Coll. Art Assn., Australian Assn. Mus., 1970-87; author studies in renaissance and modern art from Impressionism to Contemporary Multicultural Art; rsch. in relationships between modern and traditional art, particularly symbols of the sacred; editor BOA: Bull. of Archives of Art Info. Ctr., 1960—, Renaissance Studies, 1963—, Muse: Newsletter of Art Edn. and Cultural Planning, 1969—, American Studies, 1970—, Images-of-Light: Painters and Sculptors as Photographers, 1974-88, Bi-Singularity: Double Images of Nonduality in World Art, 1979—, Leonardo Studies, 1980—, Sacred Spaces: World Architecture & Symbolism, 1976—, Authenticity: Newsletter of Art and Sci. of Authentication, 1980—, Poësis: A Rev. of Poetry by Artists, 1987-93, Shama: Shamanism & Art, 1991—, Iconography of Infinity: Essays on Art and Philosophy, 1992—; planner various cultural instns. including Internat. Study Ctr., N.Y.C., Mus. Modern Art, Greenwich Village Hist. Preservation Dist., N.Y.C., Fine Arts Mus., San Francisco, Urban Planning Think Tank, San Francisco, Exploratorium, San Francisco, Bay Area Conservation Ctr., San Francisco, Archives Am. Art, San Francisco, Ft. Mason Ctr., San Francisco, Headlands Ctr. Arts, Golden Gate Nat. Recreation Area, Nat. Pk. Svc., Sausalito, Yerba Buena Ctr. Arts, San Francisco, J. Paul Getty Mus., Malibu, Louvre Mus., Paris, Humboldt Art Mus., Eureka, Calif. Indian Mus. and Cultural Ctr., Golden Gate Nat. Recreation Area, Nat. Park Svc., San Francisco.

Mem. Coll. Art Assn., Am. Assn. Mus., Internat. Coun. Mus. (tng. com.), Soc. of Archtl. Historians, Nat. Soc. of Lit. and the Arts, World Print Coun. Avocations: printmaking, poetry, collecting prints and illustrated books, publishing private press portfolios and books of poetry.

GRAHAM, LOIS CHARLOTTE, retired educator; b. Denver, Mar. 20, 1917; d. James Washington and Martha Wilhemina (Raukohl) Brewster; m. Milton Clinton Graham, June 30, 1940 (dec.); children: Charlotte, Milton, Charlene, James. Student, Okla. City U., 1935-36; AB, Ouachita Bapt. U., 1939; postgrad., U. Nev., Reno, 1953, 63, 68, Ark. State U., 1954, 59. Cert. tchr., Colo., Nev., Ark. Tchr. Fairmount Sch., Golden, Colo., 1939-40, Melbourne (Ark.) Sch., 1940-41, Blytheville (Ark.) Jr. H.S., 1944-45, Hawthorne (Nev.) Elem. Sch., 1952-81; substitute tchr. Mineral County Sch. Dist., Hawthorne, 1988-94; sr. resource cons. dept. geriatrics U. Nev.-Reno Med. Sch., 1988-90, del. to Rural Health Conf., Hawthorne, 1990; officer Mineral County Tchrs. Assn., 1955-65; ad hoc com. Nev. State Tchrs., 1965. Mem. Mineral County Emergency Planning Com., 1991—; asst. to pres. High Sch. PTA, Hawthorne, 1958, Elem. PTA, Hawthorne, 1961; pianist, choir dir., tchr. various chs., 1927—; active Older Am. Friends of Libr. Recipient Disting. Svc. award. Mem. AAUW (membership v.p. 1988-91, pres. 1991-92, 94-96), AARP (pres. 1995-98), Ret. Pub. Employees of Nev. (membership v.p. 1994-96, pres. 1995—), Older Ams., Friends Libr., Delta Kappa Gamma (v.p. 1991-92). Republican. Baptist. Avocations: volunteer work, reading, writing, knitting, crochet. Home: PO Box 1543 Hawthorne NV 89415-1543

GRAHAM, WILLIAM AUBREY, JR., real estate broker; b. Montgomery, Ala., Dec. 7, 1930; s. William Aubrey and Nina Judson (Jenkins) G.; m. Carol Fletcher, Aug. 15, 1953; children: William G., Carol Anne. BS in Bldg. Constrn., Auburn U., Ala., 1956. Lic. real estate broker, gen. contractor. V.p. Meadow Corp., Montgomery, Ala., 1956-60; pres. Graham Constrn. Co., Montgomery, 1960-65; engr. Portland Cement Assn., Orlando, Fla., 1965-69; gen. mgr. bldg. Punta Gorda Isles, Inc., Punta Gorda, Fla., 1969-72; sales mgr. Punta Gorda Isles, Inc., Punta Gorda, 1972-78; pres. Punta Gorda Realty, Inc., 1978—; chmn. bd. dirs. Southwest Fla. Bank N/A; bd. dirs. v.p. Coral Harbor Enterprises, Punta Gorda, 1978—; pres. Judson Corp., Punta Gorda, 1980—. Bd. dirs., pres. YMCA, Charlotte County, Fla., 1978-88, United Way, Charlotte County, 1979-90, Fla. Internat. Air Show, Charlotte County, 1981—, pres., 1983-96, chmn. bd. dirs., 1996—; bd. dirs., v.p. Spl. Tng. and Rehab., Charlotte County, 1983—, chmn., 1990—, bd. dirs. U.S. Selective Svc. System, 1983, chmn. 1997—. Mem. Nat. Assn. Realtors, Fla. Assn. Realtors, Nat. Assn. Home Builders, Charlotte County Home Builders Assn., VFW, Am. Legion, Elks, Kiwanis (bd. dirs., pres. Punta Gorda 1979—, Citizen of Yr. award 1983, Kiwanian of Yr. award 1990, 98). Republican. Episcopalian. Avocations: golf, tennis. Home: 500 Bal Harbor Blvd Punta Gorda FL 33950-5291 Office: Punta Gorda Realty Inc 1601 W Marion Ave Punta Gorda FL 33950-3202

GRAHAM, WILLIAM B., pharmaceutical company executive; b. Chgo., July 14, 1911; s. William and Elizabeth (Burden) G.; m. Edna Kanaley, June 15, 1940 (dec.); children: William J., Elizabeth Anne, Margaret, Robert B.; m. Catherine Van Duzer, July 23, 1984. SB cum laude, U. Chgo., 1932, JD cum laude, 1936; LLD, Carthage Coll., 1974, Lake Forest Coll., 1983; LLD (hon.), U. Ill., 1988; LHD, St. Xavier Coll. and Nat. Coll. Edn., 1983; LHD (hon.), Barat Coll., 1997, DePaul U., 1998. Bar: Ill. 1936. Patent lawyer Dyrenforth, Lee, Chritton & Wiles, 1936-40; mem. Dawson & Ooms, 1940-45; v.p., mgr. Baxter Internat., Inc., Deerfield, Ill., 1945-53, pres., 1953-71; CEO Baxter Internat., Inc., Deerfield, 1960-80; chmn. bd. Baxter Internat., Inc., Deerfield, Ill., 1980-85, sr. chmn., 1989-95, chmn. emeritus, 1995—; prof., chair Weizmann Inst. Sci., Rehoboth, Israel, 1978; lectr. U. Chgo., 1981-82. Chmn. bd. dirs. Lyric Opera Chgo.; bd. dirs. Big Shoulders, Wendy Will Care Fedn., Chgo. Hort. Soc.; trustee Orchestral Assn., U. Chgo., Evanston (Ill.) Hosp.; past pres. Cmty. Fund of Chgo. Recipient V.I.P. award Lewis Found., 1963, Disting. Citizen award Ill. St. Andrew Soc., 1974, Decision Maker of Yr. award Am. Statis. Assn., 1974, Marketer of Yr. award AMA, 1976, Found. award Kidney Found., 1981, Chicagoan of Yr. award Chgo. Boys Club, 1981, Bus. Statesman of Yr. award Harvard Bus. Sch. Club Chgo., 1983, Achievement award Med. Tech. Svcs., 1983, Disting. Fellows award Internat. Ctr. for Artificial Organs and Transplantations, 1982, Chgo. Civic award DePaul U., 1986, Internat. Visitors Golden Medallion award U. Ill., 1988, Chgo. medal U. Chgo., 1992, Laureate award Lincoln Acad. Ill., 1992, Lyric Opera Carol Fox award, 1992, Good Scout award N.E. Coun. Boy Scouts Am., 1993, Making History award Chgo. Hist. Soc., 1996, Depaul U. Dr. Humane Letters award, 1998; recognized for pioneering work Health Industry Mfrs. Assn., 1981; inducted Jr. Achievement Chgo. Bus. Hall of Fame, 1986, Modern Healthcare Hall of Fame, 1994, Art Alliance Legend award, 2000. Mem. Am. Pharm. Mfrs. Assn. (past pres.), Ill. Mfrs. Assn. (past pres.), Pharm. Mfrs. Assn. (past chmn., award for spl. distinction leadership 1981), Chgo. Club (past pres.), Commonwealth Club, Comml. Club, Indian Hill Club, Casino Club, Old Elm Club, Seminole Club, Everglades Club, Bath and Tennis Club, Links Club, Phi Beta Kappa, Sigma Xi, Phi Delta Phi. Home: 40 Devonshire Ln Kenilworth IL 60043-1205 Office: Baxter Internat Inc 1 Baxter Pkwy Deerfield IL 60015-4625

GRAHAM, WILLIAM PIERSON, investment banker, entrepreneur; b. East St. Louis, Ill., Feb. 19, 1935; s. William Schley and Opal Elizabeth (Gray) G.; m. Margaret Newton McDowell, Sept. 30, 1961; children: Lisa, Heather, Jennifer. BS, U. Ill., 1956. With IBM Corp., 1956-69, asst. to pres., 1967-68, dir. mktg. comml. industries data processing div., 1968-69; exec. v.p. EDP Tech., Inc., Washington, 1969-71, pres., CEO, 1971-73; pres. Washington Profl. Group, 1973-81; pres. SRC Corps. Equisource Source Corps; mng. dir. Pierce Investment Banking, Inc.; dir., mem. exec. com. Cornerstone R.E.I.T., 1993-96; chmn. bd. Paradigm Integration Corp., Empowernet, Inc. Asst. for domestic programs White House, Washington, 1966-67; chmn. bd. dirs. Congl. Mgmt. Found.; mem. fgn. service profl. devel. rev. group Dept. State, 1976; mem. U.S. Adv. Com. Vocat. Edn., 1968-69, U.S. Fed. Adv. Com. Employment Security, 1968-71, Com. for Excellence in Govt.; panel cons. Edn. Profl. Devel. Act, HEW, 1969-71; del. German Am. Forum, Bonn, Berlin, 1975; chmn. parents assn. Sidwell Friends Sch., Washington, 1976-78; vice chmn. fin. adv. com. Nat. Com. for Effective Congress, 1976-77. Served with AUS, 1957. White House fellow, 1966-67. Mem. White House Fellows Assn. (pres. Assn. and Found. 1973-74). Home and Office: 3238 O St NW Washington DC 20007-2842

GRAHN, GERTRUD LOUISE, nursing educator; b. Malmoe, Sweden, Dec. 9, 1930; d. Carl-Gustaf Sven and Elsa Wilhelmina (Duvander) Dagobert; m. Gunnar Grahn, Aug. 8, 1953 (div. 1993); 1 child, Eva. RN, Uppsala Coll. Sch. Nursing, Sweden, 1959; RNT, Teachers Coll., Sweden, 1966; Specialized Tchr., Uppsala U., Sweden, 1975, PhD in Edn., 1987. Operating theatre nurse Uppsala Acad. Hosp., 1959-62; nurse tchr. Uppsala Coll. Sch. Nursing, 1962-67, dir. studies, 1968-86; sr. lectr. Lund U., Sweden, 1987-95, rsch. appointment, 1987-95, dir., dept. head care rsch. unit, 1987-95; assoc. prof. Lund. U., Sweden, 1995—; sci. com. European Conf. Clin. Oncology, 1985-91; expert European Union, Brussels, 1989-91; cons. European Coll. Cancer Care, 1990-95, EONS Standing Com. for Edn., 1995-97. Contbd. articles to profl. jours. Recipient Disting. Merit award EONS, 1995. Mem. The Swedish Cancer Soc. (rsch. bd. dirs. 1989-95), Internat. Soc. Nurses in Cancer Care (bd. dirs. 1990-92), Cancer Nursing Soc., European Oncology Nurses Soc. (Disting. Merit award 1995), Internat. Soc. for Nurses in Cancer Care. Achievements include research in patient education, psycho-soc. aspects of patient care, nursing education and palliative care; development and implementation of a program on cancer patient education in Europe, core curriculum for cancer nursing education in Europe, and development and implementation of an education program on caring for patients with dementia. E-mail: gertrud.grahn@telia.com. Home and Office: Kurland 55, S-23193 Trelleborg Sweden

GRAHN, LARS EVERT, publishing executive; b. Stockholm, Sweden, June 7, 1941; s. Evert Reinhold and Maria Matilda (Björkman) G.; m. Margareta Evangeline Gustavsson, July 16, 1963; children: Linda, Sara, Love. BA, U. Stockholm, 1965. Lectr. U. Stockholm, 1967-70; asst. prof. Stockholm Sch. Journalism, 1971-77; vis. prof. Scandinavian studies U. Tex., Austin, 1973; editor, editor-in-chief Bonniers förlag, Stockholm, 1977-80, asst. pub., 1980-82; pub., mng. dir. Bokförlaget Legenda, Stockholm, 1982-89; mng. dir., group CEO Bokförlaget Natur och Kultur, Stockholm, 1989—; bd. dirs. TV4, 1991—, Böckernas Klubb, 1992—, chmn., 1992-99. Co-author: (book) Studier i dagens svenska, 1971, Programarbetarens dilemma, 1976; lit. critic of various mags. and newspapers, 1967-80. Mem. Swedish PEN Club (sec. 1985-87), Swedish Pubs. Assn. (bd. dirs. 1987—, chmn. 1999—). Office: Bokförlaget Natur och Kultur, Karlavägen 31 Box 27323, S-102 54 Stockholm Sweden

GRAINGER, INÉS PAULINA, adult educator; b. Apóstoles, Misiones, Argentina, June 28, 1942; came to Zimbabwe, 1973; d. Luis and Miguelina (Ryndycz) Pasteknik; m. Donald Howard Grainger, May 23, 1973. Diploma in tchg., Tchr. Tng. Coll., Corrientes, Argentina, 1959; MEd, U. Nac. Litoral, Santa Fé, Argentina, 1965; MPad, Ludwig Maximilian U., München, Germany, 1972, PhD, 1973; Diploma, Internat. Air Transport Assn., 1991. Tchr. secondary edn. Apóstoles, Misiones, 1960-78; lectr. U. Nac. de Córdoba, Argentina, 1978, U. Zimbabwe, Harare, 1979-85; pvt. practice cons. in tng. programs, 1985—; dir. DSP Assocs., Harare, 1996—; tng. and devel. mgr. Zimbabwe Inst. Mgmt., Harare, 1989-92, bd. dirs. Trustee, bd. dirs. Cath. U. Zimbabwe, 1996-98; bd. dirs. Nat. Manpower Adv. Coun., 1999—, Harare Poly. Adv. Coun., 2000—; pres. St. John Ambulance Cadets, Zimbabwe, 1976-2000; exec. mem., bd. dirs. Adult Literacy Orgn. of Zimbabwe, 1994-97; trustee Don Grainger Meml. Trust, 2000—, The Three Golden Keys Found., 2000—; bd. govs. Ranche House Coll., 2000—; min. plenipotentiary for Republic of Zimbabwe Internat. Parliament for Safety and Peace, 2000—. Decorated dame Order St. Constantine the Great, dame grand cross Order of St. Lazarus, officer Order of St. John of Jerusalem; selected La Dama del Mundial of World Soccer Cup, Cordoba, 1978; named Best Spkr. of the Yr., Zimbabwe C. of C., 1996; scholar Gov. Provincia de Misiones, 1967, Missio LMV, 1969-72, Rottenburg Ordinariat, 1972-73, others. Mem. Assn. Project Mgrs. (trustee 1996-99), Zimbabwe Inst. Mgmt. (bd. dirs. 1995-99, Adult Literacy Orgn. of Zimbabwe (bd. dirs. 1990-95). Roman Catholic. Avocations: amateur radio, tennis, swimming. Fax: 263-4-304267. E-mail: dgrainger@mango.zw. Office: DSP Associates, Box HG 18 Highlands, Harare Zimbabwe

GRAJCZYK, ANDREAS WILHELM, media researcher, consultant; b. Rheydt, Germany, Feb. 20, 1966; s. Hermann Josef and Irmgard (Amend) G. Grad., U. Düsseldorf, Germany, 1989; diploma in psychology, Aachen (Germany) U., 1993. Broadcasting co. rschr., media cons. Südwestrundfunk, Baden-Baden, Germany, 1994—. Mem. N.Y. Acad. Scis. Office: Südwestrundfunk, Hans-Bredow-Strasse, 76522 Baden-Baden Germany

GRALLO, RICHARD MARTIN, research psychologist; b. Winthrop, Mass., Feb. 15, 1947; s. Frederick Michael and Jennie A. (Ferrario) G. AB, Boston Coll., 1969; MS (John A. Lyons fellow), MIT, 1972; MA, NYU, 1976, PhD, 1988. Instr. philosophy Goddard Coll., Plainfield, Vt., 1974; prof. edn. Cohen Coll., N.Y.; adj. prof. applied psychology NYU. Knighted Order of St. John of Jerusalem, 1986. Fellow Inst. for Rational-Emotive Therapy, N.Y., Nat. Acad. Ednl. Rsch., Ass. for Advancement of Ednl. Rsch. (pres. divsn. fellows); mem. Phi Delta Kappa. Home: PO Box 368 Fanwood NJ 07023-0368

GRAMBOW, RICHARD F., construction engineer, consultant; b. N.Y.C., July 20, 1916; s. Charles H. and Mary (Rohr) G.; m. Dreda V. Grambow, Dec. 17, 1955; children: Richard F. Jr., David G., Steven C. BS in Marine Engring. and Naval Arch., Webb Inst. Naval Arch., 1937. Assoc. naval arch. Dept. Navy, N.Y., 1938-42; chief engr., naval arch. Marinship Corp., Sausalito, Calif., 1942-46; exec. engr. Bechtel Corp., San Francisco, 1946-48; chief engr. Indsl. Divsn. Bechtel Corp., L.S., 1948-54; chief project coord., mgr. Internat. Divsn. Bechtel Corp., San Francisco, 1954-62; project mgr. Bechtel/W.K.E., Johannesburg, South Africa, 1962-66; mgr. ops. Internat. Power, Indsl., and Mining Divsn. Bechtel Corp., San Francisco, 1966-68, v.p. for Internat. Mining and Metals Divsn., 1968-72, v.p. for comml. bldg. and land ops., 1972-76, ret., 1976-78, cons., 1978—; v.p. Bechtel Corp., Bechtel Internat. Ltd., Bechtel Pacific Corp., Pacific Bechtel Corp., Bechtel Panama, Bechtel Internat. Corp., Bechtel Nuclear Corp.; archtl. projects in Korea, Thailand, Australia, The Philippines, Malaysia, Japan, Sweden, South Africa, Mauretania, Eng., France, Spain, Zambia, Argentina, Brazil, Can., Pakistan, among others. Mem. planning commn. City Govt., Sausalito, Calif., 1958-61; mem. Sr. Citizens Adv. Group, San Juan County, 1977-80. Mem. Soc. Naval Archs. and Marine Engrs. (life). Avocations: photography, computer sciences. Home: 1052 East Ave Napa CA 94559-2147

GRAMMENOS, DIMITRIOS, archaeologist, director; b. Thessaloniki, Greece, July 4, 1947; s. Vasilios and Vasiliki (Koulouna) G. BA in Archaeology, U. Thessaloniki, 1971, PhD in Prehistoric Archaeology, 1985. Archaeologist 16th Ephorate of Prehistoric and Classical Antiquities, Thessaloniki, 1973-74, 80-92, 93—, 18th Ephorate of Prehistoric and Classical Antiquities, Kavala, 1974-80; archaeologist 15th Ephorate of Prehistoric and Classical Antiquities, Larisa, 1992-93, dir., 1995—. Author books and articles about Neolithic and Bronze Age in North Greece, poetry books. With Greek Army, 1971-73. Mem. Greek Soc. Writers. Home: 4 Iasonos St, Thessaloniki 54633, Greece Office: Archaeol Mus Thessaloniki, 6 Andronikou St, Thessaloniki 54621, Greece

GRAMMIG, ROBERT JAMES, lawyer; b. Oceanside, Calif., June 15, 1956; s. Richard Adolf and Mary Elizabeth (Spisak) G.; m. Laurel Jean Lenfestey, Aug. 10, 1996. BA, U. Pa., 1978, MA, 1978; JD, Harvard U., 1981. Bar: Fla. 1982, D.C. 1986, U.S. Dist. Ct. (mid. dist.) Fla. 1982, U.S. Ct. Appeals (11th and 5th cirs.) 1982, U.S. Supreme Ct. 1985. Law clk. to Hon. Thomas A. Clark U.S. Ct. Appeals (5th and 11th cirs.), Atlanta, 1981-82; assoc. Holland & Knight, Tampa, Fla., 1982-88, ptnr., 1989—. Bd. dirs. Child Abuse Coun., Tampa, 1993-97; mem. Leadership Tampa, 1994-95; Sec. Tampa Bay Internat. Trade Coun., 1994, vice chmn., 1995. Mem. Tampa Bay Coun. on Fgn. Rels., German Am. C. of C., U.S.-Austrian C. of C., Phi Beta Kappa. Republican. Roman Catholic. Home: 21 Bahama Cir Tampa FL 33606-3317 Office: Holland & Knight 400 N Ashley Dr Ste 2300 Tampa FL 33602-4322

GRAMSCH, ERNESTO VICENTE, physics educator; b. Vina del Mar, Chile, Apr. 5, 1961; s. Ernesto Roberto and Maria Edith (Labra) G.; m. Angela Calvo; children: Ernesto, Benjamin, Tristan. MS in Physics, U. Chile, 1986; PhD, CUNY, 1992. Rsch. asst. Brookhaven Nat. Lab., Upton, N.Y., 1986-92; applications engr. Advanced Photonix, Camarillo, Calif., 1992-94; applications engr., dir. UDT Sensors, Hawthorne, Calif., 1994-95; asst. prof. U. Santiago, 1995—; cons. eV Products, Yaphank, N.Y., 1991-92. Asst. editor: Phys. Rev., 1989-91; contbr. articles to profl. jours. Mem. SPIE. Roman Catholic. Home: Luis Beltran 1811 Apt 605, 1240 Nunoa Nunoa, Santiago Chile Office: U Santiago Dept Fisica, Ave Ecuador, 3493 Casilla 307 Santiago Chile

GRÁNÁSY, LÁSZLÓ, physicist; b. Budapest, Hungary, Feb. 15, 1955; s. József and Anna (Pázmándi) G. Diploma, Eötvös U., Budapest, 1979, PhD, 1981; candidate of sci., Hungarian Acad. Scis., Budapest, 1989. Sci. coworker Ctrl. Rsch. Inst. for Physics, Budapest, 1981-89; sr. sci. co-worker Rsch. Inst. for Solid State Physics, Budapest, 1989—; Szechenyi prof. Tech. U. Budapest, 2000—; Humboldt rsch. fellow Deutsche Forschungsanstalt Luft und Raumfahrt, Cologne, Germany, 1992-93; Brit. Coun. Sci. fellow U. Sheffield, Eng., 1997. Contbr. more than 100 articles to sci. jours. and conf. procs. Recipient award for Young Scientists, Hungarian Acad. Scis., 1989, also Physics award, 2000. Mem. Eötvös Phys. Soc. Research interests include theory of phase transformations, nucleation, growth, phase field/density functional theory. Avocations: sailing, playing guitar, tennis. Office: Hungarian Acad Scis, PO Box 49, Rsch Inst Sld St, H-1525 Budapest Hungary

GRANASZTOI, GYORGY, historian; b. Budapest, Hungary, Mar. 28, 1938; s. Pal and Lucy (Rózsaffy) G.; m. Katalin Gyorffy, Aug. 10, 1966; children: Peter, Olga. MSc, Eötvös U., 1963, PhD, 1973, prof. habil., 2000. Prof. Gyor H.S., Hungary, 1963-65; sec. cultural affairs Inst. Cultural Rels., Hungary, 1965-68; rsch. fellow Inst. History, Hungary, 1968-83; vis. prof. U. Lyons, France, 1983-85; prof. Eötvös U., 1985—; dir. Inst. for Ctrl. Europe, 1995-2000, Inst. Teleki Lászlo for Internat. Rels. and Ctrl. Europe, 2000; amb. of Hungary, NATO, 1990-94; vis. prof. U. Louvain, Belgium, 1979-80; vis. prof. EHESS, Paris, 1986-90. Author: The Urban History of Medieval Hungary, 1980. Trustee Collegium Budapest Inst. Advanced Study, 1990—. Wissenschatscholleg Berlin fellow, 1996-97. Avocations: music, rowing, American literature 1930-90. Office: Inst Teleki László, Szilagyi E Fasor 22c, 1125 Budapest Hungary

GRANATH, OLOF ERIK TRYGGVE, museum administrator; b. Boras, Sweden, Nov. 1, 1940; s. Per Olof Tryggve and Maggie Birgitta (Wastlund) G.; children: Rebecca, Adam. B.A., U. Stockholm. Art critic, Dagens Nyheter, Stockholm, 1964-79; chief editor Konstrevy, Stockholm, 1965-68; tchr. Royal Acad. Art Sch., Stockholm, 1965-68; dir. Moderna Museet Stockholm, 1979-89; dir. Swedish Nat. Art Mus., 1989—. Author: Another Light-Swedish Art since 1945, 1974, 2d edit., 1982, Utblikar över konst och konsnärer, 1979, Olle Kås- ett konstärsporträtt, 1980, Erik Dietmanenstöring fiskar stör, 1987, Per Kirkeby- einen Raum schaffen, 1990, Slutbok- tio år med Moderna museet, 1991. Commr. Swedish participation Youth Biennal, Paris, 1967, Venice, 1968. Mem. Internat. Council Museums. (mem. internat. com., dir. 1983—, pres. 1986-89). Office: Nat Mus, Box 16176, S-103 24 Stockholm Sweden

GRANATH, PER MAGNUS, Internet business executive; b. Uddevalla, Sweden, Nov. 28, 1966; s. Rune and Eva (Jonsson) G.; m. Hara Phitidis, 1999. MSc, Chalmers U. Tech., Göteborg, Sweden, 1989, Licentiate in Engring., 1996, doctor philosophy, 1998. Structural engr. VBK, Göteborg, 1991-93; rsch. asst. Chalmers U. Tech., Göteborg, 1993-98; simulations engr. Semcon, Sweden, 1999-2000; gen. mgr. Planitis.Net, Nicosia, Cyprus, 2000—; vis. scholar U. Sydney, 1997-98. Contbr. articles to profl. jours. Avocations: sailing, scuba diving. Office: Semcon ATC, Norra Langebergsgatan 4, 421 32 Frölunda Sweden

GRANATI, DIANE ALANE, ophthalmic nurse; b. Bethlehem, Pa., Sept. 23, 1952; d. William Edward and Martha Lou (Bradford) Reichard; m. Joseph P. Granati, June 15, 2000. Diploma, Abington (Pa.) Meml. Hosp., 1973. Cert. RN in ophthalmology. Med.-surg. nurse St. Luke's Hosp., Bethlehem, 1973-76; ophthalmic nurse physician's office, Pitts., 1976-77, Everett & Hurite Ophthalmic Assocs., Pitts., 1977-80; exec. dir. Assocs. in Ophthalmology, Inc., Pitts., 1980—; speaker in field. Contbr. articles to profl. jours. Mem. NAFE, Founders Soc., Am. Soc. Ophthalmic Registered Nurses, Abington Nurses Alumnae, Am. Soc. Ophthalmic Adminstrs. Home: 116 Kenyon Rd Pittsburgh PA 15205-1719 Office: 500 Lewis Run Rd Ste 218 Pittsburgh PA 15122-3057 also: 125 Daugherty Dr Ste 320 Monroeville PA 15146-2749 also: Town Centre Bldg 10475 Perry Hwy Ste 315 Wexford PA 15090-9274 Address: 4140 Brownsville Rd Ste 237 Pittsburgh PA 15227-3339 also: 2 W Main St Ste 508 Uniontown PA 15401-3403

GRANATO, CATHERINE (CAMMI GRANATO), professional hockey player; b. Downers Grove, Ill., Mar. 25, 1971. Student, Providence Coll., R.I., 1989-93, Concordia U., 1994-97. Hockey player U.S. Nat. Team, 1992—. Recipient ice hockey Gold medal Olympic Games, Nagano, Japan, 1998. Office: USA Hockey Inc 1775 Bob Johnson Dr Colorado Springs CO 80906-4090

GRANCIU, IOAN, engineer; b. Nasaud, Bistrita, Romania, May 22, 1929; s. Dumitru and Firoana (Anton) G.; m. Otilia Gavris, June 1954. Diploma in Engring., Coll. Agr., Arad, Romania, 1953; postgrad., U. Wis., 1960-61; D Agronomy, Coll. Agronomy, Cluj, Romania, 1970. Ext. Dist., Bistrita, Romania, 1953-60; tech. dir. Ministry Agr., Bucuresti, 1960-62; sci. rschr., animal breeding Rsch. Inst., Bucuresti, 1962—; dir. Ministry Agr., Bucurest, 1960-62; chief of dept. Rsch. Inst., Balotesti, Romania, 1962-97. Author: Grupele Sanguine La Animale, 1973; co-author: Cartea Specialistului in Crest. Animal, 1967; contbr. articles to profl. jours., brochures. Fellow Romanian Soc. Animal Sci.; mem. Agr. Acad./Bucuresti, Internat. Soc. Animal Blood Gr. Rsch., Am. Assn. Animal Sci. Roman Catholic. Avocations: lectr. sci. lit., philatelie, tourism. Home: Ghita Padureanu 2, 71411 Bucuresti Romania Office: Rsch Inst Bovine Breeding, 8113 Balotesti/Ilfov Romania

GRAND, MARCIA, civic worker; b. N.Y.C., Aug. 9, 1933; d. Irving and Dorothy (Miller) Kosta; m. Richard Grand, Jan. 27, 1952. Student, U. Ariz., 1950-52, 59-60. Docent, coord., docent trainer Tucson Mus. Art, 1965-71; bd. dirs., 1972-79, chmn. edn. com., 1975-79; v.p., sec. Richard Grand Found., 1966-80; pres., 1980—. Bd. dirs., sec. U. Ariz. Found., 1979-80, v.p., 1986-87, chmn. exec. com., 1986-87; mem. spl. com. office of chair U. Ariz., 1987-92; bd. dirs. Tucson Airport Authority, Greenfield Schs., 1977-82; bd. fellows Ctr. Creative Photography, 1984-98, chmn., 1993-98, mem.-at-large, bd. dirs. Tucson Mus. Art League, 1977-78; bd. trustees San Francisco Art Inst., 1995—. Nominated for YWCA Woman on the Move award, 1982; recipient Cmty. Svc. award Mortar Bd., 1978, Disting. Citizen award U. Ariz. Coll. Fine Arts, 1979. Office: 127 W Franklin St Tucson AZ 85701-1020

GRAND, RICHARD D., lawyer; b. Danzig, Feb. 20, 1930; came to U.S., 1939, naturalized, 1944; s. Morris and Rena Grand; m. Marcia Kosta, Jan. 27, 1952. BA, NYU, 1951; JD, U. Ariz., 1958. Bar: Ariz. 1958, Calif. 1973, U.S. Supreme Ct. 1973; cert. specialist in injury litigation Ariz. Bd. Legal Specialization. Dep. atty. Pima County, Ariz., 1958-59; pvt. practice trial law Tucson, 1959—; founder, 1st pres. Inner Circle Advocates, 1972-75; founder Richard Grand Found., 1966, now chmn.; hon. pres. Richard Grand Soc., 1997—. Contbr. articles to legal publs. Mem. bd. visitors law sch. Ariz. State U. Recipient citation of honor Lawyers Coop. Pub. Co., 1964. Fellow Am. Acad. Forensic Scis., Internat. Soc. Barristers; assoc. mem. Internat. Med. Soc. Paraplegia, Am. Coll. Legal Medicine; mem. ABA (vice-chmn. com. govtl. liability law, sect. of tort and ins. practice 1986-87), Pima County Bar Assn., N.Y. State Trial Lawyers Assn., Calif. Trial Lawyers Assn., Am. Bd. Trial Advs. (cert. in civil trial advocacy), Brit. Acad. Forensic Scis., President's Club of U. Ariz., Richard Grand Soc. (hon. pres.), Bohemian Club. Address: 127 W Franklin St Tucson AZ 85701-1020

GRANDCOLAS, PHILIPPE, entomologist, researcher; b. Granville, Manche, France, May 7, 1964; s. Jean and Denise (Hote) G.; m. Laure Desutter, Jan. 2, 1992. MS, U. Paris XI, Orsay, France, 1985; PhD, U. Rennes (France), 1991. Rsch. scientist CNRS, Rennes, 1993-96, Mus. Paris, 1996—. Editor-in-chief: Memoires du Muséum national d'Histoire Naturelle; contbr. articles to profl. jours. Attaché Mus. Natural History, Paris, 1988—. Recipient Prix Pesson Société Entomologique de France. Fellow Willi Hennig Soc.; mem. The Orthopterists' Soc. (Rentz award 1993), Société Francaise de Systematique (councillor). Office: Lab Entomologie Mus Nat Hist, 45 rue Buffon, 75005 Paris France

GRANDHENRY, FRANCIS HENRI, judge; b. Villers-Aux-Tours, Liege, Belgium, Feb. 5, 1950; s. Victor and Simone (Haillot) G.; m. Claire Hansenne, Aug. 11, 1973; children: Stephanie, Yves. Lic. en Droit, U. Liege, 1974. Avocat Barreau, Liege, 1974-86; justice of the peace Vise, 1986—. Echevin, Commune de Neupre, 1977-81. Home and Office: 10 Rue Duchêne, B 4120 Neupré Liege, Belgium

GRANDIN, TEMPLE, industrial designer, science educator; b. Boston, Aug. 29, 1947; d. Richard McCurdy and Eustacia (Cutler) G. BA in Psychology, Franklin Pierce Coll., 1970; MS in Animal Sci., Arizona State U., 1975; PhD in Animal Sci., U. Ill., Urbana, 1989; D (hon.), McGill U., 1999. Livestock editor Ariz. Farmer Ranchman, Phoenix, 1973-78; equipment designer Corral Industries, Phoenix, 1974-75; ind. cons. Grandin Livestock Systems, Urbana, 1975-90, Fort Collins, Colo., 1990—; lectr., asst. prof. animal sci. dept. Colo. State U., Fort Collins, 1990—; chmn. handing com. Livestock Conservation Inst., Madison, Wis., 1976—; surveyor USDA. Author: Emergence Labelled Autistic, 1986, Recommended Animal Handling Guidelines for Meat Packers, 1991, Livestock Handling and Transport, 1993, 2nd edit., 2000, Thinking in Pictures, 1995, Genetics and the Behavior of Domestic Animals, 1998, Beef Cattle Behavior Handling and Facilities Design, 2000; contbg. editor Meat and Poultry mag., 1987-98; contbr. articles to profl. jours.; patentee in field. Recipient Meritorious Svcs. award Livestock Conservation, Madison, Wis., 1986, Disting. Alumni award Franklin Pierce Coll., 1989, Industry Innovators award Meat Mktg. and Tech. Mag., 1994, Brownlee award for internat. leadership in sci. publ. promoting respect for animals Animal Welfare Found. of Canada, 1995, Harry Roswell award Scientists Ctr. for Animal Welfare, 1995, Humane Ethics in Action award Geraldine R. Dodge Found., 1998, Forbes award

Am. Meat Assn., 1998, Founders award Am. Soc. Prevention Cruelty Animals, 1999, Humane award Am. Vet. Med. Assn., 1999; named One of Processing Stars of 1990 Nat. Provisioner, 1990, Woman of Yr. in Svc. to Agr. Progressive Farmer, 1999, Humane award Am. Vet. Med. Assn., 1999. Mem. Autism Soc. Am. (bd. dirs. 1988—, Trammel Crow award 1989), Am. Soc. Animal Sci. (Animal Mgmt. award 1995), Am. Soc. Agrl. Cons. (bd. dirs. 1981-83), Am. Soc. Agrl. Engrs., Am. Meat Inst. (supplier mem., Industry Advancement award 1995), Am. Registry of Profl. Animal Scis. Republican. Episcopalian. Achievements include design of stockyards and humane restraint equipment for major meat packing companies in the U.S., Canada and Australia. Home: Grandin Livestock Systems 2918 Silverplume Dr Apt C3 Fort Collins CO 80526-2402 Office: Colo State U Animal Sci Dept Fort Collins CO 80523-0001

GRANDINI, CARLOS ROBERTO, physicist, researcher; b. Bauru, Sao Paulo, Brazil, Apr. 19, 1963; s. Carlos Grandini and Edi Perazzi; m. Nádia Alves, Jan. 10, 1990; 1 child, Núbia Alves. Physicist, UFScar, São Carlos, Brazil, 1986; M. U. São Paulo, São Carlos, Brazil, 1988, Sci. Dr., 1993. Aux. prof. UNESP, Bauru, Brazil, 1988; asst. prof. UNESP, Bauru, 1988-93, asst. dr. prof., 1993—, dean physics dept., 1998—. Mem. Am. Phys. Soc., Soc. Brasileira Física. Avocations: swimming, soccer, car racing, stamps. Office: UNESP, Av Eng Luiz Edmundo C Coube S/N, 17033360 Bauru Sao Paulo, Brazil

GRANDJEAN, MICHEL LOUIS, media executive; b. Bellegarde, Ain, France, Feb. 21, 1942; s. Denis and Madeleine (Gillot-Flagez) G.; m. Michele Bernardin, Aug. 2, 1967; children: Olivier, Anne, Edouard. Degree, Essec, France, 1965. Asst. brand mgr. Unilever-Lintas, Paris, 1968-70; media cons. Havas, Paris, 1970-82; mng. dir. Havas Conseil, Paris, 1982-88; CEO Mediapolis, Paris, 1988-2000; pres. MPG, France, 2000—; bd. dirs. Mediametrie, Paris, 1993—. Co-author: Le Publicitor, 1983. Mem. Mediametrie Found. (founding mem.). Office: Mediapolis Immeuble Galilee, 11 Sq Leon Blum, 92806 Puteaux France

GRANDMONT, JEAN-MICHEL, economist, researcher; b. Toulouse, France, Dec. 22, 1939; s. Jancu Wladimir and Paule (Cassou) Grunberg; m. Annick Duriez, Dec. 23, 1967 (div. May 1978); children: Celine, Juliette; m. Josselyne Bitan, 1979. Lic. scis., U. Paris, 1961; degree in engring., Poly., Paris, 1963, Ponts et Chaussées, Paris, 1965; PhD in Econs., U. Calif., Berkeley, 1971; doctorate (hon.), U. Lausanne, 1990. Research assoc. Cermap, Paris, 1965-68; research assoc. then dir. research Centre D' Etudes Prospectives Et De Recherches En Economie Mathematique Appliquees A la Planification, Paris, 1970-96; rsch. dir. Centre de Recherches en Economie et Statistique, Paris, 1996—; rsch. assoc. then dir. Ctr. Nat. Rsch. Scientific, Paris, 1970—; dir. sci. Group Assn. pour le Developpement de la Recherche en Economie et Statistique, Paris, 1986-89; maitre de confs. Polytechnique, Paris, 1977-92, prof., 1992—, chair dept. econs., 1997-2000. Author: Money and Value, 1983; editor: Nonlinear Economic Dynamics, 1987, Temporary Equilibrium, 1988; contbr. articles to sci. jours.; assoc. editor various profl. jours. including Econometrica, Jour. Econ. Theory, Jour. Math. Econs., 1973—. Served to lt. with French mil., 1960-63. Named Clarendon lectr. Oxford U., 1987; recipient Alexander von Humboldt Found. Rsch. award, 1992, Palmes Academiques French Min. Edn., 1995. Fellow The Econometric Soc. (Walras-Bowley lectr. 1984, pres. 1990); mem. AAAS (fgn. hon.), European Econ. Assn., Found. de France (mem. sci. com. 1984-90), Acad. Europe, Am. Econ. Assn. (hon.), Internat. Econs. Assn. (exec. com. 1992-99), French Assn. Econ. Scis. (exec. com. 1992-2000). Avocations: skiing, swimming. E-mail: grandmon@ensae.fr. Fax: 33 0 1 41 17 60 46. Office: CNRS-Crest, 15 Blvd Gabriel Peri, 92245 Malakoff Cedex France

GRANDOLINI, GIULIANO, pharmacy educator; b. Torgiano, Perugia, Italy, Mar. 6, 1930; s. Augusto Grandolini and Antonia Martelli; m. Grazia Maria Vallone, Aug. 3, 1961; children: Gloria M., Antonella G., Gabriella R. Degree in Pharmacy, U. Perugia, 1953; PhD in Pharm. Chemistry, Rome, 1963. Assoc. prof. U. Perugia, 1960-80, full prof., 1980—, pres., dean chem. and pharm. tech., 1981-94, dir. 1st chim. farm. tecn. farm., 1982-87. Author: Fitofarmacia. Impiego Razionale delle Droghe Vegetali, 1996, 2nd edit., 1999. Mem. ADRITELF (v.p.), Internat. Soc. Heterocyclic Chemistry, Soc. Chimica Italiana, Am. Chem. Soc. E-mail: ggrandol@unipg.it. Fax: 39-075-5855135. Office: U Perugia, Via del Liceo 1, 06123 Perugia Italy

GRANDPIERRE, ATTILA, astrophysicist; b. Budapest, July 4, 1951; s. Endre K. Grandpierre and Endréné (Rideg) Erzsébet. Diploma, Roland Eötvös U., Budapest, 1974; DS, Polytech. U., Budapest, 1977; Cand. of Phys. Scis., Hungarian Acad. of Scis., Budapest, 1984. Asst. tchr. Polytech. U., Budapest, 1974-81; aspirant Hungarian Acad. of Scis., Budapest, 1981-84; rsch. asst. geophys. dept. Roland Eötvös U., Budapest, 1984-87; chief rschr. Konkoly Observatory, Budapest, 1987—; mem. Com. of the Evolution of Matter, Hungarian Acad. of Scis., Budapest, 1988—; dir. Internat. Rsch. Team of the Club of Budapest of Collective Consciousness Rsch., 1985—. Author tech. papers in field; mem. editl bd. World Futures: The Jour. of Gen. Evolution, The Noetic Jour. Mem. Scientific and Med. Network, Soc. for Scientific Exploration. Office: Hungarian Acad of Scis, Konkoly Thege ut 13-17, H-1525 Budapest Hungary

GRANGIER, RENE MAURICE, ophthalmologist; b. Mascara, Algeria, Apr. 15, 1940; s. Henri and Germaine (Bouillet) G.; m. Emmanuelle Anne Tissot, Dec. 21, 1968; children: Anne Claire, Geraldine. MD, U. Lyon, France, 1968. Mil. dr. French Army, 1969—; advanced to col. mil. hosps., 1985, ret., 1998; ophthalmologist mil. hosps., Paris, Nantes, Dijon., Lyon. Contbr. articles to profl. jours. Home: 24 Ave FreresLumiere, 69008 Lyon France

GRANHOLT, ERLING, retired educator; b. Sandefjord, Norway, June 17, 1925; s. Wilhelm and Inga Pauline (Lystad) G.; m. Olga Alfrida Andersson; children: Miriam, Borgar, Aud, Ingar and Jostein (twins). Chmn. Sandefjord Riksmålsforening, Norway, 1966-78, Labour Confedn., Sandefjord, Norway, 1969-74, Pedagogisk Samfunn, Sandefjord, Norway, 1970-80, Sandefjord Sch. Coun., Norway, 1982-83, Human-Etisk Forbund, Sandefjord, 1992-97; ret.; pres. Riksmålsforbundet, Norway, 1988-90. Mem. Town Coun., Sandefjord, 1983-91; mem. County Shire Coun., Vestfold, Norway, 1987-91. Mem. N.Y. Acad. Scis. Avocations: painting, genealogy, language, philosophy, history. Home: Råstadveien 55, 3228 Sandefjord Norway

GRANIC, MATE, Croatian government official; b. Baska Voda, Sept. 19, 1947; m. Jadranka Granic; 3 children. MD, Zagreb U. Physician Vuk Vrhovac Inst. Diabetes Endicrinology and Metabolic Diseases Sch. Medicine Zagreb U., 1975-79, head clin. dept. Vuk Vrhovac Inst., 1979-85, prof., dep. dir., 1985-89, vice dean faculty of medicine, 1989, dean, 1990—. v.p. Croatian Dem. Union, dep. prime minister, 1991—, minister fgn. affairs, 1993—. Office: Office Fgn Minister 7-8, Nikole Subica Zrinskog Sq, 10000 Zagreb Croatia*

GRANIELA-RODRIGUEZ, MAGDA, educator, writer; b. Cabo Rojo, P.R.. BA, U. P.R., Mayaguez, 1977; AM, U. Ill., 1979, PhD, 1987. Instr. U. P.R., Mayaguez, 1985, asst. prof., 1987-90, assoc. prof., 1990-95; prof. U. P.R., 1995—; dir. writing lab. U. P.R., 1987-92. Author: Como raiz dilatada a un sueno, Santo Domingo: Alfa y Omega, 1990, El papel del lector en la novela mexicana contemporanea, Washington, D.C.: Scripta Humanistica, 1991, Gramatica Ancestral Aguadilla: Mester, 1999; (with others) Conflictos Culturales en la Literatura Contemporanea, 1993; Mujeres 98 Antologia de poesia femenina puertorriqueña, 1998; editor: Linea Plural, 1986-87; author poems; contbr. articles to profl. jours. Member Foster Parents Internat., Ecuador, 1985—, NARAL, 1983—; mem. disasters relief com. ARC, 1986-87, Foster Parent for World Vision, 1996—. NEH fellow, 1988; recipient Teaching award U. P.R., 1988. Mem. ASCD, MLA, Acad. Arts and Scis., Iberoamerican Inst., Union of Concerned Scientists, Pen Club of P.R., Phi Kappa Phi, Alpha Delta Kappa.

GRANILLO OCAMPO, RAUL ENRIQUE, Argentine government official; b. La Rioja, Argentina, Jan. 18, 1948; m. Nelida Barros Reyes; 3 children. Degree in Law, Nat. Univ. La Plata, Argentina; MA in Internat. Comparative Law, So. Methodist U.; PhD in Juridical Studies, U. Buenos Aires. Chief justice Supreme Court of La Rioja, 1985-86; legal/tech. sec. Pres. Menem (Nat. Cabinent position), 1989-91; prof. comml. law and social econ. history La Rioja Provincial U.; prof. constnl. and adminstrv. law Catholic U., Buenos Aires; amb. to U.S. Govt. of Argentina, Washington, 1993-97; minister of justice Govt. of Argentina, 1997—; mem. Commn. on reforming the Code of Civil, Comml., Labor and Mining Procedures of La Rioja; mem. bd. dirs. Nat. Inst. Pub. Adminstrn.; pres. Fundacion Integracion; legal advisor to Nat. Mortgage Bank and Province of La Rioja Ednl. Coun.; dir. Nat. Inst. Pub. Adminstrn.; pres. 1st Supreme Ct. of Argentine Republic Meeting. Author: Justice, 1984, The Federal System and the Economic Development, 1985, Distribution of Risks in Administrative Contracting Practices, 1990, Narcotraffic, The Tragedy of the End of the Century, 1993, Contract on International Purchase and Sale of Goods, 1994, Social Concertation, Democratic Coincidences, The Relations Between Argentina and the United States, 1989-1995: A New Era, 1996. Mem. Internat. Law Assn., Argentine Coun. for Internat. Rels. (cons. mem.), La Rioja Bar Assn. (v.p.), Argentine Coun. for Fgn. Rels. Office: Ministerio de Justicia, Funcacion Integracion, Sarmiento 440, 1041 Buenos Aires Argentina

GRANLUND, LIS, curator; b. Copenhagen, Feb. 18, 1925; arrived in Sweden, 1947; d. Einar Carl Rosenberg and Thyra Bothilla (Sørensen) R.; m. Nils Torsten Granlund, Dec. 21, 1947; children: Elsebeth Welander-Berggren, Anette Maria Granlund. Certificate, Cambridge (Eng.) U., 1963; BA, Stockholm U., 1966, MA, 1968; PhD, Uppsala (Sweden) U., 1971. Amanuensis Nat. Mus., Stockholm, 1965-66; asst. keeper Stockholms Auktionsverk, 1966-68; curator Nordic Mus., Stockholm, 1968-76; keeper depts. edn., textiles Royal Collections, Sweden, 1976-90; lectr., scientist Stockholm. Author: Jewellery, 1972; contbr. articles to profl. jours. Bd. dirs. DANA Found., Stockholm, 1976-2000; mem. Royal Princely Table Com., 1989—; v.p. Ethnographical Mus. Friends, Stockholm, 1990—; counsellor Denmark's House Found., Stockholm, 1993—. Recipient Order Al Merido Civil, H.M. King of Spain, 1979, Order of Lion, Pres. Finland, 1981, Gold medal Seraphim Class, H.M. King of Sweden, 1985, Order Dannebrog , H.M. Queen of Denmark, 1985. Mem. Scandinavian Mus. Assn., Internat. Coun. Mus. Applied Arts (pres. 1981-88), Swedish Acad. Orgn.

GRANÖ, OLAVI JOHANNES, geography educator; b. Helsinki, Finland, May 27, 1925; s. J. Gabriel and Hilma (Ekholm) G.; m. Eeva Kaleva, 1953; 2 children. Student, Turku and Helsinki U.; PhD, Helsinki U.; PhD (hon.), Torun U., Poland, Abo Akademi, Turku and Tartu, Estonia. Asst. prof. geog. Helsinki U. and Helsinki Sch. Econs., 1948-57; assoc. prof. geog. Turku U., 1958-61, prof., 1962-84, chancellor, 1984-94; pres. Archipelago Rsch. Inst., 1965-84; pres. Finnish Nat. Rsch. Coun. for Scis., 1964-69; pres. Cen. Bd. Rsch. Councs., Acad. Finland, 1970-73; mem. Sci. Policy Coun., 1964-74; pres. Adv. Com. for Rsch. Nordic Coun. Ministers, 1976-82, Coun. of the Inst. Migration, 1987-99, hon. pres., 2000; fellow (one of twelve) Acad. Finland, 1980; vis. fellow Clare Hall, Cambridge U., 1982. Mem. Royal Geog. Soc. (hon. corr.), Acad. Europaea, Geog. Soc. South Sweden (hon.), Geog. Soc. Turku (hon.), Swedish Acad. Scis., Finnish Acad. Scis. (pres. 1994-95). Home: Sirppitie 1A, 20540 Turku Finland Office: Turku U, Dept Geography, 20014 Turku Finland

GRANOTT, NIRA, psychology researcher; b. Petah-Tikva, Israel; came to U.S., 1987; d. Jacob and Celia Granott; children: Guy A. Farber, Bali Farber. MA, Tel Aviv U., 1983; EdM, Harvard U., 1988; PhD, MIT, 1994. Multi-media project dir. Ednl. TV, Tel-Aviv, 1974-80; sr. analyst, software developer Control data Corp., Tel-Aviv, 1983-86; asst. prof. psychology U. Tex. at Dallas, Richardson, 1993-95, 97—, dir. microdevel. lab., 1993—; vis. prof. psychology and lectr. edn. Harvard Grad. Sch. Edn., Cambridge, Mass., 1996-97; grant cons. Harvard U., 1995-96. Co-editor: Microdevelopment-Transition Processes in Development and Learning, 2000. Rsch. grantee NSF, 1999, Tex. Higher Edn. Bd., 2000, Timberlawn Rsch. Found., 1999. Mem. Am. Psychol. Soc., Soc. for Rsch. on Child Devel. Avocations: painting, photography, dancing, yoga. Office: Univ of Texas at Dallas PO Box 830688 Richardson TX 75083-0688

GRANQVIST, HAKAN RAGNAR AXEL, Swedish diplomat; b. Mariestad, Sweden, Jan. 2, 1935; s. K. Ragnar and Lilly (Lundstedt) G.; m. Lilian Sellgren, 1960 (div.); children: Peter R.H., Christian H. BA in Law, U. Uppsala, Sweden, 1960. With Swedish Fgn. Svc., 1961—, asst. under sec., 1979-84; minister plenipotentiary Swedish Embassy, London, 1984-89; amb. to Iran, Swedish Embassy, Teheran, 1989-92; amb. to Argentina, Paraguay and Uruguay, Swedish Embassy, Buenos Aires, 1994-97; amb. to Chile, Swedish Embassy, Santiago, 1997—. Home and Office: UD/Santiago, 10335 Stockholm Sweden

GRANQVIST, RAOUL JOHANNES, English literature educator, writer; b. Karleby, Finland, Jan. 11, 1940; arrived in Sweden, 1967; s. Duvald J. and Karin V. (Wentus) G.; div. 1982; children: Johanna, Tina. MA, Åbo Acad., Finland, 1966; PhD, Uppsala U., Sweden, 1975. Lectr. Haparanda Grammar Sch., Sweden, 1967-76; asst. prof. Luleå U., Sweden, 1976-81; assoc. prof. English lit. Umeå U., Sweden, 1981-97; prof. dept. comm. studies Linkoping U., Sweden, 1997-98; prof. Eng. lit. Umeå U., Sweden, 1998—. Author: The Reputation of John Donne, 1975, Imitation as Resistance, 1995, Revolution's Urban Landscape: Bucharest Culture and Postcommunist Change, 1999; editor: Canonization and Teaching of African Literature, 1990, Major Minorities: English Literature in Transit, 1993, Culture in Africa, 1993, Preserving the Landscape of Imagination: Children's Literature in Africa, 1997, Svenska Överord, 1999. Dep. bd. Amnesty Internat., Sweden, 1978-82. Office: Umeå U, Dept Modern Langs/English, S-90187 Umeå Sweden

GRANROSE, JOHN THOMAS, philosophy, psychology and religion educator; b. Miami, Fla., Nov. 5, 1939; s. Sylvester and Kathryn Irwin (Bradfield) G.; children: Karen, Kathleen, Jonathan. Student, Fla. So. Coll., 1957; BA, U. Miami, 1961; postgrad., U. Heidelberg, Germany, 1961-62; MA, U. Mich., 1963, PhD, 1966. Instr. U. Mich., 1964-66; asst. prof. U. Ga., 1966-71, assoc. prof., 1971-82, prof. philosophy, 1982-93, prof. emeritus, 1993—; tng. candidate, C. G. Jung Inst., Switzerland, 1987-96, dir. studies, 1998—; pres. Western Conf. on Teaching Philosophy, 1976-78; bd. dirs. Ga. Endowment for Humanities, 1982-85. Contbr. articles, revs. to profl. jours.; editor books; editor Newsletter on Tchg. Philosophy, 1976-79. Vestryman Emmanuel Episcopal Ch., 1980-82. Recipient various awards for tchg.; Nat. Woodrow Wilson fellow, Danforth Found. assoc., Fulbright grantee. Mem. Am. Philos. Assn., Am. Pscyhol. Assn., C.J. Jung Soc. of Atlanta, AAUP (pres. U. Ga. chpg. 1971-72), Soc. Values in Higher Edn., Iron Arrow, Blue Key, Phi Kappa Phi, Omicron Delta Kappa. Democrat. Home: Zweiackerstrasse 42, CH-8053 Zurich Switzerland Office: CG Jung Inst, Hornweg 28, CH 8700 Kuesnacht Switzerland

GRANSER, HARALD, geophysicist; b. Vienna, June 15, 1958; s. Gerhardt and Viktoria (Kottbauer) G.; m. Raluca Todorescu, Apr. 16, 1989; children: Laura Letitzia, Sonja Victoria. PhD, U. Vienna, 1983. Rsch. assoc. U. Vienna, 1983-85; sr. geophysicist Robertson Rsch., Llandudno, N. Wales, 1986-90, OMV-AG, Vienna, 1990—; part-time lectr. for geophysics U. Vienna, 1996—. Assoc. editor EAEG, 1988-92, tech. advisor 1992—; contbr. articles to profl. jours. Mem. Soc. Exploration Geophysics, European Assn. of Exploration Geophysicists, Am. Assn. Petroleum Geologists, European Assn. Geoscientists and Engrs., Osterreichische Mineralolverwaltung-Aktiengesellschaft. Avocations: skiing, scuba diving. Home: Schonbrunner Allee 47, A-1120 Vienna Austria Office: OMV-AG, Gerasdorfer Str, A-1210 Vienna Austria

GRANSTRÖM, GÖSTA P.B., physician, researcher; b. Stockholm, Apr. 7, 1950; s. Bertil K.J. and Ingeborg A. (Svensson) G.; m. Elisabeth M.F. Eliason, June 17, 1972 (dec. 1995); children: Monica, Mikael. DDS, U. Gothenburg, Sweden, 1975, MD, 1982, PhD. Rschr. dept. histology Göteborg U., 1970-81; hosp. registrar ENT clin. Mölndal (Sweden) Hosp., 1982-88; clin. tutor ENT Clinic Sahlgrenska Hosp., Gothenburg, 1989-90, cons. ENT Clin., 1990-93, chief phys. ENT div., 1993-99, dir. hyperbaric unit, 1993-99; prof. dept. otolaryngology, head and neck surgery Götenborg U., 1999—; vis. prof. 35 univs., U.S. and Europe, 1988-99; dir. morphological lab. dept. otolaryngology, 1998—. Co-author: Advanced Osseointegration Surgery, 1992, others; author more than 400 sci. articles and papers; mem. editorial bd. Acta Otolaryngol., Stockholm, 1993-99, others. Served to lt. Swedish Air Force, 1982-98. Recipient Pres.'s award Am. Assn. for ENT-Head and Neck Surgery, 1988, Sido prize Societas Orthodontique, Turino, Italy, 1989, Politzer prize, Maastricht, Netherlands, 1991, D. Laskin award, 1999; Linné scholar, Stockholm, 1968. Fellow Royal Soc. Medicine, Scandinavian Assn. for Oral and Maxillofacial Surgery, European Undersea Biomed. Soc., Swedish Med. Assn., Swedish Dental Assn., Swedish Assn. for Otolaryngology; mem. Soc. for Odontology and Stomatology (treas. 1990—). Avocations: scuba diving, downhill skiing, long distance running, gliding, modern music. E-mail: gosta.granstrom@orlss.gu.se. Home: Muraregatan 14, SE-431 66 Mölndal Sweden Office: Sahlgrenska U Hosp, Dept Otolaryngology, S-413 45 Gothenburg Sweden

GRANT, ARTHUR GORDON, JR., lawyer, educator; b. New Orleans, May 16, 1945; s. Arthur Gordon and Martha (McCutchon) G.; children: Arthur Gordon III, Kathryn S., Douglas M. BA, U. N.C., 1967; JD, Tulane U., 1970. Bar: La. 1970, U.S. Ct. Appeals (5th cir.) 1970, U.S. Dist. Ct. (ea. and mid. dists.) La. 1970, U.S. Dist. Ct. (we. dist.) La. 1970, U.S. Ct. Appeals (11th cir.) 1981, U.S. Supreme Ct. 1990, U.S. Dist. Ct. (so. dist.) Tex. 1998. Assoc. Montgomery, Barnett, Brown, Read, Hammond & Mintz, New Orleans, 1970-73, ptnr., 1973—; admiralty and maritime law instr. U. New Orleans Sch. Naval Architecture, 1990—; bd. dirs. Am. Boat and Yacht Coun., Millersville, Md., 1990-98. Author: Recreational Craft, Jurisdiction, Claims and Coverage, 1989; contbg. author: Recreational Boating Law, 1992, Benedict on Admiralty, Vol. 8, 7th edit., 1995. Bd. govs. Propellor Club Port of New Orleans, 1989-90, 92-94. Mem. La. Bar Assn., Soc. Naval Architects and Marine Engrs., Maritime Law Assn. U.S. (vice chmn. recreational boating com. 1990-94), Bar Assn. 5th Fed. Cir., Southeastern Admiralty Law Inst., So. Yacht Club, Thomas More Inn of Ct., Pass Christian Yacht Club. Episcopalian. Avocations: hunting, fishing, boating, Civil War history. E-mail: ggrant@monbar.com. Office: Montgomery Barnett Brown Read Hammond & Mintz 3200 Energy Ctr New Orleans LA 70163

GRANT, DONALD MARCUS, alcohol policy specialist; b. Inverness, U.K., Sept. 21, 1945; came to U.S., 1994; s. George Henry Grant and Kathleen Mary Gilchrist; m. Anne Elizabeth Stephens, 1967 (div. 1987); m. Courtney Mireille O'Connor, Feb. 15, 1992; children: Rachel, Josie, Marika, Kasya. BA, Cambridge (U.K.) U., 1967, DES, 1968, MA, 1970. Dir. Alcohol Edn. Ctr., London, 1973-83; sr. scientist WHO, Geneva, Switzerland, 1984-94; pres. Internat. Ctr. for Alcohol Policies, Washington, 1994—. Author, editor 20 books and numerous articles to profl. jours.; author (as Tom Gilchrist): Committed Agent, 1985. Democrat. Avocations: cross country skiing, fiction, travel. Home: 2506 Cliffborne Pl NW Washington DC 20009-1512 Office: ICAP 1519 New Hampshire Ave NW Washington DC 20036-1203

GRANT, DOUGLAS, publisher; b. Jan. 6, 1918; s. Robert and Ierne G.; m. Enid Whitsey; three children. DLitt, U. St. Andrews. Dir. Bracken House Publs., 1963-67, Port Seton Offset Printers, 1965-75, Br. Jour. Ednl. Psychology, 1970-91; ednl. cons. Scottish Acad. Press Ltd., 1991—. Office: Scottish Acad Press Ltd, 22 Hanover St, Edinburgh Midlothian EH2, Scotland

GRANT, IAN FRASER, magazine and book publisher; b. Wellington, New Zealand, Mar. 15, 1940; s. Colin Fraser and Joyce Edith (Frost) G.; m. Diane Elizabeth Bentley, July 16, 1966; children: Matthew, Nicholas, Katie. BA, Victoria U. of Wellington, 1986. Copywriter, creative dir. Wellington Advt. Agy., 1961-65; founding editl./mktg. dir. Nat. Bus. Rev., Wellington, 1970-83; mktg. dir. New Zealand Book Trade Orgn., Wellington, 1981-83; dir. New Zealand Book Mktg. Coun., Wellington, 1984-86; mktg. dir., bd. dirs. Profile Publs., Auckland, New Zealand, 1986—; pub. cons., then assoc. pub. GP Publs., Wellington, 1987-93; pub. cons. Fraser Books, Masterton, New Zealand, 1984—. Author: Bali: Morning of the World, 1970, Journey Through a Landscape, 1976, The Unauthorized Version (A Cartoon History of New Zealand), 1980, rev. edit., 1987, Out of the Woods (The Restructuring and Sale of New Zealand's State Forests), 1993, North of the Waingawa (Masteron Borough and County Councils 1877-1989), 1995, The Smallfarming Revolution (New Beginnings in Rural New Zealand), 1998, False Prophets (A Light Roasting of New Zealand's Sacred Cows), 1998, Wairarapa, 2000. Founder, chmn. New Zealand Cartoon Archive Trust, Nat. Libr., Wellington, 1992-99, exec. chmn., 2000—; coun. Auckland U. Tech., 2000—. Avocations: golf, organic farming, reading, films.

GRANT, ISABELLA HORTON, retired judge; b. L.A., Sept. 24, 1924; d. John Daniel and Hannabelle (Horton) Grant. BA, Swarthmore Coll., 1944; MA, UCLA, 1946; JD, Columbia U., 1950; LLD (hon.), Molloy Coll., 1976. Jr. profl. asst. OSS, Washington, 1944-45; economist Inst. Indsl. Relations, UCLA, 1946-47, Office Price Stblzn., Los Angeles, 1951-52; ptnr. Livingston, Grant, Stone & Kay, San Francisco, 1953-79; judge Mcpl. Ct., San Francisco, 1979-82, Superior Ct., San Francisco, 1982-97; ret. 1997. Bd. dirs. Kid's Turn, Pocket Opera. Fellow ABA; mem. Am. Arbitration Assn., San Francisco Ethics Commn. (chair 1999), San Francisco Bar Assn. (bd. dirs. 1978-79), Acad. Matrimonial Lawyers (pres. No. Calif. chpt. 1976), Assn. Family and Conciliation Cts. (pres. Calif. chpt. 1987-89), Nat. Coll. Probate Judges, Queen's Bench (pres. 1964), Calif. Tennis Club, Phi Beta Kappa.

GRANT, JOAN JULIEN, artist, poet; b. Cornwall, Ont., Can., Apr. 15, 1934; d. John Duncan Julien and Winnifred Josephine McCormick; m. Douglas MacDougal Grant, Sept. 24, 1955; children: Stephen John, Ann Elizabeth, D. Arakaki, Abigail Jennifer, David King. AA, West L.A. C.C., 1975; BFA, Otis Art Inst., 1977, MFA, 1979. Instr. Plymouth (N.H.) State Coll., 1998. Author, editor: Terrestis, 1995. Mem. CLCC Citizens for a Livable Culver City, 1998-2000. Avocations: reading, book discussion groups, walking, hiking. Home: 4274 LeBourget Ave Culver City CA 90232

GRANT, JOHN M., civil engineer; b. Inverness, Scotland, June 20, 1936; s. Donald and Euphemia (MacCallum) G.; m. Moira Burgess; children: Christy, Grigor, Rory. Diploma in tech., Heriot Watt U., Edinburgh, Scotland, 1956, Imperial Coll., London, 1972. Engr. Logan Contracting, U.K., 1956-60, Ove Arup, Edinburgh, 1961-65, Alexander Gibb, Nairobi, Kenya, 1965-72, Ove Arup, U.K., 1972-80; assoc. Ove Arup Partnership, U.K., 1980-95; gen. mgr. Arup Hellas, Athens, Greece, 1995—. Avocations: counseling, private pilot. Office: Arup Hellas, Craigellachie, Strathpeffer 1V14 9BW, United Kingdom

GRANT, LEE (LYOVA HASKELL ROSENTHAL), actress, television and film director; b. N.Y.C., Oct. 31, 1931; d. A.W. and Witia (Haskell) Rosenthal; m. Arnold Manoff (dec.); 1 dau., Dinah; m. Joseph Feury; 1 dau., Belinda. Student, Julliard Sch. Music, Neighborhood Playhouse Sch. Theatre, Met. Opera Ballet Sch. Stage debut as child in L'arocolo, Met. Opera House, N.Y.C., 1934; Broadway appearances include Detective Story (Critics Circle award 1949), Lo and Behold, A Hole in the Head, Wedding Breakfast; toured with The Maids (Obie award), Electra, Silk Stockings, St. Joan, Arms and the Man, Prisoner of Second Avenue; with road co. Two for the Seesaw, The Captains and the Kings, N.Y. Shakespeare Festival; motion pictures include Detective Story, 1952 (best actress Cannes Film Festival), Storm Fear, 1956, Middle of the Night, 1959, Affair of the Skin, The Balcony, 1963, Divorce American Style, 1967, Valley of the Dolls, In the Heat of the Night, 1968, Marooned, 1970, There Was a Crooked Man, 1970, The Landlord, 1970, Plaza Suite, 1971, Shampoo, 1975 (Acad. award for best supporting actress), Voyage of the Damned, 1976, Airport '77, 1977, The Swarm, 1978, The Mafu Cage, 1978, Damien-Omen II, 1978, When You Comin' Back, Red Ryder, 1979, Little Miss Marker, 1980, Charles Chan and the Curse of the Dragon Queen, 1981, Visiting Hours, 1982, Teachers, 1984, The Big Town, 1987, Defending Your Life, 1991, Under Heat, 1994, The Substance of Fire, 1996, It's My Party, 1996, The Amati Girls, 2000, Dr. T and the Women, 2000; TV series include Search for Tomorrow, 1953-54, Fay, 1975, Peyton Place (Emmy award for best supporting actres 1966), White Fang, 1993, Mulholland Drive, 1999; TV movies include Night Slaves, 1970, The respectfull Prostitute (BBC), Neon Ceiling (Emmy award), Ransom for a Dead Man, Lieutenant Shuster's Wife, 1972, Partners in Crime, 1973, What Are Best Friends For?, 1973, Perilous Voyage, 1976, The Spell, 1977, The Million Dollar Face, 1981, For Ladies Only, 1981, Thou Shalt Not Kill, 1982, Bare Essence, 1982, Will There Really Be A Morning?, 1983, The Highjacking of the Achille Lauro, 1989, She Said No, 1990, Something to Live For: The Allison Gertz Story, 1992, In My Daughter's Name, 1992, Citizen Cohn, 1992 (Emmy nomination, Supporting Actress -

miniseries, 1993); dir. TV spl. Shape of Things, 1973; dir. play Private View, 1983; dir. (feature film) Tell Me A Riddle, 1980, Women of Willmar, 1982, Feature A Matter of Sex, 1983, Nobody's Child, 1986 (Dirs. Guild Am. award), Down and Out in America, 1987 (Acad. award), No Place Like Home, 1989, (feature comedy) Staying Together, 1989; dir. documentary Women on Trial, 1992, Breast Cancer Say it! Fight it! Cure it!, 1997; dir. TV film Season's of the Heart, 1994, Reunion, 1994, Sing Me The Blues, Lena, 1994. Recipient Congl. Arts Caucus award U.S. Govt., 1983, Lifetime Achievement award Women in Film, 1989.

GRANT, MALCOLM JOHN, law and economics educator, writer; b. Oamaru, New Zealand, Nov. 29, 1947; s. Francis William and Vera Jessica (Cooke) G.; m. Christine Endersbee, July 13, 1974; Nikolas, Joanna, Thomas. LLB, U. Otago, New Zealand, 1970; LLM, U. Otago, 1973, LLD, 1986. Barrister and solicitor, New Zealand, 1970. Lectr. law Otago U., New Zealand, 1971-72, Southampton U., New Zealand, 1972-86; prof. law U. Coll. London, 1986-91; prof. land economy Cambridge U., 1991—; profl. fellow Clare Coll., Cambridge, Eng., 1991—; chmn. U.K. Agr. and Environment Biotech. Commn., 2000—. Author: Urban Planning Law, 1982, Permitted Development, 1996, Singapore Planning Law, 1999, Environmental Court Report, 2000; editor: Ency. of Planning Law and Practice, 6 vols., 1981—; co-editor: Ency. of Environ. Law, 8 vols., 1992—. Chmn. Local Govt. Commn. for Eng., 1996—. Mem. Royal Inst. Chartered Surveyors (hon.), Royal Town Planning Inst. (hon., Barrister Middle Temple 1998—). Avocations: music, opera, electronic gadgets. Office: Clare Coll, Cambridge CB2 1TL, England

GRANT, SIR MATTHEW ALISTAIR, food products company executive; b. Mar. 6, 1937; s. John and Jessie G.; m. Judith Mary Dent, 1963; three children. With Unilever, 1958-63, J. Lyons, 1963-65, Connell May & Steavenson, 1965-68; dir. Fine Fare, 1968-72; mng. dir. Oriel Foods, 1973-77; chmn. Safeway (formerly Argyll Group), England, 1977-96; chair, CEO Safeway (formerly Argyll Group), 1988-93, chair, 1993-96; gov. Bank of Scotland, 1998-99, chmn. Scottish & Newcastle plc, 1997-2000, now dep. chmn.;vis. prof. Sterling U., 1984-91, Strathclyde U., 1994—; chmn. food policy com. Retail Consortium, 1986-89; bd. dirs. Mktg. Coun., 1995—, vice chmn., 1996—; adv. com. Listed Cos., 1990-93; mem. coun. Scottish Coun. Devel. & Industry, 1994-98. Pres. Nat. Grocers Benevolent Fund, 1987-89; trustee Nat. Mus. Scotland, 1991—. Mem. Inst. Grocery Distbn. (pres. 1991-92), Advt. Assn. (pres. 1989-93). Avocations: books, paintings, horses. Office: Scottish & Newcastle PC, 50 E Fettes Ave, Edinburgh EH4 1RR, Scotland

GRANT, MERWIN DARWIN, lawyer; b. Safford, Ariz., May 7, 1944; s. Darwin Dewey and Erma (Whiting) G.; m. Charlotte Richey, June 27, 1969; children: Brandon, Taggart, Christian, Brittany. BA in Econs., Brigham Young U., 1968; JD, Duke U., 1971. Bar: Ariz. 1971, U.S. Dist. Ct. Ariz., U.S. Dist. Ct. (we. dist.) Tex., U.S. Ct. Appeals (5th, 7th, 8th, 9th and 10th cirs.), U.S. Tax Ct., U.S. Supreme Ct. Pres. Merwin D. Grant, P.C., Phoenix, 1977—; ptnr. Beus, Gilbert & Morrill, Phoenix, 1984-93; pres. Grant, Williams & Dangerfield P.C., Phoenix, 1994—. Guest condr. Phoenix Symphony Orch., 1989. Bd. dirs. Grand Canyon coun. Boy Scouts Am., Phoenix, 1974-76, Maricopa Hosp., Health Sys. Bd., 1997—, Ariz. Motorsports Charitable Found.; pres., bd. dirs. Golden Gate Settlement, Phoenix, 1975-80, 84-88, Phoenix Internat. Raceway Charities, Ariz. Acad. Decathalon Assn., exec. com., 1999—; charter mem. Rep. Presl. Task Force, Washington, 1984—; exec. bd.dirs. Ariz. Acad. Decathlon Assn., 1999—. Fellow Ariz. Bar Found.; mem. ABA (litigation sect.), Assn. Trial Lawyers Am., Kiwanis (bd. dirs. Phoenix chpt. 1972-79). E-mail: grant@phxlaw.com. Office: Grant Williams & Dangerfield 302 N 1st Ave Phoenix AZ 85003-1500

GRANT, MICHAEL, retired university president, author; b. London; arrived in Italy, 1966; s. Maurice Harold and Muriel Ethel (Jörgensen) G.; m. Rut Anne-Sophie Beskow, Aug. 2, 1994; children: Jan Patrick Michael, Antony Harold. Litt.D, Trinity Coll., Cambridge, Eng., 1936; LLD (hon.), D. Litt. (hon.). Fellow Trinity Coll., Cambridge, 1938-49; rep. Brit. Coun., Turkey, 1948-45; dep. dir. European divsn. Brit. Coun., 1945-48; prof. humanity Edinburgh (Scotland) U., 1938-49; vice chancellor U. Khartoum, 1946-48; pres., vice chancellor Queen's U., Belfast, No. Ireland, 1948-59. Author numerous books including Constantine the Great, 1993-94, The Greek and Roman Historians, 1995. Capt. Brit. Army, 1939-40. Decorated Order of Brit. Empire, comdr. Brit. Empire, Premio del Mediverraneo, Florence, Premio, Mazara del Vallo, Italy, 1983, Pres.'s Gold Medal for Edn., Sudan, 1977. Mem. Am. Numismatic Soc. (corr.), Royal Numismatic Soc. (past pres.), Virgil Soc. (past pres.).

GRANT, MICHAEL ERNEST, educational administrator, institutional management educator; b. L.A., June 6, 1952; s. Ernest Grant and Shirley Ruth (George) G. BA in Spanish, Calif. State U., Long Beach, 1974, MA in Edn. Adminstrn., 1978; EdD, Pepperdine U., 1984. Cert. elem., secondary, and community coll. tchr., bilingual and cross-cultural edn., adminstr. Tchr. kindergarten through adult edn. Long Beach Unified Sch. Dist., 1975-83, tchr. 5th grade, 1975, tchr. 6th grade, 1975-76, bilingual multicultural specialist, 1976-78, tchr. 6th, 7th and 8th grades, 1978-79, mgmt. program specialist, 1979-80, adminstr., program specialist, 1980-81, vice prin., 1981-83; asst. prof. tchr. edn. Calif. State U., San Bernardino, 1986-88; prin. dir. IMPACT/TEACH, assoc. prof. ednl. psychology and adminstrn. Calif. State U., Long Beach, 1988-91; pres., founder Mykulphone-An Empowerment Through Edn. Project, Beverly Hills, 1991—; Spanish instr. Calif. Disting. Sch., Beverly Hills, 1993—; asst. part-time instr. tchr. edn. Grad. Sch. Edn., Calif. State U., Long Beach, 1983-86; pres., CEO Mykulphone, 1999—. Contbr. articles to profl. jours. Pepperdine U. scholar, 1983-84; Calif. State U. grantee, 1988-89, 89-90, 89-91. Mem. NEA, Assn. Calif. Sch. Adminstrs., Nat. Assn. Tchr. Educators, Nat. Coun. States In-Svc. Edn., Nat. Black Congress Faculty, Calif. Faculty Assn., Calif. State Intersegmental Coordination Coun., Calif. Black Faculty and Staff Assn., Calif. Assn. Tchr. Educators, Calif. Edn. Rsch. Assn., Intersegmental Coordinating Coun. Democrat. Baptist. Avocations: Shotokon karate (black belt), acting, dancing, singing, songwriting. Home and Office: Ste 1220 270 N Cañon Dr Beverly Hills CA 90210-9999

GRANT, NANCY MARIE, marketing professional, journalist; b. Tilden, Nebr., Jan. 2, 1941; d. William Gerald and Evelyn Marie (Baughman) Whitford; m. Marvin Ostberg, 1961 (div. 1969); children: Jill Marie Ostberg Bennett, Carrie Ostberg Chun; m. Richard Grant, 1973 (div. 1975). BA in Journalism, U. Nebr., 1963; postgrad., U. Oreg., 1968; MBA, Portland State U., 1978; postgrad., U. Wash., 1979-83; diploma, Bailie Sch. Broadcasting, Seattle, 1984; postgrad., Seattle Cen. C.C., 1992, Computer & Bus. Tng. Inst., Bellevue, Wash., 1993. Internship gen. assignment reporter Lincoln (Nebr.) Jour., 1962-63; asst. state editor Lexington (Ky.) Leader, 1963; freelance writer Shreveport Times, AP, Natchatoches, La., 1964; info. rep. 1 & 2 Univ. Oreg. News Bur., Old Oreg. Alumni Mag., Faculty Staff Newsletter, Eugene, 1965-70; dir. pub. rels. U. Portland, Oreg., 1971; info. rep. 3 Oreg. Hwy. Div. and Motor Vehicles, 1972-77; founder, bus. mgr. Grant Mktg., Seattle, 1979; exec. dir., founder Wash. Neurol. Alliance, Seattle, 1985—. Editor U. Oreg. Faculty-Staff Newsletter, 1969; editor, writer U. Portland Alumni Mag., 1970, Hwy Newsletter and film, 1971-77. Lobbyist, newsletter editor Wash. Neurol. Alliance; mem. Gov.'s Com. on Disability Issues and Employment, 1983-86; bd. dirs. Wash. Assembly, 1983-86, Highland Community Ctr., Bellevue, Wash., 1984-86. Recipient Hearst award, 1963, No. 1 in country for hwy. pub. affairs event, 1973. Mem. NAFE, LWV (Seattle and Princeton, N.J.), Am. Assn. Women Bus. Owners (Seattle and Princeton), Internat. Platform Assn. Democrat. Unitarian. Avocations: hiking, climbing, bicycling, swimming. Home and Office: Nassau Arms Apts 285 Franklin Ave Princeton NJ 08540-2716

GRANT, PHYLLIS MOORE, elementary education educator; b. Gordonsville, Ala.; d. William Jr. and Millie James (Black) Moore; m. James Grant, Sept. 5, 1970 (div. July 1987; children: Valarie Joy, Anne Sajo. BS in Music Edn., Ala. State U., Montgomery, 1964; MA in Elem. Edn., Eastern Mich. U., 1972, MA in Music Edn., 1978; EdS, Oakland U., Rochester, Mich., 1980; MA in Ednl. Adminstrn., Eastern Mich. U., 1992; PhD, Columbia Pacific U., 1996, EdD, 1997. Cert. elem. and secondary tchr., ednl. adminstr., Mich. Sec. Alpha Alpha chpt. Gamma Phi Delta Sorority Alpha Alpha chpt., Montgomery, 1964-67; union rep. Huron Valley Assn., Milford, Mich., 1986-90; sec. Ala. State U. Alumni, Detroit, 1992—; test coord. Huron Valley Schs./Oxbow Elem. Sch., White Lake, Mich., 1990—; tchr. Huron Valley Sch. Dist., Highland, Mich., 1967—; tutor-tchr. Marygrove Coll., White Lake, 1967—. Sunday sch. tchr. New Hope Missionary Bapt. Ch., Southfield, Mich., 1977—, pianist, 1985—, dir., 1987—, coord. Sunday sch. programs, 1988—. Mem. ASCD, AAUW, Mich. Edn. Assn. (Svc. award 1986, 88), Huron Valley Edn. Assn. (Merit award 1974, 77), Nat. Staff Devel. Coun., Gamma Phi Delta sorority (Alpha Theta chpt.). Avocations: singing, reading, travel, volleyball, writing poetry. Home: 27076 Aberdeen St Southfield MI 48076-3667 Office: Huron Valley Schs 100 Oxbow Lake Rd White Lake MI 48386-2621

GRANT, ROSS ALAN, banker; b. Waimate, New Zealand, Apr. 1, 1947; arrived in Australia, 1970; s. Raymond Errol and Winifred Margaret (Judge) G.; m. Josephine Mary Boney, Apr. 23, 1983. BS with honors, Otago (New Zealand) U., 1967; M of Commerce with honors, Canterbury U., 1969; MBA, U. NSW, Sydney, Australia, 1975. Sys. analyst Comalco Ltd., 1971-73, project analyst, 1973-75; dir. Macquarie Bank Ltd., Sydney, 1975-86; exec. chmn. Jonray Holdings Ltd., Sydney, 1986-88; dir. Grant Samuel & Assocs. Pty. Ltd., Sydney, 1988—; chmn. Byvest Advisors Group, Sydney, 1986—; dep. chmn. Sydney Aquarium Ltd., 1993—. Author: Guide to Management Buy-Outs in Australia and New Zealand, 1987. Avocations: skiing, wine. Home: 10 Loombah Rd Dover Heights, Sydney 2030 NSW, Australia Office: Grant Samuel & Assocs Pty Ltd, Level 30/52 Martin Pl, Sydney 2000 NSW, Australia

GRANT, RUSSELL PORTER, JR., lawyer; b. Ft. Sill, Okla., Nov. 5, 1943; s. Russell Porter and Jimmie (Bell) G.; m. Janice Rae Lockley, Nov. 19, 1966; 1 child, Russell Porter III. BS, U.S. Mil. Acad., 1966; JD, U. Miss., 1974. Bar: Miss. 1974, U.S. Dist. Ct. (no. dist.) Miss. 1974, U.S. Ct. Appeals (5th cir.) 1980, U.S. Dist. Ct. (so. dist.) Miss. 1992. Ptnr. Patterson & Patterson, Aberdeen, Miss., 1974-80; petroleum landman Aberdeen, 1980-81; ops. landman Hughes & Hughes Oil and Gas, Jackson, Miss., 1981-84; mgr. gas contracts Hughes Ea. Petroleum, Ltd., Jackson, 1984-88; corp. counsel Hughes Ea. Petroleum, Inc., Jackson, 1988-89; pvt. practice Jackson, 1989-90, 91; assoc. Overstreet & Kuykendall, Jackson, 1990-91; ptnr. McKibben, Grant & Assocs., Jackson, 1991-95; mem. legal com. Interstate Oil and Gas Compact Commn., Oklahoma City, 1992—; speaker Oil and Gas Inst., U. Ala., 1990, natural gas seminar Miss. Natural Gas Assn., 1986. Co-chair exec. com. Monroe County Rep. Party, Aberdeen, 1980; pres. Aberdeen Exch. Club, 1978-79; mem. Monroe County (Miss.) Port Authority, 1979-80. Capt. U.S. Army, 1966-72. Named Outstanding Com. Chair, Aberdeen C. of C., 1979. Mem. Miss. Oil and Gas Lawyers (pres. 1986-87), Miss. Assn. Petroleum Landmen (v.p. 1987-88, pres. 1994-95), Miss. Bar (chmn. natural resources sect. 1988-89), Am. Assn. Profl. Landmen (cert. profl. landman), The Federalist Soc., Nat. Lawyers Assn. Episcopalian. Avocations: art, architecture, gardening, music, history. Home and Office: 1818 Aztec Dr Jackson MS 39211-6503

GRANT, SUSAN IRENE, lawyer; b. N.Y.C., Apr. 27, 1953; d. Walter Arnold and Beatrice L. (Thalheimer) G.; m. Brian A. King, June 24, 1990; 1 child, Alexander Grant King. BA, NYU, 1974; JD, Columbia U., 1977. Bar: N.Y. 1978, U.S. Dist. Ct. (so. and ea. dists.) N.Y. 1978. Assoc. Law Offices of Rita Eredics, Esq., Flushing, N.Y., 1977-78; staff atty. The Dreyfus Corp., N.Y.C., 1978-85; asst. gen. counsel Prudential-Bache Securities Inc., N.Y.C., 1985-89, asst. v.p., 1986-89; asst. gen. counsel, assoc. v.p. Prudential Mut. Fund Mgmt., Inc., N.Y.C., 1987-89; asst. counsel First Investors Corp., N.Y.C., 1989-94; sr. counsel, chief compliance officer Royce & Assocs., N.Y.C., 1994-96; sr. atty. Van Eck Assocs. Corp., N.Y.C., 1996-98, Weil, Gotshal & Manges LLP, N.Y.C., 1998—. Mem. ABA, N.Y. State Bar Assn. Home: 11045 Queens Blvd Forest Hills NY 11375-5501 Office: Weil Gotshal & Manges LLP 767 5th Ave New York NY 10153-0119

GRANTHAM, KIRK PINKERTON, lawyer, insurance company executive; b. Tupelo, Miss., Oct. 12, 1941; s. Homer Kirk and Lucile (Pinkerton) G.; m. Damaris Dodson, Aug. 25, 1964 (div. 1980); 1 child, Dodson Kirk; m. Cheryl Norman, Apr. 25, 1983; 1 child, Tyler Kirk. B in Pub. Adminstrn., U. Miss., 1963, JD, 1966. Bar: Miss. 1966, Fla. 1971; cert. real property law and wills, trusts and estate planning. Estate tax atty. IRS, W. Palm Beach, Fla., 1966-72; ptnr. Day, Grantham & Hess, Lake Worth, Fla., 1972-81; assoc. Shutts & Bowen, Lake Worth, 1981-86; pvt. practice, West Palm Beach, 1986—; pres. Std. Title Ins. Agy., Inc., West Palm Beach. Pres. Palm Beach County Heart Assn., 1991. Sgt. USAR, 1966-72. Recipient Leadership award YMCA, 1987. Mem. Fla. Bar Assn., ABA, Miss. Bar Assn., Lake Worth Bar Assn. (pres. 1978), Tuskawillow Club. Republican. Episcopalian. Office: 1860 Forest Hill Blvd West Palm Beach FL 33406-6086

GRANTSEV, VLADIMIR IVANOVICH, physicist; b. Jcherbinino, USSR, Sept. 13, 1943; s. Ivan Arsentievich Grantsev and Sofia Dmitrievna Pavelko; m. Ludmila Andreevna Murashko, Aug. 9, 1971; children: Ivan, Dmitri. Grad., Kyiv State U., USSR, 1965; postgrad., Inst. Physics, Kyiv, 1968; D in Physics, Inst. Nuclear Rsch., Kyiv, 1977; grad., Kyiv High Mgmt. U., 1989. Engr. Inst. Physics, 1965-70; sci. group leader Inst. Nuclear Rsch., 1970-78, sr. scientist collaborator, 1978-84, chief engr. accelerator, 1984-94, accelerator lab. leader, 1994-96, sr. scientist collaborator, 1996—. Author: Applied Nuclear Spectroscopy, 1971, Problems of Nuclear Physics and Cosmic Rays, 1986, A Man and Christian World Out-look, 1997; contbr. articles to profl. jours. Sr. lt. USSR Army, 1971-73. Recipient 1500 Age of Kyiv medal, 1982, Veteran of Work medal, 1995. Mem. N.Y. Acad. Scis. Avocations: tourism, plane gliding, piloting plane, parachute jumping. Home: Geroev Dripra St 30 #11, 254214 Kyiv Ukraine Office: Inst Nuclear Rsch, prosp Nauki 47, 252028 Kyiv Ukraine

GRANZOTTI, JOÃO ANTONIO, pediatrics educator; b. Franca, Brazil, May 14, 1942; s. Antonio and Delma Martins Granzotti; m. Clélia Agostini, Jan. 6, 1968; children: Fábio, Leandro. MD, U. São Paulo, Ribeirão Prêto, Brazil, 1968, MS, 1973, PhD, 1975. Cert. pediat. cardiology. Intern U. Sao Paulo Hosp., 1968; resident Ribeirão Preto U. Sch. Medicine, São Paulo, 1969-70; rsch. assoc. U. Ill., Chgo., 1982-83; prof. dept. pediat. faculty medicine Hosp. das Clinicas Campus, U. São Paulo, Ribeirão Prêto, 1975—. Contbr. articles to profl. jours. Fellow Am. Acad. Pediat.; mem. Pediat. Soc. Avocation: tennis. Home: Rua Guarantã 356, 14040-190 Ribeirão Prêto SP, Brazil Office: U São Paulo Dept Peds, Av Bandeirantes 3900, 14040-900 Ribeirão Prêto SP, Brazil

GRARDEL, BRUNO EDWARD, physician; b. Cambrai, Nord, France, Oct. 27, 1959; s. Francis and Chantal (Boutry) G.; m. Florence Campion, Mar. 27, 1981; children: Germain, Victor, Sidonie, Alice, Felix. BS, Baudimont, Arras, France, 1977; Internat., Hosp. and Univ. Ctr., Lille, France, 1983. MD. Intern Hosp. Lille, 1983-87, Hosp. Angers, France, 1985, Hosp. Paris, 1986; adjoint chief of svc. Hosp. Berck, France, 1987-95; rheumatologist Office Arras, France, 1995—; rheumatologist Hosp. Berck, 1987-95; rschr. in biomaterials, Bone Rsch. Inst., Berck, 1987-95. Contbr. articles to profl. jours. Pres. Bleriot Club, Le Touquet, 1990-95. Mem. Soc. Francaise de Rhumatologie. Roman Catholic. Avocation: sand yachting. Fax: 03 21 71 97 39. Office: 16 Rue D Amiens, 62000 Arras France

GRAS, PIM WILLEM, radio producer, journalist, jazz historian; b. Amsterdam, The Netherlands, Dec. 16, 1933; s. Simon Petrus and Jozina Wilhelmina (Jongeneel) G.; m. Christina Petronella Rappange, Mar. 14, 1959; children: Thijs, Caroline. Grad. in tchg., Kweekschool, Amsterdam, 1954. Tchr., Amsterdam, 1954-61; newsreader, editor ANP/NOS, Hilversum, The Netherlands, 1961-91; jazz producer NOS Radio, Hilversum, 1968-93; japp producer Concertzender, Amsterdam/Hilversum, 1993—; bd. dirs. Dutch Jazz Archive, Amsterdam, 1980—; clarinet, saxophone player in traditional jazz bands. Author: Jazz uit het historisch archief, 1974; chief editor NJA Bull., 1991—; contbr. articles to Dutch jazz periodicals; recorded with The New Orleans Seven, 1956-58, Charley's novelty orch. The Crwths, 1967-68, Spiegle Willcox, 1992, 94. Office: Dutch Jazz Archive, Prins Hendrikkade 142, 1011 AT Amsterdam The Netherlands

GRASCHEW, GEORGI BORISLAWOW, natural scientist, chemist, coordinator; b. Samokov, Bulgaria, July 2, 1946; arrived in Germany, 1987; s. Borislav and Vera (Genev) G.; m. Penka Dimitrowa, Jan. 14, 1975; 1 child, Borislawa. Grad., Tech. U. Dresden, 1973, Dr. Rer. Nat., 1974. Sci. asst. Nat. Cancer Ctr., Bulgaria, 1974-81, 84-86; project coord. Inst. Medicine, KfA, Jülich, Germany, 1982-83; sci. coord. various projects German Cancer Rsch. Ctr., 1987-92; with surg. rsch. unit OP 2000 Robert Roessle Clinic, Max Delbrueck Ctr. Molecular Medicine, Berlin, 1993—; patentee in field. Contbr. articles to profl. jours. Mem. Internat. Photodynamic Assn., Max Delbrueck Club Molecular Medicine. Avocations: music, painting. E-mail: graschew@mdc-berlin.de. Office: SRU OP2000 Robert Roessle Clinic Chante Humboldt Univ, Lindenberger Weg 80, 13122 Berlin Germany

GRASHCHENKOV, SERGEY IVANOVICH, physics educator; b. Leninsk-Kuznetsk, Russia, June 19, 1961; s. Ivan Sergeevich and Valentina Nikanorovna (Tatarenkova) G.; m. Natalia Eugenevna Panskova, July 10, 1982; children: Margarita, Elena. Diploma, Pedagogical Inst., Smolensk, 1983; Candidate Sci., Pedagogical Inst., Moscow, 1990. Tchr. Gagarin, Russia, 1983-86, Pskov (Russia) Pedagogical Inst., 1990—. Avocation: aikido. Office: Pskov Pedagogical Inst, Faculty Physics & Math, 180760 Pskov Russia

GRASHIN, ANATOLIY FEODOROVICH, physicist, educator; b. Moscow, May 6, 1932; s. Feodor Georgievich Grashin and Antonina Ivanovna Aleeva; m. Nataly Pavlovna Andrusenko, Nov. 4, 1972 (div.); children: Sergey, Olga, Varvara; m. Maria Pavlovna Andrusenko, May 8, 1992; 1 child, Peter. MS, Moscow Engring. Physics Inst., 1956, DSc, 1960; D in Physics and Math., Higher Attestation Commn. USSR, 1970. Cert. prof. theoretical physics Higher Attestation Commn. USSR, 1972. Asst. prof. Moscow Engring. Physics Inst., 1956, lectr., 1956-59, head of rsch., 1977—; sci. worker Inst. for Theoretical and Exptl. Physics, Moscow, 1959-66; prof. Moscow Regional Pedagogical Inst., 1966-77; mem. methodol. coun. Ministry of Edn., USSR, 1969-78, tech. coun., 1983-88; mem. expert coun. Univ. People's Friendship of Russia, 1978—. Author: Quantum Mechanics, 1974; contbr. articles to profl. jours. Mem. Soc. ZNANIE (methodol. coun. 1970-80), N.Y. Acad. Scis. Avocations: sports, classical music. Fax: 7-095-324-21-11. E-mail: grashin@cyber.mephi.ru. Office: Moscow Engring Physics Inst, Kashirskoe sh 31, 115409 Moscow Russia

GRASS, GÜNTER (WILHELM), writer; b. Danzig, Oct. 16, 1927; m. Anna Margareta Grass, 1954; children: Franz, Raoul, Laura, Bruno; m. Ute Grunert, 1979. Studied sculpture with Sepp Magesh, painting with Otto Pankok, Kunstakademie, Dusseldorf, 1949; studied sculpture with Sepp Mages, painting with Otto Pankok, Acad. Fine Arts, Berlin, 1953; D.H.C. (hon.), Kenyon Coll., Berlin, 1965, Harvard U., Berlin, 1976. Began as a writer of poems, dramatic scenes, also worked as a drummer and washboard accompanist with jazz band; lectr., reader Harvard U., Yale U., Smith Coll., Goethe House, Poetry Center YM-YWHA, 1964. Author: (plays) Hochwasser, 1957, Onkel, Onkel, 1958, Noch Zehn Minuten bis Buffalo, 1959, Beritten und Zurück, 1959, Die bösen Köche, 1961, Goldmäuchen, 1964, Die Plebejer Proben den Aufstand, 1966, Four Plays, 1967, Davor, 1969, Theaterspiele, 1970, Die Blechtrommel als Film, 1979; (fiction) Die Blechtrommel, 1959, Katz und Maus, 1961, Hundejahre, 1963, Geschichten, 1968, Örtlich betäubt, 1969, Aus dem Tagebuch einer Schnecke, 1972, Der Butt, 1977, Das Treffen in Telgte, 1979, Kopfgeburten; oder die Deutschen sterben aus, 1980, Die Rättin, 1986, Tierschutz, 1990, Unkenrufe, 1992; (poetry) Die Vorzüge der Windhühner, 1956, Gleisdreieck, 1960, Selected Poems, 1966, März, 1966, Ausgefragt, 1967, Danach, 1968, Die Schweinekop Fsülze, 1969, Gesammelte Gedichte, 1971, Mariazuehren/Hommageàmarie Inmary praise, 1973, Liebe geprüft, 1974, Mit Sophie in die Pilze gegangen, 1976, In the Egg and Other Poems, 1977, Kinderlied: Verse and Etchings, 1982, Nachruf auf einen Handschuh, 1982, Ach, Butt, dein Mächen geht böseaus, 1983, Mädchen, pfeif auf den Prinzenl, 1984, Aua, zum Fürchten Mannomann, 1985, Gedichte, 1985, Die Rättin, 1985, Die Gedichte 1955-1986, 1988, Tierschutz, 1990; (screenplays) Katz und Maus, 1967, Die Blechtrommel, 1979; (ballet scenarios) Fünf Köche, 1957, Stoffreste, 1959, Die Vogel Scheuchen, 1970; (radio plays) Zweiunddrei ssig Zähne, 1959, Noch Zehn Minuten nach Buffalo, 1962, Eine öffentliche Diskussion, 1963, Die Plebejer proben den Aufstand, 1966, Hochwasser, 1977; (others) Die Ballerina, 1963, Rede über das Selbstverständliche, 1965, Der Fall Axel C. Springer am Beispiel Arnold Zweig, 1967, Briefe Überdie Grenze, 1968, Über meinen Lehrer Döblin und andere Vorträge, 1968, Über das Selbstverständliche, 1968, Dokumente zur politischen Wirkung, 1971, Der Schriftsteller al Bürger-eine Siebenjahresbilanz, 1973, Der Bürger und seine Stimme, 1974, Denkzettel: Politische Reden und Aufsätze 1965-76, 1978, Aufsätze zur Literatur, 1980, Zeichnen und Schreiben das bildnerische Werk des Schriftstellers Günter Grass (2 vols.), 1983-85, Die Vernichtung der Menschheit hat begonnen, 1983, Widerstand lernen: Politische Gegenreden, 1980-1983, 1984, On Writing and Politics 1967-1983, 1985, Erfolgreiche Musterreden für den Bürgermeister, 1986, In Kupfer, auf Stein, 1986, Werkausgabe in zehn Bänden (10 vols.), 1987, Es war einmal ein Land, 1987, Zunge Zeigen, 1988, Skizzenbuch, 1989, Meine grüne Wiese: Kurzprosa, 1989, Wenn wir von Europa Sprechen: ein Dialog, 1989, Alptraum und Hoffnung, 1989, Deutscher Lastenausgleich, 1990, Totes Holz: ein Nachruf, 1990, Deutschland, einig Vaterland? Ein Streitgespräch, 1990, Er Folgreiche Mustergrussworte und Musterbriefe für Bürgermeister und Kommunalpolitiker, 1990, Droht der deutsche Einheitsstaat?, 1990, Ein Schnäppchen namens DDR, 1990, Schreiben nach Auschwitz, 1990, Gegen die verstreichende Zeit, 1991, Vier Jahrzehnte, 1991. Served with German Mil. Service, 1943-45. Recipient Süddeutscher Rund Funk Lyrikpreis, 1955, Gruppe 47, 1958, City of Bremen prize, 1959, Critics prize, Germany, 1960, Fgn. Book prize, France, 1962, Büchner prize, 1965, Fontaine prize, 1968, Heuss prize, 1969, Mondello prize, Palermo, 1977, Carl von Ossiersky medal, 1977, Internat. Lit. award, 1978, Viareggio-Versilia prize, 1978, Majkowski medal, 1978, Vienna Lit. prize, 1980, Feltrinelli prize, 1982, Leonhard Frank Ring, 1988, Karel Capek prize Czech Republic, 1994, Nobel prize for Lit., 1999. Mem. Berlin Acad. Fine Arts. Roman Catholic.

GRASSER, KARL-HEINZ, minister of finance; b. Klagenfurt, Jan. 2, 1969. M Social and Econ. Scis., U. Klagenfurg, 1992. Mgr. European integration and tourism Austrian Freedom Party, 1992-93, sec. gen., 1993-94; 2d dep. gov. in charge of tourism, trade and industry Carinthia; dist. party chief City of Klagenfurt, 1996-98; v.p. joint appli8cation com. Carinthia, Friuli-Julia-Venetia and Slovenia, 1998; fed. min. finance Austria, 2000—. Office: Fed Ministry Fin, Himmelpfortgasse 8, 1015 Vienna Austria*

GRASSET, ETIENNE ALFRED, pharmaceutical executive; b. Neuilly sur Seine, France, Mar. 6, 1951; s. Emile Octave and Simone (Mehuys) G.; m. Daniele Jaqueline Gayat, Oct. 9, 1971; children: Melanie, Celine. MS, U. Paris VI, Paris, 1976; MD, Paris-St. Antoine, Paris, 1977. Lic. pediatrician, France. Resident Paris U. Hosp., Paris, 1975-79; fellow U. Tex., Houston, 1979-81; rsch. investigator Nat. Inst. Med. Rsch., Inserm, France, 1981-85; mem. R & D team Roussel-Uclaf Nutrition, Puteaux, France, 1985-86; assoc. dir. Cephac Clin. Rsch., Creteil, 1986-88; head med. group Jouveinal Lab., Fresnes, 1988; dir. med. devel. Roussel UCLAF Nutrition, Puteaux, 1988-93; med. mgr. enteral nutrition ClinTec, Velizy, 1993-94; sci. dir. Labs. Effik, Bievres, 1994—; attending physician Paris Hosp., France, 1981—. Contbr. articles to profl. jours. Avocations: literature, history, architecture. Home: 54 Pass Enfants du Paradis, F 92100 Boulogne Billancourt France Office: Labs Effik, Burospace 7, 91571 Bièvres France

GRASSMANN, RALPH KARL CHRISTIAN, biologist, educator; b. Erlangen, Bavaria, Germany, Aug. 23, 1957; s. Hans Christian and Anneliese (Stegmaier) G.; m. Martina Bongers; children: Thilo, Stephan, Mathias. PhD, U. Erlangen, 1989, MD, 1993. Asst. prof. U. Erlangen, Nurnberg, Germany, 1993—. Contbr. articles to profl. jours. Recipient Robert Koch award City of Claustal-Zellerfeld, 1997. Fax: 09131-85-22-101, 26493. Home: Bothmerstrasse 57, D-90480 Nürnberg Germany

GRASTHU, LAKSHMINARAYANA, retired English educator; b. Kurnool, India, May 2, 1937; s. Venkata Swamy and Veeramma Grasthu; m. Shanthamma Temera, Jan. 3, 1964 (dec. 1977); children: children: M. Tulasi, Venkata Ramana; m. Ramanamma Ramallakota, Sept. 7, 1977; children: G.V. Chalapathi, G.L. Padmavathi. BA, Osmania U., Kurnool, 1960; MA, Osmania U., Hyderabad, India, 1963. Cert. in English lang. tchg. Lectr. English Arts & Sci. Coll., Jadeherla, India, 1963-65; lectr. English Osmania U., Hyderabad, 1965-83, reader English, 1983-91, prof. English, 1991-97, head dept. English, 1996-97; ret., 1997. Author: Poet Saints of India, 1996, The Quest, 1997, Wanderlust, 1998. Avocation: reading and writing poetry in English and Telugu. Home: 21/106/1 Kusum Kunji, Dilsukh Nagar, Hyderabad 500 060, India

GRATALO, JOHN, JR., mortgage banker, business owner; b. Sommerville, N.J., May 2, 1963; s. John and Anna Mae (Tylka) G. BS in Fin., DePaul U. Banker Sears Mortgage Corp., Libertyville, Ill., 1987-94; sr. loan officer Lincoln Home, Bloomingdale, Ill., 1994—; owner The Cichlid Hideout, Northbrook, Ill.; loan officer First Chgo. Mortgage, 1994—. Mem. Philipino-Am. C. of C. (officer 1996—), Indak Dance Club. Roman Catholic. Avocation: rare exotic tropical fish. Home: 1108 Whitfield Rd Northbrook IL 60062-3947

GRATIER, JEAN-PIERRE, geology educator; b. Barraux, Isere, France, June 28, 1948; s. Emile and Marie Gratier; m. Danielle Branger, Aug. 28, 1982; children: Pierre, Remi. MS, U. Grenoble, France, 1971; PhD, U. Grenoble, 1973. Asst. prof. U. Rabat, Morocco, 1973-76; asst. prof. U. Grenoble, 1976-86, prof., 1986-92, 93—, asst. to pres. of univ. for earth and plantary scis., 1995-97; rsch. scientist U. Calif., Santa Barbara, 1992-93; dir. Alpine Fedn. Earth Scis., CNRS, Grenoble, 1996-98; head earth and planetary scis. dept. French Ministry Edn. and Rsch., Paris, 1998-99; cons. in field. Contbr. articles to profl. jours. Mem. Geol. Soc. France, Geol. Soc. London, Am. Geophys. Union. Office: LGIT IRIGM, U Grenoble BP53X, 38041 Grenoble France

GRATTON, ROBERT, diversified financial services company executive; b. Montreal, Que., Can., Oct. 23, 1943; s. Bernard and Judith (Dufour) G.; m. Nicole Marcil, Aug. 1966; 3 children. LLL, U. Montreal; LLM, London Sch. Econs. & Polit. Sci.; MBA, Harvard U. Bar: Que. 1967. Asst. to Hon. Paul Gérin-Lajoie Quebec City; with Credit Foncier, COO, pres., CEO; chmn., pres., CEO Montreal Trust; pres., CEO Power Fin. Corp., 1989—, also bd. dirs.; chmn. Great-West Life & Annuity, U.S., Investors Group Inc.; bd. dirs. Power Corp. Can., Great-West Life, London Ins. Group, London Life Assurance Co., Pargesa Holding S.A. Mem. Mt. Royal Club, St.-James's Club, St.-Denis Club. Office: Power Fin Corp, 751 Victoria Sq, Montreal, PQ Canada H2Y 2J3

GRAU, GÉRARD, oceanographer; b. Auxerre, Yonne, France, Nov. 22, 1927; s. Bernard and Geneviève (Bertrand) G.; m. Odile Jactat, June 24, 1960; children: Cécile, François, Héléne, Nicolas. Engr., Ecole Centrale, Paris, 1950; Lic. in Sci., Paris U., 1951; Ingénieur géologue, ENSPM, Rueil, France, 1952; PhD, Calif. Inst. Tech., Pasadena, 1957. Rsch. engr. Inst. Français du Pétrole (IFP), Rueil, 1957-61, dir. rsch. geophysics divsn., 1962-85; sci. advisor to the pres. Inst. Français du Petrole (IFP), Rueil, 1986-93; prof. Ecole Techniques Avancées, Paris, 1971-93; prof. Inst. Océanographique, Paris, 1975—, dir., 1992—. Editor/author: Le Filtrage en Sismique, 1966, Seismic Filtering, 1971; editor proc. EAEG workshops: Practical Aspects of Seismic Inversion, 1990, 91; author: La Recherche Pétrolière, 1990; contbr. over 80 articles to profl. jours.; patentee in field. Recipient Medal, French Oceanography Soc., 1973; decorated Ordre du Mérite, French Govt., 1980. Mem. European Assn. Exploration Geophysicists (hon., pres. 1976-77, editor-in-chief 1988-94, Schlumberger award 1963), European Assn. for Tech. of Hydrocarbons (pres. sci. coun. 1989-93), Com. Nat. Français de Géodésie et Géophysique (v.p., pres. 1986-94). Office: Institut Océanographique, 195 Rue St-Jacques, 75005 Paris France

GRAU, JEAN ELIZABETH, retired insurance agent; b. New Orleans, June 8, 1932; d. Adolph Eugene and Katherine Caroline (O'Nion) Grau; divorced; children: Steven, Marilyn, Laurence, Lorraine. BEd, Loyola U. of New Orleans, 1953, MS, 1972. Cert. tchr., La. Tchr. French and English Notre Dame Acad., Washington, 1954-55; tchr. French Orleans Parish Pub. Sch. Dist., New Orleans, 1953-54, 72-86; pvt. ins. agt., New Orleans, 1980-95; tchr. gifted students Plaquemines Parish Pub. Schs., 1987-89; tchr. French East Baton Rouge, La., 1989-90, St. Charles Parish, La., 1990-91; registered rep. Jackson Nat. Fin. Svcs., New Orleans, 1993-95, ret., 1995. Author numerous poems, contbr. poetry to Scimitar and Song Anthology, Yearbook Modern Poetry, Reflections of Light Anthology, Nat. Libr. Poetry Anthologies, Word of Mouth Anthology, America at the Millennium, newspapers, mags. Pres. Aurora-Hyman-Kabel Civic Orgn., New Orleans, 1982—, del. Pres.' Council of Civic Orgns., 1984—; adv. bd. Algiers Community Network, 1985-86; active Algiers Priorities Conv., 1986, Non-Pack Police Support Group, West Bank Action Com. Mem. Codofil, France-Amerique, Am. Assn. Tchrs. French, La. Edn. Assn., L'Athenee Louisinais, Internat. Platform Assn., New Orleans Poetry Forum, La. Poetry Soc., Kappa Kappa Iota (hon.), Delta Epsilon Sigma (hon.), Kappa Delta Pi (hon.). Republican. Roman Catholic. Avocations: ham radio, violin, sewing, bicycling, gardening. Home and Office: 1601 Kabel Dr New Orleans LA 70131-3633

GRAU, MANUEL, mechanical engineer; b. Caracas, Venezuela, Jan. 4, 1954; s. Manuel and Ana (Torres) G.; m. Jessinia C. Bastidas, Sept. 16, 1978; children: Ana Karina, Ivette Katherine, Manuel Alejandro. BS in Mech. Engring., U. Del Zulia, Venezuela, 1978; MSc in Mech. & Aerospace Engring., U. Va., 1991. From facilities engr. to rotating equipment engring. supr. Lagoven, Venezuela, 1978-98; rotating equipment engring. supr. PDVSA, Venezuela, 1998-99, mgr. facilities engring., 1999—. Office: PDVSA E&O Av Libertador, Ctr Petolero Torretama 6-43, Maracaibo Edo Zulia Venezuela

GRAUDAL, NIELS ALBERT, medical researcher; b. Copenhagen, June 8, 1953; s. Hans Nikolaj Kjeldsen and Maren Ane Dorthea (Sigsgaard) G.; children: Asta, Thorbjørn, Helga; m. Gesche Jürgens; children: Daphne, Hemming, Louise. MB, U. Aarhus, Denmark, 1980. Registrar Univ. Hosp. of Aarhus, 1980; registrar Univ. Hosps. of Copenhagen, 1981-89, sr. registrar, 1989-97; assoc. prof. U. Copenhagen, 1990-94; rschr. Nat. Univ. Hosp., Copenhagen, 1997-2000; sr. registrar Gentofte Hosp., Hellerup, Denmark, 2000—; cons. Gentofte Hosp., Copenhagen, 1992—. Contbr. articles to profl. jours. Recipient award Consul-Gen. V.J. Glückstadt Found., Copenhagen, 1987, The Aage and Edith Dyssegaard Found., Copenhagen, 1998, Nycomed Nordic Rheumatology award, 2000. Mem. Danish Soc. Internal Medicine, Danish Soc. Pulmonary Medicine. Home: H P Ørumsgade 35, DK-2100 Copenhagen Denmark Office: Gentofte Hosp/Rheumat U605, Neils Andersens Vej 65, DK-2900 Hellerup Denmark

GRAUER, GAY SHERRARD MEREDITH (SHERRY GRAUER), artist; b. Toronto, Ont., Can., Feb. 20, 1939; d. Albert Edward and Shirley (Woodward) G.; m. John Keith-King, Feb. 12, 1971; children: Callum, Jonathan, Max. Student, Wellesley Coll., 1956-60, Ecole du Louvre, Paris, 1958-59; BFA, San Francisco Art Inst., 1964. One-woman shows include Mary Frazee Gallery, West Vancouver, Can., 1964, Bau-Xi Gallery, 1965, 67, 68, 70, 75, 76, 80, 83, 85, 87, 89, 90, 92, 97, Loyola Bonsecours Ctr., Montreal, Can., 1968, Jerrold Morris Gallery, Toronto, 1969, Véhicule Art Inc., Montreal, 1973, Surrey (B.C.) Art Gallery, 1980, Women in Focus Gallery, Vancouver, 1987, Art Gallery of the So. Okanagan, 1987; group exhbns. include Can. Group Painters, 1965-68, Montreal Mus. Fine Arts and Can. Pavilion Expo, 1978, Nine out of Ten Hamilton Art Gallery, 1973, Nat. Gallery Can, 1975, B.C. Prov. Coll., 1978-79, Vancouver Art Gallery, 1986, Charles H. Scott Gallery, Vancouver, 1985, ARTROPOLIS, Vancouver, 1993; commns. include World Wide Internat. Travel Office, Vancouver, 1969, U. B.C., 1972, Dept. Pub. Works Ottawa, 1976, Can. Tng. Inst., 1978; represented in various pub. and pvt. collections include Vancouver Art Gallery, Can. Coun. Art Bank, Musée d'Art Contemporain, Montreal, Nat. Gallery Can. Trustee Vancouver Art Gallery, 1974-76, hon. sec., 1975-76; founding bd. mem. Arts, Scis. and Tech. Ctr., Vancouver, 1980-83. Mem. Royal Can. Acad. Arts, Can. Artists' Rep./Front des Artistes Canadiens, Can. Conf. Arts, Royal Vancouver Yacht Club. Avocation: reading. Address: 106 8828 Heather St, Vancouver, BC Canada V6P 3S8

GRAUER, MANFRED, computer engineering educator, researcher; b. Herzberg/Elster, Brandenburg, Germany, Aug. 17, 1945; s. Erich and Lieselotte (Wilkniss) G.; m. Monika Schaarschmidt, Feb. 1, 1969; children: Juliane, Thomas. Diploma in Engring., Moscow Inst. Tech., 1970; DEng., U. Merseburg, Germany, 1975, DSc, 1979. Univ. asst. U. Merseburg, 1970-75, scientist, 1975-81; scientist Internat. Inst. Applied Systems Analysis, Laxenburg, Austria, 1981-84; prof. Inst. of Informatics, Berlin, 1984-86, U. Dortmund, Germany, 1987-88; prof. U. Siegen, Germany, 1988—, dean of faculty, 1993-95, v.p., 1997—. Editor: (book) Interactive Decision Analysis, 1984, Plural Rationality, 1985, Large-Scale Modelling, 1986, Parallel Computing, 1991; author: Multimedia, 1996. Office: U Siegen, Holderlinstr 3, D-57068 Siegen Germany

GRAUERT, JOHANNES (HANS GRAUERT), mathematics educator; b. Haren, Ems, Germany, Feb. 8, 1930; s. Clemens Grauert; m. Marie-Luise Meyer, 1956; 2 children. Student, U. Mainz, Germany, U. Munster, Germany, ETH, Zurich, Switerland; attended, Inst. for Advanced Study, Princeton U., 1957-59, Inst. des Hautes Etudes, Paris, 1959; hon. degree, U. Bayreuth, U. Bochum, U. Bonn, Germany. Prof. math U. Göttingen, Germany, 1959—; pres. Göttingen Acad. Scis., 1992-96; mem. supervisory bd. Inst. des Hautes Etudes, Paris, 1976-82. Author 10 books; contbr. articles to profl. jours. Mem. Acad. Göttingen, Acad. Mainz, Acad. Catania, Acad. Leopoldina, Acad. Europaea, Acad. Bayern (von Staudt prize 1991). Office: U Göottingen, Bunsenstrasse 3-5, 37073 Göttingen Germany

GRAVES, JENNIFER A. MARSHALL, genetics educator; b. Adelaide, Australia, Nov. 24, 1941; d. Theo John and Ann (Nicholls) Marshall; m. John Wagner Graves, July 16, 1966; children: Alison, Erica. BS, Adelaide U., 1962, MS, 1967; PhD, U. Calif., Berkeley, 1971. Lectr. La Trobe U., Melbourne, Australia, 1971-77, sr. lectr., 1978-85, reader, 1986-91, prof., 1991—. Editor: Mammals From Pouches and Eggs, 1990, Sex Chromosomes and Sex Determining Genes, 1993; contbr. over 190 articles to profl. jours. Fulbright scholar Internat. Edn. Found., 1965-71; recipient Sir Ronald A. Fisher award U. Adelaide, 1963, Ian Potter grants Ian Potter Found., Melbourne, 1988, 92, Ormonde Lectureship, U. Queensland, Brisbane, 1990, numerous govt. and pvt. grants. Fellow Australian Acad. Scis.; mem. Genetics Soc. Australia (v.p. 1993-94, pres. 1994—), Cell Biology Soc. Victoria (pres. 1981-83), Australian and New Zealand Soc. for Cell Biology (pres. 1984-85), Am. Soc. Human Genetics, Royal Soc. Victoria, others. Avocations: songwriter, singer. Office: La Trobe U, Dept Genetics, Bundoora VIC 3083, Australia

GRAVES, JOSEPH SCOTT, economics and management consultant; b. St. Louis, Apr. 20, 1948; s. Joseph Whitaker Jr. and Mary Frances (Scott) G.; m. Elizabeth Mather, Oct. 16, 1983; 1 child, Lindsay Mather. BA in Math., Chem. Engring., M in Chem. Engring., Rice U., 1971; MS in Indsl. Adminstrn., Carnegie Mellon, 1973, PhD in Ops. Rsch., 1978. Process design engr. Hudson Engring. Corp. (now part of McDermott Internat.), Houston, 1969-71; asst. prof. Washington U., St. Louis, 1974-78; prin. Resource Planning Assoc., Washington, 1978-84; mng. dir. Putnam, Hayes & Bartlett, Inc., Washington, 1984-99; sr. v.p. PHB Hagler Bailly, Inc., Washington, 1999—; spkr. in field. Author: Transmission Services Costing Framework, 1995; contbr. articles to profl. jours. Treas. Potomac Overlook Owners Assn., Washington, 1983-84. Mem. IEEE, Inst. for Ops. Rsch. and Mgmt. Scis. (chmn. computer sci. tech. 1977-78), Strategic Mgmt. Soc. (charter), Engr.'s Club St. Louis, Beta Gamma Sigma, Tau Beta Pi. Episcopalian. Avocations: sports, music, biking, camping. Office: PHB Hagler Bailly Inc 1776 Eye St NW Ste 500 Washington DC 20006-3700

GRAVES, KAREN LEE, high school counselor; b. Twin Falls, Idaho, Dec. 9, 1948; d. Isaac Mason and Agnes Popplewell; m. Frederick Ray Graves, Apr. 2, 1987. BA, Idaho State U., 1971; MEd, Coll. of Idaho, 1978. Cert. tchr. secondary edn., english 7-12, vocat. home econs. 7-12, pupil pers. svcs. K-12, Idaho. Tchr. Filer (Idaho) Sch. Dist., 1971-74, 76-80, Twin Falls (Idaho) Sch. Dist., 1974-76; counselor Mountain Home (Idaho) Sch. Dist., 1980—, dept. chairperson, dir.; bldg. coord. student assistance program, parent newsletter, parent vols., mem. multi-disciplinary team. Sponsor mem. Rocky Mountain Elk Found. Mem. NEA, ACA, ASCD, Am. Sch. Counseling Assn., Idaho Counseling Assn., Idaho Sch. Counseling Assn., Idaho Edn. Assn., Idaho Affiliation Supervision and Curriculum Devel., Mountain Home Edn. Assn. Avocations: painting ceramics, crafting, reading, crossword puzzles. Home: 1105 Maple Dr Mountain Home ID 83647-2027 Office: Mountain Home H S 300 S 11th E Mountain Home ID 83647-3235

GRAVES, NORMAN JOHN, geography educator, writer; b. Sainte Adresse, France, Jan. 28, 1925; arrived in Eng., 1935; s. George Alfred and Andrée Adèle (Carrel) G.; m. Mireille Camillle Dourguin, July 28, 1950; children: Helene Monica, Francis Alan (twins). BSc in Econs., London Sch. Econs., 1949; MA, Inst. Edn., London, 1957, PhD, 1964. Tchr. East Ham Grammar Sch., London, 1950-54; geog. tchr. Borough Beaufoy Tech. Sch., London, 1954-58; head dept. geog. Malory Sch., London, 1958-60; lectr. U. Liverpool, 1961-63; sr. lectr. Inst. Edn. U. London, 1963-74, reader, 1974-78, prof., 1978—, pro-dir., 1984-90. Author: Geography in Secondary Education, 1972, Curriculum Planning in Geography, 1979, Geography in Education, 3d edit., 1984, The Education Crisis, 1988; editor, author: Initial Teacher Education, 1990, Working for a Doctorate, 1997. Fellow Royal Geog. Soc. (Victoria medal 1993); mem. Internat. Geog. Union (chair commn. on geog. edn. 1972-80), Geog. Assn. (pres. 1978-79). Avocations: walking, gardening. Office: Inst Edn, 20 Beford Way, London WC1H 0AL, England

GRAVES, RICHARD PERCEVAL, author; b. Brighton, Sussex, Eng., Dec. 21, 1945; s. John Tiarks Ranke nd Mary (Wickens) G.; m. Anne Katharine Fortescue, 1970 (div. 1988); children: David John Perceval, Philip Macartney, Lucia Mary. MA, Oxford (Eng.) U., 1967. Schoolmaster Arnold Lodge, Leamington Spa, Eng., 1968, Harrow Sch., London, 1969, Holme Grange, Wokingham, Eng., 1969-71, Ellesmere (Eng.) Coll., 1971-73; author, 1973—. Author: (biographies) Lawrence of Arabia and His World, 1976, A.E. Housman: The Scholar-Poet, 1980, The Brothers Powys, 1983, Robert Graves: The Assault Heroic (1895-1926), 1986, Robert Graves: the Years with Laura (1926-1940), 1990, Richard Hughes, 1994, Robert Graves and the White Goddess (1940-1985), 1995. Councillor Whittington Parish Coun., 1973-80, Oswestry Borough Coun., 1976-83, Shropshire Cmty. Health Coun., 1987-91. Hawthornden fellow, 1999. Mem. Soc. Authors. Avocations: watching films, talking to strangers in bars. E-mail: Richard.Graves@btinternet.com. Home and Office: 26 Hills Ln, Shrewsbury SY1 1QU, England

GRAVETT, PETER JAMES, hematologist, medical administrator; b. London, Nov. 17, 1946; s. James Cyril and Lily Elsie (Ainsworth) G.; m. Maureen Elizabeth Dolan, June 6, 1975; 1 child, Thomas James. MB, BChir, London U., 1969. Commd. Royal Army Med. Corps, 1969, advanced through grades to lt. col., ret., 1984; house surgeon Farnborough Hosp., Kent, Eng., 1969, house physician, 1970; sr. house officer Colcester Mil. Hosp., Essex, Eng., 1970; with Her Majesty's Forces, 1970-73, Royal Army Med. Corps, 1973-80; cons. hematology Queen Elizabeth Mil. Hosp., 1980-84, The London Clinic, 1985—; med. dir. stemcell transplant unit The London Clinic, 1998—. Author: Use of English in Alternative Medicine, 1993; contbr. articles to profl. jours.; editl. com. Internat. Jour. Aromatherapy, 1999—. Mem. nat. exec. Brit. Tai Chi Chuan Assn., London, 1994. Fellow Royal Soc. Medicine, Royal Coll. Pathologists; mem. Royal Coll. Surgeons, Brit. Blood Transfusion Soc., Assn. Clin. Pathologists, Brit. Soc. Hematology. Office: London Clinic Hematol Dept, 1 Park Square West, London NW1 4LJ, England

GRAVING, RICHARD JOHN, law educator; b. Duluth, Minn., Aug. 24, 1929; s. Lawrence Richard and Laura Magdalene (Loucks) G.; m. Florence Sara Semel; children: Daniel, Sarah. BA, U. Minn., 1950; JD, Harvard U., 1953; postgrad., Nat. U. Mex., 1964-66. Bar: Minn. 1953, N.Y. 1956, U.S. Dist. Ct. (so. dist.) N.Y. 1956, Pa. 1968, U.S. Dist. Ct. (we. dist.) Pa. 1968, Tex. 1982, U.S. Dist. Ct. (so. dist.) Tex. 1982. Assoc. Reid & Priest, N.Y.C., 1955-61, Mexico City, 1961-66; v.p. Am. & Fgn. Power Co., Inc., Mexico City, 1966-68; atty. Gulf Oil Corp., Pitts., 1968-69, Madrid, 1969-73, London, 1973-80, Houston, 1980-82; pvt. practice London, 1982-84; prof. law South Tex. Coll., Houston, 1983—. With U.S. Army, 1953-55. Mem. Am. Soc. Internat. Law. Home: 8515 Ariel St Houston TX 77074-2806 Office: Inst Transnat Arbitration 1303 San Jacinto St Houston TX 77002-7013

GRAVITZ, MELVIN A., clinical psychologist; b. Balt., Dec. 8, 1927. BA, George Washington U., 1950, MA, 1951; PhD, Adelphi U., 1955. Diplomate Am. Bd. Profl. Psychology (pres. 1980-81), Am. Bd. Psychol. Hypnosis (pres. 1975-78), Am Bd. Forensic Psychology. Intern clin. psychology Springfield State Hosp., Sykesville, Md., 1953-54; clin. psychologist County Health Dept., Tampa, Fla., 1955-57; chief clin. psychologist Dept. Pub. Health D.C., 1957-64; pvt. practice Washington, 1964—; clin. prof. psychiatry George Washington U., Washington, 1966—. Contbr. numerous chpts. to books and articles to profl. jours. Named Disting. Practitioner Nat. Acad. Practice, 1982. Fellow Am. Soc. Clin. Hypnosis (pres. 1978-79), APA (coun. rep. 1988-91, 98-99, pres. divsn. hypnosis). Avocation: collecting antique books in psychology and hypnosis. Office: 1325 18th St NW Ste 105 Washington DC 20036-6511

GRAW, LEROY HARRY, purchasing and contract management company executive; b. Dupree, S.Dak., Jan. 10, 1942; s. Harry Fred and Luella (Eichmann) G.; m. Kyong Hee Yuk, Sept. 25, 1969 (div. Feb. 1979); 1 child, Natasha; m. Anat Harari, July 3, 1981; children: Byron, Karen. BS, U.S. Mil. Acad., 1964; M Commerce, U. Richmond, 1974; EdD, U. So. Calif., 1980. Govt. contracting officer worldwide, 1971-88; mgr. govt. contracts Fluor Corp., Dallas, 1988-89; mgr. contracts Superconducting Super Collider, Dallas, 1989-95; dir. contract adminstnr. Los Angeles County MTA, L.A., 1995-96; pres. Internat. Resource Mgmt. Assocs., Upland, Calif., 1996—; ccons., Dallas, 1991-95; adj. prof. U. Dallas, 1990-95, U. Calif., Riverside, 1996—, UCLA, Westwood, 1996—, Keller Grad. Sch., 1997—. Author: Service Purchasing, 1994, Cost/Price Analysis, 1994; editor: Global Purchasing, 1990; contbr. articles to profl. jours. Dist. commr. Boy Scouts Am., Portland, Oreg., 1987, mem. troop com. troop 608, La Crescenta, 1997. Capt. U.S. Army, 1964-70, Vietnam. Recipient dist. award of merit Boy Scouts Am., Honolulu, 1985. Fellow Nat. Contract Mgmt. Assn. (cert., chpt. pres. 1997—); mem. Nat. Assn. Purchasing Mgmt. (cert., nat. officer 1992—). Avocations: skiing, hiking, camping, chess. Home and Office: 1667 N Vallejo Way Upland CA 91784-1934

GRAY, CAROL HICKSON, chemical engineer; b. Atlanta, Jan. 3, 1958; d.Ronald Allen and Charlotte Patricia (Blitch) Hickson; m. Randy Lee Gray, June 25, 1983; children: Amanda Christine, Stephanie Lee, Jamie Noel. BSChemE, Ga. Inst. Tech., 1979. Process engr. Air Products and Chems., Inc., Calvert City, Ky., 1979-83, sr. process engr., 1983-86, sr. prodn. engr., 1986-87, prin. prodn. engr., 1987-89; engring. supr. Air Products and Chems., Inc., Pasadena, Tex., 1990-92; lead engr. Air Products and Chems., Inc., Calvert City, Ky., 1992-93, area supr., 1993-95; area supt. Westvaco Corp., Wickliffe, Ky., 1996—. Mem. NAFE, Internat. Platform Assn. Avocations: bicycling, photography. Office: Westvaco Corp 2025 Beech Grove Rd Wickliffe KY 42087-9010

GRAY, CHARLES ELMER, lawyer, rancher, investor; b. Elvins, Mo., July 23, 1919; s. Grover P. and Martha Elizabeth (Sullivan) G.; m. Beulah Henrich Gray, July 4, 1942; children—Karen Lee, Cecilia Jean, Bette Sue, Marsha Dawn. Student, Flat River Jr. Coll., 1937-38, U. Hawaii, 1940-41; LL.B., Washington U., St. Louis, 1947. Bar: Mo. 1947. Pvt. practice St. Louis, 1947—; ptnr. Gray and Ritter; gen. counsel, dir. United Mo. Bank, St Louis; mem. Mo. Appellate Jud. Commn.; mem. rules com. Supreme Ct. Mo., 1970-81. Served to capt. USAF, 1939-45. Fellow Internat. Acad. Trial Lawyers (dir.), Am. Coll. Trial Lawyers, Internat. Soc. Barristers (state chmn., dir.); mem. ABA, Mo. Bar Assn., St. Louis Bar Assn., Lawyers Assn. St. Louis (v.p. 1954, bd. govs., Honor award 1977), Harbour Ridge Yacht Club (commodore 1991-92), Phi Delta Phi. Home: PO Box 709 PO Box 709 Farmington MO 63640-0709 Office: Gateway One on the Mall 701 Market St Fl 8 Saint Louis MO 63101-1850

GRAY, CHARLES ROBERT, lawyer; b. Kirksville, Mo., Aug. 22, 1952; s. George Devon and Bettie Louise (McCormick) G.; m. Dana Elizabeth Kehr, June 1, 1974; children: Jennifer, Jessica, Marcus, Gregory, Victoria. BS, N.E. Mo. State U., 1974; JD, U. Mo., Kansas City, 1978. Bar: Mo. 1978, Va. 1993, U.S. Dist. Ct. (we. dist.) Mo. 1978, U.S. Ct. Appeals (fed. cir.) 1992, U.S. Ct. Appeals (4th cir.) 1995, U.S. Supreme Ct. 1981; cert. mediator; cert. hearing officer Va. Supereme Ct., 1997. Pvt. practice Parkville, Mo., 1978-81; asst. pub. defender 5th Judicial Cir. Ct. Mo., St. Joseph, 1978-79; pub. defender 6th Judicial Cir. Ct. Mo., Platte City, 1981; asst. dist. counsel Army Corps of Engrs., Kansas City, 1981-82, Vicksburg, Miss., 1982-83; chief counsel space shuttle, MX missile U.S. Army, Vandenberg AFB, Calif., 1983-85; chief counsel troop support agy. U.S. Army, Ft. Lee, Va., 1985-87; fraud counsel Def. Gen. Supply Ctr. Dept. of Def., Richmond, Va., 1987-93; pvt. practice, Chester, Va., 1993-99; owner Pvt. Jud. Svcs., Inc., Chester, 1993—; asst. atty. gen. Atty. Gen.'s Office State of Va., 1999—; adj. prof. St. Leo Coll., Ft. Lee, 1986-91, John Tyler Coll., Chester, Va., 1994—. Mem. Selective Svc. Draft Bd., Brookfield, Mo., 1972-74; pres. Old Towne Parkville Assn., 1979-81, Chester (Va.) Youth Sports Boosters, 1989-91; den leader Boy Scouts Am., Chester, 1991—. Victor Wilson honor scholar, 1977; recipient Am. Jurisprudence award Coop-Bancroft-Whitney, 1989. Mem. ATLA, Am. Arbitration Assn. (mem. nat. panel arbitrators 1994—, mem. govt. disputes panel 1995—, mem. constrn. panel 1995—, mem. comml. panel 1995—), Def. Rsch. Inst. (approved mem. panel on mediation and arbitration), Mo. Bar Assn., Va. Bar Assn., Va. Trial Lawyers Assn. Methodist. Avocations: coaching youth sports, cub scouts, softball, tennis, basketball. Home: 3813 Terjo Ln Chester VA 23831-1839 Office: Pres Presiding Ofcl PO Drawer B Chester VA 23831

GRAY, CLARENCE JONES, foreign language educator, dean emeritus; b. June 21, 1908; s. Clarence J. Sr. and Elsie (Megill) G.; m. Jane Love Little, Aug. 25, 1934 (dec. June 1998); children: Frances Gray Adams (dec. Nov. 1997), Kenneth Stewart. BA, U. Richmond, 1933; MA, Columbia U., 1934; postgrad., Centro de Estudios Historicos, Madrid, summer 1935; EdD, U. Va., 1962; LLD, U. Richmond, 1979. Underwriter Aetna Life and Casualty, 1925-30; instr. Spanish Columbia U., 1934-38; gen. sec., mem. exec. council Instituto de las Espanas en los Estados Unidos, 1934-39; instr., sec. dept. Romance langs. Queens Coll., N.Y.C., 1938-46; (on mil. leave 1943-46); dean students U. Richmond, Va., 1946-68, assoc. prof. modern langs., 1946-62, prof., 1962-79, emeritus, 1979—, dean adminstrv. svcs., 1968-73, exec. asst. to pres., 1971-79, dean adminstrn., 1973-79, emeritus, 1979—, spl. cons. to pres., 1979-91, spl. cons. to chancellor, 1991—; editor bull., 1968-74, moderator U. Richmond-WRNL Radio Scholarship Quiz program, mem. bd. Univ. Assos. Cons., Commn. on Coll., So. Assn. Coll. and Schs. Trustee Inst. Mediterranean Studies. Contbr. articles to profl. jours. Served from lt. to lt. comdr., USNR, 1943-46. Recipient Nat. Alumni award for disting. svc. U. Richmond. Mem. MLA, NEA, Am. Assn. Tchrs. Spanish, Am. Assn. for Higher Edn., Newcomen Soc. N. Am., Inst. Internat. Edn. (cert. meritorious svc.), English-Speaking Union, Legion of Honor, Order of De Molay, Country Club of Va., Colonnade Club, Masons, Rotary, Phi Beta Kappa (Epsilon chpt. sec. emeritus, historian), Phi Delta Kappa, Kappa Delta Pi, Omicron Delta Kappa (nat. sec. gen. council 1966-72, Disting. Svc. key 1968, nat. chmn. scholarship awards 1972-78), Alpha Psi Omega, Phi Gamma Delta (award for disting. and exceptional svc.), Alpha Phi Omega, Phi Beta Kappa Assocs. (life). Home: Azalea Bldg Ste 327 1717 Bellevue Ave Richmond VA 23227-3961

GRAY, DENIS PEREIRA, physician, educator; b. Exeter, Devon, Eng., Oct. 2, 1935; s. Sydney Pereira and Alice Evelyn (Cole) G.; m. Jill Margaret Hoyte, Apr. 28, 1962; children: Peter Pereira Gray, Penelope Pereira Gray, Elizabeth Allen, Jennifer Pereira Gray. BA, Cambridge U., 1957, MBBChir, 1960. Gen. practitioner Exeter, 1962—; sr. lectr. Exeter U., 1973-86, prof. gen. practice, 1986—, dir. postgrad. med. sch., 1987-97, dir. postgrad. edn.; gen. practice, 1975-2000; chmn. Joint Com. on Postgrad. Tng. for Gen. Practice, 1995-97, Conf. of Acad. Orgs. in Gen. Practice, 1995—. Co-author: Running a Practice, 1976; author: Training for General Practice, 1982; co-author/editor: Psychiatry and General Practice Today, 1994; hon. editor acad. monographs; contbr. articles to profl. jours. Trustee The Nuffield Trust. Recipient OBE Her Majesty the Queen, 1981. Fellow Royal Coll. Gen. Practitioners (hon. editor Jour. of RCGP 1972-80, chmn. of coun. 1987-90, pres. 1997—), Royal Soc. of Medicine. Mem. Christian Ch. of Eng. Avocation: reading modern history. Home: 9 Marlborough Rd, EX2 4TJ Exeter England Office: Saint Leonards Med Practice, 34 Denmark Rd, EX1 1SF Exeter England

GRAY, DONALD ALLAN, computer software technical recruiting; b. Palo Alto, Calif., Jan. 27, 1964; s. Thomas Leighton and Audrey May G. BS, U. So. Calif., 1987. Corp. trainer Computer Solutions, Internat., L.A., 1987-89; regional sales mgr. V.I. Corp., Newport Beach, Calif., 1989-91; internat. sales dir. Talarian Corp., Mountain View, Calif., 1991-96; pres. Blast Interactive, Inc., San Francisco, 1996—; bus. plan devel. mgr. Occidental Petroleum, L.A., 1988-89, Armand Hammer Mus. Art and Cultural Ctr. Avocation: polo. Home and Office: 268 Bush St Ste 3432 San Francisco CA 94104-3503

GRAY, FESTUS GAIL, electrical engineer, educator, researcher; b. Moundsville, W.Va., Aug. 16, 1943; s. Festus P. and Elsie V. (Rine) G.; m. Caryl Evelyn Anderson, Aug. 24, 1968; children: David, Andrew,

Daniel. BSEE, W.Va. U., 1965, MSEE, 1967; PhD, U. Mich., 1971. Instr. W.Va. U., Morgantown, 1966-67; asst. prof. Va. Poly. Inst. and State U., Blacksburg, 1971-77, assoc. prof., 1977-82, prof., 1983—; vis. scientist Rsch. Triangle Inst., N.C., 1984-85; faculty fellow NASA, 1975; cons. Inland Motors, Radford, Va., 1980, Rsch. Triangle Inst., 1987—; researcher Rome Air Devel. Ctr., N.Y., 1980-81, Naval Surface Weapons Ctr., Dahlgren, Va., 1982-83, Army Rsch. Office, 1983-86, NSF, 1991-93, 98—, ARPA, 1993-96, Wright-Patterson AFB, 1995-99; publs. chmn. Internat. Symposium on Fault Tolerant Computing, Ann Arbor, Mich., 1985. Co-author: Structured Logic Design with VHDL, 1993, VHDL Representation and Synthesis, 2d edit., 2000; contbr. articles to sci. jours. Assoc. treas. Northside Presbyn. Ch., Blacksburg, 1986—, bd. deacons, 1980-83; coach S.W. Va. Soccer Assn., Blacksburg, 1980-86; asst. scoutmaster Boy Scouts Am., 1990—. Grantee NSF, Office NAval Rsch., NASA, Adv. Rsch. Projects Agy; Teaching fellow U. Mich., 1967-70. Mem. IEEE (chpt. chmn. 1979-80), Computer Soc. IEEE, Sigma Xi. Democrat. Achievements include research on fault tolerance, diagnosis, testing and reliability issues for VLSI, distributed and multiprocessor computer architectures, modeling and synthesis with VHOL, modeling and design with hardware description languages. Home: 304 Fincastle Dr Blacksburg VA 24060-5036 Office: Va Poly Inst and State U Blacksburg VA 24061-0111

GRAY, GEORGE, mural painter; b. Harrisburg, Pa., Dec. 23, 1907; s. George Zacharias and Anna Margaret (Barger) G. Ed., Harrisburg Tech. H.S., Phila., 1927-30, Acad. Fine Arts, Wilmington, Del., 1931-33, Art Students League, N.Y.C., Howard Pyle Sch. Illustration, Wilmington. Designer stage scenery, N.Y.C., 1926; invited to sketch scenes of army life in various forts and camps; tchr. anatomy and figure constrn. while attending art classes, Phila., Wilmington, later staff artist, U.S. Inf. Jour., U.S. Cav. Jour., Washington, N.Y. Nat. Guardsmen, Pa. N.G. Mag., mural painter patron, Gen. J. Leslie Kincaid, pres., Am. Hotels Corp., N.Y.C., 1934—; murals exhibited in hotels throughout U.S., including MacArthur of Battan, Hotel Jefferson-Clinton, Syracuse, N.Y.; Gen. George Rogers Clark, Louisville; 3 murals Hist. L.I, Suffolk County Savs. and Loan Bank, Babylon, L.I., Pony Express Nat. Meml. Mus., St. Joseph, Mo.; mural painting Brooklyn Bridge, Seamen's Ch. Inst., N.Y.C.; hist. picture map, Hotel Huntington, L.I., portraits and paintings in pvt. collections, U.S. and abroad; mil. artist, Engring. Bd., Ft. Belvoir, Va., combat artist, U.S. Coast Guard Hdqrs., Washington, originator, chmn., Navy Art Cooperation and Liaison Com. of Salmagundi Club. Founder, chmn. Coast Guard Art Program Salmagundi Club. Recipient Meritorious Pub. Svc. citation Dept. Navy, 1964; Louis E. Seley NACAL award, 1970; medal of honor Salmagundi Club, 1973; George Gray award U.S. Coast Guard, 1983. Life fellow Royal Soc. Arts (London); mem. Soc. Illustrators, Am. Mil. Inst., Am. Soc. Marine Artists, Co. Mil. Collectors and Historians, Nat. Soc. Mural Painters, Am. Vets. Soc. Artists, Am. Artists Profl. League, Nat. Hist. Soc. (founding mem.), Assn. Mil. Surgeons U.S., Navy League U.S. (Commodore Club), U.S. Naval Inst., Armed Forces Mgmt. Inst., Artists Fellowship, Arts Club (Washington), Salmagundi Club of N.Y. (originator, chmn. COGAP, Coast Guard art program of club). Address: Salmagundi Club 47 5th Ave New York NY 10003-4303

GRAY, HERBERT ESER, Canadian government official; b. Windsor, Ont., Can., May 25, 1931; s. Harry and Fannie G.; ed. Kennedy Coll. Inst., Windsor, McGill U. Grad. Sch. Commerce, Montreal, Que., Can., Osgoode Hall Law Sch., Toronto, Ont.; m. Sharon Sholzberg, July 23, 1967; children: Jonathan, Elizabeth Anne. Mem. Ho. of Commons for Windsor W., Ottawa, Ont., 1962—, chmn. standing com. on fin., trade and econ. affairs, 1966-68, served as Parliamentary sec. to Min. of Fin., 1968-69, named min. without portfolio, 1969, min. of nat. revenue, 1970-72, min. of consumer and corp. affairs, 1972-74, min. of industry, trade and commerce, 1980-82, min. regional econ. expansion, 1982-84, pres. of Treasury Bd., 1982-84, opposition ho. leader, 1984-90, dep. leader opposition, 1989-90, leader opposition, 1990, fin. critic off. opposition, 1979, 91-93, leader gov. Ho. Commons, solicitor gen. of Can., 1993-97, dep. prime min., 1997—; min. Millennium Bur. Can., 1998—; has served as mem. Can. dels. to various internat. confs. on econ. and other matters; del. IMF and World Bank meetings, 1967, 69, 70; co-chmn. Can. Del. to OECD Ministerial meeting, 1970; leader Can. Del. to Commonwealth Fin. Mins. meeting, 1970. Windsor pres. Jaycees, 1961-62. Club: Richelieu. Lodge: B'nai Brith. Office: House of Commons, Rm 209-S Centre Block, Ottawa, ON Canada K1A 0A6

GRAY, JAMES L., investment company executive; b. Jackson, Mich., Apr. 10, 1948; s. Biscoe LaFayette, Jr. and Margaret Anne (Hurley) G.; M. Mary Elizabeth Gaynon, Mar. 2, 1968 (div. July 1978); 1 child, Bennett Lee; m. Christine J. Smith, July 16, 1994. BA in History, U. Wis., 1972, MA in History, 1974, MA in Libr. Sci., 1975; MIM, Am. Grad. Sch. of Internat. Mgmt., Glendale, Ariz., 1977; JD, So. Tex. Coll. Law Texas A&M U., Houston, Tex., 1986. Trust officer Southwest Fla. Banks, Inc., Fort Myers, Fla., 1977-80; assoc. nat. trust examiner U.S. Treasury Dept./Comptroller of the Currency, Washington, 1980-82; asst. v.p. First City Nat. Bank of Houston, 1982-88; sr. v.p., mgr. trust divsn. First Nat. Bank in Albuquerque, 1988-92; chief operating officer MFR, Inc., N.Y.C., 1992-94; 1st v.p. Concord Holding Corp., N.Y.C., 1994-95; sr. v.p. Schroder Fund Advisors, N.Y.C., 1995-99; v.p. Schroder Capital Mgmt./Internat. Inc.; mem. sales and mktg. com. Investment Co. Inst., Washington, 1996-99; sr. v.p. Brandywine Asset Mgmt., Inc., Wilmington, Del., 199-2000; dir. Scudder Investments, Inc., N.Y.C., 2000—; sales and mktg. com. Investment Co. Inst., Wash., 1996—; bd. dirs. N.Mex. Estate Planning Coun., Albuquerque, 1989-92. Author: The Southwest Securities Transfer Association Reference Manual, 1985. Bd. dirs. Presbyn. Healthcare Found., Albuquerque, 1990-92, N.Mex. Repertory Theater, Albuquerque, 1989-92. Mem. SR, SAR (treas. N.Y. treas. 1997—), Union Club/N.Y., West Side Tennis Club (N.Y.C.). Episcopalian. Avocations: tennis, swimming, golf, gardening, history. E-mail: james gray@scudder.com. Home: 240 E 47th St Apt 31E New York NY 10017-2138 also: 59 Pheasant Close W Southampton NY 11968-3062 Office: Scudder Investments Inc 345 Park Ave New York NY 10154

GRAY, JAN CHARLES, lawyer, business owner; b. Des Moines, June 15, 1947; s. Charles Donald and Mary C. Gray; 1 child, Charles Jan. BA in Econs., U. Calif., Berkeley, 1969; MBA, Pepperdine U., 1986; JD, Harvard U., 1972. Bar: Calif. 1972, D.C. 1974, Wyo. 1992. Law clk. Kindel & Anderson, L.A., 1971-72; assoc. Halstead, Baker & Sterling, L.A., 1972-75; sr. v.p., gen. counsel and sec. Ralphs Grocery Co., L.A., 1975-97; pres. Am. Presidents Resorts, Custer, S.D., Casper/Glenrock, Wyo., 1983—; owner Big Bear (Calif.) Cabins-Lakeside, 1988—; pres. Mt. Rushmore Broadcasting, Inc., 1991—; owner Sta. KGOS/KERM, Torrington, Wyo., 1993—, Sta. KRAL/KIQZ, Rawlins, Wyo., 1993—, Sta. KZMX, Hot Springs, S.D., 1993—, Sta. KFCR, Custer, S.D., 1992—, Sta. KQLT-FM, Casper, Wyo., 1994—, Sta. KASS-FM, Casper, 1995—, Sta. KVOC-AM, Casper, 1997—, KAWK-FM, Rapid City, S.D., 1997—, KHOC, Casper, Wyo., 1998—; judge pro tem L.A. Mcpl. Ct., 1977-85; instr. bus. UCLA, 1976-85, Pepperdine MBA Program, 1983-85; arbitrator Am. Arbitration Assn., 1977-97; media spokesman So. Calif. Grocers Assn., 1979-90, Calif. Grocers Assn., 1979-97, Calif. Retailers Assn., 1979-97; real estate broker, Calif., 1973—. Contbg. author: Life or Death, Who Controls?, 1976; contbr. articles to profl. jours. Trustee South Bay U. Coll. Law, 1978-79; mem. bd. visitors Southwestern U. Sch. Law, 1983—; mem. L.A. County Pvt. Industry Coun., 1982-96, exec. com. 1984-88, chmn. econ. devel. task force, 1986-89, chmn. mktg. com. 1991-93; mem. L.A. County Martin Luther King, Jr. Gen. Hosp. Authority, 1984—; mem. L.A. County Aviation Commn, 1986-92, chmn., 1990-91; L.A. Police Crime Prevention Adv. Coun., 1986—; Angelus Plaza Adv. Bd., 1983-85; bd. dirs. RecyCAL of So. Calif., 1983-89; trustee Santa Monica Hosp. Found., 1986-91, adv. bd., 1991—; mem. L.A. County Dem. Cen. Com., 1980-90, L.A. City Employees' Retirement System Commn., 1993—; del. Dem. Nat. Conv., 1980. Recipient So. Calif. Grocers Assn. award for outstanding contbns. to food industry, 1982, appreciation award for No on 11 Campaign, Calif./Nev. Soft Drink Assn., 1983; Tyler Price Meml. award Mex.-Am. Grocers Assn., 1995, Radio Affiliate of Yr.-Classic Rock ABC, 1998. Mem. ABA, Calif. Bar Assn., L.A. County Bar Assn. (exec. com. corp. law depts. sect. 1974-76, 79—, chmn. 1989-90, exec. com. barristers sect. 1974-75, 79-81, trustee 1991-93, jud. evaluation com. 1993—, nominating com. 1994), San Fernando Valley Bar Assn. (chmn. real property sect. 1975-77, L.A. Pub. Affairs Officers Assn., L.A. World Affairs Coun., Calif. Retailers Assn. (supermarket com.), Food Mktg. Inst. (govt. rels. com. 1977-97, benefits coun. 1993-97, chmn. lawyers and economists 1993-95), So. Calif. Bus. Assn. (bd. dirs. 1981—, mem. exec. com. 1982—, sec. 1986-91, chair 1991—), Town Hall L.A., U. Calif. Alumni Assn., Ephebian Soc. L.A., Harvard Club of So. Calif., L.A. Athletic Club, Petroleum Club, Casper Country Club, Phi Beta Kappa. Home: 2793 Creston Dr Los Angeles CA 90068-2209 Office: PO Box 2515 Casper WY 82602-2515 also: PO Box 3328 Hollywood CA 90078-3328

GRAY, SIR JOHN (ARCHIBALD BROWNE), medical physiologist; b. Mar. 30, 1918; s. Archibald Gray; attended Cheltenham Coll.; Clare Coll., Cambridge (Eng.) U., Univ. Coll. Hosp.; B.A., 1939; M.A., 1942; M.B., B.Chir., 1942; Sc.D., 1962; D.Sc. hon., Exeter, 1985; m. Vera Kathleen Mares, 1946; 2 children. Service research for MRC, 1943-45, mem. sci. staff of MRC at Nat. Inst. for Med. Research, 1946-52, 2d sec. Med. Research Council, 1966-68, sec., 1968-77, dep. chmn., 1975-77, mem. external sci. staff MRC, Marine Biol. Assn. Labs., Plymouth, Eng., 1977-83; in physiology Univ. Coll., London U., 1952-58, prof. physiology, 1959-66; chmn. com. Med. Rsch. EEC, 1972-75. Served as surg. lt. RNVR, 1945-46. Fellow Royal Soc., Royal Coll. Physicians, Inst. Biol.; mem. Marine Biol. Assn. (coun. 1969-78, v.p. 1989), Freshwater Biol. Assn. (coun. 1981-88 pres. 1983-88, v.p. 1988). Contbr. articles, mainly on sensory recptors and sensory system, to profl. jours. Office: care Royal Soc, 6 Carlton House Ter, London SW1Y 5AG, England

GRAY, JOYCE, tax specialist; b. Sinton, Tex., Jan. 20, 1949; d. Charlie Ernest and Agnes Webster Simmons; m. Johnnie Neal Gray, Aug. 20, 1966; children: James Stephen, John Samuel. BS in Bus., Liberty U., 1995. Registered tax assessor-collector; cert. sch. tax adminstr. Typist U.S. Automobile Assn., San Antonio, 1966; clk. USAF, San Antonio, 1966-67, clk.-receptionist, 1967-68; clk.-receptionist Social Security Adminstrn., San Angelo, Tex., 1968-70; dep. sheriff, tax assessor, collector Irion County, Mertzon, Tex., 1973-82, dep. tax assessor, collector, 1982-84, tax assessor, collector, 1985—. Co-editor Sherwood Siftings, 1996; pub. Irion County Cmty. News, 1998—; history columnist Spring Creek News, 1991-98. Regional faculty mem. Am. Heart Assn., San Angelo, 1998—; v.p. Irion County Hist. Soc., Mertzon, 1973—; coord. County Govt. Week, Mertzon, 1990—; mem., vol. Ft. Concho Nat. Hist. Landmark, San Angelo, 1991—. Mem. Tax Assessor-Collectors Assn. Tex. (pres. 1999-00), Daughters of Republic Tex. (Ft. Concho chpt., registrar and past pres. 1988—, State Essay award 1991), Pocahontas DAR, '48 Study Club (pres. 1998—). Democrat. Baptist. Avocations: genealogy, reading, collecting Texas history, books before 1800, Christian books. E-mail: jgrayins@aol.com. Home: 598 Lindell Ave Mertzon TX 76941-6423

GRAY, JULIE ELIZABETH, plant scientist, educator; b. London, July 11, 1962; d. Graham Frederick and Frances Pamela (Fenn) Knapp; m. David John Gray, Oct. 29, 1988; children: Isabella Sarah, William David. BSc in Biochemistry with honors, Liverpool (Eng.) U., 1983; PhD in Agrl. Sci., Nottingham (Eng.) U., 1989. Royal Soc. rsch. fellow Melbourne (Australia) U., 1989-90; univ. rsch. fellow U. Nottingham, 1990-93; lectr. biotech. Sheffield (Eng.) U., 1993—; vis. scientist CSIRO, Australia, 1989; vis. prof. Nat. Sch. Agronomy, Toulouse, France, 1991-92. Contbr. numerous articles to profl. jours.; patentee in field. Rsch. grantee AFRC, 1994-97, Nuffield Found., 1994-96, BBSRC, 1998—, Royal Soc., 1994, 98. Mem. Am. Soc. Plant Physiologists, Biochem. Soc., Soc. Exptl. Biology. Avocations: cycling, swimming, tennis. Office: U Sheffield Dept Molec Biol, Firth Ct Western Bank, Sheffield S10 2UH, England

GRAY, LEONARD CHARLES, hospital administrator, geriatrician; b. Melbourne, Victoria, Australia, Mar. 27, 1950; s. Leslie Leonard and Elizabeth Rose (Brown) G. MB, Melbourne U., 1973, B in Surgery, 1973, M in Medicine, 1983. Asst. geriatrician Mt. Royal Hosp., Melbourne, 1982; gen. mgr. Bundoora Extended Care Ctr., Melbourne, 1982-95; prof., dir. chief aged care & rehab. North Western Health, 1999—. Author: Geriatric Medicine, 1992. Fellow Royal Australian Coll. Physicians, Australian Coll. Health Svc. Execs.; mem. Australian Soc. for Geriatric Medicine (sec. 1986-90, pres. 1993-95), Victorian Hosps. Assn. (hon. bd. dirs. 1992-95). Office: Bundoora Extended Care Ctr, 1231 Plenty Rd Bundoora, Melbourne VIC 3083, Australia

GRAY, NANCY ANN OLIVER, college administrator; b. Dallas, Apr. 23, 1951; d. Howard Ross and Joan (Dawkins) Oliver; m. Doyle P. Gray, Nov. 24, 1973 (div. Jan. 1985); children: Paul, Jeff, Scott; m. David Nelson Maxson, Oct. 5, 1985. BA, Vanderbilt U., 1973; MEd, North Tex. State U., 1975; postgrad., Vanderbilt U., 1976-79. Cert. fund raising exec. Tchr. Highland Park High Sch., Dallas, 1973-75; chmn. drama dept. Harpeth Hall Sch., Nashville, 1975-77; assoc. dir. devel. Vanderbilt U., Nashville, 1977-78, assist. dean students, 1978-80; dir. spl. gifts U. Louisville, 1982-86; dir. major gifts Oberlin (Ohio) Coll., 1986-90; dir. capital programs The Lawrenceville (N.J.) Sch., 1990-91; v.p. devel. and univ. rels. Rider U., Lawrenceville, 1991-98; v.p. sem. rels. Princeton (N.J.) Theol. Sem., 1998-99; pres. Converse Coll., Spartanburg, S.C., 1999—; cons. United Way, Cleve., 1988-90, Oberlin Coll., 1990, Princeton Project '55, 1992-93; guest lectr. Vanderbilt U., Nashville, 1987-88. Trustee Princeton Theol. Sem., 2000—, Spartanburg Day Sch., 2000—, Oberlin Libr., 1989, Oberlin Sch. Endowment Bd., 1988-90, Oberlin Early Childhood Ctr., 1986-88, Vanderbilt U., Nashville, 1973-77; bd. dirs. Vanderbilt U. Alumni Assn., Nashville, 1984-85, George Washington coun. Boy Scouts Am., 1996-99, Brevard Music Ctr., 1999—; mem. Jr. League, 1984-89, various coms. Named Outstanding Young Woman of Am., 1982, Outstanding Woman Achievement, Lorain County (Ohio) YWCA, 1988. Mem. Nat. Soc. Fund-Raising Execs. (pres. Louisville chpt. 1985-86), Coun. for Advancement Support to Edn. (conf. presenter). Home: 488 Connecticut Ave Spartanburg SC 29302-2158 Office: Converse Coll 580 E Main St Spartanburg SC 29302-1931

GRAY, NICHOLAS FREDERICK, environmental engineer; s. John Cecil and Jean (Sparrow) G.; m. Lucy Doyle; two children. BS, London U., 1975; MS, Salford U., Eng., 1976; PhD, Sheffield U., Eng., 1980; MA, Dublin U., 1982, DSc, 1993. Chartered biologist; chartered water engr. Lectr./prof. Trinity Coll., Dublin, 1979—; cons. in field. Author: (books) Biology of Wastewater Treatment, 1989, Activated Sludge Theory and Practice, 1990, Drinking Water Quality Problems and Solutions, 1994, Calidad del agua potable, 1996, Water Technology, 1999; co-author: The Coliform Index and Waterborne Disease, 1997; contbr. over 150 tech. and rsch. articles to profl. publs. Fellow Linnean Soc. of London, Trinity Coll. Dublin; mem. Inst. of Biology, Instn. of Water and Environ. Mgmt. Mem. Ch. of Ireland. Avocations: horses, bldg. and restoring houses, gardening. Office: Trinity Coll/U Dublin, Dept Civil Structural Engr, Dublin 2, Ireland

GRAY, OSCAR SHALOM, lawyer; b. N.Y.C., Oct. 18, 1926. BA, Yale U., 1948, JD, 1951. Bar: Md. 1951, D.C. 1952, U.S. Supreme Ct. 1952. Atty.-adviser legal adviser's office U.S. Dept. State, Washington, 1951-57; sec. Nuclear Materials and Equipment Corp., Apollo, Pa., 1957-64, treas., 1957-67, v.p., 1964-71, dir., 1964-67; spl. counsel Presdl. Task Force on Communications Policy, Washington, 1967-68; cons. U.S. Dept. Transp., Washington, 1967-68, acting dir. office environ. impact, 1968-70; sole practice Washington, 1970—, Balt., 1971—; adj. prof., professorial lectr. Law Ctr. Georgetown U., Washington, 1970-71; lectr. Cath. U. Am., Washington, 1970-71; assoc. prof. U. Md., Balt., 1971-74, prof., 1974-93, Jacob A. France prof. of torts, 1993-96, prof. emeritus, 1996—; vis. prof. U. Tenn., 1977. Author: Cases and Materials on Environmental Law, 1970, 2d edit., 1973, supplements, 1974, 75, 77; (with F. Harper and F. James Jr.) The Law of Torts, 2d edit., 1986, semi-ann. supplements, 1987-99, 3d edit., vol. 1, 1996; (with H. Shulman and F. James Jr.) Cases and Materials on the Law of Torts, 3d edit., 1976; contbr. articles to legal jours. Mem. ABA, Am. Law Inst. (adviser Restatement of the Law, Third, Torts: Products Liability), D.C. Bar Assn., D.C. Fedn. of Civic Assns. (parliamentarian 1991-99), Selden Soc. (state correspondent Md.), Order of Coif, Phi Beta Kappa. Office: 500 W Baltimore St Baltimore MD 21201-1701

GRAY, PAUL EDWARD, academic official; b. Newark, Feb. 7, 1932; s. Kenneth Frank and Florence (Gilleo) G.; m. Priscilla Wilson King, June 18, 1955; children: Virginia Wilson, Amy Brewer, Andrew King, Louise Meyer. SB, MIT, 1954, SM, 1955; Sc.D., Mass. Inst. Tech., 1960. Mem. faculty MIT, 1960-71, 90—, Class of 1922 prof. elec. engring., 1968-71, dean Sch. Engring., 1970-71, chancellor, 1971-80, pres., 1980-90; mem. MIT Corp., 1971—, chmn., 1990-97; dir. Boeing Co., Seattle, Eastman Kodak Co., Rochester; dir. NVest, L.P., Boston. Trustee Wheaton Coll., Norton, Mass., 1971-97, trustee emeritus 1997—, chmn. bd. trustees, 1976-87. 1st lt. AUS, 1955-57. Fellow IEEE (life, publs. bd. 1969-70), Am. Acad. Arts and Scis.; mem. NAE (treas. 1994-01), AAAS, Mex. Nat. Acad. Engring. (corr.), Sigma Xi, Eta Kappa Nu, Tau Beta Pi, Phi Sigma Kappa. Mem. United Ch. Christ. Office: MIT Dept Elec Engring 77 Massachusetts Ave Cambridge MA 02139-4307

GRAY, PAUL WESLEY, university dean; b. Cicero, Ill., Jan. 30, 1947; s. Harry B. and Audrey (Tong) G.; m. Rachel E. Boehr, June 3, 1967; children: John M., Janel E., Robert B. BA, Faith Baptist Bible Coll., Ankeny, Tex., 1970; ThM, Dallas Theol. Sem., 1975; MS in Libr. Sci., East Tex. State U., 1977, EdD, 1980; MA, Tex. Woman's U., 1989. Dorm dir. Buckner Baptist Benevolences, Dallas, 1971-75; dir. community living residence IV Dallas County Mental Health/Mental Retardation, Dallas, 1975-78; cataloger W. Walworth Harrison Pub. Libr., Greenville, Tex., 1978-81; v.p. Golden Triangle Christian Acad., Garland, Tex., 1979-83; dir. libr. LeTourneau U., Longview, Tex., 1983-88; dean computer svc. and univ. libr. Azusa (Calif.) Pacific U., 1989—. Mem. ALA, Calif. Libr. Assn., So. Calif. Area Theol. Libr. Assn., Foothill Libr. Consortium. Republican. Baptist. Office: Azusa Pacific U 901 E Alosta Ave Azusa CA 91702-2769

GRAY, PHILIP HOWARD, retired psychologist, educator; b. Cape Rosier, Maine, July 4, 1926; s. Asa and Bernice (Lawrence) G.; m. Iris McKinney, Dec. 31, 1954; children: Cindelyn Gray Eberts, Howard. M.A., U. Chgo., 1958; Ph.D., U. Wash., 1960. Asst. prof. dept. psychology Mont. State U., Bozeman, 1960-65; assoc. prof. Mont. State U., 1965-75, prof., 1975-92; ret., 1992; vis. prof. U. Man., Winnipeg, Can., 1968-70, U. N.H., 1965, U. Mont., 1967, 74, Tufts U., 1968, U. Conn., 1971; pres. Mont. Psychol. Assn., 1968-70 (helped write Mont. licensing law for psychologists); chmn. Mont. Bd. Psychologist Examiners, 1972-74; spkr. sci. and geneal. meetings on ancestry of U.S. presidents; presenter, instr. grad. course on serial killers and the psychopathology of murder; founder Badger Press of Mont., 1998. Organizer folk art exhbns. Mont. and Maine, 1972-79; author: The Comparative Analysis of Behavior, 1966, (with F.L. Ruch and N. Warren) Working with Psychology, 1963, A Directory of Eskimo Artists in Sculpture and Prints, 1974, The Science That Lost Its Mind, 1985, Penobscot Pioneers vol. 1, 1992, vol. 2, 1992, vol. 3, 1993, vol. 4, 1994, vol. 5, 1995, vol. 6, 1996, Mean Streets and Dark Deeds: The He-Man's Guide to Mysteries, 1998, Ghoulies and Ghosties and Long-leggety Beasties: Imprinting Theory Linking Serial Killers, Child Assassins, Molesters, Homosexuality, Feminism and Day Care, 1998; contbr. numerous articles on behavior to psychol. jours.; contbr. poetry to lit. jours. With U.S. Army, 1944-46. Recipient Am. and Can. research grants. Fellow AAAS, APA, Am. Psychol. Soc., Internat. Soc. Rsch. on Aggression; mem. NRA (life), SAR (v.p. Sourdough chpt. 1990, pres. 1991-2000, trustee 1989, 00, v.p.-gen. intermountain dist. 1997-98, pres. state soc. 1998-99), Nat. Geneal. Soc., New Eng. Hist. Geneal. Soc., Gallatin County Geneal. Soc. (charter, pres. 1991-93), Deer Isle-Stonington Hist. Soc., Internat. Soc. Human Ethology, Descs. Illegitimate Sons and Daus. of Kings of Britain, Piscataque Pioneers, Order Desc. Colonial Physicians and Chirugiens, Flagon and Trencher, Order of the Crown of Charlemagne, Bozeman Rifle and Pistol Club. Republican. Avocations: collecting folk art, first and signed editions of novels, pistol shooting. Home: 1207 S Black Ave Bozeman MT 59715-5633

GRAY, SIMON JAMES HOLLIDAY, writer, educator; b. Oct. 21, 1936; s. James Davidson and Barbara Cecelia Mary (Holliday) G.; m. Beryl Mary Kevern, 1965 (div. 1997); 2 children. Student, Westminster Sch., Dalhousie U., Halifax, N.S.; M.A., U. Cambridge. Supr. English U. B.C., 1960-63; sr. instr., 1963-64; lectr. Queen Mary Coll., U. London, 1965-84. Author: (novels) Colmain, 1963, Simple People, 1965, Little Portia, 1967, A Comeback for Stark, 1968, Breaking Hearts, 1997, (non-fiction) An Unnatural Pursuit and Other Pieces, 1985, How's That For Telling 'Em Fat Lady, 1988, Fat Chance, 1995; (plays) Wise Child, 1968, Sleeping Dog, 1968, Dutch Uncle, 1969, The Idiot, 1971, Spoiled, 1971, Butley, 1971 (Evening Standard award), Otherwise Engaged, 1975 (Best Play, New York Drama Critics' Circle, Evening Standard award), Plaintiffs and Defendants, 1975, Two Sundays, 1975, Dog Days, 1976, Molly, 1977, The Rear Column, 1978, Close of Play, 1979, Quartermaine's Terms, 1981, Tartuffe, 1982, Chapter 17, 1982, The Common Pursuit, 1984, Plays One, 1986, Melon, 1987, Hidden Laughter, 1991, The Holy Terror, 1992, Cell Mates, 1995, Simply Disconnected, 1996, Life Support, 1997, Just the Three of Us, 1997, The Late Middle Classes, 1999; (TV movies) After Pilkington, 1987, Quartermaine's Terms, 1987, Old Flames, 1990, They Never Slept, 1991, The Common Pursuit, 1992, Running Late, 1992, Unnatural Pursuits, 1993, Femme Fatale, 1993, (film) A Month in the Country; (radio plays) The Rector's Daughter, 1992, With A Nod and A Bow, 1993, Suffer the Little Children, 1993. Mem. Dramatists Guild. Office: care Judy Daish Assocs, 2 St Charles Place, London W10 6EG, England

GRAY, VIVIENNE JOAN, classicist, educator; b. Auckland, New Zealand, Oct. 29, 1947; m. Evan Towns Gray. BA, U. Auckland, 1969, MA, 1970; PhD, U. Cambridge, U.K., 1974. From lectr. to sr. lectr. U. Auckland, 1974-87, prof. dept. classics, 1987—. Author: The Character of Xenophon's Hellenica, 1989, The Framing of Socrates, 1998. Rhodes fellow Lady Margaret Hall, Oxford, Eng., 1979-80. Office: Dept Classics, U Auckland, Auckland New Zealand

GRAYBEAL, BARBARA, editor, writer; b. Mountain City, Tenn., Sept. 21, 1935; d. Claude Harold and Ruby Lucille (Hodge) G.; m. Lewis N. Kremer, June 7, 1958 (div.); m. Charles L. Ring, May 8, 1982. BA magna cum laude, Marietta Coll., 1957; grad. Pub. Procedures Course, Radcliffe Coll., 1957. With New Yorker mag., N.Y.C., 1957-58; assoc. editor Saturday Evening Post, Phila., 1958-62, Episc. mag., Phila., 1962-69; asst. editor Luth. mag., Phila., 1971-72; instr. journalism Temple U., Phila., 1972-81; founding editor CGA World mag., 1980-82, sr. editor, 1982-83. Editor, writer: Fast and Fresh (by Julie Dannanbaum), 1981, The CGA Cookbook, 1984; editl. cons. Good Ideas for Decorating; contbr. articles, photographs and poetry to various publs. Mem. com. interpretation and promotion, dept. overseas missions Nat. Coun. Chs., 1966-68; mem. Phila. Dem. Com., 1968; bd. dirs., sec. Friends of Free Libr. Phila.; bd. dirs. N.C. Sch. Arts, The Assocs. of N.C. Sch. Arts, 1983-86; lay reader Episc. Ch. Mem. AAUW (pres. br.), Women in Comms. (v.p. chpt.), Marietta Coll. Alumni Assn., Internat. Platform Assn., Phi Beta Kappa, Sigma Delta Chi, Alpha Xi Delta. Address: 1525 Woods Rd Apt 106 Winston Salem NC 27106-3135

GRAY-BUSSARD, DOLLY H., energy company executive; b. Wilmington, Del., July 29, 1943; d. Henry Odell and Dorothy (Knotts) Gray; m. Robert William Bussard, Mar. 17, 1981; stepchildren: Elise Bright Chisholm, William Bussard, Robert L. Bussard, Virginia B. Barausky. BA in History and English Lit., U. Calif., San Diego, 1984; MA in History, Georgetown U., 1990. Coord. Organ. Human Devel., San Diego, 1977-78; owner, prin. Hello Dolly, La Jolla, Calif., 1978-80; ptnr. Linda Chester Lit. Agy., La Jolla, 1978-80; owner, pres. Unicorn Literary Agy., La Jolla, 1980-85; pres., chmn. bd. Energy/Matter Conversion Corp., San Diego, Calif., 1988—; vis. lectr. writers' confs. U. Calif., San Diego, 1979-81. Co-author: The Best of San Diego, 1981. Mem. Artists Cir., Santa Fe Chamber Music Festival; bd. dirs., v.p. N.Mex. Ctr. for the Book. Mem. NAFE, Am. Hist. Assn., Phi Alpha Theta. Episcopalian. Avocations: book collecting, skiing. Office: EMC2 Ste 103 9705 Carroll Center Rd San Diego CA 92126-6505

GRAYCAR, ADAM, federal agency administrator; b. Oct. 29, 1946; m. Elizabeth Percival, 1987; 2 children. BA, U. NSW, Sydney, Australia, 1968, PhD, 1974, DLitt, 1991. Lectr. polit. sci. U. New South Wales, Sydney, 1970-72; sr. lectr. social adminstrn. Flinders U., Adelaide, Australia, 1973-80; dir. social policy rsch. ctr. U. New South Wales, Sydney, 1980-85; commr. for aging Govt. of South Australia, Adelaide, 1985-90; CEO ministry of higher edn. Govt. South Australia, Adelaide, 1990-94; dir. Australian Inst. Criminology Fed. Govt. Australia, Canberra, 1994—; invited expert Social Policy and Labour Mkt. Workshop, Paris, 1991; chair Australian Heads of Govt. Violence Prevention Awards, 1994—. Author: Social Policy: An Australian Introduction, 1977, (with Adam Jamrozik) How Australians Live: Social Policy in Theory and Practice, 1989, 2d edit., 1993, (with Satyanshu Mukherjee) Crime and Justice in Australia, 1997, others; editor: Money Laundering: Risks and Countermeasures, 1996, Protecting Superannuation from Criminal Exploitation, 1996; contbr. more than 100 articles to profl.

jours. Fellow Australian Inst. Mgmt. Avocations: walking, reading. Office: Australian Inst Criminology, GPO Box 2944, Canberra ACT 2601, Australia

GRAYDON, FRANK DRAKE, retired accounting educator, university administrator; b. Ovalo, Tex., Feb. 11, 1921; s. Alonzo Otis and Jennie Lewis (Drake) G.; m. Mary Elizabeth Galt, June 16, 1943; children: Geoffrey Galt, David Drake. BBA, Tex. Tech. Coll., 1941; MBA, Northwestern U., 1943. CPA, Tex. Pub. acct. David Himmelblau & Co., Chgo., 1942-44; lectr. in acctg. Northwestern U., Chgo., 1942-44; instr. acctg. Tex. Tech. Coll., 1944-45; chief acct. U. Houston, 1945-46; asst. prof. acctg. U. Tex., 1946-50; with fin. statement sect. Cen. Controllers Office Ford Motor Co., Dearborn, Mich., 1950-51; budget examiner Agencies of Higher Edn., Legis. Budget Bd., Austin, Tex., 1951-55; fin. planning staff Temp. Commn. on Higher Edn., Austin, Tex., 1954-55; budget dir. and prof. acctg. U. Tex. System, Austin, 1955-90, spl. counsel budget and fin., Office of the Chancellor, 1990-93; budget dir. emeritus U. Tex. System, 1993—; prof. acctg. emeritus U. Tex., Austin, 1993—. Mem. AICPAs. Home: 8158 Ceberry Dr Austin TX 78759-8743 Office: Univ of Tex System 601 Colorado St Austin TX 78701-2904

GRAYESKI, MARY LYNN, chemist, foundation administrator. BS in Chemistry, Kings Coll., 1974; PhD in Analytical Chemistry, U. N.H., 1982. Tchg., rsch. asst. U. N.H., Durham, 1979-82; asst. prof. Seton Hall U., S. Orange, N.J., 1982-87, assoc. prof., 1987-93, chair chemistry dept., 1991-93; program officer Rsch. Corp., Tucson, 1993—; mem. govning. bd. Ea. Analytical Symposium, N.J., 1985-93. Contbr. over 30 articles to profl. jours. Vol. ACTION/VISTA, Midland, Tex., 1975; vol. recruiter ACTION, San Francisco, 1976; vol. ACTION/Peach Corps, Ghana, 1977-78; judge Internat. Sci. and Engring. Fair, 1996. Mem. Am. Chem. Soc., Delta Epsilon Sigma. Office: Rsch Corp 101 N Wilmot Rd Ste 250 Tucson AZ 85711-3361

GRAYSON, ZACHARY LOUIS, lawyer; b. Phila., Aug. 18, 1959; s. Harry and Shirley (Bogdanoff) Garfinkel; m. Marcia Caren Anstandig, Aug. 4, 1985; children: Ariel Michal, Avi Tzvi, Alexander Shmuel Yosef. BA, U. Pitts., 1985, JD, 1988. Bar: Pa. 1988, U.S. Dist. Ct. (ea. dist.) Pa. 1988, U.S. Dist. Ct. (ea. dist.) Mich. 1998, U.S. Ct. Appeals (3d cir.) 1998. Lectr. U. Pitts., 1983-84; speechwriter Israeli cultural rep. to greater Pitts. area, 1984-86; trial atty. spl. ops. unit div. enforcement Commodity Futures Trading Commn., Washington, 1988-89; assoc. Cozen and O'Connor, Phila., 1989-92; assoc. Wolf, Block, Schorr and Solis-Cohen, Phila., 1992-96, ptnr., 1996-97; gen. counsel Atlas Comms., Ltd., Blue Bell, Pa., 1997-99; partner EPA&M, LLC, 1999—; spl. counsel Pa. Ins. Commr., 1992-99. Trustee, v.p. Jewish Publ. Soc., 1993—; mem. 71st Precinct Community Coun., Bklyn., 1979, Pitts. Conf. Soviet Jewry, 1981; bd. dirs. Zionist Orgn. Am., Pitts., 1982-83; mem. bd. mng. dirs. Labor Zionist Ednl. Ctr., Pitts., 1986-89, Internat. Assoc. Jewish Lawyers and Jurists, 2000—; pres. Bnai Brith Justice Lodge, 1996-97, founder, trustee Project Justice, 1996—; trustee Associated Friends of Beth Rivkah Schs. Mem. ABA (task force on ins. insolvency 1994—, judicial selection and investment com.), Internat. Assn. Jewish Lawyers and Jurists (bd. dirs.), Pa. Bar Assn., Phila. Bar Assn. Jud. Selection Investment Com. Jewish. Office: EPA&M 1835 Market St Fl 28 Philadelphia PA 19103-2929 also: Fl, Moscow 123100, Russia

GRAYSTON, CLARE, solicitor; b. Birkenhead, Eng., Dec. 18, 1960; d. Ernest and Patricia (McKellar) G. BA in Law & French with honours, Keele U., Staffordshire, Eng., 1982. Articled clk. Lewis Silkin, London, 1983-85, asst. solicitor, 1985-87, ptnr., 1987—, head of corp. dept., 1999—. Contbg. author: Butterworths Encyclopaedia of Forms and Precedents, 5th edit., 1992; gen. editor: Kluwer Law International Sale of Private and Public Companies by Auction, 1996, Protection of Minority Shareholders, 1997. Dir. Women in Film and TV (U.K.), London, 1991-98, co. sec., 1991—; trustee Living Earth Found., London, 1994-96. Mem. Assn. Women Solicitors, Law Soc. Eng. & Wales, Westminster Law Soc., Assn. Internat. des Jeunes Avocats (v.p. 1995-97). Office: Lewis Silkin, Windsor House 50 Victoria St, London SW1H 0NW, England

GRAZIANI, JEANNE PATRICIA, healthcare administrator, consultant; b. Cooperstown, N.Y., Jan. 7, 1957; d. Jospeh Patrick and Catherine Lucey (Kelly) Killian; children from previous marriage, Jessica Patricia Johnson, Christina Catherine Johnson; m. Anthony E. Graziani, Sept. 5, 1992. AS, SUNY, Farmingdale, 1982; BS, SUNY, Stony Brook, 1984; postgrad., St. John's U., Jamaica, N.Y., 1998—. Registered respiratory therapist Nat. Bd. Respiratory Care; lic. respiratory therapist State N.Y. Clinician IV, neonatal and pediat. specialist Univ. Hosp., Stony Brook, 1984-87; supervising pulmonary function technologist Syosset (N.Y.) Cmty. Hosp., 1987-95; mgr. credentialing, adminstr. clin. performance improvement Queens-L.I. Med. Group, P.C., Uniondale, N.Y., 1995-96; quality stds. mgr. Vytra Healthcare, Melville, N.Y., 1996-99; healthcare project mgr. FIND/SVP, N.Y., 1999—; mem. Nat. Bd. Respiratory Care. Mem. Am. Heart Assn., Am. Lung Assn., Happauge, N.Y., 1987—. Recipient honors award, cert. appreciation McMahon Svcs. for Children, N.Y.C., 1991. Mem. NAFE, Nat. Pks. and Conservation Assn., Nat. Assn. Healthcare Quality (cert.). Republican. Mem. Christian Ch. Avocations: songwriting, singing, bicycling, horseback riding, gardening. Office: FIND/SVP 625 Avenue Of The Americas Fl 2 New York NY 10011-2095

GRAZIANO, CRAIG FRANK, lawyer; b. Des Moines, Dec. 7, 1950; s. Charles Dominic and Corrine Rose (Comito) G. BA summa cum laude, Macalester Coll., 1973; JD with honors, Drake U., 1975. Bar: Iowa 1976, U.S. Dist. Ct. (no. and so. dists.) Iowa 1978, U.S. Ct. Appeals (8th cir.) 1977, U.S. Supreme Ct. 1988. Law clk. to Hon. M. D. Van Oosterhout U.S. Ct. Appeals (8th cir.), Sioux City, Iowa, 1976-78; pvt. practice Dickinson, Mackaman, Tyler & Hagen, P.C., Des Moines, 1978-98; with Office of Consumer Advocate, Iowa Dept. Justice, Des Moines, 1999—. Mem. Gov.'s Task Force on Quality and Efficiency in Government, 1999—. Mem. ABA, Iowa Bar Assn. (chair specialization com. 1993-96, chair adminstrv. law sect. 1996-99), Order of Coif, Phi Beta Kappa. Home: 500 44th St Des Moines IA 50312-2408 Office: 310 Maple St Des Moines IA 50319-0063

GRAZIANO, PHILLIP P., jeweler; b. Bklyn., July 8, 1935; .. Peter Louis Graziano and Mary Josephine San Filippo. Student, Temple U., U. Colo. Denver Tech. Inst.; Police officer USAF, U.S., Can.; jeweler Image Jewelry, N.Y.C.; Paper Box Co.

GRAZIOSI, MASSIMO, film industry executive; b. Rome; s. Silvio and Maria (Valenza) G.; m. Marcella Rossi, Jan. 9, 1962; children: Maurizia, Massimiliano. BA, NYU, 1954. Sales mgr. Metro Goldwyn Mayer, Italy, 1965; mng. dir. 20th Century Fox, Italy, 1965-68; pres. for internat. Avco Embassy, Italy, 1968-85; chmn., v.p. European supr. Walt Disney, London, 1985-88; pres. Castle Rock Internat (Turner Broadcasting), London, 1988-97, Spring Internat., London, 1997—. Roman Catholic. Avocations: painting, arts, golf. Office: Spring Internat UK Ltd, 85 Wimpole St, W1M 8AJ London England

GRCIC, JOSEPH, philosophy educator; b. Olib, Dalmatia, Croatia; s. Ljubo and Matija Grcic. BA, City Coll. of CUNY, 1974; PhD, U. Notre Dame, 1980. Postdoctoral fellow U. Fla., Gainesville, 1985-88; prof. philosophy Ind. State U., Terre Haute, 1996—; lectr. in field. Author: Rawls and the Social Contract, 1980, Ethics and Political Theory, 2000; author, editor: Moral Choices, 1989; editor: Perspectives on the Family, 1990; contbr. articles to profl. jour N.Y. State Regents scholar. Mem. Am. Philos. Assn., Am. Soc. for Polit. and Legal Philosophy, Internat. Assn. for Philosophy of Law and Social Philosophy, Phi Beta Kappa. Avocations: travel, photography. E-mail: pigrcic@root.indstate.edu. Office: Ind State U Root Hall Terre Haute IN 47809

GREASER, CONSTANCE UDEAN, automotive industry executive; b. Jan. 18, 1938; d. Lloyd Edward and Udean Greaser. BA, San Diego State Coll., 1959; postgrad., U. Copenhagen Grad. Sch. Fgn., 1963, Georgetown U. Sch. Fgn. Svc., 1967; MA, U. So. Calif., 1968; exec. MBA, UCLA, 1981. Advt., publicity mgr. Crofton Co., San Diego, 1959-62; supr. Mercury Publs., Fullerton, Calif., 1962-64; supr. engring. support svcs. divsn. Arcata Data Mgmt., Hawthorne, Calif., 1964-67; mgr. computerized typesetting dept. Continental Graphics, L.A., 1967-70; v.p., editl dir. Sage Publs., Inc., Beverly Hills, Calif., 1970-74; head publs. RAND Corp., Santa Monica, Calif., 1974-90; mgr. svc. comms. Am. Honda Motors Co., Torrance, Calif., 1990—. Co-author: Quick Writer-Build Your Own Word Procesing Users Guide, 1983, Quick Writer-Word Processing Center Operations Manual, 1984; editor: Urban Research News, 197-74; mng. editor: Comparative Polit. Studies, 1971-74; contbr. articles to various jours. Mem. nat. com. Million Minutes of Peace Appeal, 1986, Nat. Info. Stds. Orgn., 1987-93, nat. com. Global Cooperation for Better World, 1988. Recipient Berber award Graphic Arts Tech. Found., 1989. Mem. Women in Bus. (pres. 1977-78), Graphic Comm. Assn. (bd. dirs. 1994-99), Soc. for Scholarly Pubs. (nat. bd. dirs.), Women in Comm., Soc. Tech. Comm. Office: Am Honda Motor Co 1919 Torrance Blvd Torrance CA 90501-2722

GREASLEY, ANDREW, computer educator; b. Radcliffe on Trent, U.K., Jan. 4, 1964; s. Peter and Fay (Plant) G.; m. Kay Dobie, Sept. 14, 1996. MBA, U. Derby, England, 1995. Rsch. asst. U. Derby, 1988-95, lectr., 1995—. Author: Operations Management in Business, 1999; (with Bocij, Chaffey, Hickie) Understanding Information Systems for Business, 1999. Mem. Soc. Computer Simulation Internat. Home: 31 Thornhill Rd, Derby DE22 3LX, England Office: U Derby, Kedleston Rd, Derby DE22 1GB, England

GREAVER, JOANNE HUTCHINS, mathematics educator, author; b. Louisville, Aug. 9, 1939; d. Alphonso Victor and Mary Louise (Sage) Hutchins; 1 child, Mary Elizabeth. BS in Chemistry, U. Louisville, 1961, MEd, 1971; MAT in Math., Purdue U., 1973. Cert. tch. Pres. Math Mentors Inc., 1962—; part-time faculty Bellarmine Coll., Louisville, 1982-94, U. Louisville, 1985—; project reviewer NSF, 1983—; advisor Council on Higher Edn., Frankfort, Ky., 1983-86; active regional and nat. summit on assessment in math., 1991, state task force on math., assessment adv. com., Nat. Assessment Ednl. Progress standards com.; charter mem. Commonwealth Tchrs. Inst., 1984—; mem. Nat. Forum for Excellence in Edn., Indpls., 1983; metric edn. leader Fed. Metric Project, Louisville, 1979-82; mem. Ky. Ednl. Reform Task Force, Assessment Com., Nat. Framework, Nat. Assessment Ednl. Progress Rev. Com.; lectr. in field. Author: (workbook) Down Algebra Alley, 1984; co-author curriculum guides. Recipient Presdl. award for excellence in math. tchg., 1983; named Outstanding Citizen, SAR, 1984; named to Hon. Order Ky. Cols.; grantee NSF, 1983, Louisville Cmty. Found., 1984-86. Mem. Greater Louisville Coun. Tchrs. of Math. (pres. 1977-78, 94-95, Outstanding Educator award 1987), Nat. Coun. Tchrs. of Math. (reviewer 1981—), Ky. Coun. Tchrs. of Math. (pres. 1990-91, Jefferson County Tchr. of Yr. award 1985), Math. Assn. Am., Kappa Delta Pi, Delta Kappa Gamma, Zeta Tau Alpha. Republican. Presbyterian. Avocations: tropical fish, gardening, handicrafts, travel, tennis. Home: 11513 Tazwell Dr Louisville KY 40241

GREAVES, DAVID JAMES, computer scientist, audio electronics consultant; b. London, Nov. 28, 1962; s. Peter James and Brenda Margaret (Hawkes) G. BA in Computer Sci., Cambridge (Eng.) U., 1985, PhD in Computer Networking, 1990. Rsch. fellow St. John's Coll. Cambridge U., 1991-95, lectr., fellow Corpus Christi Coll., 1995—; founder Virata Corp., 1993. Mem. editl. bd. IEEE Network Mag., 1996—. Mem. IEEE. Anglican. Avocation: music making. Home and Office: Corpus Christi Coll, Cambridge U, Cambridge CB2 1RH, England

GREAVES, IRENE ETHEL, international business educator; b. Bradford, Yorkshire, Eng., June 3, 1948; d. Wallace Harvey and Vera (Moorhouse) Whincup; m. Robert Richard Greaves, Dec. 30, 1978; 1 child, Rosemary Irene Whincup. Diploma of fgn. corr., Bradford Coll., 1968; BA with honours in Linguistics-French, U. Leeds, Eng., 1983; MSc in Info. Mgmt., U. Lancaster, Eng., 1988; City and Guilds tchr.'s cert., Huddersfield (Eng.) Poly., 1988. Various adminstrv. positions U. York, Eng., 1968-77; export mgr. Annmed, importers and exporters, Skipton, Eng., 1985-86; sr. lectr. Leicester (Eng.) Poly., 1989-91; sr. lectr. internat. bus. U. Ctrl. Lancashire, Preston, 1991—; mgmt. cons. Internat. Stock Exch., London, 1988; tutor Rsch. Couns. Grad. Schs., Eng., 1990—; external examiner U. Westminster, London, 1993-97, Groupe ESC Rennes, France, 1995—, Demontfort U., Leicester, 1995-98, 99—, Leeds Met. U., 1995-99; lectr. EFMD Small Bus. Seminar, Vaasa, Finland, 1996, AIB Conf., Stirling, U.K., 1999, Euronet Conv., Ljubljana, Slovenia. County councillor Airedale divsn. Conservative Party, North Yorkshire, 1997—. Mem. Acad. Internat. Bus. Unitarian. Avocations: travel, reading novels in original language, gardening. Office: U Ctrl Lancashire, Internat Bus Acctg Dept, Preston PR1 2HE, England

GREAVES, JOHN ALLEN, lawyer; b. Kansas City, Mo., Feb. 18, 1948; s. John Allen Greaves and Nancy Lee (Farmer) Greaves-Meltzer; m. Sharon Louise Peace Ventura, Dec. 23, 1967 (div. Mar. 1971); 1 child, Karen Christine Greaves Calogne; m. Jerri Lynn Crawford, Sept. 5, 1981. BA in Polit. Sci., U. Mo., 1976; MPA, JD with honors, Drake U., 1992. Bar: Iowa 1992, U.S. Dist. Ct. (so. dist.) Iowa 1992, Calif. 1994, U.S. Dist. Ct. (no. and cen. dists.) Calif. 1994, U.S. Dist. Ct. (so. and ea. dists.) Calif . 1995, U.S. Dist. Ct. N.Mex. 1995, U.S. Ct. Appeals (9th cir.) 1995, U.S. Dist. Ct. (no. dist.) N.Y. 1996, U.S. Dist. Ct. S.C. 1995, U.S. Ct. Appeals (4th and 10th cirs.) 1996; lic. airline transport pilot. Pres., CEO VIPilot Svcs., Inc., Kansas City, 1980-83; pilot Air Illinois, Carbondale, Ill., 1983-84, Wright Airlines, Cleve., 1983-84, ComAir Airlines, Cin., 1984-88; jud. law clk. to Hon. Arthur E. Gamble Iowa Dist. Ct., Des Moines, 1990-91; pvt. practice Des Moines, 1992-94; assoc. Baum, Hedlund, Aristei, Guilford & Downey, L.A., 1994—; mem. plaintiffs' steering com. Atlantic S.E. Airlines crash, Carrollton, Ga., 1995. Mem. ABA (mem. forum on air and space com.), ATLA, Airline Pilots Assn. (coun. 37, chmn. contract adminstrn. com. 1985-87, Disting. Svc. award), Lawyer/Pilot Bar Assn., State Bar Calif., State Bar Iowa, Iowa Trial Lawyers Assn., Delta Theta Phi. Avocations: aviation, snow and water skiing, boating and sailing, tennis, golf. Home: 3664 May St Los Angeles CA 90066-3606 Office: Baum Hedlund Aristei Gilford & Downey 12100 Wilshire Blvd Ste 950 Los Angeles CA 90025-7107

GREAVES, STANLEY JOSEPH, artist, educator; b. Georgetown, Demerara, Guyana, Nov. 23, 1934; arrived in Barbados, 1987; s. John and Priscilla Lydia (Whyte) G.; m. Barbara Klien, Aug. 6, 1960 (div. Oct. 1984); children: André, Sonya and Fiona (twins), Natasha; m. Alison Chapman-Andrews, Aug. 10, 1985. BA in Fine Art (hons.), U. Newcastle-upon-Tyne, Eng., 1967, diploma in art edn., 1968; MFA, Howard U., 1980. Tchr. Sacred Heart Primary, Georgetown, 1952-57; art tchr. secondary sch. St. Stanislaus Coll., Georgetown, 1957-62; art tchr. Berbice H.S., New Amsterdam, Guyana, 1968-71; art tchr. secondary sch. Queen's Coll., Georgetown, 1971-75; head divsn. creative arts U. Guyana, 1975-87; asst. chief examiner arts and crafts Caribbean Exams. Coun., Barbados, 1977-92. One-person shows include Caribbean Festival of Creative Arts, Georgetown, 1972, Barbados Mus., 1989, 90, Queen's Park Gallery, Bridgetown, Barbados, 1993, Nat. Gallery, Castellani House, Georgetown, 1994; exhibited in group shows at San Paulo Biennial, Brazil, 1971, Coltejar Biennial, Colombia, 1972, Casa de Las Americas, Havana, Cuba, 1977, Wilfredo Lam Ctr., Havana, 1986, Santo Domingo Biennial, 1992, 94, 96, Cuenca Biennial, Ecuador, 1998, South London Gallery, 1999. Mem. bd. trustees Nat. Art Collection, Guyana, 1993. Recipient 1st prize for sculpture, 1970, 90, 91, Guyana, Gold medal for painting, Barbados, Golden Arrow award Nat. Awards Com., Govt. Guyana, 1975, Gold medal for painting Santo Domingo, 1994; Fulbright scholar, 1979. Avocations: reading, playing classical guitar, writing poems, picture frame making, swimming. Home: # 2 Chelsea Gardens, Saint Michael Barbados

GREAVES, STUART, agrochemical company executive; b. Huddersfield, Eng., Mar. 21, 1953. BSc in Chemistry, U. Manchester Inst. Sci. Tech., Eng., 1974. Tech. mgr. A.H. Marks, Bradford, Eng., 1974-81; gen. mgr. Farmco, Perth, Australia, 1981-85; mng. dir. Martin Industries Ltd., Nottingham, Eng., 1986-96; dir. corp. devel. Micro Flo Co., Lakeland, Fla., 1996—. Mem. Royal Soc. Chemistry (charted chemist), Royal Australian Chem. Inst. (chartered chemist), N.Y. Acad. Scis., Am. Chem. Soc. Office: Micro Flo Co PO Box 5948 Lakeland FL 33807-5948

GREBENNIKOV, ANDREI VIKTOROVICH, radio engineer, researcher, educator; b. Uzhgorod, Ukraine, May 3, 1956; s. Viktor Kuzmich and Nina Petrovna (Gerasimova) G.; m. Galina Vasilevna Zhukova, Feb. 20, 1980. MS, Moscow Phys. Tech. Inst., 1980; PhD in Radio Engring., Tech. U. Comm. and Informatics, Moscow, 1991. Engr., mil. unit, Moscow, 1980-83; jr. sci. rschr. All-Union Electrotech. Inst., Moscow, 1983-88; sr. sci. rschr. Moscow Tech. U. Comm. and Informatics, 1988-98, assoc. prof. solid-state radioengring. and microelectronics, 1996-98; mem. tech. staff Inst. Microelectronics, Singapore, 1998—. Contbr. articles to sci. jours. Mem. IEEE, Microwave Theory and Techniques Soc., Popov's Sci. Soc. Avocations: travel, photography, pets, sports. Office: VLSI Inst Microelectronics, 11 Science Park Rd Sci P II, Singapore 117685, Singapore

GRECHKO, ALEXANDER TIMOFEEVICH, pharmacologist; b. Polonnoe, Ukraine, May 10, 1949; arrived in Russia, 1968; s. Timofey Feoktistovich and Inna Vasilievna (Kozyr) G.; m. Valentina Alexandrovna Petrova, Oct. 7, 1972; 1 child, Nikolay. Grad., Mil. Med. Acad., Leningrad, Russia, 1974, MD, 1992; PhD, Internat. Inform. Acad., Moscow, 1998. Chief lab. exptl. pharmacology Mil. Med. Acad., St. Petersburg, 1978-95, chief lab. exptl. physiology, 1994-96, sci. counselor, 1996—. Contbr. articles to profl. jours. Mem. Russian Soc. Pharmacologists, N.Y. Acad. Sci. Avocations: self-defense, sports. Office: Mil Med Acad, Lebedev str 6, 194044 Saint Petersburg Russia

GRECO, ADOLPH MARIO, retired management consultant; b. Cairo, Feb. 26, 1931; arrived in Australia, 1951; s. Vincent and Gaetana G.; m. Laura, May 1, 1954; children: Raymond Paul, Robert Vincent. Diploma in mech. engring., ICS, 1958; diploma in tech. prodn. engring., BIET, 1971. Machinist Borg Warner Ltd., Australia; tool designer, methods engr. C.C. Industries Pty., Australia; tool & machine designer British Motor Corp., Australia; profn. engr. Mc Culloch, Australia, works mgr.; mfg. mgr. Howard Rotavator, Australia; mgmt. mfg. cons. A Greco & Assocs., Australia, 1983—; rschr. and lectr. in field. Contbr. articles to profl. jours/. Recipient Nat. award Instn. Prodn. Engrs. Australia, 1985. Fellow Soc. Mfg. Engrs. (offshore internat. dir. 1997—); mem. Computer Automated Sys. Assn. (charter), Robotics Internat., Robot Inst. Am. (charter). Baptist. Avocation: soccer. Home: 51 Gazania Rd, Faulconbridge 2776, Australia

GRECO, MARIO, physicist, educator; b. Ravello, Italy, Sept. 8, 1941; children: Susanna, Elisabetta, Carlo Manuel. Degree in Physics, U. Rome, 1964, Prof. in Theoretical Physics, 1971. Rschr. Frascati Nat. Lab., Italy, 1966-97, leader theory divsn., 1972-76, 81-84; leader divsn. rsch. Frascati Nat. Lab., 1984-89; prof. theoretical physics U. Pavia, Italy, 1990-93, U. L'Aquila, Italy, 1994, U. Rome III, 1995—; vis. scientist CERN, Geneva, 1972, 78, 79, 82, 90, 2000, SLAC, Stanford, 1973, 74, 84; vis. prof. U. Marseille, France, 1981-88; dir. Physics Meetings of Aoste Valley, 1987—. Editor: Procs. Physics Meeting of Aoste Valley, 1987—; contbr. articles to profl. jours. Home: Via Tagliamento 20, 00198 Rome Italy Office: Univ Rome III, V. Vasca Navale 84, 00146 Rome Italy

GREDEL, ROLAND, astrophysicist; b. Schwetzingen, Germany, Dec. 9, 1957; s. Robert and Katharina (Fuchs) G.; m. Cécile Loup, Sept. 6, 1997; 1 child, Sophie. PhD, Ruprecht-Karls, Heidelberg, Germany, 1987. Fellow Smithsonian Astrophys. Obs., Cambridge, Mass., 1986-87; astronomer European So. Obs., Santiago, Chile, 1988-90; rschr. U. Cologne, Germany, 1990-91; astronomer European So. Obs., Santiago, 1991-98; dir. Calar Alto Obs., Heidelberg, 1998—. Editor: (book) The Galactic Center, 1996; contbr. articles to profl. jours. Mem. Internat. Astron. Union, Internat. Soc. for Optical Engring., Astronomy Soc. Avocations: yoga, chess, mountaineering. Home: Jesus Durban Remon 2 2o, Apartado Correos 511, 04080 Almeria Spain Office: Max-Planck Inst Astronomy, Königstuhl 17, 69117 Heidelberg Germany

GREDESKUL, SERGEY ANDREW, physicist, educator; b. Sverdlovsk, Russia, Mar. 12, 1942; arrived in Israel, 1991; s. Andrew Boris and Bella (Pesis) G.; m. Victoria Semenenko; 1 child, Tatyana. MS, Kharkov (Ukraine) State U., 1964; PhD, Low Temperature Inst. Kharkov, 1970, DS, 1990. Rschr. Physics Tech. Inst., Kharkov, Ukraine, 1968-72, Low Temperature Inst., Kharkov, 1972-91; prof. dept. physics Ben Gurion U. of Negev, Beer Sheva, Israel, 1991—; assoc. prof. Kharkov State U., 1972-91; sr. rschr. Inst. Indsl. Math., Beer Sheva, 1991-93; cons. Internat. Jour. Low Temperature, Kharkov, 1993-97, 2000—. Co-author: Vvedenie v teoriu neuporyadochennykh system, 1982; co-author: Introduction to the Theory of Disordered Systems, 1988; co-editor: L.V. Shubnikov, 1990. Recipient State prize Ukrainian State Com. on Sci. and Technique, 1985. Mem. Israel Phys. Soc. Avocations: classical music, playing piano, collecting hippopotamuses. Home: 50 HaGoren Str, 80300 Ofaqim Israel Office: Dept Physics, Ben Gurion Univ of Negev, 84105 Beer Sheva Israel

GREDZENS, SANDRA MAY PILLSBURY, art educator; b. Mpls., Sept. 30, 1949; d. Robert Kinsey and Elizabeth Anne (Massie) Pillsbury; m. David Inesis Gredzens, Nov. 25, 1989; stepchildren: Tabatha, Alex. AA, Stephens Coll., 1971; BFA, U. Calif. Santa Cruz, 1980; MEd, Hamline U., 1995. Cert. elem. and secondary educator. Lay-out artist Monterey (Calif.) Peninsula Herald, 1973-75; tchr.'s aide spl. edn., substitute tchr. Pacific Grove (Calif.) Unified Sch. Dist., 1978-82; educator art Shattuck-St. Mary's Sch., Faribault, Minn., 1982-84; tchr. elem. Woods Acad., Maple Plain, Minn., 1986-87; tchr. elem. art, art cons. Anoka (Minn.)-Hennepin Ind. Sch. Dist., 1987-97; tchr. elem. sch. Lake Superior Sch. Dist., Two Harbors, Minn., 1997—. Exhibited in group shows at Grant Marais Art Colony, 1986-98, Itasca Art Assn. Exhbn., 1996, 95, Sally Brown Collaborative Art Exhbn., 1995. Mem. Nat. Art Educators Am., Art Educators Minn., Delta Phi Delta. Republican. Lutheran. Avocations: painting, hiking, church activities, photography. Office: Mary MacDonald Elem Sch 99 Edison Blvd Silver Bay MN 55614-1254

GREEN, ANDRÉ, psychoanalyst, consultant; b. Cairo, Mar. 12, 1927; arrived in France, 1946; s. Felix and Sarina (Barcilon) G.; m. Muguette Lymboussis, May 17, 1950; children: Olivier, Laurent, Christophe; m. Litza Guttieres, May 13, 1989. MD, U. Paris, 1957; D (hon.), U. Coll. London, 1979, U. Buenos Aires, 1994. Dir. Paris Psychoanalytic Inst., 1970-73; pres. Paris Psychoanalytic Soc., 1986; v.p. Internat. Psychoanalytic Assn., 1975-77; prof. Univ. Coll., London, 1979-80; hon. prof. U. Buenos Aires. Author: Oh Private Maddress, The Fabric of Affect in Psychoanalysis, 1999, The Work of the Negative, 14 French books. Recipient Mary Sigourney prize, 1997. Address: 9 Ave du l'Observatoire, 75006 Paris France

GREEN, ANDREW JOHN, zoology researcher; b. Urmston, Eng., Mar. 24, 1964; arrived in Spain, 1993; s. Frank and Mary (Buckle) G.; m. Caroline Elizabeth Smith, Oct. 28, 1989. BA in Zoology, Oxford (Eng.) U., 1985, MA in Zoology, 1988, PhD in Zoology, 1989. Rsch. officer Wildfowl and Wetlands Trust, Slimbridge, U.K., 1989-93; Royal Soc. European Sci. Exchange Programme fellow Estacion Biologica de Doñana, Seville, Spain, 1993-94; postdoctoral fellow Estacion Biologica de Doñana, Seville, 1995-97, sr. rschr., 1998—; dep. chair threatened waterfowl specialist group World Conservation Union-Species Survival Commn., 1990-92, chair threatened waterfowl specialist group, 1992-99, mem. captive breeding specialist group, 1991-99; bd. mem. Wetlands Internat., Wageningen, The Netherlands, 1992-99. Author: Status and Conservation of the White-Winged Wood Duck, 1992, Status and Conservation of the Marbled Teal, 1993; editor Threatened Waterfowl Specialist Group News, 1990-99; contbr. articles to profl. jours. Christopher Welch scholar U. Oxford, 1985; grad. student fellow Smithsonian Instn., Panama, 1987. Mem. Survival Internat., Friends of the Earth. Avocations: walking, traveling, languages, natural history, Eastern philosophy. Office: Estacion Biol de Donana, Avda Maria Luisa S/N, 41013 Sevilla Spain

GREEN, BETTY NIELSEN, education educator, consultant; b. Copenhagen, Apr. 30, 1937; came to U.S., 1979; d. Alfred Christian Josef and Lilly Nielsen; m. Philip Irving Green, Apr. 16, 1962; children: Ruth, Erik, Nils. AA in Fgn. Lang., Daytona Beach C.C., 1981; BA in Liberal Arts, U. Ctrl. Fla., 1986; MS in TESOL, Nova Southeastern U., 1988; EdD in Curriculum and Instrn., U. Ctrl. Fla., 1994. Cert. tchr., Fla.; cert. TESOL trainer, Fla. Tchr. TESOL, program mgr. English Lang. Inst. Daytona Beach C.C., Fla., 1986-91; tchr. TESOL, fgn. lang. specialist Volusia County Schs., Daytona Beach, 1991—; tchr. trainer, facilitator Nova Southeastern U., Ft. Lauderdale, Fla., 1991—; cons. TESOL, Ormond Beach, Fla., 1991; adj. faculty, Daytona Beach, 1997—. Author, editor Teaching Assistant Manual, 1987; editor Unitarian Universalist Soc. newsletter, 1987—, religious editl. dir., 1996—. Pres. Unitarian Universalists, Ormond Beach, 1982-84, N.E. Cluster Unitarian Universalists, Volusia, 1982-86; pres., v.p. S.E. Unitarian Universalists Sem. Inst., Blacksburg, Va., 1985-89. Mem.

TESOL, Sunshine State TESOL (mem.-at-large 1999—), N.E. Fla. TESOL (pres. 1995—), ASCD, Nat. Coun. Tchrs. of English, Fla. Fgn. Lang. Assn., Fgn. Lang. Adminstrn. & Mgmt. Edn. (sec. 1995-97, pres. 1998), Fla. Assn. Bilingual Edn. Suprs. (sec. 1995), Fla. Consortium on Multicultural Edn. (chair), Phi Kappa Phi, Kappa Delta Pi. Democrat. Avocations: foreign languages, research on second language and multi-cultural educations, music, travel. Home: 771 W River Oak Dr Ormond Beach FL 32174-4641 Office: Volusia County Schs 729 Loomis Ave Daytona Beach FL 32114-4723

GREEN, DAVID, manufacturing company executive; b. Chgo., Mar. 22, 1922; s. Harry B. and Carrie (Scheinbaum) G.; m. Mary I. Winton, June 15, 1951; children: Sara Edmond, Howard Benjamin, Jonathan Winton. BA in Econs., U. Chgo., 1942, MA in Social Scis., 1949. Mgr. Toy Co., Chgo., 1946-54; founder, chmn., pres. Quartet Mfg. Co., Skokie, Ill., 1954-90, chmn., prin. officer, 1990-97; pres. Colleague, Inc., Booneville, Miss., 1967-87; chmn. bd. and cons. DG Group, Chgo., 1977—; chmn. Quartet Ovonics, 1986-97; mem. vis. com. on coll. and student activities, vis. com. to divsn. social scis., U. Chgo., vis. com. on the Coll. & student activities, vis. com. to the divsn. of the social scis. Spl. cons. to White House-Trade Expansion Act, Washington, 1962; chmn. Winnetka Caucus (Ill.), 1971; chmn. Ill. state Dan Walker for Gov., 1972, 76; spl. asst. to Gov. for intergovtl. relations, Ill., 1973-77; mem. pres.'s coun., coll. vis. com. U. Chgo.; pres.'s circle Chgo. Botanic Garden, playwright's circle Stratford Festival; founder dir. circle Steppenwolf Theatre Co.; governing mem. Chgo. Symphony Orch., Art Inst. Chgo. Served with U.S. Army, 1942-45, PTO. Recipient 1st Non-Smoking Office Bldg. award Skokie Clean Air Coalition, 1987; named Office Products Divsn. Man of Yr., Richard Karasik Humanitarian award, UJA, 1997. Mem. Bus. Products Industry Assn., Office Products Wholesale Assn. (Office Product Mfr. of Yr. award 1989, 93, 94), Chgo. Soc. of Clubs, Metropolitan (Chgo.), Bay Colony (Naples, Fla.). Home: 311 Woodley Rd Winnetka IL 60093-3740 Office: 650 Dundee Rd Ste 456 Northbrook IL 60062-2758 also: 200 E Delaware Pl Apt 22D Chicago IL 60611-5798

GREEN, EDWARD FRANCIS, manufacturing executive; b. Malden, Mass., Sept. 5, 1952; s. John Patrick and Mary Eleanor (Cahill) G.; m. Eugenia Bonita Tolla, Oct. 13, 1974; 1 child, Tanya Celeste. BS, Northeastern U., 1977; MBA, Babson Coll., 1983; advanced cert. mgmt. studies, Boston U., 1986. Supr. machine shop GE Power Generation, Lynn, Mass., 1974-77; mfg. and quality engr. GE Lighting, Lexington, Ky., 1977-78; buyer GE Motors, Springfield, Mo., 1978-79; mgr. machine shop ops. GE Aircraft Engines, Lynn, Mass., 1979-84, mgr. quality and tech. planning, 1984-86, mgr. purchased material quality, 1986-88, mgr. prodn. and inventory control, 1988-89, engine program mgr., 1989-91; mfg. program mgr. GE Aerospace, Pittsfield, Mass., 1991-92; dir. mfg. Rome (N.Y.) Cable Corp., 1992-94; plant mgr. Chicago Pneumatic Tool Co., Utica, N.Y., 1994-96, Emerson Power Transmissions-Rollway Bearing, Syracuse, N.Y., 1996—. Active Boy Scouts Am., Oneida County, N.Y., 1993—. Mem. GE Apprentice Alumni Assn., Manufacturers Assn. Ctrl. N.Y. (bd. dirs. factory mgmt. coun. 1992—), K.C., Crystal Cmty. Club (treas. 1979—), Rome C. of C. Republican. Roman Catholic. Avocations: sport fishing, home remodeling, automobile restoration, skiing, golf. Home: 23 Stonebridge Rd New Hartford NY 13413-5516 Office: Emerson Power Transmission Rollway Bearing 7600 Morgan Rd Liverpool NY 13090-3433

GREEN, FRANCIS WILLIAM, investment consultant, former missile scientist; b. Locust Grove, Okla., Mar. 17, 1920; s. Noel Francis and Mary (Lincoln) G.; m. Alma J. Ellison, Aug. 26, 1950 (dec. Sept. 1970); children: Sharmon, Rhonda; m. Susan G. Mathis, July 14, 1973 (div. July 1979). BS, Phoenix U., 1955; MS in Elec. Engring., Minerva U., Milan, Italy, 1959; MS in Engring., West Coast U., L.A., 1965. With USN Guided Missile Program, 1945-49; design and electronic project engr. Falcon missile program Hughes Aircraft Co., Culver City, Calif., 1949-55; sr. electronic engr. Atlas missile program Convair Astronautics, San Diego, 1955-59; sr. engr. Polaris missile program Nortronics divsn. Northrop, Anaheim, Calif., 1959-60; chief, supr. electronic engring. data sys. br. Tech. Support divsn. Rocket Propulsion Lab., USAF, Edwards AFB, Calif., 1960-67, dep. chief tech. support divsn., 1967-69; tech. advisor Air Force Missile Devel. Ctr., Holloman AFB, N.Mex., 1969-70, 6585 TestGroup, Air Force Spl. Weapons Ctr, Holloman AFB, 1970-78; pvt. investment cons., 1978—; mem. bd. examiners U.S. CSC; mem. Pres.'s Missile Site Labor Rels. Com.; cons. advanced computer and data processing tech. and systems engring.; mem. USAF Civilian Policy Bd. and Range Comdrs. Coun.; maj. gen., comdr. 2d brigrade State Milit. Forces; comdr. State Mil. Forces, 1989—. Contbr. articles to profl. jours. Served as pilot USAAF, 1941-47. Fellow AIAA; mem. IEEE, Nat. Assn. Flight Instrs., N.G. Assn. U.S. Home and Office: 2345 Apache Ln Alamogordo NM 88310-4851

GREEN, GEOFFREY FREDERIC, academic publishing administrator; b. Bradford, U.K., Aug. 22, 1947; s. George Hanson and Elizabeth (Kershaw) G.; m. Ellen Clare Hughes, Nov. 25, 1974; children: Emily Anais, Christopher George. MA, U. Edinburgh, Scotland, 1970, PhD, 1975. Pub. dir. T&T Clark Ltd., Edinburgh, 1975-89, mng. dir., 1989—. Mem. New Club Edinburgh, Carlton Cricket Club Edinburgh. Home: 35 Dick Pl, Edinburgh EH9 2JA, Scotland United Kingdom Office: T&T Clark Ltd, 59 George St, Edinburgh EH2 2LQ, Scotland United Kingdom

GREEN, GERARD LEO, priest, educator; b. Batavia, N.Y., July 27, 1928; s. George Leo and Marian (Powers) G. BS, Mt. St. Mary's Coll., 1952; MA, St. Bonaventure U., 1958; postgrad., U. Notre Dame, summers 1961-62, U. Buffalo, 1965-66; EdM, SUNY, 1968. ordained priest Roman Catholic Ch., 1956;. Lab technician Eastman Kodak Co., 1947-48; chemist Xerox Co., 1952; parish asst. Diocese Buffalo, 1956-59; instr. chemistry Bishop Turner H.S., Buffalo, 1959-74, dir. sci., 1959-70, 72-74; adminstr. Our Lady of the Rosary Parish, Wilson, N.Y., 1968; adminstr. St. Barnabas Parish and Sch. Depew, N.Y., 1973-75, pastor, 1976-90; prelate of honor, 1984, mem., supr., leader tng. team, 1979-90; pastor Sts. Peter and Paul Parish, Hamburg, N.Y., 1990-99; mem. sci. curriculum com. Dept. Edn. Diocese Buffalo, 1960-70, chmn. diocesan chemistry textbook evaluation com., 1961-70, mem. diocesan pastoral coun. for handicapped, 1976-82, sec. 1978-79, diocesan regional coord., 1979-80, mem. diocesan fin. com., 1984-94, diocesan priests coun., 1990-99, mem. diocesan coll. of consultors, 1994-99; active Diocesan Cons. Parish Computers, 1983-98, Diocesan Bd. Priests Retirement, 1985-91, 99—, Diocesan Cemetary Bd., 1994—, Sch. Bd. St. Francis H.S., 1992-98; diocesan bd. dirs. for TV prodn. 1986-94; chaplain Hyview Fire Co., 1976-81, Cheektowaga Police PBA, 1976-90, West End Fire Co., 1977-90, Depew Village Fire Co., 1980-88. Contbr. articles to profl. publs. Mem. Western N.Y. Sci. Congress Com., 1960-74, sec., 1968, co-chmn. 1969, chmn. 1972-73, state chmn. 1970; mem. gen. chemistry exam. com. N.Y. State Edn. Dept., 1970-73; mem. Maryvale Schs. Planning Bd., 1977-79; cons. sci. facilities in secondary schs.; mem. local IUE-AFL-CIO Scholarship Fund Com., 1968-71; mem. dist. com. Boy Scouts Am., Buffalo, 1957-74; bd. dirs. Tifft (Conservation) Farm, 1978-82, Hamburg Meals on Wheels, 1999-00; active Nat. Cath. Cemetary Conf., N.Y. State Fire Chaplains. With AUS, 1946-47. Recipient Disting. Svc. award in sci. edn., 1975, Justice and Charity award First Cath. Charities, 1999, Cure of ARS award Outstanding Priest, 1999. Mem. Sci. Tchrs. Assn., N.Y. (dir. 1971-73), Nat. Cath. Edn. Assn., Order of Arrow, KC. Address: 9686 Oak Grove Dr Angola NY 14006-8904

GREEN, GUY STEPHEN MONTAGUE, governor Tasmania; b. Launceston, Tasmania, July 26, 1937; s. Clement Francis Montague and Beryl Margaret Jenour (Williams) G.; m. Rosslyn Mary Marshall, Dec. 21, 1963; children: Jill, Ruth, David, Christopher. LLB with honors, U. Tasmania, 1960. Bar: Supreme Ct. Tasmania, 1960. Ptnr. Ritchie & Parker Alfred Green & Co., Tasmania, 1963-71; apptd. magistrate Tasmania, 1971-73, chief justice, 1973-95, lt. gov., 1982-95, gov., 1995—; law faculty mem. U. Tasmania, 1974-85; chmn. Tasmanian com. Duke of Edinburgh's award in Australia, 1975-80; Tasmanian regional com., 1975-80, dep. nat. chmn., 1980-85; dir. Winston Churchill Meml. Trust, 1975-85; chmn. Coun. Law Reporting, 1978-85; chancellor St. John Ambulance Australia, 1991-95; dep. prior, 1995—, priory exec. officer, 1984-91, pres. Tasmanian coun., 1984-92; chancellor U. Tasmania, 1985-95. Apptd. comdr. Royal Victorian Order, 2000. Apptd. Knight Commdr. Most Excellent Order of the British Empire, 1982, Knight of Grace in Most Venerable Order of the Hosp. of St. John of Jerusalem, 1985, Companion in the Gen. Divsn. of Order of Australia, 1994. Mem. Australian Inst. Jud. Adminstrn. (dep. chmn. 1986-88, coun. 1984-88), Tasmanian Club. Home: Govt House, Hobart TAS 7000, Australia

GREEN, HARRY EDWARD, electrical engineer, private consultant, educator; b. Adelaide, Australia, Feb. 11, 1935; s. Harry Edward and Alice Green; m. Helen Claire Rees, Nov. 25, 1961. B of Engring., U. Adelaide, 1957, M of Engring., 1964; PhD, Ohio State U., 1968. Registered profl. engr. Various positions Weapons Rsch. Establishment, Dept. of Supply, Salisbury, Australia, 1958-65, sr. rsch. scientist, applied physics div., 1968-69; prin. rsch. scientist Ctrl. Studies Establishment, Dept. of Supply, Canberra, Australia, 1970-72; prof., head dept. elec. and electronic engring. Univ. Coll., U. New South Wales, Campbell, Australia, 1972-86; chief div., high frequency rdar div. Surveillance Rsch. Lab., Dept. Def., Salisbury, 1986-91; dean Faculty of Engring. U. Adelaide, Australia, 1991-95; adj. rsch. prof. U. South Australia, 1995—; dir. AITEC Pty. Ltd., Adelaide, 1993-94; bd. dirs. Coop. Rsch. Ctr. for Power Generation from Low-Rank Coal, Melbourne, 1993-94. Contbr. numerous articles to profl. jours. Mem. South Australia State coun. Liberal Party of Australia, Adelaide, 1991—. Recipient John Madsen medal Instn. of Engrs., Australia, 1978, 99, Norman VW Hayes medal Instn. Radio and Electronics Engrs., Australia, 1981, Centennial medal IEEE, 1984. Fellow Instn. of Engrs. (various offices), Instn. Radio and Electronics Engrs. (coun. 1984); mem. IEEE (sr.; dir. Region 10 1983-84), Australian Joint Svcs. Staff Coll. Assn., Assn. Old Crows (assoc.), Sigma Xi. Home: 11a Bradfield St, Burnside 5066, Australia Office: Inst Telecomm Rsch, Mawson Lakes Blvd, Mawson Lakes SA 5095, Australia

GREEN, JENS-PETER, academic administrator; b. Bernburg, Saxony-Anhalt, Germany, Mar. 30, 1950; s. John Erik and Gisela (Barthel) G.; m. Hanna Elisabeth Braun, Mar. 30, 1972; children: Bjoern, Anke. State Exam Theology/English, Johannes-Gutenberg/U. Mainz, Germany, 1974, ThD, 1979. Tchr. Werner-Heisenberg Gymnasium, Heide, Germany, 1977-78, Ulrichsgymnasium, Norden, Germany, 1978; asst. U. Osnabrueck/Vechta, Germany, 1978-80; tchr., trainer, lang. cons. English lang. Gymnasium Antonianum, Vechta, 1980-87; lang. cons., German lang. cons. Wis. Dept. of Pub. Instrn., Madison, Wis., 1987-90; head of gymnasium sect. Lower Saxony Inst. of Insvc. Tng., Hildesheim, Germany, 1990-93; prin. Altes Gymnasium, Oldenburg, 1993—. Author: (book) Krise und Hoffnung. Der Evolutionshumanismus Julian Huxleys, 1981; co-author: (book) German for Communication: A Teacher's Guide, 1990, English G 2000 A3, 1999, English G 2000 A4, 1999; editor: Garrison Keillor: News from Lake Wobegon, 1995; co-editor: Britain and America. Images and Perspectives, 1997; contbr. articles to profl. jours. Avocations: cycling, hiking, reading. Home: Hoppenriekels 43B, 26125 Oldenburg L Saxony, Germany Office: Altes Gymnasium, Theaterwall 11, 26122 Oldenburg L Saxony, Germany

GREEN, JILL I., dance educator, researcher; b. Bklyn., June 19, 1954; d. Charles M. and Selma Z. (Stein) Green. BS summa cum laude, Bklyn. Coll., 1976; MA, NYU, 1981; PhD, Ohio State U., 1993. Lic. tchr. dance K-12, N.C., tchr. Kinetic Awareness. Dance instr. NYU, N.Y.C., 1981; dance tchr. Pub. Sch. 46, Bronx, N.Y., 1981-83; dance and movement instr. Lee Strasberg Theatre Inst., N.Y.C., 1983-86; dance tchr. Sheepshead Bay H.S., Bklyn., 1985-89; movement and relaxation specialist Columbus (Ohio) Psychol. Ctr., 1989-92; tchg. assoc. Ohio State U., Columbus, 1989-92, lectr., 1992-93; movement and body awareness educator Columbus Somatics Ctr., 1992-93; asst. prof. dance U. N.C., Greensboro, 1993—, coord. dance edn. program, 1993—; cons. for dance curriculum N.C. State Dept. Instrn., Raleigh, 1995-96; editl. cons. Ind. U. Press, 1995-96. Contbr. chpt. to book, articles to profl. jours. Vol. tchr. Very Spl. Arts Festival, Greensboro, 1994—, N.C. 4-H Coun., Greensboro, 1993—; demonstration classes N.C. Pub. Schs., 1993—; ednl. facilitator for homeless women WINGS Ctr. for SelfDiscovery, Columbus, 1992-93. New Faculty grantee, 1993-95; Dance Connections grantee Cmty. Found. Greater Greensboro, 1997; Ctr. for Study of Social Issues grantee, 1997—, U. N.C. Tchg. Excellence award, Sch. of Health and Human Performance, 1998. Mem. Nat. Dance Assn., N.C. Dance Alliance (bd. dirs. 1996-98), Congress on Rsch. in Dance (bd. dirs. 1998—), The Somatics Soc., Natl. Dance Edn. Assn., Am. Ednl. Rsch. Assn. Office: U NC at Greensboro Dept Dance PO Box 26169 Greensboro NC 27402-6169

GREEN, JOAL FEKETE STAFFORD, library media specialist; b. Geissen, Germany, June 20, 1948; d. Alfred Emery and Joanna Plowden Fekete; m. Carl Andrew Stafford, Aug. 1, 1970 (div. 1982); children: Drew, Sarah; m. Earl Alexander Green, July 31, 1992; children: Earl III, Staci. BA, U. Ctrl. Fla., 1970, MEd, 1974. Reference libr. Fla. Technol. U., Orlando, 1970; English tchr. Orange County Pub. Schs., Orlando, 1970-71, media specialist, 1970-80, 82—. Mem. NEA, Fla. Edn. Assn., Classroom Tchrs. Assn., Fla. Assn. Media Educators, Orange County Assn. Ednl. Media, Phi Delta Kappa. Roman Catholic. Avocations: reading, going to the beach, traveling, antique shopping. Home: 3331 Carla St Orlando FL 32806-7405 Office: Evans HS 4949 Silver Star Rd Orlando FL 32808-4539

GREEN, JOHN LAFAYETTE, JR., education executive; b. Trenton, N.J., Apr. 3, 1929; m. Harriet Hardin Hill, Nov. 8, 1962; 1 child, John Lafayette III. BA, Miss. State U., 1955; MEd, Wayne State U., 1971; PhD, Rensselaer Poly. Inst., 1974. Asst. to treas. Internat. Paper Co., 1955-57; mem. faculty U. Calif., Berkeley, 1957-65; v.p. U. Ga., Athens, 1965-71, Rensselaer Poly. Inst., Troy, N.Y., 1971-76; exec. v.p. U. Miami, 1976-80; sr. v.p. U. Houston, 1980-81; pres. Washburn U., Topeka, Kans., 1981-88; exec. dir. Assn. Collegiate Bus. Schs. and Programs, Overland Park, 1988-95; pres., chmn. bd. dirs. Strategic Planning/Mgmt. Assocs., Inc., Overland Park, Kans., 1981—; chmn. bd., CEO, Internat. Assembly for Collegiate Bus. Edn., Overland Park, 1997—; past pres. Kansas City and Topeka chpts. Planning Forum. Author: Budgeting, 1967, (with others) Cost Accounting, 1969, Administrative Data Processing, 1970, Strategic Planning, 1980, Strategic Planning: A System for Businesses, 1986, A Strategic Planning System for Higher Education, 1987, Strategy Development and Implementation for Banks, 1988, co-author: Outcomes Assessment in Higher Education Linked to Strategic Planning and Budgeting, 1997. Bd. dirs. Boy Scouts Am., Topeka, 1983-85. With U.S. Army 1951-53. Recipient Disting. Kansan of Yr. in Pub. Adminstrn. award Topeka Capital Jour., 1984, Kans. Pub. Adminstr. of Yr. award Am. Soc. Pub. Adminstrn., 1984, Disting. Exec. award Mktg. Exec. Kans., 1984, Edn. Leader's Hall of Fame award, 1995. Mem. AAUP, Conf. Bd., Am. Mgmt. Assn., Fin. Execs. Inst., Demographics Inst., Masons, Shriners, Royal Order of Jesters, Phi Delta Kappa, Beta Alpha Psi, Phi Kappa Phi, Pi Kappa Alpha, Delta Sigma Pi. Republican. Presbyterian. (elder, deacon). Avocations: golf, tennis. Home: 12018 Connell Dr Overland Park KS 66213-2526 Office: PO Box 25217 Shawnee Mission KS 66225-5217

GREEN, JONATHAN P., biologist, educator; b. N.Y.C., June 16, 1935; s. Harold and Bernice Targer G.; m. Joy Schochet, Aug. 30, 1959; children: Alexander, Stefan. BS, Pa. State U., 1957; PhD, U. Minn., 1963. Postdoctoral fellow Johns Hopkins U., Balt., 1963-64; asst. prof. Brown U., Providence, R.I., 1964-71; lectr. U. Malaya, Kuala Lumpur, Malaysia, 1971-78; assoc. prof. Reed Coll., Portland, Oreg., 1978-79; prof. Roosevelt U., Chgo., 1978—. E-mail: jgreen@roosevelt.edu. Home: 828 W George St Chicago IL 60657-5114 Office: Roosevelt Univ 430 S Michigan Ave Chicago IL 60605-1394

GREEN, JOSEPH LIBORY, lawyer; b. St. Louis, Mar. 20, 1960; s. Joseph Richard and Kathleen Ann Green; m. Sherry Michelle Fedder, Oct. 7, 1989; children: Bryan Smith, Samantha Joe Green, Jacob Fedder Green, Jacqueline Michelle Green. BSBA, Truman State U., 1982; JD, St. Louis U., 1987. Bar: Mo. 1988, U.S. Dist. Ct. (ea. dist.) Mo. 1993, U.S. Dist. Ct. (we. dist.) Mo. 1996, U.S. Ct. Appeals (8th cir.) 1998, U.S. Supreme Ct. 1998. Asst. pub. def. St. Joseph (Mo.) Pub. Def.'s Office, 1988; chief trial atty. St. Louis County Pub. Def.'s Office, Clayton, Mo., 1989-90; capital litigation atty. Mo. State Pub. Def.'s Office, St. Louis, 1990-93; assoc. Wittner, Poger, Rosenblum & Spewak, P.C., Clayton, 1993-96; sole practitioner St. Charles, Mo., 1996; ptnr. Baerveldt, Bagsby, Lee & Green, L.L.C., St. Charles, 1996—. Dem. candidate for county prosecutor, St. Charles, 1994, 98. Mem. Nat. Assn. Criminal Def. Lawyers, Mo. Assn. Criminal Def. Lawyers. Office: Baerveldt Bagsby Lee & Green LLP 566 1st Capitol Dr Saint Charles MO 63301-2726

GREEN, LAURA LORRAINE, foundation administrator; b. Denver, Nov. 23, 1924; d. Jack Wayne and Anna Laura (Cheney) Skiles; m. James Edward Green, Aug. 12, 1945 (dec. 1987); 1 child, Sharon Lee Payne. Grad. high sch., Santa Monica, Calif. Payroll Hanson Glove Factory, Milw., 1943-45; credit interviewer Broadway Dept. Store Orgn., Anaheim, Calif., 1956-57; sect. divsn. mgr. Hughes Aircraft Co., Fullerton, Calif., 1957-61; sec., payroll J.T. Murphy Carpet Co., San Jose, Calif.; owner 49er Trailer Ranch/RV & Mobile Home Park, Columbia, Calif., 1963-70; dir. adminstr. Sheriffs Aux. Vols., Tucson, 1988-92; retired. Mem. Ariz. County Attys. and Sheriffs Assn., Order of Ea. Star, Fraternal Order Police. Democrat. Methodist. Avocations: collecting stamps and antiques.

GREEN, LESLIE JOHN MACKIE, law educator; b. Bridge of Weir, Scotland, Nov. 27, 1956; s. Robert F. Green and Elizabeth Laird Mackie. BA with honors, Queen's U., Kinston, Can., 1978; MPhil, U. Oxford, Eng., 1980, PhD, 1984, MA, 1984. Fellow Lincoln Coll. Oxford, 1982-85; prof. Osgoode Hall Law Sch. York U., Toronto, Can., 1985-99. Editor: Law and the Community, 1989; author: Authority of the State, 1990; mem. editl. bd. Can. Jour. Law and Jurisprudence, 1989-99. Avocation: music. Fax: 416-736-5736. Office: Osgoode Hall Law Sch, 4700 Keele St, Toronto, ON Canada M3J 1P3

GREEN, LORA MURRAY, immunologist, researcher, educator; b. Redfield, S.D., Feb. 8, 1955; d. Everett k. and Marlene Y. (Palm) Murray; m. Timothy W. Green, Jan. 24, 1976; 1 child, Keigm W. BS in Biochemistry, U. Calif., Riverside, 1981, MS in Biochemsitry, 1982, PhD in Immunology, 1987. Fellow in immunology U. Calif., Riverside; fellow in cell biology Loma Linda (Calif.) U.; rsch. immunologist JL Pettis VA Med. Ctr., Loma Linda, 1991—; assoc. prof. medicine Loma Linda Med. Ctr., 1996—; bd. dirs. Dept. Micro and Molecular Genetics, Loma Linda; rschr. on radiation effects of thyroid NASA. Contbr. articles to profl. jours. Grantee VA, 1991-94, Loma Linda, 1995-96. Fellow Am. Assn. Immunology, Assn. Cell Biologists. Achievements include research in the role of the target tissue in autoimmune disease. Office: Loma Linda U Radiobiology Dept 11175 Campus St Loma Linda CA 92350-1700

GREEN, LOUIS FERDINAND, historian, educator; b. Saint Cloud, Paris, France, Sept. 4, 1929; arrived in Australia, 1940; s. Russell and Louie (Cowling) G.; m. Juanita Florence Crook, Mar. 31, 1951 (div. 1972); children: Karen, Natalie, Martin; m. Louise McOwan Powell, Feb. 2, 1979; children: Lucian, Antonia. BA, U. Queensland, 1951; MA, U. Adelaide, 1961; PhD, Monash U., 1989. Rsch. officer Dept. Def., Melbourne, Australia, 1951-57; tutor history U. Adelaide, 1958-60; lectr. history U. Tasmania, 1961-66; sr. lectr., reader history Monash U., Clayton, Australia, 1967-94. Author: Chronicle into History, 1972, Castruccio Castracani, 1986, Lucca Under Many Masters, 1995. Fellow Australian Acad. Humanities. Home: 82 Millswyn St, South Yarra Victoria 3141, Australia Office: Monash Univ History Dept, Clayton Victoria 3168, Australia

GREEN, MINO, engineering educator; b. N.Y.C., Mar. 10, 1927; arrived in Eng., 1934; s. Alexander and Elizabeth Rachel (Gorodetsky) G.; m. Diana Mary Allen, Sept. 12, 1951; children: David Mino Allen, Penelope Susan. BS, Durham (Eng.) U., 1948, PhD, 1951, DSc, 1965. Chartered engr. Group leader MIT, Cambridge, Mass., 1951-55; divsn. head rsch. Zenith Radio Corp., Chgo., 1955-60; assoc. dir. electrochem. lab. U. Pa., Phila., 1960-62; mng. dir. Zenith Radio Rsch. Corp. (U.K.) Ltd., London, 1962-72; reader Imperial Coll., London, 1972-83, prof., 1983-92; prof. emeritus, sr. rsch. fellow Imperial Coll. U. London, 1992—; cons. SIV, Italy, 1993-97, MMC, Japan, 1999-2000; vis. prof. Bradford U., Eng., 1965-72; cons. to various indsl. orgns., 1956—. Editor: (book) Solid State Surface Science, Vols. I to III, 1969-73; contbr. rsch. articles to profl. jours.; patentee in field. Fellow Instn. Elec. Engrs.; mem. Hurlingham Club. Avocation: hill walking. Home: 55 Gerard Rd, Barnes London SW13 9QH, England Office: Imperial Coll Elec Engring Dept, Exhibition Rd, London SW7 2BT, England

GREEN, PATRICIA PATAKY, school system administrator, consultant; b. N.Y.C., June 18, 1949; d. William J. and Theresa M. (DiGianni) P.; m. Stephen I. Green, Dec. 7, 1975. BS, U. Md., 1971, MEd, 1977, PhD, 1994. Tchr. Prince George's County (Md.) Pub. Schs., 1971-83; elem. instrnl. adminstrv. specialist Thomas Stone Sch., Mt. Ranier, Md., 1984-85, Glenridge Sch., Lanham, Md., 1984, Greenbelt (Md.) Ctr. Sch., 1983-84, Prince George's County Pub. Schs., 1985-91; prin. Columbia Park Sch., Landover, Md., 1985-91; asst. supt. Prince George's County Pub. Schs., 1991-95, assoc. supt., chief divsn. adminstr., 1995-2000, assoc. supt for pupil svcs., 1999—, acting dep. supt. for instrn., 2000—; cons. nationwide sch. systems; presenter in field. Editor, writer (newsletter) Tooth or Consequences, 1980—; featured in numerous mags. and on TV shows; contbr. articles to profl. jours. Apptd. commr. Prince George's Commn. for Children, Youth, and Families. Recipient Nat. Sch. Recognition award U.S. Dept. Edn., 1988, Outstanding Adminstr. award Prince George's County C. of C., 1990, Outstanding Rsch. award Md. Assn. Supervision and Curriculum Devel., 1995, Outstanding Educator award Prince George's County, 1983, Spotlight on Prevention award Md. State Atty. Gen., 1998. Mem. NAESP (Excellence of Achievement award 1988), ASCD, NEA, Nat. Sch. Bds. Assn., Nat. Assn. Secondary Sch. Prins., Am. Ednl. Rsch. Assn., Phi Kappa Phi. Kappa Delta Pi. Avocations: landscape gardening, photography, reading, writing, bicycling.

GREEN, PAUL JOHN, independent critic; b. Seattle, July 27, 1936; s. Howard William and Ruth Yeo G. BA in French, Seattle Pacific Coll., 1957; MA in English Lit., U. Wash., 1958; M of Libr. Sci., U. Calif., Berkeley, 1968; PhD in Lit. Studies, Wash. State U., 1981. Teaching asst. English U. Wash., Seattle, 1963-66; instr. English Ctrl. Wash. U., Ellensburg, 1966-67; rsch. asst. U. Calif., Berkeley, 1967-68; asst. serial libr. U. Oreg., Eugene, 1968-69; teaching asst. English Wash. State U., Pullman, 1974-76; ind. critic Spokane, Seattle, Pullman, 1981—. Author: The Life of Jack Gray: An Education in Living and in Love, 1991; contbr. articles to profl. jours. With USNR, 1953-65. Mem. AAUP, Am. Comp. Lit. Assn. Modern Lang. Assn., Internat. Platform Assn. Avocations: reading, writing, research. Home: 630 NE Maiden Ln Apt 10 Pullman WA 99163-4155

GREEN, PHYLLIS HARTMAN, writer, playwright; b. Pitts., June 24, 1932; d.Victor Geyer and Phyllis (Sailer) Hartman; m. Robert Bailey Green, Aug. 15, 1959; children: Sharon Buell, Bruce. BS in Edn, Westminster Coll., 1953; MEd, U. Pitts., 1955. Writer, playwright, 1972—. Author: The Fastest Quitter in Town, 1972, Nantucket Summer, 1974, Ice River, 1975, Wild Violets, 1977, Grandmother Orphan, 1977, Mildred Murphy, How Does Your Garden Grow?, 1977, Walkie-Talkie, 1978, Nicky's Lopsided, Lumpy, But Delicious Orange, 1978, A New Mother for Martha, 1978, Gloomy Louie, 1980, Bagdad Ate It, 1980 (Calif. Young Reader Medal 1984), The Empty Seat, 1980, Uncle Roland, The Perfect Guest, 1983, Eating Ice Cream with a Werewolf, 1983 (Maud Hart Lovelace award 1989), Bummer Summer, 1988, Chucky Bellman Was So Bad, 1991; playwright: Deer Season, 1980, Physically Handicapped Singles Dance, 1983, Acapulco Holiday, 1988. Named Best Actress in Del., Del. Play Festival, 1956.

GREEN, PNINA, physician; b. Odorhei, Romania, June 19, 1947; arrived in Israel, 1961; d. Menahem and Magdelena (Jankowitch) Roth; m. Yosef G.; 4 children. MD, Sackler Med. Sch., Tel Aviv U., Israel, 1972; PhD, Weizmann Inst. Sci., Israel, 1995. Deputy chief internal medicine RMC, Israel, 1997—; lectr. Tel Aviv U., Israel, 1997—. Contbr. articles to profl. jours. Mem. ISSFAL, Israel Soc. Internal Medicine, Israel Soc. Atherosclerosis. Office: Rabin Med Ctr, Beilinson Campus, 49100 Petah-Tikva Israel

GREEN, ROSARIO, federal official. Degree in Internat. Rels., Nat. Autonomous U. Mexico; M in Econs., El Colegio de Mexico. Min. fgn. affairs Mexicoan Govt.; prof. Nat. Autonomous U. Mexico. Author over ten books; contbr. articles to profl. jours. Amb. to GDR; under-sec. fgn. affairs; ofcl. UN, 1994; sec. fgn. affairs. Fax: 52 5 327 3025. Office: Ministry Fgn Affairs, Ricardo Flores Magon Num 1, 06995 Mexico City DF, Mexico*

GREEN, RUTHANN, marketing and management consultant; b. Streator, Ill., July 14, 1935; d. John Joseph and Edna Marie (Peters) G. BS in Edn., U. Ill., 1957. Elem. tchr. Jefferson Sch., Davenport, Iowa, 1957-59; tchr. Hinsdale (Ill.) Jr. High Sch., 1959-62; ednl. cons. Harcourt Brace & World, Chgo., 1962-63; exec. sec. Everpure, Inc., Oakbrook, Ill., 1963-68; ednl. cons.

Houghton Mifflin Co., Europe, 1968-69, Palo Alto, Calif., 1969-77; sr. mktg. mgr. Houghton Mifflin Co., Boston, 1977-87; v.p., nat. sales mgr. Riverside Pub. Co., Chgo., 1987-89; v.p., dir. mktg. McDougal, Littell & Co., Evanston, Ill., 1990-92; v.p., gen. mgr. Open Court Pub. Co., Chgo., 1992-94; pres. Peters & Green, Inc. Seminars & Bus. Devel., Chgo., 1994—. Author: WSIL: Why Should I Listen, 1987, 93, A Garfield Memoir, 1995. Bd. dirs. Ritchie Tower Condo Assn. Recipient Svc. award Am. Arbitration Assn., 1987, Golden Reel of Excellence Internat. TV Assn., 1983. Mem. Am. Mktg. Assn., Nat. Assn. Women Bus. Owners, Internat. Reading Assn., People for Am. Way, Common Cause, Am. Arbitration Assn., Urban Gateways (bd. dirs.). Avocations: reading, fitness activities, travel, art. Home and Office: 1310 N Ritchie Ct Apt 21A Chicago IL 60610-8405

GREEN, STEPHEN J., cardiovascular surgeon; b. Apr. 5, 1954. AB, Dartmouth Coll., 1976; MD, Tufts U., 1980. Intern then resident North Shore Univ. Hosp./Cornell, 1980-83; fellow in cardiology North Shore Univ. Hosp., 1983-85; assoc. prof. medicine NYU; assoc. dir. Cardiac Cath Labs North Shore Hosp., Manhasset, N.Y., chmn. cardiovascular svcs., performance improvement; adj. assoc. prof. medicine Cornell U. Office: North Shore Univ Hosp Divsn of Cardiology 300 Community Dr Manhasset NY 11030-3801

GREEN, SUZANNE, nurse; b. Bennington, Vt.; m. Arthur Edward Green; children: Jeannie, David, Tammie. Diploma in tchg.-supervision nursing, McGill U., Montreal, Que., Can.; BS in Cmty. Health Nursing, Russell Sage Coll. RN, N.Y., Mass., Vt., R.I., Colo. Staff nurse N.E. Deaconess Hosp., Joslin Clinic, Boston, Denver Gen. Hosp., Royal Victoria Hosp., Montreal, Pawtucket (R.I.) Meml. Hosp.; staff nurse, asst. head nurse S.W. Vt. Med. Ctr., Bennington; staff nurse, float nurse VAMC, Canandaigua, N.Y.; instr. LPNs State Vt./Dept. Edn., Bennington; staff nurse, supr. Bennington Area Home Health Agy.; instr. C.C. Vt., Bennington; adj. instr. RN program Finger Lakes C.C., Canandaigua, N.Y., LPN program Dept. Edn., State of N.Y., Flint; owner Green's Individualized Ednl. System. Author: Dyslexic Spel-Wel Dictionary, 1991, Green's Language Laterality Learning Literacy Guide, 1996, Dyslexic Smal Simpl Dictionary, 1999; creator high risk infant program, Bennington Home Health, 1980. Chmn. Bennington County Pres. Coun. Children, 1980; tutor Literacy Vols., Ontario County, N.Y., 1991-99, CPR/Heart Saver, Bennington, 1980-84; leader Webelos, Boy Scouts Am., Bennington, 1976-77; bd. dirs. Domestic Violence Project, Bennington, 1980, Reading Is Fundamental, Bennington, 1978-79, Teen Age Advocacy, Bennington, 1980; co-chmn. Water Intoxication Project/VAMC, Canandaigua, N.Y., 1995. Mem. Lady Shriners, Sigma Theta Tau. Republican. Avocations: golf, gardening, swimming, painting, writing poetry.

GREEN, TAMMIE, golfer; b. Somerset, Ohio, Dec. 17, 1959. Degree in recreation, Marshall U. Prof. golfer, 1986—; mem. exec. com LPGA, 1992-94. Named Rookie of Yr. LPGA, 1987; 6 career wins including 1989 du Maurier Ltd. Classic, Healthsouth Palm Beach Classic, Rochester Internat., 1993, Youngstown-Warren LPGA Classic, 1994, Sprint Titleholder Champion, Gaintt Eagle LPGA Classic, 1997, LPGA Corning Classic, 1998. Avocations: fishing, gardening, horseback riding, sports. Home: 4990 Township Road 147 NE Somerset OH 43783-9753 Office: 3990 Twp Rd 147 Somerset OH 43783*

GREENACRE, ROGER TAGENT, priest; b. E. Barnet, Eng., Nov. 17, 1930. BA, U. Cambridge, Eng., 1952, MA, 1956; postgrad., Cath. U. Louvain, Belgium, 1961-62. Ordained as deacon Ch. of Eng., 1954, as priest, 1955. Curate All Sts.' Hanworth, London, 1954-59; chaplain, lectr. Ely (Eng.) Theol. Coll., 1959-60; chaplain, asst. master Summer Fields Sch., Oxford, Eng., 1960-61; curate St. Mark's, Mayfair, London, 1962-63; chaplain Liddon Ho., London, 1963-65; chaplain St. George's Anglican Ch., Paris, 1965-75, rural dean, 1970-75; canon Chichester Cathedral, Sussex, Eng., 1975-2000, chancellor, 1975-77, precentor, 1977-2000; ret., 2000; priest-in-charge St. Michael's, Beaulieu-sur-Mer, France, 2000—; mem. gen. synod Ch. of Eng., 1980-85, 87-95; past mem. Liturgical Comm., Com. Roman Cath. Rels. Co-author: The Sacrament of Easter, 1989; author: The Catholic Church in France, 1996; contbr. to books, including Oil of Gladness, 1993, L'Esprit de l'Europe, vol. 2, 1993. Named Officer Nat. Order of Merit, Pres. French Republic, 1998, Chaplain of Jurisdiction and Officer Companionate of Merit, St. Lazarus Jerusalem, 2000. Fellow Internat. Pontifical Marian Acad. (corr.). Avocations: travelling, cultural, artistic and religious information on France.

GREENAWALD, GLENN DALE, social studies trainer, curriculum developer, researcher; b. Pitts., May 26, 1947; s. Glenn Victor and June (Scheller) G. BA, U. Pitts., 1969; MA, U. Minn., 1973; DA, Carnegie-Mellon U., 1978. Cert. social studies tchr., Pa. Tchr. Anoka (Minn.)-Hennepin Sch. Dist., 1969-70, Hempfield Sch. Dist., Greensburg, Pa., 1970-75; teaching asst., rsch. asst. Carnegie-Mellon U., Pitts., 1975-78; staff assoc. Social Sci. Edn. Consortium, Boulder, Colo., 1978-82, 87-91; dir. social studies W.Va. Dept. Edn., Charleston, 1982-85; dir. Learning Improvement Svcs., Nederland, Colo., 1985—; dir. Ctr. for Teaching Social Sci. U. No. Colo., Greeley, 1991-93; exec. dir. Colo. Close Up, 1985—. Author: (with Betty Dillon Peterson) Staff Development in the Social Studies, 1979, Washington Close Up Current Issues Teachers Guide, 1990, The Railroad Era, 1991. Mem. Amnesty Internat., Sierra Club, Legal Def. Fund, Colo. Mountain Club. Recipient numerous grants. Mem. ASCD, Nat. Coun. for Social Studies (chmn. archives com. 1990—, co-chmn. citizenship com. 1981), Coun. of State Social Studies Specialists; Coll. and Univ. Faculty Assembly, Social Studies Specialist Assn., Wash. Coun. for Social Studies, Colo. Coun. for Social Studies (regional dir. 1992, pres. 1994-96), Phi Delta Kappa. Avocations: running, backpacking, hiking, biking. Home and Office: 2020 Oak Ave Boulder CO 80304-1320

GREENAWALT, WILLIAM SLOAN, lawyer; b. Bklyn., Mar. 4, 1934; s. Kenneth William and Martha Frances (Sloan) G.; m. Jane DeLano Plunkett, Aug. 17, 1957 (div. May 1986); m. Peggy Ellen Freed Tomarkin, Oct. 31, 1987; children: John DeLano, David Sloan, Katherine Downs. AB, Cornell U., 1956; LLB, Yale U., 1961. Bar: N.Y. 1962, U.S. Dist. Ct. (so. and ea. dists.) N.Y. 1962, U.S. Ct. Apls. (2d cir.) 1962, U.S. Supreme Ct. 1966. Assoc. Sullivan & Cromwell, N.Y.C., 1961-65; N.E. regional legal svcs. dir. U.S. Office Econ. Opportunity, N.Y.C., 1965-68; assoc. Rogers & Wells, N.Y.C., 1968-69, ptnr., 1969-77, sr. ptnr., 1977-81; sr. ptnr. Halperin, Shivitz, Eisenberg, Schneider & Greenawalt, N.Y.C., 1981-86, Eisenberg Honig Fogler Greenawalt & Davis, N.Y.C., 1986-91, Bangser Klein Rocca & Blum, N.Y.C., 1991-93, Loselle Greenawalt Kaplan Blair & Adler, N.Y.C., 1993-97, Loselle Greenawalt Kaplan & Blair, N.Y.C., 1997-99, Meyer Greenawalt Taub & Wild, LLP, N.Y.C., 1999—; lectr. in field. Bd. editors: Yale Law Jour., 1959-61; contbr. articles in field to profl. jours. Chmn. bd. dirs. Applied Resources, Inc., N.Y.C., 1968-70; chmn. Cmty. Aid Employment of Ex-Offenders, Westchester, N.Y., 1971; pres. Westchester Legal Svcs., 1971-74, bd. dirs., 1975-91; mem. N.Y. State Gov.'s Task Force on Elem. and Secondary Edn., 1974-75; mem. Pres. Carter's Task Force on Criminal Justice, 1976; mem. adv. coun. N.Y. State Senate Dems., 1978—; asst. and acting treas. N.Y. State Dem. Party, 1990-96, vice chair, 1996—, mem. state com., 1974—; chair Greenburgh Dem. Party, 1997—; mem. Greenburgh Recreation Commn., 1976-83, Dem. Statewide Spl. Commn. on Polit. Ethics, 1986-87, Statewide Spl. Commn. on Election Law and Campaign Spending Reform, 1989-95; pres. Westchester Crime Victims Assistance Agy., 1981-82; commr. Taconic State Pks., Recreation and Hist. Preservation Commn., 1984-96, chmn., 1989-96; vice chmn. N.Y. State Coun. on Pks., Recreation and Hist. Preservation, 1989-94; moderator Scarsdale Congl. Ch., 1988-90; mem. Westchester County Parks, Recreation and Conservation Bd., 1998—; mem. Westchester County Execs. Transition Team on Planning, 1997. Lt. comdr. USN, 1956-58, with Res., 1961-68. Fellow N.Y. Bar Found.; mem. ABA, Am. Arbitration Assn. (mem. panel comml. arbitrators 1977—), N.Y. State Bar Assn. (chmn. com. on availability of legal svcs. 1968-70, chmn. action unit 3 1979-81, chmn. spl. commn. on alternatives to jud. resolution of disputes 1981-85), Assn. of Bar of City of N.Y., Nat. Legal Aid and Defenders Assn., Sphinx Head, Aleph Samach, County Tennis Club Westchester (Scarsdale, N.Y., pres. 1979-80), Yale Club (Yale Law jour. 1959-61), Phi Alpha Delta, Chi Psi. Democrat. Congregationalist. Home: 24 Lewis Ave Hartsdale NY 10530 Office: Meyer Greenawalt Et Al 230 Park Ave Rm 2525 New York NY 10169-2599

GREENAWAY, JOHN MOORE, physician, consultant; b. Sydney, Australia, Aug. 29, 1928; s. Sir Thomas Moore and Lady Lavinia (Figtree) G.; m. Judith Anne Ryan, Nov. 19, 1955; children: Timothy, Sally-Anne, Simon, Nicholas, Katharine, Jonathan. MB, BS, U. Sydney, 1951. Resident, registrar Royal Prince Alfred Hosp., Sydney, 1951-56; registrar London Hosp., 1957; rsch. fellow Kings Coll. Hosp., London, 1958-59; cons. physician Hornsby Dist. Hosp., Sydney, 1962-86; vis. med. officer Royal Prince Alfred Hosp., Sydney, 1960-2000; tutor U. Sydney, 1960-2000, hon. life mem. faculty medicine, 1994—; chief med. officer Australian Reinsurance Co., 1965-97. Co-author: Hormones in Blood, 1961. Fellow Royal Australian Coll. Physicians, Royal Coll. Phys.; mem. Diabetes Soc. Australia, Endocrine Soc. Australia, Royal Sydney Golf Club, Australian Club. Avocations: tennis, music. Home: 5 Yarranabbe Rd, Darling Point Sydney 2027, Australia Office: 231 Macquarie St, Sydney NSW 2000, Australia

GREENAWAY, PAUL RAYMOND, gallery director; b. Sydney, Australia, June 30, 1955; s. Raymond Lindsay and Junette (Phillips) G. Degree in fine arts, South Australian Sch. Art, 1977; diploma in restoration, Inst. Art Restoration, 1981. Lectr. Chamberwell Sch. Art, London, 1979-80; artists-in-residence Edith Cowan U., Perth, Australia, 1981; lectr. art history Chisholm Inst., Melbourne, Australia, 1982, Newcastle (Australia) U., 1983, 85; lectr. art S. Australian Sch. Art, Adelaide, 1986; artist-in-residence Sepik Govt., Papua, New Guinea, 1987-88; lectr. art U Gujarat, Ahmedabad, India, 1989; lectr. art theory N.A.S.A., Adelaide, 1990-93; dir. Greenaway Art Gallery, Adelaide, 1991—; mem. adv. com. Cultural Industries Com., South Australia, 1994; commr. for ARCO-Australia in Madrid, 2002. Visual exhbns. include 15 One-man shows, 1976-90. Mem. Australian Comml. Gallery Assn., South Australian Visual Arts Com. (bd. dirs. 1993—), Spanish C. of C. (founding mem. 1993—). Home and office: 39 Rundle St Kent Town, Adelaide 5067, Australia

GREENBERG, ALAN COURTNEY (ACE GREENBERG), stockbroker; b. Wichita, Kans., Sept. 3, 1927; s. Theodore H. and Esther (Zeligson) G.; m. Kathryn Olson, June 27, 1987; children: Lynn, Theodore. Student, U. Mo., 1949. With Bear Stearns & Co., N.Y.C., 1949—, gen. ptnr., 1958—, chmn. bd., CEO, 1978-93, chmn. exec. com., sr. mng. dir., 1993—. Winner Nat. Bridge Championship, 1977; recipient Horatio Alger award, 1997. Mem. Soc. Am. Magicians, Harmonie Club, Bond Club, Deep Dale Club. Office: Bear Stearns Co 245 Park Ave New York NY 10167-0002

GREENBERG, BARRY MICHAEL, talent executive; b. Bklyn., Nov. 9, 1951; s. Aaron Herbert and Alice Rhoda (Strauss) G.; m. Susan Kay Greenberg, Feb. 19, 1990; 1 child, Samuel Jacob; 1 child by previous marriage: Seth Grahame-Smith. BA, Antioch U. Dir. B'nai B'rith, Phila., 1976-80; acting dir. Jewish Nat. Fund, L.A., 1980-81; chmn. Celebrity Connection, Beverly Hills, Calif., 1981—; co-founder Beverly Hills Air Force Co.; ptnr. U.S. Film Force Co. Emeritus mem. Air Force adv. bd. USAF; mem. Wilshire cmty. police adv. bd. L.A. Police Dept.; fin. co-chair, past chair Cmty.-Police Adv. Bd. Summit; mem. 50th Anniversary of WWII com. U.S. Dept. Def.; mem. pub. safety steering com. L.A. 4th Councilmanic Dist.; mem. exec. bd. CDC Bus. Responds to AIDS program; co-founder Windsor Watch; adv. bd. Windsor Sq. Assn.; charter past pres. entertainment industry unit B'nai B'rith. With USAF, 1969-75. Recipient Chief of Chaplains Meritorious Svc. award, USAF. Mem. Def. Orientation Conf. Assn., Air Force Pub. Affairs Alumni Assn. Jewish. Avocations: pilot, music. Office: Celebrity Connection 4311 Wilshire Blvd # 300 Los Angeles CA 90010-3713

GREENBERG, BENJAMIN, physician; b. N.Y.C., Sept. 10, 1914; s. Moses and Beatrice (Kasten) G.; children: William Michael, Harvey Herman, Barry Edward. BA, Ind. U., 1936; MD, U. Edinburgh, Scotland, 1941. Intern Maimonides Hosp., N.Y.C., 1942-43; resident in surgery Maimonide Hosp., N.Y.C., 1943-44; pvt. practice N.Y.C., from 1946. Contbr. articles to profl. jours. Bd. dirs. Rockwood Park Security Assn.; chmn. adv. bd. Rep. Party; mem. Inner Circle Nat. Rep. Party, mem. Round Table; mem. Citizens Ambassador Program. Recipient Medal of Freedom award Sen. Rep. Party, 1994. Mem. AMA, Am. Acad. Family Practice, Am. Acad. Sports Medicine and Rsch., Rockwood Park Civic Assn. (bd. dirs. 1960-70), POan Am. Med. Assn., N.Y. State Med. Assn., Queens County Acad. Medicine. Republican. Jewish. Avocations: tennis, golf, photography.

GREENBERG, HELAINE IRIS, volunteer; b. Chgo., July 31, 1943; d. Arnold Sheldon and Adele Schaffner; m. George Howard Greenberg, June 12, 1966 (dec. Mar. 1994); children: Lauren, Leslie, Jason. BA in Tchg., U. Ill., 1965; MA in Journalism, U. Wis., 1975. graphics and publs. com. Jr. League Reno, 1982-84, mktg. com., 1983-84; candidate selection com. Women's Polit. Caucus, 1984; govs. appointee Truckee Meadows Human Svcs. Adv. Com., 1985-87; bd. dirs. Reno H.S. Boosters, 1986-87; trustee, sec. Biggest Little City Com., 1987-90; rec. sec., bd. mem. St. Mary's Hosp. Guild, 1987; no. Nev. chairperson Smoke-free Class of 2000, 1988-90; cmty. bd. mem. Sanford Ctr. for Aging, U. Nev., Reno, 1995—; tchr. positive aging classes Eldercollege, U. Nev., Reno., Silver Connection St. Mary's Hosp., Lake Tahoe Wellness Conf. for Srs., 1997—. E-mail: hgsunshine@aol.com.

GREENBERG, HINDA FEIGE, library director; b. Bayreuth, Germany, Feb. 26, 1947; came to U.S., 1951; d. Samuel Leon and Sima (Schampagnere) F.; m. Joseph Lawrence, July 6, 1968; children: David Micah, Jacob Alexander. BA, Temple U., 1969; MLS, Rutgers U., 1981; PhD, Drexel U., 1999. Assoc. librarian Ednl. Testing Svc., Princeton, N.J., 1981-86; dir. info. ctr. Carnegie Found., Princeton, 1986-97; dir. info. svcs. Robert Wood Johnson Found., Princeton, 1997—.

GREENBERG, IRA ARTHUR, psychologist; b. Bklyn., June 26, 1924; s. Philip and Minnie (S.) G.; m. Martha Estella Cantrell, 1949 (div. 1950); m. Judith Linda Burgard-Rials, 1952 (div. 1954); m. Monita Ruth Niborod, 1961 (div. 1965). BA in Journalism, U. Okla., 1949; MA in English, U. So. Calif., 1962; MS in Counseling, Calif. State U., L.A., 1963; PhD in Psychology, Claremont (Calif.) Grad. Sch., 1967; Grad., Marine Corps Inst.'s Command and Staff Coll., 1992. Editor Ft. Riley (Kans.) Guidon, 1950-51; copy editor, reporter Columbus (Ga.) Enquirer, 1951-55; reporter Louisville Courier-Jour., 1955-56, L.A. Times, 1956-62; free-lance writer L.A., Montclair, Camarillo, Calif., 1960-69, 76—; counselor Claremont Coll. Psychol. Clinic and Counseling Ctr., 1964-65; lectr. psychology Chapman Coll., Orange, Calif., 1965-66; psychologist Camarillo State Hosp., 1967-69, supervising psychologist, 1969-73, part-time clin. psychologist, 1973-93; part-time asst. prof. edn. San Fernando Valley State Coll., Northridge, Calif., 1967-69, lectr. psychodrama, social welfare U. Calif. Extension Divsn., Santa Barbara, 1968-69; vis. prof. edn. U. Nev., Reno, 1977—; vol. psychologist Free Clinic, L.A., 1968-70; staff dir. Calif. Inst. Psychodrama, 1969-71; tng. cons. Topanga Ctr. for Human Devel., 1970-75, bd. dirs., 1971-74, faculty Calif. Sch. Profl. Psychology, 1970-80; founder, exec. dir. Behavioral Studies Inst., mgmt. cons., L.A., 1970—; pvt. practice cons. in psychology, psychodrama, hypnosis, 1970—; founder, exec. dir. Psychodrama Ctr. for L.A., Inc., 1971—, Group Hypnosis Ctr., L.A., 1976—; prodr., host TV talk show Crime and Pub. Safety, Century Comm., Channel 77, 1983—. Author: Psychodrama and Audience Attitude Change, 1968; editor, author: Psychodrama: Theory and Therapy, 1974, Group Hypnotherapy and Hypnodrama, 1977. Vol. humane officer State of Calif., 1979-89; res. officer L.A. Police Dept., 1980-86; bd. dirs. Humane Educators Coun., 1982-86; mem. Nat. Coun. Employer Support of Guard and Res., 1998—. With AUS 11th engr. combat bn. XXI Corps, Seventh Army ETO, 1943-46; USAR, 1950-51, sgt. first class 2000; capt. Calif. State Mil. Res., 1986-93, maj., 1993-2000; lt. col. U.S. Svc. Command, 2000—. Fellow Am. Soc. Clin. Hypnosis, Am. Soc. Group Psychotherapy and Psychodrama; mem. Am. Psychol. Assn., Calif. Psychol. Assn., L.A. County Psychol. Assn., So. Calif. Soc. Clin. Hypnosis (pres. 1977-78), Group Psychotherapy Assn. So. Calif. (pres. 1987-88), So. Calif. Psychotherapy Affiliation (dir. 1976-85), Am. Soc. Psychical Rsch., Assn. Rsch. and Enlightenment, Peace Officers Assn., L.A. County, Acad. TV Arts and Scis., Nat. Acad. Cable Programming, UDT/SEAL Assn., Navy Amphibious Scouts and Raiders Assn., 11th Engr. Combat Battalion Assn., 78th Infantry Divsn. Assn., VFW, Am. Legion, Jewish War Vets., State Def. Forces Assn. Am., State Def. Forces Assn. Calif., Mensa, Am. Zionist Fedn., NRA, Calif. Rifle and Pistol Assn., SW Pistol League, Animal Protection Inst. Am., L.A. SPCA, Hebrew Nat. Orphan Home Alumni Assn., Sigma Delta Chi. Clubs: Sierra, Greater L.A. Press; B'nai B'rith; Beverly Hills Gun. Office: BSI & Group Hypnosis Ctr 8939 S Sepulveda Blvd Ste 318 Los Angeles CA 90045-3605

GREENBERG, JACOB HASKELEVICH, chemist; b. Odessa, Ukraine, USSR, Jan. 29, 1938; arrived in Israel, 1992; s. Haskel Borisovich Greenberg and Rosalia Yakovlevna Khromchenko; m. Tatyana Borisovna Ilina, Sept. 24, 1961; children: Tony, Andy. Diploma, Cen. Musical Sch./Tchaikovsky State Conservatoire, Moscow, 1956; MSc, Inst. Chem. Tech., Moscow, 1962; PhD, Inst. Gen. Inorganic Chemistry, Moscow, 1966, DSc, 1989. Jr. scientist Inst. Gen. Inorganic Chemistry, Moscow, 1962-66, rsch. scientist, 1966-75, sr. scientist, 1975-89, leading scientist, 1989-92; sr. scientist Hebrew U., Jerusalem, 1993-99, prof., 1999—; cons. Trucks and Tractors Corp., Moscow, 1985-90, PLATAN Elec., Moscow, 1985-91, URIGAL Tech., Rehovot, Israel, 1994—, II-VI Inc., Saxonburg, Pa., 1996—, IMARAD Imaging Sys., Ltd., Rehovot, 1998—. Co-author 5 books; patentee in field; contbr. over 150 articles to profl. jours. Named Rschr. of Yr., USSR Acad. Sci., 1967, 76, 88, 91; recipient EXPO-USSR medal, 1977, 89. Mem. AAAS, Am. Chem. Soc., N.Y. Acad. Scis., Israel Assn. Crystal Growth. Avocations: classical music, literature, athletics. Home: 14 6 Hatziltzal St, 98370 Maale Adumim Israel Office: Dept Inorganic Chemistry, Hebrew U, 91904 Jerusalem Israel

GREENBERG, JUDITH ANN, real estate developer; b. Pitts., July 8, 1951; d. Jack Zachary and Mary Adele (Chayet) G.; m. Manny Schechter, Feb. 18, 1990. BBA, SUNY, Binghamton, 1972. Account exec. Wells, Rich, Greene, N.Y.C., 1972-73, Weltin Advt., Atlanta, 1973-74, Grey Advt., N.Y.C., 1974-76; account supr. N. W. Ayer, N.Y.C., 1976-82; mng. dir. Core Resource (Hong Kong) Ltd., Hong Kong, 1982-92; pres. Elysse of Key West (Fla.) Inc., 1993—, Elysee Investments of Key West Inc., 1995—, Key West MJM Inc., 1996—; pres., gen. mgr. Hollywood (Fla.) Hotels Mgmt. Inc., 1996—; pres. Hollywood Realty Investors Inc., 1997—, 130 Duval St Inc., Key West, 1998—, Planet of Key West Inc., 1998—. Mem. Downtown Hollywood Bus. Assn. (v.p. 1996-98), Hollywood C. of C. Jewish. Office: Ramada Inn Hollywood 1925 Harrison St Hollywood FL 33020-5017

GREENBERG, LENORE, public relations professional; b. Flushing, N.Y.; d. Jack and Frances Orenstein. BA, Hofstra U.; MS, SUNY. Dir. pub. rels. Bloomingdale's, Short Hills, N.J., 1977-78; dir. comms. N.J. Sch. Bds. Assn., Trenton, 1978-82; dir pub. info. N.J. State Dept. Edn., Trenton, 1982-90; assoc. exec. dir. Nat. Sch. Pub. Rels. Assn., Arlington, Va., 1990-91; pres. Lenore Greenberg & Assocs., Inc., 1991—; adj. prof. pub. rels. Rutgers U. Freelance feature writer N.Y. Times. Mem. bd. assocs. McCarter Theatre, Princeton, N.J.; mem. Franklin Twp. Zoning Bd. Adjustment; mem. Franklin Twp. Human Rels. Commn.; chair Somerset County LWV; instr. Bus. Vols. for the Arts. Recipient award Am. Soc. Assn. Execs., award Women in Comms., award Internat. Assn. Bus. Communicators; Gold Medallion awrd Nat. Sch. Pub. Rels. Assn. Mem. Pub. Rels. Soc. Am. (accredited; pres. N.J. State chpt., nat. nominating and accreditation coms., Silver Anvil award), Nat. Health/Edn. Consortium. Home and Office: 30971 Carrara Rd Laguna Niguel CA 92677-2757

GREENBERG, MAURICE RAYMOND, insurance company executive; b. N.Y.C., May 4, 1925; s. Jacob and Ada (Rheingold) G.; m. Corinne Phyllis Zuckerman, Nov. 12, 1950; children: Jeffrey W., Evan G., L. Scott, Cathleen J. Pre-law cert., U. Miami, Fla., 1948; LLB, N.Y. Law Sch., 1950, also JD (hon.); JD (hon.), New Eng. Sch. Law, 1970, Bryant Coll., Middlebury Coll., Brown U., Pace U. Bar: N.Y. 1953. With Continental Casualty Co., 1952-60; joined Am. Internat. Group Inc., N.Y.C., 1960—, pres. subs. Am. Home Assurance Co., 1962-67, pres., CEO, 1967—, chmn. bd., CEO, 1989—; mem. Bus. Roundtable, pres.'s adv. com. Trade Policy and Negotiations; vice-chmn. Ctr. for Strategic and Internat. Studies; chmn. U.S.-China Bus. Coun.; vice-chmn. Coun. on Fgn. Rels.; founding chmn. U.S.-Philippine Bus. Com.; chmn. emeritus NYH, 1995; bd. govs. N.Y. Hosp. Bd. govs. N.Y. Hosp.; mem. Pres.'s adv. com. on trade negotiations Ctr. for Strategic and Internat. Studies, mem. bus. roundtable. Capt. U.S. Army, ETO, Korea. Decorated Bronze Star. Mem. N.Y. Bar Assn., The Asia Soc. (chmn.), Police Athletic League, City Athletic Club, Sky Club, India House, Lotos Club, Harmonie Club, Georgetown Club (washington). Office: Am Internat Group Inc 70 Pine St New York NY 10270-0002

GREENBERG, MYRON SILVER, lawyer; b. L.A., Oct. 17, 1945; s. Earl W. and Geri (Silver) G.; m. Shlomit Gross; children: David, Amy, Sophie, Benjamin. BSBA, UCLA, 1967; JD, 1970. Bar: Calif., 1971, U.S. Dist. Ct. (middle dist.) Calif. 1971, U.S. Tax Ct. 1977; cert. splst. in taxation law bd. legal specialization State Bar Calif.; CPA, Calif. Staff acct. Touche Ross & Co., L.A., 1970-71; assoc. Kaplan, Livingston, Goodwin, Berkowitz, & Selvin, Beverly Hills, Calif., 1971-74; ptnr. Myron S. Greenberg, a Profl. Corp., Larkspur, Calif., 1982—; professorial lectr. tax. Golden Gate U.; instr. U. Calif., Berkeley, 1989—; mem. taxation law adv. commn. Calif. Bd. Legal Specialization, 1998—, vice-chair, 2000. Author: California Attorney's Guide to Professional Corporations, 1977, 79; bd. editors UCLA Law Rev., 1969-70. Mem. San Anselmo Planning Commn., 1976-77; mem. adv. bd. cert. program personal fin. planning U. Calif., Berkeley, 1991—. Mem. AHA (bd. dirs. Marin county chpt. 1984-90, pres. 1988-89), ABA, AICPAs, L.A. County Bar Assn., Marin County (Calif.) Bar Assn. (bd. dirs. 1994-2000, pres. 1999), Real Estate Tax Inst. Calif. Cont. Edn. Bar (planning com.), Larkspur C. of C. (bd. dirs. 1985-87). Democrat. Jewish. Office: # 205 700 Larkspur Landing Cir Larkspur CA 94939-1711

GREENBERG, PHILIP ALAN, lawyer; b. Bklyn., Aug. 2, 1948; s. Harry and Jeannette (Nataf) G. BA cum laude, Bklyn. Coll., 1970; JD, N.Y.U., 1973. Bar: N.Y. 1974, U.S. Dist. Ct. (ea. and so. dists.) N.Y. 1975, U.S. Ct. Appeals (2d cir.) 1975, U.S. Supreme Ct. 1977 N.J. 1988. Assoc. Kamerman & Kamerman, N.Y.C., 1973-78, ptnr., 1978-82; ptnr. Segal, Liling, Erlitz & Greenberg, N.Y.C., 1982, Segal, Liling & Greenberg, N.Y.C., 1982-84, Segal & Greenberg, N.Y.C., 1984; mng. ptnr. Segal, Post, DeMott & Crow, N.Y.C., 1985, Segal, Greenberg, McDonald & Maher, N.Y.C., 1985-86, Segal, Greenberg & McDonald, N.Y.C., 1986-87, Segal & Greenberg, N.Y.C., 1987-93, Bizar & Martin, N.Y.C., 1993-95; ptnr. Wallman Greenberg Gasman & McKnight, N.Y.C., 1995—; mem. faculty para legal Sobelsohn Sch. Trustee Congregation Emunath Israel, 1984—, chmn. law and ins. com., 1987—. Mem. ABA (com. mem., lit. mem.), N.Y. Bar Assn., Assn. of Bar of City of N.Y., Mason (Maimonides-Marshall #739, master), Masters & Wardens Assn. (past pres. 6th Manhattan 1990-91), Internat. Assoc. Tribune, Phi Alpha Delta. Democrat. Jewish. Home: 7 Francisco Ave Little Falls NJ 07424-2316 Office: Wallman Greenberg Gasman & McKnight 350 5th Ave Ste 3000 New York NY 10118-3022

GREENBERG, WILLIAM MICHAEL, psychiatrist; b. Bklyn., Oct. 19, 1946; s. Benjamin Greenberg and Marilyn (Berger) Hamberg; m. Wendy Faith Megerman, June 14, 1992. BA, Queens Coll., 1968; postgrad., U. Medicine & Dentistry N.J., 1974-76; MD, Albert Einstein Coll. Medicine, 1978. Diplomate Am. Bd. Psychiatry and Neurology and bd. cert. in geriatric psychiatry, forensic psychiatry and addiction psychiatry; cert. clin. psychopharmacology. Computer programmer Western Electric Co., N.Y.C., 1970-73; rsch. asst. Bklyn. Jewish Hosp., 1973-74; resident in psychiatry Bronx (N.Y.) Mcpl. Hosp. Ctr., 1978-83, house staff pres., 1981-82; acting med. dir. Met. Ctr. for Mental Health, N.Y.C., 1983; staff psychiatrist Bronx Psychiat. Ctr., 1983-84; dir. psychiatry clinic North Cen. Bronx Hosp., 1984-88; psychiatrist, cons. Montefiore Mental Health Svcs. at Rikers Island, East Elmhurst, N.Y., 1985-86; pvt. practice Bronx, 1985-88; chief psychiatrist, attending staff mem. Bergen Pines County Hosp. (now Bergen Regional Med. Ctr.), Paramus, N.J., 1988-96, dir. of psychiat. rsch., 1993-2000, interim med. dir. psychiatry, 1996-98, dir. psychiatry residency tng. program, 1997-2000, mem. spkr.'s bur., 1988-2000, chmn. instnl. rev. bd., 1996-2000; attending psychiatrist Nathan Kline Inst., 2000—, Rockland Psychiat. Ctr., 2000—; pvt. practice, N.J., 1997—; attending psychiatrist Nathan Kline Inst. for Rsch., Rockland Psychiat. Ctr., Orangeburg, N.Y., 2000—; asst. clin. prof. Albert Einstein Coll. Medicine, Bronx, 1988-90; vis. asst. prof. Med. Coll. Pa., 1990-94; adj. asst. prof. Med. Coll. Pa. and Hahnemann U., 1994-2000, adj. assoc. prof., 2000—; prin. investigator for clin. drug trials. Asst. editor Community Psychiatrist, 1985-89; mem. editorial bd. Einstein Quar. Jour. Biology and Medicine, 1987—; contbr. articles to profl. jours.; reviewer profl. jours., books. Union rep. Com. Interns and Residents, N.Y.C., 1979-81; speaker's bur. Physicians for Social Responsibility, N.Y.C., 1982-84. Rock Sleyster Meml. scholar AMA, 1977; recipient Bergen Pines Psychiatry

Residency Teaching award, 1991, Psychiatrist Recognition award N.J. Alliance for the Mentally Ill, 1996. Mem. AAAS, APHA, Am. Psychiat. Assn., Am. Assn. Cmty. Psychiatrists, Assn. for Advancement of Philosophy and Psychiatry, North Jersey Psychiat. Soc. (pres. 1998-99). Avocations: analytic philosophy, meditation, computers, photography. Office: Bergen Regional Med Ctr Divsn Psychiatry Paramus NJ 07652

GREENBERGER, I. MICHAEL, lawyer; b. Scranton, Pa., Oct. 30, 1945; s. David and Betty (Kabatchnick) G.; m. Marcia Devins, July 19, 1969; children: Sarah Devins, Anne Devins. AB, Lafayette Coll., 1967; JD, U. Pa., 1970. Bar: D.C. 1971, U.S. Dist. Ct. D.C. 1971, U.S. Ct. Appeals (D.C. cir.) 1971, U.S. Supreme Ct. 1975. Law clk. to Judge Carl McGowan U.S. Ct. Appeals for D.C. Circuit, Washington, 1970-71; legis. asst. to U.S. Congresswoman Elizabeth Holtzman, 1972-73; atty., advisor Office of Criminal Justice, Office U.S. Atty. Gen., 1973; assoc. Shea & Gardner, Washington, 1973-77, ptnr., 1977-97; dir. divsn. of trading and markets U.S. Commodity Futures Trading Commn., 1997-99; counselor to U.S. Atty. Gen., 1999, prin. dep. assoc., atty. gen., 1999—; bd. govs. D.C. Bar 1995-98, com. on legal ethics, 1993-95; mem. D.C. Cir. Adv. Com. on Procedures, 1983-89; mem. steering com. D.C. Pro Bono Partnership, 1994-97, Lafayette Coll. Leadership Coun., 1994-99; mediator office of cir. exec. U.S. Cts. for D.C., 1989—; mem. D.C. Cir. Jud. Conf., 1983—; legal cons. Software Engring. Inst., Carnegie-Mellon U., 1986-87; mem. steering com. Pres.'s Working Group on Fin. Mkts., 1997-99; mem. hedge fund task force Internat. Orgn. of Secs. Commrs., 1999. Editor-in-chief U. Pa. Law Rev., 1969-70; contbr. articles to profl. jours. Bd. dirs. Washington Legal Clinic for the Homeless, 1993-98, Am. Rivers, 1993-98, sec., 1995-98; bd. dirs. MIT Enterprise Forum Washington, 1984-87, Advanced Tech. Assn. Md., 1985-87, D.C. Prisoners' Legal Svc. Project, 1997-98. Mem. Am. Law Inst., Phi Beta Kappa. Address: 2757 Brandywine St NW Washington DC 20008-1041

GREENBLATT, DEANA CHARLENE, elementary education educator; b. Chgo., Mar. 13, 1948; d. Walter and Betty (Lamasky) Beisel; BEd., Chgo. State U., 1969; MA in Guidance and Counseling, Roosevelt U., 1973; m. Mark Greenblatt, June 22, 1975. Tchr., counselor Chgo. Pub. Schs., 1969-75, City Colls. of Chgo. GED-TV, 1976; tchr. Columbus (Ohio) Pub. Schs., 1976-86; tchr. Chgo. Pub. Schs., 1993—; participant learning exchange, Chgo. Active B'nai B'rith; vol. Right-to-Read, Columbus; mem. Community Learning Exchange, Acad. Yr. in U.S.A. Com. Counselor, 1989—. Columbus. Cert. tchr. K-9, Ill., Ohio; cert. personnel guidance, Ill., Ohio; cert. Chgo. Bd. Edn. Mem. Am. Personnel and Guidance Assn., Internat. Platform Assn., B'nai B'rith Women Club (chpt. v.p.). Democrat. Home: 3820 W Touhy Ave Lincolnwood IL 60712-1026

GREENBLATT, MIRIAM, writer, editor, educator; b. Berlin; came to U.S., 1927; d. Gregory and Shifra (Zemach) Baraks; m. Howard Greenblatt (div. 1978). BA magna cum laude, Hunter Coll.; postgrad., U. Chgo., Spertus Coll. Editor Am. People's Ency., Chgo., 1957-58, Scott Foresman & Co., Chgo., 1958-62; pres. Creative Textbooks, Chgo., 1972—; tchr. New Trier H.S., Ill., 1978-81. Author: (with Chu) The Story of China, 1968, (with Cuban) Japan, 1971, The History of Itasca, 1976, (with others) The American People, 1986, James Knox Polk, 1988, Franklin Delano Roosevelt, 1989, John Quincy Adams, 1990, (with Welty) The Human Expression, 1992, The War of 1812, 1994, Cambodia, 1995, (with Jordan and Bowes) The Americans, 1996, (with Lemmo) Human Heritage, 1999, Hatshepsut and Ancient Egypt, 2000, Alexander the Great and Ancient Greece, 2000, Augustus and Imperial Rome, 2000, Peter the Great and Tsarist Russia, 2000; edit. cons. Peoples and Cultures Series, 1976-78; subject area cons. World Geography and Cultures, 1994; contbg. editor A World History, 1979. V.p. Chgo. Chpt. Am. Jewish Com., 1977-79, mem. nat. exec. coun., 1980-84; treas. Glencoe Youth Svcs., 1981-83. Mem. Nat. Assn. Scholars, Ill. Coun. Social Studies. Jewish. Address: 2754 Roslyn Ln Highland Park IL 60035-1408

GREEN-DORSEY, JEAN AUDREY, information systems executive; b. Cleve., Oct. 27, 1940; d. Sydney Howard and Bennie Irene (Blake) Green; m. William R. Dorsey, Nov. 1, 1980. BA, L.I. U., 1962. With IBM, N.Y.C., 1966-72; mktg. mgr. office automation Olivetti, N.Y.C., 1972-80; dep. dir. N.Y.C. Mgmt. Info. Sys., 1981-85; computer sys. mgr. Inter-agy. Task Force, N.Y.C., 1985-86; pres. Inst. Mgmt. Devel., N.Y.C., 1986—; dir. PolySoft Systems Inc.; sr. cons. Inst. Mgmt. Devel., 1980—; exec. prodr., host Management Matters, 1998—; founder Managementmatters.org, Inc., 2000; adv. editor Hearst Pubs., 1981—, Today's Office, 1986—, others; lectr. in field; bd. dirs. Nat. Inst. Mgmt.; bd. dirs., tech. advisor Am. Inst. Urban Psychol. Studies, 1996—. Bd. dirs. Fair Harbor Com. Assn., 1981—; co-dir. Westgate Tenants Assn., co-chair legal com., 1998—, chair, 1999; leader Citizen Amb. Program People to People office automation del. to People's Rep. China, 1988; mem. exec. bd. Cmty. Bd. #7. Mem. Assn. Computing Machinery, Assn. Info. Sys. Profls. (pres. N.Y.C. chpt., leader sci. and technology del. to People's Rep. China 1988). Clubs: Soroptimists Internat., The Club at N.Y. World Trade Ctr. E-mail: dorsey@managementmatters.org. Office: PolySoft Systems Corp 1425 4th St SW Washington DC 20024-2235

GREENE, ADDIE SLAUGHTER, systems analyst, technical writer; b. Santa Barbara, Calif., Jan. 12, 1942; d. John Slaughter and Emily Huntington (Hamilton) G.; m. Peter Frederick Eastman, Feb. 22, 1964 (div. Apr. 1979); children: Addie Susan, Peter John (name now Trout Fishing In America). BA in English Lit., Pomona Coll., 1963; AS in Computer Sci., Santa Barbara City Coll., 1985. Copy editor L.A. Times, 1963-66, Columbus (Ga.) Ledger, 1966-67, Japan Times, Tokyo, 1968, South Bay Daily Breeze, Torrance, Calif., 1969, Santa Barbara News-Press, 1969-70, 73-76; publs. mgr. McDonald Douglas Helicopters, Playa del Rey, Calif., 1985; documentation analyst Mission Linen Supply, Santa Barbara, 1986—. Contbr. numerous articles to lit. publs. Mem. Santa Barbara Choral Soc., 1977-99. Democrat. Avocations: bridge, yoga, swimming, gardening, running. Home: 4262 Highway 99 S Ashland OR 97520-9035 Office: Mission Linen Supply 717 E Yanonali St Santa Barbara CA 93103-3235

GREENE, ARTHUR E., retired microbiologist; b. Phila., Aug. 8, 1923; m. Doris M. G., Aug. 9, 1953; children: Marcia Greene Bergman, Karol Greene Budgick. AB, U. Pa., 1947; MS, Phila. Coll. Pharmacy and Sci., 1950, DSc, 1952. V.p. rsch. and sci. Coriell Inst. Med. Rsch., Camden, N.J., 1986-92; ret., 1992. With U.S. Army, 1942-45. Home: 37 S Syracuse Dr Cherry Hill NJ 08034-1237

GREENE, CLAYTON, JR., administrative judge, educator; b. Md., Jan. 22, 1951; s. Clayton Sr. and Evelyn Greene; m. Janice Elizabeth Butler, Dec. 21, 1974; children: Clayton III, Jonathan. BA in History, U. Md., 1973, JD, 1976. Bar: Md. 1977, Ct. Appeals, Md., 1977, U.S. Bankruptcy Ct., 1978, U.S. Dist. Ct., Md., 1978, Supreme Bench Balt. City, 1978, Anne Arundel County Bar Assn., Md., 1978, D.C. 1980, Ct. Appeals D.C., 1980. Law clerk Anne Arundel County Pub. Defender T. Joseph Touhey Jr., Md., 1974-76, various firms, Md., 1976-77; asst. county solicitor Anne Arundel County, Md., 1977-78; sole practioner Md., 1977-88; asst. pub. defender Anne Arundel County, 1978-85, dep. pub. defender, 1985-88, assoc. judge dist. ct., 1988-90, adminstrv. judge dist. ct., 1990-95, assoc. judge circuit ct., 1995-96, adminstrv. judge 5th Jud. Cirduit, 1996—; bd. dirs. Anne Arundel County Offender Aid and Restoration, Md., 1978-79; title ins. agent, 1980-88; mock trial judge citizenship law related edn. program, 1988-93; tchr. MICPEL trial adv. course, trial procedures for law enforcement officers, 1990-95; lectr. Anne Arundel C.C., Md., 1990-98, Jud. Inst. Md.; mem. standing com. practice and procedures Ct. Appeals, 1991-95; ex-oficio mem. Anne Arundel County Criminal Justice Coordinating Coun., 1993-95; co-chmn. Ad Hoc com. for implementation of family law divsn., 1997—; spkr. in field. asst. coach St. Jane Frances Clinic Soccer League, 1986, Arthur Slade basketball, 1988, Severna Park Green Hornets basketball, 1988, coach Arthur Slade basketball, 1994; mem. Gender Equality Com., 1990-92. Recipient Pub. Svc. award U. Md., 1987, Govs. Citation, 1988, Civic Betterment award Frontiersmen's Internat., 1989, cert. appreciation Kiwanis Club of Odenton, Morris H. Blum Humanitarian award, 1995. Mem. Hall United Meth. Ch. (bd. dirs. 1978-86, mem. bldg. com. 1984-87, trustee 1978-86), Anne Arundel County Bar Found., Md. (dir. 1993). Avocations: tennis, basketball, altosaxaphone, clarinet. Office: AA County Circuit Ct 7 Church Cir Annapolis MD 21401-1935

GREENE, EDWARD ALLEN, retired public affairs executive; b. Waco, Tex., May 25, 1926; s. James Floyd and Marie Louise (DuPré) G.; m. Elizabeth Ann Love, Oct. ll, 1952; children: Edward Allen Jr., Deborah Ann Greene Lord, Judith Love Greene Murray, Philip James. BA, George Washington U., 1950. Reporter Washington Evening Star, 1950-52; asst. pub. rels. Assn. Gen. Contractors Am., Washington, 1952-58; pub. affairs asst. Am. Waterways Operators, Washington, 1958-60; pub. info. specialist USPHS, Washington, 1960-61; pub. affairs office interim dep. U.S. Army C.E., Washington, 1961-91. Author: D-Day: The Greatest Invasion, 1969. V.p. Park View Citizens Assn., 1968, pres., 1969-70, 85-86, 93-94; vol., chief pub. rels. officer ARC-Walter Reed Hosp., Silver Spring, 1999—. Recipient U.S. Army Engrs. Comdrs. award for civilian svc., 1991. Mem. Contrsn. Writers Assn. (pres. 1977-78, Silver Hard Hat award 1989). Republican. Roman Catholic. Avocations: swimming, travel, bridge, music, eleven grandchildren. Home: 3226 Park View Rd Chevy Chase MD 20815-5644

GREENE, GRAHAM CARLETON, former publishing executive; b. Berlin, June 10, 1936; s. Hugh Carleton Greene and Helga Mary (Guinness) Connolly; m. Judith Margaret Gordon Walker, Dec. 28, 1957 (div.); m. Sally Georgina Horton, 1976; 1 son. MA, Univ. Coll., Oxford U., 1957. With Secker & Warburg, pubs., 1958-62; dir. Jonathan Cape Ltd., London, 1962-90, chmn., 1970-88; chmn. Australasian Pub. Co. Pty. Ltd., 1969-88, Chatto, Bodley Head & Jonathan Cape Australia Pty., Ltd., 1977-88; dir. Greene King Plc, 1979—, Random House Inc., 1987-88, Random House UK Ltd., 1988-90; mem. council Pubs. Assn., 1969-88, pres., 1977-79; mem. Book Devel. Council, 1970-79, dep. chmn., 1972-73, dep. chmn. Nat. Book League, 1971-74, chmn., 1974-76. Mem. gen. com. Royal Lit. Fund, 1975; mem. Brit. Council Bd., 1977-88; mem. Arts Council Working Party Sub-com. Public Lending Right, 1970; mem. Paymaster Gen.'s Working Party Pub. Lending Right, 1970-72; trustee The Trollope Soc., 1989—, Brit. Mus., 1978—, chmn. trustees, 1996—; chmn. Gt. Britain China Ctr., 1986-97, v.p., 1997—; chmn. mus. and galleries commn., 1991-96, The British Mus. Co., 1988—; dir. Ed Victor Ltd., 1991—, Rosemary Sandberg, Ltd., 1991—, Henry Sotheran, Ltd., 1990—, Open Coll. Arts, 1990-97, Jupiter Internat. Green Investment Trust PLC, 1989—; dir. Garsington Opera Ltd., 1996—, adv. com., 1990-96; chmn. Nat. Book Com., 1994-95; gov. Compton Verney House Trust, 1995—; dir. London Merchant Securities, 1996—. Decorated Chevalier de l'Ordre des Arts et des Lettres, comdr. Order Brit. Empire. Office: 6 Bayley St Bedford Sq, London WC1B 3HB, England

GREENE, HINDA MARSHA, osteopath, educator; b. Phila., Dec. 14, 1949; d. Charles Stanford and Adele (Eskin) G. BA, Western Coll., Oxford, Ohio, 1970; MA, Glassboro (N.J.) State Coll., 1972; postgrad., 1975-76; DO, Phila. Coll. Osteo. Medicine, 1980; postgrad., Fairleigh Dickinson U., Teaneck, N.J., 1974-75. Cert. Am. Acad. Osteo. Internists, Am. Acad. Osteo. Emergency Physicians; cert. ACLS, PALS, ATLS, FAAOEM, FAAOIM, FACFME. Intern Parkview Hosp., Phila., 1980-81; resident in internal medicine Albert Einstein Med. Ctr., Phila., 1981-84; attending physician in internal medicine, 1986-91, attending physician in emergency medicine, 1983-85; house physician Northeastern Hosp., Phila., 1982-84, St. Joseph's Hosp., Phila., 1982-84; asst. med. dir. disaster com., vice chmn. attending staff Met. Hosp., Phila., 1984-86, Met. Hosp. Springfield Divsn., Phila., 1989-91; pvt. practice Phila., 1987-91; asst. staff Cleveland Clinic Fla., Ft. Lauderdale, 1991-92; assoc. staff Cleveland Clinic Fla., 1992-94, full staff, 1994-96; med. dir. HRMC, Emergency Medicine, 1996—; v.p., ECS, clin. affairs HRMC, Energy Medicine, 1999; v.p., mgr. affairs ECS, 1999—; clin. prof. Phila. Coll. Osteo. Medicine, 1987-91; sect. chief dept. internal medicine Episcopal Hosp., Phila., 1988-91; mem. infection control com. Cleveland Clinic Hosp., 1995, mem. critical care com., 1993-94, mem. instnl. rev. bd. com.; bd. dirs. Broward Family Svc. Agy.; lectr., presenter in field. Contbr. chpts. to books, articles to Prevention Mag., others. Med. dir. Advanced Educators, 1995-98; sports phys. examiner Broward County High Schs., Broward C.C., 1993. Recipient N.J. Music Edn. Assn. awards, 1959-63; named Outstanding Pianist of Yr. TV Network and Music Assn., São Paulo, Brazil, 1962. Fellow Am. Acad. Osteo. Internists (v.p. 1982-93, pres.-elect 1993-94, pres. 1994-95), Am. Acad. Osteo. Emergency Medicine (bd. examiner 1993—); mem. AMA, ACP, Am. Osteo. Assn., Am. Assn. Osteo. Specialists (pres. 1994, bd. dirs. 1994—), Am. Assn. Osteo. Internists (sec./treas. 1981-82), Pa. Med. Soc., Pa. Osteo. Med. Assn., Phila. County Med. Soc., Lambda Omicron Gamma (sec./treas. 1994-95, pres. Caduceus chpt. 1978-79), Phi Delta Kappa. Avocations: music, art, sports, drama, fishing. Home: 207 NE Lakeview Dr Apt 1210 Sebring FL 33870-3155

GREENE, JIMMIE WALKER, county judge; b. Detroit, May 21, 1928; s. Rease Victor and Pearl Ailene Walker G.; m. Lois Ann Renfro, Nov. 22, 1977; children: Dixie, Wally, Jimmie II, Patrick. Student, U. Md. Commd. 2d lt. USAF, 1947, advanced through grades to mastersgt; with USAF, various locations, 1947-70; postmaster U.S. Postal Svc., Honey Bee, Ky., 1974-77; county judge, exec. McCreary County, Ky., 1978-81, 90—. Contbr. articles to McCreary County Record, 1971—. Recipient Americas Hometown Leadership award Walmart, 1997. Mem. VFW, DAV, McCreary County C. of C. (founder), U. Ky. Fellow's Soc., Am. Legion. Republican. Baptist. Avocations: camping, boating, fishing, hiking. Home: HC 84 Box 298 Parkers Lake KY 42634-9724 Office: McCreary County Ct House Ct House Sq PO Box 579 Whitley City KY 42653-0579

GREENE, KAREN SANDRA, actress, educator, singer; b. N.Y.C., Jan. 7, 1942; d. Nathan and Natalie (Barashick) Stein; m. Richard Greene, July 1, 1962 (div. 1980); children: Barry Randall, Lauren Jennifer. BA, U. Conn., 1988. Singer, dancer, Broadway actress N.Y.C., 1960-62; pres., educator Karen Greene Studios, A Class Act, Tigre Prodns., Norwalk, Conn., 1962—; pres. Front Row Ctr. for Performing Arts, 1993—; pres., dir. voice On Stage Acad., Ltd., Westport, Conn., 1982-84; dir., educator theater arts Westport YMCA, 1981-85; educator Temple Shalom, Norwalk, 1975-87; dir. theater arts Bridgeport (Conn.) Jewish Ctr., 1985; dir. Norwalk Jewish Ctr., 1985, Wilton (Conn.) Children's Theater, 1988-90; educator music and drama St. Luke's Sch., New Canaan, Conn., 1989-90; educator voice, acting, adult edn. Norwalk and Westport (Conn.) Bds. Edn., 1990—; dir., educator Curtain Call, Stamford, Conn., 1996—. Voiceover artist nat. performing tours; dir., vocalist soc. band Shades of Greene. Founding mem., chmn. Norwalk Soc. for Arts, 1999; coord. Southwestern Conn. Women's Issues Conf., 1988; active women's equal rights, pro-choice, NOW, Women's Empowerment, Fairfield County, Conn.; active animal rights advocate; Conn. rep. Friends of Animals, others; founding mem., sec. The Greater Norwalk Coun. of the Arts, Conn., 1996—; dir., educator improvisation conquering stage fright program Norwalk H.s., 1999—; educator, dir. Westport (Conn.) Summer Teen Mus. Theater, 19990—, Greenwich (Conn.) Acad., 1997—. Mem. NOW, AFTRA, SAG, Actor's Equity Assn., Internat. Platform Assn., Internat. TV Assn., Women's Empowerment, N.E. Anti-Vivisect. Soc. (Conn. rep.), People for the Ethical Treatment of Animals (Conn. rep.), Greenpeace (Conn. rep.). Avocations: art, animals, holistic healing, Reiki II, Mariel. Home and Office: 4 Suburban Dr Norwalk CT 06851-1612

GREENE, KARL ANTHONY, neurosurgeon; b. Ann Arbor, Mich., July 11, 1960; s. Thomas Samuel Harrison Jr. and Johnnye Lee (Branch) G. BS in Pharmacology with honors, U. Mich., 1981; MD, Stanford (Calif.) U., 1989, PhD, 1989. Diplomate Nat. Bd. Med. Examiners; cert. ACLS, ATLS. Intern in gen. surgery Phoenix Integr Surg. Residency Program, 1989-90; resident in neurol. surgery Barrow Neurol. Inst., Phoenix, 1990-96; inst. neuroscis, chief divsn. neurosurgery Conemaugh Meml. Med. Ctr., Johnstown, Pa., 1996—. Contbr. numerous articles to profl. jours. Recipient James H. Robinson, M.D. Meml. award in surgery Nat. Med. Fellowships, 1989, Henry J. Kaiser Family Found. merit scholar, 1989, Upjohn Travel award Internat. Neurotrauma Soc., 1993, John R. Green, M.D. resident rsch. award Ariz. Neurosurg. Soc. Annual Meeting, 1994; grantee Nat. Inst. of Mental Health, 1985-86, 86-87. Mem. Physicians for Social Responsiblity, Soc. for Neurosci., Am. Soc. for Neurochemistry (Young Investigator Travel award 1989), N.Y. Acad. Sci., Am. Assn. Neruol. Surgeons, Congress Neurol. Surgeons, NAACP. Office: Conemaugh Meml Med Ctr Dvsn Neurosurgery 1086 Franklin St # E301 Johnstown PA 15905-4305

GREENE, KAY C., psychologist, author; b. Yankton, S.D., July 10, 1939; d. Fred Orin and Evelyn Irene (Sundy) Green. B.Mus. in Edn., U. Nebr., 1962; MA in Psychology, New Sch. Social Rsch., 1980, PhD in Clin. Psychology, 1983. Lic. psychologist, Md., N.Y., D.C.; ordained deacon Fifth Ave. Presbyn. Ch., N.Y.C., 1997. With Gulf States Utilities, Beaumont, Tex., 1963-64, Tatham, Laird & Kudner, N.Y.C., 1965-66; mgmt. cons. John Wiersma Cons., Washington, 1966; advt. coord. Sullivan Stauffer Colwell & Bayles, N.Y.C., 1966-67; acting supr., ticket agt., svc. rep. Am. Airlines, N.Y.C., 1967; exec. sec. to v.p./chief engr. WPIX-TV, N.Y.C., 1967-71, adminstrv. asst. to news chief, 1971-72; office mgr. Lawrence Letter Svc., N.Y.C., 1973-78; clin. psychologist in pvt. practice N.Y.C., 1985—; regional trainer APA HOPE (HIV) Project, 1992—; tchr. music, English, spl. edn. MacArthur Jr. H.S., Beaumont, 1964-65; student music tchr. U. Nebr. Exptl. H.S., Lincoln, 1961-62; lectr. in field; condr. seminars in field; appeared on Donahue, Good Morning New York, Kelly and Co., Survival into the 21st Century, Turning Inward; radio shows include The Alan Colmes Show, WABC, N.Y., Alan Colmes, WPIX, N.Y., Open Session, Ben Reese, WNYE, N.Y., From Head to Heart, WXLO, N.Y., Foundation Focus, WNEW, N.Y., Wellness Workshop, WNWK FM, N.Y., others; pres. Bridge of Change; sr. rep. UN Hdqrs. for World Fedn. Mental Health, 1990-95, organizer various confs., keynote spkr. various internat. confs. past staff therapist/sr. staff psychologist Fifth Ave. Ctr. for Counseling and Psychotherapy, N.Y.C.; rep. UN Hdqrs. for Internat. Coun. of Psychologists, 1996—; adj. asst. prof. St. Francis Coll., Bklyn. Coll., 1997-98; vis. assoc. prof. Lincoln Ctr. Fordham U., N.Y.C., 1997-98, adj. assoc. prof., 1998; adj. assoc. prof. Pace U., N.Y.C., 1999—; vice chair NGO/DPI exec. com. UN Hdqs., 1998—, chair, 2000—; interim exec. dir. Millennium NGO Forum UN Hdqrs., 1998-99. Contbr. articles to profl. jours. Named Internat. Woman of the Yr. in recognition of svcs. to mental health Internat. Biog. Centre, 1993-94; recipient Disting. Leadership award Internat. Directory of Disting. Leadership. Mem. APA (Nat. AIDS task force 1988—, fellow internat. divsn. 52 1999), AFTRA, Authors Guild, Authors League, Internat. Coun. of Psychologists (sec.-gen. 1997—, rep. UN hdqrs. 1996—), Internat. Platform Assn., C.G. Jung Found. for Analytical Psychology, N.Y. Acad. Sci., N.Y. State Psychol. Assn. (pres.-elect acad. divsn. 1999), Screen Actors Guild, Soc. for Psychol. Study of Social Issues, World Assn. for Psychosocial Rehab. (rep. UN Hdqs. 1998—), World Fedn. Mental Health, Sigma Alpha Iota (Kappa chpt.), Pi Kappa Lambda, Psi Chi. Avocations: piano, photography, pets, painting, cooking. Home and Office: 30 Waterside Plz Apt 13E New York NY 10010-2630

GREENE, MAURICE, Olympic athlete. Defeated Carl Lewis Tex. Relays, 1995; 3 Gold Medals World Championships, Seville, 1999; 2 Gold Medals Sydney, 2000. Holder record time Grand Prix meet, Athens, 1999, world's fastest man, Sydney, 2000; became first man to win both 100 and 200 meter races at World Championship, 1999. Office: USA Track and Field Team One RCA Dome Ste 140 Indianapolis IN 46225*

GREENE, RENEE JUDITH, industrial psychology consultant; b. Charleston, S.C., Mar. 20, 1955; d. George and Sylvia R. (Ginsberg) Greene; m. Michael Fish, Mar. 29, 1986; children: Brandon Abraham, Gilah Ilana. BS, U. Fla., 1976; MS in Human Services, Nova U., 1986. Dir. Dixie council B'nai B'rith Youth Orgn., Charleston, 1976-78; dir. youth activities Charleston Jewish Community Ctr., 1976-78; asst. dir. Fla. region B'nai B'rith Youth, Orlando, 1978-80; dir. Southeast region, dept. youth activities United Synagogue Am., Plantation, Fla., 1980-83; recruiting mgr. Office Specialists, Miami, Fla., 1983-89; cons. to med. practices and hosps., 1989—. Adv. chair Country Isles Elem. Sch., 1997-98, Everglades Elem. Sch., 1998. Recipient Star of Deborah award B'nai B'rith, 1973. Mem. NAFE, Jewish Youth Dirs. Assn. (dir. 1981-82), S.E. Psychol. Assn. (assoc.), Nat. Alzheimer's and Related Diseases Assn. (assoc.), Nat. Assn. Temp. Services (chpt. pub. rels. com., v.p. South Fla. chpt. 1986, acting pres. 1986, sec. 1987—). Jewish. Avocations: art, writing, music. Home: 5600 SW 195th Ter Fort Lauderdale FL 33332-1223 Office: 1304 SW 160th Ave Ste 339 Sunrise FL 33326-1902

GREENE, RICHARD THADDEUS, bank executive; b. Charleston, S.C., July 18, 1918; s. Richard and Martha (Black) G.; m. Virginia L. Lea; children: Cheryll Y., Richard I. Jr. BS, Hampton U., 1938; D in Comml. Scis. (hon.), St. Johns U., 1992. Asst. treas. Citizen's & Southern Bank & Trust Co., Phila., 1938-41; rep., bus. mgr. Assoc. Pubs., Inc., N.Y.C., 1945-58; nat. advt. rep., sec./bus. mgr. Interstate United Newspapers, N.Y.C., 1958-60; exec. asst. to pres. Carver Fed. Savs. Bank, N.Y.C., 1960, mgr. Bklyn. office, 1961, asst. sec., mgr. Bklyn. office, 1961-63, asst. v.p., mgr. Bklyn. office, 1963-66, v.p., mgr. Bklyn. office, 1966-68, exec. v.p., 1968, pres., dir., 1969-95; bd. dirs. finance com. HUDC, Fin. Svcs. Corp., Harlem Urban Devel. Corp., N.Y.C. Partnership Inc., Thrift Assns. Svc. Corp., Fed. Home Loan Bank N.Y.; bd. advisors Black Enterprise. Former bd. dirs. Am. Savs. & Loan League, Inc., Queens Coun. on the Arts, Uptown C. of C., United Way of Tri-State, N.Y. Urban League, Inc.; trustee George E. Meares Meml. Scholarship Fund; former trustee Citizen's Budget Commn., N.Y.C.; Bd. dirs., chmn. fin. com. Apollo Theatre Found.; elder Westminster Presbyn. Ch. Maj. U.S. Army, 1941-45. Recipient Outstanding Citizen award N.Y. Recorder, Citizenship award Bklyn. HOme for the Aged, Achievement award for contbn. to community Cornerstone Bapt. Ch., Bklyn., Black Bank Pres. award Westminster Presbyn. Ch., Jamaica, N.Y., Citation of Appreciation award Abyssinian Bapt. Ch., N.Y.C., Professionalism & Excellence in Banking award Urban Bankers Coalition Inc., Banking award Harlem Commonwealth Coun., Booker T. Washington award N.Y. Hampton Alumni Club Inc. Mem. N.Y. League of Savs. Insts. (legis. com.), Harlem Bus. Alliance, Nat. Freedom Day Assn., One Hundred Black Men Inc., N.Y. Hampton Alumni Club, Omega Psi Phi (Man of Yr. award, Citizen of Yr.), Sigma Pi Phi.

GREENE, STEPHEN CRAIG, lawyer; b. Watertown, N.Y., Apr. 27, 1946; s. Harold Adelbert and Mildred Esther (Baker) G.; m. Nancy Jean Adams, Mar. 28, 1965; children: Kathryn, Stephen, Hilary. AB, Syracuse U., 1967, JD, 1970. Bar: N.Y. 1971, U.S. Tax Ct., 1977. Asst. to pres. SUNY, Oswego, 1970-73; assoc. firm Leyden E. Brown, Oswego, 1973-75; ptnr. Brown and Greene, 1976-81; pvt. practice law, 1981—. Bd. dirs. Found. Corp. Legal Studies, Inc., 1968-70, United Way of Oswego County, Inc., 1985-88, Campbell's Point Assn., 1994-96, Oswego Hosp., 1981-2000, mem. exec. com., 1985-2000, pres., 1996-98; pres. Oswego Health, Inc., 1997—; town atty. Oswego, 1972—; counsel Oswego County Bd. Realtors, 1978—; mem. Oswego County Rep. com., 1974-85, counsel, 1980-83; gen. counsel Express Abstract Co., 1992-95. Recipient Inst. Counsel, 1970. Mem. ABA, N.Y. Bar Assn., Oswego County Bar Assn., Greater Oswego C. of C. (bd. dir. 1980-87), Oswego Country Club (counsel 1977-81), Masons, Shriners, Phi Delta Phi. Home: 611 W 1st St Oswego NY 13126-4137 Office: 85 W Bridge St Oswego NY 13126-2011

GREENE, WILLIAM HENRY, economics educator, software engineer; b. Phila., Jan. 16, 1951; s. Richard Bernard and Margaret Helen Greene; m. Joanne Samela, June 1975 (div. 1982); m. Lynne Nancy Rosenthal, Feb. 20, 1983; children: Lesley, Elizabeth, Allison, Julianna. BS, Ohio State U., 1972; MA, U. Wis., 1974, PhD, 1976. Prof. Cornell U., Ithaca, 1976-81; sr. cons. Nat. Econ. Rsch. Assocs., N.Y.C., 1981-82; prof. dept. econ. Stern Sch. Bus., NYU, N.Y.C., 1982-96, chair dept. econ., 1996—; pres. Econometric Software, Inc., Plainview, N.Y., 1981—; cons. Am. Express, N.Y.C., 1992-96, Readers Digest, Pleasantville, N.Y., 1993-97, Ortho Biotech, Rahway, N.J., 1996-98. Author: Econometric Analysis, 4th edit., 2000; contbr. over 50 articles to profl. jours.; author computer software NLOGIT/LIMDEP, 1980-99. Mentor Intel Talent Search, N.Y.C., 1997-99; bd. dirs. Global Kids, N.Y.C., 1996-99. Fellow Jour. Econometrics, NYU, also scholar. Mem. Am. Stats. Assn., Am. Econ. Assn., Econometric Soc. E-mail: wgreene@stern.nyu.edu. Office: NYU Stern Sch Bus 44 W 4th St New York NY 10012-1106

GREENE-MERCIER, MARIE ZOE, sculptor; b. Madison, Wis., Mar. 31, 1911; d. Louis J.A. and Zoé (Lassagne) Mercier; m. Wesley Hammond Greene, June 21, 1937; children: Steven Hardy, Richard Stuart, Roger Hammond. AB, Radcliffe Coll., 1933; postgrad., New Bauhaus, Chgo., 1937-38. Exhibited solo shows Southwest Mo. State Coll., 1950, Argent Gallery, N.Y.C., Hohenberg Gallery, Chgo., 1951, 53, Layton Gallery, Milw., 1951, Westwinds Bookshop, Duxbury, Mass., 1951, Newton Ctr. Women's Club, 1950, Art Inst. Chgo., 1955, Chgo. Pub. Libr., 1956, Am. Inst. Archs., Chgo., 1957, Paris Galerie Duncan, 1963, Florence Galleria d'arte Arno, 1965, Rome Galleria Numero, 1966, Milan Numero, 1966, Venice Numero, 1966, S.Stefano, 1968, Milan Gian Ferrari, 1969, Trieste Centro Italo Americano, 1968, 70, Venice La Fenice, 1969, Athens, New Forms, 1970, Perpignan, Main de Fer, 1971, Rome, Artivisive, 1972, Chgo.

Met. Structures Inc., 1974, Centre Noroit, Arras, France, 1977, Amerika Haus, West Berlin, 1977, Galerie Musée de Poche Paris, 1978, Maison Française, Chgo., 1979, 83, Stad Bad Homburg v.d. Höhe, 1979, Amerika Haus, Stuttgart, 1979, Alliance Francaise de Washington, 1980, Skulpturenpark Mus., Bad Nauheim Fed. Republic Germany, 1986, Oberhessisches Mus., Giessen, Fed. Republic Germany, 1986, Galerie Loehr, Frankfurt, Fed. Republic Germany, 1991; exhibited in group shows Art Inst. Chgo., 1947, 48, 52, 55, Boson Mus. Arts, 1950, Am. Fedn. Arts, 1953, Mus. Contemporary Art, Chgo., 1968, Paris Salon d'Automne, 1962, 1971, 72, 73, 74, Salon des Beaux Arts, Salon des Independants, 1952, de la Jeune Sculpture, 1966, Salon de Mai, 1973, 74, 75, 76, 77, 78, 86, London Royal Inst. Galleries, 1954, Trieste II Exhbn. Sacred Art, 1966, Legnano, Pagani Found., 1966, 69, 70, 71, 72, Campo S. Moisé, Commune di Venezia, 1970, 72, Florence Biennale, 1971, 1st Sculpture Triennale, Paris, 1978, UNESCO, Paris, 1979, La Found. Nat. Arts Graphiques et Plastiques, Paris, 1979, Bauhaus Archiv Mus., W. Berlin, 1979, Capitol Children's Mus., Washington, 1980-81, Kurhausgarten, Bad Homburg, 1979, 80, 81, Moholy-Nagy, New Vision for Chgo., Ill. State Mus., Springfield & Chgo., 1990, 4-town travelling show Arras, France, 1990-91, Internat. Exhibition Frankfurt Kunstmesse, Galerie Loehr, 1991, Annual Mem. Show Arts Club Chgo., 1948-94; represented in permanent collections at Roosevelt U., Radcliffe Coll., S.W. Mo. State Coll., Grinnell Coll., Randolph Macon Coll., Bauhaus-Archiv Mus., Berlin, Mus. Modern Art, Venice, Stone Container Corp., 1st Nat. Bank, Chgo., Internat. Film Bur., 1st Bapt. Ch., Chgo., Bloomington, Ind., Musée des Sables, Barcarès, France, 1971, Govt. Bldg., Homburg-Saar, 1974, C.E.S. Verlaine, Arras, France, Centre Noroit, Arras, 1978, Western Ill. U., 1979, David and Alfred Smart Gallery, U. Chgo., permanent sculptures and collages Oberhessisches Mus., Giessen, Germany, 1995—; mem. U.S. del. 9th Congress Internat. Artists Assn., UNESCO, Stuttgart, W. Germany, 1979. Recipient Silver medal and 1st prize Composition, 1968, Gold medal, grand prize modern sculpture, Cannes, Semaines Internat. de la Femme, 1969, Hors Concours, Nice, 1970, Grand prix Humanitaire de France, médaille de vermeil, ler Prix Internat. de Sculpture, Mérite Belgo-Hispanique Palmes d'Or, Festival de St. Germain-des-Prés, Paris, 1975; USIS West Berlin grantee, 1977; Stadt Bad Hamburg v.d. Höhe grantee, 1979, Mary Mildred Sullivan award Randolph-Macon Coll., 1985, The Radcliffe College Alumnae Assn. Recognition awd. for visual arts, 1998. Author: Trieste, 101 Disegni, 1969; Venezia, 101 Disegni, 1970; Salzburg, 101 Zeichnungen, 1970; Editrice Libreria Internazionale Italo Svevo Trieste, 1969; Editor: Mussa, Italo, Marie Zoe Greene-Mercier Rome, Sifra, 1968, Art Internat., 1978, Public Art New Directions, 1981, Contemporary Women Sculptors, 1986, Am. Women Sculptors, 1990; contbr. to mags. Memoir, Leonardo Magazine, 1982; Reminiscences, Harvard Crimson, 1983. Mem. Renaissance Soc. (hon. mem. U. Chgo.), Arts Club of Chgo., Artists Equity Ass. (pres., chgo. chpt. 1959-62). Home: 1232 E 57th St Chicago IL 60637-1613 Office: New Forms, 9a Valaoritou St, Athens Greece also: Sifra Editrice 93 V, Ugo de Carolis Rome Italy also: Monika Beck Gallery, Schwarzenacker, Saar HAB 3121 Homburg Germany

GREENE OSTER, SELMAREE, medical anthropologist and researcher; b. Phila., Feb. 17, 1949; d. Boisey and Elizabeth (Lewis) Greene; m. Gerald Oster, Apr. 11, 1973 (dec. Oct. 1995); 1 child, Alexander S. BS in Anthropology and Biollgy, U. Pa., 1969, CUNY, 1973; MSc, CUNY, 1979, PhD, 1980. Clin. lab. cert., N.Y. Tchr. U.S. Peace Corps, Washington, 1975-77; med. rschr. Mt. Sinai Sch. Medicine, N.Y.C., 1978-88; pres., exec. officer Oster Children's Fund, N.Y.C., 1996—. Contbr. articles to sci. jours. Peace activist UN NGO Peace Action, N.Y.C., 1998—. Tropical medicine grantee Friends of Children of Haiti, 1984-90. Mem. Am. Soc. Clin. Pathologists (lic. lab. pathologist and clinician). Democrat. Roman Catholic. Avocations: horseback riding, swimming. Fax: 609-871-5799. Home: Ground Fl Apt 241 W 11th St New York NY 10017 Office: Peace Action Edn Rm 4050 866 United Nations Plz New York NY 10017

GREENER, ANTHONY, food and beverage company executive; b. 1940. Dir. Reed Internat., 1990-98, Reed Elsevier, 1993-98; chmn. Diageo plc, 1997-2000, U. Industry Ltd., London, 2000—. Office: Univ for Industry, 88 Kingsway, Holborn London WC2B 6AA, England

GREENGARD, PAUL, neuroscientist; b. N.Y.C., Dec. 11, 1925; married; 3 children. AB, Hamilton Coll., 1948; PhD, Johns Hopkins U., 1953. NSF fellow in neurochemistry U. London (Eng.)Inst. Psychiatry, 1953-54; Nat. Found. Infantile Paralysis fellow U. Cambridge (Eng.) Molteno Inst., 1954-55; Paraplegia Found. fellow Nat. Inst. Med. Rsch., Eng., 1955-56; fellow Nat. Inst. Neurological Diseases and Blindness, 1956-58; dir. biochemistry dept. Ciba-Geigy Rsch. Labs., 1958-67; prof. pharmacology and psychiatry Yale U. Sch. Medicine, New Haven, 1968-83; Andrew D. White prof.-at-large Cornell U., Ithaca, N.Y., 1981-87; Vincent Astor prof. Rockefeller U., N.Y.C., 1983—; vis. scientist Nat. Heart Inst., 1958-59; vis. assoc. prof. Albert Einstein Coll. Medicine, 1961-68, vis. prof., 1968-83; vis. prof. Vanderbilt U., 1967-68; Harvey Soc. lectr., 1980; lectr. in field. Recipient Dickson prize and medal in medicine U. Pitts., 1977, Ciba-Geigy Drew award, 1979, Biol. and Med. Scis. award N.Y. Acad. Scis., 1980, 3M Life Scis. award Fedn. Am. Socs. Exptl. Biology, 1987, Bristol-Myers award for disting. achievement in neurosci. rsch., 1989, Goodman and Gilman award in receptor pharmacology, 1992, Karl Spencer Lashley prize Am. Philos. Soc., 1993, Biochem. Soc. Thudichum medal, 1996, Charles A. Dana Found. award for pioneering achievements in health, 1997, Met. Life Found. award for med. rsch., 1998, Ellison Med. Found. Sr. Scholar award, 1999, Mayor of N.Y.C.'s award for excellence in sci. and tech., 1999, Nobel Prize, 2000. Mem. NAS (award in neuroscis. 1991), Am. Acad. Arts and Scis., Soc. for Neurosci. (Grass lectr. 1986, Gerard prize 1994), Nat. Alliance for Rsch. on Schizophrenia and Depression (Lieber prize Outstanding Achievement Schizophrenia Rsch. 1996), Am. Neurol. Assn. (hon.). Office: Rockefeller U 1230 York Ave New York NY 10021-6399

GREENHALGH, DAVID, statistics educator, consultant, researcher; b. Manchester, Lancashire, U.K., July 14, 1959; s. Clifford and Freda G. BA in Math., U. Cambridge, 1980, cert. in math. with distinction, 1982, MA in Math., 1982, PhD in Operational Rsch., 1984. Med. rsch. coun., rsch. tng. fellow Dept. Pure and Applied Biology, Imperial Coll., London, 1984-86; lectr. in statistics dept. of math. U. Strathclyde, Glasgow, U.K., 1986-89, lectr. in statistics dept. stats. and modelling sci., 1989-97, sr. lectr., 1997—; dir. Aleo Plating Ltd., Liverpool, U.K., 1989-93; cons. Pub. Health Lab. Svc., Colindale London, 1990-99; vis. rschr. Dept. Math. and Computer Sci., U. Veszprem, Hungary, 1996, 97, Centrumvoor Wiskunde en Informatica, Amsterdam, The Netherlands, 1994, Inst. for Med. Biometry, U. Tübingen, Germany, 1990, Dept. Math. Sofia Med. U., 1999; spkr. in field. Editor Jour. of Biol. Systems, 1996—; guest editor Jour. of Theoretical Medicine, 1999; contbr. articles to profl. jours. Sr. scholarship Emmanuel Coll., 1979, 79. Fellow Royal Statis. Soc.; mem. Operational Rsch. Soc., Soc. for Math. Biology. Avocations: squash, hillwalking, traveling. Home: Flat 3F3 125 Bell St, Collegelands, Merchant City, Glasgow G4 OTE, United Kingdom Office: U Strathclyde Dept Stats, 26 Richmond St, Glasgow G1 1XH, United Kingdom

GREENHALGH, ROGER MALCOLM, vascular surgeon, medical educator; b. Derbyshire, Eng., Feb. 6, 1941; s. John Greenhalgh and Phyllis (Poynton) Flint; m. Karin Maria Gross, July 30, 1964; children: Stephen John, Christina Elizabeth. BA, Cambridge (Eng.) U., 1963, MB, MBChir, 1966, MA, 1967, MD, 1983. House surgeon, sr. house officer St. Thomas Hosp., London, 1967-69; sr. registrar, lectr. St. Bartholomew's Hosp., London, 1972-76; sr. lectr. surgery Charing Cross Hosp. Med. Sch., London, 1976-81; prof. surgery, chmn. Charing Cross and Westminster Med. Sch., London, 1989-97, dean, 1993-97; chmn., dir. surgery Hammersmith Hosps. Trust, London, 1994-98; prof. surgery U. London, 1981—; prof. surgery, head dept. Sch. Medicine Imperial Coll., London, 1997—; mem. Med. Rsch. Coun. Health Svcs. Pub. Health Bd., 1998—; chmn., dir., trustee European Soc. Vasc. Surgery Ltd., 1987—; chmn. Riverside Med. Coun., London, 1992-93; mem. Coun. Assn. Surgery Gt. Britain and Ireland, 1993—; chmn. European Bd. Surgery Qualification, 1995—. Editor: Maintenance of Arterial Reconstruction, 1991, Vascular Surgical Emergencies, 1992, Surgery for Stroke, 1993, Vascular and Endovascular Surgical Techniques, 3d edit., 1994, Vascular Imaging for Surgeons, 1995, Trials & Tribulations of Vascular Surgery, 1996, Inflamatory and Thrombic Problems in Vascular Surgery, 1997, The Indications in Vascular and Endovascular Surgery, 1998, The Durability of Vascular and Endovascular Surgery, 1999, Vascular and Endovascular Opportunities, 2000. Mem. health svcs. bd. dirs. Med. Rsch. Found., 1998—. Grantee Brit. Heart Found., 1988, Med. Rsch. Coun., 1989, Nat. Health Svc. Rsch. and Devel. Health Tech. Assessment, 1999. Fellow Royal Coll. Surgeons (Eng., sec.-gen., chmn.); mem. Assn. Internal Vascular Surgeons (sec.-gen. 1983—), European Union Med. Specialists (pres. 1998—), Vascular Surgical Soc. of Great Britian and Ireland (pres. 1999-2000). Anglican. Avocation: tennis. Office: Charing Cross & Westminster, Med Sch, London W6 8RC, England

GREENIDGE, CARL BARRINGTON, international public servant, economist; b. New Amsterdam, Berbice, Guyana, Mar. 3, 1949; s. Cecil Cappel and Stella Leonie Ruperta (Hoppie) Greenidge; children: Kwesi, Coalla, Tara. BA in Econs. with honors, U. Exeter, U.K., 1971; MPhil in Econs., U. London, Eng., 1974. Rsch. asst., tutor Wye Coll., U. London, England, 1972-74; lectr. in econs. U. Guyana, Georgetown, 1974-78; chief planning officer, sec. to the state planning bd. State Planning Commn., Georgetown, 1978-80; econ. adviser Office of the Pres., Govt. Guyana, Georgetown, 1981; min. of fin. and planning Govt. Guyana, Georgetown, 1983-85, mins. fin., 1983-92; dep. sec. gen., sec. gen. ad interium Secretariat of African, Caribbean & Pacific Group States, Brussels, 1992-2000; dir. Tech. Ctr. for Agrl. and Rural Coop., 2000—; cons. economist Aubrey Barker Assocs., Georgetown, 1975-79; rsch. fellow Inst. Social and Econ. Rsch., U. West Indies, Jamaica, 1987; co-pres. coun. mins. European Cmty. and African, Caribbean and Pacific Group States, Brussels, 1989-90; mem. Inter Regional Network on Privatization, UN Devel. Project, N.Y., 1991—; mem. adv. bd. Regulatory Policy Rsch. Ctr./Inst., Hertford Coll., Oxford (Eng.) U., 1993—; vice chmn. European Ctr. for Devel. Policy Mgmt., 1995-96, European Forum on Internat. Coop., 1997-2000. Author: Empowering a Peasantry in a Caribbean Context, 2000, (with others) Privatisation: A Global Perspective, 1993; contbr. articles to profl. jours. Mem. Internat. Inst. of Pub. Fin., Agrl. Econs. Soc., Am. Econs. Assn. Avocations: gliding, cricket, squash, music. Office: CTA, Postbus 380, 6700 AJ Wageningen The Netherlands

GREENIDGE, CHARLES WOSELEY, surgeon; b. Bridgetown, Barbados, Dec. 28, 1929; s. Charles Woseley and Pauline Mary (O'Brien) G.; m. Margaret Mary Reynolds-Lewis Greenidge, Dec. 31, 1957; 1 child Charles Woseley. B in Medicine and Surgery, U. Coll. West Indies, 1956. House officer U. Hosp. West Indies, Jamaica, 1956-58; casualty officer Hackney Hosp., London, 1961-62, orthopedic house officer, 1962-63; sr. house officer Royal London Homeopathic Hosp., London, 1963-64, registrar in surgery, 1964-65; locum registrar Preston & Chorley HMC, 1965-67; cons. surgeon St. Joseph Hosp., St. Peter, Barbados. 1967-82, Sunny Lodge Clin., St. Peter, Barbados, 1982—. Recipient Silver Medal in Ob/Gyn, UCH-WI, 1956. Fellow Royal Soc. Medicine, Royal Coll. Surgeons of Eng. Roman Catholic. Avocations: gardening, reading, listening to music. Home: Dene Hollow St Lucy, Barbados West Indies Office: Sunny Lodge Clin, Queen St, Speightstown Barbados West Indies

GREENLEE, JOHN W., electric cooperative executive; b. Kansas City, Mo., Jan. 16, 1946; s. Otis and Ethel Ruby (Reeves) G.; m. Wilma Jean Lutes; children: Dawn, Diane, Shelly, Tom. AA in Bus. Adminstrn., Highland (Kans.) C.C., 1967; BS in Bus., Kans. State Tchrs. Coll., 1969. Staff acct. USDA-REA, Washington, 1969-72, field acct., 1972-78; mgr. acctg. svcs. Ea. Iowa Light & Power, Wilton, 1978-81, divsn. mgr. acctg., 1981-90; asst. gen. mgr. East River Electric Power Coop., Madison, S.D., 1990-91; mgr., CEO, Gascosage Electric Coop., Dixon, Mo., 1992—. Bd. dirs. Dixon Sr. Citizens Ctr., 1994—; mem. Com. of Fifty, Ft. Leonard Wood, Mo., 1996-99; mem. task force on regional growth Mo. Dept. Econ. Devel., Ft. Leonard Wood, 1997; mem. Dixon Area Cmty. Devel. Com., chmn., 1999. Mem. Dixon C. of C. (v.p. 1994-96, pres. 1997-00), Lions (pres. Dixon 1994-96). E-mail: greenlee@usmo.com. Office: Gascosage Electric Coop PO Drawer G Dixon MO 65459

GREEN MACIAS, ROSARIO, United Nations official. Sec. fgn. rels. Govt. Mex., Mexico City, 1990-98, now min. fgn. affairs, 1998—. Office: 2 UN Plz 28th Fl New York NY 10017*

GREENSHIELDS, RAYMOND, financial services company executive; b. Sydney, N.S.W., Australia, June 27, 1947; s. Arthur Ronald and Nancy Ellen (Donnelly) G.; m. Marilyn Joy Greenshields, Dec. 23, 1967; children: Kathryn, Fiona, Amy. B Commerce in Econs. with merit, U. N.S.W., Sydney, Australia, 1971; Assoc., Securities Inst. Australia, Sydney, 1972; AEP Kellog Sch., Northwestern U., 1990. Clk. AMP Soc., Sydney, 1967-69, investment analyst, 1969-71, comml. loans officer, 1971-72, investment officer, 1972-79, mgr. share investments, 1979-84, mgr. portfolio investments, 1984-88, chief funds mgr., chmn. investment policy com., 1988-91; mng. dir. AMP Asset Mgmt. plc, London, 1991-95; chf. gen. mgr. retail fin. svs. AMP Society, 1996-97; chmn. AMP Bank Ltd., London, 1998-99; mng. dir. AMP fin. svcs. AMP Society, 1998-99; chmn. Investment and Fin. Svcs. Assn., 1998-99; dir. Australian Svcs. Network, 1999—; chmn. ICC Working Party on Barriers to Internat. Portfolio Investment, 1992-93; bd. dirs. Cen. Queensland Coal Assocs. Joint Venture, 1977-91, Australian Bus. in Europe Ltd., 1992-95. Mem. adv. com. treasury functions N.S.W. Govt., Sydney, 1988-91; dir. Bayswater Coal, 1982-91; mem. policy com. Tomago Aluminum Project, 1980-91. Mem. Cook Soc., Inst. Dirs., Royal Sydney Yacht Squadron, Australian Club, City of London Club. Avocations: sailing, bushwalking, tennis, travel.

GREENSPAN, ALAN, central banker, economist; b. N.Y.C., Mar. 6, 1926; s. Herman Herbert Greenspan and Rose Goldsmith. BS summa cum laude, NYU, 1948, MA, 1950, PhD, 1977. Pres., CEO Townsend-Greenspan and Co., Inc., N.Y.C., 1954-74, 77-87; cons. Council Econ. Advisers, 1970-74, chmn., 1974-77; cons. Congressional Budget Office, 1977-87; mem. Pres.'s Econ. Policy Adv. Bd., 1981-87; chmn. Nat. Commn. on Social Security Reform, 1981-83; mem. Task Force on Econ. Growth, 1969, Pres.'s Fgn. Intelligence Adv. Bd., 1983-85; commn. on an All-Vol. Armed Force, 1969-70; commn. on Fin. Structure and Regulation, 1970-71; sr. adviser panel on econ. activity Brookings Instn., 1970-74, 77-87; chmn. bd. govs. Fed. Res. System, 1987—; mem. bd. economists Time mag., 1971-74, 77-87. Bd. overseers Hoover Instn. on War, Revolution and Peace, 1973-74, 77-87. Recipient John P. Madden medal, 1975, Pub. Svc. Achievement award, 1976, William Butler Meml. award, 1977. Fellow Nat. Assn. Bus. Economists (past pres.), Hillcrest Country Club, Met. Club, Century Country Club, Harmonie Club. Office: Federal Reserve System Office of Chmn 20th & C St NW Washington DC 20551-0001

GREENSPAN, JOHN S., dental and medical educator, scientist, administrator; b. London, Jan. 7, 1938; came to U.S., 1976; s. Nathan and Jessie (Dion) G.; m. Deborah, Dec. 1962; children: Nicholas J., Louise C. BSC in Anatomy with 1st class honors, U. London, 1959, B in Dental Surgery, 1962, PhD in Exptl. Pathology, 1967; ScD (hon.), Georgetown U., 1990. Licentiate in dental surgery Royal Coll. of Surgeons of Eng. Asst. house surgeon in conservation and periodontology Royal Dental Hosp. London, 1962; asst. lectr. oral pathology Sch. of Dental Surgery Royal Dental Hosp. of London, U. London, 1963-65, lectr. oral pathology Sch. of Dental Surgery, 1965-68, sr. lectr. oral pathology Sch. of Dental Surgery, 1968-75; prof. oral biology and oral pathology Sch. of Dentisty, U. Calif., San Francisco, 1976—, vice chmn. dept. oral medicine and hosp. dentistry, 1977-82, chmn. div. oral biology, 1981-89, coord. basic scis. Sch. of Dentistry, 1982-96; chmn. dept. stomatology U. Calif., San Francisco, 1989—; cons. oral pathology St. John's Hosp. and Inst. of Dermatology, London, 1973-76; cons. dental surgeon St. George's Hosp., 1972-76; prof. dept. pathology Sch. Medicine U. Calif., San Francisco, 1976—; dir. U. Calif. AIDS Specimen Bank, San Francisco, 1982—, U. Calif. Oral AIDS Ctr., San Francisco, 1987—; assoc. dir. dental clin. epidemiology program U. Calif., San Francisco, 1987—; dir. U. Calif. AIDS Clin. Rsch. Ctr., San Francisco, 1992—; Burroughs Wellcome vis. prof. Royal Soc. Medicine, U.K., 1996-97; presenter, lectr. Author: (with others) Opportunistic Infections in Patients with the Acquired Immunodeficiency Syndrome, 1989, Contemporary Periodontics, 1989, Gastroenterology Clinics of North America, 1988, Perspectives on Oral Manifestations of AIDS, 1988, AIDS: Pathogenesis and Treatment, 1988, others; contbr. articles to profl. jours.; editorial cons. Achives of Oral Biology, 1968—, Jour. of Calif. Dental Assn., 1980—; editorial adv. bd. Jour. of Dental Rsch., 1977—; editorial bd. AIDS Alert, 1987-89, Brit. Dental Jour., 1998—; sr. editor Oral Diseases, 1994-98. Rsch. grantee NIH-Nat. Inst. Dental Rsch., 1978-82, 86—, U. Calif. Task Force on AIDS, 1983—, rsch. com. Royal Dental Hosp., London, 1964-76, Med. Rsch. Coun. of U.K., 1974-77, chmn. U. Calif. San Francisco Acad. Senate, 1983-85; Nuffield dental scholar, 1958-59; fellow Am. Coll. Dentists, 1982—, AAAS, 1985—; recipient Seymour J. Kreshover Lecture award Nat. Inst. Dental Rsch., NIH, 1989, Rsch. in Oral Biology award Internat. Assn. Dental Rsch., 1992. Fellow Royal Coll. Pathologists, Royal Coll. Surgeons Faculty of Dental Surgery, Inst. Medicine of Nat. Acad. Scis.; mem. ADA, AAAS, Am. Assn. Dental Rsch. (pres. 1988-89), Internat. Assn. Dental Rsch. (pres. 1996-97), Royal Soc. Medicine (U.K.), Pathological Soc. (U.K.), Oral Pathology Soc. (U.K.), Am. Acad. Oral Pathology, Bay Area Tchrs. Oral Pathology, Internat . Assn. Oral Pathologists, San Francisco Dental Soc., Calif. Dental Assn., Calif. Soc. Oral Pathologists Histochem. Soc., Am. Assn. Pathologists. Avocations: skiing, gardening, travel, wine. Office: U Calif Dept Stomatology PO Box 422 San Francisco CA 94143-0001

GREENSPAN, MICHAEL EVAN, lawyer; b. White Plains, N.Y., Jan. 18, 1967; s. Leon Joseph and Irene (Gordon) G.; m. Diane Gloria Blum, July 2, 1989; children: Daniel, Marc, Julia. BA magna cum laude, Temple U., 1988, JD, 1991. Bar: N.Y. 1992, U.S. Dist. Ct. (so. and ea. dists.) N.Y. 1992, U.S. Dist. Ct. Conn. 1992, U.S. Ct. Appeals (2d cir.) 1993, U.S. Ct. Appeals (11th cir.) 1996. Assoc. Greenspan, Jaffe & Rosenblatt, White Plains, 1991-92; ptnr. Greenspan & Greenspan, White Plains, 1992—; mem. com. civil practice laws and rules State Bar N.Y.; Temple U. del. Symposium on the Presidency, Washington, 1987. Mem. exec. com. Loucks Track & Field Games, White Plains, 1991—. Recipient Lewis F. Powell Jr. medallion Am. Coll. Trial Lawyers Assn., 1991, James J. Manderino award Phila. Trial Lawyers Assn., 1991. Mem. ATLA, N.Y. Trial Lawyers Assn., Barristers Soc., N.Y. State Bar Assn. (contbg. editor ins. and compensation law sect. Automobile Liability Newsletter 1997—), Westchester County Bar Assn., White Plains Bar Assn., Westchester Track and Field and Cross-Country Ofcls. Orgn., Golden Key, Order of Omega, Phi Beta Kappa, Pi Sigma Alpha, Phi Alpha Theta, Delta Tau Delta. Republican. Jewish. Avocations: officiating high school track and field, race walking, basketball. Office: Greenspan & Greenspan 34 S Broadway Ste 605 White Plains NY 10601-4428

GREENSPON, ROBERT ALAN, lawyer; b. Hartford, Conn., Apr. 17, 1947; s. George Arthur and Shirley Jean (Shelton) G.; m. Claire Alice Stone, Aug. 21, 1971; children: Colin Haynes, Alison Shelton. AB, Franklin and Marshall, 1969; JD, Columbia U., 1972. Bar: Conn. 1973, N.Y. 1998, U.S. Dist. Conn. 1973, U.S. Ct. Appeals (2d cir.) 1983. Assoc. Robinson & Cole, Hartford, Conn., 1972-78; ptnr. Robinson & Cole, Hartford, 1978-81, Stamford, Conn., 1981-86; sr. v.p., gen. counsel Guinness Peat Aviation Corp., Stamford, N.Y.C., N.Y.C., Shannon, Ireland, 1985-92; ptnr. Latham & Watkins, N.Y.C., 1992—. Contbr. articles to profl. jours. Mem. ABA (comml. fin. services, aircraft fin.), Conn. Bar Assn., N.Y. State Bar Assn., Internat. Bar Assn., Southwestern Legal Found. (bd. advisors internat. and comparative law ctr.). Home: 49 Old Farm Rd Darien CT 06820-6119 Office: Latham & Watkins 885 3rd Ave Fl 10 New York NY 10022-4834

GREENSTEIN, EDWARD L., biblical studies educator; b. Rockville Centre, N.Y., Jan. 18, 1949; arrived in Israel, 1996; s. Samuel H. and Goldie (Kliegman) G.; m. Beverly Gribetz, Sept. 24, 1986; children: Batsheva, Avi. BA, Columbia U., 1970; BHL, Jewish Theol. Sem., N.Y.C., 1970, MA, 1974; PhD, Columbia U., 1977. Prof. Jewish Theol. Sem., 1976-96, Tel Aviv U., 1996—; vis. prof. Columbia U., N.Y.C., 1975-78, 82-83, 85-87, 87-91, Yale U., New Haven, 1987, 90, Union Theol. Sem., N.Y.C., 1979-80, 87, Bar-Ilan U., Israel, 1996-99; chair Columbia U. Seminar for Study of Hebrew Bible, 1987-90. Author: (book) Essays in Biblical Method and Translation, 1989; co-author: (book) The Timetables of Jewish History, 1993; co-editor: (book) The State of Jewish Studies, 1990; co-compiler: (reference book) The Hebrew Bible in Literary Criticism, 1986; editor, co-editor: Jour. of Ancient Near Ea. Soc., 1974—; editor: SBL Semeia Studies, 1988-93. Guggenheim Meml. fellow, 1992-93, NEH sr. rsch. fellow, 1991-92, Guastella fellow, 1996-99. Mem. World Union of Jewish Studies (bd. dirs. 1997—), Soc. Bibl. Lit. (mem. 3 steering coms. 1983—). Office: Tel Aviv U, Dept of Bible, 69978 Ramat Aviv Israel

GREENSTEIN, MERLE EDWARD, import and export company executive; b. Portland, Oreg., June 22, 1937; s. Sol and Tillie Germaine (Schnitzer) G.; m. Nasi Jenab; 1 child, Todd Aaron. BA, Reed Coll., 1959. Pres. Acme Trading and Supply Co., Portland, 1963-82; chmn. MMI Group, Portland, 1982-91, Internat. Devel. Assocs., Portland, 1991—; com. mem. ISRI, Washington, 1987-89; mem. dist. export coun. U.S. Dept. Commerce, 1980—, mem. first USA trade Missions to Vietnam, 1996. Chmn. fin. Portland Opera, 1966; bd. dirs. Met. YMCA, 1964-67; del. to China, State of Oreg. Ofcl. Trade Mission, 1979; chmn. Western Internat. Trade Group, 1981-82; mem. State of Oreg. Korea Commn., 1985-90; fin. chmn. Anne Frank exhibit, Portland; joint chmn. bldg. campaign Oreg. Mus. Sci. and Industry; bd. dirs. Waverly Children's Home; bd. cons. Unilearn Corp., Oreg. Youth Leadership Sem.; chmn. fin. Oreg. Holocaust Mem.; mem. Food Bank Relocation Com.; mem. property task force com. Oreg. Food Bank, also mem. capital campaign cabinet. Recipient President's E for Export, U.S. Dept. Commerce, 1969; named Citizen of the Week, City of Portland, 1953. Mem. Rolls Royce Owners Club (London), City Club, Tualatin Country Club, Masons, Shriners. Avocations: antique autos, Arabian horses, cross country skiing. Office: Internat Devel Assocs 6731 NE 47th Ave Portland OR 97218-1205

GREENSTEIN, RICHARD HENRY, lawyer; b. Newark, June 29, 1946; s. Jacob Harold and Florence G.; m. Irene Beth Polishuk, July 4, 1973; children: Suzanne Beth, Jonathan Henry. AB, Rutgers Coll., 1968; JD, Boston U., 1971. Bar: N.J. 1971, U.S. Dist. Ct. N.J. 1971, U.S. Supreme Ct. 1985. Law clk. Superior Ct. N.J., Elizabeth, 1971-72; asst. county prosecutor Union County Prosecutor, Elizabeth, 1972-74; assoc. atty. Mandel, Wysoker, Sherman, et al, Perth Amboy, N.J., 1974-77, Fox and Fox, Newark, 1977-83; ptnr. Kein, Pollatschek & Greenstein, Union, N.J., 1983—; atty. Young Astronauts N.J. Inc., 1989—; mem. ethics com. Supreme Ct. Dist. N.J., 1991-95. Lighting dir. Wash. Sch. PTA Show, Westfield, N.J., 1985-94. Mem. Exchange Club Union (pres.-elect, dir. 1983—). Jewish. Avocations: skiing, hiking, reading. Home: 743 Saint Marks Ave Westfield NJ 07090-2035 Office: Kein Pollatschek & Greenstein 2042 Morris Ave Union NJ 07083-6028

GREENSTOCK, SIR JEREMY, diplomat. Permanent rep. of U.K. to UN, N.Y.C. Office: UK Mission to UN PO Box 5238 New York NY 10150-5238

GREENWALD, ANDREW ERIC, lawyer; b. N.Y.C., May 31, 1942; s. Harold and Lillian G.; m. Paula S., Aug. 20, 1967; children: Brooke Ellen, Karen Michelle. BS, U. Wis., 1964; JD, Georgetown U., 1967. Bar: D.C. 1968, Md. 1969, U.S. Ct. Appeals Md. 1969. Lawyer Nat. Labor Rels. Bd., Washington, 1967-68; asst. corp. counsel D.C. Govt., 1968-69; shareholder Joseph, Greenwald & Laake PA, Greenbelt, Md., 1969—; past mem. dept. family and cmty. devel. U. Md. Contbr. articles to profl. jours. Active adv. com. Georgetown U. Continuing Legal Edn., 1991, Georgetown U. Law Ctr. Alumni Bd., 1995. Mem. ATLA (chmn. tort sect. 1985), ABA, Nat. Inst. Trial Advocacy, Am. Bd. Profl. Liability Attys., Am. Bd. Trial Advocates, William B. Bryant Inn, Am. Inns of Ct. Office: Joseph Greenwald & Laake PA 6404 Ivy Ln Ste 400 Greenbelt MD 20770-1407

GREENWALD, DANIEL JACK, III, lawyer; b. Mpls., Dec. 2, 1949; s. Daniel Jack Jr. and Alta Jean (Peterson) G.; m. Gail Bernadette McNaught, Oct. 5, 1980; children: Daniel Jack IV, Shannon Maryjean. BA cum laude, U. Minn., 1971, JD cum laude, 1976. Bar: N.Y. 1977, D.C. 1980. Assoc. Chadbourne & Parke, N.Y.C. and Washington, 1976-84; ptnr. Chadbourne & Parke, Washington, 1985-89; resident ptnr. Chadbourne, Parke & Afridi, Dubai, United Arab Emirates, 1986-89; gen. counsel, v.p. corp. finance Arabian Gen. Investment Corp., Dubai, 1989-92; mng. ptnr. Greenwald & van de Kraats, Dubai, 1989—. Contbr. articles to profl. jours. Legal v.p. Am. Bus. Coun. Dubai, 1986-87, exec. v.p., 1987-88, pres., 1989-92; vice-chmn. Am. Bus. Couns. of the Gulf Countries, 1990-92. Mem. ABA, Internat. Bar Assn., World Trade Club, Emirates Golf Club, Baker's Dozen Club. Republican. Lutheran. Avocations: photography, traveling, exploring, outdoor sports. Office: Greenwald & van de Kraats, PO Box 23927, Dubai United Arab Emirates

GREENWELL, ROGER ALLEN, scientist; b. Santa Maria, Calif., Mar. 4, 1941; s. George C. and Bessie Florence (Sutton) G.; m. Jeannine Pendleton, July 25, 1969; 1 child, George Eli. AA, Hancock Jr. Coll, 1961; BS, Calif. Poly. Coll., 1968; MS, U.S. Internat. U., 1974, DBA, 1981. Mathematician Naval Weapons Ctr., China Lake, Calif., 1968; ops. research analyst Corona, Calif., 1969-70; ops. research analyst Comdr. Naval Forces Vietnam, 1968-69; mathematician Naval Electronics Lab. Ctr., San Diego, 1970-77; scientist Naval Ocean Systems Ctr., San Diego, 1977-84; v.p., dir. advanced tech. divsn. Sci. and Engring. Assoc., Inc., 1984—; cons. fiber optics and econ. analysis; mem. NATO Research Study Group, 1983—. Served with U.S. Army, 1964-67. Decorated Bronze Star. Mem. AIAA, IEEE, ACS, Internat. Soc. Optical Engrs., Ops. Research Soc. Am., Inst. Mgmt. Sci., Soc. Allied Weight Engrs., Optical Soc. Am. Home: 3778 Eagle St San Diego CA 92103-3958 Office: Ste 102 7545 Metropolitan Dr San Diego CA 92108-4402

GREENWOOD, ANTONY BARON, lawyer; b. Sydney, Australia, Aug. 9, 1940; s. Wilfred and Violet Claire (Easton) G.; m. Wendy Lynn Martin, Nov. 16, 1985; children from previous marriage: Jeremy, Philip. LLB, U. Sydney, 1965. Asst. commr. Corp. Affairs Commn., New South Wales, 1971-79; commr. Nat. Cos. and Securities Commn., Australia, 1980-87; ptnr. Blake Dawson Waldron, Melbourne, Australia, 1987—; dep. chmn. compliance com. Crown Ltd., 1998—; mem. legal reference gourp Bus. Coun. Australia, 1990-97; chmn. cos. and bus. orgns. com. Law Inst., 1990—. Australian editor: International Securities Regulation, 1984—; mem. editl. bd. Australian Corp. Law, 1990—. Bd. dirs. Fairfield Pub. Hosp., 1994-95; mem. cos. and securities law rev. com. Ministerial Coun. for Co. Law, Australia, 1984-90; mem. coun. Ridley Coll., U. Melbourne, 1989-93; trustee Corp. Trustees of Gen. Synod of Anglican Ch. of Australia, 1978—. Churchill fellow, 1973. Home: 23 Rushall Crescent, North Fitzroy 3068, Australia Office: Blake Dawson Waldron, L39/101 Collins St, Melbourne 3000, Australia

GREENWOOD, FRANK, information scientist; b. Rio de Janeiro, Mar. 6, 1924; came to U.S., 1935; s. Heman Charles and Evelyn (Heyns) G.; m. Mary Mallas, Oct. 24, 1972; children: Margaret, Ernest, Nicholas. BA, Bucknell U., 1950; MBA, U. So. Calif., 1959; PhD, UCLA, 1963; hon. doctorate, Commonwealth Open U. Brit. VI, 1999. Cert. systems profl., project mgmt. profl. Various positions The Tex. Co., U.S., Africa and Can., 1950-60; assoc. prof. U. Ga., Athens, 1961-65; chmn. dept. computer sys. Ohio U., Athens, 1966-76; dir. computer ctr. U. Mont., Missoula, 1977-84; prof. mgmt. info. sys. Southea. Mass. U. (now U. Mass.), North Dartmouth, 1985-89, Ctrl. Mich. U., Mt. Pleasant, 1990-93; pres. Greenwood & Assocs., Ltd., Bloomfield Hills, Mich., 1993; instr. on-line grad. classes Internat. Sch. of Info. Mgmt. U. Denver, Denver, 1998—; instr. on-line clases Ednl. Svcs. Inst. Internat., Arlington, Va., Jones Internat. U., Englewood, Colo. Author: Casebook for Management and Business Policy: A Systems Approach, 1968, Managing the Systems Analysis Function, 1968; (with Nicolai Siemens and C.H. Marting Jr.) Operations Research: Planning, Operating and Information Systems, 1973; (with Mary Greenwood) Information Resources in the Office Tomorrow, 1980, Profitable Small Business Computing, 1982, Office Technology: Principles of Automation, 1984, Business Telecommuncations: Data Communications in the Information Age, 1988, Introduction to Computer-Integrated Manufacturing, 1990, How to Raise Office Productivity, 1991, Meeting the Challenges of Project Management: A Primer, 1998; columnist: Computerworld mag., 1972-73, The Daily Record, 1982-83, (with Mary Greenwood) Herald News, 1986, The Beacon, 1986, Morning Sun, 1990-93; contbr. monographs, articles to profl. jours. and chpts. to books. Sgt. AUS, 1943-45. UCLA Alumni scholar, 1961; Ford Found. fellow, 1962-63. Mem. Wamsutta Club (New Bedford, Mass.). Episcopalian. Avocation: exercise. Home and Office: 7426 Deep Run Apt 1322 Bloomfield Hills MI 48301-3844

GREENWOOD, JEREMY JOHN, book publisher; b. Cairo, Mar. 30, 1936; s. Basil Proctor and Stephanie Kathleen (Davidson-Houston) G.; m. Annabel Elizabeth Carlile, Oct. 23, 1963; children: Simon, Elinor, Gemma. BA, U. Cambridge. Dir. trade Cassell & Co. Book Pubs., London, 1961-66, 77-81; owner Quiller Press Ltd., London, 1981—. Author: Sefton, 1983. 1st lt. King's Dragoon Guards, 1954-58. Mem. Calvary and Guards Club. Avocations: tennis, foxhunting, shooting, golf. Office: Quiller Press, 46 Lillie Rd, London SW61TN, England

GREENWOOD, JOEN ELIZABETH, economist, consultant; b. Mineral Point, Wis., Aug. 29, 1934; d. John Edward and Lillian Laile (Rohr) G. BS, MA, U. Wis., 1956, 57; postgrad., Newnham Coll. Cambridge U., Eng., 1961-62; diploma in advanced mgmt. program, Harvard Bus. Sch., 1983. Instr. econs. Wellesley (Mass.) Coll., 1962-68; sr. assoc. Charles River Assocs., Boston, 1968-79, v.p., 1979—; mem. bd. editors Energy Jour., 1979-83. Co-author: Folded, Spindled and Mutilated: Economic Analysis and U.S. v. IBM, 1983; contbr. to profl. publs. Mem. Commonwealth of Mass. Pub. Health Coun., Boston, 1973-79. Earhart fellow U. Calif.-Berkeley, 1960-61; Fulbright scholar U.K., 1961-62. Mem. Internat. Assn. Energy Economists (v.p. 1978-84, exec. v.p. 1981-84), Nat. Coal Coun., U. Wis. Alumni Assn. (bd. dirs. 1987-93), Wis. Alumni Assn. Greater Boston (pres. 1987-89), Boston Club, Harvard Club, Phi Beta Kappa. Home: 11 Ellery Sq Cambridge MA 02138-4227 Office: Charles River Assocs 200 Clarendon St Fl 33 Boston MA 02116-5092

GREENWOOD, JOHN EDWARD DOUGLAS, investment banker, lawyer; b. Blundell Sands, Lancashire, Eng., Mar. 4, 1923; came to U.S., 1948; s. Arthur and Mabel (Hunt) G.; m. Charlotte Elizabeth Sabey, May, 25, 1946; children: Marcia Barbara Hunt, Douglas Charles William. B in Econs. with 1st class honors, McGill U., 1948; JD, Yale U., 1951. Bar: N.Y. 1952. Jr. legal assoc. Milbank, Tweed, Hope & Hadley, N.Y.C., 1951-52, Chadbourne, Hunt, Jaeckel & Brown, N.Y.C., 1952-54; with legal dept. Creole Petroleum Corp., N.Y.C., 1954-55; assoc. corp. fin. Bacon Stevenson & Co., N.Y.C., 1955-59; v.p. E.F. Hutton & Co., N.Y.C., 1959-60; pres., founder Can. Alpha Lessors Ltd., Mont., Can., 1960-63; ptnr., sr. v.p. Eastman Dillon Union Securities, N.Y.C., 1963-72; prin. Blyth Eastman Dillon & Co., N.Y., 1972-78; pvt. investor, 1978—; chmn., pres. Greenwood Corpfin, Inc.; fin. advisor Promia Inc., San Francisco; fin. advisor Laughng Yak.Com, San Francisco. Mem. Rep. Boosters Club, N.Y., 1965—; patron Winslow Therapeutic Riding, Inc., warwick, 1982—, Warwick Hist. Soc., 1984—; sec., dir. Friends of McGill, Inc., N.Y., 1952-60; treas., trustee Tuxedo Park (N.Y.) Sch., 1961-63; U.S. rep. (fin.) Intertnat. Atomic Energy Agy. World Confs., Copenhagen and Paris, 1975, Stockholm, 1976, Salzberg, 1977; charter mem. Global Telecomm. Soc., Washington. With Royal Can. Navy, 1941-45, Comms. Intelligence. Mem. Am. Nuclear Energy Coun. (bd. dirs. Washington 1976-78), Atomic Indsl. Forum, Global Telecomms. Soc. (charter), Links Club of N.Y., Univ. Club. of Montreal, Racquet and Tennis Club of N.Y., Tuxedo Club of Tuxedo Park, N.Y., Capitol Hill Club of Wahsington, Bond Club of N.Y. Episcopalian. Avocations: opera, shooting, riding, skiing, golf. Office: 19 Park Ave Warwick NY 10990-1702

GREER, ALAN GRAHAM, lawyer; b. El Dorado, Ark., May 31, 1939; s. Arthur W. and Marie (Ross) G.; m. Patricia A. Seitz, Aug. 14, 1981. BS, U.S. Naval Acad., 1961; JD, U. Fla., 1969. Ptnr. Richmnan, Greer Weil Brumbaugh, Miami, Fla., 1969—; chmn. emeritus WLRN Pub. Radio and TV Sta.; bd. dirs. Camillus Ho. Past chmn. Dade County Coun. Arts and Scis.; past mem. Fla. State Task Force on Water Issues, Gov.'s Bus. Adv. Coun. on Edn.; co-chmn. site selection com. Dem. Nat. Com., 1992, also trustee. With USN, 1961-67. Fellow Internat. Soc. Barristers, Am. Coll. Trial Lawyers; mem. ABA (standing com. on professionalism), Fla. Bar Assn. (cert., past chmn. internat. law com.). Home: 224 Ridgewood Rd Miami FL 33133-6614 Office: Richman Greer Weil Brumbaugh Miami Ctr 10th Fl 201 S Biscayne Blvd Miami FL 33131-4332

GREER, GORDON BRUCE, lawyer; b. Butler, Pa., Feb. 17, 1932; s. Samuel Walker and Winifred (Fletcher) G.; m. Nancy Linda Hannaford, June 14, 1959; children: Gordon Bruce, Alison Clark. BA, Harvard U., 1953, JD cum laude, 1959. Bar: Wis. 1959, Mass. 1961. Assoc. Foley, Sammond & Lardner, Milw., 1959-61; assoc. Bingham Dana LLP, Boston, 1961-67, ptnr., 1967-97, of counsel, 1997—; lectr. Boston U. Sch. Law. Editor Harvard Law Rev. Vos. 71, 72. Maj. USAFR. Mem. Mass. Bar Assn., Boston Bar Assn., Brae Burn Country Club, Harvard Club (Boston). Republican. Home: 45 Fieldmont Rd Belmont MA 02478-2606 Office: Bingham Dana LLP 150 Federal St Boston MA 02110-1713

GREER, MACK VARNEDOE, physician; b. Valdosta, Ga., July 29, 1927; s. Lloyd Barton an dJulie Winn (Varnedoe) G.; m. Betty Dame English, Dec. 27, 1951; children: Betty June, Mack Varnedoe. AB, Emory U., 1951; MD, Med. Coll. Ga., 1960. Diplomate Am. Bd. Family Practice. Adjustor Crawford & Co., ins. adjusters, Atlanta, 1951-52; math. and sci. tchr., football coach Clinch County (Ga.) and Waycross (Ga.) h.s., 1952-55; rotating intern Bapt. Meml. Hosp., Jacksonville, Fla., 1960-61; gen. practice medicine and surgery, Homerville, Ga., 1961-72; mem. staff South Ga. Me.d Ctr., 1972—, chief staff, 1980; coll. physician, assoc. prof. biology Valdosta State U., 1972-95, emeritus prof., 1995—. Former bd. dirs. Valdosta Girls Club. Served with USMCR, World War II, 1950-51, ret. capt. M.C. USNR. Fellow Am. Acad. Family Practice; mem. AMA, Ga. Med. Assn., South Ga. Med. Soc., Valdosta Touchdown Club, Valdosta Country Club, Pi Kappa Alpha, Alpha Kappa Kappa. Presbyterian. Home: 912 S Lakeshore Dr Valdosta GA 31605-7911

GREER, MARSHA ADAIR, health facility administrator; b. Nowata, Okla., Aug. 12, 1940; 1 child, Joe Tom Adair. ADN, Odessa Coll., 1990. Cert. gerontol. nurse. Dir. nurses Long Term Care Avalon, Odessa, Tex., 1989-90; psychiat. nurse Glenwood Hosp., 1990-92; dir. nurses, owner West Tex. Nursing Affiliation and Health Care Enterprises, Odessa, 1990—; instr. nursing Odessa Coll., 1991-93; nurse supr. Parks Good Samaritan, Odessa, 1994-96; dir. nursing long term care Kermit (Tex.) Health Care Ctr., 1998; nurse supr. Ector Country Juvenile Detention Ctr., Odessa, 1998-99; RN cons. Sr. Life Care, 1993; dir. nurses long term care Crane County Care Ctr., 1993; instr. ARC, 1994; insvc. coord. Monahans Care Ctr., 1994. Mem. ANA, Tex. Nurses Assn. Office: W Tex Nursing Affiliation 2817 Jb Sheppard Odessa TX 79764

GREER, RAYMOND WHITE, lawyer; b. Port Arthur, Tex., July 20, 1954; s. Mervyn Hardy Greer and Eva Nadine (White) Swain; m. Pamela V. Brown; children: Emily Ann, Sarah Kelly, Jonathan Collin. BA magna cum laude, Sam Houston State, 1977; JD, U. Houston, 1981. Assoc. Hoover, Cox & Shearer, Houston, 1980-83, Hinton & Morris, Houston, 1983-85; pvt. practice Houston, 1985-86; prin. Morris & Greer, P.C., Houston, 1986-90, Raymond W. Greer & Assocs., P.C., Houston, 1990-98, Rigg & Greer, Houston, 1998—; lectr. in field; mem. dist. 4 grievance com. State Bar Tex. Mem. adv. com. Enterprising Girls Scouts Beyond Bars, San Jacinto coun., 1996-98. Recipient Outstanding Alumnus award, Dept. English, Sam Houston U., 1986, Disting. Alumni Alpha Chi., 1996. Mem. ABA, State Bar Tex., Houston Bar Assn., Fort Bend County Bar Assn., Rotary (Houston asst. chmn. fresh start com. 1996-97—, chmn. fresh start com. 1997-98, dir. 1998—), Alumni Assn. (2d v.p., chmn. membership com., combined charter and membership com. 1995-96, 1st v.p. 1996-97, pres. 1997-98, immediate past pres. 1998-99), Sam Houston State U. Avocations: golf, reading. Office: Rigg & Greer 13333 Southwest Fwy Ste 100 Sugar Land TX 77478-3545

GREFEN, PAUL WILLEM, computer scientist, researcher; b. Heerlen, Limburg, The Netherlands, Apr. 18, 1963; s. Johan Jozef and Elisabeth (Vondenhoff) G.; m. Maria Henrica Coonjers, Dec. 18, 1986. Degree in engring., U. Twente, 1986, PhD, 1992. Sys. analyst U. Twente, 1985-86, asst. prof., 1986-87, 92-98, assoc. prof., 1998—, rschr., 1987-92; vis. scholar Stanford (Calif.) U., 1994; mem. program com. internat. confs. of various profl. orgns. Editor, author: Database Support for Workflow Management, 1999, Workflow Management, 2000; contbr. articles to profl. jours. including IEEE Knowledge and Data Enginrg., Distributed and Parallel Databases. Office: U Twente Dept Computer Scis, PO Box 217, 7500 AE Enschede The Netherlands

GREGER, JANUSZ STEFAN, biochemist, educator; b. Baranowicze, Poland, Jan. 8, 1932; s. Stefan Marian and Stefania Irena (Białkowska) G.; m. Krystyna Maria Mika, Feb. 28, 1968; children: Paulina, Maciej. MD, Med. U., Lodz, Poland, 1955, PhD, 1966, D in Med. Sci., 1980. From asst. to prof. Med. U., Lodz, Poland, 1955-90, prof., head dept. biochemistry, 1990—, vice dean, 1981-86, dean, 1986-90, vice-rector, 1990-93, dir. subfaculty pub. health, 1993—. Co-author 4 textbooks. Min. Health award 1985, 91, 93, 97, State Agy. Atomistics award, 1987. Mem. Polish Biochem. Soc., Polish Med. Soc., Lodz Scientific Soc., N.Y. Acad. Scis. Avocations: classical music. Home: Narutowicza 91, 90 139 Łódź Poland Office: Dept Biochemistry, Lindleya 6, 90 131 Łódź Poland

GREGERSEN, R(OALD) GEORGE, newspaper publishing executive; b. Copenhagen, Mar. 14, 1935; came to U.S., 1948; s. Richard Vilhelm and Eva (Giertsen) G.; m. Gayle Froerer Richards, May 1, 1964 (div. 1978); m. Penney Losse, Dec. 21, 1982; children: Mary Anne Georgia, John Christian. Student, U. Utah, 1953-55. Pres., CEO Mortgage Investment Corp., Salt Lake City, 1955-68; pres., CEO Gregersen & Co., Salt Lake City, 1968-74; pub., CEO The Enterprise (weekly), Salt Lake City, 1974—. Editl. writer The Enterprise, 1974—. Bd. dirs. Utal Mil. & Vets. Affairs com., Salt Lake City, 1982-92. Named Utah Mil. Citizen of Yr., 1986; recipient Assn. U.S. Army Exceptional Svc. award, 1990. Mem. Alta Club (bd. dirs. 1993-96), Rotary. Republican. Episcopalian. Avocation: flyfishing. Home: 1427 Circle Way Salt Lake City UT 84103-4433 Office: Enterprise Newspaper Group Inc 136 S Main St Ste 721 Salt Lake City UT 84101-1676

GREGG, BILLY RAY, seed industry executive, consultant; b. Taylorsville, Miss., Aug. 31, 1930; s. Hinds and Lillie Mae (Moore) G.; m. Mary Frances Barber, Aug. 12, 1950 (div. Jan. 1987); children: Kathryn, Patricia, Lisa; m. Orawan Chonlavorn, Dec. 20, 1988; 1 child, Nathan Paul. AA, Perkinston (Miss.) Jr. Coll., 1950; BS, Miss. State U., 1954, MS, 1956, PhD, 1968; postgrad., Wash. State U., 1957-63. Asst. prof. Wash. State U., Pullman, 1956-63; mgr. Ala. Crop Improvement Assn., Auburn, Ala., 1964-66; seed technologist Miss. State U., 1966-68; chief party/processing specialist seed improvement project U.S. AID, New Delhi, India, 1968-72; chief party and seed specialist seed project U.S. AID, Brasilia, Brazil, 1972-74; chief, seed industry devel. specialist U.S. AID, Bangkok, 1977-87; seed industry devel. specialist U.S. AID, Cairo, 1987-93; chief party and seed industry specialist IDB and GOB Agiplan Project, Brasilia, 1974-76; seed industry specialist Internat. Plant Breeders, Maringa, Parana, Brazil, 1976, Interam. Agrl. Sci. Inst., Brasilia, 1976-77, seed industry devel. specialist internat. programs Miss. State U., 1993—; cons./advisor on seed tech. matters, mgmt., quality control and industry devel. nat. govts., pvt. cos., World Bank, Interam. Devel. Bank, FAO, GTZ, U.S. AID in more than 80 countries, 1960-95. Contbr. over 500 articles to profl. jours.; author 2 books. With U.S. Army, 1950-52; ETO. Indian Soc. Seed Technologists fellow, 1987. Mem. Kiwanis Internat. (dir., Kiwanian of the Yr. 1968), Agrl. Sci. Soc. Thailand (hon.), Wash. State Crop Improvement Assn. (hon. life), Phi Kappa Phi, Sigma Xi, Phi Theta Kappa. Buddhist. Avocations: vegetable and flower gardening, writing, travel. Home: PO Box 1756 Starkville MS 39760-1756

GREGG, DAVID, III, investment banker; b. N.Y.C., Jan. 29, 1933; s. David Gregg and Virginia (Wyckoff) Macgregor; m. May Foster Bowers, Dec. 21, 1963 (div. Apr. 1984); children: Justine Simms Barkstrom, David; m. Sarah Choate Massengale, Dec. 8, 1984. Assoc. Eastman Dillon Union Securities & Co., N.Y.C., 1959-67, ptnr., 1967-69; v.p. Blyth & Co., Inc., N.Y.C., 1969-72; 1st v.p. Blyth, Eastman, Dillon & Co., N.Y.C., 1972-73; exec. v.p. Overseas Pvt. Investment Corp., Washington, 1973-77; mng. dir. Pierce Internat., Ltd., Washington, 1978-85, Pierce Investment Banking Corp., 1985-97, Pierce Fin. Corp., Arlington, Va., 1986-2000; sr. advisor Pierce Fin. Corp., Arlington, 2000—; chmn. bd. dirs. Gator Broadcasting Corp., Del., 1986—; trustee Calvert Tax Free Res. Fund, 1978-83; dir. No. Ireland and Border Counties Trade and Investment Coun., 1994-98; dir. Monument Funds, 2000—. Served with U.S. Army, 1955-57. Mem. Onteora Club (Tannersville, N.Y.) (dir. 1969-72), Chesapeake Bay Yacht Club (Easton, Md.), Amateur Ski Club N.Y. Republican. Episcopalian.

GREGG, JUDD, senator, former governor; b. Nashua, N.H., Feb. 14, 1947; m. Kathleen MacLellan, 1973; children—Molly, Sarah, Joshua. A.B., Columbia U., 1969; J.D., Boston U., 1972, LL.M., 1975. Bar: N.H. 1972. Ptnr. Sullivan, Gregg and Horton, Nashua, N.H.; mem. 97th-100th Congresses from 2d N.H. dist., Washington, 1981-89; governor of N.H., Concord, 1989-93; U.S. Senator from N.H., 1993—; mem. Budget/Appropriations Com.; chmn. Appropriations Subcom. on Commerce, Justice, State, Judiciary; chmn. Labor and Human Resources Subcom. on Children & Families; mem. N.H. Gov.'s Exec. Coun., 1978-80. Pres. Crotched Mountain Rehab. Found. Mem. ABA, N.H. BAr Assn., Nashua Bar Assn. Office: US Senate 393 Senate Russell Bldg Washington DC 20510-0001

GREGG, MARIE BYRD, retired farmer; b. Mount Olive, N.C., Jan. 12, 1930; d. Arnold Wesley and Martha (Reaves) Byrd; m. Robert Allen Gregg, July 11, 1953; children: Martha Susan, Kathryn Elizabeth, Kenneth Allen. BA in Elem. Edn., Furman U., 1951. Tchr. 3rd grade Greenville (S.C.) City Schs., 1951-53; med. social worker Ctrl. Carolina Rehab. Hosp., Greensboro, N.C., 1959-61; window display designer Kerr Rexall Drugs, Durham, N.C., 1960's; shop owner Something Else Antiques, Lima, Ohio, 1979-81; farm owner Mt. Olive, 1978-92. Democrat. Methodist. Avocations: antique collecting, traveling, reading, interior decorating. Home and Office: 212 Baucom Park Dr Greer SC 29650-2972

GREGOR, DOROTHY DEBORAH, librarian; b. Dobbs Ferry, N.Y., Aug. 15, 1939; d. Richard Garrett Heckman and Marion Allen (Richmond) Stewart; m. A. James Gregor, June 22, 1963 (div. 1974). BA, Occidental Coll., 1961; MA, U. Hawaii, 1963; MLS, U. Tex., 1968; cert. in Library Mgmt., U. Calif., Berkeley, 1976. Reference libr. U. Calif., San Francisco, 1968-69; dept. libr. Pub. Health Libr. U. Calif., Berkeley, 1969-71, tech. services libr., 1973-76; reference libr. Hamilton Libr., Honolulu, 1971-72; head serials dept. U. Calif., Berkeley, 1976-80, assoc. univ. libr. tech. svcs. dept., 1980-84, univ. libr., 1992-94; ret., 1994; chief Shared Cataloging div. Libr. of Congress, Washington, 1984-85; univ. libr. U. Calif.-San Diego, La Jolla, 1985-92, OCLC asst. to pres. for acad. and rsch. libr. rels., 1995-98; instr. sch. libr. and info. studies U. Calif., Berkeley, 1975, 76, 83; cons. Nat. Libr. of Medicine, Bethesda, Md., 1985, Ohio Bd. Regents, Columbus, 1987; trustee Online Computer Libr. Ctr., 1988-96; dir. Nat. Coordinating Com. on Japanese Libr. Resources, 1995-98. Mem. ALA, Libr. Info. Tech. Assn., Program Com. Ctr. for Rsch. Librs. (bd. chair 1992-93, Hugh Atkinson award 1994).

GREGOR, JAMES ANDREW, architect; b. Beirut, Lebanon, Apr. 9, 1962; s. Bryan Clunie and Farida Suzanne Assir. BA in Arch. with honors, Oxford (Eng.) Sch. Arch., 1983, diploma CSD, 1986, diploma arch., 1986. Rschr. Tribohesion, London, 1986-87; arch. ADP, Henley on Thames, Eng., 1987-88; archtl. ptnr. Andrew Gregor & Ptnr., Wiesbaden, Germany, 1988—. Mem. Royal Inst. Brit. Archs. (diploma arch.), Chartered Soc. Designers. Avocations: philosophy, snowboarding, sailing, reading. Fax: 00 49 611 87221. E-mail: 100407,2214@aol.com. Office: Andrew Gregor & Ptnr, Ruedesheimer Strasse 24, 65197 Wiesbaden Germany

GREGOR, JIRI, mathematician, educator; b. Chrlice, Czech Republic, Jan. 21, 1930; s. Jacob and Bozena G.; m. Gertruda Denska, Jan. 19, 1952; two children. Degree in engring., Czech Tech. U., Prague, 1952, DSc, 1992. From asst. prof. to full prof. math. Tech. U. Prague, 1952—; sr. lectr. U. Khartoum, Sudan, 1968-70. Mem. IEEE.

GREGOR, PAVEL, cardiologist; b. Policka, Svitavy, Czech Republic, Jan. 12, 1952; s. Robert and Marie (Stylova) G.; m. Marie Lysakova, June 19, 1977; children: Martin, Pavlina. Dr., Charles U., 1976, DSc, 1992. Physician Hosp. Kralovske Vinohrady, Prague, Czech Republic, 1976-81, cardiologist, 1981—; asst. prof. 3rd Sch. of Medicine, Prague, 1981-91, assoc. prof., 1991-95, prof. medicine, 1995—, head dept. of cardiology, 1991—. Author: Echocardiography, 1983 (Prize Presidium Czech Med. Soc., Ann. award of pub. 1984), 2d edit., 1991 (Prize Czech Soc. Cardiology 1991), Hypertrophic Cardiomyopathy, 1992 (Prize Czech Lit. Found. 1992), Cardiology, 1994. Mem. academical senate 3rd Sch. of Medicine, 1990-95, 98—. Fellow European Soc. of Cardiology; mem. Czech Soc. Cardiology. Roman Catholic. Avocations: motorcycling, books. Office: Cardio Ctr 2d Internal Clin, Srobarova 50, 10034 Prague 10, Czech Republic

GREGORI, JOSÉ, minister of justice; b. Sao Paulo, Oct. 13, 1930; s. Henrique Jr. and Esther Paraventi Gregori. Chief of staff Agrarian Reform Ministry, Brazil, 1987, Ministry Social Affairs, Brazil, 1988; chief of of staff Ministry of Economy, Brazil, 1992; various positions Ministry of Justice, Brazil, 1992-96, min. of justice, 1997—; cons. Volkswagen do Brazil, Sao Paulo, 1964-66. Office: Ministry of Justice, Esplanada dos Ministerios, 70064900 Brasilia DF Brazil*

GREGORIAN, VARTAN, academic administrator; b. Tabriz, Iran, Apr. 8, 1934; came to U.S., 1956; s. Samuel B. and Shushanik G. (Mirzaian) G.; m. Clare Russell, Mar. 25, 1960; children: Vahe, Raffi, Dareh. Grad., Coll. Armenian, 1955; BA, Stanford U., 1958, PhD, 1964; hon. degree, Boston U., 1983, Brown U., 1984, Jewish Theol. Seminary, 1984, SUNY, 1985, Johns Hopkins U., 1987, NYU, 1987, U. Pa., 1988, Dartmouth Coll., 1989, Rutgers U., 1989, CUNY, 1990, Tufts U., 1994. From instr. to assoc. prof. history San Francisco State Coll., 1962-68; assoc. prof. UCLA, 1968; from assoc. prof. to prof. U. Tex., 1968-72, dir. spl. programs, 1970-72; Tarzian prof. Armenian and Caucasian history U. Pa., Phila., 1972-80; dean U. Pa. (Faculty Arts and Scis.), 1974-78, provost, 1978-80; pres. N.Y. Pub. Libr., 1981-89; prof. New Sch. Social Rsch., N.Y.C., 1984-89; prof. History and Near Eastern studies NYU, 1984-89; pres., prof. History Brown U., Providence, 1989-97; pres. Carnegie Corp., N.Y.C., 1997—. Author: The Emergence of Modern Afghanistan, 1880-1946, 1969. Bd. dirs. Aaron Diamond Found., 1990-97, Brookings Instns., 1994-97, Inst. for Internat. Edn., 1989-95, Internat. League of Human Rights, 1984-97, Inst. for Advanced Study, 1987—, J. Paul Getty Trust, 1988—, Aga Khan U., 1995—, Human Rights Watch, 1996—; chmn. bd. visitors Grad. Sch. and Univ. Ctr., CUNY, 1984-90; bd. trustees Mus. Modern Art, 1994—. Decorated Officier de l'Ordre des Arts et Lettres (France), Grand Oficial Ordem Infante D. Henrique Portuguese Govt., 1995; recipient Danforth E.H. Harbison Teaching award 1969, Cactus Teaching award 1971, award of distinction Phi Lambda Theta and Phi Delta Kappa, 1980, Silver Cultural medal Italian Ministry Fgn. Affairs, 1977, Gold medal of honor City and Province of Vienna, Austria, 1976, 1st Disting. Humanist award Pa. Humanities Coun., 1983, Nat. Fellowship award Fellowship Commn., Phila., 1984, Gold medal Nat. Inst. Social Scis., 1985, Disting. Svc. to the Arts award Third St. Music Sch. Settlement, 1997, Disting. Svc. to Pub. Edn. award N.Y. Acad. Pub. Edn., 1998, Friends of the Arts award Town Hall, 1998; fellow Social Sci. Rsch. Coun., 1960, Ford Found. Fgn. Area Tng., 1960-62, Am. Coun. Learned Socs.-Social Sci. Rsch. Coun., 1965, John Simon Guggenheim Found., 1971-72, Social Sci. Rsch. Coun., 1971-72, Am. Coun. Edn., 1973. Fellow Acad. Arts Scis., Am. Philos. Soc.; mem. Am. Antiquarian Soc., Am. Hist. Assn. (program chmn. 1972), Am. Philos. Soc. (grantee 1965, 66), Internat. Fedn. Libr. Assns. (co-chmn. program com. 1985), Assn. Advancement Slavic Studies (program chmn. Western Slavic Conf. 1967), Mid-East Studies Assn., Coun. Fgn. Rels., Grolier Club, Round Table, Century Club, Econ. Club, Phi Beta Kappa. Office: Carnegie Corp Office of the Pres 437 Madison Ave Fl 27 New York NY 10022-7001

GREGORY, CALVIN, insurance service executive; b. Bronx, N.Y., Jan. 11, 1942; s. Jacob and Ruth (Cherchian) G.; m. Rachel Anna Carver, Feb. 14, 1970 (div. Apr. 1977); children—Debby Lynn, Trixy Sue; m. 2d, Carla Deane Deaver, June 30, 1979. AA, L.A. City Coll., 1962; BA, Calif. State U.-L.A., 1964; MDiv, Fuller Theol. Sem., 1968; MRS, Southwestern Sem., Ft. Worth, 1969; PhD in Religion, Universal Life Ch., Modesto, Calif., 1982; DDiv (hon.), Otay Mesa Coll., 1982. Notary pub., real estate lic., casualty lic., Calif.; ordained to ministry Am. Baptist Conv., 1970. Youth minister First Bapt. Ch., Delano, Calif., 1964-65, 69-70; youth dir. St. Luke's United Meth. Ch., Highland Park, Calif., 1969-70; tchr. polit. sci. Maranatha High Sch., Rosemead, Calif., 1969-70; aux. chaplain U.S. Air Force 750th Radar Squadron, Edwards AFB, Calif., 1970-72; pastor First Bapt. Ch., Boron, Calif., 1971-72; ins. agt. Prudential Ins. Co., Ventura, Calif., 1972-73, sales mgr., 1973-74; casualty ins. agt. Allstate Ins. Co., Thousand Oaks, Calif., 1974-75; pres. Ins. Agy. Placement Svcs., Thousand Oaks, 1975—; head youth minister Emanuel Presbyn. Ch., L.A., 1973-74; owner, investor real estate, U.S., Wales, Eng., Can., Australia. Counselor YMCA, Hollywood, Calif., 1964, Soul Clinic-Universal Life Ch., Inc., Modesto, Calif., 1982. Mem. Apt. Assn. L.A., Life Underwriter Tng. Coun., Forensic Club (L.A.), X32 Club (Ventura, Calif.), Kiwanis (club spkr. 1971). Republican. Office: Ins Agy Placement Svc PO Box 4407 Thousand Oaks CA 91359-1407

GREGORY, CEDRIC ERROL, retired mining engineer; b. Adelaide, Australia, Aug. 17, 1908; s. William Henry and Metha (Zimmermann) G.; m. Rachel Marion Jean Grant, Feb. 6, 1935; children: Roger, Graham (dec.),

Paul (dec.), Heather, Anne. BE, U. Adelaide, 1931, BA, 1944; B Econs., ME, U. Queensland, Australia, 1960, PhD, 1966. Chartered profl. engr., Australia; registered profl. engr., Colo. Field engr. Western Mining Corp., Western Australia, Australia, 1933-34; supt., mine mgr. Ctrl. Norseman Gold Corp., Western Australia, 1934-37; asst. underground mgr. Gt. Boulder Mine, Western Australia, 1937; gen. supt. mines New Guinea Goldfields, 1938-40; gen. mgr. Adelaide Chem. & Fertilizer Co., 1947-50; sr. lectr., assoc. prof. U. Queensland, 1957-67; prof. Colo. Sch. Mines, Golden, 1968; sr. rsch. prof. U. Idaho, 1968-74; vis. prof. Va. Poly. Inst. and State U., Blacksburg, 1974-77, King Abdulaziz U., Jeddah, Saudi Arabia, 1977-83; ret., 1983. Author: Explosives for North American Engrs., 1973 3d edit. 1984, Explosives for Engineers, 1960 4th edit., 1993, Rudiments of Mining Practice: A Concise Hist ory of Mining, 1982, All Around the World in Eighty Years, 1995. Capt. Royal Australian Engrs., Australian Imperial Forces, 1942-46, PTO. Mem. Inst. Engrs. (Australia), Soc. Mining Engrs., Playboy Club, Sigma Xi. Avocations: writing, traveling, student wellbeing. Home: 17 Meridian Gardens Mill Rd, Buderim Qld 4556, Australia

GREGORY, COLEMAN GEORGE, lawyer; b. Toronto, Ont., Can., Jan. 16, 1960; came to U.S., 1965; s. Thomas and Joan Gregory; m. Esther Louise-Toby Brodsky, June 19, 1983; 1 child, Joseph. BA, U. Calif., Berkeley, 1982; JD, Harvard U., 1986. Bar: N.Y. 1987, Paris 1992. Assoc. Sherman & Sterling, N.Y.C and Paris, 1986-92; v.p., legal counsel BHF Bank AG, N.Y.C., 1992-99; sr. v.p., gen. counsel BHF (U.S.) Capital Corp., N.Y.C., 1999—. Mem. ABA, Bar of N.Y.C., Harvard Law Sch. Alumni Assn. Office: BHF Capital Corp 590 Madison Ave New York NY 10022-2524

GREGORY, JAMES ALEXANDER, editor, writer, retired; b. Marshall, Mich., Apr. 11, 1930; s. Alexander and Chrissoula (Shoupilla) G. B of English with honors, U. Mich., 1951, MA in English, 1952. Publicist Columbia Pictures, N.Y.C., 1956; press book editor-in-chief RKO Radio Pictures, N.Y.C., 1956-57; editor-in-chief Movieland and TV Time, N.Y.C., 1958-61; West Coast editor, writer Silver Screen, Screenland, Movieland, TV Time, L.A., 1960s; staff reporter Nat. Enquirer, 1974-76, freelance writer, 1976-80; editor Landscape and Irrigation, Van Nuys, Calif.; sr. editor Arbor Age, 1984-91, ret., 1992. Author: The Lucille Ball Story; co-author The Wallaces of Alabama with George Wallace, Jr.; editor: The Elvis Presley Story. Lt. (j.g.) USN, 1953-55. Democrat. Avocations: art and autograph collector.

GREGORY, JOHN MICHAEL, urologist; b. Jax, Fla., Feb. 21, 1939; s. John Wellington and Anna Louise (Mahoney) G.; m. Helen Louise Theus, Aug. 12, 1961; children: Louise, Katherine, Michael Jr. BS, U. Ala., 1961; MD, Tulane U., 1964. Intern McCleod Infirmary, Florence, S.C., 1964-65; surg. asst. Byrne Inst., Columbia, S.C., 1965-66; fellow in urology Mayo Clinic, Rochester, Minn., 1968-72; pvt. practice Memphis Urology Group, 1972-78, Urology of Athens, Ga., 1978—. Capt. U.S. Army, 1966-68. Mem. Am. Assn. Clin. Urologists, Am. Urologic Assn. (house of dels. 1997—), Ga. Urologic Assn. (pres. 1997), Athens County Club (pres. 1995-96), Athens City Club (pres. 1988-89), Cornerstone Soc. (co-chmn. membership com. 1992—). Republican. Episcopalian. Avocation: golf. Home: 634 Milledge Cir Athens GA 30606-4366 Office: Urology of Athens 195 King Ave Ste 2 Athens GA 30606-2991

GREGORY, MARIAN FRANCES, educator, counselor, principal; b. Gary, Ind., Apr. 24, 1919; d. August Robert and Agnes Mae (Sturgess) Kuhn; m. Robert Wayne Gregory. BS in Edn., Ind. U., 1941; MA in Counseling, Columbia U., 1960. Elem. tchr. Bremen (Ind.) Schs., 1941-46; elem. tchr. Gary Pub. Schs., 1947-56, tchr. remedial reading, 1956-68; elem. prin. Spaulding and Lincoln schs., Gary, 1968-74; student tchr. cons. Ind. U., Bloomington, 1974-91; sec. Heritage Motors, Hammond, Ind., 1974. Author articles on DAR genealogy. Mem., poll watcher LWV, Hammond, 1980-95, 98; mem. Master Gardners Purdue U., Crown Point, Ind., 1977—; elder Presbyn. Ch. Mem. AAUW (pres. 1956-57), DAR, Bus. and Profl. Women's Club (pres. 1957-58), N.W. Ind. Women's Club (1st v.p. 1994-96), Delta Kappa Gamma, Kappa Kappa Kappa. Avocations: genealogy, gardening, stock market, history, swimming. Home: 2238 Ridge Rd Highland IN 46322-1562

GREGORY, MYRA MAY, religious organization administrator, educator; b. N.Y.C., Sept. 21, 1912; d. Thomas and Anna (Collins) G. Diploma, Maxwell Tchrs. Tng. Sch., Bklyn., 1933; BS in Edn., Bklyn. Coll., 1940, MA in History, 1952. Cert. music tchr. Tchr. N.Y.C. Bd. Edn., Bklyn., 1943-75; social worker Berean Bapt. Ch., Bklyn., 1932-48, supr., 1932-94, fin. sec. Sunday sch., 1935-94; bd. dirs. Berean-Vacation Bible Sch., Bklyn., 1935-86; tchr. Protestant Coun., N.Y.C., 1940-81; bd. dirs. Recreation Bedford-Stuyvesant Area Project, Bklyn.; dir. seminar Christian Teaching, Bklyn., 1974-86, 1990—. Bd. mgrs. Bklyn. Sun. Sch. Union, 1974—; bd. dirs. Bklyn. Divsn. Coun. of Chs. 1974—, pres., 1984-86, bd. dirs. Sunday Sch. Union, 1974—. Named Tchr. of Yr. Cmty. Sch. Bd. Dist. 14 N.Y.C. Bd. Edn., Bklyn., 1973, Outstanding Tchr., Stuyvesand divsn., Bklyn. Sunday Sch. Union, 1977, Educator/Leader Berean Bapt. Ch., 1977; recipient Ecumenism citation Borough Pres.'s Office, Bklyn., 1985, Religious Educator citation Bklyn. Ch. Women United, Inc., 1993, Cmty. Svc. awrd Mayors Office, N.Y.C., 1993, Ecumenical Svc./Educator Honors Office the Coun. City of N.Y., 1994, Lifetime Achievement award Bklyn. Coll., 1995, Outstanding Svc. award Coun. Chs. the City of N.Y., 1995, Leadership/Educator Citation Borough Pres. Office, Bklyn., 1999, Educator/Svc. Citation Berean Baptist Ch., 2000. Mem. ASCD, Am. String Tchrs. Assn., Am. Viola Soc., Assn. Childhood Edn. Internat., Orgn. Am. Historians, Ctr. Study of Presidency, Assn. Bible Tchrs., Music Tchrs. Nat. Assn., Nat. Orch. Assn., Schomburg Ctr. Rsch. Black Culture. Democrat. Avocations: string ensemble, drama, writing.

GREGORY, PETER JOHN, soil scientist, educator; b. Ramsgate, Eng., July 19, 1951; s. Joseph Henry and June Rosamund (Unsted) G.; m. Jane Sandra Crump, July 21, 1973; children: Thomas Joseph, George Edward. BSc, U. Reading, Eng., 1972; PhD, U. Nottingham, Eng., 1977. Fellow Inst. Biology. Lectr. U. Reading, 1980-89; prin. rsch. scientist Commonwealth Scientific and Indsl. Rsch. Orgn. (CSIRO), Perth, Australia, 1990-93; prof. soil science U. Reading, 1994—, dean faculty agr. and food, 1996-98; pro-vice-chancelor rsch., 1998—; leader GCTE Focus 3, Agr., Forestry and Soils, Eng., 1995—. Editor: Root Development and Function, 1987, Soils in the Urban Environment, 1991, Crop Production on Duplex Soils, 1992. Sci. Rsch. fellow Nuffield Found., U.K., 1988. Mem. Inst. Profl. Soil Scientists. Avocations: gardening, folk dancing.

GREGORY, ROBERT JOHN, public policy educator; b. Wellington, New Zealand, Jan. 27, 1944. BA with honors, Victoria U., Wellington, 1974, PhD, 1980; MPA, Harvard U., 1978. Assoc. prof. pub. policy and adminstrn. Victoria U. Recipient Sam Richardson award Inst. Pub. Adminstrn. Australia, 1996. Office: Victoria U, PO Box 600, Wellington New Zealand

GREGORY, ROBERT JOHN, psychologist, educator; b. Elmira, N.Y., Aug. 28, 1938; arrived in New Zealand, 1983; s. John R. Gregory and Mary Ann Gursky; m. Rosalee S. Smith, 1962 (div. 1970); children: Judi, Wendy; m. Janet E. Nicholson, July 4, 1975; 1 child, Mary Ann. BA, Cornell U., 1960; MA, Syracuse U., 1964, PhD, 1968. Registered psychologist, New Zealand. Dir. Drug Action Wake County, Raleigh, N.C., 1971-73; postdoctoral fellow dept. psychiatry Med. Ctr. Duke U., Durham, N.C., 1973-75, rsch. assoc. dept. anthropology, 1975-78; sr. rsch. assoc. Cornell U., Ithaca, N.Y., 1978-80; asst. prof. Marshall U., Huntington, W.Va., 1980-83; sr. lectr. Massey U., Palmerston North, New Zealand, 1983—; mem. bicultural com., equal employment opportunity dept. psychology Massey U., 1994-98, info. tech. com., 1998—; mem. adv. bd. DIS/Info. Newspaper, Palmerston North, 1994-96; bd. dirs. Audrey Green Info. Ctr., Environ. Growth & Goodwill Trust. Contbr. numerous articles to profl. jours. Bd. mgmt. Workbridge Inc., New Zealand, 1989-92; nat. exec. com. Disabled Persons Assembly, New Zealand. With U.S. Army, 1961, USNG, 1961-67. USPHS postdoctoral rsch. fellow, 1973-75. Mem. APA (internat. com. rehab. psychology 1992-94), Guillain Barre Found Internat. (liaison 1992—). Avocations: tree farming, stamp collecting, writing, Trout fishing. E-mail: R.J.Gregory@massey.ac.nz. Office: Sch Psychology, Massey U, Palmerston North New Zealand

GREGORY, THOMAS BRADFORD, mathematics educator; b. Traverse City, Mich., Dec. 13, 1944; s. Philip Henry and Rhoda Winslow (Hathaway) G.; m. Deirdre Dianne Mason, July 15, 1995. BA, Oberlin (Ohio) Coll., 1967; MA, Yale U., 1969, M of Philosophy, 1975, PhD, 1977. Lectr. Ohio State U., Mansfield, 1977-78, asst. prof. math., 1978-84, assoc. prof. math., 1984—. Reviewer: Math. Revs., 1984—; contbr. articles to profl. jours. Active Mansfield (Ohio) Symphony Chorus, 1977—, Presbytery Youth Ministries Com., New Philadelphia, Ohio, 1980-87, Ohio State U. Community Singers, Mansfield, 1985—; mem. Presbytery Biblical Authority task force, 1994-95; bd. dirs. Lay Acad. Religion, Wooster (Ohio) Coll., 1997—; commd. lay min. Presbytery of Muskingum Valley, New Philadelphia, Ohio, 1998—. Comdr. USNR, 1969-96. Fellow NSF, Washington, 1967; hon. fellow U. Wis., Madison, 1987-88, 92. Fellow Phi Beta Kappa; mem. Am. Math. Soc. (translator 1974-82), Ohio Coun. Tchrs. Math., Am. Soc. Naval Engrs., Res. Officers Assn., Naval Res. Assn., Navy League, Sigma Xi. Avocations: classical piano, singing. Home: 411 Overlook Rd Mansfield OH 44907-1533 Office: Ohio State U 1680 University Dr # O-15 Mansfield OH 44906-1547

GREGORY, WILTON D., bishop; b. Chgo., Dec. 7, 1947; s. Wilton and Ethel Duncan G. Student, Niles Coll., Loyola U., Chgo., St. Mary of Lake Sem., Mundelein, Ill., Pontifical Liturgical Inst., Sant'Anselmo, Rome; D in Sacred Liturgy, Pontifical Liturgical Inst., Sant'Anselmo, Rome, 1980. Ordained priest Roman Cath. Ch., 1973, ordained bishop, 1983. Aux. bishop, Chgo., 1983-93; Bishop of Belleville, 1994—; spkr. in field. Author in field. Avocations: travel, music, racquetball, golf. Address: Chancery Office 222 S 3rd St Belleville IL 62220-1916

GREGORY-ROBERTS, JOHN CHARLES, ophthalmologist; b. Sydney, N.S.W., Australia, June 19, 1942; s. Frederick and Corona (Booth) G.-R.; m. Cynthia Anne Arnold, Mar. 16, 1974; children: Simon, Emily, Nicholas, Lucy. BSc, U. Sydney, 1965, MB, BChir, 1970. Resident med. officer Sydney Hosp., 1970-72; sr. ho. officer Kings Coll. Hosp., London, 1973; vis. fellow U. Calif., San Francisco, 1977; registrar Sydney Eye Hosp., 1974-76, hon. ophthalmologist, 1978-86, cons. ophthalmologist, 1986—; hon. ophthalmologist Royal Inst. for Deaf and Blind Children, Sydney, 1978—, dir., 1990—. Contbr. articles to sci. publs. Gov. med. found. U. Sydney, 1990—; mem. bd. mgmt. Sydney Eye Hosp. Found., 1985-97; trustee Centennial Pk. Trust, Sydney, 1985-89, chmn. bicentennial com., 1987-88. Fellow Royal Coll. Ophthalmologists, Royal Australian Coll. Ophthalmologist, Royal Australasian Coll. Surgeons. Avocations: classical music, opera, antiques, skiing, tennis. Home: 23 Jersey Rd, Woollahra, NSW Sydney 2025, Australia Office: Harley Pl Level 5, 251 Oxford St, NSW Bondi Junction 2022, Australia

GREGOW, TORKEL, federal judge. Justice, pres. Supreme Ct. Sweden. Office: Högsta domstolen, Box 2066, SE-103 12 Stockholm Sweden

GREGSON, ANTHONY KNIGHT, farmer; b. Melbourne, Victoria, Australia, Mar. 31, 1945; m. Jane Enid Mary Cannon (dec. Oct. 1992); children: Thomas Knight, James Knight. BSc with 1st class honors in Chemistry, U. Melbourne, 1968, PhD in Inorganic Chemistry, 1972, DSc, 1985. ICI postdoctoral fellow U. Oxford, U.K., 1971-74; lectr./sr. lectr./assoc. prof. U. New Eng., Armidale, N.S.W., 1974-81; vis. prof. chemistry U. N.C., Chapel Hill, 1979; farmer Warracknabeal, Australia, 1981—; bd. dirs. Rural Fin. Corp. of Victoria, Melbourne, Plant Health Australia; mem., bd. trustees CIMMYT, Mex., 1996—; chmn. Coop. Rsch. Ctr. Molecular Plant Breeding, Adelaide, Australia, 1998—. Contbr. articles to profl. jours. Pres. Wimmera Cmty. Coll. Tech. and Further Edn., Horsham, 1994-96. Fellow Australian Inst. Mgmt., Royal Australian Chem. Inst.; mem. Royal Inst. Chemistry, Am. Chem. Soc., Rotary (pres. and chmn. 1988-89, dist. rep.). Avocations: skiing, travel, wine. Home and Office: Box 197, Warracknabeal VIC 3393, Australia

GREGSON, ROBERT ANTHONY MILLS, mathematical psychologist; b. Bury, Lancashire, Eng., Apr. 12, 1928; s. Robert Gregson and Emmy Mills; m. Elsie Diana Millican, July 23, 1955; children: Katharine, Jeremy. BSc in Engring., U. Nottingham, Eng., 1951; BSc with honors, U. London, 1956, PhD, 1961; DSc, Australian Nat. U., Canberra, 1998. Chartered psychologist. Rschr. aircraft industry, Coventry, Eng., 1951-54; comptr. Ops. Rsch., London, 1957-63; assoc. prof. U. Canterbury, New Zealand, 1963-67, prof., 1967-80; prof. U. New Eng., Australia, 1980-91; vis. fellow Australian Nat. U., 1991-97, math. psychologist, 1997—; vis. prof. Stockholm U., 1966-75, Tech. U. Braunschweig, Germany, 1984, various other univs. in Europe. Author: Psychometrics of Similarity, 1975, Time Series in Psychology, 1983, Nonlinear Psychophysical Dynamics, 1988, N-Dimensional Nonlinear Psychophysics, 1992, Cascades and Fields in Perceptual Psychophysics, 1995. Fellow Acad. Social Scis. Australia, Australian Psychol. Soc., Brit. Psychol. Soc., New Zealand Psychol. Soc., Royal Statis. Soc. Avocations: philately, model railroads. Office: Australian Nat U, Divsn Psychology, Canberra ACT 0200, Australia

GREIFELD, KATHRIN, anthropologist, consultant; b. Stuttgart, Germany, Apr. 5, 1956. BS, U. Karlsruhe, 1975; MA in Anthropology, U. Frankfurt, 1980, PhD, 1984. Scientist Mus. Anthropologie, Frankfurt, Germany, 1985-87; mng. dir. Volksmund, Frankfurt, 1988-90; prof. U. Salamanca, Spain, 1991-92; asst. prof. U. Heidelberg, Germany, 1993—; programme advisor Evaluation, Planning, Orgn., Svc., Health Consultancy, Bad Holmburg, Germany, 1995-97; ind. internat. health cons., 1998—; prof. U. Heidelberg, 1990—.

GREIFFENHAGEN, MARTIN O.W., retired political science educator; b. Bremervörde, Germany, Sept. 30, 1928; s. Gustav and Elisabeth (Friese) G.; m. Karin Hillmann, 1960 (div. 1970); m. Sylvia Buck, July 12, 1971; children: Kathrin, Hans. PhD, Heidelberg (Germany) U., 1956. Exec. dir. profl. assn., Essen, 1956-58; asst. lectr. polit. sci. U. Wilhelmshaven, Germany, 1958-62; prof. polit. sci. Lüneburg (Germany) U., 1962-65; dir. Inst. Polit. Sci. Stuttgart (Germany) U., 1965-90; ret., 1990. Author: The Dilemma of Conservatism in Germany, 1971, Freedom Against Equality?, 1975, The Actuality of Prussia, 1981; co-author (with Sylvia Greiffenhagen): A Difficult Country, 1993 (Polit. Book of Yr. prize 1994), Politische Legitimität in Deutschland, 1997. Home: Im Heppacher 13, D-73728 Esslingen Germany Office: Polit Sci Inst U Stuttgart, Kepler Str 17, D-70174 Stuttgart Germany

GREINER, JAMES RALPH, lawyer; b. Sacramento, Calif., May 10, 1955; s. Ralph James and Lucille Shirley (Miracle) G. BA, U. Calif., Davis, 1977; JD, McGeorge U., 1983. Extern Calif. Supreme Ct., San Francisco; with Bolling, Walter & Gawthrop, Sacramento, Rodney A. Klein, Sacramento; assoc. Shea & Smith, Sacramento, Montague & Cochrane, Sacramento; pvt. practice law Sacramento, 1990—; mock trial coach Rio Americano H.S., speaker The Amer. Assoc. of Law Libraries 1996 natl. conference, The Amer. Inns of Court 1996 natl. conference; dist. 2 repbd. govs. Calif. State Bar, co-chair com. on comms. and mem. rels. bd. govs., mem. legal and fin. com. bd. govs.; CJA panel rep. Fed. Ct. (ea. dist.), Calif. Recipient Edn.-Bus. Partnership award Calif. State U., Sacramento, 1998. Mem. ABA, Assn. Trial Lawyers Am., Assn. Fed. Def. Attys., Sacramento County Bar Assn. (pres. 1998, 1st v.p., 2d v.p., sec./treas., pres.'s award 1994, chair law day com. 1990-97, chair membership com. 1994-97, chair Mardi Gras com. 1994 , chair lawyer referral and info. svc. 1992-93, conf. dels. 1991-97, Sacramento lawyer policy com. 1991-98, cmty. edn. com. 1992-97, membership directory com. 1992-97, judiciary com. 1993 , bench bar media com. 1993-98, chair events com. 1995-97, indigent def. panel 1991 , pictorial dir. 1993-98, mem. bar found. 1994 , Sacramento county bd. of law libr. 1995), State Bar Calif. (criminal justice sect.), Calif. Pub. Defenders Assn., Consumer Attys. Calif., Capitol City Consumer Attys., Anthony M. Kennedy Am. Inn of Ct., Milton L. Schwartz Inn of Ct. Office: 555 University Ave Ste 290 Sacramento CA 95825-6511

GREINER, WALTER ALBIN ERHARD, physicist; b. Neuenbau, Germany, Oct. 29, 1935; s. Albin and Elsa (Fischer) G.; m. Barbara Chun; children: Martin, Carsten. MS, U. Darmstadt, Fed. Republic Germany, 1959; PhD, U. Freiburg, Fed. Republic Germany, 1961; DSci (hon.), U. Witwatersrand, South Africa, 1982, U. Beijing, 1990, U. Tel Aviv, 1991, U. Louis Pasteur, Strasbourg, France, 1991, U. Bucharest, 1992, Kossuth Lajos U., Debrecen, 1997. Rsch. asst. U. Freiburg, 1961-62; asst. prof. U. Md., 1962-64; prof. theoretical physics U. Frankfurt, Fed. Republic Germany, 1965—; dir. Inst. Theoretical Physics, 1965—; guest prof. at numerous univs.; adj. prof. Vanderbilt U.-Oak Ridge Nat. Lab., 1975—; hon. prof. U. Beijing, 1990; permanent sci. cons. Gesellschaft fur Schwerionenforschung, Darmstadt. Author: (with others) Nuclear Theory, Nuclear Models Vol. 1, 1970, Excitation Mechanism of Nuclei Vol. 2, 1970, Theory of the Nucleus Vol. 3, 1972, 3d edition, 1987-89, Theoretische Physik Vols. 1-10, 1974-89; editor: Jour. of Physics, 1975-89. Recipient Max Born prize Inst. Physics, 1974, Otto Hahn prize, 1982, Alexander von Humboldt medal, 1998; named officier dans l'ordre palmes academique, 1999. Mem. European Physics Soc., Am. Physics Soc., Sci. Soc. Johann Wolfgang Goethe U., Eötvös Lorand Soc. Hungary (hon.), Acad. Sci. Romania (hon.), Lions. Office: 8-10 Robert Mayer Strasse, D-60054 Frankfurt Germany

GREIS, ORTWIN, scientist; b. Magdeburg, Germany, May 7, 1941; s. Johann and Ida (Dengler) G.; m. Karin Lücker, Jan. 23, 1943. Dr.rer.nat. in chemistry, U. Freiburg, 1976; Dr.rer.nat.habil.(crystallography), U. Heidelberg, 1980. Sci. asst. U. Freiburg, Germany, 1972-76; postdoctoral Flinders U., Adelaide, Australia, 1977-78; sr. rsch. assoc. Tex. A&M U., 1978-79; sr. scientist U. Heidelberg, Germany, 1979-80; prof. chemistry U. Petroleum and Minerals, Dhahran, Saudi Arabia, 1981-86; head of ctrl. divsn. electron microscopy Tech. U. of Hamburg-Harburg, Germany, 1987—. Editor: Jour. of Classical Russian Philately; contbr. numerous articles to profl. publs. Mem. German Soc. Chemists, German Soc. Crystallographers, German Soc. Electron Microscopy, Soc. for Classical Russian Philately (pres.), Internat. Assn. Philatelic Experts (expert for Zemstvo philately). Avocations: bridge, philately, literature. E-mail: greis@tu-harburg.de. Home: Brandheide 16, 21224 Rosengarten Germany Office: Tech U Hamburg-Harburg, Eissendorfer Str 42, 21071 Hamburg Germany

GREISENEGGER, WOLFGANG, university official. Rector Vienna U. Office: Vienna Univ, Dr Karl Luegar Ring 1, A-1010 Vienna Austria*

GREISIGER, ARTHUR EUGENE, JR., writer, designer, producer, director, performer; b. Germantown, Pa., June 9, 1954; s. Arthur Eugene and Ruth (Kletzing) G.; m. Sandra Ruth Snitz, 1985. AA in Mass Media/Cinema, Bucks County Community Coll., 1980. Owner, operator Just Vairs, 1972—; owner, operator Image of the Mind, Doylestown, Pa., 1977-80, Boston, 1980-81, Dublin, 1981-85, Hollywood, 1985-88; owner, operator Image of the Mind Studios, New Hope, Pa., 1988—; theatrical, cinematic and photographic design; mech., archtl., spacial design, operational systems analysis; budgeting prodn. svcs., cons. gen. print advt., project devel. packaging. Author, designer: (multi-media prodns.) I Am Alpha and Omega, Journey to the Alpha and the Omega, 1985, Visions of Creation, 1987; writer, producer, dir. (stage and film work) Nunc Licet, 1987; filmmaker (short films) The World May Never Understand, DelAware Unlimited, New Hope, 1983-85, The case of the Question...Who?, It's justlike Jumping, Under My Feet, Kundalini, Born of Divine Love, Untitled, (documentary) You're Not Getting the Point!; Divergence; prodr. various short films, promotional videos; screenwriter (feature films) Celestial Manifesto, 1975, Milady Grael, 1982, others; photographer, writer (portfolio book) Spiritual Perceptions of Photography; numerous gallery exhbns.; numerous outdoor community festival designs, 1st Ann. Christian Summer Festival, John Ford Theatre, Hollywood; pub. photographic posters, post cards and various products. Mem. Dramatists Guild, Film Five Co-op, Am. Theatre Assn. Mem. Ch. of the New Jerusalem. Club: Corvair Soc. Avocations: flute, hiking, bicycling, kyacking, hot rodding. Office: Image of the Mind Studios PO Box 655 New Hope PA 18938-0655

GREITZER, EDWARD MARC, aeronautical engineering educator, consultant; b. N.Y.C., May 8, 1941; s. Arthur O. and Harriet G.; m. Helen Moulton, Nov. 24, 1966; children: Mary Lee, Jennifer Elizabeth. BA, Harvard U., 1962, MS, 1964, PhD, 1970. Asst. project engr. Pratt & Whitney divsn. United Techs., East Hartford, Conn., 1969-76; indsl. fellow commoner Churchill Coll., Cambridge U., Eng., 1975-76; asst. prof. MIT, Cambridge, 1977-79, assoc. prof., 1979-84, prof., dir. Gas Turbine Lab., 1984-96, H.N. Slater prof. aero. and astronautics, 1988—, assoc. head dept., 1996—; sr. rsch. engr. United Techs. Rsch. Ctr., East Hartford, 1976-77, dir. aeromech., chem. & fluid sys., 1996-98; Royal Soc. guest fellow, SERC vis. fellow, overseas fellow Churchill Coll., Cambridge U., 1983-84; vis. fellow Japan Soc. for Promotion of Sci., 1987, Peterhouse, Cambridge U., 1990-91; mem. aeronautics adv. com. NASA, 1990-94; mem. sci. adv. bd. USAF, 1992-96. Contbr. articles to profl. jours., handbooks. Recipient T. Bernard Hall prize Instn. Mech. Engrs., London, 1978, Exceptional Civilian Svc. award USAF, 1996. Fellow AIAA (Air Breathing Propulsion Best Paper award 1987), Nat. Acad. Engring., ASME (gas turbine award 1977, 79, 96, Freeman scholar in fluids engring. 1980, bd. dirs. Internat. Gas Turbine Inst. 1993-98, chmn. 1996-97, chmn. turbomachinery com. 1989-91, chmn. gas turbine scholar selection com. 1989-93, turbomachinery com., Best Paper award 1991, 92, 95, Aircraft Engine Tech. award 1995, Controls and Diagnostics com. Best Paper award 1998). Avocations: jogging, photography, rock climbing. Home: 77 Woodridge Rd Wayland MA 01778-3611 Office: MIT Dept Aeronautics & Astronautics Bldg 31-264 Cambridge MA 02139

GREKOVA, MAYA DIMITROVA, sociology educator; b. Sofia, Bulgaria, Sept. 4, 1954; d. Dimitar Konstantinov and Katina Rangelova (Bratoeva) G.; m. Valentin Rangelov Stanoev, Aug. 17, 1975 (div. May 1984); 1 child, Elitza Valentinova Stanoeva. Grad. in philosophy, Sofia U., 1976, PhD, 1986. Sociologist dept. sociology Sofia U., 1978-85, asst. prof. dept. sociology, 1985-94, dozent dept. sociology, 1995—, head dept. sociology, 1999—; expert Open Soc. Fund, Sofia, 1994-98, Ptnrs. Fund, Sofia, 1993—. Author: From Custom to Law, 1991, I and the Other, 1996; contbr. articles to profl. jours. Office: Sofia U Dept Sociology, Tzar Osvoboditel str 15, 1504 Sofia Bulgaria

GRELL, LEWIS ADAM, association executive; b. New Castle, Pa., June 15, 1932; s. Adam Lewis and Mildred Mae (Barris) G.; m. Pamela L., June 9, 1961; children: Lewis Jr., Holly, Lynn, Jon. BS in Elem. Edn., Slippery Rock Coll., 1953; MEd, U. Pitts., 1957, EdD, 1963. Tchr. New Castle (Pa.) Sch. Dist., 1953, 55-59, prin., 1959-63; prin., dir. summer sch. Oak Park (Ill.) Elem. Sch. Dist., 1963-66; asst. supt. Am. Sch. Internat. Sch. of Hague, The Netherlands, 1966-68; supt. Eden (N.Y.) Cen. Schs., 1968-72, Am. Sch. of Hague, 1972-81, Hamburg (N.Y.) Cen. Sch. Dist., 1981-89; exec. dir. Assn. Advancement Internat. Edn., New Wilmington, Pa., 1989—; chmn. Mid. States Accrediting Com., Frankfurt, Germany, 1987, European Coun. Internat. Schs., London, 1978-80; cons. Am. Sch. Brasilia, Brazil, 1987, Internat. Sch., Helsinki, 1985-88, Caracas Internat. Sch., Venezuela, 1986-88. Contbr. articles to profl. jours. Chmn. Western N.Y. Fin. and Legis. Com., Lancaster, 1983-85. With USN, 1953-55. Avocations: showing American saddlebred horses, playing softball, refereeing basketball games. Office: Westminster Coll Assn. Advancement of Internat Edn Thompson House New Wilmington PA 16172-0001

GRELON, BERNARD, lawyer, educator; b. Mar. 13, 1945; s. Andre and Leone (Fouch) G.; m. Katherine Deligny, Oct. 21, 1967; children: Mathilde, Sarah. Dr. Law, U. Paris, 1976, Agrege des Facultes de Droit, 1980. Asst. Faculty of Law, Paris, 1973-80; prof. Faculty of Law, Amiens, 1981-90; ptnr. Berlioz & Co., Paris, 1978—; prof. law U. Paris-Dauphine, 1990—. Author: Les Entreprises de Service, 1978. Mem. Assn. Henri Capitant, Assn. Internat. de Droit Economique, Assn. des Cabinets D'Avocats Avocation Internat. Avocations: golf, yachting, tennis. Office: Berlioz & Co, 68 Boulevard de Courcelles, Paris France 75017

GRENELL, JAMES HENRY, retired manufacturing company executive; b. Mpls., Feb. 19, 1924; s. Harrison Morton and Harriet Elizabeth (Kuch) G.; m. Naomi Betty Callerstrom, Sept. 15, 1945; children—Bonita (Mrs. Michael Wolfe), Suzanne Naomi, Andrea Bergine. BBA, U. Minn., 1947; postgrad. Advanced Mgmt. Program, Harvard U., 1974. With Honeywell Inc., Mpls., 1951-86; accountant Honeywell Inc., 1951-56, div. controller, 1956-68, group controller, 1968-71, asst. corp. controller, 1971-74, v.p., controller, 1974-82, v.p., staff exec., 1982-86; Instr. Mgmt. Inst. U. Wis.-Madison, 1960-69, Inst. Tech. U. Minn., Mpls., 1963-65; asso. dir. Mgmt. Center U. St. Thomas, 1959-69. Contbr. articles to profl. jours. Bd. dirs. Mpls. Soc. for Blind, 1963-71, pres., 1970-71; bd. dirs. U. Minn. Coll. Bus. Alumni Bd., 1975-82; mem. Acctg. Adv. Coun. U. Minn., 1977-83. Served to 1st lt. 1943-46, ETO. Decorated 4 Battle Stars, U.S. Army. Mem. Fin. Execs. Inst., Alpha Kappa

Psi, Harvard Club of Ariz., Harvard Club of Minn., Ariz. Club. Republican. Home: 10056 E Calle De Cielo Scottsdale AZ 85258-5652 also: 1201 Skyview Flagstaff AZ 86004-8718

GRENESTEDT, JOACHIM LENNART, educator; b. Uppsala, Sweden, Apr. 23, 1964; s. Edvard Lemmard Matameal and Marie-Louise Signa Öjvindsdotter Grenestdt; m. Chiharu Tokura; children: Ken, Scott. MSc in Engring. Physics, Royal Inst. Tech., Stockholm, 1987, PhD, 1992, Docent, 1996. Rsch. fellow Brown Boveri & Cie Rsch. Ctr., Switzerland, 1987, Asea Brown Boveru Corp. Rsch., Baden, Switzerland, 1989-90; rsch. assoc. Kyoto (Japan) U., 1987-89; vis. rschr. Japan Nat. Aerospace Lab., Tokyo, 1990-91; rsch. assoc. dept lightweight structures Royal Inst. Tech., 1991-92, sr. rsch. engr. dept. aeronautics, 1992-98; CEO Ancos, 1991-2000; assoc. prof. Lehigh U., Bethlehem, Pa., 2000—; vis. scholar divsn. engring. and applied scis. Harvard U., 1996; part-time rschr. Mid Sweden U., Östersund, 1998—. Patentee stopper for composite ships; contbr. numerous articles to profl. jours. Cpl. Royal Swedish Army, 1985-86. Recipient award Royal Swedish Acad. Scis., Tech. Dr. Marcus Wallenberg award, Saab-Scania award. Mem. ASME, Internat. Soc. Structural and Multidisciplinary Optimization, Materials Rsch. Soc., N.Y. Acad. Scis., Soc. Naval Architects and Marine Engrs., Soc. for Sandwich Constrn., Sigma Xi. Avocations: flying, hang gliding, scuba diving, sailing. E-mail: jog5@lehigh.edu. Office: Lehigh U Mech Engring & Mechs 533 Packard Lab 19 Memorial Dr W Bethlehem PA 18015

GRENFELL, GLORIA ROSS, community volunteer; b. Redwood City, Calif., Nov. 14, 1926; d. Edward William and Blanch (Ross) G.; m. June 19, 1948 (div. Nov. 15, 1983); children: Jane, Barbara, Robert, Mary. BS, U. Oreg., 1948, postgrad., 1983-85. Coll. bd., retail sales Meier & Frank Co., Portland, Oreg., 1945; book sales retailer J.K. Gill & Co., Portland, Oreg., 1948-50; advisor Mt. Hood Meadows Women's Ski Program, Oreg., 1968-78; corp. v.p. OK Delivery System, Inc., Oreg., 1977-82; ski instr. Willamette Pass, Oreg., 1983-85, Mt. Shasta, 1986; Campfire girls leader Portland, 1958-72; freelance journalist Marina, Calif., 1988. Mem. Assn. Jr. League Internat., 1957-87; mem. Monterey County Mental Health Commn., 1994—, No. Mariposa County History Ctr., Calif. Recipient Golden Poles award Mt. Hood Meadows, 1975. Mem. Soc. Profl. Journalists, Profl. Ski Instrs. Am., U.S. Ski Assn., Calif. State Sheriffs' Assn. (assoc.), Monterey History and Art Assn., Monterey Sports Ctr., Carmel Women's Club, Mariposa County C. of C., Monterey Bay Area Nat. Alumnae Panhellenic (Woman of Yr. award 1999), Order Ea. Star, DAR (Commodore Sloat chpt.), Mortar Bd., Kappa Alpha Theta. Democrat. Episcopalian. Home: 3128 Crescent Ave Lot 9 Marina CA 93933-3131

GRENIER, BERNARD, pediatrician, infectious disease consultant; b. Onzain, France, Aug. 11, 1925; s. Marcel and Madeleine (Brechoire) G.; m. Nicole Farinaux, Sept. 14, 1955; children: Olivier, Vincent, Benedicte, Marie-Helene, Delphine. Intern Hopitaux Paris, 1952-56; agrege infectious disease U. Tours, France, 1961-68, prof., 1968—; chief pediatric service Hopital, U. Tours, 1972—; mem. Bur. Nat. Internat., Paris, 1980—, Commn. Sci. Univ., Paris, 1983—. Author: Evaluation de la decision medicale, 3d edit., 1999; editor: Pilly Maladies Infectieuses, 1971, Pediatrie en Poche, 1979, Pratique Med. Pediatrie, 1982; co-author: Pechere's: Les Infections, 1979, 83. Decorated Nat. Order of Merit, officer Order Acad. Palms (France). Mem. Soc. Path. Infectious League Francaise (treas.) 1975), Assn. Enseign Path. Infections. Home: 34 rue de Loches, 37000 Tours France Office: Centre de Pediatrie, 49 Bd Beranger, 37000 Tours France

GRÉNMAN, REIDAR AXEL, otorhinolaryngologist, head and neck surgeon; b. Helsinki, Dec. 10, 1951; s. Lars Werner and Elisabeth Hortensia (Hornborg) G.; m. Seija Elisa Eskelinen, Dec. 17, 1977; 3 children. MD, U. Turku, Finland, 1977, PhD, 1985. Diplomate in medicine, specialist in otorhinolaryngology. Gen. practitioner several mcpl. health svcs., Finland, 1977-78; asst. prof. Turku U., 1988-89; mem. staff Turku U. Ctrl. Hosp., 1989-96, sr. staff mem., 1996—; mem. med. faculty U. Turku, 1975-78; mem. adminstrv. coun. U. Turku, 1977-78. Mem. Finnish Med. Assn. (adminstrv. coun. 1980-85, regional chmn. 1989—), Finnish Soc. for Otorhinolaryngology (bd. dirs. 1993-98), Am. Acad. Otolaryngology, Am. Assn. for Cancer Rsch., Collegium Oto-Rhino-Laryngologium Amicitiae Sacrum. Fax: 358-2-2613550. Office: Turku U Ctrl Hosp, Dept Otorhinolaryngology, FIN20520 Turku Finland

GRENZEBACH, WILLIAM SOUTHWOOD, nuclear engineer, consultant, historian; b. Chgo., Sept. 5, 1945; s. William Southwood Sr. and Edla (Edin) G.; m. Judith Samuels, June 16, 1968 (div. Feb. 1978). BA, Grinnell Coll., 1967; MA, Brandeis U., 1970, PhD in Comparative History, 1978; MS in Engring., Boston U., 1988; MS in Indsl. Engring., Northeastern U., Boston, 1988. Cert offshore drilling rig supt., U.S. Geol. Survey; cert. in offshore rescue, Govt. of Newfoundland. Mgr. Greyhound Lines East, Boston, 1970-77; engring. technician Sylvester Assocs., Rockland, Mass., 1977-78; subsea engr. ODECO, Inc., New Orleans, 1978-81; project mgr. SEDCO, Inc., Dallas, 1981-85; rsch. assoc. dept. energy Northeastern U., 1987-89; with Applied Mgmt. Cons., Assonet, Mass., 1989-90; sr. nuclear engr. Yankee Atomic Electric Co., Bolton, Mass., 1990-92; applied mgmt. cons. Assonet, Mass., 1992-95, British Stds. Instn., Reston, Va., 1995—; cons. Palisades Nuclear Power Sta., Covert, Mich., 1989, Peach Bottom/Limerick (Pa.) Power Sta., Delta and Limerick, 1989-90, Fitzpatrick Station, Lycoming, N.Y., 1992, Indian Point III, Buchanan, N.Y., 1993, New Brunswick Power Commn., Fredricton, 1990, New Eng. Med. Ctr., 1994-95; mem. Conf. Group on Ctrl. European History. Author: Germany's Informal Empire in East-Central Europe, 1988; contbr. articles to profl. publs.; author: (computer software) Reactor Coolant Expert System, 1988 (Copywrite award 1990). Supporter Friends of Cohasset (Mass.) Libr., 1978-83; mem. Cohasset Hist. Soc., 1978-83. Fellow U. Calif., San Diego, 1967-68, Brandeis U., Waltham, Mass., 1968-71, German Acad. Exch. Svc., Bonn, West Germany, 1971-72, Inst. for European History, Mainz, West Germany, 1972-74, Brandeis U., 1974-75. Mem. AAAS, Am. Nuclear Soc., Am. Soc. Quality, Inst. Indsl. Engrs., Soc. for Risk Analysis, Marine Tech. Soc., Soc. for History of Tech., Statis. Process Control Soc. Avocations: historical writing, reading, SCUBA diving, horseback riding. Office: 325 Huntington Ave Boston MA 02115-4401

GRESS, ESTHER, editor; b. Copenhagen, Aug. 20; d. Gustav Ferdinand and Anna Maria (Ekberg) Hansson; 1 son, Claus Gress. LittD (hon.), 1984. Mentor Westermann's Forlag, Copenhagen, 1959-50, Dansk Rim-Ordbog, Politikens Forlag, Copenhagen, 1950, newspaper Berlingske Tidende, 1950-88; editor Vor Tids Konversations Leksikon Supplement Aschehoug Dansk Forlag, Copenhagen, 1943-48; editor other publs. of Berlingske OfficinA/S, including Radiolytteren, Landet and Berlingske Aftenavis; Danish Acad. consul of Accademia d'Europa, Naples, 1982. Author: Skal, 1974, Liv, 1977, Ville—Vejen i Vejen, 1979, Det sker-måske, 1982, 85, Det gik, 1983, Raise (with English poems), 1984, Grow (with English poems), 1989, 2d edit., 1991, Raise/Telegu (with English and Indian poems), 1989, En ny begyndelse, 1992, Hvad du gør mod andre, 1997, Konfetti, 2000, Håb og Mod i det 21.Århundrede (trans. of Daisaku Ikeda), 2000; contbr. poems in 27 langs. to various anthologies, papers, and lit. mags. in Denmark and art mags. in Eng., U.S., Italy, Switzerland, Austria, Korea, India, Portugal, Thailand, Japan, Egypt, Australia, Turkey, Greece, Taiwan, Brazil, Israel; poems set to music in Danish, English, Italian. Recipient awards U.A., Italy, India, Eng., Taiwan, Grand Prix Mediterranee Etoiles d'Europa Trofeo Italia, Naples, 1989; named guest of honor N.Y. Poetry Forum, 1983, Poet Laureate Journalist with Laurel Wreath, N.Y., 1987, A.B.I. Woman of Yr., 1990; decorated grand dame Knights of Malta, 1984; in Guinness Book of World Records, 1999, as Danish poet translated into most langs. Mem. World Poetry Soc. Intercontinental, United Poets Laureate Internat., Accademia Internazionale di Lettere, Scienze, Arti Virgiglio-Mantegna, Danish Authors Assn., Danish Press Hist. Assn., Danish Publicistklub, Danish Press Staff ASsn., Internat. Acad. Poets, N.Y. Poetry Forum, Inc., Nat. Fedn. State Poetry Socs., Inc. (N.Y.), Internat. Acad. Poets, Accademia Internazionale Leonardo da Vinci, Danish PEN, Tivoli-Clubben af 1868. Home: 27 Ny Strandvej, 3050 Humlebaek Denmark

GRETZ, KARL FREDERICK, training consultant, writer; b. Phila., June 27, 1947; s. William Edward and Janis Claire Gretz; m. Ingegärd Strömberg, Nov. 25, 1975; children: Michael, Anna, Maria, Sara. BA in History and Polit. Sci., Tufts U., 1973, MEd in Counseling and Guidance, 1974; PhD in Ednl. Psychology, Brigham Young U., 1978. Asst. adj. prof. CUNY, Staten Island, 1981-82; pvt. practice marriage and family therapist Staten Island, 1978-83; staff psychologist Staten Island Hosp., 1979-83; fin. cons. Merrill Lynch & Co., Manhattan, 1983-85; sr. tng. cons. Merrill Lynch & Co., Princeton, N.J., 1985-88; pres. Gretz Assocs. & Assocs., Bensalem, Pa., 1988—; mng. dir. Drozdeck & Gretz Assocs. (formerly Tng. Groups Internat.), Bensalem, 1990-2000. Co-author: (with Steven. R. Drozdeck) Consultative Selling Techniques for Financial Professionals, 1990, The Effective Manager: Being the Best in Financial Sales Management, 1991, Empowering Innovative People: How Managers Challenge, Channel and Control the Truly Creative and Talented, 1992, The Broker's Edge: How to Sell Securities in Any Market, 1995, Professional Selling: A Consultative Approach, 1996, Managing Your Business for Success: A Guide for the Financial Consultant, 1997; contbr. articles to profl. jours. Capt. Spl. Forces U.S. Army, 1966-69, Viet Nam. Mem. LDS Ch. Office: 4431 Remo Crescent Rd Bensalem PA 19020-2931

GRETZKY, WAYNE DOUGLAS, retired hockey team executive; b. Brantford, Ont., Can., Jan. 26, 1961; s. Walter and Phyllis G.; m. Janet Jones, July 16, 1988; 3 children: Paulina, Ty Robert, Trevor Douglas. Center Peterborough Petes, Jr. Ont. Hockey Assn., 1977-78, Sault Ste. Marie Greyhounds, 1977-78, Indpls. Racers, World Hockey Assn., 1978, Edmonton Oilers (Alta., Can.), NHL, 1988, Los Angeles Kings, NHL, 1988-96, Saint Louis Blues, NHL, 1996; center N.Y. Rangers, NHL, 1996-99, ret., 1999; investor Los Arcos Sports LLC/Phoenix Coyotes, 1999—; player NHL All-Star game, 1980-86, 1988-94; mem. Stanley Cup championship teams, 1984, 85, 87, 88. Player NHL All-Star first team, 1980-92, 1990-91; named Rookie of Yr. World Hockey Assn., 1978-79, Sportsman of Yr. Sports Illus., 1982, Sporting News NHL Player of the Year, 1980-81, 86-87, Sporting News All-Star team, 1980-81, 86-87, 90-91, Sporting News Man of the Year, 1981, All-Star game MVP, 1983, 89, Canadian Athlete of the Year, 1985, Dodge Performer of the Year, 1984-85, 1986-87; recipient Art Ross Meml. trophy NHL, 1981-87, 89-90, 90-91, 93-94, Conn Smythe trophy, 1985, 88, William Hanley trophy, 1977-78, Lemms Family award, 1977-78, Hart Meml. trophy, 1974-80, Lady Byng Meml. tropy, 1979-80, 90-91, 91-92, 93-94, Lester B. Pearson award, 1982-82, 84-85, 86-87, Emery Edge award, 1983-84, 84-85, 86-87, Lester Patrick trophy, 1993-94; holder NHL career scoring record. Achievements include being the record holder for points, goals, assists, overtime assists and others. Office: c/o Phoenix Coyotes Cellular One Ice Den 9375 E Bell Rd Scottsdale AZ 85260-0101

GREVE, HENRICH ROLLEF, management educator, researcher; b. Stavanger, Norway, Jan. 1, 1966; s. Arent H. and Solveig I. (Saboe) G.; m. Takako Fujiwara, Aug. 29, 1992; children: Jan Tomoya, Ryo Egil. Grad., Sch. Econ. & Bus. Adminstrn., Bergen, Norway, 1989; MA in Sociology, Stanford (Calif.) U., 1993, PhD in Bus., 1994. Rschr. Found. for Rsch. in Econ. and Bus. Adminstrn., Bergen, 1995; asst. prof. U. Tsukuba, Japan, 1995-98; assoc. prof. U. Tsukuba, 1998—. Contbr. articles to profl. jours. including Am. Jour. Sociology, Strategic Mgmt. Jour., others. Sailor 1st class Royal Norwegian Navy, 1989-90. Fulbright fellow Fulbright Commn., 1990; rsch. grantee Ministry of Edn., Japan, 1996—. Mem. Am. Sociological Assn., Acad. of Mgmt., Strategic Mgmt. Soc. Office: U Tsukuba, Inst Policy Planning Sci, Ibaraki Tsukuba-shi 305-8573, Japan

GREVEN, MICHAEL THOMAS, political science educator; b. Hamburg, Germany, Mar. 7, 1947. MA, U. Bonn, 1972, PhD, 1973; PD, U. Paderborn, 1975. Reader U. Jle-Jfe, Nigeria, 1977-78; prof. U. Marburg, Germany, 1978-91, U. Darmstadt, Germany, 1991-95, U. Hamburg, Germany, 1995—; vis. prof. CSIR, New Delhi, India, 1982-83, U. Leipzig, Germany, 1990-91, Inst. for Höhere Studien, Vienna, 1994, U. Toronto, Canada, 1997-98. Author: Systemtheorie und Gesellschaftsanalyse, 1974, Parteien und Politische Herrschaft, 1977, Parteimitglieder, 1987, Kritische Theorie und Historische Politik, 1994, Die Politische Gesellschaft, 1999, Kontingenz und Dezision, 2000. Bd. dirs. Com. for Grundrechte and Dem., 1979-89; chmn. German Polit. Sci. Assn., 1994-97; chair rsch. com. Polit. Philosophy, IPSA, 1991-97. Office: U Hamburg Inst Polit Sci, Allendeplatz 1, 20146 Hamburg Germany

GREVILLE, ANTHONY EDEN, mining executive; b. Pretoria, South Africa, Dec. 21, 1921; s. Stanley Eden and Doreen Ellen (Sands) G.; m. Patricia Mary Hamlyn, Mar. 28, 1947 (div. 1978); children: Roderick, Morley, Damon, Justin, Virginia; m. Hendrina Jacoba Kidson, Dec. 21, 1978; children: Derick, Christoff, Barend. BSc, U. South Africa, Pietermaritzburg, 1947; BSc with honors, Natal U., Durban, South Africa, 1952; MSc, Natal U., 1954. Chartered engr. Rsch. scientist South African Govt., Pretoria, 1948-49; lectr. Natal U., 1950-52; cons. Asbestos Mines, Pietersburg, South Africa, 1952-53; field mgr. Rio Tinto Corp., Namibia, South Africa, 1953-55; mgr. R & D & W Base Minerals/Zimco Group, Johannesburg, South Africa, 1956-76; chmn. Kimony (Pty) Ltd., Johannesburg, 1976—; vis. scientist Ill. U., Urbana, 1965; cons. Transvaal Graphite, Ltd., Germiston, South Africa, 1977, Cullinan Minerals, Ltd., Olifantsfontein, South Africa, 1981. Editor (sci. and tech. jour.) Gemini, 1972-75; patentee in field. Mem. com. Progressive Movement, Johannesburg, 1987; chmn. Prince Albert (South Africa) Ratepayers Assn., 1995. Served with South African mil., 1940-45. Fellow Geol. Soc. London; mem. Geol. Soc. South Africa, Insn. Mining and Metallurgy. Mem. Dem. Party. Episcopalian. Avocation: musicology.

GRÉVISSE, FERNAND, judge; b. Boulogne-Billancourt, France, July 28, 1924; m. Suzanne Seux, Dec. 1, 1958; children: Christine Grévisse Cazeneuve, Françoise Grévisse Vautrin. Student, École Nat. Adminstrn., 1948-50. Apptd. auditeur Conseil d'Etat, 1949, Maitre des Requêtes, 1956; dep. commr. govt. Plenary Assembly, 1954-57, commr. govt. Plenary Assembly, 1957-60; apptd. head Office of Min. Justice, 1959; dir. civil affairs and the seal Min. of Justice, 1960; dir.-gen. water resources and forests Ministry of Agriculture, 1964-65, dir.-gen. rural areas, 1965-66; dep.-chair Nat. Forestry Office; head Office of Min. State in charge of civil svc., 1967; dir.-gen. adminstrn. and civil svc. dept. Govt. Sec.-Gen., 1967-71; mem. Conseil d'Etat, 1973—, chair pub. works sect., 1984-88, hon. chair, 1988—; prof. Inst. études politiques, Paris, 1977-80; chair Centre études supérieures du mgmt. pub., 1977-79; judge European Communities Ct. Justice, 1981-82, 88-94. Decorated Médaille militaire, Croix de guerre; named Comdr. Légion d'honneur, Comdr. Ordre nat. du Mérite.

GREWAL, PARWINDER S., biologist, researcher; b. Dharour, Punjab, India, May 26, 1961; came to U.S., 1991; s. Joginder S. and Amarjit K. (Sekhon) G.; m. Sukhbir K. Battu, Feb. 22, 1987; children: Parbir, Sharanbir. BS with honors, Punjab Agrl. U., Ludhiana, India, 1981, MS in Nematology, 1983; PhD in Zoology, U. London, 1990; DIC Nematology, Imperial Coll., London, 1990. Scientist Indian Coun. Agrl. Rsch., Solan, 1984-87; higher sci. officer Horticulture Rsch. Internat., Littlehampton, Eng., 1987-91; postdoctoral rsch. assoc. Rutgers U., New Brunswick, N.J., 1991-93; mgr. nematode rsch. Biosys, Inc., Palo Alto, Calif., 1993-95; rsch. leader Biosys, Inc., Columbia, Md., 1995-97; asst. prof. Ohio State U., Wooster, 1997—; mem. Mich. State Legislature Task Force, 1995. Contbr. chpts. to books, numerous articles to profl. jours. Recipient Team award for Environ. Achievement, Her Majesty the Queen, 1993, Young Scientist of Yr. award U.K. Mushroom Growers Assn., 1991. Mem. Soc. Nematologists, European Soc. Nematologists, Entomol. Soc. Am., Assn. Applied Biologists, Afro-Asian Soc. Nematologists (exec. bd. 1990—, editorial bd. 1990—). Avocations: running, travel, gardening. Office: Dept Entomology Ohio State U 1680 Madison Ave Wooster OH 44691-4114

GREY, GEORGE CHRISTOPHER, technology company executive; b. London, Nov. 25, 1961; s. John Egerton and Patricia Grey (Hanna) G. BA, Cambridge (Eng.) U., 1982. Engring. mgr. Torch Computers, Cambridge, 1982; cons. Charterhouse Japhet Plc, London, 1983; dir. Tadpole Tech. Plc, Cambridge, 1984-92, CEO, 1992-96; CEO Geofox Ltd., Cambridge, 1996-99, Psion Inc., Boston, 2000—. Mem. IEEE. Avocations: golf, basketball, films. Office: Psion Inc 150 Baker Ave Concord MA 01742-2117

GREY, MARY CECILIA, theologian; b. Houghton-le-Spring, England, June 16, 1941; d. Frederick Hugh and Norah Agnes (McArdle) Hughes; m. Nicholas Richard Grey, July 25, 1964; children: Clare, Eleanor, Stephen, Benedict. MA, U. Oxford, England, 1963; BS in Theology, Cath. U. Louvain, Belgium, 1977, MA in Religious Studies, 1977, PhD in Theology, 1987. Tchr. classics St. Mary's Convent, Middlesbrough, England, 1963-65; tchr. religious edn. Comprehensive Sch., Stevenage, England, 1979-80; lectr. theology St. Mary's Coll., U. Surrey, London, 1980-89; prof. feminism & Christendom Cath. U., Nijmegen, The Netherlands, 1988-93; prof. contemporary theology U. Southampton, England, 1993-97; scholar-in-residence Sarum Theol. Coll., Salisbury, England, 1997—; hon. prof. U. Wales at St. David's, Lampeter, 1998, D.J. James chair in pastoral theology U. Wales, Lampeter. Author: Redeeming the Dream, 1989, The Wisdom of Fools, 1993, Beyond the Dark Night, 1997, Prophecy and Mysticism, 1997, The Outrageous Pursuit of Hope, 2000; contbr. articles to profl. jours. Co-dir. Wells for India, England, 1987—; founder, mem. Cath. Women's Network, London, 1984—. Mem. European Soc. Women in Theol. Rsch. (pres. 1989-91), Cath. Theol. Soc. Gt. Britain (com. mem. 1992-93). Roman Catholic. Avocations: hill walking, violin, writing poetry, local history. Office: Sarum Coll, 19 the Close, Salisbury England

GRGAS, STIPE, literature and sociology educator; b. Sibenik, Croatia, Mar. 30, 1951; s. Mladen and Ljubica Grgas; m. Jagoda Krnic, Sept. 10, 1980; children: Zoran, Kresimir. BA in Philosophy, U. Zagreb, Croatia, 1974, MA in Philosophy; PhD, U. Zagreb, 1984. H.S. tchr. Drnis, Croatia, 1979-80; asst. faculty of philosophy U. Zadar, Croatia, 1980-84, asst. prof., 1984-94, assoc. prof., 1994—. Author: Nietzsche and Yeats, 1987; author: Construction of Nature, 1993; editor jour. Glasje. Roman Catholic. Avocations: tennis, jogging. Home: Davorina Bazjanca 13, 23000 Zadar Croatia Office: Faculty of Philosophy, Obala P Kresimira IV 2, 23000 Zadar Croatia

GRIBBLE, CHARLES EDWARD, editor, Slavic language educator; b. Lansing, Mich., Nov. 10, 1936; s. Charles P. and Elizabeth K. G. B.A., U. Mich., 1957; A.M., Harvard U., 1958, Ph.D., 1967; postgrad. Moscow State U., 1960-61. Instr., asst. prof. Russian, Brandeis U., Waltham, Mass., 1961-68; asst. prof. Slavic langs. Ind. U., Bloomington, 1968-75; assoc. prof. Slavic langs. Ohio State U., Columbus, 1975-89, prof. Slavic lang., 1989—, chairperson of dept., 1990-96; pres., editor Slavica Pubs., Inc., Columbus, 1966-97; vis. assoc. prof. Slavic langs. U. Va., 1977. Woodrow Wilson fellow, 1957-58, Am. Council Learned Socs. fellow, 1972; Internat. Rsch. and Exchanges Bd. grantee, 1960-61, 72, 80, Fulbright grantee, 1987. Mem. Am. Assn. Advancement of Slavic Studies, Am. Assn. Tchr. of Slavic and E. European Langs. (Disting. Contribution to the Profession award 1992), Linguistic Soc. Am., MLA, Linguistic Soc. Europe, S.E. European Studies Assn., Phi Beta Kappa. Author: Russian Root List, 1973, A Short Dictionary of 18th-Century Russian, 1976; editor-in-chief Folia Slavica, 1977-88; editor: Studies Presented to Professor Roman Jakobson by His Students, 1968, Medieval Slavic Texts, vol. 1, 1973; contbr. articles to scholarly jours. Office: Ohio State U Slavic Lang 1841 Millikin Rd Rm 232 Columbus OH 43210-1229 also: PO Box 14388 Columbus OH 43214-0388

GRIBBS, ROMAN S., judge, former mayor of Detroit; b. Detroit, Dec. 29, 1925; s. Roman and Magdeline (Widziszewski) Grzyb; children: Paula, Carla, Christopher, Rebecca, Elizabeth. B.S. magna cum laude, U. Detroit, 1952, LL.D., 1954. Bar: Mich. 1954. Tchr. law and acctg. U. Detroit, 1953-56; asst. pros. atty. Wayne County, Mich., 1956-64; pvt. practice law Shaheen, Gribbs & Shaheen, 1964-66; presiding referee Traffic Ct., 1966-68; sheriff Wayne County, 1968-69; mayor of Detroit, 1970-73; partner firm Fenton, Nederlander, Dodge, Barris & Gribbs, 1974; adj. prof. U. Mich., 1974; dir. Bank of Commonwealth, 1974-75; judge Wayne County Circuit Ct., 1975-82, chief judge pro tem, 1980-82; judge Mich. Ct. Appeals, 1983—; lectr. Mich. Jud. Inst., 1980—; mem. Presdl. Commn. CD Adv. Commn., 1970-74. Trustee U. Detroit, 1974-80; commr. Mich. Commn. on Inter-govtl. Rels., 1989—; bd. dirs. Thomas M. Cooley Law Sch., 1991—. Served as sgt. AUS, World War II. Mem. Nat. League of Cities (pres. 1973), Mich. Judges Assn. (bd. dirs. 1978—, pres. 1992—), U.S. Conf. Mayors (trustee), Mich. Conf. Mayors (pres.), Delta Sigma Phi, Blue Key. Democrat. Roman Catholic.

GRIEBEL, GUY, psychopharmacologist, researcher; b. Haguenau, Alsace, France, Dec. 18, 1966; s. Rene and Jacqueline Griebel. BS, Louis Pasteur U., Strasbourg, France, 1988, MS, 1989, PhD, 1993. Rschr. U. Hawaii, 1993-94; team leader Sanofi-Synthelabo, Bagneux, France, 1995—; rschr. U. Canterbury, Christchurch, New Zealand, 1995. Contbr. articles to profl. jours. Grantee Human Frontier Sci. Program, 1994, Humboldt Found., 1995. Mem. Soc. for Neurosci. Avocations: computers, working out, reading, movies. Office: Sanofi-Synthelabo, 31 Ave P V-Couturier, 92220 Bagneux France

GRIEG, EDUARD EMILLIAN, physician; b. Bucharest, Romania, Sept. 20, 1966; arrived in Norway, 1997; s. Radu and Ortansa (Turlea) G.; m. Zanina Zilic, Sept. 20, 1997. BS in Engring., UCLA, 1987; MD, U. Gothenburg, Sweden, 1997. System analyst De La Rue Printrak, Anaheim, Calif., 1988-89; attending occupational medicine Norway, 1997—. Address: Welhavensgt 2, PO Box 1042, 1603 Fredrikstad Norway

GRIEGO, JUAN LAWRENCE, federal agency administrator; b. Española, N. Mex., Apr. 9, 1963; s. Juan Santiago Griego and Marcia Kay (Clapper) Richardson; m. Katherine Therese McReynolds, Sept. 15, 1981 (div. Oct. 15, 1986); 1 child, John; m. Philippa Marie Sanchez, Jan. 11, 1992; children: Marisa, Eliana. BS in Civil Engring., N. Mex. State U., 1986. Project mgr. U.S. Dept. Energy, Los Alamos, N. Mex., 1986-92; project mgmt. br. chief U.S. Dept. Energy, Los Alamos, 1992-94, profl. project mgr., team leader project mgmt. office, 1994—; sec.-treas. Fast Ditch, Inc., Vallecitos, N. Mex., 1997—. Lt. col. N.Mex. Nat. Guard. Mem. Nat. Guard Assn. U.S., Project Mgmt. Inst. (cert. profl. project mgr., v.p. programs Otowi chpt., 1996-97). Avocations: farming, ranching, auto sports, skiing. Home: 1151 Calle Verde Espanola NM 87532-3385 Office: US Dept Energy 528 35th St Los Alamos NM 87544-2201

GRIER, PHILLIP MICHAEL, lawyer, former association executive; b. Quitman, Ga., Aug. 31, 1941; s. Phillip Moore and Helen Dale Parrish (Cottingham) G. BA, Furman U., 1963; JD, U. S.C., 1969. Bar: S.C. 1969, U.S. Dist. Ct. S.C. 1969, U.S. Ct. Appeals (4th cir.) 1972, U.S. Supreme Ct. 1978, U.S. Ct. Appeals (fed. cir.) 1985. Assoc. Haynsworth, Perry, Bryant, Marion & Johnstone, Greenville, S.C., 1969-70; asst. to pres. U. S.C., Columbia, 1969, staff counsel, 1970-74, gen. counsel, 1974-79; exec. dir., CEO Nat. Assn. Coll. and Univ. Attys., Washington, 1979-96; cons. Fulbright & Jaworski, Washington, 1996—; bd. dirs. Am. Coun. Edn., 1992-94; mem. adv. bd. Ctr. for Constl. Studies, U. Notre Dame and Mercer U., 1981-92; mem. secretariat of nat. higher edn. orgns. Nat. Ctr. for Higher Edn., Washington, 1979-96. Author: (with Joseph P. O'Neill) Financing in a Period of Retrenchment: A Primer for Small Private Colleges, 1984. Editor: The Corporate Counsellors Deskbook (Non-Profit Organizations Supplement), 1983; editor, contbg. author: Legal Deskbook for Administrators of Independent Colleges and Universities, 1982, 83, 84; editor Coll. Law Digest, 1980-96; mem. editorial adv. com. West Pub. Co., St. Paul, 1980-96; editorial bd. Jour. Coll. and Univ. Law, U. Notre Dame, Ind., 1979-96. With U.S. Army, 1963-66, USAR, 1966-74. Mem. Order of St. John, Soc. Colonial Wars, St. Nicholas Soc. of N.Y., Mil. Order Fgn. Wars, Ancient and Honorable Artillery Co., City Tavern Club (bd. govs. 1992—, sec. 1994, v.p. 1996-99), Cosmos Club (legal affairs com. 1986-90, com. reciprocity 1988-90, house com. 1990-95, chmn. 1992-95). Office: 5th Fl 801 Pennsylvania Ave NW Washington DC 20004-2615

GRIESCHE, JOACHIM, materials researcher, crystallographer; b. Berlin, Germany, Jan. 19, 1961; s. Hans-Joachim and Irene (Siepert) G. Diploma in Crystallography, Humboldt U., Berlin, Germany, 1986, PhD, 1989. Postdoc Acad. Scis., Berlin, 1989; scientist Humboldt U., Berlin, 1990-96; assoc. Pro-Web Soc., Berlin, 1996-97; scientist Inst. Semiconductor Physics, Frankfurt, Germany, 1997-99, Inst. Solar Technologies, Frankfurt, Germany, 1999—. Contbr. over 25 articles to profl. jours. Avocations: skiing, electronics, computer science. Home: Dietzgenstr 59, 13156 Berlin Germany Office: Inst Solartechnologies, Im Technologiepark 7, 15236 Frankfurt Germany

GRIESCHE, ROBERT PRICE, hospital purchasing executive; b. Berkeley, Calif., July 21, 1953; s. Robert Bowen and Lillian (Price) G.; m. Susan Dawn Albers, June 8, 1985 (div. Apr. 1989); 1 child, Sara Christine. AA, Coll. of the Canyons, Valencia, Calif., 1984. Warehouse supr. John Muir Hosp., Walnut Creek, Calif., 1973-82; purchasing mgr. Henry Mayo Newhall Hosp., Valencia, 1982-85; materials mgr. Foothill Presbyn. Hosp., Glendora, Calif., 1985-87; materials mgmt. dir. Huntington Meml. Hosp., Pasadena, Calif., 1987-96; sys. dir. purchasing So. Calif. Healthcare Sys., Pasadena, 1996—;

chmn. Huntington Employee Campaign, 1990-92. V.p. Coll. of Canyons Found., Valencia, 1985-90. Named to Outstanding Young Men of Am., 1988. Mem. Am. Soc. Healthcare Materials Mgmt., Calif. Cen. Svc. Assn. (charter). Republican. Presbyterian. Avocations: swimming, gardening, photography. Home: 3651 Cosmos Ct Palmdale CA 93550-5748 Office: So Calif Healthcare Sys 1300 E Green St Pasadena CA 91106-2606

GRIESENBACH, UTA, geneticist; b. Eitorf/Sieg, Germany, Jan. 28, 1964; d. Günter and Hannelore (Teitscheid) G.; 1 child, Caja Christina. Diplom Thesis, U. Bonn, 1991, PhD, 1996. Rsch. asst. Hosp. for Sick Children, Toronto, Ont., Can., 1992-96, postdoctoral rsch. fellow, 1996-97; rsch. fellow Nat. Heart and Lung Inst., London, 1997—. Contbg. author: Molecular Biology and the Lung, 1998, Non-Viral Vectors for Gene Therapy, 1999; contbr. articles to profl. jours. German Cystic Fibrosis Found. fellow, 1992, 93, Deutscher Akademischer Austausch dienst fellow, 1994, The Wellcome Trust fellow, 1999. Office: NHLI Dept Gene Therapy, Manresa Rd, London SW3 6LR, England

GRIESINGER, CHRISTIAN, chemist, educator; b. Ulm, Germany, Apr. 5, 1960; s. Karl Krist and Christa Helene (Scheller) G. Chemistry Diploma, U. Frankfurt, Germany, 1984, PhD, 1986. Prof. chemistry U. Frankfurt, 1990—, dir. Inst. for Organic Chemistry, 1991-97; dir. Max Planck Inst. for Biophys. Chemistry, Göttingen, 1999. Assoc. editor Jour. Magnetic Resonance, 1997—; contbr. over 100 articles to profl. jours. Recipient Award for Best Book in Chemistry, Fond. des Chemischen Industrie, 1996, Sommerfeld prize Bayerische Akademie der Wissenschaften, 1997, Leibniz prize Deutsche Forschungsgemeinschaft, Bonn, 1998. Avocations: tennis, jogging, piano, skiing. Office: Inst for Organic Chemistry, Marie Curie Str 11, 60439 Frankfurt Germany

GRIESINGER, FRANK, physician; b. Ulmdonau, Germany, Apr. 5, 1960; s. Karl and Christa (Scheller) G. MD, Med. Sch., Frankfurt, Germany, 1987; PhD, U. Gottingen, Germany, 1999. Resident U. Frankfurt, Germany, 1986-87, U. Munster, Germany, 1990-92; sr. resident U. Gottingen, Germany, 1992-98, attending physician, 1998—. Fellow U. Minn., Mpls., 1987-90. Mem. Am. Soc. Hematology, German Soc. Internal Medicine (Frerichs prize 1998), Internat. Assn. Lung Cancer. Office: U Gottingen, Robert Koch Str 40, 37075 Gottingen Germany

GRIESS, DANIEL, science educator, consultant; b. Colmar, France, May 4, 1936; s. Henri and Hélène (Dietrich) G.; m. Monique Blache, May 28, 1962; children: Olivier, Nathalie. DVM, U. Toulouse, France, 1961, Agregation, 1970. Asst. prof. Nat. Vet. Sch., Toulouse, 1962-73, prof., 1973-92, chmn. dept. nutrition, 1992—; vis. prof. Nat. Vet. Sch., Tunis, Tunisia, 1976-90; expert in field. Editor: Rev. Vet. Medicine, 1976-92. Sr. lt. vet. svc. French Army, 1960-62, Sahara. Decorated Chevalier Palmes Acads., French Ministry Edn., 1981. Roman Catholic. Home: 95 Ch des Coteaux, F 31780 Castelginest France Office: Nat Vet Sch, 23 Ch Capelles, 31076 Toulouse Cedex 3, France

GRIESSER, GERD HANS-WERNER, surgeon, educator, retired; b. Stuttgart, Germany, July 31, 1918; s. Hans and Dora (Krug) G.; m. Frowine Griesser-Leyh, Nov. 8, 1991. MD, Friedrich-Wilhelm U., Berlin, 1942; Habilitation in Surgery and Med. Stats., Eberhard Karl U., Tübingen, Germany, 1959. Resident, then sr. resident County Hosp., Illertissen, Germany, 1945-51; guest surgeon Univ. Hosp. Zurich, Switzerland, 1951; resident in surgery Univ. Hosp., Tübingen, 1952-59, dep. dir. dept. surgery, 1960-64; guest surgeon Karolinska Sjukhus, Stockholm, 1953; prof. med. informatics and stats. Christian Albrecht U., Kiel, Germany, 1964-86, pres., 1979-85; dir. Inst. Med. Informatics and Stats., Christian-Albrecht U., Kiel, 1964-79, mem. senate, 1967-73, dean med. faculty, 1972-74. Author, editor: Realization of Data Protection in Health Information Systems, 1977, Data Protection in Health Information Systems—Considerations and Guidelines, 1980, Data Protection in Health Information Systems—Where Do We Stand?, 1983; contbr. over 120 articles on cardiac surgery and hospital info. sys. to nat. and internat. publs.; patentee heart-lung machine (3). Chmn. Schleswig-Holsteinian Cancer Soc., Kiel, 1968-84, State Health Coun. of Schleswig-Holstein, Kiel, 1968-92; vice chmn. Cancer Soc., Stuttgart, 1960-64. Capt. med. corps German Mil., 1941-45, Russia. Decorated Cross of Merit 1st degree, Knight's Cross of Order of Merit (Germany); recipient Silver Core award Internat. Fedn. for Info. Processing, 1978. Mem. N.Y. Acad. Scis., Internat. Med. Informatics Assn. (bd. dirs. 1977-83, chmn. working group on privacy and security in health info. sys. 1976-84), Anglo-German Med. Soc., German Soc. Surgery, German Soc. Med. Informatics, Biostats. and Epidemiology, Assn. Computing Machinery, Biotst. Achievements include design, development and introduction of the computer-based hospital information system. Home and Office: Schleswig-Holstein, Barstenkamp 51, D-24113 Molfsee Germany

GRIEVES, FOREST LESLIE, political science educator; b. Beatty, Nev., Sept. 19, 1938; s. William Arthur and Alice Louise (Parman) G.; m. Irmgard Katharina Spengler, Mar. 31, 1963; children: Kevin Michael, Emily Katharina. BA in Polit. Sci., Stanford U., 1960; MA in Polit. Sci., U. Nev., 1964; PhD in Govt., U. Ariz., 1967. Tchg. assoc. U. Ariz., Tucson, 1964-67; asst. prof. Western Ill. U., Macomb, 1967-69; asst. prof. polit. sci. U. Mont., Missoula, 1969-72, assoc. prof., 1972-76, prof., 1976—, dept. chmn., 1990-91, 97—; guest prof. U. Saarlandes, Saarbrücken, Germany, 1978-79, 81; scholar-diplomat U.S. Dept. State, Washington, 1980; participant Friedrich Ebert Found. Seminar, Saarbrücken, 1982, Konrad Adenauer Found.-U.S. Dept. State Seminar, Bosen, Germany, 1982; Fulbright sr. lectr., Germany, 1978-79. Author: Supranationalism and International Adjudication, 1969, Conflict and Order, 1977; editor: Transnationalism in World Politics and Business, 1979; contbr. over 100 articles to profl. jours. and encys. 1st lt. U.S. Army, 1960-62. Rsch. grantee NEH, 1973, German Acad. Exch. Svc., 1978, 87; rsch. fellow Alexander von Humboldt Found., Germany, 1979, 81; Fulbright-Hays sr. scholar, Germany, 1984, 98. Mem. German Studies Assn. E-mail: fgrieves@selway.umt.edu. Office: U Mont Dept Polit Sci Missoula MT 59812-0001

GRIEZ, ERIC JACQUES, psychiatrist, medical educator; b. Ixelles, Brussels, Feb. 5, 1947; s. Marc Roger Griez; m. Annick Marie-France Durand (dec. Dec. 1988); 1 child, Thibault. PhB, U. Leuven, Belgium, 1968, MD, 1973; PhD, U. Maastricht, The Netherlands, 1984. Cert. neuropsychiatrist, Belgium; psychiatrist, The Netherlands. Lectr. U. Maastricht, 1979-84, asst. prof., 1984-96, prof., 1996—; invited assoc. prof. U. Nantes, France, 1995-97; exec. dir. European Cert. in Anxiety and Mood Disorders, 1989—; bd. dirs. Grad. Sch. Exptl. Psychopathology, The Netherlands, 1996. Avocation: private pilot. Office: U Maastricht, PO Box 616, 6200 MD Maastricht The Netherlands

GRIFFEY, KEN, JR. (GEORGE KENNETH GRIFFEY, JR.), professional baseball player; b. Donora, Pa., Nov. 21, 1969. Grad. high sch., Cin. Outfielder Seattle Mariners, 1987-99, Cin. Reds, 1999—. Recipient Gold Glove award, 1990-96; named to All-Star team, 1990-95, All-Star game MVP, 1992, , Sporting News Am. League Silver Slugger team, 1991, 93-94, 96 Sporting News All-Star team, 1991, 93-94. Office: Cincinnati Reds 100 Cinergy Fld Cincinnati OH 45202-3543

GRIFFIN, BETTY JO, elementary school educator; b. Monroe, La., Jan. 12, 1947; d. Julia Odell (Foster) Calhoun; divorced; 1 child, James Odell Griffin, Jr. BA, So. U., 1969; MA, San Francisco State U., 1975; PhD, LaSalle U., 2000. Cert. elem. tchr., Calif. Tchr. lang. arts Oakland (Calif.) Unified Sch. Dist., 1970-73, Garfield Elem. Sch., 1973-77; Garfield Elem. Sch., Stonehurst Elem. Schs., 1977-96; splty. prep. libr. and lang. arts tchr. Webster Acad., 1996—. Trustee Allen Temple Bapt. Ch., Oakland, Calif., 1987—; lit. tutor Delta Sigma Theta, Oakland, 1990—; chairperson African Am. Chain Read In, 1995—. Recipient Libr. Protection Fund award State Dept. Edn., 1997, Leadership award Dem. Nat. Com., 1997. Mem. NAACP, NEA, Oakland Edn. Assn. (bd. dirs.), Calif. Tchrs. Assn. (coun. of edn. 1996), Nat. Alliance Black Sch. Educators, Delta Sigma Theta, Phi Delta Kappa. Democrat. Avocations: reading, helping others, public speaking. Home: 2559 Oliver Ave Oakland CA 94605-4820

GRIFFIN, CHRISTOPHER OAKLEY, healthcare professional, humanities educator; b. Memphis, Apr. 27, 1970; s. Charles Ray Griffin and Gladys Lee (Oakley) Slappey. BA in English, Miss. Coll., 1992; MA in English, Baylor U., 1996; M in Humanities, U. Dallas, 1998. Tchg. asst. dept. English, Baylor U., Waco, Tex., 1993-95; hosp. worker Baylor Med. Ctr. at Irving, Tex., 1996-98; co-founder, dir. project devel. ReCare, Inc., Austin, Tex., 1999—; mem. adj. faculty Brookhaven Coll., Dallas, 1998. Author of poetry, criticism, philosophy. Presdl. scholar Miss. Coll., Clinton, 1988-92. Avocation: guitar.

GRIFFIN, DONALD WAYNE, diversified chemical company executive; b. Evansville, Ind., Mar. 1, 1937; s. Pauline Marie (Rahm) G.; m. Kristanya Johnson; children: Kristanya Anne, Kirstin Alyson. Student, Ind. U., 1954-57; BSBA, Evansville Coll., 1961. Sales rep. organics and explosives Olin Corp., Knoxville, Tenn., 1961-62; sales rep., dist. sales mgr. brass sales dept. Olin Corp., Indpls., 1964-69; dist. sales mgr. Milw., 1969-73; asst. to dir. field sales, s.w. region sales mgr. East Alton, Ill., 1973-77, dir. field sales, 1977-80, dir. internat. bus. devel., 1980-81; v.p. mktg. brass group Olin Corp., East Alton, 1981-83, pres. brass group, 1983-85, pres. Winchester group, 1985-86, pres. def. systems group, 1986-87, exec. v.p., pres. def. systems, 1987-93, vice chmn. bd. ops., 1993-94; pres., CEO, chmn. Olin Corp., Norwalk, Conn., 1996—; bd. dirs. Riverbend Bancshares, Inc., Ill. State Bank, East Alton, Olin Corp., Rayonier, Inc., Rayonier Forst Resources Co. Bd. dirs. Leadership Coun. S.W. Ill., Edwardsville, 1984—, Alton Meml. Hosp., Ill., 1983-89, St. Louis Regional Growth Assn., 1986-89. Mem. Assn. U.S. Army, Am. Def. Preparedness Assn., Navy League U.S. (life), Am. Soc. Metals, Small Arms Ammunition Mfrs. (bd. dirs. 1985—), S.W. Ill. Indsl. Assn. (bd. dirs. 1985—), Ill. C. of C. (bd. dirs. 1985-89), Wildlife Mgmt. Inst. (bd. dirs. 1986—), Nat. Shooting Sports Found. (bd. dirs. 1985—, trustee Buffalo Bill Hist. Ctr. 1991—), Chem. Mfrs. Assn. (bd. dirs. 1994—). Office: Olin Corp 501 Merritt 7 Ste 1 Norwalk CT 06851-6261

GRIFFIN, JAMES ANTHONY, bishop; b. Fairview Park, Ohio, June 13, 1934; s. Thomas Antohny and Margaret Mary (Hanousek) G. BA, Borromeo Coll., 1956; JCL magna cum laude, Pontifical Lateran U., Rome, 1963; JD summa cum laude, Cleve. State U., 1972; DHL (hon.), Ohio Dominican Coll., 1994. Ordained priest Roman Catholic Ch., 1960, bishop, 1979; asso. pastor St. Jerome Ch., Cleve., 1960-61; sec.-notary Cleve. Diocesan Tribunal, 1963-65; asst. chancellor Diocese of Cleve., 1965-68, vice chancellor, 1968-73, chancellor, 1973-78, vicar gen., 1978-79; pastor St. William Ch., Euclid, Ohio, 1978-79; aux. bishop Diocese of Cleve.; vicar of western region Diocese of Cleve., Lorain, Ohio, 1979-83; bishop Diocese of Columbus (Ohio), 1983—; mem. clergy relations bd. Diocese of Cleve., 1972-75, mem. clergy retirement bd., 1973-78, mem. clergy personnel bd., 1979-83. Author: (with A.J. Quinn) Thoughts for Our Times, 1969, Thoughts for Sowing, 1970, (with others) Ashes from the Cathedral, 1974, Sackcloth and Ashes, 1976, The Priestly Heart, 1983, Reflections on the Law of Love, 1991, Summary of the New Catholic Catechism, 1994. Bd. dirs. Holy Family Cancer Home, 1973-78; trustee St. Mary Sem., 1976-78; bd. dirs., mem. pension com. Cath. Cemeteries Assn., 1978-83; bd. dirs. Meals on Wheels, Euclid, 1978-79; vice-chancellor Pontifical Coll. Josephinum, 1983—; bd. dirs. Franklin County United Way, 1984-90; chmn. bd. govs. N.Am. Coll., Rome, Italy, 1984-88; chmn. Mayor's Coun. on Youth, 1986-90; treas. Cath. Relief Svc. Bd., 1988-91, pres., 1991-96; co-chair Columbus Cmty. Rels. Commn., 1992-95; mem. America's Promise, Columbus, 1997—. Decorated Knight of the Holy Sepulchre, 1993; recipient Human Rights award Anti-Defamation League B'nai B'rith, 1987, Gov.'s award State of Ohio, 1994, Jessing award Pontifical Coll., 1993, Don Bosco medal, 1997, N.G. Minuteman award, 1999, Columbus Urban League Cmty. Svc. award, 1999. Mem. Am. Canon Law Soc., Columbus Bar Assn. (chmn. jud. advt. com. 1987-91, Liberty Bell award 1989).

GRIFFIN, JO ANN THOMAS, retired financial planner, tax specialist; b. Dallas, July 20, 1933; d. John Baxton and Joan Marion (Ament) Thomas; m. John Barrett Brown, June 29, 1963 (div. 1972); children: John Barrett Jr., Daniel Thomas; m. Thomas Reese Griffin, Jan. 25, 1976; stepchildren: Gregory Crawford, Kevin Bradley. BA, U. Miss., 1955; BS magna cum laude, Lamar U., 1964; MEd, U. Del., 1972. Cert. fin. planner; enrolled agt. U.S. Treas. Dept. SSite mgr. Motivational Ctr., Inc., Wilmington, Del., 1976-78; asst. dir. Indochinese social svcs. Assoc. Cath. Charities, New Orleans, 1978-79; dir. continuing edn. St. Mary's Dominican Coll., New Orleans, 1979-80; with fin. mgmt. U.S. Dept. Agr., New Orleans, 1981; tax auditor IRS, New Orleans, Phila., Del., 1981-86; revenue agt. IRS, Wilmington, Del., 1986-87; tax specialist Horty & Horty, CPA's, Wilmington, 1986-87; quality control H&R Block, Wilmington, 1992-94; counselor Svc. Corps Ret. Execs., Wilmington, 1994-96; dir. Wilmington River-City Com., 1997-2000. Docent Winterthur, New Orleans Mus. Art, Wilmington and New Orleans, 1966-85; sustaining mem., advisor Jr. League Wilmington, 1989-92, 98—, mem. cmty. adv. bd., 1998—; lay reader, mem. oureach com. Episc. Ch. Diocese of Del., Wilmington, 1971—; counselor Svc. Corps. Ret. Execs., Wilmington, 1992; regent Vieux Carre chpt. DAR, New Orleans, 1984; bd. dirs. Neighborhood Watch, New Orleans, 1983-85, Waterfront Coalition, Inc., 1998-2000; sec., mem. exec. bd. Henrietta Johnson Med. Ctr., 1998—; treas., exec. bd. Civil War Round Table of Wilmington, Inc., 1999—; bd. dirs. Common Cause Del., 2000—, Del. Medicare and Medicaid Fraud Project, 2000—; CASA vol. Family Ct., State of Del., 2000—. Recipient Grad. Scholarship award AAUW, 1971, Sustained Superior Performance award IRS, New Orleans, 1984, Spl. Achievement award IRS, Wilmington, 1988, 89, Customer Svc. awards, 1989, 90. Mem. Am. Soc. Women Accts. (sec. 1986-89), Del. Valley Soc. Cert. Fin. Planners, Wilmington Tax Group, Estate Planning Coun. Del., Wilmington Women in Bus., Rotary, Blue and Gold Club, Mortar Bd., Phi Kappa Phi. Democrat. Episcopalian. Home: 900 N Broom St Apt 16 Wilmington DE 19806-4546

GRIFFIN, JOHN PARRY, clinical pharmacologist; b. Cardiff, U.K., May 21, 1938; s. David and Phyllis May (John) G.; m. Margaret Cooper, Mar. 31, 1962; children: Jane Rachel, Ruth Catherine, Timothy David. BSc with 1st class honors, Royal London Hosp. Med. Coll., 1959, PhD, 1961, MB BBS, 1964. House physician, house surgeon Royal London Hosp.; physician, house surgeon Poplar Hosp., King George V Hosp., Ilford; lectr. physiology King's Coll., London, 1965-67; hon. clin. asst. respiratory physiology Brompton Hosp., 1967-75; head clin. rsch. Riker 3M Labs., 1967-71; sr. med. officer medicines divsn. DHSS, 1971-76; med. assessor Medicine Commn., 1977-84; prin. med. officer medicines divsn. DHSS, 1976-77, sr. prin. med. officer, profl. head medicines divsn., 1977-84; dir. Assn. Brit. Pharm. Industries, 1984-94; faculty Scripps Med. Rsch. Ctr., San Diego, 1997-98; WHO cons., 1996-99; cons. Dept. Health Taiwan and IRPMA, 1995; Thomas Young lectr. and gold medallist St. George's Hosp., London, 1992; vis. lectr. U. Copenhagen, 1986, Drug Info. Assn., Atlanta, 1985; vis. prof. dept. pharmacology U. Rochester, 1979; vis. lectr. dept. indsl. pharmacy U. Lyon, France, 1976-78, 91, dept. pharmacology Rene Descartes U., Paris, 1977, U. Calif., Irvine, 1968; vis. prof. U. Surrey, Eng., 2000—; hon. cons. Lister Hosp. Stevenage, 1975—; exec. bd. Faculty Pharm. Medicine of Royal Coll. Physicians, London, Edinburgh and Glasgow, 1993—, chmn. bd. examiners for Faculty of Pharm. Medicine, 1976—; examiner toxicology Royal Coll. Pathologists, U.K., 1982—. Author: Manual of Adverse Drug Interactions, 5th edit., 1997; editor: Iatrogenic Diseases, 3d edit., Drug Induced Emergencies, Medicines: Regulation, Research and Risk, 2d edit., Internat. Medicines Regulations, A Forward Look to 1992, The Textbook of Pharmaceutical Medicine, 4th edit., 2000; editor in chief Adverse Drug Reactions and Toxicol. Revs.; mem. editl. bd. Worldwide Pharmacy Rev., Europe Drug and Device Report; contbr. articles to profl. jours. Recipient Lethby prize in biochemistry, 1958, Buxton prize in anatomy and physiology, 1958, George Riddoch prize in neurology, 1962; Yarrow Travelling Rsch. fellow U. Stockholm and U. Marburg, Germany, 1960-61. Fellow Royal Coll. Physicians, Royal Coll. Pathologists, Royal Soc. Medicine; mem. Brit. Pharm. Soc. (clin. pharmacology sect.). Fax: 01438-716029. Home: Quartermans, Digswell Ln, Welwyn Herts AL6 0SP, England

GRIFFIN, LARRY DON, English language educator, poet, college administrator; b. Vinita, Okla., Oct. 12, 1951; s. Grandville Rassler and Ethel Lina (Linam) G.; m. Melissa Ann Hearn, Feb. 25, 1978 (div. 1983); 1 child, Blake Edward. BA, Northeastern State U., Tahlequah, Okla., 1973; MA, U. Okla., 1975, PhD, 1989. Prof. English Midland (Tex.) Coll., 1981-97, chmn. fine arts and comm. studies div., 1991-97; prof. English, dean arts and scis. Dyersburg (Tenn.) State C.C., 1997—. Mem. NAACP, Walt Whitman Birthplace Assn., Walt Whitman Assn., Am Anti-Slavery Group, Coll. English Assn. (bd. dirs.), Masons (sr. steward). Democrat. Methodist. Avocations: ballet, gathering samphire, collecting bultos. Home: Bishop House 518 E Court St Dyersburg TN 38024-4714 Office: Dyersburg State CC 1510 Lake Rd Dyersburg TN 38024-2450

GRIFFIN, LUANNE MARIE, automotive corporation executive; b. Pitts., Dec. 19, 1961; d. Louis F. and Bernadette (Piekarski) Chapman; m. James E. Griffin, July 19, 1997. BA, Thiel Coll., 1983; MA, George Washington U., 1987. Sr. legis. asst. U.S. Rep. Thomas Ridge, Washington, 1983-87; English instr. Japan Min. Edn., Kagoshima, 1987-88; congrl. liaison Embassy of Japan, Washington, 1989-93; trade policy analyst Powell, Goldstein, Frazer & Murphy, Washington, 1993-95; mgr. govt. affairs Nissan N.Am., Inc., Washington, 1995—. Mem. Women in Internat. Trade., Washington Internat. Trade Assn., Tenn. State Soc. (bd. dirs.). Republican. Roman Catholic. Office: 196 Van Buren St Ste 450 Herndon VA 20170-5337

GRIFFIN, MIRIAM TAMARA, history educator; b. N.Y.C., June 6, 1935; arrived in Gt. Britain, 1957; d. Leo and Fanny (Natelson) Dressler; m. Jasper Griffin, Sept. 10, 1960; children: Julia, Miranda, Tamara. BA, Barnard U., 1956; MA, Radcliffe U., 1957; BA with 1st class honors, Oxford (Eng.) U., 1960, PhD, 1968. Tchg. fellow Harvard U., 1960-61; Fulford rsch. fellow St. Anne's Coll., Oxford, 1961-67; Barbara Craig tutorial fellow in ancient history Somerville Coll., Oxford, 1967—; Common U. Fund lectr. in ancient history Oxford U., 1968—; tutor in ancient history Trinity Coll., Oxford, 1990—; cons. Loeb Classical Libr., Harvard U., 1990. Author: Seneca, A Philosophy in Politics, 1976, Nero, The End of A Dynasty, 1984 (Nat. Book Club selection 1984); editor: Philosophia Togata I, 1989, II, 1997, Cicero: On Duties, 1991; joint editor Clarendon Ancient History Series, 1986—. Mem. Coun. Roman Soc., Oxford Philos. Soc., Inst. for Advanced Study. Avocations: music, reading, travel. Office: Somerville Coll, Oxford OX2 6HD, England

GRIFFIN, O. DANIEL, JR., reporter, writer, photographer, audio engineer, videographer; b. Portsmouth, Va., Oct. 26, 1960; s. Otto Daniel Sr. and Mary Lee (Gee) G. Student, Norfolk State U., 1980-83; BS in Fin., BA in Mass Media, Hampton U., 1986; BS in English, Old Dominion U., 1986; MFA in Film, Syracuse U., 1988. Lic. FCC. Audio & video engr. Afram Fest, Norfolk, Va., 1980—, Ujoma Fest, Portsmouth, Va., 1980—, Hampton Jazz Fest, Hampton, Va., 1980—; telecomm. engr. officer USAFNG, 1980—; audio engr. Sta. WOWI-FM, Norfolk, Va., 1984—, Star Prodn., Norfolk, Va., 1988—; promotion, pub. rels. rep. McDonald's, Portsmouth, Va., 1987; writer, reporter Citizens Press Am., Portsmouth, 1985—; asst. sport reporter Sta. WAVY-TV, Portsmouth, 1985—, Sta. WTKR-TV, Norfolk, 1987-93, Sta. WVEC-TV, Norfolk, 1991-92; owner Griffin's Photography, Audio & Video Post-Prodn. Inc., Portsmouth, 1987—, Step Above Post Prodn. Co.; writer, reporter Journal & Guide, Norfolk, 1988; mentor/computer programmer, writer, engr. Popular Hall Elem., 1992—; audio/video/light engr. cons. Treetop Co., Portsmouth, Va., 1993—; photographer Glamour Shots, Chesapeake, Va., 1996—, The New Jour. and Guide, Norfolk, 1995—; cameraman Manor High Band, Portsmouth, 1985-88; audio engr. Hal Jackson's Talent Teens, Norfolk, 1984—; photographer Pre-Teen Pageant, Portsmouth, 1987; producer, dir. Va. Beach Joint Cable Ctr., 1990—, Quiet Storm Soundtrack, Sta. WOWI-FM, Norfolk, 1984; owner, producer, dir., writer Step Above Post Prodn. Co., Portmouth, Va., 1990—; asst. sport reporter Sta. WVEC-TV, Norfolk, 1991—; producer, dir. Va. Beach Joint Cable Ctr., 1990-91. Actor play Momma Don't, audio engr./mem. stage crew In Times Like These; audio & video engr. Play Just Us, 1997—, Summer in Suffolk, 1997—; contbr. articles popular mags., 1986—. Named one of Outstanding Young Men Am., 1988. Mem. Black Filmmaker Assn., Nat. Rec. Soc. Arts and Sci., Hampton Roads Black Media Prof. Assn., Citizens Press of Hampton Roads, Norfolk State U. Alumni Band, Hampton U. Alumni Band, Yearbook Club, Newspaper Club. Baptist. Avocations: reading, music, plays, bowling, running, modeling. Home: 1425 Horne Ave Portsmouth VA 23701-3126 Office: Sta WVEC-TV 613 Woodis Ave Norfolk VA 23510-1017

GRIFFIN, ROBIN HENRY, archivist; b. Pointe á Pierre, S Fernando, Trinidad and Tobago, Nov. 4, 1935; arrived in New Zealand, 1962; s. Robert Leake and Frances Margaret (Langton) G.; m. Judith Rose Harris, Jan. 12, 1975 (div. Aug., 1989); m. Gail Irene Ferrif, May 14, 1992; step children: Michael, Nicholas and Benjamin Hamblin. BA, U. London, Eng., 1961; Diploma in Edn., Victoria U. of Wellington, New Zealand, 1966, BEd, 1972. Diploma in tchg. Christchurch, New Zealand. Asst. master Atkinson Rd. Secondary Modern Sch., Newcastle Upon Tyne, Eng., 1961, Spotswood Coll., New Plymouth, New Zealand, 1963-66, St Patrick's Coll., Silverstream, Upper Hutt, New Zealand, 1967-71; vocat. guidance officer Dept. Edn., Lower Hutt, New Zealand, 1971-72; archivist Bank of New Zealand, Wellington, 1972-90; editor Nat. Register of Archives & Manuscripts, Wellington, New Zealand, 1990-91; archivist Auckland (New Zealand) City Coun., 1992-93, Auckland Coll. of Edn., 1993—; convener New Zealand Archtl. & Tech. Archives Com.; presenter in field. Author: Bank of New Zealand Banknotes (1861-1934), 1987; many booklets for Bank of New Zealand, and numerous leaflets explaining displays in the Bank's Archives Mus.; pub. Robin's Letters to Granny: Letters to the New Zealand Herald, 1995, Technical Education in England and New Zealand...to 1970, 1997, (poems) The Haiku and the Pappygod, 2000; contbr. articles to profl. jours. Vol. archivist Auckland Pub. Libr., Auckland City Coun. Archives. Auckland Coll. of Edn. Rsch. grantee, 1995. Mem. Archives and Records Assn. of New Zealand, New Zealand Soc. Archivists, Auckland Archtl. Assn. (life), New Zealand Archeol. Assn., Soc. Archtl. HIstorians of Australia and New Zealand, West Indian Soc. Self Pub. Assn. (New Zealand) Inc., Self-Publishing Assn. of New Zealand. Avocations: archtl. history, heraldry, Irish history, Caribbean history. Home: 10 Charlton Ave, Auckland 1003, New Zealand

GRIFFIN, ROGER DAVID, history educator, researcher; b. Birmingham, Eng.; s. Robert and Joan Muriel (Harbour) G.; m. Mariella Demartini, Aug. 28, 1982; 1 child, Vincent Quentin Gregory. BA in Modern Langs. with 1st honors, Oxford (Eng.) U., 1970, PhD in Social Scis., 1989. Rsch. asst. in history Oxford Poly., 1972-76, lectr. in history, 1975-80, sr. lectr. in history, 1980-93; prin. lectr. in history Oxford Brookes U., 1993—, prof. modern history, 1997—; coll. lectr. in German, Oriel Coll., Oxford, 1972—; lectr., pub. spkr. on nationalism, racism, ecology and democracy. Author: The Nature of Fascism, 1991, Fascism, 1995, International Facism, 1998; contbr. chpts. to books, articles to profl. jours. Avocation: parenthood. Office: Oxford Brookes U, Dept History, Oxford OX3 0BP, England

GRIFFIN-ROLLO, JEAN (BARBARA JEAN GRIFFIN-ROLLO), marketing professional; b. Pasadena, Calif., May 20, 1943; d. DeWitt James and Jean Marie (Donald) Griffin; m. Rodney C. Holst, Mar. 22, 1969 (div. May 1975); 1 child, Justin D. Griffin-Holst. BA cum laude, San Jose State U., 1967. Designer integrated cir. mask Fairchild Semicondr., Mountain View, Calif., 1967-69; sr. custom integrated cir. mask designer Nat. Semicondr., Santa Clara, Calif., 1969-71; sr. specialist Advanced Micro Devices, Sunnyvale, Calif., 1971-75; mgr. mask design and computer-aided design groups Precision Monolithics, Santa Clara, 1975-76; mgr. analog mask design and graphic services Signetics Corp., Sunnyvale, 1976-82; dist. mgr. tech. mktg. Computervision Corp., Santa Clara, 1982-84, dist. mgr. sales, 1984-85, mgr. distbr. sales, 1985-87; dir. U.S. field mktg. Sun Microsystems Inc., Mountain View, 1987—; bd. dirs. U.S. Thin Film Products, Inc., Campbell, Calif. Mem. NAFE, AAUW, Navy League U.S., San Francisco Mus. Modern Art, St. Francis Yacht Club (San Francisco), Commonwealth Club of San Francisco. Republican. Avocations: sailing, skiing, refurbishing antique furniture, painting, photography. Office: Sun Microsystems Inc 2550 Garcia Ave Mountain View CA 94043-1100 Address: 9577 E Raindance Trl Scottsdale AZ 85262-1123

GRIFFITH, CLARK DEXTER, risk management professional; b. Suffern, N.Y., Dec. 21, 1965; s. William Fredrick Jr. and Lillian Griffith. BA in Econs. and Japanese, San Diego State U., 1991; M Internat. Affairs and Fin., Columbia U., 2000, cert. East Asia Study, 2000. Realtor Elegado Realty & Prudential Calif. Realty, San Diego, 1988-92; coord. import housing projects Sotetsu Real Estate Co., Ltd., Yokohama, Japan, 1991-97; regional mgr. Intradex Corp., Pearl River, N.Y., 1995-2000; project mgr. pvt. client group Merrill Lynch Internat., 1999; with risk mgmt. GE Capital, 2000—; customer svc. rep. Wells Fargo Bank, San Diego, 1988-90; cons. Kirin

Breweries, Inc., Yokohama, 1989, Nichiei Co., Ltd. Yokohama, 1990, Perillo-Griffith Travel Svc., Pearl River, N.Y., 1976-86; lectr. Am. Assn. State Colls. and Univs. Japan Studies Inst. Nat. Summer Inst., 1998, 2000. Contbr. articles to profl. jours. Mem. Am. C. of C. in Japan (vice chmn. trade expansion com. 1992-97, chmn. import housing sub-com. 1995-97), Japan Studies Assn. (founder, pres. 1989-91). Avocations: scuba diving, golfing, jet skiing, snow skiing, reading. Home: 992 Route 9W S Nyack NY 10960-4916 Office: GE Capital 2840 Broadway 130 New York NY 10025-7816

GRIFFITH, GARY ERNEST, public affairs executive; b. Ft. Worth, Mar. 14, 1948; s. Ernest Clay and Doris Blanche (Jones) G.; m. Jacqueline Teresa McGaha, Mar. 12, 1970; children: Victoria, Amanda. BA, U. Tex., 1970. Fin. dir. Clements for Gov., Dallas, 1978; alumni assn. dir. SMU, Dallas, 1979-80; communications dir., ptnr. Trammell Crow Co., Dallas, 1981-86; pres. Tex. Analyst Inc., 1987; v.p. pub. affairs Epic Healthcare Group, Dallas, 1988-94; prin. Jefferson Ptnrs., Dallas, 1994—. Active Commn. on Jud. Conduct, Austin, Tex., 1988-91; bd. dirs. Child Care, Dallas, 1983-89, Tex. Optometry Bd., Austin, 1982-87, Dallas Ballet, 1987-88, Dallas Summer Musicals, 1996—; active Dallas Pk. Bd. Mem. N.Am. Interfraternity Conf., Rotary (found. pres.), Sigma Phi Epsilon (nat. pres.), Project Am. (nat. pres.). Home: 6930 Lakewood Blvd Dallas TX 75214-3556

GRIFFITH, JULIA MARY, microbiologist; b. Sydney, Jan. 29, 1942; d. John Andrew and Barbara Burton (Cleland) La Nauze; m. Ian Peter Griffith, Mar. 7, 1970 (div. May 1987); children: Jacqueline Clare, Joanna Elizabeth. BS, U. Melbourne, 1963, MS, 1965; DPhil, Australian Nat. U., 1970. Rsch. asst. U. Melbourne (Australia), 1970, sr. tutor, 1971, part-time tutor, 1975-86; microbiologist State Pub. Health Lab., Melbourne, 1992—; state rep. Nat. Neisseria Network, Australia, 1994—. Co-author: Target Sites of Fungicide Action, 1992; contbr. scientific articles to profl. jours. Mem. Flemington Cmty. Health Ctr. Com., Melbourne, 1978-83; sec. Flemington Primary Sch. Parents' Assn., Melbourne, 1980-83; mem., newsletter editor Ascot Vale Neighbourhood Watch Com., Melbourne, 1993—; mem. Ascot Vale Resident's Assn., Melbourne, 1995—. Postdoctoral fellow U. Cambridge (Eng.), 1972-73, Rsch. fellow U. Melbourne, 1987-92, Nat. Rsch. fellow Commonwealth Australia, Melbourne, 1989-90; recipient Rsch. fellowship for women with career interruptions U. Melbourne, 1990-92. Mem. Australian Soc. Microbiology. Avocations: gardening, genealogy, classical music, fine arts, walking. Home: 25 Queens Ave, Melbourne 3032, Australia Office: U Melbourne, Microbiol Diagnostic Unit, Melbourne 3052, Australia

GRIFFITH, LONZO, JR., technology specialist, educator, farmer; b. Lynnville, Ky., Nov. 20, 1948; s. Elisha Lonzo and Dorthy Lorene G.; m. Diane Louise Tucker, Dec. 21, 1969. BS, Murray State U., 1971, MS, 1980; postgrad., U. Mo., Rolla, 1984-85. Cert. sci., chemistry, physics, math., computer sci. tchr., Fla., sci., math., computer sci. tchr., Ky. Assembler, machinist Midland Ross Corp., Paris, Tenn., 1977-80; tchr. Palmersville (Tenn.) H.S., 1980-81; instr. U. Tenn., Martin, 1981-84; tchr. Pahokee (Fla.) H.S., 1985-86; tchr. Clewiston (Fla.) H.S., 1986-96, technology specialist, tchr., 1996—; mem. tech. com. Henry County Bd. Edn., LaBelle, Fla., 1996—; local tech. rep. Fla. Internet Resource Network, Tallahassee, 1996—. Recipient First Place Ky. award Nat. Corn Growers Assn., 1999, Second Place U.S. award, 1999. Mem. NEA, Henry County Edn. Assn., Fla. Assn. for Computers in Edn., Fla. Tchg. Profession. Democrat. Baptist. Avocations: fishing, carpentry, stamp collecting. Home: 711 Bowden Rd Clewiston FL 33440-5004 Office: Clewiston HS 1501 S Francisco St Clewiston FL 33440-5016

GRIFFITH, MELVIN EUGENE, entomologist, public health official; b. Lawrence, Kans., Mar. 24, 1912; s. George Thomas and Estella (Shaw) G.; m. Pauline Sophia Bogart, June 23, 1941. AB, U. Kans., 1934, AM, 1935, PhD, 1938; postgrad., U. Mich., summers 1937-40. Instr. zoology N.D. Agrl. Coll., Fargo, 1938-39, asst. prof., 1939-41, assoc. prof., 1941-42; commd. officer USPHS, 1943-71; malaria control entomologist State Dept. Health, Oklahoma City, 1943-46, communicable disease ctr. entomologist, 1946-51; chief malaria adviser ICA, Bangkok, Thailand, 1951-60; assoc. dir. Malaria Eradication Tng. Ctr., Kingston, Jamaica, 1960; regional malaria advisor SE Asia, AID, New Delhi, 1960-62, Near East and SE Asia, AID, 1962-64; dep. chief malaria eradication br. AID, Washington, 1964-67; chief SE Asia, AID, Washington, 1967-71; ret. as capt., 1971; assoc. prof. zoology scis. U. Okla., Norman, 1946-52, prof. 1952-56; cons. Office of Health, AID, Washington, 1971-75. Contbr. articles and monographs on entomology, malaria control and pub. health. Recipient citation for disting. svc. U. Kans., 1962. Mem. Am. Pub. Health Assn., Am. Soc. Tropical Medicine and Hygiene, Am. Soc. Limnology and Oceanography, Entomol. Soc. Am., Explorers Club, N.Y. Acad. Scis., Siam Soc., Phi Beta Kappa, Sigma Xi. Address: PO Box DG Williamsburg VA 23187-3550

GRIFFITH, RICHARD LATTIMORE, lawyer; b. Abilene, Tex., Feb. 8, 1939; s. Richard Allan and Lorayne (Lattimore) G.; m. Sarah Brewster, Feb. 16, 1963 (dec. 1979); 1 child, Grey; m. Betsy Brooks, Apr. 19, 1980. BA, U. Okla., 1961; LLB, U. Tex., 1963. Bar: Tex. 1965, U.S. Dist. Ct. (no. dist.) Tex. 1966, U.S. Ct. Appeals (5th cir.) 1981, U.S. Dist. Ct. (ea. dist.) Okla. 1976, U.S. Dist. Ct. (we. dist.) Okla. 1967. Ptnr., chmn. health law sect. Cantey & Hanger, Ft. Worth, Tex., 1965—; chmn. Health Law Sect. State Bar of Tex., 1988. Co-author: Texas Hospital Law, 1988, 3d edit., 1998; contbr. articles to profl. jours. 1st lt. U.S. Army, 1963-65. Fellow Am. Coll. Trial Lawyers, Tex. Bar Found. (life); mem. Am. Bd. Trial Advocates (chpt. pres. 1985, state chmn. 1995), Def. Counsel Trial Acad. (faculty), Coll. of State Bar of Tex., Def. Rsch. Inst. (bd. dirs. S.W. region), Tex. Assn. Def. Counsel (v.p. 1984-85, regional v.p. 1986-88, 92-93), Tarrant County Bar Assn., Tex. Bar Assn. Eldon Mahon Inn of Ct. (emeritus). Avocations: gardening, fishing, hunting, cooking. Home: 6332 Curzon Ave Fort Worth TX 76116-4604 Office: Cantey & Hanger 2100 Burnett Plaza 801 Cherry St Ste 2100 Fort Worth TX 76102-6898

GRIFFITH, ROBERT CHARLES, allergist, educator, planter; b. Shreveport, La., Jan. 9, 1939; s. Charles Parsons and Madelon (Jenkins) G.; m. Loretta Dean Secrist, July 15, 1969; children: Charles Randall, Cameron Stuart, Ann Marie. BS, Centenary Coll., 1961; MD, La. State U., 1965. Intern, Confederate Meml. Med. Ctr., Shreveport, 1965-66, resident in internal medicine, 1966-68; fellow in allergy and chest disease, instr. U. Va. Med. Sch. Hosp., Charlottesville, 1968-70; practice medicine specializing in allergies, Alexandria, La., 1970-72, The Allergy Clinic, Shreveport, 1972; pres. Griffith Allergy Clinic, Shreveport, 1973—; faculty internal medicine La. State U., 1972—; owner, planter Riverpoint Plantation, Caddo Parish, La. and Miller and Lafayette Counties, Ark. Bd. dirs. Caddo-Bossier Assn. Retarded Citizens, 1977-84, Access (formerly Child Devel. Ctr.), Shreveport, 1979-85; mem. (life) NRA, med. adv. com., spl. edn. adv. com. Caddo Parish Sch. Bd., 1977-89; mem. commission on missions and social concerns First Methodist Ch., 1981-84, mem. adminstrv. bd., 1981-84; mem. med. panel for transfer Caddo Parish Sch. Bd., 1974-94; mem. adopt a flag program Confederate Meml. Mus. New Orleans; co-chair Loyola Fund Drive, 1994-95. Served to maj. M.C., U.S. Army, 1965-71. Recipient Physician of the Yr. award Shreveport-Bossier Med. Assts., 1984. Fellow Am. Coll. Asthma, Allergy and Immunology, Am. Coll. Chest Physicians (assoc.), Am. Thoracic Soc.; mem. AMA, SAR (chpt. surgeon 1994—), Am. Acad. Allergy, Asthma and Immunology, Am. Legion, Jamestowne Soc., So. Med. Assn., La. Med. Soc., Shreveport Med. Soc. (allergy spokesman 1984—), La. Allergy Soc. (charter; past pres.), U. Va. Med. Alumni Assn. (life), Pace Soc. Am., La. State U. Med. Alumni Assn., Confederate Soc. Am., Heritage Preservation Assn., League of the South (charter, sustainer), League of the South La. (bd. dirs.), Legion South, Am. Legion (Viet Nam), Mil. Order Stars and Bars, Order of So. Cross, Shreveport C. of C., Kappa Alpha, Methodist. Lodges: Masons (32 degree). Clubs: Shreveport Country, Petroleum of Shreveport, Shreveport, Ambs., Cotillion, Royal, Plantation, Shriners (El Karruba Temple), Jesters, Les Bon Temps., Demoiselle Club. Home: 7112 E Ridge Dr Shreveport LA 71106-4749 also: Riverpoint Plantation Ida LA 71044

GRIFFITH, ROBERT DEAN, military careerman, registered nurse; b. McAllen, Tex., Jan. 6, 1962; s. Roger Leroy and Susan Lynn (Disney) G.; m. Dianne Mary Clark, July 6, 1995; children: Lee Austin, Jayna Lynn. BSN magna cum laude, Old Dominion U., 1996, Degree in Biology and Chemistry. Enlisted E-1 USN, 1980; commd. ensign USN Naval Nurse Corps, 1996; student US Naval Schs., Gt. Lakes, Ill., 1980-81; profl. USS Monongahela, Norfolk, Va., 1981-82, Naval Spl. Warfare, Norfolk, 1982-93; RN Nat. Naval Med. Ctr., Bethesda, Md., 1996—, mem. staff edn. com. surg. ward, 1996-98; mem. staff ICU Nat. Naval Med. Ctr., Bethesda, 1998-99, unit mgr. cardiac rehab., 1999—. Mem. AACN, Emergency Nurses Assn., Old Dominion U. Alumni Assn., Sigma Theta Tau, Phi Kappa Phi. Avocations: family time, reading, running, bicycling, camping. Office: Nat Naval Med Ctr 8901 Wisconsin Ave Bethesda MD 20889-0001

GRIFFITH, STEVEN FRANKLIN, SR., lawyer, real estate title insurance agent and investor; b. New Orleans, July 14, 1948; s. Hugh Franklin and Rose Marie (Teutone) G.; m. Mary Elizabeth McMillan Frank, Dec. 9, 1972; children: Steven Franklin Jr., Jason Franklin. BBA, Loyola U., New Orleans, 1970, JD, 1972. Bar: La. 1972, U.S. Dist. Ct. (ea. dist.) La. 1975, U.S. Ct. Appeals (5th cir.) 1975, U.S. Supreme Ct. 1976. With Law Offices of Senator George T. Oubre, Norco, La., 1971-75; sole practice Destrehan, La., 1975—. Pres. 29th Jud. Dist. Bar Assn., 1979—. Fellow La. State Bar Found.; mem. ABA, ATLA, La. State Bar Assn. (ho. of dels. 1987—), La. Trial Lawyers Assn., New Orleans Trial Lawyers Assn., Fed. Bar Assn., St. Charles Parish Bar Assn. (pres. 1999—), Lions. Democrat.

GRIFFITH, YOLANDA EVETTE, professional basketball player; b. Chgo., Mar. 1, 1970; d. Harvey G.; 1 child, Candace Michelle. Student, Fla. Atlantic, 1993. Player Chgo. Condors, Long Beach StingRays, Germany, 1994-96; forward Sacramento Monarchs WNBA. Named ABL Defensive Player of Yr., 1997-98; recipient MVP award, 1999. Avocations: softball, music. Office: Sacramento Monarchs Arco Arena One Sports Pky Sacramento CA 95834

GRIFFITHS, DALE CHARLES, real estate executive; b. Nuneaton, Warickshir, Eng., Jan. 12, 1968; s. Brian Charles and Kay Rosalyn (Knight) G. BSc with honors in Urban Estate Survey, U. Nottingham, Eng., 1989; MA in European Property Devel., U. Newcastle, Eng., 1994. Property surveyor Connel Wilson, Leicester, 1987-89; cons. Weatherall Green Smith, Frankfurt, Germany, 1994-95, Hammerson, Frankfurt and Berlin, 1995—; investment cons. First Fin. Direct, Germany, 1998—; event organizer, 1995—. Author: Frankfurt Office Market, 1994. Mrm. Royal Inst. Chartered Surveyors (assoc. Deutsche Verband). Avocations: skiing, travel, diving, tennis, event organizing. Home: Charlottenstrasse 81, 10969 Berlin Germany Office: Griffiths Consult, Mainlust Str 18, 60329 Frankfurt Hessen, Germany

GRIFFITHS, HUGH DUNCAN, electrical engineer; b. Bournemouth, Dorset, Eng., Mar. 22, 1956; s. Gordon Hugh and Morag Gordon (Nicholson) G.; m. Morag Shearer Kirkwood, Mar. 25, 1989; children: Sian Helen, Alexandra Rose. MA in Physics, U. Oxford, 1978; PhD in Electronic Engring., U. London, 1986, DSc in Electronic Engring., 2000. Chartered engr. Eng., European engr. Scientist Plessey Roke Manor, Eng., 1978-81; rsch. assoc. U. Coll., London, 1982-85, lectr., 1985-93, prof., 1993—; mem. exec. com. Save Brit. Sci., U.K., 1996—; commissioning editor Microwave Series, Chapman and Hall, 1996—. Editor: IEE Proceedings on Radar, Sonar and Navigation, 1994—; contbr. articles to profl. jours. Recipient Young Scientist award Internat. Union Radio Sci., 1990, Fred Nathanson Meml. Radar Engr. of Yr., IEEE, AESS, 1996. Fellow IEEE, Instn. Elec. Engrs., Inst. Acoustics, Royal Acad. Engring. Mem. Labour Party. Avocations: food and wine, sports. Home: 5A Fellows Rd/Hampstead, London NW3 3LR, England Office: Dept EE Engring/Univ Coll London, Torrington Place, London WCIE 7JE, England

GRIFFITHS, JOHN LIEBIG, retired foreign service officer, marketing consultant; b. L.A., Nov. 10, 1929; s. John Francis Griffiths and Jane Elizabeth Liebig; m. Graciela Baccara, June 24, 1966 (div. Sept. 1998); children: John, Alessandra, Glenn; m. Marguerite Trechter Giddings, Jan. 29, 1999. BA, UCLA, 1954; grad., U. So. Calif., 1958, Armed Forces Staff Coll., Norfolk, Va., 1969. Various positions in fgn. svc. USIA/State Dept., Washington and Latin Am., 1960-88; internat. programs advisor U. So. Calif., L.A., 1994-97; internat. mktg. cons., Albuquerqe and L.A., 1998—. Mem. Sister Cities Found., Latin Am. and Albuquerque, 1975-96, Ptnrs. of the Ams., Latin Am. and Washington, 1970-88. Lt. USNR, 1954-58. Decorated Order of Morazán, Govt. of Honduras for Humanitarian Svc., 1975, Hon. Col. State of La. Mem. Am. Fgn. Svc. Assn., Ret. Officers Assn., Rotary Internat., Am. C. of C., Sigma Chi. Republican. Presbyterian. Avocations: linguistics, educational counseling for international exchange programs. Home: 251 S Medio Dr Los Angeles CA 90049-3911

GRIFFITHS, JOSEPHINE IVY, writer; b. Enfield, Middlesex, Eng., Mar. 6, 1939; arrived in Australia, 1953; d. Joseph Edward and Ivy Agnes (Wright) Swain; m. Bernard Frederick Griffiths, July 22, 1961; children: Bronwen Joy, Madlen Holly Elain. BA, U. Western Australia, Perth, 1981; B of Divinity with honors, Melbourne Coll. Divinity, Victoria, Australia, 1986; MPhil, U. Western Australia, 1988. cons. in field. Author: (books) The Reclaiming of Wisdom, 1994, Seeking Sophia, 1996. Home: 4A Western Ave, Yokine 6060, Australia

GRIFFITHS, ROBERT IRWIN, neuromuscular physiologist, researcher; b. Dandenong, Victoria, Australia, Sept. 12, 1954; s. Kenneth Raymond and Hilda Phyllis (Haslam) G.; m. Denise Lorraine Palmer, Dec. 20, 1975; children: Benjamin John, James Kenneth, Thomas Peter. BSc, Monash U., Clayton, Australia, 1975, PhD, 1984. Heritage fellow U. Calgary, 1984-87; rsch. scientist Monash U., Clayton, 1988-89, nat. SIDS coun. rsch. fellow, 1990-94, rsch. fellow, 1995; dir. Inst. Sport and Exercise Sci. James Cook U., Townsville, 1996-99; dir. exercise medicine Monash U., Melbourne, 1999—; cons. Axon Instruments, San Francisco, 1988—; invited participant WHO Global Strategy Meeting on SIDS, Sydney, 1992. Author: (with others) Axon Guide for Electrophysiology and Biophysics, 1993; contbr. articles to profl. jours. including Jour. Physiology and Proceedings of Royal Soc. of London; contbr. McGraw-Hill Yearbook of Sci. and Tech., 1995. Mem. Internat. Soc. Biomechanics, Australian Soc. for Med. Rsch., Sports Medicine Australia, Am. Coll. Sports Medicine. Office: James Cook U, Monash Univ Exercise Med, IRD Level 5 Monash Med Ctr, Clayton VIC 3168, Australia

GRIFFITHS, TREVOR, playwright; b. Manchester, Eng., Apr. 4, 1935; s. Ernest and Ann (Connor) G.; m. Janice Elaine Stansfield, 1960 (dec. 1977); m. Gillian Cliff, 1992; 3 children. BA with honours, Manchester U., Eng., 1955. Edn. officer BBC, London, 1965-72; tchr., lectr. in Manchester, Eng., 1957-65; further edn. officer BBC, 1965-70. Author: (radio plays) Jake's Brigade, 1969, The Big House, 1969, (stage plays) The Wages of Thin, 1969, Occupations, 1970, Apricots and Thermidor, 1971, (with others) Lay By, 1971, Sam Sam, 1972, The Party, 1973, Comedians, 1975, (new English version) The Cherry Orchard (Anton Chekhov), 1977, (with others) Deeds, 1978, Oi for England, 1982, Real Dreams, 1984, Piano, 1990, The Gulf Between Us, 1992, Thatcher's Children, 1993, Who Shall be Happy?..., 1995, (TV series) Adam Smith, 1972, Bill Brand, 1976, The Last Place on Earth, 1985, (TV plays) All Good Men, 1974, Absolute Beginners, 1974, Through the Night, 1975, Sons and Lovers, 1981, Country, 1981, Hope in the Year Two, 1994; screenwriter: (films) Reds, 1981, Fatherland, 1986, (children's book) Tip's Lot, 1972; screenwriter, dir. Food for Ravens, 1997. With inf. Brit. Army, 1955-57. Office: Peters Fraser & Dunlop, Drury House 34-43 Russel St, London WC2B 5HA, England

GRIGAS, JONAS, physicist; b. Kabeliai, Lithuania, Apr. 10, 1938; s. Pranas and Ona (Valentukeviciute) Grigas; m. Rita Morkunaite, July 27, 1963; children: Asta, Ruta. MS, Vilnius U., 1961, PhD, 1968; DSc, Inst. Physics, Riga, 1980. Engr. Inst. Radiomeasurements, Vilnius, Lithuania, 1961-63; asst. prof. physics Vilnius U., 1963-70, head lab. microwave spectroscopy of ferroelectrics, 1965—, assoc. prof. radiophysics, 1970-82, prof. radiophysics, 1982—, dept. head, 1988-93; vis. prof. physics Atomic Rsch. Ctr., Bombay, 1988, Shizuoka U., Hamamatsu, Japan, 1989, Metz (France) U., 1990, 92, 94, ETH, Zurich, 1992, 94, Iowa U., Ames, 1995, 98, Wroclaw U., Cracow U., 1988, 93, 96. Author: Microwave Dielectric Spectroscopy of Ferroelectrics and Related Materials, 1996; patentee in field; contbr. over 160 articles to profl. jours.; mem. editl. bd. Lithuanian Jour. Physics, 1982—, Sci. and Life, 1992—. Recipient Lithuanian Nat. Sci. and Tech. award, 1986, Lithuanian Nat. Sci. award, 1996. Mem. Lithuanian Acad. Scis. Roman Catholic. Avocation: beekeeping. Home: B Sruogos str 36-24, 2040 Vilnius Lithuania Office: Vilnius U Dept Physics, Sauletekio Ave 9/3, 2040 Vilnius Lithuania

GRIGGER, JANE ELIZABETH, earth science educator, photographer; b. Phila., June 7, 1947; d. John Casimer and Rozanne Marie (Peters) G. BS in Geology, Bucknell U., 1969; EdM in Earth Sci. Edn., Temple U., 1971. Tchr. secondary sci. Bensalem Twp. Sch. Dist., Cornwells Heights, Pa., 1970-72, Princeton Regional Schs. (N.J.), 1972-75; tchr. middle sch. earth sci. and math. Princeton Day Sch., 1975—; tchr. ptnrs. in edn. geology program Princeton U., 1985, photographer jours. Troop advisor S.E. Pa. coun. Girls Scouts U.S.A., 1969—; photographer Girl Scout Internat. Event, 1975, 76. Mem. Phila. Geol. Soc., Field Conf. Pa. Geologists, N.J. Sci. Tchrs. Assn., Roster Women Geoscis., N.J. Earth Scis. Tchrs. Assn., Nat. Assn. Geology Tchrs., Bucknell Alumni Club. Episcopalian. E-mail: jane grigger@pds.k12.nj.us. Home: 64-13 Ravens Crest Plainsboro NJ 08536 Office: Princeton Day Sch PO Box 75 Princeton NJ 08542-0075

GRIGGS, EMMA, management executive; b. Cleveland, Ark., Feb. 8, 1928; d. James and Frazier (Byers) Wallace; m. Augusta Griggs, Mar. 20, 1954 (dec.); children: Judy A., Terri V. Grad. H.S., Chgo. Pres., CEO Burlington No. Inc., Inglewood, Calif., 1986—. Republican. Avocations: reading, gardening, housekeeping.

GRIGGS, RUTH MARIE, retired journalism educator, writer, publications consultant; b. Linton, Ind., Aug. 11, 1911; d. Roy Evans Price and Mary Blanche (Hays) P.; m. Paul Philip Griggs, Aug. 4, 1940. BS, Butler U., 1933; postgrad. U. So. Calif., 1938, Northwestern U., 1939; MA, U. Wyo., 1944. Cert. tchr. journalism, English, speech, bus. edn. Travel writer Indpls. Star, 1927-37; summer reporter Worthington Times, Ind., 1928-33; journalism, speech tchr. Warren Cen. High Sch., Indpls., 1937-37; tchr. bus. edn., journalism Greene Twp. High Sch., South Bend, Ind., 1937-38; tchr. journalism, English, bus. edn. Howe High Sch., Indpls., 1938-46; tchr. journalism Butler U., Indpls., 1946-48, evenings 1972-76; dir. publs. Broad Ripple High Sch., Indpls., 1948-77; summer journalism workshop instr. numerous univs. 1949-80. Author: History of Broad Ripple, 1968; co-author: Handbook for High School Journalism, 1951; Teacher's Guide to High School Journalism, 1965, Marquette Memoirs, 1996. Dow Jones Newspaper Fund fellow U. Minn., 1967; named Nat. Journalism Tchr. of Yr. Wall Street Jour., 1968, Woman of Achievement Woman's Press Club of Ind., 1984; recipient Rabb award Women's Press Club of Ind., 1988, Disting. Alumni award Butler U. Alumni Bd., 1989. Mem. Journalism Edn. Assn. (v.p., pres. 1963-69, Towley award 1965), Women in Communications (pres. Indpls. 1969-70, Wright award 1969, Kleinhenz award 1978), Nat. Fed. Press Women (youth projects bd. 1979-87, Recognition award 1991), Columbia Scholastic Press Assn. (Gold Key award 1964, Golden Crown 1975, life mem. 1977), Ind. High Sch. Advisers Assn. (pres. 1972, Sengenberger award 1965), Delta Zeta (Ind. Woman of Yr. 1984). Republican. Presbyterian. Home: 8140 Township Line Rd Apt 3405 Indianapolis IN 46260-5863

GRIGNON, GÉRARD EUGÈNE JOSEPH, government official of Saint Pierre-et-Miquelon; b. Saint-Pierre-et-Miquelon, Apr. 16, 1943; s. René Grignon and Jeanne-Louise Janil. Student, Inst. Régional d'Éducation Physique & Sportive Bordeaux; law degree, U. Rennes; teaching cert. phys. edn. & sports. Prof. Teachers Coll., Rennes, 1967-71; dir. cultural ctr. & sports Saint Pierre and Miquelon, 1972-79, 81-83; prof. phys. edn. École des Beaux-Arts, Paris, 1980; mgr. youth & sports Saint Pierre and Miquelon, 1984-86; dep. UDF, Saint Pierre and Miquelon, 1986-88; dep. Saint Pierre and Miquelon, 1988-95, pres., gen. coun., 1995—; dept. to French Nat. Assembly Govt. of Saint Pierre and Miquelon. Dir. Le Vent de la Liberté, 1986—. Mem. Parti Socialiste. Avocation: theatre. Office: care Parti Socialiste, 97500 Saint-Pierre Saint Pierre and Miquelon Address: Palais Bourbon, Casier de la Poste, 75355 Paris 07 SP, France*

GRIGOLYUK, EDWARD IVANOVICH, mathematician; b. Moscow, Dec. 13, 1923; s. Ivan Iosivovich G. and Marie Timopheevna Shpak; m. Ludmila Nicolaevna Bajanova, 1960; 1 child, Marie. Student, Moscow Aviation Inst., 1944, candidate tech. scis., 1947; D Tech. Scis., Acad. USSR, 1951. Engr. technologist aircraft constrn. Tchr. Moscow Aviation Inst., 1944-47, Moscow High Tech. Sch., 1946-50; tchr. Inst. Mechanics Acad. Scis. USSR, 1951-59; tchr. Moscow State U., 1954-58, head dept. Inst. Mechanics, 1966—; tchr. Moscow Automechanics Inst. Tech. U., 1977—; dep. head lab. Inst. Hydrodynamic, Novosibirsk, USSR, 1959-65; head lab. Inst. Irf. Acad. USSR, 1952-81. Author: 31 books; editor: 51 books; redactor Ref. Jour. Mechanics; contbr. 310 papers to profl. jours.; inventor in field. Recipient Order Sign of Honour, 1975, State Prize of the USSR, 1975, Order Friendship of Peoples, 1986, Medal of V.N. Chelonej, 1987, 89, 94, Medal M.M. Bondarjuk Fen. Aircraft Sport USSR, 1991, Medal of P.L. Kapitsa Russian Acad. Natural Scis., 1996, Medal of S.P. Korolev, 1998, Diploma of V.N. Chelonej for "Outstanding Contribution in Creation and Mastering of Cosmic Space", 1998. Corresponding mem. Acad. Sci. USSR, Internat. Acad. Astronomics (prof. 1959). Avocations: philosophy, literature, Russian poetry. Home: Flat 391 Corpus 3 House 48, 4 Vavilov St, 117333 Moscow B333, Russia Office: Moscow Automechanics Inst, Bolsheja Semenovskaja 38, 105830 Moscow Russia

GRIGORESCU, MARIUS, physicist, researcher; b. Pitesti, Arges, Romania, Dec. 14, 1958; arrived in Canada, 1997; s. Florea Grigorescu and Maria (Ionescu) Esanu; m. Violeta Tanasa, July 1, 1985 (div. Dec. 1996). MS, Faculty of Physics, Bucharest, Romania, 1985; D in Physics, Inst. Atomic Physics, Bucharest, Romania, 1992. Physicist Inst. Atomic Physics, Bucharest, 1985-88, rschr., 1988-95, sr. rschr., 1995-97; rsch. assoc. Mich. State U./Nat. Superconducting Cyclotron Lab., East Lansing, 1992-93; vis. prof. Ctr. d'Etudes Nucléaires de Bordeaux Gradignan, Bordeaux, France, 1995. Contbr. articles to profl. jours. Rsch. fellow NATO, Deutscher Akademischer Austauschdienst, Bonn, Germany, 1997, Ctr. Internat. des Etudiants et Stagiaires, Paris, 1993; grantee Soros Found., Bucharest, 1992, 96. Mem. N.Y. Acad. of Scis., Am. Chem. Soc. Roman Catholic. Avocations: music, reading, swimming, photography, Christian meditation. Home: 227 Cathcard St Apt 105, London, ON Canada N6C 3M8

GRIGORIADIS, NIKOLAOS CHRISTOS, neurologist, researcher; b. Veria, Imathia, Greece, Nov. 4, 1964; s. Christos and Chrissoula (Tekidou) G.; m. Constantina Panagiotis Simeonidou, Sept. 22, 1995. MD, Med. Sch., Thessaloniki, Greece, 1989; PhD in Exptl. Physiology, Mil. Acad., Thessaloniki, 1989. Physician 401 Mil. Hosp., Athens, 1989-90, 424 Mil. Hosp., Thessaloniki, 1992-93, 96&; resident in neurology Ahepa U. Hosp., Thessaloniki, 1993-96; rsch. fellow Lab. Exptl. Physiology, Thessaloniki, 1992-97; vis. rschr. Hadassah U., Jerusalem, 1997; cons. neurologist 424 Mil. Hosp., 1996-97; rsch. asst. Aristotle U., Thessaloniki, 1997; lectr. in neurology in Med. Sch. Thessaloniki, Greece, Mai, 1998; rsch. asst. in neuroimmunology Hadassah U. Jerusalem, Mai, 1999. Author: Pediatric Neurology, 1996. Capt. Greek Armed Forces, 1989—. Recipient 1st award 3d Panhellenic Sci. Symposium Med. Students, 1993, 11th No. Greece Med. Congress, 1996, Hon. Oral Presentation award 4th Interlaken's Ivig Internat. Symposium, 1996. Mem. AAAS, European Neurosci. Assn., Hellenic Multiple Sclerosis Assn. Christian Orthodox. Avocations: painting, swimming, music, cinema, theater. Home: Mousson 15, GR-55236 Thessaloniki Greece Office: Ahepa Hosp Dept Neurology, Stilp Kyriakidi Str 1, GR-54636 Thessaloniki Greece

GRIGORIEV, SERGEI ALEKSANDROVICH, political scientist, researcher; b. Moscow, Feb. 16, 1957; came to U.S., 1991; s. Aleksandr Mironovich Grigoriev and Antonina Nikolayevna Barinova-Sitnikova; m. Valentina M. Maliukovskaya, Nov. 14, 1975 (div. June 1986); 1 child, Helen S. Grigoriev-Pogosyan; m. Elena Borisovna Kostritsyna, June 3, 1989. MA in History, Regional Studies, Langs., Moscow State U., 1979; MPA, Harvard U., 1993; PhD in Interdisciplinary Studies, Tufts U., 1996. Exec. sec. Soviet Chinese Friendship Assn., 1979-84; sr. exec. N.Am. sect. Communish Party of the Soviet Union, Moscow, 1984-90; asst. press spokesman Office Pres. USSR, Moscow, 1990-91; fellow in residence Princeton (N.J.) U., 1991-92; fellow Harvard U., Cambridge, Mass., 1992, sr. rsch. assoc., 1992—, exec. dir. Russian fellows program, 1996-99; vis. prof., lectr. Northeastern U., Boston, 1992-96; cons. ABC News, N.Y.C., 1991-92; cons., lectr. Leigh Bur., Sommerfille, N.J., 1991-94; adviser, cons. to chmn. All-Russian TV and Radio Broadcasting Co., Moscow, 1999—; adviser CNN, 2000, Eruasia Group Moscow Trip, 2000. Contbr. articles to newspapers and profl. jours. Cons. Yeltsin for Pres. Campaign, Boston, Moscow, 1996,

City Legislature Election, 1998, TV-Ctr., Moscow, 1998; advisor to Hon. Sergei V. Yastrzhembsky, Dep. Premier Moscow City Govt., 1998-99, Hon. Sergei V. Kiriyenko, leader New Force Movement, 1999. Mem. Am. Acad. Polit. Sci. Home: 110A Inman St Cambridge MA 02139-1206 also: # 108 Prospect Mira Apt 342, 124626 Moscow Russia Office: Ria Vesto News Agy, # 4 Zubovsky Blvd, 124626 Moscow Russia

GRIGORIEVA, GALINA MIRON, physicist; b. Moscow, May 23, 1938; d. Miron Solomon Rachlin and Antonina Michael Michailova; m. Yuri Vladimir Grigoriev, June 1, 1962; 1 child, Dmitri Yuri. MS in Physics, Moscow State U., 1961; DSc Tech. State Rsch. Prodn. Enterprise, Kvant, Moscow, 1968. Jr. rschr. State Rsch. Prodn. Enterprise Kvant, Moscow, 1961-64, sr. engr., 1964-67, sr. rschr., 1967-73, head of lab., 1973—. Author: (with L. B. Kreinin) The Effect of Space Radiation on Solar Cells, 1979, (with A. J. Akishin, S. N. Vernov et al) The Model of Space, 1983; contbr. articles to sci. jours. Mem. symphonic orch. Russian Acad. Scis. Recipient State medal for labor achievements, 1983, Yuri A. Gagarin medal of Cosmonautics Fedn., 1987. Mem. Cen. House of Scientists, Russian Acad. Scis. Avocation: playing violin. Home: 15/2 Apt 92 Garibaldi St, 117335 Moscow Russia Office: State Rsch Prod Enter Kvant, 3d Mytischinskaya St 16, 129626 Moscow Russia

GRIGOROIU, GABRIELA, educator, researcher; b. Piatra Neamt, Romania, Sept. 12, 1954; d. Mircea and Maria Veronica (Florea) Cernescu; m. Mircea Agenor Grigoroiu, Nov. 14, 1981; children: Mircea-Mihai, Cristiana Diana. Cert. Applied Linguistics, The Bell Sch. of Langs., Norwich, U.K., 1976; degree in English & French, U. Bucharest, 1978, cert. tchr. English, 1981; cert. 2nd degree in teaching, 1987; cert. in-svc. tchr.-trainer, Coll. St. Mark & St. John, Plymouth, Eng., 1993. Tchr. English High Sch. #2, Bals, Romania, 1978-90, High Sch. #8, Craiova, Romania, 1990-91; lectr., tchr. trainer U. Craiova, 1991—. Author: Try One of My Activities, 1999, Trainerella in Search of King Arthur's Court, 1999, TP Observation Booklet, 1999; contbr. articles to profl. jours. Exeter scholar, 1994. Fellow ELTECS; mem. TETA/IATEFL, ESSE. Home: Lapus-Arges, Bloc D11 Ap 2 Of Postal 5, 1100 Craiova Dolj, Romania Office: Univ of Craiova, A I Cuza #13, 1100 Craiova Dolj, Romania

GRIGORYAN, VALDIMIR, research scientist, consultant; b. Konstantinovka, Ukraine, Jan. 10, 1953; came to U.S., 1996; s. Sergey Arshavir and Nadezhda Zinavor (Badalyan) G.; m. Ovsanna Grigoryan, Feb. 8, 1979; children: Gevorg, Armine. MS, Yerevan State U., 1975; PhD, Inst. Radio-Engrng./Elec., Moscow, 1981. Rsch. asst. Bjurakan Astrophys. Obs., Armenia, 1975-76; jr. rsch. scientist Donetsk Inst. Physics and Tech., Ukraine, 1976-78, Yerevan Physics Inst., 1981-84; sr. rsch. scientist Laser Technique Corp., Yerevan, 1984-92; leading rsch. scientist IRE-POLUS Corp., Moscow, 1992-96; rsch. asst. prof. U. Md., Balt., 1996-2000; sr. engr. II Corvis Corp., Columbia, Md., 2000—; cons. Virtual Photonics, Inc., Berlin, 1998-2000. Contbr. articles to profl. jours. Internat. Sci. Found. grantee, 1995, 96. Mem. Optical Soc. Am. Office: Corvis Corp PO Box 9400 7015 Albert Einstein Dr Columbia MD 21046-1707

GRIGORYEV, PETER YAKOVLEVICH, gastroenterologist; b. Nizhnij Irginsk, Russia, Oct. 16, 1924; s. Jakov and Appolinarija (Chesnokova) G.; m. Emilija Yakovenko, Feb. 23, 1970. MD, Med. Inst. Khabarovsk, 1949, M in Med. Sci., 1951; DSc, Med. Inst. Tomsk, 1966. Head therapy dept. Main Railway Hosp., Khabarovsk, Russia, 1951-68; rector Med. Inst., Blagoveschensk, Russia, 1969-77; prof. 2d Med. Inst., Moscow, 1977-80; head gastroenterology dept. Med. U., Moscow, 1980—; chief gastroenterologist Ministry of Health of Russian Fedn. Author: Chronic Gastritis, 1993, Treatment of Digestive Organ's Diseases, 1993, Information Guide on Gastroenterology, 1996, Diseases of Digestive Organs, 1997, Clinical Gastroenterology, 1998. Mem. Russian Gastroenterol. Soc., Soc. War Invalids. Office: Russian State Med U, Ostrovitjanova st 1, 117437 Moscow Russia

GRIGORYEV, VLADIMIR ALEXANDROVICH, space communication systems educator; b. Novocherkassk, Rostov, Russia, July 1, 1966; s. Alexandr Ivanovich and Larisa Vladimirovna (Kurilekh) G.; m. Galina Stepanovna Troc, July 1, 1988; 1 child, Helen. CantTechScis, Mogaysky Acad., Leningrad, Russia, 1993; D'TechScis, Mogaysky Acad., St. Petersburg, Russia, 1999. Cert. in radio engrng. Engr. in comm. sect. Mgmt. Ctr. of Flights, Moscow, 1988-89, comdr. comm. sect., 1989-91; tchr. Mogaysky Mil. Space Acad., Leningrad, 1993-96; sr. tchr. Mogaysky Mil. Engrng. Sapce Acad., St. Petersburg, 1999—; cons. NII TM, St. Petersburg, 1997-98, Cert. Lab. Norma, St. Petersburg, 1997-99; cons. NII Engrng., Moscow, 1992-97, NII Comm., Moscow, 1998-2000. Author monograph; contbr. articles to Radio-engrng. and Electronics, Antenna, others. Lt.-col. Mogaysky Mil. Space Acad., 1983-99. Christian. Avocations: classical music and jazz, football. Home: Belloostrovskaya 31 fl 65, St Petersburg 197342, Russia Office: Mogaysky, Mil Engrng Space Acad, St Petersburg Russia

GRIGORYEVA, MARGARET VASILYEVNA, academy administrator, linguist; b. Kharkov, Ukraine, July 7, 1936; d. Vasily Pavlovich and Vera Ivanovna (Guseva) Steshenko; m. Valery Georgievich Lyubiev, May 8, 1969; 1 child, Grigoryev Igor Valeryevich. Philologist, Kharkov (Ukraine) State U., 1963; M of Linguistics, Lviv (Ukraine) State U., 1975; asst. prof., U. Fgn. Langs., Moscow, 1983; prof. High Certifying Commn., Moscow U., 1990. Cert. linguist. Lectr. fgn. langs. dept. Kharkov Engr. Pedagog. Acad., 1963-73, head German lang. chair, vice-dean, 1973-78; head fgn. langs. dept. Ukrainian Acad. Pharmacy, Kharkov, 1978—. Author: (textbooks) German for Pharmacy Students, 1990, 94, French for Pharmacy Students, 1994, 97, English for Pharmacy Students, 1994, 97, (books) German-Russian Minimum Vocabulary for Pharmacy Students, 1988, Russian-French Phrase-Book, 1992, Russian-English Phrase-Book, 1992, Russian-German Phrase Book, 1992, German for Students of 3-4 Years, 1995; patentee in field. Mem. Ukrainian Acad. Scis. and Technol. Cybernetics (head linguistics dept.), N.Y. Acad. Scis. Avocations: traveling, theater, reading historical literature. Home: Staritsky Str 15 Flat 148, 310018 Kharkov Ukraine Office: Ukrainian Acad Pharmacy, Pushkinskaya Str 53, 310002 Kharkov Ukraine

GRIGSBY, MARVELL A., JR., security company administrator, consultant; b. Santa Monica, Calif., May 24, 1954; s. Marvell Grigsby; m. Kay Grigsby, June 1986; children: Amber, Nelson. BA, Pepperdine U., 1976. Cert. Thx tech. V.p. Unique Protection Svcs., 1976-83; security cons. Don Cornelius Prodn., L.A., 1983—, Am. Music Awards, L.A., 1985—, Am. Comedy Awards, L.A., 1989—. Mem. Am. Soc. Indsl. Security, Security Consultants Assn. E-mail: Marvellg@aol.com. Home: PO Box 67933 Los Angeles CA 90067-0933

GRIJALVA-CHON, JOSE MANUEL, oceanologist, researcher; b. Hermosillo, Mexico, Nov. 13, 1959; s. Manuel and Herlinda (Chon-Felix) G.; m. Reina Castro-Longoria, May 17, 1986; children: Jessica, Marisol. B in Oceanology, U. Baja California, Ensenada, Mex., 1985; MS, Ctr. Sci. Rsch. & Higher Edn., Ensenada, Mex., 1986; DSc, 1995. Prof. U. Sonora, Mex., 1986—; vis. rschr. Ocean Rsch. Inst. Tokyo U., 1992. Contbr. articles to profl. jours. Recipient Nat. Researchers Sys. grant Ministry Edn., Mexico City, 1989-94, Manuel Caboz Meml. scholarship Inter-Am. Tropical Tuna Commn., La Jolla, Calif., 1993, nat. Award of Oceanographic Rsch. Inter-Secretariat Oceanographic Rsch. Commn., Mexico City, 1995. Mem. Sea of Cortez Rschrs. Assn. (sec. 1997—), Mexican Oceanologist Assn., Mexican Soc. Planktology, Acad. Marine Scis. (pres. 2000—). E-mail: mgrijal@guayacan.uson.mx. Office: Universidad de Sonora-Dictus, Rosales y Ninos Heroes s/n, 83000 Hermosillo Mexico

GRILL, VALDEMAR ERIK, endocrinologist, educator; b. Gothenburg, Sweden, Jan. 7, 1941; s. Erik Robert and Margrethe (Reimann) G.; m. Birgitta Charlotta Waernulf, Oct. 25, 1975; children: Helena, Elisabet, Kristina. MD, Karolinska Inst., Stockholm, 1969, PhD, 1975, docent, 1978. Cert. specialist in endocrinology, gen. internal medicine. Med. tng. Karolinska Hosp., Stockholm, 1969-78, assoc. prof. endocrinology, sr. physician, 1982-92; vis. scientist Northwestern U., Chgo., 1978-79; asst. prof. Karolinska Inst., 1979-82; rschr., assoc. prof. Swedish Med. Rsch. Coun., Stockholm, 1993-96; prof. dept. medicine U. Hosp. Trondheim, Norway, 1996—; head diabetes sect. Karolinska Hosp., Stockholm, 1987-95; head endocrine sect. U. Hosp. Trondheim, Norway, 1996—; adj. prof. Karolinska Inst., 1999—; cons. Novartis Co., Norway, 1999—, Pfizer Co., Norway, 1999—; lectr. in field. Contbr. over 140 articles to profl. jours.; editor: The Pathogenesis of Noninsulin Dependent Diabetes Mellitus, 1988. Grantee Swedish Med. Rsch. Coun., 1978—, Juvenile Diabetes Found., 1989, Norwegian Med. Rsch. Coun., 1996—. Mem. Royal Norwegian Sci. Soc., Norwegian Diabetes Assn. (mem. working com. profl. bd. 1997—, mem. adv. bd. Diabetologia jour. 1996-99). Avocation: outdoor life. Office: U Hosp Trondheim, Dept Medicine Sect Endocrin, N-7006 Trondheim Norway

GRIM, PATRICK NEAL, philosopher, educator; b. Pasadena, Calif., Oct. 29, 1950; s. Elgas Shull Grim and Dorathy Mae O'Neal; m. Kriste Taylor, 1978 (div. 1987); m. L. Theresa Watkins. AB in Philosophy and Anthropology, U. Calif., Santa Cruz, 1971; BPhil, U. St. Andrews, 1975; PhD, Boston U., 1976. Mellon faculty fellow Wash. U., St. Louis, Md., 1977-78; from asst. prof. to prof. SUNY, Stony Brook, 1978-94, prof., 1994—. Author: The Incomplete Universe, 1991, The Philosophical Computer, 1998; editor: The Philosopher's Annual, Vols. 1-21, 1979-99, Philosophy of Science and the Occult, 1982, 91; contbr. articles to profl. jours. Fulbright fellow, St. Andrews, Scotland, 1971-72, Mellon Faculty fellow Washington U., St. Louis, 1977-78. Fellow Acad. of Tchr./Scholars; mem. Internat. Assn. Philosophy of Law, Am. Philosophical Assn. Avocations: art, music. E-mail: pgrim@notes.cc.sunysb.edu. Home: Toad Hall 99 Swezey St Patchogue NY 11772 Office: Dept of Philosophy Suny At Stony Brk Stony Brook NY 11794-0001

GRIMALDI, JEAN-CLAUDE, systems engineering and projects administrator; b. Poitiers, France, May 6, 1947; s. Jean-Darius and Elisabeth (Himbert) G.; m. Marie-Gabrielle Brucker, July 3, 1975; children: Jean-Philippe, Jean-Michel, Marie-Noelle. Grad. in Engrng. and Mfg., Ecole Centrale De Paris, 1969; diploma, Inst. Controle De Gestion, Paris, 1982. Sr. project mgr. Jeumont-Schneider, Paris, 1970-79, mgmt. contr., 1979-82; adminstrv. and fin. dir. Compagnie Etudes & Realisation en Cybernétique Industrielle, Paris, 1982-86; R&D mgr. Autoroutes Paris-Rhin-Rhone, Dijon, France, 1987-93; tech. advisor to gen. mgr. Autoroutes Paris-Rhin-Rhone, Paris, 1993-94; Global Sys. Mobile radiotéléphone program mgr. Soc. Française du Radiotéléphone, Paris, 1994-95; dir. supply and indsl. partnerships Soc. Française du Radiotéléphone-Cegetel, Paris, 1995-97; dir. strategic projects Oracle Cons. France, Paris, 1997—; com. chmn. Confedn. Française Habitat Urbanisme Amenagement du Territoire, Paris, 1990-94; mem. tech. com. Assn. Française Normalisation-Bur. Normalisation Esploitation Voirie and Transports, Paris, 1987-94; mem. Groupe Transport 2000, Paris, 1992. Author: Passeport pour la Téléphonie Mobile, 1999; contbr. articles to profl. jours. Recipient Mgr. of Yr. in Telecom. and Networks award Inst. Nat. Télécom.-Ctr. Nat. Industries et Techniques Télécom.-IDG, Paris, 1992, Must of France for Integrated Computing award Zenith Data Sys., Lyon, France, 1993. Achievements include design and creation of industrial automaton; automatic reading of car's license plates; automatic detection of incidents on highways; design and creation of a wide area "Information Highway". Avocations: literature, manual works, music, video, programming. Home: 20 Rue Gambetta, Puteaux F92800, France Office: Oracle Cons France, 89 ave François Arago, F92732 Nanterre Cedex France

GRIMALDI, MICHEL, law educator, consultant; b. Paris, Sept. 4, 1949; s. Pierre and Colette (Susini) G.; m. Sophie Hellebranth, June 5, 1975; children: Cyril, Laure, Emmanuel. Lic. es Lettres, U. Sorbonne, Paris, 1969; D en Droit, U. Paris II, 1977; Agregation en Droit, 1978. Prof. U. Limoges, 1978-81; prof. U. Paris XIII, 1981-84, U. Paris XII, 1984-90, U. Paris II, 1990—. Author: La Nature Juriique de l'Institution Contractuelle, 1977, Successions, 1996, Droit Patrimonial de le Famille, 1997, Libéralités, Partages d'ascendants, 2000; contbr. articles to profl. jours. Roman Catholic. Home: 17 Rue de l'Annonciation, 75016 Paris France Office: U Paris II, 12 Place du Panthéon, 75005 Paris France

GRIMBLE, MICHAEL JOHN, industrial engineering educator; b. Grimsby, Eng., Oct. 30, 1943; s. Reginald Parsons and Queenie (Pearson) Grimble; m. Wendy Huntley, July 30, 1966; children: Clare Louise, Andrew Michael. BSc with hons., Rugby (Eng.) Coll., 1970; MSc, U. Birmingham, Eng., 1971, PhD, 1974, DSc, 1982; BA with hons., Open U., 1978. Chartered Engr., Eng. Apprentice CIBA Geigy, Grimsby, Eng., 1959-66; design engr. GEC Elec. Projects, Rugby, Eng., 1974-75; sr. lectr., reader Sheffield (Eng.) Polytech., 1975-81; prof. in Indsl. Systems U. Strathclyde, Glasgow, Scotland, 1981—; tech. dir. Indsl. Sys. and Control Ltd., Glasgow, 1990—. Author: (books) Optimal Control: Stochastic Estimatation Theory, 1988, Robust INdustrial Control, Optimal Design Approach for Polynomial Systems, 1994. Recipient Internat. Sci. Festival award, 1993. Fellow IEEE, Inst. Elec. Engrs. (chartered engr., Heaviside Premium 1978), Inst. Measurement and Control (Honeywell Internat. medal 1991), Inst. Math. and Applications, Royal Soc. Edinburgh. Avocations: theatre, reading, travel, family time, country walks. Office: U Strathclyde, 50 George St, Glasgow G1 1QE, Scotland

GRIMBY, GUNNAR LARS, physician, researcher; b. Stockholm, Apr. 6, 1933; s. Paul and Mary (Holm) Grimby; div.; children: Lars, Hans, Anna Ekman Grimby; m. Agneta Elisabet Holström, Mar. 31, 1985. MD, Göteborg (Sweden) U., 1960, PhD in Med. Sci., 1962; specialization in clin. physiology, specialization in rehab. medicine. Med. diplomate. Resident Sahlgrenska U. Hosp., Göteborg, 1960-65, cons., 1966-72; assoc. prof. Göteborg U., 1973-83, prof., 1983-99; chmn. expert com. on rehab. Swedish Bd. Health and Social Welfare, 1994-98. Editor-in-chief Scandinavian Jour. Rehab. Medicine, 1999—; contbr. over 300 articles to profl. publs.; contbr. chpts. to books. Bd. dirs. Coll. Phys. Edn., Stockholm, 1995-97. Sr. rsch. fellow Harvard Sch. Pub. Health, 1965-66. Fellow Royal Coll. Physicians; mem. Swedish Soc. Rehab. and Phys. Medicine (vice chmn. 1990-93, chmn. 1994-95), European Bd. Phys. Medicine and Rehab. Avocations: skiing, outdoor activities, boating. Office: Sahlgrenska U Hosp., Dept Rehab Medicine, S 41345 Göteborg Sweden

GRIMES, COLIN, management consultant; b. Eng., July 14, 1937; m. Norma Lily Coverdale, Aug. 4, 1957. BA, U. Keele, Eng., 1958; DMS, Anglian Regional Mgmt. Centre, Eng., 1981. Cert. meetings mgmt. Tchr., lectr. various schs. and colls., Eng., 1958-65; edn. officer Ministry Edn., Uganda, 1965-74; chief adminstrv. officer Southend Coll. Tech., Eng., 1974-81; CEO Inst. Packaging, Eng., 1981-85; prin. Assn. Enterprises, Eng., 1985—; cons. Brit. Know Now Fund, Ukraine, 1995—. Editor Care Home Proprietor, Private Care Clarion, 1987—, Association, 1994; cons. editor Mktg., Press and Pub. Rels. jours., 1994. Mem. European Soc. Assn. Execs. (bd. dirs. 1994—), Lions Internat. (charter pres. 1994-95), European Cert. Assn. Mgmt., Soc. of Assn. Execs. Avocations: photography, crosswords, travel. Office: Assn Enterprises, 840 Melton Rd, LE4 8BN Thurmaston Leicester, England

GRIMES, CRAIG ALAN, electrical engineering educator; b. Ann Arbor, Mich., Nov. 6, 1956; s. Dale Mills and Janet LaVonne (Moore) G.; m. Elizabeth Carol Dickey, 1998. BS in Physics, Pa. State U., 1984, BSEE, 1984; MS, U. Tex., 1985, PhD, 1990. Engr. Applied Rsch. Labs., Austin, Tex., 1981-83; pres. Crale, Inc., Austin, 1985-90; rsch. scientist Lockeed Rsch. Labs., Palo Alto, Calif., 1990-92; dir. advanced materials lab. Southwall Techs., Palo Alto, Calif., 1992-94; asst. prof. dept. elec. engring. U. Ky., Lexington, 1994-98, assoc. prof., 1998-2000; Frank J. Derbyshire prof. U. Ky., 2000—, dir. Ctr. for Micro-Magnetic and Electronic Devices, 2000—; rsch. asst. U. Tex., Austin, 1985-88, teaching asst., 1987-90; cons. Eastman Kodak, San Diego, 1989, Storage Tech., Boulder, Colo., 1989, Read-Rite, Fremont, Calif., 1994, AT&T Bell Labs., Murray Hill, N.J., 1995; mem. Clark County Rural Electric Coop. Co-author: Essays on the Formal Aspects of E&M Theory, 1992, Advanced Electromagnetism: Foundation, Theory and Applications, 1995; contbr. articles to profl. jours. Active Nature Conservancy, 1988-95, Austin Triathletes, 1987-90. Mem. AAAS, IEEE, Bluegrass Masters. Achievements include 6 patents, 2 pending in field; development and manufacture of permeameters, magnetic measurement tools for high frequency permeability measurements; development of size independent antennae. E-mail: grimes@engr.uky.edu. Home: 525 Mccalls Mill Rd Lexington KY 40515-9719 Office: U Ky Dept Elec Engring 453 Anderson Hl Lexington KY 40506-0001

GRIMES, HEILAN YVETTE, publishing executive; b. Hamilton, Ohio, Sept. 16, 1949; d. J and Claudette (Hinkle) G. Grad., New Eng. Sch. Photography, 1987. Founder, pres. Dot & Line Graphics, 1975—, Color Computer Weekly, 1982—, Hollow Earth Pub., 1983—. Author: Norse Mythology, 1984, Legend of Niebelungenlied, 1984, Using QuarkXPress 3.3, 1994, Beginning Internet, 1994, Filemaker Pro Developer's Guide, 1997; founder Byte Mag., 1974, Macpower Mag., 1993. Recipient various photographic awards and grants. Democrat. Avocations: magic, juggling, hiking, traveling. E-mail: yvettegr@hotmail.com. Office: PO Box 1355 Boston MA 02205-1355

GRIMES, JAMES GORDON, geologist; b. Kenosha, Wis., Mar. 18, 1951; s. James Gordon Bennett Jr. and Alyce Louise (Gannaway) G. BS in Earth Sci., U. Wis., Parkside, 1974; MS in Geology, Mich. Tech. U., 1977. Registered profl. geologist, Tenn. Geologist nat. uranium resource evaluation project Union Carbide Corp. Nuclear Div., Oak Ridge, Tenn., 1977-84; geol. cons. UCC-ND Mercury Task Force, Oak Ridge, 1983; geologist Lockheed Martin Energy Systems Inc., Oak Ridge, Tenn., 1984-99; tech. mgr. Y-12 plant Meterol. Info. Support System, 1987-96. Mem. AAAS, Am. Statis. Assn., Am. Meteorol. Soc., Am. Mgmt. Assn., Am. Water Resources Assn., Nat. Weather Assn., Geol. Soc. Am., Am. Nuc. Soc., Air and Waste Mgmt. Assn., Internat. Assn. Math. Geology.

GRIMES, JOYCE METTS, librarian; b. Columbia, S.C., Dec. 6, 1946; d. Carlisle Eusebius and Ruth (Cannon) Metts; m. Jimmy W. Grimes, Apr. 24, 1971; children: J. Bartley, J. Reid. BS, Limestone U., Gaffney, S.C., 1985; MLIS, U. S.C., 1997. Cert. assoc. profl. mgr., real estate. Broker S.C. Real Estate Commn., Columbia, 1985—; legis. libr. S.C. Gen. Assembly. Mem. Toastmasters (sec.-treas. 1999—).

GRIMES, MARGARET WHITEHURST, artist, educator; b. New Bern, N.C., June 5, 1943; d. Alan Pendleton and Margaret (Whitehurst) G. BA, Gov. State U., 1975, MA, 1976; postgrad., Notre Dame U., 1977; MFA, U. Pa., 1980. Instr. drawing and design Thornton C.C., Chgo., 1974-79; prof. painting and drawing Western Conn. State U., Danbury, 1980—, asst. chair, 1991-92, coord., master fine arts program, 2000; guest lectr./critic Vt. Coll. of Norwich U., Montepelier, 1995-96, Vt. Studio Ctr., Johnson, 1995, Tanglewood Inst., Lenox, Mass., 1997, S.V.A. Conf. on Liberal Arts and the Edn. of Artists, 1997, Ctrl. Conn. State U., New Britain, 1997, Weir Farm Nat. Hist. Site, Wilton, Conn., 1998. Co-editor New Art Assn. Newsletter, 1971; one woman shows include Green Mountain Gallery, N.Y., 1979, Blue Mountain Gallery, N.Y., 1980-2000, Fischbach Gallery, N.Y., 1986, Moravian Coll., Bethlehem, Pa., 1990, Western Conn. State U., 1990, 98, Ctrl. Conn. State U., 1997, Washington Art Assn., 1990, 2000; three-person show Provincetown Group Gallery, Mass., 1987; exhibited in group shows at Internat. Women's Art Festival, Walker Art Inst., 1976, Woodmere Mus., Phila., 1977, Provincetown Art Mus., Mass., 1978, Reading Mus., Pa., 1983, Queens Mus., N.Y., 1983, Rahr-West Mus., Manitowac, Wis., 1983, Columbus (Ohio) Mus. of Art, 1987, Katherina Rich Perlow Gallery, 1987, 88, 89, 76th Am. ann. show Newport (R.I.) Mus., 1988, Erector Sq. Gallery, New Haven, Conn., 1994, Kline Gallery, 1994, Creiger-Dane Gallery, Boston, 1995, Park Ave. Atrium, N.Y.C., 1995, Wilmington (Del.) Ctr. for Contemporary Art, 1996, Conn. State U. biennial, 1987-99, Blue Mountain Gallery, 1980-2000, Bachelier-Cardonsky Gallery, Kent, Conn., 1996, 97, 98, Philbrook Museum, Tulsa, Okla., Ringling Museum of Art, Sarasota, Fla., Davenport Museum, Iowa, 1999-2000; represented in permanent collections at Pitts. Plate Glass Co., Conn. Ins. Group, N.Am. Christian Sci. Ch. Ctr., Boston, U.S. Tobacco Co., Bellevue Hosp., N.Y. Recipient Disting. Lectureship award Henry Barnard Found., 1990; rsch. grantee in painting Conn. State U., 1985; named Disting. Prof. Conn. State U., 1992. Mem. AAUP (grantee 1986, 90, 91, 93), Coll. Art Assn. Home: 27 Wykeham Rd Washington CT 06793-1308

GRIMES, RUTH ELAINE, city planner; b. Palo Alto, Calif., Mar. 4, 1949; d. Herbert George and Irene (Williams) Baker; m. Charles A. Grimes, July 19, 1969 (div. 1981); 1 child, Michael; m. Roger L. Sharpe, Mar. 20, 1984; 1 child, Teresa. AB summa cum laude, U. Calif., Berkeley, 1970, M in City Planning, 1972. Rsch. and evaluation coord. Ctr. Ind. Living, Berkeley, 1972-74; planner City of Berkeley, 1974-76, sr. planner, 1983—, analyst, 1976-83; bd. dirs. Vets. Asssistance Ctr., Berkeley, pres., 1978-93; bd. dirs. Berkeley Design Advocates, treas., 1987-94. Author: Berkeley Downtown Plan, 1988; contbr. numerous articles to profl. jours. and other publs. Bd. dirs. Berkeley-Sakai Sister City Assn., 1994—, pres., 1995-97, Ctr. Ind. Living. Honored by Calif. State Assembly Resolution, 1988; Edwin Frank Kraft scholar, 1966. Mem. Am. Inst. Cert. Planners, Am. Planning Assn., Mensa, Lake Merrit Joggers and Striders (sec. 1986-89, pres. 1991-93), Lions Internat. (bd. dirs. Berkeley club 1992-94, 2000—, v.p. 1997-98, pres. 1998-99, chair membership com. 1999-2000), U. Calif. Coll. Environ. Design Alumni Assn. (bd. dirs. 1992-98, treas. 1994-96, disting. alumnus com. 1997—). Avocation: long distance running. Home: 1330 Bonita Ave Berkeley CA 94709-1925 Office: City of Berkeley 2121 Mckinley Ave Berkeley CA 94703-1519

GRIMES-FREDERICK, DOROTHEA D., communications executive; b. New Orleans; d. Morris and Rosemary (Birch) Grimes; m. John H. Frederick. BS in Physics, So. U., Baton Rouge; EDD, Rutgers U., 1980. Mem. tech. staff. Bell Labs., 1980-85; engrng. tech. mgr. Bell Labs., Middletown, N.J., 1985-88; product assurance tech. dir. Bell Labs., Parsippany, N.J., 1989-93; dir. bus. devel. AT&T, Middletown, 1993-95; internat. mkt. mgr. Lucent Techs., Basking Ridge, N.J., 1995-97, dir. global bus. ops., 1997-99; dir. e-bus. competitive insight Lucent Techs., 1999—. Contbr. articles to profl. jours. Mem. Exec. Women's Forum, Summit, N.J., 1988, bd. dirs., 1989-93. Mem. NAACP, Nat. Platform Assn., C. of C.

GRIMM, CLAYFORD THOMAS, architectural engineer, consultant; b. Buchannon, W.Va., July 31, 1924; s. Clayford Thomas and Genevieve Fallon Grimm; m. Elide Lucy Medone, Dec. 27, 1946; 1 child, Rose Marie. BArchE, Cath. U. Am., 1949. Sr. lectr. archtl. engrng. U. Tex., Austin, 1969-91; pres. Clayford T. Grimm, P.E., Inc.; cons. archtl. engrs., Austin. Contbr. over 168 articles to profl. jours. Pres. Serra Club, Austin, 1970-71. With AUS, 1943-46. Fellow ASTM (Walter C. Voss award 1994), ASCE (life); mem. The Masonry Soc. (hon., Pres. award 1995), Constrn. Specifications Inst. (spl. award edn.), Brit. Masonry Soc. (hon.). Republican. Roman Catholic. Home: 1904 Wooten Dr Austin TX 78757-7702

GRIMSELL, COLIN PETER, hotel executive, consultant; b. London, Jan. 10, 1934; arrived in South Africa; s. Reginald Henry and Doris May (Simpkins) G.; m. Ruby Lillian Lee, May 22, 1954 (div. 1978); children: Jane Catherine, Sarah Helen, Victoria Louise; m. Tersia Leiding, June 24, 1978; children: Laura Julie, Amelia Ann. Mgr. Royal Sportsman Hotel, Portmadoc, North Wales, 1964-66, Royal Hotel Ltd, Ventnor, Isle of Wight, 1966-71; gen. mgr. Both Worlds, Gibraltar for Trust Houses Forte Internat., 1971-72, Five Star Apollonia Beach Hotel, Cyprus, 1972-73, Reina Cristina, Algeciras, Spain, 1974, Malibu Hotel, Durban, South Africa, 1974-79; hotel ops. mgr So. Sun Hotels, Cape Town, South Africa, 1979-80, regional mgr., 1980-81; group purchasing mgr. So. Sun Hotels, Johannesburg, 1981-84, dir. group svcs., 1984-89; dir. quality control So. Sun Hotels, Holiday Inns, Johannesburg, 1989-92; dir., owner Hotel Performance Cons., Johannesburg, 1992—; dir. South African Trainers, Cons. and Svc. Providers to Hospitality Industry, 1996-99; bd. mem. Hospitality Industries Tng. Bd., South Africa, 1998-99; com. mem. Tourism Bus. Coun. South Africa, 1998-99. Author: Stocks Hotels Policy and Procedure Manual, 1996-99, Michelangelo Hotel (Johannesurg) Operating Manual, 1997; editor: Stocks, Hotels, Casino Division, Table Procedures; joint author: Hotel and Resort Design and Development Procedures, 1998. Flight lt. RAF, 1952-56. Avocation: African Game Watching. Office: Hotel Performance Cons, PO Box 417, Riveria, Johannesburg 2128, South Africa

GRIMSSON, OLAFUR RAGNAR, President of Iceland; b. Isafjordur, Iceland, May 14, 1943; married; 2 children. BA in Econs. and Polit. Sci., Manchester U., 1965, PhD in Polit. Sci., 1970. Mem. Econ. Coun. Iceland, 1966-68; bd. mem. Progressive Party's Youth Fedn., 1966-73; exec. bd. mem. Progressive Party, 1971-73; bd. mem. Icelandic Broadcasting Svc., 1971-75; prof. polit. sci. U. Iceland, 1973-92; alt. mem. parliament Govt. of Iceland, 1974, 75, chmn. exec. bd. Liberal and Left Alliance, 1974-75, rep. Reykjavik parliament, 1978-83, rep. Reykjanes, 1991-96, chmn. Parliamentary Group of People's Alliance Party, 1980-83, mem. Parliamentary Assembly of Coun. of Europe, 1980-84, 95, alt. rep. Reykjavik, 1984, 85, alt. rep. Rykjanes, 1987-90, leader People's Alliance Party, 1987-95, 91-96, min. fin., 1988-91; to Pres.

of Iceland, Reykjavík, 1996—; vice chmn. Icelandic Security Commn., 1979-90. Office: Office Pres, Sóleyjargarta 1, 150 Reykjavik Iceland

GRIMSTON, MALCOLM CHARLES, science educator; b. Cleethorpes-Lincolnshire, England; s. Arnold and Ena (Wilcox) G. BA with honors, Open U., Milton Keynes, England, 1993; MA, Magdalene Coll., Cambridge, England, 1979. Chemistry tchr. Stowe Sch., Buckingham, England, 1980-83, Millfield Sch., Somerset, England, 1983-87; dir. public presentations UK Atomic Energy Authority, London, 1987-92; energy issues adviser British Nuclear Industry Forum, London, 1992-95; sr. rsch. fellow Imperial Coll. Ctr. for Environ. Tech., London, 1995-99, Royal Inst. Internat. Affairs, Chatham House, London, 1999—. Author: Chernobyl & Bhopal Ten Years On, 1997, Leukemia and Nuclear Establishments, 1999, Coal as an Energy Source, 1999; contbr. articles to profl. jours. Gov. Sheringdale Sch., London, 1994—; councillor West Hill Ward Wandsworth Borough Coun., London, 1994—; chmn. housing com., 1997-98, edn. com. 1998—. Mem. Conservative Party. Avocations: singing, bridge, squash. Home: 67 Trevelyan Rd, SW179LR London England Office: Royal Inst Internat Affairs, 10 St James's Sq Chatham Ho, SW14 4LE London England

GRIMWADE, FREDERICK SHEPPARD, finance company executive; b. Melbourne, Victoria, Australia, June 23, 1958; s. Frederick Sheppard and Joan Elizabeth (Rich) G.; m. Alexandra Jane Fry, Oct. 7, 1989; children: Frederick Sheppard, Mary Elizabeth, Olivia Rose, Russell Richard. LLB with honors, B Comm, Melbourne U., 1981; diploma, Securities Inst. of Australia, Melbourne, 1983; MBA, Columbia U., 1985. Solicitor Mallesons Stephen Jaques, Melbourne, 1981-83; summer assoc. McKinsey & Co., Melbourne, 1984; assoc. Goldman Sachs & Co., N.Y., 1985-87; assoc., v.p. Goldman Sachs (Australia), Sydney, 1988-89; co. sec., gen. mgr. shareholder rels. Western Mining Corp. Ltd., Melbourne, 1989-95; group co. sec., gen. mgr. legal affairs Colonial, Melbourne, 1996-98; gen. mgr. corp. devel. Colonial First State Investments, 1998—, head pvt. capital, 2000—. Fellow Inst. Corp. Mgrs., Secs. and Adminstrs. Ltd., Securities Inst. of Australia; mem. Australian Club, Melbourne Club. Avocations: farming, skiing. Office: Colonial, 330 Collins St, Melbourne Victoria 3000, Australia

GRIMWADE, RICHARD LLEWELLYN, lawyer; b. Chgo., Apr. 26, 1945; s. Eric Illingworth and Pauline J. (Crandall) G.; m. Alexandra M. Galbraith, Feb. 22, 1981; children: Eric Montgomery, Sarah Elizabeth. BA, Lawrence U., 1967; JD cum laude, U. Wis., 1971. Bar: Wis. 1971, N.Y. 1971, Ill. 1978, Calif. 1981, U.S. Dist. Ct. (so. and ea. dists.) N.Y., 1971, U.S. Dist. Ct. (no. dist.) Wis., 1971, U.S. Dist. Ct. (no. dist.) Ill., 1978, U.S. Dist. Ct. (ctrl. dist.) Calif., 1981, U.S. Ct. Appeals (2d cir.) 1971, U.S. Ct. Appeals (7th cir.) 1978, U.S. Ct. Appeals (9th cir.) 1981. Atty. Davis Polk, N.Y.C., 1971-75; ptnr. Barton Klugman, L.A., 1983-93; pvt. practice L.A., 1993—. Mem. U. Wis. Law Rev., 1969-71. Bd. mgrs. Ketchum Downtown YMCA, L.A., 1991-97; trustee Reform L.A. Pub. Schs. (LEARN), 1993-97. Recipient 3 Am. Jurisprudence awards for evidence, legis., and acctg. and law Bancroft-Whitney, 1970. Mem. State Bar Calif., State Bar Wis., State Bar N.Y., State Bar Ill., Rotary L.A. (bd. dirs. 1991-93, sec. 1994), Toastmasters (Best Spkr. award, Best Performer award 1996, Best Table Topics award 1997), Order of Coif. Avocations: gardening, poetry, running, public speaking, history. Office: MCI Center 700 S Flower St Ste 1100 Los Angeles CA 90017-4113

GRINDE, KJELL, oil company executive; b. Bergen, Norway, Aug. 1, 1929; s. Lars and Hanna (Birkeland) G.; divorced; children: Lars, Eva; m. Anneliv Hoset; stepchildren: Cèline, Vilde. MS in Civil Engring., Tech. U. Norway, Trondheim, 1954. Scientific asst. Tech. U. Norway, 1954-56; control engr. Snowy Mt. Hydro-Electric Authority, New South Wales, Australia, 1956-58; site engr. Norconsult A.S., Ethiopia, 1958-61; resident mgr. Norconsult A.S., Lagos, Nigeria, 1961-64; mktg. dir. Norconsult A.S., Oslo, Norway, 1964-69; mng. dir. Norconsult A.S., 1969-81; tech. dir. Saga Petroleum, A.S., Oslo, 1981-87; dir. corp. staff Saga Petroleum, A.S., 1987-94; owner Grinde Sr. Cons., 1994—; bd. dirs., pres. Internat. Fedn. Cons. Engrs., The Hague, The Netherlands, 1973-81; chmn. bd. Norwegian Petroleum Cons., 1975-80; chmn. bd. Sr. Expert Group. Recipient Honors award Norwegian Natural Scis. Rsch. Coun., 1979. Mem. Norwegian Polytech. Soc., Norwegian Acad. Tech. Scis., Norwegian Soc. Profl. Engrs., Norwegian Petroleum Soc. Home and OFfice: Hanna Winsnesgt 1, 3014 Drammen Norway

GRINDE, TURID VOGT, psychologist, researcher; b. Trondheim, Norway, Nov. 23, 1923; d. Fredrik and Signe (Fjalstad) Vogt; m. Hans Grinde, Jan. 4, 1946; children: Geir, Bjørn, Gunner. Candidate of psychology, U. Oslo, 1948; MPH, U. Calif., Berkeley, 1976. Rsch. asst., lectr. U. Oslo, 1949-51; clinician, rschr. Ctr. Inst. Cerebral Palsy, Oslo, 1960-66; sch. psychologist Baerum, Norway, 1967-69; cons. Ministry Health and Social Affairs, Oslo, 1969-79, head of child welfare, 1979-83; project mgr. Nordic Coun. of Ministers, 1983-89; sr. rschr. Ministry of Children and Family Affairs, Oslo, 1989—, Norwegian Social Rsch., Oslo, 1989—; organizer, participant Nordic and internat. confs. Author: Children and Child Welfare in the Nordic Countries, 1989, The Knowledge Base of Child Welfare, 1993, Child Welfare Complaints and Legal Rights, 1996; contbr. articles to profl. jours. Main author proposal law for psychologists, Norwegian Parliament, 1972. Mem. APA (affiliate), Norwegian Psychol. Assn. (chmn. 1963-65, 68-69), Norwegian Rschrs., Internat. Soc. Prevention Child Abuse and Neglect, Assn. Child Psychology and Psychiatry. Avocations: family activities, outdoor activities, travel. E-mail: Turid.V.Grinde@isa/.mo. Home: Gml Drammensvei 184 B, 1336 Sandvika Norway Office: Norwegian Social Rsch, Munthes gt 29, 0260 Oslo Norway

GRINDEA, DANIEL, international economist; b. Galatz, Romania, Feb. 23, 1924; came to U.S., 1975; s. Samy and Liza (Kaufman) Grünberg; m. Lidia Bunaciu; 1 child, Sorin. MS in Econs., Inst. Econ Scis., Bucharest, Romania, 1948; MLaw, Faculty of Law, Bucharest, 1948; PhD in Econs., Inst. Fin. and Planning, St. Petersburg, Russia, 1953. Assoc. prof. econs. various univs., Bucharest, 1953-69, prof. econs., 1969-75; cons. State Planning Com., 1953-56, Ministry of Fin., 1956-68; mem. Sci. Coun. of Ctrl. Statis. Office, 1956-68; internat. economist Republic Nat. Bank of N.Y., N.Y.C., 1976-78, sr. internat. economist, dept. head, 1978-79, v.p., sr. internat. economist, 1979-84, sr. v.p., chief economist, 1984-89, sr. cons., 1990-95; pres. Romanian-Am. C. of C., N.Y.C., 1990-92; sr. advisor U.S. Congl. Adv. Bd., 1988; prof., elected mem. sci. coun. l'Ecole Supérieur des Scis. Commls. d'Angers, France, 1989; mem. econ. adv. bd. Inst. Internat. Fin., Washington, 1988; invited vis. prof. l'Institut Internat. de la Planification de l'Edn., UNESCO, Paris, 1973; mem. adv. group Com. on Asian Econ. Studies, 1983. Contbr. articles on forecasts in field to U.S. and internat. publs.; papers presented to profl. confs. in U.S., France, Sweden, Ireland, Bulgaria, Romania. Recipient 1st prize in econ. rsch. Ministry of Edn., Romania, 1969, Book award Am. Romanian Acad. Art and Scis., 1995, 98, emeritus mem., 1998. Achievements include correct predictions on world economy and individual countries; special research regarding the transition period to a free market economy in the ex-communist European countries.

GRINDLE, WILLIAM HENRY, music educator, church musician; b. Bangor, No. Ireland, Oct. 2, 1935; s. Harry Edward and Agnes Jean (Atkinson) G.; m. Heather Marianne Loane, Aug. 6, 1968; children: Hannah, Rachel. BA, Queen's U., Belfast, No. Ireland, 1957, MA, 1980; MusB (1st Class), Trinity Coll., Dublin, 1978, PhD, 1985; ARSCM, Royal Sch. Ch. Music, Croydon, Surrey, Eng., 1977; LRAM diploma, Royal Acad. of Music; ARCM diploma, Royal Coll. of Music. Tchr. French and music Friern Barnet Grammar Sch., London, 1961-62; organist, choirmaster Bangor Parish Ch., 1962-64; organist, master of the choristers Belfast Cathedral, 1964-75; tchr. music Ashleigh House Girls' Sch., Belfast, 1973-75; sr. lectr. in music Stranmillis Coll., Belfast, 1975-91, head dept. music, 1991-98, ret., 1998; mem. com. Down, Dromore and Connor Diocesan Organ Scholarship Mgmt. Bd.; tutor organ-playing course Armagh Ch. Choir Union; examiner Royal Irish Acad. Music, Dublin; adjudicator, lectr., workshop facilitator; music cons. Irish Ch. Hymnal Rev. com. Author: Irish Cathedral Music, 1989; contbr. articles to Ch. of Ireland Gazette, The Organists Rev.; pub. compositions include Prelude on the tune University for organ, 1976, What is that Light? Carol for SATB and organ, 1988. Mem. Belfast Music Festival Com.; diocesan rep. Royal Sch. Ch. Music. Recipient Prout and Stewart prize Trinity Coll., 1978; John Vine Meml. Bursary grantee Belfast Mus. Festival, 1960. Fellow Trinity Coll. of Music, Royal Coll. Organists (John Brooke Meml. prize for choir-tng. 1963); mem. Ulster Soc. Organists and Choirmasters (pres. 1986-87), Royal Sch. Ch. Music (assoc.). Anglican. Avocations: reading, gardening, walking, spectator sports. E-mail: harry.grindle@talk21.com. Home: 37 Cairnburn Crescent, Belfast BT4 2HU, Northern Ireland

GRINDLEY, BRUCE ALAN, real estate agency executive; b. Woking, England, Mar. 1, 1948; s. Ernest and Ivy (Mummery) G. Brokerage clk. Leslie & Godwin, Lloyds Brokers, London, 1965-67; from enquiry clk. to br. mgr. Abbey Life, London, Croydon, Crawley, England, 1967-86; dir. Sunway Properties, Tenerife, Spain, 1986-94, Tenerife Property Shop, 1994—. Recipient Winner Best Internat. Estate Agt. Gold award 1996-97, Best Internat. Residential Estate Agent, 1997-98, Best Spanish Estate Agent Gold award, 1998-99, 99-2000. Fellow Life Ins. Assn.; mem. Internat. Real Estate Inst., Nat. Assn. Estate Agts. Office: Tenerife Property Shop SL, 117 Puerto Colon, Playa de las Americas Adeje Tenerife, Spain

GRINNELL, JOSEPH FOX, financial company executive; b. July 4, 1923; s. Robert L. and Mary King G.; m. Marjorie Volwiler, Aug. 24, 1946; children: Stephen F., Christine K. Burcham, James W. BA, Yale U., 1945; JD, Northwestern U., 1949. Bar: Ill. 1949, U.S. Dist. Ct. (no. dist.) Ill. 1949, Minn. 1954. Assoc. Winston-Strawn, Chgo., 1949-54; sr. v.p. law Investors Diversified Svcs., Mpls., 1954-83; of counsel Pepin Dayton Herman Graham & Getts, Mpls., 1983-87. Bd. dirs. Guthrie Theater, Mpls., 1970-71, Minn. Orch. Assn., Mpls., 1976-78; bd. dirs., chmn. Minn. Pollution Control Agy., Mpls., 1973-81. Served to lt. (j.g.) USN, 1942-46, PTO. Democrat. Presbyterian. Home: 6101 Idylwood Dr Minneapolis MN 55436-1232

GRINO, RENE SUDARIO, educator; b. ILoilo Province, The Philippines, June 24, 1947; s. Elenito Golenda and Rosaline (Sudario) G.; m. Benecia Gapasin Vanderwoude, July 23, 1970 (div. June 1985); children: Jonathan, Rene Jr., Christopher, Allan. BS in Edn., Notre Dame U., Cotabato City, The Philippines, 1968; MS in Edn., PLM2, 1980; EdD, U. So. Mindanao, 1997. Instr. Mindanao Inst. Tech., Kabacan, Cotabato, 1970-80; asst. prof. U. So. Mindanao, Kabacan, Cotabato, 1980-89, assoc. prof., 1990-97, assoc. prof. V, 1997—. Advisor Boy Scouts of the Philippines, Cotabato, 1975—; instr. Philippine Nat. Red Cross Orgn., Cotabato, 1975—; vol. Philippines Red Cross. 1st lt. Philippine Army, 1980-81, capt. res., 1998. Decorated Mil. Merit medal, 1996; recipient Outstanding Jaycee of the Yr. award Golden Grain Jaycees, 1983; Sci. Found. of the Philippines scholar, 1980-81. Mem. Masons, AFP Reservists (bd. dirs. 1990-97, Outstanding Reservist of the Yr. 1998). Avocations: practical shooting, mountaineering, forest conservation, cross country biking. Home: Univ of So Mindanao, Cottage #01, Kabacan Cotabato, The Philippines

GRINSTEIN, YURY ISAYEVICH, physician; b. Achinsk, Russia, Apr. 21, 1950; s. Isay Borisovich and Yelisaveta Vasilyevna (Torgashina) G.; m. Alla Rudolfovna Zeliger, Feb. 2, 1979; children: Igor, Ann. PhD, Cen. Rsch. Inst. Hematology, and Blood Transfusion, Moscow, 1985; MD, Siberian Med. U., Tomsk, Russia, 1994; Prof., Med. Acad., Krasnoyarsk, Russia, 1995. Student Med. Inst., Krasnoyarsk, Russia, 1969-75; intern Regional Clin. Hosp., Krasnoyarsk, Russia, 1975-76; nephrologist Regional Clin. Hosp., Krasnoyarsk, 1976-80; asst. lectr. Med. Inst., Krasnoyarsk, 1980-92, asst. prof., chair internal diseases N2, 1992-94; prof., head of chair of therapy Med. Acad., Krasnoyarsk, 1994—; vice-rector on postgrad. edn. Med. Acad., Krasnoyarsk, 1996-98; supr. Regional Ctr. Intensive Cardiology and Cardiac-Vascular Surgery, Krasnoyarsk, 1998—. Author: (book) The Diagnosis and Treatment of Glomerulonephritis, 1995; inventor in field. Grantee Georg Soros Internat. Scientific Fund. Mem. European Renal Assn., N.Y. Acad. Scis. Home: 147-44, Krasnoyarsky Rabochy Str, 660093 Krasnoyarsk Russia Office: Med Acad, P Zheleznyak Str 1, 660022 Krasnoyarsk Russia

GRINYER, PETER HUGH, business educator, management consultant; b. London, Mar. 3, 1935; s. Sydney George and Grace (Forhals) G; m. Sylvia Joyce Boraston, 1958. BA, U. Oxford, 1957, MA, 1961; PhD in Applied Econs., London Sch. Econs., 1968. Sr. managerial trainee Unilever plc, London, 1957-59; p.a. to CEO, mgr. prodn. planning and stock control E.R. Holloway Ltd., Welwyn Garden City, Eng., 1959-61; from asst. lectr. to sr. lectr. Hendon Coll. Tech., London, 1961-64; lectr. The City U., London, 1964-69, sr. lectr., 1969-72, reader, 1972-74, prof. bus. strategy, 1974-79; Esmee Fairbairn prof. U. St. Andrews, Scotland, 1979-93; prof. emeritus and part-time U. St. Andrews, 1993—, vice-prin., 1985-87, acting prin., 1986, chmn. mgmt. inst., 1989-95; vis. prof. Stern Sch. Bus. NYU, 1996—, mem. univ. grants sub-com. mgmt. & bus. studies, 1979-85. Co-author: Corporate Models Today, 1975, 2nd edit., 1979, From Private to Public, 1977, Turnaround: The Fall and Rise of Newton Chambers, 1979, Sharpbenders, 1988, Organising Strategy: Sun Tzu Business Warcraft, 1994; mem. editl. bd. Strategic Mgmt. Jour., Managerial and Decision Economics, Jour. Gen. Mgmt.; contbr. 60 articles to profl. jours. em. Scottish Legal Aid Bd., Edinburgh, 1991-2000; mem. appeals tribunal panel C competition Commn., 2000—. Mem. Brit. Acad. Mgmt., Acad. Mgmt. (USA). Baptist. Avocations: golf, mountain walking, gardening, music. Home: 60 Buchanan Gdns, KY16 9AL Saint Andrews Fife, Scotland Office: U St Andrews Dept Mgmt, North St, KY16 9AL Saint Andrews Fife, Scotland

GRINYOV, BORIS VICTOROVICH, science administrator; b. Kharkov, Ukraine, Apr. 1, 1956; s. Victor Borisovich and Nataliya Fedorovna (Kurinaya) G.; m. Tatyana Volislavovna Vovna, Oct. 16, 1976; children: Tatyana, Victoriya. Diploma in physics, Kharkov State U., 1978, Candidate Phys. Math. Scis., 1985, D in Tech. Scis., 1994. Jr. rsch. worker Kharkov State U., 1978-82; sr. rsch. worker Inst. for Single Crystals, Kharkov, 1987-88, head lab., 1992-93, sci. sec., 1993-94, dir. sci. and rsch. dept. alkali halide crystals, 1995-96, gen. dir. sci. and tech. concern, 1997—; head working group of sci. and tech. collaboration Rsch. and Tech. Orgn. NATO, Ukraine; dep. head working group Internat. Collaboration on Physics of High Energy; mem. Nat. Commn. Ukraine in UNESCO Affairs. Author: (with V.P. Seminozhenko) Scintillation Detectors of Ionizing Radiation for Heavy Conditions of Application, 1993, (with L.V. Atroschenko, S.F. Burachas, L.P. Gal'chinetsky) Crystals of Scintillators and Detectors of Ionizing Radiation Based on Them, 1998; mem. editl. bd. Functional Materials Jour.; contbr. articles to profl. jours. Recipient State Prize of Ukraine on Sci. and Tech., 1996. Mem. Nat. Acad. Sci. Ukraine (corr.). Achievements include 54 patents in field. Avocations: driving, fishing. Office: State Com for Sci, Shevchenko Ave 16, 252030 Kiev Ukraine

GRIP, CARL-ERIK, research metallurgist; b. Åtvidaberg, Sweden, June 22, 1940; s. Erik Konrad and Maj Elisabeth (Johansson) G.; m. Ingalill Anita Hoffner, Apr. 5, 1969; children: Niklas, Helena. MSc, Royal Inst. Tech., 1966, D of Engring., 1971, PhD, 1998. Rsch. and devel. engr. Metallurg. Rsch. Plant, Luleå, Sweden, 1966-71; rsch. and devel. engr. Norrbotten Steel Ltd., Luleå, 1971-74, sect. leader, 1974-76, rsch. and devel. dept. mgr., 1976-86; mgr. energy optimization SSAB (formerly Norbotten Steel Ltd.), Luleå, 1987-92, sr. rsch. metallurgist, 1992—. Contbr. articles to profl. jours. Capt. Swedish Army Res., 1960-95. Mem. CF Trade Union (pres. 1981-88, v.p. 1988—), Iron and Steel Inst. of Japan, Iron and Steel Soc., Jernkontoret (bd. dirs. rsch. energy area 1990—). Home: Vallstengatan 7, S 97342 Luleå Sweden Office: SSAB Tunnplåt AB, S97188 Luleå Sweden

GRIPPA, LUIGI, chemical engineer; b. Milan, May 15, 1942; s. Lodovico and Domenica (Franzoni) G.; m. Vittoria Maria Compostella, May 20, 1967; children: Pietro, Stefano. D in Chem. Engring., Poli. Milano, 1966. Prodn. mgr. Lepetit, Italy, 1973-78, project mgr., 1979-80; dir. engring. Dow Chem., Italy, 1981-86; tech. dir. Italy, 1990-94; project mgr. Biochimica del Salento, Italy, 1987-89; engring. mgr. Hoechst Marion Roussel, Italy, 1995-99; engr. dir. Aventis Pharma, Italy, 2000—; tchr. Poli. Milan, 1972-74, courses for project mgrs., Rotterdam, The Netherlands, 1989-94. Contbr. articles to profl. jours. Mem. Ordine Ingegneri Milano, Alpine Club. Avocations: numismatics, alpinism, gardening. Home: Via Sismondi 53, 20133 Milan Italy Office: Aventis Pharma, Via R Lepetit 8, 20020 Lainate Italy

GRISAR, JOHANN MARTIN, retired research chemist; b. Görlitz, Germany, July 10, 1929; came to U.S., 1955, naturalized, 1962; s. Charles Martin and Dora (Stoess) G.; m. Carol Lee Hanson, Jan. 2, 1960 (div. Aug. 1981); children: Caia, Margot, Paul; m. Gabriele L. von Oettingen, June 25, 1983. Diploma in chemistry, Swiss Fed. Inst. Tech., Zurich, 1954; PhD, MIT, 1959. Rsch. chemist Marion Merrell Dow Inc. (formerly Wm. S. Merrell Co.), Cin., 1963-81, Strasbourg, France, 1981-93; ret., 1993. Contbr. articles to profl. jours.; inventor, patentee in field drug rsch. Mem. Am. Chem. Soc. Home: 7 Rue de Mulhouse, 67160 Wissembourg France

GRISHAM, ANDREW FLETCHER, aerospace engineer, consultant; b. Nashville, Feb. 23, 1937; s. Albert Harding and Gladys Katella (Harmon) G.; m. Marilyn Jean Crerar, Sept. 2, 1967; children: David Andrew Fletcher Grisham, Mary Kathryn Grisham Wright, Elizabeth Ann Grisham Volz. BSCE, Vanderbilt U., 1958; MSCE, U. Calif., Berkeley, 1960, post-grad., 1958-60. Civil engring. tchg. asst. U. Calif., Berkeley, 1958-59; sr. structural engr. Boeing Co., Seattle, New Orleans, 1958-73; sr. specialist engr. Boeing Co., Renton, Everett, Wash., 1973-82; prin. engr. Boeing Space Group/Marine Sys., Kent, Renton, Wash., 1982-89; sr. prin. engr. Boeing Mil. Airplane Group, Seattle, 1989-94; cons. Boeing Comml. Airplane Group, Seattle, 1989-94, Boeing Def. and Space Group Rsch., Seattle, 1994-96; cons. The Raisbeck Group, Rockwell Internat., Seattle, 1977, Superior Design Co., Bellevue, Wash., 1994-96, The Boeing Co., Bellevue, 1994-96; instr. finite element methods Boeing grad. engr. tng., Kent, Wash., 1979; chmn. cross-corp. maj. structural analysis sys., Boeing Co., Phila., Wichita, Kans., Renton, Wash., Kent, Wash., Everett, Wash., Seattle, 1988-91. Author: (Boeing mainframe sys. handbooks and software) Interfaced Structural Analysis System, 1965-87, (Boeing workstation sys. handbooks and software) Multidisciplinary Design, Analysis and Optimization System, 1987-96; author papers. Chmn. worship and music com. Trinity Methodist Ch., Seattle, 1969-75, mem. Rep. precinct com., Seattle, 1978-86, ch. organist, Seattle, 1954-73. U. Calif. grantee NSF, 1959-60; A.J. Dyer scholar Vanderbilt U., 1954-58, scholar U. Calif., 1958-60. Mem. Seattle Prof. Engring. Employees Assn., Queen City Yacht Club, Holiday Ramblers, Tau Beta Pi. Republican. Nazarene. Achievements include devel. of Boeing finite element pre- and post-processors for modeling, optimization and commonality analysis for joint (Marine, Navy, Air Force) strike fighter; developed methods for nonlinear geometric analysis of Apollo Saturn booster tank penetrations, and for analysis, including post buckling in aerospace structural finite element models for multiple load conditions using pre-strains. Avocations: travel, boating, music, politics, 9 year restoration of 1961 Rolls Royce Silver Cloud S2. Home and Office: 8713 Golden Gardens Dr NW Seattle WA 98117-3942

GRISHAM, JOHN, writer; b. Jonesboro, Ark., Feb. 8, 1955; m. Renee Jones; children: Ty, Shea. BS, Miss. State U., 1977; JD, U. Miss., 1981. Bar: Miss. 1981. Practiced law Southaven, Miss., 1981-91; mem. Miss. Ho. Reps., 1984-90. Author: A Time to Kill, 1989, The Firm, 1991, The Pelican Brief, 1992, The Client, 1993, The Chamber, 1994, The Rainmaker, 1995, The Runaway Jury, 1996, The Partner, 1997, The Street Lawyer, 1998, The Testament, 1999. Office: Doubleday Pub 1540 Broadway New York NY 10036-4039

GRISHAM, LARRY RICHARD, physicist; b. Henderson, Tex., Feb. 2, 1949; s. James Marion and Eva Fay (Powell) G.; m. Jacqueline Lea Criswell, June 24, 1972; children: Austin Nathanial, Rachel Nicole, Hilary Jane. BS in Physics, U. Tex., 1971; PhD in Physics, Oxford (Eng.) U., 1974. Postdoctoral fellow Princeton (N.J.) U., Plasma Physics Lab., 1974-75, staff rsch. physicist, 1975-82, rsch. physicist, 1982-89, prin. rsch. physicist, 1989—, head beam physics, 1988—; cons. Northrop Corp., L.A., 1985, Phys. Dynamics, La Jolla, Calif., 1986-88, Teledyne Brown Engring., Huntsville, Ala., 1989—; mem. and chmn. various rev. panels U.S. Army Strategic Def. Command, 1986—. Contbr. numerous articles to profl. jours. Mem. N.J. Rhodes Scholar Selection Com., Morristown, 1986—. Recipient Tex. Exes Centennial Honored Alumnus award U. Tex., Austin, 1985, Wolfson Grad. award, 1972; winner Westinghouse Sci. Talent Search, Washington, 1967; Rhodes scholar, 1971; Woodrow Wilson fellow, 1971, invited rsch. fellow Japan Atomic Energy Rsch. Inst., 1996. Mem. AAAS, Am. Phys. Soc., Phi Beta Kappa. Methodist. Achievements include research in energy confinement properties of tokamak plasmas as a fuction of major and minor radius; physics and technology of high power neutral beam systems physics of excited nuclear states. Avocation: hiking. Home: 2 Dennick Ct Princeton NJ 08540-2202 Office: Princeton Univ Plasma Physics Lab PO Box 451 Princeton NJ 08543-0451

GRISHCHENKOV, VLADIMIR GERMANOVICH, microbiologist, researcher; b. Kharkov, Ukraine, Aug. 8, 1948; s. German Leont'evich Grishchenkov and Vera Markovna Ravich; m. Elena Alekseevna Pukhlij, Oct. 5, 1973 (div. Oct. 1980); 1 child, Mary; m. Nina Georgievna Koretskaja, Jan. 1, 1981; children: Ann, Georgij, Konstantin. Diploma, State U., Kharkov, 1972; PhD in Biology, All-Union Inst. Genetics, Moscow, 1980. Jr. rschr. Russian Acad. Scis., Inst. Biochem./Physiol. Microorganisms, Pushchino, 1979-85, rschr., 1985-95, sr. rschr., 1995—; assoc. prof. Pushchino State U., 1996—; vice-chmn. lab. of biology plasmids Russian Acad. Scis., Inst. Biochem. and Physiol. Microorganisms, Pushchino, 1980—. Contbr. articles to profl. jours.; inventor in field. Grantee Internat. Soros Found., 1994, Fulbright Found., 1997-98. Mem. Russian Genetic Soc. Mem. Jabloko party. Avocations: tennis, traveling. Home: Mikrorajon B dom 29 Kv 41, 142292 Pushchino Russia Office: Inst Biochem/Phys Microorg, Prospekt Nayki 5, 142292 Pushchino Russia

GRISHIN, ANATOLY MIKHAILOVICH, mechanics educator; b. Saratov, Russia, Feb. 20, 1939; s. Mikhail Nikolaevich Grishin and Antonina Ferdorovna Burmistrova; m. Samoylova Grishin, Aug. 8, 1962 (div.); children: Valery, Dmitry; m. Lyudmila Gavrilovna Grishina. Diploma in mechanics, Saratov State U., 1961; PhD in Physics and Math., Tomsk (Russia) State U., 1967, DSc in Physics and Math., 1976. Tutor dept. theoretical mechs. Saratov Poly. Inst., 1961-63; sr. lectr. dept. theoretical mechs. Tomsk (Russia) State U., 1966-67, asst. prof., 1967-71, sr. scientist, 1971-73; head sector aerothermochemistry Rsch. Inst. Applied Math. and Mechs., Tomsk State U., 1973-75, head lab. aerothermochemistry, 1977-80; head dept. phys. mechs. Tomsk State U., 1980—, dean faculty mechs. and math., 1977-80; dir. edn. and rsch. ctr. on reactive media mechs. and ecology, 1995—, dissertational coun., 1975—; Soros prof., Internat. Sci. Edn. Program, Russia, 1994—. Author: Mathematical Modeling of Forest Fires and New Methods of Fighting Them, (edited F. Albini in English), 1997 (Tomsk award 1997); co-author: Physical Gas Dynamics of Reactive Media, 1985 (Moscow award 1985), Conjugate and Non-Stationary Problems of Reactive Media Mechanics, 1984 (Novosibirsk award 1984). Honored scientist of Russian Federation, 1999—. Mem. Tomsk Soc. Mech. Scientists and Thermophysicist (chmn. 1993—), Russian Nat. Com. on Theoretical and Applied Mechanics, 1985—. Avocations: picking mushrooms, symphonies, detective stories, theater. E-mail: fire@fire.tsu.tomsk.su. Office: Tomsk State U, Lenin 36, 634050 Tomsk Russia

GRISHIN, YURI PETROVICH, electronics educator, researcher; b. Leningrad, Russia, Aug. 22, 1939; s. Piotr Ivanovich and Anastasia Pimenovna (Drozdova) G.; m. Tatiana Aleksejevna Lavrentieva, Jan. 28, 1961; 1 child, Olga Yurievna. BSc, Leningrad Elec. Engring. Inst., 1962, PhD, 1969, DSc, 1985. Rsch. engr. Leningrad Elec. Engring. Inst., 1962-66, from lectr. to sr. lectr. dept. radioelectronic sys., 1970-87; prof. Leningrad Elec. Engring. Inst., St. Petersburg, 1987-92; chief rsch. lab. short range navigation and landing sys. Leningrad Elec. Engring. Inst., 1986-92; prof. faculty elec. engring. Bialystok (Poland) Tech. U., 1992—; cons. numerous electronic equipment firms, Moscow and St. Petersburg, 1972-92. Co-author: Application of Microprocessors to Radioelectronic Systems, 1982, Fault-Tolerant Dynamic Systems, 1985, 3 textbooks. Named Hon. Radio Engr. of USSR, 1990; grantee Russian Ministry of Edn., 1993, Com. Sci. Rsch., 1993-98, Polish Rsch. Com., 1995, 96, 98—. Mem. IEEE, Russian Sci. Soc. Radioengring., Electronics and Telecom., N.Y. Acad. Scis. Mem. Orthodox Ch. Avocations: music, history, bicycling, hiking. Office: Tech U Bialystok, Wejska 45A, 15-351 Bialystok Poland

GRISI, JEAN-YVES, sales and marketing executive; b. Nice, France, Dec. 19, 1965; s. Rene and Yvonne (Duran) G. Grad., Nat. Telecomms. Sch., Paris; MBA, INSEAD. Sales mgr. SDP, Paris, 1985-87; cons. Andersen Cons., Paris, 1987-89; from tgn. ctr. mgr. to bus. solutions group dir. Microsoft, Les Ulis, France, 1991—. Avocations: tennis, travel. Home: 107 Rue Blomet, Paris France 75015 Office: Microsoft, 18 Ave de Quebec, 91957 Les Ulis France

GRISMORE, ROGER, physics educator, researcher; b. Ann Arbor, Mich., July 12, 1924; s. Grover Cleveland and May Aileen (White) G.; m. Marilynn

Ann McNinch, Sept. 15, 1950; 1 child, Carol Ann. BS, U. Mich., 1947, MS, 1948, PhD, 1957; BS in Computer Sci., Coleman Coll., 1979. From asst. to assoc. physicist Argonne (Ill.) Nat. Lab., 1956-62; assoc. prof. physics Lehigh U., Bethlehem, Pa., 1962-67; specialist in physics Scripps Inst. Oceanography, La Jolla, Calif., 1967-71, 75-78; prof. physics Ind. State U., Terre Haute, 1971-74; from mem. staff to sr. scientist JAYCOR, San Diego, 1979-84; lectr. Calif. Poly. State U., San Luis Obispo, 1984-92, rsch. prof., 1992—, lunar sample investigator, 1994—. Contbr. numerous articles to profl. jours. Served as ensign USNR, 1945-46, PTO. Mem. Am. Phys. Soc., Am. Geophys. Union, N.Y. Acad. Scis., Sigma Xi. Achievements include co-discovery of the radioisotope silver-108m in the general marine environment, and development of the technique of radiosilver dating. Home: 535 Cameo Way Arroyo Grande CA 93420-5574 Office: Calif Poly State U Dept Physics San Luis Obispo CA 93407

GRISOGONO, BRANKO, atmospheric physics educator, researcher; b. Virovitica, Slavonia, Croatia, July 30, 1959; s. Grga and Ivka (Novački) G. BS in Natural Scis. and Math., U. Zagreb, Croatia, 1983, MS in Natural scis. and Math., 1987; PhD in Physics, U. Nev., 1992; cert., Office Naval Rsch., 1996. Technician U. Zagreb, 1983, tchg. asst., 1984-86, rsch. asst., 1987-89; rsch. asst. Desert Rsch. Inst., U. Nev., Reno, 1989-92, postdoctoral fellow, 1992; postdoctoral fellow Uppsala (Sweden) U., 1993-95, asst. prof. atmospheric physics, 1995-96, assoc. prof., 1996-97; asst. prof. dynamic meteorology Stockholm U., 1997—. Co-author: USA-Croatia Scientific Cooperation, 1995; contbr. articles to sci. jours., including Jour. Atmospheric Scis., Jour. Applied Meteorology, Quar. Jour. Royal Meteorol. Soc., Jour. Geophys. Rsch. With Yugoslav Army, 1986-87. Mem. Am. Geophys. Union, Royal Meteorol. Soc. (U.K.). Office: Stockholm U, Dept Meteorology, S-10691 Stockholm Sweden

GRISSINO-MAYER, HENRI DEE, research scientist; b. Monterrey, Calif., Dec. 24, 1954; s. Keith Alva and Sigrid Leota (Mayer) Summers. BS, U. Ga., 1985, MS, 1988; PhD, U. Ariz., 1995. Tchg. asst. U. Ga., Athens, 1985-88, rsch. asst., 1986, map rm. asst., 1988; grad. rsch. assoc. U. Ariz., Tucson, 1988-95, rsch. assoc. Lab. Tree-Ring Rsch., 1995-97; asst. prof. Valdosta State U., 1997-00, U. Tenn., 2000—; mem. com. Internat. Tree-Ring Data Bank, Boulder, Colo., 1988—, internet list mgr., 1988—; group leader N.Am. Dendroecological Fieldweek, Ft. Collins, Colo., 1991—; internet list mgr. Biogeography Speciality Group, Tucson, 1992—. Adv. editl. bd. Dendrochronologia jour., 1999—; assoc. editor Jour. of Ariz.-Nev. Acad. of Sci., 1999—; contbr. articles to profl. publs., chpt. to book.; programmer software in field. Sci. grantee USDA Forest Svc., 1990-94, Nat. Park Svc., 1991-95, NOAA, 1992—, SWCA, Inc., 1996—, NSF, 1998—; recipient Alton A. Lindsey award Nat. Park Svc., 1998. Mem. Assn. Am. Geographers, Assn. Pacific Coast Geographers, Ariz./Nev. Acad. Sci., Ariz. Archeol. and Hist. Soc., Assn. Southwestern Naturalists, Internat. Tree-Ring Soc. (sec. 1999—), Ga. Acad. Sci. Avocations: camping, hiking, rare books. Office: U Tenn Dept Geography Knoxville TN 37996-0001

GRIVEAU, JEAN-FRANCOIS, biologist; b. Rennes, France, June 8, 1964; s. Guy and Marie (Joly) G.; m. Marie-Jeanne Bousseau, Aug. 21, 1988; children: Anne-Lise, Helene. BS, U. Rennes, 1986, MS, 1988, PhD, 1994. Co-in charge Unité de Biologie de la Reproduction, Rennes, 1996—. Mem. European Soc. Human Reproduction & Embryology, French Soc. Andrology, BLEFCO, CECOS. Home: 53 rue de la Pommerais, 35136 Jacques de Pa Pajde France Office: Unite de Biologie Reproduction, 1 bis rue de la Cochardiere, 35000 Rennes France

GRIVNA, MICHAL, epidemiologist, educator, administrator; b. Prague, Czech Republic, Apr. 26, 1960; s. Vasil and Ekaterina (Maximovic) G. MD, Charles U., Prague, 1985; state exam. in pediats., Prague, 1989; MPH, Va. Commonweath U., 1993; state exam. in hygiene of children/adol., Prague, 1997. Postgrad. fellow Charles U., Prague, 1985-89; rsch. asst. dept. preventive medicine Med. Coll. Va.-Va. Commonwealth U., Richmond, 1992-93; epidemiol. analyst Dept. Health, Commonwealth of Va., Richmond, 1993; asst. prof. Charles U., Prague, 1983—; dir. Ctr. for Childhood Injury Epidemiology and Prevention, Prague, 1997—. Author: (booklet) The Methodology of Injury Prevention on Community Level, 1999; editor: (newsletter) Actualities in Childhood Injury Prevention, 1996—. Mem. APHA, Czech Pediat. Soc. (chmn. childhood injury prevention bd. 1996), European Safe Cmty. Network (bd. dirs. 1999), Internat. Soc. for Child and Adolescent Injury Prevention. Avocations: classical music, traveling. Office: Ctr Childhood Injury Epidem, U Uvalu 84, 15006 Prague 5, Czech Republic

GRIZZARD-BARHAM, BARBARA LEE, artist; b. Roanoke, Va., Apr. 4, 1935; d. Alton Lee and Mable (Jewell) Grizzard; m. Charles Thomas Barham, Sr., June 25, 1955; children: Charles Thomas, Christopher. BS, Va. Commonwealth U., 1971, postgrad. Educator Colonial Heights (Va.) Sch. Sys., 1971-88; represented by Agora Gallery, N.Y.C. exhibited in solo shows at Wakefield (Va.) Ctr. for Arts, 1993, 94, Petersburg (Va.) Area Art League, 1993, 95, 2000, Rappahannock Westminster-Canterberry Gallery, 1995, Assn. for Visual Artists Gallery, Chattanooga, 1999, Rappahanock Westminster Canterberry Gallery, Va., 1999, Williamsburg Regional Libr./Gallery/Theater Complex, Va., 1999; group shows include Richmond Jewish Cmty. Ctr., 1991, 93, Rappahannoc Art League Show, 1995, Assoc. Artists Winston-Salem, 1991, 92, 96, Hoyt Inst. Fine Arts, pa., 1998, Fredericksburg (Va.) Creative Ctr. Art, 1999, richmond (Va.) Creative Ctr. Art, 199, Richmond (Va.) Women's Caucus for Art, 1999-2000, Shockoe Bottom (Va.) Art Ctr., 1999-2000. Recipient awards for art. Mem. Petersburg Area Art League, Shockoe Bottom Art Gallery, 1708 Art Gallery, Va. Mus. Art, Whitney Mus. Art, Mus. Modern Art. Republican. Episcopal. Avocations: investing, amateur genealogist, breeding Am. Cocker Spaniels champions, piano, Civil War tours. Home: 701 Forestview Dr Colonial Heights VA 23834-1116

GRKOVIĆ, VOJIN RADOVAN, engineering educator; b. Čačak, Serbia, Yugoslavia, Apr. 1, 1947; s. Radovan Vojin and Andjelija Miodrag (Cvetković) G.; m. Svetlana Radivoj Polimac, Dec. 20, 1970; children: Milica, Radovan, Veljko. BSc, Mech. Faculty, Belgrade, Yugoslavia, 1970, MSc, 1974, PhD, 1984. Engr., designer Energoproject, Belgrade, 1974-75; fellow engr. Mech. Faculty, Belgrade, 1975-77; chief engr. Kolubara B, Lazarevac, Yugoslavia, 1977-84, tech. dir., 1984-95; assoc. prof. Faculty Tech. Scis., Novi Sad, Yugoslavia, 1988-94, prof., 1994—; gen. dir. Birach, Zvornik, Bosnia Herzegovina, 1998-2000; assoc. prof. Faculty Tech. Scis., Novisad, 1988-94, prof., 1994—. Author: Technological Fundaments of District Heating Turbines, 1995, District Heating of Belgrade By Out of City Located Thermal Power Plants, 1996, Bus. Rehabilitation of Industrial Systems, 2000. Mem. N.Y. Acad. Scis., Yugoslav Soc. Thermal Engrs. (pres. 1993-97), Belgrade Union Profl. Engrs. (pres. 1994-98). Avocations: tennis, skiing, hunting. Office: U Novi Sad Faculty Tech Sci, Trg Dositeja Obradovica 6, 21000 Novi Sad Yugoslavia

GROBLER, JAN PETRAS, company executive; b. Vereniging, Gauteng, South Africa, Feb. 8, 1967; s. Jan Petrus and Marta Margaretha (Bierman) G.; m. Debbie Ann Craig, Dec. 15, 1995. B of Commerce, U. Stellenbosch, South Africa, 1988, LLB, 1990, MBA, 1992. Cert. advocate. Legal advisor Sarlan, South Africa, 1993-94; CEO Curato-Mgmt. Svcs., Johannesburg, South Africa, 1995—, Curator Group, South Africa, 1999—; dir. Catalyst Consulting, South Africa, 1996—, Zenith Tech. Cons., South Africa, 1998—; trustee Wauru Trust, South Africa, 1996—, Tavin Flame Trust, South Africa, 1996—. Co-author: (manual) Curator Franchise Manual, 1999; co-developer: (software) Task Modeler, 1999. Cpl. South African Air Force, 1992. Recipient Higher Diploma Game Ranging, Allenby, 1997. Fellow Inst. Life and Pension Advisors. Avocations: game farming, back-packing, scuba, reading. Office: Curator Mgmt Svcs, PO Box 3993, 2060 Johannesburg Gauteng, South Africa

GROCE, JAMES WILTON, insurance agent; b. Ft. Worth, June 26, 1942; s. Charles Tilmon Sr. and Mary Elizabeth G.; m. Patricia Louise Groce, July 5, 1943; children: Lisa Michelle Groce Russell, James David Groce. BBA, Tex. Wesleyan U., 1972; MBA, Tex. Christian U., 1975. Cert. life and health ins. Tex. Owner, mgr. Airport Garage, Ft. Worth, 1961-65; info. sys. Tex. Pacific Mo Pac R.R., Ft. Worth, 1965-67; railway engr. Santa Fe, Ft. Worth, 1967-69; prodn. controll scheduler Bell Helicopter Textron, Ft. Worth, 1969-75; buyer Bell Helicopter Internat., Bedford, Tex., 1975-76; local rec. agt. State Farm Ins., 1977—. Officer Gideon's Internat., Ft. Worth, 1967-2000; leader, coach YMCA Indian Guide Program and Athletics, Ft. Worth, 1976-79, 94-99; leader, counselor Royal Amb. Program, NRHBC, Ft. Worth, 1978-83; coach pee-wee football Richland Youth Assn., N.Richland Hills, Tex., 1981-83. Mem. Assn. Life Underwriters, Richland Hill Masonic Lodge. Republican. Baptist. Avocations: motorcycling, youth and childrens sports programs, camping, fishing, boating. Home: 7640 Lake Highlands Dr Fort Worth TX 76179-2806 Office: 1060 W Pipeline Rd Ste 108 Hurst TX 76053-4732

GROCH, MARK WALTER, medical physicist; b. Chgo., Feb. 1, 1949; s. Julian Paul and Rose Agnes (Trhlik) G.; m. Enid Marie Draus, Dec. 5, 1970; children: Carolyn Marie, Paul John. BS cum laude, DePaul U., 1971, MS, 1973; PhD, Rush U., 1994. Rsch. group leader Searle Diagnostics, Des Plaines, Ill., 1973-82; sect. dir. nuclear physics Rush Presbyn. St. Luke's Med. Ctr., Chgo., 1982-90; from rsch. mgr. to project leader Siemens Med. Sys., Hoffman Estates, Ill., 1990-94; assoc. prof. radiology Northwestern U. Med. Sch., Chgo., 1995—; sr. med. physicist Northwestern Meml. Hosp., Chgo., 1994—; pres. Digital Imaging Software Cons., Inc., Lisle, Ill., 1985-89; prof. med. physics Rush U., 1982-95; cons. in field. patentee in field. Coach basketball Bethany Luth. Sch., Naperville, Ill., 1988-97; chmn. bd. edn. St. John's Luth. Sch., Mt. Prospect, Ill., 1980-83; vol. West Suburban Human Soc., Downers Grove, Ill., 1998—. Grantee Nat. Cancer Inst., 1986. Mem. Soc. Nuclear Medicine, Am. Soc. Nuclear Cardiology. Lutheran. Avocations: fishing, softball, golf. Office: Northwestern U 251 E Huron St Chicago IL 60611-2908

GRODZKI, TOMASZ, surgeon; b. Szczecin, Poland, May 13, 1958; s. Stanislaw Grodzki and Aleksandra (Szymanska) Grodzka; m. Joanna Rozewicka, April 28, 1984; children: Katarzyna, Anna. MD, Med. Acad., Szczecin, Poland, 1983, PhD, 1991. Asst. Thoracic Surgery Dept., Szczecin, 1983-91, sr. asst., 1991-95, head dept., 1995—; dir. hosp. Hosp. Zdunowo, Szczecin, 1998—. Contbr. articles to profl. jours. Mem. health commn. City Coun., Szczecin, 1991-95; v.p. Found. Transplantology, Szczecin, 1994—. Recipient Pomeranian award Gov. Province, 1997. Fellow European Bd. Cardiothoracic Surgeons; mem. European Assn. Cardiothoracic Surgery, European Soc. Thoracic Surgeons, Polish Thoracic Surgeons Club (v.p. 1997—). Roman Catholic. Avocations: tennis, skiing, travelling, literature. E-mail: grodzki@grodzki.szczecin.pl. Home: 37 Hubalczykow, 70-776 Szczecin Poland Office: Regional Hosp Lung Diseases, 4 Sokolowskiego, 70-891 Szczecin Poland

GROEGER, VIKTOR, physicist, educator; b. Vienna, Austria, July 1, 1946; s. Rudolf and Elise (Hammer) G.; m. Heide Goedl, June 24, 1972; children: Herbert, Ulrich. PhD, U. Vienna, 1973. From asst. to lectr. U. Vienna, Austria, 1972—. Home: Promenadeg 57, A-1170 Wien Austria Office: Inst Material Physics, Strudlhofg 4, A-1090 Wien Austria

GROEN, BERNIE GERARDUS, computer specialist; b. Amsterdam, The Netherlands, Mar. 5, 1955; arrived in Australia, 1959; s. Bernardus L. and Maria G.; m. Jennifer Lynette Morley, July 29, 1978; children: Jamie, Jessica, Benjamin. Mem. tech. support staff CSIRO, Armidale, Australia, 1981-85; mgr. Tandy Electronics, Armidale, 1985-89; computer specialist Osborne, Armidale, 1989-90, U. New Eng., Armidale, 1990—. Author: Introduction to MS Dos, 1992, revised edit., 1993. Mem. IEEE (affiliate). Avocations: computer design and implementation, rock climbing, electronics, space related image processing. Office: Faculty Econs Bus and Law, Armidale NSW 2351, Australia

GROENHEIM, HENRI ARNOLD, psychologist, consultant; b. Bklyn., Oct. 18, 1927; s. Herman and Suzanna May (Bierman) G.; m. Gail Thacker, June 29, 1957; children: Lisa Gail, Gary Thomas. BA in Psychology, Pa. State U., 1950; MA in Counseling, George Washington U., 1954; PhD in Counselor Edn., Fla. State U., 1968. Lic. psychologist Md. State Bd. Examiners of Psychologists. Sch. counselor Brookville (Pa.) Jr.-Sr. H.S., 1950-51; dean of boys Derry Twp. Jr.-Sr. H.S., Hershey, Pa., 1951-52; sch. counselor Frederick (Md.) H.S., 1952-54; counselor Nurnberg Am. H.S., Germany, 1954-55; sch. counselor Kenwood Sr. H.S., Balt., 1955-61; sch. counselor, guidance dept. chair Overlea Sr. H.S., Balt., 1961-66; coll. counselor Catonsville C.C., Balt., 1968-69; assoc. prof. Johns Hopkins U., Balt., 1970-74; assoc. prof. psychology Towson State U., Balt., 1969-94; cons. psycholog. testing Divsn. Rehab. Svcs., Balt., 1973—, Disability Determination Svcs., Balt., 1973—, Kennedy Inst., Balt., 1985-86, Balt. City Pub. Schs., 1990-98; sr. counseling profl. mentor dept. counseling George Washington U., 1996—; med. staff allied health profl. Harford Meml. Hosp., Harford County, Md. Contbr. articles to profl. jours.; moderator TV program, 1987. Bd. dirs. Cmty. Counseling & Resource Ctr., Cockeysville, Md., 1985-90; com. mem. State Democratic Election Com., Balt., 1994. Recipient Sparks medal for outstanding scholarship Pa. State U., 1948. Fellow Md. Psychol. Assn. (ins. com.); mem. APA, Balt. Psychol. Assn., Johns Hopkins Club, Rotary (Aberdeen, Md.). Avocations: swimming, travel, golf. Home and Office: 526 St Francis Rd Baltimore MD 21286-1325

GROENIGEN, JAN-WILLEM VAN, soil scientist, researcher; b. Den Helder, The Netherlands, Sept. 23, 1970; s. Jan Cornelis Van and Jaantje Laurina Van (Vam Dem Berg) G.; m. Ernestine Hadeweij Maters, July 2, 1999. MSc, Wageningen (The Netherlands) U., 1994, PhD, 1999. Rschr. Wageningen U., 1994-95; PhD fellow ITC, Enschede, The Netherlands, 1995-99; postdoctoral fellow U. Calif., Davis, 1999—. Contbr. articles to profl. jours. Mem. Soil Sci. Soc. Am., Dutch Soil Sci. Soc. Mem. Dutch Reformed Ch. Avocations: reading, swimming, gardening. Office: Univ Calif Dept Agronomy 1 Shields Ave Davis CA 95616-5271

GROENINK, RIJKMAN WILLEM JOHAN, banker; b. Den Helder, The Netherlands, Aug. 25, 1949. Law Studies, Utrecht U., The Netherlands, 1972; Bus. Adminstrn., Manchester Bus. Sch., England, 1973. With ABN AMRO Holding N.V., Amsterdam, The Netherlands, 1974—; mng. dir., Netherlands ABN AMRO Holding N.V. (formerly AMRO Bank), Amsterdam, The Netherlands, 1988-2000; chmn. ABN AMRO Holding N.V., Amsterdam, The Netherlands, 2000—. Office: ABN AMRO Bank NV, PO Box 283, Amsterdam 1000 EA, The Netherlands*

GROEZINGER, LELAND BECKER, JR., investment professional; b. San Francisco, Dec. 6, 1941; s. Leland Becker Sr. and Clara Catherine (Hudson) G. BS and BA, U. Ariz., 1964, MS in Fin., 1967. Asst. legis. adv. Leland B. Groezinger Sr., Sacramento, 1970-78; personal investor Sacramento, 1978—. Mem. Episcopal Cmty. Svcs. for the Diocese of No. Calif., Sacramento, 1983-91, bd. dirs., 1984-91, treas., 1985-91; mem. Sacramento Traditional Jazz Soc., Sacramento, 1985—, bd. dirs., 1992-00, treas., 1994-95, v.p., 1996-97, pres. 1998-99. Republican.

GROGAN, STANLEY JOSEPH, educational and security consultant; b. N.Y.C., Jan. 14, 1925; s. Stanley Joseph and Marie (Di Giorgio) G.; m. Mary Margaret Skroch, Sept. 20, 1954; 1 child, Mary Maureen. AA, Am. U., 1949, BS, 1950, MA, 1955; grad., Fed. Emergency Mgmt. Agy. Staff Coll., 1970; degree, Indsl. Coll. Armed Forces Air War Coll., 1972; MS, Calif. State Coll., Hayward, 1973; EdD, Nat. Christian U., 1974. Personal asst., recruitment asst. CIA, Washington, 1954-56; disting. grad. acad. instr., allied officer course Maxwell AFB, Ala., 1962; asst. prof. air sci. U. Calif., Berkeley, 1963-64, Chabot Coll., 1964-70, Oakland Unified Sch. Dist., 1962-83, Hayward Unified Sch. Dist., 1965-68; instr. ednl. methods, edn. rsch. methods of instrn. Nat. Christian U., 1975—, Nat. U. Grad. Studies, Belize, 1975—; pres. SJG Enterprises, Inc., cons., 1963—; cons. pub. rels., 1963—; bd. dirs. We T.I.P., Inc., 1974. Contbr. articles to profl. jours. and newspapers. Asst. dir. Nat. Ednl. Film Festival, 1971. With AUS, 1945; lt. col. USAFR, 1948-76; col. Calif. State Mil. Res. Decorated Air medal with oak leaf cluster, Korean Svc. medal with four battle stars, UN Svc. medal; recipient citation Korea, 1963; RCVP Korean Vets. Assn. medal, 1994; named to Hon. Order Ky. Cols. Commonwealth of Ky., 1970, Outstanding Secondary Educators of Am., 1972. Fellow Internat. Inst. of Security and Safety Mgmt.; mem. NRA (life), VFW (life), DAV (life), Am. Def. Preparedness Assn. (life), Internat. Inst. Security and Safety Mgmt. (regional v.p. 2000—, Veteran of Millennium award 2000), Assn. Nat. Def. and Emergency Resources (bd. dirs. 1995-98), Night Fighter Assn. (nat. publicity chmn. 1967), Air Force Assn. (life), Res. Officers Assn. (life), Phi Delta Kappa, Am. Soc. Indsl. Security (cert. protection profl.), Nat. Def. Exec. Res./FEMA, Marines Meml. Home: 2585 Moraga Dr Pinole CA 94564-1236

GRÖGLER, THOMAS, materials scientist, researcher, manager; b. Schweinfurt, Germany, Dec. 27, 1969; s. Rudolf and Renate (Schmid) G.; m. Claudia Derenbach, 1999. Diploma in engring., Erlangen (Germany) U., Nürnberg, 1995, PhD in Engring., 1998. Rschr. U. Erlangen-Nürnberg U., 1995-98; material group mgr. Siemens AG, Nürnberg, 1998-99; project mgr. internat. procurement office Siemens Ltd., Bombay, 1999-2000; project mgr. mergers and acquisitions Siemens AG, Nürmberg-Moorenbrumm, 2000; mgr. strategic mktg. Siemens AG, Fürth. Contbr. articles to profl. jours. and symposium procs. (award Japanese Soc. Solid Oxide Fuel Cells 1995). Mem. Convent of U. Erlangen-Nürnberg, 1991-92. Avocations: sailing, golf, history. Home: Hofmannstr 11, D-91052 Erlangen Germany Office: Würzburgerstr 121, D-90766 Fürth Germany

GROH, DONNA H., healthcare administrator; b. Carlisle, Pa.; d. Richard W. and Helen Louise (Matthews) Hunsecker; m. Martin C. Groh; children: Kevin, Erin. Diploma, Bryn Mawr Hosp. Sch. Nursing, 1971; BSN, U. Pa., 1978, MSN, 1982. Staff nurse ICU Bryn Mawr (Pa.) Hosp., 1971-76; asst. head nurse Children's Hosp. Phila., 1977-79, head nurse pediatric ICU, 1979-81; dir. nursing, critical care svcs. Children's Hosp., L.A., 1982-90; COO Irvine (Calif.) Med. Ctr., 1991-97; dir. of opers. and bus. devel. Am. Assn. Crit. Care Nurses, 1997-2000; mgmt. cons., 2000—. Mem. AACN, Am. Soc. Assn. Execs., Am. Orgn. Nurse Execs., Orgn. Nurse Execs. Calif., Sigma Theta Tau.

GROISMAN, VITALIY, physician; b. Nikolaev, Ukraine, USSR, May 6, 1939; s. Alexander and Maria (Feldstein) G.; m. Valentina Grebennikova, Dec. 5, 1962; 1 child, Irine. Student, Mil. Navy Med. Coll., Odessa, USSR, 1957-59, Stavropol (USSR) Med. Inst., 1962-67. Stomatological surgeon Stomatological Clinic, Togliatti, USSR, 1967-68; head physician Stomatological Clinic, Togliatti, 1968-86; asst. dir. health protection and sport AvtoVAZ, Togliatti, 1980-82; head physician Hosp., Togliatti, 1982—; pres. Med.-Scientific Firm, Togliatti, 1991—; coach (hon.) Firm "Vizavi", Russia, 1972—; founder pyramid therapy. Author: Myself and the People Around, 1999; contbr. over 20 articles to med. jours.; 12 patents. Dep. City of Dyma, Togliatti, 1993—. Recipient 45 diplomas, medals Internat. Acrobatics Fedn., 1972-93; named Hon. Dr. Russia, 1997—. Mem. Rotary Internat, N.Y. Med. Acad. Avocations include: travel, developing alternative medicine. Office: City Hosp # 1, Oktybrskaya St 68, 445009 Togliatti Samarskaya Oblast, Russia

GROLLMAN, JULIUS HARRY, JR., cardiovascular and interventional radiologist; b. L.A., Nov. 26, 1934; s. Julius Harry and Alice Carolyn (Greenlee) G.; m. Alexa Jule Silverman, May 20, 1959; children: Carolyn, David, Elizabeth. BA, Occidental Coll., 1956; MD, UCLA, 1960. Diplomate in radiology and vascular and interventional radiology Am. Bd. Radiology. Intern L.A. VA Hosp., 1960-61; resident in radiology UCLA Med. Ctr., 1961-64; chief cardiovascular radiology Walter Reed Gen. Hosp., 1965-67; chief cardiovascular radiology Ctr. Health Svcs. UCLA, 1967-78; chief cardiovascular and interventional radiology Little Company of Mary Hosp., Torrance, Calif., 1978—; clin. prof. radiol. sci. UCLA, 1978—. Contbr. over 130 articles and papers to profl. jours., and 9 chpts. to books. Fellow Soc. for Cardiac Angiography and Interventions (trustee 1992-95), Am. Coll. Radiology, Coun. Cardiovascular Radiology, Am. Heart Assn., Soc. Cardiovascular and Interventions Radiology; mem. AMA, Am. Roentgen Ray Soc., Radiol. Soc. N.Am., Western Angiographic and Interventional Soc. (pres. 1976-77), N.Am. Soc. for Cardiac Imaging (pres. 1991-92). Republican. Presbyterian. Office: Little Company of Mary Hosp Dept Radiology 4101 Torrance Blvd Dept Torrance CA 90503-4664 also: RPM 100 Oceangate Ste 1000 Long Beach CA 90802-4347

GROMET-ELHANAN, ZIPPORA, biochemist, researcher; b. Poland, Nov. 21, 1931; Arrived in Israel, 1936; d. Naftali and Rachel (Landau) Gromet; m. Shmuel Elhanan, Feb. 19, 1957; children: Binyamin, Ofra. MSc, Hebrew U., 1955, PhD, 1960. Mem. faculty Weizmann Inst. Sci., Rehovot, Israel, 1960—, prof., 1985—, chmn. dept. biochemistry, 1987-90; vis. scientist cell physiology, U. Calif., Berkeley, 1964-65, dept. microbiology Ind. U., Bloomington, 1974-75; vis. prof. Cornell U., Ithaca, N.Y., 1985, Johns Hopkins U., Balt., 1992, 96; mem. organizing com. Internat. Congress Photosynthesis, Rehovot, 1974, internat. sci. com. Conf. on Primary Electron Transp. and Energy Transduction in Photosynthetic Bacteria, Brussels, 1976; chmn. Aharon Katzir-Katchalsky conf., Rehovot, 1991; mem. internat. adv. com. 7th EBEC, Helsinki, 1992. Mem. editl. bd. Photosynthesis Rsch., 1980-85, Jour. Bioenergetics and Biomembranes, 1992—; contbr. articles to profl. jours., chpts. to books. Grantee Israeli Sci. Found., 1982-84, 90-93, 93-96, U.S.-Israel Binat Sci. found., 1975-81, 84-87, 90-93, 97—; fellow C.F. Kettering Found., 1964-65. Mem. Israeli Biochemistry and Molecular Biology Soc. (com. mem. 1977-79, 84-85), Israeli Soc. Microbiology, Am. Soc. Microbiology. Jewish. Office: Weizmann Inst Sci Dept, Biological Chemistry, Rehovot 76100, Israel

GROMOV, EVGENY MIKHAILOVICH, physicist, researcher, educator; b. Nizhny Novgorod, Russia, Sept. 1, 1956; s. Mikhail Vasiljevich and Klavdia Petrovna (Mazina) G.; m. Julia Vladimirovna Kazakova, Dec. 24, 1982; children: Ksenia, Kirill. MSc, U. Nozhny Novgorod, 1978, PhD, 1984; DSc in Physics and Math, Nizhny Novgorod Radiophys., 1993; Sozos prof., Open Soc. Inst., Russia, 1997, 98, 99. Jr. rschr. Inst. Applied Physics, Russian Acad. Sci., Nizhny Novgorod, 1978-84, rschr., 1984-92, sr. rschr., 1992-96, leading rschr., 1996—; assoc. prof. Nizhny Novgorod State Tech. U., 1989-96, prof., 1996—. Contbr. articles to profl. jours. Avocations: sports. E-mail: gromov@hydro.appl.sci-nnov.ru. Fax: 7 (8312) 365-976. Office: Inst Applied Physics RAS, Uljanov St 46, 603600 Nizhny Novgorod Russia

GROMOV, VLADIMIR VSEVOLODOVICH, physical chemist; b. Samara, Russia, June 22, 1931; s. Vsevolod Mijhailovich and Ida Eduardovna (Mell) G.; m. Margarita Ivanovna Karinskaya, Jan. 2, 1956; children: Nataliya Vladimirovna, Vsevolod Vladimirovich. PhD, Inst. Phys. Chemistry, Moscow, 1958, DS in Chemistry, 1970; DS in Physics, Acad. Natural Sci. Russia, 1991. Had lab. Inst. Phys. Chemistry Acad. Scis., Moscow, 1971—. Contbr. more than 400 articles to profl. jours.; author 9 monographs. Avocations: travel, sports, carving. e-mail: gromov@lpc.issi.ru.; fax: 333-7056. Home: Flat 269, Osirovityanova Str 31, 117279 Moscow Russia Office: Inst Phys Chemistry, Leninsky Prospect 31, 117915 Moscow Russia

GROMOVA, ELIZAVETA SERGEEVNA, chemist, researcher, educator; b. Rostov-on-Don, Russia, Jan. 18, 1944; d. Sergey Semenovich and Evgeniya Vassiljevna (Khokhlova) G.; m. Yurii Vladimirovich Zernii; children: Eugenii, Andrey. Master's degree, Moscow State U., 1966, PhD, 1970, DSc, 1989, prof., 1993. Young rsch. worker Moscow State U., 1970-74, asst. prof., 1974-78, sr. rsch. worker, 1978-89, leading rsch. worker, 1989-98, prof., 1998—. Contbg. author: Physico-Chemical Methods in Molecular Biology, 1978; mem. editl. bd. Moleculyarnaya Biologia; contbr. articles to profl. jours. Recipient award Howard Hughes Med. Inst., 1995. Mem. Biochem. Soc. Russia. Avocations: tennis, skiing, gardening. Office: Dept Chemistry, Moscow State Univ, 119899 Moscow W-234, Russia

GRON, JOHAN PETER LEO, research scientist; b. Purmo, Finland, Feb. 9, 1966; s. Leo Johannes and Anita Irene (Soderman) G.; m. Marika Anneli Peuhkuri, Aug. 14, 1993; 1 child, Sofia. MS in Chem. Engring., Abo Akademi U., Finland, 1993, Tech. Lic. in Chem. Engring., 1997, Tech. Dr. in Chem. Engring., 1998. Rsch. scientist Abo Akademi U., 1993-95; deputy process rsch. mgr., process rsch. engr. Valmet Corp., Jarvenpaa, Finland, 1995-96, deputy product devel. mgr., sr. product devel. engr., 1996-98; rsch. mgr. Valmet Corp., Jaruenpaa, 1998—; adj. prof. Abo Akademi U., 1998—; project scientist Iggesund (Sweden) Paperboard Corp., 1993-96. Co-author: (book) Paper Making Science and Technology, Vol. 11, 2000; patentee in field; contbr. articles to profl. jours. Mem. Tech. Assn. Pulp and Paper Industry, Finnish Paper Engrs. Assn., Engring. Soc. in Finland. Home: Vattuangsvagen 6A, 02360 Esbo Finland Office: Valmet Corp/Paper Finishing, Sys Divsn/Wartsilankatu 100, 04400 Jarvenpaa Finland

GRØN, ØYVIND, physicist, educator; b. Oslo, Norway, Mar. 11, 1944; s. Ragnar Geelmuyden and Edith Magdalena (Aalholm) G.; m. Margit Synnøve Saether, June 30, 1973; children: Ragnar, Anders, Olav, Jon Martin. Cand. real, U. Oslo, 1973, PhD, 1990. Tchr. Bjørknes Skole, Oslo, 1968-81; rsch. asst. U. Oslo, 1979-85, prof., 1993—; lectr. Oslo Coll. Engring., 1985-92, prof., 1992—. Contbr. over 85 articles to profl. jours. Recipient Rsch. prize Illustrert Vitenskap Scandinavia, 1988, King's Gold medal, Norway, 1988. Mem. Norsk Fysisk Selskap. Avocations: philately, walking through the forest. Home: Teiebaerstien 37, 1349 Rykkinn Norway Office: Oslo Coll, Cort Adelers Gt 30, N 0254 Oslo Norway

GRONCHI, DIVO, banker; b. Pisa, Italy, Jan. 21, 1939; m. Anna Maria Alocchi; 2 children. Degree in econs., U. Florence, 1963. With Banca Toscana, 1958-87, exec., mgr., 1967-86, dep. ctrl. mgr., 1986-88; balance sheet and planning area mgr., ctrl. mgr. Banca Monte dei Paschi di Siena SpA, 1988-93, substitute ctrl. mgr., 1993—; dir. gen. Banca dei Paschi di Siena SpA, Siena, Italy, 1996-2000, CEO, 2000—; chmn. Monte Paschi vita, Ticino Assicurazioni; bd. dirs. Instituto Sao Paulo di Torino Spa, Instituto Mobiliare Italiano SpA, Associazione Banaria Italiana. Decorated Grand Officer and Ticino Vita Comdr. of Order of Merit of Italian Republic. Mem. ICLE (pres.). Avocation: the sea. Office: Banca Monte Del Paschi Di Siena Spa, Piazza Salimbeni 3, 53100 Siena Italy*

GRÖNDAHL, FREDRIK BROR, marine biologist, educator; b. Solna, Stockholm, Mar. 26, 1960; s. Birger Allan Gröndahl and Maud Ingerd (Svennborg) Nasser; m. Katarina Gun Strömberg, Jan. 10, 1987; children: Nikolaj Gröndahl, André Gröndahl. PhD, U. Göteborg (Sweden), 1988. Marine biologist The Royal Swedish Acad. Scis., Stockholm, 1982-88; postdoctoral rschr. U. Wash., Seattle, 1989-90; asst. prof. marine biology The Royal Inst. Tech., Stockholm, 1991—. Avocations: diving, traveling, bird watching. Home: Alfagelstigen 6B, S-45033 Grundsund Sweden Office: Royal Inst Tech, S-10044 Stockholm Sweden

GRONDINE, ROBERT FRANCIS, lawyer; b. Milford, Mass., Jan. 29, 1952; s. Albert Francis and Mary Roselma (Credit) G.; m. Aiko Morii, June 28, 1979; 1 child, Michelle Morii. AB, Dartmouth Coll., 1974; postgrad., Cornell U., 1974-75, Harvard U., 1979-80; JD, Boston U., 1980. Bar: N.Y. 1981, Mass. 1981, U.S. Dist. Ct. (ea. and so. dists.) N.Y. 1981, Calif. 1990, D.C. 1991. Assoc. Baker & McKenzie, N.Y.C., 1980-82; assoc. Baker & McKenzie, Tokyo, 1982-86, ptnr., 1986-92; ptnr. White & Case, L.L.P., Tokyo, 1992—. Mem. Am. C. of C. in Japan (bd. govs. 1994-95, 98, v.p. 1996, 1999, pres. 2000). Office: White & Case LLP, 1-19-1 Kandanishikicho, Chiyoda-ku 101-0054, Japan

GRONDONA, JESÚS MATEOS, neurobiologist, educator; b. Malaga, Spain, Feb. 9, 1965; s. Juan and Isabel (Grondona) Mateos; m. Mercedes Jimenez; children: Erica, David. D in Biol. Scis., U. Málaga, Spain, 1992. Assoc. prof. U. Malaga, 1996-99, prof., 1999—. Author: The Subcommissurel Organ, 1992; contbr. articles to profl. jours. Mem. Iberica Assn. Comparative Endocrine. Avocation: photography. Office: Univ Malaga, Dept Animal Biology, 29071 Malaga Spain

GRÖNEMEYER, DIETRICH H.W., radiologist, medical educator; b. Clausthal-Zellerfeld, Germany, Nov. 12, 1952; s. Wilhelm Karl-Dietrich and Hella Carin (von Hunnius) G.; m. Christa Enste, Oct. 21, 1977; children: Till, Friederike, Laura Charlotta. MD, U. Kiel, Germany, 1981; PhD, U. Witten-Herdecke, Mulheim an der Ruhr, Germany, 1990. Asst. prof. biomed. tech. Biomed. Tech. U., Kiel, 1978-82; asst. prof. radiology U. Kiel, 1982-84; asst. prof. radiology U. Witten-Herdecke, 1984-88, asst. med. dir. thoracic clinic, 1987-88, dir. Inst. of Diagnostic and Interventional Radiology,, 1988-90, chmn. Inst. Diagnostic and Interventional Radiology, 1990-96, asst. prof., 1988-90, assoc. prof., 1990-96, chmn. med. computer sci., 1990-96, prof. radiology, 1996—, chmn. dept. radiology and microtherapy, 1997—; dir. Muelheim Krankenhaus Inst., Germany, 1988-96, Rsch. Devel. Ctr. Microtherapy, Germany, 1990—, R & D Ctr. Minimally Invasive Therapy, Berlin, 1995-97; vis. prof. Harvard U. Med. Sch., Boston, 1996. Editor: Interventionelle Computer Tomographie, 1989, Interventional Computed Tomography, 1990; mem. editl. bd. Minimally Invasive Therapy, 1991—, Open Field MRI, 1999, Medicine in Deutschland, 2000; co-editor Medizin im Bild, 1995-96. Avocations: reading, writing, sports, traveling, family. Office: U Witten-Herdecke Inst Microtherapy, Universitätsstr 142, 44755 Bochum Germany also: U Witten-Herdecke, Alfred Herrhausenstrasse 50, 58448 Witten Germany

GRONER, LISSY, member of European parliament; b. Langenfeld, Germany, May 31, 1954. Mem. European Parliament, Germany, 1989—; mem. Group of the Party of European Socialists; mem. com. on culture, youth, edn., the media and sport, com. on women's rights and equal opportunities, com. on employment and social affairs; mem. European Parliament to the Joint Assembly of the Agreement between the African, Caribbean and Pacific States and the European Union (ACP-EU). Office: ParkstraBe 15, D-91413 Neustadt/Aisch Germany

GRÖNIG, HANS ERNST, physicist; b. Mönchengladbach-Rheydt, NW, Germany, Feb. 10, 1931; s. Fritz and Elly Erna (Leisel) G.; m. Ingeborg Erna Mustert, May 7, 1960. Diploma in Physics, U. Tech., Aachen, Germany, 1956, D in Physics, 1960, D Habilitation in Mechanics, 1967; D (hon.), Yokohama (Japan) Nat. U., 1996; diploma (hon.), Lavrentyev Inst. Hydrodynamics, 1998. Rsch. asst. U. Tech., 1956-61, sr.. rsch. asst. dept. mechanics, 1963-67, prof. high temperature gasdynamics, 1967-96, head shock wave lab., 1971-96; prof. emeritus, 1996; postdoctoral fellow Calif. Inst. Tech., Pasadena, 1961-62; guest prof. Yokohama (Japan) Nat. U., 1981, 94, 96, Shock Wave Rsch. Ctr., Sendai, Japan, 1991, 97, Taiwan U., 1993; hon. prof. East China Inst. Tech., Nanjing, 1990, Chongqing (China) U., 1993. Editor: Shock Tubes and Waves, 1988; editor-in-chief Jour. Shock Waves, 1995. Mem. AIAA, Am. Acoustical Soc., German Phys. Soc., German Aerospace Soc. Achievements include patent for Nanospark. Home: An der Höhe 21, 52076 Aachen Germany Office: U Tech Aachen Shock Wave Lab, Templergraben 55, 52056 Aachen Germany

GRONKIEWICZ-WALTZ, HANNA, lawyer, banker. Pres. Nat. Bank of Poland. Office: Narodowy Bank Polski, ul Świętokrzyska 11/21 POB 1011, 00-919 Warsaw Poland

GRØNMO, SIGMUND HAROLD, sociology educator; b. Sømna, Norway, Mar. 28, 1947; s. Ivar and Irene Elisabeth (Dale) G.; m. Vigdis Bjørknes, July 20, 1993; children: Roy, Tone. Magister Artium, U. Oslo, 1971. Rsch. asst. Inst. for Social Rsch., Oslo, 1972-74; rsch. fellow Norwegian Fund for Market and Distbn. Rsch., Oslo, 1975-76, rsch. dir., 1976-88; prof. sociology U. Oslo, 1978-88; prof. Norwegian Sch. Mgmt., Oslo, 1989; prof. sociology U. Bergen, Norway, 1990—; vis. prof. Dalhousie U., Halifax, Canada, 1983, Ill. St. U., 1986-87, U. Calif., Berkeley, 1993-94; dept. chair dept. sociology U. Bergen, 1990-92, vice dean faculty social scis., 1991-92, dean, 1996-98, vice-rector, 1999—. Author: Military Views, Interests and Attitudes among Norwegian Officers 1918-1970, 1975, Consumer, Market, and Society: Perspectives and Results from Social Scientific Consumer Research, 1984, Consumer Influence in Society. A Framework for Empirical Studies, 1991, Society, University, and World Community, 1997; contbr. articles to profl. jours. Mem. Norwegian Student Soc. (hon.). Office: U Bergen, Dept Sociology, N-5007 Bergen Norway

GRONOUWE-HIDDINK, RIET HENDRICA JACOBA MARIA, cytologist, hematologist; b. Gorssel, The Netherlands, Oct. 31, 1944; d. Aaldert D.J. Hiddink and Jacoba P. Leuveninck; m. Derk H. Gronouwe. BA, Tech. Lab. Sch., Deventer, The Netherlands, 1965. Lab. technician Deventer Hosp., 1965-68, Deventer Ziekenhuil, 1967—. Fellow Internat. Acad. Cytology; mem. Volksparty Voor Vryheid En Democratie (sec.). Home: Molenenk, 131BL Wjhe The Netherlands Office: Deventer Ziekenhuil, Fesevurstraat 7, 7400 GC Deventer The Netherlands

GRÖNROOS, MATTI, obstetrician/gynecologist, educator, retired; b. Turku, Finland, Jan. 20, 1931; s. Alex Gustaf and Katri Irene (Lindholm) G.; m. Leena Annikki Hyry; children: Liisa, Juha, Jouko, Petri. Lic. in Medicine, Turku (Finland) U., 1957, MD, 1965, Docent in Ob/gyn., 1966. Asst. to physician in ob/gyn., surgery and medicine Ctrl. Hosp. Turku, 1954-58, resident in ob/gyn., 1959-64, asst. chief physician, chief physician, 1961-74, chief physician in gynecol. oncology, 1975-86; chief physician in outpatient clinic Finnish Cancer Assn., Turku, 1975-86; prof., head dept. ob/gyn. U. Ctrl. Hosp. Turku, 1986-93, ret., 1993; rsch. asst. dept. anatomy Turku U., 1958-59, dept pathology, 1965-73; coordinating chief physician for mass screenings for cervical, endometrial and breast cancers, Turku dist., 1963-85; postdoctoral fellow in reproductive endocrinology U. Calif., San Francisco, 1982; rsch. scientist Hormone Lab., Radium Hosp., Karolinska Hosp., Stockholm, Hammersmith Hosp., London, Radiumhospital, Oslo, 1960, 62, 65, 67, 71. Contbr. articles to profl. jours. Congress sec. 16th Scandinavian Congress o Ob/gyn., 1970; sec. gen. Scandinavian Assn. Ob/gyn., 1970-75, 76-83; mem. nat. com. for cancer prevention Finnish Cancer Assn., 1973-93, del., 1977-93; chmn. Finnish Assn. Ob/gyn., Helsinki, 1988-89. Lt. Finland Med. Corps, 1957-58/. Recipient Silver medal for merit Ministry of Edn., Finland, 1978, Silver medal Finnish Ice Hockey Assn., 1982, Prof. Honoris Causa, Ministry Edn., Finland, 1982. Mem. World Assn. Gynecol. Cancer Prevention (hon.), Am. Geriatrics Soc. (hon.), Finnish Assn. Ob/gyn. (hon.). Avocations: Archipelago of Turku, pictorial art, ice hockey.

GRØNTVEDT, TORBJØRN, orthopaedic surgeon, educator; b. Ørland, Norway, Aug. 7, 1949; s. Oddvar Hilding and Klara Ovedie Grøntvedt; m. Randi Moe (div. Feb. 1994); children: Hans Ove, Nina, Karin. MD, U. Copenhagen, 1977; PhD, Univ. Trodheim, Norway, 1996; PhD in Orthop. Surgery, Norwegian U. Sci. and Tech., 1996. Intern Sundsvall, Sweden, 1977-79; resident in gen. surgery Trondheim Univ., Trondheim, Norway, 1980-84, resident in orthopaedic surgery, 1984-88; cons. orthopaedic surgery Trondheim Univ. Hosp., Trondheim, 1988—; asst. prof. orthopaedic surgery Trondheim Univ. Hosp., 1995—; orthopaedic rschr., Mpls., 1994. Author: Training for All, 1994, Treatment of Acute and Chronic Anterior Cruciate Ligament Injuries: A Clinical and Biomechemical Study, 1996. Lt. Norwegian Air Force, 1979-80. Recipient Norwegian Orthopaedic Assn. Rsch. award, 1992, Smith and Nephew's Arthroscopy Rsch. award, 1993, Vital Sports Medicine Rsch. award, 1993. Mem. Norwegian Sports Medicine Assn. (pres. 1993). Avocations: fishing, hunting, cross-country skiing, jogging, reading. Office: Trondheim Univ Hosp, Dept Orthopaedic Surgery, 7006 Trondheim Norway

GROOM, ARTHUR JOHN RICHARD, political science educator; b. Lincoln, United Kingdom, July 5, 1938; s. Richard George Pearmain and Edna (Wheatley) G.; m. Antoinette Rosemarie Corti, Apr. 17, 1971; children: Anna, Helen. BS in Econs., London U., 1959; MA, Lehigh U., 1961; D of Polit. Sci., Geneva U., 1974; PhD (hon.), Tampere U., 2000. Lectr. U. Coll., London, 1965-77; prof. U. Kent, Eng., 1978—; bd. dirs. Ctr. for Conflict Analysis, U.K.; bd. acad. coun. for the UN System, 1994-97; chmn. European Standing Group on Internat. Rels., 1990-98, Internat. Studies Coord. Com., 1998—; exec. com. European Consortium for Polit. Rsch., 1997—. Co-editor: Contemporary International Relations, 1994, Frameworks for International Cooperation, 1990, The UN at the Millennium: The Principal Organs, 2000; co-author: International Relations: Then and Now, 1991. Mem. Brit. Internat. Studies Assn. (chmn. 1990-92), Royal Commonwealth Soc., Internat. Studies Assn. (v.p. 1997-98, governing coun. 1998-2000). Avocations: opera, music, travel, wine. Office: Dept Polit/ Internat Rels, Rutherford Coll/U Kent, CT2 7NX Canterbury United Kingdom

GROOM, JEREMY RICHARD, stockbroker; b. Chislehurst, Kent, Eng., May 2, 1948; s. Peter Farrant and Anne (Dainty) G.; m. Jennifer Brooke, Apr. 9, 1983; children: Camilla, Pelham. MA in Modern Hist. with hons., Lincoln Coll., Oxford, Eng., 1967-70. Asst. stockbroker Myers & Co., London, 1971; stockbroker Seymour Pierce Co., London, 1972-77, ptnr., 1977-87; dir. Seymour Pierce Butterfield, London, 1987-94, Brewin Dolphin & Co., Marlborough, Eng., 1994—. Past chmn. London Concert Choir. Mem. Securities Inst., Marylebone Cricket Club. Avocations: theater, music, cricket. Home: Bachelor's Mead Horton, Devizes SN10 3NB, England Office: Brewin Dolphin & Co, Cross Keys House The Parade, Marlborough SN8 1NE, England

GROOMBRIDGE, BRIAN HUGHES, retired adult education educator; b. London, Apr. 24, 1926; s. Gerald Hughes and Jane Miriam (Smith) G.; m. Yvonne Barbara Watkins (div. 1962); children: Nicholas, Helen; m. Joy Samuel, Nov. 24, 1964; children: Edward, Timothy, Joseph. MA, Cambridge (Eng.) U., 1951; PhD (hon.), U. Helsinki, Finland, 1990; D Univ (hon.), Open U., U.K., 1994. Prin. Latchworth Adult Edn., Settlement, U.K., 1951-53, The Percival Guildhouse, Rugby, U.K., 1953-55; freelance contract, rsch. and broadcasting BBC ITV Various, U.K., 1955—; dep. dir. Nat. Inst. Adult Continuing Edn., U.K., 1964-68; head ednl. programs Ind. Broadcasting Auth., U.K., 1968-76; prof. adult edn. and dir. dept. extra mural studies U. London, 1976-89; mem. planning com. Open U., U.K., 1966-68; mem. Com. of Inquiry Into Adult Edn., U.K., 1970-74, Internat. Evaluation Team, Ministry Edn., Finland, 1996. Author: Education and Retirement, 1960, Television and the People, 1972, Real Voices: Social Action Broadcasting, 1994. Founder, chmn. U. of the Third Age in London, 1982; chmn., trustee Rights & Humanity, U.K., 1985-95; chmn. Nat. Policy Devel. Group on the Arts, U.K., 1990-92, Local Polit. Orgn., Richmond Upon Thames, 1995-97, The Scarman Trust, U.K., 1996-99. Decorated Knight of the White Rose of Finland, Pres. of Finland, 1999. Mem. Royal Commonwealth Soc., Brit. Libr., Nat. Trust. Liberal Democrat. Avocations: chamber music concerts, walking in Richmond Park. Home: 11 Deanhill Rd, London SW14 7DQ, England

GROOMS, HENRY RANDALL, civil engineer; b. Cleve., Feb. 10, 1944; s. Leonard Day and Lois (Pickell) G.; m. Tonie Marie Joseph; children: Catherine, Zayne, Nina, Ivan, Ian, Athesis, Shaneya, Yaphet, Rahsan, Dax, Jevay, Xava. BSCE, Howard U., 1965; MSCE, Carnegie-Mellon U., 1967, PhD, 1969. Hwy. engr. D.C. Hwy. Dept., Washington, 1965; structural engr. Peter F. Loftus Corp., Pitts., 1966; structural engr., engring. mgr. Rockwell Internat. (now Boeing), Downey, Calif., 1969—. Contbr. articles to profl. jours. Scoutmaster Boy Scouts Am., Granada Hills, Calif., 1982-87; basketball coach Valley Conf., Granada Hills, 1984—; coach Am. Youth Soccer Orgn., Granada Hills, 1985-90, 94—; tutor Watts Friendship Sports League, 1989—; co-founder Project Reach Scholarship Found., 1993. Recipient Alumni Merit award Carnegie-Mellon U., 1985; named Honoree Black History Project Western Res. Hist. Soc., 1989. Fellow Inst. Advancement Engring. (Outstanding Engring. Vol. award, 1999); mem. ASCE, Tau Beta Pi, Sigma Xi. Office: Boeing Mail Code H013-C326 5301 Bolsa Ave Huntington Beach CA 92647-2099

GROOTENHUIS, PETER, mechanical engineer, educator; b. July 31, 1924; s. Johannes Christiaan and Anna Christina (van den Bergh) G.; m. Sara Joan Winchester, Aug. 7, 1954; children: Hugh John, Carol Felicity. Diploma, Imperial Coll., London, PhD, DSc in Engring. Apprentice to asst. project engr. Bristol (Eng.) Aero Engine Co., 1944-46; lectr. in mech. engring. Imperial Coll., 1946-59, reader in mech. engring., 1959-72, prof. in mech. engring., 1989—, sr. rsch. fellow in mech. engring., 1989—; founder, later tech. dir. Derritron Electronics Ltd., 1960—; dir. Derriton Environ. Systems. Ltd., 1981-84; ptnr. Grootenhuis Allaway Assocs. (cons. engrs.), 1969-92; cons. Binnie and Ptnrs., 1962-64, Royal Armament R & D Establishment, 1963-64, Absorbit Ltd., 1964-69, City of London Corp., 1964-91, Arup Assocs., 1965-67, MOD, 1965-84, Esso Chems. Ltd., 1968, 71, Union Electrica Madrid, 1976-81; mem. spl. adv. bd. in ergonomics U. London, 1966-89, BSI Coms., 1967—; mem. joint Inst. Mech. Engrs./Dutch Working Pty. on Edn., 1979-81; external examiner Coll. Tech. Dublin, 1971-79, U. Lagos, Nigeria, 1972-75, U. Bristol, 1979-81. Contbr. over 70 articles to profl. jours.; mem. editl. adv. bd. Jour. Environ. Engring., 1969-89 (chmn. 1974-89). Fellow Inst. Mech. Engrs., Soc. Environ. Engrs. (founding mem., pres. 1964-67), City of London, Guild of London Inst., Fellowship of Engring., Royal Aero. Soc. (assoc.), Royal Acad. Engrs.; mem. Inst. of Metals, Brit. Acoustical Soc. (now Inst. Acoustics, mem. provisional coun. 1964-66), Knightsbridge Br. Cons. Pty. Assn. (chmn. Imperial Coll. wine com. 1975-89), Old Centralians (pres. 1988-89), Athenaeum. Avocations: gardening, sailing. Office: Imperial Coll Mech Engring, Exhibition Road, London SW7 2BX, England

GROOT KOERKAMP, PETER W.G., scientist, researcher; b. Zuidelijke Ysselmeerpolders, The Netherlands, Dec. 23, 1964; s. Jan and Diny (Berghuis) Groot Koerkamp; m. Ellen Wilms; children: Ragnar, Quiryn. MSc, Agrl. U., Wageningen, The Netherlands, 1990, PhD, 1998. Rschr., project leader, sr. scientist Inst. Agr. and Environ. Engring., Wageningen, 1990—. Contbr. articles to profl. jours. Mem. Am. Soc. Agrl. Engring., Wrolds Poultry Sci. Assn., European Agrl. Engring. Soc. Achievements include patent in field. Office: Inst Agrl & Environ Engring, PO Box 43, 6700 AA Wageningen The Netherlands

GROOVER, SANDRA MAE, business executive; b. Ft. Ord, Calif., Sept. 10, 1955; d. Ralph Hillis Jr. and Joanne (Hodges) G.; m. L. Scott Butterfield, Mar. 16, 1985 (div. July 1991). AS in Bus. Adminstrn., No. Va. C.C., Alexandria, 1983; BS in Behavioral Sci., Nat. Louis U., 1990; MBA in Mgmt. Policy and Orgnl. Behavior, Case Western Res. U., 1992—. Mgr. credit, collection Kay Jewelers Inc. (acquired by Sterling, Inc.), Alexandria, 1976-80, mgr. accounts payable, 1980-84, exec. asst. to sr. v.p., 1984-86, dir. inventory control, 1986-87, div. v.p. mdse. ops., 1987-90; v.p. distbn. Sterling, Inc., Akron, Ohio, 1990-96; v.p. mdse. support ops. Mayor's Jewelers, Inc., Coral Gables, Fla., 1996-97; v.p. distbr. Aurafin Corp., Sunrise, Fla., 1997-2000, mgmt. cons., 2000—. Mem. Gemological Inst. Am. (grad. gemologist), Case Western Res. U. Alumni Assn. (pres. South Fla. chpt. 1997—), Mensa. Republican. Avocations: reading, art application, gemology, scuba diving. Home: 20425 NE 10th Court Rd N Miami Beach FL 33179-2523

GROPPENBACHER, DOUGLAS J., real estate investment broker, consultant; b. Fresno, Calif., Nov. 23, 1942; s. Wilfred Charles and Olga Josephing (Balestra) G.; m. Nancy Lee G., Aug. 29, 1964; children: Joseph, Richard, Amy, David. BBA, U. Portland, 1964; MBA, Ariz. State U., 1973. Cert. Internat. Property Specialist, 1998, Cert. Comml. Investment Mem. 1986, Nat. Assn. Realtors. V.p., bd. dirs. Amerco Inc., Phoenix, 1964-75; CEO SafGuard, Inc., Tempe, Ariz., 1975-76; pres. Investment Svcs., Inc., Phoenix, 1976-88; assoc. broker Centre Real Estate Co., Phoenix, 1988-93, Terra Comml. Real Estate, Phoenix, 1993-95, RE/MAX Comml. Investment, Scottsdale, Ariz., 1995—; select coms. Ariz. Dept. Real Estate, Phoenix. Chmn. parents adv. com., McClintock H.S., Tempe, 1982-84; mem. select coms. Tempe Union H.S., 1980-84; co-founder Basic Athletic Sports Injury orgn., 1987-97; mem. bd. Ariz. Football Fedn., 1996-98; pres. McClintock Pop Warner Football, 1976-78. Recipient Realtor of Yr. award Phoenix Assn. Realtors, 1992. Mem. Nat. Assn. Realtors (comml. com. 1993—, bd. mem., past pres. ctrl. Ariz. chpt.), Scottsdale Assn. Realtors (vice chmn. to chmn. comml. 1995-99), Tau Omega. Republican. Roman Catholic. Avocations: woodworking, fly fishing. E-mail: dougg@sarweb.com. Office: RE/MAX Comml Investment 7110 E Mcdonald Dr Ste A1 Scottsdale AZ 85253-5426

GROPPER, ALLAN LOUIS, lawyer; b. N.Y.C., Jan. 25, 1944; s. Jerome F. and Susan M. (Weingarten) G.; m. Jane Evangelist, Aug. 10, 1968 (dec. Feb. 1999); 1 child, Andrew. BA, Yale U., 1965; JD, Harvard U., 1969. Bar: N.Y. 1969, U.S. Dist. Ct. (so. and ea. dists.) N.Y. 1971, U.S. Ct. Appeals (2d cir.) 1971, U.S. Supreme Ct. 1974. Atty. Civil Appeals Bur., Legal Aid Soc., N.Y.C., 1969-71; assoc. White & Case, N.Y.C., 1972-77, ptnr., 1978—. Bd. dirs. Browning Sch., 1990—, pres., 1997—; bd. dirs. Legal Aid Soc., 1990—, v.p., 1996—; bd. dirs. N.Y. Lawyers for Pub. Interest, 1990—. Mem. ABA (bus. bankruptcy com.), Assn. of Bar of City of N.Y. (v.p. 1995-96, mem. exec. com. 1991-96, chmn. 1994-95), N.Y. State Bar Assn. (bankruptcy law com. 1984—). Home: 115 Central Park W New York NY 10023-4153 Office: White & Case 1155 Ave of Americas New York NY 10036-2787*

GROS, XAVIER EMMANUEL, non-destructive testing engineer, consultant; b. Agen, France, Dec. 16, 1968; s. Robert Louis and Gisèle (Vigouroux) G. Diploma, U. Bordeaux, France, 1990; BS with honors, Sheffield (Eng.) City Poly., 1991; MS, Robert Gordon U., Aberdeen, Scotland, 1992, PhD, 1995. Non-destructive testing consultant Dunlop SP, Birmingham, Eng., 1995, Thor Ceramics, Eng., 1995, Schlumberger, Paris, 1995; rsch. fellow Kyushu U., Kasuga, Japan, 1996-99, European Inst. for Advanced Materials, 1999—. Author: NDT Data Fusion, 1996, 2d edit., 1997. Lt., Arme du Train, 1995-96, France. Recipient spl. prize, 6th European Conf. Non-Destructive Testing, Nice, France, 1994. Mem. IEEE, Brit. Inst. Non-Destructive Testing, ASNT. Achievements include fusion of multisensor non-destructive testing data, and eddy current testing of composites. Home and Office: Independent NDT Ctr, 14 rue G. Brassens, F-33520 Bruges Gironde, France

GROSDEVA, TSONKA IVANOVA, nuclear energy industry executive; b. Sofia, Bulgaria, Mar. 21, 1956; arrived in France, 1974; d. Ivan Savov and Borislava Stefanova (Iossifova) G.; 1 child, Diane. MSc, U. Paris VI, 1979; PhD, U. Paris XIII, 1983. Cons. Renault Car Factory, Paris, 1979-82; human factors analyst Nuclear Safety Authority, Paris, 1983-87; rschr. Nuclear Generation (Electricité de France), Paris, 1987-91, sr. inspector, 1992-98, project mgr. in nuc. generation field, 1998—; mem. design team JET-European project, Oxford, Eng., 1987; organizer 7th European Ann. Manual Human Decision Making, Paris, 1988; advisor World Assn. Nuclear Operators, Kozloduy, Bulgaria, 1991-92. Mem. editl. bd. EDF Jour., Paris, 1989-91. Mem. French Nuclear Assn. (symposium organizer 1986). Avocations: photography, cooking, gardening. Home: 10 Pl des Impressionnistes, 92 500 Rueil-Malmaison France Office: Electricite de France, 1 Place Pleyel, 93282 Saint-Denis Cedex, France

GROSE, ANDREW PETER, foundation executive; b. Washington, July 16, 1940; s. Peter Andrew and Mildred (Holston) G.; m. Jacqueline Stamm, Aug. 17, 1963; children: Peter Andrew II, Tracey Christine. BS with high honors, U. Md., 1962, MA, 1964. Mem. legis. staff Fla. Ho. of Reps., Tallahassee, 1972-74; rsch. dir. Nev. Legislature, Carson City, 1974-83; chief of staff Office of Gov. Nev., Carson City, 1983-87, dir. econ. devel., 1984-90; dir. Western region Coun. of State Govt., San Francisco, 1990-95; pres. Westrends, 1990-95; CFO Pub. Policy Inst. Calif., 1995—; mem. exec. com. Nat. Conf. State Legislatures, Denver, 1982-83. Author: Florida Model City Charter, 1974; mem. editl. bd. Nev. Rev. of Bus. and Econs., Reno, 1976-90. Chair trustees Temple United Meth. Ch., San Francisco, 1998—. Capt. USAF, 1964-70, to brig. gen., Res. Recipient Spl. citation Nev. Libr. Assn., Carson City, 1981. Mem. Air Force Assn., Res. Officers Assn., Nat. Assn. State Devel. Agys. (1st v.p.), Western Govt. Rsch. Assn. (pres. 1993-95), Kiwanis (pres. 1981-82, bd. dirs. 1994-97, treas. 1997—). Democrat. Home: 405 Hazelwood Ave San Francisco CA 94127-2129 Office: Public Policy Inst Calif 500 Washington St Ste 800 San Francisco CA 94111-2934

GROSE, ELINOR RUTH, retired elementary education educator; b. Honolulu, Apr. 23, 1928; d. Dwight Hatsuichi and Edith (Yamamoto) Uyeno; m. George Benedict Grose, Oct. 19, 1951; children: Heidi Diane Hill, Mary Porter, John Tracy, Nina Evangeline. AA, Briarcliff Jr. Coll., 1948; postgrad., Long Beach State U., 1954-55; BS in Edn., Wheelock Coll., Boston, 1956; MA in Edn., Whittier Coll., 1976. Cert. tchr., Mass., N.Y., Calif. Reading tchr. Cumberland Head Sch., Plattsburgh, N.Y., 1968-70; master tchr. Broadoaks Sch., Whittier (Calif.) Coll., 1971; reading tchr. Phelan/Washington Schs., Whittier, 1971-73; elem. tchr. Christian Sorensen Sch., Whittier, 1977-94, ret., 1994; cons. Nat. Writing Projet, 1987—, South Basin Writing Project, Long Beach, 1987—; team tchr. first Young Writers' Camp, Long Beach State U., 1988. Author: Primarily Yours, 1987, Angel Orchid Watercolor, 1994. First v.p. Women's League of Physicians Hosp., Plattsburgh, 1970; photo historian of Acad. for Judaic, Christian and Islamic Studies at 6th Assembly World Coun. of Churches, Vancouver 1983, UCLA, 1994—, MIT, 1999—, Abraham Symposium, Istanbul, Turkey, 2000. Named Companion of the Order of Abraham, 1987. Mem. AAUW (assoc. in dialogue 1996—), NEA, Calif. Tchrs. Assn., Whittier Elem. Tchrs. Assn., English Coun. of Long Beach, Acad. Judaic, Christian and Islamic Studies (named companion Order of Abraham 1987), Orange County Soc. Calligraphy. Presbyterian. Avocations: travel, painting, gardening, gym. Home: Museum Heights 171 N Church Ln # Ln619 Los Angeles CA 90049-2000

GROSE, VERNON LESLIE, corporation executive; b. Spokane, Wash., June 27, 1928; s. Wesley Grose and Pearl Quantz; m. Phyllis Jean Heine, Apr. 14, 1951; children: Rhonda Susan Chumley, Brenda Ruth Tutmarc, Lynnda Lorelle Owens, Wesley Paul, Bradley Wayne, Nanette Jill Shotwell. BS in Physics, Whitworth Coll., 1950; MS in Sys. Mgmt., U. So. Calif., L.A., 1967; DSc (hon.), So. Calif. Coll., 1973. Applied physicist The

Boeing Co., Seattle, 1952-59; dir. reliability Litton Industries, Woodland Hills, Calif., 1959-62; dir. applied tech. Northrop Ventura, Rancho Conejo, Calif., 1962-64; chief of reliability Rocketdyne divsn. N.Am. Aviation, Van Nuys, Calif., 1964-66; v.p. Tustin Inst. Tech., Santa Barbara, Calif., 1967-81; chmn. Omega Universal Inc., Woodland Hills, 1981-83; presdl. apptd. mem. Nat. Transp. Safety Bd., Washington, 1983-84; expert cons. White House Assignment to NASA Chief Engr., Washington, 1984-85, White House Assignment to EPA Assoc. Adminstr. for R&D, Washington, 1985-86; chmn. Omega Sys. Group Inc., Arlington, Va., 1986—; adj. prof. U. So. Calif., L.A., 1967-69, U. So. Calif., Ramstein, Germany, 1967, U. So. Calif., Madrid and Seville, Spain, 1968-69, George Washington U., Washington, 1969-85; mem. safety adv. group for space flight NASA, Huntsville, Ala., 1969-70; expert lectr. Am. Soc. Safety Engrs., Des Plaines, Ill., 1980-91; expert commentator more than 300 TV interviews, 1988—. Author: (book) Managing Risk: Systematic Loss Prevention for Executives, 1987; contbr. numerous articles to profl. jours. Dir. Nat. Aviation Show and Aerospace Exhbn., L.A., 1966, Whitworth Coll. Alumni Assn., Spokane, 1968-70, So. Calif. Coll., Costa Mesa, 1972-75, Calif. Crime Technol. Rsch. Found., Sacramento, 1972-75; sys. specialist Calif. Coun. on Criminal Justice, Sacramento, 1971-73; mem. Gov.'s Select Com. on Law Enforcement Problems, Sacramento, 1972-73; commr. Calif. Curriculum Devel. Commn., Sacramento, 1972-75. Capt. USAF, 1951-72. Fellow AIAA (assoc.); mem. IEEE (sec.-treas. sys. sci. and cybernetics group 1965-70), NAS (panel on human error in merchant marine safety 1972-75, com. on rsch. needs to reduce maritime collisions, rammings, and groundings 1978-81, panel on causes and prevention of grain elevator explosions 1978-81). Republican. Episcopalian. Avocations: history, music, Christian education, philosophy of science. E-mail: vgrose@omegainc.com. Home: 1101 S Arlington Ridge Rd Arlington VA 22202-1951 Office: Omega Sys Group Inc 1400 S Joyce St Arlington VA 22202-1872

GROSECLOSE, JAY C., civil engineer, consultant; b. Aug. 10, 1951; s. J.C. and V. Faye (Owen) G.; m. Earlene Sue Clay, May 28, 1977. BSCE, N.Mex. State U., 1974; postgrad., Kans. U., 1978-80. Registered profl. engr., Mo., N.Mex. Project engr. Black & Veatch Cons. Engrs., Kansas City, Mo., 1974-80; project engr., mgr. Scanlon & Assocs. Inc., Santa Fe, 1980-82; staff profl. engr. N.Mex. Interstate Stream Commn., Santa Fe, 1982—, dep. chief, 1992—; engr. adv. Colorado River Basin Salinity Control Forum Work Group, 1990—, adv. coun. alt. mem., 1997—; engr. adv. Upper Colo. River Commn. Engr. Adviser, 1990—; Pacific Southwest Inter-Agy. Com. Alt., 1990—; engring. adviser Rio Grande Compact Commn., 1997-98, Can. River Commn., 1990—, Interstate Stream Commn. Water Conservation Com., 1996; N.Mex. Regional Water Planning Coord., 1996-98. Ofcl. Kansas City Bapt. Assn. Youth Basketball League, 1976-80; deacon 1st Bapt. Ch. Santa Fe, sec.-treas., 1982, vice-chmn., 1983, chmn., 1988, chmn. missions and evangelism com., 1988, outreach dir., 1988-89. Named as one of Outstanding Young Men of Am., 1980. Mem. Am. Water Works Assn., Gideons Internat. (pres. Santa Fe 1983, v.p. Santa Fe 1984-86, treas. Santa Fe 1987-89, meml. chmn. 1990—), Phi Kappa Tau. Democrat. Home: 120 Calle Don Jose Santa Fe NM 87501-2363 Office: NMex Interstate Stream Commn State Capitol Bataan Bldg Santa Fe NM 87503-0001

GROSECLOSE, LYNN HUNTER, lawyer; b. Marion, Va., Apr. 22, 1943; s. Byron Glen and Wilma Comer G.; m. Sharon L. Pair; children: Seth, Zachery, Meredith. BA, Emory & Henry Coll., 1964; postgrad., Emory U., 1964-65; JD, U. Va., 1970. Bar: Fla. 1971, U.S. Dist. Ct. (mid. dist.) Fla. 1972, U.S. Ct. Appeals (5th cir.) 1980, U.S. Ct. Appeals (11th cir.) 1981, Colo. 1993. Prof. Orlando Jr. Coll., Fla., 1965-67; atty. Langston & Massey, Attys., Lakeland, Fla., 1971-75; ptnr. Sprott & Groseclose, Attys., Lakeland, 1975-80, Jacobs, Valentine, Groseclose, Lakeland, 1980-84, Lane, Trohn, Bradenton, Fla., 1984-96, Brown, Clark, Sarasota, Fla., 1996-99, Thompson, Goodis, Thompson, Groseclose & Richardson, Sarasota, 1999—. Sr., jr. warden St. Davids Episcopal Ch.; pres., bd. dirs. Vols. in Svc. to Elderly, Gulfcoast Legal Svcs., Sarasota Manatee Legal Aid. Mem. Sarasota County Bar Assn., Manatee County Bar Assn., Colo. Bar Assn., Fla. Def. Lawyers Assn., Fedn. Ins. and Corp. Counsel, Fla. Bar Found. (legal assistance to poor com. 1997—). Democrat. Avocations: history, remodeling, golf. Home: 7512 Preserves Ct Sarasota FL 34243-3700 Office: Thompson Goodis Thompson Groseclose & Richardson 100 Wallace Ave Ste 240 Sarasota FL 34237-6042

GROSECLOSE, WANDA WESTMAN, retired elementary school educator; b. Clarks, Nebr., Oct. 5, 1933; m. B. Clark Groseclose; children: D. Kim, Byron C. Jr., Eric P., A. Glenn. B degree, Brigham Young U., 1976; M in Tchg., St. Mary's Coll., Moraga, Calif., 1981. Cert. tchr., Calif., life credential. 5th grade tchr. Brentwood (Calif.) Union Sch. Dist., 1977-97; ret.; art tchr., mentor tchr. Contra Costa County Program of Excellence. Author: American Music in Time, In the Shadow of Our Ancestors. Mem. human rels. bd. dirs. City of Livermore, Calif., 1968-70. Republican. Mem. LDS Ch. Avocations: oil painting, sewing, gardening, genealogy. Home: 83 Payne Ave Brentwood CA 94513-4701

GROSHEV, VLADIMIR PAVLOVITCH, economics educator, bank executive; b. Chebenky, Orenbourg, USSR, Jan. 20, 1940; s. Pavel Kuzmitch and Anna Pavlovna G.; m. Margarita Prokopievna Teplukhina, Nov. 5, 1960; children: Larisa, Tatiana. Diploma, Tomsk (USSR) Poly. Inst., 1964; D, Acad. Social Scis., Moscow, 1984. Sr. lectr. Tomsk (USSR) Poly. Inst., 1962; prof. Russian Econ. Acad. named after Plekhanov, 1987—, rector, 1987-90; bd. dirs. Magnitogorsk Metallurgic Works, Zavod Imeni Degtyareva Plant, Kovrov; chmn. bd. Sameco joint stock co.; chmn. supervisory coun. Inkombank, 1988—;. Author: Strategy of Overcoming the Cirsis and Reforming the Russian Economy in the 1996-2000 and the Period Up To 2005, 1995; editor: Investment Project Business Plan-The Entrepreneur's Sketch Book, 1996, Personnel Training for a Market Economy, 1996, Personnel Training for Small Business, 1997. Chmn. bd. Groshev Fund nonprofit charity orgn., 1995—. Res. maj. Russian Army. Recipient Order Znak Pocheta, Presidium Supreme Soviet of USSR. Mem. Russian Union Industrialists and Entepreneurs (v.p. 1997—), Russian Econ. Acad. (chmn. bd. trustees 1990—), Acad. Mgmt. and the Market (pres. 1990—), Club Inkombank Founders. Avocations: handicraft, artistic wood-working, building the house, gardening. Office: Joint Stock Bank Inkombank, 41 Zatsepa Oul, 113 054 Moscow Russia

GROSJEAN, HENRI J.E., biochemist, researcher; b. Brussels, Feb. 5, 1941; arrived in France, 1991; s. Albert M.J. and Denise (Wihl) G.; m. Eliane Gubin (div.); children: Philippe, Isabelle. Grad. in chemistry, U. Brussels, 1964, PhD in Biochemistry, 1969. From asst. to assoc. prof. U. Brussels, 1970-89, prof., 1990-91; dir. rsch. Structural, Enzymology and Biochemistry Lab. Nat. Ctr. Sci. Rsch. (CNRS), Gif-sur-Yvette, France, 1991—; vis. prof. U. Strasbourg, France, 1988, U. Umea, Sweden, 1990. Contbr. over 120 articles to profl. jours., chpts. to books; mem. editl bd. European Jour. Biochemistry, 1988-92; jour. referee. Recipient Jean Stas prize Royal Acad. Sci., Belgium, 1970, Ann. Councourse prize of Sci. Acad. Sci. in Belgium, 1986; Internat. fellow NIH-Yale U., 1974-75. Mem. Am. Soc. Microbiology, Belgian Soc. Biochemistry, French Soc. Biochemistry, European Molecular Biology Orgn., RNA Soc. U.S., French Soc. Biophysics. Fax: 33 1 6982 3129. E-mail: grosjean@lebs.cnrs.gif.fr. Office: CNRS Stru-Enzym-Biochem Lab, 1 Ave de la Terrasse, F-91198 Gif-sur-Yvette France

GROSJEAN, NATHALIE, physical measurements technician; b. Lyon, France, July 15, 1965; d. Pierre and Anne-Marie (Bouchon) G. Diploma in phys. measurements, U Inst. Tech., Grenoble, France, 1986. Technician METRAFLU, Ecully, France, 1986-92; engr. asst. Nat. Ctr. Sci. Rsch., Ecully, 1992—. Avocations: walking, mountain climbing, mountain biking, reading, music. Office: UCB/CNRS Ctrl Sch Lyon, Lab Mechs Fluids-Acoustics, 69131 Ecully France

GROS LOUIS, KENNETH RICHARD RUSSELL, university chancellor; b. Nashua, N.H., Dec. 18, 1936; s. Albert W. and Jeannette Evelyn (Richards) Gros L.; m. Dolores K. Winandy, Aug. 28, 1965; children: Amy Katherine, Julie Jeannette. BA, Columbia U., 1959, MA, 1960; Ph.D. (Knapp fellow), U. Wis., 1964. Asst. prof. Ind. U., Bloomington, 1964-67, assoc. prof. English and comparative lit., 1967-73, prof., 1973—, assoc. chmn. comparative lit. dept., 1967-69, assoc. dean arts and scis., 1970-73, chmn. dept. English, 1973-78, dean arts and scis., 1978-80, v.p., 1980-88, chancellor, 1988—; v.p. acad. affairs, 1994—; bd. dirs. Anthem, Inc.; exec. coun. acad. affairs Nat. Assn. Univ. and Land Grant Colls., 1986-97—, bd. dirs. Bd. dirs. Editor Yearbook of Comparative and Gen. Lit., 1968—, Vol. I: Literary Interpretations of Biblical Narratives, 1974, Vol. II, 1982; contbr. articles to profl. jours. Bd. dirs. Assoc. Group, 1983-95, Anthem Blue Cross and Blue Shield, 1995—; mem. Ind. Com. Humanities, chmn., 1980-81; chmn. Com. on Instnl. Coop., 1986-2000; mem. Nat. Commn. on Libr. Preservation and Access, 1986-93; vice chmn., bd. dirs. Ctr. for Rsch. Librs., 1986—, chmn. bd. dirs., 1987-88. Recipient Disting. Teaching award Ind. U., 1970. Mem. MLA, Nat. Coun. Tchrs. English, AAUP, Phi Beta Kappa. Home: 4965 E Heritage Woods Rd Bloomington IN 47401-9313 Office: Ind U Bryan Hall Rm 100 Bloomington IN 47405

GROSMAN, ALAN M., lawyer; b. Mar. 13, 1935; s. Charles M. and Grace (Fishman) G.; m. Bette Bloomenthal, Dec. 27, 1967; children, Ellen, Carol. BA, Wesleyan U., 1956; MA, Yale U., 1957; JD, N.Y. Law Sch., 1965. Bar: N.J. 1965, U.S. Dist. Ct. N.J. 1965, U.S. Supreme Ct. 1969. Ptnr. Grosman & Grosman and predecessors, Millburn, N.J., 1965—; asst. prosecutor Essex County, N.J., 1968-69; prosecutor Millburn, 1981—; mem. family part practice com. N.J. Supreme Ct., 1984-88, mem. dispute resolution task force, 1987-88, com. on women in the cts., 1991-93; chmn. N.J. World Trade Coun., 1975-77, dir., 1978—; lectr. in field. Reporter New Haven Jour., 1959-60, Newark Evening News, 1961-62; author: New Jersey Family Law, 1999; contbr. articles to profl. jours. Mem. ABA (chmn. alimony, maintenance and support com. family law sect. 1983-87, editor ABA Family Law Quar. 1993—), N.J. State Bar Assn. (exec. editor N.J. Family Lawyer 1980-91, mem. exec. com. family law sect. 1980—, chmn. sect. 1987-88, appellate practice com. 1995—), Am. Acad. Matrimonial Lawyers (pres. N.J. chpt. 1983-85, nat. bd. govs. 1984-88, editor Jour. AAML 1980-90), Essex County Bar Assn. (chmn. family law com. 1970-72), N.Y. Law Sch. Alumni Assn. (bd. dirs. 1988-98), Millburn-Short Hills Rep. Club, Inc. (counsel 1988—), Phi Beta Kappa. Address: 75 Main St Ste 205 Millburn NJ 07041-1322

GROS-PIETRO, GIAN MARIA, economics educator; b. Turin, Italy, Feb. 4, 1942. Degree in econs., U. Turin. Tchr. prodn. econs. Sch. Indsl. Adminstrn. U. Turin, 1965-72, prof. indsl. econs., 1974—, full prof. indsl. policy and econs., 1994—; rschr. CERIS-Istituto di Ricera sull'Impresa e lo Sviluppo, Nat. Rsch. Coun., 1965-72, dir., 1977-80; coord. plan for instrumental mechs. Ministry of Industry, Italy, 1977-80; econ. cons. Italian Union Machine Tool Constructors, 1983; mng. dir. Fincimu. rep. Ministry Public Investment; bd. dirs. Cogesta, Nat. Roadways Corp.; mem. various sci. couns.; v.p. sci. com. Nomisma. Author numerous texts in field. Bd. dirs. U. Turin, 1985. Mem. Nat. Inst. for Fgn. Trade, Soc. Italiana degli Economisti. Office: Corso Unione Sovietica 281b, 3, 4, e 5 Piano, I-10134 Turin Italy*

GROSS, AXEL, physics educator; b. Lüneburg, Niedersach, Germany, Dec. 30, 1961; s. Dieter and Sigrid (Stoye) G.; m. Daniella Koopmann, June 10, 1995. Physics diploma, U. Göttingen, Germany, 1990; PhD, Tech. U. Munich, 1993, Habilitation, 1999. Staff scientist Fritz Haber Inst., Berlin, 1993-98; assoc. prof. physics Tech. U. Munich, 1998—. Contbr. articles to sci. jours., including Phys. Rev. Letters, Surface Sci. Rep. Mem. AAAS, German Phys. Soc. Office: Tech U Munich, Physics Dept T30, D-85747 Garching Germany

GROSS, FRANCK RENÉ CLAUDE, marketing professional; b. Argenteuil, France, Apr. 11, 1961; s. Jacques and Liliane (Chuinard) G.; m. Marie-Dominique Gross, Sept. 4, 1981 (div. Apr. 1994); children: Elsa, Jean Felix; m. Joanna Fisher, May 22, 1998; 1 child, Owen. Tech. cert. in piping and boilerwork, 1978. lic. tech. boiler maker, France. Sales engr. E.G. Com., Paris, France, 1987-89; co. mgr. Eclosia, Montrouge, France, 1989-94; cons. Rueil Malmaison, Montrouge, France, 1994-97; sales engr. Bva Myfra, Montrouge, France, 1997-98; mktg. mgr. Adobe Sys., Noisy le Grand, France, 1998—. Recipient Black Belt, First Dan Aikido, 1996. Avocation: aikido. Office: Adobe Sys France, 2 Rue du Centre, 93 885 Noisy le Grand France

GROSS, GIL, radio talk show host, columnist; b. Kew Gardens, N.Y., Apr. 11, 1948; s. William and Ruth (Rose) G.; m. Rhoda Gail Bodzin, Oct. 5, 1980; 1 child, Spencer Darrow. Anchor, reporter NBC News, N.Y.C., 1975-78, WCBS, N.Y.C., 1978-81, RKO, N.Y.C., 1981-84, ABC News, N.Y.C., 1985-87; host The Gil Gross Show WABC, N.Y.C., 1987-89, WOR, N.Y.C., 1989-91, CBS, N.Y.C., 1992-98; morning drive host WWDB-Radio, Phila., 1999—. Exec. prodr. The Bob Berkowitz Show; syndicated columnist Gross Point. Bd. dirs. Cmty. Access, N.Y.C., 1985-91. Jewish.

GROSS, HANNS, history educator; b. Stockerau, Austria, June 20, 1928; came to U.S., 1961; s. Arthur and Gabriele (Schneider) G.; m. Bonnie Jean Rotter, July 20, 1991. BA with honors, U. London, 1950; AM, U. Chgo., 1963, PhD, 1966. Tchr. Emmanuel Grammar Sch., Swansea, Wales, 1950-61; tutor Bible Coll. Wales, Swansea, 1950-61; asst. prof. So. Ill. U., Carbondale, 1966-67; asst. prof., assoc. prof. history Loyola U., Chgo., 1967-78, prof., 1978-99, emeritus, 1999—. Author: Empire and Sovereignty, 1973, Rome in the Age of Enlightenment, 1990. Elder Moody Ch. Mem. Am. Hist. Assn., Am. Soc. for Legal History, Am. Soc. for 18th Century Studies, Conf. on Faith and History, Soc. Italian Hist. Studies. Avocations: travel, walking, conversation. Office: Loyola U Dept History 6525 N Sheridan Rd Chicago IL 60626-5344

GROSS, JOHANN, physician, biochemist; b. Klosdorf, Romania, May 5, 1939; arrived in Germany, 1949; s. Wilhelm and Mathilde (Schenker) G.; m. Margaretha Görgner, Dec. 22, 1962; children: Torsten, Solveigh. Diploma, Charité Humboldt U., Berlin, 1965, MD, 1966, Specialist in Biochemistry, 1970, Habilitation in Medicine, 1974. Rsch. asst. inst. biochemistry Humboldt U., Berlin, 1965-73, sr. asst. pediatric clinic, 1974-82, docent pediatric clinic, 1978-80; prof. Inst. Pathol. and Clin. Biochemistry, Berlin, 1980—, dir., 1983-95. Contbr. 265 articles to profl. jours. Internat. Fedn. Clin. Chemistry grantee, Mexico City, 1978, WHO grantee, Milton Keynes, Eng., 1979. Mem. German Soc., German Soc. Clin. Chemistry and Lab. Medicine, Biochem. Molecular Biology, Molecular Biology Rsch. Lab. Avocations: music, theater, sports, gardening. Home: Dolgenseestrasse 14, Berlin 10319, Germany Office: Spandauer Damm 130, Berlin 14050, Germany

GROSS, JONATHAN, poetry educator; b. N.Y.C., Nov. 20, 1962; s. Theodore Lawrence and Selma Dora Gross; m. Jacqueline Russell, Mar. 20, 1993; 1 child, Shiri Nicole. BA, Haverford Coll., 1985; PhD, Columbia U., 1992. Adj. prof. NYU, 1991-92; Coll. of New Rochelle, N.Y., 1991-92; asst. prof. DePaul U., Chgo., 1992-98, assoc. prof., 1998—. Compiler Keats Shelley Jour. Bibliography, 1997-99; musician Scrap Metal Soul, Chgo., 1996-99. Meyer Fund fellow Huntington Libr., 1994; travel grantee Am. Coun. Learned Socs., 1994. Mem. MLA, Byron Soc. Jewish. Home: 3812 N Whipple St Chicago IL 60618-3522

GROSS, JOSEPH H., lawyer, educator; b. Tel Aviv, Feb. 28, 1934; s. Woolf and Mali (Timberg) G.; m. Zvia Armon, July 21, 1959; children: Raz, Aeyal, Vardit. LLB, Tel Aviv U., 1955, LLM, 1958; PhD, U. London, 1962. Bar: Israel 1959, N.Y. 1989. Legal advisor Discount Bank Investment Co., Tel Aviv, 1963-76; assoc. dean Law Sch. Tel Aviv U., 1973-78; head of law firm Prof. Joseph Gross, Hodak, Greenberg & Co., Tel Aviv, 1979—; vis. scholar Harvard U. Law Sch., Boston, 1977; chmn. com. on mergers Govt. of Israel, 1975-77, mem. com. to reform co. law, 1985-94, chmn. adv. bd. govt. cos., 1986-91; bd. dirs. Ta'agidim Ltd., Sano Ltd., Ramot Ltd.; chmn. Carmel Bank Ltd., Bloostein-Genosar Ltd.; chmn. Disciplinary Ct. of Tel Aviv U., mem. ct. appeals on mergers and monopolies; mem. pub. com. on taxing nonprofit orgns. Israel Income Tax Authority, 1989-90. Author: Israel's Company Law, 1970, Company Promoters, 1972, Israel Securities Law, 1973, Directors in Government Companies, 1977, Tax Planning of Investments, 1984, Corporation Tax, 3 edits., 1987, V.A.T., 1987, Directors and Officers of Corporations, 1989, Director's Manual, 9th edit., 1999; editor: Economic and Social Aspects of Israel, 1989, The New Companies Law, 1999, 2d edit., 2000. Maj. Israeli Army, 1954-57. Mem. Israel Bar Assn. (chmn. contract law com. 1987-95). Home: 10 Berkovitz St, 64238 Tel-Aviv Israel Office: 23 King Shaul Blvd, 64367 Tel Aviv Israel

GROSS, LAURA ANN, marketing and communications professional, acupuncturist, herbalist; b. Kew Gardens, N.Y., July 11, 1948; d. Melvin Fredericks and Harriette (Levy) G. BA, Boston U., 1970; MA, Columbia U., 1974; MS, Pacific Coll. Oriental Medicine, Pacific Coll. Oriental Medicine, 1996. Staff writer Am. Banker, N.Y.C., 1974-82, assoc. editor, 1982-88; dir. fin. svcs., instns., communications Am. Express Travel/Related Svcs. Co., N.Y.C., 1988-89; dir. sales promotion and pub. rels. Am. Express Travelers Cheque Group/Am. Express Travel Svcs., N.Y.C., 1989-92; dir. strategic bus. comm. Am. Express Travel Related Svcs., N.Y.C., 1992-93; pres. Strategic Comm. Cons., N.Y.C., 1993—; founder Alternative Ctr. for Natural Healing, 1997—; spkr. fin. svcs. and Chinese medicine. Author, editor consumer surveys and articles. Recipient editorial awards Pannell Kerr Forster, 1984, N.E. Bus. Press Editors, 1986, N.Y. Bus. Press Editors, 1987, first Boston U. Coll. of Liberal Arts Young Alumni award, 1985. Mem. Acupuncture Soc. N.Y., Bank Mktg. Assn., Promotion Mktg. Assn. (Spire award 1991), Pub. Rels. Soc. Am. (Silver Anvil award 1990, Big Apple award 1992, Creativity in Pub. Rels. award 1993). Avocations: fiction writing, travel, snorkeling.

GROSS, LILLIAN, psychiatrist; b. N.Y.C., Aug. 18, 1932; m. Harold Ratner, Feb. 4, 1961; children: Sanford Miles, Marcia Ellen. BA, Barnard Coll., 1953; postgrad., U. Lausanne, Switzerland, 1954-56; MD, Duke U., 1959. Diplomate Bd. Pediatrics, Am. Bd. Psychiatry and Neurology, Am. Bd. Child Psychiatry. Intern Kings County Hosp., Bklyn., 1959-60, resident, 1967-70, psychiatrist devel. evaluation clinic, 1970-72; resident Jewish Hosp., Bklyn., 1960-62; physician in charge pediatric psychiat. clinic Greenpoint (N.Y.) Hosp., 1964-67; pvt. practice pvt. practice, Great Neck, N.Y., 1970—; clin. instr. psychiatry Downstate Med. Ctr., Bklyn., 1970-74, clin. asst. prof., 1974-99; lectr. in psychiatry Columbia U., 1974-99; psychiat. cons. N.Y.C. Bd. Edn., 1972-75, Queens Children's Hosp., 1975-96; mem. med. bd. Camp Sussex (N.J.), 1963—, Saras Ctr., Great Neck, N.Y., 1977—. Child psychiatry fellow Kings County Hosp., 1969-70, pediatric psychiatry fellow, 1962-63. Fellow Am. Acad. Pediatrics, Am. Acad. Child Psychiatry, N.Y. Soc. Clin. Hypnosis (past pres.); mem. AMA, Bklyn. Psychiat. Assn., Bklyn. Pediatric Soc. (sr. mem.), Nassau Pediatric Socs., Soc. Adolscent Psychiatry, N.Y. Coun. Child Psychiatry, Am. Med. Women's Assn. (Nassau, pres. 1985-86, 95-96), N.Y. Kings County Med. Socs., N.Y. Soc. Clin. Hypnosis (pres. 2000—), Internat. Soc. Study of Multiple Personality and Dissociation (founder, pres. L.I. component study group). Home and Office: 55 Blue Bird Dr Great Neck NY 11023-1001

GROSS, MECHTHILD MARIA, women's health nurse; b. Fulda, Hessen, Germany, Apr. 6, 1964; d. Winfried and Maria (Schubert) G. Cert. midwife, U. Frauenklinik, Tuebingen, Germany, 1991; MD in Psychology, U. Konstanz, Germany, 1995; PhD, U. Bremen, Germany, 2000. RN. Asst. lectr. U. Bremen, Germany, 1995-98; cons. and lectr. in field. Author: Scientific Thinking in Midwifery Education, 1995, Giving Birth-A Time Related Process, 2000; editor German Midwifery Lit. Svc., 1993—; co-editor: The Midwife, 1998—, A Guide to Effective Care in Pregnancy and Childbirth, German edit., 1998; contbr. articles to profl. jours. Mem. German Assn. Midwives (bd. dirs. conf. 1990—), Internat. Coun. Midwives (rsch. com.). Avocation: choir. E-mail: gross@uni-bremen.de.

GROSS, MICHAEL ROBERT, writer, editor; b. N.Y.C., July 16, 1952; s. Milton and Estelle (Murov) G.; m. Barbara Hodes, June 21, 1986. BA, Vassar Coll., Poughkeepsie, N.Y., 1974. Music columnist Andy Warhol's Interview, N.Y.C., 1973-74; contbg. editor Circus Mag., N.Y.C., 1973-76; editor-in-chief Rock Mag., N.Y.C., 1976-78, Fire Island News, N.Y.C., 1978; sr. copywriter Bantam Books, N.Y.C., 1978-80; columnist Photo Dist. News, N.Y.C., 1981-83; contbg. editor East Side Express, N.Y.C., 1983-84; contbg. editor, columnist Manhattan, Inc., N.Y.C., 1984-85; reporter, columnist N.Y. Times, N.Y.C., 1985-88; contbg. editor N.Y. Mag., N.Y.C., 1988-94; commentator CBS This Morning, N.Y.C., 1992-93; sr. writer Esquire Mag., N.Y.C., 1994-95; contbg. editor Tatler mag., London, 1994-99; writer at large GQ Mag., N.Y.C., 1996-00; contbg. editor N.Y. Mag., N.Y.C., 1997-00, Travel and Leisure mag., N.Y.C., 1997—; sr. editor George Mag., N.Y.C., 2000. Author: Robert Plant, 1975, Bob Dylan, 1978, Model: The Ugly Business of Beautiful Women, 1995; co-author: The Rock Yearbook, 1980, Temple Kent, 1982, Shattered Mask, 1983, Precious Objects, 1984, My Generation: Fifty Years of Sex, Drugs, Rock, Revolution, Glamour, Greed, Valor, Faith and Silicon Chips, 2000; contbr. articles to profl. jours. Mem. Am. Soc. Journalists and Authors, Authors Guild. Office: Ellen Levine Lit Agy 15 E 26th St New York NY 10010-1505

GROSS, PATRICK WALTER, business executive, management consultant; b. Ithaca, N.Y., May 15, 1944; s. Eric T. B. and Catharine B. (Rohrer) G.; m. Sheila Eve Proby, Apr. 12, 1969; children: Geoffrey Philipp, Stephanie Lovell. Student, Cornell U., 1962-63; B in Engring. Sci., Rensselaer Poly. Inst., 1965; MSE in Applied Math., U. Mich., 1966; MBA, Stanford U., 1968. Cons. info. mgmt. operation Gen. Electric Co., Schnectady, 1965-67; sr. staff mem. Office Sec. Def., Washington, 1968-69, spl. asst., 1969-70; founder, prin. exec. officer, chmn. exec. com. Am. Mgmt. Systems, Inc., Arlington, Va., 1970—, also bd. dirs.; also bd. dirs.; chmn. bd. dirs. Medlantic Enterprises, Inc., 1988-94, Baker and Taylor Holdings, Inc., 1994—, dir., 1992—, Medlantic Healthcare Group, Capital One Fin. Corp., Landmark Sys. Corp., Powersim Corp., Computer Network Tech. Corp.; adv. coun. Stanford Grad. Sch. of Bus., 1999—, Ctr. for Strategic and Internat. Statis., 1998—. Trustee Washington Hosp. Ctr., 1977-87, Sidwell Friends Sch., 1980-88, 92—, Wolf Trap Found. Performing Arts, 1997—, Com. for Econ. Devel.; mem. exec. com., treas. Youth for Understanding, 1984-90, 93—, vice chmn., 1996—, Youth for Understanding Found., Germany, 1989—; mem. Econ. Policy Coun. UNA-USA, mem. Coun. on Competitiveness, Fed. City Coun., Washington, 1992—; bd. dirs. Wolf Trap Fund. for the Performing Arts, 1997—; mem. adv. bd. Ctr. Strategic Internat. Studies; adv. coun. Stanford Grad. Sch. Bus.; adv. bd. Stanford Inst. for Econ. Policy Rsch. Mem. Fgn. Policy Assn. (bd. govs., bd. dirs., mem. exec. com. 1977-86, 87—), World Affairs Coun. Washington (bd. dirs., founding vice chmn. 1980-91, chmn. 1991—), Coun. Excellence in Govt. (bd. dirs. 1996—, v. chmn. 1999—), Jamestown Found. (bd. dirs. 1997—), Coun. Fgn. Rels., Washington Inst. Fgn. Affairs, Internat. Inst. Strategic Studies (London), World Econ. Forum (Geneva), Econ. Club Washington, Nat. Economists Club, Aspen Inst. Soc. Fellows, Pilgrims of U.S., Smithsonian Luncheon Group, Met. Club Washington, Chevy Chase Club, Univ. Club N.Y.C., Useless Bay Country Club (Wash.), Sigma Xi, Tau Beta Pi. Home: 7401 Glenbrook Rd Bethesda MD 20814-1327 Office: Am Mgmt Sys Inc 4050 Legato Rd Fairfax VA 22033-4087

GROSS, PETER ALAN, epidemiologist, researcher; b. Newark, Nov. 18, 1938; s. Meyer P. and Nathalie (Bass) Denburg) G.; m. Regina Teri Gittlin, May 30, 1964; children: Deborah Karen, Michael Philip, Daniel Brian. BA cum laude, Amherst Coll., 1960; MD, Yale U., 1964. Diplomate Am. Bd. Internal Medicine. Intern Yale-New Haven Hosp., 1964-65, jr. resident, 1965-66; sr. resident Peter Bent Brigham Hosp., Boston, 1968-69; research and edn. assoc. Va Hosp., West Haven, Conn., 1971-73, acting chief infectious disease sect., 1972-73; chief infectious disease sect. VA Hosp., West Haven, Conn., 1973-74; chief infectious disease sect. Hackensack (N.J.) U. Med. Ctr., 1974—, chmn. dept. medicine, 1980—, chmn. med. bd., 1986; prof. medicine N.J. Med. Sch., Newark, 1981—, vice chmn. dept. medicine, 1994—; assoc. clin. prof. medicine Columbia U. Coll. Physicians and Surgeons, N.Y.C., 1971-81, asst. clin. prof., 1974-77; asst. prof. medicine Yale U. Sch. Medicine, New Haven, 1971-74; ad hoc reviewer rsch. grants NIH, Nat. Inst. Allergy and Infectious Diseases; investigator Ctr. for Biologic Evaluation and Rsch. FDA, 1974-95; mem. clin. indicators task force Joint Commn. on Accreditation of Healthcare Orgns., 1987-89, chmn. pneumonia clin. adv. panel, 1999. Author: Gram Strain Recognition, 1975, 2d edit., 1980, Managing Your Health, 1991; assoc. editor: Clinical Performance and Quality Health Care; mem. editorial bd. Jour. Clin. Microbiology, 1980—, Infection Control, 1980-90; mem. editl. bd. Managed Care, 1998—; editl. adv. bd. Joint Commn. Jour. Quality Improvement. Served to lt. comdr. USPHS, CDC, 1966-68. NIH fellow Yale U., 1969-71. Fellow Infectious Diseases Soc. Am. (clin. affairs com., past chair practice guidelines com., councillor 2000—); mem. ACP (task force on adult immunization), Am. Acad. Microbiology, Am. Soc. Virology, Am. Soc. Microbiology, Soc. Healthcare Epidemiologists Am. (councillor 1986-88, v.p. 1992, pres.-elect 1993, pres. 1994, past pres. 1995), Assn. Profs. Medicine. Office: Hackensack U Med Ctr Dept Internal Medicine Hackensack NJ 07601

GROSS, RICHARD BENJAMIN, lawyer; b. Santa Monica, Calif., Sept. 26, 1947; s. Edward L. and Adele P. Gross; m. Pamela McGovern, June 1, 1985; 1 child, Hannah McGovern. Student, UCLA, 1965-68; BA, U. Calif., Berkeley, 1970; JD, Harvard U., 1973; postgrad., Cambridge (Eng.) U., 1973-74. Bar: N.Y. 1975, U.S. Dist. Ct. (so. dist.) N.Y. 1975, U.S. Ct. Appeals (2d cir.) 1975, Ill. 1987. Assoc. White & Case, N.Y.C., 1974-77; assoc. counsel Am. Express Co., N.Y.C., 1977-82; sr. v.p., gen. counsel and sec. Citicorp Diners Club, Inc., Chgo., 1982-90; sr. v.p., gen. counsel Citicorp Ins. Group, Inc., N.Y.C., 1990-91; sr. v.p., gen. counsel, sec. Ambac Fin. Group, Inc., N.Y.C., 1991-98; mng. dir., gen. counsel U.S. Trust Corp., N.Y.C., 1998—. Bd. dirs. Randall's Island Sports Found., 1999—. Mem. ABA (com. of corp. gen. counsel, com. on fed. regulation of securities, com. on banking), N.Y. Bankers Assn. (mem. lawyers adv. com., mem. govt. rels. com., mem. govt. affairs coun.), N.Y. State Bar Assn., Assn. of the Bar of the City of N.Y., Am. Soc. Internat. Law, Am. Soc. Corp. Secs., Am. Corp. Counsel Assn., Am. Bankers Coun., Fin. Svcs. Roundtable (mem. lawyers coun., govt. affairs coun.). Fax: (212) 852-1310. Office: US Trust Corp 114 W 47th St New York NY 10036-1510

GROSS, RICHARD CHILDREY, radiologist; b. Phila., Feb. 26, 1943; s. Richard Dana and Rachael (Childrey) G.; m. Carrol Ann Gallihue, June 2, 1968; children: Carson Haven, Dana Richard, Rachael Marie. BS, Pa. State Univ., 1964; MD, Jefferson Medical Coll., 1969. Diplomate Am. Coll. Radiology, Am. Coll. Radiology in Vascular and Intercentional Radiology. Intern Harrisburg (Pa.) Polyclinic Hosp., 1969-70; resident in radiology St. Mary's Hosp. & Medical Ctr., San Francisco, 1973-75; resident in radiology Univ. Calif., San Francisco, 1975-76, fellow in cardiovascular radiology, 1976-77; radiologist Roseville (Calif.) Radiology, 1977-97, Radiological Assocs. of Sacramento, Sacramento, Calif., 1997—; CEO Roseville Imaging Medical Group, 1990-97. Contbr. articles to profl. jours. With U.S. Army, 1970-72, Vietnam. Decorated Bronze Star US Army, 1971. Avocations: skiing, mountain climbing, hiking, gardening. E-mail: rgoss@rcsis.com. Fax number: 916 791 2861. Home: 6402 Eureka Rd Granite Bay CA 95746-9648 Office: Roseville Imaging Ctr 1130 Conroy Ln Ste 100 Roseville CA 95661-4154

GROSS, RICHARD WILSON, lawyer; b. Morgantown, W.Va., May 17, 1948; s. Glem Richard and Margery Jean (Wilson) G.; children: Amy Kathleen, Shawn Patrick, Shannon Christine, Shealy Cathleen. BFA, West Va. U., 1971; JD, U. Miami, 1975; postgrad., Fla. Internat. U., 1977. Bar: Fla. 1975, U.S. Dist. Ct. (so. dist.) Fla. 1989. Dir. econ. and community devel. City of Hialeah, Fla., 1974-81, asst. city atty., 1981-86, dep. city atty., 1986-90; mng ptnr. Wetzel and Gross, Hialeah, Fla., 1990-98; pvt. practice Hialeah, 1998—. Mem. Fla. Bar. Assn., Miami Springs C. of C. (pres. 1991-92). Democrat. Roman Catholic. Home: PO Box 111302 Hialeah FL 33011-1302 Office: 39 E 6th St Hialeah FL 33010-4845

GROSS, RONALD MARTIN, forest products executive. BA, Ohio State U., 1955; MBA, Harvard U., 1960. With Battelle Meml. Inst., Columbus, Ohio, 1957-58, Champion Internat., 1960-68; with Can. Cellulose Co. Ltd., Vancouver, B.C., 1968-78, pres., CEO, dir., 1973-78; pres., COO ITT Rayonier, Inc., Stamford, Conn., 1978-81, pres., CEO, 1981-84, chmn., pres., CEO, 1984-96; chmn., CEO, 1996-98, chmn. emeritus, 1999—; bd. dirs. Rayonier Inc., Pittston Co., Corn Products Internat. Office: 6 Landmark Sq Ste 400 Stamford CT 06901-2704

GROSS, STANLEY CARL, marketing consultant; b. Bklyn., Apr. 3, 1938; s. Sidney and Estelle Gross; m. Anita Jackson, Oct. 3, 1971; 1 child, Amanda Rae. BA, Bklyn. Coll., 1959; MBA, St. John's U., 1966; PhD in Mktg. and Orgn. Devel., Union Exptl. Colls. and Univs., 1978. Sales rep. Avery Products Co., N.Y.C., 1959-62; v.p. sales Ranger Rsch., Inc., N.Y.C., 1962-68; v.p. mktg. Brian Lloyd Co. Inc., N.Y.C., 1969-71; pres. Stan Gross Assocs. Inc., Haverford, Pa., 1971—; pvt. practice mktg. Marketing Maps; instr. Phila. Community Coll., 1973, Manor Jr. Coll., 1974; asst. prof. mktg. Rider Coll., 1975-81; keynote speaker Mature Mktg. Inst., N.Y.C. Author: Reconstituting Advertising Effectiveness, 1979, Market Directed Corporate Effectiveness, 1983, Marketing Maps, 1986, The Inner Mind of the Mature Market, 1989, Marketing Strategy is Best Achieved Through Inner Mind Marketing Maps, 1994, Advertising Learning: To Add a 92 Percent Assurance that the Marketer's new Planned Band Advertisement and Campaign Will Be Successful or Not, 1995, The Five Feelings That Determine the Prescriptions Physicians Write, 2000; contbr. articles to profl. jours. With USAR, 1960-65. Recipient Pub. Svc. award Delaware County (Pa.), 1978, Faculty Adv. award Mktg. Club, Rider Coll., 1976. Mem. Am. Mktg. Assn. (awards 1979, 80), Assn. for Consumer Rsch. Republican. Jewish. Home and Office: 518 Waldron Park Dr Haverford PA 19041-1928

GROSS, STANLEY MERHL, chiropractor; b. Breese, Ill., June 27, 1953; s. Walter Frank and Priscilla Dean (Myers) G.; m. Katherine Ferlisi, June 27, 1993; children: Timothy, Carisa, Geno, Zachary. BS in Biomed., Washington U., St. Louis, 1982; PhD, Harvard U., 1983; BS in Biology, Logan Coll., Chesterfield, Mo., 1986, D Chiropractic, 1988. Diplomate Advanced Chiropractic Technique; cert. acupuncture Community Chiropractic Ctr. Pvt. practice, chief staff Community Chiropractic Ctr., O'Fallon, Mo., 1988—; instr., lectr. Logan Coll. Chiropractic, Chesterfield, Mo., 1988—. Author: Bio-Synergistic Integration, 1984, The Physician Within, 1997. Dir. Ankylosing Spondytitis Assn., St. Louis, 1988—; alderman ward II, St. Paul, Mo., 1993—. Recipient Star Scholarship Logan Alumni Assn., Chesterfield, 1987. Mem. Acad. Advancement Sci., Am. Chiropractic Assn., Toastmasters Internat. (Most Able award 1992). Avocations: gardening, swimming, fishing. Home: 1707 Old Highway 79 O'Fallon MO 63366-4319 Office: 305A O Fallon Plz O'Fallon MO 63366

GROSS, STEFAN, literary historian; b. Aachen, Germany, Oct. 5, 1954. MA, U. Aachen, 1979; PhD, U. Paderborn, Germany, 1984, habilitation, 1995. Asst. U. Paderborn, 1980-94, asst. prof., 1996—. Author: E.R. Curtius and die Deutsche Romanistik, 1980, Maurice Maeterlincks Frühe Stücke, 1984, Luis Buñuel: Simon of the Desert, 1996; editor: Maeterlinck: Psychologie des Songes, 1985. Home: An Der Warmen Pader 1, 33098 Paderborn Germany Office: Univ Paderborn, Warburger Str 100 FB 3/3, D-33098 Paderborn Germany

GROSS, STEPHEN RANDOLPH, accountant; b. Newark, Oct. 8, 1947; s. Edward Thomas and Frances (Randolph) G.; m. Barbara Louise Schutz, June 14, 1969 (div. Jan. 1981); children: David Randolph, Matthew Jeffrey; m. Tami Marie Haddad, Dec. 30, 1999. AB, Duke U., 1970. CPA, Ga.; cert. fraud examiner, valuation analyst, Ga. From staff acct. to ptnr. Lester Witte & Co., Atlanta, 1970-74; ptnr. Lester Witte & Co., Chgo., 1974-79, nat. dir. tng., 1978-79, exec. com.; founder, mng. ptnr. HLB Gross Collins, Atlanta, 1979—; trustee Saloman Smith Barney Mutual Funds; bd. dirs. Hotpalm.com, Inc., 9keys.com, Inc, Vertica Software, Inc., ebank.atlanta, Anderson Calhoun, Ltd., Super Corp., Inc., United Telesis, Inc.; treas. Henry Aaron Enterprises, Inc., Milw.; v.p. Coventry Holding Group, Inc., Decatur, Ga.; sec. Carint of NA, Milan. Active Atlanta Symphony Orch., 1975—, High Mus. Art, Atlanta, 1985—, Ga. Pub. Policy Found., 1991—. Mem. AICPA, Ga. Soc. CPAs, Nat. Assn. Cert. Valuation Analysis, Assn. Cert. Fraud Examiners, Inst. Bus. Appraisers, Cherokee Town amd Country Club, Chaine des Rotisseurs (Paris), Ravinia Club, Reynolds Plantation Club. Episcopalian. Home: 175 River North Dr NW Atlanta GA 30328-1111 also: 2956 Lake Rd Pebble Beach CA 93953 Office: Gross Collins & Cress PC 2625 Cumberland Pkwy SE Ste 400 Atlanta GA 30339-3993

GROSS, SUSAN LYNN, administrative assistant; b. Chgo., Dec. 27, 1952; d. William Theodore and Avis Dianne (Boothman) G. Sec. to asst. buyer Sears Roebuck & Co., Chgo., 1971-74, sec. to buyer, 1974-76, sec. to mktg. mgr., 1976-79, exec. sec. to asst. v.p., 1979-90, adminstrv. asst. to fin. mgr., 1990-95; adminstrv. asst. to v.p. credit fin. Sears Roebuck & Co., Hoffman Estates, Ill., 1995—. Mem. Nat. Mus. Women in Arts (charter). Avocations: drawing, calligraphy, knitting, reading, swimming. Office: Sears Roebuck & Co 3333 Beverly Rd Hoffman Est IL 60192-3322

GROSS, TERRY R., radio producer, host; b. Bklyn., Feb. 14, 1951; s. Irving and Anne (Abrams) G.; m. Francis Davis, 1996. BA, SUNY, Buffalo, 1972, MEd, 1974; DLitt (hon.), Drexel U., 1989; LittD (hon.), Haverford Coll., 1998. Exec. prodr., host Fresh Air Sta. WHYY Radio, Phila., 1975—. Recipient Best Live Program award Corp. for Pub. Broadcasting, 1981, award Ohio State, 1987, Disting. Alumni award SUNY, Buffalo, 1993, Peabody award, 1994, First Amendment award Ford Hall Forum, 1997, Gracie award Nat. Radio Personality, Am. Women in Radio & Television, 1999. *

GROSSE, HARALD, theoretical physicist, educator; b. Vienna, Austria, July 15, 1944; s. Günter and Magdalena (Miesbauer) G.; m. Adelheid Hoch, June 28, 1974; children: Barbara, Claudia, Alexandra. PhD, U. Vienna, 1971, diploma, 1973, docent, 1980, habilitation, 1986. Asst. U. Vienna, 1974-80, docent, 1980-86, univ. prof., 1986—; project leader Erwin-Schrödinger Inst., Vienna, 1993-96. Editor: (series) Texts and Monographs in Physics; author: Models in Statistical Physics and Quantum Field Theory, 1988; co-author (with Andre Martin): Particle Physics and the Schrödinger Equation, 1997; contbr. over 150 articles to scientific jours. Mem. Internat. Assn. Math. Physics, Austrian Phys. Soc. (Boltzmann prize 1981), Erwin-Schrödinger Inst. Soc., Internat. Adv. Com. Avocations: jogging, skiing. Office: U Vienna, Boltzmanngasse 5, A-1090 Vienna Austria

GROSSER, ALFRED, retired political science educator; b. Frankfurt, Germany, Feb. 1, 1925; arrived in France, 1933, naturalized, 1937.; s. Paul and Lily (Rosenthal) G.; m. Anne-Marie Jourcin; children: Jean, Pierre, Marc, Paul. Agrege, nat. competition, 1947; dr Etat lettres et sciences humaines, U. Sorbonne, Paris, 1970. Asst. dir. UNESCO, Germany, 1950-51; asst. prof. German civilization U. Paris, 1951-55; prof. Inst. Polit. Studies, Paris, 1956-92; dir. studies and research Nat. Found. Polit. Sci., Paris, 1956-92, prof. emeritus; vis. prof. Sch. Advanced Internat. Studies, Johns Hopkins U., Bologna, Italy, 1955-69; Kratter vis. prof. modern European history Stanford U., 1964-65; prof. politics Ecole Polytechnique, Paris, 1973-95, Ecole Hautes Etudes Commerciales, 198-95; pres. Info. and Research Ctr. on Contemporary Germany, Paris, 1982—. Recipient Peace prize Union German Pubs., 1975. Mem. Internat. Polit. Sci. Assn. (exec. com. 1967-73, v.p. 1970-73), French Assn. Polit. Sci. (bd. dirs. 1965-94), Inst. Etudes Politiques (pres. sci. council 1986-92). Home: 8 rue Dupleix, 75015 Paris France

GROSSI, FILIPPO, industrial engineer; b. San Remo, Imperia, Italy, Aug. 21, 1921; s. Francesco Paolo and Giulia (Scribani Rossi) G.; m. Silvana Peterlongo, Mar. 16, 1972; 1 child, Francesca. Dr. Engring., Politechnique Lausanne, 1945, Politecnico Torino, 1946. Gen. mgr., mng. dir., pres. Techint SpA, Milan, 1948-88; pres. Techint Finanziaria SRL, Milan, 1988—; pres. Sacma SpA, Milan, 1946-78, Techint Engring. Co., Lugano, Switzerland, 1978-92, Pomimi Farrel SpA, Castellanza, Varese, Italy, 1987-92; v.p., pres. Snia Techint SpA, Rome, 1977-91; v.p. Camer di Commercio Milan, Moscow, 1989—; mem. Italian com. Internat. Vienna Coun., Rome, 1988—; mem. panel 121 Congrès Nat. ded Sociétés Historiques Scientifiques, Nice, 1996. Author: Généalogie and History of the astronomes Cassini and Maraldi. Col. Italian Air Force, 1941-43. Recipient In-Arch Inst. Naz. Architettura, 1967, Interpetrol D'Oro Mostra Internat. Petrolio Ambiente, 1973, Cittadimo Benemerito City of San Remo, 1990. Mem. AIM, Assn. Dimore Storiche Italiane, Monticello (Italy) Golf Club. Avocations: golf, sailing, skiing, astronomy. Office: Techint Finanziaria SRL, Via Monte Rosa 93, 20149 Milan Italy

GROSSIN, WILLIAM, sociology educator, researcher; b. Tavers, France, Nov. 13, 1914; s. Louis and Cesarine (Mariot) G.; m. Marguerite Dorlanne, Apr. 13, 1936; children: Robert, Jacques, Daniel. D in Sociology, Sorbonne U., Paris, 1965, PhD, 1972. master primary sch. La Chapelle Vendomoise, 1938-39; lt. mil., 1939-45; journalist Paris, 1946-60; redactor Nat. Ctr. Sci. Rsch., Paris, 1962-68; prof. sociology U. Nancy, France, 1968-83. Author: L'Enjeu de L'Automation, 1958, L'Automatisation, 1960, Les Temps de La Vie Quotidienne, 1974, Des Resignes aux Gagnants, 1977, Pelliculture Americaine (poetry), 1990, La Creation de l'Inspection des Travail, 1992, Pour une Science des Temps, 1997; contbr. articles to profl. jours. Fellow Assn. des Sociologues de langue Francaise, Assn. Internat. de Sociologie (inst. prof.); mem. citizens of World. Avocation: foreign languages. Home: 79 Rue des Eaux Bleues, 45190 Tavers France Office: Nat Ctr Sci Research, 13 Quai Anatole France, Paris France

GROSSMAN, DAVID, editor, translator; b. Phila., Oct. 16, 1947; s. Joseph and Ruth (Weiss) G.; m. Miriam Gelbman, Mar. 15, 1970; children: Yehuda Haim, Devorah, Yona Zev, Tehilla, Shira. BA in English, CCNY, 1969; MS in Psychol. Guidance, L.I. U., 1972, MLS, 1973. Cert. journalist, Israel. Freelance editor Israel, 1974—; editor Szold Inst., Jerusalem, 1974-80; instr. Jerusalem Coll., 1981—; freelance translator Israel, 1981—; contact ELEAS-English Lang. Editors' Assn., Jerusalem, 1987—; dir. On-Target Cons., Jerusalem; lectr. on computer-based editing and translation; moderator internat. forum on Jewish and Hebrew lang. and linguistics. Co-editor: Current Index to Israeli Jours. in Edn., 1974-80; editor/translator numerous books, articles and theses; contbr. articles to profl. jours. Pres. Assn. of Americans and Canadians for Aliyah, 1973-74; mem. Ramot Cmty. Coun., Jerusalem, 1975-80. Recipient scholarships L.I. U., Bklyn., 1971-72, L.I., 1972-73. Avocations: free loans of computers to neophytes in computerized editing or translating; dir. retraining program for computer-based editing and translating; moderator professional advancement groups.

GROSSMAN, JEROME, non-profit organization executive, educator; b. Boston, Aug. 23, 1917; s. Maxwell Bernard and Mary Jeanette (Radin) G.; m. Roslyn Yetta Gruber, June 7, 1942; children: Daniel Jefferson, Marilyn Jean, Richard Adam. BA, Harvard U., 1938. Pres. Mass. Envelope Co., Somerville, 1944-75; pres. Coun. for a Livable World, Boston, 1980-91, chmn., 1991—; lectr. Tufts U., 1978—; commentator sta. WCRB Waltham, Mass., 1978—; pres. Coun. Livable World Edn. Fund, 1980-91; mem. Gov.'s Com. Econ. Effects Arms Race Mass. Economy, 1985—; arbitrator N.Y. Stock Exch., 1992—. Contbr. articles to profl. jours. Pres. PTA Coun., Newton, Mass., 1960-62; mem. Newton Charter Reform Comm., 1969; dir. Educators for Social Responsibility, Cambridge, Mass.; trustee Mass. Civil Liberties Union Found., Boston, 1977—; campaign mgr. Hughes for Senate, Cambridge, Mass., 1962; founder Polit. Action Peace, 1962, chmn., 1962-71; elected del. Mass. Dem. State Conv., 1962, 82, 84, 86, 90; dir. Nat. New Dem. Coalition, 1968—; nat. dir. adminstrn. McCarthy for Pres., Washington, 1968; chmn. Com. ReElect Congressman Robert F. Drinan, 1970-80; mem. Dem. Nat. Com., 1972-80; del. Dem. Nat. Conv., 1972, 76, 80; del. Dem. Nat. Conv., 1972, 76, 80; mem. Mass. Dem. State Com., 1972-80, bd. dirs. affirmative action com., 1975-78; mem. steering com. Mass. McGovern for Pres., 1972; elected mem. Dem. Nat. Platform Com., 1976; pres. Wellesley Com. Nuclear Weapons Freeze, 1981-84; treas. Peace Polit. Action Com., 1982—. Jewish. Club: Wightman Tennis (Weston, Mass.). Home: 65 Grove St Apt 347 Wellesley MA 02482-7821 Office: Coun for a Livable World 110 Maryland Ave NE Washington DC 20002-5626

GROSSMAN, MARC, diplomat; b. L.A., Sept. 23, 1951; s. Melvin and Estelle Grossman; m. Mildred Patterson, May 29, 1982; 1 child, Anne. BA, U. Calif., Santa Barbara, 1973; MSc in Internat. Rels., London Sch. Econs./Polit. Sci., 1974. Polit. officer U.S. Embassy, Islamabad, Pakistan, 1977-79; staff asst. Bur. Near Eastern and South Asian Affairs U.S. Dept. State, 1979-80; dep. spl. adviser to Pres. Carter The White House, Washington, 1980; chief profl. staff State Dept. Transition Team, 1980; country officer for Jordan Dept. of State, 1981-83; polit. officer U.S. Mission to NATO, 1983; dep. dir. pvt. office of sec. gen. NATO, 1984-86; exec. asst. to dep. sec. Dept. State, 1986-89; dep. chief U.S. Mission in Turkey, 1989-92; exec. sec., spl. asst. to sec. Dept. of State, Washington, 1993-94; U.S. amb. to Turkey Dept. of State, Ankara, 1995-97; asst. sec. for Europe and Can. affairs Dept. of State, Washington, 1997-98, asst. sec. European affairs, 1998-2000, dir. gen. Fgn. Svc., 2000—. Mem. Am. Friends of the London Sch. of Econs., Army and Navy Club (Washington). Avocations: reading, travel, sports.

GROSSMANN, FRIEDRICH KARL WILHELM, phytopathology educator, researcher; b. Stuttgart, Germany, Mar. 16, 1927; s. Friedrich and Hedwig Klara (Sautter) G.; m. Hannelore Müller, Sept. 23, 1955; children: Georg, Martin. Diplom-Landwirt, U. Hohenheim, Stuttgart, 1950, DrAgr, 1953; Habil, U. Göttingen, Germany, 1962. Asst. U. Göttingen, 1953-63; prof. in ordinary U. Giessen, Germany, 1963-70, dean Faculty Agr., 1969-70; prof. phytopathology and plant protection U. Hohenheim, 1970-90, dean Faculty of Agrl. Scis. I, 1979-81, prof. emeritus, 1990—. Editor Zeitschrift für Pflanzenkrankheiten und Pflanzenschutz, 1973-88; contbr. more than 150 articles to sci. jours. Served with German Air Force, 1944-45. Recipient Adventurers in Agrl. Sci. award of distinction, 1979, Bundesverdienstkreuz Pres. Fed. Republic of Germany, 1990; Otto-Appel-Denkmünze Found. grantee, 1990. Mem. Deutsche Phytomedizinische Gesellschaft (hon.; pres. 1971-75, Anton-de-Bary medal 1997), Am. Phytopathol. Soc., Deutsche Botanische Gesellschaft, Internat. Soc. Plant Pathology (pres. 1978-83). Home: Tiefer Weg 63, 70599 Stuttgart Germany

GROSSMANN, HANS HENNING, dermatologist; b. Hamburg, Germany, June 27, 1939; arrived in Tanzania, 1977; s. Hans and Magdalene (Mehlert) G.; m. Herma Claussen, Mar. 27, 1969; children: Malte, Falk, Ole. MD, U. Hamburg, 1969, cert. in dermato-venereology, 1974, cert. in tropical medicine, 1986. Cons. Pub. Health Authority, Hamburg, 1974-77, Kilimanjoro Christian Med. Coll., Tumaini U., Moshi, Tanzania, 1977-85, 90—, German Found. Internat. Devel., Berlin, Tanzania, 1986-90; congress co-chmn. Pafcoderma, 1981; chief organizer Internat. Pre-World Congress, 1987; facilitator, dir., prof. Regional Dermatology Tng. Ctr., Moshi, 1997, bd. dirs. Editor: Dermatology in Basic Health Services, 1988. Bd. dirs. Found. for Internat. Dermatology Edn., 1997—, Internat. Found. for Dermatology, N.Y., 1989—. Recipient Presdl. citation Internat. League Dermatol. Soc., Sydney, 1997, Castellani-Reiss medal WHO-Collaborating Ctr. for Dermatology, Leprosy and Sexually Transmitted Diseases, 1999. Fellow Am. Acad. Dermatology; mem. Internat. Soc. Dermatology (v.p. 1994—), African Assn. for Dermatology (coun. mem. 1991—). Green Party. Lutheran. Avocations: research in island iogeography, ornithology, forest biology, traditional medicine. Home and Office: Regl Dermatology Tng Ctr, Pvt Bag, Moshi Tanzania

GROSSMANN, RONALD STANYER, lawyer; b. Chgo., Nov. 9, 1944; s. Andrew Eugene and Gladys M. Grossmann; m. Jo Ellen Hanson, May 11, 1968; children: Kenneth Frederick, Emilie Beth. BA, Northwestern U., 1966; JD, U. Mich., 1969. Bar: Oreg., 1969. Law clk. Oreg. Supreme Ct., Salem, 1969-70; assoc. Stoel Rives Boley Jones & Grey, Portland, Oreg., 1970-76, ptnr., 1976—. Mem. ABA, Oreg. Bar Assn. Office: Stoel Rives LLP 900 SW 5th Ave Ste 2600 Portland OR 97204-1268

GROSSMANN, VOJTECH EDUARD, pharmacologist, toxicologist; b. Vlcovice, Czech Republic, Feb. 2, 1922; s. Vilem and Josefa (Skrabalova) G.; m. Vera Marie Cespivova, Sept. 27, 1947; children: Irena, Vojtech. DM, Chalres U., 1949. Asst. prof. Med. Mil. Acad., Hradec Kralove, Czech Republic, 1951-58; prof. pharmacology Med. Faculty, Hradec Kralove, Czech Republic, 1958-72; sr. researcher Charles U., Hradec Kralove, Czech Republic, 1972-90, Inst. Exptl. Biopharmacy, Hradec Kralove, Czech Republic, 1990—; head dept. pharmacology Med. Mil. Acad., 1951-58, 58-72; head IV dept. Inst. Exptl. Medicine Acad. Sci., 1985-90. Author: Science of Drugs, 1961, 63, Pharmacology, 1959; co-author: Drugs in Clinical and Preclinical Trials, 1994; inventor/patentee in field. Mem. com. new drugs Ministry of Health, Prague, 1953-85. Recipient Golden medal Czech Acad. Sci., 1992, Purkinje medal Czech Med. Soc., Prague, 1981. Mem. Czech Republic Pharm. Soc., Czech Soc. Pharmacology and Toxicology (hon.), Czech Soc. Biochemistry and Molecular Biology, Czech Nuclear Med. Assn. (hon.), N.Y. Acad. Scis. Avocation: painting. Home: Svendova 1041, 50002 Hradev Kralove Czech Republic Office: Inst Exptl Biopharm, Heyrovskeho 1207, 50002 Hradec Kralove Czech Republic

GROSVENOR, GILBERT MELVILLE, journalist, educator, business executive; b. Washington, May 5, 1931; s. Melville Bell and Helen (Rowland) G.; m. Donna C. Kerkam, June 16, 1961 (div.); children: Gilbert Hovey II, Alexandra Rowland; m. Wiley Jarman, June 1, 1979; 1 child, Graham Dabney. BA, Yale U., 1954; D in Pub. Svc. (hon.), George Washington U., 1983; LHD (hon.), U. Colo., 1983, Curry Coll., 1984; LLD (hon.), Coll. of Wooster, Ohio, 1983; LHD (hon.), Coll. William and Mary, 1987, Miami U., Oxford, Ohio, 1988, Syracuse U., 1989, R.I. Coll., 1991, Old Dominion U., 1993, Longwood Coll., Worcester, Mass., 1997. With Nat. Geog. Soc., 1954—, trustee, 1966—, v.p., 1966-80, assoc. editor, 1967-70, editor, 1970-80, pres., 1980-96, chmn. bd. dirs., 1987—; bd. dirs. Chevy Chase Bank, FSB, Marriott Internat., Inc., Saul Ctrs., Inc., Ethyl Corp.; former fellow Yale Corp. Trustee Nat. Wildflower Rsch. Ctr., Fed. City Coun., B.F. Saul Real Estate Trust, Saul Ctrs., Inc., Wildlife Conservation Soc.; past vice chmn. Pres.'s Commn. Ams. Outdoors; chmn. emeritus, found. bd. Alexander Graham Bell Assn. for Deaf; bd. dirs. Conservation Fund, Environmentors Project, Dian Fossey Gorilla Fund Internat.; bd. visitors Duke U. Nicholas Sch. Environ.; former bd. visitors Coll. William and Mary; ann. corp. mem. Children's Hosp.; former mem. Pres.'s Commn. Environ. Quality; mem. Washington Cathedral Bldg. Com. Recipient Editor of Year award Nat. Press Photographers Assn., 1975, Disting. Achievement award U. So. Calif. Sch. Journalism and Alumni Assn., 1977, Pres. medal George Washington U., 1993, Golden Plate award Am. Acad. Achievement, 1996. Mem. Assn. Am. Geographers, Explorers Club (citation of merit 1997), Newcomen Soc., Alfalfa Club, Alibi Club, Cosmos Club, Chevy Chase Club (Md.). Office: Nat Geog Soc 1145 17th St NW Washington DC 20036-4701*

GRÓSZ, ANDOR, ophthalmologist; b. Győr, Hungary, Dec. 23, 1951; s. Sándor and Sándorné (Tóth) G.; m. Ljudmilla Gorbunova, May 25, 1975; 1 child, Éva. MD, Kirov Mil. Med. Acad., 1977, specialist in ophthalmology, 1985, specialist in aeromedicine, 1989, PhD, 1992. Head of med. svc. Hungarian Def. Forces, Börgönd, Hungary, 1979-83; sr. ophthalmology Hungarian Def. Forces, Kecskemét, Hungary, 1986-97, head of aeromed. rsch. dept., 1997—, chief air surgeon, 1997—; guest lectr. Semmelweis Med. U., Budapest, 1996—; guest lectr. HIETE Med. U., Budapest, 1996—; qualification as lectr. at Zriny Miklós Def. U. Budapest, 1998, hon. lectr., 1998—; mem. Nat. Bd. Qualification in Aeromedicine. Editl. bd. Honvédorvos; author: A Visual Performance Test, 1986. Col. Aeromed. Hosp., 1997. Recipient Dr. Papolczy Ferenc Found. award 1988. Mem. Hungarian Soc. of Aviation and Space Medicine (gen. sec.), Hungarian Acad. of Sci., Psychophysiology in Ergonomics, Aerospace Med. Assn., Internat. Soc. of Ocular Trauma. Avocation: traveling. Home: 29 II/25 Dózsa György, 6000 Kecskemét Hungary Office: HDF Aeromed Hosp, 17 Balaton U, 6000 Kecskemét Hungary

GROTH, JOHN HENRY CHRISTOPHER, pastor, author, academic administrator; b. Waterloo, Iowa, June 26, 1954; s. Ulrich F. and Ruth E. (Kangas) G.; m. Cheryl A. Johnson, June 17, 1987; children: John Ross, Eric Samuel, Rebecca Nicole. BA, Wartburg Coll., 1976; MDiv, Wartburg Theol. Sem., 1981; STM, Trinity Luth. Sem., Columbus, Ohio, 1992; postgrad., Bapt. Coll. Am., 1999—. Ordained to ministry Lutheran Ch., 1982. Interim pastor St. John Luth. Ch., Preston, Iowa, 1981-82; pastor St. John Luth. Ch., Lithopolis, Ohio, 1982-88, Old St. Paul Luth. Ch., Newton, N.C., 1988-93, Eastside Bible Ch., Newton, N.C., 1993—; founder, pres. Carolina Christian Coll. Author: (book) Ritual Legalism and Morality, 1993; editor: The Soul Winner's Log, 1996—. Bd. dirs. Prison Ministry, Catawba, Maiden, N.C., 1989-93; exec. bd. dirs. Crisis Pregnancy Ctr., Hickory, N.C., 1989-93; founder Christian Athletic Assn., Newton, 1991. E-mail: johng@abts.net. Home: 310 W 8th St Newton NC 28658-3132 Office: Eastside Bible Ch Carolina Christian Coll 725 E 11th St Newton NC 28658-1865

GROTHE, WERNER GÜNTHER, mathematician; b. Halle, Saale, Germany, Feb. 16, 1949; s. Walter and Irmgard (Hädicke) G.; m. Carola Regine Winkler, July 30, 1979; children: David Jonathan, Eva Alina. Degree in Math., U. Karlsruhe, Germany, 1973. Rschr. in obstetrics U. Heidelberg, Germany, 1974-89, rschr. in devel. info. sys. for hosps., 1989—. Author: Ein Informationssystem für die Geburtshilfe, 1984. Avocations: biking, swimming, Yoga, family. Office: Univ Klinikum, Tiergartenstr 15, 69121 Heidelberg Germany

GROTTA, SANDRA BROWN, interior designer; m. Louis William Grotta. Pres. S.G. Interiors, New Vernon, N.J., 1964—. Mem. Am. Soc. Interior Designers.

GROUNDSTROEM, KAJ WALTER EDVARD, cardiologist, consultant; b. Helsinki, Uusimaa, Finland, May 11, 1950; s. Hans Edvard Vilhelm and Elli Eila Elina (Vaarala) G.; m. Carola Margareta Eklund; children: Carita, Edvard, Fredrik. MD, Helsinki U., 1977; PhD, Oulu (Finland) U., 1991. Specialization in internal medicine, 1985, cardiology, 1986. Gen. practitioner Ylitornio, Finland, 1978-79; registrar in internal medicine Kalix, Sweden,

1980-81; registrar in internal medicine and cardiology Oulu U. Ctrl. Hosp., 1981-86; cons. in cardiology Tampere U. Hosp., 1987—; chmn. Medicinar-klubben Thorax Helsingfors, Finland, 1975. Conbtr. chpt. to book Advances in Echo Imaging Using Contrast Enhancement, 1993; contbr. articles to med. jours. including British Med. Jour., Jour. Am. Soc. Echocardiography. With Finnish Mil., 1977-78. Rsch. fellow Western Gen. Hosp., Edinburgh, 1991-92. Mem. Finnish Cardiac Soc. (asst. sec. 1996-97, sec. 1998-2000). Office: Tampere U Hosp Dept Medicin, 33520 Tampere Finland

GROVE, JEFFREY SCOTT, family practice physician; b. Paxton, Ill., Sept. 21, 1964; s. Ronald Edwin and Delores Ann (Martensen) G.; m. Karen Beth Hanlon, June 17, 1989; 1 child, Garrett Jeffrey. BS in Biology, Fla. So. Coll., 1986; DO, Southeastern Coll. Osteo Med., North Miami Beach, Fla., 1990. Diplomate Am. Bd. Quality Assurance and Utilization Rev. Physicians; bd. cert. family practice and in geriatrics. Intern Suncoast Hosp., Largo, Fla., 1990-91, resident in family practice, 1991-93; pvt. practice Sun-Coast Family Med. Assocs., Largo, 1993—; med. dir. Barrington Properties, Largo, 1994-97, Oak Manor Nursing Ctr., Largo, 1993—, Drew Village Nursing Ctr., Clearwater, Fla., 1996-99, Highland Pines Nursing Ctr., 1999-2000; rep.-at-large exec. com. Suncoast Hosp., 1995—, chief adminstrv. resident, 1992-93, family practice teaching staff, geriatrics program dir., 1993-96, faculty devel. com., 1994—, legal compliance comm., 1998—; mem. quality assurance/utilization rev. com., 1993—, med. dir. of quality assurance/utilization rev. dept., 1995—, legal compliance com., 1998—; bd. dirs. Suncoast Cmty. Care PHO, Largo, 1994-98, med. dir., 1998; clin. asst. prof. family medicine Nova Southeastern U. Coll. Osteo. Medicine, North Miami Beach, 1994-2000, clin. assoc. prof., 2000—; clin. instr. Kirksville Coll. Osteo. Medicine, 1993—; bd. trustees SunCoast Hosp. Found., 1996—, SunCoast Hosp., 1998—; regional med. dir. Tampa Bay for Elder Health. Vice-chmn. bd. trustees SCH Found., 1997-98, chmn. bd. trustees SCH Found., 1998-99. Named to Outstanding Young Men of Am.; recipient Disting. Trustee award SCH Found., 2000. Mem. Am. Osteo. Assn., Fla. Osteo. Med. Assn., Am. Coll. Osteo. Family Physicians (trustee 1997—, chair membership com. 1997-99, treas. 1999—), Nova Southeastern U. Coll. Osteo. Medicine Alumni Assn. (v.p. 1999—), Pinellas County Osteo. Med. Soc. (bd. govs. 1995—, treas. 1996-99), Nat. Eagle Scout Assn. (life), Scouting Res. Republican. Methodist. Avocations: golf, stamp collecting, travel, snow skiing. Home: 301 Osceola Rd Clearwater FL 33756-1453 Office: SunCoast Family Med Assocs 360 Clearwater Largo Rd N Largo FL 33770-2335

GROVE, MYRNA JEAN, elementary education educator; b. Bryan, Ohio, Oct. 24, 1949; d. Kedric Durward and N. Florence (Stombaugh) G. Student, Bowling Green State U., 1970-71; BA in Edn., Manchester Coll., 1971; postgrad., U. No. Colo., 1974-76, Purdue U., 1977, St. Francis Coll., Ft. Wayne, Ind., 1986, Coll. Mount St. Joseph, Ohio, 1986; MLS, Kent State U., 1999. Cert. elem. tchr., Ohio. Tchr. elem. sch. Bryan City Schs., 1972—. Author: Asbestos Cancer: One Man's Experience, 1995, Legacy of One-Room Schools, 1999; editor newspaper column Education Today, 1975-82, newsletter N.W. Ohio Emphasis, 1981-83 (award 1981). Dir., violinist Bryan String Ensemble, 1981—; organist Trinity Episc. Ch., Bryan, 1979-89; active Lancaster Mennonite Hist. Soc., Hans Herr Found.; trustee Bryan Area Cultural Assn., 1984-89; bd. dirs. William County Cmty. Concerts. Jennings scholar Martha Holden Jennings Found., Bowling Green State U., 1982-83. Mem. ALA, NEA (Ohio del., state contact 1986-87), Am. Booksellers Assn. (assoc. mem.), Ohio Edn. Assn. (presenter 1984, del. global issues 1986, sec. N.W. Ohio Tchrs. Uniserv. 1975-78), Ohio Assn. Gifted Children, Bus. and Profl. Women Ohio (individual devel. com. 1986-90, speaking skills cert. 1987), Ohio Libr. Coun., Ohioana Libr. Assn., N.W. Ohio Manchester Coll. Alumni Assn. (past pres.), Bryan Edn. Assn. (exec. com., pres. 1985-86), Williams County Geneal. Soc., Williams County Hist. Assn., P. Buckley Moss Soc., Trees of Life (v.p. 1994-99, region moss docent), Alpha Delta Kappa (pres. 1996-98), Alpha Mu. Avocations: collecting dolls, playing piano, organ and violin, reading, travel.

GROVE, NOEL RANDALL, writer; b. South English, Iowa, Jan. 25, 1938; s. George William and Miriam Helen G.; m. Deanna Sue Goering, Aug. 16, 1958 (div. Feb. 1978); children: Lisa, Amy, Elizabeth; m. Barbara Ann Payne, July 31, 1982; 1 child, Eleni. BA in Eng., McPherson Coll., 1959. English, speech tchr. Inman (Kans.) H.S., 1959-61; reporter McPherson (Kans.) Sentinel, 1961-64; reporter, night editor Hutchinson (Kans.) News, 1964-66; picture editor Newspaper Enterprise Assn., Cleve., 1966-67; capitol correspondent Newspaper Enterprise Assn., Washington, 1967-69; writer National Geographic, Washington, 1969-94; freelance writer Middleburg, Va., 1994—; charter bd. mem. Bicycle Fedn., Washington, 1975—, founding bd. mem. Soc. Environmental Journalists, 1990-93. Author: Wild Lands for Wildlife, 1984, Preserving Eden, 1992, Birds of North America, 1995, Atlas of World History, 1997, Living Planet, 1999, Range of Light, 1999. Democrat. Protestant. Home: PO Box 1016 Middleburg VA 20118-1016

GROVE, ROBIN ALEXANDER JOHN, solicitor; b. Bedford, Bedfordshire, England; s. Barrie Peter and Annie G. Law LLB with honors, Cardiff (Wales) U., 1992; Law Soc. finals, Guildford (Eng.) Law, 1993. Solicitors Practicing Cert. Trainee solicitor Laytons, London, 1994-96, asst. solicitor, 1996—. Dir. Elmbridge Housing Trust, Esher, Eng., 1999. Mem. Walton and Weybridge Roundtable (treas. 1996-99). Avocations: cricket, golf, wine tasting. Office: Laytons, 76 Bridge Rd Hampton Ct, KT8 9HF London Surrey, England

GROVER, ROSALIND REDFERN, oil and gas company executive; b. Midland, Tex., Sept. 5, 1941; d. John Joseph and Rosalind (Kapps) Redfern;m. Arden Roy Grover, Apr. 10, 1982; 1 child, Rosson. BA in Edn. magna cum laude, U. Ariz., 1966, MA in History, 1982; postgrad. in law, So. Methodist U., Dallas. Libr. Gahr H.S., Cerritos, Calif., 1969; pres. The Redfern Found., Midland, 1982—; ptnr. Redfern & Grover, Midland, 1986—; pres. Redfern Enterprises Inc., Midland, 1989—; chmn. bd. dirs. Flag-Redfern Oil Co., Midland. Sec. park and recreation commn. City of Midland, 1969-71, del. Objectives for Convocation, 1980; mem., past pres. women's aux. Midland Cmty. Theatre, 1970; chmn. challenge grant bldg. fund, 1980, chmn. Tex. Yucca Hist. Landmark Renovation Project, 1983, trustee, 1983-88; chmn. publicity com. Midland Jr. League, Midland, Inc., 1972, chmn. edn. com., 1976, corr. sec., 1978; 1st v.p. Midland Symphony Assn., 1975; chmn. Midland Charity Horse Show, 1975-76; mem. Midland Am. Revolution Bicentennial Commn., 1976; trustee Mus. S.W., 1977-80, pres. bd. dirs., 1979-80; co-chmn. Gov. Clements Fin. Com., Midland, 1978; mem. dist. com. State Bd. Law Examiners; trustee Midland Meml. Hosp., 1978-80, Permian Basin Petroleum Mus., Libr. and Hall of Fame, 1989—. Recipient HamHock award Midland Cmty. Theatre, 1978. Mem. Ind. Petroleum Assn. Am., Tex. Ind. Producers and Royalty Owners Assn., Petroleum Club, Racquet Club (Midland), Horseshoe Bay (Tex.) Country Club, Phi Kappa Phi, Pi Lambda Theta. Republican. Office: PO Box 2127 Midland TX 79702-2127

GROVES, COLIN PETER, anthropologist, educator; b. London, June 24, 1942; arrived in Australia, 1974; s. Harold Victor and Dorothy Mary Catherine (Edwards) G.; m. Phyllis Rose Dance, Jan. 26, 1977. BS, U. Coll., 1963; PhD, Royal Free Hosp. Sch. Medicine, 1966. Asst. prof. U. Calif., Berkeley, 1966-68; rschr. Reader's Digest Spl. Books, London, 1969; demonstrator Cambridge (United Kingdom) U., 1969-73; lectr. Australian Nat. U., Canberra, 1974-78, sr. lectr., 1979-88, reader, 1989—. Mem. editl. bd. Jour. Human Evolution, 1985-90, Internat. Jour. Primatology, 1988—, Zool. Rsch., 1993—, Cryptozoology, 1988—; author: Gorillas, 1970, Horses, Asses and Zebras in the Wild, 1974, A Theory of Human and Primate Evolution, 1989; contbr. articles to profl. jours. Rsch. grantee Nat. Geographic Soc., 1972, Australian Rsch. Coun., 1975, 1994, 2000. Fellow Royal Anthrop. Inst.; mem. Am. Soc. Mammalogists, Bombay Natural History Soc., Deutsches Gesellschaft fur Saugetierkunde, Malayan Nature Soc., N.Y. Acad. Sci., Australian Skeptics. Avocations: wildlife watching, music appreciation, reading, classics. Home: 250 Dryandra St, O'Connor 2602, Australia Office: Australian Nat U, Dept Archaeology Anthropolo, Canberra 0200, Australia

GROVES, SHERIDON HALE, orthopedic surgeon; b. Denver, Mar. 5, 1947; s. Harry Edward Groves and Dolores Ruth (Hale) Finley; m. Deborah Rita Threadgill, Mar. 29, 1970 (div. Apr. 1980); children: Jason, Tiffany; m. Nanely Marie Lamont, July 1, 1980 (div. Dec. 1987); 1 child, Dolores; m. Elaine Robbins, Feb. 7, 1991. BS, U.S. Mil. Acad., 1969; MD, U. Va., Charlottesville, 1976. Commd. 2nd lt. U.S. Army, 1969, advanced through grades to maj., 1979, ret., 1992; surg. intern U.S. Army, El Paso, Tex., 1976-77, resident in orthop. surgery, 1977-80; staff orthop. surgeon U.S. Army, Killeen, Tex., 1980-83; ret. U.S. Army, 1992; staff emergency physician various emergency depts. State of Tex., 1983-84, 87; emergency dept. dir. Victoria (Tex.) Regional Med. Ctr., 1984-86; med. dir. First Walk-In Clinic Victoria, 1986-87; tchr. U. Tex. Med. Br., Galveston, 1986-90; emergency dept. dir. Gulf Coast Med. Ctr., 1988-89; with Amerimed Corp., 1990-92, Primedex Corp., 1992-93; clinic med. dir, staff orthop. surgeon Pain Relief Network, 1993-99; ret., 1999—; lectr. Spkrs. Bur., Victoria, 1984-86, Cato Inst., Ludwig Von Mises Inst. Host radio talk show, 1996-97; contbr. articles to profl. jours. Mem. Victoria Interagy. Coun. Sexual Abuse, 1984-86; treas. bd. dirs. Youth Home Victoria, 1986-90; vol. Bible tchg. Calif. Penal Sys. Recipient Physician's Recognition award, AMA, 1980, 83, 86, 89, 92, 95. Fellow Am. Acad. Neurologic and Orthop. Surgeons; mem. Soc. Mil., Orthop. Surgeons, Am. Coll. Emergency Physicians, Tex. Med. Found., Assn. Grads. of U.S. Mil. Acad. (life), Am. Assn. Disability Evaluation Physicians, Coalition of Med. Providers, Am. Coll. Sports Medicine, Am. Running and Fitness Assn. (cert. of recognition 1987), Internat. Coll. Surgeons (pres., vice regent), Internat. Martial Arts Assn., Hurricane Sports Club of Houston, Smithsonian Assocs., So. Calif. Striders Track Club. Avocations: track and field masters (3-time nat. champion), martial arts.

GROVES-GIDNEY, GAVRIELLE, consultant geophysicist; b. Bklyn., July 28, 1956; arrived in U.K., 1982; d. Jerome E. and Lillian (Slesar) Gleich; m. Mark N. Groves-Gidney, Dec. 31, 1982 (div. 2000). BA in English Lit. magna cum laude, SUNY, Fredonia, 1977; MSc in Geology, W.Va. U., 1982. Chartered geologist. Geologist Cities Svc., Tulsa and Houston, 1982; geophysicist Arco Oil, London, 1984-88; sr. geophysicist Union Tex. Petroleum, London, 1988-90; staff geophysicist Det Norske Oljeselskap, London, 1990-92; cons. geophysicist Kent, Eng., 1992-2000; freelance author Kent, 1992—; freelance cons., 2000—; staff geophysicist Exploration Geoscientists Ltd., Goudhurst, Eng., 1997—; grad. tchg. asst. W.Va. U., 1979-82; sec. Exploration Geoscis. Ltd., Kent, 1991—. Author: The Last Assignment, 1997. W.Va. Geol. Survey grantee, 1978. Fellow Geol. Soc.; mem. Soc. Authors, Pen Internat., Tunbridge Wells Writers Cir. (Ann Warboys award 1995). Avocations: guitar and vocals, local and architectural history, gardening and garden design, travel, research.

GROZDOVA, IRINA DMITRIEVNA, biochemist, researcher; b. Moscow, May 30, 1946; d. Dmitry Mitrophanovich Grozdov and Irina Vladimirovna Pavlova; m. Vladimir Sergeevich Prasolov, June 15, 1967 (div. Mar. 1979); children: Katherine, Vladimir; m. Nickolay Sergeevich Melik-Nubarov, Jan. 15, 1993. PhD, Moscow State U., 1977. Jr. rschr. Moscow State U., 1977-85, sr. rschr., 1997—; sr. rschr. Inst. Organic Chemistry, Moscow, 1985-88, Rsch. Ctr. Molecular Diagnostic and Therapy, Moscow, 1988-97. Contbr. articles to profl. jours. Democrat. Fax: 7(095)939-01-74. E-mail: grozdova@mail.ru. Home: Chasovaya 27/12 apt 32, 125315 Moscow Russia Office: Moscow State U, Leninskiy Gory, 119899 Moscow Russia

GROZEVA, EKATERINA ILIEVA, science administrator, chemist; b. Plovdiv, Bulgaria, June 21, 1945; d. Ilia Dimitrov and Maria Dimitrova Stoilova; m. Dimo Boitchev Grozev, May 20, 1973; children: Boian Dimov, Mladen Dimov. Diploma, Plovdiv, 1969; PhD, High Inst. Chemistry Tech., Sofia, Bulgaria, 1987. Technologist Bulgarska rosa, Karlovo, Bulgaria, 1969-72; technologist Rsch. Inst. Perfumery and Cosmetic, Plovdiv, 1972-90, head lab. fine organic synthesis, 1990-92, dir., 1992-94; mgr. Dr. Grozeva-Aromsa Ltd., Plovdiv, 1995—; Spkr. at confs. Contbr. articles to profl. jours. Mem. Union Dem. Forces. Mem. Union Scientists, Club Bus. Women, Inst. Food Technologists. Avocations: traveling, books. Office: Dr Grozeva-Aromsa Ltd, Bul Svoboda 36, 4000 Plovdiv Bulgaria

GRUBBS, CONWAY E., marine company executive; b. Tribbey, Okla., Mar. 26, 1918; s. Harvey Kendrick and Ida Irene (Wright) G.; m. Clyde Laverne Mason, Aug. 23, 1941; children: Jimmy Conway, Barri Lynn. Student, Northeastern Okla. A&M Coll., 1937-38. Mgr. ops., mgr. mktg., gen. mgr, v.p., dir. Caribbean, Ctrl. and So. Am. Chgo. Bridge & Iron Co., Oakbrook, Ill., 1955-69, asst. mgr. marine ops., dir. underwater welding rsch., 1969-76; mgr. worldwide underwater constrn. Chgo. Bridge & Iron Co., Prairieville, La., 1976-79; pres., owner D&W Underwater Welding Svc., Inc., Baton Rouge, 1979-84; dir. underwater welding R & D Global Divers and Contractors, Inc., Lafayette, La., 1984—; cons. U.S. Nat. Rsch. Coun., U.S. Dept. Interior; chmn. exec. com. Joint Industry Underwater Welding Devel. Program. Contbr. articles to profl. jours. With USAAF, 1941-44. Mem. Am. Welding Soc. (chmn. coms., tech. rep., Meritorious Award for Outstanding Achievements in the Science of Welding 1987), Internat. Inst. Welding (chmn., del.). Achievements include patents for Method of Underwater Welding Using Pressurized Welding Electrode Transfer Capsule and Dry Welding Electrode Insitu Storage, Viewing Scope for Turbid Environment and Use in Underwater Welding, and Method of Underwater Welding Using Viewing Scope; major advancements in underwater 'wet' welding. Office: Global Divers & Contractors PO Box 10840 New Iberia LA 70562-0840 Address: 7414 Prairie Dr Greenwell Springs LA 70739-3055

GRUBER, DORIS MARIA, obstetrician/gynecologist, educator; b. Neunkirchen, Austria, Jan. 24, 1968; d. Harald and Gertraud (Abseher) G. MD, U. Vienna, 1992. Mem. Austrian Menopause Soc., Austrian Soc. Sterility and Fertility, European Menopause and Anodropause Soc. Roman Catholic. Fax: 0043-1-40400-2817. E-mail: doris.gruber@akh-wien.ac.at. Office: U Vienna Gen Hosp, Währinger Gürtel 18-20, 1090 Wien Austria

GRUBER, EVA MARIA, physician; b. Ried, Innkreis, Austria, May 24, 1964; d. Johann and Maria (Mayer) G. MD, U. Innsbruck, Austria, 1990. Resident Cmty. Hosp. Austria, 1990-93; fellow U. Innsbruck, 1993-95, U. Vienna, Austria, 1995-97; rsch. fellow Harvard U. Med. Sch., Boston, 1997-99; asst. in anesthesia U. Vienna, 1999—. Contbr. articles to profl. jours. including Annals of Thoracic Surgery and Anesthesia Analgesia. Rsch. grantee Max Kade Found., 1997. Office: Dept Cardiothor VASC Anes, Waehringer Guertel 18-20, A-1090 Vienna Austria

GRUBER, GEORGE MICHAEL, accountant, financial systems consultant; b. Euclid, Ohio, Sept. 9, 1951; s. George and Cecilia Marie (Cantwell) G.; m. Alice Armas Peralta, June 22, 1985; 1 child, Christian Alexander. BS in Acctg. and Fin., San Francisco State U., 1983, MBA in Fin., 1991. Letterpress printer Custom Printing Assocs., San Francisco, 1973-78; voucher examiner U.S. Dept. Labor, San Francisco, 1980-81; teamster United Courier, Inc., San Francisco, 1979-81; bookkeeper, tile setter Curry Tile, Albany, Calif., 1982; sr. staff acct., fin. analyst Marriott Corp. divsn. Farrells Restaurants Inc., San Francisco, 1983-85; asst. contr. Bay Area Seating Svc., Oakland, Calif., 1985-87; mgr. acctg. and fin. divsn. Grand Met. Plc (Pillsbury) The Häagen Dazs Co. Inc., Hayward, Calif., 1987-90; corp. contr. Andronico's Park & Shop Inc., Albany, Calif., 1991; div. contr. Core-Mark Internat., Hayward, 1991-93; founder, owner Gruber Fin. Sys. Svcs. (GFS), 1993—; mid-Pacific regional fin. acctg. contr. DFS, L.P., Tamuning, Guam, 1993-95; CFO, treas. Tool&Garden.com, 1999-2000; guest lectr. fin. San Francisco State U., 1990-91. Coach Willie Mays Youth Baseball, San Francisco; league umpire. With USMC, 1969-72, Vietnam. Mem. Inst. Mgmt. Accts. (v.p. edn. 1991-92, pres. 1992-93, cert. of appreciation 1992-93), Nat. Soc. Pub. Accts., VFW, Am. Legion. Avocations: cycling, archery, pistol, martial arts (Tang Soo Do). Email: GGruber@PacBell.net. Home and Office: Gruber Fin Svcs Co 432 Congo St San Francisco CA 94131-3111

GRUBER, JONAS, chemistry educator, researcher; b. Sao Paulo, Brazil, Dec. 15, 1957; s. Isaac and Haia (Eisenfish) G.; m. Maria Silvia Martins de Souza, Jan. 7, 1995. B of Chemistry, U. Sao Paulo, 1984, PhD in Organic Chemistry, 1991; postgrad., Queen Mary & Westfield Coll., London, 1992-93. Cert. in chemistry. Lectr. chemistry U. Sao Paulo, 1990-91, prof., 1991—; cons. to various industries, Brazil, 1984—; councilor Chem. Inst., U. Sao Paulo, 1996—. Contbr. papers to profl. jours. Rsch. grantee Fundacao Amparo Pesquisa Estado Sao Paulo, Conselho Nacional Desenvolvimento cientifico Tecnologico, Financiadora Estudos Projetos. Mem. AAAS, Brazilian Chem. Soc., Brazilian Chem. Assn., N.Y. Acad. Scis. Avocation: philately.

GRUBER, LOREN CHARLES, English language educator, writer; b. Carroll, Iowa, Sept. 17, 1941; s. Maurice Deputy and Harriett Helen (Brynteson) G.; m. Irene Ellen Olson, Mar. 5, 1967 (div. 1980); children: Elizabeth Gruber Shinall, Stephen, Margaret; m. Meredith Adair Crellin, Jan. 22, 1983 (div. 1999). BA, Simpson Coll., 1963; MA, Western Res. U., 1964; PhD, U. Denver, 1972. English instr. Grove City (Pa.) Coll., 1964-66, Simpson Coll., Indianola, Iowa, 1966-69; tchg. asst. U. Denver, 1968-69, tchg. fellow, 1969-70; from asst. to assoc. prof. Simpson Coll., Indianola, 1970-82; chief exec. cons. Stanley, Barber, Southard, Brown and Assocs., San Diego, 1982-83; account exec. Sta. KJEM-AM and K-95-FM, Bentonville, Ark., 1983-87; mgr., news dir. Sta. KQIS-FM, Clarinda, Iowa, 1987-89; asst. prof. English N.W. Mo. State U., Maryville, 1989-93, interim dir. composition, 1992-93; prof. English and mass comm. Mo. Valley Coll., Marshall, 1993—, chair mass comm., 1995-98, chair English dept., 1996-98, dean divsn. arts and humanities, 1998—; reviewer Choice, Middletown, Conn., 1973-82. Gen. editor In Geardagum Series, 1974-82, 91-92; editor-in-chief: (with Meredith Crellin Gruber and Gregory K. Jember) Essays on Old, Middle, Modern English and Old Icelandic, 1999; bibliographer Neuphilologische Mitteilungen, Helsinki, Finland, 1978-82; bus. mgr. Laurel Rev., 1989-93; assoc. editor Lyrical Iowa, 1999-2000; contbr. articles to profl. jours., poetry, short fiction to magazines. Founding pres. Indianola Writers Workshop, 1972; sec. Indianola Fine Arts Commn., 1973; state del. Iowa Rep. Party Conv., Des Moines, 1976, 80, 88; hon. mem. 4-H, Page County, Iowa, 1988; bd. dirs. Writers Hall of Fame, 1995-98; founder Mid-Mo. chpt. Writers' Hall of Fame, 1996-98. Mem. Medieval Acad. Am. (life, mem. endowment campaign com. 1995-96), Soc. for Advancement Scandinavian Studies (life), Soc. for New Lang. Study (exec. sec. 1973-82, 91-92), Mo. Writers Guild (bd. dirs. 1992—, editor News 1992-94, 2nd v.p. 1993-94, 1st v.p. 1994-95, pres. 1995-96), Soc. Children's Book Writers and Illustrators, Iowa Poetry Assn. (pres. 1980-82, 88-92), Bentonville/Bella Vista Ark. Kiwanis (pres. 1985-86, lt. gov.'s award 1986, Merit and Spl. award 1986), Clarinda Iowa Rotary (pres. pro-tem 1989), Mo. Writers' Guild (Marshall chpt., charter), Kiwanis (bd. dirs. Marshall chpt. 1999—), Sigma Tau Delta (publs. and handbook com. 2000—). Republican. Episcopalian. Avocations: fishing, hunting, ornithology, travel. Home: PO Box 217 Marshall MO 65340-0217 Office: Mo Valley Coll Dept Of English Marshall MO 65340

GRUBER, RONALD P., plastic surgeon, researcher; b. London, Apr. 13, 1941; came to U.S., 1946; s. Paul Pinkas and Edith (Lieblein) G.; m. Gloria Lynn Rubel, June 4, 1967; children: Alicia, Brandon, April, Amanda. BA in Speech, U. Calif., Berkeley, 1962; MD, U. Calif., San Francisco, 1966. Diplomate Am. Bd. Plastic Reconstructive Surgery. Intern Maimonides Med. Ctr., N.Y.C., 1966-67; resident in gen. surgery Montefiore Med. Ctr., N.Y.C., 1967-68; resident in surgery U. Calif., San Francisco, 1970-71; resident in surgery Stanford U. Med. Ctr., 1971-73, chief resident in plastic surgery, 1973-74; chief clin. and exptl. br. Edgewood (Md.) Arsenal Biophysics Lab., 1968-70; Bank of Am. fellow Stanford (Calif.) U., 1971-72, clin. asst. prof., 1996—; assoc. staff Alta Bates Hosp., Berkeley, 1974—; active staff Summitt Hosp., Oakland, 1974—; chief of plastic surgery, Providence Hosp., Oakland, 1974—. Cons. Annals of Plastic Surgery, 1986—, Plastic & Reconstrucive Surgery, 1992—, Reg. Edition Aesthetic Plastic Surgery Jour.; co-author: Rhinoplasty: State of the Art, 1993; contbr. numerous articles to scientific jours., including Plastic & Reconstructive Surgery, Aesthetic Surgery, Annals of Plastic Surgery, Clin. Plastic Surgery, others; presenter in fields of plastic surgery rsch. and physics rsch.; co-author numerous videos; contbr. numerous chpts. to books. Major, U.S. Army, Edgewood Arsenal, Md., 1968-70. Recipient rsch. grant to study x-ray penetrability of silicone, Plastic Surgery Edn. Found., 1991. Mem. AAAS, AMA, ACS, Royal Soc. Medicine, Am. Physicians Fellowship Inc., Internat. Coll. Surgeons, Am. Soc. Plastic and Reconstructive Surgeons, N.Y. Acad. Scis., Internat. Soc. Study of Time, Am. Soc. Aesthetic Plastic Surgery, Am. Soc. Maxillofacial Surgeons, Am. Assn. Plastic Surgeons (by invitation), Am. Physics Soc., Calif. Med. Assn., Alameda Contra Costa County Med. Assn., Calif. Soc. Plastic Surgeons, Rhinoplasty Soc. (pres. 1999-2000). Achievements include development of the periareolar subpectoral augmentation mammaplasty; pioneer of the open rhinoplasty. Office: East Bay Aesthetic Plastic Surgery Ctr 3318 Elm St Oakland CA 94609-3012 also: 911 Moraga Rd Ste 201 Lafayette CA 94549-4500

GRUBHOFFER, LIBOR, research scientist, educator; b. Policka, Czech Republic, Apr. 30, 1957; s. Jindrich and Vlasta (Leinweberova) Grubhoffer; (div.); children: Vendula, Marek. MS, Charles U. Prague, 1981; PhD, Czechlosvak Acad. Scis., 1987. Rsch. asst. Rsch. Inst. Organic Synteses, Pardubice, 1982-83, Inst. Sera and Vaccines, Prague, 1983-85; rsch. asst. Inst. Parasitology, Ceske Budejovice, 1985-87, rsch. scientist, 1987-93; dir. Acad. Sci. Czech Rep. Inst. Parasitology, Ceske Budejovice, 1994—; assoc. prof. U. South Bohemia, Ceske Budejovice, 1997—. Contbr. over 65 articles to profl. jours. Mem. Internat. Soc. for Devel. of Comp. Immunology. Roman Catholic. Avocations: hiking, cross country skiing, roller blade skating, ice hockey, bowling. Office phone: 420-38 5300351. Office: Inst Parasitology, Acad Sci of Czech Republic, 37005 Ceske Budejovice Czech Republic

GRUBIC, ADRIANNE, journalist; b. Morristown, N.J., Mar. 2, 1975; d. Roger Allen and Janice Faye Grubic. BA, Auburn U., 1997; M Mass comms., U. S.C., 1998. Grad. asst. S.C. Press Assn., Columbia, 1997-98; intern WGNX-TV, Atlanta, 1998; sports copy editor Marietta Daily Jour., 1999-2000. Mem. Soc. Profl. Journalists (publs. chmn. 1997), Assn. Women in Sports Media, Omega Phi Alpha (comms. dir. 1997—). Avocations: running, basketball, web design, volunteering, rollerblading. E-mail: krinklefish@mindspring.com. Home: 2255 Lenox Rd NE Apt A24 Atlanta GA 30324-4313

GRUBIC, ZORANA, immunobiologist; b. Split, Dalmatia, Croatia, May 10, 1963; d. Zoran and Tonka (Poljak) G. Biologist, U. Zagreb, Croatia, 1986, MS, 1991, PhD, 1997. Rsch. asst. Nat. Referral Organ Transplantation and Tissue Typing Ctr., Zagreb, 1987-91, rschr., 1991—. Mem. European Found. Immunogenetics, Croatian Immunology Soc. (HID). Office: Nat Ref Organ Transpl Ctr, Kišpaticeva 12, HR-10000 Zagreb Croatia

GRÜBLER, ARNULF MARIAN, regional planner; b. Graz, Styria, Austria, Feb. 1, 1955; s. Georg and Maria (Puntigam) G. MA, Tech. U., Vienna, Austria, 1985, PhD, 1989. Rsch. asst. energy programme Internat. Inst. Applied Systems Analysis, Laxenburg, Austria, 1978-83, rsch. asst. gas study project, 1985, rsch. scholar dynamics of tech & environ. compatabile energy, 1986—; intern industry dept. World Bank, Washington, 1984; mem. expert group indsl. transformation Internat. Social Sci. Coun. Programme, 1994-95; lectr. Vienna U., 1990-91, Leoben U., 1998—; cons. Environ. Policy Divsn. World Bank, Washington, 1991-92, GM, Warren, Ohio, 1994-95, UN, N.Y.C., 1995-96; lead author Intergovtl. Panel on Climate Change, 1994—. Mem. editl. bd. Jour. Indsl. Ecology, 1996—, Tech. Forecasting and Social Change, 1995—; author: The Rise and Fall of Infrastructures, 1990, Diffusion of Technologies and Social Behavior, 1991, Environment and Development, 1994, Global Energy Perspectives to 2050, 1995, Technology and Global Change, 1998. Grantee Austrian Electricity Bd., Vienna, 1987-89, Ctrl. Rsch. Inst. for Electric Power, Tokyo, 1994—, European Communities, Brussels, 1996—. Mem. Russian Acad. Natural Scis. (fgn.). Avocations: technology history, viticulture. Office: Internat Inst Applied, Systems Analysis, A-2361 Laxenburg Austria

GRUBMULLER, HELMUT, physicist; b. Munich, Germany, July 31, 1965; s. Karl-Heinz and Emmy (Lingl) G.; m. Brigitte Sonja Gumberger, Sept. 13, 1991; children: Julia, Diana. BSc, Tech. U. Munich, 1990, PhD in Physics, 1994. Software developer MS Microsys., Munich, 1984-91; vis. scientist Beckman Inst. Univ. Ill., Urbana, 1991; sr. rsch. asst. Ludwig Maximilians U., Munich, 1994-98; cons. Spektrum Verlag, Heidelberg, Germany, 1994. Mem. AAAS, German Physics Soc., Molecular Graphics Soc., German Biophysics Soc. (mng. bd. 1996—). Avocations: computer graphics, quantum mechanics. Office: Max-Planck Inst Theor Molec Bio, Am Fassberg 11, D-37070 Göttingen Germany

GRUBNIK, VLADIMIR VLADIMIROVICH, surgeon; b. Odessa, Ukraine, Mar. 22, 1950; s. Vladimir and Tamara (Gorbaneva) G.; m. Tatyana Ananevna Zolotaryova, Apr. 27, 1979; 1 child, Alexandra. MD, Med. U. Odessa, 1973, PhD, 1975; DSc, Med. U. Kiev, 1987. Surgeon Odessa Dist. Hosp., 1973-75; surgeon, prof. surgery, chief surgery dept. Med. U. Odessa,

1975—. Author: (with Hoholya, Saenko, Dotsenko) Clinical Course and Treatment of Acute Ulcers of the Digestive Tract, 1989; (with V.M. Mavrodi) Physiotherapy in Surgery, 1995; (with others) Lasers for Surgery, 1998, (with V.N. Sokolov) Breast Diseases, 1999, (with V.N. Zaporojan) Vidioendoscopic Surgery and Gynecology, 1999, (with A.A. Shalimov, Joel Horowitz) Chronic Pancreatitis, 2000, (with A.A. Shalimov) Infection Control in Surgery, 2000, (with V.A. Tsepkolenko) Plastic Aesthetic Surgery, 2000; contbr. articles to profl. jours; patentee in field. Recipient Govt. prize in sci., 1990. Mem. European Assn. Endoscopic Surgery, Russian Assn. Endoscopic Surgery, N.Y. Acad. Scis. Home: 148/2 Schors St #12, 65036 Odessa Ukraine

GRUCHALLA, MICHAEL EMERIC, electronics engineer; b. Houston, Feb. 2, 1946; s. Emeric Edwin and Myrtle (Priebe) G.; m. Elizabeth Tyson, June 14, 1969; children: Kenny, Katie. BSEE, U. Houston, 1968; MSEE, U. N.Mex., 1980. Registered profl. engr., Tex. Project engr. Tex. Instruments Corp., Houston, 1967-68; group leader EG&G Washington Analytical Services Ctr., Albuquerque, 1974-88; sr. staff engr. EG&G Energy Measurements Inc., Albuquerque, 1988-94; engrng. specialist Allied Signal FM&T, Albuquerque, 1994—; cons. engrng., Albuquerque; lectr. in field, 1978—; expert witness in field; presenter sci. testimony before Ho. of Reps. Sci. Com., 1996. Contbr. articles to tech. jours.; patentee in field. Judge local sci. fairs, Albuquerque, 1983—. Served to capt. USAF, 1968-74. Recipient R&D 100 award, 1991, Gen. Mgr.'s Vision award Dept. Energy, 1994. Mem. IEEE, Instrumentation Soc. Am., Planetary Soc., N.Mex. Tex. Instruments Computer Group (pres. 1984-85), Electric Auto Assn. (v.p. Albuquerque chpt. 1994—), Sigma Xi, Tau Beta Pi, Eta Kappa Nu. Avocations: electro-optics, photography, woodworking. Office: Allied Signal KCD PO Box 5250 Albuquerque NM 87185-5250

GRUDER, YARON E., foundation administrator. Dir. gen. The Wolf Found., Herzlia, Israel. Office: The Wolf Found. PO Box 398, Herzlia BET46103, Israel*

GRUEBER, NILS HEINRICH AUGUSTIN, retired German diplomat, international law educator; b. Schwaebisch Gmünd, Germany, July 3, 1933; s. Edgar Herbert and Marianne (Peclard) G.; m. Fatiha Guidoum, Mar. 23, 1967; children: Karim, Carsten, Nadja. 1st state exam. in law, Freiburg (Germany) U., 1958; 2d state exam., Stuttgart, Germany, 1964; LLD, U. Zurich, Switzerland, 1962. With Fgn. Office, Bonn, 1965-98; retired, 1998. Mem. Self Realization Fellowship, 1953—. Decorated Order of Rising Sun (Japan), Order of Merit (Egypt). Fellow Existential Psychologische Bildungsstätte Todtmoos-Rütte (bd. dirs. 1980-85). Avocations: classical piano, oriental philosophy, science of religion, tennis, classical music. Home: 1-14 Motoyama Chikusaku, Nagoya 464-0036, Japan Office: Meijo U, 1-501 Shiogamaguchi, Nagoya 468-8502, Japan

GRUEN, MICHAEL STEPHAN, lawyer; b. L.A., Mar. 25, 1942; s. Victor and Elsie Caroline (Krummeck) G.; m. Susanna Lloyd, July 18, 1964; m. Vanessa Elisabeth Ahlfors, Jan. 3, 1976; children: Madeleine, Alexis, Viveca; stepchildren: Stefan, Sebastian. BA cum laude, Harvard U., 1963; LLB, UCLA, 1966. Bar: Calif. 1966, N.Y. 1967, U.S. Ct. Appeals (2d cir.) 1976, U.S. Supreme Ct. 1975, U.S. Dist. Ct. (so. and ea. dists.) N.Y. 1986. Assoc. Paul, Weiss, Rifkind, Wharton & Garrison, N.Y.C., 1966-69, Gilinsky, Stillman & Mishkin, N.Y.C., 1969-70, Wolf, Popper, Ross, Wolf & Jones, N.Y.C., 1970-74; gen. counsel Bio-Med. Scis., Inc., Fairfield, N.J., 1974-75; pvt. practice N.Y.C., 1975-80; mem. Gruen & Muskin, N.Y.C., 1980, Gruen, Muskin & Thau, N.Y.C., 1981-88, Gruen, Gilliatt & Livingston, N.Y.C., 1989-90, Gruen & Livingston, N.Y.C., 1990-97, Gruen & Farrelly LLP, N.Y.C., 1998—. Contbr. articles to legal and gen. publs. Bd. dirs. Boys' Athletic League, 1966-82, Columbia Land Conservancy, 1986—, pres., 1988-91; dir. N.Y. Landmarks Conservancy, 1972-94, adv. coun., 1994-97; chmn. Historic Dists. Coun., 1974-79; bd. advisors Prep. Divsn. Bklyn. Coll. Ctr. for Performing Arts, 1980-83; mem. law com. Mcpl. Art Soc., 1987—; pres. Riverside Dems., N.Y.C., 1971-72. Mem. ABA (litig. sect.), N.Y. State Bar Assn., Assn. of Bar of City of N.Y. Office: 500 5th Ave Ste 5225 New York NY 10110-5299

GRUENDLER, PETER, chemistry educator; b. Rosswein, Saxonia, Germany, Apr. 26, 1940; s. Willy and Martha (Herzog) G.; m. Regina Kohn, Dec. 28, 1963; children: Grundler, Kai. Diploma in Chemistry, U. Leipzig, Germany, 1965, Dr.rer.nat., 1969, Dr.rer.nat.habil, 1984. Scientific asst. U. Leipzig, 1966-70, sr. asst., 1970-85, docent, 1985-88; prof. analytical chemistry U. Rostock, Germany, 1988—; dir. dept. analytical and environ. chemistry, Rostock, 1988. Coun. mem. U. Rostock, 1990-96, sr. faculty mem., 1992-96; adv. bd. Friedr.-Ebert Found., Bonn, Germany, 1992—. Mem. Group Electroanalysis in German Chem. Soc. Office: Rostock Univ/Chem Dept, Buchbinderstrasse 9, D-18051 Rostock Germany

GRUENWALD, JAMES HOWARD, association executive, consultant; b. Cin., Aug. 30, 1949; s. Howard Francis and Geraldine Emma (Mueller) G. BS, Xavier U., 1971. Cert. profl. in recreation and leisure svc., Ill. Rep. pub. rels. Cath. Youth Orgn., Cin., 1969-72; sales rep. Spade Trucking Co., Cin., 1972-73; field rep. Ohio Dept. Transport, Columbus, 1973-76; editl. sales rep. Cin. Suburban Newspaper, 1977-79; nat. exec. dir. Say Soccer USA, Cin., 1979-93; co-founder, exec. dir. U.S. Indoor Soccer Orgn., 1985-93, 1985-90; bd. dirs. Buckeye Men's Baseball, Cin., 1982-90, chmn., 1982-86, 89-90; dir. Amateur Athletic Union, Indpls., 1983-85; nat. membership coord. Am. Youth Soccer Orgn., L.A., 1993—; cert. trainer Am. Coaches Effectiveness Program, Champaign, Ill., 1983-92. Editor Touchline jour., 1980-92, Parents Guide to Soccer, 1985-92. Adv. bd. Church Parish, Cin., 1974-76. Recipient cmty. svc. award State of Mich., 1986. Mem. Nat. Coun. Youth Sports Dirs., Nat. Recreation and Parks Assn., Mich. Recreation and Parks Assn. (cmty. svc. award 1986), Soc. for Non Profits. Avocations: hiking, reading, writing, teaching, conducting workshops. Home: 11986 Cedarcreek Dr Cincinnati OH 45240-1550 Office: 12501 Isis Ave Hawthorne CA 90250-4149

GRUFFAT, JEAN-CLAUDE, banker; b. Lyon, France, Nov. 6, 1944; came to U.S., 1987; s. Jean-Marius and Marie-Antoinette (Coquand) G.; m. Christiane Linz, June 11, 1969; children: Stephane, Sabine. M in Polit. Sci., U. Lyon, 1968, PhD in Law, 1972; Stanford Exec. Program, Standford U., 1987. Bar: Lyon, 1966. With Banque de l'Indochine, Paris, 1973-74; head treasury, personnel and adminstrn. Banque Indosuez, Bangkok, Thailand, 1974-78; agy. mgr. Banque Indosuez, Al Khobar, Damman, Saudi Arabia, 1978-81; regional mgr. for West Coast Banque Indosuez, Djeddah, Saudi Arabia, 1981-83; regional mgr. for Hong Kong, China and Macau Banque Indosuez, Hong Kong, 1983-87; regional mgr. for N.Am. Banque Indosuez, N.Y.C., 1987—; exec. v.p., global head, sr. regl. officer for Americas Indosuez Capital, 1994; market mgr. Citibank, Paris, 1998—; bd. dirs. Levesque Beaubien Geoffrion, Montreal; conseiller du commerce Exterieur de la France, 1984—; mem. Paris exec. com. Banque Indosuez, 1993, chmn. Asia exec. com., 1996; market mgr. for France, global relationship banking Citibank N.A. Bd. dirs. French Inst./Alliance Francaise, N.Y.C., 1989—. Mem. Inst. Internat. Bankers (trustee 1989-94), Hong Kong Club, Econ. Club N.Y., Cercle De L'Union Interalliee-Paris. Avocations: reading, jogging, music. Office: Citibank, 19 Le Parvis, 92073 Paris La Defense France

GRUGULIS, IRENA, educator; b. Wolverhampton, Britain, Jan. 6, 1965; d. Janis Izidors and Angharad Stella (Jones) G. BA with honors, Bristol U., 1986; PhD, Warwick U., Britain, 1996. Investment banker; writer comedy sketches BBC Radio; lectr. in employment studies Manchester Sch. of Mgmt., UMIST, Britain, 1996—. Editl. bd. Personnel Rev., 1998—; contbr. articles to profl. jours. Rsch. grant Econ. and Social Rsch. Coun., 1994-96, 99—, European Regional Devel. Fund, 1998. Fellow Skope (assoc.); mem. Manchester Indsl. Rels. Soc. (coun. mem. 1999—), British Univs. Indsl. Rels. Assn. (nat. exec. 1998—). Avocations: bridge, cooking, reading, black and white movies, yoga. Office: Manchester Sch Mgmt UMIST, PO Box 88, Manchester M60 1QD, Britian

GRUHL, ANDREA MORRIS, librarian; b. Ponca City, Okla., Dec. 9, 1939; d. Luther Oscar and Hazel Evangeline (Anderson) Morris; m. Werner Mann Gruhl, July 10, 1965; children: Sonja Krista, Diana Krista. BA, Wesleyan Coll., 1961; MLS, U. Md., 1968; postgrad., Johns Hopkins U., 1970-71, U. Md., 1968, 71-73, Oxford U., 1996. Tchr. Broward County, Fla., Dept. Def. Montgomery County, Md., 1961-66; libr. Prince Georges County (Md.) Pub. Libr., 1966-68, 81-83, U. Md., College Park, 1970-72; art. history rschr. Joseph Alsop, Washington, 1972-74; libr. Howard County Pub. Libr., Columbia, Md., 1969-70, 74-79; European exch. staff Libr. of Congress, Washington, 1982-86; cataloger fed. documents GPO, Washington, 1986-93, supervisory libr., 1993—; women's program adv. com., processing dept. rep. Libr. of Congress, 1983-86, mem. ofcl. Libr. of Congress delegation to Internat. Fedn. Libr. Assn. ann. conf., Munich, 1983, Chgo., 1985; state del. White House Conf. on Librs., 1978, 90. Indexer, editor: Learning Vacations, 3d edit., 1980; editor: Federal Librarian, 1994-99; LCPA Index to Libr. of Congress Info. Bull., 1984. Trustee Howard County (Md.) C.C., 1989-95, Howard County Pub. Libr., Columbia, Md., 1979-87; publ. chmn. LWV Howard County, 1974, bd. dirs., 1996-97; citizens rep. Howard County, exec. bd. Balt. Regional Planning Coun. Libr. com., 1976-79; Friends of Libr., Howard County, pres., 1976; vol. Nat. Gallery Art Libr., Washington, 1978-80. Mem. ALA (councilor 1997—, co-chair coun. caucus 2000—, fed. libr. round table 1988—, v.p. 1997-98, pres. 1998-99, editor 1994-99, IFLA rep. 1996—, govt. documents roundtable 1996—), Assn. Libr. Collections and Tech. Svcs. Libr., Adminstrn. and Mgmt. Assn. (planning and evaluation libr. svcs. 1996-97), Libr. Info. Tech. Assn., D.C. Libr. Assn. (co-chair mgmt. interest group 1996-97), Assn. Coll. and Rsch. Librs., Internat. Fedn. Libr. Assns. and Instns. (sect. on cataloging internat. std. bibliographic description/cartographic materials working group 1999—), UN Assn. (Nat. Capitol area chpt., membership com., Md . telephone chair 1992-94), Art Librs. Soc. N.Am. (coord. mems.' publ. exhbn. 1980-82), Libr. Congress Profl. Assn. (coord. ann. staff art shows 1982-83, chair libr. sci. interest group 1985-87), Libr. Congress Am. Fedn. State County and Mcpl. Employees Union (program chair 1984-86), Md. Libr. Assn. (pres. trustee divsn. 1982-83), Md. Assn. C.C. Trustees (sec. 1991-92, bd. dirs. 1992-93), Md. Assn. C.C. (bd. dirs. 1992-95), Beta Phi Mu. Democrat. Lutheran. Home: 5990 Jacobs Ladder Columbia MD 21045-3817 Office: Govt Printing Ofc Washington DC 20401-0001

GRUHL, JAMES, energy scientist, artist; b. Milw., Apr. 9, 1945; s. Alfred and Helen (Vanderveer) G.; m. Nancy Lee Huston, July 4, 1974; children: Amanda Natalie, Steven Christopher. BS, MIT, 1968, MS, 1968, PhD, 1973. Lectr. MIT, 1969-83; rsch. scientist MIT Energy Lab., Cambridge, 1973-83, program mgr., 1978-83, rsch. affiliate, 1984; sci. adv. bd. U.S. EPA, 1986-93; energy cons. U.S. Congress, rsch. insts., internat. energy industries, 1973—. Ednl. counselor MIT, 1978—. Represented by Sanders Galleries, Tucson. Recipient Silver Beaver award Boy Scouts Am., 1986, numerous art awards, 1990—; NSF grantee. Mem. IEEE, AAAS, Math. Programming Soc., MIT Alumni Assn. (officer 1978—), Tau Beta Pi, Eta Kappa Nu. Achievements include research on uncertainties and validity of analytic models, validity of government and industry energy policy models, and climate change models. Office: Gruhl Assocs PO Box 36524 Tucson AZ 85740-6524

GRULIOW, AGNES FORREST, artist, educator; b. Davenport, Iowa, July 5, 1912; d. James Lindsay and Agnes (Johnston) F.; m. Leo Gruliow, Sept. 25, 1945; children: Frank Forrest, Rebecca Agnes Lindsay. BA, Antioch Coll., Yellow Springs, Ohio, 1938; student, Art Students League, N.Y.C., 1963-66. Resident dir. Am. Peoples Sch., N.Y.C., 1937-41; asst. nat. sec. Nat. Fedn. Settlements, N.Y.C., 1941-43; assoc. pers. dir.,asst. prof. Antioch Coll. Extramural Sch., Yellow Springs, 1943-45; index designer-editor Current Digest of Soviet Press, Washington and N.Y.C., 1949-53; freelance editor N.Y.C., 1954-57; tchr. art City & Country Sch., N.Y.C., 1966-68; hostess Am. Friends Svc. Com. Internat. Seminar, Oestgeest, The Netherlands, 1960, Poughkeepsie, N.Y., 1961; sr. vis. fellow Woodrow Wilson Found., 1977-80; proprietor art studio N.Y.C., 1961-69, Worthington, Ohio, 1970-72; art therapy asst. Harding Hosp., Worthington, 1970-72. One-woman show at Antioch Coll., 1967; group show Herndon Gallery, Yellow Springs, Ohio, 2000. Pres. Columbia U. Greenhouse Nursery Sch., N.Y.C., 1954-59; bd. mem. Open Door Day Care Ctr., N.Y.C., 1954-59; mem. founding and adv. bd. East Harlem Tutoring Program, N.Y.C., 1965-73; mem. bd. Columbus Area Internat. Program, 1970-72, 79-87, sec., 1981, pres., 1982-85, chair adv. bd., 1983-87; del. Nat. Bd. Coun. Internat. Programs, Cleve., 1981-83; mem. bd. Cmty. Svc., Inc., Yellow Springs, 1981-99. Mem. Am. Assn. Slavic Studies, Columbus Coun. World Affairs, Columbus Meml. Soc., Columbus Mus. Art, Ohio Hist. Soc., South Ctrl. Ohio Preservation Soc., UNA, UNICEF, World Federalist Assn. Ctrl. Ohio (membership sect. 1987-94), Crichton Club (Columbus), Order Eastern Star. Home: 163 E Lane Ave Columbus OH 43201-1212

GRUM, JANEZ, mechanical engineering educator; b. Ljubljana, Slovenia, Oct. 28, 1946; s. Janez and Helena Grum; m. Darinka Moskon, Sept. 10, 1976; children: Tanja, Gregor, Matej. BSc in Mech. Engrng., U. Ljubljana, 1969, MSc in Mech. Engrng., 1973, PhD in Mech. Engrng., 1977. Rsch. engr. R&D sect. Saturnus, Ljubljana, 1970-71; teaching asst. dept. mech. engrng. U. Ljubljana, 1971-78, asst. prof. materials sci. and tech. of materials, 1978-84, assoc. prof. materials sci. and tech. of materials, 1984-96, prof. materials sci. and tech. of materials, 1996—, head dept. heat treatment lab., 1978—, head material testing lab., 1988—, vice dean dept. mech. engrng., 1989-93, head dept. tech. of materials, 1993—; mem. sci. com. 5th European Conf. on Non-Destructive Testing, Sarajevo, 1991, 4th Internat. Conf. Trends Devel. of Machine Design and Techs, Zenica, Bosnia, and Herzegovina, 1996, Conf. Laser Material Processing, Croatian Soc. Heat Treatment, Opatija, Croatia, 1995; mem. organizing com. 3d European Symposium for Stereology, Ljubljana, Slovenia, 1981; corr. mem. Internat. Inst. Prodn. Engring. Rsch., 1982-85; vice dean U. Mech. Engrng., 1989-93; mem. coun. U. Commn. Prešeren awards Students Rsch. Achievements, 1989-91, 93—; mem. internat. sci. rev. com. 4th Internat. Conf. and Rev. Com., 1997, 5th Internat. Sci. Conf. Prodn. Engring., Opatija, Croatia, 1999; mem. sci. bd. 2d. Internat. Conf. Trends Devel. of Machine Design and Techs, Zenica, Bosnia, and Herzegovina, 1995, 1st Symposium Revitalization and Modernization Metal Industry of Bosnia and Herzegovina, Bihać, 1997; mem. programme com. MATRIB'99, Trogir, Croatia, 1999; mem. conf. sci. com., expert Conf. Trends in Devel. Machinery and Associated Tech., Zenica, 1998; cons. Železarna Ravne, Železarna Štore, Železarna Jesenice, Slovenia, Železarna Sisak, Croatia, TAM Maribor, Slovenia, IMPOL Slovenstra Bistrica, Slovenia, ISKRA Semič, ISKRA Železniki, Slovenia, ETA Cerkno, Slovenia, IPLAS Koper, ITAS Kočevje, PAPIRNICA Vevče, Slovenia, SATURNUS, Ljubljana, KOVINARSKA, Ljubno, TOMOS, Koper, LITOSTROJ, Ljubljana, TITAN, Kamnik, Slovenia, Industrija kugličnih ležajeva, Beograd, Serbia; cons. in field. Co-author: Materials for Engineers, 1987, 89, 91, 93, 95; editor exec. editl. bd. Acta Stereologica, 1982; mem. editl. bd. 3d European Symposium for Stereology, 1981—; co-editor jour. News Soc. Non-Destructive Testing, 1993—; author over 300 papers, 140 reports. Mem. IEEE, ASM Heat Treating Soc. (mem. internat. organizing com. 3d Internat. Conf. Quenching and Control of Disortion 1999), Am. Soc. Metals, Am. Welding Soc., Am. Soc. Heat Treating, Am. Soc. Non Destructive Testing, Am. Ceramic Soc., Deutsche Gesselschaft fur Materialkunde EV Oberursel, Internat. Soc. Sterology, Slovene Soc. for Nondestructive Testing (v.p. 1982—, editor procs. 1985, 90, 97, 98), Slovene Soc. for Stereology and Image Processing (v.p. 1992—), N.Y. Acad. Scis. (active), Brit. Inst. Nondestructive Testing, Materials Rsch. Soc., European Materials Rsch. Soc., European Powder Metallury Assn., ABI Rsch. Assn. (dep. gov.), Internat. Biog. Ctr., Minerals-Metals-Materials, Soc. Exptl. Mechs. Achievements include research in: heat treating, laser processing and analysis of materials, nondestructive testing of materials, mechanical testing of materials, metaalography and microstructures, others. Fax: 386 61 218 567. E-mail: janez.grum@fs. uni-lj.si. Home: Studenec 13, 1260 Ljubljana-Polje Slovenia Office: U Ljubljana Fac Mech Engr, Askerceva 6, 1000 Ljubljana Slovenia

GRUM, MIKKEL, agronomist, plant breeder; b. Baghdad, Iraq, Dec. 12, 1962; arrived in Colombia, 1992; s. Anders and Mette Brøndum; m. Lisbeth Riis, June 18, 1994. MS, Royal Vet. Agrl. U., Copenhagen, 1988; PhD, RVAU, Copenhagen, 1993. Cons. CARE-Danmark, Copenhagen, 1988; rsch. mgr. Royal Vet. Agrl. U., Vaini, Tonga, 1989-92; assoc. scientist RVAU, Cali, Colombia, 1992-94; assoc. scientist Internat. Plant Genetic Resources Inst., Cali, Colombia, 1994-97, Nairobi, Kenya, 1997—.

GRUMLEY, LARRY TYLER, secondary education educator; b. Racine, Wis., Nov. 9, 1951; s. Robert Larry and Maxine (Short) G.; children: Lisa Marie, Daniel Alan. BS in English, Drake U., 1974; MA, Edinboro U., Pa., 1982. Tchr. in english NSW/TAFE, Grainville, Australia, 1989; sr. lectr. Educational Assistance, Melbourne, Australia; asst. prof. U. Western Sydney, Milpena, Australia, 1988-91; sr. tchr. NSW/BOS, Sydney, 1990—; sr. tchr. english Our Lady Mercy Coll., Parramatta, Australia, 1984-95; head english dept. C. McAuley Sr. H.S., Westmead, Australia, 1996—; sr. examiner New S. Wales Bd. Studies, Sydney, 1991—; guest lectr. Vanis, 1990—. Author: (book) General Studies in Focus, 1995, Comprehension 7&8, 9&10, 1997, Multiple Choice Comprehension, 1997, All Texts Study Guide, 1998, Poetry Workbook for 7&8, 1999, Poetry Workbook for 9&10, 1999, Poetry Workbook for 11&12, 1999, New All Texts Study Guide, 2000, Area of Study-Changing Self, 2000. V.p. Wattsburgh Tchrs. Assn., 1980-93; union rep., OLMC, Australia, 1994-96. Grantee Human Rights Commn., Australia, 1985-86. Mem. Modern Languages Assn., English Tchrs. Assn. Avocations: sports, horses, writing. Home: 5 Molyneaux Ave, 2147 Kings Langley Australia Office: Catherine McAuley HS, Dancy Rd, 2145 Westmead Australia

GRÜMM, JOHANN J., physicist, international officer; b. Melk, Austria, Oct. 25, 1919; s. Joseph J. and Theresia M. (Bauer) G.; m. Elfriede M. Altmann, mar. 1, 1921; 1 child, Hans-Richard. DrPhil, U. Vienna, 1949. Dept. head Simmering Graz Pauker Ltd., Vienna, 1958-61; head Inst. for Reactor Devel. Stüdienges für Atomenergie, Vienna, 1961-71; sci. dir. Nuclear Rsch. Ctr., Seibersdorf, Austria, 1971-78; dep. dir. gen. IAEA, Vienna, 1978-83, sci. advisor, 1984-87. Author: (autobiography) Three Lives, 1992; author/co-author books on reactor theory, 1958-83; contbr. articles to profl. jours. Decorated hon. cross 1st class for arts and scis. Austrian Govt., 1975. Fellow Am. Nuclear Soc. (hon. mem.); mem. Austrian Phys. Soc., Deutsche Kerntechnische Gesellschaft (hon.). Home: Joanelligasse 7/9, A1060 Vienna Austria

GRÜN, RAINER WOLFGANG, research scientist; b. Duisburg, Germany, Apr. 14, 1956; s. Paul and Ursula (Ketteler) G.; m. Fiona Marian Silver, May 18, 1990; children: Harriet Sarah, Robin Adair. Diploma, U. Köln, Germany, 1982, Dr. rer. nat., 1985; DSc, Australian Nat. U., 1997; Habilitation, U. Cologne, 1998. Rsch. asst. U. Köln, Germany, 1982-83, rsch. assoc., 1983-85; postdoctoral fellow McMaster U., Hamilton, Ont., Can., 1985-87; rsch. assoc. U. Cambridge, Eng., 1987-89, sr. rsch. assoc., 1989-92; fellow Australian Nat. U., Canberra, 1992-94, sr. fellow, 1994-98, dir. Quaternary Dating Rsch. Ctr., 1992—, prof., 1998—, head environ. geochemistry and geochronology, 2000—; head thermoluminescence/epectron spin resonance lab., Cambridge U., 1987-92. Author: (book) ESR Dating, 1989; editor Quaternary Geochronology, 1994—. Active Clare Hall Coll., Cambridge. Office: Rsch Sch Earth Scis, Australian Nat U, Canberra ACT 0200, Australia

GRUNBAUM, MARIANNE HETTNER, artist; b. Freiberg, Germany, Nov. 6, 1894; came to U.S., 1937; d. Franz and Anna (Stuebel) Hettner; m. Franz Victor Grunbaum, Oct. 27, 1919 (dec. Dec. 1980); children: Elizabeth Lord, Werner Grunbaum. Student, U. Heidelberg, Germany, 1914-16, U. Houston, 1914-16. One-woman shows DuBose Gallery, Houston, 1971, Roberto Molina Gallery, Houston, 1980-92; exhbns. include New Accessions U.S.A., Colorado Springs, Colo., 1954 (Smith Coll. acquired oil painting for permanent collection), Tex. Fine Arts Assn., Laguna Gloria Art Mus., Austin, Tex., 1955, Nat. Arts Club, N.Y.C., 1967, Laguna Gloria Art Mus., Austin, Tex., 1974, Wash. State U., 1984, Cheney Cowles Meml. Mus., Spokane, 1986. Represented in permenant collections Smith Coll. Mus. of Art, Crossed Sqares Cheney Cowles Meml. Mus., Spokane, Wash., pvt. collections including De Menil collection, Houston; contbr. book The Best of Acryllic Painting, 1996.

GRUNBERG, ROBERT LEON WILLY, nephrologist; b. Bucharest, Romania, July 23, 1940; came to U.S., 1972, naturalized, 1977; s. William A. and Isabelle L. (Rosen) G.; m. Donna M. Fishman, Oct. 19, 1975; children: Wendie I., Andrea B. MD, U. Orleans-Tours, France, 1969. Diplomate Am. Bd. Internal Medicine, Am. Bd. Nephrology; cert. hypertension specialist in clin. hypertension. Intern, then resident in cardiology Vichy (France) Hosp., 1968-72; resident in internal medicine Albert Einstein Med. Ctr., Phila., 1972-74; fellow in nephrology-hypertension Hahnemann Univ. Hosp., Phila., 1974-76, sr. clin. instr. then asst. clin. prof. div. nephrology, 1976; pvt. practice medicine specializing in nephrology Allentown, Pa., 1976—; attending physician St. Luke's Hosp., Bethlehem, Pa., Lehigh Valley Ctr. (now Lehigh Valley Hosp.), Allentown; attending charge divsn. nephrology Easton (Pa.) Hosp.; courtesy staff Hahnemann Univ. Hosp.; dir. Renal Dialysis Ctr. at Easton (Pa.) Hosp., 1989; chief dialysis Warren Hosp., Phillipsburg, N.J., 1999. Fellow ACP; mem. AMA (Physician's Recognition award 1975, 79, 82, 85, 88, 89-92, 92-95, 95-98, 2001), Pa. Med. Soc., Am. Soc. Nephrology, Am. Soc. Artificial Internal Organs, Internat. Soc. Hypertension, Am. Soc. for Parenteral and Enteral Nutrition, Internat. Soc. for Artificial Organs, Internat. Soc. Nephrology, Assn. for Advancement of Med. Instrumentation, Internat. Soc. for Peritoneal Dialysis, Nat. Kidney Found., N.Y. Acad. Scis. Office: 50 S 18th St Easton PA 18042-3912 also: 401 N 17th St Allentown PA 18104-5034

GRUNDHOEFER, HORST PETER, sociologist, educator; b. Muenster, Germany, July 26, 1939; s. Peter Michael and Margarete (Rau) G.; m. Barbara Boehm, Oct. 23, 1970. Tchr. Sch. for Apprentices, Cologne, Germany, 1966-70; lectr. Tech. Coll., Cologne, 1970-71; prof. U. Applied Scis., Cologne, 1971—. Author: Consumer Attitudes and Behavior in the Context of Family Structure, 1982; contbr. articles to profl. jours. Mem. German Assn. Mktg. Lectrs. Office: U Applied Scis Cologne, Mainzer Str 5, D-50678 Cologne NRW, Germany

GRUNDLAND, JGNACY MAREK, biochemist, astrophysicist; b. Warsaw, Poland, Nov. 8, 1913; s. Treneusz and Daniela Grundland; m. Anna Maria Lisiewicz, May 12, 1934; 1 child, Jacek; m. Stephania Helman, Sept. 3, 1939 (dec. 1955); 1 child, Alfred Michel. MD, Faculty of Medicine, Paris, 1939; Cert. in Chemistry/Physics, U. Toulouse, France, 1941; Docent in Biochemistry, Polish Acad. Scis., 1958. Attaché Nat. Sci. Rsch. Ctr., Paris, 1939-55, head of rsch., 1955; docent Polish Acad. Scis., 1956-58; pvt. scientist in biochemistry/astrophysics Warsaw, 1958—. Contbr. numerous articles to profl. jours. Mem. N.Y. Acad. Scis., Planetary Soc. Avocation: fine arts. Home: pl Hallera 10 M 109A, 03-464 Warsaw Poland

GRUNDMANN, DAVID, surgeon; b. Munich, Germany, Oct. 19, 1946; arrived in Australia, 1952; s. Henniech and Anna (Ginzburg) G.; children from previous marriage: Adam Robert, Lisa Rachel. MBBS, U. Melbourne, 1970. Jr. resident St. Vincent's Hosp., Melbourne, Australia, 1971-72; sr. resident, dep. supt. Sale (Australia) Hosp., 1972-73; pvt. practice, Melbourne, 1973-76; surgeon Fertility Control Clinic, Melbourne, 1976-82; founder, med. dir. Planned Parenthood of Australia, 1983—; pvt. practice Townsville Clinic—, 1983, Rockhampton Clinic, 1987—, Brisbane Clinic, 1990—, Necastle Clinic, 1994—, Melbourne Clinic, 1998; invited participant sterilisation program, West Bengal, 1988. Contbr. articles to profl. jours. and profl. meetings. Commonwealth scholarship Med. Sch. Melbourne U. Fellow Australian Coll. Biomed. Scientists; mem. Internat. Soc. Abortion Drs. (founding; pres.), Internat. Soc. Gynecol. Endoscopy, Australasian Assn. for Vol. Sterilisation, Assn. Reproductive Health Profls., Australian Inst. for Health Law and Ethics, Abortion Provider Fedn. Australia (pres. 1991-93), Children By Choice (life), Am. Assn. Gynecol. Laparascopists, Nat. Abortion Fedn. USA, Family Planning Assn. Queensland (life), Australian Soc. for Ultrasound in Medicine, Am. Inst. for Ultrasound in Medicine, Medico Legal Soc. Queensland. Jewish. Avocations: flying, snow skiing, scuba diving, tennis, collecting Australian art. E-mail: david-doc@bigpond.com. Home: Windermere Towers Brett's Wharf, 13/27 Harbour Rd Apt 13, Hamilton QLD 4007, Australia Office: Planned Parenthood Australia, 8 Campbell St, Brisbane 4006, Australia

GRUNDSTRÖM, LEIF THOMAS INGEMAR, tumor biology educator; b. Skellefteå, Sweden, Dec. 21, 1953; s. Ingemar and Rut (Boström) G.; m. Christine Anne Klöpfer, Mar. 23, 1985; children: Eric, Caroline, Robert. Dr.'s degree, Umeå (Sweden) U., 1981, MD, 1982. Amanuensis Umeå Univ., 1975-81, lectr., rsch. asst., 1981-82, rsch. asst., docent, 1984-86, lectr., 1992-94, prof. tumor biology, 1994—; scientist Natural Sci. Rsch. Coun. of Sweden, Umeå, 1986-92. Contbr. articles to profl. jours. Mem. Swedish Cancer Soc. (priority com. microbiology and immunology, alternate sci. bd. 1992—); Swedish Soc. for Med. Rsch. (alternate scientific bd. 1989—). Office: Umeå U Dept Applied, Cell and Molecular Biology, S-901 87 Umeå Sweden

GRUNENBERG, ALFONS, chemist; b. Wanne-Eickel, Germany, July 30, 1954; s. Bruno and Maria (Klein) G.; m. Ivana Valkova, July 17, 1985; children: Alexander, Verena. Diploma in chemistry, U. Essen, Germany, 1983; DSc, U. Essen. Lab. mgr. Bayer AG, Dormagen, Germany, 1986-89, Wuppertal, Germany, 1989—. Contbr. articles to profl. jours.; inventor in field. Home: Gneisenaustr 15, D-41539 Dormagen Germany Office: Bayer AG, Friedrich-Ebert-Str 217-333, D-42096 Wuppertal Germany

GRUNENWALD, DOMINIQUE HENRI, thoracic surgeon; b. Chateauroux, Indre, France, Oct. 9, 1949; s. Joseph Marie and Therese Helene (Randouyer) G.; m. Sophie Marie Rerolle, June 23, 1973; children: Alice, Celine, Etienne, Josephine. MD, U. Paris, 1973, postgrad., 1990. Intern Hosp. Paris, 1976-80, chief Surg. Clinic, 1982-86; pvt. practice thoracic surgery Am. Hosp. Paris, 1986-92; thoracic surgeon CMC Pte de Choisy, Paris, 1986-92; chief thoracic dept. Institut Montsouris, Paris, 1996—; prof. thoracic and cardiovasc. surgery U. Paris, 2000—; prof. Extranjero de la Escuela de Graduados Asociacion Medica Argentina, 1995, European Sch. Oncology, 1995; surg. cons. Institut Gustave Roussy, Villejuif, 1990; expert judicaire Cour d'Appel de Paris, Tribunal Administratif de Paris. Mem. Coll. Francais Chirurgie Thoracique et Cardio-Vasculaire, Coll. Medicine Hopitaux de Paris, European Assn. Cardio-Thoracic Surgery, Am. Soc. Clin. Oncology, Acad. Chirurgie, Soc. Thoracic Surgeons, Gen. Thoracic Surg. Club, Frency Soc. Thoracic and Cardiovasc. Surgery (v.p.). Roman Catholic. Avocation: sailing. Office: Inst Mutualiste Montsouris, Inst Mutualiste Montsouris, 42 Blvd Jourdan, 75014 Paris France

GRUNER, ELISSA L., meteorologist; b. Chgo., Oct. 27, 1963; d. Claus D. and Irene A. Gruner. BA in Physics, Knox Coll., 1984; postgrad., U. Freiburg, Germany, 1982-83; MS in Atmospheric Scis., U. Ill., 1987. Rsch. assoc. U. Wis., Madison, 1987; instr. geography No. Ill. U., De Kalb, 1988; weekend meteorologist Sta. WLUC-TV, Marquette, Mich., 1988-89, Sta. KGAN-TV, Cedar Rapids, Iowa, 1993-94; chief meteorologist Sta. KHQA-TV, Quincy, Ill., 1989-93; morning meteorologist Sta. WRTV-TV, Indpls., 1994-96; morning meteorologist Sta. KXTV-TV, Sacramento, 1996-99, environ. reporter, 1999, chief meteorologist, 1999—. Recipient award for literacy promotion Mo. TV Coun., 1992, award for best weather segment and story No. Calif. Regional TV and Radio News Dirs. Assn., 2000. Mem. Am. Meteorol. Soc. (Seal of Approval award). E-mail: elynn@kxtv.com.

GRÜNEWALD, BJÖRN MIKAEL, employers' organization administrator, educator, consultant; b. Stockholm, Sweden, Mar. 2, 1940; s. Isaac and Märta (Grundell) G.; m. AnnBritt Jonsson, June 2, 1962; children: Kent, Axel, Andreas, Tobias. Diploma, Naval Acad., Stockholm, 1960; student, Royal Inst. Tech., 1961-63; diploma in bus. adminstrn, Stockholm Sch. Econs., 1968; postgrad., U. Uppsala, Sweden, 1969; diploma in pers. mgmt., Swedish Mgmt. Group, Stockholm, 1976; diploma, Military Staff and War Coll., Stockholm, 1986-87. Sec. student union U. Stockholm, 1967-68; rschr. Swedish Nat. Union of Students, Stockholm, 1968-70; sec. Fedn. Swedish Industries, Stockholm, 1970-71; with Swedish Employer's Confederation, Stockholm, 1971-93, sr. v.p., 1988-93, dir. Brussels office, 1991-93; sr. advisor multi-disciplinary team ctrl. and eastern Europe Internat. Labour Orgn., Budapest, Hungary, 1993-98; prin. officer employer's activities Europe Internat. Labour Orgn., Geneva, Switzerland, 1998—. Contbr. articles to profl. jours. Bd. dirs. Nat. Swedish Bd. Edn., Stockholm, 1978-81, 84-86, Nat. Swedish Bd. Univs. and Colls., Stockholm, 1983-88, chmn. adv. bd., 1986-88; chmn. edn. com. BIAC; adv. OECD, Paris, 1988-93; chmn. Jt. Found. Higher Sch. Bus. Nat.-Louis U., Nowy Saczs, Poland, 1992—. Recipient Polish Order of Merit, 1991. Mem. World ORT Union of London (exec. com. 1982-91), Swedish ORT of Stockholm (pres. 1981-91), Rotary Club (pres. 1984-85), Swedish Naval Res. Officers Assn. (pres. 1991-94). Home: Box 364, S 18424 Åkersberga Sweden

GRUNFELD, FRED, law educator; b. Aarle-Rixtel, The Netherlands, June 21, 1949; s. Hans Siegfried and Wilma (Van Dam) G.; m. Marij Van den Bosch, Oct. 11, 1978; children: Joram, Samme. MSc, Free U., 1975; PhD, U. Maastricht, 1991. Rschr. Inst. Population Rsch., The Netherlands, 1976-81; rsch. assoc. in internat. studies Leyden U., 1981-83; lectr. internat. orgns. Webster U., Leyden, 1984-85, U. Limburg, Maastricht, 1984-95; assoc. prof. internat. rels. U. Maastricht, 1995—; mem. The Netherlands, 1996—; bd. dirs. Human Rights Ctr., Maastricht, 1994—; dir. for The Netherlands of European Masters in Human Rights and Democratization. Author: Political Opinions in Lelystad, 1977, The Netherlands and the Middle East, 1984, The Netherlands and Near East, 1991; co-editor: The Right to Restitution, Compensation and Rehabilitation for Victims of Gross Violations of Human Rights and Fundamental Freedoms, 1992, The Legitimacy of the United Nations: Towards an Enhanced Legal Status of Non-State Actors, 1997, Human Rights Violations: A Threat to International Peace and Security, 1998, The Effectiveness of United Nations Economic Sanctions, 1999, Human Rights from Exclusion to Inclusion: Principles and Practice, 2000, Rendering Justice to the Vulnerable, 2000. Treas. Dutch Acads. for Peace in the Middle East, 1989—. Mem. Dutch Soc. Internat. Affairs, Jewish Lawyers and Jurists, Acad. Coun. on UN Sys. Mem. Labour Party. E-mail: f.grunfeld@ir.unimaas.nl. Home: Bosscherweg 185, 6219 AA Maastricht Limburg, The Netherlands Office: Maastricht U, Bouillonstraat 3 PO Box 616, 6200 MD Maastricht Limburg, The Netherlands

GRÜNFELD, VERONICA, physicist, educator; b. Buenos Aires, Mar. 14, 1935; d. Markus David and Edith (Buzasi) G.; children: Susana, Blas, Ana. Physicist, Instituto Balseiro, Argentina, 1958; PhD in Physics, U. Cuyo, Argentina, 1961; postgrad., U. Calif., Berkeley, 1962-64. Rschr. Atomic Energy Commn., Argentina, 1960-96; lectr. Instituto Balseiro, Bariloche, Argentina, 1964-79, assoc. prof. physics, 1982-99, dir. Office of Continuing Edn., 1997—; lectr. U. Calif., Davis, 1980-81; cons. Min. of Edn., Argentina, 1994-98, Nat. Sci. Agy., Argentina, 1996-98; organizer Tchr. Workshops for Sci. Tchrs., Bariloche, 1989-99. Author: Physics in Medicine and Biology, 1990; dir./author video: Teaching: An Argentine Experience, 1994 (Patagonia prize 1995); contbr. articles to profl. jours. Sec. Local Civic Coun., Playa Bonita, Bariloche, 1986-90, pres., 1998-99. Recipient Snowstar award Assn. of Bus. and Profl. Women, 1989. Mem. Am. Assn. Physics Tchrs., Am. Assn. Physics in Medicine. Avocations: writing fiction, poetry and history of science. E-mail: grunfeld@cab.cnea.gov.ar. Office: Instituto Balseiro, Av Bustillo 9500, 8400 Bariloche Rio Negro, Argentina

GRUNSCHLAG, TONI, pianist, researcher; b. Vienna, Austria; came to U.S., 1939; d. Morris Grunschlag and Celia Reichmann-Reinharz. Diploma, Vienna Conservatory, Austria, 1938, State Acad.; studies with Robert Casadesus, U.S.A. formed two-piano recital and touring team with sister Rosi, 1942—; researched, performed and recorded rare pieces for two pianos, internat., 1956-82; instr. Bellas Artes Sch., Mexico City, 1981-83; recorded with VOX, Vienna, 1968, CRI, N.Y.C., 1983, 20th Century Music, 1991. Rec. artist Sonata, 1991, Phantasie, 1991, Coal-Scuttle Blues, 1991—, music by Starer, Martinu and Otto Lüning. Recipient Kreisler prize Vienna State Acad., 1938. Mem. Chamber Music Am. Avocation: collecting antiques. Home: 230 W 107th St New York NY 10025-3038

GRUNTENKO, NATALIA EVGENIEVNA, cytology and genetics researcher; b. Novosibirsk, Russia, May 29, 1969; d. Evgeniy Vladimirovich and Inga Yurievna (Rauschenbach) G.; m. Alexey Vladimirovich Kochetov, July 22, 1988; 1 child, Darya. MSc, Novosibirsk State U., 1991; PhD, Inst. Cytology and Genetics, Novosibirsk, 1996. Probationer-rschr. Inst. Cytology and Genetics, Novosibirsk, 1991-92, staff jr. rschr., 1992-96, staff rschr., 1996-97, staff sr. rschr., 1997—. Contbr. articles to profl. jours. Russian Acad. Scis. grantee, 1997. Mem. Vavilov's Soc. Geneticists and Selectionists. Christian. Avocation: poetry. E-mail: nataly@bionet.nsc.ru. Office: Inst Cytology and Genetics, pr-t Lavrentieva 10, Novosibirsk 630090, Russia

GRUOL, MARY CATHERINE SCHUETZ, human resources executive; b. Huntingburg, Ind., May 24, 1946; d. Hubert John Schuetz; m. Peter Raymond Gruol, Aug. 15, 1970; children: Michael, Jeffrey. Cert. x-ray tech., St. Mary's Sch. Nursing, 1965; student, IBM Edn. Ctr., 1967-70, Framingham State Coll., Northeastern Coll.; MEd, Cambridge Coll., 1994. Project mgr. MIS Barnett Computing Co., Jacksonville, Fla., 1971-75; sr. sys. analyst William Underwood Co., Westwood, Mass., 1975-80; co-owner Topside Properties, Chatham, Mass., 1985-89; pres. Bobbin Hollow Inc., Amherst, Mass., 1989-91; cons. Lighthouse Capital Mgmt., Boston, 1991-93; dir. ops. and human resources Bus. Matters, Inc., Waltham, Mass., 1993-96; pres., owner New Venture Solutions, Bedford, Mass., 1996-97; v.p. human resources MathSoft, Inc., Cambridge, Mass., 1997-00; chief adminstrv. officer, v.p. Thinking Investments, Inc., Waltham, Mass., 2000—. Mem. N.E. Human Resources Group, N.E. Human Resources Assn., 128 Venture Capital Group, Aero Club of New Eng. Home: 64 River Ridge Sudbury MA 01776-1428

GRUPP, HARIOLF WOLFGANG, physicist, economist; b. Ellwangen, Germany, July 3, 1950; s. Georg and Maria Anna (Lang) G.; m. Annette Schmalenstroer, Apr. 30, 1979; children: Sebastian, Tillmann, Friedrun. Diploma in physics, U. Heidelberg, Germany, 1975, Doctorate, 1978; Doctorate in Econs., Tech. U., Berlin, 1997. Asst. prof. U. Heidelberg, 1978-80; sr. rschr. Parliament, Bonn, Germany, 1980-83, Fed. Govt., Bonn, 1984; dir. Fraunhofer Inst. Sys. and Innovation, Karlsruhe, Germany, 1985—; prof. U. Karlsruhe, 2000—. Author: Delphi Report, 1995. Founder Energy & Environment Rsch., Heidelberg, 1977. Recipient Fraunhofer prize Fraunhofer Soc., 1988. Mem. Internat. Schumpeter Soc. (bd. mgrs. 1996—), Sci. Coun. Avocations: volleyball, piano, gospel choir. Office: Fraunhofer Inst Sys Innovat, Breslauer Strasse 48, D-76139 Karlsruhe Germany

GRUSS, RALF, strategy consultant; b. Tegernsee, Bavaria, Germany, Apr. 7, 1972; s. Walter and Heidi (Loidl) G. Student, U. Mass., 1994, London Sch. Econs., 1996; diplom wirtschaftsingenieur, U. Karlsruhe, Germany, 1996. Bus. analyst Arthur D. Little, Wiesbaden, Germany, 1997-98; cons. Arthur D. Little, Wiesbaden, 1998-99, mgr., 2000—. Office: Arthur D Little, Gustav Stresemann-Ring 1, 651859 Wiesbaden Germany

GRUSSMANN, WOLF-DIETRICH, lawyer, researcher; b. Innsbruck, Tyrol, Austria, Jan. 24, 1958; s. Oswald and Brünnhilde (Gordes) G.; m. Danielle Lellinger, Sept. 7, 1996; children: Philip, Mischa. M, U. Salzburg, Austria, 1980, D, 1991. Lectr. pub. law and polit. sci. U. Salzburg, 1983-88; lectr. U. Padova, Italy, 1983-84; probationer Dist. & Regional Ct., Salzburg, 1987; asst. prof. U. Salzburg, 1992-98; assoc. Fed. Chancellery Constl. Svc., Vienna, Austria, 1992-93; functionary, prin. adminstr. European Commn., Brussels, 1998; lectr. Fed. Acad. Pub. Adminstrn., Vienna, 1991-98; mem. Austrian Stds. Inst., Vienna, 1992-98; del. Uncitral, Vienna, 1993; vice-chair Fed. Procurement Control Commn., Vienna, 1994-98; chair pers. com. U. Salzburg, 1997-98. Author: Adolf Julius Merkl, 1989, co-editor, 1993, 95. Recipient Leopold Kunschak Appreciation award Leopold Kunschak Bd. Curators, Vienna, Austria, 1991. Mem. Austrian Lawyers Convent. Avocations: billiards, blues, tennis. Office: European Commn DG XIII, Ave de Beaulieu 31, B-1160 Brussels Belgium

GRUTMAN, JEWEL HUMPHREY, lawyer, writer; b. N.Y.C., Mar. 13, 1931; d. Robert and Gladys Humphrey; m. Robert W. Bjork, June 26, 1954 (div. Apr. 22, 1975); 1 child, Bruce Bjork; m. Roy Grutman, Oct. 30, 1975 (wid. 1994); m. Fredrick Yonkman, July 4, 1998. BA magna cum laude, Mt. Holyoke Coll., 1952; LLB, Columbia U., 1955. Bar: N.Y., U.S. Dist. Ct. (So. Dist.) N.Y. 1971, U.S. Dist. Ct. (ea. dist.) N.Y. 1974, U.S. Dist. Ct. Conn. 1984, U.S. Supreme Ct. 1984. Atty. Debevoise & Plimpton, N.Y.C., 1954-60; ptnr. Eaton Van Winkle, N.Y.C., 1976-79, Grutman Greene & Humphrey, N.Y.C., 1979—. Co-author: (with CD-ROM) The Ledgerbook of Thomas Blue Eagle, 1994 (Christopher award 1995, Internat. Reading Assn. award), (CD-ROM) The Journey of Thomas Blue Eagle, 1995 (Best Project award Intermedia, Asia, 1995, Creative NGee ANN Disting. award 1995, EMMA award best visual content 1996), The Journal of Julia Singing Bear, 1995; asst. prodr., editor (ednl. film on art) Where Time is a River (1st prize Women's Film Festival); contbr. photograph illustrations: The Reforming Power of the Scriptures, 1996; developer series of designs based on Native Am. art; contbr. articles to mags. and newspapers. Dir. Inwood Ho., N.Y.C., 1970-80; past mem. various coms. Mt. Holyoke Coll.; mem. com. sr. advisors N.Y. Commn. for Internat. Bus. and UN, 1997; past chmn. com. to establish Barbara Black Fellowship at Columbia U. Law Sch.; past pres. 85th St. Playground Assn., N.Y.C.; active supporter The Children's Storefront, Harlem, N.Y.C., N.Y. Jr. League. Mem. Assn. Bar of City of N.Y., The Stanwich Club (Greenwich, Conn.), Sombrero Golf Club (Marathon, Fla.). Avocations: opera, golf, tennis, poetry.

GRUTTER, ALEXANDRA SARA, marine biologist, researcher; b. N.Y.C., Aug. 9, 1963; arrived in Australia, 1991; d. Theodore Edmund and Marie Claire (Vermeyen) G.; m. Mark A. Johnson, July 21, 1990. BA in Aquatic Biology summa cum laude, U. Calif., Santa Barbara, 1989; PhD in Marine Biology, James Cook U., Townsville, Australia, 1995. Scuba instr. Ocean Odyssey, Kauai, Hawaii, 1983-87; lab. technician U. Calif., Santa Barbara, 1989-90; postdoctoral fellow dept. parasitology U. Queensland, Brisbane, Australia, 1996-99; rsch. fellow Australian Rsch. Coun. dept. zoology and entomology, 2000—. Contbr. articles to profl. jours. including Bio Sci., Nature, others. Australian Rsch. Coun. fellow, 1997-99. Mem. Am. Soc. Parisitology, Am. Soc. Ichthyologists and Herpetologists, Coral Reef Soc. Avocations: scuba diving, windsurfing. Office: U Queensland, Dept Zoology and Entomology, Brisbane QLD 4072, Australia

GRÜTZMEIER, SVEN SAHLGREN, health clinic administrator, physician; b. Norresundby, Denmark, Sept. 20, 1950; arrived in Sweden, 1977; s. Anton Grützmeier and Ingegärd Sahlgren. MD, Aarhus (Denmark) U., 1977; specialist internal medicine/hematology, Linköping (Sweden) U., 1986, specialist clin. chemistry, 1989. Lic. physician. Resident Main Hosp., Norrköping, Sweden, 1977-81, Univ. Hosp., Linköping, 1981-89; dir. Gay Men's Health Clinic, Linköping, 1985-91; specialist Gay Men's Health Clinic-South Hosp., Stockholm, 1990—; asst. dir. Gay Men's Health Clinic, Stockholm, 1992—; cons. Stockholm County Orgn. against AIDS, Stockholm, 1990—, Mus. Natural History, 1994—, Maria Regina Hospice, 1994—, med. dir., 1994—; arranger Yearly Gay Health Confs. Physicians, 1988—. Contbr. articles to med. jours. Arranger confs. for physicians and dentists on health issues for gay men and lesbians, 1988—; med. support cons. Worldpridem, Stockholmpridefestivals, 1988—. Recipient Gold Medal award Royal Soc. Pro Patria, 1998. Fellow European Soc. Med. Oncology, Swedish Hematol. Soc., N.Y. Acad. Scis.; mem. AAAS, Swedish Gay Physicians (pres. 1988—), Royal Soc. Pro Patria. Avocations: opera, ballet, cooking, history, trains. Office: Gay Men's Health Clinic, Dept Dermatology South Hosp, S-118 83 Stockholm Sweden

GRUYITCH, LYUBOMIR TIHOMIR, engineering educator; b. Belgrade, Serbia, Oct. 29, 1939; arrived in South Africa, 1992; s. Tihomir O. and Mariya A. (Peychitch) G.; m. Krunitza M. Savitch, Jan. 26, 1964; children: Yelena, Djordje. Diploma mech. engring., Faculty Mech. Engring., Belgrade, 1963, DSc, 1972; MS, Faculty Electrical Engring., Belgrade, 1970; Doctor (hon.), U. Sci. and Engring., Lille, France, 1984. Asst. Faculty of Mech. Engring., Belgrade, 1964-74, asst. prof., 1974-79, assoc. prof., 1979-88, prof., 1988-92; AECI prof. of control Dept. Electrical Engring., Durban, South Africa, 1992-93; prof. Ecole Nat. D'Ingenieurs, Belfort, France, 1993-99, U. Tech., Belfort-Montbeliard, 1999—; rsch. assoc. Dept. Electrical Engring., Santa Clara, Calif., 1971; vis. prof. U. Notre Dame, 1988-89, U. La., Baton Rouge, 1989-90, Ecole Centrale de Lille; chmn. chair of automatic control, 1982, 83, 90-92. Inventor new lyapunov method based stability theory, gen. nonlinear sys. tracking theory;, stability theory on time-varying sets of nonlinear and large-scale sys.; co-inventor natural tracking controller; discovery of a new physical principle, generalizations in the relativity theory containing Lorentz-Einstein results as special, singular cases, basis for a new relativity theory; contbr. articles to profl. and sci. jours. Ind. candidate Pres. of the Republic of Serbia, 1990; pres. of Senate Faculty of Mech. Engring., 1982-84. Recipient Belgradian Young Math. award City of Belgrade and Ednl. Coun. of Serbia, 1958, Jurema award Yugoslav Assn. for Regulation, Automation and Measurements, 1988, Air Force Acad. award for Tchg. Superior Yugoslav Air Force Acad., 1988. Mem. IEEE (sr.), Assn. of Serbia for Sys. Automatic Control and Measurement (founder 1981), Am. Math. Soc., Internat. Fedn. of Automatic Control, Soc. for Indsl. and Applied Math. Avocations: football, swimming, rowing, tennis, literature. Home: 1 Rue Marcel Paul, 90000 Belfort France Office: U Tech Belfort-Montbeliard, Site Belfort, 90010 Belfort France

GRUZBERG, ILYA A., physicist, researcher; b. Perm, Russia, Nov. 25, 1963; came to U.S., 1992; s. Aleksandr A. and Lyudmila A. Gruzberg; m. Anna A. Dobritsa, Aug. 3, 1996. Diploma, Perm State U., 1985; MS in Physics, Yale U., 1994, PhD in Physics, 1998. Rsch. asst. Perm State U., 1985-88; asst. lectr. Perm Poly. Inst., 1988-92; tchg. asst. Yale U., New Haven, 1992-94, rsch. asst., 1994-98; postgrad. rschr. Inst. for Theoretical Physics, U. Calif., Santa Barbara, 1998—. Contbr. articles to profl. jours. Mem. Am. Phys. Soc. Avocations: books, music, singing. E-mail: ilya@itp.ucsb.edu. Fax: 805-893-2431. Office: Inst for Theoretical Physic Univ Calif Santa Barbara CA 93106-4030

GRYGAR, JIRI, astrophysicist; b. Dziewietlice, Poland, Mar. 17, 1936; s. Josef and Hedvika (Stojanova) G.; m. Libuse Kalasova, Sept. 17, 1981; children: Helena, Vi't, Lukas. BSc, Masaryk U., 1957; MSc, Charles U., 1959; PhD in Astrophysics, Czechoslovak Acad. Sci., 1963. From scientist to prin. scientist Astronomical Inst., Ondrejov, Czechoslovakia, 1963-80; prin. scientist Inst. Physics, Rez, Czechoslovakia, 1980-91, Prague, Czech Republic, 1991—; chmn. sci. coun. grant agy. Czech Acad. Sci., Prague, 1991-93. Recipient Comenius medal Fed. Govt. Czechoslovakia, 1992, Kisch award Czech Writer's Assn., 1992, Kalinga prize UNESCO, 1996; minor planet named in his honor Grygar, 1996. Mem. Czech Astronomical Soc. (chmn. 1992-98), Internat. Astronomical Union, Czech Learned Soc., European Astronomical Soc. Office: Czech Acad Sci Inst Physics, Na Slovance 2, CZ 182 21 Prague Czech Republic

GRYNING, SVEN-ERIK GORM, air pollution scientist; b. Naestved, Denmark, June 9, 1948; s. Dan and Grete (Sørensen) G.; ptnr. Susanne Maria Sidoroff, 1976; children: Morten Nikolaj Sidoroff, Mikkel Peter Sidoroff. MS, Tech. U. Denmark, 1972, PhD, 1982. Mem. scientific staff health physics Risø Nat. Lab., Denmark, 1974-77; mem. scientific staff physics Risø Nat. Lab., 1977-84, mem. scientific staff meteorology and wind energy, 1984-92, sr. scientist, 1992—; engr. cons. in pollution, Denmark, 1974; adj. dir. rsch. Swedish Def. Rsch. Establishment, 1992-96; chmn., convener NATO/CCMS Internat. Tech. Conf. Series on Air Pollution Modelling and its Applications, 1992—; project leader Øresund experiment, 1982-90; chmn. exec. com. Nopex, 1992—; mem. sci. panel on atmospheric chemistry European Commn., 1995—. Editor: Air Pollution Modeling and its Application X, 1994, XI, 1996, XII, 1998, XIII, 2000; guest editor: Jour. Atmospheric Environment, Jour. Agrl. and Forest Meteorology, Theoretical and Applied Climatology. Grantee Nordic Coun. Mins., 1992, 96, NATO, 1993, 95, 97, European Commn., 1994, 96. Mem. Danish Meteorol. Soc. (dep. chmn. 1991—), European Assn. Sci. of Air Pollution (hon. sec. 1992—, editor workshop proceedings 1997, EURASAP/NORDFOSK proceedings 1988). Home: Haraldsborgvej 120, DK-4000 Roskilde Denmark Office: Risø Nat Lab, DK-4000 Roskilde Denmark

GRYSEELS, BRUNO MARIA AUGUSTA JAN, tropical disease scientist; b. Ukkel, Brabant, Belgium, June 10, 1954; s. Karel and Marie-Thérèse (Remy) G.; m. Annie Lanclus; children: Charlotte, Sophie, Mira. MD, U. Ghent, Belgium, 1979; D Tropical Medicine and Hygiene, Inst. Tropical Medicine, Antwerp, Belgium, 1979; PhD, U. Leiden, Belgium, 1990. Staff mem. U. Zaire/ITM, Kinshasa, 1980-81; dir. Programme d'Etude et Contrôle de la Schistosomiase, 1982-86, Programme de Lutte contre les maladies transmissibles, Burundi, 1983-86; lectr. dept. parasitology U. Leiden, The Netherlands, 1986-92, assoc. prof., 1993-95; dir. Prince Leopold Inst. Tropical Medicine, Antwerp, 1995—; mem. steering com. Schistosomiasis WHO/TDR, 1990-95, mem. task force environment and tropical medicine, 1994-95; mem. expert com. on control of schistosomiasis WHO, 1993; cons. WHO, World Bank, 1992—, others. Recipient Royal Medal for Courage and Self-Sacrifice, Belgium, 1975, Commemorative Fund award Am. Soc. Tropical Medicine and Hygiene, 1985. Office: Prince Leopold Inst Trop Me, Nationalestraat 155, 2000 Antwerp Belgium

GRYSPOLAKIS, JOACHIM NICOLAS, mathematics educator; b. Athens, Greece, Oct. 31, 1947; s. Nicolas and Theofano (Hrysovergi) G.; m. Dimitra Korakianitou, Feb. 21, 1951; children: Theophano, Nicolas. Diploma, U. Thessaloniki, Greece, 1970; postgrad., U. Houston, 1973-74; MSc, Wayne State U., 1975, PhD, 1976. Tchg. asst. U. Houston, 1973-74; tchg. asst. Wayne State U., Detroit, 1974-75, rsch. fellow, 1975-76; asst. prof. U. Sask., Saskatoon, Can., 1976-78; lectr., spl. scientist U. Crete, Greece, 1978-84; prof. Tech. U. Crete, 1984—; v.p. Tech. U. Crete, Chania, 1989-93, vice rector fin. and planning and rsch.; vis. rsch. scholar U. Ala., Birmingham, 1994-95; mem. Nat. Com. for Evaluation of Greek Univs., 1993, Nat. Exam. Com. for Admission Greek Univs., 1990-91; mem. com. for evaluation of proposals Greek Univs., 1995—, mem. Com. of Ministry of Edn. for Evaluation of Grad. Programs of Greek Univs., 1996; spkr. in field. Author: Differential and Integral Calculus I, 1984, 3d edit., 1994, Differential and Integral Calculus II, 1985, 3d edit., 1994, also lecture notes; referee jours. Am. Math. Soc., Houston Jour. Math., Zentralblatt für Mathematik, Bull. Greek Math. Soc.; contbr. over 60 articles to profl. jours. and conf. procs. With Greek Army, 1970-72. Recipient Grand Cross, Orthodox Patriarch of Constantinoupolis, 1992, Hon. Diploma, Rotary Club, 1994, Union Greek Writers, 1995; grantee Nat. Rsch. Coun. Can., 1977-79, Nat. Rsch. Found. Greece, 1979-81. Mem. Greek Math. Soc. (mem. governing bd. 1979-82), Am. Math. Soc., Hist., Archeol. Soc. Greece. Greek Orthodox. Avocation: collecting Greek art. E-mail: mgrysp@thalis.aml.tuc.gr. Office: Tech U Crete, Chania Campus, 73100 Crete Greece

GRYTSENKO, ANATOLIY, retired military officer, researcher; b. Bagachivka, Ukraine, Oct. 25, 1957; s. Stepan and Anna Grytsenko; m. Liudmila Masalitina, Aug. 2, 1978; children: Alex, Svetlana. MBS, Air Force Inst., Kiev, Ukraine, 1979, PhD, 1984; student, U.S. Air War Coll., Montgomery, Ala., 1993-94. Cert. in elec. engring., automatic control theory, nat. security. Commd. officer Air Force, Ukraine, 1974-99; head maintenance group Air Force Regt., Ohtirka, Ukraine, 1979-81; instr. automatic flight control and nav. sys. Air Force Inst., Kiev, Ukraine, 1984-92; from sr. staff officer to dep. head analytical office MoD Mil. Edn. Directorate, Kiev, 1992-94; dir. concepts and analysis divsn. Gen. Staff Rsch. Ctr., Kiev, 1994-96; dir. mil. security and def. studies divsn. Nat. Rsch. Ctr. for Def. Techs. and Mil. Security, Kiev, 1996-97; head analytical svc. Nat. Security and Def. Coun. Staff, Kiev, 1997-99; ret. Air Force, 1999; pres. Ukrainian Ctr. for Econ. and Polit. Studies; cons. nat. security and def. com. Ukraine's Parliament, Kiev, 1996-2000. Author: several books, some 100 articles; chief editor Nat. Security and Def. Mag., 1999—. Head mil. com. Atlantic Coun. of Ukraine, Kiev, 1996—; mem. expert group Ukraine Parliament, 1996-98. European fellow Ctr. for European Security Studies, Groningen, Netherlands, 1996-98; NATO fellow, Kiev, 1998-2000. Eastern Orthodox. Avocations: chess, travel, reading, soccer. E-mail: grytsenko@uceps.com.ua. Home: apt 344, 8-B Trostianetskaya St, Kiev Ukraine 254091 Office: Ukrainian Ctr Econ/Polit, 9 Prorizna St Apt 20, Kiev Ukraine 01034

GRYZODUB, OLEKSANDR IVANOVICH, chemist; b. Konstantinovka, Donetsky, Ukraine, Dec. 27, 1948; s. Ivan Petrovich Gryzodub and Salima Pastchenko; m. Helena Andreyevna Seraya, Jan. 8, 1972. MS, State U. Kharkov, 1971, PhD, 1982; DS, State Ctr. for Drug Sci., Kharkov, 1990. Rschr. State Ctr. for Drug Sci., Kharkov, 1971—, lab. head, chief sci. cons., 1989—; prof. State Ctr. for Drug Sci., Kharkov, 1996—; dep. chmn. Pharmacopoeia, Kharkov, 1992—; co-head program Devel. Generic Drugs in Ukraine, 1991-96; sci. chief devel. Ukrainian Pharmacopoeia. Mem. N.Y. Acad. Scis., AOAC Internat. Avocations: history, karate, guitar. Fax: 0572-19-93-83. E-mail: gryzodub@phukr.kharkov.ua. Office: State Ctr for Drug Sci, 33 Astronomicheskaya Str, 61085 Kharkov Ukraine

GRZANKA, LEONARD GERALD, writer, consultant; b. Ludlow, Mass., Dec. 11, 1947; s. Stanley Simon and Claire Genevive Grzanka; m. Christine Duncan Pearson, May 15, 1997. BA, U. Mass., 1972; MA, Harvard U., 1974. Asst. prof. Gakushiun U., Tokyo, 1975-78; pub. rels. specialist Pacific Gas and Electric Co., San Francisco, 1978-80; sales promotion writer Tymshare Transaction Svcs., Fremont, Calif., 1980-81; account exec. The Strayton Co., Santa Clara, Calif., 1981-82; mng. editor Portable Computer Mag., San Francisco, 1982-84; prin. Grzanka Assocs., San Francisco, 1984-86; San Francisco bur. chief Digital News, 1986-91; battery program cons. Bevilacqua Knight Inc., Oakland, Calif., 1991-97; freelance writer, cons., 1997—; staff asst. Electric Power Rsch. Inst./U.S. Advanced Battery Consortium, Palo Alto, Calif., 1991-96; lectr. Golden Gate U., San Francisco, 1985-87. Author: Neither Heaven Nor Hell, 1978; translator, editor: (art catalog) Masterworks of Japanese Crafts, 1977; translator: (book chpt.) Manajo: The Chinese Preface to the Kokinwakashu, 1984 (Literary Transl.

award 1984), Spanish translation, 1994. Sgt. USAF, 1965-69. Fellow Danforth Found., 1974. Mem. United Anglers Calif., Harvard Club of San Francisco (bd. dirs. 1984-88, Cert. Appreciation 1986, 88), Phi Beta Kappa, Phi Kappa Phi. Avocations: writing, fishing. Home: 2909 Madison St Alameda CA 94501-5426

GRZYBOWSKI, ANDRZEJ, actor, architect; b. Warsaw, Sept. 1, 1930; s. Stefan and Alexandra (Holubiczko) G.; Maria Cichocka, July 7, 1952 (dec. Aug. 1988). Magister of Art, Theatre High Sch., Warsaw, 1952. Interior arch. Actor Teatr im Jaracza, Olsztyn, Poland, 1952-53, Teatr Polski, Opole, Poland, 1953-55, Teatr Artos, Warsaw, 1955-56, PTZM, Warsaw, 1956-60, Teatr Syrena, Warsaw, 1960-62, Teatr Ludowy, Warsaw, 1962, Teatr Komedia, Warsaw, 1962-64, Teatr Cwilkinskiei, Warsaw, 1965-70, Teatr, Bielsko-Biala, Poland, 1970-74, Teatr Wspolczesny, Warsaw, 1974-95. Illustrator: Arabiens Pferde, Allahs liebste Kinder, 1972, Araber in Europa, 1982, Karety, Bryczki i Uprzeze, 1995; prin. works include interior in Royal Castle, Warsaw, other buildings. Mem. Polish Horse Soc., Polish Heraldry Soc. Roman Catholic. Avocations: horseback riding. Office: Andrzej Grzybowksi Arch, Lwowska 11 m 5, Pl, 00-660 Warsaw Poland

GRZYBOWSKI, ANDRZEJ EDWARD, mayor, ophthalmologist; b. Poznań, Poland, Oct. 19, 1968; s. Zbigniew Edward and Marta (Szczepańska) G.; m. Małgorzata Maria Szareyko, Aug. 28, 1993; children: Ignacy, Antoni. MD, Karol Marcinkowski U., Poznań, 1993, PhD, 1997, Degree in Ophthalmology, 1998. Postgrad. staff Dept. Pathophysiology, Poznań, 1993-97; resident Dept. Ophthalmology, Poznań, 1995-98, post-doctoral fellow, 1997-98; dep. mayor City of Poznań, 1998—. Author: Advances in Evoked Potentials, 1998; contbr. articles to profl. jours. Mem. Internat. Soc. for Clin. Electrophysiology Vision, Am. Acad. Ophthalmology, Assn. for Rsch. in Vision and Ophthalmology. Roman Catholic. Avocations: basketball, tennis, Russian literature. Office: City Hall, 17 Kolegiacki Sq, 60-967 Poznań Poland

G.-TÓTH, LÁSZLÓ, ecologist researcher; b. Budapest, Hungary, May 26, 1954; s. László and Margaret (Glász) T.; m. Judit Padisák, 1978; children: Marcell, Franciska. Cert. biologist, Eötvös Loránd U., Budapest, Hungary, 1979, Dr. Univ., 1980; PhD, Com. Sci. Qualification, Budapest, Hungary, 1989. Sci. rsch. worker Hungarian Acad. Sci., Biol. Inst., Tihany, Hungary, 1979-89, sr. scientist, 1989—; JSPS Mambusho fellow Shinshu U. Sch. Med. Sci., Matsumoto, Japan, 1994-96. Author: (book) Four Months Research on the Ocean; mem. editl. bd. Jour. Plankton Rsch., 1989—, Limnetcica, 1994—; contbr. numerous sci. publs. to internat. jours. Ministry of Edn. in Paris postdoctoral fellow U. Rennes, 1992-93; Shinshu U. Sch. Allied Medicine grantee, 1994-96. Mem. Internat. Soc. of Limnology, Hungarian Acad. Sci. (adviser mem ecol. com. 1992—, microbiology com. 1994—). Avocations: collection of antique science books and color Japanese wood-block prints from the Edo-period. Home: Szent Donát U 5, H-8229 Csopak Hungary Office: Hungarian Acad Scis, Balaton Limnological Rsch Inst, H-8237 Tihany Hungary

GU, BENXI, physics educator, researcher; b. Haian, Jiansu, China, Aug. 21, 1945; s. Liangqi Gu and Quangming Zhang; m. Cunzhu Li, Feb. 20, 1971; 1 child, Jing. MSc in Physics, Nanjing (China) U., 1981. Vis. investigator Ruhr U., Bochum, Germany, 1985-88; asst. Nanjing U., 1969-80, lectr. physics, 1980-85, 89-90, assoc. prof., 1991-93, prof., 1994—. Contbr. over 100 articles to sci. jours., including Phys. Rev., Applied Physics Letters, Jour. Applied Physics. Recipient awards for progress in sci. and tech. and natural sci., China, 1993, 98. Office: Nanjing U, Dept Physics, Nanjing 210093, China

GU, JUN, computer scientist, educator; b. Nanjing, Jiang Su, China; arrived in Can., 1989; s. Xu Sheng Gu and Xiang Chai Lü; m. Wei Wang, July 14, 1982; children: John Gu, Mond Gu. BSEE, U. Sci. and Tech. of China, Hefei, 1982; PhD in Computer Sci., U. Utah, 1989. Asst. prof. elec. and computer engring. U. Calgary (Can.), 1989-90, assoc. prof. elec. and computer engring., 1990-94, prof. elec. and computer engring., 1994-2000; prof. dept. computer sci. Hong Kong U. Sci. and Tech., 2000—; cons. various govt. agys. and indsl. cos., worldwide, 1989—. Assoc. editor Jour. of Global Optimization, 1994—, Internat. Jour. on Artificial Intelligence Tools, 1994—, Jour. Combinatorial Oprimization, 1999—; mem. adv. bd. International Book Series on Combinatorial Optimization, 1996—; patentee in field. Recipient VLSI Circuit Design award, 1987; Presdl. Rsch. fellow U. Utah, 1986, 88. Mem. IEEE (sr.; assoc. editor Computer Soc. Press Bd. 1995-97, assoc. editor-in-chief Computer Soc. Press Bd. 1997—, assoc. editor Transactions on Knowledge and Data Engineering, 1996—, Transactions on VLSI Sys., 1998—, Design Automation award 1988, 89, 93), ACM, Inst. of Space and Terrestrial Sys. (life), Am. Assn. for Artificial Intelligence. Avocations: reading, writing, traveling, sports.

GU, NIU-FAN, psychiatrist, educator; b. Shanghai, China, Sept. 19, 1937; s. Henrrey and Yao-Ying (Wu) G.; m. Ying-Ming Zhao, Apr. 15, 1967; 1 child, Yi-Jiong. MD, Shanghai Med. U., 1959; sr. adminstr., Shanghai Mgmt. U., 1982; clin. pharmacologist, U. Milano, Italy, 1981. V.p. Shanghai Inst. Mental Health, 1985-94; head dept. psychiatry Shanghai Med. U., 1994—; pres. Shanghai Mental Health Cen., 1994-98; dir. WHO Collaborating Cen., 1995—; dir. clin. pharmacology Ministry Pub. Health, 1997—. Editor: Chinese Jour. Psychiatry, Beijing, 1990—, Chinese Jour. of New Drug and Clin. Remedies, 1989—; Chief-editor: (books) Handbook of Psychotropics, 1993, Psychotropics, 1998; Editor-Author: (books) Comprehensive Textbook Internal Medicine, 1983. Bd. dirs. Chinese Soc. Drug Abuse, 1994—. Recipient Shanghai Sci. and Tech. award, Shanghai Health Bureau, 1993, Advanced Scientific award, Ministry of Pub. Health, 1997. Mem. Chinese Med. Assn., Chinese Genetics Assn., Chinese Mgmt. Assn. (adminstrv. com. head.). Avocations: musci, travel. Office: Shanghai Mental Health Cen, 600 Wan Ping Nan Rd, 200030 Shanghai China

GU, QU-MING, chemist; b. Chengdu, Sichuan, China, Sept. 13, 1958; came to the U.S., 1989, naturalized citizen; s. Tong-Xin Gu and Zhai-yi Jiang; m. Ya-lan Lu, Feb. 15, 1985; 1 child, Shelley. BS, Sichuan U., Chengdu, 1982; MS, West China U. Med. Sci., Chengdu, 1985; PhD, U. Wis., 1994. Rsch. asst. West China U. Med. Scis., Chengdu, 1982-85, lectr., rschr., 1986-89; rsch. assoc. U. Wis., Madison, 1985-86, rsch. asst., 1989-94, postdoctoral rschr., 1994-95; postdoctoral rschr. SUNY, Stony Brook, 1995-96; rsch. scientist Lipitek Internat., San Antonio, 1996; sr. rsch. chemist Hercules Inc., Wilmington, Del., 1996—. Contbr. articles to profl. jours. Pre-doctoral fellow Bristol-Myers-Squibb Co., N.J., 1992-94. Mem. ACS Organic Chemistry, Chinese Chem. Soc. (Outstanding Rsch. award 1987). Achievements include synthesis and structural determinatino of cyclic ADP-ribose; synthesis of new compounds; development of specialty chemicals, bio-organic chemistry and biotechnology; patentee in field. Avocations: swimming, track and field, music. E-mail: qgu@herc.com. Office: Hercules Inc 500 Hercules Rd Wilmington DE 19808-1599

GU, YUANCHAO, biomedical engineer, geneticist; b. Shanghai, People's Republic of China, Nov. 21, 1952; came to U.S., 1985; s. Zhi Fang and Yiming (Zhu) G.; m. Li Hao, July 30, 1980; 1 child, Liang. MD, Tongji Med. U., Wuhan, People's Republic of China, 1977. Rsch. assoc. Med. Coll. Ga., Augusta, 1985-92; biochemistry & genetic technologist II dept. genetics & molecular biology Emory U., Atlanta, 1993—; CEO Charles Internat. Inc., Atlanta, 1999—. Mem. AAAS. Achievements include research on two new and different quadruplicated globin gene arrangements; detection of a new hybrid globin gene among African Americans; research on the gene expression and the promoter function from different promoter point mutation in globin gene and sickle cell disease, the function and structure of Guanylate cyclase-A/Atrial natriuretic factor receptor gene, mental retardation and Down's syndrome. Home: 6400 Glenbrook Dr Tucker GA 30084-8704 Office: Charles Internat Tucker GA 30084

GUAJARDO, ELISA, counselor, educator; b. Roswell, N. Mex., Nov. 13, 1932; d. Alejo Najar and Hortensia (Jiminez) Garcia; m. David Roberto Guajardo, Oct. 15, 1950; 1 child, Elsie Edith. BS, Our Lady of the Lake U., 1962, MEd, 1971; MA, Chapman U., 1977. Cert. tchr., adminstr., counselor, Calif. Elem. tchr. San Antonio (Tex.) Sch. Dist., 1962-63; tchr. social sci. Newport Mesa Sch. Dist., Costa Mesa, Calif., 1963-67; tchr. social sci. Orange (Calif.) Unified Sch. Dist., 1967-70, project dir., 1970-71, tchr. English, 1972-73, counselor, 1973—; pres. Bilingual, Bicultural Parent Adv. Bd., Orange, Calif., 1971-72; reader bilingual projects Calif. State Dept. Edn., Orange, 1971-72; vis. lectr. We. Wash. Univ., Bellingham, 1972-73; mem. curriuculum and placement couns., Orange Unified Sch. Dist., 1973-78, 95-96. Author: (Able)Adaptations of Bilingual/Bicultural Edn, Fed. Project Proposal. Mem. NEA, AAUW, Calif. Tchrs. Assn., Orange Unified Edn. Assn, Hon., Alpha Chi, Our Lady of Lake U., Tex. chpt. Democrat. Mem. Assemblies of God Church. Avocations: choir and solo singing, piano, marimba, organ. Home: 335 E Jackson Ave Orange CA 92867-5743 Office: Canyon HS 220 S Imperial Hwy Anaheim CA 92807-3945

GUALAZZINI, GIUSEPPE ERNESTO, human resources executive; b. Fornovo di Taro, Parma, Italy, Sept. 20, 1959; s. Mario and Giuseppina (Bonomi) G.; m. Elena M. Bonora, Sept. 10, 1988; children: Anna, Luca. Tech. diploma, G. Feltrinelli, Milan, Italy, 1978. Orgnl. devel. analyst AGIP S.p.A., Milan, 1981-86; orgnl. sys. project leader Alivar S.p.A., Milan, 1986-87; staffing mgr. Boehringer Ingelheim Group, Milan, 1987-89; human resources mgr. Italy, Turkey and Greece. GE Med. Sys., Monza, Italy, 1989-96; human resources mgr. Italy and Greece Danzas S.p.A., Grandate, Italy, 1996—. Mgr. restructuring plan, 1994, 95 (CEO awards). With Italian Spl. Athletic Light Inf. Corps., 1979-80. Mem. AMA. Home: Via Caracciolo 77, 20155 Milan Italy Office: Danzas SpA, Via Mantero 8, 22070 Grandate Italy

GUAN, DAGAO, metallurgical engineer; b. Guangfeng, Jianxi, China, Dec. 20, 1932; s. Fusheng Guan and Xiyin Liu; m. Yuexian Fang, Aug. 18, 1959; children: Fangli, Fangzheng, Fangzhong. Grad., Cen. South Univ. Tech., Changsha, China, 1956. Sr. engring. diplomate, China. Technician, sect. chief Tech. Sect. of Shanghai Nonferrous Metals Co., 1956-59; technician, group chief No. 1 Dept. of Shanghai Nonferrous Metals Rsch. Inst., Shanghai, 1960-77, engr., dept. chief, 1978-82; sr. engr., dept. chief No. 8 Dept. of Shanghai Nonferrous Metals Rsch. Inst., Shanghai, 1983-86; prof., chief editor Shanghai Metals, 1986-93; prof., adviser Shanghai Nonferrous Metals, 1994—; mem. precious metals br. of new materials plan group Nat. Sci. and Tech. Com. of China, Beijing, 1978—, precious metals plan group of China Nat. Nonferrous Metals Industry Corp., Beijing, 1978—; cons. Chongqing Instrument Materials Rsch. Inst. of Machine Industry Ministry of China, 1987—; corr. com. editing and screening com. of Jour. of Functional Materials, Chongqing, 1997—. Inventor: Study on the Preparation of Ultrapure Germanium (7N grade) by Chemical Process, 1958 (Sci. and Tech. award Shanghai City Govt. 1959), Study on the High Precision Resistor Material Used in Wide Temperature, 1973 (award China countrywide sci. conf. 1978), Study on the Longevous Material Used in the Recorder Motors, 1987 (3rd award of Electronic Industry Ministry of China, 1989); chief editor: Shanghai Metals, 1986 (award of excellent grade 1992). Participant People's Polit. Cons. Conf., Xinya Hotel, Shanghai, 1959, People's Congress, Xinya Hotel, 1959; rep. Nat. Sci. and Tech. Conf., Beijing Hotel, 1959; rep. Shanghai Sci. and Tech. Conf., Friendship Hall, 1963. Mem. China Soc. of Instrument Materials (bd. dirs. 1990—), Shanghai Soc. of Nonferrous Metals (bd. dirs. 1986—), others. Avocations: reading Chinese poetry and newspaper, music, TV, swimming. Home: 403 Rm No 102/Guyang Rd N, 201600 Songjiang/Shanghai China Office: Shanghai Youse Jingshu, Box 600-402/245 Changshi Rd, 201600 Songjiang/Shanghai China

GUAN, JOSEPH SENG KEE, corporate trainer, consultant; b. Malacca, West Malaysia, Aug. 14, 1945; arrived in Singapore, 1950; s. Francis Yong Boon and Josephine Hye Neo (Teoh) G.; m. Dorothy Siew Lian Khoo, Oct. 1, 1994. B in Music Edn., U. Tulsa, 1976, M in Music Edn., 1977; PhD, Tex. A&M U., 1994. Cert. hypnotherapist, Am. Bd. Hypnotherapy. Tchr. St. Joseph's Instn., Singapore, 1968-74, 78-84, ednl. adminstr., 1984-87; ednl. adminstr. St. Patrick's Sch., Singapore, 1988-91, East View Secondary Sch., Singapore, 1995-96; corp. trainer Joseph Guan and Assocs., Singapore, 1997—; trainer Cath. Schs. Coun., Singapore, 1986-91. Facilitator Internat. Office Cath. Edn., Rome, 1986-88. Mem. Changi Sailing Club, Superbowl Golf and Country Club, Kappa Delta Pi. Roman Catholic. Avocations: travel, sailing, reading. Office: Joseph Guan and Assocs, 2-C Jalan Pesawat, 619359 Singapore Singapore

GUAN, MING, product development manager; b. Wuzhou, Guangxi, China, Dec. 22, 1958; arrived in Singapore, 1989; s. Xiao-Xie Guan and Hui-Qiong Li; m. Joanne Siok Wan Tay, Oct. 1, 1988; children: Yang Yue, Yang Sheng, Yang Ze. BS, Guangxi Normal U., 1982; PhD, U. Exeter, Eng., 1989. Postdoctoral fellow Diagnostic Biotech., Singapore, 1990-91; rsch. assoc. Diagnostic Biotech. Pte. Ltd., Singapore, 1992-93; rsch. assoc. Genelabs Diagnostics Pte. Ltd., Singapore, 1994, rsch. scientist, 1995, mgr. quality control, 1996—, mgr. product devel., 1997—. Contbr. articles to books and profl. jours.; patentee in field. Recipient Overseas Rsch. Students Ors award scheme Com. Vice-Chancellors and Prins. of U. of U.K., 1986-88; overseas scholar Edn. Commn., China, 1985-86. Mem. AAAS, Am. Soc. Microbiology, Faculty Club, Nat. U. Singapore. Avocations: swimming, creative writing, Wei Qi. Office: 85 Science Park, Science Park Dr, Singapore 118259, Singapore

GUAN, XIAOJUN, research computer scientist; b. Jan. 27, 1960; came to U.S., 1985; s. Zhuo Guan and Shuhua Wang; m. Peijie Long, July 23, 1987; children: Alan, Eric. BS, Jilin (China) U., 1982; MS, Mont. State U., 1988; PhD, Wash. State U., 1990. Postdoctoral fellow Oak Ridge (Tenn.) Nat. Lab., 1990-92, rsch. assoc., 1992-94, staff scientist, 1994-96; sr. cons. Glaxo Wellcome Inc., Research Triangle Park, N.C., 1996—. Contbr. chpt. to book, articles to profl. jours. E-mail: xg42498@glaxowellcome.com. Office: Glaxo Wellcome Inc 5 Moore Dr Research Triangle Park NC 27709

GUANGCHUN, XU, editor in chief. Minister, state administration of Radio, Film & TV Govt of China, Beijing, 2000S. Office: State Administration Radio Film & TV, 2 Fuxing Menwai St, 100866 Beijing China*

GUANG SHENG, CHENG, microbiologist, consultant; b. Nanchang, Jiangxi, China, Oct. 10, 1937; s. Zhong Xuan Cheng and Duan Rou Tao; m. Ying Yun Wei, Feb. 4, 1975; 1 child, Wei Yi. BS, Peking U., Beijing, 1958. Asst. rschr. Chinese Acad. Scis., Beijing, 1958-78, rschr., 1978-85, assoc. prof., 1985-94, rsch. prof., 1994—. Editor: Proceedings in Analytical Microbiology, 1988, Dictionary of Fermentation Industry, 1991; author: History of Biology in Ancient China, 1990. Mem. revolutionary com. Chinese Kuoming Tong. Fellow Inst. Microbiology Chinese Acad. Scis., China Assn. Sci. and Tech., Chinese Soc. Microbiology (sec. gen. 1991—). Avocations: reading, stamp collecting. Home: Zhong Guam Cum Buld B12-106, Beijing 100080, China Office: Inst Microbiology, Chinese Acad Scis, Beijing 100080, China

GUANGUN, GU, academic administrator; b. Changzhou, Jiangsu, China, Jan. 1940. Grad., Nanjing Inst. Technology. Former dir. Southeast U. Computer Network and Telecomms. Inst.; former chmn. dept. computer sci. and engring. Southeast Univ., Nanjing, China, former v.p., pres.; mem. Chinese Scientific Rsch. Network, Spl. Commn. on Chinese Edn. and Chinese Edn. Networking. Author five books including first Chinese textbook on computer networking, 1980; developer X.25 telecomm. controller, 1988; developer China's first urban OSI network and EDI system; contbr. articles to profl. publs. Named Nat. Outstanding Young Scholar, All-China Excellent Educator, Model for All-China Edn. System; recipient Advanced prize for Educators Baoshan Steel Works, People's Tchr. medal, awards State Scientific Congress, others. Mem. Chinese Computer Assn. (deputy dir. network commn.), Jiangsu Provincial Scientific Assn., others. Office: Southeast Univ, Si Pai Lou 2, Nanjing 210096, China*

GUANI, ALBERTO, diplomat; b. Montevideo, Uruguay, Apr. 9, 1959; came to U.S., 1996; s. Alberto Antonio Guani and Mercedes Amarilla. M in Internat. Rels., State U. Montevideo. Tchr. English Alianza Cultural Uruguay, Montevideo; advisor to polit. dept. Fgn. Ministry of Uruguay. Contbr. articles to newspaper. Mem. Uruguayan Journalist Assn. Office: Mission of Uruguay to UN 747 3rd Ave Fl Dave21 New York NY 10017-2803

GUAN-RONG, QI, astronomy educator; b. Jiangsu, China, Oct. 3, 1940; s. Qi and Zu (Xiu-lan) Yi-jun; m. Wu Gui-fang; children: Tao, Yan, Yee. BSc, Nanking U., 1966. Asst. rschr. Shaanxi Observatory, Xian, 1966-77, assoc. prof., 1978-86, prof., 1986—, dep. dir., 1987-89, dir., 1989—. Author: Time Measurement, 1983, Handbook of Astronomy and Physics, 1983, The Time, 1985, The Fundamentals of Time Measurement, 1999, The Nature of Time, 2000; editor: The Radio Navigational Signals, 1989. Recipient Sci. Tech. Spl. prize Academia Sinica, 1987, 1st Nat. Sci. Rsch. prize Nat. Com. Sci. and Tech., 1988. Mem. Chinese Astronomy Soc. (v.p. 1989-95), Shaanxi Astronomy Soc. (v.p. 1988—), Internat. Astronomy Union. Avocations: literature, bridge. Office: Shaanxi Astron Observatory, PO Box 18 Lintong Xian, 710600 Shaanxi China

GUANZON, RICARDO SOTELO, physician, educator; b. Bantog, Asingan, Philippines, Nov. 19, 1956; s. Rafael Vasquez and Rosario (Sotelo) G. BS in Psychology, U. Philippines, Diliman, 1978; MD, U. Philippines, Manila, 1982; MA in Edn., Pangasinan State U., Philippines, 1994; EdD, Pangasinan State U., 2000. Med. diplomate. Sch. physician coll. faculty Divine Word Coll., Urdaneta, 1987—; med. dir. Guanzon Med. Clinic, Asingan, Philippines, 1986—; cons. medicine Urdanta Dist. Hosp., Philippines, 1988-95; cons., chmn. dept. family medicine Region 1 Med. Ctr., Dagupan City, Philippines, 2000—; chmn. dept. family medicine Virgen Milagrosa U., San Carlos City, Philippines, 2000—; cons. family medicine, neuropsychology Dagupan Doctors Villaflor Hosp., Dagupan City, Philippines, 1993—, chmn. dept. family medicine, 2000. Editor-in-chief Filipino Family Physician Jour., 1993-2000. Fellow Guardia de Honor Hija de Maria, Asingan, Pangasinan. Recipient AFP award for excellence Surgeon Gen., 1985, fellowship Brit. Coun., U. Coll. London, 1998, Brit. Med. Jour., 1998. Fellow Philippine Acad. Family Physicians (nat. dir. 1993—, pres. 1998-2000); mem. Philippine Soc. Microbiology and Infectious Diseases, Philippine Soc. Tchrs. Family Medicine. Avocations: bowling, swimming, film-watching, volleyball, reading magazines. Home: 53 Costes St Poblacion East, Pangasinan Philippines Office: Dagupan Doctors Mayombo Dis, Villaflor Meml Hosp, Dagupan City 2400, Philippines

GUARDIA, GILBERTO F., civil engineer; b. Panama City, Republic Panama, Feb. 13, 1930; s. Tomas Guardia and Licia Fabrega; m. Teresa Garcia de Paredes, Dec. 17, 1949; children: Teresita, Gilberto Jose, Juan Ignacio. BS in Civil Engring., U. Santa Clara, 1950. Registered profl. engr., Fla., Republic Panama. Estimator Ministerio Obras Pub., Panama City, 1950-51; pvt. practice Panama City, 1950-51; civil engr. div. engring. Panama Canal Co., Panama City, 1951-52; structural engr. Diaz & Guardia, Panama City, 1952; pres., chief exec. officer Empresas Diaz & Guardia, S.A., Panama City, 1952-90; adminstr. Panama Canal Commn., Balboa, Republic Panama, 1990-96; chmn. bd. Banque Nat. Paris, Panama City, 1996—; bd. dirs. Cia Azuc la Estrella, S.A., Panama City. Dir. Inst. Latin Am. Estudios Avanzados, Panama City, 1986; chmn. founding bd. govs. City Club, Panama, 1996—; bd. trustees City of Knowledge, Panama, 1995—. Recipient Comendatori Order St. Silvestre, Pope Paul VI, 1968. Fellow ASCE; mem. Am. Concrete Inst., Am. Soc. Profl. Engrs., Soc. Panama Architectural Engrs., Camara Panama Contrn. (bd. dirs. 1951), Soc. Panama Ejecutivos Empresa (bd. dirs. 1960), Camara Comercio Indsl. Panama (bd. dirs. 1968). Roman Catholic. Office: Calesa Via Ric J Alfaro, Balboa Panama

GUARDIOLA, PHILIPPE, physician, researcher; b. Orleans, Loiret, France, Aug. 8, 1966; s. Rene and Michele Guardiola. B, David Angers, France, 1984; diploma in biotechnology, Paris VII, 1997, diploma in hematology, 1999. Chief clin. asst. Hosp. St. Louis, Paris, 1999—. Contbr. articles to profl. jours. Mem. European Group Blood and Marrow Tranplantation, Assn. Internal Hematology. Avocations: tennis, skiing, painting, piano. Office: Hosp St Louis, 1 av claude vellefaux, 75475 Paris CEDEX 10, France

GUARNO, PETER GARY, consumer products company executive; b. White Plains, N.Y., July 25, 1952; s. Peter Vincent and Betty Omejean (Baker) G. BS, Elizabeth Seton Coll., 1976. V.p., CFO, auctioneer White Plains Auction Rms., 1976-80; pres., CFO, auctioneer Westchester County Auctions, Larchmont, N.Y., 1981-88; pres., CFO 7-11 Corp, Larchmont, 1988-92, Schmieg & Kotzian Custom Furniture, Mamaroneck, N.Y., 1990-96; CEO, CFO Judgement Review Group, White Plains, 1996—; CEO, CFO Antique Advt. Network, White Plains, 1996—. E-mail: gman725@webtv.net.

GUBAIDULLIN, AMIR ANVAROVICH, mechanical engineer, educator; b. Kazan, Tatarstan, Russia, Aug. 4, 1947; s. Anvar Garifovich and Gulzifa Sitdikovna (Sundukova) G.; m. Nailya Abdullovna Galeeva, July 1, 1971; children: Askar, Alia. MSc in Math. with honors, Kazan State U., 1970; PhD in Physics and Maths., Moscow State U., 1977; DSc in Physics and Maths., Tyumen (Russia) State U., 1992. Cert. in maths. Asst. lectr. Kazan State U., 1970-73; postgrad. fellow Moscow State U., 1974-77; asst. prof. Ufa (Russia) Aviation Inst., 1977-86; head of lab. Tyumen Inst. Mechanics Multiphase Sys., Russian Acad. Scis., 1986-95, dir., 1995—; vis. prof. Royal Inst. Tech., Stockholm, 1997; sr. rschr. Ufa br. Russian Acad. Scis., 1977-86; prof. Tyumen State U., 1986—. Contbr. articles to profl. jours. Recipient diploma Siberian br. Russian Acad. Scis., 1997, 99, Gov. Tyumen Region, 1999; rsch. and travel grantee Russian Found. for Basic Rsch., Russian Govt., Russian Ministry of Edn., Internat. Sci. Found., Deutsche Forschungsgemeinschaft, NATO Sci. Com., European Mechanics Soc., 1992—. Mem. European Mechanics Soc., Info. Ctr. for Multiphase Flow, Russian Acad. Natural Scis. (v.p. Tymen br. 1996), Russian Acad. Scis. (gen. assembly of Siberian br. 1995—). Avocations: swimming, skiing, traveling, music. Fax: 7 3452 243648. E-mail: timms@sbtx.tmn.ru. Home: Zavodskaya St 1 App 2, Tyumen 625048, Russia Office: TIMMS, Taymirskaya St 74, Tyumen 625000, Russia

GUBAIDULLIN, DAMIR ANVAROVICH, engineering educator; b. Kazan, Russia, Dec. 6, 1957; s. Anvar Garifovich and Gulzifa Sitdikiovna (Sundukova) G.; m. Lyailya Haidarovna Vafina, July 24, 1981; 1 child, Dilya. MS, Kazan State U., 1980; PhD, Moscow State U., 1988; DS, Tuymen State U., Russia, 1994. Rschr. Kazan State Pedagogical Inst., Russia, 1980-83, Kazan Phisiko-Tech. Inst., 1987-91; exec. sec. Inst. Mech. Engring., Kazan, 1991-95; head dept., prof. Kazan Br. Moscow Power Engring. Inst., Kazan, 1995-98; dir. Inst. Mech. Engring., Kazan, 1998—. Contbr. articles to profl. jours. Grantee Russian Found. for Basic Rschs., Moscow, 1997, Pres. of Russian Fedn., Moscow, 1996, Internat. Sci. Found., N.Y., 1993. Mem. N.Y. Acad. Sci., Inst. Mech. Engring., Order of Friendship of Russian Fedn. Avocations: music, sports. Office: Inst Mech Engr/Russian Acad, Lobachevsky St 2/31, 420111 Kazan/Tatarstan Russia

GUBBAY, ANTHONY ROY, judge; b. Manchester, Eng., Apr. 26, 1932; arrived in Zimbabwe, 1958; s. Henry Ezra and Gracia (Djeddah) G.; m. Alice Wilma Sanger, Dec. 8, 1962; children: David Owen, Nicholas Henry John. BA, U. Witwatersrand, Johannesburg, South Africa, 1952; MA, Cambridge (Eng.) U., 1955, LLM, 1956; hon. doctorate, U. Essex, Eng., 1994. Bar: South Africa, 1957, So. Rhodesia (now Zimbabwe) 1958. Apptd. sr. counsel Rhodesia, 1974; apptd. pres. Spl. Income Tax, Patents Tribunal, Fiscal and Valuation Cts., 1974-77; apptd. judge High Ct., Rhodesia, 1977-83, Appeal Supreme Ct., Zimbabwe, 1983-90; chief justice Supreme Ct., Zimbabwe, 1990—; chmn. Legal Practitioners Disciplinary Tribunal, Zimbabwe, 1983-90, Jud. Svc. Commn., Zimbabwe, 1990—; mem. Permanent Court Arbitration; patron Commonwealth Magistrates and Judges Assn.; mem. com. Reference Group on the Promotion of the Human Rights of Women and the Girl Child Through the Judiciary, 1997. Recipient Great Cross of the Rio Branco Order Brazilian Govt., 1999. Fellow Jesus Coll., Cambridge (hon. 1992—); mem. Oxford and Cambridge Soc. Zimbabwe (pres. 1983—), Hon. Soc. Lincoln's Inn (hon. bencher 1997), Harare Club. Avocations: classical music, philately, tennis. Office: Supreme Ct Zimbabwe, PO Box CY870 Casueway, Harare Zimbabwe

GUBERN, ROMAN, education educator; b. Barcelona, Spain, Aug. 8, 1934. PhD, U. Autónoma, Barcelona, Spain, 1978. Prof. Calif. Inst. Tech., Pasadena, 1975-77, U. So. Calif., L.A., 1977, U. Autónoma, Barcelona, 1977—; prof. emeritus U. Lima, Peru, 1995—; guest rschr. MIT, 1971-72; dean faculty info. scis. supra U. Autónoma, Barcelona, 1987-88; dir. Inst. Cervantes, Rome, 1993-95, Symposium on New Tech. and Cultural Life, Madrid, 1984; founding mem., prof. EINA Sch. Comm., Barcelona, 1967-70; pres. Nat. Commn. for the Evaluation Rsch., Spain, 1992-93. Author: Iconic Messages in Mass Culture, 1974, The Computerized Ape, 1987 (Fundesco award 1986), The Opulent Glance-Expoloration of the Modern Iconosphere, 1987, Benito Perojo. Pioneerism and Survival, 1994 (Film History award

1994, Jean Mitry award 1995), From Bisons to Virtual Reality, 1996. Hon. com. Internat. Assn. for Visual Semiotics, 1991. Recipient Poly. U. Valencia medal, 1986, Palmes Acad. award French Republic, 1993. Mem. AAAS, Spanish Assn. Film Historians (pres. 1991-96), Royal Acad. Fine Arts, N.Y. Acad. Scis. Home: Calle Hurtado 32, 08022 Barcelona Spain

GUBERT, RENZO, sociology educator; b. Primiero, Italy, Aug. 11, 1944; s. Giuseppe and Corinna (DelMarco) G.; m. Maria Silvia Zecchini, July 10, 1971; children: Daniele, Chiara, Giacomo, Maddalena, Elisa, Giuseppe, Francesco, Martino, Ester. M. U. Sociology, Trento, Italy, 1969. Prof. Cath. U., Milan, 1974-82, U. Trento, 1974-80, 80—; mem. Italian Parliament, Rome, 1994-96, senator, 1996—; v.p. def. com. Italian Senate, Rome, 1996-99; vis. prof. Ecole des Hautes Etudes en Sciences Sociales, Paris, 1990; dir. dept. social theory, history and rsch. U. Trento, 1984-90, 91-92; mem. steering com. European Values Study Group, Tilburg, 1989—; v.p. Opera U., Trento, 1983-87. Author: La Situazione Confinaria, 1972, L'Identificazione Etnica, 1976; co-author, editor: L'Appartenenza Territoriale Tra Ecologia E Cultura, 1992, Persistenze e Mutamenti Dei Valori Degli Italiani Nel Contesto Europeo, 1992, La Specificitá Culturale di una Regione Alpina nel Contesto Europeo, 1997, La via Italiana alla Postmodernita, Verso una Nuova Architettura dei Valori, 2000; editor: Annali di Sociologia-Soziologisches Jahrbuch, 1992—. mem. Italian Sociol. Assn. (v.p. 1987), Assn. Parlamentare Amici Della Cina (pres. 1994—), Parliamentary Assn. Friends of China, Internat. Inst. Sociology, Internat. Sociol. Assn. Roman Catholic. Avocations: agriculture, mountaineering, bees. Home: Loc Grotta 52, 38050 Villazzano Italy Office: U Trento, Via Verdi 26, 38100 Trento Italy

GUBIN, GENNADYI DMITRIEVICH, biologist, educator; b. Tyumen, Russia, Aug. 20, 1928; s. Dmitriy Fadeevich and Maria Vasilievna (Dolgorukaya) G.; m. Svetlana Victorovna Dumcheva, Aug. 20, 1969; 1 child, Denis. Med. Diplomate, Ekat. Med. Inst., Ekaterinburg, Russia, 1952, Candidate of Med. Scis., 1956; MD, St. Petersburg Med. Inst., Russia, 1972; Prof., Tyumen Med. Acad., 1973. Med. diplomate. Aspirant biology dept. Ekaterinburg Med. Inst., 1952-55, asst. rschr., 1956-60, docent biology dept., 1960-63; head of dept. of med. biology and genetics Tyumen Med. Acad., 1963-99, dean of med. and pharm. faculty, 1963-67, vice-rector for edn., 1968-73; head of cen. methodical com., Tyumen Med. Acad., 1963-73, asst. of the head of C.M.C., 1973-99, chief of CMC for med./biol. scis., 1963-99; active mem. of scientific com. for chronobiology, Com. Russian Acad. Med. Sci., Moscow, 1982-99. Author: (books) Diurnal Rhythms of Biological Processes, 1980, Biological Rhythms and Alcohol, 1986, Chronostructure and Environment, 1998; inventor: Guidebook for Chronobiology and Chromomedicine, 1989. Decorated Badge of Honor, USSR Govt., Moscow, 1976, medal for Elaboration of Oil and Gas Industry, 1978; included at Golden Fund of the Russian Scis. for Cycles Study, Stavropol, 1996. Mem. N.Y. Acad. Sci., Russian Acad. for Natural Sci. Russian Orthodox. Office: Tyumen Med Acad, Odesskagya 52, 625023 Tyumen Russia

GUBLER, MARIE-LOUISE ELISABETH, theology educator; b. Zurich, Switzerland, Sept. 29, 1939; d. Gustav-Adolf and Anne-Marie Louise (Ruedin) G. D of Theology, U. Fribourg, Switzerland, 1976. Tchr. math., biology Sil, Switzerland, 1961-67; tchr. religion, math. Zurich, Switzerland, 1971-79; prof. biblical theology Menzingen, Switzerland, 1980—; prof. New Testament Catechetical Inst.; prof. biblical theology Luzern, Switzerland, 1991—. Author: Die Fruehesten Deutungen des Todes Jesu, 1977, Juden und Christen Die fremden Brueder, 1981, Der Name der Jungfrau war Maria, 1989, Wer Waelzt uns den Stein vom Grab, 1996, Im Haus der Pilgerschaft, 1999. Mem. Internat. Theol. Revue, Diakonia. Roman Catholic. Avocations: painting, literature, cooking. E-mail: mlgubler@d-planet.ch. Home: Aabachstrasse 341, 6300 Zug Switzerland

GUCCIONE, JOYCE E., securities company executive; b. Chgo., June 23, 1954. CFP, Coll. Fin. Planning, Denver, 1994. V.p. Everen Securities Inc., Gurnee, Ill., 1990—; cons. Ill. State Treas. Office, 1997—; fin. planner, investment advisor, ins. broker, charter pres. Italian Am. War Vets. Ladies Aux.; radio anchor WJJG-AM 1530; adv. ICAN/Ednl. IRA, 1998—. Contbr. articles to mags. Mem. adv. bd. Ill. Coll. Accts. Network, 1993—. Roman Catholic. Office: 1st Union Securities Inc 5101 Washington St Ste 4 Gurnee IL 60031-2974

GUCER, SEREF, chemsistry educator, researcher; b. Gelibolu, Canakkale, Turkey, Oct. 5, 1946; s. Hüsamettin and Seniha Gucer; m. Sema Konyaly, Mar. 2, 1977; 1 child, Cem. BSc, Ege U., Izmir, Turkey, 1967, MSc, 1970, PhD in Chemist, 1971. Tchg. asst. Ege U., 1967-76, asst. prof., 1976-83; prof. chemistry Inönu U., Malatya, Turkey, 1983-95, head dept., 1983-86, 88-92, vice rector, 1984-86, 88-92; prof. chemistry Uludag U., Bursa, Turkey, 1995—, head dept., 1998—. Editor: Metal Speciation in the Environment, 1990 (NATO award 1988); contbr. articles to sci. jours., including Zeitschrift Analytical Chemistry. Mem. Bursa City Coun., 1998. 2d lt. Turkish Air Force, 1975. Rsch. grantee German Acad. Exch. Svc., Dortmund, 1972-74, Karlsruhe, 1990, Belgium Nat. Rsch. Coun. grantee Antwerp U., 1988, TUBIKAK-DOPROG rsch. grantee U. Warsaw, Poland, 1997. Mem. AAAS, Turkish Chem. Soc., European Microbeam Analysis Soc., Bursa Turkish-German Soc., Rotary (sec. Malatya 1991-92). Avocations: travel, stamp collecting. Fax: 90 224 4428022. E-mail: sgucer@uludag.edu.tr. Office: Uludag U, Izmir yolu 10 km Gorukle, Bursa 16059, Turkey

GUCKENHEIMER, DANIEL PAUL, financial advisor; b. Tel Aviv, Oct. 10, 1943; s. Ernest and Eva Guckenheimer; m. Helen Sandra Fox, Dec. 21, 1969; children: Debra Ellen, Julie Susan; came to U.S., 1947, naturalized, 1957. BBA in Fin., U. Houston, 1970; cert. hosp. adminstrn., Trinity U., San Antonio, 1973. Asst. adminstr. Harris County Hosp. Dist., Houston, 1970-76; pres. Mid Am. Investments, Kansas City, Kans., 1976; exec. dir. Allen County Hosp., Iola, Kans., 1977-78; comml. loan officer Traders Bank, Kansas City, Mo., 1979; v.p. and mgr. Traders Ward Pkwy. Bank, 1980; v.p., mgr. installment loans Traders Bank, 1981, v.p., comml. loan officer, 1982; sr. v.p., mgr. comml. loans United Mo. Bank South, 1982-91; sr. v.p., mgr. lending United Mo. Bank, N.A., 1991-93; pres. Guckenheimer Financial Svcs. 1993—. Bd. dirs. Robert Morris Assocs., 1988-92. Bd. dirs. Food Distbn., Inc., 1983-88, Crime Stoppers Greater Kansas City, 1989—; clinic adminstr. 190th USAF Clinic, 1977-84; Served with USAF, 1962-66, maj. Res., ret. Mem. N.G. Assn., Olympic Soc., Internat. Platform Assn., Assn. Mil. Surgeons U.S., Mil. Order World Wars, B'nai Brith (v.p. 1982-83, pres. 1984-85, treas. 1986-95). Home: 8439 W 113th St Shawnee Mission KS 66210-2437

GUCZI, LASZLO, educator; b. Szeged, Hungary, Mar. 23, 1932; s. Janos and Julianna (Deak) G.; m. Gyorgyi Huszti, July 20, 1956; 1 child, Gabor (dec.). BS, U. Szeged, Hungary, 1955, PhD, 1959; PhD, Hungarian Acad. Sci., Budapest, 1968, DS, 1976; D.habil., Tech. U., Budapest, 1995. Prof., head dept. phys. chemistry Tech. U., Budapest, 1980-90, prof., head dept. surf. sci. catal., 1990—; editor Elsevier, Amsterdam, 1980—, mem. editl. bd., 1983-93; chmn. IOICC, Budapest, 1988-92, 8SHHC, Budapest, 1993-95. Author: Hydrocarbon Catal., 1978 (State prize 1983, Republic's Order Officer Cross 1993). Rsch. fellow Isotope Lab., 1956-59, Radiat. Chem. Group, 1959-61, Catalyst Group, 1961-80. Mem. Hungarian Catalysis Club (sec. 1970-80), Hungarian Petrochem. Soc. (sec., chmn. 1972-83), Hungarian Chem. Soc., Divsn. Petroleum Chemistry, Inst. Isotope & Surface Chemistry. Home: 4 Matyas Kiraly u, H-1121 Budapest Hungary Office: Inst Isotope & Surface Chem, Konkoly Thege M u 29/33, H-1121 Budapest Hungary

GUDER, WALTER GEORG, physician; b. Krauthausen, Dueren, Germany, Jan. 7, 1938; s. Walter Otto and Irma (Dresel) G.; m. Malve Manitius, May 8, 1965; children: Andreas, Tassilo. MD, Ludwig-Maximilian U., Munich, 1966. Various to clin. chemist, prof. clin. biochemistry Munich, 1978—. Editor: Biochemical Nephrology, 1978; editor/author: Molecular Nephrology; author: Samples: From the Patient to the Laboratory, 1996; editor supplemental Kidney Internat., 1994; editor-in-chief European Jour. Clin. Chemistry Clin. Biochemistry, 1984-90; editor: Jour. Kidney Internat. Mem. German Soc. Clin. Chemistry (pres. 1984-87), N.Y. Acad. Sci., Am. Assn. Clin. Chemistry. Office: Inst Klin Chem Bogenhausen, Englschalkinger StraBe 77, D-81923 Munich Germany

GUDERJAN, THOMAS HAROLD, archaeologist, educator; b. Toluca, Ill., July 27, 1954; s. Harold August and Marie Guderjan. BA, So. Ill. U., 1976; MA, So. Meth. U., 1983, PhD, 1988. Dir. exhibits Inst. Texan Cultures, U. Tex., San Antonio, 1983-86, sr. rsch. assoc., 1986-91; exec. dir. Maya Rsch. Program, San Antonio, 1990—; asst. prof. archaeology St. Mary's U., San Antonio, 1992-2000; asst. prof. Tex. Christian U., Ft. Worth, 2000—; lectr. Calif. Acad. Sci., Applied Physics Lab. Johns Hopkins U., Pre-Columbian Sco. Washington, others. Author or co-author books, book chpts., also articles in field. Mem. Mayor's Japan coun. City of San Antonio, 1987; advisor Youth Odyssey, Corpus Christi, Tex., 1986—; sponsor U.S. study for several Ctrl. Am. students. Fulbright fellow, Belize, 1990. Fellow Explorers Club; mem. Alamo Pre-Columbian Soc. (bd. dirs. 1988—). Democrat. Avocations: scuba diving, hiking, exploring. E-mail: guderjan@hotmail.com. Office: Maya Rsch Program 2800 N University Dr Fort Worth TX 76129-0001

GUDJONSSON, SIGURDUR, fish biologist; b. Reykjavik, Iceland, Aug. 5, 1957; s. Gudjon Juliusson and Audur Jorundsdottir; m. Gudridur Gudfinnsdottir, Aug. 19, 1981; chidlren: Gudjon, Gunnar, Arnar, Birkir. BSc, U. Iceland, 1980; MSc, Dalhousie U., Halifax, N.S., Can., 1983; PhD, Oreg. State U., 1991. Rschr. Marine Rsch. Inst., Reykjavik, 1980-81; sr. scientist Inst. Freshwater Fisheries, Reykjavik, 1985-88, head ecology divsn., 1988-97; dir. Inst. of Freshwater Fisheries, 1997—. Office: Inst Freshwater Fisheries, Inst Freshwater Fisheries, Vagnhofdi 7, 110 Reykjavik Iceland

GUDKOV, ALEXANDER VLADIMIROVICH, urologist; b. Omsk, Russia, Nov. 9, 1951; s. Vladimir Ivanovich and Anna Terentjevna (A-trochenko) G.; m. Tatjana Konstantinovna Turapina, Apr. 1, 1972 (div. 1984); 1 child, Vladimir; m. Natalia Leonidovna Chukina, Aug. 17, 1984; 1 child, Sergey. Degree, Med. Inst., Omsk, 1975, Med. Inst., Omsk, 1976, Siberian Med. U., Tomsk, Russia, 1981; cand. med. scis., Siberian Med. U., Tomsk, Russia, 1989. Emergency physician Omsk, 1975-76; urologist Regional Clin. Hosp., Omsk, 1976-79, U. Clinics, Tomsk, 1981-86; chief urologist Regional Clin. Hosp., Tomsk, 1986-94; head urological dept. Siberian Med. U., Tomsk, 1994—. Author: Operative Treatment Syndrome Fraley, 1989; editor: Actual Questions of Urology, 1998; contbr. articles to profl. jours.; patentee in field. Mem. Tomsk Regional Assn. Russian Urologists (chmn. 1986—). Avocations: hunting, fishing, shooting. Home: 1 Tchernikla Str 127-128, 634063 Tomsk Russia Office: Siberian Med Univ, Moskowsky Tract 2, 634050 Tomsk Russia

GUDLAUGSSON, KRISTJAN LOFTSSON, journalist; b. Akranes, Iceland, Jan. 4, 1949; arrived in Norway, 1983; s. Gudlaugur Maggi Einarsson and Nanna Eliasdottir; m. Soffia Snorradottir, Aug. 2, 1967 (div. June 1982); children: Astasigridur, Nannakatrin; m. Marit Wilhelmsen, Aug. 16, 1985; 1 child, Kristjan Mimir Kristjansson. BA in History and Chinese, U. Lund, Sweden, 1980. Cert. journalist, Norway. Instr. U. Reykjavik, Iceland, 1980-81; corr. Radio Iceland, Beijing, 1982-93; news editor Rogalands Avis Stavanger, Norway, 1986-91; instr. journalism U. Stavanger, 1994-95; journalist Rogalands Avis Stavanger, Norway, 1992-93, 96—. Contbr. essays to China and We, 1984—. Sec. gen. Communist Party Iceland, 1975-79; chmn. Chinese-Icelandic Friendship Assn., 1976-78; dep. mem. Stavanger City Coun., 1991-95. Named hon. citizen Dubrovnic City Coun., 1993. Mem. Norwegian Assn. Journalists. Mem. Labor Party Norway. Avocations: chess, golf, history, languages. Home: Øvre Stokkavei 57, 4023 Stavanger Rogaland, Norway Office: Rogalands Avis, Box 322, Hillevågsveien 104, 4001 Stavanger Norway

GUDMUNDSDOTTIR, THORUNN, lawyer; b. Reykjavik, Iceland, July 9, 1957; d. Gudmundur Ingvi Sigursson and Kristin Thorbjarnardottir. Candidatus Juris, U. Iceland, 1982; LLM, Cornell U., Ithaca, N.Y., 1983. Dep. judge Dalasysla Magistrate, Iceland, 1982; pvt. practice Reykjavik, 1983—; lectr. U. Iceland Law Sch., 1993—. Mem. ABA, Icelandic Law Assn. (v.p. 1989-90), Icelandic Bar Assn. (bd. dirs. 1988-91, pres. 1995-97), Icelandic Maritime Law Assn., Internat. Bar Assn., Scandinavian Law Forum (bd. dirs. 1990—). Mem. Ind. Party. Avocation: mountain hiking. Office: Lex Law Offices, Sundagardar 2, 104 Reykjavik Iceland

GUDMUNDSEN, OLA, physiologist; b. Oslo, Norway, July 9, 1958; s. Per Olaf and Ase (Winther) G.; m. Bente Schatten, June 26, 1992; children: Espen, Rasmus, Mikkel. CandMag, U. Oslo, 1984, MSc, 1986, DSc, 1994. Scientist U. Oslo, 1986-94; CRC Medstat Rsch. A/S, Lillestrøm, 1994-95; mng. dir. Scandinavian Clin. Rsch. A/S, Kjeller, 1995—. Mem. Drug Info. Assn., N.Y. Acad. Sci., Am. Heart Assn. Avocation: music. Home: Røyskattlia 6, 2743 Harestva Norway Office: Scandinavian Clin Rsch A/S, PO Box 135, N-2007 Kjeller Norway

GUDMUNDSON, CLAES RICHARD, physician, researcher; b. Halsingborg, Sweden, Feb. 20, 1933; s. Richard Fredrik and Elisabeth Nilla (Persson) G.; m. Agneta Gunnarsdotter Jacobsson, Mar. 30, 1958; children: Amelie, Christian, Annika, Ingela. BS, U. Lund, 1953, PhD, 1956, MD, 1963. Rschr. orthopaedic surgery Malmoe, 1963-73; rschr. biochemistry U. Lund, 1965-73; physician Pvt. Clinic, Kristianstad, 1976—; cons. Swedish Road Dept., Stockholm, 1976-84. Contbr. articles to profl. jours. Home: Fridarpsvagen 111-4, 29194 Kristianstad Sweden

GUDMUNDSSON, FINNBOGI, library administrator; b. Reykjavik, Iceland, Jan. 8, 1924; s. Gudmundur Finnbogason and Laufey Vilhjalmsdottir; m. Kristjana P. Helgadottir, Oct. 1, 1955 (dec.); 1 child, Helga Laufey. Cand. mag., U. Iceland, 1949, Dr. phil., 1961. Assoc. prof. U. Man., Winnipeg, Can., 1951-56; lectr. Icelandic Univs., Oslo and Bergen, 1957-58; tchr. Iceland Reykjavik Gymnasium, 1958-64, U. Iceland, Reykjavik, 1962-64; dir. Nat. Library of Iceland, Reykjavik, 1964-94. author: Sveinbjörn Egilsson's Translations of Homer, 1960, Stephan G. Stephansson in Retrospect: Seven Essays, 1982, The Humour of Snorri Sturluson, 1991; contbr. articles to profl. jours]; editor: Orkneyinga saga, 1965; Selected Letters Written to Stephan G. Stephansson I-III, 1971-75, Arbok Landsbokasafns, 1964-93, Andvari, 1968-82; Poets' Letters to Gudmundur Finnbogason, 1987. Mem. Icelandic Studies Soc. (chmn. 1962-64), Icelandic Research Librarians (chmn. 1966-73), Icelandic Patriotic Soc. (pres. 1967-82), Nordinfo (bd. dirs. 1976-79), Icelandic Nat. League (hon.), Icelandic Libr. Assn., Rotary (sec. 1983-84). Lutheran.

GUDMUNDSSON, SIGURDUR, physician, medical director; b. Reykjavik, Iceland, Sept. 25, 1948; m. Sigridur Snaebjornsdottir; children: Gudmundher, Ingvi, Bryndis, Kristin. Cand.Med. et Chir., U. Iceland, 1975; MD, U. Wis., 1981; PhD, U. Iceland, 1993. Resident U. Wis., Madison, 1975-81; clin. instr. U. Wis. Hosp., Madison, 1983-85; cons. in internal medicine and infectious diseases Borgarspitalinn, Reykjavik, 1985-93; cons. in internal medicine and infectious diseases Landspitalinn, Reykjavik, 1993-98, co-dir. biomed. comm., 1995-98, prof. medicine, 1998-99, med. dir. health, 1998—; docent in internal medicine U. Iceland, 1989-98, faculty dean for postgrad. med. edn., 1993-98. Contbr. 10 chpts. to books and some 90 articles to profl. jours. Recipient Best Tchr. award Icelandic Med. Student Assn., 1996, Tchr. of Yr. award, 1996, award for best rsch. contbn. Med. Sch. Sci. Bd., 1997. Mem. Iceland Sci. Acad., Am. Soc. for Microbiology, Infectious Disease Soc. Am., Scandinavian Soc. Antimicrobial Chemotherapy, Brit. Soc. for Antimicrobial Chemotherapy. Office: Directorate of Health, Laugavegur 116, IS-150 Reykjavik Iceland

GUDRA, TADEUSZ (THADDEUS GUDRA), telecommunications educator, acoustics educator; b. Granice-Laski, Kepno, Poland, Oct. 16, 1946; s. Stanisław and Victoria (Boruch) G.; m. Teresa Maria Przewłocka, Oct. 17, 1970; children: Agnes, Margaret. MS in Engring., Wroclaw (Poland) U. Tech., 1970, PhD, 1981. Engr. Wroclaw U. Tech., 1970-81, tutor, 1981-83, assoc. prof., 1984—, head ultrasonic dept. Inst. Telecomm. and Acoustics, 1990—; assoc. prof. Consejo Superior de Investigationes Cientificas, Madrid, 1990; dozent Inst. Physics, W. Goethe U., Frankfort au Main, Germany, 1995; engr. Aeg-Telefunken, Mannheim, Germany, 1970—. Co-author: Fundamentals of Ultrasonic Technology, 1990 (award 1991), Measurement Ultrasonic Devices, 1991 (award 1992); contbr. articles to profl. jours.; patentee in field. Pres. Inst. Trade Union, Solidarity, Wroclaw U. Tech., 1980-89. Recipient award Ministry Sci. and Edn., Warsaw, 1986; grantee Polish Com. Sci. Rsch., Warsaw, 1995-97, Com. Sci. Rsch., Warsaw, 1998-2000. Mem. Polish Elec. Engrs. Assn., Polish Acoustical Soc. (awards 1975, 91, 94 95 96, 97), Polish Med.-Physics Assn. (v.p. 1995-98), European Fedn. Orgns. for Med. Physics. Roman Catholic. Avocations: music, playing guitar, tennis, skiing, mountain tourism. Office: Inst Telecomm & Acoustics, Wybrzeze Wyspianskiego 27, 50370 Wroclaw Poland

GUEAR, CHRISTOPHER THOMAS, state agency administrator; b. Ft. Dix, N.J., Dec. 25, 1967; s. Thomas Samuel and Eleanor Kathleen Guear. BA in Polit. Sci., Elizabethtown Coll., 1990; MPA, Pa. State U., Harrisburg, 1992. Pub. finance analyst N.J. Election Law Enforcement Commn., Trenton, 1993-94, compliance officer, 1995—. Dorothy Forney Meml. scholar Elizabethtown Coll., 1989. Mem. Pi Sigma Alpha, Phi Alpha Theta. Avocations: vexilology, volleyball, hockey.

GUEBENLIAN, SHAHÉ, international affairs consultant; b. Adana, Turkey, Sept. 25, 1920; arrived in Eng., 1968; s. Setrak and Repega (Gomidassian) G.; m. Iris Kathleen Russell. Editor The Sunday Mail, Nicosia, Cyprus, 1948-51; stringer Reuters, AFP, INS, 1948-53; staff corr. in the Middle East Reuters London, Cyprus, 1953-63; mgr. for East and Ctrl. Africa Reuters, Nairobi, 1963-68; mgr. for Africa Reuters, London, 1968-77, mgr. for Africa, the Middle East and the Caribbean, 1969-77, mgr. pub. rels.a nd publicity, 1977-82; cons. Cyprus News Agy., Nicosia, 1983-97; mem. panel assessors The Reuter Found., 1984—; vis. lectr. internat. affairs and journalism City U., London, 1984, 85; vis. lectr. journalism Internat. Inst. for Journalism, Berlin, 1985-94; vis. lectr. journalism and news agy. mgmt. All-China Journalism Syndicate, Beijing, 1985; media cons. Armenian Embassy, London, 1992—; cons. on Pan-African news agy. project UNESCO, Paris and Dakar, Senegal, 1993-95. Author: Blueprints for National News Agencies of Kenya, Kuwait, The Gulf, Oman, 1974-77; compiler, editor: Democracy on Trial, 1974; compiler Blueprint for Pana, 1994. Recipient Gen. Svc. medal Royal Air Force, London, 1957, Insignia of the Order of Menelik, The Emperor of Ethiopia, Addis Ababa, 1972, Honor award Ohio U., Athens, 1987, Disting. Contbn. to Internat. Journalism award Reuters Found., 2000/. Mem. Internat. Friendship League (nat. v.p. U.K. 1992—). Avocations: travel, languages, Oriental cuisine, chamber music. Home and Office: Penthouse B, Ross Court Putney Hill, London SW15 3NZ, England

GUEDES-VIEIRA, MANUEL JOSE, insurance executive; b. Lisbon, Portugal, Apr. 4, 1943; s. Evaristo Guedes and Carlota (Silva) V.; m. Maria de Sao José Picciochi Alves, Dec. 8, 1995. MA, Tech. U., 1968. Jr. economist Office of the Prime Minister, Lisbon, 1968-69; economist Centro de Estudos de Planeamento-Econs. Rsch. Ctr., Lisbon, 1972-76, exec. dir., 1976-79; chief of staff Ministry of Planning, Lisbon, 1979; chief of staff of min. Office of Min. of Fin., Lisbon, 1985-88; asst. Ministry of Fin. and Planning, Lisbon, 1980-82; head of divsn., underwriter Companhia de Seguros de Crédito-Credit Ins. Co., Lisbon, 1982-85; dep. chair bd. dirs. Inst. de Seguros de Portugal-Inst. for Ins. Regulation, Lisbon, 1988-94; exec. dir. Credit Ins. Co., 1994—; dir. Portugal RE, 1996—; mem. NATO Sci. Bd., 1980-84; chmn. bd. Auditors-Tranquilidade, Lisbon, 1986-88, ins. group Coun. European Union, 1992; co-chmn. 100th meeting European Ins. Suprs., 1993, Ins. Co. European Union; mem. adv. bd. Oporto Rail System Bur., 1977-91; ., Nat. Assn. Ins. Commrs., others. Author: (with others) Plano Director Coimbra, 1971; contbr. articles to profl. jours. Founder Assn. Portugal Amigos Caminhos de Ferro, 1980—; bd. dirs. Fundo Extraodinário do Reconstrucão de Chiado, Lisbon, 1988-94; ch. warden St. Paul's Parish and mem. of the perm. comm. of the Synod, Portuguese Episcopalian Ch. Lt. Portuguese Army, 1969-72.worked with OECD Ins. Co., Nat. Assn. Ins. Commrs., others;. Fellow Sociedade de Geografia de Lisboa, Orgn. for Econ. Cooperation and Devel. Ins. Com., Portuguese Inst. for Ins. Supervision, Econs. Rsch. Ctr., Automovel Club de Portugal, Internat. Assn. Ins. Fraud Agys. Avocations: railroading, public law, government management, reading literature. Fax: (351-2) 791 3847. Office: COSEC SA, Av Da Republica 58, P-1069-057 Lisbon Portugal

GUEDJ, CYRIL SYLVAIN, telecommunications company research and development engineer; b. Gravelines, France, Nov. 19, 1968; s. Richard and Yveline (Sabau) G.; m. Eugénie Martinez; 1 child, Fanny. ME, U. Caen, 1992, MS, 1992; MBA, Bus. Adminstrn. Inst. (Institut d'Adminstrn. des Entreprises), 1992; PhD, U. Paris, 1997; post doctoral fell., U. Delaware, 1998. Tng. engr. in optoelectronics Thomson, France, 1992; mil. rschr. Atomic Energy Bur. CEA, France, 1992-93; R&D engr. Alcatel Alsthom Rsch., France, 1994-97; rschr. DRET, Orsay, France, 1993-94; physicist Paul Scherrer Inst., Villigen, Switzerland, 1999; comms. mgr. LEE, Caen, 1990-91; rep. adminstrn. bd. ISMRA-ENSI, Caen, 1990-91, rep. perfection. coun., 1990-91; doctorate Fundamental Electronics Inst., Orsay, 1993-97; post-doctorate fellow U. Del., 1998. Contbr. articles to profl. jours.; patentee in field. Mil. rschr. Atomic Energy Br., 1992-93. Recipient European-Material Rsch. Soc. award, 1995. Mem. French Nuclear Energy Soc., French Elec. and Electronics Soc., French Phys. Soc. Avocations: sailing, computers, art. Home: 4 Rue Robert Thomas, 91400 Saclay France Office: Alcatel Alsthom Rsch, Route de Nozay, 91460 Marcoussis France

GUELIN, PIERRE JOSE, research director; b. Le Havre, Seine Mar-, itime France, Aug. 2, 1936; s. Jean Aime and Jeanne Georgette (Mercier) G.; m. Andree Marie-Claire Perrier Guelin, Mar. 14, 1963; 1 child, Richard. B in Engring., E.N.S.G., 1960; PhD, U., 1962; DSc, Chairmanship: L. Neel, 1970. Rsch. dir. C.N.R.S., Grenoble, 1966—. Contbr. articles to prof. jours. Lt. Engrs. Mers-El-Kebir, 1964-65. Avocations: solo sailing. Office: Lab Sols Solides Structures, Domaine U BP 53, 38041 Grenoble Cedex 9 France

GUELINCKX, PAUL JULIEN, plastic surgery educator; b. Tienen, Brabant, Belgium, Apr. 21, 1956; s. Jan J. Guelinckx and Maria Elvira Kempeneers; m. Hilde Elise Vanrusselt, July 6, 1979; children: Peter, Isabelle. Premed. degree, Limburg U. Ctr., Belgium, 1976; DMS, Katholik U. Leuven, Belgium, 1981, specialist in plastic surgery, 1987, PhD in Muscle Physiology, 1988. Specialist in plastic and reconstructive surgery, hand surgery and microsurgery; bd. cert. Belgian Soc. Plastic and Reconstructive Surgery. Clin. supr. plastic surgery Univ. Hosp., Louvain, 1987-89, adj. supr. plastic surgery, 1989-91, adj. clin. head plastic surgery, 1991-93, prof. plastic and reconstructive surgery, 1995—; chief of clinic Acad. Hosp., Maastricht, The Netherlands, 1993-95; prof. surgery KUL, Louvain, 1995-97; rsch. cons. BAKKEN Rsch. Ctr., Maastricht, 1988-95. Contbr. articles to med. jours. Mem. Round Table nr. 21, Tienen, Belgium, 1984-88, Christian Dem. Party, Belgium, 1989—. Recipient Travel award for exptl. work on microneurovascular muscle transplantation, 1987, 1st prize Group Advancement Microsurgery, 1980. Mem. Internat. Microsurgery Soc., European Assn. Plastic and Reconstructive Surgery, Am. Soc. Plastic and Reconstructive Surgeons. Avocations: horseback riding, jogging, swimming. Home: Broekstraat 24, 3300 Tienen Brabant, Belgium Office: U Z Louvain, Herestraat 49, 3000 Louvain Brabant, Belgium

GUELLUY, PHILLIPE, diplomat; b. 1941; m. Claire Guelluy; 2 children. Sec. to French Embassy Tokyo, 1971-75; sec. to Perm. French Del. to NATO, 1975-78; strategic affairs asst. Ministry of Fgn. Affairs, 1978-79; adviser French Embassy, Madrid, 1979-83; dep. dir., then chief of staff strategic affairs Fgn. Affairs Ministry, France, 1983-91; amb. to Norway Oslo, 1992-95; diplomatic adviser Minister of Def., Ministry of Def., 1995-97; chief of staff Ministry of Fgn. Affairs, 1997-98; French Perm. Rep. to NATO Brussels, 1998—. Decorated Chevalier of Legion of Honor of Nat. Order of Merit, France. Office: NATO Hdqrs, Blvd Leopold III, 1110 Brussels Belgium*

GUELZOW, MARTIN GERHARD ERNST, television production company executive, producer; b. Luebeck, Germany, Oct. 26, 1959; s. Hartmut and Gerda (Jeckeln) G.; m. Brigitte Wette, June 15, 1990. Law student, U. Bonn, Germany, 1983-87. Sr. exec. prodr., authorized signatory Fremantle, Cologne, Germany, 1993-96, mng. dir., 1996-98; mng. dir. Fremantle Mktg. GmbH, Cologne, Germany, 1996-98, SKOPOS Social and Mktg. Rsch. Inst., Cologne, Germany, 1996-98, DasEreignisReich Event Agy., Cologne, Germany, 1997-98, Endemol Entertainment Prod., Gmbh, Cologne, 1998—, Dictum Factum Film un Fernselproduktions GmbH, Huerth, 1999—. Avocations: tennis, diving, travel, collecting old watches. Office: Dictum Factum Film and Fen Sehrprodns GmbH, Ander Hasenkaule 1-7, 50354 Huerth Germany

GUEMBEL, HERMANN OSKAR CORNELIUS, surgeon; b. Landstuhl, Germany, May 15, 1957; s. Woldgang Fritz Hermann and Liselotte Charlotte (Arnoldi) G.; m. Brigitte Rita Mack, Apr. 21, 1995; children:

Nikolai, Till. MD, U. Sch. Frankfurt, Germany, 1986. Resident U. Eye Clinic, Frankfurt, Germany, 1986-90, cons., 1990-00; assoc. prof. ophthalmology, head dept. ophthalmology Bundeseschr-Krankenhans Uem. Author: Liposomes in Ophthalmology and Dermatology, 1993, Schutzimpimpfungen und Reisemedizin, 1994, In Fekhonen in der Augenheilkunde, 1999. Avocations: travel, hunting, hiking, family activities. Office: U Eye Clinic, Main Theodor-Stern-Kai 7, 60590 Frankfurt Germany

GUENTHER, KENNETH ALLEN, business association executive, economist; b. Rochester, N.Y.; s. Walter K. and Erna (Ahrenz) G.; m. Lilly Hoesli, Jan. 11, 1964; 1 child, Christine R. B.A. cum laude, U. Rochester, 1957; postgrad., Johns Hopkins U. Sch. Advanced Internat. Studies, 1957-58, Rangoon Hopkins Ctr., Burma, 1958-59, Yale U., 1959-60. Internat. economist Dept. Commerce, Washington, 1960-65; fgn. service officer Dept. State, Washington, 1965, 68-69, Santiago, Chile, 1966-68; spl. asst. to Senator Jacob Javits U.S. Senate, Washington, 1969-73; exec. dir. Inter-Am. Devel. Bank, Washington, 1973-74; asst. spl. trade rep. White House, Washington, 1974-75; asst. to bd. govs. Fed. Res System, 1975-79; assoc. dir. Ind. Bankers Assn. of Am., Washington, 1980-82, exec. dir., 1982-85; exec. v.p., 1985—, dir.; bd. dirs. Ind. Cmty. Bankers Am., Cmty. Banking Network Inc., Ind. Cmty. Bankers Securities Corp. Inc., Ind. Cmty. Bankers Bancard Inc., Ind. Cmty. Bankers Fin. Svcs. Inc.; mem. Fin. Instns. Adv. Com. on the Golden Dollar. Contbr. articles on banking to profl. jours. Mem. adv. com. on The Golden Dollar, U.S. Mint, 1999-2000. With U.S. Army, 1961-66. Recipient spl. achievement award Fed. Res. System, 1977, presdl. pen for work on Monetary Control Act, 1980, electronic funds transfer achievement award U.S. Treasury, 1995. Mem. Breton Woods Com., Russian Am. Bankers Forum (bd. overseers 1993), Small Bus. Adminstrn. (nat. adv. coun. 1994-2000), Social Compact (bd. dirs. 1994-99), Exchequer Club, Kenwood Country Club. Home: 4513 Dalton Rd Bethesda MD 20815-3732

GUERIN, CHRISTIAN JEAN MARIE, ophthalmologist; b. Grenoble, France, Mar. 14, 1947; s. Andre Gabriel and Colette Marie (Jay) G.; m. Catherine Bernadette Munch, June 2, 1973; children: Sandra, Cedric. MD, U. Lyon, 1976. Intern Vinatier Hosp., Lyon, France, 1971, Jean 23 Hosp., Lyon, 1972; resident specializing in ophthalmology Croix Rousse Hosp., Lyon, 1972-73, 74-76; practice medicine specializing in ophthalmology Venissieux, France, 1977-78, Altkirch, France, 1980—; ophthalmologist Community Clinic, Pierre Benite, France, 1978-80, Community Clinic for Lepers, Meched, Iran, 1973-74. V.p. Walkers of Heimersdorf, 1987; mem. Pupil's Parents of Pub. Teaching, Altkirch, 1987. Mem. Union Opthalmologists, Practising Group Altkirch, Fedn. Functional French Drs., Soc. Self-Taught Men, Tennis Club (Altkirch). Roman Catholic. Avocations: reading, personal research, sciences, philosophy. Office: 5 rue de L'Hotel de Ville, 68130 Altkirch France

GUERIN, DANIEL FRANÇOIS, ophthalmologist, surgeon; b. Bondy, Paris, France, Apr. 13, 1948; s. Maurice and Jeanine (Mautref) G.; m. Gabrielle Jeanne Rubia de la Herreda, Jan. 22, 1972; children: Brice, Fabien. Diploma in ophthalmology, U. Paris VI, 1978. Eye surgeon Found. Rothschild, Paris, 1975-92, eye surgeon asst., 1980-92; eye surgeon Clinique Aulnay, Aulnay Sous Bois, France, 1978-97; tchg. attache Med. Faculty Paris, 1983. Inventor: Intra Ocular Lens Forceps, 1982, Cannulas for Eye Surgery, 1983-92, Trephine for Conical Cutting Corneas, 1989, Intraocular Lens, 1990. Mem. French Ophthalmology Soc., European Soc. of Ophthalmology, European Soc. of Ophthalmalic, Plastic and Reconstructive Surgery (cand.). Avocation: oil painting. Office: Clin D'Aulnay, 28-36 Ave du 14 Juillet, 93604 Aulnay Sous Bois France

GUÉRITÉE, NICOLAS, endocrinologist; b. Bucharest, Romania, Dec. 29, 1920; s. Virgile-Georges and Marie-Antoinette (Gebhardt) G.; m. Gabriela Rizescu, Dec. 6, 1944 (div. 1954); 1 child, Jean-Claude; m. Lucienne Suzanne Taillebois, July 24, 1954; children: Catherine, Virginie. MD, U. Med. Sch., Bucharest, 1944, Faculté de Médecine, Paris, 1952. Pvt. practice medicine specializing in endocrinology Paris, 1957-85; cons. in endocrinology Hosp. of Nanterre, Paris, 1958-66, Endocrine Dept. Faculty of Medicine La Pitié-Salpétrière, Paris, 1960-85; head med. dept. French Sub. of Schering A.G. Berlin, Paris, 1949-58; head rsch. dept. Lab. Théramex SA, Monaco and Paris, 1958-75; bd. dirs. Laboratoire Théramex SA, 1975-99; expert WHO, 1958; mem. French Nat. Com. of Qualification of the Endocrinologists, 1976-85; founder, exec. ann. Journees Francaises de'Endocrinologie Clinique, 1980—; pres. EEC Specialist Sect. of Endocrinology, 1989-94; mem. exec. com. European Bd. Endocrinology, 1994—. Founder, chief editor La Revue Francaise d'Endocrinologie Clinique, 1960-2000; inventor steroid compounds. Mem. French Nat. Union of Endocrinologists (founder, exec. pres. 1960-91), Societe Francaise d'Endocrinologie, Am. Soc. Bone and Mineral Rsch., Soc. for Study of Reprodn., Endocrine Soc. (Am.). Christian Orthodox. Avocation: fly fishing.

GUERMONPREZ, DAMIEN, banker; b. Lille, Nord, France, Feb. 1, 1963; s. Michel Guermonprez and Annie Vernier; m. Marie-Flore Bertin, June 27, 1992; children: Alexandra, Eleonore, Ines. MS in Fin., U. Lille, 1987; M in Fin., Essec, Cergy, 1989; MBA, Harvard U., 1995. Fin. mgr. Renault Credit Internat., Boulogne, France, 1989-93; dir. fin. svcs. Europe Case, Paris, 1995-99; mng. dir. Banque Accord, Lille, 1999—. Mem. Harvard Bus. Sch. Club of France. Avocations: skiing, golf. Fax: 33328385791. E-mail: dguermonprez@mba1995.hbs.edu. Home: 18 ave François Roussel, 59170 Croix France Office: Banque Accord, 4/6 rue Jeanne Maillotte, 59110 La Madeleine France

GUERNSEY, NANCY PATRICIA, mechanical engineer; b. Oct. 12, 1955; d. Orville Wendell and Dorothy Elizabeth (Maccia) Guernsey. BE in Mech. Engring., Manhattan Coll., Riverdale, N.Y., 1977; MS in Nuclear Engring., Poly. U., 1986. Cert. aircraft single engine pilot. Asst. engr. sys. engring. Grumman Aerospace Co., Bethpage, N.Y., 1977-83; engr. product support govt. support sys. divsn. Harris Corp., Syosset, N.Y., 1983-86; pub. health engr. Nassau County Dept. Health Bureau water pollution control, Mineola, N.Y., 1987-88; project engr. N.Y.C. Dept. Trans. Divsn. Bridges, Bur. Design, 1988—. Mem. ASME, The Ninety-Nines (sect. air age edn. chmn. 1982-84), Aircraft Owners and Pilots Assn., Mensa. Republican. Presbyn. Home: 6 Brookview Ln Manalapan NJ 07726-3886 Office: NYC DOT divsn of Bridges Bureau of Design 2 Rector St Fl 6 New York NY 10006-1819

GUERNSEY, THOMAS FRANKLIN, law educator; b. Battle Creek, Mich., Nov. 3, 1951; s. Richard L. and Ruth F. (Davis) G.; m. Kathe A. Klare, June 22, 1974; children: Alison, Adam. BA with distinction, U. Mich, 1973; JD cum laude, Wayne State U., 1976; LLM, Temple U., 1980. Bar: N.H. 1976, Va. 1983, U.S. Supreme Ct. Instr. law Vt. Law Sch., Royalton, 1976-78; asst. gen. counsel Temple Legal Aid Office, Phila., 1978-80; asst. prof. law T.C. Williams Sch. Law, U. Richmond (Va.), 1980-83, assoc. prof., 1983-86, assoc. dean, 1992-95, prof., 1986-96; dean, prof. law So. Ill. U., Carbondale, 1996—, interim vice chancellor acad. affairs, provost, 1999-2000; mediator Offender Aid and Restoration Community Mediation Project, 1984—; cons. Calif. Bd. Bar Examiners, San Francisco, 1984—, Nat. Conf. of Bar Examiner, Chgo., 1992—; master Am. Inns of Ct., Ill., 1996—. Author: Admissibility of Evidence in Virginia, 1990, Problems and Simulations in Evidence, 1991, 2d edit. 1995, Trial Practice, 1991, Special Education Law, 1993, A Practical Guide to Negotiation, 1996; sr. assoc. editor Wayne Law Rev., 1974-76; also articles. Mem. ABA (chmn. competition com. 1983—). Avocations: scuba diving, water skiing. Home: 2914 W Alveria Dr Carbondale IL 62901-5227 Office: So Ill U Sch of Law Carbondale IL 62901-6804

GUERRA, VASCO LEITÃO, educator, researcher; b. Torres Vedras, Portugal, Dec. 12, 1968; s. Orlando Mateus and Maria Eugenia (Leitão) G.; m. Antonia Bacelar Lopes, Feb. 22, 1992; 1 child, André Lopes Guerra. Degree in physics, Inst. Superior Técnico, Lisbon, Portugal, 1991, MSc in physics, 1994. Asst. lectr. math. dept. Inst. Superior Técnico Centro Fisica de Plasmas, Lisbon, 1991-93, asst. lectr. physics dept., 1993-94, asst. physics dept., 1994-98, asst. prof., 1998—. Contbr. articles to profl. jours. Mem. Amnesty Internat., Portugal, 1994. Office: Ctr Fisica de Plasmas, Inst superior Técnico, 1049-001 Lisbon Portugal

GUERREIRO, RENATO NAVARRO, telecommunications executive; married; 3 children. BBA, IESE. Ptnr. McKinsey & Co.; CEO Temecommunicaroes Brasileiras, S.A., Brasilia, Brazil; pres. Anatel (Nat. Agy. Telcom.); dir. Bankers Trust, Spain. Office: Agy Nat Telecom, SAS Quadra 6, CEP 70 Brasilia 313-900, Brazil*

GUERRERO, JOSE, advertising executive; b. Barcelona, Oct. 17, 1948; s. Jose G. and Carmen Santos; m. Teresa Darbra, Sept. 21, 1972; 1 child, Mireia. Advtsg. Degree, Spanish Sch. New Careers, Barcelona, 1972; M in Advtsg. and Comml. Direction, Mktg. and Adminstrn. High Sch., Barcelona, 1975; advtsg. strategies and agy. mgmt., U. Chgo., 1980. Acct. exec. Danis, Barcelona, 1969-72; acct. dir. MMLB, Barcelona, 1972-75; gen. dir. Barcelona McCann Erickson, Barcelona, 1975-84, gen. dir. Spain, 1984-87; pres. TBWA Espana, Barcelona, 1988-95, Wilkens-Vaquero-Guerrero, Barcelona, 1995-97, Guerrero & Ptnrs., Barcelona, 1998—; gen. dir. Advtsg. Festival San Sebastian, Madrid, 1997—. Pvt. Svc. Corps., 1970-71. Mem. Spanish Asn. Advtsg. Agys. (vice-chmn.), Advtsg. Assn. Catalonia (mem. mgmt. bd. 1985—). Avocations: sailing, golf, reading, travel. Office: Guerrero & Ptnrs, Balmes 76 2o 2o, 08007 Barcelona Spain

GUERRERO, JULEN, soccer player; b. Portugalete, Spain, Jan. 7, 1974. Attacking midfielder Athletic Bilboa, Spain; forward Spain. Winner 2 World Cups, 1994, 98. Address: Real Fedn Espanola Futbol, Calle Alberto Bosch 13, 347 Madrid E-28014, Spain*

GUERRERO-IGEA, FRANCISCO JAVIER, physician, researcher; b. Suances, Spain, Feb. 19, 1955; s. Alberto and Maria Luisa (Igea) G.; m. Isabel Arantave, June 7, 1990; children: Paloma, Julia. Med Lic, Valladolid (Spain) U., 1979; MD, Granada (Spain) U., 1988. Resident in internal medicine Rio Hortega Hosp., Valladolid, 1975-79, Faculty of Medicine, Granada U., 1983; family physician Spanish State Health Svc., Sedella-Salares, Malaga, Spain, 1984-86; internal medicine physician Andalusian Health Svc., Baza, Granada, 1986-87; internal medicine specialist Motril (Spain) Hosp., Andalusian Health Svc., 1988-93; family medicine physician Health Ctr. of Motril-Este, Andalusian Health Svc., 1988-93; internal medicine specialist Riotinto Hosp., Minas de Riotinto, Spain, 1993—; rsch. dir. family medicine health ctr. Andalusian Health Svc., La Vinuela, 1984-86, Motril-Este, 1990-91. Contbr. articles to profl. jours. Mem. Internat. Soc. Arteriosclerosis, Nat. Soc. Arteriosclerosis, Nat. Soc. Internal Medicine, Nat. Soc. Infectious Diseases and Clin. Microbiology. Avocations: computer science, playing guitar, athletics, tennis. E-mail: fguerreroi@meditex.es. Office: Riotinto Hosp, Los Cantos St s/n, Minas de Riotinto Huelva, Spain 21660

GUERRERO-ROMERO, JESUS FERNANDO, internist, researcher; b. Durango, Mexico, Mar. 7, 1955; s. Vicente Guerrero and Beatriz Romero; m. Martha Rodriguez, May 3, 1974; Fernando, Martha Jeanette. Student, State U., Durango, 1980, State U., Durango, 1981; internist, Ministry of Health, Mexico, 1988; diplomate in med. rsch., Nat. U. Mexico, 1994. Acad. sec. Sci. and Humanity Coll. State U., Durango, 1976-79, sec. conflicts Acad. Union, 1979-81, dir. CCH, 1981-83, cons. chief rector's office, 1987-88; fellow internal medicine Ministry Health Mexico, U. Durango, 1983-88; internist Gen. Hosp. Mexican Social Security Inst., 1988-93, 96—; rsch. coord. Mexican Social Security Inst., Durango, 1993-96, chief med. rsch. unit, 1998—; nat. rschr. level 1 Investigators Nat. Sys. Mexican Fed. Govt., 1999—. Mem. editl. bd. Jour. Invest Med. Health Sys., 1994-96; contbr. articles to profl. jours. Recipient A.H. Robins award A. H. Robins Mexico, 1980. Mem. Am. Coll. Physicians, Mexican Internal Medicine Assn. (titular, 1st pl. Nat. Clin. Rsch. award 1993, 96, 99), Mexican Diabetes Fedn. (titular, 1st pl. Nat. Clin. Rsch. award 1999), Am. Diabetes Assn. (profl.). Avocations: chess, athletics. Home: Siqueiros 225 Esq/Castaneda, 34000 Durango Mexico Office: Mexican Sch Security Inst, Av La Normal S/N, 34070 Durango Mexico

GUERRINI, VINCENT HENRY, research veterinarian, journal editor; b. Limerick, Ireland, May 26, 1952. MVSC, U. Pretoria, South Africa, 1983; PhD, U. Queensland, St. Lucia, Australia, 1985, MS in Computer Sci., 1999. Tutorial fellow U. Queensland, Brisbane, Australia, 1982-85; rsch. officer Queensland Dept. Primary Industries, Brisbane, Australia, 1985-87; prin. rsch. scientist Pestsearch, Brisbane, Australia, 1988-92; sr. rsch. scientist Worksafe, Sydney, Australia, 1992-94; dir. Pestsearch, 1994—; lectr. dept. biology U. So. Queensland, Toowoomba, 2000—; lectr. U. Sydney, 1993. Editor-in-chief Online Jour. Veterinary Research, 1996—, Online Jour. Bioinformatics; contbr. articles to profl. jours. Recipient Australian meat rsch. grants, 1983-85, rsch. and devel. grants Australian Woolboard, Melbourne, 1985-87, Medisearch Internat., Brisbane, 1988-92. Mem. AAAS, IEEE, Internat. Soc. for Free Radical Rsch. Avocations: tennis, bodybuilding, swimming, computers, Internet. Office: U South Queensland, Dept Biology, QLD Toowoomaal Qld 4350, Australia

GUERS, CHRISTIAN ALAIN, information systems specialist; b. Santiago, Chile, Mar. 21, 1964; s. Henri Louis and Lucie Rose (Galaz) G. Ingeniero en Informatica, U. Tecnica Federico Santa María, Valparaiso, Chile, 1987. Cert. engr. info. sys. Sys. cons. Dipac-Manta, Quito, Ecuador, 1988; sys. analyst Banco de Chile, Santiago, 1988-90; sys. engr. Bancosorno, Santiago, 1990-93; info. sys. mgr. Nike, Santiago, 1993-99; regional tech. mgr. Nike Inc., Beaverton, Oreg., 1999—. Founder, dir. Intersoft jour., 1984. Mem. IEEE-Computer Sci., Assn. Computing Machinery. Avocations: sports, short story writing. Office: Nike Inc 1 SW Bowerman Dr Beaverton OR 97005-0979

GUERTIN, LAURA ANN, geology educator; b. Springfield, Mass., July 9, 1970; d. Raymond Andre and Judith Elizabeth (Surprenant) G. BA, Bucknell U., 1992; PhD, U Miami (Fla.) RSMAS, 1998. Tchg. asst. Bucknell U., Lewisburg, Pa., 1992, U. Miami, Coral Gables, Fla., 1992-96; sr. lectr. Mary Washington Coll., Fredericksburg, Va., 1998-2000; acad. advisor U. Colo., Boulder, 2000—. Contbr. articles to prof. jours. Vol. Hands-On-Miami, 1996-98. Recipent merit award Am. Assn. Petroleum Geologists, 1997; grantee Texaco, 1997. Mem. Geol. Soc. Am., Am. Assn. Petroleum Geologists, Soc. Sedimentary Geology, Sigma Xi. Avocations: music performance, outdoor activities. Office: PO Box 3532 Boulder CO 80307-3532

GUESGEN, HANS WERNER, computer science educator, researcher, consultant; b. Bonn, Germany, Apr. 24, 1959; arrived in New Zealand, 1992; s. Werner and Elsbeth (Palm) G.; m. Gabriele Groebe, Aug. 11, 1984; children: Mirjam, Maike, Marni. Diploma in info., U. Bonn, Germany, 1983; D in Natural Scis., U. Kaiserslautern, Germany, 1988; Dr Habil., U. Hamburg, Germany, 1993. Sci. rschr. German Nat. Rsch. Ctr. for Computer Sci., St. Augustin, Germany, 1983-92; lectr. U. Auckland, New Zealand, 1992-95, sr. lectr., 1995-2000; assoc. prof. U. Auckland, 2000—; project head GMD, St. Augustin, Germany, 1985-89; fellow Internat. Computer Sci. Inst., Berkeley, Calif., 1989-90; dir. grad. studies U. Auckland, 1994—. Author: Consat: A System for Constraint Satisfaction, 1989; co-author: A Perspective of Constraint Based Reasoning, 1992; editor: Technische Expertensysteme, 1988; contbr. articles to profl. jours. Grantee German Fed. Ministry Rsch. and Tech., 1985-89, U. Auckland, 1993-2000. Mem. Am. Assn. for Artificial Intelligence. Avocations: scuba diving, hiking, reading, working with wood. Office: U Auckland Computer Sci Dept, Private Bag 92019, Auckland New Zealand

GUESON, EMERITA TORRES, obstetrician, gynecologist; b. Angeles City, Philippines, Jan. 4, 1942; came to U.S., 1964; d. Lina (Torres) Gueson. AA, U. Sto. Tomas, Manila, Philippines, 1958, MD, 1963. Resident in ob-gyn. Phila. Gen. Hosp., 1966-71; attending physician Nazareth Hosp., Phila., 1973—, Holy Redeemer Hosp., Meadowbrook, Pa., 1983—; bd. dirs. Physicians Who Care; lectr. healthcare issues to consumer groups, Phila. Author: Doctors Under Fire, 1989, Scales of Justice: Exploring the Wilderness of Health Care and Society's Moral Conscience, 1992, Do HMO's Cut Costs...and Lives, 1997, Survival Guide for HMO Patients, 1997; pub. ThereseVision Publs.; also med. writer, screenplay writer, line dir., prodr. Fellow ACOG, ACP; mem. AMA, Pa. Med. Soc., Philadelphia County Med. Soc., Pro-Life Ob.-Gynecologists (charter). Avocations: writing, painting, refinishing furniture. Office: 3336 Aldine St Philadelphia PA 19136-3802 also: Holy Redeemer Med Ctr Med Bldg Ste 311 Meadowbrook PA 19046

GUEST, BRIAN MILTON, lawyer; b. Vineland, N.J., Mar. 18, 1948; s. Edmund James Jr. and Vivian D. Guest. AB in Polit. Sci. with distinction, Rutgers U., 1970; JD, Boston U., 1973. Bar: N.J. 1973, U.S. Dist. Ct. N.J. 1973, U.S. Supreme Ct. 1978, U.S. Ct. Appeals (3d cir.) 1981; diplomate N.J. Mcpl. Govt. Law, 1994. Assoc. Hartman & Schlesinger, Mt. Holly, N.J., 1973-78; ptnr. Hartman & Schlesinger, Mt. Holly, 1978-82, Bookbinder & Guest, Burlington, N.J., 1982-83, Bookbinder, Guest & Domzalski, Burlington, 1983-90, Guest, Domzalski, Kurts & Langraf, Burlington, 1990-91, Guest, Domzalski, Kurts, Landgraf & McNeill, Burlington & Cherry Hill, N.J., 1991-94, Kearns, Vassallo, Guest & Kearns, Willingboro, N.J., 1994—; pres. Raritan Sigma Phi Epsilon Corp., New Brunswick, N.J., 1983-89, trustee, 1982-92. Bd. dirs. Drenk Mental Health Svcs., Inc., pres. bd. trustees, 2000—; trustee 1st United Meth. Ch., Moorestown, N.J., 1995-97, Meml. Health Alliance, 1999-00, Virtua Health Sys. Ambulatory Svcs., 2000—, sec. bd., 2000—. Mem. ABA, Trial Attys. N.J., N.J. Bar Assn. (gen. counsel del. 1983-86), Burlington County Bar Assn. (trustee 1982-84), Burlington County C. of C. (bd. dirs. 1987—, treas. 1989, v.p. 1990, pres. 1991), Masons (worshipful master Mt. Holly club 1982), Rotary, Sigma Phi Epsilon (trustee 1982-91). Office: Kearns Vassallo Guest & Kearns 630 Beverly Rancocas Rd Willingboro NJ 08046-3736

GUETHENKE, GUNNAR KARL-HEINZ HERMANN, engineering researcher; b. Rostock, Germany, Feb. 29, 1972; s. Dietmar and Hilde (Ruge) G. Diploma engring., bus. mgmt., Rheinisch Westfaelisch Tech., Aachen, Germany, 1997. Cert. in engring. and mgmt. Rschr. Fraunhofer Gesellschaft, Aachen, 1997—. Contbr. articles to profl. jours.; patentee in field. Recipient Henry Ford award Ford Motor Co., 1998, Eurodrive award SEW AG, 1999. Fellow Studienstiftung des Deutschen Volkes, Daimler-Chrysler Scholarship. Avocation: golf.

GUEULLE, PATRICK, engineer, author; b. Sainte Adresse, France, Sept. 2, 1954; s. Pierre and Suzanne (Malapert) G. Elec. engr., U. Le Havre, 1973; superior English, SPLEF, 1975; engr., EFREI, 1976. Engr. Le Havre, 1977—, journalist, 1973—, author, 1977—; lectr. U. Le Havre, 1981-84; tchr. C. of C., Le Havre, 1983-89; engr. Matra, Velizy, France, 1976. Author 30 books; contbr. articles to tech. jours. Sec. A.U.V.A., Le Tilleul, France, 1996-97. With French Navy, 1976-77. Mem. OMPP. Avocations: photography, hiking, boating. Office: BP 279, F-76055 Le Havre France

GUEVARRA, MANUEL ROBINSON, artist, retired military officer; b. San Roque, Cavite, The Philippines, June 17, 1931; s. Jose Andico and Frances (Robinson) G.; m. Carol Ann Bennett, June 15, 1963; children: Mark Bennett, Christian Benjamin. AA, Valencia Coll., 1979. Actor Cor-Qui Films Inc., Manila, 1950-51; enlisted USN, 1953, advanced through grades to chief petty officer, ret., 1976; procurement specialist Naval Tng. Ctr., Orlando, Fla., 1977-79; supr. dist. ops. USPS, Orlando and Lake Mary, Fla., 1979-97; sculptor Crealde Sch. of Arts, Winter Park, Fla., 1997—. Prin. works include The General, 1997, Winston Churchill, 1997, George Patton, 1997; works exhibited at Art-Works Gallery and Studio, Oviedo, Fla. Com. mem. St. Stephen's Ch., Winter Springs, Fla., 1989-90; counselor Boy Scouts Am., Winter Park, 1976-78. Mem. Fleet Res. Assn., Nat. Assn. Postal Suprs., Fil-Am. Club of Ctrl. Fla. (auditor, v.p. 1976-78). Democrat. Roman Catholic. Avocations: sculpture, stamp collecting, coin collecting, gardening, carpentry.

GUEZ, JEAN-CLAUDE, management consultant; b. Hasnon, Nord, France, Aug. 4, 1943; s. Robert J. and Marie H. (Duhamel) G.; m. Martine Baccot, July 1965 (div. June 1971); 1 child: Nathalie; m. Micheline S. Chatelain, July 27, 1974; 1 child: Valerie. MS, Ecole Poly., Paris, 1965. Asst. Andersen Consulting, Paris, 1967-69, sr. cons., 1969-72, mgr., 1972-79, ptnr., 1979-89, mng. ptnr., 1989-99; ret., 1999; dir. tech. svcs. France, Andersen Consulting, Paris, 1991-96, mgn. dir. european tech. svcs., Paris, 1990-99; mng. dir. European Travel Industry Svcs., Paris, 1997-99; non-exec. bd. mem. Ocean Group, London, Ci3S, Paris. Active Aide et Action charity orgn., Paris, 1985—, Am. Hosp. Fundraising Orgn., Neuilly-s-Seine, France, 1992—. Served to lt. French air force, 1965-66. Mem. French GUIDE (chmn. DB sect. 1972-80). Roman Catholic. Avocations: SCUBA diving, water sports, making movies, travel, music. Home: 172 Boulevard Bineau, 92200 Neuilly-sur-Seine France Office: Andersen Cons, 55 Ave George V, F-75379 Paris 8, France

GUEZZANE, SAЇD, electrical engineer; b. Algiers, Algeria, Oct. 17, 1955; s. Boualem and Zakia (Hermouche) G.; m. Chafia Kayouche; children: Meriem, Amina. Student, U. Algiers, Algeria, 1974-76, Ecole Polytech. d'Algiers, Algeria, 1976-78, Ecole Polytech. Grenoble, France, 1978-80. Chief of project Sonelgaz, Algers, Algeria, 1982-88, Sonitra, Algers, Algeria, 1988-90; chief of project in renewable energy Sonelgaz, Algers, 1990-2000. With Transmission Unit Algerian Army, 1980-82. Avocations: music, sports, reading. Home: 13 Rue Mohamed Douba, Hussein Dey Algiers Algeria Office: Sonelgaz, 2 Blvd Col Krim Bel Kacen, Algiers Algeria

GUFFI, MICHELE EMILIO ALFREDO, cardiothoracic surgeon, consultant; b. Roveredo, Switzerland, Oct. 26, 1961; s. Giancarlo and Myriam Ida (Pattani) G.; m. Eliete Araujo Fernandes, Jan. 24, 1995; 1 child, Sofia. MD, U. Lausanne, Switzerland, 1986. Clinic res. Surgery Clinic, Lucerne, Switzerland, 1987, Fribourg, Switzerland, 1988-89; clinic res. Clinic of Gen. and Orthopaedic Surgery, Lugano, Switzerland, 1990-91; cardiovasc. surg. resident Beneficencia Portuguesa, São Paulo, Brazil, 1991-93; fellow in cardiothoracic surgery U. Ala., Birmingham, 1993; vis. physician Nat. Heart Lung Inst., London, 1994; staff surgeon Univ. Hosp. Lausanne, 1994-95; cons. surgeon Columbia Hosp. de la Tour, Geneva, 1996—. Contbr. articles to profl. jours.; inventor in field. With Swiss Army, 1980-90, Fribourg. Mem. N.Y. Acad. Scis., Iternat. Soc. for Artificial Organs, Swiss Med. Fedn. Roman Catholic. Avocations: piano, old motorbikes, swimming.

GUGEL, M. SUE, artist; b. Van Wert, Ohio, Nov. 22, 1938; d. Merlin Harvey Smith and Margaret Ann Louise Miller; m. Lorenz Walter Gugel, Dec. 28, 1959 (dec. 1980); children: Scott, Craig, Kristina. Studied with David Humphreys Miller, 1957; student, U. N.Mex., 1965-67, U. Alaska, 1967-71. Tchr. art therapy ARC, El Paso; art tchr. Shiva Paint Co., El Paso, 1972-74, Officers Club, El Paso, Fairbanks, Alaska, 1975-80, Umpqua C.C., 1975—; art tchr. spl. arts, disabilities Umpqua Valley Arts Ctr. Group shows include Rickerts Gallery, Newport, Oreg., Tolly's Art and Antiques, Oakland, Oreg., Art Mill Gallery, Roseburg, Oreg., Umpqua Valley Art Ctr., Roseburg; represented in permanent collections including Bapt. State Conv. Bldg., Anchorage, Pioneer Hall of Fame, Burrough Pub. Libr., Fairbanks, Alaska, Roseburg Forest Products, Trent Colleges, Wash., Oreg., others. Charter mem. Nat. Mus. Women in the Arts. Mem. Fairbanks Art Assn. (pres., award), Umpqua Valley Arts Assn. (pres., award), Nat. Soc. Lit. and the Arts, Willamette We. Artists Assn. Republican. Avocations: music, politics. E-mail: lindaf@teleport.com. Home: PO Box 367 Dillard OR 97432-0367

GUGGENHEIM, HANS GEORG, journalist, writer; b. St. Gallen, Switzerland, Mar. 30, 1927; s. Karl Benno Guggenheim and Nelly Berta Zollikofer; m. Anne-Grete Schonneman-Jensen, March 2, 1974; 1 child, Maria-Helena. Maturitat, Kantons Schule, St. Gallen, 1946; postgrad., U. Zurich, U. Hamburg, U. Geneva, Sorbonne, Paris. Tour mgr. Globus Gateway, Switzerland, 1963-70, Am. Express, USA, 1970-95; pvt. practice Ardeche, France, 1946—. Author: Around the World in 80 Ways, 1979, (play) The Last Days, 1963. Designated Chgo. Ambassador City of Chgo., 1979; named hon. citizen Atlanta, disting. vis. Dade County. Avocations: theater, literature, music, painting. Home and Office: Tour de Bressac, F 07400 Alba-la-Romaine France

GUGGENHEIM-BOUCARD, ALAN ANDRE ALBERT PAUL EDOUARD, business executive, international consultant; b. Paris, May 12, 1950; came to U.S., 1981, naturalized, 1991; s. Jacques and Micheline (Raffalovich) Guggenheim; m. Suzanne Marton, Mar. 20, 1974; 1 child, Valerie. BS, U. Paris, 1971; MSCE, Ecole Speciale des Travaux Publics, Paris, 1974; MBA in Finance, U. Paris, 1975; grad., French Command-Gen. Staff Res. Coll., 1981. Asst. prof. math. Nat. Sch. Arts and Architecture, Paris, 1972-75; civil engr. Societe Routiere Colas, Paris, 1976-77, French Antilles, 1977-78; chief exec. officer, exec. dir. C.R.P.G., Pointe A Pitre, Guadeloupe, 1978-81; chief exec. officer, chmn. San Joaquin Software Systems, Inc., Stockton, Calif., 1982-86, CalCar Investment Svcs., Inc., Newbury Park,

Calif., 1983—; chmn., CEO CYCOM Tech. Corp., 1996—; CEO NagraStar, Englewood, Colo., 2000—; bd. mem. Sucmanu, Paris, 1976-82; bd. of organizers Pacific State Bank, Stockton, Calif., 1985-87. Exec. Editor newsletter L'Action Universitaire, 1970-76. Mem. French Res. Policy Rev. Bd., Paris, 1971-77; mem. Ventura County Rep. Cen. Com., Rep. Presdl. Task Force, Rep. Campaign Coun.; mem. bd. Calif. Rep. Assembly; candidate Rep. 37th Assembly Dist., Calif.; mem. cen. com. Calif. Rep. Party, 1992—. Maj. French Res., 1981. Recipient Gold Medal Omnium Technique Holding, 1975. Fellow Engr. and Scientist France; mem. AAAS, ADPA, Assn. U.S. Army, Rotary, KC. Roman Catholic. Avocations: skiing, boating, classical music. E-mail: aguggenheim@cis-tech.com. Home: 7139 S Espana Way Aurora CO 80016 Office: 90 Inverness Cir E Englewood CO 80112

GUGGENHEIMER, TOBIAS IMMANUEL SIMON, architect; b. Basel, Switzerland, Jan. 30, 1953; s. Heinrich Walter and Eva Augusta (Horowicz) G.; m. Lisa Ann Shapiro, June 27, 1976 (div. 1999); children: Anna Bella, Leanora Margaret. BA in Lit., SUNY, Binghamton, 1975; MArch, U. Colo., 1985. Registered architect, N.Y., N.J. Pres. Tobias Guggenheimer Arch., P.C., Dobbs Ferry, N.Y., 1991—; educator Pratt Inst. Sch. of Architecture, Bklyn., 1987-99; asst. prof., dir. interior design program Marymount Coll., Tarrytown, N.Y., 1999—; lectr. various univs., mus. Author: (books) A Taliesin Legacy: The Architecture of Frank Lloyd Wright's Apprentices, 1995; contbg. editor: Jour. of Taliesin Fellows, 1996-97; archite ct: (restorations) Frank Lloyd Wright's Serlin Residence, 1996-97, Frank LLoyd Wright's Reisley Residence, 1999, (bldgs.) Mittman Residence, Spearfish, S.D., 2000, (renovations) Yannuzzi Residence, Tuxedo Park, N.Y., 1997-99, Malek Residence, 1999, Shore Residence, 1999, Howe Bldg., 2000, Holtz-Lamb Residence, 2000. Cons. Village Tuxedo Park, 1999. Mem. Nat. Coun. Archtl. Registration Bds. Home: 445 Broadway Apt 2cc Hastings-on-Hudson NY 10706-2318 Office: Tobias Guggenheimer Archs 145 Palisade St Dobbs Ferry NY 10522-1617

GUGGENHIME, RICHARD JOHNSON, lawyer; b. San Francisco, Mar. 6, 1940; s Richard E. and Charlotte G.; m. Emlen Hall, June 5, 1965 (div.); children: Andrew, Lisa, Molly; m. Judith Perry Swift, Oct. 3, 1992. AB in Polit. Sci. with distinction, Stanford U., 1961; JD, Harvard U., 1964. Bar: Calif. 1965, U.S. Dist. Ct. (no. dist.) Calif. 1965, U.S. Ct. Appeals (9th cir.) 1965. Assoc. Heller, Ehrman, White & McAuliffe, 1965-71, ptnr., 1972—; spl. asst. to U.S. Senator Hugh Scott, 1964; bd. dirs. Comml. Bank of San Francisco, 1980-81, Global Savs. Bank, San Francisco, 1984-86, North Am. Trust Co., 1996-99. Mem. San Francisco Bd. Permit Appeals, 1978-86; bd. dirs. Marine World Africa USA, 1980-86; mem. San Francisco Fire Commn., 1986-88, Recreation and Parks Commn., 1988-92; chmn. bd. trustees San Francisco Univ. High Sch., 1987-90; trustee St. Ignatius Prep. Sch., San Francisco, 1987-96. Mem. Am. Coll. Probate Counsel, San Francisco Opera Assn. (bd. dir.), Bohemian Club, Wine and Food Soc. Club, Olympic Club, Chevaliers du Tastevin Club (San Francisco), Thunderbird Country Club (Rancho Mirage, Calif.). Home: 2621 Larkin St San Francisco CA 94109-1512 Office: Heller Ehrman White & McAuliffe 333 Bush St San Francisco CA 94104-2806

GUGLIELMETTI, ROBERT JOSEPH, science educator; b. Marseille, France, Dec. 23, 1937; s. Félix and Marie-Antoinette (Traversa) G.; m. Marie-Claude Sabiani, Aug. 3, 1963; children: Eric, Franck. Baccalaureate, Lycee Thiers, Marseille, 1956; 1st cycle, U. Marseille, 1958, MSc, 1960, Thesis of Scis. in Chemistry, 1967; dr. hon. causa, U. Rostov, Russia, 1995. Asst. U. Marseille, 1967-68, maitre asst., 1968-71; maitre de confs. U. Brest, France, 1971-78, prof., 1978-83; prof. U. Marseille, 1983—; dir. Inst. U. Tech., Brest, 1980-83; dir. CNRS Lab., Brest, 1978-83, Marseille, 1995-99. Editor: Organic Photochromic and Thermochromic Compounds, 1998-99; contbr. chpts. to books. Recipient Chevalier des Palmes Acad. Edn. Nat., 1989, Officier des Palmes Acad. Edn. Nat., 1996. Mem. Soc. Francaise Chimie (pres. region PACA 1994-98), Soc. Chimie Suisse. Avocations: footing, cycling, mechanical sports. Home: 6 Impasse Belle Fontaine, 13009 Marseille France Office: U Mediterranee Faculte Scis, 163 Av de Luminy, 13288 Marseille France

GUGLIELMINO, LUCY MARGARET MADSEN, education educator, researcher, consultant; b. Charleston, S.C., Feb. 20, 1944; d. Robert Allen and Margaret Webb (Rodgers) Madsen; m. Paul Joseph Guglielmino, July 31, 1965; children: Joseph Allen, Margaret Rose. BA in English magna cum laude, Furman U., 1965; MEd in English and Edn., Savannah Grad. Ctr., 1973; EdD in Adult Edn., U. Ga., 1977. Tchr. English various pub. schs., Mass., N.J., S.C., Ga., 1965-72; vis. asst. prof. adult and cmty. edn. Fla. Atlantic U., Boca Raton, 1978-87, asst. prof., 1987-88, assoc. prof., 1988-90, prof., 1991—, chmn. dept. edn. leadership, 1991-94, dir. Melby Cmty. Edn. Ctr., 1994—; cons. AT&T, Motorola, Westvaco, S.E. banks, 1979—; bd. dirs. South Fla. Ctr. for Edn. Leaders. Author: Adult ESL Instruction: A Sourcebook, 1991, Community Education and Florida's Future: Proceedings of the Commissioner's Summit, 1997; co-author: Administering Programs for Adults, 1997; author (adult form) Self-Directed Learning Readiness Scale, 1978, 3 other forms and translations into 10 other langs., 1979-94, Learning Preference Assessment (self-scoring format for business), 1991; contbr. over 80 articles to profl. jours., chpts. to books. Mem. Fla. Literacy Coalition, 1990—, Riviera Civic Assn., 1979—, Commn. on Status of Women. Recipient Tchr. of Yr. award Coll. Edn., Fla. Atlantic U., 1990, Outstanding Achievement award 1991, Presdl. Merit award, 1993, Profl. Excellence award, 1998; named to Fla. Adult and Cmty. Edn. Hall of Fame, Fla. Adminstrs. Adult and Cmty. Edn., 1992; numerous grants, 1979—. Mem. AAUW, Nat. Cmty. Edn. Assn., Am. Assn. for Adult and Continuing Edn., Commn. Profs. Adult Edn. (chmn. self-directed learning task force 1987-88, 90-91), Fla. Adult Edn. Assn. (bd. dirs. 1989-90), Phi Kappa Phi, Phi Delta Kappa. Episcopalian. Avocations: reading, swimming, biking, flower arranging, gardening. Home: 734 Marble Way Boca Raton FL 33432-3007 Office: Fla Atlantic U ED251 777 Glades Rd Boca Raton FL 33431-6424

GUHA, ABHIJIT, engineering educator, researcher; b. Calcutta, India, Apr. 14, 1962; s. Ashimananda and Kamal Rani (Nag) G. B of Mech. Engring., Jadavpur U., Calcutta, India, 1984; M of Engring., Indian Inst. Sci., Bangalore, 1986; PhD, Trinity Coll., U. Cambridge, England, 1990. Engr. Devel. Cons., Calcutta, India, 1986; lectr. dept. aerospace engring. U. Bristol, England, 1995—; Prince of Wales Scholar, Trinity Coll., Univ. of Cambridge, Eng., 1986-89; Nehru Scholar (hon.), India, 1986-89. Author: Two-Phase Flows with Phase Transition VKI Lecture Series, 1995; contbr. articles to profl. jours. Prince of Wales scholar Trinity Coll., U. Cambridge, 1986-89, Nehru scholar, India, 1986-89; fellow Gonville & Caius Coll., U. Cambridge, 1990-94. Mem. Inst. Engrs. Avocations: charity fund raising, guitar, literary activities, reading, television. Office: U Bristol Dept Aerospace, Univ Walk, Bristol BS8 1TR, England

GUHA, BIMALENDU, science educator; b. Barisal, East Bengal, India, Jan. 14, 1945; s. Satish Chandra Guha and Sucharu Bala; m. Rita Das, Dec. 4, 1979; 1 child. BS, City Coll., Calcutta, India, 1965; M of Tech., Indian Inst. Tech., Madras, PhD in Metall. Engring., 1988. Sr. sci. officer Indian Inst. Tech., Madras, 1989-94, asst. prof., 1994—. Mem. Indian Inst. Metals. Avocations: reading scientific fiction, philosophy, walking. Office: Indian Inst Tech, Metallurgical Engring Dept, Madras 600036, India

GUHATHAKURTA, MEGHNA, social science educator, researcher, writer; b. Dhaka, Bangladesh, Aug. 11, 1956; d. Jyotirmay and Basanti (Datta) G. MSS, Dhaka (Bangladesh) U., 1979; PhD, York (Eng.) U., 1990. Prof. Dhaka (Bangladesh) U., 1984—, chairperson dept. internat. rels., 1998-2000; Rsch. assoc. Ctr. Social Studies, Dhaka, 1980—; rsch. fellow Ctr. Policy Dialogue, Dhaka, 1995—; mem. coun. Rawoo, The Netherlands, 1997—. Author: The Politics of British Aid Policy Formation, 1990; assoc. editor: Jour. Social Studies, 1980—; co-editor: (anthology) SAARC: Beyond State-Centric Cooperation, 1992, (anthology) Living on the Edge: Essays on the CHT, 1997 (FriedrichNaumann Stiftung 1997); editor: (anthology) Contemporary Feminist Perspectives, 1997. Mem. com. war criminal trial Nirmul Com., Dhaka, 1992—; mem. Nat. Com. Protection of Fundamental Rights in the CHT, Dhaka, 1991—. Recipient Fgn. and Commonwealth Office award Fgn. Office, Eng., 1987-90. Mem. Bangla Acad. (life). Avocations: writing, dancing, broadcasting. Home: 52c Dhaka Univ Qtr, Dhaka 1000, Bangladesh Office: Dhaka U, Dept Internat Rels, Dhaka 1000, Bangladesh

GUHA-THAKURTA, RAJEEB, financial planner; b. London, July 23, 1969; s. Pradip Kumar and Kishwar Jehan (Khan) G.-T. BA with honors, Strasbourg U., 1991. Assoc. KDR Fin. Svcs., Ascot, United Kingdom, 1992—, ptnr., 1996—. Mem. Life Ins. Assn. (achievement forum 1996—), Charity Crusaders Soccer Club (chmn., pres. 1994-98), Thames Valley C. of C., Million Dollar Round Table (ct. table). Mem. Conservative Tory Party. Avocations: charity fundraising, soccer, tennis, film and theater. Home: Seema Llanvair Dr, Ascot Berkshire SL5 9LW, England Office: KDR Fin Svcs, 61B Willis House, Ascot Berkshire SL5 7HP, England

GUI, JIN KANG, information engineer; b. Shanghai, China, June 29, 1946; s. Jin Fa and Zao Di (Zhou) G.; m. Tong Liu, Jan. 1975 (div. Feb. 1993); 1 child, Qi Dong. Diploma, Shanghai Jiao Tong U., 1968, MSc, 1980; D in Tech., Helsinki U. Tech., 1993. Mech. engr. Machinery Factory, Harbin, China, 1968-78; computer automated design researcher Shanghai Jiao Tong U., 1978-80; lectr. Harbin Shipbuilding Engring. Inst., 1981-86; rsch. asst. U. Trondheim, Norway, 1987-91; rsch. scientist Helsinki U. Tech., 1990-94; vis. scientist Fraunhofer Inst. Computer Graphics, Darmstadt, Germany, 1994-95; European Union-tech. coord. VTT Mfg. Tech., Espoo, Finland, 1995-97; European Union-project mgr. MET, Helsinki, Finland, 1997-98; rsch. scientist VTT Info. Tech., Espoo, Finland, 1998—. Mem. IEEE, Computer Soc. Avocations: painting, Chinese/Shanghai opera, Chinese cooking. Home: Kääntöpiiri 2 A 35, 02210 Espoo Finland Office: VTT Info Tech, PO Box 1203, FIN02044 Tekniikante 4 B Espoo Finland

GUICHARD, ANDRE PIERRE, direct mail order executive; b. Paris, Dec. 6, 1924; s. Désiré and Marthe Guichard; m. Helene Juliard, May 1, 1945; 1 child, Jean-Pierre. Clk. Soveda, Paris, 1946-47, CWB, Paris, 1947-52; mgr. Delattre & Frouard, Paris, 1952-55; dir. Saxby, Paris, 1955-72; chmn., CEO Manutan, Paris, 1972-94, chmn. supr. bd., 1994—; non-exec., chmn./dir. Key Indsl. Equipment, Verwood, U.K. Lt. Tanks, 1945-47. Office: Manutan, 32 Bis Blvd de Picpus, 75012 Paris France

GUICHEMERRE, ROGER, French literature educator; b. Corbeil, France, Jan. 24, 1924; s. Charles F.J. and Lucie Henriette (Golbéry) G.; m. Annie Soulié, May 11, 1967; children: Jean-Pierre, Marie. Lic es Lettres, U. Paris Sorbonne, 1946, agrégation és lettres, 1947, Doctorat és lettres, 1971. Prof. Lycées, Rouen and Paris, 1948-63; asst. prof. U. Paris Sorbonne, 1963-69; prof. U. Poitiers, France, 1969-86; prof. 17th century French lit. U. Paris, 1986-93, prof. emeritus, 1993—; vis. prof. U. N.Mex., Albuquerque, 1982-94. Author: La Comédie avant Molière, 1972 (prix de l'Académie 1972), La Comédie classique, 1978, La Tragi-comédie, 1981, Quatre poètes du XVIIe siècle, 1990, Visages du théatre franç du XVIIo Siècle, 1994, Dom Carlos et autres nouvelles françaises du XVIIo Siècle, 1995. Decorated officier des Palmes Académiques. Roman Catholic. Avocations: Romance languages and literature, painting. Home: 18 rue des Sources, 92350 Le Plessis-Robinson France Office: U Paris IV-Sorbonne, 1 rue Victor Cousin, 75005 Paris France

GUIDA, HAROLD SEYMOUR, architect; b. San Gabriel, Calif., Dec. 17, 1941; arrived in Australia, 1981; BArch, Ariz. State U., 1966; MArch in Urban Design, UCLA, 1968. Architect Mitchell/Giurgola Architects, 1968-73, assoc., 1974-80, ptnr., 1980-88; ptnr. Mitchell/Giurgola & Thorp Architects, Australia, 1980—; adj. prof. Temple U., Phila., 1974-81, Calif. State Polytechnic U., Pomona, 1988-89. Design architect: Australian Capital Territory Legislative Assembly Building, 1994 (Royal Australian Inst. Architects Canberra medallion 1996), Allen Allen and Hemsely Law Offices, Sydney, 1993 (Royal Australian Inst. Architects Nat. Interior Architecture award 1994), ANA Hotel Sydney, 1992 (Spl. Mention for Outstanding Structures, Fedn. Internat. de la Precontrainte 1994), Brit. High Commn., Canberra, 1997, Waterfront Residential Complex, Kowloon Sta., Hong Kong, 2000; design coord.: Parliament House, Canberra, Australia, 1988 (Sir Zeiman Cowen award Royal Australia Inst. of Architects 1989). Councillor Royal Australian Inst. of Architects, 1991-96, v.p. ACT chpt. 1992-96, mem. nat. awards jury, 1983, 87-88. Recipient Disting. Achievement award Coll. of Architecture and Environ. Design, Ariz. State U., 1985. Fellow Royal Australian Inst. Architects; mem. AIA (com. mem. Phila. 1976-78). Office: MGT Archs, Franklin St/Endeavour House, Manuka CAN 2603, Australia also: PO Box 3634, Manuka ACT 2603, Australia

GUIDA, PAT, information broker, literature chemist; b. Highland Park, Mich.; d. Wilfred Bernard and Patricia Mary (Kelly) Graham; m. Edward Silvio Guida, Aug. 29, 1965; children: Niels Bohr, Eric Bohr. Student, Regis Coll., 1946-48, Rutgers U., 1952-55; BS cum laude, Fairleigh Dickinson U., 1961. Asst. librarian Warner-Lambert Research Inst., Morris Plains, N.J., 1961-64; librarian Reaction Motors Div. Thiokol, Denville, N.J., 1964-69; mgr., info. ctr. Foster D. Snell Div., Booz Allen & Hamilton Inc., Florham Park, N.J., 1969-80; pres. Pat Guida Assocs., Fairfield, N.J.; mem. Sci. Adv. Bd. EPA, Washington, 1978-82, Library Com. Chemists Club, N.Y.C., 1983-89. Editor: Chemical Digest, 1971-74. Pres. PTA, Sparta, N.J., 1959-60. Mem. Inst. Food Technologists (profl.). Avocations: theatre, West Highland white terriers, music, travel. Office: 24 Spielman Rd Fairfield NJ 07004-3412

GUIDO, GIANLUIGI, consumer researcher, consultant; b. Cutrofiano, Lecce, Italy, Sept. 26, 1963; s. Pasquale G. and Lidia Ligori. DSc, Libera U. Internat., Rome, 1987; M of Internat. Bus. Adminstrn., U.S. Internat. U., San Diego, 1990; PhD, U. Cambridge (Eng.), 1996. Commercialist Dr. U. Bari (Italy); official auditor, 1992. Rschr. Inst. San Paolo, Turin, Italy, 1987-88, U.S. Internat. U., San Diego, 1989-90; prof. mgmt. U. Lecce, Italy, 1990-93; rsch. scientist U. "La Sapienza", Rome, 1994—; pres. Guido Mktg. Rsch., Lecce, 1998—; prof. mktg. Scuola Superiore Sant'Anna U. Pisa, Italy, 1996-97, U. Padua, Italy, 1998—, U. Lecce, 1999—; bd. dirs. Soc. Pub. Transp., Lecce, 1995-99; researcher Inst. Adriano Olivetti Di Studi Per La Gestione Dell' Economia e Delle Aziende-Olivetti, Ancona, Italy, 1987; fin. cons. Ente Partecipazioni Finanziamento Industria Manifatturiera, Rome, 1988; rschr. Libera U. Internat., Rome, 1998—, rschr., Univ. of Lecce, Italy, 1999—. Author: The Financial Innovations of Interest Rate Swaps, 1988, Marketing and Distribution: Strategies for a Changing Europe, 1991, The Economy of the Titles Market, 1994, A Theory of In-Salience on Consumer Awareness, 1996, Consumer as a Product, 1997, Methodological and Operative Aspects of the Marketing Research Process, 1999, Business Economics and Management: Principles, Frames and Models, 2000, The Salience of Marketing Stimuli, 2000. Supporter Children Internat., N.Y., 1989—. Rotary scholar Rotary Found., 1989, Brit. Coun. scholar, 1993; grantee Inst. European Adminstrn. Affairs Internat. Scholarship, France, 1992. Mem. Am. Mktg. Assn., Assn. Consumer Rsch., Italian Assn. Marketing Rsch. (ordinary mem.). Avocations: playing violin, composing, writing novels, enigmatography. Home: 13 Via Trento e Trieste, 73024 Maglie Lecce, Italy Office: Guido Mktg Rsch, 2 Via La Marmora, 73100 Lecce Italy

GUIDOUX, RENÉ, scientist, physician, researcher; b. Aigle, Vaud, Switzerland, Sept. 21, 1936; s. André and Enrica (Delgrosso) G.; m. Lucienne Grassi, June 24, 1967; children: Yvan, Myriam. MD, U. Lausanne, Switzerland, 1964. Rsch. fellow dept. pharmacology U. Lausanne, 1964-71, 75-76; rsch. fellow dept. pharmacology U. Pa., Phila., 1972-73, rsch. fellow dept. biochemistry and biophysics, 1974; scientist Nestlé Rsch. Ctr., Lausanne, 1976—. Contbr. articles to profl. publs.; patentee in field. Mem. Swiss Pharmacology and Toxicology Soc., Swiss Nutrition Rsch. Soc., N.Y. Acad. Scis. Home: Ave de Beaumont 24, 1012 Lausanne Switzerland Office: Nestec Ltd/CRN, Vers-chez-les-Blanc, CH-1000 Lausanne Switzerland

GUIGOU, ELISABETH, French government official; b. Marrakesh, Morocco, Aug. 6, 1946; d. Georges Vallier and Jeanne Flecchia; m. Jean-Louis Guigou, 1966; 1 child. Grad., U. Rabat, U. Montpellier; postgrad., Ecole Nat. d'Adminstrn. Civil servant Ministry of Fin. Govt. of France, 1974, with Office of Treas., 1974-75, with Office of Banks, 1976-78, with Office of Fin. Mkts., 1978-79, fin. attaché Embassy, London, 1979-81, head Office for Europe, Am. and Asia Treas., 1981, tech. counselor Office of Min. Economy and Fin., 1982, tech. counselor, 1982-88, with Office of Pres. of Republic, 1988-90, min. Del. European Affairs, 1990-93, mem. Regional Coun. Provence Alpes Cote-d'Azur, 1992—, mem. European Parliament, 1994—, now min. of justice, 1997S; dep. chair fin. com. VIIth Plan, 1975-78; maitre de confs. Inst. d'Etudes Politiques, Paris, 1976; sec.- gen. interministerial com. European Econ. Cooperation, 1985-90. Author: Pour Les Européens, 1994, Etre Femme en Politique, 1997,. Office: 13 Place Vendome, 75042 Paris Cedex, France

GUIGOV, KRASSIMIR BORISSOV, health management administrator, toxicologist; b. Russe, Bulgaria, July 25, 1943; s. Boris Guigov Hadjiiliev and Lubitza Ivanova Parmakova; m. Maria Trendafilova, Sept. 27, 1970; children: Trendafil, Lilia, Renette. MD, Med. Acad., Sofia, Bulgaria, 1969, specialization in disaster medicine, 1974, specialization in mil. toxicology, 1974; PhD, Mil. Med. Acad., Sofia, 1985. Hosp. physician Mil. Acad. Medicine, 1970-76, med. asst., 1976-83, chief of svc., 1983-85, chief of sect., 1986-90, asst. prof. medicine, 1989, chief of dept., 1990-97, v.p., 1991-94; med. rels. Amb. of Bulgaria in Tunisia, 1997—; cons. Ministry of Health, Sofia, 1983-97, Ministry of Def., Sofia, 1985-97, Ministry of Environment, Sofia, 1985-95, Prime Min. of Bulgaria, 1990-96. Author books, articles and instrns. in field. Col. Mil. Med. Acad., 1988-97. Mem. Internat. Soc. Disaster Medicine, Nat. Disaster Med. Soc. of USA (hon.), Disaster Med. Soc. Bulgaria (v.p. 1991), N.Y. Acad. Scis. Orthodox. E-mail: tedi@nat.bg. Home: Mladost 3 Block 376 ap 62, 1712 Sofia Bulgaria Office: Amb of Bulgaria in Tunisia, Belvedere BP 28, 1002 Tunis 1002, Tunisia

GUIJUN, ZHUANG, marketing specialist, educator; b. Jiaonan County, China, Apr. 4, 1960; parents Zhuang Peiyuan and Zhang Zhiying; m. Zhou Xiaolian, July 23, 1988; 1 child, Zhuang Mengzhou. B in Econs., Shaanxi Inst. Fin. & Econs., Xi'an, China, 1984, M in Mktg., 1989; postgrad., City U. Hong Kong, 1997—. Lectr. Shaanxi Inst. Fin. & Econs., 1984—; vis. scholar Manchester Bus. Sch., England, 1994-96; cons. Xi'an Mktg. Rsch. Ltd., 1995—, Kaiyuan Dept. Store, Xi'an, 1995—. Soldier People's Liberation Army, China, 1977-80. Mem. Chinese Mktg. Assn., Chinese Mktg. Assn. Univs., Shaanxi Mktg. Assn. Avocations: table tennis, basketball, travel. Office: Shaanxi Inst Fin Econs, Xi'an, Shaanxi China 710061

GUILHERME, LUIZ-ROBERTO GUIMARÃES, soil scientist, educator; b. Uberlândia, Brazil, Aug. 25, 1964; s. Roberto and Maria-Therezinha (Rodrigues) G.; m. Cristina Hermeto Gueno, Dec. 1, 1990; 1 child, Fernanda. BS, ESAL, Lavras, Brazil, 1986, MSc, 1990; PhD, Mich. State U., 1997. Tech. asst. Brazilian Assn. Fertilizer Difusion, Sã Paulo, 1989-91; asst. prof. Fed. U. Lavras, 1991-97, assoc. prof., 1997—, chair dept. soil sci., 1992-93, Univ. Dean of Extension pro-rector, 1997—; cons. in field; grad. fellow Mich. State U., 1996; proposal reviewer in field. Co-author: Soil Fertility Guide, 1999; reviewer jours. Scientia Agricola, Pesquisa Agropecuária Brasileira, Revista Ciência e Agrotecnologia, Revista Brasileira de Ciência do Solo. Mem. Environ. Dev. City Coun., Lavras, 1992-93, 98—; mem. Quality Control Program on Siol Analysis, Profert-MG, Brazil, 1991-93. Rsch. scholar Nat. Coun. Sci. and Tech. Devel., 1998—, CNPq scholar, 1986, 87-88, 93-97; recipient award Brazilian Mininstry Edn., 1999, cert. of honor Rotary Club Lavras, 1988. Mem. Am. Chem. Soc., Soil Sci. Soc. Am., Brazilian Soc. Soil Sci. (coord. permanent tech. com. divsn. soil chemistry and mneralogy 1991-93, Franz Wilhelm Dafert award 1994), Internat. Union Soil Sci., Phi Kappa Phi. Avocations: jogging, piano, guitar, travel, cooking. Office: Fed U Lavras, Campus UFLA CP 37, 37200000 Lavras MG Brazil

GUILIANI CURY, HUGO M., economist, consultant; b. Puerto Plata, Dominican Republic, May 25, 1940; s. Juan Guiliani and Nadime Cury; m. Milady D. Coronado, July 28, 1968; children: Joanna, Maria Teresa, Laura. B in Econs., U. Miami, 1962; diploma in planning econs., Inst. L.Am. Planification, Chile, 1963; diploma in mgmt., Rsch. Inst. Mgmt. Sci., Delft, The Netherlands, 1964; D in Econs. (hon.), Inst. Las Americas, San Juan, P.R., 1980. Head devel. dept. Corp. Indsl. Devel., Santo Domingo, Dominican Republic, 1962-66; tech. dir. Corp. Pub. Enterprises/Corde, Santo Domingo, 1967-77; pres., chief exec. dir. Nat. Paper Industry, Dominican Republic, 1978-81; min. of treasury Dominican Govt., 1984; gov. Ctrl. Bank Dominican Republic, 1984-86; prof. U. Santo Domingo, 1967-78; pres. Banco Continental, Santo Domingo, 1987-98, Banco Nat. Constrn., Santo Domingo, 1987-98, Guiliani Cury and Assocs., Santo Domingo, 1998—. Author of nine books, 1978-87. Bd. dirs. Found. Dominican Desarrollo, 1981-83. Recipient Order of Cristobal Colon, Dominican Govt., 1986; named Outstanding Young Men of the Country, Jaycees Assn., Santo Domingo, 1977, Outstanding Dominican Economist Past 30 Yrs., Coll. Dominican Economist, 1997. Fellow Internat. Bankers Assn.; mem. Delta Sigma Pi. Roman Catholic. Avocations: sports, horse riding, jogging. Home: Eps-P-3188 PO Box 25261 Miami FL 33102-5261 Office: Guiliani Cury Assocs Inc, Nicolas De Bari 8, Santo Domingo Dominican Republic

GUILLAMA-ALVAREZ, NOEL JESUS, healthcare company executive; b. Havana, Cuba, Nov. 30, 1959; came to U.S., 1966; s. Jesus Mario Guillama and Rosa Maria Alvarez Guillama; m. Elayne Z. Cueto, Oct. 30, 1967; 1 child, Jahziel Mikhail Guillama. Student, Palm Beach C.C., Lake Worth, Fla., 1978-80; BS in Bus. Adminstrn., Pacific We. U., L.A., 1992; postgrad., MIT, 1997-99. Cert. bldg. contractor, Fla.; lic. real estate broker, mortgage broker, gen. ins. agt. Dir. programing Teleprompter Corp., West Palm Beach, Fla., 1976-79; pres., CEO JMG Holdings Inc, Palm Beach, Fla., 1980-90; v.p. ops. Quality Care Networks, Boca Raton, Fla., 1990-95; v.p. devel. Medpartners, Inc., Birmingham, 1995; pres., CEO Met. Health Networks, Boca Raton, 1995-2000; chmn., mng. ptnr. Millenium Capital Ptnrs., Boca Raton, 1997—; chmn. QuantumMed.com, Inc., Royal Palm Beach, Fla., 1999—; chmn., CEO Tektonica, inc., Royal Palm Beach, 2000—; vice chair Palm Beach County Adv. Bd., West Palm Beach, 1990-92; co-founder, vice chair Lake Worth Cmty. Devel. Corp., 1990-92; co-founder, dir. Project Lake Worth, 1989-92. Writer weekly column Palm Beach Latino Newspaper, 1991-92. Recipient award Leukemia Soc. Am., 1979, Chin de Plata award Todo Mag., Miami, Fla., 1978. Mem. Am. Fin. Assn., Am. Coll. Healthcare Execs. (assoc.), Med. Group Practice Assn. Avocations: scuba diving, tennis, golf, fishing. Office: 5100 Town Center Cir Ste 560 Boca Raton FL 33486-1070

GUILLAUME, GILBERT, judge; b. Bois-Colombes, France, Dec. 4, 1930; s. Pierre and Berthe (Brun) G.; m. Marie-Anne Hidden; children: Elisabeth, Marc, Helene. Diploma, Institut d'Etudes Politiques, Paris, 1951, Ecole Nationale D'Adminstrn., Paris, 1956. Mem. Conseil D'Etat, Paris, 1957-97; legal adviser French Civil Aviation Dept., Paris, 1968-79; dir. legal affairs Orgn. Econ. Cooperation and Devel., Paris, 1979, French Ministry Fgn. Affairs, Paris, 1979-87; judge Internat. Ct. of Justice, Hague, The Netherlands, 1987—, pres., 2000—; arbitrator Internat. C. of C., Internat. Ctr. for Settlement of Investments Disputes. Contbr. articles to profl. jours. Decorated officier of Legion of Honor. Mem. Permanent Ct. of Arbitration, French Br. of Internat. Law Assn. (chmn. 1989—), French Soc. Air and Space Law (chmn. 1976-80), French Soc. Internat. Law (vice chmn. 1987—), Academie de Marine, Institut de droit internat. Home: 36 rue Perronet, 92200 Neuilly-sur-Seine France Office: Internat Ct Justice, Peace Palace, Carnegieplein 2, 2517 KJ The Hague The Netherlands

GUILLAUME, PHILIPPE, museum administrator; b. Beijing, July 25, 1934; s. Jules and Elisabeth (Wittouck) G.; m. Monique Aboville, Feb. 15, 1958; children: Emmanuel, Francois, Agnes, Dominique; m. Shirîn Malek-Mansour Kadjar, Aug. 1, 1980; 1 child, Philippe. Lic. en droit, U. Paris, 1955; PhD, U. Louvain, Belgium, 1957. With Belgian Diplomatic Svc., 1960, Kingston, Jamaica and, Santo Domingo, 1962-64, Bonn, Germany, 1965-69, Warsaw, 1969-71, Paris, 1971-74, Tehran, 1974-75, Brussels, 1975-86; prof. in geopolitics for businessmen Institut Supérieur de Commerce St. Louis, 1988-99, United Bus. Inst., 1988-99; chmn. Brussels European Mus. Contemporary Art, 1999—. Fax: 32-2-640-29-24. Home and Office: 10 Rue de la Vallee, B-1050 Brussels Belgium

GUILLAUMONT, ROBERT, retired chemist, educator; b. Lyon, France, Feb. 26, 1933; s. Jean and Alexandrine (Masbou) G.; m. Nicole Parent, Dec. 15, 1958; children: Cyrille, Elisabeth. Licence es scis., Faculty of Scis., Paris, 1957, PhD, 1966. Asst. in radiochemistry Faculty of Scis., Paris, 1958-67; asst. prof. chemistry Faculty of Scis., Orsay, France, 1967-72, prof., 1972-98, retired, 1998; head radiochemistry group Nuclear Physics Inst., Orsay, 1979-90; head standing group radwaste mgmt. Ministry of Industry, 1986—; mem. numerous French nat. coms., 1973—. Author: Protactinium 1974, Fundamentals of Radiochemistry, 1993; contbr. articles to chemistry and radiochemistry mags. With French Army, 1960-62. Recipient Ordre Nat. du Merite Ministry of Industry, 1989. Mem. French Acad. Scis. (corr. mem. chemistry sect.). Home: 7 E Branly, F91 120 Palaiseau France

GUILLAUSSEAU, PIERRE JEAN, physician, educator; b. Ville d'Avray, France, June 23, 1948; s. Jean François and Paule Thérèse (Chevrel) G.; m.

Claudine Jeanne Scholer, Nov. 20, 1970; children: Valérie, Nicolas, Axelle. MD, Faculty of Medicine, Paris, 1977. Diplomate in internal medicine, diabetes and endocrine diseases. Intern in internal medicine, diabetes and endocrine diseases Assistance Publique, Paris, 1973-77, asst., 1977-81; hosp. physician Hopital Lariboisiere, Paris, 1984—; prof. Faculty of Medicine, Paris, 1990—; mem. coun. Mediterranean Group for study of Diabetes, 1995-96, v.p., 1998, gen. vice chair, 2000. Mem. French-Speaking Assn. for Study of Diabetes (gen. sec. 1992-94), European Assn. for Study of Diabetes (coun. 1990-92), French Diabetes Assn. (mem. coun. 1987-96), Rotary (pres. Paris 1999-2000). Avocations: sailing, tennis, prehistory and ethnology. Home: 16 rue de Passy, 75016 Paris France Office: Hopital Lariboisiere, 2 rue Ambroise Pare, 75010 Paris France

GUILLEMIN, ROGER C. L., physiologist; b. Dijon, France, Jan. 11, 1924; came to U.S., 1953, naturalized, 1963; s. Raymond and Blanche (Rigollot) G.; m. Lucienne Jeanne Billard, Mar. 22, 1951; children: Chantal, Francois, Claire, Helene, Elizabeth, Cecile. B.A., U. Dijon, 1941, B.Sc., 1942; M.D., Faculty of Medicine, Lyons, France, 1949; Ph.D., U. Montreal, 1953; Ph.D. (hon.), U. Rochester, 1976, U. Chgo., 1977, Baylor Coll. Medicine, 1978, U. Ulm, Germany, 1978, U. Dijon, France, 1978, Free U. Brussels, 1979, U. Montreal, 1979, U. Man., Can, 1984, U. Turin, Italy, 1985, Kyung Hee U., Korea, 1986, U. Paris, Paris, 1986, U. Barcelona, Spain, 1988, U. Madrid, 1988, McGill U., Montreal, Can., 1988, U. Claude Bernard, Lyon, France, 1989, Laval U., Quebec, Can., 1996, Sherbrooke U., Quebec, 1997, U. Franche-Comté, France, 1999. Intern, resident univs. hosps. Dijon, 1949-51; asso. dir., asst. prof. Inst. Exptl. Medicine and Surgery, U. Montreal, 1951-53; asso. dir. dept. exptl. endocrinology Coll. de France, Paris, 1960-63; asst. prof. physiology Baylor Coll. Medicine, 1953-57, assoc. prof., 1957-63, prof., dir. labs. neuroendocrinology, 1963-70, adj. prof., 1970—; resident fellow, chmn. labs. neuroendocrinology Salk Inst., La Jolla, Calif., 1970-89, adj. rsch. prof., 1989-94; Disting. Scientist Whittier Inst., 1989-97, med. and sci. dir., 1993-94; adj. prof. medicine U. Calif., San Diego, 1995-97; disting. prof. Salk Inst., La Jolla, Calif., 1997—. Decorated chevalier Legion d'Honneur (France), 1974, officer, 1984; recipient Gairdner Internat. award, 1974; U.S. Nat. Medal of Sci., 1977; co-recipient Nobel prize for medicine, 1977; recipient Lasker Found. award, 1975; Dickson prize in medicine, 1976; Passano award sci., 1976; Schmitt medal neurosci., 1977; Barren Gold medal, 1979; Dale medal Soc. for Endocrinology U.K., 1980, Ellen Browning Scripps Soc. medal Scripps Meml. Hosps. Found., 1988, Disting. Scientist award Nat. Diabetes Rsch. Coalition. Fellow AAAS; mem. NAS, Am. Physiol. Soc., Am. Peptide Soc. (hon.), Assn. Am.Physicians, Endocrine Soc. (pres. 1986), Soc. Exptl. Biology and Medicine, Internat. Brain Rsch. Orgn., Internat. Soc. Rsch. Biology Reprodn., Soc. Neuro-scis., Am. Acad. Arts and Scis., French Acad. Scis. (fgn. assoc.), Academie Internationale de Medecine (fgn. assoc.), Swedish Soc. Med. Scis. (hon.), Academie des Scis. (fgn. assoc.), Academie Royale de Medecine de Belgique (corr. fgn.), Internat. Soc. Neurosci. (charter), Western Soc. Clin. Rsch., Can. Soc. Endocrinal Metabolism, (hon.), Club of Rome. Office: The Salk Inst 10010 N Torrey Pines Rd La Jolla CA 92037-1099

GUILLERMOND, GABRIEL GEORGES, physician; b. Nice, France, Oct. 22, 1925; s. Georges Fernand and Yvonne Henriette (Chaskin) G.; m. Nelly Cannebotin, Sept. 5, 1953 (Oct. 1971); m. Marguerite Bondin, June 17, 1972; 1 child, Florence. Lic. in Sci., Sci. Inst., 1950; DM, Montpellier Med. Sch., 1952; Diploma of Labour Medicine and Profl. Diseases, Med. U., Marseille, France, 1981. Pvt. practice physician, internal medicine Nice, 1952—; physician Brit. Am. Hosp., Nice, 1952-72; sworn doctor Edn. Ministry, Nice, 1972—; labour medicine, metilliand diseases French Rys., Soc. Social Organisms Edn. Ministry, Nice, 1965—. Club: Babriel L'Annonciateur. Lodge: Lions (hon. mem.). Home and Office: 47 Rue Marechel Joffre, 06000 Nice France

GUILLET, JACQUES ANDRE, physician, medical researcher; b. Cauterets, France, Apr. 16, 1948; s. Auguste Victor and Gloria (Otal) G.; m. Catherine Michele Casse, Jan. 17, 1979; children: Audrey Valerie, Cecile Pauline. MD, Faculty Medicine, Bordeaux, France, 1978. Resident physician Bordeaux San. Region, Agen, France, 1973-78; resident pediatrics Faculty Medicine, Bordeaux, 1979, resident biophysics, biology, 1984; resident nuclear medicine Nat. Inst. Nuclear Scis. and Techs., Paris, 1980, lectr., 1988; resident biophysics nuclear Bordeaux II U., 1982-86; medicine lectureship Pellegrin Hosp., Bordeaux, 1982-86; biologist, head depts. biophysics, nuclear medicine St Esprit Hosp, Agen, France, 1985—; lectr. Conservatoire Nat. Arts et Metiers, Agen, 1984—, Nat. Edn. Ctr. for Radiol. Risks, 1994—; head rsch. ctr. Radioactivity Rsch./Supervision Ctr., Agen, 1994-99; bd. dirs. Hosp. Centre, Agen, 1991-94; hon. mem., med. advisor French Assn. Thyroid Patients, 2000—. Author: Nuclear Medicine and Biology: 5 books in French, 1984-93, Prostatic Specific Antigen, 1987-88, Atlas of Bone Scintigraphy, 1993, Thyroid autoantibodies, 1997; contbr. more than 300 articles to profl. jours. Recipient awards Amersham-Buchler, Europe, 1983, French Soc. Nuclear Energy, Sfen, Paris, 1992. Mem. European Assn. Nuclear Medicine, French Soc. Biophysics, French Soc. Radio Protection, Pediatric Nuclear Medicine, Concerted Activity in Nuclear Medicine, French Assn. Thyroid Patients (hon., med. adv., 2000—). Office: Hosp St Esprit, Rt de Villeneuve, 47923 Agen France

GUILLET, JEAN PIERRE, physicist; b. Puy de Dôme, France, Apr. 11, 1937; s. Roger and Elise (Champagnol) G.; m. Liliane Cazenave, Feb. 27, 1965 (div. Nov. 1972); m. Paulette Ferracci; children: Thierry, Francois. Diploma in Sci., U. Clermont-Ferrand, France, 1958; Diploma in Electronic Engring., Ecole Superieure d' Elec., Paris, 1960; Radiophysicist, Ctr. Physique Atomique, Toulouse, France, 1979. Cert. radiophysicist. Engr. Meudon Observatory, Meudon, France, 1960-64, TELCO Biomed., Paris, 1965-67, Tranchant Electronique, Paris, 1969-71, SNIAS, Paris, 1971-72, CIT-ALCATEL, Paris, 1974-76; radiophysicist Inst. Paoli-Calmettes, Marseille, France, 1976-97; freelance journalist, l'Usine Nouvelle, 1976-86; tchr. Ecole Superieure d'Ingenieurs, Marseille, 1976—, Ecole de Manipulateurs de Radiologie, Marseille, 1989-96., Lycée St. Vincent de Paul, Marseille, 2000—. Author: Reseaux actifs. Filtres., 1971, Amplificateurs de signaux biologiques, 1972, Abrege de Physique Radiotherapique, 1994, Manual de Fisica de Radioterapia, 1996. Soldier French artillery, 1964. Mem. Soc. Ingenieurs Ecole Superieure Electricite, Soc. Physiciens d'hopitaux, Mediterranee Physique Medicale, Société Française de Physique, European Phys. Soc. Avocations: novel writing, Bonsai, microinformatic, protection and study of European twisted beeches. Home: 35 Bd Paul Riquet, Bouches du Rhone, 13012 Marseille France Office: Inst Paoli-Calmettes, 232 Bd de St Marguerite, Bouches du Rhone, 13009 Marseille France

GUILLONNEAU, BERTRAND, urologist, surgeon; b. Paris, Feb. 5, 1959; s. Andre and Solange (Molere) G.; m. Marianne Chatriot, May 12, 1985; children: Gaspard, Pauline, Pierre. ND, 1985. Resident U. Hosp., Nantes, France, 1983-90, asst., 1990-93; urologist Montsouris Inst., Paris, 1993—; rschr. in field. Contbr. articles to profl. jours. Mem. European Assn. Urology, French Assn. Urology. Office: Inst Montsouris, 42 Blvd Jourdan, 75014 Paris France

GUILLOT, JACQUES LOUIS ELIE, veterinarian; b. Saint Etienne, France, June 11, 1968; s. Henri Guillot and Rose Messina; m. Cécile Lamas; children: Chloé, Coline, Solal. Diploma in vet. medicine, Vet. Coll. Alfort, France, 1991; diploma in med. mycology, Inst. Pasteur, Paris, 1993; PhD in parasitology, Creteil, 1995. Asst. Vet. Coll. Alfort, 1991-95, asst. prof., 1995—; small animal dermatology practice, 1998—. Contbr. articles to profl. publs. Mem. Internat. Soc. Human and Animal Mycology, European Confedn. of Med. Mycology. Office: Ecole Veterinaire d'Alfort, 94704 Maisons Alfort Cedex France

GUILMET, GEORGE MICHAEL, cultural anthropologist, educator; b. Seattle, Feb. 8, 1947; s. Michael D. and Avis M. (Digerness) G.; m. Glenda J. Black, May 24, 1980; children: Michelle R., Douglas J. BS in Metallurg. Engrng., U. Wash., Seattle, 1969; MA in Anthropology, U. Wash., 1973; PhD in Anthropology, UCLA, 1976. Lectr. anthropology Calif. State U., Bakersfield, 1976-77, program dir. urban anthropology internship program, 1977-78; asst. prof. comparative sociology U. Puget Sound, Tacoma, Wash., 1977-82; assoc. prof. U. Puget Sound, Tacoma, 1982-88, prof., 1988—; reader dept. anthropology UCLA, 1974-75; rsch. cons. dept. psychiatry UCLA, 1975-76; rsch. assoc. Nat. Ctr. Am. Indian Alaska Native Mental Health Rsch., U. Colo., 1986—; disting. vis. prof. anthropology San Diego State U., 1991; grant reviewer NIMH, Bethesda, 1991, 92; spkr. in field. Author, co-author: (chpts.) Research in Philosophy and Technology, vol. 8, 1985, Technology and Responsibility: Philosophy and Technology, vol. 3, 1987, Behavioral Health Issues among American Indians and Alaska Natives: Explorations on the Frontiers of the Biobehavioral Sciences, 1988, Native America in the Twentieth Century: An Encyclopedia, 1994, (rsch. monograph) The People Who Give More, 1989; contbr. articles to profl. jours.; keyboardist, vocals Brave New World; singles released include It's Tomorrow, 1967. Evaluation cons. Chief Leschi Sch., Puyallup Tribe Indians, Tacoma, 1989, 96—, vol. musician Puyallup Tribe Indians, Tacoma, 1996, 97, cultural needs assessment cons., 1996-97, juvenile justice program cons., 1997-98. Kaiser Aluminum Chem. Corp. scholar, 1968-69; grantee Carnegie Found., 1974, U. Puget Sound, 1977-79, 83-84, 86, 88, 89, 91, 93. Fellow Am. Anthrop. Assn. (bd. dirs. coun. anthropology edn. 1983-85); mem. Soc. Psychol. Anthropology, Soc. Philosophy Tech., Fedn. Small Anthropology Programs, Pacific N.W. Historians Guild. Home: 1211 S Tyler St Tacoma WA 98405-1135 office: Dept Comparative Sociology U Puget Sound Tacoma WA 98416-0001

GUIMARAES, CLAUDIA TEIXEIRA, plant geneticist; b. Sete Lagoas, Brazil, June 26, 1968; d. Paulo Martins Guimaraes and Evangelina Teixeira da Costa Guimaraes. BS in Agrl. Engring., Fed. U. Vicosa, Brazil, 1991, MS in Genetics and Plant Breeding, 1993, PhD in Genetics and Plant Breeding, 1999. Rschr. Embrapa Maize and Sorghum, Sete Lagoas, 1999—. Contbr. chpt. to book, articles to profl. jours. Mem. Brazilian Soc. Genetics (Young Geneticist award 1999). Avocation: scuba diving. E-mail: claudia@cnpms.embrapa.br. Office: Embrapa Maize and Sorghum, PO Box 151, Sete Lagoas 35701, Brazil

GUIMARAES, ROMEU CARDOSO, evolution researcher, molecular biology educator; b. Belo Horizonte, Brazil, July 29, 1943; s. Miguel Fernandes and Anita Cardoso Guimaraes; m. Alexandrina Magalhaes, Nov. 29, 1969. MD, Fed. U. Minas Gerais, Belo Horizonte, 1965, PhD in Pathology, 1970; full prof. genetics, Sao Paulo State U., 1987. Assoc. rschr. U. Tex., Austin, 1970-73, U. Kent, Canterbury, Eng., 1981-82, Free U. Berlin, 1988-89, Weizmann Inst. Sci., Rehovot, Israel, 1989-90; prof. Sao Paulo State U., Botucatu, Brazil, 1976-93; assoc. prof. Fed. U. Minas Gerais, Belo Horizonte, 1993—. Author: In Search of Illusions, 1994, also book chpts., articles. Named Illustrious Son of Belo Horizonte, Pub. Profs. Assn., 1997; sr. rsch. fellow Nat. Rsch. Coun., Brasilia, Brazil, 1984-99. Mem. Internat. Soc. for Study of Origin of Life, Sao Paulo State Acad. Sci., Acad. Medicine Minas Gerais. Fax: 55-31-274-4988. E-mail: romeucg@icb.ufmg.br. Home: 414/1002, Ave Assis Chateaubriand, 30150101 Belo Horizonte Brazil Office: U Fed de Minas Gerais, Inst Ciencias Biologicas, 31270901 Belo Horizonte Brazil

GUIMARAES, RUI MANUEL, cardiologist; b. Braga, Portugal, Jan. 1, 1951; s. Manuel C. and Julia G. Guimaraes; m. Paula G. Goncalves; 1 child, Pedro; m. Zelia Costa-e-Silva, Feb. 3, 1992. MD, Faculdade Medicina Lisboa, Lisbon, Portugal, 1979. Intern Civil Hosps. Lisbon, 1979-86, asst. ICU, 1986—; cons. Hosp. St. Louis, Lisbon, 1987—, Hosp. Inst. Urologia, 1997. Contbr. articles to sci. jours. Fellow Portuguese Soc. Cardiology (Young Investigator's award 1984), Soc. Internat. Medicine; mem. Order of Physicians. Home: Pr Ilha Faial 12-1, 1000-168 Lisbon Portugal Office: R Jose Falcao 47 R/C, 1000-184 Lisbon Portugal

GUINE, RAQUEL PINHO FERREIRA, chemical engineer, educator; b. Coimbra, Portugal, June 12, 1968; d. Jose Victor Domingos Ferreira and Maria Rosa Pinho Domingues G. Lic. faculty sci. and tech., U. Coimbra, 1991, MChemE, 1997. Asst. 1st tchr. Poly. U., Viseu, Portugal, 1994-97, asst. 2d tchr., 1997-98, asst. prof., 1998—. Mem. editl. bd. Terra fertil, 1997. Pres. U. Choir, Coimbra, 1992-93. Mem. Engrs. Profl. Assn., Portuguese Chemistry Soc., Assn. Indsl. Devel. Viseu. Avocations: singing, painting, aerobics. Home: N 87, Estrada dos Pereiros, 3040-093 Coimbra Portugal Office: ESAV, Campus Politecnico Repeses, 3500 Viseu Portugal

GUINIER, DANIEL, security firm executive; b. Montluçon, Auvergne, France, July 20, 1944; s. Lucien and Camille (Bonnefoy) G.; 1 child, Sébastien. DSc, PhD, U. Strasbourg, France, 1979. Cert. bio-computing, info. sci. and computer security. Supr. lab. computer ctr. Nat. Rsch. Coun. (CNRS), Strasbourg, France, 1974-83; rsch. assoc. Nat. Rsch. Coun., 1985-89; vis. prof. Naval Postgrad Sch., Monterey, Calif., 1983-84; pres., cons. OSIA: Orgn. and Advanced INfo. Sys., Strasbourg, 1990—; lectr. (IMI) U. Compiègne, France, 1992—, U. Strasbourg, IECS, 1993—, IAE, 1995, Nancy II. Author: People Identification by Biometrics, 1991, Security and Quality of Information Systems-Systemic Approach, 1992, Catastrophe Management, Contingency Plans, 1994; patentee in field. Expert in info. sys. security for the Cts. of Justice, France, 1991—. Region Alsace grantee, France, 1990. Mem. IEEE-Computer Soc., Assn. for Computing Machinery, Inst. Internal Auditors, N.Y. Acad. Scis. Avocations: music, mineralogy. Office: OSIA, OSIA, BP 86, F67034 Strasbourg Cedex 2, France

GUINN, STANLEY WILLIS, lawyer; b. Detroit, June 9, 1953; s. Willis Hampton and Virginia Mae (Pierson) G.; m. Patricia Shirley Newgord, June 13, 1981; children: Terri Lanae, Scott Stanley. BBA with high distinction, U. Mich., 1979, MBA with distinction, 1981; MS in Taxation with distinction, Walsh Coll., 1987; JD cum laude, U. Mich., 1992. CPA, Mich.; cert. mgmt. acct., Mich. Tax mgr. Coopers & Lybrand, Detroit, 1981-87; tax cons. Upjohn Co., Kalamazoo, 1987-89; litigation atty. Brobeck, Phleger & Harrison, 1992-94, Coughlan, Semmer & Lipman, San Diego, 1994-95; consumer fin. atty. Bank Am. NT & SA, San Francisco, 1995-98, GreenPoint Credit, LLC, San Diego, 1998—. Served with USN, 1974-77. Mem. AICPA, ABA, Calif. State Bar Assn., Inst. Cert. Mgmt. Acctg., Phi Kappa Phi, Beta Gamma Sigma, Beta Alpha Psi, Delta Mu Delta. Republican. Mem. Christian Ch. Avocations: tennis, racquetball, running. E-mail: stan.guinn@greenpoint.com. Home: 3125 Crystal Ct Escondido CA 92025-7763 Office: GreenPoint Credit 10089 Willow Creek Rd San Diego CA 92131-1603

GUINSBURG, PHILIP FRIED, alcohol and substance abuse counselor; b. N.Y.C., Sept. 13, 1946; s. Theodore and Elena (Fried) G.; m. Debrah Josias Guinsburg, June 15, 1968; children: Mark, Michael. BA, Columbia Coll., 1968; MA, U. N.D., 1970, PhD, 1973. Diplomate Am. Bd. Med. Psychotherapy; lic. alcohol and drug abuse counselor. Clin. dir. Nashville Drug Treatment Ctr., Dede Wallace Ctr., 1973-78; pvt. practice Nashville, 1974—; asst. clin. prof. psychiatry Vanderbilt U., Nashville, 1987-93; cons. Crisis Intervention Ctr., 1974-99; pres. Dreammakers, Inc., Nashville, 1989-91, bd. dirs., 1982—; cons. Campus For Human Devel. Baseball coach Brentwood (Tenn.) Civitan Little League, 1982-92. Mem. Am. Counseling Assn., Am. Group Psychotherapy Assn., Am. Acad. Psychoterhapists (chair continuing edn., treas.), Assn. for Spiritual, Ethical and Religious Values in Counseling, Nat. Assn. Alcoholism and Drug Abuse Counselors, Tenn. Assn. Alcohol and Drug Abuse Counselors (pres.). Jewish. Avocations: gardening, sports, gourmet foods. Home: 8121 Maryland Ln Brentwood TN 37027-7341 Office: 2313 21st Ave S Nashville TN 37212-4908

GUIOT, PIERRE, business development director in life sciences; b. Belgium, 1947; married; 1 child. Degree in Chem. Engring. with honors, Meurice Inst. Chemistry, Brussels, 1969, postgrad., 1970; MS in Theoretical Physics with honors, Free U. Brussels, 1972-76; PhD in Biophysics with honors, Cath. U. Louvain, Belgium, 1976-81; post-univ. tng. in mkt. mgmt., ICHEC, Brussels, 1987. Cert. prof. chemistry, high tech level, INPET-Brussels, 1971-72; cert. prof. physics, coll. level, Free U. Brussels, 1976; cert. official supplier med. devices, INAMI-Brussels, 1986. Asst. Meurice Inst. Chemistry, 1970-71; sr. investigator U. Louvain, 1976-83; new products promotion mgr./Europe Medtronic Holland, 1984-85; prodn. mgr. Sopar Biochem, 1986-87; internat. dir. comml. devel. and regulatory affairs Reilly Chemicals, 1989—. Editor C.R.C. Press, Inc., U.S.; contbr. numerous articles to profl. jours. Recipient Charles Meurice award 1969, 1st Laureate Interuniv. Competition in Physics, 1977, Pierre Bruylants award, U. Louvain, 1982, Stas award Belgian Royal Acad. Scis., 1982. Mem. N.Y. Acad. Scis. Home: rue Cramat 31, B-7181 Petit-Roeulx-lez Nivelles, Belgium

GUIOT-POULET, ANNE-LAURE, research scientist; b. Lyon, Rhône, France, May 15, 1963; d. Philippe Edgar-Augustin Guiot and Catherine Jeanne Legorgeu. Vet. degree, Nat. Sch. Lyon, 1985; PhD in Immunology, Claude Bernard Lyon, 1997. Cert. vet. Vet. practitioner France, 1985-90; chief of projects Merial, Lyon, 1993—. Home: 2 place des 4 Vierges, 69110 Sainte Foy Les Lyon France Office: Merial, 254 rue M Merieux BP 7009, 69342 Lyon France

GUIRALDENQ, PIERRE-HENRI, physical metallurgy educator; b. Paris, Apr. 2, 1934; s. Paul-Henri and Elise (Jeanjean) G.; m. Anne-Marie Clemence, Sept. 5, 1964; 1 child, Pierre-Marie. Lic. es Scis. Physiques, U. Marseille, 1958; dip., Inst. Saclay, 1959; D es Sc. Physiques, U. Paris, 1964. Rsch. attaché CNRS, Paris, 1963-64; engr. CAFL, St Etienne, France, 1964-68; prof. Ecole Centrale de Lyon, Ecully, France, 1968-99, head dept. phys. metallurgy, 1968-89, head rsch. CNRS unit, 1978-90; head ctr. micro analysis Ecole Centrale de Lyon - U. Lyon, Ecully, Lyon, France, 1975-85; sci. cons. French Ministry Def.-Navy, Paris, 1987-; head indsl. edn. Dept. of Ecole Centrale de Lyon, 1995-99; prof. emeritus U. Lyon, France, 1999—. Author: Dental Metallurgy, 1981, Diffusion in Materials, 1984, Emile Boren (1871-1956): Space and Time of a Life Through Two Centuries, 1999. With French Navy Mil. Svcs., 1961-63. Decorated Order of Merit, Order of Acad. Distinction (France); recipient medal Le Chatelier, Soc. Devel. Industries, 1988, medal of engaged mil. svcs. Fellow Soc. Francaise de Metallurgie et des Materiaux (medal Rist 1965, medal Reaumur 1985), Académie des Scis. Lyon (laureate). Roman Catholic. Home: 16 Rue du Prieuré, 69130 Ecully Rhone, France Office: Ecole Centrale de Lyon, 36 Ave de Collongue, 69131 Ecully Rhone, France

GUIRARDELLO, REGINALDO, engineering educator; b. Valinhos, Brazil, Aug. 23, 1961; s. Orlando Sobrinho and Verônica (Rossi) G.; m. Edinêis De Brito, June 30, 1990. BSc, UNICAMP, Campinas, Brazil, 1983, MSc, 1988; PhD, U. Wis., 1993. Cert. in chem. engring. Rschr. Codetec, Campinas, 1984-87; instr. UNICAMP, Campinas, 1987-88, asst. prof., 1993—. Contbr. articles to profl. jours. Mem. AAAS, Brazilian Assn. Chem. Engring. Office: Univ Estadual de Campinas, Coll Chem Engring, 13083970 Campinas Brazil

GUIRGUIS SALEH, OSIRIS WANIS, biophysicist, researcher; b. Cairo, Egypt, Feb. 21, 1956; s. Wanis Guirguis Saleh and Alice Spiro Salama; m. Mary Khatchik Kamberian, Aug. 21, 1983; children: Christina, Anais. BSc in Physics, Cairo U., 1976, MSc in Solid State Physics, 1980, PhD in Radiation Physics, 1987. Demonstrator dept. physics Faculty of Sci., Cairo U., Giza, Egypt, 1976-80, asst. lectr. dept. physics, 1980-82, asst. lectr. dept. biophysics, 1982-87, lectr. dept. biophysics, 1987-94, assoc. prof. dept. biophysics, 1994-2000, prof. dept. biophysics, 2000—; lectr. in field. Contbr. numerous articles to profl. jours. Mem. Egyptian Biophys. Soc. E-mail: osiriswg@frcu.eun.eg, osiriswg@hotmail.com. Home: 14 Hassan Mazhar St, Heliopolis 11341, Egypt Office: Cairo U Faculty of Sci, Dept Biophysics, Giza Egypt

GUITTAR, LEE JOHN, retired newspaper executive; b. St. Louis, May 4, 1931; s. LeRoy and Edna Mae (Johnston) G.; m. Elizabeth Madden Shedrick, Aug. 23, 1980; children—David Lee, Stephen Joseph, Mitchell John, Jeanne Marie, Richard Laughran; step-children: Elisabeth F. Shedrick, Kathryn S. Shedrick, Daniel C. Shedrick. AB, Columbia U., 1953; postgrad., U. Mass., 1962; MA, Columbia U., 1993. With Gen. Electric Co., 1955-65; mgr. community and govt. relations programs Gen. Electric Co., N.Y.C., 1963-65; mgr. employee and pub. relations Tidewater Oil Co., N.Y.C., 1965-66; from personnel dir. to circulation dir. Miami (Fla.) Herald, 1967-71; v.p., bus. mgr. Detroit Free Press, 1972-74, v.p., gen. mgr., 1974-75, pres., dir., 1975-77; pub. Dallas Times Herald, 1977-80; Publisher The Denver Post, 1980-83; chmn. Denver Post, 1983; pres. U.S.A. Today, 1984-86; v.p. group exec. newspapers The Hearst Corp., N.Y.C., 1986-98; editor, pub. San Francisco Examiner, 1995-98, ret., 1998. Lt. (j.g.) USNR, 1953-55, Korea. Mem. Farm Neck Golf Club (Martha's Vineyard, Mass.), Phi Beta Kappa. Republican. Roman Catholic.

GUIZANI, MOHSEN MOKHTAR, computer educator; b. Oueslatia, Kairouan, Tunisia, Feb. 9, 1961; s. Mokhtar Saleh and Mobarka Saleh G.; m. Saida Omar Garsallaoui, Aug. 3, 1989; children: Nadra, Fatma, Maher, Zainab, Sara. BSEE, Syracuse U., 1984, MSEE, 1986, MS in Computer Engring., 1987, PhD in Computer Engring., 1990. Teaching asst. Syracuse (N.Y.) U., 1984-87, rsch. asst., 1986, teaching fellow, 1988, teaching assoc., 1988-89; assoc. prof. U. Mo., 1997-99; chmn. computer sci. dept. U. W. Fla., 1999—. Contbr. articles to profl. jours. Recipient scholarship Syracuse U., 1985; rsch. grantee in field. Mem. IEEE (sr.), Assn. for Computing Machinery, Tau Beta Pi. Avocations: reading, sports. Office: U W Fla Dept Computer Sci 11000 University Pkwy Pensacola FL 32514-5750

GUIZOL, CHRISTIAN YVES MARIE, manufacturing company executive; b. Algiers, Algeria, Sept. 16, 1929; s. Marius and Marie-Thérèse (Fleuriot) G.; m. Blandine Savalle, July 26, 1958; children: Hélène, Roselyne, Catherine. Grad. engr., Cen. Sch. Arts and Mfrs., 1953; student, Nat. Higher Sch. Mining, Paris, 1954-55. Engr. French Overseas Mining Bur., Bumifom, 1955-60; various missions French Equatorial Africa, Western Pakistan, 1958-59; engr. Comilog, Moanda, Gabon, 1960; mining engr. Cie de Mokta Djebel Djerissa, Tunisia, Grand Lahou Manganese Mines, Ivory Coast, Compagnie des Mines d'Uranium de Franceville, Gabon, 1968-71; dir. bldg. materials dept. Imerys, Paris, 1974-92. Mem. Union Nat. des Productuers de Granulats (hon. pres.), Encem (pres.), Fedn. Francaise des Tuiles er Briques (hon. pres.), Soc. Industry Minerale. Home: 51 Ave Jean Jaures, 94230 Cachan France Office: SIM, 17 rue St Severin, 75005 Paris France

GULACSI, MIKLOS, physicist, researcher; b. Cluj, Romania, May 16, 1960; arrived in Australia, 1995; s. Miklos and Erzsebet (Kovacs) G.; m. Melinda Buzogany, Apr. 28, 1984 (div. Oct. 1992); 1 child, Szabolcs; m. Sonia Alessandra Gherdevich, Dec. 10, 1993. MSc, U. Babes-Bolyai, Cluj, 1984; MPhil, Internat. Sch. Advanced Stds., Trieste, Italy, 1989, PhD, 1991. Staff rsch. physicist Inst. Isotopic and Molecular Tech., Cluj, 1984-88; postgrad. rsch. fellow Internat. Sch. for Advanced Studies, Trieste, 1988-91; postdoctoral rsch. assoc. Los Alamos Nat. Lab., 1991-93, rsch. assoc., 1993-95; Queen Elizabeth II fellow Australian Nat. U., Canberra, 1995—; cons. Los Alamos Nat. Lab., 1995—; invited lectr. internat. confs., workshops, and schs., 1983—. Assoc. editor, mem. editl. bd. Philos. Mag., 1995—; contbr. numerous articles to physics jours. Recipient acad. award Romanian Acad. of Scis., 1985. Mem. Am. Phys. Soc., N.Y. Acad. Scis. Avocation: classical music. Office: Australian Nat U Inst Advanced Studies, Dept Theoretical Physics, Canberra ACT 0200, Australia

GULACSI, ZSOLT, physicist; b. Cluj, Romania, Jan. 14, 1955; arrived in Hungary, 1993; s. Miklos and Erzsebet (Kovacs) G.; m. Katalin Vajda, Mar. 31, 1984; children: Zsolt, Balazs. PhD, U. Babes-Bolyai, Cluj, Hungary, 1985; habilit., U. Lajos Kossuth, Debrecen, 1995. Rschr. Inst. Isotopic and Molecular Tech., Cluj, 1984-90; rsch. fellow Inst. for Theoretical Physics, Aachen, Germany, 1991-92; assoc. prof. physics Lajos Kossuth U., Debrecen, Hungary, 1993—; referee for western sci. jours., Hungarian Nat. Rsch. Found., 1995—. Contbr. articles to profl. jours. Alexander von Humboldt Rsch. fellow, 1991-92, Prof. Szecsenyi fellow Hungarian Min. Edn., 1997; Internat. Ctr. for Theoretical Physics grantee, Trieste, Italy, 1986-92; Physics award Romanian Acad. Scis., 1985. Mem. N.Y. Acad. Scis., Am. Phys. Soc., Humbold Club for Hungarian ex Homboldt Fellows, Lorand Eotvos Phys. Soc. Avocations: gardening, reading, classical music. Office: Lajos Kossuth U Dept Theor Phys, Poroszlay ut 6/c POB 5, H-4010 Debrecen Hungary

GULACSY, ISTVAN, surgeon; b. Ungvar, Hungary, Oct. 6, 1942; s. Istvan and Margit (Steierer) G.; m. Eva Volgyes, Oct. 19, 1972; children: Attila, Reka.; Grad. med. sch., St. Petersburg, 1966; PhD, U. Budapest, 1981. Surgeon Med. Sch., Pecs, Hungary, 1967-73; anesthesiologist Med. Sch., Zurich, 1973-74; rschr. Med. Sch., Leningrad, 1976-80; asst. prof. Med. Sch., Pecs, 1981-87; vis. prof. Med. Sch., Charlotte, N.C., 1987, Amsterdam, 1989; gen. surgeon Med. Sch., Pecs, 1970-96; assoc. prof. cardiac surgery Heart Inst., Baranyr, Hungary, 1996—. Surgeon Coun. Sanitary Politics, Budapest, 1994. Lt. Nat. Army, Pecs, 1970-92. Avocations: gardening, stamp collecting, foreign languages. Home: Vasut u 30, 7831 Pellerd Baranya, Hungary Office: Heart Inst, Ifjusag Str 13, 7624 Pecs Baranya, Hungary

GULATI, KAVITA, pharmacologist; b. Delhi, India, Nov. 16, 1962; d. Ved Prakash and Krishna (Dua) Kheterpal; m. Nityan Gulati, Jan. 13, 1989; children: Vedika, Raghav. BSc in Human Biology with hons., All India Inst. Med. Scis., Delhi, 1983, MSc in Drug Assay, 1985; PhD in Pharmacology, U. Coll. Med. Scis., Delhi; PhD in Alternative Medicine (Hon.), Open Internat. U., 1988. Asst. rsch. officer Inst. Hist. Medicine and Med. Rsch., Delhi, 1985-88; rsch. asst. Guy's Hosp., London, 1989; sr. rsch. fellow U. Coll. Med. Scis., Delhi, 1989-90, sr. resident, 1990-93; scientist All India Inst. Med. Scis., Delhi, 1995—; lectr. Hamdard Coll. Pharmacy, Delhi, 1986-88; cons. Nat. Poisons Info. Ctr., Delhi, 1995—. Co-author: Elements in Health and Disease, 1987; contbr. articles to profl. jours. Delhi Police Dept. scholar, 1980-83. Mem. Indian Pharm. Soc. (life, Achari prize 1992), Internat. Found. Alternative Medicine, Indian Soc. Promotion Medicinal Aromatic Plants, N.Y. Acad. Scis. Avocations: reading, traveling, skiing, music. Home: B 159 Vivek Vihar, Delhi 110095, India Office: All India Inst Med Scis, Ansari Nagar, Delhi 110029, India

GULATI, SANJEEV, pediatric nephrologist; b. Shimla, India, June 25, 1963; s. Darshan Lal and Nirmal G.; m. Kiran Verma, Apr. 4, 1992; children: Shrea, Srishti. MB, BChir, Maulana Azad Med. Coll., New Delhi, 1985; MD, PGIMER, Chandigarh, India, 1990; DM, Sanjay Gandhi Post Grad. Inst., Lucknow, India, 1994. Diplomate Nat. Bd., India. From jr. to sr. resident Postgrad. Inst. Med. Edn. and Rsch., Chandigarh, 1987-91; from sr. resident to sr. rsch. assoc. Sanjay Gandhi Post Grad. Inst., Lucknow, 1991-96, asst. prof., 1996—; renal fellow Royal Children Hosp., Melbourne, Australia, 1996. Contbr. articles to profl. jours. Pediat. Nephrology fellow Melbourne U., 1996, Royal Coll. Pediat. & Child Health fellow, London, 1997; recipient Bansal Oration & Gold medal Indian Soc. Nephrology, 1997, St. Achar Gold medal Indian Acad. Pediat., 1999. Mem. Internat. Pediat. Nephrology Assn., Internat. Soc. Nephrology, Transplantation Soc. Hindu. Avocations: philately, reading. Home: H No 77 Type IV, 226 014 Lucknow India Office: Sanjay Gandhi Post Grad Ins, Raebareli Rd, 226 014 Lucknow India

GULATI, VIPIN, accountant; b. New Delhi, India, Nov. 3, 1953; came to U.S., 1982; s. Har Kishan Lal and Shakuntalarani (Sachdeva) G.; m. Raman Bais, July 24, 1986; children: Sheena, Shawn. Diploma hotel mgmt., Inst. Hotel Mgmt., Bombay, India, 1976; BA, U. Delhi, 1979; MBA, U. Rajasthan, Jaipur, India, 1981. CPA, Mich. Gen. mgr. Hotel Kandhari, Vijayawada, India, 1979-81; mgr. food and beverage Holiday Inn, Agra, India, 1981-82; acct. Irving Kaplan, Farmington Hills, Mich., 1983-87, S.B. Malerman P.C., Southfield, Mich., 1987-88; chief fin. officer Heidi's Salon, Birmingham, Mich., 1989-90; pres. Vipin Gulati, CPA, P.C., Bingham Farms, Mich., 1990—. Fellow AICPA, Mich. Assn. CPAs, Sports Club (West Bloomfield, Mich.). Avocations: tennis, golf, traveling. Home: 1961 Golf Ridge Dr Bloomfield Hills MI 48302-1724

GULBINOWICZ, HENRYK ROMAN CARDINAL, archbishop; b. Wilno, Poland, Oct. 17, 1928; s. Antoni and Waleria (Gajewska) G. Grad. Theol. Sem. Bialystok, Poland; Dr.Theology, Catholic U., Lublin, Poland; D honoris causa Pope Faculty Theology, Wrocław, Poland, 1996. Ordained priest Roman Catholic Ch., 1950, consecrated bishop, 1970, elevated to cardinal, 1985. Titular bishop, apostolic adminstr. Archdiocese of Bialystok, 1970-76, archbishop of Wroclaw, Poland, 1976—, elevated to Sacred Coll. of Cardinals, 1985. mem. Congregation for Ea. Chs., Congregation Clergy Affairs, Congregation for Evangelization of Nations. Mem. Civitate Wratislaviensi Donatus (hon.).*

GÜLER, ERDEN, pharmacy educator, consultant; b. Eskisehir, Turkey, July 24, 1943; s. Turgut Mehmet and Suzan (Koçak) G.; m. Rana Karpat, July 7, 1969; children: Ihsan, Zeynep. Degree in pharmacy, Ankara (Turkey) U., 1967; PhD, Istanbul (Turkey) U., 1976. Asst. in pharmacy Anadolu U., Eskisehir, 1970-71; asst. in pharmacy Istanbul U., 1971-79, postdoctoral asst., 1979, asst. prprof. pharmacy, 1983-89; prof. pharmacy Anadolu U., 1989—; head pharmacists in Eskisehir region, 1970-72; head dept. pharm. tech., Eskisehir, 1984—; mem. pharm. scis. com., Ankara, 1986-90. Editor Acta Pharmaceutica Turcica; editor: Interaction Between Drugs, Foods, Alcohol and Contact Lenses; editor: Drug Index, 1996-97. 1st lt., Mil. Depo., Ankara, 1967-69. Mem. Turkish Pharmacists Assn. Ankara, Turkish Pharmacists Assn. Eskisehir, N.Y. Acad. Scis. Home: Suleyman Cakir Cd Isin, I Sitesi 131 /5, Eskisehir Turkey Office: Anadolu U, Eczacilik Fakultesi, Eskisehir 26470, Turkey

GÜLER, INAN, electrical engineer, lecturer; b. Gümüsova, Düzce, Turkey, June 30, 1956; s. Sabri and Ayse (Tavacioglu) G.; m. Nihal Fatma Özemir, May 21, 1982; children: Eyüp, Pinar. BSc, Erciyes U., 1981; MSc, Mid. East Tech. U., 1985; PhD, Tech. U. Istanbul, 1990. From rsch. asst. to asst. prof. Erciyes U., Kayseri, Turkey, 1983-93; assoc. prof. Kahramanmaras (Turkey) Sütcü Imam U., Kahramanmaras, Turkey, 1993-97; assoc. prof. Gazi U., Ankara, Turkey, 1997-99, prof., 1999—, head electronics/computers, 1998—; vice-dean tech. edn. faculty Gazi U., Ankara, 1997-2000; cons. higher edn., coun. indsl. tng. World Bank, Ankara, 1995-97. Contbr. articles to profl. jours. With Turkish Army, 1990. Grantee Turkish Petroleum Found., 1988. Mem. AAAS, Chamber Elec. Engrs., N.Y. Acad. Scis. Islamic. Avocations: driving, mountain climbing, computers. E-mail: iguler@tef.gazi.edu.tr. Home: Baris Sitesi 3B-12-26, 06530 Ankara Bilkent, Turkey Office: Dept Electronics/Computers, Gazi Univ Tech Edn Faculty, 06500 Ankara Besevler, Turkey

GULESEN, OZDEMIR, medical educator; b. Kirsehir, Turkey, Mar. 26, 1936; s. Ibrahim and Muzeyyen (Ersoy) G.; m. Aysil Serbetci, Feb. 26, 1963; 1 child. MD, U. Ankara, Turkey, 1961. Teaching mem. Pub. Health Sch., Ankara, Turkey, 1965—; asst. prof. Diyarbakir U. Med. Faculty, Turkey, 1969-75, prof. pub. health, 1976-76; prof. pub. health Uludag U. Med. Faculty, Bursa, Turkey, 1976—; head dept. Pub. Health Med. Faculty, Bursa, 1980-94; dep. dean, 1978-80; dep. dean Med. Faculty, Diyarbakir, 1975-76; dir. Nursing Coll., Bursa, 1977-78. Author: Medical Vital Statistics, 1966, Epidemiology, 1983, Modern Epidemiology, 1996. Lt. Turkish Mil., 1966-68. WHO scholar, London, 1963. Mem. Turkish Med. Assn. Moslem. Avocations: reading, travel. Home: Doktorlar Sitesi 9, 16370-05 Bursa Turkey Office: Uludag U, Uludag U, Tip Fakultesi Halk Sagligi, 16059 Bursa Turkey

GULGOWSKI, PAUL WILLIAM, German language, social science, and history educator; b. Oberhausen, Germany, July 4, 1940; s. Paul and Katharina (van Look) G.; m. Heide Anna Maria Hegenscheidt, July 6, 1989; children: Audrey-Annette, Paul William. BSc, U. Tex., El Paso, 1970; MA, Marquette U., 1992; PhD, U. Bremen, Germany, 1981. Cert. tchr., social sci., German and history. Commd. 2d lt. U.S. Army, 1970, advanced through grades to maj., 1981; gen. staff officer, comdr. combat and support forces U.S. Army, worldwide, 1970-80; polit. advisor, forces comdr. U.S. Army, Germany, 1980-82; prof. German U.S. Mil. Acad., West Point, N.Y., 1982-85; personal rep. of NATO Land Forces comdr., Heidelberg, Germany, 1985-87; ret. U.S. Army, 1987; lectr. German and fgn. lang. study methodology U. Wis., Whitewater, 1993—. Author: U.S. Military Government in Germany, 1983, Flucht aus Ostpreussen, 1986; author articles. Chief historian USCG Aux., Washington, 1992-94; comdr. northwestern USCG 9th, 1994—; v.p. Wis. Profl. Edn. & Info. Coun., 1997-99, pres., 2000—. Decorated D.S.M. with four oak leaf clusters; comdr.'s cross German Order of Merit. Mem. Phi Kappa Phi. Roman Catholic. Avocations: classical music, literature, skiing, boating, travel. Home: PO Box 180347 Delafield WI 53018-0347

GULISASHVILI, ARCHIL, mathmatician, educator; b. Tbilisi, Georgia, Russia, Apr. 14, 1947; came to U.S., 1991; s. Boris and Gulizar (Mamatsashvili) G.; m. Olga A. Molchanova; 1 child, Mikhail. PhD, Tbilisi State U., Russia, 1972, DSc, 1989. Scientist Inst. Math., Georgian Acad. Scis., Tbilisi, 1972-91; vis. prof., rsch. scientist, leading rschr. Boston U., 1992-94; vis. prof. Cornell U., Ithaca, N.Y., 1994-95; vis. assoc. prof. Howard U., Washington, 1995-96; assoc. prof. Ohio U., Athens, 1996—. Contbr. articles to profl. jours. Avocations: poetry, music. E-mail: guli@bing.math.ohiou.edu. Office: Ohio Univ Dept Math Athens OH 45701

GULJANS, ANDREJS, judge. Chmn. Supreme Ct. of Latvia. Office: Brivibas bulv, 34 Riga 1511, Latvia*

GULKIS, SAMUEL, astronomer; b. West Palm Beach, Fla., Feb. 3, 1937; s. Nathan and Beatrice Gulkis; m. Marjorie Cohen, June 16, 1963; 1 child, Susan Renee. B in Aero. Engring., U. Fla., 1960, M in Physics, 1963, PhD in Physics, 1965. Asst. prof. Cornell U., Ithaca, N.Y., 1967-68; rsch. scientist Cornell U., Arecibo, P.R., 1965-67; sr. rsch. scientist Jet Propulsion Lab., Pasadena, Calif., 1968—; co-investigator Planetary Radio Astronomy Ex on Voyager, NASA, 1975—, COBE Spacecraft, NASA, 1985—; prin. investigator MIRO-Rosetta, European Space Agy., 1996. Co-editor, author: Coherent Detection at Millimeter Wavelengths; contbg. author: Atmospheric Remote Sensing. Mem. Internat. Astron. Soc., Phi Beta Kappa. Office: Jet Propulsion Lab 4800 Oak Grove Dr Pasadena CA 91109-8001

GULLEDGE, SANDRA SMITH, publicist; b. Great Lakes, Ill., July 6, 1949; d. Dennis Murrey and Olga (Grosheff) Smith. BS, Northwestern U., 1971; MA, Annenberg Sch Comm., U. So. Calif., 1986. Columnist Camarillo Daily News, Calif., 1971-76; editor Fillmore Herald, Calif., 1976-78; pub. info. officer Oxnard Union High Sch. Dist., Calif., 1980-82, Ventura County Cmty. Coll. Dist., 1982-83; pub. rels. dir. Murphy Orgn., Oxnard, Calif., 1983-84; editor Forum and Solutions GTE, Irving, Tex., 1988-89; mktg. spec. USAA Alliance Svc., San Antonio, 1995-99.

GULLI, CHRISTIAN ANDRE MARIE, electronics company executive; b. Tunis, Tunisia, Nov. 25, 1958; arrived in France, 1961; s. Vincent and Christiane (Vidal) G.; m. Rosario Medina; children: Nicolas, Celia, Thomas. M Electronics, Faculty Limoges, France, 1981; DEA in acoustics, Faculty Bordeaux, France, 1983; PhD in Sci., Toulouse, France, 1986, habilitation in sci. rsch., 1997. Rschr. Thomson Sintra Asm, Brest, France, 1986-90; rschr., mgr. Sextant Avionique, Bordeaux, France, 1990—; S&I mgr. Sextant Avionique, Bordeaux, 1993-95, new techs. mgr., 1995-98; bus. devel. dir. component maintenance Sogerma Aerospatiale, Bordeaux, 1998—; mem. NATO/RSG10, Brussels, 1993. Patentee in field. Mem. IEEE. Avocations: chess, diving, skiing, fishing. Office: Sogerma Aerospatiale, Aeroport de Merignac BP2, 33701 Merignac France

GULLIKSSON, ANDERS GUNNAR, executive search firm executive; b. Herrljunga, Sweden; s. Gunnar and Margit Gulliksson; m. Ann-Sofi Elisabet Kandell, Mar. 5, 1988; children: Anna, Karin. MA, Uppsala U., Sweden. Account mgr. Lintas, Stockholm, 1969-72; mktg. mgr. B&W Stormarunader, Malmö, Sweden, 1972-78; gen. mgr. Tiger Rang, Uddevalla, Sweden, 1979-88; mng. ptnr. Korn/Ferry, Stockholm, 1989—. Avocations: art, music, sports. Office: Korn/Ferry Internat, Jakobsbergsgatan 7, 111 44 Stockholm Sweden

GULLO, LOUIS JOSEPH, reliability engineer; b. Woodside, N.Y., Sept. 9, 1958; s. Louis N. and Theresa A. Gullo; m. Diane S. Gullo, Dec. 12, 1985; children: Louis Joseph Jr., Stephanie Marie, Catherine Faye, Christina Terese. BSEE, U. Conn., 1980. Elec. engr. Tex. Instruments, Inc., Dallas, 1984-86; design assurance engr. ISC Def. Systems, Lancaster, Pa., 1986-88; prin. reliability engr. Honeywell, Inc., Tampa, Fla., 1988-89; tech. staff engr. Honeywell, Inc., Phoenix, Ariz., 1996—; prin. reliability engr. Group Technologies Corp., Tampa, 1989-96; mem. reliability adv. bd. Honeywell, Inc., Phoenix, 1996—; mem. Partnership for RMS Stds., Washington, 1999—. Stds. editor IECQ-CMC Avionics Working Group, Seattle, 1998—; contbr. articles to profl. jours. With U.S. Army, 1980-84, maj. USAR, 1984—. Decorated Army Commendation medal. Avocations: outdoor recreation, golf, softball. Home: 9440 Listow Ter Boynton Beach FL 33437-2716 Office: Honeywell Inc 21111 N 19th Ave Phoenix AZ 85027-2700

GULMANN, CLAUS CHRISTIAN, judge. Judge Ct. Justice European Communities, Luxembourg, 1994-. Office: Ct Justice European Communities, Palais de la Cour de Justice, L-2925 Luxembourg Luxembourg*

GÜLSOY, TANSES YASEMIN, advertising agency executive; b. Verdun, France, Feb. 19, 1963; d. Turgut and Tuna (Bugday) B. BA in English and Am. Lit., Pomona Coll., 1985; MA in Journalism and Mass. Comm., NYU, 1988. Rsch. asst. Harry Frank Guggenheim Found., N.Y.C., 1986-88; advt. copywriter Manajans/Thompson, Isbanbul, Turkey, 1989—, dir. internat. advt., 1997—. Author: An English-Turkish Dictionary of Advertising, 1999. Scholar Pomona Coll., 1982-85, Honnold fellow for grad. study, 1985; fellow Harry Frank Guggenheim Found., 1986-88. Mem. Am. Mktg. Assn., Turkish Soc. for Opinion and Mktg. Rsch., Turkish Assn. for Advt. Copywriters, NYU European Alumni Group, Pomona Coll. Alumni Vols., Robert Coll. Alumni Assn. (bd. dirs. 1994-96). Avocation: lexicography. Home: Adnan Saygun Cad 71/10, I.Ulus, 80600 Isbanbul Turkish Office: Manajans/Thompson, Buyukdere Cad 191, Levent, 80509 Istanbul Turkey

GULUBOVA, MAYA VLADOVA, pathologist, educator; b. Rouzhintzi, Vidin, Bulgaria, May 19, 1958; s. Vlado Zhivkov and Veneta Simeonova (Nizamska) G.; m. Krassimir Bernardov Ignatov, Aug. 4, 1985; 1 child, Maria Magdalena. MD, Med. Faculty, Sofia, Bulgaria, 1983; diploma in pathology, Med. Acad., Sofia, Bulgaria, 1989; PhD, Med. Acad., 1999. Gen. practitioner Regional Hospital, Svishtov, Bulgaria, 1984; asst. Med. Inst., Stara Zagora, Bulgaria, 1984-88; sr. asst. Med. Inst., Stara Zagora, 1989-92; prin. asst. Trakia U., Stara Zagora, 1993—. Author: Immunology and Its Impact on Infections, 1995; contbr. articles to profl. jours. Lt. Med. Forces Bulgaria, 1982. Mem. Assn. Young Med. Scientists in Europe, Internat. Med. Assn. Bulgaria, Union Med. Balkanique. Home: Armeiska Str 16 E 2, 6003 Stara Zagora Bulgaria Office: Med Faculty Trakia U, Armeiska Str 11, 6000 Stara Zagora Bulgaria

GULYA, ERNÖ, oncologist; b. Olaszliszka, Hungary, July 16, 1939; m. Ilona Tóth, Dec. 4, 1971 (dec. 1977); m. Edit Herczeg, Nov. 24, 1979; 1 child, Ernö. Med. diploma, U. Med. Sch., Budapest, 1964; PhD, Hungarian Acad. Sci., Budapest, 1981. Cert. in internal medicine, oncology, occupl. medicine. Asst. dr. County Hosp., Szolnok, 1964-65, Cen. Hosp. of Ministry of Justice, 1965-69; asst. dr. Cen. Hosp. of Ministry of Interior, Budapest, 1969-81, 1st asst., 1981-84, head physician, 1984-90, chief oncologist, head physician, 1990—; chmn. breast cancer com. Cen. Hosp. Ministry of Interior, Budapest, 1984, mem. rsch. ethical com., 1996; vis. fellow Christie Hosp. Paterson Lab., Manchester, Eng. Author: (book) Hematopoietic Cell Transplantation on Experimental Animals, 1981; contbr. chpts. to books; inventor in field. Coll. sec. Coll. of H.S., Sárospatak, 1954-57; presidium's mem. Sport Club, Semmelweis U. Med. Sch., Budapest, 1959-64. Mem. Hungarian Soc. for Hematology, Exptl. Hematology, Oncology, Chemotherapy, Physiology, Senology, Internal Medicine, European Stem Cell Club. Avocation: tennis. Home: Erdöalja u 2, 1037 Budapest Hungary Office: Cen Hosp Ministry Interior, Városligeti-fasor 9, 1071 Budapest Hungary

GULYAKEVICH, OLGA VLADIMIROVNA, chemist, researcher; b. Moscow, Jan. 26, 1949; d. Vladimir Ivanovich and Elena Nikolaevna (Bichkova) G.; m. Alexander Leonidovich Mikhal'chuk, June 16, 1978; 1 child, Polina Alexandrovna. Student, Byelorussian State U., Minsk, 1971, Marxism-Leninizm U., Minsk, 1974, Byelorussian Acad. Sci., 1989. Fieldworker Inst. Physico-organic Chem. Byelorussian Acad. Scis., Minsk, 1971-73, jr. rsch. worker, 1973-74, 1974-89; rsch. worker Inst. Bio-Organic Chemistry Byelorussian Acad. Scis., Minsk, 1989-97; head rsch. worker Inst. Bio-organic Chemistry Belarus Acad. Sci, Minsk, 1997, 1998—. Inventor in field; contbr. articles to profl. jours. Mem. Byelorussian Knowledge Soc., Pharmacol. Soc. Avocations: theatre, tourism, recreational activities. Home: 22/12 Sverdlov Str, Minsk 220050, Belarus Office: Inst Bioorganic Chemistry Belarus Nat Acad Scis, 5/2 Acad Kuprevich, Minsk 220141, Belarus

GULYANI, BHARAT BHUSHAN, chemical engineer, educator, researcher; b. Rishikesh, U. Pradesh, India, Dec. 28, 1962; s. Bhagwan Dass and Krishna Kumari (Arora) G. BE, U. Roorkee, India, 1984, ME, 1987, PhD, 1999. Prof. scientist C.B.R.I., Roorkee, 1989-91; sr. rsch. fellow U. Roorkee, 1991-95, rsch. assoc., 1996—. Mem. AIChE, Am. Chem. Soc. Avocations: creative writing, poetry, philosophy, music. Home: 579 IDPL Township, Rishikesh 249202, India Office: U Roorkee, Dept Chem Engring, Roorkee 247667, India

GULYAS, LORAN, sociology educator; b. Ravenna, Ohio, July 17, 1952; s. Dennis and Phyllis Ann Gulyas; m. Linda Beznoska, May 3, 1980 (div. Feb. 1985); m. Sara Lynn Hruby, Mar. 21, 1998. BA in Sociology, Hiram (Ohio) Coll., 1974; MA in Sociology, U. Notre Dame, 1975. Dir. inpatient svcs. Murtis H. Taylor Mental Health Ctr., Cleve., 1981-85; dir. aftercare svcs. Lake County Mental Health Ctr., Mentor, Ohio, 1985-95; asst. prof. sociology Lakeland C.C., Kirtland, Ohio, 1995—; program dir. human svcs. Lakeland C.C., Kirtland, 1998—. V.p. bd. dirs. Lake County Mental Health Assn., Painesville, Ohio, 1987-90; mem. housing com. Lake County Alcohol and Drug Addiction and Mental Health Svcs. Bd., 1990—; bd. dirs. Extended Housing, Painesville, 1996—. Named Profl. of Yr., Bridges, Lake County, Ohio, 1994; recipient oustanding mgmt. award Inst. for Creative Living, Cleveland Heights, Ohio, 1980. Mem. Nat. Orgn. Human Svcs. Educators. Avocations: backpacking, hiking, rock collecting. Office: Lakeland C C 7700 Clocktower Dr Kirtland OH 44094-5198

GULYAYEV, GENNADY IVANOVICH, researcher; b. Dniepropetrovsk, Ukraine, Jan. 19, 1926; s. Ivan Nickitovich and Olimpiada Yakovlevna (Shamova) G.; m. Sophiya Leonidovna Bykova, June 15, 1950; 1 child, Yury. Engr. diploma, Inst. of Steel, Moscow, 1948; Candidate of Sci. in Tech., Metallurgical Inst., Dniepropetrovsk, 1955; DSc in Tech., All-Union Sci. Rsch. Inst. Metall. Machinarybuild, Moscow, 1978. Rolling master South Tube Works, Nickopol, Ukraine, 1948-52; sr. rschr. Tube Inst., Dniepropetrovsk, 1955-59, chief of lab., 1959-66, dep. dir., 1966-91, mgr. dept., 1991—; leader of postgrad. Tube Inst., Dniepropetrovsk, 1961-96; dep. chmn. Tech. Soc., Dniepropetrovsk, 1973-91. Author: Quality of Electrowelded Tubes, 1978; author, editor: Pressing of Steel Tubes and Profiles, 1973, Technology of Reducing and Sizing Tubes, 1975; contbr. articles to profl. jours. Recipient Two Orders and 10 medals of the USSR, Moscow, 1946-99, Gold medal State Prize of the USSR, Moscow, 1967, Gold medal prize Coun. Ministry of the USSR, Moscow, 1982; named Honoured Doer of Sci. of Urkaine, Kiev, 1990. Mem. Iron and Steel Soc. U.S.A., N.Y. Acad. Scis. Avocations: collecting post cards of Old Yekaterinoslav (Dniepropetrovsk). Fax: 380 562 464566. Home: 52 Sevastopol'skaya St, 10 Dniepropetrovsk 49010, Ukraine Office: State Tube Inst, 1a Pisarzhevsky St 5, Dniepropetrovsk 49600, Ukraine

GUMEROV, FARID MUHAMEDOVICH, physicist, researcher; b. Kazan, Russia, June 15, 1952; s. Muhamed Usmanovich Gumerov and Galia Shaihramovna Valeeva; m. Gusel Isaevna Kulikova, Nov. 16, 1985. Degree, Inst. Chem. Tech., Kazan, 1974, MS, 1979, DSc, 1992. Jr. lectr. Inst. Chem. Tech., Kazan, 1978-87, prof. asst., 1987-93, prof., 1993—; dean mech. engring. faculty State U. Techs., Kazan, 1995-96, head dept. theoretical basis of heat technics, 1996—, dir. asst., 1996—. Contbr. numerous articles to profl. jours. Mem. Internat. Acad. Refrigeration (academician), N.Y. Acad. Scis. Office: Kazan State Tech U, Karl Marx St 68, Tartastan Kazan 420015, Russia

GUMIŃSKI, CEZARY, chemistry educator, researcher; b. Warsaw, Poland, Mar. 23, 1944; s. Wacław and Stefania (Wegner) G.; m. Barbara Tenderenda, Feb. 1, 1969; 1 child, Jan. MS, U. Warsaw, 1967, DSc, 1975. Asst. dept. chemistry U. Warsaw, 1967-75, adj., 1975-93, sr. lectr., 1993—. Co-author, co-editor: Metals in Mercury, 1986 (award Ministry of Edn. 1987), Intermetallics in Mercury, 1992, Metals in Liquid Alkali Metals, 1996; contbr. over 75 articles to Jour. Phase Equilibria, 1990—. Mem. Am. Soc. Materials (category editor), Polish Chem. Soc., IUPAC (solubility commn.). Avocations: music, hi-fi equipment. Home: Przybylskiego 11 m 74, 02777 Warsaw Poland Office: U Warsaw Dept Chemistry, Pasteura 1, 02093 Warsaw Poland

GUMMESSON, EVERT NILS, business educator; b. Trollhättan, Sweden, Jan. 18, 1936; s. Gunnar and Ingeborg Sofia (Hallberg) G.; m. Antonia J. M. Jansen, Oct. 23, 1965; children: Charlotte, Madelene. MBA, Stockholm Sch. Econs., 1965; BA, Stockholm U., 1970, PhD, 1977. Mktg. mgr. Reader's Digest, Stockholm, 1965-68; sr. cons., dir. PA Cons. Group, Stockholm, 1968-82; ptnr. Stockholm Cons. Group, 1982-88; sr. cons., dir. Cicero Mgmt., Stockholm, 1989-90; prof. U. Gothenburg and U. Karlstad, Sweden, 1986-91; prof., rsch. dir. U. Stockholm, 1992—; dir. IHM Bus. Sch., Gothenburg, 199--95. Author: Total Relationship Marketing, 1999, Qualitative Methods in Management Research, 2000; contbr. articles to profl. jours.; mem. editl. adv. bd. 10 jours. Sgt. Infantry, 1956-57. Recipient The Chrisottander prize Sch. Higher Edn. in Comms. and Veckans Affarer, 1999. Fellow World Acad. Productivity Sci.; mem. Swedish Inst. Quality (mem. scientific bd. 1997—), Internat. Svc. Quality Assn. (dir. 1991-96), N.Y. Acad. Scis., Rotary (pres. 1997-98). Avocations: gardening, hiking, parachuting, paragliding. Home: Forsetevägen 10, SE-18267 Djursholm Sweden Office: Stockholm U, Sch Bus, SE-10691 Stockholm Sweden

GUMPEL, PETER ERIC, investment banker, lawyer; b. Boston, Mar. 31, 1955; s. Henry J. and Edelgarde V. (von Asseburg) G.; m. Evelyn Petros, Sept. 2, 1989. BA, Colgate U., 1977; postgrad., St. Gallen Sch. Econs, Switzerland, 1977-78; JD, Columbia U., 1981. Bar: N.Y. 1982, Mass. 1989. Assoc. Reid & Priest, N.Y.C., 1981-84, Reboul, MacMurray, Hewitt, Maynard & Kristol, N.Y.C., 1984-88; assoc. Hutchins & Wheeler, Boston, 1988-91, of counsel, 1991-93; dir. Raiffeisen Investment AG, Vienna, Austria, 1992-98; mem. mng. bd. Raiffeisen Investment AG, 1998—, also bd. dirs.; mem. supr. bds. various subsidiaries in Eastern Europe. Contbr. articles to profl. publs. Fulbright scholar, Switzerland, 1977. Mem. Mass. Bar Assn., Assn. of Bar of City of N.Y. Office: Reisnerstrasse 30, A-1030 Vienna Austria

GUMPPERT, KARELLA ANN, federal government official; b. N.Y.C., Oct. 16, 1942; d. Leonard Lewis and Florence M. Gumppert. AB in Polit. Sci., George Washington U., 1963, postgrad., 1963-65. Lic. in real estate sales, Md., 1984. Jr. editor to Bd. Govs. Fed. Res. Sys., Washington, 1966-67; editl. asst. Jour. of Maritime Law and Commerce, N.Y.C., 1969-71; adminstr. NYU Law Sch., N.Y.C., 1968-73; law asst. White & Case and other firms, N.Y.C., Boston, Hartford, 1974-80; vol. asst. U.S. Presdl. Inaugural Com., Washington, 1981; confidential asst. The White House Staff, Washington, 1981; publs. asst. Congressional Budget Office, Washington, 1982-84; credit summarizer Xerox Corp., Arlington, Va., 1985-86; asst. in govtl. affairs Mut. Omaha, Washngton, 1988; land law adjudicator U.S. Dept. Interior, Anchorage, 1991—. Author, illustrator: (children's book) An Adventure, 1949; founding editor lit. mag. Springboard, 1959; mem. editorial bd., copy editor newspaper Amicus Curiae, 1964-65. Charity asst. Girl Scouts U.S.A., N.Y.C., 1952-54, Christian Assn., N.Y.C., 1959-61, Wesley Found., Washington, 1962-63; vol. asst. N.Y. Rep. County Com., 1959-62, Conn. Reps. State Com., Hartford, 1979-80. Recipient numerous scholarships, 1957-60. Mem. NAFE, Nat. Trust for Hist. Preservation, Nat. Audubon Soc., Women's Nat. Rep. Club, Anchorage Opera Assn., Library of Cong. Assocs. (founding mem.). Avocations: music, nostalgia, travel, theatre, sports.

GÜMÜSALAN, YAKUP, anatomist; b. Bursa, Turkey, Dec. 16, 1963; s. Hasan and Fevziye (Acar) G.; m. Nermin Cemberci, Aug. 14, 1993; children: Suad Mert, Gulsah Saadet. MD, Ankara (Turkey) U., 1988; postgrad in anatomy, Hacettepe U., Ankara, 1990-92. Capt. Gülhane Mil. Med. Acad., Ankara, 1988—, faculty dept. anatomy, 1992-97; assoc. prof. anatomy KSU Sch. Medicine, K.Maras, 1998—. Contbr. articles to profl. jours. Muslim. Office: KSU Sch Medicine K Maras, KSU Tip Fak Hastane Cd #32, 46050 K Maras Turkey

GUNALINGAM, BRINTHAPAN BRENDAN, cardiologist; b. Jaffna, Sri Lanka, Sept. 22, 1969; arrived in Australia, 1971.; s. Sangarapillay and Pragaspathy Sabaratnam. MBBS, Sydney (Australia) U., 1993, FRACP, 1997; ECFMG, 1998. Intern Gosford Hosp., Gosford, Australia, 1993; resident med. officer R.N.S.H., Sydney, 1994; med. registrar Royal North Shore Hosp., Sydney, 1995-97; cardiology registrar St. Vincent's Hosp., Sydney, 1998-99, fellow in interventional cardiology, 1999—. Fellow Royal Australian Coll. Physicians, 1998-99;winner Fiji Nat. Oratory Contest, 1982, Fiji Jr. Tennis Chamionship, 1980. Mem. Australian Med. Assoc. Hindu. Avocations: tennis, cricket, skiing, guitar. Home: 7 Rokeva St, Eastwood NSW 2122, Australia Office: St Vincents Hosp, Darlinghurst 2010, Australia

GUNALP, ILHAN RIZA, ophthalmologist, educator; b. Istanbul, Turkey, July 24, 1940; s. Ihsan and Nimet (Affan) G.; m. Zeren Unsal, July 17, 1967; children: Burak, Caglar. MD, Univ. Med. Sch. Ankara, 1967, specialist in ophthalmology, 1970. Resident Ankara Med. Faculty, 1967-70, from asst. prof. to assoc. prof., 1970-82, prof. ophthalmology, 1982—; dir.

Ophthalmology Dept., Ankara, 1998—. Mem. Human Rights Assn., 1999. Lt. Turkish Med. Corps, 1972-73. Mem. Ophthalmology Soc., N.Y. Acad. Scis. Home: Cinnah Caddesi, 06680 Ankara Turkey Office: Ankara Med Faculty, Mamak Caddesi, Ankara Cebeci, Turkey

GUNARTO, HARY, computer science educator, researcher; b. Solo, Indonesia, June 7, 1954; s. Radix Koesnan; m. Ely Yuliana, Apr. 20, 1981; children: Paramita, Marsha. BS, Gadjah Mada U., Yogyakarta, Indonesia, 1978; MS, U. Wis., Pullman, 1984; PhD, Wash. State U., 1988. Lectr. Gadjah Mada U., Yogyakarta, 1979-82; rsch. asst. Wash. State U., Pullman, 1987-88, postdoctoral lectr., 1988-89; head R&D computing ctr. Gadjah Mada U., Yogyakarta, 1989-93, assoc. prof., 1994—; cons. Dept. Higher Edn. Indonesia, 1991-94; head of electronics lab. Gadjah Mada U., Yogyakarta, 1991—, mem. univ. rsch. coun., 1993-95. Author: Monte Carlo Methods and Simulation, 1994, Business Forecasting with Computers, 1996; editor: JJF Physics Jour., 1993; referee: Internat. Jour. VLSI Design, 1989-90; contbr. sci. papers to profl. jours. Pres. Indonesian Student Assn. in USA, Pullman, 1985. Super Semar-Govt. fellow Gadjah Mada U., 1975, Indonesian Govt. fellow, 1982. Mem. IEEE, Himpunan Fisikawan Indonesia, Assn. for Computing Machinery. Avocations: reading, bicycling, camping. Office: Gadjah Mada U, Fak Mipa Sekip Unit 3, 55281 Yogyakarta Indonesia

GUNAWAN, BAMBANG, payment system executive; b. Cirebon, Indonesia, Oct. 10, 1958; s. Waloeyo and Sukoríní Pringgokusumo; m. Hana Farida, Apr. 25, 1992; children: Isthi Prasasya, Mardika Parama. Diploma, Nat. Hotel & Tourism Inst., Bandung, Indonesia, 1983; MBA, Inst. Pengembangan Managewen, Jakarta, Indonesia, 1988. Br. mgr. PT. Blue Inter Globe Corp., Medan, Indonesia, 1983-85; ops. mgr. PT. Blue Inter Globe Corp., Jakarta, Indonesia, 1985-87; head merchants svcs. Am. Express, Jakarta, Indonesia, 1989-93, head corp. svcs., 1993-97; dir., country mgr. MasterCard Internat., Jakarta, Indonesia, 1997—. Avocations: reading, travel, golf. Home: Jl Bumi Asih II A3/11, Bumí Karang Indah, 12440 Jakarta Indonesia Office: Mastercard Internat, Jakarta Stock Exch Bldg, 12190 Jakarta Indonesia

GUNDEL, JANOS, agronomist; b. Budapest, Hungary, Oct. 1, 1941; s. Ferenc and Maria (Szekelyhidy) G.; m. Zsuzsanna Balogh, 1998; children: Gabriella, Karoly. MS in Agr., U. Agrl. Scis. Hungary, 1963; PhD of Agr., Hungarian Acad. Scis., 1990; hab. dr. of agrl. scis., Pannon U., 1996; Dr. h.c., Debrecen U., 1999. Agronomist Rsch. Inst. Vegetable Prodn., Kecskemet, Hungary, 1963-67; asst. rschr. Nat. Quality Control Inst. Compound Feed Prodn., Budapest, Hungary, 1967-68; rschr., dir. Rsch. Inst. Animal Breeding and Nutrition, Herceghalom, Hungary, 1968—; hon. asst. prof. U. Agr. Scis., Gödöllö, Hungary, 1988; vis. prof. U. Agrl. Scis., Debrecen, Hungary, 1996; pres. sci. com. animal prodn. Hungarian Agrl. Ministry, 1985—. Co-author, co-editor: Design of Experiments in Animal Production, 1982; editor-in-chief Hungarian Jour. Animal Prodn., 1990—; editl. adv. bd. Livestock Prodn. Sci. Fellow Cochran Found., 1992, Eisenhower Exch., 1996. Mem. Hungarian Assn. Agrl. Rschrs., Hungarian Assn. Biologist, Nat. Geog. Roman Catholic. Avocations: tennis, swimming, kayaking, reading. E-mail: jgundel@atk.hu. Office: Rsch Inst Animal Breeding and Nutrition, Gesztenyes ut 1, 2053 Herceghalom Hungary

GUNDERMANN, KNUT-OLAF, hygienist, microbiologist, educator; b. Magdeburg, Germany, Oct. 22, 1933; s. Werner and Charlotte (Bohne) G.; m. Karin Möller. MD, U. Kiel, Germany, 1958, Habilitation, 1969. Asst. Inst. Biochemistry U. Kiel, 1960-62, asst. Inst. Hygiene, 1962-69, sr. asst. Inst. Hygiene, 1970-74, prof. Inst. Hygiene, 1974-76; prof. dir. U. Berlin, 1976-80; prof. dir. Inst. Hygiene and Environ. Medicine U. Kiel, 1980-2000; head, bd. dirs. U. Hosp., 1987-99. Author: Environment and Health, 1997; editor, co-author: Lehrbuch der Hygiene, 1991; editor-in-chief Internat. Jour. Hygiene and Environ. Medicine, 1980-99. Chmn. Union for Health Promotion, Schleswig-Holstein, Germany, 1977-95. Mem. German Soc. Hygiene and Microbiology (pres. 1993-94, Ferdinand Cohn medal 1999), Am. Soc. Microbiology, Soc. Hosp. Infection (London), German Soc. Hosp. Hygiene, German Soc. Nature Scientist and Physicians. Office: U Kiel Inst Hygiene, Brunswiker str 4, 24105 Kiel Germany

GUNDERSON, BRENT MERRILL, lawyer; b. Vernal, Utah, Apr. 16, 1960; s. Merrill Ray and Betty Velate (Norton) G.; m. Julie Phillips, Oct. 28, 1983; children: Adam Brent, Jeremy Phillip, Matthew Norton, Hannah, Rachel, Mariah, Kayla, Jacob Elden. BA, Brigham Young U., 1984; JD, Columbia U., 1987. Bar: Ariz. 1987, U.S. Dist. Ct. Ariz. 1987, U.S. Tax Ct. 1994. Ptnr. Brown & Bain, Phoenix, 1987-96; pvt. practice Mesa, Ariz., 1996—; pres. Ariz. Mgmt. Soc., Phoenix, 1996-97. Asst. dist. commr. Boy Scouts Am., Mesa, Ariz., 1994-97, scoutmaster troop 611, Mesa, 1991-94, troop 761, Mesa, 1999—, chair varsity scout com., 1997-98; precinct capt. Mesa Rep. Precincts 47 & 17, 1988-94; cubmaster pack 761, Boy Scouts Am., 1998-99. Recipient Mesa Dist. award of Merit, 1997, Scoutmaster award of Merit Boy Scouts Am., 1992, named to Scout Leader Hall of Fame, 1993, Scouting Family Hall of Fame, 1999. Mem. Am. Immigration Lawyers Assn. (v.p. Ariz. chpt. 1992-93, Maricopa County Bar Found. (bd. dirs. 1991-95), East Valley Estate Planning Coun. (bd. dirs. 1997—, pres. 1999-2000), Am. Immigration Lawyers Assn., Ariz. Mgmt. Soc. (bd. dirs. 1997—). Mem. LDS Ch. Avocations: backpacking, fishing, China. Office: Gunderson & Denton PC 123 N Centennial Way Ste 150 Mesa AZ 85201-6747

GUNDERSON, STEVEN ALAN, anesthesiologist; b. Rockford, Ill., Feb. 9, 1949; s. Donald Hans and Margaret E. (Johanson) G.; m. Tina A. Anstedt, May 29, 1976; children: Kelly, Kimberly, Tory, Erin. AS, Rock Valley Coll., 1969; BA, Drake U., 1972, postgrad., 1972-74; DO, Coll. Osteopathic Medicine, Des Moines, Iowa, 1977. Diplomate Am. Bd. Anesthesia. Staff anesthesiologist Rockford (Ill.) Anesthesia Assn., 1984—; clin. faculty Rockford Sch. Medicine, 1986—; chmn. anesthesia dept. Swedish Am. Hosp., 1992-94; adminstr., med. dir. Rockford Ambulatory Surg. Ctr., 1994—. Served to lt. comdr. USN, 1978-81. Fellow Am. Coll. Anesthesiologists; mem. AMA, Internat. Anesthesia Rsch. Soc., Am. Coll. Physician Execs., Federated Ambulatory Surgery Assn. (bd. dirs., mem. exec. com. 1998—), Ill. State Med. Soc., Freestanding Surgery Ctr. Assn. (bd. dirs. 1996—), Winnebago Med. Soc., Rockford Country Club. Republican. Lutheran. Avocations: biking, fishing, swimming, wood working, reading. Office: Rockford Anesthesiologists Assn 2202 Harlem Rd # 200 Loves Park IL 61111-2754

GUNDLACH, KARSTEN KURT HELMUTH, maxillofacial surgery educator; b. Hamburg, Germany, May 8, 1943; s. Kurt A.E.M. and Gisela (Krug von Nidda) G.; m. Kathrin Specht, Dec. 3, 1971; children: Kaspar O., Kristina F. MD, Heidelberg (Germany) U., 1969; DDS, Hamburg (Germany) U., 1971; MSD, U. Minn., Mpls., 1974; PhD, Hamburg U., 1980; diploma in Maxillofacial Surgery, 1978, diploma in Facial Plastic Surgery, 1981. Resident Country Hosp., Grafenau, Germany, 1971-72; instr. U. Minn., Mpls., 1972-74; resident U. Hamburg, 1974-83, prof., 1983-92; prof., chmn. Rostock (Germany) U., 1992—; lectr. Sch. Logopedics, Hamburg, 1979-92, Sch. Dental Assistance, Hamburg, 1990-92. Author: Missbildungen des Kiefergelenkes, 1982; co-editor: Proceedings of 3rd Symposium Riga-Rostock, 1995, Proceedings of 3rd Rostock Symposium on Clefts of Lip, Alveolus and Palate, 1997, also 4th and 5th Symposium, 1999. V.p. Hamburg Polo Club, 1984-92. Recipient awards Arbeitsgemeinschaft Kieferchirurgie, Germany, 1977, 78. Mem. German Assn. Cranio-Maxillofacial Surgery (media dir. 1996—, Wassmund preis 1982), European Assn. Craniomaxillofacial Surgery (editor-in-chief jour. 1999—), Am. Soc. Plastic Surgeons, German Cleft Palate Assn. (bd. mem. 1996—), Am. Cleft Palate-Craniofacial Assn., Am. Soc. Maxillofacial Surgeons, German Assn. Plastic Reconstructive Surgery. Avocations: tennis, field hockey. Office: Rostock U Dept Maxillofac Surg, Strempelstrasse 13, 18057 Rostock Germany

GUNDU RAO, P., pharmacist; b. Alur, A.P., India, Mar. 5, 1935; d. Srinivasa Rao and Kamala Padakandla; m. Narmada Rao Kowligi, July 4, 1964; children: Lakshmi, Usha, Krishna. B.Pharm., Banaras Hindu U., 1955, M.Pharm., 1956; Dr.rer.nat., Friedrich Schiller U., Jena, Germany, 1962; Diploma in German, Leipzig U., 1959. Cert. pharmacist, India. Lectr. Birla Inst. Tech. & Sci., Pilani, India, 1957-59, reader, 1962-68; dir. Coll. Pharmacy, Manipal, India, 1968-78; prof. Addis Ababa U., Ethiopia, 1978-84; prin. Coll. Pharm., Manipal, 1984-95; dir. R&D Divi's Labs. Ltd., Hyderabad, India, 1995—; cons., inspector Pharmacy Coun. India, 1964-76, 85-95; hon. lectr. German, MGM Coll., Udupi, India, 1968-78. Editor Indian Jour. Pharm. Edn., 1975-78, 86-95; author: Inorganic Pharmaceutical Chemistry, Bio Chemistry for Pharmacy Students; contbr. articles to profl. jours. Pres. Manipal Consumers Co-Operative Soc., 1969-72. Recipient Visishta Seva Medal, Coll. Chest Physicians, 1995. Fellow Acad. Gen. Edn.; mem. Indian Pharm. Congress (organising sec. 1971-72, 90), Assn. Pharmacy Tchrs. India, Controlled Release Soc., Indian Pharm. Assn., Rotary Club of Udupi (pres. 1989-90). Avocations: Internet exploring, popular science writing, travel, fine arts. Office: Divi's Labs Ltd, Dharam Karan Rd Ameerpet, Hyderabad 500 016, India

GÜNDÜZ, AHMET KAAN, ophthalmologist; b. Ankara, Turkey, Aug. 18, 1963; s. Turgut and Necla (Suner) G. MD, Hacettepe U., 1988. Ophthalmologist Numune State Hosp., Ankara, Turkey, 1994-96; clin. instr. ophthalmology Ankara U. Eye Clinic, 1996—; fellow Wills Eye Hosp. Oncology Svc., 1996. Contbr. articles to profl. jours. With Turkish Mil., 1993. Edn. grant Tübitak, Ankara, 1978-88. Mem. Turkish Ophthalmology Assn., Internat. Ocular Inflammation Soc., Am. Acad. Ophthalmology. Avocations: aviation, marine, cars & motoring, reading, cinema. Home: GMK Bulvari 116/3, 06570 Ankara Turkey Office: Ankara U Eye Clinic, Ankara Turkey

GUNDUZ, GONUL, chemical engineer; b. Dikili, Izmir, Turkey, Apr. 29, 1951; d. Hasan and Ayse Obus Tufan; m. Erol Gunduz, Swpt. 21, 1984; 1 child, Umut. BS in Chemical Engrng., Ege U., Izmir, Turkey, 1972; MS in Chemical Engrng., Ege U., 1973, PhD, 1979. From asst. prof. to prof. Ege U., Izmir, Turkey, 1982—. Author: Differential Equations and Applications, 1995; contbr. articles to profl. jours. Mem. Am. Chem. Soc., Nat. Geographic Soc., Chamber Chemical Engrng., Soc. Heat Science and Tech. Avocations: music, travel, photography. Office: Ege U Fac of Engring, Chem Engring Dept, 35100 Bornova Turkey

GUNDUZ, MEHMET, otolaryngologist, cancer genetic researcher; b. Inli, Nigde, Turkey, Jan. 10, 1967; s. Sevket and Keziban (Ozkan) G.; m. Esra Dinçsoy, Aug. 15, 1993; children: Etka, Ihsan, Taha. MD, Hacettepe U. Med. Sch., Ankara, Turkey, 1990; postgrad., Okayama (Japan) U., 1997—. Resident dept. otolaryngology Hacettepe Med. Sch., Ankara, 1990-94; otolaryngologist Nigde Nat. Hosp., 1994-95, dir. dept. otolaryngology, 1994-95; rschr. Wakayama (Japan) Med. Coll., 1995-97. Coord. Turkish Med. Jour., Ankara, 1993-94; contbr. articles to Otolaryngologic Emergency, Archives of Otolaryngology Head and Neck Surgery, European Jour. Cancer Rsch., others. Chief Turkish-Japanese and Ctrl. Asia Culture Ctr., Okayama, 1997—. Rotary Club scholar, 1986-87; Monbusho scholar, 1995—. Avocations: music, reading. E-mail: mgunduz@cc.okayama-u.ac.Jp. Home: Shimoifuku Nishimachi 7-32, Iwai Sankopo 707, Okayama 700-0054, Japan Office: Japan U Med Sch/Otolaryng, 2-5-1 Shikatacho, Okayama 700-8558, Japan also: Sahinali mah Stadyum arkasi, Olimpiyat sok Gunduz Apt 2, Nigde Turkey

GUNGE, NORIO, yeast geneticist, educator; b. Nagasaki, Japan, May 24, 1929; s. Masaji and Michiko Gunge; m. Teru Umeda, Dec. 20, 1956; children: Mariko, Takao. Grad., Kyushu (Fukuoka, Japan) U., 1953; PhD, Tokyo U., 1965. Sr. researcher Dai-Nippon Sugar Mfg. Co., Yokohama, Japan, 1953-74, Mitsubishi-Kasei Inst. of Life Scis., Tokyo, 1975-85; prof. Kumamoto (Japan) Inst. Tech., 1985—; vis. prof. Ruhr U., Bochum, Germany, 1985. Contbr. articles to sci. jours.; mem. editorial bd. Yeast jour., 1985-93. Mem. Am. Soc. for Microbiology, Genetic Soc. Am., Molecular Biology Soc. Japan, Japan Soc. for Bioscis., Biochemistry and Agrochemistry (councilor 1986—). Home: Tokuo 271-57, Kumamoto 861-55, Japan Office: Kumamoto Inst of Tech, Ikeda 4-22-1, Kumamoto 860, Japan

GUNGER, RICHARD WILLIAM, lawyer; b. Auburn, N.Y., Aug. 7, 1963; s. William Bruce and Lita Patricia G.; m. Barbara Jean Taber, Nov. 24, 1984; children: William Robinson, James Taber. BA magna cum laude, Alfred U., 1985; JD cum laude, Syracuse U., 1988. Bar: N.Y. 1989, U.S. Dist. Ct. (no. dist.) N.Y. 1991, U.S. Dist. Ct. (we. dist.) N.Y. 1993, U.S. Supreme Ct. 1993. Assoc. Albert D. DiGiacomo, Syracuse, N.Y., 1988-89, Cuddy, Durgala & Timian, Auburn, N.Y., 1989-90; atty. pvt. practice, Auburn, N.Y., 1990—; bd. dirs. Cayuga Counseling, Auburn. Alan L. Ponyman scholar, 1985. Mem. ABA, N.Y. State Bar Assn. Cayuga County Bar Assn., KC. Office: 5 Court St Auburn NY 13021-3713

GUNGWU, WANG, historian, academic administrator; b. Surabaya, Indonesia, Oct. 9, 1930; s. Fo Wen and Yien (Ting) W.; m. Margaret Ping-Ting Lim, 1955; children: Shih-chang, Lin-chang, Hui-chang. BA with honors, U. Malaya, Singapore, 1953, MA, 1955; PhD, U. London, 1957. From asst. lectr. to lectr. U. Malaya, 1957-59; lectr. U. Malaya, Kuala Lumpur, 1959-61, sr. lectr., 1961-63, dean of arts, 1962-63, prof. history, head of dept., 1963-68; prof. Far Ea. history, head of dept. Australian Nat. U., 1968-75, 80-86, prof. emeritus, 1989—, dir. rsch. Sch. Pacific Studies, 1975-80; vice-chancellor U. Hong Kong, 1986-95; dir. East Asian Inst. Nat. U. Singapore, 1997—; John A. Burns disting. vis. prof. history U. Hawaii, 1979, Rose Morgan vis. prof. history U. Kans., 1983; faculty prof. faculty of arts and social scis. Nat. U. Singapore, 1998—; disting. professorial fellow Inst. S.E. Asian Studies, Singapore, 1996—. Author: The Nanhai Trade, 1958, 98, A Short History of the Nanyang Chinese, 1959, The Structure of Power in North China During the Five Dynasties, 1963, China and the World Since 1949, 1977, Community and Nation, 1981, Dongnanya Yu Huaren (Southeast Asia and the Chinese), 1987, The Function of History, 1990, China and the Chinese Overseas, 1991, The Chineseness of China, 1991, The Chinese Way; China's Position in the International Relations, 1995, China and Southeast Asia: Myths, Threats, and Culture, 1999, The Chinese Overseas: From Earthbound China to the Quest for Autonomy, 2000; gen. editor East Asian Historical Monographs Series for Oxford U. Press (30 vols.), 1968-95; editor Malaysia: A Survey, 1964, Self and Biography: Essays on the Individual and Society in Asia, 1975, (with D. Leslie and C. Mackerras) Essays on the Sources for Chinese History, 1974, (with C.K. Leung and J. Cushman) Hong Kong: Dilemmas of Growth, 1980, (with M. Guerrero and D. Marr) Society and the Writer: Essays on Literature in Modern Asia, 1981, (with J. Cushman) Changing Identities of Southeast Asian Chinese since World War II, 1988, Hong Kong's Transition: (with Wong Siu-lun) A Decade after the Deal, 1995, Global History and Migrations, 1997, Xianggang shi xinbian (Hong Kong History: New Perspectives), 1997, (with Wong Siu-lun) Hong Kong in the Asia-Pacific Region: Rising to the New Challenges, 1997, (with Wong Siu-lun) Dynamic Hong Kong: Business and Culture, 1997, (with John Wong) China's Political Economy, 1998, (with Wang Ling-chi) The Chinese Diaspora: Selected Essays, 1998, (with John Wong) Hong Kong in China: The Challenges of Transition, 1999, (with John Wong) China: Two Decades of Reform and Change, 1999, (with Zheng Yongnian) Politics and Society in Post-Deng China, 2000; councillor, editor jour. Nanyang Hseuh-hui (Singapore); v.p., editor jour. Royal Asiatic Soc. Malayan Branch, 1962-68; contbr. articles to profl. jours. and collected vols. on Asian history. Mem. Commn. Inquiry on Singapore Riots, 1964-65, Com. on Australia-Japan Rels., 1980-81, exec. councillor, Hong Kong, 1990-92; mem. exec. coun. World Wildlife Fund for Nature, Hong Kong, 1987-95; chmn. Environment Pollution Adv. Com., Hong Kong, 1988-95, Coun. Performing Arts, Hong Kong, 1989-95, Australia-China Coun., 1984-86; bd. dirs. East Asian History Sci. Found. Ltd., Hong Kong, 1987-95; co-patron Asia-Link, U. Melbourne, 1994—; chmn. Asia-Pacific Coun., Griffith U., Brisbane, 1997; mem. Nat. Heritage Bd., 1997-99, advisor, 1999—; bd. dirs. Nat. Arts Coun., 1996—; mem. Nat. Libr. Bd., 1997—. Rockefeller fellow U. London, 1961-62, sr. vis. fellow, 1972, vis. fellow All Souls Coll., U. Oxford, 1974-75. Fellow Australian Acad. of Humanities (pres. 1980-83), Royal Soc. of Arts London (hon. corr. mem. for Hong Kong 1987-95); mem. Academia Sinica, Internat. Assn. Historians of Asia (pres. 1964-68, 88-91), Internat. Soc. for Study of Chinese Overseas (pres. 1991—), East-West Ctr. Honolulu (internat. adv. panel), Inst. S.E. Asian Studies Singapore (regional coun. mem. 1982—), Assn. S.E. Asian, Instns. of Higher Learning (adminstrv. bd. 1987-89, v.p. 1991-93), Chinese U. of Hong Kong (coun. 1986-95), Inst. East Asian Polit. Economy (bd. dirs. 1989-97, chmn. 1996-97), Asia-Australia Inst. Coun., Asia Soc. Coun., Internat. Inst. Strategic Coun., Social Sci. Rsch. Coun. (bd. dirs. 1999—),. Avocations: music, reading, walking. Home: #08-02 Ardmore Park, Singapore Singapore Office: East Asian Inst, Nat U Singapore Kent Ridge, Singapore Singapore

GUNIN, ANDREI GERMANOVICH, reproductive endocrinologist; b. Nizhnii Novgorod, Russia, Dec. 1, 1965; s. German and Alla (Peshkova) G. MD, Chuvash State U., 1988; PhD in Philosophy, 2d Moscow Med. Inst., 1990; D in Sci., Moscow People Friendship U., 1997. Resident in ob-gyn. Cheboksary City Maternity Hosp., Russia, 1988-89, ob/gyn, 1989—; from asst. prof. to prof. Med. Inst. Chuvash State U., Cheboksary, 1990—. Mem. Internat. Soc. Neuroendocrinology, N.Y. Acad. Scis. E-mail: drgunin@yahoo.com. Home: PO Box 86, 428034 Cheboksary Russia

GUN'KO, VLADIMIR MOISEEVICH, research physicist; b. Dnipropetrovsk, Ukraine, Nov. 13, 1951; s. Moisey Nikiforovich and Nina Tiriopheevna (Maslova) G.; m. Lyudmila Grigoreevna Limarenko, Aug. 13, 1976; 1 child, Vladimir. Grad. in physics, State U., Dnipropetrovsk, 1973; PhD in Chem. Sci., Inst. Phys. and Organic Chem., Kiev, Ukraine, 1983. Engr. Dnipropetrovsk State U., 1973-76; sr. engr. Inst. Phys. and Organic Chemistry, 1976-78, jr. rschr., 1978-85; sr. rschr. Inst. Surface Chemistry, Kiev, 1985-91, head of lab., 1991-96, leading rschr., 1996—; project leader Sherwin-Williams Co., U.S., 1993-95. Editor (spl. issue) Colloid Surfaces, 1995; contbr. articles to profl. jours. Grantee Internat. Sci. Found., 1993, Swiss Nat. Sci. Found., 1996—. Avocations: cycling, underwater hunting, body-building. Home: Bulvar Perova 48/192, 02183 Kiev Ukraine Office: Inst Surface Chemistry, 17 General Nauurov St, 03164 Kiev Ukraine

GUNN, ALBERT EDWARD, JR., internist, educator, lawyer, administrator; b. Port Washington, N.Y., Oct. 31, 1933; s. Albert Edward and Esther Frances (Williams) G.; m. Joan Marie Jacoby, May 18, 1968; children: Albert Edward III, Emily Williams Gunn Hebert, Andrew Robert, Clare Margaret, Catherine Ann, Philip David. BS, Fordham Coll., 1955, LLB, 1958; MB BCh BAO, Nat. U. Ireland, Galway, 1967. Bar: N.Y. 1958, D.C. 1972; diplomate Am. Bd. Internal Medicine. Owner, agt. Albert E. Gunn Ins. Agy., Port Washington, 1953-65; intern Montefiore Hosp., N.Y.C., 1967-68; resident in medicine Roosevelt Hosp., N.Y.C., 1968-70; USPHS trainee in neurology U. Rochester, N.Y., 1970-72; asst. dir. govtl. rels. AMA, Washington, 1972-74; med. dir. Geriat. Svcs. Suffolk County, Hauppauge, N.Y., 1974-75; med. dir. Rehab. Ctr., U. Tex./M.D. Anderson Cancer Ctr., 1975-88, chief rehab. sect., 1988-93, chief geriat. sect., 1993—, dep. chmn. dept. internal med. spltys., 1998—; asst. prof. medicine U. Tex. Med. Sch., Houston, 1976-80, assoc. prof., 1980-2000, prof., 2000—, also assoc. dean for admissions; med. dir. Region IV, Tex. Med. Found., 1986-93; del.-at-large White House conf. on Handicapped Individuals, 1977; pres. Mus. Med. Sci., 1990; cons. CDC, Legal Svcs. Corp., Nat. Libr. Medicine. Co-author: Rehabilitation of the Cancer Patient, 1976, AIDS in Africa, 1988; editor, contbg. author: Cancer Rehabilitation, 1984; mem. editl. bd. Cancer Bull., 1977-90, Gerontology and Geriatrics Edn., Linacre Quar.; contbr. articles to profl. jours. Mem. nat. adv. health coun. HEW, 1974-75; mem. adv. com. Nat. Inst. Law Enforcement and Criminal Justice, Law Enforcement Assistance Adminstrn., U.S. Dept. Justice, 1974-76; mem. bd. regents Nat. Libr. Medicine, NIH, 1983-87, chmn., 1986-87, chmn. lit. selection tech. adv. com., 1988-91; bd. dirs. Right to Life Advs., 1977-78, Tex. Med. Ctr. Libr., 1990. With USAF Strategic Air Command, 1958-61, capt. Res., 1961-75. Fellow ACP; mem. Tex. Med. Assn. (trustee ins. trust, chmn. bd. trustees 1997-99), Harris County Med. Soc. (exec. bd. 1986-90, v.p. 1998), Royal Coll. Physicians London (licentiate), Royal Coll. Surgeons Eng., Houston Acad. Medicine (bd. dirs. 1986-90, pres. 1990), Houston Bar Assn., D.C. Bar, Cath. Med. Assn. (regional bd. dirs. 1992—, Thomas Linacre award 1997), Sons of Union Vets. of Civil War, Am. Legion, KC, Army and Navy Club, Cosmos Club, Drs. Club (Houston). Roman Catholic. Home: 2329 Watts St Houston TX 77030-1139 Office: U Tex MD Anderson Cancer Ctr 1515 Holcombe Blvd Houston TX 77030-4009

GUNN, MOREY WALKER, JR., secondary education educator, choir director, organist; b. Orangeburg, S.C., June 23, 1939; s. Morey Walker Sr. and Marjorie (Dusek) G.; m. Sheila Dianne Taylor, Nov. 26, 1994; 1 child, Andrew Walker. BA in Music, Furman U., 1961, MA, 1967. Cert. specialist music edn. tchr., S.C. Band dir. Holly Hill (S.C.) H.S., 1961-65, Orangeburg H.S., 1965-71, Greer (S.C.) H.S., 1971-73, Ft. Johnson H.S., Charleston, S.C., 1973-77, Berkeley County Schs., Goose Creek, S.C., 1978-92; organist St. Andrews United Methodist ch., 1992—. Mem. Nat. Rep. Senatorial Com. 1978-97; deacon 1st Presbyn, Ch., 1965-71; elder James Island Presbyn. Ch., 1974-76, 78-80, choir dir., organist, 1965-94; organist St. Andrews United Meth. Ch., Orangburg, S.C., 1994—; bd. dirs. excellence in teaching award com. Charleston County Youth Symphony, 1975; bd. dirs. Charles Towne Landing Band Festival Com., 1988-89. Mem. Am. Guild Organists, Sertoma Club (bd. dirs. 1989-90), Kiwanis Club (bd. dirs. 1997—, sec. 1998-99, pres. 1999-2000, Disting. sec. 1999, Disting. Kiwanian award 1998-2000), Hibernian Soc., Elks, Phi Mu Alpha (hon. life). Avocations: dancing, reading, dining out, table tennis, collecting seascape prints. Home: 2 Waters Edge Ct Charleston SC 29414-7327

GUNN, S. JEANNE, writer, natural healer; b. Janesville, Wis., Feb. 28, 1939. Cert. Reiki master, massage therapy, aromatherapy, Ayurveda, iridology; ordained minister. Office mgr. constrn. co., 10 yrs; developer Bodywork & Co., Virginia Beach, Va., 1992, Sacred Earth Ctr., Virginia Beach, 1994. Author: Reiki and Beyond Healing Manual, 1994, also Reiki instrn. booklets, 1994, Natural Healing-Alternative Resources for Total Health, 1999, Calamity Coyote and Her Desert Friends series, 2000; also poems; editor several orgn. newsletters; contbr. articles to newspapers and tng. manuals interior designer, painter greeting cards; designer wall hangings. Active PTA; troop leader Girl Scouts U.S.A.; den mother Boy Scouts Am.; girls softball coach; vol. hosp. and ch.; seminar developer Teen Imagines; founder Talk of Towne. Recipient award for outstanding media person in cmty. Talk of the Towne. Mem. Toastmistresses (past pres.). Avocations: writing poetry, gardening, walking, painting, quilting. E-mail: wddancer@yahoo.com. Office: Sacred Earth Ctr 6255 E Avon Lima Rd Avon NY 14414-9556

GUNNARSSON, BIRGIR ISLEIFUR, bank executive, former parliamentarian; b. Reykjavík, Iceland, July 19, 1936; s. Gunnar E. Benediktsson and Jórunn Isleifsdóttir; m. Sonja Backman, Oct. 6, 1956; children:Björg Jóna, Gunnar Jóhann, Ingunn Mjöll, Lilja Dögg. Diploma in law, U. Iceland, 1961. Cert. adv. to Supreme Ct., 1967. Leader Youth Soc. of Independance Party, Reykjavík, 1959-62; sec. gen. Independence Party Youth Fedn., Reykjavík, 1961-63; sole practice Reykjavík, 1963-72; mayor City of Reykjavík, 1972-78; chmn. exec. com. Independence Party, 1979-87; member Parliament, Can., 1979-91; 2nd dep. speaker Althing (Lower House of Parliment), 1983-87; minister Ministry of Culture and Edn., Can., 1987-88; gov. Cen. Bank Iceland, 1991—; chmn. Com. Heavy Industry, 1983-87. Bd. dirs. Civil Aviation Bd., 1984-87; mem. City Coun. Reykjavík, 1962-82. Mem. Rotary Internat. Home: Fjölnisvegur 15, 101 Reykjavik Iceland also: Sedlabanki Islands, Kalkofnsvegur 1, 101 Reykjavik Iceland

GUNNARSSON, MAGNUS, consulting company executive, economist; b. Raykjavik, Iceland, Sept. 6, 1946; s. Gunnar and Kristin (Valdimarsdottir) M.; m. Gunnhildur Gunnarsdottir, July 5, 1968; children: Adalheidur, Gunnar Kristinn. Grad., Icelandic Comml. Coll., Reykjavik, 1967; postgrad., U. Iceland, Reykjavik, 1971, MIT, 1980. V.p. fin. Union of Icelandic Fish Producers, Reykjavik, 1971-73; mng. dir. Hafskip Shipping Co., Reykjavik, 1973-75, Eagle Air/Icelandic Charter Airlines, Reykjavik, 1976-81; v.p. Esso Oil Iceland, Reykjavik, 1981-83; mng. dir. Confedn. of Iceland Employers, Reykjavik, 1983-86, Union of Icelandic Fish Producers, Reykjavik, 1986-94; pres. Capital Cons., Reykjavik, 1994—; chmn. bd. Nord Morus, France, 1991-94, Haraldur Bödvarsson Ltd., Akranes, Iceland, 1991-95, French-Icelandic Ltd., Akranes. Editor The Icelandic Student Mag., 1968, Eimreioin, 1972-75; contbr. articles to newspapers and mags. Chmn. bd. Icelandic Export Coun., 1986-94, Icelandic Fisheries Com., 1989-93, French-Icelandic Trade Coun., 1990-93, Coalition of Fisheries Nations, 1992-93; chmn. task force to reconstruct Icelandic fishing industry, 1992-94; chmn. bd. Icelandic Fisheries Devel. Fund, Confedn. Icelandic Employers, 1992-95. Home: Thernunes 10, 210 Garoabaer Iceland Office: Capital Cons, Kringlan 5, North Tower, 103 Reykjavik Iceland

GUNNELS, LEE O., retired finance and management educator, manufacturing/research company director, inventor; b. Huntington Park, Calif., Sept. 11, 1933; s. LeRoy O. and Marrion W. Gunnels; m. Laura Gunnels, Nov. 7, 1958; children: Cornelia, Amelia, Sarah. BA in Math./Physics, U. Hawaii, 1960; MBA, Xavier U., Cin., 1970. Nuclear physicist Bettelle Meml. Inst., Columbus, Ohio; ret. assoc. prof. fin. and mgmt. Muskingum Tech. Coll., Zanesville, Ohio; past chmn. faculty senate Muskingum Tech. Coll., Zanes-

ville; inventor, developer Gunnels Rsch. LLC; chmn. bd. dirs. Pallet Systems and Mgmt. Corp., Inc., Zanesville (Ohio) Pallet, Inc. Contbr. articles to various publs. Home: 1849 Drugan Ct SW Reynoldsburg OH 43068-8181 also: Stoney Meadow Farms Zanesville OH 43701

GUNNER, MURRAY, Jewish organization administrator; b. N.Y.C., Mar. 26, 1918; s. Abraham and Sadie (Schnee) G.; m. Pearl O. Katz, June 12, 1949; children: Marilyn Ruth, Janet Marie. BS, CCNY, 1938; MSW, Columbia U., 1946; cert., Hebrew U., 1971. Cert. social worker. Social worker, acting supr. N.Y.C. Dept. Welfare and Camp LaGuardia, 1940-45; adminstrv. asst. Coun. House, St. Louis, 1946-50; program dir. Jewish Community Ctr., Hartford, Conn., 1950-54; exec. dir. Jewish Community Ctr., Newburgh, N.Y., 1954-62, Bklyn., 1962-66, Yonkers, N.Y., 1966-83; cons. Jewish Community Ctr., Jewish Fedn., 1983-89; exec. dir. Jewish Coun. of Yonkers, 1989—; cons. Hudson River Mus., Elizabeth Seton Coll., 1989-89; co-chmn. commn. of synagogue rels. United Jewish Appeal Fedn., N.Y.C., 1980-81, co-chmn. Jewish Community Ctrs., 1981-82; co-chair adult edn. com. Greystone Jewish Ctr., Yonkers, 1980-82, bd. dirs., 1978-80. Contbr. author to various books. mem. Charter Revision Commn., Yonkers, 1979, Mayor's Holocaust Commn. Yonkers, 1979, Mayor's Com. on Jewish Affairs, Yonkers, 1990—, Yonkers Crime Commn., 1975, Yonkers Mental Health Coun., 1978-83; bd. dirs. Yonkers United Way, 1981-83; mem. Mayor's Cmty. Rels. Com., Yonkers, 1992—; exec. com. Edn. 2000, Yonkers, 1992—; mem. adv. com. to senator N.Y. State Sena, 1997—, Mentoring Com. for Youth at Risk, 1993—; bd. dirs. Cmty. Planning Agy., Yonkers, 1992—; task force City/County Youth Violence; mem. Mayor's Commn. on AIDS, 1997—; mem. cmty. planning coun. Substance Abuse Prevention Com., 1997—; mem. shared decision making commn. Gorton H.S., 1997; mem. exec. com. Yonkers Mayor's Cmty. Rels. Commn., 1997; mem. edn. com. Yonkers City Coun., 1998—; chair Yonkers Flag Day Commn., 1998; mem. Yonkers Family and Cmty. project Columbia U., 1998; mem. N.Y. State Assemblyman Adv. Com., 1997; mem. Yonker Mayor's Health Comm., 1998-99, Older Adult Task Force, Substance Abuse Task Force; mem. older adults com. Yonkers Mayor Health Commn., 1999; apptd. mem. partnership com. Yonkers Bd. Edn., 1999; bd. dirs. Greystone Jewish Ctr. Recipient Israel Cummings award Commn. on Synagogue Rels. Fedn., 1963, cert. of merit, 1992, Am. Com. on Italian Migration, 1992, cert. of recognition for outstanding svc. and contbns. Charles Gorton H.S., Yonkers, 1995, Yonkers Martin Luther King Commn. award, 1995, Cmty. Svc. award Mayor of City of Yonkers, 1995, Multi-Cultural Edn. award Yonkers Pub. Schs., 1998; honored for cmty. svc. Jewish Coun. Yonkers Bd. Dirs., City of Yonkers, County of Westchester, U.S. Congress, Rockland County YM-YWHA, 1998; Murray Gunner Day named in his honor City of Yonkers, 1983, County of Westchester, 1983; named guest of honor Westchester chpt. Am. Heart Assn., 1997. Mem. NASW (Gold Care mem.), Rotary (chair pub. rels. com. 1988—, chair cmty. svcs., bd. dirs. 1993-94, Paul Harris fellow 1994). Home: 10 Gateway Rd Yonkers NY 10703-1200 Office: Jewish Coun of Yonkers 584 N Broadway Yonkers NY 10701-1731

GUNNERSON, DEBRA ANN, piano teacher; b. Detroit, Apr. 30, 1955; d. Robert James and Marjorie Jane (Page) Robinson; m. Gary Lee Gunnerson, May 22, 1976; children: Adam Lee, Julie Ann, Carrie Ann, Aaron Lee. BA in Piano Performance, George Mason U., 1976, MA in Piano Performance, 1991. Nat. cert. piano tchr. Music Tchrs. Nat. Assn. Pvt. tchr. piano, Chantilly, Va., 1971—; asst. adj. prof. George Mason U., Fairfax, 1990-91; pianist Kennedy Ctr., Washington, 1973, Nat. Cathedral, Washington, 1973, McLean (Va.) Symphony, 1990. Scholar George Mason U., 1973. Mem. No. Va. Music Tchrs. (yearbook chmn. 1993-95, chmn. judged recital 1995-97, pres.-elect 1999-2001), Fairfax West Music Fellowship (historian 1996-97), Springfield Music Club (membership chmn. 1994-95, pres. 1997-99, historian 1999-2001); chmn. Chamber Music at Home Friday Morning Music Club, 1998—. Avocation: walking. Home and Studio: 4509 Hazelnut Ct Chantilly VA 20151-2415

GUNNING, JAN WILLEM, economics educator; b. Breda, The Netherlands, Jan. 7, 1949; s. Johannes H. and Hermine M.E. (Swellengrebel) G.; m. Louisa Johanna Schepers, May 19, 1973; children: Joost, Krik. MA, U. Groningen, The Netherlands, 1972; PhD, U. Oxford, Eng., 1980. Rsch. fellow U. Groningen, 1972-73; economist World Bank, Washington, 1973-78; rschr. U. Oxford, 1978-80; vis. prof. U. Brussels, 1980-82; divsn. chief, dir. Econ. and Social Inst., Amsterdam, The Netherlands, 1982-93; prof. devel. econs. Free U., Amsterdam, 1987—; prof. econs., fellow St. Antony's Coll., Oxford (Eng.) U., 1998-2000, dir. Ctr. for Study African Econs., 1998-2000; cons. in field; mng. editor Jour. African Econs., Oxford, 1992—; dir. Amsterdam Inst. Internat. Devel., 2000—; mem. Nat. Adv. Coun. on Devel. Coop., The Hague, The Netherlands, 1987-97. Author: Peasants and Governments, 1989, Controlled Open Economies, 1990, Trade Shocks in Developing Countries, 1999; contbr. articles to profl. jours. Fulbright scholar, 1966. Mem. Am. Econ. Assn., Royal Econ. Soc., Reveil Hist. Assn. (pres. 1994—). Avocations: history, playing flute, sailing, rowing. Home: Straatweg 24, 3621 BX Breukelen The Netherlands Office: Dept Ecpms 4 Azig, De Boelelaan 1105, 1081 HV Amsterdam The Netherlands

GUNNOE, NANCY LAVENIA, food executive, artist; b. Southside, Tenn., Jan. 7, 1921; d. Edgar Hatton and Clara Sharp (McCurdy) Thompson; m. Raymond Glen Gunnoe, Dec. 6, 1941; children: Lynn Thompson Gunnoe Sheets, Paul Randall (dec.), Joy Virginia Gunnoe Woodrum. Student, Austin Peay Coll., 1939, U. Charleston, 1973-87, 91. Cashier Kroger Co., Charleston, W.V., 1939-40; with Superior Laundry & Cleaning, Charleston, 1940-41; file clk. Hancock Oil Co., Oakland, Calif., 1942; office clk. Office Price Adminstrn., Stockton, Calif., 1943; sec.-treas. R.G. Gunnoe Farms Inc., Charleston, 1947—. Exhibited at local orgns. Mem. Nat. League Am. Pen Women, Inc., Allied Artists W.Va., Univ. Charleston Builders, Kanawha Valley Hist. and Preservation Soc., Charleston Woman's Club, Sunrise Mus. Republican. Avocations: china painting, porcelain sculpture. Home: 2040 Oakridge Dr Charleston WV 25311-1112 Office: 2115 Oakridge Dr Charleston WV 25311-1409

GUNSEL, SELDA, chemical engineer, researcher; b. Istanbul, Turkey, Nov. 10, 1958; d. Nejat and Hikmet (Suntekin) G.; m. Donald Lee Pferdehirt, June 6, 1987; children: Melisa, Lara. BSc in Chem. Engring., Istanbul Tech. U., 1981; MSc in Chem. Engring., Pa. State U., 1983, PhD in Chem. Engring., 1986. Advanced rsch. engr. Pennzoil Prods. Co., The Woodlands, Tex., 1986-90, sr. rsch. engr., 1990-94, rsch. assoc., 1994-97, sr. rsch. assoc., 1997-98, dir. tech. devel., 1999-2000, v.p. tech. devel., 2000—. Editor: Current Research in Tribology in North Am., 1993; mem. editl. rev. bd. CRC Handbook Lubrication and Tribology, Vol. III; mem. editl. bd., Jour. of Lubrication Sci.; Assoc. editor, Lubrication Engrg. Jour., contbr. articles to profl. jours. Mem. Am. Chem. Soc., Am. Soc. Heating, Refrigeration, Air Conditioning Engrs., Soc. Automotive Engrs. (Excellence in Oral Presentation 1996, chmn. lubricant rsch. award bd. 1997—), Soc. Tribologists and Lubrication Engrs. (Captain Alfred E. Hunt award 1998, bd. dirs. 1996—, instr. edn. courses 1990, 97, 99), Sigma Xi, Phi Lambda Upsilon. Achievements include patents for non-aqueous lamellar liquid crystalline lubricants, liquid crystal-surfactant technology; contributions in the field of lubrication science and tribology; leadership in the advancement of knowledge and application of science and lubrication and tribology; research in areas of thermal/oxidative stability of lubricants, friction/wear mechanisms in boundary and elastohydrodynamic lubrication, vapor-phase lubricants, liquid crystal lubricants, refrigeration lubricants. Office: Pennzoil Prods Co Tech Ctr 1520 Lake Front Cir The Woodlands TX 77380-3632

GUNTER, BRADLEY HUNT, capital management executive; b. Norfolk, Va., Dec. 8, 1940; s. J.A. and Virginia (Whalen) G.; m. Susan Mason Hart, Dec. 27, 1962 (div. 1977); children: Bradley Hunt, Valerie Mason; m. Anne A. Macon, Nov. 7, 1985 (dec. 1994); 1 child, Bradford Macon Gunter; m. Meredith Laura Strohm, Dec. 16, 1994. BA, U. Richmond, 1962; MA, U. Va., 1963, PhD, 1969. Instr. Washington and Lee U., Lexington, Va., 1967-69; asst. prof. Boston Coll., 1969-71; corp. sec. Fed. Res. Bank, Richmond, Va., 1971-80; pres. Bartleby's Inc., Richmond, 1980-85; dir. found. rels. U. Va., Charlottesville, 1985-86; investment broker Scott and String fellow, Richmond, 1987-89; mng. dir. Scott & Stringfellow Capital Mgmt., Richmond, 1989-97, pres., CEO,, 1977-2000; pres. Scott & Stringfellow Capital Mgmt., LLC, Richmond, 2000—; cons. NEH, Washington, 1975-80. Author: Studies in The Waste Land, 1971, Guide to T.S. Eliot, 1970, Checklist of T.S. Eliot, 1969; contbr. articles to profl. jours. Vestryman St. Paul's Ch., Richmond, 1975-78; chmn. fund drive United Way, Richmond, 1980; mem. arts and scis. alumni coun. U. Va., also mem. Emeritus Soc.; bd. dirs. St. Christopher's Sch. Found., Richmond, 1981-85, Richmond Ballet, Big Bros. Richmond Inc., Va. Found. for Humanities and Pub. Policy, Elk Hill Farm; trustee St. Paul's Endowment Fund, Inc., United Way Greater Richmond; pres. Arts Coun. Richmond, Hist. Richmond Found., Poe Found.; bd. dirs., chmn. U. Va. Cancer Ctr., U. Va. Health Scis. Coun., U. Va. Libr. Bd. Mem. Richmond Assn. Bus. Economists, Assn. for Investment Mgmt. and Rsch., U. Va. Alumni Assn. (chpt. pres. Richmond 1981), Va. Soc. Mayflower Descs. (bd. dirs.), Country Club Va., Colonnade Club, Focus Club, Univ. Club, Farmington Country Club, Phi Beta Kappa, Omicron Delta Kappa. Episcopalian. Avocation: tennis. Office: Scott & Stringfellow Capital Mgmt LLC 310 4th St NE Ste 100 Charlottesville VA 22902-5266

GÜNTER, PETER, physics educator; b. Zurich, Sept. 28, 1944; s. Fritz and Emma (Notter) G.; m. Carolina Carmen Medrano. Diploma in physics, Swiss Fed. Inst. Tech., Zurich, 1971, PhD, 1976, venia legendi, 1982. Rsch. assoc. Swiss Fed. Inst. Tech., 1971-76, 1st asst., 1976-79, sr. 1st asst., 1980-82, privatdozent, 1982-87, prof. exptl. physics, 1987—, head nonlinear optics lab., 1987—, head inst. quantum electronics, 1990-92. Co-author: Organic Nonlinear Optical Materials, 1995, Laser Induced Dynamic Gratings, 1978; co-editor five books on photorefractive effects, materials and applications, and electrooptics and nonlinear optics; mem. editl. bd. numerous profl. jours. Fellow Optical Soc. Am.; mem. IEEE Quantum Electronics and Applications Soc., Swiss, European and Am. Phys. Socs. Office: ETH-Zurich, Inst Quantum Electronics, CH-8093 Zurich Switzerland

GUNTER, WILLIAM DAYLE, JR., physicist; b. Mitchell, S.D., Jan. 10, 1932; s. William Dayle and Lamerta Berniece (Hockensmith) G.; m. Shirley Marie Teshera, Oct. 24, 1955; children: Maria Jo, Robert Paul. BS in Physics with distinction, Stanford U., 1957, MS, 1959. Physicist Ames Rsch. Ctr. NASA, Moffett Field, Calif., 1960-81, asst. br. chief electronic optical engring., 1981-85; pvt. practice cons. Photon Applications, San Jose, Calif., 1985-98, Modesto, Calif., 1998-2000; owner virtual business Photon Applications, Modesto, 2000—. Patentee in field; contbr. articles to profl. jours. With U.S. Army, 1953-55. Recipient Westinghouse Sci. Talent Search award, 1950; Stanford U. scholar, 1950. Mem. IEEE (sr.), Am. Phys. Soc., Optical Soc. Am., Planetary Soc., Nat. Space Soc., NASA Alumni League. Office: Photon Applications 3701 Rosanne Ln Modesto CA 95356-9416

GÜNTHER, BRUNO GUILLERMO, physiology educator; b. Osorno, Chile, Mar. 26, 1914; s. Karl and Amely (Schaffeld) G.; m. Elena Beckdorf, Jan. 18, 1946; children: Bruno, Teresa. MD, U. Chile, Santiago, 1939. Med. diplomate. Instr. U. Chile, Santiago, 1939-40, prof., 1967-75; prof. U. Chile, Valparaiso, Chile, 1955-66; asst. prof. U. Concepción, Chile, 1941-44, prof., 1945-54, 76-93. Editor: (textbook) Physiopathology, 1963; contbr. numerous articles to profl. jours. Home: Pedro de Valdivia 072, Dept 501 Providencia, Santiago Chile

GUNTHER, ELLEN SOZANNE, treasurer; b. Beckley, W.Va., Feb. 23, 1947; d. Reginald St.Clair and Glida Mae (Banas) Meyers; m. Walter Lee Radcliff, Apr. 1, 1967 (div. Jan. 1972); 1 child, Michael Shane Radcliff; m. Jesse Ward Gunther, Feb. 23, 1992. AA, Coll. W.Va., 1989; B (regents), Bluefield State U., W.Va., 1993; MS, Marshall U., 2000. Owner, hairdresser Raymonds Beauty, Beckley, W.Va., 1966-85; bursar Coll. W.Va., Beckley, 1985—. Democrat. Methodist. Avocations: gardening, sewing, playing basketball. E-mail: elleng@cwv.net. Home: 120 Reservoir Rd Beckley WV 25801-4316 Office: Coll West Va PO Box AG 609 S Kawanha St Beckley WV 25802

GUNTHER, ROBERT DAVID, physiologist, educator; b. Teeneck, N.J., May 27, 1953; s. Maxwell David and Dorothy Eleanor G.; m. Joan Diane Starratt, Aug. 11, 1979; children: Cory Ann, Mitchell David. BS in Biology and Chemistry, U. Miami, 1976; PhD in Physiology, U. Calif. Los Angeles, 1981. Postdoctoral rschr. U. Calif. Los Angeles, 1982; asst. rsch. physiologist Ctr. Ulcer Rsch. and Edn., Los Angeles, 1986; asst. prof. U. Calif. Los Angeles, 1988; assoc. prof./dept. chair Daemen Coll., Amherst, 1988—. Recipient Morton Grossman-Smith Kline Beckman fellowship, Ctr. Ulcer Rsch. and Edn., 1983, 86; grantee NIH, 1981-82. Mem. N.Y. Acad. Sci., Am. Assn. Advancement Sci. Avocations: guitar, tropical fish. Fax: 716-839-8516. E-mail: rgunther@daemen.edu. Office: Daemen Coll 4380 Main St Amherst NY 14226-3544

GUNTHER, WILLIAM DAVID, university administrator, economics educator; b. Balt., Oct. 11, 1940; s. Geneva (Gee) G.; m. Irene Leveja Reineks, Jan. 8, 1966; children: William B., Kristine A., Jennifer R. BS, Kent State U., 1962, MA, 1965; PhD, U. Ky., 1969. Asst. prof. econs. U. Ala., Tuscaloosa, 1968-72, assoc. prof. econs., 1972-76, prof. econs., 1976—, assoc. dean for rsch., 1988-98; dean sch. bus. U. So. Miss., Hattiesburg, 1998—. Contbr. articles to profl. jours. Fulbright scholar Fulbright Commn., 1972, Faculty fellow USAF, 1979. Mem. Assn. Coll. Honor Socs. (exec. coun. 1983—), Nat. Assn. Bus. Economists, Am. Econs. Assn., So. Regional Sci. Assn. Avocations: bicycling, coin collecting, paper money collecting. Office: U So Miss PO Box 5021 Hattiesburg MS 39406-1000

GUNTINAS LICHIUS, ORLANDO, surgeon, otolaryngologist; b. Leverkusen, Germany, May 12, 1967; s. Jaime and Ursula (Lichius) Guntinas; m. Julia Warnking, Nov. 23, 1995; children: Josephine, Mathilda. MD, U. Cologne, 1994, PhD, 1994, ENT specialist degree, 1998, speech specialist degree, 1999; degree in plastic surgery. Resident ENT dept. U. Cologne, 1994-98, staff surgeon, 1998—. Grantee Fritz ter Meer Found., Bayer AG, 1992. Avocations: German literature, painting. Office: ENT Dept HNO-Klinik, Joseph Stelzmann Strasse 9, D-50924 Koln Germany

GUNTY, CHRISTOPHER JAMES, newspaper editor; b. Hometown, Ill., Oct. 13, 1959; s. Harold Paul and Therese Agnes (Kohs) G.; m. Nancy Louise Blanton, July 10, 1982; children: William, Amy, Timothy. BA, Loyola U., Chgo., 1981. Circulation mgr. The Chgo. Catholic, 1981-83, assoc. mnging. editor, 1983, mng. editor, 1983-85; editor, mng. editor The Catholic Sun, Phoenix, 1985-96; assoc. pub. The Cath. Sun, Phoenix, 1996—. Author: He Came to Touch Us, 1987; co-author videotape script The Pope in Arizona, 1987; contbg. author: (anthologies) Freedom of Journalist, 1990, Mission and Future of the Catholic Press, 1998; contbr. articles to spl. Catholic news svcs. as well as papers where employed. Mem. Fiesta Bowl Com., Phoenix, 1987-92; bd. dirs. Catholic Journalism Scholarship Fund, 1990—, pres., 1995-96, 99—. Named Honoree Summer U. Internat. Cath. Union of the Press, Switzerland, 1988. Mem. Cath. Press Assn. (bd. dirs. 1988-99, sec. 1990-92, v.p. 1994-96, pres. 1996-98, St. Francis de Sales award 2000), Assoc. Ch. Press, Ariz. Newspapers Assn., Soc. Profl. Journalists. Roman Catholic. Avocations: bicycling, sci. fiction. Office: The Catholic Sun 400 E Monroe St Phoenix AZ 85004-2336

GUO, BOWEI, combustion and thermal science educator, consultant; b. Luoyang, Henan, China, May 19, 1933; s. Zhaoshu and Hongyi (Xu) G.; m. Yuqin Wang, Jan. 24, 1957; children: Hong, Ying, Qing. BS, Northeastern U., Shenyang, China, 1953, MS, 1955. Asst. prof. Northeastern U., 1956-59, lectr., 1960-79, assoc. prof., 1980-84, dir. Inst., 1981-85, vice dean, 1984-88, prof., 1985—. Author: Fuel and Combustion, 1984 (Textbook of Excellence 1988), Advanced Combustion Technologies, 1994; contbr. articles to profl. jours.; patentee in field. Recipient Advanced Tchr. award Metallury Ministry of China, 1986, Outstanding Contbg. Scientist award Govt. Shenyang City, 1989. Mem. China Mech. Engring. Soc. (advanced mem.), China Indsl. Furnace Soc. (vice chmn. 1985-97), Energy Soc. Liaoning Province (standing mem. coun. 1978—), China Thermal Engring. Soc. (head combustion com. 1979-85), Thermophysics Soc. Liaoning Province (vice chmn. 1986-96). Avocations: music, Do "Taijiquan". Home: Apt 241 Bldg 13-3 Wanghulu, 110006 Shenyang China Office: Northeastern Univ, 110006 Shenyang China

GUO, HOUYANG, physicist researcher; b. Gushi, Henan, People's Republic of China, May 15, 1965; s. Zhongli and Xifeng (Rao) G.; m. Xiao-Ling Li, Aug. 8, 1988; children: Monica, Emma. B of Phys. Engring., Hefei U. of Tech., China, 1985; MSc, Inst. of Plasma Physics, Hefei, China, 1988; PhD, U. Québec, Montréal, Can., 1993. Postdoctoral fellow Centre Canadien de Fusion Magnétique, Montréal, Can., 1993-94; rsch. assoc. JET Joint Undertaking, Oxford, Eng., 1994-96, rsch. scientist, 1996—; responsible officer for diagnostics JET Joint U., 1994-96, physicist in charge, 1995—; experimental session leader JET Joint Undertaking, 1998-99; sr. rsch. scientist, project leader U. Wash., 1999—. Contbr. articles to profl. jours.; inventor in field. Recipient Postdoctoral fellowship Nat. Fusion Program of Can., 1994-96, Young Scientist Travel award ISCS World Lab., 1993, scholarship Agreement of Chinese Edn. Com. and Québec High Edn. Com., 1988-90. Mem. Am. Phys. Soc. Office: Redmand Plasma Physics Lab Univ Wash 14700 NE 95th Ste 100 Redmond WA 98052

GUO, JAMES ZHIQIANG, engineer. BS, Nanjing U., 1982; MS, Zhejiang U., 1985; PhD, Oreg. State U., 1994. Lic. profl. engr. Lectr., rsch. assoc. Fuzhou U., 1985-89; rsch./tchg. asst. Oreg. State U., Corvallis, 1989-94; cons. PMIC, Philomath, Oreg., 1993-94; R&D engr. Hewlett-Packard Co., Corvallis, 1995-99, sr. quality engr., 1999—. Mem. Phi Kappa Phi. E-mail: james guo@hp.com. Office: Hewlett-Packard Co 1000 NE Circle Blvd Corvallis OR 97330-4241

GUO, JIAN DONG, chemist, educator; b. Beijing, Sept. 25, 1945; s. Xu Feng and Zhao Rui (Wang) G.; m. Xiao Lin Xu, Feb. 9, 1972; 1 child, Fan. Diploma, Peking U., Beijing, 1969; postgrad., Swiss Fed. Inst. Tech., Zürich, 1987-94. Engr. Chem. Plant, Heng Shui, China, 1971-80; tchr. U. of Air, Beijing, 1980-87; vis. scholar Swiss Fed. Inst. Tech., 1987-94; assoc. prof. chemistry Peking U., 1994-99; prof. chemistry and physics Peking U., $D, 1999—; reviewer Chinese Physics Letters, Beijing, 1998—. Contbr. articles to profl. jours. Avocations: music, literature. Office: Peking Univ, Dept Physics, Beijing 100871, China

GUO, JONG-SHENQ, mathematics educator; b. Tainan, Taiwan, Dec. 25, 1956; s. Chun-Fu and Rey-Feng (Chang) g.; m. Yung-Jen Lin, July 1, 1985; children: Karen, Henry. BS, Nat. Taiwan Normal U., 1980; MSc, Purdue U., 1987; PhD, U. Minn., 1989. Assoc. prof. Nat. Tsing Hua U., Hsichu, Taiwan, 1989-94; vis. scholar U. Minn., Mpls., 1992-93; prof. Nat. Tsing Hua U., 1994-95, Nat. Taiwan Normal U., Taipei, 1995—; mem. panel of math. Nat. Sci. Coun., Taipei, 1996-98. Editor Bull. Nat. Taiwan Normal U., 1996, 2000—; contbr. articles to profl. jours. Mem. Math. Soc. Republic of China (acad. com. 1998), N.Y. Acad. Scis., U. Minn. Alumni Assn., Nat. Geog. Soc., Phi Tau Phi, Phi Kappa Phi. Avocations: tennis, music. Office: Nat Taiwan Normal U, 88 Sec 4 Ting Chou Rd, 117 Taipei Taiwan

GUO, KANG-XIAN, physicist, educator; b. Xichang City, Sichuan, Peoples Republic of China, Nov. 24, 1964; s. Ming-Gang and Zheng-Fen (Xiao) G.; m. Zhong-Hong Mao, June 1, 1991; 1 child, Ai-Xin. BS, Sichuan U., 1988, MS, 1991; PhD, Shanghai Jiao-Tong U., 1994. Lectr. Guangzhou Normal U., 1994-96, prof., 1997—; Mem. Chinese Ctr. Advanced Sci. and Tech. World Lab., Beijing, 1993-96. Contbr. articles to profl. jours. Avocations: fishing, cooking. Office: Guangzhou Normal U, Dept Physics, Guangzhou 510400, Peoples Republic of China

GUO, LIN-SONG, science educator; b. Putian, Fujian, China, Sept. 11, 1962; parents Jiaqi Guo and Jinjin Lin; m. Qiuhua Yu, Oct. 16, 1992; 1 child, Yuxin Yu. BSc, Zhejiang U., Hangzhou, China, 1983, MSc, 1990, PhD, 1998. cert. univ. tchr. Asst. engr. Guizhou Motorcycle Corp., Guiyang, China, 1983-87; lectr. Zhejiang U., Hangzhou, China, 1990-97. Avocations: badminton, swimming, bridge. Fax: 852-27888423. E-mail: melsguo@cityu.edu.hk.

GUO, MENG XIONG, science educator; b. Lao Ting, He Bei, China, Dec. 5, 1929; s. Yu Xuan Guo and Shu Zhen Gao; m. Guo Ha Li, Sept. 7, 1963; children: Nan, Ying. BS, N.E. Coll. Engring., Shen Yang, China, 1955. Asst. prof. Beijing Coll. Mining and Tech., 1955-59, lectr., 1960-80; assoc. prof. China U. Mining and Tech., Beijing, 1980-85, prof., 1985—; tech. supr. and advisor Chem. Plant, Beijing, China, 1984—; pres. Beijing Whisker Composite Materials Ltd. Co., Beijing, 2000—. Author: Flotation, 1989; mem. editl. bd. Jour. Chem. Mining Techniques, 1984-95; patentee in field. Activist rep. The Congress of Youth Socialist Constrn. Activities of the Whole Country, 1958. Named Advanced Worker, Mcpl. Party Com. and People Com. of Beijing City, 1960; recipient Third Class award, Ministry of Coal Industry, Beijing, 1988, Encouragement of Sci. and Tech. award, Spl. Subsidy, The State Coun., Beijing, 1992. Mem. Assn. Coal Processing and Utilization, Inst. Composite Materials China, Hong Kong Worldwide Inventors Assn. Avocations: Taijiquan, Qigong exercises. E-mail: Guonan@public.east.cn.net. Office: China U Mining & Tech, D11 College Rd, Beijing 100083, China

GUO, MIN-LIANG, biochemist, educator; b. Yudu County, Jiangxi, China, Sept. 18, 1964; s. Cheng-Fa and Yun-xiu (Liu) G.; m. Qin Xu, Dec. 25, 1991; 1 child, Xiu-yuan. BS, Jiangxi Agrl. U., Nanchang, China, 1985; MS, Jiangsu Agrl. Coll., Yangzhou, China, 1988. Asst. Jiangsu Agrl. Coll., 1988-91, asst. prof., 1991-93, asst. prof., dir. lab., 1993-95; asst. prof., dir. lab. Yangzhou U., Yangzhou, China, 1995-97; assoc. prof., dir. lab. Yangzhou U., 1997—; liaison Jiangsu Biochemistry Soc., 1992-97; hon. vis. scientist Monash U., Clayton, Vic., Australia, 1998-99. Editor: Book of Biochemistry, 1993; contbr. articles to profl. jours. Rsch. grantee Scientific Com. of Jiangsu, 1994, Yangzhou U., 1997, Ednl. Com. of Jiangsu, 2000. Mem. AAAS, N.Y. Acad. Scis., Chinese Soc. for Biochemistry and Molecular Biology, Jiangsu Biochemistry Soc. (councilor 1997—). Office: Biochemistry Lab Coll Bio-, Sci/Biotech Yangzhou U, Jiangsu Province 225009, China

GUO, PEIXUAN, molecular virology educator; b. Chaoyang, Guangdong, China, Apr. 4, 1951; came to U.S., 1983; s. Yongjian Guo and Huifang Zhang; m. Mar. 29, 1981; children: Yinyin, Sida. DVM, Foshan (Guangdong) Vet. Coll., 1978; MS in Microbiology, South China Agr. U., Guangzhou, 1981; PhD in Microbiology and Genetics, U. Minn., 1987. Guest rschr. U. Basel, Switzerland, 1985; rsch. scientist II N.Y. State Dept. Health, Albany, 1987-88; vis. scientist NIH, Bethesda, Md., 1988-89; asst. prof. Purdue U., West Lafayette, Ind., 1990-93, assoc. prof., 1994-97; prof. molecular virology Purdue U., West Lafayette, 1998—; ad hoc mem. study sect. on biomed. and behavioral rsch facilities, NIH, 1997; chmn. search com. for tenure-track faculty, 1994-95; chmn. workshop of 3d Asia-Pacific Congress Med. Virology, Beijing, 1994; chmn. Workshop of Vaccines and Vaccine Vectors Internat. Congress Vet. Virology, Interlake, Switzerland, 1994; chmn. workshop viral structure and assembly, Internat. Symposium Molecular Virology, Xian, China, 1996, Beijing, 1998; advisor Inst. Microbiology Chinese Acad. Scis. Contbr. over 50 articles to profl. jours. including Sci., Procs. NAS, Jour. Molecular Biology, Jour. Virology, RNA, Molecular Cell, Gene, Nuc. Acid Rsch., Virology and Viral Genes; editor seminars in virology, 1994. Recipient 1st award NIH, 1993, Pfizer Disting. Faculty award for rsch. excellence, 1995; Purdue U. faculty scholar, 1999; grantee Solvay, 1991-93, Integrated Biotech. Corp., 1991-94, NIH, 1992—, NSF, 1997—. Mem. AAAS, Am. Soc. Virology, Am. Soc. Microbiology, Am. Soc. Biochemistry and Molecular Biology, Soc. Chinese Bioscientists in Am., RNA Soc. Achievements include discovery of a small viral RNA novel and essential in viral DNA packaging leading to the opening of a new area of research; successful assembly of infectious double-stranded DNA virion of ø29 in vitro with recombinant proteins and synthetic nucleic acids; design of a novel strategy for high efficient inhibitiion of ø29 virion assembly and by the use of a mutant RNA with two functional domains and multile-copy involvement in viral DNA packaging; development of particle vaccines, subunit vaccines with multiple gene products, and recombinant vaccines of ILT virus; development of new methods for the quantification of stoichiometry for intermediate reactions; discovery of a hexameric molecular motor composed of 6 RNA molecules. Office: Purdue U Cancer Ctr Purdue Univ HAN5B-036 Purdue University IN 47907

GUO, QIXIN, scientist, electrical engineering educator; b. Shanghai, China, Jan. 28, 1964. BS, Toyohashi U. Tech., Japan, 1990, M Engring., 1992, DEng, 1996. Asst. prof. elec. engring. Saga (Japan) U., 1992-97, assoc. prof., 1997—. Contbr. articles to profl. jours. Office: Saga U, Honjo 1, Saga 840-8502, Japan

GUO, QIZHONG, engineering educator, researcher; b. Guangdong, China, Oct. 8, 1962; came to U.S., 1984; m. Xiaolan Wang; 1 child, Lillian. B of

Engring., Tianjin (China) U., 1982; MS, U. Minn., 1987, PhD, 1991. Registered profl. engr., Minn. Rsch./tchg. asst. U. Minn., Mpls., 1985-91, rsch. assoc., 1991-92; R&D engr. Lemna Corp., St. Paul, 1992; asst. prof. Rutgers U., Piscataway, N.J., 1992-98, assoc. prof., 1998—; mem. tech. adv. steering com. Barnegat Bay Nat. Estuary Program, Trenton, N.J., 1996—; mem. tech. adv. com. Whippany Watershed Project, Trenton, 1996—. Contbr. articles to profl. jours. Mem. ASCE, Am. Waterworks Assn., Am. Geophysical Union, Am. Water Resources Assn. (U. Minn. student chpt. pres. 1990-91), Water Environ. Fedn. Achievements include research in solutions to hydraulic problems in deep tunnel project for Greater Chicago; revealing environmental problems that may occur as a result of processing hazardous waste derived fuel in cement kilns; developing a new method for quantifying freshwater input and flushing time in estuaries. Office: Rutgers Univ 623 Bowser Rd Piscataway NJ 08854-8014

GUO, SHENG MING, retired history educator; b. Zhengjiang, Jiangsu, China, Dec. 25, 1915; came to U.S., 1989, naturalized, 1996; s. Dun Xue Guo and Xiao Chun Wu; m. Hong Yi Wang, Jan. 24, 1945; children: Victor Kuo, John Kuo, Meide Guo. BA in History, Nat. Ctrl. U., Chongching, China, 1938; MA, Ctrl. Inst. Polit. Sci., Chongching, 1941; postgrad., Tulane U., 1949. Vice consul Chinese Consulate, New Orleans, 1945-47, acting consul, 1948-50; prof. history Kuangsi (China) U., 1951-53, Hunan (China) U., 1953-56, East China Normal U., Shanghai, 1957-89; advisor Chinese Assn. Medieval History, Beijing, 1976—, Shanghai Assn. Social Sci., 1983—; U.S. State Dept. vis. prof., Georgetown U., Harvard U., U. Chgo., Stanford U., also others, 1983. Author: A Survey of Western Historiography, 1983 (State prize 1985), An Outline of World Civilization, 1989 (State prize 1991); editor-in-chief: Dictionary of World History, 1986; editor History of Foreign Countries in Ency. Sinica, 1987. Presbyterian. Avocation: gardening.

GUO, WEINONG, research associate; b. Suzhou, People's Republic China, July 24, 1968; s. Xicang and Jiaming (Zhang) G.; m. Yumei Yu, Apr. 13, 1994. MD, Suzhou Medical Coll., People's Republic China, 1991; PhD, Nagoya Univ., Japan, 1997. Cardiologist 2nd Affiliated Hosp. of Suzhou Medical Coll., People's Republic China, 1991-93; postdoctoral fellow Nagoya Univ., Japan, 1997-98; rsch. assoc. Washington Univ., St. Louis, Mo., 1998—; invited reviewer Joun. of Molecular and Cellular Cardiology, 1997—, Cardiovascular Rsch., 1997—. Contbr. articles to profl. jours. Recipient fellowship Am. Heart Assn., 1998—, rsch. grant Japan Heart Found., 1997-98. Mem. Am. Heart Assn., Biophys. Soc., Japanese Circulation Soc. E-mail: wguo@molecool.wustl.edu. Office: Washington Univ Box 8103 660 S Euclid Ave Saint Louis MO 63110-1093

GUO, XIN, materials science educator; b. Yichun, Jiangxi, China, Jan. 21, 1967; s. Chunhai Guo and Furong Wen; m. Nan Jia, Feb. 28, 1993; 1 child, Sijia. BS, Huazhong U. Sci. Tech., Wuhan, China, 1988, PhD, 1992. Asst. prof. Wuhan (China) U. Tech., 1993-95, assoc. prof., 1995-97; assoc. prof. Huazhong U. Sci. Tech., Wuhan, 1997-2001; guest scientist Max-Planck-Inst., Stuttgart, Germany, 1998-2001. Contbr. articles to profl. jours. Home: Robert-Koch Str 102, 70565 Stuttgart Germany Office: Max-Planck Inst Festkorperf, Heisenbergstr 1, 70569 Stuttgart Germany

GUO, XIN KANG, mathematics educator; b. Shanghai, People's Republic of China, Feb. 10, 1938; s. Zai and Li Juan (Wang) G.; m. Ying Zhu Chen, Nov. 28, 1967; 1 child, Jin. Grad., Fudan U., Shanghai, 1961. Asst. prof. dept. math. Guangxi U., Nanning, Peoples Republic of China, 1961-77, lectr., 1978-84, assoc. prof., 1985-89, prof., 1990—, vice-dir., 1981-84, vice-dir. dept. sci. rsch., 1984-88, dir. Inst. Math. and Computer Software, 1989—; Reviewer Math. Revs., 1988—. Contbr. articles on boundary value problems of partial differential equations to profl. jours. Recipient Sci. Progressive Prize, Guangxi Province Govt., Nanning, 1985, Brilliant Sci. Article Diploma, Guangxi Province Fedn. Sci., Nanning, 1988, Excellent Textbook Prize, Guangxi U., Nanning, 1988, Excellent Teaching Prize, Guangxi U., Nanning, 1989. Mem. Chinese Soc. Indsl. and Applied Math. (councillor 1990—), Am. Math. Soc., Math. Soc. People's Republic of China. Home and Office: Guangxi U, Dept Math, Nanning Guangxi, China

GUO, XIN-HENG, physicist; b. Beijing, Jan. 15, 1964; parents Shang Xin Guo and Zhi Ying Zheng; m. Lan Li, Feb. 27, 1989; 1 child: Dao-Shi. B in Physics, U. Sci. & Technology China, 1986; PhD, Inst. High Energy Physics, Beijing, 1991. Vis. scholar U. Wuppertal, Germany, 1991; postdoctoral rschr. Inst. Theoretical Physics, Beijing, 1992-94, assoc. prof., 1994-99; sr. participant Internat. Ctr. Theoretical Physics, 1995; postdoctoral fellow Hiroshima U., Japan, 1996; rsch. assoc. spl. rsch. ctr. subatomic structure of matter U. Adelaide, Australia, 1997—. Mem. Chinese Soc. Physics. Office: Spl Rsch Ctr Subatomic SM, Level 4 10 Pulteney St, Adelaide SA 5005, Australia

GUO, XUANCHANG, sculptor, educator; b. Ching Qing, China, Dec. 25, 1953; came to U.S., 1993; s. Han Zhong Guo and Fangbi Liu; m. Qun Cao, Jan. 31, 1982 (div.); 1 child, Dao Xi Guo; m. Hong Zhao, May 16, 1996; 1 child, Shirley D. BA in Art, Sichuan Fine Art Inst., Chong Qing, China, 1982; student, Sichuan Fine Art Inst., 1978-82. Mem. staff Chong Qing (China) Ctr. Co., 1968-71; prof. Sichuan Fine Art Inst., Chong Qing, China, 1981-91; rschr. Germany Kassel U. Art Dept., Kassel, 1991-92; master sculptor Sculpture USA, L.A., 1993. Creator Logo Sculpture of Chamber, 1995 (Pres. appreciation award), monument Sun President in US, 1997 (L.A. award of art achievement 1997); portrait statues include George Bush, 1991, Bill Clinton, 1996, Arnold Schwarzenegger, others; public sculptures include Monument of the Longmuch, Sichuan, China, 1989, Journey to the West, China Town, Las Vegas, Nevada, 1994, The Silk Way, Las Vegas, 1996, Sun Zhong Shan in Am.-1911, L.A., 1997, 300 foot statue of Deng Xiao Ping in China, 1999; permanent displays include Nat. Art Mus., Beijing, Sichuan Art Mus., Chong Qing, China; exhibitions include Art Exhibition for six Famous Sculptors of China, Hong Kong, 1991, 14th World of Art Under One Roof, N.Y.C., 1992, Asian Art Exhibition, Korea, 1994, Nat. Chinese Sculpture Exhibition, Beijing, 1995, Sculpture Exhibition of Guo XuanChang, L.A., 1996; editor Calligraphy and Painting Collection of Eminent Chinese of Worldover, 1998. Recipient The Columbus Gold award L.A., 1994, Outstanding award Fine Art Assn. of China, 1994, Sculpture Achievement award L.A., 1998; featured in books including Selected Sculpture by Guo XuanChang, 1987, Encyclopedia of Living Artists, 1992, The World Famous Chinese Artists Almanac, 1996, The Eloqent Sculpture of Guo XuanChang, 1997, Calligraphy and Painting Collection of Eminent Chinese of World Over, 1998. Mem. World Assn. Chinese Artists (v.p. 1997, art achievement award 1997), Internat. Sculpture Ctr., China Sculpture Rsch. Inst. (dir. 1987), City Sculpture USA (pres. 1992). Avocations: outdoor sports, music, movies. E-mail: city@gus.net. Fax: (626) 333-8679. Home: 16151 La Monde St Hacienda Heights CA 91745-4253

GUO, YIZHU, chemist; b. Nankang, Jiangxi, China, May 9, 1967; came to U.S., 1996; s. xiuyan Guo and Bingfeng Feng; m. xia Jiang, Apr. 19, 1997. BS, Jiangxi (China) U., 1989; M, Changchun Inst. Applied Chemistry, Jinlin, China, 1992, PhD, 1995. Grad. rsch. asst. Changchun Inst. Applied Chemistry/Chinese Acad. Scis.; rsch. asst. Changchun Heat-Shrinkable Materials Co., Jilin; rsch. scientist U. P.R., San Juan, 1996-99, U. Calif., Berkeley, 1999—; cons. Chungchun Shrinkable Materials Factory, Jinlin, 1993-96. Rsch. fellow Dept. Energy, 1996, NIH, 1998, U.S. Navy Rsch. Office, 1999. Mem. Am. Chem. Soc., Sigma Xi. Office: U Calif Berkeley Dept Chem Engring 201 Gilman Hall Berkeley CA 94720-1401

GUO, YONG-MING, mechanical engineering researcher, educator; b. Shaoyang, China, Aug. 25, 1955; parents: Zhi-Ping Guo and Yi-Ping Jin; married; 1 child, Wen-Fang. BSc, Northwestern Poly. U., Xi'an, China, 1981; MSc, Chongqing (China) U., 1985; PhD, U. Electro-Comm., Tokyo, 1994. Lectr. Nanjing (China) U. Aeronautics and Astronautics, 1985-90; asst. prof. U. Electro-Comm., Tokyo, 1994-95, Kagoshima (Japan) U., 1995—. Contbr. articles to profl. jours. Mem. Japan Soc. for Tech. of Plasticity. Avocations: sports, music, computers, movies. Office: Kagoshima U Dept Mech Engr, Korimoto 1-21-40, Kagoshima 890-0065, Japan

GUO, ZHIXIONG, mechanical engineer; b. Hunan, China. BS, Tsinghua U., 1989, MS, 1991, PhD, 1995. Lectr. Tsinghua U., Beijing, 1994-95; rschr. KAIST, Taejon, South Korea, 1995-96; from rschr. to rsch. assoc. Tohoku U., Sendai, Japan, 1996-99; rsch. scientist Poly. U., Bklyn., 1999—. Mem. Japan Soc. Mech. Engrs. Office: Poly U Mech Engring Dept 333 Jay St Brooklyn NY 11201-2907

GUOZHANG, XIE, physicist, educator; b. Feng Cheng, Jiangsi, China, June 18, 1929; s. Xie Jufong and Cao Dengu; m. Wu Hezheng; children: Xie Ling, Xie Meiling. B Engring., Tsing Hua U., Beijing, 1951. Rschr. Inst. Applied Physics Acad. Sci. of China, Beijing, 1951-58; rschr. Inst. Chem. Engring. and Electro-Mechanics, Changzhou, China, 1958-65; sr. engr., rschr. The Semiconductor Factory, Changzhou, China, 1965-85; prof. physics Hehai U., Changzhou, 1985-95; prof. physics, dir. Inst. Micromechanism Tech., Changzhou, 1995—; adv. Acad. Sci. Hong Kong, Am. Biographical Inst., Internat. Biographical Ctr., Eng.; dep. dir. gen. Acad. Sci. Hong Kong. Author: The Translation Skill on Science and Technology English, 1987, The Fabrication and Application of Micromechanism, 1991; contbr. over 100 articles to profl. jours. Mem. Electronic Assn. (bd. dirs. 1982), Tsing Hua U. Alumni Assn. (bd. dirs. Changzhou br. 1981—). Achievements include discovering a metastable phase in AB alloy and the invention of a new technique for fabricating high temp CMOS. Avocations: chess, physical training. Address: 85-2-301 S Lao Don Xin Cun, Changzhou, Jiangsu 213001, China

GUPTA, AJIT, civil engineer; b. Meerut City, India, Sept. 8, 1946; s. Indra Kumar and Nirmal (Goel) G.; m. Saroj Jain, Mar. 13, 1971; children: Amit, Anuj. BTech with honors, IIT, Kharagpur, India, 1970. Site engr. Holst & Co., Watford, England, 1970-71; sr. site engr. William Press, London, 1971-74; mng. dir. Rapid Engring. Co. Pvt. Ltd., New Delhi, 1974—. E-mail: rapidcoat@vsnl.com. Home: D-701 Kaveri Apts Alaknanda, New Delhi 110 019, India Office: Rapid Engring Co Pvt Ltd, 112 DSIDC Phase 1 Okhla, New Delhi 110020, India

GUPTA, ASHOK KUMAR, physicist, researcher; b. Shahjahanpur, U.P., India, Jan. 1, 1944; s. Surendra Datt and Savitri Devi G.; m. Usha Gupta, Mar. 6, 1967; children: Vivek, Manish. BSc, Agra U., India, 1962; MSc, Banaras Hindu U., India, 1964; MS, Case Inst. Tech., Cleve., U.S., 1969; PhD, Case Western Reserve U., Cleve., U.S., 1971. Rsch. assoc. Case Western Reserve U., Cleve., 1971-73; sci. officer BHEL, Hyderabad, India, 1974-77; sr. scientist Nat. Phys. Lab., New Delhi, India, 1977-83, asst. dir., 1983-88; sr. asst. dir. Nat. Phys. Lab., New Delhi, 1988-91, dep. dir., 1991-96, scientist (dir. grade), 1996—. Editor: (book) Progress in High Temperature Superconductivity Vol. 16, 1988; contbr. over 100 papers to profl. jours, 18 chpts. to books; presenter 100 rsch. papers at sci. seminars or symposiums. Fellow Indian Cryogenics Coun. (Merit scroll, 1978, A.N. Chatterlee Meml. medal, 1990), Metrology Soc. India; mem. Materials Rsch. Soc. India (life mem., MRSI-ICSC award 1992), Indian Physics Assn. (life mem.), Semiconductor Soc. India (life mem.), Indian Sci. Congress Assn. (life mem.). Avocations: photography, reading literature. Home: DII/4 NPL Colony, New Rajendra Nagar, New Delhi 110060, India Office: Nat Phys Lab Cryogen Divsn, Dr KS Krishnan Rd, New Delhi 110012, India

GUPTA, BAL K., physicist, researcher; b. Meerut, India, May 1, 1954; came to U.S., 1992; s. Deepchand and Kunti Gupta; m. Sarita Gupta, June 17, 1979; children: Shilpa, Pratyush. PhD, Indian Inst. Tech., New Delhi, 1978. Sr. design engr. Indian Inst. Tech., 1978-90; rsch. scientist Aarhus (Denmark) U., 1990-92; rsch. assoc. Ohio State U., Columbus, 1992-95; staff engr. Seagate Tech., Mpls., 1995-98; prin. engr. Read-Rite Corp., Fremont, Calif., 1998—. Author: Solar Selective Surfaces, 1981, translated into Russian, 1984, Handbook of Tribology: Materials, Coatings, & Surface Treatments, 1991; contbr. over 45 articles to profl. peer-reviewed jours.; patentee in field. E-mail: balgupta@home.com. Home: 4356 Diavila Ave Pleasanton CA 94588-8376

GUPTA, BALDEV RAJ, linguistics educator, writer; b. Chhamal, Sialkot, Pakistan, July 8, 1942. MA in Sanskrit, Phi Univ., 1963; MA in Punjabi, Punjabi U., 1976, postgrad. diploma in French, 1971; PhD in Linguistics, Panjabi U., 1975. Tchr. Tamil, Ctr. Continuing Edn., Jammu, 1979-82, coord. Tamil courses, 1999—; prof. Punjabi, U. Jammu, 1986—, head dept., 1989-91, 93-96, 99—. Author: (in Punjabi) Sheik Farid Di Bhasha, 1976, Bhasha Vigyan Te Punjabi Bhasha Di Banar, 1981, Bhasha Vigyan, Lipi Aur Lok Sahit, 1985, (short stories) Rachama Samarpan, 1993, Jammu Kashmir Vich Prakaskit Panjabi Sahit, Bhashagat Chinian, 1991, (in Hindi) Bhasha Vigyan, (in English) Indian Linguistics Punjabi Tamil Phonology; translator Tamil into Punjabi, Tamil into Hindi, Jammu and Kashmir; contbr. numerous articles to linguistic jours. Mem. linguistic instns. Office: U Jammu, A-20 New Univ Campus, 180 006 Jammu India

GUPTA, BRAJ BANSH PRASAD, endocrinology educator; b. Awari, Bihar, India, Feb. 15, 1959; s. Hardeo Prasad and Khatrani Gupta; m. Laxmi Gupta, Feb. 24, 1978; children: Poonam, Nilima, Rekha. Degree, Adarsh Seva Vidyalaya Coll., India, 1974; BSc with honors, Banaras Hindu U., India, 1976, MSc in Zoology, 1978, PhD, 1982. Rsch. assoc. Banaras Hindu U., Varanasi, India, 1983-84; lectr. North Eastern Hill U., Shillong, India, 1985-90; reader North Eastern Hill U., Shillong, 1990—. Contbr. articles to profl. jours. Rsch. fellow DAAD, Germany, 1989-91, sr. fellow, 1995; fellow Zool. Soc., Calcutta, 1999. Mem. European Soc. Comparative Endocrinology, Asia and Oceania Soc. Comparative Endocrinology, Indian Soc. Gen. and Comparative Endocrinology (life), Soc. Reproductive Biology and Comparative Endocrinology (life), Indian Soc. Environ. Endocrinology (life), Indian Pineal Rsch. Group (life), Indian Soc. Chronobiology (life). Hindu. Avocations: gardening, music, writing, football, driving. Office: Dept Zoology, North Eastern Hill U, Shillong 793022, India

GUPTA, BRAJMOHAN DAS, publisher; b. Varanasi, India, Sept. 25, 1940; s. Krishnadas and Bela (Bahu) G.; m. Asha Gupta, Feb. 28, 1963; children: Archana, Taru, Jaya, Shilpa, Sachin Kumar. B Comm., Banaras Hindu U., Varanasi, 1961. Dir. Chowkhamba Sanskrit Series Office, Varanasi. Home: K37/118 Gopal Mandir Ln, 221001 Varanasi India Office: Chowkhamba Sanskrit Series, K37/99 Gopal Mandir Ln, 221001 Varanasi India

GUPTA, CHHITAR MAL, research scientist; b. Bharatpur, Rajasthan, India, Sept. 1, 1944; s. B. L. and C. G.; m. Savita Khandelwal, June 26, 1970; children: Manish, Nivedita. BS, Rajasthan U., 1964, MS, 1966; PhD, Agra U., 1969. Postdoctoral fellow Inst. Molecular Biology, Calif., 1973-75; rsch. assoc. MIT, Cambridge, 1975-78; scientist CDRI, Lucknow, India, 1978-92; dir. IMT, Chandigarh, India, 1992-97, CDRI, Lucknow, India, 1997—; vis. scientist MIT, Cambridge, 1981; scientist SRF, JRF, CDRI, Lucknow, 1966-73. Recipient Bhatnagar prize CSIR, Delhi, 1985, Ranbaxy Rsch. award Ranbaxy Rsch. Found., Delhi, 1985, others. Fellow Indian Acad. Scis., Nat. Acad. Scis. Office: Cen Drug Rsch Inst, Cahttar Manzil MG Marg, 226001 Lucknow India

GUPTA, DHARMA PRAKASH, mathematics educator, researcher; b. Thakurdwara, Moradabad, India, July 27, 1928; arrived in Can., 1988; s. Bhikhari Lal Agarwal and Ram Pyari; m. Shashi Prabha, Dec. 3, 1953; children: Priti, Stuti, Aparna. BSc, U. Allahabad (India), 1948, MSc, 1950, DPhil, 1959, DSc, 1972. Chartered mathematician Inst. Maths. and Its Applications, Eng. Asst. prof. U. Sagar (India), 1952-61; lectr. in maths. Regional Engring. Coll., Allahabad, India, 1961-63, reader in maths, 1963-72, prof. maths., 1972-77, 79-80; prof., head Higher Petroleum Inst., Tobruk, Libya, 1977-79; prof., head dept. engring. scis. U. Tech., Brega, Libya, 1980-88; vis. prof. Toronto U., 1988-95; vis. scientist Calgary (Can.) U., 1972; vis. prof. Kuwait U., 1981, Lakehead U., Thunder Bay, Can., 1990, York U., Toronto, 1991-92; supr. thesis, 1970-96, adv. Contbr. 50 articles to math. jours., 150 revs. Mathematical Reviews, USA, Zentralblatt fur Math., Germany, 1961-96. Fellow Inst. Math. and Its Applications; mem. Allahabad (India) Math. Soc. (pres.), Indian Sci. Congress (life), Indian Sci. Congress (life), Indian Math. Soc. (life mem.), Am. Math. Soc., Rotary Club (Allahabad), Vigyan Bharati (chief coordinator). Home: 19/2 Hastings Rd, 211001 Allahabad 211001, India

GUPTA, DINESH CHANDRA, accountant, educator; b. Mandsaur, India, Feb. 15, 1962; s. Bagdiram Ji and Dhapu (Bai) G.; m. Sarita Gupta, May 24, 1987; children: Sandeep, Sneha. BCom, Vikram U., Ujjain, India, 1982, MCom, 1984; MPhil, Devi Ahilya U., Indore, India, 1989, PhD, 1999. Chartered acct. Asst. prof. Govt. Coll., Badnawar, India, 1986-96, Govt. Postgrad. Coll., Mandsaur, India, 1996—. Office: Govt Post Grad Coll, Mandsaur India

GUPTA, GIRDHARILAL SADURAM, economics educator; b. Talchiri, India, May 1, 1941; s. Saduram and Narmada S. (Gupta) G.; m. Lalita Girdharilal, Jan. 30, 1963; children: INdu, Jaya, Manish. BA, M.S. U., Baroda, India, 1962, MA, 1964; PhD, Johns Hopkins U., 1970. Lectr. econs. Indian Inst. Mgmt., Ahmedabad, 1970—; vis. prof. Ill. State U., Normal, 1982, 83, 85-86, 90; prof. U. Sains Malaysia, 1993-94, 97-98; vis. scholar Indsl. Credit and Investment Corp. India, Bombay, 1976; cons. Resource Mgmt. Corp., Bethesda, Md., 1968, Managerial Econs., 1988. Co-author: Managerial Economics: Concepts and Cases, 1977, Teching Manual for Managerial Economics: Concepts and Cases, 1978, Marine Fish Marketing in India, 1984, Inland Fish Marketing in India, 1985; contbr. numerous articles to U.S., Malaysian and Indian jours. Mem. bd. studies in econs./mgmt., acad. couns. and adv. bds. several Indian univs.; cons. various govt. and pvt. orgns., including food and agr. orgns., Internat. Coop. Alliance and Res. Bank of India; mem. sales tax adv. com. Govt. of Gujarat, 1977-78. Johns Hopkins U. fellow; Indian Govt. scholar; Univ. Merit scholar; gold medalist. Mem. Indian Econometric Soc. (exec. com. 1978-79, 89-90), Indian Econ. Assn., Gujarat Econ. Assn., Rajasthan Econ. Assn. Avocations: indoor sports, badminton. Office: Indian Inst Mgmt, Ahmedabad, Gujarat 380015, India

GUPTA, HARI MOHAN, physicist, educator; b. Bhinmal, Rajasthan, India, Oct. 21, 1944; arrived in Brazil, 1976; s. Radhe Mohan and Kamala Devi (Mital) G.; m. Indu Mital, Dec. 6, 1970; children: Charu, Navin. BSc, Jodhpur U., 1963, MSc, 1965; PhD, Udaipur U., 1971. Asst. prof. Udaipur (India) U., 1965-76; vis. prof. Univ. Fed. do Espirito Santo, Vitoria, Brazil, 1976-79, Inst. de Fisica e Quimica de São Carlos- U. São Paulo, San Carlos, Brazil, 1979-81; asst. prof., assoc. prof. UNESP, Rio Claro, Brazil, 1981-95; prof. UNESP, Rio Claro, 1995—. Contbr. articles to profl. jours. Mem. Soc. Brazilian Physicists. Achievements include studying current voltage characteristics of Schottky Barriers, tunneling in metal insulator metal structures. Home: Av 5 No 940, 13500380 Rio Claro SP, Brazil Office: IGCE Dept Physics, Rua 10 No 2527, 13500230 Rio Claro SP, Brazil

GUPTA, KANTESH, mathematics educator, researcher; b. Khatauli, India, July 10, 1949; d. Vishambher Sahai and Moorti (Devi) G.; m. Kamal K. Mittal; children: Aasheesh, Ankur, Anshul. MSc, Meerut U., 1976, MPhil, 1981; PhD, Rajasthan U., Jaipur, 1988. Lectr. S.S. Jain Subodh Degree Coll., Jaipur, 1979-83; lectr., reader Malaviya Regional Engring. Coll., Jaipur, 1983—; papers presented 1st Internat. Conf. on Vibration Problems of Math. Elasticity, Jalpaiguri, 1990, annual conf. Indian Math. Soc., Muzzafarpur, 1993, Indian Sci. Congress Assn., Jaipur, 1994. Author: Advanced Mathematics for Engineers, 1996; contbr. articles to profl. jours. including Acta Ciencia India, Proceedings Indian Nat. Sci. Acad., Indian Jour. Tech., India Jour. Pure Applied Math., Ganita Sandesh, among others. Mem. Indian Sci. Congress Assn., Indian Math. Soc., Indian Soc. for Tech. Edn., Am. Math. Soc., London Math. Soc., Rajasthan Ganita Parishad. Home: 4/30 Malviya Nagar, Jaipur 302017, India Office: Malviya Regional Engr Coll, Dept Math, Jaipur India

GUPTA, KISHAN CHAND, psychologist; b. Alawal Pur, Punjab, India, Mar. 19, 1932; came to U.S., 1972; s. Shri Mela Ram and Bhagwanti Gupta; m. Raj Kumari Aggarwal, Dec. 7, 1955; children: Shailesh, Neeraj. BA, Punjab U., India, 1952; BE, Jamia Millia Islamia U., New Delhi, 1954; MA in Psychology, Aligarh Muslim U., India, 1959; postgrad. cert. in counseling psychology, Cen. Bur. Edn. and Vocat. Guidance, 1961; course in vocat. rehab., Gov. India Ministry of Employment and Tng., New Delhi, 1962; D of Spl. Edn., U. Liverpool, England, 1970. Cert. psychologist, Coun. Nat. Register Health Svc. Providers Psychol., Ohio; lic. psychologist, Ohio. Head Tchrs. Tng. Dept., Rhotak, India, 1954-55; sr. tchr. psychology Tchrs. Tng. Inst. Panjab Civil Svc., India, 1955-61; regional sch. counselor Divisional Insp. Schs., Ambala, India, 1961; employment counselor Sub-Regional Employment Exch., Patiala, India, 1961-63; clin. psychologist child guidance clinic coll. nursing Ministry of Health, New Delhi, 1963-72, dir. child guidance clinic coll. nursing, 1966-69; staff psychologist, adminstrn. specialist V Western Res. Psychiat. Hosp., Northfield, Ohio, 1972—; mem. faculty of arts Delhi U., India, 1965-68; sec. Delhi Soc. for the Welfare of Retarded Children, 1966-70; part-time cons. Family Life Ctr., New Delhi, 1970-72; part-time faculty Cuyahoga Cmty. Coll., Cleve., 1972-73; faculty psychologist N.E. Clergy Tng. Inst., Hawthornden State Hosp., 1972-75; cons. S.E. Cmty. Mental Health Ctr., Cleve., 1974-75; part-time psychologist Shaker Heights, Ohio, 1974-78. Contbr. articles to profl. jours. Cons., clin. dir. Lorain County Ctr. for Youth Services, 1979-83. Recipient Commonwealth scholarship U. Liverpool, U.K., 1969-70. Hindu. Home: 1875 Surrey Pl Gates Mills OH 44040-9757 Office: North Coast Behavioral Health Svcs South Campus PO Box 305 Northfield OH 44067-0305

GUPTA, LAXMAN DAS (GAHOI VAISH), utility executive; b. Kanpur, India, Nov. 30, 1947; s. Babu Ram and Ganga Devi Gupta; m. Shashi Kala Mahendru, Jan. 5, 1973; children: Ruchi, Nidhi. BSc in Engring., Kanpur U., 1969; M in Tech., Indian Inst. Tech., Bombay, 1972; diploma in mktg., Maharaja Sayaji Rao U., Baroda, India, 1975. Trainee elec. engr. Jkrayon, Kanpur, 1969-70; devel. engr. Jyoti Ltd., Baroda, 1972-75; sr. engr. Engrs. India Ltd., New Delhi, 1975-80; dep. gen. mgr. Nat. Thermal Power Corp. Ltd., New Delhi, 1980—; cons. Gautam Electric Motors, New Delhi, 1975-80; mem. vis. faculty Indian Engring. Inst., New Delhi, 1975-80; ptnr. Coral Consultants, New Delhi, 1975-80; mediator Lawyers Engaged in Alternative Dispute Resolution (LEADR), Australia, 1999—. Pres. NTPC Housing Soc., Faridabad, India, 1990-93, GV Assn., Delhi, 1992-95; gen. sec. Saket Enclave SFS Assn., Delhi, 1993-94. Mem. IEEE (India and U.S.). Avocations: chess, tracking, gardening, travel, reading, music. Home: C-14/2 DDA SFS Flats Saket, New Delhi 110 017, India

GUPTA, MANOJ, materials scientist, educator; b. New Delhi, Dec. 28, 1961; s. Ramesh Chand and Rajdulari (Singhal) G.; m. Neerja Goel, June 27, 1993; 1 child, Neelabh. B in Engring., Visvesveraya Regl. Coll. Engr., Nagpur, India, 1984; M in Engring., Indian Inst. Sci., Bangalore, 1987; PhD, U. Calif., Irvine, 1992. Rsch./sales engr. Encon Thermal Engrs., New Delhi, 1984-85; project engr. Aero. Devel. Agy., Bangalore, 1987-88; rsch./tchg. asst. U. Calif., 1989-92; postdoctoral fellow U. Alta., Can., 1992; pool officer Nat. Phys. Lab., New Delhi, 1993; assoc. prof. materials sci. Nat. U. Singapore, 1993—; cons. in field; rep. of Singapore at Asian-India workshop on advanced materials Nat. Sci. and Tech. Bd., 1995. Contbr. more than 100 articles to internat. jours., conf. procs. Recipient Gold medal Indian Inst. Sci., 1987, award at ann. metallography competition APMI/MPIF, San Francisco, 1992; rsch. grantee Ameritherm Inc., 1989; selected as amb. from Singapore by Minerals, Metals and Materials Soc. Bd., U.S., 1997. Mem. Minerals, Metals and Materials Soc., Singapore Microscopy Soc. Hindu. Avocations: skating, racket games, recreational hiking. Office: Nat Univ Singapore Dpet MPE, 10 Kent Ridge Crescent, Singapore 129788, Singapore

GUPTA, MUNISHWAR NATH, biochemistry educator, researcher; b. New Delhi, June 25, 1948; s. Maharaj Kishore and Jal Devi Gupta; m. Sulbha Karandikar, Jan. 17, 1975; 1 child, Chetan. BSc, Delhi U., 1967; MSc, Indian Inst. Tech., Delhi, 1969; PhD, Indian Inst. Sci., Bangalore, 1975. Lectr. Indian Inst. Tech., Delhi, 1975-83; asst. prof. Indian Inst. Tech., 1984-90, prof., 1990—; vis. prof. U. Minn., 1978-79, U. Compiegne, France, 1996; rsch. assoc. Mass. Inst. Tech., 1988, Chemistry Ctr., Lund, Sweden, 1990. Editor: Thermostability of Enzymes, 1993; mem. editl. bd. Bioseparation; contbr. numerous articles to profl. jours. Nat. Sci. Talent Search fellow Nat. Coun. Ednl. Rsch. & Tng., India, 1964-73. Mem. Soc. Biol. Chemists (life). Office: Dept Chemistry IIT, Hauz Khas, New Delhi 110016, India

GUPTA, NARENDRA KUMAR, electrical engineering educator; b. Arrah, Bihar, India, Sept. 11, 1947; arrived in Eng., 1970; s. Bishwa Nath and Janaki (Devi) G.; m. Chandra Kala, Dec. 15, 1976; children: Vikas Kumar, Aditya Kumar. BSc Elec. Engring., Ranchi U., India, 1969; postgrad. diploma in Tech. Sci. Elec. Power Engring., U. Manchester Inst. Sci. Tech., Eng., 1972, PhD, 1986; M in Tech. Power Electronics, Brunel U., Eng., 1976; MBA, Napier U., Edinburgh, 1996. Practical trainee Agartala Power House, Tripura, India, 1970; elec. and tech. planning asst. Staveleys Ltd., Atherton, Eng., 1970-71; applications engr. grade I and II Gec-General Signal Ltd., London, 1972-76; devel. engr. grade I and II Gec-General Signal

Ltd., Manchester, Eng., 1976-78; sr. asst. engr. Nchanga Consolidated Copper Mines, Kitwe, Zambia, 1978-80; devel. engr. grade III, prin. engr. in theoretical studies Gec-General Signal Ltd., Manchester, Eng., 1980-87; lectr. dept. elec., electronics and computer engring. Napier U., Edinburgh, Scotland, 1987—; com. mem. edn. and tng. BNCE, London, 1990-96; ednl. devel. and svcs. com. mem. Napier U., Edinburgh, 1993-96. Mem. IEEE USA (sr. mem.), IEE London (chartered engr., com. mem. edn. and tng. 1990-97, chmn. 1996-97, vice-chmn. editl. adv. panel Engring. Sci. and Edn. Jour., mem. editl. adv. panel Engring. Mgmt. Jour., mem. profl. gorup com. M6 bus. mgmt. in the marketplace, vice-chmn. sci. edn. and mgmt. sect.), Inst. Rlwy. Signal Engrs. London,. Hindu. Avocations: reading, swimming, gardening, meeting people. Home: 66 Langton View East Calder, West Lothian EH53 ORA, Scotland Office: Sch Engring Napier U, 10 Colinton Rd, Edinburgh EH10 5DT, Scotland

GUPTA, NARINDER KUMAR, mechanical engineer, educator; b. Mirpur, India, Aug. 22, 1942; s. Krishan Lal and Pushpa Gupta; m. Rashmi Gupta; children: Shivanshu, Shalav. BS in Physics, J&K U., 1960; BSME, Regional Engring. Coll., Srinagar, 1966; PhD, Indian Inst. Tech., Delhi, 1973. Assoc. lectr. Regional Engring. Coll., Srinagar, India, 1967-68; from rsch. fellow to assoc. prof. Indian Inst. Tech., New Delhi, 1968-86, prof., 1987—; visitor Cambridge (U.K.) U., 1977, 81, UMIST, U.K., 1988, 90, 92, 93, 96; AvH fellow Ruhr U., Bochum, Germany, 1981, 85, 90; vis. prof. Sci. U., Tokyo, 1991, U. Cape Town, South Africa, 1996; Erskine fellow U. Canterbury, New Zealand, 1995. Editor: Plasticity and Impact Mechanics, 1993, 96; co-editor: Stress Waves in Solids, 1973, Large Deformations, 1978, 84; mem. editl. adv. bd. Internat. Jour. Impact Engring., Internat. Jour. Mech. Scis., Internat. Jour. Crashworthiness, Internat. Jour. Thin-walled Structures; contbr. articles to profl. jours. Recipient Padamshri, Govt. India, Humboldt rsch. award. Fellow Indian Nat. Acad. Engrs., Nat. Acad. Scis. (India), Aero. Soc. India, Instn. of Engrs.; mem. Indian Internat. Centre, Indian Soc. Theoretical and Applied Mechanics (life, pres. 1995-97), Indian Soc. Mech. Engring. (life, pres. 1996-98, 98-2000), Indian Soc. Tech. Edn. (life), Soc. Indsl. and Applied Math. (life), Indian Soc. Advancement Material and Process Engring. (life), Aeronautical Soc. India (life), Soc. Engring. Sci. Avocations: painting, classical Indian music. E-mail: nkgupta@am.iitd.ernet.in. Home: 36 West Ave, iit Delhi, Hauz Khas, New Delhi 110 016, India Office: Dept Applied Mechanics, Indian Inst Tech Hauz Khas, New Delhi 110 016, India

GUPTA, NIRMAL, gynecologist and obstetrician, educator; b. Nasirabad, India, July 29, 1950; d. Chand Mal and Vimla Gupta; m. Ramesh Chandra Gupta, Jan. 19, 1976; children: Tanu Shri, Mayank. Student, Maharani Coll., Jaipur, India, 1967; MBBS, Sawai Mansingh Med. Coll., Jaipur, 1972, MS in Gynecology and Obstetrics, 1976. Clin. tutor gynecology and obstetrics Ravinder Nath Tagore Med. Coll., Udaipur, India, 1976-77; asst. prof. gynecology and obstetrics Sawai Man Singh Med. Coll., Jai[ur, 1977-78, Jawaharlal Nehru Med. Coll., Ajmer, India, 1978-97; asst. prof. gynecology and obstetrics Govt. Med. Coll., Kota, India, 1997-98, assoc. prof., 1998—; cons. Ravindra Nath Tagore Med. Coll., 1976-77; sr. cons. Sawai Mansingh Med. Coll., 1977-78, J.L.N. Med. Coll., 1978-97, Govt. Med. Coll., 1997—. Author: Therapeutic Apheresis, 1997, Artificial Orgnas, 1998; contbr. articles to profl. juors. Surgeon, Mobile Surg. Camps in Rural Areas, Udaipur, 1976-97; gynecologist Family Welfare Programme, Udaipur, 1976-97; gynecologist and obstetrician Health Camps, Ajmer, 1978-97. Mem. Fedn. Gynecol. and Obstet. Socs. India, Indian Socs. Apperess, Indian Med. Assn. Avocations: guitar, badminton, reading. Home: Gulab Bagh, Sheetla Mata Temple, 305001 Ajmer, Rahasthan India Office: Med Coll Kota, Mahaveer Nagar, 234 005 Kota, Rajasthan India

GUPTA, NIRMAL KUMAR, marketing educator, consultant; b. Kota, Rajasthan, India, Aug. 20, 1961; s. Pooran Prakash and Satya Wati (Goyal) G.; m. Parvinder Kaur, Oct. 9, 1994. BSc, U. Rajasthan, Jaipur, 1980, MSc in Physics, 1982, MBA, 1984, PhD, 1988. Asst. prof. U. Rajasthan, Jaipur, 1984-86; rsch. assoc. Indian Inst. Mgmt., Ahmedabad, India, 1987-88; assoc. prof. S.P. Jain Inst. Mgmt., Mumbai, India, 1989-90, Mgmt. Devel. Inst., Gurgaon, India, 1990-94; prof. S.P. Jain Inst. Mgmt., Mumbai, 1994-96, program dir., 1995-96, chmn. mktg. area, 1995-96, mktg. educator, 1997—. Editor: Managing Transition, 1994, Management Research, 1994. Recipient best case writing award Assn. Indian Mgmt. Schs., 1992, 93, best rsch. paper award, 1992, 93, Best Tchr. award, 1994. Fellow Acad. Mktg. Sci.; mem. Am. Mktg. Assn., N.Am. Soc. Mktg. Edn. in India (bd. dirs.), Soc. Mktg. Advances. Avocations: national chess playing, cricket, wildlife conservation, missionary work. Home: T-13 IIM Campus, Vastrapur, Ahmedabad 380 015, India

GUPTA, PRATIBHA, medical educator; b. Vanasthali, India, Oct. 9, 1946; d. Prakash Chandra and Savitri Devi (Bindal) Goyal; m. Chandra Prakash Gupta, Dec. 4, 1973; two children. MB, BChir, Rajasthan U., India, 1968, MD, 1976. Demonstrator UCMS & GTB Hosp., Delhi, 1971-78, lectr., 1978-80, 82-86, reader, 1987-94, prof., 1995—; lectr. Kufa Coll. Medicine, Iraq, 1980-82; vis. scientist Respiratory Divsn., London, 1986; rsch. scientist Royal Infirmary Hosp., London, Glasgow, Scotland, 1988. Author: Dusty Dawn, 1996; co-editor, author: Fundations and Frontiers, 1994; cnotbr. chpts. to books. Pres. Bharat Vikas Parishad, East Delhi Br., 1988. Recipient award All India Sci. Contest Envirotech., Delhi, 1995; Fulbright scholar Sch. Medicine, 1993-94. Fellow Internat. Med. Sci. Acad.; mem. Nat. Acad. Med. Scis., Assn. Physiologists and Pharmacologists (life, H.H. Loeschake 1988), Indian Assn. Occupational Health (life), Internat. Soc. Environ. Epidemiology. Home: E-14 Hosp Res Campus, Delhi 110095, India Office: UCMS & GTB Hosp, Dilshad Garden, Delhi 110095, India

GUPTA, PRAVEEN, insurance company executive; b. Jaipur, Rajasthan, India, Sept. 7, 1956; s. Anand Swaroop and Tushti (Bharadwaj) G.; m. Medha Desai, Sept. 4, 1983; children: Amiya, Vandana. BA, Sch. Basic Scis.-Humanities, Udaipur, India, 1975; MA, St. Stephen's Coll., Delhi, India, 1977. Divsnl. mgr. New India Assurance Co. Ltd., Baroda, 1988-91; br. mgr. New India Assurance Co. Ltd., Bangkok, 1991-93; mgr. New India Assurance Co. Ltd., Hong Kong, 1993-2000, Gen. Accident plc, London, 1998; rep. office Gen. Accident plc, Mumbai, India, 1998-2000; gen. mgr. bus. devel. Allianz AG, Bombay, India, 2000—; alt. bd. dirs. Asian Hull Syndicate, Hong Kong. Exch. fellow Rotary Found., 1984. Fellow Ins. Inst. India (D. Subrahmaniam award 1990, S.K. Desai Meml. award 1995), Chartered Ins. Inst. (assoc.). Avocations: reading, nature walks, music, creative writing. E-mail: praveengupta56@hotmail.com. Home: B-404 Eternia Hiranandani Gardens, Powai Mumbai 400 076, India Office: 125 Maker Chambers VI, Nariman Point Bombay 400 076, India

GUPTA, RADHA RAMAN, chemistry educator, editor, researcher; b. Rajgarh, Alwar, India, Aug. 18, 1941; s. Goverdhan Dass and Sampati Devi G.; m. Vimla Gupta; children: Vandana, Archana, Rajni, Lokesh Mohan. BSc, Raj Rishi Coll., Alwar, India, 1961; MSc in Chemistry, U. Rajasthan, Jaipur, India, 1963, Cert. in Modern European Langs., 1967, PhD in Chemistry, 1968. Asst. prof. Rajasthan U., 1968-86, assoc. prof. chemistry, 1986—; rschr. Munich (Germany) U., 1981-82, Aix Marseille (France) III U., 1980-81; vis. scientist Kiel (Germany) U., 1985, Sarbrücken (Germany) U., 1991; NRC vis. lectr. several univs. in Brazil, 1996; Cancer fellow Cancer Rsch. Lab., Auckland, New Zealand, 1990; mem. Internat. Adv. Bd. for Reversal of Drug Resistance, Szeged, Hungary, 1995-96; mem. Internat. Biog. Ctr., Eng.; mem. internat. com. Phenothiazines and Structurally Related Compounds, 1989-93, chmn., 1993-96. Author: Heterocyclic Chemistry, Vols. I and II, 1998; editor, author 5 vols. in Landolt Börnstein Series, 1997, 98, 2000; editor-in-chief Heterocyclic Comms., 1995—; editor, author for several internat. monographs. Grantee UGC, CSIR, Internat. Orgns., ICMR, others. Mem. Internat. Soc. Heterocyclic Chemistry, Indian Sci. Congress, Internat. Soc. Antimicrobal Activity of Non-Antibiotics. Home: 10A Vasundhara Colony, 302018 Jaipur India Office: U Rajasthan Dept Chemistry, Gandhi Nagar, 302004 Jaipur India

GUPTA, RAJ KUMAR, physics educator, researcher; b. Narwana, Haryana, India, June 18, 1938; s. Basant Lal and Kamla Devi; m. Shashi P. Gupta, June 22, 1965; children: Rahul, Rathin. BA, Panjab U., Chandigarh, India, 1959, BSc with honours, 1961, MSc with honours, 1962, PhD, 1967. Lectr. fellow Alexander von Humboldt Stiftung, Germany, 1973-76; reader physics Viswa Bharti, Santiniketan, India, 1977-78; prof. physics Panjab U., 1987—; assoc. mem. Internat. Ctr. Theoretical Physics, Trieste, Italy, 1981-93; guest prof. J.W. Goethe U., Frankfurt, Germany, 1993-95; W.E. Heraeus guest prof. J.-L. U., Giessen, Germany, 1991-92; vis. fellow chemistry dept. U. Newcastle upon Tyne, Eng., 1994. Co-editor: Heavy Elements and Related New Phenomena, 2 vols., 1999; contbr. articles to profl., gen. and internat. jours., rev. articles at internat. and nat. confs. Recipient Hari Om award and gold medal Shri H.C. Shah Rsch. Endowment; Postgrad. fellow Nat. Rsch. Coun. Can., 1965-69, UNESCO-IAEA fellow Internat. Ctr. Theoretical Physics, 1971, Univ. Grants Commn. India nat. fellow Panjab U., 1993-95; rsch. grantee Volkswagen Stiftung, Germany. Mem. Indian Phys. Assn. (exec. com. 1981-86), Indian Assn. Physics Tchrs. (life), Nat. Soc. Sci. Crafts and Creative Arts (chn. 1997—, Nat. Sci. Day award). Hindu. Avocations: reading, writing, discussion. Home: 418 Sector 37A, Chandigarh 160036, India Office: Panjab U, Physics Dept, Chandigarh 160014, India

GUPTA, RAJAT KUMAR, lawyer, accountant; b. New Delhi, Apr. 22, 1960; came to U.S., 1970; s. Ravindra Kumar and Rama G. BBA, Rutgers Coll., New Brunswick, N.J., 1978-82; JD, Rutgers U., Newark, 1985-88. Bar: N.J. and Pa. 1989, U.S. Tax Ct. 1992; lic. CPA. Staff acct. Borrelli & Assoc's., Highland Park, N.J., 1983-84, S. Kirschenbaum & Co., CPA, East Brunswick, N.J., 1984-85; tax assoc. Coopers & Lybrand, Princeton, N.J., 1988-89; pvt. practice atty. New Brunswick, 1989-98; sr. assoc. Spevack & Cannan, P.A., Iselin, N.J., 1998—; vol. Acct's. for the Public Interest, N.J., 1991—; mentor Rutgers Law Sch., Seton Hall Law Sch., Asian and Pacific Law Students Assn. Prodn. editor Rutgers Computer & Technology Law Jour., 1987-88, Cannonball-One Lap of America, 1988: contbr. articles to profl. jours. Arbitrator Better Bus. Bur., Newark, 1986-87; vol. atty. Rutgers U. Off Campus Housing Ctr., 1996—; mem. com. on character N.J. Supreme Ct., 1997—. Mem. ABA, Asian and Pacific Lawyers Assn. N.J., N.J. State Bar Assn, mem. Middlesex Co. Bar Assn. Hindu. Avocations: tennis, travel, photography, astronomy. Office: Spevack & Cannan PA 525 Green St Iselin NJ 08830-2618

GUPTA, RAJEEV KUMAR, computer software consultant; b. Ujjain, India, Jan. 14, 1968; s. Anil Kumar and Ved Vati Gupta; m. Kiran R. Gupta, June 15, 1992; 1 child, Sagar. B in Computer Sci. and Engring., Kamla Nehru Inst. Tech., Sultanpur, India, 1989; diploma in devel. econs., Indira Gandhi Inst. Devel. Rsch., 1991; diploma in Gemology, Indo-Am. Soc., Bombay, 1996. Rsch. analyst, asst. Indira Gandhi Inst. Devel. Rsch., Bombay, 1990-94; cons. Nortel No. Telecom, Dallas, 1994-97, MCI Telecom., Colorado Springs, Colo., 1997-98, Lucent Techs., Warren, N.J., 1998-99, Security Industry Automation Ctr., Bklyn., 1999-2000; with Lehman Bros., 2000—. Mem. IEEE Computer Soc. (sr.), Nat. Geog. Soc., Indian Sci. Congress Assn., United Writers Assn., World Wide Fund Nature. Avocations: astronomy, amateur radio, bird watching, writing. Fax: 732-926-8149. Office: Internet Archs Inc 80 Royal Dr # 314 Piscataway NJ 08854-3017

GUPTA, RAJENDRA KUMAR, meterologist, remote sensing technologist educator; b. Alwar, Rajasthan, India, Feb. 18, 1946; s. Jagadish Prasad and Kailash Rani Gupta; m. Shashi Bala Gupta; children: Sweta, Shilpa. BSc, U. Rajasthan, Jaipur, India, 1965, MSc in Physics, 1967; PhD in Physics, Jawaharlal Nehru Technol. U., Hyderabad, India, 1991. Lectr. dept. edn. Govt. of Rajasthan, 1967-70; sr. sci. asst. Indian Inst. Tropical Meteorology, Pune, 1970-72, jr. sci. officer, 1972-79; head sys. engring. and meteorology cell Nat. Remote Sensing Agy., Hyderabad, 1979-82, head satellite meteorology sect., 1982-88, head tng. group, 1988—; chmn. Nat. Symposium in Advanced Techs. in Meteorology, 1995; organizer UN/ESCAP workshop on remote sensing and sustainable development, 1996; convenor nat. seminar Can. Internat. Devel. Agy and European Space Agy. on microwave remote sensing; main sci. organizer, editor Cospar Symposiums, Washington, 1992, Nagoya, Japan, 1998, Warsaw, 2000; presenter numerous confs., symposia in field. Contbr. numerous articles to profl. jours., chpts. to books; inventor in field. Fellow Andhra Pradesh Acad. Scis., Inst. Electronics and Telecomm. Engrs., Indian Geophys. Union; mem. Indian Meteorol. Soc. (life, nat. exec. coun. 1993-97), Indian Soc. Remote Sensing (life), Indian Nat. Cartographic Assn. (life). Avocations: management and economics, social welfare activities. Home: E-8 NRSA Housing Complex, Manovikasnagar Hashmathpet, Secunderabad 500 009, India Office: Nat Remote Sensing Agy, Balanagar, Hyderabad 500 037, India

GUPTA, RAM NIWAS, research mathematician, educator; b. Delhi, India, July 15, 1942; s. Hukam Chand and Misri Devi Gupta; m. Usha Kumari Jain, June 19, 1976; children: Madhuri, Shalini. BA, Ramjas Coll., 1961, MA in Math., 1963; PhD of Math., Delhi U., 1967. Lectr. Ramjas Coll., Delhi, 1963-68; asst. prof. U. Fla., Gainesville, 1968-69, UCLA, 1969-70; reader, prof. Punjab U., Chandigarh, India, 1970—; vis. prof. Simon Fraser U., Burnaby, Can., 1990-91. Mem. Am. Math. Soc., Indian Math. Soc., Indian Sci. Congress Assn. Avocations: walking, gardening. Office: Dept Math, Panjab Univ Dept Math, Chandigarh 160014, India

GUPTA, RAMESH CHANDRA, medical educator, epidemiologist, researcher; b. Bharatpur, India, July 25, 1948; s. Suraj Bhan and Sampati Devi Gupta; m. Nirmal Gupta, July 29, 1950; children: Tanushri, Mayank. MBBS, Sawai Man Singh Med. Coll., Jaipur, India, 1971, MD, 1975. Clin. tutor in medicine Sawai Man Singh Med. Coll., 1975-76, Ravindra Nath Tagore Med. Coll., Udaipur, India, 1976-77; asst. prof. medicine Jawahar Lal Nehru Med. Coll., Ajmer, India, 1978-89; assoc. prof. medicine J.L.N. Med. Coll., Ajmer, India, 1989-96, prof. medicine, 1999—; prof. medicine Kota (India) Med. Coll., 1996-99; cons. physician Med. Coll. Jaipur, Udaipur, 1975—; med. tchr. Med. Coll. Jaipur, Ajmer, and Kota, 1975—, rschr., 1975—; dir. med. unit Jawahar Lal Nehru Med. Coll., 1993-96, 99—, Med. Coll. Hosp. Kota, 1996—. Contbr. articles to profl. jours. Med. cons. and epidemiol. rschr. Mobile Surg. Camp, rural areas of Rajasthan, India, 1976-95. Travel grantee U.G.C., New Delhi, 1995, Japan Soc. Apheresis, Nagasaki, 1997, Kyoto, 1996. Fellow Indian Coll. Physicians; mem. Internat. Soc. Apheresis (travel grantee 1996, Kyoto), Internat. Soc. Artificial Organs, Indian Med. Assn. (Best Worker award 1984), Assn. Physicians of India (joint sec. 1984-85), Indian Soc. Transplantation, Indian Soc. Apheresis (pres. 1993—). Avocations: golf, reading. Fax: 0145-422375. Home: Gulab Bag, Near Sheetla Mata Temple, Ajmer 305001, India Office: Medical College, Rang Bari Rd, Kota India

GUPTA, RISHAB KUMAR, medical association administrator, educator, researcher; b. Nagina, Utter Pradesh, India, Apr. 18, 1943; came to U.S., 1965; s. Sahu Harbans Lal and Chandravati (Devi) G.; m. Mridula Gupta, May 2, 1972; children: Arvind, Anita. MSc, G.B. Plant U., Pantnagar, India, 1965; MS, PhD, Rutgers U., 1968. Asst. rsch. oncologist UCLA Sch. Medicine, 1972-75, assoc. rsch. oncologist., 1975-79, asst. prof., 1979-81, assoc. prof., 1981-85, prof., 1985-92; v.p., dir immunodiagnosis John Wayne Cancer Inst., Santa Monica, Calif., 1992—; mem. study sect. NIH, Bethesda, Md., 1989-92; spl. grant reviewer Med. Rsch. Coun. Can., 1991. Editorial bd. Contemporary Oncology, 1991—; Contbr. articles to med. jours. Pres.'s fellow Am. Soc. for Microbiology, 1967; Rsch. grantee Calif. Inst. for Cancer Rsch., UCLA, 1973-75, U. Calif. Cancer Rsch. Com., 1973, 74, 81, Nat. Cancer Inst/NIH, 1981-90. Mem. Am. Assn. for Cancer Rsch., Am. Assn. Immunologists, Am. Soc. for Clin. Oncology, Am. Acad. Microbiology, Am. Soc. Microbiology. Achievements include definition, isolation, and characterization of tumor associated antigens that are immunogenic in cancer host from cultured and biopsy tumor cells; development of monoclonal antibodies to these antigens and untilization of these in immunoassays to detect the antigens in body fluids of cancer patients and determine their clinical significance in terms of immunodiagnosis and immunoprognosis. Home: 7118 Costello Ave Van Nuys CA 91405-3307 Office: John Wayne Cancer Inst 2200 Santa Monica Blvd Santa Monica CA 90404-2302

GUPTA, ROHIT BHRAM, chemical engineer; b. Bombay, July 3, 1969; s. Bhram Sarup and Santosh Bhram (Aggarwal) G.; m. Priti Rohit Gupta, Dec. 6, 1994. B Engring., U. Mass., 1992. Project head Ducon Equipment Pvt. Ltd., Bombay, 1992-94, dir. market devel., 1994-97; mng. dir. Peenar Tech. (divsn. Nuwave Pvt. Ltd.), Mumbai, India, 1997—. Avocations: sports, music, reading. Home: 6 Alpana, 2d Fl, Pedder Rd, Bombay 400 026, India Office: Peenar Tech, PO Box 9316, Cumballa Hill Mumbai 400 026, India

GUPTA, SANJAY, psychiatrist; b. Bombay, Sept. 24, 1959; s. Parkash Ram and Sarla Rani; m. Sadhna Kayastha, Jan. 14, 1992; 1 child, Sheila. MD, The U. Delhi, India, 1984. Diplomate Am. Bd. Psychiatry and Neurology, Am. Bd. Forensic Examiners, Am. Bd. Addiction Medicine, Am. Bd. Forensic Medicine, Am. Bd. Geriat. Psychiatry, Am. Bd. Adolescent Psychiatry. Resident in psychiatry SUNY, Syracuse, 1987-91; rsch. fellow U. Iowa Hosps. and Clinics, Iowa City, 1991-94; asst. prof. psychiatry U. Nebr., Omaha, 1994-95; clin. assoc. prof. psychiatry health scis. ctr. SUNY Health Scis. Ctr., 1996—; clin. assoc. prof. dept. psychiatry U. Buffalo, 1997—; rschr. brain imaging U. Iowa, 1991-94; examiner Am. Bd. Psychiatry & Neurology Examinations, 1993-95; bd. advisors profl. standards Am. Bd. Forensic Medicine, Springfield, Mo., 1995-96; dir. psychiatry Olean (N.Y.) Gen. Hosp., 1995—, chmn. dept. psychiatry, 1997—; spkr. in field. Contbr. articles to profl. jours. Travel fellow Am. Coll. Neuropsychopharmacology, 1992. Mem. Am. Psychiat. Assn., Am. Assn. Geriatric Psychiatrists, Am. Bd. Forensic Examiners, Internat. Soc. Neuroimaging in Psychiatry, Am. Assn. Physicians from India, U. Iowa Alumni Assn. Hindu. Achievements include involvement in trials of new drugs for schizophrenia. Office: Psychiatric Network Olean Gen Hosp W 2221 W State St Olean NY 14760-1921

GUPTA, SANTOSH KUMAR, chemical engineer, educator; b. Allahabad, India, July 19, 1946; s. Har Swarup and Durgawati Rani Gupta; m. Sulochana Agrawal, July 11, 1970; children: Aatmeeyata, Akanksha. B Tech., Indian Inst. Tech., Kanpur, 1968; PhD, U. Pa., 1972. Postdoctoral fellow U. Pa., Phila., 1972-73; asst. prof. chem. engring. Indian Inst. Tech., 1973-80, prof., 1980—, head chem. engring. dept., 1987-89; vis. prof. U. Notre Dame, Ind., 1985-87, Nat. U. Singapore, 1998-99, U. Wis., Madison, 1999-2000; referee rsch. papers in field; mem. editl. bd. Jour. Polymer Engring., 1995—, Indian Chem. Engr., 1994-95; cons. editor textbook series in chem. engring. Allied Pubs., 1993-98; series editor IITK, 1993-2000; mem. chem. engring. rsch. adv. com. Indian Petrochems. Corp. Ltd., Vadodara, 1984-90; mem. program adv. com. for thrust area funding in chem. engring. Dept. Sci. and Tech., New Delhi, 1984; lectr., cons. in field. Author: Reaction Engineering of Step-Growth Polymerization, 1987, Numerical Methods for Engineers, 1995; contbr. over 160 articles to profl. jours. Recipient Herdillia award for excellence in rsch. Indian Inst. Chem. Engrs., 1987. Fellow Indian Acad. Scis. Avocation: poetry. Office: Indian Inst Tech, Dept Chem Engring, Kanpur 208016, India

GUPTA, SATISH KUMAR, scientist, researcher; b. Chhachhrauli, Haryana, India, Apr. 20, 1953; s. Gur Prasad and Satya Rani Gupta; m. Rita Gupta, Dec. 4, 1980; children: Ashish, Manish. BSc, Delhi (India) U., 1973; MSc, All India Inst. Med. Scis., Delhi, 1976; PhD, All India Inst. Med. Scis., New Delhi, 1983. Cert. scientist. Rsch. officer Nat. Inst. Immunology, Delhi, 1982-85, sr. rsch. officer, 1985-89, from staff scientist IV to staff scientist V, 1989-98, staff scientist VI, 1998—; short-term cons. WHO, Dir, Korea, 1992; vis. scientist Inst. Pasteur, Paris, 1984, Lab. Molecular Biology, Medical Rsch. Coun., Cambridge, Eng., 1990, 92, 93; vis. fellow Jones Inst. Reproductive Medicine, Norfolk, 1987-88. Editor: (books) Immunology: Perspectives in Reproduction and Infection, 1991, Prospects of Zona Pellucida Glycoproteins, 1996, Reproductive Immunology, 1999; inventor in field. Recipient Indian Nat. Sci. Acad. Young Scientist Acad. medal, 1982, Shakuntala Amir Chand prize Indian Coun. Medical Rsch., 1984, Shanti Swarup Bhatnagar prize CSIR, 1997. Fellow Nat. Acad. Scis. Allahabad, 1994, Indian Acad. Scis., 1999; mem. Internat. Soc. Immunology of Reproduction (coun. mem. 1998-01). Avocations: listening to music, gardening. E-mail: skgupta@nii.res.in. Home: N-47 Greater Kailash-I, New Delhi 110048, India Office: Nat Inst Immunology, Aruna Asaf Ali Marg, New Delhi 110 067, India

GUPTA, SATYA PRAKASH, chemistry educator, researcher; b. Gonda, India, June 20, 1945; s. Gur Prasad and Banarasa (Devi) G.; m. Kanak Lata Mittal, Nov. 22, 1972; children: Salil Prabhakar. BSc, Allahabad U., India, 1965, MSc, 1967, D Phil, 1971. Sr. vis. mem. TIFR, Bombay, 1971-73; asst. prof. BITS, Pilani, 1973-82, assoc. prof., 1982-90, prof., 1990—. Author: Quantum Biology, 1996; inventor in field of drug design. Recipient Ranbaxy award Ranbaxy Rsch. Found, 1989. Fellow Nat. Acad. Sci. Avocation: reading. Home: B 323 B Vidya Vihar, Pilani 333031, India Office: Birla Inst Tech and Sci, Dept Chemistry, Pilani 333031, India

GUPTA, SATYANDRA KUMAR, mechanical engineering educator, researcher; b. Mathura, India, July 25, 1967; s. S.N. and Sushma Gupta; m. Sanyukta Purwar, June 3, 1994; 1 child, Swati Gupta. BE in Mech. Engring., Roorkee (India) U., 1988; MTech in Prodn. Engring., Ind. Inst. Tech., Delhi, 1989; PhD in Mech. Engring., U. Md., 1994. Scientific officer, Numerical Control Lab. Indian Inst. Tech., Delhi, 1990; rsch. assoc., Inst. Systems Rsch. U. Md., College Park, 1994; project scientist, Robotics Inst. Carnegie Mellon U., Pitts., 1995-96, rsch. scientist, Robotics Inst., 1996-98, adj. asst. prof. indsl. adminstrn., 1997-98; asst. prof. mech. engrg. Inst. Systems Rsch., U. Md., 1998—, assoc. dir. Computer Integrated Mfg. Lab., 1998—; guest rschr. NIST, 1999—; invited spkr. numerous seminars, 1993—; various offices numerous ASME Confs., 1994—, including papers chair Design for Mfg. conf., 1999, exhibit chair Design Engring. tech. conf., 2000. Contbr. chpts. to books, numerous articles to profl. jours. and conf. procs.; patentee in field; guest editor spl. issue Computer Aided Design Jour., 2000. Mem. ASME (awards and honors chair design for mfg. com., Best Paper awards 1994, 99), Soc. Mfg. Engrs. Fax: 301-314-9477. E-mail: skgupta@eng.umd.edu. Office: U Md 2135 Martin Hl Bldg 088 College Park MD 20742-0001

GUPTA, SUDHIR, immunologist, educator; b. Bijnor, India, Apr. 14, 1944; came to U.S., 1971; s. Tej S. and Jagdishwari Gupta; m. Abha, Jan. 28, 1980; children: Ankmalika Abha, Saurabh Sudhir. MD, King George's Med. Coll., Lucknow, India, 1966, PhD, 1970. Diplomate Am. Bd. Allergy and Immunology, Am. Bd. Diagnostic Lab. Immunology, Clin. Immunology Bd., Royal Coll. Physicians and Surgeons Can. Intern King George's Med. Coll., Lucknow, 1966, resident in medicine, 1967-70; teaching faculty fellow dept. medicine Tufts U. Med. Sch., Boston, 1971-72; vis. fellow in medicine Columbia U., N.Y.C., 1972-74; rsch. fellow Sloan-Kettering Inst. Cancer Rsch., N.Y.C., 1974-76, asst. prof., 1976-78, assoc. prof., 1978-82; instr. Cornell U., N.Y.C., 1976-77, asst. prof., 1977-79, assoc. prof., 1979-82; prof. medicine U. Calif., Irvine, 1982—, prof. microbiology and molecular genetics, 1984—, prof. pathology, 1986—, prof. neurology, 1988—, vice chair Dept. Medicine, 1994—; mem. adv. panel FDA, Washington, 1989—; sci. advisor Inst. Immunopathology, Kohn, Germany, 1990—; mem. allergy-immunology subcom. NIH, Bethesda, Md., 1985-89; vis. prof. Hematologic Rsch. Found., Roslyn, N.Y., 1992. Editor-in-chief Jour. Clin. Immunology, 1980—; editor: Immunology of Clinical and Experimental Diabetes, 1984, Mechanisms of Lymphocyte Activities and Immune Regulation I-VII, 1985-98, New Concepts in Immunbodeficiency Diseases, 1993, Multidrug Resistance in Cancer, 1996, Immunology of HIV Infections, 1996. Pres. Nargis Dutt Meml. Found., So. Calif., 1990; vice-chair AIDS Task Force, Orange County (Calif.) Med. Assn., 1987-95; mem. Indo-Am. Republican Club, Orange County, 1991—. Recipient Arthur Manzel Rsch. award R.A. Cooke Inst., N.Y.C., 1976, Outstanding Achievement award in med. scis. Nat. Fedn. Asian Indians in N.Am., 1986, Lifetime Achievement award Jeffrey Modell Found., N.Y.C., 1990, Disting. Scientists award Assn. Scientists Indian Origin in Am., 1994, Disting. Physician award Indian Med. Assn. Master ACP; fellow Royal Coll. Physicians and Surgeons Can., Am. Soc. Medicine (London); mem. Am. Assn. Immunologists. Achievements include description of the presence of K+ channels in human T cells, their role in T cell function and assn. with exptl. autoimmune diseases, reversal of multidrug resistance of cancer cells by cyclosporin A both in vitro and in vivo, described a new human intracisternal retrovirus associated with CD4+ cell deficiency without HIV infection; increased apoptosis in T cells in human aging. Fax: 949-824-4362. E-mail: sgupta@uci.edu. Office: U Calif Dept Medicine C240 Med Sci I Irvine CA 92697-0001

GUPTA, SURAJ NARAYAN, physicist, educator; b. Haryana, India, Dec. 1, 1924; came to U.S., 1953, naturalized, 1963; s. Lakshmi N. and Devi (Goyal) G.; m. Letty J.R. Paine, July 14, 1948; children: Paul, Ranee. MS, St. Stephen's Coll., India, 1946; PhD, U. Cambridge, Eng., 1951. Imperial Chem. Industries fellow U. Manchester, Eng., 1951-53; vis. prof. physics Purdue U., 1953-56; prof. physics Wayne State U., Detroit, 1956-61, disting. prof. physics, 1961-99; disting. prof. physics emeritus Wayne State U., 1999—; researcher on high energy physics, nuclear physics, relativity and gravitation. Author: Quantum Electrodynamics, 1977. Fellow Am. Phys. Soc., Nat. Acad. Scis. of India. Achievements include quantum theory with negative probability and quantization of the electromagnetic field; flat-space

interpretation of Einstein's theory of gravitation and quantization of the gravitational field; regularization and renormalization of elementary particle interactions; development of the theory of bound states in quantum electrodynamics and quantum chromodynamics; mass matrix formulation of quark mixing and CP violation in weak interactions; investigation of phenomena at supercollider energies. Home: 30001 Hickory Ln Franklin MI 48025-1566 Office: Wayne State U Dept Physics Detroit MI 48202

GUPTA, SURESH CHAND, physicist, researcher; b. New Delhi, June 2, 1943; s. Duli Chand and Saraswati Devi Gupta; m. Jyotsna Goel, May 8, 1970; children: Neeraj, Anuradha. BSc with honors in Physics, U. Delhi, India, 1962, MSc in Physics, 1964, PhD, 1974. Cert. solid state physicist. Jr. sci. officer Solid State Physics Lab., Delhi, 1965-71, sr. sci. officer II, 1971-78, sr. sci. officer I, 1978-83, scientist D, 1983-87, scientist E, 1987-93, scientist F, 1993—, group head, 1987-93, additional dir., divisional head, 1993—. Contbr. articles to profl. jours., chpt. to book. Commonwealth postdoctoral fellow Commonwealth Scholarship Commn., Durham (Eng.) U., 1974-75, Alexander von Humboldt Found. fellow, Fraunhofer Inst., Freiburg, Germany, 1981-82; vis. fellow Royal Soc. London, Strathclyde (Scotland) U., 1991, 95. Mem. Indian Assn. Crystal Growth (life), Materials Rsch. Soc. India, Soc. Photo-Optical Instrumentation Engrs. Avocations: sports (cricket, badminton), music, reading sports magazines. Home: B-3/26 Safdarjung Enclave, Delhi 110029, India Office: Solid State Physics Lab, Lucknow Rd, Delhi 110054, India

GUPTA, UMA, psychology researcher, consultant; b. Meerut, India, Feb. 15, 1957; d. Jai Prakash and Subhashini Gupta. BA in Psychology with honors, Meerut U., 1975, MA in Psychology, 1978, MPhil in Psychology, 1979, PhD in Psychology, 1983. Jr. rsch. fellow Meerut U., 1983-84; gen. postdoctoral fellow Banaras Hindu U., Varanasi, India, 1986-88, Univ. Grants Commn. rsch. scientist A, 1988-93, Univ. Grants Commn. rsch. scientist B, 1993—. Editor: Advances in Psychopharmacology, Neuropsychology and Psychiatry, 1991, Advances in Environmental Toxicology and Social Ecology, 1992, Caffeine and Behavior: Current Views and Research Trends, 1999; contbr. articles to profl. jours.; asst. editor Pharmacopsychoecologia, 1988-93, editor, 1994—. Mem. Pharmacopsychoecol. Assn. (life), Indian Acad. Applied Psychology (life). Avocations: Indian music, Hindi poetry, acting, cooking. Home: c/o Prof BS Gupta Banaras Hindu U, Old D/5 Jodhpur Colony, Varanasi 221005, India Office: Banaras Hindu U, Dept Basic Prin Inst Med Scis, Varanasi 221005, India

GUPTA, VIJAY KUMAR, dairy scientist, researcher, educator, consultant; b. Shahabad Markanda, Haryana, India, Jan. 3, 1953; s. Suraj Bhan and Bhagwanti Devi Gupta; m. Ruby Gupta, June 26, 1980; children: Candy, Dipti. BSc in Dairying, Nat. Dairy Rsch. Inst., Karnal, India, 1973, MSc in Dairying, 1976, PhD in Dairying, 1982. Cert. dairy technologist. Tech. asst. Composite Milk Plant, Ludhiana, India, 1974; scientist S-1, asst. prof. Nat. Dairy Rsch. Inst., Karnal, 1977-84, scientist S-2, assoc. prof., 1984-85, sr. scientist, assoc. prof., 1986—; rschr. Nat. Dairy Rsch. Inst., Karnal, 1977—, tchr., 1978—, cons., 1980—. Inventor in field; contbr. rsch. articles to profl. jours. German Acad. Exch. Svc. fellow, 1985-86, German Acad. Exch. Svc. Reinvitation fellow, 1993; grantee Deutsche Gesellschaft fur Technische Zusammenarbeit, 1997. Mem. Indian Membrane Soc. (life), Assn. Food Scientists and Technologists India (life), Indian Dairy Assn. (life), Agrl. Rsch. Svc. Scientists Forum (life), Internat. Dairy Fedn. Group F 41. Avocations: computer operation, chess, carrom. Home: House #468 Sector 6, 132001 Karnal Haryana, India Office: Nat Dairy Rsch Inst, Dairy Tech Divsn, 132001 Karnal Haryana, India

GUPTA, VINOD KUMAR, internist, researcher, ethicist; b. Jaipur, India, Mar. 23, 1954; s. Dharam Prakash and Saran (Malhotra) G.; m. Anjali Dhankani, May 10, 1979; 1 child, Vivek Gupta. MB BS, U. Rajasthan, 1976, MD, 1980. Jr. resident All India Inst. of Med. Scis., New Delhi, 1977-78; registrar in gen. medicine J.L.N. Med. Coll., Ajmer, India, 1978-79, sr. registrar in gen. medicine, 1979-80; cons. physician Panacea Med. Clinic, Delhi, 1980-85; gen. physician, med. dir. Emirates Diagnostic Clinic, Dubai, United Arab Emirates, 1985-87; specialist physician Al Rasheed Med. Clinic, Dubai, 1988-89; physician Dubai Police, 1989—. Author: Spirit of Enterprise, 1990 (Rolex award 1990); contbr. articles to profl. jours. Recipient Cert. of Merit Ministry of Edn. and Youth Svcs., Govt. of India, 1970-71, Lala Ramchander Meml. award, 1970-71, Merit scholarship Bd. of Secondary Edn., 1970-71, U. Rajasthan, 1973-75, Prize for Courteous Behavior and Svc. to Cmty. Rotary Internat., 1985, New Century award Barons 500, 1999, Leaders for the New Century. Achievements include creation of new theory of origin of migraine from the eye; elucidation of adaptive role of magnesium depletion, with special reference to the myocardial cell in acute myocardial infarction; reformation of ethical norms for handling of scientific correspondence by journal editors and conducting clinical trials in humans. Avocations: badminton, instrumental music, visiting foreign lands, philosophy, swimming. Office: Dubai Police Med Svcs, PO Box 12005, Dubai United Arab Emirates

GUPTHAR, ABINDRA SUPERSAD, biotechnologist, educator; b. Durban, South Africa, Oct. 11, 1961; s. Supersad and Urmilla (Boodhram) G. BSc, U. Durban-Westville, 1983, BSc with hons., 1984; MSc, U. Witwatersrand, South Africa, 1985; PhD, U. Witwatersrand, 1989. Jr. lectr. U. Witwatersrand, 1988; lectr. U. North, South Africa, 1989-90; lectr. U. Durban-Westville, 1991, sr. lectr., 1992-96, assoc. prof., 1997—. Contbr. articles to profl. jours. Mem. South African Biochem. Soc., Electron Microscopy Soc. So. Africa. Mem. African Nat. Congress. Avocations: sports, fishing, modern music. Office: U Durban Westville, P/Bag X54001, Durban 4000, South Africa

GURA, SARIT, artist; b. Tel-Aviv, May 19, 1952; d. Haim and rachel (Lipschitz) Shelein; children: Tal, Adi, Omer. Student art, 1976-80. Tchr. art Bd. of Edn., Tel-Aviv, 1996—. Artist-painter, 1971—; designer, prodr. of bronze, Tel-Aviv, 1995—; exhibited masks Sotheby's, Israel, 1995; design/sculpture and accessories in different medias, 1993—, Art Expo, N.Y., 1996, 98; auctions Engel Gallery, Opal Gallery, Kishon Gallery; pvt. exhbn. Soho, N.Y., 1991; restoration of miniatures, 1972-77. Jewish. Home and Office: Kam St 55/3, Tel Aviv Israel

GURAYA, SARDUL SINGH, zoology educator, researcher; b. Village Kotmajlis, Punjab, India, Oct. 12, 1930; s. Banta Singh and Nihal Kaur G.; m. Surinderpal Kaur, Mar. 11, 1962; children: Gurmeet, Harmeet, Rupa. BSc with honors, Punjab U., 1954, MSc with honors, 1956, PhD, 1959, DSc, 1971; PhD (hon.), Internat. U. Found., 1988. Asst. prof. Gorakhpur (India) U., 1960-62; postdoctoral fellow Population Coun., N.Y.C., 1962-64; pool officer CSIR, New Delhi, 1965-66, scientist emeritus, 1992-96; reader Udaipur (India) U., 1966-71; prof. Punjab Agrl. U., Ludhiana, India, 1971-92; prof. emeritus Punjab Agrl. U., Ludhiana, 1996-2000; head zoology dept. Punjab Agrl. U., Ludhiana, 1972-86; dean Coll. of Basic Scis. and Humanities, 1986-90; nat. lectr. UGC, Govt. of India, 1976-77; dir. ICMR Advance Regional Rsch. Ctr. in Reproductive Biology, 1982-91; mem. various adv. and expert coms. nat. and internat. scientific and ednl. orgns. and couns. Author 10 books; mem. editl. bd. various jours.; contbr. over 27 chpts. to books and over 375 articles to profl. jours. Recipient Gold medal 5th Internat. Congress of Animal Reproduction and Artificial Insemination, 1968, Bhatnagar prize, Bgsanti Devi-Amir Chand prize, various prestigious prizes and awards; fellow INSA, NAAS, NASC, FPAS. Mem. INSA (exec. coun. 1986-89), NAAS (exec. coun. 1991-98), Internat. Cell Rsch. Orgn., Nat. Com. for Rsch. on Human Reproduction, Exec. Ind. Soc. of Comparative Endocrinology, Ind. Soc. Invertebrate Reproduction, Soc. of Reproduction and Fertility. Avocations: long walks, observation of plants and animals in their natural habitats, fast cycling. Home: 32G Sarabha Nagar, 14001 Ludhiana India Office: Punjab Agrl U, Dept Zoology, 141104 Ludhiana India

GÜRÇINAR, YUSUF, architect, educator; b. Adana, Turkey, Mar. 2, 1954; s. Kemal and Neriman (Altinbüken) G.; m. Suna Kenanoğlu, July 2, 1992; children: Elif, Begüm. BS in Arch., Acad. Arch. and Engring., Ankara, 1979; M in Engring., Stuttgart (Germany) Tech. U., 1983, D in Engring., 1988. Chief designer U.S. Archtl. Office, Ankara, 1977-79; designer Jean Marie Hewig Arch. Office, Fareberswille, France, 1981-83, Dr. Stern GMBH Office, Obereslingen, Germany, 1982-83; lectr. Inst. Bldg. Economy, Stuttgart Tech. U., 1988-89; chmn. dept. arch. Çukurova U. Faculty Arch. and Engring., Adana, 1989-92, chmn. dept. int. arch., 1994—; assoc. prof. Çukurova U. Faculty Arch. and Engring., 1995; mem. Chamber of Archs. and Engrs., Ankara, 1989-92; vice chmn. Com. of Preservation of Cultural and Natural Heritage, Adana, 1991-95; mem., editor Environ. Rsch. Appl. Cent., Çukurova U., Adana, 1991-92; chmn. Com. on Environ. Studies, Adana Municipality, 1991-92, Adana Coop. Orgn. Ctr., 1993-95. Designer Misurata Twp. of Iron and Steel Complex at Weidleplan Archtl. Office, Stuttgart, 1977-79, Mosque and Cultural Ctr. projects, Fareberswille, France, 1981-83, Tech. Pk. Heidelberg Detail Project and Application, 1984, prefabricated mfr. of guard rails of stairways for Wilhelm Müssig Factory, 1986-87, archtl. projects of Çukurova U. Yumurtalik Rsch. Ctr., Adana, 1991, Satellite Town of Tchr., 1993, Satellite Town 4328 Bldg., 1994, 144 Residence 1st Phase of 1071 Bldg. Kadirli Satellite Town, 1995, Japanese Tea Ho. for Bot. Garden, Çukurova U., 1995, 58 residence and shopping ctr. 2d phase of 1071 Bldg. Kadirli Satellite Town, 1996, Adminstrn. Bldg. and Glass Ho. for Bot. Garden Çukurova U., 1996, Tech. Rsch. Ctr. Çukurova U., 1996; contbr. articles to profl. jours. Mem. adminstrv. com. Bot. Garden, Çukurova U., 1995. Res. officer Turkish Mil., 1983. Islamic. E-mail: yusgun@cu.edu.tr. Avocations: swimming, chess. Home: Çukurova Univ, Camlitepe Lojmanlari E Blok, 01330 Adana Balcali, Turkey Office: Çukurova U, Dept Interior Architecture, Adana Balcali, Turkey

GUREL, CIGDEM SECKIN, electronics engineer, researcher; b. Ankara, Turkey, Dec. 10, 1969; s. Ömer Lutfi and Asiye Gurel. BSc, Hacettepe U., Ankara, 1991, MSc, 1995; PhD, Hacettepe U., 2000. Rsch. asst. Hacettepe U., 1991—; rschr. Rsch. Found., Hacettepe U., 1997-98, Govt. Planning Orgn., Ankara, 1998—. Contbr. articles to profl. jours. PhD scholar Sci. and Tech. Rsch. Coun. Turkey, 1992-99. E-mail: cigdem@hacettepe.edu.tr. Home: 205 Sokak, 06374 Ankara Eryaman, Turkey Office: Hacettepe Univ Beytepe, Campus/Elec Engring Dept, 06532 Ankara Beytepe, Turkey

GUR'EV, NIKOLAI VICTOROVICH, chemist; b. Sovetskaya Gavan, Russia, Aug. 28, 1956; s. Victor Nikolaevich and Tatiana Nikolaevna (Sevruk) G. BS, St. Petersburg Inst. Tech., 1978, MS, 1979, DSc, 1984; postgrad., St. Petersburg State U., 1998—. Jr. rsch. scientist Scientific Ctr. S.I. Vavilov State Optical Inst., St. Petersburg, 1984-86, sr. rsch. scientist, 1986—; cons. to students St. Petersburg Inst. of Tech., Russia, 1987-94. Inventor in field; contbr. articles to profl. jours. Named Internat. Man of Yr., 2000. Mem. N.Y. Acad. Scis. Home: Tallinnskay St 12-49, 195196 Saint Petersburg Russia Office: Vavilov State Optical Inst, Babushkin St 36/1, 193171 Saint Petersburg Russia also: State U, Universitetskii St 2 Him, 198904 Saint Petersburg Russia

GUREVICH, AARON JA, historian; b. Moscow, Russia, May 12, 1924; m. Esther, 1945 (dec. Aug., 1997); 1 child, Elena. PhD, Moscow U., 1946; DSc (hon.), Lund U., 1992, Adam Mickiewicz U., 1996. Lector, prof. Pedagogical Inst., Tver, Russia, 1950-66; rschr. Inst. Philosophy, Moscow, 1966-69, Inst. Gen. History, Moscow, 1969—; prof. Moscow Lomonosov U., 1989—, Russian Univ. Humanities, 1993—. Author: Categories of Medieval Culture, 1985, Medieval Popular Culture, 1988, Historical Anthropology of the Middle Ages, 1992, The Origins of European Individualism, 1995. Home: Apt 100, 3 Malo-Moskovskaya, 129164 Moscow Russia

GUREVICH, ALEXANDER VICTOR, physicist, researcher; b. Moscow, Sept. 19, 1930; s. Victor Ber and Sofia Abraham (Tseitlin) G.; m. Galina Dmitrii Karelova, Feb. 27, 1955; children: Elena, Tatiana. MD, Moscow U., 1952; PHD, Lebedev Inst. Physics, Moscow, 1957, DSc, 1964. Cert. tchr. Chem. Coll., Schelkovo, 1952-53; jr. rschr. Inst. Terrestial Magnetism, Troitsk, 1954-57; jr. rschr. Lebedev Inst. Physics, Moscow, 1957-64, sr. rschr., 1964-79, group leader, 1979-94, dir. theoretical dept., 1994—; vis. prof. Köngle Stockholm U., 1987, Md. U., 1990, 91, 93, 95, Leicester (Eng.) U., 1991, 94; hon. Sacler prof. Tel-Aviv U., 1991; hon. Upson prof. Cornell U., Ithaca, N.Y., 1993; group leader Max-Planck Inst. Aeronomie, Germany, 1992-97. Author: Space Physics with Artificial Satellites, 1965, Nonlinear Phenomena in the Ionosphere, 1978, Physics of the Pulsar Magnetosphere, 1993, Physics of Microwave Discharge, 1997. Recipient Appleton prize Royal Soc. and URSI, 1990. Mem. Acad. Sci. USSR (corr., Landau prize 1980, Mandelstam prize 1993). Jewish. Avocations: skiing, mountain climbing. Home: Bolotnikovskaya 40-4-79, 113209 Moscow Russia Office: Lebedev Inst Physics, Leninskii Prospect 53, 117924 Moscow Russia

GUREVICH, ALEXANDR ILYICH, molecular biologist, researcher; b. Kursk, Russia, May 21, 1927; s. Ilya Efimovich and Maria Israilevna (Rashkovskaya) G.; m. Alexandra Vladimirovna Prochnova, July 1, 1953. Cand. Chem. Scis., Inst. Elemento-organic Comp., Moscow, 1961; Doctor of Chem. Scis., Shemyakin Inst. Bioorg. Chem., Moscow, 1973. Chemist, technologist Chemico-Pharm. Plant, Moscow, 1948-54; rschr. Zelinsky Inst. Organic Chemistry, Moscow, 1958-60; sr. rschr. Shemyakin Inst. Bio-Organic Chemistry, Moscow, 1960-87, leading rschr., 1988—. Coauthor: Chemistry of Antibiotics, vol.. I and II, 1961, Proteins and Peptides, 1995; contbr. articles to profl. jours. Home: ul Miklukho-Maklaya 65-4-44, 117342 Moscow Russia Office: Shemyakin Inst Bioorg Chem, ul Miklukho-Maklaya 16-10, 117871 Moscow Russia

GUREVICH, GRIGORY MANOVICH, physicist, researcher; b. Moscow, Nov. 28, 1935; s. Man Moiseevich Gurevich and Fanya Solomonovna Polyakova; m. Irina Fyodorovna Klementovich, Feb. 24, 1958; 1 child, Elena Grigoryevna. Student, Moscow State U., 1953-59; PhD, Lebedev Phys. Inst., Moscow, 1975. Jr. rsch. scientist Rsch. Inst. Instrumentation for Thermal Energetics, Moscow, 1959-62, Lebedev Phys. Inst., Russian Acad. Scis., Moscow, 1962-70; jr. rsch. scientist, sr. rsch. scientist, head of sect. Inst. for Nuclear Rsch., Russian Acad. Scis., Moscow, 1970—; guest scientist Moscow State U., 1984-97, Joint Inst. Nuclear Rsch., Dubna, Russia, 1984-99, Charles U., Prague, Czech Republic, 1989-98, Leuven (Belgium) U., 1996. Contbr. articles to profl. jours. Recipient Vet. medal City Coun. Moscow, 1987, Medal of Moscow, Pres. Russian Fedn., 1997. Mem. N.Y. Acad. Scis. Avocations: windsurfing, skiing. Fax: (095) 1352268. E-mail: gurevich@cpc.inr.ac.ru. Office: Inst Nuclear Rsch, 60th October Anniversary 7a, 117312 Moscow Russia

GUREVITCH, PAVEL SEMENOVICH, anthropologist, educator; b. Ulan-Ude, Russia, Aug. 13; s. Semen Moiseevich and Revekka Anufrievna (Mendelevich) G.; m. Eugenia Antonovna, Apr. 8, 1959; 1 child, Kristina. MA in Philology, Urals U., 1955; PhD, Moscow State U., 1965. Head editl. bd. Pravda Buriatii newspaper, Russia, 1955-61; editor-in-chief Burgitian TV, 1961-62; asst. editor-in-chief All-Union Radio & TV, Russia, 1965-70; sr. rschr. Sci. Coun. Modern Fgn. Philosophy, 1970-84; head dept. Inst. Philosophy, Russian Acad. Scis., 1984—; dean psychoanalytical dept. Moscow Inst. Psychology and Sociology, 1998—; prof. Inst. Social Scis., 1980-82. Author: Social Mythology, 1983, Is Mysticism Reborn?, 1984, Adventures of the Image, 1991, Philosophical Anthropology, 1997. Mem. Moscow Psychoanalytical Assn. (pres. 1997—), Union Journalists, Acad. Humanties Rsch. (v.p. 1995), Internat. Acad. Informatization. Avocations: soccer, classical singing. Office: Inst Philosophy, 14 Volkhonka St, 119842 Moscow Russia

GURGULINO DE SOUZA, HEITOR, government organization consultant; b. São Lourenço, Brazil, Aug. 1, 1928; arrived in Japan, 1987; s. Arthur Gurgulino and Catarina Sachser de Souza; m. Lilian Maria Quilici, Jan. 6, 1960; children: Carlos Eduardo, Gustavo Alberto. BS in Math., U. Mackenzie, São Paulo, Brazil, 1949, Lic., 1950; postgrad., Aeronautics Inst. Tech., São Paulo, 1951-55, U. Kans., 1955-56; doctorate (hon.), Autonomous U. Guadalajara, Mex., 1986, Fed. U. Espirito Santo, Vitoria, Brazil, 1987; D. Law (hon.), Calif. State U., 1997. Head of unit Orgn. of Am. States, Washington, 1962-69; rector Fed. U. São Carlos, São Paulo, 1970-74; dir. Ministry of Edn. and Culture, Brasilia, Brazil, 1972-74, Nat. Coun. for Sci. and Technol. Devel. (CNPq), Brasilia, 1975-78; pres. Grupo Univ. Latino-Americano (GULERPE), Brasilia and Caracas, Venezuela, 1985-87; rector UN U., Tokyo, 1987-97; spl. advisor to dir.-gen. UNESCO, Paris, 1997-99; chmn. Interam. Com. on Sci. and Tech. of OAS, Washington, 1974-77; mem. Fed. Coun. Edn., Brasilia, 1982-87. Contbr. ency. chpt.: International Encyclopedia of Higher Education, 1978; co-editor: Science Policy-Ed. Perspectiva, 1974. Recipient Order of Ednl. Merit, Ministry of Edn., 1973, Order of Rio Branco, Ministry of Fgn. Affairs, 1974. Mem. Brazilian Physics Soc., Brazilian Soc. Advancement of Sci., Am. Phys. Soc. Avocations: sailing, swimming, music. Fax: 33-1-5658-0780.

GURIAN, MAL, telecommunications executive; b. N.Y.C., Nov. 17, 1926; s. George Joseph and Rose (Graff) G.; m. Gloria Dickler; children: Randy Harlan, Nancy Ellen Newman. Ptnr. Mal Gurian Assocs., N.Y.C., 1946-77; v.p. Radio Telephone Corp., N.Y.C., 1960-83; sr. v.p. Aerotron, Inc., Raleigh, N.C., 1965-81; v.p. Oki Advanced Comm., Hackensack, N.J., 1981-84; pres. Oki Telecom, Fairlawn, N.J., 1984-88, Cartell, Inc., Romulus, Mich., 1988, Cellcom Cellular Corp., Fairfield, N.J., 1989-91; CEO Universal Cellular, Inc., Anaheim, Calif., 1992; chmn., CEO Global Link Comm., Inc., Irvine, Calif., 1993—; pres., CEO Authentix Network, Inc., Tucson, 1995-98, chmn., 1998—; pres. Ea. Profl. Photographers Assn., N.Y.C., 1951-53; exec. advisor TRW Wireless Commn., Sunnyvale, Calif., 1994; advisor Sims Comms., Inc., Delray Beach, Fla., 1994-98; arbitrator Am. Arbitration Assn., 1994—; bd. dirs. N.E. Digital Networks, Inc., Melville, N.Y., Rangestar Internat., San Jose, Calif. Life mem. Old Tappan (N.J.) First Aid Corp., 1966—. Cpl. USMC, 1943-46. Decorated Air medal; recipient Alexander S. Popov Hon. Medal award St. Petersburg Electrotech. U., Russia, 1995. Fellow and life mem. Radio Club Am. (life mem., v.p. 1976-92, exec. v.p. 1993, pres. 1994, pres. emeritus 1995—, Spl. Svcs. award 1986, Sarnoff citation 1988, Fred Link award 1989); mem. Am. Assn. Pub. Safety Comm. Officers, Nat. Assn. Bus. and Ednl. Radio (bd. dirs. 1977-84, Chmn.'s award 1986).

GURIRAB, THEO-BEN, Namibian government official; b. Usakos, Namibia, Jan. 23, 1938; married; 3 children. Tchrs. diploma, Augustinium Tng. Coll., Okahandja, Namibia; BA, Temple U., 1969, MA in Internat. Rels. Former rep. to N.Am. SWAPO, until 1972, mission chief to UN, 1972-77, former sr. advisor to pres., party spokesman; sec. for fgn. affairs Politburo, from 1986; former mem. senate for Namibia UN Inst.; mem. Constituent Assembly, 1989—; min. fgn. affairs Namibia, Windhoek, 1991—. Office: Min Fgn Affairs Govt Bldg 4 Fl, PvtBag 13347 Robt Mugabe Av, Windhoek Namibia*

GURLAND, HANS JUERGEN, internist, nephrologist; b. Riga, Latvia, Apr. 26, 1930; arrived in Germany, 1939; s. Ernst and Hedwig (Stahl) G.; m. Barbara Zimmermann, May 13, 1963 (div. 1987); 1 child, Christof.; m. Baerbel Schmidt, July 23, 1987. Student, U. Muenster, Westfalia, Germany, 1951-54; MD, U. Munich, Bavaria, Germany, 1957, prof. Internal Medicine, 1979. Diplomate German Bd. Internal Medicine and Nephrology. Chief dept. nephrology Klinik Grosshadern U. Munich, 1974-95; med. dir. Kuratorium Dialyse and Nierentransplantation, Neuried, Germany, 1995-97; mem. med. adv. bd. The Extramural Grant Program, Baxter, McGaw Park, Ill., 1989-91. Author of more than 400 publs.; editor: 10 books, 16 chpts. in books; mem. editl. bd. Kidney Internat., 1975-78, Artificial Organs, 1977-91, Life Support Systems, 1982-87, Blood Purification, 1983-98, Zeitschrift f. Urologie u. Nephrologie, 1984-90, Plasma Therapy and Transfusion Sci., 1984-98, Jour. Clin. Aphresis, 1984-98, Biomaterials, Artificial Cells and Artificial Organs, 1986-98, Internat. Jo our. Artificial Organs, 1988-94, Jour. of Nephrology, 1988—, Artificial Organs Today, 1989-98, Infusionstrhapie und Transfusionsmeizin, 1992-99, Advances in Renal Replacement Therapy, 1993-98. Named Hon. Mem. Czech Soc. Nephrology, 1988, Austrian Soc. for Artificial Organs, 1989, Polish Soc. Nephrology, 1992. Fellow Royal Coll. Physicians Edinburgh; mem. German Soc. Clin. Nephrology (coun. 1971-84), German Soc. Process and Chem. Engring. (bd. dirs. 1978-87), Internat. Soc. for Artificial Organs (pres. 6th world congress Munich 1987, pres. soc. 1990-92, Internat. Faculty for Artificial Organs (sen. mem. faculty 1990—, tenure prof. faculty 1992—), European Dialysis and Transplantation Assn. (chmn. registration com. 1969-76, coun. mem. 1971-74), European Soc. for Artificial Organs, (pres. 1994-96). Home: Nanette-Streicher-Strasse 5, D-86199 Augsburg Germany

GURLEY, ELISABETH ANNE, art historian, educator, writer; b. Boston, Mar. 5, 1927; arrived in Switzerland, 1994; d. Harold Coleman and Julia Josephine (Finnin) Ryan; m. Franklin Louis Gurley, June 17, 1950. Student, Boston U., 1947; BSc, Mass. Coll. Art, 1948, BFA (hon.), 1993; student, U. Paris and Ecole du Louvre, 1963-64. Supr. art edn. pub. elem. and high schs., Canton and Stoughton, Mass., 1948-49, pub. elem. and jr. high schs., Dedham, Mass., 1949-51; tchr. Avery Sch., Dedham, 1951-52; teen page editor Detroit News, 1956; juvenile editor Va. Kirkus Lit. Svc., 1957-58. Contbr. numerous articles on art history to profl. jours., newspapers and mags., 1970—; subject of articles in Life mag., 1952, La Liberte newspaper, Switzerland, 1988; paintings exhibited Zagora, Thessaly, Greece, 1992. Address: 1626 Romanens, Fribourg Switzerland

GURLEY, FRANKLIN LOUIS, lawyer, military historian; b. Syracuse, N.Y., Nov. 26, 1925; Swiss national, 1994 (dual nationality); s. George Bernard and Catherine Veronica (Moran) G.; m. Elizabeth Anne Ryan, June 17, 1950. A.B., Harvard U., 1949, J.D., 1952. Bar: Mass. 1952, N.Y. 1956, Ill. 1956, Mich. 1956, D.C. 1956. Fgn. service staff officer Dept. State, Washington and Germany, 1953-55; atty. N.Y. Central R.R. Co., 1955-56; asst. dist. atty. New York County, 1956-57; atty. firm Dewey, Ballantine, Bushby, Palmer & Wood, N.Y.C., 1957-63; gen. counsel, sec. IBM Europe Corp., Paris; also mng. atty. IBM Corp., Armonk, N.Y., 1963-68; sr. v.p., gen. counsel Nestle S.A., Vevey, Switzerland, 1968-83; spl. legal adv. Nestle S.A., Vevey, 1984-85; internat. legal cons., 1985—. Author: 399th in Action in World War II, 1946, (play) King Philip's War, 1952; chief editor Beachhead News (Germany), 1945-46; contbr. articles to profl. and mil. jours. Pres. Tappan Landing Assn. Tarrytown N.Y. 1958-60. Served with inf. AUS, 1944-46, ETO. Decorated Bronze Star, Combat Inf. Badge; 7th Army mile run champion, 1945; set West Point and Heptagonal 1000-yard records in track, 1948. Mem. SAR (sec., bd. mgrs. N.Y. chpt. 1957-63, founding mem. Swiss chpt. 1970), 100th Inf. Divsn. Assn. (historian 1984—). Home and Office: 1626 Romanens, Fribourg Switzerland

GURLING, HUGH MALCOLM, research scientist; b. London, May 6, 1950; s. Kenneth John and Nora (Sempill) G.; m. Meryl Joan Dahlitz; children: Holly, Laurel, Alisdair. MB BS, U. London, 1973, MD, 1989, MPhil, 1979. House physician, house surgeon King's Coll., London, 1973-74; sr. house officer Guy's Hosp., London, 1974-76; registrar Maudsley Hosp., London, 1976-79; lectr. Inst. Psychiatry, London, 1980, sr. lectr., 1984-86; reader molecular psychiatry U. Coll., London, 1989, prof. molecular psychiatry, 1996. Assoc. editor Psychiatric Genetics, 1989-99. Mem. Am. Soc. Human Genetics, NHS Support Fedn. Avocations: squash, windsurfing, politics. Office: Molecular Psychiatry Lab, 46 Cleveland St, London W1P 6DB, England

GURRI, GARCIA FRANCISCO DELFIN, research anthropologist; b. N.Y.C., Apr. 13, 1960; s. Delfin Gaspar Gurri and Guadalupe Maria Garcia. BA in Anthropology, NYU, 1985; MA in Anthropology, Ariz. State U., 1990; PhD in Anthropology, Ind. U., 1997. Investigator C INVESTAV, Unidad Merida, Mex., 1989-94; investigator A Ecosur, San Cristobal, Mex., 1997-99, coord., 1999—. Contbr. articles to profl. jours. and conf. procs. Home: St 12 # 339 San Roman, 24000 Campeche Mexico Office: Ecosur, St 10 # 3 264 X 61 Centro, 24000 Campeche Mexico

GURRIA TREVINO, JOSÉ ANGEL, Mexican government official; b. Mexico, May 8, 1950. BA in Econs., Nat. Autonomous U., 1972; MA in Pub. Fin., Leeds U., Eng.; studentInternat. Rels., U. So. Calif.; student Fin., Harvard U. Analyst Fed. Electricity Commn., Mexico, 1968-71; pvt. sec. to Sec. Gen. Fed. Dist. dept. Govt. of Mexico, Mexico City, 1971-74, pvt. sec. to dir. gen. pub. fin. dept.; permanent rep. Internat. Coffee Orgn., London, 1976-78; adv. pub. debt. Secretariat of Treasury, Mexico, 1978, dir. pub. debt., 1979; dir. gen. pub. credit, negotiator pub. fgn. debt Govt. of Mexico, Mexico City, 1983-88, undersec. internat. fin., negotiator free trade treaty, 1989-93; dir. gen. Nat. Bank for Fgn. Trade, Mexico, 1993-94; sec. fgn. affairs Govt. of Mexico, Mexico City, from 1995, now sec. fin. and pub. credit; Mem. Com. Internat. Affairs, Modernization and Ideology. Institutional Revolutionary Party. Office: Palacio Nacional ler, Patio Ctrl 3d Fl, Of 3045, 06606 Mexico City Mexico*

GURRY, DESMOND LEO, pediatrician; b. Edinburgh, Scotland, Dec. 23, 1933; s. Leo John and Mary Catherine (Snigg) G.; m. Patricia Ann Currie, Mar. 24, 1962; children: Karen, Tania, Ian. Matriculation, Xavier Coll., Melbourne, Australia, 1950; MBBS, U. Melbourne, 1956. Diploma of Child Health, London; diplomate Am. Bd. Pediatrics. Resident med. officer Prince Henry's Hosp., Melbourne, 1957-59; resident Princess Margaret Hosp. for Children, Perth, 1959-60; sr. house officer Children's Hosp., Sheffield, U.K.,

1965; registrar Alder Hey Children's Hosp., Liverpool, U.K., 1965-66; resident in pediatrics Case Western Res. U., Cleve., 1966-67; sr. lectr. in pediatrics U. Western Australia, Perth, 1969—; fellow Hosp. for Sick Children, Toronto, Can., 1973; vis. physician U. Childrens Hosp., Erlangen, Germany, 1976-77, Munich, 1980, Muenster, Germany, 1983-84, Beijing Children's Hosp., China, 1989-90, 94-95. Co-author: (book) Sea Stingers, 1986; co-editor: (book) The Impact of the Past upon the Present, 1992; contbr. articles and editorials to profl. jours.; author/guest editor: World Pediatrics and Child Care, 1985-86. Pediatrician, famine relief team Ethiopian Med. Action, Wollo Province, 1973-74; pres. Non-Smokers Movement of Western Australia, 1986-89; chmn., subcom. on neglect Western Australian Advisory and Coord. Com. on Child Abuse; councillor Australian Soc. of the History of Medicine, 1989—. Flt. lt. Royal Australian Air Force, 1957. Recipient stipends German Acad. Exch. Svc. (DAAD), Erlangen, 1976, Munich, 1980, Muenster, 1984. Fellow Royal Australian Coll. of Physicians; mem. Royal Coll. of Physicians/London, Australian Coll. of Edn., Internat. Coll. Pediatrics. Avocations: swimming, bush-walking, music, photography. Office: U Western Australia/Pediats, Princess Margaret Hosp Children, 6008 Perth Australia

GÜRS, KARL AUGUST, physicist; b. Frankfurt am Main, Germany, Nov. 5, 1927; s. Karl Hermann Albert and Katharina Anna (Bernhardt) G.; m. Ursula Emilie Preuschen, Apr. 7, 1960; children: Inge, Karl, Irmgard, Ursula. MS in Physics, Johann Wolfgang Goethe U., Frankfurt am Main, 1954; PhD, Johann Wolfgang Goethe U., 1959. Scientific asst. Frankfurt U., 1956-59, hon. prof., 1972; lab. mgr. Siemens AG, Munich, 1960-66; dept. mgr. Battelle Inst., Frankfurt, 1967-84, sr. rsch. leader, 1984-86; pvt. practice Eschborn, Germany, 1986—. Author: Laser, 1970, Optical Spectra of Ce and Pr in Solids, 1993, Optical Spectra of Nd in Solids, 1997; co-author: Halbleitertabellen, 1964, Laser, 1969, Table of Laser Lines in Gases and Vapors, 1976, 3d edit., 1980; patentee in field; contbr. over 50 articles to profl. jours. Mem. German Physical Soc., Physics Assn., Assn. Univ. Tchrs. Avocations: collection and preparation of fossils. Home & Office: Weissdornweg 23, 65760 Eschborn Germany

GÜRSES, METIN, physics educator; b. Hacibektas, Turkey, Apr. 2, 1945; s. Ismail and Selvi (Erdogan) G.; m. Ünsal Erdogan, Dec. 8, 1969; children: Derya, Can. BSc, Middle East Tech. U., Ankara, Turkey, 1969, MSc, 1972, PhD in Physics, 1975, habilitation, 1981. Asst. prof. physics Middle East Tech. U., 1976-79; vis. rschr. in physics Yale U., New Haven, 1973-75; vis. scientist Max-Planck Inst. for Astrophysics, Munich, 1979-81; sr. rschr. Tubitak Inst. Basic Scis., Gebze, Turkey, 1982-88; prof. physics Cukurova U., Adana, Turkey, 1988-91; prof. math. Bilkent U., Ankara, 1991—; chmnb. math. dept. Bilkent U., 1991-94; invited lectr. in field. Contbr. over 60 articles to refereed internat. jours., including Phys. Rev. Letters, Jour. Math. Physics, Jour. Classical and Quantum Gravity, and others. With Turkish Armed Forces, 1975, Ankara. Recipient Sedat Simavi Sci. award, Istanbul, Turkey, 1986, Encouragement award for Young Scientists, Tubitak, Ankara, 1984; Alexander von Humboldt fellow, Bonn, Germany, 1979, 87; sr. assoc. Internat. Ctr. Theoretical Physics, Trieste, Italy, 1997. Mem. Am. Math. Soc., Am. Phys. Soc., Internat. Soc. Gen. Relativity and Gravitation (life mem.), Turkish Phys. Soc., Turkish Math. Soc., Turkish Acad. Scis. Avocations: chess, table tennis. Office: Bilkent Univ, Dept Math, 06533 Ankara Turkey

GURUL, AYDIN, naval officer; b. Ankara, Turkey, May 13, 1948; s. Refet and Nermin (Köslü) G.; m. Bennur Ersoy, Aug. 11, 1978; children: Aysin, Atilla. BS, Naval Acad., Istanbul, 1969. Ensign, capt. Turkish Navy, 1967-95, rear adm., 1995—. Office: Dz H O Komutani, Prensipler Baskani, 81704 Ruzia Istanbul Turkey

GURUMURTHY, PREMA, medical researcher; b. Chennar, India, Sept. 10, 1943; d. Kumara Swamyiyer and Kunthalambal Ramakrishnan; m. Swaminathan Gurumurthy, June 12, 1977; children: Priya, Prakash. BSc in Chemistry, S.I.E.T. Women's Coll., Madras, India, 1963; MSc in Biochemistry, U. Madras, 1965; PhD in Biochemistry, Indian Inst. Sci., Bangalore, 1975. Med. diplomate. Postdoctoral rsch. scholar dept. pharmacology U. Minn., Mpls., 1983-84; jr. rsch. fellow Tb Chemotherapy Ctr./Indian Coun. Med. Rsch., Madras, 1965, rsch. asst., 1965-67, asst. rsch. officer, 1967-70, 74-77, sr. rsch. officer, 1977-83, dep. dir., head dept. biochemistry, 1983—; supr.-guide U. Madras, Chennai, India, 1993; examiner in field. Author: Textbook of Pharmaceutical Science; contbr. articles to profl. jours. Recipient award Indian Contress, 1996. Mem. Soc. Biol. Chemistry India, Am. Bibliographic Soc. Avocation: music (giving concerts). Home: 21 Thirumalapai Pillai Rd, T Nagar, Chennai 600017, India Office: Dept Biochemistry (HOD), Tb Rsch Ctr, Chetput, Chennai 600031, India

GURVICH, VICTOR ALEXANDER, physicist, engineer; b. Moscow, Dec. 24, 1951; s. Alexander and Galina (Shtykanova) G.; m. Irina Makarova, Apr. 29, 1988; children: Marina, Yury. MS in Mech. Engring., Moscow Inst. Electronics, 1974; PhD in Med. Engring., Inst. of Med. Devices, Moscow, 1986. Engr. Russian Rsch. Inst. for Light Engring., Moscow, 1974-77; chief lab. x-ray image intensifiers Mosroentgen, Inc., Moscow, 1977-92; gen. mgr. Alvim R&D Ltd., Jerusalem,, 1993-98, Toronto, Ont., Can., 1998—; head project Ministry of Industry and Trade, Jerusalem, 1995-98; scientific sec. Mosroentgen, Inc., Moscow, 1982-92. Patentee in field; contbr. articles to profl. jours. Inventor State Com. on Discoveries and Inventions Affairs, 1986; silver medalist Exhbn. of Econ. Achievement, USSR, 1985; recipient diploma Internat. Tech. Exhbns. in Plovdiv, Bulgaria, 1985, and Leipzig, Germany, 1987. Mem. Am. Assn. Physicists in Medicine, Russian Assn. Physicists in Medicine, N.Y. Acad. Scis., Israeli Assn. New Entrepreneurs, N.Y. Acad. Scis. Avocations: tourism, guitar, poetry. E-mail: vgurvich@pathcom.com. Office: 39 Slender Fernway, Toronto, ON Canada M2J 4P4

GURVITZ, MILTON SOLOMON, psychologist; b. Buffalo, Nov. 27, 1919; m. Sylvia Klein, June 20, 1948; children: Lynda Irene, Robert. BS, SUNY, Buffalo, 1941; MA, NYU, 1948, PhD, 1950. Diplomate in clin. psychology and psychoanalysis Am. Bd. Profl. Psychology. Psychologist USPHS Hosp., Lewisburg, Pa., 1942-46, Ctr. for Psychol. Services, N.Y.C., 1947-48; chief psychologist Hillside Hosp.-L.I. Jewish Med. Ctr., Glen Oaks, N.Y., 1949-55; clin. assoc. prof. Adelphi U., Garden City, N.Y., 1950-55; cons. psychologist Jewish Cmty. Svcs. L.I., 1955-61; pvt. practice psychology Great Neck, N.Y., 1950-87; dir. Great Neck Consultation Ctr., 1960-85, dir. emeritus, 1986—; cons. Conn. Commn. on Alcoholism, 1947-53; clin. prof. postdoctoral program in psychoanalysis, chmn. child and adolescent faculty Adelphi U., 1968-87; pvt. practice psychology Sarasota, Fla., 1987; cons. psychologist Sarasota Child Protection Team, 1990, Jewish Family Svc. Sarasota, 1991—; active med. staff Sarasota Meml. Hosp., 1992; cons. psychologist Fla. State U.-Asolo Film Conservatory, 1993—. Author: Dynamics of Psychological Testing, 1950. Fellow APA, Am. Acad. of Clin. Psychology, Soc. Pers. Assessment; mem. Nat. Psychol. Assn. for Psychoanalysis (sr.). Jewish. Fax: 941-366-0200. E-mail: drmiltpsyc@aol.com. Home: 1111 N Gulfstream Ave Sarasota FL 34236-5593 Office: 5 S Gulfstream Ave Sarasota FL 34236-8907

GUSDON, JOHN PAUL, JR., obstetrics and gynecology educator, physician; b. Cleve., Feb. 13, 1931; s. John and Pauline (Malencek) G.; m. Marcelle Deiber, June 6, 1956 (dec. 1979); children: Marguerite, John Phillip, Veronique; m. R. Carolyn Gallager Aycock, July, 1989. BA, U. Va., 1952, MD, 1959. Diplomate Am. Bd. Ob-Gyn. Rotating intern U. Hosps. Cleve., 1959-60, resident, 1960-64; instr. ob-gyn. Sch. Medicine, Case Western Res. U., Cleve., 1964-66, asst. prof., 1967; asst. prof. ob-gyn. Bowman Gray Sch. Medicine, Wake Forest U., Winston-Salem, N.C., 1967-70, assoc. prof., 1970-74, prof., 1974-90, prof. emeritus, 1990—; staff IHS Hosps. Contbr. articles to sci. jours., chpts. to books. Lt. USN, 1952-55, Korea. Recipient John Horsley Meml. award U. Va., Charlottesville, 1968, Pres. award South Atlantic Assn. Ob-Gyn., 1973. Fellow ACOG (Pres. award 1970, 72), Am. Assn. Immunology; mem. Am. Soc. Immunology of Reproduction (founder, pres. 1981-84), Am. Gynecol. and Obstet. Soc. Republican. Roman Catholic. Avocations: reading, fishing, amateur boxing, cooking.

GUSE, ANDREAS H., biochemist; s. Klaus E.U.H. and Ingeborg (Sonnet) G.; m. Jutta E. Kietzke; children: Nick Linus, Jil Vivian. Diploma in Biology, U. Hamburg, Germany, 1987, Dr.rer.nat., 1990; Pvt. docent, U. Hamburg, 1994; Dr.med.habil., U. Erlangen, Germany, 1993. Rsch. asst. U. Hamburg, 1987-90; rsch. assoc. Max-Planck-Soc., Erlangen, 1990-93; sr. rsch. assoc. U. Hosp., Hamburg, 1993—. Contbr. articles to profl. jours. Rsch. grantee Deutsche Forschungsgemeinschaft, 1993, 94, 96, 98, 99, Wellcome Trust, 1997, Deutscher Akademischer Austauschdienst, 1999, Werner-Otto prize, 1999, Roche Molecular Biochems. Rsch. award, 2000. Mem. Gesellschaft f. Biochemie u. Molekularbiologie, Deutsche Gesellschaft für Zellbiologie, The Calcium Club, European Calcium Soc. Avocation: sports. Office: Univ Krankenhaus Eppendorf, Grindelallee 117 4 OG, D-20146 Hamburg Germany

GUSEV, ALEXANDER, geophysicist; b. Moscow, Feb. 5, 1945; s. Alexander Gusev and Dina Sharevsky; m. Eugenia Knyazeva, Apr. 25, 1975; 1 child, Maria. BSM in Physics, U. Moscow, 1967; candidate sci., USSR Acad. Sci., Moscow, 1978; DS, Russian Acad. Sci., Moscow, 1994. Jr. rschr. Inst. Physics of Earth, Petropavlovsk-Kamchatsky, Russia, 1967-73; sr. rschr., chief lab. Inst. Volcanology, Petropavlovsk-Kamchatsky, 1974-91; learned sec., chief lab. Inst. Volcanic Geology and Geochemistry, Petropavlovsk-Kamchatsky, 1991-93, 96—; sr. rschr. Inst. Geofisica U. Nat. Autonoma Mex., Mexico City, 1994-95. Mem. editl. bd. jour. Volcanology and Seismology, 1979-89; contbr. articles to profl. jours.; compiler, inventor earthquake prediction techniques. Home: 3 Piip Blvd Flat # 51, 683006 Petropavlovsk-Kamcha Russia Office: Inst Volcanic Geology, 9 Piip Blvd, 683006 Petropavlovsk-Kamcha Russia

GUSEV, ANATOLY ALEXANDROVITCH, space physicist, software analyst; b. Ivanteevka, Moscow, Russia, Mar. 15, 1949; s. Alexandra Nikolaevna Guseva; m. Galina Ivanovna Pugacheva, Sept. 12, 1972. Bachelor's, Moscow Engring.-Phys. Inst., 1972; MS, Acad. Scis., Moscow, 1972; PhD, Moscow State U., 1985. Cert. in exptl. nuclear physics engring. Engr. Inst. Electromechanics, Moscow, 1972-75; sr. engr. Inst. Nuclear Physics Moscow State U., 1975-80, jr. investigator Inst. Nuclear Physics, 1980-85, sr. investigator Inst. Nuclear Physics, 1985-95; vis. prof. U. Estadual do Campinas, Brazil, 1993—; prin. investigator high-energy electron experiment onboard Intercosmos-17 satellite, Moscow, 1976-78. Contbr. articles to profl. jours. Sr. lt. Russian Army Res., 1980—. Recipient Medal of URSS Indsl. Progress Exhbn., Coun. Min. USSP, 1978. Mem. European Geophys. Union, Brazilian Soc. Physics., Russian Acad. Sci. (prin. splst. Inst. Space Rsch. 1999—). Avocations: classical music, literature, sports. Fax: 55(19)7885512. Office: Unicamp/IFGW/DRCC, Cidade U Barao Geraldo, 13083970 Campinas Brazil

GUSEV, EVGENY LEONIDOVICH, mathematician, educator; b. Yakutsk, Sakha, Russia, May 14, 1952; s. Leonid Andreevich and Galina Petrovna (Kurova) G. Grad., Irkutsk State U., 1974, Irkutsk State U., 1984; DSc in Physics and Math., Russian Acad. Scis., Moscow, 1991. Programming engr. Engring. Plant, Byshkek, 1974-76; mathematician Yakut Geol. Dept. Russian Acad. Scis., Yakutsk, 1976-78, aspirant Yakut Sci. Ctr., 1978-81, head lab., 1981-93, main sci. worker, 1993—; prof. math. Yakut U., 1991; dir. Inst. Technogenic Hazard Forecasting, Yakutsk, 1997. Author: Mathematical Methods of Interference Filters' Optimization, 1987, Mathematical Methods of Layer Structures' Synthesis, 1993; contbr. articles to profl. publs. Grantee Russian Fund Fundamental Rsch., 1995, 96, 97. Mem. N.Y. Acad. Scis., Internat. Geog. Soc. Avocations: sports, travel, music, philosophy. Home: Oiunskaya Str 20/1 Apt 55, 677013 Yakutsk Sakha, Russia Office: Yakut Sci Ctr Russian Acad, Petrovsky Str 2, 677891 Yakutsk Sakha, Russia

GUSEV, NIKOLAI BORISOVITCH, biochemist, researcher; b. Moscow, June 27, 1948; s. Boris Ivanovich and Valentina Nikolaevna (Guseva) Lushin. MSc, Moscow State U., 1971, PhD, 1975, ScD, 1987. Jr. rsch. fellow Moscow State U., 1974-81, sr. rsch. fellow, 1981-84, assoc. prof., 1984-91, prof., 1991—. Contbr. articles to profl. jours.; editl. bd. Biochemistry, 1994—. Grantee Internat. Sci. Found., 1994-95, Wellcome Trust, London, 1996-99; named Soros Prof., Internat. Soros Sci. Edn. Program, 1997, 98, 99, 2000. Mem. Russian Biochem. Soc., N.Y. Acad. Scis. Avocation: music. Office: Moscow State U, Dept Biochem Sch Biology, 119899 Moscow Russia

GUSEV, VITALYI, physicist; b. Moscow, Apr. 3, 1956. MA in Physics, Moscow State U., 1979, PhD in Physics, 1982, ScD in Physics, 1991. Rschr. Moscow State U., 1979-86, asst. prof., 1986-90, assoc. prof. physics, 1990-98; prof. U. Maine, LeMans, France, 1998—. Co-author: (with A. Karabutov): Laser Optoacoustics, 1991. Recipient Lenin Consomol prize in sci. and tech. Ctrl. Com. of All-Union Communist Youth Orgn., 1987; Humboldt fellow Alexandre von Humboldt Found., 1993-95.

GUSEV, VLADIMIR GEORGIYEVICH, physicist, researcher; b. Novoskbirsk, Russia, Apr. 20, 1939; s. Georgiy Ivanovich and Nina Jakovlevna (Miljarchik) G. Student, Tomsk, Russia, 1963. Faculty mem. State Univ., Tomsk, 1964—. Contbr. articles to profl. jours. Mem. N.Y. Acad. Scis. Home: Mokrushina 20-52, 634045 Tomsk Russia Office: Tomsk State Univ, Lenina 36, 634050 Tomsk Russia

GUSEV, YEUGENIY MIKHAILOVICH, research scientist; b. Moscow, Nov. 1, 1947; s. Mikhail Mikhailovich and Taisiya Timofeevna (Mordashova) G.; m. Elena Nikolaevna Moskvina, Nov. 19, 1977 (div. Aug. 1990); children: Mikhail, Yeugeniy; m. Klara Vasilievna Plyuscheva, Nov. 15, 1992. MSc, Moscow Phys. Engring. Inst., 1972; PhD, Russian Acad. Agrl. Sci., St. Petersburg, 1979; D in Biol. Sci., Moscow State U., 1993. Cert. engring.-physicist, hydrologist, agrl. physicist. Engr. Sci.-Product Co. Red Star, Moscow, 1972-74; postgrad. staff Water Problems Inst., Russian Acad. Sci., Moscow, 1974-77, jr. rschr., 1978-81, sr. rschr., 1981-89, head lab., 1989—; mem. sci. coun. Water Problems Inst., Russian Acad. Sci., 1979—; educator Ecol. Lyceum N232, Moscow, 1992-93; cons. Inst. Agrl. Modernization, Shijiazhuang, China, 1996. Author: Formation of Soil Water Regime and Resources for the Winter-Spring Period, 1993; mem. editl. bd. Jour. Hydrol. and Hydromechanics, 1997—; contbr. articles to profl. jours. Grantee U.S. Dept. State, Washington, 1993, Internat. Sci. Found., N.Y.C., 1993, Govt. of Russia, Moscow, 1994, 97, Russian Found. Basic Rsch., Moscow, 1995, 98, Russian Found. Basic Rsch. and Internat. Sci. Found., 1995. Mem. N.Y. Acad. Sci. Avocations: mini-soccer, tennis, drawing. E-mail: gusev@iwapr.msk.su. and sowa@online.ru. Home: Apt 45, Marshala Nedelina St 4, 121596 Moscow Russia Office: Water Problems Inst RAS, Gubkina St 3, 117971 Moscow Russia

GUSHEE, DAVID PAUL, religious studies educator; b. Frankfurt, Germany, June 17, 1962. BA, Coll. William and Mary, 1984; MDiv, So. Bapt. Sem., 1987; PhD, Union Sem. N.Y., 1993. Prof. So. Bapt. Sem., Louisville, 1993-96; prof., dir. Union U., Jackson, Tenn., 1996—; mem. ethics study commn. Bapt. World Alliance, McLean, Va., 1996-2000, sec. ethics study commn., 2000—. Author: The Righteous Gentiles of the Holocaust, 1994; co-author: A Bolder Pulpit: Reclaiming the Moral Dimension of Preaching, 1998; editor: Preparing for Christian Ministry, 1996; mem. editl. bd. Prism mag.; local columnist Jackson Sun, 1996—. Named one of Outstanding Young Men of Am., 1996; recipient Christian Journalism award Evang. Press Assn., 1991, 92, 97, Outstanding Young Religious Leader award Jaycees, Jackson, 1998. Mem. Am. Acad. Religion, Soc. Christian Ethics (convener Evang. ethics interest group 1996—), Phi Beta Kappa (Alpha chpt.). Avocations: baseball, movies. Fax: 901-668-9756. E-mail: dpgushee@usit.net.

GUSHEL', NIKOLAI PETROVICH, mathematics educator; b. Crimea, Russia, May 25, 1949; s. Piotr Feoktistovich and Kseniya Mikhailovna (Gorpinich) G.; m. Revekka Zalmonovna Skopets, Dec. 15, 1973 (div. Mar. 1987); 1 child, Marina; m. Nataliya L'vovna Halova, Oct. 22, 1988; 1 child, Andrei. Grad. in math., Crimean Pedagogical Inst., 1971; postgrad., Yaroslavl Pedagogical Inst., USSR, 1973-76; Cand Math. Sci., Leningrad Dept. Math. Inst. Acad. Scis., USSR, 1983. Tchr. math. and physics Zorkinskaya Secondary Sch., Crimea, 1971-72; asst. lectr. Yologda (USSR) Pedagogical Inst., 1976-80; asst. prof. math. Yaroslavl br. Corr. Inst. Transport Engring., 1980—; reviewer Math. Abstracts, Moscow, 1980—; asst. prof. Yaroslavl Pedagogical Inst., 1992—. Contbr. articles to math. jours. Served with Soviet Army, 1972-73. Avocation: market gardening. Home: 21 Trufanova Apt 158, 150063 Yaroslavl Russia Office: Corr Inst Transport Engrs, Moskovskii Prospect 151, 150048 Yaroslavl Russia

GUSHUE, PETER BOLAND, historian, educator; b. Bronxville, N.Y., Oct. 18, 1954; s. Joseph Thomas and Catherine Fleming G. MBA, Western New Eng. Coll., 1983; MA, Ga. State U., 1991; PhD in Latin Am. History, U. Ala., 1997. Instr. German Shelton State C.C., Tuscaloosa, Ala., 1994-95; vis. prof. Towson State U., Md., 1996; vis. asst. prof. Auburn (Ala.) U., 1997-98; asst. prof. Christopher Newport U., Newport News, Va., 1998—. Mem. Am. Hist. Assn., Southeastern Coun. Latin Am. Studies, Conf. Latin Am. History. Presbyn. email: pegushue@cnu.edu. Avocations: golf, foreign languages, baseball, football, hockey. Office: Christopher Newport U 1 University Pl Newport News VA 23606-2949

GUSMANI, ROBERTO, linguist; b. Novara, Piedmont, Italy, Oct. 18, 1935; s. Giuseppe and Adele (Negri) G.; m. Ivinia Gorra, Apr. 20, 1961; children: Laura, Paola. Dr.Phil., U. Milan, 1958; Libera Docenza, Min. of Edn., Italy, 1964. Asst. prof. U. Erlangen, Germany, 1958-64; prof. U. Messina, Italy, 1964-72, U. Trieste, Italy, 1972-78; prof. linguistics U. Udine, Italy, 1978—, dean faculty modern lang., 1978-81, rector, 1981-83, head dept. Linguistics & Classical Philology, 1999—. Author: Lydisches Wörterbuch, 1964, Neue Epichorische Schriftzeugnisse aus Sardis, 1975, Saggi Sull' Interferenza Linguistica, 1986, Itinerari Linguistici, 1995. Mem. Italian Soc. Glottology (pres. 1976-78). E-mail: roberto.gusmani@dgfc.uniud.it. Office: Univ Udine, Dept Glottologia, 33100 Udine Italy

GUSSAKOVSKAYA, MAYA ALEXANDROVNA, biologist, researcher; b. Moscow, Sept. 15, 1937; d. Alexandr Stephanovich and Claudia Prokophievna (Gussakovskaya) Chnikina; m. Igor Michailovich Zimin, Oct. 19, 1973. Degree in biol. scis., Moscow State U., 1968, Doctorate, 1985. Rschr. Lomonosov State U., Moscow, 1959—. Contbr. articles to profl. jours. Recipient award Internat. Sci. Found., 1996. Mem. Internat. Assn. Sexual Plant Reproduction Rsch., Internat. Soc. Plant Physiologist, Russian Bot. Soc. Home: Academic Varga 26 110, 117133 Moscow Russia Office: Lomonosov State Univ, Vorobievy Gory, 119899 Moscow Russia

GUSSENHOVEN, CARLOS HENRICUS, linguist; b. Amsterdam, July 19, 1946; s. Carel Aloysius and Maria Josepha (de Haan) G.; m. Thelma Pondaag; children: Karel, Otto. MA, U. Amsterdam, 1971; Doctorate, U. Nijmegen, The Netherlands, 1984. Lectr. U. Nijmegen, 1971-95, prof., 1995—; vis. prof. U. Calif. Berkeley, 1991. Co-author: (textbook) The Pronunciation of English, 1976, English pronunciation for Student Teachers, 1981, Understanding Phonology, 1998, others. Sec. Foresight Commn. for the Modern Langs., The Hague, 1993. Grantee Netherlands Orgn. for Scientific Rsch., Stanford U., 1986, Fulbright, U. Calif., Berkeley, 1995. Mem. Linguistic Assn. of Am., Linguistic Assn. of Gt. Britain, Nederlandse Vereniging voor Algemene Taalwetenschap, 1980—. Office: Univ Nijmegen, Erasmusplein 1, Nijmegen 6525 HT, The Netherlands

GUSTAFSON, ERIC WILLIAM, business consultant, conservationist; b. Monterrey, Mex., Feb. 12, 1945; s. Bertel and Elenor (Ceder) G.; m. Mina Villarreal, June 16, 1973; children: Eric Alain, Karini, Elyn Michelle. BS, Duke U., 1966; MBA cum laude, Monterrey Inst. Tech., 1970; PhD, U. Mass., 1975. Founder, dir. ITESM, 1971-73, Univ. Tchg. Excellence Ctr. and LASCA Computer Degree, Monterrey, 1973-74; from strategic planning mgr. to internat. v.p. Cuauhtemoc Brewing Co., Monterrey, 1975-80; internat. dir. Femsa/Visa Group, Monterrey, 1980-82; nat. v.p. Ducks Unltd. of Mex. Wildlife Conservation Orgn., 1982-97; ptnr. Metroalianza SA, 1998—; assoc. World Bus. Coun. Sustainable Devel., Switzerland, 1991—, pres. U.S.-Mex. C. of C., NE Mexico, 1996—; founder, ptnr. Craidero Estrella, S.A., 1999; cons. U. Nuevo Leon, 1975-76, Clemente Jacques Food Corp.; Mex. rep. Can./U.S./Mex. Trilateral Wildlife Com., 1997; rep. of Mex. at UNCED World Summit Brazil, 1992, rep. of Mex. on N.Am. Waterfowl Mgmt. Plan, 1995—. Author: Organization and Development of Teaching Improvement Center, 1975, Eco-efficiency and Sustainable Development, 1992; ; editor: Mexico: Monterrey and You, 1984. pres. bd. dirs. Am. Sch. Found., Monterrey, 1988-90; nat. bd. dirs. Mex. Nat. Coun. Parks and Res., 1996; Mex. rep. N.Am. Waterfowl Mgmt. Plan, 1995—; active Conservation Mex., 1999. Recipient Excellence in Environment Spain-Mex. award, 1995; N.Am. Wetlands Conservation Act grantee, 1999; Ford Found. scholar, Nat. Coun. Sci. & Tech. Mex. scholar. Mem. Valle Alto Golf Club, Casino de Monterrey, U.S.-Mex. C. of C. (pres. 1996—), Phi Kappa Psi. Avocations: hiking, hunting, tennis, horseback riding, golf. E-mail: karini@usa.net. Fax: (528) 356-5010. Office: Arbol 182 Santa Engracia, Garza Garcia Nuevo Leon 66267, Mexico

GUSTAFSON, GÖSTA, physicist; b. Helsingborg, Sweden, Feb. 18, 1941; s. Erik and Astrid (Berglund) G.; m. Lena Ekholm, Dec. 27, 1963; children: Sven, Erik, Boel, Johan. PhD, Lund (Sweden) U., 1971. Fellow NORDITA, Copenhagen, 1969-72; rsch. assoc., docent Lund U., 1972-88, prof., 1991—; rschr. Swedish Sci. Rsch. Coun., Lund, 1988-91. Mem. Royal Physiographic Soc. Home: Vapenkroken 46, 22647 Lund Sweden Office: Lund U Dept Theor Physics, Sölvegatan 14A, 22362 Lund Sweden

GUSTAFSON, KENT D., broadcast executive, consultant. Student, U. Wis., Stevens Point. Gen. mgr. Children's Broadcasting, Mpls.; v.p., CEO Polusin, Inc., Chgo., Polnet Comm. Ltd., Chgo. Recipient Media Excellence (ethnic) award State of Ill., 1997, 98, Exceptional Polish Broadcasting, 1999. Avocation: aviation. Office: Polnet Communications Ltd PO Box 144 Wauconda IL 60084-0144

GUSTAFSON, LEWIS ALLAN, engineering geologist; b. Lansing, Mich., Dec. 12, 1931; s. Palmer Leonard and Erma Beryl (Washburn) G.; m. Mary Joanne Porter, Oct. 1, 1955; children: Lori, Steven, Leslie. BS in Geology, Mich. State U., 1955, MS in Geology, 1960; postgrad., U. Minn., 1974. Cert. engring. geologist, Oreg., Calif. Staff geologist Walla Walla Dist. U.S. Army Corps Engrs., 1963-68, Omaha Dist. U.S. Army Corps Engrs., Omaha, 1968-74; resident geologist RIRIE Dam U.S. Army Corps Engrs., Idaho Falls, 1974-75; chief, geology sect. Portland Dist. U.S. Army Corps Engrs., 1975-81; divsn. geologist North Pacific Divsn. U.S. Army Corps Engrs., Portland, 1981-88; chief geologist Hdqtrs. U.S. Army Corps of Engrs., Washington, 1988-92; cons. engring. geologist Bend, Oreg., 1992—. Lt. U.S. Army, 1956. Mem. Soc. Am. Mil. engrs., Assn. Engring. Geologists, Am. Underground Constrn. Assn., U.S. Com. on Large Dams. Avocations: hunting, shooting, fishing, hiking, history. Home: 1275 NE Paula Dr Bend OR 97701-6058

GUSTAFSON, ROBERT ALLEN, pediatric cardiothoracic surgeon; b. Keyser, W.Va., Dec. 6, 1950; s. Oscar Harold and Jacqueline (Simmons) G.; m. Lisa Lynn, Aug. 11, 1973; children: Ashley Lynne, Lindsey Michelle, Jeffrey Andrew. AA, Potomac State Coll., 1970; BA, W.Va. U., 1972, MD, 1976. Diplomate Am. Bd. Surgery, Am. Bd. Thoracic Surgery. Intern in gen. surgery W. Va. U. Med. Ctr., Morgantown, W. Va., 1976; asst. resident in gen. surgery W. Va. U. Med. Ctr., Morgantown, 1977-80, chief resident in gen. surgery, 1980-81, fellow in thoracic surgery, 1981-83; fellow pediatric cardiothoracic surgery Boston Children' Hosp., Boston, 1983; chief pediatric cardiac surgery W.Va. U., Morgantown, 1984—, asst. prof. surgery, 1984-87, assoc. prof. surgery and pediatrics, 1987-94, prof. surgery and pediatrics, 1994—; surgeon-in-chief W. Va. U. Children's Hosp., Morgantown, 1997—, Children's Hosp. W.Va. U., 1997—; vis. prof. Allegheny Gen. Hosp., Pitts., 1988, 1995, Johns Hopkins U., 1990. Manuscript reviewer Annals of Thoracic Surgery, 1990—, Jour. of Thoracic and Cardiovascular Surgery, 1995—; contbr. articles to profl. jours. Participating surgeon Internat. Rotary Club Gift of Life Project, N.Y.C., 1985—. Recipient Presdl. award So. Thoracic Surg. Assn., 1988, Alumni Achievement award Potomac State Coll., 1990, Innovation Achievement award W.Va. Univ. Hosp., 1994, High Performance Leadership award, 1998, Miracle Maker award Children's Miracle Network, 1996. Fellow ACS, Am. Acad. Pediatrics; mem. AMA, Am. Assn. Thoracic Surgery, W.Va. Chpt. ACS (state councilor 1990-94, 96-99), W.Va. Med. Assn. (program com. 1991-97), Monongalia County Med. Soc., Southeastern Surg. Congress, Internat. Soc. Pediatric Cardiovascular Surgery, So. Thoracic Surg. Assn., Soc. Thoracic Surgeons, Surg. Sect. Am. Acad. Pediatrics, Lunar Soc. for Congenital Heart Surgery, W.Va. Chpt. Am. Acad. Pediatric, Am. Heart Assn., ARC, Am. Cancer Soc., Habitat for Humanity, Interplast, Inc., Cousteau Soc., Nature Conservancy, W.Va. Audubon Soc., Project Hope, W.Va. Spl. Olympics Inc. Republican. Methodist. Avocations: golf, tennis, travel. Office: W Va U Sch of Medicine Dept of Surgery PO Box 9238 Morgantown WV 26506-9238

GUSTAFSON, ROBERT ERIC, artistic director; b. N.Y.C., Oct. 7, 1935; s. Eric Theodore and Ebba Marie (Johnson) G. BA, Queens Coll., 1957; MFA, Carnegie Tech., 1959. Founder, artistic dir. Apollo Muses Ctr. for the Arts, Peapack, N.J., 1983—; curator selected exhbns. Cooper-Hewitt Mus., N.Y.C., 1978, Libr. and Mus. of the Performing Arts Lincoln Ctr., 1980. Author, lectr.: Court Theatres of Europe, 1982, Cinderella is a Man, Autobiography, 1998; columnist (Gannett newspapers) Classical Notes, 1995-98; cameo performances in the N.J. Ballet, others on stage, TV and cinema. Avocations: collecting art and porcelains, hiking, international travel, creating beautiful environments. Home: Riverview Box 16 Peapack NJ 07977

GUSTAFSSON, ANDERS HÅKAN, animal nutritionist, consultant; b. St. Lundby, Sweden, Oct. 27, 1954; s. Evald and Maj (Lundahl) G.; m. Maud Romney; children: Rickard, Magnus. MS in Agr., Swedish U. Agrl. Scis., Uppsala, 1983, PhD in Agr., 1993. In-svc. tng. Swedish Assn. Livestock Breeding and Prodn., Eskilstuna, 1991, 92, 95. Rsch. asst., dept. animal nutrition and mgmt. Swedish U. Agrl. Scis., 1983; cons. Swedish Assn. Livestock Breeding and Prodn., 1984-93; mng. dir. Dala-Gävle Livestock Co-operative, Bollnäs, Sweden, 1993-95; R & D staff Swedish Dairy Assn., 1995—; cons. dairy and beef cattle prodn., Co-operative Ext. Orgn., Värmland county, Sweden, 1983; rsch. scholar Ohio Agrl. R & D Ctr., Ohio State U. dept. animal sci., 1990; mem. bd. Milk Test and Grading Lab. No. Sweden (NMF), 1993-95. Mem. Am. Dairy Sci. Assn., Nordic Assn. Agrl. Scientists. Home: Rasbo, Jarstadal, S-755 96 Uppsala Sweden Office: Swedish Dairy Assn, SLU, S-753 23 Uppsala Sweden

GUSTAFSSON, BENGT S.H., agriculturist, scientist; b. Vissefjarda, Kalmar, Sweden, Oct. 10, 1930; s. Sture B.M. and Berta A.L. (Franzen) G.; m. Ewy G. Svensson, Apr. 24, 1963; children: Niklas, Martin. BS, Agr. U. Uppsala, 1956; MS, U. Ill., 1964; PhD, Purdue U., 1969. Rschr. Agr. U. Lund, Sweden, 1956-62; rsch. asst. U. Ill., Purdue U., Urbana, West Lafayette, 1962-65; head rsch. divsn. Agr. U. Lund, 1965-95; attaché Swedish Embassy, Washington, 1982-84. Contbr. chpts. in books and articles to profl. jours. Rsch. fellow Kellogg Found., 1962. Mem. Royal Swedish Acad. Agr. Lutheran. Avocation: gymnastics.

GUSTAFSSON, LARS ERIK EINAR, writer, educator; b. Västerås, Sweden, May 17, 1936; came to U.S., 1983; s. Einar H. and Lotten Margaretha (Carlson) G.; m. D. Alexandra Chasnoff, Nov. 6, 1982; children: Benjamin, Karen. PhD, Uppsala (Sweden) U., 1978. Editor-in-chief Bonniers Pub. House, Stockholm, 1961-72; rsch. fellow Ctr. Advanced Studies, Bielefeld, Germany, 1980-81; Aby Warburg rsch. prof. Warburg Found. U. Hamburg, Germany, 1997-98; bd. dirs. Svenska Dagbladet Found.; bd. regents Uppsala (Sweden) U., 1994-97; adj. prof. U. Tex., Austin, 1983—; Jamail Disting. prof., 1998—. Author numerous novels and poetry collections. John Simon Guggenheim Meml. fellow of poetry, 1993. Mem. Acad. of Arts (Berlin), Acad. Scis. and Lit. (Mainz, Germany), Royal Swedish Acad. Engring. (Stockholm), Bavarian Acad. Fine Arts (Munich). Avocation: painting. Office: U Tex Austin Dept Philosophy Austin TX 78712

GUSTAFSSON HEMPEL, CHRISTINA, jewelry company executive; b. Szeged, Hungary, Jan. 23, 1945; d. George Running Horse Beauchamps and Elsa Marianne (Gustafsson) Kvarnström; m. Patrick Le Guehennec, Oct. 2, 1972 (div. July 1975); children: Malin, Sofie, Abbe, Jonathan, Elin. Student, Uppsala U., Sweden, 1987-90; degree, Läromästaren, Uppsala, 1994; student, Bolands Computerschool, 1996—, Webdesigner Sch., 1997-98, EKEBY Journalist Media Sch., 1998. Sec. County of Stockholm, 1963-68; tchr. Fetco's Art Sch., Stockholm, 1969-71; sec. Gota Bank of Stockholm, 1972-74; dir. catering Tromsö (Norway) Seafood Co., 1974-77; guide The Domëch., Uppsala, 1978-82; tchr. presch. Eriksbergs Child Care Ctr., Uppsala, 1983-87; with Merlite Ind., Inc., Uppsala; art tchr. Upsala Artschool, Uppsala, 1994—; owner Esmeralda Gallery, Old Town Stockholm, 1995—; journalist, webdesigner IT framjandet, 1997—; mgr. Boland-TBV Computer Sch., IT-Network Sys. Sch., Uppsla, 1999-2000; network systems adminstr. TBV, Uppsala, 2000—; mem., sec. Uppsala Data IT-Vega, 1997—. Author: Lyrics in Poetanthology: 200 About 2,000, Astrate edit., 1999—; contbr. articles and photos to newspapers, 2000—. Field worker Sisters of Mercy, Stockholm, 1968-72; mem. Swedish UNICEF, 2000—, Greenpeace, 1999—. Mem. Animal Rights, Swedish Save the Children, Swedish Red Cross, Amnesty Internat. Democrat. Avocations: music, theater, art, travel, polar dogs. E-mail: scillha@hotmail.com. Home and Office: Merlite Inds Inc, Glimmervägen 7A, 75241 Uppsala Sweden

GUSTAVSON, ROYSTON ROBERT, musicologist, consultant; b. Brisbane, Queensland, Australia, Sept. 11, 1964; s. Robert Ward and Jill (Dempster) G. BA with honors, U. Queensland, Australia, 1986; PhD, U. Melbourne, Australia, 1998; MBA, U. Melbourne, 2000. Examiner Australian Music Exam. Bd., Brisbane, 1989-92; rsch. asst. U. Melbourne, 1994-97, rsch. fellow, 1998-99; freelance rschr., cons. Melbourne, 2000—; chair Australian Com. Répertoire International De Littérature Musicale, 1996-99. Author: (with others) New Grove Dictionary of Music and Musicians, 2nd rev. edit., 2000, Oxford Companion to Australian Music, 1997, eight articles to profl. jour.; editor: (music score with H. Reeder) Historic Australian Operas # 2, 1994, jour. Australasian Music Research, 1996-98; mem. editl. com. Context: Jour. Music Rsch., 1992; mem. adv. com. Musicology Australia, 1996-99. Grantee Deutscher Akademischer Austauschdienst, Berlin, 1993. Mem. Musicological Soc. Australia (nat. com. 1990—, exec. sec. 1992-94, convenor Source Studies study group 1993-95, Musicology prize Victorian Chapter, 1996), Internat. Musicological Soc., Gesellschaft Für Musikforschung, Am. Musicological Soc. Anglican. Avocations: singing in choirs, swimming, chess. Home and Office: PO Box 4229, 3052 Parkville VI, Australia

GUSTERSON, BARRY AUSTIN, pathologist; b. Colchester, Essex, Eng., Oct. 24, 1946; s. Joseph Austin and Doris Edith (Fairweather) G.; m. Ann Josephine Davies, Dec. 2, 1972; children: Philip, Rosalind, Ruth. BSc in Physiology, St. Bartholemew's Hosp., London, 1967; MB, BChir, St. Bartholemew's Hosp., 1976; BDS, Royal Dental Hosp., 1972; PhD, Inst. Cancer Rsch., 1980. Sr. clin. scientist, cons. Ludwig Inst. Cancer Rsch., London, 1983-86; chmn. sect. cell biology and exptl. pathology Inst. Cancer Rsch., London, 1986-2000, prof. histopathology, 1986-2000; prof. pathology U. Glasgow, Scotland, 2000—; cons. histopathology Royal Marsden Hosp., London, 1984-2000; founding dir. Toby Robins Breast Cancer Rsch. Ctr., London, 1998-2000; dir. pathology Internat. Breast Cancer Study Group, Bern, Switzerland, 1995—; chmn. pathology group Orgn. European Cancer Insts., Geneva, Switzerland, 1992-96, faculty bd. mem., 1992-96; faculty bd. mem. European Soc. Mastology, Milan, Italy, 1994—. Contbr. chpts. in books and articles to profl. jours. Fellow Pathol. Soc. Gt. Britain and Ireland (com., Oakley lectr. 1986); mem. Brit. Soc. Cell Biology. Socialist. Avocations: antique English glass and furniture, gardening, walking, reading. Office: Univ Glasgow Pathology Dept, Western Infirmary, Glasgow G11 6NT, Scotland

GUT, RAINER E., banker; b. Baar, Switzerland, Sept. 24, 1932; s. Emil Anton and Rosa (Müller) G.; m. Josephine Lorenz; 4 children. Ed., Cantonal Sch. Zug. Gen. ptnr. Lazard Freres & Co., N.Y.C., 1968-71; chmn., CEO Swiss-Am. Corp., N.Y.C., 1971-73; dep. mem. exec. bd. Credit Suisse, Zürich, 1973-75; exec. bd. mem. Credit Suisse, Zurich, 1975-77, spkr. exec. bd., 1977-82, pres. exec. bd., 1982-83, chmn., 1983—; chmn. Nestlé S.A., Vevey, Switzerland; bd. dirs. Nestlé, Vevey, Sofina, Brussels, Pechiney, Paris, Union Carbide Corp., Danbury, Conn., Daimler-Benz Holding, Zurich; chmn. Credit Suisse First Boston, 1988; chmn. CS Holding, 1986-96, Credit Suisse Group, 1997—, WATT, 1998. Office: Nestlé SA, Avenue Nestle 55, CH-1800 Vevey Vaud, Switzerland*

GUT, WLODZIMIERZ, chemist; b. Krakow, Poland, May 2, 1949; s. Joseph and Genevieve (Malek) G.; m. Casimire Hajdas, July 7, 1973; two children. MSc, Jagiellonian U., 1973, DSc, 1984; postgrad., Econ. Acad., 1999. Tram driver Mcpl. Traffic Co., Cracow, 1972-76; scientific asst. Inst. Meteorology & Water Mgmt., Cracow, 1974-79; tutor Inst. Forensic Rsch., Cracow, 1983-97; pension and quality sys. specialist pharm. manufacture ESPEFA, Cracow, 1999—. Mem. Polish Toxicol. Soc., Polish Chem. Soc., Internat. Assn. Forensic Toxicology. Roman Catholic.

GUTCHÉ, GENE, composer; b. Berlin, July 3, 1907; came to U.S., 1925; s. Maximillian and Flora (von Zerbst) G.; m. Marion Frances Buchan, Dec. 1, 1935. M.A., U. Minn.; M.A. (creative scholar), 1950; Ph.D. (creative scholar), State U. Iowa, 1953. Guggenheim fellow, 1963-65. Contbr. articles to profl. jours.; World premieres include Piano Concerto Opus 24, Mpls. Summer Session, 1956, Third String Quartet Opus 12 No. 3, Arts Quartet, 1958, Holofernes Overture Opus 27 No. 1, Mpls. Symphony, 1959, Rondo Capriccioso Opus 21, N.Y. Chamber Orch., 1960, Concertino for Orch. Opus 28, Mpls. Summer Session, 1961, Fourth String Quartet Opus 29 No. 1, Fine Arts Quartet, 1962, Symphony IV Opus 30, Albuquerque Symphony, 1962, Timpani Concertante Opus 31, Oakland Symphony, 1962, Symphony V for Strings Opus 34, Chautauqua Festival, 1962, Bongo Divertimento Opus 35, St. Paul Chamber Orch., 1962, Raquel Opus 38, Tulsa Philharmonic, 1963, Genghis Khan Opus 37, Mpls. Symphony, 1963, Rites in Tenochtitlàn Opus 39, St. Paul Chamber Orch., 1965, Gemini Opus 41, Mpls. Summer Session, 1966, Hsiang Fei Opus 40, Cin. Symphony, 1966, Rites in Tenochtitlàn Opus 39 No. 1, New Orleans Symphony, 1967, Classic Concerto for Chamber Orch. Opus 44, St. Paul Chamber Orch., 1967, Aesop Fabler Suite Opus 43, Fargo-Moorhead Symphony, 1968, Epimetheus USA Opus 46, Detroit Symphony, 1969, Symphony VI, Opus 45, Detroit Symphony, 1971, Icarus, Opus 48, Nat. Symphony, 1976, Bi-Centurion, Opus 49, Rochester Philharmonic, 1976, Perseus & Andromeda XX, Opus 50, Cin. Symphony, 1977, Helios Kinetic, Opus 52, Fla. Philharmonic, 1978, Akhenaten, Opus 51, Milw. Symphony, 1980, Opus 51, No 2, St. Louis Symphony, 1983; European premieres include Symphony V for Strings, Opus 34, Radio-TV Luxembourg, 1968, Violin Concerto, Opus 36, Orch. Stabile Trieste, 1969, Bongo Divertimento, Opus 35, Munich Philharmoniker, 1967, Hsiang Fei, Opus 40, Oslo Philharm., 1970, Epimetheus U.S.A., Opus 46, Stockholm Philharm., 1969, Genghis Khan, Opus 37; also recs. (Recipient Minn. State Centennial prize 1958, Luria award 1959, prize Albuquerque Nat. Composition 1962, prize Oscar Esplá Internat. Composition 1962, XVI Premio Cittá di Trieste 1969, Louis Moreau Gottschalk Gold medal 1970, XIX Premio Cittá di Trieste 1972), commd. works include, St. Paul Philharmonic, 1962, St. Paul Arts and Scis., 1965, regents U. Minn., 1966, Fargo-Moorhead Symphony, 1967, St. Paul Chamber, 1967, Detroit Symphony, 1969, Nat. Symphony Orch., 1975, Rochester Philharmonic, 1976, Cin. Symphony Orch., 1977, Fla. Philharmonic, 1978,, Milw. Symphony, 1980 (nationwide broadcast of Akhenaten, Opus 51 by NPR/N/C radio 1980, by St. Louis Symphony Orch. on Nat. Pub. Radio, 1983). NEA Bicentennial grantee, 1976, 77, 78; Ford Found. rec. grantee, 1976; Grantee Copland Found., 2000. Address: Regus Pub 10 Birchwood Ln Saint Paul MN 55110-1601

GUTEKUNST, THOMAS FERDINAND, information technology consultant; b. Basel, Switzerland, Jan. 15, 1966; s. Ferdinand and Renate (Baumann) G.; m. Antoinette Werthemann, Aug. 6, 1992; children: Ariane, Lukas, Nathalie. Diploma in computer sci., ETH, Zürich, 1991, PhD, 1995. Rsch. asst. ETH, Zürich, 1991-92, project mgr., 1992-95; project mgr. Swiss Bank Corp., Basel, Switzerland, 1995-97; assoc. dir. Swiss Bank Corp., Basel, 1997-2000; dir. UBS AG, Zurich, 2000—. Contbr. articles to profl. jours. 1st lt. Swiss Army, 1985-96. Recipient Best PhD Thesis award GI/ITG-Fachgruppe Kommunikation und Verteilte Systeme of the German Gesellschaft für Informatik, 1995. Mem. IEEE, Assn. Computing Machinery, E.E. Zunft zu Hausgenossen, Basel. Home: Spalentorweg 51, 4051 Basel Switzerland

GUTERRES, ANTONIO MANUEL DE OLIVEIRA, prime minister of Portugal; b. Santos-o-Velho, Lisbon, Portugal, Apr. 30, 1949. Grad. in electronic engring., Superior Tech. Inst. Lisbon. Chmn. indsl. planning divsn. Cabinet of Sines Region, Portugal, 1973; founder, v.p. Portuguese Assn. Consumer Protection, 1973-74; asst. lectr. Inst. Superior Tecnico, Lisbon, 1973-75; mem. nat. and polit. commn. Socialist Party, Portugal, 1974; asst. to min. without portfolio Mario Soares, chief of cabinet of Sec. of State for Industry, asst. to Min. Fins. Govt. of Portugal, 1974-75, dep. Portuguese Parliament, 1976-83, 85, chmn. parliamentary com. economy and fin., 1977-79, mem. Mcpl. Assembly Fundao, 1979, chmn. parliamentary com. regional planning, local authorities and environment, 1985-88, mem. nat. bur. Socialist Party, 1986-88, pres. parliamentary group of Socialist Party, 1986-91, mem. coun. of state, 1991, leader Socialist Party, v.p. Socialist Internat., co-chmn. African Com., 1992, prime min., 1995—; mem. European Integration Com., 1976-79; mem. parliamentary assembly Coun. of Europe, 1981-83; dir. strategic devel. IPE, 1984-85. Office: Office of Prime Min, Office of Prime Min, Rua da Imprensa a Estrela 2, 1249-064 Lisbon Portugal also: Embassy Rep of Portugal 2125 Kaloranu Rd NW Washington DC 20008*

GUTHEIL, IRENE ANDERMAN, social work educator, researcher; b. St. Louis, June 17, 1944; d. Sam and Lillian Ruth Anderman; m. John Gordon Gutheil, June 9, 1968 (dec.); children: David Arthur, Robert Douglas. BA, Brandeis U., 1966; MS, Columbia U., 1968, D Social Welfare, 1988. Lic. social worker, N.Y. Psychiat. social worker Karen Horney Clinic, N.Y.C., 1968-69; social work cons. New Rochelle (N.Y.) Nursing Home, 1973-76, 77-83, Westledge Extended Care Facility, Peekskill, N.Y., 1973-84; social worker Geriatric Assocs., Montefiore Med. Ctr., Bronx, N.Y., 1986; adj. instr. Fordham U. Grad. Sch. Social Svc., N.Y.C., 1982-84, prof., 1987—; dir. Ravazzin Ctr. for Social Work Rsch. in Aging Fordham U. Grad. Sch. Social Svc., Tarrytown, N.Y., 1995—; adj. instr. Mercy Coll., Dobbs Ferry, N.Y., 1981-83; mem. human svcs. adv. bd. Actors Fund Am., N.Y.C., 1989-92; mem. rsch. adv. bd. Found. for Long Term Care, Albany, N.Y., 1997—; mem. adv. bd. Health Avcs. for Older People, N.Y.C., 1998—; bd. dirs. Aging in Am., Bronx, 1998—. Contbg. author: (with R. Chernesky) Adult Psychopathology: A Social Work Perspective, 1999; editor: Work with Older People: Challenges and Opportunities, 1994; contbr. articles to profl. jours., including Jour. Gerontol. Social Work, Social Work. Grantee Fordham U., 1991, Grotta Found., 1999, Fan Fox and Leslie R. Samuels Found., 1999. Fellow Gerontol. Soc. Am. (postdoctoral fellow 1989); mem. NASW, Coun. on Social Work Edn., Am. Soc. on Aging, Assn. for Gerontology in Social Work Edn., State Soc. on Aging N.Y. (exec. bd. 1992-94, 98-99). E-mail: gutheil@fordham.edu. Office: Fordham U Grad Sch Social Svc Neperan Rd Tarrytown NY 10591

GUTHEINZ, JOSEPH RICHARD, JR., lawyer, federal agency official; b. Camp Lejune, N.C., Aug. 13, 1955; s. Joseph R. Sr. and Rita A. (O'Leary) G.; m. Lori Ann Bentley, Jan. 16, 1976; children: Joseph, Christopher, Michael, Jim, Bill, Dave. AS, AA, Monterey Peninsula Coll., Calif., 1975; BA, Calif. State U., Sacramento, 1978, MA, 1979; postgrad., U. Calif., Davis, 1979-80; grad., U.S. Army Tactical Schs., 1980, U.S. Army Flight Sch., 1984; MS in Sys. Mgmt., U. So. Calif., 1985; JD, S. Tex. Coll. Law, 1996. Bar: Tex. 1997, U.S. Dist. Ct. (so. dist.) Tex. 1997, U.S. Vets. Ct. Appeals 1998, U.S. Armed Forces Ct. Appeals 1998, U.S. Ct. Appeals (5th, 10th, 11th cirs.) 1998, U.S. Ct. Appeals (fed. cir.) 1998, U.S. Tax Ct. 1998; lic. FAA comml. pilot; cert. fraud examiner; cert. tchr., Calif. Officer U.S. Army, Kitzigen, Fed. Rep. Germany, 1980-82; capt., mil. intelligence officer U.S. Army, Stuttgart, Fed. Rep. Germany, 1982-84; capt., aviator U.S. Army, Ft. Polk, La., 1984-86; spl. agt. civil aviation security FAA, Oklahoma City, 1986-87; spl. agt. U.S. Dept. Transp., Denver, 1987-90; sr. spl. agt. Office Insp. Gen. NASA, Houston, 1990—; pvt. practice atty. Houston, 1996—; instr. Ctrl Tex. Coll., Nelligan, Fed. Rep. Germany, 1983; guest spkr. Internat. Bus. Forum, 1995, Assn. Govt. Accts., 1996; task force leader Nine Agy. Fed. Omniplan, 1992-96; chief NASA OIG investigator, Russian Mir Space Stas. fire and collision, 1997, Op. Lunar Eclipse, 1998-00; task force leader Fed. Agy. Investigation, Rockwell Internat/Boeing N. Am. and United Space Alliance, 2000, others. Briefed Pres. Yeltsin's econ. advisors, 1995. Recipient Letter of Commendation, FBI dir. Louis Freeh, 1995, NASA Exceptional Svc. medal, 2000, Pres.'s Coun. for Integrity and Efficiency Career Achievement award, 2000; named Hon. Lt. Gov. Okla., 1987; Merit scholar S. Tex. Coll. Law; recipient Tex. Spl. Commendation U.S. Atty. Office So. Dist., 1996. Mem. ATLA, Assn. Certified Fraud Examiners, Tex. Bar Assn. Republican. Roman Catholic. Avocations: reading, pistol shooting, volleyball, chess, weight lifting. Office: NASA Johnson Space Ctr Crim Invest Code W-Js Bldg 265 2101 Nasa Rd 1 Houston TX 77058-3691 also: 205 Woodcombe Dr Houston TX 77062-2537

GUTHKE, KARL SIEGFRIED, foreign language educator; b. Lingen, Germany, Feb. 17, 1933; came to U.S., 1956, naturalized, 1973; s. Karl Hermann and Helene (Beekman) G.; m. Dagmar von Nostitz, Apr. 24, 1965; 1 child, Carl Ricklef. MA, U. Tex., 1953; PhD, U. Göttingen, Germany, 1956; MA (hon.), Harvard U., 1968. Faculty U. Calif., Berkeley, 1956-65; prof. German lit. U. Calif. at Berkeley, 1962-65, U. Toronto, Ont., Can., 1965-68; prof. German lit. Harvard U., 1968-78, Kuno Francke prof. German art and culture, 1978—; vis. prof. U. Colo., 1963, U. Mass., 1967; vis. fellow Sidney Sussex Coll., Cambridge U., Nat. Rsch. Ctr., Wolfenbüttel, Inst. for Adv. Studies, U. Edinburgh, Humanities Rsch. Ctr., Australian Nat. U., Canberra. Author: Englische Vorromantik und deutscher Sturm und Drang, 1958, (with Hans M. Wolff) Das Leid im Werke Gerhart Hauptmanns, 1958, Geschichte und Poetik der deutschen Tragikomödie, 1961, Gerhart Hauptmann: Weltbild im Werk, 1961, rev. edit., 1980, Haller und die Literatur, 1962, Der Stand der Lessing-Forschung: Ein Bericht über die Literatur, 1932-1962, 1965, Modern Tragicomedy: An Investigation into the Nature of the Genre, 1966, Wege zur Literatur: Studien zur deutschen Dichtungs-und Geistesgeschichte, 1967, Hallers Literaturkritik, 1970, Die Mythologie der entgötterten Welt: Ein literarisches Thema von der Aufklärung bis zur Gegenwart, 1971, Das deutsche bürgerliche Trauerspiel, 1972, 5th rev. edit., 1994, G.E. Lessing, 3d edit., 1979, Literarisches Leben im 18. Jahrhundert in Deutschland und in der Schweiz, 1975, Das Abenteuer der Literatur, 1981, Haller im Halblicht, 1981, Der Mythos der Neuzeit, 1983, Erkundungen, 1983, Das Geheimnis um B. Traven entdeckt, 1984, B. Traven: Biographie eines Rätsels, 1987, The Last Frontier: Imagining Other Worlds, 1990, Letzte Worte, 1990, B. Traven: The Life Behind the Legends, 1991, Last Words, 1992, Trails in No-Man's Land, 1993, Die Entdeckung des Ich, 1993, Schillers Dramen, 1994, Ist der Tod eine Frau, 1997, The Gender of Death, 1999, Der Blick in die Fremde, 2000, also others; transl.: Die moderne Tragikomödie: Theorie und Gestalt, 1968; editor: Haller, Die Alpen, 1987; co-editor: (Hanser) Gotthold Ephraim Lessing, Werke, 1970-72, Joh. H. Füssli, Sämtliche Gedichte, 1973, B. Traven: Briefe aus Mexiko, 1992, Lessing Yearbook, Colloquia Germanica, Twentieth Century Literature, German Quarterly. Honored in History and Literature: Essays in Honor of Karl S. Guthke, 2000. Fellow Humanities Rsch. Ctr., Canberra Australia, Inst. Advanced Studies, Edinburgh, Scotland, Rsch. Ctr., Wolfenbuttel; mem. Lessing Soc. (past pres.), Inst. Germanic Studies (London corr. fellow). Office: Harvard U Dept German Cambridge MA 02138

GUTHRIE, CHARLES, NATO official, military officer; b. U.K., Nov. 17, 1938; m. Kate Guthrie; 2 children: David, Andrew. Grad., Royal Mil. Acad., 1959. Commd. Welsh Guards Ministry of Def., U.K., 1959, advanced through grades to gen., early assignments include troop comdr., squadron comdr., 1959-72, mil. asst. to Chief of Gen. Staff, 1975-76, brigade maj. Household Divsn., 1976-77; comdr. 1st bn. Welsh Guards Ministry of Def., U.K., Germany and No. Ireland, 1977-80; col. Gen. Staff, Ministry of Def. Ministry of Def., U.K., 1980-81, comdr. 4th Armoured Brigade, 1981-85, gen. comdg. officer 2d Infantry Divsn., 1985, col. command Intelligence Corps, 1986-87, asst. chief of Gen. Staff, 1987-89, comdr. 1st British corps, 1989-92, comdr. No. Army Group, comdr.-in-chief British Army of Rhine, 1992-93, adc gen., 1993—, chief of def., 1994—. Avocations: skiing, horses, tennis. Office: Armed Forces, Main Bldg Whitehall, London SW1A 24B, UK also: NATO Hdqrs, Blvd Leopold III, 1110 Brussels Belgium*

GUTHRIE, DIANA FERN, nursing educator; b. N.Y.C., May 7, 1934; d. Floyd George and A. May (Moler) Worthington; m. Richard Alan Guthrie, Aug. 18, 1957; children: Laura, Joyce, Tammy. AA, Graceland Coll., 1953; RN, Independence (Mo.) Sanitarium, 1956; BS in Nursing, U. Mo., 1957, MS in Pub. Health, 1969; EdS, Wichita State U., 1982; PhD, Walden U., 1985. RN, Mo., Kans.; lic. profl. counselor, Kans.; cert. in stress mgmt. edn.; cert. clin. hypnosis; cert. holistic nursing; cert. healing touch; advanced RN practitioner; lic. marriage and family therapist. Instr. red cross U.S. Naval Sta., Sangley Point, Philippines, 1961-63; acting head nurse newborn nursery U. Mo., Columbia, 1963-64, birth defect nurse dept. pediat., 1964-65, nursing dir. clin. research ctr., 1965-67, research asst., 1967-73; diabetes nurse specialist Sch. Medicine U. Kans., Wichita, 1973—, asst. then assoc. prof. Sch. Medicine, 1974-85, prof. dept. pediat. and psychiatry Sch. Medicine, 1985-99, prof. emeritus, 2000; prof. dept. nursing Kans. U. Med. Ctr., Wichita, 1985-99, ret., 1999; nurse cons. diabetes Mo. Regional Med. Program, Columbia, 1970-73; nat. advisor Human Diabetes Ctr. for Excellence, Lexington, Ky., 1982-90, Phoenix, 1983-92, Charlottesville, Ky., 1990-95; adj. prof. Sch. Nursing Wichita State U., 1985—. Author: Nursing Management of Diabetes, 1977, 4th edit. 1997, The Diabetes Source Book, 1990, 4th edit., 1999, Alternative and Complementary Diabetes Case, 2000; contbr. articles to profl. jours. Mem. health adv. bd. Mid-Am. All Indian Ctr., Wichita, 1978-80; bd. dirs. Wichita Urban Indian Health Clinic, 1980-82; bd. trustees Graceland Coll., Lamoni, Iowa, 1996—. Fellow Am. Acad. Nursing; mem. ANA, APHA, Am. Diabetes Assn. (affiliate bd. dirs. 1979-83, pres. Kans. affiliate 1980-81, 90-91, Outstanding Educator award 1979, Regional Outstanding Svc. award 1984), Am. Assn. Diabetes Educators (Kans. area Disting. Svc. award 1999), Am. Assn. Med. Psychotherapists (profl. adv. bd. 1985—), Am. Diabetes Assn. (Kans. area profl. edn. and youth com. 1988—), Sigma Theta Tau (Exemplary Recognition award Epsilon Gamma chpt. 1996, Disting. Svc. award 1999). Democrat. Mem. Reorganized LDS Ch. Avocations: harp, piano, oil painting, crafts, reading. E-mail: dguthrie@kumc.edu. Office: 200 S Hillside Wichita KS 67211-2127

GUTHRIE, FRANK ALBERT, chemistry educator; b. Madison, Ind., Feb. 16, 1927; s. Ned and Gladys (Glick) G.; m. Marcella Glee Farrar, June 12, 1955; children: Mark Alan, Bruce Bradford, Kent Andrew, Lee Farrar. AB, Hanover Coll., 1950; MS, Purdue U., 1952; PhD, Ind. U., 1962. Mem. faculty Rose-Hulman Inst. Tech., Terre Haute, Ind., 1952—, assoc. prof., 1962-67, prof. chemistry, 1967-94, prof. emeritus, 1994—, chmn. dept., 1969-72, chief health professions adviser, 1975-94; Kettering vis. lectr. U. Ill., Urbana, 1961-62; vis. prof. chemistry U.S. Mil. Acad., West Point, N.Y., 1987-88, 93-94, admissions coord., 1989—; vis. prof. chemistry Butler U., spring 2000. Mem. exec. bd. Wabash Valley council Boy Scouts Am., 1971-87, adv. bd., 1988—, v.p. for scouting, 1976; selection chmn. Leadership Terre Haute, 1978-80. Served with AUS, 1945-46. Recipient Silver Beaver award Boy Scouts Am., 1980. Fellow Ind. Acad. Sci. (pres. 1970, chmn. acad. found. trustees 1986—); mem. Am. Chem. Soc. (sec. 1973-77, editor directory 1965-77, chmn. divsn. analytical chemistry 1979-80, chmn. 1958, counselor Wabash Valley sect. 1980—, local sect. activities com. 1982-86, nominations and elections com. 1988-94, sec. 1992-94, coun. policy com. 1995, constn. and bylaws com. 1996—, steering com. for Joint Ctrl.-Gt. Lakes Regional Meetings, Indpls., 1978, 91, vis. assoc. com. profl. tng. 1984—, chmn. analytical chemistry exam. inst. std. exam. 1994), Coblentz Soc., Midwest Univs. Analytical Chemistry Conf., Hanover Coll. Alumni Assn. (pres. 1974, Alumni Achievement award 1977), Sigma Xi (treas. Wabash Valley chpt. 1994-98), Phi Lambda Upsilon, Phi Gamma Delta, Alpha Chi Sigma (E.E. Dunlap scholarship selection com. 1986—, chmn. 1990—, dir. expansion 1995-99, profl. rep. 1997—). Presbyterian. Club: Masons (32 deg.). Home: 120 Berkley Dr Terre Haute IN 47803-1708 Office: Rose Hulman Inst Tech 5500 Wabash Ave Terre Haute IN 47803-3999

GUTHRIE, RANDOLPH HOBSON, JR., plastic surgeon, consultant; b. N.Y.C., Dec. 8, 1934; s. Randolph Hobson and Mabel Edith (Welton) G.; m. Beatrice Mills Holden, Mar. 20, 1965; children: Randolph Hobson III, Michael Phipps, Philip Holden. AB, Princeton U., 1957; MD, Harvard U., 1961. Intern N.Y. Hosp., N.Y.C., 1961-62, resident, 1962-63, 69-71, chief resident, 1971; resident St. Luke's Hosp., N.Y.C., 1963-66, chief resident, 1966—; chief plastic & reconstructive surgery svc. Meml. Sloan-Kettering Cancer Ctr., N.Y.C., 1971-77; chief dept. plastic and reconstructive surgery N.Y. Downtown Hosp., N.Y.C., 1979-2000; asst. prof. Cornell U. Med. Coll., 1971-74, assoc. prof., 1974-89, prof., 1989—; asst. attending surgeon, N.Y. Hosp., 1971-74, assoc. attending surgeon, 1974-89, attending surgeon, 1989—; attending surgeon Sloan-Kettering Cancer Ctr., 1977-93, cons., 1994—. Author: The Truth About Breast Implants, 1994; co-author: Reconstruction and Esthetic Mammoplasty, 1989; contbr. articles to profl. jours., books. Pres. East River Med. Found., N.Y.C., 1970-80, Acacia Found., N.Y.C., 1980-94; alumni dir. St. Paul's Sch., Concord, N.H., 1979-83, form agt., 1983-87, term trustee, 1985-89, life trustee, 1989-94; trustee Episcopal Sch., N.Y.C., 1976-84; bd. dirs. Am.-Italian Found. Cancer Rsch., N.Y.C., 1985-94; bd. dirs., treas. Save Venice, Inc., 1985-89, pres., 1989-97, chmn., 1997—; trustee N.Y. Downtown Hosp., 1985-92, Isabella Stewart Gardner Mus., Boston, 1998—. Maj. M.C. AUS, 1966-69. Decorated Cavaliere nel 'Ordine Al Merito della Repubblica Italiana; rsch. fellow Sloan Kettering Cancer Ctr., 1971-77. Mem. ACS, Plastic Surgery Rsch. Coun., Am. Geriatrics Soc., Am. Soc. Plastic and Reconstructive Surgeons, Pan Am. Med. Soc., N.Y. Soc. Plastic and Reconstructive Surgery, N.Y. Med.

Soc., Med. Soc. County N.Y., Herbert Conway Soc., Doubles Club, Century Club, Knickerbocker Club (N.Y.C.). Home and Office: 15 E 74th St New York NY 10021-2604

GUTIERREZ, CARL T. C., governor; b. Agana Heights, Guam, Oct. 15, 1941; s. Tomas Taitano Gutierrez and Rita Benavente Cruz; m. Geraldine Chance Torres, 1963; children: Carla Stahl, Tommy, Hannah. Mem. Senate Guam, beginning 1972, spkr., chmn. of ways and means com., chmn. HUD; vice chmn. rules com., tourism com., transp. com.; gov. Guam, Agana, 1994—. Roman Catholic. Address: PO Box 2950 Agana GU 96932-2950

GUTIÉRREZ, ELISA DE LEÓN, languages educator; b. Mercedes, Tex., July 30, 1931; d. Juventino and Felipa (Sanchez) de León; children: Richard, Laura, Carlos, Daniel, Emilio F. Jr., Martha. BA, U. Tex., 1952, MEd, 1972, PhD, 1985. Registered med. technologist. Chief med. technologist Dr. Rodriguez Hosp., Rio Grande City, Tex., 1953-60; biology tchr. Rio Grande City H.S., 1953-64; exec. dir. Cmty. Action Program Starr County, Tex., 1965-67; specialist divsn. dir. bilingual edn. Tex. Edn. Agy., Austin, 1972-95; planner Ark. Dept. Edn., Little Rock, 1995—. Mem. Tex. Assn. Bilingual Edn. (legis. chmn. 1998-99), Am. Soc. Clin. Pathologists (registered). Roman Catholic. Avocations: reading. Home: 6309 Treadwell Blvd Austin TX 78757-4321

GUTIERREZ, FRIAS MARCELO ARTURO, civil engineer; b. Cordoba, Argentina, May 31, 1931; s. Arturo Deadth and Maria Clarz (Frias) G.; m. Lidia Mabel Salazar, June 25, 1960; children: Marcelo Andres, Sergio. Degree in civil engring., U. Cordoba (Argentina), 1957. Resident engr. Agua & Elec. Power, Viedma, Argentina, 1957-60; civil engr. Water Devel. Dept., Viedma, 1960-67; sr. tech. officer FAO/ONU, Rome, 1967-84; cons. Water Devel. Dept., Viedma, 1985-92. Mem. ASCE, Oxford Club (life). Roman Catholic.

GUTIERREZ, HORACIO TOMAS, concert pianist; b. Havana, Cuba, Aug. 28, 1948; came to U.S., 1961; s. Tomas A. and Josephine (Fernandez) G.; m. Patricia A. Asher, July 1, 1972. Diploma, Juilliard Sch. Music, 1970; Doctorate (hon.), Cath. U. Am., 1999. Made debut at age 11 with Havana Symphony Orch., 1959; performed recitals and with major symphony orgns. throughout world; appeared in Music Nights, BBC-TV, London, PBS, U.S.; tours. of U.S., Can., Europe, S.Am., Israel, USSR; recs. of Liszt, Tschaikowsky, Schumann, Rachmaninoff, Prokofiev, Grieg, and Brahms on EMI, Angel, Telarc, Chandos Records. Recipient 2d prize Tschaikowsky Competition, 1970; recipient Avery Fisher award for outstanding achievement in music, 1982. Office: Cramer/Marder Artists 127 W 96th St Apt 13B New York NY 10025-6430 also: 3436 Springhill Rd Lafayette CA 94549-2535*

GUTIERREZ-CARRETERO, ENCARNACION, cardiac surgeon, researcher; b. Seville, Spain, May 19, 1966; d. Jesús Gutierrez-Rodrigo and Encarnación Carretero-Morales; m. Rafael Bello-Puentes; 1 child, Rafael Bello-Gutierrez. Licenciate of medicine, U. Seville, 1991, MD, 1997. Med. resident Hosp. Virgen Del Rocio, Seville, 1992-96, exptl. rschr., 1992—, asst. prof., 1993—, cardiovasc. surgeon, 1997. Author: Guia de Formacion de Especialista, 1995. Mem. Spanish Soc. Cardiovasc. Surgery, Spanish Soc. Surg. Rsch. Avocations: paddling, walking, reading, music. Home: Av Emilio Lemos 19 6 3M, 41020 Seville Spain also: C Emilio Lemos, Edificio Covandonga 6 3M, 41020 Seville Spain

GUTIÉRREZ DEL ÁLAMO, JOAQUÍN M., mathematics educator; b. Madrid, June 27, 1948; s. Joaquín G. and María JÉsus Gil. Lic. in math., U. Complutense Madrid, 1971, D Math., 1990; lic. in history, U. Paris, 1981. Asst. prof. U. Polit. Madrid, 1982-83, 84-90, assoc. prof., 1990—; prof. Inst. Estella (Spain), 1983-84; vis. prof. Univ. Coll. Dublin, Ireland, 1994. Contbr. articles to profl. jours. Roman Catholic. Office: ETSI Indsls Dept Math, C José Gutiérrez Abascal 2, 28006 Madrid Spain

GUTIERREZ-MORLOTE, JESÚS, physician, cardiologist; b. Santander, Cantabria, Spain, Mar. 27, 1949; s. Jesus Gutierrez and Blanca Morlote; m. Ana Lobato. MD, U. Valladolid, Spain, 1973; PhD, U. Cantabria, 2000. Provincial dir. Ministry of Pub. Health, Salamanca, Spain, 1984-87, gen. dir. pub. health, 1990-91, gen. dir. human resources and orgn., 1992, gen. dir. profl. orgn., 1992-93, gen. sec. of health, 1993-94; gen. dir. pub. health Castilla-La Mancha, 1987-89. Author of numerous works on coronary disease. E-mail: mivgmj@humv.es. Office: Hosp U Marques Decilla, Avenida Valdecilla s/u, Santander Cantabria, Spain

GUTIN, BERNARD, physiology and education educator; b. N.Y.C., Aug. 26, 1934; m. Chelley Shaner, June 30, 1958; children: Glenn, Linda. Student, Hofstra Coll., 1953-54, Cortland State Coll., 1957-58; AB, Hunter Coll., 1960; MA, PhD, NYU, 1965. Grad. asst. NYU, 1960-61; asst. prof. Hunter Coll., 1961-68; prof. Tchr. Coll. Columbia U., 1968—; physiologist Cardiac Rehab. Ctr. Montefiore Hosp., 1973-80, Inst. of Environ. Stress U. Calif., Santa Barbara, 1975; dir. physiology Weight Control Ctr. Holy Name Hosp., Teaneck, N.J., 1980-83; dir. Ctr. for Health Promotion, 1982-84, Div. of Health Sci., 1987-89; vis. scientist Hosp. for Spl. Surgery, 1989-90; emeritus prof. Applied Physiology and Edn. Tchrs. Coll. Columbia U., 1991; prof. pediatrics and physiology Ga. Prevention Inst. Med. Coll. of Ga. Assoc. editor Rsch. Quar., 1976-80; reviewer Medicine & Science in Sports and Exercise, Internat. Jour. of Sports Medicine, Internat. Jour. of Obesity, Jour. Am. Med. Assn., New Eng. Jour. of Medicine, Jour. of Pediatrics, Jour. of Applied Physiology Pediatrics, Obesity Rsch., Pediatric Exercise Sci. Mem. exercise com. N.Y. Heart Assn., 1978-87, Food and Nutrition Coun. of Greater N.Y., 1983-85. Athletic scholar, Hofstra U., Grad. Tuition scholar NYU. Fellow Am. Coll. Sports Medicine; mem. AAHPER (rsch. coun. 1971), Am. Alliance for Health, Phys. Edn., and Recreation, N.Y. Acad. Scis., N.Am. Assn. for Pediatric Exercise Sci., Am. Inst. Nutrition, Am. Soc. for Clin. Nutrition, North Am. Assn. for Study of Obesity, Am. Acad. Kinesiology and Phys. Edn. Democrat. Home: 724 Somerset Way Augusta GA 30909-3131 Office: Med Coll Ga Ga Prevention Inst Augusta GA 30912-3710

GÜTING, RALF HARTMUT, computer science educator; b. Lünen, Germany, May 9, 1955; s. Hans-Friedrich and Hildegard (Kroh) G.; m. Edith Ermert, Apr. 1, 1977; children: Nils, Helge. MS in Computer Sci., U. Dortmund, Germany, 1981, PhD in Computer Sci., 1983; postgrad., McMaster U., Hamilton, Ont., Can., 1981-82. Rsch. asst. U. Dortmund, 1981-87, asst. prof., 1987-89; prof. U. Hagen, Germany, 1989—; vis. rschr. IBM Almaden Rsch. Ctr., San Jose, Calif., 1985-96. Author: Datenstrukturen und Algorithmen, 1992, (with M. Erwig) Übersetzerbau, 1999. Evangelical Christian. Avocations: music, tennis. Office: Fern Univ Hagen, Praktische Informatik IV, D-58084 Hagen Germany

GUTLEB, ARNO CHRISTIAN, veterinarian, researcher; b. Klagenfurt, Carinthia, Austria, May 3, 1962; m. Barbara Rainer; children: Tobias, Helena. Dipl.Tzt., U. Vet. Medicine, Vienna, Austria, 1980, PhD, 1995. Asst. U. Vet. Medicine, Vienna, 1989-94, 95-97; postdoctoral fellow Wageningen Univ., Wageningen, The Netherlands, 1994-95, 97-00; postdoc Wageningen Univ., The Netherlands, 2000—. Mem. Internat. Union for Conservation of Nature (editor Otter Specialist Group Bull.), Soc. Environ. Toxicology and Chemistry, Soc. Environ. Contamination and Toxicology. Home: Parallelweg 4, NL6861EK Oosterbeek The Netherlands Office: Toxicology Sect WUR, Tuinlaan 5, NL6703HE Wageningen The Netherlands

GUTMAN, HAIM, surgical oncologist, researcher; b. Haifa, Israel, Jan. 27, 1952; s. Abraham and Rachel (Seltzer) G. MD magna cum laude, Tel Aviv Sch. Medicine, Israel, 1976. Med. diplomate, surgeon. Intern Sapir Med. Ctr., Kfar Saba, Israel, 1975-76; R & D officer Israel Def. Forces/Med. Corps, 1977-81; resident in surgery Beilinson Campus Rabin Med. Ctr., Petach Tikva, Israel, 1981-87; sr. surgeon Beilinson Campus Rabin Med. Ctr., Petach Tikva, 1987-91, attending surgeon, surg. oncologist Beilinson Campus, 1993—, chairperson melanoma and soft tissue tumor bds., 1994, chmn. quality assurance com., 1993-94, mem. Helsinki com., 1995-96, mem. resuscitation ad-hoc com., 1996; postdoct. surg. oncology fellow M.D. Anderson Cancer Ctr., Houston, 1991-93; sr. lectr. dept. surgery Sackler Sch. Medicine Tel Aviv U., 1996. Mem. editl. bd.: Oncology Report, 1993, The Cancer Jour., 1993; contbr. numerous articles to profl. jours. Maj. Israel Def. Forces Med. Corps. Res., 1969—. Grantee Israel Cancer Assn., 1995, 98, 99, Schauder Fund, 1997-98; IPF scholar Am. Physicians Fellowship for Medicine in Israel, 1991-92, 92-93, Sima Weisman scholar, 1992, Smithkline-Beecham Annual Surg. Oncology scholar, 1992, Surg. Oncology scholar Israel Cancer Assn., 1991-92, 92-93. Mem. Israel Med. Assn. (Surg. Oncology scholar 1991-92, mem. specialization and edn. com. scientific coun.), Israel Surg. Soc. (edn. com. 1988), Israel Soc. Surg. Oncology (mem. scientific com. 1995), Am. Assn. Cancer Rsch., N.Am. Surg. Oncology Group, Soc. Surg. Oncology, European Soc. Surg. Oncology. Office: Rabin Med Ctr/Beilinson Cam, Dept Surgery, 49100 Petach Tikva Israel

GUTMAN, LUCY TONI, school social worker, educator, counselor; b. Phila., July 13, 1936; d. Milton R. and Clarissa (Silverman) G.; divorced; children: James, Laurie. BA, Wellesley Coll., 1958; MSW, Bryn Mawr Coll., 1963; MA in History, U. Ariz., 1978; MEd, Northwestern State U., 1991, MA in English, 1992; postgrad., U. So. Miss., 1992—. Cert. sch. social work specialist, Nat. Bd. Cert. Counselor; diplomate in clin. social work; cert. secondary tchr., La.; cert. counselor, La.; cert. Acad. Cert. Social Workers, La. Bd. Cert. Social Workers. Social worker Phila. Gen. Hosp., 1963-65; sr. social worker Irving Schwartz Inst. Children and Youth, 1965-66; sr. psychiat. social worker Child Study Ctr. Phila., 1966-68; chief social worker Framingham (Mass.) Ct. Clinic Juvenile Offenders, 1968-72; dir. clinic, supr. social work Tucson East Cmty. Mental Health Ctr., 1972-74; coord. spl. adoptions program Cath. Social Svcs. So. Ariz., Tucson, 1974-75; social worker Met. Ministry, 1983; supr. social work Leesville (La.) Mental Health Clinic, 1984; sch. social worker Vernon Parish Sch. Bd., Leesville, 1984—; cons. Nashua (N.H.) Cmty. Coun., 1969-72; adj. instr. English, sociology, Am. and European history Northwestern State U., Ft. Polk, La., 1984—; part-time counselor River North Psychol. Svcs., Leesville, 1989-92; presenter La. Sch. Social Workers Conf., 1986, 87, Ann. Conf. NASW, 1987, 88, La. Spl. Edn. Conf., 1988, La. Conf. Tchrs. English, 1991, 94, So. Assn. Women Historians, 1994, Mid-Am. Conf. History, 1997, Conf. Contemporary So. Women's Lit., 1997, La. Hist. Assn. Conf., 1998. Contbr. articles to profl. jours. Nat. Soc. Colonial Dames scholar, 1978-79; fellow Pa. State, 1961-62, NIMH, 1962-63. Mem. NASW (diplomate), La. Hist. Assn., So. Hist. Assn., So. Assn. Women Historians, Gamma Beta Phi, Phi Alpha Theta, Phi Kappa Phi. Home: 2004 Allison St Leesville LA 71446-5104

GUTMAN, RICHARD EDWARD, lawyer; b. New Haven, Apr. 9, 1944; s. Samuel and Marjorie (Leo) G.; m. Jill Leslie Senft, June 8, 1969 (dec.); 1 child, Paul Senft; m. Rosann Seasonwein, Dec. 10, 1987. AB, Harvard U., 1965; JD, Columbia U., 1968. Bar: N.Y. 1969, U.S. Ct. Appeals (2d cir.) 1969, U.S. Dist. Ct. (so. and ea. dists.) N.Y. 1975, U.S. Supreme Ct. 1982, Tex. 1991. Counsel Exxon Corp., N.Y.C., 1978-90; Dallas, 1990-91; asst. gen. counsel Exxon Corp., Dallas, 1992-99, Exxon Mobil Corp., Dallas, 1999—; pres. 570 Park Ave Apts., Inc., N.Y.C., 1984-89, past bd. dirs. Fellow Am. Bar Found. (life); mem. ABA (fed. regulation securities com., vice chmn. 1995-98), Am. Law Inst., N.Y. State Bar Assn. (exec. com. 1983-86, 93—, securities regulation com. 1980—, chmn. 1993-97, treas. bus. law sect. 2000), Assn. of Bar of City of N.Y. (securities regulation com. 1980-81, 83-86), Dallas Bar Assn., Coll. of the State Bar of Tex., N.A.M. (corp. fin. and mgmt. com.), Harvard Club (N.Y.C., admissions com. 1983-86, chmn. 1985-86, nominating com. 1986-87, bd. dirs. 1988-91, v.p. 1990-91), Harvard Club (Dallas, bd. dirs. 1998—).

GUTMANN, RAMON MAXIMO, gerontologist; b. Buenos Aires, May 2, 1943; s. Abraham Jacob and Hildegard (Springer) G.; m. Fortune Mizraji, Aug. 13, 1963 (div. Mar. 1968); 1 child, Adrian Rodolfo; m. Luisa Acrich, Jan. 6, 1973; children: Juan Martin, Dalia Irene. MS in Social Work, U. Buenos Aires, 1974, degree sociology; PhD in Social Psychology, U. Kennedy, Buenos Aires, 1978; cert. in advanced gerontology, Yeshiva U., N.Y.C., 1980. Dir. Social Svcs. Jewish Community, Buenos Aires, 1968-78; exec. dir. Coordinating Coun. of Jewish Social Svcs., Buenos Aires, 1968-96; prof. social gerontology U. Buenos Aires; ad honorem advisor for gerontol. programs Sec. of Third Age, 1993—; v.p. for Latin Am. and the Caribbean Internat. Fedn. on Aging, 1993—. Author books; contbr. more than 100 articles to profl. jours. Hon. advisor Partido Blanco de los Jubilados, 1991-93. Mem. Gerontol. Soc. of Am., Internat. Psychogeriatric Assn., Assn. Gerontol. Buenos Aires (v.p. 1992-94), Gerontol. Soc. of Argentina (spl. mem.), Gerontol. Soc. of Entre RiosArgentina (mem. emeritus). Avocation: tennis. E-mail: gutmann@ciudad.com.ar.

GUTMANN, VALENTIN, physician; b. Bucharest, Romania, Nov. 14, 1954; s. Felix and Sofia G.; m. Jeanet Walter, July 6, 1981; 1 child, Beny. MD, Inst. Medicine and Pharmacy, Bucharest, 1980. Med. diplomate. Resident in internal medicine Univ. Hosp., Bucharest, 1980-83; family physician various rural clins., Romania, 1983-86; chief resident Barzilay Hosp., Ashqelon, Israel, 1986-89; family physician Sick Found. of Nat. Workers, Yavne, Israel, 1989—. Mem. N.Y. Acad. Scis. Avocation: keyboard playing.

GUTOWICZ, MATTHEW FRANCIS, JR., radiologist; b. Camden, N.J., Feb. 23, 1945; s. Matthew F. and A. Patricia (Walczak) G.; m. Alice Mary Bell, June 27, 1977; 1 child, Melissa. BA, Temple U., 1968; DO, Phila. Coll. Osteo. Medicine, 1972. Diplomate Am. Bd. Radiology, Am. Bd. Nuclear Medicine. Intern Mercy Hosp., Denver, 1972-73; resident in diagnostic radiology Hosp. of U. Pa., Phila., 1973-76, fellow in nuclear medicine, 1976-77; chief dept. radiology and nuclear medicine Fisher Titus Med. Ctr., Norwalk, Ohio, 1977—; pres. Firelands Radiology, Inc., Norwalk, 1977—. Republican. Roman Catholic. Avocations: photography, tennis, scuba diving. Home: 23 Patrician Dr Norwalk OH 44857-2463

GUTOWSKI, JUERGEN, physics educator; b. Hamburg, Germany, Dec. 23, 1955; s. Helmuth and Irene (Gladysz) G.; m. Antje Gerhartz, Aug. 27, 1982; 1 child, Angelo. Diploma in physics, Tech. U. Berlin, 1982, D in Natural Scis., 1985, habilitation, 1988. Sci. asst. Tech. U. Berlin, 1982-85, asst. prof. physics, 1985-91; prof. physics U. Bremen, Germany, 1991—, vice rector, 1995-97, dean physics and elec. engring., 1998—. Editor Procs. Internat. Conf. on II-VI Compounds, 1989. Mem. German Phys. Soc., European Phys. Soc., Deutscher Hochschulverband. Protestant. Office: U Bremen Inst Solid St Phys, PO Box 330 440, D-28334 Bremen Germany

GUTSALYUK, VALARY MICHAEL, food engineering educator, researcher; b. Ocnitsa, Moldova, Mar. 26, 1952; s. Michael Ephim and Anna Gregory (Shimanskaya) G.; m. Yurij Ludmila Kvashenko, Mar. 4, 1962 (div. 1991); 1 child, Tatyana. Degree in Engring., Food Engring. Inst., Kyiv, 1973, PhD, 1983, DS, 1996. Rsch. engr. Food Engring. Inst., Kyiv, 1973-77, scientific worker, 1977-83, asst. prof., 1983-92; assoc. prof. Food Technologies U., Kyiv, 1992-97, prof., 1997—; mgr. FILTOCON Venture, Kyiv, 1991—; sec. Ukrainian Nat. Com. Heat-Mass Transfer, 1996—. Contbr. articles to scientific jours.; inventor in field. Mem. N.Y. Acad. Scis., Nat. Geographic Soc., Ukrainian Membrane Soc. Avocations: music, sports. Office: Ukrainian State U Food T, 68 Vladimirskaya St, 252033 Kyiv Ukraine

GUTSOL, ALEXANDER FYODOROVICH, physicist, researcher; b. Magnitogorsk, Russia, Dec. 1, 1958; s. Fyodor Issidorovich and Elena Venidiktovna (Fedorenko) G.; m. Natalya Nikolaevna Kiryukhina, Oct. 27, 1979; children: Kirill Alexandrovich, Ksenia Alexandrovna. Engr., Phys.-Tech. Inst., Moscow, USSR, 1982, PhD, 1985. Rschr. Inst. Chemistry and Tech./Kola Sci. Ctr./Russian Acad. Scis., Apatity, Russia, 1985-90, sr. rschr., 1990—; vis. scientist Tampere (Finland) U. Tech., 1998, 2000, TNO, Apeldoorn, The Netherlands, 1998, SINTEF, Trondheim, Norway, 1997, TAN Ceramics Ltd., Migdal Haemek, Israel, 1996. Contbr. articles to profl. jours.; patentee in field. Recipient poster award 5th European Conf. on Thermal Plasma Processes, 1998; Urgent grantee Internat. Sci. Found., 1994, Nordic Coun. Mins. grantee, 1997, grantee Acad. Scis. Finland, 1998, 2000, Russian Found. Basic Rsch., 1998. Home: Kozlova St 5-12, 184200 Apatity Russia Office: Inst Chemistry and Tech, Fersman St 14, 184200 Apatity Russia

GUTSTEIN, CAROL FEINHANDLER, realtor; b. Chgo., Aug. 31, 1941; d. Emanuel Joshua and Rose (Paster) Feinhandler; m. Solomon Gutstein, Sept. 3, 1961; children: Jonathan, David, Daniel, Joshua. BS in Edn., Loyola U., 1962; MA in Spl. Edn., DePaul U., 1969. Cert. comml. investment mem.; grad. residential real estate; cert. comml. real estate. Spl. cons. Mayor's Office of Sr. Citizens and Handicapped, Chgo., 1977-79; realtor C-21 Shoreline, Evanston, Ill., 1982-84, Matanky, Chgo., 1985, Hallmark & Johnston, Chgo., 1986-95, L.H. Properties, Ltd., Lincolnwood, Ill., 1996—; cons. Nursing Homes, Chgo., 1978-80. Compiler, editor Community Resources for the Disabled Person in the Chicago Metropolitan Area, 1978. Active campaigner Paul Simon for Senate campaign, 1984-85, 89-90; mgr., dir. Aldermanic campaigns, Chgo., 1975, 79, 95; del. 11th Congrl. Dist. Dem. Nat. Conv., 1980; mem. Dist. 1 Chgo. Sch. Coun., 1989-91. Fellowship Northwestern U., 1962. Mem. WCR (bd. dirs. 1997-98), CCIM (bd. dirs. 1997-2000), Camp Ramah (bd. dirs. 1985-2000), Hadassah (corr. sec. 1998, bd. mem. 1999). Democrat. Jewish.

GUTTHAL, STEPHAN DIRK, management consultant; b. Berlin, Jan. 10, 1969; s. Joachim and Karin (Günther) G. Diploma in engring., Tech. U. Berlin, 1994, D of Engring., 1999. Lectr. Tech. U. Berlin, 1991-94, rsch. asst., 1994-98; intern Siemens Med. Systems, Iselin, N.J., 1994; cons. Andersen Consulting, Berlin, 1998—; freelance software developer, Berlin, 1993-94; freelance cons., Berlin, 1996-98. Author: Chances and Risks in the Express Freight Industry, 1999; contbr. articles to profl. jours. Winner Berlin Bus. Championship, McKinsey & Co., 1997. Avocations: collecting classical records, backpacking, travel. Office: Andersen Consulting, Cicerostrasse 21, D-10709 Berlin Germany

GUTTMANN, ANTHONY JOHN, mathematics educator; b. Melbourne, Australia, Apr. 8, 1945; s. Laszlo and Anna Guttmann; m. Susette Veronica Wise, Dec. 4, 1967; children: Jacki, Laurence. BS, U. Melbourne, 1965, MS, 1967; PhD, U. NSW, Australia, 1969. Lectr. U. Newcastle, Australia, 1971-73, sr. lectr., 1974-75, assoc. prof., 1976-83, prof., dean math. faculty, 1984-86; reader U. Melbourne, 1987-88, prof., 1989—, head dept. math., 1993-94, dep. dean, 1994-95. Author: Programming and Algorithms, 1977; contbr. numerous articles to profl. jours. Recipient numerous rsch. grants Australian Rsch. Coun., 1968—. Fellow Australian Math. Soc. (coun., Hannan medal 1999), Soc. for Indsl. and Applied Math. Avocations: running, reading, triathlon. Office: U Melbourne Dept Math & Stats, Swanson St, Parkville 3010, Australia

GUTTMANN, KARL, consulting mechanical engineer; b. Vienna, Austria, May 11, 1919; came to U.S., 1949; s. Otto and Friederike (Kraus) G.; m. Clarice Brown, Jan. 18, 1954 (div. May 1955); m. Ethel Weiner, Jan. 31, 1958 (dec. Feb. 1990); 1 child, Steven O.; m. Frances Binnington, Aug. 1993. ME with honors, Vienna State Coll. Engring., 1938. Registered profl. engr., Calif., Oreg., Wis., D.C., Utah. Vice pres. Kasin, Guttmann & Assocs., San Francisco, 1956-77; pres. Guttmann & MacRitchie, San Francisco, 1977-98; prin. Guttmann & Blaevoet, San Francisco, 1998—. Mem. Calif. Bldg. Safety Bd., 1986-93; mem. San Francisco Seismic Hazard Evaluation Com., 1978-86; tech. adviser Calif. Energy Commn., 1981. Fellow ASHRAE (life mem.; pres. Golden Gate chpt. 1960-61; Disting. 50 Yr. Mem. award 2000); mem. Am. Assn. Energy Engrs. Home: 389 Upper Ter San Francisco CA 94117-4517 Office: Guttmann & Blaevoet 55 Hawthorne St Ste 400 San Francisco CA 94105-3910

GUTTY, GIANFRANCO, insurance company executive. CEO Assicurazioni Generali, dep. chmn., mng. dir. Office: Assicurazioni Generali, Assicurazioni Generali, Piazza Duca degli Abruzzi 2, 34132 Trieste Italy*

GUTWIRTH, JACQUES, anthropologist; b. Antwerp, Belgium, 1926. LittD, U. Paris, 1969. Dir. rsch. Cen. Nat. Recherche Sci., Ivry Cedex, France, 1982—; prof. anthropology Paris V, 1983—. Author: Vie Juive Traditionnelle, 1970, Les Judeo-Chretiens d'Aujourd'Hui, 1987, C Eghise Electronipue, 1998. Mem. Assn. Francaise de Sociologie Religieuse (pres. 1981-83), Soc. d'Ethnologie Francaise (v.p. 1983-87). Home: Am Eiserner Schlag 3, D 60431 Frankfurt France Office: Cen Nat Recherche Sci, Musee l'Homme, 94204 Ivry Cedex France

GUTZMAN, PHILIP CHARLES, aerospace executive, logistician; b. Salmon, Idaho, June 23, 1938; s. Lester Theodore and Mildred Cordelia (Hinchey) G.; m. Karen Diane Withington, June 17, 1957 (div. Sept. 30, 1957); m. Linda Ann Young, Aug. 28, 1960; children: Kevin Raeder, Lance. BS, U. Ariz., 1962, BA, 1962; MPA, U. Okla., 1977. Cert. Profl. Logistician. Hardrock miner Calera Mining Co., Cobalt, Idaho, 1955; enlisted U.S. Army, 1955-62, commd. 2d lt., 1962, advanced through grades to maj., 1970; supr. logistics engring. Gen. Dynamics Land Systems, Detroit, 1983-84, chief advance systems, 1984-85; ops. mgr. Gen. Dynamics Svcs., St. Louis, 1985-87, dir. ground elec., 1987-88; dep. program mgr. Gen. Dynamics Svcs., Taif, Saudi Arabia, 1988-89; dir. logistics Gen. Dynamics Svcs., Detroit, 1989-91, program mgr. Saudi Arabian Tank program, 1992-93; sr. cons. Shipley Assocs., Boise, 1994—; adj. prof. mgmt. Boise State U., 1995. Author: Dictionary of Military Acronyms, 1990; contbr. numerous mil. articles to profl. jours., 1972—. Decorated Bronze Star (3), Purple Heart (5), Air medal, Meritorious Svc. medal (2), Cross of Gallantry with Palm. Mem. Soc. Logistics Engrs. (chpt. chmn. 1990-93, bd. dirs. 1992). Republican. Avocations: judo, fishing, reading. Office: Shipley Assocs 111 E 200 S Farmington UT 84025-2315

GUTZOW, IVAN STOYANOV, chemist; b. Sofia, Bulgaria, May 31, 1933; s. Stoyan Ivanov and Maria Magdalena (Guldan) G.; m. Danja Dimitrova Kateva, July 15, 1962; 1 child, Stoyan. Chem. Engr., Tech. U., Sofia, 1959; D Chem. Sci., Bulgarian Acad. Scis., 1972. Chemist Inst. Phys. Chemistry Bulgarian Acad. Sci., Sofia, 1959-62, rsch. asst. Inst. Phys. Chemistry, 1962-74, rsch. prof. Inst. Phys. Chemistry, 1974-98, head of dept. crystal growth Inst. Phys. Chemistry, 1989-93, head dept. amorphous materials Inst. Phys. Chemistry, 1997-2000; editor-in-chief Jour. Bulgarian Chem. Comms., 1990-96; part-time lectr., prof. chem. faculty, U. Sofia, 1979-84, U. Bourgas, 1985-93, Tech. U. Sofia, 1992-97; vis. prof. physics of glass, U. Rostock, Germany, 1990, glass sci., Alfred U., N.Y., 1992, 98, 99U. Jena, Germany, 1995-97, Fed. U. Sao Carlos, Brazil, 1995. Co-author: (with J. Schmelzer) The Vitreous State, 1995; editor: Acad. Publs./Sofia, 1994, Thin Films and Phase Transformation Surfaces, 1994, Proc. Vakna Conf. on Glass and Ceramics, 1995, 97, 99; contbr. numerous articles to profl. jours. Recipient award Ministry of Edn., Sofia, 1968, award in chemistry Union Bulgarian Scientists, Sofia, 1984, Order of St. Cyril and Method, Sofia, 1974. Mem. German Glass-Tech. Union, Internat. Commn. on Glass, Bulgarian Acad. Sci. Avocations: hobby gardener, mountain climbing. Office: Inst Chem/Bulgarian Acad, Acad G Bonchev Str Block 11, 1113 Sofia Bulgaria

GUUL-SIMONSEN, FRODE, SR., research scientist; b. Haderslev, Denmark, Mar. 13, 1934; s. Arthur and Maren (Schmidt) Guul-S.; m. Ulla Mathiesen, Apr. 15, 1964; children: Lisbeth, Merete. BSME, Engring. Coll., 1958, degree European engr., 1992. Lectr. The Engring. Coll., Copenhagen, 1958-59; rsch. engr. Privat Co., Haderslev, Denmark, 1959-62, Nat. Inst. Agrl. Engring., Bedford, 1963, Sch. Europe, London, 1963; scientist Rsch. Inst., Horsens, Denmark, 1963-94, dep. head dept., sr. rsch. scientist, 1994—. 1st class Army's Tech. Corps, 1958-59. Mem. European Fedn. Nat. Engring. Assns., The Soc. of Danish Engrs. E-mail: FrodeG.Simonsen@agrsci.dk. Home: Husoddevej 66, DK-8700 Horsens Denmark Office: Danish Inst Agrl Scis, Schuttesvej 17, DK-8700 Horsens Denmark

GUVENIR, HALIL ALTAY, computer scientist, educator; b. Bursa, Turkey, Nov. 16, 1957; s. Halit and Nuriye (Kale) G.; m. Nuray Abacioglu, July 29, 1989; children: Ayca, Alp. BS, Istanbul (Turkey) Tech. U., 1979, MS, 1981; PhD, Case Western Res. U., 1987. Rsch. asst. Istanbul Tech. U., 1979-82; knowledge engr. Case Western Res. U., Cleve., 1985; asst. prof. Hacettepe U., Ankara, Turkey, 1987-88; asst. prof. Bilkent U., Ankara, 1988-94, assoc. prof. computer sci., 1994—; vice chair dept. computer engring. Bilkent U., 1997—; cons. Tantalus Inc., Cleve., 1987, Aselsan, Ankara, 1989, Capital Mkt. Bd. Turkey, Ankara, 1991-92. Contbr. articles to profl. jours. Turkish Ministry Edn. scholar, 1982-87, The Sci. and Rsch. Coun. Turkey grantee, 1995-97. Mem. AAAI, Assn. Computing Machinery (chmn. Bilkent chpt. 1992—). Avocations: swimming, cycling, photography. Office: Computer Engring Info Sci, Sch Computer Engring, Bilkent U, 06533 Ankara Turkey

GU XIULIAN, Chinese government official; b. Nantong, Jiangsu, China, 1936. Degree in metallurgy, Shenyang Metall. and Mech. Sch, China, 1961. Technician Gansu Jinchuan Non-Ferrous Metals Corp., China, 1962-67;

mem. sci. and tech. info. divsn. Ministry of Textiles, China, 1968-72; vice min. of state planning commn. Beijing People's Govt., 1973-82; gov. Jiangsu Prov., China, 1983-89; min. chem. industry Beijing People's Govt., 1989-98; vice president All-China Women's Federation, Beijing, 1998S. Mem. Communist Party of China, 1956—, alternate mem. Ctrl. Com., 1977-82, elected to Ctrl. Com., 12th Party Congress, 1982; dep. sec. Jiangsu Communist Party, 1989—. Office: ACWF, 15 Jian Guomen St, Beijing 100730, China*

GUY, DAVID MAURICE, academic administrator; b. Wellington, New Zealand, Oct. 30, 1944; s. Alan Charles and Enid Helen (Ashcroft) G.; children: Sheralyn May, Stephen David. BA with honors, Victoria U., Wellington, 1966; DipEdSt, U. Waikato, Hamilton, New Zealand, 1975, MEd, 1978; EdD, U. B.C., Can., 1982. Tchr. Heretaunga Coll., New Zealand, 1968-70; head dept. Mahurangi Coll., New Zealand, 1971-73; dir. continuing edn. U. Waikato, 1973-93, dir. cmty. and external rels., 1993-99, dir. external rels., 1999—; chmn. Nat. Coun. Adult Edn., 1989-92, Waikato Inst. Leisure Sport Studies, 1999—; ops. mgr. Tauranga U. Coll., 1997—. Mem. Cmty. Assistance Program, Hamilton, Hamilton Cmty. Arts Coun., Trade Union Edn. Authority, Wellington. Recipient Commemoration medal Govt. of New Zealand, 1990. Office: U Waikato, Pvt Bag 3105, Hamilton New Zealand

GUY, ELEANOR BRYENTON, writer; b. Pitts., Sept. 6, 1930; d. Lloyd Charles and Verda Eleanor (Hooper) Bryenton; m. Daniel Sowers Guy, Dec. 22, 1962; children: Stanley, Sharon. BA, Ohio Wesleyan U., 1953. Program dir. Cleve. Met. YWCA, Lakewood, Ohio, 1953-56, ctr. dir., 1956-57; residence dir., mem. faculty St. Luke's Hosp. Sch. Nursing, Shaker Heights, Ohio, 1957-59; pers. asst., counselor Acacia Mutual Life Ins. Co., Washington, 1959-62; admissions counselor Ohio No. U., Ada, 1963-64; freelance writer, photographer Kenton (Ohio) Times, 1984-88, Ada Herald, 1988-96; coord. external affairs, editor the Writ, Pettit Coll. of Law, Ohio No. U., 1995-96. Sec. bd. trustees, chmn. pub. rels. com. Ada Pub. Libr., 1982-86; mem. pub. rels. com., bd. dirs. Hardin County Alcohol and Drug Abuse Ctr., Kenton, 1989-92; chmn. publicity Town and Gown Planning Com., Ada, 1988; tchr., mem. co-chair edn. com., mem. missions com., mem. adminstrv. coun. local ch., mem. centennial com., publicist, 1985—, lay del. to West Ohio Ann. conf., 1998—. Mem. AAUW (pres. local br. 1978-80), Ohio No. U. Women (parliamentarian, pub. rels. chair Christmas Arts Festival 1990-96), P.E.O. (v.p. 1994-96, sec. 1998-99), Twice Ten Art Club (pres. 1984-85, 90-91, 97-98, sec. 1988-89, 99—). Methodist. Avocations: photography, travel, music.

GUY, KEITH WILLIAM ARTHUR, marketing professional, engineering executive; b. Frilford Heath, Berkshire, Eng., Dec. 14, 1943; s. Kenneth Leonard and Margaret (Rose) G.; m. Penelope Ann Gresner, Apr. 5, 1968 (div. July 1990); children: Tabitha Kate, Victoria Rose, Hannah Roberta; m. Kathryn Elizabeth Franklin, May 25, 1991. BSc, Imperial Coll., London, 1965, MSc, 1966, PhD, 1978. Mgr., staff engr. Air Products Ltd., Walton-on-Thames, Eng., 1970-77, mgr. design, 1977-81, mgr. process and proposals, 1981-85, gen. mgr. tech., 1985-89; mktg. dir. Air Products Plc, Walton-on-Thames, 1990-99; mem. bd. Interdisciplinary Rsch. Ctr., Imperial Coll., 1989—; mem. bd. PEC of Sci. and Engring. Rsch. Coun., Eng., 1990—, chmn. chem. engring. com., 1991—. Contbr. articles on engring. to profl. jours. Chmn. Mitcham and Morden Conservative Assn., London, 1984-89, v.p., 1990—. Fellow Royal Acad. Engrs., City and Guilds of London Inst., Instn. Chem. Engrs. (chmn. London br. 1985-87, v.p. 1999—). Conservative. Anglican. Avocations: books, bridge, music, travel, golf. Office: IAC Kings Bldg, Smithsquare Westminster, London SWIP 3JJ, England

GUY, MATTHEW TODD, county official; b. Denver, Dec. 18, 1970; s. Willard Ray and Carol Ann Guy; m. Tara Lynn Guy, June 26, 1993. BA in Polit. Sci., Ctrl. Coll., 1993; MPA, U. Colo., 1996. cert. trainer Am. Taekwondo Assn., Lakewood, Colo., 1998-2000, sch. owner, Pueblo, Colo., 2000. Adminstrv. aide dept. pub. works City of Boulder, Colo., 1994-96; sr. legis. auditor State Colo. Auditor's Office, Denver, 1996-97; dir. student fin. resource ctr. Met. State Coll., Denver, 1997-2000; dir. records ops. dept. transp. El Paso County, Colorado Springs, Colo., 2000—. Chair Water and Sewer Bd., Englewood, Colo., 1996-98; city coun. candidate City Coun., Englewood, 1997. Mem. Am. Coll. Pers. Assn., Nat. Assn. Coll. and Univ. Bus. Officers, Coll. Pers. Assn. Colo. Avocations: hockey, mountain climbing, martial arts. E-mail: mrguy@atataekwondo.com. Home: 44 S Golfwood Dr W Pueblo West CO 81007-3672

GUY, MILDRED DOROTHY, retired secondary school educator; b. Brunswick, Ga.; d. John and Mamie Paul (Smith) Floyd; m. Charles H. Guy, Aug. 18, 1956 (div. 1979); 1 child, Rhonda Lynn. BA in Social Sci., Savannah State Coll., 1949; MA in Am. History, Atlanta U., 1952; postgrad., U. So. Calif., U. Colo. Tchr. social studies L.S. Ingraham H.S., Sparta, Ga.; tchr. English and social studies North Jr. H.S., Colorado Springs, 1958-84, ret., 1984; cooperating tchr. Tchr. Edn. Program, Col. Coll., 1968-72. Fund raiser for Citizens for Theatre Auditorium, Colorado Springs, 1979; bd. dirs. Urban League, 1971-75; del. to County and State Dem. Conv., 1972, 76, 80, 84, 92, 96; mem. Pike's Peak C.C. Coun., 1976-83; mem. Colo. Springs Opera Coun. of 500, 1984-88; mem. nominating com. Wagon Wheel coun. Girl Scouts U.S.A., 1985-87; active Fine Arts Ctr., Pikes Peak Hospice; mem. St. John's Bapt. Ch., former sanctuary choir mem.; mem. Svcs. of Charity (local and nat.); life mem. Friends of Colorado Springs Pioneers Mus. Recipient Viking award North Jr. H.S., 1973, Woman of Distinction award Girl Scouts Wagon Wheel Coun., 1989, 94; Outstanding Black Woman of Colorado Springs award, 1975; named Pacesetter, Atlanta U., 1980-81, Outstanding Black Educator of Yr., Black Educators of Dist. II, Colorado Springs, 1984, Outstanding Ednl. Svc. award Colo. Dept. and State Bd. Edn., 1983, Dedicated Svc. award Pikes Peak C.C., 1983, Outstanding Cmty. Leadership award Alpha Phi Alpha, 1985, Action award Colo. Black Woman for Polit. Action, 1985, Sphinx award, 1986; named in recognition sect. Salute to Women, Colorado Springs Gazette Telegraph, 1986; Wall of Fame honoree Nat. Women's Hall of Fame, 1997. Mem. LWV (Colo. chpt.), Negro Hist. Assn. Colorado Springs, Women's Found. Colo., NAACP (life), Golden Heritage (life), NEA, AAUW, Colo. Coun. Social Studies Assn. Study Afro-Am. Life and History, Women's Ednl. Soc. Colo. Coll. (bd. mgrs. 1992-98), Colo. Springs Pioneers Mus. (life), Alpha Delta Kappa, Alpha Kappa Alpha (pres. Iota Beta Omega chpt. 1984-85, Chpt. Pres. award 1985). Home: 3132 Constitution Ave Colorado Springs CO 80909-2177

GUYARD, MARIUS-FRANCOIS, French literature educator; b. Paris, Mar. 18, 1921; s. Marius and Jeanne (Chabrillat) G.; m. Francoise Bordier, 1947; 4 children. D ès L, U. Paris, Sorbonne. Prof. U. Athens, 1955-57; prof. Strasbourg (France) U., 1957-63, vice chancellor, 1970-76; cultural counsellor French Embassy, U.K., 1963-65; prof. French Lit. U. Paris, Sorbonne, 1965-67, 80-90, prof. emeritus, 1990—; vice chancellor U. Montpellier (France), 1967-69, U. Amiens, 1969-70, U. Lyon (France), 1976-80; chmn. Conf. des Recteurs Français, 1975-78; mem. Franco-Brit. Coun., 1972-99. Author: La Grande-Bretagne dans le roman francais, 1954, Recherches Claudéliennes, 1964, D'un romantisme l'autre, 1992—; edits. of Lamartine, Hugo, 1958-2000, Claudel de Gaulle; numerous contbns. to revs. critical anthologies. Decorated Legion d'honneur, comdr. Ordre Nat. du Mérite, comdr. Ordre des Palmes Académiques, chevalier des Arts et Lettres (France); comdr. Orange=Nassau (Netherlands); officier Merite Italien.

GUYER, CHARLES GRAYSON, II, psychologist; b. High Point, N.C., May 22, 1949; s. Charles Grayson Sr. and Mildred Louise (Wrokman) G.; m. E.R. Ward, June 24, 1986; children: Charles Grayson III, Jarvis Griffith. BA, Appalachian State U., 1972, MA, 1974; EdD, Coll. William & Mary, 1978. Bd. cert. in counseling psychology and family psychology Am. Bd. Profl. Psychology. Resident No. Wyo. Mental Health, Buffalo, 1978-80; pvt. practice High Point, N.C., 1980-83, pvt. practice, Greensboro, N.C., 1988-98; chief sch. psychologist Perquimans County Schs., Hertford, N.C., 1998—; pres. Am. Bd. Family Psychology, 1992-94, bd. dirs., 1991-93. Contbr. articles to profl. jours., chpts. to books. Lt. USN, 1983-88. Fellow APA, Am. Soc. Clin. Hypnosis (chair ethics com. 1993-97), Acad. Family Psychology, Acad. Counseling Psychology (pres. 1993-95, Irving I. Sector award for the advancement of clin. hypnosis 1997); mem. Am. Group Psychotherapy Assn., Nat. Assn. Sch. Psychologists, Va. Acad. Clin. Psychologists, Va. Psychol. Assn., N.C. Soc. Clin. Hypnosis, N.C. Sch. Psychology Assn., Guilford County Psychol. Assn. (treas. 1997-98), Soc. Clin. Exptl. Hypnosis. Methodist. Avocations: running, reading. Home: 371 Great Hope Church Rd Hertford NC 27944

GUYNES, DEMI See MOORE, DEMI

GUYNN, RANDALL DAVID, lawyer; b. L.A., Oct. 13, 1957; married; 7 children. BA in Econs. with highest honors, Brigham Young U., 1981; JD, U. Va., 1984. Bar: N.Y. 1987, D.C. 1988. Law clk. to Judge J. Clifford Wallace U.S. Ct. Appeals 9th Cir., San Diego, 1984-85; law clk. to Justice William H. Rehnquist U.S. Supreme Ct., Washington, 1985-86; assoc. Davis Polk & Wardwell, N.Y.C., 1986-93, ptnr., 1993—; co-head Fin. Instns. Group, 1996—. Author: U.S. Disclosure Standards for Banks, 1998, Modernizing Securities Pledging Laws, 1996, Foreign Bank Aquisitions of U.S. Banks, 1995; exec. editor Va. Law Rev., 1983-84. Mem. ABA, Internat. Bar Assn. (chmn. com. on modernizing pledging laws 1994-2000), Order of Coif. Republican. Mem. LDS Ch. Avocation: photography. Office: Davis Polk & Wardwell 450 Lexington Ave Fl 31 New York NY 10017-3982

GUYON, ETIENNE MARIE, physics educator; b. Paris, Mar. 31, 1935; s. Pierre and Colette (Parot) G.; m. Marie Yvonne Mainguy, Dec. 21, 1957; children: Anne, Aude, Antoine, Emmanuel. Grad., Ecole Normale Superieure, Paris, 1959, DSc, 1964. Rsch. assoc. CNRS, Orsay, France, 1961-67; prof. U. Paris, Orsay, 1968—; dir. Palais de la Découverte, Paris, 1988-90, Ecole Normale Superieure, Paris, 1990—. Author: Mixing and Disorder, Physical Hydrodynamics, Physics of Granular Matter; contbr. articles profl. jours. Decorated officer Legion of Honor, officer Order of Merit. Fellow Am. Phys. Soc. Avocations: cross country skiing and racing, mountaineering. Home: 24 rue Ronsard, 91470 Limours France Office: Ecole Normale Superieure, 45 rue d'Ulm, 75005 Paris France

GUYOT, ALAIN M., researcher, consultant; b. Toulon, France, Dec. 3, 1931; s. Joseph Marie and Elisabeth (Putinier) G.; m. Evelyne Angles D'Auriac, Apr. 15, 1961; children: Constance, Franck, Etienne, Laurent, Edouard, Christiane. Ingenieur, Ecole Polytechnique, Paris, 1952; PhD, U. Lyon, France, 1957. With Centre Nat. de la Recherche Scientifique, Lyon, 1953—, dir. rsch., 1967-86, dir. rsch. (exceptional class), 1986-96, emeritus, 1996; cons. Soc. Industrielle des Liaisons Electriques, Montereau, France, 1962-95, Essences-Lubrefiants Fransais, Paris, 1966—, Ugine-Kuhlman, Paris, 1967-75, Inst. F. Petrole-Ecole Nat. Superieure Petrole Moteurs, Rueil, France, 1991—. Editor: Polyvinyl Chloride, 1977, Frontiers in Advanced Polymers, 1987; editor periodical, 1993. Mem. Am. Chem. Soc. Roman Catholic. Avocation: walking. Home: 6 Quai de Serbie, Lyon 69006, France Office: Centre Nat Recherche Scientifique-LCPP, CPE-Lyon BP 2077, Villeurbanne 69616, France

GUZAK, KAREN JEAN WAHLSTROM, artist; b. Cambridge, Mass., May 21, 1939; d. Ernest E. and Kathryn E. (Kemp) Wahlstrom; m. Steven V. Guzak, Aug. 29, 1959 (div. 1983); children: Gretchen, Christopher, Lauren. BS, U. Colo., 1961; BFA, Cornish Sch. Allied Arts, Seattle, 1976. Pres. Karen Guzak Inc., Seattle, 1982—. One-woman shows include Foster White Gallery, Seattle, 1981, 84, 87, 89, 91, 94, 96, 98, 2000, Davidson Galleries, Seattle, 1981, 84, 87, Tom Luttrell Gallery, San Francisco, 1981, Harris Gallery, Houston, 1982, Laura Russo Gallery, Portland, Oreg., 1987, 89, 91, 96, Musee Hyacinth Rigaud, Perpignan, France, 1988; exhibited in group shows at Bklyn. Mus., 1981, Brentwood Gallery, St. Louis, 1982, Seattle Art Mus., 1983, San Francisco Mus., 1983, Portland Art Mus., 1985, Davidson Gallery, 1992, Stifel Fine Arts Ctr., Wheeling, W.Va., 1993, Bellevue (Wash.) Art Mus., 1988, 90, 95, 96, DeCordova Mus., 1991, Purdue U., 1995, U. Brighton, Eng., 1997, Bronx Mus., 1987, Portland Art Mus., 1997; represented in permanent collections Portland Art Mus., Jundt Mus. Gonzaga U., Brooklyn Mus., N.Y.C. Libr. Print Collection, Pratt Inst., City of Seattle, King County Wash., South Seattle C.C.; pub. comms. So. Oreg. State Coll., King County Coun. Chambers, South Seattle C.C. Bd. commrs. King County Arts Commn., Seattle, 1981-86, commr., 1984-85; mem. arts adv. com. METRO Arts Program, Seattle, 1985-91; bd. dirs. Ctr. Contemporary Art, 1987-88; mem. contemporary coun. Seattle Art Mus., 1990-96; pres., developer Sunny Arms Coop., Seattle, 1988-90; co-developer, pres. Union Arts Coop., Seattle, 1992-93; pres. bd. dirs. Artist Trust, Seattle, 1996—. Boettcher scholar Univ. Colo., 1957-61; recipient Housing Designs that Work award Seattle Design Commn., 1991, Home of Yr. award Seattle Times and AIA, 1994. Democrat. Home & Office: Karen Guzak Inc 230 Avenue B Snohomish WA 98290-2841

GUZEK, JAN WOJCIECH, physiology educator; b. Lublin, Poland, Mar. 28, 1924; s. Józef and Maria (Pelczarska) G.; m. Barbara Moskalewska, Oct. 24, 1952 (dec. Nov. 10, 1980); children: Anna Maria, Maria Magdalena, Wojciech Józef. Grad. in medicine, Jagellonian U., Kraków, Poland, 1951; MD, U. Lódź, Poland, 1962; habilitation in human physiology, U. Lódz, Poland, 1968. Asst. lect. dept. gen. pathology, faculty of medicine U. Kraków, 1949-60; sr. lectr., reader, asst. prof. dept. physiology U. Lódź, 1960-74, vice dean Sch. Medicine, 1972, dep. dir. Inst. Physiology and Biochemistry, Sch. Medicine, 1973-74, prof.-in-ordinary, head dept. pathophysiology, 1974-94, prof. emeritus, part-time faculty mem., 1994—; mem. com. for physiol. scis. Polish Acad. Scis., 1984—, mem. com. for basic med. scis., 1987-93, com. for clin. pathophysiology, 1984-87, com. for cell pathophysiology, 1987-90. Editor, co-author textbooks in field, 1970, 80, 85, 90, 92, 98, 2000; translator Hans Selye: The Stress of Life, Polish edit., 1960; contbr. articles to profl. publs. Mem. Internat. Parliament for Safety and Peace, Palermo, Italy, 1991—; mem. sci. coun. Ministry of Health, Warsaw, Poland, 1985-87. Rsch. fellow Free U., Brussels, 1963, U. Copenhagen, 1972, hon. rsch. fellow U. Coll. London, 1988; recipient Tchr. of Merit award State Coun. Poland, 1973, Chevalier of Polonia Restituta, State Coun. Poland, 1980, Sci. award Ministry of Health, Warsaw, 1987, 94, Hon. diploma, medal Charles U. Med. Faculty, 1994, Napoleon Cybulski award Polish Physiol. Soc., 1996; named Knight Sovereign Mil. Templar Order, Jerusalem, 1991; selected World Intellectual, Internat. Biog. Ctr., 1993, Man of Yr., Am. Biog. Inst., 1994; nominated Internat. Cultural Diploma of Honor, Am. Biog. Inst., 1994. Mem. Polish Physiol. Soc. (hon.; pres. 1984-90, v.p. 1996—, chmn. hist. commn. 1996—), Polish Endocrinol. Soc., Internat. Soc. Neuroendocrinology, Internat. Brain Rsch. Orgn., European Neuroendocrine Soc., European Pineal Soc., Internat. Soc. Pathophysiology (charter mem., chmn. ednl. commn., mem. coun. 1991-98), Soc. Pathol. Physiology/GDR (corr.), Learned Soc. Lodz (pres. med. br. 1991-97, mem. coun. 1994-96, v.p. 1996—), Gen. Sikorski's Inst. Polish History (London), Czech Med. Soc. J.E. Purkyne (hon.), Bulgarian Assn. of Clin. and Exptl. Pathophysiology (hon. mem.), N.Y. Acad. Scis. Roman Catholic. Avocations: science in history, classical painting, old Polish maps, walking. Home: ul Narutowicza 120 m 2, 90-145 Lodz Poland Office: Sch Medicine Dept Pathophys, ul Narutowicza 60, 90-136 Lodz Poland

GUZMAN, ANGEL ESTEBAN, physician; b. Capital, Mendoza, Argentina, Mar. 16, 1951; s. Angel Teodoro Guzmán and Maria Carmen Camargo; m. Norma Mercedes Llaver, Jan. 2, 1976; children: Isteban Matias, Maria Pavla, Leandro Gabriel. Physician, U. Nat. Cuyo, Argentina, 1975; phlebolopist, U. El Salvador, Buenos Aires, 1981. Jr. surgeon Hosp. Ferrovizio, Mendoza, 1976-81, phlebolopist, 1981-87, head phlebology svc., 1987-91; phlebolopist Hosp. Italiano, Mendoza, 1985-87, head phlebology svc., 1987—. Contbr. sci. articles to profl. jours. Recipient 1st Nat. prize Assn. Med. Ferrovizia, 1989. Mem. Internat. Soc. Lymphology, Argentine Med. Assn., Med. Coll., Coll. Venous Surgery (pres. 1993-95, sec. 1995-98), Soc. Phlebology (pres. 2000-2001), Am. Congress Phlebology (nat. hon. mem.). Avocations: cycling, tennis, philosophy, music, tourism. Office: Plastic Surgery Clinic, Emilio Civit 356, 5500 Mendoza Argentina

GUZMAN, LINDA ANN, educator; b. Queens, N.Y., May 17, 1969; d. Roberto and Nancy (Aleman) G.; 1 child, Jacquelyn Nikole. BS, Fla. Internat. U., 1995, MS, 1996. Cert. tchr., Fla. Tchr. Miami Dade County Pub. Schs., Miami, 1995-98; area resource tchr. Palm Beach County Schs., 1998—; sr. staff mem. Camp Lohikan, Lake Como, Pa., summer 1998, 99. Mem. Coun. for Children with Behavior Disorders, Coun. Exceptional Children (professionally recognized spl. educator 1999), Zool. Soc Fla., Fla. Internat. U. Alumni Assn., Phi Kappa Phi, Golden Key. Roman Catholic. Avocations: playing piano, travel. Office: Palm Beach County Schs Area 3 ESE 1601 N Tamarind Ave West Palm Beach FL 33407-6231

GUZMAN, MIGUEL A., surgeon; b. Mazatlan, Sinaloa, Mex., Jan. 14, 1936; s. Miguel C. and Carmen (Elizondo) G.; m. Rosa Maria Garcia Hallatt, July 7, 1962; children: Miguel, Juan Carlos, Francisco, Fabian, Rosemary, Fernando. MD, U. Nacional Autonoma Mexico, Mexico City, 1960. Intern Trinity, Kansas City, 1961-62; resident in surgery Creighton U., Omaha, 1962-66; cons. U.S. Consulate, Mazatlan, 1967—; designed physician Immigration Can. Embassy. Fellow ACS, Consevo Mexicano Surgery; mem. Assn. Mexicana Gen. Surgery, El Cid Golf and Country Club. Roman Catholic. Avocations: golf, piano music. Home: 513 Roosevelt, 82000 Mazatlan Mexico Office: PO Box 490, 1808 Nelson, 82000 Mazatlan Mexico

GUZY, MARGUERITA LINNES, middle school education educator; b. Santa Monica, Calif., Nov. 19, 1938; d. Paul William Robert and Margarete (Rodowski) Linnes; m. Stephen Paul Guzy, Aug. 25, 1962 (div. 1968); 1 child, David Paul. AA, Santa Monica Coll., 1959; student, U. Mex., 1959-60; BA, UCLA, 1966, MA, 1973; postgrad. in psychology, Pepperdine U., 1988-92; cert. bilingual competence, Calif., 1994. Cert. secondary tchr., quality review team ednl. programs, bilingual, Calif. Tchr. Inglewood (Calif.) Unified Sch. Dist., 1967—, chmn. dept., 1972-82, mentor, tchr., 1985-88; clin. instr. series Clin. Supervision Levels I, II, Ingelwood, 1986-87; clin. intern Chem. Dependency Ctr., St. John's Hosp., Santa Monica, 1988-92; lectr. chem. and codependency St. John's Hosp., Santa Monica, 1992—; tchr. Santa Monica Coll., 1975-76; cons. bilingual edn. Inglewood Unified Sch. Dist., 1975—, lead tchr. new hope program at-risk students, 1992; cons. tchr. credentialing fgn. lang. State of Calif., 1994; sch. rep. restructuring edn. for state proposal, 1991-93; mem. Program Quality Rev. Team Pub. Edn., Calif., 1993; mem. Supt.'s Com. for Discrimination Resolution, 1994-95, tech. com. for integrating multimedia in the classroom, 1997—. Author: Elementary Education: "Pygmalian in the Classroom", 1975, English Mechanics Workbook, 1986. Recipient Teaching Excellence cert. State of Calif., 1986; named Tchr. of Yr., 1973, 88. Mem. NEA, Calif. Tchrs. Assn., Inglewood Tchrs. Assn. (local rep. 1971-72, tchr. edn. and profl. svcs. com. 1972-78), UCLA Alumnae Assn. (life), Prytanean Alumnae Assn. (bd. dirs. 1995-96, 1960's rep., 2d v.p. membership 1996-98). Republican. Avocations: reading, travel, swimming, dancing, cooking. Office: Monroe Magnet Mid Sch 10711 S 10th Ave Inglewood CA 90303-2015

GVOSDOWICH, NICOLAI WASIL, mathematician, educator; b. Wileica, Belorus, Feb. 10, 1953; s. Wasil and Nadja Gvozdowich; m. Galina Alexsandr Niconchik; children: Elena, Wasil. Degree, Minsk State Pedagogical U., Belorus, 1973. Tchr. math. Minsk, 1973-74; reader dept. math., head dept. math. Minsk State Pedagogical U., 1974—. With Russian Army, 1974-75. Avocations: swimming, car trips. Office: State Pedagogical Univ, Sovetskaja St 18, 220809 Minsk Belarus

GWALTNEY, CORBIN, editor, publishing executive; b. Balt., Apr. 16, 1922; s. Howell Corbin and Margaret (Bell) G.; m. Doris Jean Kell, July 13, 1946 (dec.); children: Margaret Kell, Jean Corbin, Thomas Stewart; m. Jean Caryl Wyckoff, June 20, 1973 (dec.). B.A., Johns Hopkins U., 1943; LHD (hon.), L.I. U., 1970; DHL (hon.), Johns Hopkins U., 1998. Instr., English Johns Hopkins U., 1946; with indsl. relations dept. Western Electric Co. and Locke div. Gen. Electric Co., 1946-49; editor Johns Hopkins Mag., 1949-59; editor, exec. dir., chmn. Editorial Projects for Edn., Inc., Balt. and Washington, 1959-78; exec. editor Chronicle Higher Edn., Washington, 1966-2000; chmn. Chronicle Higher Edn., 2000—; exec. editor Chronicle of Philanthropy, 1988—, chmn., 2000—. Served with AUS, 1943-45. Recipient Robert Sibley award Am. Alumni Council, 1951, 56, 59, Disting. Service to Higher Edn. awards Columbia U. Alumni Fedn., 1964, Disting. Service to Higher Edn. awards Am. Coll. Public Relations Assn., 1971; George Polk award for edn. reporting, 1979. Home: 5104 Brookview Dr Bethesda MD 20816-1602 also: 4755 Bayfields Rd Harwood MD 20776-9576 Office: Chronicle Higher Edn 1255 23rd St NW Ste 700 Washington DC 20037-1146

GWANZURA, LOVEMORE, microbiologist educator, researcher; b. Marondera, Zimbabwe, Dec. 9, 1954; s. Tinarwo Zonde and Janet (Nhamoinesu) G.; m. Christine Nyirongo, Jan. 30, 1981; children: Chipo, Karen, Tapiwa. BS, U. Zambia, Lusaka, 1978; MPhil, U. Zimbabwe, Harare, 1995. Med. lab. technologist Ministry of Health, Lusaka, 1977-81, Harare, 1981-82; sr. asst. chief med. lab. scientist Pub. Health Lab., Harare, 1982-84; sr. med. lab. scientist U. Zimbabwe, 1985-94, lectr., 1994-98, prof., 1998—; cons. Irish Govt., 1997; cons., investigator Zimbabwe AIDs Prevention Project, Harare, 1993—; mem. Internat. Union Microbiology Socs., Harare, 1992—. Contbr. articles to profl. jours. Recipient Zimbabwe S.K. Med. Scientist of Yr. award, 1997; grantee Fogarty Found., 1990, Internat. Atomic Energy Agy., 1995. Fellow Zimbabwe Inst. Med. Lab. Scis.; mem. Zimbabwe Immunology Soc. (v.p. 1997-98). Roman Catholic. Avocations: football, squash, tennis, movies. Office: Med Lab Scis U Zimbabwe, Box A178, Avondale, Harare Zimbabwe

GWARTNEY, PATRICIA ANNE, sociology educator; b. Glendale, Calif., Mar. 30, 1951; d. Robert Alan and Marilyn Arline (Sanborn) G.; m. Stanley Morshead Gibbs, July 31, 1971 (div. Feb. 1994); children: Loren, Spencer; m. George Gordon Goldthwaite Jr., Apr. 29, 1995; children: Emily Eleanor, Lisa Margaret, Adam Michael. AB, U. Calif., Berkeley, 1973; MA, U. Mich., 1979, PhD, 1981. Asst. prof. U. Oreg., Eugene, 1981-88, assoc. prof., 1988-96, prof. sociology, 1996—, affiliate Ctr. for Study of Women in Soc., 1984—, founding dir. Oreg. Survey Rsch. Lab., 1992—. Contbr. articles to profl. publs.; editl. bd. Jour. Marriage and the Family, 1995-97. Cons. Task Force on Gender Fairness Oreg. Supreme Ct., 1996-98. Fulbright fellow U. Auckland, New Zealand, 1986. Mem. AAAS, AAUP, Am. Sociol. Assn., Pacific Sociol. Assn. (coun.), Population Assn. Am. Democrat. Congregationalist. Home: 2875 Spring Blvd Eugene OR 97403-2510 Office: U Oreg Dept Sociology Eugene OR 97403-1291

GWARY, DANIEL MUSA, science educator; b. Kwajaffa, Borno, Nigeria, June 29, 1959; s. Musa Angili and Halima Musa (Hemman) G.; m. Shatu Daniel Bassi, Dec. 26, 1985; children: Michael, Ishaya, Kefas, Esther. BSc, U. Maiduguri, Nigeria, 1982; MSc, U. Wales, Bangor, 1985, PhD, 1989. Tchr. cmty. sch. Itele, Nigeria, 1982-83; agr. evaluation officer Agrl. Devel. Programme, Maiduguri, 1983; grad. asst. U. Maiduguri, 1983-84, asst. lectr., 1985-88, lectr. II, 1989-92, sr. lectr., 1992—; resident scientist Ctr. for Arid Zone Studies, Maidiguri, 1993—; cons. UN, Geneva, Switzerland, 1998-2001; rsch. coord. Nat. Rsch. on Groundnut, Maiduguri, 1998-2000. Contbr.: (book) Livestock Atlas of the Lake Chad Basin, 1996; contbr. articles to profl. jours. Vice-chmn. Chapel of Grace, Maiduguri, 1999—; treas. Devel. Assn., Kwajaffa, 1999—; sec. Local Govt. Subcom., Hawul, Nigeria, 1994-96; adviser Student Assn., Uni-Maid, Nigeria, 1993-95. Recipient Young Scientist Rsch. award Royal Soc. London, 1996-97, Commonwealth Fellowship award, 1991, 92; study fellow U. Maiduguri, 1984-88. Mem. West African Farming Sys., Nigerian Soc. for Plant Protection, Brit. Mycol. Soc. Avocations: football, table tennis, traveling, community service. Home: R40 U Maiduguri PO Box 4053, Maiduguri Borno, Nigeria Office: U Maiduguri Dept Sci, Bama Rd PMB 1069, Maiduguri Borno, Nigeria

GWYNN, ANTHONY KEITH (TONY GWYNN), professional baseball player; b. L.A., May 9, 1960; m. Alicia; children: Anthony, Anisha Nicole. Student, San Diego State U. Player minor league teams Walla Walla and Amarillo, Hawaii, 1981-82; outfielder San Diego Padres, 1982—. Winner Nat. League batting title, 1984, 87, 88, 89, 95; recipient Gold Glove award, 1986-87, 89-91; mem. All-Star team, 1984-87, 89-96; named MVP N.W. League, 1981, Sporting News Nat. League Silver Slugger team, 1984, 86-87, 89, 94, Sporting News Nat. League All-Star Team, 1984, 86-87, 89, 94. Office: San Diego Padres Qualcomm Stadium PO Box 2000 San Diego CA 92112-2000

GY, PIERRE MAURICE, sampling consultant and expert; b. Paris, July 25, 1924; s. Felix and Clemence (Gourdain) G.; m. Sylvia Duchesne, 1946; children: Genevieve, Anne, Caroline. Degree in chem. engring., Paris Sch. Physics & Chemistry, 1946; PhD in Physics, U. Nancy, 1960, PhD in Math., 1975. Chem. engr. CMCF, Congo, 1946-49; rsch. engr. Minerais & Metaux, Paris, 1949-52, from head mineral processing labs to tech. mgr., 1952-62; ind. sampling cons. Cannes, France, 1963—; founder, chmn. Internat. Sampling Inst. Author: Sampling of Particulate Materials: Theory and Practice, 1979, 2d edit., 1982, Heterogeneite- Echantillonnage- Homogeneisation, 1988,

Sampling of Heterogeneous & Dynamic Material Systems, 1992, Sampling for Analytical Purposes, 1998, others. Recipient medal Mining and Metall. Inst. Japan, 1958, 2 gold medal Soc. de L'Industrie Minerale, 1963, 76, Lavoisier medal French Soc. Chemistry, 1995. Mem. AAAS, Am. Inst. Mining Engrs. (hon.), Can. Inst. Mining and Metallurgy, N.Y. Acad. Scis., Can. Inst. Mining and Metallurgy. Avocations: photography, mountain climbing. E-mail: gy@pierregy.com. Home and Office: 14 Av Jean-de-Noailles, 06400 Cannes France

GYALPO, (NYILOG-GYARI) PEMA, international relations educator, TV commentator; b. Nyagrong, Tibet, June 18, 1953; arrived in Japan, 1965; s. Nima and Norzin Yuldron (Nyilogtsang) G.; m. Tsering Dolma Basar, 1982. BLL, Asia U., 1975; postgrad., Sophia U., Tokyo U. of Fgn. Langs.; PhD, Natl. U. Liaison officer H.H. The Dalai Lama, Japan, 1975-80, rep., 1980-90; vis. lectr. Tokushoku U., Tokyo; vis. prof. Gifu (Japan) Women's U., 1994, prof., 1996—; dir. Tibet Culture Ctr. Internat., Tokyo, 1975—; advisor All Japan Students Cultural Coun., 1996—, Nat. U., Mongol, 1996—, Japan Inner Culture Found., 1995—, others. Recipient Letter of Appreciation Amb. of Nepal, 1974, Amb. of Mongol, 1996, Best Tutor award All Japan Pvt. Tutors Assn., 1998; co-winner Best Translators award Japan Translators Assn., 1995. Mem. TRSH Center (bd. dirs. 1997—), JIGA (bd. dirs.), JEPA (advisor, hon.), Japan Internat. Studies Assn., Ajia Sekei Gakkai, Writers and Novelists Club (1st fgn. mem.), Japan Indian Goodwill Assn. (dir. 1997—), others. Democrat. Buddhist. Avocations: reading, writing. Office: Pema Ltd, 4-F-3-12-6 chome Shimbashi, Minatoku 140, Japan

GYEKENYESI, JOHN PAUL, mechanical engineer; b. Nagykanizsa, Hungary, May 16, 1938; came to U.S., 1951; s. George Laszlo and Katherine (Korcsmar) G.; m. Erika Eva Sari, June 17, 1961; children: John, Thomas, Andrew. BSME, Case Inst. Tech., 1961, MSME, 1966; PhD in Mechanics, Mich. State U., 1972. Registered profl. engr., Ohio. Test engr. Ohio Crankshaft Co., Cleve., 1961-62; design engr. NASA-Lewis Rsch. Ctr., Cleve., 1962-72, rsch. engr., 1972-82, sr. scientist structures, 1982-85, rsch. mgr. structures, 1985-99; rsch. mgr. structures NASA-Glenn Rsch. Ctr., Cleve., 1999—; cons. in structures Sari Corp., Cleve., 1978-90. Contbr. over 70 articles to profl. jours., chpts. to books. Pres. Ohio Soccer Assn., Cleve., 1992—. Recipient Yr.'s Best Paper in Structures award NASA, 1986, 91, Software of Yr. award NASA, 1994, Excellence in Tech. Transfer award Consortium of Fed. Labs., 1994, R&D 100 award, 1995, Excellence in Engrng. award NASA, 1996. Mem. ASME (ceramics com. 1990—, Best Paper in Ceramics award 1987, 97, EDI Tech. Innovation award 1998), ASTM (ceramics com. 1985—), Am. Ceramic Soc. (structural ceramics 1987—), ASM Internat. Roman Catholic. Achievements include development of computational techniques by applying the method-of-lines in analytical fracture mechanics to obtain new solutions to 3-D crack problems; first to devel. gen. purpose ceramic component life prediction software (CARES); rsch. in failure mechanisms in ceramic matrix composites. Avocations: soccer, table tennis. Office: NASA Glenn Rsch Ctr 21000 Brookpark Rd Cleveland OH 44135-3191

GYENES, GÁBOR, physician; b. Budapest, Dec. 14, 1959; s. George and Marianne (Ferenczi) G.; m. Erika Müllner, July 13, 1991; children: Balázs, Dóra. MD, Semmelweis U. Med. Sch., 1984; postgrad., Karolinska Inst., 1994-97. Asst. prof. 3rd Dept Med. Semmelweis Med. U., 1984-98; clin. fellow adult cardiology U. Toronto, Ont., Can., 1998—. Author: Pharmindex Kompendium, 1995, Hypertension: Data and Facts, 1997; editor: Cardiology, 2000. Sgt. Hungarian Army, 1985-86. Recipient Eminent Young Scientist award Internat. Rsch. Promotion Coun., 2000. Mem. Hungarian Soc. of Cardiology, Hungarian Soc. Internal Medicine, Can. Cardiovascular Soc. Avocations: rock and classical music, tennis, soccer. Office: Toronto Gen Hosp, 200 Elizabeth St, Toronto, Canada

GYENGE, ANDRÁS, diplomat; b. Budapest, Dec. 29, 1950; s. Zoltán and Zoltánué (Nagy Margit) G.; m. Zsuzsanna Szuroczki (div. July 1998); children: Balázs, Dóra; m. Anikó Nagy, Aug. 15, 1998. Student, U. Internat. Rels., Moscow, 1974, U. Econ. Scis., Budapest, 1982-83; Dr. Econ. Scis., 1993. 3d sec. Embassy of Hungary, Mozambique, 1976-81; 2d sec. Embassy of Hungary, Portugal, 1986-90; amb. Embassy of Hungary, Lisbon, 1996—; head dept. Coun. of Europe (MFA), Budapest, 1992-96; spl. advisor on minority issues Min. of FA, Budapest, 1994-96. Avocations: tennis, wine collecting. Office: Embassy of Hungary, Cda Sto Amaro 85, 1379-072 Lisbon Portugal

GYLL, JOHN SÖREN, company executive; b. Skorped, Västernorrland, Sweden, Dec. 26, 1940; s. Josef and Gertrud G.; m. Lilly Margareta Hellman, 1974; 3 children. Higher cert. exam. and univ. degrees. Mktg. mgr., v.p. Rank-Xerox AB, 1963-77; pres. Uddeholm-Sweden, 1977-79, exec. v.p., 1979-81; pres., CEO Uddeholm-Sweden, 1981-84, Procordia AB, Stockholm, 1984-92, AB Volvo, Göteborg, Sweden, 1992-97; bd. dirs. AB Volvo, SCA AB, Skanska AB, SKF AB. Mem. Royal Swedish Acad. Engring. Scis., Fedn. Swedish Industries (chmn.), Swedish Employers Fedn. (bd. dirs.). Avocations: hunting, golf, skiing. Office: AB Volvo, PO Box 7724, SE10395 Stockholm Sweden

GYLLENHAMMAR, PEHR GUSTAF, finance company executive, retired automobile company executive, writer; b. Gothenburg, Sweden, Apr. 28, 1935; s. Pehr and Aina (Kaplan) G.; m. Christina Engellau; children: Cecilia, Charlotte, Oscar, Sophie. MLaw, U. Lund, 1959; MD (hon.), U. Gothenburg, 1981; TechD (hon.), Brunel U., 1987; Ed (hon.), Tech. U. Nova Scotia, 1988; DSocSci (hon.), U. Helsinki, 1990; LLD, U. Vt. With Ins. Co. Amphion, 1961-64; asst. adminstrv. mgr. Ins. Co. AB Skandia, 1965-66, v.p., 1966, dep. mng. dir., 1968-70, mng. dir., chief exec., 1970; mng. dir., CEO AB Volvo, Gothenburg, 1971-83, chmn., CEO, 1983-90, exec. chmn., 1990-93; also bd. dirs. AB Volvo; chmn. CGU plc, 1998—; mng. dir. Lazard Freres & Co. LLC; chmn. bd. Swedish Ships Mortgage Bank; sup. bd. Lagardére SCA; chmn. Reuters Founders Share Co. Ltd. Author 5 books. Office: CGNU plc St Helens, 1 Undershaft, London EC3P 3DQ, England

GYOHTEN, TOYOO, economist; b. Yokohama, Japan, 1931; married; 2 children. BA in Econs., U. Tokyo, 1955; postgrad., Princeton U., U.S.A., 1956-58. With Ministry Fin., Tokyo, 1955-89, Japan Desk, Internat. Monetary Fund, Washington, 1964-66; spl. asst. to pres. Asian Devel. Bank, Manila, Philippines, 1966-69; dir. gen. Internat. Fin. Bur., Ministry of Fin., Tokyo, 1984-86; vice min. fin. for internat. affairs Ministry of Fin., Tokyo, 1986-89; with The Bank of Tokyo, Ltd. (merged with Mitsubishi Bank Ltd.), Tokyo, 1991—; chmn. bd. dirs. The Bank of Tokyo, Ltd., Tokyo, 1992-96; sr. advisor The Bank of Tokyo-Mitsubishi, Ltd., 1996—; spl. advisor to Prime Minister of Japan, 1998; pres. Inst. for Internat. Monetary Affairs, 1995—; chmn. working party III OECD, Paris, 1988-90; vis. prof. Harvard U., 1990, Princeton U., 1990-91, U. St. Gallen, Switzerland, 1991; trustee Princeton in Asia, N.J.; mem. adv. panel East African Devel. Bank, Uganda, Asia Pacific Adv. Comm., N.Y. Stock Exch.; mem. exec. com. Trilateral Comm., N.Y., Paris, Tokyo; mem. Com. on Fgn. Exch. and Transactions, internat. coun. The Asia Soc., N.Y., Group of Thirty, Washington. Coauthor: (with Paul Volcker) Changing Fortunes, 1992. Office: Inst Internat Monetary Aff, 1-3-2 Nihombashi-Hongokucho, Chuo Tokyo 103-0021, Japan

GYÖRGY, LOVÁSZ, geographer, educator; b. Budapest, Hungary, May 23, 1931; s. János Lovász and Julianna Remmler; m. Magdolna Straub, 1955; 1 child, Lovász György. PhD in Geoscis., Hungarian Acad. Scis., Budapest, DSc in Geoscis. Rschr. Transdanubian Sci. Inst., Pécs, Hungary, 1957-73, sec. dir., 1973-78; head of sci. lab. Geosci. Rsch. Inst., Budapest, 1978-88; head phys. geography dept. Janus Pannonius U., Pécs, 1988-97, prof. phys. geography, 1997—. Author: Geological Processes of Southeastern Transdanubian Surface, 1972, Physical Geography of Baranya County, 1977, Physical Geography of Hungary, vol. I, 1994, vol. II, 1997. Mem. Hungarian Geography Assn., Hungarian Acad. Sci. (degree com. 1958-70, geography com. 1996—). Avocations: hiking, music. Home: Papnövelde str 19, H-7621 Pécs Hungary Office: U Pécs, Ifjusóg Str 6, H-7601 Pécs Hungary

GYÖRGYDEÁK, ZOLTÁN BARNABÁS, chemistry educator; b. Gyula, Békés, Hungary, July 11, 1942; s. Zoltán and Lenke (Némedi) G.; m. Erzsébet Olajos, July 3, 1965; children: Judit, Anikó. Cert. chemist, L. Kossuth U., Debrecen, Hungary, 1965, PhD, 1971. Rsch. fellow Rsch. Group Antibiotics, Hungarian Acad. Sci., Debrecen, 1965-88, sr. rsch. fellow, 1988-91; assoc. prof., docent dept. organic chemistry Faculty of Scis. U. Debrecen, Debrecen, 1991—; Scholar German Acad. Exch. Fellowship, Hamburg, Germany, 1971-72, Humboldt scholar Alexander Humboldt Found., Hamburg, 1983-84, Legerlotz Found. scholar, Zurich, Switzerland, 1986-88. Author: Monosaccharide Sugars, 1998; contbr. articles to profl. jours.; patentee in field. Home: Kápolna u 3, H-2093 Budajenö Hungary

GYÖRY, ÁKOS ZOLTAN, medical educator; b. Budapest, Hungary, Sept. 29, 1935; s. Albert Bela and Eleonora Maria (Dingha) Á; m. Ingelore Elisabeth Rubenow, Dec. 2, 1961; children: Karin, Ingrid, Stephan. MBBS, U. Sydney, Australia, 1961, MD, 1971, DSc, 1991. C.J. Martin rsch. fellow Max Planck Inst. Biophysics, Frankfurt, Germany, 1969-71; vis. fellow Hosp. U. Penn., Phila., 1972; sr. rsch. fellow dept. physiology U. Sydney, 1972-74, sr. lectr., 1974-77, assoc. prof., 1977-91; dir. Renal Lab., Royal North Shore Hosp.-U. Sydney, 1975—, prof. medicine, head dept., 1991—. Contbr. over 150 articles to med. jours. and books. Mem. acad. bd. U. Western Sydney, 1989-94. Fellow Royal Australasian Coll. Physicians; mem. Am. Physiol. Soc. Avocations: carpentry, wood carving, stamp collecting. E-mail: azgy@med.su.oz.au. Home: 23 Lowry Cr, Saint Ives NSW 2075, Australia Office: U Sydney, Dept Medicine, Sydney NSW 2006, Australia

GYULAI, PÉTER LÁSZLÓ, agrozoologist; b. Miskolc, Hungary, May 26, 1950; s. László and Lászlóné (Szucs Erzsébet) G. Biologist-chemist degree, Kossuth L. U., Debrecen, Hungary, 1974, doctorate, 1978. Head lab. Plant Prot. Stat., Miskolc, Hungary, 1974-88, agrozoologist, 1988—. Co-author: Fauna of the Bükk Nat. P., 1993, Noctuidae of Mongolian Expeditions, 1999. Mem. Hungarian Entomologist Soc., Soc. Europaea Lep. Greek Catholic. Avocations: owlet moths of Asia, mountain climbing. Home: Melyvolgy 13/A, 3530 Miskolc Hungary Office: Plant Health & Soil Conv, Blaskovics 24, 3501 Miskolc Hungary

GYULEV, VLADIMIR GENKOV, manufacturing executive; b. Assenovgrad, Plovdiv, Bulgaria, Nov. 18, 1944; s. Genko Dimitrov and Macry (Hachova) G.; m. Bozhidara Ivanova Kousheva; children: Vladimir, Mira. BS, Tech. U. Sofia, 1970, PhD, 1975. Engr. Inst. Info., Rennes, France, 1975-76; rschr. Bulgarian Acad. Scis., Sofia, 1977-82; dep. dir. United Plants for Memory Drives, Stara Zagora, Bulgaria, 1983-84, Assembly Automation Plant, Plovdiv, Bulgaria, 1984-86; dir. gen. COMTEK Co., Plovdiv, 1987-90; pres. CO-TEK, Sofia, 1990—. Inventor in field. Home: 6 13th of March Str, 1040 Sofia Bulgaria Office: CO-TEK, 122 Vassil Levsky Bld, 1527 Sofia Bulgaria

GZELL, IAN VITALY, barrister; b. Brisbane, Australia, May 28, 1941; s. Vitaly and Lorna Margaret (Martin) G.; m. Sylvia Rose Butts, Feb. 14, 1964; children: Catherine Helen Furby, Angela Margaret Cusack, Justine Louise, Cecelia Elizabeth. BA with honors, U. Queensland, Brisbane, 1964, LLB, 1965, BCom, 1974. Bar: Queensland 1965, Papua New Guinea 1973, N.S.W. 1985, Western Australia 1986, South Australia 1992, Victoria 1992, No. Territory, 1992, Australian Capital Territory, 1992, Tasmania, 1992, New Zealand 1995, Singapore, Fiji, Solomon Islands; Queen's Counsel Queensland, 1977, N.S.W., 1986, We. Australia, 1987, South Australia, 1992, Australian Capital Terr. 1992, Vic. 1993, Tasmania 1993. Pvt. practice Brisbane, Australia, 1965, Sydney, 1990; chmn. bd. dirs. Counsels Chambers Ltd.; bd. dirs. Internat. Disputes Ctr. Pty. Ltd.; spkr., rschr. in field revenue law. Contr. articles to profl. jours. Chmn. Queensland Philharmonic Orch., 1978-90, Queensland Theatre Co., 1985-90, Lang. Rd. Residents Assn., 1993-95, Centennial Pk. Residents Assn., 1994-95; dir. Arts Coun. N.S.W., 1994—, pres., 1999—, Regional Arts Australia, 1999—; consultative com. Centennial Pk. and Moore Pk. Trust Cmty., 1994-95; planning and fin. com. Queensland of Commonwealth Schs. Commn., 1978-79; mem. com. Commonwealth Tertiary Edn. Commn., 1980-83; bd. dirs. Lyric Opera Queensland, 1981-84, Queensland Symphony Orch., 1986-89. Mem. Internat. Tax Planning Assn., Internat. Fiscal Assn., Internat. Acad. Estate and Trust Law, Law Coun. Australia (taxation com. 1986—), Comml. Law Assn. Australia (pres. 1994-96), Taxation Inst. Australia (pres. 1985-86), Australian Club, Tattersalls Club, The Lakes Golf Club. Avocations: golf, opera, theatre, music. Home: 110 Lang Rd Centennial Pk, Sydney 2021, Australia Office: 174 Phillip St 5th Fl, Sydney 2000, Australia

HANGODY, LÁSZLO, physician, orthopedic consultant, surgeon; b. Kiskunhalas, BacsKiskun, Hungary, May 20, 1958; s. László Hangody and Margit Bartfai; m. Katalin Bucher; children: László, György, András. MD, Semmelweis Med. Sch., Budapest, Hungary, 1982; PhD, Hungarian Scientific Acad., Budapest, Hungary, 1994. Asst. surgeon Uzsoki Hosp., Budapest, 1982-86, orthopedic surgeon, 1986-88, cons. orthopedic and trauma surgeon, 1988-94; sr. cons. orthopedic and trauma surgeon Sanitas Pr. Clin., Budapest, 1991—, Uzsoki Hosp., Budapest, 1994—; PhD instr. Semmelweis Med. Sch., Budapest, 1999—; cons. surgeon Haynal Imre Med. Sch., Budapest, 1996—, Semmelweis Med. Sch., 1996—, Smith and Nephew Endoscopy Co., Andover, Mass., 1996—, Zalaegerszegi H.S. of Phys. Edn., 1998—, Surgicraft Ltd., Redittch, U.K., 1998—. Editl. bd. Jour. of Orthpedic and Trauma; contbr. articles to profl. jours.; patentee in field. 1st Prize winner EFORT, 1993. Mem. Hungarian Arthroscopy Soc. (sec. 1996), Internat. Cartilage Repair Soc. (exec. bd. 1997), Hungarian Orthopedic Soc. (exec. bd.), Hungarian Trauma Soc. (exec. bd. 1999), ESSKA (1st prize winner 1994, 96). Roman Catholic. Avocations: sports, music, literature, fishing. Home: Törökvész Str 44D, 1025 Budapest Hungary Office: Uzsoki Hosp Orth/Trauma Dep, Mexikói Str 62, 1145 Budapest Hungary

HA, DONG HAN, physicist, researcher; b. Taegu, Korea, May 3, 1959; s. Tae Bo and Sook Hee (Joo) H.; m. Eun Mi Kim, Oct. 23, 1991; children: Hebin, Yoonbin. BS in Physics, Kyungbook Nat. U., Taegu, 1981; MS in Physics, Korea Advanced Inst. Sci. and Tech., Seoul, 1985, PhD in Physics, 1989. Rsch. asst. Korea Advanced Inst. Sci. and Tech., 1985-89; sr. rschr. Korea Rsch. Inst. Stds. and Sci., Taejon, 1989-97, prin. rschr., 1997—; part-time lectr. Dankook U., Seoul, 1987-89; guest rschr. Electrotech. Lab., Tsukuba, Japan, 1991-92, 1995. Contbr. articles to profl. jours. Mem. Korean Phys. Soc. Avocations: travel, cycling, Internet. Home: Nare Apt 105-1005, Jonmeendong, Yusong Taejon 305 390, Republic of Korea Office: KRISS, PO Box 102, Yusong Taejon 305 600, Republic of Korea

HA, HYUN-JOON, chemistry educator; b. Jinju, Kyungnam, Korea, Nov. 18, 1959; s. Won-Sik and Young-chae (Chang) H.; m. Jung-Mi Yang; children: Sungmin, Sungkyun. BS, Seoul Nat. U., 1982; Phd, Brown U., 1987. Rsch. assoc. Stanford (Calif.) U., 1987-88; sr. rsch. scientist KIST, Seoul, 1988-91; cons. KIST Seoul, 1992-93; dept. chmn. Hankuk U., Kyonggi-do, Korea, 1993-96; sec. ICHC, Seoul, 1996-97; vis. rsch. prof. Cambridge (Eng.) U., 1993; founder, CEO ChemBioNex Co., Ltd., 2000. Referee editl. bd. Organic Chem. Jour., 1999—; contbr. articles to profl. jours. Sec. Brown Club in Korea, Seoul, 1989—. Mem. Am. Chem. Soc., Korean Chem. Soc. (sec. planning 1999), N.Y. Acad. Scis. Budhist. Avocations: tennis, movies, travel.

HA, HYUNJUNG, biologist, edcutaor; b. Milyang, Korea, Jan. 25, 1957; child of Changsik Ha and Sunhee Bae; m. Taisun Hyun, Aug. 1, 1987; children: Jiwon, Jihee. BS, Seoul (Repubic Korea) Nat. U., 1981; MS, Korea Advanced Inst. Sci. & Tech. Dept. of Life, 1985; PhD, U. Ala., 1992. Rschr. Genetic Engring. Rsch. Ctr., Seoul, 1985-87; rsch. fellow Mass. Gen. Hosp., Boston, 1993-94, Beth Israel Hosp., Boston, 1993-94; sr. scientist Korea Rsch. Inst. Bioscience and Biotechnology, Taejon, 1994-96; asst. prof. Chungbuk Nat. U., Cheongju, Korea, 1996—; cons. Bioneer Corp., Cheongwon, Korea, 1998—. With Republic of Korea Army, 1981-82. Mem. Korean Soc. Immunology (mem. editl. bd. 1996-97), Microbiological Soc. Korea (mem. editl. bd. 1999—), Korean Soc. Molecular Biology, Biochemical Soc. Korea. Fax: 82-0431-267-2306. Office: Chungbuk Nat U, Heungduk Gu, Kaesin-dong, Cheongju 361-763, Republic of Korea

HA, QUANG PHUC, engineering educator, researcher; b. Binh Dinh, Vietnam, Jan. 1, 1958; s. Thong Ha and Muoi Thi Tran; m. Hoa Thi Ngoc Nguyen, Sept. 29, 1996; children: Thi Ngoc Hien, Thi Ngoc An. BEE, Ho Chi Minh City Poly., Vietnam, 1980; PhD, Moscow Power Engring. Inst., 1992, U. Tasmania (Australia), 1997. Chartered profl. engr. Lectr. Pedagogical U. Tech., Ho Chi Minh City, Vietnam, 1980-88; postdoct. Moscow Power Engring. Inst., 1988-92; lectr. U. Tasmania (Australia), 1993-94; sr. rsch. assoc. U. Sydney, 1997—. Contbr. articles to profl. jours., chpts. to books. Mem. Inst. Engrs. Australia. Buddhist. Home: 51 East St, Lidcombe NSW 2141, Australia Office: Dept Mechanical/Mechatronic Engring, U Sydney J07, Sydney 2006 NSW, Australia

HA, YEONG-HO, electrical engineering educator, consultant; b. Kyungnam, Korea, Aug. 10, 1953; came to U.S., 1979; s. Sang-Tae and So-Ok Lee; m. Haesook Jung, May 3, 1979; children: Theodore Tae-Eun, June Jung-Eun. BS, Kyungpook Nat. U., Taegu, Korea, 1976, MS, 1978; PhD, U. Tex., 1985. Chmn. dept. biomed. engrng. Kyungpook Nat. U., 1991-92, dir. sch. affairs Grad. Sch. Industry,, 1992-93, vice dean planning and coordination, 1997-98, prof., 1986—; cons. LG Electronics, Kumi, Korea, 1987—; dir. Taegu Software Ctr., 1997—. Author: Digital Signal Analysis, 1990, PC Fortran Programming, 1990; contbr. articles to profl. jours.; patentee in apparatus for compensation for image display characteristics. Mem. com. YMCA, Taegu, 1990—; chmn. Ventur Capital Mirae Angel Club, 1997—. With Korean Army, 1977. Mem. IEEE (Taegu sect. chmn. 1998—), Inst. Electronics Engrs. Korea (trustee 1998—, Meritorious svc. award 1995). Avocation: golf. E-mail: yha@ee.knu.ac.kr. Fax: 82-53-957-1194. Home: 966-7 Jisan-Dong, Taegu 706-090, Korea Office: Kyungpook Nat Univ, 1370 Sankyuk-Dong, Taegu 702-701, Korea

HAACK, RICHARD WILSON, retired police officer; b. Chgo., July 7, 1935; s. Arthur Frank and Mildred Ann (Meyer) H.; m. Ruth Marie Tietz, May 27, 1972; children: Laura Marie, Karl Richard. Grad., Sheriff's Police Acad., Cook County (Ill.), 1967; AS, Triton Coll., 1973; cert., Chgo. Police Acad., 1974; BA, Lewis U., 1975; MA, Northeastern Ill. U., 1979; BS in Bus. Adminstrn., Elmhurst Coll., 1982. Shipping clk. Am. Furniture Mart, Chgo., 1955-60; quality control insp. Nat. Can Co., Chgo., 1961-67; police officer Northlake (Ill.) Police Dept., 1967-92, watch comdr. patrol divsn., 1978-85, dept. chief of police, 1986-87, in-svc. tng. coord., 1991-92, retired, 1992; realtor Internat. Realty World-Norton & Assocs., 1984-87. Author Ency. Am. Judiciary; contbr. articles to profl. publs. Mem. Bill Bruce fundraising com. Aid Assn. Luths., Christ Evang. Luth. Ch., Northlake, 1981-82, mem. Gala Varsity Show, 1982, chmn. evang. bd., 1981-85, ch. rep. Internat. Luth. Laymen's League, 1984—, pub. rels. dir., usher, 1873-85; choir Apostles Luth Ch., 1985-87; membership chmn. Redeemer Luth. Ch. Men's Club, 1995-99; dir., emcee German-Am. Police Assn. Oktoberfest, 1980—, chmn. entertainment, 1984—; coach Northlake Little League baseball team, 1985; trustee Northlake Police Pension Fund, 1997—; active March of Dimes-Mothers March, 1997-99. Served with USMC, 1952-55, Korea, with res. 1955-60. Recipient John Edgar Hoover Meml. Gold medal, 1987, numerous letters of commendation, competitive shooting awards. Mem. NRA, Internat. Assn. Chiefs of Police, Ill. Police Assn. (life), Fraternal Order Police (life, sec.-treas. Perri-Nagle Meml. Lodge 18 1977-85), St. Jude Police League, Nat. Police Officers Assn., Internat. Police Assn. (life), German/Am. Police Assn. (life, bd. dirs 1980—), Combined Counties Police Assn., Internat. Juvenile Officers Assn., Ill. Juvenile Officers Assn., Ill. Police Assn. (life), Emerald Soc. Ill. Irish/Am. Police Assn., Northeastern Ill. U. Alumni Assn. (bd. dirs. 1980-86), Am. Polit. Sci. Assn., Schwaben Verein, N.W. Real Estate Bd., Leyden Real Estate Bd. (inner circle 1984-87), Sharkhunters, Internat. Platform Assn., Realtors Polit. Action Com. Ill. (inner circle 1984-87), Am. Legion. Ret. and Disabled Police of Am., Kaire Ind. Distbr., Die Hard Cub Fans, Moose Lodge, Korean War Vets.-Navy League. Republican. Home: 244 E Palmer Ave Northlake IL 60164-1735 Office: 55 E North Ave Northlake IL 60164-2518

HAAG, RALPH-GERALD, economist, diplomat; b. Strasbourg, France, Feb. 17, 1956; married; 2 children. MS in Engring. Sci., Ecole Centrale de Paris, 1979, PhD Qualifiying Exam., 1981; MS in Mgmt., U. Calif., Berkeley, 1985. Expert tech. coop. Lat. Am. French Ministry of Fgn. Affairs, 1981-83; programme mgmt. officer UN, Luanda, Angola, 1985-87; programme mgmt. adviser UN, N.Y.C., 1987-88; logistics adviser, observer UN, Managua, Nicaragua, 1990; orgn. and planning adviser UN, Port-au-Prince, Haiti, 1990; mgmt. and logistics adviser UN, Rangoon, Burma, 1991; sr. coord. Internat. Assistance Programmes UN, Vienna, Austria, 1992-93; dep. coord. UN ind. sec. Joint Internat. Observers Group UN, Kampala, Uganda, 1994; regional dir. designate, sr. mgmt. adviser UN, Vienna, 1994-95; dir. regional office West and Ctrl. Africa UN, 1995-96; head diplomatic mission, amb. plenipotentiary UN, Dakar, Senegal, 1995-96; sr. adviser to spl. rep. sec.-gen., de facto chief of staff UN, Dushanbe, Tajikistan, 1997-98; prof., researcher Strasbourg U./Ensais, 1988-89; prof. in charge bus. adminstrn. dept. ISEG, Strasbourg, 1989-92; dir. gen., CEO Net Deals Internat.-NDI, Strasbourg, 1998—; v.p. San.Sat, Managua, 2000—; cons. Internat. Olympic Com., L.A., 1984; acad. apointee U. Calif., Berkeley, 1985; dir., CEO French TMVE, N.Y.C., 1987-88; spl. advisor to pres. and CEO The Bang Group, Sarreguemines, France, 1996-97. Rotary scholar Rotary Found., 1983. Mem. Rotary Internat. (Amb. of Goodwill 1984), European Engr. Avocations: golf, reading. Home: Domaine du Golf Green Vill, 20 rue de Londres, F-67610 Strasbourg La Wantzenau, France

HAAG, RUDOLF, theoretical physicist; b. Tubingen, Germany, Aug. 17, 1922; s. Albert and Anna (Schaich) H.; m. Kaethe Fues, July 19, 1948 (dec. Jan. 1991); children: Albert, Friedrich, Elisabeth, Ulrich; m. Barbara Klie, Apr. 27, 1992. Diploma in physics, Stuttgart U., 1948; PhD, Munich U., 1951; DSc (hon.), U. Marseille, 1979. Lectr. Munich U., Germany, 1954-56; vis. prof. Princeton U., N.J., 1957-59; prof. physics U. Ill., Urbana, 1960-66; prof. physics Hamburg U., Germany, 1966-87, prof. emeritus, 1987—. Author: Local Quantum Physics, 1992; contbr. articles to profl. jours.; editor Communications in Math. Physics, 1964-90. Mem. German Phys. Soc. (Max Planck medal 1970), Internat. Assn. Math. Physics (Henry Poincaré prize 1997). Home: Waldshmidtstr 4b, D-83727 Schliersee Neuhaus Germany

HAAK, ALEX JOHAN HENRI, architect, educator; b. Haarlem, The Netherlands, Feb. 9, 1930; s. Willem Adriaan and Elisabeth Wilhemina Hendrika (Ten Hooven) H. Engr., U. Tech., Delft, 1957, Harvard U., Delft, 1958. Dir. Architekten Buro Prof Ir.Haak BNA BV, Delft, 1960—; lectr. interior design U. Tech., Delft, 1960-79, prof. interior design, 1980-91; guest lectr. Ball State U., 1965, Birmingham Poly. (Eng.), 1974—; advisor archtl. firms. Author: Mens en Maat, 1980, Muizen achter het behang, 1991. Served to lt. Netherlands Royal Engrs., 1959-60. Hon. fellow AIA; mem. Alliance of Dutch Architects. Roman Catholic. Lodge: Rotary. Office: Architektenburo Prof Haak BNA BV, Oude Delft 159, 2611 HA Delft The Netherlands*

HAAKONSEN, BENT, diplomat; b. Denmark, Jan. 10, 1936; m. Kirsten Haakonsen; 1 child. Joined Ministry Fgn. Svc., 1961; served Ministry Fgn. Svc., Bonn, 1964-67; permanent rep. to EEC Brussels, 1972-74; amb. to Czechoslovakia, 1978-79; head Danish del. to CSCE Madrid, Spain, 1980-81; under-sec. for trade rels. Govt. of Denmark, 1983-86, permanent under-sec. of state, 1986-91; permanent rep. UN, N.Y.C., 1991-95; amb. to Germany Bonn, 1995-99, Berlin, 1999—. Address: Royal Danish Embassy, Rauchstrasse 1, D-10787 Berlin Germany

HAAN, CHAN-HOON, architectural engineering educator, acoustic design consultant; b. Seoul, Republic of Korea, Mar. 2, 1961; s. Young-dong and Duck-hee (Min) H.; m. Mi-kyong Park, May 16, 1987; children: Kee-woong, Kee-sup. BEng in Arch., Hongik U., 1983; MEng in Arch., Yonsei U., 1985; PhD, U. Sydney, 1994. Registered archtl. engr., Korea. Acoustic designer Archiban Archs. & Assocs., Seoul, 1986-88; project mgr. LG Indsl. Sys. Co., Seoul, 1988-89; acoustic engr. RTA Cons. Engrs. Co., Sydney, Australia, 1990-91; tutor U. Sydney, 1991-92; lectr. Yonsei U., Seoul, 1994-96; assoc. prof. Chungbuk Nat. U., Chongju, Korea, 1994—; head chmn. Dept. Archtl. Engring., Chunbuk Nat. U., 1998—; mem. adv. com. Inchon (Korea) Internat. Airport, 1996—; mem. judging com. Archtl. Bd., City of Chongju, 1997-99, Archtl. Competition Bd., 1998-99; treas. Korean Inst. Architects, 1997-98. Prin. works include: Seoul Arts Ctr., 1988 (Outstanding Archtl. Work award 1988), (as acoustical cons.) Korean High-Speed Railway Stations, 1996 (Outstanding Archtl. Work, 1998), Inchon Internat. Airport, 1998; contbr. articles to profl. jours. Mem. policy adv. com. City of Chongju, 1998; leader ch. choir Sondang Presbyn. Ch., 1995—. Lt. 3d Military Divsn., 1985-86. Named Outstanding Artist of Yr. in Arch., The Fedn. of Artistic and Cultural Orgn. of Korea, 1998. Mem. Acoustical Soc. Korea (exec.), Archtl. Inst. Korea, Korean Inst. Architects. Avocations: photography, travel, attending classical music concerts. Home: 106-502 Samik Apt Gasin-dong, 361-240 Chongju Chungbuk, Republic of Korea

Office: Chunkbuk Nat U, Dept Archtl Engrs, 361-763 Chongju Chungbuk, Republic of Korea

HAAR, ANA MARIA FERNÁNDEZ, advertising and public relations executive; b. Oriente Province, Cuba, Mar. 25, 1951; came to U.S., 1960, naturalized, 1970; d. Gilberto and Esmeralda Emiliana (Diaz) Fernández. Grad., Miami Dade Community Coll., 1971; student, Barry Coll., 1972-78. Adminstrv. asst. thru asst. v.p. nat. accounts Flagship Bank, Miami Beach, Fla., 1971-77; v.p. comml. lending Jefferson Nat. Bank, Miami Beach, 1977-78; pres. IAC Advt. Group, Miami, 1978—; instr. Miami Dade Community Coll. Women in Mgmt. Program, 1980-81; hostess Sta. WPBT Program Viva; exec. com. World Trade Ctr., Miami. Mem. Dade County Commn. on Status of Women, 1979-82; chmn. Econ. Devel. Task Force of Commn. on Status of Women, 1979-82; bd. dirs. Downtown Miami Bus. Assn., 1979-82; bd. dirs., chmn. Human Capital Group, New Am. Alliance. Recipient Gran Orden Martiana of Cuban Lyceum for excellence in community svc., 1976, Up and Comers award South Fla. Bus. Jour., 1988; named one of 100 Most Influential Hispanics Hispanic Bus. Mag. Mem. Advt. Fedn. Greater Miami, Greater Miami Advt. Fedn. (bd. dirs.), Asociación de Publicitarios Latino-Americanos (v.p.), Japan Soc. (bd. dirs.), Miami Beach C. of C. (hon. life, trustee), Greater Miami C. of C., Hispanic Heritage Festival Com., Cuban Women's Club (past pres.), Assn. Hispanic Advt. Agys. (pres. 1998-99). Office: IAC Advt Group 2725 SW 3rd Ave Miami FL 33129-2335

HAARDE, GEIR HILMAR, government official; b. Reykjavik, Iceland, Apr. 8, 1951; s. Tomas and Anna (Steindorsdottir) H.; m. Patricia A. Mistretta, June 5, 1975 (div. 1982); children: Ilia Anna, Sylvia; m. Inga Jona Thordardottir, June 19, 1987; 1 stepchild, Borgar Thor; children: Helga Lara, Hildur Maria. BA in Econs., Brandeis U., 1973; MA in Internat. Relations, Johns Hopkins U., 1975; MA in Econs., U. Minn., 1977. Head div. Ctrl. Bank Iceland, Reykjavik, 1977-83; spl. asst. to Min. Fin. Reykjavik, 1983-87; mem. Icelandic Parliament, Reykjavik, 1987—, min. fin., 1998—; lectr. U. Iceland, 1979-83; chmn. Parliamentary Group, 1991-98. Chmn. organizing com. World Handball Championship, Iceland, 1995; v.p. Conservative Party, 1999—. Lutheran. Home: Granaskjol 20, 107 Reykjavik Iceland Office: Icelandic Parliament, Althingi, 150 Reykjavik Iceland

HAARER, DIETRICH, physicist, educator; b. Stuttgart, Germany, June 23, 1938; s. Theodor Karl and Mathilde (Kaysser) H.; m. Arnhild Beduhn, Oct. 1, 1967; children: Franziska, Johannes, Stefanie. Physicist, U. Stuttgart, 1966, PhD, 1969. Postdoctoral fellow, rschr. IBM, San Jose, Calif., 1970-75; mgr. IBM, San Jose, 1975-80; prof. U. Bayreuth, Germany, 1980—; cons. German Chem. Co., 1981—. Co-author: (textbook) Spektroskopie Amorpher and Kristalliner Festkorper, 1995; mem. editl. bd. Chem. Physics, 1996—, Advanced Materials. Recipient Max Planck award Alexander von Humboldt Found. and Max Planck Soc., 1992. Mem. German Phys. Soc., German Chem. Soc., Am. Phys. Soc., European Phys. Soc. Avocations: music, reading. Office: Physikalisches Inst, Univ Bayreuth, D-95440 Bayreuth Germany

HAARMAN, HERMAN ROELOF, management consultant, real estate advisor; b. Voorst, Holland, Dec. 19, 1953; m. Annemieke Quaadquas, Apr. 15, 1977 (div. 1987); children: Robbert, Allard, Marlies. MS, Tech. U. Delft, Holland, 1981. Cert. archtl. engr.; master real estate. Project mgr. Reyenga-Postma, Voorburg, Holland, 1977-78, Verhave-lugt, The Hague, Holland, 1978-79; architect FC de Weger, Rotterdam, Holland, 1980-81; town planner Rijksgebouwendienst, The Hague, 1981-82; real estate advisor Ministry of Housing, The Hague, 1983-89; dir. EG-Beraad Bouw, The Hague, 1989-98; dir. sustainable bldg. Ministry of Housing, The Hague, 1998—. Editor, head author EU-Bulletin Constrn. Sector, 1989-98. Candidate D66, Zoebermeer, Holland, 1994; mem. Town Coun., Rijnwoude, 1998—. Office: EG Beraad Bouw, Min Housing/Spatial Plan, PO Box 2095, 2500 EZ The Hague The Netherlands

HAAS, ALOIS, retired chemistry educator, researcher, consultant; b. Czernowitz, Romania, Jan. 3, 1932; arrived in Germany, 1940; s. Franz Josef and Anna Christine (Schäfer) H.; m. Claudia Margit Kussin, July 20, 1968; children: Julia, Sebastian. Diploma in chem. engring., State Engring. Sch., Essen, Germany, 1955; D of Natural Scis., Tech. U., Aachen, Germany, 1960; PhD, DSc, U. Cambridge, Eng., 1962; PhD (hon.), Jagiellonian U., Cracow, Poland, 1989, U. Poly. Temesvar, Romania, 1998, Russian Acad. Scis., Novosibirsk, 1998. Habilitation U. Göttingen, Germany, 1962-65; from docent to prof. inorganic chemistry Ruhr U., Bochum, Germany, 1965-69; dean, pro-dean chem. faculty Ruhr U., 1971-73, 87-90; hon. prof. Tongje U., Shanghai, 1984; coord. European Union-TMR project, 1998—. Author, editor: Gmelin Handbook of Inorganic Chemistry Perfluoroorganoelement Chemistry, 18 vols., 1974-97; contbr. numerous articles to profl. jours. Mem. Max Planck Soc., MPI Kohleforschung, Mulhaim Internat. (corr.), Ukrainian Nat. Acad. Sci. (fgn.), Royal Soc. Chemistry, Am. Chem. Soc., German Cambridge Soc. Avocations: sports, music, travel. Home: Gräfin-Imma-St 39, 44797 Bochum Germany Office: Ruhr U Bochum, FNO 0341036, D 44780 Bochum Germany

HAAS, EILEEN MARIE, homecare advocate; b. Pitts., Feb. 27, 1948; d. Michael Joseph and Bridget Agnes (Connolly) McNulty; m. Jerry Albert Haas, July 19, 1975; 1 child, Melissa. Student, York Coll. of Pa., 1975-78, Messiah Coll., Grantsville, Pa., 1978-80. Clk. Exch. Bur. Pitts., 1966-67; debt. collector Nat. Account Sys., Pitts., 1967-71; preadoptive advocate Hershey, Pa., 1983-84, Phila., 1984-85; homecare advocate Dillsburg, Pa., 1985-88, Deer Lodge, Mont., 1988-92, Gibsonia, Pa., 1992—; interpreter svcs. St. Victors Ch., Bairdsford, Pa., 1992—; presenter Harrisburg (Pa.) Area C.C., 1985, Pa. Soc. Respiratory Therapy, Ctrl. Pa. chpt., 1985; co-presenter Coun. Exceptional Children, Salt Lake City, 1997; rschr. in pulmonary rehab. With USN, 1971-74. Mem. DAV, Am. Soc. Deaf Children, Coun. Exceptional Children, Assn. Severe Handicaps, Profl. Networking for Excellence in Svc. to Deaf and Hard of Hearing. Republican. Roman Catholic. Avocations: deaf education research, dysphagia research, writing, needlepoint, knitting. Home: 90 Kaufman Rd Gibsonia PA 15044-7950

HAAS, GILBERT ALAIN, physician; b. Paris, Aug. 20, 1937; s. Claude Raymond and Juliette-Rose (Richner) H.; Luna-Olga, Mar. 14, 1946; 1 child, Olivier. Student, Med. U. Paris, 1958-66, MD, 1972. Extern Paris Hosp., intern; with The Am. Hosp., Paris; pvt. practice Paris. Served as lt. with French Army. Home and Office: 60 Rue Saint-Andre des Arts, 75006 Paris France

HAAS, LU ANN, counselor; b. Waterloo, Iowa, Oct. 16, 1956; d. Leonard Edward and Naomi Lee (Binley) H.; divorced; children: Shauna Lee Haas, Nicholas William Smith. AAS, Ctrl. Tex. Coll., 1986; BA magna cum laude, Mt. mercy Coll., 1992; MA, U. Iowa, 1993. Cert. rehab. counselor; cert. lay spkr. Meth. Ch. Ind. truck driver, 1982-83; night supr. Four Oaks-John Mcdonald Residential Treatment, Monticello, Iowa, 1991-92; security officer RA-CO Security Co., 1993-94; substance abuse counselor Area Substance Abuse Coun., Anamosa, Iowa, 1993-94; counseling psychologist Dept. Vets Affairs, Cin., 1994-96, Dallas, 1996-97; mentor host program Fairfield Elem. Sch., Copperas Cove, Tex., 1994-97; ret., 1997; spkr. in field; cons. in field. Unit sec. United Meth. Women. Sgt. U.S. Army, 1975-81, 83-87. Leonard A. Miller scholar, 1993. Mem. ACA, Nat. Rehab. Assn., Am. Rehab. Counseling Assn., Nat. Rehab. Counseling Assn. (sec./treas. 1997, 98, bd. dirs. 1995, 96, membership chmn. 1995-97), Tex. Rehab. Counseling Assn., Disabled Am. Vets. (life), U. Iowa Alumni Assn., Kappa Gamma Pi (liaison Mt. Mercy Coll.), Am. Legion, Vietnam Vets. Am. (assoc. Miami Valley (Ohio) chpt.). Democrat. Methodist. Avocations: crocheting, reading, writing. Home: 1404 Janet Ln Copperas Cove TX 76522-1228

HAAS, PETER M., political science educator; b. Oakland, Calif., Jan. 23, 1955; s. Ernst B. and Hildegarde Haas; m. Julie Zuckman, Apr. 28, 1986; 1 child, David. BA (hons.), Univ. Mich., 1977; PhD, Mass. Inst. Tech., 1986. Teaching fellow Harvard Univ., 1984, 85; marine policy rsch. fellow Marine Policy Ctr. Woods Hole Oceanographic Inst., 1986-87; asst. prof. political sci. dept. Univ. Mass., Amherst, 1986-92; project dir. Ctr. for Internat. Affairs Harvard Univ., 1990-92; assoc. prof. political sci. dept. Univ. Mass., 1992-98, prof. political sci. dept., 1998—; vis. asst. prof. Yale Univ. Political Sci. dept. 1986; editorial bd. Jour. of European Public Policy, 1999—, Global Environmental Politics, 1999—; adj. rsch. fellow Ctr. for Sci. and International Affairs Harvard Univ., 1990—; presenter at numerous confs. Author: Knowledge, Power and International Policy Coordination, 1997, Institutions for the Earth: Sources of Effective International Environmental Protection, 1993, Saving the Mediterranean: The Politics of International Environmental Cooperation, 1990; contbr. numerous articles to profl. jours.; and book chpts. Recipient rsch. fellowship German Marshall Fund, 1992, Peace and World Security Studies Program, Hampshire Coll., 1989, 99, Nat. Sci. Found. 1990, 92, Rockefeller Brothers Fund Project grant, 1991 and others. E-mail: Haas@polsci.umass.edu. Office: Univ Mass political sci dept 214 Thompson Hall Amherst MA 01003

HAAS, ROBERT LANCE, surgeon, consultant; b. N.Y.C., Oct. 7, 1933; s. Kalman and Ruth Haas; m. Lois Feldman, Apr. 14, 1957; children: Kara, Robyn, Bradley, Felice. BS in Biology, Ohio State U., 1953; DDS, Columbia U., 1957, MPH, 1973. Diplomate Am. Bd. Oràl & Maxillofacial Surgery. Intern in maxillofacial surgery Harlem Hosp., N.Y.C., 1958; resident in maxillofacial surgery Grasslands Hosp., Valhalla, N.Y., 1960; pvt. practice; assoc. attending maxillofacial surgeon N.Y. Med. Coll.-Grassland Hosp., Valhalla, Bronx (N.Y.)-Lebanon Med. Ctr., Fordham-Misericordia Med. Ctr., The Bronx; attending maxillofacial surgeon Royal Hosp., The Bronx; attending surgeon, chief maxillofacial surgery & dentistry Newark Beth Israel Med. Ctr., dir. out-patient dept. Contbr. articles to profl. jours. Adminstrv. judge City of Tampa. Fellow Am. Coll. Oral & Maxillofacial Surgeons, Am. Acad. Cosmetic Surgeons, Internat. Soc. Oral & Maxillofacial Surgeons, Am. Dental Soc. Anesthesiology, Internat. Assn. Study Pain, Am. Pain Soc.; mem. APHA, state and local affiliates of ADA, Internat. Assn. Maxillofacial Surgery, Hillsborough County Hosp., Am. Assn. Oral & Maxillofacial Surgeons, Nat. Ctr. Health Edn. (charter assoc.), Alpha Omega. Home: 17627 Nathans Dr Tampa FL 33647-2273

HAASE, ASHLEY THOMSON, microbiology educator, researcher; b. Chgo., Dec. 8, 1939; s. Milton Conrad and Mary Elizabeth Minter (Thomson) H.; m. Ann DeLong, 1962; children: Elizabeth, Stephanie, Harris. BA, Lawrence Coll., 1961; MD, Columbia U., 1965. Intern Johns Hopkins Hosp., Balt., 1965-67; clin. assoc. Nat. Inst. Allergy and Infectious Disease, Bethesda, Md., 1967-70; vis. scientist Nat. Inst. Med. Rsch., London, 1970-71; chief infectious disease sect. VA Med. Ctr., San Francisco, 1971-84, med. investigator, 1978-83; prof. microbiology U. Minn., Mpls., 1984-99, head dept., 1984—, Regent's prof., 1999—; mem. fellowship screening com. Am. Cancer Soc., San Francisco, 1978-81; mem. UNESCO Internat. Cell Rsch. Orgn., India, 1978; mem. nat. adv. coun. Nat. Inst. Allergy and Infectious Diseases, 1986-91, mem. task force on microbiology and infectious diseases, 1991, merit investigator, 1989—, chair AIDS rsch. adv. com., 1993-96, chmn. vaccine subcom.; Javits neurosci. investigator Nat. Inst. Neurol. and Communicative Disorders and Stroke, 1988-95; chmn. panel on AIDS, U.S.-Japan Coop. Med. Sci. Program, 1988-95; mem. OAR AIDS Rsch. Evaluation Working Group, 1995-96; mem. adv. com. for career awards in biomed. scis. Burroughs-Wellcome Fund, 1995—; trustee Lawrence U., 1997—. Editor: Microbial Pathogenesis, 1988-94; contbr. articles on AIDS pathogenesis and other topics in neurovirology to profl. jours. Recipient Lucia R. Briggs Disting. Achievement award Lawrence Coll., 1990. Mem. Am. Soc. Microbiology, Assn. Am. Physicians, Am. Soc. Clin. Investigation, Am. Soc. Virology, Assn. Med. Schs. Microbiology Chmn., Infectious Diseases Soc. Am., Nat. Multiple Sclerosis Soc. (adv. com. 1978-84), Phi Beta Kappa, Alpha Omega Alpha. Democrat. Home: 14 Buffalo Rd Saint Paul MN 55127-2136 Office: U Minn Dept Microbiology 420 Delaware St SE Minneapolis MN 55455-0374

HAASE, GERALD MARTIN, pediatric surgeon; b. Shanghai, Jan. 29, 1947; s. Warner A. and Jean E. Haase; children: Sean Hale, Ryan Eric, Jessica Ann; m. Peggy Newman. BA, Johns Hopkins U., 1968; postgrad., Wayne State U. Med. Sch., 1968-70; MD, Tufts U., 1972. Diplomate Am. Bd. Surgery. Resident in surgery U. Colo., Denver, 1972-74, 75-77; resident in pediat. surgery Children's Hosp., Boston, 1974-75; fellow pediat. surgery Children's Hosp., Columbus, Ohio, 1977-79; practice medicine Denver Pediat. Surgeons, 1979—; chmn. dept. pediatric surgery Childrens Hosp., Denver 1980-91; cons. pediatric surgeon Fitzsimons Army Med. Center, Aurora, Colo., 1982-96; clin. asst. prof. surgery U. Colo. Health Sci. Center, Denver, 1979-84, assoc. prof. 1985-91, prof. 1992—; chmn. surg. steering com.; group V chmn. Children's Cancer Group, bd. dirs. Am. Cancer Soc., 1990-96. Mem. AMA, ACS, Denver Med. Soc., Colo. Med. Soc., Am. Acad. Pediatrics, Am. Pediat. Surg. Assn. (chmn. cancer com. 1995-98), Soc. Surg. Oncology, Internat. Soc. Pedit. Oncology, Nat. Childhood Cancer Found. (med. and sci. adv. bd.), Internat. Coll. Surgeons, Internat. Soc. Pediat. Surg. Oncology (charter mem.), Extracorpeal Life Support Orgn. (charter mem.), Am. Soc. Clin. Oncology, Am. Burn Assn., Pacific Assn. Pediat. Surgery, N.Y. Acad. Sci., Sigma Phi Epsilon, Delta Phi Alpha. Office: Professional LLC 1056 E 19th Ave # B190 Denver CO 80218-1007

HAASE, GUNTER, optics scientist educator; b. Gelsenkirchen, Germany, July 23, 1918; s. Gustav and Emma (Bock) H.; m. Elisabeth Scholl; 1 child, Wolfgang. Dr. rer. nat., Univ., Frankfurt, Germany, 1941, Dr. phil. nat. habil., 1944. Prof. Univ., Frankfurt, Germany, 1954; dir. Dept. Photographic Sci. of Univ., Frankfurt, 1961-70; prof. Technische U., Mûnich, 1970—, dir. inst. for photographic sci., 1970-89; dir. inst. for photographic sci. Inst. for Chemistry of Info. Recording, Mûnich, 1986-89; emeritus Technische U., Mûnich, 1989—; dir. Sect. Sci. and Techniques of German Soc. Photographic Sci., Köln, Germany, 1970-77. Author, editor: Photographic Science, Vol. I-III, 1968; author: Physik für Mediziner, 1968; contbr. articles to profl. jours. Recipient Golden Needle, German Soc. Photography, 1995. Mem. Deutsche Physikalische Gesellschaft, Deutsche Gesellschaft für Angewandte Optik, Optical Soc. Am., Soc. for Imaging Sci. and Technology, Internat. Soc. for Optical Engring., Gesellschaft Deutscher Naturforscher und Ärzte.

HAASE, MICHAEL EIK, publisher; b. Copenhagen, Nov. 4, 1957; s. Niels J Haase and Juliane Marie (Michelsen) Larsen; m. Frances Ann Buchschacher, July 15, 1997; children: Chinie, Ronja, Sebastian. Mktg. assoc. Press, Maanedsbladet, Copenhagen, 1987-90; mktg. dir. P. Haase & Son Forlag, Copenhagen, 1990-96, pub., 1996—. Office: P Haase & Sons Pubs, Lövstraede 8 2 TV, 1152 Copenhagen Denmark

HAA'SZ, GYÖRGY JENS, drilling company executive; b. Stridóvár, Hungary, Sept. 27, 1944; s. Jenö and Jenöné (Boldog) Szabó; m. Györgyné Kerkay, Apr. 17, 1970; 1 child, Gabriella. Diploma in drilling tchnician, Drilling & Prodn. Coll., Nagykanizsa, Hungary, 1963; MSc in Petroleum Engring., U. Heavy Indstry, Miskolc, Hungary, 1968. Drilling engr. Transdadubian Drilling Co., Gellenhaza, Hungary, 1968-74; drilling rig mgr. Transdadubian Drilling Co., Iraq, 1974-78; drilling contracting mgr. KFV Oil & Gas Co., Nagykanizsa, 1979-88, mgr. bus. devel., 1988-90; mktg. dir. ROTARY Drilling Co., Nagykanizsa, 1990-95, dir. internat. ops., 1995—; drilling rig mgr. KFV-Nikex Drilling Co., Libya, 1984; turbo crew chief Hungarian Blowout Specialists, Kuwait, 1991; project mgr. ROTARY Drilling Co., Damascus, Syria, 1997, Nagykanizsa, 1998. Recipient Excellent Miner award Ministry Industry, 1976, 86, Excellent Innovator award, 1983. Mem. Hungarian Assn. Miners, 1968. Avocations: sailing, gardening. Home: Sugár u. 6, H-8800 Nagykanizsa Hungary Office: ROTARY Drilling Co, Erzsébet tér 22, H-8800 Nagykanizsa Hungary

HAAVARDSSON, FRIDTHJOV, finance executive; b. Bodoe, Norway, June 10, 1937; s. Haavard and Inga (Nilsen) Hanssen; m. Aagot Holm, Aug. 6, 1966; children: Ingeborg, Nils F. MA in Econs., McGill U., Montreal, Can., 1962; MBA, Norwegian Sch. Bus. and Econs., Bergen, 1961. 1st sec. Ministry of Industry, Oslo, 1963-64; jr. expert UNTAB, Jakarta, Indonesia, 1964-65; sec. Norwegian Shipowners Assn., Oslo, 1965-68; treas. Lorentzens Reder Co., Oslo, 1968-70; asst. dir. Fred Olsen & Co., Oslo, 1970-79, fin. dir., 1979—, also bd. dirs.; bd. dirs. Bonheur asa, Fnd. Olsen Energy ASA, Loki ASA, Ganger Rolf asa, Oslo; vice chmn. Aker Group, Oslo, 1980-84, Wideroes Flyveselskap, Oslo, 1982-89; chmn. Det Bergenske Dampskipsselskad, Bergen, 1983-84. Avocations: skiing, golf, tennis, music. Home: Nordengveien 34, 1396 Billingstad Norway

HAAVISTO, HEIKKI JOHANNES, retired Finnish government official; b. Turku, Finland, Aug. 20, 1935; s. Urho and Alli Haavisto; m. Maija Rihko, Nov. 14, 1964; children: Antti, Erkki, Ilkka. MS in Agr., U. Helsinki, Finland, LLM, D in Agr. and Fgn.; PhD (Hon.), U. Turku, Finland; D in Agr. and Forestry (hon.), U. Helsinki, Finland, Dr.Vet. (hon.). Head of dept. Oy Vehnä Ab, 1963-66; sec.-gen. Ctrl. Union of Agrl. Prodrs. and Forest Owners, Helsinki, 1966-75, pres, 1976-94; min. fgn. affairs Govt. of Finland, Helsinki, 1993-95; mem. adminstrv. coun. Osuukunta Metsäliitto, Helsinki, 1976-93, vice chmn., pres., 1976-83; chmn. delegation Finn. Coop. Pellervo, Helsinki, 1979—; vice chmn. adminstrv. coun. Ctrl. Union Coop. Banks, Helsinki, 1985-93; active Internat. Policy Coun. on Agr. and Trade, Washington, 1988-94; chmn. adminstrv. coun. Raisio Group, 1987-96, chmn. bd. dirs. 1997—. Mem. Centre Party of Finland. Address: Hintsa, 21200 Raisio Finland

HABAKKUK, JOHN HROTHGAR, economic historian; b. Barry, Wales, May 13, 1915; s. Evan Guest and Anne (Bowen) H.; MA, St. John's Coll., Cambridge U., 1940; m. Mary Elizabeth Richards, Aug. 8, 1948; children: David, Alison, Kate, Lucy. Fellow, Pembroke Coll., Cambridge U., 1938-50, univ. lectr. Faculty Econs. and Politics, 1946-50; vis. prof. Harvard U., 1954-55, U. Calif., Berkeley, 1962-63; prof. econ. history, fellow All Souls Coll., Oxford U., 1950-67, fellow, 88—; prin. Jesus Coll., 1968-84, vice chancellor univ., 1973-77; pres. Univ. Coll., Swansea, 1975-84; trustee Rhodes Scholarships, 1977-86; mem. Adv. Coun. Pub. Records, 1958-70, Social Sci. Rsch. Coun., 1967-71, Royal Hist. Manuscripts Commn., 1977-85. Chmn. Oxfordshire Health Authority, 1982-84. Created knight bachelor, 1976; hon. fellow Pembroke and St. John's colls., Cambridge U., Jesus Coll., Oxford, Univ. Coll. Swansea, 1991. Fellow Brit. Acad.; mem. Royal Hist. Soc. (pres. 1977-80). Author: American and British Technology in the 19th Century, 1962; Population Growth and Economic Development since 1750, 1970, Marriage, Debt and the Estate System, 1994; co-editor: Economic History Review, 1950-60, Cambridge Economic History, Vol. VI, 1965. Home: 28 Cunliffe Close, Oxford OX2 7BL, England Office: All Souls, Oxford OX1 3DW, England

HABANEC, IVAN PAUL, management consultant; b. Piestany, Slovakia, Apr. 14, 1934; arrived in England, 1969; s. Otto F. and Beatriz (Kotikova) H.; 1 child, Susan; m. Olga Patricia Montoya, Aug. 17, 1985; children: Steven, Lucia. MBA, Prague Sch. Econs., 1963. Mgr. UUSTE, Prague, Czech Republic, 1964-69; cons. Whitehead Group, London, 1969-73; mgr. Bechtel, Saudi Arabia, 1973-85; freelance cons. London, 1985—; cons. UN, Malaysia, Laos, Ghana, 1988-91, Price Waterhouse, Prague, 1991-92, European Cmty., Warsaw, 1992-93, World Bank, Moscow, 1994-95, Russian Min. of Economy, 1996-97, Hosp. Restructuring Fund, Republic of Georgia, 2000; advisor Russian Found. Legal Reform, 1998-2000. Fellow Inst. Mgmt. Cons. Conservative. Avocation: current affairs. Home: 151 Dartmouth Rd, London NW2 4EN, England

HABANSKY, BETH JUDITH, speech language pathologist; b. Bridgeport, Conn., Dec. 13, 1966; d. Ronald John and Patricia Ann Habansky. Student, U. St. Andrews, Scotland, 1986-87; BA, Bryn Mawr Coll., 1988; MS, Columbia U., 1992. Cert. clin. competency speech lang. pathology Am. Speech-Lang. Hearing Assn.; lic. speech lang. pathology. Secondary mortgage investment supr. Citytrust Co., Bridgeport, 1988-89; secondary mortgage investment coord. Centerbank, Waterbury, Conn., 1989; asst. tchr. Coop. Ednl. Svcs., Fairfield, Conn., 1990; speech-lang. pathologist, coord. cognitive rehab. program Easter Seals Southwestern Conn., Stamford, 1992-94; staff speech-lang. pathologist New Milford (Conn.) Hosp., 1994-95, speech-lang. pathology mgr., 1995—. On-line supr. Pain Relief Ctr., 1997-98. Mem. Brain Injury Assn., Conn. Brain Injury Assn. Fax: 860-210-7400. Office: New Milford Hosp 21 Elm St New Milford CT 06776-2993

HABBE, KARL ALBERT, retired geography educator; b. Celle, Germany, Mar. 15, 1928; s. Walter and Marianne (Schmoldt) H.; m. Ebba Seiffert, Dec. 19, 1958; children: Dorothee, Joachim, Ulrich. Grad., U. Freiburg, 1954, D in Natural Scis., 1957, Habilitation, 1965. Asst. U. Freiburg, 1958-66, pvt. dozent, 1966-70; Wiss. Rat U. Erlangen, 1970-73, prof., 1973-93, ret., 1993. Author: Das Flurbild des Hofsiedlungsgebiets im Mittleren Schwarzwald am Ende des 18 Jahrhunderts, 1960, Die wuermzeitliche Vergletscherung des Gardasee-Gebietes, 1969, Zur geomorphologischen Kartierung von Blatt Groenenbach-Probleme, Beobachtungen, Schlussfolgerungen, 1986, Die aeolischen Sandablagerungen vor dem Stufenhang der Noerdlichen Frankenalb-Probleme, Beobachtungen, Schlussfolgerungen, 1997. Home: Haenflingweg 3, D-91056 Erlangen Germany Office: U Erlangen-Nuernberg, Dept Geography Kochstr 4, D-91054 Erlangen Germany

HABEEB, HABEEBA HUSSAIN, library director; b. Male, Republic of Maldives, Sept. 9, 1930; d. Hussain Habeeb and Shahima Shamsuddin; m. Abdulla Zubair, May 18, 1923; children: Ibrahim, Shafeea, Shahida. Grad. High Sch. Urdu Medium, Osmania, Hyderabad, India, 1948; grad. High Sch. English Medium, Holy Family Convent, Colombo, Sri Lanka, 1952. Cert. librarian. Asst. prin. Govt. Service, Male, Maldives, 1956-62; sec. Prime Minister's Office, Male, 1962-67, Foreign Affairs, Male, 1968-70, Transp. Dept. Govt. Service, Male, 1974-78, Aid Dept. Ministry of Justice Govt. Service, Male, 1974-75; librarian Nat. Library, Male, 1978-86, deputy dir., 1986-90; dir., 1990-95, dir. gen., 1995—. Author: Mohammed Thakurufaan The Great, 1990; co-author: Innovation in Primary School Construction, 1986; translator: How to Write Short Stories, 1984, other works from Urdu to Dhivehi and English to Dhivehi; editor Jour., Niru Libr. newsletter, Children's Club mag.; contbr. articles to cultural publs. Recipient Pres.'s award Gold Pen, Presdl. award for 25 yrs. govt. svc., Presdl. Encouragement award. Mem. Nat. Ctr. for Linguistic and Hist. Rsch. (adv. mem.). Home: Mandoovilla 8 Bodutulah St, Male Machchangolhi 20-03, Republic of Maldives Office: Nat Libr, 59 Majeedi Magu Galolhu, Male 20-24, Maldives*

HABEL, HELMUT HEINRICH, electronic engineer; b. Hollabrunn, Noe, Austria, Aug. 6, 1956; s. Helmut K. and Annemarie (Holzer) H.; m. Ruth M. Lehenbauer, Oct. 25, 1983; children: Harald, Heike. Diplom Ingenieur, Tech. U., Vienna, Austria, 1984. Student asst. Tech. U., Vienna, Austria, 1980-84, asst., 1984-92; tchr. Tech. High Sch. 10, Vienna, Austria, 1987—; ptnr. Light & Motion, Vienna, Austria, 1992—. Inventor electronic controller for el-lamps. Mem. IEEE, Electromagnetic Compatibility Soc. (vice-chmn. Austria sect.). Achievements include inventor of electronic balast for cold cathode tubes. Home and Office: Paulusgasse 13, A-1030 Vienna Austria

HABERHAUER, GEORG FRANZ, chemist, educator; b. Klagenfurt, Carinthia, Austria, Oct. 1, 1969; s. Franz L. and Heidrun (Hofmeister) H.; m. Christina Troyer, Aug. 30, 1997. MSc, U. Tech., Vienna, Austria, 1991, PhD, 1994. Rsch. asst. U. Tech., Vienna, 1991-92; rsch. scientist U. Frankfurt, Germany, 1992-95; rschr. Austrian Rsch. Ctrs., 1995—; lectr. U. Tech., Vienna, 1997—, Agrl. U., Vienna, 1999—. Mem. German Chem. Soc., Am. Chem. Soc. Avocations: skiing, hiking, wine. Home: Neubaugasse 5/11, A-1070 Vienna Austria

HABERMAN, CHARLES MORRIS, mechanical engineer, educator; b. Bakersfield, Calif., Dec. 10, 1927; s. Carl Morris and Rose Marie (Braun) H. BS, UCLA, 1951; MS in Mech. Engring., U. So. Calif., 1954, MS in Aeronautical Engring., 1960. Lead, sr. and group engr. Northrop Aircraft, Hawthorne, Calif., 1951-59, cons., 1959-61; asst. prof. to prof. mech. engring. Calif. State U., L.A., 1959-91; cons. Royal McBee Corp., 1960-61. Author: Engineering Systems Analysis, 1965, Use of Computers for Engineering Applications, 1966, Vibration Analysis, 1968, Basic Aerodynamics, 1971. Served with AUS, 1946-47. Mem. Am. Soc. Engring. Edn. Democrat. Roman Catholic.

HABERMAS, JÜRGEN, philosopher, sociologist; b. Düsseldorf, Germany, June 18, 1929; s. Ernst and Grete (Koettgen) H.; m. Ute Wesselhoeft, Aug. 1955; children: Tilmann, Rebekka, Judith. PhD, U. Bonn, Germany, 1954; AM, Inst. Sozialforschung, 1959; Habilitation, U. Marburg, Germany, 1961; D (hon.), New Sch. for Social Rsch., N.Y.C., 1980, Hebrew U. Jerusalem, 1989, U. Buenos Aires, 1989, U. Hamburg, 1989, Reichsuniv. Utrecht, 1990, Northwestern U., 1991, U. Athens, 1993, U. Tel Aviv, 1995, U. Bologna, 1996, U. Paris, 1997, U. Cambridge, England, 1999. Asst. prof. Inst. Social Rsch., 1959; prof. philosophy U. Heidelberg, Germany, 1961-64; prof. philosophy, sociology U. Frankfurt, Germany, 1964-71; dir. Max Planck Inst., Starnberg, 1971-83; prof. philosophy U. Frankfurt, 1983-94, prof. emeritus, 1994—; vis. prof. grad. faculty New Sch. for Social Rsch., N.Y.,

Inst. for Humanities Wesleyan U., U. Calif. Santa Barbara, Haverford Coll., U. Pa., Phila., Coll. France Paris, Northwestern U., Evanston, Ill., U. Calif. Berkeley, lectr., Princeton U., Cornell U., Harvard U., Nat. U. Seoul. Contbr. articles to profl. jours. Recipient Hegel prize, 1974, Sigmund Freud prize Deutschen Acad. Sprache und Dichtung, 1976, Ordentliches Mitglied, 1983, Adorno prize, Mitglied Inst. Internat. Philosophy, 1980, Geschwister Scholl prize, 1985, Wilhelm Leuschner medal, 1985, Sonning prize, 1987, Ordentliches Mitglied Acad. Europaea, 1988, Karl Jaspers prize, 1995, Culture Prize Landes Hessen, 1999, Helmholtz medal Berlin-Brandenburgische Akademie der Wissenschaften, 2000. Mem. Am. Acad. Arts and Scis. (hon.), Brit. Acad. Sci. (fgn.). Home: Ring-str 8B, D82319 Starnberg Germany

HABETHA, KLAUS OTTO PAUL, mathematics educator; b. Berlin, Feb. 14, 1932; s. Hugo and Katharina (Sauer) H.; m. Jutta H.E. Treuchel, Apr. 7, 1962; children—Anke, Jorg. Abitur, Oberschule, 1950; Sec. Tchrs. Exam, Freie U. Berlin, 1957; Dr.rer.nat., Freie U. Berlin, 1959; Habilitation, Tech. U. Berlin, 1962. Rsch. asst. Tech. U. Berlin, 1957-62, privatdozent, 1962-66, Wiss. rat. and prof., 1966-69; guest prof. Chalmers Inst. Tech., Gothenburg, Sweden, 1967-68; full prof. math. U. Dortmund, 1969-75, RWTH Aachen, 1975-97, prof. emeritus, 1997—, dean faculty of sci., 1982-84, vice rector, 1984-87, rector, 1987-97; v.p. German Rector's Conf., 1996-98. Author: Hohere Mathematik fur Ingenieure and Physiker, 3 vols., 1976-79. Contbr. articles to profl. jours. Editor Complex Variables jour., 1982—. Mem. Am. Math. Soc., Berliner Mathematische Gesellschaft, Deutsche Mathematiker-Vereinigung. Avocation: stamp collecting. Home: Hangstrasse 35, D-52076 Aachen Germany Office: Rheinisch-Westfalische Tech Hochschule, Templergraben 55, D-52056 Aachen Germany

HABGOOD, JOHN STAPYLTON, archbishop; b. Stony Stratford, England, June 23, 1927; s. Arthur Henry and Vera (Chetwynd-Stapylton) H.; m. Rosalie Mary Ann Boston, June 7, 1961; children: Laura, Francis, Ruth, Adrian. BA, Cambridge U., 1948, MA, 1952, PhD, 1953; DD (hon.), U. Durham, Eng., 1975, Cambridge U., 1985, Aberdeen U., 1988, Huron U., 1990, Hull U., 1991, Oxford U., 1996, Manchester U., 1996; DHL, York Coll., 1995. Ordained to priesthood Ch. of Eng., 1955. Demonstrator in pharmacology Cambridge U., Eng., 1950-53, fellow King's Coll., 1952-55; vice prin. Westcott House, Cambridge, 1956-62; rector St. John's Episcopal Ch., Jedburgh, Scotland, 1962-67; prin. Queen's Coll., Birmingham, Eng., 1967-73; bishop of Durham, Eng., 1973-83; archbishop Ch. of Eng., York, Eng., 1983-95. Author: Religion and Science, 1964, A Working Faith, 1980, Church and Nation in a Secular Age, 1983, Confessions of a Conservative Liberal, 1988, Making Sense, 1993, Faith and Uncertainty, 1997, Being a Person, 1998, Varieties of Unbelief, 1999. Hon. fellow, King's Coll., Cambridge, 1986. Privy councillor; life peer, 1995—. Club: Athenaeum (London). Home and Office: 18 The Mount, Malton North Yorkshire Y017 7ND, England

HABIB, ELIAS EDOUARD, surgeon, researcher; b. Beyrouth, Liban, July 24, 1955; arrived in France, 1981; s. Edouard Nakhlé and Odette Georges (Chehade) H.; m. Noha Soubhi Chéhab, June 14, 1981; children: Marianne Nada, Cyril Nabil. MD, U. Lyon, 1981; CU Chirurgie, U. Paris VI, 1987; DU Chir Coelio, U. Paris XI, 1996. Intern Paris, 1981-86; attaché spécialiste Hosp. R. Ballanger, Aulnay, France, 1986-89, asst., 1989-93, practicien hospitalier, 1993—; pres. ARCIF, Paris, 1999—. Contbr. chpts. to books, articles to profl. jours. Mem. Internat. Soc. Surgery, European Hernia Soc., Thoracic and Cardiovasc. Surg. Soc. of the French Lang., French Soc. Surg. Endoscopy, Ile de France Assn. for Rsch. en Surgery. Home: 181 Bld Pasteur, 94360 Bry Sur Marne France Office: Hopital R Ballanger, Bld R Ballanger, 93602 Aulnay Sous Bois France

HABIB, IBRAHIM WAHBY, computer networks engineer, educator, consultant; b. Cairo, Aug. 16, 1959; came to U.S., 1988; s. Wahby Mohamed and Salwa Kamel Habib. BSEE, Ain Shams U., Cairo, 1981; MSEE, Poly. U. N.Y., 1984; PhD in Elec. Engring., CUNY, 1991. Cons. N.J., N.Y., 1998—; assoc. prof. CUNY, 1999—; part-time tech. cons. AT&T, 1998—. Guest editor IEEE JSAC, IEEE Comms. Mag.; contbr. articles to profl. jours. Mem. IEEE (sr.; reviewer 1991—, editor 1993-97, mem. tech. program com.). Achievements include patent pending Adaptive Allocation of Resources in Communication Networks. Fax: (212) 650-8249. E-mail: eeiwh@eemail.engr.ccny.cuny.edu. Office: CUNY Elec Engring Dept 137 St and Convent Ave New York NY 10031

HABIB, KHALED JAWAD, research scientist; b. Kuwait City, Kuwait, Sept. 5, 1959; s. Jawad Mobbarak and Zakia K. H.; m. Anh N. Tran Lam, 1978; children: Anwer, Lila, Sarah. BS in Mech. Engring., N.C. State U., 1981; MS in Chem. Engring. and Materials Sci., U. Okla., 1985; PhD in Chem. and Materials Engring., U. Iowa, 1988. Assoc. researcher Kuwait Inst. Scientific Rsch., 1981-88, assoc. scientist, 1988-93, rsch. scientist, 1993—; postdoct. fellow in chem. engring. Tech. U. Aachen (Germany), 1991-92; tech., scientific cons. for local industries, Kuwait, 1992—. Contbr. articles to profl. jours.; inventor in field. Grantee Winter Coll. on Optics, 1993, NATO, 1994; recipient Brit. Chevening award Govt. of Gt. Britain, 1995, award in engring. sci. Kuwait Found. Advancement of Sci. Mem. Nat. Assn. Corrosion Engring., Am. Soc. Metals, SPIE (Optical Engring. Soc.). Avocations: lecturing, travel, running, language, reading. Office: Kuwait Inst Sci Rsch, PO Box 24885 Materials Appl, 13109 Safat Kuwait

HABIB, MIR-MOHAMED, physician; b. India, Feb. 21, 1961; s. Sanaullah Mir-Mohamed and Shazad Begum; m. Sajida Habib, Feb. 22, 1941; children: Zubair, Uwais, Samiha, Suhail. MBBS, Kidpane Med. Coll., Madras, India, 1970; DSc, London U., 1974. Tutor in anatomy Med. Sch., Madras, India, 1970-71; with Lancaster (Australia) Gen. Hosp., 1971, Suubuny Med. Ctr., Melbourne, 1971-72; gen. practitioner Dr. Habib Surgery, Campbellfield, Australia, 1972—. Mem. Royal Australian Coll. of Gen. Pracitioners, Northern Divsn. of Gen. Practice. Muslim. Avocations: meeting friends, traveling. Office: Mirzuss, 347 Barry Rd, Campbellfield VIC 3061, Australia

HABIBI, HASSAN EBRAHIM, Iranian government official; b. 1937. Student sociology and law, France; student, Theol. Coll.; PhD in Law. Min. culture and higher edn., 1979; mem., later spokesman Revolutionary Coun.; mem. Supreme Coun. Edn. and Cultural Revolutionary Hdqrs.; min. justice Govt. of Iran, Teheran, 1984-89, 1st v.p., 1989—. Author: Inamate. Office: Office of the Pres, Palestine Crossroad, Pastor Ave, Tehran Iran*

HABIBI, SOHEIL, electrical engineer; b. Tehran, Iran, Aug. 24, 1964; p. Nureddin Habibi and Farideh Sinaie. MSc in Electronics, Norwegian Inst. Tech., Trondheim, Norway, 1990; PhD in Elec. Engring. and Electronics, Keio U., Tokyo, 1996. Rsch. fellow NTU, Singapore, 1996-97; process engr. SensoNor, Horten, Norway, 1997-98; project mgr. SensoNor, Horten, 1998—; project mgr. European Union. Contbr. articles to profl. jours. Scholar Nordic Min. Chamber, Copenhagen, 1989, Monbusho scholar Japanese Govt., Tokyo, 1992-96. Mem. IEEE Electron Device Soc., Am. Vacuum Soc. Mem. Baha'i Faith. Achievements include inventor of photochemical etching of InGaAs/InAIAs using HBr and 172nm Excimer lamp; research in fabrication technology for high frequency device manufacturing characterization of ultraviolet excited Br*-radical etching of InGaAs/InAIAs material system, fabrication technology for high frequency device manufacturing dry sequential process of photochemical etching and surface passivation of In0.52Al).48As using HBr and H2S. E-mail: soheil.habibi@sensonor.no. Fax: 47 3303 5105. Home: Parkvn 17, N-3080 Holmestrand Norway Office: SensoNor asa, PO Box 196, N-3192 Horten Norway

HABIB-NASSIF, ANNE-MARIE, internist; b. Beirut, Lebanon, Aug. 17, 1960; d. Robert and Ruth (Neff) N.; m. Alexis Habib; 2 children. MD, U. St. Joseph, Lebanon, 1986. Diplomate Am. Bd. Internal Medicine. Resident in internal medicine Roosevelt Hosp., N.Y.C., 1987-90; postdoctoral residency fellow Columbia U., N.Y.C., 1990; renal fellow Mt. Sinai Hosp., N.Y.C., 1990-92; asst. physician Pitie-Salpetriere, France, 1992-93; asst. rsch. fellow Hammersmith Hosp., London, 1998—. Avocations: tennis, skiing, cycling, swimming. Office: Hammersmith Hosp, London SW10 9LP, England

HABICHT, JEAN-PIERRE, public health researcher, educator, consultant; b. Geneva, Dec. 15, 1934; s. Max H. and Elizabeth (Peterson) Herzog; m. Pat Hinxman, Jan. 3, 1959 (div. Oct. 1990); children: Heidi, Christopher, Oliver; m. Gretel H. Pelto, June 13, 1997. MD, U. Zurich, 1962, Dr. Med., 1964; MPH, Harvard U., 1968; PhD, MIT, 1969. Cert. in clin nutrition Am. Bd. Nutrition. Biochem. rsch. asst. Merck, Sharpe & Dohme, Rahway, N.J., 1958-59; pediat. intern Children's Hosp. Med. Ctr., Boston, 1965-66; med. officer WHO, Guatemala, 1969-74; prof. maternal and child health U. San Carlos, Guatemala, 1972-74; spl. asst. Nat. Ctr. for Health Stats., Washington, 1974-77; James Jamison prof. nutritional epidemiology Cornell U., Ithaca, N.Y., 1977—; cons. pub. health issues nat. and internat. govts., profl. agys., 1975—; mem. expert com. on nutrition WHO, Geneva, 1975—, mem. com. on epidemiology and disease prevention, 1986-89; mem. epidemiology and disease control study sect. NIH, Washington, 1980-83; mem. food and nutrition bd. NAS, Washington, 1981-84, mem. com. evaluation of Women Infant and Child nutrition risk criteria, 1994-96, mem. com. internat. nutrition, 1994-97; mem. com. uses dietary reference intakes Inst. Medicine NAS, 1997—; mem. adv. group coordinating subcom. on nutrition UN, 1983-89, chmn., 1986-87; mem. joint nutrition monitoring and evaluation com. HHS-USDA, 1982-86; chmn. expert com. phys. status: Use and Interpretation of Anthropometry, WHO, 1991-93; mem. steering com. on low birth weight UNICEF, 1999—. Contbr. articles to profl. jours., chpts. to books. Fellow Am. Coll. Epidemiology; mem. APHA, Am. Soc. Clin. Nutrition, Am. Soc. Nutritional Scis. (Kellogg prize 1994, Atwater Meml. lectr. 1998, Conrad A. Elvehjem award 1999), Soc. for Epidemiologic Rsch., Internat. Epidemiol. Assn., Internat. Soc. Rsch. on Human Milk and Lactation (mem. exec. com. 1995-96), Sigma Xi, Gamma Sigma Delta, Delta Omega. Office: Cornell U Div Nutritional Sci Savage Hall Ithaca NY 14853

HABON, EDUARDO VAÑO, JR., mechanical engineer; b. Cebu City, The Philippines, Jan. 22, 1960; s. Eduardo Filipinas Sr. and Casiana Bonghanoy (Vaño) H.; m. Josephine Alegado, Nov. 7, 1988; children: Edjellen Faith, April Rose, Judie Ann, Edward Joseph, Eduardo III. BS in Mech. Engring., U. San Jose, Recoletos, 1981. Cert. mech. engr. Lube oil and fuel prep. engr. Atlas Consolid. Mining and Devel. Corp., Toledo City, The Philippines, 1982-90; preventive maintenance engr., safety & loss control officer Atlas Consolid. Mining and Devel. Corp., Toledo City, 1990-93, operation shift engr., 1993-94; preventive maintenance svc. engr., safety and health officer Toledo Power Co., 1994—; aux. cons. Consumers Generation-Magellan Cogeneration Inc., Cavite City, The Philippines, 1994, 97; commissioning engr. Rizal (The Philippines) Cement Ins., 1993. Mem. Lutopan chpt. Couples for Christ, Toledo City, Cebu. Mem. Philippine Soc. Mech. Engrs. (Toledo City chpt.). Avocations: playing chess, basketball, cycling, reading books, hiking. Fax: 032-322-6041. E-mail: evhabon@tpc.com.ph. Home: Ocy9ou Das, Toledo City 6038, The Philippines Office: Toledo Power Co-CPS, Bo Sigpit, Toledo City 6038, The Philippines

HABRUN, BORIS, veterinarian; b. Zagreb, Croatia, Dec. 14, 1966; s. Branko and Marija (Bonomi) H. DVM, Vet. Faculty, Zagreb, 1993, MSc, 1996, PhD, 1999. Younger asst. Croatian Vet. Inst., Zagreb, 1994-97, asst., 1997-99, higher asst., 1999—. Mem. Croatian Vet. Assn. Avocations: sailing, skeet shooting, hunting. Fax: 385 1 619 08 41. Home: Ilica 510, 10090 Zagreb Croatia Office: Croatian Vet Inst, Savska c 143 PO Box 883, 10000 Zagreb Croatia

HABSIEGER, LAURENT THIERRY, mathematician, researcher; b. Paris, May 20, 1963; s. Guy Lucien Habsieger and Michelle Juliette Martin Revel. M, U. Paris, 1985; PhD, U. Strasbourg, France, 1987. Rsch. assoc. Inst. Math. and Its Applications, Mpls., 1987-88; prof. U. Que., Montréal, Que., Can., 1988-90; rsch. assoc. Nat. Ctr. Sci. Rsch., France, 1990—; mem. sci. bd. U. Bordeaux, France, 1996-2000; cons. Maths en Jeans, France, 1996—. Mem. Soc. Math. France, N.Y. Acad. Scis. Avocations: badminton, tennis, skiing, philately. Office: A2X U Bordeaux 1, 351 cours de la Liberation, F-33405 Talence France

HABUKA, HITOSHI, engineering educator; b. Kisakata, Akita, Japan, Mar. 25, 1957; s. Toshikazu and Katsuko (Kikuchi) H.; m. Satoko Ito, Apr. 19, 1986; children: Satoru, Rie. BS, Niigata (Japan) U., 1979; MS, Kyoto (Japan) U., 1981; DS, Hiroshima (Japan) U., 1996. Rschr. R&D Ctr., Shin-Etsu Handotai Co., Ltd., Annaka, Japan, 1981-95; mgr. R&D Ctr., Shin-Etsu Handotai Co., Ltd., Annaka, 1995-2000; assoc. prof. dept. material sci. chem. engring. Yokohama Nat. U., Japan. Contbr. articles to profl. jours. Mem. AAAS, Japan Soc. Applied Physics, Soc. Chem. Engrs., The Electrochem. Soc., Am. Chem. Soc. Avocations: listening to music. Office: Yokohama Nat U, 79-5 Tokiwadai Hodogaya, Yokohama 240-8501, Japan

HABUSH, ROBERT LEE, lawyer; b. Milw., Mar. 22, 1936; s. Jesse James and Beatrice (Liebenberg) H.; m. Miriam Lee Friedman, Aug. 25, 1957; children: Sherri Ellen, William Scott, Jodi Lynn. BBA, U. Wis., 1959, JD, 1961. Bar: Wis. 1961, U.S. Dist. Ct. (ea. and we. dists.) Wis. 1961, U.S. Ct. Appeals (7th cir.) 1965, U.S. Supreme Ct. 1986. Pres. Habush, Habush, Davis & Rottier, S.C., Milw., 1961—; lectr. U. Wis. Law Sch., Marquette U. Law Sch., State Bar Wis., other legal orgns. Author: Cross Examination of Non Medical Experts, 1981; contbr. articles to legal jours. Capt. U.S. Army, 1959-75. Mem. ATLA (bd. govs. 1983-86, pres. 1986-87), ABA, Internat. Acad. Trial Lawyers (bd. dirs. 1983-87, 91-92), Internat. Soc. Barristers, Nat. Coll. Advocacy, Nat. Bd. Trial Advs., Am. Bd. Trial Advs., Am. Soc. Writers on Legal Subjects, Wis. Bar Assn., Wis. Acad. Trial Lawyers (pres. 1968-69), Inner Circle Advs., Trial Lawyers for Pub. Justice, Roscoe Pound Found. Office: Habush Habush Davis & Rottier 777 E Wisconsin Ave Ste 2300 Milwaukee WI 53202-5381

HACEK, LAURA I. GARCIA, administrative assistant; b. Chgo.. AA, Wright Coll., Chgo., 1997; student, Georgetown U., 1998—. Meetings & events asst. mgr. Am. Acad. Facial, Plastic and Reconstructive Surgery, Alexandria, Va., 1998—; freelance photographer Reflections Photography, Falls Church, Va., 1998—. Artist: Georgetown Jour., 1999, ARC newsletter, 1996. Vol. mem. ARC adv. bd., Chgo., 1995-98. Vol. Dem. party, Chgo., 1995, YMCA, Chgo., 1993-98. Recipient Bronze Congl. Medal of Honor, 1985. Mem. Latino Civil Rights Orgn. Avocations: photography, art, volunteering, internat. affairs. E-mail: lhacek@aafprs.org. Home: PO Box 6564 Arlington VA 22206-0564 Office: Am Acad Facial Plastic & Reconstructive Surgery 310 S Henry St Alexandria VA 22314-3524

HACHET, PASCAL ANDRÉ, psychologist, writer; b. Montreuil Dous Bois, France, Apr. 11, 1962; s. Jacques and Josette (Fouquoire) H.; m. Amal Mahmoud El Sayed, June 30, 1990. M in Psychology, U. Paris, 1988, student, 1989, 90, PhD in Psychoanalysis, 1994. Licensed psychologist. Psychologist Sato-Picardie, Beauvais, France, 1990—; lectr. Univ. Reims, France, 1992-95, Univ. Paris, 1994-96, Ecole des Psychologues Praticiens, Paris, 1998—; expert European Coun., France, 1993; rschr. Nat. Assn. Rsch. Psychology, Paris, 1992; supr. pubs. European Assn. Exchanges and Studies in Drug Addiction, Beauvais, 1995-97. Author: Les Psychanalystes et Goethe, 1995, Les Toxicomanes et leurs Secrets, 1996, Dinosaures sur le divan, psychanalyse de "Jurassic Park", 1998, Le Mensonge Indispensable, du trauma social au mythe, 1999, Ces Ados qui fument des joints, 2000, Psychanalyse de Rahan, le fantôme psychique d'un héros de BD, 2000, Cryptes et Fantorres in psychanalyse, 2000. Mem. European Assn. Psychoanalysis. Avocation: athletics. Home: 213 Blvd Davout, 75020 Paris France Office: Sato-Picardie, 2 rue Achille Sirouy, 60000 Beauvais France

HACHICHOU, NABIL MAHMOUD, engineering executive; b. Sidon, Lebanon, July 25, 1957; s. Mahmoud Wafic and Raeifeh Abdul-Latif (Wehbe) H. BEE, Am. U., Beirut, Lebanon, 1980. Elec. engr. ACE, Beirut, Lebanon, 1980-84; tech. mgr. Saudi Oger, Riyadh, Saudi Arabia, 1984—. Mem. IEEE, Instrument Soc. Am. Muslim. Avocations: reading, stamp collecting, walking. Office: Saudi Oger Ltd, PO Box 708, Abha Saudi Arabia

HACK, ALBERTO GERMAN, chemistry educator, consultant; b. Rosario, Argentina, May 27, 1937; s. Valentin Luis and Catalina Elisa (Theler) H.; m. Angelina Paula Bruls, Feb. 26, 1965; 1 child, Angela Diana. Grad. in chem. engring., U. Litoral, Santa Fe, Argentina, 1961. Asst. Technische Hochschule Aachen, Germany, 1962-65; asst. prof. U. del Sur, Bahia Blanca, Argentina, 1965-68; titular prof. chem. engring. U. Rosario, Argentina, 1969—; exec. sec. APOSGRAN, Rosario, 1986—; S.Am. rep. Internat. Assn. Cereal Sci. and Tech., Rosario, 1996—. Home: Pje Alvarez 1564, 2000 Rosario Santa Fe, Argentina Office: APOSGRAN, Cordoba 1402, 2000 Rosario Santa Fe, Argentina

HACKER, GERHARD WOLFGANG, medical/clinical biologist, histochemist, endocrinologist; b. St. Florian am Inn, Austria, Apr. 15, 1956. Diploma in Endocrinology and Pathology, U. London, 1985; PhD in Zoology and Biochemistry, U. Salzburg, Austria, 1982. Rsch. fellow U. London, 1983-84; asst. Salzburg Gen. Hosp., 1987-92; head immunohistochemistry and biochemistry unit Landeskliniken, Salzburg, 1987—; asst. U. Salzburg, 1982-83, assoc. prof., 1988-96, gen. sec. Med. Rsch. Coord. Ctr., 1995—, prof. histochemistry, histology and endocrinology, 1997—; rsch. fellow U. Uppsala, Sweden, 1986, 92; guest prof. U. Xi'an, China, 1989; vis. prof. Deborah Rsch. Inst., Brown Mills, N.J., 1993; assoc. pres. Internat. Conf. on Modern Methods in Analytical Morphology, Atlantic City, 1995. Editor: Modern Methods in Analytical Morphology, 1994, Gold and Silver Staining: Techniques in Molecular Morphology, 2000; assoc. editor Cell Vision, 1993-98, Applied Immunohistochemistry and Molecular Morphology, 1999—. Pres. Internat. Workshop, Salzburg, 1992; sci. sec. Congress of Comparative Endocrinology, Salzburg, 1988. Recipient Doppler prize Salzburg Govt., 1983, 1st prize for ear-nose-throat rsch. Soc. for ENT, 1993, 1st prize for med. rsch., Salzburg Govt., 1994. Mem. European Neuropeptide Club (Austria), Nat. Soc. Histotech. (U.S.), Austrian Neurosci. Assn. (bd. dirs. 1993—), Mid. European Soc. for Alternative Methods. Avocations: musician, computers, animal welfare. E-mail: g.hacker@lkasbg.gr.at. Office: Gen State Hosp, Landeskliniken Salzburg, Inst Pathol Anat (LKA), A-5020 Salzburg Austria

HACKER-KLOM, URSULA BEATE, radiobiologist; b. Muenster, Germany, July 27, 1953; d. Paul A.E. and Irmgard D. (Schilling) H.; m. Ralph D. Klom; children: Jan F., Meike K. PhD, U. Muenster, 1991. Rsch. asst. U. Tex., Houston, 1978-79; scientific employee U. Muenster, Germany, 1973-82; asst. lectr. Inst. of Radiation Biology, Muenster, 1982-91; asst. prof. Clinic of Radiobiology, Muenster, 1993—; tchr. High Sch., Muenster, 1976—, Pub. High Sch., Muenster, 1991-92. Mem. German Soc. of Cytometry, ESTRO, German Soc. of Radiology, Nat. Radiation Protection Bd., Inst. of Radiology. Home: Schöppingenweg 53, D-48149 Münster Germany Office: Inst Radiobology, Robert-Kock-Str 43, D-48149 Münster Germany

HACKETT, GRANT, Olympic athlete; b. Southport, Australia, May 9, 1980. Recipient Gold medal 1500-meter freestyle Sydney Olympics, 2000; winner 1500-meter Atlanta Olympics, 1999; set new world record 200-meter freestyle Australia's nat. championships, 1999. Office: Australian Swimming Inc, PO Box 940, Dickson ACT 2602, Australia*

HACKETT, IAN JAMES, social science educator, charity administrator; b. Bromborough, Eng., May 16, 1946; s. James Henry and Gladys Jean (Dixon) H.; m. Nadine Ruth Eynon, Dec. 30, 1972 (div. 1976); Su Mita Bose, July 30, 1981. BSc, U. Manchester Inst. Sci. Tech., Eng., 1967; MSc, Univ. Coll. North Wales, Bangor, 1971, PACE, 1972; BA in Law, Thames Valley U., London, 1980. Tchr. Ysgol Dyffryn Ogwen, Gwynnedd, Wales, 1972-73; rsch. chemist U. Saskatchewan, Can., 1973-74; head chemistry Ellen Wilkinson H.S., London, 1974-82; head sci. Salvatorian Coll., Harrow, Eng., 1982-89; dep. head Internat. Sch. London, 1989-99; dir. One World Trust, London, 1993-99; head Internat. Sch. London, 1999—; in-svc. tng. cons., lab. design cons. Internat. Sch. London, Internat. C.C., 1987-89. Author: The Spring of Civilization, 1973, Beyond Sovereignty, 1985; founding editor/publisher (alternative global news mag.) Earth, 1975-77, Malta; founding editor (ednl. charity news mag.) One World, 1995—. Chair Assn. World Federalists U.K., 1991-92, treas. 1983-93; sec. Labour Party Br., Ealing Common, London, 1975-77. Mem. London Internat. Schs. Assn. (in-svc. com. 1994—), Holmes Place Health Club. Mem. World Federalist Movement. Avocations: cycling, swimming, scuba-diving. Home: 1 Kenilworth Rd, Ealing London W5 5PB, England Office: One World Trust, 7 Millbank, London SW1P 2JA, England and: Internat Sch London, 139 Gunnersbury Ave, London W3 8LA, England

HACKETT, JOHN PETER, dermatologist; b. N.Y.C., Feb. 10, 1942; s. John Thomas and Helen (Donohue) H.; m. Carol A. Hedden, July 27, 1968; children: John, Elizabeth, Susanne. AB, Holy Cross Coll., 1963; MD, Georgetown U., 1967. Diplomate Am. Bd. Internal Medicine, Am. Bd. Dermatology. Intern Georgetown U. Hosp., 1967-68, resident, 1968-69; fellow Johns Hopkins Hosp., 1972-75, chief resident, 1975; practice medicine specializing in dermatology Seattle, 1975—; chmn. bd. dirs. NW Dental Ins. Co., 1989-92; clin. asst. prof. dermatology U. Wash., 1976-88, clin. assoc. prof., 1988—; active staff Swedish Hosp., Providence Hosp.; cons. Wash. State Dept. Labor and Industries, 1992—; pres. Psoriasis Treatment Ctr., Inc., 1978-80; cons. physician Children's Orthopedic Hosp. Contbr. articles to profl. jours. Bd. dirs. Mercer Island Boys and Girls Club, 1976-81, Seattle Ctr. for Blind, 1979-80, N.W. Chamber Orch., 1983-86. Served to lt. condr. USNR, 1969-71. Mem. Am. Acad. Dermatology, Seattle Dermatol. Soc. (pres. 1981-82), Soc. Investigative Dermatology, Am. Contact Dermatitis Soc., Wash. State Med. Soc., King County Med. Soc. (chmn. media rels. com. 1977-80, grievance com. 1991—), Wash. Physicians Ins. Exch. (chmn. actuarial subcom. 1983-85, chmn. subscribers adv. com. 1986-90, audit com. 1988-92, fin. com. 1990-92), Wash. Athletic Club, Seattle Yacht Club, Columbia Tower Club, Marine Corps Meml. Office: 925 116th Ave NE Ste 266 Bellevue WA 98004-4601

HACKL, GUIDO, medical editor; b. Vienna, Jan. 2, 1920; s. Karl and Luise (Reichmann) H.; m. Eleonore Jahn, Jan. 4, 1951; 1 child, Susanne. Diplomkaufmann, Wirtschafts U., Vienna, 1940; Dr der Handels Wissenschaft, Vienna, 1940. Mem. Psychotechnicat Inst., Vienna, 1937—, leader, 1958—; trainee Human Rels. in U.S., 1954; pres. Arbeitsgemeinschaft fur Psychotechnik in Österreich, 1959—; Aufsichtsrat der Schiffswerfte Korneuburg, 1962-74; leader control dept. Bundeskanzleramt Wien, 1974-80. Author: Charakterbild des Menschen, 1950, Methoden der Personal-Auslese, 1954, Moderne Vorgesetzten Schulung, 1963, Charakterkunde, 1970, Besprechungstechnik, 1971; editor Jour. Mensch Arbeit, 1958—. Recipient Goldenes Verdienstzeichen, Republik Österreich, 1956, Grosses Ehrenzeichen, Republik of Österreich, 1975, Grosses Silbernes Ehrenzeichen, Republik of Österreich, 1982. Mem. Mensa Austria (pres. 1982-97). Avocation: stamp collecting. Home: Vegag 4, A-1190 Wien Austria

HACKL, MAXIMILLIAN, banker; b. Munich, Dec. 20, 1924. With Bayerische Vereinsbank AG, Munich, 1951—, chmn. supervisory bd., 1990—; hon. chmn. supervisory bd. Hypo Vereinsbank, Munich, 2000—; dep. chmn. supervisory bd. Lowenbrau AG, Munich; mem. supervisory bd. Siemens AG, Munich; mem. adminstrv. bd. Landwirtschaftliche Rentenbank, Frankfurt am Main; mem. adv. bd. Berlinische Lebensversicherung AG, Berlin and Weisbaden; chmn. Bayerischer Bankenverband e V., Munich; mem. bd. Bundeverband deutscher Banken e.V.; mem. senate Max-Planck-Gesellschaft zur Forderung der Wissenschafte e.V. Munich. Avocations: classical music, skiing. Office: Hypo Vereinsbank, Am Tucher Park 16, 80538 Munich Germany*

HACKNEY, HOWARD SMITH, retired county official; b. Clinton County, Ohio, May 20, 1910; s. Volcah Mann and Gusta Anna (Smith) H.; B.S. cum laude, Wilmington Coll., 1932; m. Lucille Morrow, June 28, 1934; children: Albert Morrow, Roderick Allen, Katherine Ann Luby. Farmer, Wilmington, Ohio; farm reporter Agrl. Adjustment Adminstrn., Wilmington, 1934-40, committeeman, 1940-52, office mgr., 1952—, county exec. dir. Agrl. Stblzn. and Conservation Service, 1961-88. Treas., dir. Clinton County Community Action Council; treas. Clinton County Council Chs.; dir. Ohio Pork Producers Coun.; trustee, mem. agrl. adv. com. Wilmington Coll.; trustee Clinton County Hist. Soc. Named to Ohio State Fair Hall of Fame, 1983, Swine Hall of Fame, 1986. Mem. Nat. Assn. Stblzn. and Conservation Service Office Employees (awards 1970, state, regional legis. cons., Agriculturist of Yr. 1987), AAAS, Soil Conservation Soc. Am., Farmers Union, Ohio Duroc Breeders Assn. (pres., dir.), Ohio Acad. Sci., Ohio Acad. History, Ohio Hist. Soc., Grange, Ohio Southdown Breeders Assn., Clinton County Farm Bur. (sec., dir.), Clinton County Agrl. Soc. (treas., dir., award 1975), Clinton County Lamb and Fleece Improvement Assn. (dir.), Clinton County Hist. Soc., Delta Theta Sigma (hon.), Masons. Republican. Quaker. Home: 2003 Inwood Rd Wilmington OH 45177-9424

HACKNEY, JACK DEAN, physician; b. Marion, Ill., Oct. 11, 1924; s. William F. and Betty (Monical) H.; m. Dorothy Anne Stublefield, Sept. 8, 1946; children: Richard W., Robert J. Student, So. Ill. Univ., 1941-43, Yale U., 1943; MD, St. Louis U. Sch. Medicine, 1948. Diplomate Am. Bd. Internal Medicine, Acad. Toxicol. Scis. Resident in internal medicine VA Hosp., St. Louis, 1949-51, White Meml. Hosp., L.A., 1953-54; rsch. assoc. Loma Linda U., L.A., 1954-57, asst. to assoc. prof., 1957-69; prof. medicine U. So. Calif., L.A., 1969-94, prof. emeritus, 1994—; dir. pulmonary lab. Rancho Los Amigos Med. Ctr., Downey, Calif., 1969-92, chief environ. health, 1970-94, emeritus, 1994—; mem. EPA Sci. Adv. Bd., Washington, 1984-86; cons., 1986-92. Editor/author: Inhalation Toxicology of Air Pollution, 1993; contbg. author: Bronchial Asthma: Mechanics and Therapeutics, 1985, 93; contbr. articles to profl. jours. Mem. air quality adv. com. Dept. Health Svcs., State of Calif., 1974-94, med. adv. panel South Coast Air Quality Mgmt. Dist., 1985-92. 1st lt. AMC, 1951-53, Korea. Recipient Calif. medal Am. Lung Assn. Calif., 1992. Fellow Am. Coll. Chest Physicians, Am. Coll. Toxicology; mem. Am. Physiol. Soc., Am. Thoracic Soc., Alpha Omega Alpha, Sigma Xi. Achievements include development of indirect method for measuring respiratory ventilation; extraction of gases from blood for Gas Chromatographic analysis; control of exposure facilities and methods to study human inhalation toxicology and use of these facilities to demonstrate ozone toxicity, adaptation to ozone, and determine exposure responses to many inhaled gas and particle pollutants. Home: 5181 Duenas Laguna Hills CA 92653-1878 Office: Environmental Health Svc RLAMC 7601 Imperial Hwy # 51 Downey CA 90242-3456

HACKNEY, ROBERT WARD, plant pathologist, nematologist, parasitologist, molecular geneticist, commercial arbitrator; b. Louisville, Dec. 11, 1942; s. Paul Arnold and Ovine (Whallen) H.; m. Cheryl Lynn Hill, June 28, 1969 (div. Dec. 1995); 1 child, Candice Colleen; m. Jacqueline Monica Eisenreich, Dec. 27, 1995. BA, Northwestern U., 1965; MS, Murray State U., 1969; PhD, Kans. State U., 1973. Postgrad. rsch. nematologist U. Calif., Riverside, 1973-75; plant nematologist Calif. Dept. Food and Agr., Sacramento, 1975-85, sr. plant nematologist, supr., 1985-89, sr. plant nematologist, 1989—; comml. arbitrator Am. Arbitration Assn., 1980—; chmn. Calif. Nematode Diagnosis Adv. Commn., Sacramento, 1981—. Assoc. editor Jour. Nematology, Annals of Applied Nematology, 2000; contbr. articles to profl. jours. Hon. dep. Sheriff, Sacramento, 1992-93. Served with USMC, 1966. NSF grantee, 1974. Mem. Soc. Nematologists, Internat. Coun. Study of Viruses and Virus Diseases of the Grape, Delta Tau Delta, Sigma Xi. Democrat. Baptist. Office: Calif Dept Food & Agriculture Plant Pest Diagnostic Ctr 3294 Meadowview Rd Sacramento CA 95832-1437

HACKS, PETER, playwright; b. Breslau, Poland, Mar. 21, 1928; s. Karl and Elly (Hermann) H.; m. Anna Elisabeth Wiede, Feb. 23, 1955. PhD, U. Munich, 1951. Author: Dramen 1-3, 1972-81, Stücke nach Stücken 1-2, 1965-85, Die Massgaben der Kunst, 1977 (Heinrich Mann prize 1981), Die Gedichte, 1988, Die Erzählungen, 1995, Die Späten Stücke, 1999. Recipient Lessingpreis, Ministerium für Kultur GDR, Berlin, 1956, Nationalpreis II Klasse, GDR Govt., 1974, I Klasse, 1977, Alex Wedding prize Acad. der Künste zu Berlin, 1993. *

HADDACKS, PAUL K., NATO official; m. Penny Haddacks; 1 child. Grad., Britannia Royal Naval Coll., Royal Naval Staff Coll., Royal Coll. of Def. Studies. Commd. ensign British Royal Navy, advanced through grades to vice-adm., 1997, jr. officer frigates and destroyers, comdr. HMNS Scimitar, 1971, navigating officer various ships, comdr. frigates Cleopatra, HMS Naiad, 1979-84, asst. dir. of Navy Plans, Ministry of Def., 1984, comdr. HMS intrepid, dep. dir. Naval Warfare, Ministry of Def., capt. of the fleet, CinC Fleet; commodore, sr. naval officer for Mid. East, comdr. maritime forces during Operation Desert Shield, 1990; asst. chief of staff policy and requirements divsn., SHAPE Royal British Navy, 1994-97; mil. rep. for U.K. to NATO Mil. Com. Brussels, 1997—. Avocations: family, travel, sailing, golf. Office: NATO Hdqrs, Blvd Leopold III, 1110 Brussels Belgium*

HADDAD, EDMONDE ALEX, public affairs executive; b. Los Angeles, July 25, 1931; s. Alexander Saleeba and Madeline Angela (Zail) H.; m. Harriet Ann Lenhart; children: Mark Edmonde, Brent Michael, John Alex. AA, Los Angeles City Coll., 1956; BA, U. Southern Calif., 1958; MA, Columbia U., 1961. Staff writer WCBS Radio News, New York, 1959-61; news commentator, editor KPOL AM/FM Radio, Los Angeles, 1961-67, dir., pub. affairs, 1967-73; exec. dir. Los Angeles World Affairs Council, 1973-84; pres. L.A. World Affairs Coun., 1984-88; deputy asst. sec. of State for Pub. Diplomacy Dept. State, U.S. Govt., Wash., 1987-88; mem. steering com., moderator Conf. environ., L.A., 1989-90; pres. Nat. Coun. World Affairs Orgns., 1981-83; pres. Radio and TV News Assn. So. Calif., 1965-66; sr. fellow Ctr. Internat. Rels., U. Calif., L.A., 1991-94; bd. dirs. Pen Ctr. USA West; apptd. by Gov. Gray Davis to Gov.'s Blue Ribbon Adv. Panel on Hate Groups, 1999—. Author: Look to the Rainbow, 1997; contbg. author: How Peace Came to the World,, 1985; founder, pub. World Affairs Jour. Quar., 1981. Bd. dirs. PEN Ctr. USA West, 1994—. Recipient Am. Polit. Sci. Assn. award for Disting. Reporting of Pub. Affairs, 1967. Mem. Am. Assn. Ret. Persons (coord. 23d congrl. dist. 1999), Friends of Wilton Park (exec. com. So. Calif.), Brit. Fgn. Office Conf. Ctr. Democrat. Avocations: writing poetry, nonfiction, and op-ed articles for newspapers, public speaking, travel. Home: 582 Pacific Cove Dr Port Hueneme CA 93041-2175

HADDAD, EDWARD RAOUF, civil engineer, consultant; b. Mosul, Iraq, July 1, 1926; came to U.S., 1990.; s. Raouf Sulaiman Haddad and Fadhila (Sulaiman) Shaya; m. Balquis Yousef Rassam, July 19, 1961; children: Reem, Raid. BSc, U. Baghdad, Iraq, 1949; postgrad., Colo. State U., 1966-67; PhD (hon.), 1995. Project engr., cons. Min. Pub. Works, Baghdad, 1949-63; arbitrator Engring. Soc. & Ct., Kuwait City, Kuwait, 1963-90; tech. advisor Royal Family, Kuwait, 1987-90; cons. pvt. practice Haddad Engring., Albuquerque, 1990-95; owner, pres. Overseas Contacts-Internat. Bus. and Consulting, Albuquerque, 1995—; organizer reps abroad, Kuwait, 1990. Pres. Parents Assn., U. N.Mex., 1995. Recipient Hon. medal Pope Paul VI of Rome, 1973, Men of Achievement award Internat. Biog. Ctr., 1994. Mem. ASCE, NSPE, ABA (assoc.), Am. Arbitration Assn. (mem. adv. bd.), Sierra Cath. Internat. (trustee), Lions (bd. dirs. 1992), Inventors Club (bd. dirs. 1992), KC (chancellor 1992). Address: 1425 Monte Largo Dr NE Albuquerque NM 87112-6378

HADDAD, GEORGE RICHARD, musician, educator; b. East End, Sask., Can., May 11, 1918; s. Richard and Labeeby (Salloum) H.; m. Lilyan Aboud, May 20, 1949; children: Constance Haddad Frecker, Diane, Carolyn Haddad Dougherty. Asso., Toronto Conservatory Music, 1931; asso. licentiate, 1941; Mus.B., U. Toronto, 1940; M.A., Ohio State U., 1954; student, Royal Conservatory Music Toronto, 1936-40, Julliard Grad. Sch., N.Y.C., 1940-43, Paris Conservatoire, 1950-52. Tchr. piano Bay View Summer Coll. Music, summers 1948-51; prof. sch. music Ohio State U., Columbus, 1952—; prof. emeritus Ohio State U., 1988—. Appeared in various recitals; guest appearances throughout, U.S., Can., Europe, 1944—, guest artist, Detroit Symphony, Toronto Symphony, Luxembourg Symphony, and others. George Haddad piano scholarship established in his honor Ohio State U., 1986. Mem. Music Tchrs. Nat. Assn., Nat. Music Guild Piano Tchrs., Ohio Music Tchrs. Assn., Musicians Union, Pi Kappa Lambda. Clubs: Faculty, Kinsmen of Can, Torch. Home: 2689 River Park Dr Upper Arlington OH 43085 Office: Sch Mus Ohio State U Columbus OH 43210

HADDAD, GEORGES JOSEPH, mathematics educator, researcher, academic administrator; b. La Goulette, Tunisia, Sept. 1, 1951; s. Henri and Odette (Bellaiche) H.; m. Elisabeth Attlan; children: Samuel, Julia, Noémie. Asst. U. Tours, 1975-76, U. Paris-Dauphine, 1976-83; maitre-asst. U. Paris, Panthéon-Sorbonne, 1983-84, prof., 1987—, pres., 1989-94, hon. pres., 1994; prof. U. Nice, 1984-87; v.p. Conf. of Pres. of Univs., 1990-92, first v.p., 1992-94; pres. Adv. Group on Higher Edn., UNESCO, 1995—. Contbr. articles to profl. jours. Office: U Paris 1 Panthéon-Sorbonne, 12 place du Panthéon, 75231 Paris Cedex 05, France

HADDAD, MENASHE, vascular surgeon; b. Tel-Aviv, Oct. 21, 1946; s. Joseph and Shoshana (Rahamim) H.; m. Helena Zeitouni, May 22, 1980; children: Asaf, Sahar, Snir. MD, Hadassah Hebrew U., Jerusalem, 1973; diploma in surgery, Tel-Aviv U., 1981. Med. diplomate; cert. gen. surgery bd., vascular surgery bd. Gen. practitioner Israel Def. Force, 1972-75; resident gen. surgery Beilinson Med. Ctr., Petah-Tikva, Israel, 1975-82, sr. gen. surgeon, 1982-86; resident in vascular surgery CHU Hopital Nord, St.-Etienne, France, 1986-87; dep. chief vascular surgery Rabin Med. Ctr.-Beilinson Campus, Petah-Tikva, Israel, 1987—; cons. Kupat-Holim, Hefer-Shomron dist., Israel, 1992, Dan-Petah-Tikva dist., Israel, 1992—. Maj. med. br. Israel Def. Force, 1972-75. Mem. Internat. Soc. Lymphology, Internat. Union Angiology, European Soc. Vascular Surgery, Soc. Surgery Vascular Langue Francaise, Internet Soc. Jewish. Avocations: computer, science fiction, parachuting. Home: 22 Bialik St, 54038 Givat-Shmuel Israel Office: Rabin Med Ctr-Beilinson Campus, Dept Vascular Surgery, 49100 Petah Tiqwa Israel

HADDEN, ROBERT DAVID MARTIN, neurologist, researcher; b. Belfast, No. Ireland, Feb. 12, 1968; s. David Robert and Diana Sheelagh Mary (Martin) H. BA, Cambridge (Eng.) U., 1989; BM, BCh, Oxford (Eng.) U., 1992; PhD, U. London, 2000. Sr. house officer in medicine Royal Victoria Infirmary, Newcastle, Eng., 1993-96; rsch. fellow in neurology Guy's Hosp., London, 1996-2000; specialist registrar in neurology West London Hosp., 2000—; rsch. collaborator U. Würzburg, Germany, 1997—; mem. med. adv. bd. Guillian-Barré Syndrome Support Group U.K., 1997—; poster presenter Am. Neurol. Assn., 1999. Contbr. articles to med. jours., including Annals Neurology, Neurology, Current Opinion in Neurology. Mem. Royal Coll. Physicians (U.K.), Assn. Brit. Neurologists (assoc.), Peripheral Nerve Soc. Avocations: kayaking, mountain biking, climbing. Home: 3 Butterworth Ter, Sutherland Walk, London SE17 3EJ, England Office: Atkinson Morleys Hosp, London SW20 0NE, England

HADERS, THOMAS MICHAEL, elementary school educator, portrait painter; b. Cin., May 7, 1956; s. John Russell and Irene Eleanor Haders. BA in Arts Edn. magna cum laude, U. Cin., 1990. Cert. tchg. visual arts, Ohio. Art educator Cin. Pub. Schs., 1991-94; tchr. Dayton Ind. Schs., 1996-98; tchr. beginning painting Cin. Recreation Com., 1999—. Roman Catholic. Avocations: painting, sculpting, drawing, gardening.

HADFIELD, MARK, engineering educator; b. Harwich, Essex, Eng., June 9, 1960; s. Alan and Dorothy Mary (Conway) H.; m. Caroline Anita Jones, Feb. 1, 1972; children: Megan, Isaac. BEng in Mech. Engring with honors, Brunel U., Eng., 1988, PhD in Tribiology, 1993. Sr. engr. AE Wellworty, Lymington, Eng., 1988-90; lectr. dept. mech. engring. Brunel U., Uxbridge, Eng., 1992-97; reader sch. design, engring. & computing Bournemouth U., Dorset, Eng., 1997—. Contbr. articles to profl. jours. With Royal Fleet Aux., 1976-84. Decorated Campaign medal Brit. Govt., 1982. Mem. Inst. Marine Engrs., Instn. of Mech. Engrs., Highcliffe Sailing Club (social sec. 1990), Theatre Group (founder, dir. 1991). Mem. Ch. of England. Avocations: sailing, family life, church. Office: Bournemouth U, Sch Design Engring Compute, Bournemouth BH1 3NA, England

HADFIELD, MICHAEL JAMES, electrical engineer; b. Waukesha, Wis., Jan. 25, 1934; s. Raymond James and Viola Emma (Hardke) H.; m. Arlene Rita Echaust, June 11, 1955 (dec. 1996); children: Steven Michael, Linda Frances, Mary Arlene (dec. 1998), Dayna JoAnne; m. Judy Kay Hadfield; children: Franklin Dennis, David Lawrence Miller. BSEE, Marquette U., 1955; postgrad., U. Wis., 1960, U. South Fla., 1968-69. Commd. USMC, 1955, advanced through grades to capt., 1965, resigned; project engr. GM, Milw., 1958-60; guidance sys. engr. Honeywell, Inc., Clearwater, Fla., 1960-93, prin. staff engr., 1991-93; mktg. mgr., program mgr. USAF, Holloman AFB, 1994-99; cons., 1999—; pres., chmn. Sta. WQXM-FM/FM Enterprises, Largo, Fla., 1968-69, Oconee Devel. Corp., Largo, Fla., 1974-93; v.p. Real Property Ctr., 1975-79; v.p. Luten Properties, Inc., 1979-93; broker-salesman Prudential Fla. Realty, Clearwater, 1993-94; mng. ptnr., assoc. fellow Belleair (Fla.) Profl. Ctr. Partnership, 1984-93. Contbr. chpts. to books, 32 articles to tech. jours. Pres. Meth. Ch. Coun. Recipient: Gold Medal AFCEA and SAME. Mem. AIAA, IEEE (program chmn., exec. com.), Assoc. Proposal Mgmt. Profls., Nat. Bd. Realtors, Fla. Bd. Realtors, Air Force Assn., Inst. of Navigation (v.p. Eastern Region, chmn. Inertial Div.), Alpha Sigma Nu, Eta Kappa Nu, Pi Mu Epsilon, Tau Beta Pi, Scabbard and Blade. Democrat. Home and Office: PO Box 1189 Cloudcroft NM 88317-1189

HADGU, TEKLU, mechanical research engineer, consultant; b. Adowa, Ethiopia, May 24, 1955; came to the U.S., 1990; s. Hadgu Araya and Belaynesh Abay; m. Dorit S. Tesfay, Feb. 6, 1999. PhD in Mech. Engring., Auckland (New Zealand) U., 1989. Steamfield engr. Ministry of Mines and Energy, Addis Ababa, Ethiopia, 1980-85; postdoctoral fellow Lawrence Berkeley (Calif.) Nat. Lab., 1992-95; staff scientist II Ecdinamics Rsch. Assocs., Albuquerque, 1995-96; environ. engr. Applied Physics Inc., Albuquerque, 1997—; geothermal cons. Geothermal Devel. Assoc., Reno, 1991; geothermal advisor Commn. Fed. D'Electricidad, Mex., 1998. Recipient Devel. Program fellowship UN, 1982, 85, Mitsubishi prize Mitsubishi, Auckland, 1982. Mem. Am. Geophys. Union, Internat. Geothermal Assn. Avocations: hot air ballooning, running. E-mail: thadgu@sandia.gov. Fax: 505-234-0061. Home: 506 W Orchard Ln Apt 15 Carlsbad NM 88220-4679 Office: Sandia Nat Labs 4100 National Parks Hwy Carlsbad NM 88220-9060

HADHOUD, MOHIY MOHAMED, electronic engineering educator, researcher; b. Esmaelia, Egypt, Sept. 8, 1953; s. Mohamed Hadhoud and Sadika (Ali) Nasar; m. Karima Abdeldaim, Jan. 23, 1983; children: Mohamed, Jasmine, Alaa. BSc, Menoufia U., 1976, MSc, 1981; PhD, Southampton (Eng.) U., 1987. Adminstr. faculty electronics U. Menoufia, 1978-81, lectr., 1981-84, assoc. prof. electronics, 1987-90, assoc. prof., 1996—; assoc. prof. Jr. Tech. Coll., Jeddah, Saudi Arabia, 1990-91, telecom. tng. expert, 1991-96; tng. expert Saudi Post Telephone and Telegraph, Jeddah, 1991-96. Contbr. articles to profl. jours. including Jour. Modern Optics. Lt. Egyptian Air Def., 1976-78. Mem. IEEE (participant circuits and systems transactions, internat. confs.), Elec. Engring. Soc. Mem. Nat. Party. Moslem. Home: El-Tomy No 10, Menouf Menoufia, Egypt Office: Menoufia U, Fac Electronic Engring, 32952 Menouf Menoufia, Egypt

HADHRI, TAIEB, mathematician, educator; b. Monastir, Tunisia, Aug. 18, 1957; s. Abdesselem and Fatma (Helali) H.; m. Monia Allegue, July 28, 1984; children: Sirine, Salim. Diploma in Engring. Sci., Ecole Polytechnique, Palaiseau, France, 1979, Ecole Nat. Ponts et Chaussees, Paris, 1981; Doctorate in Engring. Scis., U. Paris 6, 1981, State Doctorate, 1986. Asst. prof. U. de Technologie de Compiegne, France, 1982-84; assoc. prof. Ecole Nat. des Ponts et Chaussees, Paris, 1982-88; rschr. Nat. Ctr. Sci. Rsch., Paris, 1984-95; prof. Nat. Engring. Sch. of Tunis, Tunisia, 1988—, Poly. Sch. of Tunisia, La Marsa, 1994—; head dept. civil engring. Nat. Engring. Sch. of Tunis, 1989-93, dir., 1995; dir. Poly. Sch. Tunisia, 1995—; rsch. cons. Hutchinson Cie, Paris, 1987-92; mem. sci. bd. Ctr. Testing and Civil Engring. Technics, Tunis, 1991—. Contbr. articles to profl. jours. Mem. Monastir City Safeguard Assn., 1996—. Decorated Order of Merit of Edn. (Tunisia), 1996; prize Pres. of Tunisian Republic for the Baccalaureat, 1975. Mem. Tunisian Astronomy Soc., Tunisian Math. Soc. (v.p. 1995-97), Tunisian Old Boys Assn. Polytechnique-France (mem. mgmt. com. 1995—), Tunisian Old Boys Assn. Ecole Nat. Ponts et Chausees. Avocations: soccer, swimming, reading. Home: App 21 Bloc A Cite Narjess, El Manar, Tunis Tunisia 1013 Office: Ecole Poly de Tunisie, Rue El Khawarizmi PO Box 743, La Marsa Tunisia 2078

HADI, MUHAMMAD NAJIB S., civil engineer, lecturer; b. Kirkuk, Iraq, Jan. 1, 1956; s. Sadraddin and Jahida H.; m. Hayfa Muhammad S. Bashir Hadi, Dec. 11, 1979; children: Reema, Ahmed. HSC, Baghdad Coll., Iraq, 1973, BS, 1977; MS, Baghdad U., Iraq, 1980; PhD, Leeds U., Eng., 1989. Civil engr. Rafidain Eng. Lab., Baghdad, Iraq, 1975-84; lectr. U. Tech., Baghdad, Iraq, 1983-85, 1989-92; rsch. asst. U. South Australia, Adelaide, 1993-94; lectr. U. Wollongong, Australia, 1994—. Grantee: ARC, 1996, 97, ESDF, 1996, 97. Mem. ASCE, Instn. of Engrs. of Australia. Avocations: swimming, walking. Office: Dept Civil Mining & Env Eng, U Wollongong, Wollongong 2522, Australia

HADINOTO, KUSUDIARSO, professional society administrator, engineering and business consultant; b. Semarang, Ctrl. Java, Indonesia, Aug. 13, 1930; s. Raden Adipati Ario and Raden Ayu A.A.K. Hadinoto; m. Retno Harsini Atmini Notosubagio, Oct. 30, 1954; children: Yana, Dion. MSEE, Tech. U., Delft, The Netherlands, 1955; Lemhannas II, Def. Coll., Jakarta, Indonesia, 1968; Sespa, Mgmt. Sch., Jakarta, Indonesia, 1970. European Ing.; European Chartered Profl. Engrs., Fédération Européenne d'Assns. Nationales d'Ingénieurs, Paris, 1988. Prof. Inst. Tech., Bandung, Indonesia, 1955-59, U. Indonesia, Jakarta, 1960-65; founder, dir. Electric Power Utility Lab., Jakarta, 1962-70; dir. Space Applications Aerospace Agy., Jakarta, 1970-77; dir. gen. mfg. industries Min. Industry, Jakarta, 1978-83; pres. Electrical Cable Mfg. Assn. APKABEL, Jakarta, 1984—; scientific adv. chief of staff Air Force, Indonesia, 1958-86; chmn. Electronic Co. Indonesia, 1978-80, Steel Constrn. Co. Indonesia, 1980-83, Integrated Textile Co. Indonesia, 1984-88, EAN Indonesia barcoding and EDI, 1993—; sr. advisor Internat. Copper Assn., 1997—. Chief editor Engring. Mag., 1958-76; contbr. articles to profl. jours. Col. Air Force, 1958-86, Indonesia. Recipient Medal Nat. Devel. Indonesian Govt., 1983. Mem. Indonesian Soc. Engrs. (chmn. Jakarta chpt. 1958-62), Royal Netherlands Inst. Engrs. (sr.). Avocations: reading, writing. Home: 5 Jalan Danau Tondano, 10210 Jakarta Indonesia Office: APKABEL Elec Cable Mfrs, Ketapang Indah B2/32 JL, Zainul Arifin Jakarta 11140, Indonesia

HADISUWARNO, RUDY HARSOJO, hairstylist, educator; b. Pekalongan, Indonesia, Oct. 21, 1949; s. Iskander Hadisuwarno and Tresna Lastari Sutedja. Student, Trisakti U. Arch., Jakarta, Indonesia, 1968; diploma in hairdressing, Vidal Sasson, England, 1973, 75. Founder Rudy Hadisuwarno Orgn., Jakarta, 1968—; pres., dir. Rudy Hadisuwarno Cosmetics, Jakarta, 1975-85; pres. commisary Rudy Hadisuwarno, Jakarta, 1985—; pres. commisary PT Rudytech, Jakarta, 1988—, Pvt. Ltd. Co. Muliatama Estetika Citra, Jakarta, 1994—; commisary PT Beautama, Jakarta, 1997—. artist, performer Singapore Hair Show, 1983, Malaysian Hair Show, 1983, ICD World Congress, 1987; editor Rudy Hadisuwarno Hairdressing Beauty Jour. Recipient Medaille Chevalier de la Chevalerie Intercoiffure Mondial, 1990, Satya Lencana Pembangunan award Pres. Rep. Indonesia, 1993, World Master of the Craft award, 1997. Mem. Art and Fashion Group Internasion (World Master Craft award 1997), Indonesia Hairdresser Beautician Assn. (v.p., 1995—), Intercoifure Indonesia (pres. 1979—). Avocations: paintings, reading, swimming, tennis. Office: Jl Puri Pesanggrahan IV/NR7, Bukit Cinere Indah, Jakarta 16514, Indonesia

HADJICOSTAS, EVSEVIOS PETROU, chemist; b. Nicosia, Cyprus, July 8, 1962; s. Petros Hadjicosta and Theopisti Constantinou Poui; m. Eleni Philiou Pipi, July 7, 1991; 1 child, Maria, 1999. BS, U. Athens, 1987; student, Mediterranean Inst. Mgmt. Quality mgr. Industry Agrochem. Products, Nicosia, 1988—; coord. quality mgmt. system ISO 9000 Premier Chem. Co. Ltd.; del. EURACHEM. Contbr. articles to profl. jours.; mem. editl. bd. Chem. News, 1992—. Mem. Pancyprian Union Chemists (sec. gen. 1996-98), Chemists Registration Com. m(sec. gen. 1997-99). Avocations: guitar, bicycling, swimming, ping-pong. Office: Premier Chem Co Ltd, 4 Olymbou St PO Box 1513, 1510 Nicosia Cyprus

HADJICOSTAS, THYRSOS, electrical engineer, consultant; b. Nicosia, Cyprus, May 18, 1962; arrived in Greece, 1995; s. Panayiotis and Eleni (Papadouris) H.; m. Angeliki Barka, June 17, 1995. BSc in engring., U. London, 1985, PhD, 1989; MBA, Brunel U., Henley, Eng., 1994. Lab. asst. U. London, 1985-89; asst. engr. Electricity Authority of Cyprus, Nicosia, 1989-91, elec. engr., 1991-94; area engr. Electricity Authority of Cyprus, Larnaca, Cyprus, 1994-95; sr. cons. KANTOR Mgmt. Consultants, Athens, 1995-97; mgr. KANTOR Mgmt. Consultants, 1997-98, dir. energy and utilities, 1999—; project assessor Higher Tech. Inst., Nicosia, 1990-94. Contbr. articles to profl. jours. V.p. U. London Assn. Cyprus, 1992-94. 2d lt. artillery Army of Cyprus, 1980-82. Recipient Overseas Rsch. Scheme grant U. London, 1986-88, Draper's Co. scholarship U. London, 1985-86, postgrad. studentship U. London, 1986-88. Mem. IEEE (sr., mem. exec. com. Cyprus sect. 1994-95), Inst. Mgmt. Avocations: sports, reading, travel. Home: 22 Dhigeni, 15341 Athens Greece Office: KANTOR Mgmt Consultants, 4 Vasilissis Sofias, 10674 Athens Greece

HADJIDEMETRIOU, JOHN DEMETRIOS, physicist educator; b. Thessaloniki, Macedonia, Greece, Nov. 29, 1937; s. Demetrios J. and Ourania A. (Papadopoulou) H.; m. Athena Georgopoulou, Apr. 11, 1966; children: Ourania, Demetrios, Chrysoula. BSc in Math., U. Thessaloniki, Greece, 1959; PhD of Physics and Astronomy, U. Manchester, Eng., 1965. Rsch. asst. Hellenic Rsch. Found., Thessaloniki, Greece, 1965-66; univ. asst. U. Thessaloniki, 1966-69, prof., chair mechanics, 1969—. Author: Theoretical Mechanics, 1982; mem. editl. bd. Astrophysics and Space Sci., 1989-95; assoc. editor Celestial Mechanics and Dynamical Astronomy, 1993—; contbr. articles to profl. jours. 2d lt. Greece Artillery, 1960-62. Mem. Internat. Astron. Union (mem. sci. organizing com. 1980-92, pres commn. 7, 2000—), European Astron. Soc. (founder), Celestial Mechanics Inst., Hellenic Astron. Soc. (vice chmn. 1992-96). Avocation: photography. Home: Leoforos OXI 19, GR55438 Thessaloniki Greece Office: U Thessaloniki Physics Dept, GR540 06 Thessaloniki Greece

HADJIEV, DIMITRE EMILOV, chemical engineer, researcher; b. Sofia, Bulgaria, July 17, 1947; s. Emil Dimitrov and Zephira Gueorguieva (Popova) H.; m. Katerina Metodieva Staneva, Jan. 15, 1978 (div. May 1992); m. Lilia Stoilova Peneva, Aug. 25, 1995; children: Elena, Emilie. BSChemE, High Tech. Sch., Sofia, 1971; PhD, Acad. Scis., Sofia, 1981; DSc, Nat. Polytechnic Inst., Toulouse, France, 1994. Rschr. Bulgarian Acad. Scis., Sofia, 1973-81, sr. rschr., 1981-87, assoc. prof., 1987-91; dir. rsch. Nat. Inst. Applied Tech., Toulouse, 1991-93; head Lab. for Environ. Engring. and Biochem. Processes U. Inst. Tech., Caen, 1993-2000, head dept. chem. engring., 1999-2000; founder chem. engring. dept. Acad. South Brittany, Lorient, France, 2000—; cons. Pharmachim, Sofia, 1979-84; head sect. hydrometall. divsn. Kremikovtzi, Sofia, 1985-89. Editor: Recent Progress in Chemical Engineering, Vol. 20, 1992; inventor phase-inversion method, three-phase cyclone, and emulsion treatment. Recipient nat. medal of tech. Ministry of Industry, 1980, hon. award Bulgarian Acad. Scis., 1980, 2000 Outstanding Scientists of the 20th Century award, Cambridge, Eng. Mem. Nat. Geographic Soc. Achievements include patents and papers concerning the design of new types of processes and apparatus for waste waters treatment, a new phase inversion method for emulsion treatments, three-phase separations, among others. Home: 49 Bd Laennec, 56100 Lorient France Office: Inst U Tech, 4 rue Jean Zay, 56325 Lorient Cedex, France

HADJIMICHAEL, GEORGHIOS COSTA, civil engineer, consultant; b. Marathovounos, Famagusta, Cyprus, June 5, 1934; s. Costas and Yianoula (Karalouka) H.; m. Stavroula Iosifidou, Apr. 23, 1861; children: Eleni, Yianoula, Haris. B of Engring., Am. U. of Beirut, 1971. Tech. asst. dept. pub. works Govt. Cyprus, 1956-71, exec. engr., cons., 1972-82; area mgr. Charilaos Apostolides & Co. Ltd., Iraq, 1982-85, Chapo Contracting, Cyprus, 1985-87; advisor claims, cons. Integrated Surveys Ltd., Kuwait, 1987-89; with G.P. Zachariades (Overseas) Ltd., 1989-91; project mgr. Bahrain Mil. Hosp., 1989-91; gen. mgr. Charilaos Apostolides & Co. Ltd., 1992-95; CEO Pygmalion Techniki Ltd., 1996—. Fellow ASCE, Profl. and Tech. Chamber of Cyprus, Cyprus Soc. Civil Engrs. and Architects. Mem. Christian Orthodox Ch. Avocations: photography, fishing, bee-keeping, philately. Home: 8A Nicou Georghiou, Pallouriotissa Cyprus Office: 28 Sofoulis St 4th Fl #404, PO Box 29071, 1620 Nicosia Cyprus

HADJIMINAS, CHRISTIAN, investment banker; b. Ouasha, Zaire, Sept. 3, 1960; s. George and Margueritte (Bosch) H.; m. Claire Tsalouchidou, Jan. 12, 1991. BA, Columbia U., 1981; MBA, U. Pa., 1983. Sr. trader Philipp Bros., Inc., London and N.Y.C., 1983-87; pres. Advanced Svcs. Group, Inc., N.Y.C., 1987-89; mng. dir. European Fin. Assocs. Ltd., Athens, Greece, 1989—; pres. European Aerospace Techs., S.A., Athens, 1992—; bd. dirs. Thalis Sensors, Theon Mobile Platforms, S.A., Athens. Avocations: helicopter flying, scuba diving. Office: European Fin Assocs, Stratigi 7, 154 51 North Psychigo Athens, Greece

HADJIMINAS, JOHN STAVROS, retired physiology educator; b. Kyrenia, Cyprus, Dec. 20, 1920; arrived in Greece, 1946; s. Stavros Minas and Styliani Stavrou (Kakopierou) H.; m. Alexandra John Paximada, May 15, 1956 (dec. June 1998); children: Stavros, Dimitris. Diploma in comml. art, Washington Sch. Art, 1939; cert. in arch., Internat. Corr. Sch., Israel, 1945; diploma in medicine, Athen's (Greece) U., 1956; MD (hon.), Athens (Greece) U., 1970, PhD (hon.), 1961; cert. in physiology, Goteborg (Sweden) U., 1966, Edinburgh (Scotland) U., 1971. Undergrad. asst. dept. exptl. physiology Athens U., 1949-56, lab. asst., 1956-63, lectr., 1963-70, reader in physiology, 1970-72, assoc. prof. exptl. physiology, 1972-82, prof. exptl.

physiology, 1982-88, ret., 1988; translator/supervisor Med. Books Pub. Co., Athens, 1960—; hon. pres. Nutricare Pub. and Counselling Co., Athens, 1988-95. Author: (in Greek) Notes on Physiology, 1954-73, elements of Physiology, 1974, Abridged Physiology, 1984-87; contbr. numerous articles to profl. jours. Recipient Gold medal of City of Athens, Mayor of Athens, 1997, Hon. Plaque and Diploma for Spl. Svcs. to Med. Edn. and Cmty., Assn. Cypriot Med. Doctors in Greece, 1997. Mem. Physiol. Soc. U.K., Anti-Cancer Soc., Med. Assn. Greece, Tectonic Instn. Greece. Avocations: painting, photography, fishing, sailing, internet. E-mail: vegas@ath.Forthnet.gr. Home: 25 Larisis Str, 115 23 Athens Greece

HADJIOLOV, DIMITER HRISTOV, histochemist, oncology educator; b. Samokov, Bulgaria, Apr. 25, 1935; s. Hristo Ivanov and Tanja Dimitrova (Dejanova) H.; m. Ilka Nikolova Vulcheva, July 13, 1958; children: Nikolai, Hristo. MD, Med. U. Sofia, Bulgaria, 1958; PhD, Med. Acad. Sofia, Bulgaria, 1965; DSc, Nat. Ctr. Oncology, Sofia, Bulgaria, 1976. Rsch. scientist Nat. Ctr. Oncology, Sofia, Bulgaria, 1960-67; asst. prof. Med. Acad., Sofia, Bulgaria, 1967-72; prof., head unit carcinogenesis Nat. Ctr. Oncology, Sofia, Bulgaria, 1972-97, prof., head unit oncopathology, 1995—; dir. Nat. Ctr. Oncology, Sofia, 1979-81; vis. prof. German Cancer Rsch. Ctr., Heidelberg, 1972-96; chief cons. Nat. Oncopathology, Sofia, 1996-97. Author: (book) Carcinogenesis, 1977, DNA Damage and Cancer, 1981; contbr. over 140 articles to profl. jours. Recipient E. Roosevelt fellowship UICC-Geneva, 1972. Bulgarian Oncol. Soc. (pres. 1979-81), Orgn. Dirs. European Cancer Insts., European Assn. for Cell Rsch., Nat. Acad. Med. Scis. Avocations: inhibition of carcinogenesis, reversion of malignancy. Home: Solunska Str 17, 1000 Sofia Bulgaria Office: Nat Ctr Oncology, Plovdivski Polo Str 6, 1756 Sofia Bulgaria

HADJIPAPAS, ANDREAS, publishing executive; b. Aphania, Cyprus, July 20, 1935; s. Anastasis and Myrofora (Papanastasi) H.; m. Anastasia Tserioti, May 1, 1960; children: Rona, Pola. Student, Tchrs. Tng. Coll., Morphou, Cyprus, 1953-54, Ind. U., 1967. Reporter Cyprus Mail, Nicosia, 1954-70; asst. editor Agon, newspaper, Nicosia, 1970-72; sr. news editor Cyprus Broadcasting Corp., Nicosia, 1972-92; pub., dir. The Cyprus Weekly, Nicosia, 1979—; dir. Cyprus News Agy., Nicosia, 1992-95; corr. UPI, Gemini New Agys., Fin. Times, London, 1972. Home: 95 Dasoupolis St, Nicosia Cyprus Office: Cyprus Weekly, PO Box 24977, Nicosia 1306, Cyprus

HADJIPATERAS, DIMITRIS CONSTANTINE, naval architect, marine consultant; b. London, Sept. 18, 1951; s. Constantine Adamantios and Stamatia Tika (Pateras) H.; m. Kyriakoula Psarros, Nov. 7, 1977; children: Tika, Marika, Constantine, Anastasia. BSc with honours, U. Newcastle-upon-Tyne, Eng., 1975. Cert. European engr. European Fedn. Nat. Engring. Assns., Paris; chartered and tech. engr. Engring. Coun., London. Marine supt. N.J. Pateras Sons Ltd., London, 1975-78; dir., tech. mgr. City Shipbrokers Ltd., London, 1978-81; marine cons., adviser Marine Mgrs. Ltd., London, 1982-94; dir. Argonaut Agys. Ltd., London, 1995; marine cons. Navtek Marine Cons., 1997—; chmn., bd. dirs. New Eagle Fin. Ltd., London, 1976-85; prin. Baltic Exch., London, 1975-80; sr. assoc. Space Studies Inst., Princeton, N.J., 1982; dir. Hadjipateras Ltd., London, 1994—. Fellow Royal Instn. Naval Architects, Inst. Marine Engrs., Inst. Dirs., Brit. Interplanetary Soc.; mem. AIAA, Soc. Naval Architects and Marine Engrs. U.S.A., Soc. Naval Architects Japan, Royal Aero. Soc. London (assoc.), N.Y. Acad. Scis., Planetary Soc. (founder), World Space Found. (founder), Nat. Space Soc. (founder L-5 Soc.), U.S. Naval Inst. Md. (assoc.). Avocations: astronautics, manned space flight, first edition books, Albert Einstein, Alpine skiing. Home: Flat 25, 6 Hall Rd, London NW8 9PA, England Office: Ulysses Marine Electronic, 10 Ely Pl, London ECIN 6RY, England

HADJISTAMOV, DIMITER, chemical engineer; b. Sofia, Bulgaria, Dec. 18, 1940; arrived in Switzerland, 1972; s. Bojan Hadjistamov and Elena Zacharieva; m. Emilia Petkova, Dec. 10, 1991. Diploma in chemical engring., Tech. U., Dresden, Fed. Republic Germany, 1967, Dr.Ing.Chem., 1971. Rsch. engr. Micafil AG, Zürich, Switzerland, 1972-73, Sarlab AG, Zürich, 1974; chem. process devel. engr. Ciba-Geigy AG, Basel, Switzerland, 1975-98; sci. specialist Ciba-Geigy AG, Basel, 1991-98; plant mgr. Ciba-Geigy AB, Schweizerhalle, Switzerland, 1983; mgr. DECE GmbH, 1999—; head rheology group, Basel, 1986-99; mem. exec. com. Swiss Rheology Group, Zürich, 1990—. Mem. Neue Schweizerische Chemische Gesellschaft, Verein Deutscher Ingenieure, Deutsche Rheologische Gesellschaft, Soc. Rheology U.S.A., N.Y. Acad. Sci. Avocations: bridge, judo, sailing. Home: Helvetierstr 15, 4125 Riehen Switzerland

HADJIYANNAKIS, EVAGELOS YIANNIS, surgeon; b. Kastelorizo, Rodos-Dodecanese, Greece, Dec. 25, 1938; s. Yiannis Vasilios Hadjiyannakis and Anastasia Evagelos Stamatiou; m. Katerina Koniavitou, Dec. 26, 1967 (div. 1994); children: Yiannis, Vasia. MD, Athens U., 1961, PhD, 1964, postgrad., 1973. House officer 1st surg. univ. clinic Laiko Hosp., Athens, Greece, 1962-64, univ. asst. 1st surg. univ. clinic, 1964-66, 1st asst. univ. clinic, 1966-68, lectr. 1st surg. dept., 1969-75, asst. prof. univ., 1973—; sr. hosp. registrar Cambridge, Eng., 1969-71; cons. 2d dept. transplant unit Tzanio Gen. Hosp., Pireus, Greece, 1975-86, 1st surg. dept. transplant unit Evagelismos Hosp., Athens, 1986—; assoc. prof. Athens U., 1983. Author: Surgical Emergencies Complications of Liver Transplantation, 1982, Kidney and Liver Transplantation, 1995, Internal Medicine: Kidney, Pancreas, Liver, Cardiac and Lung Transplantation; contbr. numerous articles to profl. jours. Pres. Kastelorizian World Assn., Pireus, Greece, 1983-90, World Transplant Athletics, Athens, 1980—; chmn. European Forum Immunosuppression, 1982, Euroepan Congress Transplant Soc., 1990. Recipient Gold medal Patriarch Athenagoras, Constantinople, 1963, Patriarch Venediktos, Jerusalem, 1980, Golden Gross Patriarch Venediktos, Jerusalem, 1978, Laudation, European Internat. Hepatobiliaery Assn. Congress Athens, 1995. Fellow Am. Coll. Vascular Surgery; mem. Hellenic Transplantation Soc. (pres.), Internat. Coll. Surgery, Transplantation Soc., N.Y. Acad. Scis., Nat. Yachting Club (Pireus), Yachting Club (Vouliagmenis), Rotary (Athens). Avocation: sculpture. Office: 10 Vasilissis Sophias Ave, 106 74 Athens Greece

HADLEY, LEILA ELIOTT-BURTON (MRS. HENRY LUCE, III), writer; b. N.Y.C., Sept. 22, 1925; d. Frank Vincent and Beatrice Boswell Eliott Burton; m. Arthur T. Hadley, II, Mar. 2, 1944 (div. Aug. 1946); 1 child, Arthur T. III; m. Yvor H. Smitter, Jan. 24, 1953 (div. Oct. 1969); children: Victoria C. Van D. Smitter Barlow, Matthew Smitter Eliott, Caroline Allison F.S. Nicholson; m. William C. Musham, May 1976 (div. July 1979); m. Henry Luce III, Jan. 1990. MD, St. Timothy's Sch., 1943. Author: Give Me the World, 1958, reprinted, 1999, How to Travel with Children in Europe, 1963, Manners for Children, 1967, Fielding's Guide to Traveling with Children in Europe,1972, rev., 1974, 84, Traveling with Children in the U.S.A., 1974, Tibet-20 Years After the Chinese Takeover, 1979, (with Theodore B. Van Itallie) The Best Spas: Where to Go for Weight Loss, Fitness Programs and Pure Pleasure in the U.S. and Around the World, 1988, rev., 1989, A Journey with Elsa Cloud, 1997, Give Me the World, 1999; assoc. editor: Diplomat mag., N.Y.C., 1964-65, Saturday Evening Post, N.Y.C., 1965-67; editorial cons. TWYCH, N.Y.C., 1985-87; book reviewer Palm Beach Life, Fla., 1967-72; consulting editor: Tricyle, The Buddhist Rev., 1991—; garden columnist Fishers Island Gazette; contbr. articles to various newspapers, mags. Mem. bd. advisors Tricycle, the Buddhist Rev., 1991—; bd. dirs. Wings Trust, Inc., Tibet House, 1995, Fishers Island Conservancy, 1995. Mem. Acad. Am. Poets, Soc. Woman Geographers (exec. council 1984—), Authors Guild, Nat. Writers Union, Nat. Press Club, PEN, Explorers Club, Central Park Conservancy, N.Y. Acad. Medicine (guest bd.), Nat. Arts Club. Home: 4 Sutton Pl New York NY 10022-3056

HADLEY, PAUL BURREST, JR. (TABBIT HADLEY), domestic engineer; b. Louisville, Apr. 26, 1955; s. Paul Burrest and Rose Mary (Ruckert) H. Grad. in Computer Ops. and Programming, No. Ky. Vocat. Sch., 1975. Floor mgr. reconciling dept. Cen. Trust Co., Cin., 1974-76; freelance photographer Ky., Ohio, Colo., 1975—; chef mgr. The Floradora, Telluride, Colo., 1978-96; domestic engr. Telluride Resort Accomodations, 1996—; pres. Tabbit Enterprises; freelance recipe writer, Telluride, 1978—. Author poetry (Golden Poet award 1989, Silver Poet award 1990); actor: (plays) Of Mice and Men, The Exercise, Crawling Arnold, A Thousand Clowns, The Authentic Life of Billy The Kid, others. Actor The Plunge Players, Telluride; v.p. Telluride Coun. for Arts and Humanities, 1989. Mem. Plan Internat. USA, Christian Children's Fund. Avocations: mountain climbing, hiking, photography, travel. Home: PO Box 923 Telluride CO 81435-0923

HADLEY, RALPH VINCENT, III, lawyer; b. Jacksonville, Fla., Aug. 20, 1942; s. Ralph V. and Clare (Cason) H.; m. Carol Fox Hadley, Sept. 18, 1993; children: Graham Kimball, Christopher Bedell, Blair Vincent. BS, U. Fla., 1965, JD, 1968. Bar: Fla. 1968, Calif. 1972. Assoc. Kurz, Toole, Taylor & Moseley, Jacksonville, 1968-69; asst. atty. gen. State of Fla., Orlando, 1972-73; ptnr. Davids, Henson & Hadley, Winter Garden, Fla., 1973-80; sr. ptnr. Hadley & Asma, Winter Garden, 1980-89, Parker, Johnson, Owen, McGuire, Michaud, & Hadley, Orlando, 1989-91, Owen & Hadley, Orlando, 1991-94, Hadley, Gardner & Ornstein, P.A., Winter Park, Fla., 1994-95; Swann, Hadley & Alvarez, P.A., Winter Park, 1995-2000; with Swann & Harley, 2000—; vice chmn. bd. dirs. Tucker State Bank, Winter Garden, 1981-88; vice chmn. bd. dirs., sec. Tucker Holding Co., Jacksonville, 1984-88; bd. dirs. BankFIRST, All Sign Products. Bd. dirs. Orange County Dem. Exec. Com., Orlando, 1974-81, Spouse Abuse, Inc., Orlando, 1975-81. Lt. comdr. USN, 1969-72, Vietnam. Recipient award of merit Orange County Legal Aid Soc., 1987, Disting. Svc. award Judge J.C. Jake Stone Legal Aid Soc., 1989, Pres. Pro Bono Svc. award Fla. Bar, 1992. Mem. ABA, Fla. Bar Assn., Calif. Bar Assn., Orange County Bar Assn. (legis. chmn. 1979, 82), Am. Inn of Ct. (master), Winter Park C. of C. (bd. dirs. 1979-80), West Orange C. of C. (bd. dirs. 1979-82), Rotary. Presbyterian. Office: 1031 W Morse Blvd Winter Park FL 32789-3715

HADZIC, NEDIM, pediatric hepatologist, consultant; b. Sarajevo, Bosnia-Herzegovina, Aug. 26, 1956; arrived in Eng., 1992; s. Izet and Emina Hadzic; m. Sanja Lagumdzija, Aug. 1, 1984; children: Miran, Nadan. MD, Med. Sch., Sarajevo, 1979; MSc, U. Sarajevo, 1985. Diplomate in medicine. Gen. practitioner Health Ctr., Sarajevo, 1981-84; trainee pediatrician Children's Univ. Hosp., Sarajevo, 1985-88; lectr. in pediatrics U. Sarajevo, 1989-91; clin. fellow in immunology Inst. of Child Health, London, 1992-93; lectr. in pediatric hepatology King's Coll. Med. Sch., U. London, 1994-95; cons. in pediatric hepatology King's Coll. Hosp., London, 1996—. Contbr. articles to profl. jours. Fellow Royal Coll. Pediatrics and Child Health; mem. Am. Assn. Study Liver Disease., European Assn. for Study Liver Disease, European Soc. of Paediatric Gastroenterology, Hepatology and Nutrition. Avocations: classical music, tennis, basketball. Home: 51 Pymers Mead, London SE21 8NH, England Office: Kings Coll Hosp Dept Child Health, Denmark Hill, London SE5 9RS, England

HAEBERLE, ERWIN JAKOB, sexologist; b. Dortmund, Germany, Mar. 30, 1936. MA, Cornell U., 1964; EdD, Inst. Adv. Study Human Sexual., San Francisco, 1977; PhD, U. Heidelberg, Germany, 1966; hon. prof., People's Hosp., Fuyang, China, 1999. Prof. Inst. for Advanced Study of Human Sexuality, San Francisco, 1977-88; rsch. assoc. Kinsey Inst., Bloomington, Ind., 1982-84; dir. info. and documentation AIDS Ctr. Fed. Health Office, Berlin, 1988-94; dir. archive of sexology Robert Koch Inst., Berlin, 1994—; vis. prof. U. Kiel, Germany, 1983-84, U. Geneva, Switzerland, 1984-85; disting. vis. prof. San Francisco State U., 1984. Author: (textbook) The Sex Atlas, 1978, (Web site) Archive for Sexology, 1998—.

HAEBERLE, ROSAMOND PAULINE, retired educator; b. Clearwater, Kans., Oct. 23, 1914; d. Albert Paul and Ella (Lough) H. BS in Music Edn., Kans. State U., 1936; MusM, Northwestern U., 1948; postgrad., Wayne State U., 1965-66. Profl. registered parliamentarian. Tchr. sch. dist., Plevna, Kans., 1936-37, Esbon, Kans., 1937-41, Frankfort, Kans., 1941-43, Garden City, Kans., 1943-44; music supr. sch. dist., Waterford Twp., Mich., 1944-47; tchr. sch. dist., Pontiac, Mich., 1947-80; ret. sch. dist., Pontiac, 1980; pres. Pontiac Fedn. Tchrs., 1961-63. Bd. dirs. Pontiac Oakland Town Hall; adv. coun. Waterford Sr. Citizens, chmn., 1990-93; pres. Oakland County Pioneer and Hist. Soc., 1992-94. Recipient Tchrs. Day award Mich. State Fair, 1963. Mem. AAUW (pres. Pontiach br. 1970-72, founds. chair Pontiac br.), Mich. Fedn. Music Clubs (state pres. 1993-95, chmn. state bylaws and citations com., pres. Tuesday musicale of Pontiac 1984-86, pres. S.E. dist. 1986-90, chmn. Music for the Blind Northeastern region 2000, chair Northeastern Regon Nat. Music Week 1996-99), Mich. Fedn. Bus. and Profl. Womens Club (Woman of Achievement award dist. IX 1994), Mich. DARS (state parliamentarian 1985-96), DAR (Gen. Richardson chpt., regent 1983-85, libr. and parliamentarian, Excellence in Cmty Svc. award 1995), Waterford-Clarkston Bus. and Profl. Womens Club (bylaws and parliamentarian), Pontiac Area Ret. Sch. Pers. (parliamentarian, pres. 1981-84), Mich. Assn. Retired Sch. Pers (Disting. Svc. award 1994), Mich. Bus. and Profl. Women's Club,(dir. dist. 10 1965-67), Pontiac Bus. and Profl. Women (pres. 1959-61, Woman of the Yr. award 1974), Pontiac Area Fedn. Women's Clubs (pres. 1976-78, 81-84), Mich. Registered Parliamentarians, Louise Saks Parliamentary Unit (pres. 1990-92), Bloomfield Rep. Women's Club (parliamentarian 1999-2000), Eastern Star, Mu Phi Epsilon, Beta Sigma Phi (life), Zeta Tau Alpha. Republican. Methodist. Avocations: travel, playing piano, reading, bell ringing, dance.

HAEBERLIN, HEINRICH RUDOLF, electrical engineering educator; b. Basel, Switzerland, Feb. 9, 1947; s. Rudolf and Bethly (Buergin) H.; m. Ruth Huerzeler, Mar. 31, 1982; children: Andreas, Kathrin. MS in Elec. Engring., Swiss Fed. Inst. Tech., Zurich, 1971, PhD in Elec. Engring., 1978. Asst. Swiss Fed. Inst. Tech., Zurich, 1971-77, asst. in chief, 1978-79; R&D engr. Zellweger Uster AG, Hombrechtikon, Switzerland, 1979-80; prof. elec. engring. Berner Fachhochschule, Hochschule fuer Technik und Architektur, Burgdorf, Switzerland, 1980—. Author: Photovoltaik-Strom aus Sonnenlicht fuer Inselanlagen und Verbundnetz, 1991; contbr. articles to profl. jours. Mem. Schweiz Elektrotechnischer Verein, Swiss Commn. for PV-Stds., Sonnenenergie-Fachverband. Achievements include contbns. to increase reliability and reduce electromagnetic interference problems of grid-connected inverters for photovoltaic installations; creation of a test ctr. for PV-inverters and PV-systems; creation and operation of the highest grid-connected PV plant in the world at Jungfraujoch (3454 m.). Office: Hochschule fuer Technik und Archit, 1 Jlcoweg, CH-3400 Burgdorf Switzerland

HAEFELINGER, GUENTER, chemist, educator; b. Freiburg im Breisgau, Germany, May 23, 1937; s. Friedrich Ernst and Anna (Wessbecher) H.; m. Brigitte Weiss, Apr. 5, 1963; children: Michael, Steffen Joerg. Diploma, Tech. Hochschule, Karlsruhe, Germany, 1962; D, U. Tuebingen, Germany, 1965; postgrad., U. Calif., Berkeley, 1965-67. Habilitation U. Tuebingen, 1967-70, akademischer rat, oberrat, 1971-73, Aussenplanmässiger prof., 1973-75, Wissenschaftlicher rat, prof., 1975-80, C3 prof. theoretical organic chemistry, 1981—. Author: Organische Chemie-Experimentalchemie II, 1986; contbr. chpts. to books. Recipient 1st prize poster exhibit Am. Urol. Assn., 1983. Mem. German Chem. Assn., World Assn. Theoretical Organic Chemists, Correlation Analysis in Chemistry. Avocations: choral music, cello, table tennis. E-Mail: guenter.haefelinger@uni-tuebingen.de. Home: Eichenweg 3, D-72076 Tübingen Germany Office: U Tuebingen Inst Org Chem, Auf der Morgenstelle 18, 72076 Tübingen Germany

HAEFFNER, ERIK AXEL, executive; b. Skutskar, Sweden, May 9, 1918; s. Axel and Karin (Borg) H.; m. Ingeborg Nenkert, Dec. 26, 1955 (dec. 1976); children: Catharine, Fredrik. Student, Gavle, Sweden, 1938, Chalmers U. Tech., 1946, Royal Inst. Tech., 1952. Rschr. FOA, Stockholm, 1946-49; leader nuclear chem. dept. Atomic Energy Co., 1950-65; rsch. dir. Innovative Co., Stockholm, 1966-71; mng. dir. Eurochem Co., Belgium, 1957-59; mng. dir. Innovation Inst., 1971-86, chmn., 1987-92. Author: Understanding innovation, 1972; contbr. articles to profl. jours.; patentee in field.

HAEGI, MARCEL, scientist, physicist; b. Geneva, Oct. 29, 1931; arrived in Italy, 1962; s. Emile and Rosa (Voegeli) H.; m. Sybilla Kool, Apr. 14, 1961; children: Vlasta, Anita, Eric, Tamara. D in Phys. Scis., U. Geneva, Switzerland, 1968. Cert. thermonuclear physicist. Scientist Univ. Geneva, Switzerland, 1960-62; scientist Euratom, Brussels, 1962-78, prin. scientist, 1978—; cons. Inst. Parliamentary Studies, Rome, 1992—. Guest editor Fusion Tech., 1994; contbr. articles to profl. jours. Mem. European Fedn. Rd. Crash Victims, Geneva, 1991—. Mem. Swiss Phys. Soc., European Phys. Soc. E-mail: mhaegi@pelagus.it. Home: via del Piscaro No 4, I-00044 Frascati Italy Office: Euratom-ENEA, via Enrico Fermi 27, I-00044 Frascati Italy

HAEMMERLE, MARKUS, economist, educator, consultant; b. Bludenz, Vorarlberg, Austria, July 24, 1956; s. Werner and Ria (Reinl) H.; m. Marlene Koch, May 4, 1984; children: Christian, Andreas, Clemens. Mag.rer.soc.oec., U. Innsbruck, Austria, 1980, Dr.rer.soc.oec., 1982. Asst. prof. U. Innsbruck, 1980-94, lectr. dept. econs., 1982-98; project mgr. Sparkasse, Dornbirn, Austria, 1983-84, Leica, Heerbrugg, Switzerland, 1988-89; mgr. Catro-Betriebsberatung, Goetzis, Austria, 1993-94; project mgr., lectr. Technikna Vorarlberg, Dornbirn, 1994-95; tchr. HAK, Feldkirch, Austria, 1995—; lectr. Mgmt. Ctr. Innsbruck, 1997—; cons. in field. Author: Basics in Finance and Accounting, 1998. Mem. Sparkasseverein, Feldkirch, 1997—. Recipient Johannes-Bisesser prize U. Innsbruck, 1982. Mem. Assn. Austrian Econ. Grads., Faculty for Social and Econ. Scis. Club. Avocations: travel, convertibles. Office: Bundeshandelsakademie, Liechtensteiner-Str 50, A-6800 Feldkirch Austria

HAENEN, ROGER EDOUARD, infection control practitioner; m. Clemence Tordeurs; children: Joeri, Ursula, Larsen, Erika. Infection control surveillance practitioner IDEWE Occupl Health Svc., Louvain, Belgium. Contbr. articles to profl. jours. Office: IDEWE Occulp Health Svc, Interleuvenlaan 58, B-3001 Louvain Belgium

HAENLEIN, HANS, architect, educator; b. Berlin, Aug. 25, 1935; arrived in Eng., 1948; s. Ernst Maria and Susanna (Carolus) H.; m. Ulrike Becker-Freyseng, May 27, 1961 (div. 1978); children: Hans-Christoph, Martin; m. Marie Harrison, Dec. 29, 1982; 1 child, Lucy. Diploma in arch., Hammersmith Coll. Art & Bldg., London, 1960. Registered arch., U.K. Prin. Hans Haenlein Archs., London, 1963—; lectr., sr. lectr. dept. arch. Regent St. Poly. (now Westminster U.), London, 1960-75; dep. head dept. arch. Poly. North London, 1975-76; head dept. arch. South Bank U., London, 1976-89, prof. arch., 1989-91; prof. arch. U. Reading, Eng., 1991—; dir., gov. Bldg. Ctr., London, 1977-85; chmn. edn. com. Constrn. Industry Coun., London, 1988-91. Prin. works include edn. and cmty. bldgs. Chmn. Hammersmith Soc., London, pres., 1985—. Decorated Mem. of Brit. Empire, Cen. Chancery of Orders of Knighthood, London, 1987. Fellow Royal Soc. Arts; mem. European Assn. for Archtl. Edn. (founder, 1st pres. 1975-80), Royal Inst. Brit. Archs. (v.p. 1987-90). Avocations: music, traveling, reading.

HAERING, KURT ARNOLD, investment executive; b. Basel, Switzerland, Jan. 16, 1941; s. Emil and Ilse (Fecht) H.; m. Helen Birrer, Sept. 7, 1973; children: Corinne, Jacqueline. Matura, Math. Naturwissenschaftl, Basel, 1961; diploma, Tech. U. Zürich, Zürich, 1967. Cert. elec. engr. Product mgr. Philips, Zürich, 1967-70; market rschr. Saarbach, Tokyo, 1971-72; area mgr. Autophon, Zürich, 1973-77; export mgr. ITT, Zürich, 1978-83; dir. Ascom, Basel, 1984-88; gen. mgr. Bakoplan, Zürich, 1989-91, Landis & Gyr (Schweiz), Zug, Switzerland, 1991—. Mem. Sch. Bd., Birmensdorf, Switzerland, 1985; active Freisinnig-Demokratische Partei, Birmensdorf, pres., 1992; pres. Baugenossenschaft, Birmensdorf, 1992. Mem. Schweizerischer Elektrotechnischer Verein (com. mem. 1996). Democrat. Avocations: cooking, hiking, photography. Home: Howielstrasse 18, 8903 Birmensdorf Switzerland

HAERTEL, RAINER MARIA, chemical company executive; b. Vienna, June 27, 1947; s. Wilhelm and Gertrude (Pölzl) H.; m. Vera A. Amon, Nov. 15, 1977; children: Daniela, Christoph R. MS, U. for Bus. Econs., Vienna, 1975. Mktg. svc. control officer Steel div. Sandvik, Vienna, 1976-77; sales and mktg. mgr. for Yugoslavia, Coromant div., Vienna, 1978-81, gen. mgr. saws and tools div., 1981-83; mgr. dir. Loctite Europa, Vienna, 1984—. Avocations: tennis, skiing, golf, arts and painting. Home: Paul-Guselstrasse 22, A2103 Langenzersdorf Austria Office: Loctite Europa GmbH, Erdbergstrasse 29, 1030 Vienna Austria

HAERTTER, SEBASTIAN GOETZ, pharmacist; b. Mainz, Germany, Aug. 6, 1964; s. Ernst Rudolf and Dorothea (Aderhold) H.; m. Dagmar Wendt, June 1, 1991; children: Isabel, Carolin. PhD, U. Mainz (Germany), 1983. Asst. prof. psychiatry U. Mainz (Germany), 1993—, specialized pharmacist for clin. chemistry, 1997—; pharmacist Hoechst AG, Germany, 1987—. Author: Wohnen in Wandel, 1981. Mem. German Soc. Pharmacology and Toxicology, Soc. of Neuropharmacology and Toxicology, German Pharm. Soc. Avocations: drums, soccer, painting, minerals, geology. Office: U Mainz, Untere Zahlbacherstrasse 8, 55131 Mainz Germany

HAEUSER, MICHAEL JOHN, library administrator; b. LaCrosse, Wis., July 5, 1943; s. Loyal Eldon and Kamilla (Brenengen) H.; m. Linda Kay Johnsrud, Aug. 31, 1968 (div. 1981); 1 child, Britton; m. Irene Jeanette Morris, June 20, 1987. BS in History, U. Wis., 1970, MA in History, 1972, MLS, 1973, cert., 1986. Readers svcs. libr. Knox Coll., Galesburg, Ill., 1973-74, head readers svcs., 1974-76; head libr. Linfield Coll., McMinnville, Oreg., 1976-81; dir. learning resources, head libr. Gustavus Adolphus Coll., St. Peter, Minn., 1981-97, coll. archivist, 1997—; co-instr. Mil. History WWII, 1979; presenter in field. Cons. to editor books for coll. librs., Choice mag.; contbr. articles to profl. jours. Chmn. Core Curriculum Rev. Task Force, Linfield Coll., 1977-7; mem. coll. libr. com. Nat. Commn. Preservation and Access, 1989, team Bibliographic Instrn., 1982—; bd. dirs. Minn. Humanities Commn., 1990-97. With U.S. Army, 1963-66. NEH fellow, 1978; grantee, 1980, 83; grantee: Japan Found., 1978, U.S. Office Edn., 1979, 80, Murdock Trust, 1979, Hearst Found., 1980, Collins Found., 1980, Nat. Archives and Records Svc., 1983, Presser Found., 1983; recipient John Cotton Dana Libr. pub. rels. award 1983, 94. Mem. ALA (selected vol. pres.' program Chgo. chpt. 1985, sec. coll. libr. sect. 1990, Outstanding Pub. Rels. 1983), Assn. Coll. And Rsch. Librs., Assn. Coll. and Resource Librs. (nat. adv. coun. libr. sect. 1985), Am. Hist. Assn., Minn. Libr. Assn. (pres. 1988-90), Minn. Assn. Libr. Friends (bd. dirs. 1990), Minn. Humanities Commn. (bd. dirs. 1991-97). Lutheran. Avocations: skiing, outdoor work, reading, traveling, association activities. Office: Gustavus Adolphus Coll Folke Bernadotte Meml Libr 800 W College Ave Saint Peter MN 56082-1485

HAFEEZ, ZEBA HASAN, dermatologist; b. Karachi, Sindh, Pakistan, Sept. 30, 1960; d. Mushtaq and Zubaida (Malik) Hasan; m. Mohsin Hafeez, Apr. 16, 1987; children: Sahar, Sarah A. MBBS, Dow Med. Coll., Karachi, Pakistan, 1984. Dermatologist Sindh Govt. Lyari Gen. Hosp., Karachi, 1990, Dow Med. Coll. Civil Hosp., Karachi, 1990—, Anklesaria Hosp., Karachi, 1990-2000; pvt. practice Karachi, 1996—; rsch. scholar U. Calif., San Francisco, 2000—. Author numerous poems; contbr. articles to profl. jours. Recipient Editors Choice award Nat. Libr. Poetry, 1996, 97, Poetry award Am. Ctr. Arts Coun., 1980-81, 87, 1st prize short story, 1984. Mem. Coll. Physicians & Surgeons Pakistan, Pakistan Assn. Dermatologists, Pakistan Med. Assn. Avocations: reading, writing poetry, music, travel. Home: 6 Margarita Terr Novato CA 94947

HAFER, THOMAS PAUL, government official; b. Reading, Pa., Aug. 22, 1955; s. Howard Stanley and Dorothy Rosalyn (Kopach) H.; m. Janeen Marie Granakis, May 2, 1987. BA in History magna cum laude, St. Joseph's U., Phila., 1977; M.Pub./Internat. Affairs summa cum laude, U. Pitts., 1978. Cert. govt. fin. mgr. Presdl. mgmt. intern Naval Sea Systems Command, Arlington, Va., 1979-81, budget analyst, 1981-84; budget analyst Office of Undersec. of Def., Washington, 1984-91, auditor, 1991-95; dep. dir. re-engring. travel transition office Dept. of Def., Washington, 1995-97; assoc. dir. fin. commerce directorate Dept. of Def., Arlington, Va., 1997-98; dep. dir. Def. Integrated Travel and Relocation Solutions Office, Rosslyn, Va., 1998—; instr. Sch. of Foxhunting. Editor-in-chief Hayes History Jour., 1976-77; contbr. articles to profl. jours. Chmn. St. Elizabeth Seton Pastoral Adv. Coun., Lake Ridge, Va., 1995—, mem. exec. bd., 1996-98; bd. dirs., hon. sec. Bull Run Hunt, Manassas, Va., 1992-94. Recipient Hammer award for reinventing govt. Office of Vice Pres., Nat. Performance Rev., 1996. Mem. Presdl. Mgmt. Intern Alumni Group, Am. Soc. Mil. Comptrollers (historian 1994), Fed. Exec. Inst. Alumni Assn. (class rep. 1988). Democrat. Roman Catholic. Avocations: fox hunting, liturgical planning, writing. Home: 14692 Stratford Dr Woodbridge VA 22193-3548 Office: Fin Policy Directorate Ste 201/203 Crystal Square #4 Arlington VA 22202-3402

HAFEZ, ABDEL-FATTAH, physics educator, researcher; b. Alexandria, Egypt, Nov. 16, 1949; s. Hafez Abdel-Rehim and Fatima Hassan (Imran) H.; m. Zeinab Abdel-Moneim, Apr. 21, 1978; children: Muhammad, Ahmad, Ibrahim. BS, Faculty Sci., Alexandria, 1972, MS, 1977; PhD, Hungarian Acad. Scis., Budapest, 1986. Demonstrator Faculty Sci., Alexandria, 1972-77, asst. lectr., 1977-87, lectr., 1987-93, assoc. prof., 1993-98, prof. radiation physics, 1998—. Referee Jour. Radiation Physics and Chemistry; contbr. papers to profl. jours. Mem. Internat. Nuclear Track Soc., Egyptian Bi-

ophysics Soc., Egyptian Phys. Soc. Avocations: listening to music, reading. Office: Alexandria U Facult Sci, Physics Dept, 21511 Alexandria Egypt

HAFEZ, ZAKI KAMAL, petroleum company executive; b. Berkit El-Saabh, Egypt, July 13, 1946; s. Kamal Hafez Shaheen and Om Mohamed Zaki Abu Zeid; m. Samiha Wagih Attiya, Feb. 19, 1976; children: Ghada, Sameh, Mohamed. B Bus., Cairo U., 1968, postgrad., 1968-70; postgrad., A.U.C., Cairo, 1997, Agip Inst., Rome, 1999. Bus. analyst Petroleum Pipeline Co., Cairo, 1968-74; purchasing head Sumed Pipeline Co., Alexandria, Egypt, 1974-78; comml. dir. Multinat. Glass Co., Cairo, 1978-82; procurement head, comml. dir. IEOC, Cairo, 1982—. Editor work sys. and procedures in purchasing for numerous cos. Mem. Commerce and Bus. Union. Home: 14 Ammar Ibn Yassir, El-Nozah Heliopolis, Cairo Egypt Office: IEOC, 2 Wadi El-nil Mohardessin, 311 Cairo Egypt

HAFF, GUY GREGORY, college educator, researcher; b. Montclair, N.J., Sept. 25, 1969; s. Guy Gordon and Sandra K. H. BS, East Stroudsburg U., 1993; MS, Appalachian State U., 1996; PhD, U. Kans., 1999. Cert. strength and conditioning specialist. Graduate asst. Appalachian State U., Boone, 1993-96; cardiac rehab. intern Appalachian State U., Boone, N.C., 1994; personal trainer Milburne (N.J.) Short Hills Athletic Club, 1995; graduate tchg. asst. U. Kans., Lawrence, 1996-99; mem. com. USA Weightlifting, 1997—; mem. Human Performance Lab., Appalachian State U., 1999—. Reviewer Strength and Conditioning, 1999—. Mem. Nat. Strength and Conditioning Assn. (scholarship 1996), Am. Coll. Sports Medicine, U.S. Weight Lifting Assn. (athletic coach). Avocations: weightlifting, computers, reading, Hiking. E-mail: gh10644@ hotmail.com. Home: PO Box 1624 Boone NC 28607-1624 Office: Appalachian State Univ 208 Broome Kirk Gym Boone NC 28608-0001

HAFFNER, ALFRED LOVELAND, JR., lawyer; b. Bklyn., Sept. 11, 1925; s. Alfred Loveland and Mary Ellen (Myers) H.; m. Mary Dolores Hyland, July 10, 1965; children: Mary Elizabeth, Anne Dolores, Jeanne Marie, Catherine Diane. BS in Engring., U. Mich., 1950, JD, 1956. Bar: N.Y. 1958, U.S. Patent and Trademark Office, 1958, U.S. Dist. Ct. (so. and ea. dists.) N.Y. 1959, U.S. Ct. Claims 1959, U.S. Ct. Appeals (fed. cir.) 1961, U.S. Supreme Ct. 1961, U.S. Ct. Appeals (2d cir.) 1962. Draftsman-engr., indsl. engr., asst. plant engr. Owens-Ill. Glass Co., Bridgeton, N.J., 1950-53, Streator, Ill., 1953-54; since practiced N.Y.C.; assoc. Kenyon & Kenyon, N.Y.C., 1957-60, Ward, McElhannon, Brooks & Fitzpatrick, N.Y.C., 1960-61; ptnr. Ward, McElhannon, Brooks & Fitzpatrick, 1961-71, Brooks Haidt Haffner & Delahunty, N.Y.C., 1971-98, Morgan & Finnegan, LLP, N.Y.C., 1998—; chmn. Nat. Coun. Patent Law Assns., 1973-74, councilman, 1971-88; mem. founding com. Nat. Inventors Hall of Fame Found., 1972, pres., 1973-74, sec., 1980-94, exec. com. 1989-94, endowment trust com., 1991-93, chmn. exhibits com., 1992-95, legal com., 1993-95, 97-98, fin. com., 1993-94, 97—, strategic planning com., 1994-97, chmn., 1995-97, sel. com., 1996-98, bd. dirs., 1972—. Served with USNR, 1943-46. Mem. ABA, N.Y. State Bar Assn., Am. Intellectual Property Law Assn., N.Y. Intellectual Property Law Assn. (sec. 1964-68, dir. 1968-70, 71-72, pres. 1970-71), Strathmore Assn. Westchester (treas. 1976-79, v.p. 1980-82, pres. 1982-83, exec. com. 1983—), Phi Gamma Delta, Phi Alpha Delta. Home: 1 Gainsborough Rd Scarsdale NY 10583-4811 Office: Morgan & Finnegan LLP 345 Park Ave New York NY 10154-0053

HAFNER, HEINZ, psychiatrist, researcher; b. Munich, Germany, May 20, 1926; s. Heinrich and Elisabeth (Gerner) H.; m. Wiltrud Ranabauer, Aug. 29, 1967; children: Gerald, Gilbert, Constantin, Sibylle. MD, Univ. Munich, 1950, PhD, 1951; MD (hon.), Univ. Helsinki, 1990; Dr.rer.soc. (hon.), Univ. Constance, Germany, 1992. Diplomate Am. Bd. Psychology, Philosophy. Prof., chmn. dept. social psychiatry Univ. Heidelberg, 1964-68, prof. psychiatry, chmn. dept. psychiatry, 1968-94; dir. Cen. Inst. of Mental Health, Mannheim, Germany, 1974-94; chmn. Schizophrenia Rsch. Unit. CIMH, Mannheim, Germany, 1994—; dir. WHO Collaborating Ctr., Mannheim, Germany, 1980-99; chmn. Fedn. Commn. on Rsch. and Edn. in Pub. Health, 1993—; v.p. Expert Commn. on Psychiatry, 1969-75; group chmn. WPA Global Programme on Fighting Schizophrenia, 1995—. Editor: Search for the Causes of Schizophrenia, 1987, Search for the Causes of Schizophrenia II, 1991, Search for the Causes of Schizophrenia III, 1995, New Research in Psychiatry, 1996, Search for the Causes of Schizophrenia IV, 1999, Gesundheit-unser Höchstes Gut?, 1999, Das Rätsel Schizophrenie, 2000. Mem. scientific coun. Fed. Rep. of German, 1976-83, chmn. exptl. com. on rsch., exptl. com. on medicine. Recipient Herrmann Simon award, 1972, Erik Stromgren medal, 1988, Joseph Zubin award Am. Psychopathological Assn., 1997, Salomon Neumann award, 1993, Rsch. Methodology award AMDP, 1998, Leader of Psychiatry award WPA, 1999, Great U. Medal, U. Heidelberg, 1993, Great Order of Merit, Federal Republic Germany, 1994. Federal Svc. Cross 1st Class, 1982. Mem. Heidelberg Acad. of Sci., German Acad. of Researchers Leopoldina, Presidential Bd. AEP. Home: Am Buchsenackerhang 27, 69118 Heidelberg Germany Office: Central Inst of Mental Heal, J5, 68159 Mannheim Germany

HAFNER, JÜRGEN, scientist, physics educator; b. Lunz am See, Austria, July 24, 1945; s. Edmund and Edith (Frömming) H.; m. Anneliese Dokreuzer, May 26, 1971; children: Thomas, Michael. Diploma in engring., Tech. U. Vienna, Austria, 1970, Dr.Techn., 1973. Rsch. asst. Tech. U. Vienna, 1971-75, docent, 1979-82, prof. theoretical physics, 1982-98, dir. Inst. Theoretical Physics, 1991-95; rsch. assoc. Max-Planck-Inst., Stuttgart, 1975-79; sr. vis. scientist U. Cambridge, Eng., 1981; prof. invité U. Grenoble, France, 1983; prof. solid state physics U. Vienna, 1998—. Author: From Hamiltonians to Phase Diagrams, 1987; editor: Liquid and Amorphous Metals, 1992; mem. editl. bd. Jour. Non-Crystalline Solids, 1990—; co-editor Europhysics Letters; contbr. over 360 articles to profl. jours., chpts. to books. Recipient Kardinal-Innitzer prize Innitzer Found., 1981, Erwin-Schrödinger prize Austrian Acad. Scis., 1995. Mem. Austrian Phys. Soc. (Ludwig-Boltzmann prize 1979), German Phys. Soc., Chem.-Phys. Assn. (pres. 1992). Office: Tech U Vienna, U Vienna, Sensen gasse 8 12, A-1090 Vienna Austria

HAFSI, MOHAMED, clinical psychology educator, psychotherapist; b. Ain Bessem, Algiers, Algeria, June 16, 1954; s. Said and Zohra (Arar) H.; m. Mitsue Sudo, Oct. 12, 1979; children: Leila, Ramy. MSc, Lyon (France) II U., 1979, DESS, 1980; PhD, Osaka (Japan) U., 1987. Cert. clin. psychologist, psychotherapist. Asst. prof. Nara (Japan) U., 1988-91, assoc. prof., 1991-93, prof., 1993—. Mem. editl. bd. Psychologia, 1997—; contbr. articles to profl. jours. Mem. UNESCO, Japan, 1997. Recipient Tableau d'Honneur, Prefecture of Rhone, France, 1979. Mem. Japanese Psychology Assn., Japanese Psychoanalysts Assn. Avocations: gardening, carpentry, soccer, fishing. Home: 267-6 Fukigaoka, Nabari-shi, Mie 518-0419, Japan Office: Nara U, 1500 Misasagi-cho, Nara-shi 631-0803, Japan

HAFSTAD, HELGE ANDREAS, aviation administrator; b. Oslo, Feb. 25, 1961; s. Gunnar A. and Karin (Aarenstrup) H.; m. Vibeke Anya Jacobsen, Aug. 1, 1997. Flight dispatcher, Sheffield Sch. Aeronautics, Ft. Lauderdale, Fla., 1987; deck officer Class 5, Oslo Teknisk Maritim, 1995. Lic. flight dispatcher FAA. Flight dispatcher Braathens S.Am. and Far East, Oslo, 1987-92, flight dispatch coord., 1992-94, sect. head flight dispatch, 1994-99, mgr. flight support, 1999—; mem. IFPS Project Team, Eurocontrol, Brussels, 1992-96; mem. EAMG Sys. Sub-Group, Eurocontrol, Brussels, 1996—. Author, editor: (newsletter) Trim, 1996—. Cpl. Royal Norwegian Air Force, 1980-87. Mem. Internat. Civil Aviation Orgn. (mem. all weather ops. group 1996-99), Internat. Air Carrier Assn. (mem. operational com. 1992—), Salda-Norway (bd. dirs. 1997—), Royal Inst. of Navigation, Barum Yacht Club. Avocations: navigation, sailing, hiking, reading. Home: Christian Michelsens gate, N-0568 Oslo Norway Office: Braathens ASA, Oksenoyveien 3, N-1330 Oslo Norway

HAFTORN, SVEIN, zoologist; b. Drammen, Buskerud, Norway, Jan. 30, 1925; s. Birger and Martha (Winsvold) H.; m. Eva Hamborgstrøm, Mar. 25, 1928; children: Jens, Sylvi, Tone, Beate. PhD, U. Oslo, 1957. Curator Kongelige Norske Videnskabers Selskab Museet, Trondheim, Norway, 1952-66; prof. U. Trondheim, 1966-90. Author: Våre fugler, 1962, Fjellfaûna, 1966, Norges fûgler, 1971, Fûglekongen, 1986. Fellow Am. Ornithol. Union (hon.), Norwegian Ornithol. Soc. (hon.); mem. Videnskapsakademiet Oslo, Kongelige Norske Videnskabers Selskab Trondheim. Home: Målsjøen, N-7540 Klaebû Norway Office: Norwegian U Sci and Tech, N-7491 Trondheim Norway

HAGA, TATSUYA, neurochemist, researcher; b. Tokyo, Feb. 14, 1941; s. Ko and Yasu (Tadokoro) H.; m. Kazuko Tsutsumi, Apr. 4, 1969. BS, U. Tokyo, PhD, 1970. Instr. U. Tokyo, 1969-74, prof., 1988—; assoc. prof. Hamamatsu (Japan) U., 1974-88. Co-author: Receptor Biochemistry, 1990; editor: G Protein-Coupled Receptors, 1999. Office: U Tokyo Faculty Medicine, 7-3-1 Hongo, Tokyo 1130033, Japan

HAGA, VIGLEIK ARNBJØRN, cultural affairs executive; b. Sandnes, Norway; s. Trygve Assaeus and Ruth Cecilie (Nygaard) H.; m. Arna Louise Jakobsen, June 24, 1972; children: Eva, Aadne Martin, Lars Peder. Cand., Rogaland Coll., 1975; Norwegian Sch. Mgrs., 1998. Tchr. Ibestad Comm., Norway, 1972-73; jr. officer of cultural affairs Rana Comm., Norway, 1977-79; sr. dir. ops. Rana Municipality, Mo i Rana, Norway, 1979-86; cinema dir. Kinoteatret, Moirana, 1986-96; exec. of cultural affairs Rana Municipality, 1996—. Cashier, Norsk Kulturforum, Oslo, 1979-87, leader ctrl. commn. 1987—, Assn. Cinema Dirs. Norway, 1989-97; bd. mem. Norwegian Cinema Assn., 1991-97; local pres. Norden Assn., 1992-96. Mem. Rana Rotary Club. Mem. Norwegian Labour Party. Lutheran. Avocations: literature, music, arts. E-mail: hvigleik@rana.kommune.no. Home: Nygata 71, 8618 Andfiskaa Norway Office: Rana Kommune, Boks 173, 8601 Mo i rana Norway

HAGAN, FRANCIS KWESI, mechanical engineer; b. Mankessim, Ghana, Jan. 23, 1944; s. Francis Thomas Kweku and Theresah Efua Atta (Imbeah) H.; m. Emelia Filicity Micah, June 20, 1975; children: Dorcas, Issabella, Sabbina, Francis, Florence, Emelia. Student, Jr. Tech. Inst., Koforidua, Ghana, 1961-63, Sch. of Mines, Tarkwa, Ghana, 1963-65; Mech. Engring. Technician, Poly.-Kumasi, Ghana, 1967-69, Poly.-Accra, Ghana, 1972-73. Technol. cert. in mech. engring. Mechanic Jute Factory, Kumasi, 1965-66, Sugar Factory, Komenda, 1969-71; tutor St. Paul Tech. Sch., Kukurantumi, Ghana, 1971-72; loco contr. Ghana Rlwys. & Harbour, Takoradi, Ghana, 1973-74; technician engr. Ghana Water & Sewerage Corp., Tamale, 1974, maint. engr./sta. mgr., 1974-82; dist. mgr. Ghana Water & Sewerage Corp., Mampong Ashanti, 1982-86; workshop mgr./project officer Ghana Water & Sewerage Corp., Ho, 1986-93, dist. mgr., 1993—. Mem. statutory planning com. Ho Dist. Assembly, 1994— . Mem. Ghana Instn. of Technician Engrs. Methodist. Avocations: music, swimming, football, table tennis, dancing. Office: Ghana Water & Sewerage Corp, Box 41, Ho Volta, Ghana

HAGAR, AUDREY SPILKER, playwright; b. Oct. 24, 1973. Student, Pitzer Coll., 1991-92; BA, Loyola Marymount U., 1996; postgrad., U. So. Calif., 1998-2000. Ptnr. Simi Starlight Ranch Co., L.A., 1998—. Author: The Mouse House, 1998 (all proceeds donated to charity); playwright: Butterflies are Insects, 1998.

HAGARE, PRASANTHI, engineering educator; b. Kakinada, Australia, Feb. 13, 1966; arrived in Australia, 1992.; d. Anand G. and Mary (Kanukala) H.; m. Hagare Dharmappa. BS, Andhra U., India, 1984; MS, Hyderabad U., India, 1986; M in Tech., Indian Inst. Tech., Bombay, 1988; PhD, U. Tech., Sydney, Australia, 1995. Project. engr. AIC, Bombay, 1988-89; rsch. assoc. AIT, Bangkok, Thailand, 1990-92, U. Tech., Sydney, Australia, 1992-94; sr. lectr. U. Tech., Sydney, 1995—; with Infotech Profls. Pty. Ltd. Contbr. articles to profl. jours. Mem. Internat. Assn. on Water Quality, Australian Water Assn., Australasian Assn. Engring. Edn. Avocations: reading, writing, gardening, sports, music.

HAGEBØ, EINAR, chemistry educator; b. Oslo, July 28, 1933; s. Asbjørn and Ragnhild (Gåsdal) H.; m. Liv Rønning, Dec. 31, 1957; children: Jan, Mads, Eva, Lena. Candidate Real, U. Oslo, 1959, PhD, 1971. Rsch. asst. U. Uppsala, Sweden, 1960-64; chemist CERN, Geneva, Sweden, 1964-69; 1st lectr. U. Oslo, 1969-91, prof., 1992—, vice head dept., 1997-99. Editor (with B. Salbu) Aspects of Nuclear Science, 1987. Mem. Norwegian Chem. Soc., N.Y. Acad. Scis. Office: U Oslo Dept Chemistry, PO Box 1033 Blindern, 0315 Oslo Norway

HAGEDORN, LINDA SERRA, education educator, researcher; b. Chgo., Dec. 12, 1951; d. Genaro Victor Serra and Ruth Bass; m. Timothy William Hagedorn, June 5, 1981; children: Aaron, Serra. BA, Elmhurst Coll., 1973; MEd, Nat. Louis U., 1990; PhD, U. Ill., Chgo., 1995. Electronic exch. engr. GTE Automatic Electric, Northlake, Ill., 1973-77; electronics instr. Triton Coll., River Grove, Ill., 1977-85; tchr. Cmty. Consol. Sch. Dist. 15, Palatine, Ill., 1985-91; rsch. assoc. Nat. Ctr. for Tchg. Learning and Assessment, Chgo., 1991-94, postdoctoral fellow, 1994-96; asst. prof. U. So. Calif., L.A., 1996—; trustee Sias U., Zhengzhou, China, 1999—. Mem. editl. bd. Rev. Higher Edn., 1999—; contbr. articles to profl. jours. Recipient Assessment for Student Devel. Rsch. award Am. Coll. Pers. Assn., 1996-97, Mertes award for excellence in cmty. coll. rsch. Assn. Calif. C.C. Adminstrs., 1997; AIR/NCES/NSF Improving Instnl. Rsch. in Postsecondary Edn. Instns. Database Inst. scholar NCES, Washington, 1997. Mem. Am. Ednl. Rsch. Assn. (bd. mem., exec. coun. 1998-2000). E-mail: lsh@usc.edu. Fax: 213-740-3889. Home: 23545 Estrella Pl Valencia CA 91355-2132 Office: Univ So Calif 3470 Trousdale Pkwy Los Angeles CA 90089-0017

HAGEL, REINHOLD ANTON, electrical engineer, researcher; b. Staffelstein, Bavaria, Germany, June 20, 1956. Diploma in engring., U. Erlangen-Nürnberg, Germany, 1983; DEng, U. Erlangen-Nürnberg, 1995. Project engr. Siemens Med. Lab., Erlangen, 1984-87; rsch. engr. U. Erlangen-Nürnberg, 1988-96; project engr. Balluff, Inc., Neuhausen, Germany, 1997-98; project mgr. TEMIC Telefunken microelectronic GmbH, Nürnberg, 1998—. Contbr. over 20 articles to profl. jours. Mem. IEEE (grantee 1994), Internat. Compumag Soc. (founding). Avocations: mechanical watches, New Mexico, music.

HAGELSTEIN, ROBERT PHILIP, publisher; b. N.Y.C., Dec. 15, 1942; s. H. Robert and E. Ann (Buhrow) H.; m. Ann G. Linguvic, Apr. 26, 1970; children: Christopher R., Jonathan W. B.A. in English Lit., L.I. U., 1964. Prodn. mgr. Johnson Reprint Corp., N.Y.C., 1965-68; editor-in-chief Johnson Reprint Corp., 1968-70; v.p. Greenwood Press, Inc., Westport, Conn., 1970-73; pres. Greenwood Pub. Group, 1973-99; pub. cons., 1999—; bd. dirs. Aldwych Press, London. Contbr. articles to scholarly and profl. jours.; author Converticalc computer software program. Mem. Info. Industry Assn., Am. Soc. Info. Sci., Spl. Librs. Assn. (George Polk Awards com.), Scholarly Pub. Assn., North Palm Beach Yacht Club, South Norwalk Boat Club.

HAGEMEYER, JÜRGEN, ecologist, educator; b. Enger, Germany, Mar. 14, 1959; s. Heinrich and Gertrud (Bunn) H. Diploma in biology, U. Bielefeld, Germany, 1985, Dr.rer.nat., 1990, Privatdozent, 1996. Rschr. Tel Aviv U., 1986-87; sci. asst. Bielefeld U., 1988-97, sr. asst., 1997—. Author: Ökophysiologische Untersuchungen zur Salz-und Cadmiumresistenz von Tamarix aphylla, 1990, Die Variabilität der Elementverteilungen im Stammholz von Bäumen, 1997; editor: (with M.N.V. Prasad) Heavy Metal Stress in Plants, 1999. Mem. Assn. Ökologie Berlin, Vereinigung Angewandte Botanik Göttingen, Internat. Assn. Ecology. Avocations: books, swimming. Office: Bielefeld U Faculty Biology, Dept Ecology, 33615 Bielefeld Germany

HAGEN, KIRK DEE, mechanical engineer, educator; b. Ogden, Utah, July 12, 1953; s. Darius and Ellen Virginia (Hicks) H.; m. Jan Rowley, June 9, 1978; children: Kathryn, Jennifer, Alec, Daniel. BS in Physics, Weber State Coll., Ogden, 1977; MSME, Utah State U., 1981; PhD in Mech. Engring., U. Utah, 1989. Sr. engr. Hercules Aerospace, Magna, Utah, 1980-86; prin. engr. Unisys Corp., Salt Lake City, 1986-92; assoc. prof. mech. engring. tech. Weber State U., Ogden, 1993—; adj. prof. engring. Salt Lake C.C., Salt Lake City, 1991-93. Author: Heat Transfer with Applications, 1999, Introduction to Engineering Analysis, 2000; contbr. articles to profl. jours. Blazer scoutleader Boy Scouts Am., Centerville, Utah, 1990-91. Mem. ASME, ASHRAE, Am. Soc. Engring. Edn., Boy Scouts Am. (varsity scoutleader), N.Y. Acad. Scis., Sigma Xi. Mem. LDS Ch. Avocations: woodworking, painting. Home: 582 N 220 E Centerville UT 84014-1836 Office: Weber State U Ogden UT 84408-0001

HAGEN, THOMAS BAILEY, business owner, former state official, former insurance company executive; b. Buffalo, Sept. 19, 1935; s. Walter B. and Isabella S. (Bailey) H.; m. Susan R. Hirt, May 31, 1958; children: Jonathan, Sarah. Student, Pa. State U., Erie, 1953-55; BS in Commerce, Ohio State U., 1957; DPubSvc (hon.), Edinboro U. Pa., 1996. With Erie (Pa.) Ins. Group, 1953-98, exec. v.p., 1976-82, pres., 1982-90, chmn., CEO, 1990-93, spl. asst. to chmn., 1993-95, also bd. dirs., 1996-98; sec. of commerce Commonwealth of Pa., 1995-96, sec. cmty. and econ. devel., 1996-97; chmn. bd. dirs. Custom Engring. Co., 1997—; chmn. Team Pa. Found., 1997—; bd. dirs. Pa. Housing Fin. Agy., GPU, Inc., Ani-Mition, Inc., St. Raymond Holdings (U.S.), Inc.; chmn. Pa. Indsl. Devel. Authority, 1995-97, Pa. Econ. Devel. Fin. Authority, 1995-97, Pa. Ben Franklin/IRC Partnership, 1995-97; chmn. bd. dirs. Verango Machine Co., Lamjen, Inc., Custom Group Industries, Ltd. Bd. dirs. Erie Philharmonic, 1962-75, pres., 1970-71; bd. dirs. Erie Coun. Navy League U.S., 1977-86; pres. Erie Tomorrow Corp., 1979-86; vice chmn., bd. dirs. Bayfront East Side Taskforce, Erie, 1978-96; bd. dirs. Erie Conf. on Community Devel., 1985-93, hon. dir., 1993—; bd. dirs. Pa. Chamber Bus. and Industry, Harrisburg, 1986-95, 99—, Pa. Econ. Devel. Partnership, 1987-94, Pa. for Effective Govt., 1987-95. Capt. USNR. Alumni fellow Pa. State U., 1988; recipient Ins. Mentor award U. Ala., 1976, Golden Baton award Erie Philharmonic, 1974, Disting. Pennsylvanian award Gannon U., 1987, Phila. C. of C., 1980, Outstanding Community Service award Multiple Sclerosis Soc., 1980, Alumni Citizenship award Ohio State U., 1981, Man of the Yr. award Erie and Chautauqua Mag., 1986, Preservationist of the Yr. award (now Otto Haas award) Pa. Hist. and Mus. Commn., 1987, Honor award Pa. Soc. Architects, 1993. Mem. Internat. Ins. Soc. (bd. dirs. 1978-92, hon. counselor award 1982), Ins. Fedn. Pa. (chmn. 1984-86), Ins. Inst. Am. (inst. for property and liability underwriters, trustee 1987-93), Griffith Found. (v.p. 1985-92, trustee 1985-95, trustee emeritus 1995—), The Pa. Soc. (pres. 1995-97, bd. dirs. 1990—). Office: 100 State St Ste 440 Erie PA 16507-1456

HAGENBUCH, RODNEY DALE, computer company executive, financial consultant; b. Saxville, Wis.; s. Herbert Jenkin and Minnie Leona (Hayward) Hagenbuch; children: Kris, Beth, Patricia; m. LaVerne Julia Scoonover, Sept. 1, 1956. BS, Mich. State U., 1980. Cert. fin. mgr. Designer Olds div. Gen. Motors, Lansing, Mich., 1960-66; institutional account exec. Merrill Lynch, Lansing, 1966-75, institutional mgr., 1975-80; sales mgr. Merrill Lynch, Columbus, Ohio, 1980-82; sr. resident v.p. Merrill Lynch, Tacoma, 1982-93, L.A., 1993-98; ret., 1998; prin. Oxford Group, 1999, Securities Expert Witness Network, 1999, Quantum Leap Inst., 1999; adv. bd. U. Wash. Sch. Bus., Tacoma; chmn. CommunityPath.com. Bd. dirs. Tacoma Club, 1989-93, treas. 1990, pres. 1993, L.A. Acad. Finance, 1993-98, L.A. United Cerebral Palsey, 1994—; adv. bd. Charles Wright, 1989-93; bd. dirs. L.A. Red Cross, 1996—; mem. econ. devel. bd. City of Tacoma, 1986-93, chmn. 1987-88; pres. Downtown Tacoma Assn., 1986; chmn. Corp. Coun. for the Arts, 1986, L.A. United Way, 1993-2000; pres. Tacoma Symphony, 1988; chmn. Human Resources Commn., Meridian Twp., 1972-74, Meridian Planning Commn., Lansing, 1964-70, Meridian Police and Fire Com., Lansing, 1964-70; pres. adv. bd. U. Wash., Tacoma, chmn. 1992; mem. State Wash. Arts Stabilization Bd., Tacoma Art Mus. Bd., sec. 1992; legis. chmn. N.W. Securities Industry Assn.; campaign chmn. Pierce County United Way Bd., 1991-92; non-resident dir. Tacoma Art Mus., 1994—, Tacoma Urban League, 1983-93; bd. mem. New L.A. Mktg. Plan; bd. mem., dist. 2 com. NASD, 1996-99; bd. govs. L.A. Town Hall, 1996; mem. fraternity of friends L.A. Music Ctr. Recipient Outstanding Citizen award Mcpl. League Pierce County, 1988; named Nat. Vol. of Yr., Urban League Western Divsn., 1987. Mem. Tacoma C. of C. (bd. dirs.), Forward Washington (bd. dirs.), L.A. Children's Hosp. Rsch. Inst. (bd. govs. 1994-99). Avocations: running, skiing. Home: 16826 Monte Hermoso Dr Pacific Palisades CA 90272-1910

HAGENMAIER, HANSPAUL, chemistry educator; b. Geislingen, Steige, Germany, Dec. 31, 1934; s. Otto and Josephine H.; m. Marianne Christian, July 21, 1962; children: Andrea, Christine, Susanne. Diplom-Chemiker, U. Tuebingen, Germany, 1961; PhD, Cornell U., 1965. Instr. Cornell U., Ithaca, N.Y., 1965-66; rsch. assoc. U. Tuebingen, Germany, 1966-73, prof. organic chemistry and biochemistry, 1974—. Inventor and patentee in field. Recipient Philip Morris Rsch. prize, 1987, European award in clean technology of the EC, 1987, Bundesverdienstkreuz, The Pres. of Germany, 1990. Mem. Gesellschaft Deutscher Chemiker. Home: Liegnitzerstr 8, D-72072 Tübingen Germany Office: U Tuebingen, Auf der Morgenstelle 18, D-72076 Tübingen Germany

HAGENSTEIN, WILLIAM DAVID, forester, consultant; b. Seattle, Mar. 8, 1915; s. Charles William and Janet (Finigan) H.; m. Ruth Helen Johnson, Sept. 2, 1940 (dec. 1979); m. Jean Kraemer Edson, June 16, 1980 (dec. 2000). BS in Forestry, U. Wash., 1938; MForestry, Duke, 1941. Registered profl. engr., Wash., Oreg. Field aid in entomology U.S. Dept. Agr., Hat Creek, Calif., 1938; logging supt. and engr. Eagle Logging Co., Sedro-Woolley, Wash., 1939; tech. foreman U.S. Forest Svc., North Bend, Wash., 1940; forester West Coast Lumbermen's Assn., Seattle and Portland, Oreg., 1941-43, 45-49; sr. forester FEA, South and Central Pacific Theaters of War and Costa Rica, 1943-45; mgr. Indsl. Forestry Assn., Portland, 1949-80; exec. v.p. Indsl. Forestry Assn., 1956-80, hon. dir., 1980-87; pres. W.D. Hagenstein and Assocs., Inc., Portland, 1980—; H.R. MacMillan lectr. forestry U. B.C., 1952, 77; Benson Meml. lectr. U. Mo., 1966; S.J. Hall lectr. indsl. forestry U. Calif. at Berkeley, 1973; cons. forest engr. USN, Philippines, 1952, Coop. Housing Found., Belize, 1986; mem. U.S. Forest Products Trade Mission, Japan, 1968; del. VII World Forestry Congress, Argentina, 1972, VIII Congress, Indonesia, 1978; mem. U.S. Forestry Study Team, West Germany, 1974; mem. sec. Interior's Oreg. and Calif. Multiple Use Adv. Bd., 1975-76; trustee Wash. State Forestry Conf., 1948-92, Keep Oreg. Green Assn., 1957—, v.p., 1970-71, pres., 1972-73; adv. trustee Keep Wash. Green Assn., 1957-95; co-founder, dir. World Forestry Ctr., 1965-89, v.p., 1965-79; hon. Dir. for Life, 1990. Author: (with Wackerman and Michell) Harvesting Timber Crops, 1966; Assoc. editor: Jour. Forestry, 1946-53; columnist Wood Rev., 1978-82; contbr. numerous articles to profl. jours. Trustee Oreg. Mus. Sci. and Industry, 1968-73. Served with USNR, 1933-37. Recipient Hon. Alumnus award U. Wash. Foresters Alumni Assn., 1965, Forest Mgmt. award Nat. Forest Products Assn., 1968, Western Forestry award Western Forestry and Conservation Assn., 1972, 79, Gifford Pinchot medal for 50 yrs. Outstanding Svc., Soc. Am. Foresters, 1987, Charles W. Ralston award Duke Sch. Forestry, 1988, Lifetime Achievement award Oreg. Soc. Am. Foresters, 1995; Honored as only surviving co-founder World Forestry Ctr., 2000. Fellow Soc. Am. Foresters (mem. coun. 1958-63, pres. 1966-69, Golden Membership award 1989); mem. Am. Forestry Assn. (life, hon. v.p. 1966-69, 74-92, William B. Greeley Forestry award 1990), Commonwealth Forestry Assn. (life), Internat. Soc. Tropical Foresters, Portland C. of C. (forestry com. 1949-79, chmn. 1960-62), Nat. Forest Products Assn. (forestry adv. com. 1949-80, chmn. 1972-74, 78-80), West Coast Lumbermen's Assn. (v.p. 1969-79), David Douglas Soc. Western N. Am., Lang Syne Soc., Hoo Hoo Club, Xi Sigma Pi (outstanding alumnus Alpha chpt. 1973). Republican. Home: 3062 SW Fairmount Blvd Portland OR 97201-1439 Office: 921 SW Washington St Ste 803 Portland OR 97205-2826

HAGER, LAURIE VINCENT, federal agency executive; b. Md., Nov. 1963; d. Phillip Gray Vincent; m. Norman William Hager, Jr., May 5, 1990; children: Amy Christine, Emily Grace. AA in Photography with honors, Montgomery Coll., Rockville, Md., 1984; BA in Mgmt. with honors, Nat. Louis U., 1993. With NOAA, Rockville, Md., 1981-83; prodn. mgr. ChromaColour Labs., Inc., Gaithersburg, Md., 1984-87; night shift supr. Camera Graphics, Inc., Alexandria, Va., 1987-88; co-lab mgr. Photocraft, Inc., Rockville, 1988-90; lab mgr. Tech. Photo, Inc., Kensington, Md., 1990-91; platemaker/film stripper Comprint, Inc., Gaithersburg, 1990-91; quality control staff Rieger Comm., Inc., Gaithersburg, 1991-93; photographer Creative Dimensions Group, Army Recruiting Command, Alexandria, 1993; office adminstr. Dept. Health and Human Svcs., Rockville, Md., 1993-94; program specialist FDA, Office Regulatory Affairs Dept. Health and Human Svcs., Rockville, 1994—; lectr. in field. Contbr. articles to profl. jours.; editor: EEPS (Electronic Entry Processing System) Manual for FDA, 1995. Bd. dirs., past pres. of assn. Village of Tall Oaks/Home Owners Assn., Mt. Airy, Md., 1993-94, pres., treas., 1996-97; councilman, sanitation dept. head Town of Mount Airy, 1998—, mem. ethics commn., 1994-98. Recipient Gold Key award Montgomery County Scholastic competition for photography, 1981, Cert. of Appreciation U.S. Dept. Commerce, 1984, Cert. of Achievement, Montgomery Coll., 1983-84, Dist. Mgr. of the Yr. award Md. Jaycees,1 994-95, Performers award Ea. Inst. Jaycees, 1994. Mem. Mt.

Airy Area Jaycees (state dir. 1997-98, chmn. bd. 1996-97, pres. 1995-96, state dir./cmty. dir. 1994-95, pub. relations program mgr. 1994-96, treas. 1993-94, writer/editor newsletter 1992-93, Team Leader award 1993, Bd. Mem. of Yr. award 1993-94, Jaycee of the Yr. 1992-93, 93-94), U.S. Jaycees (Ambassadorship 1999), Md. Mcpl. League, Internat. Thespian Soc. (life), Phi Theta Kappa. Avocations: home crafts, gardening, decorating, raising children, community charity work.

HAGER, LOUISE ALGER, retired chaplain; b. Spokane, Wash., Dec. 15, 1923; d. Russel S. and Thelma Ella (Geib) Alger; m. Bernard Coe, Nov. 16, 1945 (dec. July 1965); children: Cynthia W., Marjorie L.; m. Onslow B. Hager, Jan. 16, 1970 (dec. Dec. 1983). BEd, Nat. Coll. Edn., 1946; M of Theol. Studies, St. Paul Sch. Theology, 1997. Kindergarten tchr. Edgewater Park Bd. Edn., Beverly, N.J., 1946-47, 59-83; pres. bd. mgrs. Cinnaminson (N.J.) Home, 1985-88; chaplain Rsch. Med. Ctr., Kansas City, Mo., 1986-88; assoc. chaplain John Knox Village, Lee's Summit, Mo., 1988-98; ret., 1998; vol. chaplain, psychogeriatric inpatient unit Sheppard Pratt Health Sys., 1999—; vol. chaplain Hollowell and Taylor Halls health care units Inpatient Nursing Svcs. at Broadmead Retirement Cmty., 1999—. Chaplain vol. Burlington County Hosp., Mt. Holly, N.J., 1987-88; lay minister. Mem. NEA, Lee's Summit Ministerial Soc., Coll. Chaplains, Am. Soc. on Aging, Mid-Am. Congress on Aging. Democrat. Quaker. Avocations: reading, piano playing, singing, sewing, walking. Home: Broadmead 13801 York Rd Apt M1 Cockeysville MD 21030-1891

HAGER, MARTIN HERMANN, bank executive; b. Vienna, Austria, May 30, 1963; s. Hermann and Renate (Grimus) H. Analyst FM Zumtobel AG, Dornbirn, Austria, 1988-90; portfolio mgmt., trading & rsch. Epple Brokerage GmbH, Vienna, Austria, 1990, Kapital & Real GmbH, Vienna, Austria, 1991-92; equity analyst Europe Raiffeisen Zentralbank, Vienna, Austria, 1993, equity analyst eastern Europe, 1994-98; CEE rsch. pub., London br. Raiffeisen Zentralbank, 1999—. Author: Kapitalmaerkte in Osteuropa, 1994, The Russian Capital Market, 1996, The Bulgarian Capital Market, 1997; contbr. articles to profl. jours. With Austrian Mil., 1992. Mem. Investclub Schottenring, Investclub Landskron (pres. 1991-92). Roman Catholic. Avocations: wind surfing, skiing, gardening, theatre, literature. Home: Neubaugasse 76/4/25, 1070 Vienna Austria Office: Raiffeisen Zentralbank, Am Stadtpark 9, 1030 Vienna Austria

HAGER, WILLI HERMANN, hydraulics educator; b. Uznach, Switzerland, July 8, 1951; s. Willi J. Hager and Ida M. Fuchs; m. Susanna S. Iten, May 17, 1951; children: Olivia, Mirjam, Caren. Degree in civil engring., Swiss Fed. Inst. Tech., Zurich, Switzerland, 1976, PhD, 1981, PD, 1994. Hydraulic engr. Kuster & Hager, Switzerland, 1976-83; rsch. engr. EPFL, Lausanne, Switzerland, 1983-88; rsch. head ETH, 1989-98, head hydraulics dept., 1999—, prof., 1998. Fellow ASCE (J.C. Stevens award 1988, best practice paper award 1994, best tech. note award 1994); mem. Internat. Assn. Hydraulic Rsch. (10th Ippen award), SIA. Avocations: collecting biographies, stamps, wines. Research interests include air-water high speed flows, dam-break waves, sewer and dam hydraulics, impulse waves scour. E-mail: hager@vaw.baug.ethz.ch. Office: VAW, ETH Zentrum, CH-8092 Zurich Switzerland

HAGERMAN, JOHN DAVID, lawyer; b. Houston, Aug. 1, 1941; s. David Angle and Noima L. (Clay) H.; m. Linda J. Lambright, June 25, 1975; children: Clayton Robert, Holly Elizabeth. BBA, So. Meth. U., 1963; JD, U. Tex., Austin, 1966. Bar: Tex. 1966, U.S. Ct. Appeals (5th cir.) 1967, U.S. Supreme Ct. 1969; cert. civil trial law, 1980-95; real estate broker Tex. Pres., owner Hagerman & Sereau, Inc., Woodlands, Tex., 1966—; condr. bank creditor rights seminars. Contbr. articles to profl. jours. Res. dep. sheriff Montgomery County, Tex.; former bd. dirs. Montgomery County Fair Assn., 1978—, Montgomery County Hosp. Dist. Found., Seven Coves Homeowners Assn. Mem. ABA, Tex. Bar Assn., Houston Bar Assn., Houston Outdoor Advtsg. Assn., Tex. Assn. Civil Trial Splsts., Tex. Assn. Bank Counsel, Comml. Real Estate Assn. Montgomery County, Petroleum Club (Houston), Woodlands Country Club, Beta Theta Pi. Republican. Avocations: swimming, tennis, jogging, shooting. Office: Hagerman & Seureau Inc 24800 Interstate 45 Ste 100 Woodlands TX 77386-1987

HAGERTY, ETHAN JAMES, electrical engineer, educator; b. Houston, Jan. 31, 1964; s. Terrence Lee and Marcia (Stevenson) H.; m. Sandra Blaine, Apr. 10, 1994. BSEE, MIT, 1985; MEE, Tex. A&M U., 1989. Registered profl. engr., Tex., Calif. Mgr. electronics divsn. Premier Engring. Co., Fremont, Calif., 1989-92; engr. Wynwood Mfg. Co., Fremont, Calif., 1992-94, WERIK & Assocs., San Diego, 1994—. Author: How to Succeed in a World of Engineering, 1991; contbr. numerous articles to profl. jours. Mem. IEEE, N.Y. Acad. Scis., Phi Kappa Pi. Democrat. Roman Catholic. Avocations: fishing, hunting, biking. Office: WERIK & Assocs 3802 Rosecrans St Ste 901 San Diego CA 92110-3114

HAGEY, WALTER REX, retired banker; b. Hatfield, Pa., July 24, 1909; s. Justus T. and Martha Mabel Hagey; m. Dorothy E. Rosenberger, Oct. 17, 1931; 1 child, Donald C. Grad., Peirce Coll., 1929; student, U. Pa., 1931-36; LLB, La Salle Extension U., 1938; STB, Temple U., 1943; grad., Stonier Grad. Sch. Banking Rutgers U., 1951; LLD, Muhlenberg Coll., 1963. With Fidelity Bank (formerly Fidelity-Phila. Trust Co.), 1929—, asst. sec., 1948—, asst. v.p., 1957-66, v.p., 1966-74. Supply pastor Eastern Pa. Synod Lutheran Ch. Am., 1950-80, treas., 1950-80, now Luth. Synod S.E. Pa.; treas. Luth. Synod Northeastern Pa., 1969-70; pres., dir. Phila. Luth. Social Union; treas. Luth. Laymens Movement for Stewardship of United Luth. Ch., 1959-63; mem. bd., exec. com. Luth. Council in U.S., 1962-74; mem. bds., treas. home missions, inner missions, Christian edn. Eastern Pa. Synod, Luth. Ch. Am., 1950-69; vice chmn. adminstrn. and fin. Luth. Ch. in Am., 1972-78, mem. bd. pensions, 1978-84, v.p. Bd. Am. Missions, 1972-78; bd. dirs., adv. bd. Muhlenberg Med. Center; bd. dirs., chmn. Prosser Found., 1968-89; bd. dirs., treas. Luth. Retirement Homes, 1978-82; mem. com. for investments Luth. Ch. in Am., 1978-82; bd. dirs., sec. Silver Spring-Martin Luther Sch., 1976-89; treas. Bethesda House, 1950-69; treas., registrar Luth. Lay Acad., 1981-96; treas. The Auxiliary-Luth. Theol. Sem. at Phila., 1986-89, The Religious Tercentenary Com., 1982-89. Mem. Am. Inst. Banking, Phila. Estate Planning Coun., Pa. Coun. Chs. (dir. 1954-70), Pa. Soc., Luth. Hist. Soc. Ea. Pa., Men of Mt. Airy Sem. (pres. 1976-86), Pa. Bible Soc. (treas., sec., pres., dir. 1971-95), Rotary, Elm Club (sec. 1951-63), Midday Club, Anglers Club (Phila.). Home: 235 N Washington St Telford PA 18969-1759

HAGFELDT, ANDERS ULF, chemist, educator; b. Norrkoping, Sweden, Feb. 16, 1964; s. Ulf Karl-Gustav and Mona Britt-Marie (Johansson) H.; m. Camelia Mihaela Dumitra-Mic, June 4, 1988; children: Mikael, Rebecka. MS, Uppsala (Sweden) U., 1989, PhD, 1993. Fellow Ecole Poly. Fed. de Lausanne, Lausanne, 1993-94; rsch. asst. Uppsala U., 1994-98, lectr., 1998—; fellow LEAD-Europe, Geneva, Switzerland, 1996—; program sec. Ångstrom Solar Ctr., Uppsala, 1997—; bd. dirs. Cluster Consortium, Uppsala. Contbr. articles to profl. jours.; patentee in field. Recipient Bjurzons premium Uppsala U., 1993, The Benzelius award Royal Soc. Scis., 1995. Avocations: playing the drums, table tennis, sailing, reading. Home: Kattgrind Skuttunge, S-74030 Bjorklinge Uppland, Sweden Office: Uppsala U Dept Phys Chem, Box 532, S-75121 Uppsala Sweden

HÄGG, CLAES, economist, educator; b. Bromma, Stockholm, Sweden, Mar. 10, 1949; s. Gösta and Mariana (Svensson) H. MBA, Stockholm Sch. Econs., 1971, PhD, 1974. Rsch. fellow Stockholm Sch. Econs., 1972-75; from asst. prof. to assoc. prof. Stockholm U., 1975—, sr. rschr., 1993—; chmn. bd. Intectus Inc., Stockholm, 1990—. Author: Stock Valuation, 1989, Real Estate, 1990, Valuation of Firms, 1991, Depreciation Charges and the Rate of Return, 1993, Real Estate Cycles, 1994, The Duration of Real Estate, 1997. Grantee Johnson Found., Stockholm, 1990, Swedish Coun. for Bldg. Rsch., Stockholm, 1993. Mem. Swedish Soc. Econs., Swedish Soc. Real Estate. Avocations: literature, fine art. Office: Stockholm U Sch Bus, 106 91 Stockholm Sweden

HÄGG, GÖRAN MIKAEL, health science researcher; b. Vänersborg, Sweden, Sept. 29, 1946; s. Herbert Karl and Elsa (Fransohn) H.; m. Ingrid Margareta Åslin; children: Ellinor, Helén. MSc, Chalmers U. Tech., Göteborg, Sweden, 1971, PhD, 1991. Rsch. engr. Swedish Rsch. Inst. for Nat. Def., Stockholm, 1971-73, Karolinska Hosp., Solna, Sweden, 1973-77, Nat. Bd. Occpl. Safety and Health, Solna, 1977-87; rsch. engr. Nat. Inst. Occupl. Health, Solna, 1987-91, sr. rschr., 1991-95; sr. rschr. Nat. Inst. for Working Life, Solna, 1996—; assoc. prof. Chalmers U. Tech., 1994; project leader Sven-Project, Stockholm, 1971-73; mng. bd. Seniam Biomed. Project, European Union, 1996-99; presenter in field. Contbr. articles to profl. jours., chpts. to books; patentee event counter. Mem. Nordic Ergonomic Soc., Internat. Soc. Electrophysiology and Kinesiology. Avocations: choral conducting, sailing. Office: Nat Inst Working Life, Programme for Ergonomics, S-11279 Stockholm Sweden

HAGGARD, WILLIAM HENRY, meteorologist; b. Woodbridge, Conn., Nov. 20, 1920; s. Howard Wilcox and Josephine Cecelia (Foley) H.; m. Blanche Woolard, Mar. 21, 1944 (div. May 1967); children: William Henry Jr., Robert H.; m. Martina Wadewitz, Oct. 1, 1967. BS in Physics, Yale U., 1942; cert. in profl. meteorology, MIT, 1942; MS in Meteorology, U. Chgo., 1946; postgrad., Fla. State U., 1958-59. Instr. meteorology N.C. State U., Raleigh, 1946-47; rsch. meteorologist U.S. Weather Bur., 1947-48; forecaster USWB Nat. Airport, 1949-50; instr. U.S. AID, Washington, 1950-51; staff weather rsch. project U.S. Navy, Norfolk, Va., 1951-54; chief adv. svcs. br. U.S. Weather Bur., Washington, 1954-59, asst. chief Office of Plans, 1960-61; dep. dir. Nat. Weather Records Ctr., Asheville, N.C., 1961; dir. Nat. Climatic Ctr., Asheville, 1963-75; pres. Climatol. Cons. Corp., Asheville, 1976-97, v.p., 1998; cons., 1999—; mem. weather com. U.S. Power Squadron, Raleigh, N.C., 1988-98. Contbr. articles to tech. jours., 1947-99. Bd. dirs. ARC, Asheville, 1965-70, United Way, Asheville, 1964-70. Capt. USN, 1942-45, with Res. 1951-54. Recipient Tech. Adminstr. award NOAA, Washington, 1970. Fellow Am. Meteorol. Soc. (cert. cons. meteorologist, bd. dirs. pvt. sector meteorology sect. 1989-92, mem. cert. cons. meteorologist bd. 1983-88), Nat. Coun. Indsl. Meteorologists (pres. 1988-89, bd. dirs. 1987-90, 94-96, sec., treas. 1994-99). Republican. Presbyterian. Avocations: sailing, photography. Office: William H Haggard CCM LLC 150 Shope Creek Rd Asheville NC 28805-9795

HAGGBLOM-AHNGER, ULLA MARJUT, engineering educator; b. Valkeakoski, Finland, May 13, 1959; d. Ingmar Erik and Evi Bertta (Mannila) H.; m. Ane Albert Ahnger, June 29, 1985; children: Erik Albert, Henrik Wilhelm. MSs in Engring., Abo Akademi, Finland, 1984, Dr. Tech., 1998. Rsch. engr. United Paper Mills, Ltd., Finland, 1985-89; lectr. Tampere Polytechnic, Finland, 1989-98; prin. lectr. Tampere Polytechnic, 1999—; presenter in field; cons. CFPA, 1998-99. Contbr. articles to profl. jours. Mem. Finnish Paper Engrs. Assn. Avocations: squash, tennis, alpine skiing. Home: Elianderinkatu 11B7, 33230 Tampere Finland Office: Tampere Polytechnic, POB 21 Teiskontie 33, 33521 Tampere Finland

HAGGERTY, ARTHUR DANIEL, stress and chronic pain management specialist; b. Bklyn., Mar. 25, 1925; s. Arthur Daniel and Sophia Edna (Stendera) H.; m. Asta Constance Gundersen, Sept. 11, 1949 (dec. May 1993); children: Donna, Mark, Lynne, Gayle. BA, L.I. U., Bklyn., 1949; MA, NYU, 1951; PhD, Western U., San Diego, 1953. Lic. psychologist, N.Y.; lic. nursing home adminstr., N.Y. Adminstr. homes for aged and blind St. John's Episcopal Hosp., Bklyn., 1956-73; prof., dir. grad program in health care adminstrn. L.I. U., Greenvale, N.Y., 1973-77; pvt. practice psychologist Boca Raton, Fla., 1977-85; dir. edn. and rsch. Palm Beach chpt. Alzheimer's Assn., Boca Raton, 1986-89; health psychologist Psychiat. and Psychol. Assocs., Atlantis, Fla., 1985-96; CEO Stress and Chronic Pain Mgmt. Sys., East Northport, N.Y., 1996-98; psychol. cons. Grace Med. Group, Bklyn., 1956-58; mem. N.Y. State Bd. Examiners Nursing Home Adminstrn., Albany, 1970-75; cons. in tng. Fla. State Commn. Criminal Justice, Tallahassee, 1982-92; cons. continuing edn. Palm Beach C.C., Lake Worth, Fla., 1982-92. Editor Long Term Care and Health Svcs. Adminstrn. Quar., 1976-80. Sgt. U.S. Army, 1944-46, PTO. Recipient Nat. Edn. award Am. Coll. Nursing Home Adminstrn., Washington, 1978. Fellow Am. Inst. Stress; mem. The Monroe Inst. (prof.), Am. Acad. Experts in Traumatic Stress. Office: Stress & Chronic Pain Mgmt Sys 423 Clay Pitts Rd East Northport NY 11731-3801

HAGGETT, PETER, geographer, researcher; b. Pawlett, Somerset, Eng., Jan. 24, 1933; s. Charles Frederick and Ethel Elizabeth (Haines) H.; m. Brenda Mavis Woodley, July 28, 1956; children: Sarah Bridget, Timothy Ian, Jacqueline Susan, Andrew Graham. BA, Cambridge (Eng.) U., 1954, PhD, 1969, ScD, 1985; DSc (hon.), Durham (Eng.) U., 1989, York U., Can., 1983; Dsc (hon.), Copenhagen U., 1999; LLD, Bristol (Eng.) U., 1986. Asst. lectr. Univ. Coll., London, 1955-57; lectr. Cambridge U., 1957-66; fellow Fitzwilliam Coll., Cambridge, 1963-66; prof. urban and regional geography U. Bristol, 1966-98, prof. emeritus, 1998—, acting vice-chancellor, 1984-85, dir. Inst. of Advanced Studies, 1995-98; chmn. history of medicine com. Wellcome Trust, Eng., 1993—; James J. Hill prof. U. Minn., 1994; Hooker disting. prof. McMaster U., Can., 1996; Erskine vis. lectr. U. Canterbury, New Zealand, 1979. Author: Locational Analysis in Human Geography, 1965, Geography: A Modern Synthesis, 1972 (Prix Internat. de Geographie 1991); co-author: Spatial Diffusion, 1981, Atlas of Disease Distribution, 1988, Island Epidemics, 2000. Mem. Univ. Grants Com., London, 1985-89; mem. Nat. Radiol. Protection Bd., Harwell, Eng., 1986-93; trustee Bristol Mcpl. Charities, 1990-97; bd. govs. Queen Elizabeth's Hosp., Bristol, 1990-97. Decorated comdr. Brit. Empire; recipient Anders Retzius Gold medal Swedish Soc. for Anthropology and Geography, 1994, Cullum medal Am. Geog. Soc., 1969. Fellow Brit. Acad. (v.p. 1995-97), Royal Geog. Soc. (life; Patron's medal 1986), Assn. Am. Geographers (Meritorious Contbn. award 1973). Methodist. Home: 5 Tun Bridge Close, Chew Magna, Avon BS40 8SU, England Office: U Bristol, Dept Geography, Bristol BS8 1SS, England

HĀGGMAN, LARSERIK AUGUST, editor-in-chief; b. Helsinki, Finland, Sept. 6, 1950; s. Erik and Alli (Jansson) H.; m. Pirkko Taipale, May 11, 1979; children: Mattias, Maria, Marika. Polit. journalist NYA Pressen, Finland, 1971-74, Yleisradio, Finland, 1974-83, Hufuudstadsbladet, Finland, 1983-87; corr. Scandinavian New Agencies, Moscow, 1987-90; editor-in-chief Nordic Couns. Monthly, Stockholm, 1990-95, Suomen Silta, Finland, 1995-98; sec. gen. Pohjola-Norden, 1998—. Mem. Finnish Polit. Journalists (chmn 1983-85). Office: Pohjda-Norden, Sibeliuksenkatu 9, 00250 Helsinki Finland

HAGHIGHI, VAHID, airline pilot; b. Teheran, Iran, Nov. 23, 1957; arrived in Sweden, 1976; s. David and Mansoureh (Mohseni) H.; m. Carita Marry-Louis Åkesson (div. 1995); children: Abraham, Madelaine. Grad. flight instrn. program, Stockholm Coll., 1988; cert. capt. B747-200, Pan Am Internat. Flight Acad., Miami, Fla., 1995; cert. capt. B747-400, N.W. Aerospace Tng. Ctr., Mpls., 1996. Nursing asst. Malmö (Sweden) Cmty., 1983-86; flight instr. Malmö Flight Sch., 1987-89; ground flight instr. various schs. Sweden, 1985-95; airline pilot Malmö Aviation Airlines, 1989—. Translator (Swedish to Perisan and English to Persian): Rules and Regulations, 1983, Aviation Metrology, 1983, Navigation, 1984, Aerodynamics, 1984, Weight and Balance, 1985, How Does an Aircraft Work?, 1985, Aviation Communication, 1986. Mem. Swedish Pilots Assn. Avocations: swimming, tennis. Home: Rudeboksv 115, 226 55 Lund Sweden Office: Malmö Aviation Airlines, Malmö Sturup Airport, Malmö Sweden

HAGI, GHEORGE, retired professional soccer player; b. Sarcele, Romania, Feb. 25, 1965. Defender Sportul Studentesc Football Club, Romania, Steaua Bucharest Football Club, Romania; winner European Super Cup, 1987; defender Real Madrid Football Club, Spain, 1990-91, Brescia Football Club, Italy, 1992-93, Barcelona Football Club, Spain, 1994-96; defender, capt. Romanian Nat. Team, 1984—; ret. Internat. Soccer, 1998; now defender Galatasaray Football Club, Istanbul, Turkey, 1996—. Named Best Player of Century, Romania, 1999. Office: Hasnun Galip Sokak N 7-9-11, Beyoglu, TR-80700 Istanbul Turkey*

HAGIHARA, AKIHITO, epidemiologist, educator; b. Ichijima, Hyogo, Japan, Feb. 21, 1954; s. Katsumi Sakamoto and Kaoru Okutani; m. Naoko Hagihara, Mar. 17, 1982; children: Seita, Kou-hey. LLB, Tohoku U., 1979; M in Med. Sci., Osaka U., 1989, MD, 1993; MPH, U. Mich., 1993. Legal staff Kansai Electric Power Co., Osaka, Japan, 1979-82, 84-87; rschr. Japan Energy Law Rsch. Inst., Tokyo, 1982-84; rsch. fellow Osaka U., 1993-95; asst. prof. Kyushu U., Fukuoko, Japan, 1995-99, assoc. prof., 1999—; assoc. prof.; dir. Health Sci. Assn., Fukuoka, 1998, Japan Soc. Health Promotion, Fukuoka, 1999—. Author: Communication in Health, 1998; contbr. articles to profl. jours. Grantee Japan Ministry Edn., 1998, Japan Ministry Health and Welfare, 1998. Mem. Japan Pub. Health Assn., Japan Assn. Hygiene. Avocations: mountaineering, gardening, golf, reading. Office: Kyushu Univ Sch Medicine, 3-1-1 Maidashi, Fukuoka 812-8582, Japan

HAGIWARA, KEIJI, pediatrician; b. Tenri, Nara, Japan, Jan. 15, 1948; s. Shiro and Fumie Hagiwara; m. Sachie Nishizima, Feb. 10, 1978; children: Fumito, Tasuku, Ryo. MD, Yamaguchi U., Ube, Japan, 1975, PhD, 1985. Med. lic., Japan. Intern Yamaguchi U. Hosp., Ube, 1975; pediatrician Yamaguchi Ctrl. Hosp., Hofu, Japan, 1976-79; sr. ho. staff Yamaguchi U. Sch. Medicine, Ube, 1979-87, lectr. dept. pediat., 1987-97, vice dir. dept. pediat., 1988-97; pediatrician Kami-Ube Pediat. Clinic, Ube, 1997—; guest rschr. Cath. U. Louvain, Brussels, 1985-87; health cons. The Japanese Sch. Brussels, 1985-87; health cons. Ministry Fgn. Affairs, 1987. Cons. Kotoshiba Elem. Sch., Ube, 1997—. Recipient Konishi award, 1989; sci. grantee Ministry Edn. Japan, Tokyo, 1989, Ministry Edn. and Culture Japan, Tokyo, 1997. Mem. Am. Soc. for Microbiology, Japan Pediat. Soc., Japan Med. Assn. E-mail: keijiha@mocha.ocn.ne.jp. Fax: 81-836-29-1156. Home: Tokiwadai 1-16-16-3, Ube 755-0097, Japan Office: Kami-Ube Pediat Clinic, Tokiwadai 1-20-2, Ube 755-0097, Japan

HAGIWARA, NAOTO, materials scientist, researcher; b. Tokyo, Aug. 7, 1968; m. Hiroko Matsuoka, May 23, 1998. B in Engring., Keio U., Yokohama, Japan, 1991, M in Engring., 1993. Researcher Tokyo Gas Co., Ltd., Tokyo, 1993—. Contbr. articles to profl. jours. Recipient Excellent Paper award Japan Gas Assn., 2000; Rsch. grantee Kato Sci. Found., 1992. Mem. Japan Soc. Mech. Engrs., Iron and Steel Inst. Japan, Soc. Material Sci. Japan (Excellent Study and Presentation award 1998). Avocations: classical music, oboe. Office: Tokyo Gas Co Ltd, 1-16-25 Shibaura Minato-ku, Tokyo 105-0023, Japan

HAGIWARA, NATHANIEL TSUTOMU, educator; b. Musashino, Tokyo, Japan, Jan. 24, 1932; s. Noboru and Shizue H.; m. Shigeko Kanh; children: Hiroko, Fumiko. MA, St. Paul U., 1959; PhD in Lit. (hon.), Cambridge (Eng.) U., 1995. Asst. prof. Senshu U., Tamaku, Kawasaki, Japan, 1966-72, prof., 1972—; vis. fellow Yale U., 1973-74; lectr. in field; vis. fellow Yale U., 1973-74. Author: A Study of Nathaniel Hawthorne, 1981, The Higher Education for New Age, 1983, Handbook for Language Laboratory, 1986, Pleasure Learning-Suggestopedia, 1997, American Folklore-Dark and Light, 1999. Councilor Adv. Coun. Met. Devel. Project Iruma City, 1993—; examiner Soc. Testing English Proficiency, Shinjuku, Tokyo, 1972—. Senshu U. fellow, 1988; Hon. PhD in Lit. 1995, Cambridge Eng.; Internat. Order of Merit, Internat. Biogral. Cent. Mem. Lang. Lab. Assn. Japan (dir. 1994—), Nathaniel Hawthorne Soc. Japan (pres. 1993-95, 1997-99), Japan Assn. Suggestopedia (pres. 1993-95, 1997-99), Pragmatics Assn. Japan (bd. dirs. 1994—), Acad. Grand Officer (lit.), Accademia Internat., Academia Del Verbano. Epsicopalian. Avocations: gardening, fishing, pen and ink drawing. Home: 4-20-6 Kyonan-cho, Musashino-shi, Tokyo 1800023, Japan Office: Senshu U, 2-1-1 Higashi-mita Tama-ku, Kawasaki-shi 214, Japan

HAGIWARA, TAKASHI, multimedia company executive; b. Tokyo, June 3, 1956; s. Yasuhiro and Masako Hagiwara; m. Fumiko Izumoto, May 19, 1985; children: Kosuke, Kenta, Nozomi. BA of Bus. Adminstrn., Sophia U., Tokyo, 1980. Legal staff Sanyo Electric Trading Co., Ltd., Osaka, Japan, 1980-82, sales staff, 1982-87; own equipment mfg. coord. Sanyo Electric Inc., Chgo., 1987-92; coord. new bus. Sanyo Electric Trading Co., Ltd., Osaka, 1992-93; sr. sales staff Sanyo Electric Co., Ltd., Oizumi, Japan, 1993-97; coord. comm. products Sanyo Electric Co., Ltd., Daito, Japan, 1997-98, U.K. sales coord., 1998-99; procurement coord. Sanyo U.K. Sales Ltd., Hertfordshire, U.K., 1999—. Mem. Kwansai Yacht Club. Avocation: sailing. Office: Sanyo Europe LTD, Sanyo House Otterspool Way, Otterspoolway Watford Herts WD2 8JX, England

HAGLAND, JAN RAGNAR, philology educator; b. Haugesund, Norway, Mar. 3, 1943; s. Johannes Johannesen and Agnes Karine H. PhD, U. Trodheim, Norway, 1985. Asst. master United World Coll., Glamorgam, Wales, 1969-70; univ. lectr. U. Trondheim, Norway, 1970-77; sr. lectr., 1977-86, prof., 1986—; vis. prof. U. Chgo., 1991, U. Coll., London, 1993, U. Iceland, 1993, St. Olaf Coll., 1991, Ecole pratique des Hautes Etudes de la Sorbonne, Paris, 2000. Author: National Government and Language Norms, 1986, Runic Finds: Sources for the History of Trade, 1986, The Frostathinglaw, 1994, Njalssaga, 1996. Dean Humanities U. Trondheim, 1987-90; chmn. Norwegian Assn. Mother Tongue Tchrs., Norway, 1982-83. Recipient Rsch. award Royal Norwegian Acad. Sci. and Letters, 1985. Mem. Royal Norwegian Acad. Sci. and Letters, Norwegian Acad. Lang. and Lit., Norwegian Assn. Lit. Translators. Avocations: sports, skiing, bicycling, hiking. Office: Norwegian U Sci and Tech, N-7491 Trondheim Norway

HAGMÜLLER, EGBERT, surgeon; b. Radolfzell, Germany, Nov. 20, 1955; s. Josef and Rita (Deggelmann) H.; m. Karola Jäkle, Sept. 11, 1982. Student, U. Bochum, 1975-77, U. Heidelberg, Germany, 1977-91; MD, U. Heidelberg, Germany, 1981, PhD, 1992; postgrad., U. Freiburg, 1980-81. Cert. vascular surgery, abdominal surgery, thoracic surgery, minimal invasive surgery, endocrine surgery. Intern Akadem Lehrkrankenhaus Singen, U. Freiburg, 1980-81; asst. physician Surg. U. Clinic Mannheim, U. Heidelberg, 1982-91, asst. med. dir., 1991-95, dep. med. dir., 1996-97; chefarzt Chirurgie Krkhs am Plattenwald Bad Friedrichshall, 1997—; prof. U. Heidelberg, 1999; cons. German Cancer Rsch. Instn., Heidelberg, 1991—, German Soc. Surgery, Munchen, 1991—, German Soc. Vascular Surgery, Munchen, 1991—. Contbr. articles to profl. jours. Mem. German Soc. Surgery (reisestipendium 1994), Internat. Soc. Surgery, Am. Assn. Cancer Rsch. Roman Catholic. Home: Donauschwabenstrasse 21, 74206 Bad Wimpten Germany Office: Surg Clin, Krkhs am Plattenwald, 74177 Bad Friedrichshall Germany

HAGOORT, JACQUES, physicist, educator; b. Woerden, The Netherlands, Apr. 8, 1942; d. Leendert Jacob and Gijsbertha Van Dijk; m. Wilhelmina Greve, Nov. 24, 1967; children: Koert, Thijs, Chiel. MS, Delft U., The Netherlands, 1966; PhD, Delft U., 1981. Rsch. physicist Shell, Netherlands, 1967-76; sr. staff reservoir engr. Shell Canada, 1976-78; group leader Shell Rsch., 1978-83; cons. Hagoort Assocs., The Netherlands, 1983—; prof. Delft U., The Netherlands, 1988—. Author: (book) Introduction to Gas Reservoir Engineering, 1988. Recipient Rossiter Raymond award, 1974, Lester C. Uren award, 1998. Mem. Soc. Petroleum Engrs., Royal Dutch Inst. Engrs. Home: Guldo Gezellelaan 90, 2611 PX Delft The Netherlands Office: Hagoort & Assocs, Gasthuislaan 51, 2611 PX Delft The Netherlands

HAGRUP, KNUT, aviation consultant; b. Bergen, Norway, Nov. 13, 1913; s. Lie-Svendsen and Ebba (Hagrup) H.; m. Esther Skaugen, Sept. 22, 1944 (dec. 1975); children: Vivi, Bente. Math dgree, 1933; grad., Coll. Royal Norwegian Air Force, 1936; Civil Engr., Darmstadt U., 1940; Dr. Laws (hon.), Pacific Luth. U., 1978; Sc. Dr. (hon.), Northrop U., 1978; Dr. econs., Hochschule fur Verkerswesen, Dresden, Germany, 1979; Dr. tech., Stockholm U., 1980. Chief technician hqrs. Eng. Dept. Royal Norwegian Air Force, 1942; chief engr. Norwegian Civil Aeros. Bd., Oslo, 1945, Scandinavian Airlines Sys., Stockholm, 1946; v.p. ops., 1951-56, v.p. engring., 1956-60, v.p. tech. and ops., 1960-62, exec. v.p. tech. and ops., 1962-69, pres., CEO, 1969-79; chmn. bd. Saab-Fairchild Airliner program, Stockholm-N.Y.C., 1980-85; cons., dir. various Scandinavian industries; dir. Hennes & Mauritz, Stockholm, Saab-Scania; cons., prof., trustee Northrop U., L.A., 1980-90; chmn. commn. air transport Internat. C. of C., Paris, 1969-85; chmn. IATA, 1974-75; Assn. European Airlines, 1975-76, chmn. Author: La Bataille du Transport Aerien, 1978, Die Heutige Weltluftfahrt, 1979, How the Aerospace Industry of Western Europe Will Survive, 1981. Served with Royal Norwegian Air Force, 1940-45. Decorated Norwegian war medal, Def. medal, Haakon VII's medal, comdr. No. Star (Sweden), Order St. Olav (Norway), grand officer Orange-Nassau (Netherlands), comdr. Legion d'Honneur (France), Brit. Def. medal, comdr. Order White Elephant (Thailand). Fellow Brit. Aero Soc.; mem. Royal Airforce Club. Home: Rte de Clémenty 37, 1260 Nyon Switzerland

HAGSTEN, IB, animal scientist, livestock consultant; b. Assens, Denmark, May 18, 1943; came to U.S., 1971, naturalized, 1980; s. Kresten and Marie (Jakobsen) H.; m. Patricia Ellen Dettman, July 13, 1968; children: Ellen Marie, Scot (dec.), Lisa R. BS, Bygholm Landbrugskole, Horsens, Denmark, 1965; MS, Royal Danish Agr. U., Copenhagen, 1971, Purdue U., 1973; PhD, Purdue U., 1975. Cert. animal scientist; diplomate Am. Coll. Animal Nutrition. Farm laborer, foreman various livestock farms, Denmark,

Eng., Germany, Can., 1958-65; tchg. asst. Royal Danish Agr. U., 1969-70; rsch. assoc. Nat. Danish Rsch. Found., Copenhagen, 1971; cons. nutritionist M.D. King Milling Co., Pittsfield, Ill., 1976-77; acting product mgr. Am. Hoechst Corp., Somerville, N.J., 1978, tech. specialist, 1977-83; profl. sales rep. Hoechst Roussel Agri-Vet. Co., Gladstone, Mo., 1983-89, tech. svc. specialist, 1989-90, sr. profl. svc. specialist, 1990-98; pres. Hagsten Enterprises, Internat., livestock cons. svc., Kansas City, Mo., 1999—; cons. Shell Farm, Inc., Ørum, Denmark, 1970-71, Agri-Bus. Tng. and Devel., Inc., Roswell, Ga., 1979-95, Nat. Renderer's Assn., Hong Kong, 1989, USDA Trade Mission, Moldova, 1995, HRVet-Asia Workshop, Thailand, 1998, Hoechst Asia, Bangkok, 1998, employee-tng., Ukraine & Moldova, 2000; adj. prof. Rutgers U., New Brunswick, N.J., 1981-84, U. Mo., Columbia, 1990-97; pres. Personal Growth Alternatives, 1982—; cert. assessor environ. assistance program Nat. Pork Prodrs. Coun. Author: Energy Metabolism Evaluations, 1971; contbr. articles to profl. jours. and popular publs. Bd. dirs. MACOS handicapped support group, Macomb, Ill., 1976-77; co-chair Cmty. Hunger Walks (CROP), Western N.J., 1978-82; mem. family curriculum bd. Lopatcong Twp. Sch., Phillipsburg, N.J., 1982; vice moderator Pilgrim Presbyn. Ch., Phillipsburg, 1980-83, elder, 1979-83, Gashland Presbyn. Ch., Gladstone, 1990-93; regional exec. bd. mem. United Marriage Encounter, Mo., Kans., 1983-95; bd. dirs. Gashland Christian Presch., 1991-93; mem. Core of Advocates, Coll. Vet. Medicine Kans. State U.; bd. dirs. Heartland Presbyn. Pro-Life, 1993—, pres., 1999-2000. Sgt. Danish King's Royal Guard, 1959-61. Mem. Danish Soc. Animal Sci., Am. Soc. Agrl. Cons. (bd. dirs. 1978-81, 92-94, 95-97, chmn. ethics com. 1992-94, sec.-treas. 1990—, Disting. Svc. award 1980), Am. Soc. Agrl. Cons. Internat. (charter), Am. Coll. Animal Nutrition (charter, diplomate), Nat. Feed Ingredient Assn., Am. Registry Profl. Animal Scientists (chmn. ethics) com. 1982-85, cert.), Greater Kansas City Scandinavian Club (bd. dirs. 1992-96). Republican. Avocations: people, gardening, travel, reading. Home and Office: 7212 N Woodland Ave Kansas City MO 64118-2263

HAGSTROM, DAVID ALAN, educational consultant, educator; b. Oak Park, Ill., Apr. 28, 1935; s. Clarence Edward and Frances (Jackson) H.; m. Nancy Booth (div. 1985); children: Susan Janan, Bruce David; m. Karen Noordhoff, May 11, 1985. BA, Grinnell Coll., 1957; MA Teaching, Harvard U., 1958; EdD, U. Ill., 1966. Cert. tchr., adminstr., Ill., Wis., Alaska. Tchr., sch. adminstr. Evanston (Ill.) Pub. Schs., 1958-75; prof. Nat. Coll. Edn., Evanston, 1975-83, U. Alaska, Juneau, Fairbanks, 1983-91; dir. Alaska Ctr. for Ednl. Leadership, Fairbanks, 1992-93; co-owner New Viewpoint Educators, 1990—; prof. Lewis and Clark Coll., Portland, Oreg., 1995—. Contbr. articles to profl. ednl. jours. Recipient Next Century Schs. award Nabisco Found., 1990, A+ Educator award U.S. Dept. Edn., 1992. Mem. ASCD. Democrat. Episcopalian. Avocations: gardening, running, camping, assisting people to create a sense of community in the workplace. Home: 4133 NE 20th Ave Portland OR 97211-5738

HAGUE, WILLIAM JEFFERSON, British politician; b. Rotherham, United Kingdom, Mar. 26, 1961; s. Timothy Nigel and Stella (Jefferson) H.; m. Ffion Jenkins, 1997. Degree in politics, econ., philosophy, Magdalen Coll., Oxford, 1982; MBA, INSEAD, 1986. Mgmt. cons. McKinsey & Co., London, 1985-88; mem. Parliament House of Commons, Westminster, England, 1989—; mem. for Richmond, Yorkshire; parliamentary pvt. sec. Chancellor of the Exchequer, 1990-93; undersec. of state Dept. Social Security, England, 1993-94, min. of state for social security and disabled people, 1994-95, sec. of state for Wales, 1995-97; leader Conservative Party, Leader of the Opposition, 1997—. Pres. Oxford Union Oxford U., 1981, Conservative Assn., 1981; chmn. Young Conservatives, South Yorkshire, England, 1977-79. Mem. Beefsteak Club. Mem. Ch. of England. Avocations: reading, walking, travel, judo. Office: House of Commons, London SW1A 0AA, England

HAHN, FRANK HORACE, economics educator; b. Berlin, Germany, Apr. 26, 1925; s. Arnold and Maria (Katz) H.; m. Dorothy Salter, 1946. BSc in Econs., London, 1945, PhD, 1951; MA, Cambridge (Eng.) U., 1960; D in Social Scis. (hon.), Birmingham (Eng.) U., 1981; DLitt (hon.), U. East Anglia, Norwich, 1984; Doctor honoris causa, U. Strasbourg, 1984; DSc in Econs. (hon.), London, 1985; D (hon.), U. York, 1991; LittD (hon.), U. Leicester, 1993; PhD (hon.), U. Athens, 1993; doctor honoris causa, De L'Univ. Paris X, Nanterre, 1999. Lectr., reader math. econs. Birmingham U., 1948-60; lectr. econs. Cambridge U., 1960-66; prof. econs. London Sch. Econs., 1967-72, prof., 1972-92, prof. emeritus, 1992; prof. ordinario U. Siena, 1989—; hon. fellow London Sch. Econs., 1989; fellow Churchill Coll., Cambridge, 1960—. Author: General Competitive Analysis, 1971, (with K.J. Arrow) The Share of Wages in the National Income, 1972, Money and Inflation, 1982, Equilibrium and Macroeconomics, 1984, Money, Growth and Stability, 1985, (with Robert Solow) A Critical Essay on Modern Macroeconomic Theory, 1995; editor: The Economics of Missing MArkets, Information, and Games, 1989; co-editor: (with Ben Friedman) Handbook of Monetary Economics, 1990; mng. editor Rev. Econ. Studies, 1965-68; assoc. editor Jour. Econ. Theory, 1971-76. Recipient Palacky gold medal Czechoslovak Acad. Scis., 1991. Fellow Brit. Acad., Econometric Soc. (pres. 1968-69), NAS (fgn. assoc. 1988), Am. Acad. Arts and Scis. (hon.), Am. Econ. Assn. (hon.), Royal Econ. Soc. (pres. 1986-89), Brit. Assn. Advancement Sci. (pres. sect. F 1990).

HAHN, HOH-GYU, chemistry researcher; b. Daejeon, ChungNam, Korea, Sept. 14, 1952; s. Meen-Hee and Myung-Jae (Cho) H.; m. Pyung-Sook Kim, Nov. 9, 1980; children: Soo-Jin, Ye-Jee. BS, Han Nam U., Deajeon, 1976; MS, Korea Advanced Inst. Sci., Seoul, 1985, PhD, 1989. Rschr. Korea Inst. Sci. and Tech., Seoul, 1978-85, sr. rschr., 1985-92, prin. rschr., 1992—; cons. Young-Jin Co., Ulsan, Korea, 1992-93, Dong-Oh Chem. Co., Ulsan, Korea, 1992—; lectr. chemistry dept. U. Seoul, 1992—. Author: Practice of Fundamental IR, NMR, Mass Spectroscopy, 1993; patentee in field. Sgt. Korean Army, 1976-78. Recipient Encouragement of Rsch. award Korea Sci. and Engring. Found., Daejeon, 1989-90; named 1st Agrl. Devel. Scientist, Ministry Agrl., Seoul, 1998; Linton scholar Han Nam U., Daejeon, 1973-76; post-doctoral fellow Oreg. State U., Corvallis, 1989-90. Mem. Internat. Soc. Heterocyclic Chemistry, Korean Chem. Seoul, Korean Soc. Pesticide Sci. Roman Catholic. Avocations: flower planting, beekeeping. Home: Jugong Apt 615-208, Sangil-dong Kangdong-ku, Seoul 134-796, Korea Office: Korea Inst Sci & Tech, Hawolkocdong 39-1, Seoul 136-791, Korea

HAHN, JEONG SANG, hydrogeologist, educator, consultant; b. Taeku, Republic of Korea, Dec. 11, 1939; s. Yong Jik Hahn and Suk Im Kim; m. Wha Ja Yoon; children: Chan, Hyok. BS, Seoul Nat. U., 1964, MS, 1978; PhD, Korea U., Seoul, 1985. Cert. groundwater profl. Assn. Groundwater Scientists and Engrs.; cert. profl. engr. in applied geology, Korea, cert. profl. engr. in geophysics, Korea. Sect. chief Han River Basin Survey Team Korea Water Resources Corp., Seoul, 1966-73; project mgr. IDA Tube Well Project, Dhaka, Bangladesh, 1973-74; exec. mgr. Jung Ang Devel. Co., Ltd., Seoul, 1974-76; exec. dir. Hankook Kun Up Constrn. Co., Seoul, 1976-78; pres. Hans Engring. Co., Ltd., Seoul, 1980-95; vis. prof. dept. geology Yonsei U., Seoul, 1995—. Author: (textbooks) Groundwater, 1983, Groundwater Hydrology, 1988, Groundwater Environment and Pollution, 1998, Risk Assessment of Contaminated Soil and Groundwater, 1998. Dir. Asian-Pacific NGO, Seoul, 1995—; tech. advisor Nat. Environ. Preservation Com., Ministry of Environment, Seoul, 1990—, Met. Landfill Assn., Kimpo, Kyong Ki-Do, 1993—; mem. Nat. River Mgmt. Com., Ministry of Constrn. and Transp., Seoul, 1995—. Served with Korean mil., 1964-66. Recipient Best Paper Acad. award Geologic Soc. of Korea, Seoul, 1988, Indsl. Medal prize Pres. of Korea, Seoul, 1993. Mem. Nat. Groundwater Assn., Korean Soc. Groundwater Environment (pres.), Korea Water Resources Assn. (bd. dirs.). Avocations: golf, Chinese checkers. E-mail: geohans@chollian.net. Fax: 82-2-5443831. Home: 304-1106 Family Apt, 150 Moonjeong-dong, Songpa-ku Republic of Korea

HAHN, KLAUS JÜRGEN, pharmaceutical research executive; b. Hindenburg, Germany, June 1, 1936; arrived in Japan, 1996; s. Erwin Paul and Gerda Dorothea (Ludwig) H.; m. Marie-Luise Homann, Oct. 10, 1965 (dec. Nov. 1989); m. Juliane Elisabeth Wohlwender, Mar. 27, 1991. Med. examination, U. Bonn, Germany, 1962; MD, U. Bonn, 1963; PhD, U. Heidelberg, Germany, 1973; extraordinary prof., U. Heidelberg, 1975. Intern Clemens August Hosp., Bitburg, Germany, 1962-64; intern Univ. Hosp., Heidelberg, 1964-65, asst. lectr. internal medicine, 1966-74; fellow in clin. pharmacology U. Mich., Ann Arbor, 1965-66; v.p. R&D Knoll AG BASF AG, Ludwigshafen, Germany, 1975-96; sr. mng. and representative dir. R&D Hokuriku Seiyaku Co. Ltd., Katsuyama, Japan, 1996—; cons. WHO, Geneva, 1964-68; pres. Soc. Pharm. Physicians, Germany, 1977-81; chmn. Internat. Fedn. Assns. Pharm. Physicians Symposium, Munich, 1980. Coauthor: Internal Medicine 1st-6th edit., 1984, Praktische Medizin von A-Z, 1993; contbr. Ullmann's Encyclopedia of Industrial Chemistry, 4th edit., 1984. Grantee in clin. pharmacology WHO, 1965; fellow faculty pharm. medicine Royl Coll. Physicians U.K., Edinburg, Glasgow, London, 1996. Office: Hokuriku Seiyaku Co Ltd, 1-1 Inokuchi 37, Katsuyama-shi Fukui 9118555, Japan

HAHN, LEWIS EDWIN, philosopher, retired educator; b. Swenson, Tex., Sept. 26, 1908; s. Edwin D. and Ione (Brewster) H.; m. Elizabeth Herring, June 30, 1932 (dec. 1991); children: Helen Elizabeth, Mary, Sharon; m. Mary Anne King, Sept. 1, 1992; children: Michael H. King, Mary Susan King. BA, U. Tex., 1929, MA, 1929; PhD, U. Calif., 1939. Tchg. fellow U. Calif., 1931-34; from instr. philosophy to assoc. prof. U. Mo., Columbia, 1936-49; prof. philosophy Washington U., St. Louis, 1949-63, chmn. dept., 1949-63; from assoc. dean to dean Washington U. Grad. Sch. Arts and Scis., St. Louis, 1953-63; rsch. prof. philosophy So. Ill. U., Carbondale, 1963-77; prof. emeritus So. Ill. U., 1977—; vis. prof., editor So. Ill. U. Libr. of Living Philosophers, 1981—; disting. vis. prof. Baylor U., 1977-80; Mem. U.S. Nat. Commn. UNESCO, 1965-67; vis. lectr. Princeton U., 1947. Author: A Contextualistic Theory of Perception, 1942, (with others) Value: A Cooperative Inquiry, 1949, Enhancing Cultural Interflow Between East & West, 1998; co-author: Guide to the Works of John Dewey, 1970; editor: Library of Living Philosophers, 1981—; co-editor: The Philosophy of Gabriel Marcel, 1984, The Philosophy of W.V. Quine, 1986, expanded edit., 1998, The Philosophy of G.H. von Wright, 1989, Charles D. Tenney's Discovery of Discovery, 1991; editor: The Philosophy of Charles Hartshorne, 1991, The Philosophy of A.J. Ayer, 1992, The Philosophy of Paul Ricoeur, 1995, The Philosophy of Paul Weiss, 1995, The Philosophy of Hans-Georg Gadamer, 1997, The Philosophy of Roderick M. Chisholm, 1997, The Philosophy of P.F. Strawson, 1998, The Philosophy of Donald Davidson, 1999. Recipient Disting. Svc. award So. Ill. U., 1993. Fellow AAAS; mem. Am. Philos. Assn. (exec. bd. 1950-54, 70-73, chmn. com. placement, available pers. 1951-54, sec.-treas. West divsn. 1949-51, sec.-treas. 1960-66, com. on internat. coop. 1967-80, history com. 1993), AAUP, Am. Soc. Aesthetics, S.W. Philos. Soc. (pres. 1955), Mo. Philos. Assn. (pres. 1949-50), So. Soc. for Philosophy and Psychology (pres. 1958-59), Ill. Philosophy Conf. (pres. 1969-71), Soc. Advancement Am. Philosophy (Herbert W. Schneider award 1998), Phi Beta Kappa. Home: 1951 N Reed Station Rd Carbondale IL 62901-7136 Office: So Ill U Dept Philosophy Carbondale IL 62901-4505

HAHN, SONG-YOP, electrical engineer, educator; b. Bukchung, Korea, Mar. 14, 1939; s. Duk-Hyung Hahn and Eul-Sum Park; m. Jung-Ok Choi, Oct. 22, 1967; children: Hekyung, Youngae, Jusun, Taekyung. BS, Seoul (Korea) Nat. U., 1963, MS, 1967; PhD, Inst. Nat. Poly. Lorraine, Nancy, France, 1979. Chartered elec. engr., U.K. From lectr. to prof. Seoul Nat. U., 1968—, head dept. elec. engring., 1981-83, assoc. dean coll. engring., 1983-85, head sch. elec. engring., 1992-94, dean coll. engring., 1995-97; vis. prof. Inst. Nat. Poly. Grenoble, France, 1985-86; dir. Ctr. Advanced Design Tech., Seoul, 1993—; bd. dirs. Korea Elec. Power Corp., Seoul, Korea Elec. Rsch. Inst., Changwon. Contbr. articles to profl. jours. Recipient Order Civil Merit-Dongbaeg medal, Rep. Korea, 1996, Univ. Lead award Soc. Mfg. Engrs., 1996, Presdl. award in engring. Rep. Korea, 1999. Fellow Inst. Elec. Engrs. U.K.; mem. Korean Inst. Elec. Engrs. (pres. 1994-95), Korea Acad. Sci. Tech., Nat. Acad. Engring. Korea, Korea Inst. Applied Superconductivity and Cryogenics (pres. 1998—), Korean Soc. Engring. Edn. and Tech. Transfer (pres. 1999-2000). Avocations: classical music, football, go, tennis, skating. Home: Jamsil Songpa, Asian Village Apt 8-1201, Seoul 138 227, Korea Office: Seoul Nat U, Kwanak PO Box 34, Seoul 151742, Korea

HAHN, TALIA ETHELEA, cell biologist; b. N.Y.C., Jan. 1, 1942; arrived in Israel, 1959; d. Charles and Rose (Katz) Cohen; m. Oleg Hahn, Apr. 5, 1971; 1 child, Dina Portugal. BSc, Bar-Ilan U., Ramat-Gan, Israel, 1964, MSc, 1968; PhD, Weizmann Inst. Sci., Rehovot, Israel, 1987. Bacteriologist Assaf Harofe Med. Ctr., Tel-Aviv, 1964-66; immunology rsch. scientist Kaplan Med. Ctr., Rehovot, 1969-83, dir. Pediat. Rsch. Inst., 1988—; lectr. Hebrew U. Med. Sch., Jerusalem, 1994—. Contbr. articles to profl. jours.; inventor in field. Mem. Com. for Advancement of Rights for Handicapped Women, Com. for Establishment of Gynecological Svcs. for Handicapped Women, Tel-Aviv and Jerusalem, 1995—. Recipient Award for Most Innovative Work on Quinolones, Rhone-Poulenc Sante, 1989. Mem. Internat. Union of Immunol. Socs., Soc. for Leukocyte Biology, Internat. Soc. for Interferon and Cytokine Rsch. Jewish. Avocations: reading, music. Home: 1 Laskov St, 76566 Rehovot Israel Office: Pediatric Rsch Inst, Kaplan Med Ctr, 76100 Rehovot Israel

HAHN, THOMAS JOONGHI, accountant; b. Seoul, Korea, Apr. 12, 1955; came to U.S., 1979; s. Sang Jin and Seong Soon (Hong) H.; m. Linda Young Kim, May 26, 1984; children: Gina K., Michael J., Catherine S. BS, U. Md., 1982. CPA, CFP. Jr. acct. VerKenteren, Anerbach & Olson, CPAs, Silver Springs, Md., 1982-83; sr. acct. Chough, Oh & Co., CPAs, Silver Springs, 1983-85; ptnr. Lee & Hahn, CPAs, Falls Church, Va., 1985-87; prin. Thomas J. Hahn, CPA, Falls Church, 1987—; bd. dirs. STG, Inc., Fairfax, Va. Host weekly radio talk show, 1996—. Recipient Svc. award Posung H. S. Alumni Assn. of Greater Washington Area, 1992. Mem. AICPA, Va. Soc. CPAs. Roman Catholic. Office: Thomas J Hahn CPA 7639 Leesburg Pike 1st Fl Falls Church VA 22043-2520

HÄHNEL, ROLAND, biochemistry educator, consultant; b. Dresden, Saxony, Germany, Oct. 5, 1931; arrived in Australia, 1961; s. Willy Emil and Johanna Louise (Nagel) H.; m. Martha Erika Thoss, Mar. 31, 1955; children: Claudia, Isabel. Diplom-chemiker, U. Halle-Wittenberg, 1955, Dr. Rer. Nat., 1958. Clin. biochemist dept. dermatology U. Halle, Saale, Germany, 1955-59; clin. biochemist dept. ophthalmology U. Frankfurt, Germany, 1959-60; rsch. fellow Queen Elizabeth II Coronation Gift Fund Trust, Perth, West Australia, 1961-68; sr. lectr. U. Western Australia, Nedlands, 1968-72, assoc. prof., 1972-97, sr. hon. rsch. fellow Ctr. Molecular Immunology and Instrum., 1998—; cons. biochemist St. John of God Hosp., Subiaco, W.A., 1989-94; clin. staff scientist Sir Charles Gairdner Hosp., Nedlands, 1989—; cons. clin. biochemist Royal Perth Hosp., 1990—; treas. Immunogenetics Rsch. Found., 1998—. Contbr. articles to profl. jours. Pres. West Australian Goethe Soc., Perth, 1975—; mem. State Adv. Panel for Translating & Interpreting, Perth, 1987-90; mem. Musica Viva Br. Com., 1998-99. Recipient Bundesverdienstkreuz 1st Class, Pres. Fed. Republic of Germany, 1982, 97; Internat. fellow USPHS, 1968, Yamagiwa-Yoshida fellow Internat. Union Against Cancer, 1978. Fellow Australian Assn. Clin. Biochemists (edn. rep. 1981-83, br. pres. 1984-85). Avocations: playing the piano, travel, reading, gardening. Home: 27 Templetonia Crescent, City Beach 6015, Australia Office: U Western Australia Ctr, Molecular Immunology Instru, Nedlands 6009, Australia

HAI, BAI YU, acoustical engineer, researcher; b. Siping, China, Apr. 25, 1941; s. Jun Feng Bai and Gui Lan Ma; m. Yu Zhen Zhao, Nov. 1, 1969; children: Bai Yun, Bai Yang. BS in Physics, Jilin U., Changchun, China, 1965. Rschr. Inst. Acoustics Academia Sinica, Beijing, 1965-71, Inst. Physics Academia Sinica, Beijing, 1972-79; vis. scholar Max-Planck Inst. Solid State Physics, Stuttgart, Germany, 1980-82; assoc. prof. physics Inst. Acoustics Academia Sinica, 1983—; vis. scholar Hong Kong City Poly., 1990. Contbr. articles to profl. jours. Recipient scholarship Max-Planck Inst., 1980-82. Fellow Acoustic Soc. China; mem. N.Y. Acad. Scis., Signal Processing Soc. Avocations: literature, art, music. Office: Academia Sinica Inst Acoust, 17 Zhongguancun St, Beijing 100080, China

HAI, SYED M. ABDUL, executive; b. Kharkuda, India, May 5, 1943; s. Syed Mushtaq and Khatoon Ahmed; m. Noor Fatima, Apr. 14, 1972; children: Anjum, Najma, Sana. BS, Karachi U., Pakistan, 1961, MS, 1963; MS, Yale U., 1966; PhD, N.Mex. State U., 1969. Dir. gen. PCSIR Labs. Complex, Karachi, Pakistan, 1996—; sec. PCSIR, Karachi, Pakistan, 1989-96, dir., 1984-99; dir. Scientific Info. Ctr., Karachi, Pakistan, 1995-96. Alexander von Humboldt fellow, Germany, 1976-77. Fellow Japan Soc. Promotion Sci., Sigma Xi; mem. Am. Chem. Soc. Avocations: chess, bridge, cricket, reading, sight seeing. Home: 26-V Block 2 PECHS, Karachi 75400, Pakistan Office: PCSIR Labs Complex, Off Univ Rd, Karachi 75280, Pakistan

HAIDER, ZULFIQAR, physician, researcher, consultant; b. Lahore, Punjab, Pakistan, May 24, 1930; s. Syed Mohammad and Safia Begum Hussain; m. Yasmin Zehra Haider; 1 child, Abid. MB BS, U. Punjab, Lahore, 1953. Resident and registrar Nat. Health Svc., Eng., 1959-65; sr. fellow Ottawa Gen. Hosp., Can., 1966-67; resident, fellow U. Md. Hosp., Balt., 1969-70; rsch. dir. Pakistan Med. Rsch. Coun., Lahore, 1970-85; assoc. prof., dir. clin. rsch. Postgrad. Med. Inst., Lahore, 1988-90; dir. Inst. Exptl. Medicine, Lahore, 1990-91; cons. physician Polyclinic Fatima Meml. Hosp., Lahore; mem. nat. panel of experts Pakistan Med. Rsch. Coun., 1980-85, hon. cons., 1996—, mem. nat. adv. panel, 1997—; coord. Hepatitis Study Group, Lahore, 1990—; advisor Soc. Family Physicians in Continuing Med. Edn. and Rsch., 1982-88. Co-author: Diabetes Mellitus in Pakistan, 1982, Hypertension: A Clinical Study in Lahore, 1985, Multicentre Study of Risk Factors for Coronary Heart Disease; mem. editl. bd. Jour. Pakistan Med. Assn., 1976-86; reviewer Pakistan Jour. Med. Rsch., 1998—; contbr. articles to profl. jours. including Diabetes, Hypertension, Lipid & Liver Diseases, among others. Fellow Pakistan Acad. Med. Scis., 1987-94. Fellow Royal Coll. Physicians (Edinburgh), Pakistan Diabetic Assn. (chmn. sci. com. 1986-92), Nat. Acad. Med. Scis. Pakistan (sec. Ctrl. Zone 1996, rsch. coord. 1996); mem. Gymkhana Club (life). Avocations: history, literature. Home: 329-S Phase II, LCCHS, Lahore Cantt Pakistan Office: Fatima Meml Hosp, Polyclinic Shadman, Lahore Pakistan

HAIG, ALEXANDER MEIGS, JR., former government official, former army officer, business executive; b. Phila., Dec. 2, 1924; s. Alexander Meigs and Regina Anne (Murphy) H.; m. Patricia Antoinette Fox, May 24, 1950; children: Alexander P., Brian F., Barbara E. Student, U. Notre Dame, 1943; B.S., U.S. Mil. Acad., 1947; M.A., Georgetown U., 1961; grad., Naval War Coll., 1960, Army War Coll., 1966; grad. hon. law degree, Niagara U.; LL.D. (hon.), U. Utah. Commd. 2d lt. U.S. Army, 1947, advanced through grades to gen., 1973, staff officer Office Chief of Staff for Ops., 1962-64, mil. asst. to sec. of army, 1964, dep. spl. asst. to sec. and dep. sec. of def., 1964-65; bn. and brigade comdr. 1st Inf. Div. U.S. Army, Vietnam, 1966-67; regtl. comdr., dep. comdt. U.S. Mil. Acad., 1967-69; mil. asst. to asst. to Pres. for Nat. Security Affairs, Washington, 1969-70; dep. asst. to pres. NSC, Washington, 1970-73; vice chief of staff U.S. Army, Washington, 1973; chief of staff White House, 1973-74; comdr.-in-chief U.S. European Command, 1974-79; supreme allied comdr. Europe SHAPE, 1974-79; ret., 1979; pres., chief oper. officer, dir. United Techs. Corp., Hartford, Conn., 1979-81; sec. state Washington, 1981-82; chmn., pres. Worldwide Assocs., Inc., 1984, pres., 1984—; bd. dirs. Am. Online, Inc., Interneuron Pharms., Inc., MGM Mirage, Inc., Metro-Goldwyn-Mayer Inc. Author: Caveat: Realism, Reagan and Foreign Policy, 1984, Inner Circles: How America Changed the World, A Memoir, 1992. Decorated D.S.C., Silver Star with oak leaf cluster, Legion of Merit with 2 oak leaf clusters, D.F.C. with 2 oak leaf clusters, Bronze Star with oak leaf cluster, Air medal with 23 oak leaf clusters, Army Commendation medal, Purple Heart U.S.; Nat. Order 5th Class; Gallantry Cross with palm; Civil Actions Honor medal 1st Class; grand officer Nat. Order of Vietnam, Republic of Vietnam; medal of King Abdel-Aziz Saudi Arabia; grand cross Order of Merit Fed. Republic Germany; recipient Disting. Svc. medal Dept. of Def.; Disting. Svc. medal U.S. Army; Man of Yr. award Air Force Assn.; James Forrestal Meml. award, Disting. Grad. award Assn. Grads. West Point. Mem. Soc. of 1st Divsn. Office: Worldwide Assocs Inc 1155 15th St NW Ste 800 Washington DC 20005-2706

HAIG, ROBERT LEIGHTON, lawyer; b. Plainfield, N.J., July 30, 1947; s. Richard Randall and Edith (Remington) H. AB, Yale U., 1967; JD, Harvard U., 1970. Bar: N.Y. 1971, U.S. Dist. Ct. (so. and ea. dists.) N.Y., U.S. Ct. Appeals (2d cir.). Assoc. Kelley Drye & Warren, N.Y.C., 1970-79, ptnr., 1980—; mem. bd. advisers Law Dept. Mgmt. Adviser, 1995—. Coauthor: Preparing for and Trying the Civil Lawsuit, 1987, 91, 94, 97, 2000, Federal Civil Practice, 1989, 93, 97, Federal Litigation Guide, 1992, 93, 94, Corporate Counsel's Guide, 1996, 97, Products Liability in New York, 1997; also contbr. chpts. to books, articles to profl. jours.; mem. bd. editors Fed. Litigation Guide Reporter, 1989—, In-House Law Practice Management, 1997—; editor-in-chief Comml. Litigation in N.Y. State Cts., 1995, Bus. and Comml. Litigation in Fed. Cts., 1998, Successful Partnering Between Insite and Outsite Counsel, 2000. Co-chair Comml. Cts. Task Force, 1995—; mem. legis. com. Com. for Modern Cts., N.Y.C., 1986—, bd. dirs., 1994—; mem. Am. Law Inst., 1998—; mem. N.Y. State Conf. Bar Leaders, exec. coun., 1988-90, dept. disciplinary com. appellate divsn., 1996—, hearing panel chair, 1999—; mem. N.Y. State Jud. Salary Commn., 1997—. Recipient award for excellence in continuing legal edn. Assn. Continuing Legal Edn. Adminstrs., 1991. Fellow Am. Bar Found. (life), N.Y. Bar Found. (life); mem. ABA (del. 1991—, standing com. on jud. selection, tenure and compensation 1995-96, com. on bus. cts. 1996—, chair subcom. on rels. between inside and outside counsel 1997—), Assn. of Bar of City of N.Y. (mem. jud. com. 1985-88, chmn., 1989-92, mem. coun. on jud. adminstrn. 1989-92, chmn. 1996-99), N.Y. County Lawyers Assn. (exec. com. 1986-95, v.p. 1986-92, pres. 1992-94, dir. 1985—, chmn. com. on supreme ct. 1984-86, chmn. fin. com. 1988-90, lectr. 1984—, pres. Found. 1992-94), N.Y. State Bar Assn. (chmn. com. on fed. cts. 1986-88, del. 1988—, chmn. comml. and fed. litig. sect. 1988-90, lectr. 1985—, exec. com. 1991-94, mem. steering com. on commerce and industry 1997—, chair com. on multi-disciplinary practice and the legal profn. 1998-99, 1st Ann. award for Disting. Pub. Svc. comml. and fed. litig. sect. 1995). Office: Kelley Drye & Warren 101 Park Ave Fl 30 New York NY 10178-0062

HAIGH, ROBERT WILLIAM, business administration educator; b. Phila., Aug. 22, 1926; s. Harry E. and Mildred (Elliott) H.; m. Jane Stanton Sheble, June 19, 1948; children: Cynthia Jane, Anne Sheble, Robert William, Barbara Lynne. Student, Muhlenberg Coll., 1944-45; AB cum laude, Bucknell U., 1948; MBA with high distinction, Harvard U., 1950, DCS, 1953. Research and teaching faculty Harvard U. Grad Sch. Bus. Adminstrn., 1950-56, asst. prof., 1953-56; asst. to pres. Helmerich & Payne, Inc., Tulsa, 1956, controller and asst. to pres., 1956-57, fin. v.p., dir., 1957-61; fin. v.p., dir. White Eagle Internat. Oil Co., 1957-60; v.p. corp. planning and devel. Standard Oil Co. (Ohio), Cleve., 1963-66; pres. Sohio Chems. & Vistron Corp. Subs., 1966-67, Sohio Chemicals and Vistron Corp. Subs., 1966-67; group v.p., pres. edn. group, dir. Xerox Corp., Stamford, Conn., 1967-72; exec. v.p. Swedlow Corp., 1973-74, pres., chief exec. officer, dir., 1974; pres. Hillsboro Assocs., 1974-75; sr. v.p. Freeport Minerals Co., 1975-76; chmn. bd., chief exec. officer Photo Quest, Inc., Cognitrex, Inc., 1977-78; dir. Wharton Applied Rsch. Ctr., lectr. U. Pa., Phila., 1978-79; Disting. prof. bus. adminstrn. Darden Grad. Sch. Bus. U. Va. Tayloe Murphy Internat. Bus. Studies Ctr., 1979-95; prof. emeritus U. Va., 1995—. Author: (with John G. McLean) The Growth of Integrated Oil Companies, 1954, Leading Virginia Industries series: Textiles and Apparel, A Business Update, 1986, Wood and Paper Products, 1987, Investment Strategies and the Plant-Location Decision: Foreign Companies in the U.S., 1989, Global Markets for Pollution-Control Equipment: An Export Opportunity for Virginia Business, 1991, Medical Products Companies in Virginia: Export Status Report. Served with USNR, 1944-45. Mem. Phi Beta Kappa, Phi Lambda Theta. Home: 404 Ednam Dr Charlottesville VA 22903-4716

HAIGHT, WARREN GAZZAM, investor; b. Seattle, Sept. 7, 1929; s. Gilbert Pierce and Ruth (Gazzam) H.; m. Suzanne H., Sept. 1, 1951; children—Paula Lea, Ian Pierce; m. Ottina Mehau, June 25, 1985. A.B. in Econs, Stanford U., 1951. Asst. Treas. Hawaiian Pineapple Co., Honolulu, 1955-64; v.p., treas. Oceanic Properties, Inc., Honolulu, 1964-67; pres., dir. Oceanic Properties, Inc., 1967-85, chmn., 1983-85; pres. Hawaii, Castle & Cooke Inc., 1983-85, Warren G. Haight & Assocs., 1985—; chmn. Molokai Ranch, Ltd., 1996—; bd. dirs. Round Hill Enterprises, Inc., Las Positas Land Co., Inc., Baldwin Pacific Properties, Inc., Hawaii Project Mgmt., Inc., Transamerica Realty Advisors, Inc., Queen Emma Corp., Queens Devel. Corp., Dole Corp., Standard Fruit and Steamship Co., Inc., Bumble Bee Seafoods, Inc. Bd. dirs. Downtown Improvement Assn., Oahu Devel. Conf., Hawaii Island Econ. Devel. Bd., Econ. Devel. Corp. Honolulu, Intellect, Inc., Hawaii Resort Developers Conf., Homeless Solutions, Inc., Mutual Housing of Hawaii, Inc.; mem. Transit Coalition, Honolulu, Govs. Com. on Econ. Futures; pres., bd. dirs. Land Use Rsch. Found. of Hawaii, Pacific Found. for Cancer Rsch., Hawaii Nature Ctr.; mem. policy adv. bd. for elderly affairs State of Hawaii. Lt. USNR, 1951-55. Mem. Housing Coalition, Calif. Coastal Council. Clubs: Outrigger Canoe, Round Hill Country,

Plaza, Pacific. Home: 319 Lala Pl Kailua HI 96734-3224 Office: 220 S King St Ste 1465 Honolulu HI 96813-4542

HAILE WELDENSAE, Eritrean government official; b. Asmara, Eritrea, Feb. 15, 1947; married; 3 children. Student, U. Addis Ababa (Ethiopia) Coll. Tech., 1965-66, 69-72, U. Asmara (Eritrea), 1992. Tchr. U. Nat. Svc., Ethiopia, 1968; head dept. info. and polit. orientation Govt. of Eritrea, 1975-77, mem. ctr. com., 1977, head dept. polit. orientation, edn. and culture, 1977-87, head dept. nat. guidance, 1987-91, head dept. economy, 1991, sec. dept. econ. affairs, 1991-92, sec. dept. econ. devel. and cooperation, 1992-93, min. finance and devel., 1993-97, min. fgn. affairs, 1997—. Office: Ministry of Fgn Affairs, PO Box 190, Asmara Eritrea

HAILEY, ARTHUR, author; b. Luton, Eng., Apr. 5, 1920; arrived in Can., 1947, naturalized, 1952, (also Brit. citizen); s. George and Elsie (Wright) H.; m. Sheila Dunlop, July 28, 1951; children: Roger, John, Mark (by previous marriage), Jane, Steven, Diane. Student elementary schs., Eng. Author: Runway Zero-Eight, 1958 (with John Castle), The Final Diagnosis, 1959, In High Places, 1962, Hotel, 1965, Airport, 1968, Wheels, 1971, The Moneychangers, 1975, Overload, 1979, Strong Medicine, 1984, The Evening News, 1990, Detective, 1997; author novels pub. in 40 langs., 160 million copies in print; author 12 internat. TV plays including No Deadly Medicine (Emmy nomination 1957); (TV series) Hotel; collected plays Close-up on Writing for Television, 1960; motion pictures include Zero Hour, 1956, Time Lock, 1957, The Young Doctors, 1961, Hotel, 1966, Airport, 1970, The Moneychangers, 1976, Wheels, 1978, Strong Medicine, 1986; (poem) A Last Request; first editor RAF aircrew tng. mag, Airclues. Air Ministry staff officer, London, 1945-47; pilot, flight lt. RAF, 1939-47; commd. RCAF Res. flight lt., 1951. Recipient Air Efficiency award RAF; subject TV program This Is Your Life, Eng., 1991. Mem. Writers Guild Am. (life), Authors League Am., Alliance of Canadian Cinema, Television and Radio Artists (hon. life), Writers Guild Can. (life). Home: Lyford Cay, PO Box N-7776, Nassau The Bahamas Office: Nancy Stauffer Assocs PO Box 1203 Darien CT 06820-1203

HAILS, ROBERT EMMET, aerospace consultant, business executive, former air force officer; b. Miami, Fla., Jan. 20, 1923; s. Daniel Troy and Jean (Burke) H.; m. Ethel Fitzgerald Gayle, Mar. 2, 1957; children: Robert Emmet Jr., Merrily Hails Joiner, Florence T. Hails Patton, Laura Hails Smith. BS in Aero. Engring., Auburn U., 1947; MS in Indsl. Engring., Columbia U., 1950; postgrad., C&CS Air U., 1955; postgrad. AMP, Harvard U. Sch. Bus., 1965. Enlisted USAAF, 1942, commd. 2d lt., 1944, advanced through grades to lt. gen., 1974, combat pilot Pacific Theater, 1944-45; assigned to SAC, 1947-48; inspector gen. Hdqrs. USAF, 1950-53; program devel. officer Marcel Dassault Mystere IV Jet Aircraft, French Air Force Am. embassy, Paris, 1953-55; air staff project officer F-104/F-105 aircraft HQ USAF, 1956-60; comdr. procurement dist. USAF, San Francisco, 1960-62; mil. asst. for weapons systems acquisition Office Sec. AF, 1962-66; system program dir. Joint USAF/USN A-7D Aircraft Engring., Devel., Test & Prodn., AF Systems Cmmd., 1966-68; dep. chief staff maintenance engring. Air Force Logistics Command, 1968-71; comdr. Def. Pers. Support Ctr. Def. Log. Agy., Phila., 1971-72; comdr. Air Logistics Ctr. USAF, Warner Robins AFB, Ga., 1972-74; vice comdr. Tactical Air Command Langley AFB, Va., 1974-75; dep. chief systems and logistics Hdqrs. USAF, Washington, 1975-77; ret. USAF, Washington, 1977; mgmt. cons. Atlanta, 1978-80; sr. v.p. internat. ops. LTV Corp., Dallas, 1980-84; pres. Hails Assocs. Inc., Macon, Ga., 1984—; mem. sci. bd. Loral Corp., Yonkers, N.Y., 1992-96. Regional exec. Boy Scouts Am.; mem. Auburn U. Alumni Engring. Coun.; bd. advisors Wesleyan Coll., 1985-90; mem. Found. Bd., Macon State Coll., 1998—. Decorated DSM with 2 oak leaf clusters, legion of Merit with 2 oak leaf clusters, Air medal with 2 oak leaf clusters; Order of Nat. Security (Korea); recipient Engring. Achievement award Auburn U., 1998. Mem. AIAA, Air Force Assn., Daedalians, Auburn U. SPADES, Army-Navy Country Club (Arlington, Va.), Idle Hour Golf and Country Club, Omicron Delta Kappa, Sigma Alpha Epsion. Roman Catholic.

HAILU, SOLOMON, international government official. Dir., exec. officer UNESCO, Santo Domingo. Office: UNESCO Santo Domingo, Aptdo Postal 25350, Santo Domingo Dominican Republic*

HAIN, JOAN E., secondary education educator; b. N.Y.C., Dec. 12, 1947; d. Kurt and Lore Goldstein; m. Barry J. Hain, May 2, 1981; 1 child, Daniel. BFA, Pratt Inst., 1970; MA, CW Post, 1975. Tchr. N.Y. State Union Tchrs., N.Y.C., 1970-00. Avocations: sculpture, drawing, painting, photography, travel. Office: Wellington C Mepham HS 2401 Camp Ave Bellmore NY 11710-3029

HAINE, THOMAS WILLIAM NICHOLAS, educator; b. Oxford, England, Feb. 23, 1967; s. Stephen Robert and Jennifer Susan (Taylor) H.; m. Barbara Jean Souter, Sept. 13, 1997. BA in Physics & Theoretical Physics, U. Cambridge, England, 1988, MA; PhD in Phys. Oceanography, U. Southampton, England, 1993. Rsch. assoc. U. Eas Anglia, England, 1993-94; lectr. U. Oxford, England, 1996-99; asst. prof. Johns Hopkins U., Balt., 2000—. Contbr. rsch. papers to profl. pubs. Rsch. grantee Natural environment Rsch. Coun., England, 1996, 97; rsch. scholar MIT, Cambridge, Mass., 1994-96; rsch. fellow Wolfson Coll, Oxford, 1996-99. Fellow Royal Meteorological Soc.; mem. Am. Meteorological Soc., Am. Geophys. Union. Office: Earth and Planetary Scis The Johns Hopkins U 301 Olin Hall The Johns Baltimore MD 21218

HAINES, DAVID H., consulting executive; b. Kane, Pa., Nov. 23, 1949; s. Joseph Harry Haines and Loma Ruth Housely; m. Rashelle Harrison, May 26, 1990; children: Steffanie, Amber, Jamie. BA in Journalism/Econs., U. Fla., 1971; MA in Internat. Econs., Am. U., 1974. Dir. western region N.Y. Times Co., San Francisco, 1975-80; nat. acct. mgr. Control Data/Source Telecomms. Corp., McLean, Va., 1980-83; dir. mktg. and sales U.S. region Context Mgmt. Sys., L.A., 1983-85; mng. dir. McGraw-Hill DRI, San Francisco, 1985-89, Maxwell/Macmillan, San Francisco, 1989-93; dir. bus. devel. Arthur Anderson LLP, San Franicsco, 1993-99; v.p. bus. devel., strategy Cotelligent Inc., San Francisco, 1999—; v. chmn., bd. dirs. APEX Computing, San Francisco, 1984—; dir., bd. dirs. Beverly Hills Releasing/Sunset Studios, L.A., 1985-00. Author: Warp Speed Marketing, 1998; contbr. articles to profl. jours. Recipient Entrepreneur of Yr. award Venture Entreprenuer Club, San Francisco, 1987; Athletic, Academic scholarship Kiwanis Club Internat., N.Y.C., 1967-71. Fellow Sales and Mktg. Executives; mem. Nat. Assn. Computer Cons., Info. Tech. Assn. Am., Pub. Rels. Soc. Am., Am. Soc. Info. Scientists, St. Vincent de Paul Soc. (bd. dirs. 1998—). Republican. Avocations: snow and water skiing, scuba diving, mountain biking, music. E-mail: dhaines@cotelligent.com. Home: 135 Stewart Dr Tiburon CA 94920-1340 Office: Cotelligent 101 California St San Francisco CA 94111-5802

HAINES, JULIAN PAUL, research scientist; b. Kingston-upon-Thames, Eng., Feb. 3, 1964; arrived in France, 1992; s. Jeremy Frederick and Lucy (Albion) H.; m. Anabel Chacon, July 20, 1989. BSc, Concordia U., Montreal, Can., 1987; PhD, McGill U., Montreal, Can., 1990. Postdoctoral rschr. U. Leicester, Eng., 1990-92; rschr. Nat. Ctr. Sci. Rsch., Meudon, France, 1992—. Referee Jour. Physics: Condensed Matter, 1996—; contbr. articles to profl. jours.; patentee in field. Recipient European High Pressure Rsch. Group award, Belgium, 1996. Office: CNRS, LPCM, 1 Place A Briand, 92190 Meudon France

HAINES, KENNETH H., television broadcasting executive; b. Spokane, Sept. 5, 1942; s. Kenneth A. and Helen Elizabeth (Evans) H.; m. Stephanie Marie Phelps, Nov. 23, 1981; 1 child, Avery Jordan. BA, Dakota Wesleyan U., 1964; MA, U. Wyo.; MS, Troy State U., 1970; EdD, Va. Tech., 1976. News dir. KORN TV, Mitchell, S.D., 1962-64; sta. mgr. KUWR Radio, Laramie, Wyo., 1965-67; gen. mgr. KLME Radio, Laramie, 1967-68; instr. flight ops. U.S. Army, Ft. Rucker, Ala., 1968-70; from dir. radio, tv, film to dir. pub. affairs, univ. rels. Va. Tech., Blacksburg, 1970-81; from dir. network ops. to exec. v.p., COO Raycom Sports, Charlotte, N.C., 1981—; bd. dirs. Charlotte Sports Commn., ACC Properties; trustee Dakota Wesleyan U. Bd. dirs. Sunshine Football Classic, 1989—, Charlotte Basketball Challenge, 1987—; tournament dir. LPGA Golf, 1997—. Named Reporter of Yr., UPI, 1967, Opperman Disting. Lectr., Dakota Wesleyan U., 1998, Outstanding TV Sports Exec., All-Am. Football Found., 1999; recipient golden award Coun. Support Higher Edn., 1978. Mem. Am. Assn. Agr. Writers, Am. Coll. Pub. Rels. Assn. (exceptional achievement award 1974), Va. Press Assn., Coun. for Advancement and Support of Edn. (pres. univ. faculty club 1980-82), Nat. Acad. TV Arts and Scis. (judge), Charlotte C. of C. (bd. dirs.), Phi Kappa Delta, Pi Delta Epsilon, Omicron Delta Kappa. Avocations: sports, photography, television, travel, reading. Home: 1909 Carmel Rd Charlotte NC 28226-5021 Office: Raycom Sports 2815 Coliseum Centre Dr Ste 200 Charlotte NC 28217-1378

HAINES, ROBERT EMMETT, technical writer, vocational educator; b. East St. Louis, Ill., Aug. 18, 1931; s. William McIllvain and Fonnie LaFont (Radford) H.; m. Mozelle Jay Hood, Jan. 9, 1959; 1 child, Mindy Ilene. BS in Edn., So. Ill. U., 1974. Cert. tchr., Ill. History tchr. Althof H.S., Belleville, Ill., 1974-76; constrn. tech. instr. Lewis and Clark Jr. Coll., Godfrey, Ill., 1977-80; constrn. tech. instr. ARAMCO, Saudi Arabia, 1981-82, tech. writer, 1983-85, ednl. devel. specialist, 1986-91. Author: Bob's View, 1995, (poetry collection) What's a Redneck and Other Poems, 1992. Mem. VFW, Masons, Shriners, Phi Theta Kappa. Republican. Avocations: writing, novels. Home: RR 1 Box 314 Altha FL 32421-9607

HAINES, THOMAS DAVID, JR., lawyer; b. Dallas, Oct. 30, 1956; s. Thomas David Sr. and Carol V. (Mullins) H.; m. Nanette Cluck, Mar. 1, 1986; children: Bennett Ann, Maison Cluck. BS in Polit. Sci., Okla. State U., 1979; JD, U. Okla., 1982. Bar: Okla. 1982, N.Mex. 1983, U.S. Ct. Appeals (10th cir.) 1983, U.S. Dist. Ct. N.Mex. 1983. Assoc. Hinkle, Cox, Eaton, Coffield & Hensley, Roswell, N.Mex., 1982-87, ptnr., 1988—. Contbg. editor N.Mex. Tort and Worker's Compensation Reporter, 1987-90, Employment Law Deskbook for New Mexico Employers, 1997, 99. Youth sponsor First United Meth. Ch., Roswell, 1986-88, chmn. stewardship com. 1990-91, chmn. adminstrv. coun., 1998-99; coach Roswell Youth Soccer Assn., 1995-98; trustee 1st United Meth. Ch., Roswell, 1996-98. Mem. State Bar Assn. N.Mex. (com. on continuing legal edn., young lawyers divsn. 1989—, mem. med.-legal rev. commn. 1988—), Chaves County Bar Assn., N.Mex. Def. Lawyer's Assn., N.Mex. Trial Lawyer's Assn., Kiwanis (Roswell club, Outstanding Club Sec. award 1993-95, pres. 1998-99, named one Outstanding Young Men in Am. 1990), Phi Delta Phi, Phi Kappa Phi. Republican. Avocations: golf, basketball, music, politics. Office: Hinkle Cox Eaton Coffield & Hensley 400 N Pennsylvania Ave Ste 700 Roswell NM 88201-4777

HAINES, WILLIAM JOSEPH, pharmaceutical company executive; b. Crawfordsville, Ind., Sept. 26, 1919; s. Burt and Lala R. (Luster) H.; m. Wilma M. Hester, June 6, 1943; children: Paula Sue Haines Curtis-Burn, Eric J. AB summa cum laude, Wabash Coll., 1940, DSc (hon.), 1970; PhD, U. Ill., 1943; grad. exec. program in bus. adminstrn., Columbia Bus. Sch., 1965. Rsch. biochemist Upjohn Co., Kalamazoo, 1943-50, head dept. endocrinology rsch., 1950-54; tech. dir. Armour Labs., Kankakee, Ill., 1954-58; v.p. dir. rsch. Ortho Pharm. Corp., Raritan, N.J., 1958-65, exec. v.p., 1965-67; vice chmn. Johnson & Johnson Internat., 1967-69; dir., mem. exec. com. Johnson & Johnson, New Brunswick, N.J., 1969-79, v.p. corp. officer sci. and tech., 1979-82; pres. Bucks-Tech Assocs., Inc. (cons. in mgmt., sci. and tech.), Doylestown, Pa., 1982—; chmn. sci. adv. com. Alliance Internat. Health Care Trust, 1983-87; former dir. Quidel Corp., La Jolla, Calif.; invited lectr. Laurentian Hormone Conf., 1952, Gordon Rsch. Conf., 1952. Contbr. numerous sci. articles to profl. jours., including pioneer paper on human requirement for essential amino acids, 1942. One of initial investigators to identify essential amino acids for human nutrition; patentee biosynthesis of adrenal cortex hormones, paper chromatography and automatic partition column chromatography of steroids. Trustee Wabash Coll., 1972-93, trustee emeritus, 1993—; trustee Hood Coll., 1975-87, vice chmn. bd., 1982-87, trustee emeritus, 1989—; Joslin Diabetes Found. Inc., Boston, 1974-79; elder Thompson Meml. Presbyn. Ch., New Hope, Pa. Recipient William E. Upjohn prize and medal, 1952, Alumni Merit award Nat. Assn. Wabash Men, 1973. Fellow AAAS, Am. Inst. Chemists; mem. Am. Chem. Soc. (med. cheistry div.), N.Y. Acad. Scis., Endocrine Soc., Am. Soc. Biol. Chemists, Soc. Chem. Industry (former chmn. Am. sect.), Pharm. Mfrs. Assn. (former chmn. R&D sec.), Assn. Rsch. Dirs., Indsl. Rsch. Inst., (dir. emeritus), N.J. Acad. Scis., Soc. Exptl. Biology and Medicine, Pacific Coast Fertility Soc., Am. Fertility Soc., Internat. Soc. Rsch. in Biology Reproduction (charter), Am. Inst. Mgmt. (exec. council), Am. Mgmt. Assn., Am. Found. Pharm. Edn. (Century Club), Ind. Covered Bridge Soc., Sons of Ind. (N.Y.C. chpt.), Chemists Club (N.Y.C.), Masons, Elks, Kiwanis (emeritus), Lake Naomi Club, Phi Beta Kappa, Phi Lambda Upsilon, Phi Kappa Phi, Sigma Xi, Alpha Chi Sigma. Republican. Home: 5 Bedford Dr Doylestown PA 18901-9463 Office: Johnson & Johnson 1 Johnson And Johnson Plz New Brunswick NJ 08933-0002

HAINS, GAÉTAN JOSEPH DANIEL ROBERT, computer scientist; b. Montreal, May 9, 1963; s. Guy and Thérèse (Guillemette) H. BSc, Concordia U., 1985; MSc, Oxford U., 1987, DPhil, 1990. Rschr. CRIM, Montreal, 1989; from asst. prof. to assoc. prof. U. Montreal, 1989-95; prof. U. Orleans, France, 1995—; dir. lab. info. fondamentale U. Orleans, 2000—; vis. prof. ENS, Lyon, France, 1994; vis. researcher Isis-Fujitsu, Japan, 1994-95. Mem. N.Y. Acad. Sci. Office: LIFO BP 6759 Batiment IIIA, Rue Leonard de Vinci, 45067 Orleans France

HAIRALD, BURNEY LESHAWN (SHAWN HAIRALD), marketing professional; b. Tupelo, Miss., July 12, 1968; s. Leroy Utley and Mary (Payne) H. AA, Itawamba C.C., Fulton, Miss., 1988; BBA in Mktg., U. Miss., 1990. Product devel. and data processor/indsl. engr. asst. PeopLoungers Mfg. Co., Inc., Nettleton, Miss., 1985-99; housing cons. So. Housing, Inc., Tupelo, 1999—; substitute tchr. Nettleton Sch. Dist., 1999—; assoc. scout Colorado Rockies, 1999—. Player/coach Tupelo Tigers semi-pro baseball team, 1998, 1999; coach Boys Baseball team Nettleton, 1998, 1999, Girls Softball team, 1991-98. Life mem. Miss. DECA Alumni (Outstanding Alumni 1989, 1990, nat. judge Denver 1991, Anaheim, Calif. 1992, Orlando, Fla. 1993). Methodist. Avocations: playing and coaching baseball, softball, football, tennis, computers, landscaping. E-mail: shairald@hotmail.com. Home: 4126A Highway 6 Plantersville MS 38862-3910 Office: Tupelo MS

HAIRAPETIAN, HRATCHIK, mathematics educator, researcher; b. Oct. 25, 1946; m. Anahit Mazgarian, 1975; children: Haik, Hasmik. Diploma in mechanics and math., Armenian State U., Yerevan, 1968, Cand Scis. in Physics and Math., 1975; D Phys. and Math. Scis., Moscow State U., 1993. Rschr. Inst. Math., Armenian Acad. Scis., Yerevan, 1971-78; assoc. prof. math. Armenian State Engring. U., Yerevan, 1979-81, lectr., 1981—, head dept. applied math., 1991-93. Contbr. articles to math. jours. Mem. Armenian Math. Soc. Avocation: playing chess. Home: Avan-Aringe 2/2, Apt 30, 375022 Yerevan Armenia Office: Armenian State Engring U, Dept Math, Teryan 105, 375009 Yerevan Armenia

HAIRE, MARJORIE FRANCES, nurse; b. Dublin, Ireland, Apr. 7, 1953; d. Cecil William and Nora Mary (Robinson) H. RN. Med. staff nurse Jersey Group Hosps., Channel Islands, 1975-76; nutrition coord. South East Asian Outreach, Loi, Thailand, 1971-81; mgr. book store Galway Christian Fellowship, Ireland, 1983-87; matron Sacred Heart Nursing Home, An Spidéal, Ireland, 1988-93; nurse Med. Ctr., An Spidéal, 1993-97; counsellor Life, Galway, 1994-95. Avocations: swimming, walking, cycling, reading. Home: Clochscoilte Beárna, County na Contae na Gaillimhe Ireland

HAIZET, PATRICK FELIX, management consultant; b. Paris, Feb. 1, 1929; s. Roger Marie and Helene Marguerite (de Marchena) H.; m. Isabelle Marie Moulin-Roussel, Feb. 14, 1957; children: Raphaela, Marie-Helene. B, U. Paris, 1949; D, Ind. U., 1950. Trainee Banque Francaise Du Commerce Extérieur, Paris, 1952-53, asst. cashier, 1953-57, dep. v.p., 1957-62, v.p., 1962-70, 1st v.p., 1970-82, exec. v.p., 1982-89; chmn., CEO Credit Francais Internat., Paris, 1989-93; cons. Coopers & Lybrand, Paris, 1988-98, Price Waterhouse Coopers, Paris, 1998-2000. Capt. French Air Force, 1951-52. Mem. St. Germain Country Club. Roman Catholic. Avocations: golf, tennis, skiing. Home and Office: 33 Ave du Marechal Maunoury, 75016 Paris France Office: Price Waterhouse Coopers, 32 Rue Guersant, 75017 Paris France

HÁJEK, VÁCLAV, microbiologist; b. Kolín, Czech Republic, July 13, 1934; s. Václav and Terezie (Kolárová) H.; m. Tatána Obletilová, July 8, 1961 (div. 1970); children: Gabriela, Michaela; m. Anna Simová, Mar. 31, 1973; 1 child, Veronika. MD, Charles U., 1960; PhD, J.E. Purkyne U., Brno, Czech Republic, 1982. Intern Divsn. Hosp., Pardubice, Czech Republic, 1960-63; sr. lectr. Med. Faculty Palacky U., Olomouc, Czech Republic, 1963-89, microbiologist, 1989—, assoc. prof., 1990-98, prof., 1998—, head microbiol. inst., 1990—; head microbiol. divsn. Tchg. Hosp., Olomouc, 1990—; head Nat. Ref. Lab. for Staphylococci, 1974-93. Contbr. articles to profl. jours. Recipient grants Internal Grant Agy., Czech Ministry of Health, 1991-94, 94—. Mem. Czech Soc. for Microbiology (internat. subcom. on taxonomy of staphylococci of internat. com. systematic bacteriology 1975—). Roman Catholic. Avocation: hiking. Office: Palacky Univ Medical Faculty, 3 Hněvotínská Str, 775 15 Olomouc Moravia, Czech Republic

HAJIVASSILIOU, CONSTANTINOS ARGYROU, pediatric surgeon, educator; b. Nicosia, Cyprus, Apr. 27, 1961; s. Argyros and Nedi (Charalambous) H.; m. Evangelia Koundourou, July 23, 1990; children: Danae, Maria. BSc with Honors, Edinburgh U., Scotland, 1984, MbChB, 1986; MD with distinction, U. Edinburgh, Scotland, 1997. Diplomate Royal Coll. Surgeons, Royal Coll. Paediatric Surgeons. Lt. Infantry, Cyprus, 1976-78; surg. trainee U. Edinburgh, 1986-88; trauma surgeon Addenbrookes Hosp., Cambridge, 1988-89; surg. rotation Glasgow, 1989-92, paediatric surg. reg., 1992-95; lectr. in surg. paediatrics R.H.S.C., U. Glasgow, 1995-98, hon. sr. lectr., 1998—, Wellcome Trust sr. lectr., 1999—; cons. Biosil Ltd., 1994—; cons. pediatric, neonatal surgery R.H.S.C., Yorkhill; sr. lectr. Wellcome Trust, U. Glasgow, 1999. Patentee in field; contbr. articles to profl. jours. Recipient Astra prize Caledonian Soc. Gastro Enterology, 1994, Surg. Rsch. prize (2) Royal Medico Chirurgical Soc., 1995, Lord Moynihan prize Assn. Surgeons of U.K. and Ireland, 1995, Scottish Surgical Paediatrician Soc. prize, 1998. Fellow Royal Soc. Medicine; mem. British Assn. Paediatric Surgeons, British Med. Assn. Avocations: electronics, radio amateur, diving, flying. Office: U Dept Surg Paediatrics, Royal Hosp Sick Children, G38SJ Yorkhill Glasgow Scotland

HAJNIS, KAREL, physical anthropology educator; b. Lany-Vasirov, Czech Republic, June 6, 1930; s. Karel and Marie (Jirkovska) H.; m. Milena Hladka (div. May 1970); 1 child, Jan; m. Anna Konickova. MA, Charles U., 1956, PhD, 1960. Asst. lectr. Charles U., Prague, 1956-59, spl. asst., lectr., 1959-67, assoc. prof., 1968-90, prof., 1990—. Author: Karel Linné, 1957, ABC Cloveka, 1977, The Concrescence of Sutures of the Cranial Vault, 1984, Growth of Czech and Slovak Children, 1989, Growth and Ontogenetic Development in Man, Vols. I-IV, 1981-94 among others; contbr. numerous articles to profl. jours. Rsch. scholarship A. von Humboldt Stiftung U. Mainz and Kiel, 1967-68. Mem. Czech Assn. Anthropology, Med. Assn. J.E. Purkyne Anatomy and Obesitology, Germany Assn. Anthropology, Current Anthropology, Internat. Assn. Human Biology, others. Home: Volsinach 2012, 10000 Prague 10, Czech Republic also: Dept Phys Edn Tech U, Halgrove 6, 46117 Liberec 1, Czech Republic

HAJOS, ZOLTAN GEORGE, chemist; b. Budapest, Mar. 3, 1926; came to U.S., 1957; s. Imre Henrik and Elizabeth Maria (Teichner) H.; m. Irene Edith Pal, Feb. 19, 1955 (dec. May 27, 1994); m. Katherine Birnbaum, june 24, 1999. MS, Tech. U., Budapest, 1947, DSc, 1949. Asst. prof. Tech. U., 1948-57; rsch. assoc. Princeton (N.J.) U., 1957-60; rsch. fellow Hoffmann-La Roche, Inc., Nutley, N.J., 1960-70; rsch. assoc. U. Vt., Burlington, 1972-73, U. Toronto, Ont., Can., 1973-74; prin. scientist R.W. Johnson Pharm. Rsch. Inst., Raritan, N.J., 1975-90. Contbg. author: Carbon-Carbon Bond Formation, 1977; contbr. articles to profl. jours. Mem. Am. Chem. Soc., Sigma Xi. Roman Catholic. Achievements include patents in field of total and asymmetric synthesis of medicinal-organic compounds; glycosides, hydrophenanthrenes, steroidal hormones, heterocyclics, (i.e. furanes, dioxanes and purines); asymmetric synthesis of chiral synthons. Home: Pauler u 2 II 21, H-1013 Budapest Hungary

HAJTMAN, BÉLA, biostatistician, consultant; b. Budapest, July 21, 1932; s. Pál and Olga (Götz) H.; m. Béláné Borbála Koós, Mar. 6, 1955; children: Agnes, Edit, Olaf. M. Math., Eötvös U., Budapest, 1955, Diploma for Tchg., 1959; Diploma of Psychology, U. Budapest, 1973, PhD, 1973. Asst. rschr. Inst. Math., Hungarian Acad. Sci., Budapest, 1954-62; rsch. worker Inst. Exptl. Medicine, Budapest, 1962-69; sr. rschr. Computing Ctr., Budapest, 1969-71; assoc. prof. Semmelweis U. Medicine, Budapest, 1971-96; ret.; lectr. stats. Eötvös U., 1964-83; cons. in field. Author: Introduction to Statistics, 1968 (Book of Yr. 1971), Mathematics for Physicians and Pharmacists, 1980; contbr. articles to profl. jours. With Hungarian Mil., 1954. Mem. Soc. for Clin. Biostats. (founder, pres. 1991—), Hungarian Biol. Soc. (pres. sect. biometrics 1990-95), Biometric Soc. (coun. mem. 1988-92), Internat. Soc. Clin. Biostats. (exec. com. 1994-96). Home: Szabolcska M u 9, H-1114 Budapest Hungary Office: Soc for Clin Biostats, PO Box 256, H-1519 Budapest Hungary

HAJTMAN, LADISLAV MICHAEL, charitable foundation executive, educator; b. Bratislava, Slovakia, July 20, 1948; came to U.S., 1968; s. Ladislav and Josephine (Kovac) H.; m. Anne Rush Gerner, July 3, 1952 (div. June 1983); 1 child, Laura Anne; m. Sandra Jean McCain, July 26, 1985. BS, Gannon U., 1973. CPA, Tex. Staff acct. Main Lafrentz & Co., Erie, Pa., 1973-76; v.p. N.Am. Group, Inc., Fairview, Pa., 1976-85; gen. mgr. Herzstein Investments, Houston, 1985—; exec. dir. Albert and Ethel Herzstein Charitable Found., Houston, 1985—; instr. Becker CPA Rev. Course, Houston, 1989—. Mem. AICPA, Tex. Soc. CPA's. Republican. Roman Catholic. Avocations: tennis, sailing, golf, skiing, reading. Home: 180 Grove Rd Kemah TX 77565-2652 Office: Albert and Ethel Herzstein Charitable Found 6131 Westview Dr Houston TX 77055-5421

HAKALA, THOMAS J(OHN), financial planner, accountant; b. Bayonne, N.J., July 6, 1948; s. John R. and Anna J. (Vida) H.; m. Marilynn Freund, Aug. 15, 1976; children: Lauren V., John C. AB in History, Georgetown U., 1970; JD, St. John's U., 1975; postgrad., NYU, 1975-80. Bar: N.J. 1975, N.Y. 1976; CPA, Tex. Supr. Weeden & Co., N.Y.C., 1970-73; mgr. Coopers & Lybrand, N.Y.C., 1975-87; sr. mgr. KPMG Peat Marwick, N.Y.C., 1987-89, ptnr., 1989-99; exec. dir. fin. planning and wealth mgmt. UBS Warburg, N.Y.C., 1999—; dir. UBS Trust Co., N.Y.C., 1999—; bd. advisers Jour. Taxation of Estates and Trusts, N.Y.C., 1990-92. Contbr. articles to profl. jours. Mem. Edison (N.J.) Republican Club, 1991—. Mem. AICPA, Ocean Beach and Yacht Club, Phi Delta Phi. Republican. Roman Catholic. Avocations: reading, history, photography, walking on beaches, swimming. E-mail: tom.hakala@ubs.com. Home: 8 Whitewood Rd Edison NJ 08820-3202 Office: UBS Warburg 10 E 50th St New York NY 10022-6831

HAKAMA, MATTI KAARLO, epidemiologist, consultant, educator; b. Oulu, Finland, Nov. 9, 1939; s. Kaarlo and Kaisa (Jaakkola) H.; m. Pirjo Sirpoma, Dec. 30, 1961; children: Annamaija, Tapani, Kaarina. MSc, U. Minn., 1966; ScD, U. Helsinki, 1970. Actuary Finnish Cancer Registry, 1961-63, head statistician, 1963-71; assoc. prof. biometry U. Helsinki, 1971-75; prof. epidemiology U. Tampere, Finland, 1975—, dir. Tampere Sch Pub. Health, 1999—; cons. in epidemiology Finnish Cancer Registry, 1971—; mem. expert adv. panel on health situation and trend assessment WHO, 1985—; rsch. prof. Finnish Cancer Inst., 1995-97; supr. divsn. epidemiology DKFZ, 1998. Contbr. articles to profl. jours. Ensigh Finnish Coastal Artillery, 1964-65. Recipient Edgar Gentilli prize Royal Coll. Gynecol. Obstetrics, 1982, Cancer Soc. Finland award, 1982, Knight First Class, Order of White Rose of Finland, 1989. Mem. Internat. Union Against Cancer (coun. mem. 1994—), Internat. Gastric Cancer Assn. (coun. mem. 1995—). Home: Hulaudentie, FIN37500 Lempäälä Finland Office: U Tampere, Tampere Sch Pub Health, FIN3301 Tampere Finland

HAKEEM, AHMED ATAUL, government executive; b. Rajbari, Bangladesh, June 30, 1952; s. Azher Uddin and Begum Rabeya (Khatun) A.; m. Shirin Majid, Jan. 28, 1979; children: Sami Ahmed Hasnayeen, Sara Raiyana Andalib. BA with honors, Dhaka U., 1973, MA in Econs., 1974; M.Social Sci., Birmingham (Eng.) U., 1987; Assoc. Cost & Mgmt. Acct., Inst. Cost & Mgmt. Accts., 1994. Rsch. supr. Bangladesh Rural Advancement Com., Sylhet, 1977; thcr. econs. Notredam Coll., Dhaka, 1977; rsch. officer Planning Commn., Dhaka, 1977-79; asst. acct. gen., dep. acct. gen. Acct. Gen.'s Office, Dhaka, 1979-83; chief accounts officer Govt. Ministries of Agr., Edn., Dhaka, 1983-91; dir. budget and dep. sec. Ministry of Fin., Dhaka, 1991—; dir. Bangladesh Jute Mills Ltd., Narshingdi. Contbr. articles to profl. jours. Dep. nat. commr. Bangladesh Scouts, Dhaka, 1988—; trustee Rabeya Azher

Child Health Found., Sajjankanda, Rajbari, Bangladesh, 1988—. Recipient Medal of Merit, Bangladesh Scouts, 1993, Bar to the Medal of Merit, 1995. Mem. Am. Econ. Assn., Inst. Cost. and Mgmt. Accts. (assoc.), Officers Club. Avocations: music, gardening, tennis, jogging, travel. Home: 71/1 Circuit House, Circuit House Rd, Dhaka Bangladesh Office: Audit Dept Audit House, 43 Kakrail Rd, Dhaka 1000, Bangladesh

HAKEEM, MUHAMMAD ABDUL, artist, educator; b. N.Y.C., Oct. 15, 1945; s. Cheveland and Ruby (Rountrea) Marshall; m. Sheron Fatima, Nov. 27, 1987. Student of sculpture and painting, Pratt Inst., Pietrasanta, Italy, 1972; BFA, Pratt Inst., 1974; MA, Tchr. Coll., 1976; MEd, Columbia U., 1980. Artist N.Y. Daily News, 1976-78; asst. technician Bklyn. Mus., 1980-81, instr. African Art, 1981; tchr. Holy Rosary Sch., Bklyn., 1982-89; arts and crafts specialist Fresh Air Fund Camp, Fishkill, N.Y., summer 1983, Camp Merrimac, Contoo Cook, N.H., summers 1986-88; tchr. art Middle Sch. 319, Bronx, N.Y., 1997-98, Denver Sch. Dist., 2000—; adj. prof. Naropa Inst., Boulder. One-man shows include Christ Hosp. Primary Care Ctr., Jersey City, N.J., 1997; exhibited in group shows at Bklyn. Mus., 1973, Lynn Kottler Galleries, 1974, Hansen Galleries, 1974, Galleries Internat., 1975, Cmty. Gallery, 1977, Waverly Gallery, Inc., 1977, Allan S. Park Gallery, 1978, Greenwich Bar and Restaurant, 1979, Macy Gallery, 1980, West Side Story, 1981, Lynn Kittler Galleries, 1981, World Trade Expo-Keane Mason Gallery, 1981, Tabor Gallery, 1982, Gallery II, St. George, Utah, 1984, Beaulahland, 1986, Morin-Miller Galleries, 1987, 89, Ednl. Alliance, 1988, Steamboat Springs (Colo.) Art Coun./Eleanor Bliss Ctr. for the Arts of the Depot (hon. mention), 1992, Boulder (Colo.) Art Ctr., 1993, Louisville (Colo.) Arts Ctr., 1993, Emmanuel Gallery-U. Colo., Denver, 1994, Cross Gallery, Boulder, 19955, Cross Gallery, Denver, 1995, Bklyn. Children's Mus., 1996, The Christ Hosp. Primary Care Ctr., 1997, Boulder Mus. Contemporary Art, 2000; works represented at Kearon-Hempenstall Gallery, Jersey City; multimedia exhbn. at Colo. History Mus., 1996. Art tchr. Lower East Side Cmty Sch., N.Y.C., 1976-77, Urban League, Bklyn., 1969 summer; counselor Office of Cath. Edn., Bklyn., 1987-88; mem. customer panel Regional Transp. Divsn. Winner Cheekwood Nat. Contemporary Painting Competition, Cheekwood Mus. Art, Tenn., 1993. Mem. Kappa Delta Pi (Kappa chpt.). Home: 2900 E Aurora Ave Apt 354 Boulder CO 80303-2242 Address: 2900 Aurora Ave Apt 354 Boulder CO 80303-2242

HAKEEM, SHAZIA TABASSUM, science educator, microbiologist, researcher; b. Karachi, Sindh, Pakistan, Dec. 29, 1971; d. Abdul Hakeem and Noorgehan (Begum) H. BSc, Abdullah Govt. Coll., Karachi, 1990; MSc in Microbiology, U. Karachi, 1993; BS, Qualification Authority, New Zealand, 1999. Cert. med. lab. technologist. Microbiologist Lab and Blood Bank, Dr. Essa, Karachi, 1989-90, 94-99; microbiologist BAQAI Med. U. Hosp., Karachi, 1991-94, rsch. officer Immunology and Infectious Disease Rsch. Lab., 1991-94; lectr. Jinnah U. Woman, Karachi, 1997—; cons. rsch. Sure Bio-diagnostics and Pharms., Karachi, 1997—; co-rschr. Hoechst Pakistan, Karachi, 1998, Iowa U., 1997-98, Bristol Myers Squibb, 1997-98, dept. pharmacogonosy Karachi U., 1998. Mng. editor The World's Food Problems, 1999. Mem. Am. Soc. Microbiology, Pakistan Soc. Microbiology, Pakistan Med. Lab. Technologists Assn., Karachi Microbiology Tchr. Soc. Avocations: reading, poetry, sketching, stamp collecting. Home: III-D 23/3 Nazimabad, Karachi 74600SND, Pakistan Office: Jinnah U Women, V-C Nazimabad, Karachi 74600SND, Pakistan

HAKIM, RÉMI JOËL, physics and astrophysics educator, researcher; b. Deauville, Calvados, France, July 26, 1936; s. Isaak Zaki Hakim and Claire Penso; m. Monique Charlotte Jafé, Mar. 13, 1962; children: Christophe, Gilles, Clèment. B in Maths., Paris U., Paris, 1954, Lic. in Maths., 1956; DSc, Paris U., Orsay, France, 1966; Diplôme d'Hèbreu, INALCO, Paris, 1987. Asst. prof. Paris U., 1961-68; prof. math. Montpellier U., France, 1968-82; prof. physics Paris 7 U., 1982-96, prof. emeritus, 1996—; rsch. assoc. CNRS, 1973—. Sgt. French Air Force, 1959-61, Algeria. Decorated Mèdaille de Maintien de l'Ordre French Air Force, 1960. Fellow French Phys. Soc. Jewish. Avocations: genealogy, painting, art history, studying Turkish, Persian, Hebrew and other Oriental languages. Office: Astrophysique Relativiste, Observatoire, 92190 Meudon France

HAKIM, SEYMOUR (SY HAKIM), writer, artist, retired secondary education educator; b. N.Y.C., Jan. 23, 1933; s. Sol and Renee Hakim; m. Odetta Roverso, Aug. 18, 1970. AB, Ea. N.Mex. U., 1957; MA, NYU, 1960; postgrad., U. Calif., Brigham Young U., U. Pa., U. Mass. Tchr. art and English various schs. in N.Mex. and N.Y., 1957-61; tchr. English and art Dept. Def. Vicenza (Italy) Am. Sch., 1962-70, tchr. English, art, and photography, 1972-94, chmn. English dept., 1973-93; ret., 1994; tchr. London Ctrl. H.S., 1971; mem. exec. bd. Italo-Britannica Assocs. Author: (play) The Sacred Family, 1970, (poems) Manhattan Goodbye, 1970, Undermoon, 1970, The Museum of the Mind, 1971, Wine Theorem, 1972, (autobiography) Substituting Memories, 1976, Iris Elegy, 1979, Balancing Act...a congruence of symbols, 1981, The Birth of a Poet, 1985, Eleanor Goodbye, 1988, Michaelangelo's Call, 1999; editor: Overseas Teacher, 1977; contbr. poems and articles to various periodicals and anthologies; one-man exhbns. of art, 1970, 73, 82-83, 86, Vicenza, 1993, N.Y.C., 1999, The Gallery Washington, 1999, Tribecca, N.Y.C., 2000; internat. group shows, 1971, 76, 78, 84, 85, 87, 89, 90, 92, 94, 95, 96, 97, N.Y.C., 1994, Phila., 1994, 95, 96, 97, N.Y.C., 1999, 2000; represented in collections in China, Romania, Japan, Eng., Korea, Germany, U.S., Internat. Biennial Print Exhibit, 1985, 87, 88, 90, 91, 92, 93, 94, 95, 96, 97, Third Egyptian Internat. Print Triennale, 1999. With AUS, 1952-54. Address: via Chiesanuova 1, 36023 Longare, Vicenza Italy

HAKIMELAHI, GHOLAM HOSEIN, chemistry educator, researcher, consultant; b. Shiraz, Fars, Iran, Jan. 1, 1954; s. Aliakbar and Kefayat (Tavasoli) H.; m. Zahra Ramezani, Jan. 1, 1975; children: Shahram, Ali. BSc in Chemistry, Nat. U., Tehran, Iran, 1972; MSc in Chemistry, Shiraz U., 1974; PhD in Chemistry, McGill U., Montreal, Quebec, Can., 1979, postdoctoral studies in Chemistry, 1979-82. Cert. tchr., Iran. Rsch. assoc. McGill U., Montreal, 1980-82; asst. prof. Shiraz U., 1982-83, assoc. prof., 1983-86, prof., 1986-91; vis. prof. Acad. Sinica, Taipei, Taiwan, 1992—; tchr. Dominican Internat. Sch., Taipei, Taiwan, 1994-99; dir. dept. chemistry Shiraz U., 1987-89; rsch. cons. Daroupakhsh Pharm. Co., Tehran, 1987-90; cons. in viral chemotherapy Saadi Hosp. Shiraz, 1988-90; hon. tchr. Shiraz schs., 1983-91. Author: Physical, Chemical and Clinical Properties of the Generic Drugs, 1989; patentee: U.S. Patent for Ester of retinoic acid and azetidinone derivatives, 1983, novel nucleotide Phosphonoamidates as anti-AIDS, 1996, Adenylates as anti-viral agents, 1996, Iranian patent for a novel procedure for indsl. prepartion of zovirax and related compounds, 1989, a new method for preparation of bitamycin, 1989, preparation of new pain killer for migraine headaches, 1989; mem. editl. bd. Jour. Sci. Iran; contbr. numerous articles to profl. jours. including Helv. Chim. Acta, Jour. Colloid and Interface Sci., Organometallics, Jour. Med. Chem. and others; presenter papers at sci. symposia. Officer Iranian Armed Forces, 1974-75. Recipient Best Rschr. award Ministry of Sci. and Edn., Iran, 1983-85, Best Inventor award, Iranian Acad. Sci., 1986, Iranian Chem. Soc. award 1990, French Med. Found. award, 1991, Best Tchr.'s award, 1997, Self Dedication award, 1998. Mem. Swiss Chem. Soc., N.Y. Acad. Scis. Avocations: gardening, sports, writing, painting, counseling. Home and Office: Inst of Chemistry, Acad Sinica, Nankang Taipei 11529, Taiwan

HÄKKINEN, MIKA, race car driver; b. Helsinki, Finland, Sept. 28, 1968. Race car driver, 1987—. 5-time Finnish karting champion, 1974-86, champion Finnish, Swedish and Nordic Formula Ford 1600, 1987, champion Opel Lotus Euroseries, 1988, runner-up Brit. GM Lotus Series, 1988, 3d pl. Japanese Grand Prix, 1993, 2d pl. Belgium, 3d pl. San Marino, Britain, Italy, Portugal and Europe, 1994, 2d pl. Italy and Japan, 1995, 3d pl., Britain, Belgium, Italy and Japan, 1995, 1st pl. European Grand Prix, 1996, 3d pl. Australia and Germany, 1997. Office: McLaren Internat Ltd Unit 22, Work Bus Park Albert Dr Sheerwater Work, Surrey GU21 5JY, England*

HAKOGI, MASUMI, economist, educator; b. Kobe, Japan, Jan. 11, 1936; s. Isamu and Sueko (Tomiyori) H.; m. Reiko Shirose, Apr. 29, 1975. BA, Osaka U. Fgn. Studies, 1959; MA, Osaka U., 1968. Staff Kyowa Rubber Industry Co., Ltd., Osaka, 1959-65; lectr. Fukushima (Japan) U., 1971-72, assoc. prof., 1973-81, prof. econs., 1982-93; prof. econs. Tohoku U., Sendai, Japan, 1993-99, Hiroshima (Japan) U. Econs., 1999—; chmn. Fukushima City Internat. Exch. Study Com., 1989-91; vice chmn. Fukushima City Internat. Exch. Cons. Com., 1990; cons. Sendai Internat. Exch. Bases Constrn. Planning Rsch., 1993-94. Co-editor: International Industrial Adjustment, 1983, Economics of the Socialist Countries, 1989. Mem. Japan Soc. Internat. Econs., Internat. Studies Assn., Univ. Assn. Contemporary European Studies. Avocations: tennis, hiking, fishing. Home: 2-492 Aza Numanoue, Fushiogami Fukushima 960-8154, Japan Office: Fac of Econs Hiroshima U, 5-37-1 Gion Asaminami-ku, 980-8576 Hiroshima City 731-0192, Japan

HAKOLA, HANNU PANU AUKUSTI, psychiatry educator; b. Lapua, Finland, Feb. 22, 1932; s. Aukusti Jalmari and Toini Kyllikki (Tikkanen) H.; m. Maija-Leena Salo, Apr. 19, 1954; children: Jouni, Marja, Jorma, Jaakko. MD, U. Turku, Finland, 1956, MA, 1960, PhD, 1972. Diploma in health adminstrn. Nat. Bd. Health, Finland, 1979. Asst. physician Neuropsychiat. Clinic, Turku, 1956-60; chief psychiatrist Harjamäki Hosp., Siilinjärvi, Finland, 1960-69, Niuvanniemi Hosp., Kuopio, Finland, 1969-83; prof. forensic psychiatry U. Kuopio, Finland, 1983-95; med. dir. Harjamaki Hosp., Siilinjärvi, 1960-69. Author: On Environmental Conditions of Criminal Psychopaths, 1959, Clinical Aspect of a New Hereditary Disease, 1972, Polycystic Lipomembranous Osteodysplasia with sclerosing Leukoencephalopathy, 1990, Duraljan Vocabulary, 1997, 1000 Duraljan Etyma, 2000; editor: Symposium on Forensic Psychiatry, 1988; inventor Carbamazepine in Schizophrenia, 1982, Duraljan Superfamily, 1989, 1000 Duraljan Etyma, 2000; editorial bd. Med. Jour. Duodecim, 1975-81; contbr. over 250 articles to profl. jours. and chpts. to books. Bd. dirs. Kuopio U. Ctrl. Hosp., 1985-89, 93—. Decorated knight Finnish Order of White Rose; comdr. Finnish Order of Lion; Paulo Found. grantee, Helsinki, Finland, 1971, Aaltonen Found. grantee, Tampere, Finland, 1973; recipient Prize, Acta Psychiat. Scandinavia, 1972. Mem. Finnish Med. Assn. (de. com. 1964—, exec. bd. 1980-84), Med. Assn. North-Savo (hon.), Rotary (pres. 1995), Avo-Puijo club 1974-75, Paul Harris fellow 1982, Blue Stone fellow 1995). Avocations: music, hunting, Joutenlahti farm. Home: Satamakatu 3 D 49, FIN-70100 Kuopio Finland Office: Niuvanniemi Hosp, FIN 70240 Kuopio Finland

HAKOSHIMA, SHIN-ICHI, business executive; b. Dec. 9, 1937. Grad., Kyushu U., 1962. With Asahi Shimbun, 1962—, assoc. editor econ. news dept., 1979-84, econ. editor, Nagoya Head Office, 1985-86, econ. editor Tokyo Head Office, 1987-89, dep. mng. editor Nagoya Head Office, 1990-91, mng. editor Seibu Head Office, 1991, mng. editor Tokyo Head Office, 1992-93, mng dir., adminstrn., 1996-97, mng. dir., CEO, 1998; sr. mng. dir., COO, 1998, pres., CEO, 1999—. Office: 5-3-2 Tsukiji, Chuo-ku, 104-8011 Tokyo Japan

HAKUO, YANAGISAWA, government official; b. Fukuroi City, Shizuoka, Japan, Aug. 1935; married; two children. Grad. Law, Tokyo U. Min. for fin. reconstruction Japan. E-mail: kisa-ishii@frc.fsa.go.jp. Office: Min of Finance, 3-1-1 Kasumigaseki, Chiyoda-ku 100-0013, Tokyo*

HAKUSHI, KAWAMURA, law educator; b. Fukuyama City, Japan, Apr. 1, 1939; s. Minoru and Misao Kawamura; m. Yukiko Kawamura; children: Seitaro, Akihisa. LLM, Chuo U., 1964. Trainee Yamaichi Securities Ltd., Tokyo, 1964-65; instr. Hakodate (Japan) U., 1967—, prof. in corp. law, 1978—, pres., 1989—. Author: The Commercial Code and Nonsense of the General Shareholders Meeting in Japan Ultrabig Company. Office: Hakodate U, Takaoka cho 51-1, Hakodate 042, Japan

HALABE, UDAYA BHATTA, civil engineering educator, researcher; b. Kathmandu, Nepal, Nov. 19, 1961; came to U.S., 1985; s. Gangadhar Bhatta and Shailaja Bhatta H.; m. Anjali Marathe; children: Esha Bhatta H., Shivali Bhatta H. BE in Civil Engring., U. Roorkee, India, 1984; M in Tech. (Civil Engring.), Indian Inst. Tech., Kanpur, India, 1985; MS in Civil Engring., MIT, 1988, MS in Mgmt., 1990, PhD in Civil Engring., 1990. Registered profl. engr., W. Va. Asst. prof. W. Va. U., Morgantown, 1990-96, assoc. prof., 1996—. Contbr. numerous articles to profl. jours.; delivered 40 sci. papers at sci. confs., and writer of over 20 rsch. reports. Mem. ASCE, ASNT, Am. Concrete Inst., Am. Soc. for Nondestructive Testing, Sigma Xi. Avocations: walking, reading, tennis, swimming. Home: 900 Alpine St Morgantown WV 26505-2603 Office: W Va U PO Box 6103 Engring Sci Bldg Rm #627 Morgantown WV 26506

HALABY, NAJEEB E., financier, lawyer; b. Dallas, Nov. 19, 1915; s. Najeeb Elias and Laura (Wilkins) H.; m. Doris Carlquist, Feb. 9, 1946 (div. 1977); children: Lisa (Queen Noor of Jordan), Christian, Alexa; m. Jane Allison Coates Frick, Oct. 1, 1980 (dec. 1996); m. Libby Anderson Cater, Dec. 1, 1997. A.B., Stanford U., 1937; student, U. Mich. Law Sch., 1937-38; LL.B., Yale, 1940; LL.D., Allegheny Coll., 1967, Loyola U., Los Angeles, 1968, Dowling Coll., 1985, Embry Riddle & Aero. U., 1993. Bar: Calif. 1940, D.C. 1948, N.Y. 1973. Pvt. practice L.A.; with O'Melveny & Myers, 1940-42; test pilot Lockheed Aircraft Corp., Burbank, Calif., 1942-43; fgn. affairs adviser to sec. def., 1948-53, dep. asst. sec. def., 1952-54; with L. S. Rockefeller and Bros., 1953-56; pres. Am. Tech. Corp.; sec.-treas., counsel Aerospace Corp.; faculty lectr. UCLA; dir. def. studies program; chmn. UCLA (1960 disarmament conf.); pvt. practice law Calif., 1959-61; adminstr. FAA, 1961-65; pres. Pan Am World Airways, 1968-72, chmn., chief exec. officer, 1969-72; pres. Halaby Internat. Corp., 1973—; chmn. Save The Children Found., 1992-98, Dulles Access Rapid Transit, Inc., 1985-98; with Nat. Ctr. for Atmospheric Rsch. Found., 1985—. Trustee Aspen Inst., chmn., Wolf Trap Found., (Va.), Jones Inst. Reproductive Biology, Flight Safety Found.; elected chmn. bd. visitors AOPA Flight Safety Found.; mem. adv. coun. Brookings Inst., Libr. of Congress, Smithsonian Instn., Nat. Gallery of Art, Stanford in Washington. Served as naval aviator USN World War II; asst. chief fighter sec. Naval Air Test Center Patuxent River, Md. Decorated Legion of Honor France; Order of Cedars Lebanon; medal of Independence Jordan; recipient Arthur Fleming award; Godfrey L. Cabot award; Monsanto Air Safety award; Glen Gilbert Air Traffic award, Nat. Air and Space Mus. trophy Smithsonian Instn., 1995. Fellow AIAA; mem. Soc. Exptl. Test Pilots, Corbey Ct., Coun. on Fgn. Rels. Clubs: Alibi, Metropolitan; Chevy Chase; Bohemian (San Francisco); Piping Rock (N.Y.C.), Explorers, Tower. Office: 175 Chain Bridge Rd Mc Lean VA 22101-1907*

HALANG, WOLFGANG ANDREAS, electrical engineer, educator; b. Essen, Germany, Oct. 4, 1951; s. H.B. Edgar and Erika Margret (Kiesendahl) H.; m. Bertha Karina Morales Velazquez, May 15, 1986; children: Andrea, Matthias. Dipl.-Math., Ruhr-U., Bochum, Germany, 1974, Dr.rer.nat., 1976; Dr.rer.nat., U. Dortmund, Germany, 1980. Sr. computer sys. engr. Coca-Cola GmbH, Essen, 1976-85; adj. prof. U. Dortmund, 1985; asst. prof. King Fahd U. Petroleum and Minerals, Dhahran, Saudi Arabia, 1985-87; vis. asst. prof. U. Ill., Urbana/Champaign, 1987-88; sr. engr. Bayer AG, Leverkusen, Germany, 1988-89; prof. and dept. head U. Groningen, The Netherlands, 1989-92; prof. Fern-U., Hagen, Germany, 1992—; vis. prof. U. Maribor, Slovenia, 1997, U. Rome II, Italy, 1999; dir. NATO Advanced Study Inst., Sint Maarten, Dutch Antilles, 1992; external examiner City U. of Hong Kong. Co-author: Constructing Predictable Real Time Systems, 1991, Real-Time Systems -- Implementation of Industrial Computerized Process Automation, 1992, A Safety Licensable Computing Architecture, 1993, Genetic Algorithms for Control and Signal Processing, 1996, Methodenlehre sicherheitsgerichteter Echtzeitprogrammierung, 1998, Sicherheitsgerichtete Echtzeitsysteme, 1999; co-editor: Real Time Computing, 1994; founder, editor-in-chief Jour. Real-Time Systems, 1989—; mem. editl. bd. 4 sci. jours.; guest editor 3 sci. jours.; contbr. over 250 articles to profl. jours., and confs. Assn. of Iron and Steel Industry scholar Düsseldorf, 1971-75, Prof. Dr.-Ing. Erich-Müller Found. scholar, 1972-75, Fed. Govt. Germany scholar, 1975-76. Mem. IEEE Computer Soc. (tech. com. on complexity in computing 1995—), Internat. Fedn. Automatic Control (chair tech. com. on real time software engring. 1996—, tech. com. on safety of computer control sys. 1996—), Wissenschaftsakademie für Kommunikations- und Informationstechnik (pres.), Verein Deutscher Ingenieure/Verein Deutscher Elektrotechniker (chair tech. com. on real-time sys. in automation 1992—), Gesellschaft für Informatik (chair tech. com. on real-time sys.). Roman Catholic. Home: Am Hange 14, D-58119 Hagen Germany Office: Fernuniversität, Faculty Elec Engring, D-58084 Hagen Germany

HALAS, STANISLAW, physicist, researcher; b. Stryjów, Poland, July 9, 1945; s. Ksawery and Karolina (Pańko) H.; m. Barbara Miroslawa Strakowska, Sept. 2, 1973; children: Piotr, Agnieszka, Jakub, Krzysztof, Joanna, Remigiusz. M in Physics, Maria Curie-Sklodowska U., Lublin, Poland, 1968, D of Physics, 1973. Tutor Maria Curie-Sklodowska U., Lublin, 1973-84, docent, 1984-91, prof., 1991-96, full prof., 1997—; head mass spectrometry lab. Maria Curie-Sklodowska U., 1984—; vis. scientist U. Calgary, Alta., Can., 1979-80. Contbr. articles to profl. jours. Recipient award Polish Acad. Scis., Warsaw, 1990, award Internat. Isotope Soc., Budapest, Hungary, 1996. Mem. Polish Phys. Soc. (pres. Lublin divsn. 1980—), European Isotope Soc. Avocations: swimming, driving. Office: Maria Curie Sklodowska U, 20-031 Lublin Poland

HALÁSZ, BÉLA, anatomist, educator; b. Kalaznó, Tolna, Hungary, July 4, 1927; s. Ármin and Irén (Ruppert) H.; m. Etelka Karácsonyi, Apr. 18, 1954; children: Etelka, Zita. MD, Med. U., Pécs, Hungary, 1954, PhD, 1966, DSc, 1972. Instr. dept. anatomy Univ. Med. Sch., Pécs, 1954-55, asst. prof., 1955-60, adj. prof., 1960-67, assoc. prof., 1967-71; prof. Med. Sch. Semmelweis U., Budapest, Hungary, 1971—, chmn. 2nd dept. anatomy, 1971-95; vice rector Med. Sch. Semmelweis U., 1973-79, pres. joint rsch. orgn. of Hungarian Acad. Sci. and Med. Sch. Semmelweis U., 1982-95. Co-author: Hypothalmic Control of the Anterior Pituitary, 1963; contbr. chpt. to: Frontiers in Neuroendocrinology, 1969; contbr. articles to sci. jours. Recipient Széchenyi prize Hungarian Govt., 1990. Mem. Am. Acad. Arts and Scis. (hon.), Am. Physiol. Soc. (hon.), Internat. Soc. Endocrinology (Ulf von Euler award 1976, G. Harris lectr. 1992), Internat. Soc. Neuroendocrinology (v.p. 1974-80), European Sci. Found. (mem. exec. coun. 1990-96), Acad. Europaea, Hungarian Soc. Endocrinology (pres. 1982-90), Hungarian Acad. Sci. (v.p. 1990-96). Lutheran. Avocations: classical music, gardening. Home: Madách Imre út 1, H-1075 Budapest Hungary Office: Semmelweis med U 2nd Dpt An, TüzoltÓ u58, H-1094 Budapest Hungary

HALASZ, GEORGE, psychiatrist, consultant; b. Budapest, Hungary, July 6, 1949; came to Australia, 1957; s. Laszlo and Alice (Klein) H. Intern Prince Henry's Hosp., Melbourne, Victoria, Australia, 1975-76; sr. house officer Brook Gen. Hosp., London, 1976; resident Beilinson Hosp., Petah Tikva, Tel Aviv, 1977; sr. house officer Middlesex Hosp., London, 1977; registrar King's Coll. Hosp., London, 1978-82; sr. registrar Maudsley, Bethlem Royal Hosp., London, 1982-84; cons. Austin Hosp., Melbourne, 1985-87, Monash Med. Ctr., Melbourne, 1987—; tutor Melbourne U., 1985—; hon. sr. lectr. Monash U., 1987-88; sr. lectr. 1988-93. Editl. bd. mem. Australian and New Zealand Jour. of Psychiatry, 1992—; editor: She Won't Be Right, Mate!, 1997, She Still Won't Be Right, Mate!, 1999. Fellow Royal Australian and N.Z. Coll. Psychiatrists; mem. Royal Coll. Psychiatrists, Eng. Avocations: traveling, reading, theater, music. Office: 30 Burke Rd Med Stes, Melbourne Victoria 3145, Australia

HALASZ, NORBERT PETER, biologist, chemist; b. Hodsag, Yugoslavia, June 28, 1942; s. Johan and Stephanie (Simandy) Haumann; m. Maria Margit Fekete, Nov. 30, 1969 (div. 1994); children: Attila, Erika; m. Maria Olasz, Feb. 25, 1995; 1 child, Gergely Kurunczi. BS in Biology & Chemistry, Jozsef A. Univ., Szeged, Hungary, 1965, PhD in Natural Scis., 1969; PhD in Biology, Acad. Scis., Budapest, Hungary, 1977, DSc in Biology, 1992. Jr. rsch. assoc. Jozsef A. Univ., Szeged, Hungary, 1965-67, rsch. assoc., 1968-69; rsch. assoc. Inst. Biophysics Hungarian Acad. Scis., Szeged, Hungary, 1970-76, sr. rsch. assoc. Inst. Biophysics, 1977-90, sr. sci. advisor Inst. Biophysics, 1991-92; sr. sci. advisor Chinoin Works, Budapest, Hungary, 1993—; head libr. sci. info. and documentation unit Chinoin Works, Budapest, 1996—; vis. scientist Karolinska Inst., Stockholm, 1975; dep. sci. dir. Inst. of Biophysics, Hungarian Acad. Scis., Szeged, 1977-80, 82-92; vis. scientist Goettingen (Germany) U., 1983-91, Yale U., New Haven, Conn., 1980-81, 89-93; head of libr., 1996—. Author: (book) The Vertebrate Olfactory System, 1990 (Award of Excellence Hungarian Acad. Sci. 1993); founder, editor-in-chief Neurobiology, 1993-95; editor: Neurobiology, 1996—. Recipient Lenhossek award for article in Acta Anatomica, 1974, Order of Labour/Silver Grade, Hungarian Govt., 1980. Mem. Hungarian Acad. Sci. (mem. neurobiology com. 1980—, sec. 1981-90), 11 other Hungarian and internat. sci. socs. Avocations: hiking, photography, reading. Office: Chinoin Works Co Ltd, To U 1-5 PO Box 110, 1325 Budapest Hungary

HALAWA, EDWARD E.H., engineer, consultant; b. G. Sitoli Nias, N. Sumatra, Indonesia, Jan. 2, 1959; s. Heziduhu and Simina H.; m. Rapital Simarmata, Apr. 22, 1988; 1 child, Yohan Kristian. BS in Mech. Engring., U. Sumatra, Medan, Indonesia, 1984; MS in Mech. Engring., U. South Australia, Adelaide, 1995. Jr. rschr. LIPI, Bandung, Indonesia, 1985-94; energy splist. APO ASEAN-Canada Solar Energy Project, Bandung, 1994-96; energy rschr. Indonesian Inst. Scis. (LIPI), Bandung, 1994—. Author: Programming in C/C and its Numerical Application, 1995; contbr. articles to profl. jours. Mem. N.Y. Acad. Scis., World Energy Council (Indonesia section), Yayasan Nilam (chmn. 1999—). Roman Catholic. Home: Kompleks Taman Sari B42, Cileunyi Bandung 40393, Indonesia Office: R&D Ctr Applied Phys LIPI, JL Cisitu Kompleks LIPI, Bandung 40135, Indonesia

HALBARDIER, SHERYL LINETTE, social studies educator, counselor; b. San Antonio, Sept. 13, 1948; d. Edward William and Barbara (Hensley) Halbardier; m. John Sterling Thompson, May 14, 1979 (div. Mar. 1982). BS in Elem. Edn., U. Tex., 1970; postgrad., Our Lady of the Lake Coll., San Antonio, 1981—; student, U. Paris, 1969. Lic. chem. dependency counselor, Tex. Substance abuse prevention specialist Edgewood Ind. Sch. Dist., San Antonio, 1986-90; rsch. asst. Univ. Health Sci./U. Tex. Health Sci. Ctr., San Antonio, 1990-92; tchr. social studies and sci. Dallas Ind. Sch. Dist., 1992-94; owner, counselor Co-A-Tots, San Antonio, 1994—; Mem. adv. bd. on writing fed. grants Edgewood Ind. Sch. Dist., 1986-88, Ara County Youth Support Ctr., Rockport, Tex., 1989. Author: Co-A-Tots, 1996. Job coach for mentally retarded Alamo Hts. Manor, San Antonio, 1995-96; aide Rep. Task Force, Washington, 1980-96. Our Lady of the Lake U. fellow, 1990. Mem. Women in Bus., Tex. Com. on Alcoholism and Drug Abuse. Avocations: jewelry making, horseback riding, swimming, computer. Address: Apt 117 8607 Jones Maltsberger Rd San Antonio TX 78216-5920

HALDANE-STEVENSON, JAMES PATRICK, minister; b. Llandaff, Wales, Mar. 17, 1910; s. Graham Morton and Jane (Thomson) Stevenson; m. Leila Mary Flack, Nov. 5, 1938 (div. 1967); children: Alan, Keith, Janet; m. Joan Talbot Smith, Aug. 6, 1983. BA, U. Oxford, Eng., 1933, MA, 1941; postgrad., U. Lausanne, Switzerland, 1934. Ordained to ministry Anglican Ch., 1935. Clk. Westminster Bank, Birmingham, Eng., 1927-30; curate Anglican Ch., Lambeth, Eng., 1935-38; commissary Archbishop Ont., 1939-44; chaplain British Army, Dunkirk, France, Cassino, Italy, Northern Ireland, 1939-55; rector Anglican Ch., Wongan Hills, Australia, 1956-59; vicar Anglican Ch. of North Balwyn, Melbourne, Australia, 1959-80; founder HSC Consultancy, 1991. Author: (as J.P. Stevenson) In Our Tongues, 1944, Religion and Leadership, 1948, Crisanzio and Other Poems, 1948, Beyond the Bridge, 1973, The Backward Look, 1976; represented in anthologies including Soldiers Also Asked, 1943, Padre Presents, 1943, Poems from Italy, 1945, Songs of Australia, 1977; contbr. Australian Encyclopaedia, Australian Dictionary of Biography, Poetry Rev., Poetry Today, Guardian, New Statesman, Spectator; Australian correspondent Le Monde, 1969-73. Mem. Athenaeum Club (life, London), Instn. Engrs. Australia, Instn. Royal Engrs. (Eng.), Melbourne Club. Home: 4/33 Bruce St, Toorak 3142, Australia Office: 36 Collins St, Melbourne 3000, Australia

HALDAR, FRANCES LOUISE, business educator, accountant, treasurer; b. Mineola, N.Y., July 2, 1948; d. Alfred Karl and Gudrun Maria (Lucks) Loschen; m. Kali S. Haldar, Feb. 29, 1972; children: Neil Alexander, Monica Joyce. AA, The Ohio Sate U., 1985, BSBA in Acctg. summa cum laude, 1989, MBA, 1991, PhD, 1999. Adminstrv. asst. Pam Am. World Airways Inc., N.Y.C., 1968-73; acct., treas. K.S. Haldar, MD, Inc., Mansfield, Ohio, 1978—; adj. prof. to assoc. prof. bus., then assoc. prof. acctg. North Cen. State Coll., Mansfield, 1991-99; acad. advisor N. Ctrl. Tech. Coll., Mansfield, 1991-98; assoc. prof. bus. N. Ctrl. State Coll., Mansfield, 1993-96, assoc. prof. acctg., 1996-99, prof. acctg., 1999-2000; asst. dean bus., math. and tech. Cuyahoga Cmty. Coll., Highland Hills, Ohio, 2000—. Mem. Am. Assn. Higher Edn., Nat. Bus. Edn. Assn., Am. Assn. C.C., Am. Acctg. Assn., Inst. Mgmt. Accts., Golden Key, Phi Kappa Phi, Beta Gamma Sigma. Avocations: reading, traveling. Office: Cuyahoga Cmty Coll 4250 Richmond Rd Highland Hls OH 44122-6104

HALDAR, SUBHAS CHANDRA, mechanical engineering educator, researcher; b. Midnapore, India, Jan. 4, 1966; s. Joydeb and Anandamayee

(Das) H.; m. Arpita Dey, Apr. 19, 1999. B of Engring., Bengal Engring. Coll., Howrah, India, 1987; MTech, Indian Inst. Tech., Madras, 1989; PhD, Indian Inst. Tech., Kharagpur, 1995. Lectr. Regional Engring. Coll., Rourkela, India, 1993-97, sr. lectr., 1997—. Contbr. articles to profl. jours. Mem. Instn. Engrs. (India), Indian Soc. Tech. Edn. Avocations: chess, music. Fax: (0091) 661-571169/572926. E-mail: schaldar@rec.ori.nic.in. Office: Regional Engring Coll, Dept Mech Engring, Rourkela Orissa 769 008, India

HALDEMAN, BRUCE, investment company executive; b. Louisville, June 23, 1936; s. Walter Newman and Jane (Norton) H.; m. Barbara Olds, Oct. 2, 1965; children: Walter N. III, Anne O. BS, Va. Mil. Inst., Lexington, 1958. Lt. USAF, Tucson, 1959-62; dist. sales mgr. Armco Steel Co., Memphis, Dallas, Richmond, Va., Greensboro, N.C., 1963-78; regional engr. Am. Wood Preservers Inst., Greensboro, 1978-83; mgr. tech. svcs. Atlantic Wood Industries, Savannah, Ga., 1984-85; v.p., then pres., CEO Kentex Mineral Co., Greensboro, 1985—. Served to maj. USAFR, 1959-76. Mem. Nat. Assn. Royalty Owners, Am. Soc. Civil Engrs., Forest Oaks Country Club, Louisville Country Club, Soc. Colonial Wars, Peyton Soc. Va., N.C. Zool. Soc., Hist. Preservation Soc. N.C. Republican. Avocations: tennis, hiking, amateur historian.

HALE, ALLAN, retired editor; b. London, May 19, 1930; s. Ernest Allan and Daisy May (Lavender) H.; m. Mirella Audley Barrett, 1963; children: Martin Edward, Annemarie Audley, Roderick Jack. Reporter Kentish Ind., London, 1953-55, South London Press, 1955-57, Kentish Times, London, 1957-60; reporter, feature writer, copy editor Manchester Evening News, London, 1960-65; writer/asst. city editor Globe-Dem. St. Louis, Mo., 1965-70; copy editor Community Newspapers, Perth, Australia, 1987-93; reporter West Australian Weekend News, Perth, 1971—; journalism fellow Stanford U., 1968. Contbr. articles to profl. jours. With Brit. Army, 1948-53. Mem. Australian Journalists Assn., Sigma Delta Chi. Avocations: reading, bush walking, astronomy, painting. Home: 83 Evandale St, Perth Australia 6014

HALE, CECIL, communications educator; b. St. Louis, Aug. 3, 1945; s. Cecil and Allean (Cunningham) H.; m. Brenda Kidd; children: Juanita, Tasha, Cecil-Jamil. Student, So. Ill. U., 1963-66; MA, Internat. U. of Comm., Washington, 1975; PhD, Union Inst., Cin., 1978; MPA, Harvard U., 1995. Lic. by FCC. Announcer, asst. gen. mgr. WMPP Radio, 1964-68; announcer XPRS Radio, L.A., 1972-74; announcer, asst. program/music dir. WNOV Radio, Milw., 1968-70, WVON Radio, Chgo., 1970-77; nat. dir., mgr. Phonogram/Mercury Records, Chgo., 1977-78; v.p. Capitol Records, Inc., Hollywood, Calif., 1978-81; prof. San Francisco State U., 1984-94, City Coll. San Francisco, 1986—; prof. Mass Media Inst. Stanford U., 1987-92; cons. N.T.A., Lagos, Nigeria, 1982-83, Gallo Winery, Inc., Modesto, Calif., 1977, Capitol Records, Inc., Hollywood, 1981-82, Congl. Caucus, Washington, 1975. Author: The Music Industry, 1990; exec. producer phono records. Recipient Key to City and City Coun. Resolution, L.A., 1980, Outstanding Tchr. award Acad. Senate, City Coll. San Francisco, 1990, San Francisco State U. Faculty award, 1986; U. Calif. fellow, 1992. Mem. ABA, NAACP, AAUP, NEA, Nat. Acad. Recording Arts and Scis., Am. Fedn. Musicians, Am. Fedn. TV and Radio Artists, Am. Fedn. Tchrs., Soc. for Values in Higher Edn., Stanford Alumni Assn., Harvard Alumni Assn., Kennedy Sch. Exec. Coun., Coun. for Black Am. Affairs (pres. 1997—), Masons, Nat. Eagle Scout Assn., Harvard Club San Francisco, Alpha Phi Alpha. Avocations: aviaton, computer science. Home: 24179 Alberta Ct Hayward CA 94545-2055 Office: City Coll San Francisco 50 Phelan Ave San Francisco CA 94112-1821

HALE, DANNY LYMAN, financial executive; b. Ft. Lauderdale, Fla., Mar. 23, 1944; s. Thomas Hatten and Marion June (Frizzell) H.; m. Reda Fay Kofahl, June 10, 1966; 1 child, Matthew Bryan. BA in Econs., Yale U., 1966. Cons. in fin. planning Gen. Electric Co., Fairfield, Conn., 1977-78; mgr. fin. stragety devel. Gen. Electric Co., Louisville, 1978-79, mgr. fin. ops., 1979-80; mgr. divsn. fin. ops. GE Credit Corp., Stamford, Conn., 1980-82, v.p., dept. gen. mgr., 1982-84; mng. dir., mgr. bus. devel. Kidder Peabody Group, N.Y.C., 1987-88; pres. chase Comml. Corp., Chase Manhattan Bank, Paramus, N.J., 1988-91; exec. v.p. U.S.F. & G. Corp., Balt., 1991, exec. v.p., CFO, 1993-98; exec. v.p., CFO Promus Hotel Corp., Memphis, 1999—. With U.S. Army, 1967-69. Republican. Congregationalist. Home: 4021 Gulf Shore Blvd N Apt 204 Naples FL 34103-2230 Office: Promus Hotel Corp 755 Crossover Ln Memphis TN 38117-4900

HALE, DAVID FREDRICK, health care company executive; b. Gadsden, Ala., Jan. 8, 1949; s. Millard and Mildred Earline (McElroy) H.; m. Linda Carol Sadorski, Mar. 14, 1975; children: Shane Michael, Tara Renee, Erin Nicole, David Garrett. BA, Jacksonville State U. Dir. product mgmt. Ortho Pharm. Corp. divsn. Johnson & Johnson, Raritan, N.J., 1978-80; v.p. mktg. BBL Microbiology Sys. divsn. Becton Dickinson & Co., Cockeysville, Md., 1980-81, v.p., gen. mgr., 1981-82; sr. v.p. mktg. and bus. devel. Hybritech, Inc., San Diego, 1982, pres., 1983-86, CEO, 1986-87; pres., CEO, bd. dirs. Gensia Sicor, Inc., San Diego, 1987-97, Women First HealthCare, Inc., 1998-2000; bd. dirs. Dura Pharms., LMA N.Am., Metabasis Therapeutics, Children's Hosp., Francis Parker Sch., U. Calif. San Diego Found., San Diego Econ. Devel. Corp., Biocom San Diego; founder CONNECT. Mem. World Pres.'s Orgn., Chief Exec.'s Orgn. Republican. Episcopalian. Home: PO Box 8925 16596 Via Lago Azul Rancho Santa Fe CA 92067 Office: Women First HealthCare Inc 12220 El Camino Real Ste 400 San Diego CA 92130-2091

HALE, GEOFFREY, research scientist; b. Chipping Sodbury, U.K., Sept. 2, 1953; s. Harold John and Christine (Fowles) H.; m. Gillian Hutson, Aug. 6, 1977; children: Alison, Christopher, Joanna. BA in Natural Sci., Cambridge (Eng.) U., 1974, PhD in Biochemistry, 1977. Rsch. asst. U. Cambridge, 1977-85, sr. rsch. assoc., 1985-95; rsch. lectr. U. Oxford, Eng., 1995-98; reader therapeutic immunology U. Oxford, 1998-2000, prof. therapeutic immunology, 2000—; rsch. dir. Therapeutic Antibody Ctr., Cambridge, 1990-95, Oxford, 1995—. Contbr. articles to profl. jours. Youth work leader St. Matthews Ch., Cambridge, 1977-85, churchwarden, 1985-91; youth work leader St. Nicholas Ch., Marston, 1997—, ch. warden, 2000—. Achievements include patentee in field. Avocation: playing keyboard instruments.

HALE, KENNETH FRANK, physicist; b. London, Feb. 6, 1929; s. Frank Edward and Gladys Florence (Groom-Howe) H.; m. M.A. Walker, Sept. 11, 1954; children: Claire, Adrienne, John. BSc in Physics with honors, London U., 1956, PhD, 1961, DSc, 1974. Mem. staff Nat. Phys. Lab., Teddington, Middlesex, Eng., 1949-72, sr. prin. sci. officer, 1972-76; sr. prin. sci. officer Nat. Martime Inst., Feltham, Middlesex, 1976-85, Brit. Maritime Tech. Ltd., Feltham, 1985-86; sr. rsch. fellow Brunel U., Uxbridge, Middlesex, 1986—. Co-author: Dynamic Experiments in the Electron Microscope, 1981; joint originator optical fibers use for crack detection and monitoring; contbr. 90 papers to scientific jours. Fellow Inst. Physics, CPhys. Avocations: tennis, squash, golf, sailing. Fax: 01895-812556. Office: Brunel U, Uxbridge UB8 3PH, England

HALE, MONICA, environmental scientist; b. London. BS, London, 1974, MS, 1999. Lectr. in biogeography Kings Coll., London, 1974-82; dir. urban spaces scheme U. North London, 1982-89; head formal edn. Coun. for Environ. Edn., Reading, Eng., 1989-92; dir. London environ. ctr. London Guildhall U., 1992-98; environ. specialist Internat. Fin. Corp., Washington, 1998; environ. tng. coord. World Bank, Washington, 1999—. Author: Ecology in Education, 1993; (with Walter Filho) Trends in Environmental Education Worldwide, 1994; (with Mohamad Soerjani) Environmental Education for Biodiversity and Sustainable Developement, 1998; (with Mike Lachowicz) The Environment, Employment and Sustainable Development, 1998. Recipient Gilcrest award for achievement U. London, 1990. Fellow Linnean Soc. London, Inst. Ecology & Environ. Mgmt. (chmn. tng. edn. and career devel. 1995—, v.p. 1998—), Royal Geographic Soc., Royal Soc. Arts; mem. Internat. Union for Conservation and Nature (edn. and comm. commn. 1996—). Avocations: photography, early music, archaeology, Russian history, American history. Office: World Bank Inst 1818 H St NW Washington DC 20433-0001

HALE, WILLIAM BRYAN, JR., newspaper editor; b. Stephenville, Tex., Apr. 26, 1933; s. William Bryan and Gladys (Tittle) H.; divorced; children: Shandra Hale Reiss, Tamara Hale Cameron, Nicholas, Sabrina. Student, UCLA, 1953-54. Police beat/courts reporter Santa Monica (Calif.) Outlook, 1953-58; gen. reporter Ontario (Calif.) Daily Report, 1958-59; criminal court writer L.A. City News Service, 1959-60; gen. reporter L.A. Times, 1960-61; reporter Houston Chronicle, 1961-62; news editor Somerset (Pa.) American, 1962-63; night editor Elmira (N.Y.) Star-Gazette, 1963-64; copy editor, investigative reporter Milw. Jour., 1964-70; Tucson corr. Time mag./Time-Life Books, 1970-71; night city editor Tucson Citizen, 1970-71; nat. desk copy editor Los Angeles Times, 1971-90; sr. lectr. U. So. Calif., 1974-88; pres. Nat. Copy Editors Sch., Thousand Oaks, Calif., 1984-90; founder and dir. Australian Sub-Editors Sch., Sydney, Australia, 1989-94. Cpl. USMC, 1951-53. Avocations: horseback riding, hiking. Home: PO Box 35128 Tucson AZ 85740-5128

HALE, WILLIAM WALLACE, III, psychologist, researcher; b. Ridgewood, N.J., Jan. 9, 1966; arrived in The Netherlands, 1985; s. William Wallace, Jr. and Joan Beverly (McLean) H.; m. Cornelia Dorothea Van Roon, June 13, 1987; children: Ian James William, Peter John Christiaan. MA, U. Utrecht, The Netherlands, 1993; PhD, U. Groningen, The Netherlands, 1997. Rschr. Acad. Hosp. Groningen, 1993-99; asst. prof. psychology U. Maastricht, 1999—. Contbr. articles to profl. jours. mem. Dutch Inst. Psychology, Am. Psychol. Assn. Office: U Maastricht Dept Med Psych, Universiteitssingel 50 Box 616, 6200 MD Maastricht The Netherlands

HALEMANE, RAJENDRA K., engineering executive; b. Ednad, Kerala, India, Feb. 27, 1965; s. Shama Bhat and Thirumaleshwari (Ambikana) H.; m. Shubhashree R. Ka, Jan. 20, 1993; 1 child, Shyamaraja Bhat. BEng, Malnad Coll. Engring., Hassan, India, 1988. Mng. ptnr. Shamson Electronics, Mangalore, India, 1987-95; ptnr. Shamson Traders, Kasaragod, India, 1990-91, Mayatronics, Puttur, India, 1993-95; mng. ptnr. Shamraj Enterprises, Mangalore, 1994—; mng. dir. Pragati Mechatronics Pvt. Ltd., Mangalore, 1994-96; ptnr. S.S. Sales Corp., Mangalore, 1995—; cons. Swastik Elecs., Neerchal, India, 1988-94, Kakunje Plastics, Manjeshwar, India, 1990-94, Sakriya Elecs., Mangalore, 1989—, Priyanka Electronics, Mangalore, 1995—. Mem. Lom Jr. C. of C. (sec. 1995, v.p. 1996-97). Achievements include the founding of formula of herbal tea. Home: 3-17-1506 Nanthoor Cross, Vivekananda Rd, Mangalore 575 002, India Office: 1 Fl Manar Complex, Balmatta New Rd, Mangalore 575 001, India

HALER, LAWRENCE EUGENE, councilman, communications educator; b. Iowa City, Iowa, Jan. 24, 1951; s. Eugene Hilbert and Mary Elizabeth (Hans) H.; m. Jenifer Lea Leitz, June 1, 1974. BA, Pacific Luth. U., 1974. Reactor operator UNC Nuclear Industries, Richland, Wash., 1974-80, lead cert. instr., 1980-81, mgr. tng. adminstrn., 1981-82, sr. ops. analyst, 1982-85; sr. specialist Gen. Physics Corp., Columbia, Md., 1985-86; sr. instr. Rockwell Hanford Ops., Richland, 1986-88; tech. instr. Westinghouse Hanford Co., Richland, 1988-89, sr. specialist instr., 1989-96, Fluor Daniel Hanford team leader, 1996-99, Fluor Daniel Hanford comm. specialist, 1999—; chmn. bd. dirs. Benton-Franklin County Bd. Health, Richland, 1994-95, Sci. and Tech. Park, Richland; vice chmn. Benton-Franklin Regional Coun. Govts., 1994. Chmn. Benton County Reps., Richland, 1976-78, state committeeman, 1988-90; councilman, mayor pro-tem City of Richland, 1990-96, mayor, 1996-2000, councilman, 2000—; chmn. Ctrl. Bus. Dist. Devel. Bd., Richland; chmn. cmty. econ. devel. steering com. Nat. League of Cities. Mem. Richland C. of C. (chmn. legis. affairs com. 1988-93), Richland Kiwanis (pres. 1994-95). Lutheran. Avocations: swimming, photography. Home: PO Box 1319 Richland WA 99352-1319 Office: Richland City Coun 505 Swift Blvd Richland WA 99352-3510

HALEVY, SIMA, dermatologist; b. Petah Tiqva, Israel, May 8, 1948; parents Shmuel and Rachel (Singalowsky) Sukenik; divorced; children: Ilit, Itai. MD magna cum laude, Tel-Aviv U., 1973. Internship Beilinson Medical Ctr., Petah Tiqva, 1972-73, residency in dermatalogy and venereology, 1974-79, sr. physician, 1980-86; cons. Kupat Holim, Tel Aviv, 1982-91; head dept. dermatology Soroka Medical Ctr., Beer-Sheva, Israel, 1986—; prof. dermatology Ben-Gurion U. of the Negev, Israel, 1992—; profl. adv. com. The Israel Medical Assn. Scientific Coun., 1990—, examination bd. specialists in skin & venereal diseases, 1990—, found. com. Ben-Gurion U., 1993—, senate mem., 1994—; mem. internat. adv. com. Archives of Dermatology, 1998. Sci. editor: Every Woman Can Be Beautiful-A Guide to Well Grooming and Appearance of Women, 1979; contbr. articles to profl. jours. Recipient Excellence of Presentation award Beilinson Med. Ctr., 1979; numerous rsch. grants, 1981-95. Mem. Israel Medical Assn., Israeli Dermatological Soc., Am. Acad. Dermatology, N.Y. Acad. Sci., Women's Dermatologic Soc., Internat. Soc. Dermatology, European Acad. Dermatology. Avocations: music, piano. Office: Dept Dermatology, Soroka U Med Ctr, 84101 Beer Sheva Israel

HALEY, JOHN DAVID, petroleum consulting company executive; b. Denver, Mar. 16, 1924; s. Peter Daniel and Margaret Dorothy (O'Haire) H.; m. Annie Loretta Breeden, June 20, 1951; children: Laura, Patricia, Brian, Sharon, Norine, Kathleen. Profl. engr., Colo. Sch. Mines, 1948. Registered profl. engr., Colo., Okla. Petroleum engr. Creole Petroleum, Venezuela, 1948-50; field engr. Texaco Inc., La., 1950-52; staff engr. Carter Oil (Exxon), Tulsa, 1954-56; petroleum cons. Earlougher Engring., Tulsa, 1956-61; v.p. prodn. Anschutz Corp., Denver, 1962-86; v.p. Circle A Drilling, Denver, 1967-78; dir. Circle A Mud, Denver, 1983-86; pres. Greylock Pipeline, Denver, 1983-86, Anschutz Pipeline, Denver, 1984-86, Haley Engring. Inc., 1987—. Mem. Pres.'s Coun., Colo. Sch. Mines, 1985—; bd. dirs. Alumni Assn., 1992-97, pres., 1995; bd. dirs. CSM Found., 1996-98; Rep. committeeman, Littleton, Colo. Lt. comdr. USNR, 1943-46, 52-54. Recipient Outstanding Alumnus award Alumni Assn., 1997. Mem. Soc. Petroleum Engrs. (bd. dirs. Denver chpt. 1965), Soc. Petroleum Evaluation Engrs. (bd. dirs. 1992-95), Ind. Petroleum Assn. Mountain States, Am. Petroleum Inst. (citation for svc.), Internat. Assn. Drilling Contractors, Rocky Mountain Oil and Gas Assn. (bd. dirs. 1988-2000), Soc. Profl. Well Log Analysts, Petroleum Club (Denver chpt.). Roman Catholic. Home: 561 E Caley Dr Littleton CO 80121-2212

HALEY, PATRICIA ANN, psychiatric therapist, school counselor, administrator; b. Waxahachie, Tex., Jan. 17, 1951; d. Bob A. and Gertie M. (Graham) H. BA, Tex. Woman's Univ., 1973, postgrad. in deaf edn., 1978; MEdin counseling and student svcs., U. North Tex., 1994. Lic. profl. counselor. Tchr. Ennis (Tex.) Ind. Sch. Dist., 1985-93; counselor Ferris (Tex.) Ind. Sch. Dist., 1994—; PRN, psychiat. therapist HCA Med. Ctr.; owner Poetic Perspectives, Waxahachie, 1988—, Jasmine's. Editor (poetry) Family Tributes, 1989, Therapeutic Poetry, 1990, Heroes and Heroines, 1991; contbg. poet (cassette) The Sound of Poetry, 1993. Mem. prof. women's adv. bd. Am. Biog. Inst. Recipient Tex. Counseling Assn. Profl. Devel. award, 1996. Fellow AAUW (interviewee cable TV show 1994); mem. ACA, Tex. Counseling Assn. (Ednl. Endowment award 1996, Profl. Devel. award 1996), Poetry Soc. of Tex., Tex. Play Therapy Assn., Tex. Sch. Counselors Assn., Kappa Delta Pi, Phi Delta Kappa, Pi Lambda Theta, Chi Sigma Iota. Avocations: singing, acting, reading, writing poetry, swimming.

HALFORD, GRAEME SYDNEY, psychology educator; b. Sydney, NSW, Australia, Nov. 11, 1937; s. Sydney Charles and Faith Olive (Aldis) H.; m. Joan Margaret Hough, 1967 (div. 1975); children: Ross (dec.), Rowena (dec.). MA, U. New Eng., Armidale, 1965; PhD, U. Newcastle, 1969. Psychology lectr. U. Newcastle, 1965-70, sr. psychology lectr., 1971-72; assoc. prof. psychology Queen's U., Kingston, 1972-75; sr. lectr. in psychology U. Queensland, Brisbane, 1975-79, reader in psychology, 1980-89, prof. psychology, 1989—. Author: The Development of Thought, 1982, Children's Understanding: The Development of Mental Models, 1993, Developing Cognitive Competence: New Approaches to Process Modelling, 1995, Mathematics Education: Models and Processes, 1995; mem. editl. bd. Psycho. Rev., 1994-2000, Human Devel., 1992-95, Internat. Jour. Behavioral Devel., 1991-97, Cognitive Sci., 1999—, Cognitive Devel., 1999—; assoc. editor: Australian Jour. Psychology, 1986-91. Fellow Acad. Social Scis. in Australia (convenor Queensland br. 1986-97), Australian Psychol. Soc., Am. Psychol. Soc.; mem. Australasian Cognitive Sci. Soc. (pres. 1995-97), Australian Acad. Sci. (nat. com. for psychology 1990-96), Wynnum-Manly Yacht Club, U. of Queensland Staff and Grads. Club. Avocations: sailing, theatre. Office: U Queensland, Dept Psychology, Brisbane QLD 4072, Australia

HALFVARSON, LUCILLE ROBERTSON, music educator; b. Petersburg, Ill., May 17, 1919; d. Harris Morton and Lucille (Fox) Robertson; m. Sten Gustaf Halfvarson, Aug. 8, 1946; children: Laura, Eric, Linnea, Mary. BA, Knox Coll., 1941; MusM, Am. Conservatory, 1969; DHL (hon.), Aurora U., 2000. Cert. tchr., Ill. Tchr. music and speech Freeman Elem. Sch., Aurora, Ill., 1941-44; choral dir. Galesburg (Ill.) Sr. H.S., 1944-46; dir. of music Our Savior Luth. Ch., Aurora, Ill., 1950-63; oratorio soloist, 1952-67; dir. of music Westminster Presbyn. Ch., Aurora, 1963-84; vocal instr. Merit Music Program, Chgo., 1982-93; ret., 1993; choir dir. 1st Meth. Ch., Galesburg, 1944-46; choral-vocal instr. Waubonsee C.C., Sugar Grove, Ill., 1967-79; organizer Jr. Coll. Music Festival, Waubonsee Coll., Sugar Grove, 1972-73; pvt. vocal instrn., Aurora, 1979—. Conductor Messiah Concert Waubonsee Coll., Paramount Arts Ctr., 1968—, 25th Concert, 1992. Co-chair Citizens Adv. Com. Paramount Arts. Ctr., Aurora, 1977-78; founder, pres. United Arts Bd. Fox Valley, 1977-82; chair Paramount Celebration Arts, 1985-86; residency dir. Met. Life Affiliate Artist, Aurora, 1982-83; bd. dirs. YWCA, 1984-91, chair corp. award com., 1994-95; dir. New Eng. Congl. Ch. Bell Choir, 1997-99. Recipient Disting. Svc. award Cosmopolitan Club, Aurora, Ill., 1983; named Woman of Year YWCA, Aurora, 1976, Disting. Alumni Knox Coll., Galesburg, Ill., 1984; Paul Harris fellow Rotary Found. of Rotary Internat., 1999. Mem. AAUW, DAR, PEO, Music Educators Nat. Conf., Am. Choral Dirs. Assn., Aurora C. of C. (Image Maker 1992), Phi Beta Kappa. Avocations: needlework, gardening, fishing, reading. Home: 1105 W Downer Pl Aurora IL 60506-4821

HALICZER, JAMES SOLOMON, lawyer; b. Ft. Myers, Fla., Oct. 27, 1952; s. Julian and Margaret (Shepard) H.; m. Paula Fleming, Oct. 3, 1987. BA in English Lit., U. So. Fla., 1976, MA in Polit. Sci., 1978; JD, Stetson U., 1981. Bar: Fla. 1982. Assoc. Conrad, Scherer & James, Ft. Lauderdale, Fla., 1982-86, ptnr., 1988-92; assoc. Bernard & Mauro, Ft. Lauderdale, 1985-86; shareholder Cooney, Haliczer, Mattson, Lane, Blackburn, Pettis & Richards, Ft. Lauderdale, 1992-96, Haliczer, Pettis & White, P.A., Ft. Lauderdale, Fla., 1996—. Mem. ABA, Fla. Bar Assn., Broward County Bar Assn., Assn. Trial Lawyers Am., Def. Rsch. Inst., Am. Acad. Healthcare Attys., Phi Kappa Phi, Pi Sigma Alpha, Omicron Delta Kappa. Democrat. Methodist. Avocations: reading, jogging. Office: Haliczer Pettis & White PA 101 NE 3rd Ave Fort Lauderdale FL 33301-1162

HALIFA, MOHAMED, bank executive. Dir.-gen. Ctrl. Bank of the Comoros, Moroni, gov. Office: Ctrl Bank of the Comoros, PO Box 405, Moroni Comoros*

HALKET, THOMAS D(ANIEL), lawyer; b. N.Y.C., July 20, 1948. SB in Physics, MIT, 1971, SM in Physics, 1971; JD, Columbia U., 1974. Bar: Mass. 1974, N.Y. 1979. Ptnr., chmn. tech. group, chmn. emerging cos. group Hughes Hubbard & Reed LLP, N.Y.C. Mem. ABA (chmn. divsn. aerospace law 1979-83, ventures and entrepreneur divsn. 1986-89, sect. sci. and tech. coun. 1982-85, program chmn. 1981-86, sec. 1985-86, vice-chmn. 1986-87, chmn. 1988-89), AAAS, AIAA (sr.), Am. Arbitration Assn. (chmn. tech. com. 1998—, computer disputes adv. com. 1992-96), Am. Phys. Soc., Bar Assn. City N.Y. (law and sci. com. 1987-90, computer law com. 1993-96, 1997-2000, tech. in law practice com. 1993-96, chmn. subcom. on software and uniform comml. code 1993-96, 97-99), Computer Law Assn. Fax: 212-422-4726. E-mail: halket@hugheshubbard.com. Office: Hughes Hubbard & Reed LLP One Battery Park Plz New York NY 10004

HALKIAS, CHRISTOS CONSTANTINE, electronics educator; b. Monastiraki, Doridos, Greece, Aug. 23, 1933; s. Constantine C. and Alexandra V. (Papapostoloy) H.; m. Demetra Saras, Jan. 22, 1961; children: Alexandra, Helen-Joanna. BSEE, CCNY, 1957; MSEE, Columbia U., 1958, PhD, 1962. Prof. elec. engring. Columbia U., N.Y.C., 1962-73; prof. electronics Nat. Tech. U. Athens, Greece, 1973—; Fulbright vis. prof. Nat. Tech. U. Athens, 1969, dir. informatics divsn., 1983-86; dir. Nat. Rsch. Found., Athens, 1983-87. Author: Electronic Devices and Circuits, 1967, Integrated Electronics, 1972, Electronic Fundamentals and Applications, 1976, Design of Electronic Filters, 1988; contbr. articles to profl. jours. Recipient D.B. Steinman award CCNY, 1956; higgins fellow Columbia U., 1958. Mem. IEEE (chmn. Greek sect. 1982-86, sr. Centennial medal 1984), European Unions Info. Soc. (tech. adv. group 1999—), Sigma Xi. Home: 4 Kosti Palama St, Paleo Psyhico, 15452 Athens Greece Office: Nat Tech U Athens, Zographou, 15773 Athens Greece

HALL, ALAN CRAIG, library director; b. Marietta, Ohio, Mar. 9, 1954; s. Harry Edward and Flossie June (Heddleston) H.; m. Barbara Ann Metzger, May 23, 1981; 1 child, Shawn Alan. BS in Edn., W.Va. U., 1976; MLS, Case Western U., 1977. With circulation dept. Washington County Pub. Libr., Marietta, Ohio, 1970-75; with govt. documents dept. Freiberger Libr., Cleve., 1976-77; dir. Delphos (Ohio) Pub. Libr., 1977-83, Pub. Libr. of Steubenville and Jefferson County, 1983—; cons. Morgan County Libr., McConnelsville, Ohio, 1992-93, Barnesville (Ohio) Pub. Libr., 1991, Reed Meml. Libr., Ravenna, Ohio, 1997-98; chair Ohio Libr. Coun., Columbus, 1994, com. rev. bd. structure, 1999, co-chair Ohio statewide resource sharing com., 1998-99. Author: Marietta's Innkeeper, 1991, The Mary Thompson Collection, 1997; editor: The Papers of A.T. Nye, 1975, Abandoned Underground Coal Mines of Jefferson County, 1991, Richmond, Ohio Cemetery Book, 1995; compiler Historic Pages Series, 1975-76; editor: Steubenville (Ohio) Bicentennial History Book, 1996-97; contbr. articles to profl. publs. Chairperson Ohio Humanities Coun., Steubenville, 1991; pres. Ret. Sr. Vol. Program, Steubenville, 1989-90; ruling elder Starkdale Presbyn. Ch., 1985-88, 94-96, 98-2000, chmn. pastor nominating com., 1996-97; mem. Cmty. Found. Jefferson County, 1999—, v.p., 2000—. Mem. ALA, Nat. Assn. Rd. Passengers, Jefferson County Hist. Soc., Steubenville Lions Club (pres. 1986-87), Ohio Libr. Assn. (pres. 1992-93, Libr. of Yr. 1989), Steubenville Rotary. Office: 407 S 4th St Steubenville OH 43952-2942

HALL, ANDREW CLIFFORD, lawyer; b. Warsaw, Poland, Sept. 16, 1944; s. Edmund and Maria (Hahn) H.; came to U.S., 1949, naturalized, 1954; children: Michael Ian, Adam Stuart, Hilary Meyers Azrael, Katie Meyers; m. Gail Meyers, 1993. BA, U. Fla., 1965, JD with high honors, 1968. Bar: Fla. 1968, U.S. Dist. Ct. (so. dist.) Fla. 1968, U.S. Dist. Ct. (no. dist.) Ga. 1971, U.S. Ct. Appeals (5th cir.) 1971, Ga. 1973, U.S. Supreme Ct. 1974, U.S. Ct. Appeals (D.C. cir.) 1974, U.S. Ct. Appeals (11th cir.) 1981. Law clk. to judge U.S. Dist. Ct.; assoc., Haas, Holland, Levison, Gilbert, Atlanta, 1970-72, Frates, Floyd, Pearson, Stewart, Miami, 1972-75; ptnr. Storace, Hall & Hauser, Miami, 1975-79, Hall & Hauser, 1979-82, Hall & O'Brien, P.A., Miami, 1982-95, Andrew Hall and Assoc., Pa., 1995-99; Hall, David and Joseph, P.A., 1999—; instr. bus. law U. Fla.; Trustee U. Fla., Coll. of Law Found. Bd. dirs. Greater Miami Jewish Fedn.; chmn., bd. trustees, bd. dirs Cen. Agy. Jewish Edn., Ash Ha Torah; mem. coun. of 100 Fla. Internat. U. Mem. ABA, Hebrew Immigrant Aid Assn. (nat. bd. mem.), Fla. State Bar, Am. Judicature Soc., U. Fla. Coll. Law Alumni (coun.), Acad. Fla. Trial Lawyers (diplomate), Assn. Trial Lawyers Am., Phi Kappa Phi, Phi Alpha Delta, Order of Coif. Democrat. Jewish. Home: 2000 S Bayshore Dr Miami FL 33133-3256 Office: Hall David and Joseph PA Att/Karen Fernandez 1428 Brickell Ave Ph Miami FL 33131-3411

HALL, ANTHONY CLIVE, land use planner, educator; b. London, Mar. 27, 1944; s. Edwin and Edith Sarah (Hinton) H. BSc, Sussex U., Brighton, Eng., 1965; MA, Oxford (Eng.) Poly., 1990; PhD, Birmingham (Eng.) U., 1996. Sch. tchr. Buckinghamshire (Eng.) County, 1966-67; rsch. asst. Manchester (Eng.) U., 1969-70; asst. planner East Sussex (Eng.) County, 1970-72; lectr. Liverpool (Eng.) Poly., 1972-74; sr. transp. planner Freeman Fox & Ptnrs., London, 1974-76; lectr. Chelmer Inst., Chelmsford, Eng., 1976-78; prin. lectr. Anglia Poly. U., Chelmsford, 1978-97, prof., 1997—. Author: Generation of Objectives for Design Control, 1990, Design Control: Towards a New Approach, 1996; contbr. articles to profl. jours. Mem. Chelmsford Borough Coun., 1995—, chmn. planning com., 1996—. Recipient Essex Chronicle Environ. Bursay award, 1991. Mem. Royal Town Planning Inst. (chmn. East Eng. br. 1996), Inst. Hwys Transp., Royal Geog. Soc. Liberal Democrat. Mem. Soc. of Friends. Avocations: travel, architecture, railways. Office: Anglia Poly U, Victoria Rd S, Chelmsford CM1 1LL, England

HALL, ANTHONY VINCENT, botany educator, systematist, conservationist; b. Bedford, Eng., Apr. 22, 1936; s. Alfred Smith and Lucy Vincentia

(Wynniatt) H.; m. Grizelda Purdie Gray, Apr. 25, 1964; children: Peter Wynniatt, Gregory Anthony, Malcolm Buchanan. BSc, U. Cape Town, Rondebosch, South Africa, 1955, BSc with honours, 1957, MSc, 1959, PhD, 1963. Rsch. asst. Rhodes U., South Africa, 1956; lectr. botany U. Cape Town, 1958-70, sr. lectr., 1970-82, assoc. prof., 1982—, asst. curator, 1958-89, keeper, 1989-96, hon. rsch. assoc. in botany, 1997—, emeritus assoc. prof., 1997—. Co-author: History of Scientific Endeavour in South Africa, 1977, Threatened Plants of Southern Africa, 1980; contbr. over 75 articles to sci. jours., chpts. to books. Chmn. Coordinating Coun. for Nature Conservation in Cape, 1970-85, Cape Peninsula Conservation Trust, 1980-85; pres. Athenaeum Trust, Cape Town, 1985-87. Recipient mayor's medal for conservation City of Cape Town, 1983, Centenary medal for conservation Cape Times, 1986; Willem Hiddingh scholar, 1960-62, grantee South African Coun. for Sci. and Indsl. Rsch., 1980-85. Fellow Royal Soc. South Africa (gen. sec. 1968-85, honours cert. 1990). Avocations: photography, travel, restoring classic cars. Office: U Cape Town Bolus Herbarium, Pvt Bag, Rondebosch 7700, South Africa

HALL, BRUCE MILNE, physician, medical educator; b. Sydney, NSW, Australia, Apr. 25, 1947; s. John James and Mary (Milne) H.; m. Suzanne Jean Hodgkinson, Aug. 8, 1984; children: Alexandra, Rachael, Madeleine. MB, BChir, Sydney U., 1970, PhD, 1980. Asst. prof. medicine MacMaster U., Hamilton, Ont., Can.; assoc. prof. Stanford (Calif.) U., 1987-91; prof. U. NSW, Sydney, 1991—; dir. dept. medicine Liverpool Hosp., U. NSW, 1991—. Chmn. Transplantation and Immunology sect. NIH, Bethesda, Md., 1988-91. Fellow Royal Australian Coll. Physicians. Avocations: gardening, skiing. Home: 14 Vernon St, Strathfield NSW 2135, Australia Office: Univ NSW, Liverpool Hosp, PO Box 103, Liverpool NSW 2170, Australia

HALL, BRYAN HOWARD, banking executive; b. San Luis Obispo, Calif., Feb. 7, 1944; s. Howard and C. Berniece (Vernon) H.; m. Gwen Marie Paton, May 30, 1975 (div. J.l. 1985); 1 child, Erika Anne; m. Patricia Anne Barry, Oct. 16, 1995. BA, Coe Coll., 1966; JD, Univ. Iowa, 1968. Spl. asst. to asst. sec. U.S. Dept. HEW, Washington, 1968-70; dir. of manpower coord. City of Des Moines, 1970-73; assoc. dir. Cen. Iowa Regional Assn. of Local Gov., Des Moines, 1973-76; exec. dir. Iowa Pers. Mgmt. Info. System State of Iowa, Des Moines, 1976-78, Iowa Legis. Privacy Task Force, Des Moines, 1978-80; coord. Iowa Episcopal Diocese, Des Moines, 1981; sr. trust examiner Iowa Dept. of Banking, Des Moines, 1982-84; mgr., v.p. Corprate Trust Dept. Bankers Trust Co., Des Moines, 1984—. Dir. Coalition for the Homeless, Des Moines, 1998—, Celtic Music Assn., Des Moines, 1994. Mem. Copr. Trust Network (adv. bd. 1997—), Nat. Assn. Bond Lawyers, Iowa State Bar Assn., Polk County Bar Assn., Iowa Gov. Practice Sect. (coun. mem. 1996-98). Office: Bankers Trust Co 665 Locust St Des Moines IA 50309-3763

HALL, CHRISTOPHER GEORGE LONGDEN, management consultant; b. Coventry, Eng., June 7, 1956; came to U.S., 1980; s. Alfred Frederick and Margaret Anne (Robinson) H.; m. Avril Jacqueline Wardell, July 31, 1982. MA, Oxford U., 1977, DPhil, 1980; MS in Bus., Columbia U., 1983. Asst. to chmn. Gold Fields Am. Corp., N.Y.C., 1980-83; pres. Hall Mgmt. Assocs., San Francisco, 1983-87, Congden and Carpenter Co., Seekonk, Mass., 1987-88; mng. dir. Petralex Stainless Ltd., Malvern, Pa., 1985-86; v.p. planning Levinson Steel Co., Pitts., 1988-89; v.p. mktg. Thypin Steel Co., N.Y.C., 1989-95; ptnr. Stafford Bus. Advisors, Portland, ME, 1995—; internat. commercial arbitrator Am. Arbitration Assn., 1991—. Author: Britain, America and Arms Control, 1921-1937, 1987, Steel Phoenix, The Fall and Rise of the American Steel Industry, 1996, Ports and Railroads of the Atlantic Northeast, 1999. Councilman City of Oxford (Eng.), 1979-81; mem. Dem. Nat. Com., 1996-97; chmn. Maine Dem. Com., 1997-99; pres. Genesis Cmty. Loan Fund; bd. dirs. Maine Coun. Chs. Mem. United Oxford and Cambridge Univs. Club (London), Nat. Arts Club (N.Y.). Episcopalian. Avocations: travel, cricket, naval history. Office: 107 Exchange St Portland ME 04101-5001

HALL, DAVID WALTER, botanist; b. New Orleans, Sept. 6, 1940; s. Walter Knowlton and Lenna Anne (Guthrie) H.; m. Tiia Reet Karell, Nov. 25, 1981; children: Alexander, Elizabeth. BS, Ga. So. U., 1965, MS, 1967; PhD, U. Fla., 1978. Diplomate Am. Bd. Forensic Examiners; cert. expert in botany; registered profl. wetland scientist. Rsch. assoc. U. Fla., Gainesville, 1971-73, asst. in botany, 1973-81, dir. plant identification and info. svc., 1981-90; sr. scientist KBN Engrng. and Applied Scis., Inc., Gainesville, 1990-96, Golder Assocs. Inc., Gainesville, 1996-97; pres. David W. Hall Cons., Inc., Gainesville, 1997—. Author: Illustrated Plants of Florida and the Coastal Plain, 1993; co-author spl. publs. Inst. Food and Agrl. Scis., U. Fla., 1987, 88, 89, 92, 2000; adj. prof. dept. civil engrng. U. Fla., 1989; contbr. or co-contbr. chpts. to: Aquatic Pest Control Applicator Training Manual, 1991, Turf Weeds and Their Control, 1994, Forensic Taphonomy: The Post-Mortem Fate of Human Remains, 1997. Bd. dirs., v.p. Fla. Tennis Found., 1992—; tennis coach Ga. So. U., 1966-67; profl. racket stringer, 1963-90; pvt. instr. tennis, 1965-90; umpire various tennis tournaments, 1963-85; dir. profl. tennis tournaments, 1964-85; condr. tennis clinics for area high schs. and coll. programs, leagues, underprivileged children; organizer, mem. City of Gainesville Tennis Adv. Bd.; founder U. Fla. Gator Tennis Boosters, 1968; bd. dirs. tennis program 300 Club, Gainesville, 1975-76, organizer, tennis chmn.; organizer, dir. Fla. intercity adult tennis league; mem. dist. 4 Cmty. Devel. Com., 1994-95; commr. tennis Gainesville Sports Coun., 1989-90. Named one of Outstanding Young Men of Am., 1973; NDEA Title IV fellow U. Fla., 1967-70; Mercer Rsch. fellow Harvard U., 1968; recipient Disting. Svc. award Fla. Assn. County Agrl. Agts., 1990, Nat. Assn. County Agrl. Agts., 1990, Disting. Alumni award dept. biology Ga. So. U., 1991, Svc. award Fla. Dept. Environ. Regulation, 1988, Svc. Leadership award Augusta Coll., 1963; ranked in various coll. and other tennis tournaments, 1960-94. Fellow Am. Coll. Forensic Examiners, Am. Acad. Forensic Scis.; mem. AAAS, Am. Soc. Plant Taxonomists, Exotic Plant Pest Coun., Assn. Southea. Biologists, Soc. Wetland Scientists, Weed Sci. Soc. Am., So. Weed Sci. Soc., Fla. Acad. Scis., Fla. Native Plant Soc. (Green Palmetto Svc. award 1987), Nat. Assn. Environ. Profls., Fla. Assn. Environ. Profls., North Fla. Bot. Soc., Fla. Weed Sci. Soc. (pres. 1987-88, sec., treas. 1984-86, bd. dirs. 1984-90, Outstanding Weed Scientist 1999), Internat. Assn. for Identification (Fla. divsn.), Internat. Weed Sci. Soc., USTA (mem. exec. bd. 1991-93, mem. dels. assembly 1991-93, mem. pres.'s com. 1989-91, active other coms.), Fla. Tennis Assn. (pres. 1989-91, 1st v.p. 1985-87, chmn. adult tennis coun. 1986-89, mem. exec. bd. 1982-95, USTA del. 1991-93, mem. Fla. Tennis Assn./USTA league appeals com. 1985-86, Man of Yr. 1984), Gainesville Area Tennis Orgn. (pres., bd. dirs. 1994-2000), Swannee River Valley Cmty. Tennis Assn. (v.p., bd. dirs. 2000—). Achievements include definition of discipline of forensic botany. Avocations: tennis, singing. Home and Office: 3666 NW 13th Pl Gainesville FL 32605-4823

HALL, DEBORAH WOODRICK, social services administrator; b. Natchez, Miss., Aug. 31, 1955; d. Herbert Lavelle Sr. and Patricia Banks Woodrick; m. David Thomas Hall, May 11, 1996. BBA, U. Miss., Oxford, 1977, MBA, 1980. Acad. program coord. U. Miss., Oxford, 1978-81; field dir., dir. pub. rels. Prairie Girl Scout Coun., Tupelo, Miss., 1981-83; dir. pub. rels. and devel. United Meth. Sr. Svcs. Miss., Tupelo, 1983-88, United Meth. Children's Home, Selma, Ala., 1988-94; exec. dir. United Way N.E. Miss., Tupelo, 1994—; pres. Miss. United Way Assn. Active, sec. City of Tupelo Better Streets Task Force, 1998; task force mem., mem. coun. on fin. and adminstrn. Miss. United Meth. Ch., 1998-99; vol., guild pres. Tupelo Cmty. Theatre, 1999; vol., sch. time friend Big Bros./Big Sisters; active All Am. City Task Force, Tupelo, 1999; covey/Franklin 7 habits facilitator CREATE Found., Tupelo. Named Woman of the Yr., Tupelo Area Bus. and Profl. Women's Club, 1995; named to Leadership Lee Class, Cmty. Devel. Found., Tupelo, 1988. Mem. Rotary Club Tupelo (club sec. 1996-97, dist. sec. 1998-99, Paul Harris fellow 1999). Methodist. Avocations: reading, scrapboooking, camping. E-mail: debbieh@dixie-net.com. Fax: 662-680-5754. Home: 127 Sesame Dr Tupelo MS 38801-8615 Office: United Way NE Miss PO Box 334 Tupelo MS 38802-0334

HALL, FLOYD, retail executive; b. Duncan, Okla., Sept. 4, 1938; m. Janet Hall; children: Larry, Karen. Student, Bakersfield Jr. Coll., So. Meth. U., Harvard U., 1977. Nat. sales mgr. Montgomery Ward, Chgo., 1966-70; v.p., regional v.p. The Singer Co., Dallas, Tex., 1970-73; pres., CEO B. Dalton Book Seller, Mpls., 1973-81; chmn., CEO Target Stores, Mpls., 1981-84, Grand Union Co., Wayne, N.J., 1984-89; also bd. dirs. Grand Union Co.; chmn., CEO The Museum Co., East Rutherford, N.J., 1989-95, also bd. dirs.; chmn., pres., CEO Kmart Corp., Troy, Mich., 1995—, also bd. dirs.; bd. dirs. Lynx Techs., Kenwood Prodns. Trustee Bklyn. Mus.; bd. dirs. Give Kids The World, Jundt Growth Fund. Served with U.S. Army. Office: Kmart Corp 3100 W Big Beaver Rd Troy MI 48084-3163

HALL, GARY, JR., Olympic athlete; b. Cin., Sept. 26, 1974. Recipient Gold medal 50-meter freestyle Sydney Olympics, 2000, 4 Gold medals Atlanta Olympics, 1996; set Am. record for 50-meter freestyle. Office: USA Swimming 1 Olympic Plz Colorado Springs CO 80909-5746*

HALL, GRACE ROSALIE, physicist, educator, literary scholar; b. Meriden, Conn., July 15, 1921; d. George John and Grace Cleora (Gleason) White; m. Eldon Conrad Hall, July 2, 1948; children: Brent Channing, Pamela Rosalie, Craig Gleason, Gordon Timothy. Spl. student, Pembroke Coll., 1940-41; BS in Chemistry, Ea. Nazarene Coll., 1946; MA in Physics, Boston U., 1946, postgrad., 1946-53; MA in English, Simmons Coll., 1975. Bookkeeper Cherry & Webb Co., Providence, 1939-42; sec. to registrar Eastern Nazarene Coll., Quincy, Mass., 1942-44, instr. physics, chemistry, 1945-46; teaching fellow physics Boston U., 1946-49; instr. physics lab. Northeastern U., Boston, 1956-57; instr. physics Simmons Coll., Boston, 1949; asst. prof. physics Eastern Nazarene Coll., Quincy, 1957-61, asst. prof. chemistry, 1969, asst. prof. phys. sci., 1974; instr. Shakespeare Barrington (R.I.) Coll., 1984; tchr. Westwood (Mass.) Sem., 1975; ch. sch. dir. 1st Parish, Westwood, 1977-81; chair sem. U. Louisville, 1988. Author: The Tempest as Mystery Play: Uncovering Religious Sources of Shakespeare's Most Spiritual Work, 1999; contbr. (with others) Webs & Wardrobes, 1987; contbr. articles to profl. jours. Dir. South County Norfolk Assn. for Retarded Citizens, 1978-79, Westwood Interfaith Coun., 1985-89; judge H.S. Sci. Fairs, North Quincy, Mass., 1960-64, 69-76, Regional Sci. Fairs, Bridgewater, Mass., 1960-62; chair City-Wide Bookfair, Quincy, 1962; pres. Ch. Women United, 1959. Recipient faculty scholarship Eastern Nazarene Coll., 1943-45; recipient Libr. Family of Yr. award City of Quincy, 1960; named to R.I. Honor Soc. Mem. MLA (session participant 1978, 84), Shakespeare Assn. Am. (seminar participant 1988-96, 2000), Christianity and Lit. Assn. (conf. participant 1984, 89-90, 95), MIT Women's League (editor activities guide and newsletter 1989—, adv. group 1998—), New Eng. Hist. Geneal. Soc., Internat. Soc. Poets, Munro Soc., Clarendon Soc., Mythopoetic Soc., Phi Delta Lambda. Avocations: children's lit., recycling, grandparenting, snorkeling . E-mail: grwhall@aol.com.

HALL, HAZEL JANE READ, information scientist, educator; b. Edinburgh, Scotland, Mar. 24, 1963; d. Paul Guy and Marianne Toulmin H.; m. Timothy Paul Read, June 27, 1987. BA with hons., Birmingham (Eng.) U., 1986; MA, U. Ctrl. Eng., Birmingham, 1993. Libr. asst. U. Birmingham, 1987; libr., info. svcs. Birmingham Poly., 1988-89; lectr. info. mgmt. Queen Margaret Coll., Edinburgh, 1989-99, Napier U. Bus. Sch., Edinburgh, 1999—; cons. Frontline, Stirling, Scotland, 1992-93. Contbr. articles to profl. jours. Mem. Libr. Assn. (assoc.), Inst. Info. Scientists (mem. coun. 1993-96, John Campbell Trust award 1994), U.K. Online User Group (mgmt. com.), Scottish Elec. Inf o. Group. Avocations: skiing, hill walking, gastronomy, writing, music. Office: Napier Univ Bus Sch, Sighthill Ct, Edinburgh EH11 9BN, Scotland

HALL, JAMES ROBERT, secondary education educator; b. Salem, Ill., Dec. 24, 1947; s. James Wesley and Patricia Joyce (Ellis) H. BS, U. Ill., 1970. Cert. secondary tchr., Ill. Tchr. Murphysboro (Ill.) H.S., 1970—. Author, compiler (tng. manual) Key Club Faculty Advisors, 1975. Sunday sch tchr. United Meth. Ch., Murphysboro, 1973-76, youth dir., 1973-76, mem. coun. on ministries, 1984—, trustee, 1984—; founder, dir. Christian Lay Coun. Youth Coffeehouse, 1973-75; mem. Murphysboro Recreation Bd., 1974-76, pres. 1975-76; cmty. amb. So. Ill. U. Area Svcs., 1975—; bd. dirs. Murphysboro Heart Fund, 1973-76, co-chmn. 1975-76; chmn. Murphysboro Muscular Dystrophy Assn., 1971-74; counsellor Little Grassy Youth Ch. Camp, 1973; mem. steering com. Murphysboro Apple Festival, 1975—, exec. com., 1983—; bd. dirs. Murphysboro United Way, 1978-83, Murphysboro Sr. Citizens Coun., 1980-83, Resource Reclamation Inc., 1979-85; vice chmn. Murphysboro Swimming Pool Project Commn., 1983-84, chmn. 1984-88; active Murphysboro Tourism Commn., 1995—; chmn. Murphysboro Mainstreet Promotions Commn., 1998—. Named on of Oytstanding Young men of Am. 1975, 84; recipient Citizenship award Sta. WTAO Radio, 1983, 84, Ann. Cmty. Svc. award Modern Woodmen Am., 1982, Citizen of Yr. award Murphysboro C. of C., 1984, Disting. Educator award Phi Delta Kappa, 1991. Mem. NEA, Ill. Edn. Assn., Murphysboro Edn. Assn., Key Club (advisor 1972—, adminstr. Ill.-Eastern Iowa dist. 1985-96, Key Club Internats. 1996, James R. Hall Achievement award 1999), Kiwanis (pres. 1977-78, lt. gov. dist. divsn. 1984-85, chmn. spl. club svcs. Ill.-Eastern Iowa dist. 1984-85, Mid. Sch. Builders Club advisor 1993—, cert. trainer 1993—, gov.-elect 1995-96, gov. 1996-97, Target 2000, long range planning com. for Key Club, Dr. Luis V. Amador medallion 1995, G. Harold Martin fellow 1996, George F. Hixson fellow Diamond 2 Levil i 1996-98). Avocations: collecting books and plates, bowling, tennis. Home: 28 Candy Ln Murphysboro IL 62966-2953 Office: Murphysboro H S 16 Blackwood Dr Murphysboro IL 62966-2937

HALL, JEAN QUINTERO, communications and history educator; b. Manila, July 28, 1946; came to U.S., 1963; d. Evan Drake Moody and Victoria (Quintero) Bombon; m. Edward Payson Hall. BA in Comm., U. Wash., 1978; MPA, U. Del., 1984. Faculty Kapiolani C.C., Honolulu, 1984-85; cmty. developer Cath. Social Svcs., Honolulu, 1985; adminstr. City & County of Honolulu, 1985-86; faculty New River C.C., Dublin, Va., 1986-90; adminstr. Radford (Va.) U., 1987-89, faculty, 1989-92; pres. Global Soc., Radford, 1989-92; ind. cons. Silver City, N.Mex., 1992-94; faculty Western N.Mex. U., Silver City, 1994—; spkr. in field; columnist Filipino-Am. J., Phoenix, 1999—. Author: Desiderate Melodies, 1990, Rizal - Our Beloved Beacon, 1996. Grantee Commonwealth Va., 1991. Mem. Pacific & Asian Comm. Assn., Asian Studies/Philippine Studies Group, Filipino Am. Educators Assn., Filipino Cultural Heritage Soc., Filipino Am. Assn. N.Mex., Sigma Iota Epsilon. Avocation: writing. Home: 20 Vista Grande Silver City NM 88061-6613

HALL, JOHN WESLEY, JR., lawyer; b. Watertown, N.Y., Jan. 28, 1948; s. John Wesley and Mary Louise Hall; m. Alison Hall; children: Justin William, Mark Daniel, Juliana Sanchez. BA, Hendrix Coll., 1970; JD, U. Ark., 1973. Bar: Ark. 1973, U.S. Dist. Ct. (ea. and we. dists.) Ark. 1973, U.S. Ct. Appeals (8th cir.) 1973, D.C. 1975, U.S. Ct. Appeals (5th cir.) 1976, U.S. Supreme Ct. 1976, Tenn. 1988, U.S. Ct. Appeals (fed. cir.) 1988, U.S. Ct. Appeals (6th cir.) 1991, Nev. 1993, U.S. Ct. Appeals (9th cir.) 1995, N.Y. 1996, U.S. Ct. Appeals (2d cir.) 1999. Dep. pros. atty., Office Pros. Atty., Little Rock, 1973-79; head career criminal divsn. Little Rock, 1978-79; law clk. Ark. Supreme Ct., Little Rock, 1974; pvt. practice, Ark. Supreme Ct., 1974—; instr. trial advocacy Ark. Pros. Attys. Assn., 1977-79; adj. prof. Sch. Law, Grad. Sch. Criminal Justice, U. Ark., Little Rock, 1985, 88, 91; speaker to lawyer and police groups. Author: Search and Seizure, 3d edit., 2000, Professional Responsibility of the Criminal Lawyer, 2d edit., 1996, Trial Handbook for Arkansas Lawyers, 4th edit., 1999; editor, author: Arkansas Prosecutor's Trial Manual, 1976-77, Arkansas Extradition Manual, 1978; editor: (with B. Scheck and P. Neufield) DNA: Understanding, Controlling, and Depleting the New Evidence of the 90's, 1990; contbr. articles to law jours. Mem. NACDL (life, bd. dirs. 1989-95, 97-000), Am. Bd. Criminal Lawyers, Assn. Responsible Lawyers, Ark. Bar Assn. (ho. of dels. 1976-79), Ark. Assn. Criminal Def. Lawyers (pres. 1987-89). Episcopalian. Home: 300 Rice St Little Rock AR 72205-6141 Office: 523 W 3d St Little Rock AR 72201-2309

HALL, KATHRYN WALT, ambassador; m. Craig Hall; 2 children, 4 stepchildren. AB in Econs., U. Calif., Berkeley, JD. Asst. city atty. Berkeley, Calif.; with Safeway Stores; pres. Kathryn Hall Vineyards, Inc., Walt Mgmt., Inc.; mng. dir., ptnr. Hall Fin. Group, Inc.; amb. to Austria Vienna, 1997—; mem. hunger adv. com. U.S. Ho. of Reps. Co-founder North Tex. Food Bank; mem. Nat. Adv. Coun. for Violence Against Women; trustee Woodrow Wilson Internat. Ctr. for Scholars; former bd. dirs., v.p. Tex. Mental Health Assn. Mem. Dallas Area C. of C., Comml. Real Estate Women, Tex. Retailers Assn. Office: The Honorable Kathryn Hall Amb Dept State 9900 Vienna Pl Washington DC 20521-9900

HALL, KIMBALL PARKER, research scientist; b. Richmond, Va., Nov. 7, 1914; s. Howard Warren and Gene (Parker) H; m. Elise LeFevre, Aug. 15, 1942; children: Katherine, Daniel, Christiane. AB with distinction and cum laude, Dartmouth Coll., 1937; PhD, Cornell U., 1942. Chemist Eastman Kodak, Rochester, N.Y., 1942-43; rsch. engr. Lockheed Aircraft, Burbank, Calif., 1943-45; rsch. dir. Coast Paint and Chem. Co., L.A., 1945-47; rsch. engr. Jet Propulsion Lab., Pasadena, Calif., 1947-55; rsch. assoc. Princeton (N.J.) U., 1956-61; founder, pres. Hall Marine Corp., Princeton, Setauket, N.Y., 1965-96; sr. rsch. scientist U.S. Naval Ordnance Sta., Indian Head, Md., 1977-92; sr. engrng. adviser Outboard Marine Corp., Waukegan, Ill., 1996—; cons. Princeton U., 1961-65, Rocket Power, Mesa, 1961-65. Contbr. articles to profl. jours. Vol. village clk., Shoreham, N.Y., 1959-61. Nat. Def. Rsch. Com. rsch. fellow Cornell U., 1940-41. Assoc. fellow AIAA; mem. Am. Chem. Soc., Sigma Xi. Episcopalian. Achievements include 10 patents for boat propulsion; research on astronautics and rocketry. Avocations: walking, swimming, bird watching, boating, photography. Office: Kimball P Hall and Assocs Wading River NY 11792

HALL, LORRAINE CHRISTINA, logistics researcher, consultant; b. Sheffield, Yorkshire, Eng., Apr. 9, 1959; arrived in Australia, 1995; d. Kenneth and Joan (Holland) H. BS in Transport Planning, Loughborough (Eng.) U., 1993; MS in Logistics and Distbn., Cranfield (Eng.) U., 1994. Residential social worker Nottinghamshire County Coun., Eng., 1978-83; receptionist Godfrey Davis, Nottingham, Eng., 1083-85; customer svc. unemall mgr. Parceline, Nottingham, 1985-93; mgr. transport sys. Safeway, Melbourne, Australia, 1995-97; rsch. fellow Monash U., Melbourne, 1997—; cons. Synergy Logistics, Melborne, 1995—. Mem. Inst. Logistics, Logistics Assn. Australia (v.p. 1999—). Avocations: show jumping, eventing, dressage, couture. Office: Synergy Logistics, PO Box 138, Wallan Vic 3756, Australia

HALL, MARCIA BROWN, art historian, educator; b. Washington, July 13, 1939; d. Charles Edward Brown and Frances Peebles Ocheltree; m. Charles Arthur Mann Hall, June 9, 1961 (div. May 1990); children: Christopher Martin, Brian Starbuck; m. Gerald Richard Hoepfner, Dec. 18, 1991. BA, Wellesley Coll., 1960; MA, Radcliffe Coll., 1962; PhD, Harvard U., 1967. Vis. lectr. Franklin & Marshall Coll., Lancaster, Pa., 1967-71; asst. prof., prof. Temple U., Phila, 1973—; dir. NEH summer seminar, Rome, 1992. Author: Renovation and Counter-Reformation: Vasari and Duke Cosimo in Santa Maria Novella and Santa Croce, 1965-77, 1979, Color and Meaning: Practice and Theory in Renaissance Painting, 1992, Michelangelo: The Sistine Ceiling Restored, 1993, After Raphael: Painting in Central Italy in the Sixteenth Century, 1999; editor, contbr.: Color and Technique in Renaissance Painting, 1987, The School of Athens, 1997; co-editor: The Princeton Raphael Conference, 1990; contbr. articles to profl. jours. Fulbright found. fellow Villa I Tatti, Harvard Ctr. for Renaissance Studies, Florence, Italy, 1963-64. Mem. Coll. Art Assn., 16th Century Studies, Renaissance Soc. Am. Home: 720 Davidson Rd Philadelphia PA 19118-4302

HALL, MARGARET JEAN (MARGOT HALL), biochemistry educator; b. Boston, Mar. 25, 1942; d. Robert King and Margaret (Wheeler) H. AB in Chemistry, French, U. N.C., 1964; MS in Chemistry, U. Denver, 1971; PhD in Biochemistry, U. N.C., 1984. Med. technologist U. N.C., Chapel Hill, 1963-65, rsch. asst., 1965-84, postdoctoral/rsch. asst., 1984-85; asst. prof. U. So. Miss., Hattiesburg, 1985-91, assoc. prof., 1991-97, full prof., 1997—. Contbr. articles to profl. jours. Fellow Am. Inst. Chemists; mem. Am. Soc. Clin. Pathologists, Am. Assn. Clinic Chemistry, Miss. Acad. Sci. (pres.-elect), Royal Soc. Chemistry. Republican. Episcopalian. Home: 104 Kensington Dr Hattiesburg MS 39402-1933 Office: U So Miss PO Box 5134 Hattiesburg MS 39406-1000

HALL, MARIE-JOYEE FAITH, Spanish and English language educator; b. Jersey City; d. Frederic Michael and Marie F. Claudia (Melè) Contey; m. Samual Xaviar Conca, Sept. 6, 1947 (dec. Nov. 1964); 1 child, Marie-Joyee Abagail Holian; m. Walter Tildon Hall (dec.). AABA, Ocean County Coll., 1969; BA, Georgian Ct. Coll., 1972. Substitute tchr. Ocean County Sch., 1968—; tchr. Kavner Sch., 1971; tchr. Spanish and English N.J. State Program, Lakewood, 1978—. Author: Tapestries-An Anthology, 1988, Narda-Nymphae del Mar, 1999, Pirate Ship, 1999, Great Sea Bird, 1999, Toy Fella and Friends (Tetralogy), Tangles of Movements and Outdoor Spoken Words, Big Store; author 15 children's books, short stories, poems. Committeewoman Bricktown Dem. Club, 1978-80. Roman Catholic.

HALL, MERRI CAROL, financial advisor; b. Buffalo, Sept. 21, 1963; d. Catherine Ann Yoerk; m. William J. Hall, Aug. 13, 1988; children: Brittany, Shelby. Student, Hofstra U. Mktg. rep. Empire Am., Buffalo, 1983-91; account exec. Empire Fin. Svcs., Williamsville, N.Y., 1991—; bd. dirs. Buffalo Postal Credit Union. Republican. Roman Catholic. Avocations: golf, softball, reading, jetskiing. Home: 4340 Rushford Dr Hamburg NY 14075-3074 Office: Empire Fin Svcs 3075 Southwestern Blvd Orchard Park NY 14127-1236

HALL, MIRIAM ELIZABETH LEWIS, psychologist, educator; b. Córdoba, Argentina, Oct. 20, 1968; came to U.S., 1987; d. Philip Christie and Rosa Elisa Dragone de Lewis; m. Todd Wesley Hall, Aug. 1, 1992; children: Brennan, Aiden. BA, Biola U., 1991, MA, 1993, PhD, 1996. Therapist Family Life Counseling and Ednl. Ctrs., Tucson, 1996-98; asst. prof. Biola U., La Mirada, Calif., 1998—. Contbg. author: Measures of Religious Behavior, 1999; contbr. articles to profl. jours.; contbg. editor Jour. Psychology and Theology, 1998—, guest editor, 1999. Bd. dirs. Narramore Christian Found., Calif., 1999—. Mem. APA, Christian Assn. for Psychol. Studies. Evangelical. Office: Biola U Rosemead 13800 Biola Ave La Mirada CA 90639-0001

HALL, PAMELA S., environmental consulting firm executive; b. Hartford, Conn., Sept. 4, 1944; d. LeRoy Warren and Frances May (Murray) Sheely; m. Stuart R. Hall, July 21, 1967. BA in Zoology, U. Conn., 1966; MS in Zoology, U. N.H., 1969, BS summa cum laude, 1982; student spl. grad. studies program, Tufts U., 1986-90. Curatorial asst. U. Conn., Storrs, 1966; rsch. asst. Field Mus. Natural History, Chgo., 1966-67; tchg. asst. U. N.H., Durham, 1967-70; program mgr. Normandeau Assocs. Inc., Portsmouth, N.H., 1971-79, marine lab. dir., 1979-81; programs and ops. mgr. Normandeau Assocs. Inc., Bedford, N.H., 1981-83; v.p. Normandeau Assocs. Inc., Bedford, 1983-85, sr. v.p., 1986-87, pres., 1987—. Mem. Conservation Commn., Portsmouth, 1977-90, Wells, Estuarine Rsch. Res. Rev.Commn., 1986-88, Great Bay (N.H.) Estuarine Rsch. Res. Tech. Working Group, 1987-89; trustee Trust for N.H. Lands, 1990-93; trustee N.H. chpt. Nature Conservancy, 1991—, chair 1995-99, chair emeritus, 1999—, trustee, 2000—, incorporator N.H. Charitable Fund, 1991-99; bd. advisors Vivamos Mejor, USA, 1990—; bd. dirs. Environ. Bus. Coun. New England, 1995—, treas. 1997—; bd. emeritus Ecosystems Inst., 1997—; commr. N.H. Land and Heritage Commn., 1998-99. Graham Found. fellow, 1966; NDEA fellow, 1970-71. Mem. Women's Transp. Seminar, The Nature Conservancy, Soc. of the Protection of N.H. Forests, The Audubon Soc., Nat. Assn. Environ. Profls., Sigma Xi. Home: 4 Pleasant Point Dr Portsmouth NH 03801-5275 Office: Normandeau Assocs Inc 25 Nashua Rd Bedford NH 03110-5500

HALL, PENELOPE COKER, magazine editor; b. Charlotte, N.C., Mar. 19, 1932; d. James Lide and Elizabeth (Boatwright) Coker; m. William Parmenter Wilson, Sept. 6, 1964 (div. 1971); 1 child, Eliza Wilson Ingle; m. Mortimer Waddhams Hall, Dec. 8, 1972; stepchildren: Dorothy, Margaret, Mary Howland, Matthew. Student, Sarah Lawrence Coll., Bronxville, N.Y., 1954. Sr. editor, biographer Cleveland Amory's Celebrity Register, N.Y.C.; prodr., commentator Wrap-Up with Mike Wallace, N.Y.C.; co-prodr., interviewer for series of hr. long spls. NBC-TV, N.Y.C.; co-host 10 Around Town Channel 10 TV, Phila.; co-host The New Yorkers Channel 5 TV, N.Y.C., 1968-70; reporter, Sunday anchor 10 O'Clock News, Channel 5, N.Y.C., 1970-73; host cable cooking show Cooking Cable, Millbrook, N.Y., 1975—; editor-in-chief Dutchess Mag., N.Y.C., 1992-98, editor-at-large, columnist, 1998—. Contbr. numerous articles to profl. jours.; author: Fancy and the Cement Patch, 1966, The Wish Bottle, 1967, Riding High, 1990. Bd. trustees Spoleto Festival, Charleston, S.C., 1997—, Coker Coll., Hartsville, S.C., 2000—. Mem. Authors League, Nat. Trust for Hist. Preservation Nat. Trust Coun., Sandanona Beagles, Millbrook Hounds, Century Club, Millbrook Golf and Tennis Club (bd. dirs. 1989-93), Cosmopolitan Club. Democrat. Episcopalian. Avocations: painting, horseback riding, boating. Home: PO Box 516 Millbrook NY 12545-0516

HALL, RALPH FREDERICK, social science educator; b. Sydney, NSW, Australia, Sept. 19, 1940; s. Edward Ralph and Edith Louisa (Emms) H.; m. Diane Narelle Everett, Jan. 15, 1965 (div. 1976); children: Lachlan Everett, Jacoba Ann, Dorinda Alison; m. Susan Gaye Moxham; 1 child, Vivienne Louisa Moxham-Hall. BA with honors, U. Sydney, 1966, MA with honors, 1968, PhD, 1971. Clk. Sydney County Coun., 1956-60; asst. acct. Dairy Farmers Coop., Sydney, 1960-64; lectr. psychology U. Sydney, 1968-72; sr. lectr. psychology U. NSW, Kensington, Australia, 1972-74, Macquarie U., 1974-75; prof. liberal and gen. studies U. NSW, Kensington, 1975-90, prof. social sci. and policy, 1991—. Author: Global Issues, 1987, Impacts, 1991, Children, Commercial Strategies and On-Line Services, 1998; assoc. editor Australian Jour. Psychology, 1979-81; contbr. articles to profl. jours. Chmn. N.S.W. Higher Sch. Cert. Gen. Studies Syllabus Com., 1981-93; mem. Higher Edn. Coun., 1994-95. Recipient U. Sydney medal, 1968, H. Tasman Lovell Meml. medallion, 1971. Mem. Australian Psychol. Soc. (sec. 1966-68), Fedn. Australian U. Staff Assn. (pres. 1988-94), Nat. Tertiary Edn. Union (life), City of Sydney Swimming Assn. (life), Leichhardt Swimming Club (life). Avocations: swimming, running, wine appreciation. Office: U NSW, Sch Social Sci and Policy, Kensington Australia 2033

HALL, RICHARD CLAYTON, retired psychologist; b. Pitts., Apr. 29, 1931; s. Clayton LeClaire and Genevieve (Gorman) H.; m. Doris Margaret Bjorkland, Aug. 26, 1963; children: Karen, Janice, Dorothy. BS in Psychology with honors, Trinity Coll., 1952; MS, U. Pitts., 1959, PhD, 1963. Rsch. psychologist Polk (Pa.) Ctr., 1963-68, dir. behavior modification programs, 1968-75, chmn. subcom. human rights for behavior mgmt. procedures, 1987-89, staff psychologist, 1989-91; ind. researcher Key West, Fla., 1975-84, Polk, Pa., 1985-95; retired, 1995. Contbr. articles to profl. jours. With U.S. Army, 1953-55. NSF Coop. Grad. fellow, 1959. Mem. Sigma Xi, Pi Gamma Mu. Democrat. Presbyterian. Avocation: soloist at ch., civic operetta groups. Home: PO Box 235 101 Elm St Polk PA 16342-1705

HALL, ROBERT ALAN, construction company executive; b. Montgomery, Ala., Oct. 30, 1958; s. Mack Luverne and Miriam (Johnston) H. BS in Commerce and Bus. Adminstrn., U. Ala., 1981. CPA, Ala., cert. internal auditor. Sr. acct. Jackson and Thornton, CPAs, Montgomery, 1981-83; sr. auditor Vulcan Materials Co., Birmingham, Ala., 1983-86, supr. internal audit, 1986-87; mgr., fin. and adminstrn. Saudi Arabian Vulcan Ltd., Jubail, Saudi Arabia, 1987-90; spl. assignments analyst Vulcan Materials Co., 1990-91; contr., treas., asst. sec. Bill Harbert Internat. Constrn. Inc., Birmingham, Ala., 1991-95, v.p., CFO, 1995-2000; v.p., CEO, sec. B.L. Harbert Internat., LLC, 2000—; presdl. appointee White House Conf. on Small Bus., 1995; mem. Pres.'s Bus. Adv. Coun., Washington, 1995—; mem. profl. adv. bd. Sch. Accountancy/U. Ala., 1991—. Charter mem. Rep. Presdl. Task Force, Washington, 1984-86; presdl. appointee White House Conf. Small Bus., 1995. Recipient presdl. achievement award Pres. Ronald Reagan, 1983, Cert. of Appreciation, Gov. of Ala., 1988; named hon. citizen City of L.A., 1984, hon. asst. atty. gen. State of Ala., 1984, hon. lt. gov. of Tex., 1995, hon. lt. gov. of Ala., 1998; named one of Outstanding Young Men of Am., 1986. Mem. AICPA, Ala. Soc. CPAs, Am. Businessmen's Assn. Saudi Arabia (bd. dirs. 1988-90), U. Ala. Sr. Execs. Club., Coll. Commerce, Hon. Order Ky. Cols. Baptist. Home: 416 Old Brook Cir Birmingham AL 35242-2658 Mailing Address: PO Box 531390 Birmingham AL 35253-1390

HALL, ROBERT EMMETT, JR., investment banker, realtor; b. Sioux City, Iowa, Apr. 28, 1936; s. Robert Emmett and Alvina (Faden) H.; m. Marna Thiel, 1969. BA, U. S.D., 1958, MA, 1959; MBA, U. Santa Clara, 1976; grad., Am. Inst. Banking, Realtors Inst. Grad. asst. U. S.D., Vermillion, 1958-59; mgr. ins. dept., asst. mgr. installment loan dept. Northwestern Nat. Bank Sioux Falls, S.D., 1959-61, asst. cashier, 1961-65; asst. mgr. Crocker Nat. Bank, San Francisco, 1965-67, loan officer, 1967-69; asst. v.p., asst. mgr. San Mateo (Calif.) br. Crocker Nat. Bank, 1969-72; v.p., western regional mgr. Internat. Investments & Realty, Inc., Washington, 1972—; owner Hall Enterprises Co., San Jose, Calif., 1976—; pres. Alamaden Oaks Realtors, Inc., 1976—; instr. West Valley Coll., Saratoga, Calif., 1972-82, Grad. Sch. Bus., U. Santa Clara (Calif.), 1981-82, Evergreen Valley Coll., San Jose, Calif. Treas. Minnehaha Leukemia Soc., 1963, Lake County Heart Fund Assn., 1962, Minnehaha Young Rep. Club, 1963. Mem. Am. Inst. Banking, Calif. Assn. Realtors (vice chmn.), Alamaden Country Club, Elks, Rotary (past pres.), KC, Beta Theta Pi. Home: 6951 Castlerock Dr San Jose CA 95120-4705 Office: Hall Enterprises 100A Crown Blvd San Jose CA 95120-2903

HALL, ROBERT JOSEPH, physician, medical educator; b. Buffalo, June 4, 1926; s. Joseph M. and Florence C. (Kirst) H.; m. Dorothy Nowak, Aug. 28, 1948; children: Thomas R., Kathleen A. Hall Noble, Mary J. Hall Stuart, Michael F., Steven E. Student, Canisius Coll., Buffalo, 1943-45; MD, U. Buffalo, 1948. Diplomate Am. Bd. Internal Medicine, Sub Bd. Cardiovascular Disease (mem. cardiovascular disease sect. 1969-75). Intern Mercy Hosp., Buffalo, 1948-49; commd. 1st lt. M.C. U.S. Army, 1948, advanced through grades to col., 1966; resident in internal medicine Walter Reed Gen. Hosp., Washington, 1949-52; resident in cardiovascular diseases Walter Reed Gen. Hosp., 1956-57; asst. cardiovascular research Walter Reed Army Inst. Research, 1957-58; service in Korea and Japan, 1952-55; chief cardiology service Brooke Gen. Hosp., Ft. Sam Houston, Tex., 1961-66, Walter Reed Gen. Hosp., 1966-69; ret., 1969; clin. assoc. prof. medicine Georgetown U. Med. Sch., 1967-69; clin. prof. medicine Baylor U. Coll. Medicine, Houston, 1969—, U. Tex. Med. Sch., Houston, 1977—; med. dir. Tex. Heart Inst., Houston, 1969-93; chmn. exec. com. profl. staff Tex. Heart Inst., 1969-93; dir. div. cardiology St. Luke's Episcopal Hosp., Houston, 1969-95; assoc. chief med. service St. Luke's Episcopal Hosp., 1970-83; dir. edn., cardiology Tex. Heart Inst. Tex. Heart Inst. and St. Luke's Episcopal Hosp., 1992—; cons. Tex. Children's, VA, Brooke Gen. hosps., M.D. Anderson Hosp. and Tumor Inst.; mem. cardiovascular study sect. NIH, 1958-61; mem. phys. evaluation team Gemini project NASA, 1958-61; mem. nat. adv. heart counseil Dept. Def., 1966-69; adv. council Mended Hearts, 1970-78. Contbr. numerous articles med. jours. Mem. President's Adv. Panel Heart Disease. Decorated Legion of Merit; recipient Disting. Alumnus award Canisius Coll., 1995. Fellow A.C.P., Am. Coll. Cardiology (gov. 1968-71-74, chmn. bd. govs. and trustee 1973-74); mem. Am. Heart Assn. (fellow council clin. cardiology; pres. Houston chpt. 1974-75, advisor corp. cabinet 1980-86), Assn. Mil. Surgeons U.S., Assn. Advancement Med. Instrumentation, Pan Am. Med. Assn. (chmn. sect. cardiovascular diseases 1978-81), Assn. Univ. Cardiologists, Tex. Med. Assn., Tex. Cardiology Club, Harris County Med. Soc., Houston Cardiology Soc. (chmn. 1976-77), Houston Soc. Internal Medicine, Alpha Omega Alpha, 1948—. Home: 5504 Sturbridge Dr Houston TX 77056-1623 Office: 6624 Fannin St Ste 2480 Houston TX 77030-2309

HALL, ROGER DAVID, management consultant, educator; b. Salford, Manchester, Eng., Mar. 5, 1943; s. Harry and Prudence Marie (Dunning) H.; m. Joan Alice Hopkins, Mar. 15, 1969; children: Caroline Elizabeth, Jonathan David. BA, Leeds U., Eng., 1965; MS, U. Manchester Inst. Sci./Tech., Eng., 1969, Salford U., Eng., 1991; PhD, Salford U., 1995; MEd, Manchester U., 1999. Mgmt. trainee Smith and Newphew, Eng., 1965-67; lectr. Stockport Coll., Eng., 1969-71, sr. lectr., 1990-99; mng. dir. Stylo Plastics, Eng., 1971-90; prin. lectr. Huddersfield U. Bus. Sch., 1999—; external verifier Inst. of Mgmt., Eng., 1994—, br. sec., 1996-98. Author: (book) Pubs of Blackley, 1980; co-author: Pubs of Swinton and Pendlebury, 1983. Magistrate, Salford, 1986—, licensing magistrate, 1987—, youth ct. magistrate, 1988—, family ct. magistrate, 1990—. Fellow Inst. Mgmt., Inst. Personnel and Devel., Royal Soc. Arts. Avocations: local history, pubs and real ale, cookery, snooker, fgn. travel. Home: 123 Hill Ln, M9 6PW Manchester England Office: Bus Sch Huddersfield Univ, Queensgate HD1 3DH, England

HALL, ROGER KINGSLEY, pediatric dental surgeon, educator; b. Melbourne, Australia, Aug. 18, 1934; s. Howard Alfred James and Ilma Winifred (Dwyer) H.; m. Jenifer Jane Johnson (div. 1972); children: Cecilia Janeta, Gabrielle Netherway, Nicholas Kingsley; m. Veronica Kertesz, Sept. 9, 1973; children: Simon Kingsley, Adam Kingsley. BDSc, U. Melbourne, 1956, MDSc, 1962. Dental officer Royal Dental Hosp., Melbourne, 1956-57; demonstrator U. Melbourne, 1958-59; registrar Eastman Dental Hosp., London, 1959-60; dir. dentistry, chief pediatric dental surgeon Royal Children's Hosp., Melbourne, 1960-98; sr. assoc. U. Melbourne, 1976-98, prin. assoc., 1999—. Author: Paediatric Oral Medicine and Pathology; contbr. articles to profl. jours. Sgt. Melbourne Univ. Regiment Nat. Svc. 1952-55. Recipient Order of Australia medal Australian Govt. and Queen Elisabeth of Eng., 1996. Fellow Royal Australasian Coll. Dental Surgeons, Internat. Coll. of Dentists; mem. Internat. Assn. Pediat. Dentistry (pres. 1985-87), Australian and New Zealand Soc. of Pediat. Dentistry (found. pres. 1973-76), Australasian Acad. Pediat. Dentistry (found. pres. 1989-95), Australian Dental Assn. (dental health svcs. com. 1996-99), Internat. Assn. of Oral and Maxillofacial Surgeons, Internat. Assn of Dental Rsch., Old Melburnians, Melbourne Cricket Club, Rotary Internat., others. Avocations: sports, food and wine, photography. Office: Royal Childrens Hosp, 575 Malvern Rd, Toorak 3142, Australia

HALL, ROLAND, philosopher, researcher; b. Hounslow, Middlesex, Eng., July 11, 1930; s. Alfred and Barbara Julia (Clarke) H.; m. Daphne Blenkiron, 1954 (div. 1991); children: Caroline, Rosalind, Xanthe; m. Roma Gillian Hutchinson, Sept. 4, 1995. BA with 1st class honors, U. Oxford, Eng., 1954, B Philosophy, 1956, MA, 1957. Asst. in logic U. St. Andrews, Scotland, 1956-57, lectr. philosophy, 1957-66, sr. lectr., 1966-67; reader philosophy U. York, Eng., 1967-94, head philosophy dept., 1979-85; contbr., editl. staff, cons. Oxford English Dictionary, 1959—. Founder, editor The Locke Newsletter: An Annual Journal of Locke Research, 1970—; author: Fifty Years of Hume Scholarship, 1978, Eighty Years of Locke Scholarship, 1983; asst. editor The Philos. Quarterly, 1961-67. Served with Brit. Army, 1949-50. Avocations: reading, music, winning literary competitions. E-mail: rh1@york.ac.uk. Home and Office: The Locke Newsletter, Summerfields The Glade, Escrick York YO19 6JH, England

HALL, STANTON HARRIS, dental educator, orthodontist; b. Boise, Idaho, Apr. 8, 1940; s. Perce and Orpha (Harris) H; m. Sharon Viola Price, June 30, 1962; children: Jennifer Ann, Camille Elaine, Matthew Ridd. MS, DDS, Northwestern U., 1967; PhD, U. Wash., 1974. Cert. orthodontist, 1977; diplomate Am. Bd. Orthodontics, 1991. Research assoc. Nat. Inst. Health, Bethesda, Md., 1974-77; assoc. prof. dept. orthodontics U. Wash., Seattle, 1979—. Contbr. articles and poetry to profl. publs. Mem., counselor stake presidency Ch. Jesus Christ Latter-Day Saints, 1984-93, bishop, 1979-84, 93—; councilman Aurora Dist. Boy Scouts Am., Seattle, 1984-87. Capt. USAF, 1967-69, comdr. USPHS, 1974-77. Fellow USPHS, 1964-67; recipient C.V. Mosby award for scholarship, Northwestern U. Dental Sch., 1967. Mem. ADA, AAAS, Wash. Assn. Dental Specialities (sec.-treas. 1988-89, pres. 1989-91), Wash. State Soc. Orthodontists (bd. dirs., publ. chmn. 1982-87, sec.-treas. 1987-88, v.p. 1988-89, pres. 1989-90), Pacific Coast Soc. Orthodontists (Wash. state dir., bd. dirs. 1994-97), Am. Assn. Orthodontists, Omicron Kappa Upsilon. Home: 4549 Thackeray Pl NE Seattle WA 98105-4841 Office: U Wash Dept Orthodontics Seattle WA 98195-0001 also: 12817 120th Ave NE Kirkland WA 98034-3001

HALL, STEPHEN JOHN GORDON, animal science educator; b. Cambridge, Eng., May 7, 1951; s. John Gordon and Anna (Grove-White) H.; m. Susan Bernice Kingsley, May 10, 1980; children: Nicola Jane Corisande, Katherine Anne Jessamy. BA, Cambridge (Eng.) U., 1973, MA, 1979, PhD, 1989. Wooldridge farm livestock rsch. fellow Animal Health Trust, U.K., 1979-82; livestock and zool. cons., 1982-92; rsch. assoc. CNRS, France, 1992-93, Cambridge U., 1993-96; rsch. fellow Overseas Devel. Inst., London, 1997; prof. animal sci. Sch. Agr. De Montfort U., Caythorpe, U.K., 1997—; cons., vis. scientist Ministry of Agr., U.K., UN Food and Agrl. Orgn., MGM Environ. Solutions Ltd., U.K., European Commn. Prin. author: 200 Years of British Farm Livestock, 1988; contbr. numerous articles to profl. jours. Mem. coun. Univs. Fedn. for Animal Welfare, U.K., 1996—. Mem. Rare Breeds Survival Trust, Chillingham Wild Cattle Assn. (mem. coun. 1989), various sci. orgns. Avocations: photography, restoring old houses, conserving biodiversity. E-mail: sjghall@dmu.ac.uk. Home: 3 Cross O'Cliff Hill, Lincoln LN5 8PN, United Kingdom Office: De Montfort U, Sch Agr, Caythorpe Grantham NG32 3EP, United Kingdom

HALL, TERESA JOANNE KEYS, manufacturing engineer, educator; b. Chanute, Kans., 1954; d. William Milton and Mary Joanne (Greve) Keys; m. Douglas Wayne Hall, Jan 31, 1986; 1 child, Benjamin Alan. BA in Industry, U. No. Iowa, 1988, MA in Tech., 1991; PhD in Indsl. Edn. and Tech., Iowa State U., 1997. Cert. mfg. engr. Dept. mgr. Cooks Inc., Waterloo, Iowa, 1974-76; grounds maintenance City of Waterloo, 1976-77; trades mechanic Deere & Co., Waterloo, 1977-79, foundry maintenance planner, 1979-82, metals analyst, 1982-84, sr. maintenance planner, 1984-87; pvt. practice Waterloo, 1988-91; instr. U. Northern Iowa, Cedar Falls, 1992-96, asst. prof., 1997-00, assoc. prof., 2000—; expert witness mfg. fabrication & safety issues; panel reviewer NSF, 1999-2000. Contbr. articles to profl. jours. Grantee NSF, 1996, 98, Tchr. Edn. Alliance, 1997. Mem. AAUW, Soc. Mfg. Engrs. (faculty advisor 1993—, Region 9 exec. bd. 1998—), Am. Mensa Ltd., Nat. Assn. Indsl. Technologists (Outstanding Prof. of Yr. for Region 2), Epsilon Pi Tau. Avocations: gardening, curriculum design. Office: U Northern Iowa Dept Indsl Tech Cedar Falls IA 50614-0001

HALL, TIMOTHY COUZENS, biology educator, consultant; b. Darlington, Durham, Eng., Aug. 29, 1937; came to U.S., 1965; s. Gilbert Leslie and Dorothea Olive (Lindemann) H.; m. Sandra Severn, Aug. 20, 1960; children: Alexandra Vikki Anna, Liza Bryony, Peter Marcus Jeremy. BSc with honors, U. Nottingham, Eng., 1962, PhD in Plant Physiology, 1965. Louis W. and Maud Hill postdoctoral fellow dept. hort. sci. U. Minn., St. Paul, 1965-66; asst. prof. horticulture U. Wis., Madison, 1966-70, assoc. prof., 1970-75, prof., 1975-82, adj. prof. biophysics and genetics, 1982-84; dir. Agrigenetics Advanced Rsch. Div., Madison, 1980-84, Agrigenetics Rsch. Corp., Boulder, Colo., 1981-84; Disting. prof., head dept. biology Tex. A&M U., College Station, 1984-92, dir. Inst. Devel. and Molecular Biology, 1992—; sr. biotech. cons. Rhône-Poulenc Agrochimie, Lyon, France, 1985—; chair, organizer Gordon Conf. on Plant Molecular Biology, 1987; cons. plant biotech. Novartis, 1997-98; co-chair, co-organizer Juan March Workshop on Chromation and DNA Modification, 1998. Editor: (with J.W. Davies) Nucleic Acids in Plants, 2 vols., 1979, (with L. van Vloten-Doting and G.S.P. Groot) Molecular Form and Function of the Plant Genome, 1985; mem. editl. bd. Oxford Surveys Plant Molecular and Cell Biology, 1983-80, Transgenic Rsch., 1991-95, Plant Jour., 1991—, Jour. Virology, 1996—; contbr. numerous articles to profl. jours., book chpts.; patentee in field. Pilot Royal Air Force, 1956-58. Grantee NIH, NSF, USDA, NATO, Rhône-Poulenc Agrochimie, Internat. Paper Co., Tex. Advanced Tech. Program, Rockefeller Found. Fellow Indian Virol. Soc.; mem. AAAS, RNA Soc., Am. Soc. for Biochemistry and Molecular Biology, Am. Soc. for Microbiology, Am. Soc. Plant Physiologists (organizer Juan March workshop on chromatin and DNA modification Madrid, 1998), Am. Soc. for Virology, Am. Phytopathol. Soc., Soc. Gen. Microbiology, Fedn. Am. Socs. Exptl. Biology, Biochem. Soc., Internat. Soc. for Molecular-Plant Microbe Interactions, Internat. Soc. Plant Molecular Biology, Soc. for In Vitro Biology, RNA Soc., Squash Club Tex. A&M U., Sigma Xi. Avocations: squash, racquetball, bridge, travel. E-mail: tim@idmb.tamu.edu. Office: Tex A&M U Inst Devel Molecular Biol College Station TX 77843-0001

HALL, TIMOTHY S., surgeon; b. Kansas City, Kans., May 6, 1955; s. Charles Raymond and Agnes Husband Hall; m. Katherine Campbell, Jan. 4, 1975; children: Elizabeth, Malloury. BA, Franklin & Marshall Coll., 1978; MD, Temple U., 1982. Diplomate Am. Bd. Thoracic Surgery. Surg. resident Johns Hopkins, Balt., 1989, fellow cardiovasc. surgery, 1991; fellow thoracic surgery Meml. Sloan Kettering, N.Y.C., 1990; thoracic surgeon U. Calif., San Francisco. Contbr. chpts. to books and articles to profl. jours. Fellow ACS; mem. Am. Coll. Chest Physicians, Soc. Thoracic Surgeons. E-mail: tshall@itsa.ucsf.edu. Office: UCSF PO Box 0118 M593 505 Parnassus Ave San Francisco CA 94143

HALLAK, JACQUES, educational administrator; b. Beirut, Jan. 29, 1937; s. Charles H.; m. Viviane; children: Michele Sophie, Bruno Charles. Diploma in econs., Centre Econ. Studies, 1961; D of Math., U. Paris, 1962; DA, U. Caen, 1972. Economist Ministry of Fin., Paris, 1960-65; sr. staff mem. IIEP/UNESCO, Paris, 1965-79; assoc. prof. U. Caen & U. Paris, 1968-79; sr. program officer UNESCO, Paris, 1980-84; sr. edn. planner UNESCO-World Bank Coop. Program, Paris, 1985-87; sr. edn. specialist, economist The World Bank, Washington, 1987-88; dir. Internat. Inst. Ednl. Planning, Paris, 1988—; asst. dir. gen. UNESCO, 1994—; dir. Internat. Bur. Edn., Geneva, 1998—; chmn. Internat. Working Group Edn., Paris, ex-officio, vice chmn. Assn. for Devel. Edn. in Africa; bd. dirs. Internat. Acad. Edn. Author: A qui profite l'ecole?, 1974, Planning the Location of Schools: An Instrument of Educational Policy, 1977, Investing in the Future, 1990. Recipient Bandera del honor (1st class) Andres Bello Venezuelan Govt., 1994, Chevalier e la Légion d'Honneur, 1999. Mem. Academia Europaea. Office: Internat Inst Ednl Planning, 7-9 rue Eugène Delacroix, 75116 Paris France*

HALLAN, STEIN IVAR, internist, researcher; b. Trondheim, Norway, Dec. 14, 1962; s. Per and Asbjørg (Ronglan) H.; m. Guri Melbø; 1 child, Per Gunnar. MD, U. Trondheim, 1988, PhD, 1999. Intern Innherred Hosp., Levanger, Norway, 1988-89, resident in medicine, 1990-91, resident in clin. chemistry, 1992-94; resident in medicine U. Hosp. Trondheim, 1995-98, cons. clin. chemistry, 1998—. Avocations: cross country skiing, fishing, music. Home: Ingrid Kiaers v 10, N-7053 Ranheim Trondheim Norway Office: U Hosp Trondheim, Dept Clin Chemistry, N-7006 Trondheim Norway

HALL-BARRON, DEBORAH, lawyer; b. Oakland, Calif., Oct. 7, 1949; d. John Standish Hall and Mary (Swinson) H.; m. Eric Levin Meadow, Feb. 1973 (div. June 1982); 1 child, Jesse Standish Meadow Hall; m. Richie Barron, 1997. Paralegal cert., Sonoma State U., Rohnert Park, Calif., 1984; JD, John F. Kennedy U., Walnut Creek, Calif., 1990. Bar: Calif. 1991. Paralegal Law Offices Marc Libarle/Quentin Kopp, Cotati, Calif., 1983-84, MacGregor & Buckley, Larkspur, Calif., 1984-86, Law Offices Melvin Belli, San Francisco, 1987-88, Steinhart & Falconer, San Francisco, 1988; mgr. Computerized Litigation Assocs., San Francisco, 1986; law clk. Morton & Lacy, San Francisco, 1989-91, assoc., 1991-96; atty. Law Offices of Charlotte Venner, San Francisco, 1996-97, Plastiras & Terrizzi, San Francisco, San Rafael, Calif., 1998, Bishop, Barry, Howe, Haney & Ryder, San Francisco, 1998-99, McLemore, Collins and Toschi, Oakland, Calif., 1999-2000, ITT Fin. Corp., San Francisco, 2000—. Atty. Vol. Legal Svcs., San Francisco, 1991-96; judge San Francisco Youth Ct., 1995-97; com. chmn. Point Richmond (Calif.) coun., 1994-96. Recipient Whiley Manuel Pro Bono award State Bar Calif., 1993. Mem. Nat. Assn. Ins. Women, Def. Rsch. Inst., Bar Assn. San Francisco (del. 4th world conf. on women 1995, chair product liability com.), Internat. Com. Lawyers for Tibet (litigation com. 1991-97, co-chair women's com.), Ins. Claims Assn. (chmn. membership com. 1994-96), Hon. Order of Blue Goose Internat., Queen's Bench (chmn. employment com. 1994-97, bd. dirs. 1996—, newsletter editor and webmaster 1999), BASF intellectual property/entertainment law). Democrat. Avocations: sailing, playing guitar and saxaphone, home brewing, mountain biking, human rights advocate.

HALLBERG, ÅKE E. L., publisher, graphic designer, educator; b. Malmö, Sweden, Mar. 3, 1935; s. Edvin F. and Maja K. (Esbjörnsson) H.; m. Solveig G. Hansson, Sept. 16, 1961; children: Björn, Irene. Degree in graphic engring., Graphic Inst., Stockholm, 1961. Printing mgr. Hallandspostens Boktr., Halmstad, Sweden, 1961-73; pub. Spektra Pub., Halmstad, 1973-97; lit. cons. Natur & Kultur, 1998—; cons., lectr., speaker in field, Sweden, Denmark, Finland. Author textbooks; contbr. articles to profl. jours. Recipient award Swedish-Am. Found., 1968, Swedish Nat. Bd. Tech. Devel., 1992, Swedish Graphic Cos. Fedn., 1996. Avocations: magic, accordion playing, music. E-mail: info@spektrastudio.se. Office: Spektra Pub, Box 7024, 3007 Halmstad Sweden

HALLBERG, LEIF YNGVE GUSTAF, medical educator; b. Lund, Sweden, June 10, 1923; s. Yngue P.B. and Inez E.J. (Larsson) H.; m. Ingrid G.A. Brandt, Sept. 25, 1945 (dec. July 1992); children: Håkan, Agneta, Bengt; m. Kerstin B. Uddgren, July 30, 1994. MD, U. Lund, 1948; PhD, U. Göteborg, 1955. Assoc prof. medicine U. Göteborg, Sweden, 1955-67; prof. medicine U. Göteborg, 1967—; med. dir. Sahlgren U. Hosp., Göteborg, 1969-75; sci. advisor Swedish Nat. Bd. Health and Welfare, 1968-89; chmn. Bd. Hematology Swedish Med. Assn., 1968-76, Bd. Internal Medicine, 1973-78; expert advisor WHO, UNICEF, FAO. Chmn. pub. Jour. Internal Medicine, 1980-93; mem. editl. bd. sci. jours.; contbr. articles to profl. jours. Recipient Internat. Danone prize of nutrition, 1999. Mem. Rotary. Avocations: golf, sailing. Home: Terrassgatan 11, 41133 Göteborg Sweden Office: Sahlgren U Hosp Dept Nutrit, Annedalsklinikerna, 41335 Göteborg Sweden

HALLBERG, ÖRJAN HANS OLOF, reliability engineer; b. Hudiksvall, Sweden, Apr. 14, 1942; s. Helge and Karin Elisabet (Olsson) H.; m. Inger Kerstin Bergendahl, Jan. 4, 1969; children: Olof, Patricia. MSEE, Chalmers Tech. U., Göteborg, 1966. Component engr. Swedish Adminstr. Telecom., Stockholm, 1966-71; reliability group mgr. ELLEMTEL, Stockholm, 1971-81; quality mgr. RIFA AB, Kista, Sweden, 1981-87; qualification vendor assesment mgr. Ericsson Telecom, Stockholm, 1987-92, quality improvement mgr., 1992—; environ. coord. Ericsson Telecom Wireline Sys., Stockholm, 1997—; tech. program mem. RELCON, Copenhagen, 1982-86; steering com. European Symposium on Reliability of Electron Devices, Failure Physics Analysis, 1992-99. Co-author: Långtidsuppförandet hos tekniska system, 1994; contbr. articles to profl. jours. Avocation: playing violin. Home: Polkavägen 14B, SE-14265 Trångsund Sweden Office: Ericsson Telecom, Tellusborgsvägen 83-87, SE-12625 Stockholm Sweden

HALLBERG, PEKKA ILMARI, chief justice; b. Joensuu, Finland, June 12, 1944; s. Reino Ilmari and Aira Annikki (Voutilainen) H.; m. Taru Salme Marjaana Ali-Melkkilä, Feb. 15, 1970; 1 child, Lauri Petteri. Cand.jur., Univ., Helsinki, 1967, Lic.jur., 1971, Dr.jur., 1978. Referendary Supreme Adminstrv. Ct., Helsinki, Finland, 1967-79; researcher Finnish Acad., Helsinki, Finland, 1973-77; legis. counsellor Ministry of Justice, Helsinki, Finland, 1977-79; justice Supreme Adminstrv. Ct., Helsinki, Finland, 1979-93, pres., 1993—. Mem. Finnish Law Soc. (chmn. 1994-98), Finnish Cultural Found. (vice chmn. 1994-95, chmn. 1995—, bd. trustees), Finnish Acad. Sci. and Letters. Home: Osuuskunnantie 75, FIN00660 Helsinki Finland Office: Supreme Adminstrv Ct, Unioninkatu 16, FIN00131 Helsinki Finland*

HALLCHURCH, TIMOTHY THOMAS, genealogist, consultant; b. Codsall, Staffordshire, Jan. 17, 1941; s. Lancelot Wallace Hallchurch and Eleanor Jane Robertsh; m. Heather Joan Charlton; children: Andrew Wallace, Philip Timothy. Grad., Royal Mil. Acad., 1961. Comdr. Queens Own, Oxfordshire Hussars, 1989-91; def. mgr. Apricot Computers, 1986-89; sales mgr. Oral Info. Systems, 1989-95; land systems sales mgr. Marconi CIS, 1996-98; dir. Oxford Hallchurch Cons., 1998—; dir. Precolor Products, Wolverhampton, 1961-80; cons. Consultancy Solutions, Ltd., 1998-2000. Author: History of a Worcestershire Family, 1998. A/lt. col. Army Royal Signals, 1969-96. Mem. Otmoor Conservative Assn. (chmn. 1990-2000), Oxfordshire Inst. of Dirs. (chmn. 1996-2000), Otmoor Archaelog. and Hist. Soc. (com. 1996-99), Army Onithol. Soc. of Expeditions Orgn., Inst. of Mgmt. (fellowship), British Computer Soc. (assoc.), Army Ornithol. Soc. Avocations: geneaology, ornithology, history, tennis, antiques.

HALLECK, DONNA P., piano teacher; b. South Boston, Va., July 16, 1955; d. Edward Nathaniel and Joyce Fears Peade; m. Allen Duaine Halleck, July 23, 1977; children: Nathaniel, Stephen, Paul, Mark. BA, Bob Jones U., 1977. Tchr. 3rd grade piano Thrifthaven Bapt. Ch. Sch., Memphis, Tenn., 1977-79, Denbigh Bapt. Ch. Sch., Newport News, Va., 1979-84; tchr. piano Ft. Washington, Mo., 1984-89, Chesapeake, Va., 1989—. Tchr. Sunday Sch., Chesapeake, Va.; active Nursing Home Min., Senkara Nursing Care, Chesapeake; poll worker Rep. Party of Md., Ft. Washington. Mem. Tidewater Music Tchr Forum (assoc. treas. 1999—). Avocation: reading. E-mail: allen-donnahalleck@juno.com.

HALLENGREN, ANDERS, writer, historian; b. Stockholm, June 19, 1950; s. Sven Gotthard and Gunvie Marianne (Blomquist) H.; m. Kerstin Löfvall, Sept. 7, 1986; children: Mia-Li, Julia. BA, MA, Stockholm U., 1972, PhD, 1994; M in Philosophy and Lit., Tchrs. Coll., Stockholm, 1974. Pres. Bokgillet Coop., Stockholm, 1977-79; fgn. affairs journalist Europe, Am., and Africa, 1981-86; vis. fellow dept. history Harvard U., Cambridge, Mass., 1980, 87, rsch. affiliate in history, 1987; dir. Inst. of Current History, Stockholm, 1990—; editor Värld och Vetande, Gothenburg, 1991-99; coord., mem. adv. coun. Transnat. Inst., Norwich, Vt. and Moscow, 1992-98; mem. com. English lang. tchg. coun. Guangxi Tchrs. U., Guilin, China, 1993; mass media cons. Medvik/Kinnevik, Stockholm, 1985-89; editl. cons. Nordiska Affärslivet, Stockholm, 1983-86; lectrs. and poetry readings in U.S., China, Russia, Can., Eng., others, 1988—; spkr. internat. meeting of writers P.E.N. Radio Yugoslavia, Belgrade, 1990, Moscow Writers Union, 1991; assoc. prof. comparative lit., dept. history of lit. and history of ideas Stockholm U.,

1999—; project dir. Nobel Found., 2000—; chmn. Nobel Copyright Group, 2000—; rsch. affiliate European Sci. Found., Strasbourg, 1999—. Author: Détente and Disruption, 1991, The Puritan Mind and the Modern Self, 1991, Deciphering Reality, 1992, The Code of Concord, 1994, What is National Literature, 1996, Gallery of Mirrors, 1998; mem. editl. bd. Parnass, 1993-96, mng. editor, 1997—; mem. editl. bd. Referens, 1974-76, Litter, 1976-77, Kooperativa Bokgillet, 1977-79, Nordiska Affärslivet, 1983-86, Världarnas Möte, 1989-95, Varld och Vetande, 1991-95, Arcana, 1994-95, Albert Bonnier Pub. Co., 1998—. Elected commr. Swedish Ch., 1997. Grantee Royal Swedish Acad. Scis., 1982, 93, Swedish Inst., 1987, 98, Stockholm U., 1980-89, 97—, K.A. Wallenberg Found., 1980, 94, Marcus and Marianne Wallenberg Found., 1994, Långman Cultural Fund, 1984, 95, The Swedish Acad., 1995. Fellow Hemingway Soc., Caribbean Studies Assn. (P.R.), N.Y. Acad. Scis., ; mem. PEN, World Assn. Writers, Union Profl. Translators, Stockholm Assn. Humanities (pres., bd. dirs.), Union Swedish Writers (grantee 1994-95), Transnat. Vladimir Solovyov Soc. (founder, coord. 1993—), St. Croix Landmarks Soc. (V.I.), Am. Acad. Religion, Lit. Soc. Sweden (mem. com. 1998—). Avocations: astronomy, archaeology, music composition. Fax: 46-8-155874, 108450. Home: Regeringsgatan 70 C, SE-11139 Stockholm Sweden Office: Stockholm U, Dept Literature, SE-10691 Stockholm Sweden

HALLET, CHARLES JOSEPH, Jesuit priest, educator, academic administrator; b. Sougné-Remouchamps, Liège, Belgium, Sept. 4, 1933; arrived in Chile, 1969; s. Célestin Pascal H. and J.M. Madeleine Paula Collard. BA, U. Cath. Louvain (Belgium), 1959; BPhil, Ecole Hautes Etudes, Le Puy, France, 1961; DD, P. U. Cath., Santiago, Chile, 1979. Ordained to Roman Catholic ch., 1965. Prof. P. U. Cath., Santiago, Chile, 1969-80, 87-89, U. Cath., Valparaiso, Chile, 1981-86; vicar of edn. Archdioces Antofagasta (Chile), 1991—; vice-grand chancellor U. Cath. Norte, Antofagasta, 1991—; dir. dept. theology U. Cath. Norte, Antofagasta, 1993—. Author: El Educador Cristiano, 1988, Répertoire des Spirituels Catholiques de Wallonie, 1990, El Beato Alberto Hurtado S.J.: su perfil espiritual, 1994, María de Magdala, la Divina Amante, 1995, Conozca a los Padres de la Iglesia, 1995, Del Big Bang...a Adán y Eva, 1996, El Profesional y la Etica hoy, 1997, Buda, Jesús o Mahoma?, 1997, La Educación Jesuita, 1998, Constructores de Humanidad, 1999, La Perfección Cristiana hoy, 1999. Decorated knight Order Leopold II, 1996. Mem. N.Y. Acad. Scis. Avocation: drawing. Home: Eduardo Orchard 1637, casilla 1147 Antofagasta Chile Office: U Catolica Norte, Av Angamos 0610, casilla 1280 Antofagasta Chile

HALLETT, CHRISTOPHER R., realtor; b. Hyannis, Mass., Apr. 8, 1966; s. Robert Nathan and Kathleen Ann Hallett. Degree in mgmt., Cape Cod C.C.; postgrad., Suffolk U. Bartender Oyster Harbors, Osterville, Mass.; realtor CB/John A. Drew, Centerville, Mass., 1992-94, CB/Murray RE, Hyannis, Mass., 1994, Prudential Premier, Centerville, Mass., 1994—. Mem. Nat. Assn. Realtors, Cape Cod & Islands Bd. Realtors, Cape Cod Fencing Club. Avocations: fencing, sailing, golf. E-mail: crhallett@yahoo.com. Home: 55 Wintergreen Cir Osterville MA 02655-1565 Office: Prudential Premier Properties 619 Main St Centerville MA 02632-2915

HALLETT, JOHN WILLIAM, surgeon, educator, former career officer; b. Wheeling, W.Va., July 6, 1947. BS, U.S. Air Force Acad., 1969; MD, Duke U., 1973. Diplomate Am. Bd. Gen. and Vascular Surgery. Commd. U.S. Air Force, 1965, advanced through grades to lt. col., ret., 1984; chief vascular surgery Wilford Hall U.S. Med. Ctr., San Antonio, 1980-84; program dir., fellow in vascular surgery Mayo Found., Rochester, Minn., 1990-97; co-dir. vascular ctr. Mayo Found., Rochester, 1990—; assoc. dean faculty affairs Mayo Med. Sch., Rochester, 1998—, prof. surgery. Author: Handbook of Patient Care in Vascular Surgery, 1982, 3d edit., 1995. Fellow ACS; mem. Internat. Soc. Cardiovasc. Surgery, Am. Surg. Assn., Soc. Vascular Surgery, Midwestern Vascular Surg. Soc. (pres. 1995-96), Peripheral Vascular Surgery Soc. (pres. 1989-90). Avocations: art, literature, motorcycles. E-mail: hallett.john@mayo.edu. Office: Mayo Clinic 200 1st St SW Rochester MN 55905-0002

HALLEUX, ALBERT MARTIN JULIEN, motor vehicle inspection company executive; b. Dison, Belgium, Nov. 18, 1920; s. Albert Julien and Marie (Lemaire) H.; Mech. Engr., U. Liege, 1945, Aero. Engr., 1955; m. Arlette Lehyme, May 20, 1967; 1 child, Emmanuel. Engr., then chief engr. Autosecurite, Verviers, 1949-74, pres., 1974—; dep. WP29 experts group Econ. Commn. for Europe, Geneva, 1962—; gen. sec. Internat. Motor Vehicle Insp. Com. CITA, 1969-92; gen. sec., founder Union Tech. Assistance for Motor Vehicles and Road Traffic, Geneva UNATAC, 1978—; v.p. Groupement des Organismes de Contrôle Automobile, Brussels, 1979-82, 86-89, pres., 1982-85; v.p. Fonds d'Etudes pour la Sécurité Routière, Brussels, 1982-85, Fonds de pré vision et d'utilité publique de l'inspection des véhicules automobiles, Brussels, 1983-85, Autosecurity Internat, pres. 1991—, Immosecurite, 1991—, Hallinvest, 1991—. Decorated chevalier Order de la Couronne, Officier de l'Ordre de Leopold. Mem. Soc. Promoting Traffic Safety. Liberal. Roman Catholic. Died. Home: 2 rue de Louvain, B-4800 Verviers Belgium Office: Ave Du Parc, Zoning Industriel de Petit-Rechain, 4800 Verviers Belgium

HALLEY, PAUL-LOUIS, food service executive; b. Cherbourg, France, Sept. 11, 1934; s. Paul-Auguste and Marthe (Brard) H.; m. Annick de Pinsun, Apr. 27, 1968; children: Olivier, Julie, Marie. Student, Ecole St. Joseph de Tivoli, Bordeaux, France, Ecole St. Louis de Gonzague, Paris, City London Coll. Mgr. sales Halley Frères, 1959-60; co-founder Promodes, S.A., 1961—, mgr. development, 1962-69, exec. dir., 1969-72, pres., CEO, 1972-99; pres. EuroCommerce, 1999—. Decorated chevalier Legion of Honor (France), commandeur Nat. Order of Merit (France), officier dans l'ordre du Mérite Agricole, France. Avocation: water sports. Office: EuroCommerce, 123-133 Rue Froissart, B-1040 Brussels Belgium*

HALLEY, PETER JOHN, research engineer, lecturer; b. Brisbane, Australia, Feb. 3, 1966. B in Chem. Engring., U. Queensland, 1987, PhD, 1993. Rsch. engr. SRI Internat., Menlo Park, Calif., 1989, SIHRC, Adelaide, Australia, 1993; assoc. lectr. U. Queensland, Brisbane, 1994-95, lectr., rsch. engr., 1995-99, sr. lectr., 1999—. Avocations: rheology and polymer processing, touch football, tennis, squash, reading. Office: U Queensland, Chem Engring Dept, Brisbane QLD 4072, Australia

HALLEZ, JEAN PAUL, surgeon; b. Paris, May 9, 1948; s. Jean and Annette (Humbert) H.; m. Martine Marie Prot, June 17, 1970; children: Charlotte, Louis-Nicolas, Ghislain. MD, U. Paris, 1977. Bd. cert. diplomate surgeon. Intern and resident Faculty Medicine Paris; chef de clinique U. Paris, 1979-81; surgeon Hetford Brit. Hosp., Paris, 1984-95, Am. Hosp., Paris, 1984—; cons. Inst. d'Endoscopie, Paris, 1986—, pres., 1989—; surgeon Inst. Nat. des Invalides, 1998—. Mem. editl. bd. Gynecol. Endoscopy, London, 1991—; inventor in field. Mem. Soc. Internat. D'Urologie, Assn. Française de Chirurgie, N.Y. Acad. Scis. E-mail: hallez@cybercable.fr. Home: 164 Rue de Courcelles, 75017 Paris France Office: Instn Nat des Invalides, 6 blvd des Invalides, 75700 Paris France

HALLGRIMSSON, JONAS, pathologist, educator; b. Iceland, Sept. 6, 1931; s. Jonsson and Thoranna (Magnusdottir) H.; M.D., U. Iceland, 1958; m. Anna Margret Larusdottir, July 3, 1954; children—Hallgrimur, Petur, Larus, Margret. Resident in pathology U. Iceland Hosp., Reykjavik, 1958-59, U. Minn. Grad. Sch., Mpls., 1959-60; intern Meml. Hosp., Worcester, Mass., 1960-61; resident in pathology Mass. Gen. Hosp., Boston, 1961-65; pathologist U. Iceland Hosp., 1965-69, chief pathologist, 1969-78, dir. dept. pathology, 1978—; assoc. prof. U. Iceland Faculty of Medicine, 1966-78, prof., chmn. dept. pathology, 1978—, dean Faculty of Medicine, 1982-84; dir. Inst. Pathology, U. Iceland, 1978—; chmn. Bd. Public Health, Gardabaer, 1970-78. Fellow Royal Soc. Medicine, 1959-60, Rockefeller Found., 1961-63, Commonwealth Fund, 1968. Mem. Icelandic Med. Assn., Am. Coll. Pathologists, Am. Soc. Clin. Pathology, European Soc. Clin. Investigation. Club: Gardar Rotary. Contbr. articles to med. jours. Home: 2 Tjarnarflot, 210 Gardabaer Iceland Office: Univ Iceland, PO Box 1465, Reykjavik Iceland

HALLIDAY, GARY MARK, immunology researcher; b. Melbourne, Victoria, Australia, Dec. 25, 1955; s. Gordon Albert and Nancy Marrion (Cochrane) H. BSc with honors, Monash U., Melbourne, Victoria, Australia, 1977, PhD, 1981. Rsch. officer U. London, 1981-83; rsch. officer U. Tasmania, Hobart, 1984-86, lectr., 1987-88; lectr. U. Sydney, NSW, Australia, 1989-91, sr. lectr., 1992-98; assoc. prof. U. Sydney, 1998—; hon. sr. lectr. pathology U. Sydney, 1992—; hon. vis. scientist Royal Prince Alfred Hosp., Sydney, 1993—. Contbr. more than 80 articles to profl. jours. and more than 5 chpts. to books. Recipient Rsch. grants Fed. and Local Grant Awarding Bodies, 1988-2000. Mem. Soc. for Investigative Dermatology, Australian Soc. for Immunology (state councillor 1987-88), Australasian Coll. Dermatologists (assoc.). Achievements include discovery of role of langerhans cells in carcinogenesis; effects of retinoic acid on UV-induced melanogenesis; sunscreen protection from uv-immunosuppression. Office: U Sydney, Dept Dermatology, Sydney 2006, Australia

HALLIDAY, IAN, astronomer; b. Lloydminster, Sask., Can., Nov. 10, 1928; s. Clarence Peter and Edith Victoria (Phillips) H.; m. Norma Lillian Mobley, July 7, 1951; children—John Douglas, Janet Elizabeth. B.A., U. Toronto, 1949, M.A., 1950, Ph.D., 1954. Sr. sci. officer Dominion Obs., Dept. Energy, Mines and Resources, Ottawa, 1952-70; sr. research officer Herzberg Inst. Astrophysics, Nat. Research Council Can., Ottawa, 1970-90, guest worker, 1990-96. Author research papers in field; editor: Jour. Royal Astron. Soc. Can, 1970-75; co-editor: Solid Particles in the Solar System, 1980. Recipient Queen's Silver Jubilee medal, 1977, Polish Medal of Merit, 1976. Fellow Royal Soc. Can.; mem. Internat. Astron. Union (pres. commn. 22 1976-79), Royal Astron. Soc. Can. (pres. 1980-82, hon. pres. 1989-93), Can. Astron. Soc., Am. Astron. Soc., Meteoritical Soc., Planetary Soc., Internat. Halley Watch (chmn. steering group 1985-90). Home: 825 Killeen Ave, Ottawa, ON Canada K2A 2X8

HALLIDAY, IAN GIBSON, physics educator; b. Kelso, Scotland, Feb. 5, 1940; s. John Alexander and Gladys (Taylor) H.; m. Ellenor Gardiner Hervey Wilson, June 28, 1965; children: Robert Alan, Katrina Ellenor. MA, Edinburgh (Scotland) U., 1961, MSc, 1962; PhD, Cambridge (Eng.) U., 1964. Instr. Princeton (N.J.) U., 1964-66; rsch. fellow Christ's Coll. Cambridge (Eng.) U., 1966-67; lectr. Imperial Coll. U. London, 1967-75, reader, 1975-90, prof., 1990-92; prof. U. Coll. Swansea, Wales, 1992—; chmn. theory com. Sci. & Engring. Rsch. Coun., 1987-91; CEO Particle Physics and Astronomy Rsch. Coun., 1998—. Editor: Frontiers of High Energy Physics, 1987; contbr. articles to profl. jours. Fellow Inst. Physics. Avocations: golf, tennis, fishing. Home: 65 Owls Lodge Ln, Swansea SA3 5DP, Wales Office: U Coll Swansea, PPARC Polaris House, North Star Ave, Swindon SN2 1SZ, Wales

HALLIDAY, JOHN MEECH, investment company executive; b. St. Louis, Oct. 16, 1936; s. William Norman and Vivian Viola (Meech) H.; m. Martha Layne Griggs, June 30, 1962; children: Richard M., Elizabeth Halliday Traut. BS, U.S. Naval Acad., 1958; MBA, Harvard U., 1964. Dir. budgeting and planning Automatic Tape Control, Bloomington, Ill., 1964-66; dir. planning Ralston-Purina, St. Louis, 1966-67, v.p. subsidiary, 1967-68, dir. internat. banking, 1967-68; v.p. Servicetime Corp., St. Louis, 1968-70; assoc. R.W. Halliday Assocs., Boise, Idaho, 1970-87; v.p. Sawtooth Comm. Corp., Boise, 1970-73, Comdr. Corp., 1979-81; pres., CEO, bd. dirs. ML, Ltd., San Francisco, 1979—, H.W.L. Inc., San Francisco, 1985-93; pres. Halliday Labs., Inc., 1980-91; exec. v.p., bd. dirs. Franchise Fin. Corp. Am., Phoenix, 1980-85; bd. dirs., v.p. Harvard Bus. Sch. Assn. No. Calif., 1980-87; pres., CEO, bd. dirs. Cycletorl Diversified Industries, Inc., 1992—; guest lectr. U. Calif. Berkeley, 1991-99, Calif. Bus.-Higher Edn. Forum, 1995-98. Pres. Big Bros. San Francisco, 1978-81; trustee, pres. U. Calif.-Santa Cruz Found., 1988—; mem. ad hoc com. on corrections Calif. State Senate, 1995-96; fellow bd. visitors and fellows viticulture and enology U. Calif., Davis, 1999. Mem. Restaurant Assn. (v.p. 1969-70), Olympic Club (San Francisco), Scott Valley Tennis Club (Mill Valley, Calif.). Republican. Episcopalian. Home: 351 Corte Madera Ave Mill Valley CA 94941-1013 Office: 55 New Montgomery St Ste 317 San Francisco CA 94105-3426

HALLIDAY, PETER ERNEST, police officer, researcher; b. London, Oct. 19, 1947; arrived in Hong Kong, 1967; s. Albert Charles and Diedre (Heywood) H.; m. Sin Ping Chau, Jan. 12, 1993; 2 children. MA, U. Birmingham, Eng., 1991; PhD, U. Hong Kong, 2000. Inspector Hong Kong Police, 1967-75, chief inspector, 1975-77, supt., 1977-83, sr. supt., 1983-88, chief supt., 1988-96, asst. commr., 1997—. Chmn. Supts. Assn., 1988-91, Ping Shan Halfway House, 1990—; group scout leader Scout Assn. Hong Kong, 1990—. Recipient Police medal for Meritorious Svc., 1980, Queen's Police medal for Disting. Svc., 1997. Mem. Mental Health Assn. Hong Kong, Hong Kong Mgmt. Assn., Hong Kong Coll. Psychiatrists (affil), Royal Asiatic Soc. (hon. editor Hong Kong br. 1995—), N.Y. Acad. Scis., Hong Kong Jockey Club. Avocations: rock climbing, history, fitness. Home: 8 Monte Villas Kau To Shan, Shatin Hong Kong Office: c/o Police Hdqs, Arsenal St, Hong Kong China

HALLIDAY, WILLIAM ROSS, retired physician, speleologist, writer; b. Atlanta, May 9, 1926; s. William Ross and Jane (Wakefield) H.; m. Eleanore Hartvedt, July 2, 1951 (dec. 1983); children: Marcia Lynn, Patricia Anne, William Ross III; m. Louise Baird Kinnard, May 7, 1988. BA, Swarthmore Coll., 1946; MD, George Washington U., 1948. Diplomate Am. Bd. Vocat. Experts. Intern Huntington Meml. Hosp., Pasadena, Calif., 1948-49; resident King County Hosp., Seattle, Denver Children's Hosp., L.D.S. Hosp., Salt Lake City, 1950-57; pvt. practice Seattle, 1957-65; with Wash. State Dept. Labor and Industries, Olympia, 1965-76; med. dir. Wash. State Div. Vocat. Rehab., 1976-82; staff physican N.W. Occupational Health Ctr., Seattle, 1983-84; med. dir. N.W. Vocat. Rehab. Group, Seattle, 1984, Comprehensive Med. Rehab. Ctr., Brentwood, Tenn., 1984-87; dep. coroner, King County, Wash., 1964-66; chmn. Hawaii Speleol. Survey, 1989-97; dir. Western Speleol. Survey, 1957-83, dir. rsch., 1983-96. Author: Adventure Is Underground, 1959, Depths of the Earth, 1966, 76, American Caves and Caving, 1974, 82, Floyd Collins of Sand Cave, 1998; co-author: (with Robert Nymeyer) Carlsbad Cavern: The Early Years, 1991; editor: Jour. Spelean History, 1968-73; contbr. articles to profl. jours. Mem. Gov.'s North Cascades Study Com., 1967-76; mem. North Cascades Conservation Coun., v.p., 1962-63; pres. Internat. Speleological Found., 1981-87, Internat. Union Speleol. Com. on Volcanic Caves, 1992-98, hon. pres. 1998—; asst. dir. Internat. Glaciospeleological Survey, 1972-76; chmn. Hawaii Speleol. Survey, 1989-97; dir. We. Speleol. Survey, 1957-83, dir. rsch., 1983-96. Served to lt. comdr. USNR, 1949-50, 55-57. Recipient medal Geol. Soc. China; named Alumnus of Yr., George Sch., 1992. Fellow Am. Coll. Chest Physicians, Nat. Speleological Soc. (hon. mem. 1965, bd. govs. 1950—), Explorers Club; mem. AMA, Internat. Assn. Hydrogeology, Nat. Trust (Scotland), Geol. Soc. Am., Mountaineers Club (past trustee), Seattle Tennis Club.

HALLIGAN, MARY A., mechanical engineer; b. Portsmouth, Ohio, Dec. 8, 1959; d. John F. and Mary Barba (Lutz) H. BS in Geology, Lamar U., 1982; BSME, U. Houston, 1992. Mech. engr. NASA/Johnson Space Ctr., Houston. Avocations: hiking, genealogy. E-mail: mary.halligan1@jsc.nasa.gov. Office: NASA/JSC Mail Code EC4 2101 Nasa Rd 1 Houston TX 77058-3691

HALLIN, MARC, mathematics educator; b. Ghent, Belgium, Apr. 23, 1949; s. Paul and Jacqueline (Maricaux) H.; m. Dominique Bertin, July 14, 1973; children: Marie, Catherine, Françoise. DSc in Math., Free U. Brussels, 1976. Full prof. math. Free U. Brussels, 1988—; corr. classe des scis. Acad. Royale de Belgique, 1999—. Pres. Conseil Wallon de la Statistique, Namur, 1997—. Recipient Prix du Statisticien d'Expression Française, Statis. Soc. Paris, 1993. Fellow Am. Statis. Assn., Inst. Math. Statistics; mem. Belgian Statis. Soc. (pres. 1993-96), Inst. de Statistique de l'Universite Libre de Brussels (pres. 1992-96), Internat. Statis. Inst. Home: 47 ave Louis Lepoutre, B-1050 Brussels Belgium Office: ISRO Univ Libre Brussels, Campus de la Plaine CP210, B-1050 Brussels Belgium

HALLISSEY, MICHAEL, strategic consultant; b. Southampton, England, Mar. 6, 1943; s. John Francis and Mary (Kendall) H. Grad., Magdalen Coll., Oxford U., Eng., 1964. Chartered acct., Eng. With Price Waterhouse, 1964-98; asst. mgr. Price Waterhouse, Melbourne, Australia, 1968, Milan, Italy, 1969; ptnr. Price Waterhouse, London, 1974-98, head practice devel., 1979-81, head strategic planning, 1981-82, head corp. fin. services, 1983-88; dir. strategy Price Waterhouse Europe, 1988-98, PricewaterhouseCoopers (formerly Price Waterhouse), 1998; vis. fellow Imperial Coll. Sci. and Tech., London, 1998—. Contbr. articles to profl. publs. Fellow Royal Soc. of Arts; mem. Inst. Chartered Accts. Eng. and Wales. Mem. Conservative Party. Mem. Ch. of Eng. Avocations: politics, sailing, music, opera. Home: 66 Waterside Point, Anhalt Rd, London SW11 4PD, England Office: Imperial Coll Sci & Tech, 53 Prince's Gate, London SW7 2PG, England

HALLIWELL, FRANCIS STEPHEN, foreign language educator; b. Wigan, Lancashire, Eng., Oct. 18, 1953; s. Francis and Joyce (Casey) H.; m. Helen Ruth Gainford, Aug. 19, 1978; children: Luke Joseph, Edmund Benjamin Toby. BA, Oxford (Eng.) U., 1976, DPhil, 1981. Lectr. Worcester Coll., Oxford, 1977-79, Jesus Coll., Oxford, 1979-80, Westfield Coll., London, 1980-82; fellow Corpus Christi Coll., Cambridge, 1982-84; reader Birmingham (Eng.) U., 1984-95; prof. Dept. Greek St. Andrews U., Scotland, 1995—; vis. prof. U. Chgo., 1990, U. Rome, 1998; vis. faculty fellow U. Calif.-Riverside, 1993. Author: Aristotle's Poetics, 1986, Plato Republic 10, 1988, Plato Republic 5, 1993, Aristophanes Birds and Other Plays, 1997. Avocations: music, golf, literature. Office: Univ of St Andrews, Dept of Greek, Saint Andrews KY16 9AJ, Scotland

HALLMANN, ARMIN, biochemist; b. Niederhatzkofen, Bavaria, Germany, Aug. 31, 1965; s. Georg and Marianne (Zieglmeier) H. Diploma in Biology, U. Regensburg, Germany, 1991, PhD, 1995. Tutor in biochem. scis. U. Regensburg, 1991—, mem. rsch. staff, rsch. scientist, 1995—, asst. prof., 1995—, educator biochem. scis., 1995—, head biochemistry/molecular biology lab, 1996—. Contbr. articles to profl. jours. Recipient scholarshp Nissen Found., Germany, 1992-94, Richard-Winter Found., Germany, 1992-95, OBAG prize, Germany, 1996, Junkmann Found., Germany, 2000. Mem. Verband Deutscher Biologen, Gesellschaft Biochemie Molekularbiologie, N.Y. Acad. Scis., Am. Soc. for Biochemistry and Molecular Biology. Home: Eichendorffstr 10, D-84056 Rottenburg Germany Office: U Regensburg/Inst Biochemie, Universitatsstr 31, D-93053 Regensburg Germany

HALLORAN, MIKE, software company executive, music publishing executive; b. Anchorage, May 17, 1954; s. Thomas Orrey and Barbara (Long) H.; m. Sylvia Thayne Edwards, Apr. 28, 1979; children: Marjorie C., Julia C. Student, San Jose State U., 1972-75. Prin. artist/condr. Gilbert & Sullivan Soc., San Jose, Calif., 1973-92; prodr./dir. PFS Prodns., San Jose, Calif., 1974-85; rec. artist MBA Records, San Jose, Calif., 1975-89; owner PF Slow Pub. Co., San Jose, Calif., 1984—; prin. double bass Santa Clara (Calif.) Symphony, 1985-89; owner PPW Wholesale Comms., San Jose, 1986—; nat. sales mgr. Distinct Corp., Saratoga, Calif., 1996—; cons. vintage/antique musical instruments, San Jose, 1980—. Columnist IAMA Jour., 1990-91. Active Santa Clara County Dem. campaign, 1994; music dir. Immanuel Luth. Ch., Los Altos, Calif., 1998—. Mem. Am. Fedn. Musicians, ASCAP. Roman Catholic. Avocations: music, cooking, film, San Francisco Opera. Home: PO Box 6840 San Jose CA 95150-6840

HALLOY, STEPHAN ROLAND PIERRE, ecologist; b. Bujumbura, Burundi, June 1, 1953; arrived in New Zealand, 1989; s. Georges Henri André Ghislain Halloy and Louise Elisa Rose Ghislaine (Fenaux) Laurent; m. María Lidia Hance, Sept. 20, 1979; children: Diana Stéphanie, Giselle Adine. B of Humanities, Nat. U. Tucumán, Argentina, 1971, M in Biol. Scis., 1978, PhD in Biol. Scis., 1983. Asst. prof. plant ecology Nat. U. Tucumán, 1983-88, asst. prof., chair phytogeography, 1985-88, assoc. prof., chair phytogeography, 1988; biodiversity program leader Ministry Agr. and Fisheries, Mosgiel, New Zealand, 1989-92, Crop and Food Rsch., Mosgiel, New Zealand, 1992-94; head dept. sci. Found. Friends of Nature, Santa Cruz, Bolivia, 1995; scientist Crop and Food Rsch., 1996—; in charge project dept. sci. and indsl. rsch. Hellaby Trust, Dunedin, New Zealand, 1986-87; vice dir. Inst. Geoscis. and Environ., Tucumán, 1988; tech. advisor Found. Friends of Nature and The Nature Conservancy, Washington, 1996, project leader World Wildlife Fund, Santa Cruz, 1997. Contbr. over 170 articles to profl. jours. New Zealand rep. Commonwealth Sci. Coun., London, 1992; advisor Bolivian Govt., La Paz, 1996; New Zealand and Bolivia rep. So. Connection, Valdivia, Chile, 1997. Recipient Travel grant Orgn. Am. States, Ecuador, 1980. Mem. World Conservation Union (species survival commn. 1993—, world commn. on protected areas 1994—), N.Y. Acad. Scis. Avocations: mountain climbing, conservation, ethics, gardening. E-mail: halloys@crop.cri.nz. FAX: 64 3 489 0674. Office: Crop and Food Rsch, PB 50034, Mosgiel Otago 9032, New Zealand

HALLUIN, ALBERT PRICE, lawyer; b. Nov. 8, 1939; children: Russell, Marcus. BA, La. State U., 1964; JD, U. Balt., 1969. Bar: Md. 1970, N.Y. 1985, Calif. 1991. Assoc. Jones, Tullar & Cooper, Arlington, Va., 1969-71; sr. patent atty. CPC Internat. Inc., Englewood Cliffs, N.J., 1971-76; counsel Exxon Rsch. & Engring. Co., Florham Park, N.J., 1976-83; v.p., chief intellectual property counsel Cetus Corp., Emeryville, Calif., 1983-90; ptnr. Fleisler, Dubb, Meyer & Lovejoy, San Francisco, 1990-92, Limbach & Limbach, San Francisco, 1992-94, Pennie & Edmonds, Menlo Park, Calif., 1994-97, Howrey, Simon, Arnold & White, LLP, Menlo Park, 1997—; pres., CEO, chmn. Halzyme Tech., Inc., 1995—. Contbr. articles to legal jours. Pres. Belle Roche Homeowners Assn., Redwood City, Calif., 1995—. Named One of Top 20 Intellectual Property Lawyers, Calif. Lawyer's mag., 1993. Mem. ABA, Am. Intellectual Property Law Assn. (chmn. chem. practice com. 1981-83, sec. 1984-85, bd. dirs. 1984-89, founding chmn. biotech. com. 1990-92), Licensing Exec. Soc., Assn. Corp. Patent Counsel, Bar Assn. San Francisco, San Francisco Patent Assn. Republican. Episcopalian. Fax: 650-463-8400. E-mail: HalluinA@Howrey.com; Halzym@Earthlink.net. Office: Howrey, Simon, Arnold & White LLP 301 Ravenswood Ave Menlo Park CA 94025-3434

HALLUITTE, BLAISE, chemical company executive; b. Paris, Aug. 18, 1943; s. Jean and Madeleine (Simonin) H.; m. Barbara Musselman, June 2, 1973; children: Jerome, Eleanore. MS, Inst. Nat. Agonomique, Paris, 1967; MBA, Columbia U., 1970. Mgmt. cons. McKinsey & Co., Paris, 1970-73; pres., CEO Canonne Mecavigor, Paris, 1974-77; CEO Calibracier, Loire, France, 1978-82; chmn., CEO Rhone-Poulenc Animal Nutrition, Antony, France, 1982-97; pres., CEO Rhodia Inc., Cranbury, N.J., 1997-98, pres. consumer spltys. divsn., 1997-98, exec. v.p. corp. strategy and bus. devel., 1999—. Trustee Internat. House, N.Y.C., 1997—. Office: Rhodia Inc CN7500 259 Prospect Plains Rd Cranbury NJ 08512-3717 Office: Rhodia SA 25 Quai Paul Doumer, 92400 Courbevoie France

HALLWORTH, ROBERT EARL, anesthesiologist; b. Phila., Feb. 13, 1946; s. Robert Earl and Birdie Louise (Huppi) H.; m. Kathryn Celia Brown, Feb. 16, 1973; 1 child, Elizabeth Ann. BS in Pharmacy, Temple U., 1969; DO, Phila. Coll. Osteo. Medicine, 1979. Diplomate Nat. Bd. Med. Examiners, Am. Osteo. Bd. Anesthesiology, Am. Acad. Pain Mgmt. Staff pharmacists Albert Einstein Med. Ctr., Phila., 1973-75; intern Suburban Gen. Hosp., Norristown, Pa., 1979-80, anesthesia resident, 1980-82; anesthesia resident Met. Hosp., Phila., 1982-83; anesthesiologist Group Anesthesia Svcs., Norristown, 1983-87, Cmty. Anesthesia Assocs., Ltd., Lancaster, Pa., 1987-99, Prime Care Desert Valley Hosp., Victorville, Calif., 1999—; program dir. anesthesia residency Cmty. Hosp. of Lancaster, 1989-99; anesthesia rep. Medicare Carrier Adv. Com., Camp Hill, Pa., 1994-99. With U.S. Army, 1971-72. Mem. Internat. Soc. Spinal Endoscopy, Am. Osteo. Assn., Am. Soc. Regional Anesthesia, Am. Osteo. Coll. Anesthesiologists (examiner 1988—), Am. Soc. Anesthesiologists, Pa. Osteo. Med. Assn. (dist. 5 rep. 1993-99), Lancaster Osteo. Med. Soc., Lancaster City and County Med. Soc., Sigma Sigma Phi. Avocations: running, skiing, motorcycling, swimming, bicycling. Home: 8461 Svl Box Victorville CA 92392-5169 Office: PrimeCare Desert Valley Med Ctr 16850 Bear Valley Rd Victorville CA 92392-5794

HALMOS, PETER, entrepreneur; b. Budapest, Hungary, July 4, 1943; came to U.S., 1951; s. George Anthony and Clara (Sacher) H.; m. Vicki Carol Knight, Dec. 31, 1978; children: Nicholas, Gregory. BS, MBA, U. Fla., 1969; postgrad., Harvard U., 1976. Chmn. bd. Safecard Svcs., Inc., Ft. Lauderdale, Fla., 1969-90, exec. mgmt. cons., 1990-92; v.p. High Plains Capital Corp., Cheyenne, Wyo., 1978-92, chmn., 1992—; chmn., CEO Credit Ln. Corp., 1990—, Passport Ins. Co., Inc., Bismark, N.D., 1990—, Your Life Pub. Corp., 1997—, PAH Corp., 1996—, Peter Halmos & Sons, Inc., 1997—, Intelligence Svcs. Corp., 1998—; chmn. Trucks, Podell, Stoll, Blank, Horowitz & Halmos Jam Music Corp., 1998—. Trustee Palm Beach (Fla.) Day Sch., 1988-91; trustee, chmn. Peter Halmos Family Found., Inc., 1984—; bd. dirs. Pinecrest Sch., Ft. Lauderdale, 1985-92; trustee Preservation Found., Palm Beach, 1988—, Palm Beach Community Chest United Way, 1988-92, Am. Cancer Soc., Palm Beach, 1988—. Independent. Episcopalian. Home: 315 Clarke Ave Palm Beach FL 33480-6126

HALMSHAW, RONALD, retired physicist; b. Heckmondwike, Yorkshire, Eng., Nov. 29, 1919; s. Harry and Louisa May (Stansfield) H.; m. Margaret Gwenda Ackroyd. BSc, London U., 1940; PhD, City U., London, 1973. From exptl. asst. to exptl. officer Ministry of Supply (now Ministry of Def.), Nottingham, Eng., 1941-48; sci. officer, then sr. sci. officer Ministry of Supply (now Ministry of Def.), London, 1948-56, prin. sci. officer, 1956-72, sr. prin. sci. officer, 1973-80; cons. H.W. Consultancies, Swansea, Eng., 1982-94; ret., 1994; presenter in field. Co-author: Physics of Industrial Radiology, 1966; author 5 textbooks on indsl. radiology and non-destructive testing, 1966, 71, 82, 87, 95; contbr. articles to profl. jours. Named Mem. of Order of Brit. Empire, 1985; recipient McMaster Gold medal Am. Soc. Non-Destructive Testing, 1995. Fellow Brit. Inst. Non-Destructive Testing (hon., pres. 1970-72), Inst. Physics (chartered). Avocations: photography, alpine gardening, walking. Home: 49 Crouch Croft, N Eltham London SE9 3HX, England

HALONEN, TARJA, Finnish government official; b. Dec. 24, 1943. Lawyer Lainvalvonta Oy, 1967-68; social welfare officer, organizing sec. Nat. Union Finnish Students, 1969-70; lawyer Ctrl. Orgn. Finnish Trade Unions, 1970—; parliamentary sec. Prime Min. Sorsa, 1974-75; mem. parliament, 1979—; second min. Ministry of Social Affairs and Health, 1987-90, Ministry of Justice, 1990-91; second min. Ministry of Fgn. Affairs, 1995-99, min. of fgn. affairs, 1999-2000; Pres., 2000—. Office: Office of President, Mariankatu 2, FIN00170 Helsinki Finland*

HALPERIN, EDWARD CHARLES, physician; b. Somerville, N.J., Nov. 15, 1953; s. Irving M. and Ruth (Jacobs) H.; m. Sharon F. Rosenblatt, Sept. 6, 1981; children: Rebecca, Jennifer, Alison. BS, U. Pa., 1975; MD, Yale U., 1979. Diplomate Am. Bd. Radiology. Intern Stanford (Calif.) U. Hosp., 1979-80; resident Mass. Gen. Hosp., Boston, 1980-83; asst. prof. Duke U., Durham, N.C., 1983-85, assoc. prof., 1985-93, prof., 1993-96, L.R. Prosnitz prof. and dept. chmn., 1996—. Author: Pediatric Radiation Oncology, 1989, 3d edit., 1999, Russian edit., 1999. Recipient Career Devel. award Am. Cancer Soc., 1986; fellow Am. Coun. on Edn., 1992. Fellow Am. Coll. Radiology. Office: Duke Med Ctr PO Box 3085 Durham NC 27715-3085

HALPERIN, GEORGE BENNETT, education educator, retired naval officer; b. N.Y.C., Aug. 7, 1926; s. George and Muryal (Lesser) H.; m. Ellen Elizabeth Barber, Dec. 18, 1957 (div. 1988); children: Gail Susan, Thomas Allyn. BS, U.S. Naval Acad., 1950; MBA, Stanford U., 1958; postgrad., Naval War Coll., Newport, R.I., 1965-66; MA in History, U. Vt., 1976; MEd, Harvard U., 1979; postgrad., Oxford U., 1987-88, St. Catherine's Coll., 1987-88. Commd. ensign U.S. Navy, 1950, advanced through grades to comdr., 1965; dir. systems and standards div. Naval Supply Ctr., Oakland, Calif., 1963-65; freight terminal officer Naval Support Activity, Danang, Vietnam, 1966-67; supply officer Naval Air Sta., Barbers Point, Hawaii, 1967-70; ret., 1970; tchr. history Stowe (Vt.) High Sch., 1972-80, asst. prin., 1975-76; tchr. John F. Kennedy Sch., Berlin, 1980-86; Chmn. Lamoille South Dist. Profl. Growth Com., 1977-78. Decorated Navy Commendation medal. Mem. U.S. Naval Acad. Alumni Assn., Army-Navy Country Club, Oxford Soc., Harvard Club (Boston), Hanover Country Club. Home: 285 Woodhaven Dr Unit 7A White River Junction VT 05001-2832

HALPERN, DAVID RODION, special education administrator; b. Ann Arbor, Mich., Mar. 29, 1951; s. Werner Israel and Edith (Winograd) H.; m. Noreen Danzo, May 28, 1972; children: Aaron Benjamin, Joseph Morris. BS, SUNY, Buffalo, 1973; MS, Nazareth Coll., 1977; cert. advanced study, SUNY, Brockport, 1985. Tchr. emotionally disturbed Rochester (N.Y.) Mental Health Ctr., 1973-78, program coord., 1981-88; tchr. emotionally disturbed Rochester City Sch. Dist., 1978-81; prin. alternative high sch. Monroe 1 Bd. Coop. Ednl. Svcs., Fairport, N.Y., 1988-98, prin. alternative edn. dept., 1998—; cons. Monroe #2 Bd. Coop. Ednl. Svcs., Rochester; mem. alternative edn. steering com. N.Y. State Dept. Edn.; mem. Reclaiming Youth Work Group Monroe County Interagy. Coun.; adj. faculty Grad. Sch. Edn., Nazareth Coll., 1994—. Photographer: A Brand Plucked From the Fire, 1986. Mem. N.Y. State Educators of the Emotionally Dist., Jewish Fedn. Bd. Dirs., Bur. Jewish Edn. (pres. 1993-95), N.Y. State Alt. Edn. Assn. (pres.-elect 1999-2001). Avocations: fishing, photography, reading science fiction and fantasy. Office: Foreman Ctr 41 Oconnor Rd Fairport NY 14450-1327

HALPERN, JACK, chemist, educator; b. Poland, Jan. 19, 1925; came to U.S., 1962, naturalized; s. Philip and Anna (Sass) H.; m. Helen Peritz, June 30, 1949; children: Janice Henry, Nina Phyllis. BS, McGill U., 1946, PhD, 1949; DSc (hon.), U. B.C., 1986, McGill U., 1997. Postdoctorate overseas fellow NRC, U. Manchester, Eng., 1949-50; instr. chemistry U. B.C., 1950, prof., 1961-62; Nuffield Found. traveling fellow Cambridge (Eng.) U., 1959-60; prof. chemistry U. Chgo., 1962-71, Louis Block prof. chemistry, 1971-83, Louis Block Disting. Service prof., 1983—; vis. prof. U. Minn., 1962, Harvard, 1966-67, Calif. Inst. Tech., 1968-69, Princeton U., 1970-71, Max. Planck Institut, Mulheim, Fed. Republic Germany, 1983—, U. Copenhagen, 1978; Sherman Fairchild Disting. scholar Calif. Inst. Tech., 1979; guest scholar Kyoto U., 1981; Firth vis. prof. U. Sheffield, 1982, Phi Beta Kappa vis. scholar, 1990; R.B. Woodward vis. prof. Harvard U., 1991; numerous guest lectureships; cons. editor Macmillan Co., 1963-65, Oxford U. Press; cons. Am. Oil Co., Monsanto Co., Argonne Nat. Lab., IBM, Air Products Co., Enimont, Rohm and Haas; mem. adv. panel on chemistry NSF, 1967-70; mem. adv. bd. Am. Chem. Soc. Petroleum Research Fund, 1972-74; mem. medicinal chemistry sect. NIH, 1975-78, chmn., 1976-78; mem. chemistry adv. council Princeton U., 1982—; mem. univ. adv. com. Ency. Brit., 1985—; mem. chemistry vis. com. Calif. Inst. Tech., 1991—; chmn. German-Am. Acad. Coun., 1993-96, chmn. bd. trustees, 1996—. Assoc. editor: Inorganica Chimica Acta, Jour. Am. Chem. Soc.; co-editor: Collected Accounts of Transition Metal Chemistry, vol. 1, 1973, vol. 2, 1977, Procs. NAS, Oxford Univ. Press, Internat. Series Monographs on Chemistry; mem. editl. bd. Jour. Organometallic Chemistry, Accounts Chem. Rsch., Catalysis Revs., Jour. Catalysis, Jour. Molecular Catalysis, Jour. Coord. Chemistry, Gazzetta Chimica Italiana, Organometallics, Catalysis Letters, Kinetics and Catalysis Letters; contbr. articles to Ency. Britannica, rsch. jours. Trustee Gordon Rsch. Confs., 1968-70; bd. govs. David and Arthur Smart Mus., U. Chgo., 1988—; bd. dirs. Ct. Theatre, 1989—. Recipient Young Author's prize Electrochem. Soc., 1953, award in catalysis Noble Metals Chem. Soc., London, 1976, Humboldt award, 1977, Richard Kokes award Johns Hopkins U., 1978, Willard Gibbs medal, 1986, Bailar medal U. Ill., 1986, Wilhelm von Hoffman medal German Chem. Soc., 1988, Chem. Pioneer's award Am. Inst. Chemists, 1991, Paracelsus prize Swiss Chem. Soc., 1992, Basolo Medal, Northwestern U., 1993, Robert A. Welch award, 1994, Henry J. Albert award Internat. Precious Metals Inst., 1995, award in Organometallic Chem. Am. Chem. Soc., 1995, Order of Merit Federal Republic of Germany, 1996. Fellow AAAS, Royal Soc. London, Am. Acad. Arts and Scis., Chem. Inst. Can., Royal Soc. Chemistry London (hon.), N.Y. Acad. Scis., Japan Soc. for Promotion Sci.; mem. NAS (fgn. assoc. 1984-85, mem. coun. 1990—, chmn. chemistry sect. 1991-93, v.p. 1993—), Am. Chem. Soc. (editl. bd. Advances in Chemistry series 1963-65, 78-81, chmn. inorganic chemistry 1985, award in inorganic chemistry 1968, award for disting. svc. in advancement of inorganic chemistry 1985, award in organometallic chemistry 1995), Max Planck Soc. (sci. mem. 1983—), Art Inst. Chgo., Renaissance Soc. (bd. dirs. 1985—), New Swiss Chem. Soc. (Paracelsus prize 1992), Am. Friends of the Royal Soc. (bd. dirs.), Sigma Xi. Home: 5630 S Dorchester Ave Chicago IL 60637-1722 Office: U Chgo Dept Chemistry Chicago IL 60637

HALPERN, VIVIAN HAIM, physicist, educator; b. London, Mar. 18, 1939; arrived in Israel, 1966; d. Joseph and Eva (Joschpe) H.; m. Eva Gluck, Dec. 12, 1965; children: Tova Rivka, Devorah, Shlomo, Noa. BS, Cambridge U., 1960; PhD, Oxford U., 1965. Rsch. fellow Imperial Coll., London, 1964-66; sr. lectr. Bar-Ilan U., Ramat-Gan, Israel, 1966-74, assoc. prof., 1974-92, prof., 1992—. Co-author: Quantitative Analysis of Physical Problems, 1981. Mem. Israel Phys. Soc. (sec. 1980-82, treas. 1988-91, sec. 1996-99). Jewish. Avocation: Torah study. E-mail: halpern@phys-net.ph.biu.ac.il. Office: Bar-Ilan U, Ramat Gan 52-900, Israel

HALPERT, DOUGLAS JOSHUA, lawyer; b. Bklyn., Nov. 9, 1962; s. Eugene and Miriam (Feigenbaum) H.; m. Yee-Wen Chen, July 22, 1989. BA in English Lit., U. Chgo., 1984; JD, Fordham Law Sch., 1988. Bar: N.Y. 1989, Ohio 1994. Immigration atty. Cohen, Swados, Wright, Hanifin, Bradford & Brett, Buffalo, 1988-94, Frost & Jacobs, Cin., 1994—. Recipient Vol. Lawyer of Yr. award Cin. Bar Assn., 1998. Mem. Am. Immigration Lawyers Assn., Cin. Bar Assn., Alumni Schs. Com. of U. Chgo. Avocations: lit., writing, movies, sports. Office: Frost & Jacobs 2500 PNC Ctr 201 E 5th St Ste 2500 Cincinnati OH 45202-4182

HALPERT, RICHARD LEE, lawyer; b. Kalamazoo, Mich., Nov. 1, 1947; s. Samuel K. and Rosalie (Zuravel) H.; m. Mary K. Sydlaske, June 24, 1973; children: David, Michael. BA, Kalamazoo Coll., 1969; JD cum laude, Ind. U., 1972. Bar: Mich. 1973, U.S. Dist. Ct. (we. dist.) Mich. 1980, U.S. Supreme Ct. 1985. Trial atty. Van Buren County Pros. Attys. Office, Paw Paw, Mich., 1972-74, Kreis, Enderle, Halpert, Borsos & Ford, Kalamazoo, 1974-82, Halpert & Koning, Kalamazoo, 1982-87, Howard & Howard, Kalamazoo, 1987-95, Halpert, Weston, Wuori & Sawusch, P.C., Kalamazoo, 1996—; lectr. in field. Co-author over 30 manuals for Inst. Continuing Legal Edn.; note editor Ind. Law Jour., 1971-72. Bd. dirs. YMCA, Kalamazoo, 1989-94, bd. trustees, 1998—, Kalamazoo County Humane Soc.; trustee Ctrl. Mich. U., Mt. Pleasant, 1981-83. Mem. ATLA, Mich. Trial Lawyers Assn., Am. Burn Assn. (spl. mem. 1983—, rehab. com. 1997—), Internat. Soc. for Burn Injuries (spl. mem. 1986—), State Bar Mich. (negligence sect., com. on profl. and jud. ethics 1980-82), Kalamazoo Bar Assn. (chmn. com. on profl. responsibility 1981-83), Phoenix Soc. for Burn Injuries (trustee, 1st v.p.), Am. Arbitration Assn. Avocations: bicycling, nature photography, hiking. Office: Halpert Weston Wuori and Sawusch PC 136 E Michigan Ave Ste 1050 Kalamazoo MI 49007-3917

HALPIN, TIMOTHY PATRICK, former air force officer; b. Worcester, Mass., Mar. 13, 1960; s. Daniel Joseph Halpin and Angelina (Ferranti) Wilkes; m. Rachel Esther Hanneman, Aug. 3, 1991; children: Alyssa Kristin, Patrick Stephan, Joseph Marvin, Nathan Erick. BBA in Mgmt., U. Mass., 1982; MBA, Embry-Riddle Aero. U., 1994; JD, Regent U., 1998. Bar: Va. 1998. Commd. 2d lt. USAF, 1982, advanced through grades to capt., 1986; instr. electronic warfare USAF, various locations, 1984-89, 93d Bomb Wing, Castle AFB, Calif., 1989-95; resigned, 1995; atty. Lambert & Lambert, 1997-2000, David J. Crandall, Martinsville, Va., 2000—. Decorated DFC, Air medal (3). Mem. VFW. Republican. Avocations: cross country and downhill skiing, ice hockey, politics, theology. Home: 215 Rives Rd Martinsville VA 24112-3828 Office: David J Crandall 110 Starling Ave Martinsville VA 24112-3806

HALSEY, JAMES ALBERT, international entertainment impresario, theatrical producer, talent manager; b. Independence, Kans., Oct. 7, 1930; s. Harry Edward and Carrie Lee (Messick) H.; m. Minisa Crumbo; children: Sherman Brooks, Gina, Cris, Woody. Student, Independence Community Coll., 1948-50, U. Kans.; doctorate of Fine Arts honoris causa, Baker Univ., 1992. Pres. Thunderbird Artists, Inc., Independence, from 1950, Jim Halsey Co., Inc., Tulsa, from 1952, Norwood Advt. Agy., James Halsey Property Mgmt. Co., Tulsa Proud Country Entertainment, Stas. KTOW/KGOW, J.H. Radio Mgmt., Cyclone Records, Tulsa Records, J.H. Lighting and Sound Co., Singin' T Prodns.; v.p. Gen. Artists Corp., Beverly Hills, Calif., 1966; chmn., chief exec. officer Century City Artists Corp., Tulsa, Nashville; personal mgr. various entertainment personalities; pres. Internat. Fedn. Festival Orgns.; mgr. Oakridge Boys, 1975; internat. jurist Golden Orpheus Festival, Bulgaria, 1981-82, 84, 88, 94; ptnr. Billboard Song Contest; cons. William Morris Agy., 1990-95; producer shows for auditoriums, fairs, rodeos, TV, internat. music fests also others in U.S. and internationally including Tulsa Internat. Music Festival, 1977-80, Neewollah Internat. Music Festival, 1981-83; gen. ptnr. Parker Ranch, Tulsa; bd. dirs. Merc. Bank and Trust, Tulsa, Citizens Nat. Bank, Independence, Farmers & Mchts. Bank, Mound City, Kans., Nashville Symphony; chmn. mus. bus. dept. Okla. City U., 1994—; lectr., speaker colls., univs., 1992—. Trustee Philbrook Art Ctr., Tulsa; bd. dirs. Thomas Gilcrease Mus. Assn., Tulsa Philharm. Assn., Roy Clark Celebrity Golf Classic, UNICEF, Nashville Symphony, Nat. Music Coun. Served with U.S. Army, 1954-56. Recipient Disting. Service award U.S. Jr. C. of C., 1959, Ambassador of Country Music award SESAC Corp., 1978, citation Cashbox Mag., 1980, citation Golden Orpheus Festival, 1982, Hubert Long award Wembley Festival, Eng., 1982, commendation Los Angeles Mayor Tom Bradley, Gov.'s medal Kans. Commn., 1986, Frederic Chopin medal Polish Artist Bur., 1987, Lifetime Achievement award Internat. Buyers Assn., 1997, Okla. Govs. award for excellence art and edn., 1998, Cherokee medal of honor Cherokee Hist. Soc., 1999; named Disting. Kansan Topeka Capital Jour.; inductee Okla. Music Hall of Fame, 2000. Mem. Country Music Assn. (bd. dirs. 1963-64, 70-71, v.p. 1979-80, Founding Pres.'s award 1985), Acad. Country Music (bd. dirs. 1969-70, 73-74, v.p. 1975-76, 78-79, 79-80, 88-89, Jim Reeves Meml. award 1977), Internat. Fedn. Festival Orgns. (Am. pres., Oscar Midem award 1982). Home: 720 N 136 Rd Mounds OK 74047-5275

HALSTED, DAVID CRANE, diplomat; b. Plainfield, N.J., Sept. 7, 1941; s. Osborne and Katharine (Patterson) C.; m. Michele Vautrain, Mar. 8, 1996; children: Edward, Sarah, David Jr., Charles. BA, Dartmouth Coll., 1963; MA, George Washington U., 1968. Dep. chief of mission U.S. Embassy, Kampala, Uganda, 1979-81; dep. dir. Vietnam, Laos, Cambodia desk State Dept., 1982-84; polit./econ. counselor U.S. Embassy, Rangoon, Burma, 1984-86; dep. dir. West African Affairs State Dept., Washington, 1986-89, dir. African Regional Affairs, 1989-91; U.S. Consul Gen. U.S. Consulate Gen., Capetown, South Africa, 1991-93; U.S. ambassador to Chad, 1996-99; team leader Vienna Office of the Inspector Gen., Rosland, Va., 1999—. Lt. (j.g.) USNR, 1963-67. Office: Office of Inspector General 1700 N Moore St Arlington VA 22209-2793

HALSTENSEN, TROND SUNDBY, immunology educator; b. Oslo, Sept. 29, 1955; s. Andreas and Rigmor (Sundby) H.; m. Kjersti Skjold Rønningen, June 30, 1984 (div. 1999); children: Victoria, Christian Fredrik, Carl Henrik. MD, U. Oslo, 1984, PhD, 1991. Intern Kristiandsund, 1984-85, Sunndalsøra, 1985-86; rsch. fellow U. Oslo, 1987-91, sr. rschr., 1991-93, sr. med. officer, 1993-98, prof., 1998—; cons. Red Cross Geriatric Home, Oslo, 1986-87. Contbr. articles to profl. jours. Recipient Anders Jahres Biomedical Rsch. prize, 1994; grantee 6th Internat. Congress Mucosal Immunology. Fellow Norwegian Soc. Immunology (bd. dirs. 1987-92, cashier 1987-92). E-mail: thalsten@odont.uio.no. Home: Trosterud vn 42, 0386 Oslo Norway Office: Inst Oral Biology U Oslo, PB 1052 Blindern, 0316 Oslo Norway

HALT, JAMES GEORGE, advertising executive, graphic designer; b. Buffalo, Feb. 16, 1937; s. Clemens George Halt and Marion Helen Smith; m. July 6, 1963; children: Shannon, Kevin, Sean, Christopher. BFA, U. Buffalo, 1961. Artist, designer Thomas Lowes Assocs., Buffalo, 1961-63, art dir., 1963-69, creative dir., 1969-77; pres., owner James Halt Graphic Design, Buffalo, 1977—; cons. Hammermill Paper Co., Erie, Pa. and Memphis, 1978—. Co-author, designer: Graphic Design USA, 1986, 89-90; designer: Trademarks USA, 1968, The Book of American Trademarks, vol. I, 1972, vol. II, 1973, Novum Gebruchsgraphik, 1980. Mem. Albright Knox Art Gallery, 1987—, Buffalo Mus. Sci., 1988—, Buffalo/Erie County Hist. Soc., 1993—, Zool. Soc. Buffalo, 1988—. Recipient Freedom Found. medal, Freedom Found. at Valley Forge, 1966, Creativity Certificate of Distinction, Art Direction Magazine Book/Show, N.Y.C., 1971, 73-79, 82-83. Mem. Art Dirs. Communicators of Buffalo (recipient over 75 awards 1961—). Democrat. Roman Catholic. Avocations: golf, woodworking, gardening. Home: 351 Springville Ave Amherst NY 14226-2857 Office: James Halt Graphic Design 166 Niagara Falls Blvd Buffalo NY 14223-3025

HALTER, H(ENRY) JAMES, JR. (DIAMOND JIM HALTER), retail executive; b. Fernandina, Fla., Feb. 28, 1947; s. Henry James and Grace (Bealey) H.; m. Wanda O'Quinn, Mar. 15, 1970; children: Jennifer, John Elizabeth, Amelia. BS in Mgmt., Valdosta State Coll., 1970. Sales mgr. Southwestern Co., Nashville, 1969; collection mgr. Fla. Title & Mortgage Co., Jacksonville, 1970-72; appraiser Richard Hamilton & Assocs., Jacksonville Beach, 1972-74; exec. v.p. Developers Investors Svc. Corp., Jacksonville, 1975-78; pres. A-Coin and Stamp Gallery, Inc., Jacksonville, 1978-81; ptnr. Jacksonville Precious Metals, 1981, Sidetrack Video Arcade Chain, Ga., 1982-84; pres. Diamond House Corp., Valdosta, Ga., 1985—, J-Mart Jewelry Outlets, Inc., Tifton, Ga., 1988-91; chmn. bd. J-Mart Jewelry Outlets, Inc., 1990-91; pres. K&H Ltd., Valdosta, 1992-94; exec. dir. Soc. for Legalization of Drugs, Valdosta, 1994-97; bus. cons., 1996—. Author: May I Help You, 1988, LIZ, Inc., 1998; voice of Ernie Beaver for nationally syndicated TV cartoon spl. Coots and Critter, 1996. Bd. dirs. Park Ave. United Meth. Ch., Valdosta, 1986-88, Alapaha coun. Boy Scouts Am., 1982—; mem. Alumni Bd. Valdosta State U.; youth spkr. Atlanta Com. for the Olympic Games, selected local hero torch bearer Olympic Games, Atlanta, 1996; co-author Olympic Awareness Award for 1996 Olympic Games, 1994-95; mem. Ga. Small Bus. Task Force. Recipient Addy award, 1980, 83, God and Svc. nat. award Meth. Ch. and BSA, Cmty. Hero Torch Bearer, Coca Cola Olympic Torch Relay, 1996; named Adm. in Ga. Navy, 1983, Outstanding Ga. Citizen, 1990. Mem. Nat. Speakers Assn., Toastmasters, Sertoma, Vigil Honor, Order of the Arrow, Rotary, Sigma Iota (pres. charter), Alpha Phi Omega. Avocations: motivational speaking, antique paper money, wiregrass Ga. history, civic speaker on Ga. history. Home and Office: 208 Breckenridge Dr Valdosta GA 31605-6402

HALTOM, CRISTEN EDDY, psychologist; b. Albion, N.Y., Oct. 22, 1948; d. Arthur Benedict and Susan (Cooper) Eddy; m. Maurice Haltom Jr., Apr. 5, 1980; children: Jhakeem, Ajemo, Rebecca. BA, Albion Coll., 1970; MS, Cornell U., 1974, PhD, 1978. Lic. psychologist, N.Y. Instr. Eisenhower Coll., Seneca Falls, N.Y., 1976, Elmira (N.Y.) Coll., 1976-77, Cornell U., Ithaca, N.Y., 1977-78; clin. psychology intern Benjamin Rush Ctr. Mental Health and Mental Retardation, Phila., 1978-79; assoc. psychologist Elmira Psychiat. Ctr., 1979-84; pvt. practice Ithaca, 1984—; lectr. and presenter in field. Co-editor: Women and Problem Drinking, 1980; author: (newsletter) Survival Guide for Parents, 2000—; contbr. articles to profl. jours. Panelist Cable Channel 7 TV, Ithaca, 1988, arts & scis. career ctr. Cornell U., 1994, 97; foster care parent tng. Tompkins Co. Dept. Social Svcs., 1997-99; presenter in field. Mem. APA, Ctrl. N.Y. Psychol. Assn., N.Y. State Psychol. Assn., World Fedn. Mental Health, Christian Assn. Psychologists. Avocations: drawing, tennis, dance, windsurfing. Office: 215 N Geneva St Ithaca NY 14850-4135

HALVERSON, STEVEN THOMAS, lawyer, construction executive; b. Enid, Okla., Aug. 29, 1954; s. Robert James Halverson and Ramona Mae (Ludke) Selenski; m. Diane Mary Schueller, Aug. 21, 1976; children: John Thomas, Anne Kirsten. BA cum laude, St. John's U., 1976; JD, Am. U., 1979. Bar: Va. 1979. Asst. project dir. ABA, Washington, 1977-79; with Briggs & Morgan, St Paul., 1980-83; sr. v.p. M.A. Mortenson Cos., Denver, 1984-99; pres., CEO Haskell Co., Jacksonville, Fla., 1999—; bd. dirs. Ctr. for New West, Lowell Whiteman Sch., Design Build Inst. Am. Co-author: Federal Grant Law, 1982, The Future of Construction, 1997; contbr. articles to profl. jours. Bd. dirs. Jacksonville Symphony. Republican. Roman Catholic. Home: 825 Mapleton Ter Jacksonville FL 32207-5204 Office: Haskell Co Haskell Bldg 111 Riverside Ave Fl 1 Jacksonville FL 32202-4950

HALVORSEN, FRED-ARNE, internist, gastroenterologist, consultant; b. Stokmarknes, Norway, Apr. 4, 1950; s. Edmund and Bergljot (Toften) H.; m. Gudlaug Seim, Aug. 6, 1977; children: Vemund, Linn Kristin. MD, U. Oslo, 1975. Specialist in internal medicine, 1985; specialist in gastroenterology, 1989. Registrar in internal medicine Ringerike (Norway) Hosp., 1978-82, Ullevaal (Norway) Hosp., 1982-83; registrar in internal medicine Buskerud Ctrl. Hosp., Drammen, Norway, 1983-87, The Nat. Hosp., Norway, 1987-88; cons. internal medicine Buskerud Ctrl. Hosp., 1988—, head, sect. gastroenterology, 1996—. Contbr. articles to profl. jours.; oral presenter in field. Home: Hoevik Terrasse 40, N-3400 Lier Norway Office: Buskerud Ctrl Hosp, Dronninggt 28, N-3004 Drammen Norway

HALWIG, J. MICHAEL, allergist; b. Denver, Apr. 15, 1954; s. John Philip and Hilda (Fuggis) H.; m. Nancy Diane Graupman, June 14, 1975; children: Courtney Elizabeth, J. Christopher. BA, Johns Hopkins U., 1975; MD, Northwestern U., Chgo., 1980. Diplomate Am. Bd. Allergy and Immunology, Am. Bd. Internal Medicine. Intern in internal medicine Northwestern U. Meml. Hosps., Chgo., 1980-81, resident in internal medicine, 1981-83; allergy fellowship Northwestern U. Med. Sch., Chgo., 1983-85; practice medicine specilizing in allergy, asthma, immunology Atlanta, 1985—; instr. Northwestern U. Med. Sch., Chgo., 1984-85, admissions amb., 1989—; clin. asst. prof. Emory U. Sch. Medicine, 1989—. bd. dirs. Am. Lung Assn. Ga., 1996—. Fellow Am. Coll. Allergy, Asthma and Immunology (allergy practice and practice guidelines com. 1992—), Am. Acad. Allergy, Asthma and Immunology (Managed Care Key Contact Network 1996—); mem. AMA, Asthma and Allergy Found. of Am. (nat. chpt. bd. dirs., chpt. rels. and devel. com. 1997—, mktg. and fundraising com. 1997—, Ga. chpt. founding mem., bd. dirs., med. dir. 1995—, chmn. med. adv. com. 1995—), Joint Coun. on Allergy and Immunology, Med. Assn. Ga. (rep. Coun. on Legislation 1989-95), Allergy, Asthma and Immunology Soc. Ga. (pres. 1993-95, v.p. 1991-93, program chmn. 1991-93, co-chmn. third party payors com. 1992—, rep. benign medicare carrier adv. com. 1993—, Gengia medicare carrier adv. com.), So. Med. Assn., Cobb County Med. Assn., Cobb Area Pediat. Soc., Wellstar Health Care Sys. (pediat. asthma task force 1996—, asthma/COPD task force 1998—), Ga. Partnership for Caring. Presbyterian. Avocations: running, listening to jazz, golf. Office: 1700 Hospital South Dr Ste 404 Austell GA 30106-8116

HAM, KAREN, musician, music educator; b. Bklyn., Apr. 13, 1952; d. Irving and Eva (Walker) H. AA, Staten Island Coll., 1974; BA, CUNY, 1978; MA, NYU, 1983; student in piano, French Conservatory Music, N.Y.C., 19905. Tchr. Assn. Black Social Workers, Bklyn., 1978-85, Bklyn. Music Sch., 1985-87; tchr., condr. Holy Innocents Sch., Bklyn., 1985—; dir. choir and music ensemble, keyboard classes. Roman Catholic. Avocations: research of American songwriters, American musical films. Office: Holy Innocents Sch 249 E 17th St Brooklyn NY 11226-4601

HAMA, AMADOU, prime minister. Prime min. Embassy of Republic of Niger, Washington. Office: Embassy of Republic of Niger 2204 R St NW Washington DC 20008-4035

HAMACHER, HORST W., mathematics educator; b. Buir, Germany, Apr. 21, 1951; s. Aloys G. and Helene G. (Hanussek) H.; m. Renate Clara Kremer, Aug. 28, 1972; children: Elke, Jens, Anna, Monika. Diploma, U. Cologne, 1977, PhD, 1980. Asst. prof. U. Cologne, 1977-81; assoc. prof. U. Fla., Gainesville, 1981-88; prof. U. Kaiserslautern, Germany, 1988—, v.p., 1994-97; dir. Ctr. for Optimization and Combinatorics, Gainesville, 1985-92; co-dir. Zentrum für Techno-und Wirtschaftsmathematik, Kaiserslautern, 1992-95, dept. head, bd. dirs., 1997—. Contbr. articles to profl. jours., chpts. to books. Mem. Inst. Ops. Rsch. and Mgmt. Sci., Math. Programming Soc., Assn. Advancement of Waldorf Pedagogic (treas. 1982-85, 91-99, trustee Gainesville chpt. 1982-85, Kaiserslautern chpt. 1991-99). Avocations: woodworking, music, reading. Home: Haselaecker 3, D-67661 Kaiserslautern Germany Office: Univ Kaiserslautern, Postfach 3049, D-67653 Kaiserslautern Germany

HAMADA, HIROSHI, electronics executive; b. Apr. 28, 1933. Student, Tokyo U., 1957. Pres. Ricoh Co. Ltd., Tokyo, 1983, chmn. bd. Avocations: tennis, go. Office: Ricoh Co Ltd, 15-5 Minami-Aoyama 1-chome, Minato-ku Tokyo 107-8544, Japan*

HAMADA, JIRO, psychologist, educator; b. Fukui, Japan, Aug. 27, 1947; s. Kazuo and Jitsuko (Hara) H.; m. Kayoko Hase, Feb. 21, 1981; children: Mariko, Eriko. BEd, Tokushima U., Japan, 1971; MEd, Osaka U. Edn., Japan, 1973; PhD, Hokkaido U., Sapporo, Japan, 1980. Instr. Hokkaido U., 1976-82; asst. prof. Tokushima U., 1982-83, assoc. prof., 1983-90, prof., 1990—. Contbr. articles to profl. jours. Mem. Japanese Psychol. Assn., Japanese Psychonomic Soc., Japanese Ergonomics Assn. (Japanese br. trustee 1995—). E-mail: hamada@ias.tokushima-u.ac.jp. Home: Babayama 47-9 Hachiman-cho, Tokushima 770-8070, Japan Office: Tokushima U Faculty, Minami-Josanjima, Tokushima 770-8502, Japan

HAMADJODA, ADJOUDJI, government official; b. Banyo, Adamaoua, Cameroon, 1937. Student, French Nat. Vet. Sch., Alfort, 1963-67; PhD in Vet. Sci., 1968; cert. in vet. medicine for tropical coun, Nat. Vet. Sch., Alfort, 1969. Adj. Ngaoundere Animal Husbandry Ctr., 1969-74; gen. dir. Corp. for Devel. and Exploitation of Animal Prodn., Cameroon, 1974-84; minister livestock, fisheries and animal industries Govt. Cameroon, Yaoundé, 1984—; min. livestock, fisheries and animal industries Govt. of Cameroon, 1999—. Mem. ctrl. com., asst. nat. treasurer Cameroon People's Dem. Movement.

Mem. Democratic People's Assembly of Cameroon. Office: Ministry Livestork, Fisheries & Animal Industry, Yaoundé Cameroon

HAMAI, JAMES YUTAKA, business executive; b. L.A., Oct. 14, 1926; s. Seizo and May (Sata) H.; B.S., U. So. Calif., 1952, M.S., 1955; postgrad. bus. mgmt. program industry exec., UCLA, 1963-64; m. Dorothy K. Fukuda, Sept. 10, 1954; 1 child, Wendy A. Lectr. chem. engring. dept. U. So. Calif., Los Angeles, 1963-64; process engr., sr. process engr. Fluor Corp., Los Angeles, 1954-64; sr. project mgr. central research dept. Monsanto Co., St. Louis, 1964-67, mgr. research, devel. and engring. graphic systems dept., 1967-68, mgr. comml. devel. New Enterprise div., 1968-69; exec. v.p., dir. Concrete Cutting Industries, Inc., Los Angeles, 1969-72; pres., dir. Concrete Cutting Internat., Inc., Los Angeles, 1972-78, chmn. bd., 1978—; cons. Fluor Corp., Los Angeles, 1970-72; dir. Intech Systems Co., Ltd., Tokyo, Cutting Industries Co., Ltd., Tokyo, Unity Five Industries, Ltd., Tokyo; internat. bus. cons. Served with AUS, 1946-48. Mem. Am. Inst. Chem. Engrs., Am. Mgmt. Assn., Tau Beta Pi, Phi Lambda Upsilon. Club: Rotary (gov. dist. 1982-83). Home: 6600 Via La Paloma Rancho Palos Verdes CA 90275-6449 Office: PO Box 700 Wilmington CA 90748-0700

HAMAJIMA, BIN, English and Japanese educator; b. Anjo, Aichi, Japan, Mar. 24, 1937; s. Kurazo and Chiyo (Inagaki) H.; BA, Meiji Gakuin U., 1960, MA, 1967, EdD (hon.), Internat. U. Found., 1988 ; m. Chieko Miyazaki, Nov. 3, 1966; children: Shinri, Nozomu, Kaori. Dir. edn. East West Cultural Inst., Chiba, 1961-68; head English dept. Shikoku Gakuin U., Kagawa, 1976-77; head English lit. dept. Shikoku Gakuin U., 1977-83, dir. univ. libr., 1986-90. Fellow Internat. Biog. Assn.; mem. Shikoku English Lang. Edn. Soc. (dir. 1975—), Japan Assn. Coll. English Tchrs., English Linguistic Soc. Japan, Phonetic Soc. Japan, Soc. for Teaching Japanese as Fgn. Lang., Japan Univ. Libr. Assn. (bd. of div. 1988-90) Internat. Rels. Com. (chmn. 1988-94), Japan-Brit. Soc. Kagawa (coun. 1992—), Japan Asian Friendship Assn., The Gideons Internat., Kagawa-Nishi Camp (capt.), Ch. Music Assn. (adv. com. 1986—). Author introduction to Variorum edit. English Bible, 1974, Bishops' Bible 1568 (facsimile edit.), 1998, History of English Bible Translations. Home: 1316-1 Harada, Zentsuji, Kagawa 765-0032, Japan Office: Shikoku Gakuin U, 2-1 3-chome Bunkyo Zentsuji, Kagawa 765-8505, Japan

HAMAKUBO, TAKAO, medical researcher; b. Muroto, Kochi, Japan, Dec. 14, 1952; s. Shozo and Wakako (Hirosue) H.; m. Mamiko Fujihara, Nov. 22, 1987; children: Takuya William, Rieko Alice, Shunji David. BS, U. Tokyo, 1975; MD, Kyoto U., 1982, D in Med. Sci., 1987. Asst. prof. Kyoto U., 1987-91, 95-96; rsch. assoc. Vanderbilt U., Nashville, 1988-93, rsch. instr., 1993-95; asst. prof. U. Tokyo, 1996-97, lectr., 1997-99, assoc. prof., 1999—. Co-author: Neuropeptides and Their Peptidases, 1987; contbr. articles to profl. jours. including Jour. of Neurosci., Am. Jour. Physiology. Recipient Erwin von Bälz prize Böehringer Ingerheim Co., Ltd., 1998. Mem. Soc. for Neurosci., Japanese Biochem. Soc. Home: 3-6-27 Iwatominami, Komae Tokyo 201 0005, Japan Office: U Tokyo RCAST, 4-6-1 Komaba Meguro, Tokyo 153 8904, Japan

HÄMÄLÄINEN, MIRJA LIISA, pediatric neurologist, researcher; b. Helsinki, Finland, July 26, 1958; d. Veikko and Kielo Tuulikki (Kietäväinen) H. MD, U. Kuopio, Finland, 1984; specialist in pediat. neurology, U. Helsinki, 1992, PhD, 1997, specialist in clin. pharmacology, 1997. Gen. practice resident various depts., various instns., Finland, 1984-87; resident in pediat. neurology U. Helsinki, 1988-92; cons. pediat. Helsinki City Maternity Hosp., 1992; cons. pediat. neurology Aurora Hosp., Helsinki, 1992; rsch. fellow U. Helsinki, 1993-96; rsch. fellow clin. pharmacology, U. Helsinki, 1993-96; specialist in pediatric neurology U. Helsinki Hosp. Children and Adolescents, 1996—. Contbr. articles to med. jours.; author: Kodin Suuri Lääkärikirja, 1995. Recipient rsch. grants Orion Corp. Rsch. Found., Found. for Non-Hosp. Care, Arvo and Lea Yippo Found., Finnish Acad., 1993-96, award for best acad. dissertation in clin. pharmacology in Finland, 1997. Mem. Finnish Assn. Pediat. Neurology (comptroller 1995—), Finnish Christian Med. Soc. (treas. 1991-93), Scandinavian Assn. for the Study of Pain, Internat. Headache Soc., Internat. Assn. Study of Pain, Am. Headache Soc. Avocations: kayaking, literature, music. Office: U Helsinki Hosp Children and Adolescents, Lastenlinnantie 2, 00250 Helsinki Finland

HAMALAINEN, SIRKKA, banker; b. Riihimäki, Finland, May 8, 1939; married; 2 children. BS in Econs., 1961, MA in Econs., 1964, licentiate of sci. econs., 1979; PhD in Econs., Helsinki Sch. Econs. and Bus. Adminstrn., 1981. Economist Bank of Finland, Helsinki, 1961-72, head of office, 1972-79, acting head, 1979-81; dir. Bank of Finland, 1982-91, gov., chmn., 1992-98; dir. econs. dept. Finnish Ministry Fin., 1981-82; mem. exec. bd. European Ctrl. Bank, 1998—. Office: ECB, Postfach 16 03 19, D-60066 Frankfurt am Main Germany*

HAMANN, DERYL FREDERICK, lawyer, bank executive; b. Lehigh, Iowa, Dec. 8, 1932; s. Frederick Carl Hamann and Ada Ellen (Hollingsworth) Hamann Geis; m. Carrie Svea Rosen, Aug. 23, 1954 (dec. 1985); children: Karl E., Daniel A., Esther Hamann Brabec, Julie Hamann Bunderson; m. Eleanor Ramona Nelson Curtis, June 20, 1987. AA, Ft. Dodge Jr. Coll., Iowa, 1953; BS in Law, U. Nebr., 1956, JD cum laude, 1958. Bar: Nebr. 1958, U.S. Dist. Ct. Nebr. 1958, U.S. Ct. Appeals (8th cir.) 1958. Law clk. U.S. Dist. Ct. for Nebr., Lincoln, 1958-59; ptnr. Baird, Holm, McEachen, Pedersen, Hamann & Strasheim, Omaha, 1959—; chmn. adv. com. Supreme Ct. Nebr., Omaha, 1986-95; chmn. bd. or chmn. exec. com. Midwestern Cmty. Banks. Past pres. Omaha Estate Planning Coun. Mem. Nebr. Bar Found. (pres. 1981-86), Nebr. Assn. Bank Attys. (pres. 1985-86). Republican. Lutheran. Avocations: boating, reading. Office: Baird Holm McEachen Pedersen Hamann & Strasheim 1500 Woodmen Tower Omaha NE 68102

HAMAOKA, TAKAFUMI, preventive medicine educator; b. Mikame-cho, Ehime, Japan, Dec. 24, 1962; s. Yoshitsugu and Mutsuko (Hamada) H.; m. Shitomi Murahashi, May 13, 1989; children: Taisei, Rina. MD, Ehime U., Matsuyama, Japan, 1989; PhD, Tokyo Med. U., 1993. Rsch. assoc. dept. biochemistry and biophysics U. Pa., Phila., 1990-91; chief instrn. dept. Tokyo Met. Health Promotion Ctr., 1993-94; rschr. Collaborating Ctr. Health Promotion Sports Medicine WHO, Tokyo, 1993—; asst. prof. preventive medicine and pub. health Tokyo Med. U., 1994—; lectr. Japan Sports Club Assn., Tokyo, 1994—, Tokyo Gakugei U., 1996; vice-chmn. Japan Triathlon Med. Com., Tokyo, 1997—; mem. editl. bd. environ. health perspectives NIH, N.C., 1997—. Author: Integration of Medical and Sports Sciences, 1992; contbr. articles to profl. jours. Com. mem. Inis. Info. Ctr., Tokyo, 1997—. Recipient Young Investigators award 1st Congress of European Coll. of Sports Sci., Niece, France, 1996, Rsch. award Tokyo Met. Govt., 1991, Grant-in-Aid award The Ministry of Edn. Sci. and Sports and Culture, 1997. Fellow Japanese Soc. Phys. Fitness and Sports Medicine, Am. Coll. Sports Medicine; mem. Internat. Soc. Non-invasive Optical Diagnosis (sci. com. 1996—), Soc. Biomed. Near Infrared Spectroscopy (sec. 1994—), N.Y. Acad. Sci. Home: 3-1-2 Minami Kasai, Edogawa-ku, Tokyo 134-0085, Japan Office: Dept Preventive Medicine, Med Univ 6-1-1 Shinjuku, Tokyo 160-8402, Japan

HAMAR, PÉTER, physiologist, researcher; b. Budapest, Hungary, May 1, 1969; s. János and Judit (Sármezei) H.; m. Boglárka Enikő Bay-Fodor, Dec. 18, 1993. MD, Semmelweis U., Budapest, 1994, PhD, 1999. Nurse Nat. Ambulance Svc., Budapest, 1989; univ. fellow Semmelweis U., Budapest, 1994—; postdoctoral fellow U. Clinic Essen, Germany, 1995-96; lectr., 1994—. Contbr. articles to profl. jours. Scholar German Acad. Exch. Svcs., 1995-96; Rschr. Exch. grantee OMFB, 1996-99; Rsch. grantee Nat. Rsch. Fund, 1997-99. Mem. European Soc. Organ Tranplantation, (Best Posters 1997), Hungarian Nephrological Soc., Hungarian Physiol. Soc. Avocations: sailing, skiing. Home: Szalmás Piroska u. 2/B, H-1068 Budapest Hungary Office: Semmelweis U Med Sch, Nagyvárad Tér 4, H-1089 Budapest Hungary

HAMARNEH, SAMI KHALAF, historian of pharmacy, medicine and science, author; b. Madaba, Jordan, Feb. 2, 1925; came to U.S., 1952, naturalized, 1957; s. Khalaf and Nura A. (Zumut) H.; m. Nazha T. Ajaj, July 4, 1948; 1 son, Faris. BSc in Pharmacy, Syrian U., Damascus, 1948; MSc in Pharm. Chemistry, N.D. State U., Fargo, 1956; PhD in History of Pharmacy and Medicine, U. Wis., 1959; DLitt (hon.), Hamdard U., Karachi, Pakistan, 1998. Curator charge divsn. med. scis. Mus. History and Tech., U.S. Nat. Mus., Smithsonian Instn., Washington, 1959-72; historian dept. sci. and tech. Nat. Mus. Am. History U.S. Nat. Mus., Smithsonian Instn., 1972-77; curator emeritus Mus. History and Tech., U.S. Nat. Mus., Smithsonian Instn., 1977—; prof. history Islamic med. scis. King Fahd Med. Rsch. Ctr./Abdulaziz U., Jeddah, Saudi Arabia, 1982-83; med. historian faculty medicine Allied Sci. Sch. Pub. Health/Yarmouk U., Irbid, Jordan, 1984-86; prof. U. Jordan, Amman, 1987-90; prof. Islamic medicine Internat. Inst. Islamic Thought and Civilization, Kuala Lumpur, Malaysia, 1993-99; ret., 1999; vis. assoc. prof. George Washington U., 1963-64; vis. prof. history of sci. U. Pa., Phila., 1969; vis. prof. U. Aleppo, Syria, 1977-79; spl. research med. scis., profl. ethics and edn. in medieval Islam. Author: Bibliography of Medicine and Pharmacy in Medieval Islam, 1964, Index of Arabic Manuscripts on Medicine and Pharmacy at the National Library of Cairo, 1967, Index of Manuscripts on Medicine and Pharmacy in the Zahiriyah Library, 1969, Temples of the Muses and a History of Pharmacy Museums, 1972, Origins of Pharmacy and Therapy in the Near East, 1973, The Physician, Therapist and Surgeon Ibn al-Quff, 1974, Catalogue of Arabic Manuscripts on Medicine and Pharmacy at Brit. Library, 1975, Directory of Historians of Arabic-Islamic Science, 1980, Pharmacy Museums USA, 1981, Health Scis. in Early Islam, Collected Papers, 2 vols., 1983-85, Background of History of Arabic Medicine and Allied Sciences, 1986, Promises, Heritage and Peace, 1986, Introduction on Al-Biruni's Book on Precious Stones, 1988, Ibn al-Quff al-Karaki's Book on the Preservation of Health, 1989, Ibn al-Quff al-Karaki's on Surgery, 1994, Directory of Historians of Islamic Medicine and the Allied Sciences, 1995, Yunani Greek Arabic-Islamic Medicine and Pharmacy During the Golden Age, 1997; editor: Jour. History Arabic Sci, 1976-80; mem. adv. bd. Hamdard Medicus, 1980—; contbr. articles to profl. jours. Recipient Star of Jordan medal, 1965; E. Kremers award for distinguished pharmaco-hist. writings, 1966, Citation of Merit, U. Wis., 1997. Mem. Inst. History Arabic Sci. (founding mem. 1976), Am. Inst. History Pharmacy (pres. 1979-81), Arab Soc. for History Pharmacy (Cairo) (founding mem. 1976), Arab Acad. of Damascus (corr. mem.), Royal Acad. for Islamic Civilization Inst. (corr. mem. 1983—). Home: 4631 Massachusetts Ave NW Washington DC 20016-2361 Office: Smithsonian Instn Nmah Rm 5003 Washington DC 20560-0001

HAMASAKI, KEITA, chemistry educator; b. Higashi-Kurume, Japan, Jan. 10, 1965; s. Yoshinori and Michiko (Yoshimoto) H. BS, Tokyo Inst. Poly., Atsugi, Japan, 1990; MS, Tokyo Inst. Tech., 1992, PhD, 1995. Rsch. assoc. Harvard U., Boston, 1995-97; prin. rsch. assoc. Tokyo Inst. Tech., Yokohama, Japan, 1997-99, asst. prof., 1999—. Mem. ACS, AAAS, Japan Chem Soc. E-mail: khamasak@bio.titech.ac.jp. Office: Toko Inst Tech, 4259 Nagatsuta B1-804, Yokohama 2268501, Japan

HAMATY, FREDERICK CLIVE, lawyer, senator; b. Kingston, Jamaica, Sept. 17, 1945; s. Munair Norman and Tatiana Helen (Shoucair) H,; m. Merle Allison Foreman, Dec. 16, 1967; children: Neil Frederick, Gillian Tatiana, Gail Allison. Grad., Jamaica Coll., Kingston, 1962, London Coll. Law, 1971. V.p. Jamal, Westmoreland Branch, Jamaica, 1974-76; chmn. Savanna-La-Mar Hosp. Regional Bd., Westmoreland & Elizabeth, Jamaica, 1977-80; sr. ptnr. M.N. Hamaty & Co., Westmoreland, Jamaica, 1981; dir., chmn. Westmoreland Environ. Devel. Co. Ltd., 1994—, Campbleton Gardens Ltd., Westmoreland, 1970. Author: Reflections of a Father by a Son, 1989. Mem. nat. exec. coun. Peoples Nat. Party, Kingston, 1994; sen. Jamaican Senate, Kingston, 1994, 97—; mem. Constitutional Commn., Kingston, 1992; appointed notary republic Island of Jamaica, 1983; appointed Queens Counsel, 1992. Mem. Jamaican Bar Assn. (coun. mem. 1991-92), Advoicates Assn., Cornwall Bar Assn. (pres. 1990-93), Rotary (pres. 1974-75), Masons. Roman Catholic. Avocations: swimming, golf, tennis. Home: Ferris Heights PO Box 7, Sevannah-La-Mar, Westmoreland Jamaica Office: M N Hamaty & Co, 103 Great George St, Westmoreland Jamaica

HAMBARDZUMYAN, VEMIR, educator; b. Vardenis, Armenia, Nov. 6, 1929; s. Vanush Ambardzumyan and Mille (Arzoyan) H.; m. Djuliet Asatryan, Feb. 27, 1960; children: Karen, Karine, Victor. PhD, Moscow, 1965, D of Tech. Sci., 1981. Engr. Enterprise Autotransport, Min. Transp., Yerevan, Armenia, 1959-61; prof. Armenian Argotech. Inst., Yerevan, 1965-81, 89-94, head chair, 1981-85; chmn. scientific lab. Traffic Safety, Yerevan, 1981-94; chmn. corp. KANXUM, Yerevan, 1989—; pres. Traffic Safety Found. Armenia, Yerevan, 1991—; prof. Moscow State Automobile Rd. Inst., 1994—, Russian U. Friendship People, Moscow, 1994—; head of chair Hydraulic Higher Sch. Algeria, Blida, 1985-89. Author: (manuals) Traffic Safety, 1997, 98, 99, General Systems Approach of Traffic Safety, 1999, Ecological Safety of Automobile Transport, 1999, Organization and Management of Traffic Safety, 1980; contbr. over 150 articles to profl. jours. Lt. Armenia Mil., 1950-54. Mem. N.Y. Acad. Sci., Internat. Acad. Ecology & Life Protection, Internat. Orgn. MORBOT (v.p. 1994—), Expert Econ. Devel. Inst. World Bank, Soc. Risk Analysis. Avocation: chess, gardening.

HAMBLEN, LAPSLEY WALKER, JR., judge; b. Chattanooga, Tenn., Dec. 25, 1926; s. Lapsley Walker Sr. and Libby (Shipley) H.; m. Claudia Royster Terrell, Mar. 20, 1971; children by previous marriage: Lapsley Walker III, Allen M., William Shipley. BA, U. Va., 1949, LLB, 1953. Bar: W.Va. 1954, Ohio 1955, Va. 1957. Trial atty. IRS, Atlanta, 1955; atty. advisor U.S. Tax Ct., 1956; ptnr. Caskie Frost Hobbs & Hamblen and predecessor firms, Lynchburg, Va., 1957-82; dep. asst. atty. gen. tax div. U.S. Dept. Justice, 1982; judge U.S. Tax Ct., Washington, 1982-92, chief judge, 1992-94, 94-96, sr. judge, 1996-2000, ret., 2000; mem. adv. bd. Va. tax rev. U. Va. Law Sch., Charlottesville, 1990—; former trustee So. Fed. Tax Inst.; former co-dir. ann. conf. on fed. taxation U. Va. Served with USN, 1945-46. Fellow Am. Coll. Tax Counsel, Am. Coll. Trust and Estate Counsel, Raven Soc., Order of Coif, Omicron Delta Kappa, Phi Alpha Delta. Presbyterian.

HAMBLETON, GEORGE BLOW ELLIOTT, management consultant; b. Balt., Dec. 20, 1929; s. John Adams Hambleton and Margaret (Elliott) Carey; m. Janet Findlay MacLaren, Mar. 17, 1962 (dec. 1991); children: Anne Carey, Charles MacLaren, James Elliott; m. Diana Lee Walker, June 29, 1998. AB, Princeton U., 1952; program for mgmt. devel., Harvard U., 1964. Various positions with Latin American div. Pan Am, 1955-62; asst. div. service mgr. Pan Am, Miami, Fla., 1963-64; dir. USSR Pan Am, Moscow, 1966-70; dir. internat. affairs Pan Am, Washington, 1971-76; dir. comml. sales Pan Am, N.Y.C., 1977-80; v.p. mktg. N.Y. Airways, N.Y.C., 1976-77; exec. dir., vice chmn. Project Orbis, Inc., N.Y.C., 1980-83; pres. Andrews MacLaren, Inc., N.Y.C., 1983-86; dep. asst. sec., dep. dir. gen. U.S. and fgn. comml. svc. Dept. Commerce, Washington, 1986-88; sr. v.p. Mgmt. Internat. Inc., Westport, Conn., 1988—; bd. dirs. Flight Found., Inc., Washington, Andrews MacLaren Ltd., Northants, Eng. Dir. Fgn. Policy Discussion Group, Washington, 1975-96; mem. N.J. Conservation Found.; mem. adv. com. East-West Trade, U.S. Dept. Commerce, 1973-79; mem. dist. export coun. U.S. Dept. Commerce, Conn., 1989-93; bd. dirs. River Blindness Found., Houston, 1990-95, Coll. of the Atlantic, Bar Harbor, Maine, 1996—. 1st lt. U.S. Army, 1952-55, Korea. Mem. Upper Raritan Watershed Assn., Brook Club (N.Y.), Met. Club (Washington), Naval and Mil. Club (London), Md. Club (Balt.), Princeton Club (N.Y.), Essex Hunt Club (Far Hills, N.J.), Union Club (N.Y.), Harvard Bus. Sch. Club (Washington, v.p. 1973-76), Wings Club (N.Y.), Soc. Colonial Wars (N.Y.). Republican. Episcopalian. Avocations: flying, fishing, skiing, running, hunting. Home: 280 Pleasant Valley Rd Mendham NJ 07945-2920 Office: Mgmt Internat Inc PO Box 943 Far Hills NJ 07931-0943

HAMBLEY, DOUGLAS FREDERICK, geological and environmental engineer; b. Toronto, Ont., Can., Jan. 14, 1950; s. Fredrick Armstrong and Gwendolyn Shannon (Plant) H.; m. Sherrie Kate Barham Hambley, May 24, 1992 (div. June 2000). BS in Mining Engring., Queen's U., 1972; MBA, Lewis U., 1986; PhD in Earth Scis., U. Waterloo, Ont., Can., 1991. Registered profl. engr., Can., Ill., Va., Pa., Md., Wis.; registered profl. geologist, Pa., Wis., Ill. Jr. engr. Iron Ore Co. of Can., Schefferville, Que., 1972-73; mining engr. trainee Falconbridge (Ont.) Nickel Mines, Ltd., Can., 1974-75; mining engr. Harrison Bradford & Assocs., Ltd., St. Catharines, Ont., 1975-76; project engr. Denison Mines, Ltd., Elliot Lake, Ont., 1977-80; sr. mining engr. Engrs. Internat., Inc., Westmont, Ill., 1980-84; mining engr. Argonne (Ill.) Nat. Lab., 1984-88; rsch. asst. U. Waterloo, Ontario, 1988; sr. cons. Dunn Geosci. Corp., West Chicago, Ill., 1989; civil/geol. engr. Argonne (Ill.) Nat. Lab., 1990-91; mgr., geo-environtl. group Nova, Environtl. Svcs., Des Plaines, 1991; project mgr. Graef, Anhalt, Schloemer and Assocs., Inc., Chgo., Ill., 1992-2000; self-employed cons., 2000—. Contbr. articles to profl. jours. Recipient Cert. of Appreciation, Office of Geologic Repositories, 1987. Mem. ASCE, Soc. Mining, Metallurgy and Exploration (chmn. Chgo. sect. 1987-88), Assn. Engring. Geologists (treas. N.C. sect. 1987-88), Can. Inst. Mining and Metallurgy, Assn. Groundwater Scientists and Engrs., Soc. Am. Mil. Engrs. (treas. Chgo. post 1996-97, 3rd v.p. 1998, 2d v.p. 1999, pres. 2000), Ill. Bd. Licensing Profl. Geologists, Ill. Engirng. Coun. (dir. 1998, v.p. 1999—). Avocations: travel, cello, guitar, folk music. E-mail: dfhambley@earthlink.net. Home: 9108 W Ballard Rd Apt 1B Des Plaines IL 60016-4986

HAMBRAEUS, BENGT, composer, educator; b. Stockholm, Jan. 29, 1928; arrived in Can., 1972; m. Enid Odenaes, Mar. 21, 1960; children: Michael, Elisabeth. Organ studies with Alf Linder, 1944-48; MA, Uppsala U., 1950, PhD, 1956, PhD (hon.), 1992. Librarian, amanuens Inst. of Musicology, Uppsala, 1948-56; program producer, head chamber music, head music prodn. Swedish Broadcasting Corp., Stockholm, 1957-72; prof. theory, musicology, organ improvisation and composition McGill U., Montreal, Que., Can., 1972-95; prof. emeritus McGill U., Montreal, Que., 1995—; lectr. in field. Composer: Giuoco del Cambio, 1952-54, Crystal Sequence, 1954, Introduzione-Sequenze-Coda, 1958-59, Constellations I-V, 1958-83, Rota, 1962-63, Transfiguration, 1962-63, Responsorier, 1964, Motetum Archangeli Michaelis, 1967, Tre pezzi per organo, 1966-67, Rencontres, 1968-70, Five Organ Pieces, 1969-75, Tides, 1974, Continuo for organ and orch., 1975, Ricordanza, 1975-76, Tornado, 1976; (broadcast opera) Sagan, 1979; Livre d'orgue, 1980-81, Sheng, 1983, Tre intermezzi, 1984, Variations on a theme by Gilles Vigneault, 1984, La passacaille errante, 1984, Quodlibet, 1984, Trio Sonata, 1985, Three Dances, 1986; (chamber opera) L'ouï-dire, 1986; Symphonia Sacra, 1986, Vortex, 1986, Mirrors, 1986-87, Five Psalms, 1987, Apocalipsis cum figuris, 1987, Echoes of Loneliness, 1988, Night Music, 1988, Cinque studi canonici, 1988, Après-Sheng, 1988, Cadenza, 1988, Dos recercadas, 1988, Litanies, 1989, Nocturnals, 1989-90, Canvas with Mirrors, 1990, Rondeau, 1991, Loitsu, 1991, Concerto for Piano and Orch., 1991-92, Missa pro organo, 1992, St. Michael's Liturgi, 1992, Organum Sancti Jacobi, 1993, Meteoros, 1993, Songs of the Mountain, The Moon, and Television, 1994, Due rapsodie, 1994, Triptyque pour orgue avec MIDI, 1994, Sonata per cinque, 1995, Klavidar, 1995, A solis ortus cardine, 1995, Quatre tableaux, 1995-96, Concentio, 1995, Concerto per corno principale ed orch, 1996, Archipel, 1996-97, FM 643765, 1997 Lukas IV: 23-30 (1998), Quintette pour Clarinette en La et Quatuor à cordes (1998), Labyrinth, 1998, Riflessioni, 1999, Le Cor Magique, 2000; pub. numerous articles, essays and books on musicol. topics from 16th to 20th centuries; also numerous works for tape, choir, orch. and organ. Recipient Royal Swedish Gold medal Litteris et Artibus, 1986, The Swedish Tribute, 1996; also numerous awards in Sweden, Denmark and Japan. Mem. Royal Swedish Music Acad., Swedish Composers Soc., Swedish Composers Performance Right Bur., Can. League Composers, Swedish Soc. Musicology. Office: McGill U Faculty of Music, 555 Sherbrooke St W, Montreal, PQ Canada H3A 1E3

HAMBRAEUS, LEIF MAGNUS, nutritionist; b. Stockholm, June 4, 1936; s. Magnus and Wera (Sandstrom) H.; m. Anna Margareta Fajerson, June 21, 1959; children: Sofia, Katarina, Torkel, Joakim. MB, Karolinska Inst., Stockholm, 1957, DMS, 1964, MD, 1967. Rsch. asst. Stockholm U., 1960-64; from asst. to acting prof. Uppsala (Sweden) U., 1965-71, prof. nutrition, 1972—; Fulbright grantee MIT, Cambridge, 1973-74; guest lectr. Gen. Foods, Can., 1975; vis. scientist Meml. U., Newfoundland, 1984. Mem. editl. bd. Nutrition Rsch., Nutritional Biochemistry, Nutrition Rsch. Rev., Annals of Nutrition and Metabolism; contbr. articles to profl. jours. Fellow Swedish Royal Acad. Agriculture and Forestry Scis., Finnish Acad. Sci. and Letters; mem. Am. Nutritional Scis., Am. Coll. Nutrition, Fedn. European Nutrition Socs. (pres. 1988-92), N.Y. Acad. Scis., Nutrition Soc. Office: Uppsala U, Dag Hammarskjold Vag 21, S-75237 Uppsala Sweden

HAMBRICK, ARLENE, school system administrator, minister; b. Chgo., Nov. 8, 1945; children: Ronald T., Anthony C. BS, Chgo. State U., 1971; MDiv, Chgo. Theol. Sem., 1981; EdD, U. Mass., 1993. Spl. edn. tchr. Chgo. Pub. Schs., 1971-81, Boston Pub. Sch., 1981-93; dir. elem. and mid. sch. Bluefield (Va.) Coll., 1993-96; sr. mgr. Appalachia Ednl. Lab., Charleston, W.Va., 1996-98; dir. Ctr. for Sch. and Cmty. Devel. North Ctrl. Ednl. Lab., Oak Brook, Ill., 1999—; mem. Mercer County Pub. Sch. Bd., Bluefield, 1992—, Tazwell (Va.) County Pub. Sch. Bd., 1993—. Contbr. articles to profl. jours. Chair, founder Attleboro, Mass. Civil Rights Commn., 1991-93. Mem. AAUW, NAACP, Assn. of Tchr. Educators (del. 1994—). Avocations: sewing, reading, jogging, collecting books about Black history, Women's history and Black Women's history.

HAMBRO, CHARLES ERIC ALEXANDER, investment company executive; b. July 24, 1930; s. Sir Charles Hambro and Pamela Cobbold; m. Rose Evelyn 1954 (div. 1976); 3 children: m. Cherry Felicity, 1976. Student, Eton. With Hambros Bank Ltd., 1952-83, mng. dir., 1957-65, dep. chmn., 1965-72, chmn., 1972-83; chmn. bd. dirs. Hambros PLC, London, 1983-97, Guardian Royal Exch. Assurance, London, 1983—; dir. P&OSN Co., GEn. Oriental Investments, San Paolo Bank Holdings; chmn. Royal Nat. Pension Fund for Nurses, 1968. Trustee Brit. Mus., 1984-94. With Coldstream Guards, 1949-51. Named Baron life Peer of Dixton and Dumbleton, County of Cloucester, 1994. Mem. White's Club, Carlton Club. Avocations: shooting, farming, forestry. Office: Guardian Royal Exch PLC, Royal Exch, London EC3V 3LS, England*

HAMBURGER, CLARA, musicologist; b. Budapest, Sept. 29, 1934; d. István and Georgette (Weiller) H.; m. Iván Kertész, July 23, 1957; 1 child, Martha. Diploma in musicology, Ferenc Liszt Music. Acad., Budapest, 1961, dr., 1981; postgrad. in mus. scis., Hungarian Acad. Scis., 1981. Librarian Hungarian Acad. Scis., Budapest, 1959-61; librarian music dept. Nat. Széchényi Library, Budapest, 1961-66; editor music books Gondolat, Budapest, 1966-90; gen. sec. Hungarian Liszt Soc., Budapest, 1992—. Author: Liszt, 1966, 2d enlarged edit., 1980 (transl. into German and English, 1987), Liszt-kalauz, 1986, Franz Liszt lettres à Cosima et à Daniela, 1996, Franz Liszt Briefwechsel mit seiner Mutter, 2000; ,contbr. articles to profl. ours. Avocation: music. Home: Deres u 12, H-1124 Budapest Hungary

HAMBYE, ANNE-SOPHIE EMMANUELLE, nuclear medicine physician; b. Brussels, Jan. 12, 1962; d. Albert Ange and Marie-Francoise Felicie (Lepiece) H.; children: Anne-Charlotte, Laurent, Guillaume. MD, U. Louvain, Brussels, 1986; PhD, Free U., Brussels, 1999. Intern U. Louvain, 1986-90, fellow in nuclear medicine, 1990-92; nuclear cardiologist Middelheim Hosp., Antwerp, Belgium; cons. Cath. U. Leuven, Belgium. Active P.S.C., Belgium, 1985—. Fellow Am. Coll. Cardiology (assoc.); mem. AAAS, European Assn. Nuclear Medicine, Am. Soc. Nuclear Cardiology, British Soc. Nuclear Cardiology, Belgian Soc. Internal Medicine, Belgian Soc. Nuclear Medicine, N.Y. Acad. Scis. Roman Catholic. Avocations: music, opera, books, history. Office: Middelheim Hosp/Nuclear Med, Med Lindendreef 1, 2020 Antwerp Belgium

HAMDA, MOHAMED EL-BEJI, banker; b. Tunis, Tunisia, May 26, 1934; married; 4 children. Student, Lycée Alaoui, Tunis, U. Econs., Paris, Ecole des Hautes Etudes Politiques, Paris. Editor Nat. Bank of Agriculture, 1960-72; asst. mng. dir. Banque Nat. Agricole, 1972-73; mgr. Arab-Internat. Bank of Investment, 1973-74; asst. mng. dir. Soc. Tunisienne de Banque, 1974-78; mng. dir. Banque Nat. de Tunisie, 1978-81, Soc. Tunisienne de Banque, 1981-84, Union Tunisienne de Banques, Paris, 1984-88; dep. gov. Banque Centrale de Tunisie, 1988-90; gov. Banque Centrale de Tunisie, Tunis, 1990—. Decorated comdr. Ordre de la République de Tunisie. Office: Ctrl Bank Tunisia, 25 Rue Hédi Nouira BP 777, 1080 Tunis Tunisia

HAMDAR, BASSAM CHARIF, agri-economics educator, consultant; b. Beirut, May 13, 1957; s. Charif Ali Hamdar and Souad Jamil Ayad; m. Lora Ann Bnkovic, Aug. 24, 1992 (div. May 1997); m. Wafa Hassen Yassin, Aug. 20, 1997; children: Mohammad, Zeinab. BS in Bus. Econs., Lebanese Am. U., Beirut, 1982; MS in Agri-Econs., Am. U. Beirut, 1984; PhD in Agri-Econs., Miss. State U., 1988. Rsch. asst. Am. U. Beirut, 1982-84, Miss. State U., Stakville, 1984-88; asst. prof. agri-econs. Am. U. Beirut, 1992—; dir. Bur. Bus. and Fin. Svcs., Beirut, 1997—. Mem. editl. bd. Internat. Jour. Supply Chain Mgmt., 1997—. Avocations: travelling, swimming, tennis.

Fax: 961-1-744460. Home: Alghobeiri, Raad St, Beirut Lebanon Office: Am U Beirut, Bliss St, Beirut Lebanon

HAMDI, ANWAR, pharmacology educator; b. Douma, Damascus, Syria, Dec. 10, 1953; s. Abdulrahman Hamdi and Samia Kaddoh; m. Hana Dara, Aug. 10, 1980; children: Abdulrahman, Jumanah, Anas, Ahmed, Osama. MD, Damascus U., 1978; PhD in Biomed. Scis., East Tenn. State U., 1990. Cert. Ednl. Commn. for Fgn. Med. Grads. Resident in surgery Coll. Medicine Damascus U.; practicing physician gen. surgery dept. Riyadh (Saudi Arabia) Cen. Hosp., 1979-83, practicing physician plastic surgery dept., 1983-86; grad. rsch. asst. dept. pharmacology James H. Quillen Coll. Medicine, Johnson City, Tenn., 1987-90; rsch. assoc. dept. neuroscis. Pennington Biomed. Rsch. Ctr. La. State U., Baton Rouge, 1990-94; asst. prof. clin. pharmacology, dept. clin. pharmacology Coll. Medicine, King Khalid U., Abha, Saudi Arabia, 1994-99; assoc. prof. clin. pharmacology Coll. Medicine, King Khalid U., Abha, 2000—; vis. asst. prof. dept. medicine Sch. Medicine, La. State U., New Orleans, 1996, 97. Author: (books) Secrets of Sleep, 1986, Disturbances of Sleep, Description and Treatment, 1986, 95, Evaluate Your Knowledge and Expertise in Pharmacology, 1998, Test Your IQ, 1999, The Universe: A Mathematical and Physical Study, 1999, The Brain: A Mathematical and Physical Study, 2000; contbr. chpts. to books and articles to profl. jours. Recipient award for outstanding presentation La. Med. and Surg. Assn., 1991, Abha Lit. Club award, 1997. Mem. Am. Fedn. for Clin. Rsch. (Trainee Travel award 1991, 92), Neurosci. Soc., Southeastern Pharmacology Soc., Syrian Med. Assn. Office: King Khalid U, Coll Medicine PO Box 641, Abha Saudi Arabia

HAMDI, MOKTAR, microbiologist, educator; b. Sidi Khlif, Tunisia, Apr. 28, 1959; s. Mohamed and Fahima Hamdi; m. Melika El Hemdi; children: Amin, Saif. MST, Provence U., Marseille, France, 1986, Engr., 1987, PhD, 1991. Rsch. lab. microbiologist Orstom, Marseille, 1988-89; rsch. biologist Biotech. Ctr., 1989-92; rschr. Paul Sabatier U., Toulouse, France, 1992-93; lectr. dept. microbiology Ecole Superior Ind. Alim, Tunis, Tunisia, 1993—; cons. in field. Contbr. articles to profl. jours.; editl. adv. bd. Bioprocess Engring., 1997—; author; several manuels of environ. and fermentation processes, 1994—; patent in field. Recipient, Chouman Found. Prize in Life Scis., 1997. Mem. Internat. Assn. Water Quality, N.Y. Acad. Scis., Tunisian Scis. Soc. Avocations: music, sports, coaching football. Office: Hiher Inst Food Industries Tunis, 58 Ave Alain Savary, 1003 El Khadra Tunis, Tunisia also: Nat Inst Applied Sci and Tech, BP 676, 1080 El Khadra Tunis, Tunisia

HAMDI, SUHAILA TALIB, chemistry educator, researcher; b. Basrah, Iraq, Dec. 9, 1949; arrived in Jordan, 1992; d. Talib Hamdi and Zahrah Naji (Issa) Hammod; m. Kais Abdul-Kareem Ebraheem; children: Omer, Zaineb. BSc, U. Basrah, 1971; PhD, U. Surrey, Eng., 1977. Asst. prof. U. Basrah, 1977-83, assoc. prof., 1983-92; vis. asst. prof. Solar Energy Rsch. Ctr., Baghdad, Iraq, 1988-89; prof. chemistry Applied Sci. U., Amman, Jordan, 1994—; cons. solar energy rsch., Baghdad, 1988-89. Author: Electrochemistry and Chemical Kinetics, 1990 (Writer's award 1990). Recipient Excellence in Tchg./Rsch. award U. Basrah, 1990. Avocations: sports, music.

HAMDY, IHAB ABDEL HAMID, business manager; b. Giza, Egypt, Mar. 23, 1971; s. Abdel Hamid Hamdy.; Grad., Port Said English Sch., Cairo, 1987. U. London, 1989, Cairo U., 1995. Credit contr. Multichoice, Egypt, 1994-96; bus. rschr. AC Nielsen Am., Egypt, 1996-98; regional mgr. RIME Info. Bur., Cairo, 1998—. Mem. Gezira Club (Sports award 1989), Auto. and Touring Club, Shooting Club (award 1990). Avocations: reading, travel, sports. Home: 1-A El Messaha St Apt 23, Giza 12311, Egypt Office: Rime Info Bur Ltd 155 Bldg, 19 El Shahid Helmy El Masry, Cairo 11361, Egypt

HAMED, MOHAMED, engineering educator; b. Suez, Egypt, Jan. 31, 1946; s. Mohamed Ahmed Nada and Tafida Ibrahim Gomaa; m. Mona Thabet Khater, Aug. 13, 1981; children: Sara, Ibrahim. BSc, Ain Shams U., Cairo, 1968; PhD, Moscow Power Inst., 1978. Staff engr. Electricity Authority, Cairo, 1969-79; lectr. Suez Canal U., Port Said, Egypt, 1978-83, asst. prof., 1983-89, head dept. elec. engring., 1985-92, vice dean for rsch. faculty of engring., 1992-93, dean., 1993, prof., 1989—; dir. computer ctr. Suez Canal U., 1990-92; cons. Ednl. Bldg. Authority, Cairo, 1993—; mem. sci. com. for staff promotion Highest Congress of Univs., Cairo, 1995—. Mem. N.Y. Acad. Scis., mem. of Amer. Assoc. for the Devel. of Scis. Islamic. Avocations: football, writing, helping others. Home: Port Fouad City, 25 El Ebour Zone, Port Said 42523, Egypt Office: Suez Canal Univ, Faculty of Engring, Port Said 42523, Egypt

HAMED, SAAB KHALIL, physician; b. Abu-Snan, Israel, Oct. 14, 1928; s. Saab Ahmed Khalil and Saab Said Shahraban; m. Saab Kamel Milhim, Sept. 27, 1963; children: Amer, Vivian, Nizar, Nali, Shahirban, Amera, Haitam. MD, Rashidia Coll., 1959. Sr. doctor Karmel, Haifa, Israel, 1960-63; pvt. practice Acre, Israel, 1966—. Mayor Kfar Abu-Snan, 1969-90. Scholarship British Coun., 1963-64, Hebrew U. Haddassah Med. Sch. Mem. Israel Med. Home: PO Box 23, 24905 Kfar Abu-Snan Israel

HAMEED, KAMRAN, pulmonologist, consultant; b. Lahore, Pakistan, Sept. 20, 1959; s. Abdul Hameed and Fahmida Shafi Dilshad; m. Asifa Razaque, Apr. 12, 187; children: Anam, Ahsan, Amna. MBBS, King Edward Med. Sch., Lahore, 1984. Med. officer to ho. officer Mayo Hosp., Lahore, 1984-89; sr. ho. officer medicine East Birmingham (Eng.) U., 1989-90; registrar, chest medicine Aberdeen (Scotland) Royal Infirmary, 1990-92, Llandough Hosp., Cardiff, Wales, 1992-93; cons. pulmonologist Hera Hosp., Makkah, Saudi Arabia, 1996, head medicine dept., head chest unit, 1996; cons. pulmonologist Al Noor Specialist Hosp., Makkah, Saudi Arabia, 1996—, dep. head medicine, head chest unit, 1996—; clin. tutor Aberdeen Med. U., 1990-92; tutor, diploma course in tuberculosis and chest diseases, Llandough Hosp., 1992-93. Contbr. articles to profl. jours. Mem. Royal Coll. Physicians, Brit. Thoracic Soc., Asian Pacific Soc. Respirology, Arab Thoracic Assn. Avocations: computers/internet, music, reading. E-mail: drkamranh@yahoo.com. Office: Al-Noor Specialists Hosp, Dept Medicine, Holy Makkah Saudi Arabia

HAMEED, MOHAMED ABDUL, oil and gas company executive; b. Hyderabad, India, July 22, 1948; arrived in Saudi Arabia, 1977; s. Aziz Mohammed Abdul Siddiqui and Iqbal Unnisa Begum; m. Kishwar Jehan Faridi, July 30, 1978; children: Mohamed Abdul Hafeez, Mohamed Abdul Moiz, Abdul Samad. B Engring. in Mech. Engring., Osmania U., Hyderabad, 1973. Mech. engr. M/S Standard Industries, Bala Nagar Hyderabad, 1971-77; piping engr. Chiyoda Internat. S.A., Riyadh, Saudi Arabia, 1977-80; project engr. Brown & Root Saudi Ltd., Al'Khober, Saudi Arabia, 1982-83; sr. project engr. Abalkhail Cons. Engrs., Al'Khober, 1983-84; project engr. Saud Consult, Dammam, Saudi Arabia, 1980-82, prin. engr., 1985-86, project mgr., 1987-91, sr. mgr., dept. head, 1992—. Mem. ASME. Avocations: reading, driving, cooking, indoor games, traveling. Office: Saud Consult, 4th St Al'Khober PO Box 1293, Dammam 31431, Saudi Arabia

HAMEED, SALMAN, finance executive; b. Rawalpindi, Punjab, Pakistan, Jan. 10, 1955; arrived in Hong Kong, 1989; s. Sheikh Mohammad Abdul and Akhtar (Nisa) H.; m. Afia Arshad, Mar. 29, 1985; children: Shanzaeh, Salman. BS with honors, Karachi U., Pakistan, 1977; postgrad., U. London. Fin. trainee Premier Tobacco Industries, Pakistan, 1978-82; acct. Premier Tobacco Industries, 1982-86, asst. mgr., 1986-87; fin. analyst Am. Express, Pakistan, 1987-88; contr. Am. Express, 1988-89; regional fin. mgr. Philip Morris Asia Inc., Hong Kong, 1989—, fin. dir., 1998—. Mem. Chartered Inst. Mgmt. Accts. (student), Inst. Cost and Mgmt. (student). Avocations: reading, charity work, photogrphy, sports. Office: Philip Morris Asia Inc, II Pacific Pl 88 Queensway, Hong Kong Hong Kong

HAMEKA, HENDRIK FREDERIK, chemist, educator; b. Rotterdam, Holland, May 25, 1931; came to U.S., 1960, naturalized, 1963; s. Dirk C. and Johanna (Mannebeck) H.; m. Charlotte C. Procacci, Aug. 2, 1972. Drs., U. Leiden, The Netherlands, 1953, D.Sc., 1956; M.A. (hon.), U. Pa., 1971. Rsch. assoc. U. Rome, Italy, 1956-57; fellow Carnegie Inst. Tech., 1957-58; rsch. physicist N. V. Philips Lamps, Eindhoven, The Netherlands, 1958-60; asst. prof. chemistry Johns Hopkins, 1960-62; assoc. prof. chemistry U. Pa., 1962-67, prof. chemistry, 1967—; disting. vis. rsch. prof. USAF Acad., 1986-87. Author: Advanced Quantum Chemistry, 1965, Introductory Quantum Theory, 1967, Physical Chemistry, 1977; Contbr. numerous articles to sci. jours. Recipient Alexander von Humboldt prize, 1981; Alfred P. Sloan Research fellow, 1963-67. Achievements include research on theory of molecular structure and optical and magnetic properties of molecules; calculations of spin-orbit and spin-spin coupling; theory of resonance optical rotation, spectral predictions. Home: 1503 Argyle Rd Berwyn PA 19312-1905 Office: U Pa Dept Chemistry Philadelphia PA 19104

HAMELIN, JOËL HUBERT, space scientist; b. Chateau-Gontier, Mayenne, France, July 31, 1948; s. Norbert François and Madeleine Charlotte (Madiot) H.; m. Monique Mélanie Hamon, Mar. 24, 1967 (div. Feb. 1987); children: Emmanuel, Yohan, Katell, Gaël; m. Christiane Yvetot, Mar. 4, 1988; 1 child, Laure. Diploma univ. tech. and electronics, Universitaire Technologie Electronique, Angers, France, 1968; diploma engr., Conservatoire des Arts & Métiers Nat., Paris, 1973. Physicist asst. U. Ctr. Scis. and Tech., Clermont-Ferrand, France, 1968-73; head electromagnetic environ. group Nat. Telecom Rsch. Ctr., Lannion, France, 1974-86; sr. engr. European Space Agy., Noordwijk, The Netherlands, 1986-91; asst. dir. gen. Space Affairs Bur., Paris, 1991-92; head space advanced techs. dept. Ministry Rsch. and Space, Paris, 1992-93; space dir. Ministry of Postal Svcs. Telecommunications and Space, Paris, 1993-98; dep. to European space coord. European Commn., Brussels, 1998—; sci. adviser Nat. Telecom. Rsch. Ctr., 1986-88, Meteorage Ltd., Paris, 1986-92. Author: (with Pierre Degauque) Compatibilité électromagnetique, 1990, Electromagnetic Compatibility, 1993; contbr. over 60 articles to profl. publs. Recipient prize paper award EMC, 1979. Mem. IEEE (sr.), Internat. Union RadioSci. (chmn. electromagnetic hoise and interference com. 1987-93, sci. coord. 1993-99). Home: 10 rue Marthe Edouard, 92190 Meudon France Office: Ministry of Space, European Commn, Rue de la Loi 200, B-1049 Brussels Belgium

HAMELIN, MICHEL, planetary science researcher; b. Paris, Apr. 8, 1944; s. Lucien and France (Haberer) H.; m. Rosa Ricondo, June 18, 1977 (div. Sept. 1994); children: Nora, Sylvia, Frédéric; m. Tamara Golova, May 19, 1995. Lic. in scis., U. Orsay, France, 1967; DEA in Plasma Physics, U. Orsay, 1968, D, 1972; D d'Etat, U. Orléans, France, 1978. Asst. Faculty of Medicine, Paris, 1969; rsch. attaché Groupe de Recherches Ionosphériques-Nat. Ctr. Sci. Rsch., St. Maur, France, 1970, Groupe de Recherches Ionosphériques-Nat. Rsch. Sci., Orléans, 1971-78; rsch. chargé Centre de Recherches en Physique de l'Environnement-Laboratoire de Physique et Chimie de 'l Environnement-Centre National de la Recherche Scientifique, Orléans, 1979-98, Centre d'étude des Environnements Terrestre et Planétaires-Centre National de la Recherche Scientifique, St. Maur, France, 1999—. Contbr. articles to profl. jours. Mem. European Geophys. Soc., Am. Geophys. Union. Avocations: mountain touring, sailing. Office: CETP-CNRS, 4 ave de Neptune, 94107 St Maur France

HAMELIN, RAYMOND ARMAND, science educator; b. Paris, May 14, 1930; s. Joseph and Marie (Thomas) H.; m. Simone Giorgio, July 18, 1956; children: Bernard, Christine, Rozenn. Agrégation Scis. Physiques, Ecole Normal Superieure, Paris, 1954; D Scis., Paris, 1960. Agrégé préparateur chimie ENS, 1955-59; scientific cons. ctrl. lab. Etablissements Kuhlmann, Levallois, 1960-62; scientific attache French scientific mission Emb. of France, U.S.A., 1962-65; scientific dir. Sté Ugine-Kuhlmann, 1965-72; adj. scientific dir. Sté Péchiney-Ugine-Kuhlmann (PUK), 1972-74; dir. Inst. Nat. Scis. Appliquées, Lyon, 1974-91; prof. U. Pierre et Marie Curie (Paris VI), France, 1974-95; ret., 1995; prof. Inst. Nat. Scis. et Techs. Nucléaires, Saclay, France, 1959-75; mem. Nat. Chemistry Com., 1971-74, 79-87; v.p. Consultative Com. Scientific Rsch. and Tech., 1973-74; sec. gen. Conf. Grandes Ecoles, 1983-91. Editor-in-chief: Energie Nucléaire rev., 1966-73; pres. editl. gen. com. Techniques de l'Ingenieur ency., 1991-96. Pres. conseil perfectionnement Ecole Polytechnique Feminine, 1993—; chmn. com. admission List of French Engrs., 1998—. Decorated Bronze Medal Youth and Sports, Govt. Ministry Youth and Sports, 1983, Silver Medal Youth and Sports, 1991, knight Legion of Hon., French Govt., 1987, officer Ordre Mérite Allemand (Germany), 1988, Presdl. medal Tufts U., 1988, officer Ordre Nat. Mérite, French Govt., 1993. Fellow N.Y. Acad. Scis.; mem. French Soc. Chemistry (sec. 1992-95, editor-in-chief L'Actualité Chimique), Internat. Union for Pure and Applied Chemistry (sec. com. chemical rsch. applied to world needs 1993—), Nat. Coun. Engrs. and Scientists France (mem. elect adminstrn. coun. 1996—). Fax: 33-1-4633 6979. E-mail: rayhamelin@aol.com. Home: 5 rue des Ursulines, 75005 Paris France

HAMER, BRIAN A., lawyer; b. Chgo., June 6, 1956. BA, Yale Coll., 1978; JD, Columbia U., 1982. With Schiff, Hardin & Waite, Chgo., Mayer, Brown & Platt, Chgo.; chief asst. corp. counsel City of Chgo. Dept. of Law; 1st dep. dir. of revenue City of Chicago, 1997—. E-mail: b.hamer@ci.chi.il.us. Office: Chicago Dept Revenue 333 S State St Ste 530 Chicago IL 60604-3900

HAMFELT, ANDREAS, computer science educator; b. Uppsala, Sweden, Mar. 19, 1960; s. Arne and Kerstin (Backström) H. LLM, MSC, Uppsala (Sweden) U., 1987, Lic. Philosophy, 1990, PhD. Lectr. Uppsala U., 1990-93, sr. lectr., 1993-95, assoc. prof., 1995-98, acting prof., 1998-2000, prof., 2000—; expert Ministry of Justice, Stockholm, 1988, 90, 91; expert evaluator Swedish Found. Internat. Coop. in Rsch. and Higher Edn., Stockholm, 1998; vis. researcher NORFA, Denmark, 1994. Contbr. articles to profl. jours. Bd. dirs. Found. Legal Info., Stockholm, 1988-98. Mem. Assn. Logic Programming. Avocations: hunting, sailing. Home: Stureg 15 A, S-75223 Uppsala Sweden Office: Dept Info Sci, Kyrkogårdsg 10, S-75120 Uppsala Sweden

HAMID, MOHAMMAD, Urdu language educator, university official; b. Chapra, Bihar, India, Dec. 1, 1940; s. Mohammad Amin and Bashirun Nisa; m. Omaima Naaz; children: Sajid Mohammad (dec.), Tabassum Hena, Rashid Mohammad. BA, Jagdam Coll., Chapra, 1960; MA in Urdu, Patna (India) U., 1962; MA in Persian, Bihar U., Muzaffarpur, 1963, PhD, 1971. Cert. journalist. Lectr. Bihar U. Rajendra Coll., Chapra, 1964, reader; prof. Urdu, Jaiprakash U., Chapra, 1991—, dir., coord. coll. devel. coun., 1998—, mem. syndicate; mem. syndicate Jaiprakash U., 1996, Bihar U., 1981, also mem. senate. Author: Talash-O-Tajziah, 1986 (Outstanding Book of Yr. award 1986), Development and Growth of Urdu Short Stories, 1986; columnist Blitz weekly, Bombay, 1980. Sec. Mazharul Haque Celebrations, Chapra, 1963—, Saran dist. Nat. Integration Com., 1981—. Grantee Univ. Grants Commn., Govt. of Uttar Pradesh. Mem. Bihar Urdu Acad., Saran Press Assn. (v.p. Chapra 1997—, pres. 1999), U. Tchrs. Assn. (pres. 1996). Avocation: reading books. Home: Karimchak, Bihar Chapra 841 301, India Office: Jaiprakash U, Dak Bangalow Rd, Bihar Chapra 841 301, India

HAMIDZADEH, HAMID REZA, mechanical engineer, educator, consultant; b. Tehran, Iran, July 22, 1952; came to U.S., 1982; s. Khodadad and Nosrat (Fassieh) H. m. Azar Mofid, July 2, 1987; children: Cyrus, Archer. BSc, Arya Meher U. of Tehran, 1974; MSc, Imperial Coll. U. London, 1975, PhD, 1978. Postdoctoral rsch. asst. Imperial Coll., London, 1978-82; lectr., assoc. mem. grad. sch. U. Md., College Park, 1982-83; asst. prof. U. So. Colo., Pueblo, 1983-86; assoc. prof. S.D. State U., Brookings, 1986-90, prof., 1990—, prin. investigator mech. engring., 1994-96; sr. design cons. Cummins Engine Co., Columbus, Ind., 1995; organizer numerous tech. confs.; rev. manuscripts of tech. books for pubs. Contbr. more than 67 articles to profl. jours. including Jour. Shock and Vibration, ASME, among others. Recipient numerous grants. Mem. ASME (sr. del NSSC com. 1988-93, regional chair bd. minority and women 1989-92, profl. devel. com. 1993-96, Faculty Advisor of Yr. 1991). Avocations: swimming, poetry. Home: 6015 S Mustang Ave Sioux Falls SD 57108-3800 Office: SD State U Dept Mech Engring 214 Crothers Engring Hl Brookings SD 57007-0001

HAMILTON, CARLOS ROBERT, JR., internist, endocrinologist; b. Houston, June 12, 1939; s. Carlos Robert and Berta (Denman) H.; m. Carolyn Burton, Aug. 12, 1961; children: Carlos R. III, Patricia Frances. BA, U. Tex., 1961; MS, MD with honors, Baylor Coll. Medicine, 1966. Diplomate Am. Bd. Internal Medicine, Am. Bd. Endocrinology and Metabolic Diseases; lic. physician, Tex. Intern in internal medicine The Johns Hopkins Hosp., Balt., 1966-67, asst. resident in internal medicine, 1967-69, chief resident in medicine, 1970-71; clin. and rsch. fellow Harvard Med. Sch./Mass. Gen. Hosp., Boston, 1969-70; asst. prof. medicine Johns Hopkins U. and Hosp., Balt., 1971-72; staff endocrinologist Wilford Hall USAF Med. Ctr., San Antonio, 1972-74; clin. prof. medicine Baylor Coll. Medicine, Houston, 1974-99; clin. prof. medicine Med. Sch. U. Tex., Houston, 1999—; cons. endocrinology and internal medicine Med. Clinic of Houston, L.L.P., 1974—; med. advisor employee benefit com. Southwestern Bell Tel. Co., 1975-93; attending physician in endocrinology Ben Taub Gen. Hosp./Baylor Coll. Medicine, 1980—; attending physician, mem. active staff The Meth. Hosp., Houston, 1974—. Contbr. articles to profl. jours. Dist. and coun. chair, area pres., regional bd. dirs., v.p. Boy Scouts Am., Houston, Atlanta, Irving, Tex., 1980—; bd. regents Tex. Woman's U., 1999—. Recipient Dist. award of merit, Silver Beaver award, Silver Antelope award, Disting. Eagle Scout award, Silver Buffalo award Boy Scouts Am., 1982-99. Fellow ACP (bd. dirs. Tex. chpt., Mead-Johnson Residency scholar 1970, bd. dirs. Tex. Acad. Internal Medicine and ACP-ASIM health and pub. policy com.), Am. Coll. Endocrinology; mem. SAR (bd. dirs. Paul Carrington chpt. 1992—, pres. 1993), Am. Soc. Internal Medicine (bd. dirs. polit. action com. 1995-98, Key Congl. Contact of Yr. 1996), Am. Assn. Clin. Endocrinologists (bd. dirs. 1995—, chair legis. and regulatory com. 1998-2000, sec. exec. com. 2000—), Tex. Med. Assn. (exec. com. polit. action com. 1989—, chair 1995, 96), Harris County Med. Soc. (bd. dirs. 1992-99, pres.-elect 1998, pres. 1999), Kiwanis (bd. dirs. Houston chpt. 1986-95, pres. 1995), Alpha Omega Alpha, Sigma Xi. E-mail: chamilton@mchllp.com. Home: 5100 San Felipe St Unit 302E Houston TX 77056-3620 Office: Med Clinic of Houston LLP 1707 Sunset Blvd Houston TX 77005-1713

HAMILTON, CHARLES RICHARD, oncologist; b. Birmingham, Warwicksh., Eng., Mar. 5, 1954; s. Hector Alexander and Carmen Teresa (Fryer) H.; m. Penelope Vivien Wickins, Sept. 29, 1979; children: Thomas, Benjamin, Matthew, Emily. M.B.B.S., Med. Sch. St. Bartholomew's. Asst. lectr. Imperial Cancer Rsch. Found., London, 1980-81; registrar St. Bartholomew's Hosp., London, 1982-84; lectr. Royal Marsden Hosp., London, 1984-87; fellow Princess Margaret Hosp., Toronto, Ont., Can., 1985-86; cons. oncologist Southampton Univ. Hosp., 1989—. Co-editor: Texbook of Clinical Oncology, 1995. Fellow Royal Coll. Radiologists, Royal Coll. Physicians. Home: Hadrian Way, Southampton SO6 7HX, England Office: Southampton Univ Hosp, Lyon St, Southampton SO9 4KY, England

HAMILTON, DARDEN COLE, state legislator, flight test engineer; b. Pitts., Nov. 28, 1956; s. Isaac Herman Hamilton and Grace Osborne (Fish) Thorp; m. Linda Susanne Moser, Aug. 7, 1976; children: Christopher Moser Hamilton, Elijah Cole Hamilton. BS in Aeronautics, St. Louis U., Cahokia, Ill., 1977; postgrad., Ariz. State U. Lic. pilot, airframe and power mechanic. Engr. McDonnell Douglas Aircraft Co., St. Louis, Mo., 1977-80; group leader, engring. Cessna Aircraft Co., Wichita, Kans., 1980-83, sr. flight test engr., 1983-85; sr. flight test engr. Allied-Signal Aerospace Co., Phoenix, 1986-92, flight test engr. specialist, 1992-98, prin. engr., 1998—; mem. Ariz. Senate, Phoenix, 1998-, vice chair transp. com., mem. appropriations com., mem. fin. com., mem. health com. Editor Family Proponent Newsletter, 1994-98. Mem. Ariz. Gov.'s Constnl. Commemoration Com., 1997-99; bd. dirs. Ariz. House and Senate Chaplaincy, 1997-98, chmn. bd. advisors, 1998—; Desert Sky precinct committeeman Glendale Rep. Com.; vol. coord. legis. dist. 16 campaign John Shadegg for Congress, 1994-96; mem. adult edn. dept. Rivers Cmty. Ch.; del. Ariz. dist. 16 Ariz. Rep. Conv., 1995—; resolutions com. Ariz. Rep. Com., Ariz. govs. mil. base retention task force, 1999—; chmn. Ariz. Senate domestic violence task force, 1999—, Ariz. Space Commn., 2000—. Mem. NRA (life, cert. instr.), Soc. Flight Test Engrs., Am. Helicopter Soc., Am. Legis. Exch. Coun., Ariz. State Rifle and Pistol Assn. (life), Ariz. Space Commn. Avocations: horses, target shooting, camping. Home: 5533 W Christy Dr Glendale AZ 85304-3889 Office: Allied-Signal Aerospace Co 111 S 34th St Phoenix AZ 85034-2802 Address: Ariz State Senate Rm 304 1700 W Washington St Phoenix AZ 85007

HAMILTON, DAVID MIKE, publishing company executive; b. Little Rock, 1951; s. Ralph Franklin and Mickey Garnette H.; m. Carol Nancy McKenna, Oct. 25, 1975; children: Elisabeth Michelle, Caroline Ellen. BA, Pitzer Coll., 1973; MLS, UCLA, 1976. Cert. tchr. library sci., Calif. Editor Sullivan Assocs., Palo Alto, Calif., 1973-75; curator Henry E. Huntington Library, San Marino, Calif., 1976-80; mgr. prodn., mktg. William Kaufmann Pubs., Los Altos, Calif., 1980-84; pres. The Live Oak Press, Palo Alto, 1984—; cons. editor, gen. ptnr. Sensitive Expressions Pub. Co., Palo Alto, 1985—; consulting dir. AAAI Press, 1994—; mng. editor and pub. AI Mag. Author: To the Yukon with Jack London, 1980, The Tools of My Trade, 1986, Making A Digital Book, 1994; contbg. editor and webmaster AAAI world-wide web site, 1995—; contbg. author Small Press jour., 1986, Making a Digital Book, 1995, (books) Book Club of California Quarterly, 1985, Research Guide to Biography and Criticism, 1986. Sec. vestry Trinity Parish, Menlo Park, 1986, bd. dirs., 1985-87; trustee Jack London Ednl. Found., San Francisco; bd. dirs. ISYS Forum, Palo Alto, 1987-96; pres. site coun., mem. supt.'s adv. com. Palo Alto Unified Sch. Dist.; mem. Wellesley Coll. Parent's Coun., 1997—. Mem. ALA, Coun. on Scholarly, Med. and Ednl. Pubs., Am. Assn. Artificial Intelligence (bd. dirs. 1984—, dir. publs.), Bookbuilders West (book show com. 1983), Author's Guild, Soc. Tech. Communication (judge 1984), Assn. Computing Machinery (chmn. pub. com. 1984), Soc. Scholarly Pubs. (program com. 1999), Sierra Club (life), Commonwealth Club, Book Club Calif. Democrat. Episcopalian. Avocations: backpacking, camping, hiking, book collecting. Office: The Live Oak Press PO Box 60036 Palo Alto CA 94306-0036

HAMILTON, HOWARD HENRY, educational administrator; b. Glen Cove, N.Y., May 27, 1935; s. Howard Henry and Josephine (Coddington) H.; m. Rosemarie Margaret Adinolfi, June 16, 1972; children: Sharon, Francis, Lyn, Marie. BS in Bus. Mgmt., Providence Coll., 1957; MS in Counseling, St. John's U., 1966. Asst. to plant mgr. Circle Wire & Cable Co., Syosset, N.Y., 1958-59; fin. adminstr. Sperry Rand, New Hyde Park, N.Y., 1959-61; asst. admissions, records, fin. aid St. John's U., Jamaica, N.Y., 1961-66; dep. dir. univ. admissions Fairleigh Dickinson U., Rutherford, N.J., 1966-91; pres. Ednl. Svcs. Internat., 1991—; founder, pres. ES: USA, Inc., 1992—; chmn. Becton Dickinson & Co., Internat. Scholarship Com. Chmn. bd. dirs. Psychotherapy Assocs., Bayonne, N.J., 1983—; advisor Circle of K. Kiwanis; pres. Kiwanis Club of Rutherford, 1980-81. Recipient Achievement award Fairleigh Dickinson U., Svc. award Korean Student Assn., 1984. Mem. Nat. Assn. Fgn. Student Advisors, Nat. Assn. Coll. Admission Counselors (Svc. award 1970-75), N.J. Assn. Coll. Admission Counselors (pres. 1981-82, Svc. award 1970-85), Middle States Assn. Collegiate Registrars and Officers of Admission (treas. 1986-87), Hotel and Restaurant Soc. (hon. life), Sigma Pi. Avocations: travel, swimming, working with college students. Home: 306 N Mountain Ave Montclair NJ 07043-1019

HAMILTON, HOWARD LAVERNE, zoology educator; b. Lone Tree, Iowa, July 20, 1916; s. Harry Stephen and Gertrude Ruth (Shibley) H.; m. Alison Phillips, Dec. 22, 1945 (dec. 1972); children: Christina Helen, Phillips Howard, Martha Jayne; m. Elizabeth Burnley Bentley, June 18, 1975; children: Elizabeth Marshall, Catherine Randolph. B.A. with highest distinction, State U. Iowa, 1937, M.S., 1938; postgrad., U. Rochester, 1938-40; Ph.D., Johns Hopkins U., 1941. Asst. prof. to prof. zoology Iowa State U., 1946-62, acting head, 1960-61, chmn. dept. zoology and entomology, 1961-62; prof. biology U. Va., 1962-82, prof. emeritus, 1982—. Author: Lillie's Development of the Chick, 1952; cons. editor, McGraw-Hill Ency. Sci. and Tech., 1962-78; mng. editor: The Am. Zoologist, 1965-70; Author: (with Viktor Hamburger) Citation Classic: A Series of Normal Stages in the Development of the Chick, 1951. Served to capt. Med. Adminstrv. Corp., AUS, 1941-45, to col. USAR, 1945-69. Mem. Am. Soc. Zoologists, Am. Soc. Naturalists, Soc. Developmental Biology, Internat. Inst. Devel. Biology, Am. Inst. Biol. Sci., Nat. Soc. Ams. of Royal Descent (pres. gen. 1974-80, hon. life pres. gen. 1980—), SAR (nat. exec. com., pres. Va. Soc. 1979-80, registrar gen. 1980-82, pres. gen. 1982-83, Minuteman award and Gold Good Citizenship medal), Order of Three Crusades 1096-1192 (historian gen. 1976-83, 1st v.p. gen. 1983—), Assn. Preservation Va. Antiquities, Va. Hist. Soc. Club: Farmington Country. Home: Jumping Branch Farm 1906 Garth Rd Charlottesville VA 22901-5411 Office: U Va Dept Biology Gilmer Hall Charlottesville VA 22901

HAMILTON, JACK RICHARD, retired social psychologist; b. Sioux City, Iowa, Oct. 19, 1940; s. Eugene Niles and Frances Maxine Hamilton. Degree in social psychology, U. Iowa, 1963. Asst. exec. dir., nat program dir. Nat. Epilepsy League, Chgo., 1969-72; ptnr. Hamilton Med. Equipment, Cedar Rapids, Iowa, 1972-85; pvt. practice bus. cons. Chgo., 1985-99; ret., 1999.

Author, dir. Chgo. Placement Program, 1970 (Citation, Pres. Lyndon Johnson 1971). Congl. liaison Nat. Assn. Med. Equipment Suppliers, Washington, 1978-85. White House grantee, 1970.

HAMILTON, JAMES DOUGLAS, economics educator; b. Denver, Colo., Nov. 29, 1954; s. Warren Bell and Alcita Victoria Hamilton; m. Marjorie Ann Flavin, Aug. 6, 1983; children: Laura Diane, Richard Gregory. BA, Colo. Coll., 1977; MA, U. Calif., Berkeley, 1981, PhD, 1983. From asst. prof. to assoc. prof. to prof. econs. U. Va., Charlottesville, 1981-92; prof. econs. U. Calif., San Diego, 1992—; vis. prof. U. Calif., San Diego, 1984-85; rsch. advisor Fed. Res. Bank, Richmond, Va., 1989-92; rsch. assoc. Nat. Bur. Econ. Rsch. Assoc. editor Jour. Econ. Dynamics and Control, 1988—, Jour. Bus. and Econ. Statistics, 1991—, Econometrica, 1992-95, Rev. Econs. and Statistics, 1993—, Jour. Money, Credit and Banking, 1993—. Grad. fellow NSF U. Calif., 1978-81; rsch. grantee NSF, 1988—. Fellow Econometric Soc.; mem. Am. Econ. Assn., Soc. Econ. Dynamics and Control. Office: U Calif San Diego Dept Econs San Diego CA 92093-0508

HAMILTON, LESLIE JAMES, oceanographer; b. Chinchilla, Queensland, Australia, Feb. 16, 1952; s. Vincent and Kathleen Browne (Langan) H.; m. Doreen Yunqi Chen, Apr. 10, 1996; 1 child, Dale. BS, James Cook U. North Queensland, Townsville, Australia, 1972; grad. diploma of phys. oceanography, U. NSW, Sydney, Australia, 1985. Exptl. officer Def. Sci. and Tech. Orgn., Sydney, 1981-88; sci. officer Australian Oceanographic Data Ctr., Sydney, 1988; profl. officer Def. Sci. and Tech. Orgn., Sydney, 1988-94, sr. profl. officer, 1994—. Contbr. articles to profl. jours. Mem. Australian Marine Sci. Orgn. Avocations: table tennis, music, bridge, traveling. Office: Def Sci and Tech Orgn, Wharf 17 Pirrama Rd, 2009 Pyrmont NSW, Australia

HAMILTON, LIAM, high court official. Pres. High Ct., Dublin, Ireland; chief justice Supreme Ct, Dublin, Ireland. Office: The High Court, Four Courts Morgan Pl, Dublin 7, Ireland also: Supreme Ct, Four Cts, Dublin Ireland*

HAMILTON, PHILLIP ALEXANDER, physicist; b. Launceston, Australia, Mar. 26, 1942; s. Robert and Hope (Brown) H.; m. Margaret Mary Atkins, Dec. 21, 1963; children: Sally Jane, Jenny Ann. BS, U. Tasmania, 1962, PhD, 1970, DSc, 1984. From lectr. in physics to pro vice-chancellor rsch. U. Tasmania, Hobart, 1965-97; pro vice-chancellor Deakin U., Victoria, 1997—. Fellow Royal Astronomical Soc., Australian Inst. Physics, Instn. Engrs. Australia. Office: Deakin U, Geelong, Victoria Australia 3217

HAMILTON, RHODA LILLIAN ROSÉN, guidance counselor, language educator, consultant; b. Chgo., May 8, 1915; d. Reinhold August and Olga (Peterson) Rosén; m. Douglas Edward Hamilton, Jan. 23, 1936 (div. Feb. 1952); remarried, Aug. 1995 (dec. 1997); children: Perry Douglas, John Richard Hamilton. Grad., Moser Coll., Chgo., 1932-33; BS in Edn., U. Wis., 1953, postgrad., 1976; MAT, Rollins Coll., 1967; postgrad., Ohio State U., 1959-60; postgrad. in clin. psychology, Mich. State U., 1971, 76, 79, 80; postgrad., Yale U., 1972, Loma Linda U., 1972; postgrad. in computer mgmt. sys., U. Okla., 1976; postgrad. in edn., U. Calif., Berkeley, 1980. Exec. sect. to pres. Ansul Chem. Co., Marinette, Wis., 1934-36; pers. counselor Burneice Larson's Med. Bur., Chgo., 1954-56; adminstrv. asst. to Ernst C. Schmidt Lake Geneva, Wis., 1956-58; assoc. prof. fin. aid Ohio State U., 1958-60; tchr. English to spkrs. of other langs. Istanbul, Turkey, 1960-65; counselor Groveland (Fla.) H.S., 1965-68; guidance counselor, psychol. cons. early childhood edn. Dept. Def. Overseas Dependents Sch., Okinawa, 1968-85; instr./lectr. early childhood Lake Sumter Jr. Coll., Leesburg, Fla., 1986-88; pres. Hamilton Assocs., Groveland, Fla., 1986—; vis. lectr. Okla. State U., 1980; co-owner plumbing, heating bus., Marinette, 1943-49; journalist Rockford (Ill.) Morning Star, 1956-58, Istanbul AP, 1960; lectr. Lake Sumter C.C., 1989—, Lake Sumter Jr. Coll., 1989. Author poetry on Middle East, 1959-64; Career Awareness, 1978; Listen Up, 1997-98. Vol. instr. U.S. citizenship classes, Okinawa, 1971-72; judge Gold Scholarships Okinawa Christian Schs., 1983, 84. Mem. Am. Fedn. Govt. Employees, Fla. Retired Educators, Order Ea. Star (organist; life mem. Shuri One in Okinawa and Trillium 208 in Wis.), Marinette Woman's Club (Wis., pres. 1949-51), Groveland Woman's Club (Fla.), Phi Delta Gamma. Episcopalian. Home: 2408 Ellsworth Way Apt 1A Frederick MD 21702-3124

HAMILTON, RICHARD A., retired military officer, aeronautical engineer; b. Romney, W.Va., Sept. 6, 1933; s. George Robert and Margaret A. Hamilton; m. Carolyn A. Kuhn, June 5, 1956; children: Robert Michael, Richard A. Jr., Amy Melissa. BS in Aero. Engring., W.Va. U., 1956; MS in Aerospace Engring., Air Force Inst. Tech., 1965. Commd. 2d lt. USAF, 1956, advanced through grades to col., 1978, ret., 1986; project mgr. Sci. Applications Internat., San Diego, 1987-92; adj. prof. Embry Riddle Aero. U., Hickam AFB, Hawaii, 1994—. Decorated Disting. Flying cross USAF, Song Be, Vietnam, 1968. Mem. Armed Forces Comm. Electronics Assn., Daedalians. Avocations: woodworking, model building, computers, electronics, tennis. E-mail: dicaham@aol.com. Home: 98-719 Iho Pl Apt 501 Aiea HI 96701-2528

HAMILTON, ROBERT OTTE, lawyer; b. Marysville, Ohio, July 27, 1927; s. George Robinson and Annette (Otte) H.; m. Phyllis Eileen Clark, Dec. 16, 1962; children: Nathan Clark, Scott Robert. AB, Miami U., Oxford, Ohio, 1950; JD, U. Mich., 1953. Bar: Ohio 1953, U.S. Supreme Ct. 1960. Sole practice, Marysville, 1953—; pros. atty. Union County, Ohio, 1957-65; city atty. City of Marysville, 1965-81. Mem. Union, Morrow and Delaware Mental Health Bd., 1957-72; pres. Marysville Jaycees, 1954; pres. Union County Hist. Assn., 1961-63; mem. Union County Republican Exec. Com., 1955-65, sec., 1955-60. Served with USN, 1945-46, to lt. (j.g.) USNR, 1946-66. Mem. ABA, Ohio State Bar Assn. (chmn. jr. bar sect. 1961, ho. of dels. 1976-86, exec. com. 1983-86), Ohio State Bar Found. (pres. 1996), Union County Bar Assn. (pres. 1960), Ohio Acad. Trial Lawyers. Lodge: Masons. Home: 432 W 6th St Marysville OH 43040-1464 Office: 116 S Court St Marysville OH 43040-1545

HAMILTON, T(HOMAS) STEWART, hospital administrator; b. Detroit; s. J.T. Stewart and Lucy Safford Hamilton; married, June 30, 1931; children: Ann Brainerd, Barbara Almy, Jeanne. AB, Williams U., 1934; ScD (hon.), Williams Coll., 1969, Trinity Coll., 1962, U. Hartford, 1976; MB, Wayne State U., 1938, MD, 1939. Gen. practice medicine Wallfleet, Mass., 1940-41; asst. dir. Mass. Gen. Hosp., Boston, 1941, 46-48; dir. Newton (Mass.)-Wellesley Hosp., 1948-62, Hartford (Conn.) Hosp., 1962-76; prof. U. Conn. Sch. Medicine, Farmington, 1976—. Home: 80 Loeffler Rd Apt G315 Bloomfield CT 06002-2290

HAMILTON-BURKE, IAN DOUGLAS, accountant; b. Bolton, Eng., Oct. 14, 1943; s. John Douglas and Jean Hamilton (Drane) B.; m. Joan Planché, July 8, 1970; children: James Patrick Ian, Victoria Roisin, Andrew Charles Raoul. Student, Liverpool Coll., 1951-60. Fellow Inst. Chartered Accts. in Eng. and Wales. Ptnr. Poulsoms, Liverpool, Eng., 1968-85, Hodgson Impey, Liverpool, 1985-90, Pannell Kerr Forster, Liverpool, 1990-91, Hamilton-Burke Dufau, Liverpool, 1991—; dir. Chrisp Hotels, Windermere, Eng., 1968-98, Minster Exec., London, 1978-86, Curtins Holdings, PLC, Liverpool, 1988—, Curtins Cons. Engrs., PLC, 1998—. Mem. com. Liverpool Marie Curie Home, 1978—; gov. Liverpool Coll., 1988—. Mem. Worshipful Co. Pipe Makers Tobacco Blenders (freeman, liveryman). Avocations: hockey, marathons, fell walking. Office: Gladstone House, 2 Church Rd, Liverpool L15 9EG, England

HAMILTON-KEMP, THOMAS ROGERS, organic chemist, educator; b. Lebanon, Ky., May 13, 1942; s. Thomas Rogers and Catherine Rose (Hamilton) K.; m. Lois Ann Groce, Sept. 13, 1980. AA, St. Catharine Coll., 1962; BA, U. Ky., 1964, PhD in Chemistry, 1970. Asst. prof. natural products chemistry U. Ky., Lexington, 1970-75, assoc. prof., 1975-85, prof., 1985—. Contbr. articles to profl. jours. Mem. AAAS, SAR, Am. Chem. Soc., Am. Soc. Hort. Sci., Filson Club, Sigma Xi, Gamma Sigma Delta. Democrat. Roman Catholic. Home: 2025 Williamsburg Rd Lexington KY 40504-3015 Office: U Ky Agrl Sci Ctr N Rm N308 Lexington KY 40546-0001

HAMILTON-MILLER, JEREMY MARCUS TOM, medical microbiology educator; b. London, Sept. 2, 1938; s. Dudley James Vincent and Pamela (Russell) H.; m. Susan Rosemary Clarke, May 1, 1965; children: Timothy James, Julia Clare. BA, U. Cambridge, U.K., 1960; PhD, U. London, 1964, DSc, 1980. Rsch. asst. Guys Hosp. Med. Sch., London, 1961-65; rsch. fellow Dunn Sch. of Pathology, U. Oxford, 1966-70, Charing Cross Hosp. Med. Sch., London, 1970-71; lectr., then sr. lectr., reader and prof. Royal Free Hosp. Sch. of Medicine, London, 1972—. Contbr. over 400 scientific articles to profl. jours. Mem. Ch. of Eng. Avocations: gardening, woodworking, home brewing. Home: 13 Belmont Rd, Twickenham Middlesex TW2 5DA, England Office: Royal Free Hosp Sch of Medicine, Pond St, London NW3 2QG, United Kingdom

HAMILTON-SMITH, ELERY, sociologist; b. Harben Vale, Australia, Dec. 28, 1929; s. Thorold Mervyn and Elizabeth Jane (Chapman) S.; m. Shirley Gertrude Mather, May 20, 1950 (div. 1969); children: Anthony, Darien, Philippa, Felicity; m. Jean Elder, Feb. 23, 1970 (div. 1984); children: Simone, Alexander; m. Angela Vaughan Millane, June 21, 1989; children: Katrina, Michelle, Amanda. AUA, Univ. Adelaide, 1956. Devel. officer Victorian Assn. Youth Clubs, Melbourne, Australia, 1959-66; cons. Edn. Divsn. Commonwealth Secretarat, London, 1972; adv. on social devel. United Nations Devel. Program, Teheran, Iran, 1974-75; prof. Royal Melbourne Inst. of Tech., Melbourne, 1977-93, La Trobe Univ., Melbourne, 1994—; mng. dir. Conservation Planning Survey Svcs., Melbourne, 1969-94, Rethink Cons. Pty. Ltd., Melbourne, 1996—. Editor: Le Jeu: Miroir De La Sociètè, 1994; author: Rethinking Dementia, 1995; author/editor: Guidelines for Cave and Karst Protection, 1997, Teaching About Dementia, 1997. Bd. dirs. Buoyancy Found., Melbourne, 1968-74; commn. Australian Frontier, Melbourne, 1968-80; active World Commn. on Protected Areas, Gland, Switzerland, 1993—. Recipient Faculty Enrichment award, Gov. Can., 1990, Thomas Ramsay scholar Mus. of Victoria, 1993-94. Mem. Australasian Assn. of Social Workers (hon. life mem.), Internat. Sociological Assn., Australian Cave Karst Mgmt. Assn. Avocations: cave exploration & rsch., environmental protection, historical rsch., cooking, reading. Office: Rethink Cons P/L, PO Box 36, 3053 Carlton South Australia

HAMIT, FRANCIS GRANGER, freelance writer; b. N.Y.C., Oct. 6, 1944; s. Harold Francis and Ethel Cordelia (Granger) H.; m. Doris Elaine Pratt Kaesser, May 31, 1974 (div. Mar. 1978). B of Gen. Studies, U. Iowa, 1972, MFA in English, 1976. Freelance writer Iowa City, Chgo., L.A., 1975—; area capt. RRS Security, Ill., 1977; sales rep. Wells Fargo Co. Inc., Chgo., 1979-80; assoc. editor Video Action Mag., Chgo., 1982; factory rep. Hoover Co., L.A., 1987-88; v.p. sales and mktg. EPIC Pvt. Security, West Covina, Calif., 1989-90. Author: Virtual Reality and the Exploration of Cyberspace, 1993; author, dir.: (play) Marlowe: An Elizabethan Tragedy, 1988; contbg. editor: Security Technology and Design Mag., 1993—, Advanced Imaging Mag., 1994—; contbr. 15th edit. Ency. Britannica, 1981-82. With U.S. Army, 1967-71, Vietnam, Germany. Mem. Am. Soc. Indsl. Security, Nat. Mil. Intelligence Assn., L.A. Sci. Fantasy Soc., Assn. Former Intelligence Officers. Democrat. Buddhist.

HAMLETT, JAMES GORDON, electronics engineer, management consultant, educator; b. Utica, N.Y.. BSEE, Syracuse U., 1947-49; BSBA, SUNY, Syracuse, 1985; MBA, City U., Seattle, 1991. Cert. profl. cons.; chartered cons.; cert. vocat. edn. tchr., N.Y.; 1st class radiotel. lic. with ship radar endorsement, FCC. Engr.-writer Warner, N.Y., Inc., Syracuse, 1952-54; vocation edn. tchr. evenings adult edn. Syracuse Cen. Tech. H.S., 1956-62; project leader GE, Syracuse, 1966-90; mgmt. cons. Syracuse, 1990—; adj. faculty City U., Seattle; pres., mgmt. cons. IntraGlobal Mgmt., Inc., Syracuse, N.Y., 1994—; lectr. City Univ. Trencin, Slovakia, 1995; steering com. Empire State Coll. SUNY, 1995—; spkr. in field. Author: Your Television Set, 1953, Engineering-Related Abbreviations, 1980-84 (VIP award 1980). Prin. Onondaga (N.Y.) Flood Control Com., 1962; tennis coach U.S. Jaycees, North Syracuse, N.Y., 1968; mem. steering com., sec., mem. exec. com. L.C. Smith Coll. Engring. and Computer Sci., Syracuse U., 1991, founding officer Alumni Assn., 1994—; keynote spkr. VA Regional Hosp., 1995. With U.S. Army, 1942-45, ETO. Recipient Cert. of Appreciation for Outstanding Dedication L.C. Smith Coll. Engring and Computer Sci. Syracuse U., 1993, Testimonial-Belgium Remembers (Battle of the Bulge), Ctr. Rsch. and Info. of Battle of Ardennes, Liége, Belgium, 1996, Citation for disting. svc. during Battle of Bulge, N.Y. State Senate Dist., 1996, N.Y. State Conspicuous Svc. medal, 1997; Bus. and Mgmt. Lectureship Ctrl. European grant, Slovakia, 1994-95. Fellow Soc. for Tech. Commn. (internat. stem mgr., mgmt. theory and practice 1980, exec. com.); mem. IEEE (life sr., exec. com. Cert. 1981, editor Syracuse Scanner 1959-69), VFW, N.Y. Acad. Scis. (cert. 1985), Am. Mgmt. Assn. Internat., Profl. Cons. Assn. Ctrl. N.Y., Am. Cons. League, Internat. Platform Assn., Syracuse GE Engrs. Assn., Greater Syracuse C. of C., Syracuse U. Alumni Assn., Am. Soc. Tng. and Devel., Empire State Coll. Alumni Assn. (pres. Syracuse area alumni/student assn.), City U. Alumni (life), Vets. Battle of the Bulge (life, historian, treas.), Order of the Engr. Avocations: tournament tennis (Wimbledon, Eng. 1969), reading management practice, music. Home: 330 Everingham Rd Syracuse NY 13205-3258

HAMLETT, TIMOTHY FLOYD, journalism educator; b. London, Sept. 16, 1945; arrived in Hong Kong, 1980; s. Bernard John and Vera Venetia (Davies) H.; m. Christine Suk Yin Cheung, Mar. 23, 1984; 1 child, M. Brunel. BA in History, Oxford (Eng.) U., 1967, diploma in edn., 1968; MA in War Studies, U. London, 1969. Sub-editor West Lancs Gazette, U.K., 1978-79; night sub-editor Newcastle Jour., U.K., 1979-80; chief sub-editor HK Std., 1980-82, Sunday Post, 1982-84; assoc. editor Hong Kong Std., 1984-87; assoc. prof. Hong Kong Bapt. U., 1988—; contbg. editor Hong Kong Bus. mag., 1988—; writer, presenter Radio TV Hong Kong, 1982—; editl. cons. Choice Comm. Internat. Ltd., Hong Kong, 1987-92; columnist South China Morning Post, Hong Kong, 1992—. Contbr. news stories to profl. publs.; radio program writer, presenter: Hong Kong Commercial Radio, 1989. Recipient Hong Kong News award (3), 1985, (2), 1986. Mem. Soc. for Prevention of Cruelty of Animals, Hong Kong Journalists Assn., Hong Kong Press Club (hon. life mem.). Office: Hong Kong Bapt U Dept Journalism, 224 Waterloo Rd, Kowloon Hong Kong

HAMLIN, ERNEST LEE, religious organization administrator, Christian education consultant; b. Sussex, Va., Dec. 9, 1943; s. Arish Lee and Elma Roseanna (Coleman) H.; divorced; 1 child, Cherry. BA, Va. Union U., 1970, MDiv, 1974; MA, Presbyn. Sch. Christian Edn., Richmond, Va., 1976. Ordained to ministry United Ch. of Christ, 1975. Asst. pastor Mt. Zion Bapt. Ch., Charlottesville, Va., 1971-79; interim pastor Jerusalem Bapt. Ch., Sparta, Va., 1980; pastor Bethesda Bapt. Ch., Colonial Heights, Va., 1981-83, Union Hill United Ch. of Christ, Sedley, Va., 1986-89; pres., CEO Christian Edn. Ministries, Richmond, 1990; pastor Emmanuel-St. Mark's United Ch. of Christ, Saginaw, Mich., 1990-92; exec. dir. Christian Edn. Ministries, Newport News, Va., 1997; sr. pastor Tubman-King Community Ch., Daytona Beach, Fla., 1992-93; interim pastor Ch. of the Open Door United Ch. of Christ, Miami, Fla., 1994; mem. corp. bd. Bd. for World Ministries, United Ch. of Christ; Christian edn. lectr. local chs., Richmond, 1974-90; counselor/chaplain Med. Coll. Va., Richmond, 1976-77; edn. cons./counselor Smithdeal-Massey Bus. Coll., Richmond, 1978; substitute tchr. Richmond Pub. Schs., 1979-83; admissions rep./ednl. cons. Rutledge Coll., Richmond, 1984. Counselor Janie Porter Barrett Sch. for Juvenile Delinquents, Hanover County, Va., 1973; house mgr. Offender Aid and Restoration Hospitality House, Richmond, 1979-87; active United Ch. of Christ Clergy Cluster, Elon Homes for Children campaign com., Covenant Assn., St. John's Mission Coun., Halifax Ministerial Assn., Halifax Habitat for Humanity, Fla. Impact, various others. Recipient Outstanding Svc. award Richmond Va. Seminary, 1986, Merit award, World of Poetry, 1990; named Honorary Chairperson United Negro Coll. Fund, 1983. Mem. United Black Christians, Acad. of Parish Clergy, Nat. Assn. Black Achievers, Kappa Alpha Psi. Office: Christian Edn Ministries 1001 41st St Newport News VA 23607-2343

HAMLIN, GEORGE L., technical writer; b. Des Moines, Aug. 25, 1939; s. George L. Hamlin and Marian E. Haven; m. Betsy A. Hamlin, June 9, 1962. BS, Iowa State U., 1961. Tech. writer Naval Ordnance Lab., White Oak, Md., 1962-69; sr. tech. writer Naval Ordnance Lab., White Oak, 1969-74, Naval Surface Weapons Ctr., White Oak, 1974-88, Naval Surface Warfare Ctr., White Oak, 1988-94, Advanced Tech. and Rsch., Burtonsville, Md., 1995—; mem. stds. com. Soc. for Tech. Comm., Washington, 1969-70; corp. planning group Dir. Navy Labs., Washington, 1976-84; tech. manual stds. com. Naval Sea Sys. Command, Washington, 1982-89; mgr. White Oak Lab. Employees Assn., 1988-93. Co-author: Packard: A History of the Motor Car and the Company, 1978 (Best Auto History Book 1979), Complete Handbook of Automobile Hobbies, 1981; sr. editor The Packard Cormorant, 1975—; contbr. articles to profl. jours. Town councilman Riverdale (Md.) Town Coun., 1971-73; police commr. Riverdale Police Dept., 1972-73; bd. dirs. Am.'s Packard Mus., Dayton, Ohio, 1996-97; trustee Packard Found., Dayton, 1998—. With U.S. Army, 1963. Recipient Excellence in Newspaper Writing award William Randolph Hearst Found., 1960. Mem. Packard Automobile Classics Inc. (trustee, v.p. internat. 1991—, Weiss trophy 1999), Soc. Automotive Historians, Profl. Car Soc. (founder, chpts. chmn. 1985—, Appreciation award 1999), Antique Automobile Club Am., Studebaker Drivers Club (regional mgr. 1966—), Theodore Roosevelt H.S. Found. Avocations: automobile restoration, Pepsi collectibles. E-mail: geohamlin@juno.com. Office: PO Box 123 Fulton MD 20759-0123

HAMLIN, HARRY ROBINSON, actor; b. Pasadena, Calif., Oct. 30, 1951; s. Chauncey Jerome and Bernice (Robinson) H.; 1 son by previous marriage, Dimitri Alexander; m. Lisa Rinna, Mar. 29, 1997. B.A., Yale U.; postgrad., Am. Conservatory Theatre, San Francisco. Performances include: (films) Movie Movie, 1979, Clash of The Titans, 1981, King of the Mountain, 1981, Making Love, 1982, Blue Skies Again, 1983, Maxie, 1985, Dinner At Eight, 1990, The Celluloid Closet, 1995, Badge of Betrayal, 1996; (TV mini-series) Studs Lonigan, Master of the Game, 1984, Space, 1985, Favorite Son, 1988, Night Sins, 1997; (TV films) Laguna Heat, 1987, Deceptions, 1990, Deadly Intentions...Again?, 1991, Deliver Them From Evil: The Taking of Alta View, 1991, Save Me, 1992, Under Investigation, 1993, Poisoned by Love: The Kern County Murders, 1993, In the Best of Families: Marriage, Pride and Madness, 1994, Tom Clancy's Op Center, 1995, Her Deadly Rival, 1995, One Clean Move, 1996, Badge of Betrayal, 1996, Allie & Me, 1997, Night Sins, 1997, Stranger in Town, 1998, Frogs for Snakes, 1998, The Hunted, 1998, Like Father, Like Santa, 1998, Quarantine, 1999, Silent Predators, 1999; (TV series) L.A. Law, 1986-91, Movie Stars, 1999—; (Broadway debut) Awake and Sing!, 1984. ITT Fulbright grantee, 1977. Office: care Larry Taub Gersh Agency Inc 232 N Canon Dr Beverly Hills CA 90210-5302

HAMLIN, WILFRID GARDINER, retired literature and philosophy educator; b. N.Y.C.; s. Talbot Faulkner and Hilda Blanche Hamlin; m. Elizabeth Brett Hamlin, June 11, 1944 (dec. Apr. 1968); 1 child, Christopher Stone. BA, Wayne U.; MA, Antioch Coll., Yellow Springs, Ohio; PhD, Union Inst., Cin. Test psychologist Johnson O'Connor Rsch. Found., N.Y.C., 1940-42, 44-46, Adjutant Gen.'s Office, N.Y.C., 1945-46; mem. faculty Goddard Coll., Plainfield, Vt., 1948-99; coll. editor Goddard Coll., Plainfield, 1975-98, mem. emeritus faculty, 1998—; edn. cons., 1950's and 60's. Author: To Start a School, 1971; editor: Teacher/School/Child, 1964. Avocations: photography, reading, theater, films, classical music. Home: PO Box 263 Plainfield VT 05667-0263

HAMLYN, PETER JOHN, neurosurgeon; b. Ashbourne, England, Aug. 10, 1957; s. David William and Paula Anne (Bowker) H.; m. Geraldine Marrie Shepherd, May 18, 1994; children: Dominic Joseph, Gabriel Louis, Bendict James. BSc, U. Coll., London, 1979, MBBS, 1982; MD, U. London, 1993. Cons. neurosurgeon St. Bartholomews Hosp., London, 1990-95; lead cons. neurosurgeon Royal Hosps. NHS Trust, London, 1995—; hon. lectr. neurosrugery St. Bartholomews Med. Ctr., London, 1990-95; chmn. British Brain & Spine Found. Trading Ltd., London, 1996—, vice chmn., 1992—; patron Headway, North England, 1992. Contbr. scientific papers to profl. jours. Rsch. fellow U. Coll. London, 1989-96. Fellow Royal Coll. Surgeons, Inst. Sports Medicine; mem. British Med. Assn., Soc. Neurol. Surgeons Britain. Avocation: sports medicine journalism. Home: 152 Harley St, London W1N 1HH, England

HAMLYN-HARRIS, GEOFFREY, writer, publisher; b. Cairns, Queensland, Australia, Nov. 16, 1921; s. Cyril Hamlyn-Harris and Maymie Ada Stevens; m. Norma Jean Collins, July 6, 1963; 1 child, Charles Hamlyn. Ed., Queensland State Edn. Dept. With Jackeroo Scottish Australian Pastoral Co., 1937-42; pvt. farmer, grazier Palmwoods/Amiens, Australia, 1946-68; overseer officer CD Storrie Grazier, Bollon, Australia, 1960-61; leading hand Kraft Foods Pty. Ltd., Brisbane, Australia, 1961-63; literary agt. Nylmah Lit. Agy., Stanthorpe, Australia, 1963-71; author, pub. Hamlyn-Harris Pubs., Stanthorpe, 1971—; manuscript appraiser, cons. Nylnah Agy., Stanthorpe, 1963-71. Author: Through Mud and Blood to Victory, 1943, reprint, 1993, 3d edit., 1999, The Blue Bead, 1989, Tales of the Neva Wer, 1995 (Xrox Fast Book awards 1943), Brothers of Empire, 1994, (verse) Australian Point of View, Another Point of View, A Point of View Too, 1994-99. Cpl. Australian Imperial Forces, 1942-46. Decorated Def. medal Australian Govt., 1945, Pacific Svc. medal, 1945, Pacific Star, 1945, 1939/45 Star, 1945, cert. of appreciation, 1985. Mem. Queensland Arts Coun., Stanthorpe Toastmaster Club (sec. 1997-98), Stanthorpe Hist. Soc. (hon. life, sec. 1963-71, mus. custodian 1991-97). Anglican. Avocations: wood sculpture, bird watching, book illustrating, style drawing, reading. Fax: 07 46 811 450. Office: Hamlyn-Harris Pub, 5 Garden St, Stanthorpe QLD 4380, Australia

HAMMAD, IHAB ADEL, dentist, educator; b. Alexandria, Egypt, Apr. 6, 1958; s. Adel M. and Esmat K. (Khattab) H.; m. Amani M. Khalil, Aug. 16, 1983; children: Shahira, Moshira, Adel. BDS, Alexandria U., 1980; cert. prosthodontics, U. Minn., 1985, MS, 1985; DSc, Boston U., 1988. Lic. dentist (prosthodontics). Instr. Alexandria U., 1981-83, asst. prof., 1988-91, assoc. prof., 1997-99, prof., 2000—; clin. asst. prof. U. Minn., Mpls., 1985-86; asst. prof. King Saud U., Riyadh, Saudi Arabia, 1991-95, assoc. prof., 1995-97; cons. prosthodontist divsn. postgrad. prosthodontics U. Minn., Mpls., 1985-86, cons. advanced gen. dentistry, 1985-86; cons. King Saud U., Riyadh, 1991-97, Alexandria U., 1997—; lectr. Saudi Dental Soc., Riyadh, 1989-92, Medina, 1997. Contbr. articles to profl. jours. Fellow Egyptian Dental Assn.; mem. Am. Acad. Fixed Prosthodontics (S.D. Tylman's award 1986), N.Y. Acad. Scis., Alexandria Sci. Dental Soc. (clinician 1980-81, 81-82). Avocations: reading, sculpturing, automobiles, soccer, fishing. Office: Alexandria U Sch Dentistry, Champollion Street Azarita, Alexandria Egypt

HAMMAD, MAHMOUD AHMAD, mechanical engineer; b. Anata, Jerusalem, Oct. 16, 1944; arrived in Jordan, 1967; s. Ahmad Abdel-Mahdy and Adeebah Ahmad (Ibraheem) H.; m. Alia Taleb Khateeb, Jan. 1, 1969; children: Amjad, Rasha, Taleb, Ahmad, Mohammad, Rani, Ala. BS in Mech. Engring., Cairo U., 1968; MS, Strathclyde U., Glasgow, Scotland, 1976, PhD, 1982. Maintenance engr. Royal Jordan Air Force, Amman, 1968-75; lectr. U. Jordan, Amman, 1976-78, asst. prof., 1983-89; assoc. prof. U. Jordan, 1994-99, prof., 1999—, head mech. engring. dept., 1999—; cons. STATS Comp., U.K., 1989-90; dir. Tng. Ctr. Abudhabi Air Force, Abu Dhabi, United Arab Emirates, 1989-90; mem. Nat. Com. of Energy Conservation, Amman, 1993; chmn. 2nd Jordanian Internat. Conf. on Mech. Engring., 1997; chmn. Com. for Engring. Certs. Evaluation, Amman, 1997—. Author: (book) Heating and Air Conditioning, 1994; contbr. articles to profl. jours. and publs. Coun. mem. Jordan Engrs. Assn., Amman, 1995—; asst. sec. gen. Alyakza P.P., 1992-93, vice-chmn. polit. office, 1992-93. Capt., squadron comdr. Royal Jordanian Air Force, 1968-75. Recipient PhD scholarship, U. Jordan, Glasgow, 1978, Sci. Week medal Higher Coun. of Sci. and Technology, Amman, 1995, Jordanian Engrs. Assn. shield, 1997, Golden medal Golden Jubilee of Pakistan, 1997, 2000 Outstanding Scientists of the 20th Century award IBC, Cambridge. Mem. ASHRAE, Internat. Inst. Refrigeration, N.Y. Acad. Scis. Achievements include being part of the first team to build a biogas prodn. and use in a Jordan farm; locally mfg. and testing of first and second generation solar cooling units. Email: hammad@fet.ja.edu.jo. Office: Univ Jordan, PO Box 13240 Aljubaiha, Amman 11942, Jordan

HAMMADEH, MOHAMAD EID, biologist; b. Talzahab, Syria, Jan. 29, 1954; arrived in Germany, 1984; s. Mahmoud and Haloum Hammadeh; m. Constanze Fischer, Dec. 29, 1997; 1 child. DVM, Aleppo U., Syria, 1977; PhD in Vet. Medicine, Giessen (Germany) U., 1988; diploma in biol. sci., Saarland (Germany) U., 1996; diploma in mgmt., Kassel (Germany) U., 1990. Vet. Agrl. Ministry, Syria, 1977-81; h.s. tchr. Morraco, 1981-82; acad. staff Giessen (Germany) U., 1983-88; head in vitro fertilization lab. Saar-

brucken (Germany) Pvt. Hosp., 1991-95; head in vitro fertilization lab. and human reproduction U. Saarland, 1995—. Contbr. articles to profl. jours. With Syrian Army, 1977-78. Islam. Avocations: anthropology, soccer, reading about history. Home: Ginster St 1, 66424 Homburg Germany Office: Dept Ob-Gyn, U Saarland, 66421 Homburg Germany

HAMMANN, PETER J.C., management and marketing educator; b. Munich, Germany, Apr. 2, 1938; s. Ernst Wilhelm and Margherita Vittoria (Euler) H.; m. Ursula Helen Seyboth, Dec. 17, 1940; children: Sabine, Christoph, Michael. Diplom-kaufmann, LMU U., Munich, Germany, 1964, Dr.oec.publ., 1965, Dr.habil., 1970. Exec. asst. Rhein Stahlwerue, Munich, Germany, 1964-66; rsch. assoc. LMU U., Munich, Germany, 1966-70; prof. Tech. U., Berlin, Germany, 1970-74, Ruhr U., Bochum, Germany, 1974—; vis. prof. MIT, Cambridge, Mass., 1972-73; dept. dean Ruhr U., 1980-81; CEO AIF, Cologne, Germany, 1986-92, mem. sci. coun., 1986—. Author: Dec.anal. in Marketing, 1975; co-author: Marketing Research, 4th edit., 2000, Management Theory, 4th edit., 1992, Purchasing, 1986. Mem. TIMS/ORSA, AMA, Schlalenbach Soc., German Mktg. Assn. (v.p. 1989-99). Avocations: literature, fine arts, music. Home: Wasserstrasse 66, D-44803 Bochum Germany Office: Ruhr U Dept Mgmt & Econs, D-44780 Bochum Germany

HAMMARSTRÖM, LARS-ERIK, physician, consultant surgeon; b. Danderyd, Sweden, Aug. 5, 1949; s. Per Olof and Clara Linnea (Svantesson) H.; m. Toki Ito, July 15, 1972; children: Christina Linnea, Clara Louise. B of Medicine, Karolinska Inst., Stockholm, 1970, MD, 1976, specialist gen. surgery, 1980; PhD, U. Lund, Sweden, 1996. Registrar Dept. Surgery Ctrl. Hosp., Eskilstuna, Sweden, 1976-81; sr. registrar Dept. Surgery Lund Hosp., 1981-96; cons. Mälarsjukhuset, Eskilstuna, 1996—; assoc. prof. Univ. Lund, Sweden, 1998. Contbr. articles to profl. jours. Recipient Adolf Kussmaul award European Soc. Gastrointestinal Endoscopy, 1980. Mem. Internat. Coll. Digestive Surgery, Swedish Surg. Soc., Scandinavian Surg. Soc., Scandinavian Assn. digestive Endoscopy. Avocation: Nippon-to (art of Japanese sword). Home: Vallmovägen 28, 240 10 Dalby Sweden Office: Mälarsjukhuset, 631 88 Eskilstuna Sweden

HAMMARSTROM, SVEN ROBERT, biochemistry educator; b. Stockholm, Jan. 8, 1945; s. Ernst Sven and Eva Linnea Hammarstrom; m. Birgitta Anna Wiklund, Apr. 4, 1970; children: Cecilia, Johan. BM, Karolinska Inst., Stockholm, 1966, MD, 1971, PhD, 1972. Rsch. asst. Royal Vet. Coll., Stockholm, 1967-72; asst. prof. Karolinska Inst., Stockholm, 1972-74, assoc. prof., 1976-86; rsch. fellow Harvard U., Cambridge, Mass., 1974-75; prof. Linkopina U., Sweden, 1986—. Contbr. about 200 articles to profl. jours. Recipient Medicinal Chemistry award U.S. Acad. of Pharm. Scis., 1980, Swedish-Belgian Cultural award Univ. Libre, Brussels, 1982; sr. Fulbright scholar, Fulbright Commn., Washington, 1994. Mem. Swedish Soc. for Biochemistry and Molecular Biology, Am. Sco. for Biochemistry and Molecular Biology, AAAS, Swedish Med. Assn. Avocations: skating, skiing, flying. Office: Divsn Cell Biology, Linkoping Univ, Linköping S-5818, Sweden

HAMM-BRUECHER, HILDEGARD, retired politician, writer; b. Essen, Germany, May 11, 1921; m. Erwin Hamm, July 28, 1956; children: Florian, Verena. D. U. Munich, 1945, State U., Lima, Peru, 1980. City councillor Munich, 1948-54; mem. state legislature Bavaria, 1950-60, 70-76; dep. minister edn. Govt. Germany, Bonn, 1967-72; minister of state Fgn. Office, Bonn, 1976-82; mem. parliament Bonn, 1976-90. Author: Freiheit ist mehr ab ein Wort, 1996, many other books. Recipient Buber-Rosenzweig medal Christlich-Jüdische Gesellschaft, 1991, Ehrenbürger der Stadt, Munich, 1995. Mem. Free Democratic Party. Avocations: swimming, skiing. Address: Staatsministerin aD, Defreggerstr 8, 81545 Munich Germany

HAMMER, CHARLES JOHN, cabinetmaker, architectural draftsman, designer; b. Phila., June 22, 1944; s. Charles Walter and Dorothy Jane Hammer; m. Judi Ann Covington, Nov. 1, 1968 (div. June 1, 1979); children: Rena Joanne, Jonathan Mark; m. Linda Elaine Hammer, June 28, 1988. Archtl. draftsman R.P. Fox, AIA, Newark, 1968-75; cattle farmer Valley Garden Farm, Appomattox, Va., 1975-86; archtl. draftsman TAG Galyean, Lewisburg, W.Va., 1988-90, Dan Hart, AIA, Lewisburg, W.Va., 1990-92; draftsman Greenbrier Archtl. Woodwork, Ronceverte, W.Va., 1992-95, cabinetmaker, 1997—. Designer, builder wood furniture, 1980—; designer, drafter personal homes, 1986—. With USMC, 1962-66. Avocations: swimming, health/fitness, reading, hiking.

HAMMER, TERENCE MICHAEL, physician; b. Chgo., May 7, 1946; s. Albert S. and Minnetta Elizabeth (Nichols) H.; 1 child, Kathryn Gyo Hammer. BS, U. Ill., 1968; MD, Stanford U., 1973. Diplomate Am. Bd. Family Practice. Intern L.A. County-U. So. Calif. Med. Ctr., 1973-74; med. dir. Long Beach (Calif.) Health Dept. Drug Program, 1974-75; resident in family medicine Contra Costa Med. Svcs., Martinez, Calif., 1975-77; pvt. practice in family medicine Redondo Beach (Calif.) Med. Group, 1977-81, Family Practice Assocs., Torrance, Calif., 1981-96, Med. Inst. Little Co. of Mary Hosp., Torrance, 1996—; lectr. in field. Bd. trustees Peninsula Edn. Found., Palos Verdes, Calif., 1991-99; bd. examiners Malcolm Baldridge Nat. Quality Awards, 1999. Mem. Am. Coll. Physician Execs., Premier Health Med. Group (pres. 1991—), South Bay Ind. Physicians Med. Group (pres. emeritus), Soc. Chief Med. Officers, Phi Beta Kappa. Lutheran. Avocations: white water rafting, skiing, modern art collecting, swimming, writing. Office: Med Inst Little Co Mary Hosp 20911 Earl St Ste 400 Torrance CA 90503-4355

HAMMERGREN, JOHN H., health/medical products executive. BSBA, U. Minn.; MBA, Xavier U. With Baxter Healthcare Corp./Am. Hosp. Corp. and Lyphomed Inc., 1981-91; pres. med./surgical divsn. Kendall Healthcare Products Co., Mansfield, Mass., 1991-96; corp. exec. v.p., pres., CEO supply mgmt. bus. McKesson HBOC, Inc., 1996-99, co-pres. & co-CEO, 1999—. Office: McKesson HBOC Inc One Post St San Francisco CA 94104*

HAMMERSLEY, DAVID ALAN, retired chemical company executive; b. Newcastle-upon-Lyme, Eng., Jan. 18, 1936; arrived in Belgium, 1970; s. Robert Stevens and Norah (Kirkham) H.; m. Jennifer Ann Cureton, Sept. 1, 1962; children: Ann Julia Trewren, Carol Judith Pritchard. BA in Natural Scis., Cambridge (Eng.) U., 1957, M of Chem. Engring., 1958, MA, 1960. Project engr. Babcock & Wilcox Atomic Energy, London, 1958-61; chem. engr. Monsanto, Ruabon, Wales, 1961-65, rubber technologist, 1965-70; mktg. mgr. Monsanto, Brussels, 1970-77, bus. dir., 1977-89, dir. mfg., 1989-95; v.p. Europe Flexsys, Brussels, 1995-99; v.p. Plastics and Rubber Inst., U.K., 1988-90; coun. mem. Chem. Industries Assn., U.K., 1991—; chmn. Monsanto Plc., U.K., 1991-95, Interco. Productivity Group, U.K., 1992—. Fellow of Instn. of Chem. Engrs. (chartered engr.), Inst. Materials Companion Inst. Mgmt. Anglican. Avocations: tennis, mountain walking, golf, skiing.

HAMMOND, CHARLES BESSELLIEU, obstetrician, gynecologist, educator; b. Ft. Leavenworth, Kans., July 24, 1936; s. Claude G. and Alice (Sims) H.; m. Peggy A. Hammond, jUne 21, 1958; children: Sharon L., Charles B. BS, The Citadel, 1957, Duke U., 1961. Diplomate Am. Bd. Ob-Gyn. Intern in surgery Duke U., 1961-62, resident in ob-gyn, 1962-63, 66-69, fellow in reproductive endocrinology, 1963-64, asst. prof. dept. ob-gyn, 1969-73, asso. prof., 1973-78, prof., 1978-81, E.C. Hamblen prof., 1981—, chmn., 1980—. Contbr. in field. Served with USPHS, 1964-66. Fellow (hon.) Royal Coll. Ob-gyn. (ad cundeum), 1998; mem. Am. Fertility Soc. (pres. 1985), Am. Coll. Ob.-Gyn. (chmn. dist. IV 1997-2000), Am. Assn. Ob-Gyn. Found. (pres. 1996—), Assn. Profs. Obstetrics and Gynecology, Am. Gynecol. and Obstet. Soc. (pres. 1993-94), Soc. Gynecol. Investigation, N.C. Med. Soc., N.C. Soc. Obstetricians and Gynecologists (pres. 1985), Am. Gynecol. Club (pres. 1994). Presbyterian. Home: 2827 Mcdowell Rd Durham NC 27705-5604 Office: Duke U Med Ctr PO Box 3244 Durham NC 27715-3244

HAMMOND, DEANNA, educator; b. Terre Haute, Ind., Feb. 13, 1945; d. DeForest and Dorothy Illen (Spaulding) H. BS in Edn., U. Houston, 1970, MEd, 1983. Cert. tchr., reading specialist, Tex. Tchr., Gregg Elem. Sch., Houston, 1970, Fairchild Elem. Sch., Houston, 1970-77, Cen. Elem. Sch., Palacios, Tex., 1977-79, Foster Elem. Sch., Houston, 1979-90, also grade chmn.; magnet coord. John E. Codwell Elem. Sch., 1990—. Block capt. crime watch Huntington Village Civic Assn., Houston, 1982; exec. bd. PTA, Foster Sch.; dir. Vols. in Pub. Schs., Foster Sch. Mem. Tex. State Council of Internat. Reading Assn., Greater Houston Area Reading Council, Congress Houston Tchrs. (bldg. rep. 1983, 85-86), Assn. Children with Learning Disabilities, Am. Assn. Ret. Persons, PTA. Republican. Clubs: Young Homemakers (Palacios); Christian Womens Fellowship (Houston). Home: 12426 South Dr Houston TX 77099-2424 Office: John E Codwell Elem Sch 5225 Tavenor Ln Houston TX 77048-2625

HAMMOND, GLENN BARRY, SR., lawyer, electrical engineer; b. Roanoke, Va., Sept. 3, 1947; s. Howard Reichard and Billie (Cromer) H.; m. Vickie McComb, Dec. 29, 1973 (div.); 1 child, Glenn Barry II. BA, Va. Mil. Inst., 1969; MBA, So. Ill. U., 1974; JD, U. Richmond, 1978; BS elec. engring., Nova Coll., 1995. Bar: Va. 1979, U.S. Dist. Ct. (we. dist.) Va. 1979, U.S. Ct. Appeals (4th cir.) 1981, U.S. Ct. Mil. Appeals 1989, Air Force Ct. Mil. Rev. 1989, U.S. Supreme Ct., 1992. Assoc. Wilson, Hawthorne & Vogel, Roanoke, 1978-79; pvt. practice Roanoke, 1979-80, 86—; atty., advisor to chief adminstrv. law judge Social Security Adminstrn., HHS, Roanoke, 1980-86; ptnr. Wooten & Hart P.C., 1995-98; pres. R.F. Cons., Inc., Roanoke, Va., 1998—; pres. LCH Broadcasting Group, Inc. Roanoke, also bd. dirs. Editor: Psychiatry in Military Law, 1988. Sr. vice comdr. Mil. Order World Wars, Roanoke, 1981. Col. JAGC, USAF, 1969-75, Res. 1975—. Mem. Air Commando Assn. (life), DAV (life), VFW (life), AFA (life), Nat. Mil. Intelligence Assn. (life), Armed Forces Comms. Electronics Assn., Nat. Orgn. Social Security Claimants Reps., Masons.

HAMMOND, HERBERT J., lawyer, mediator, arbitrator; b. Santa Fe, May 19, 1951; m. Myra Hammond; children: Ariel, Joy. BS magna cum laude, U. N.Mex., 1973; JD, NYU, 1976. Bar: Tex. 1977, U.S. Patent and Trademark Office 1977. Sr. ptnr. Thompson & Knight, Dallas. Contbr. to law jours. Mem. State Bar Tex. (vice chmn. com. on computerization of the profession 1989-92, chair computer sect. 1994-95, newsletter editor computer sect.), Am. Intellectual Property Law Assn., Dallas Bar Assn. (chair intellectual property sect. 1998), Phi Beta Kappa, Phi Kappa Phi, Kappa Mu Epsilon. Office: Thompson & Knight 1700 Pacific Ave Ste 3300 Dallas TX 75201-4693

HAMMOND, ISAAC WILLIAM, physician, epidemiologist; b. Cape Coast, Ghana, Mar. 17, 1951; s. Charles Williams and Beatrice Hammond; m. Marilyn Barker, June 11, 1977 (div. May 1981); 1 child, Allotey; m. Hoora Rahimi, Aug. 31, 1982; children: Mohammed, Mustafa, Reza, Mahjub, Sarah. BS, Calif. State U., 1976; MPH, Ind. State U., 1979; PhD, U. Okla., 1982; MD, U. Fla., 1989. Fellow U. Okla. Health Sci. Ctr., Oklahoma City, 1979-82; NIH fellow Cornell U. Med. Ctr., N.Y.C., N.Y., 1982-84; intern, resident Emory U. Med. sch., Atlanta, 1989-92; resident Tulane U. Med. Sch., New Orleans, 1992-93; staff physician, dir. hypertension clin. VA Med. Ctr., New Orleans, 1993-96; adj. assoc. prof. Tulane U. Sch. Pub. Health & Tropical Medicine, 1994-98; pres., dir. clin. rsch., dir. outcomes rsch. and disease state mgmt. Am. Rsch. Assocs., 1996—; reviewer FDA, 1996-98, Eli Lilly & Co., 1998—; assoc. prof. Ind. U., 1999—, U. North Tex., 1997—. Grantee NIH, Astra-Merck, Am. Heart Assn., WHO, Nat. Heart, Lung & Blood Inst. Mem. AMA, Am. Coll. Physicians, Am. Fedn. Clin. Rsch., Am. Soc. Hypertension, Am. Soc. Internal Medicine, Internat. Soc. Hypertension in Blacks, Nat. Med. Assn., N.Y. Acad. Sci., Royal Soc. Health, Soc. Epidemiol. Rsch., Soc. Gen. Internal Medicine, So. Med. Assn. Office: Am Rsch Assocs PO Box 3572 Carmel IN 46082-3572

HAMMOND, JANE LAURA, retired law librarian, lawyer; b. nr. Nashua, Iowa; d. Frank D. and Pauline Hammond. BA, U. Dubuque, 1950; MS, Columbia U., 1952; JD, Villanova U., 1965, LHD, 1993. Bar: Pa. 1965. Cataloguer Harvard Law Libr., 1952-54; asst. libr. Sch. Law Villanova (Pa.) U., 1954-62; libr. Sch. Law, Villanova (Pa.) U., 1962-76; prof. law Sch. Law Villanova (Pa.) U., 1965-76; law libr., prof. law Cornell U., Ithaca, N.Y., 1976-93; adj. prof. Drexel U., 1971-74; mem. depository libr. coun. to pub. printer U.S. Govt. Printing Office, 1975-78; cons. Nat. Law Libr., Monrovia, Liberia, 1989. Fellow ALA; mem. ABA (coun. sect. legal edn. 1984-90, mem. com. on accreditation 1982-87, mem. com. on stds. rev. 1987-95), PEO, Coun. Nat. Libr. Assn. (sec.-treas. 1971-72, chmn. 1979-80), Am. Assn. Law Librs. (sec. 1965-70, pres. 1975-76). Episcopalian. Office: Cornell U Sch Law Myron Taylor Hall Ithaca NY 14853

HAMMOND, KEVIN, computer scientist, educator; b. Ipswich, Suffolk, Eng., June 17, 1962; s. Brian Keith and Maureen (Clarke) H. BSc with honors, U. East Aglia, Norwich, Eng., 1983, PhD, 1989. Rsch. asst. Glasgow (Scotland) U., 1989-92, rsch. fellow, 1992-95; lectr. St. Andrews (Scotland) U., 1995—. Author: Parallel SML: A Functional Language and Its Implementation in Dactl, 1989; editor: Research Directions in Parallel Functions Programming, 2000. Scottish Office for Econ. Devel. rsch. fellow Royal Soc. Edinburgh, 1992; rsch. grantee U.K. Engring. and Phys. Scis. Rsch. Coun., 1993, 98, Brit. Coun., 1999, 2000. Mem. Assn. for Computing Machinery. Avocations: mountain climbing, early music, running, board games. Office: U St Andrews Computer Sci, North Haugh, Saint Andrews KY16 9SS, Scotland

HAMMOND, LISA A., oncologist, researcher; b. Lima, Peru, Aug. 28, 1958; d. Benjamin Berry and Patricia Feid Thelin; m. Kevin Lee Hammond, Oct. 29, 1994. BA, Stephens Coll., 1979; M in Internat. Mgmt., Am. Grad. Sch. Internat. Mgmt., 1982; MD, U. Tex., San Antonio, 1991. Intern U. Tex. Health Sci. Ctr., San Antonio, 1991-92, resident internal medicine, 1992-94, oncology fellow, 1994-97, instr. oncology, 1997-98; clin. rschr. Inst. for Drug Devel., San Antonio, 1998—; bd. dirs. Am. Cancer Soc., San Antonio. Choir mem. Wayside Chapel; alt. del. Tex. Rep. Conv., 1998. Recipient Fellowship award Pharmacia Upjohn, 1997; Clin. oncology fellow scholar Am. Cancer Soc., 1994-95; Berlex Oncology Found. scholar, 1997. Mem. Am. Soc. Clin. Oncology, Am. Assn. Cancer Rsch., S.W. Oncology Group, Tex. Soc. Med. Oncology, San Antonio Cancer Inst. E-mail: lhammond@saci.org. Office: Inst Drug Devel/CTRC 7979 Wurzbach Rd # 271 San Antonio TX 78229-4427

HAMMOND, RAYMOND WILLIAM, pharmacotherapy specialist; b. Port Arthur, Tex., May 16, 1944; s. Woodrow Wilson and Anna Mary (Brockman) H.; m. Sandra Louise Borel, Feb. 1, 1964; children: Cynthia Lynn, Jeffrey Carl. BS in Pharmacy, U. Houston, 1973; PharmD, U. Tenn. Ctr. Health Scis., 1981. Lic. pharmacist, Tex., Okla., N.Mex.; cert. Pharmacotherapy Specialist, 1991—. Staff pharmacist USPHS Hosp., S.I., N.Y., 1974-75; dep. chief pharmacist Med. Ctr. Fed. Prisoners, Springfield, Mo., 1975-77, USPHS Outpatient Clinic, Savannah, Ga., 1977-78; chief USPHS Outpatient Clinic, 1978-79; chief pharmacist USPHS Outpatient Clinic, Port Arthur, Tex., 1981; pharmacist USPHS Indian Hosp., Whiteriver, Ariz., 1981-83; asst. chief inpatient clin. pharmacy services W.W. Hastings Indian Hosp., Tahlequah, Okla., 1983-91; chief customer svc. and quality assurance br. divsn. Supply Mgmt. Indian Health Svc., Albuquerque, 1991-94; asst. prof. pharmacy, experiential programs coord.; dir. drug utilization rev. program Coll. Pharmacy, U. N.Mex., 1994-97; clin. pharmacy corrd. Sierra Med. Ctr., El Paso, Tex., 1997-98; clin. assoc. prof. pharmacy coop. pharmacy program U. Tex., Austin and El Paso, 1998-99; assoc. dean practice programs Coll. Pharmacy U. Houston, 1999—; clin. resource speaker SW Okla. State U. Sch. Pharmacy, 1984-91; adj. asst. prof. Northeastern State U. Coll. of Optometry, Tahlequah, Okla., 1986-90; adj. assoc. prof., 1991; mem. adv. bd. Cherokee County Elder Care. Contbr. chpt. to book and articles to profl. jours. Mem. instl. rev. bd. NE State U., Tahlequah, 1985-91; bd. dirs. Cherokee County Hospice Assn., 1986-87. Capt. USPHS, 1974-94. Fellow Am. Coll. of Clin. Pharmacists; mem. Am. Soc. Health Systems Pharmacists, Tex. Soc. Health-Sys. Pharmacists, N.Mex. Soc. Hosp. Pharmacists (pres. 1997), Commd. Officers Assn. USPHS, Mensa, Rho Chi. Democrat. Roman Catholic. Avocations: photography, backpacking, computer science, fishing, beer and winemaking. Home: 3015 Marble Falls Dr Pearland TX 77584-7067

HAMMOND, VERNON FRANCIS, school administrator; b. Grand Rapids, Mich., Sept. 27, 1931; s. Rodney Clyve and Wylida Helen (Bonner) H.; m. Anne Louise Seeley, Dec. 10, 1954; children: Michelle, Milissa, Milanie, Michael. BA, Bob Jones U., 1959, MA, 1960; postgrad., Butler U., 1968-69, Pepperdine U., 1969-72; MEd, Lynchburg Coll., 1975. Cert. ednl. adminstrn. Tchr., coach, vice prin. Cen. Bapt. Schs., Anaheim, Calif., 1963-68; tchr. Indpls. Christian Acad., 1968-69; tchr., coach Faith Bapt. Schs., Canoga Park, Calif., 1969-72; prin. Lynchburg (Va.) Christian Acad., 1972-75, Bethany Christian Sch., Troy, Mich., 1975-84, Heart to Heart Christian Acad., Phoenix, 1984-88; adminstr. Temple Christian Schs., Lakeland, Fla., 1989-97; girls head basketball coach Temple Christian Sch., 1990-97; instr. Ind. Bapt. Coll., Indpls., 1968-69, Lynchburg Bapt. Coll., 1973-75; sec.-treas. Mich. Assn. Christian Schs., Troy, 1982-83; bd. dirs. Western Fellowship Christian Schs., Phoenix, 1985-88; conv. spkr. Christian Edn. Assn., S.E., Pensacola, Fla.; founder, pres. V and A Enterprises, 1994—. Del. Mich. Rep. Conv., 1980, 82; precinct del. Mich. Rep. Party, Troy, 1980-84; precinct leader Ariz. Rep. Party, Phoenix, 1986-89; bd. dirs. Bethany Villa, Troy, 1975-84. With USN, 1951-55. Coach of Fla. Christian Girls Conf. State Championship Basketball Team, 1993-94. Mem. adv. bd. Sketch Erickson Nat. Ministries, Lakeland, Fla., 1995—. Avocations: reading, gardening, woodworking, coaching.

HAMMOND, WALTER EDWARD, aerospace engineer; b. Austin, Tex., Feb. 26, 1947; s. John Hays and Carmela Sierra (Abadiano) H.; m. Suzanne Scott Adams, Aug. 18, 1971; children: W. Scott, Anne E., David J., Michael C. MS, U. Tex., 1973; MBA, Tex. A&M U., 1982, D Engring., 1984. Registered profl. engr. Ala. Mem. tech. staff Rocketdyne Divsn. Rockwell Internat., Canoga Park, Calif., 1976-79; prin. systems analyst Teledyne Brown Engring., Huntsville, Ala., 1983-86; level III assoc. Booz, Allen & Hamilton, Inc., Huntsville, 1987-88; sr. aerospace engr. Thiokol Corp., Huntsville, 1989; supr. Systems Analysis Br. Sverdrup Technology, Inc., Huntsville, 1989-93; dir. coml. practices and partnerships Nat. Technology Transfer Ctr., Wheeling, W.Va., 1996; spl. projects engr. Hernandez Engring., Inc., Huntsville, 1999-2000; sr. engr. Pace & Waite, Inc., Hunstville, 2000—; mem. secretariat Air Force Scientific Adv. Bd., Washington, 1999—; cons. Akbay Assocs., Inc., Athens, Ala., 1994-98. Author 2 books on space transp. systems; contbr. articles to profl. jours. Corr. sec. Hispanic Heritage Assn. of North Ala., Huntsville, 2000. Decorated Commendation medal USAF, others. Fellow AIAA (assoc., bd. dirs. 1976—, Spl. Svc. award 1986); mem. Res. Officers' Assn. (life), Air Force Assn., Brit. Interplanetary Assn. Republican. Methodist. Avocations: jogging, snow skiing. E-mail: Walter.Hammond@msfc.nasa.gov. Office: Pace & Waite Inc Mail Code PWI NASA Marshall Flight Ctr Huntsville AL 35812

HAMMOND-BLESSING, DIANN A., elementary education educator; b. Cedar Rapids, Iowa, May 24, 1943; d. Russell Irving and Ola Arline (Leonard) Hammond; m. Dale Fredrick Blessing, June 10, 1979. BA in Edn., U. Wyo., 1966, MEd, 1973. Cert. elem. tchr., Colo. Tchr. German and social studies Deaver-Frannie Schs., Deaver, Wyo., 1966-68, Alliance (Nebr.) City Schs., 1968-70; tchr. elem. Jefferson County Schs., Arvada, Colo., 1971—; del. Colo. Del. Assembly, 1974-79; sec. Argonauts Investment Group, 1986-87, v.p., 1989, pres., 1990, treas.-elect, 1993, treas., 1994. Co-author curriculum units Our Changing Langauge, 1978. mem. Record Keeping Task Force, Jefferson County, Colo., 1974-75, 84; del. Dem. County and State Convention, Colo., 1976, 80; mem. polit. action com. Jefferson County Schs., 1979-80; precint chair Dem. Com., Colo., 1984. Mem. NEA, AAUW (editor newspaper 1985-87), PTA, Internat. Reading Assn. (Colo. coun., Colo. Edn. Assn., Colo. Reading Assn., Jefferson County Edn. Assn. (mem. com., rep. 1973-82, 94-95, 96-97, 97-98, bd. dirs. 1974-79), Jefferson County Internat. Reading Assn., Instrnl. Profl. Devel. Avocations: special event and interior decorating, assembly and design of clothing, elegant crafts. Home: 6626 S Yukon Way Littleton CO 80123-3070 Office: Warder Elem Sch 7840 Carr Dr Arvada CO 80005-4420

HAMMOND-PARKER, STEPHEN, business executive; b. Wellington, New Zealand, Oct. 5, 1944; arrived in Hong Kong, 1985; s. William Parker and Marion Hammond; m. Kristina Georgieff; children: Andre Stephen, Luisa Kristina. Assoc. dir. J.H. Minet Aviation divsn., London, 1976-78; mng. dir. Internat. Airline Passengers Assn., London, 1978-82; pres. Internat. Airline Passengers Assn., Dallas, 1981-83; mng. dir. Assn. Bus. travellers, Sydney, Australia, 1982—, Frequent Bus. Travellers Club, Hong Kong, 1986—; bd. dirs. So. Cross, London, 1983. Avocations: music, golf, squash. Home: 21B 2 Brady St, Mosmart NSW 2088, Australia Office: ABT, PO Box 1163, North Sydney NSW 2059, Australia

HAMMOND-STROUD, DEREK, baritone; b. London, Jan. 10, 1926; s. Herbert William and Ethel Louise (Elliott) Stroud. Student, Trinity Coll. Music, London, 1937-38. roles include Alberich in The Ring, Beckmesser in Der Meistersinger, Papageno in The Magic Flute, Tonio in Il Paliacci, Faninal in Der Rosenkavalier, Bartolo in Barber of Seville, also Rigoletto and Falstaff; appearances include: Glyndebourne Festival Opera, 1959-60, Sadlers Wells Opera Co., 1961-71, Royal Opera Covent Garden, 1971-89, Met. Opera, N.Y.C., 1977—, Netherlands Opera, 1977-80, Teatro Colón, Buenos Aires, 1981, Nat. Theatre, Munich, 1983; appeared in concerts Europe, U.S.A.; prof. singing Royal Acad. Music, London, 1974-90; recs. for E.M.I., RCA, Phonogram, Célèbre Records, Symposium. Decorated Order Brit. Empire, 1987; recipient Sir Charles Santley Meml. Gift Worshipful Co. Musicians, 1988; hon. fellow Trinity Coll. Music, 1982. Mem. Inc. Soc. Musicians, Royal Acad. Music (hon.). Home: Muswell Hill, 18 Sutton Rd, London N10 1HE, England

HAMMONS, THOMAS JAMES, electrical engineering consultant, engineering educator; b. Northampton, Eng.; s. Herbert Richard and Cynthia Gladys (Warwick) H. BSc in Engring., Imperial Coll., 1957, AGGI, City and Guilds Coll., 1957; PhD, DIC, Imperial Coll., 1961; doctorate in engring., World U., 1986. Chartered engr., Eng.; registered European engr., Fedn. Nat. Engring. Assns. in Europe. Engr., systems engring. dept. AEI, Manchester, 1961-62; faculty heavy elec. engring. U. Glasgow, 1962—; prof. elec. and computer engring. McMaster U., Hamilton, Ont., Can., 1978-79; vis. scientist U. Saskatchewan, Can., summer 1979; cons. Mawdsleys Ltd., Dursley, Gloucesterhire, U.K., 1965-78, NSHEB, Edinburgh, U.K., 1965-70, GEC, Stafford, U.K., 1975-85; mem. Internat. Conf. High Voltage Networks (CIGRE); elec. power engring. cons. Contbr. more than 300 articles to profl. jours. Grantee Atomic Engergy Authority, 1963-64, South of Scotland Electricity Bd. Fellow IEEE (chair UKRI sect. 2000, chair power engring. chpt. UKRI sect., chair internat. practices for energy devel. and power generation, past chair PES task force on harmonising stds. worldwide, past chair PES sta. control com., past mem. internat. com. stds. bd. 1995-96, tech. coun. PES, 1993-97); mem. Power Engring. Soc. IEEE (Disting. Svc. award 1996), Industry Application Soc. IEEE, Instn. Mech. Engrs. U.K., Instn. Diagnostic Engrs. U.K. Fax: 44 141 330 4808. E-mail: T.Hammons@ieee.org. Home: Clairmont 11c Winton Dr, Glasgow G12 OPZ, Scotland Office: U Glasgow, Glasgow G12 8QQ, Scotland

HAMNER, MARVINE PAULA, aerospace engineer, researcher; b. Kansas City, Mo., Nov. 20, 1956; d. David Wilson and Sarah May (Brooks) Talbot; m. Robert Jefferson Hamner, Dec. 24, 1973; children: Erinn Nicole, James Robert. BS, MIT, 1990; MS, Purdue U., 1993; DSc, Washington U., St. Louis, 1999. Sr. specialist engr. The Boeing Co., Seattle, 1990-98; engring. sect. supr. Aero. Scis. and Tech. group Applied Physics Lab, Johns Hopkins U., 1999—; founder, engr. Leading Edge Technologies, Newton, Mass., 1995—; adj. prof. Washington U., 1998-99. Mem. AIAA, Am. Phys. Soc., 99s Inc. Avocation: flying. Home: 12040A Little Patuxent Pkwy Columbia MD 21044-4819

HAMORI, JOZSEF, neuroscientist; b. Fegyvernek, Szolnok, Hungary; s. Rudolf and Julia (Milassin) H.; m. Iren Somfai, Aug. 6, 1955 (div. 1977); children: Maria, Eszter; m. Anna Tompa, Feb. 11, 1978; children: Barbara, Mate. MSc, Elte U., Budapest, 1955, PhD, 1958; ScD, Hungarian Acad., Budapest, 1972. Jr. research fellow Med. Sch., Dept. Anatomy, Pecs, Hungary, 1955-58, rsch. fellow, 1958-63; sr. rsch. fellow Semmelweis U., Budapest, 1963-72; prof. anatomy Semmelweis U., 1972—; prof. zoology Janus Pannonius U., Pecs, 1989—; Sec. Degree Acad. Qualifying Com., Budapest, 1987—; rector Pecs U., 1992-94, min., 1998-2000, chmn. sci. policy coun., 2000—. Author: From Neurons to Thinking, 1982, One Brain - Two Minds?, 1985, Brain in Danger, 1988. Recipient Acad. award, Hungarian Acad. Scis., 1972, Szeichenyi award, 1994. Mem. Neurobiology Assn. Hungary (pres. 1988—), Internat. Brain Rsch. Orgn. (governing com.), Hungarian Acad. Sci. Roman Catholic. Avocations: history, arts, garden-

ing. Home: Erkel u 89, 2092 Budakeszi Hungary Office: Dept Anatomy, Tuzolto u 58, 1450 Budapest Hungary

HAMOUR, ABUOBEIDA A., infectious diseases physician; b. Bangunarti, Sudan, July 13, 1958; s. Abdelaal Hamour and Naylah Saeed Mirghani; m. Suhair Saeed Khalid, Dec. 24, 1987; children: Naylah, Ahmed, Omer. MB BChir, Faculty of Medicine, Khartoum, Sudan, 1981; MSc, U. Manchester, Eng., 1993. Intern, med. resident Khartoum Tchg. Hosp., 1981-83; med. resident Coventry & Norwich (Eng.) Hosp., 1984-87; med. registrar Norwich Hosp., 1988-90; lectr. in communicable diseases U. Manchester, 1991-98; cons. in infectious diseases and tropical medicine Al-Hada Armed Forces Hosp., Taif, Saudi Arabia, 1998-2000, King Fahd Armed Forces Hosp., Jeddah, Saudi Arabia, 2000—. Author: (book) Bailliere's Clinical Infectious Diseases, 1996. Mem. European Coll. Physicians London, Am. Soc. Microbiology, European Soc. Clin. Microbiology and Infectious Diseases. Muslim. Avocations: reading, travel, country walking. Office: King Fahd Armed Forces Hosp, PO Box 9862, Jeddah 21159, Saudi Arabia

HAMPE, JOHANNES A., economist, educator; b. Troppau, Czechoslovakia, Nov. 4, 1940; s. Johannes and Maria (Peiker) H.; m. Sigurlaug Saemundsdottir, Dec. 28, 1976; 1 child, Bjorn. Diploma in econ., U. Munich, 1966, Dr. rer. pol., 1976. Lectr. econs. U. Munich, 1976—. Author: Introduction to Urban Economics, 1988, Economics, 1991, 3d. edit., 1993, Schriften der Vereins fur Socialpolitik, 1987. Bd. dirs. Munich Forum, 1974—, Assn. Promotion Rsch. on Urban and Regional Economics, 1990. Mem. Am. Econ. Assn., European Econ. Assn., German Econ. Assn., Acad. Regional Sci. and Planning (assoc.). Roman Catholic. Office: U Munich, Dept Econ, D 80539 Munich Germany

HAMPEL, KLAUS ERICH, retired gastroenterologist; b. Leipzig, Germany, Mar. 18, 1932; s. Erich and Maria (Baldus) H.; m. Antje Marianne Dierks, 1965; 1 son, Dierk Johannes. MD, SUNY, Stony Brook, 1960; habil., Free U., Berlin, 1967. Med. asst. Med. Clinic, Free U., Berlin, 1960-67; lectr., sr. registrar Free U. Med. Sch., 1967-69, prof., head gastroent. unit, 1969-97, head diet sch., 1977-97; dean U. Klinikum Charlottenburg, 1976-78; ret., 1997. Author papers on cytogenetics, hematology, gastroenterology, ethical problems in medicine. Mem. European Assn. Gastroenterology and Endoscopy (pres.), Am. Gastroenterol. Assn. (sr.). Address: 7 Schopenhauerstrasse,, 14129 Berlin Federal Republic Germany

HAMPEL, SIR RONALD (CLAUS), retired chemicals executive; b. Shrewsbury, Eng., May 31, 1932; s. Karl Victor Hugo and Rutgard Emil Klothilde (Hauck) H.; m. Jane Bristed Hewson, 1957; children: Katharine, Andrew, Rupert, Peter. MA in Modern Langs. and Law, U. Cambridge, Eng., 1955. Joined Imperial Chem. Industries PLC, 1955, v.p. Ams., 1973-80, gen. mgr. comml., 1977-80, chmn. paints divsn., 1980-83, chmn. agrochemicals, 1983-85, dir., 1985-99, COO, 1991-93, dep. chmn., CEO, 1993-95, chmn., 1995-99; chmn. United News & Media plc, London, 1999—; outside dir. Powell Duffryn PLC, 1983-88, Comml. Union PLC, 1988-95, Brit. Aerospace PLC, 1989—, Alcoa, 1995—; mem. adv. bd. Teijin, 1999—; mem. listed cos. adv. com. London Stock Exch., 1996-99; mem. nominating Com. N.Y. Stock Exch., 1996-98. Mem. exec. com. Brit. N.Am. Com., 1987-95; mem. European Round Table, 1995-99; mem. U.K. coun. INSEAD, 1994-99; chmn. com. corp. governance, 1996-99; mem. adv. com. Karlpreis Aachen. 2d lt. Royal Arty., Brit. Army, 1951-52. Created knight bachelor, 1995; hon. fellowship Corpus Christi Coll., Cambridge, 1996. Fellow Royal Soc. Arts; mem. Brit. Inst. Mgmt. (companion), All Eng. Lawn Tennis Club (com.). Anglican. Avocations: tennis, golf, skiing. Office: United News & Media plc, 245 Blackfriars Rd, London SE1 9UY, England

HAMPER, ROBERT JOSEPH, marketing executive; b. Chgo., May 20, 1956; s. Robert William and Barbara Jean Hamper. BSBA with honors, Ill. State U., 1977, MBA with honors, 1979; ABD, Northern Ill. U., 1999. Fin. mgr. Ill. Bell, Chgo., 1979-82; staff mgr. AT&T, Basking Ridge, N.J., 1982-84; mem. tech. staff Bell labs., Homedale, N.J., 1983-84; sr. staff. mgr. market analysis Ameritech Svcs., Schaumburg, Ill., 1985-87; dir. strategic planning Ameritech Corp., Chgo., Ill., 1987-90; pres. R.J. Hamper Bus. Cons., River Forest, Ill., 1981—, mgr. investment fund, 1990—; asst. prof. fin. and mktg. Dominican U., River Forest, 1983-98; adj. prof. fin. Loyola U., Chgo., 1988—; seminar presenter in field; career counselor, 1985—. Author: Developing a Profitable Marketing Plan: Text and Cases, 1987, Marketing and Planning Forms, 1987, Strategic Market Planning, 1990, 92, 94, 95, 97, 99, Handbook for Proposal Writing, 1995, 97, 98, 2000; contbg. author: College Business Math, 1995, 97, 99; contbr. articles to profl. jours. Mem. Am. Mktg. Assn. (exec.), Am. Mgmt. Assn., Fin. Mgmt. Assn., Am. Fin. Assn., Am. Hosp. Assn. Home and Office: 730 Clinton Pl River Forest IL 60305-1914

HAMPL, JAROSLAV ALOIS, biochemist, researcher; b. Brno, Czech Republic, July 2, 1935; s. Alois and Marie (Sekorova) H.; m. Jana Zelinkova, Feb. 4, 1961; 1 child, Jaroslav. MA, U. Brno, 1958, DSc, 1968; PhD, U. Košice, Slovak Republic, 1976. Chemist food industry, Brno, 1958-60, State Commerce Inst., Brno, 1960-62; rschr. Vet. Rsch. Inst., Brno, 1962—, head biophys. dept., 1976-89. Contbr. articles to profl. jours. Grantee Ministry of Agr., Czech Republic, 1995, Ministry of Industry, Czech Republic, 1997. Mem. Czech Biochem. Soc. Avocations: theatre, sports. Office: Vet Rsch Inst, Hudcova 70, 621 32 Brno Czech Republic

HAMPSON, CHRISTOPHER, former chemical industry executive; b. Sept. 6, 1931; s. Harold Ralph and Geraldine Mary Hampson; m. Joan Margaret Cassils Evans, 1954; 5 children. BChemE, McGill U., 1952. V.p. Can. Industries, 1956-78, sr. v.p., 1982-84; gen. mgr. planning Imperial Chem. Industries, 1978-82; mng. dir., CEO ICI Australia, 1984-87; exec. dir. Imperial Chem. Industries, 1987-94; chmn. bd. dirs. Yorkshire Electricity Group, 1994-97, RMC Group PLC, 1996—, Brit. Biotech. PLC, 1998—; Bd. dirs. SNC-Lavalin Group, Montreal, TransAlta Corp., Calgary, Can., BG plc. Mem. Hurlingham Club, York Club (Toronto, Ont., Can.), Boodle's. Avocations: tennis, skiing. Office: RMC Group PLC, RMC House, Coldharbour Ln/Thorpe Egham, Surrey TW20 8TD, England

HAMPSON, THOMAS R., investigations company executive; b. Warrensburg, Mo., Sept. 19, 1947; s. Richard Hampson and Margaret Jane King; m. Linda Pribula, Aug. 24, 1974; children: Erik, Jennifer, Mark. BA in Polit. Sci., U. Ill., Chgo., 1973. Lic. detective, Ill. Intelligence analyst USAF, Western Europe, 1965-69; investigator Ill. Legis. Investigating Commn., Chgo., 1973-76, sr. investigator, 1977-78, chief investigator, 1979-83; pres., founder Search Internat., Inc., Schaumburg, Ill., 1983—. Bd. dirs. Chgo. Crime Commn., 1987—. With USAF, 1965-69. Mem. World Assn. Detectives, Soc. Competetive Intelligence Profls., Exec. Club of Chgo. Republican. Avocations: outdoor activities, hunting, camping, computer applications. Office: Search Internat Inc 1870 N Roselle Rd Ste 105 Schaumburg IL 60195-3100

HAMPTON, CHRISTOPHER JAMES, writer; b. Horta, Fayal, The Azores, Jan. 26, 1946; s. Bernard Patrick and Dorothy Patience (Herrington) H.; m. Laura Margaret De Holesch, May 15, 1971; children: Alice Jane, Mary Ann. M.A. in Modern Langs., New Coll., Oxford, Eng., 1968. Resident dramatist Royal Ct. Theatre, London, 1968-70. Author: (plays) When Did You Last See My Mother?, 1966, Total Eclipse, 1968, rev., 1981, The Philanthropist, 1970 (Evening Standard award, Plays and Players London Critics Best Comedy award 1970), Savages, 1973 (Plays and Players Best Play award 1973, L.A. Drama Critics Circle award 1974), Treats, 1976, Tales from Hollywood, 1982 (Evening Standard award 1983), White Chameleon, 1991, Alice's Adventures Underground, 1994; (book and lyrics of musical with Don Black) Sunset Boulevard, 1993 (Tony awards 1995); (teleplays) Able's Will, The History Man (from Malcolm Bradbury) BBC, 1981, The Price of Tea, 1984, Hotel Du Lac (from Anita Brookner) BBC, 1986 (BAFTA Best TV Film award 1987), The Ginger Tree (Oswald Wynd); (play adaptations) The Portage to San Cristobal of A.H. by George Steiner, Les Liaisons Dangereuses by Choderlos de Laclos, 1985; (translator) Marya (PBY Isaac Babel) 1967, Uncle Vanya (Chekhov) 1970, Ghosts (Ibsen) 1978, The Prague Trial (Chereau and Mnouchkine) 1980, Art (Yasmina Reza) 1996 (Scott Montcrieff prize 1997), An Enemy of the People (Ibsen) 1997, The Unexpected Man (Yazmina Reza) 1998. Tales from the Vienna Woods by Ödön von Horváth, Don Juan Comes Back from the War by Ödön von Horváth, Faith, Hope and Charity by Ödön von Horváth, The Wild Duck by Henrik Ibsen, Tartuffe by Molière, Hedda Gabler by Henrik Ibsen, A Doll's House by Henrik Ibsen; (screenplays) A Doll's House, 1973, Tales From the Vienna Woods, 1979 (Screen International award 1980), The Honorary Consul, 1983, The Good Father, 1986 (Prix Italia 1988), Wolf at the Door, 1986, Dangerous Liaisons, 1988 (Best Adapted Screenplay Acad. award, Best Adapted Screenplay award Writers Guild of Am.), Mary Reilly, 1996, Total Eclipse, 1995; dir., screenwriter: Carrington, 1995 (Spl. Jury prize Cannes Film Festival 1995), The Secret Agent, 1996; translator from French to English, Broadway play Art. Fellow Royal Soc. Lit.; mem. Dramatists Club (London).

HAMPTON, JAMES ANTONY, psychologist, educator; b. Sheffield, Yorkshire, England, Aug. 21, 1951; s. Antony Barmore and Helen Patricia (Lockwood) H.; m. Robin Andrea Richmond, July 15, 1972; children: Adam, Saskia, Max. BA in Natural Scis. with honors, Cambridge U., 1972; PhD in Psychology, U. Coll. London, 1976. Rsch. fellow U. Coll. London, 1976-77; lectr. SL City U., London, 1977-90, reader, 1990-96, prof., 1996—; vis. prof. Stanford U., 1984-85, U. Chgo., 1995-96; cons. Civil Svc. Commn., English, 1985, Internat. Psychoanalytical Assn., 1990-95; examiner Brit. Psychol. Soc., 1984-89. Contbr. articles to profl. jours. Recipient PG studentship Med. Rsch. Coun., England, 1972-75; Sr. Rsch. scholar Fulbright Commn., 1995-96. Mem. Psychonomics Soc. U.S., European Soc. Philosophy & Psychology (com. mem. 1999), Cognitive Sci. Soc. U.S. Avocations: music, French countryside, cooking. Office: City U Dept Psychology, St John St, London EC1V 0HB, England

HAMPTON, MARIAN ELIZABETH, theatre educator; b. Springfield, Ill., Dec. 27, 1934; d. John Kavanaugh and Caroline Ruth (Schafer) Cox; m. Charles Christy Hampton, Jr., Dec. 22, 1957 (div. Dec. 1980); children: Helen Caroline, Charles Christy III. BFA, Ill. Wesleyan U., 1956; MFA, Yale U., 1959; PhD, Internat. Coll., L.A., 1979. Instr. drama Allegheny Coll., Meadville, Pa., 1959-63; instr. theatre San Francisco State U., 1972-76; drama tchr. Athenian Sch., Mount Diablo, Calif., 1976-78; asst. prof. U. Tenn., Knoxville, 1979-84; from asst. to assoc. prof. U. Tex., Austin, 1985-95; prof. theatre Ill. State U., Normal, 1995—, head acting area, 1995-98. Author: Singing for Actors, 1984; editor, contbr.: The Vocal Vision, 1997. Founder, pres. Cmty. Coalition on Edn., San Francisco, 1970; mem. Edn. Voucher Feasibility Steering Com., San Francisco, 1971; candidate Sch. Bd., San Francisco, 1972. Recipient Rsch. awards U. Tex. and Ill. State U., 1987, 89, 98; named Miss Ill., Miss Am. Pageant, Atlantic City, 1955; scholar Nat. Alpha Lambda Delta, Ill. Wesleyan U., 1953. Mem. SAG, AFTRA, Assn. for Theatre in Higher Edn. (mem. governing coun. 1997-99, chair profl. devel. com. 1997-99), Voice and Speech Trainers Assn. (pres. 1994-96), Actors' Equity Assn., PEO (Ill. chpt. JV), Phi Kappa Phi. Democrat. Methodist. Avocations: reading, hiking. E-mail: mhampto@aol.com. Home: 2107 Case Dr Bloomington IL 61701-1442 Office: Ill State Univ Dept Theatre PO Box 5700 Normal IL 61790-0001

HAMPTON, PHILLIP JEWEL, artist, educator; b. Kansas City, Mo., Apr. 23, 1922; s. Cordell Bernard Daniels and Goldie Kelley Powell; m. Dorothy Louise Smith, Sept. 28, 1946 (dec. Oct. 1986); children: Harry James, Robert Keith. Student, Drake U., 1947-48; BFA, Kansas City U., 1951; MFA, Kansas City Art Inst., 1952. Dir. art program Savannah (Ga.) State Coll., 1952-69; prof. art So. Ill. U., Edwardsville, 1969-92, emeritus prof. fine arts, 1992—; artist, spl. projects Hampton Studio, Edwardsville, 1992—; dir. day camp City of Kansas City Recreation, 1952; art cons. U.S. GSA, East St. Louis, Ill., 1995-98; curator 2 spl. exhbns. St. Louis Artists' Guild, 1998—. Author: (catalogs) 3d World Drawings, 1979, Schemata of Ethnic Minority Artists, 1980; artist book/promotional materials Symphony Kids, KFUO-99FM, 1996; exhibited in one-man show at So. Ill. U., Edwardsville Gallery, 2000; represented in permanent collection at St. Louis Art Mus. Mem. adv. bd. West Broad YMCA, Savannah, 1966-69; bd. dirs. United Fund, Edwardsville, 1971-74; mem. Citizens Adv. Coun. Dist. 7, Edwardsville, 1973-75. Recipient Gov.'s award for best-in-show Ill. State Fair Profl. Art Exhbn., 1990, others. mem. St. Louis Art Mus., Art St. Louis, St. Louis Artists' Guild. Presbyterian. Avocations: reading, writing, chess, market studies. Home: 832 Holyoake Rd Edwardsville IL 62025-2315

HAMWAY, SARY M., management consultant; b. Alexandria, Egypt, Oct. 28, 1950; s. Mahmoud A. Hamway and Omayma I. Omara; m. Madiha I. Zaki, May 24, 1991; children: Youssef, Yara. B, Helwan U., Cairo, 1987, MS, 1990. Tchg. asst. Helwan U., Cairo, 1987-91; sales and mktg. dir. Badkook Co., Jeddah, Saudi Arabia, 1991-95; mng. dir. Franchise Devel. Svcs., Jeddah, 1995—; lectr. Helwan U., Cairo, 1987-91, Andalus Tech., Jeddah, 1998-99; spkr. Coun. C. of C., Jeddah, 1999. Mem. Arab Bus. Assn., Saudi Mgmt. Assn. Avocations: reading, travel, swimming. Office: Franchise Devel Svcs, 221 Hael St, Jeddah 21411, Saudi Arabia

HAMYLTON-JONES, KEITH, diplomat, writer; b. London, Oct. 12, 1924; s. George and Gertrude (Mitchell) Jones; m. Eira Morgan, Aug. 26, 1953; 1 child, Alison. BA, MA, Oxford (Eng.) U., 1950. 3d sec. H.M. Fgn. (Diplomatic) Svc., Warsaw, 1950; 2d sec. Lisbon, 1953-56; 1st sec. Manila, 1956-59; head of chancery and H.M. consul Montevideo, 1962-67; head of chancery Rangoon, 1967-68; asst. head S.E. Asia dept. Fgn. Office, London, 1968-70; H.M. consul-gen. Lubumbashi, 1970-72; counsellor Fgn. Office, London, 1973-74; H.M. amb. San Jose, Costa Rica, 1974-79; amb. Tegucigalpa, Honduras, 1975-78, Managua, Nicaragua, 1976-79; ret.; Expdn. leader Operation Raleigh, Costa Rican Rain Forest, 1985. Author: (under pen name Peter Myllent) The Ideal World, 1972. Capt. H.M. Welsh Guards, 1943-46, ETO. Decorated Companion of the Most Disting. Order of St. Michael and St. George, 1979. Avocations: reading, research, writing, historic house and garden maintenance, walking. Home: Morval House, Morval, Cornwall PL13 1PN, England

HAMZA, GÁBOR, law educator; b. Budapest, Hungary, Feb. 22, 1949. MD, Hungarian Acad. Scis., 1983, PhD, 1975. Bar: Hungary, 1972. Asst. prof. law Eötvös Loránd U., Budapest, 1971-77, sr. asst. prof. law, 1977-80, assoc. prof. law, 1980-84, prof. law, dir. Inst. Roman and Comparative Law, 1984—; vis. prof. U. Rome, 1986, 87, 88, 89, U. Parma, Italy, 1988, U. Salerno, 1989, European U. Inst. Florence, Italy, 1990, Syracuse (N.Y.) U., 1991, U. Paris V, 1994-95, U. Paris XII, 1993-96, U. Memphis, 1995; Fulbright vis. prof. Benjamin N. Cardozo Sch. Law, N.Y.C., 1989-90; guest lectr. in field; rsch. fellow U. Munich, 1976-77, U. Rome, 1979, U. Cologne, Germany, 1980-81, U. Frankfurt am Main, Germany, 1989, Swiss Inst. Comparative Law, Lausanne, 1996. Editor-in-chief Anglo-Am. Legal Studies, Acta Facultatis Politico-Iuridicae Universitatis de Rolando Eötvös nom, Publicationes Instituti Juris Romani Budapestinensis und Studien zum römischen Recht in Europa. Mem. Inst. Internat. Droit Inspiration et Expression Francaises, Am. Soc. Internat. Law, Am. Fgn. Law Assn., Orgn. Am. Historians, Soc. Jean Bodin, Soc. Internat. Histoire Droit, Assn. Henri Capitant, Consejo Europeo Investigaciones Sociales sobre L.A., Centro Internat. Ricerche Giuridiche, Lab. Storia Constituzionale Antoine Barnave, Vereinigung für Verfassungsgeschichte, Hungarian Lawyers Assn. Home: Fadrusz u 28, H-1114 Budapest Hungary Office: ELTE Romai Jogi Tanszék, Egyetem ter 1-3, H-1053 Budapest Hungary

HAMZA, GÜNTER, engineering company executive; b. Vienna, Aug. 14, 1940; s. Ignaz and Herta (Zinnauer) H.; m. Eva Pecinowsky; children: Christine, Andreas. Diploma in engring., U. Tech., Vienna, 1969. Mem. research and devel. staff Siemens AG, Vienna, 1969-70; authorized signatory Bacher Elektronische Geräte, Vienna, 1970-74; mgr. mktg. and sales SAT Schrack, Vienna, 1974-85; mng. dir. SAT Systeme für Automatisierungstechnik, Vienna, 1985—. Contbr. articles to profl. jours. Mem. Internat. Electrotech. Commn. (mem. various coms.). Avocations: music, photography, skiing, surfing, sailing. Home: Silbergasse 25, A-1190 Vienna Austria Office: Systeme für Automatisievumgstechnik, Ruthnergasse, A-1210 Vienna Austria

HAMZA, MILOS, hotel executive; b. Slany, Czech Republic, May 2, 1922; s. Vaclav and Ruzena Hamza; m. Jirina Hamza. Student, Commercial Coll., Czech Republic, 1942. Exec. Hilton Hotels, Inc., Chgo., 1950-55, Sheraton Hotels Inc., Cin., 1955-60; gen. mgr. Dinkler Hotels, Inc., Atlanta, 1960-68; pres. Milo Enterprises Inc., Tampa, Fla., 1968-80, Milos Hamza, Sarasota, Fla., 1980—. Home: 2301 Gulf Of Mexico Dr Unit 75N Longboat Key FL 34228-3218

HAN, BO-YING, material scientist, researcher; b. Shanghai, China, Jan. 19, 1963; s. Zhongrong and Jiahui (Zhu) H.; m. Wei Zhao, May, 1996. BS, Fudan U., Shanghai, 1984, MS, 1987; PhD, U. Pierre et Marie Curie, Paris, 1993. Rsch. asst. Fudan U., Shanghai, 1987-90, U. Pierre et Marie Curie, Paris, 1990-93; rsch. investigator U. Namur, Belgium, 1993-95; rsch. scientist U. Bourgogne, Dijon, France, 1995; rsch. assoc. dept. chem. engring./materials sci. U. Minn., Mpls., 1995- . Author: Handbook of Contemporary Science and Technology, 1989; contbr. articles to profl. jours. Mem. Am. Phys. Soc., Materials Rsch. Soc. Home: 421 Washington Ave SE Minneapolis MN 55455-0373 Office: Univ of Minn Dept. Chem Engring/Mat Sci Minneapolis MN 55455

HAN, BUXIN, psychologist; b. Feixi County, China, Oct. 24, 1966; s. Rongzhang Han and Xiulan Zhou; m. Li Gao, Jan. 20, 1995; 1 child, Lingwei. BS, Anhui Coll. Traditional Chinese Med., Hefei, China, 1986, MS, 1989; PhD, Chinese Acad. Scis., 1993. Physician-in-charge Hua Gang Hosp., Feixi County, 1989-90; from asst. prof. to assoc. prof. Chinese Acad. Scis., Beijing, 1993—. Grantee Chinese Natural Sci. Found., Beijing, 1997—. Mem. Chinese Psychol. Soc. (dep. sec.-gen. 1997—). Avocations: painting, calligraphy, pop music. Office: Inst Psychology Chinese Acad Scis, Beishatan, 100101 Beijing China

HAN, CHINGPING JIM, industrial engineer, educator; b. Shanghai, People's Republic China, Aug. 24, 1957; came to U.S., 1983; s. Bao-San Zhang and Xiao-xian Han; m. Man-xia Maria Zhang, Feb. 22, 1982; children: George, Elaine. PRC, BSME, Dalian Inst. Tech., Dalian, 1982; MS in Indsl. Engring., Pa. State U., 1985, PhD, 1988. Asst. prof. mfg. systems engring. Fla. Atlantic U., Boca Raton, 1988-93, assoc. prof. and assoc. dir. mfg. systems engring., 1993—. Contbr. articles to profl. jours., procs. Avocations: classical music, travel. E-mail: han@fau.edu. Home: 19571 Black Olive Ln Boca Raton FL 33498-4827 Office: Dept Mech Engring Fla Atlantic Univ 777 Glades Rd Boca Raton FL 33431-6498

HAN, HUIWAN, physician, researcher, biochemist educator; b. Beian, China, July 18, 1942; d. Weizhen Han and Lirong Sun; m. Weijin Jin, Sept. 20, 1969; 2 children. B, Beijing Med. Coll., 1967. Physician Hosp. Forest Agy., Gansu Provcince, China, 1968-75; rsch. asst. Inst. Biophysics Acad. Sinica, Beijing, 1976-79, asst. rsch. prof. Inst. Biophysics, 1980-88, asst. rsch. prof. Inst. Chemistry, 1992-93, assoc. prof. Inst. Chemistry, 1993-99, rsch. prof. Inst. Chemistry, 2000—; vis. scholar U. Los Andes, Merida, Venezuela, 1989-90, U. Minn., Mpls., 1991; cons. Inst. Internat. Med. Hong Kong Acad. Scis., 1999; sr. vis. scholar Fundign Office Key Lab. Edn. Ministry Tsinghua U., 1999; academician Inst. Oriental Celebrity, Loudi, China, 1999—; project prof. Inst. Internat. Chinese Med. Coll., 2000—. Mem. Chinese Scientist Club (hon., bioanalytical sect.), Sigma Xi. Achievements include 2 patents; inventor of Microscope Image Processing System of Automated Discrimination in Cancered Cells. Avocations: music appreciation, tourism, biography, sewing and weaving. Home: I-1201 Rm, 1st Apt Inst Devel Biology, Beijing 100080, China Office: Chinese Acad Scis Inst Chem, No. 2 N 1st St, Beijing 100080, China

HAN, JEONG-IN, researcher; b. Seoul, Korea, Jan. 19, 1961; s. Nam-Won Han and Weol-Kyung Kim; m. Gi-Seon Ko, Nov. 18, 1991; children: Dae-Hyun, Dong-Hyun. BS with highest honors, Yonsei U., Seoul, 1983; MS, Korea Adv. Inst. Sci. & Tech., Seoul, 1985, PhD, 1989. Sr. rschr. Samsung Electronic Co., Kiheung, KyungGi, Korea, 1989-92, Korea Electronics Tech. Inst., Osan, KyungGi, Korea, 1992—; advisor Sinwoo-Aimsak Co., Seoul, 1991—, Bomoon Trading Co., Seoul, 1992—, Daehyun Tech., Seoul, 1995—; cons. Daewon Electronics Co., 1992—, Woongsan Electronics Co., Seoul, 1997—; mem. strategic planning com. G-7 Nat. Project for Flat Panel Display, 1994-95; mem. orgn. com. G-7 Nat. Project for Flat Panel Display, 1995—; mem. exec. com. Asia Display '98, 1997—; mem. Samsung Human Tech. Prize, 1997—; vis. prof. Kyung Gi U., 1998—; head of elec. devices rsch. ctr. KETI, 1999—, tech. adv. soft pixel, 2000—, tech. adv. of trans dream, 2000—, tech. adv. of Sai Hyup Tech., 2000—, tech. adv. soft & Touch, 1999—, tech. adv. Yang Yang Ind. Inc., 1998—. Patentee in field. Pvt. Korean Mil. Res., 1983-92. Scholar Korea Govt., 1983-85, 85-89. Avocations: Badook, electronic entertainment, singing, sports. Home: 103-803 Olympic Family Apt, Moon Jung-Dong Song Pa-Ku, Seoul 138-767, Korea

HAN, JUN, computer scientist, researcher; b. Shanghai, China, Mar. 11, 1958; arrived in Can., 1996; s. Jihui Han and Guixian Xia; m. Xiaomin Chen, Apr. 6, 1985; 1 child, Zheng. MSc, China Textile U., Shanghai, 1989; PhD, U. Dortmund, Germany, 1997. Rsch. asst. U. Dortmund, 1993-96; postdoctoral rsch. fellow U. Toronto, Can., 1997; software designer No. Telecom, Brampton, Ont., Can., 1997-98; software designer large vocabulary speech recognition Nortel Networks Multimedia Application Ctr., Toronto, Ont., Can., 1998—. Author: Optimization of Feedforward Neural Networks, 1996. Recipient 1st prize Internat. Comp. Signal Analysis & Processing by Intelligent Techniques, Germany, 1996. Mem. IEEE, IEEE Computer Soc. Avocations: basketball, swimming. Office: Nortel Networks Multimed App Ctr, 522 University Ave, Toronto, ON Canada M5G 1W7

HAN, KWAN-HEE, industrial engineer, educator; b. Incheon, Korea, Feb. 4, 1959; s. Sang-Jib and Jeong-Hae (Ye) H.; m. Jae-Seon Lee; children: Kyu-Min, Su-Jin. BS, Ajou U., 1982; MS, Korea Advanced Inst. of Sci. and Tech, 1984, PhD, 1996. Sect. mgr. of MIS Daewoo Electronics Co., Ltd., Seoul, 1984-89, sect. mgr. CIM, 1989-94, dept. mgr. CIM, 1995-96, gen. mgr. rsch. inst., 1996-99; prof. indsl. sys. Gyongsang Nat. U., Korea, 2000—. Contbr. articles to profl. jours. Mem. IEEE, Assn. Computing Machinery. Avocations: tennis, climbing. Home: 102-707 Hyundae Apt, Chojundong Chinju, Gyeongnam 660-360, Republic of Korea Office: Dept Indsl Engring, 900 Gazwa-Dong Chinju, Gyeongnam 660-701, Republic of Korea

HAN, KYONGHO, electrical engineering educator; b. Seoul, Korea, June 25, 1959; s. Shinwook Han and Moonok Lim. BS, Seoul Nat. U., 1982, MS, 1984; PhD, Tex. A&M U., 1992. Rschr. KTA, Seoul, 1985-87; sys. adminstr. Tex. A&M U., College Station, 1989-92; sr. rschr. ETRI, Taejon, Korea, 1992-93; asst. prof. Dankook U., Seoul, 1993-98, assoc. prof., 1999—. 2d lt. 3d Army Acad., 1984-85. Mem. IEEE. Avocations: music, travel, tennis, driving. Office: Dankook U Dept Elec Engring, Hannamdong Yongsanku, Seoul Republic of Korea

HAN, LIYING, physics educator; b. Beijing, China, Sept. 25, 1928; d. Zhucun and Huiyun (Tong) Han; m. Lianchu Gu, Jan. 1, 1954; 1 child, Congzhong. BSc, Beijing U., 1950. Tchr. Beijing U., 1950-52; lectr. Tsinghua U., Beijing, 1953-58, asst. prof., 1958-60, assoc. prof., 1960-65, dir. rsch. sect., 1965-76, prof., 1980; cons. Beijing Peoples Govt., 1982-86. Author: Vacuum Science and Its Applications, 1982; inventor in field of optical thin films. Mem. China Electronic Soc., Beijing Optical Soc. (dir. 1982—), China Vacuum Soc. (dir. 1979-83), China Optronic Soc. (dir. 1985-96). Avocations: music, travel, reading, gardening. Home: Westsouth 17 Bldg No 2-103, 100084 Beijing China Ofifce: Tsinghua U, Dept Applied Physics, 100084 Beijing China

HAN, MAN JUNG, chemistry educator; b. Chinju, Kyungnam, Korea, Nov. 28, 1935; s. Sung and Dan Dong (Ha) H.; m. Moon Suk Cho, Feb. 28, 1968; children: Il Ah, Kyung Ah, Soong Koo. BS, Seoul Nat. U., Korea, 1960; MS, Mainz U., Germany, 1968, PhD, 1970. Rsch. assoc. U. Mich., Ann Arbor, 1971-73; sr. scientist Agy. for Def. Devel., Seoul, 1973-75; prof. chemistry Ajou U., Suwon, Korea, 1978—, dean acad. affairs, 1981-83; dir. Polymer Rsch. Ctr. Ajou U., 1987—; advisor Ministry Sci. and Tech., Korea, 1981-87. Vice chmn. bd. trustees Korea Inst. for Chem. Tech. Recipient Leetaekyu award for Sci., 1998, Korean Nat. award for sci., 1999. Mem. Korean Polymer Soc. (pres. 1993—), Am. Chem. Soc., Korean Chem. Soc. (pres. macromolecule chem. divsn. 1988-90), N.Y. Acad. Scis. Home: 324-901 Hunyang Shibum Apt, Bundang Sungnam Kyunggi 461-030, Republic of Korea Office: Ajou Univ, Dept Applied Chemistry, Suwon 441-749, Republic of Korea

HAN, MYUNG-MOOK, computer scientist, educator; b. Seoul, Korea, Sept. 29, 1957; s. Doo-Ick and Mi-Ja (Lee) H.; m. In-Hee Song, July 12, 1991; 1 child, Sun-Mee. B of Engring., Yonsei U., Seoul, 1980; MS, N.Y. Inst. Tech., 1987; PhD, Osaka (Japan) City U., 1997. Chmn. honor com.

Yonsei U., 1979-80; rschr. Osaka City U., 1991-92; postdoctoral rschr. Korea Rsch. Found., Seoul, 1997-98; prof. KyungWon U., Songnam, Korea, 1998—; spl. rschr. Yonsei U., 1997—. Contbr. articles to profl. jours. 1st lt. Korean Army, 1980-82. Mem. IEEE, Korea Fuzzy Logic and Intelligent Systems Soc. (dir. 1998—), Inst. Electronics, Info. and Comm. Engrs., Korea Info. Sci. Soc. E-mail: mmhan@mail.kyungwon.ac.kr. Fax: 031-750-5273. Home: 413-602 Kkachi-Maul, Lotte Apt 63 GuMee-Dong, Songnam 463500, Republic of Korea Office: KyungWon Univ, San 65 Bokjung-Dong Sujung, Songnam 461-701, Republic of Korea

HAN, OKSOO, pianist, music educator; b. Seoul, Korea, June 18, 1938; d. Kyung-Seok H. and Young-Hwan Kim; m. Won-Hoon Park, Sept. 25, 1971; children: Suzanne, Thomas. BA, Ewha Women's U., Seoul, Korea, 1960; MA, Cin. Conservatory Music, 1962; DMA, William Penn Coll., 1983. Artist Eric Semon Mgmt., N.Y.C., 1965-72; prof. L.I. U., 1966-75, Kyunghee U., Seoul, Korea, 1976-78, Dankook U., Seoul, Korea, 1983—; dir. Korean chpt. World Piano Competition, Cin., 1987—; chmn. Han Romanson Internat. Piano Competition, Seoul, 1994—; jury Tchaikovsky, Prokofiev, Cin. Internat. Competitions, others, 1987—. Soloist Carnegie Recital Hall, 1964, European Debut Recitals, 1964 (recording) My Favorite Chopin, 1991. Recipient Cultural Merit citation Korean Govt., 1967; named Musician of Yr., Seoul, 1982. Mem. Am. Music Scholarship Assn. (bd. dirs. 1987—). Home: 17-29 Kookee-Dong Chongroku, Seoul 110-011, Korea Office: Dankook U, San 8 Hannam-Dong, Seoul 140-210, Korea

HAN, RUI, pharmacologist; b. Teiling, China, Mar. 8, 1929; s. Chang-he and G.C. (Chou) H.; m. Su-de Zhou, July 7, 1956; children: Hong, Tao. MD, Sheng Yang Med. Coll., China, 1951; PhD, Chinese Union Med. Coll., China, 1960; PhD (hon.), Toyama Med. & Pharm. U., Japan, 1995. Assoc. prof. Inst. Materia Medica, China, 1978-80, 82-85, prof., 1985—; vis. assoc. prof. Mt. Sinai Sch. Medicine, 1980-82; vis. prof. Toyama Med. & Pharm. U., Japan, 1994-95; dep. dir. Inst. Materia Medica, 1978-83; ad hoc cons. WHO, Geneva, 1978; sci. cons. Nanking Inst. Materia Medica, 1984-88; prin. investigator new anticancer drug studies N-formyl sarcolysin, harringtonine, homoharringtonine, glyciphosphoramide Ministry Pub. Health Award, China, 1978-86. Editor: Cancer Chemoprevention & Drug Treatment, 1991; mem. editl. bd. Chinese Jour. Cancer, Chinese Jour. Cancer Rsch., Chinese Med. Sci. Jour. Recipient Outstanding Scientist award Ministry Pub. Health, 1990, State Coun., 1991. Mem. Soc. Exptl. Biology & Medicine, Cell Kinetic Soc., N.Y. Acad. Scis. Home: Bldg 12 Gate A, Fan Cheng Yuan Dist 1, Beijing Fang Zhuang 100078, China Office: Chinese Acad Med Scis Inst Mt Md, Xian Nong Tan St, Beijing 100050, China

HAN, SANG-CHUL, drama educator; b. Seoul, Sept. 28, 1936; s. Hack-Su Han and Un-Nyon Lee; m. Ju-Jee Kim; 2 children. BA, Yonsei U., Seoul, 1961, MA, 1965. Lectr. Yonsei U., Seoul, 1968-76, Chungju (Korea) U., 1976-78; asst. prof. Sacred Heart Women's U., Buchon, Korea, 1978-83; prof. Hallym U., Chunchon, Korea, 1984—; vis. prof. Columbia U., N.Y.C., 1982-83; chairperson English, Hallym U., Chunchon, 1984-87, dean gen. edn., 1994; bd. dirs. Hallym U. Theatre, Chunchon. Contbr. drama revs. to profl. publs. Recipient 5th award of culture and arts Seoul Shinmoon, 1988, Dramatic Activities honor Jour. Auditorium, 1994. Mem. Internat. Theatre Critics Assn. Korea (v.p. 1986-91, pres. 1993-95). Home: Yonhee Dong 112-33, 120-110 Seoul South Korea Office: Hallym U English, 200-702 Chunchon South Korea

HAN, SEHWAN, medical educator; b. Seoul, South Korea, May 28, 1959; s. Ik-Sik and Hye-Ja (Kim) H. BS, Seoul Nat. U. Coll. Medicine, 1985, MS, 1994, PhD, 1996. Lic. in medicine, Korea, 1985. Intern Seoul Nat. U. Hosp., 1985-86, resident, 1990-94, fellow in surgery, 1994-95; asst. prof. surgery Inje U., Seoul, 1995-2000, assoc. prof. surgery, 2000—. Contbr. articles to profl. jours. Capt. Korean Army, 1986-89. Mem. Internat. Soc. Surgery, N.Y. Acad. Sci., Internat. Hepato-Pancreato-Biliary Assn. Home: Sucho-gu, 599-7 Umyon-dong, Seoul South Korea Office: Inje Univ Sangeye Palk Hosp, 761-1 Sangeye-Dong, 139-707 Seoul South Korea

HAN, SEUNG-SOO, diplomat; b. Chunchon, Republic Korea, Dec. 28, 1936; m. Soja Han; 2 children. BA, Yonsei Univ., Seoul, Republic Korea, 1960; MPA, Seoul Nat. Univ., 1963; DPhil in Econs., U. York, Eng., 1968. Fellow, lectr. econs. U. York, Eng., 1965-68; rsch. officer dept. applied econs. Cambridge (Eng.) U., 1970-88; prof. econs. Seoul Nat. U., 1985-86; chmn. Korea Trade Commn., 1987-88; min. trade and industry Govt. Republic Korea, 1988-92; amb. to U.S. Govt. Republic Korea, Washington, 1993-94; chief of staff to the pres. Seoul, 1994-95; dep. prime min., min. fin. and economy, 1996-97; vis. prof. dept. internat. rels. U. Tokyo, 1986-87; mem. Nat. Assembly, 1988-92, 1996-2000, 2000—. Author 8 books; contbr. articles to profl. jours. Fulbright vis. scholar Harvard U., 1986-87. Office: Nat Assembly, 1 Yoidodong, Seoul Korea

HAN, SHAOWEI, geomatics educator; b. Linghai, Liaoning, China, Feb. 6, 1965; s. Wanjin Han and Guiyun Zhang; m. Ping Wang, Dec., 1990; children: Ning, Jenny. BSc, Wuhan U. Surveying & Mapping, China, 1986, MSc, 1989; PhD, U. NSW, Australia, 1997. Assoc. lectr. Wuhan Tech. U. Surveying & Mapping, 1989-90, 91-92, lectr., 1992-93, assoc. prof., 1993-94; rsch. asst. Hong Kong Poly. U., 1990-91; lectr. U. NSW, 1997-99, sr. lectr., 1999—. Author: Carrier Phase-Based Long Range GPS Kinematic Positioning, 1997; contbr. articles to jours. in field; inventor in field. Recipient prize U.S. Inst. Navigation, 1995, 96, Inst. Surveyors, Australia, 1996. Mem. IEEE, Am. Geophys. Union, Inst. Navigation, Internat. Assn. Geodesy (spl. study group 1.157 1995-99, study group 1.154 1995-99, chmn. spl. study group 1.179 1999-03). Office: Sch Geomatic Engring, U NSW, Sydney NSW 2052, Australia

HAN, YOUNGYEARL, communication theory educator; b. Seoul, Korea, June 10, 1938; s. Gilyong Han and Yonghyun Min; m. Eunmo Kim, June 18, 1971; children: Sanghoon, Yesung, Sangmin. BS, Seoul Nat. U., 1960; MS, U. Mo., Rolla, 1976, PhD, 1979. Rsch. scientist Korea Inst. Sci. and Tech., Seoul, 1969-70; vis. prof. comm. U. Colo., Colorado Springs, 1988-89; rsch. engr. Siemens Halske, Berlin, 1991-94; vis. prof. comm. Oreg. State U., Corvallis, 1995-96; prof. comm. theory Hanyang U., Seoul, 1980—; cons. Ministry of Interior, Seoul, 1981-91, Ministry of Comm., Seoul, 1989-94; dir. Korea Ednl. Indsl. Found., Seoul, 1990-92; prin. cons. Korea Patent Bur., Seoul, 1993—. Author: Information Theory, 1985; editor: Jour. of Korea Inst. of Comm., 1983-85; patentee in field. Chief steering com. Asia-Pacific Comm. Conf., Seoul, 1992. Presdl. citation Govt. of Korea, 1993. Mem. IEEE (sr.), Korea Inst. of Comm. (v.p. 1991-94, sr. v.p. 1995). Roman Catholic. Avocations: gardening, music. Office: Hanyang U Dept Elec Comm Engring, Sungdong-ku, Seoul 133-791, Republic of Korea

HAN, ZHI-QUAN, physicist, researcher; b. Beijing, China, Mar. 25, 1940; d. Ji-yuan and Hua-xin (You) H.; m. Tian-jin Wang, June 7, 1967; children: Jing-dong, Fan. Ed., U. Sci. and Tech. of China, Beijing, 1963. Technician North China Inst. Electro-Optics, Beijing, 1963-68; engr. S.W. Inst. Applied Magnetics of China, Mianyang, 1968-84, sr. engr., 1987-88, rschr., 1988—; vis. scholar Ohio State U., Columbus, 1984-86; vis. prof. Xian Comm. U./Electronics, China, 1993. Recipinet Nat. Women's banner Nat. Dem. Women Union, 1979, Advanced Person of Sci., Ministry of Electronic Industry, 1982; Guang-hua grantee, 1993. Mem. Chinese Inst. Electronics. Home: No 356 Mian Zhou South Rd, Mianyang Sichuan 621000, China Office: SW Inst Appled Magnetics, PO Box 105, Mianyang Sichuan 621000, China

HAN, ZHUBIN, federal judge. Procurator-gen. Supreme People's Procuratorate, Beijing. Office: Sup Peoples Procuratorate, 147 Beiheyan Dr, Beijing 100726, China*

HANAI, FUMIHIKO, orthopedist; b. Ama gun, Aichi, Japan, Mar. 2, 1957; s. Kiyotaka and Suzuko (Itou) H.; m. Haruko Yamada, Nov. 3, 1987; children: Yuki, Shyouhei. M, Shiga U. Med. Sci., 1983; MD, Nagoya City U., 1993. Staff orthopedic dept. Nagoya City (Japan) U., 1983-84, 87-88, Toyokawa City (Japan) Hosp., 1984-85, Komaki City (Japan) Hosp., 1985-87; chief orthopedic dept. Inabe Kousei Hosp., Mie, Japan, 1988-99, Inabe Orthop. Clinic, 1999—; rschr. Siga U. Med. Sci., 1990—. Author: Spine, 1996, Neuroscience Research, 1993, Pain Research, 1993, Clinical Orthopedics and Related Research, 1998. Mem. Japanese Orthopedic Assn., Japan Spine Rsch. Soc., Japanese Soc. Study of Pain. Avocations: skiing, diving. Home: Sasaohigashi, Toin Town, Mie Hokuseichyo Inabe 511-0232, Japan Office: Inabe Orthop Clinic 3176-1, Yamada Toin Town, Mie Hokuseichyo Inabe Mie 511-0251, Japan

HANAI, RYO, molecular biologist, educator; b. Himeji, Hyogo, Japan, Jan. 13, 1962; s. Satoshi and Michiko (Umetani) H. BSc, U. Tokyo, 1984, MSc, 1986, PhD, 1989. Postdoctoral fellow Harvard U., Cambridge, Mass., 1989-92, rsch. assoc., 1992-96; lectr. in molecular biology Rikkyo U., Tokyo, 1996-98, assoc. prof., 1998—. Mem. Japanese Soc. Molecular Biology, Biophys. Soc. Japan, Biochem. Soc. Japan.

HANAMIRIAN, VARUJAN, mechanical engineer, educator, journalist, publisher; b. Istanbul, Turkey, June 23, 1952; s. Kurgin and Etil Sona (Azat) H. Dip. in Mech. Engring., U. Stuttgart, Fed. Republic Germany. Postal mgr. Foto Annemie, Stuttgart; tchr. Berlitz Sch., Stuttgart; creative dir. Unver Werbeagentur, Stuttgart; scientific asst. Fraunhofer-Gesellschaft, Stuttgart; course leader Volkshochschule, Stuttgart; educator, cons.; translator various govtl. and pvt. instns. and offices. Mem. adv. bd. Produktion weekly. Organizer Orgn. Com. EM 1986, Stuttgart; interviewer various market rsch. assn.; adminstr. various offices. Mem. Verein Deutscher Ingenieure. Club: Allgemeiner Deutscher Automobil, München. Avocation: chess.

HANAMURA, TOSHIHIRO, engineer; b. Shizuoka, Japan, Jan. 30, 1956; s. Genki and Katsu (Yokohata) H.; m. Ikuko Matsuoka, Nov. 3, 1987; 1 child, Narihiro. B in Engring., Nagoya U., Japan, 1978, M in Engring., 1980; PhD in Sci., U. Va., 1983. Sr. rschr. Nippon Steel Co., Kawasaki, Japan, 1984—. Contbr. articles to profl. jours. Mem. Japan Inst. Metals, Materials Rsch. Soc., Iron and Steel Inst. Japan. Avocation: tennis.

HANAN, LAURA MOLEN, artist; b. Ft. Monmouth, N.J., Jan. 30, 1954; d. Richard Eugene Molen and Agnes Arlene (Stahlhacke) Rose; m. John Morris Hanan, Apr. 26, 1985; 1 child, Whitney Anne. BS, U. Calif. Berkeley, 1978; BA in Journalism, Humboldt State U., 1980; AOS in Visual Comm., Northwest Coll. Art, 1992. Reporter, city editor Contra Costa Sun, Moraga, Calif., 1980-81; sports reporter, photographer The Canby (Oreg.) Herald, 1981-82; sr. technical writer MDS Qantel Bus. Computers, Hayward, Calif., 1982-84; bus. mgr., owner, designer Hanan Constrn. and Design Co., Inc., Alameda, Calif., 1986-90; dir. admissions Northwest Coll. Art, Poulsbo, Wash., 1992-93; fine artist, graphic artist Laura Hanan Art, Gig Harbor, Seattle, Wash., 1993—; owner, rennovator Sage Equities, 2000; creative dir. Pacific Pipeline, Kent, Wash., 1992-93; co-owner The Watermark Gallery, Village Art Gallery, Freighthouse Gallery, Gig Harbor, Tacoma, 1993-96; art dir., cons. Exec. Office Svcs., Gig Harbor, Beaverton, Oreg., 1996-97. Exhibited in group shows Emerald City Fine Art Gallery, Seattle, 1996-97, Nicholas Joseph Fine Art, N.Y.C., 1997-98, Hastings-Ray Gallery, Southern Pines, N.C., 1997—, Peninsula Br. Libr., Gig Harbor, 1994, 95, 96, Tacoma Art Mus., 2000; represented in permanent collection Pierce County Libr., also pvt. collections. Recipient First Place prize Peninsula Art League, 1995, 2d place, 1996, 3d place, 1997, Peoples Choice award Peninsula Art League, 1997; accepted for 1999 Tacoma Art Mus. juried fundraiser, for 25th anniversary "The Night Tacoma Danced", 2000. Avocations: graphic art, weight lifting, sewing, computers, walking.

HANANI, MENACHEM, physiologist, biology educator; b. Petah-Tikvah, Israel, July 29, 1945; s. Joseph and Hassia (Weisfish) H.; m. Pnina Shatil, June 16, 1974; children: Yair, Yael. BSc, Hebrew U., Jerusalem, 1968, MSc, 1970, PhD, 1976. Instr. Hebrew U., Jerusalem, 1974-76; rsch. fellow NIH, Bethesda, Md., 1976-78; hon. fellow U. Coll., London, 1979, 82; head Lab. Exptl. Surgery Hadassah U. Hosp., Jerusalem, 1979—; rsch. assoc. Mayo Clinic, Rochester, Minn., 1984, 86, 93, 95-96, 98-99; chmn. neurobiology tchg. divsn. Hebrew U., Jerusalem, 1995-98. Editor: Presynaptic Regulation of Neurotransmitter Release, 1991; contbr. articles to profl. jours. Rsch. grantee US-Israel Binat. Sci. Found., 1988, 91, 95, 99, Israel Sci. Found., 1988, 94; Wellcome Found. fellow, London, 1979, 82. Mem. Am. Physiol. Soc. Office: Hadassah U Hosp, Mount Scopus, 91240 Jerusalem Israel

HANAPPE, PAUL CLEMENT, transportation executive, consultant; b. Fayt, Hainaut, Belgium, May 22, 1931; s. Carl and Blanche (Andries) H.; m. Odile Dumas, July 8, 1967; children: Cyrille, Florence. D in Law, Louvain U., Belgium, 1953, degree in econs. sci., 1954; MA in Econs., Princeton U., 1960. Lawyer Barreau, Mons, Belgium, 1953-61; chief of projects Soc. of Techniques and Econ. Study, Paris, 1961-69; rsch. dir. Soc. d'Econ. et de Math. Afflipuer-Metra Int., Paris, 1969-77; prof. Archtl. Sch., Brussels, 1978—; dir. Higher Inst. Urbanism and Urban Renovation, Brussels, 1978-82; rsch. dir. Nat. Inst. Rsch. of Transp. and Sec., Paris, 1982—; vis. prof. Erasmus U., Rotterdam, The Netherlands, 1977-78. Author: Une Image de La France en 2000, 1971, Les Firmes Multinationales, 1972; Industries in Europe, 1973, Industrial Ports, 1980; mem. editorial bd. Transport Revs., 1984, Questions, 1987, Research, Transport, Security, 1988. Pres. Assn. Montparnasse Residents, Paris, 1973-75. Recipient Knight of the Crown, King of Belgium, 1976. Mem. Future Studies Fedn. (founder 1974), Internat. Assn. Ports and Harbours, Union of City Planners of Belgium. Home: 20 Rue CDT R Mouchotte, 75014 Paris France Office: INRETS, 2 Av Gen Malleret-Joinville, 94114 Arcueil France

HANASSAB, SHAHRAM SAMUEL, electronics executive, engineer; b. Tehran, Iran, Sept. 21, 1955; arrived in Eng., 1971; s. Nourullah and Parvindokht Hanassab; m. Tannaz Elghanian, Apr. 6, 1995. BSc with honors, U. London, 1977, PhD, 1983; MSc, U. Wales Inst. Sci. and Tech., 1979. Lectr. U. London, 1982-84; sales mgr. Global Import/Export Ltd., London, 1979-81; mng. dir. Global Sales Ltd., London, 1981-85, Hanaco Ltd., London, 1985—. Contbr. articles to profl. jours. including Internat. Jour. Cybernetics. Mem. Inst. Mgmt., Cybernetics Soc. Jewish. Avocations: reading books and journals, travel, chess, computer programs, history. Office: Hanaco Ltd, 198 City Rd, London EC1V 2PH, England

HANAU, KENNETH JOHN, III, venture capitalist; b. Ridgewood, N.J., Apr. 30, 1965; s. Kenneth John Jr. and Carol Lee (Rossner) H.; m. M. Ranson Smith, June 4, 1994; children: Lindsay Lee, Hollin Ranson. BA magna cum laude, Amherst Coll, 1988; MBA, Harvard U., 1993. CPA, Vt. Assoc. Coopers & Lybrand, Boston, 1989-90; asst. to pres. K&H Corrugated Case Corp., Walden, N.Y., 1990-91; assoc. Morgan Stanley & Co., Inc., N.Y.C., 1993-94; prin. Weiss, Peck & Greer, Private Equity Ptnrs., LLC, N.Y.C., 1994—; Bd. dirs. K&H Corrugated Case Corp., Walden, N.Y., Shelter Distbn., Inc., Indpls., Richelieu Foods, Inc., Northbrook, Ill., Color Assocs., Inc., St. Louis, Lionheart Newspaper Inc., Fort Worth, Tex., Regent Comm., Inc., Covington, Ky., Village Voice Media, LLC, N.Y.C., Masters Inst., Inc., San Jose, Calif. Mem. Siwanoy Country Club, Harvard Club N.Y.C., Madison Beach Club, Hay Harbor Club (Fishers Island, N.Y.). Avocations: reading, music, golf. E-mail: Ken.Hanau@wpginvest.com. Home: 21 Gladwin Pl Bronxville NY 10708-2201 Office: Weiss Peck Greer LLC One New York Plaza New York NY 10004

HANAUER, CARL MORTON, storage company executive; b. Newark, Sept. 9, 1936; s. Leonard Gustave and Ruth (Mehr) H.; m. Paula Bernstein, June 30, 1959 (div. June 1965); 1 child, Lisa Gail; m. Lynn Ann Landman, Sept. 1, 1979; children: Alexis, Zachary. PhD in Fin., Pacific West U., L.A., 1959. Pres. Rental Property Svc. Corp., L.A., 1966-83; mng. dir. Abacus Self Storage, London, 1983-88, Self Storage Svcs. Ltd., London, 1988-95, Internat. Storage Mgmt. Ltd., Walton-on-Thames, Surrey, Eng., 1995—; chmn. Hanauer & Sons Investments, Inc., N.Y.C., 1967—. Avocation: growing orchids. Home: Heatherfield Cottage, Queens Rd, Surrey Waybridge KT13 0AH, England Office: Internat Storage Mgmt Ltd, New Zealand Ave, Surrey Walton-on-Thames KT12 1PL, England

HANAWA, TOSHIYA, economics educator; b. Tokyo, Sept. 9, 1931; s. Tsunetaro and Torae Hanawa; m. Saeko Mizuno, Oct. 20, 1960. BA, Hitotsubashi U., Kunitachi, Tokyo, 1955, MA, 1957, PhD, 1979. Lectr. Tokyo Gakugei U., 1960-63, assoc. prof., 1963-69; assoc. prof. Hitotsubashi U., Kunitachi, Tokyo, 1969-72, prof., 1972-95, prof. emeritus, 1995—; prof. Chuo U., Tokyo, 1995—. Author: Money and Monetary Economy, 1980, Monetary Economics, 1982. Mem. Japan Soc. Monetary Econs. (pres. 1992-94), Sci. Coun. Japan. Home: Minami Chiyoda-ku, 2-6-13-503 Kudan, Tokyo 102-0074, Japan Office: Chuo U, 742-1 Higashinakano, Tokyo Hachioji 192-03, Japan

HANAWA, YOSHIKAZU, automotive executive; b. Tokyo, Mar. 14, 1934. BA in Econs., Tokyo U., 1957. With Nissan Motor Co. Ltd., Tokyo, 1957—, dir., 1985-88, mng. dir., 1988-90, exec. mng. dir., 1990-91, exec. v.p., 1991-96; pres. Nissan Motor Corp, Tokyo, 1996—, Now CEO. Office: Nissan Motor Co Ltd, 6-17-1 Ginza, Chuo-ku Tokyo 104-8023, Japan*

HANCOCK, CHARLES CAVANAUGH, JR., scientific association administrator; b. Riverside, Calif., Oct. 19, 1935; s. Charles Cavanaugh and Mary Elizabeth (Riordan) H.; children: Christopher Alan, Stephen Edward. B.S. in Chem. Engring, Stanford U., 1958; M.S. in Indsl. Engring, Tex. Tech U., 1967. Commd. 2d lt. U.S. Air Force, 1958, advanced through grades to lt. col., 1974; worldwide locations in research and devel. and logistics, to, 1979, ret., 1979; exec. officer Am. Soc. Biochem. and Molecular Biology, Bethesda, Md., 1979—; also mgr. Jour. Biol. Chemistry.; gen. sec. 17th Congress of Biochemistry and Molecular Biology; bd. dirs. Chem. Heritage Found., 1993-94. Decorated Meritorious Service medal with 3 oak leaf clusters. Mem. AAAS, Inst. Indsl. Engrs. (sr.), Coun. Engring. and Sci. Soc. Execs., Conv. Liaison Coun. (chmn. 1991-92), Profl. Conv. Mgmt. Assn., Coun. Sci. Editors, Soc. Scholarly Pub., Sigma Xi, Alpha Pi Mu, Univ. Club San Diego. Club: Univ. Club. Office: Am Soc Biochem & Molecular Biology 9650 Rockville Pike Bethesda MD 20814-3998

HANCOCK, ELEANOR IRIS MARGARETE, history lecturer; b. Hobart, Australia, Feb. 13, 1956; d. William Frederick and Eva Maria Jutta (Brinck) H.; m. Edward Barrington Wilson, Feb. 10, 1979 (div. Jan. 1995); m. Gunther Erich Rothenberg, Apr. 2, 1995. BA, Australian Nat. U., Canberra, 1978; MA, Victoria U. Wellington, New Zealand, 1983; PhD, Australian Nat. U., Canberra, 1989. Clerical officer Dept. Prime Minister and Cabinet, Canberra, 1978-79; diplomat Dept. Fgn. Affairs, Canberra, 1979-80; third sec. Australian High Commn., Wellington, New Zealand, 1980-83; diplomat Dept. Fgn. Affairs, Canberra, 1983-84; tutor U. Coll. U. New South Wales, 1984-88; lectr. to sr. lectr. Monash U. Melbourne, 1988—. Author: The National Socialist Leadership and Total War, 1941-1945, 1992.

HANCOCK, JOHN MICHAEL, biologist; b. Ipswich, Suffolk, Eng., Feb. 26, 1954; s. Ronald Henry and Margaret Molly (Dunt) H.; m. Elizabeth Banerjee. BSc with honors, Kings Coll., London, 1975; PhD, Edinburgh (Scotland) U., 1980. Postdoctoral asst. Max-Planck-Inst. Molecular Genetics, Berlin, 1978-82, Imperial Coll., London, 1982-85; postdoctoral assoc. Cambridge (Eng.) U., 1985-91; rsch. fellow Australian Nat. U., Canberra, 1991-94; group head Med. Rsch. Coun., Clin. Scis. Ctr., London, 1994-2000; reader Royal Holloway U. London, 2000—; hon. lectr. Imperial Coll., 1994. Editor: Chartwatch mag.; contbr. articles to profl. jours. (numerous citations 1988—). Mem. Soc. Molecular Biology and Evolution, Internat. Soc. Molecular Evolution, U.K. Genetical Soc. Avocations: collecting CDs, guitar. Office: Royal Holloway U London, Dept Computer Sci Egnam, Surrey TW20OEX, England

HANCOCK, WILLIAM FRANK, JR., management consultant; b. Richmond, Va., Jan. 4, 1942; s. William Frank and Gladys Elizabeth (George) H.; m. Donna G. Hosmer, May 18, 1968; children: Peter James, Jeffrey William, Jennifer Beth. BBA, U. Iowa, 1964; MBA, U. Pa., 1966; postgrad., Columbia Pacific U. CPA, CLU, CPCU, CMA, CDP. Exec. asst. to exec. v.p. John Hancock Mutual Life Ins. Co., Boston, 1966-69; mgmt. cons. Keane Assocs., Boston, 1969-74, regional mgr., 1974-75; v.p., gen. mgr. comml. sys. SofTech, Inc., Waltham, Mass., 1975-79; dir. internat. sales and field ops. Nixdorf Computer Co., Burlington, Mass., 1979-80; mgr. mktg. Digital Equipment Corp., 1980-84, electronic commerce mgr., 1984-97; mgmt. cons. electronic commerce Grant Thornton LLP, 1997-98; mgmt. cons., nat. electronic commerce practice Ernst & Young, LLP, 1998-2000; prin. IBM, 2000—; adj. prof. acctg. and fin. Grad. Sch. Bus., Northeastern U., Boston, 1966—, sr. instr. acctg. Grad. Sch. Bus. Babson Coll., Wellesley, Mass, 1985—. Treas. Pilgrim Ch.; trustee Sherborn Libr.; chmn. Sherborn coun. Boy Scouts Am. With U.S. Army, 1967-72. Recipient Outstanding Teacher of Yr. Awd., Northeastern Univ., 1989. Mem. AICPA, Data Processing Mgmt., Nat. Assn. Accts., Assn. Computing Machinery, Boston C. of C., Exec. Club Boston, Wharton Alumni Club, U. Iowa Alumni Assn. Congregational. Home: 24 Dexter Dr Sherborn MA 01770-1124 Office: IBM Corp 404 Wyman St Waltham MA 02451

HANCOCK, WILLIAM MARVIN, computer security and network engineering executive; b. Portsmouth, Va., Feb. 10, 1957; s. William H. and Marjorie E. (Davis) H. BA in Computer Sci., Thomas A. Edison Sr. Coll., 1992; MS in Computer Sci., Greenwich U., 1993, PhD in Computer Sci., 1994. Cert. info. systems security profl., network expert. Programmer Tex. Instruments, Dallas, 1972-74; cons. Digital Equipment Corp., Dallas, 1979-82; div. analyst Standard Oil of Ohio, Dallas, 1982-84; v.p. engring. New Leaf Techs., Arlington, Tex., 1984-90, Network 1 Inc., Arlington, 1990-94; exec. v.p. and chief tech. officer Network 1, Boston, 1990-2000; v.p. security, chief security officer Exodus Comm., Inc., Arlington, 2000—; U.S. network expert Am. Nat. Stds. Inst., N.Y.C., 1985-87; stds. editor Internat. Orgn. for Stds., Geneva, 1986-88. Author: Designing and Implementing Ethernet Networks, 1988, Network Concepts and Architectures, 1989, Issues and Problems in Computer Networks, 1990, Advanced Ethernet/802.3 Management and Performance, 1992, Computer Consulting is a Very Funny Business, 1993, Designing and Implementing ATM Networks, 1994, Applied Networking, 1996, Advanced Network Architecture, 1996, Everything You Wanted to Know About Networks But Were Afraid to Ask, 1998, Windows-NT Network Security, 1998, Networking Explained, 1999, Network Security Concepts, 2000, Practical Guide to Network Security, 2000; editor-in-chief Computers and Security Mag.; columnist Network Security Mag. With USN, 1974-79. Recipient Arnold Fletcher award, 1992. Mem. IEEE, NSOR, ANSI, Internat. Computer Security Assn., Digital Equipment Computer Users Soc. (Tech. Excellence award 1992), Assn. for Computing Machinery, Computer Security Inst. Achievements include design of over 4300 computer networks. Six-time world aikido champion. Office: Exodus Comm Inc 4101 Vistaview Ct Arlington TX 76016-6404

HANDA, HIROSHI, molecular biology educator; b. Nakatsu, Oita, Japan, Oct. 22, 1946; s. Toyomi and Kikue H.; m. Sachiko, Nov. 11, 1973; children: Gen, Kan, Sou. MD, Keio U., 1972, DMS, 1976. Rsch. assoc. U. Tokyo, 1976-77; postdoctoral fellow NIH, Bethesda, Md., 1977-78, MIT, Boston, 1978-80; rsch. assoc. U. Tokyo, 1980-84, assoc. prof., 1984-91; prof. Tokyo Inst. Tech., 1991—; head dept. biomolecular engring. Tokyo Inst. Tech., 1993—; dir. Gene Rsch. Ctr., Yokohoma, 1997—. Recipient Kitasato prize, 1991, Teshima prize, 1994, Yazaki prize, 2000. Mem. AAAS, Am. Soc. Microbiology, Japanese Biochem. Soc. (councilor 1991—), Molecular Biology Soc. Japan (com. 1993—). Avocations: ceramics, drawing, ice hockey. Home: 1-17-16 Sakurajosui, Setagaya 156, Japan Office: Tokyo Inst Tech, 4259 Nagatsuda, Midori 227, Japan

HANDA, JUNICHI, management consultant; b. Tokyo, Feb. 13, 1957; s. Hideo and Sumiko Handa; m. Yukiko Fukushima; children: Maiko, Ryutaro. BA, U. Tokyo, 1979; MBA, Harvard U., 1987. Sr. mgr. Tonen Corp., Tokyo, 1979-87, Mc Kinsey & Co.,Inc., Tokyo, 1988-95; v.p. A.T. Kearney, Tokyo, 1995—. Author: IT Management, 1999; contbr. articles to profl. jours. Avocations: histories of Japan and China.

HANDEL, WILLIAM KEATING, advertising and sales executive; b. N.Y.C., Mar. 23, 1935; s. Irving Nathaniel and Marguerite Mary (Keating) H.; m. Margaret Inez Sitton; children: William Keating II, David Roger. BA in Journalism, U. S.C., 1959, MA in English Lit., 1960. Account supr. Ketchum, MacLeod & Grove, Pitts., 1960-67; mgr. advt. and pub. rels. ITT Gen. Controls, Glendale, Calif., 1967-80; mgr. corp. comm. Fairchild Camera and Instrument Corp., 1980-84; dist. mgr. Cahners Pub. Co., 1984-90; western regional sales mgr. Quality Publ. Co., 1990—; pub. rels. counsel Calif. Pvt. Edn. Schs., 1978-87; chmn. exhibits Mini/Micro Computer Conf. Bd. dirs. West Valley Athletic League, L.A. chpt. USMC Scholarship Found.; pub. rels. cons. Ensenada, Mexico Tourist Commn., 1978; chmn., master of ceremonies USMC Birthday Ball, L.A., 1979-82. With USMC, 1950-53. Decorated Silver Star, Bronze Star, Purple Heart (4), Navy Commendation medal with combat V; recipient Pub. Svc. award L.A.

Heart Assn., 1971-73. Mem. Bus. and Profl. Advt. Assn. (cert. bus. communicator, past pres.), 1st Marine Divsn. Assn., Navy League (bd. dirs.), AdLinx Golf Club of So. Calif., Torrey Pines Golf Club, Griffith Pk. Golf Club, Nueva España Boat Club, Bajamar Country Club, Ensenada Country Club, Baja Country Club, Ensenada Fish and Game Club (Baja, Mex.), U. S.C. Alumni Club (founder/pres. L.A. chpt.), Sigma Chi (chpt. adv.). Republican. Roman Catholic. Home: 2428 Badajoz Pl Carlsbad CA 92009-8044

HANDELMAN, DORON, patent attorney, physicist; b. Bucharest, Romania, Aug. 10, 1955; arrived in Israel, 1961; s. Benjamin and Madelene (Kindler) H.; m. Anat Prober, Feb. 5, 1980; children: Amir, Limor. BSc in Math. and Physics, Tel-Aviv U., 1980, MSc in Physics, 1986. Project officer Israel Def. Force, Tel-Aviv, 1979-84; software engr. Decision Sys. Israel, Givat-Shmuel, 1984-86, project engr., 1986-92, cons., 1992-95; patent atty. Sanford T. Colb and Co., Advs. and Patent Attys., Rehovot, Israel, 1994-96; ind. patent atty. and cons. Givatayim, Israel, 1996—; founder, dir. Eatech Advanced Food Tech., Haifa, Israel, 1995—, Dauphin Biotech. Promotion, Hertzlia, Israel, 1994—. Contbr. articles to profl. jours.; patentee in various fields. Con. Givatayim (Israel) City Hall, 1995-96. Recipient award for improvement of a libr. of physics related software programs Israel Aircraft Industries, 1990, award for improvement of an electro-optical software program Israel Aircraft Industries, 1990. Mem. IEEE (sr.), N.Y. Acad. Scis. Office: Doron Handelman, PO Box 473, 53103 Givatayim Israel

HANDELSMAN, DAVID JOSHUA, endocrinologist, researcher; b. Melbourne, Victoria, Australia, Apr. 16, 1950; s. Salomon and Sulamit (Kagan/Gershon) H.; m. Penelope Louise Hoskins, Aug. 8, 1986; children: Timothy, Nicholas, Elizabeth. MB, BS, U. Melbourne, 1974; PhD, U. Sydney, NSW, Australia, 1984. Resident med. officer Royal Prince Alfred Hosp., Sydney, 1975-77, endocrinology registrar, 1978-79; rsch. fellow U. Sydney, 1980-83; NHMRD rsch. fellow Med. Rsch. Coun., U. Sydney, 1985-86, Wellcome sr. rsch. fellow, 1987-89; rsch. fellow UCLA, 1984-85; prof. reproductive endocrinology and andrology, 1996—; found. dir. ANZAC Rsch. Inst., Concord Hosp., U. Sydney; dir. dept. andiology Concord Hosp. Contbr. articles to profl. jours. Fellow RACP; mem. Endocrine Soc., Am. Andrology Soc., Am. Fertility Soc., Australian Soc. Reproductive Biology, Endocrine Soc. Australia. Avocations: mathematics, family, work. Home: 18 N Arm Rd, Middle Cove, NSW Sydney 2068, Australia

HANDEREK, JAN MICHAL, physicist, educator; b. Lodygowice, Krakow, Poland, Sept. 9, 1934; s. Jan and Filomena (Jakubiec) H.; m. Irena Szczepanik; 1 child, Ewa. MS, High Pedagogical Sch., Katowice, Poland, 1957; D Physics, Acad. Mining and Metallurgy, Crakow, Poland, 1964; Postgrad., Jagiellonian U., Crakow, Poland, 1968. Dr.'s Diploma; Diploma of Qualifying for Asst. Prof.; Diploma of Prof.'s Title. Asst., adj. High Pedagogical Sch., Katowice, Poland, 1957-68; asst. prof., holder of chair Silesian U., Katowice, Poland, 1968-76, assoc. prof., vice-dean, 1976-89, prof., 1989—; vis. prof. U. Metz (France), 1989, 91, 95; cons. European Orgn. Nuclear Rsch., Geneva, 1988-96, U. Milan/Nat. Inst. Nuclear Physics, 1995—. Author, co-author monographs; contbr. 135 articles to sci. jours. Recipient State Distinction Pres. of State, 1973, 78, Medal of Edn. Min. Edn., 1993, Scientific awards, Min. Edn., 1972, 78, 87. Roman Catholic. Avocations: tourism. Office: Inst Physics Silesian U, Univerytecka 4, 40 007 Katowice Poland

HANDLER, KENNETH VICTOR, banker; b. Toronto, Aug. 12, 1952; s. Maurice and Freda (Inwald) H.; m. Solange Moussa, July 21, 1976; children: Sharon, Karen, Natalie. BSc, Hebrew U., Jerusalem, Israel, 1978. Mgr. br. unit Israel Discount Bank Ltd., Tel Aviv, 1982-86, mgr. fgn. trade desk, tng. ctr., 1986-88, mgr. documentary credits, import dept., 1988-95, mgr. local guarantees credit divsn., 1995—; bank rep. Israel nat. com. Internat. C. of C., Tel Aviv, 1986-94; bank rep. Israael-Can. C. of C., Tel Aviv, 1986-88, Israel-Brit. C. of C., Tel Aviv, 1988-95. Hon. treas. Israel-Brit. C. of C., 1995-2000. Tank comdr. Israeli Def. Forces, 1970-73. Mem. Israel Squash Assn. (vice-chmn.). Avocations: reading, music, squash, tennis, football. Office: Israel Discount Bank Ltd, 27 Yehuda Halevy St, 65136 Tel Aviv Israel

HANDLER, THOMAS JOSEPH, solicitor; b. Budapest, Hungary, May 25, 1938; arrived in Australia, 1948; arrived in U.K., 1965; s. Nicholas and Lily (Singer) H.; m. Adrienne Marxreiter, May 25, 1970; children: Rebecca Louise, Sophie Melinda. BA, Sydney (Australia) U., 1958, LLB, 1962. Solicitor NSW, Australia, 1962, Eng., 1966. Articled clk., solicitor W.C. Taylor & Scott, Sydney, 1959-65; solicitor Simmons & Simmons, London, 1965-67; solicitor Baker & McKenzie, London, 1978-99, ptnr. (adminstrv. ptnr. 3 occasions), 1973-97; cons., 1997-99; trustee Found. for Internat. Environ. Law & Devel., London, 1993—; mediator, Ctr. for Dispute Resolution, London, 1995—; mediator, Mediation U.K.'s Camden Mediation Svc., London, 1994—; mem. European adv. com. Ctr. for Pub. Resources, U.S., 1996. Mem. editl. bd., then sr. editl. advisor (jour.) Environment Law Brief, 1993-95; legal cons. (jour./newsletter) ELFline, 1994—; editor, contbr.: Regulating the European Environment, 1989, 2d edit., 1993, 3d edit., 1997. Mem. exec. com. Environ. Law Found., London, 1994—; mem. bd. Environ. Coun., London, 1996-98; chmn. Environ. Resolve, London, 1995-98. Winner Classical Soc. NSW Latin Reading Competition, 1955. Avocations: Maine Coon cats, arts, reading, gardening, cross-country skiing.

HANDLEY, LEON HUNTER, lawyer; b. Lakeland, Fla., Sept. 9, 1927; s. Driskle Hubert and Mamie (Denmark) H.; m. Mary Virginia Wolfe, May 2, 1953; children: Leon Hunter, Mary Ellen, Laura Catherine, Leann Virginia. BSBA with honors, U. Fla., 1949, JD, 1951. Bar: Fla. 1951, U.S. Dist. Ct. (so. dist.) Fla. 1952, U.S. Dist. Ct. (mid. dist.) Fla. 1962, U.S. Supreme Ct. 1956, U.S. Ct. Appeals (5th cir.) 1960, U.S. Ct. Appeals (11th cir.) 1981. Pres. Gurney & Handley, Orlando, Fla., 1951—; bd. dirs. Orlando/Tampa Cracker Groves, Inc., Orlando, 1964—; v.p., bd. dirs. So. Indsl. Savs. Bank, Orlando, Claude H. Wolfe, Inc., Orlando, 1969—; pres., chmn. bd. dirs. Mine & Mill Supply Co., Lakeland, 1966—; gen. counsel, life dir., past pres. Cen. Fla. Fair; chmn. bd. trustees Sta. WMFE-TV. Pres. Chesley Magruder Charitable Trust; elder Presbyn. Ch. Warrant officer U.S. Maritime Svc., 1945-46, ETO; sgt. U.S. Army, 1946-48, Korea; capt. USAFR, 1949-59. Fellow Am. Coll. Trial Lawyers; mem. ABA, Am. Bd. Trial Advocates (Fla. Trial Lawyers of Yr. 1966, advocate), Orange County Bar Assn. (past pres.), Fla. Bar Assn. (past pres. sta. jr. bar sect., bd. govs. 1959-60), Fedn. Ins. and Corp. Counsel, Internat. Assn. Def. Counsel, Assn. Def. Trial Attys., Trial Attys. Am., Am. Judicature Soc. (listed Best Lawyers in Am.), Pres.'s Coun. (founder U. Fla. chpt.), Citrus Club, Orlando Country Club, Univ. Club, Masons (grand orator Fla. 1982, 86), K.T., Shriners, Scottish Rite (33d degree, insp. gen. hon. 1979), Rotary (pres. Orlando chpt. 1984, Paul Harris fellow), Travelers' Century Club, Fla. Blue Key (pres. 1951), Phi Delta Phi, Alpha Tau Omega (pres. U. of Fla. chpt. 1951), Phi Kappa Phi, Alpha Kappa Psi, Beta Gamma Sigma (U. Fla. Hall of Fame). Republican. Avocations: jogging, handball. Home: 1800 Turnberry Ter Orlando FL 32804-6015 Office: Gurney & Handley 225 E Robinson St Ste 450 Orlando FL 32801-1905

HANDLEY, VERNON GEORGE, conductor; b. Enfield, Eng., Nov. 11, 1930; s. Vernon Douglas and Claudia Lillian Handley; m. Barbara Black, 1954 (div.); 2 children; m. Victoria Parry-Jones (div.); 2 children; m. Catherine Newby, 1987; 1 child. Student, Oxford U., Guildhall Sch. of Music; hon. doctorate, U. Surrey, 1980; D of Music (hon.), Liverpool U., 1992. Condr. Oxford U. Mus. Club and Union, 1953-54, Oxford U. Dramatic Soc., 1953-54, Tonbridge Philharm. Soc., 1958-61, Guildford Philharm. Orch. and Choir, 1962-83; assoc. condr. London Philharm. Orch., 1983-86, guest condr., 1966-72; prof. orch. and conducting Royal Coll. Music, 1966-72; prin. condr. Ulster Orch., 1985-89, Malmö Symphony Orch., 1985-89; prin. guest condr. Liverpool Philharm. Orch., 1989-94, condr. emeritus; prin. guest condr. Melbourne Symphony Orch., 1993-95; chief condr. W. Australian Symphony Orch., 1994-96; assoc. condr. Royal Philharm. Orch., 1994—, guest condr., 1961-94, numerous others; toured Germany, 1966, 80, South Africa, 1974, Holland, 1980, Sweden, 1980, 81, Australia, 1986; numerous recs. Recipient Arnold Bax Meml. medal for conducting, 1962, Hi-Fi News Audio award, 1982, Gramophone Record of Yr., 1986, 89, Brit. Phonographic Industry award, 1988; named Condr. of Yr., Brit. Composer's Guild, 1974; fellow Goldsmith's Coll., London, 1987. Mem. Royal Philharm. Soc. (hon.). Avocations: bird photography, building furniture. Office: Royal Philharm Orch, 16 Clerkenwell Green, London EC1R 0DP, England also: 4 Addision Bridge Place, London W14 8XP, England*

HANDLING, PIERS GUY PATON, arts executive; b. Calgary, Alta., Can., July 21, 1949; s. William Douglas and Margaret Joan (Garrod) H. BA with honors, Queen's U., Kingston, 1971. Dir. rsch. and info. Can. Film Inst., Ottawa, 1975-76, dir. publs., 1976-79, assoc. dir., 1980-81; sessional lectr. Carleton U., Ottawa, 1981-83, Queen's U., Kingston, 1984; dep. dir., artistic dir. Festival of Festivals, 1987-94; dir. Toronto (Can.) Internat. Film Festival Group, 1994—. Author: Canadian Feature Films 1913-1969, part 3 1964-69, 1976, The Films of Don Shebib, 1978; author, editor: Self Portrait: Essays on the Canadian and Quebec Cinemas, 1980, The Shape of Rage: The Films of David Cronenberg, 1983, L'Horreur interieure: Les films de David Cronenberg, 1990. Avocations: skiing, climbing, tennis, squash. Home: 84 Langley Ave, Toronto, ON Canada M4K 1B5 Office: 16th Fl, 2 Carlton St, Toronto, ON Canada M5B 1J3

HANDLIR, JIRI VLADIMIR, headmaster; b. Brno, Czech Republic, Oct. 15, 1946; s. Jaromir Handlir and Drahomira (Tvaruzkova) Bulickova; m. Dana De Diana Boro, July 24, 1969 (div. 1971); m. Dagmar Dvorakova, July 12, 1973; children: Petr, Irena. Student, Tech. Coll., Brno, 1966; MSc, U. Brno, 1971; PhD, Inst. Tech., Brno, 1986. Rschr. Zbrojovka Brno, 1972-84; sr. rschr. Tesla Kolin, Brno, 1984-90; headmaster Tech. Coll., Brno, 1990—; assoc. prof. Inst. Tech., Brno, 1985—. Author: Operations Research, 1989, Systems Identification, 1991, The Use of Evolution Program for Learning of Artificial Intelligence Systems, 1996, Management, 1998; author photography post cards, calendars, 1977—. Cpl. Czechoslovakia mil., 1971-72. Mem. Computer Soc. of IEEE, N.Y. Acad. Scis., Press Club. Avocations: photography, tennis, skiing, mountaining. Home: Maresova 8, Brno 602 00, Czech Republic Office: ISS, Purkynova 97, Brno 612 00, Czech Republic

HANDRICH, KLAUS DIETER, physicist, researcher, educator; b. Hoyerswerda, Saxonia, Germany, Sept. 7, 1939; s. Max and Magdalena (Bartuschka) H.; m. Ludmilla Wasiljewa, June 25, 1963 (div. May 1983); children: Lars, Evelyn; m. Roswitha Wuttke, May 30, 1985; 1 child, Adriano. Diploma in physics, U. Leipzig, Germany, 1962, PhD in Physics, 1967; habilitation, Tech. U., Dresden, Germany, 1973. Asst. lectr. Tech. U., Dresden, 1967-75; univ. lectr. Tech. U. Merseburg, 1975-89; prof. theoretical physics Tech. U., Ilmenau, Germany, 1989—; head dept. theoretical physics I Tech. U., Ilmenau, 1989, dir. Inst. Physics, 1990-92; referee Physica Status Solidi, Berlin, 1973; vice-dir. dept. physics Tech. U., Merseburg, Germany, 1980-86. Author: (with S. Kobe) Amorphe Ferro-and Ferrimagnetika, 1980 (award Tech. U. Merseburg 1983); editor: (in German) Elektricheskie kristalli, 1972, La matière à l état solide, 1987. Mem. Deutsche Physikalische Gesellschaft Bad Honnef. Avocations: physics, classical music. Home: Buchenstrasse 11, 98693 Ilmenau Germany Office: Tech U Ilmenau Inst Physics, Weimarer Strasse 25, 98684 Ilmenau Germany

HANDS, ERIC WILLIAM, civil engineer, electrical engineer, researcher; b. Oakland, Calif., Sept. 27, 1943; s. Richard Ford Hands and Esther Mae (Larson) Hazelet; m. Monica Louise Ulery, 1968 (div. 1973); 1 child, Lars Michael Foxen; m. Sherrill Ann Gardner, 1977 (div. 1985); 1 child, Lief Forrest. Student, U. Calif., Davis, 1975-80, U. Wash., 1981-82, 84, Griffin Bus. Coll., 1983; BS in Liberal Studies, U. State N.Y., Albany, 1984. Engr.-in-tng., Calif., 1985. Engring. technician, software developer Naval Undersea Warfare Engring. Sta., Keyport, Wash., 1980-81; engr., carpenter, sales profl. various orgns., 1984—; real estate/ins. sales staff Channel Islands Real Estate/Metropolitan Ins., Port Hueneme, Camarillo, Calif., 1985; civil engr. Martin, Northart & Spencer, Santa Barbara, Calif., 1985-86, Dept. Pub. Works, County of Santa Barbara, 1986-87; owner, tech. cons. Silver Fox, Seattle, 1999—. Author, editor: Energy and Resources, 1976. Contbg. mem. Dem. Nat. Com., 1993; hon. mem. Rep. Nat. Com., 1992. With USN, 1961-64, U.S. Army Res., 1982-88, USNR, 1988—, U.S. Merchant Marine, 1991-2000. Mem. IEEE, ASCE, NSPE, N.Y. Acad. Scis. E-mail: eds2@se-anet.com. Home: 5035 15th Ave NE Apt 205 Seattle WA 98105-4335 Office: Silver Fox Ste 1339 4739 University Way NE Seattle WA 98105-4412

HANDS, TERENCE DAVID (TERRY HANDS), theater and opera director; b. Jan. 9, 1941; s. Joseph Ronald and Luise Berthe (Kohler) H.; m. Josephine Barstow, 1964 (div. 1967); m. Ludmila Mikaël, 1974 (div. 1980); 1 child; life ptnr. Julia Lintott; 2 children. BA in Eng. Lang. and Lit. with honors, Birmingham (Eng.) U., 1962, DLitt (hon.), 1988; diploma with honors, RADA (Royal Acad. of Dramatic Art), 1964; DLitt (hon.), Middlesex U., 1997. Founder, artistic dir. Liverpool (Eng.) Everyman Theatre, 1964-66; artistic dir. RSC Theatreground, 1966-67; from assoc. dir. to artistic dir. Royal Shakespeare Co., England, 1967-91, dir. emeritus, 1991—; cons. Comedie Francaise, 1975-80, Clwyd Theatr Cymru, dir., 1997— contbr. to Theatre 72, Playback pubs.; translator of plays. Dir.: (plays) Hamlet, 1994, Merry Wives of Windsor, 1995, The Pretenders, 1996, The Royal Hunt of The Sun, 1996, The Importance of Being Ernest, 1997, A Christmas Carol, 1997, Equus, 1997, The Journey of Mary Kelly, 1998, The Seagull, 1998, The Norman Conquests, 1998, Macbeth, 1999, 12th Night, 1999, Under Milk Wood, 1999, Macbeth (Broadway), 2000, others. Recipient Chevalier des Arts et des Lettres, 1975, Pragnell Shakespeare award 1991. Fellow Shakespeare Inst. (hon.). Office: Clwyd Theatr Cymru, Mold Flintshire, North Wales CH7 1YA, England

HANDSAKER, JERROLD LEE, lawyer; b. Ames, Iowa, Apr. 12, 1950; s. Vernon Glenn and Hyllis Elenor (Ullestad) H.; m. Janet Marie Gregg, June 25, 1976; children: Melissa Ann, Lori Beth. BS in Indsl. Adminstrn., Iowa State U., 1972; JD, Drake U., 1975. Bar: Iowa 1976, U.S. Tax Ct. 1976, U.S. Dist. Ct. (so. dist.) Iowa 1976, U.S. Dist. Ct. (no. dist.) Iowa 1982, U.S. Supreme Ct. 1987. Assoc. Bloethe Law Firm, Victor, Iowa, 1976-78; lawyer Hattery-Handsaker Law Firm, Nevada, Iowa, 1978-79; ptnr. Parker & Handsaker Law Firm, Nevada, 1979-89; assoc. Buchanan Dotson Buchanan Bibler & Buchanan, Algona, Iowa, 1989-90; ptnr. Buchanan Bibler Buchanan Handsaker & Gabor, Algona, Iowa, 1991-98, of counsel, 1998-99; pres., CEO Innovative Lighting Inc., Algona, 1993—, Oak Lake Home Owners Assn. Algona, 1990-94; bd. dirs. Mirenco Inc., 1998—. Contbr. article to popular boating mag.; patentee motorized telescopic boat light, 1994, self-concealing landscape lights, 1995. Recipient Maynard Speece award for most popular new invention Minn. Inventors Congress, Redwood Falls, Minn., 1994. Mem. ABA, Nat. Marine Mfrs.'s Assn., Iowa State Bar Assn., Kossuth County Bar Assn. (treas. 1991-98), Am. Boating and Yachting Coun., Kiwanis Club of Algona (bd. dirs., pres. 1997). Republican. Lutheran. Avocations: golf, swimming, volleyball, flying. Home: 62 Smith Cir Algona IA 50511-5004 Office: Innovative Lighting Inc PO Box 494 Algona IA 50511-0494

HANDY, ROBERT TRUMAN, association administrator, finance consultant; b. Portland, Oreg., May 1, 1941; s. Royal Sheppard and Eloise (Yeager) H.; m. Linda Rose Andreas, Aug. 26, 1967 (div. 1976); 1 child, Heather Andreas Handy Zimmerman; m. Janet Lee Ward, Jan. 14, 1979; stepchildren: Christopher W. Ward, Elizabeth Leigh Ward Schmidt. BS in History, Polit. Sci., Portland State U., 1969, MA in Am. Diplomatic History, 1971. Dir. community svcs. Coll. of the Mainland, Texas City, Tex., 1972-74, dir. internat. programs, 1975-76; founder and exec. dir. Gulf Coast World Affairs Coun., 1976-84; exec. dir. Houston World Trade Assn., 1984-88; pres. Devel. Resources Internat., Houston, 1988-99; exec. dir. Brazoria County Hist. Mus., Angleton, Tex., 1992-99; registered rep. SWS Fin. Svcs., Houston, 1999—; adj. faculty Alvin (Tex.) C.C., 1994-98. Pub., editor Jour. Fgn. Affairs; internat. editor In Between Mag.; book reviewer Houston Chronicle. Bd. dirs. Galveston County Community Action Coun., Galveston, Tex., 1973, La Marque (Tex.) Aid and Guidance Coun., 1979; mem. La Marque Econ. Devel. Coun., 1980; del. European Community Visitors Program, Belgium, Fed. Republic Germany, France, Eng., 1981; chmn. Galveston County Coun. of Chambers, 1988; appointee European Community "Team 1992", 1989. With USN, 1959-62. Mem. Brazosport C. of C. (chmn. internat. com. 1992-93). Democrat. Avocations: racquetball, jogging. Home: 2910 Frostwood Cir Dickinson TX 77539-4207 Office: 18333 Egret Bay Blvd Houston TX 77058-3839

HANDZEL, ZEEV THEODOR, immunologist, allergist. MD, Hebrew U., Jerusalem, 1964. Rsch. fellow NIH, Bethesda, Md., 1971-73; sr. physician dept. pediat., dep. chmn. Kaplan Hosp., Rehovot, Israel, 1974-82, head clin. immunology and allergy unit, 1982—; dir. Pediatric Rsch. Inst. Pediat. Rsch. Inst., Rehovot, 1990—; dir. clin. trials with Thymic Humoral Factor, 1977-87; sr. lectr. pediat. Hebrew U. and Hadassah Med. Sch., Jerusalem, 1979, assoc. prof., 1983; vis. scientist Pasteur Inst. London Sch. Tropical Medicine, London, Paris, 1986-87, U. Wis. Clin. Ctr., 1994-95. Editor: Allergy, 1996; contbr. articles to profl. jours. Grantee Agis Industries, 1991, Heiser Found. for Leprosy, 1992, Israeli League against Tb, 1994-96, Israel Ministry Health, 1999-2000; recipient AIDS Rsch. Internat. award World Acad. Population and Health Scis., 1987, Internat. Rsch. Project on Susaptibility to Tb. Mem. Internat. AIDS Soc., European Soc. of Immunodeficiency (rep., pres.-elect), Am. Acad. Allergy and Clin. Immunology, Israel Soc. Allergy and Clin. Immunology, N.Y. Acad. Scis. Office: Pediatric Rsch Inst, Kaplan Hosp, 76100 Rehovot Israel

HANEBALY, ELAÏDI, mathematics educator; b. Casablanca, Morocco, Nov. 1, 1942; s. Mohammed and Fatna (Moukat) H.; m. Zoubida Kanbar, Apr. 3, 1981; children: El Mehdi, Meryem, Hasnae. BA, Lahlou, Casablanca, Morocco, 1962; lic., Scis. U., Rabat, Morocco, 1969; Doctorat, Scis. U., Bordeaux, France, 1979; Doctorat d'ETAT, Pau U., France, 1988. Asst. facutly of scis. U. Mohammed V, Rabat, Morocco, 1972-79, maitre asst. faculty of scis., 1979-88, maitre of confs. faculty of scis., 1988-92, prof. faculty of scis., 1992—; reviewer in math. CAL Reviews, U.S., 1984—. Contbr. articles to profl. jours. Gen. sec. Syndicated Nat. de L'enseignement Superieur, Rabat, 1979-81. Mem. Am. Math. Soc. Office: Univ Mohammed V, Dept Math, BP 1014 Rabat Morocco

HANEDA, HISAO, construction company executive; b. Nishinomiya, Japan, Jan. 8, 1940; s. Seisaku and Sumiko (Nakamura) H.; m. Kazuko Tane, Apr. 27, 1969; children: Izumi, Kaori. B in Engring., U. Tokyo. Engr. boiler designing sect. Shin-Mitsubishi Industries, Ltd., Kobe, Japan, 1963-64, Mitsubishi Heavy Industries Ltd., Kobe, 1964-71; engr. utility boiler engring. sect. Power Systems Hdqrs., Tokyo, 1971-74, sr. engr., 1974-81, project mgr., 1981, mgr. boiler devel. group, 1981-88, dep. gen. mgr. energy system engring. dept., 1991-93, gen. mgr. products devel. dept., 1993-95; dep. mgr. thermal power dept. Kobe Shipyard and Machinery Works, 1988-90; gen. mgr. thermal power dept. Toden Kogyo Co., Ltd., 1995; gen. mgr. Futtsu Works, Toden Kogyo Co., Ltd., 1995-97, dir., gen. mgr., 1997-99; dir., gen. mgr quality assurance dept., 1999—; mem. Rsch. Com. for High Efficiency Energy System Model using Unused Energy, Tokyo, 1991-93, Rsch. Com. for Efficient Utilization Possibility of Waste Heat from Factory, Tokyo, 1992-93, Specialist Com. of City of Kobe's ECOTOPIA 2000 Planning Conf., 1992-93, Fuel Cell Com. of New Energy Industry Conf., Tokyo, 1993, Yokohamaologies Concil, Yokohama, 1997—. Editor: Mitsubishi Heavy Industries Tech. Rev., 1983—; patentee boiler, Sliding Pressure oncethrough boiler. Recipient West Meml. award U. Tokyo, 1963, Grand Tech. award Okochi Meml. Found., 1991. Mem. ASME (Prime Mover Com. award 1977), Japan Soc. Mech. Engrs. (Outstanding Tech. Achievement award 1985), Instn. Mech. Engrs. (corr., Edwin Walker prize 1996), Japan Boiler Assn., Japan Ex-Libris Soc., Internat. Ukiyo-e Soc., Japan Netherlands Inst., Niigata Soc. History. Buddhist. Avocations: collecting books, pottery, and ex libris, photography, travel. Home: 188-7 Nakakibogaoka Asahiku, Yokohama 241, Japan Office: Toden Kogyo Co Ltd, 1-3-13 Takanawa, Minato-ku Tokyo 108-0074, Japan

HÁNEK, PAVEL, surveying educator; b. Prague, Czechoslovakia, Sept. 12, 1944; s. Václav and Ružena (Franclová) H.; m. Ludmila Říhová, Aug. 9, 1974; children: Dagmar, Pavel. Cert. technician, Tech. Sch. Surveying, 1962; diploma in engring., Czech Tech. U., Prague, 1967, PhD, 1980, habil.asst. prof., 1987, 97. Exec. technician State Rwys., Prague, 1967-71; lectr. faculty civil engring. Czech Tech. U., 1971-87, asst. prof., 1987—; guest asst. Tech. U., Graz, Austria, 1978; cons. HSC-P Hánek, Prague, 1990—. Author, co-author books, textbooks, ency. in field; patentee in indsl. surveying; contbr. numerous articles to profl. publs. Recipient medal Prague Underground, 1983. Mem. Czech Union Surveying (mem. com. 1997—), Nat. Com. Internat. Fedn. Surveyors. (nat. del. 1990—). Avocations: classical music, history of surveying. E-mail: hanek@fsv.cvut.cz. Office: CTU Civil Engr Spl Geodesy, Thákurova 7, CZ 16629 Prague 6, Czech Republic

HANEKE, DIANNE MYERS, education educator; b. San Francisco, Feb. 23, 1941; d. Wayne and Dorothy (Johnson) Myers; m. John Paul Haneke, Apr. 10, 1965; children: Mark, Debra, Julie. BA in Social Sci., Edn., So. Calif. Coll., 1964; MS in Edn., SUNY, Albany, 1971, cert. advanced studies, 1990, postgrad., 1990—, PhD in Reading, 1998. Cert. elem., social studies and reading tchr., N.Y. Reading specialist Greenville (N.Y.) Elem. Sch., 1971-72, 84-85, Durham (N.Y.) Elem. Sch., 1972-74, Cairo (N.Y.) Durham Schs., 1979-82, 86-89; counselor Capital Area Christian Counseling, Delmar, N.Y., 1980-81; instr. psychology Columbia Greene C.C., Hudson, N.Y., 1982-83; reading specialist Hunter (N.Y.)-Tannersville Schs., 1985-86; instr. edn. and reading Mt. St. Mary Coll., Newburgh, N.Y., 1990-92; asst. prof. reading edn. Concordia U., Austin, Tex., 1993—, dir. field work experiences, 1993—. Author: A Woman After God's Own Heart, 1982, A View From the Inside: An Action Plan for Gender Equity in New York State Educational Administration, 1990. Instr. water safety ARC, 1978-91; host parents Youth for Understanding, 1984-85, 88-89; leader, resource person Girl Scouts Am., 1978-90. Myers-Haneke Edn. scholar So. Calif. Coll., 1971—; recipient Alumnus of Yr. award So. Calif. Coll., 1979, Disting. Contbr. award So. Calif. Coll. Alumni Assn., 1988, Disting. Svc. award So. Calif. Coll. Edn. Dept., 1988, So. Calif. Coll. Alumni Assn., 1994. Mem. ASCD, Am. Ednl. Rsch. Assn., Assn. Tchr. Educators, Capital Area Reading Coun., Christian Educators' Assn. Internat., Coll. Reading Assn., Nat. Reading Conf., Internat. Coun. Tchrs. English, Tex. State Reading Assn., Delta Kappa Gamma, Phi Delta Kappa. Republican. Avocations: swimming, tennis, vocal and instrumental music, travel, Special Olympics. Office: Concordia Univ Edn Divsn 3400 Interstate 35 N Austin TX 78705-2799

HANEKE, ECKART, dermatologist; b. Neustettin, Germany, Sept. 30, 1941; s. Helmut Hans-Georg and Hildegard W. (Fritze) H.; m. Elisabeth Maria Gutschmidt, Mar. 8, 1978; 1 child, Tilman. MB, U. Halle, Germany, 1966, MD, 1968; PhD, U. Erlangen, Germany, 1978. Resident dept. dermatology U. Halle, 1967-71, sr. resident dept. dermatology, 1971-73; asst. prof. dept. dermatology U. Erlangen, 1975-80, clin. prof. dept. dermatology, 1980-86; prof., chmn. dept. dermatology Ferdinand Sauerbruch Klinikum Hautklin, Wuppertal, Germany, 1986—; cons. dept. dermatology U. Erlangen, 1975-80, lectr. dermatology, 1976-86, sr. cons., 1980-86; dir. dept. dermatology Ferdinand Sauerbruch Klinikum Hautklin. Author: Burning Mouth Syndrome, 1980 (in German). Mem. German Soc. Dermatology (bd. dirs. 1995-2000), European Nail Soc. (pres. 1999—), European Soc. Dermatol. Surgery (pres. 1995—), North-Rhine Westfalia Dermatol. Soc. (pres. 1988-96), German Soc. Dermatopathology (pres. 1996-98). Office: Klinikk Bunaes, Lokkeasveien 3, 1300 Sandvika Norway

HÁNĚL, LADISLAV, zoologist; b. Hradec Králové, Czech Republic, Mar. 15, 1960; s. Ladislav Háněl and Eva (Ondrušková) Kopůnková. MSc, Charles U., Prague, Czech Republic, 1985; PhD, Czechoslovak Acad. Scis., Prague, 1991. Rschr. Acad. Scis. Czech Republic, České Budějovice, 1984—. Contbr. articles on zoology and ecology to sci. jours. Mem. Czech Zool. Soc., N.Y. Acad. Scis., European Soc. Nematologists. Home: Netolická 20/1176, CZ-37005 České Budějovice Czech Republic Office: Inst Soil Biology, Acad Sci, Na Sádkách 7, CZ-37005 České Budějovice Czech Republic

HANES, FRANK BORDEN, author, farmer, former business executive; b. Winston-Salem, N.C., Jan. 21, 1920; s. Robert March and Mildred (Borden) H.; m. Barbara Mildred Lasater, Dec. 3, 1942 (dec. Feb. 1990); children: Frank Borden, Nancy Hanes White, Robin March Hanes-McGregor; m. Jane Craig, July 3, 1991. BA, U. N.C., 1942; DHL, St. Andrew's Presbyn. Coll., 1992. Columnist, feature writer, reporter, copy editor Winston-Salem Jour. and Sentinel, 1946-49; vice chmn., dir. Mchts. Devel. Co., shopping center, Winston-Salem, 1956-64; dir. Chatham Mfg. Co., Elkin, N.C., Hanes Cos., Winston-Salem. Author: Abel Anders, 1951, The Bat Brothers, 1953, The Fleet Rabble, 1961, Journey's Journal, 1958, Jackknife John, 1964, The Seeds of Ares, 1977, The Garden of Nonentities, 1983. Chmn. com. for endowed professorships U. N.C., 1965-67; chmn. Friends of U. N.C. Library, 1966-68, Old Salem, Inc., 1968-70, Summit Sch., 1959-62; pres. Winston-Salem Operetta Assn., 1949-50, Winston-Salem Arts Council, 1955-56, N.C. Lit. and Hist. Assn., 1973-74; mem. bd. visitors U. N.C., 1980-86; chmn. Arts and Sci. Found., 1976-90; vice chmn., trustee John Motley Morehead

Found.; chmn. John W. and Anna Hodgin Hanes Found.; bd. govs. U. N.C. Press; mem. bd. N.C. Soc.; bd. dirs. N.C. Children's Home Soc., N.C. Zool. Soc. With USNR, 1942-45. Recipient Roanoke Chowan award for poetry N.C. Lit. and Hist. Assn., 1953, award Winston-Salem Arts Coun., 1957, Cum Laude Soc. award Woodberry Forest Sch., 1961, Sir Walter Raleigh award for fiction, 1961, Disting. Alumnus award U. N.C., 1975, Disting. Svc. medal U. N.C., Alumni Assn., 1978, Ragan award for contbns. to fine arts, 1985, William R. Davie award U. N.C. Bd. Trustees, 1989, Fortner award ror contbns. to writers and cmty. St. Andrew's Presbyn. Coll., 1995. Mem. P.E.N., N.C. Writers Conf. (chmn. 1951-52), N.C. Quarter Horse Assn. (pres. 1963-64), Order of Gimghoul (pres. 1940-42), Order of Minotaur (pres. 1940-41), Sigma Alpha Epsilon. Clubs: Rotarian. (Winston-Salem), Old Town (Winston-Salem); Rancheros Visitadores (Santa Barbara, Calif.); Roaring Gap (N.C.) (pres. 1976-78); Rainbow Springs (Macon County, N.C.). Home: 1057 W Kent Rd Winston Salem NC 27104-1131

HANES, JOHN WARD, sculptor, civil engineer consultant; b. San Francisco, June 5, 1936; s. Ward Herbert and Ruth Florence (Jacks) H.; m. Virginia Rae Meadows, Nov. 27, 1957 (div. Feb. 1966); children: Derek S., Kim R., Mark A.; m. Meda Lee Walter, June 29, 1968; 1 child, Ward W. BS in Engring., U. Calif., Davis, 1979. Registered civil engr., Calif. From engr. technician to civil engr. Soil Conservation Svc., USDA, Berkeley, Calif., 1960-79; civil engr. Soil Conservation Svc., USDA, Davis, 1979-83, hydraulic engr., 1983-90; sculptor, consulting civil engr. Boonville, Calif., 1990—; CEO Hanes Ranch, Inc., Boonville, 1999—. Pres. Santa Rosa (Calif.) Ski Club, 1971. Mem. Gualala Arts Ctr., Mendocino Arts Ctr., Nat. Sculpture Soc. Avocations: private pilot, multi media art, hunting, camping, fishing. Home: Box 510 29000 Mountain View Rd Boonville CA 95415

HANES, RALPH PHILIP, JR., former textiles executive, arts patron, cattle farmer; b. Winston-Salem, N.C., Feb. 25, 1926; s. Ralph Philip and Dewitt (Chatham) H.; m. Joan Audrey Humpstone, Jan. 14, 1950 (dec. Jan. 1983); m. Mary Charlotte Metz, Dec. 23, 1984. Grad., Woodberry Forest Sch., 1944; student, U. N.C., 1944-46; B.A., Yale U., 1949; L.H.D. (hon.), St. Andrews Coll., Laurinburg, N.C., 1981; DFA (hon.), N.C. Sch. of Arts, 1987; HHD (hon.), Wake Forest U., 1990. With Hanes Co., Inc. (formerly Hanes Dye and Finishing Co.), Winston-Salem, N.C., 1950-93; pres. Hanes Dye and Finishing Co., 1965-68, chmn. bd., 1968-88, chmn. emeritus, 1988-93; chmn. bd. Ampersand, Inc., 1976-85; mem. coun. of sr. fellows Salzburg Seminars in Am. Studies. Cons. editor Performing Arts Rev., 1981-85, Jour. Arts Mgmt. and Law, 1981-86; editorial adv. bd. Art Economist, 1982-86. Bd. dirs. (apptd. by Pres. J.F. Kennedy) Nat. Cultural Ctr. for Performing Arts, 1962-65; mem. (apptd. by Pres. L.B. Johnson) Nat. Council Arts, 1965-70, mem. adv. music panel, 1970-72; bd. dirs. Am. Symphony Orch. League, 1958-61, Moravian Music Found., 1963-65; founder, mem. bd. visitors N.C. Sch. Arts, 1985—; trustee Salem Coll., 1961-64; bd. dirs. Jargon Soc. Inc., 1968—, pres., 1968-75; founder N.C. State Arts Coun., chmn. 1964-66; founder Ams. for the Arts (formerly Am. Coun. Arts), bd. dirs., 1960-69, pres., 1964-66, vice chmn., 1967-69; bd. visitors Barter Theatre, State Theatre of Va., 1967-75; mem. nat. adv. com. Brevard Sch. Music, 1969-74; trustee, exec. com. N.C. Sch. Arts, 1966-78; mem. nat. adv. com. Am. Crafts Coun., 1970-72, Appalachian Trail Conf., 1973-76; assoc. fellow Jonathan Edward Coll., Yale U., 1971-74; chmn. Yale U. Council Com. on Music, 1970-73; bd. dirs. Nat. Audubon Soc., 1972-78, John W. and Anna H. Hanes Found., 1974—, So. Appalachian Highlands Conservancy, 1974-78, Old Salem, Inc., 1974-77, Isaak Walton League Am., 1974-78, Nature Conservancy, 1975-79, (apptd. by Pres. Gerald Ford) Kennedy Center for the Performing Arts, 1975-80; mem. internat. council Mus. Modern Art, 1978-93; bd. dirs. Salzburg Seminar of Am. Studies, 1978-82, Spoleto Festival, 1979-86, 87-93; arts cons. govts. of, Austria, 1978, P.R., 1978; bd. dirs. Nat. Council Friends of Kennedy Ctr., 1975-80, Nat. Mus. Am. Art, Renwick Gallery, 1976-89, Alliance for Arts Edn., 1976-79; mem. exec. com. Nat. Coun. for Arts and Edn., 1976-79; mem. adv. coun. on arts Fed. Res. Bank of Richmond (Va.), 1977-78; bd. dirs. Am. Land Trust, 1976-93, Bus. Com. for Arts, 1980-86, Arena Stage, Washington, 1990-93; mem. Gov.'s Coun. Bus., Arts and Humanities, 1977-85; mem. fine arts com. Fed. Res. Bank of Washington, 1979-81; mem. adv. bd. Pauline Koner Dance Consort, 1977-80; bd. dirs. Arts Internat., 1981-85, Arts Resources Corp., 1981-83; adv. com. Am. Farmland Trust, 1983-97; mem. internat. coun. N.Y.C. Ballet, 1984-86; chmn. Am. Art Forum, 1986-87, bd. dirs. 1986-90; bd. dirs. Arena Stage, 1990-92; com. mem. State of N.C. Award, 1993, Yr. of Mountains Commn., N.C., 1995-96; corporate mem. Woods Hole Oceanog. Inst., 1994-98; mem. founding com. Agri-Rsch. Extension Network of N.Am., 1995-97; mem. coun. advisors Blue Ridge Pky., 1998—; exec. com. Ambs. for the Arts, NEA, 1999—; chmn. cabinet Spl. Olympics World Games, 1999, trustee emeritus Kennedy Ctr. for the Arts, D.C., 1999—, bd. govs. Nat. Com. for the New River, N.C., Va., W.Va.,1999—. Named Young Man of Yr. Winston-Salem Jaycees, 1958, Young Man of Yr. N.C. Jaycees, 1958, Hon. Comdr., USS N.C., 1998; recipient Chmn.'s award NEA, 1966, Gov.'s award for preservation of natural area, 1969, pub. svc. award State of N.C., 1976, Morrison award for the Arts, 1977, Swan award, Tenn., 1970, N.C. Soc. of N.Y.C. award, 1979, Cmty. Svc. award Winston-Salem Urban League, 1979, Conservation award Isaac Walton League Am., 1982, award for disting. svc. to arts Nat. Gov.'s Assn., 1982, N.C. Gov.'s award in fine arts, 1982, awards Winston-Salem chpt. NAACP, 1983, Nat. Medal of Arts Amb. for the Arts presented by Pres. George Bush, 1991, award Piedmont Opera Theatre, 1992; tribute Nat. Arts Club, N.Y.C., 1995, Southeastern Ctr. for Contemporary Arts Leadership award, 1998, Winston-Salem Arts Coun. Young Leadership award, 2000. Mem. Am. League Anglers, Potomac Appalachian Mountain Club, S.E. Coun. on Founds., Trout Unltd., World Bus. Coun., Appalachian Consortium, East African Wildlife Soc., Isaac Walton League, Nat. Wildlife Fedn., N.Am. Mycological Assn., Pa. Acad. Fine Arts, Ut Prosim Soc., Royal Soc. Arts, Wilderness Soc., Walpole Soc., Appalachian Trail Conf., Century Assn. (N.Y.C.), Yale Club (N.Y.C.), Lotos Club (N.Y.C.), Met. Club (Washington), Peale for Visual Arts (Phila.), Piedmont Club, Twin City Club, Cane River Club, Bohemian Club, Currituck Club, Roaring Gap. Home: PO Box 1704 Winston Salem NC 27102-1704 Office: Hanes Cos Inc PO Box 202 Winston Salem NC 27102-0202

HANES, URSULA, sculptor; b. Toronto, Ont., Can., Jan. 18, 1932; d. Charles Samuel and Theodora Burleigh (Auret) H.; m. David John Fry, Aug. 30, 1956 (div. 1968); m. Daniel P. Guthrie, 1976 (div. 1981); children: Rachel Sabina, Simon David, Tanya Amanda, Timothy Jeremy John. Student, Cambridge Sch. Art, 1951, Art Student's League, N.Y.C., 1953, Columbia U., 1953; Diploma in Child Study, U. Toronto, 1954. audio-visual cons. I.D.R.C., Republic Du Mali, West Africa, 1971-72; co-founder Les Ateliers Fourwinds, Internat. Art Ctr., 1995. One-woman show Musée du Nouveau Monde, La Rochelle, France, 1990, Arles, 1991, 92, Fontvieille, 1993, Galerie Conseil Général, Aix-en-Provence, 1992, Hotel de Manville, Les Baux de Provence, 1999, Galerie d'Art, Beaucaire, 2000; exhibits include Columbia U., 1953, New Eng. Soc. Artists, 1953, Ont. Soc. Artists, 1954-62, Royal Can. Acad. Arts, 1955, 57, 59-62, Stratford Festival, 1955, Young Can. Contemporaries, 1957, Can. Nat. Exhibit, 1956, 59-60, Saxe Gallery, Toronto, 1980, L'Art Du Temps, Mouries, 1997, Galerie Mas d'Arnaud, St. Martin-de-Crau, 1999; sculpture and batik exhbns. Lanzarote, Canary Islands, Spain, 1969-75; commns. include San Juan Bautista, Calif., 1983. Mem. Sculptors' Soc. Can. (pres. 1964-65), Ont. Soc. Artists, Royal Can. Acad. Arts. Avocations: reading, theatre, dance arts. E-mail: redwinds4@aol.com. Address: Les Ateliers Fourwinds, La Juliere, 13930 Aureille France

HANEY, JAMES KEVIN, lawyer; b. New Brunswick, N.J., Apr. 11, 1966; s. James Alexander and Caroline Martha (Smolinski) H.; m. Elaine M. (Larsen), June 25, 1995. BA, U. Pa., 1988; JD with honors, St. John's U., 1991; MBA, Seton Hall U., 1998. Bar: N.J. 1991, U.S. Dist. Ct. N.J. 1991, N.Y. 1992, U.S. Ct. Appeals (3d and fed. cirs.) 1998, U.S. Supreme Ct. 1998, U.S. Dist. Ct. (so., ea., we., and no. dists.) N.Y. 1999, U.S. Ct. Internat. Trade, 1999, U.S. Ct. Claims, 1999, U.S. Ct. Mil. Appeals, 1999, U.S. Tax Ct. 1999. Twp. engring. inspector East Brunswick (N.J.) Twp., 1986-89; law clk. to Hon. June Strelecki N.J. Superior Ct., Monmouth County, 1991-92; assoc. Magee, Pagano & Isherwood, Wall, N.J., 1992-93, Zucker, Facher & Zucker, West Orange, N.J., 1993-99, Gilberg & Kiernan, Parsippany, N.J., 1999-2000, Wong Fleming, Edison, N.J., 2000—. Mem. ABA, Assn. Def. Trial Attys., Def. Rsch. Inst., N.J. Def. Assn., N.J. State Bar Assn., N.Y. State Bar Assn., Ctrl. N.J. Alumni Club U. Pa., St. John's Alumni Assn., Phi Delta Phi. Address: Gilberg & Keiekman 140 Littleton Rd Ste 201 Parsippany NJ 07054-1867

HANGARTNER, THOMAS NIKLAUS, medical physicist, educator; b. Brunnen, Switzerland, Aug. 9, 1949; came to U.S., 1985; s. Josef Paul and Gertrud Maria (Bärlocher) H.; m. Elisabeth Ruth Everts, Oct. 18, 1975; children: Lilian Regina, Angelica Danielle. Diploma in phys. ETH, Swiss Fed. Inst. Tech., Zurich, 1975, Dr. Sc. nat., 1978. Rsch. assoc. Swiss Fed. Inst. Tech., 1978-79; rsch. assoc. U. Alta., Edmonton, Can., 1979-80, asst. prof. biomed. engring., 1981-82, assoc. prof., 1982-85; assoc. prof. biomed. engring., medicine and physics Wright State U., Dayton, Ohio, 1986-94, prof., 1994—; reviewer NIH, Washington, 1986—. Contbr. articles to profl. publs.; patentee in field. Capt. Swiss Army, 1983—. Alta. Heritage Found. for Med. Rsch. scholar, 1981, 83, 86; recipient cert. of merit Radiol. Soc. N.Am., 1989. Mem. Am. Assn. Physicists in Medicine (mem. diagnostic radiology com. 1988-92), Am. Inst. Physics, Am. Soc. for Bone and Mineral Rsch., Nat. Osteoporosis Found. (U.S.), Nat. Osteoporosis Soc. (U.K.), N.Y. Acad. Scis. (life), Handyman Club of Am. (life), Tau Beta Pi (Emiment Engr. 1998—). Achievements include patents for method and apparatus for evaluation of cortical bone by computed tomography, method and apparatus for evaluation of structural width and density by computed tomography. Home: 1900 Kresswood Cir Dayton OH 45429-1151 Office: Wright State U Biomed Imaging Lab 1 Wyoming St 504 East Bldg Dayton OH 45409-2722

HANGEN, WILLIAM J., retired business executive; b. St. Louis, Mar. 28, 1931; s. William M. and Mabel Josephine (Jinkerson) H.; m. Shirley Mae Diebal, June 13, 1953; children: William Eric, Lori Jean Young, Jill Marie Mask, Kurt David. Student, Washington U., St. Louis, 1948-51; BS, U. Mo., 1953; postgrad., Wayne State U., 1957-62. Chemist, pigments dept. E.I. duPont de Nemours & Co., Newark, 1955-56; materials engr. missle divsn. Chrysler Corp., Detroit, 1956-64; engring. and mgmt. positions elec. products and advanced products divsns. Sheldahl, Inc., Northfield, Minn., 1964-83, v.p., gen. mgr. elec. products divsn., 1970-76, sr. v.p., gen. mgr. indsls. group, 1976-80, exec. v.p., 1980-83; dir. exec. search, bd. dirs. Moli-D Cos., Inc., 1983-91, chief fin. officer, 1986-91; gen. mgr. food products divsn. Ryt-Way Industries, Northfield, Minn., 1991-94. Contbr. to profl. jours. Corp. rep. Inst. Printed Circuits, 1970—, bd. dirs., 1974-76, treas., 1976-78, v.p., 1978-80, pres., 1980-82, mem. program com., 1975-79, chmn., 1977-79, chmn. fin. com., 1978, chmn. long range planning com., 1978-80. Served with Ordnance Corps AUS, 1953-55. Mem. Am. Chem. Soc., Walter's Lake Property Owners Assn. (pres. 1962-64), Alpha Chi Sigma, Optimist Club (v.p. Waterford, Mich. 1963-67), Northfield Golf Club, Northfield Hockey Assn. Republican. Lutheran. Home: 4992 90th St E Northfield MN 55057-4347

HANHIMAKI, JUSSI MARKUS, historian, researcher; b. Espoo, Finland, Feb. 3, 1965; s. Jussi Kalervo and Hilkka Doris (Uuskallio) H.; m. Holli Tina Schauber, June 17, 1990. BA, Tampere Univ., Tampere, Finland, 1987; MA, Boston Univ., 1988, PhD, 1993. Lectr. MIT, Cambridge, 1990-91; researcher USIP, Washington, 1991-92; asst. prof. Bishop's Univ., Lennoxville, Can., 1992-93; rsch. fellow Harvard Univ., Cambridge, 1993-94, Ohio Univ., Athens, 1994-95; lectr. LSE, London, 1995-2000; grad. prof. Inst. of Internat. Studies, Geneva, 2000—. Author: Scandinavia and the United States: An Insecure Friendship, 1997, Containing Coexistence: America, Russia, and the "Finnish Solution", 1997, Rinnakkaiseloa patomassa: Yhdysvallat ja Paasikiven linja, 1948-56, 1996. Recipient Charles Warren fellow Harvard Univ., 1993, Peace scholar U.S. Inst. Peace, 1991, fellow Nobel Inst., 1997. Mem. Soc. Historians of Am. Fgn. Rels., Am. Historical Assn., Finnish Historical Soc. Avocations: tennis, jogging. Office: Rue de Lausanne 132, CH-1211 Geneva 21, Switzerland

HANIFEN, RICHARD CHARLES, bishop; b. Denver, June 15, 1931; s. Edward Anselm and Dorothy Elizabeth (Ranous) H. B.S., Regis Coll., 1953; S.T.B., Cath. U., 1959, M.A., 1966; J.C.L., Pontifical Lateran U., Italy, 1968. Ordained priest Roman Catholic Ch., 1959; asst. pastor Cathedral Parish, Denver, 1959-66; sec. to archbishop Archdiocese Denver, 1968-69, chancellor, 1969-76; aux. bishop of Denver, 1974-83; 1st bishop of Colorado Springs, Colo., 1984—. Office: Bishop Colo Springs 29 W Kiowa St Colorado Springs CO 80903-1403

HANIHARA, KAZURO, anthropologist, educator; b. Kitakyushu-shi, Japan, Aug. 17, 1927; s. Yumijiro and Chitoshi (Okubo) H.; m. Kazuko Kimura, Nov. 15, 1953; children: Yumio, Tsunehiko. BS, U. Tokyo, 1951, D of Sci., 1957. Lectr. Sapporo Med. Coll., Japan, 1956-58; assoc. prof. Sapporo Med. Coll., 1958-72; prof. U. Tokyo, 1972-88, Internat. Rsch. Cen. Japanese Studies, Kyoto, 1987-93; vis. prof. U. Chgo., 1959-60, 1968; disting. vis. prof. Az. State U., Tempe, 1984; vice-dir. Internat. Inst. for Advanced Studies, Kyoto, 1994-96; trustee Kobe Coll., Nishinomiya, Japan, 1999—. Editor: (books) The Minatogawa Man, 1982, The Origin and Past of Modern Humans as Viewed from DNA, 1995; Author: (books) Population History of the Japanese, 1995, Faces of the Japanese, 1999. Recipient Culture Prize, The Kyoto Shimbun, 1984. Fellow Internat. Inst. Advanced Studies. Avocations: photography, audio-listening, computer programming.

HANIKA, JIŘÍ, chemical engineering; b. Prague, Czech Republic, Oct. 31, 1944; s. Jiri and Anna (Bolehovská) H.; m. Eva Maresová, Aug. 23, 1973; children: Jiri, Jana. MSc, Inst. Chem. Tech., Prague, 1966, PhD, 1972, DSc, 1987. Cert. chem. engr., chem. tech. Rsch. asst. Inst. Chem. Tech., Prague, 1972-76, asst. prof., 1977-83, assoc. prof., 1984-95, prof. chem. engring., 1996—, vice dean faculty chem. tech., 1985-90, dean faculty chem. tech., 1990-91. Co-author: Handbook of Heat and Mass Transfer, 1986, Catalytic Hydrogenation, 1986; contbr. articles to profl. jours. Mem. Czech Soc. Indsl. Chemistry (vice-chmn. 1989-97, chmn. 1997—), Czech Soc. Chem. Engring. (com. mem. 1993—), European Fedn. Chem. Engring. (working party on chem. reaction engring. 1991—). Avocations: classical music, cross country skiing, astronomy. Home: V udolí 5/36, CZ-16500 Prague 6, Czech Republic Office: Inst Chem Tech, Technická 5, CZ-16628 Prague 6, Czech Republic

HANIN, LEONID GRIGORIĬ, mathematician, educator; b. Leningrad, Oct. 2, 1956; arrived in Israel, 1991; s. Grigorii Alexandr and Miriam Meer (Babkova) H.; m. Marina Tsalya Kazakevich, May 25, 1985; children: Mark, Boris. MS in Math. and Math. Edn., Leningrad State U., 1978; PhD, Steklov Math. Inst., 1985. Engr., mathematician Glavzapstroy, Leningrad, Russia, 1978-83; asst. prof., sr. rsch. fellow Inst. R.R. Engring., Leningrad, 1985-90; rschr. Technion-Israel Inst. Tech., Haifa, 1991-94, adj. asst. prof., 1992-93, adj. assoc. prof., 1993-94; asst. prof. Idaho State U., Pocatello, 1997-99, assoc. prof., 1999—; vis. assoc. prof. Mich. Technol. U., Houghton, 1994-95, Wayne State U., Detroit, 1995-97. Co-author: Biomathematical Problems in Optimization of Cancer Radiotherapy, 1994. Recipient Golden medal for excellent successes in learning Russian Ministry of Edn., 1973, Prize for Russian Nat. Students' Rsch. Work Competition, 1978, Outstanding Rschr. award Idaho State U. 1999-2000. Office: Idaho State U Dept Math Pocatello ID 83209-0001

HANINEC, PAVEL, neurosurgeon, researcher, educator; b. Prague, Czech Republic, Mar. 29, 1958; s. Stefan and Anna (Neumann) H.; m. Jana Nepeřilová, June 13, 1958; children: Michal, Zuzana. MD, Fac. Gen. Medicine, Prague, 1983, PhD, 1989. Asst. dept. anatomy Faculty Gen. Medicine, Charles U., Prague, 1979-89, asst. dept. neurosurgery 1st Med. Faculty,, 1989-97, asst. prof., 1997, head, asst. prof. dept. neurosurgery 3d Med. Faculty, 1998—; asst. dept. neurosurgery U. Montpellier, France, 1991-92. Contbr. articles to profl. jours. Vice pres. Found. for Devel. Neurosurgery, Prague, 1997. Mem. Czech and Slovak Anatomical Soc., Czech and Slovak Neurosurg. Soc., N.Y. Acad. Sci. Avocations: skiing, hunting, visual art. Home: Kvetnoveho Vitezstvi 1361, 14900 Prague 4, Czech Republic Office: Charles U 3d Med Faculty, Srobárova 50, 10000 Prague 10, Czech Republic

HANISKO, JOHN-CYRIL PATRICK, electronics engineer, physicist; b. Detroit, Mar. 17, 1937; s. John Joseph and Pauline Victoria (Vrabel) H. BEE, U. Detroit, 1963, MSEE, 1965; MA, Wayne State U., 1972, PhD in Physics, 1988. Engr. Burroughs, Detroit, 1962-65; rsch. engr. Boeing, Seattle, 1965-67; sr. engr. Eastman Kodak, Rochester, N.Y., 1967-68; staff engr. Kent-Moore Corp., Warren, Mich., 1971-73; rsch. engr. Udylite, Warren, 1973-75; cons. Southfield, Mich., 1975-76; project engr. Bendix, Troy, Mich., 1976-80; staff engr. TRW, Farmington Hills, Mich., 1980-94; sr. engr. Eaton Corp., Southfield, Mich., 1994—. Contbr. articles to profl. jours. Mem. Cath. League for Civil and Religious Rights, N.Y., Nat. Tax Limitation Com., Washington, Nat. Right to Life Com., Washington. Named Design of Yr. EDN Mag., 1977. Mem. IEEE (sr.). Roman Catholic. Achievements include 13 patents for Electrical Control Apparatus for Internal Combustion Engines, for Sequential Injection Timing Apparatus, for Voltage Controlled Oscillator Having Ratiometric and Temperature Compensation, for Automotive Anti-theft Device, for brake-sensor signal processing, for resistive brake lining wear and temperature sensing system, for method and apparatus for trimming gain of an accelerometer, for method and apparatus for detecting operational failure of a digital accelerometer, for single-wire brake sensing system, for apparatus and method for testing an acceleration sensur, for brake actuator service limit sensor for single-lamp brake status indicator system. Home: 21888 Murray Crescent Dr Southfield MI 48076-1619 Office: Eaton Corp 26201 Northwestern Hwy Southfield MI 48076-3926

HANJALIC, KENAL, physics educator, researcher; b. Sarajevo, Bosnia, Nov. 30, 1939; arrived in The Netherlands, 1994; s. Arif and Hanjalic and Izeta Hadziselimović, July 21, 1966; children: Alan, Aida. Dipl. Ing., U. Sarajevo, 1964; MSc, U. Birmingham, Eng., 1966; PhD, U. London, 1970, DSc (hon.), 1999. Prof. U. Sarajevo, 1971-93, dir. Inst. for Process, Power and Environ. Engring., 1980-84, dean mech. engring., 1984-85; mayor City of Sarajevo, 1985-87; min. for sci., tech. and info. Govt. of Bosnia Herzegovina, Sarajevo, 1987-91; prof. Mich. Technol. U., Houghton, 1993-94; prof. physics, sect. head Delft (The Netherlands) U. Tech., 1994—. Author: Dynamics of Compressible Fluid Flow, 1978; editor Mathematical Modeling in Energy Systems, 1990, Expert Systems and Computer Simulations in Energy Engineering, 1992, Turbulence, Heat and Mass Transfer, Vol. I, 1995, Vol. II, 1997, Vol. III, 2000. Recipient rsch. award Max Planck Found., 1992. Mem. ASME, Acad. Scis. Bosnia Herzegovina, Am. Phys. Soc., IAHR. Avocations: classical music, skiing, tennis. Office: Delft U Tech, Lorentzweg 1, 2628 CJ Delft The Netherlands

HANKE, HARTMUT, physician; b. Sindelfingen, Germany, Oct. 24, 1961; s. Josef and Luise (Stauch) H.; m. Sybille Göhler; children: Theresa, Greta. MD, U. Tübingen, Germany, 1988. Postdoctoral fellow dept. physiology U. Tübingen, 1988-89, internal fellow dept. cardiology, 1990-92, rsch. fellow Inst. Social Medicine, 1993-94; internal fellow divsn. cardiology U. Ulm, Germany, 1994—, specialist in internal medicine, 1997, specialist in clin. cardiology, 1999; sr. physician in cardiology, 1999—; cons. exptl. cardiology U. Ulm, 1994—. Contbr. articles to profl. jours. Recipient Rudolf Thauer award German Soc. Cardiology, 1992. Mem. Am. Heart Assn. (mem. coun. arteriosclerosis 1994—). Avocations: jogging, sailing. E-mail: hartmut.hanke@medizin.uni-ulm.de. Office: U Ulm Divsn Cardiology, Robert Koch Str 8, 89081 Ulm Germany

HANKEN, JAMES, biologist; b. N.Y.C., July 14, 1952; s. William Hanken and Miriam (Geller) Gertz; m. Sally Esther Susnowitz, Sept. 1, 1984; children: Daniel, Alexandra. AB, U. Calif., Berkeley, 1973, PhD, 1980. Killam postdoctoral fellow Dalhousie U., Halifax, Can., 1980-83; asst. prof. U. Colo., Boulder, 1983-90, assoc. prof., 1990-94, prof. biology, 1994-99; prof. biology Harvard U., Cambridge, Mass., 1999—; assoc. editor Jour. of Morphology, Boulder, 1988—; panel mem. NSF, Washington, 1996—; editor Am. Zoologist, Boulder, 1996-98; lectr. Uppsala (Sweden) U., U. Calif., Berkeley. Editor (3 books) The Skull, 1993. Fellow AAAS; mem. Soc. Integrative and Comparative Biology, Herpetologists League, Soc. for Study of Evolution. Achievements include work on biology of neotropical salamanders, evolution and development of the vertebrate skull. Office: Harvard U Dept Organism & Evol Bio Cambridge MA 02138

HANKINS, HESTERLY G., III, computer systems analyst, inventor, educator; b. Sallisaw, Okla., Sept. 5, 1950; s. Hesterly G. and Ruth Faye (Jackson) H. BA in Sociology, U. Calif., Santa Barbara, 1972; MBA in Info. Systems, UCLA, 1974; postgrad., Golden Gate U., 1985-86, Ventura Coll., 1970, Antelope Valley Coll., 1977, La Verne U., 1987, NRI McGraw-Hill Sch. Writing, Washington, 1993—; PhD (hon.). Cert. community coll. tchr., Calif. Applications programmer Xerox Corp., Marina Del Rey, Calif., 1979-80; spl. asst. to CEO Naval Air Sta. of Moffett Field, Mountain View, Calif., 1984-85; mgr. computer systems project Pacific Missile Test Ctr., Oxnard, 1985-88; mgr. computer systems project MIS Def. Contract Adminstrn. Svcs. Region, L.A., 1988-94, ret., 1994; instr. writing Nat. U., Inglewood, Calif., 1994—; instr. bus. West Coast U., Camarillo, Calif., 1985; core adj. faculty Nat. U., L.A., 1988—; lectr. bus. Golden Gate U., Los Altos, Calif., 1984; instr. computer sci. Chapman Coll., Sunnyvale, 1984, Ventura (Calif.) Coll., 1983-84; lectr. tchr. computers De Anza Coll.; cons. L.A. Police Dept., Allison Mortgage Trust Investment Co.; minority small bus. assn. cons. UCLA. Author: Campus Computing's Accounting I.S. As A Measurement of Computer Performance, 1973, Campus Computer, 1986, Network Planning, 1986, Satellites and Teleconferencing, 1986, Quotable Expressions and Memorable Quotations of Notables, 1993, Idea Bank, 1993, Product Rating System, 1993, Training Base Model, 1993, Sound Seal/Shield, 1994, My Biographical Profile. Mem. St. Paul United Meth. Ch., Oxnard, Calif., 1986-87; fundraiser YMCA Jr. Rodeo, Lake Casitos, Calif.; key person to combine fed. campaign United Way. Named One of Outstanding Young Men in Am., U.S. Jaycees, 1980. Mem. Nat. Assn. Accts., Calif. Assn. Accts., Intergovtl. Coun. on Tech. Info. Processing, Assn. Computing Machinery (Smart Beneficial Suggestion award 1984), IEEE Computer Soc., Fed. Mgrs. Assn., Friends of Culver City Libr., Alpha Kappa Psi (sec. 1972-73). Democrat.

HANKÓ, ZOLTÁN GYÖRGY, hydraulic engineer, researcher; b. Budapest, Hungary, Feb. 3, 1925; s. Géza and Anna (Szabó) H.; m. Lenke Fórizs, Jan. 27, 1951; children: Álmos, Zsombor. Civil Engr., U. Tech., Budapest, 1948; D Engring., U. Bldg. and Traffic, Budapest, 1963. Cert. hydraulic engr., Hungary. Chair hydraulic structures U. Tech., Budapest, 1948-58, asst. prof., 1948-50, 1st asst., 1950-58; sr. rsch. assoc. Water Resources Rsch. Ctr. Plc, Budapest, 1958-62, dir. hydraulic lab., 1962-75, sci. adv., 1975—. Contbr. articles to profl. jours. Active Vitális Prize Awarding Com., Budapest, 1980—. Recipient Kisköre River Barrage award, Budapest, 1972, Flood Fighting award Nat. Water Authority, Budapest, 1954. Mem. Hungarian Hydrological Soc. (hon., presdl. coun. 1993—, Pro Aqua award 1992), Internat. Assn. Hydraulic Rsch. (past sec. nat. com.). Home: Csaba utca 16/A, H-1122 Budapest Hungary Office: Vituki Plc, Kvassay Jenő út 1, H-1095 Budapest Hungary

HANKS, GEORGE CAROL, JR., lawyer; b. Breaux Bridge, La., Sept. 25, 1964; s. George Carol and Quenola Reese Hanks; m. Stacey L. Hanks, Apr. 29, 1995. JD, Harvard U., 1989; BA summa cum laude, La. State U., 1986. Bar: Tex. 1989, U.S. Dist. Ct. (so. dist.) Tex. 1992, U.S. Ct. Appeals (5th cir.) 1993, U.S. Dist. Ct. Ariz. 1994. Judicial law clk. Houston, 1989-91; assoc. atty. Fulbright & Jaworski, Houston, 1991-96; shareholder Wickliff & Hall PC, Houston, 1996—; panel chmn. grievance com., spl. disciplinary counsel Coll. State Bar Tex., Houston, 1993—. Contbr. articles to profl. jours. Bd. dirs. Big Bros. and Big Sisters, Houston, 1995-97. Fellow Houston Bar Assn.; mem. Fed. Bar Assn., Tex. Assn. Def. Counsel, Houston Bar Found., Coll. of State Bar of Tex. Avocations: aviation, ice hockey, scuba diving. Home: 12035 E Circle Dr Houston TX 77071-3602 Office: Wickliff & Hall 1000 Louisiana St Ste 5400 Houston TX 77002-5006

HANLEY, FRED WILLIAM, librarian, educator; b. Booneville, Miss., May 13, 1939; s. John Martin and Ethel May (Robertson) H.; m. Bethany Nell Holt, June 21, 1971; children: Seth Patrick, Cassandra May. BS, Lambuth Coll., Jackson, Tenn., 1961; MDiv, Meth. Theol. Sch., Delaware, Ohio, 1964; MA in History, Ariz. State U., 1966, MA in Counseling, 1968. Cert. secondary tchr., Ariz. Assoc. pastor Prospect Street Meth. Ch., Marion, Ohio, 1961-64; tchr. history Phoenix Union High Sch. Dist., 1965-74, curriculum coord., 1974-78, chmn. English dept., 1978-89, varsity cross country coach, 1978-80, chmn. libr. dept., 1989—, chmn. tech. com., 1991—, varsity golf coach, 1980-89, 99—. Editor Ariz. Health Svcs. jour., 1965. Bd. dirs. Wesley Found., Tempe, Ariz., 1964-69; vol. Am. Cancer Soc., Phoenix, 1985-91; chmn. Phoenix Symphony Guild Symphonette Orch., 1993—; mem. exec. com. Phoenix Symphony Guild Orchestral Tng. Program, 1994—; libr. Phoenix Symphony Guild, 1998—. Recipient Tchr. of Yr. award West High Sch., Phoenix, 1969, Disting. Alumnae award Lambuth Coll., 1979. Mem. ALA, NEA, Ariz. Edn. Assn., Ariz. Libr. Assn., N. Cen. Assn. of Sec. Schs. Accreditation Team for Ariz., Nat. Coun. Tchrs. English., Phi Alpha Theta. Democrat. Avocations: marathon running, golf, hiking. Home: 10411 W

Flower St Avondale AZ 85323-4403 Office: Alhambra High Sch 3839 W Camelback Rd Phoenix AZ 85019-2598

HANN, WILLIAM MATHIS, chemist, researcher; b. Pittman, N.J., Apr. 15, 1945; s. William Mathis Hann and Helen Scott (King) Watts; m. Christina Freeburger, Aug. 1, 1981; children: Marlene A., Matthew A., Cynthia A. BS in Chemistry, LaSalle U., Phila., 1974. Sr. rsch. technician Rohm and Haas Co., Spring House, Pa., 1973-75, rsch. scientist, 1976-85, sr. rsch. scientist, 1985-88, group leader water treatment, 1988—; mem. steering com. Understanding Asia, Spring House, 1996-98; symposium co-chair Corrosion 97, 1996-97, Corrosion 98, 1997-98; symposium vice-chair Corrosion 93, 1992-93, chmn. corrosion 89, 1988-89. Contbr. articles to profl. jours. Mem. Nat. Assn. Corrosion Engrs. Achievements include development of immunoassay detection technique for ppm levels of water soluble polymers; developed well-known Acumer and Optidose dispersant product lines, which are sold world wide; primary inventor of ten U.S. patents covering dispersants and corrosion inhibitors. Avocations: sailing, scuba diving, travel, reading. Office: Rohm and Haas Co 727 Norristown Rd Spring House PA 19477

HANNA, ADEL SHAFIK, dermatologist, venereologist, consultant; b. El-Menia, Egypt, Jan. 19, 1947; s. Shafik Hanna and Evon Kamel (Hendy) Demian; m. Faten Kamel Badawy, Jan. 25, 1981; children: Sherif, Sally. MD, U. Alexandria, Egypt, 1970, diploma Skin and Venereology Disease, 1978; MS in Pub. Health, High Inst. Pub. Health, 1992. Med. diplomate in dermatology and Sexually Transmitted Disease and AIDS. House officer MOH Hosps., Alexandria, 1971-72, registrar, 1973-78, speciaist skin and venereology disease, 1978-83; gen. practitioner Rural Health Ctrs., Tanta, Egypt, 1972-73; head skin and venereology disease dept. El-Moassat Hosp., Alexandria, 1984-85; clin. adminstr. Alexandria Skin and Venereology Disease Clinic, Alexandria, 1986-88; cons. health ins., Alexandria, 1989-96; cons., dir. MOH, Alexandria, 1997—. Mem. Egyptian AIDS Prevention Soc. Avocations: music, travel, reading. Home: El Moaskar El Romany, Dobat Mostafa Kamel Bldg 11, Alexandria Egypt Office: 12 Bobastes St, Celeopatra Hamamat, Alexandria Egypt

HANNA, MURAD SAMI, industrial minerals company executive, financial consultant; b. Atbara, Sudan, Apr. 23, 1952; s. Sami Hanna Butros and Eugunee Khalil Abdelmalak; m. Eman Fawzi Awad, Oct. 28, 1978; children: Amal, Reymon, Maryann. BSc in Acctg., U. Khartoum, Sudan, 1975, BSBA with honors, 1976. Cert. acct. Saudi Arabia. Chief acct. Lektro Co., Khartoum, Sudan, 1976-78, Polytra Co., Khartoum, Sudan, 1980-81; sr. cost acct. Sudanese Steel Products, Khartoum, Sudan, 1978-80; fin. contr. Albilad Movenpick Hotel, Jeddah, Saudi Arabia, 1981-83; mng. dir. Arab Leasing Co., Riyadh, Saudi Arabia, 1983-86; mng. dir., chief exec., financial cons. Saudi Indsl. Minerals Co., Saudi Arabia, 1986—. Author: Sudanese Commercial Banks Investments, 1976. Fellow Arab Soc. Cert. Pub. Accts., Inst. Comml. Mgrs., Inst. Profl. Mgrs. Coptic Orthodox. Avocations: swimming, hunting. Office: Saudi Indsl Minerals Co, PO Box 26649, Riyadh 11496, Saudi Arabia

HANNA, TERRY ROSS, lawyer, small business owner; b. Wadsworth, Ohio, May 17, 1947; s. Harry Ross and Geraldine (Frensley) H.; m. Max Anna Hindes, Jan. 20, 1968; children: Travis, Taylor, Molly. BBA, U. Okla., 1968, JD, 1972; LLM, NYU, 1973; MA in Bibl Studies, Dallas Theol. Sem., 1988. Bar: Okla. 1972, U.S. Tax Ct. 1974, U.S. Ct. Appeals (10th cir.) 1979, U.S. Supreme Ct. 1989; CPA, Okla. Mem. McAfee & Taft, Oklahoma City, 1972-80; pres. P 356 Inc., Oklahoma City, 1980—; of counsel Crowe & Dunlevy, Oklahoma City, 1987—; owner Mo Jo Video, 1995—; spl. lectr. Oklahoma City U. Sch. Law, 1974-75. Editor Okla. U. Law Rev., 1970-72. Mem. internat. com. Boy Scouts Am., 1988—; dir. U.S. Found. for Internat. Scouting, Irving, 1989—. Baden-Powell fellow World Scout Found., 1988—; recipient Silver Beaver award Boy Scouts Am., 1988. Mem. Okla. Bar Assn. (pres. taxation sect. 1978-79), Sports Lawyers Assn., Order of Arrow (lodge advisor 1989—), Kappa Sigma (chpt. advisor 1974-75), Phi Delta Phi (magister 1972). Republican. Mem. Christian Ch. Avocations: coach, patch collector, fishing, softball, computers. Home: 2600 W Coffee Creek Rd Edmond OK 73003-3326 Office: Crowe & Dunlevy 1800 Mid America Towers Oklahoma City OK 73102

HANNAFORD, PETER DOR, public relations executive, writer; b. Glendale, Calif., Sept. 21, 1932; s. Donald R. and Elinor (Nielsen) H.; m. Irene Dorothy Harville, Aug. 14, 1954; children: Richard Harville, Donald R. II. AB, U. Calif., 1954. Acct. exec. Helen A. Kennedy Advt., 1956; v.p. Kennedy-Hannaford, Inc., San Francisco and Oakland, Calif., 1957-62; pres. Kennedy-Hannaford, Inc., 1962-67, Pettler & Hannaford, Inc., Oakland, 1967-69; v.p. Wilton, Coombs & Colnett, Inc., 1969-72; pres. Hannaford & Assocs., Oakland, 1973; asst. to Gov. of Calif.; dir. pub. affairs Govs.' Office, 1974; chmn. bd. Hannaford Co., Inc. (formerly Deaver & Hannaford, Inc.), 1975-95; mng. dir. The Franklin Firm, Washington, 1996-98; pub. Ferndale (Calif.) Enterprise, 1996-98; pres. Hannaford Enterprises Inc., 1998—; nat. pres. Mut. Advt. Agy. Network, 1968-69; vice chmn. Calif. Gov.'s Consumer Fraud Task Force, 1972-73; bd. dirs. Eberle Comms. Group Inc. Author: The Reagans: A Political Portrait, 1983, Talking Back to the Media, 1986 (Japanese edit. 1990); co-author: Remembering Reagan, 1994, Recollections of Reagan, 1997, My Heart Goes Home: A Hudson Valley Memoir, 1997, The Quotable Ronald Reagan, 1998, The Essential George Washington, 1999. Mem. Alameda County Rep. Ctrl. Com., Rep. State Cttl. Com. Calif., 1968-74, The Commonwealth Fund's Commn. on Elderly People Living Alone, 1986-91; Rep. nominee for U.S. Congress, 1972; governing bd. Tahoe Regional Planning Agy., 1973-74; trustee White House Preservation Fund, 1981-89, pub. rels. adv. com. USIA, 1981-92; bd. dirs. Am. Alternative Found., 1984—, Washington Internat. Horse Show, 1986-91; mem. adv. com. Mt. Vernon, 1991-96; mem. bd. of session Georgetown Presybn. Ch., Washington, 1999—. 1st lt. Signal Corps, U.S. Army, 1954-56. Mem. Univ. Club (N.Y.C.), Cosmos Club, Potomac Polo Club, Theta Xi. Presbyterian. Office: Hannaford Enterprises Inc Ste 800W 1299 Pennsylvania Ave NW Washington DC 20004-2400

HANNAY, DAVID HUGH ALEXANDER, diplomat; b. London, Sept. 28, 1935; s. Julian G. Hannay; m. Gillian Rosemary Rex, May 9, 1961; children: Richard, Philip, Jonathan, Alexander. Degree in History, New Coll., Oxford, Eng., 1959. With Fgn. Office, 1959—, Brit. Embassy, Tehran, Iran, 1960-61; third sec. Kabul, 1961-63; second sec. Fgn. Office, 1963-65; second then first sec. U.K. Del. to European Coms., Brussels, Belgium, 1965-70; first sec. U.K. Negotiating Team with European Coms., 1970-72; chef de cabinet to Sir Christopher Soames v.p. of Commn. of European Coms., 1973-77; head Energy, Sci. and Space dept. Fgn. and Commonwealth Office, 1977-79, head Middle East dept., 1979; asst. under sec. of state for European Community matters, 1979-84; min. Washington, 1984-85; amb. and U.K. permanent rep. European Communities, Brussels, 1985-90; amb. and U.K. permanent rep. on security coun. UN, 1990-95; spl. rep. Cyprus, 1996—, non-exec. dir. chime comms., 1996—; non-exec. dir. AEGIS Group, 2000—. Mem. Ct. and Coun. Birmingham U., 1998—, Coun. Britain in Europe, 1999—. Lt. Brit. Army, 1954-56. Decorated CMG Her Majesty the Queen of Eng., 1981, KCMG, 1986, GCMG, 1995. Mem. Travellers Club. Avocations: traveling, gardening, photography.

HANNAY, DAVID RAINSFORD, general practice physician, educator; b. London, Jan. 3, 1939; m. Janet Mary Gilliat; 3 children. MB, B of Surgery, Cambridge (Eng.) U., 1965, MA, 1966; PhD, U. Glasgow, Scotland, 1975; MD, Cambridge U., 1982. Jr. hosp. dr. London and Manchester, Eng., 1964-68; lectr. Glasgow U., 1968-75, sr. lectr., 1975-84; gen. practitioner Dumfries and Gallaway Health Bd., Scotland, 1984-86, 2000—; prof. gen. practice U. Sheffield, Eng., 1986-96, emeritus prof., 1997—; hon. prof. Crichton Campus Glasgow U., Scotland, 1999—. Author: The Symptom Iceberg, 1974, Lecture Notes on Medical Sociology, 1988; contbr. over 90 articles to profl. jours. Fellow Royal Coll. Gen. Practitioners, Faculty Pub. Health Medicine. Avocations: playing bagpipes, sailing, tennis.

HANNEQUIN, PASCAL PAUL, physician; b. Vouziers, Ardennes, France, Jan. 19, 1958; s. Gabriel Firmin and Genevieve Marie (Soide) H.; m. Beatrice Marthe Masson, June 27, 1981; children: Charlotte, Lucie, Timothee. MD, Faculty Medicine, Reims, France, 1982, physician in nuclear medicine, 1985; D in Physics, Faculty Physics, Reims, France, 1989. Nuclear medicine asst. Cancer Inst., Reims, France, 1982-89; nuclear medicine practitioner Ctr. D'Imagerie Nucleaire, Annecy, France, 1989—. Inventor in field. Mem. Soc. Nuclear Medicine. Home: Allee du bouverat, 74290 Menthon St Bernard France Office: Ctr D'Imagene Nucleaire, 4 Chemin tour de la Rein, 74000 Annecy France

HANNERS, G(ARY) DALE, retired psychological mental health professional; b. Leachville, Ark., Sept. 16, 1942. BS, Memphis State U., 1966; MS, Ark. State U., 1968; PhD, U. Memphis, 1995. Lic. psychol. examiner, Ark.; cert. sch. psychologist. Tchr. Memphis Pub. Schs., 1964-65; with personnel dept. Sears, Roebuck and Co., Memphis, 1965-66; supr. client svcs. Abilities Unltd., Jonesboro, 1966-70; rehab. counselor State of Ark., Jonesboro, 1970-74, psychol. examiner, 1979—; psychologist, human resources cons., 1994—; pvt. practice cons. human svcs., Ark., 1970-79; cons. Little People Am., Calif. Mem. Am. Psychol. Assn. (assoc.), Ark. Psychol. Assn., Ark. Sch. Psychol. Assn., Civitan (sec.-treas. Jonesboro chpt. 1967-70). Republican. Baptist. Avocations: music, reading, farming, landscaping. Home: 2113 Club Cv Jonesboro AR 72401-6100

HANNIBALSSON, JON BALDVIN, Icelandic ambassador; b. Isafjordur, Iceland, Feb. 21, 1939; m. Bryndis Schram; four children. MA in Econs., U. Edinburgh, Scotland, 1963; postgrad., U. Stockholm, Stockholm, 1963-64; diploma in Ednl. Studies, U. Iceland, 1965; postgrad., Harvard U. European Studies, 1976-77. Tchr. Reykjavik (Iceland) High Sch., 1964-70; headmaster Isafjordur (Iceland) Coll., 1970-79; chief editor Althydubladid, Reykjavik, 1979-82; M.P. Iceland, Reykjavik, 1982-98; min. fin. Govt. of Iceland, Reykjavik, 1987-88, min. for fgn. affairs and external trade, 1988-95; amb. to U.S., Can. and Mex., Embassy of Iceland, Washington, 1998—; chmn. Social Dem. Party of Iceland, 1984-96; pres. Coun. of Mins. of the European Free Trade Assn., 1989, 91, 94. Dep. mem. Reykjavik City Coun., 1966-67; chmn. Union of High Sch. and Coll. Tchrs., 1966-68; mem. Town Coun. of Isafjorour, 1971-78 (chmn. 1975-76). Named Hon. Citizen, Vilnius, Lithuania, 1995. Mem. North Atlantic Coun. Mins. Office: Embassy of Iceland 1156 15th St NW Ste 1200 Washington DC 20005-1733

HANNING, GARY WILLIAM, utility executive, water company executive, consultant; b. Sherman, Tex., Aug. 30, 1942; s. William Homer and Mary Maxine (Harshbarger) H.; m. Robin Dale Smith, June 8, 1974; children: TJ, Lorissa Diane. BS, Rollins Coll., 1974; MBA, Stetson U., 1976. Mgr., co-owner Hanning Water Systems, Denison, Tex., 1963-66; engring. technician Gen. Dynamics, Ft. Worth, 1966-67; engr. supr. Bendix Field, Pasadena, Calif., 1967-70; engr. Philco-Ford Corp., Cape Kennedy, Fla., 1970-73, Jet Propulsion Lab., Pasadena, Calif., 1973-74; sect. mgr. Planning Rsch. Corp., Kennedy Space Ctr., 1974-77; pres. S.S.S. Water Systems, Inc., Denison, 1978-83, Texoma Svcs. Corp., Pottsboro, Tex., 1980-99, Tanglewood Water Co., 1994-99; exec. Tecon Water Cos. Inc., 1999—; bd. dirs. Ind. Water and Sewer Co. Tex. Inc., Austin, Boy Scouts Am., Circle Ten, Dallas; entrepreneur Bells Discount Supply, Tex., 1983-87; adv. bd. MD Productivity, Austin, 2000—. Contbr. articles to profl. jours. Mem. City Coun., Pottsboro, Tex., 1992—. With USN, 1960-63. Mem. State Bar of Tex. (grievance com. 1999—), Tanglewood Golf Assn. (sec.-treas. 1992), Am. Legion, C. of C. Mem. Ch. of Christ. Avocations: inventing, camping, reading, golfing, boating, hunting. Office: Tecon Water Cos Inc 1437 Georgetown Rd Pottsboro TX 75076-6907

HANNINK, D. BRADLEY, financial company executive; b. Modesto, Calif., May 8, 1955; m. Maren Choate; children: Mia, Caleb. MS in Counseling summa cum laude, U. San Francisco, 1985; MS in Fin. Planning, Coll. Fin. Planning, Denver, 1998. Assoc. pastor Rosedale Bible Ch., Bakersfield, Calif., 1985-87; fin. advisor Am. Express Fin. Advisors, Bakersfield, 1987—; guest spkr. and trainer fin. edn. svcs. Bectel and Chevron Corp., Bakersfield. Bd. dirs. Bakersfield Meml. Hosp. Mem. Rotary (bd. dirs.). E-mail: Brad.x.Hannink@aexp.com. Office: Am Express Fin Advisors 5500 Ming Ave Ste 252 Bakersfield CA 93309-4625

HANNON, LEO FRANCIS, retired lawyer, educator; b. Boston, June 29, 1926; s. Bernard Francis and Elsie A. (Byrne) H.; m. Marion Ryan, June 7, 1958 (dec.); children: Elizabeth, James, Patricia, Jane. BS, Boston Coll., 1951; LLB, Georgetown U., 1958. Bar: D.C. 1958, U.S. Dist. Ct. D.C. 1958. Spl. agt. Office of Naval Intelligence, Washington, 1953-59; sr. atty. Nat. Labor Rels. Bd., Phila., 1960-69; mng. counsel labor security and benefits E.I. DuPont Co., Wilmington, Del., 1969-90; tchr. U. Del., Newark, 1991-95; mem. Bus. Roundtable Litigation Com., N.Y., Washington, 1980-90. Author: Legal Side of Private Security, 1992; contbr. articles to profl. jours. Bd. mem. Contact USA, Harrisburg, Pa., 1993-96; vol. Seamen's Ctr., Wilmington, Del. With USN, 1944-46, 51-53. Avocations: writing, travel, golf. Home: 1211 Hilltop Ave Wilmington DE 19809-1625

HANNUM, DAVID LAWRENCE, business consultant, training specialist; b. Detroit, May 6, 1945; s. John Andrew and Ruth (Life) H.; m. Mary Ellen Oltesvig, Apr. 19, 1968; children: James K., Charles M. BS, Regis Coll., Denver, 1982; MBA, Fairleigh Dickinson U., 1984; M cert. in project mgmt., George Washington U., 1991. Instr. Mich. Bell., Detroit, 1971-78, mgr. tng., 1978-80; with course devel. dept. AT&T, Denver, 1980-82; systems test mgr. AT&T, Parsippany, N.J., 1982-84; project mgr. AT&T, Morris Plains, N.J., 1984-89; mgr. tng. AT&T, South Plainfield, N.J., 1989-91; networking cons. AT&T G1S, Atlanta, 1991-96; owner, chief cons. DLH Cons., 1996-97; cons. eB Networks, 1997-2000; CEO Network Solutions, Inc., 2000—; co-owner Pocono Craft Loft, Tannersville, Pa., 1986-92; trainer Engring. Soc. Detroit, 1979; assoc. prof. County Coll. of Morris, Dover, N.J., 1984-85. Author various computer tng. courses. Leader, trainer, commr. Boy Scouts Am., Mich., Colo., N.J., Pa., 1975-90. With USNR, 1962-63. Mem. IEEE, IEEE Computer Soc. (assoc. editor, columnist Micro mag. 1982-86), ASTD, Profl. Picture Framers Assn. Avocations: handcrafts, woodworking, fishing, travel, community activities. Home and Office: 100 Marthas Cv Fayetteville GA 30215-5137

HANRAHAN, FIONNUALA M., librarian; b. Dublin, Ireland, 1955; d. Sean and Mona (Norton) H. Diploma in libr. and info. sci., Libr. Assn., London, 1977; BA, U. Coll. Dublin, 1986; M in Libr. and Info. Sci., U. Wales, 1992. Librarian Dublin Corp., 1978, sr. librarian, 1979-81; divsnl. librarian Dublin County Coun., 1981-85; dep. city and county librarian Dublin Corp., 1985-96; county librarian Wexford (Ireland) County Coun., 1996—. Editor An Leabharlann, The Irish Library, 1994-99. Chmn. Nat. Childrens Book Festival, 1984-87; sec. Dublin Heritage Group, 1989-96. Mem. Libr. Assn. Ireland (assoc.) (hon. sec. 1987-92, v.p. 1992-97).

HANS, MEYER, bank executive; b. Apr. 20, 1936. Student, U. St. Galen. Joined Swiss Nat. Bank, Zurich, 1965; mem. governing bd. Swiss Nat. Bank, 1985, vice chmn. governing bd., 1988-96, chmn. governing bd., 1996—, pres. Office: Swiss Nat Bank, Borsenstr 15, 4388 Postfach 8022 Zurich, Switzerland*

HANS-ADAM, II, Prince of Liechtenstein; b. Feb. 14, 1945; s. Prince Franz Josef II and Princess Gina; m. Countess Marie Aglae Kinsky von Wchinitz und Tettau, 1967; 3 sons, 1 dau. Grad., Sch. Econs. and Social Scis., St. Gallen, Switzerland, 1969. Exec. authority of Liechtenstein, 1984—, succeeded father as reigning prince, 1989—. Address: Schloss Vaduz, FL-9490 Vaduz Fürstentum Liechtenstein

HANSBURY, STEPHAN CHARLES, lawyer; b. Mt. Holly, N.J., Nov. 3, 1946; s. Charles Clark and Kathryn Irene (Meyer) H.; m. Sharon Buckley; children: Elizabeth Kathryn, Jillian Judith, Stephanie Clark. BA, Allegheny Coll., 1968; MBA, Fairleigh Dickinson U., 1973; JD, Seton Hall U., 1977; cert. civil trial atty., Supreme Ct. N.J., 1989. Bar: N.J. 1977, U.S. Dist. Ct. (no. dist.) N.J. 1977, U.S. Supreme Ct. 1982. Dir. spl. programs Bloomfield (N.J.) Coll., 1968-71; dir. fin. aid Monmouth Coll., West Long Branch, N.J., 1971-72; asst. adminstr. Morris View, Morris Plains, N.J., 1972-78; assoc. Hansbury, Martin & Knapp, Morris Plains, 1978-87, pres., 1987-92; ptnr. Kummer Knox, Naughton & Hansbury, Parsippany, N.J., 1992-99, pres., 1996-97; ptnr. Cooper, Rose & English, LLP, 2000—; mem., gen. counsel Cheshire Home, Florham Park, N.J., 1978—, Ciba-Geigy Corp., Summit, N.J., 1980-92. Legis. aide Assemblyman Arthur Albohn, Morristown, N.J., 1980-83; mem. Morris County Bd. of Social Svcs., 1989-96, chmn. 1992-94; bd. dirs. Colonia Symhony. Mem. ABA, N.J. Bar Assn., Morris County Bar Assn. (trustee 1987-90), Rotary (pres. 1998-99), Morristown Club. Republican. Episcopalian. Avocations: tennis, golf, reading. Office: Cooper Rose & English LLP 480 Morris Ave Summit NJ 07901-1523

HANSDOTTIR, HELGA, geriatrician; b. Reykjavik, Iceland, Aug. 15, 1959; d. Hans Jetzek and Alfheidur Lindal; m. Kristinn Gudbrandur Hardarson; children: Kristinsson, Theodor, Magnus. MD, U. Iceland, 1987. Diplomate Iceland Bd. Geriatric Medicine; bd. cert. internal medicine with added qualifications in geriatric medicine. Rotating intern The Nat. Hosp. Iceland and Reykjavik City Hosp., 1987-89; resident Reykjavik City Hosp., 1989-91; intern U. Conn., 1991-92, resident in internal medicine, 1992-94, fellow in geriatrics, 1994-96, instr. in medicine, 1996-97; attending physician Reykjavik City Hosp., 1997—. Mem. Am. Geriatric Soc., Icelandic Physician Assn. Avocations: arts, hiking. Home: Tjarnargotu 24, 101 Reykjavik Iceland

HANSELAAR, ANTONIUS G.J.M., pathologist; b. Tilburg, N. Brabant, The Netherlands, Mar. 20, 1953; s. A. and J. (Smulders) H.; m. Ellen C.A.M. Van Loevezijn, Dec. 27, 1983; children: Caspar, Rogier. MD, U. Nijmegen, The Netherlands, 1980, PhD, 1990. Resident dept. pharmacol. toxicology and pathology U. Nijmegen, The Netherlands, 1981-82; resident in pathology U. Hosp., Nijmegen, 1982-86, pathologist, asst. prof., 1986-90, 92-95; rschr. U. Calif., San Francisco, 1990-91, BCCA/Cancer Imaging, Vancouver, Can., 1991-92; assoc. prof. cytopathology U. Nijmegen, 1995—; head cytopathology U. Hosp., Nijmegen, 1992-98; cons. Dutch Nat. Health Ins. Coun., 1995—; coord. pathologist Found. Prevention Cervical Cancer, East Netherlands, 1998—; cons. Found. Des-Ctr., 1994—. Author: DNA-Cytometry of Cervical Intraepithelial Neoplasia, 1990; contbr. articles to profl. jours. Capt. Dutch Royal Army, 1980-81. Fellow John Jambor Knowledge Fund, Vancouver, 1992, Dutch Cancer Soc., 1991, NATO, 1990. Mem. Netherlands Soc. Pathology (chmn. 1994—). Roman Catholic. Avocations: field hockey, golf, sailing. Office: Univ Hosp Nijmegen/Path Dpt, PO Box 9101, 6500 HB Nijmegen The Netherlands

HANSELL, PHYLLIS SHANLEY, nursing educator, researcher, consultant; b. N.Y.C., Jan. 3, 1947; s. Peter James and Jewell Mae (Altis) S.; m. Robert Lewis Hansell, June 16, 1984; children: Benjamin, Christopher. BS, Fairleigh Dickinson U., 1972; MEd, Columbia U., 1975, EdD, 1981. RN. Staff nurse Mountainside Hosp., Montclair, N.J., 1967-69; head nurse N.Y. Med. Coll., N.Y.C., 1970-72, clin. instr., 1972-75; instr. Seton Hall U., South Orange, 1975-77, asst. prof., 1977-79, prof. nursing, 1986-94, 96—, dir. nursing rsch., 1986-94, dept. chair, 1996-99, acting dean, 1999-2000, dean Coll. Nursing, 2000—; dir. nursing rsch. Meml. Sloan Kettering, N.Y.C., 1984-86. Contbr. articles to profl. jours., chpt. to book. Bd. dirs. Jr. League, Montclair, 1992-94, chair grants and corp. devel., chair Newark Teen Arts Festival, Montclair and Newark, 1994-95. Recipient Gov.'s merit award Gov. N.J., 1994. Fellow Am. Acad. Practice (Disting. Practitioner 2000); mem. ANA (chair rsch., Gov.'s award 1994), N.J. State Nurses Assn. (mem. coun., rsch. award 1994), Sigma Theta Tau (v.p. Gamma Nu chpt. 1994-96, rsch. award 1983). Avocations: opera, ballet, skiing, tennis. Office: Seton Hall U 400 S Orange Ave South Orange NJ 07079-2697

HANSEN, BARBARA L., English educator; b. Indpls., Sept. 27, 1935; d. Joseph Martin and Ruth Edna Hansen. BS in Edn., Ball State U., 1963, MA in English, 1964, PhD in English, 1971. Grad. tchr. Ball State U., Muncie, Ind., 1963-64; instr. English Ball State U., Muncie, 1964-67, doctoral fellow, 1967-68, instr. English, 1969-72; asst. prof. English U. Cin., 1972-78, assoc. prof. English, 1978-90, prof. English, 1990—. Author: Picking Up the Pieces: Healing Ourselves After Personal Loss, 1991, rev. edit., 1993, The Strength Within: Cultivate Habits of Wholeness, Hope, and Joy, 2000; co-author: (with Rebecca McDaniel) Developing Sentence Skills, 1990, Simplified Sentence Skills, 1997; contbr. articles to profl. jours. Recipient Outstanding Handicapped Student award Venture Club, 1962, Midwest Handicapped Profl. Woman of Yr. award Pres.'s Com. for the Handicapped, 1972. Avocations: reading, writing, counseling. Office: U Cin-RWC 9555 Plainfield Rd Cincinnati OH 45236-1007

HANSEN, CHARLES MEDOM, chemist; b. Louisville, Sept. 16, 1938; s. Kristian and Alma (Jensen) H.; m. Kirsten Lyck, June 23, 1967; children: Susan, Kristian, Michael. BCHE, U. Louisville, 1961; MS, U. Wis., 1962; lic. techn., Tech. U. Denmark, Copenhagen, 1965, dr. techn., 1967. Sr. rsch. assoc. PPG Industries, Pitts., 1968-76; dir. Scandinavian Paint and Printing Ink Rsch. Inst., Horsholm, Denmark, 1976-85; sr. scientist Hempel Marine Coatings, Copenhagen, 1985-87, Force Inst. (formerly Danish Isotope Ctr.), Copenhagen, 1988—; mem. tech. adv. bd. Internat. Conf. on Organic Coatings, Athens, Greece, 1980-90. Author: (handbook) Hansen Solubility Parameters—A User's Handbook, 1999; contbr. articles to profl. jours. Named Pioneer of Polymer Sci., Polymer News, 1984, Disting. Alumnus U. Louisville, 1998. Mem. Danish Acad. Tech. Scis., Danish Soc. Polymer Tech. (pres. 2000—). Achievements include the devel. of Hansen Solubility Parameters to predict affinity-solvency, polymer compatibility, adsorption on surfaces, permeation, etc. Avocations: bicycling, woodsmanship, hiking. Home: Jens Bornøsvej 16, 2970 Hørsholm Denmark Office: 345 Park Alle, DK 2605 Brondby Denmark

HANSEN, CHARLES MORTON, genealogy editor, retired military officer; b. Huntington Park, Calif., Sept. 27, 1933; s. Andrew Hansen and Lena S. Andrew. BA in History, UCLA, 1955; MA in History, San Francisco State U., 1985. Commd. 2d lt. U.S. Army, 1955, advanced through grades to col., 1977; platoon leader U.S. Army, Korea, 1957-59; sr. adv. U.S. Army, Viet Nam, 1965-66; bn. comdr. U.S. Army, Korea, 1969-70; ret. U.S. Army, 1982; contbg. editor The Am. Genealogist, 1988—; editor The Genealogist, 1996—. Contbr. articles to profl. jours. Decorated Legion of Merit, Bronze star, Combat Infantry Badge, Cross of Gallantry Republic of Vietnam; recipient Coddington award for Merit New England Hist. Geneal. Soc., 1995. Fellow Am. Soc. of Genealogists; mem. Soc. of Genealogists (London), Heraldry Soc. (London), Soc. Heraldica Scandinavia (Denmark), Ninth Infantry Regiment Assn., Harbor Point Racquet Club. Methodist. Avocation: tennis. Home: 25 Rodeo Ave Apt 22 Sausalito CA 94965-1783

HANSEN, CHRISTOPHER AGNEW, lawyer; b. Yakima, Wash., Dec. 10, 1934; s. Raymond Walter and Christine F.M. (Agnew) H.; m. Sandra Ridgely Pindell, Aug. 4, 1959; Anne Ridgely, Christopher Agnew Jr., Eric Bruce. BS, Cornell U., 1957; JD, U. Md., 1963. Bar: Md. 1963, U.S. Supreme Ct. 1973, U.S. Ct. Appeals (4th cir.) D.C. 1978. Law clk. Cir. Ct. for Balt. County, Towson, Md., 1960-63; assoc. Piper & Marbury, Balt., 1963-74; of counsel Casey, Scott, Canfield & Heggestad PC, Washington, 1982-93; ptnr. Constable, Alexander & Skeen, Towson, 1984-86, Parks, Hansen & Ditch, Towson, 1986-94; of counsel Heggestad & Weiss, PC, Washington, 1993—; pvt. practice Towson, 1974-83, 95—. With U.S. Army, 1957-60. Mem. ABA, D.C. Bar, Md. State Bar Assn., Bar Assn. Balt. County, Balt. City Bar Assn., Phi Alpha Delta. Episcopalian. Home: 800 Hatherleigh Rd Baltimore MD 21212-1614

HANSEN, DEIRDRE DORIS, ethnomusicologist, educator, researcher; b. Piet Retief, South Africa, Aug. 16, 1938; Heinrich Theodor Jes and Muriel (Galt) H. Licentiate Performer in Pianoforte, Trinity Coll. Music, London, 1957, Licentiate Tchr. Pianoforte, 1961; M in Music, Rhodes U., Grahamstown, South Africa, 1962, 68; PhD in Ethnomusicology, Witwatersrand U., Johannesburg, South Africa, 1982. Music tchr. Victoria Girls H.S., Grahamstown, 1962; rsch. officer Inst. Social and Econ. Rsch., Grahamstown, 1963-66; relief lectr., music Rhodes U., 1979-80, lectr., piano, 1980-82; sr. lectr. U. Cape Town, South Africa, 1982—; sr. bursar, African Studies, Witwatersrand U., 1967-71; ethnomusicology rschr., 1969-76, 78-80; pvt. music tchr., Howick, KwaZulu, 1976-78; curator Kirby Collection, U. Cape Town, 1982—; invited to attend panel of adjudicators, Samro postgrad. indigenous African music study, S. Africa, 2000. Solo pianist South African Broadcast Corp., Grahamstown, 1963-66; contbr. articles to profl. jours. Guest spkr. B. Tyamzashe Celebration, Bisho Eastern Cape, 1970; vis. lectr. U. Durban-Westville, Kwazulu-Natal, 1996; guest spkr., Heritage Day of the Xhosa Nat., Eastern Cape Dept. Edn. Culture, Alice, 1996. Named Hon. Dau. Thembu Nat., homestead Chief Mtirharha, Eastern Cape, 1969. Mem. Soc. Ethnomusicology, Smithsonian (assoc.). Mem. Inkatha Freedom Party. Christian. Avocations: piano playing, embroidery, water-color painting, photography. Home: Plumstead, Carlsheim 105 Woodley Rd, Cape Town 7800, South Africa Office: U Cape Town Faculty Music, P/Bag Rondebosch 7701 C, Cape Town 7700, South Africa

HANSEN, DONALD MARTY, journalist, retired accountant; b. Elmhurst, Ill., July 6, 1935; s. Donald Joseph Hansen and Vivian Leona (Bourgart) Guthrie; m. Rose Ann Baumeister, Aug. 12, 1961 (div.); children: Teresa Lynn, Donna Louise, David Lawrence, Daniel Leonard. Assoc. in Acctg., Racine Tech., 1970. Drill press operator J.I. Case Co., Racine, Wis., 1964-70; acct. Scott Petersen Meat Co., Chgo., 1974-95, Crosby Freezer, Inc., Chgo., 1995-2000; ret., 2000; editor, pub. Don Hansen's Nat. Weekly Football and Basketball Gazettes, Brookfield, Ill., 1987—; columnist USA Today Online, 1998—; editor, pub. Don Hansen's Ann. 52-page Football SchedulesBooklet, 2000—; stringer Football News, Miami, 1981—, The Sporting News, St. Louis, 1987—, USA Today, Arlington, Va., 1987—; mem. Melberger award selection com. Downtown Wilkes-Barre Touchtown Club, 1993—; mem. com. for NCAA Divsn. III Player of the Yr., John Gagliardi award, 1993—. Editor, pub. Don Hansen's Annual 52-Page Football Schedules Booklet, 2000—; contbr. articles to profl. jours. Originator, promoter, operator annual summer wrestling tournament Oak Park-River Forest (Ill.) H.S., 1978-80; mem. selection com. Farm All-Am. Football Team, 1999—; mem. selection com. NCAA Divsn. II Hall of Fame Football, 1999—. With USN, 1952-54. Recipient Leadership trophy Chase Park (Chgo.), 1947, Celebrity Cert. of Appreciation ARC, 1992, Statistician of the Yr. Oak Park-River Forest H.S., 1981. Mem. CO-SIDA Coll. Sports Info. Dirs. Am. Republican. Mem. Assembly of God Ch. E-mail: fbgazette@thc.to; don@donhansen.com. Home: Apt 10 5613 King Arthur Ct Westmont IL 60559-2269 Office: Don Hansen's Nat Weekly Football Gazette PO Box 305 Westmont IL 60559-0305

HANSEN, FLEMMING, economics educator, marketing consultant; b. Copenhagen, July 16, 1938; s. Arne and Grethe (Christensen) H.; m. Birgit Hallum Andersen; children: Morten, Jan, Karin. MBA, Copenhagen Sch. Bus. Adminstrn. and Econs., Denmark, 1962, PhD, 1967; postgrad., Columbia U., 1962-63; D of Econs., Lunds U., Sweden, 1972. With WA-Reklame/Mktg. I/S, Denmark, 1960-64; asst. prof. Copenhagen Sch. Bus. Adminstrn. and Econs., 1964-67, prof., 1977—; assoc. prof. Whitemore Sch. Bus. Adminstrn. and Econs. U. N.H., 1967-70; prof. Aalborg U. Ctr., Denmark, 1974-77; chmn. dept. mktg. Copenhagen Bus. Sch., 1987-90; vis. prof. UCLA, 1986; bd. dirs. BRF-Kaedit, Copenhagen, Callup A/S, Copenhagen; part-owner, bd. dirs. AIM A/S, 1970-89, owner, 1973-90. Author: Consumer Choice Behavior, 1972, Scaling: Measurements in the Social Sciences, 1979, Studies of Communication Efforts, 1985; contbr. articles to profl. jours.; editor: Advances in Consumer Research, 1997. Vice chmn. ESOMAR, Amsterdam, The Netherlands, 1980-86, EMAC, Brussels, 1986-94; pres. Rsch. Coun., Copenhagen, 1999—; chmn. Forum for Advt. Rsch., Copenhagen, 1998—. Cpl. Danish Army, 1963-64. Recipient award A.C. Nielsen Found., 1963, prize Dansk Ekhueruslius, 1974. Mem. Assn. Consumer Rsch., Rep. Coun., Royal Danish Shooting Soc. Avocations: history, golf, tennis, bridge, literature. Home: Ordrupgaardvej 12, 2920 Charlottenlund Denmark Office: Copenhagen Bus Sch, Solbjerg Plads 3 3, 2000 Copenhagen Denmark

HANSEN, GERD, economist; b. Pansdorf, Germany, Jan. 1, 1938; s. Wilhelm and Kathe (Hardt) H.; m. Renate Lentin, Aug. 28, 1964. Diploma, U. Kiel, Germany, 1962; D Polit. Sci., U. Hamburg, Germany, 1966, Dr.habilitation, 1971. Prof. U. Frankfurt, Germany, 1972-79, U. Kiel, Germany, 1979—. Author: Methodenlehre der Statistik, 1974, Quantitative Wirtschafts forschung, 1993; contbr. articles to profl. jours. Mem. German Statis. Soc. Avocation: music. Home: Seeblick 1, D24245 Kirchbarkau Germany Office: U Kiel, Wilhelm-Seelig Platz 7, D24098 Kiel Germany

HANSEN, GLEN ARTHUR, scientist, researcher; b. Thermopolis, Wyo., June 28, 1961; s. Glen Arthur and Ilene Lois (Haynes) H.; m. Paula Dee Rathbun, May 23, 1998. AAS in Petroleum Engring. Tech., Casper Coll., 1982; BS in Petroleum Engring., U. Wyo., 1985; MS in Mech. Engring., U. Nebr., 1991; PhD in Computer Sci., U. Idaho, 1996. Rsch. asst. U. Nebr., Lincoln, 1989-90, tchg. asst., 1990-91; sr. engr. Idaho Nat. Engring. Lab., Idaho Falls, 1991-95, engring. specialist, 1995-96; tech. staff mem. Los Alamos Nat. Lab., 1996—, project leader, 1997—; prin. investigator Los Alamos (N. Mex.) Nat. Lab., 1998—. Mem. IEEE, ASME, Am. Nuclear Soc. (Idaho chpt.), Soc. Indsl. Applied Math., Assn. Computing Machinery. Home: 945 San Ildefonso Rd # 57 Los Alamos NM 87544-2849 Office: Los Alamos National Lab PO Box 1663 Los Alamos NM 87545-0001

HANSEN, H. JACK, management consultant; b. Chgo., Mar. 28, 1922; s. Herbert Christian John and Laura Eliabeth (Osterman) H.; m. Joan Dorothy Norum, Nov. 28, 1980; children: Marilyn Joan, Gail Jean, Mark John, Jacquelyn Lee. BSME, Ill. Inst. Tech., 1944. Cert. mgmt. cons. Mech. and indsl. engr. Harper Wyman Co., Chgo., 1944-51; chief indsl. engr. Shakeproof divsn. Ill. Tool Works, Des Plaines, 1951-53; cons., prin. A.T. Kearney & Co., Chgo. and N.Y.C., 1953-71; pres. H.J. Hansen Co., Elburn, Ill., 1971—; acting. mfg. enring. mgr. European operation Hobart Corp., 1974-78; owner, mgmt. cons. Hansen Mgmt. Search Co., Mt. Prospect, Ill., 1980-93. Pioneerd use of Should Cost studies for U.S. Dept. Def., conceptualized and developed procedure for gain sharing productivity improvement; active turnaround cons., 1992—. Mem. Planning Commn., Village of Elburn, 1995-97, trustee, 1997—, chmn. Pers. Commn., mem. Fin. Commn., mem. Pub. Works Commn.; pres. Good Shepherd Luth. Ch., Des Palines, Ill., 1988-90, Men's Club, 1987-90; active mem. mcpl. legis. com. DuKane Valley Coun. With AUS, 1945-46. Mem. Inst. Mgmt. Cons. (founding), Methods-Time Measurement Assn. (bd. dirs. 1964-70, pres. 1967-68), Am. Arbitrtion Assn., Soc. Advancement Mgmt. (past bd. dirs.), coun. for Internat. Progress in Mgmt. (past bd. dirs.), Found. Internat. Progress in Mgmt. (past bd. dirs.), Econ. Devel. Com., Elburn C. of C. Office: H J Hansen Co 317 Prairie Valley St Elburn IL 60119-8977

HANSEN, HANNE SAND, radiotherapist, consultant, oncologist; b. Copenhagen, June 26, 1936; d. Hans Marius and Gudrun Thyra (Sand) H. Med. diploma, U. Copenhagen, 1962, MD, 1975. Specialist in radiotherapy, 1971; specialist in oncology, 1989. Intern, registrar Svendborg, 1963, various hosps., Copenhagen, 1967-68; registrar, sr. registrar Radium Ctr. of Copenhagen, 1964-67, 69-73, cons. radiotherapist, 1973—; registrar oncologic dept. Lund, Örebro, Sweden, 1967-68; sr. registrar Royal Marsden Hosp., London, 1968-69; cons. radiotherapist oncologic dept. Nat. U. Hosp., Copenhagen, 1990—; mem. Nordic CART, 1984—, European Union EU-LIMA, 1988, Nordic Assn. Clin. Physics, 1992. Contbr. articles to profl. jours. Recipient Scandinavian Soc. Med. Radiology traveling scholarship, 1968, Acta Radiologica donation, 1970, Am. Cancer Soc. traveling scholarship, 1972, William Nielsen donation, 1977. Mem. Scandinavian Soc. for Head-Neck Oncology (bd. dirs.), Danish Soc. Oncology (rep. in European Radiology Assn. 1987, ICR 1992), Danish Soc. of Head and Neck Oncology (chmn. 1984-96). Home: Toftekaersvej 42, 2820 Gentofte Denmark Office: Rigshospitalet, Blegdamsvej 9, 2100 Copenhagen Denmark

HANSEN, HANNE WILHELM, publicist, agent; b. Copenhagen, Jan. 23, 1927; d. Suend Wilhelm and Lissen Wilhelm (Bendix) H. Dir. Nordiska Strakosch Theater, Copenhagen, 1978—. Office: Nordiska Strakosch Theater, Gothersgade 11 4, 1123 Copenhagen Denmark

HANSEN, HANS CHRISTIAN, environmental chemist; b. Lindknud, Denmark, Apr. 12, 1959; s. Niels Holger and Karen (Bruun) H.; m. Birthe Poulsen; 3 children. MSc, Agrl. U., Copenhagen, 1987, PhD, 1991. From rsch. asst. to prof. Agrl. U., Copenhagen, 1987—. Office: Chemistry Dept, Thorvaldsensvej 40, DK-1871 Frederiksberg Denmark

HANSEN, HAROLD B., JR., principal; b. Sewickley, Pa., July 3, 1955; s. Harold B. and Mary Clara (VanderVort) H.; m. Patty Jo Gabhart, Sept. 19, 1976; children: Jeremiah James, Joshua Andrew, Esther Beth, Christopher Seth. BA in Elem. Edn., Purdue U., 1980; MA in Sch. Adminstrn., Western N.Mex. U., 1987. Cert. secondary lang. arts and spl. edn. tchr., TESL tchr., instrnl. leader, sch. adminstr., elem. tchr., coach, N.Mex. Resource rm. tchr. Flossmoor/Homewood (Ill.) Pub. Schs., 1981, Newcomb (N.Mex.) H.S., 1981-82; tchr. self-contained spl. edn. Chester (Mont.) Pub. Schs., 1982-84; adminstr., prin., tchr. Bennett (Colo.) Bapt. Ch. Sch., 1984; propr., tutor Hemispheric Learning Tutorial Svcs., 1982—; tchr. resource room, coach cross county, wrestling, track and field Gallup-McKinley County Pub. Schs., Tohatchi/Navajo Reserv., N.Mex., 1985-90; elem. tchr. phys. edn. and health, at-risk tchr. Tohatchi Elem. Sch. Gallup-McKinley County Pub. Schs., Tohatchi, 1990-98, 5th grade track & field head coach, 1991-98, 5th grade boys' and girls' basketball asst. coach, 1995-98; prin. Smith Lake Elem. Sch., Gallup-McKinley County Pub. Schs., 1998—; mem. various sch. coms. Gallup-McKinley County Pub. Schs., 1990-98; seminar leader on hemispherecity; dep. registration officer McKinley County, N.Mex., 1986—. Past pres. Village of Hope, substance abuse tng. ctr.; co-founder, past bd. dirs. Christian Home Educators Assn.; dir. Approved Workmen Are Not Ashamed; coord. Jump Rope for Heart, Am. Heart Assn.; mem. Coun. for Curricular Excellence, McKinley County; TESOL rep. for Western N.Mex. U.'s Gallup Grad. Ctr.'s Adv. Coun., 1997—. Named to Outstanding Young Men of Am., 1987. Mem. ASCD, N.Mex. Assn. Health, Phys. Edn., Recreation and Dance, Christian HomeEducators Assn., Aesthetic Realism Found. Fax: 505-786-5542. E-mail: HaniibaazH@aol.com. Home: PO Box 100 Smith Lake NM 87365-0100

HANSEN, JAY, professional organization executive; b. Verdun, France, Jan. 27, 1960; s. John and Patricia (Ettipio) H.; m. Susy Olivera, Feb. 14, 1989; 1 child, Chaska. BA in Polit. Sci., San Diego State U., 1985. Legis. dir. Rep. Jim Bates, Washington, 1985-89, Rep. Bob Clement, Washington, 1989-96; dir. transportation programs Am. Cons. Engrs. Coun., Washington, 1996-98; v.p. govt. affairs Nat. Asphalt Pavement Assn., Washington, 1998—; bd. dirs. Am. Hwy. Users Alliance, Washington, 1999—; transportation com. U.S. C. of C., Washington, 1999—; mem. Nat Quality Initiative, Washington, 1996—. Mem. Am. Soc. Assn. Execs. (effective lobbying award 1997). Home: 3308 Jones Bridge Rd Chevy Chase MD 20815-5735

HANSEN, JOHN HERBERT, university administrator, accountant; b. Milw., Mar. 20, 1945; s. John Herbert and Elsie F. (Patri) H.; m. Christina Ann Laniey, Sept. 5, 1970. BBA, U. Wis., 1969; M in Acctg., U. Ill., 1973. CPA, Wis. Dir. treas. svcs. Marquette U., Milw., 1973—. With USAF, 1970-73. Mem. Am. Inst. CPA's, Milw. Bond Club. Republican. Club: Merrill Hills Country. Avocations: golf, gardening. Office: Marquette U PO Box 1881 Milwaukee WI 53201-1881

HANSEN, JORN DINES, physics educator; b. Copenhagen, July 30, 1940; s. Hakon and Gerda Kirsten (Johansen) H.; m. Lis Montandon, Aug. 7, 1965; children: Karin, Marianne. Cand. Mag., U. Copenhagen, 1965. Tchg. asst. U. Copenhagen, 1965; fellow CERN, Geneva, 1965-73; rsch. asst. prof. U. Ill., Urbana, 1970-72; postdoctorate fellow U. Copenhagen, 1973-77, assoc. prof., 1977-88, prof., 1988-93, 1993—; mem. Danish Cern Com., Denmark, 1982-99, ACCU/CERN, Geneva, 1979-80, Recfa/CERN, Geneva, 1981-85, 88-93; bd. mem. NBI, Copenhagen, 1985-93; responsible for all physics studies, U. Copenhagen, 1999—. Home: Lyngskraenten 29, 2840 Holte Denmark Office: Niels Bohr Inst, Blegdamsvej 17, 2100 Copenhagen Denmark

HANSEN, KENNETH D., lawyer, ophthalmologist; b. Seattle, Mar. 26, 1947; s. George R. and Elaine D. (Jacobsen) H.; m. Barbara Caleen, Oct. 8, 1976; 1 son, David Scott. BS in Psychology, U. Wash., 1969, JD, 1972, MD with honors, 1976. Bar: Wash. 1972, Mich. 1977, Ill. 1984, D.C. 1986, U.S. Supreme Ct. 1981; diplomate Am. Bd. Ophthalmology. Legal counsel Assn. Wash. Bus., Olympia, 1972-73; asst. atty. gen. State of Wash., Seattle, 1973-74; v.p., gen. counsel N.W. Med. Rsch. Found., Seattle, 1976-86; pres. Internat. Health Found., 1986—; intern medicine U. Mich. Hosp., Ann Arbor, 1977, resident in ophthalmology, 1978-80; sr. med. staff Henry Ford Hosp., Detroit, 1981-82; dir. ophthalmology Carbondale (Ill.) Clinic, 1983-86, chmn. dept. surgery, gen. counsel, 1984-86; clin. asst. prof. ophthalmology and med. humanities So. Ill. U., Carbondale, 1983-86; clin. asst. prof. ophthalmology U. Md., Balt., 1986—; med.-legal adv. com. U. Mich. Hosp. System; cons. Nat. Def. Med. Coll., China; charter coun. mem. practicing physicians adv. coun. to Sec. of U.S. Dept. Health and Human Svcs., 1992-97; internat. med.-legal lectr. Assoc. editor Trauma, 1995—, Wash. Law Rev., 1971-72; contbr. articles to legal and med. profl. jours., publs. Recipient U. Wash. Med. Thesis Award, Gold Medal Egyptian Med. Syndicate, 1986; William Wallice Wilshire Meml. scholar; Anna C. Dunlap Meml. scholar; Grad. Rsch. fellow, 1975—; recipient Red Rose award Soc. Rsch. Adminstrs., 1989. Fellow Am. Coll. Legal Medicine (jud. coun., model statutes com., Pres.'s award 1989), Internat. Coll. Surgeons; mem. ABA, AMA, Wash. State Bar Assn., Mich. Bar Assn., Ill. Med. Soc. (med.-legal coun.), Ill. Bar Assn., Mich. Med. Schs. Coun. Deans (med.-legal adv. com.), Mich. Ophthalmology Soc. (Rsch. award 1981), Am. Acad. Ophthalmology, D.C. Bar Assn., Phi Delta Pi, Phi Eta Sigma, Pi Sigma Epsilon. Baptist. Home: 6501 Bright Mountain Rd Mc Lean VA 22101-1701 Office: 901 N Stuart St Ste 210 Arlington VA 22203

HANSEN, KLAUS, English language educator; b. Berlin, Jan. 12, 1934; s. Georg and Käthe (Weber) H.; m. Barbara Butte, Apr. 15, 1967; 1 child, Dagmar. Dr.Phil., Humboldt U., Berlin, 1962, Dr.Sc.Phil., 1975. Diplomate in English and German philology. Univ. asst. Humboldt U., Berlin, 1958-69, sr. asst., 1969-74, asst. prof., 1974-78, full prof. English lang., 1978-99; prof. emeritus, 1999—; dean philological faculty Humboldt U., Berlin, 1990-93, mem. acad. senate, 1990-98. Author: Abriss der modernen englischen Wortbildung, 1964, 5th edit., 1979; co-author: Englische Phonetik, 1975, 10th edit., 1996, Englische Lexikologie, 1982, 3d edit., 1990, Die Differenzierung des Englischen in nationale Varianten, 1996. Office: Humboldt U Berlin, Unter den Linden 6, D-10099 Berlin Germany

HANSEN, LARS MAERSK, geologist, consultant; b. Korsor, Denmark, Sept. 8, 1946; arrived in Sweden, 1966; s. Tage and Asta Maersk (Holm) H.; m. Ulla Wänstrand, Mar. 21, 1970; children: Sigrid, Tor. BSc, Univ. Uppsala, Uppsala, Sweden, 1981, lic., 1992. Cons. Trias Geology, Uppsala, 1983-89, Golder Assocs., Uppsala, 1989-94, Vattenfall Hydropower, Stockholm, 1994-96, Golder Assocs., Uppsala, 1996—. Contbr. articles to profl. jours. Fellow IMM, The Engr. Coun. Avocations: sailing, Tango. Office: Golder Assocs, Bjorkgatan 73, S75323 Uppsala Sweden

HANSEN, LAURITS LYDEHOJ, scientist; b. Allerslev, Denmark, Feb. 14, 1947; p. Paul Harry and Ella Rigmor (Petersen) H. Candidate of Agronomy, Royal Vet. and Agrl. U., Copenhagen, 1973, PhD, 1995. Cert. sr. scientist. Scientist dept. pigs and horses Danish Inst. Animal Sci., Copenhagen, 1974-84, Foulum, Denmark, 1984-95, Foulum, 1995-97; sr. scientist dept. animal product quality Danish Inst. Agrl. Scis., Foulum, 1997—. Author: Housing Systems for Pig Production, 1993 (St. Antonius award 1994); contbr. chpt. to book. Pvt. Bornholms Vfrn, 1973-74. Avocations: breeding of English Pointers for field trail, hunting and fishing, history. E-mail: LauritsLydehoj.Hansen@agrsci.dk. Fax: 45 89991564. Home: Vingevej 33, DK-8830 Orum Jutland, Denmark Office: Danish Inst Agrl Scis, Rsch Ctr Foulum, DK-8830 Foulum Jutland, Denmark

HANSEN, MAGNUS BANG, special education administrator, consultant; b. Kalvehave, Sjaelland, Denmark, May 24, 1936; s. Harry and Lilly (Bang) H.; m. Asta Bang Hansen, June 28, 1958; children: Gitte, Hannah, Jens. Grad., Seminarium, Skaarup, 1958; EdD, Marlborough U., Honolulu, 1999. Tchr. Cmty. Korsør, 1958-62, Cmty. Langeland, 1962-65; headmaster Sigrid Undset Sch., Kalundborg, Denmark, 1965-98; 1st lt. Danish Army, Holbaek, 1961-71; editor Sa-Materialer, Copenhagen, 1976-84; pres. Union of Dirs. of State Spl. Schs., Denmark, 1970-85; pres., educator Social Sys. Export, Latvia, Lithuania, Greece, Ireland, Hungary, Germany, Belgium, Sweden, Great Britain, 1991-97; pres. Dirs. Coll. Vestsjelland, 1992-98. Author: FRA Gamle Bakkehus, 1982; editor: Children with Psychotic Behavior, 1981; developer sandpit table for wheelchairs; contbr. articles to profl. jours. Mem. Town Coun. Kalundborg, 1974-81. Recipient Medal of Merit in Silver Her Majesty the Queen of Denmark, 1998. Mem. Lions Club (dir., advisor 1983-85, pres. Kalundborg 1986-87, 96-97, Dir.'s award 1985, Membership award 1994). Mem. Conservative Party. Lutheran. Avocation: ornithology. Address: Mollabakken 16, DK 4400 Kalundborg Danmark

HANSEN, MICHAEL VESTERGAARD, scientist; b. Copenhagen, Apr. 8, 1953; s. Einer and Helene (Vestergaard) H.; m. Jette Holm (div. 1980); children: Marie, Einar; m. Ingrid Aldehag, Aug. 22, 1987; children: Emma, Sofia, Karl. MD, Copenhagen U., 1978; PhD, Linkoping U., Sweden, 1989, D Med. Sci., 1989; Assoc. Prof., Lund U., Sweden, 1998. Resident Hosp., Lulea, 1978-85; sr. resident Hosp., Linkoping, 1985-90; sr. urologist Hosp., Fredrikstad, 1990-91, Halmstad, 1991-98; dir. scientific affairs Abbott, Scandinavia, 1998—. Contbr. more than 20 articles to profl. jours. Mem. Scandinavian Urol. Assn., Internat. Continence Soc., Internat. Soc. for Tech. Assessment in Health Care. Lutheran. Office: Abbott Scandinavia, PO Box 509, 16929 Solna Sweden

HANSEN, OTTO, veterinarian, scientist, educator; b. Nyborg, Funen, Denmark, Dec. 7, 1937; s. Oluf and Marie (Carlsen) H.; m. Aase Bust Petersen, July 29, 1972; children: Lasse, Toke. DVM with hons., Royal Vet. Agrl. U., Copenhagen, 1963, PhD, 1969; DMSc, Aarhus (Denmark) U., 1984. Asst. vet. surgeon Als, Denmark, 1964-66; asst. prof. Aarhus U., 1969-72, assoc. prof., 1972—; prof. Royal Vet. Agrl. U., Copenhagen, 1985-86; vice chmn. inst. physiology Aarhus U., 1978-80, chmn., 1987-88; mem. Biomembrane Rsch. Ctr., 1987-95. Contbr. over 100 articles to profl. publs. Dep. Nat. Com. Environ. Protection, Dept. Hadsten, 1987—. With Med. Corp. Denmark Mil., 1963-64. Recipient Found. Promotion Vet. Sci. award, 1981, 83, 85, 89, 91, numerous awards for papers. Mem. Am. Physiol. Soc., Soc. Gen. Physiologists. Home: Langskovvej 4, DK 8370 Hadsten Jutland, Denmark Office: Aarhus U Dept Physiology, Ole Worms Alle 160, DK 8000 Århus Jutland, Denmark

HANSEN, PETER, international organization executive. Under sec.-gen. Commr.-Gen. of UNRWA, N.Y.C. Address: PO Box 140157, Amman 11814, Jordan

HANSEN, TORBEN INGEMANN, lawyer; b. Frederiksberg, Denmark, Dec. 7, 1936; s. Carl Johannes and Inger (Ingemann) H.; m. Randi Andersen. Candidatus Juris, U. Copenhagen, Denmark, 1961. Bar: Denmark 1967, High Ct. 1971, Supreme Ct. 1976. Officer of the crown Ministry of Edn. and Ministry of Fin., Denmark, 1961-67; pvt. practice Copenhagen, 1967—. Corr. Euromoney Internat. Fid. Law File, 1990. Legal asst. Chief. Mil. Prosecutor, 1962-63; mem. Pub. Rent Control Bd., Frederiksberg, 1974; lay jduge Housing Tribunal, Copenhagen, 1978-92; city counsellor City of Frederiksberg, 1985-89. Decorated knight of Dannebrog, 1999. Mem. Internat. Bar Assn., Danish Bar Assn., Lloyd's of London (underwriter 1986-92)), Rotary Internat., Frederiksberg Rotary (pres. 1988-89, Paul Harris fellow 1995). Conservative. Avocations: sailing, skiing, tennis. Home: Emanuel Olsens Vej 9, 2000 Frederiksberg Denmark Office: Ingemann Meurs-GerkenSchiersing, Amaliegade 42, 1256 Copenhagen Denmark also: 26 bd Raspail, F75007 Paris France

HANSEN, VAGN LUNDSGAARD, mathematics educator; b. Vejle, Denmark, Sept. 27, 1940; s. Hans and Emma (Lundsgaard) H.; m. Birthe Broeng, July 25, 1964; children: Hanne, Helle, Martin. Candidatus Scientiarum, U. Aarhus, Denmark, 1966; PhD, U. Warwick, Eng., 1972. Asst. prof. math. U. Aarhus, 1966-69; assoc. prof. U. Copenhagen, 1972-80; prof. Tech. U. Denmark, Lyngby, 1980—; vis. prof. U. Md., College Park, 1986. Author: Braids and Coverings, 1989, Geometry in Nature, 1993, Shadows of the Circle, 1998, Fundamental Concepts in Modern Analysis, 1999; editor: Collected Mathematical Papers of Jakob Nielsen, 1986. Mem. Danish Acad. Natural Scis. (pres.), Danish Sci. Rsch. Coun. (vice chair 1993-95, 96-98), Danish Math. Soc., Am. Math. Soc., London Math. Soc., Société Mathématique de France. Home: Broensholmdalsvej 18, DK-2980 Kokkedal Denmark Office: Tech U Denmark, Dept Math Bldg 303, DK-2800 Lyngby Denmark

HANSEN, WENDELL JAY, clergyman, gospel broadcaster; b. Waukegan, Ill., May 28, 1910; s. Christian Hans and Anna Sophia (Termansen) H.; m. Bertelle Kathryn Budman, Mar. 9, 1933 (dec. Jan. 6, 1956); 1 child, Sylvia Marie; m. Eunice Evaline Irvine, Nov. 2, 1957; 1 child, Dean. Grad., Cleve. Bible Coll., 1932; AB, William Penn U., 1938; postgrad., Gletch Berg Skule, Switzerland, 1939; MA, U. Iowa, 1940, PhD, 1947. Ordained to ministry Recorded Friends, 1936, Evang. Reformed Ch., 1944. Pastor chs., Grinnell, Iowa, Mpls., Iowa City, 1934-47; evangelist with talking and performing birds, 1946—; past mgr. gospel radio stas. Two Rivers, Wis., Menomonie, Wis., Peru, Ind., Wabash, Ind., East St., Louis, Ill., Indpls., 1952—; pres., chmn. of bd. WESL Inc., East St. Louis, 1962—; cons. radio and TV, 1970—, appointed adv. com. to Indpls. Prosecutor, 1986; Appeared on Fuji Network, Tokyo and Channel X, London. Author: How to Steer Clear of Drugs; contbr. articles to popular mags. Dir. St. Paul Inter-racial Work Camp, 1939; chmn. Minn. Joint Refuge Com., 1940-41; trustee Lorine L. Reynolds Found., 1995—. Recipient honor citation Internat. Assn. Broadcasters, 1980; Boss of Yr. award Hamilton County Broadcasters, 1979, award Boys Town, 1983, award Women of Faith, St. Louis, 1984. Mem. Internat. Platform Assn., Internat. Assn. Christian Magicians, Ind. Bird Fanciers, East St. Louis C. of C. (bd. dirs. 1981-86), Pi Kappa Delta. Club: Ind. Pigeon (best exotic bird award 1969, 75, 80). Lodge: Kiwanis (East St. Louis bd. dirs. 1980-84). Republican. Quaker.

HANSEN-FLASCHEN, JOHN HYMAN, medical educator, researcher; b. Hamilton, Ohio, June 25, 1950; s. Steward Samuel and Joyce (Davies) Flaschen; m. Susan Lauretta Hansen, Aug. 22, 1951; children: Lynn, Lauren. AB, Brown U., 1972; MD, NYU, 1976. Diplomate in internal medicine, pulmonary medicine, critical care medicine Am. Bd. Internal Medicine. Resident in medicine U. Pa., Phila., 1976-79, chief resident in medicine, 1980-81, pulmonary fellow, 1979-80, 81-82, attending physician, 1982—, asst. prof. medicine, 1982-87, assoc. prof., 1988-98, prof., 1999—, dir. edn. and tng. programs in pulmonary and critical care, 1983-90, dir. pulmonary and critical care divsn., 1990-98, chief pulmonary, allergy and critical care divsn., 1998—, dir. Penn Lung Ctr., 1996—. Mem. editl. bd. Clin. Pulmonary Medicine, Respiratory Medicine, UpToDate; editor Respiratory Biology and Disease, Ency. Britannica; editor Respiratory Cluster, Ency. Britannica; contbr. articles to profl. jours. Mem. steering com. Nat. Emphysema Treatment Trial, 1997—. Recipient Spl. Investigator award Am. Heart Assn., 1982-84, Lindback Tchg. award U. Pa., 1999, 3 other tchg. awards; Measey Found. fellow, 1982-83. Fellow ACP, Am. Coll. Chest Physicians, Coll. Physicians Phila.; mem. Am. Thoracic Soc. (chmn. postgrad. edn. com. 1995—, clin. problems long range planning com. 1997-99), Soc. for Critical Care Medicine, Soc. for Bioethics Consultation, Laennec Soc. Phila. (pres. 1990-91), Drinker Soc. for Critical Care in Phila. (founder, 1st pres. 1988-90), Sigma Xi, Alpha Omega Alpha. Democrat. Home: 365 Penn Rd Wynnewood PA 19096-1401 Office: Hosp of U Pa 873 Mahoney Bldg 3400 Spruce St Philadelphia PA 19104-4206

HANSENNE, MICHEL, European parliamentary administrator; b. Mar. 23, 1940. M.p. Belgium, 1974-89; min. French culture, 1979-81, min. employment and labor, 1981-88, min. civil svc., 1988-89; dir. gen. Internat. Labor Office, Geneva, 1989-99; mem. European Parliament Brussels, 1999—. Author: Emploi les scenarios du possible; un garde-fou pour la mondialisation. Office: European Parliament, 60 rue Wiertz, 1047 Brussels Belgium

HANSFORD, NATHANIEL, academic administrator, lawyer; b. Columbia, S.C., Oct. 16, 1943; s. Bradley Richard and Ernestine (Stokely) H.; m. Frances Fincher, Sept. 19, 1970; children: Nathaniel F., Mary Frances. BS, U. Ga., 1965, JD, 1968; LLM, U. Mich., 1980. Bar: Ga., Ala. Law clk. Judge Lewis R. Morgan U.S. Dist. Ct., Newnan, Ga., 1968-70; assoc. Mitchell & Mitchell, Dalton, Ga., 1973-75; dean, prof. Sch. Law U. Ala., Tuscaloosa, 1975-88; pres. North Ga. Coll. and State U., Dahlonega, Ga., 1999—; bd. dirs. Synovus Fin. Corp., Columbus, Ga., Cohulta Bank, Chatsworth, Ga. Author: Alabama Equity, 1984, UCC Transaction Guide, 1988, Sales, Leases & Bulk Sales, 1989. Bd. vis. U. Ga. Sch. Law. Capt. U.S. Army, 1970-73, col. USAR, 1973-94. Fellow Am. Bar Found., Ala. Bar Assn.; mem. Order of Coif, Kiwanis (treas. Tuscaloosa chpt. 1976-82), Rotary, Phi Beta Kappa. Office: North Ga Coll and State U 32 College Cir Dahlonega GA 30597-0001

HANSFORD, STEPHEN JOHN, marketing executive; b. Hampton Court, Middlesex, Eng., Oct. 22, 1949; s. John Vincent and Pamela (Jelly) H.; m. Linda June Abbott, Aug. 12, 1972 (div. Mar. 1990); children: Claire Louise, James Peter; m. Grania Margaret-Mary Lewis, July 20, 1992; 1 child, Holly. Chartered Inst. Marketing. Domestic sales mgr. Brit. Gas, Reading, Eng., 1967-79; mng. dir. SSL Mktg. Ltd., Southampton, Eng., 1979-88, Concept Ltd., Winchester, Eng., 1988-93; head internat. bus. Uponor Ltd., Derbyshire, Eng., 1994-98, divisional gen. mgr., 1998-2000; free-lance interim mgr.-dir., mgmt. cons., 2000—; cons. SAPCO, Paris, 1981-88, Roberts Gordon, Buffalo, N.Y., 1985-88. Pub. (jours.) The Yachter, 1984-88, Homelife, 1985-88. Mem. Inst. Mktg., Royal Southampton Yacht Club (com. mem.). Avocation: sports.

HANSHEW, LOUISA EMILY, fundraiser; b. Phila., Feb. 3, 1955; d. Joseph and Elizabeth (Morris) H.; 1 child, Chelsea. BS, Drexel U., 1976. Dir. individual giving Drexel U., Phila., 1982-86; dir. devel. Pa. Ballet, Phila., 1986-87; dir. corp. giving Hahnemann U., Phila., 1987-89; centennial coord. Drexel U., Phila., 1989-92; dir. devel. Albert Einstein Healthcare Found., Phila., 1992-93, Meth. Hosp., Phila., 1993-96; v.p. devel. The Devereux Found., Devon, Pa., 1996—; pres. Louisa Hanshew and Assocs., Maple Glen, Pa., 1997—. Mem. Nat. Soc. Fund-Raising Exec., Am. Mktg. Assn., Coun. for the Advancement and Support of Edn. Office: 1719 Rittenhouse Sq Philadelphia PA 19103-6109

HANSHUANG, SHAO, biotechnology researcher; b. Hunan, Xiangyin, China, Dec. 10, 1968; s. Shao Hegao and Xu Juying; m. Li Jihong, Sept. 27, 1995. Bachelor, Jilin U., Changchun, China, 1992; Master, South China U. Tropical Agr., 1997. Asst. Nat. Key Biotech. Tropical Crops, Danzhou, China, 1992-96, asst. rschr., 1997—. Contbr. articles to profl. jours. Avocations: basketball, table tennis, swimming. Office: Nat Key Biotech Lab, Chengxi Rd, Haikou Hainan 571101, China

HANSJURGENS, BERND, economist; b. Olpe, Germany, May 12, 1961; s. Heinrich and Gisela (Burghaus) H.; m. Daniela Hornhardt, Mar. 12, 1992; children: Kim, Torben, Ivo. Master, U. Marburg, Germany, 1986, PhD, 1991. Rsch. asst. U. Marburg, 1987-92, asst. prof., 1992-98, prof., 1999—. Author: Ecotaxation and the Tax System, 1992 (Albert Osswald prize 1992), Ecotaxation and Innovation, 1996. Mem. German Econ. Assn. Avocation: soccer. Home: Borngasse 1, 35085 Ebsdorfergrund Germany Office: Univ Halle, Universitatsring 3, 06108 Halle Germany

HANSLEY, LEE, art gallery owner, curator; b. Roanoke Rapids, N.C., Jan. 11, 1948; s. Lonnie L. and Kathleen (Crumpler) H. Student, U. N.C., 1966-70. City editor The Daily Herald, Roanoke Rapids, 1970-73; editor The Northampton News, Jackson, N.C., 1973-75, Roanoke-Chowan News-Herald, Ahoskie, N.C., 1976, Halifax (N.C.) County This Week, 1976-78, The Suburbanite Newspaper, Winston-Salem, N.C., 1978-80; exhbns. curator Southeastern Ctr. Contemporary Art, Winston-Salem, 1980-86; pub. rels. dir. WUNC Radio, Chapel Hill., N.C., 1986-91; ind. cons. Durham (N.C.) Arts Coun., 1992; proprietor Lee Hansley Gallery, Raleigh, N.C., 1993—; cons. art exhibits Duke U. Law Sch., Durham, 1995—. Curator: Edith London: A Retrospective, 1992; editor: (exhbn. catalogs) Award in Visual Arts, 1981, 83, 86, Durham Art Guild 50th Anniversary Catalogue, 1998. Mem. Raleigh Arts Commn., 1989-95, chmn., 1991-93; mem. Durham Art Guild, 1991-97; bd. dirs. City Gallery, Raleigh, 1989-93, Theatre Devel. Bd., N.C. State U., 1999—; pub. rels. bd. Nat. Pub. Radio, Washington, 1989-91; mem. City of Raleigh Pub. Art Com., 1989—. Recipient Gen. Excellence award N.C. Press Assn., Chapel Hill, 1978, Investigative Reporting award, 1978. Mem. N.C. Mus. Art., Mus. Modern Art, Smithsonian Instn., Weatherspoon Gallery, Ackland Art Mus. Democrat. Avocations: gardening, non-fiction, art collecting. Home: 804 N King Charles Rd Raleigh NC 27610-1628 Office: Lee Hansley Gallery 225 Glenwood Ave Raleigh NC 27603-1404

HANSLÍK, EDUARD JOSEF, scientist; b. Prague, Czech Republic, Sept. 26, 1941; s. Eduard and Ružena (Teichová) H.; m. Vlasta Marie Čížková, Dec. 5, 1968; 1 child, Vlasta. MSc in Engring., Tech. U., Prague, 1969, PhD, 1980. Cert. internat. higher hydrol. course Moscow State Lomonosov U., 1975. Technician T.G. Masaryk Water Rsch. Inst., Prague, 1959-69, scientist, 1969-84, head radio-ecol. dept., 1985-94, sr. scientist, project mgr., 1995—; mem. interdepartmental radon commn. Ministry of the Environment, Prague, 1994-99, chmn. com. for radon and other natural radionuclides, 1994—; chmn. nat. adv. bd. for radiol. methods Czech Standardization Inst., Prague, 1996—; mem. com. for doctor degrees Charles U., Prague, 1999. Editor (conf. procs.) Radionuclides and Ionizing Radiation in Water Mgmt., 1978, 82, 85, 88, 90, 93, 96, 99. Mem. Soc. for Water Pollution. Achievements include patent for method for removal of radium from water by sand filtration. Avocations: literature, mountain touring. E-mail: eduard_hanslik@vuv.cz. Home: Klánova 72, 147 00 Prague 4, Czech Republic Office: TG Masaryk Water Rsch Inst, Podbabská 30, 160 62 Prague 6, Czech Republic

HANSON, DAVID BIGELOW, construction company executive, engineer; b. Cambridge, Mass., Feb. 24, 1946; s. David B. Jr. and Kathleen M. (Roscoe) H.; m. Colleen Marie Barrett, Oct. 31, 1969; children: Matthew Joseph, Joshua David. BS in Civil Engring., U. Mass., 1968; postgrad., Templeton Coll., 1989. Supt. Bechtel Corp., San Francisco, 1968-71; project engr. Dwight Bldg. Co., Hamden, Conn., 1971-74; cost engring. mgr. HBE Corp., St. Louis, 1974-79, dir. project devel., 1979-81, v.p., 1982-84; v.p. Bassett Constrn. Co., Pueblo, Colo., 1981-82; dir. procurement and estimating Turner Internat. Industries, Inc., N.Y.C., 1984-85, v.p. procurement and estimating, 1986, v.p., gen. mgr., 1986-89; v.p., gen. mgr. Healthcare div. Turner Constrn. Co., N.Y.C., 1989-91; v.p., gen. mgr. Turner Constrn. Co., Detroit, 1991-95; sr. v.p. Walbridge Aldinger Co., Detroit, 1995—; bd. dirs. Met. Realty Corp., 1994-2000; vice-chmn. constrn. procurement com. Mich. Minority Bus. Devel. Coun., 1995—. Mem. adv. bd. Regional Alliance for Minority and Women Businesses, N.Y.C., 1989-91; bd. dirs. Boys Hope, 1994—, Detroit Music Hall, 2000—. Mem. ASCE, NSPE, Assn. Gen. Contractors (internat. constrn. com. 1987-89, chmn. Detroit EEO com. 1992-99, bd. dirs. Detroit chpt. 1994-95, 98—, treas. 1999, v.p. 2000), Constrn. Innovation Forum (bd. dirs. 1992-95, mem. exec. com. 1993-95), Engring. Soc. Detroit, Greater Detroit C. of C. (bd. dirs. 1993—), Assn. of African Am. Bus. and Contractors (adv. bd. dirs. 1993—), Detroit Golf Club (bd. dirs. 1999—), Econ. Club of Detroit. Office: Walbridge Aldinger Co 613 Abbott St Detroit MI 48226-2521

HANSON, DIANE CHARSKE, management consultant; b. Cleve., May 15, 1946; d. Howard Carl and Emma Katherine (Lange) Charske; m. William James Hanson, June 30, 1973. BS, Cornell U., 1968; MS, U. Pa., 1989. Home service rep. Rochester Gas and Electric, N.Y., 1968-70; home economist U. Conn., Storrs, 1970-72; job analyst personnel dept. State of Conn., Hartford, 1972-73; sales rep. Ayerst Labs., Waterbury, Conn., 1973-80, sales trainer, 1979-80; dist. sales mgr. Phila., 1980-87; pres. Creative Resource Devel., W. Chester, Pa., 1986—; developer, pres. Womens Referral Network, West Chester, 1987-89. Vice-pres., bd. dirs., aux. pres. Chester County Soc. for Prevention Cruelty to Animals, 1986-97, pres. bd. dirs., 1992-94, mem. exec. com., 1994-95. Mem. ASTD (v.p. comm. Phila./Delaware Valley chpt. 1991-92, pres. Del. chpt. 1999—), Internat. Soc. for Performance Improvement (v.p. programs Great Valley chpt. 1993-94, pres.-elect 1995, pres. 1996), Pa. State Tech. Devel. Ctr. (bd. dirs. 1991-92), Assn. Quality and Participation, Phila. Soc. for Human Resources, Phila. Human Resources Planning Group, Phila. Orgn. Devel. Network, Chester County Human Resources Assn. (program chair 1991-92), Greater Valley Forge Human Resources Assn. (bd. dirs. 1993-94). Avocations: skiing, tennis, gardening, sailing, exercise. E-mail: hanson@team-doctor.com. Home and Office: 824 W Strasburg Rd West Chester PA 19382-1927

HANSON, DORENE KAY, engineering draftsman; b. Lemmon, S.D., Jan. 22, 1960; d. Donald Patrick Hanson and Joyce E. Van Cleave. Assoc. Degree in Tech. Drafting, Black Hills State Coll., 1981. Rodman U.S. Geol. Survey, Independence, Mo., 1978-79, 81-83; janitor Bison (S.D.) Sch. Dist., 1979-80; transp. aide S.D. Transp. Dept., Belle Fourche, 1980-81; engring. draftsman III Western Area Power Adminstrn., Watertown, S.D., 1983—. Vol. Spl. Olympics, Watertown, Kampeska Days Com., Watertown, 1985-94. Recipient Cert. of Excellence, Source One Mgmt., Inc., Watertown, 1990, Kampeska Day Spirit award Kampeska Day Com., Watertown, 1991. Avocations: stamps, arts and crafts, volleyball, bowling. E-mail: cockerspaniel-lover@excite.com and dhanson@wapa.gov. Fax: 605-882-7409. Office: Western Area Power Adminstrn 1330 41st St SE Watertown SD 57201

HANSON, GERALD EUGENE, oral and maxillofacial surgeon; b. Lincoln, Nebr., July 18, 1947; s. Gerald Stephen and Ferne Althea (Russell) H. DDS, MPH, Loma Linda U., 1973; oral & maxillofacial surgery cert., U. Minn., 1976. Diplomate Am. Bd. Forensic Dentistry. Pvt. practice Palm Desert, Calif., 1976-78, Las Vegas, Nev., 1978—; mem. com. edn. & rsch. Eisenhower Med. Ctr., Rancho Mirage, Calif., 1977, dir. continuing dental edn. program, 1977-78; chief divsn. oral & maxillofacial surgery Sunrise Hosp., 1984-94, Columbia Mountain View Hosp., 1995—. Rep. environ. reference com. joint policy coun. APHA, Washington, 1977; bd. dirs. Clark County chpt. Am. Cancer Soc., 1979-83; chmn. oral cancer screening clinics Jaycees State Fair & Annual Health Fair, Las Vegas, 1981; adv. bd. Clark County C.C., Las Vegal, 1979; mem. Nev. State Bd. Health, 1990-95; treas., bd. dirs. Am. Assn. Oral and Maxillofacial Surgery Found., 1995—. Fellow Pierre Fauchard Acad., Internat. Coll. Dentists, Western Soc. Oral & Maxillofacial Surgeons (bd. dirs. 1981-83, 91-97, pres. 1995-96), Am. Assn. Oral & Maxillofacial Surgeons (trustee Dist. VI 1984-88, Nev. del. 1979-83, sec.-treas. 1988-91), Am. Coll. Dentistry; mem. ADA (chmn. sci. session 1982, mem. coun. hosp. affairs 1985-89, AAOMS rep. interprofl. rels. com. 1987), Nev. Dental Assn. (co-chmn. group care & hosp. svcs. com. 1979-84, Clark County del. Ho. Dels. 1980-84, pres. 1987), Am. Coll. Oral & Maxillofacial Surgeons, Nev. Soc. of Oral and Maxillofacial Surgeons (pres. 1983-85), Am. Assn. Oral and Maxillofacial Surgery Found. (bd. dirs. 1995—), Las Vegas Execs. Assn., Clark County Aviation Assn. (pres. 1999), Clark County Dental Soc. (pres. 1982-83). Avocations: flying, antique airplane collecting, music, diving, skiing. Office: 2585 S Jones Blvd Ste 1A Las Vegas NV 89146-5604

HANSON, GERALD WARNER, retired county official; b. Alexandria, Minn., Dec. 25, 1938; s. Lewis Lincoln and Dorothy Hazel (Warner) H.; m. Sandra June Wheeler, July 9, 1960; 1 child, Cynthia R. AA, San Bernardino Valley (Calif.) Coll., 1959; BA, U. Redlands (Calif.), 1979; MA, U. Redlands, 1981; EdD, Pepperdine U., 1995. Cert. advanced metrication specialist. Dep. sealer San Bernardino (Calif.) County, 1964-80, div. chief, 1980-85, dir. weights and measures, 1985-94; CATV cons. City of Redlands, 1996—, City of Yucaipa, 1998-99; substitute tchr. Redlands Unified Sch. Dist., 1996—. Chmn. Redlands Rent Rev. Bd., 1985-99; bd. dirs. House Neighborly Svc., Redlands, 1972-73, Boys Club, Redlands, 1985-86; mem. Redlands Planning commn., 1990-98. With USN. Fellow U.S. Metric Assn. (treas. 1986-88, 92—); mem. NRA (life), Nat. Conf. on Weights and Measures (life, asst. treas. 1986-94), Western Weights and Measures Assn. (life, pres. 1987-88), Calif. Assn. Weights and Measures Ofcls. (life, 1st v.p. 1987), Calif. Rifle and Pistol Assn. (life), Masons, Shriners, Kiwanis (treas. Redlands club 1983-95), Over the Hill Gang (San Bernardino, newsletter editor 1998-2000). Avocations: golf, digital photography, mechanics, microcomputers. Home: 225 E Palm Ave Redlands CA 92373-6131

HANSON, LORD JAMES EDWARD, industrialist; b. Jan. 20, 1922; s. Robert and Louisa Ann (Rodgers) H.; m. Geraldine Kaelin, 1959; 2 children: Robert William, John Brook, 1 stepchild, Karyn. Exec. chmn. Hanson PLC, London, 1965-97, chmn. emeritus, 1998—. Office: 1 Grosvenor Pl London SW1X 7JH, England

HANSON, SIR JOHN GILBERT, academic administrator; b. Sheffield, Yorkshire, England, Nov. 16, 1938; s. Gilbert Fretwell and Gladys Margaret (Kay) H.; m. Margaret Clark, Aug. 25, 1962. BA, U. Oxford, England, 1961, MA, 1964; DLitt (hon.), Oxford Brookes U., 1995, U. Humberside, 1996, U. Greenwich. Asst. prin. War Office, London, 1961-63; asst. rep. British Coun., Madras, India, 1963-66; rep. British Coun., Bahrain, 1968-72; dep. controller edn. and sci. divsn. British Coun., London, 1972-75, controller fin. divsn., 1979-82, dep. dir. gen., 1988-92, dir. gen., 1992-98; trainee ME Ctr. Arab Studies, Lebanon, 1966-68; counsellor British Embassy, Tehran, 1975-79; min. British High Commn., New Delhi, India, 1984-88; warden Green Coll., U. Oxford, Eng., 1998—; patron GAP, 1989-97; mem. governing coun. Soc. S. Asian Studies, 1989-93, Sch. Oriental and African Studies, U. London, 1991-99; mem. Franco-British Coun., 1992-97; coun. mem. UK-Japan 2000 Group, 1993-97, Vol. Svc. Overseas, 1993-97. Trustee Charles Wallace (India) Trust, 1998—; chmn. U.K. Overseas Student Affairs Com., 1999—. Hon. fellow Wadham Coll., Oxford, 1997, St. Edmund's Coll., Cambridge, 1998—. Mem. Brit. Skin Found. (pres. 1997—). Avocations: books, music, sport, travel. Office: Wardens Lodgings, Green Coll Woodstock Rd, Oxford OX2 6HG, England

HANSON, JOHN KOW, accountant; b. Ctrl. region, Ghana, Sept. 10, 1942; s. Kwaw Anstill and Mary Araba (Sawyerr) H.; m. Margaret Bennet-Lartey, Sept. 30, 1967; children: Edmund, Yvonne, Margaret-Effie, Jacqueline Hanson. BA in Econs. with honors, U. Sheffield, Eng., 1972. Acct. Spear & Jacksons, Sheffield, Eng., 1972-73; acct. Ghana Sugar Estates Ltd., Accra, 1974-75, chief acct., 1976-77, fin. contr., 1977-82, mng. dir., 1982-90; pub., mng. editor Bus. & Fin. Times, Accra, 1991—; dir. Celebrity Golf Club, Tema, Ghana,1986—, Charterhouse Farms Ltd., Accra, 1980—. Pub., mng. editor Bus. and Fin. Times, 1989 (Best Newspaper 1992). Mem. Grand Lodge Ersleaces (past master Tema Lodge 1991-92), Lodge of Perfection (prin. sojourner Royal Arch chpt. 1989—), Rose Croix 180 (Ghana Ebenezer chpt.), Dist. Grand Lodge Ghana (std. bearer 1994—). Avocations: golf, reading, writing, music, soccer. Home: PO Box 1500, Tema Ghana Office: Bus & Fin Times, PO Box 2157, Accra Ghana

HANSON, KAIDO, academic administrator; b. Vyru, Estonia, Sept. 20, 1936; s. Paul and Hedviga (Kunnapu) H.; m. Olga Novitskaya; 1 child, Pavel. MD, U. Tartu, Estonia, 1961; PhD in Roentgenology-Radiology, Ctrl. Rsch. Inst., Leningrad, Russia, 1964, DS, 1973. Lectr., chair biochem. U. Tartu, Estonia, 1964-66; head lab. biochem. Ctrl. Rsch. Inst. Roentegeology — Radiology, Leningrad, Russia, 1966-75, head dpet. radiobiology & biotech., 1975-87; head dept. molecular oncology, prof. N.N. Petrov Rsch. Inst. Oncology, Leningrad, Russia, 1988-91; acting dir., prof. N.N. Petrov Rsch. Inst. Oncology, St. Petersburg, Russia, 1991-99; dir. N.N. Petrov Rsch. Inst. Oncology, St. Petersburg, 1999—. Author of 4 books. Mem. Scientific Coun. IARC. Office: N N Petrov Rsch Inst, 68 Leningradskaya, 189646 Saint Petersburg Russia

HANSON, KENT BRYAN, lawyer; b. Litchfield, Minn., Sept. 17, 1954; s. Calvin Bryan and Muriel (Wessman) H.; m. Barbara Jane Elenbaas, Aug. 24, 1974; children: Lindsay Michal, Taylor Jordan, Chase Philip. AA with high honors, Trinity Western Coll., 1974; BA, U. B.C., Vancouver, 1976; JD magna cum laude, U. Minn., 1979. Bar: Minn. 1979, U.S. Dist. Ct. Minn. 1980, U.S. Ct. Appeals (8th cir.) 1980, U.S. Dist. Ct. (we. dist.) Wis. 1983, Wis. 1985, U.S. Ct. Appeals (9th cir.) 1989, U.S. Dist. Ct. Ariz. 1992, Ohio 1993, Calif. 1994. Assoc. Grossman, Karlins, Siegel & Brill, Mpls., 1979-81, Gray, Plant, Mooty, Mooty & Bennett, Mpls., 1981-85; ptnr. Bowman & Brooke, Mpls., 1986-95; CEO Hanson, Marek, Bolkcom & Greene, Ltd., Mpls., 1996—. Bd. dirs. Inner City Boys Club, Ctrl. Free Ch., Mpls., 1979-81; 12th ward del. Mpls. Dem. Farmer Labor Com. Conv., 1982; mem. exec. bd. Ctrl. Free Ch., Mpls., 1986; chair exec. bd. Ctrl. Community Ch., 1993-96. Mem. ABA, State Bar Assn. Wis., Minn. Def. Lawyers Assn., Minn. State Bar Assn., Hennepin County Bar Assn., Calif. State Bar Assn., State Bar of Ohio, Def. Rsch. Inst. Avocations: classical music, golf, tennis, computers, theology. Office: Hanson Marek Bolkcom & Greene Ltd 2200 Rand Tower 527 Marquette Ave Minneapolis MN 55402-1302

HANSON, MARCI JILL, educator; b. Wendell, Idaho, Aug. 28, 1948; d. H. Max and Maxine Nancy Hanson. BS, U. Oreg., 1970; MS, Pa. State U., 1974; PhD, U. Oreg., 1978. Rsch. scientist Ednl. Testing Svc., Princeton, N.J., 1978-79; lectr. San Francisco State U., 1979-82, prof. spl. edn., 1982—; program dir. San Francisco Spl. Infant Svcs., 1979-95. Author: Teaching the Infant with Down Syndrome, 1977, 2d edit., 1987; co-author: (with E.W. Lynch) Early Intervention: Implementing Child and Family Services for Infants and Toddlers Who Are At Risk or Disabled, 1989, 2d edit., 1995, Developing Cross-Cultural Competence, 1992, 2d edit., 1998; editor: Atypical Infant Development, 1984, 2d edit., 1996. Mem. Calif. Assn. Profs. Early Childhood Spl. Edn. (co-chair 1997-98), Nat. Assn. Edn. Young Children, Am. Assn. Mental Retardation, Coun. Exceptional Children (divsn. early childhood), Soc. Rsch. in Child Devel., Phi Beta Kappa. Office: Dept Spl Edn 1600 Holloway Ave San Francisco CA 94132-1722

HANSON, MILTON, manufacturing executive, consultant; b. Vulga, S.D., May 2, 1954; s. Robert and Rose Hanson; m. Maureen Hanson, Mar. 29, 1980; children: Eric, Ryan, Rose. BSEE, Calif. State U., L.A., 1982. Dir. engring. Emerson, Carson, Calif., 1980-86; v.p. On-Line Power, Commerce, Calif., 1986—. E-mail: mhanson001@aol.com. Office: On-Line Power 5701 Smithway St Los Angeles CA 90040-1507

HANSON, OWEN JERROLD, computer science educator; b. Petworth, Sussex, Eng., Jan. 2, 1934; s. Lawrence and Edith Audrey (Waller) H.; m. Barbara Maria Teresa Srodzinska, Aug. 14, 1965 (div.); children: Annette Maria, Ilona Constance; m. Lena Diane Hall, 1996. BA, Cambridge (Eng.) U., 1957, MA, 1961; MSc, U. London, 1970; PhD, City U., London, 1986. Works metallurgist Wilkinson Sword Co., U.K., 1957-60; mgr. works lab. Gillette Industries, U.K., 1960-64; sr. systems engr. IBM UK Ltd., 1964-70; sr. lectr. City U., London, 1970-88, prof., head dept., 1988-99; cosn. UNESCO, IBM (East Europe), 1974—; mgr. dir. DuoDisc Ltd., U.K., 1990—. Author: Basic File Design, 1978, Design of Computer Data Files, 1982, 2d edit., 1988, Essentials of Computer Data Files, 1985; editor, author (with others): Keeping Computers Under Control, 1975. Capt. Purley Lawn Tennis Club, U.K., 1963-70; helper Disabled Swimming Club, U.K., 1971-81; mem. Parliamentary IT Com., U.K., 1987—. Mem. Assn. for Computing Machinery, IEEE, South London Harriers. Conservative. Avocations: tennis, competitive running, squash, walking, reading. Office: Middlesex Univ, Bounds Green Rd, London N11 2NQ, England Home: 24 The Drive Wallington, Surrey SM6 9LX, United Kingdom

HANSON, RICK, psychologist; b. Stillwater, Okla., Oct. 21, 1952; s. William Roderick and Helen Louise Hanson; m. Jan Hanson, Feb. 14, 1982; children: Forrest, Laurel. BA summa cum laude, UCLA, 1974; MA in Psychology, Rosebridge Inst., 1986; PhD in Psychology, Wright Inst., 1991. Lic. psychologist, Calif. Pres. Together Seminars, L.A., 1977; seminar leader, mgr. Earthplay, Inc., L.A., 1978-80; risk analyst Stan Kaplan Assocs., Newport Beach, Calif., 1980-81; pvt. practice bus. cons. Sausalito, Calif., 1981-82; pres. Body of Knowledge, Mill Valley, Calif., 1983-85; mgmt. cons., prin. Peak Mgmt., San Rafael, Calif., 1985-92; pvt. practice psychology San Rafael, 1992—. Columnist Family Matters, 1992—. Pres., bd. dirs. Family Works, San Rafael, 1995; spkr. Marin county Mother's Clubs, schs., 1992—. U. Calif. Presdl. scholar, 1973; named Best Family Therapist Pacific Sun Poll, 1995. Mem. APA, AAAS, Soc. for Exploration of Psychotherapy Integration, Phi Beta Kappa. Avocations: rock climbing, hiking, reading. Office: 610 D St San Rafael CA 94901-3708

HANSON, WENDY KAREN, chemical engineer; b. Mpls., May 29, 1954; d. Curtis Harley Hanson and Patricia Lou (Vogler) Schweiger. BS, U. Minn., 1976; BA, U. Colo., Denver, 1984; postgrad., U. Calif., La Jolla, 1984-87. Chem. technician Shasta Beverages, Mpls., 1977-78, Conwed, Roseville, Minn., 1978-80; geologist Century Geophys. Corp., Grand Junction, Colo., 1980, Tooke Engring., Grand Junction, 1980-82; sr. scientist Sci. Ventures, San Diego, 1987-96; engr. Parker-Hannifin Corp., San Diego, 1996-97. Patentee magnesium separation from Dolomitic phosphate by sulfuric acid leaching. Judge San Diego (Calif.) Sci. and Engring. Fair, 1987-96; leader, publs. editor San Diego (Calif.) Wilderness Assn., 1989-97. Avocations: backpacking, gardening, spitoon collecting.

HANSSON, BILL STEFAN, ecology and neurobiology educator, researcher; b. Jonstorp, Sweden, Jan. 12, 1959; s. Rune Allan and Lisa Dorotea (Persson) H.; m. Susanne Erland, Feb. 2, 1993; two children: Otto Rune, Agnes Susanna. BSc, Lund U., Sweden, 1982, PhD, 1988. Rsch. asst. Lund U., 1988, asst. prof., 1990-92, assoc. prof., 1992-95, tenured assoc. prof., 1995-2000, prof., 2000—; rsch. assoc. U. Ariz., 1989-90; committeemem. Swedish Natural Sci. Coun., Stockholm, 1996—. Author: Insect Olfaction, 1999; contbr. articles to profl. jours., chpt. to book. Recipient Takasago prize in Olfactory Rsch., 1998, fellow STA, Japan, 1997. Avocations: hunting, sports, scuba diving. E-mail: bill.hansson@ekol.lu.se. Home: Stationstigen 16, S-24563 Hjarup Sweden Office: Lund U Dept Ecology, Solvegatan 37, S-22362 Lund Sweden

HANSSON, CARITA G., dermatologist, educator, consultant; b. Sweden, 1947. MD, U. Gothenburg, Sweden, 1973, PhD, 1988. Cons. dept. dermatology Sahlgrenska U. Hosp., Gothenburg, 1988—; assoc. prof. dermatology U. Gothenburg, 1996—. Fellow Skin Cancer Assn. (hon.); mem. Swedish Wound Healing Soc. (bd. dirs. 1995—). Office: Derp Dermatology, Sahlgrenska Univ Hosp, 413 45 Göteborg Sweden

HANSSON, LARS MAGNUS NILS, physician; b. Stockholm, Sept. 16, 1925; s. Nils and Hedvig (Bergström) H.; m. Margareta Osvald, Mar. 22, 1951; children: Göran, Magnus. MD, Karolinska Institutet, Stockholm, 1954. Cert. specialist in internal medicine, heart diseases and geriatrics. Physician Med. Clinic, Karolinska Hosp., 1954-55, Med. Clinic, St. Eriks Hosp., Stockholm, 1955-65; head physician Högdalens Hosp., Stockholm, 1965-72; head physician Geriatric Clinic Nacka Hosp., 1972-79, Rosenluns Hosp., 1979-90; head physician all geriatric hosps. in south area, Stockholm, 1972-88; physician in pvt. practice Stockholm; bd. dirs. Danvikshem, 1981-96, Stockholms Sjukhem, 1984-2000. Mem. Rotary Stockholm-Klara (pres. 1995-96). Avocations: sailing, archipelago life.

HANSSON, ULRIKA TRESSA, librarian; b. Lund, Sweden, May 27, 1949; d. Yngve B. Hansson and Ruth S. Sjövall. BA, U. Lund, 1972. Librarian; cons. Swedish Soc. Against Painful Experiments on Animals, 1982—; pres., chmn. bd. dirs. Swedish Fund for Rsch. without Animals, 1992-96, mem. ethical rev. com., 1982-92; alternatives com. Swedish Nat. Bd. for Exptl. Animals, 1995—. Contbr. articles to profl. jours. Office: Soc Agst Painful Anim Exper, Gamla Huddingevägen 437, SE-12542 Alvsjo Sweden

HANTON, E. MICHAEL, public and personnel relations consultant; b. Gary, Ind.; s. Zachary and Maria (Suciu) H. AB, Ind. U., 1951, MA, 1955; grad., USAF Air War Coll., 1968. Various prodn. positions U.S. Steel Corp., Gary, 1940-41, 50; prodn. contr. Douglas Aircraft Corp., Santa Monica, Calif., 1946-47; classified advt. mgr Weaver Pub. Co., Santa Monica, 1947-48; reporter Muncie (Ind.) Evening Press, 1952, Gary Post-Tribune, 1952-53; head cashier Office Lake County Treas., Gary, 1955-60; pub. and pers. rels. cons. Gary, 1960—, Plattsburgh, N.Y., 1968—; asst. prof. State U. Coll. Arts & Scis., Plattsburgh, 1966-67; cons. community rels. and fund raising. Author: The New Nurse, 1973. With USAAF, 1941-45, USAF active res. 1945-69, ret. Decorated Air medal, Purple Heart. Mem. Am. Med. Writers Assn., Assn. Edn. in Journalism and Mass Communications, Health Scis. Comm. Assn., Am. Acad. Advt., Nat. League Nursing, Gary C. of C., Plattsburgh C. of C., Air Force Assn., Res. Officers Assn., Nat. Arts Club, Steel Club, Caterpillar Club, Flying Boot Club. Office: PO Box 803 Plattsburgh NY 12901-0803

HANTSCHMANN, PEER, medical educator; b. Kiel, Germany, Oct. 2, 1966; s. Norbert and Jutta (Costede) H.; m. Katharina Grundmann, Apr. 17, 1993; children: Fidelia Thea, Tamina Frieda. Student, U. Ratisbone, 1987-89, U. Wuerzburg, 1989-92; MD, U. Wuerzburg, 1994; med. diplomate, U. Munich, 1992-93. Resident dept. ob-gyn. Munich, 1993-98, lectr. dept. ob-gyn., 1998—; cons. Vulvovaginal Neoplasma Group of Germany, 1998—. Contbr. articles to profl. jours., chpt. to book. Scholar Gynecologic Oncology Study Group of the German People, 1990-93; recipient best candidate presentation award ISSVD Exec. Coun., 1997. Mem. Internat. Soc. for Study of Vulvovaginal Disease, European Coll. for Study of Vulvar Diseases, German Gynecologists, Gynecologic Oncology Study Group, Gynocologic Pathology Study Group. Evangelical. Avocations: playing flute, squash. Office: Dept Ob-Gyn, Maistrasse 11, 80337 Munich Germany

HANUMAIAH, B(ELIGIRAIAH), physics educator; b. Chamarajanagar, India, Aug. 18, 1948; m. Uma, June 22, 1981; children: H.C. Murali, H. Rachna. BSc, Mysore U., India, 1970, MSc, 1972; PhD, Moscow State U., 1981. Lectr. Govt. Coll., Mandya, India, 1972-76; rsch. Moscow State U., 1976-81; lectr. Maharani's Sci. Coll., Mysore, India, 1982; reader Karnatak U., Dharwad, India, 1982-91, prof., 1991—. Contbr. articles to profl. jours. Pres. Bharat Jnana Vignana Parishat, Dharwad, 1996—; treas. Citizen Forum, Dharwad, 1986-90. Mem. Indian Soc. Radiation Physics (life), Indian Assn. Phys. Tchrs. (life), Internat. Radiation Physics Soc. Avocations: badminton, reading, gardening, administration, research. Office: Karnatak U, Dharwad 580 003, India

HANUMANTHACHARI, JUTURU, mathematics educator, researcher; b. Tirupati, India, May 12, 1942; s. Juturu Anjaneyachari and Juturu Sakuntalamma; m. Juturu Muni Ratna, June 7, 1962; children: Anjani Kumari, Radha Vijaya, Nagarjun. BSc, S.V. Univ., Tirupati, 1962, MSc, 1964, PhD, 1975. Lectr. math. A.C. Coll., Guntur, India, 1964-66; tutor S.V. U., 1966-68, lectr., 1968-75, reader, 1975-85, prof., 1985—, head Dept. Math., 1985-87, chmn. bd. studies math., 1993-96, dean Sch. Math. and Phys. Scis., 1998—, vice prin. scis., 1999—; reviewer Am. Math. Soc., 1994—. Editor: (textbook) Mathematics for B.A., 1992; editl. bd. Southeast

Asian Bull. Math., 1994—; contbr. articles to profl. jours. Vice-prin. S.V. U. Coll. Arts and Scis., 1999—. Rsch. grantee S.V. U., 1994; recipient Best Tchr. award Govt. Andhra Pradesh, 2000—. Mem. Indian Math. Soc. (coun. 1988-90, life), S.V. U. Tchr.'s Assn. (pres. 1989-90). Avocations: magazines, films. Home: No 6 Arjun Apts KV Layout, Tirupati 517507, India Office: Dept Math, University Rd, Tirupati 517502, India

HANUŠ, TOMÁŠ, urologist, consultant; b. Prague, Czechoslovakia, July 1, 1951; s. František and Jiřina (Rufferová) H.; m. Eva Skrbková, Oct. 14, 1976; children: Alena, Věra, Petr. MD, Charles U., Prague, 1975, PhD, 1987. Resident in surgery Liberec (Czechoslovakia) Hosp., 1975-76; resident in urology Tchg. Hosp., Prague, 1976-83; asst. dept. urology Postgrad. Inst., Prague, 1983-93; assoc. prof. 1st med. faculty dept. urology Charles U., 1993—; vice dean 1st med. sch. Charles U., Prague, 1999—; chmn. Czech IncoForum, 2000—. Author: (textbook) Voiding Disorders, 1991; co-author: (textbook) Female Incontinence, 1992; contbr. chpts. to books and articles to profl. jours. Mem. Czech Urol. Soc. (pres. 1993—), Internat. Continence Soc. (chmn. sci. com. 1994), European Assn. Urology (nat. del. 1999—). Mem. Ch. of Brethren. Avocations: tourism, music, basketball. Office: Charles Univ Dept Urology, U nemocnice 2, 12800 Prague 2 Czech Republic

HANUŠ, VLADIMÍR, cosmetics researcher; b. Olomouc, Moravia, Czech Republic, Mar. 8, 1945; s. Emanuel and Antonie (Štenclová) H.; m. Pavla Krčková, Aug. 21, 1970 (div. 1980); 1 child, Marek. D Natural Sci., U. Olomouc, Czech Republic, 1970. Chief dept. prodn., quality control Inst. Cosmetic, Prague, Czech Republic, 1970-90, chief dept. devel. cosmetic products, 1973—; chief dept. cosmetic rsch. Inst. Med. Cosmetic, Prague, 1973—; chief dept. cosmetic prodn. Inst. Med. Cosmetics, Prague, 1996—, work safety inspector, 1980-90. Inventor method of production of mink oil hydrolysates for use in cosmetics, use of mink oil in cosmetics and pharmacy, cosmetic, pharm. and detergent product, use of mink oil in cleansing cosmetic products, other patents in field; contbr. articles to profl. jours. Recipient Hon. Diploma Ministry of Health, 1981, Inst. Nat. Health, 1982, 83. Mem. Cosmetology Soc., Gardener Club. Avocations: tennis, cooking, gardening. Home: Amforová 1902, 155 00 Prague 5, Czech Republic Office: Inst Med Cosmetic, Bohuslava ze Švamberka 6, 140 00 Prague Czech Republic

HANUSCHAK, LEE NICHOLAS, physician; b. Warren, Ohio, Dec. 22, 1947; s. Michael and Clorinda (Rossi) H.; m. Hulcine Zdunski, Oct. 29, 1977; children: Gregor, Dulcinea. AB cum laude, Harvard Coll., 1969; MS, EES, Stanford U., 1971; MD, Case Western Reserve U., 1977. Stanford U., Palo Alto, Calif., 1969-73; NIH fellow, 1970-71; lectr. Med. Sch. Stanford U., Palo Alto, Calif., 1971-72; assoc. physician div. diabetes and metabolism Pa. Hosp., Phila., 1992—; pvt. practice in internal medicine and diabetes Phila., 1987—; clin. assoc. U. Pa. Sch. Medicine, 1980—; rsch. supr. Garfield Duncan Found., Phila., 1980-86; cons. internal medicine Wills Eye Hosp., Phila., 1981-91; founder, pres. Med. Decision-Making, Inc., Ardmore, Pa., 1986-88; med. dirs. Travelers Health Network, Phila., 1986-88; med. dir., founder Pa. Found., Phila., 1987—. Contbr. Diabetes Fact Book, 1981, Conn's Current Therapy, 1982; inventor computer program for adjustment of insulin doses. Recipient numerous corp. grants, 1980-86. Mem. ACP, Am. Diabetes Assn., Am. Soc. Internal Medicine, Harvard/Radcliffe Club of Phila. (schs. com.). Office: 829 Spruce St Philadelphia PA 19107-5752

HANUSHEK, ERIC ALAN, economics educator; b. Lakewood, Ohio, May 22, 1943; s. Vernon F. and Ruth (Hostetler) H.; m. Nancy L. Keleher, June 11, 1965 (div.); children: Eric Alan, Megan E. B.S., U.S. Air Force Acad., 1965; Ph.D. in Econs., MIT, 1968. Sr. staff economist Coun. Econ. Advisers, Washington, 1971-72; assoc. prof. USAF Acad., Colo., 1972-73; sr. economist Cost of Living Coun., Washington, 1973-74; assoc. prof. econs. Yale U., New Haven, 1975-78; dir. pub. policy analysis U. Rochester, N.Y., 1978-83, prof. econs. and polit. sci., 1978-2000, chmn. dept. econs., 1982-87, 88-90, dir. W. Allen Wallis Inst. Polit. Economy, 1992-99; rsch. assoc. Nat. Bur. Econ. Rsch., 1996—; Hanna sr. fellow Hoover Instn. Stanford (Calif.) U., 2000—; dep. dir. Congl. Budget Office, Washington, 1984-85; mem. com. nat. stats. Nat. Rsch. Coun., 1992-98; cons. World Bank 1984—, U.S. Com. on Civil Rights, 1986-89. Author: Education and Race, 1972, (with J. Jackson) Statistical Methods for Social Scientists 1977, (with C. Citro) Improving Information for Social Policy Decisions, 1991, (with R. Harbison) Education Performance of the Poor, 1992, Making Schools Work, 1994, (with J. Banks) Modern Political Economy, 1995, (with N. Maritato) Assessing Knowledge of Retirement Behavior, 1996, (with Dale W. Jorgenson) Improving America's Schools, 1996, (with Constance F. Citro) Assessing Policies for Retirement Income, 1997. Served to capt. USAF, 1965-74. Disting. vis. fellow Hoover Instn., Stanford U., 1999-2000. Mem. Internat. Acad. Edn., Assn. Pub. Policy Analysis and Mgmt. (v.p. 1986-87, pres. 1988-89), Am. Econ. Assn., Econometric Soc., Am. Statis. Assn. Office: Stanford U Hoover Instn Stanford CA 94305-6010

HANZAWA, SATOSHI, industrial engineer, researcher; b. Chiba, Japan, May 23, 1960; s. Akira and Kazuko (Okada) H. MSc, Tokyo U. Agr. and Tech., 1985. Rschr. Marine Biology Inst., Simidzu, Japan, 1990-92, Tosoh Corp., Ayase, Japan, 1985-89, 93—. Author: Encyclopedia of Bioprocess Technology, 1999, Technologies and Markets of Industrial Enzymes, 1999. Achievements include patents in field. Avocations: fishing, motorcycles. Office: Tosoh Corp, 2743-1 Hayakawa, Kanagawa Ayase-shi 252-1123, Japan

HAO, KUANG-TSAI, publishing executive; b. Taipei, Taiwan, Apr. 3, 1961; s. Shi-Chun and Wu-Ju Hao. BA, Cheng-Chi U., Taipei, 1983. Chief editor ECHO Pub. Co., Taipei, 1985-87; dep. editl. dir. Yuan-liou Pub. Co., 1987-92; mng. editor Grimm Press, 1992—; mem. jury Bologna Internat. Book Fair, 1996; mem. com. Jane Goodall Inst.-Taiwan, Taipei, 1997. Author, editor: (children's book) The Giant and Spring, 1993 (award Biennale Illustrations Bratislava 1993); editor: (children's books) Reminiscences of Beijing, 1994, (award Bologna Internat. Book Fair 1994), The Honest Thief, 1994 (Catalónia Internat. prize 1994), Illustrated Shakespeare Series, 1996 (Best Design in Brazil award 1996), Much Ado About Nothing (Catalónia Internat. prize 1997). Named Best Pub., Biennale Illustrations Bratislava, 1995; recipient awards 1995-98 Bologna Children's Book Illustration Exhbn. Mem. Internat. Bd. on Books for Young People. Avocations: music, travel. Office: Grimm Press Ltd Sec 2, 6F No 20 Hsin-Sheng Sth Rd, Taipei Taiwan

HAO, LAWRENCE KAHOLO, state official, clinical hypnotherapist; b. Paahau, Hawaii, Aug. 24, 1937; s. Louis Kanoa and Mona Doris (Kaholo) H.; m. Ramona Kay Newton, Apr. 15, 1960; children: Debra Lynn Kelani, Melanie Pualani, Lance Kanoa, Sean Lani Newton. BS, Ind. U., 1962, MS, 1970. Cert. internat. travel agt., pvt. pilot, scuba, charter boat capt., USCG. Recreational therapist Beatty Meml. Hosp., Westville, Ind., 1962-63; tchr. Russiaville (Ind.) Elem. Sch., 1963-65; tchr. phys. edn. Western Elem. Sch., Russiaville, 1965-67; aquatic dir. Ea. H.S., Greentown, Ind., 1967-69; grad. asst. Ind. U., Bloomington, 1969-70; asst. prof. Western Ill. U., Macomb, 1970-72, U. Hawaii, Honolulu, 1973-76; asst. coord. hwy. safety Hawaii Dept. Transp., Honolulu, 1972-76, adminstr. motor vehicle safety, 1976—. Mem., chmn. Med. Adv. Bd. Hawaii, 1972—, Hawaii Hwy. Safety Coun., 1972—, Lt. Sheriff reserve program Sheriff Dept. State of Hawaii, 1984—. With USAR, 1956-62. Mem. MADD (profl.), Am. Assn. Motor Vehicle Adminstrs. (profl., regional rep. 1978—), Nat. Hwy. Traffic Safety Adminstrn. (profl., regional rep. 1972—). Avocations: swimming, spear and sport fishing, scuba diving, ukulele. Fax: 808-832-5830.

HAO, LING YUN, biotechnologist; b. Beijing, China, Jan. 30, 1969; d. Guo Hua Huan; m. Xin Ming Wang, Feb. 22, 1994; 1 child, Tuo Shi. B, Beijing Med. U., China, 1992; PhD, Oita Med. U., Japan, 1997. Med. Diplomate. Rschr. EBARA Rsch. Co., Ltd., Fujisawa, Japan, 1997—. Recipient fellowship Japanese Monbushyou, 1993-97. Avocations: TV, travel. Office: EBARA Rsch Co Ltd, 2-1 Honfujisawa 4-chome, 251-8502 Fujisawa-shi Japan

HAQ, IHSAN UL, Arabic language educator; b. Rawalpindi, Pakistan, Dec. 8, 1952; s. Abdul and Ansar (Saboor) H.; m. Ruqayya Surwar, May 16, 1976; 1 child, Munira. BA, U. Sindh, Pakistan, 1972; MA, U. Karachi, Pakistan, 1974, PhD, 1989; Higher Diploma in Linguistics, Saudi Arabia U. Lectr. U. Karachi, 1977-84, asst. prof., 1984-93, assoc. prof., 1993-95, prof., 1995—, chair dept. Arabic, 1994-98; bd. dirs. Sheikh Zayid Islamic Ctr., Karachi, 1994-96. Author: Quaranic Language Course, 1984, Muslim Personal Law in Quran, 1982, Shah Hmadan and His Contribution in Kashmir, 1992; co-author: (course books) Arabic and Islamic Studies, 1996-99. Recipient Acad. Shield, U. Brunei, 1992, Sirah award Ministry of Religious Affairs, 1982, Shah Hamadan award Govt. of Kashmir, 1987; named hon. citizen, Kansas City. Mem. Karachi Univ. Club, Islamic Soc. Singapur, Arabic Soc. Karachi (life). Avocations: reading, listening to music, poetry. E-mail: ihsanhq@super.net.pk. Office: Dept Arabic, U Karachi, Karachi Pakistan

HAQ, KAISER MOHAMED HAMIDUL, English educator, author; b. Dhaka, Bangladesh, Dec. 7, 1950; s. Mohamed Azharul and Hamida (Begum) H.; m. Rowshan Haq, Nov. 21, 1976 (dec. Jan. 1999). BA with honors, Dhaka U., 1972, MA, 1973; PhD, Warwick U., Coventry, Eng., 1982. Lectr. in English Dhaka U., 1975-82, asst. prof. English, 1982-85, assoc. prof. English, 1985-91, prof. English, 1991—. Author of poems; mem. editorial bd. Form: A Mag. of the Arts, 1984-86; contbr. articles to profl. jours. Mem. Asiatic Soc Bangladesh, Bangladesh Assn. for Am. Studies. Avocations: aerobics, yoga, isometrics. Office: Dhaka Univ, English Dept, 1000 Dhaka Bangladesh

HAQ, RUKHSANA, publishing executive; b. Nairobi, Kenya, May 4, 1956; d. Rafiq and Balqis Chaudhry; m. Shaqur Ul Haq, Oct. 17, 1976. MBA, USIU, Nairobi, 1986. Dir. Camerapix Publ., Nairobi, 1989-96, mng. dir., 1996—. Avocations: reading, design work, physical fitness. Home: PO Box 45048, Nairobi Kenya Office: Camerapix Publ Internat Ltd, PO Box 450487, Nairobi Kenya

HAQUE, IFTIKHAR, electrical engineer; b. Lahore, Punjab, Pakistan, Jan. 4, 1961; s. Abdul and Zeenat Firdous (Khokhar) H.; m. Anila Taizeen, Aug. 19, 1984; children: Meera, Alyzeh. BSEE, U. Tex., 1985. Asst. adminstrv. mgr. ICI Pakistan Ltd., Karachi, 1987-89, asst. plant mgr., 1989-91, materials mgr., 1991-92; materials mgr. Gillette Pakistan Ltd., Karachi, 1992-95; inventory mgr. Banawai Indsl. Group, Jeddah, Saudi Arabia, 1995-96, purchasing mgr., 1996-98; dir. purchasing and logistics Siemens Can. Ltd., Ont., 1998—; cons. Meconsult, Karachi, 1992. Contbr. articles to profl. jours. Mem. Pakistan Students Fedn., 1979. Mem. Am. Prodn. and Inventory Control Soc. (mem.-at-large), Purchasing Mgmt. Assn. Can. (assoc.), Karachi Gymkhana (life), Nat. Assn. Purchasing Mgmt. Avocations: scuba diving, swimming, tennis, snooker. Home: 6321 Tenth Line West, Mississauga, ON Canada L5N 5T5 Office: Siemens Can Ltd, 2185 Derry Rd W, Mississauga, ON Canada L5N 7A6

HAQUE, KAZI MAINUL, import, export executive; b. Arpara, Faridpur, Bangladesh, July 16, 1957; s. Kazi Obaidul Haque and Mosammat Mahmuda Khatun. Higher Secondary Sch. Cert., Kamarkhali Coll., Faridpur, 1975, BA, 1977; MA in Bengali Lit., Dhaka (Bangladesh) U., 1979. Airfreight mgr. Enem Express, Ltd., 1980-90; owner, mng. dir. Arch Logistics Svcs. Ltd., Dhaka, 1991—. Mem. Nafta Internat. Club. Avocations: travelling, gardening, reading, writing. Office fax: (880-2) 8321531/Home fax: 880 2 9118406. E-mail: arch@bangla.net. Office: Arch Logistics Svcs Ltd, 40/3 Inner Circular Rd Fl 3, Box 2775 Dhaka 1000, Bangladesh

HAQUE, MOHAMMED MOMINUL, banking executive; b. Dhaka, Bangladesh, Jan. 1, 1970; s. Mohammad Zahurul and Momtaz (Begum) H. Diploma in Commerce, Dhaka Govt. Comml. Inst., 1988; BA, Dhaka U., 1991; MSS, Nat. U., 1996. Handball player Dhaka, 1984-87; liaison officer VI South Asian Fedn. Games, Dhaka, 1993; personal asst. to mng. dir. Bangladesh Shilpa Bank, Dhaka, 1991—. Mem. Chatra Oykka Forum, Dhaka, 1987-88, Annay, Dhaka, 1989-90. Mem. Surjakar Ujjal Boys Club, Out Market Share Trade Assn. Avocations: travel, music. Fax: 88-02-9562061. Home: 4/A/1 Hatkhola Rd 1st Fl, Tikatuli Dhaka 1203, Bangladesh Office: Bangladesh Shilpa Bank Head Office, GPO Box 975 8 Dit Ave, Dhaka Bangladesh

HAQUE, MOHAMMED SHAHIDUL, electrical engineer; b. Dhaka, Bangladesh, May 12, 1965; came to U.S., 1991; s. Shamsul and Hafiza H.; m. Aynun Naher, June 14, 1994; children: Afsara, Sakib. BSEE, Bangladesh U. Engring. & Tech., Dhaka, 1989; MSEE, U. Ark., 1992, PhD, 1997. Tchg. asst., dept. elec. engr. Bangladesh U. Engring. and Tech., 1990; rsch. asst., dept. elec. engr. U. Ark., Fayetteville, 1991-92; sr. rsch. asst. U. Ark., 1993-97, rsch. asst. prof., 1997; process devel. engr. Novellus Systems Inc., San Jose, 1997-99, process mgr. 300 mm PECVD program, 2000—; lectr. in field. Contbr. articles to Jour. Applied Physics, Solar Energy Materials and solar Cells, Jour. Elec. Materials, others. Mem. IEEE, Electrochemical Soc. Islamic. Achievements include research in microelectronic materials for solar cell applications and multichip module packaging technology; invention of a low temperature silicon solar cell fabrication process; contribution to understanding and quality improvement of chemical vapor deposited silicon dioxide and diamond dielectric films. Avocations: music, philately, photography. Home: 2200 Monroe St Apt 1001 Santa Clara CA 95050-3434 Office: Novellus Sys Inc 3970 N 1st St San Jose CA 95134-1501

HAQUE, SHAHUDUL, protective service official; b. Noakhali, Bangladeshi, Apr. 2, 1946; s. Kazi Sultan Alam and Mosammat Tajunnessa Begum; m. Sharmin Haque, May 21, 1978; children: Shahnaz Zerin, Farnaz Zerin. BA, Panjab U., 1968. Asst. supt. of police Bangladesh Police, 1976-77, additional supt. of police, 1977-78, supt. of police, 1978-82, asst. inspector gen. of police, 1982-85; dep. inspector gen. police Chittagong range, Bangladesh, 1986-87; prin. Police Acad., Saradah, Bangladesh, 1987-89; dep. inspector-gen. of police Khulna Range, Bangladesh, 1989-92; acting police commr. UNTAC, Cambodia, 1993—; dep. inspector gen. of police Dhaka, Bangladesh, 1993-94; police commr. Chittagong Met. Police, 1994-96; additional inspector gen. police Police Hdqs., Dhaka-Bangladesh, 1996—. With Pakistan Army Armoured Corps, 1968-74, Bangladesh Army Armoured Corps, 1974-76. Mem. Rotary Club. Islam. Avocations: reading, gardening. Office: Establishment Ministry, Officer on Spl Duty, Dhaka Bangladesh

HARA, HEIHACHIRO, applied mathematician; b. Okayama, Japan, Sept. 24, 1946; s. Katsuji and Katsuko (Kamoi) H.; m. Tomoko Katayama, Mar. 29, 1974; children: Soichiro, Mikijiro. B Engring., Okayama U., Japan, 1969; MS, U. Wales, Swansea, U.K., 1978; PhD, Hiroshima U., Japan, 1989. Rschr. Mitsui E & S Co. Tamano Lab., Japan, 1969-90; assoc. prof. Shimane U., Japan, 1990-95; prof. Kawasaki U. of Med. Welfare, Japan, 1995—. Author: (books) Finite Element Method in Engineering Science, 1983, Foundation of Boundary Element Method with Fortran Programs, 1985, An Introduction to Numerical Method by FORTRAN, 1986, An Invitation to Finite Element Method, 1995. Mem. Math. Soc. Japan, Am. Math. Soc. Office: Kawasaki U Med Welfare, 288 Matsushima, 701 0193 Kurashiki Japan

HARA, KAZUO, retired psychologist, educator; b. Osaka, Japan, Mar. 11, 1929; s. Senkichi and Masako (Usami) H.; m. Kazue Ishikawa, June 11, 1959; children: Marie, Naoto. BA, San Jose State U., 1953, MA, 1954; PhD, Stanford U., 1960. Asst. dept. physiology Stanford U., 1958-61; instr. Internat. Christian U., Tokyo, 1961-63, asst. prof., 1963-66, assoc. prof., 1966-73, prof. psychology, 1973-94, chmn. Grad. Sch. Edn., 1992-94; prof. psychology Asia U., Tokyo, 1994-99, v.p. acad. affairs, 1997-99; prof. emeritus Internat. Christian U., 1994. Mem. APA, Japan Psychol. Assn. (editor 1969-91), Japan Soc. Liberal and Gen. Edn. (bd. dirs., chief editor 1992-95). Methodist. Home: 4-6-33 Nozaki, Mitaka, Tokyo 181-0014, Japan

HARA, MIKAE, artist, educator; b. Osaka, Japan, Oct. 16, 1951; d. Michio and Sachi Hara. BFA, Osaka U. Arts, 1974; MFA, Calif. Coll. Arts & Crafts, 1986. Lectr. Osaka (Japan) U. Arts, 1987-98, asst. prof., 1999—; vis. prof. Calif. Coll. Arts and Crafts, 2000. One-woman shows include Galerie Petites Formes, Osaka, Japan, 1987-2000, Sumi Gallery, Okayama, Japan, 1987, 91, 92, 93, others; group shows include Auckland New Zealand Mus., 1989, Victoria Arts Ctr., Melbourne, Australia, 1990, Galerie Petites Formes, 1990, Sumi Gallery, 1990, Banchou Gallery, Tokyo, 1990, Liberal Art, Hiroshima, Japan, 1990, Prix Arts Electronica Linz, 1990, 91, 92, Gallery Fukuoka, Fukuoka, Japan, 1991, Kyoto Daimaru Art Gallery, 1992, Ebert Gallery, San Francisco, 1989, 90, 91, 92, 94, 95, 96, 98, 2000, others; represented in permanent collections including Victorian Art Ctr. Mem. Assn. for Computing Machinery. Avocations: movies, musicals, jazz music. Office: Osaka Univ Arts, 469 Higashiyama Kanan-cho, Minamikawachi Osaka, Japan

HARA, YORIKO, Japanese literature researcher; b. Shimonoseki, Yamaguchi, Japan, Sept. 22, 1963; d. Yoshihiko and Kumiko (Imamura) H. BA, Baiko Jo Gakuin U., Shimonseki, 1986, MA, 1988, PhD in, 1996. Cert. in Japanese classical and comparative lit. Tchr. high sch. Japan, 1989-92; asst. dept. Japanese lang. and lit. Baiko Jo Gakuin U., 1994-96; lectr. Ind. State U., Terre Haute, 1996-97; art commentator, Japan, 1999—. Translator Sarashina Nikki, 2000. Home: 8-4 Ishigami-cho, Yamaguchi-ken Shimonoseki-ghi 751-0825, Japan

HARADA, HAJIME, lawyer; b. Tokyo, Sept. 10, 1947; s. Jiro and Yukiko (Takahashi) H.; m. Akiko Kawada, Apr. 1981; 1 child. LLB, Tokyo U., 1970; student, Legal Rsch. Ctr. Supreme Ct., Tokyo, 1974. With Export-Import Bank Japan, Tokyo, 1970-72; assoc. Iwata Law Firm, Tokyo, 1974-82, Kido & Ikeda Law Firm, Tokyo, 1982-93; ptnr. Kido, Ikeda & Harada Law Firm, Tokyo, 1993-99, Kido & Harada Law Firm, Tokyo, 1999—; statutory auditor Koken Co., Ltd., Tokyo, 1997—, Fuji Xerox Learning Inst. Inc., 2000—. Contbr. articles to profl. jours., including Jurist, Jour. Japanese Inst. Internat. Bus. law, Copyright. Mem. Japan Fedn. Bar Assns., Japan Patent Attys. Assn., Licensing Execs. Soc. Japan. Avocation: driving. Office: Rm 828, New Kokusai Bldg, 4-1 3 chome Marunouchi, Chioduku Tokyo 100-0005, Japan

HARADA, NORIO, software engineer, researcher, educator; b. Aichi, Japan, Feb. 12, 1945; s. Iwao and Tomiko Harada; m. Reiko Harada, Oct. 31, 1971; children: Shin, Satoshi. BS, Nagoya U., Nagoya-Shi, Japan, 1967, MS, 1969; D Engring., Kyoto U., Kyoto-Shi, Japan, 1979. Rschr. Nippon Electric Co. Ltd., Kawasaki-Shi, Kanagawa, Japan, 1969-82, rsch. supr., 1982-84; rsch. mgr. NEC Corp., Kawasaki-Shi, 1984-87; mgr. NEC Corp., Minato-Ku, Tokyo, 1987-91, chief engr., 1991-96; prof. computer sci. Takushoku U., Tokyo, 1996—. Contbr. articles to profl. jours. Recipient Yonezawa Meml. Paper award, 1985. Mem. IEEE, AAAS, Assn. Computing Machinery, Math. Soc. Japan, Inst. Electronics, Info. and Comm. Engrs. Japan (Excellent Paper award 1985, 88), Info. Processing Soc. Japan, N.Y. Acad. Scis. Buddhist. Avocations: mathematics, tennis, reading, research. Home: 18-5 Yokoyamadai 1-Chome, Sagamihara-Shi Kanagawa 229-1121, Japan Office: Takushoku U Hachioji-Shi, 815-1 Tatemachi, Tokyo 193-0985, Japan

HARADA, TERUICHI, medical educator; b. Osaka, Japan, Oct. 24, 1958; s. Masaaki and Hisae (Minamide) H.; m. Chikage Saisyo, Apr. 9, 1989; 3 children. B in Medicine, Osaka City U., 1987; MD, Saitama Med. Sch., 1998. Resident in plastic surgery Osaka City U., 1987-90, rschr., 1998—; asst. doctor critical care medicine Saitama (Japan) Med. Ctr., 1990-98; cons. welfare group for the children with facial disfigurement, Osaka, 1998—. Author: Textbook of Industrial Medicine, 1998. Mem. Japanese Assn. of Acute Medicine (councilor of capital branch 1997—), Japan Shock Soc. (councilor 1998—), Japan Burn Assn. (councilor 1999—), Internat. Soc. for Burn Injuries, Am. Burn Assn. Avocations: essayist, classical musician, scuba diving. Office: Plastic Surg, Osaka City U, Abenoku Asahi 1-4-3, Osaka 545-8585, Japan

HARADA, YASUO, educational administrator; b. Kure, Japan, May 31, 1931; s. Masao and Yoshie (Kitsutaka) H.; m. Yuki Sakamoto Harada, Apr. 17, 1961; 1 child, Masashi. Student, Hiroshima U. Sch. Medicine, Japan, 1957, postgrad., 1959-63; PhD, Hiroshima U., Japan, 1963. Medical diplomate. Assoc. prof. Hiroshima U., Japan, 1967-78, prof., 1978-93; dir. Hiroshima U. Hosp., Japan, 1984-88; dean sch. of medicine Hiroshima (Japan) U., 1990-93, pres., 1993—; collaborator Acta Otolaryngologica, Stockholm, Sweden; editor: ENT Jour., Jour. Otolaryngology, Can.; assoc. editor Auris Nasus Larynx, Tokyo. Author: The Vestibular Organs, 1988, Atlas of the Ear by Scanning Electron Microscopy, 1983. Recipient Gold prize Indian Neurootological Equilibrium Soc., 1987, Bárány Gold medal Bárány Soc. Meeting and Uppsala U., Sweden, 1994, Medal with Purple Ribbon Japanese Govt., 1995. Mem. Internat. Bárány Soc., Collegium-Otorhinolaryngologicum Amicitae Sacrum, Polizer Soc. Home: Koami-cho 2-1, Hiroshima 730-0855, Japan Office: Hiroshima U, Kagamiyama 1-3-2, Higashi-Hiroshima 739-8511, Japan

HARAGUCHI, MIKIMARO, artist, educator; b. Shimodate, Ibaraki, Japan, Jan. 30, 1945; s. Kojiro and Shige H.; m. Hizuko Kajiura, Oct. 31, 1973; 1 child, Asami. BA, Nat. Tokyo Geijutsu Daigaku, MA; student, Ecole Nat. Superieure. From part-time lectr. to prof. Sugino Women's Coll., Tokyo, 1982-95, prof., 1995—. Exhbns. include Seville, Spain, 1992, Montreal Can., 1994, Tukuba Mus. Art, 1996; patentee in field. Mem. Rainforest Found. Japan. Avocations: walking, kendo. Home: 3-9-305 Kodan, Kitamoto-shi 364-0023, Japan Office: Sugino Womens Coll, 406019 Kamiosaki, Shinagawa-ku TOkyo Japan

HARAHAP, RUSTAM EFFENDI, gynecologist; b. Gunungsitoli, Indonesia, Aug. 9, 1937; s. Amir Gani Malioth and Nurmalam Dalimunthe Harahap; m. Soelistijo Rini Sardjono, July 14, 1964; children: Berlin, Donald, Piepong. MD, U. Indonesia, Jakarta, 1964, splty. in ob.-gyn., 1970, PhD, 1983. Physician Amboina (Indonesia) Hosp., 1964-66; with dept. ob/gyn U. Indonesia, 1966-70, cons., lectr., 1970-83; pvt. practice Jakarta, 1983—; with M.D. Anderson Hosp. and Tumor Inst., Houston, 1970. Author: Gynecological Cancers, 1983; contbr. articles to profl. jours. Recipient IBC Golden Scroll of Excellence award, Twentieth Century Achievement award. Fellow Internat. Biog. Assn., Am. Biog. Inst. Rsch. Assn.; mem. AAAS, Indonesian Med. Assn., Indonesian Assn. Ozone Therapy, Internat. Med. Soc. for Ozone Therapy, Indonesian Soc. Obstetricians and Gynecologists, Nat. Geog. Soc., Internat. Soc. for Preventive Oncology, N.Y. Acad. Sci., World Orgn. Family Drs., Planetary Soc., Order Internat. Fellowship. Avocations: music, videography, astronomy. E-mail: rehara@hotmail.com. Home: 36B Wisnu Str Witana Harja, Pamulang 15417, Indonesia Office: B30-31, 2 Suryopranoto Harmoni Plz, Jakarta 10130, Indonesia

HARALAMBIDES, MARINA, violinist, educator; b. Athens, Greece, Dec. 21, 1970; d. Vassos and Vassiliki (Moutoyianni) H.; m. George Panos Lelakis, Feb. 23, 1997. LRAM, Royal Acad. Music, London, 1993, Profl. Cert., 1994. Violinist Greek Radio Symphony Orch., Athens, 1995-96, Athens State Symphony Orch., 1996—; violin prof. F. Nakas Conservatory, Athens, 1996—, chamber music prof., 1998—; violinist Orch. of Colours, Athens, 1995—, Orch. Enarmonia, Athens, 1997—. Violin soloist various recitals, concerts, confs., 1995—. Greek Orthodox. Home: 40 El Venizelou St, Ag Paraskevi, Paraskevi Athens 153 41, Greece

HARALDSSON, ANDERS, computer scientist, educator; b. Stockholm, Dec. 12, 1946; m. Eva Rosenlund; children: Karin, Anna. BS in Math. and Computer Sci., Uppsala (Sweden) U., 1969; PhD in Computer Sci., Linköping (Sweden) U., 1977. Rsch. asst. Uppsala U., 1969-76; assoc. prof. Linköping U., 1977—, chmn. dept. computer and info. sci., 1990-99; chmn. undergrad. programs in computer sci. and tech. Linköping Inst. Tech., 1999—. Author: LISP-details, 1975, Programming Pascal, 1978, Programming LISP, 1993. Home: Westmansgatan 4, S-582 46 Linköping Sweden Office: Linköping U, Dept Computer and Info Sci, S-581 83 Linköping Sweden

HARALDSSON, PER-OLLE, physician; b. Lund, Sweden, Jan. 8, 1949; s. Harald Nils and Greta Lilly (Andersson) Olsson; m. Dina de O'Pinheiro; 1 child, Vincent, 1999. MD, U. Lund, Sweden, 1975; PhD, Karolinska Inst., Stockholm, 1991, Docent, 1996. Physician, dept. otorhinolaryngology Karolinska Hosp., Stockholm, 1985—; assoc. prof. docent Karolinska U., 1996—. Fellow Royal Soc. Medicine (U.K.); mem. European Acad. Facial Plastic Surgery (v.p. 1995—), European Rhinologic Soc., European Sleep Rsch. Soc. E-mail: po@haraldsson.nu. Office: Dept Otorhinolaryngology, Karolinska Hosp, S-171 76 Stockholm Sweden

HARALD V, King of Norway; b. Feb. 21, 1937; s. King Olav V and Crown Princess Märtha; m. Sonja Haraldsen, Aug. 29, 1968; 2 children: Märtha Louise, Haakon Magnus. Ed., U. Oxford, Eng. Office: HM The King of Norway, Royal Palace, N-0010 Oslo Norway

HARAMUNDANIS, KATHERINE LEONORA, information scientist, writer; b. Boston, Jan. 25, 1937; d. Sergei Illarionovich and Cecilia Helena (Payne) Gaposchkin; m. John Haramundanis, Mar. 6, 1958; children: George John, Sergei Edward. BA, Swarthmore Coll., 1958; MS in Computer Sci., Boston U., 1997. Rsch. assoc. Smithsonian Astrophys. Obs., Cambridge, Mass., 1958-74; tech. writer Wang Labs., Lowell, Mass., 1974-77; cons. writer Digital Equipment Corp., Nashua, N.H., 1977-98; info. architect Compaq Computer Corp., 1998—; judge Soc. for Tech. Comm., 1989, 92. Author: Cecilia Payne-Gaposchkin: An Autobiography and Other Recollections, 1984, 2nd edit., 1996, The Art of Technical Documentation, 1992, 97, Exploring Workstation Applications, 1996; (with C. Payne-Gaposchkin) Introduction to Astronomy, 1970; contbr. articles to profl. jours. Recipient Spl. Svc. award Smithsonian Instn., 1966, Merit award Smithsonian Astrophys. Obs., 1972. Mem. AAAS, IEEE Computer Soc., Assn. for Computing Machinery (treas. Spl. Interest Group for Sys. Documentation 1993-96, chair 1997—), IEEE Profl. Comm. Soc., Soc. for Tech. Comm. (exec. coun. 1993-95), Assn. Computational Linguistics, Linguistic Soc. Am., Am. Astron. Soc., Am. Archeol. Soc., Am. Soc. Oriental Rsch. Home: PO Box 1365 Westford MA 01886-4865

HARASAWA, RYO, microbiology educator; b. Chiba, Japan, Dec. 11, 1947; s. Hiroshi and Tsuru (Ohno) H.; m. Sumie Kobayashi, Oct. 26, 1975; children: Mikito, Mariko. DVM, Azabu U., Sagamihara, Japan, 1973; PhD, U. Tokyo, 1978. Lic. veterinarian, Japan. Sr. scientist Inst. Phys. and Chem. Rsch. (RIKEN), Wako, Japan, 1979-84; assoc. prof. microbiology Miyazaki (Japan) U., 1984-89, U. Tokyo, 1989—; vis. fellow NIH, Bethesda, Md., 1980-82; vis. scientist U. Ala., Birmingham, 1988. Recipient Vet. Sci. award Japan Soc. Vet. Science, 1990. Avocation: making and playing the violin. Home: Itabashi-ku, Komone 4-2-4, Tokyo 173-0037, Japan Office: U Tokyo Faculty Medicine, Hongo 7-3-1, Bunkyo-ku, Tokyo 113-0033, Japan

HARAT, MAREK, neurosurgeon, researcher; b. Libi—ż, Poland, Aug. 9, 1958; s. Stanisław and Ludwika (Starzycka) H.; m. Ewa S—kowska, June 26, 1981; children: Agata, Maciej. MD, Mil. Med. Acad., Łódź, Poland, 1983, PhD, 1988, assoc. prof., 1997. Asst. dept. neurosurgery Mil. Med. Acad., Łódź, 1985-88, sr. asst. dept. neurosurgery, 1988-94; head dept. neurosurgery Mil. Clin. Hosp., Bydgoszcz, Poland, 1994—; v.p. Pomeranian sect. Polish Neurosurg. Soc., 1997, mem. exec. com., 1998; chmn. Polish Stereotactic and Functional Neurosurg. Soc., 1998; mem. exec. com. European Soc. for Stereotactic and Functional Neurosurgery, 1999. Contbr. articles to profl. jours. Col. Mil. Health Svc. Grantee Found. for Polish Sci., 1998, Com. for Sci. Rsch., Poland, 1999. Mem. World Fedn. Neurosurg. Socs., Internat. Neurotrauma Soc., European Assn. Neurosurg. Socs. Roman Catholic. Avocations: skiing, cycling, classical music, opera. Home: Widok 79, 85-357 Bydgoszcz Poland Office: Mil Clin Hosp, Powstancow Warszawy 5, 85-681 Bydgoszcz Poland

HARAVE, MAHESHAPPA DEVANNA, engineering educator; b. Chamarajanagar, Mysore, India, May 15, 1960; s. Devanna Mallappa Harave and Mahadevamma Madappa Heggadahalli; m. Usharani Sambamurthy Horalavadi, June 15, 1989; 1 child, Madhurya. B in Engring., N.I. Engring., Mysore, 1983; M in Tech., S.J. Coll. Engring., Mysore, 1987; postgrad., IISC, Bangalore, India. Lectr. S.J. Coll. Engring., Mysore, 1983-91, sr. lectr., 1991—. Contbr. articles to profl. jours. Avocations: writing poetry, singing, chess. Home: Harave, Mysore India Office: S J Coll Engring, Manasa Gangothri, Mysore 570006, India

HARB, PHYLLIS, realtor; b. Nurenberg, Germany, Apr. 11, 1956; came to U.S., 1956; d. Samuel Lewis Serra and Joyce Joan Schuessler; m. George Harb, July 1, 1989; children: Kristen Nicolle, Jinan Noel. AA, Glendale Coll., 1984. Sr. underwriter Sears Savings Bank, 1979-82; loan officer L.A. Fed. Savings, 1982-87; v.p. loan adminstrn. BSC Mortgage (subs. Sterling Bank), 1986-89; realtor Dilbeck Realtors, 1989-92; realtor, mktg. specialist MacGregor Realty, 1992-99, REMAX, 1999—; instr. Banking Inst., 1987-89. Address: MacGregor Realty 200 W Glenoaks Blvd Ste 100 Glendale CA 91202-3621

HARBAUGH, DANIEL PAUL, lawyer; b. Wendell, Idaho, May 18, 1948; s. Myron and Manuelita (Garcia) H. BA, Gonzaga U., 1970, JD, 1974. Bar: Washington 1974, U.S. Dist. Ct. (ea. dist.) Wash. 1977, U.S. Ct. Appeals (9th cir.) 1978. Asst. atty. gen. State of Wash., Spokane, 1974-77; ptnr. Richter, Wimberley & Ericson, Spokane, 1977-83, Harbaugh & Bloom, P.S., Spokane, 1983—; bd. dirs. Spokane Legal Svcs., 1982-86; bd. govs. LAWPAC, Seattle, 1980-92. Bd. dirs. Spokane Ballet, 1983-88; chpt. dir. Les Amis du Vin, Spokane, 1985-88; mem. Spokane County Civil Svc. Commn., 1991—, chmn., 1999—, Gonzaga U. Pres' Coun., 1991—. Mem. ATLA, Wash. State Bar Assn. (spl. dist. counsel 1982-95, mem. com. rules for profl. conduct 1989-92, mem. legis. com. 1995-96), Spokane County Bar Assn. (chair med.-legal com. 1991), Wash. State Trial Lawyers Assn. (v.p. 1988-89, co-chair worker's compensation sect. 1992, 93, spl. select. com. on workers' corp. 1990—, forum 1994—, vice-chmn. 1994-97, mem. legis. com. 1995-98), Nat. Orgn. Social Security Claimants Reps., Internat. Wine and Food Soc. (pres. local chpt. 1989-91, cellar master 1994-96), Empire Club, Spokane Club, Spokane Country Club (adminstrv. com. 1995-98, chmn. 1991-98, trustee 1996-99, sec.-treas. 1997-98, pres. 1998-99, ex-officio 1999-2000, long range planning com. 1999—), Alpha Sigma Nu, Phi Alpha Delta. Roman Catholic. Office: Harbaugh & Bloom PS PO Box 1461 Spokane WA 99210-1461

HARBECK, WILLIAM JAMES, real estate executive, lawyer, international consultant; b. Glenview, Ill., Dec. 16, 1921; s. Christian Frederick and Anna (Gaeth) H.; m. Jean Marie Allsopp, Jan. 20, 1945; children: John, Stephen, Timothy, Mark, Christopher. B.A., Wabash (Ind.) Coll., 1947; J.D., Northwestern U., 1950. Bar: Ill. 1950. Land acquisition atty. Chgo. Land Clearance Commn., 1950-51; regional real estate dir. Montgomery Ward & Co., Chgo., 1951-68; asst. to pres., dir. corp. facilities Montgomery Ward & Co., 1968-70, v.p., dir. facilities devel., 1970-81; v.p. Montgomery Ward Devel. Corp., 1972-81; pres., chief exec. officer Montgomery Ward Properties Corp., 1974-81; pres. William J. Harbeck Assocs., 1981-90; bd. dirs. Randhurst Corp., 1972-90, mem. exec. com., 1975-81. Mem. editorial bd. profl. jours.; contbr. articles to profl. jours. Bd. dirs. Chgo. Lawson YMCA, 1973-89, chmn. devel. com., 1979-89, mem. exec. com., 1985-89; bd. dirs. Greater North Michigan Ave Assn., Chgo., 1979-81; chmn. constrn. com. Chgo. United, 1979-81; co-chmn. Chgo. Bus. Opportunities Fair, 1980-81; mem. real estate com. Chgo. Met. YMCA, 1982-89, chmn. Bldg. Task Force, 1985-90; mem. pres.'s coun. Concordia U., River Forest, Ill., 1969-87, mem. bd. regents, 1987-96, mem. strategic planning com., 1989-91; bd. trustee Concordia U. Found., 1996-97; mem. planning com. Inst. for Philanthropic Mgmt., 1985-89; youth Bible and Bethel instr. Redeemer Luth. Ch., Highland Pk., Ill., 1965-89, congregation pres., 1968-70, 85-87, chmn. ch. growth com., 1982-89; mem. Eternal Shepherd Luth. Ch., Salem, S.C., 1990-99, bd. elders, 1991-96, chmn., 1993-96, mem. St. Peters Lutheran Ch., Arlington Heights, IL, 1999—; trustee Luth. Ch. Mo. Synod Found., 1975-76, 81-90, bd. mems., 1992-98, mem. Synodical mission study commn., 1974-75, mem. dist. rsch. and planning com., 1981-90, mem. task force on synodical constn. by-laws and structure, 1975-79; bd. mems. Luth. Ch. ext. fund, 1989-92; mem. rsch. and planning com. No. Ill. Dist. Luth. Ch. Mo. Synod, 1984-89; nat. mem. Luth. Ch. Ext. Fund. Bd., 1992-96; sponsor Luth. Chs. for Career Devel., 1979-88; corp. chmn. U.S. Bond drive, Chgo., 1976; chief crusader Chgo. Crusade Mercy, 1976-78; divsn. chmn. Chgo. Cerebral Palsy campaign, 1977-78. Lt. (j.g.) USNR, 1942-46. Mem. Ill. Bar Assn., Internat. Coun. Shopping Ctrs. (bd. dirs. 1972-78, exec. com. 1975-78, govt. affairs com. 1977-89, awards com. 1980-83, urban com. 1980-83, lectr. 1969-89), Luth. Layman's League, Alpha Sigma Kappa, Phi Alpha Delta. Home and Office: 1376 Village Dr Arlington Heights IL 60004-8104

HARBERG, ALBERT JUSTUS, association executive; b. Aland, Finland, Nov. 28, 1925; s. Julius Ferdinand and Anna Brynhilda (Lundell) H.; m. Ebba Nordberg, Oct. 17, 1950. M, Aland Naval Inst., Mariehamn, Finland, 1950; diploma in econs., Swedish Acad. Comm., Helsinki, 1960. Ships officer Gustaf Erikson, Mariehamn, Finland, 1946-59; mng. dir. 5 shipping cos., Mariehamn, Finland, 1961-66; sec. Aland Shipowners Assn., Mariehamn, Finland, 1967-74, mng. dir., 1974-89. Author of books on maritime history; contbr. articles to profl. jours. Mem. Aland Shipowners Assn., Mariehamn Rotary, Aland Nautical Club (chmn. 1984-92). Lutheran. Avocations: reading, English, maritime history, outdoor activities.

HARBERGER, ARNOLD CARL, economist, educator; b. Newark, July 27, 1924; s. Ferdinand C. and Martha (Bucher) H.; m. Ana Beatriz Valjalo, Mar. 15, 1958; children: Paul Vincent, Carl David. Student, Johns Hopkins U., 1941-43; MA, U. Chgo., 1947, PhD, 1950; Doctor honoris causa, U. Tucuman, 1979, Cath. U. Chile, 1988, Tech. U. Cen. Am., 1989. Asst. prof. polit. economy Johns Hopkins U., 1949-53; asso. prof. econs. U. Chgo., 1953-59, prof., 1959—, chmn. dept., 1964-71, 75-80, Gustavus F. and Ann M. Swift disting. svc. prof., 1977-91, prof. emeritus, 1991—, dir. Ctr. Latin Am. Econ. Studies, 1965-92; vis. prof. MIT (Ctr. Internat. Studies), New Delhi, 1961-62, Econ. Devel. Inst., IBRD, 1965, Harvard U., 1971-72, Princeton U., 1973-74, UCLA, 1983, 84, U. Paris, 1986; prof. econs. UCLA, 1984—; cons. IMF, 1950, 89, U.S. Pres.'s Materials Policy Commn., 1951-52, U.S. Treasury Dept., 1961-75, Com. Econ. devel., 1961-78, Planning Commn., India, 1961-62, 73, Pan Am. Union, 1962-76, Dept. State, 1962-76, Cen. Bank, Chile, 1965-70, Dominican Republic, 1989, Nicaragua, 1990, China, 1995, Ecuador, 1996, Planning Dept., Panama, 1963-77, Colombia, 1969-71, Nicaragua, 1990, Indonesia, 1997—; cons. Ford Found., 1967-77, Planning Commn., El Salvador, 1973-75, Budget and Planning Office, Uruguay, 1974-75, Can. Dept. Regional Econ. Expansion, 1975-77, Econ. Min. Argentina, 1994—, Fin. Ministry, Bolivia, 1976, Mex., 1976—, Econ. Adv. Office, Russia, 2000; cons. Can. Dept. Employment and Migration, 1980-82, Indonesian Ministry Fin., 1981-82, 86, 97—, Can. Dept. Fin., 1982-88, Can. Dept. Industry, Sci. and Tech., 1991—, Chinese Ministry Fin., 1983; ministry fin., Malawi, 1988, Venezuela, 1989, Colombia, 1991, 94, Dominican Republic, 1996, 97; mem. internat. adv. coun. Inst. Internat. Studies, Stanford U., 1991—; v.p., chmn. adv. coun. Inst. for Policy Reform; cons. Office Econ. Adviser to the Pres. Russia, 2000. Author: Project Evaluation, 1972, Taxation and Welfare, 1974; Editor: Demand for Durable Goods, 1960, The Taxation of Income from Capital, 1968, Key Problems of Economic Policy In Latin America, 1970, World Economic Growth, 1985; contbr. sci. papers to profl. jours. and govt. publs. With AUS, 1943-46. Guggenheim fellow; Fulbright scholar; faculty rsch. fellow Social Sci. Rsch. Coun.; Ford Found. faculty rsch. fellow, 1968-69. Fellow Econometric Soc., Am. Acad. Arts and Scis., Am. Econ. Assn. (disting., mem. exec. com. 1970-72, v.p. 1992, pres.-elect 1996, pres. 1997, disting. fellow 1999), Western Econ. Assn. (v.p. 1987-88, pres. 1989-90), Royal Econ. Soc., Nat. Tax Assn., NAS, Phi Beta Kappa. Home: 136 Buckskin Rd Bell Canyon CA 91307-1125 Office: UCLA PO Box 951477 405 Hilgard Ave Los Angeles CA 90095-9000

HARBESON, JOHN WILLIS, political science educator; b. New Brunswick, N.J., Sept. 14, 1938; s. Robert Willis and Gladys (Evans) H.; m. Ann Elizabeth Warmoth, Aug. 25, 1963; children: Eric John, Kristen Lynne. BA cum laude, Swarthmore (Penn.) Coll., 1960; MA, U. Chgo., 1962; PhD, U. Wis., 1970. From asst. prof. to prof. polit. sci. U. Wis.-Parkside, Kenosha, 1967-85, chair divsn. social scis., 1975-79, 82-85, dir. internat. studies, 1977-79; prof. polit. sci. CUNY, 1985—, dir. internat. studies, 1985-88, chair. dept. polit. sci., 1999—; lectr. U. Nairobi, Kenya, 1966-67; vis. prof. Addis Ababa U., Ethiopia, 1973-75; prof. Land Tenure Ctr., U. Wis., Madison, 1976-85; sr. social sci. analyst Agy. Internat. Devel., 1979-82; professorial lectr. Johns Hopkins U., Washington, 1980-82; adj. prof. Columbia U., N.Y.C., 1990-92; sr. advisor Agy. for Internat. Devel. for Democracy and Governance Issues in Ea. and So. Africa, 1993-95; Jennings Randolph sr. fellow U.S. Inst. of Peace, 1998-99. Author: Nation Building in Kenya, 1973, Ethiopian Transformation, 1988; author, editor: Military in African Politics; author, co-editor: Africa in World Politics, 1991, 3d edit., 2000, Civil Society and the State in Africa, 1993, Responsible Government: The Global Challenge, 1993; contbr. 65 articles to profl. jours. Chairperson Congl. campaigns, Racine, Wis., 1970, 72, Dem. Party, Croton-On-Hudson, N.Y., 1989-91; elected village trustee Croton-on-Hudson, 1991-93; pres.'s coun. U. Ill., 1992—. Recipient Meritorious Svc. award Agy. of Internat. Devel., 1980, Rsch. award J.D. and C.T. MacArthur Found., 1991; fellow Am. Coun. of Learned Socs., 1989, Rockefeller Found., 1966. Mem. ACLU (sec. Racine-Kenosha chpt. 1972-74), Am. Polit. Sci. Assn., African Studies Assn., Nat. Urban League (bd. dirs. Racine chpt. 1971-73), Swarthmore Coll. Alumni Coun. Episcopalian. Avocations: tennis, organ and piano playing, reading, singing. Home: 5 Valley Trl Croton On Hudson NY 10520-2213 Office: Convent and 138th Cuny New York NY 10031

HARBISON, PETER DESMOND, former magazine editor, archaeologist, historian; b. Dublin, Jan. 14, 1939; s. James Austin and Sheelagh Helen (MacSherry) H.; m. Edelgard Soergel, Dec. 6, 1969; children: John, Maurice, Ronan. BA, MA, Univ. Coll., Dublin, 1959; DPhil, Philipps U., Marburg, Germany, 1964; postgrad., Albert Ludwigs U., Freiburg, Germany, 1961. Archaeologist Irish Tourist Bd., Dublin, 1966-84, edit. publicity officer, 1984-86; editor Ireland of the Welcomes mag., Dublin, 1986-95; chmn. Nat. Monuments Adv. Coun., Dublin, 1986-90. Author: Guide to the National Monuments of Ireland, 1970, Pre-Christian Ireland, 1988 (British Archaeol. Book award 1988), Pilgrimage in Ireland, 1992, The High Crosses of Ireland, 1992, The Golden Age of Irish Art, 1999 (also French, German and Italian edits.), The Crucifixion in Irish Art, 2000, others; contbr. articles to acad. and profl. jours.; co-author: (with Jacqueline O'Brien) Ancient Ireland, 1996. Fellow Soc. of Antiquaries of London, Trinity Coll. Dublin (hon.); mem. Royal Irish Acad. (v.p. 1992-93, coun. mem. 1993-96, 97—, hon. acad. editor 1995—), Royal Hibernian Acad. Arts (hon., prof. Archeology 1999—), Friends of the Nat. Collections of Ireland (sec. 1971-76), German Archaeol. Inst., Kildare St. and Univ. Club (wine coms.). Avocations: archaeology, travel, music. Home: 5 Saint Damians Loughshinny, Skerries Co Dublin Ireland

HARBOE-HANSEN, HANS, naval editor, writer; b. Holbaek, Denmark, Apr. 27, 1923; s. Egede and Kirstine (Soenderby) Harboe-Hansen; m. Annie Holst Nielsen, Nov. 20, 1970; 1 child, Christian; m. Lykke Elsebeth Raae, Sept. 12, 1951 (div. Oct. 1970); children: Peter, Bente. Commd. officer Royal Danish Navy, 1941, advanced through grades to capt., 1967, ret., 1974; cons. Contraves Italiana, Rome, 1976-83; naval editor Def. Sys. Internat., Sterling Publs., London, 1994-98, Def. Procurement Analysis, Highbury House Comm., London, 1998—. Contbr. articles to profl. jours. Decorated knight Order of Dannebrog, knight 1st grade Order of Dannebrog (Denmark). Mem. U.S. Naval Inst. (life), Naval Lts. Assn. (life), Naval Officer's Club (life). Lutheran. Home: Hjortevaenget 230, DK-2980 Kokkedal Denmark Office: Highbury House Comm, 1-3 Highbury Station Rd, London N9 1SE, England

HARBOURT, CLIFFORD MARK, lawyer; b. Trenton, N.J., June 13, 1947; s. Clifford Bozarth and Elizabeth Kathleen (Fesko) H.; m. Louise Marie Pastore, June, 1970; children: Clifford John, Matthew Evan. BS in Econs., Villanova (Pa.) U., 1969; JD, Duquesne U., Pitts., 1973; LLM, Georgetown U., 1977. Sr. technician reviewer Chief Counsel IRS, Washington, 1973—.

HARCOURT, WENDY JANE, editor, development organization executive; b. Adelaide, Australia, Apr. 16, 1959; arrived in Italy, 1988; d. Geoffrey Colin and Joan Margaret (Bartrop) H.; m. Mark Keese, Dec. 2, 1978 (div. 1985); m. Claudio Sardoni, Dec. 18, 1989; children: Caterina Sardoni, Emma-Claire Sardoni. BA, U. Adelaide, 1979, BA with honors, 1981; PhD in History, Australian Nat. U., 1987. Lectr. Canberra (Australia) Coll. of Advanced Edn., 1983-84; assoc. editor, program coord. Soc. for Internat. Devel., Rome, 1988-92, assoc. editor, program dir., 1993-95, editor, program dir., 1995—; cons. culture and comm. sectors UNESCO, Paris, 1994-99, Inst. Edn., Hamburg, Germany, 1997, WHO, Geneva, 1999-00, UNFPA-EU, 2000; cons. OECD Devel. Ctr., Paris, 1996-97; guest lectr. Schumacher Coll., Eng., 1997, UN Staff Tng. Coll., 1998, World U. for Women, Hamburg, 2000; rsch. coord. Swiss Nat. Sci. Found., 1994-97. Editor: Feminist Perspectives on Sustainable Development, 1994, Power Reproduction and Gender, 1997, Women @ Internet: Creating New Cultures in Cyberspace, 1998, Jour. of Soc. for Internat. Devel., 1994—, Quar. Bull. Women in Devel. Europe, 1988-94. Coord. Women and Environment Group, Europe, 1991-94, Women and Health Group, Rome, 1993-94; mem. Adolescent Reproductive Health, Rome, 1996-97; mem. steering group, rsch. coord. Women in Devel. Europe, 1988-97, Rockefeller Project Politics of Place, 2000—; mem. adv. bd. Turin UN Staff Tng. Ctr., 1997. Commonwealth postgrad. scholar Australian Govt., 1982-86. Avocations: writing poetry, swimming, reading about international affairs. Home: Via Livorno 36, 00162 Rome Italy Office: Soc for Internat Devel, Via Panisperna 207, 00184 Rome Italy

HARCROW, E. EARL, lawyer; b. Carrizozo, N.Mex., Mar. 4, 1954; s. James Earl and Nettie (McInnes) H.; m. Julie A., Apr. 16, 1987; children: Ashley Nicole, James Earl. BS, Tex. Tech. U., 1976, JD, 1979. Bar: Tex. 1979, U.S. Dist. Ct. (no. dist.) Tex., U.S. Ct. Appeals (5th cir.) 1979. Asst. dist. atty. Lubbock (Tex.) Dist. Atty. Office, 1979-80, Tarrant Dist. Atty. Office, Ft. Worth, 1980-83; ptnr. Shannon, Gracey, Ratliff & Miller, Ft. Worth, 1985-99; mng. ptnr. Shannon, Gracey, Ratliff & Miller, 1995-96, ptnr. in charge of tech., 1996-99; ptnr. Haynes & Boone, Ft. Worth, 1999—; gen. counsel Dallas Ft. Worth Med. Ctr., 1990—. Bd. dirs. Planned Parenthood North Tex., 1987-92; fellow Tex. Bar Found., 1991—. Office: Haynes and Boone LLP 201 Main St Ste 2200 Fort Worth TX 76102-3126

HARDALUPAS, YANNIS, engineering educator, researcher; b. Volos, Greece, Aug. 22, 1960; arrived in U.K., 1984; s. Triantafillos and Andromahi (Hatziioannou) H.; m. Evdokia Simigdala, Jan. 1, 1990; children: Mahi, Phillios-Simon. Degree in Mech. Engring., Nat. Tech. U. Athens, 1984; PhD, Imperial Coll., London, 1989. Rsch. asst. dept. mech. engring. Imperial Coll., 1984-87, 88-91, rsch. fellow dept. mech. engring., 1991-93, 94, Engring. and Phys. Scis. Rsch. Coun. advanced rsch. fellow, 1994—, lectr. in thermofluids, dept. mech. engring., 1998—. Contbr. numerous articles to profl. jours.; patentee in field. Recipient awards, scholarships and grants. Mem. AIAA, Greek Chamber Engring., Combustion Inst. (Brit. sect.), Soc. Automotive Engrs. (assoc.). Christian Orthodox. Avocations: tennis, squash. Office: Imperial Coll/Mech Engring, Exhibition Rd, London SW7 2BX, England

HARDAWAY, ERNEST, II, oral and maxillofacial surgeon, public health official. BS, Howard U., 1957, DDS, 1966, cert. in oral and maxillofacial surgery, 1972; MPH, Johns Hopkins U., 1973. Intern, then chief resident oral and maxillofacial surgery Howard U. Med. Ctr., Washington, 1969-72; asst. prof., mem. attending staff Howard U. Coll. Medicine and Med. Ctr., Washington, 1974—; with Bur. Quality Assurance, HHS, Washington, 1974-77; various adminstrv. positions Bur. Med. Services and Health Services Adminstrn., USPHS, 1977-80; dep. commr., then commr. pub. health City of Washington, 1982-84; acting v.p. fin. and adminstrv. affairs Mile Sq. Health Ctr., Inc., 1984; asst. to regional health adminstr. Fed. Employee Occupational Health Program, 1985; exec. v.p. Fed. Employee Occupational Health Program, Chgo., 1986—; mem. profl. staff Com. on Ways and Means, U.S. Ho. of Reps., 1972; spl. asst. to dir. Office Policy Planning and Evaluation, HEW, 1973; presenter at numerous profl. meetings. Contbr. articles to dental jours. Mem. D.C. Emergency Med. Care Adv. Com., D.C. Long-Term Planning Group, 1983, D.C. Health Coordinating Council, D.C. Commn. on Homelessness, 1984; mem. adv. bd. Rosemont Health Ctr., 1984; sec. D.C. Commn. on Licensure to Practice Healing Art, 1983; bd. dirs. United Black Fund, 1984, Potomac Valley Myastenia Gravis Found., 1984. Global Community Health fellow HEW, 1971, Louise C. Ball fellow, 1969; recipient Meritorious Service award USPHS, 1982, J.B. Johnson Nursing Ctr. award, 1983, Outstanding Service placque D.C. Village Choir, 1984, Disting. Service cert. Concerned Citizens for Alcohol Abuse, 1984, Whitman-Walker award for AIDS effort, 1984, Exceptional Accomplishment award Regional Health Adminstr., 1987. Fellow Am. Assn. Oral and Maxillofacial Surgeons (ho. of dels. 1977-80), Internat. Coll. Dentistry, Royal Soc. Health, Acad. Dentistry Internat., Am. Coll. Dentistry; mem. ADA (cons. council hosp. dental care 1976-77), D.C. Soc. Oral and Maxillofacial Surgeons (sec.-treas. 1979-81), Nat. Dental Assn. (Dentist of Yr. 1983, 1st ann. Disting. Service award 1984), Omicron Kappa Upsilon, Chi Delta Mu, Sigma Pi Phi. Home: 88 W Schiller St Apt 1204 Chicago IL 60610-2037

HARDAWAY, TIMOTHY DUANE, basketball player; b. Chgo., Sept. 1, 1966. Grad., U. Tex. at El Paso, 1989. With Golden State Warriors, 1989-95, Miami Heat, 1995—. Named to NBA All-Rookie team, 1990, All-Star team, 1991, 92, 93. Office: Miami Heat SunTrust Int'l Ctr One SE 3rd Ave Ste 2300 Miami FL 33131

HARDEE, LEWIS JEFFERSON, JR., theater educator; b. Wilmington, N.C., Jan. 17, 1937; s. Lewis Jefferson and Dorothy (Dosher) H. BA, U. N.C., 1959, MA, 1971. Instr. Am. Acad. Dramatic Arts, N.Y.C., 1970-84; asst. prof. Wagner Coll., S.I., N.Y., 1984-89, assoc. prof., 1989-95, prof., 1995-2000; prof. emeritus Wagner Coll., S.I., 2000, S.I., N.Y., 2000—; head theatre dept., prodr. Wagner Coll., S.I., 1995-99; music dir., composer in residence Penny Bridge Players, Bklyn., 1981-84, music dir. Wagner Coll. Theatre, S.I., 1984-94. Author: A Brief History of the Lambs, 1997; composer Revolution!; composer, author, lyricist The Prince and the Pauper, 1978, revised, 1992, Treasure Island, 1979, Christopher Columbus, 1981, 92, Christopher Columbus His Story, 1991, Hansel and Gretel, 1981, Nothing to Hide, 1983, Robin Hood, Build Me A Bridge, 1983, Goldilocks, 1983, Sweet Land of Liberty, 1986, The Little Prince, 1987, Three Southern Families, A History, 1994; editor, The Lambs Script, 1997; co-author: Nothing to Hide, 1983; editor: The Lambs, 1997. Bd. dirs. The Lambs, N.Y.C., 1987—, historian, 1996—, corr. sec., 1998—; bd. dirs. Inter-Cities Performing Arts, Inc., Union City, N.J., 1988-89, Brunswick Performing Arts Ctr., Inc., Southport, N.C., 1989-94. With U.S. Army, 1960-62. Grantee Meet the Composer, Inc., 1982, N.C. Coun. for Arts, 1976; recipient Award of Merit Eleanor Gay Lee Gallery Found., 1983; Parade Grand Marshall, N.C. Fourth of July Festival, 1998. Mem. ASCAP, Dramatists Guild, Assoc. Artists Southport (hon. life), Omicron Delta Kappa. Avocation: history. Home: 320 E 57th St New York NY 10022-2948 Office: Wagner Coll Grymes Hill Staten Island NY 10301

HARDEN, ANITA JOYCE, nurse; b. Jackson, Tenn., May 17, 1947; d. Percy Lawrence and Marjorie (Robinson) H.; 1 child, Brian Robinson Weir. BSN, Ind. U., 1968, MBA, 1989; MSN, Ind. U.-Purdue U., Indpls., 1973. Staff nurse Indpls. Hosps., 1968-71; instr. Ind. U. Sch. Nursing, 1973-75; dir. continuing care Gallahue Mental Health Ctr., Indpls., 1975-80; mgr. psychiatry Cmty. Hosp., Indpls., 1980-87, product line mgr. for psychiat. and mental health svcs., 1986—; dir. psychiat. svcs. Cmty. Hosp. North, 1987-89, v.p., 1990-94; exec. dir. mental health svcs. Cmty. Hosps. of Ind., Inc., 1989-90; exec. dir. mental health St. Vincent-Cmty. Health Network, 1994-96; exec. dir. behavioral care svcs. Cmty. Hosps. Indpls., 1996—; clin. asst. prof. Ind. U., 1977-82, clin. assoc. prof., 1982—; clin. assoc., trainer Suicide Prevention Svc., Indpls., 1974-77; chmn. adv. bd. de-institutionalization project Cen. State Hosp., Indpls., 1978-79. Contbr. articles to profl. jours. Mem. Ind. County Cmty. Mental Health Ctr., 1979-80; bd. dirs. Marion County Mental Health Assn., Indpls. Zoo; bd. dirs. Alternatives in Madison County, Jackson-Peoples Living Ctr. Recipient Outstanding Achievement in Professions award Ctr. Leadership Devel., 1981, Clin. Excellence award Ind. U. Sch. Nursing, 1989. Mem. Ind. U. Alumni Assn., Christian Women's Fellowship, 500 Festival Assocs., Greater Indpls. Orgn. Nurse Execs. (v.p.), Coalition 100 Black Women (bd. dirs.), Neal-Marshall Aumni Club, Alpha Kappa Alpha, Sigma Theta Tau, Chi Eta Phi. Mem. Christian Ch. (Disciples of Christ). Home: 7607 Newport Bay Dr Indianapolis IN 46240-3370 Office: 7150 Clearvista Dr Indianapolis IN 46256-1695

HARDEN, PATRICIA KEEGAN, financial aid officer; b. Rye, N.Y., May 18, 1937; d. Vincent L. and Eleanor C. Keegan; m. David O. Harden, Apr. 15, 1978. BS, Simmons Coll., 1958. Dir. fin. aid Simmons Coll., Boston, 1970-78; asst. mgr. Capt.'s Quars. Inn, Saba, Netherlands Antilles, 1977-81; dir. fin. aid Endicott Coll., Beverly, Mass., 1981-84, Emmanuel Coll., Boston, 1984-96; fin. aid coord. Urban Coll. Boston, 1997—; cons. Mass. Higher Edn. Assistance Group, Newton, 1998—, Butera Sch. Art, Boston, 1999—. Vol. asst. Beacon Hill Civic Assn., Boston, 1992-94. Mem. Mass. Assn. Student Fin. Aid (pres. 1992-95). Office: Urban Coll Boston 178 Tremont St Boston MA 02111-1006

HARDENBERG, ALEXANDER JOHAN, entrepreneur; b. Hengelo, The Netherlands, Dec. 28, 1969; s. Hans and Nel Hardenberg. BBA, Europkan U., The Netherlands, 1996, MBA, 2000. Former CEO, fin. specialist premium wholesaler, Rotterdam, The Netherlands; entrepreneur Hardenberg Group, The Netherlands, 1996—. Avocations: tennis, squash, skiing, kickboxing. E-mail: Ajh.group@inter.nl.net. Office: Hardenberg Beheer BV, Calandstraat 85, 3125 BA Schiedam The Netherlands

HARDICSAY, GABOR, physician; b. Budapest, Hungary, Nov. 10, 1947; s. Gabor and Maria (Kajtar) H.; m. Ilona Magyar, Apr. 6, 1974; children: H. Eva, H. Zsofia. MD, Semmelweis Med. U., Budapest, Hungary, 1972. Re-

sident County Hosp., Zalaegerszeg, Hungary, 1972-73; resident Merenyi Gen. Hosp., Budapest, Hungary, 1974-77, asst., 1978-80; chief med. officer Civil Aviation Authority, Budapest, Hungary, 1980—; cons. in field. Contbr. articles to profl. jours. Fellow Aerospace Med. Assn.; mem. Internat. Acad. Aviation Space Medicine (selector 1999), Austrian Flight Acad. (hon.). Avocations: music, cooking, collecting woodcut/copperplate. Home: Eszek u 9-11 IV.01, H-1114 Budapest Hungary Office: Civil Aviation Authority, Ferihegy Airport PO Box 41, H-1675 Budapest Hungary

HARDIE, ALAN, food products company executive; b. Edinburgh, Scotland, Nov. 10, 1950; s. Frederick and Catherine (Mavor) H.; m. Morvern Cameron Mackay, June 30, 1973; children: Stuart, Caroline. BSc, Edinburgh U., 1972. Mng. dir. Standard Brands, Tunis, Tunisia, 1976-79; dir. mfg. Nabisco Brands, Toronto, 1979-84; mng. dir. Nabisco La Favorita, Caracas, Venezuela, 1984-90; v.p. R.J. Reynolds Internat., Geneva, 1990-92; pres. Nabisco Mexico, Mexico City, 1992-94; chmn., prin. shareholder Paterson Arran Ltd., Livingston, Scotland, 1994—; dir. Career Devel. Edinburgh and Lothian Ltd., 1995—. Avocations: golf, hiking, travel. Office: Paterson Arran Ltd, The Royal Burgh Bakery, EH54 5DN Livingston Scotland

HARDIE, DAVID GRAHAME, biochemist, educator; b. Liverpool, Eng., Apr. 25, 1950; s. Grahame McLean and Bertha Tyson (Kinnish) H.; m. Linda Margaret Walton, May 7, 1977; children: Stuart, Duncan, Calum, Iain. BA, Cambridge (Eng.) U., 1971, MA, 1974; PhD, Heriot-Watt U., Scotland, 1974. Rsch. asst. Portsmouth (Eng.) Poly., 1974-75; from rsch. asst. to reader biochemistry Dundee (Scotland) U., 1975-90, prof., 1994—; cons. Oncogene Sci., N.Y., 1991-92; grant com. Sci. and Enging. Rsch. Coun., 1993-94; pers. chmn. cellular signalling Dundee U., 1994. Author: Biochemical Messengers, 1991; editor: Protein Phosphorylation, 1993, 2d edit., 1999; co-editor: Multidomain Proteins-Structure and Evolution, 1986, The Protein Kinase Facts Book, 1995; mem. editl. bd. European Jour. Biochemistry, 1987-92, Biochem. Jour., 1989-96. Recipient numerous grants for rsch., 1977—. Fellow Royal Soc. Edinburgh; mem. Biochem. Soc. (editl. bd. 1989—), Brit. Diabetic Assn. Avocations: walking, sailing. Office: Dundee Univ, Dundee U, Sch Life Scis, DD1 5EH Dundee Scotland

HARDIE, GEORGE GRAHAM, casino executive; b. Cleve., Aug. 19, 1933; s. William M. and Helen (Graham) H.; children: George Graham Jr., Jennifer. With sales dept. Hardie Bros., Pitts., later various mgmt. positions, operator dist. sales agys.; owner, driver, trainer, racer standardbred horses, 1963—; owner, mgr. Profile, Inc., Las Vegas, 1973—; founder, mng. ptnr. Bell Gardens Bicycle Club Casino, 1984-94; mayor City of Cathedral City, Calif., 1988-90, mayor pro tem, 1990-92; owner, mgr. Profile Comm. Inc., 1990—, Hardie's Korn Kettle Inc., 1990—; owner, mgr. investment and acquisitions co. Lodestar Internat. Inc. (formerly The Hardie Group), 1990—; owner Emerald Meadows Ranch, 1989—. Active cmty. and civic affairs. Recipient Congl. award, 1987; commendation L.A. County Suprs., 1987, L.A. County Office Dist. Atty., 1987; resolution Calif. Senate, 1987, cert. of recognition City of Bell Gardens, 1987; named Man of Yr. Variety Boys & Girls Club of the Desert, 1996. Mem. Calif. Harness Drivers Guild (past pres.), Western Standardbred Assn. (past bd. dirs.), Golden State Greyhound Assn. (organizer, pres. 1973), Bell Gardens C. of C. (pres. 1986). Office: Hardie Group Inc Lodestar Internat Inc 1350 E Flamingo Rd # 347 Las Vegas NV 89119

HARDIE, JAMES CARL, college administrator, consultant; b. Pitts., June 10, 1922; s. Stanley Frank and Helen Katherine (Wassel) H.; m. Emma Kathryn Cepko, Jan. 28, 1956; children: James Matthew, Lynn Anne. BA, U. Pitts., 1943, ML, 1948. Counselor U. Pitts., 1946; dir. housing, head men's dormitories Carnegie Inst. Tech., Pitts., 1946-47; dir. athletic publicity U. Pitts., 1947-48; dir. campaign Ketchum, Inc., Pitts., 1948-57; dir. devel., v.p. Case Inst. Tech., Cleve., 1957-67; v.p. Case We. Res. U., Cleve., 1967-69; cons. to more than 60 non-profit instns. Cleve., 1969—. Chmn. bd. Jennings Found. Yardstick Project, 1968-81; founder Corp. 1% Program for Higher Edn., 1961-69; trustee George S. Dively Found., 1985-97. Lt. U.S. Army, 1943-45. Decorated Purple Heart; recipient Disting. Svc. award Ohio Coun. Fund-Raising Execs., 1988, Citation Coun. Fin. Aid to Edn., 1979; named Outstanding Profl. Nat. Soc. Fund-Raising Profls., 1991. Mem. Union Club Cleve., Grand Harbor Country Club (Fla.), Grenelefe Country Club (Fla.), Omicron Delta Kappa, Delta Sigma Rho. Republican. Avocations: golf, reading, gardening, piano, writing. Home and Office: 245 Springdale Ln Moreland Hls OH 44022-1343 also: 1508 Ocean Dr Apt 103 Vero Beach FL 32963-5346

HARDIE, KIM RACHAEL, microbiologist, researcher; b. London, June 28, 1965; d. Jeremy Michael and Margaret Isobel (Drinkwater) H.; m. William Reid, May 1, 1999. BSc in Biol. Scis. with honors, Leicester (Eng.) U., 1987; PhD in Biol. Scis., Cambridge (Eng.) U., 1990. Cert. molecular biologist. Post-doctoral rschr. U. Nottingham, Eng., 1991-92, U. Victoria, B.C., Can., 1992-94; post-doctoral fellow Inst. Pasteur, Paris, 1994-96; post-doctoral fellow Nottingham U., 1996-98, lectr., rsch. fellow, 1998—. Editor: Methods in Microbiology: Bacterial Pathogens, 1998; contbr. articles to profl. jours., including Molecular Microbiology, EMBO Jour. Fellow EMBO, Paris, 1995, BSAC, Nottingham, 1998. Mem. SGM, ASM, Biochem. Soc. Avocations: cats, hiking, embroidery. Office: Nottingham U, University Park, Nottingham NG9 2RD, England

HARDIE BOYS, SIR MICHAEL, New Zealand governor-general; b. Wellington, New Zealand, Oct. 6, 1931; s. Reginald and Edith May (Bennett) H. B.; m. Edith Mary Zohrab, 1957; 4 children. Student, Wellington Coll., 1944-48, Victoria U. Coll., 1949-54; LLD (hon.), Victoria U. Wellington, 1997. Pvt. practice barrister, solicitor, 1954-80; councillor, pres. Wellington Dist. Law Soc., 1974-79; judge High Ct., 1980-89; mem. Ct. of Appeal, 1989-95; gov.-gen. New Zealand and C-in-C of New Zealand, 1995—. Hon. fellow Wolfson Coll., Cambridge; Knight Grand Cross of Most Disting. Order of St. Michael and St. George, 1995, Knight Grand Companion of New Zealand Order of Merit, 1996. Mem. Gray's Inn (hon. bencher). Avocation: outdoors. Office: Government House, Private Bag, Wellington New Zealand Office: Govt House, Pvt Bag, Wellington New Zealand

HARDIN, ANN, marriage and family therapist; b. Findlay, Ohio, Aug. 2, 1947; d. Richard Clair and Ethelyn Lois (Miller) Webber; m. John Westley Hardin, Dec. 6, 1969; children: David Jason, Christopher John. AA in Mgmt./Supervision, L.A. Met. Coll., Guam, 1981; BSW, U. Mo., 1984, MSW, 1985. Cert. clin. social worker; lic. master social worker, Ariz., individual, marriage and family therapist, Guam. Bookkeeper, cashier Pub. Fin. Corp., Findlay, Ohio, 1965-66; office mgr. Grange Mut. Casualty Co., Findlay, 1967-68; exec. br. fed. govt., Washington, 1969; office mgr. Animals Hosps., Inc., Vallejo, Calif., 1970-73; dir. Option, Inc./Project Concern Internat., San Diego, Calif., 1975-78; counselor Navy Family Svc. Ctr., Guam, 1985-92; family therapist client svcs. and family counseling divsn. Superior Ct. Guam, 1992—; faculty U. Guam/Sch. of S.W., 1990-91, 96-97, 98-99; mem. Gov.'s Task Force on Child Sexual Abuse, 1986-90, Gov.'s Task Force on Suicide, Guam, 1990, Gov.'s Task Force on Domestic Violence, 1993—; presenter confs. in field, including Joint World Congress of Internat. Fedn. Social Workers and Internat. Assn. Schs. of Social Work, 1996. Adult leader Young Christian Life, Guam, 1985-91; team presentor Cath. Engaged Encounter, Guam and Mo., 1982-92; founder Sexually Assaulted Female Enrichment Group, Multiagy. Sexual Abuse Treatment Group, Women Survivors of Ptnr. Abuse Group, Sexually Assaulted Female Edn. and Recovery Group. Named Outstanding Grad. Student, Sch. of Social Work, Columbia, Mo., 1985. Mem. NASW (clin. social worker), Guam Assn. of Social Workers (Social Worker of Yr. 1991, v.p. 1993-94, conf. chairperson 1994, 98), Guam Assn. Marriage and Family Therapists (v.p. 1990-91), Acad. Cert. Social Workers, Am. Counseling Assn., Assn. for Specialists in Group Work, Am. Assn. Christian Counselors, Mizzow Alumni Assn. Roman Catholic. Home: PO Box 4324 Agana GU 96932-8324

HARDIN, GARRETT, biology educator; b. Dallas, Apr. 21, 1915; s. Hugh and Agnes (Garrett) H.; m. Jane Swanson, Sept. 7, 1941; children: Hyla, Peter, Sharon, David. ScB, U. Chgo., 1936; PhD, Stanford U., 1941. Staff mem. Carnegie Instn., Washington and Palo Alto, Calif., 1942-46; prof. biology U. Calif., Santa Barbara, 1946-78, emeritus, 1978—. Author: Biology: Its Principles and Implications, 1949, 2d edit., 1966, Biology: Its Human Implications, 1949, Nature and Man's Fate, 1959, Population, Evolution and Birth Control, 1964, Birth control, 1970, Exploring New Ethics for Survival, 1972, Stalking the Wild Taboo, 1973, Mandatory Motherhood, 1974, Managing the Commons, 1977, The Limits of Altruism, 1977, Promethean Ethics, 1980, Naked Emperors, 1982, Filters against Folly, 1985, Living Within Limits, 1993, The Ostrich Factor, 1998; (classic essay) The Tragedy of the Commons, 1968. Office: U Calif Dept Biol Sci Santa Barbara CA 93106

HARDIN, HAL D., lawyer, former United States attorney, former judge; b. Davidson County, Tenn., June 29, 1941. BA, Middle Tenn. State U., 1966; JD, Vanderbilt U., 1968; postgrad., State Jud. Coll., Reno, 1976. Bar: Tenn. 1969, D.C. 1983, Tex. 1990, U.S. Ct. Claims, 1983, U.S. Tax Ct., 1983, U.S. Ct. Mil. Appeals, 1983, U.S. Supreme Ct., 1973. Fingerprint technician FBI, 1961; dir. St. Louis Job Corps Ctr., 1968; asst. dist. atty. Nashville, 1969-71; pvt. practice, 1971-75; presiding judge Nashville Trial Cts., 1976-77; judge Spl. Ct. of Appeals, 1977; U.S. atty. Middle Dist. Tenn., 1977-81; practice law Nashville, 1981—; instr. govt. Aquinas Coll., Tenn. State Coll., 1975-76; adj. instr. fed. sentencing, criminal practice and procedure Nashville Sch. Law, 1994-2000. Bd. dirs. Leadership Nashville, 1983, Capital Case Resource Ctr., 1988-95, Nat. Assn. Former U.S. Attys., 1993-96; vol. Peace Corps, Colombia, S.Am., 1963-65. Named one of Best Lawyers in Am., 1993-2000. Fellow Tenn. Bar Found.; mem. Nashville Bar Assn. (bd. dirs. 1983-85, v.p. 1985), Ky. Bar Assn., Tenn. Bar Assn. (gen. counsel 1982-90), D.C. Bar, Tex. Bar Assn., Tenn. Criminal Def. Attys., Am. Bd. Trial Advs. (sec. Tenn. chpt. 1987, nat. bd. dirs. 1988-89, pres. Tenn. chpt. 1990), Inns of Ct. (master), 6th Cir. Jud. Coun. (life mem.). Office: 218 3d Ave N Nashville TN 37201

HARDIN, PAUL, III, law educator; b. Charlotte, N.C., June 11, 1931; s. Paul and Dorothy (Reel) H.; m. Barbara Russell, June 8, 1954; children: Paul Russell, Sandra Mikush, Dorothy Holmes. AB, Duke U., 1952, JD, 1954; LHD (hon.), Clemson U., 1970; LLD (hon.), Coker Coll., 1972; LittD (hon.), Nebr. Wesleyan U., 1978; LLD (hon.), Adrian Coll., 1987, Monmouth Coll., 1988; HHD (hon.), Wofford Coll., 1989; LLD (hon.), Rider Coll., 1990; LHD (hon.), Duke U., 1994. Bar: Ala. 1954. Practiced in Birmingham, 1954, 56-58; asst. prof. Duke Law Sch., 1958-61, assoc. prof., 1961-63, prof., 1963-68, univ. trustee, 1969-74, 1995—; pres. Wofford Coll., Spartanburg, S.C., 1968-72, So. Methodist U., Dallas, 1972-74, Drew U., Madison, N.J., 1975-88; chancellor U. N.C., Chapel Hill, 1988-95, chancellor emeritus, prof. law, 1995—; interim pres. U. Ala., Birmingham, 1997; vis. prof. U. Tex., summer 1960, U. Pa., 1962-63, U. Va., 1974; dir. Smith Barney mut. funds, Italy Fund, Inc. Author: (with Sullivan, others) The Administration of Criminal Justice, 1966, (with Sullivan) Evidence, Cases and Materials, 1968; contbr. articles to profl. jours. law revs. Chmn. Human Relations Com., Durham, N.C., 1961-62; mem. gen. conf. United Meth. Ch., 1968, 76, 80, 84; pres. Nat. Assn. Schs. and Colls. of United Meth. Ch., 1984; chmn. Nat. Commn. on United Meth. Higher Edn., 1975-77. Served with CIC, AUS, 1954-56. Mem. Carnegie Found. for Advancement Teaching (bd. dirs. 1990-98), Order of Coif, Phi Beta Kappa.

HARDING, ANN MARGARET, economics educator; b. London, May 18, 1958; arrived in Australia, 1970; d. Arthur Phillip and Margaret Mary (Kirby) H.; m. John Sekoranja, July 1, 1995; children: James, Jack. B of Econs. with honors, Sydney (Australia) U., 1983; PhD, London Sch. Econs., 1990. With Depts. Social Security, Health and Family Svcs. and Treas., 1981-92; prof. applied econs. and social policy, inaugural dir. Nat. Ctr. for Social and Econ. Modelling, U. Canberra, Australia, 1993—; various sr. rsch. and policy analyst positions, Australia. Author: (book) Lifetime Income Distribution and Redistribution, 1993; editor: (book) Microsimulation and Public Policy, 1996; author numerous articles and book chpts. U.K. Commonwealth PhD scholar Brit. Coun., 1987-90, scholar Sydney U., 1977-79, , 83. Fellow Acad. Social Scis. in Australia; mem. Internat. Assn. Rsch. on Income and Wealth, Econs. Soc. Australia, Australian Assn. for Social Rsch. Office: U Canberra, Belconnen ACT 2601, Australia also: 170 Haydon Dr, Bruce ACT 2617, Australia

HARDING, JOHN EDMOND, engineering educator, academic administrator; b. Sutton, Surrey, Eng., Nov. 22, 1948; s. William Gordon and Alice Eleanor (Burke) H.; m. Patricia Anne Wigfull, Jan. 7, 1978; children: Emma Philippa, Laura Anne. BSc in Civil Enging., Imperial Coll., London, 1970, MSc, diploma, 1971, PhD, 1975. Lectr. structural enging. Imperial Coll., 1978-85, prof., 1985—; pro vice chancellor U. Surrey, Guildford, Eng., 1991—, head dept. civil enging., 1997—; mem. U.S. Structural Stability Rsch. Coun., 1988—; mem. working group European Conv. for Constructional Steelwork, 1982—. Editor: Bridge Management, 3 vols., 1990, 93, 96; (design manual) Constructional Steel Design—An International Guide, 1992; editor Internat. Jour. Constructional Steel Rsch., 1980—; hon. editor Structures and Bldgs. Procs. of Instn. Civil Engrs., 1991-96; contbr. numerous articles to profl. jours., papers to profl. confs. Mem. governing bd. Tormead Sch., Guildford, Surrey, 1994—, Reigate (Surrey) Coll., 1995—, St. Mary's Univ. Coll., Strawberry Hill, Twickenham, Middlesex, Eng., 1996—. Fellow Instn. Structural Engrs. (cert.), Instn. Civil. Engrs. Office: Univ Surrey, Dept Civil Enging, Surrey Guildford GU2 5XH, England

HARDING, MARIE, ecological executive, artist; b. Glen Cove, N.Y., Nov. 13, 1941; d. Charles Lewis and Marie (Parish) H.; m. John P. Allen, Jan. 29, 1965 (div. Oct., 1991); 1 child, Eden A. Harding. BA, Sarah Lawrence Coll., 1964; postgrad., Arts Students League, N.Y.C., 1965. Founder Synergia Ranch Ctr. for Wellness, Innovation, Retreats and Confs., Santa Fe, 1969; founding mem., actress Theater of All Possibilities, Santa Fe, 1971-86; founding mem., dir. Inst. Ecotechnics, Santa Fe, also London, 1974—; bd. dirs. Synopco Corp., N. Mex., 1974-81; bd. dirs., founding mem. Savannah Systems Pty., Ltd., Kimberly region, Australia, 1976—, Outback Sta. Pty. Ltd., Kimberly region, Australia, 1976-94; chair, dir. EcoWorld, Inc., Santa Fe, 1982-94; dir., founding mem., CFO Space Biospheres Ventures, Biosphere 2, Ariz., 1984-94; chair, CEO Oceans Expdns., Inc., 1986-92; pres. ecol. and biosphere R&D/implementation project Global Ecotechnics Corp., Santa Fe, 1994—; pres. Decisions Team, Inc. Ecol. Project Mgmt., Ariz., 1994—, Syneco LLC at Synergia Ranch, retreats and confs., Santa Fe; particpant in constrn. and fin. Capt. R. Heraclitus rsch. vessel, Oakland, Calif., 1974; bd. dirs. Hotel Vajra, Kathamdu, Nepal, 1976-94, Caravan of Dreams Performing Arts Ctr., Ft. Worth, 1983-94, Synergetic Press, London and Ariz., 1984—. Artist: paintings shown in exhibitions San Francisco, London, Ft. Worth, Santa Fe, Biosphere 2, Ariz., 1979-93, Biosphere 2 Paintings Exhbn., London, 1996; project dir., artist mural project History of Jazz, Dance, Theater, Ft. Worth, 1982-83; producer, dir. (films) Bryon Gysin Loves ya, Project Charlie, The Search, Synergia History, Planet Earth Conf. Vol. Swallows, Madras, India, 1964, Project Concern, Vietnam, Hong Kong, 1964-65; artist, founder, trustee October Gallery Trust, internat. artists forum, London, 1979; mem. Planetary Coral Reef Found., Inc., 1993—. Mem. Friends of Tibet. Avocations: ecological project implementation, endangered lifestyles/cultures, painting, landscape gardening, retreat faciliatation, martial arts. Home and Office: Synergia Ranch 26 Synergia Rd Santa Fe NM 87501-0052

HARDING, RAY MURRAY, JR., judge; b. Logan, Utah, Nov. 23, 1953; s. Ray M. Sr. and Martha (Rasmussen) H.; children: Michelle, Nicole, Justin. BS, Brigham Young U., 1975; JD, J. Reuben Clark Law Sch., 1978. Bar: Utah 1978. Ptnr. Harding & Harding, American Fork and Pleasant Grove, Utah, 1978-85; owner Harding & Assoc., American Fork and Pleasant Grove, 1986-95; judge Utah County 4th Jud. Dist. Ct., 1995—; atty. Lindon City and Pleasant Grove City, Utah, 1983-95, Alpine City, 1985-94, American Fork, Utah, 1985-95. Bd. trustees Utah Valley State Coll., 1986-95, chmn., 1991-93. Named Businessman of Yr., Future Bus. Leaders of Am., 1983. Mem. ABA, ATLA, Utah State Bar Assn., Utah Trial Lawyers Assn., Utah County Bar Assn. Avocations: skiing, scuba diving, hiking, hunting, travel. Home: 11165 Yarrow Cir Highland UT 84003-9598 Office: Utah County 4th Judicial Dist Ct 125 N 100 W Provo UT 84601-2849

HARDING, WAYNE EDWARD, III, software company executive, accountant; b. Topeka, Sept. 29, 1954; s. Wayne Edward and Nancy M. (Gean) H.; m. Janet Mary O'Shaughnessy, Sept. 5, 1979 (div. Mar. 1985); m. Karen Ruttan, Oct. 10, 1987. BS with honors in Bus. Adminstrn., U. Denver, 1976, MBA, 1983. Ptnr. HKG Assocs., Denver, 1976-77; staff auditor Peat, Marwick, mitchell & Co., Denver, 1976-78; auditor Marshall Hornstein, P.C., Wheat Ridge, Colo., 1978-79; sr. auditor Touche Ross & Co., Denver, 1979-80; controller Mortgage Plus Inc., 1980-81; sec.-treas. Sunlight Systems Energy Corp., 1980-81; ptnr. Harding, Newman, Sobule & Thrush, Ltd., Denver, 1981-82; pvt. practice specializing in microcpmputer applications Harding, Newman, Sobule & Thrush, Ltd., 1982-89; acct., v.p. Great Plains Software, Fargo, N.C.; also dir., CPA ptnr. rels.; founder Discount Computer Rentals, Inc., 1985; dir. Harding Transp., Harding Tech. Leasing, Crown Parking Products; co-founder Glass Group, Inc., SysTrust Svcs., Inc. (chmn.); lectr. to various profl. groups on computer tech. Mem. editl. bd. Practical Acct., Mag., 1995-98; contbr. articles to profl. jours. Class agt., mem. alumni coun. Phillips Exeter Acad., Exeter, N.H., 1973-83, class agt., 1993-98; bd. dirs., treas. legal Ctr. Handicapped Citizens, Denver, 1979-80; vol. Denver Bridge, 1984-85. Mem. AICPA (instr., mem. tech. rsch. com. 1994-97, high tech. task force 1998, mem. info. tech. exec. com. 1998-99, mem. e-bus. task force 1999—, spl. recognition award 2000), Colo. Soc. CPAs (chmn. CPE com. 1987-89, instr., bd. dirs. 1994-97, v.p. 1996-97, pres.-elect 2000, exec. v.p. 2000—), Beta Alpha Psi, Pi Gamma Mu, Beta Gamma Sigma. Libertarian. Home and Office: 5206 S Hanover Way Englewood CO 80111-6240

HARDJO, ELIEZER HERNAWAN, business and educational consultant; b. Kuningan, Indonesia, Apr. 17, 1949; m. Eny Setiowati; 3 children. MBA, European U., Belgium, 1987; PhD in Bus. Adminstrn., Kennedy Western U., Boise, 1994, JD in Bus. Law, 1994; PhD in Mgmt., Pacific Western U., Hawaii, 1994, U. Berkley, Mich.; EdD, St. George U., U.K., 1999. Cert. mgr. Inst. Cert. Profl. Mgrs.; cert. profl. cons. Fin. and adminstrn. mgr. P.T. Eurindo Combined, Rhone Poulenc, France, 1971-74; dep. gen. mgr., Max Factor divsn. mgr. P.T. Timur Laut, 1974-80; gen. mgr. P.T. Farteco Indonesia/The Lactose Co., New Zealand, 1981-83; mng. dir. P.T. Seta Sari Farma/Alcapharm, The Netherlands, 1983-88; gen. sales dir. P.T. Dua Berlian/S.C. Johnson & Son, 1988-90; gen. mgr. Salim Group, Jakarta, 1990-2000, Heavenspring Consulting Co., Jakarta, 2000—; internat. faculty mem. Kennedy Western U., Boise, Idaho. Mem. Internat. Christian C. of C. (nat. pres. Indonesia chpt. 1998). Office: Jal Pegangsaan Indah Barat, BI/8 Pondok Gading Utama, Jakarta 14240, Indonesia

HARDMAN, GEORGE LYNN, psychiatrist; b. Phila., May 11, 1941; s. George A. Jr. and Hazel E. H. BA cum laude, Harvard Coll., 1962, MD, 1966. Diplomate in psychiatry and forensic psychiatry Am. Bd. Psychiatry and Neurology. Co-dir. delinquency sect. Judge Baker Guidance Ctr., Boston, 1973-83; dir. diagnostic project McLean Hosp., Belmont, Mass., 1983-90; psychiatrist Brockton (Mass.) Multi-Svc. Ctr., 1990—. Contbr. articles to profl. jours. Avocations: photography, travel, early music. E-mail: GLHARDMAN@aol.com. Home: PO Box 1019 123 Nason Hill Rd Sherborn MA 01770-1233

HARDMEIER, CHRISTOF FELIX, religious studies educator; b. Zurich, Switzerland, Nov. 2, 1942; s. Ernst Heinrich and Hanna Henriette (Mueller) H.; m. Ursula Johanna Elisabeth Paschke, Mar. 23, 1968; children: Martin-Ernst, Ruth-Anna. Theol. degree, U. Zurich, 1968; PhD in Theology, U. Heidelberg, Germany, 1975; postdoctoral lecturing qualification, Church Coll. Bethel, Bielefeld, Germany, 1988. Cert. prof. Old Testament studies. Asst. for Old Testament studies U. Heidelberg, 1972-77; lectr. Old Hebrew lang. Church Coll. Bethel, Bielefeld, 1977-93; prof. Old Testament studies U. Greifswald, Germany, 1993—. Avocations: photography, mountaineering, jazz, classical music. Fax: 0049 3834 580620. Office: U Greifswald Faculty Theol, Rubenowplatz, D-17487 Greifswald Germany

HARDNER, CRAIG MARTIN, tree geneticist; b. Melbourne, Vic., Australia, Nov. 4, 1962; s. Robert Fredrick and Nancy Helen (McKinnon) H.; m. Ylva Katarina Bohm; children: Aili, Tove. BSc, U. Melbourne, 1986; BSc with honors, U. Tasmania, 1993, PhD, 1997. Plant physiologist CELBI, Portugal, 1987; quantiative geneticist Swedish Agrl. U., Uppsala, Sweden, 1988-90; rsch. scientist Victorian Dept. Conservation and Environ., Australia, 1990; vis. scientist U. Wis., Madison, 1990; tree geneticist CSIRO, Brisbane, Australia, 1996—; welfare officer U. of Tasmania Student Union, Hobart, 1995; head of students Peninsula Sch., Mteliza, Australia, 1981. Author: (with others) Forest Conservation Genetics, 1997. Mem. Soc. for the Study of Evolution. Avocations: sailing, skiing, music, politics, bagpipes. Home: 94 Park Rd, Yeronga 4104, Australia Office: CSIRO Divsn Plant Industry, Saint Lucia 4067, Australia

HARDWICH, GERALD CARLTON, marketing research executive; b. Syracuse, N.Y., Sept. 4, 1943; s. Carlton Stuart and Harriette Mae (Wiltsie) H.; m. Diane Melanie Pearce, Aug. 20, 1966; children: Elizabeth Ann, James Matthew. BS, U. Md., 1967; MBA, U. Cin., 1968. Distbn. analyst Shell Chem. Co., N.Y.C., 1968-69; sr. mktg. planner, product planner, analyst Mattel, Inc., South Plainfield, N.J., 1969-72; dir. mktg. rsch. Mohaasco Corp., Amsterdam, N.Y., 1972-79, Tupperware Home Parties, Orlando, Fla., 1979-93; v.p. Mktg. Directions and Rsch., Longwood, Fla., 1993—; pres. Consumer Mktg. Insights, 1997—. Deacon Montclair (N.J.) Ctrl. Presbyn. Ch., 1970-72; bd. dirs. Fla. Symphony Orch., Orlando, 1980-82; asst. scoutmaster Citrus coun. Boy Scouts Am., 1982—; elder, trustee Wekiva Presbyn. Ch., Longwood, 1983-85. NSF scholar, 1960; Ward J. McDowell scholar, U. Cin. fellow, 1967-68. Mem. Am. Mktg. Assn. (v.p., pres., nat. com.), U. Cin. Alumni Assn. (chpt. pres. 1970-92), Quill and Scroll, Alpha Delta Sigma (pres. chpt. 1966-67). Republican. Office: Mktg Directions & Rsch 6 Old Post Rd Longwood FL 32779-3033

HARDWICK, KEVIN DALE, protective services official; b. Cin., Feb. 16, 1960; s. Clyde U. Jr. and Marian D. (Seichrist) H.; m. Cynthia Susan Sunderman, Oct. 19, 1985; children from previous marriage: Kevin, Andrew, Adam, Patrick. Student, U. Cin., 1978-82. Emergency med. tech., Ohio, Ky.; fire inspector, Ohio, Ky.; paramedic, Ky.; fire investigator, Ohio, Ky. Fire inspector, capt. New Burlington Fire Dept., Cin., 1978-82; fire safety officer, asst. fire inspector Cin./No. Ky. Internat. Airport, 1982—; fire investigator, coord. Boone County (Ky.) Fire Investigation, 1994—; instr. Fire Dept. Instrs. Conf., Indpls., 1995, 96; mem. adv. com. Fire Dept. Safety Officer, Quincy, Mass., 1995—. Author: The Voice, 1994, 95, 96, 97; contbr. articles to profl. jours. Recipient Appreciation award Cin. FBI Agts., 1988, Ferrara Firefighting, 1994. Mem. Masons, Scottish Rite, Shriners. Avocations: softball, motorcycles, travel, fire truck design. Home: 1568 Covered Bridge Rd Cincinnati OH 45231-2425 Office: Cin/No Ky Internat Airport Fire Dept PO Box 752000 Cincinnati OH 45275-2000

HARDWICK, MICHAEL JOHN, lawyer; b. Chester, Eng., Dec. 24, 1958; s. Frank and Audrey (Marchington) H.; m. Moira Margaret Neilson, June 22, 1985; children: Paul Richard, Rosanna Clare, Mark William, Kirsty Anne. MA, Univ. Coll., Oxford, Eng., 1980; LLM, Gonville and Caius Coll., Cambridge, Eng., 1981. Solicitor of Supreme Ct. Asst. solicitor Linklaters & Paines, London, 1984-91, ptnr., 1991—. Co-author: Taxation of Companies and Company Reconstructions, 7th edit., 1998, Tax Advice for Company Transactions, 1992. Sec. circuit property com. West London Mission, London, 1986-88; treas. Flitwick Parochial Ch. Coun., Bedfordshire, Eng., 1989-90. Tapp postgrad. scholar Gonville and Caius Coll., 1981; recipient Alfred Syrett prize City of London Solicitor's Co., 1982. Mem. Law Soc. (internat. tax sub-com. 1991—, revenue law com. 1998—, chmn. corp. tax subcom. 2000—), City of London Law Soc. (mem. rev. law com. 1991—, chair 1998—). Church England. Avocations: cross country skiing, sports, mountain walking. Office: Linklaters & Alliance, One Silk St, London EC2Y 8HQ, England

HARDY, BARBARA GLADYS, English literature educator, critic, writer; b. Swansea, Eng., June 27, 1924; d. Maurice and Gladys Emily (Abraham) Nathan; m. Ernest Dawson Hardy, 1946 (dec.); children: Julia, Kate. BA, U. Coll., London, 1946; MA, U. Coll., 1948; D.Univ. (hon.), Open U., 1980. Lectr. Birkbeck Coll., London, 1950-65, prof., 1970-89; prof. Royal Holloway Coll., London, 1965-70, Birkbeck Coll., 1970-89; prof. emeritus U. of London, 1989—; dir. Yeats Sch., Sligo, Eng., 1991; hon. prof. Univ. Coll., Swansea, 1991—. Author: The Novels of George Eliot, 1959, The Appropriate Form, 1964, The Moral Art of Dickens, 1970, The Exposure of Luxury, 1972, A Feading of Jane Austen, 1975, Tellers and Listeners, 1975, The Advantage of Lyric, 1977, Particularities: Readings in George Eliot, 1982, Forms of Feeling in Victorian Fiction, 1985, Narrators and Novelists, 1987, Swansea Girl, 1994, Henry James, The Later Writing, 1996, London Lovers, 1997, Shakespeare's Storytellers, 1998, 99, Thomas Hardy Imagining

Imagination, 2000, Dylan Thomas An Original Language, 2000; contbr. articles to profl. jours. Fellow Birkbeck Coll., Holloway Coll., U. Wales, Swansea; Brit. Acad. rsch. grantee, 1987. Mem. MLA (hon.), Welsh Acad. (hon.). Mem. Labour Party. Avocations: walking, acting. Office: Birkbeck Coll, Malet St, London WC1, England

HARDY, BEN(SON B.), orchid nursery executive; b. Oakland, Calif., Nov. 22, 1920; s. Lester William and Irene Isabell (Bliss) H. Student pub. schs., Oakland, Calif., Concordia, Calif.; grad. photo. Intelligence Sch., Denver, 1949. Served as enlisted man U.S. Navy, 1942-48; joined USAF, 1948, advanced through grades to capt., 1957; with 67th Reconnaisance Squadron Korea, 1951-52; Hdqrs. Squadron Thule AFB, 1956; resigned, 1957; material requirements analyst-coord. Teledyne Ryan Aero. Co., San Diego, 1958-73, 83-98, ret., 1998; dispatcher-coord. Cubic Western Data Co., San Diego, 1977-80; owner-ptnr. orchid nursery. Pres. Exotic Plant Soc., 1976-78, 81-84, San Diego Gesneriad Soc., 1978; dir. 23d Western Orchid Congress, 1979. Author: (with John Klemme) The Orchid Badge Collector's Guide, 1993. Decorated Bronze Star; recipient Letter of Commendation NASA, also others. Mem. Am. Orchid Soc. (life), N.Z. Orchid Soc., San Diego County Orchid Soc. (life, pres. 1972-73, 75-76), Pacific Orchid Soc. Hawaii, Hoya Soc. Internat. (pres. 1981-83, 95—), Cymbidium Soc. Am., Orchid Digest Corp., Auckland Orchid Club, Orchid Badge Club Internat. (found. 1988, pres. 1991—), VFW (life). Home: 9443 E Heaney Cir Santee CA 92071-2919

HARDY, DAVID MALCOLM, bank executive; b. Westcliff-on-Sea, Essex, England, July 16, 1955; s. Roy and Mary (Ebsworth) H.; m. Maureen Ann Petherick, Aug. 1, 1981 (div. Jan. 1995); children: Matthew James Cranmer, Joanna Louise; m. Marion Dorothy Brazier, July 14, 1995. Various positions Barclays Bank PLC, Eng., 1973-81; mgr. Barclays Merchant Bank, London, 1981-85; seconded to London Clearing Ho., 1985-87, CEO., 1987—; non-exec. dir. Internat. Petroleum Exch., 1993-99, The Futures and Options Assn., 1993—, London Commodity Exch., 1991-96, ICCH Ltd., 1991—. Named Freeman, City of London, 1995. Fellow Assn. Corp. Treasurers; mem. Chartered Inst. Bankers (assoc.). Avocations: golf, photography. Office: The London Clearing Ho, 33 Aldgate High St, London EC3N 1EA, England

HARDY, DAVID WILLIAM, executive; b. Wilmslon, England, July 14, 1930; s. John Herbert and Amy Doris (Bacon) H.; m. Rosemary Stratford Collins, Sept. 11, 1957; children: Sarah Elizabeth, Alexander David. Grad., Wellington Coll., Berkshire, England, 1947. Dir. Funch Edye Co., Inc., 1954-64; v.p. Imperial Tobacco, 1964-70; fin. dir. Taterlyle, England, 1972-77; exec. dir. Ocean Transport, England, 1977-83; chmn. Globe Investment Trust, England, 1983-90, London Docklands Devel. Corp., 1988-92, Bankers Trust Investment Mgmt. Ltd., 1992-94; chmn. trustees Nat. Maritime Mus., 1995—; chmn. Marine Gen. Mut. Life Assurance, 1985-99, Traffic Rsch. Lab., 1996—. Deputy chmn. London Transp., 1984-87; chmn. Docklands Light Railway, 1984-87; pres. Blackwall Poplar Dist. Rowing Club, 1992—; vice chmn. St. Katherine and Shadwell Trust, 1992—. 2d lt. English Mil., 1953-54. Avocations: fly fishing, shooting, rugby, rowing. Office: Nat Maritime Mus, Greenwich, London SW10 9NF, England

HARDY, JACKIE NORMAN, physics educator; b. Danville, May 18, 1946; s. Norman Linwood and Estelle David Hardy; m. Margaret Oakes Hardy, Dec. 16, 1967; children: Kevin Bryan, Keith Anderson. BS in Agrl. Engrng., Va. Polytech. Inst., 1968. Physics tchr., coach Tunstall H.S., Dry Fork, Va., 1968—. Mem. NEA (v.p. local chpt.). Baptist. Avocations: science, volleyball, golf. Home: 2721 Golf Club Rd Danville VA 24540-7783 Office: Turnstall HS 100 Trojan Cir Dry Fork VA 24549-2300

HARDY, JOHN DENIS, paediatrician consultant; b. Kenilworth, Warwickshi, Eng., July 29, 1939; arrived in Abu Dhabi, 1996; s. William Irvine and Elizabeth Douglas Chaundy (Thompson) H.; m. Margaret Mary Byrne, Nov. 28, 1970; children: Timothy Mark, Nicholas John-Denis, Jennifer Ann. M.B.B.S., London U., 1963. House physician and surgeon various hosps., 1963-65; house surgeon in obs. Rochford, Essex and H.P. Paediatrics, London, 1965-66; house physician Acton gen. Hosp., London, 1967; paediatric registrar/med. registrar Princess Alexandra Hosp., Harlow, Essex, 1968-70; paediatric registrar Addenbrookes Hosp., Cambridge, 1970-72; sr. paediatric registrar Royal Free Hosp., London, 1972-74, 75-76; leukaemia rsch. fellow Hosp. for Sick Children, London, 1974-75; cons. paediatrician Harlow, Essex, 1976-90; chief paediatrics King Faisal Mil. Hosp., Khamis Mushay, Saudi Arabia, 1990-91; chief paediat. Armed Forces Hosp., Wadi al Dawasir, Saudi Arabia, 1992-94; chief paediat./cons. paediatrician, hon. clin. assoc. prof. Faculty Medicine and Health Scis., Tawam Hosp., Al Ain, Abu Dhabi, 1996—. Contbr. over 20 articles to profl. jours. Hon. sec. N.E. Thames Regional Paediatric adv. Com.; mem. BPA coun., 1989-90. Recipient Prox Access Roxburgh prize, 1963, Grade C Merit award N.E., Thames Regional Health Authority, 1986. Fellow Royal Coll. Physicians (London and Edinburgh), Royal Coll. Pediat. and Child Health; mem. Brit. Med. Assn. Neonatal Soc., BBS, RCS, Dobst RCOG, DCH. Ch. of Eng. Avocations: writing, running, tennis, squash, chess. Office: Towam Hosp, POB 15258, Al Ain Abu Dhabi United Arab Emirates

HARDY, RALPH W. F., biochemist, biotechnology executive; b. Lindsay, Ont., Can., July 27, 1934; s. Wilbur and Elsie H.; m. Jacqueline M. Thayer, Dec. 26, 1954; children: Steven, Chris, Barbara, Ralph (dec.), Jon. BSA, U. Toronto, 1956; MS, U. Wis.-Madison, 1958, PhD, 1959; DSc (hon.), U. Guelph, 1997. Asst. prof. U. Guelph, Ont., Can., 1960-63; research biochemist DuPont deNemours & Co., Wilmington, Del., 1963-67, research supr., 1967-74, assoc. dir., 1974-79, dir. life scis., 1979-84; pres. Bio Technica Internat., Inc., Peoria, Ill., 1984-86; pres., CEO Boyce Thompson Inst., Inc., Ithaca, N.Y., 1986-95; dep. chmn. Bio Technica Internat., Inc., 1986-90, cons., bd. dirs., 1990-99; pres. Nat. Agrl. Biotech. Coun., Ithaca, N.Y., 1996—; mem. exec. com. bd. agr. NRC, 1982-88, mem. commn. life scis., 1984-90, bd. biology, 1984-90, com. on biotech, 1988-95, chmn. com. 1993-94, bd. sci. technol. internat. devel., 1990-93, chmn. com. on biol. control, 1992-95, chmn. com. on biol. nitrogen fixation, 1992-94, chmn. com. on natural products, 1996-97; mem. com. genetic experimentation Internat. Coun. Sci. Union, 1981-95; chmn., founder Nat. Agrl. Biotech. coun., 1988-93; mem. sci. adv. com. U.S. Dept. Energy, 1991-95; mem. alt. agr. rsch. comml. bd. USDA, 1992-96, mem. and corp. sec. alt. agrl. rsch. comml. corp., 1996-2000; mem. Can. reallocations com. NSERC, 1997-98; mem. Can. Found. for Innovation, 1998-99; bd. dirs. Biocap, Can. Author: Nitrogen Fixation, 1975, A Treatise on Dinitrogen Fixation, 3 vols., 1977-79; contbr. over 150 articles to sci. jours. Mem. biotech. exec. bd. Cornell U., 1986-95, adv. coun. Vet. Coll., 1989-96; mem. gov. bd. Cornell Ctr. for Environment, 1991-95. Recipient Gov. Gen.'s Silver medal, 1956, Sterling Henricks award 1986; WARF fellow, 1956-58; DuPont fellow, 1958-59. Mem. Indsl. Biotech. Assn. (bd. dirs. 1986-89), Agr. Rsch. Inst. (bd. govs. 1988-91), Am. Chem. Soc. (exec. com. biol. chemistry divsn. 1978-81, Del. award 1969), Am. Soc. Biol. Chemists and Molecular Biologists, Am. Soc. Plant Physiology (exec. com., treas. 1974-77), Am. Soc. Agronomy, Am. Soc. Microbiology. Episcopalian.

HARDY, SALLY JANE, association director; b. Wallasea, Wirral, U.K., June 3, 1962; d. Alan Anthony and Margaret Therese (Hyland) Parkinson; m. Michael Graham Hardy, Oct. 6, 1989; children: Oscar Michael, Florence Margaret. Student, Loughborough U., 1980-83. Mem. Inst. of Chartered Secs. and Adminstrs. Scientific officer Econ. and Social Rsch. Coun., London, 1983-84, higher scientific officer, 1984-86; exec. sec. Regional Studies Assn., London, 1986-90, dir., 1990—; Mem. com. Central London YMCA, 1994-96. Editor: (book) An Enlarged Europe: Regions in Competition, 1995, Unemployment and Social Exclusion, 1997; editor social sci./report, London, 1994-97. Fellow Royal Soc. Arts. Avocations: slalom canoeing, badminton, windsurfing. Office: Regional Studies Assn, PO Box 2058, BN25 4QU Seaford United Kingdom

HARDY, WAYNE RUSSELL, insurance and investment broker; b. Denver, Sept. 5, 1931; s. Russell Hinton and Victoria Katherine (Anderson) H.; m. Carolyn Lucille Carvell, Aug. 1, 1958 (July 1977); children: James Russell Hardy, Jann Miller Hardy. BSCE, U. Colo., 1954; MS in Fin. Svcs., Am. Coll., 1989. CLU; chartered fin. cons. Western dist. mgr. Fenestra, Inc., San Francisco, 1956-63; ins. and investment broker John Hancock Fin. Svs., Denver, 1963—, Wayne R. Hardy Assocs., Denver, 1963—; speaker convs. and sales seminars, 1977, 81, 84, 85, 89; v.p. CLU assn. John Hancock, 1979-80, chmn. agt.'s adv. com., 1983-84; active State of Colo. Ins. Adv. Bd., 1991-93; profl. model, actor J.F. Images Agy., Denver, 1964-89. Chmn. Colo. Coun. Camera Clubs, Denver, 1962; bd. dirs. Porter Charitable Found., Denver, 1983-85; deacon, class pres. South Broadway Christian Ch., 1961-65; mem. Denver Art Mus., Denver Botanic Gardens, Rocky Mountain Estate Planning Coun., Mensa, Alliance Francaise. Capt. U.S. Army, 1954-56, Korea, USAR, 1956-80. Mem. Am. Soc. CLU and ChFC (pres. Rocky Mountain chpt. 1990-91), Nat. Assn. Life Underwriters (pres. Denver chpt. 1983-84, Nat. Quality award 1968—, expert witness ins. litigation, Disting. Life Underwriters award 1970-83), Nat. Football Found. (bd. dirs. Denver chpt. 1992—), Screen Actors Guild, Million Dollar Round Table (life), U. Colo. Alumni (bd. dirs. 1990-92), U. Colo. Alumni C Club (bd. dirs. 1972-74), Univ. Club, Greenwood Athletic Club, Village Tennis Club, Rocky Mountain Optimist Club (pres. 1984-85). Republican. Avocations: tennis, photography, foreign languages, art, travel. Home and Office: 6178 E Hinsdale Ct Englewood CO 80112-1534

HARDY, WILLIAM ROBINSON, lawyer; b. Cin., June 14, 1934; s. William B. and Chastine M. (Sprague) H.; m. Leslie Warrington Bailey, Apr. 16, 1999; children from previous marriage: Anita Christina, William Robinson Jr. AB magna cum laude, Princeton U., 1956; JD, Harvard U., 1963. Bar: Ohio 1963, U.S. Supreme Ct. 1975. Life underwriter New Eng. Mut. Life Ins. Co., 1956-63; assoc. Graydon, Head & Ritchey, Cin., 1963-68, ptnr., 1968-98; mem. panel comml. arbitrators Am. Arbitration Assn., 1972—, mem. panel large complex case program, 1993—, panel of mediators, 1993—, comml. arbitrator tng. faculty, 1998—; reporter joint com. for revision of rules of U.S. Dist. Ct. for So. Dist. Ohio, 1975, 80, 83, mem., 1990—. Bd. dirs. Cin. Union Bethel, 1968-82, pres., 1977-82, emeritus, 1982—; bd. dirs. Ohio Valley Goodwill Industries Rehab. Ctr., Cin., 1970—, pres., 1981-92; mem. Cin. Bd. Bldg. Appeals, 1976—, vice chmn., 1983, chmn., 1983—; pres. Hamilton County (Ohio) Alcohol and Drug Addiction Svcs. Bd., 1990-92; trustee Substance Abuse Mgmt. and Devel. Inc., 1998-99. Capt. USAR, 1956-68; maj. gen. Ohio Mil. Res., insp. gen., 1988-89, TJAG, 1989-93, dep. comdr., 1993-96, comdr., 1996—. Recipient award of merit Ohio Legal Ctr. Inst., 1975, 76, Ohio Commendation medal, 1999. Mem. ABA, AAAS, Ohio Bar Assn., Cin. Bar Assn., Ohio Acad. Trial Lawyers, 6th Cir. Jud. Conf. (life), Ohio Soc. Colonial Wars (gov. 1979), Princeton (N.Y.C.) Club, Interlachen Club (Winter Park, Fla.), Phi Beta Kappa. Mem. Ch. of Redeemer. Office: 432 Walnut St Ste 206 Cincinnati OH 45202-3909

HARE, CLARE KEAN, aeronautical and aerospace engineer, consultant; b. N.Y.C., July 10, 1962; s. Peter Hewitt and Daphne Joan Hare. BS in Math., BS in Engring., Harvey Mudd Coll., 1984; MS in Aero. and Astronaut. Engring., Stanford U., 1985. Engr. mission engring. Hughes Aircraft, El Segundo, Calif., 1985-87, engr. sys. test, 1987-88, lead sys. engr., 1988-90; controls engr. Hughes Aircraft, Reston, Va., 1990; mgr. Hughes Aircraft, El Segundo, 1991-95; cons. on software and comm., Manhattan Beach, Calif., 1995-99; payload operation mgr. Astrolink Internat., Manhattan Beach, 1999—. Contbr. articles to Am. Jour. Econs. and Sociology. Mem. AAAS. E-mail: clarksterh@earthlink.net. Home and Office: 740 13th St Apt 23 Manhattan Beach CA 90266-4868

HARE, DAVID, playwright; b. St. Leonards, Sussex, Eng., June 5, 1947; s. Clifford Theodore and Agnes (Gilmour) H.; m. Margaret Matheson, Aug. 1970 (div. 1980); children: Joe, Lewis, Darcy; m. Nicole Farhi, 1992. MA, Cambridge U., 1968. Founder Portable Theatre, 1968, Joint Stock Theatre Group, 1974, Greenpoint Films, 1983; assoc. dir. Royal Nat. Theatre, London, 1984-88, 89-97. Author: (plays) Slag, 1970 (Evening Standard Drama award 1970), The Great Exhibition, 1972, (with Howard Brenton) Brassneck, 1973, Knuckle, 1974 (John Llewlyn Rhys award 1975), Teeth 'n' Smiles, 1975, (with others) Deeds, 1978, Plenty, 1978 (N.Y. Drama Critics Circle Best Fgn. Play award 1983, Best Play Tony award nominee 1983), A Map of the World, 1982 (Dramalogue award), (with Brenton) Pravda, 1985 (Evening Standard Drama award 1985, Plays and Players best play award 1985, City Limits best play award 1985), The Bay at Nice, 1986, Wrecked Eggs, 1986, The Knife, 1987, The Secret Rapture, 1988 (Plays and Players Best Play award 1988, Drama mag. Best Play award 1988, Drama Desk Best Play award nominee 1990), Racing Demon, 1990, 93, 95 (Olivier Best Play award 1990, Time Out Theatre award 1990, Plays and Players best play award 1990, London Critics Circle Best Play award 1990, Tony award nominee 1996), Murmuring Judges, 1991, 92, 93, The Absence of War, 1993, Skylight, 1995, 96, 97 (Olivier Best Play award), Amy's View, 1996, 97, 98, 99, The Judas Kiss, 1997, 98, Via Dolorosa, 98, 99; (adaptations) Fanshen (William Hinton), 1975, Rules of the Game (Luigi Pirandello), 1971, 92, The Life of Galileo (Bertolt Brecht), 1994, Mother Courage and Her Children (Brecht), 1995, Ivanov (Anton Chekhov), 1997, The Blue Room (Schnitzler), 1998; plays performed U.S.-Broadway, Pub. Theatre, N.Y.C., Goodman Theatre, Chgo., Arena Theatre, Washington, Lincoln Ctr., and other places; (TV films) Man Above Men, 1973, Licking Hitler (Brit. Acad. Film and TV Arts Best Play award 1978), Dreams of Leaving, 1980, Saigon: Year of the Cat, 1983, Heading Home, 1990, The Absence of War, 1995; (screenplays) Plenty, 1985, Wetherby, 1985 (Golden Bear award best film Berlin Film Festival 1985), Paris By Night, 1988, Strapless, 1989, Damage, 1992, The Secret Rapture, 1993, Feasting with Panthers, 1995; (essays) Writing Lefthanded, 1991, Asking Around, 1993; dir: (theatre) Inside Out, 1968, Christie in Love, 1969, Purity, 1969, Fruit, 1970, Blow Job, 1971, England's Ireland, 1972, Brassneck, 1973, The Pleasure Principle, 1973, The Provoked Wife, 1973, The Party, 1974, Teeth 'n' Smiles, 1975, Weapons of Happiness, 1976, Devil's Island, 1977, Plenty, 1978, Total Eclipse, 1981, A Map of the World, 1983, Pravda, 1985-86, King Lear, 1986, The Bay at Nice and Wrecked Eggs, 1986-87, The Knife, 1987, The Secret Rapture, 1989, The Designated Mourner, 1996; (films) Wetherby, 1985, Paris by Night, 1989, Strapless, 1989, (TV) Licking Hitler, 1978, Dreams of Leaving, 1980, Heading Home, 1992, The Designated Mourner, 1996, Heartbreak House. 1997; (opera libretto) The Knife, 1988; author: (books) Writing Left-handed, 1991, Asking Around, 1993, Acting Up, 1999. Fellow Royal Soc. Lit.; mem. Officiers de l"ordre des Artes et Lettres, Dramatists Club. Office: c/o Casarotto Ramsay, 60 Wardour St, London W1, England

HARENCAK, PAUL, III, quality assurance professional; b. Paterson, N.J., Dec. 2, 1955; s. Paul and Maria (DeLuca) H.; m. Michele Bina, Oct. 28, 1979; children: Nicole, Dana. BS in Biology Scis., Rutgers U., 1977. Engring. Marcal Paper Co., Elmwood Park, N.J., 1977; v.p. Facile Holdings Inc., Paterson, N.J., 1977—; owner Riverside Acquistions Inc., 1998—. Contbr. articles to profl. jours. Grantee Nat. Endowment Scis., 1976-77. Mem. Am. Chem. Soc., Am. Soc. Quality Control, Greater Paterson C. of C. (chmn. bd.), Commerce and Industry Assn. N.J. (bd. dirs.). Office: Facile Holdings Inc 185 6th Ave Paterson NJ 07506-1559

HAREZI, ILONKA JO, financial company executive, consultant; b. Princeton, Ind., Jan. 17, 1949; d. Joseph and Helen Marie Fullop; m. John O. Schofield, Jan. 14, 1971 (div. Dec. 1982); 1 child, Franceska; m. Courtland Reeves, Sept. 26, 1986; children: Bryan, Katharine. Grad., Chgo. Sch. Design, 1969. Mktg. ptnr. Fullop and Assocs., 1983-85; founder, sec., treas. Kinetic Energy Ltd., 1985-90; freelance set designer Ilonka Creative Environments, 1974-84; founder, v.p. Harezi Internat., 1980-84; founder, sec., treas. Elf Cocoon Corp., 1984-86; founder, pres., chmn. Elf Cocoon Internat. Ltd., 1985-92; founder, pres. Elfworks, Inc., 1991-94, Elfworks, Nev., 1994-96; pres., dir. Allied Fund for Capital Appreciation, Inc., 1998—; interviewed by radio, TV, and newspapers on design and extremely low frequency electromagnetic tech.; presenter tech. sems. on ELF and scalar phenomena. Contbr. articles to profl. jours. Bd. dirs. Inst. for Higher Human Learning Potential, Phila., 1979. Mem. NAFE, Am. Inst. Interior Designers, Women's Internat. League for Peace and Freedom, Nat. Assn. Against Health Fraud, Knights of Malta (dame), Knights of Africa (dame), U.S. Acad. Polit. Sci., ACLU, Am. Craft Coun. Office: ELF Tesler St Rt 1 Saint Francisville IL 62460

HARF, PATRICIA JEAN KOLE, syndicated columnist, educational consultant, lecturer, clinical and behavioral psychologist, family therapist; b. Berea, Ohio, Oct. 14, 1937; d. Paul Frederic and Mena (Labordes) Kole. BS in Edn. with honors, Baldwin-Wallace Coll., Berea, Ohio, 1959; MS in Edn. with honors, U. Akron, 1966; D in Edn. cum laude, Ariz. State U., 1972; PhD, London Inst. Applied Rsch., 1995; HHD, World Acad., 1994; PhD, London Inst. Applied Rsch., 1995. Rsch. Ednl. Rsch. Coun. Am., 1967-69; tchr. Berea City Schs., Cleve. and Parma, Ohio, 1969-73; asst. prof. Cleve. State U., 1975—; corr., columnist, freelance writer, syndicated columnist Universal PressChronicle-Telegram, Elyria, Ohio, 1986-89; owner Harf Family Counselors, Berea, Ohio, 1993—; ednl. cons. State of Ohio Bd. Edn. and Gov., 1997—; syndicated columnist Universal Press, Cleve. Plain Dealer; diagnostician of reading difficulties; trustee Coalition for Children's Media; cons. learning disabilities; guest lectr.; TV guest appearances; court appointed spl. cons. for juveniles, 1996-97; mem. Reading Enrichment for Adult Devel.; mem. Coun. of Higher Learning; cons., adult juror Kids First Coalition for Quality Children's Media; advisor, cons. to Juvenile Cts. of Clyahoga County. Author teaching materials and tchr. and children's texts; contbr. articles to profl. jours. ; also advisor to book pubs. and magazines. Pres. Berea Hist. Soc., World Found. Successful Women; mem. Cleve. Orch. Women's Com., Nat. Mus. Women in Arts, Coun. Exceptional Children, Ohio Town Forum, Ohio Arts Festival, com. 500 Project READ; advisor Cleve. Radio and TV Coun.; tutor Project Learn, Cleve.; mem. Berea Rep. Precinct Com.; founder Preventive Parenting; dep. senator Internat. Parliament Safety & Peace Italy; mem. Children's TV Workshop, 1995-96; trustee United Meth. Childrens Found. and Home, 1996-97, Berea Children's Home. Named Intellectual Woman of Yr., 1991-92, Emminent fellow in Universe of Mankind, 1994, Ohio Ednl. Woman of Yr., Ohio Educator of Yr. and Outstanding Educator, Outstanding Citizen Berea C. of C., Outstanding Berea High Grad. awd., 1997; Ohio Edn. Woman of Yr., 1991, Most Admired woman of Yr., 1993, Lifetime Fellow and Hon. Prof. Australian Inst. for Coordinated Rsch., 1995; recipient Women's Inner Cir. of Achievement award, 1992, Woman of Yr. commemorative medal Order of Internat. Fellowship, 1994, Excellence in Journalism award 1990-93, World Lifetime Achievement award, 1996, Gold Star award Am. Soc. for Outstanding Volunteerism, 1995; named baroness Royal Order Bohemian Crown, 1994. Mem. NEA, NOW, AAUW, LWV, Am. Writers Assn, Am. Women in Radio and TV, Inc., Soc. Profl. Journalists (Excellence in Journalism award 1990, Ohio Live, Woman Source directory 1998-00), Women in Journalism, Assn. Tchrs. of Learning Disabilities, Am. Assn. Women in Bus., Berea C. of C. (Outstanding Citizen 1965), Bus. Profl. Women Assn., Australian Inst. Coordinated Rsch. (fellow, hon. prof.), Berea Hist. Soc., Berea Bus. and Profl. Women, Women in Comm. Inc., Internat. Women's Media, Internat. Reading Assn. (cons. and writer for reading tchrs.), Ohio Edn. Assn. (Woman of Yr. in Comms. 1991), Internat. Platform Assn., World Found. of Successful Women, Nat. Assn. Women (Internat. Leaders in Achievement award 1996), Profl. Educators Assn., Learning Disability Assn., Nat. Assn. Psychologists, Ohio Assn. Psychologists, Nat. Assn. Women in the Arts, Western Res. Rep. Women's Assn., S.W. Women Rep. Assn., Kiwanis (sec., v.p.), Berea Rep. Club (Mayoral Volunteerism award 1987), Press Club of Cleve. (award 1996), Cleve. Women's City Club, Cleve. Orch. Women's Soc., U. Akron Alumni Assn., Berea H.S. Alumni Assn., Berea Town Forum, Berea C. of C., Baldwin Wallace Alumni Assn., Baldwin Wallace Women's Club, Berea Town Forum. Republican. Methodist. Avocations: reading, golf, flower arranging, politics, crafts. Home: PO Box 81720 Cleveland OH 44181-0720

HARGETT, DAVID RAYMOND, gemologist; b. New Haven, June 4, 1953; s. Raymond Edward and Mary (Nolan) H. Grad., Gemol. Inst. Am., 1977; BS in Bus. Mgmt., Econs., NYU, 1986. Cert. gemologist Am. Gem Soc. Mgr. GIA-Gem Trade Lab., N.Y.C., 1977-93; prin., pres. David Hargett, Inc., N.Y.C., 1993—. Contbg. editor Gems & Gemology Mag., Santa Monica, 1988-95; contbr. articles to profl. jours. Vol. Lawyers Com. for Human Rights, 1992—. Mem. N.Y. Acad. Scis., Am. Gem Soc. (cert.), N.Y. Mineral. Club (bd. govs. 1988—, program chmn. 1988—), Turtle Bay Assn., GIA Alumni Assn. Achievements include rsch. in cause of color diamonds; design of various lab. instruments. Office: David Hargett Inc 140 E 46th St Apt 6G New York NY 10017-2621

HARGITAI, ROBERT, mining engineer, consultant, educator; b. Tatabanya, Komarom, Hungary, Nov. 1, 1962; s. Istvan Hargitai and Károlyné Koska (Brassai Melinda); m. Maria Brath; children: Eszter, Robert. MSc in Mining Engring., U. Miskolc (Hungary), 1989, PhD in Geol. Scis., 1994; PhD in Tech. Scis., Hungarian Acad. Scis., 1992. Rschr. Hungarian Acad. Scis., Budapest, Hungary, 1989-92; sr. lectr. U. Miskolc (Hungary), 1992-95; head dept. informatics BZ Rsch. Ctr. for Applied Scis., Miskolc, 1995; mgr. Hungarian nat. DGPS project Hungarian Nat. Army Technol. Dept., Budapest, 1996; French govt. scholar, Paris Mining Acad., 1990-91; World Bank scholar, U. Wollongong, Australia, 1995-96; cons. Hungarian Nat. Army, 1996—; vis. prof. U. Miskolc, 1996—, Geodesical High Sch., Szekesfehervar, 1996—, Mining Dept. Colo. Sch. Mines, 1998. Sgt. Hungarian Army, 1981-84. Recipient Gold medal Hungarian Credit Bank for Hungarian Tech. Devel., 1986. Mem. Australian Geog. Soc., Hungarian Acad. Sci. (spatial informatics com. 1995—, computerscis. in the mining com. 1995—), Internat. Assn. Math. Geology. Avocations: rock-climbing, surfing, diving, mountaineering. Home: PO Box 142, H-8000 Szekesfehervar Hungary Office: Rigo U 10, H-8002 Szekesfehervar Hungary

HARGRAVE, ROBERT WARREN, hair styling salon chain executive; b. Meridian, Miss., Sept. 15, 1944; s. George Herbert and Clara (Gibson) H.; m. Janeice Stodghill, Dec. 23, 1967; 1 child, Jennifer Lyn. Student, Tyler Jr. Coll., 1963-65; BS, Baylor U., 1967; postgrad., East Tex. State U., 1968. Lic. nursing home adminstr., Tex. Nursing home adminstr. ARA-Nat. Living Ctrs., Waco, Tex., 1969-71; dir. personnel and spl. programs ARA-Nat. Living Ctrs., Houston, 1971-75; exec. v.p. ARA-Geriatrics, Colo., Tex, 1975-79; founder, owner 16 hair styling salons San Antonio Enterprises, Inc., 1979—; tchr. nursing home adminstrn., McLennan Community Coll., Waco, 1970, mem. steering com. to establish nursing home license program, 1970; mem. Nat. Bd. Salon Franchises, Cutco Insutries, Inc., N.Y.C., 1985-87, pres. Direct Licensees' Assn., 1991-92; adv. com. Tex. Cosmetology Commn., 1994—. Mem. adv. bd. cosmetology dept. South San High Sch., 1987—, adv. coun. for career and tech. edn. N. East Ind. Sch. Dist., 1994—. Mem. Am. Salon Assn., Tex. Salon Assn., San Antonio Salon Assn., Tex. Nursing Home Assn. (chpt. pres. 1970), Colo. Health Care Assn. (del. for nat. fire safety 1978), Am. Health Care Assn., Nat. Parks and Recreation Assn., Nat. Therapeutic Recreational Soc., Gideons Internat. Avocations: boating, fishing. Office: San Antonio Enterprises Inc PO Box 792627 San Antonio TX 78279-2627

HARGREAVES, DAVID WILLIAM, communications company executive; b. Akron, Ohio, May 4, 1943; s. William B. and Helen Grace (Slusser) H.; m. Sandra Jean Tessier, Sept. 4, 1965; children: Kristen Elizabeth, Cinda Anne, Gregory David. BSEE, U. Maine, Orono, 1965; MBA, U. Rochester, 1967. Sales engr. Mobile Communications div. Gen. Electric, Lynchburg, Va., 1970-74, mgr. systems projects, 1974-75, mgr. systems bids/proposals, 1975-78; mgr. internat. mktg. Gen. Electric Powerline Carrier Bus., Lynchburg, 1978-80; gen. mgr. Gen. Electric Microwave Link Operation, Owensboro, Ky., 1980-84; mng. dir. Alpha Telecom div. Alpha Industries, Methuen, Mass., 1984-86; pres. Dynatech Tactical Comms. Inc. (formerly Controlonics Corp.), Nashua, N.H., 1986-97; pres., CEO DTC Comms. Inc., Nashua, 1997—; condr. seminars in field. Contbr. articles to profl. jours. Chmn. bd. Gen. Electric United Way Pacesetter campaign, Lynchburg, 1978; advisor Jr. Achievement project bus., Owensboro, 1982, 83. Served to capt. U.S. Army, 1968-70, Vietnam. Decorated Bronze Star, D.S.C., 1970. Mem. Am. Mktg. Pres.'s Assn., Massibesic Yacht Club, Eta Kappa Nu, Tau Beta Pi. Republican. Avocations: sailing, skiing, amateur radio. Home: 191 Buttrick Rd Hampstead NH 03841-2183 Office: DTC Comms Inc 75 Northeastern Blvd Nashua NH 03062-3128

HARGROVE, ROY BELMONT, III, stockbroker; b. Farmville, Va., Sept. 2, 1958; s. Roy Belmont Jr. and Margaret Ann (Heaton) H.; m. Cynthia Ann Metcalf, Aug. 9, 1980; children: Roy B. IV, Katherine Allyn. BS, Lynchburg Coll., 1980, MBA, 1985. CFP. Account exec. Wheat First Securities, Williamsburg, Va., 1980-86, investment officer, 1986-88, v.p., investment officer, 1988-94; sr. v.p. Wheat First Butcher Singer, Williamsburg, 1994—; br. mgr. Williamsburg office Wheat First Union, Williamsburg, 1996—. Trustee Endowment, Williamsburg Bapt. Ch., 1990-99, chmn. ofcl. bd., 1988, Sunday sch. tchr., 1990-98; founding bd. dirs., past chmn. Hospice Support Care of Williamsburg, 1982-91, 95—; fundraiser Am. Cancer Soc., Williamsburg, 1992—; mem. local com. Kingsmill chpt. Ducks Unltd., 1982-90; coach Williamsburg Recreation Jr. Basketball Program, 1994—; bd. dirs. Williamsburg Landing Retirement Cmty., 1996—; mem. budget and fin. com. Kingsmill Comty. Svc. Assn., 1996-2000; bd. dirs. Hampton Roads Acad., 1999—. Recipient Disting. Alumni award Prince Edward Acad., 1998. Mem. Kiwanis. Avocations: golf, skiing, fishing.

Home: 104 Thomas Cartwright Williamsburg VA 23185-8904 Office: Wheat First Union 275 Mclaws Cir Williamsburg VA 23185-5649

HARHUT, CHESTER T., judge. BS in acctg., bus., Bethell Coll.; JD, Univ. Pitts., 1995. Judge Lackawanna County Ct., 1987-96, Family Ct. Lackawanna County Ct., 1996—; bd. dirs. Lackawanna Jr. Coll. Former pres., bd. trustees Everhart Mus. Mem. Nat. Coun. Juvenile and Family Ct. Judges, Pa. Trial Judges Assn. (mem. family divsn., officer, co-chair legis. liaison com.). Office: Lacka County Ct House 200 N Washington Ave Scranton PA 18503-1524

HARIG-KOLLESCH, JUTTA, philologist, researcher, retired; b. Stettin, Germany, Nov. 7, 1933; d. Paul and Hedwig (Unruh) Kollesch; m. Georg Harig, Feb. 21, 1969 (dec. Aug. 1989). PhD, Martin-Luther U., Halle, Germany, 1961; DrSc in Philosophy, Humboldt U., Berlin, 1970. Head Corpus Medicorum Graecorum Acad. Scis., Berlin, 1961-98. Author: Galen, On the organ of smell, 1964, Studies in the pseudogalenic Medical Definitions, 1973, Aristotle, On motion of animals; On locomotion of animals, 1985. Mem. Deutsches Archäologisches Inst. (corr.). Home: Albertinenstr 18, D-13086 Berlin Germany

HARIJAN, RAM, technology transfer researcher; b. Keecheri, Kerala, India, June 3, 1938; s. Narayanan and Devaki (Amma) Nambiar; m. Lakshmi VP, Aug. 19, 1977; 1 child, Pooja Devi. BA with honors, Madras U., India; MA with award, Southampton U., Eng.; PhD, Reading U., Eng. Lectr. Kerala (India) U.; mining officer Singareni Collieries, India; sch. tchr. Barnstaple Grammar Sch., Eng.; lectr. Bosworth Coll., Eng.; tutor cons. Open U., Eng.; researcher Centre for Studies in Tech. Transfer, Eng.; involved in rsch. which influenced the computerisation policies of Indian Govt., 1985-89; vis. prof. U. Madras, 1982, Calicut U., 1985. Chmn. North Devon Dist. Labour Party, 1972-77, North Devon Assn. Racial Equality, 1978-80; vol. social worker Helping the Disabled and Disadvantaged. Avocations: bridge, chess. E-mail: ramh55@hotmail.com. Home: 30 Norfolk Rd, Desford Leicester LE9 9HR, England

HARILELA, DAVID JETHANAND, enterpreneur; b. Hong Kong, Apr. 25, 1949; s. George Naroomal Mirchandani and Chandra Jethanand (Parmanand) H.; m. Avisha Devidas Ladharam, Apr. 9, 1956; children: Divia, Davina, Sheeva. BSc, U. So. Calif., 1974. Gen. mgr. Harilela's Emporium, Hong Kong, 1977-87, pres., 1987—; pres. Harilela (George) Ltd., Hong Kong, 1990—; CEO David Harilela Group of Cos., Hong Kong; licensing cons.; specialist in licensing. Singer, songwriter: China Mail (9th Best Band in Asia 1969). Avocations: songwriting, poetry, basketball. Office: D Harilela Group of Cos, 29-43 Ashley Rd 2Fl Rm201-5, Kowloon Centre, Hong Kong

HARIRI, V. M., arbitrator, mediator, lawyer, educator. BS, Wayne State U.; JD, Detroit Coll. Law; LLM, London Sch. Econs. and Polit.Sci.; diploma arbitration, Reading (Eng.) U. Pvt. practice internat. and domestic bus. law Detroit; drafting com. Republic of Kazakhstan Code on Arbitration Procedure, Free Econ. Zone Legislation, Republic of Belarus; instr. internat. comml. arbitration Chartered Inst. Arbitrators, Am. Arbitration Assn. Fellow Chartered Inst. Arbitrators (exec. com. N.Am. br., co-founder); mem. ABA, Internat. Bar Assn., Am. Soc. Internat. Law, Am. Arbitration Assn., London Ct. Internat. Arbitration, World Jurist Assn., Mich. Trial Lawyers Assn. Office: 325 N Center St Ste E3 Northville MI 48167-1244

HARIU, TAKASHI, engineering educator, researcher; b. Sendai, Miyagi, Japan, Mar. 28, 1939; s. Fumio Tendo and Sumi Hariu. BS, Tohoku U., Sendai, Japan, 1961, M.Engring., 1964, Dr.Engring., 1967. With Hitachi Ltd., Kokubonji, Japan, 1961-62; rsch. assoc. Tohoku U., Sendai, 1967-71, assoc. prof., 1971-95; prof. engring. Ibaraki U., Hitachi, 1995—; sr. rsch. assoc. U. Newcastle-upon-Tyne, Eng., 1972-74; cons. rschr. U. Roorkee, India, 1980, Tech. U. Darmstadt, Germany, 1985. Author: Optoelectronic Devices, 1990; editor, author: Low Temperature Epitaxial Growth of Semiconductors, 1991. Mem. 153d com. Japan Soc. for the Promotion of Sci., 1988-98. Mem. IEEE (sr. mem.), Japan Soc. Applied Physics, Inst. Electronics, Info. and Comm. Engrs. Japan. Avocations: Go, music, tennis. Home: Ayukawa-cho 6-9-21-403, Hitachi 315, Japan Office: Ibaraki Univ, Nakanarusawa 4-12-1, Hitachi 316, Japan

HARKARVY, BENJAMIN, artistic director. Artistic dir. Royal Winnipeg (Can.) Ballet, 1957-58; artistic dir., founder The Netherlands Dance Theatre, 1959-69; artistic dir. Harkness Ballet, N.Y.C., 1969-70, Dutch Nat. Ballet, The Netherlands, 1970-71, Pa. Ballet, Phila., 1972-82; freelance choreographer various ballet cos., 1982-91; artistic dir. dance divsn. Juilliard Sch., N.Y.C., 1992—; dir. ballet project Jacob's Pillow, 1983-89. Choreographer ballets Time Passed Summer, Recital for Cello and 8 Dancers, Cinque Madrigali, Frames. Office: Juilliard Sch 60 Lincoln Center Plz New York NY 10023-6588

HARKER, DEBRA P., marketing educator; b. London, Aug. 22, 1959; arrived in Australia, 1989; d. Patrick and Patricia May Dickson; m. Michael Harker, Dec. 15, 1989; 1 child, Amy Rose. PhD, Griffith U., Brisbane, Australia, 1995; BA in Bus. with honors, South Bank U., London, 1988. Cert. practicing marketer Australian Mktg. Inst. Sales and mktg. officer Credit Protection Assn., London, 1983-85; market rsch. cons. KPMG Peat Marwick McLintock, Birmingham, Eng., 1988-89; market rsch. exec. AGB:McNair Market Rsch., Brisbane, 1990-92; rsch. asst. Griffith U., Brisbane, 1992-93, assoc. lectr. mktg., 1995-97; sr. lectr. mktg. U. of the Sunshine Coast, Maroochydore South, Queensland, Australia, 1996—. Mem. Australian Consumers Assn. (com. mem. 1999—), Advt. Stds. Bur. (cons. 1998—). Avocations: reading, opera, surf life saving, sports. Fax: 617 5430 1231. E-mail: dharker@usc.edu.au. Home: Waringa 4 Caribbean Ct, Castaways Beach, Queensland 4567, Australia Office: U of the Sunshine Coast, LMB4 Faculty of Bus, Maroochydore South 4558, Australia

HARKES, JOHN, professional soccer player; b. Kearny, N.J., Mar. 8, 1967; m. Cindy; children: Ian, Lauren. Student, U. Va. With U.S. Nat. Team, 1987—, capt.; midfielder West Ham United English Premier League, 1995-96; midfielder, capt. D.C. United Team, 1996-99; midfielder Derby County Football Club, New England Revolution, Foxboro, Mass., 1999—. Named Player of Yr., Mo. Athletic Club, 1987, Player of Yr., Atlantic Coast Conf., 1987, Most Valuable Player, U.S. Cup, 1990, First Am. to play in F.A. Cup Final, 1993, First Am. to score goal in Coca-Cola League Cup Final, 1993, C0-Most Valuable Player, Copa Am., 1995. Achievements include captaining D.C. United to first-ever MLS Championship, 1996, scoring English League's Goal of Yr., 1990. Office: New England Revolution Foxboro Stadium Rte 1 Foxboro MA 02035

HARKIN, DANIEL JOHN, controller; b. Bradenton, Fla., Mar. 29, 1955; s. John Lewis and Stella Marie (Durand) H.; m. Theresa Ann Ford; children: Erin Kathleen, Shaun Ford. BBA, Fla. Atlantic U., 1975. CPA, Fla. Controller Vis. Home Health Svc., Boca Raton, Fla., 1975-78; CPA Cherry Bekaert & Holland, Ft. Lauderdale, Fla., 1978-85; controller Griffin Bros. Co., Inc., Davie, Fla., 1985-90, L.W. Rozzo, Inc., Pembroke Pines, Fla., 1990—. Contbr. articles to profl. jours. Fla. univ. faculty scholar Fla. Atlantic U., 1972-75. Mem. AICPA, Fla. Inst. CPAs (mem. com. 1980-91, adv. com. MAS 1990-91, speaker 1984), Nat. Assn. Accts., Nat. Inst. Tax Profls., Smithsonian Instn., Inst. Mgmt. Accts., Greenpeace, Roscicrucian Order AMORC. Roman Catholic. Avocations: computer systems and programming, gardening, boating, philosophy, teaching. Home: 1834 SW 21st St # 2 Fort Lauderdale FL 33315-1833 Office: L W Rozzo Inc 17200 Pines Blvd Hollywood FL 33029-1505

HARKNESS, DAVID DALGLEISH, patent administrator; b. Bootle, Lancashire, Eng., Feb. 26, 1939; s. Walter and Sarah (Arnold) H.; m. Jean Sundewall, Aug. 3, 1968; children: Helen, Andrew. Diploma in dyeing, Leeds (Eng.) U., 1961, BSc with honors, 1962. Examiner U.K. Patent Office, London, 1962-72, sr. examiner, 1972-80; chief examiner European Patent Office, Munich, 1980-89, directorate advisor, 1989-94, mem. bd. appeals, 1994-2000. Avocations: walking, gardening, bridge. Office: European Patent Office, Erhardtstrasse 27, 80331 Munich Germany

HARKNESS, MABEL GLEASON, retired librarian; b. Oil City, Pa., Jan. 20, 1913; d. Charles Wilcox and Mabel Amy (Fulton) Gleason; m. Benjamin Olney, Mar. 23, 1946 (dec. 1963); m. Bernard Emerson Harkness, Sept. 5, 1964 (dec. 1980). AB, U. Rochester, 1935, MA, 1962. Cert. libr., N.Y. Libr. Stromberg-Carlson Co., Rochester, N.Y., 1942-51, Garden Ctr. Rochester, 1953-67, Monroe County (N.Y.) Bookmobile, 1952-53; now ret.; vol. cataloger Geneva (N.Y.) Hist. Soc.; editor Gleam mag., Rochester Poetry Soc., 1945, Engr.'s Notebook, Stromberg-Carlson Co., 1946-50, Garden Ctr. Bull., 1955-67; co-founder, past pres. Western N.Y. chpt. Spl. Librs. Assn., 1945. Compiler: Harkness Seedlist Handbook 1986 (Worth award for bot./hort. writing Am. Rock Garden Soc.), 2d edit., 1993; contbr. articles on horticulture and local history to various publs. Trustee Keuka Coll., Keuka Park, N.Y., 1971-80, now emeritus. Mem. AAUW (life), Am. Rock Garden Soc. (life), Alpine Garden Soc. (Eng.), Scottish Rock Garden Club (life). Republican. Episcopalian. Avocations: musicology, architectural history. Home: 5169 Pre Emption Rd Geneva NY 14456-9736

HARKNESS, R. KENNETH, restaurant chain executive; b. Warren, Ohio, Aug. 22, 1949; s. Roy K. and Yvonne D. (Howitt) H.; m. Marianne Loprete, Sept. 28, 1974 (div. Apr. 1999); 1 child, Austin Blaine. BS in Bus., Rutgers U., 1972, MBA in Acctg., 1973. Pres., chief exec. officer N.Y. Sub Inc., Dallas, 1974-81, 85—, Fox Hunt Realty, Inc., Far Hills, N.J., 1981-85, Kenco Restaurants, Inc., Dallas, 1987—. Mem. University Park Master Plan Com. Mem. Nat. Restaurant Assn., Tex. Restaurant Assn., Rep. Inner Circle. Episcopalian. Fax: 214-522-3920. Office: NY Sub Inc 3411 Asbury St Dallas TX 75205-1844

HARLAN, NORMAN RALPH, construction executive; b. Dayton, Ohio, Dec. 21, 1914; s. Joseph and Anna (Kaplan) H.; m. Thelma Katz, Sept. 4, 1955; children: Leslie, Todd. Indsl. Engring. degree, U. Cin., 1937. Chmn. Am. Constrn. Corp., Dayton, 1949, Harlan, Inc., realtors. Mem. Dayton Real Estate Bd., Ohio Real Estate Assn., Nat. Assn. Real Estate Bds., C. of C., Pi Lambda Phi. Home: 303 Glenridge Rd Kettering OH 45429-1631 Office: Am Constrn Corp 2451 S Dixie Dr Dayton OH 45409-1861

HARLAN, PATRICK RAYMOND, entertainer; b. Great Falls, Mont., Nov. 14, 1970; arrived in Japan, 1993; s. Patrick Raymond Harlan and Nancy Kathleen Day. BA, Harvard Coll., 1993. Level 1 Japanese Proficiency cert. Tchr., curriculum creator IB Am. Club, Fukui, Japan, 1993-95; freelance actor, narrator, disc jockey Tokyo, 1996—; comedian Have Mercy Inc., Tokyo, 1997—; radio host Japan Broadcasting Corp., Tokyo, 1997—; radio disc jockey Inter FM, Tokyo, 1999—; weekly TV caster TBS TV Justs, 1999—. Appeared in TV dramas Strange Tales of this World, 1996, Bakayaro Special, 1999, movies Blister, 1998. Named Grand Champion of Comedy, Tokyo FM, 1999. Mem. Harvard Club Japan. Avocations: volleyball, ping pong, chess, motorcycling, reading. Home: 105 Senriso 10 Samoncho, Shinjuku Tokyo 160-0017, Japan

HARLAN, RAYMOND CARTER, communication executive, writer, consultant; b. Shreveport, La., Nov. 13, 1943; s. Ross E. and Margaret (Burns) H.; m. Nancy K. Munson, 1966 (div. 1978); children: Kathleen Marie, Patrick Raymond; m. Sarah J. Kinzel, 1979 (div. 1982); m. Linda Frances Gerdes, Mar. 30, 1985; stepchildren: Kimberly Jo Gillis, Kellie Leigh Raffa, Ryan William Gerdes. BA in Speech and Drama cum laude, Southwestern U., 1966; MA in English, U. Tex., 1968; MA in Speech & Theatre Arts, Bradley U., 1976. Commd. 2d lt. USAF, 1968, advanced through grades to maj., 1980, ret., 1988; pres. ComSkills, Aurora, Colo., 1988-2000; mgr. AT&T Broadband, 2000—; asst. prof. Bradley U., Peoria, Ill., 1972-76; instr., asst. prof., course dir. Air Force Acad., Colorado Springs, 1976-81; asst. prof. Air Force Inst. Tech., Dayton, Ohio, 1987-88; internat. trainer Inst. for Internat. Rsch., London, 1990-92; presenter in field. Author: The Confident Speaker, 1993; co-author: Telemarketing That Works, 1991, Interactive Telemarketing, 1995; contbr. articles and revs. to profl. jours. Decorated Air Force Commendation medal with three oak leaf clusters, Air Force Meritorious Svc. medal with one oak leaf cluster; recipient George Washington Honor Medal Freedom Found., 1983, Leo A. Codd award Am. Def. Preparedness Assn., 1st Prize ann. poetry contest Ariz. State Poetry Soc., 1979. Mem. ASTD, Soc. for Tech. Comm., Assn. Air Force Missileers. Lutheran. Avocations: skiing, cycling, gardening. Office: AT&T Digital Media Ctr 4100 E Dry Creek Rd Littleton CO 80122-3729

HARLAN, ROSS EDGAR, retired utility company executive, writer, lecturer, consultant; b. Poteau, Okla., July 11, 1919; s. Edgar Leslie and Leola (Carter) H.; m. Margaret Burns, May 31, 1942; children: Raymond Carter, Rosemary, Marvin Allen, Scott Lee. Student, Southeastern Okla. State U., 1937-38, Eastern Okla. State Coll., 1938-39; B.S.B.A., Okla. State U., 1941; postgrad., Harvard U., 1942. Mem. faculty, coach Poteau High Sch., 1945-46, Poteau Jr. Coll., 1945-46; with Okla. Gas & Electric Co., Oklahoma City, 1946-85, mgr. rates and contracts dept., 1954-64, v.p., 1964-78, sr. v.p. div. mgmt., 1978-80, sr. v.p. adminstrn. and public affairs, 1980-85; ret.; ind. cons., writer Oklahoma City, 1985—; cons. spl. books div. Reader's Digest, 1985—; mem. bd. govs. Ea. Okla. State Coll. Devel. Found. Author: Strikes, 1946, Frontier Oklahoma-The Twin Territories, 1994. Pres. Okla. Council on Econ. Edn., 1977-79; bd. govs. Nat. Wrestling Hall of Fame, 1977-85; pres. adv. bd. Okla. State U. Coll. Bus. Assos.; mem. adv. bd. Okla. State U. Tech. Inst.; bd. govs. Okla. State U. Found. Served with Army N.G., 1937-38; to lt. col. USAAF, 1941-46. Named to Okla. State U. Coll. Bus. Hall of Fame, 1980, Eastern Okla. State Coll. Hall of Fame, 1992; recipient George Washington Honor medal Freedoms Found. Am., 1970, Disting. Alumnus award Okla. State U., 1979; named Boss of Yr., Nat. Secs. Assn., 1977; charter mem. Poteau (Okla.) Athletic Hall of Fame. Mem. Oklahoma City C. of C., Toastmasters Internat. (comm. and leadership award 1985), Am. Legion, VFW, Mil. Order of World Wars (Silver Patrick henry medallion 2000), Disabled Am. Vets., Beta Gamma Sigma. Methodist. Home and Office: 2639 N Eagle Ln Oklahoma City OK 73127-1166

HARLAN, SUSAN JORDAN, artist, educator; b. Frankfurt, Germany, Mar. 7, 1950; d. Edwin McFreeland and Doris Jordan Harlan; m. Richard Daniel Maughn, May 3, 1985; 1 child, Jordan. BFA, U. Miami, 1973, MFA, 1975; postgrad., Hampshire Coll., 1975-76. Tchg. asst. U. Miami, 1973-75; instr. Pensacola Jr. Coll., 1975-79; adj. prof. U. South Fla., 1979-80; fed. and supreme ct. trial artist CBS and Washington Post, Washington Times, 1981-84; editl. cartoonist, trial artist USA Today, 1984-87; instr. Corcoran Sch. Art, 1988-92; assoc. prof. art Portland State U., 1992—; vis. prof. St. Mary's Coll., Md., 1985; artist resident Sitka Ctr. for Art and Ecology, Otis, Oreg., 1996. Author: Songlines, 1993; one-woman shows include Gallery K, Washington, 1989, 91, Arnold & Porter, Washington, 1989, Jones Troyer Fitzpatrick Gallery, Washington, 1991, 93, 94, Emerson Gallery, Washington, 1992, Nat. Mus. Women in the Arts, Washington, 1993, Elizabeth Leach Gallery, Portland, 1994, 95, 96, 99, Sherry Frumkin Gallery, Santa Monica, Calif., 1995, 97, 2000, Troyer Fitzpatrick Gallery, Washington, 1997, 2000, Clark Coll., Vancouver, Washington, 1999; group exhbns. include Richmond Arts Coun., 1989, Strahmore Hall, Balt., 1990, Md. Hall of Arts, 1990, Linn Munson Williams Proctor Inst. and Mus., Utica, N.Y., 1990, Gallery K, Washington, 1991, Galerie d'Art Contemporain, Chamalieres, Paris, 1991, Anderson Gallery, Va. Commonwealth U, 1993, Daidan Theol. Sem., Washington, 1993, Comus Gallery, Portland, 1993, N.D. Mus., Grand Forks, 1994, Nat. Mus. Women in the Arts, Washington, 1994, Forum for Contemporary Art, St. Louis, 1995, Irvine (Calif.) Fine Arts Ctr., 1996, Elizabeth Leach Gallery, Portland, 1996, Pensacola (Fla.) Jr. Coll., 1997, others; represented in permanent collections J. Paul Getty Mus., L.A., Nat. Gallery Art, Washington, Victoria Albert Mus., London, Walker Art Mus., Mpls., Nat. Mus. Women in the Arts, Washington. Tchr. Self Enhancement Ctr. Youth at Risk, Portland, 1998. Grantee Nat. Mus. Women in the Arts Fellowship, Washington, 1993. Mem. Coll. Art Assn. E-mail: sjharlan@aol.com. Office: Portland State Univ PO Box 751 Portland OR 97207-0751

HARLECH, PAMELA, journalist; b. N.Y.C., Dec. 18, 1934; d. Ralph Frederick and Irene Georgia (Talmey) Colin; m. Lord Harlech, 1969; 1 chld, Pandora Beatrice Ormsby Gore. BA, Finch Coll. Features editor Vogue Mag., N.Y.C., 1961-64; editor Am. Vogue Mag., London, 1964-69; contbg. editor food column Brit. Vogue, London, 1969-84. Author: Feast Without Fuss, 1976, Pamela Harlech's Practical Guide to Cooking, Entertaining and Household Management, 1981, Vogue Book of Menus, 1984. Bd. govs. Royal Sch. Needlework, London, 1979-85; mem. Welsh Arts Coun., Cardiff, Wales, 1982-85, South Bank Bd., 1985-94, Arts Coun. Gt. Britain, 1986-90; trustee Victoria and Albert Mus., London, 1985-94; v.p., pres., Am. Friends Covent Garden, London, 1978-94; chmn. English Nat. Ballet, 1990-2000, Women's Playhouse Trust, 1982-94; chmn. devel. Theatre Mus., 1998—.

HARLEMAN, JOHANNES HENDRIKUS, experimental pathologist; b. Rotterdam, The Netherlands, Sept. 9, 1953; s. Johannes H. Harleman and Elisabeth J. Steenbergen; m. Helene Maria Bijloo, Feb. 27, 1976; children: Eden J.F., Marie C.E. DVM cum laude, State U. Utrecht, The Netherlands, 1977; PhD, U. Ill., 1982. Bd. cert. in Vet. Pathology, Toxicologic Pathology, and Toxicology, The Netherlands. Rsch. assoc. U. Ill., Urbana-Champaign, 1978-82; pathologist Ciba Geigy AG, Basel, Switzerland, 1982-83; sr. pathologist Smith Kline & French, Welwyn, U.K., 1983-86; head of pathology ASTA Medica AG, Halle, Germany, 1986-99; head toxicology-pathology Novartis Pharma AG, Basel, 1999—; Co-author (Internat. Agy. Rsch. on Cancer, WHO) International Classification of Rodent Tumors-Haematopoietic System, 1993, International Classification of Rodent Tumors—Male Genital System, 1997, International Classification of Rodent Tumors—Female Genital System, 1997; editorial bd. mem. Toxicologic Pathology, 1997—. Bd. mem. Christian Reformed Ch., Champaign, 1980-81, Christliche Gemeinschaft Bielefeld, 1992-99. Mem. German Soc. Toxicologic Pathology (v.p. 1992—), Soc. Toxicologic Pathology, Royal Netherlands Vet. Assn., Phi Kappa Phi. Christian Reformed Church. Avocations: tennis, squash, cooking, hiking, reading. E-mail: johannes.harleman@pharma.novartis.com. Office: Novartis Pharma AG, WSH 2881 PO5, CH-4002 Basel Switzerland

HAR-LEV, MOTI (MORDECHAI HAR-LEV), electrical engineer; b. Oradea, Romania, Feb. 4, 1954; arrived in Israel, 1964; s. Odette Kotigaru-Keilin, Feb. 3, 1987; children: Shay, Liad, Hila, Alon, Coral. BSc, Ben Gurion U., Israel, 1981; MSM, Boston U., 1997. Engr. ELTA, Israel, 1981-85, team leader, 1985-86, sys. engr., 1986-88, project mgr., 1988-95, programs mgr., 1995—. Avocations: collecting stamps, collecting coins. Office: ELTA, PO Box 330 DEP 3445, 77102 Ashdod Israel

HARLEY, IAN, executive. With Abbey Nat. plc, London, 1977—, fin. dir., 1993-96, CEO, 1997—; non-exec. dir. First Nat. Fin. Corp., 1995, Rentokil; group chief exec. Scottish Mut. Assurance. Office: Abbey Internat, Baker St, London NW1 6XL, England*

HARLEY, JOHN HENRY, accountant, financial advisor; b. London, Aug. 3, 1952; s. Hugh Rosborough Swanzy and Brenda Patricia (Thompson) H.; m. Sylvia Mary Harley, Sept. 4, 1976; children: Michael, Jeremy, Sarah. Grad., Wycliffe Coll., Stonehouse, Eng., 1969. Articled clk. Spicer & Pegler, Cardiff, Wales, 1969-73, sr. auditor, 1973-74; sr. auditor, mgr. Price Waterhouse, Johannesburg, South Africa, 1974-79; sr. audit mgr. Price Waterhouse, London, 1979-84, ptnr., auditor, 1984-90, ptnr., head MA London, 1990-92; ptnr. in charge Netherlands CF Price Waterhouse, Rotterdam, The Netherlands, 1992-95; head European MA Price Waterhouse, London and Frankfurt, 1995-97; head global corp. fin. Infocomms., entertainment and media Price Waterhouse (now Price Waterhouse Coopers), London, 1997-2000; global leader of corp. fin. for the technology/comms. sector Ernst & Young, London, 2000—. Author: European Cultures Guide, 1997. Mem. com. of honor European Union Chamber Orch., Exeter, Brussels, 1991—. Fellow Inst. of Chartered Accts. in Eng. and Wales; mem. Chartered Accts. of South Africa (assoc.), Lamberhurst Golf Club. Mem. Ch. of England. Avocations: golf, tennis, skiing. Office: Ernst & Young, 1 Lambeth Palace Rd, London SE1 7EV, England

HARLLEE, MARY BETH, social worker, educator; b. Statesville, N.C., Apr. 20, 1946; d. Zimmie Edward and Anna Beth (Morrison) Tharpe; m. Thomas Cannon Harllee, Nov. 12, 1972. AA, Mitchell Jr. Coll., 1966; BA, Catawba Coll., 1968; MEd, U. N.C., Charlotte, 1977; MSW, U. S.C., Columbia, 1990. Lic. social worker, N.C., S.C.; cert. domestic violence profl. Child welfare specialist City of Danville, Va., 1968-72; personnel cons. Golden Door, Charlotte, 1972-74; reading specialist, program coord. Learning Found., Charlotte, 1974-76; human svcs. asst. City of Charlotte, 1977-87; svc. rep. Kelly Svcs., Charlotte, 1987-88; social worker S.C. State Hosp., Columbia, 1989-90, Harris Psychiat. Hosp., Anderson, S.C., 1990—; founder, chair Darlington County Task Force on Child Abuse, 1999—; dir. Project Cope, Hartsville, S.C., 1995—; adj. prof. Coke Coll., Hartsville, S.C., 1995—. Chair social com. N.C. Literacy Bd., Charlotte, 1984-88; mem. gov.'s Adv. Bd. Alzheimer's Assn. Named Social Worker of Yr. Dept. Health and Environ. Control, Florence, S.C., 1992, 95. Mem. Nat. Assn. Clin. Social Workers. Democrat. Avocations: dance, cooking, writing poetry, reading. Office: Harris Psychiat Hosp PO Box 2907 Anderson SC 29622-2907

HARLOW, ERNEST, portfolio manager; b. Leek, Staffordshire, England, Apr. 1, 1927; s. Ernest and Alice Ann (Rogers) H. Portfolio mgr. Ernest Harlow, Cheshire, England; bd. dirs. Ernest Harlow Cheshire. Avocation: fishing. Home: Dye House/Rushton Spencer, nr Macclesfield, Cheshire England

HARLOW, TIMOTHY NEAL, physician; b. Cheadle Hulme, Cheshire, Eng., Sept. 26, 1956; s. Donald Francis and Irma Sylvia Harlow; m. Caroline Anne Hely-Hutchinson, Oct. 20, 1979; children: Alastair, Jennifer. B.Medicine, B.Surgery, Birmingham (Eng.) Med. Sch., 1982; Diploma in Child Health, Royal Coll. Physicians/Surgeon, 1984. House officer Sandwell Hosp., 1982, Good Hope Hosp., 1983; sr. house officer Dudley Rd. Hosp., 1984-86; gen. practice registrar Bromsgrove, Eng., 1986-87; gen. practice medicine Coll. Surgery, Cullompton, Eng., 1987—; examiner, surgeon St. John's Amb., 1987—; asst. med. officer, dep. leader Oundle Mountaineering Exptn. to China, 1982; mem. Birmingham Med. rsch. Expeditionary Soc. Exptn., 1982. Patentee in field. Mem. Lost Valley Mountaineering Assn. (founding mem.). Liberal Democrat. Buddhist. Avocations: mountaineering, scuba diving, skiing, medical journalism. Office: College Surgery, College Rd, Cullompton EX15 1TG, England

HARMAN, DONALD LEE, nurse, educator, consultant; b. Titusville, Pa., Mar. 22, 1948; s. William Ceska and Eva Louise (Matha) H. BS in Edn., Edinboro Coll., 1970, MEd, 1972; AAS in Nursing, Ohio U.-Zanesville, 1977; MS, U. Wis., 1993. RN, Ohio, Ill., Wis. Dir. out-patient svcs. Spencer Hosp., Meadville, Pa., 1974; in-svc. instr. Guernsy Meml. Hosp., Cambridge, Ohio, 1974-77; instr. in med., surg., and pediat. nursing Blessing Hosp., Quincy, Ill., 1977-79; pediat. staff nurse Rush Presbyn. St. Luke's Hosp., Chgo., 1979; camp nurse Young Men's Jewish Coun., Chgo., 1979; emergency rm. nurse Henrotin Hosp., Chgo., 1979, intravenous therapist, 1980; head instr. med. surg. nursing Sch. Nursing Madison (Wis.) Gen. Hosp., 1980-81, dir. nursing Edn., 1981-86; dir. mktg. and sales Epic Sys. Corp., 1986-88; tng. and devel. coord. Hazleton Labs. Am., Inc., Madison, Wis., 1988-89, asst. mgr. clin. rsch. unit, 1989-90; instr. Madison Area Tech. Coll., 1988-92; staff nurse U. Wis., Madison, 1990-94; charge nurse Mendota Mental Health Inst., 1990-94; clin. nurse specialist Citation Computer Syss. Inc., 1993-97; sr. clin. sales cons. HealthVISION Corp., 1994-98; clin. cons., instr. Eclipsys Corp., 1999—; pres., bd. dirs. CommonHealth Co.; del. to China U.S. Healthcare Systems, 1987; cons. HMOS Computer Systems, 1994-95, Citation Computer Systems, 1995-96, HealthVision Corp., 1996-98, Transition Systems, Inc., 1998, Eclipsys Corp., 1999—. Author: Energy-For All Reasons Facilitator's Guide. Recipient Copper Cup award, Madison Gen. Hosp., 1983. Mem. NEA (life). Methodist.

HARMAN, WILLIAM BOYS, JR., lawyer; b. Newport News, Va., June 5, 1930; s. William Boys and Helen (Conner) H.; children: Susan Carol, Thomas Scott, Ann Carrington. AB, Coll. William and Mary, 1951, JD, 1956; LLM, Georgetown U., 1960. Bar: Va. 1956, D.C. 1961. Tax atty. Gen. Motors Corp., Detroit, 1956-58; atty. Office Chief Counsel, IRS, Washington, 1958-59, Office of Tax Legis. Counsel, U.S. Treasury Dept., Washington, 1959-61; atty. firm Cummings & Sellers, Washington, 1961-62; asso. gen. counsel Am. Life Conv., Washington, 1962-67; gen. counsel Am. Life Conv., 1968-72; v.p. law Am. Life Ins. Assn., 1973-75; exec. v.p. Am. Council Life Ins., 1976-78; partner firm Sutherland, Asbill & Brennan, Washington, 1978-85, Davis & Harman, Washington, 1985—. Served with USCGR, 1952-54. Mem. ABA, Va. State Bar, D.C. Bar Assn., Assn. Life Ins. Counsel, Am. Law Inst., SAR, William and Mary Law Sch. Assn., Order of Coif, Washington Golf and Country Club, Metropolitan Club, Phi

Beta Kappa, Phi Alpha Delta, Sigma Alpha Epsilon. Home: 3839 N Tazewell St Arlington VA 22207-4568 Office: Davis & Harman Ste 1200 1455 Pennsylvania Ave NW Washington DC 20004-1034

HARMANEC, PETR, astronomer; b. Kolin, Praha, Czech Republic, Sept. 18, 1942; s. Jaroslav and Olga (Tomková) Kratochvíl; m. Dagmar Nováková (div. 1981); children: David, Jakub; m. Irena Havlová, Oct. 14, 1982; children: Petr Bernas, Václav Havel. RNDr., Charles U., Prague, Czech Republic, 1964; PhD, Czechoslovak Acad. Scis., Prague, Czech Republic, 1969, DSc, 1991; postgrad. student, Acad. Scis. Astron. Inst., Ondřejov, 1964-69. Astronomer Acad. Scis. Astron. Inst., Ondřejov, Czech Republic, 1969-91; dep. dir. Acad. Scis. Astron. Inst., Ondřejov, 1991-94, astronomer, 1994—; chmn. coun. scis. Acad. Scis., Prague, Czech Republic, 1997-2000; dir. Inst. of Astronomy, Charles U., Prague, 1999—. Contbr. 171 original astronomical papers, 1964—; editor Proceedings of European Meeting Internat. Astron. Union on Astrophysics, 1987; co-editor Internat. conf. proceedings Workshop on Rapid Variation of Early Type Stars, 1983. Mem. Internat. Astron. Union. Avocations: photography, jogging. Home: Reznická 7, 110 00 Praha 1 Bohemia, Czech Republic Office: Inst AStronomy Charles U, v Holesovickach 2, CZ-18000 Praque 8 Bohemia, Czech Republic

HARMANT, MICHAEL JEAN, aerospace executive; b. Fumel, France, May 10, 1944; came to Belgium, 1984; s. Emile François and Jeanne Marie-Therese (Weiss) H.; m. Yvonne Henriette Bonfill, July 17, 1972; children: Fabrice, Joanne, Maïté. Masters, ENSAM, Paris, 1965. Registered profl. engr. Mgr. mining ops. Miferma, Mauretania, France, 1967-70; edn. cons. Euratec-Paris, Algers, Algeria, 1970-73; asst. gen. mgr. Equipments Mechaniques Specialises, Paris, 1973-82; pres. gen. mgr. Etablissements Pierre Roch, Luneville, France, 1982-84; COO Adrien de Backer, Brussels, 1984-87; gen. mgr. SKF-Applications du Roulement, Thomery, France, 1987-89, Sonaca S.A., Gosselies, Belgium, 1989-96; cons., 1996-97; sec. gen. Soc. Ingénieurs Arts et Métiers, Paris, 1997—; chmn. bd. dirs. Ataena S.A., Jumet, Belgium; dir., bd. dirs. Gebecoma, BDIG, Belgospace, Uwec and others, Brussels; chmn. aircraft sectoral group AECMA, Enterprises Wallonnes de L'Aeronautique. Author (manual) Methodology of Modern Maintenance, 1971; editor (periodical) Contact, 1990—; pub. (monthly) Arts Et Métiers Mag., 1997; patentee in fields of systems and process equipment. Recipient Doyen Dutravail award Ministere Du Travail, Brussels, 1994. Mem. Exec. Club. Avocation: private pilot. Home: 3 place Gabriel-Fauré, 94510 La queue-en-Brie France Office: 9 bis Avenue d'Iena, 75783 Paris France

HARMANTZIS, FOTIOS C., computer scientist, engineer; b. Stavli, Evritania, Greece, May 17, 1973; s. Christos F. and Anna G. (Bletsas) H. BSc in Computer Sci., U. Crete, Heraklion, 1995, MSc in Computer Sci., 1997; grad., U. Pa., U. Toronto, Ont., Can. Undergrad. trainee Computer Ctr. U. Crete-Found. for Rsch. and Tech.-Hellas, Heraklion, 1992-93; undergrad. rsch. asst. Inst. Computer Sci.-Found. for Rsch. and Tech.-Hellas, Heraklion, 1993-95, grad. rsch. asst., 1995-97, mem. telecom. and networks groups, 1994-97; tchg. fellow U. Pa., Phila., 1997-98; rsch. fellow, tchg. fellow U. Toronto, 1998-99; trainer State Inst. Vocation Tng., Heraklion, 1996. Contbr. rsch. articles to profl. jours. Rsch. asst. ACTS Project Cashman, 1995-97, RACE-II Project Topic, 1993-94; Connaught scholar U. Toronto, 1998-99. Mem. IEEE, IEEE Comms. Soc., Assn. for Computing Machinery, Informs, Sigma Xi. Avocations: music, art history, travel, reading.

HARMATZ, DAVID, biochemist; b. Jerusalem, Aug. 19, 1943; s. Abraham and Rebecca Harmatz; 2 children: Yael, Guy. BSc, Hebrew U., 1966, MSc, 1968, PhD, 1973. Vis. rsch. fellow Sloan-Kettering Cancer Inst., N.Y.C., 1973-75; resident rsch. assoc. NASA Ames Rsch. Ctr., Moffett Field, Calif., 1976; core facility mgr., scientist Hebrew U. Life Scis., Jerusalem, 1984—; vis. prof. dept. biochemistry U. Wyo., Laramie, 1984—.

HARMELINK, HERMAN, III, clergyman, author, educator, ecumenist; b. Sheldon, Pa., Dec. 26, 1933; s. Herman II, and Thyrza (Eringa) H.; m. Barbara Mary Conibear, Aug. 11, 1959; children: Herman IV Alan, Lindsay Alexandra (Mrs. Richard L. LeMay, Jr.). BA cum laude, Central Coll., 1954; MA, Columbia U., 1955; postgrad., U. London, 1955; MDiv, New Brunswick Theol. Sem., 1958; World Coun. Chs. scholar, U. Heidelberg, 1959; STM magna cum laude, Union Theol. Sem., N.Y.C., 1964, MPhil, 1978. Ordained to ministry Reformed Ch. Am., 1959. Min. Cmty. Ch., Glen Rock, N.J., 1959-64, Woodcliff Cmty. Ch., Woodcliff-on-Hudson, N.J., 1964-71, Reformed Ch., Poughkeepsie, N.Y., 1971—; adj. faculty in philosophy SUNY, Marist Coll.; chaplain Holland-Am. Line; vice-chmn. Faith and Order Commn., Nat. Coun. Chs., 1976-79, mem. Commn. on Regional and Local Ecumenism, 1981-84; pres. Synod of N.J., 1969; chmn. interch. rels. Ref. Ch. Am., 1964-71; chmn. Ecumenical Rels. Commn. Internat. Coun. of Cmty. Chs., 1994—; del. 18th Plenary Consultation on Ch. Union, St. Louis, 1999; pres. Dutchess Interfaith Coun., 1977-78, devel. retirement cmty. com., 1989—, bd. dirs.; del. gen. coun. World Alliance Ref. Chs., Frankfurt, 1964, Nairobi, 1970; adv. Gen. Assembly World Coun. Chs., Uppsala, Sweden, 1968; U.S. del. 50th Anniversary Faith and Order Commn., Lausanne, Switzerland, 1977; del. Nat. Coun. Chs. Gen. Assembly, 1999—. Author: Ecumenism and the Reformed Church, 1968; The Reformed Church in New Jersey, 1969; Another Look at Frelinghuysen and His Awakening, 1969; contbg. author to Piety and Patriotism, 1976, Vision from the Hill, 1984, The Livingston Legacy, 1987. Trustee Peter A. Lindsay Trust Imperial Coll. U. London; trustee St. Francis Hosp., exec. com. of bd., joint conf. com., chmn. planning com.; bd. dirs. Dutchess County Arts Coun., 1976-80, Bardavon 1869 Opera House, 1978-79; mem. allocation and planning divsn. United Way of Dutchess County; mem. Dutchess County Execs. Com. on Med. Ethics; sec. bd. dirs. Rehab. Programs, Inc., 1977-79; bd. dirs. Anderson Ednl. Found., Collingwood Repertory Theatre, 1978-80, Mid-Hudson Meml. Soc., 1981-84; pres. Poughkeepsie Generating Cmty., 1974—; bd. dirs. Literacy Vol. of Dutchess County, pres. 1987-89; bd. dirs. Literacy Vols. Am., N.Y., chmn. pers. comm., mem. program com., pres.-elect, 1992-93, pres. 1993-96, bd. dirs. nat. bd. Lit. Vols. Am.; Poughkeepsie Rural Cemetery, chmn. fin. com.; pres. Ranfurly Library Svc. of N.Y. Inc., Town of Poughkeepsie Dem. Com., Dutchess County Dem. Com.; participant U.S.-S. African Leader Exchange Program, 1971; adv. bd. Wartburg Luth. Svcs., 1993—; chmn. Anderson Sch. Wine Showcase; ecumenical adv. del. Presbyn. Ch. Gen. Assembly, Long Beach, Calif., 2000. Lt. USNR, 1957-61. Fulbright Travel grant to Germany, 1958-59. Mem. N.Am. Acad. Ecumenists, Am. Soc. Ch. History, Presbyn. Hist. Soc., Poughkeepsie C. of C., Dutchess Interfaith Coun., Dutchess County Clergy Club, Dutchess County Hist. Soc. (life, bd. dirs. 1974-78), Poughkeepsie Rotary (pres. 1977-79, sec. 1979—, sec. Dist. 721, 1980-81, gov. 1982-83, chmn. World Community Svc., Rotary Internat. Coun. on Legis., Monte Carlo, 1983, Rotary Internat. pres.'s rep. to dist. confs. 1984, 88, Paul Harris fellow, sect. leader internat. conv., Portland, 1990), Lumanites (sec.-treas.), 251, Poughkeepsie Social Reading Club (past pres.), Circumnavigators Club (N.Y.C.), The Club, Travelers Century Club (life mem.), Fjord Club, Mil Order Fgn. Wars of U.S. (life vet. companion, chaplain, mem. coun. N.Y. commandery), Fulbright Assn. (life), St. George's Soc. N.Y. (life), Chevalier du Tastevin (France), Royal Overseas League (London), Friends of St. George's and Descendants of the Knights of the Garter (life, Windsor), The English Speaking Union, The Co. of Pastors, Witherspoon Soc.

HARMON, DAVID EUGENE, optometrist, geneticist; b. Greeneville, Tenn., July 27, 1951; s. Carl Eugene and Kathryn Elizabeth (Colyer) H. BS, U. Tenn., 1973, MS, 1975; PhD, U. Ga., 1978; OD, New Eng. Coll. Optometry, 1989; computer cert., Carson-Newman Coll., 2000. Fellow U. Ga., Athens, 1978, U. Fla., Gainesville, 1979; vis. asst. prof. So. Ill. U., Carbondale, 1980-82; asst. prof. Clemson (S.C.) U., 1982-85, assoc. prof., 1985; internist VA Hosp., Boston, 1988, Children's Hosp., Boston, 1988-89, Dimock Community Health Ctr., Boston, 1989; eye specialist Morristown, Tenn., 1989—; geneticist Morristown, 1989—; genetic cons. Nigerian Govt., 1980—. Contbr. articles to profl. jours. Mem. Sunday sch. Trinity United Meth. Ch., Greeneville, 1954—; sch. rep. New Eng. Coll. Optometry, 1987; coach nat. winning dairy cattle judging team, 1980, 81. Recipient Breeder All-Am. Dairy Animal award Am. Guernsey Cattle Club, 1973, Nat. 4-H Pub. Speaking award, 1969, Nat. 4-H Leadership award, 1970. Mem. Am. Optometric Assn., Am. Dairy Assn., Am. Soc. Animal Sci., Tenn. Optometric Assn., So. Coun. Optometrists, Am. Holstein Assn., Morristown C. of C., New Eng. Coll. Optometry Alumni Assn. (life), Lions Club Morristown, Sigma Xi, Alpha Zeta. Avocations: camping, hiking, table tennis. Home and Office: 131 N Henry St Morristown TN 37814-4626

HARMON, GEORGE MARION, academic administrator; b. Memphis, Aug. 12, 1934; s. George Marion and Madie P. (Foster) H.; m. Bessie W. Porter, Dec. 27, 1958; children: Nancy R., Mary K., Elizabeth T., George Marion III. BA, Rhodes Coll., 1956; MBA, Emory U., 1957; DBA, Harvard U., 1963. Market rsch. analyst Continental Oil Co., Houston, 1957; rsch. assoc. Harvard U., 1960-63; asst. prof. Coll. Bus. Adminstrn., dir. Salzberg Meml. Transp. Program Syracuse U., N.Y., 1963-66; sr. assoc. sys. econs. divsn. Planning Rsch. Corp., Washington, 1966-67; prof., chmn. dept econs. and bus. adminstrn., dir. continuing edn. program in econs. and bus. adminstrn. Southwestern U. (name changed to Rhodes Coll.), Memphis, 1967-74; prof., dean divsn. bus. and mgmt. W.Va. Coll. Grad. Studies, Charleston, 1974-75; prof., dean Sch. Bus. and Mgmt. Saginaw Valley State Coll., University Center, Mich., 1975-78; pres. Millsaps Coll., Jackson, Miss., 1978-2000, prof. emeritus, sr. counsel spl. projects, 2000—; mem. faculty fin. Sch. Banking of the South, La. State U., 1968-72; dir. Audio Visual Sys., Inc., Tenn., 1970-72; v.p., treas. Allen Industries, Inc., Tenn., 1970-72; co-founder, v.p. Computer Survey Sys., Inc., Tenn., 1972-73; bd. dirs., chmn. exec. compensation com. MacCarty Farms, Inc., Magee, Miss., 1982-95; bd. dirs. Entex, Inc., Houston, 1981-99; mem. So. Regional Edn. Bd., Atlanta, 1994-98; bd. dirs. Union Planters Bank of Miss. Contbr. articles on bus. adminstrn. to profl. jours. Bd. dirs. Fayetteville-Manlius Cen. Sch. Dist., N.Y., 1961-63, John Houston Wear Found., Jackson; trustee, chmn. pers. and labor rels. com. Saginaw Osteo. Hosp., 1977-78; bd. dirs. Jackson Symphony Orch. Assn., 1981-85, Miss. Opera Assn., 1981-86; chmn. So. Colls. and Univs. Union, 1983-88, Miss. Found. Ind. Colls., 1982; univ. senate United Meth. Ch., 1990-2000; comm. and sec. Jackson Internat. Airport Authority, 1991-97; chmn., bd. dirs. Jackson Med. Edn. Dist., 1998—. Mem. NCAA (coun. 1986-92), Jackson C. of C. (bd. dirs. 1981-84; chmn. bd. dirs. Jackson Med. Dist. 1998-99), Soc. Internat. Bus. Fellows, Jackson Country Club, Univ. Club, Capitol City Club, Harvard Club (N.Y.C.), Rotary, Phi Beta Kappa, Beta Gamma Sigma, Omicron Delta Kappa. Methodist. Home: 104 Adderbury Ct Ridgeland MS 39157-8709 Office: Millsaps Coll 1701 N State St Jackson MS 39210-0002

HARMON, SHERRY LYNN, computer software company executive; b. Houston, Mich., May 8, 1953; d. James Henry and Marriel Harriet Butler; m. Stewart J. Throop, July, 1973 (dec. Sept. 1978); m. Gary Michael Harmon, May 27, 1988. BS, Mich. State U., 1977, MA with honors, 1979. Salesperson, sales mgr., br. mgr. Lanier, Honolulu, 1979-82; sales mgr. Data Gen., Honolulu, 1982-84; strategic sales mgr. Digital Equipment, Culver City, Calif., 1984-88, channels mgtg. staff, 1990-91; regional mgr., dir. sales Grid Systems/AST, L.A., 1988-90; dir. channels mktg. Interleaf Inc., Chgo., 1991-95; dir. channels Xerox, InConcert, Chgo., 1995-97; v.p. channel sales iManage Inc., San Mateo, Calif., 1997—. Artist wood block print: Snow, 1971, conceptual art: 1953 Michigan, 1978; graphic artist (invention) Spectrometer, 1979. Avocations: sewing, photography, working on automobiles.

HARMOND, RICHARD PETER, historian, educator; b. N.Y.C., Mar. 19, 1929; s. William and Violet (Makein) H. BA, Fordham U., 1951; MA, Columbia U., 1954, PhD, 1966. Assoc. prof. St. John's U., N.Y.C., 1957—. Co-author: Long Island as America, 1977; co-editor: Technology in the 20th Century, 1983, Biographical Dictionary of American and Canadian Naturalists and Environmentalists, 1997; editor: (newsletter) L.I. Archives Conf., 1982-99; assoc. editor: L.I. Hist. jour., 1988—; contbr. articles to profl. jours. and other publs. With U.S. Army, 1951-53. Mem. Orgn. Am. Historians, Soc. History of Tech., Theodore Roosevelt Assn. (trustee 1994—), Phi Alpha Theta (paper prize com. 1994-97). Office: St John's U Hist Dept Jamaica NY 11439-0001

HARMS, STEVEN ALAN, lawyer; b. Detroit, Feb. 15, 1949; s. Herbert Rudolph and Elsa Jane (McClelland) H.; m. Nancy Gayle Banta, June 26, 1971; children: Jennifer Elizabeth, Heather Lynn, Robin Ann. BA, Hope Coll., 1970; JD, Detroit Coll. Law, 1975. Bar: Mich. 1975, U.S. Dist. Ct. (so. dist.) Mich. 1975, U.S. Ct. Appeals (6th cir.) 1982; bd. cert. creditors rights specialist. Ptnr. Muller, Muller, Richmond, Harms, Myers & Sgroi, P.C., Birmingham, Mich.; sec. gen. practice session State Bar Mich., 1982-83; mediator Oakland County Cir. Ct., 1990—; lectr. in field; adj. prof. Bus. Law Walsh Coll., Troy, Mich., 1990—. Author: Successful Collection of a Judgement, 1981, Rights of Commercial Creditors, 1982, Post Judgement Collection, 1988, Handling the Collection Case in Michigan, 1989, rev. edit., 1999; co-author: Attorney Fee Agreements, 1995, contbg. editor Michigan Business Formbook, 1997, rev. edit., 2000, Michigan Civil Procedure, 1997; editor: General Practitioner, State Bar Mich., 1978-82. Bd. dirs. fin. com. YMCA, North Oakland County, Mich., 1987—, chmn. bd., 1990-91. Republican. Club: Pearson Yacht Owners Assn. (commodore 1988-90), Hunter Sailing Assn. (vice commodore 1985-86, commodore 1987-88). Office: Muller Muller Richmond Harms Myers & Sgroi PC 33233 Woodward Ave Birmingham MI 48009-0903

HARNER, MICHAEL JAMES, anthropologist, educator, author; b. Washington, Apr. 27, 1929; s. Charles Emory and Virginia (Paxton) H.; m. June Knight Kocher, 1951; children: Teresa J., James E.; m. Sandra Ferial Dickey, 1966. A.B., U. Calif., Berkeley, 1953, Ph.D., 1963. Asst. prof. Ariz. State U., Tempe, 1958-61; from sr. mus. anthropologist to assoc. rsch. anthropologist and asst. dir. Hearst Mus. Anthropology U. Calif., Berkeley, 1961-66; from vis. assoc. prof. to assoc. prof. Columbia U., N.Y.C., 1966-70; from assoc. prof. to prof. grad. faculty New Sch. Social Research, N.Y.C., 1970-87, chmn. dept. anthropology, 1973-77; internat. tchr. shamanism, 1977—; founder, dir. Ctr. for Shamanic Studies, Norwalk, Conn., 1979-87; founder, pres., bd. dirs. Found. for Shamanic Studies, Mill Valley, Calif., 1985—; researcher Harvard U. Upper Gila expdn., 1948, Upper Amazon basin, 1956-57, 60-61, 64, 69, 73, Western N.Am., 1951-53, 59, 65, 76, 78, Lapland, 1983, 84, Can. Arctic, 1987; vis. assoc. prof. U. Calif., Berkeley, 1971, 72, vis. prof., 1975; vis. assoc. prof. Yale U., New Haven, 1970; co-organizer 1st Internat. Congress on Shamanism, Moscow, 1999. Author: The Jivaro: People of the Sacred Waterfalls, 1972, 2d edit., 1984, Music of the Jivaro of Ecuador, 1972, Cannibal, 1979, The Way of the Shaman, 1980, 3d edit., 1990; editor: Hallucinogens and Shamanism, 1973; cons. editor: Revision Mag. Social Sci. Rsch. Coun., Doherty Found., Am. Mus. Nat. History fellow. Fellow AAAS, Am. Anthrop. Assn., Royal Anthrop. Inst. G.B. and Ireland, N.Y. Acad. Scis. (co-chmn. anthropology sect. 1980-81); mem. Am. Ethnol. Soc., Soc. Am. Archaeology, Soc. Ethnohistory, Assn. Transpersonal Psychology, Internat. Transpersonal Assn. (bd. dirs. 1982-85, 89-91), Assn. for the Anthropology of Consciousness, Xat Medicine Men's Soc., Inst. Andean Studies, Explorers Club (fellow). Office: Found for Shamanic Studies PO Box 1939 Mill Valley CA 94942-1939

HARNER, TIMOTHY R., lawyer; b. Clarkson, N.Y., Sept. 1, 1955; s. Roy Seymour and Helen Belle (Dowden) H.; m. Suzanne Lee Daggs, May 22, 1982; children: Sarah, Andrew. BA, Houghton Coll., 1977; JD cum laude, Harvard Law Sch., 1980. Bar: N.Y., 1981. Law clk. U.S. Ct. Appeals 2nd Cir., N.Y.C., 1980-81; assoc. Nixon, Hargrave, Devans & Doyle, Rochester, N.Y., 1981-85; gen. counsel Upstate Farms Coop., Inc., LeRoy, N.Y., 1985—; dir. Palmer Food Svcs., Rochester. Editor: Harvard Law Rev., 1978-79, devel. officer, 1979-80. Trustee, sec. Roberts Wesleyan Coll., Rochester, 1989. Mem. Am. Corp. Counsel Assn. (past pres. Ctrl. and Western N.Y. chpts. 1997). Republican. Methodist. Avocations: astronomy, golf, jogging. Office: Upstate Farms Coop Inc 7115 W Main Rd Le Roy NY 14482-9352

HARNEY, JEAN LENORE, physician; b. St. Kitts, West Indies; d. John Leonard and Mae Elizabeth (Woolward) H.; m. Derrick Dickinson, Dec. 1, 1955 (div. 1960). MPH, Harvard Sch. Pub. Health, Boston, 1957. Med. officer St. Kitts, 1953-60; med. officer health Govt. Barbados, 1960-69; med. officer Pan-Am. Health Orgn./WHO, Venezuela, Belize, Antigua, 1969-75; chief med. officer Govt. Barbados, 1975-85; project mgr. Carribbean Assn. Environ. Health Officers, Barbados, 1985-89; health cons. Barbados, 1990—; hon. assoc. lectr. U. West Indies, Barbados. Recipient award for contribution in preventive medicine Caribbean Assn. Environ. Health Officers, 1988, Disting. Svc. award Caribbean Pub. Health Assn., 1994, Outstanding Career in Medicine award U. West Indies, Barbados BAMP CME, 1999.

HARNEY, MARY, government official; b. Ballinasloe, Ireland, Mar. 1953. Mem. Dublin County Coun., 1979-91, Tail Eireann, 1981; co-founder Progressive Democrats, 1985; min. environmental protection Ireland, 1989-93; leader Progressive Dems., 1993; dep. prime min. Ireland, 1997—; spokesperson on justice, equality and law reform. Office: Office of Prime Min, Upper Merrion St, Dublin 2, Ireland*

HARNISCH, JÖRG-HENNER, economist; b. Halle, Germany, Feb. 27, 1949; s. Heinz and Sigrid Harnisch; m. Svetlana Treskova, June 1, 1999; 1 child. Proficiency in English cert., Cambridge (Eng.) U., 1970; 1st staatsexamen, 1975, 2d staatsexamen, 1977. Lectr. U. Mass Media and Fgn. Lang. Tchg., Marburg, Germany, 1975, U. Didactics and Methodics in English, Bremen, Germany, 1977-78; sr. lectr. Athenäum Scriptor.Hain.Hanstein.Jüd.Verlag, Konigsten, Germany, 1978-79; dir. Inst. Cultural and Econ. Analyses, Fulda, Germany, 1988-99. Author: (books) The Theories of Language and the Science of Language, 1974, Foreign Language Teaching Theories with Teaching Material and Analyses, 1977, Financial and Economic Analyses of Great Britain, 1988-90, The Philosophies of Pragmatism in the USA in the 20th Century, 1990-92. Advisor World U. Svc., 1967, 68; advisor to various univ. polit. and acad. groups, 1969-74. Mem. Internat. Rsch. Coms. on Sociolinguistics (lectr. 1992), Internat. Comm. Studies U.S. (lectr. 1996), Crossroads in Cultural Studies (lectr. 1998), Univ. Sports Club and Team. Avocations: sports, reading. Home: Rhönstrasse 13, 36037 Fulda Hessen, Germany

HARNISCH, RÜDIGER, linguist, educator, researcher; b. Ludwigsstadt, Germany, May 10, 1955; s. Carl G. and Marianne (Däumler) H.; m. Felicitas Schwierz, May 28, 1982; children: Philipp, Veit. MA, U. Bayreuth, Germany, 1982, PhD, 1986, PhD habilitation, 1998. Rschr. linguistic Minorities Rsch. Project, Bayreuth, 1984-88; lectr. U. Bayreuth, 1988-94, 98—; rschr. Zentrum für Allgemeine Sprachwissenschaft, Berlin, 1996-98; vis. lectr. Ecole Normale Supérieure, Yaoundé, Cameroon, 1990, Karl-Franzens-Univ., Graz, Austria, 1999; cons. Dialektsituation im Grenzgebiet, Bayreuth and Jena, Germany, 1990—, Sprachatlas von Nordostbayern, Bayreuth, 1986—; rschr. Diachronische Adäquatheitsbedingungen für Grammatiktheorien, 2000—, Morphologische Markiertheit und Kimplexitüt in Sprachwandel. Author: Natürliche Generative Morphologie und Phonologie, 1987, Grundform-und Stamm-Prinzip in der Substantivmorphologie, 1997; co-editor: Festschrift Robert Hinderling, 1995, (series) Bayreuther Beiträge zur Dialektologie, 1989—, (handbook) Mitteleuropäische Sprachminderheiten, 1996. Grantee Friedr-Naumann-Stiftung, 1982-84, Deutsche Forschungsgemeinschaft, 1994-96. Fellow Johann-Andreas-Schmeller-Gesellschaft (sec. 1979-99); mem. Jean-Paul-Gesellschaft, Deutsche Gesellschaft für Sprachwissenschaft. Avocation: fencing. Home: Sterntalerring 25/b, D-95447 Bayreuth Germany Office: Univ Bayreuth, Germanistische Linguistik, D-95440 Bayreuth Germany

HAROUN, ELTAHIR MOHAMED, veterinary pathology educator, researcher; b. Elobeid, Sudan, July 1, 1945; s. Mohamed Haroun Adam and Fatima Basheer Mohamed; m. Fatima Elameen Elshareef, June 23, 1977; children: Elgasim, Mohamedelameen, Afaf, Najat, Elrasheed. BVSc, U. Khartoum, Sudan, 1970, MVSc, 1975; PhD, U. Edinburgh, 1979. Asst. rsch. officer Vet. Rsch. Lab., Khartoum, 1970-72; tchg. asst. U. Khartoum, 1973-75, lectr. vet. pathology, 1979-84; rsch. fellow U. P.R., 1984-85; from assoc. prof. to prof. vet. pathology U. King Saud, Saudi Arabia, 1985—, head dept. vet. medicine, 1986-93; cons. King Abud Al Aziz City of Sci. and Tech., Saudi Arabia, 1989-95. Contbr. articles to profl. jours.; author, translator books. Mem. Sudan Vet. Assn. (sec., mem. editl. bd.), Saudi Biol. Soc. Office: King Saud Coll Agr/Vet Med, Gassim Br PO Box 1482, Buraydah Gassim, Saudi Arabia

HARPER, DAVID BENJAMIN, microbial biochemistry researcher; b. Hitchin, U.K., Aug. 13, 1942; s. John Childs and Rosemary Helen (Flawn) H. BSc with honors, U. Bristol, 1964; PhD, Wye Coll., 1967. Chartered chemist U. London. Rsch. fellow Sci. Rsch. Coun. Queen Mary Coll., 1967-68; Nat. Rsch. Coun. fellow Prairie Regional Lab., Saskatoon, Can., 1968-70; Wellcome rsch. fellowship U. Newcastle Upon-Tyne, U. Kent, U.K., 1970-72; lectr. to sr. lectr. Queen's U. of Belfast, U.K., 1973-88, reader, 1988-92, prof., 1992—. Contbr. articles to profl. jours. Fellow Royal Soc. of Chemistry; mem. Soc. of Chem. Industry, Soc. of Gen. Microbiology, Am. Soc. for Microbiology. Avocations: gardening, tree planting, cacti collecting, bee keeping. Office: Dept Food Sci Queens U, Newforge Lane, Belfast BT9 5PX, United Kingdom

HARPER, GREGORY SCOTT, research scientist; b. Brisbane, Queensland, Australia, Aug. 7, 1958; s. Edward George and Laurel Nichol (Barnes) H.; m. Catherine Mary Leach, Oct. 3, 1981; children: Alexander Scott, Elise Prue. BSc, U. Queensland, Brisbane, 1981; PhD, Monash U., Melbourne, Australia, 1985; GDip in Tech. Mgmt., Deakin U., Geelong, Australia, 1999. Lab. asst. U. Queensland, 1980; Fogarty internat. fellow NIH, Bethesda, Md., 1984-87; rsch. scientist Wenner-Gren Found., Uppsala (Sweden) Found., 1987-88; fellow Adelaide (Australia) Children's Hosp., 1988-92; rsch. biochemist Commonwealth Sci. and Indsl. Rsch. Org., Brisbane, 1992—; specialist in sci. commercialization. Author of monographs reviews and sci. papers. Recipient Overseas Study award Meat Rsch. Corp., 1994; Traveling fellow Australia-New Zealand Found., 1995, Invitational fellow Japan Soc. for the Promotion of Sci., 1996, Ctrl. Queensland U. fellow; grant Dept. Industry Sci. and Tourism, Australian Govt., 1998, 2000; chair 15th Australian Conf. Biotech., 2000. Mem. Australian Soc. Biochemistry and Molecular Biology Inc., Assn. Profl. Engrs., Scientists and Mgrs., Matrix Biology Soc. Australia and New Zealand, Inc. (sec.), Australian Biotechnology Assn. (sec. Queensland br.), Crondar Pty. Ltd. (dir., founder). Presbyterian. Avocations: yachting, camping, woodworking. E-mail: gregory.harper@tag.csiro.au. Office: U QLd, Commonwealth Sci & Indsl Gehrmann Labs, ST Lucia 4072, Australia

HARPER, SHIRLEY FAY, nutritionist, educator, consultant, lecturer; b. Auburn, Ky., Apr. 23, 1943; d. Charles Henry and Annabelle (Gregory) Belcher; m. Robert Vance Harper, May 19, 1973 (dec. Mar. 2000); children: Glenda, Debra, Teresa, Suzanna, Cynthia. BS, Western Ky. U., 1966, MS, 1982. Cert. nutritionist and lic. dietitian, Ky. Dir. dietetics Logan County Hosp., Russellville, Ky., 1965-80; cons. Western State Hosp., Hopkinsville, Ky., 1983-84, instnl. dietetic adminstr., 1984-88; dietitian Rivendell Children's Psychiat. Hosp., Bowling Green, Ky., 1988-90; instr. nutrition Western Ky. U., Bowling Green, 1990-92; cons. Auburn (Ky.) Nursing Ctr., 1976-95, Belle Meade Home, Greenville, Ky., 1980—, Brookfield Manor, Hopkinsville, Ky., 1983—, Sparks Nursing Ctr., Central City, Ky., 1983—, Muhlenberg Cmty. Hosp., Greenville, 1989-2000, Russellville (Ky.) Health Care Manor, 1978-83, 92—, Westlake Cumberland Hosp., Columbia, Ky., 1993—, Franklin-Simpson Meml. Hosp., Franklin, Ky., 1993—; nutrition instr. Madisonville (Ky.) Cmty. Coll., 1995-98. Mem. regional bd. dirs. ARC of Ky., Frankfort, 1990-96; vice chair ARC of Logan County, 1992-93, chmn., 1993-96, 97—; bd. dirs. Logan County ARC United Way, 1993—; co-chair adv. coun. devel. disabilities Lifeskills, 1992-93, adv. coun. Lifeskills Residential Living Group Home, 1993—, human rights adv. coun., 1994—; chair Let's Build our Future Campaign; nutrition del. Citizen Am. Program to USSR, 1990; adv. chair for vocat. edn., Russellville; mem. adv. coun. for home econs. and family living, We. Ky. U., 1990-93; bd. dirs. ARC of Logan County for United Way, 1993—; del. 24th Internat. Congress on Arts and Comm., Oxford (Eng.) U., 1997. Recipient Outstanding Svc. award Am. Dietetic Assn. Found., 1993, Outstanding Svc. award Barren River Mental Health-Mental Retardation Bd., 1987, Svc. Appreciation award Logan-Russellville Assn. for Retarded Citizens, 1987, Internat. Woman of Yr. award for contribution to Nutrition and Humanity, Internat. Biographical Assn., 1993-94, World Lifetime Achievement award Am. Biographical Inst., 1995; inaugurated Lifetime Dep. Gov., Am. Biographical Rsch. Bd., 1995, Pres.'s award ARC of Logan County, 1996, award of excellence Oxford, Eng. Internat. Congress on Arts and Comm., Internat. Sash of Acad., Am. Biograph. Inst., 1997. Mem. Am. Dietetic Assn., Nat. Nutrition Network, Ky. Dietetic Assn. (pres. Western dist. 1976-77, Outstanding Dietitian award 1984), Bowling Green-Warren County Nutrition Coun., Nat. Ctr. for Nutrition and Dietetics (charter), Ky. Nutrition Coun., Logan County Home Economist Club (sec. 1994-95, v.p. 1995-96, pres. 1996-97), Internat. Biog. Assn., Internat. Platform Assn., Gerontol. Nutritionist, Oncology Nutrition, Diabetes Care and Edn., Dietitians in Nutrition Support, Dietitians in Gen. Clin. Practice, Cons. Dietitians in Health Care, Edn. of Health Profls., Phi

Upsilon Omicron (pres. Beta Delta alumni chpt. 1994-96, Outstanding Alumni award 1997). Avocations: music, drawing and art, poetry, reading, cake decorating. Home and Office: 443 Hopkinsville Rd Russellville KY 42276-1286

HARPER, VESTA TAMORA, lawyer, paralegal educator; b. Vicksburg, Miss., Sept. 25, 1971; d. Gregory Duwayne and Sara Susette (Jackson) H. BS, Alcorn State U., 1993; MBA, Tex. Tech. U., 1996, JD, 1996. Bar: Tex. 1997. Extern Criminal Dist. Ct. No. 2, Dallas, 1989; legal rsch. asst. West Tex. Legal Svcs., Lubbock, 1995; staff atty. West Tex. Legal Svcs., Ft. Worth, 1998—; contract atty. Exec. Secretariat Sch., Dallas, 1997—; pvt. practice law, Dallas, 1997-98; extern 5th Dist. Ct. Appeals, Dallas, 1997; contract atty. Southeastern Paralegal Inst., Dallas, 1998. Mem. ABA. Home: 9433 Timberleaf Dr Dallas TX 75243-6123 Office: West Tex Legal Svcs 600 E Weatherford St Fort Worth TX 76102-3264

HARRACH, BALAZS, virologist, researcher; b. Mosonmagyarovar, Hungary, Apr. 5, 1952; s. Walter and Judit (Kovats) H.; m. Maria Benko, June 21, 1975; children: Borbala, Nora. DVM, U. Vet. Sci., Budapest, 1975; PhD, Hungarian Acad. Scis., Budapest, 1988. Jr. scientist Vet. Med. Rsch. Inst. Hungarian Acad. Scis., Budapest, 1975-78, scientist, 1979-89, sr. scientist, team leader, 1992-2000, dir., 2000—; vis. fellow Inst. Plant Pathology U. Minn., St. Paul, 1978-79; vis. fellow Inst. Virology, U. Glasgow, Scotland, 1987-88, U. Saskatchewan, Saskatoon, Can., 1990-92. Mem. editl. bd. Acta Veterinaria Hungarica, 1997—; author: (with others) Adenovirus Methods and Protocols, Vol. 21, 1998, Methods in Molecular Medicine, Vol. 24; contbr. articles to profl. jours. including Virology, Jour. Gen. Virology, Archives of Virology, Acad. Press. Recipient silver medal Nat. Exhbn. on Agr. and Food Industry, 1985, Outstanding Innovator award Hungarian Acad. Scis., 1986; rsch. grantee PHARE-ACCORD, European Union, 1993-94. Mem. Hungarian Microbiol. Soc., European Soc. for Vet. Virology. Avocations: travel, skiing, nature, computers. Office: Hungarian Acad Scis Vet Med, Rsch Inst, Hungaria krt 21, H-1143 Budapest Hungary

HARRAP, STEPHEN BRIAN, physiology educator; b. Melbourne, Victoria, Australia, Feb. 10, 1955; s. Brian Sinclair and Ruth Alma (Jarrett) H.; m. Shelley Ann Guckert, May 14, 1957; children: Nicholas, Jeremy, Laura. MB, BS, U. Melbourne, 1978, PhD, 1986. Commonwealth Med. fellow Glasgow, U.K., 1986; Neil Hamilton Fairley fellow Nat. Health & Med. Rsch. Coun. U. Melbourne, 1987-89; sr. lectr. Monash U., Melbourne, 1990-95; R.D. Wright fellow, NHMRC U. Melbourne, 1990-95, prof. physiology, 1995—, head dept. physiology, 1996—; trustee High Blood Pressure Rsch. Found. Australia, 1994—; cons. physician Austin Hosp., Melbourne, 1989-94, Royal Melbourne Hosp., 1995—. Pacific Rim regional editor Clin. Sci., 1995—; contbr. articles to profl. jours. Rsch. Project grant Nat. Health and Med. Rsch. Coun., Australia, 1989—, Rsch. Program grant Victorian Health Promotion Found., 1990-99. Fellow Royal Australasian Coll. Physicians, High Blood Rsch. Coun. Australia (program sec. 1993-95, exec. com. 1993-99), Coun. for High Blood Pressure Rsch. of Am. Heart Assn., Internat. Soc. Hypertension. Avocations: debating, surfing, golf, violin, photography. Office: Univ Melbourne, Dept Physiology, Victoria 3010, Australia

HARRAR, RICHARD EARLE, nurse; b. Needham, Mass., Oct. 29, 1951; s. Earle Larzelier and Barbara (Chandler) H.; m. Nancy Gass Sias, Mar. 30, 1979 (div. 1982); m. Linn Kat, 1991. BS in Nursing cum laude, Alderson-Broaddus Coll., 1987; postgrad., U. Pitts., 1993-94. RN, N.H. Emergency room technician Greater Southeast Community Hosp., Washington, 1974-75, Suburban Hosp., Bethesda, Md., 1975-76; physician's asst. Atlantic Internat. Corp., Riyadh, Saudi Arabia, 1976-77; policeman Town of Thomaston, Maine, 1977-78, 81-83; phlebotomist Leonard Morse Hosp., Natick, Mass., 1978-80; phlebotomy supr. The Faulkner Hosp., Boston, 1980-81; staff nurse Broaddus Hosp. Assn., Philippi, W.Va., 1984-87, nurse mgr. dept. Vet. Affairs, 1987-90; staff nurse emergency room Reddington-Fairview Hosp., Skowhegan, Maine, 1990-91; emergency rm. shift supr. Security Forces Hosp., Riyadh, Saudi Arabia, 1991-92, critical care nurse dept. vets. affairs, 1992-95; critical care nurse Springfield Vt. Hosp., 1996-97, Yale New Haven Hosp., 1997-98, Dartmouth-Hitchcock Med. Ctr., Lebanon, N.H., 1998—; mem. nursing curriculum com. Alderson-Broaddus Coll., Philippi, 1985-87. Vol. nurse ARC Blood Drive, W.Va., 1986. Decorated Nat. Def. Service Medal. Mem. AACN, Broaddus Hosp. Grad. Nurses Assn., Alderson-Broaddus Coll. Grad. Nurses Assn. Avocations: piano, organ, reading, sailing, foreign travel. Home: 33 Sky Line Ter Claremont NH 03743 Office: Dartmouth- Hitchcock Medical Center Coronary Care Unit Lebanon NH 03766

HARRE, GEORGE, retired chief justice. Chief justice Cayman Islands; ret., 1998. Home: Les Rousses, F-07460 Saint Paul le Jeune France

HARRELL, CARLTON (BENJAMIN CARLTON HARRELL), columnist, retired editor; b. Mamie, N.C., Oct. 1, 1929; s. Taylor Smith Jr. and Nellie Augusta (Gallop) H.; m. Audrey (Jeanine) Tarkenton, Apr. 26, 1952; children: Melissa Ann, Sheila Lynn. Student, U. N.C., 1947-49. Reporter Daily Advance, Elizabeth City, N.C., 1950-52, 53-56, Goldsboro (N.C.) News-Argus, 1956-57; reporter Durham (N.C.) Sun, 1957-64, state editor, 1964-65, asst. city editor, 1965-69, city editor, 1969-72, mng. editor, 1972-90; assoc. editor Herald-Sun, Durham, 1991-96, editor emeritus, columnist, 1996—. 2d lt. U.S. Army, 1952-53. Mem. Am. Soc. Newspaper Editors, Hist. Preservation Soc. Durham. Office: Herald Sun 410 Argonne Dr Durham NC 27704-1428

HARRELL, CAROLYN LAWTON See KILGORE, CAROLYN HARRELL

HARRELL, DAVID EDWIN, JR., history educator; b. Jacksonville, Fla., Feb. 22, 1930; s. David Edwin and Marilyn Mildred (Lee) H.; m. Adelia Francis Roberts, Sept. 6, 1955; children—Mildred Susan, David Edwin III, Elinor Elizabeth, Marilyn Lee, Harold Robert. B.A., David Lipscomb Coll., 1954; M.A., Vanderbilt U., 1958, Ph.D., 1962. Asst. prof. East Tenn. State U., 1961-64, assoc. prof., 1964-66; assoc. prof. U. Okla., 1966-67, U. Ga., 1967-70; prof. U. Ala. at Birmingham, 1970-75, univ. scholar, 1975-81, 85-90, chmn. dept. history, 1970-74, 85-87; disting. prof. U. Ark., 1981-85; dir. Am. Studies Rsch Ctr., Hyderabad, India, 1993-95; Daniel F. Breeden eminent scholar Auburn U., 1990—; disting. USIA lectr., Bangladesh, 1993, 96, Sri Lanka, 1994, 95, Indonesia, 1994, Nepal, 1995, Egypt, 1995. Author: Quest for a Christian America, 1966, White Sects and Black Men in the Recent South, 1971, The Social Sources of Division in the Disciples of Christ, 1973, All Things Are Possible: The Healing and Charismatic Revivals in Modern America, 1975, Oral Roberts: An American Life, 1985, Pat Robertson: A Personal Religious and Political Portrait, 1987, The churches of Christ in the Twentieth Century, 1999; editor: Varieties of Southern Evangelicalism, 1981, Indian Jour. Am. Studies, 1993-95; contbr. articles to profl. jours. Recipient author's awards for best articles East Tenn. Hist. Soc., 1966, author's awards for best articles Mo. Hist. Soc., 1969, ambassadorial citation, India, 1995; sr. Fulbright scholar, Hyderabad, India, 1993-95, Allahabad, India, 1976-77. Fellow Inst. for Ecumenical and Cultural Research; mem. Am. Hist. Assn., Orgn. Am. Historians, So. Hist. Assn., Am. Acad. Religion, Am. Soc. Church History, Disciples of Christ Hist. Soc., Indian Assn. Am Studies. Home: PO Box 704 Auburn AL 36831-0704 Office: Auburn U History Dept 310 Thatch Hall Auburn AL 36849-5207

HARRELL, MARGARET ANN, writer, editor, dream researcher, photographer; b. Greenville, N.C., Sept. 25, 1940; d. John Henry and Rosa Lee Harrell; m. Jean-Marie Mensaert, Feb. 25, 1970 (dec. 1990). BA in History magna cum laude, Duke U., 1962; MA in Contemporary Brit. and Am. Lit., Columbia U., 1964; postgrad., U. N.C., 1976, Carl Jung Inst., Zurich, Switzerland, 1984-87; cert. practitioner of basic applications of psycho-dynamic systems, Inst. Human Devel., Ghent, 1992; tchg. diploma, Light Body Internat., Ter Duinen, Belgium, 1993/99. Moderator Ford Found. summer courses in Greek classics Columbia U., N.Y.C., 1963; copy editor, asst. editor Random House Pubs., N.Y.C., 1965-68; dance instr., 1969; sec. Euro-clear, Brussels, 1972-75; asst. to psychologist, dream rschr., 1983-84; co-organizer US and Indian workshops and lectrs. Belgium, 1993—; editor, 1968—; contbr. poetry reading Am. Book Week, Leuven, Belgium, 1992; participant Internat. Poetry Festival, Belgium and Romania, 1992; del. Culture Building Stone for Europe, 2002, Brugge, Belgium, 1993, Athens, 1994; mem. computer parapsychology project U. Amsterdam, 1994; with James Clark Maxwell Project, 2000; contbr. Internat. Drama Festival, Sibiu, Romania, 1995, 96; guest lectr. Sibiu U., 1995; coord. internat. Mus. Exhbn. on Life of Jan Mensaert, 1995—; presenter, panelist Internat. Parapsychol. Assn. conv., 1995. Author: Marking Time with Faulkner: A Study of the Symbolic Importance of the Mark and of Related Actions, 1999, Love in Transition: Voyage of Ulysses--Letters to Penelope, Vol. I, II, III, 1996, Vol. IV, 1998; contbr. to book of poetry: When the Wide Sky is Falling, 1993; contbr. papers to Spl. Collections Libr. U. Iowa, 1993; tri-annual columnist The Epiphanies & the Mystery, Exceptional Human Experience News, 2000—. Sponsor Save the Children, 1985—; co-organizer Introduction of South Indian Tamil Siddha tradition into Belgium. Fellow MacDowell Colony, 1969, 70, 73. Mem. Am. Soc. for Psychical Rsch., The Planetary Soc., Mars Underground, Romanian Cure Hist. Archeological Soc. (hon. mem.). Avocations: T'ai chi, energy studies, art, photography, computers. Home: 46 Lunevillelaan, 3300 Tienen Belgium

HARRELL, SAMUEL MACY, agribusiness executive; b. Indpls., Jan. 4, 1931; s. Samuel Runnels and Mary (Evans) H.; m. Sally Bowers, Sept. 2, 1958 (div.); children: Samuel D., Holly Evans, Kevin Bowers, Karen Susan, Donald Runnels, Kenneth Macy. B.S. in Econs., Wharton Sch., U. Pa., 1953. Pres., chmn. bd., chief exec. officer, chmn., exec. com. Early & Daniel Industries, Cin., 1971—; chmn. bd., chmn. exec. com. Early & Daniel Co., Cin., 1971—; chmn. bd., chief exec. officer, chmn. exec. com. Tidewater Grain Co., Phila., 1971—; dir. Harriman Inst. Columbia U.; bd. dirs. Wainwright Bank & Trust Co., Wainright Abstract Co., Nat. Grain Trade Council, U.S. Feed Grains Council; mem. Chgo. bd. Trade. Contbg. author: The Status of Agribusiness in Russia and the CIS. Dir. Harriman Inst., Columbia U. With AUS, 1953-55. Mem. Nat. Assn. Cert. Valuation Analysts, Inst. Bus. Appraisers, Am. Soc. Farm Mgrs. & Rural Appraisers, Am. Soc. Agrl. Cons., Internat. Bus. Brokers Assn., Young Pres.'s Orgn., U. Pa. Alumni Assn. (past pres.), Terminal Elevator Grain Mchts. Assn. (dir.), Millers Nat. Fedn. (dir.), Assn. Operative Millers, Am. Soc. Bakery Engrs., Am. Fin. Assn., Council on Fgn. Relations, Fin. Exec. Inst., N.Am. Grain Export Assn. (dir.), Mpls. Grain Exchange, St. Louis Mchts. Grain Exchange, Buffalo Corn Exchange, Delta Tau Delta (Past prs. Ind. alumni). Presbyterian. Clubs: Columbia, Indpls. Athletic, Woodstock, Traders Point Hunt, Dramatic, Players, Lambs (Indpls.); Racquet (Phila.); University (Washington and N.Y.C.). Lodges: Masons, Rotary. Home: 9495 Whitegate Ln Cincinnati OH 45243-1647 Office: EDI Internat Inc PO Box 43400 Cincinnati OH 45243-0400

HARRELSON, CLYDE LEE, secondary school educator; b. Baton Rouge, Nov. 20, 1946; s. Hezzie Clyde and Marguerite Lucille (Tucker) H. BA, Southeastern La. U., 1968; MA, La. State U., 1974, EdS, 1980, postgrad., 1981; postgrad., So. U., 1982. Cert. social studies and English tchr., prin., supr., La. Tchr. English, East Baton Rouge Parish Sch. Bd., 1970—; tchr. English, McKinley Mid. Magnet Sch., Baton Rouge, 1982—, now dean of students; mem. Mid. Sch. Lang. Arts Curriculum Com. Mem. Arts Coun. Greater Baton Rouge, Found. for Hist. La., La. Preservation Alliance, Nat. Trust for Hist. Preservation, Colonial Williamsburg Found., NCCJ, Cmty. Assn. for Welfare Sch. Children, La. Dem. Com., Nat. Dem. Com.; mem. East Baton Rouge Parish Dem. exec. com., 1981-85, 96—. Mem. NEA, ASCD, Nat. Coun. Tchrs. English, La. Coun. Tchrs. English, East Baton Rouge Coun. Tchrs. English, East Baton Rouge Parish Dem. Exec. Com., La. Assn. Educators, East Baton Rouge Parish Assn. Educators, Kiwanis, Phi Delta Kappa. Episcopalian. Home: 3710 Prescott Rd Baton Rouge LA 70805-5055

HARRER, KLAUS DIETER, management consultant; b. Ried, Austria, Dec. 8, 1963. Degree in mgmt., U. Econs., Vienna, 1988. Mgmt. cons. Czipin & Ptnr., Austria, 1989-91; mng. ptnr. Czipin & Ptnr., Hungary, 1991-98, Prague, Czech Republic, 1994-98; mng. dir. Plaut Cee, Vienna, Budapest, Prague, 1999—; mgr. Regional Ctr., mng. dir. Plaut Cee, Poland, Czech Republic, 1999—, Hungary, 1999—; regional ctr. mgr., mng. dir. Plaut Internat. Mgmt. Cons., Vienna, Budapest, Prague, 1999—; advisor The Economist Group/Bus. Ctrl. Europe, Vienna, 1996—; mem. adv. bd. Richter Shoes Ltd., Linz, Austria. Recipient award Sallinger Fund, 1988, award Austrian Auditing Corp., 1988. Mem. Fedn. Austrian Industries. Home: Koronafurt v 9, H-1165 Budapest Hungary Office: Plaut Cee Vienna, Modecenterstrasse 14, A-1030 Vienna Austria

HARRICE, NICHOLAS CY (NICHOLAS PSIHARIS), commercial radio and television announcer; b. Chgo., Mar. 1, 1915; s. Peter and Vasiliki (Anargyros) Psiharis; child by previous marriage, Lincoln Peter; m. 2d, Helena Seroy, Dec. 12, 1959; 1 child, Melanie Samantha. Student Sch. Commerce, Northwestern U., 1934-38. Concession barker Chgo. World's Fair, 1934; with Samuel Insull ABC Network, 1935; announcer, copywriter, newsman, programmer Sta. WLS, Chgo., 1936-42; news broadcaster Sta. WGN, Chgo., 1942-45; freelance comml. announcer N.Y.C., 1945—; contract comml. announcer "and, they are mild!" segment Pall Mall cigarette advt. campaign for radio and TV, 1946-70; product spokesman for GM, Proctor & Gamble, DuPont Co., Miller Brewing Co., Alka-Seltzer, Kaiser-Fraser; host Adventures Sherlock Holmes, 1947-49; announcer radio programs for Walter Winchell, Grand Cen. Sta., Cavalcade of Am., The Big Story, H.V. Kaltenborn, Wednesday Night Fights, William L. Shirer, RCA Victor Show, The Thin Man, Quick as a Flash; producer What's the Good Word; co-starred (with Ginger Rogers) Cavalcade of Am., NBC, 1951; pres. Stair Mountain Prodns. Recipient Sargent Oratorical award, 1935; Clio award, 1962; 1st place Gold medal sabres Ill. Fencers League, 1936; mem. champion sabre team Amateur Fencers League Am., 1935. Mem. SAG (bd. dirs. 1966-69), AFTRA (bd. dirs. 1956-60), Friars Club, Lambs Club, Deru Club, Lynx Club. Address: PO Box 189 Kelly WY 83011-0189

HARRIES, ANTHONY DAVID, physician, consultant; b. Singapore, Malaysia, Aug. 19, 1950; s. James Ronald Harries and Margaret Ingram (Cousins) H.; m. Margo Ann Sevastopulo, Jan. 6, 1973; children: Katherine, Nicola, John. MB, B of Surgery, Cambridge (Eng.) U., 1975, MA, 1976, MD, 1984. House office Eng., 1975-76, sr. house officer, 1976-79; registrar in medicine Cardiff, Wales, 1979-81, rsch. fellow in gastroenterology, 1981-83; lectr. Liverpool (Eng.) Sch. Tropical Medicine, 1983-91; Foundation prof. medicine Med. Sch., Malawi, 1991—; cons. Tb WHO, Geneva, 1994—; vis. prof. medicine, Cape Town, South Africa, 1992—. Author: 100 Clinical Problems in Tropical Medicine, 1987, TB/HIV: A Clinical manual, 1996; asst. editor Malawi Med. Jour., 1991-95. Recipient Rsch. grants WHO, Malawi, 1994—, Joint UN Programme in HIV/AIDS, Malawi, 1996, Overseas Devel. Adminstrn., U.K., Malawi, 1996. Fellow Royal Coll. Physicians London, Royal Soc. Tropical Medicine Malawi (local sec. 1991—), Royal Soc. Medicine. London. Avocations: squash racquets, travel, reading. Home: Roydon Cottage Old High Rd, Roydon IP22 3XJ, United Kingdom Office: Brit High Commn ODA TB, PO Box 30042 Lilonswe 3, Lilonswe 3, Malawi

HARRIETT, JUDY ANNE, medical equipment company executive; b. Walterboro, S.C., July 22, 1960; d. Billy Lee and Loretta (Rahn) H. BS in Agrl. Bus./Econs., Clemson U., 1982. Sales rep. III Monsanto Corp., Atlanta, 1982-85; surg. stapling rep. Ethicon, Inc., Johnson & Johnson Corp., Somerville, N.J., 1985-87; acct. exec. ALARIS Med. Sys., San Diego, 1987—; regional tng. coord. Imed Corp., San Diego, 1992-93, Alaris Med Sys, San Diego, 1993—; mem. pres. adv. panel, 1991, 92, mem. pres. club, 1993. Author: Time and Territory Management, 1984. Com. mem. Multiple Sclerosis Fund Raising Benefit, Knoxville, Tenn., 1988, 89, Women's Ctr. Benefit, Knoxville, 1990. Mem. NAFE, Pres.'s Club (life). Republican. Avocations: golf, reading, snow skiing, water skiing, travel. Home: 18701 Vineyard Point Ln Cornelius NC 28031-7993 Office: ALARIS Med Sys 10221 Wateridge Cir San Diego CA 92121-2733

HARRIGAN, RICHARD GEORGE, salesperson; b. Joliet, Ill., Feb. 12, 1952; s. William Francis and Margaret (Ruettiger) H.; m. Patricia Rae Bowman, Aug. 12, 1989; children: Michelle Freeman, Kimberly Freeman; children from a previous marriage: Jennifer Harrigan, Michelle Harrigan, Richard Harrigan, Sarah Harrigan, Samantha Harrigan. AS in Heating and Refrigeration, Joliet Jr. Coll., 1980. Salesman G.W. Berkheimer, Gary, Ind., 1978-92; owner, operator East-West Ent., Hobart, Ind., 1992—. Mem. IBR, NHAW. Roman Catholic. Avocation: travel. E-mail: riksearch@aol.com. Office: East-West Ent PO Box C Hobart IN 46342-0016

HARRINGTON, ANTHONY STEPHEN, lawyer, diplomat; b. Taylorsville, N.C., Mar. 9, 1941; s. Atwell Lee and Louise (Chapman) H.; m. Hope Reynolds, Sept. 25, 1971; children: Adam Reynolds, Michael Addison. AB, U. N.C., 1963; LLB, Duke U., 1966. Bar: N.C. 1966, D.C. 1968, U.S. Supreme Ct. 1970. Asst. dean Duke Law Sch., Durham, N.C., 1966-68; assoc. Hogan & Hartson, Washington, 1968-73, ptnr., 1974-99; U.S. amb. to Brazil Am. Embassy Brasilia, 2000—; bd. dirs. Ovation, Inc., Ctr. for Democracy, SouthernNet Inc., Southeastern Metal Products, Werres Corp., Rosemount Ctr.; co-chair Nat. Alliance to End Homelessness; vice-chmn. Pres. Fgn. Intelligence Adv. Bd., 1993-99; mem. Commn. on Roles and Capabilities of Intelligence Cmty., 1995; chmn. Pres.'s Intelligence Oversight Bd., 1994-99. Gen. Counsel Clinton/Gore Presdl. Campaign, 1992, Dem. Nat. Com., Washington, 1981-85. Episcopal. Clubs: Met., City (Washington). Avocations: politics, reading, gardening, tennis. Home: Ratcliffe Manor 7768 Ratcliffe Manor Ln Easton MD 21601-7432 also: 701 Pennsylvania Ave NW Washington DC 20004-2608 Office: Am Embassy Brasilia Unit 3500 APO AA 34030-3500

HARRINGTON, BRUCE MICHAEL, lawyer, investor; b. Houston, Mar. 12, 1933; s. George Haymond Harrington and Doris (Gladden) Maginnis; m. Anne Griffith Lawhon, Feb. 15, 1958; children: Julia Griffith, Martha Gladden, Susan McIver. B.A., U. Tex., 1960, J.D. with honors, 1961. Bar: Tex. 1961, U.S. Dist. Ct. (so. dist.) Tex. 1962, U.S. Ct. Appeals (5th cir.) 1962, U.S. Supreme Ct. 1973. Assoc. Andrews & Kurth and predecessor firm, Houston, 1961-73, ptnr., 1973-84; dir. Offenhauser Co., Houston, Allied Metals, Inc., Houston. Trustee St. John's Sch., Houston, 1981-92, chmn. bd., CEO, 1986-92; chmn. bd. Covenant House, Tex., 1991-95; trustee St. Luke's Episcopal Hosp., Tex. Med. Ctr., Houston, 1983-86; bd. dirs. YMCA Bd. Mgmt., Am. Cancer Soc., 1992-94, Ctr. for Hearing and Speech, 1993, chmn. bd., 1995-98; vice chmn. Gateway Found., 1993-95; mem. adv. com. Assn. Governing Bds. of Colls. and Univs. Mem. ABA, Nat. Assn. Ind. Schs. (chmn. trustee com.), Ind. Schs. Assn. S.W. (chmn. trustee com., bd. exec. com.), Tex. Bar Assn., Houston Bar Assn., The Mil. and Hosp. Order of St. Lazarus, The Venerable Order of St. John (U.K.), The Order of Saints Maurice and Lazarus (Savoy), Houston Country Club, Petroleum Club, Houston Club, Phi Delta Phi, Order of Coif. Republican. Episcopalian. Home: 3608 Overbrook Ln Houston TX 77027-4128

HARRINGTON, DONALD JAMES, university president; b. Bklyn., Oct. 2, 1945; s. John Joseph and Ruth Mary (Cummings) H. BA, Mary Immaculate Sem., Northampton, Pa., 1969, MDiv, 1972, ThM, 1973; LLD (hon.), St. John's U., 1985; postgrad., U. Toronto, 1980-82; PhD (hon.), Fu Jen U., Taipei, Taiwan, 1994; DHum (hon.), Am. U. Rome, 1994, Dowling Coll., 1996. Ordained priest Roman Catholic Ch., 1973. Instr. Niagara U., Niagara University, N.Y., 1973-80, dir. student activities, 1974-77, dean student activities, 1977-80, exec. v.p., 1981-84, pres., 1984-89; pres. St. John's U., Jamaica, N.Y., 1989—; bd. dirs. The Bear Stearns Cos., Inc., 1993—, Commn. Ind. Colls. and Univs., Albany, N.Y., 1987-89; mem. bd. Cath. edn. Diocese of Buffalo, 1987-89. Trustee Niagara U., 1984—, St. John's U., 1986—, DePaul U., 1988-91, Sem. Immaculate Conception, 1990-97, Res. Group, 1988—, Sisters Hosp., Buffalo, 1988-89; chair adv. com. Love Canal Land Use, 1988-89; bd. dirs., mem. exec. com. Commn. Ind. Colls. and Univs., 1991—; chair Big East Athletic Conf., 1994-97; mem. sanctity of life com. Diocese of Bklyn., 1990-97; chair Western N.Y. Consortium for Higher Edn., 1988-89, mem. exec. com., 1985-89; mem. adv. bd. New Yorkers Caring for N.Y.-N.Y. Med. Coll., 1998—; mem. Commr.'s Coun. on Higher Edn., 1998—. Mem. Assn. Cath. Colls. and Univs. (bd. dirs. 1997—). Office: St John's U Office of Pres 8000 Utopia Pkwy Jamaica NY 11439-0001*

HARRINGTON, DONALD SZANTHO, clergy member; b. Newton, Mass., July 11, 1914; s. Charles Elliot Marshall Harrington and Leita Lancaster Hersey; m. Vilma Juliana Szantho, Mar. 28, 1939; children: Ilona Vilma, Francis David; m. Aniko Szantho, July 29, 1984; children: Aniko Kinga, Enikö. AB, U. Chgo., 1938; BD, Meadville/Lombard Theol., Chgo., 1938; DD, Meadville/Lombard Theol., 1964; student, U. Leiden, Holland, 1938-39; STD, Starr King Theol., Berkeley, Calif., 1959; DD, Ecumenical Theol. Inst., Claj-Napoca, Romania, 1978. Min. First Unitarian Ch., Hobart, Ind., 1936-38, Peoples Liberal Ch. Chgo., 1939-44; founding min. Beverly Unitarian Fellowship, Chgo., 1942-44; min. Cmty. Ch. N.Y., 1944-82, min. emeritus, 1982—; chair Ctr. Advanced Study Religion and Sci., Chgo.m Coun. Internat. & Pub. Affairs, N.Y.C., 1990—. Author: As We Remember Him: Jesus, Jewish Reformer, 1964, Religion in an Age of Science, 1965, Modern Humanity In Search of a Myth, 1987, Outstretched Wings of the Spirit, 1980. Founding chair Am. Com. on Africa, N.Y.C., 1950-60; co-chair, founder Unitarian Universalist Advance, Black and White Action, 1965; chmn. Liberal Party N.Y., 1965-85; del. at large N.Y. State Constitutional Convention. Harriet Otis Craft fellow Meadville/Lombard Theol., Leiden, 1938-39. Mem. Sigma Pi Phi, Unitarian Universalist Min. Assn. Avocations: hiking, swimming, reading. Home: PO Box 432 2700 Arrowhead Ln Peconic NY 11958-1603 Office: Cmty Church 10 Park Ave New York NY 10016-4338

HARRINGTON, HELMI STRAHL, musician, educator; b. Bad WÖrishofen, Germany, May 22, 1945; d. Hans Klaus and Hanni Schorn Strahl; m. Robert C. Harrington (div. Jan. 1988); children: Hanni Helmi Harrington Van Zandt, Charles Robert; m. Duane Sellman (dec. Dec. 1995). AA, Del Mar Jr. Coll., Corpus Christi, Tex., 1966; MusB in Performance, U. Houston, 1967, MusM in Music Lit. and Performance, 1968; PhD in Musicology, U. Tex., 1977. Owner Accordion-Concertina Music, Duluth, Minn., 1989—; head accordion-concertina repair dept. Red Wing Tech. coll., Duluth, 1992, 93; head Accordion-Concertina Repair and Technician's Sch., Duluth, 1994—. Concert pianist, 1966-73; leader Duluth Accordionaires, 1991; founder, dir. Accordion-Concertina-Music-Ensemble. Curator World Accordions Mus. Mem. Accodionists and Tchrs. Guild (bd. dirs. 1981—), Am. Accordionists Assn., Nat. Music Tchrs. Assn., Minn. Music Tchrs. Assn. Avocations: dog training, wood carving. Home: 13412 Washburn Dr Burnsville MN 55337-2164 Office: Accordion Concertina Repair Technicians Sch 2801 W 1st St Duluth MN 55806-1713

HARRINGTON, JOHN JOSEPH, lawyer; b. Richmond, Va., Apr. 21, 1961; s. Daniel Joseph and Carolyn (Slattery) H.; m. Peg Dawson, Sept. 6, 1997. BA, Vanderbilt U., 1983; MA, Brown U., 1985; JD, U. Tenn., 1992. Bar: Va. 1993, Tenn. 1995. Fgn. svc. officer U.S. Dept. State, Washington; jud. law clk. to Hon. Charles D. Susano Jr. Knoxville, Tenn., 1994-95; assoc. atty. Waller Lansden Dortch & Davis, Nashville, 1995-98; sr. counsel Bridgestone/Firestone, Inc., Nashville, 1998—. Mem. Am. Corp. Counsel Assn. (v.p. 1999—), Omicron Delta Kappa, Pi Sigma Alpha. Avocations: hiking, biking, tennis, astronomy. Fax: 615-872-1490. Office: Bridgeston Firestone Inc 50 Century Blvd Nashville TN 37214-3672

HARRINGTON, LORI LYNN, social services administrator; b. Jackson, Mich., May 31, 1970; d. Patrick John and Sharon Ann Nagy; m. David Charles Harrington, Jr., July 31, 1993. BA in Psychology, St. Mary's Coll., Notre Dame, Ind., 1992; MSW, We. Mich. U., 1996. Profl. child interviewer Child & Family Advocacy Ctr., Elkhart, Ind., 1992-96, program coord., 1996-99; exec. dir. Mental Health Assn., Elkhart, Ind., 1999—; adv. bd. midwest region Children's Advocacy Ctr., St. Paul, 1999. Mem. NASW, Am. Profl. Soc. Abuse of Children (founding bd. mem., treas., v.p. 1996-98), Elkhart C. of C. (leadership academy 1999-2000). Democrat. Roman Catholic. Avocations: reading, dance, cultural events, wine tasting, home improvement. Office: Mental Health Assn in Elkhart County 421 S 2d St Ste 340 Elkhart IN 46516

HARRINGTON, MARY EVELINA PAULSON (POLLY HARRINGTON), religious journalist, writer, educator; b. Chgo.; d. Henry Thomas and Evelina (Belden) Paulson; m. Gordon Keith Harrington, Sept. 7, 1957; children: Jonathan Henry, Charles Scranton. BA, Oberlin Coll., 1946; postgrad., Northwestern U., Evanston, Ill., Chgo., 1946-49, Weber State U., Ogden, Utah, 1970s, 80s; MA, U. Chgo.-Chgo. Theol. Sem., 1956. Publicist Nat. Coun. Chs., N.Y.C., 1950-51; mem. press staff 2d assembly World Coun. Chs., Evanston, Chgo., 1954; mgr. Midwest Office Communication, United Ch. of Christ, Chgo., 1955-59; staff writer United Ch. Herald, N.Y.C., St. Louis, 1959-61; affiliate missionary to Asia, United Ch. Bd. for World Ministries, N.Y.C., 1978-79; freelance writer and lectr., 1961—; corr. Religious News Svc., 1962—; prin. lectr. Women & Family Life in Asia

series to numerous libs., Utah, 1981, 81-82; pub. rels. coord. Utah Energy Conservation/Energy Mgmt. Program, 1984-85; tchr. writing Ogden Cmty. Schs., 1985-89; adj. instr. writing for publs. Weber State U., 1986—; instr. Acad. Lifelong Learning, Ogden, 1992—, Eccles Cmty. Art Ctr., Ogden, 1993-94; dir. comm. Shared Ministry, Salt Lake City, 1983-97; chmn. comm. Intermountain Conf., Rocky Mountain Conf., Utah Assn. United Ch. of Christ, 1970-78, 82—, Ind. Coun. Chs., 1960-63; dir. comm. United Chs., 1971-78, Christ Congl., Ogden, 1980—; chmn. comm. Ch. Women United Utah, 1974-78, Ogden rep., 1980—, hostess Northern Utah, 1998. Editor: Sunshine and Moonscapes: An Anthology of Essays, Poems, Short Stories, 1994, (booklet) Family Counseling Service: Thirty Years of Service to Northern Utah, 1996; contbr. numerous articles and essays to religious and other publs. Pres. T.O. Smith Sch. PTA, 1976-78, Ogden City Coun. PTA, 1983-85; assoc. dir. Region II, Utah PTA, Salt Lake City, 1981-83, mem. State Edn. Commn., 1982-87; chmn. state internat. hospitality and aid Utah Fedn. Women's Clubs, 1982-86; v.p. Ogden dist., 1990-92, pres. Ogden dist., 1992-96, state resolutions com., 1996—; trustee Family Counseling Svc. No. Utah, Ogden, 1983-95, emeritus trustee, 1995—; Utah rep. to nat. bd. Challenger Films, Inc., 1986—; state pres. Rocky Mountain Conf. Women in Mission, United Ch. of Christ, 1974-77, sec., 1981-84, vice moderator Utah Assn., 1992-94. Recipient Ecumenical Svc. citation Ind. Coun. Chs., 1962, Outstanding Local Pres. award Utah PTA, 1978, Outstanding Latchkey Child Project award, 1985, Cmty. Svc. award City of Ogden, 1980, 81, 82, Celebration of Gifts of Lay Woman Nat. award United Ch. of Christ, 1987, Excellence in the Arts in Art Edn. award Ogden City Arts Commn., 1993, Spirit of Am. Woman in Arts and Humanities award Your Cmty. Connection, Ogden, 1994; Utah Endowment for Humanities grantee, 1981, 81-82. Mem. Nat. League Am. Penwomen (chmn. Utah conv. 1973, 11 awards for articles and essays 1987-95, 1st pl. news award 1992, 1st pl. short stories 1997, 3d pl. articles 1997), AAUW (state edn. rep. 1982-86, parliamentarian Ogden br. 1997—), League of Utah Writers (Publ. Quill award 1998). Democrat. Avocation: building miniature world of peace each Christmas by family in the home. Home and Office: 722 Boughton St Ogden UT 84403-1152

HARRINGTON, MICHAEL BALLOU, health economist, systems engineer; b. Denver, Sept. 26, 1940; s. Theodore Charles Ballou and DeEtte June (Krastetter) H.; m. Mary Lynn Kijanka, Nov. 17, 1978; 1 child, Meredith Ballou. MS, U. Calif., Irvine, 1969, PhD (NDEA fellow), 1972. With Fgn. Service, Dept. State, 1972-74, Arthur Young & Co., 1975-78; sr. health economist/systems engr. GEOMET Technologies, Inc., Gaithersburg, Md., 1978-80; group leader The Mitre Corp., 1980-87, lead scientist, 1987-96, prin. info. tech. economist, 1997—; adj. prof. Grad. Inst. Bus. and Pub. Affairs, Washington, George Mason U., Fairfax, Va. With USMC, 1958-61. Mem. numerous profl. socs. Club: Potomac Valley Srs. Track. Avocation: writing. Contbr. articles to profl. jours.

HARRINGTON, MICHAEL GERARD, biochemistry educator, researcher; b. Cork, Ireland, Jan. 8, 1930; s. Cornelius H. and Martha Young; m. Joyce Mary O'Brien, Jan. 4, 1954; children: Deidre, Margot, Michael, Finola, Maeve. BS, U. Coll., 1950, MS, 1951; PhD, Nat. U. Ireland, 1954. Lectr. biochemistry U. Coll. Dublin, 1954-63, prof. biochemistry, 1964-93, prof. emeritus, 1993—; assoc. prof. physiology Med. Sch. Tufts U., Boston, 1963-64; fellow WHO, Stockholm, 1965; extern examiner Al-Fateh Med. U., Tripoli, Libya, 1973-95; chmn. Nat. Accreditation Bd., Ireland, 1987-96; cons. Mater Misericordiae Hosp., Dublin, 1975—; chmn. Nat. Com. for Biochemistry, 1970-74. Contbr. articles to profl. jours. Fellow Inst. Biology Ireland, Inst. Chemistry Ireland; mem. Milltown Golf Club (mem. com. 1971-73). Roman Catholic. Avocations: golf, photography. Home: 36 Avoca Hall, Blackrock Dublin, Ireland

HARRINGTON, NANCY REGINA O'CONNOR, volunteer; b. Chgo., Oct. 28, 1928; d. John Roland and Ethel Catherine (Constable) O'Connor; m. James Edward Harrington, Sept. 8, 1951; children: Mary Beth Grayson, Janet Gaines, Gail, Nancy Chartier. BA in art edn., Rosary Coll., River Forest, 1946-50. Cert. art tchr., Ill. Artist Chgo. Park Dist., 1949; art tchr. Chgo. elem. schs., 1951-52; color coord. homes Palos Park (Ill.) Builder, 1957-58; vol. Art Inst. of Chgo., 1980-86. Exhibited in Loyola Ramble, 1970s, Wilmette, 1960s, Palos Park, Ill., Evergreen Park, Ill., Chgo., Osprey, Fla., 1990s, Glenview, Ill., 1980s, 1990s. Bd. mem. Acad. Our Lady H.S. Alumni Bd., 1960's; pres. Mothers Club, v.p. Parents Club Regina Dominican H.S., Wilmette, Ill., 1972-73; vol. Judge Robert Downing Dem. Party, Glenview, Ill., 1974; 1st forelady of criminal ct. Cook County Ct. Sys., Chgo., 1980s; assoc. mem. Art Inst. Chgo., 1990—; vol. Resurrection House Daycare Ctr. for Homeless, Sarasota, Fla., 1993-98, Juvenile Diabetes Found., 1998—; colleague Ringling Mus. Art, Sarasota, 1994—; gen. chair Beaux Arts Festival, The Oaks C.C., 1996; mem. women's bd. Rosary Coll., 1990-98; hostess Hist. Spanish Pointe Fla. Luncheon, 1998, 99; mem. women's bd. dirs. Dominican U., 1997—. Recipient medallion Regina Dominican H.S. Mothers Club, 1972-73, Kemeny Lion medallion Art Inst. Chgo., 1980s, Resurrection House medallion, 1999; Honored vol. Sarasota Arts Coun., 1992. Mem. AAUW, Natl. Heritage Soc., North Shore Country Club (gen. chairperson 9-hole golf 1986, gen. chairperson art festival, 1996), Oaks Country Club (mem. garden club, 1991—, ad hoc archtl. rev. bd., 1991-92, women's bd., 1993, Dominican Univ. Women's Bd., 1997—, vol. Juvenille Diabetes Found., Sarasota, Fla. 1998, 99, Hostess of Mrs. Potter Palmer Luncheon Historic Spanish Pointe, Osprey, Fla., Ringling Sch. of Art and Design Libr.; chair Art Seminar of 25th Internat. Congress on Arts and Comm., New Orleans, 1998; attendee, singer choir 26th Internat. Congress Arts and Commn., Lisbon, 1999; gen. chairperson art festival, 1995—, gen. chairperson Oaks Celebrates Arts, 1994, chairperson Art Club, 1993-94; founder Art Appreciation Club, 1993, Artist of Month Column (author) 1994—); founding mem. Nat. Women's Art Museum. Roman Catholic. Avocations: travel, reading, aquacize, opera, duplicate bridge. Home: 210 Saint James Park Osprey FL 34229-9065

HARRINGTON, PETER TYRUS, emergency management company executive, public relations consultant, author, photographer; b. N.Y.C., Aug. 28, 1951; s. Don and Gerry S. (Spolane) H. BA, Union Coll., 1973, MA in Am. Labor, 1975. Spl. investigator U.S. Dept. of Commerce, 1970; staff dir. N.Y. State Assembly, N.Y.C., 1971-73; editl. staff mem., writer, photographer Nat. Geographic Mag., Washington, 1974-76; ptnr. Don Harrington Assocs., Wilton, Conn., 1977—; pres. Harrington Comm., Wilton, 1980—; pub. affairs officer Fed. Emergency-Mgmt. Agy., Washington, 1983—, Fed. Catastrophic "Red" Team, 1996-97; exec. officer Hurricane Andrew recovery, 1992-94; chief-of-staff to chmn. County Bd. Commrs., Dade County, Fla., 1994-95; cons. IBM, Armonk, N.Y., 1984-85; contbr. GE Capitol Corp.; contbg. editor Taxfax Mktg. Mag., 1985—; spl. cons. So. Conn. Newspaper Syndicate (Greenwich Time, Stamford Advocate); cons. Expeditions Inc., New Canaan, Conn., 1987-88; contbg. corr. Los Angeles Times, Washington Post Syndicate. Author: The Last Cathedral, 1979 (Book of Yr. award 1979), Never Too Old, 1981; author and photographer, The Sailing Chef, 1978, Maine, 1989; contbr. Murdock, Travel Marketing, Intrepid, Discovery, People, Yankee, Video and TV Guide mags., Smithsonian, Arizona Republic, Chicago Tribune, N.Y. Times, Wall Street Journal, Miami Herald, Boston Herald; contbr. and photographer of many articles with expertise in Amazon and Polar Region. Scoutmaster troop, Boy Scouts Am., Albany, N.Y., 1971-73; exec. dir. ACLU, Albany, 1972-73; mem. bd. Annapolis Youth Ctr., Md., 1978; past pres. Wilton Summer Playshop, 1972—; mem. adv. bd. ARC, Conn. Recipient Pub. Svc. Citation, Fed. Govt., 1985, Metro-Dade (Fla.), 1993. Fellow Author's Guild, Nat. Press Found., Soros Found.; mem. Writers Union, Nat. Press Club, Legis. Councils Assn., Nat. Press Photographers Assn., Am. Soc. Mag. Photographers. Office: Don Harrington Assocs 271 Wilson Ave Satellite Beach FL 32937-2933

HARRINGTON, ROBERT DUDLEY, JR., printing company executive; b. Worcester, Mass., Dec. 19, 1932; s. Robert Dudley and Anne Victoria Harrington; m. Melissa Banks Hubner, Mar. 25, 1978 (div.). AB, Brown U., 1955; MBA, Columbia U., 1957. With Morgan Guaranty Trust Co., N.Y.C., 1957-59; v.p. Faulkner, Dawkins & Sullivan, N.Y.C., 1959-69; pres. Printers Express Co., Inc., Greenwich, Conn., 1976—. Trustee, mem. Woods Hole Oceanographic Instn. Corp., pres. Assocs. Mem. N.Y. Yacht Club, Edgartown Yacht Club, Round Hill Club, Edgartown Reading Rm., Holland Lodge, Athelstan Lodge, The Pilgrims, Edgartown Yacht Club (past commodore). Office: Printers Express Co Inc 333 Greenwich Ave Greenwich CT 06830-6505

HARRINGTON, WALTER HOWARD, JR., judge; b. San Francisco, Aug. 14, 1926; s. Walter Howard and Doris Ellen (Daniels) H.; BS, Stanford, 1947; JD, Hastings Coll., U. Calif., 1952; m. Barbara Bryant, June 1952 (div. 1973); children: Stacey Doreen, Sara Duval; m. 2d, Hertha Bahrs, Sept. 1974. Admitted to Calif. bar, 1953; dep. legislative counsel State of Calif., Sacramento, 1953-54, 55; mem. firm Walner & Harrington, Sacramento, 1954; dep. dist. atty. San Mateo County, Redwood City, Calif., 1955-62; pvt. practice in Redwood City, 1962-84; judge San Mateo County Mcpl. Ct., 1984-90, Superior Ct., 1990-96. Chmn., San Mateo County Criminal Justice Council, 1971-76, San Mateo County Adult Correctional Facilities Com., 1969-71; pro tem referee San Mateo County Juvenile Ct., 1967-72. Ensign USNR, 1944-46. Mem. San Mateo County Bar Assn. (pres. 1969, editor publs. 1964-74), State Bar Calif. (editorial bd. 1968-81, vice chmn. 1969, 74-75, chmn., editor 1975-76), San Mateo County Legal Aid Soc. (pres. 1971-72), Order of Coif, Delta Theta Phi. Republican. Episcopalian. Office: Hall of Justice 400 County Ctr Redwood City CA 94063-1655

HARRINGTON-LLOYD, JEANNE LEIGH, interior designer; b. L.A.; d. Peter Valentine and Avis Lorraine (Brown) Harrington; m. James Wilkinson, Dec. 17, 1966 (div. Mar. 1976); m. David Lloyd, Nov. 27, 1985. BS in Psychology, U. Utah, 1984; cert., Salt Lake Sch. Interior Design, 1985; MS in Mgmt., Marylhurst Coll., 1990. With Mary Webb-Davis Agy., L.A., 1970; model, actress McCarty Agy., Salt Lake City, 1983-85; contract designer Innerspace Design, Salt Lake City, 1985-89; space planning and utilization mgr. U.S. Bancorp, Portland, Oreg., 1991-99. Mem. ASID, Internat. Interior Design Assn., Internat. Facilities Mgmt. Assn. Democrat. Avocations: travel, art history, reading, weight training, riding dressage. Home: 7077 Surfbird Cir Carlsbad CA 92009-4018

HARRIS, ALAN WILLIAM, physicist, researcher; b. Birmingham, Eng., Feb. 25, 1952; s. John William and Betty May (Chambers) H.; m. Ute Isolde Schweikhardt, Sept. 9, 1988; 1 child, Samantha Marie. BSc, U. Leeds, Eng., 1973, PhD, 1977. Postdoctoral fellow Max Planck Inst. for Astronomy, Heidelberg, Germany, 1977-80; rsch. scientist Rutherford Appleton Lab., Chilton, Eng., 1980-83; U.K. resident astronomer Internat. Ultraviolet Explorer Satellite European Space Agy., Madrid, 1983-86; mgr. U.K. Quick-Look Facility for Rosat X-ray Astronomy Satellite Rutherford Appleton Lab., Chilton, Eng., 1986-89, Max Planck Inst. for Extraterrestrial Physics, Munich, 1989-92; dep. divsn. leader German Aerospace Ctr., Dept. Planetary Exploration, Berlin, 1992—. Contbg. author: (with G. Sonneborn) Exploring the Universe with the IUE Satellite, 1987, A Decade of UV Astronomy with the IUE Satellite, 1988, (with H.U. Zimmermann) Databases and On-Line Data in Astronomy, 1991; contbr. articles to profl. jours. Recipient Group Achievement award NASA, 1991; Asteroid 7737 Sirrah named in his honor, 1999. Fellow Royal Astron. Soc.; mem. Internat. Astron. Union, European Geophys. Soc. E-mail: alan.harris@dlr.de. Office: DLR Dept Planetary Explor, Rutherfordstrasse 2, D-12489 Berlin Germany

HARRIS, BRIAN NICHOLAS, surveyor; b. Wantage, U.K., Dec. 21, 1931; s. Claude and Dorothy H.; m. Rosalyn Marion Caines, Mar. 18, 1961; children: Suzanne Nicole, Jennifer Ellen. Surveyor Insignia Richard Ellis Chartered Surveyors, London, 1953-61; ptnr. Richard Ellis St. Quintin Chartered Surveyors, London, 1961—, chmn., 1984-93; mem. Australia New Zealand Trade Com., London, 1991-2000. Chmn. bldg. com. Mus. in Docklands; hon. propr. advisor to the Order of St. John; mem. Friends of Royal Opera, House and the Guildhall Sch. of Music and Drama; corp. mem. Glyndebourne; chmn. Heathrow Airport, 1993-99; common councillor for the Broad Street Ward, 1996—, mem. planning and transp., music and drama coms.; sheriff City of London, 1998-99. Fellow Royal Soc. Encouragement of Arts, Mfrs., and Commerce; mem. Internat. Ct., Brit. C. of C. (bd. dirs., dep. pres. 1994-98), London C. of C. (bd. dirs. 1989-96, pres. 1992-94, trustee edn. trust 1990-96, chmn.-elect 2000), Australian and New Zealand C. of C. (chmn. 1996-98), Britain Australia Soc. (dep. chmn. 2000—), Broad Street Ward Club, Worshipful Co. of Glaziers and Painters of Glass Ct. of Assts., Guild of Freemen of the City of London, Co. of World Trades, Flyfishers Club, Tandridge Golf Club. Avocations: gardening, flyfishing, golf, opera. Home: Grants Paddock Grants Ln, Limpsfield RH8 0RQ, England Office: Insignia Richard Ellis, 107 Cheapside, London EC2V 6MX, England

HARRIS, CHAUNCY DENNISON, geographer, educator; b. Logan, Utah, Jan. 31, 1914; s. Franklin Stewart and Estella (Spilsbury) H.; m. Edith Young, Sept. 5, 1940; 1 child, Margaret (Mrs. Philip A. Straus, Jr.). AB, Brigham Young U., 1933; BA, Oxford U., 1936, MA, 1943, DLitt, 1973; postgrad., London Sch. Econs., 1936-37; PhD, U. Chgo., 1940; DEcon (honoris causa), Catholic U., Chile, 1956; LLD (honoris causa), Ind. U., 1979; DSc (honoris causa), Bonn U., 1991, U. Wis., Milw., 1991. Instr. in geography Ind. U., 1939-41; asst. prof. geography U. Nebr., 1941-43; asst. prof. geography U. Chgo., 1943-46, assoc. prof., 1946-47, prof., 1947-84, prof. emeritus, 1984—, dean social scis., 1955-60, chmn. non western area programs and internat. studies, 1960-66, dir. ctr. for internat. studies, 1966-84, chmn. dept. geography, 1967-69, Samuel N. Harper Disting. Svc. prof., 1969-84, spl. asst. to pres., 1973-75, v.p. acad. resources, 1975-78; del. Internat. Geog. Congress, Lisbon, 1949, Washington, 1952, Rio de Janeiro, 1956, Stockholm, 1960, London, 1964, New Delhi, 1968, Montreal, 1972, Moscow, 1976, Tokyo, 1980, Paris, 1984, Sydney, Australia, 1988, Washington, 1992, The Hague, 1996; v.p. Internat. Geog. Union, 1956-64, sec.-treas., 1968-76; mem. adv. com. for internat. orgns. and programs Nat. Acad. Scis., 1969-73, mem. bd. internat. orgns. and programs, 1973-76; U.S. del. 17th Gen. Conf. UNESCO, Paris, 1972; exec. com. div. behavioral scis. NRC, 1967-70; hon. cons. geography Libr. of Congress, 1974-80, mem. coun. of scholars, 1980-83, Conseil de la Bibliographie Géographique Internationale, 1986-94. Author: Cities of the Soviet Union, 1970; editor: Economic Geography of the U.S.S.R, 1949, International List of Geographical Serials, 1960, 71, 80, Annotated World List of Selected Current Geographical Serials, 1960, 64, 71, 80, Soviet Geography: Accomplishments and Tasks, 1962, Guide to Geographical Bibliographies and Reference Works in Russian or on the Soviet Union, 1975, Bibliography of Geography, Part I, Introduction to General Aids, 1976, Part 2, Regional, vol. 1, U.S., 1984, A Geographical Bibliography for American Libraries, 1985, Directory of Soviet Geographers 1946-87, 1988; contbr. Sources of Information in the Social Sciences, 1973, 86, Encyclopedia Britannica, 1989, Columbia Gazetteer of the World, 1998; contbg. editor: The Geog. Rev., 1960-73, Soviet Geography, 1987-91, Post-Soviet Geography and Economics, 1992-99, emeritus 2000—; hon. editor Urban Geography, 1984—; contbr. articles to profl. jours. Life mem. vis. com. U. Chgo. Libr. Recipient Alexander Csoma de Körösi Meml. medal Hungarian Geog. Soc., 1971, Lauréat d'Honneur Internat. Geog. Union, 1976; Alexander von Humboldt Gold Medal Gesellschaft für Erdkunde zu Berlin, 1978; spl. award Utah Geog. Soc., 1985; Rhodes scholar, 1934-37. Fellow Japan Soc. Promotion of Sci.; mem. Assn. Am. Geographers (sec. 1946-48, v.p. 1956, pres. 1957, Honors award 1976), Am. Geog. Soc. (coun. 1962-74, v.p. 1969-74; Cullum Geog. medal 1985), Am. Assn. Advancement Slavic Studies (pres. 1962, award for disting. contbns. 1978), Am. Acad. Arts and Scis., Social Sci. Rsch. Coun. (bd. dir. 1959-70, vice-chmn. 1963-65, exec. com. 1967-70), Internat. Coun. Sci. Unions (exec. com. 1969-76), Internat. Rsch. and Exchs. Bd. (exec. com. 1968-71), Nat. Coun. Soviet and East European Rsch. (bd. dir. 1977-83), Nat. Coun. for Geog. Edn. (Master Tchr. award 1986); hon. mem. Royal Geog. Soc. (Victoria medal 1987), Geog. Socs. Berlin, Frankfurt, Rome, Florence, Paris, Warsaw, Belgrade, Japan, Chgo. (Disting. Svc. award 1965, bd. dir. 1954-69, 82-90), Polish Acad. Scis. (fgn. mem.). Home: 5550 S South Shore Dr Apt 906 Chicago IL 60637-5033 Office: U Chgo Com on Geog Studies 5828 S University Ave Chicago IL 60637-1515

HARRIS, CURTIS W., minister, mayor; b. Surry County, Va., July 1, 1925; s. Sandy and Thelma Margaret Washington Harris; m. Ruth Jones, Feb. 20, 1946; children: Curtis Jr., Kenneth, Joanne, Michael, Karen, Michelle. Student, Va. Union U.; cert. in clin. tng. for pastors, Med. Coll. Va.; DD (hon.), Va. Sem. and Coll., 1972, LLD (hon.), 1983. Ordained minister Bapt. Ch., 1959. Pastor 1st Bapt. Ch., Bermuda Hundreds, Va., 1959-61, Union Bapt. Ch., Hopewell, Va., 1961—, Gilfield Bapt. Ch., Ivor, Va., 1961-85. Mayor City of Hopewell, 1997—, mem. city coun., 1986—; nat. bd. dirs., pres. Va. State unit So. Christian Leadership Conf., 1963-98; advisor Hopewell Action Coun.; mem. U.S. Com. on Civil Rights; active Petersburg Ministers Conf., Va. Bapt. Conv., Bapt. Gen. Conv.; past pres. Hopewell chpt. NAACP, Carter G. Woodson PTA; past pres., sec. Hopewell Ministerial Assn.; past nat. pres. Moses Life Ins. Assn.; past supt., tchr. Union Bapt. Sunday Sch.; past vice chmn. Va. State Adv. Com. to U.S. Commn. on Civil Rights; past exec. sec. and moderator Bethany Bapt. Assn. and Allied Bodies; past counselor non-boarding students Va. State U.; past exec. dir., bd. dirs. Va. Coun. on Human Rels. Recipient Recognition award Va. state unit So. Christian Leadership Conf., 1967, Rosa Parks award nat. unit, 1981, Inspirational award Va. unit, 1981, Centennial Cmty. Recognition award, 1982, Martin Luther King Jr. Cmty. Svc. award Va. state unit, 1983, Unmatched Determination award nat. bd., 1992, Appreciation award Emporia/Greenville chpt., 1992; Outstanding Svc. award Ushers Union of Hopewell, 1969, cert. of appreciation, 1986; Outstanding Citizenship award Va. Coun. on Social Welfare, 1971, Citizen of Yr. award Alpha Kappa Alpha, 1971, 88, Outstanding Svcs. and Deeds to Mankind award Little Gilfield Ch., Ivor, 1971, Man of Yr. award Petersburg chpt. Nat. Assn. Negro Bus. and Profl. Women, 1971, cert. of recognition Zion Bapt. Ch., 1978, Dedicated Svc. award Pres. Bd. Visitors and Faculty of Va. State Coll., 1978, cert. of appreciation Floyd E. Kellam H.S., Virginia Beach, 1982, Cmty. Spirit award Tabernacle Bapt. Ch., 1982, Alumni award Carter G. Woodson H.S., 1983, Cmty. Rels. award Prince William County br. NAACP, 1986; named Parade marshal Hopewell Christmas Parade, 1978, Citizen of Yr., Petersburg Consistory # 144 Masons, 1982, Outstanding Achievement award Citizens of Hopewell, 1989, Support of Children award City of Hopewell Sch. Bd., 1990, Martin Luther King Jr. Legacy award Alpha Phi Alpha, 1992, Jon D. Strother Human Rights award, 1994, cert. of appreciation U.S. Army Quartermaster Ctr. and Sch., Ft. Lee, Va., 1995, Lifetime Svc. to Fellowmen award Surry County Citizens Forum, 1995, Majestic Leader award Lott Carey Bapt. Fgn. Mission Conv., 1995, Real Dream aw. Home: 209 Terminal St Hopewell VA 23860-2940 Office: City of Hopewell 300 N Main St Hopewell VA 23860-2740

HARRIS, D. ALAN, lawyer; b. Oak Park, Ill., Mar. 4, 1949; s. E.B. and M.A. (Solberg) H.; m. Marcella Ruble, July 13, 1985. AB, U. Ill., Urbana, 1970, JD, 1973. Bar: Ill. 1974, U.S. Dist. Ct. (no. dist.) Ill. 1974, U.S. Ct. Appeals (7th cir.) 1975, U.S. Ct. Appeals (3rd cir.) 1984, Calif. 1990. From assoc. to ptnr. Freeman, Freeman & Salzman, Chgo., 1974-81; sole practice Chgo., 1981-89; ptnr. Harris & Ruble, Chgo., 1990—, L.A., 1997—; spl. dep. atty. gen. Commonwealth of Pa., 1981-97. Mem. ABA, Ill. Bar Assn., Chgo. Bar Assn. Club: Union League (Chgo.). Office: 1625 Woods Dr Los Angeles CA 90069-1633

HARRIS, EDWARD A., producer, writer, director; b. Elizabeth, N.J., Dec. 14, 1946; s. Howard E. and Bernice W. Harris; m. Chris Garrison, May 16, 1987. Student music composition and theory, U. Okla., 1964-67, L.A. C.C., 1977, UCLA, 1978. Singer, songwriter, 1962—; pres., exec. prodr. Myriad Prodns., L.A./Atlanta, 1965—; creative dir. Myriad Graphics, L.A., 1976-95; prodr., assoc. dir. Columbia Music Hall, Hartford, Conn., 1972-75; film and TV prodr., 1971—; multi-media entertainment cons., Los Angeles, 1977-95; field producer Good Morning Am., also Good Night Am., ABC-TV, 1975-77; exec. prodr., dir. The Act Factory, L.A., 1977-83; sr. ptnr. Myriad-Fritz Prodns., L.A., 1977-83; v.p. Sports Prodns., Am. Videogram, Inc., L.A., 1986-87; ptnr. Myriad/Knox Prodns., L.A., 1987-92, H-two-O Prodns., L.A., 1987-92; exec. prodr. The Gateway Group, San Francisco, 1974-75; dir. Performance Evaluation Workshop, L.A. Songwriter's Expo, 1978-83; co-dir. SPVA Performing Arts Workshop, L.A., 1980; exec. dir. Nat. Sports Found., L.A./Atlanta, 1993—. Composer over 30 songs; exec. prodr.: (TV show) The National Sports Tributes, 1991—; prodr.: (TV sports mag.) The Clubhouse, 1982-88, (TV series) Boating World, ESPN, 1987-92. Pres. Wintonbury Mall Mchts. Assn., Bloomfield, Conn., 1971-72. Mem. Am. Fedn. Musicians, AGVA, Internat. Assn. Sports Muss. and Halls of Fame, North Am. Sport Libr. Network, Nat. Ctr. Non-Profit Bds., Soc. for Preservation of Variety Arts, Alpha Epsilon Pi, Kappa Kappa Psi.

HARRIS, E(LEANOR) LYNN(E), religious studies and literature educator; b. Villa Park, Ill., July 7; d. Robert Carl and Karin Elizabeth (Peterson) Karlström. BA, U. Chgo., MA; MDiv, No. Bapt. Theol. Sem., 1975; D of Ministry, Chgo. Theol. Sem., 1980; PhD, NYU, 1980. Ordained min. United Ch. of Christ, 1987. Prof. U. Ill. Chgo., 1970—; interim min. Union Congl. Ch., Moline, Ill., 1997; min. Glen Ellyn (Ill.) Congl. Ch., 1987-89; night ministry, Chgo., 1999, 2000; adj. faculty religious studies Loyola U., Chgo.; adj. faculty English Ind. U. Northwest, DePaul U., Ill. Benedictine U.; sec. Bd. Christian Witness in Soc., 1984-88; mem. seminaries com. Chgo. Met. Assn., United Ch. Christ; active Night Ministry, Chgo., summers 1999, 2000; presenter in fields. Author: The Mystic Spirituality of A.W. Tozer, A Twentieth Century American Protestant, 1992; contbr. poems and articles to profl. jours. Recipient Lucia Queen of Light award City of Chgo., 1970. Mem. MLA, Am. Acad. Religion, Soc. Sci. Study Religion, Am.-Scandinavian Found., Chgo. Metro. Assn. (seminaries com.), Mensa. Avocations: art, music, travel, folk dancing, camping. Home: PO Box 412 Wheaton IL 60189-0412

HARRIS, EMILY LOUISE, special education educator; b. New London, Conn., Nov. 16, 1932; d. Frank Sr. and Tanzatter (McCleese) Brown; m. John Everett Harris Sr., Sept. 10, 1955; children: John Everett Jr., Jocelyn E. (dec.). BS, U. Conn., 1955; MEd, Northeastern U., 1969. Cert. tchr. elem. spl. subject sci., Mass., spl. subject reading, secondary prin., elem. prin. Tchr. New Haven Sch. Dept., 1957-59, Boston Sch. Dept., 1966-68, Natick (Mass.) Sch. Dept., 1969-72; cert. nurse's asst. The Hebrew Rehab. Ctr., Roslindale, Mass., 1973-75; spl. edn. educator Boston Sch. Dept., 1975-76, 78—, support tchr., 1976-78; site coord. Tchr. Corps., 1977-81; leader, coleader Harvard U. Student Tchrs. at Dorchester H.S. Sem., 1995—; tchr. adviser Future Educators Am. Dorchester H.S. Editor, compiler: Cooking With the Stars, 1989. Mem.-del. Mass. Fedn. Tchrs., Boston, 1993-96; elected rep. AFL-CIO (Boston Tchrs. Union), 1986-96; registrar of voters Dorchester (Mass.) H.S., 1986—; adv. bd. New England Assn. Schs. and Colls., 1980-93; 1st v.p., bd. dirs. League of Women for Comty. Svcs., Boston, 1976-80, Cynthia Sickle-Cell Anemia Fund, Boston, 1976-80. Recipient Tchg. award Urban League Guild Mass., 1993. Mem. AAUW, Zeta Phi Beta (Zeta of Yr. 1994), Alpha Delta Kappa, Kappa Delta Pi, Order Ea. Star (past worthy matron Prince Hall chpt. 1983-84), Delta Omicron Zeta, Phi Delta Kappa. Baptist. Avocations: reading, sewing. Home: 36 Dietz Rd Hyde Park MA 02136-1134

HARRIS, FREDERICK JOHN, foreign language and literature educator; b. N.Y.C., July 29, 1943; s. Frederick and Anna (Guttmann) H. BA, Fordham U., 1965; MA, Columbia U., 1966, PhD, 1969. Asst. prof. Fordham U., N.Y.C., 1970-79, assoc. prof., 1979-84, prof. French and comparative lit., 1984—, chmn. divsn. humanities, 1979-85, chmn. dept. modern langs. and lits. (bi-campus), 1995-99; bd. dirs. Fordham U. Press, N.Y.C.; mem. adv. com. Krieg und Literatur/War and Literature. Author: André Gide-Romain Rolland: Two Men Divided, 1973, Encounters with Darkness: French and German Writers on World War II, 1983; contbr. articles to profl. jours. Mem. MLA, PEN Am. Ctr., Am. Assn. Tchrs. French, Internat. Comparative Lit. Assn., Am. Comparative Lit. Assn., Assn. des Amis d'André Gide, Société des Professeurs Français et Francophones d'Amérique (bd. dirs. 1995-98), Stewart Hall (v.p. 1989-90, bd. dirs.). Roman Catholic. Office: Rose Hill Campus Lincoln Center Campus Fordham U New York NY 10023

HARRIS, GUY HENDRICKSON, chemical research engineer; b. San Bernardino, Calif., Oct. 2, 1914; s. Edwin James and Nellie Mae (Hendrickson) H.; m. Elsie Mary Dietsch, Mar. 15, 1940; children: Alice, Robert, Mary, Sara. AA, San Bernardino Valley Coll., 1934; BS, U. Calif., Berkeley, 1937; AM, Stanford U., 1939, PhD, 1941. Analytical chemist Shell Devel. Co., Emeryville, Calif., 1937-38; organic chemist William S. Merrell Co., Cin., 1941-45; rsch. chemist Fiber Bd., Emeryville, 1945-46; from organic chemist to assoc. scientist The Dow Chem. Co., Pittsburg, Calif., 1946-62; assoc. scientist The Dow Chem. Co., Walnut Creek, Calif., 1964-82; sr. lectr. U. Ghana, Legon Accra, 1962-64; chmn. dept. chemistry John F. Kennedy U., Orinda, Calif., 1964-69; pvt. practice cons. Concord, Calif., 1982-88; rsch. engr. U. Calif., Berkeley, 1988—. Contbr. K & O Encyclopedia Chem. Tech., 1959, 70, 84, 97, Reagents in Mineral Tech., 1990. Fellow AAAS, Royal Soc. Chemistry; mem. AIME, Soc. Mining Engrs. (disting. mem.), Bus. Men's Fellowship USA, The Commonwealth Club, Sigma Xi. Roman Catholic. Achievements include 51 patents in field of mineral processing reagents in particular Z200 (R) agricultural chemicals and process for manufacture. Home: 1673 Georgia Dr Concord CA 94519-1921 Office: Univ California 386 Evans Hall # 1760 Berkeley CA 94720-3861

HARRIS, IAN LOUIS, economist, writer, accountant; b. London, Aug. 28, 1962; s. Peter and Renee H. BA with hons. in Econs. & Law, U. Keele, England, 1984. Chartered accountant. Edn. and welfare officer U. of Keele, England, 1984-85; trainee acct. Newman Harris & Co., London, 1985-88; mgmt. cons. BDO Consulting, London, 1988-94; dir., mng. dir. Z/Yen Ltd., London, 1994—; dir. Financial Lab., London, 1996—, Weathersure, London, 1999—; financial adv. Taskforce 2000, London, 1996—; initiative gov. The Childrens Soc., England, Wales, 1998—. Co-author: (with Michael Mainelli) Clear Business Cuisine, 2000; writer songs and sketches; contbr. articles to profl. jours. Avocations: writing, theatre, music, cooking, cricket. Home: 12 Clanricarde Gardens, W2 4NA London England Office: Z/Yen Ltd, 5-7 St Helens Place, EC3A 6AU London England

HARRIS, JAMES RIDOUT, retired communications executive; b. Lockhart, Tex., Apr. 14, 1920; s. Walter Karl and Hortense (Ridout) H.; m. Frances Elizabeth Wiley, June 23, 1943; children: Richard Wells, Betty Anne, Beverly Jean. B.S., U. Richmond, 1941; M.E.E., Poly. U., 1948; postgrad. Williams Coll., summer 1959; Engr. Chesapeake & Potomac Telephone Co., Richmond, Va., 1941-42; with Bell Telephone Labs., N.Y. and N.J., 1942-82, dir. data communications, 1961-65, dir. customer switching and govt. communications, 1965-71, dir. customer equipment studies center, 1971-81, dir. data network spl. studies ctr., 1981-82; dir. spl. studies ctr. AT&T Info. Systems Labs., 1983. Developed pioneer solid state computing equipment, 1950, world's earliest transistor-based computing equipment; supervised devel. world's earliest high speed transistor-based computer, Bell Labs, 1953; patentee computing, communications and solid state cirs.; directed preparation of Engineering and Operations in the Bell System, 1977. Recipient George R. Stibitz Computer Pioneer award, 1999. Mem. IEEE (sr., adminstrv. com. of computer soc. 1962-65), Am. Phys. Soc., Soc. Automotive Engrs., Phi Beta Kappa, Sigma Xi. Presbyterian (elder, trustee, pres. corp.). Home: 8 Dogwood Ln Rumson NJ 07760-1412

HARRIS, JEFFREY SAUL, physician, executive, consultant; b. Pitts., Mar. 13, 1949; s. Aaron Wexler and Janet Mary (Wexler) Harris; m. Mary V. Anderson, Jan. 2, 1981; children: Sarah Ariel, Noah Aaron, Susannah Leia. BS in Molecular Biophysics/Biochemistry, Yale U., 1971; MD, U. N.Mex., 1975; MPH, U. Mich., 1982; MBA, Vanderbilt U., 1988. Diplomate Am. Bd. Preventive Medicine in Occupl. Medicine and Gen. Preventive Medicine, Am. Bd. Emergency Medicine, Am. Bd. Medicine Quality, Am. Bd. Ind. Med. Examination; lic. Md., Calif., Tenn., Alaska. Gen. med. officer USPHS, Juneau, Alaska, 1976-78; clin. dir. S.E. Alaska Native Health Corp, Juneau, 1978-79; asst. to commr. Tenn. Dept. Health and Environ., Nashville, 1980-83; dir. health care mgmt. Northern Telecom Inc., Nashville, 1983-88; pres. HDM, Inc., Nashville, 1988-90; med. dir. Aetna Health Plans of Tenn., Nashville, 1990-91; nat. leader practice, health strategy Alexander & Alexander Cons. Group, San Francisco, 1991-94; chief prevention, health and disability officer Indsl. Indemnity, San Francisco, 1994-97; pres. J. Harris Assocs., Inc., Mill Valley, Calif., 1979—; pres., CEO Med-Fx, Inc., 1999—; mng. ptnr. The Hofmann Health Care Group, 2000—. Author: Strategic Health Management, 1994, Best Practices in Occupational Medicine, 2000; author, editor: Occupational Medicine Practice Guidelines: Evaluation and Management of Common Health Problems and Functional Recovery in Workers, 1997, Quick Reference to Practice Guidelines in Occupational Medicine, 1999, Managed Care in Occupational Medicine, 1998; author, co-editor: Managing Employee Health Care Costs, 1992, Manual of Occupational Health and Safety, 1992, 96, 2000, Health Promotion in the Work Place, 1994, 2000, Integrated Health Management, 1998; mem. editl. bd. Am. Jour. Health Promotion, 1985—, Occupl. Environment Med. Report, 1988—; contbg. editor JAMA, Internat. Jour. Occupl. Environ. Health, Am. Jour. Pub. Health, 1988—, Jour. Internat. Occupl. Environ. Health; contbr. articles to profl. jours. Fellow Am. Acad. Family Practice, Am. Coll. Occupl. Environ. Medicine (dir., chmn. practice guidelines com. 1992-98, Presdl. award 1996), Am. Coll. Preventive Medicine, Am. Coll. Med. Quality, Am. Bd. Ind. Med. Examiners. Avocations: skiing, running, playing music, painting, writing children's stories. E-mail: jharrismvl@aol.com and jeff harris@medfx.net. Home: 386 Richardson Way Mill Valley CA 94941-4053 Office: J Harris Assocs Inc and Med-Fx PO Box 1087 Mill Valley CA 94942-1087

HARRIS, JOCELYN MARGARET, English educator; b. Dunedin, New Zealand, Sept. 10, 1939; d. Windsor Norman and Margaret Constance (Garrett) Wood; children: James de Gall, Louise Marie. MA, U. Otago, Dunedin, 1961; PhD, London, 1969. Lectr. U. Otago, 1971-94, prof., chair, 1995—. Author: Samuel Richardson, Sir Charles Grandison, 1972, Samuel Richardson, 1987, Jane Austen's Art of Memory, 1989; author, editor: (with Tom Keymer) Samuel Richardson's commentary on Clarissa, 1749-65, Vol. 1, 1998. Joint founder Dunedin Collective for Women, 1972. Mem. Am. Soc. 18th Century Studies, Australasian and Pacific 18th Century Soc. (pres. 1983-90). Office: U Otago English Dept, Albany St, Dunedin New Zealand

HARRIS, JOE FRANK, former governor; b. Cartersville, Ga., Feb. 16, 1936; s. Grover Franklin and Frances (Morrow) H.; m. Elizabeth Carlock Harris, June 25, 1961; 1 son. Joe Frank, Jr. BBA, U. Ga., 1958; LLD (hon.), Woodrow Wilson Coll. Law, 1981, Asbury Coll., 1983, Morris Brown Coll., 1983, LaGrange Coll., 1987, Mercer U., 1987. Sec.-treas. Harris Cement Products, Inc., Cartersville, 1958-79; pres. Harris Georgia Corp., Cartersville, 1979-83; mem. Ga. Gen. Assembly, 1965-83; gov. State of Ga., 1983-91; prof., Disting. Exec. fellow Ga. State U., Atlanta, 1993—. Bd. regents Univ. Sys. Ga., 1999—. Served with U.S. Army, 1958. Democrat. Methodist. Home: 712 West Ave Cartersville GA 30120-3441

HARRIS, JOHN LEONARD, chemical engineering educator, researcher; b. Sydney, Australia, Mar. 14, 1944; s. Leonard Roy and Elsie Clare (O'Connell) H.; m. Gail Denise Rogers, July 3, 1943; children: Alyse Gay, Lenae Janel, Dacia Loryn, Bryce James. B in Engring., U. NSW, Sydney, 1966; PhD, U. NSW, 1972. Ops. rsch. analyst CRA, Melbourne, Australia, 1970-73; rsch. engr. J.R. Norman & Assocs., Sydney, 1973-74; process engr. Altona Petrochem. Co., Melbourne, 1974-75; lectr., sr. lectr. chem. engring. Royal Melbourne Inst. Tech. U., 1975—; sec. Chemeca 87 Organizing Com., Melbourne, 1988-90; expert witness Dept. Environ. Protection, Perth, Australia, 1993-94. Contbr. articles to profl. jours., confs. on the topic of membrane processing and catalytic reactions. Mem. Instn. Chem. Engrs. (chartered engr.), Instn. Engrs. Australia (chartered profl. engr.). Avocations: tennis, golf, swimming, family activities. Office: RMIT U, 124 Latrobe St PO Box 2476V, Melbourne 3001, Australia

HARRIS, JUNE LEATRICE, education coordinator, administrator; b. South Mills, N.C.; d. Charlie Cyphus and Emma Jane (Griffin) H. BS, N.C. Ctrl. U.; MA, Atlanta U.; PhD, U. Md. Profl. staff Com. Edn. and Labor Rep. William L. Clay, Washington, 1983-94; tchr. Balt. Pub. Schs., Mo. Coll., St. Louis, Mo., U. D.C., Washington, Elizabeth City (N.C.) State U.; edn. policy coord. Com. on Edn. and the Workforce, 1994—. Author: Excellence in Education. Recipient Recognition award State Occupl. Info. Coordinating, Salt Lake City, 1990. Mem. Mich. Edn. Assn., D.C. Vocat. Edn., Phi Delta Kappa, Delta Sigma Theta. African Methodist Episcopal Zion Church. Avocations: basketball, golf, reading. Office: US Ho Reps 1107 Longworth Bldg Washington DC 20515-0004

HARRIS, LEROY S., mechanical engineer; b. Phila., Apr. 5, 1924; s. Philip H. and Isabella (Roseberg) H.; m. Florence Schwab, Mar. 26, 1950; children: Andrew, Joel. BS, Pa. State U., 1945, MS, 1946; postgrad., U. Pa., 1954-56, Villanova U., 1954-55; MBA, Temple U., 1957. Registered profl. engr., Pa., Ohio, Calif., N.H., Ill. Mech. engr. Baldwin Loco Works, Eddystone, Pa., 1946-48, U.S. Naval Boiler and Turbine Lab., Phila., 1948-50, Bell Aircraft Corp., Buffalo, 1950-52; asst. prof. mech. engring. Villanova (Pa.) U., 1953-56; mgr. R&D Schutte & Koerting Co., Cornwells Heights, Pa., 1957-68; chief engr. Am. Chain and Cable Co., York, Pa., 1968-69; asst. pres. K-G Industries Inc., Rosemont, Ill., 1969-74; v.p. gen. mgr. Am. Tara Corp., Chgo., 1974-76; dir. engring. Morrison Knudsen Corp., Cleve., 1976-93; pres. cons. engring. L.S. Harris Corp., Cleve., 1993—. Author more than 50 tech. papers. Fellow ASME (v.p. 1979-82, vice chmn. R&D 1988-90, chmn. environtl. affairs 1976-79, chmn. process industries divsn. 1966-70, Centennial medal 1980, Dedicated Svc. medal 1993); mem. Cleve. Engring. Soc., Loss Execs. Assn., Nat. Fire Protection Assn., Masons, Sigma Tau. Achievements include 33 U.S. and fgn. patents. Home: 23285 Pheasant Ln Westlake OH 44145-4358 Office: LS Harris Corp 20545 Center Ridge Rd Cleveland OH 44116-3423

HARRIS, MARILYN, retired academic administrator; b. N.Y.C.; d. Bernard and Rose (Block) Hochberg; m. Seymour J. Harris; children: Randall (dec.), April. AB summa cum laude, CUNY-Hunter Coll., 1945; MS, Iowa State U., 1947. Mem. faculty dept. math and stats. Hunter Coll., N.Y.C., 1946-48; sys. analyst, statistician market rsch. svcs. GE, N.Y.C., 1962-67; biostatistician comprehensive child care project Einstein Med. Sch., N.Y.C., 1967-69; asst. to dean, acting dir. computer ctr. Baruch Coll. CUNY, 1969-72; dir. data collection and evaluation office univ. mgmt. data Ctrl. Office, CUNY, 1972-74; dir. mgmt. info. sys. Bklyn. Coll., CUNY, 1974-79, dir. pers. svcs., 1979-85, asst. v.p. human resources and adminstrv. svcs., 1985-89, bd. dirs. Bklyn. Ctr. Performing Arts, 1982-89, chair seat campaign, 1984-86; Docent Pollock/Krasner House, East Hampton, L.I., 1995-97. Bd. dirs. Project Greenhope, 1988-93; vol. mgmt. cons. Women in Need, 1988-94, bd. dirs., 1989-92, sec. exec. com., 1990-92; bd. dirs. Women's City Club, 1990-97, active homeless project, 1989-91, mem. emergency task force, 1992-93, v.p. ops., 1993-94; active Womanspace of Gt. Neck, 1989, mem. exec. com.-at-large, 1990-94, mem. adv. bd., 1994-96; adv. bd. Omsbudservice of Nassau County, 1991—. Recipient Excellence award Art League Nassau County, 1994, Helen Nobel award of merit Nat. Art League, 1996, Gold medal 1st pl., 1996, Silver medal, 1997. Mem. Artists Network Great Neck (Hon. Mention awards), Artist Alliance of L.I., Phi Beta Kappa, Phi Kappa Phi, Pi Mu Epsilon. Home: 9 Knightsbridge Rd Great Neck NY 11021-4569

HARRIS, MARION HOPKINS, former government official; b. Washington, July 27, 1938; d. Dennis Cason and Georgia (Greenleaf) Hopkins; m. Charles E. Harris, July 1957 (div. 1964); 1 child, Alan E. MPA, U. Pitts., 1971; M in Mgmt. Sys., U. So. Calif., 1984, DPA, 1985. Dir. program planning Rochester Urban Renewal Agy., N.Y., 1971-72; exec. dir. Fairfax County Redevel. and Housing Authority, Fairfax, Va., 1972-73; dep. dir. housing mgmt. HUD, Detroit, 1973-75; pres.; mng. auditor GAO, Washington, 1979-80; sr. field officer of housing, Washington, 1979-89, dir. evaluation divsn. adminstrn., USHUD, 1989-91, asst. prof. Dept. Bus. and Pub. Adminstrn. Bowie State U., Md., 1991—, pres. Leo Group, Mgmt. Cons., 1995—; prof. grad. sch. mgmt. & tech. U. Md. U. Coll., 1997—. Bd. dirs. S.W. Neighborhood Assembly, Washington, 1979-80; commr. S.W. Adv. Neighborhood Commn., Washington, 1986; mem. pub. adv. com. Washington Coun. Govts., 1985-87; mem. consumer adv. bd. Wash. Suburban Sanitary Com., 1989—; bd. dirs. Bowie State U. Found., 1991—; mem. transition team Gov. State of Md., 1995; mem. Md. Gov.'s Workforce Investment Bd., 1996—. Recipient Outstanding Peormance award HUD, 1984; Carnegie-Mellon mid-career fellow, 1970; Ford Found. travel-study awardee, 1970. Mem. Am. Acad. Soc. and Polit. Sci., U. So. Calif. Doctoral Assn., LWV (exec. bd. Washington 1983-84). Roman Catholic. Avocations: ballroom dancing, foreign travel, swimming. E-mail: mhharris@erols.com. Home: 10947 Swansfield Rd Columbia MD 21044-2727 Office: Leo Group Mgmt Consultants 6006 Greenbelt Rd Ste 248 Greenbelt MD 20770-1019

HARRIS, MARK STEPHEN, telecommunications executive; b. Epping, Essex, Eng., Jan. 30, 1966; s. Norman Russell and Beryl Jean (Spencer) H. BS in Physics with honors, U. Birmingham, Eng., 1989. Bus devel. analyst BT plc, Felixstowe, Eng., 1989-90; bus. ops. support mgr. BT plc, Ipswich, Eng., 1990-91, sr. svc. mgmt. cons., 1991-93, bus. devel. mgr., 1993-95; product mktg. mgr. BT plc, Felixstowe, 1995; bus. product devel. mgr. Cable London, 1996-97; data products dept. mgr. NB3, Springfield, Eng., 1997-98; founder, dir. Streetparty Ltd., Ipswich, Eng., 1998—; project leader Eurescom, Heidelberg, Germany, 1991-93. Founder Mid-Suffolk Countryside Vols., Stowmarket, Eng., 1986, Innercity Youth Club, Birmingham, Eng., 1987, Street Party, Charity, Felixstowe, 1992. Mem. IEEE, Inst. Mgmt., Inst. Physics, Instn. Elec. Engrs. (chartered), Inst. Logistics & Transport, Inst. Dirs. Avocations: marathon running, mountaineering, violin, contryside conservation, musical composition. Home: 7 Mellis Ct, Felixstowe Suffolk, England IP112YQ

HARRIS, MARY ANN, school media specialist, storyteller, consultant; b. Moultrie, Ga., June 10, 1946; d. James Bobby and Mary Ola (Rooney) Brooks; m. John W. Harris, July 29, 1972; children: Paul, Justin. BS, Knoxville Coll., 1969; MA, Wayne State U., 1971; EdD, Nova U., 1986. Gerontology field supr. Case Western Res. U., Cleve., 1972-73; program dir. Fairhill Mental Health Ctr., Cleve., 1973-74; adj. instr. Cuyahoga Community Coll., Cleve., 1975-80; dir. sr. citizen ctr. City of Cleve., 1980-81; devel. officer Cleve. Adult Tutorial, 1981-86; research project assoc. U. Mich., Ann Arbor, 1986—; pres. E. Cleve. (Ohio) Bd. Edn., 1998—; gerontology cons. Council for Econ. Opportunities, Cleve., 1981-83, Project Rainbow, Cleve., 1980—. Author: Grandparent Stuff-Riddles About Growing Old, 1985. Vol. Arthritis Found., Cleve., 1985-86; mem. East Cleve. Bd. Edn., 1979—, v.p., pres. 1998; precinct committeeman East Cleve. Dem. Party, 1984—; pres. Ohio Caucus of Black Sch. Bd. Grantee Adminstrn. on Aging, 1979, Cuyahoga County Commisioners Office, 1985; recipient Mother of Yr. award Cleve. Call and Post Newspaper, 1984. Mem. Nat. Alliance of Black Sch. Educators, NAACP (chmn. com. 1985-86), Ohio Sch. Bds. Assn. (pres. N.E. region 1995), Alpha Kappa Alpha (2d v.p. Cleve. 1985-86). Democrat. Avocations: creative writing, bowling, sewing. Home: 1326 E 143rd St Cleveland OH 44112-2542 Office: East Cleveland Bd Edn 15305 Terrace Rd East Cleveland OH 44112-2933

HARRIS, MARY EMMA, art historian, landscape designer; b. Kinston, N.C., July 11, 1943; d. Aubrey Eugene and Dorothy (Rouse) H. BA, Greensboro Coll., 1965; MA, U. N.C., 1974; cert. landscape design & comml. hort., N.Y. Bot. Garden, 1991. Mem. edn. dept. Detroit Inst. Art, 1969-70; rsch. dir. Black Mountain Coll. Rsch. N.C. Mus. Art, Raleigh, 1970-73; ind. scholar N.Y.C., 1973—, pvt. practice landscape designer and horticulturist, 1992—; chair, project dir. Black Mountain Coll. Project, Inc., N.Y.C., 1999—. Author: The Arts at Black Mountain College, 1987, Remembering Black Mountain College, 1996. Named Disting. Alumna Greensboro Coll., 1988; recipient Cmty Svc. award Pks. Coun., 1999; Ind. Scholar grantee NEH, 1973, 79. Mem. Assn. Ind. Historian Art (treas.). Home: 42 Grove St Apt 33 New York NY 10014-5376 Office: Black Mountain Coll Project Inc Village Sta PO Box 607 New York NY 10014-0607

HARRIS, MATTHEW NATHAN, surgeon, educator; b. N.Y.C., Dec. 20, 1931; s. Saul and Deborah (Moskowitz) H.; m. Frances Wicentowski, June 27, 1954; children: Amy Rachel, Julie Rebecca, Daniel Charles. BA, NYU, 1952; MD, Chgo. Med. Sch., 1956. Diplomate Am. Bd. Surgery, Nat. Bd. Med. Examiners; lic. physician, N.Y. Intern Bellevue Hosp. Ctr., N.Y.C., 1956-57, resident in gen. surgery, 1957-58, 60-63; sr. clin. trainee in cancer USPHS, N.Y.C., 1963-64; instr. anatomy NYU, N.Y.C., 1966-68, dir. elective surg. anatomy, 1973-74; prof. surgery, dir. surg. oncology NYU Sch. Medicine, N.Y.C., 1979—; vis. surgeon Bellevue Hosp. Ctr.; attending surgeon Tisch Hosp.; cons. and lectr. in field.; cons. surgeon Manhattan V.A. Hosp. Contbr. articles to Jour. ACS, Breast Disease, Cancer, Annals Surgery, Radiology, N.Y. State Jour. Medicine, Cancer Rsch., Surgery, Jour. Lab. Investigations, others. Capt. USAR, 1958-60, Korea. Chgo. Med. Sch. scholar, 1955. Fellow ACS (cancer liaison fellow, N.Y. state chmn.); mem. AMA, Am. Soc. Clin. Oncology, Am. Assn. Clin. Anatomists, Am. Radium Soc., N.Y. Cancer Soc., N.Y. Surg. Soc. (pres. 1991-92), N.Y. Med. Soc., N.Y. Met. Breast Cancer Group, Soc. Surg. Oncology, N.Y. Cancer Programs Assn., Inc., Pan-Am. Med. Soc., Soc. Cons. Armed Forces, 38th Parallel Med. Soc. (Korea), Pan Pacific Surg. Assn., Internat. Pigment Cell Soc., Assn. Cancer Edn., Assn. Academic Surgery, So. Alumni Bellevue Hosp., Chgo. Med. Sch. Alumni Assn., Alpha Omega Alpha, Sigma Xi, Beta Lambda Sigma. Achievements include research in cytologic evaluation breast diseases by stereoactic aspiration, malignant melanoma vaccine, primary surgical management malignant melanoma. Office: NYU Med Ctr 530 1st Ave New York NY 10016-6402

HARRIS, MICALYN SHAFER, lawyer, educator; b. Chgo., Oct. 31, 1941; d. Erwin and Dorothy (Sampson) Shafer. AB, Wellesley Coll., 1963; JD, U. Chgo., 1966. Bar: Ill. 1966, Mo. 1967, U.S. Dist. Ct. (ea. dist.) Mo. 1967, U.S. Supreme Ct. 1972, U.S. Ct. Appeals (8th cir.), 1974, N.Y. 1981, N.J. 1988, U.S. Dist. Ct. N.J., U.S. Ct. Appeals (3d cir.) 1993. Law clk. U.S. Dist. Ct., Mo., 1967-68; atty. The May Dept. Stores, St. Louis, 1968-70, Ralston-Purina Co., St. Louis, 1970-72; atty., asst. sec. Chromalloy Am. Corp., St. Louis, 1972-76; pvt. practice St. Louis, 1976-78; atty, CPC Internat., Inc., 1978-80; divsn. counsel CPA N.Am., 1980-84, asst. sec., 1981-88; gen. counsel S.B. Thomas, Inc., 1983-87; corp. counsel CPC Internat., Englewood Cliffs, NJ, 1984-88; assoc. counsel Weil, Gotshal & Manges, N.Y.C., 1988-90; pvt. practice, 1991; v.p., sec., gen. counsel Winpro, Inc., 1991—; arbitrator Am., Arbitration Assn., NYSE, NASD, The Aspen Ctr. Conflict Mgmt.; adj. prof. Lubin Sch. Bus. Pace U. Mem. consultative groups Restatement of Agy. and UCC Article 2. Mem. ABA (gov. bd. Ctr. Profl. Responsibility and Ch., publs. com., bus. law sect., past chair corp. counsel com., chair corp. comm. subcom., past chair subcom. counseling the mktg. function, mem. securities law com., tender offers and proxy statements subcom., legal bus. ethics com., chair task force on e-mail privacy, vice chair subcom. on computer software contracting, task force on electronic contracting, task force on conflicts of interest, ad hod com. on tech., strategic planning com.), N.Y. State Bar Assn. (securities regulation com., technology law com., chair subcom. on licensing, task force on shrink-wrap licensing, exec. com., bus. law sect.), N.J. Bar Assn. (computer law com.), Assn. Bar City N.Y., Bar Assn. Metro St. Louis (past chair TV com.), Mo. Bar Assn. (part chmn. internat. law com.), Am. Corp. Counsel Assn. N.Y. (mergers and acquisitions com., corp. law com.), N.J. Gen. Coun., Computer Law Assn. Address: 625 N Monroe St Ridgewood NJ 07450-1206

HARRIS, MICHAEL GENE, optometrist, educator, lawyer; b. San Francisco, Sept. 20, 1942; s. Morry and Gertrude Alice (Epstein) H.; m. Dawn Block; children: Matthew Benjamin, Daniel Evan, Ashley Beth, Lindsay Meredith. BS, U. Calif., 1964, M in Optometry, 1965, D in Optometry, 1966, MS, 1968; JD, John F. Kennedy U., 1985. Bar: Calif., U.S. Dist. Ct. (no. dist.) Calif. Assoc. practice optometry Oakland, Calif., 1965-66, San Francisco, 1966-68; instr., coord. contact lens clinic Ohio State U., 1968-69; asst. clin. prof. optometry U. Calif., Berkeley, 1969-73, dir. contact lens extended care clinic, 1969-83, chief contact lens clinic, 1983—, assoc. clin. prof., 1973-76, asst. chief, then assoc. chief contact lens svc., 1970—, lectr., then sr. lectr., 1978—, vice chmn. faculty Sch. Optometry, 1983-85, 95—, prof. clin. optometry, 1984-86, clin. prof., 1986—, dir. residency program, 1993-95, asst. dean, 1994-95, assoc. dean, 1995—; John de Carle vis. prof. City U., London, 1984; vis. rsch. fellow U. NSW, Sydney, Australia, 1989; sr. vis. rsch. scholar U. Melbourne, Victoria, Australia, 1989, 92; pvt. practice optometry, Oakland, 1973-76; mem. ophthalmic devices panel, med. device adv. com. FDA, 1990—, interim chair, 1994; lectr., cons. in field; mem. regulation rev. com. Calif. Bd. Optometry; cons. hypnosis Calif. Optometric Assn., Am. Optometric Assn.; cons. Nat. Bd. Examiners in Optometry, Soflens divsn. Bausch & Lomb, 1973—, Barnes-Hind Hydrocurve Soft Lenses, Inc., 1974-87, Pilkinton-Barnes Hind, 1987-94, Contact Lens Rsch. Lab., 1976—, Wesley-Jessen Contact Lens Co., 1977—, Palo Alto VA, 1980—, Primarius Corp., Cooper Vision Optics Alcon, 1980—; co-founder Morton D. Sarver Rsch. Lab., 1986; Max Shapero meml. lectr., 1995. Editor current comments sect. Am. Jour. Optometry, 1974-77; editor Eye Contact, 1984-86; assoc. editor The Video Jour. Clin. Optometry, 1988—; cons. editor Contact Lens Spectrum, 1988—; author: Contact Lenses: Treatment Options for Ocular Disease, Contact Lenses for Pre & Post-Surgery; editor: Problems in Optometry, Special Contact Lens Procedures; Contact Lenses in Ocular Disease, 1990; mem. hon. internat. editl. bd. Contact Lens and Anterior Eye Jour.; contbr. chpts. to books, articles to profl. publs.; author various syllabi. Planning commr. Town of Moraga, Calif., 1986, vice-chmn., 1987-88, chmn., 1988-90; mem. Town Coun., Moraga, 1992—, vice mayor, 1994-95, mem. Medi-Cal. adv. planning commn., 1993-95, chair, 1994—, with Managed Care commn., 1995—, chair, 1996—; mem. city county rels. com. Contra Costa County, Calif.; planning commr. City of Pleasant Hill, Calif., 1999—; founding mem. Young Adults divsn. Jewish Welfare Fedn., 1965—, chmn., 1967-68; commr. Sunday Football League, Contra Costa County, 1974-78; chmarer mem. Jewish Cmty. Ctr. Contra Costa County; founding mem. Jewish Cmty. Mus. San Francisco, 1984; Para-RAbbinic, Temple Isaiah, Lafayette, Calif., 1987, bd. dirs., 1990; life mem. Bay Area Coun. for Soviet Jews, 1976; bd. dirs. Jewish Cmty. Rels. Coun. Greater East Bay, 1979—, Campolindo Homeowners Assn., 1981-85; pres. student coun. John F. Kennedy U. Sch. Law, 1984-85; grantor Michael G. Harris Family Endowment Fund, U. Calif., Dr. Michael G. Harris Tchg. award U. Calif. Named Alumnus of Yr., U. Calif. Sch. Optometry, 1999; U. Calif. fellow, 1971; Calif. Optometric Assn. scholar, 1965, George Schneider meml. scholar, 1964. Fellow Am. Acad. Optometry (diplomate cornea and contact lens sect., chmn. contact lens papers, mem. contact lens com. 1974—, vice chmn. contact lens sect. 1980-82, chmn. sect. 1982-84, immediate past chmn. 1984-86, chmn. jud. com. 1989—, chmn. bylaws com. 1989—), Assn. Schs. and Colls. Optometry (coun. on acad. affairs), AAAS, Prentice Soc. (pres.-elect 1994-96, pres. 1996—); mem. ABA, Assn. for Rsch. in Vision and Ophthalmology, Am. Optometric Assn. (proctor 1969—, cons. on hypnosis, mem. contact lens sect., mem. position papers com., mem. com. on ophthalmic stds., subcom. on testing andertification, cons. editor Jour.), Calif. Optometric Assn., Assn. Optometric Contact Lens Educators, Am. Optometric Found., Mexican Soc. Contactology (hon.), Nat. Coun. on Contact Lens Compliance, Internat. Soc. Contact Lens Rsch., Calif. State Bd. Optometry (regulation rev. com.), Calif. Acad. Scis., U. Calif. Optometry Alumni Assn. (life), Contrac Costa Bar Assn., Mus. Soc., JFK U. Sch. Law Alumni Assn., Benjamin Ide Wheeler Soc. U. Calif., B'nai B'rith, Mensa, Robert Gordon Sproul Assn. U. Calif. Democrat. Office: U Calif Sch Optometry Berkeley CA 94720-0001

HARRIS, MILDRED CLOPTON, clergy member, educator; b. Chgo., May 27, 1936; d. Jordan and Willa Mildred Clopton; m. Herbert Curlee Harris, Feb. 4, 1928. BA, DePaul U., 1957; MA, Columbia U., 1963, Governors State U., 1975; MPS, Loyola U., Chgo., 1985; D in Min., Bible Inst. Sem., Plymouth, Fla., 1985. Ordained to ministry Ind. Assemblies of God. Tchr. Gary (Ind.) Pub. Schs., 1957-93; founder, pres. God First Ministries, Chgo., 1978—; organizer Chgo. March for Jesus, 1995-97. Author: Traits of an Intercessor, 1991, Educating Your Child God's Way, 1991, The Productive Prayer Guide, 1991; exec. prodr. (cassette) tribe of Judah En Danse, 1995-96 (ASCAP award); host (TV show) Born Again, (radio show) WYCA 92.3, WCFJ 1470 AM. Bd. dirs. Midwestern U., Chgo., 1989-97, Goodman Theater, Chgo., 1994—, Make a Wish Found., Chgo., 1994-97, Windows of Opportunity, Chgo., 1997—; mem. exec. adv. com. Chgo. Housing Authority, 1995-99, commr., 1999—; overseer Gary (Ind.) Educators for Art, 1990—. Recipient CHANCE award Chgo. Housing Authority, 1998, Seniors-Gladys Reed award, 1998; Mary Herrick scholar Du Sable H.S. Alumni, 1998. Mem. ASCAP, Nat. Soc. Fundraising Execs., Religious Conf. Mgmt. Assn., Nat. Coun. Negro Women (life), Union League Club Chgo., Chgo. Ill. Links Inc. Avocations: traveling, interior decorating. Home: 7246 S Luella Ave Chicago IL 60649-2514

HARRIS, MILES FITZGERALD, meteorologist; b. Brunswick, Ga., Feb. 2, 1913; s. James Madison and Louise (Fitzgerald) H.; m. Marguerite Bertice Leonard, May 13, 1938; children: Ann Louise, Theresa Geraldine, Emily Leland. BSc in Meteorology, NYU, 1944, MSc in Meteorology, 1957. Weather observer U.S. Weather Bur., Macon, Ga., 1932-35, Savannah, Chattanooga., Macon,, Washington, 1937-42; cadet/clk. South Atlantic Steamship Line, Savannah, 1935-37; meteorologist U.S. Weather Bur., Washington, 1944-45; hurricane forecaster U.S. Weather Bur., San Juan, P.R., 1945-48; spl. projects meteorologist U.S. Weather Bur., Washington, 1948-51, rsch. meteorologist, 1951-61, head editing and pub. br., 1961-66; phys. scientist, chief Sci. Info. Br. Environ. Sci. Svcs. Adminstrn., Washington, 1966-70; editor Mon. Weather Review, 1968-70; editor Am. Meteorol. Soc., Boston, 1970-83, ret., 1983; Editor, writer, cons. Earth Sci. Curriculum Project, Boulder, Colo., 1964-67. Author: Man Against Storm, 1962, Getting to Know the World Meterological Organization, 1966, Opportunities in Meteorology, 1972, Investigating the Earth, 1967-84, (with Marguerite L. Harris, Eleanor V. Spiller and Mary Carr) John Hale, A Man Beset by Witches, 1992; contbg. author Ency. Earth Scis., 1976. Mem. Am. Meteorol. Soc. Democrat. Congregationalist. Avocations: local history, writing and research on John Hale, The Salem Witchcraft Trials. Home: 40 Lothrop St Beverly MA 01915-5150

HARRIS, PAMELA SUE, rehabilitation physician; b. Emporia, Kans., May 27, 1962; d. Thomas Lee and Janet Kaye (Dant) Fitzpatrick; m. Thomas Wayne Harris, Dec. 19, 1987; children: Emily Elizabeth, Bethany Elaine. BA with honors in Human Biology, U. Kans., 1984, MD, 1988. Diplomate Am. Bd. Phys. Medicine and Rehab. Resident U. Kans., 1988-92; assoc. med. dir. Bethany Rehab. Ctr., Kansas City, Kans., 1992-96;

rehab. med. dir. Providence Med. Ctr./St. John Hosp., Kansas City, 1996-98; pvt. practice rehab. medicine Kansas City, 1992—. Fellow Am. Acad. Phys. Medcine and Rehab.; mem. AMA, Kans. Med. Soc., Kiwanis (chmn. internat. com. young children Priority One 1997-99, mem. internat. com., 1996-97, chmn. Kans. dist. 1994-97). Avocations: cross stitch, crafts, flower arranging.

HARRIS, PENNY SMITH, fundraising consultant; b. Old Town, Maine, Apr. 6, 1941; d. Owen Halbert and Louise Marion (Whitten) Smith; m. Parker Fred Harris, June 22, 1963 (div. 1992); children: Susan Leslie, Nancy Lynne. BS in Sociology, U. Maine, 1963; MS in Bus. Mgmt., Husson Coll., 1984. Social worker Elizabeth Lund Home, Burlington, Vt., 1964-65; pub. sch. tchr. Essex Junction, Vt.; asst. dir. devel., corp. support mgr. Maine Pub. Broadcasting Network, Bangor, 1985-89; dir. devel. Eastern Maine Healthcare, Bangor, 1989-94; dir. healthcare campaign N.E. Health, Rockland, Maine, 1994-97; sr. assoc. Copley Davenport Co., Inc., Wenham, Mass., 1997-98, M. Davenport Assocs., 1998—. Trustee Maine Pub. Broadcasting Corp., 1991-95, Maine Coast Artists, 1993—, U. Maine System, 1991—; mem. task force on campaign fin. Senator George Mitchell, Augusta, Maine, 1983; mem. All Am. City selection award jury Nat. Civil League, N.Y.C., 1987; bd. dirs. Greater Bangor United Way, 1990-93. Mem. LWV (pres. Bangor-Brewer chpt. 1979-81, state pres. 1982-85, nat. bd. dirs. 1986-88, sec. nat. bd. dirs. 1988-90, project dir. TV polit. debates Bangor 1982, project dir. Nat. Security and You Conf., Portland, Maine 1983), U. Maine Alumni Assn. (v.p. bd. dirs. 1991-93), Greater Portland C. of C. Democrat. Methodist. Avocations: skiing, travel, hiking, biking. Home and Office: PO Box 2862 S Portland ME 04116-2862

HARRIS, RACHEL LOUISE, therapeutic radiographer, researcher; b. Liskeard, Cornwall, Eng., Jan. 22, 1965; d. Clark and Rosamund Lilian (Doidge) Badham; m. Trevor Wayne Harris, May 30, 1987. Diploma in therapeutic radiography, Portsmouth Sch. Radiography, 1988; MSc in Social Rsch., Plymouth (Eng.) U., 1993. Radiographer Cornwall Health Authority, Truro, Eng., 1988-89; sr. II Plymouth Health Authority, 1990-94, supt. rsch. radiographer in oncology, 1995—; conf. presenter in field. Contbr. articles to profl. jours. Mem. Coll. Radiographers, European Soc. Therapeutic Radiology and Oncology (com.). Anglican. Avocations: walking dogs, fishing, reading. Office: Plymouth Oncology Ctr, Derriford Hosp, Plymouth PL6 8DH, England

HARRIS, RAYMOND JESSE, retired government official; b. Van Buren, N.Y., Dec. 28, 1916; s. Francis Elbert and Anna Marie (Selinsky) H.; m. Rosalba Emilia Prestianni, Jan. 7, 1950 (dec. 1989). A.B., Harvard U., 1940, postgrad., 1940-42; postgrad., U. Pa., 1952-54, 59-60. Corr. drafter U.S. State Dept., Washington, 1947; vice consul Am. consulate palermo, Italy, 1947-50, Munich, Germany, 1950-51; personnel technician, information officer City of Phila., 1952-59, administrv. asst. to water commr., 1959-79; ret., 1979; Republican committeeman 59th ward City of Phila., 1986-98. Served with USAAF, 1942-45; ETO. Named Water Dept. Supr. of Year, 1971, 72, 73, 76; recipient Ted Moses award Pa. Water Pollution Control Assn., 1978. Mem. Am. Water Works Assn., Archeol. Inst. Am., Amnesty Internat. USA, Nat. Trust Historic Preservation, Pa. Hist. Soc., Acad. Polit. Sci., Am. Anti-Vivisection Soc., Planetary Soc., Harvard of Phila. Club, Germantown Rep., Preservation Alliance Greater Phila. Home: 275 W Tulpehocken St Philadelphia PA 19144-3209

HARRIS, RHODRI, electronics engineer; b. Exeter, Devon, England, Nov. 1, 1968; s. Tegwyn and Iris (Morgan) H. B in Technology, Plymouth Coll., 1989; B in Engring., Southampton U., 1992, postgrad., 1992-99. Sys. specialist NDS, Southampton, 1995—; sys. engring. cons. Tandberg TV, 1999—. Mem. IEEE. Home: 15 Waldegrave Close, SO19 9RY Southampton England

HARRIS, ROBERT DALTON, history educator, researcher, writer; b. Jamieson, Oreg., Dec. 24, 1921; s. Charles Sinclair and Dorothy (Cleveland) H.; m. Ethel Imus, June 26, 1971. BA, Whitman Coll., Walla Walla, Wash., 1951; MA, U. Calif., Berkeley, 1953, PhD, 1959. Tchg. asst. U. Calif., Berkeley, 1956-59; instr. history U. Idaho, Moscow, 1959-61, asst. prof., 1961-68, assoc. prof., 1968-74, prof. history, 1974-86, prof. emeritus, 1986—. Author: (Book) Necker, Reform Statesman of Ancient Regime, 1979, Necker & Revolution of 1789, 1986. 1st lt., U.S. Army, 1942-46; Ballet Folk of Moscow, Idaho, (bd. dirs., 1971-73), Historian, First United Methodist Church, Moscow, Idaho, 1989—. Mem. Am. Hist. Assn., Am. Assn. of U. Prof. Democrat. Methodist. Avocations: social dancing, violinist. Home: 928 E 8th St Moscow ID 83843-3851

HARRIS, ROBERT GAYLEN, art director, graphic designer, illustrator; b. Tacoma, Nov. 29, 1960; s. Gaylen Amon and Janelle Lee (Hinton) H.; m. Chelene Hope Ward, Sept. 24, 1988 (div. Nov. 1995). AD, Tacoma C.C., 1981; student, Brigham Young U., 1981-84. Graphic artist Phone Directories, Provo, Utah, 1983-84; graphic designer Clark Pub., Tacoma, 1984-89; art dir. Bringhurst Corp., Tacoma, 1989-98; owner Images, Tacoma, 1987—, Art Haus Harris Gallery, Tacoma, 1997—; art dir. Web-X, Tacoma, 1998—; pres. Art Haus, Inc., Tacoma; curator The Pierce County Playwrights Festival, Tacoma, 1995-97; cons. in field. Designer holiday poster Tacoma C. of C., 1991-97; designer fire safety poster Tacoma Fire Dept., 1992; designer food safety awareness posters Domani Labs., Tacoma, 1997; mem. Tacoma Art Mus., Seattle Art Mus., Bellevue Mus. Art. Named regional winner Corel/Egghead Software Nat. Design Contest, 1995, 2nd place original concept-digital PIP Corp. Masters Competition, 1998; winner Corp. Identification Corel $3,000,000 World Design Contest, 1996, abstract category Dec.-Jan. Corel 10th World Design Contest, 2000, cover art/article Corel User, May 2000; featured artist Reader Gallery, Corel Mag., Mar. 1996, June 1998. Mem. Allied Artists Am. Avocations: painting, writing, reading, computing, travel. Home and office: 1119 E 53d St Apt D Tacoma WA 98404-2720

HARRIS, ROBERT JAMES, adult education educator; b. London, Mar. 10, 1947; s. Charles William and Lucy Dorothea (Weller) H.; m. Janet Nuttall Horne, Feb. 23, 1974; children: Ruth Emily, Amelia Mary, George Robert William. BA, U. Leeds, Eng., 1969; MA, McMaster U., Hamilton, Ontario, Can., 1970. Lectr. Brunel U., London, 1975-77, U. Leicester, Eng., 1977-87; prof. U. Hull, Eng., 1987—, pro-vice chancellor, 1993-98. Co-author: (book) Welfare, Power and Juvenile Justice, 1987, Secure Accommodation in Child Care, 1993; author: (book) Crime, Criminal Justice and the Probation Service, 1991; co-editor: (book) Probation Around the World: A Comparative Study, 1995. Chmn. Humberside Child Protection Com., Hull, Eng., 1988-91; mem. Home Office Probation Tng. Adv. Group, London, 1991-97; coun. mem. Cancer Relief Macmillan Fund, London, 1993-96; acad. auditor Quality Assurance Agy. for Higher Edn., Birmingham, 1997—. Avocations: book collecting, travel, the arts. Home: 10 Luralda Wharf, London E14 3BY, England Office: U Hull, Dept Politics & Asian Studies, Hull HU6 7RX, England

HARRIS, ROY JAY, JR., editor, business journalist; b. St. Louis, Oct. 2, 1946; s. Roy Jay and Ruth Dorothy (Schofer) H.; m. Andrea McKenna (dec.); children: David McKenna Harris, Roy Jay Harris III. BS in Journalism, Northwestern U., 1968, MS in Journalism, 1971. Staff reporter The Wall Street Jour., Pitts., 1971-74; staff reporter The Wall Street Jour., L.A., 1974-88, dep. bur. chief, 1988-95; sr. editor CFO Mag., Boston, 1996—. With U.S. Army, 1969-70. Mem. Soc. Am. Bus. Editors and Writers, Soc. Profl. Journalists, Am. Soc. Bus. Press Editors. Office: CFO Mag 253 Summer St Fl 3 Boston MA 02210-1118

HARRIS, SANDRA JEAN, linguist, educator; b. Davenport, Iowa, Dec. 16, 1939; arrived in Eng., 1964; d. Denzil and Meta (Belz) Nelson; m. David John Harris, Aug. 15, 1964; children: Mark, Paul. BA in English summa cum laude, U. Iowa, 1961; MA in English, U. Mich., 1962; PhD in Linguistics, U. Nottingham, Eng., 1981. Cert. tchr., Iowa. Lectr. Nottingham (Eng.) Coll. of Edn., 1965-75; sr. lectr. Trent Polytech., Nottingham, 1975-83; prin. lectr. Nottingham Polytech., 1983-85; dept. head Nottingham Trent U., 1985—, dean faculty of humanities, 1989-95, dean grad. studies, 1995—; mem. editl. bd. Over Here: European Journal of American Culture, 1992-2000. Author: Language Projects: An Introduction to Language Study, 1979; co-author: (with others) Managing Language: The Discourse of Corporate Meetings, 1997, The Languages of Business: an International Perspective, 1997; also articles in academic jours. Mem. bd. govs. Nottingham High Sch. for Girls, 1993—; treas., mem. Nat. Exec. U.K. Coun. for Grad. Edn., 1999—. Named Woodrow Wilson fellow, U.S., 1961, Horace Rackham fellow U. Mich., 1962. Fellow Royal Soc. Arts, London, English Assn. (founding, hon.); mem. Brit. Assn. Applied Linguistics, Brit. Assn. Am. Studies, Phi Beta Kappa. Avocations: walking, collecting antique china. Office: Nottingham Trent U, Faculty of Humanities, Nottingham NG11 8NS, England

HARRIS, SANDRA M., psychology educator; b. Hollandale, Miss., Jan. 11, 1959; d. Edna Lee McMeans; m. Frank A. Mileto, Sept. 7, 1997. AA in Bus. Mgmt., San Bernardino Valley Coll., 1983, AS in Math., 1987; AAS in Avionics Tech., C.C. of the Air Force, 1987, AAS in Instr. Tech., 1990; BA in Gen./Exptl. Psychology, Calif. State U., 1989, MA in Gen./Exptl. Psychology, 1990; MS in Sch. Psychometry, Auburn U., 1998, PhD in Ednl. Psychology, 1999. Cert. total quality mgmt. instr. and facilitator. Grad. rsch. asst. Calif. State U., San Bernardino, 1989-91; chief evaluation br. USAF, San Bernardino, 1990-91, chief world affairs br., 1991-92, mgr. USAF, San Bernardino, 1992-93; developer Airman Leadership Airman Leadership Sch. Program, 1992-93; developer Airman Leadership Sch. Program, chief faculty devel. USAF, Montgomery, Ala., 1993-94, supt. assoc. programs team, 1994-95, interactive courseware systems instrnl. systems designer, ednl. reviewer, 1995-96, instrnl. systems designer, 1996-97; psychometrics grad. rsch. asst. Ednl. Testing Svc., Auburn, Ala., 1997-99; diversity awareness tng. facilitator Auburn City Schs., 1998-99; interactive courseware lead instrnl. systems designer Cubic Applications, Inc., 1997—; asst. prof. psychology Troy State U. Montgomery, Montgomery, 1999—; statis. cons. Troy State U. Montgomery, 1995, mem. adj. faculty, 1994-98; mem. adj. faculty Chapman U., Calif., 1993; presenter in field. Sgt. USAF, 1977-97. Honoree San Bernardino Child Participation Presch. Program, 1986, Fontana Youth Edn. Motivation Program, 1993; recipient Mil. Excellence award Noncommd. Officers' Assn., 1991, Recognition Ribbon, USAF, 1992, Commendation medal with 4 oak leaf clusters, 1996, Meritorious Svc. medal with 1 oak leaf cluster, 1997; named Instr. of Yr., Air Mobility Command, 1991, Sr. Noncommd. Officer of Yr., USAF, 1992, one of 12 Outstanding Airmen of Yr. for Air Mobility Command, 1992, Vol. of Yr., 63d Mission Support Squadron, 1993. Mem. APA, AAUW, Am. Ednl. Rsch. Assn., Nat. Assn. Sch. Psychologists, Nat. Coun. on Measurement in Ednl, Psychometric Soc., Mid-South Ednl. Rsch. Assn. Home: PO Box 241842 Montgomery AL 36124-1842 Office: Troy State U Montgomery CEP Dept PO Box 4419 Montgomery AL 36103-4419

HARRIS, SIDNEY EUGENE, dean, management educator; b. Atlanta, Ga., July 21, 1949; s. Nathaniel and Marian (Johnson) H.; m. Mary A. Styles, July 24, 1971; 1 child, Savaria Brandy Harris. BA in Mathematics, Morehouse Coll., 1971; MS in Ops. Rsch., Cornell U., 1975, PhD, 1976. Mem. tech. staff Bell Telephone Labs., Holmdel, N.J., 1973-78; asst. prof. Ga. State U., Atlanta, 1978-82, assoc. prof., 1982-87; prof. mgmt. Claremont (Calif.) Grad. Sch., 1987-97, dean, 1991-96; bd. dirs. Svc. Master Corp., Chgo. (cons.); bd. dirs. Family Savs., L.A., chair audit com., 1991-97, compensation com.; bd. dirs. Total System Svcs., Macon, Ga., Lanier Worldwide, Atlanta, Transamerica Investors, L.A.; cons. Coca-Cola Co., Atlanta, 1991—, AT & T, IBM, Xerox Corp. Hewlett Packard, BellSouth, Svc. Master, Chgo. Editor MIS Quar., 1991; contbr. articles to profl. jours.; author, co-author to several books; lectr. in field. Bd. dirs. Peter F. Drucker Non-Profit Found., N.Y.C., 1991—; vice chmn. L.A. County Productivity Commn., L.A., 1991; bd. trustees Menlo Coll.; mem. Family Support Adv. Bd., 1990. Recipient Vol. Svc. award Nat. Computer Com. Bd., 1985. Mem. Sigma Xi, Beta Gamma Sigma. Avocations: tennis, jogging, sailing. Office: Ga State U J Mack Robinson Coll Bus University Plaza Atlanta GA 30303

HARRIS, STUART INNES, construction equipment engineer, marketing professional; b. N.Y.C., Feb. 2, 1928; s. John David and Rose Marie (Fatt) H.; m. Susan Margiotta, Dec. 4, 1954 (div. Feb. 1971); children: Douglas Keith, Gail Harris Nichols, Patricia Ann. BS in Mining Engring., Lehigh U., 1951; MS in Liberal Studies, U. Pa., 1984. Registered profl. engr., N.J., Del., Ala.; accredited inspector test cranes and derricks U.S. Dept. Labor. Projects engr. N.Y. Trap Rock Corp., West Nyack, 1951-52; line officer USN, 1952-55; sales engr. Keasbey & Mattison, Ambler, Pa., 1955-58; v.p. Vacuum Concrete Corp. of Am., Phila., 1958-60; engring. control analyst RCA, Moorestown, N.J., 1960-62; sales engr. COMAD Equipment Corp., Moorestown, 1962-63, State Equipment Corp., Phila., 1963-65; CEO, owner Stuart I. Harris Constrn. Equipment, Haddonfield, N.J., 1965—; mgr. ea. distbn. ctr. Clark Equipment Co., Benton Harbor, Mich., 1970-74; sr. crane engr. Phila. Naval Shipyard, 1980-90; sales rep. Alex Lyon & Son, Bridgeport, N.Y., 1992—; heavy equipment expert cons. Tech. Adv. Svc. for Attys., Blue Bell, Pa., 1973—. Mem. Friends Hosp. Corp., Phila., 1978—; chmn. property com. Haddonfield Friends Meeting, 1995—; charter mem. Charles Custis Harrison Soc., U. Pa., 1995—. Lt. comdr. USNR, 1951-54, Korea. Recipient Legion of Honor award The Chapel of Four Chaplains, Valley Forge, Pa., 1980. Mem. ASME, Soc. of Mining, Metallurg., and Petroleum Engrs., Cooper River Yacht Club (over 100 racing trophies). Republican. Mem. Soc. of Friends. Office: Stuart I Harris Constrn Equipment PO Box 255 Haddonfield NJ 08033-0217

HARRIS, SUSAN A., travel agent; b. L.A., Nov. 27, 1958; arrivedin Eng., 1997; d. David and Sonia Pearl (Laveter) H.; m. Marcus Russell, May 22, 1997. BA, U. Calif., Santa Barbara, 1980. Travel agt. Revel Travel, Beverly Hills, Calif., 1981—. Avocations: tennis, shopping, travel.

HARRIS, THOMAS SARAFEN, management consultant; b. Middletown, Ohio, Dec. 17, 1947; s. William Sellers and Ellen Marion (Sarafen) H.; children: Anna Wooldridge, Julie; m. Véronique Ponchet de Langlade. BA, Johns Hopkins U., 1969, postgrad., 1969-72. Trainee Brakeley, John Price Jones, Inc., N.Y.C., 1972-74, account mgr./v.p., 1974-78; directeur svc. internat. Equip'Contact SARL, Paris, 1978-80; mng. dir. Thos. Harris & Associates, London, Paris, Essen, Rome, Amsterdam, N.Y.C., 1980-89; founder, mng. dir. cons. Harris & Co., London, Paris, Essen, Rome, Amsterdam, N.Y.C., 1989-94; dir. Harris Internat., Inc., N.Y.C., 1994—; mem. internat. adv. bd. Interphil, 1982-91; chmn. World Fundraising Coun., 1991-94, sec. commn. ethics, 1994—; mgr. Harris the Virtual Cons. firm, 1996—. Author: The Tao In Fund Raising, 1992, International Fund Raising, 1999; contbr. articles to profl. pubis. Mem. Inst. Fund Raising Mgrs. Democrat. Avocations: solo ocean sailing, cooking, yoga. Home and Office: 10 rue d'Alesia, 75014 Paris France

HARRIS, VIOLAINE KATHLEEN, molecular biologist; b. Idaho Falls, Idaho, Feb. 1, 1971; d. Walter John Harris and Laurence Coint-Bavarot Dearien. BA, U. Colo., 1993; PhD, Georgetown U., 1998. Cancer student rsch. fellow U. Colo. Cancer Ctr., Denver, 1992; rsch. asst. U. Pa., Phila., 1993-94; fellow Georgetown U., Washington, 1998-2000, Mt. Sinai Med. Ctr., N.Y.C., 2000—. Recipient Predoctoral Tng. award Pharm. Mfrs. Assn. Found., Washington, 1997; Predoctoral fellow U.S. Army Breast Cancer Rsch. Program, 1996, Postdoctoral fellow Susan Komen Found. in Breast Cancer, Dallas, 1999. Mem. AAAS, Phi Beta Kappa. Avocations: modern and jazz dance, rollerblading, jogging. E-mail: violaine harris@hotmail.com.

HARRIS, WARDELL W., minister; b. Madison, Ark., May 26, 1941; s. Oze Jr. and Mary E. (McDonald) H.; m. Ora Lee Davis, Oct. 5, 1963; children: Coral A., Steven C. Student, Philandes-Smich Coll., 1961, Grace Christian Coll., 1975, Moody Bible Inst., 1982, Ashland Sem., 1985. Ordained to ministry Ch. of God in Christ, 1982. Supr. Orange Sch. Dist., Cleve., 1964—; asst. pastor Jonas Temple Ch. of God in Christ, Cleve., 1978—; pastor-founder Greater Harvard Ave. Ch. of God in Christ, Cleve., 1986—; mem. state ordination bd. Ch. of God in Christ, 1985—, state asst. dean seminars, 1987—, mem. gen. assembly, 1984, elders coun., 1984; dean State Sunday Sch., Cleve., 1975—. Pres. Street Club, Warrensville Heights, 1978; mem. Warrensville Heights Band Boosters, 1980. Home and Office: 23307 Felch St Cleveland OH 44128-5217

HARRIS, WARREN LYNN, development engineer; b. Albuquerque, May 8, 1966; s. Jerry Dale and Viola Guadalupe (Gutierrez) H., m. Clarissa cosgrove, April 1, 1998, 1 child: Tiffany Bellan. BS, Ariz. State U., 1988. Programming mgr. I.P.C. Computer Svcs., Inc., Tempe, Ariz., 1985-89; software sys. engr. Intel Corp., Chandler, Ariz., 1990; dir. software R & D Pics, Inc., Tempe, 1990-91; dir. software R & D parics divsn. Ansoft Corp., Tempe, 1991-94; devel. engr. Ansoft Corp., Phoenix, 1994—. Mem. IEEE, Assn. for Computing Machinery, Mortar Bd., Golden Key, Upsilon Pi Epsilon. Avocations: racquetball, model building, chess, pool, Star Trek collecting. Office: Ansoft Corp 4949 W Phelps Rd Glendale AZ 85306-1426

HARRIS, WAYNE MANLEY, lawyer; b. Dec. 28, 1925; s. George H. and Constance M. Harris; m. Diane C. Quigley, Sept. 30, 1978; children: Wayne, Constance, Karen, Duncan, Claire. LLB, U. Rochester, 1951. Bar: N.Y. 1952, U.S. Supreme Ct. 1958. Ptnr. Harris, Chesworth & O'Brien (and predecessor firms), Rochester, N.Y., 1958—; drafter 5 laws passed in N.Y. State. Pres. Delta Labs, Inc. (non-profit environ. lab.) Adopt-A-Stream program, 1971—, Friends of Bristol Valley Playhouse Found., 1984-87, Monroe County Conservation Coun. Inc., 1956-61, v.p., 1984-87; v.p. Powder Mills Pk. Hatchery Preservation Inc., 1993-95, pres., 1995—. With combat inf., Germany, 1944-46. Decorated Bronze Star; recipient Sportsman of Yr. award Genesee Conservation League, Inc., 1960, Conservationist of Yr. award Monroe County Conservation Coun., Inc., 1961, Kiwanian of Yr. award Kiwanis Club, 1965, Livingston County Fedn. of Sportsmen award, 1966, N.Y. State Conservation Coun. Nat. Wildlife Fedn. Water Conservation Conservationist of Yr. award, 1967, Rochester Acad. Sci. Hon. Fellowship award, 1970, Conservation award Nat. Am. Motor Corp., 1971, Meritorious Leadership in Civic Devel. award Rochester C. of C., 1972, Svc. award Rochester Against Intoxicated Drivers, 1989, Vol. Conservationist of Yr., N.Y. State Conservation Coun. Inc., 2000. Mem. ATLA, N.Y. State Trial Lawyers Assn., AIDA Reins. and Arbitration Soc., Indsl. Mgmt. Coun., Wild Turkey Fedn. Home: 60 Mendon Center Rd Honeoye Falls NY 14472-9363 Office: Harris Chesworth & O'Brien 1820 East Ave Rochester NY 14610-1829

HARRIS, WHITNEY ROBSON, lawyer, educator; b. Seattle, Aug. 12, 1912; s. Olin Whitney and Lily (Robson) H.; m. Jane Freund Foster, Feb. 14, 1964; 1 child, Eugene Whitney; m. Anna Galakatos, Jan. 8, 2000. AB magna cum laude, U. Wash., 1933; JD, U. Calif., 1936; LHD (hon.), McKendree Coll., 1999. Bar: Calif. 1936, U.S. Supreme Ct. 1945, Tex. 1953, U.S. Ct. Mil. Appeals 1955, Mo. 1964. Pvt. practice L.A., 1936-42; trial counsel U.S. Chief of Counsel, Nuremberg, 1945-46; chief legal advice br. U.S. Mil. Govt. for Germany, 1946-48; prof. law So. Meth. U., 1948-54; staff dir. legal service and proc. Com. Orgn. Exec. Br. Govt., 1954; exec. dir. ABA, 1954-55; solicitor for Tex. Southwestern Bell Telephone Co., Dallas, 1955-63; gen. solicitor Southwestern Bell Telephone Co., St. Louis, 1963-65; pvt. practice St. Louis, 1965-89; arbitration judge, 1993—; sr. counselor Mo. Bar Assn., 1987; lectr. UCLA, Stanford U., Washington U., Wellesley Coll., U. Denver, Reed Coll., U. Wash., Claremont Coll., Boston Coll., Williams Coll., So. Meth. U., U. Mo., McKendree Coll., Ga. State Coll., Occidental Coll., U. S.C. Author: Family Law, 1953, Tyranny On Trial, 1954, 3d edit. 1999, Legal Services and Procedure, 1955; (with others) Law, Culture and Values, 1989; contbr. numerous articles to profl. jours. including Ency. Brit., 1954, The Internat. Lawyer, 1986, Washington U. Law Quar., 1987, U. Toledo Law Rev., 1992. With USN, 1942-46. Decorated Legion of Merit, Order of Merit Officer's Class (Germany), Medal of the War Crimes Commn. (Poland); named nat. outstanding fund raising vol. Nat. Soc. Fund Raising Execs., 1985. Mem. ABA (chmn. internat. law sect. 1953-54, chmn. adminstrv. law sect. 1960-61), Japan-Am. Soc. St. Louis (pres. 1978-80, Disting. Svc. award 1995), Naval War Coll. Found. (grad. level), Order of Coif, Phi Beta Kappa, Phi Kappa Psi, Delta Theta Phi. Achievements include establishing Jane and Whitney Harris Rsch. Libr. at Winston Churchill Meml. and Libr., Fulton, Mo., 1980, Jane and Whitney Harris Reading Rooms at St. Louis Country Day Sch., 1980, and at Washington U., 1985, Jane and Whitney Harris Ann. Rsch. Fellowship in Arthritis at Washington U. Sch. Medicine, 1989, Whitney Robson Harris collection on Third Reich at Washington U., 1980, Jane and Whitney Harris Ann. Lecture on Tropical Ecology at U. Mo. St. Louis, 1991, Jane and Whitney Harris Secret Garden at Mo. Botanical Garden, 1993, Jane and Whitney Harris Child Care Facility at Jr. League, St. Louis, 1994, Jane and Whitney Harris Anniversary Garden, Forest Park, St. Louis, 1999, Jane and Whitney Harris Japanese Garden, Mo. Botanical Garden, St. Louis, 1999. Home: 2818 Stonington Pl Saint Louis MO 63131-3417

HARRIS, WILEY LEE, financial services executive; b. Lynchburg, Va., Jan. 15, 1949; s. Willie M. Harris; m. Thelma E. Thomas, June 28, 1991. BS in Indsl. Sociology, Yale U., 1971. Human resources trainee GE, Lynchburg, 1972-74; equal employment opportunity mgr. GE, 1974-77; human resources mgr. GE Info. Svcs. Co., Chgo., 1977-79, Rockville, Md., 1979-87; compensation mgr. GE Capital, Stamford, Conn., 1987—. Mem. NAACP, Lynchburg, 1980—. Recipient Civic Achievement award NAACP, Lynchburg, 1986, Employment Achievement, State of Va., Richmond, Va., 1980. Mem. Internat. Assn. for Employee Benefits, Am. Compensation Assn., Am. Soc. for Personnel Adminstrn. Republican. Office: GE Capital 260 Long Ridge Rd Stamford CT 06927-1600

HARRISON, ALVIN, Olympic athlete; b. Orlando, Fla., Jan. 20, 1974. Student, Hartnell Coll. Winner Gold Medal 4X400 meter relay U.S.A. Track and Field Team, Sydney, 2000. Office: USA Track and Field One RCA Dome Ste 140 Indianapolis IN 46225*

HARRISON, BETTINA HALL, retired biology educator; b. Foxboro, Mass.; d. Malcolm Bridges and Rita Louise (Busiere) Hall; m. John W. Harrison, July 12, 1941 (dec.); children: John W., Deborah, Christine. BS, U. Mass., 1939; AM, Radcliffe Coll., 1940; PhD, Boston U., 1968. Faculty Lasell Jr. Coll., Auburndale, Mass., 1940-41, 52-56, Maine Mills Lab., 1941-43, 49-51; with Cen. Main Hosp., 1943-45; faculty biology U. Mass., Boston, 1967-96, ret., 1996. Contbr. articles to profl. jours. Life corporator Boston Mus. Sci. Named Outstanding Tchr., U. Mass./Boston, 1986. Mem. N.Y. Acad. Sci., New Eng. Soc. Electron Microscopy (pres. 1963-64), AAAS. Home: 19 Priscilla Ln Medford MA 02155-1516

HARRISON, CALVIN, Olympic athlete; b. Orlando, Fla., Jan. 20, 1974. Student, Hartnell Coll. Winner Gold Medal 4X400 meter relay U.S.A. Track and Field Team, Sydney, 2000. Office: USA Track and Field Team One RCA Dome Ste 140 Indianapolis IN 46225*

HARRISON, DAVID J., sales professional; b. Palo Alto, Calif., Oct. 16, 1958; arrived in Eng., 1998; s. Richard Alan and Barbara Ann (Frank) H.; m. Anne Francoise Magral, May 29, 1997; 1 child, Paul. BA, U. Conn., 1980; MBA, St. Xavier Coll., Chgo., 1995; MA, U. So. Calif., 1998. With sales dept. Filmstar, L.A., 1990-91, CLT, Luxembourg, 1996, Shock, Eng., 1998; with sales dept., acct. Grendes & Troye, France, 1991-96; programmer Ellipse, France, 1997; with sales dept. 2-Match, London, Eng., 1999—. Democrat. Jewish. Avocation: collecting alarm watches. Home: St Edmunds Ter, 18 St Edmunds Ct, London NW8 7QL, England Office: 2-Match, 18 Bretton Pl, London W1, England

HARRISON, DEREK, retired personal care industry executive, inventor, journalist; b. Oswaldtwistle, Lancashire, Eng., Jan. 5, 1929; s. Percival and Elizabeth Alice (Bamber) H.; m. Joyce (Joy) Alice Whitaker, June 11, 1955; children: Nicholas, Carole Miller. Student, Regional Coll. Art, 1947-52, Manchester U., 1947-52. Asst. mgr. Moorside Laundry, Swinton, 1955-57; mgr. Moorside Laundry, 1957-71, prin., 1971-; ret., 1986, cons., 1986—; chmn. Manchester Br. Inst. Mgmt., 1996-99, v.p. 1999—; mem. Trafford Park Quality Forum, 1994, Laundry Wages Coun., 1972-88, nat. exec. coun. Assn. Brit. Laundry, Cleaning & Rental Svcs., 1984-87. Patentee in field. Chmn. Brit. Diabetic Assn. (Salford), 1995—; mem. exec. coun. Manchester C. of C. & Industry, 1996; gov., registrar Bridgewater Sch., Worsley, 1971, 72, 73, 74; liveryman Worshipful Co. of Launderers, London, 1980; sr. lectr. Hollings Coll., Manchester, 1962; mem. Laundry Wages Coun., London, 1972-88. With Army—Royal Engrs., 1948-55. Recipient Freedom of the City of London, 1979, Drummond Cup U. Manchester, 1947, 48, Ernest Albinson award for journalism Guild of Cleaners and Launderers, 1999. Life mem. City Livery Club (Liveryman of the City of London 1980), Manchester U. Motor Club (v.p. 1969-70); mem. Guild of Cleaners & Launderers (hon. v.p. 1978, dep. master Coll. of Fellows 1989—), Automobile Assn. (hon. life. mem.). Avocations: travel, gardening, photography. Home: 5 Woodlands Ave, Swinton, Manchester M27 0DJ, England

HARRISON, EARL DAVID, lawyer, real estate executive; b. Bryn Mawr, Pa., Aug. 25, 1932; divorced; 1 child, H. Jason. BA, Harvard U., 1954; JD, U. Pa., 1960. Bar: D.C. 1960. Pvt. practice Washington; exec. v.p. Washington Real Estate Corp., Washington, 1986-94; pres. EDH Assocs., Inc., 1994—. Capt. U.S. Army, 1954-57. Decorated Order of Rio Branco (Brazil); Order of Merit (Italy). Mem. ABA, Internat. Coun. Shopping Ctrs., D.C. Bar Assn., Washington Assn. Realtors, Greater Washington Comml. Assn. Realtors, Nat. Assn. Realtors, Nat. Restaurant Assn., Met. Washington Restaurant Assn., Coun. Internat. Restaurant Brokers (v.p., gen. coun.), Harvard Club, Nat. Press Club. Office: 1077 30th St NW Apt 706 Washington DC 20007-3834

HARRISON, JAMES WILBURN, gynecologist; b. Martin, Tenn., Mar. 23, 1918; s. Woodie and Georgia Harrison; m. Babs Wise Dudley, Jan. 29, 1948; children: James Wilburn Jr., James Michael, Babs Suzanne, Linda Denise. Student, U. Tenn., Martin, 1936-37, U. Tenn., Knoxville, 1937-38; MD, U. Tenn., Memphis, 1941; grad., U.S. Army Staff Coll., Ft. Leavenworth, Kans., 1972. Diplomate Am. Bd. Ob-gyn. Asst. resident Brooke Gen. Hosp., Ft. Sam Houston, Tex., 1947; chief surgery Station Hosp., Clark AFB, Philippines, 1948-49; resident, sr. resident Letterman Gen. Hosp., San Francisco, 1949-51; advanced through grades to col. U.S. Army, resigned, 1954; chief staff St. Michael Hosp., Texarkana, Ark., Wadley Regional Med. Ctr., Texarkana, Tex., So. Clinic, Texarkana, Ark.; asst. clin. prof. ob.-gyn. U. Ark. Coll. Medicine, Little Rock. Chmn. Bowie County Child Welfare Bd.; mem. N.E. Tex. Mental Health Bd. With USAR, 1955-78, ret. 1979. Decorated Army Commendation medal, Legion of Merit. Fellow ACS (life), ICS (life), Am. Coll. Ob-gyn. (life), Assn. Mil. Surgeons U.S. (life), Tex. Soc. Ob-gyn. (life); mem. AMA (life), Tex. Med. Assn., Northridge Country Club (founding), Alumni Assn. U.S. Army Command and Gen. Staff Coll., Tri-State Med. Soc. (pres. 1960s), Am. Legion, AMA Sr. Phyicians, Tex. 50 Yr. Club. Methodist. Avocations: collecting, travel, military history. Home: 4009 Pecos St Texarkana TX 75503-2857

HARRISON, JONATHAN, philosophy educator; b. West Derby, Liverpool, Eng., Sept. 22, 1924; s. Edward Albert and Dorothy Marshall (Williams) H.; m. Jean Bradbury (dec. 1969); children: Roger Marshall, Kate Elizabeth, Timothy James, John Edward; m. Antonia Gransden, 1978. BA in Politics, Philosophy and Econs., Corpus Christi Coll./Oxford U., 1945, MA, 1952. Lectr. in philosophy U. Durham, Eng., 1947-59; sr. lectr. in philosophy U. Edinburgh, 1959-64; prof. philosophy U. Nottingham, Eng., 1964-88; prof. philosophy Northwestern U., Chgo., 1968. Author: Our Knowledge of Right and Wrong, 1971, reprinted, 1993, Hume's Moral Epistemology, 1976, Hume's Theory of Justice, 1981, A Philosopher's Nightmare and Other Stories, 1985, Time-Travel for Beginners and Other Stories, 1988, Ethical Essays, Vols. I, II, III, Avebury, 1993-95, Essays in Metap hysics and the Theory of Knowledge, Vols. I, II, Avebury, 1995-96, God, Freedom and Immortality, Avebury, 1999; editor, introduction and top notes Challenges to Morality, 1993; contbr. numerous articles to profl. jours. Mem. Mind Assn. (past pres.), Royal Inst. Philosophy (mem. coun.). Avocations: walking, reading, music. Home: 10 Halifax Rd, Cambridge CB4 3PX, England

HARRISON, JUDITH ANNE, human resources executive; b. N.Y.C., Aug. 15, 1954; d. William Russell and Lucille Kathleen Harrison; m. Brian Taylor Jarvis, Sept. 18, 1993. BA, CCNY, 1976. Bus. mgr. creative svcs. Burson-Marsteller, N.Y.C., 1976-80; creative ops. mgr. mktg. and comm. Arthur Young, N.Y.C., 1981-84; dir. collateral svcs. advt. and promotion CBS, N.Y.C., 1984-86; dir. mktg. comm. Media Gen., N.Y.C., 1986-87; pres. J.A. Harrison Comm., N.Y.C., 1988-92; v.p. The Fry Group, N.Y.C., 1992-96; v.p. human resources Ruder Finn, N.Y.C., 1997-99; s.r. v.p. Ruder Finn, 1999—. Mem. Pub. Rels. Soc. Am., Soc. Human Resource Mgmt., Am. Women in Radio and TV (bd. dirs. N.Y. chpt. 1990-91), World Studio Found. (bd. dirs. 1998—). Office: Ruder Finn 301 E 57th St New York NY 10022-2900

HARRISON, LEONARD CHARLES, medical educator, researcher; b. Sydney, NSW, Australia, Dec. 24, 1944; s. Reginald James and Veronica Kathleen (Barton) H.; m. Dianne Pilgrim, Dec. 3, 1966 (div. 1991); children: Michael, Paul, Rachael, Johanna, Kristen; m. Margo Carole Austin, June 26, 1993. MB BS, U. NSW, Sydney, 1968; MD, U. Melbourne, Australia, 1976, DSc, 1986. Sr. lectr. dept. medicine U. Melbourne/Royal Melbourne Hosp., 1973-76, assoc. prof., 1981-87; C.J. Martin fellow physician diabetes br. NIH, Bethesda, Md., 1976-80; prof., dir. Burnet Clin. Rsch. unit Walter and Eliza Hall Inst. Med. Rsch./Royal Melbourne Hosp., Melbourne, 1987—; head divsn. autoimmunity and transplantation Royal Melbourne Hosp.; dir. Diabetes Australia Rsch. Ltd., 1991-98, Amkaid Pty. Ltd., Melbourne, 1990-99; mem. ethics com. Nat. Health and Med. Rsch. Coun., 1981-84; mem. bd. med. rsch., bd. postgrad. edn. Royal Melbourne Hosp., 1981—. Editor: Receptor Biochemistry and Methodology, 1980; contbr. over 350 articles to profl. jours.; patentee methods for diagnosis and treatment of autoimmune diseases. Recipient Wellcome Med. for med. rsch. Wellcome Co., 1985; grantee NIH, 1995, 2000, Juvenile Diabetes Found. Internat., 1995, 2000. Fellow Royal Australasian Coll. Physicians (Susman medal 1987), Royal Coll. Pathologists Australasia; mem. Australian Soc. Immunology, Australian Soc. Med. Rsch. (bd. dirs. 1981-84), Australian Diabetes Soc. (sec. 1986-88, pres. 1988-90, Kellion medal 1992. Kellion Lectr./Award 2000). Avocations: writing, sailing, Italian culture, tennis. Office: Walter & Eliza Hall Inst, Royal Parade Parkville, 3050 Melbourne Victoria, Australia

HARRISON, MARION EDWYN, lawyer; b. Phila., Sept. 17, 1931; s. Marion Edwyn and Jessye Beatrice (Cilles) H.; m. Carmelita Ruth Deimel, Sept. 6, 1952; children: Angelique Marie (Mrs. Kevin B. Bounds), Marion Edwyn III, Henry Deimel. BA, U. Va., 1951; LLB, George Washington U., 1954, LLM, 1959. Bar: Va. 1954, D.C. 1958, Supreme Ct. 1958. Spl. asst. to gen. counsel Post Office Dept., 1958-60, assoc. gen. counsel, 1960-61, mem. bd. contract appeals, 1958-61; ptnr. firm Harrison, Lucey & Sagle (and predecessors), Washington, 1961-78, Barnett & Alagia, 1978-84; ptnr. Scott, Harrison & McLeod, 1984-86, Law Offices Marion Edwyn Harrison, Washington, 1986—; mem. coun. Adminstrv. Conf. U.S., 1971-78, sr. conf. fellow, 1984-88; mem. D.C. Law Revision Commn., 1975-92; lectr. Nat. Jud. Coll., Reno, 1979, La. State U. Law Sch., Aix-en-Provence, 1987, 89, Tulane U. Law Sch., Crete, 1997, Hofstra U. Law Sch., Nice, 1999, Pa. State U. Dickinson Law Sch., Vienna, 2000; adv. dir. NationsBank, N.A., 1987-93. Contbr. articles to profl. publs.; editor-in-chief Fed. Bar News, 1960-63; mem. editorial bd. Adminstrv. Law Rev., 1976-89. Trustee AEFC Pension Fund, Chgo., 1986-92; pres. Young Rep. Fedn. Va., 1954-55; mem. Va. Rep. Cen. Com., 1954-55; bd. visitors Judge Adv. Gen. Sch., Charlottesville, Va., 1976-78; chmn. Wolf Trap Assn., 1984-87; bd. dirs. Wolf Trap Found., 1984-88; pub. mem. USIA Insp. Mission, Argentina, 1971. Officer AUS, 1955-58. Decorated Commendation medal. Fellow Am. Bar Found. (life); mem. ABA (chmn. sect. adminstrv. law 1974-75, ho. of dels. 1978-88, bd. govs. 1982-86, chmn. com. on fgn. and internat. orgns. 1986-87, lawyers in govt. com. 1980-82), FBA (nat. coun. 1966-82), Inter-Am. Bar Assn., Bar Assn. D.C. (chmn. adminstrv. law sect. 1970-71, bd. dirs. 1971-72), George Washington U. Law Assn. (pres. 1974-77), Smithsonian Instn. (nat. bd. dirs. 1991-97), Federalist Soc., Soc. Mayflower Desc., Washington Golf and Country Club, Met. Club, Nat. Lawyers Club (Washington), Farmington Country Club (Charlottesville, Va.), Gainey Ranch Golf Club (Scottsdale, Ariz.), Knight of Malta. Republican. Roman Catholic. Home: 4111 N Ridgeview Rd Arlington VA 22207-4617 also: 7222 E Gainey Ranch Rd Scottsdale AZ 85258-1529 Office: 1700 K St NW Ste 700 Washington DC 20006-3813 also: 107 Park Washington Ct Falls Church VA 22046-4519 also: Falkenstrasse 14, 8008 Zurich Switzerland

HARRISON, MICHAEL, lawyer; b. May 27, 1957; s. Michael Sr. and Jane (Venable) H.; m. Nina Lucas Harrison, Oct. 19, 1996. BA with honors, Rutgers Coll., 1982; JD, Harvard, 1985. Bar: U.S. Dist. Ct. N.J. 1986. Atty. Clapp & Eisenberg, N.J., 1985-86, Kelley Drye and Warren, N.Y.C., 1986-87, Schnader, Harrison, Segal & Lewis, Phila., 1987-92; cer. practice, 1992; v.p., gen. counsel Groupe Danone N.Am., Stamford, Conn., 1992—; asst. adj. prof. N.Y. U. Mgmt. Inst., 1993—. bd. dirs. Jr. Achievement Southwestern, Conn., 1996—, vice chmn. devel., 1997. Sgt. USMC, 1975-80; capt. USAR, 1997—. Mem. ABA, Nat. Bar. Assn., N.J. State Bar Assn., Westchester County Bar Assn. Mem. Carpatho Rusyn Orthodox Ch. Office: 208 Harbor Dr Stamford CT 06902-7467 also: 120 White Plains Rd Tarrytown NY 10591-5526

HARRISON, MICHAEL JAY, physicist, educator; b. Chgo., Aug. 20, 1932; s. Nathan J. and Mae (Nathan) H.; m. Ann Tukey, Sept. 1, 1970. A.B., Harvard, 1954; M.S., U. Chgo., 1956, Ph.D., 1960. Fulbright fellow and H. Van Loon fellow in theoretical physics U. Leiden, Netherlands, 1954-55; NSF fellow U. Chgo., 1957-59; research fellow math. physics U. Birmingham, Eng., 1959-61; asst. prof. Mich. State U., East Lansing, 1961-63; assoc. prof. Mich. State U., 1963-68, prof., 1968—, faculty grievance officer, 1972-73, dean Lyman Briggs Coll., 1973-81, adj. prof. community health scis., 1988-93, adj. prof. epidemiology, 1993—; vis. research physicist Inst. Theoretical Physics, U. Calif., Santa Barbara, 1980-81; with Air Force Cambridge Research Center, summer 1953, M.I.T. Lincoln Lab., summer 1954, RCA Sarnoff Lab., summers 1961-63; physicist Westinghouse Labs., summer 1956; cons. RCA Lab., 1961-64, United Aircraft Co., 1964-66, U.K. Atomic Energy Authority, Harwell Lab., summer 1960, Thailand project in Bangkok, Mich. State U.-AID, summer 1968; vis. research affiliate theoretical biology and biophysics, Los Alamos Nat. Lab., 1987-88. Contbr. articles to U.S., fgn. profl. jours. Am. Council on Edn. fellow U. Calif., Los Angeles, 1970-71. Fellow Am. Phys. Soc.; mem. AAUP (chpt. treas. 1966-67), N.Y. Acad. Scis., Harvard Club of Ctrl. Mich. (pres. 1988-93), Rotary, B'nai B'rith, Phi Beta Kappa, Sigma Xi. Jewish. Avocations: hiking, travel, photography. Home: 277 Maplewood Dr East Lansing MI 48823-4746 Office: Mich State U Physics Dept East Lansing MI 48824

HARRISON, PATRICK WOODS, lawyer; b. St. Louis, July 14, 1946; s. Charles William and Carolyn (Woods) H.; m. Rebecca Tout, Dec. 23, 1967; children: Heather Ann, Heath Aaron. BS, Ind. U., 1968, JD, 1972. Bar: Ind. 1973, U.S. Dist. Ct. (so. dist.) Ind. 1973, U.S. Dist. Ct. Nebr. 1982, U.S. Supreme Ct. 1977. Assoc. Goltra, Cline, King & Beck, Columbus, Ind., 1972-73; ptnr. Goltra & Harrison, Columbus, 1973-78; pvt. practice Columbus, 1979-80; ptnr. Cline, King, Beck and Harrison, Columbus, 1980-85, Beck, Harrison & Dalmbert, Columbus, 1985—; Ind. Jud. Nominating Commn. nominee Ind. Supreme Ct., 1984. With U.S. Army, 1968-70. Fellow Ind. Trial Lawyers Assn. (bd. dirs. 1984, emeritus dir. 1999, Co-Trial Lawyer of Yr. 1999); mem. Am. Trial Lawyers Assn. Republican. Baptist. Avocation: golf. Home: 14250 W Mount Healthy Rd Columbus IN 47201-9309 Office: Beck Harrison & Dalmbert 320 Franklin St Columbus IN 47201-6732

HARRISON, RICHARD ANTHONY, solar physicist; b. Solihull, U.K., Sept. 1, 1956; s. Anthony Robin and Margaret Jean (Gibbons) H.; m. Belinda Janet Nunn, May 10, 1986; children: Ross Alexander, Rozanna Victoria. BS with honors, U. Birmingham, Eng., 1979, PhD, 1983. SERC rsch. fellow space rsch. dept. U. Birmingham, 1983-84; long term vis. scientist High Altitude Obs. Nat. Ctr. for Atmospheric Rsch., Boulder, Colo., 1985-86; higher sci. officer astrophysics divsn. Rutherford Appleton Lab., Chilton, Eng., 1986-89, sr. sci. officer astrophysics divsn., 1989-93, prin. sci. officer astrophysics divsn., 1993—, head solar physics, 1999—. Editor on solar atmosphere Jour. Annales Geophysica, 1991-95; gen. editor Com. on Space Rsch. (COSPAR) Info. Bull., Paris, 1991—; contbr. numerous rsch. papers to internat. jours. and publs. Fellow Royal Astron. Soc.; mem. Internat. Astron. Union, European Geophys. Soc. (v.p. 1993-95).

HARRISON, RICHARD DEAN, minister, counselor; b. Gaffney, S.C., Oct. 15, 1952; s. Wiley H. and Georgia Ann (Earwood) H.; m. Sandra Kay Parris, Oct. 16, 1970; children: Kathryn Hope, Richard Dean Jr. BA, U. S.C., 1973, MAT, 1975; MDiv, So. Bapt. Theol. Sem., 1986, DMin, 1990. Ordained to ministry So. Bapt. Conv., 1985. Pastor English Bapt. Ch., Stephensport, Ky., 1985-87, Rehoboth Bapt. Ch., Gaffney, 1987-92; counselor Cherokee Mental Health and Counseling Ctr., Gaffney, S.C., 1992—; pastor Lando (S.C.) Bapt. Ch., 1997—. Chaplain Gaffney Jaycees, 1977-79, Asbury-Rehoboth Vol. Fire Dept., Gaffney, 1989—; bd. dirs. Piedmont Community Action Agy., Spartanburg, S.C., 1979-81. Mem. Breckinridge Bapt. Assn. (exec. com. 1985-87), Broad River Bapt. Assn. (exec. com., dir. Sunday sch. 1987-92). Home: 117 Stacy Dr Gaffney SC 29341-1433 Office: Cherokee Mental Health and Counseling Ctr 125 E Robinson St Gaffney SC 29340-2444

HARRISON, RUSSELL SAGE, political science educator, consultant; b. Southport, N.C., Feb. 24, 1944; s. Russell S. and Julia (Grayson) H. BA, Duke U., 1966; PhD, U. N.C., 1971. Asst. prof. polit. sci. Rutgers U., Camden, N.J., 1971-77, assoc. prof. polit. sci., 1977—, chmn. dept. polit. sci., 1997-99; project dir. Camden County Mgmt. Audit, 1995-96, Professionalization of County Govt., Camden, 1991-92. Author: Inequality of Public School Finance, 1977. Cons. South Jersey Port Authority, Salem (N.J.) Port Authority, N.J. Dept. Transp., Fed. Econ. Devel. Adminstrn., N.J.; trustee Cadbury Retirement Cmty., Camden, 1995-98, asst. sec., 1995-98; active Soc. of Friends, clk., 1998—. Mem. Am. Polit. Sci. Assn., Am. Soc. Pub. Adminstrn., Northeastern Polit. Sci. Home: 301 Plantation Dr Cinnaminson NJ 08077-4308 Office: Rutgers U Dept Political Sci Camden NJ 08101-0020

HARRISON, STEVEN J., English educator; b. Long Beach, Calif., May 19, 1956; s. Edward A. and Ruth E. Harrison. BA, Calif. State U., Fullerton, 1980, MA, 1995. English teacher Rialto (Calif.) Jr. H.S., 1981-84, Magnolia Jr. H.S., Chino, Calif., 1984-94, Woodcrest Jr. H.S., Ontario, Calif., 1994—; mentor tchr. Woodcrest Jr. H.S., 1997-99. Mem. Calif. Art Club. Democratic. Avocations: art collecting, antiquing, reading, gardening. E-mail: Jishbug@earthlink.com. Home: 2192 Edinboro Ave Claremont CA 91711-1966

HARRISON, WILLIAM BURWELL, JR., banker; b. Rocky Mount, N.C., Aug. 12, 1943; s. William Burwell and Katherine (Spruill) H.; m. Anne MacDonald Stephens, Dec. 7, 1985; children Katherine Adams, Anne Stephens. AB in Econs., U. N.C., Chapel Hill, 1966, spl. student in bus. adminstrn., 1966-67; Sr. Mgmt. Program, Harvard Bus. Sch., Vevey, Switzerland, 1979. Trainee Chem. Bank, N.Y.C., 1967-69, Mid-South corp. and corr. banking group, 1969-74, West Coast corp. and corr. banking group, 1974-76; dist. head, Western regional coord. Chem. Bank, San Francisco, 1976-78; regional coord., sr. v.p. Chem. Bank, London, 1978-82, sr. v.p., divsn. head Europe, 1982-83; exec. v.p. U.S. corp. divsn. Chem. Bank, N.Y.C., 1983-87, group exec. banking and corp. fin. group, 1987-90, vice chmn. instl. banking, 1990—; vice chmn. Global Bank, 1992—; vice chmn. Chase Manhattan Corp., N.Y.C., 1995—, chmn., CEO, 2000—; bd. dirs. Dillard Dept. Stores, Little Rock, Merck & Co., Inc., Whitehouse Station, Miss., Banco Gen. Negocios, Buenos Aires; mem. bd. advisors N.C. Outward Bound Sch., Asheville; mem. Bretton Woods Com. Trustee Carnegie Hall; bd. dirs. United Cerebral Palsy of N.Y.C., Inc., United Negro Coll. Fund, Inc.; trustee Central Park Conservancy; mem. bd. visitors Kenan Flagler Bus. Sch.; mem. bd. overseers Sloan-Kettering Cancer Ctr., 1999—. Mem. Fin. Svcs. Roundtable, Bus. Roundtable, Bus. Coun., Blind Brook Club, Racquet Club, Links Club, Round Hill Club, Nat. Golf Links Am., Field Club Greenwich, Golf Club Purchase. Episcopalian. Avocations: athletics, traveling.

HARROLD, DENNIS EDWARD, lawyer; b. Los Angeles, Nov. 7, 1947; s. Edward Adron and Helen Lucille (Morrison) H.; m. Mary Ann Padgett, Oct. 21, 1972; children: Teresa Lauren, Derek Christopher. BS, Ind. U., 1969; JD, 1972. Bar: Ind. 1972, U.S. Dist. Ct. (so. dist.) Ind. 1972, U.S. Ct. Mil. Appeals 1972, U.S. Ct. Appeals (7th cir.) 1982, U.S. Supreme Ct. 1986. Pub. defender Shelby Superior Ct., Shelbyville, Ind., 1976-77; assoc. Adams & Cramer, Shelbyville, 1976-78; sec. Soshnick, Bate and Harrold, P.C., 1979-85; sec. Bate, Harrold & Bate, P.C., Shelbyville, 1985-96, McNeely, Stephenson Thopy and Harrold, 1996—; sch. bd. atty. Shelbyville Central Schs., Ind., 1978—; atty. Shelby County office of family and children 1987-96; sch. bd. atty. Blue River Career Programs, 1994—. Mem. adv. bd. Salvation Army. Shelbyville, 1982-92. Served to capt. U.S. Army, 1972-76, Korea. Named Hon. Mem. Bar Republic of Korea, Ministry of Justice, Seoul, 1975. Fellow Ind. Bar Found.; mem. ABA, Ind. State Bar Assn. (ho. of dels. 1982-85), Shelby County Bar Assn. (pres. 1990-91), Indpls. Bar Assn., Assn. Trial Lawyers Am., Nat. Sch. Bds. Assn. Council Sch. Attys., Internat. Legal Soc. Korea, Ind. Trial Lawyers Assn., Ind. Pub. Defender Council, dir. Shelby County C. of C., pres. 1996-97, trustee Shelby Rural Elec. Cmty. Fund, Inc. Lions, Elks. Republican. Roman Catholic. Home: 2481 N Richard Dr Shelbyville IN 46176-9487 Office: 30 E Washington St Ste 400 Shelbyville IN 46176-1351

HARROP, WILLIAM CALDWELL, retired ambassador, foreign service officer; b. Balt., Feb. 19, 1929; s. George A. and Esther (Caldwell) H.; m. Ann G. Delavan, Aug. 22, 1953; children—Mark D., Caldwell, Scott N., George H. AB, Harvard U., 1950; postgrad., Grad. Sch. Journalism U. Mo., 1953-54; fellow, Woodrow Wilson Sch., Princeton U., 1968-69. Fgn. Service officer, 1954-93; vice consul Palermo, 1954-55; 2d sec. Rome, 1955-58; internat. relations officer Dept. State, 1958-63; 1st sec. Brussels, 1963-66; consul Lubumbashi, Congo, 1966-68; dir. Office Research for Africa, Dept. State, Washington, 1969; dep. chief mission Am. embassy, Canberra, Australia, 1973-75; U.S. ambassador to Guinea, 1975-77, dep. asst. sec. of state for Africa, 1977-80, ambassador to Kenya and Seychelles, 1980-83; insp. gen. Dept. State and Fgn. Service, 1983-86; ambassador to Zaire, 1987-91, Israel, 1992-93; ret., 1994; chmn. Am. Fgn. Svc. Assn., 1970-73, bd. dirs.; bd. dirs. Assn. for Diplomatic Studies and Tng., Am. Acad. Diplomacy. Served with USMCR, 1951-52. Recipient Dept. State Merit Service award, 1968, Presdl. Disting. Service award, 1985, State Dept. Disting. Service award, 1987. Mem. Am. Acad. Diplomacy (bd. dirs.), Washington Inst. Fgn. Affairs, Fly Club (Cambridge, Mass.), Met. Club (Washington), Chevy Chase (Md.) Club. Address: 3615 49th St NW Washington DC 20016-3214

HARSANYI, GABOR, microelectronics educator, researcher; b. Budapest, Hungary, Mar. 20, 1958; s. Gabor and Vera (Mikosevich) H.; m. Agnes Homor, June 26, 1981 (div. 1991); m. Eva Bato, Mar. 12, 1993. MS, Tch. U. Budapest, 1981, Cert. in Engring., 1983, Doctor, 1984; PhD, Hungarian Acad. Scis., Budapest, 1992. Rsch. mgr. MEV Co., Budapest, 1981-84; asst. prof. Tech. U. Budapest, 1984-88, adj. prof., 1988-92, assoc. prof., 1992—; fellowship Japan Internat. Cooperation Agy., Tokyo, 1990; rsch. fellow Fla. Internat. U., Miami, 1996; cons. Tekmar Ltd., Essen, Germany, 1993, Automotive Sys. Lab., Inc., Farmington Hills, Mich., 1996, Whirlpool-Europe, Cassinetta, Italy, 1996. Author: Polymer Films in Sensor Applications, 1995, Sensors in Biomedical Applications, 2000; editor: MCM/C/Mixed Technologies and Thick Film Sensors, 1995, MCM and Sensor Technologies, 1996; patentee in field of thick film gas sensors and uric acid sensors. Sgt. Hungarian Nat. Army, 1976-77. Mem. Internat. Microelectronics and Packaging Soc. (Europe tech. program com. 1990—, Hungary pres. 1993-94, Best Paper of Session award 1992, fellow 1998). Roman Catholic. Avocations: tourism, travelling. Home: 36 Zsokavar, H-1157 Budapest Hungary Office: Dept Electronics Tech, Budapest U Tech and Econ, H-1521 Budapest Hungary

HARSANYI, JOHN CHARLES, economics educator; b. Budapest, Hungary, May 29, 1920; came to U.S., 1961; s. Charles and Alice H.; m. Anne Klauber, Jan. 2, 1951; 1 child, Tom Peter. Dr. Phil., U. Budapest, Hungary, 1947; MA, Sydney U., Australia, 1953; PhD, Stanford U., 1959; DSc (hon.), Northwestern U., 1989. Univ. asst. U. Budapest, Hungary, 1947-48; lectr. in econs. U. Queensland, Brisbane, Australia, 1954-56; vis. asst. prof. Stanford U., Calif., 1958; sr. fellow Australian Nat. U., Canberra, 1959-61; prof. econs. Wayne State U., Detroit, 1961-63; prof. bus. adminstrn. U. Calif., Berkeley, 1964-90, prof. emeritus, 1990—. Author: Essays on Ethics, Social Behavior and Scientific Explanation, 1976, Rational Behavior and Bargaining Equilibrium, 1977, Papers in Game Theory, 1982, (with Reinhard Selten) A General Theory of Equilibrium Selection in Games, 1988; editl. bd. Internat. Jour. Game Theory, Games and Econ. Behavior; contbr. numerous articles to profl. publs., 1953—. Co-recipient Nobel Prize in Econs., 1994; NSF grantee, 1963-85; fellow Ctr. Advanced Study in Behavioral Scis., Stanford, Calif., 1965-66. Fellow Econometric Soc., Am. Acad. Arts and Scis., Am. Econ. Assn. (disting.); mem. NAS. Office: U Calif Haas Sch Bus Berkeley CA 94720-0001

HARSANYI, KALMAN, pharmaceutical company executive, educator; b. Budapest, Aug. 25, 1927; s. Miksa and Jozsa (Frank) H.; m. Eva Benedek, Sept. 13, 1975; children: Miklos, Zsofia; m. Edit Szabo, Apr. 1958 (div. 1974); 1 child, Gabor. Chem. Engr., Polytechnic U., Budapest, 1949; PhD, Hungarian Acad., Budapest, 1959. Asst. to first asst. Organic Chemistry, 1949-60; rsch. dep. leader Chinoin Pharm. Works, Budapest, 1960-63, 70-77, head of rsch., 1963-70; head of rsch. dept. II G. Richter Chem. Works, 1977-92, head of rsch. group VII, 1992-97, rschr., 1998—; Titular prof. Poly. U., Budapest, 1989—. Patentee; contbr. about 70 articles to profl. jours. Gold laureate inventor, Hungarian govt., 1970-87; recipient Zemplen prize Hungarian Acad., 1992, Gabor prize for creative tech. works, Novofer Found. for Tech. and Intellectual Creation, 1996. Mem. Hungarian Acad. (commn. organic chemistry 1979-92), heterocyclic chemistry 1972—, com. med. chemistry 1995—). Avocation: gardening. Office: Chem Works Gedeon Richter, PO Box 27, H-1475 Budapest Hungary

HARSEV, EMIL MANOLOV, bank executive; b. Dimitrovgrad, Bulgaria, Oct. 19, 1961; married; 2 children. MA in Fin., U. for Nat. and World Econonomy, Sofia, Bulgaria, 1987, PhD, 1989. Asst. dept. fin. and credit U. for Nat. and World Economy, 1987-91, rsch. sec. dept. fin. and credit, 1990-91; exec. dir., dep. gov. Bulgarian Nat. Bank, Sofia, 1991-93; mng. ptnr. Harsev Co. Unltd., Sofia, 1993—; chmn. mng. bd. Mineralbank, Sofia, 1991-92; chmn. Commn. Unification and Bank Stds., 1992-98; sr. advisor com. econ. policy Bulgaria Parliament, 1990-91; mem. MB Mineral Bank, 1991-96, MB Credit Bank, Sofia, 1993-95, MB Bulgarian-Russian Investments Bank, Sofia, 1994-96, spl. advisor to govt., 1993-95; prof. U. Plovdiv, 1996-97; cons. in field. Author: Economy in Transition, 1990, Evolution of Money, 1991, Manual of Bank Accounting, 1992, Manual of Bank Operations, 1996; contbr. over 150 articles to profl. jours. Recipient Global Leader of Tomorrow award World Econ. Forum, 1997. Office: Harsev Co Unltd, 109 Vassil Levsky Ave, 1000 Sofia Bulgaria

HARSHMAN, DALE RICHARD, physicist; b. Honolulu, Aug. 13, 1956; s. Richard Eugene and LaVonne Olive Harshman; m. Sandra Joan Harshman, Feb. 2, 1985; 1 child, Joshua Dale. BSc, Pacific Lutheran U., 1978; MSc, Western Wash. U., 1980; PhD, U. B.C., Vancouver, Can., 1986. Rsch. assoc. U. B.C., 1980-86, postdoctoral fellow, 1986; postdoctoral fellow Bell Labs., Murray Hill, N.J., 1986-88, mem. tech. staff., 1988-97; exec. v.p., dir. sci. rsch. Physikon Rsch. Corp., Lynden, Wash., 1997—; vis. prof. U. Notre Dame, Ind., 1999—, Ariz. State U., Tempe, 1999—; cons. U.S. Dept. Energy, Arlington, Va., 1992; spkr. in field. Contbr. numerous articles to profl. jours. Grantee U.S. Dept. Energy, 1995-98. Mem. Am. Phys. Soc. Avocations: robotics, bike riding, poetry, music, fishing. E-mail: drh@physikon.net. Office: Physikon Rsch Corp PO Box 1014 Lynden WA 98264

HART, DABNEY GARDNER, environmental scientist; b. Jackson, Miss., Dec. 3, 1940; d. Malcolm Everett and Nancy Elizabeth (Parrish) Gardner; m. Charles Willard Hart, Jr., June 9, 1962. AB, Bryn Mawr (Pa.) Coll., 1962, MA, 1970; MS, Am. U., 1984, PhD, 1989. Biologist Acad. of Natural Scis., Phila., 1962-73, spl. projects editor, 1973-75; sr. writer/editor Mitre Corp., McLean, Va., 1975-76, tech. staff, 1976-80, group leader, 1980-98; participant Breeden-Archibold-Smithsonian Biol. Survey of Dominica, 1963, 65; mem. sci. adv. com. EPA, 1978-82. Author: The Ostracod Family Entocytheridae, 1974; contbr. numerous articles to profl. jours. Mem. Jr. League, Phila., Washington. Rsch. grantee NSF, 1962-73. Mem. AAAS (sr. scientist and engr.), Bryn Mawr Coll. Alumnae Assn., Cosmos Club (Washington, chair admissions com. 1996—), Explorers Club. Avocations: travel, needlework. Office: Mitre Corp 7525 Colshire Dr Ste 100 Mc Lean VA 22102-7508

HART, GURNEE FELLOWS, investment counselor; b. Chgo., Apr. 26, 1929; s. Percival Gray and Marguerite May (Fellows) H.; m. Marjorie Walker Leigh, Apr. 23, 1966. BA cum laude, Pomona Coll., 1951; MBA, Stanford U., 1955; vis. scholar, Jesus Coll., Cambridge, Eng., 1994-95. With Willis & Christy, L.A., 1955-65; investment counsel Scudder, Stevens & Clark, Inc., L.A., 1965-67; with Scudder, Stevens & Clark, N.Y.C., 1967—, ptnr., 1972-85, mng. dir., 1985-94, adv. mng. dir., 1994—. Bd. dirs. Lincoln Ctr. for the Performing Arts, Inc., 1981-86, N.Y. Philharmonic, 1974—, vice-chmn., exec. com., 1976-96, trustee, 1988—; chmn. Friends of N.Y. Philharm., 1975-82; bd. dirs., v.p. Berkshire Farm Ctr. and Svcs. for Youth, 1972-83; trustee Pomona Coll., 1982—; bd. dirs., treas. Am. Friends of Cambridge U., 1997—; bd. dirs. Cambridge U. Devel. Office in U.S., Inc. 1st lt., inf. U.S. Army, 1951-53, Korea. Decorated Bronze Star. Mem. St. Andrew's Soc. State of N.Y., Soc. Mayflower Desc., Century Assn., Univ. Club, Knickerbocker Club, Indian Harbor Yacht Club (Greenwich, Conn.),

Phi Beta Kappa. Republican. Episcopalian. Home: 133 E 64th St New York NY 10021-7045

HART, JAMES WARREN, university administrator, restaurant owner, former professional football player; b. Evanston, Ill., Apr. 29, 1944; s. George Ezrie and Marjorie Helen (Karsten) H.; m. Mary Elizabeth Mueller, June 17, 1967; children: Bradley James and Suzanne Elizabeth (twins), Kathryn Anne. B.S., So. Ill. U., 1967. Quarterback St. Louis Cardinals Profl. Football Team, 1966-83, Washington Redskins Profl. Football Team, 1984; radio sports personality Sta. KMOX, 1975-84, Sta. KXOK, 1985-86; sports analyst Sta. WGN Radio, Chgo., 1985-89; athletics dir. So. Ill. U., Carbondale, 1988-99; assoc. chancellor for external affairs So. Ill. U., 1999—; head coach So. Ill. Spl. Olympics, 1973-90, Mo. Spl. Olympics, 1976-78; co-owner Dierdorf & Hart's Steak House (2 locations), St. Louis. Co-author: The Jim Hart Story, 1977. Gen. campaign chmn. St. Louis Heart Assn., 1974-88; hon. chmn. St. Louis Sr. Olympics, 1986-88; bd. dirs. Carbondale Conv. and Tourism Bur., Carbondale Main St. Com. Named Most Valuable Player in Nat. Football Conf., 1974, Most Valuable Player with St. Louis Cardinals, 1973, 75, 78, Man of Year St. Louis Dodge Dealers, 1975, 76, Man of Year Miller High Life, 1980, So. Ill. U. Sports Hall of Fame, 1978, Mo. Sports Hall of Fame, 1998; recipient Brian Piccolo Meml. Humanitarian award Nat. YMCA, 1981. Mem. AFTRA, Fellowship Christian Athletes, Nat. Football League Players Assn. (Byron White award 1976). Republican. Office: So Ill U 207 Anthony Hall Carbondale IL 62901-4312

HART, JOHN EDWARD, lawyer; b. Portland, Oreg., Nov. 21, 1946; s. Wilbur Elmore and Daisy Elizabeth (Bowen) H.; m. Bianca Mannheimer, Mar. 29, 1968 (div. 1985); children: Ashley Rebecca, Rachel Bianca, Eli Jacob; m. Serena Callahan, Nov. 9, 1991; 1 child, Katelyn Elizabeth. Student, Oreg. State U., 1965-66; BS, Portland State U., 1971; JD, Lewis and Clark Coll., 1974. Bar: Oreg. 1974, U.S. Dist. Ct. Oreg. 1974, U.S. Ct. Appeals (9th cir.) 1975. Ptnr. Schwabe, Williamson and Wyatt, Portland, 1973-92, Hoffman, Hart & Wagner, Portland, 1992—; adj. faculty U. Oreg. Dental Sch., 1987—; legal cons. Oreg. Chpt. Obstetricians, Gynecologists, Portland, 1985—, Am. Cancer Soc. Mammography Project, 1987—. Contbr. articles to profl. jours. Co-chmn. Alameda Sch. Fair, Portland, 1983. With U.S. Army, 1967-68. Mem. ABA, Am. Coll. Trial Lawyers, Am. Bd. Trial Advocates (pres. 1995) Am., Inns of Ct., Oreg. State Bar Assn., Oreg. Assn. Def. Counsel (pres. 1989), Multnomah Athletic Club. Democrat. Presbyterian. Avocations: jogging, weight lifting, outdoor activities. Office: Hoffman Hart & Wagner 1000 SW Broadway Ste 2000 Portland OR 97205-3072

HART, JOHN FRASER, geography educator; b. Staunton, Va., Apr. 5, 1924; s. Freeman H. and Jean. B. (Fraser) H.; m. Meredith A. Davis, Feb. 5, 1949; children: Richard L., Meredith A. AB, Emory U., 1943; MA, Northwestern U., 1949, PhD, 1950. Asst., then assoc. prof. U. Ga., 1949-55; from asst. prof. to prof. Ind. U., 1955-67; exec. sec. Assn. Am. Geographers, 1965-66; prof. geography U. Minn., Mpls., 1967—; vis. prof. Clansfield State Coll., 1976-77; Disting. vis. prof. East Carolina U., 1977; Fulbright lectr. U. Lille (France), Durham U., 1960. Mem. editorial adv. bd. Geog. Rev., 1976—, Jour. Geography, 1985-88, Focus, 1988—; contbr. articles to profl. publs. With USNR, 1943-46. Recipient medaille de l'Université de Liège, 1960, Platinum Plow U. Minn. geography students, 1971; named Friend of S.D. Geography, 1979, Chevalier du Ordre du Bleuet D'Or, Chicoutimi, Que., Can., 1989. Fellow Am. Geog. Soc., Royal Geog. Soc., Royal Scottish Geog. Soc.; mem. Assn. Am. Geographers (editor annals 1970-75, citation for meritorious contbns. 1969, councilor West Lakes divsn. 1976-79, pres. 1979-80, hon. life mem. Southea. divsn., Lifetime Achievement award 1987, J.B. Jackson prize 1991), Can. Assn. Geographers (councillor 1974-77), Inst. Brit. Geographers, Nat. Coun. Geog. Edn. (award for teaching geography 1971). Home: 4505 Drexel Ave Edina MN 55424-1131 Office: U Minn Geography Dept Minneapolis MN 55455

HART, JOHN WILLIAM, theology and ecology educator; b. N.Y.C., Oct. 5, 1943; s. Thomas Esmond and Veronica Frances (Merz) H.; m. Jane Helen Morell, Aug. 16, 1975; children: Shanti, Daniel. BA, Marist Coll., 1966; STM, Union Theol. Sem., 1972, MPhil, 1976, PhD, 1978. Dir. Heartland Project, Midwestern Cath. Bishops, 1979-81; asst. prof. religious studies Mt. Marty Coll., Yankton, S.D., 1981-82; assoc. prof. religious studies Coll. of Great Falls (Mont.), 1983-85; prof. theology Carroll Coll., Helena, Mont., 1985—; vis. asst. prof. religion Howard U., Washington, 1978-79; dir., founder environtl. studies program Carroll Coll., 1997—; lectr. in field in 22 states in U.S., Brazil, Can., Italy, Switzerland, Eng., 1980—. Author: The Spirit of the Earth: A Theology of the Land, 1984, Ethics and Technology: Innovation and Transformation in Community Contexts, 1997; ghost author various ch. documents, 1979—; contbr. articles to profl. publs., chpts. to books. Del. Internat. Indian Treaty Coun., Geneva, 1987, 90, UN Internat. Human Rights Commn., Templeton Oxford Sems. in Sci. and Christianity, 1999—. Recipient Templeton Sci.-Religion award, 1995; Danforth Found. fellow, 1973-74; NEH grantee, 1985, 86; AAR/Lilly Tcgh. Scholar in Religion, 1997-98. Mem. Soc. Christian Ethics, Am. Acad. Religion. Democrat. Roman Catholic. Office: Carroll Coll Theology Dept Helena MT 59625-0001

HART, JOSEPH THOMAS CAMPBELL, lawyer; b. Orange, N.J., May 23, 1936; s. Maurice I. and Anne G. (Campbell) H. AB, Fordham U., 1958, JD, 1961. Bar: N.Y. 1962, U.S. Dist. Ct. (so. and ea. dists.) N.Y. 1966, U.S. Ct. Appeals (2d cir.) 1974, U.S. Ct. Appeals (5th cir.) 1983. Assoc. Dewey, Ballatine, Bushby, Palmer & Wood, N.Y.C., 1962-65; assoc. Fulton, Rowe, Hart & Coon, N.Y.C., 1965-71, ptnr., 1971—; sec. The G. Unger Vetlesen Found., N.Y.C., 1987, The Ambrose Monell Found., N.Y.C., 1994. Mem. Assn. of the Bar of the City of N.Y. Office: Fulton Rowe Hart & Coon One Rockefeller Plaza New York NY 10020

HART, KEVIN ARTHUR, justice of the peace; b. Anaconda, Mont., Jan. 27, 1962; s. Donald Franklin and Katherine Marie (Longfellow) H.; m. Stacey Lynn Boyer Guindon, Sept. 5, 1987; children: Eric J., Devin S. Grad., San Francisco Coll. Mortuary Sci., 1981; student, Mont. Tech., 1981-83. Mortician Longfellow Funeral Home, Anaconda, 1984-89, Sun Land Mortuary, Sun City, Ariz., 1989-91; nurses aide Mont. State Hosp., Warm Springs, 1991-92; correctional officer Mont. State Prison, Deer Lodge, Mont., 1992-95; justice of the peace Anaconda-Deer Lodge County, 1995—. Sec.-treas. Kiwanis, Anaconda, 1982-85, v.p., 1988-89. Mem. Nat. Judges Assn., Mont. Magistrate Assn. (dist. chmn. 1995-99). Roman Catholic. Avocation: family activities. E-mail: adlcjp@imine.net. Home: 1110 Heather Dr Anaconda MT 59711-2634 Office: Justice Ct Anaconda-Deer Lodge County 800 Main St Anaconda MT 59711-2950

HART, MARGARETA, audit director, researcher; b. Stockholm, Sweden, Aug. 22, 1944; Immigrated to Finland, 1945.; d. Ragnar and Greta (Edstrand) Lihr; m. Horst Hart; 1 child, Malin. PhD, Gothenburg U., Sweden, 1984. Rsch. asst. Swedish Radio, Sweden, 1966-68, Gothenburg U., Sweden, 1970-76; sr. auditor Nat. Audit Office, Sweden, 1976-78; rsch. asst. Gothenburg U., 1979-83; audit dir. Nat. Audit Office, Sweden, 1990—. Avocations: sailing, skiing, traveling. Home: Grindav 1, 18533 Vaxholm Sweden Office: National Audit Office, PO Box 45070, 10430 Stockholm Sweden

HART, MELISSA ANNE, state senator; b. Pitts., Apr. 4, 1962; d. Donald P. and Albina Simone Hart. BA, Washington and Jefferson Coll., 1984; JD, U. Pitts., 1987. Pa. state senator, atty.; chmn. Sen. Fin. Com.; vice chmn. Sen. Urban Affairs & Housing Com.; bd. dirs. C.C. Allegheny County, Pitts. Cancer Inst., SWPA Vets. Home Adv. Coun. Bd. dirs. Vietnam Vets. Leadership Program; bd. trustees U. Pitts. Mem. Pa. Bar Assn., Allegheny County Bar Assn., North Suburban Builders Assn. Republican. Office: Pa State Senate State Capitol LM 171 Harrisburg PA 17120

HART, PAMELA HEIM, banker; b. Chgo., July 14, 1946; d. Gordon Theodore and Leah Almira (Gardner) Heim; m. William Richard Hart, July 8, 1972 (div. 1979); 1 child, Elizabeth Alyson. BA, DePauw U., 1968; MA in Tchg., Washington U., St. Louis, 1970; M in Mgmt., Purdue U., 1982. Chartered bank auditor; cert. bank compliance officer. Tchr. history University City (Mo.) H.S., 1969-74; tchg. asst. Purdue U., Hammond, Ind., 1980-82, guest faculty, 1983-84; auditor Continental Bank NA, Chgo., 1984-86, legal and regulatory compliance specialist, 1986-88, asst. auditor, 1988-92, sr. portfolio risk analyst, 1992-94; with asset securitization group Bank of Am. (formerly Continental Bank NA), Chgo., 1994-98; v.p. capital raising products Bank of Am., Chgo., 1994-99, v.p. pvt. bank strategic planning and projects, 1999—. Trustee Forest Ridge Acad., Schererville, Ind., 1987-88; mem. vestry St. Paul Episc. Ch., Munster, Ind., 1982-92, jr. warden, 1998, 99; active LWV. Mem. Chartered Bank Auditors Assn., Chicagoland Compliance Assn. (bd. dirs., treas. 1987-88), Cert. Bank Compliance Officer Assn. (exam. com. mem. 1992-96), P.E.O. Avocations: needlework, travel, reading. E-mail: hartpamela55555@aol.com. Home: 910 Ridge Rd Munster IN 46321-1750 Office: Bank of Am 231 S La Salle St Chicago IL 60604-1407

HART, PAUL VINCENT, JR., emergency and family medicine physician, inventor; b. Estherville, Iowa, Sept. 28, 1950; s. Paul Vincent and Florence Mary (Gehringer) H.; m. Susan Murphey, Sept. 27, 1989. BS, Iowa State U., 1972; MD, Creighton U., 1976. Diplomate Am. Bd. Emergency Medicine. Resident in gen. surgery U. Minn., Mpls., 1976-77; emergency physician Wheeling (W.Va.) Med. Ctr., 1977-79; pvt. practice family practice and emergency medicine, Kansas City, Kans., 1979-84, Westwood, Kans., 1985—; v.p. Organ Design & Mfg., Westwood, 1989—. Co-patentee liver assist devices. Mem. AMA, Am. Acad. Family Physicians. Republican. Roman Catholic. Home: 2813 W 51st St Westwood KS 66205-1748

HART, RICHARD WESLEY, religious organization administrator, pastor; b. Greensboro, N.C., Feb. 21, 1933; s. Shelly Monroe and Virginia (Boaz) H.; m. 1954; (div. May 1969); children: Richard Wesley Jr., Larry Earl, Howard Clayton; m. Shirleen Atkins Chance, Aug. 16, 1997. BDiv, Toccoa Falls (Ga.) Coll., 1951; DDiv, Evang. Christian Sem., 1966. Regional dir. Am. Evang. Christian Chs., Fontana, Calif., 1958-66; pres. Evang. Christian Chs., San Bernardino, Calif., 1966-83; founder, dir. Reidsville (N.C.) Urban Ministry, 1983—. Mem. Rep. Nat. Com., Washington, 1991—; establisher AGAD Scholarship Fund, 1992. Mem. Am. Vets. Avocations: coin and old currency collector. Home and Office: 2125 Smith St Reidsville NC 27320-6513

HART, ROBERT CLYNTON, biology educator; b. Chingola, Copperbelt, Zimbabwe, July 21, 1947; s. Robert Kidson and Eileen Grace H.; m. Rei van den Berg, July 2, 1969; children: Susan Nicola, Philippa Jane. BS with honors, U. Natal (South Africa), Pietermaritzburg, 1968; DSc, 1994; PhD in Sci., Rhodes U., Grahamstown, Ea. Cape, South Africa, 1974. Rsch. officer Inst. Freshwater Studies Rhodes U., Grahamstown, Ea. Cape, South Africa, 1969-77; sr. rsch. officer Rhodes U., Grahamstown, 1978-81, Barclays Nat. Bank profl. postgrad. limnology, 1982-87, intermitent acting dir. Inst. Freshwater Studies, 1983-86, dir. Inst. Freshwater Studies, 1986-87; sr. lectr. U. Natal, Pietermaritzburg, 1987-89, assoc. prof., 1990-93, prof., 1994—; mem. scientific steering com. Coun. Scientific and Indsl. Rsch., Pretoria, South Africa, 1979-84. Author, co-author, editor: Inland Waters of Southern Africa. An Ecological Perspective, 1990; contbr. articles to profl. jours. univ. senate rep. bd. trustees Albany Mus., Grahamstown, 1983-87. Recipient Scientific Rating award Found. Rsch. Devel., 1984, 88, 94, 98, rsch. operating funds CSIR/Found. Rsch. Devel., 1982—. Mem. Internat. Assn. Theoret. and Applied Limnol. (nat. rep. 1990-95), Limnol. Soc. So. Africa (hon. sec. 1975, 82-84), Internat. Limnol. Assn. (mem. limnology in developing countries com. 1998—, mem. editl. panel 1998—). Avocations: photography, birding, wilderness, aviation. E-mail: HartR@nu.ac.za.

HART, RUSS ALLEN, telecommunications educator; b. Seguin, Tex., June 30, 1946; s. Bevelly D. and Hattie V. (Reeh) H.; m. Judith Harwood, 1984 (div. 1986); m. Patricia Barrios, Mar. 22, 1987. BA, Tex. Tech. U., 1968; MA, U. Ariz., 1976; PhD, U. Wyo., 1984. Chief cinematographer, producer-dir. dept. med-TV-film, health sci. ctr. U. Ariz., Tucson, 1973-77; instr., coord. ednl. TV and cinematography U. Wyo., Laramie, 1977-81; assoc. prof., dir. biomed. communication Mercer U., Macon, Ga., 1981-84; prof., dir. instructional telecommunications Calif. State U., Fresno, 1984-92, prof., assoc. dir. computing, comm. and media svcs., 1992-95, prof., assoc. dir. Acad. Innovation Ctr., 1995-98, prof. mass comm., 1998—, dir. grad. program, 2000—; condr. ednl. confs.; tech. cons. for distance edn. Contbr. articles to profl. jours. Served to capt. USAF, 1968-73. Recipient Cert. Merit, Chgo. Internat. Film Festival, 1975, 1st pl. INDY Indsl. Photography award, 1976, 2d pl. INDY Indsl. Photography award, 1975, Silver plaque Chgo. Internat. Film Festival, 1978, Winner of case study competition Internat. Radio and TV Soc., 1989, Bronze Telly award, 1992-93, 95, Crystal Shooting Star award, 1993, 94, Cine Golden Eagle award, 1994. Mem. Assn. for Ednl. Comms. and Tech. (rsch. session chmn. 1983), Am. Assn. Adult and Continuing Educators (mem. eval. task force 1986), Broadcast Edn. Assn., Health Sci. Comms. Assn. (mem. continuing edn. subcom. 1983), Biol. Photog. Assn. (film judge 1975), Alliance for Distance Edn. in Calif. (founding mem. 1991), Ednl. Telecom. Consortium of Ctrl. Calif. (founding mem. 1993), Phi Delta Kappa, Phi Kappa Phi. Office: Calif State U Mass Comm & Journalism Fresno CA 93740-0001

HART, SEAN LEE, pharmaceutical executive, consultant; b. Kansas City, Mo., June 3, 1969; s. Wayne Lawrence and Judy (Carnagie) H.; m. Katie Christine Willcox, July 29, 1995. BS in Biochemistry, U. Kans., 1991; MBA in Mktg., Webster U., 1998. Clin. rsch. assoc. Berger Boyer & Assoc., Kansas City, Mo., 1992-94, project leader, 1994-95, CEO, 1995—; cons. Ethical Review Com., Kansas City, 1992—; mem. adv. bd. Power Hypertension Study, Kansas City, 1997-98, ACT Osteoporosis Trial, Kansas City, 1998—. Bd. dirs. Alumni Bd. Barstow, Kansas City, 1998—. Mem. Drug Info. Assn., Assocs. Clin. Rsch. Profls. Presbyn. Avocations: golf, scuba diving. E-mail: sean@bergerboyer.com. Office: Berger Boyer & Assocs 2018 Baltimore Ave Kansas City MO 64108-1914

HART, WILLIAM LEE, IV, legislative staff member; b. Anchorage, Alaska, Oct. 8, 1971; s. William Lee III and Barbara Lee H.; m. Vicki Marie Kinney, May 23, 1998. BA in History, U. Idaho, 1994. Sales rep. Bill Hart & Assoc., Meridian, Idaho; 1st Congl. Dist. field rep. Craig for Senate, Boise, Idaho, 1996; campaign mgr. Ron Crane for State Treas., Meridian, 1997-98; press sec. U.S. Senator Larry Craig, Washington, 1998—. Mem. Alpha Kappa Lambda (dir. corp. bd. Alpha Phi chpt. 1994—, Alumni of Yr. 1996). Republican. Episcopalian. Home: Apt D Auburn Ct Alexandria VA 22305-2936 Office: SH 520 Us Senator Larry Craig Washington DC 20510-0001

HARTAL, OREN MICHAEL, engineering executive; b. Jerusalem, Mar. 22, 1940; s. Pinhas and Esther (Goner) H.; m. Elisheva Cohen, Nov. 12, 1963; children: Adi, Yael, Tamar, Na'ama. BSc in Elec. Engring., Technion, Haifa, Israel, 1966, MSc in Elec. Engring., 1976. Lic. electronic engr. specializing in electro-magnetic compatibility. Electromagnetic compatibility engr., sect. head Rafael, Haifa, Israel, 1966-90, head electromagnetics sect., 1992-97, head electromagnetics directorate, 1997-98, chief scientist, 1999—; dir. engring. R.B. Enterprises, Pa., 1983-84, 90-91; exper on electromagnetic compatibility United Nations Devel. Program, Madras, India, 1990-93; chief engr. Lightning Elimination Assocs., Downey, Calif., 1977-78; cons. elec. industries, Israel, 1972—; electromagnetic compatibility educator many orgns., Israel, U.S., India, 1972—; electromagnetic compatibility Stds. coord., com. mem. Bur. Stds., Tel-Aviv, 1972-90. Author: EMC By Design, 1990. Recipient Cert. of Appreciation, Archs. and Engrs. Assn. Israel, Tel Aviv, 1992. Mem. IEEE Israel (sr., chmn. electromagnetic compatibility sect. 1986-92, cert. of achievement 1992), URSI Israel (chmn. commn. E on radio noise and interference 1986—), Internat. Union Radio Scientists, Nat. Assn. Radio and Telecomm. Engrs. Avocations: playing the clarinet in chamber music, travel emphasizing nature, ancient history and anthropology. E-mail: hartalo@hotmail.com. Home: 20 Zipornim St, 36066 K Tivon Israel Office: Rafael Armament Devel Auth, PO Box 2250, 31021 Haifa Israel

HARTBERG, WARREN KEITH, biologist, educator; b. Watseka, Ill., Jan. 24, 1941; s. Warren Eugene and Marie Isabelle Hartberg; m. Rebecca Crosby, Feb. 2, 1964; children: Gretchen Mackenzie, Adam, Joanna Meek. AB, Wabash Coll., 1963; MS, U. Notre Dame, 1965, PhD, 1968. Entomologist, geneticist WHO, Dar es Salaam, Tanzania, 1968-70; from asst. prof. to assoc. prof. Ga. So. Coll., Statesboro, 1970-80, coord. Inst. Anthropology & Parasitology, 1971-83, acting head biology, 1979-80, prof., 1980-86; chmn., prof. Baylor U., Waco, Tex., 1986—; cons.Internat. Ctr. Insect Physiology and Ecology, Mombasa, Kenya, 1970-77. Contbr. articles to profl. jours. chmn. bd. dirs. In-as-Much Project, Inc., Statesboro, 1975-76; bd. dirs. Bullock County Wildlife Club, Statesboro, 1983-85. Fellow Tex. Acad. Scis.; mem. Am. Mosquito Control Assn., Soc. Vector Ecology, La. Mosquito Control Assn., Tex. Mosquito Control Assn. (bd. dirs. 1991-99, sec., 1991, v.p. 1995-97, pres. 1998), Sigma Xi. Avocations: model railroading, fishing, military history. Home: 13000 Sandalwood Dr Waco TX 76712-3136 Office: Baylor U Biology Dept Waco TX 76798

HARTER, GEORGES, architect, urban planning consultant; b. Hanoi, Vietnam, Dec. 6, 1942; s. Eugene Louis and Georgette Henriette (Silvestre) H.; m. Jeannine Marie Schilling, July 24, 1971; children: Nicolas, Magali. Diploma in Fine Arts, Nat. Sch., 1969; Diploma in Urban Planning, Paris U., 1970. Registered architect, France. Architect, urban planner B.E.R.U., Paris, 1969, French Mission in Zaire, Kinshasa, 1970; tchr. architecture Housing & Urban Planning Agy., Paris, 1971-73, tchr. urban planning, head studies sector, 1973-75, cons., 1977-79; new town project mgr. Regional S.W. Devel. Authority, San Pedro, Ivory Coast, 1975-76; chmn.'s cons. Devel. & Cooperation Agy., 1980-85; architect, designer, 1986—; pres. Galmier SA, 1990-94; internat. projects dir. L'EDA, Paris, 1996—; tchr. Paris VIII U., 1973-80, Paris VII U., 1979-80; cons. The World Bank, Abidjan, Ivory Coast, 1980, Adma-Opco, 1980. Author: Housing in Developing Countries, 1975, Land Plotting in Developing Countries, 1977, Facilities in Developing Countries, 1984. Recipient award Engrs. and Scientists France Soc., 1981. Avocations: collecting old shares and bonds, collecting African and Oriental bracelets.

HARTER, JOHN J., economic analyst; b. Canyon, Tex., Jan. 31, 1926; s. Ralph E. and Grace S. Harter; m. Irene T. Harter, May 25, 1957; children: Tian, Tonia, Lal. BA, U. So. Calif., 1948, MA, 1953; M of Econ., Harvard U., 1963. Lectr. in history U. So. Calif., L.A., 1948-53; fgn. svc. officer, assignments in S. Africa, Chile, Thailand, Geneva Dept. of State, Washington, 1954-83, oral historian, 1983-99; conf. affairs officer Fgn. Svc. Assn., Washington, 1989-96; freelance writer, cons. Washington, 1983—; declassifier Agy. for Internat. Devel., Washington, 1998—. Author: The Language of Trade, 1984. Sec., mem. vestry Am. Ch., Geneva, 1969-70. Mem. Diplomatic and Consular Officers Ret. Democrat. Episcopalian. E-mail: jjitharter@aol.com. Home: 1664 Valencia Way Reston VA 20190-4976

HARTER, LAFAYETTE GEORGE, JR., economics educator emeritus; b. Des Moines, May 28, 1918; s. Lafayette George and Helen Elizabeth (Ives) H.; m. Charlotte Mary Toshach, Aug. 23, 1950; children—Lafayette George III, James Toshach, Charlotte Helen. B.A. in Bus. Adminstrn, Antioch Coll., 1941; M.A. in Econs, Stanford, 1948, Ph.D., 1960. Instr. Menlo Coll., Menlo Park, Calif., 1948-50; instr. Coll. of Marin, Kentfield, Calif., 1950-60; prof. econs. dept. Oreg. State U., 1960-85, prof. emeritus, 1985—, chmn. dept., 1967-71; mem. panel arbitrators Fed. Mediation and Conciliation Svc., 1965-84, Oreg. Conciliation Svc., 1967-84; mem. Univ. Ctrs. for Rational Alternatives. Author: John R. Commons: His Assault on Laissez-faire, 1962, Labor in America, 1957, Economic Responses to a Changing World, 1972; editorial bd. Jour. Econ. Issues, 1981-84. Assoc. campaign chmn. Benton United Good Neighbor Fund, 1970-72, campaign chmn., v.p., 1972-73, pres., 1973-74, vice chmn.; pub. mem. Adv. Commn. on Unemployment Compensation, 1972, 73, chmn., 1974-78; Bd. dirs. Oreg. Coun. Econ. Edn., 1971-89; pub. mem. local profl. responsibilities Oreg. State Bar Assn., 1980-83; pub. mem. Oreg. Coun. on Ct. Procedures, 1985-93, bd. mem. Community Econs. of Corp., Community Econ. Stabilization Corp. Lt. comdr. USNR, 1941-46. Mem. AAUP, Am. Arbitration Assn. (pub. employment disputes panel 1970-92), Am. Western Econ. Assns., Indsl. Rels. Rsch. Assn., Am. Assn. for Evolutionary Econs., Oreg. State Employees Assn. (v.p. faculty chpt. 1972, pres. 1973), Am. Assn. Ret. Persons (pres. local chpt. 1992-93), Corvallis Retirement Village (fin. com., bd. dirs.). Democrat. Mem. United Ch. of Christ (moderator 1972, 73; mem. fin. com. Oreg. conf. 1974-82, dir. 1978-81, mem. personnel com. 1983-85). Home: 3755 NW Van Buren Ave Corvallis OR 97330-4952

HARTLEY, DAVID MINOR, physicist, research scientist; b. Uniontown, Pa., Aug. 26, 1968; s. Harold Minor and Brenda Joyce (Wilson) H.; m. Amy Elizabeth Meyer, Sept. 29, 1990; children: Devin Minor Meyer, Abigail Elizabeth Meyer. BS in Physics with honors, W.Va. U., 1990; MS in Physics, U. Md., 1992, PhD in Physics, 1996. Broadcast engr. Radio Sta. KOLL, Gillette, Wyo., 1985-87; undergrad. rsch. asst. plasma physics lab. W.Va. U., Morgantown, 1988-90; assoc. mem., tech. staff Computer Scis. Corp., Greenbelt, Md., 1993; tchg. asst. U. Md., Balt., 1990-94, rsch. asst., 1993-96; rsch. scientist, program mgr. Dynamics Tech., Inc., Arlington, Va., 1996—; instr. U. Md., Balt., 1992-96, grad. physics curriculum adv. com., 1994-95; analyst Lynx Techs., Inc., Fairfax, Va., 1995-96; rschr. U. Md., 1996; speaker in field. Contbr. articles to profl. jours. Mem. Am. Phys. Soc., Sigma Pi Sigma. Republican. Presbyterian. Achievements include research in tunneling theory of site-specific negative-ion formation and decay at surfaces, mathematical modelling of HIV epidemic, experimental verification of periodic pulling in nonlinear oscillators. Avocations: observational astronomy, extra-class amateur radio license, martial arts, history. Home: 14220 Greenspan Ln Rockville MD 20853-2509 Office: Dynamics Tech Inc 1555 Wilson Blvd Ste 320 Arlington VA 22209-2405

HARTLING, PETER, writer, journalist; b. Chemnitz, Germany, Nov. 13, 1933; s. Rudolf and Erika (Hantzschel) H.; m. Mechthild Maier, 1959; 4 children. Student Gymansium Nurtingen/Neckar. Journalist, 1953—; lit. editor Deutsche Zeitung und Wirtschaftszeitung, Stuttgart and Cologne, 1955-62; editor of mag. Der Monat, 1962-70, also co-pub.; editor, mng. dir. S. Fischer Verlag, Frankfurt, 1968-74; editor Die Vater, 1968. Author: Yamins Stationem, 1955, In Zeilen zuhaus, 1957, Palmstrom grusst Anna Blume, 1961, Spielgeist-Spiegelgeist, 1962, Niembsch oder Der Stillstand, 1964, Janet, 1966, Das Familienfest, 1969, Gilles, 1970, Ein Abend, Eine Nacht, Ein Morgen, 1971, Zwetti-Nachprufung einer Errinerung, 1973, Eine Frau, 1974, Holderlin, 1976, Anreden, 1977, Hubert oder Die Ruckkehr nach Casablanca, 1978, Nachgetragene Liebe, 1980, Die dreifache Maria, 1982, Das Windrad, 1983, Felix Guttmann, 1985, Waiblingers Augen, 1987, Der Wanderer, 1988, Herzwand, 1990, Schubert, 1992, Das Land das ich er fand, 1993, Das Wandernde Wasser, 1994, Bozena, 1994, Schumanns Schatten, 1996, Horizonttheater, 1997, Grosse Kleine Schwester, 1998. Recipient Literaturpreis des Deutschen Kritikerverbandes, 1964, Literaturpreis des Kulturkreises der Deutschen Industrie, 1965, Literarischer Forderungspreis des Landes Niedersachsen, 1965, Prix du Meilleur livre estranger, Paris, 1966, Gerhart Hauptmann Preis, 1971, Deutscher Jugendbuchpreis, 1976, Stadtschreiber von Bergen-Enkheim, 1978-79, Hoelderlin-Preis, 1987, Andreas-Gryphius-Preis, 1990, Stadtschreiber von Mainz, 1995; named Prof. honoris causa Grosses Bundesverdienstkreuz, 1996. Mem. PEN, Akademie der Wissenschaften und der Literatur Mainz, Akademie der Kunste Berlin, Deutsche Akademie fur Sprache und Dichtung Darmstadt. Address: Finkenweg 1, D-64546 Morfelden Germany

HARTMAN, ALAN FRAZIER, estate planning specialist; b. Rushville, Ind., Sept. 30, 1947; s. Cecil R. and Theodotia (Frazier) H.; m. Catherine Elizabeth Loman, July 7, 1969; children: Michael, Lauren. BS in Bus., Ind. U., 1970. CLU; ChFC. Brokerage sales mgr. Mfr.'s Life, Atlanta, 1974-79; spl. agt. Northwestern Mutual Life, Atlanta, 1979-84; regional dir. Southwestern Life and Phila. Life, Hilton Head, S.C., 1984-86; assoc. gen. agt. Ctrl. Benefits Planners, Hilton Head, 1986-92; estate planning specialist Merrill Lynch, Pierce, Fenner & Smith, Macon, Ga., 1992-95; fin. cons. Wheat, First, Butcher, Singer, Hilton Head Island, S.C., 1995-96, Cmty. Bank. Mktg., Macon, Ga., 1996-97; v.p. Prudential Securities, Atlanta, 1997-98; regional v.p. Insured Investor Group, Macon, 1998—; cons. Atlanta, 1997—. Fund raiser Med. Ctr. Found., 1992-2000, bd. dirs. 1992-93; bd. dirs. charitable estate planning Macon Symphony, 1992-93; vol. charity and ins. First Presbyn. Ch., Hilton Head, 1990-91. Mem. Macon Estate Planning Coun., Albany Estate Planning Coun., Atlanta Estate Planning Coun., Atlanta CLU, Nat. CLU, Masons (Palestine lodge #486). Republican. Presbyterian. Avocations: tennis umpire, barbershop quartet. Home: 1173 Oakcliff Rd Macon GA 31211-1329 Office: Estate Planning Consultants 901 Washington Ave Ste 1 Macon GA 31201-6720 Office: Insured Investor Group PO Box 4984 Macon GA 31208-4984

HARTMAN, CHARLES EDWARD, engineer; b. South Bend, Ind., Sept. 16, 1947; s. Charles E. and Rosemary G. (Geiger) H.; m. Terri A. Portolese, Aug. 30, 1969; children: Chas E., Chris A. BSCE, Purdue U., 1970. Product engr. Uniroyal, Inc., Mishawaka, Ind., 1970-72; environtl. engr.

Ausco Products, Inc., Benton Harbor, Mich., 1972-82, product engr., 1982—. Avocations: jogging, sports, music, computers. Home: 5432 S Roosevelt Rd Stevensville MI 49127-9574

HARTMAN, GÖRAN LARS, ecologist, researcher, educator; b. Uppsala, Sweden, July 13, 1958; s. Lars Olov and Ulla Birgit (Ohlson) H.; m. Lisa Sjöström, July 5, 1997. BSc, U. Uppsala, 1984; PhD, Swedish Univ. Agr. Sci., Uppsala, 1994. Dir. studies Swedish Univ. Agrl. Scis., Uppsala, 1996—. Contbr. articles to profl. jours., books. Avocations: fishing, hunting, music, gardening. Home: Tiundagatan 63, 752 30 Uppsala Sweden Office: Swedish U Agrl Sci, Dept Conserv Biology Box 7002, 750 07 Uppsala Sweden

HARTMAN, JEFFREY EDWARD, pastor; b. Nyack, N.Y., June 23, 1959; s. Edward Harold and Constance Ruth (Gibbs) H.; m. Cynthia Lynn Chason, Aug. 14, 1982; children: Joshua Jefferson, Jeremiah Jordan, Julia Lyndsay. BS, Liberty U., 1982; postgrad., Westminster Theol. Sem., 1984-87, Trinity Evang. Div. Sch., 1990; MDiv, Princeton Theol. Sem., 1998; M in Sacred Theology, Yale U., 2000; postgrad., Harvard U., 2000. Ordained to ministry, 1985. Assoc. pastor Maranatha Bapt. Ch., Gainesville, Ga., 1982-84; pastor Christ Community Ch., Newfield, N.J., 1984—; baseball head coach Cumberland Christian Sch., Vineland, N.J., 1991-95; chaplain Newcomb Med. Ctr., Vineland, 1987—. Founder, editor, columnist: Newfield Neighbors newspaper, Newfield, N.J., 1988—. Co-founder, bd. dirs. Compassion Crisis Pregnancy Ctr., Clayton, N.J., 1986-90, chmn. bd. dirs. 1990-95. Recipient John Finley McLaren prize in Bibl. theology Princeton Theol. Sem., N.J., 1997. Office: Christ Community Ch 201 Salem Ave Newfield NJ 08344-9074

HARTMAN, ROSEMARY JANE, retired special education educator; b. Gainesville, Fla., Aug. 24, 1944; d. John Leslie and Irene (Bowen) Goddard; m. Alan Lynn Gerber, Feb. 1, 1964 (div. 1982); children: Sean Alan, Dawn Julianne Silva, Lance Goddard; m. Perry Hartman, June 27, 1992. BA, Immaculate Heart Coll., 1967; MA, Loyola U., 1974. Cert. resource specialist. Tchr. L.A. Unified Schs., 1968-78; resource specialist Desert Sands Unified Sch. Dist., Palm Desert, 1978-83; resource specialist Palm Springs Unified Schs., 1983-99, retired, 1999. Co-author: The Twelve Steps of Phobics Anonymous, 1989, One Day At A Time in Phobics Victorious, 1992, The Twelve Steps of Phobics Victorious, 1993; founder Phobics Victorious, 1992. Mem. Am. Assn. Christian Counselors (charter), Nat. Assn. of Christian Recovery, Anxiety Disorders Assn. Am. Office: Phobics Victorious PO Box 695 Palm Springs CA 92263-0695

HARTMAN-IRWIN, MARY FRANCES, retired language professional; b. Portland, Oreg., Oct. 18, 1925; d. Curtiss Henry Sabisch and Gladys Frances (Giles) Strand; m. Harry Elmer Hartman, Sept. 6, 1946 (div. June 1970); children: Evelyn Frances, Laura Elyce, Andrea Candace; m. Thomas Floyd Irwin, Apr. 11, 1971. BA, U. Wash., 1964-68; postgrad., Seattle Pacific, 1977-79, Antioch U., Seattle, Wash., 1987, Heritage Inst., Seattle, Wash., 1987. Lang. educator Kennewick (Wash.) Dist. # 17, 1970-88; guide Summer Study Tours of Europe, 1971-88. Sec. Bahai Faith, 1971-99, libr., 2000, Pasco, Washington, 1985-88; trustee Mid. Columbia coun. Girl Scouts U.S. Fulbright scholar, 1968. Mem. NEA, Wash. Edn. Assn., Kennewick Edn. Assn., Nat. Fgn. Lang. Assn., Wash. Fgn. Lang. Assn., Literacy Coun. (literacy tutor Tillamook Bay C.C.). Avocations: painting, sewing, writing essays and short stories. Home: PO Box 247 Netarts OR 97143-0247

HARTMANN, ANDREAS, toxicologist, researcher; b. Nordenham, Germany, May 9, 1964; s. Heino Wilhelm and Waltraud (Rastetter) H.; m. Karin Lieselotte Bitter, Sept. 9, 1994; children: Julia Katharina, Sina Marie. Master's degree, U. Oldenburg, Germany, 1989, diploma, 1992; PhD in Human Genetics, U. Ulm, Germany, 1996. Eurotox registered toxicologist. Cons. U. Oldenburg, 1991-92; postdoctoral fellow U. Ulm, 1996, U. Calif., San Francisco, 1996-98; toxicologist Novartis Pharma, Basel, Switzerland, 1998—; sec. GUM, Heidelberg, Germany, 1998—; councillor EEMS, Basel, 1999—. Author: (book chpts.) Exercise and Oxygen Toxicity, 1999, DNA Repair Protocols, 1999; contbr. articles to profl. jours. Recipient Young Scientist award EEMS, 1999; postdoctoral fellow DFG, 1996. Avocations: endurance sports, triathlon. Office: Novartis Pharma AG, WSH 2881 5 14, 4002 Basel Switzerland

HARTMANN, ANN W., financial planner; b. Detroit, Mar. 5, 1941; d. Robert Allan and Eunice Elizabeth (Seitz) Wilson; m. James Cline Hartmann, July 18, 1970 (dec.); m. Richard W. Brockmeyer, Oct. 1, 1994 (div. 1999). BA, Montclair State Coll., 1962; MBA in Fin., Rutgers U., 1975. CLU; chartered fin. cons. Tchr. Bloomfield (N.J.) Bd. Edn., 1962-63; administr. Girl Scouts USA, Pa., Mich., 1963-72, YWCA of Am., N.J., Ohio, 1972-77; dir. fin. and field personnel Sycor, Inc., Ann Arbor, Mich., 1977-79; sr. cons. Health Systems Group, Ann Arbor, 1979-80; fin. planner Hartmann & Assocs., Toledo, 1980—; adj. faculty U. Toledo, 1983-87, Lourdes Coll., Sylvania, Ohio, 1987-98; faculty Cigna/Lincoln Nat. Edn. Events, 1984—; speaker in field. Editor: (newletter) Money Talks, 1982—. 1st v.p. Girls Clubs of Am., N.Y.C., 1985-87; pres. Maumee Valley Girl Scout Coun., Toledo, 1990-97; nat. aquatic sch. staff instr., trainer ARC, Mich., Pa., 1974-80. Named Hines award Honoree Nat. Bd. Child Welfare, 1986. Mem. Am. Arbitration Assn. (comml. panel, NASD arbitrator), Soc. Fin. Svc. Profls. (pres. Toledo chpt. 1988-90, nat. bd. dirs. 1993-96, nat. nominating com. 1996-97, sec. 1998-99, treas. 1999-2000, pres.-elect 2000—), Toledo Assn. Life Underwriters (v.p. 1991-94, pres. elect 1994, pres. 1995), Toledo Estate Planning Coun. (bd. dirs. 1992-98), Zonta Club Toledo I (bd. dirs. 1987-88). Republican. Methodist. Avocations: sailing, bridge, needlework. Office: Hartmann & Assocs 6635 W Central Ave Toledo OH 43617-1029

HARTMANN, ERVIN, physicist, researcher; b. Ujpest, Hungary, Apr. 18, 1935; s. József and Erzsébet (Szabo) H.; m. Erzsébet Skulteti, Aug. 2, 1965; 1 child, Tünde. Diploma in Physics, Eötvös U., Budapest, Hungary, 1953-58; PhD, Moscow Inst. Steel and Alloys, 1968; DSc, Hungarian Acad. Scis., Budapest, Hungary, 1988. Scientific researcher Tech. U., Budapest, Hungary, 1958-75, Rsch. Lab. for Crystal Physics, 1976—; prof., 1990—; guest researcher Max Planck Inst. for Solid State Rsch., Stuttgart, Fed. Rep. Germany, Inst. Crystallography, Moscow, Ioffe Inst., St. Petersburg. Co-author: Laboratory Manual on Crystal Growth, 1972, Physics of Electrolytes, 1972, Crystal Growth (in Hungarian), 1986; author: An Introduction to Crystal Physics, 1984. Recipient Presdl. award Hungarian Acad. Scis., Budapest, Hungary, 1986, Gyulai award R. Eötvös Phys. Soc., 1998. Mem. Internat. Orgn. for Crystal Growth (councillor), Hungarian Com. for Crystal Growth (chmn.). Home: Frakno u 28/a, H-1115 Budapest Hungary Office: Inst Rsch Solid State Physics, Konkolythege 29-33, H-1121 Budapest Hungary

HARTMANN, PETER CLAUS, historian, educator; b. Munich, Mar. 28, 1940; s. Alfred and Manfreda (Knote) H.; m. Beate Just, Sept. 29, 1972; children: Pia, Emanuel, Aurelia, Patrick. D in Philosophy, U. Munich, 1967, D in Philos. Habil., 1976; Doctorat d'U., Sorbonne U., Paris, 1969. Research asst. German Hist. Inst., Paris, 1970-81; privatdozent U. Munich, 1978-81; prof. modern history U. Regensburg, Fed. Republic Germany, 1981; prof. modern and Bavarian history U. Passau, Fed. Republic Germany, 1982-88; prof. modern history U. Mainz, Fed. Republic Germany, 1988—. Author: Pariser Archive, Bibl. u. Dokumentationszentren, 1976, Geld als Instrument Europ. Machtpolitik im Zeitalter d. Merkantilismus, 1978, Steuersystem d. Europ. Staaten a. Ende d. ancien Regime, 1979, Karl Albrecht-Karl VII, 1985, Franz. Gesch. 1914-45, 1985, Französ Verfassungsgesch. d. Neuzeit, 1985, Bayerns Weg i. d. Gegenwart, Vom Stammesherzogtum z. Freistaat heute, 1989, Der Jesitenstaat in Südamerika 1609-1768, 1994, Französ, Könige und Kaiser d. Neuzeit, 1994; Regionen in d. Frühen Neuzeit, 1994, D. Mainzer Kurfürst als Reichserzkanzler, 1997, D. Bayerische Reichskreis (1500 bis 1803), 1997, Gesch. Frankreichs, 1999. Office: U Mainz, Saarstr 21, D-55099 Mainz Germany

HARTMANN, ROBERT TROWBRIDGE, newspaper executive, counselor; b. Rapid City, S.D., Apr. 8, 1917; s. Miner Louis and Elizabeth (Trowbridge) H.; m. Roberta Sankey, Jan. 17, 1943; children: Roberta H. Brake, Robert S. A.B., Stanford U., 1938. Reporter Los Angeles Times, 1939-41, 45-48, editorial writer, 1948-54, chief Washington bur., 1954-63; chief (Mediterranean and Middle East Bur.), 1963-64; FAO info. adviser Washington, 1964-65; editor Republican Conf. U.S. Ho. Reps., 1966-69; minority sgt.-at-arms U.S. Ho. Reps., 1969-73; chief staff to the Vice Pres., 1973-74; counsellor (with cabinet rank) to Pres. Gerald R. Ford, 1974-77; sr. research fellow Hoover Instn., Stanford U., 1977—; trustee Gerald R. Ford Found., 1981—; mem. U.S. Ho. of Reps. Mission to Peoples' Republic of China, 1972. Author: Palace Politics, An Inside Account of the Ford Years, 1980. Asst. to permanent chmn. Rep. Nat. Conv., 1968, 72; bd. visitors U.S. Naval Acad., 1977-80. Served from ensign to lt. comdr. USN, 1941-45, PTO; now capt. USNR, ret. Recipient Sigma Delta Chi Distinguished Service award for Washington Corrs., 1957; Better Understanding citation English Speaking Union of U.S., 1958; Overseas Press Club citation, 1961; Freedoms Found. citation, 1963; Distinguished Eagle Scout award Boy Scouts Am., 1975; Reid Found. fellow, 1951. Mem. Navy League, Hammer and Coffin Soc., Delta Chi, Sigma Delta Chi, Delta Sigma Rho. Mem. Ch. of Christ. Clubs: Nat. Press (Washington), Army and Navy (Washington), Capitol Hill (Washington); Mil. Order of the Carabao, Chevaliers du Tastevin; Country Club of St. Croix (V.I.). Home: 5001 Baltimore Ave Bethesda MD 20816-1607

HARTMANN, ULRICH, diversified financial services company executive; b. Berlin, Aug. 7, 1938; married; 2 children. Law student, Munich, Berlin and Bonn, 1958-67. Auditor Tereuarbeit AG, Düsseldorf, 1967-71; asst. to bd. mgmt. Deutsche Leasing AG, Frankfurt, 1971-72; corp. counsel VEBA Kraftwerke Ruhr AG, Gelsenkirchen, 1973-75; head bd. office and pub. rels. VEBA AG, Düsseldorf, 1975-80; mem. bd. mgmt. Nordwestdeutsche Kraftwerke AG, Hamburg, 1980-85, Preussenelektra AG, Hannover, 1985-89; mem. bd. mgmt. VEBA AG, 1989—, CFO, mem. bd. mgmt., 1990—, CEO, chmn. bd. mgmt., 1993—; chmn. supervisory bd., co-chmn. bd. mgmt., CEO E.ON, Gelsenkirchen; chmn. supervisory bd. Müncheneückversicherungs-gesellschaft AG, Munich, RAG Aktiengesellschaft, Essen, Germany; consul gen. Norway, 1993—. Office: E ON, Alexander von Humboldt Str, 45896 Gelsenkirchen Germany*

HARTMANN, WERNER, animal geneticist, researcher; b. Schessinghausen, Germany, Feb. 10, 1927; s. Friedrich and Luise (Masbruch) H.; m. Renate Merck Hartmann, Nov. 3, 1956 (widowed Oct. 1991); children: Franz-David, Michael, Luise, Christof. Diploma in Agr., U. Gottingen, Germany, 1952, D. in Agr., 1954; postgrad., Iowa State U., 1954-56. Rschr. Max-Planck Inst., Mariensee, Germany, 1956-60; head broiler breeding Lohmann Co., Cuxhaven, Germany, 1960-70; head poultry genetics Fed. Rsch., Celle, Germany, 1970-92; cons. Animal Breeding Ctr., Godollo, Hungary, 1963-68, FAO of UN, Rome, 1972-74, FAO Poultry Program, Poznan, Poland, 1975-81; chmn. European Working Group Poultry Breeding Genetics, 1976-86. Author: Worlds Poultry Science Journal, 1985, British Poultry Science, 1988, Diseases of Poultry, 1992, Worlds Poultry Science Journal, 1997. Recipient G. Mendel Meml. medal. Acad. of Sci., Brno, Czechoslovakia, 1965. Mem. Worlds Poultry Sci., Animal Breeding Soc., Animal Genetics Sci. Assn., Polish Soc. Zootechnics (hon.). Lutheran. Avocations: jogging, sauna, collecting old books and coins. Fax: 05141-381849. Office: Inst fur Kleintierforschung, Dornbergstr 25/27, 29223 Celle Germany

HARTMANN-JOHNSEN, OLAF JOHAN, internist; b. Aalesund, Norway, Aug. 22, 1924; s. Odd and Helga Elisabeth (Hartmann) Johnsen; m. Mary Essil Archibald, 1956 (dissolved 1968); children: Sally, Helga Elisabeth; m. Mary Eldbjørg Hestad, May 23, 1969; children: Olaf Johan, Else Margrete. MB, BS, U. Queensland (Australia), 1956; MD, Oslo U., 1974. Physician Royal Brisbane (Australia) Hosp., 1956-63, Oslo U. Hosp., 1964-65, Bundaberg Gen. Hosp., 1966, Hornsby Dist. Hosp., 1967-70, Upton Hosp., Slough, Eng., 1970, Blacktown Dist. Hosp., 1971-73, Ullevål Hosp., 1974-77, Vesfn Hosp., 1977-78, Kragerø Hosp., 1978-79; physician-in-chief St. Joseph's Hosp., Porsgrunn, 1979-82; cons. physician, chief med. officer Nesset County, 1982-91; govt. med. officer, 1982-91; communal med. officer RAuma County Aandalsnes, 1991-92; staff physician Psychiat. Hosp., Hjelset, 1993-98; tutor in medicine U. Oslo Med. Sch., 1975-77 cons. in gen. practice and cmty. med., 1991—. Contbr. articles to med. jours. Served with Norwegian Air Force, 1942-47. Decorated King Haakon VII medal, Norwegian War Svc. medal, several Brit. campaign medals, medaille de la France Liberee. Mem. Norwegian Med. Assn., Coll. Norwegian Internists, N.Y. Acad. Scis. Conservative. Lutheran. Home: Ranvik, 6460 Eidsvaag Norway

HARTNELL, GEORGE GORDON, radiologist; b. Oxford, Eng., July 19, 1952; came to U.S., 1991; s. Francis George and Margaret Eileen Hartnell. BSc in Anatomy, U. Bristol, 1973, MB ChB, 1976. Lic. Mass., Md. Intern Can. Red Cross Meml. Hosp., Taplow, Bucks, Eng., 1976-77, St. Martin's Hosp., Bath, Avon, Eng., 1977; resident Can. Red Cross Meml. Hosp., Taplow, 1978-79; registrar Harefield (Eng.) Hosp., Middlesex, 1979-81, West Middlesex U. Hosp., Isleworth, Eng., 1981-83; resident radiology Hammersmith Hosp., London, 1983-85, sr. registrar, 1985-87; lectr., cons. U. Bristol, Eng., 1987-90; dir. cardiac radiology Deaconess Hosp., Boston, 1991-93, dir. cardiovasc. and interventional radiology, 1994-96; dir. cardiovasc. and interventional radiology Beth Israel Deaconess Med. Ctr., Boston, 1996-98, Baystate Med. Ctr., Springfield, Mass., 2000—; assoc. prof. radiology Harvard Med. Sch., Boston, 1991-98; assoc. dir. CDVL Johns Hopkins Hosp., dir. cardiovascular MRI, 1998-2000; assoc. prof. radiology Johns Hopkins U. Med. Sch., 1998-2000; dir. cardiovascular interventional radiology Baystate Medical Ctr., Springfield, Mass. Author: Film Viewing—Cardiovascular System, 1990; editor: (with others) SCVIR Syllabus 8: Noninvasive vascular imaging with ultrasound, computed tomography and magnetic resonance, 1997; contbr. over 400 sci. publs. and rev. articles on cardiovasc. imaging. Grantee Johns Hopkins Hosp. and Alexandria Hosp., 1985, Bristol and Weston Health Authority, 1989, 90, Cordis Ltd., 1989. Fellow Royal Coll. Radiologists, Cardiovascular and Interventional Soc. Europe, Am. Coll. Cardiology, Am. Heart Assn. (Coun. on Cardiovascular Radiology), Soc. Cardiovascular and Interventional Radiology; mem. Royal Coll. Physicians of U.K., N.Am. Soc. Cardiac Imaging, Assn. Univ. Radiologists, Brit. Inst. Radiology, Brit. Med. Assn., Radiol. Soc. N.Am. Office: Baystate Medical Ctr Dept Radiology Chestnut St Springfield MA 01101

HARTNETT, MAURICE A., III, state supreme court justice; b. Dover, Del., Jan. 20, 1927; s. Maurice and Anna Louise (Morris) H.; m. Elizabeth Anne Hutchinson, Aug. 21, 1965; 1 child, Anne Elizabeth. Student, Washington Coll.-Chestertown, Md., 1946-47; BS, U. Del.-Newark, 1951; postgrad., Georgetown U., 1951; JD, George Washington U., 1954; EdM, U. Del., 1956. Bar: Del. 1954, U.S. Dist. Ct. Del. 1957, U.S. Supreme Ct. 1959. Pvt. practice law Dover, Del., 1955-76; exec. dir. Del. Legis. Ref. bur., Dover, 1961-69; vice chancellor Del. Ct. Chancery, Dover, 1976-94; justice Del. Supreme Ct., 1994—; code revisor Del. Rev. Code Commn., 1961-72; commr. Nat. Conf. Com. Uniform State Laws, Chgo., 1962—, sec., exec. com., 1977-83; chmn. State Tax Appeal Bd., Wilmington, Del., 1973-76. Served with U.S. Army, 1945-46. Mem. ABA, Del. Bar Assn., Kent County Bar Assn. (pres. 1974), Am. Law Inst. Democrat. Home: 144 Cooper Rd Dover DE 19901-4926 Office: Del Supreme Court 55 The Grn Dover DE 19901-3611

HARTNETT, THOMAS ROBERT, III, lawyer, author; b. Sioux City, Iowa, July 19, 1920; s. Thomas R. and Florence Mary (Graves) H.; m. Betty Jeanne Dobbins, Mar. 3, 1943; children: Thomas Robert Joseph, Jeanine Elizabeth, Dennis Edward, Glenn Michael. Student, Trinity Coll., 1937-39; LLB, U. So. Calif., 1948. Bar: Tex. 1948, U.S. Dist. Ct. (no. dist.) Tex., 1949, U.S. Ct. Appeasl (5th cir.) 1954, (10th cir.) 1955, (11th cir.) 1983, U.S. Supreme Ct., 1957. Pvt. practice Dallas, 1948-88; of counsel Hartnett Law Firm, Dallas, 1988—. Author: The Root of the Whys-On the Internet, 1998. With USAAF, 1939-45. Mem. State Bar Tex., Dallas Bar Assn. Republican. Roman Catholic. Home: 5074 Matilda St Apt 224 Dallas TX 75206-4268 Office: 4900 Thanksgiving Tower 1601 Elm St Dallas TX 75201-7254

HARTNETT, WILL FORD, lawyer; b. Austin, Tex., June 3, 1956; s. James Joseph and Emily (High) H.; m. Tammy Lynn Cotton, Dec. 7, 1996; 1 child, Will. BA, Harvard U., 1978; JD, U. Tex., 1981. Bar: Tex. 1981, U.S. Ct. Appeals (5th cir.) 1985, U.S. Supreme Ct. 1985; cert. in Estate Planning and Probate Law Tex. Bd. Legal Specialization. Assoc. Turner & Hitchins, Dallas, 1981-82; ptnr. The Hartnett Law Firm, Dallas, 1982—; bd. dirs. Tex. Guaranteed Student Loan Corp., Austin, 1987-90. Co-author: Annual Survey of Wills and Trusts, 1986. Mem. Tex. Ho. of Reps., 1991—; vice-chmn. House Jud. Affairs Com., 1995—. Fellow Am. Coll. Trust and Estate Coun., Tex. Bar Found.; mem. SAR, Dallas Bar Assn., Mensa, Harvard Club Dallas (bd. dirs., treas. 1983-95), Rotary. Republican. Roman Catholic. Home: 4722 Walnut Hill Ln Dallas TX 75229-6354 Office: The Hartnett Law Firm 4900 Thanksgiving Tower Dallas TX 75201

HARTOUGH, HOWARD DALE, JR., pharmaceutical company executive; b. Phila., Dec. 10, 1943; s. Howard Dale and Cornelia (Tysse) H.; m. Pamela Hibbitt, June 9, 1969; children: Hugh, Lynn. BChemE, Ga. Inst. of Tech., 1966; MBA, U. Utah, 1975. Plant engr. Degussa, Frankfurt, Germany, 1966-70; sr. cons. Divo Inmar GmbH, Frankfurt, 1971-75; comml. devel. specialist Dart Industries Inc., Paramus, N.J., 1975-79; mgr. worldwide mktg. rsch. Borg Warner Chems., Parkersburg, W.Va., 1979-88; dir. bus. devel. Chemfirst Inc., Jackson, Miss., 1988-92; mgr. bus. devel. Catalytica Inc., Mountain View, Calif., 1992-97; dir. purchasing Catalytica Pharmas. Inc., Greenville, N.C., 1997—. Mem. Town coun., North Hills, W.Va., 1988; chmn. Friends of W.Va. Pub. Radio, Charleston, 1988; founder, chmn. Artsbridge Inc., Parkersburg, 1986; pres., founder East Carolina Jr. Volleyball Club, Greenville, 1999. Mem. Nat. Assn. Purchasing Mgmt., Comml. Devel. and Mktg. Assn., Lic. Exec. Soc. Episcopalian. Avocations: genealogy, coin collecting, golf. Office: Catalytica Pharmas Inc Intersection of US 264 and US 13 Greenville NC 27834

HARTQUIST, THOMAS WILBUR, astrophysicist; b. Redwood City, Calif., May 3, 1954; arrived in Eng., 1998; s. John N. and Ethel M. (Burke) H. BA, Rice U., Houston, 1974; AM, Harvard U., 1975, PhD, 1978. Postdoctoral rsch. asst. Harvard-Smithsonian Ctr. Astrophysics, Cambridge, Mass., 1978-79; postdoctoral rsch. fellow dept. physics and astronomy U. Coll. London, 1979-80; rsch. scientist Max Planck Inst. Astrophysics, Garching, Germany, 1980; Royal Soc. Jaffé Donation fellow dept. physics and astronomy U. Coll. London, 1980-83; asst. prof. astronomy dept. physics and astronomy U. Md., College Park, 1983-84; sr. rsch. scientist Max Planck Inst. extraterrestrische Physics, Garching, Germany, 1985-98; lectr. dept. physics and astronomy U. Leeds, Eng., 1998-99, reader dept. physics and astronomy, 1999-2000, prof. astrophysics, dept. physics and astronomy, 2000—. Editor: Molecular Astrophysics, 1990, (with A.J. Willis) Astrophysical and Laboratory Plasmas, 1996, (with D.A. Williams) The Molecular Astrophysics of Stars and Galaxies, 1998; author: (with D.A. Williams) The Chemically Controlled Cosmos, 1995; contbr. articles to profl. jours. Bart J. Bok prize lectr. Harvard U. dept. astronomy, Cambridge, Mass., 1987; hon. mem. Robin Bluebeard Page Class at Munich Art Acad., 1995-98. Office: U Leeds, Dept Physics & Astronomy, Leeds LS2 9JT, England

HARTSHORNE, TIMOTHY SCOTFORD, psychology educator; b. Oneida, N.Y., Nov. 15, 1948; s. Marion Holmes and Ruth (Scotford) H.; m. Sheila Kyle Berenson (div.); children: Joshua Keiles, Nathan Scotford; m. Nancy Ellen Salem, June 13, 1988; children: Michael David Salem, Jacob Holmes, Katherine Swift, Seth McClellan, Aaron Proctor. BA in Sociology with honors, Grinnell Coll., 1970; MA in Counseling and Guidance cum laude, Colgate U., 1973; PhD in Ednl. Psychology, U. Tex., 1979. Cert. sch. psychologist, Kans., nat.; registered profl. counselor, Kans.; nat. cert. counselor. Psychiat. technician Broadlawn Hosp., Des Moines, 1970-72; dir. guidance De Sales High Sch., Utica, N.Y., 1973-74; asst. prof. Wichita State U., 1978-89; assoc. prof. psychology Cen. Mich. U., 1989-97, prof. psychology, 1997—, dept. chair, 1995—; part-time instr. Austin (Tex.) Community Coll., 1977-79; vis. lectr. Pitts. State U., 1986, 92, 93; test field coord. Am Guidance Svc., Inc., 1978-79, Charles E. Merrill Pub. Co., 1984; cons. Keystone Area Edn. Agy., Elkader, Iowa, Cedarvale Adolescent Treatment Unit, 1989; chair Gov. State of Kans. Conf. on Edn. for Parenthood, 1982; mem. Commn. on Edn. for Parenthood, 1982-89; mem. adv. com. Kans. State Network, 1983; mem. test evaluation com. Wichita Pub. Schs., 1986-87; vis. rsch. fellow Renwick Coll., Sydney, Australia, 1996. Author: Ethics and Law for School Psychologists, 1991, 3rd edit., 1998; (with others) Best Practices in School Psychology, 1985, Children's Needs: Psychological Perspectives, 1987; contbr. articles to profl. jours. Bd. dirs. Wichita Youth Home, 1979-82; founder Parenting Edn. Network, 1982; coord. Mid-Mich. chpt. The Compassionate Friends, 1998—. Named Outstanding Young Man Am. U.S. Jaycees, 1981; NIMH traineeship, 1974-75. Mem. AACD, Am. Psychol. Assn., Nat. Assn. Sch. Psychologists (state del. 1982-85, regional dir. 1985-89), Am. Edn. Rsch. Assn., N.Am. Soc. Adlerian Psychology. Democrat. Avocations: family history, travel, creative writing. Home: 918 S Brown St Mount Pleasant MI 48858-3608 Office: Cen Mich U Psychology Dept Mount Pleasant MI 48859

HARTWELL, LELAND HARRISON, geneticist, educator; b. Los Angeles, Oct. 30, 1939; s. Majorie (Taylor) H.; m. Theresa Naujack. BS, Calif. Inst. Tech., 1961; PhD, MIT, 1964. Postdoctoral fellow Salk Inst., 1964-65; asst. prof. U. Calif., Irvine, 1965-67, assoc. prof., 1967-68; assoc. prof. U. Washington, Seattle, 1968-73, prof., 1973—; pres., dir. Fred Hutchison Cancer Rsch. Ctr., Seattle, 1997—; rsch. prof. Am. Cancer Soc., 1990—. Recipient Eli Lilly award, 1973, NIH Merit award, 1990, GM Sloan award, 1991, Hoffman LaRoche Mattia award, 1991, Gairdner Found. Internat. award, 1992, Simon Shubitz award U. Chgo., 1992, Brandeis U. Rosenstiel award, 1993, Sloan Kettering Cancer Ctr. Katherine Berkan Judd award, 1994, Genetics Soc. of Am. medal, 1994, MGH Warren Triennial prize, 1995, Keith Porter award Am. Soc. Cell Biology, 1995, Carnegie Mellon Dickson award, 1996, Louisa Gross Horwitz prize Columbia U., 1995, Albert Lasker Basic Med. Rsch. award Albert and Mary Lasker Found., 1998, Brinker Internat. award for basic sci. Susan G. Komen Breast Cancer Found., 1998, Disting. Alumni award Calif. Inst. Tech., 1999, City of Medicine award, 1999, medal of honor Am. Cancer Soc., 1999; Guggenheim fellow, 1983-84; Am. Bus. Cancer Rsch. grantee, 1983—; Am. Cancer Soc. scholar; laureate Passano Found., 1996. Mem. NAS, AAAS, Am. Soc. Microbiology, Am. Soc. Cell Biology, Genetics Soc. Am. (pres. 1990). Office: Fred Hutchinson Cancer Rsch Ctr 1100 Fairview Ave N Seattle WA 98109-4417*

HARTZ, STEVEN EDWARD MARSHALL, lawyer, educator; b. Cambridge, Mass., July 11, 1948; s. Louis and Stella (Feinberg) H.; m. Janice Lindsay, June 12, 1976. A.B. magna cum laude, Harvard Coll., 1970; J.D. U. Chgo., 1974. Bar: N.Y. 1975, U.S. Dist. Ct. (so. and ea. dists.) N.Y. 1975, Fla. 1979, U.S. Dist. Ct. (so. dist.) Fla. 1979, U.S. Ct. Appeals (2d cir.) 1975, U.S. Tax Ct. 1979, U.S. Ct. Appeals (5th cir.) 1979, U.S. Ct. Appeals (11th cir.) 1981, U.S. Supreme Ct. 1979, U.S. Dist. Ct. (mid. dist.) Fla. 1984. Assoc. Cleary, Gottlieb, Steen & Hamilton, N.Y.C., 1974-79; asst. U.S. atty. U.S. Dept. Justice, Miami, Fla., 1979-82, dep. chief criminal div., chief fraud and pub. corruption sect. 1981-82; sole practice, Miami, Fla., 1982-90; of counsel Akerman, Senterfitt & Eidson, P.A., Miami, 1980, ptnr./shareholder, 1991—; lectr. dept. English, U. Miami 1984, adj. assoc. prof., 1985-86. Co-author: Housing, A Community Handbook, 1973. Vol. atty. M.F.Y. Legal Services, N.Y.C., 1978. Recipient Dirs.' award U.S. Dept. Justice, 1981; Fulbright Hays scholar, 1970. Mem. ABA, Fla. Bar, Assn. Bar City N.Y., N.Y. State Bar Assn., Fed. Bar Assn., Dade County Bar Assn., Nat. Assn. Criminal Def. Lawyers, Phi Beta Kappa. Office: One Southeast 3rd Ave 28th Fl Miami FL 33131-4943

HARTZELL, IRENE JANOFSKY, psychologist; d. Leonard S. and Annelies Janofsky; 1 child, Mark Adam. BA, U. Calif., Berkeley, 1963, MA, 1965; PhD, U. Oreg., 1970. Lic. psychologist, Wash. Psychologist Lake Washington Sch. Dist., Kirkland, Wash., 1971-72; staff psychologist VA Med. Ctr., Seattle, 1970-71, Long Beach, Calif., 1973-74; dir. parent edn. Children's Hosp., Orange, Calif., 1975-78; clin. psychologist Kaiser Permanente, Woodland Hills, Calif., 1979-94; clin. instr. pediats. U. Calif. Irvine Coll. Medicine, 1975-78. Author: The Study Skills Advantage, 1986; contbr. articles to profl. jours. Intern Oreg. Legis., 1974-75. U.S. Vocat. Rehab. Adminstrn. fellow U. Oreg., 1966-67, 69. Mem. APA, Pi Lambda Theta.

HARUTA, HISAYOSHI, economist, educator, consultant company executive; b. Shizuoka, Japan, Feb. 14, 1943; s. Yukio Hamada and Toshi Haruta; m. Setsuko Ohara, Mar. 15, 1971; children: Masato, Takeru. BA, Tokyo U., 1966, PhD, 1991; MA, U. Pa., 1971. Chief policies and planning sect. UN Commn. Human Settlements, Nairobi, 1980-82; chief govt. Office Trade Ombudsman, Tokyo, 1983; chief economist Japan Ctr. Econ. Rsch., Tokyo, 1983-85; chief internat. affairs sect. Econ. Planning Agy., Tokyo, 1985-87, dir. nat. acctg., 1989-91; dir. planning divsn. Nat. Land Agy., Tokyo, 1987-89; dir. small bus. adminstrn. Ministry of Industry and Trade, Tokyo, 1991-92; prof. Nagoya (Japan) U., 1992-95; pres. Avant Assocs. Inc., Tokyo,

1995—; prof. Grad. Sch. Bus. Adminstrn. Tama U., Tokyo, 1999—; vis. prof. Grad. Sch. Internat. Devel. Nagoya U., 1999; internat. trade netotiator Econ. Planning Agy., 1985-87; chmn. Nagoya Regional Office Japan Archtl. Inst., 1995-96; vis. prof. Grad. Sch. Internat. Devel. Nagoya U., 1999. Author: Urbanization and Social Change, 1995 (Ministry of Edn. grant 1994); co-author: Political Theory and Public Policies, 1998; dir. book: Global Report on Human Settlements, 1987 (UN grant). Advisor com. on nat. devel. plan Prime Min.'s Office, Tokyo, 1996-99; advisor com. on environ. impact assessment act Environ. Agy., Tokyo, 1994-96; chmn. City Ctr. Renewal Commn., Nagoya Mcpl. Govt., 1994-95. Ford Found. scholar, 1969; UNESCO grantee, 1984. Mem. Am. Econ. Assn. Zen Buddhist. Home: 2-3-2 Mejirodai Bunkyo-ku, Tokyo 1120015, Japan Office: 2-1-5 Shibuya Shibuya-ku, Tokyo 1500002, Japan

HARVAN, SEAN C., marketing executive; b. Monsey, N.Y., Nov. 25, 1970. BS in Polit. Sci., Ariz. State U., 1993. Devel. officer, dir. prospect rsch. The Rockefeller U., N.Y.C., 1994-96; project dir. Interpub. Group of Cos., Inc., N.Y.C., 1997-98, McCann Erickson, Tokyo, 1999—; cons. Asahi Breweries Ltd., Tokyo, 1999—. Republican. E-mail: sean harvan@japan.mccann.com. Home: 4-5-32 Minami Azabu, Minato-ku, Tokyo 106-0047, Japan Office: Shin Aoyama Bldg East, 1-1-1 Minami-Aoyama, Tokyo 107-8679, Japan

HARVEY, ANDRE, sculptor; b. Hollywood, Fla., Oct. 9, 1941; s. Edmund H. and Jeanne C. (Bright) H.; m. Roberta R. Rush, Jan. 12, 1964. BA, U. Va., 1963. Sculptor Rockland, Del., 1971—. Exhbns. include: Images of Am. Exhbn., Moscow, London, Paris, The Internat. Ctr. for Wildlife Art, Gloucester, U.K., Nat. Sculpture Soc., N.Y.C., NSS Port of History Mus., Phila., Nat. Acad. of Design, N.Y.C., Tiffany & Co., N.Y.C., Nat. Audubon Soc., N.Y.C., Hunter Mus., Chattanooga, Brandywine River Mus., Chadds Ford, Pa., Gibbes Art Gallery, Charleston, S.C., Phila. Flower Show, Longwood Gardens, Kennett Square, Pa., Contemporary Sculpture at Chesterwood, Stockbridge, Mass., Palazzo Mediceo, Seravezza, Italy, others; selected pub. collections include: The Frederik Meijer Gardens, Grand Rapids, Mich., Brandywine River Mus., Chadds Ford, Pa., Botanic Garden Ctr. & Conservatory, Ft. Worth, Tex., MBNA Am., Wilmington, Del., Nature in Art Trust, Gloucester, U.K., U. Va., Charlottesville, Del. Art Mus., Wilmington, Greenville Mus., S.C., The Jockey Club, Washington, Crown Controls Corp., New Bremen, Ohio, others; specific bronze sculptures include: The Sunbathers, Gamecock: Floyd's Finest, The Phoenix, First Light, Helen, Chloe and Lucinda, Scent of Honeysuckle, Water's Edge, Morning Glory, others. Recipient Joel Meissner award Nat. Sculpture Soc., N.Y.C., 1980, Tallix Foundry award, 1989. Fellow Nat. Sculpture Soc.; mem. Nature in Art Trust, Artist's Equity, Internat. Sculpture Ctr. Avocation: automobile preservation. Home: PO Box 8 Rockland DE 19732-0008

HARVEY, CYNTHIA, ballet dancer; b. San Rafael, Calif.; m. Chris Murphy, 1990. Studied with Christine Walton, The Novato Sch. Ballet; student, San Francisco Ballet Sch., Marin Ballet Sch., Sch. Am. Ballet Theatre, N.Y.C., Am. Ballet Theatre Sch., N.Y.C., Nat. Ballet Sch. Can., Toronto. With Am. Ballet Theatre, N.Y.C., 1974, soloist, 1978-82, prin. dancer, 1982-86, 1988—; prin. dancer Royal Ballet, London, 1986-88; artistic coord. Am. Ballet Theatre Summer Intensives; guest tchr. worldwide; guest artist The Royal Ballet, The Birmingham Royal Ballet, Stuttgart Ballet. Creator: role of Gamzatti in La Bayadere; appeared in Swan Lake, Don Quixote, Sleeping Beauty, Giselle, Raymonda, Ballet Imperial, Coppelia, Etudes, Manon, Romeo and Juliet, La Sylphide, Les Sylphides, Symphony Concertante, Symphonic variations, Theme and Variations. Recipient John Anthony Bitson award, 1973. Office: care Am Ballet Theatre 890 Broadway 3rd Fl New York NY 10003*

HARVEY, DIANA KARANIKAS, writer; b. Chgo.; d. Alexander and Helen Karanikas; m. Jackson Harvey, June 13, 1992. BA, Northwestern U.; MFA, Am. Film Inst. Hollywood historian various t.v. documentaries. Author: Marilyn Monroe, 1999; co-author: (with J. Harvey) Dead Before Their Time, 1996, Neil Diamond, 1996, Barbra Streisand, 1997, Katharine Hepburn, 1998; creator, co-exec. prodr. Serious Moonlight, 1999; prodr. stage plays; appeared in numerous stage plays and motion pictures. Co-founder Artists in Action, L.A. Mem. SAG, Actors Equity Assn., Writers Guild Am. West. Office: c/o Original Artists 9465 Wilshire Blvd # 340 Beverly Hills CA 90212-2612

HARVEY, GLORIA-STROUD, physician assistant; b. Washington, D.C., Apr. 16; d. Robert W. and Ruth Elizabeth (Brown) Stroud; m. Jimmy Lawrence Harvey; children: Dana, Daman, Byron, Justin. BS, U. Md., 1968; physician asst. cert., Howard U., 1977. Physician asst. Weaver Clinic, Ahoskie, N.C., 1977-80, Western State Hosp., Staunton, Va., 1980-84, Walter Reed Army Med. Ctr., Washington, 1984-91, John Amsted Hosp., Butner, N.C., 1991—, U. N.C., Chapel Hill, 1991—; physician asst. Aroyga, Durham, N.C., 1992—, Maria Parham Hosp., Henderson, N.C. Bd. dirs. Unique Builders, Henderson N.C., 1994-95, Cultural Initiatives, 1995. Mem. Am. Bus. Women's Assn., N.C. State-Employed Physician Assts.' Assn. (chmn. 1994), Triangle Assn. for Physician Assts., N.C. Assn. for Physician Assts. Methodist. Home: 2693 Hidden Spring Ln Oxford NC 27565-6146

HARVEY, JACQUELINE MARY MELROSE, health facility administrator; b. Brisbane, Australia, July 14, 1968; d. Maxwell Melrose Harvey and Mary Yvonne (Ford) Fereday. BE, James Cook U., Townsville, Australia, 1989; grad. diploma in libr. sci., Queensland U. Tech., Brisbane, 1992, MEd, 1998, grad. cert. mgmt., 1999. Tchr. Innisfail (Australia) H.S., 1990-91; med. rsch. officer Mater Hosps., Brisbane, 1993-97, spl. projects officer, 1998—. Contbr. articles on early human devel. to profl. jours. Mem. Australian Inst. Mgmt. Avocations: swimming, photography, painting, reading.

HARVEY, JOHN ARTHUR, nuclear physicist; b. Saskatoon, Sask., Can., Dec. 14, 1921; naturalized U.S. citizen; married; 2 children. BSc, Queen's U., Ont., Can., 1945; PhD in Physics, MIT, 1950. Physicist Atomic Energy Can., Ltd., 1945-46; rsch. asst. MIT, 1946-50; assoc. physicist Brookhaven Nat. Lab., 1951-55; physicist Oak Ridge Nat. Lab., 1955-93, dir. linear accelerator, 1965-93, retired, 1993, cons., 1993—; rsch. prof. U. Tenn., 1995—. Fellow Am. Phys. Soc. (sec.-treas. divsn. nuc. physics 1966-86). Home: 108 Ogontz Ln Oak Ridge TN 37830-3905 Office: Oak Ridge Nat Lab PO Box 2008 Oak Ridge TN 37831-2008*

HARVEY, JOHN COLLINS, physician, educator; b. Youngstown, Ohio, Sept. 11, 1923; s. J. Paul and Mary J. (Collins) H.; m. Adele Dillon, Nov. 26, 1949; children: Elizabeth V.R. (Mrs. Charles Yon), John Collins Jr., William Charles II, Amy L.R. (Mrs. L. F. Reese), Margaret J.B. (Mrs. Gregory Granitto). Grad., Phillips Exeter Acad., 1941; BS, Yale U., 1944; MD, Johns Hopkins U., 1947, MLA, 1968; MAS, Johns Hopkins, 1974; MA, St. Mary's U., 1975, PhD in Theology, 1988; DSc (hon.), Barry U., 1992. Diplomate: Am. Bd. Internal Medicine. Successively house officer, asst. resident, resident Osler Med. Service, Johns Hopkins Hosp., 1947-53, physician, 1953-73; successively instr., asst. prof., asso. prof., prof. medicine Johns Hopkins, 1953-73; prof. medicine Georgetown U., Washington, 1973-89, prof. medicine emeritus, 1989—; sr. rsch. scholar Kennedy Inst. of Ethics, Georgetown U., Washington, 1989—, Ctr. for Clin. Bioethics, Georgetown Med. Ctr., 1993—; Vis. prof. medicine U. Ibadan, Nigeria, 1964; hon. assoc. prof. medicine Guy's Hosp., London, 1973. Co-editor: Catholic Perspectives on Medical Morals, Catholic Studies in Bioethics; Contbr. articles to profl. publs. Mem. various local, state and nat. govt. med. adv. coms.; trustee Washington Home for Incurables; mem. med. adv. com. Sacred Congregation for Causes of Saints, Holy See, Vatican City. Col. (ret.) M.C., USAR. A. Blaine Brower Traveling fellow ACP to Guy's Hosp. London, 1956; sr. scholar Kennedy Inst. Ethics, Georgetown U., 1973-89. Fellow ACP (master), APHA; mem. AAAS, AMA, Am. Clin. and Climatol. Assn., Biophys. Soc., Johns Hopkins Soc. Scholars, Peripatetic Club, Tudor and Stuart Club (Balt.), Yale Club (N.Y.C.), Chevy Chase Club, Cosmos Club, Knights of St. Gregory, Knights of Malta, Phi Beta Kappa, Sigma Xi, Alpha Omega Alpha. Republican. Roman Catholic. Home: 12610 Three Sisters Rd Potomac MD 20854-6359 Office: Georgetown U Med Ctr Bldg D Ctr Clin Bioethics Rm 234 4000 Reservoir Rd NW Washington DC 20007-2145

HARVEY, KAREN L., professional organization administrator. MSN, U. Colo., Denver, 1977. Dir. edn. Assn. Profls. in Infection Control and Epidemiology, Inc., Washington, 1995—. Musician (CD) Kairos: Spirits' Time, 1999. Address: Assn Profls in Infection Control and Epidemiology Inc 1275 K St NW Ste 1000 Washington DC 20005-4006

HARVEY, MORRIS LANE, lawyer; b. Madisonville, Ky., Apr. 22, 1950; s. Morris Lee and Margie Lou (Wallace) H.; m. Mary Topel; children: Morris Lane Jr., John French, Laura Kathleen. BS, Murray State U., 1972; JD, U. Ky., 1974. Bar: Ill. 1975, U.S. Dist. Ct. (so. dist.) 1979. Assoc. Hanagan & Dousman, Mt. Vernon, Ill., 1975-77; ptnr. Feiger, Quindry, Molt & Harvey and successor firms, Fairfield, Ill., 1977-85; sole practice Fairfield, 1986-97, Mt. Vernon, 1997—; instr. Frontier C.C., Fairfield, 1977-79; spl. asst. atty. gen. State of Ill., Fairfield, 1977-82; Ill. pres. Woodman of World Life Inst. Soc., 1985-87; mem. nat. fraternal com., 1987-89, nat. legis. com., 1989-93, nat. jud. com., 1993-97. Recipient Outstanding Young Man Am. U.S. Jaycees, 1978, 81, 89. Mem. ABA, Ill. Bar Assn., Assn. Trial Lawyers Am., Ill. Trial Lawyers Assn., Am. Judicature Soc. Home: 5 Webster Hill Est Mount Vernon IL 62864-2346 Office: 2029 Broadway St Mount Vernon IL 62864-2910

HARVEY, PATRICIA JEAN, special education administrator, retired; b. Newman, Calif., Oct. 27, 1931; d. Willard Monroe and Marjorie (Greenlee) Clougher; m. Richard Blake Harvey, Aug. 29, 1965; children: G. Scott Floden, Timothy P. BA, Whittier Coll., 1966, MA, 1971. Resource specialist Monte Vista High Sch. and Whittier (Calif.) High Sch., 1977-98; dept. chair spl. edn. Whittier (Calif.) High Sch., 1982-94; ret., 1998. Author: (tchrs. manual) The Dynamics of California Government and Politics, 1970, 90; co-author: Meeting The Needs of Special High School Students in Regular Education Classrooms, 1988. Active Whittier Fair Housing Com., 1972; pres. Women's Aux. Whittier Coll., 1972-73, sec., 1971-72; historian Docian Soc. Whittier Coll., 1963-64, pres. 1965-66. Democrat. Episcopalian. Home: 424 E Avocado Crest Rd La Habra CA 90631-8128 Office: The Learning Advantage Ctr 13710 Whittier Blvd Ste 206 Whittier CA 90605-4407

HARVEY, PETER MARSHALL, podiatrist; b. Lubbock, Tex., Nov. 12, 1941; s. Marshall and Betty (Compton) H.; BS, Tex. Tech. U., 1962; grad. Ill. Coll. Podiatric Medicine, 1966; m. Sue Kadane, Feb. 1, 1981; children by previous marriage—Jason, Jacob; stepchildren—Chris Robertson, Jill Robertson, Brent Robertson; m. Debby Williams, 1997; 1 stepchild, Cameron Rodriguez. Intern, Community Hosp., Lubbock, Tex., 1966-67; practice podiatry specializing in foot surgery, Wichita Falls, Tex., 1967—; bd. dirs. Podiatry Ins. Co. Am. Mem. Am. Podiatric Med. Assn. (Tex. del. to ho. of dels. 1985—), Tex. Podiatry Med. Assn. (dir. 1975—, pres. 1982-83, Svc. award 1978), Am. Coll. Foot and Ankle Surgeons (assoc.). PICA (chmn. claims com. 1984—). Republican. Fax: 940-723-4646. E-mail: mharvey@cyberstation.net. Office: 1612 10th St Wichita Falls TX 76301-4390

HARVEY, RONALD K., writer, researcher; b. Kearney, Neb., July 17, 1945; s. Clinton L. and Hazel R. (Perkins) H. AA in Radio and TV, City Coll. of San Francisco, 1973; BA in Broadcasting Comms. (cum laude), San Francisco State U., 1975. Bus. analyst Dun & Bradstreet, Inc., Omaha, San Francisco, 1968-70; teaching asst. in radio & TV City Coll. of San Francisco, 1971-74; dir. vets. counseling office Associated Students SFSU, 1973-95; news and pub. affairs producer KPFA Berkeley, 1973-84; writer, rschr. Pacific Rsch., 1984—; dir. Vets. Peace Com., San Francisco, 1973-75; program dir. Campus Radio Station, Kearney, Nebr., 1968. Author: Poems With No Judgement, 1986, Short Stories, 1980, Children's Stories, 1984, (screenplay) Pray for Peace, 1987; writer: The Road to Wounded, 1973, Studies in Space Law, 2000. Recipient George Washington Honor medal Valley Forge Found., 1966. Mem. Am. Heritage Soc. E-mail: rh22222222@aol.com. Home and Office: Fill This Out 5380 W 78th Pl Apt 8 Arvada CO 80003-2638

HARVEY, SUSAN, company executive; b. Harpenden, Eng., July 3, 1943; d. Gordon and Dorothy Bailey (Rudd) Bone; m. Robin John Harvey, July 3, 1971 (div. 1999); 1 child, Tom. MA with honors, Edinburgh (Scotland) U., 1968; diploma in conf. interpreting, London, 1971. Sec. gen. 1976 World Orienteering Championships, 1974-76; mng. dir. Harvey Map Svcs. Ltd., Doune, Scotland, 1977—; bd dirs. Alt. Outdoors, Scotland, 1990-2000, McLaren Cmty. Leisure Centre Ltd., 1999—; convennor Doune and Deanston Cmty. Futures Steering Group, 1999—. Bd. dirs. Countryside Commn. for Scotland, 1988-92, Scottish Alliance for Women's Tng., 1991-94, Rural Stirling Partnership, Scotland, 1992-96, S.E. region Scottish Natural Heritage, 1992-96. Mem. Scottish Orienteering Assn. (pres. 1979-80), Internat. Orienteering Fedn. (pres. 1994—, Silver Pin of Honor 1990), Internat. Masters Games Assn. (mem. bd. govs. 1995—). Avocations: gardening, carpentry, walking, guitar, orienteering. Home: Mile End, FK16 6BJ Doune Perthshr, Scotland Office: Harvey Map Svcs Ltd, 12-16 Main St, FK16 6BJ Doune Scotland

HARVIN, CHARLES ALEXANDER, III, state legislator, lawyer; b. Sumter, S.C., Feb. 7, 1950; s. Charles Alexander Harvin, Jr. m. Cathy Jane Brand; 1 child, Mary Franklin; Grad. in history and polit. sci. Baptist Coll., Charleston, S.C., 1972, Augusta Law Sch., 1976; hon. degree Sherman Chiropractic Coll., Spartanburg, S.C., 1979, Francis Marion Coll., 1986; LLD (hon.) Charleston So. Univ., 1988. Mem. S.C. Ho. of Reps., 1976—, asst. majority leader, majority whip, 1978-82, majority leader, 1982—, mem. ways and means com., vice chmn. rules com., majority leader Emeritus Ho. of Reps., S.C., 1987—. Pres. Bapt. Coll. Young Dems., 1970-72; officer Charleston County Young Dems., 1971-72; chmn. 6th Congl. Dist. Young Dems., 1975-76; life mem. S.C. Young Dems.; chmn. Clarendon County Dem. Com.; vice chmn. S.C. Dem. Com., 1976-78, also mem. exec. com.; del. Dem. Nat. Conv., 1984; mem. S.C. Gov.'s Agr. Study Com.; U.S. Constn. Bicentennial Commn., 1985—; trustee S.C. Hall of Fame; vice chmn. alumni bd. Bapt. Coll., 1975-76; bd. visitors Clemson U., 1977-78,.Med. Univ. S.C., 1986-87, Charleston So. Univ., 1988-90. Maj. USNG. Recipient Outstanding Service award Charleston County Young Dems., 1972, S.C. Young Dems., 1977; Disting. Service award S.C. Dem. Com., 1981; appreciation award S.C. Tech. Edn. Colls., 1981; Legislator of Yr. award S.C. Young Dems., 1982, S.C. Student Legislature, 1981, S.C. State Library Bd., 1982, S.C. Assn. for Deaf, 1985; award S.C. Coun. for Exceptional Children, 1982, S.C. Agrl. Cmty., 1982; Outstanding Legislator Service award United Parcel Svc., 1984; Disting. Svc. award Bapt. Coll. of Charleston Alumni Assn., 1984, also numerous other awards and commendations. Mem. ABA, Am. Judicature Soc., S.C. Trial Lawyers Assn., Clarendon County Farm Bur., Clarendon County Hist. Soc. (v.p. 1983-84, pres. 1985-86), S.C. State Employees Assn., NAACP, Huguenot Soc. of S.C., First Families of S.C., Alpha Phi Omega (life). Lodges: Masons, Shriners. Office: South Carolina Ho of Reps PO Box 11867 Columbia SC 29211-1867

HARVITT, ADRIANNE STANLEY, lawyer; b. Chgo., May 15, 1954; d. Stanley and Maryln (Loye) H.; m. Donald Martin Heinrich, Aug. 27, 1977; children: Patrick Loye, Christina Marie. AB, U. Chgo., 1975, MBA, 1976; JD with honors, Ill. Inst. Tech., 1980. Bar: Ill. 1980, U.S. Dist. Ct. (no. dist.) Ill. 1980, U.S. Ct. Appeals (7th cir.) 1985, (9th cir.) 1988, U.S. Supreme Ct. 1985, Wis. 1993. Fin. analyst Bell & Howell Co., Chgo., 1976-77; trial atty. U.S. Commodity Futures Trading Commn., Chgo., 1980-83; assoc. Hannafan & Handler, Chgo., 1983-85; ptnr. Harvitt & Gekas, Ltd., Chgo., 1985-97, Harvitt & Assoc., Ltd., Milw., 1997-98; ptnr. pub. svc. spl. prosecutor Milw. County Dist. Atty.'s Office, 1998; v.p., assoc. gen. counsel Stephens Inc., Little Rock, 1999-2000; adj. prof. securities regulation U. Ark. Sch. of Law, Little Rock, Ark., 1999. Mem. Law Rev. Chgo.-Kent Coll. Law, 1979-80. Mem. ABA, Ill. Bar Assn. (article hon. mention 1982), Chgo. Bar Assn., Assn. Women Lawyers, U. Chgo. Alumni Assn. (svc. citation 1995, bd. govs. 1996-98), U. Chgo. Women's Bus. Group (v.p. 1988-90), U. Chgo. Women's Bd., Art Inst. Chgo. Avocations: skiing, swimming, scuba diving.

HARWOOD, ELEANOR CASH, librarian; b. Buckfield, Maine, May 29, 1921; d. Leon Eugene and Ruth (Chick) Cash; m. Burton H. Harwood, Jr., June 21, 1944 (div. 1953); children: Ruth (Mrs. Wiliam R. Cline), Eleanor, James Burton. BA, Am. Internat. Coll., 1943; BS, New Haven State Tchrs. Coll., 1955. Libr. Rathbun Meml. Libr., East Haddam, Conn., 1955-56; asst. libr. Kent (Conn.) Sch., 1956-63; cons. Chester (Conn.) Pub. Libr., 1965-71. Author: (with John G. Park) The Independent School Library and the Gifted Child, 1956, The Age of Samuel Johnson, LLD, Remember When, 1987, (essay) Growing Up in Chester, 1993, Moosley Yours, 1996. Mem. United Ch. Lt. (j.g.) USNR, 1944-46, WWII. Recipient medal Am. Theater-Victory. Mem. ALA, Conn. Libr. Assn., Chester Hist. Soc. (trustee 1970-72), DAV, Am. Legion, Am. Legion Aux., Soc. Mayflower Descs., Appalachian Mountain Club. Home: 10 Maple St # 255 Chester CT 06412-1316

HASAN, MASOOD, company executive; b. Lucknow, British India, Oct. 13, 1925; s. Said and Nadirah (Ghani) H.; m. Rafia Hakim, Dec. 27, 1953; children: Naveed, Nada. BS with honors, Punjab U., Lahore, 1945, MS with honors, 1946; MS in Chem. Engring., Case Western Res. U., Cleve., 1949; Diploma in Indsl. Tng., Jose. E. Seagram & Sons, Louisville, 1950. Registered chem. engr. Internat. fellow Jos E. Seagram & Sons, Inc., Louisville, 1949-50; mgmt. trainee Unilever, Ltd., U.K., 1950-51; asst. prodn. mgr. Lever Bros. Pakistan, Ltd., 1951-53; dir. Wazirali Industries, Ltd., Pakistan, 1953-64; mng. dir. EWP Computer Svcs., Ltd., Pakistan, 1964-67, United Cons., Ltd., Pakistan, 1967-73; sec. Ministry of Def. Prodn., Govt. of Pakistan, Rawalpindi, 1973-77; chmn. Fed. Mgmt. Devel. and Inspection Commn., Pakistan, 1977-78; mng. dir. Emmay Assocs. Pvt., Ltd., Lahore, 1978—. Pres. Chand Bagh Found., Lahore, 1986—, Engring. Cons. Assn. of Pakistan, Lahore, 1990—. Fellow Pakistan Inst. of Chem. Engrs., Instn. of Engrs.; mem. (emeritus) Am. Inst. Chem. Engrs., Am. Chem. Soc. Avocations: writing, reading. E-mail: emmay@brain.net.pk. Office: Emmay Assocs Pvt Ltd, 90 B6 Canal Park Gulberg 2, 54660 Lahore/Panjab 54660, Pakistan

HASAN, SARAH, editor; b. Kuwait, Kuwait, Feb. 11, 1971; came to U.S., 1990; d. Mohammed Farhatullah and Munira Iqbal Sayeed; m. Kamran Hasan, Aug. 21, 1993; children: Yusrah D., Imaan D., Dunya D. BA in Polit. Sci./Econs./Internat. Study, So. Meth. U., 1995. Project mgr., client svcs. mgr., pub. co. profiles Nasser-Norsig & Assocs., Dallas, 1996-97; beauty cons. Mary Kay Cosmetics, Fairfax, Va., 1998—; editor Internat. Med. Pub., McLean, Va., 1999—. Author: (book) "Rasmein" Family Customs, 2000. Mentor/tchr. Jr. Achievement, Dallas, 1994-95; campaign mgr. Internat. Student Body, Dallas, 1993-95; judge Model UN, Chgo., 1994; active UNICEF. So. Meth. U. scholar, 1993-95. Mem. Internat. Club (v.p. 1993-95), Golden Key, Omicron Delta Epsilon. Muslim. Avocations: interior design, sewing, painting, stamp collecting. Home: 13276 Maple Creek Ln Centreville VA 20120-6108

HASAN BABU, HAFIZ MOHAMMAD, computer engineering educator, researcher; b. Lalpur, Bangladesh, Feb. 10, 1966; s. A.K.M. and Anwara (Begum) Yunus Pramanik; m. Setara Rosion, Oct. 6, 1995. MS in Computer Sci. and Engring., Tech. U. Brno, Czech Republic, 1992; PhD in Computer Sci. & Elecs., Kyushu Inst. Tech., Japan, 2000. Lectr. Microland, Bangladesh, 1992-93; lectr. Khulna U., Bangladesh, 1993-99, asst. prof., 1999—; bd. dirs., cons. Computer Acad., Rangpur, Bangladesh, 1994—; examiner Dhaka U., Bangladesh, 1994-95; rschr. Kyushu Inst. Tech., Japan, 1995-97. Contbr. articles to profl. jours. Vol. tchr. to illiterate Bangladesh Govt., Lalmonirhat, 1982; blood donation participant Rangpur Samity, 1986. Fellow Deutscher Akademischer Austauschdient, Germany, 1995. Mem. IEEE, Bangladesh Computer Soc. (assoc.). Avocations: sightseeing, gardening, table tennis, music, fishing. Home: c/o AKM Yunus Pramanik, Senpara, Rangpur 5400, Bangladesh

HASANOGLU, ALPER, physician, physiologist; b. Istanbul, Turkey, Oct. 26, 1967; s. Serafettin and Faize (Gürsoy) H.; m. Çigdem Ceylan, Apr. 17, 1999. Dr., Cerrahpasa Med. Sch., Istanbul, 1991, Physiology, 1998. Med. diplomate. Emergency dr. State Hosp., Corlu, Turkey, 1991-95; asst. dr. Physiology Inst.-Cerrahpasa, Istanbul, 1995-98, Psychiatrische Uni Poliklinik Kantonhosp., Basel, Switzerland, 1999—. Recipient II prize Türk Fizyolijik Bilimler Dern., 1998. Mem. Soc. Neurosci., Nat. Soc. Epilepsy, N.Y. Acad. Scis. Avocations: psychiatry, neuroscience, poetry, football. Home: Oberer Rheinweg 23, 4058 Basel Switzerland Office: Psychiat Uni Poliklinik, Pepersgraben 4, 4031 Basel Switzerland

HASAPIS, XENOPHON, marketing professional; b. Nicosia, Cyprus, Aug. 1, 1954; s. Christos and Erato (Poullidou) H.; m. Victoria Aphrodite Sakkiadou, July 10, 1993; 1 child, Christos. BS, U. London, 1978, PhD, 1981. Comml. dir. SAP Hellas, Athens, 2000—; brand mgr. Procter & Gamble, Athens, 1981-85; mktg. mgr. Procter & Gamble, Geneva, 1985-87; mktg. dir. Xerox, Athens, 1987-89; client svcs. dir. J.N. Leoussis Advt., Athens, 1989-97; mktg. dir. Papaellinas Mass, Athens, 1997-2000; cons. in field. U. London scholar, 1979-81. Mem. Brit. Inst. Mgmt., Greek Inst. Mgmt. Greek Orthodox. Home: 8 Lordou Vironos, 15127 Athens Greece Office: SAP Hellas SA, 20 Effinidon Str, 17564 Athens Greece

HASCHKE, MICHAEL ROGER, geologist; b. Ravensburg, Germany. BS, U. Wuerzburg, Germany, 1992; MS, SUNY, Albany, 1994; Doctorate, Free U. Berlin, 1999. Science-com Mediatraining, Ravensburg, 1995-96; rsch. asst. Free U. Berlin, 1996-99, postdoctoral fellow, 1999—. Contbr. sci. papers to profl. jours. Recipient postdoctoral stipend Free U. Berlin, 1999; scholar SUNY-Albany, 1994-95; Sigma Xi rsch. grantee, 1994, Benevolent Soc. Rsch. grantee SUNY-Albany, 1994. Mem. Am. Geophys. Union (rschr.). Avocations: sailing, boxing, spinning. Fax: 49 030 7759078. E-mail: mrh@zedat.fu-berlin.de. Home: Absenreuterweg 28, 88213 Ravensburg Germany Office: Tel Aviv U, Dept Geophysics, 69978 Tel Aviv Israel

HASE, MASASHI, physicist, researcher; b. Toyama, Japan, Dec. 20, 1965; s. Hiroshi and Akiko (Yoshida) H.; m. Yukari Matsuo, Feb. 17, 1996. B Engring., U. Tokyo, 1989, M Engring., 1991, D Engring., 1994. Cert. solid state physics, especially, quantum spin sys. Postdoctoral rschr. Dept. Edn., Tokyo, 1994-95, Inst. Phys. and Chem. Rsch., Wako, Japan, 1995-96; rschr. Nat. Rsch. Inst. Metals, Tsukuba, Japan, 1996—; lectr. Sophia U., Tokyo, 1994-95. Contbr. articles to profl. jours. Recipient award Toyama Found., 1995. Avocations: golf, travel, reading. Office: Nat Rsch Inst Metals, 1-2-1 Sengen, Tsukuba 305-0047, Japan

HASE, MUNEAKI, physicist, researcher; b. Tondabayashi, Osaka, Japan, Aug. 6, 1969; p. Hideo and Kyoko Hase. Bachelors Degree, Osaka (Japan) U., 1993, Masters Degree, 1996, Doctors Degree, 1998. Postdoctoral staff Osaka U., Suita, 1998-99; rschr. Nat. Rsch. Inst. Metals, Tsukuba, Ibaraki, Japan, 1999—. Recipient ICL '99 Young Rschr. award Generation of Coherent THz Phonons in GeTe Ferroelectrics, Osaka, 1999. Mem. Phys. Soc. Japan, Am. Phys. Soc. (jr.). Avocations: skiing, camping. E-mail: hasedon@nrim.go.jp. Fax: 81-298-59-2801. Office: Nat Rsch Inst for Metals, Sengen 1-2-1, Tsukuba Ibaraki 305-0047, Japan

HASE, TSUNAO, chemistry educator, researcher; b. Osaka, Japan, July 14, 1925; s. Kumataro and Gen (Kumada) H.; m. Kazue Harada, July 23, 1960; children: Shiori, Makoto. BSc, Osaka U., 1949, DSc, 1962. Asst. Osaka City U., 1949-62, lectr., 1962-65, asst. prof., 1965-67; prof. chemistry Kagoshima (Japan) U., 1967-91, prof. emeritus, 1991—, dean Faculty Sci., 1983-87; hon. prof. Inst. Tech. and Higher Study Monterrey, Mex., 1984, Xiangtan U., China, 1994. Mem. Chem. Soc. Japan (chief Kyushu br. 1990-91). Home: Meiwa 1-3-1, Kagoshima 8900024, Japan Office: Kagoshima U Faculty Sci, Korimoto 1-21-35, Kagoshima 890-0065, Japan

HASEBE, NORIO, civil engineering educator; b. Gifu, Japan, Feb. 1, 1942; s. Ryozo and Sadako (Imai) H.; m. Misako Isobe, Mar. 29, 1975; children: Fumi, Siho, Takuya. Bachelor's degree, Nagoya (Japan) Inst. Tech., 1964, Master's degree, 1969; Doctoral degree (hon.), Tokyo U., 1974. Civil engr. Shimizu Constrn., Japan, 1964-67; from asst. to lectr. to assoc. prof. Nagoya Inst. Tech., 1969-84, prof., 1984—; chmn. dept. civil engring. Nagoya Inst. Tech., 1991-93. Co-editor: Stress Intensity Handbook, vols. 1, 2 1987, vol. 3, 1992; contbr. more than 185 articles to profl. jours. Mem. ASCE, Japanese Soc. Civil Engrs., Japanese Soc. Mech. Engrs., Japanese Soc. Materials Sci. Avocations: tennis, ski. Home: Umesato 2-14-15, Midoriku Nagoya 458-0001, Japan Office: Nagoya Inst Tech, Gokisocho Showaku, Nagoya 466-8555, Japan

HASEEB, KHAIR EL-DIN, economist, statistician; b. Mosul, Iraq, Aug. 1, 1929; married; 3 children. BA in Econs. and Commerce, U. Baghdad, Iraq, 1954; MSc in Econs., London Sch. Econs., 1957; PhD Nat. Income, U. Cambridge, Eng., 1960. Civil servant Ministry of Interior, Iraq, 1947-54; head Rsch. Stats. Dept. Iraq Oil Co., Baghdad, Iraq, 1959-60; lectr. U. Baghdad, 1961-63; dir. gen. Iraq Fedn. Industries, 1960-63; gov., chmn. of bd. Ctrl. Bank Iraq, 1963-65; pres. Ctrl. Organization Banks, 1964-65; acting pres. Econ. Orgn., Iraq, 1964-65; assoc. prof. Econs. Dept. U. Baghdad, 1965-71, prof. Econs., 1971-74; chief Programme and Co-ordination Unit UN-Econ. Commn. Western Asia, 1974-75, Natural Resources, Sci. and Tech. Divsn., 1976-1984; acting dir. gen. Ctr. Arab Unity Studies, Lebanon, 1978-83, dir. gen., 1983—; chmn. bd. Social Security Organization, 1963-65, alternate gov. Iraq Internat. Bank Reconstruction Devel., 1963-65; gov. Iraq Internat. Monetary Fund, 1963-65; mem. bd. dirs. Iraq Nat. Oil Co., 1967-68; sec. gen. Arab Nat. Conf., 1991—. Author: The Nat. Income of Iraq, 1953-61, 64, Workers Participation in Mgmt. in Arab Countries (1971 Arabic), Sources of Arab Economic Thought in Iraq, 1900-71 (1972 co-ed., Arabic), Arab Monetary Integration (1982 ed.), The Arabs and Africa (1985ed.), The future of the Arab Nation, 1991, Arab-Iranian Relations (1998 ed.); numerous articles pub. E-mail: info@caus.org.lb. Fax: 961 1865 548. Office: Ctr for Arab Unity Studies, Lyon Str Hamra POB 113-6001, Beirut Lebanon

HASEEBUDDIN, SYED, scientist, researcher; b. Hyderabad, India, Aug. 9, 1970; s. Syed Hasnuddin and Fathimunnisa Begum; m. U.K. Firdous. BSc, Kakatiya U., Warangal, India, 1991, MSc, 1993; PhD, Osmania U., Hyderabad, 1997. Rsch. fellow Indian Inst. Chem. Tech., Hyderabad, 1993-97; devel. mgr. AR&D, paints divsn. ICI India Ltd., Mohali, 1997—. Contbr. articles to sci. and profl. jours. Recipient Young Scientist award Indian Coun. Chemists, 1994, Sr. Rsch. fellowship C.S.I.R., New Delhi, 1995, Indian Paint Assn. award, 1997. Mem. Oil Technologists Assn. India, Oil & Colour Chemists Assn. Eng., N.Y. Acad. Scis., Surface Coatings Internat. (complimentary). Avocations: reading, painting, travelling, music. Fax: 091-0172-253191. Home: D No 13-7-89 Yellam Bazaar, Warangal 506 002, India Office: Innovation Ctr A-42 Ph VIII, Focal Pt SAS Nagar, Dist Ropar 160059, India

HASEGAWA, AKIRA, retired science educator; b. Tokyo; m. Miyoko Hasegawa; children: Tomohiro, Atsushi, Akiko. B of Engring., Osaka (Japan) U., 1957, M of Engring., 1959; PhD, U. Calif., Berkeley, 1964; DSc, Nagoya (Japan) U., 1967. Assoc. prof. Osaka U., 1964, prof., 1991-98, ret., 1998; disting. mem. tech. staff Bell Labs, 1968; ret., 1991. Author: (books) Optical Solutions in Fibers, 1989, One World of Lao Tsu and Modern Physics, 1990, Space Plasma Physics, 1990, Solutions in Optical Communications, 1995. Recipient Rank award Brit. Govt., 1991, Da Vinci Excellent prize Henessy Louis Vetton, Paris, 1995, Computer and Comm. award Nippon Elec. Corp., 1995. Fellow IEEE (Quantum Electronics award 1999), Am. Phys. Soc. (Maxwell prize 2000); mem. Rotary.

HASEGAWA, HIROSHI, marketing professional educator; b. Otsuka, Japan, Sept. 18, 1960; s. Masaaki and Sayoko (Inoue) H.; m. Tomoko Nakano, Jan. 18, 1995; children: Yu, Sawako. B, Meiji U., Tokyo, 1984; M, Waseda U., Tokyo, 1987; postgrad., Aichgakuin U., Nagoya, Japan, 1991. Asst. prof. Asahi U., Hozumi, Japan, 1991-94; assoc. prof. Asahi U., Hozumi, 1994—; rsch. scholar U. Tex. Austin, 1995-96. Author: (books) Basic Distribution Terms Handbook, 1999, Marketing Universe, 1998, Marketing, 1994, Green Marketing, 1993. Avocation: tennis. Office: Aichi Inst Tech, 1247 Yachigusa, Yagusa-cho 470-0392, Japan

HASEGAWA, JUNICHI, computer science educator; b. Tatebayashi, Japan, Dec. 21, 1951; s. Yasutoshi and Tomiko (Tabei) H.; m. Kimiko Shishido, Mar. 7, 1982; children: Sayaka, Yuuki, Asumi. BE, Nagoya (Japan) U., 1974, ME, 1976, D in Engring., 1979. Rsch. asst. Nagoya U., 1979-86, lectr., 1986-87; assoc. prof. Chukyo U., Toyota, Japan, 1987-88, prof., 1988—; gen. chmn. MIRU '98, Tokyo, 1997-98. Co-author: Fundamental Techniques of Image Processing, 1986, Computer-Aided Diagnosis of Medical X-Ray Images, 1994. Mem. Inst. Elecs. Info. and Comm. Engrs. (paper reviewer 1989—, editl. sec. transactions), Info. Processing Soc. Japan (sec. SIG-CV 1992-94, chmn. SIG-CV 1997-98, paper reviewer 1998—), Japanese Soc. Med. Imaging Tech. (paper awards 1991, 96, 98), Japan Soc. MEBE (councilor Tokai br. 1985—, paper award 1997). Avocations: soccer, skiing. Office: Chukyo U, 101 Tokodachi Kaizu-cho, Aichi Toyota 470-0393, Japan

HASEGAWA, YASUJI, French language educator; b. Ōsaka-shi, Japan, Oct. 7, 1929; s. Ta'ichirō and Koma (Kamitani) H.; m. Yaé Ta'ichi, Mar. 1959 (dec. 1993). Diploma in French, Ōsaka Fgn. Langs. Sch., 1950; Lic. of Letters in French Lit., Kyoto (Japan) U., 1953. 1st sec., tchr. Inst. Franco-japonais du Kansai, Kyoto, 1953-60; instr. French Tôka'i U., Tokyo, 1960-66; asst. prof. Tôka'i U., Hiratsuka, Japan, 1966-75, prof., 1975-80, prof. Fgn. Langs. Teaching Ctr., 1980-95; prof. Inst. Oceanography Tôka'i U., Shimizu, Japan, 1983-91; prof. Inst. High-Tech. Tôka'i U., Numazu, Japan, 1991-95. Author textbook, 1982; contbr. articles to profl. jours. Mem. Soc. French Lang. and Lit., Japan Soc. French Lang. Teaching. Buddhist. Avocations: walking, skiing, classical music, history of Japan. Home: 2241-14 Minami-Yana, Hadano-shi 257-0003, Japan

HASEGAWA, YUKIHIRO, physician; b. Tokyo, Jan. 10, 1957; s. Kiyoshi and Momoyo (Hayashi) H.; m. Chizuko Mori; children: Akitoshi, Takahiro. MD, Keio U., Tokyo. Resident Tokyo Met. Kyose Children's Hosp., Tokyo, 1982-84, chief endocrinology, 1992—. Author: Turner Female, 1999, Let's Learn Pediatric Endocrinolog, 1999. Recipient Novo Nordisk Growth award, Tokyo, 1998; Endocrinology fellow Tokyo Met. Kiyose Children's Hosp., 1984-92. Mem. Japan Endocrine Soc., Japan Pediatric Endocrine Soc., The Endocrine Soc. Office: Tokyo Met Childrens Hosp, 1-3-1 Umezono Kyose, Tokyo 204-8756, Japan

HASEK, DOMINIK, professional hockey player; b. Pardubice, Czech Republic, Jan. 29, 1965. Goaltender Buffalo Sabres, 1992—. Recipient Vezina Trophy, 1994, 95, 96, 97, 98, Hart Trophy, 1996-97, 97-98, Lester B. Pearson award, 1997. Office: Buffalo Sabres Marine Midland Arena One Seymour H Knox III Plaza Buffalo NY 14203

HASELDEN, CLYDE LEROY, librarian; b. Latta, S.C., Aug. 26, 1914; s. Hampton Berry and Mary Beulah (Allen) H.; m. Erva Lee Buchanan, Dec. 3, 1940 (dec. Apr. 15, 1982); 1 dau., Janice Charlotte. B.A., Furman U., 1938; B.S. in L.S, Columbia U., 1939; M.A., U. Chgo., 1948. Fellow reference dept. City Coll. N.Y., 1938-39; reference asst. U. Ark., 1939-43; assignee Civilian Pub. Service, 1943-46; librarian Parsons Coll., Fairfield, Iowa, 1947-50, Baldwin-Wallace Coll., 1950-59, Lafayette Coll., 1959-80; coll. and univ. library bldg. cons. Fellow Council on Library Resources, 1972. Contbr. articles to profl. jours. Mem. A.L.A., Ohio Coll. Assn. (pres. 1954-56), Pa. Library Assn., Assn. Coll. and Research Libraries (pres. Phila. 1965-67), AAUP, Phi Kappa Phi. Home: 15193 Village Dr Wilmington NC 28401-7530

HASENFUSS, IVAR, zoology educator; b. Jekabpils, Zemgale, Latvia, May 23, 1932; arrived in Germany, 1941; s. Georg and Elisabeth (Schmidt) H.; m. Inge Koltzer, Apr. 1, 1966. D Natural Scis., U. Erlangen, Germany, 1958. Asst. instr. U. Fribourg, Switzerland, 1962-64; asst. instr. U. Erlangen, 1965-79, lectr. zoology, 1971-80; prof. U. Erlangen-Nürnberg, 1980-94; ret., 1994. Author: Larvalsystematik der Zünsler, 1960; contbr. articles to sci. jours., including Zoologische Jahrbücher, Zeitschrift für Morphologie und Ökologie der Tiere, Zoomorphologie, Zoomorphology. Avocation: studies in insects. Home: Karlsbader Strasse 9, D-91083 Baiersdorf Germany

HASHEM, HASHEM HUSSEIN, computer systems executive; b. Dakar, Senegal, Mar. 30, 1949; m. Maud Stephan, 1976; children: Tarek, Abbas, Jad. MS in Engring., St. Joseph U., 1974. Tech. mgr. Pan Arab Computer Ctr., 1978-88; regional mgr. Team Internat., 1988-92; gen. mgr. Internat. Computer & Comm. Systems, Beirut, Lebanon, 1992—. Mem. Order of Engrs. (Lebanon). Office: Internat Computer Systems, Beirut 136007, Lebanon

HASHIDA, MITSURU, pharmaceutical sciences educator; b. Osaka, Japan, Dec. 18, 1951; s. Wataru and Yukiko (Ajiro) H.; m. Itsuko Miki, Nov. 2, 1975; children: Yasuhiko, Nobuhiko, Taeko. BS, Kyoto (Japan) U., 1974, MS, 1976, PhD in Pharm. Scis., 1977. Asst. prof. pharm. scis. Kyoto U., 1980-83, assoc. prof., 1983-92, prof., 1992—. Baned Pharm. Scientist of Yr., Internat. Pharmacy Fedn., 1998. Fellow Am. Assn. Pharm. Scientists; mem. Acad. Pharm. Scis. and Tech. Japan (award 1999), Controlled Release Soc. (mem.-at-large), Japan DDS (standing dir. 1994—). Home: 41-1 Shimogamominamichanoki-cho, Sakyo-Ku, Kyoto 606-0845, Japan Office: Kyoto U Grad Sch Pharm Scis, Sakyo-ku, Kyoto 606-8501, Japan

HASHIMOTO, AKIHIRO, engineering educator; b. Yokohama, Kanagawa, Japan, July 6, 1949; s. Yoshikazu and Michiko (Itoh) H.; m. Yoshiko Kikuchi, Nov. 19, 1981. B of Engring., Tokyo Inst. Tech., 1972, M of Engring., 1974, D of Engring., 1981. Rsch. assoc. U. Tsukuba, Japan, 1981-85; asst. prof. U. Tsukuba, 1985-94, assoc. prof., 1994-99, prof., 1999—. Contbr. articles to profl. jours. Office: U Tsukuba Inst Policy and Planning Scis, Tennodai 1-1-1, Tsukuba Ibaraki 305-8573, Japan

HASHIMOTO, DAIJO, surgeon, physician; b. Chang Chen, Jilin, Japan, Jan. 7, 1944; s. Motofumi and Masuko (Shirakawa) H.; m. Masako Yabuki, June 22, 1972; children: Chigusa, Motomu, Nahoko, Sumire. MD, Tokyo U., 1968, PhD, 1979. Resident, attending surgeon Mitsui Meml. Hosp., Tokyo, 1969-73; faculty surgery Tokyo U., 1973-76, faculty pathology, 1976-78; asst. prof. Hamamatsu (Japan) Med. Coll., 1980-84; assoc. prof. Tokyo U. Hosp., 1984-89; chief surgeon Tokyo Met. Police Hosp., 1989-99; prof. Saitama (Japan) Med. Coll., 2000—. Author: Advanced Techniques in Gasless Laparoscopic Surgery, 1995; contbg. author: Novel Regional Therapies for Liver Tumor, 1995, Lasers in Gastroenterology, 1989; contbr. articles to med. jours.; patentee in field. Rsch. grantee Japanese Govt., 1982, 96, 97. Mem. Japanese Assn. Laser Medicine and Surgery (counsillor 1985—), Gasless Laparoscopic and Endoscopic Surgeons' Soc. (chmn., founder), Internat. Computer Aided Soc. (bd. dirs. 1992—). Avocations: ocean cruises, golf, hunting. Home: Nishikata 2-8-7, Bunkyo-ku Tokyo 113-0024, Japan Office: Saitama Med Coll, 1981 Tsujidou-machi, Saitama Kamoda Kawagoe-shi 350-8550, Japan

HASHIMOTO, HIROAKI, economics educator; b. Tokyo, Mar. 20, 1944; s. Keiji and Kocho (Tachi) H.; m. Kaoru Isozaki, Oct. 23, 1982; children: Akiko, Ayumi, Meika. Degree, Chuo U., Tokyo, 1969, Keio U., Tokyo, 1971; postgrad. Sch. Arts and Scis., U. Pa., 1976-78. Lectr. econs. Asia U., Tokyo, 1975-81, assoc. prof., 1981-89, prof., 1989—. Mem. Japanese Econ. Assn., Japan Statis. Soc. Home: 4-25-13 Machiya, Shiroyama, Kanagawa Tsukuigun T220-0101, Japan Office: Asia Univ, 5-24-10, Sakai, Musashinoshi, Tokyo 180-8629, Japan

HASHIMOTO, PAULO HITONARI, anatomy educator, physician; b. Amagasaki, Hyogo, Japan, Mar. 23, 1930; s. Sohei and Otei (Asakura) H.; m. Maria Elizabeth Yoshiko Inoue, May 5, 1960; children: Yoneichi, Kazuko, Hideko, Muneaki, Narutoshi. Intern, Osaka U., 1953-54; MD, Osaka (Japan) U., 1953, DMSc, 1960. Instr. Med. Sch. Osaka U., 1957-60, asst. prof., 1960-65, assoc. prof., 1965-74, prof. anatomy, 1974-93, hon. prof., 1993—; prof. Koshien U., Japan, 1993-98; postdoc. fellow Harvard Med. Sch., Boston, 1963-65. Contbr. articles to profl. jours. Mem. AAAS, Am. Assn. Anatomists, Am. Soc. for Cell Biology, Internat. Brain Rsch. Orgn., N.Y. Acad. Scis., Japanese Assn. Anatomists (hon.), Japanese Soc. Electron Microscopy, Japanese Soc. for Microcirculation (coun.). Roman Catholic. Avocation: vocal music.

HASHIMOTO, SHIGEHIRO, biomedical engineer; b. Tokyo, June 14, 1956; s. Moritsugu and Yoshiko (Nakajima) H.; m. Chisato Fukuoka, Jan. 22, 1984; children: Haruka, Saori. B.Engring., Tokyo Inst. Tech., 1979, M.Engring., 1981, MD, 1987, Dr.Engring., 1990. Cert. 1st class high sch. tchr. Rsch. assoc. Kitasato U., Sagamihara, Japan, 1981-89, asst. prof., 1989-94; assoc. prof. biomed. engring. Osaka (Japan) Inst. Tech., 1994—. Author: Introduction to Biosystems Engineering, 1996, Introduction to Biomedical Measurement Engineering, 2000; co-author: Implant Materials in Biofunction, 1988, Microcirculation Annual, 1991. Ministry of Edn., Sci. and Culture of Japan grantee for encouragement of young scientists, 1984-85, 88-93. Mem. Japanese Soc. Artificial Organs (councilor 1985-2000), Japanese Soc. for Biomaterials (councilor 1996—), Internat. Soc. Artificial Organs (reviewer 1988—), Japan Internat. Assn. for the Exchange of Students for Tech. Experience (auditor 1986-94, dir. 1994-99). Achievements include research studies in the effect of shear rate in blood flow on clot growth and erythrocyte destruction in the artificial heart. E-mail: hasimoto@elc.oit.ac.jp. Office: Osaka Inst Tech, Elec Engring Ohmiya 5-16-1, Asahi-ku Osaka 535-8585, Japan

HASHIMOTO, TOHRU, life science educator; b. Kumamoto, Japan, Feb. 3, 1930; s. Sueki and Setsu (Minami) H.; m. Fusako Sakuma, Apr. 25, 1958 (div. Mar. 1973); 1 child, Kenji; m. Yoshiko Sakamoto, Jan. 29, 1977; 1 child, Eri. BS, Tohoku U., Sendai, 1955; MSc, U. Tokyo, 1957, DSc, 1961. Lectr. Musashi U., Tokyo, 1960-63; postdoctoral U. Calif., Davis, 1962-63; asst. U. Tokyo, 1963-70; rsch. scientist Inst. for Phys. and Chem. Rsch., Wako, Japan, 1970-86; prof. Kobe (Japan) U., 1986-93; prof. dept. life sci. Kobe Women's U., 1993—; mem. rsch. project evaluation com. Ministry of Environment of Japan, Tokyo, 1989-99. Contbr. 68 articles to profl. jours. Mem. Japan Soc. Plant Physiology, Am. Soc. Plant Physiology. Buddhist. Avocations: skiing, playing violin in a quartet. Home: 9-45-101 Uozakiminami, 5-chome, Higashinada-ku, Kobe 6580025, Japan Office: Kobe Women's U, Higashisuma, Suma-ku, Kobe 6548585, Japan

HASHIMOTO, TORU, bank executive; b. Okayama, Japan, Nov. 19, 1934; m. Haruko Hashimoto; two children. Grad., Tokyo U., 1957. With Fuji Bank, Ltd., Tokyo, 1957, asst. gen. mgr. Internat. Divsn. II, 1979-80, dep. gen. mgr. Shimbashi br., 1980, asst. chief mgr. exec. secretariat, 1980, spl. asst. to pres. Exec. Secratariat, 1980, joint gen. mgr. internat divisn., 1982-1984; exec. v.p. Heller Internat. Corp., 1984-86; head office gen. mgr. internat. credit divsn. Fuji Bank, Ltd., Tokyo, 1986, gen. mgr. internat. credit divsn., also bd. dirs., 1986, mng. dir., 1987-90, dep. pres., 1990-91, pres., 1991—, former pres., CEO, chmn. bd. Fulbright scholar, U. Kans., 1959-1960. Avocations: reading, golfing. *

HASHIMOTO, TSUNEYUKI, materials scientist; b. Zentsuji, Kagawa, Japan, July 31, 1950; s. Saburo and Fujie (Takagi) H.; m. Ayako Gomi, Mar. 20, 1980; 1 child, Takanori. BSc, U. Tokyo, 1974, MSc, 1976, DSc, 1979. Rschr. Hitachi (Ibaraki, Japan) Ltd., 1979-89, sr. rschr., 1989—; vis. scientist Argonne (Ill.) Nat. Lab., 1984-85. contbr. articles to profl. jours. Mem. Phys. Soc. Japan, Japan Inst. Metals, Atomic Energy Soc. Japan. Avocations: music, skiing. Office: Hitachi Ltd Hitachi Rch Lab, 7-1-1 Omika-Cho, Ibaraki Hitachi 319-1292, Japan

HASHIMOTO, YOSHIKAZU, chemist, educator; b. Tokyo, July 2, 1927; s. Takashi and Misao H.; m. Reiko Hashimoto, Apr. 3, 1959; children: Kazuhiko, Otohiko. B, Keio U., Tokyo, 1951, PhD, 1963. From asst. prof. to assoc. prof. Keio U., Tokyo, 1951-72, prof., 1972-93, prof. emeritus, 1993—; mem. China joint environ. project Keio U.-Chengdu City, 1990—, guest Ctr. for Area Studies, 1993—; vis. rsch. assoc. MIT, Cambridge, 1963-65; cons. Japan Hwy. Pub. Corp., Tokyo, 1975-84; founder Jack East Asia Air Surveillance Network (JACK Network), 1991; guest Ctr. Area Studies, 1993—. Recipient Environ. Agy. award, Japan, 1996. Mem. Japan Soc. Air Pollution (bd. dirs. 1985-92, award 1992), Chem. Soc. Japan, Am. Chem. Soc. Home: 6-17-15 Todoroki, Tokyo 158-0082, Japan Office: Ctr Area Studies Keio U, 2-15-45 Mita Minato-ku, Tokyo 108-8345, Japan

HASHIMOTO-GOTOH, TAMOTSU, molecular biologist, educator; b. Tsuyama, Okayama, Japan, Sept. 27, 1946; s. Nobutoshi Gotoh and Haruko Harada; adopted s. Muneo Hashimoto and Chiyoko (Ikeda) Hashimoto; children: Yoh-ichi, Lynn, Akira. BS, Tohoku (Japan) U., 1971; MS, Kyushu (Japan) U., 1974, DSc, 1977; DMS, Kyoto Prefectural U. Medicine, Japan, 1996. Rsch. fellow in medicine Osaka (Japan) U., 1977; rsch. fellow Dartmouth Med. Sch., Hanover, N.H., 1977-79; Max-Planck Inst. für Molekulare Genetik, West Berlin, Germany, 1979-81; rsch. scientist Deutsches Krebs Forschungs Zentrum, Heidelberg, Germany, 1981-83; sr. rsch. scientist pharm. rsch. labs. Hoechst Japan, Kawagoe, Saitama, 1983-90; assoc. prof. Kyoto (Japan) Prefectural U. Med., 1991—; vis. lectr. Kyoto U. Faculty Integrated Human Studies, 1995—. Co-author: Current Perspectives on Molecular and Cellular Oncology; contbr. articles to profl. jours. Grantee Mitsuiseimei Rsch. Found., 1991, Japan Osteoporosis Found., 1997. Mem. Am. Soc. Microbiology, Japan Soc. for Molecular Biology, Japan Soc. for Bone and Mineral Research, Alexander von Humboldt Club. Avocation: music of J.S. Bach. Address: DBMG RINDG, Kyoto Prefecture U Medicine, Kamigyo-Ku Kyoto 602-8566, Japan

HASHIRO, MAKOTO, dermatologist, psychodermatologist; b. Nishinomiya, Japan, Mar. 23, 1962; s. Susumu and Yukiko (Hosoda) H. MD, Osaka (Japan) U., 1986, PhD, 1991. Cert. specialist in dermatology; bd. cert. in psychosomatic medicine. Staff dept. dermatology Osaka U. Sch. Medicine, Osaka, 1986-87; dermatologist, psychodermatologist Minoh (Japan) City Hosp., 1991-94, Kansai Rohsai Hosp., Amagasaki, Hyogo, Japan, 1994—; lectr. Osaka U. Sch. Medicine, Japan, 1999—. Mem. Japanese Dermatol. Assn., Japanese Soc. for Investigative Dermatology, Japanese Soc. of Psychosomatic Medicine (cert.), Japanese Soc. of Hypnosis. Avocations: photography, aviation, traveling. Office: Kansai Rohsai Hosp Dermatol, 3-1-69 Inabasou, Amagasaki 660-8511, Japan

HASHIZUME, MAKOTO, surgeon; b. Kitakyushu, Fukuoka, Japan, Jan. 8, 1953; s. Eisuke and Kiyoko (Higuchi) H.; m. Tamiko Saku, Feb. 11, 1985; 1 child, Rika. MD, Kyushu U., Fukuoka, 1979, PhD, 1984. Cert. Japan Surg. Soc., Japanese Soc. Gastroenterol. Surgery. Resident dept. surgery II Kyushu U. Hosp., Fukuoka, 1979-80, sr. resident dept. surgery II, 1984-85; rsch. asst. prof. dept. surgery Hahnemann U. Sch. Medicine, Phila., 1985-86; chief dept. of surgery Fukuoka City Hosp., 1986-87; asst. prof. dept. of surgery II Kyushu U., Fukuoka, 1990-98, assoc. prof. dept. surgery II, 1998-99; prof., chmn. dept. disaster and emergency medicine Grad. Sch. Med. Scis., Kyushu U., Fukuoka, 1999—; vice-dir. Assn. Fukuoka Social Ins. Care, 1993-94; mem. program com. Soc. Am. Gastrointestinal Endoscopic Surgeons, Calif., 1994-95. Inventor in field; editor Hepato-Gastroenterology, 1995—; mem. editl. bd. Japan Soc. for Endoscopic Surgery, 1995—; inventor in field. Recipient Prize of the Pres., Japanese Soc. Gastroenterol. Surgery, 1993. Fellow ACS; mem. Japanese Soc. Gastroenterol. Surgery (mem. com.), Japan Gastroenterol. Endoscopy Soc. (mem. com.), Internat. Assn. for Study of Liver, Internat. Soc. Surgery, Internat. Gastro-Surg. Club, Soc. Am. Gastrointestinal Endoscopic Surgeons, Japan Soc. for Endoscopic Surgery (com. mem.), Japan Soc. for Portal Hypertension (com. mem.), N.Y. Acad. Sci. Avocation: music. Fax: 81-92-642-6224. E-mail: mhashi@dem.med.kyushu-u.ac.jp. Office: Kyushu U Grad Sch Med Scis, 3-1-1 Maidashi, Higashi-Ku, Fukuoka 812-8582, Japan

HASHMI, FARRUKH SIYAR, psychiatrist; b. Sept. 12, 1927; s. Ziaullah Quereshi and Majida Mufti; m. Shahnaz Hashmi, Feb. 11, 1972; children: Zia, Mahnaz, Noreen. MB BS, Punjab U.; dipl. psychol. medicine, King Edward Med. Coll., Lahore, Pakistan. Asst. med. officer for health Berwickshire, 1957; scholar Volkart Fedn., Switzerland, 1958-60; registrar Uffculme Clinic and All Saints Hosp., 1960-63; rsch. fellow dept. of psychiatry U. Birmingham, 1969; cons. psychiatrist W. Birmingham Helath Authority, 1969-92; psychotherapist HM Prison, Stafford, 1973-92; cons. psychiatrist Eating Disorders Unit S, Warwick Mental Health Svcs.; cons. trans-cultural psychiatry The Woodbourne Clinic, Birmingham, 1992—; home sec.'s adv. com. on race, 1976-81; commr. Commn. for Racial Equality, 1980-86; mem. working party of cmty. and race rels. tng. Home Office Police Tng. Coun., 1982-83; GMC mem. Tbnl. on Misuse of Drugs, 1983-92; adv. con. C of E Bd. for Social Responsibility, 1984-86; regional adv. com. BBC, 1970-77; chmn. Psychiatric Divsn. W Birmingham Health Dist., 1977-83, 89. Author: Pakistani Family in Britain, 1965, Psychology of Racial Prejudice, 1966, Mores Migration and Mental Illness, 1966, Community Psychiatric Problems Among Birmingham Immigrants, 1968, In a Strange Land, 1970, Measuring Psychological Disturbance in Asian Immigrants to Britain, 1977, Oriental Club, Rotary Internat., Edgbaston Priory (Birmingham). Mem. Health and Welfare Adv. Panel Nat. Com. on Commonwealth Immigrants, 1966-81; founder, chmn. Iqbal Acad. Coventry Cathedral, 1972-86; mem. Warley Area Social Svcs. Sub com., 1973-81; mental health svcs. com. RHA, 1976-92. Decorated officer Order Brit. Empire Her Majesty the Queen, 1974. Mem. World Psychiat. Assn., Overseas Drs. Assn. U.K., World Fedn. for Mental Health. Avocations: writing, reading, music. Home: 5 Woodbourne Rd, Edgbaston, Birmingham B15 3QJ, United Kingdom Office: Woodburne Priory Hosp, 21 Woodbourne Rd, Edgbaston Birmingham B15 3QJ, England

HASHMI, SYED AZHAR RASHEED, polymer engineer; b. Kanpur, India, June 25, 1962; s. Mohammad Rasheed Sahir and Jamila Begum H.; m. Seema Perveen, Feb. 12, 1989; 1 child, Rafey. BTech, Harcourt Butler Tech. Inst., Kanpur, 1983, MTech, 1987; MS, Birla Inst. Tech. & Sci., Pilani, India, 1992; PhD in Applied Chemistry, Barkatullh U., Bhopal, India, 1997. From prodn. engr. to process & quality control incharge Madhya Pradesh United Polypropylene Ltd, Mandideep, India, 1984-88; scientist B Regional Rsch. Lab., Bhopal, India, 1988-93, scientist C, 1993-98, scientist El, 1998—; cons. in field. Patentee in field; contbr. articles to profl. jours. Japan Internat. Coop. Agy. fellow, Japan, 1994-95. Mem. Instn. Engrs., Material Rsch. Soc. India (treas. Bhopal chpt.), Indian Plastics Inst. Islam. Avocations: literature, chess, cricket. Home: D-15 RRL Campus, 462026 Bhopal India Office: Regional Rsch Lab, Hoshangabad Rd, 462026 Bhopal India

HASHMI, ZIAUDDIN SYED, microbiologist; b. Peshawar, Pakistan, Feb. 24, 1960; s. Ruknuddin Syed and Zahida Khatoon (Abdul Wahab) H.; m. Shameem Fatima, Nov. 12, 1962; children: Abdullah, Faseeha. MS, U. Karachi, 1983; PhD, U. Otago, 1993. Microbiologist Haj Rsch. Ctr., Jeddah, Saudi Arabia, 1983; lectr. U. Umm Al-Qura, Makkah Al-Mukarramah, Saudi Arabia, 1984-88; demonstrator U. Otago, Dunedin, New Zealand, 1988-92; postdoctoral fellow U. Sydney, 1993-94; mgr. R&D BOMAC Labs. Ltd., Auckland, New Zealand, 1994-99; mgr. regulatory affairs BOMAC Labs., 2000—; course cons. Auckland Univ. Tech., 1994—, vice pres., Pakistan Assn. New Zeland Inc. Contbr. articles to profl. jours. Merit scholar U. Grants Com. New Zealand, 1990-92; recipient Glaxo prize Australian and New Zealand Microbiology Socs., 1992. Mem. Brit. Inst. Regulatory Affairs, Australian Soc. for Microbiology, New Zealand Orgn. Quality. Islam. E-mail: ziahashmi@hotmail.com. Avocations: reading, jogging. Home: 31 Watson Pl, Papatoetoe, Manukau City, Auckland New Zealand Office: BOMAC Labs Ltd, Wiri Station Rd, Manukau City 1701, New Zealand

HASKAYNE, RICHARD FRANCIS, petroleum company executive; b. Calgary, Alta., Can., Dec. 18, 1934; s. Robert Stanley and Bertha (Hesketh) H.; m. Lee Mary Murray, 1958 (dec. 1993); m. Lois P. Heard, 1995. B.Comm., U. Alta., 1956; postgrad., U. Western Ont., 1968, LLD; LLD, U. Calgary, U. Alta. Chartered acct., Alta. With Riddell, Stead & Co., chartered accts., Calgary, 1956-60; corp. acctg. supr. to v.p. fin. Hudson's Bay Oil & Gas Co., Ltd., Calgary, 1960-73; compt. Canadian Arctic Gas Study Ltd., 1973-75; sr. v.p. to pres. Hudson's Bay Oil & Gas Co. Ltd., Calgary, 1975-81; pres., chief exec. officer Home Oil Co., Ltd., Calgary, 1981-91, also bd. dirs.; chmn. bd. NOVA Corp., Calgary, 1992-98; pres., CEO, bd. dirs. Interprovencial Pipe Line Co., 1987-91, Interhome Energy, 1989-91; bd. dirs. Fording Inc., Crestar Energy Inc., Alta. Energy Inc., Weyerhaeuser Co.; chmn. bd. TansAlta Corp., 1996-98, TransCan. Pipelines Ltd., 1998—, MacMillan Bloedel Ltd., 1996-99. Chmn. bd. govs. U. Calgary, 1990-96. Recipient award Officer of the Order of Can., 1997. Fellow Fin. Execs. Inst., Inst. Corp. Dirs.; mem. Calgary Petroleum Club (past pres.), Calgary Golf and Country Club, Earl Grey Golf Club, Ranchmen's Club, U. Calgary Chancellor's Club, The York Club, Libr. Club, Commerce Club, Alta Inst. Chartered Accts., Kappa Sigma. Office: 2030 Bankers Hall 855 2d St SW, Calgary, AB Canada T2P 4J8

HASKELL, BARBARA, curator; b. San Diego, Nov. 13, 1946; d. John N. and Barbara (Freeman) H.; m. Leon Botstein; children: Clara Haskell Botstein, Maxim Haskell Botstein. BA, UCLA, 1969. Asst. registrar Pasadena (Calif.) Art Mus., 1969, curatorial asst., 1970, asst. curator, 1970, assoc. curator, 1970-72, curator painting and sculpture, 1972-74; curator painting and sculpture Whitney Mus. Am. Art, N.Y.C., 1975—. Author: Arthur Dove, 1974, Marsden Hartley, 1980, Milton Avery, 1982, Blam! The Explosion of Pop, Minimalism and Performance 1958-64, 1984, Georgia O'Keefe: Works on Paper, 1985, Ralston Crawford, 1985, Charles Demuth, 1987, Red

Grooms, 1987, Donald Judd, 1988, Burgoyne Diller, 1990, Agnes Martin, 1992, Joseph Stella, 1994, The Am. Century: Art and Culture, 1900-1950. Named Woman of Yr., Mademoiselle mag., 1973. Office: Whitney Mus Am Art 945 Madison Ave New York NY 10021-2701

HASKELL, PAUL HEGER, executive recruitment company executive; b. N.Y.C., July 6, 1934; arrived in France, 1964; s. John Henry Farrell and Paulette (Heger) H.; m. Francoise Gallimard, Mar. 14, 1964 (div. Nov. 1976); children: Stephen, Frederick; m. Veronique Simenel, Oct. 30, 1980 (div. Feb. 1994); m. Mariella Giannetti, July 7, 1994. BA, Harvard U., 1956, MBA, 1960. Cons. McKinsey & Co., Inc., N.Y.C., Geneva, Paris, 1960-69; head Paris office A.T. Kearney, Paris, 1970-72; corp. contr. Rhone Poulenc Group, Paris, 1973-76; dir. pers. Booz, Allen & Hamilton Internat., Paris, 1977-79; ptnr. Berndtson Internat., Paris, 1980-96; pres. Hashell & Co., 1996—. Mem. exec. com. Reps. Abroad, Paris, 1968—. Lt. (j.g.) USN, 1956-58. Mem. Am. C. of C. (bd. dirs. 1970-85), Franco-Am. C. of C. (bd. dirs. 1979—), Am. Club Paris (exec. com. 1975-80), Polo Club Paris. Roman Catholic. Avocations: tennis, golf, skiing. Home: 25 Rue de Chazelles, 75017 Paris France

HASKINS, CHARLES GREGORY, JR., lawyer; b. Chgo., Jan. 27, 1951; s. Charles G. and Ellen Barbara (Essman) H.; m. Gail Beaubien Ferbend, June 14, 1987; 1 child, Charles Robert. BA, U. Ill., 1972; JD, John Marshall Law Sch., 1976. Bar: Ill. 1976, U.S. Dist. Ct. (no. dist.) Ill. 1976. Assoc. George J. Cullen, Ltd., Chgo., 1976-82; shareholder George J. Cullen & Assoc., Ltd., Chgo., 1982-89, Cullen, Haskins, Nicholson & Menchetti, Chgo., 1989—. Mem. ATLA, Workers Compensation Lawyers Assn. (bd. dirs. 1986-96, pres. 1989), Ill. Bar Assn., Ill. Trial Lawyers Assn. (bd. mgrs. 1989—, treas. 1997, co-chmn. Workers Compensation com. 1991—, co-editor Case Notebook 1992—), Chgo. Bar Assn. (cham. indsl. commn. com. 1987-88), Workplace Injury Litigation Group (bd. dirs. 1997—). Democrat. Roman Catholic. Avocations: golf, water skiing, snow skiing. Office: Cullen Haskins Nicholson & Menchetti 35 E Wacker Dr Ste 1760 Chicago IL 60601-2271

HASKINS, CHRISTOPHER ROBIN, food products executive; b. May 30, 1937; s. Robin and Margaret Haskins; m. Gilda Horsley, 1959; 5 children. BA, Trinity Coll., Dublin, Ireland. With Ford Motor Co., Dagenham, 1960-62; with No. Foods (formerly No. Dairies), Hull, Humberside, Eng., 1962—, chmn. bd. dirs., 1986—. Mem. Commn. for Social Justice, 1992-94; trustee Runnymede Trust, 1989—, Demos, 1993—. Avocations: farming, cricket, writing, politics. Home: Quarryside Farm Skidby, nr Cottingham, Hull East Yorkshire HU16 5TG, England Office: No Foods PLC, Beverly Ho St Stephens Sq, Hull East Yorkshire HU1 3XG, England*

HASLE, KARL-FREDERIK, ambassador; b. Copenhagen, Nov. 3, 1926; arrived in France, 1992; s. Henning and Inge (Flach) H.; m. Birte Joensen, May 13, 1954; children: Louise, Frederik. Law, U. Copenhagen, 1952; diploma, Inst. Sci., Paris, 1953. Head of sect. Ministry of Fgn. Affairs, Copenhagen, 1953; served Yugoslavia, Romania, Turkey and N.Y.C.; min. embassy Coun. of Europe, Paris, 1977-81; amb. to Monocco, 1982-84; amb. UNESCO, Paris, 1984-86; amb. to Argentina, 1986-92; chmn. award com. for yearly cultural prize Läkerol's Kultur Prize, Copenhagen, 1976-97. Named Chevalier of Dannebrog Order, 1978, Grand Cross, Agentina, 1992, Chili, 1991. Home: Residence Les Longs Pres, 43 Chemin du Châtelard, 01220 Divonne les Bains France

HASLEGRAVE, MARIANNE, medical association administrator; b. London, England, Nov. 2, 1942; d. William Alexander and Joan Frances Harvey; m. David Brian Huggard, Aug. 31, 1968 (div. Jan. 1982); 1 child, Richard; m. James Edward Haslegrave, May 7, 1982. BA, Durham (England) U., 1964; MA, Queens (N.Y.) Coll., 1977. Coord. NGO Forum, World Conf., N.Y.C., 1979-80; liaison officer UN Conf., N.Y.C., 1981; cons. Internat. Planned Parenthood Fedn., London, 1985-88; gen. sec. Internat. Fedn. Bus. Profl. Women, London, 1988-91; dir. Commonwealth Med. Assn., London, 1992—; del. Internat. Conf. Population Dev., Cairo, 1994; cons. WHO, Geneva, 1994-96, UN Population Fund, Amman, Jordan, 1996; convenor Advocacy for Women's Health Group, London, 1993—; organizer NSO Forum on Follow Up, Internat. Conf. on Population and Devel., The Hague, 1999. Author: (with others) Human Rights, 1988. Mem. AAUW (N.Y. chpt.), Brit. Fedn. Women Grads. (v.p. 1985-88, coord. internat. rels. 1995-99), Internat. Fedn. Univ. Women (mem. com.). Office: CMA, BMA House Tavistock Sq, London WC1H 9JP, England

HASNER, ROLF KAARE, management consultant; b. Oslo, Mar. 15, 1919; s. Harald Alexander and Henny (Christensen) H.; m. Edel Jensen, May 26, 1956; children: Richard, Nina. Grad., Norwegian Mil. Acad., 1939; MBA, Norwegian U. Commerce & Social Scis., 1943, U. Chgo., 1947. Clk. Nat. Bank of Norway, Oslo, 1940-41; econ. A.S. Lilleborg Fabrikker, Oslo, 1943-45; bus. cons. N.Y.C., 1951-57; exec. v.p. Globe Slicing Machine Co., Inc., Stamford, Conn., 1957-65; prin. owner, exec. v.p., bd. dirs. Globe Slicing Machine Co., Inc., Stamford, 1965-87, fin. cons., 1987—. Bd. dirs. Norwegian Am. Mus., Decorah, Iowa; elder bd. Luth. Ch., Greenwich Conn.; bd. dirs. Greenwich Coun. Boy Scouts Am. Served with Armed Forces, Norway, 1940-45. Scholar Rockefeller Found., 1946-47, Internat. House of Chgo., 1946-47. Mem. Norwegian Am. C. of C. Internat. (pres. 1985-87), Skytop (Pa.) Club, Greenwich Skating Club, Greenwich Country Club, Greenwich Rotary (pres. 1978-79, bd. dirs.). Home: Bobolink Ln Greenwich CT 06830

HASPL, MIROSLAV, orthopedic surgeon; b. Samobor, Croatia, Apr. 22, 1953; s. Adolf and Agnes (Pesek) H.; m. Željka Hundrić, Oct. 14, 1978; children: Helena, Ana. MD, U. Zagreb, Croatia, 1976, postgrad., 1985. Registrar Hosp., Varazdin, Croatia, 1979-85; sr. registrar dept. orthopedic surgery U. Zagreb, 1985-92, head dept., 1992—, assoc. prof., 1996—. Author 6 books in field; contbr. over 100 articles to profl. jours. Mem. SICOT, EFORT, ESSKA, Croatian Orthopedic Assn. (sec. 1998). Avocations: skiing, fishing, tennis. Home: Golubovećka 20, 10000 Zagreb Croatia Office: Dept Orthoped Surgery, Salata 6, 100000 Zagreb Croatia

HASRAT, MASHOOQ ALI KHAN, media specialist; b. Lucknow, India, July 10, 1943; s. Islam Ali and Khairun (Nisa) Khan; m. Shamim Fatima, Dec. 3, 1972; children: Tasneem, Sameer, Rizwan, Nida, Anum, Furqan. Grad., Karachi (Pakistan) U., 1965, M in Sociology, 1969. Urdu newswriter Radio Pakistan, Karachi, 1970-72; Urdu lang. expert Fgn. Langs. Press, Beijing, 1973-77; press officer Nat. Press Trust, Islamabad, Pakistan, 1978-86, mgr., 1987-88, gen. mgr., 1989—. Author books; contbr. articles to profl. jours. Avocations: reading books, magazines, newspapers, television, visiting hill stations. Office: Nat Press Trust H No 4, St No 31, Sector G-6/2, Islamabad 44000, Pakistan

HASSAN, ALADIN ABDEL-AZIZ, biochemist, toxicologist, researcher; b. Cairo, Egypt, Sept. 17, 1933; s. Abdel-Aziz Abu-zeid and Safia Zaki (Goher) H.; m. Meral Tarhan, Mar. 30, 1989. BSc in Chemistry, U. Cairo, 1953; PhD in Chemistry, U. Berne, Switzerland, 1960. Assoc. prof. Atomic Energy Authority, Cairo, 1961-66; rsch. assoc. U. N.C., Raleigh, 1966-67, CDC Dept. Health, Miami, Fla., 1967-69; pesticide toxicologist Rhodia, Inc., New Brunswick, 1969-72; prof. Atomic Energy Authority, Cairo, 1973-77; tech. officer UN FAO/IAEA, Vienna, Austria, 1977-95; cons. to more than 20 developing countries UN FAO/IAEA, Vienna, 1977-95. Author, rsch. coord.: DDT in the Tropics, 1994, Bound Pesticide Residues in Grain, 1992, Nature of Pesticide Residues in Grain, 1990; contbr. articles to profl. jours. including Jour. Environ. Sci. and Health. Recipient State Chemistry prize Egyptian Ministry of Sci., 1966. Muslim. Avocations: tennis, chess, theater, travel. Home: Graben 31/21, 1010 Vienna Austria

HASSAN, ALLEN CLARENCE, lawyer, physician, surgeon, educator; b. Red Oak, Iowa, Mar. 29, 1936; s. Oman Diab Hassan and Dorothea Tuttle. DVM, Iowa State U., 1962; MD, U. Iowa, 1966; JD, Lincoln U., 1978. Bar: Calif. 1981, U.S. Dist. Ct. (ea. dist.) Calif. 1981, U.S. Supreme Ct. 1981; diplomate Am. Bd. Family Practice, Am. Bd. Sports Medicine. Intern Mt. Zion Hosp., San Francisco, 1966-67; residency Mendolino State Hosp. Psychiatry, Talmage, Calif., 1967-70; sole practice Sacramento, Calif., 1981—; clin. instr. family practice, U. Calif., Davis, 1976-86. Author: Failure to Atone, 1969, Diagnosis and Treatment of Brain and Spinal Cord Trauma, 1992, True Story of a Jungle Surgeon in Vietnam. Served as sgt. USMC, 1954-57, comdr. USCG. Fellow Coll. of Legal Medicine; mem. AMA, Am. Acad. Family Physicians (program chmn. 1973-76, sec., treas. 1974, 75, pres. 1975-76), Calif. Bar Assn., Calif. Trial Lawyer Assn., Calif. Med. Assn. Avocations: reading, jogging, golf, flying, scuba diving. Home: 401 Bret Harte Rd Sacramento CA 95864-5602 Office: 2933 El Camino Ave Sacramento CA 95821-6012

HASSAN, ATA MOHD, power and generation company executive, researcher; b. Halhul, Hebron, Palestine, May 7, 1927; s. Mohammad Salem and Rifqa Fatima (Abdullah) H.; m. Najdah Nimati Amasheh, Nov. 21, 1941; children: Jommana, Hania, Mona, Ata Jr. BSc, Roosevelt U., Chgo., 1952; MS, U. Cin., 1958, PhD, 1966. Cert. rschr. in polymer phys. chemistry, rschr. in material sci. and seawater desalination. Sch. prin. Govt. Palestine, Jerusalem, 1946-50; sci. tchr. Govt. Syria, Hama, 1950-52; technician Chgo. Med. Sch., 1953-56; rschr. Strietmann/Keebler, Cin., 1958-64; sr. rschr. Armstrong World, Lancaster, Pa., 1964-76, KISR, Kuwait City, 1976-84; gen. mgr. DDS, Denmark, 1985-87; head R&D dept., rsch. Saline Water Conversion Corp., Jubail, Saudi Arabia, 1988—; rsch. asst. Kuwait Inst. for Sci. Rsch.; prin. sci. tchr. Edn. Dept., Palestine, Syria, 1946-52; rschr., head of dept. in seawater desalination, Mid. East, 1976—. Author: (book chpts.) Plastics Polymer Science and Technology, 1952, CRC Critical Review in Polymer and Macromolecular Science, 1971, Desalination Encyclopedia, 1999; contbr. over 100 papers and presentations to profl. jours. and confs.; patent pending in field. Mem. Social and Charity Clubs, U.S. and Kuwait, 1945-54. Mem. Internat. Desalination Assn. (Outstanding Rschr. Desalination 1999, Ida award), Am. Chem. Soc., Am. Physical Soc., Exch. Club (pres. 1975-76). Muslim. Avocations: travel, investing, photography, gardening, history. Home: 8270-2 Avenida Navidad San Diego CA 92122 Office: Saline Water Conversion Cor, Box 8269, Al-Jubail Saudi Arabia

HASSAN, EZZELDIN OSMAN, obstetrics/gynecology educator; b. Dakahlia, Egypt, Sept. 28, 1930; s. Osman Hassan; m. Nafisa Massoumi, Aug. 10, 1973; 1 child, Mohamed. MB BChir, Cairo U., 1953, D of Ob-Gyn., 1961. House officer Cairo U. Hosp., 1953-54, resident, 1955-57; cons. ob-gyn. Ministry of Health, Cairo, 1958-60; from lectr. to asst. prof. Mansoura U., 1961-72, prof., chmn., 1973-90, prof., 1991—. Author: (books) Contraceptive, 1962, Fertility Care Manual, 1980, Fertility Care Bulletin, 1985. Office: Egyptian Fertility Care Soc, 2 (A) Mahrouky St, 12612 Mohandeseen Cairo, Egypt

HASSAN, HANY IBRAHIM, engineering consultant; b. Cairo, Egypt, Feb. 2, 1965; s. Hassan and Nadia (Sand) Ibrahim. BS, Cairo U., 1987, MS, 1991; PhD, Tokyo U., 1997. Instr. Cairo U., 1987-91, asst. tchr., 1991-94; engr. Nippon Koei Co., Ltd., Tokyo, 1997—. Office: Nippon Koei Co Ltd, 2-5 Kojimachi, Tokyo 102-0083, Japan

HASSAN, HOSNI MOUSTAFA, microbiologist, biochemist, toxicologist and food scientist, educator; b. Alexandria, Egypt, Sept. 3, 1937; came to U.S., 1961; s. Moustafa Hosni and Sania M. (El-Hariri) H.; m. Awatif El-Domiaty, July 12, 1961 (div. May 1983); children: Jehan, Suzanne; m. Linda C. McDonald, Dec. 16, 1992; 1 child, Nora Elizabeth. BSc, Ain Shams U., Cairo, 1959; PhD, U. Calif., Davis, 1967. Asst. prof. Cairo High Polytech. Inst., 1968-70, U. Alexandria, 1970-72; vis. prof. McGill U., Montreal, 1972-74; rsch. asst. prof. U. Maine, Orono, 1974-76; rsch. assoc. biochemistry Duke U. Med. Ctr., Durham, N.C., 1976-79; assoc. prof. McGill U. Med. Sch., Montreal, 1979-80; assoc. prof. N.C. State U., Raleigh, 1980-84, prof., 1984-93, prof., head microbiology dept., 1993—, head dept. microbiology, interim head toxicology dept., 1999—. Mem. editl. bd. Free Radicals in Biology and Medicine, 1984—; author: (chpts.) Enzymatic Basis of Toxicology, 1980, Biological Role of Copper, 1980, Advances in Genetics, 1989, Stress Responses in Plants, 1990, FEMS Microbiol. Reviews, 1994, Lung Biology Series, Vol. 15, 1997, others; author/co-author over 100 rsch. publs. fellow NIH, 1967, Fulbright sr. fellow, Paris, 1987-88; NIH-NSF grantee N.C. State U., 1982, 83-93. Fellow Am. Inst. Chemists, Sigma Xi; mem. Am. Soc. Biol. Chemists and Molecular Biology, Am. Soc. for Microbiology (pres.-elect and pres. N.C. chpt. 1993-95). Democrat. Achievements include discovery of the toxicity and mutagenicity of oxygen free radicals and the protective role of the antioxident enzymes superoxide dismutases and hydroperoxidases; the mechanism of regulation of the synthesis of the enzyme Mn-superoxide dismutase and catelases in bacteria. E-mail: hosni hassan@ncsu.edu. Home: 2637 Freestone Ln Raleigh NC 27603-3950 Office: NC State U Microbiology Dept PO Box 7615 Raleigh NC 27695-0001

HASSAN, RASHID MEKKI, economics educator; b. Karima, Northern, Sudan, Feb. 22, 1953; s. Mekki and Dihaiba Abdin (Ahmed) H.; m. Entisar Osman Abdalla, Oct. 2, 1986; children: Mekki, Hatim, Mohamed. BS with honors, U. Khartoum, Sudan, 1977, MS, 1983; MS, Iowa State U., 1988, PhD, 1989. Agrl. economist Min. of Agr., Khartoum, 1977-79; grad. asst. U. Khartoum, 1980-82; tchg. asst. U. Juba, Sudan, 1983-84; grad. asst. Iowa State U., Ames, 1984-86, grad. rsch. assoc., 1986-89; Rockefeller Found. fellow Internat. Maize and Wheat Rsch. Ctr., Nairobi, Kenya, 1989-91; economist CIMMYT, Nairobi, 1991-95; prin. economist CSIR, Pretoria, 1995-97; assoc. prof. U. Pretoria, 1997-98; prof. and chair environ. econs. U. Pretoria, S. Africa, 1998—. Editor: (books) Maize Technology: AGIS Application, 1998, Accounting for Environmental Values, 1999; assoc. editor: Agrekon, 1998—; contbr. articles to profl. jours. Social Sci. Rsch. fellow Rockefeller Found., 1989, World Food Inst. scholarship, 1988. Mem. Internat. Soc. Ecology Economics, Am. Agrl. Econ. Assn., Internat. Assn. Agrl. Economists, Gamma Sigma Delta, Phi Kappa Phi. Muslim. Avocations: soccer, reading, touring.

HASSAN, SAYED MOHAMMED, analytical chemist; b. Cairo, Oct. 18, 1944; came to U.S., 1988; s. Mohammed Hassan Ali; m. Souad Ali Shaaban, July 12, 1973; children: Wael, Ghada, Hany. B Pharmacy and Pharm. Chemistry, U. Cairo, 1966, M Pharm. Sci., 1973, PhD in Pharm. Sci., 1975. Drug control analyst Nile Co. for Pharms., Cairo, 1966-67, Drug Control and Rsch. Ctr., Cairo, 1967-74; asst. lectr. to prof. and head dept. analytical chemistry Faculty of Pharmacy, Al-Mansoura, Egypt, 1974-88; prin. rsch. chemist DynCorp/U.S. EPA, Athens, Ga., 1988-95; mgr. chem. instrumentation dept. crop and soil scis. Coll. Agrl. and Environ. Scis., U. Ga., Athens, 1996—; cons. Nat. Orgn. Drug Control and Rsch., Cairo, 1976-88, Kahira Co. for Chem. and Pharm. Industries, Cairo, 1987-88. Contbr. articles, revs. to profl. jours. Recipient Abdul Hameed Shoman award Shoman Found., Jordon, 1984. Mem. AAAS, Am. Chem. Soc., N.Y. Acad. Scis., Assn. Ofcl. Analytical Chemists, Egyptian Biochem. Soc., Chem. Soc. Egypt, Pharm. Soc. Egypt, Sigma Xi. Avocations: stamp collecting, fishing, walking, chess, computer programming.

HASSAN, SHAWKY MOHAMED, chemistry educator; b. Elmansoura, Dakahlia, Egypt, June 11, 1943; s. Mohamed Hassan Gabr and Ensaf Abbas Ali; m. Hayam Mohamed Abo-Elnaga, Feb. 18, 1971; children: Rania, Ahmed, Mohamed. BS with honors, U. Assiut, Egypt, 1963; PhD, Petroleum Inst., Moscow, 1970. Demonstrator Assiut U., Egypt, 1963-65; rschr. Nat. Rsch. Ctr., Cairo, 1965-73; lectr. Mansoura U., Egypt, 1973-76; assoc. prof. Mansoura U., 1976-80, prof. phys. chemistry, 1980—, head chem. dept., 2000—; dean, founder Sci., Domiatt, Egypt, 1985-91; cons. Domiatt Gov., Domiatt, 1986-91; mem. Supreme Promotion com. for Univs. Staff, Cairo, 1990-93; head phys. chemistry divsn., Faculty of Sci., Mansoura, 1997—. Ofcl. rep. Egyptian Govt., Internat. Conf. on Tropical Ozone and Atmospheric Changes, Penang, 1990; mem. exec. coun. Domiatt, Egypt, 1986-91; mem. Supreme Edn. Coun., Domiatt, 1987-91; mem. environ. protection com., Domiatt, 1991. Moslem. Avocations: strolling, reading, exploration. Office: Fac Sci Dept Chemistry, Mansoura Univ PO Box 35516, Mansoura Egypt

HASSAN, TOGHRILLE PETER, governmental relations consultant; b. Hyderabad, India, June 2, 1944; s. Khurshid and Mary (Tarachand) H.; m. Doreen Fernes, June 10, 1971; 3 children. M, U. Andhra Pradesh, India, 1968. Mgr. corp. affairs Voltas Ltd., Delhi, India, 1978-82; v.p. Maker Group, Delhi, 1983-90; resident dir Essar Group, Delhi, 1991-97; advisor Nagarjuna Group, Delhi, 1998—. Mem. India Internat. Centre, New Delhi, 1995—, India Habitat Centre, New Delhi, 1997—. Mem. Indo-Am. C. of C., Punjab Harayana C. of C., Delhi Golf Club. Avocations: reading, listening to music, group discussion. Home: D/64 Panchsheel Enclave, New Delhi 111 017, India

HASSAN, WAJAHAT UL, rheumatologist, consultant; b. Attock, Punjab, Pakistan, Mar. 24, 1958; arrived in Eng., 1987; s. Ijaz Ul and Zubaida (Bagum) H.; m. Sharon Ann Scott, Feb. 6, 1990; children: Aqeel, Saadia. MB BChir, Kingedwar Coll., Lahore, Pakistan, 1984; MD, Newcastle (Eng.) U., 1996. Med. officer Mayo Hosp., Lahore, 1984-85; sr. house officer Nat. Health Svc., Sunderland, Eng., 1988-89, registrar, 1988-90; rsch. registrar Rheumatology Dept., Sunderland, 1990-93; sr. registrar Leicester (Eng.) Royal Infirmary, 1993-95; cons. rheumatologist Nat. Health Svcs., Sunderland, 1995—; cons. rheumatologist Leicester Royal Infirmiry. Contbr. papers to med. jours. Fellow Royal Coll. Physicians, Brit. Rheumatology Soc. Muslim. Avocations: cricket, squash, computing. Home: 15 Mill Hey Ave, Lancashire FY6 8DR, England Office: Cons Rheumatologist, Leicester Royal Infirmary, LEI 5WW Leicester England

HASSANAIN, AHMED HANY ABDEL HAMID KAMAL, environmental chest physician, educator, consultant, researcher; b. Cairo, Aug. 23, 1955; s. Abdel Hamid Kamal Ahmed and Habiba Mokhtar (Qamah) H.; m. Maha Osman Elshenawe, Dec. 22, 1983; children: Habiba, Mohamed. MB, BCh, Ain Shams U., Cairo, 1979, MS, 1988, PhD, 1991. Commd. 1st lt. Egyptian Med. Corps, 1979, advanced through grades to col., 2000; resident Ministry Health, 1980-83; house officer-specialist Respiratory D Hosp., Cairo, 1979-88, registrar, 1988-91, head respiratory function lab., 1991-95; dir. Mollak Army Hosp., Ismailia, Egypt, 1995-96; cons. environ. scis. Army Med. Corps, Cairo, 1995—; head chest disease and allergy dept. Maadi Armed Forces Hosp., Cairo, 1995—; asst. prof. Mil. Med. Acad., Cairo, 1996—; cons. Army Med. Corps, 1994—; head relief group Sini floods Army Med. Corps, Egypt, 1988; mem. relief group, Mission to Iran, 1990. Contbr. articles to profl. jours. with interest in math. modelling of lung function and air pollution, environ. and defence and strategy. Mem. Egyptian Respiratory Soc. (assoc.), Brit. Thoracic Soc. (assoc.). Muslim. Avocations: reading in sciences and arts, writing novels and scenarios for TV and film. Fax: 202-5256339. Home: 8 Ismail Mohy El Din, 11341 Heliopolis Cairo Egypt Office: Maadi Armed Forces Hosp, Kornish El Nile, Cairo Egypt

HASSANAL BOLKIAH, HIS MAJESTY MUI'ZZADDIN WADDAULAH, Sultan of Brunei; b. Darussalam, Brunei, July 15, 1946; s. Sultan Omar Ali Saifuddin; m. Rajah Isteri Anak Saleha, 1965; 6 children; m. Pengiran Isteri Hajjah Mariam, 1981, 1 child. Student, Victoria Inst., Kuala Lumpur, Malaysia, 1961-63, Royal Mil. Acad., Sandhurst, Eng., 1963-67. Apptd. crown prince and heir apparent for State of Brunei, 1961; ruler of state, sultan, 1967—, prime min., 1984—, min. fin. and home affairs, 1984-86, min. of def., 1986—. Hon. capt. Coldstream Guards, 1968. Office: Office of HM The Sultan, Bandar Seri Begawan 1000, Brunei*

HASSAN BIN TALAL, Crown Prince of Jordan; b. Amman, Jordan, Mar. 20, 1947; brother of the late King Hussein of Jordan; m. Sarvath, 1964; children: Rahma, Sumaya, Badiya, Rashid. BA, Christ Ch., Oxford U. Hon. gen. Jordanian Army; pres. Higher Coun. for Sci. and Tech.; co-patron Islamic Acad. Scis.; founder Royal Sci. Soc., Bilad Al-Sham Conf., Al Al-Bait Found., Royal Inst. for Interfaith Studies. Author: A Study on Jerusalem, 1979, Palestinian Self-Determination, 1981, Search for Peace, 1984. Co-chmn. Ind. Commn. on Internat. Humanitarian Issues. Mem. Royal Sci. Soc. Jordan (founder 1970, chmn.). Address: Majlis el Hassan, Royal Palace, Amman Jordan

HASSANE, MAHAMAT HASSANE, veterinary scientist; b. Ndjamena, Chad, Dec. 24, 1955; s. Mahamat Hassane Adam and Amina Moussa; m. Rosemary Wanjiru Ikonya, Dec. 20, 1985; 1 child, Abderahman. MSc in Vet. Studies, Karl Marx U., Leipzig, German Dem. Republic, 1980; Dr. medicinae veterinariae, Ludwig Maximillian U., Munich, Fed. Republic Germany, 1983; PhD, U. Sierra Leone, Freetown, 1992; MBA, Kenyatta U., Nairobi, Kenya, 1999. Cert. in vet. medicine, Chad, Kenya. Rsch. asst. Inst. Parasitology, Tropical Medicine and Infectious Disease, Munich, 1981-83; rsch. fellow Internat. Lab. for Rsch. on Animal Diseases, Nairobi, Kenya, 1984-86, Internat. Ctr. Insect Physiology and Ecology, Nairobi, 1987-90; postdoctoral rsch. assoc. dept. zoology Seattle U., 1990; postdoctoral rsch. fellow Internat. Ctr. Insect Physiology and Ecology, Nairobi, 1990-94, scientist, 1984-98; prin. scientist, dir. Ctr. Recherche Environ. et Devel. Durable au Tchad, Ndjamena, 1999—; cons. Internat. Ctr. Insect Physiology and Ecology, Nairobi, 1988; di. Contbr. rsch. articles to profl. jours. Vice-chmn. African Regional Postgrad. Programme in Insect Sci. Network, Nairobi, 1997-98; project coord. Assn. Tchadienne Pour la Protectione de l'Environment (ATUPE). Otto Benecke Stiftung scholar, 1980-83, PhD scholar Deutscher Academischer Austauch Dienst (DAAD), German Acad. Exch./African Regional Postgrad. Programme in Insect Sci. (ARPISS), 1987-90. Mem. Internat. Soc. Chem. Ecology, Internat. Assn. Camel Practitioners and Rschrs., Assn. Veterinaires Tchadiens, East African Wildlife Soc., Kenya Inst. Mgmt. Muslim. Avocations: sightseeing, reading, walking. Fax: 00-235-521771. E-mail: hmahamat@intnet.td. Office: Ctr Recherche Environ Devel, Avanue Numeiry, Ndjamena BP 853, Chad

HASSANEIN, MUHAMMAD MEDHAT, federal official. Min. of fin. Egypt, 1999—. Office: Ministry of Fin, Lazougli Square, Cairo Egypt*

HASSEL, JAMES CRAIG, counselor; b. Wilkes-Barre, Pa., Nov. 15, 1960; s. Robert Ward and Eleanor I. (Krommes) H. BS, King's Coll., Wilkes-Barre, Pa., 1987; MS, U. Scranton, 1990. Cert. addictions counselor. Peer counselor N.E. Pa. C.I.L., Scranton, 1988-90; rehab. counselor United Rehab. Svcs., Wilkes-Barre, 1990; drug and alcohol counselor Cath. Soc. Svc., Wilkes-Barre, 1990-98, Serento Gardens, Hazleton, Pa., 1998, Children's Svc. Ctr., Wilkes-Barre, Pa., 1999, Greenway Ctr., Henryville, Pa., 1999, Clem-Mar House, Inc., Edwardsville, Pa., 2000—. Home: 50 Waller St Wilkes Barre PA 18702

HASSELHOFF, DAVID, actor; b. Balt., July 17, 1952; m. Catherine Hickland (div.); m. Pamela Bach; children: Taylor-Ann, Hayley Amber. television appearances include: (series) The Young and the Restless, 1975-82, Semi-Tough, 1980, Knight Rider, 1982-86; exec. prodr., star Baywatch, (NBC) 1989-90, (syndicated) 91—, Baywatch Nights, 1995—; (movies) Griffin and Phoenix: A Love Story, 1976, Pleasure Cove, 1979, The Cartier Affair, 1984, Bridge Across Time, 1985, Perry Mason: The Case of the Lady in the Lake, 1988, Knight Rider the Movie, 1988, Panic at Malibu Pier, 1989, Knight Rider 2000, 1990, Ring of the Muskateers, 1992, Avalanche, 1994, Gridlock, 1996, Nick Fury, 1997, Shaka Zulu: The Citadel, 1999, Diamond Hunters, 1999; films include: Starcrash, 1979, Starke Zeiten, 1988, W.B. Blue and the Bean, 1989 (also co-prodr.), The Final Alliance, 1989, Legacy, 1998, The Big Tease, 1999, The Target Shoots First, 2000, Layover, 2000; albums include Looking for Freedom, 1989 (Platinum), Crazy for You, 1991 (Gold), David, 1991 (Gold), Everybody's Sunshine, 1992 (Gold), You Are Everything, 1993 (Gold), Du, 1994, Best of David Hasselhoff, 1995, David Hasselhoff, 1995, Hooked on a Feeling, 1997, Magic Collection, 2000; (video) Baywatch: Forbidden Paradise, 1995. Office: care Jan McCormack 11342 Dona Lisa Dr Studio City CA 91604-4315

HASSELMO, NILS, academic administrator, linguistics educator; b. Kola, Sweden, July 2, 1931; came to U.S., 1958; s. A. Wilner and Anna Helena (Backlund) H.; m. Patricia June Tillberg, Oct. 25, 1958; children: Nils Peter, Michael Erik, Anna Patricia. Fil. mag., Uppsala U., 1956, Fil. lic., 1962, PhD (hon.), 1979; BA, Augustana Coll., Ill., 1957, DHL (hon.), 1995; PhD, Harvard U., 1961; LHD (hon.), North Park Coll. Theol. Sem., 1992. Asst. prof. Swedish Augustana Coll., Rock Island, Ill., 1958-59, 61-63; from assoc. prof. to prof. Scandinavian langs. and lit. U. Minn., Mpls., 1965-83, 88—, chmn. Scandinavian langs. and lit., 1970-73; dir. U. Minn. Ctr. for N.W. European Langs. and Area Studies, Mpls., 1970-73; assoc. dean U. Minn. Coll. Liberal Arts, Mpls., 1973-78; v.p. for adminstrn. and planning U. Minn., Mpls., 1980-83; sr. v.p. acad. affairs, provost U. Ariz., Tucson, 1983-88, prof. English and linguistics, 1983-88; pres. U. Minn., Mpls., 1988-97, Assn. Am. Univs., Washington, 1998—; vis. com. dept. Germanic langs. and lit. Harvard U., Cambridge, Mass., 1981-86; trustee Nat. Merit Scholarship Corp., 1992-97. Author: Amerikasvenska, 1974, Swedish America: An Introduction, 1976; editor: Perspectives on Swedish Immigration, 1978. Bd. dirs. Swedish Council Am., 1978—, chmn. bd. 1999—; bd. dirs. Walker Art Ctr., 1989-95; mem. Gov.'s Task Force on Technology and Improvement of

Employment, Minn., 1982-83; mem. bd. overseers Mpls. Coll. Art & Design, 1982-83; trustee Am. Scandinavian Found., 1992—. Served to sgt. Royal Signal Corps, Swedish Army, 1951-54. Fulbright-Hays fellow, 1968; decorated Royal Order of North Star Sweden, 1973; recipient King Carl XVI Gustaf's Bicentennial medal in Gold Sweden, 1976, Swedish-Am. of Yr. award Swedish Govt. and Vasa Order Am., 1991, Ellis Island medal of honor, 1993. Mem. MLA, Soc. for Advancement Scandinavian Study (pres. 1971-73), Linguistic Soc. Am., Vetenskaps-Societeten, Royal Gustavus Adolphus Acad., Swedish-Am. Hist. Soc. (chmn. bd. 1984-86), Nat. Assn. State Univs. and Land Grant Colls. (exec. com. Acad. Affairs Coun. 1986-88, chmn. coun. pres. and chancellors 1992-93, chair bd. 1994-95), Univ. Rsch. Assn. (trustee 1993-97).

HASSETT, JAMES MANNING, small business owner, psychology educator; b. N.Y.C., June 22, 1947; s. John and Jean (Manning) H.; m. Patricia Ann Dugan, Nov. 26, 1977; 1 child, Eileen. BS in Psychology, Fordham U., 1969; MA in Psychology, Harvard U., 1971, PhD in Psychology, 1975. Asst. prof. Wellesley (Mass.) Coll., 1974-75, Boston U., 1974-84; assoc. editor Psychology Today, N.Y.C., 1977-80; cons. editor Addison-Wesley Pub., Reading, Mass., 1984; rsch. psychologist Sci. Systems, Inc., Cambridge, Mass., 1984-85; pres. Brattle Systems, Inc., Arlington, Mass., 1985—. Author: A Primer of Psychophysiology, 1978, Psychology in Perspective, 1984, (with others), 2d edit., 1989; contbr. articles to profl. jours. NSF fellow, 1969; recipient Sci. Writers award ADA, 1978; recipient Small Bus. Prime Contractor award of excellence SBA, 1997; named Prime Contractor of Yr. for New Eng. SBA, 1999. Office: Brattle Systems Inc 1100 Massachusetts Ave Arlington MA 02476-4332

HASSETT, PATRICK JOHN, airline pilot; b. Chgo., Mar. 17, 1958; s. John J. and Gerrie A. (Tubacki) Carrabine. BS in Aero. Sci., Embry-Riddle Aero. U., 1980, MS in Aero. Sci., 1985; MS, U. So. Calif., 1982. Lic. FAA airline transport pilot, flight instr. airplane, helicopter, glider, FAA flight engr., dispatcher, mechanic; Argentine pilot rated, Peruvian pilot rated, Saudi pilot rated, FCC G.R.O.L. w/radar; USCG rated mcht. marine capt. Commd. 2d lt. U.S. Army, 1980; advanced through grades to capt., 1984; army pilot, capt. U.S.A. Aviation Ctr., Ft. Rucker, Ala., 1981-85; army test pilot Eighth Army, Korea, 1985-86, 501st M.I., Korea, 1986-88; pilot Eastern Airlines, Miami, Fla., 1989-91, Rich. Internat. Airways, Miami, Fla., 1991-92, Saudi Arabian Airlines, Jeddah, Saudi Arabia, 1992-99; L1011 pilot Nova Air of Sweden, Stockholm, 1999; A300 pilot, CRM instr. Tradewinds Airlines, 1999—; scouting asst. dist. commr., Daytona, Fla., 1976-80, Ft. Rucker, Ala., 1982-85; accident prevention counselor FAA, Ft. Rucker, 1982-85; V.I.P. dispatcher, instr., 1988 Seoul Olympic Com., 1988; media/VIP lot mgr. NBC/Atlanta Com. Olympic Games, 1996. Contbr. numerous articles to profl. publs. Mem. CAP. Recipient Medal of Merit for Saving Life, 1976, 84, Air medal and Aerial Achievement medal USAF, 1991. Mem. Internat. Soc. Air Safety Investigators, Aviation Psychologists Assn. Avocations: collecting World War I, World War II and East German militaria, photography, master scuba diving (divemaster). Home: 715 Schilling Dr Dyer IN 46311-2351

HASSMÉN, PETER KARL, psychology educator, researcher, author; b. Stockholm, Sept. 13, 1956; s. Karl-Axel and Marianne Elin (Elwing) H. BSc, Stockholm U., 1983, PhD, 1991. Rsch. asst. N.Mex. State U., Las Cruces, 1987-88; rsch. asst. Stockholm U., 1983-88, doctoral position, 1988-91, asst. prof. psychology, 1991-92, assoc. prof., 1992—, dir. unit sport psychology, 1996—; cons. Karolinska Hosp., Stockholm, 1994—. Author: Analysis of Variance, 1996, Be a Smart Exerciser, 1999; contbr. articles to sci. jours., including Psychosomatic Medicine, Nutrition, Med. Sci. Sport Exercise, Acta Physiologica, Sport Psychologist, Jour. Sport Scis. Grantee Swedish Ctr. for Sports Rsch., 1989—, Swedish Sports Rsch. Coun., 1994—, also over 30 grants, including U.S. Army Rsch. Inst. Mem. European Group for Rsch. into Elderly, Internat. Soc. Psychophysics, Internat. Soc. Behavioral Medicine. Avocations: photography, writing, painting. Office: Stockholm U, Dept Psychology, SE106 91 Stockholm Sweden

HASSONA, WALID HASSAN, dentist, surgical research scientist; b. Ebshan, Egypt, May 18, 1964; s. Hassan El Saied Hassona and Hosnia M. Fahmy El Deeb. D of medicine, Alexandria Med. Sch., Egypt, 1980, oncology specialist, 1985, cancer rsch. scientist, 1989; gen. dentist, Alexandria Dental Sch., Egypt, 1994. Gen. dentist Lotus Point, Damanhour, 1974—, Walid Pharmacy, Kafr El Shiekh, Egypt, 1976—, Empire Valley, Kafr El Shiekh, 1980—; gen. practitioner Alexandria U. Hosp., 1980-85, cons. oncologist, 1985-89; gen. dentist Ev-Lp Hosp., Damanhour, Egypt, 1994—; cancer rsch. scientist Alexandria U. Hosp., 1989-95. Inventor Al-Araby Mag., 1987. Mem. Up To Date Ctr., Dr.'s Club, The Am. Ctr. (libr. mem.), Internat. Union Against Cancer/Switzerland, Japan Cancer Soc., German Cancer Soc., Am. Assn. Oral and Maxillofacial Surgeons, Up-to-Date Ctr., Dr.'s Club, The Am. Ctr. Al Wafd Polit. Party. Islamic. Avocations: reading, writing, light and classical music, tennis, yoga. Home: 9 Osman Ben Afan St, Damanhour 22111, Egypt Office: Empire Valley, El Sheikh 33716, Egypt

HASTEY, SHARI ROSE, nonprofit organization administrator; b. New Westminster, B.C., Jan. 5, 1946; d. Gilbert Charles and Norma Gertrude (Booth) Clark; m. Allen Barbour, Sept. 3, 1966 (dec. Jan. 1969); m. Kenneth Gerald Hastey, Sept. 21, 1972 (dec.); children: Timothy, Stephen, Cynthia, Karen. Postgrad. in counseling, Fuller Sem.; tng. programs in violence prevention, tng. programs in cultural diversity, tng. in gang awareness. Head counselor, regional co-dir. Young Life Urban Camps, 1976-83; exec. dir. Cmty. Partnership for Youth (CPY), Monterey, Calif., 1993—; ptnr. D&H Assocs., co-owner M.E.S. Ragz, 1991-92; owner Consider It Done, 1990-94; mem. Am. Reads Task Force, 1998—; wedding cons. Chair. adv. bd. Salvation Army, 1987-94; chair bd., mem. basic needs com., cmty. rels. com. Monterey County Homeless Coalition, 1988-92; mem. adv. com. Fort Ord Task Force, 1991-92; bd. dirs. Healthy Start, 1992—, Jim Tunney Youth Found., 1994—. Recipient Outstanding Cmty. Svc. award Sun St. Cts., Inc. 1994, Outstanding Vol. Svc. award Monterey County Vol. Ctr., 1991, Vol. of Yr., 1992, Vol. Appreciation Key to City, Seaside, 2000; named Woman of Achivement, Seaside Bus. and Profl. Women's Club, Woman of Distinction, Soroptimists Internat., 1990; honoree City of Seaside, 1998. Mem. NAACP (life), League United Latin Am. Citizens. Office: Cmty Ptnrshp Youth PO Box 42 Monterey CA 93942-0042

HASTIE, JOHN DOUGLAS, lawyer; b. Guthrie, Okla., Dec. 9, 1939. BA, U. Okla., 1961, LLB, 1964. Bar: Okla. 1964. Atty. Hastie and Kirschner, Oklahoma City, 1974-96; adj. prof. Coll. of Law U. Okla., 1982-90, 2000—; atty. Andrews Davis Legg Bixler Milsten and Price, Oklahoma City, 1996—; adviser and lectr. in field. Contbr. articles to profl. jours. Capt. U.S. Army, 1964-66. Mem. ABA, Okla. Bar Assn., Oklahoma County Bar Assn., Assn. of Bar of City of N.Y., Am. Coll. Real Estate Lawyers, Anglo-Am. Real Property Inst., Am. Law Inst., Am. Coll. Mortgage Attys., Internat. Bar Assn. Home: 1704 Windham Ct Norman OK 73071-7351 Office: Andrews Davis Legg Bixler Milsten and Price 401 W Main St Ste 444 Norman OK 73069-1319

HASTINGS, CHESTER RAY, education educator, director student services; b. San Antonio, Tex., Oct. 29, 1928; s. Albert C. and Flora B. (Ballard) H.; m. Elva J. Davidson, Aug. 27, 1960; children: Terri Lynn, Stephen, Allison Anne. BS, S.W. Tex. State U., 1949, MEd, 1955; PhD, U. Tex., 1964. Lic. profl. counselor, Tex. Tchr. social studies Harlandale H.S., San Antonio, Tex., 1945-54, Alamo Heights Jr. H.S., San Antonio, 1954-55, Armed Forces Dependent Schs., Germany and Japan, 1955-58, Brackenridge H.S., San Antonio, 1958-60; dir. guidance and student svcs. Del Mar Coll., Corpus Christi, Tex., 1961-66; dean and v.p. McLennan C.C., Waco, Tex., 1966-88; prof. edn. adminstrn. Sch. Edn., Baylor U., Waco, Tex., 1988—; dir. student svcs. program and collegiate scholars of practice doctoral progam; mem. summer seminar in acad. adminstrn. Tex. Assn. Colls., San Antonio and Coll. Sta., Tex., 1967; mem. Nat. com. of Coll. Placement and Guidance Exams. Coll. Bd., Princeton, N.J., 1969-70; mem. com. on sch. and coll. practice So. Assn. of Schs. and Colls., Atlanta, 1969-72; adv. com. Area Agy. on Aging, Waco, Tex., 1987-88, Tex. Higher Edn. Coord. Bd. Affirmative Action Com., Austin, 1984-86. Pres. N.W. Rotary Club, Waco, Tex., 1977-78; v.p. and charter mem. Eastside Rotary Club, Waco, 1967-69; bd. trustees The Art Ctr., Waco, 1980-88, chair edn. adv. com. Heart of Tex. Private Industry Coun., Waco, 1986-88; administrator Founds. in Edn. U. Tex., Austin, 1959. Recipient Nat. Def. Edn. Act fellowship in guidance and counseling, U. Tex., Austin, 1969, fellowship in Jr. Coll. Adminstrn. Kellogg Found., 1960-61, 1962-63. Mem. ASCD, Am. C.C. Assn., Am. Counseling Assn., Am. Coll. Pers. Assn., Tex. Counseling Assn., Phi Delta Kappa (pres. Baylor chpt. 1990-91). Avocations: gardening, travel. Home: 504 Kiowa Ln Waco TX 76706-5135 Office: Baylor U Sch Edn Waco TX 76748

HASTINGS, DAVID JOHN, management consultant; b. Norwich, Eng., Feb. 20, 1932; s. Stanley Gordon and Leila Mary (Pick) H.; m. Jean Edrich, June 21, 1956; children: Roger Jonathan, Carol Joanne. Student, King Edward VI, Norwich, 1939-48. Trainee Dougill & Hastings Ltd., Norwich, 1950-54, warehouse dir., 1955-68, joint mng. dir., 1968-80; chmn. Soc. Associated Factors in Europe, London, 1978-80; sr. ptnr. DJ Assocs., Salhouse, Eng., 1980—; dir. Norwich Sport Village, 1988-94; dir. Anglia Housing Group, London, 1991-95. Leader Broadland Dist. Coun., Norwich, 1983-87, vice chmn., 1987-89, chmn., 1989-91; vice chmn. Meml. Trust divsn. USAF Am. Libr., 1990—; trustee Norfolk Heritage Fleet Trust, 1997. Nat. Svc. Royal Air Force, 1950-52, Germany; observer-lt. Royal Observer Corps, 1954-88, Eng. Recipient medal of merit, Scout Assn., 1970, Commdr. in Chief RAF Strike Command commendation, 1976. Mem. Freeman Guild of Air Pilots and Air Navigators, Royal Aero Club (Gold award 1990), U.S. Confederate Air Force (col. 1992), Royal Ocean Racing Club, Horning (Eng.) Sailing Club (Commodore 1963). Mem. Church of England. Avocations: flying, sailing, skiing, family, photography. Office: DJ Assocs, Salhouse, Norfolk NR13 6RQ, England

HASTINGS, ELISA KIPP, English language educator; b. L.A., May 14, 1956; d. Charles F. and Margaret Heaney) Kipp; m. Robert Allan Hastings Jr., July 18, 1987; 1 child, Trevor Carlyle. BA in Theatre Arts, Calif. State U., Northridge, 1978; postgrad., Calif. State U., Dominguez Hills, 1996—. Cert. single subject credential English, English lang. devel. Tchr. Horance Mann Jr. H.S., L.A., 1983-88, Bell Gardens (Calif.) H.S., 1988-92; tchr. Bellflower (Calif.) H.S., 1993—, sch. site coun., 1994-96; festival judge Drama and Shakespeare Festivals, L.A., 1990-92; judge regional speech competition, Cypress, Calif., 1995; mem. curriculum devel. com. Bellflower Sch. Dist., 1996—; advisor Calif. Scholarship Fedn., 1994-96. Prodr., dir.: (video prodn.) Tartuffe, 1991; dir. sch. plays and festivals, 198-96; freelance writer pubs. including Shasta Bus. Jour. Sponsor Christian Children's Fund, 1984-96; mem. Klanwatch-So. Poverty Law Ctr., 1990-96; guild mem. Shakespeare Festival, L.A., 1995-96; mem. Copii Lumii Children's World. Recipient Cert. of Appreciation Sch. Site Coun., Bellflower H.S., 1996. Mem. Writer's Forum in Redding, RESOLVE Nat. Mem. Unity Ch. Avocations: literature-reading and writing, attending theatre and movies, travel. Home: 119 W Mariposa Ave Stockton CA 95204-3623 Office: Bellflower HS 15301 Mcnab Ave Bellflower CA 90706-4101

HASTINGS, JOHN JACOB, writer, lyricist, consultant, activist; b. Walla Walla, Wash., Oct. 7, 1953; s. Frederic William and Margaret Mary (McElliggot) H. AA, Walla Walla C.C., 1976; BFA, Ea. Wash. U., 1979. Mgr. Monroe Cigar Co., Chgo., 1980-83; prof. Harry Truman C.C., Chgo., 1981; farmer Touchet, Wash., 1986-99. Author: Four Score Seven, 1995; (poetry) Playing Possum, 1995, Back on the Stack, 1998, Linda's Lullaby in Heaven, 1998, Penultimate Glory, 1998, Excellent annus, 1998, EiRiECAIM, 2000; lyricist: Hilltop Records, Hollywood, Calif., 1997-98. Cons. Nat. Orgn. Dems., 1975-2000; precinct com. mem. Walla Walla (Wash.) County Dem. Ctrl. Com., 1992-99, mem. Dem. Nat. Com., 1998, Dem. Senatorial campaign, 1998, Westchester County Dem. Party, 2000—; activist Peace Movement, Walla Walla and Bellingham, Wash., 1977-86; mem. MADD, ACLU. Mem. Nat. Geographic Soc., Nat. Trust for Hist. Preservation, Walla Walla Pioneers Hist. Soc. (faculty mem.), Nat. Assn. Women in Arts (assoc.), Smithsonian Instn., Libr. Congress (assoc.), Ea. Wash. U. Alumni, Nat. Parks and Conservation Assn. Wilson Ctr., Handyman's Club Am., Nature Conservancy, Hastings Art Soc. (pres, C.L.O.), N.Y. Acad. Polit. Sci., N.Y. Acad. Sci. Roman Catholic. Avocations: letter writing, conservationist, tree planter. Home and Office: PO Box 854 Mohegan Lake NY 10547-0854

HASUE, KAZUO, chemistry educator; b. Ohmiya, Saitama, Japan, Apr. 10, 1947; s. Setsuko and Saburo (Ohsawa) H.; m. Akemi Saito, Jan. 17, 1980. BS, Waseda (Japan) U., 1971, MS, 1973; DEng, Nihon (Japan) U., 1991. Rsch. assoc. Nat. Defense Acad., Japan, 1973-92, lectr., 1992-94, assoc. prof. chemistry, 1994-99, prof., 1999—. Contbr. articles to profl. jours. Recipient ICT award Fraunhofer Inst. for Chem. Tech., Germany, 1990. Mem. Japan Indsl. Explosives Soc. (award 1984), Chem. Soc. Japan, Internat. Pyrotechnics Soc. Office: Nat Defense Acad Dept Chem, 1-10-20 Hashirimizu, Yokosuka Kanagawa 239-8686, Japan

HASUMI, SHIGEHIKO, academic administrator; b. Tokyo, Apr. 29, 1936. BA, U. Tokyo, 1958, MA, 1960; PhD, U. Paris, 1965. Asst. faculty letters U. Tokyo, 1966-68; lectr. Rikkyo U., 1968-69, assoc. prof., 1969-70; lectr. faculty arts & scis. U. Tokyo, 1970-73, assoc. prof., 1973-88, prof., 1988-97, dir. grad. sch. arts & scis., 1993-95, dean faculty arts & scis., 1993-95, v.p., 1995-97, pres., 1997—; lectr. in field. Author: Against the Japanese Language, 1977, On Soseki Natsume, 1978, Doucault, Deleuze, Derrida, 1978, Peotics of Image, 1979, Mythology of Cinema, 1979, On Kanzaburo Oe, 1982, Directed by Yasujiro Ozu, 1983, Macime Du Damp or Invention of the Mediocrity, 1988, Lectures on Hollywood Film History, 1993; co-author: Yasujiro Ozu Story, 1989. Mikio Naruse or Design for Living, 1990; editor: Foucault's Century, 1993, Lumiere's Century, 1995; contbr. articles to profl. jours. Office: 7-3-1 Hongo, Bunkyo-ku Tokyo 113-8654, Japan*

HASUND, SVEIN HARALD, mechanical engineer; b. Oslo, Norway, Sept. 25, 1942; came to U.S., 1965; s. Inge and Ingeborg Pauline (Kreftung) H.; child from previous marriage, Monica; m. Pauline Grace MacDonald Beith; children: Ian, Craig. AI in Mech. Engring., Schous Tech. Sch., Oslo, Norway, 1965; BSME, U. Colo., 1967; MSME, Stevens Inst. Tech., 1970. Registered engr.-in-tng., Colo. Estimator, controls engr. Exxon Rsch. & Engring., Florham Pk., N.J., 1967-74; cost schedule supervisor Exxon Rsch. & Engring., Alaska, 1974-77; project control supr. Exxon Rsch. & Engring., Florham Pk., 1977-81; supervising engr. Arco Alaska Inc., Anchorage, 1981-83, project. mgr., 1983-88, dir. engring. and projects, 1988-95; owner SHH Consulting, 1995—; project dir. Roche Carolina, Inc., 1996. Webelos leader Boy Scouts Am., Anchorage, 1982-83, asst. troop leader, 1984-85; foster parent State of Alaska, Anchorage, 1984-93; bd. dirs., pres. Anchorage Ski Club, 1984-90; bd. dirs. Anchorage Organizing Com., Winter Olympics, 1988-91, tech. com. cons., 1989; bd. dirs., treas. Anchorage Youth Symphony, 1990-91; mem. Mcpl. Budget Adv. Commn., Anchorage, 1988-95. Sgt. C.E., Norwegian Army, 1961-63. Recipient Chmn.'s award C. of C., Anchorage, 1988; Paul Harris fellow Rotary Internat., 1992. Mem. Soc. Petroleum Engrs., Rotary Internat. (youth exch. officer 1988-95), Tau Beta Pi. Avocations: skiing, tennis, gardening, reading. Home: 2036 Emerson Ln Superior CO 80027-8330

HASUNUMA, KOHJI, biologist, educator; b. Tokyo, Nov. 12, 1943; s. Chiyoji and Fumie Hasunuma; m. Miyako Abe, Mar. 14, 1971; children: Madoka Rai, Itaru. BS in Biol. Sci., Tokyo U., 1966, MS in Biol. Sci., 1968, DSc in Biol. Sci., 1971. Rsch. assoc. Tokyo U., 1971-79; assoc. prof. Nat. Inst. Basic Biology, Okazaki, Japan, 1979-90; prof. Yokohama (Japan) City U., 1990—; vis. rschr. Carnegie Instn. Washington (D.C.), 1990; mem. Com. Natural Sci. in Nat. Inst. Academic Degree, 1994—. Author: (with H. Hirano) Signal Transduction in Plants (in Japanese), 1996, (with N. Kimura and S. Tokunaga) Signal Transduction of Light (in Japanese), 1999; mem. editl. bd. Internat. Jour. Cell Biology, Cytologia, 1991—; contbr. papers to profl. jours.; reviewer in field; hon. theme editor Ency. Life Support Sys., UNESCO, 1999—. Mem. N.Y. Acad. Scis., Internat. Biog. Ctr. (life fellow 1998—, dep. dir. gen. 1998—) (Cambridge), Am. Biog. Inst. (life fellow 1998—, dep. gov. 1998—, rsch bd. adv. 1998—). Achievements include: detection of orthophosphate repressible cyclic phosphodiesterases (cPDase) in the mycelia of Neurospora crassa, circadian oscillation of the concentrations of cAMP and cGMP in the mycelia of N. crassa, and in Lemna paucicostata 381, the stimulation of flowering when cGMP was administered to it, 2 species of cyclic phosphodiesterases activation by heating and by $Mg2+$; isolatation of mutants in the cPDases, cpd-1 and cpd-2 with reduced activities also in the adenylate cyclase resulting in the reduced concentrations of cAMP in the mycelia; development of a hypothesis that mutual regulation of concentrations of 2d messengers including cAMP, cGMP, cytosolic free $Ca2+$ concentration, diacyl glycerol and inositol trisphosphate may constitute underlying mechanism of circadian rhythm (supported by rsch.), in vitro systems to analyze molecular mechanism of light signal transduction. Fax: (home) 0427-99-6045; (office) 045-820-1901. E-mail: hasunuma@tb3.so-net.ne.jp; kohji@yokohama-cu.ac.jp. Home: 438-7 Tsuruma, Machidashi Tokyo 194-0004, Japan Office: Yokohama City U Kihara Inst Biol Rsch, 641-12 Maioka-cho, Totsuka-ku Yokohama 244-0813, Japan

HATA, IRA FRANCIS, technology company executive; b. Santa Monica, Calif., Apr. 4, 1962; s. Hugo Masami and Grace Sachiko (Nishimura) H.; m. Mari Linda Kimura; children: Anna, Justin, Emyle. Student, UCLA, 1982-84, Calif. State U., 1980-82. Dir. procurement Far East N.Am. Philips Co., N.Y.C., 1988-90; pres. Advanced Strategies Corp., Tokyo, 1990-92; assoc. pub. Ziff-Davis Japan Ltd., Tokyo, 1993-94; dir. direct ad sales Internat. Data Group, Tokyo, 1994-95; pres. Roadrunner Tech. Inc., Yokohama, Japan, 1997—; exec. mktg. dir. Datamasa Corp., Tokyo, 1986-87. Democrat. Buddhist. Avocations: karate, basketball, scuba diving, golf, tennis. Office: Roadrunner Tech Inc, 4-1-11-503 Eda Minami, Tsuzuki-ku Yokohama 224-0007, Japan

HATA, KENJIRO, insurance company executive. Chmn. Meiji Life Ins. Co., Tokyo. Office: Meiji Life Ins Co, 2-1-1 Marunouchi Chiyoda-ku, Tokyo 100-0005, Japan*

HATADA, KAZUYUKI, mathematician, educator; b. Maebashi, Gunma, Japan, Dec. 23, 1951; s. Kiyoshi and Tokiko Hatada; m. Kumiko Yoshikawa, Dec. 15, 1985; 1 child, Hidehiko. BS, U. Tokyo, 1974, MS, 1976; DSc, U. Tokyo, 1979. Rsch. fellow faculty sci. U. Tokyo, 1979-80; assoc. prof. dept. math. faculty edn. Gifu U., Gifu City, Japan, 1981-99, prof., 1999—; vis. prof. U. Paris XI, autumn 1993. Contbr. articles to profl. math. jours. Recipient Insignia of Dedications, Cambridge, 1988, Silver medal, 1989, Gold medal for 1st 500, 1990, The Internat. Order of Merit, 1990, Internat. Man of Yr. award, 1991-92, 95-96, 20th Century award for Achievement, 1993, Global Distinction award, 1994-95, The Golden Scroll of Excellence, 1997, Internat. Cultural Diploma Honor, 1988; named Albert Einstein Internat. Acad. Found. honoree, 1998. Mem. World Inst. Achievement (life), Math. Soc. Japan, Am. Math. Soc. (reviewer), Astron. Soc. Japan. Achievements include proofs of the 10 new congruences enjoyed by the eigenvalues of Hecke operators on SL(2,Z); discovery that the Hecke rings as representations act naturally on the integral homology groups and ladic cohomology groups of suitable smooth projective toroidal compactifications of the higher dimensional modular varieties through correspondences and the investigation of properties on this; gave new sharp estimates of the eigenvalues of Hecke operators on Siegel cusp forms; obtained the new expressions of the local zeta functions of the compactified Hilbert modular schemes in terms of the action of the Hecke rings; study of the parabolic cohomology, others. Home: 6-2 Chiyoda 2 chome, Maebashi Gunma 371-0022, Japan Office: Gifu U Dept Math Fac Edn, 1-1 Yanagido Gifu City, Gifu 501-1193, Japan

HATADA, KOICHI, polymer chemistry educator; b. Osaka, Japan, Dec. 15, 1934; s. Yoshio and Yoshi (Jyo) H.; m. Michiko Sawada, Oct. 15, 1961; children: Izuho, Naoki, Tatsuya. BSc in Chemistry, Osaka (Japan) U., 1957, MSc in Polymer Chemistry, 1960, DSc, 1965. Rsch. assoc. Daicel Co. Ltd., Saitama, Japan, 1957-64; asst. prof. faculty engring. sci. Osaka U., Toyonaka, Japan, 1964-67, assoc. prof. faculty engring. sci., 1967-83; postdoctoral fellow U. Mass., Amherst, 1973-74; prof. faculty engring. sci. Osaka U., Toyonaka, 1983-98, dean Faculty of Engring. Sci., 1994-96; prof. of applied physics and chemistry Fukui (Japan) U. of Tech., 1998—; prof. emeritus Osaka U., 1998—; senator Osaka U., 1994-96, v.p., 1997-98. Author: (with Kitayama and Vogl) Macromolecular Design of Polymeric Materials, 1997. Recipient award for disting. svc. in advancement of polymer sci. Soc. Polymer Sci., Japan, 1995. Mem. Chem. Soc. Japan, Soc. Polymer Sci. Japan (head Kansai br. 1990-92, bd. dirs. 1991-94, v.p. 1992-94), Am. Chem. Soc., Japan Soc. Analytical Chemistry, Adhesion Soc. Japan. Home: 3-4-11 Asahigaoka, Ikeda 563-0022, Japan Office: Fukui U Tech Faculty Engr, 3-6-1 Gakuen, Fukui 910-8505, Japan

HATANAKA, MASAKAZU SHOICHI, virology educator; b. Osaka, Kansai, Japan, Mar. 23, 1933; s. Kazuo and Yasue (Sakai) H.; m. Kazuko Fujimoto, Apr. 10, 1963; children: Iwao, Takeshi, Melissa, Rachel, Brooke. MD, Kyoto (Japan) U., 1958, PhD, 1963. Diplomate. Rsch. assoc. Kyoto U., 1963-68; scientist Case Western Res. Med. Sch., Cleve., 1964-65, Salk Inst., San Diego, 1965-67, NIH, Bethesda, Md., 1967-70, Flow Labs., Rockville, Md., 1971-75; expert, sect. head Nat. Cancer Inst., Bethesda, 1975-80; prof. Kyoto U., 1980-95, dir. Inst. for Virus Rsch., 1991-95, prof. emeritus, 1996—; dir. Shionogi Inst. Med. Sci., Osaka, 1995-2000; exec. v.p. Shiongi & Co., Osaka, 1997-2000, adviser, 2000—; rep. U.S.-Japan AIDS Com., Tokyo, 1990—, France-Japan AIDS com., Tokyo, 1990—, Italy-Japan Biotech. Com., Tokyo, 1989—; expert cons. NIH, Bethesda, 1975-80, Fogarty scholar-in-residence, 1995—; vis. prof. INSERM, Pasteur Inst., Paris, 1977. Editor: FEBS Letters, Amsterdam, 1991-95, Microbial Pathogenesis, London, 1991—, Vivus Genes, Dordrecht, 1987-95, Viral Immunology, 1996—; contbr. articles to profl. jours. Mem. evaluation com. Ministry of Health and Welfare, Japan, 1990-98, Ministry Fgn. Affairs, Japan, 1986-95, Agt. of Sci. and Tech., Japan, 1984. Grantee Mitsubishi Found., Tokyo, 1983, Yamada Sci. Found., Osaka, 1989, Uehara Meml. Found., Tokyo, 1989; Fogarty scholar-in-residence NIH, 1995—. Mem. Japanese Biochem. Soc. (bd. dirs.), Japanese Cancer Soc., Japanese Virus Soc. (pres. 1997), Japanese AIDS Soc. Home: 1405 Nakano-cho, 5-13-3 Miyakojima, Osaka 534-0027, Japan Office: Shionogi & Co, 5-12-4 Sagisu Fukushima, Osaka 553-0002, Japan

HATANO, MASAMI, humanities educator; b. Ama-Gun, Aichi, Japan, Feb. 11, 1940; s. Shozo and Chiyo (Okada) H.;m. Toyoko Shibata, Nov. 23, 1969; children: Masatoshi, Masaaki. BEd, Mie U., 1962; MA, Hiroshima U., 1965, postgrad., 1965-68. Tchr. Owase (Mie, Japan) Sr. High Sch., 1962-63; asst. instr. faculty edn. Mie U., 1968-69, instr., 1969-70, assoc. prof., 1970-78, prof., 1978-83, prof. faculty humanities and social scis., 1983-95, prof. emeritus, 1995—; prof. Aichi Gakuin Jr. Coll., 1995—, prof. English, dean, 1996—; chief translator Mitsubishi Rayon Co. Ltd., Ohtake, Hiroshima, 1967; chairperson Mie U. Internat. Exch. Programs, Tsu, Mie, 1983-90, chairperson subcom., 1991-95; vis. prof. Mich. State U., East Lansing, 1977; interviewer Soc. of Testing English Proficiency, Tokyo, 1977—; bd. trustees Aichi Gakuin U. Compiler, commentator: The Hidden Dimension, 1977, To Room Nineteen, 1978; author: (with others) Nihongo ni Natta Gaikokugo Jiten, 1983, Dreams in Macbeth, 1983m, Toward International Orientation in Education, 1984, Tarquin's Ravishing Strides, 1987, Hamlet as a Scholar, 1993, The World of Doris Lessing - With Special Reference to To Room Nineteen, 1996, A World of Doris Lessing, 1998, A Look at International Academic Cooperation Between Universities and Colleges, 1998, Short Stories of Doris Lessing (Japanese transl.), 2000. Recipient Scholarships, Japanese Ministry Edn. East-West Ctr., Tokyo and Honolulu, 1972-73, Honolulu, 1977. Mem. English Lit. Soc. Japan, Shakespeare Soc. Japan. Buddhist. Avocations: international travel, golf. Office: Jr Coll Divsn Aichi Gakuin, 1-100 Kusumoto Chikusa-ku, Nagoya-City Aichi 464-8650, Japan

HATCH, MARK BRUCE, software engineer; b. Lynn, Mass., July 20, 1959; s. Carroll Bruce and Claire Adelle (Sherys) H. BS, U. Mass., 1981; MS, U. Mass., Lowell, 1990. Cons. Bassook & Brisk, Wayland, Mass., 1988-90; dir. R&D Toltran Ltd., Lake Zurich, Ill., 1990-94; pres. Minisoft Systems Design, Lynn, Mass., 1994-98; sr. analyst/client server New England Computer, Wakefield, Mass.; dir. ops. Web Knowlogy, LLC, Wakefield, Mass., 1998—; sr. software engr. One Core Fin. Network, Inc., Woburn, Mass., 1998—, Lava Storm Inc., Waltham, Mass., 2000—; instr. computer sci. North Shore C.C., Lynn, Mass., 1988—. Mem. Internat. Asns. Machine Trans., Assn. Machine Trans. in Americas. Achievements include U.S. and fgn. patents for improved trans. system in the field of machine trans. based on a multi-lingual approach to computer analysis; design on a complete lang.-ing, multi-lingual machine trans. system, integrated client-server svcs. to implement translation techniques in an open systems environment. Home: 67 Mudge St Lynn MA 01902-1215 Office: One Core.com 800 W Cummings Park Ste 2800 Woburn MA 01801-6359

HATCH, ROSS RIEPERT, weapon system engineering executive; b. N.Y.C., Sept. 6, 1934; s. Aylmer Roscoe and Ebba (Riepert) H.; m. Phyllis Anne Hess, July 21, 1961; children: Robert Ross, Michael Aylmer. BS in Engring., U.S. Naval Acad., Annapolis, Md., 1956; MS in Engring. Electronics, U.S. Naval Postgrad. Sch., Monterey, Calif., 1964; MS in Fin. Mgmt., George Washington U., 1972. Commd. ensign USN, 1956, advanced through grades to capt., 1977, ret., 1985, dept. head destroyers, cruisers, ice-breakers, 1956-71; commanding officer guided missile destroyer USS Semmes (DDG-18), Charleston, S.C., 1971-72; commanding officer guided missile cruiser USS Belknap (CG-26), Norfolk, Va., 1979-82; head missile br. Office of Chief Naval Ops., Washington, 1972-76; program mgr. Naval Sea Sys. Command, Washington, 1976-79; dir. combat sys. Naval Sea Sys. Command, 1982-85; strike/cruise missile program mgr. Applied Physics Lab.-Johns Hopkins U., Laurel, Md., 1985-96, asst. dept. head power projection dept., 1996-99; weapon systems cons. Editor procs. Precision Strike Tech. Symposium, 1990-98. Scout master Boy Scouts Am., 1972-75. Recipient Legion of Merit, Sec. of Navy, Arlington, Va., 1985; Hatch Outcrop Antartica named in his honor U.S. Bd. of Geographic Names, Washington, 1962. Mem. IEEE, Am. Soc. Naval Engrs., Precision Strike Assn. (bd. dirs. 1988—), U.S. Naval Inst., Glacer Soc. (advisor 1999—). Republican. Episcopalian. Avocations: photography, studio art glass, computers, travel. Home: 9538 Helenwood Dr Fairfax VA 22032-2006

HATCHER, JOE BRANCH, executive search consulting company executive; b. Ft. Worth, July 28, 1936; s. W. Joe and Jessie Mae Hatcher; m. Irma Gail Collins, Apr. 18, 1957; children: Gregory Layne, Geoffrey Alan, Gailyn. BA, U. Wichita, 1960; MA, U. Kans., 1967, PhD, 1968. Mem. English lit. faculty Baker U., Baldwin City, Kans., 1966-74; asst. to pres. Park Coll., Kansas City, Mo., 1974-75; v.p. Albion (Mich.) Coll., 1976-81; pres. Hendrix Coll., Conway, Ark., 1981-91; vice chmn. 1st Comml. Bank, Little Rock, 1992-95, also bd. dirs., 1992-95; cons. Hatcher & Assocs., Conway, Ark., 1995—; of couns. AST/BRYANT, Conway, 1995—. Bd. dirs. Ark. Coun. for Econ. Edn. Mem. Conway C. of C. Methodist. Avocation: tennis. Office: 916 Heather Cir Conway AR 72032-9395

HATCHER, PETER JOHN, educational psychologist, researcher; b. London, July 9, 1943; s. Peter Raymond and Amelia Violet (Heyward) H.; m. Janet Chambers, Aug. 26, 1967; children: Justine Simone, Julian Peter. BA with Honors in Psychology, U. Durham, Eng., 1966; MSc in Ednl. Psychology, U. Newcastle-upon-Tyne, Eng., 1975; DPhil in Psychology, U. York, Eng., 1992. Rsch. asst. Med. Rsch. Coun., London, 1967-68; spl. edn. tchr. Redbridge Edn. Authority, London, 1968-70; tchr. Bahamas Govt., 1970-73; ednl. psychologist Cumbria Edn. Svc., U.K., 1975-78, 84-96; lectr. psychology U. Ctrl. Queensland, Australia, 1979-83; rsch. fellow U. York, 1996-98; sr. ednl. psychologist Cumbria Edn. Svc., 1996-98; sr. lectr. psychology of edn. U. York, 1998—; Editl. bd. Jour. Dyslexia, Chichester, U.K., 1995—; contbr. articles to profl. jours. Recipient Dina Feiterson rsch. award Internat. Reading Assn., 1998. Fellow Brit. Psychol. Soc. (assoc.); mem. Assn. Edn. Psychologists. Avocations: cycling, walking, music, photography. Office: Univ of York Dept Psych, Heslington, York Y010 5DD, England

HATCHER, STEPHANIE D., accountant; b. Vinita, Okla., July 12, 1966; d. Lowell Craig and Linda Marie H. BS in Acctg., Okla. State U., 1988. CPA. Staff auditor Bank of Am., Dallas, 1988-90, trust asst., 1990-92, trust officer, 1992-94, asst. v.p., 1994-98; supervising sr. tax divsn. KPMG, LLP, Dallas, 1998—. Chmn. fin. com. First Bapt. Ch., Arlington, Tex., 1997—. Mem. AICPA, Tex. Soc. CPAs. E-mail: shatcher@kpmg.com. Office: KPMG LLP 8200 Brookriver Dr Dallas TX 75247-4069

HATEGAN, CORNEL, physicist, researcher; b. Ohaba-Matnic, Romania, Aug. 17, 1940; s. Nicolae and Lia (Albu) H.; m. Dora Tanchis, Oct. 9, 1965; 1 child, Alina. Diploma in physics, U. Bucharest, 1964; PhD in Physics, Inst. Atomic Physics, Bucharest, 1973. Rschr. Inst. Atomic Physics, Bucharest, 1964-70, sr. rschr., 1973—; Humboldt rschr. U. Erlangen-Nurnberg, Germany, 1970-71; guest scientist Physics Tech. Inst., Harkov, 1978-82, U. Munich, 1989-95. Mem. editl. bd. Romanian Rep. Physics, 1992—, Procs. Romanian Acad., 2000—; contbr. articles to profl. jours. including Physics Letters. Recipient Hurmuzescu prize Romanian Acad., 1976. Fellow Inst. Physics (London); mem. Romanian Physics Soc. (pres. nuclear physics divsn. 1990—), Romanian Acad., N.Y. Acad. Scis., Humboldt Club. Romanian Orthodox. Avocation: predictive behavior models in contemporary geopolitics. Home: Str Diligentei 30, RO-74321 Bucharest Romania Office: Inst Atomic Physics, Magurele PO Box MG-6, 76900 Bucharest Romania

HATELY, WILLIAM, retired radiology consultant; b. Edinburgh, Scotland, Dec. 19, 1935; s. William Williamson and Janet Favard (Roxburgh) H.; m. Gillian Massot, Sept. 19, 1959; children: Ruth, Diane. MB, BChir, Edinburgh U., 1958, Diploma in Med. Radiodiagnosis, 1964. Accredited diagnostic radiologist. Intern Royal Infirmary, Edinburgh, 1958-59, sr. house officer, 1962-64, registrar, 1964-65; intern Ea. Gen. Hosp., Edinburgh, 1959; sr. registrar Westminster Hosp., London, 1965-67; fellow in radiology Hosp. of St. Raphael, New Haven, Conn., 1967-68; dir. X-ray dept. The London Clinic, 1976-98; cons. radiologist Royal London Hosp., 1968-98; ret., 1998; pres. British Inst. of Radiology, London, 1992-93; cons. mem. Tower Hamlets Dist. Health Authority, London, 1986-90; sr. examiner Royal Coll. of Radiologists, London, 1989; radiographers bd. Coun. for Profl. Supplementary to Medicine, London, 1985-98. Contbr. articles to profl. jours. Squadron leader RAF med. br. 1959-62. Mem. British Med. Assn. Avocation: travel. Home: 4 Hitherwood Dr, London SE19 1XB, England

HATFIELD, JAMES ALLEN, theater arts educator, administrator; b. Marion, Ind., May 1, 1953; s. Frederick Marion and Mary Josephine (Murray) H.; m. Teresa Faye House, Mar. 28, 1977; 1 child, Edward Everett. BS, Ball State U., 1974, MA, 1975; PhD, Wayne State U., 1981. Asst. prof. Oakland U., Rochester, Mich., 1978-83; assoc. prof. Jackson (Miss.) State U., 1983-86; assoc. prof., chmn. theater dept. Butler U., Indpls., 1986-90; prof., dir. theater dept. U. Tex., Tyler, 1990—; bd. dirs. Opera South, 1984-86; mem. Performance evaluation com. Miss. Arts Commn., Jackson, 1983-86; vice-chair Tex. Kennedy Ctr./Am. Coll. Theatre Festival, 1992-95, state chair, 1996-99. Dir., designer: (operas) Lost in the Stars, 1987, The Marriage of Figaro, 1988, The Merry Widow, 1989, The Great Soap Opera, 1990; (plays) My Sister in This House, 1988 (Am. Coll. Theatre Festival nomination), Another Antigone, 1991 (Am. Coll. Theatre Festival N.E. Tex. Cert. of Excellence), The Doctor in Spite of Himself, 1991, Thymus Vulgaris, 1991, Antigone, 1992, Habeas Corpus, 1992, The Norman Conquests, 1992, Getting Married, 1993, Anatol, 1993, Old Times, 1993, La Ronde, 1994, As You Like It, 1994, You Never Can Tell, 1994, Oleanna (Am. Coll. Theatre Festival Critics Choice Cert. of Excellence), 1994, Oleanna, 1995, KC/ACTF Region VI Production, Later Life, 1995 The Heiress, 1995, 3 Courtelines, 1995, Lettice & Lovage, 1995, Best of Friends, 1996, Phaedra, 1996, Octavia, 1996, Mrs. Klein, 1996, A Midsummer Night's Dream, 1997, Love Letters, Ravenscroft, 1998, The School for Wives, 1998, Love Letters, 1998, Mandrake, 1999, Molly Sweeney, 1999, Indiscretions, 1999, Mandrake, 1999; (mus. theater prodns.) Candide, 1987, Sunday in the P George, 1988, Marry Me a Little, 1989 (Am. Coll. Theatre Festival Nomination), Two by Two, 1993, Candide, 1998, Kismet, 2000. State chmn. Kennedy Ctr./Am. Coll. Theatre Festival, 1996-99; bd. govs. The Assn. for Theatre in Higher Edn., 1997-99. Recipient medal of excellence in lighting Am. Coll. Theatre Festival, 1978, Outstanding Tchg. award U. Tex. Chancellor's Coun., 1993, KC/ACYF Bronze medal for excellence in theatre, 1999. Mem. AAUP, Am. Fedn. Musicians, Assn. for Theatre in Higher Edn. (governing coun.), U.S. Inst. for Theatre Tech., Ind. Theatre Assn., Speech Communication Assn., Assn. Communication Adminstrn., Soc. Stage Dirs. and Choreographers, Tex. Ednl. Theatre Assn., Am. Alliance for Theatre and Edn., South West Theatre Assn. Avocations: photography, graphic design, sailing. Office: U Tex Dept Theater PO Box 8152 Tyler TX 75711-8152

HATFIELD, JESSICA LYNN, media company executive; b. Cape Town, South Africa, Jan. 17, 1957; d. Alan Francis and Dorothy Pamela (Boal) Orange; m. Graham Hatfield, July 22, 1974; children: Carey Anne, Mark Alan. Owner Bracknell Catering Svcs., Berkishire, Eng., 1974-80; account mgr. White Knight, London, 1980-81; mgr. Hartin Kemp Estate Agts., Buckinghamshire, 1985-88; bus. devel. mgr. Euroelectrics, London, 1988-90, Advance Mktg., Buckinghamshire, 1990-91, Trans World Group, Hertfordshire, 1991-94; chmn., CEO The Media Vehicle PLC, London, 1994—. Recipient FMCG Best Sales Promotion award Incentive Today mag., London, 1993. Mem. Home House (founder). Avocations: motor racing, adventuring, reading, music, fundraising. Office: The Media Vehicle Group Plc, 17/18 Great Pulteney St, London W1R 3DG, England

HATFIELD, JIM GAIL, safety engineer; b. Huntington, W.Va., Apr. 21, 1941; s. Ode and Bertha M. (Ross) H.; m. Wynonia Jean Mitchem, May 27, 1961 (dec.); children: Carrie, Julia, Timothy, Daniel, Summer, James; m. Tammy Elizabeth McDaniel, June 6, 1998. Student, Fla. Jr. Coll., 1986, U. N.Mex., 1987. Account specialist Huntington (W.Va.) Alloys Inc., 1961-80; owner Hatfields Constrn. Co., Yulee, Fla., 1981-82; safety supr. Brown & Root Constrn. Co., Houston, 1982-88; corp. safety dir. Davis H. Elliot Co., Inc., Roanoke, Va., 1989-98; safety dir. Red Simpson, inc., Yulee, Fla., 1999—; defensive driving course instr. Nat. Safety Coun., Roanoke, 1990—. Pub. rels. dir. Am. Diabetes Assn., Silver City, N.Mex., 1987-88. Recipient Citizenship award DAR, Huntington, W.Va., 1956. Mem. Am. Soc. Safety Engrs., Safety Coun. S.W. Va., World Safety Orgn. Avocations: camping, fishing, travel, photography, boating. Office: Red Simpson Inc 21 Santa Barbara St Yulee FL 32097-5653

HATHAWAY, LYNN MCDONALD, education advocate, administrator; b. N.Y.C., Mar. 28, 1939; d. William Douglas IV and Dorothy Edna (Homan) McDonald; m. Earl Burton Hathaway II, July 7, 1962; children: Earl Burton III, Amanda McDonald Joyner. BA, Bryn Mawr Coll., 1960. Editl. asst. Mademoiselle mag., N.Y.C., 1960-61; adminstrv. asst. Peace Corps office Nat. Coun. Chs., N.Y.C., 1961-62; vice chmn. cmty. rsch. N.Y. Jr. League, 1969-70; editor, chmn. N.Y. Entertains cookbook, 1973-74; edn. chair London Svc. League, 1979-80; pres., dir. London Svc. League, Jr. League, 1980-82; ind. writer, editor London, 1983. Bd. dirs. Friends of Ferguson Libr., Stamford, Conn., 1988, mem., rec. sec., v.p., pres., 1988-95, trustee, 1996—, sec. bd. trustees, 1995—, continuing chair student life com.; trustee, mem. exec. com., chair student life com. Conn. State U. Sys., 1991—, sec. bd. trustees, 1999. Mem. Bryn Mawr Alumnae Assn. (pres. London 1983-86, internat. councillor 1988-90). Episcopalian. Fax: 203-359-2511. E-mail: lynnhath@aol.com. Home: 50 Old North Stamford Rd Stamford CT 06905-3961

HATHCOCK, JOHN EDWARD, vocalist; b. Memphis, Sept. 6, 1955. BA in Psychology, Memphis State U. (now U. Memphis), 1986; studied with Dr. David Williams, U. Memphis, 1992-97; studied with Ethel Maxwell, 1982-98. Singer, performer, composer opera and sacred classical music, vocal coach, 1999—; pres. Position Prodns., 1988-90; pres., founder Soaring Spirit Music, 1996—. Author: Seasons of Wonder, 1995; author poems; patentee in field; exec. prodr., vocal performer Grace: The Eternal Song. Mem. Bellevue Choir, 1991-92, Memphis Vocal Arts Ensemble, 1993, The Heritage Found. Recipient Mr. Wheelchair Am. award, 1990, Man of Yr. award Happi Internat. Talent, Trailblazer award City of Memphis, 1990. Mem. Gospel Music Assn. (profl.), Beethoven Club (dir. pub. rels. 1993), Internat. Platform Assn., Heritage Found., Internat. Soc. Poets. Baptist. Fax: 901-683-6805.

HATHORNE, GAYLE GENE, musician, genealogical educator, writer; b. Concordia, Kans., Sept. 3, 1953; d. Richard and R. Virginia (Huscher) Hathorne; 1 child, Amanda Kimberly. BMusic, Manhattan Sch. Music, N.Y.C., 1976; Artist's Diploma, Karajan Akademie, Berlin Philharm. Orch., 1980; student, Mars Hill (N.C.) Coll., 1989-90, Blue Ridge C.C., Flat Rock, N.C., 1991, 92. Backstage hornplayer Bayreuth (Germany) Festival, 1977; 3d/1st solo hornist Stadt. Orch., Solingen, Germany, 1980-88; genealogy instr. Blue Ridge C.C., 1999—; pvt. horn tchr., Hendersonville, 1989—; substitute tchr. music and German, Henderson County Pub. Schs., 1988-98. Sr. editor Tarheel Tattler, 1994-96, River Ramblings, 1994-96; editor Kuykendall Gazette, 1996-97; performer on CDs/cassettes; extra in film 28 Days, 1999. Nat. Fedn. Music Clubs nat. scholar, 1971. Mem. DAR (state pub. rels. N.C. Soc. 1997-99, organizing regent Abraham Kuykendall chpt. 1996), Children of Am. Revolution (organizing sr. pres. French Broad River Soc. 1992, state libr. 1996-98). Democrat. Avocations: genealogical research, photography, travel, writing, listening to opera. Home: 346 Stoney Mountain Rd Hendersonville NC 28791-2085

HATLEVOLL, REIDULV, oncologist; b. Baerum, Norway, Apr. 2, 1935; s. Nils and Marit (Lindgren) H.; m. Svanhild Hagen, Mar. 28, 1958; children: Helge, Øyvind, Trond, Ingunn, Hilde. MD, U. Oslo, 1960. Cert. specialist in radiology and oncology. Registrar Regional Hosp., Trondheim, Norway, 1963-68; registrar Norwegian Radium Hosp., Oslo, 1968-73, cons., 1973—. Contbr. articles to profl. jours. Lt. Norwegian Air Force, 1962-63. Mem. Norwegian Med. Assn. (bd. mem. jr. doctors 1964-68), Norwegian Oncol. Soc., European Soc. Therapeutic Radiology and Oncology. Lutheran. Avocations: outdoor life, skiing. Home: Ramstadas vn 24, 1363 Høvik Norway Office: Norwegian Radium Hosp, Montebello, 0310 Oslo Norway

HATO, TSUNEHIRO, researcher; b. Nagoya, Aichi, Japan, Apr. 30, 1963; s. Tsunenori and Yoko Hato; m. Mitsue Hato, 1999. BS, Nagoya (Japan) U., 1987, MS, 1989, PhD, 1992. Cert. in engring. Rschr. Fujitsu Ltd., Atsugi, Japan, 1992—. Inventor High Tc Josephson Junction with Indium-Tin-Oxide barrier; contbr. articles to profl. jours. Active Ngo Save the Africa fund-raising campaign, 1997. Recipient Inose Sci. award Assn. for Promotion of Elec. Electronic and Info. Engring., 1988, Most Impressive Presentation award Internat. Workshop on High-Temperature Superconducting Electron Devices, 1994. Mem. Japan Soc. of Applied Physics, New Superconducting Materials Forum (committeeman). Avocations: skiing, tennis, mountain climbing, cooking. Office: Fujitsu Ltd, 10-1 Morinosato Wakamiya, Atsugi 243-0197, Japan

HATTENBACH, LARS OLOF, ophthalmologist, researcher; b. Frankfurt am Main, Germany, July 12, 1963; s. Karl Olof and Ingeborg (Schulz) H. MD, Johann Wolfgang Goethe U., Frankfurt, Germany, 1990. Cert. Ednl. Commn. for Fgn. Med. Grads.; bd. cert. ophthalmology. Intern dept. internal medicine Johann Wolfgang Goethe U. Hosp., Frankfurt, 1991-92; resident dept. ophthalmology Johann Wolfgang Goethe U. Hosp., Mainz, Germany, 1992-93; resident dept. ophthalmology Johann Wolfgang Goethe U. Hosp., Frankfurt, 1993-94, 95-98, sr. physician retina specialist/retinal surgeon, 1998—; resident Franz-Volhard Clinic Max Delbruck Ctr. Molecular Medicine, Humboldt U. Hosp., Berlin, 1994-95. Reviewer Ophthalmologica, 1998—; contbr. articles to profl. jours. Vol. paramedic German Red Cross, Frankfurt, 1983-84; ambulatory care mission Ophtalmo Sans Frontieres, Cameroon, Africa, 1996. Recipient Dr. Heinz and Helene Adam award, 1997, award Rhein-Main Opthalmol. Soc., 1998; Johann Wolfgang Goethe U. Rsch. grantee, 1997, August Scheidel Rsch. grantee, 1998, Dr. Paul and Cilli Weill Rsch. grantee, 1999. Mem. European Cmty. Ophthalmic Rsch. Assn., Assn. for Rsch. in Vision and Ophthalmology, German Ophthalmol. Soc. Avocations: skiing, sailing. Office: JW Goethe Univ, Theodor-Stern-Kai 7, 60590 Frankfurt am Main Germany

HATTESTAD, TRINE, Olympic athlete; b. Lorenskog, Norway, Apr. 18, 1966; 2 children. Winner title javelin World Championships, 1993, 97; winner Bronze medal javelin Atlanta, 1996; 3rd place javelin World Championships, 1999; winner javelin Bislett Games, set world record Oslo, 2000; winner Gold medal javelin Sydney, 2000. Office: Norges Fri-idrettsforbund, Karl Johansgt 2, Oslo 1 0154, Norway*

HATTORI, AKIRA, economics educator; b. Kasaoka, Japan, July 8, 1949; s. Setsuo and Chiho Hattori; m. Mizue Tsurufuji, Mar. 21, 1981; children: Yasuyuki, Tomoko. BA, Kagawa U., Takamatsu, Japan, 1972; MA, Kyushu U., Fukuoka, Japan, 1974; PhD, Kyushu U., 1977. Rsch. fellow dept. econs. Kyushu U., Fukuoka, 1977-79; vis. scholar Stanford (Calif.) U., 1987, 92; prof. internat. polit. economy and fgn. exch. Fukuoka (Japan) U., 1987—; mem. com. peace studies Sci. Coun. Japan; co-rschr. Inst. Statis. and Math., Ministry Edn., 2000. Co-author: World Economy and International Trade, 1985, Disarmament, Economic Conversion and Management of Peace, 1991, Economic Issues of Disarmament, 1993; editor: International Finance, 1986; co-editor: International Economic Policy Coordination in the 1990's, 1991; Disarmament and Reconstructuring of the World Economy after the End of the Cold War, 1994, the Economics of International Security, 1994, The Economics of Disarmament and International Security, 1995, Arms Spending, Development and Security, 1995, Disarmament and Security Toward the Next Century, 1996, New Economic Era and Global Governance, 1997, Economic Structure in Asian Countries and Peace, 1998, Security and Economics in Asian Countries, 1999; contbr. articles to profl. publs. Bd. dirs. Economists Allied for Arms Reduction, N.Y.C., 1993—, gen. sec., Japan, 1989—; mem. internat. adv. bd. Mahatma Ghandi Internat. Tng. Ctr. Conflict Prevention & Mgmt., India. Fellow Acad. of Polit. Sci.; mem. Am. Econ. Assn., Royal Econ. Soc., Am. Polit. Sci. Assn., Nat. Geog. Soc., Western Econ. Assn. Internat., Japan Soc. Money and Banking. Home: 1-6-31-103 Jonan Ku, Higashiaburayama, Fukuoka 814-0155, Japan Office: Faculty Commerce Fukuoka U, 8-19-1 Nanakuma, Jonan Ku Fukuoka 814-0180, Japan

HATZIALEXANDROU, ELENA, leisure center director; b. Thessaloniki, Greece, Nov. 1, 1967; d. Apostolos and Eli (Alexandridou) H. Diploma, Thessaloniki Bus. Sch., 1988, diploma in acctg., 1989; MBA, Middlesex U., London, 1993; postgrad. diploma, Westminster Univ., London, 1991; postgrad., Royal Coll. of Art, London, 1996. Sales rep. Macedonian Sun Hotel Leisure and Shopping Ctr., Thessaloniki, 1986-87, internal auditor, 1988-89, hotel mgr., 1992-93, dir., 1994-97, also bd. dirs.; mktg., sales mgr., adminstr. Warner Bros. Village Roadshow, 1997-98; dir., ptnr. Mango's Studios, 1999; mng. dir. Papandreou Prodns., 1999-2000; owner, dir. Aroma Export-Imports, Thessaloniki, 1994-98; owner, bd. dirs. Hotel/Leisure Ctr., 1992—. Photographer Ena Mag., 1989; prodr. Safe Sex, 1999, Deep Pink, 2000, Crying, 2000—; exec. prodr. Risoto, 2000; mng. dir. Safe Picture, 2000. Mem. Cultural Devel. of Thessaloniki, 1994. Mem. Halkidiki Hotel Assn. (bd. dirs. 1993-94), Hellenic Inst. of Mgmt., Assn. of MBA's, Nautical Club of Thessaloniki, London New Producer Alliance. Avocations: life drawing, photography, philosophy, water skiing, travelling.

HAU, HARALD, business educator; b. Fulda, Hessen, Germany, Oct. 23, 1966; s. Horst and Margarete (Wolf) H.; m. Laurence Plazenet, Oct. 4, 1997; 1 child, Pierre-Hadrian. BA, U. Bonn, 1990; MA, U. Va., 1991; PhD, Princeton U., 1996. Lectr. Woodrow Wilson Sch., Princeton U., 1995-96; asst. prof. ESSEC-Grad. Bus. Sch., 1996-99, assoc. prof., 1999-2000; assoc. prof. fin. INSEAD Bus. Sch., Fontainebleau, France, 2000—; rsch. affiliate Ctr. for Econ. Policy Rsch., London, 1999—. Contbr. articles to profl. jours. With German Army, 1986-87. Recipient Studienstiftung des deutsohen Volkes, Germany, 1988-92; Herman Schlosser fellow, 1992-95, Bradley fellow, 1993-95. E-mail: harald.hau@insead.fr. Office: INSEAD-Sch Bus, Blvd de Constance, 77305 Fontainebleau Cedex, France

HAU, MICHEL, historian, educator; b. Reims, France, July 16, 1943; s. Jean and Germaine (Appert) H.; m. Nicole Delcleve, Dec. 21, 1973; children: Stephane, Sophie. Maitrise, U. Paris, 1966; Diplome, Inst. Etudes Polit., Paris, 1966; Doctorat, U. Paris, 1985. Asst. U. Strasbourg, France, 1970-74, asst. prof. contemporary history, 1984-87, prof. contemporary history, 1987—. Author: La Croissance de la Champagne, 1976, L'industrialisation de l'Alsace, 1987, Histoire economique de l'Allemagne XIX-XX, 1994, La Maison De Dietrich, 1997. Served with French Army, 1969-70. Mem. Soc. des Amis des Univs. Acad. Strasbourg (sec. gen. 1986—), Soc. Histoire Moderne etr Contemporaine. Roman Catholic. Office: U Strasbourg 2, Palais Univ, 67000 Strasbourg France

HAUBER, FREDERICK AUGUST, ophthalmologist; b. Pitts., July 3, 1948; s. Michael H. and Cecilia (Azinger) H.; m. Cathy Lu Rosellini, Aug. 3, 1981; children: Elizabeth Alexandra, Natalia Fredericka. BS in Microbiology cum laude, U. Pitts., 1970; MD, U. Tenn., 1974. Intern U. South Fla., Tampa, 1975, resident in ophthalmology, 1982; pvt. practice Pasco Eye Inst., New Port Richey, Fla., 1983—; asst. clin. prof. U. South Fla., Tampa, 1984—; rechr., spkr. in field, 1990—; cons. Optimed, Inc. Contbr. articles to profl. jours. Advisor health care cost containment com., Tarpon Springs, Fla., 1988; founder Pasco County Diabetes Assn.; mem. bd. counsellors U. Tampa. Fellow ACS, Am. Acad. Ophthalmology; mem. Southeastern U.S. Debate Soc. Achievements include patent for achromatic intraocular lens; first to insert glaucoma pressure regulator; development of binary optical intraocular lens, color vision eye chart system. Office: Pasco Eye Inst 5347 Main St New Port Richey FL 34652-2506

HAUENSTEIN, KAREN, physician's assistant, critical care nurse; b. Brigham City, Utah, Jan. 18, 1963; d. DeWayne Edgar and Vaudis Jennie (Yates) H.; m. Donald Pope Arnett, Apr. 12, 1997; 1 adopted child, Cory Dee Arnett. Degree in nursing, Weber State U., Ogden, Utah, 1983; cert. physician asst., U. Utah, 1995. RN, Utah. Staff nurse Ecclesiastical Mission, Bolivia, S.Am., 1984-85, McKay Dee Hosp., Ogden, 1983-89; critical care registered nurse LDS Hosp., Salt Lake City, 1989-95; physician asst. Dr. William T. Graff, St. George, Utah, 1995-97, Utah Dept. Juvenile Corrections, St. George, 1996-97, Red Cliffs Family Medicine, St. George, 1997-99; physician asst., clin. staff faculty So. Utah U., Cedar City, 1999—. Vol. Am. Cancer Soc., 1995—, Am. Heart Assn., 1994—. Sterling scholar Deseret News-Salt Lake City, 1980, acad. scholar Weber State U., 1983, Utah Bur. Rural Health, 1993. Fellow Am. Acad. Physician's Assts.; mem. AACN, Bus. and Profl. Women (Young Career Woman 1997), Elks. Avocations: children, animals, music, poetry, hiking. Home: 4071 W 25 N Cedar City UT 84720-8051 Office: Valley View Pediat 150 E Altamira Dr Ste 1000 Cedar City UT 84720-3562

HAUER, JAMES ALBERT, lawyer; b. Fond du Lac, Wis., Apr. 3, 1924; s. Albert A. and Hazel M. (Corcoran) H.; children: Stephen, John, Paul, Christopher, Patrick. BCE, Marquette U., 1948, LLB, 1949; bank mgmt. cert., Columbia U., 1957, U. Wis., 1959. Bar: Wis., U.S. Dist. Ct. (ea. dist.), U.S. Ct. Appeals (9th cir.), U.S. Dist. Ct. (fed. dist.) 1958. Patent counsel Ira Milton Jones, Milw., 1949; chief counsel Wauwatosa Realty, Milw., 1950-57; v.p. Wauwatosa (Wis.) State Bank, 1957-67; pres. Milw. We. Bank, 1967-69, Prem Constrn. Co., Milw., 1969-73; pvt. practice Elm Grove, Wis., 1973-86, Sun City, Ariz., 1986—. Pres., bd. dirs. Sunshine Svc., Sun City, Meals on Wheels, Sun City. With USMCR, 1942-45. Mem. Wis. Bar Assn., Ariz. Patent Law Assn. (charter). Roman Catholic. Office: 9915 W Royal Oak Rd # Gh1078 Sun City AZ 85351-3163

HAUER, JEROME M., city official; b. Manhattan, N.Y., Oct. 31, 1951; s. Milton and Rose Hauer; m. Glenda Hauer; 1 child, Michael. BA, NYU, 1976; MPH, Johns Hopkins U., 1978. Rsch. assoc. divsn. cardiac surgery Johns Hopkins Hosp., Balt., 1976-78; assoc. adminstr. Red Cross Blood Svcs., 1978-80; various positions IBM, 1983-87; dep. dir. Emergency Med. Scs., N.Y.C., 1987-88, spl. asst. to exec. dir., 1988-89; commr. State of Ind., Indpls., 1989-96; dir. N.Y.C. Office Emergence Mgmt., 1996—; reachback cons. USMC, 1998; reviewer Heart and Lung Jour. Critical Care, 1987; lectr., presenter in field. Author: (with others) Auto-Transfusion, 1981, Current Problems in Surgery, 1982, Autotransfusion Units: Guideline Report, 1983, Advanced Emergency Care for Paramedic Practice, 1992; contbr. more than 30 articles to profl. jours. including Emergency Medicine, Resident and Staff Physician, Circulation, among others; mem. editl. bd. Natural Disaster Mgmt. Jour., 1998. Mem. exec. com. Interagy. Coun. Drugs, State Ind., 1989, vice chmn. state emergency response com., 1989-92; chmn., bd. dirs. Ind. Pub. Safety CInst., 1990-94; vice chmn., bd. dirs. Ctrl. U.S. Earthquake Consortium, 1990; chmn. The Leadership Coalition for Global Bus. Protection, 1997; mem. sci. adv. for hazardous materials response FBI, 1997; mem. Am. Heart Assn., Am. Lung Assn. Recipient bronze award Internat. Film and TV Festival, 1986, Legion of Hoosier Heros award Mil. Dept. Ind., 1994, Ind. Commendation medal for Exceptional Meritorious Svcs., Ind. Nat. Guard, 1994, Sagamore of the Wabash award, Gov. Evan Bayh, 1994, Outstanding Alumnus of Yr. Pub. Health Practice, Soc. Alumni Johns Hopkins U. Sch. Hygiene and Pub. Health, 1995, Disting. Alumni award NYU, 1997, Hon. Legion award N.Y.C. Police Dept., 1998; named Man of Yr. Fire Safety Dirs. N.Y.C., 1999. Fellow Internat. Soc. Hematology; mem. Nat. Emergency Mgmt. Assn. (regional v.p., treas. 1990), Nat. Assn. State EMS Dirs. (govt. affairs com. 1993-95), Nat. Fire Protection Assn. (tech. com. on disaster mgmt. 1993-95), Internal Security Assn., Assn. Contingency Planners, Am. Soc. for Indsl. Security, Ind. Arson and Crim Assn. (hon.), Internat. Assn. Fire Chiefs, Internat. Rescue and Emergency Care Assn., Acad. Surg. Rsch., Am. Soc. Hosp. Based Emergency Air Med. Svc., N.Y. Acad. Scis., Assn. Mil. Surgeons U.S., Internat. Soc. Blood Transfusion, Internat. Soc. Thrombosis and Haemostatis, Mass. Assn. Blood Banks. Office: Office Emergency Mgmt 7 World Trade Ctr Fl 23 New York NY 10048-2301

HAUER, THOMAS, philosopher; b. Čeladná, Czech Republic, Jan. 21, 1963; s. Thomas Hauer and Dobroslava (Melichaříková) Matochová; m. Věra Zálešák, Mar. 8, 1985 (div. 1988); 1 child, Thomas; m. Stanislava Dorda, 1989; children: Agata, Michel. MA, Masaryk U., Brno, Czech Republic, 1990, PhD, 1996. Lectr. metalurgy U. Mining and Metalurgy, Ostrava, Czech Republic, 1991-94; chair Inst. Philosophy U. Mining and Metalurgy, Ostrava, 1995—; lectr. U. Mining and Metalurgy, Tech. U. Ostrava; lectr. dept. philosophy U. Ostrava. Author: Wandering is not Gaping/Postmodernism and the Natural World, 1995, Inquiry as Recontextualization, 1996. Mem. N.Y. Acad. Scis. Avocations: literature, internet, farming. E-mail: Tomas.Hauer@vsb.cz. Fax: 0042 69 663 33 07. Home: Zvoníčkova 158, 715 00 Ostrava Michalkovice Czech Republic Office: Univ Mining and Metalurgy, 17 Listopadu, 708 33 Ostrava Czech Republic

HAUG, MARIUS NYGAARD, investment company executive; b. Oslo, Nov. 23, 1960; s. Bjørn and Agnes (Nygaard) H.; m. Hege Johanna Andenes; children: Tønnes, Agnes. M of Laws, U. Oslo, 1988. Inspector The Banking Ins. and Securities Commn., Oslo, 1988-91, gen. coun., 1994-97; legal advisor The Ministry of Fin., Oslo, 1991-92; exec. officer EFTA Surveillance Authority, Geneve and Brussels, 1992-94; legal dir. Norges Bank Investment Mgmt., Oslo, 1997-99, head of legal and compliance, 1999—. Avocation: golf. Home: Dyrlandsveien 11, 0875 Oslo Norway Office: Norges Bank Investment Mgmt, PO Box 1179, 0107 Oslo Norway

HAUG, THOMAS PETER, communications executive; b. Weiningen, Zürich, Switzerland, Sept. 11, 1964; s. Werner A. and Gertrud (Weber) H.; m. Alessandra Christina Berger, Sept. 21, 1990; children: Alexander Thomas, Sarah Christina. Degree in Bus. Economy and Adminstrn., Polytecnicum, Berne, Switzerland, 1990; Corp. Fin. Evening Programme, London Bus. Sch., 1992. Info. tech. project mgr. Frama Ltd., Switzerland, 1987-89, dir. bus. devel., 1993-95, CEO, 1996—; mng. mgr. Frama (UK) Ltd., Eng., 1990-92. Mem. Eurobit (bd. dirs.), Employers Assn. Berne (mem. exec. bd.), London Bus. Sch. Alumni Assn. Avocations: tennis, skiing, family activities. Office: Frama Ltd, Kalchmatt, 3438 Lauperswil Berne, Switzerland

HAUGAARD, MARK, social theorist; b. Copenhagen, June 8, 1961; s. Erik Christian and Myrna Lita (Seld) H.; m. Rhoda Patricia Clarke, July 7, 1987; 1 child, Vanessa. BA, Trinity Coll., Dublin, 1984, MPhil, 1985, PhD, 1991. Lectr. U. Coll., Dublin, 1991-94; Newman scholar Univ. Coll., Dublin, 1994-97; lectr. Nat. U. Ireland, Galway, 1997—. Author: The Constitution of Power, 1997, Structures Restructuration and Social Power, 1992. Newman scholar, 1994-97. Avocations: sailing, politics, music. Office: Dept Politics/Sociology, Nat Univ Ireland, Galway Ireland

HAUGGAARD-NIELSEN, ANDERS BOE, structural engineer; b. Esbjerg, Denmark, Feb. 18, 1968; s. Henrik Boe and Else (Hindsgavl Madsen) H.; m. Pernille Hauggard; 1 child, Louise. MSc, DTU, Copenhagen, 1993, PhD, 1997. Structural engr. Ramboll, Copenhagen, 1997-99, Mobilix, Copenhagen, 1999—. Home: Fuglegardsvej 34 B, 2820 Guentofte Denmark Office: Prags Blvd 80, 2300 Copenhagen Denmark

HAUGHEY, EDWARD ENDA, pharmaceuticals executive; b. Drogheda, Ireland, Jan. 5, 1944; s. Edward and Rose (Traynor) H.; m. Mary Gordon Young, Jan. 5, 1972; children: Caroline Philippa, Edward Gordon Shannon, James Quinton Stewart. Grad., Christian Bros. Sch., Dundalk, Ireland; D in Bus. Adminstrn. (hon.), Internat. Mgmt. Inst., 1992; LLD (hon.), Nat. U. Ireland, 1996. Chmn., CEO Norbrook Labs. Ltd., Newry, Northern Ireland, 1969—; bd. dirs. Bombardier Shorts PLC, Northern Ireland, Bank of Ireland Mgmt., Northern Ireland, Ballyemond Castle Farms, Northern Ireland, Norbrook Holdings, Northern Ireland. Patentee low-pain injection of oxytetracycline for veterinary use. Sentator Upper Ho. Irish Parliament, Dublin, 1994, reapptd., 1997; hon. consul for Chile in Northern Ireland, 1992. Decorated Order of Brit. Empire for Svcs. to Industry, 1986, Gran Ofcl. Order Bernardo O'Higgins, Chile, 1994. Fellow Irish Mgmt. Inst. (hon.), Royal Coll. Surgeons Ireland (hon.); mem. Farmers Club (London), Reform Club (Belfast, Northern Ireland), Savage Club (London). Mem. Fianna Fail party. Avocations: fishing, shooting, studying architectural history. Office: Norbrook Labs Ltd, Station Works, Camlough Rd, BT35 6JP Newry Northern Ireland

HAUGLAND, JERRY LEE, accounting educator; b. Sutherland, Nebr., Aug. 26, 1941; s. Jacob Reinertsen and Louise Anna (Burklund) H.; m. Susan Warrell, July 24, 1982; children: Charles, Michael. BSBA, U. Nebr., 1962, MA, 1966; PhD, Okla. State U., 1975. Cert. mgmt. acct. Instr. S.E. Mo. State U., Cape Girardeau, 1966-73, asst. prof., 1973-75, assoc. prof., 1975-79, prof., 1979—, coord. MBA program, 1976-86; bd. dirs. Haugland Ranch Inc., Sutherland, 1984—; acctg. program cons. Northeastern State U., Tahlequah, Okla., 1989. Book reviewer Scott, Foresman and Co., 1993, Prentice Hall, 1993, John Wiley and Co., 1993, South-Western, 1995, Richard D. Irwin, 1997; contbr. articles to profl. jours. Treas. Optimist Club, Cape Girardeau, 1975, 76. Recipient Outstanding Svc. award Alpha Kappa Psi, 1978, Outstanding Svc. award Beta Gamma Sigma, 1997. Mem. Am. Acctg. Assn. (state chairperson 1977, membership com. 1981), Mo. Assn. Acctg. Edn. (bd. dirs. 1976-78, v.p. 1979, pres. 1980), Beta Alpha Psi. Office: SE Mo State Univ One University Pla Cape Girardeau MO 63701

HAUGLAND, SUSAN WARRELL, education educator, consultant; b. Portland, Oreg., Aug. 29, 1950; d. George William and Commery Wallace (Coleman) Warrell; m. Jerry Lee Haugland, July 24, 1982; children: Charles, Michael. BS in Child Devel., Oreg. State U., 1972; PhD in Psychology, Saybrook Inst., 1976. Cert. family and consumer scis. Dir., head tchr. Lafayette Co-op Nursery Sch., Detroit, 1973-75; handicapped svcs. coord. OutWayne County Head Start, Wayne, Mich., 1975-76; asst. prof. child devel. Va. Poly. Inst. and State U., Blacksburg, 1976-79; prof. emeritus child devel. S.E. Mo. State U., Cape Girardeau, 1979-99, prof. emeritus, 1999—; pres. K.I.D.S. & Computers, Inc., Cape Girardeau, 1999—; prof. early childhood edn. The Met. State Coll. of Denver, 2000—; dir. Ctr. for Child Studies, Cape Girardeau, 1979-99, Kids Interacting with Devel. Software, Cape Girardeau, 1985—; chair Human-Environ. Studies, Cape Girardeau, 1990-93; judge Developmental Software Awards, 1991—, Child Mag. Awards, 1992-99. Author: Helping Young Children Grow, 1980, Developmental Evaluations of Software for Young Children, 1990, Young Children and Technology: A World of Discovery, 1997, Haugland Developmental Software Scale, 1997, Haugland/Gertzog Developmental Scale for Web Sites, 1998; dept. editor Early Childhood Education Jour., 1992—; mem. editl. bd. Jour. Computing in Childhood Edn.; contbr. numerous articles to profl. jours. Grantee numerous orgns.; recipient Gov.'s award for Teaching Excellence, 1996. Mem. Assn. for Childhood Edn. Internat., Nat. Assn. for Edn. Young Children, Nat. Assn. for Early Childhood Tchr. Educators, Tech. and Young Children Caucus (software chair), Nat. Assn. Family and Consumer Scis., Omicron Nu, Phi Kappa Phi. Democrat. Methodist. Avocations: reading, travel, cooking, bicycling. Office: KIDS & Computers Incs 2143 Bellridge Pike Cape Girardeau MO 63701-1866

HAUKE, GUILLERMO, science educator; b. Zaragoza, Spain, Feb. 7, 1965; s. Guillermo Hauke and Magdalena Bernardos; m. Ana Cristina Altemir, Aug. 14, 1998; 1 child, Maria. Degree in engring., Centro Politecnico Superior, Zaragoza, Spain, 1989; PhD, Stanford U., 1995. Assoc. prof. Centro Politénico Superior, 1995—, coord. fluid mechs. dept., 1998-2000; cons. in field. Co-author: Finite Element Flow Simulation, 1998, Numerical Modelling of Hydrodynamic Systems, 1999; contbr. articles to profl. jours. Fulbright grantee, 1989-93; recipient 2d nat. award Ministry Edn. and Sci., 1990. Roman Catholic. Avocations: skiing, windsurfing, classical music, travel.

HAUN, JACOB, JR., electrical engineer; b. Richmond, Va., Mar. 15, 1932; . Jacob and Eleanor Hollingsworth (Grabill) H.; m. Eloise Clymer, June 18, 1960 (div. 1973); children: Jacob III, Harvie Clymer, Frank Hollingsworth; m. Marlene Rubin Walker (div.); children: Noah Isaiah, Joshua David; m. Diane Lynn Gardner. BEE, U. Va., 1953; MBA, Harvard U., 1955; MD, Med. Coll. Va., 1972. Avocations: flying, skiing, back packing, rock climbing, whitewater rafting. Home: 644 Kern Springs Rd Woodstock VA 22664-3210

HAUNER, MILAN LOTHAR, historian; b. Gotha, Germany, Mar. 4, 1940; came to U.S., 1980; s. Vilem Bohumir Hauner and Gertrud Jacob; m. Magdalena Hauner Slavikova, Sept. 1971; children: Katherina, Anushka, Thomas. MA, PhD, Charles U., Prague, Czechoslovakia, 1962; PhD, U. Cambridge, Eng., 1972. Rsch. assoc. St. Anthony's Coll., Oxford, Eng., 1971-74; rschr. Amnesty Internat., London, 1974-76; rsch. fellow German Hist. Inst., London, 1976-80; vis. prof. U. Wis., Madison, 1980-84, hon. fellow, 1985—; fgn. policy analyst Radio Liberty, Munich, 1988-89; vis. prof. U. Calif., Berkeley, 1990, Georgetown U., Washington, 1991-92; dir. E. European studies Woodrow Wilson Ctr., Washington, 1990-91; Fulbright vis. prof. U. Leipzig, Germany, 1998-99. Author: India in Axis Strategy, 1981, Hitler: A Chronology of His Life and Time, 1983; co-author: Afghanistan and the Soviet Union, 1989, What is Asia to us?, RRussia's Asian Heartland, 1990, 92. Short-Term grantee IREX, 1992, 95, 97; Hooper Internat. fellow Fgn. Policy Rsch. Inst., 1994-95; Fulbright grant, 1998-99, Ford Found. grant, 1981-82. Mem. Am. Assn. for the Advancement of Slavic Studies, Internat. Inst. Strategic Studies. Avocations: traveling, swimming, skiing. Home: 5013 Risser Rd Madison WI 53705-1366 Office: Dept HIstory U Wis Madison WI 53706

HAUPT, GUENTHER KURT, chemical engineer; b. Detmold, Germany, Aug. 20, 1948; s. Gerhard and Ingeborg (Seidel) H.; m. Ingrid Scharrer, Oct. 24, 1969; children: Stefan, Oliver. Diploma, U. Erlangen, 1973. Acad. asst. U. Erlangen, Germany, 1973-81; asst. mgr. Siemens AG, Erlangen, 1981—. Home: Bismarckstrasse 3, 90491 Nürnberg Bavaria, Germany Office: Siemens AG, Freyeslebenstrasse 1, 91058 Erlangen Bavaria, Germany

HAUPTMAN, AHARON, mechanical engineer, technology-foresight researcher; b. Wroclaw, Poland, Sept. 1, 1948; came to Israel, 1957; s. Moshe and Laura (Melzer) H.; m. Tzipora Hershko, Sept. 14, 1976; children: Nadav, Tomer. BSc, Technion, Haifa, Israel, 1971; MSc, Tel Aviv U., 1979, PhD, 1986. Rschr., tchr. Tel Aviv U., Israel, 1977-86; rsch. fellow Caltech, Pasadena, Calif., 1986-87; lectr., rschr. Tel Aviv U., 1987-89; sr. rschr. Interdisciplinary Ctr. Technol. Analysis & Forecasting, Tel Aviv, 1988—. Home: 2-B Haneveim St, 47279 Ramat Hasharon Israel

HAUPTMAN, HERBERT AARON, mathematician, educator, researcher; b. N.Y.C., Feb. 14, 1917; s. Israel and Leah (Rosenfeld) H.; m. Edith Citrynell, Nov. 10, 1940; children: Barbara, Carol Hauptman Fullerton. BS in Math., CCNY, 1937; MA, Columbia U., 1939; PhD, U. Md., 1955, PhD (hon.), 1985; PhD (hon.), CCNY, 1986, U. Parma, Italy, 1989, D'Youville Coll., 1989, Bar-Ilan U., Israel, 1990, Columbia U., 1990, Tech. U., Lodz, Poland, 1992, Queen's U., Kingston, Ont., Can., 1994, Niagara U., 1996, U. Toledo, 1999. Statistician U.S. Census Bur., Washington, 1940-42; civilian instr. electronics and radar U.S. Army Air Force, Boca Raton, Fla., 1942-43, 46-47; physicist, mathematician Naval Rsch. Lab., Washington, 1947-70; mathematician Hauptman-Woodward Med. Rsch. Inst., 1970-72, exec. v.p., rsch. dir., 1972-85, pres., rsch. dir., 1985-87, pres., 1988—, also bd. dirs., 1972-94, 99—; prof. biophys. scis. SUNY, Buffalo, 1970—, prof. computer scis., 1992—; chmn. N.Y. State Inst. on Superconductivity, 1988-98; mem. sci. adv. bd. BioCryst, 1989—; math. instr. U. Md., 1958-70; chmn. Inter Congress Symposium Direct Methods in Crystallography, Buffalo, 1976; pres. Assn. Ind. Rsch. Insts., 1979-80; mem. U.S. Nat. Com. for Crystallography, 1979-81, 82-85, 88, 89. Author: (with J. Karle) Solution of the Phase Problem., 1953, Crystal Structure Determination: The Role of the Cosine Seminvariants, 1972; editor: Dir. Methods in Crystallography, Proceeding of the 1976 Intercongress Symposium, 1978; contbr. chpts. to books, articles to profl. jours. Trustee Buffalo Gen. Hosp., 1990-96; chmn. communications com. Philos. Soc. Washington, 1966-67, corr. sec., 1967-69, pres., 1969-70. Served to lt. (jg.) USNR, 1943-46. Sr. fellow for travel, lectures and rsch. in Italy NATO, 1973; grantee NSF, 1972-92, grantee NIH, 1992—; recipient Belden prize (gold medal) in Math., 1935, RESA award in Pure Scis., 1959, Citizen of Yr. award Buffalo Evening News, 1986, Schoelkopf award Am. Chem. Soc., 1986, Gold Plate award Am. Acad. Achievement, 1986, Nat. Libr. Medicine medal, 1986, Law Sch. award Maimonides Chabad House, 1986, others, (with J. Karle) Patterson award, 1984, Nobel Prize in Chemistry, 1985; honoree Western New York Man of Yr. Buffalo C. of C., 1986, YMCA Dinner, 1986, 90th Nobel Ann. Dinner, 1991; inductee Nobel Hall Mus. Sci. and Industry, 1986, Townsend Harris Hall of Fame, 1989, U. Md. Alumni Hall of Fame; guest of honor Roswell Park Meml. Inst., 1985, YMCA Luncheon, 1986, others; invited guest Am. Nobel Convocation, 1987, 88, Weizmann Nat. Dinner, 1988, others. Fellow Washington Acad. Scis., Jewish Acad. Arts and Scis. (medal 1986); mem. AAAS, Am. Math. Soc., Am. Phys. Soc., Am. Crystallographic Assn. (mem. Fankuchen award com. 1988), Math. Assn. Am., U.S. Nat. Acad. Scis., Cosmos Club, Saturn Club (guest of honor 1985), Phi Beta Kappa, Sigma Xi (sec. Buffalo chpt. 1971-72). Avocations: stained glass art, swimming, hiking. Office: Hauptman Woodward Med Rsch 73 High St Buffalo NY 14203-1149

HAUSCHILD, DOUGLAS CAREY, optometrist; b. Manchester, Conn., Oct. 3, 1955; s. Vernon Francis and Barbara Gwendolyn (Rose) H.; 1 child, Chelsea Anna. BA in Biology magna cum laude, Wesleyan U., 1977; OD, New Eng. Coll. Optometry, 1981. Clinician Boston Eye Clinic, 1978-81; assoc. Drs. Todd, Todd & Hauschild, Hendersonville, N.C., 1981-84; owner, optometrist Weaverville (N.C.) Eye Assocs., 1984—, Asheville (N.C.) Eye Care Assocs., 1985—; clinician Walter Reed Army Med. Ctr., 1980, West Roxbury VA Med. Ctr., 1981, NEWENCO Pediatric/Geriatric Sply. Clinic, 1981; nominee Buncombe County Bd. of Health. Contbr. health articles to newsletters. Mem. Henderson County Bd. Health, 1983-85; actor Asheville Community Theatre, 1988—; instr. phys. edn. Evangel. Chapel Christian Acad., Asheville, 1985-86; mem. Bent Creek Bapt. Ch. Choir, Soloist; leader Bent Creek Bapt. Ch. Care Group, 1987-91; choir mem., soloist St. Eugene's Roman Cath. Ch., 1992—; mem. St. Eugene's Pastoral Coun., 1995—, chair, 1997-98, choir, 1993—, cantor, 1999—. Fax: (828) 645-7279. E-mail: shapsight@msn.com. Mem. Am. Optometric Assn., So. Coun. Optometrists, N.C. State Optometric Soc., Mtn. Dist. Optometric Soc., Am. Pub. Health Assn., Lions (past pres.), KC, Elks, Beta Sigma Kappa, Delta Tau Delta. Republican. Avocations: photography, animal husbandry, gardening, theater, numismatics. Office: Weaverville Eye Assocs PO Box 1628 Weaverville NC 28787-1628

HAUSCHKE, DIETER ANDREAS, biostatistician, researcher; b. Witten, Germany, Mar. 4, 1955; s. Karl and Josephine (Thomas) H.; 1 child, Andreas. MS, U. Dortmund, Germany, 1982, PhD, 1986; Habilitation in Biometry, U. Dortmund, 1999. Cert. biometry in medicine. Lectr. U. Göttingen, Germany, 1982-86; scientist Byk Gulden GmbH, Konstanz, Germany, 1986-92, head of dept. biometry, 1992—; assoc. prof. U. Dortmund, 1999—; lectr. U. Hannover, Germany, 1994-99. Contbr. articles to profl. jours. including Internat. Jour. Clin. Pharmacology Ther. Toxicology, Pulmonary Pharmacology, Drug Inf. Jour., Biometrika, Statistics in Medicine; mem. editl. bd. Internat. Jour. Clin. Pharmacology and Therapeutics. Capt. Mil. Police, 1973-75. Mem. Internat. Biometric Soc. (prize to promote young scientists in field of biometry German region 1991), Internat. Soc. Clin. Biostats., Am. Statis. Assn., Drug Info. Assn., European Environ. Mutagen Soc., Assn. of Applied Human Pharmacology. Office: Byk Gulden Pharms, Byk-Gulden-Str 2, 78467 Konstanz Germany

HAUSEL, WILLIAM DAN, economic geologist, martial artist; b. Salt Lake City, July 24, 1949; s. Maynard Romain and Dorthy (Clark) H.; children: Jessica Siddhartha, Eric Jason. BS in Geology, U. Utah, 1972, MS in Geology, 1974. Astronomy lectr. Hansen Planetarium, Salt Lake City, 1968-72; rsch. asst. U. Utah, 1972-74; tchg. asst. U. N.Mex., Albuquerque, 1974-75; project geologist Warnock Cons., Albuquerque, 1975; geologist U.S. Geol. Survey, Casper, Wyo., 1976-77; staff geologist Geol. Survey of Wyo., Laramie, 1977-81, dep. dir., 1981-91, sr. econ. geologist, 1991—; assoc. curator mineralogy Wyo. State Mus., Cheyenne, 1983-90; cons. Western Gold Exploration and Mining, Anchorage, 1988, 89, Chevron Resources, Georgetown, Mont., 1990, Fowler Resources, Philipsburg, Mont., 1992, Bald Mountain Mining, U.S., 1993, A and E Diamond Exploration, Calif., 1993, Echo Bay Exploration, Diamond Exploration, U.S., 1994; instr. diamond exploration methods, U. Wyo., 1988, 94, Wyo. Geol. Assn., 1993, N.Am. Exploration, 1994, MK Gold, 1996; state rep. JUKO-KAI Internat., Wyo., 1994; U.S. dir. open divsn., Shorin-Ryu Karate 1996, open divsn. head, Shorin-Ryu Karate and Kobudo (Juko-kai Internat.), 1997—; instr. martial arts dept. phys. edn., U. Wyo., 1993—, Campus Shorin-Ryu Karate and Kobudo Club, 1977—. Author: Partial Pressures of Some Lunar Lavas, 1972, Petrogenesis of Some Representative Lavas, Southwestern Utah, 1975, Exploration for Diamondiferous Kimberlite, 1979, Gold Districts of Wyoming, 1980, Ore Deposits of Wyoming, 1982, Geology of Southeastern Wyoming, 1984, Minerals and Rocks of Wyoming, 1986, The Geology of Wyoming's Precious Metal Lode and Placer Deposits, 1989, Economic Geology of the South Pass Greenstone Belt, 1991, Economic Geology of the Cooper Hill Mining District, 1992, Mining History and Geology of Wyoming's Metal and Gemstone Districts, 1993, Geology Mining Districts and Ghost Towns of the Medicine Bow Mountains, 1993, Diamonds, Kimberlite and Lamproite in the United States, 1994, Pacific Coast Diamonds-An Unconventional Source Terrane, 1995, Economic Geology of the Seminoe Mountains Greenstone Belt, 1994, The Great Diamond Hoax of 1872, 1995, Geology and Gold Mineralization of the Rattlesnake Hills, Granite Mountains, Wyoming, 1996, Copper, Lead, Zinc, Molybdenum and Associated Metal Deposits of Wyoming, 1997, Diamonds and Mantle Source Rocks in the U.S., with Special Emphasis on the Wyoming Craton, 1998, Water Training Techniques for Martial Artists, 1998, Diamond Fever, 1999, Gemstones and Other Unique Minerals and Rocks of Wyoming, 2000; contbr. more than 400 articles to sci. and profl. jours. and contbr. to 6 books. Grantee NASA, 1981, Office of Surface Mining, 1979, U. Wyo., 1981-92, U.S. Geol. Survey Coop. Geol. Mapping Initiative, 1985-88, 98, Union Pacific Resources, 1991-94, State of Wyoming Diamond Rsch. grantee, 1998-2000; recipient Pres.'s Cert. Excellence Am. Assn. Petroleum Geologists, 1992, Outstanding Contributions award Wyo. Geol Assn., 1992, Prospector's Best Friend award Rocky Mountain Prospector's and Treasure Hunter's Assn., 1998, Grandmaster Instr. of the Yr. award World Karate Union, 1998, Open Shorin-Ryu Instr. of the Yr. award JKI, 1998; named Laramie Lyceum Disting. Lectr., 1994, Disting. Lectr. Dept. Geology and Geophysics, U. Wyo., 1998; named to World Karate Union Hall of Fame, 2000, Millennium Hall of Fame, 1998. Mem. Wyo. Geo. Assn., Wyo. Profl. Geologists, U. Utah Geology Club (pres. 1969-71), Laramie Bushido Dojo Karate (pres. 1985-88), U. Wyo. Campus Shotokan Karate Club (instr. 1988-93), Shorin-Ryu Karate and Kobudo Club (U. Wyo. Campus headmaster 1993—), Juko-Kai Internat., Seiyo-no Shorin-Ryu Karate Kobudo Kai Assn. Avocations: karate (9th degree black belt soke), jujutsu and other martial arts (7 black belts including Juko-Kai Interat. Samurai and Juko-Kai Internat. Prof. Martial Arts), Soke Shodai (Grandmaster) of Seiyo-no Shorin-Ryu Karate and Kobudo, sketching. Home: 4238 Grays Gable Rd Laramie WY 82072-6911 Office: Geol Survey Wyo PO Box 3008 Laramie WY 82071-3008 also: Shorin Ryn Karate & Kobudo Club Univ Wyo PO Box 3625 Laramie WY 82071-3625

HAUSER, BERNICE WORMAN, inter-campus director; b. N.Y.C., Sept. 13, 1932; d. Aaron and Rose (Dunkel) Worman; m. A. Daniel Hauser, June 13, 1953; children:Mitchell Alan, Lisa Ann Hauser Pinero. BA cum laude, Hunter Coll., 1953, MS, 1956; MS in Adminstrn. and Supervision, CUNY, 1978. Tchr. Yonkers Pub. Schs., N.Y.C., 1953-54, N.Y. Pub. Schs., N.Y.C., 1954-60; primary sci. tchr., cons. Pub./Parochial/Ind. Schs., N.Y.C., 1960-72; tchr., primary sci. chair Walden Sch., N.Y.C., 1972-80, coord. student tchrs., 1980-88, curriculum cons., prin. sci. chair, 1988-91; asst. to headministress Horace Mann Sch., N.Y.C., 1991-93, dir. inter-campus activities, 1993—; cons. Scholastic Publs., N.Y.C., 1980—; bd. dirs. CUNY Pub.-Pvt. Schs. Partnership Coun. Author: How to Help Your Child at Home with Science, 1991, the Cat in the Hat Comes Back, 1997, You're the Apple of My Eye, 1998, (adoption issues) Am. Baby, 1984; primary cons. articles Tchr. Clearinghouse for Sci., 1987—; editor: Horace Mann Bull., 1993—; contbr. articles to Ind. Sch., Bull. of Sci. Tech & Soc., Parents League Bull., others. Mem. parks coun. Ctrl. Park Conservancy, 1970—; mem. Citizens Com. For Better N.Y., N.Y.C., 1980—; cons., speaker and writer Adoptive Parents Com., N.Y.C., 1975—; trustee, v.p., nominating chair Louis Wise Svcs. for Children, N.Y.C., 1976—. Recipient Impact II award Exxon, 1987, Jeremy Rifkin award NASTS, 1991; honoree United Jewish Appeal for Disting. Vol. Svc. to Louise Wise Svcs., 1998. Fellow Phi Delta Kappa; mem. AAUW, ASCD, Nat. Sci. Tchrs. Assn. (presenter 1985—), Nat. Assn. Ind. Schs., Nat. Assn. Sci. Tech. and Soc., Assn. Tchr. Ind. Schs. (program chairperson), N.Y. Assn. Ind. Schs. (liaison), Hunter Coll. High Sch. Alumni Assn. (past pres), Phi Beta Kappa, Epsilon Pi Tau, Cum Laude Soc. Avocations: indoor gardening, theater, opera, reading, writing. Office: Horace Mann Sch 231 W 246th St Riverdale NY 10471-3430

HAUSER, HARRY RAYMOND, lawyer; b. N.Y.C., July 12, 1931; s. Milton I. and Lillian (Perlman) H.; m. Deborah Marlowe, Aug. 6, 1954; children: Mark Jeffrey, Joshua Brook, Bradford John, Matthew Milton. AB, Brown U., 1953; JD, Columbia U., 1959. Bar: N.Y. 1959, Mass. 1963, Wash. 1972. Practice in N.Y.C., 1959-61, Boston, 1962—; atty. Sperry Rand Corp., 1959-61, Hotel Corp. Am., N.Y.C., 1961-62; v.p., sec., gen. counsel Hotel Corp. Am., 1962-70; mem. firm Gadsby & Hannah, 1971—. Life trustee Temple Israel, Boston; pres., dir. N. Bennett St. Sch.; trustee, gen. counsel The Boston Harbor Assn., Inc. Mem. ABA, N.Y. State Bar Assn., Mass. Bar Assn., D.C. Bar Assn., Internat. Bar Assn., Brown U. Club. Home: 1175 Chestnut St #2 Newton Upper Falls MA 02464-1336 Office: Gadsby & Hannah 225 Franklin St Boston MA 02110-2804

HAUSER, MARKUS, computer scientist; b. Karlsruhe, Germany, Apr. 1, 1967; s. Werner and Britta (Zeisig) H.; 1 child, Nina. Dr.Ing., U. Dresden, Germany, 1998. Rschr. U. Karlsruhe, Germany, 1992-94; sr. rschr. U. Dresden, Germany, 1994-98; sr. rschr., mgr. CAX/STEP ProSTEP GmbH, Germany, 1998—; facilitator CAX Implementor Forum www.cax-if.org. Author, editor: Forum Bauinformatik, 1997; co-author: PDM Schema Usage Guide; contbr. articles to profl. jours. Mem. Gesellschaft Info. Avocations: cycling, squash, tennis, artificial intelligence. Home: Am Bongert 5, 56242 Marienrachdorf Germany Office: ProStep GmbH, Julius Reiber Str 15, D-64293 Darmstadt Germany

HAUSER, THOMAS, marketing executive; b. Augsburg, Germany, May 30, 1967; s. Heinrich Kaspar and Sigrid Edith (Warzel) H. Diploma in bus., U. Augsburg, 1993; postgrad., European Bus. Sch., Germany, 1997—. Cons. Sultan & Hausner Malerei-Gestaltung-Design, Augsburg, 1992-93; trainee AES Werbeagentur GmbH, Augsburg, 1993; trainee, editor, product mgr. KOGNOS Verlag GmbH, Stadtbergen, Germany, 1994-95; mktg. mgr. MAN Roland Druckmaschinen AG, Augsburg and Offenbach, Germany, 1995—; cons. U. Augsburg, 1993-94, lectr. Author: Crisis PR for Companies, 1994; editor: Market and Service Oriented Management for Associations, 1995; contbr. chpts. to books, articles to profl. jours. Mem. Promotion Fedn. Mktg. U. Munich, Am. Mktg. Assn., Internat. Gutenberg Fedn., German Mktg. Assn. Avocations: arts and culture, writing, travel, spirit of the age. Home: Buergermeister-Ulrich-Str 8, 86199 Augsburg Germany Office: MAN Roland AG Corp Mktg, Stadtbachstrasse 1, 86135 Augsburg Germany

HAUSER-CRAM, PENNY, developmental psychologist; b. Detroit, Mar. 29, 1947; d. John Eugene and Dorothy Jane Hauser; m. Bestor Cram, June 14, 1969; children: Slater Ernesto, Lacey Barbara. BS, Denison U., 1968; MA, Tufts U., 1976; EdD, Harvard U., 1983. Asst. prof. Wellesley Coll., Wellesley, Mass., 1982-84; dir. Eliot-Pearson Children's Sch., Tufts Univ., Medford, Mass., 1984-87; assoc. prof., dir. program in devel. and ednl. psychology Boston Coll., Chestnut Hill, Mass., 1990—. Author: Essays on Educational Research, 1983, Early Education in the Public Schools, 1991. Recipient Excellence in Rsch. award Boston Inst. for the Devel. of Infants and Parents, Mass, 1992. Office: Boston College Campion Hall Chestnut Hill MA 02167

HAUSLER, RUDOLF HEINRICH, research chemist; b. Zurich, Switzerland, Apr. 9, 1934; came to U.S., 1963; s. Robert Ruppert and Elsa (Figi) H.; m. Barbara Louise Corsaw, Feb. 5, 1972; 1 child, Natasha Louise. diploma chem. engring., Swiss Fed. Inst. Tech., Zurich, 1958, D.Tech.Scis., 1961. Research chemist, project leader Battelle Meml. Inst., Geneva, 1961-63; research chemist, research assoc. Universal Oil Products Co., Des Plaines, Ill., 1963-76; tech. dir. Gordon Lab., Inc., Great Bend, Kans., 1976-79; sr. research chemist corp. research and devel. Petrolite Corp., St. Louis, 1979-81, prin. investigator, 1981-86, research fellow, 1986-91; sr. engring. advisor Mobil R&D Corp., Dallas, 1991-96; co-owner, v.p. tech. BJB Co., Post, Tex., 1996—; pres. Corro-Consulta; cons. in field of corrosion in nuc. energy generation, in oil and gas prodn.; investor in oil and gas prodn.; lectr. in

field. Registered profl. engr., Calif. Author, co-author 3 books. Mem. Electrochem. Soc. (chmn. Chgo. sect. 1967-68, councilor 1972—), Nat. Assn. Corrosion Engrs. (chmn. Chgo. sect. 1974-75, Outstanding Achievement award 1990), Chgo. Tech. Socs. Council (chmn. 1974-75), Am. Chem. Soc., Am. Soc. Metals. Unitarian-Universalist. Author, patentee in field. Office: Corro Consulta PO Box 357 7804 Pencross Lane Dallas TX 75248-3109

HAUSMAN, WILLIAM RAY, fund raising and management consultant; b. Bradford, Pa., Apr. 22, 1941; s. Raymond Harvey and Eleanor Janet (Freeman) H.; m. Rosalyn Schmidt, Aug. 16, 1963; children: Valerie Noelle, Stephanie Carol. AB, Wheaton Coll., 1963; MA, Trinity Evang. Div. Sch., 1966, DD (hon), 1981; postgrad., North Park Theol. Sem., 1968-69; EdM, Harvard U., 1977. Ordained to ministry Evang. Covenant Ch., 1971. Minister Christian edn. Glen Ellyn (Ill.) Covenant Ch., 1966-69; from registrar, dir. admissions to assoc. dean Trinity Evang. Div. Sch., Deerfield, Ill., 1969-80; pres. North Park Coll. and Theol. Sem., Chgo., 1980-86; from cons. to group mgr. Donald A. Campbell & Co., Inc., Chgo., 1986-94, v.p. ea. regional mgr., 1994—, sr. v.p., 1995—; bd. dirs. InTrust mag. Bd. dirs. Rockport Chamber Music Festival. Mem. Nat. Soc. Fund Raising Execs. (cert. 1989), Lehigh County Hist. Soc., Coun. Advancement and Support Edn., New Eng. Hist. Geneal. Soc. Office: Campbell & Co Eastern Regional Office 85 Eastern Ave Ste 305 Gloucester MA 01930-1869

HAUSMANN, MICHAEL, physicist; b. Ludwigshafen, Germany, May 21, 1957; s. Kurt and Gisela (Helm) H.; m. Vera Müller, Sept. 7, 1991; children: Annkatrin, Margarethe. Diploma in physics, U. Heidelberg, 1984, D of Natural Scis., 1988, habilitation, 1996. Postdoctoral Inst. of Applied Physics, Heidelberg, Germany, 1988-92, scientific asst., 1992-99; instr. Inst. of Molecular Biotechnology, Jena, Germany, 1999—. Contbr. articles to profl. jours.; inventor in field. Mem. SPIE, German Phys. Soc., Soc. Biol. Radiation Rsch., German Soc. Cytometry. Home: Paul-Loebe-Str 6a, D-67071 Ludwigshafen Germany Office: Inst of Molecular Biotech, Beutenbergstr 11, D-07745 Jena Germany

HAUSNER, JOHN HERMAN, judge; b. Detroit, Oct. 31, 1932; s. John E. and Anna (Mudrak) H.; m. Alice R. Kieltyka, Aug. 22, 1959. Ph.B. cum laude, U. Detroit, 1954, M.A., 1957, J.D. summa cum laude, 1966. Bar: Mich. 1967, U.S. Ct. Appeals (6th cir.) 1968, U.S. Supreme Ct. 1971, U.S. Tax Ct. 1976, U.S. Ct. Claims 1976, U.S. Ct. Mil. Appeals 1976. Tchr. Detroit Pub. Schs., 1954, 56-59; tchg. fellow U. Cin., 1959-61; instr. U. Detroit, 1961-74; sole practice U. Detroit, Detroit, 1967-69; asst. U.S. atty. Detroit, 1969-73; chief asst. U.S. atty. ea. dist. Mich., 1973-76; judge 3rd Jud. Cir. Mich., Wayne County, 1976-94; ret. 3d Jud. Cir. Mich., Wayne County, 1994, 1994; lectr. Law Sch.; faculty adviser Nat. Jud. Coll., 1978-79. Author: Sebastian, The Essence of My Soul, 1982; contbr. articles to Detroit Advertiser. Active Civic Searchlight. Served with U.S. Army, 1954-56. Mem. Fed. Bar Assn. (mem. exec. bd. Detroit chpt. 1976-82), State Bar Mich., Mich. Retired Judges Assn., Blue Key, Alpha Sigma Mu. Republican. Home: 22433 Louise St Saint Clair Shores MI 48081-2034 also: 8420 E Desert Palm Tucson AZ 85730-4723

HAUSSELT, JÜRGEN HEINRICH, materials science educator, research administrator; b. Nürnberg, Germany, May 21, 1946; s. Karl and Pauline (Boss) H.; m. Elisabeth B. Schneider, Nov. 5, 1971; 1 child, Susanne E. Diploma in physics, U. Erlangen, Germany, 1971, PhD in Materials Sci., 1975; habilitation, U. Freiburg, Germany, 1996. Asst. prof. materials sci. U. Erlangen, 1975-77; postdoctoral asst. Stanford (Calif.) U., 1976-77; scientist/rschr. Degussa AG, Hanau, Germany, 1977-83; dir. Degussa Inc., N.Y.C., 1983-84; dept. head rsch. Degussa AG, Hanau, 1984-88, dir. rsch., 1989-93; head rsch. inst. Rsch. Ctr. Karlsruhe, Germany, 1993—; prof. materials sci. U. Freiburg, 1996—; chmn. sci.-tech. coun. Rsch. Ctr. Karlsruhe, 1997—. Co-editor: Edelmetalltaschenbuch, 1995; author and co-author more than 20 patents in field; contbr. over 60 articles to internat. scientific publs. Mem. German Soc. Materials (mem. bd.). Avocation: motoryachting. Office: Inst Materials Science, PO Box 3640, D-76021 Karlsruhe Germany

HAUSSER, DOMINIQUE, public health physician; b. Geneva, 1955. MD, U. Geneva, 1981; MS in Cmty. Health, U. Montreal, 1986; PhD, U. Lausanne, 1987. Rschr. U. Mali, Bamako, 1982, U. Inst. Social and Preventive Medicine, Lausanne, Switzerland, 1984-93; sr. rschr. Swiss Fed. Inst. Tech., Lausanne, 1993—; dir. nat. rsch. program AIDS Swiss Nat. Rsch. Found., 1988-97; cons. WHO, Geneva, 1985-96, UNICEF, Burundi, 1992-94; co-chmn. scientific com. 12th World AIDS Conf., Geneva, 1998; chmn. 10th internat. conf. reduction of harm related to drugs, Geneva, 1999; cons. Pompidou Group-Coun. of Europe, 1995-99. Editor: Psychosocial and Cultural Aspects of AiDS, 1994—; contbr. articles to profl. jours. Active Parliament, Geneva, 1993—. Avocations: sailing, computer science. Office: Swiss Federal Inst Tech, IREC/CP555, CH-1001 Lausanne Switzerland

HAUSSER, MICHEL JEAN, literature educator; b. Paris, Nov. 8, 1928; s. Jacques Henri and Suzanne Louise (Jodry) H.; m. Ginette Anik Effantin, May 7, 1953; children: Isabelle, Dominique. Arts degree, Sorbonne, Paris, 1951; agrégation, Paris, 1957; arts doctorate, U. Paris 7, 1978. Grammar sch. tchr. Nat. Edn., French Equatorial Africa, 1952-59; univ. asst., dean Arts Faculty, Brazzaville, 1959-65; asst. prof. U. Bordeaux 3, France, 1965-78, prof., 1978-96. Author: Essai sur la poétique de la négritude, 1986, Pour une poétique de la négritude, 1988-92, Littératures francophones: Afrique noire, 1998; editor: Ecrire la liberté, 1991. Recipient Mérite congolais Pres. of the Congo Republic, 1965; named officer Nat. Edn. Min., 1978. Avocation: music. Home: 1 rue du Vélodrome, 33200 Bordeaux France Office: U Michel de Montaigne-Bordeaux 3, Domaine Univ, 33405 Talence France

HAUSSONNE, F. JEAN-MARIE, educator; b. Paris, Apr. 9, 1947; s. Maurice and Raymonde (Geray) H.; m. Marie-Therese, 1969; children: Yves Marie, Anne Cecile. Degree in ceramic engring., E.N.S.C.I., Sevres, France, 1970; PhD, U. Caen, 1983. Engr. C.N.E.T. France Telecom, France, 1973-94; prof. U. Caen, France, 1994—. Author: Sol-gel Films, 1994; author, editor: Batio Base Materials for Capacitors, 1994; contbr. articles to profl. jours.; patentee in field. Mem. SEE, Am. Ceramic Soc. Avocations: sailing, music. Office: LUSAC, Site Univ BP 78, 50130 Outeville France

HAUSTEIN, KNUT-OLAF FRIEDRICH, clinical pharmacologist, researcher, educator; b. Dresden, Saxonia, Germany, Sept. 20, 1934; s. Friedrich Paul Max and Irmgard (Schwalm) H.; m. Heidi Martha Maria König, July 14, 1967; children: Andreas Michael, Maria Christine. MD, U. Leipzig, Germany, 1957; Habilitation, Med. Acad., Erfurt, Germany, 1967. Cert. clin. pharmacologist. Pharmacologist Arzneimittelwerk, Dresden-Radebeul, Germany, 1957-61; physician Bezirkskrankenhaus, Dresden-Friedrichstadt, Germany, 1961-67; pharmacologist Inst. Pharm. Toxicol. Med. Acad., Erfurt, Germany, 1972-85; clin. pharmacologist, head Inst. Clin. Pharm. Med. Acad., Erfurt, 1985-93, U. Jena, Erfurt, 1994-99; guest prof. clin. pharmacology U. Erlangen-Nürnberg, Germany, 1995-97; founder Inst. Nicotine Rsch. & Smoking Cessation, Erfurt, Germany, 1999—. Contbr. chpts. to books, more than 190 articles to sci. jours. pres. Kulturbund e. V., Erfurt/Thuringia, 1990-92; active Goethe-Gesellschaft, Weimar, 1975—. Mem. N.Y. Acad. Scis., Deutsche Gesellschaft f. Pharmakologie u Toxikologie (sect. clin. pharmacology), German Soc. Clin. Pharmacology, German Soc. Nicotine Rsch. (head). Roman Catholic. Avocations: classical music, literature, fine arts. Office: Inst Nicotine Rsch & Smoke, Johannesstrasse 85-87, D-99084 Erfurt Germany

HAUSTGEN, THIERRY RENÉ CAMILLE, psychiatrist; b. Vanves, H de Seine, France, Feb. 29, 1956; s. Gérard and Thérèse (Willocquet) H. MD, U. Paris, 1983, specialist in Psychiatry, 1990. Cert. med. expert Rouen Tribunals, 1987, Paris Tribunals, 1992. Intern in psychiatry Paris Region Hosps., 1981-85; hosp. practitioner in mental health svcs. Ctr. Hosp. Specialisé, Evreux, France, 1985-91, Pub. Establishment of Sanity, Ville-Evrard, Seine SD, France, 1991; cons. Ctr. Med. Psychol., Montreuil, Seine SD, 1991. Author: (books) Psychiatric Observations and Certificates in the 19th Century, 1985, Mood Bipolar Disorders, 1995, A History of Psychotic Disorders, 1997; also contbr. articles to Synapse; L'Evolution Psychiatrique; Annales Med.-Psychol., 1985-97, (Prize Synapse 1986). Mem. Coll. Synapse, Paris, L'Evolution Psychiatrique (corr.), Soc. Medico-Psychologique, Paris (corr.). Avocations: history, literature, classical music. Office: Ctr Med-Psychologique, 77 Rue Victor Hugo, 93100 Montreuil Seine SD, France

HAUTEPIERRE, JEAN See **TISSERAND, JEAN-PAUL PHILIPPE**

HAUW, LIE GIOK See **SUDYATMIKO, DJOKO**

HAVASS, MIKLÓS, computer company executive; b. Szeged, Hungary, Apr. 23, 1940; s. Zoltan and Judit (Polner) H.; m. Maria Toth, Aug. 1, 1970; children: Norbert, Nikolett, Zsombor. PhD in Math., Jate U., Szeged, 1963. Rschr. Pmszi, Budapest, 1963-65; head of dept. Nimigüszi, Budapest, 1965-72; pres. Szamalk, Budapest, 1972—. Recipient E. Fenyes medal Hungarian Cen. Stats. Office, 1990, L. Aschner medal for mgr. of yr. 1997, D. Gabor medal 1998, Gy. Ostrowski medal 1999, Pro Scientia Transsylvanica medal 2000. Mem. IEEE, Hungarian Computer Soc. (pres. 1990-93, J. von Neumann medal 1978), Fedn. Tech. and Sci. Socs. (pres. 1994-98, medal 1994), Hunagi (pres. 1996-99). Avocations: music, books, history, philosophy. Home: Mexikoi 52/b, H-1145 Budapest Hungary Office: Etele u 68, H-1115 Budapest Hungary

HAVEL, IVAN MILOŠ, computer scientist; b. Prague, Czechoslovakia, Oct. 11, 1938; s. Václav Maria and Božena (Vavrečková) H.; m. Květa Vašková, 1968 (div. Mar. 1984); children: Vojtěch, Prokop; m. Dagmar Lantayová, May 15, 1986. Degree in engring., Czech Tech. U., Prague, 1966; MS, PhD, U. Calif., Berkeley, 1971; CSc, Czech Acad. Scis., Prague, 1974. Rsch. scientist Inst. Automation and Info. Theory, Czech Acad. Sci., 1972-79; programmer M.E.T.A., Prague, 1982-90; dir. Ctr. for Theoretical Study Charles U., Prague, 1990—, assoc. prof., 1992—; mem. bd. Inst. Software Tech., UN U., Macau, 1993-98; mem. sci. bd. Acad. Scis. of Czech Republic, Prague, 1993-97. Author: Robotika, 1980, Arsemid, 1997, Otevrene oci a zvednute oboci, 1998, Svatojansky vylet, 1999; editor-in-chief jour. Vesmír, 1990—; contbr. articles t profl. jours. Mem. coun. Civic Forum, Prague, 1989-90. Mem. Academia Europea, Club of Rome. Office: Ctr for Theoretical Study, Jilská St 1, 11000 Prague 1 Czech Republic

HAVEL, VACLAV, Czech government official, playwright; b. Prague, Czechoslovakia, Oct. 5, 1936; s. Václav M. and Božena (Vavrečková) H.; m. Olga Splíchalová, July 9, 1964 (dec. Jan. 1996); m. Dagmar Veškrnová, Jan. 4, 1997. Student, Czech Tech. Coll., Prague, 1955-57, Acad. Mus. Arts, Prague, 1966; hon. degree, York U., Toronto, 1982; D honoris causa, U. Toulouse, France, 1982, U. Lyon, France, 1984, U. Columbia, N.Y.C., 1990, Hebrew U., Jerusalem, 1990, U. of F. Palacky, Charles U., U. of J.A. Komensky, Czechoslovakia, 1990, LeHigh U., Bethlehem, Pa., 1991, U. Brusel, 1991, Harvard U., 1995, U. New South Wales, Australia, 1995, Vilnius U., Lithuania, 1996, Trinity Coll., Dublin, 1996, Bar-Ilan U., Ramat Gan, Israel, 1997, Taras Shevchenko Nat. U., Kiev, Ukraine, 1997, U. Jordan, Amman, 1997, U. Glasgow (U.K.), 1998, U. Oxford (U.K.), 1998, U. Pretoria (South Africa), 1998, U. St. Thomas, Minn., 1999, U. Manitoba, Winnipeg, Can., 1999. Technician chem. lab., 1951-55; scenery technician ABC Theatre, Prague, 1959-60; dramatic adviser, asst. producer, author Theatre on Railings, Prague, 1960-68; mem. Club Engaged Non-Party Mems., 1968; chmn. Club Ind. Writers, 1968; imprisoned 4 times, spent nearly 5 years in prison, 1977-89; pres. Czechoslovakia, Prague, 1989-92; now pres. Czech Republic, Prague, 1993—. Author: Antikódy, 1964, Letters to Olga, 1983, O lidskou identitu, 1984, Disturbing the Peace, 1986 (Polit. Book of Yr. Friedrich-Elbert-Found. 1990), Do ruznych stran, 1989, Speeches, 1990, Open Letters: Selected Writings 1965-90, Summer Meditations, 1991, Dear Citizens, 1992, Václav Havel 92 & 93, 1994, 95, 96, Art of the Impossible, 1997, Toward a Civil Society, 1994, (with others) The Power of Powerless, 1986, Václav Havel or Living in Truth, 1986, others, (plays) The Garden Party, 1963, The Memorandum, 1965 (Off Broadway award The Village Voice 1968), The Increased Difficulty of Concentration, 1968 (Off Broadway award The Village Voice 1970), The Beggar's Opera, 1972, Audience, 1975, Private View, 1975, The Mountain Hotel, 1976, Protest, 1979, The Mistake, 1983, Largo Desolato, 1984, Temptation, 1985, Redevelopment, 1987, Tomorrow!, 1988; contbr. essays to profl. jours. With Czechoslovakian Army, 1957-59. Recipient Austrian State prize for European lit., 1969, Jan Palach prize, 1981, Erasmus prize, 1986, Prize of Liberty, 1989, Olof Palme prize, 1989, Simon Bolivar prize UNESCO, 1990, Charlemagne prize, Sonning prize, Averell Yearriman Democracy award, B'nai Brith prize, Freedom award, Raoul Wallenberg Human Rights award, 1991, Order of White Eagle, Indira Gandhi prize, Phila. Liberty medal, Jackson H. Ralston prize, 1994, The Dutch Freedom Fighters medal Geuzenpenning Found., Netherlands, 1995, The Catalonia Internat. prize Catalonian Inst. Mediterranean Studies, Barcelona, Spain, 1995, Future of Hope award, Hiroshima, Japan, 1995, European Statesman award Inst. for East-West Studies, N.Y.C., 1997, Le Prix Special Europe award Internat. Assn. Theatrical Critics, France, 1997, J. William Fulbright prize Washington, 1997, Peace and Democracy award Burma, 1997, Compostela Group prize, Spain, 1998, First Decade award Gazeta Wyborcza, Poland, 1999, The Open Sociedy prize, Hungary, 1999, Gold Adalbud prize, Slovkia, 1999, others. Achievements include leading the Czech "Velvet Revolution." E-mail: president@hrad.cz. Office: Kancelar Prezidenta Republiky, 119 08 Prague Czech Republic

HAVELANG, JOAO, sports association administrator; b. Rio de Janeiro, May 8, 1916. D in Law. Pres. Confederaçao Brasileira de Desportos, 1958-74, FIFA, 1974-98; hon. pres., ret.; mem. Internat. Olympic Com., 1963—; pres. COMETA S.A.; dir. various co., schs. Recipient Cavalier of the Legion d'Honneur, France, Order of Spl. Merit in Sports, Comdr. of the Cavaliers Orden Infante Dome Henrique, Cavalier Vasa Orden, Sweden, Grand Cross of Elizabeth the Cath., Spain; nominated Nobel Peace Prize, 1988. Office: FIFA House, PO Box 85, 8030 Zurich Switzerland*

HAVENS, EDWIN WALLACE, manufacturing executive; b. Rockville Center, N.Y., Mar. 5, 1950; s. Edwin Wallace and Helen Marie (Lamb) H.; m. Maria Antonia Gorgone, Sept. 20, 1980; 1 child, Brian Patrick. BA, Hofstra U., 1973. Nat. svc. mgr. Garrard U.S.A., Plainview, N.Y., 1975-79; product mgr. TDK Electronics, Garden City, N.Y., 1979-83; tech. mgr. Fuji Photo Film, N.Y.C., 1983-84, Maxell Corp. Am., Moonachie, N.J., 1984-87; nat. sales mgr. SKC Am. Inc., East Rutherford, N.J., 1987-89; dept. mgr. SKC Am. Inc., Mount Olive, N.J., 1989-95, divsn. mgr., 1995-96, gen. mgr., 1996-98, dir., 1998—. Editor: Viewpoint, 1995; author: (comic strip) The Korea Side, 1987—. Active Spring St. Mchts. Assn., Newton, N.J., 1994-97. Mem. Video Software Dealers Assn., Internat. Recording Media Assn. (bd. dirs. 1993—, mem. environ. com. 1993—, mem. seminar com. 1993—, mem. statis. com. 1993—), Vision Fund of Am. Mgmt. (coun. 1997—). Avocations: deep sea fishing, horseback riding. Office: SKC Am Inc 850 Clark Dr Budd Lake NJ 07828-4313

HAVENS, TIMOTHY JOHN, physicist; b. Bismark, N.D., Feb. 1, 1956; s. Harold Lloyd and Luanne Virginia (Cowan) H.; m. Janine Louise Ley, June 19, 1981; children: Garrett Wade, Stanley McKay, Luke Timothy. BS, Eckerd Coll., 1980; PhD, Coll. of William and Mary, 1985. Asst. prof. physics Francis Marion U., Florence, S.C., 1985-90; summer rsch. fellow Med. U. S.C., Charleston, 1986; sr. engr. GE Med. Systems, Florence, S.C., 1990—. Contbr. articles to Phys. Rev. Letters, IEEE Trans. on Mag., Jour. of Applied Sci.; patentee in field. Grantee NSF, 1990, Fed. Edn. for Scon. Security Act. Mem. Am. Phys. Soc., S.C. Acad. Sci. Home: 1208 Madison Ave Florence SC 29501-4254 Office: GE Med Systems PO Box 100539 Florence SC 29501-0539

HAVERKAMP, RICHARD GERARD, chemistry educator; b. Palmerston North, New Zealand, Jan. 8, 1961; s. Derk Jan and Rosine Patricia (Johnson) H. BSc with honors, Victoria U. of Wellington, New Zealand, 1982; PhD, U. Auckland, New Zealand, 1992. Plant chemist Colgate Palmolive Ltd., Petone, New Zealand, 1983; process/rsch. coord. Fletcher Challenge Ltd., Wellington, 1985-89; rev. sec. Dept. Sci. and Indsl. Rsch., Wellington, 1990; postdoctoral fellow U. Toronto, Can., 1992-95; vis. scientist SINTEF, Trondheim, Norway, 1994; dir. Rsch. Ctr. for Surface and Materials Sci., Auckland, New Zealand, 1995-98; vis. rschr. Aluminum Pechiney, Voreppe, France, 1996; sr. lectr. Massey U., Palmerston North, New Zealand, 1998—; cons. to industry, New Zealand, 1995—. Patentee alumina concentration measuring device. Mem. AIME, New Zealand Inst. Chemistry (sec. Manawatu br. 1986—), Inst. Profl. Engrs. New Zealand, Royal Soc. New Zealand, Electrochem. Soc. Avocations: mountaineering, tramping, caving, kayaking, beekeeping.

HAVERKORN V. RIJSEW, MICHIEL JOHAN, medical microbiologist, infectious diseases consultant; b. Oudenrijn, The Netherlands, Sept. 12, 1932; s. Carel Theodoor Haverkorn van Rijsewijk and Johanna Huberta Wackie Eysten; m. Elisabeth Eckebus; children: Alice, Karel, Marijke, Paul. PhD in Medicine, U. Leiden, The Netherlands, 1963, MD, 1965; grad. in med. microbiology, Erasmus U., Rotterdam, The Netherlands, 1977. Mem. staff dept. infectious diseases U. Leiden, The Netherlands, 1964-75; mem. staff dept. med. microbiology Univ. Hosp., Rotterdam, The Netherlands, 1975-77; biol. safety cons. Tech. U., Eindhoven, The Netherlands, 1981-94; head Regional Pub. Health Lab., Veldhoven, The Netherlands, 1985-96; Winsbury White lectr. Royal Soc. Medicine, London, 1993. Author: Diagnostic Compass, Microbiology, 1997; editor: Sterptococcal Disease and the Community, 1974, Interpretation of Laboratory Reports in Medicine, 1996. Mem. Am. Soc. Microbiology, Am. Soc. Human Genetics, Internat. Epidemiological Assn.

HAVERKOS, HARRY WILLIAM, epidemiologist; b. Cincinnati, Jan. 17, 1951; s. Harry C. and Vivian Mary H.; m. Lynne Mazella, Oct. 22, 1977; children: H. Daniel, Kathryn Jan, Colleen Vivian. BS in Preprofl. Studies, U. Notre Dame, 1973; MD, Med. Coll. Ohio, 1976. Med. epidemiologist Ctrs. Disease Control, Atlanta, 1981-84; health sci. adminstr. NIH, Bethesda, 1984-98; staff physician Walter Reed Army Med. Ctr., Washington, 1989—; med. officer Food and Drug Adminstrn., Rockville, Md., 1998—; capt. U.S. Pub. Health Svc., 1981—. Fax: 301-827-2510. E-mail: haverkosh@cder.fda.gov. Office: Food and Drug Adminstrn 5600 Fishers Ln Rockville MD 20857-0001

HAVERLY, DOUGLAS LINDSAY, librarian, historian; b. Stamford, N.Y., Apr. 16, 1925; s. De Forest Ward and Amy Elizabeth (Lindsay) H. Student, Albany Bus. Coll., 1948, Alfred U., 1948-49, Russell Sage Coll., 1950-52. With N.Y. State Libr., Albany, 1949-77; with Bur. Testing N.Y. State Dept. Edn., Albany, 1978-82; ret., 1982; pres., curator Donald C. Ringwald Marine Navigation Ltd., Albany, 1987—. With USN, 1943-54. Mem. Steamship Hist. Soc. (budget dir. 1973-76, bd. dirs. 1977-80, organizer Hudson Valley chpt. 1974, chmn. 1975-78, libr. 1990-93), Hudson River Maritime Ctr., Sons and Daus. of Pioneer Rivermen, Palatines to Am. (historian N.Y. chpt. 1991-95), Herkimer (N.Y.) Hist. Soc., Schoharie County Hist. Soc. (life), Clan Lindsay Assn. USA Inc. (charter), N.Y. Hist. Soc., Ulster County Geneal. Soc., Van Aken/Auken Newsletter. Avocation: genealogy. Home and Office: DC Ringwald Marine Nav Ltd 23 Wedgewood Dr Loudonville NY 12211-1940

HAVILAND, MARLITA CHRISTINE, elementary school educator; b. Moses Lake, Wash., Sept. 4, 1952; d. Marvin Curtis and Delita F. (Grout) McCully; m. James A Haviland, June 18, 1971. BS in Edn., So. Nazarene U., Bethany, Okla., 1973; MA in Edn., No. Ariz. U., 1987. Cert. elem. tchr., Ariz., Colo., ESL, basic edn., spl. edn. tchr., c.c., Ariz., early childhood edn., Colo.. Elem. tchr. St. Paul (Ark.) Pu. Sch., Twin Wells Indian Sch., Sun Valley, Ariz., Navajo Gospel Mission, Kykotsmovi, Ariz., Shonto (Ariz.) Boarding Sch. (now Shonto Prep Sch.); instr. Northland Pioneer Coll., Diné Coll.; coord. Sch. Wide Book Fair.; coach Accelerated Schs.; local chair North Ctrl. Assn. Coord. Children Inc., Shonto. Mem. Nat. Fedn. Fed. Employees (past pres., sec.-treas., steward), Nat. Sci. Tchrs. Assn., Ariz. CADRE, Alpha Nu, Phi Kappa Phi. Home: PO Box 7427 Shonto AZ 86054-7427

HAVLÍČKOVÁ, HELENA ANNA, plant physiologist, researcher; b. Náchod, Czech Republic, May 22, 1941; d. Antonín and Anna (Teichmanová) Elsner; m. Jiří Václav Havlíček, Oct. 21, 1965; children: Jiří, Jan. RNDr, Charles U., Prague, 1966; PhD, Czech Acad. Sci., Prague, 1972. Rschr. Acad. Sci. Czech Republic, Prague, 1966-67; rschr. Rsch. Inst. Crop Product, Prague, 1967-72, ind. rschr., 1972—; head team of Plant Resistance to Insect Pests, Prague, 1993—; lectr. biotech. stress Faculty Sci., Charles U., 1990—; lectr. plant resistance to insects Agronomy U., Prague, 1990—. Contbr. over 120 articles to profl. jours. Mem. Exptl. Plant Biology Assn., ESA, FESPP. Avocations: literature, music. Home: Velvarská 43, 160 00 Prague 6, Czech Republic Office: Rsch Inst Crop Prod, Drnovská 507, 161 06 Prague 6, Czech Republic

HAVNER, KERRY SHUFORD, civil engineering and solid mechanics educator; b. Huntington, W.Va., Feb. 20, 1934; s. Alfred Sidney and Jessie May (Fowler) H.; m. Roberta Lee Rider, Aug. 28, 1954; children: Karen Elese Smith, Clark Alan, Kris Sidney. BSCE, Okla. State U., 1955, MS, 1956, PhD, 1959. Registered prof. engr., Okla. Stress analyst Douglas Aircraft Co., Tulsa, 1956; from instr. to asst. prof. civil engring. Okla. State U., Stillwater, 1957-62; sr. stress and vibration engr. Garrett Corp., Phoenix, 1962-63; sect. chief solid mechs. rsch. missile/space systems divsn. McDonnell-Douglas Corp., Santa Monica, Calif., 1963-68; lectr. civil engring. U. So. Calif., L.A., 1965-68; from assoc. prof. to prof. civil engring. N.C. State U., Raleigh, 1968-82, prof. civil engring. and materials sci., 1982-99, prof. emeritus, 1999—; sr. vis. dept. applied math. and theoretical physics U. Cambridge, 1981, 89. Author: Finite Plastic Deformation of Crystalline Solids, 1992; contbg. author: Mechanics of Solids, The Rodney Hill 60th Anniversary Volume, 1982; contbr. articles to Jour. Applied Math. and Physics, Jour. of Mechs. and Physics of Solids, Acta Mechanica, Procs. and Phil. Trans. Royal Soc., others; bd. editors Mechs. of Materials, Internat. Jour. Plasticity. 2d lt. U.S. Army, 1961, 1st lt. USAR. Rsch. grantee NSF, 1971, 74, 76, 78, 81, 83, 87, 91, 94; vis. fellow Clare Hall, 1981; recipient Melvin R. Lohmann medal Okla. State U., 1994. Fellow ASCE (sec. engring. mechs. divsn. 1983-85, chmn. 1987-88, chmn. engring. mechs. adv. bd. 1990-91, chmn. TAC-CERF awards com. 1991-94; assoc. editor Jour. Engring. Mechs. 1981-83), Am. Acad. Mechanics (assoc. editor Mechanics, 1991-97); mem. ASME, Soc. Engring. Sci., Soc. Indsl. and Applied Math., Sigma Xi. Democrat. Methodist. Achievements include research in theories and analyses of anisotropic hardening and finite deformation in crystalline materials, particularly metals. Home: 3331 Thomas Rd Raleigh NC 27607-6743 Office: NC State U PO Box 7908 Raleigh NC 27695-0001

HAVSTEEN, JAKOB HENRIK, financial executive; b. Copenhagen, Jan. 4, 1950; m. Pia Havsteen, Apr. 28, 1973. MS in Econs., Copenhagen Bus. Sch., 1979. Acct. Copenhagen, 1975-78; fin. contr. B&W Electronics, Copenhagen, 1978-80; fin. mgr. Herdsgan/Mannequines, Copenhagen, 1980-86; fin. mgr. Diners Club Denmark, Copenhagen, 1986, fin. dir., 1986-88, gen. mgr., CEO, 1988-92; fin. dir. AEG-Denmark, Copenhagen, 1992-94; gen. mgr. Difko Adminstrn. A/S, Copenhagen, 1994-95; gen. mgr., CEO Difko Danish Investment Found.%, 1995—. Mem. regional bd. Conservative Party, Denmark, 1989-96. Home: Agiltevej 8, 2970 Hoersholm Denmark Office: Danish Investment Found, 31 G Nyhaun, 1051 Copenhagen Denmark

HAVU, NIILO, pathologist; b. Soujärvi, Finland, May 1, 1936; s. Nicolai and Martta (Määränen) H.; m. Ulla Margareta Svedung, May 8, 1965. B in Medicine, U. Uppsala, 1958, Licentiate in Medicine, 1963, MD, 1963; PhD, U. Umeå, 1969. Med. Diplomate Pathology, Cytology. Assoc. prof. pathology U. Umeå, 1970-86, acting prof. pathology, 1969; acting prof. pathology U. Linköping, 1970-74; head dept. pathology Astra AB, Södertälje, 1973-89; sr. expert toxicologist Astra/Astrazeneca, Södertälje, 1989—; assoc. prof. pathology Karolinska Inst., Stockholm, 1986—. Author: (book) Sulfhydryl Inhibitors and Pancreatic Islet Tissue, 1969. Lt. Army/Air Force, Stockholm, 1956-81. Fellow The Swedish Med. Soc., Royal Soc. Medicine; mem. Internat. Acad. Pathology. Avocations: astronomy, chorus, botany, paleoanthropology. Home: Hackvagen 7, S-15137 Sodertalje Sweden Office: Astrazeneca/RS, Gartuna, S-15185 Sodertalje Sweden

HAWASH, MICHAEL ANDREW, lawyer; b. Middlesbrough, Eng., Mar. 30, 1966; came to U.S., 1981; s. Ralph Hawash and Linda (Burnip) Kuschel. BA in History, U. Tex., 1990, BA in Govt., 1991; JD, U. Houston, 1994. Bar: Tex. 1994, U.S. Dist. Ct. (so., no., ea., and we. dists.) Tex. 1995, U.S. Ct. Appeals (5th cir.) 1996, U.S. Dist. Ct. (ea. dist.) La. 1996. Assoc. Meyer Orlando & Evans PC, Houston, 1993-2000, Verner Liipfert Bernhard McPherson and Hand, Chartered, Houston, 2000—. Mem. ABA, Fed. Bar Assn., Maritime Law Assn., State Bar Tex., Houston Young Lawyers Assn., Houston Bar Assn., Computer Game Developers Assn., Phi Delta Phi, Phi Kappa Psi. Home: 6206 Taggart St Unit A Houston TX 77007-2051 Office:

Verner Liipfert Bernhard McPherson and Hand 1111 Bagby St Ste 4700 Houston TX 77002-2543

HAWAWINI, GABRIEL ALFRED, finance educator; b. Alexandria, Egypt, Aug. 29, 1947; arrived in France, 1965; s. Alfred Goubrane and Renee (Eddi) H.; m. Marci Serene Garber, July 16, 1977; children: Alfred, Alana. MS in Chem. Engring., Ecole Nat. Superieure de Chimie de Toulouse, France, 1972; MBA, NYU, 1974, PhD, 1977. Asst. prof. fin. NYU, N.Y.C., 1977-79; assoc. prof. CUNY, 1979-81; prof., head dept. fin. European Inst. Bus. Adminstrn. (INSEAD), Fontainebleau, France, 1981-87, Yamaichi prof. fin., 1988-96, assoc. dean, dir. Euro-Asia Ctr., 1988-97, also bd. dirs. and bd. dirs. Euro-Asia Ctr., assoc. dean for devel., 1998-2000, dean, 2000—; vis. prof. fin. Wharton Sch., U. Pa., Phila., 1987-88; Henry Grunfeld chaired prof. investment banking. Author: European Equity Markets, 1984, Mandatory Financial Disclosure and Capital Market Equilibrium, 1987, The Transformation of the European Financial Services Industry: From Fragmentation to Integration, 1989, Mergers and Acquisitions in the U.S. Banking Industry, 1991, Finance for Executives: Managing for Value Creation, 1999; editor Finance, 1985-94; contbr. numerous aticles to profl. jours. Recipient Money Marketeers Internat. award NYU, 1975, Presdl. award Baruch Coll., CUNY, 1982, Helen Kardon Moss Anvil Wharton Sch., 1988. Mem. Am. Fin. Assn., Am. Econ. Asns., French Fin. Assn. (v.p. 1985-92). Avocation: travel. Home: 21 Bourg-Tibourg, 75004 Paris France Office: INSEAD, Blvd de Constance, 77305 Fontainebleau France

HAWE, DAVID LEE, manufacturing consultant; b. Columbus, Ohio, Feb. 19, 1938; s. William Doyle and Carolyn Mary (Hasig) H.; m. Margret J. Hoover, Apr. 15, 1962; children: Darrin Lee, Kelly Lynn. Lic. real estate broker, Calif. Project mgr. ground antenna systems W.D.L. Labs., Philco Corp., 1960-65; credit mgr. for Western U.S. Am. Hosp. Supply Corp., Burbank, Calif., 1965-74; owner, mgr. Hoover Profl. Equipment Co., Contract Health Equipment Co., Guasti, Calif., 1974-75; pres. Baslor Care Svcs.; owner convalescent homes Santa Ana, Calif., 1975-80; pres. Application Assocs., 1980—; CEO Xiron Inc., 1985—; bd. dirs., chmn. bd. dirs. Xiron, Inc.; dir. Medisco Co., Casa Pacifica, Broadway Assocs. Bd. dirs. Santa Ana Cmty. Convalescent Hosp., 1974-79, pres. 1975-79. With USN, 1954-56. Mem. Am. Vacuum Soc. Republican. Roman Catholic. Home: 18082 Hallsworth Cir Villa Park CA 92861-4503

HAWES, JUSTIN ALEXANDER, corporate executive; b. Johannesburg, Gauteng, S. Africa, Apr. 12, 1968; s. Alexander Dixon and Rowena Anne Philip H.; m. Heather Glynn Volck, Nov. 13, 1999. BCom, Witwaterand U., Johanesburg, 1989, B Acctg., 1990, higher Diploma in taxation, 1996. Chartered acct., S. Africa. Trainee acct. Arthur Andersen, Johannesburg, 1992-94; cons. Destag, Bensheim, Germany, 1994-95; gen. mgr. MegaPro Fin., Johanesburg, 1995-96; CEO First Focus Mgmt., Johanesburg, 1996—; non-exec. dir. Donau Design Co., Johannesburg, 1998-99, Afrityre, 1999—; fin. dir. Granite Plus, Cape Town, S. Africa, 1995-99; dir. Scan Display, Johannesburg, 1996—; dir. First Focus Fin., 1996—; dir. E Granite, 1999—. Treas. United Dem. Movement, Johannesburg, 1998-99, parliamentary candidate, 1999; chmn. Jhb Chartered Acct., 1992-93, provincial candidate, 1999. Mem. S. African Inst. of Chartered Accts., Commerce Student Coun. (v.p., pres. 1988-89), Rand Athletic Club (treas. 2000—). Mem. United Dem. Movement, Anglican. Avocations: roadrunning, golf, birdwatching, hiking, cricket. Office: First Focus Mgmt, Pvt Bag x 7000, Parklands Johannesburg 2121, South Africa

HAWK, KATHLEEN PATRICIA, broadcast consultant; b. Butler, Pa., Feb. 12, 1945; d. Allen Clarence and Betty Ruth (Wilson) Pollock; m. Robert Ferdinand Hawk, Dec. 31, 1966; 1 child, Allen Robert. BSc, Parsons Coll., Fairfield, Iowa, 1966. Ind. internat. radiofrequency/microwave cons. Butler, Pa., 1990—; invited reviewer U.S. Congress, Office of Tech. Assessment, Wireless Technologies and the Nat. Info. Infrastructure, 1995; participant numerous seminars, confs., telecomms. adv. com.; mem. elec. sensitivity network. Author: Case Study in the Heartland, 1996; freelance writer Pitts. Post Gazette; contbr. articles to profl. jours. Worthy advisor Rainbow Girls, 1961; mem. Nat. Coalition of Citizens and Pub. Ofcls. for Local Control; founding mem. Cellular Phone Task Force; bd. dirs. Delbert Parkinson Christian Cancer Coalition. Mem. Bioelectromagnetics Soc., Butler Natural Living Group, 1000 Club, Butler Country Club, 36 Year Card Club, Am. Legion Aux., Am. Golf Hall of Fame. Republican. Achievements include rsch. on human and animal health in close proximity to telecomms. facilities. Avocations: gourmet cooking, crafts, sports, pub. speaking, politics. Home and Office: 122 Thornwood Dr Butler PA 16001-3442

HAWKE, PAUL HENRY, historian; b. Canton, Ohio, Mar. 9, 1958; s. Richard Carl and Sara (Hemming) H.; m. Gaynel O. Allen, May 2, 1987; children: Cailean Stewart, Angela Janette. BA in History, Geography, Hist. Preservation, Mary Washington Coll., 1982; postgrad., Temple U., 1983, U. Ark., 1984-85; MA in History and Heritage Preservation, Ga. State U., 1993. Park tech. Petersburg (Va.) Nat. Battlefield, 1978-81; intern Fredericksburg (Va.) and Spotsylvania Nat. Mil. Park, 1981-82; park ranger Independence Nat. Hist. Park, Phila., 1982-83; park historian Pea Ridge (Ark.) Nat. Mil. Park, 1983-85; historian Southeast Regional Office, Atlanta, 1985-95; S.E. coord. Am. Battlefield Protectio Program, Atlanta, 1991-95, Civil War sites adv. commn. staff, 1991-93; coord. Nat. Historic Landmarks Program, Atlanta, 1986-95; chief interpretation and resources mgmt. Shiloh (Tenn.) Nat. Mil. Park, 1995-2000; chief Am. Battlefield Protection Program, Washington, 2000—. Co-author: Civil War Battlefield Guide, 1991; editor The Parapet: Newsletter of the Civil War, 1992—; asst. editor, author: Jour. of Civil War Fort Study Group, 1994. Water safety chmn. Am. Nat. Red Cross, Benton County, Ark., 1984-85, water safety instr., Canton, Ohio, 1975-80, Fredericksburg, Va., 1980-82, small craft safey inst., Benton County, Ark., 1984-85, Canton, 1975-80. Named Ky. Col., Gov. of Ky., 1992. Mem. Civil War Fortification Study Group (sec., treas.), Coast Def. Study Group, Assn. of Nat. Park Rangers, Assn. for Preservation of Civil War Sites, Nat. Trust for Hist. Preservation, Civil War Trust, Soc. of Mil. Historians. Avocations: swimming, travel, movies, military history, sports. Home: 6314 Morning Dew Ct Clarksville MD 21029-1150 Office: Nat Park Svc Am Battlefield Protection 800 N Capitol St NW Ste 330 Washington DC 20002-4244

HAWKEN, PATTY LYNN, retired nursing educator, dean of faculty; b. Wheaton, Ill., July 13, 1932; d. Leonard William and Betty (Stock) H. BSN, U. Mich., 1956; MSN, Case Western Res. U., 1962, PhD, 1970. Instr. U. Mich., Ann Arbor, 1956-57, Highland Hosp., Oakland, Calif., 1957-59; from instr. to assoc. prof., assoc. in adminstrn. Case Western Res. U., Cleve., 1960-71; assoc. prof. Emory U., Atlanta, 1971-72, prof., dir., 1972-74; dean, prof. U. Tex. Health Sci. Ctr. Sch. Nursing, San Antonio, 1974-97, ret., 1997. Contbr. articles to profl. jours. Bd. dirs. Wesley Cmty. Ctr., San Antonio, 1986, 89; mem. United Way Allocation Com., San Antonio, 1987; adv. com. Trinity U. Health Care Adminstrn., San Antonio, 1984-97, VA Dean's Com., San antonio, 1982-97. Recipient Nurse of Yr. award Tex. Nursing Assn., San Antonio chpt., 1985, Disting. Alumni award Case Western Res. U., 1991, U. Mich., 1995; named to Women's Hall of Fame. Mem. ANA (cabinet on edn. 1986-88), Nat. League Nursing (pres. 1989-91, Disting. Svc. award 1991), Am. Assn. Colls. of Nursing (com. on edn. 1986-88), Commns. Grads. Fgn. Nursing Schs. (trustee, pres. 1983-85), Am. Acad. Nursing (bd. govs. 1994-97), San Antonio 100 Club, Internat. Women's Forum (San Antonio pres. celebration, Hall of Fame 1994-97). Avocations: snorkeling, swimming. Home: 1826 Fallow Run San Antonio TX 78248-2000

HAWKER, GEOFFREY FORT, arbitrator, civil engineer, barrister; b. London, Dec. 20, 1929; married; 2 daus. BSc in Engring., U. London, 1950. Called to Bar Gray's Inn, 1970; chartered civil engr. Design, fabrication, erection, adaptation gen. steel struct Aston Constrn. Co. Ltd., 1945-50; with nat. svc. Royal Engrs., Gold Coast Colony, 1951-52; with power sta. contracts, design Volta Bridge, sea def. Sir William Halcrow & Ptnrs., Seaford and Ghana, 1953-59; with hydro-electric project Mitchell Constrn. Co. Ltd., Iverness-shire, Scotland, 1960-61; with head office Rendel Palmer & Tritton, Oldbury Nuclear Power Sta., Gloucestershire, Eng., 1961-63; opened office Chadwick, O'hEocha and Assocs., London, 1963-64; pvt. practice London, 1964—. Co-Author: A Guide to Commercial Arbitration under the 1979 Act, 1980, The ICE Arbitration Procedure, 1983, The ICE Arbitration Practice, 1986, The ICE Minor Works Contract-A Guide and Commentary, 1992. Svc. in Territorial Army. Fellow Inst. Civil Engrs., Royal Acad. Engrs., Inst. Structural Engrs., Chartered Inst. Arbitrators; mem. Am. Arbitration Assn., Swiss Arbitration Assn., Internat. Bar Assn., Worshipful Co. Arbitrators (liveryman), Worshipful Co. Engrs. (liveryman), Soc. Engrs. and Scientists of France, Internat. Fedn. Cons. Engrs., London Ct. Internat. Arbitration, Swiss Arbitration ASsn., Bahrain Ctr. for Internat. Comml. Arbitration. Office: 46-48 Essex St, London WC2R 3GH, England

HAWKINS, DAVID RAMON, psychiatrist, writer, researcher; b. Milw., June 3, 1927; s. Ramon Nelson and Alice-Mary (McCutcheon) H.; m. Susan Humphrey; children: Lynn Ashley, Barbara Catherine. BS, Marquette U., 1950; MD, Med. Coll. Wis., Milw., 1953; PhD, Columbia Pacific U., 1995. Med. dir. North Nassau Mental Health Ctr., Manhasset, N.Y., 1956-80; dir. rsch. Brunswick Hosp., L.I., N.Y., 1968-79; pres. Acad. Orthomolecular Psychiatry, N.Y.C., 1970-80; dir. Inst. Spiritual Rsch., Sedona, Ariz., 1979-88, The Rsch. Inst., Sedona, 1988—; pres. Attractor Rsch., Sedona, 1989—, Veritas Pub., Sedona, 1995—; chmn. Inst. Advaned Theoretical Rsch., 1993—; guest lectr. U. Notre Dame, Harvard U., U. Mich., 1970-88, U. Calif., San Francisco, 1997; Landsberg lectr. U. Calif. San Francisco Med. Sch., 1997; guest on TV news and interview shows including McNeal-Lehrer, Barbara Walters, Today, 1972-76; chief of staff Mingus Mountain RTC, 1995; cons. psychiatrist MJL Hosp., Cottonwood, Ariz., 1995; cons. USN, Dept. Health Edn. Welfare, Congress. Author: (with Linus Pauling) Orthomolecular Psychiatry, 1973, Force vs. Power, 1995; contbr. articles to profl. jours. With U.S. Navy, 1945-46, PTO. Decorated knight Sovereign Order St. John of Jerusalem, Danish Crown; Rsch. grantee N.Y. State Dept. Mental Hygiene, annually, N.Y. State Legis., 1967-87; recipient Mosby Book award, 1953. Mem. AMA, APA, Ariz. Med. Soc., Ariz. Psychiat. Soc., Alpha Omega Alpha. Avocations: inventing, designing, woodcraft, dance, architecture. Office: Rsch Inst 151 Keller Ln Sedona AZ 86336-9748

HAWKINS, DAVID ROLLO, SR., psychiatrist; b. Springfield, Mass., Sept. 22, 1923; s. James Alexander and Janet (Rollo) H.; m. Elizabeth G. Wilson, June 8, 1946; children: David Rollo Jr., Robert Wilson, John Bruce, William Alexander. B.A., Amherst Coll., 1945; M.D., U. Rochester, N.Y., 1946. Intern Strong Meml. Hosp., Rochester, 1946-48; Commonwealth Fund fellow in psychiatry and medicine U. Rochester, 1950-52; instr. psychiatry U. N.C. Sch. Medicine, 1952-53, asst. prof., 1953-57, asso. prof. psychiatry, 1957-62, prof., 1962-67; prof., chmn. dept. psychiatry U. Va. Sch. Medicine, 1967-77, Alumni prof. psychiatry, 1967-79, asso. dean, 1969-70; psychiatrist-in-chief U. Va. Hosp., 1967-77; prof. psychiatry Pritzker Sch. Medicine, U. Chgo., 1979-90, U. Ill., 1990—; clin. prof. psychiatry U. N.C., Chapel Hill, 1992—; dir. liaison and consultation svcs. dept. psychiatry Michael Reese Hosp., Chgo., 1979-87, chmn., 1987-92; assoc. attending physician N.C. Meml. Hosp., Chapel Hill, 1952-62, attending physician, 1962-67; cons. Watts Hosp., Durham, 1952-67, VA Hosp., Fayetteville, N.C., 1956-67, Eastern State Hosp., Williamsburg, Va., 1971—, VA Hosp., Salem. Va., 1969-79, mem. deans com., 1971-77; spl. rsch. fellow Inst. Psychiatry, U. London, 1963-64, Fogarty internat. rsch. fellow, 1976-77, U.S.-USSR and Romania health exch. fellow, 1978. Rev. editor Psychosomatic Medicine, 1958-70; assoc. editor Psychiatry, 1970-92. Mem. small grants com. NIMH, 1958-62; mem. nursing rsch. study sect. NIH, 1965-67; mem. Gov.'s Commn. Mental, Indigent and Geriatric Patients, 1968-72; mem. rsch. evaluation com. Va. Dept. Mental Hygiene and Hosps., 1970-73; mem. behavioral sci. test com. Nat. Bd. Med. Examiners, 1970-73. Served as capt. M.C., AUS, 1948-50. Fellow Am. Coll. Psychoanalysts (charter bd. regents 1979-81, treas. 1989-91, pres.-elect 1992, pres. 1994), Am. Psychiat. Assn.; mem. AAUP, Am. Psychosomatic Soc. (mem. coun. 1959), AMA, Group for Advancement Psychiatry (bd. dirs. 1987-89), Assn. Am. Med. Colls. (coun. acad. socs. 1973-78), Am. Psychoanalytic Assn., Am. Coll. Psychiatrists, AAAS, Va. Psychoanalytic Soc., Washington Psychoanalytic Soc., Chgo. Psychoanalytic Soc., N.C. Psychoanalytic Soc., Ill. Psychiat. Soc. (coun. 1981-82, pres.-elect 1987, pres. 1988-90), Soc. Neurosci., Am. Assn. Chmn. Depts. Psychiatry (sec.-treas. 1971-73, pres. 1974-75), Sleep Rsch. Soc., Nat. Bd. Med. Examiners (exam. com. 1983-87), Phi Beta Kappa, Sigma Xi, Alpha Omega Alpha. Address: 405 Deming Rd Chapel Hill NC 27514-3207

HAWKINS, ELLIS DELANO, manufacturing executive, insurance executive, gaming executive; b. Princeton, Ark., Feb. 13, 1941; s. Eddie and Anne Beadie (Smith) H.; m. Vera Mae Smith, Aug. 19, 1969 (div. Sept. 1979); children: Angela, Stacey, Rhonald. AA, Shorter Jr. Coll., 1958; BBA, Calif. Coast U., 1981, MBA, 1983. Cert. in statis. process control; lic. ins. agt., Ill. Operator drill press Choctaw Inc., Poyen, Ark., 1962-65; supr. Chrysler Corp., Detroit, 1965-76, Alcan Aluminum, Terre Haute, Ind., 1976-86; Borg-Warner, Chgo., 1986-91, ins. exec., 1991—; pres., chief exec. officer Jes-El-Ed Inc., Chgo., 1980—; also bd. dirs. Jes-El-Ed Inc.; bd. dirs., sec. Idlewild Civic Investment, Inc.; prodn. mgr., photographer St. James Trumpet, 1989; mem. bd. rsch. advisors ABS Inc., 1993. Scoutmaster Boy Scouts Am. Troop 53, Malvern, Ark., 1962; solicitor United Found., Detroit, 1971; life mem. NAACP. With USN, 1958-62. Recipient Commendation Letter Tribune Star, 1986, Appreciation Letter, M.L. King Convocation Com., 1986. Mem. Am. Legion (chmn. Spl. Olympics 1982-89, Plaque 1985, Cert. of Appreciation 1989), Idlefellows Social Club. Democrat. Avocations: golf, bowling, short verse writing; profl. freelance photographer.

HAWKINS, JOHN, writer; b. N.Y.C., May 15, 1941; s. Baseem and Valentine (Orfali) Trabulsi; m. Nadine Thomas, Nov. 6, 1971; 1 child, Robert Trabulsi. BS in Acctg. and Fin., CUNY, Bklyn., 1967. Cert. instr. NRA. Tax acct. Morris & McVeigh, N.Y.C., 1959-67; stockbroker Walston & Co., N.Y.C., 1967-71; self-employed various bus., N.Y.C., 1971-94; writer West Palm Beach, Fla., 1994—. Author: Bells of Revenge, 1995, Jack's Place, 1996. Mem. Am. Numismatic Assn. (life) Masons, Cedars of Lebanon.

HAWKINS, LORETTA ANN, secondary school educator, playwright; b. Winston-Salem, N.C., Jan. 1, 1942; d. John Henry and Laurine (Hines) Sanders; m. Joseph Hawkins, Dec. 10, 1962; children: Robin, Dionne, Sherri. BS in Edn., Chgo. State U., 1965; MA in Lit., Governor's State U., 1977, MA in African Cultures, 1978; MLA in Humanities, U. Chgo., 1998. Cert. tchr., Ill. Tchr. Chgo. Bd. Edn., 1968—; lectr. Chgo. City Colls., 1987-89; tchr. English Gage Park H.S., 1988—; Mem. steering com. Mellon Seminar U. Chgo., 1990; tchr. adv. com. Goodman Theatre, Chgo., 1992, mem. cmty. adv. coun., 1996—; spkr. in field. Author: (reading workbook) Contemporary Black Heroes, 1992, (plays) Of Quiet Birds, 1993 (James H. Wilson award 1993), Above the Line, 1994, Good Morning, Miss Alex; contbr. poetry, articles to profl. publs.; featured WTTW-Educate, 1996. Santa Fe Pacific Found. fellow, 1988, Lloyd Fry Found. fellow, 1989, Andrew W. Mellon Found. fellow, 1991, Ill. Arts Coun. fellow, 1993; Cmty. Arts Assistance Program Award grantee Chgo. Dept. Cultural Affairs; recipient Feminist Writers 3d pl. award NOW, 1993, Zora Neale Hurston-Bessie Head Fiction award Black Writer's Conf., 1993, numerous others; featured on WTTW-TV Educate, 1996. Mem. AAUW, Nat. Coun. Tchrs. English (spkr. conv.), Am. Fedn. Tchrs., Women's Theatre Alliance, Dramatists Guild of Am., Internat. Women's Writing Guild. Avocations: films, coins, reading, walking. Home: 8928 S Oglesby Ave Chicago IL 60617-3047 Office: Gage Park HS 5630 S RockwellAve Chicago IL 60629

HAWKINS, PAMELA LEIGH HUFFMAN, biochemist; b. Washington, Oct. 7, 1950; d. Lauria Carl and Maryalice (Flinner) Huffman; m. James Lee Hawkins, Mar. 7, 1981 (div. Aug. 1993). BS in Biochemistry, Va. Polytech. Inst. & State U., 1972; MS in Biochemistry, Pa. State U., 1975. Sci. info. specialist Informatics, Inc., Rockville, Md., 1972; asst. rsch. scientist Union Carbide Corp., Tarrytown, N.Y., 1975; assoc. rsch. scientist Am. Hosp. Supply Corp., Gibbstown, N.J., 1976-78; rsch. scientist Am. Hosp. Supply Corp., Miami, Fla., 1978-85; R & D scientist Baxter Healthcare Corp., Miami, 1985-95, sr. rsch. scientist, 1993-95; prin. scientist Sigma Diagnostics, St. Louis, 1995—. Contbr. articles to profl. jours. Recipient Baxter Diagnostics Tech. award for Thromboplastin-IS, 1990, Baxter Internat. Tech. award, 1991. Mem. Internat. Soc. Thrombosis and Hemostasis, Am. Chem. Soc., Mortar Bd., Phi Sigma, Gamma Sigma Delta, Phi Lambda Upsilon. Lutheran. Achievements include U.S. and European patent for fresh blood (unfixed) hematology control, 3 U.S. and 1 European patents for improved extraction methods for preparing thromboplastin reagents, patent for thromboplastins for recombinent tissue factor, U.S. patent for thromboplastin reagents based on recombinent technology, production of thromboplastin IS, Innovin, various others. Office: Sigma Diagnostics 545 S Ewing Ave Saint Louis MO 63103-2991

HAWKSWORTH, BRIAN MICHAEL, investment company executive; b. Durban, South Africa, Dec. 13, 1935; s. Alan William and Kathleen (Perry) H.; m. Audrey Denise Mackenzie, Mar. 4, 1961 (div. Mar. 1989); children: Michael John, Sally Denise; m. Louie Barbara Du Toit, Nov. 19, 1993. Cert. in theory of acctg., U. Natal, Durban, 1960. Chartered acct. Trainee Murray Smith Berend Noyce Accts., Durban, 1954-59; acct. Deloitte & Touche, Durban, 1959-60, Annan Dexter, London, 1960-61; ptnr. Ernst & Young, Johannesburg, South Africa, 1962-96; dir. South Africa Inst. Race Relations, Inst. Internat. Affairs, Johannesburg, 1996—, Associated Ore & Metal Corp., Ltd., Johannesburg, 1996—, Thebe Investments (Pty.) Ltd., 1997—. Fellow Inst. Dir. (chmn. 1988—); mem. Comml. Fin. Accts., South Africa Inst. Chartered Accts. (mem. coun. 1983-86). Presbyterian. Avocations: tennis, bird watching, classical music, gardening. Home: 29 College Ave, Sandton 2021, South Africa

HAWLADER, SARWAR HOSSAIN, plant breeder; b. Bhandaria, Pirojpur, Bangladesh, May 14, 1960; s. Abul Kashem Hawlader and Zohora Begum; m. Zebun Nessa; children: Sabrina, Farzana, Aadnan. BSc in Agr. with honors, Bangladesh Agrl. U., 1981, MSc in Agr., 1984; PhD, Inst. Postgrad. Studies Agr., 1995. Sci. officer Bangladesh Agrl. Rsch. Coun., Dhaka, 1983, Agrl. Rsch. Sta., Thakurgaon, 1983-91; sr. sci. officer Bangladesh Agrl. Rsch. Inst., Gazipur, 1991-98; program coord. Asia Vegetable R&D Ctr., Dhaka, 1998-99; prin. sci officer, head Bangladesh Rice Rsch. Inst., Bhanga, Faridpur, 1999—; adj. faculty Inst. Postgrad. Studies in Agr., 1995—, rsch. supr., 1996—; reviewer Bangladesh Jour. Agrl. Rsch., 1995—, Bangladesh Jour. Plant Breedingand Genetics, 1996—. Contbr. 50 articles to sci. and profl. jours. Mem. Plant Breedingand Genetics Soc. Bangladesh (life, organizing sec.1997-98), Bangladesh Assn. for Advancement of Sci., Bangladesh Soc. Horticultural Scis. Muslim. Avocations: games, gardening, fishing, travel. Home: Village and Post Chinguria, Police Sta, Pirojpur Bhandaria 8550, Bangladesh Office: Bangladesh Rice Rsch Inst, Bhanga Fardipur 7830, Bangladesh

HAWLEY, DONALD FREDERICK, retired diplomat; s. Mr. and Mrs. F.G. Hawley; m. Ruth Morwenna Graham Howes, 1964. MA, New Coll., Oxford, Eng., 1946; DLitt (hon.), U. Reading, 1994. Mem. Sudan Judiciary, 1947, chief registrar, registrar gen. marriages, 1951; mem. HM Fgn. Svcs., 1955, fgn. office, 1956; polit agt. Trucial States HM Fgn. Svcs., Dubai, 1958; head chancery Brit. Embassy, Cairo, 1962; counsellor, head chancery Brit. High Commn., Lagos, Nigeria, 1965; counselor Brit. Embassy, Baghdad, Iraq, 1968; HM consul-gen. Brit. Embassy, Muscat, 1971; ambassador to Oman Brit. Embassy, 1971-75; asst. under sec. of state FCO, 1975-77; Brit. high commr. to Malaysia, 1977-81; vis. fellow dept. geography Durham U., 1967; mem. London adv. com. Hong Kong and Shanghai Banking Corp.; chmn. Ewbank Preece Group, 1982-86, spl. advisor, 1986-96; pres. coun. Reading U., 1986-94. Author: Handbook for Registrars of Marriage and Ministers of Religion, 1963, Courtesies in the Trucial States, 1965, The Trucial States, 1971, Oman and its Renaissance, 1977, rev. edit., 1995, Courtesies in the Gulf Area, 1978, Manners and Correct Form in the Middle East, 1984, 2d edit., 1996, Sandtracks in the Sudan, 1995, Sudan Canterbury Tales, 1999, Desert Wind and Tropic Storm, 2000. Gov. ESU, 1989-95; pres. Sudan Def. Force Dinner Club. Served with Brit. Armed Forces, 1941. Recipient Hon. DCL, Durham, 1997; decorated Knight Comdr. Order St. Michaels, Order St. George. Mem. Ctr. for Brit. Soc., Brit. Malaysian Soc. (chmn., 1983-95, v.p. 1993—), Sudan Pensioners Assn. (chmn.), Royal Soc. for Asian Affairs (chmn.), Order of The Brit. Empire, Travellers Club, Beefsteak Club. Avocations: tennis, travel, gardening. Home: Little Cheverell House, near Devizes, Wilts SN10 4JJ, England

HAWLEY, HAROLD PATRICK, educational consultant; b. Paducah, Ky., Jan. 8, 1945; s. Mathew Mark and Mae (Herndon) H.; m. Ann Dunbar, 1971 (div. 1982); Lucrecia Thomas, Aug. 27, 1983; children: Cherise, Charlotte. AA, Paducah Jr. Coll., 1965; BA, U. Ky., 1968; MS, Ind. U., New Albany, 1974; EdD, Ind. U., Bloomington, 1977; postgrad., Mary Baldwin Coll., 1988, Ala. A&M U., 1996. Liaison to adjutant gen. 5th army U.S. Army, Ft. Carson, 1970, Bien Hoa, Vietnam, 1969-70; English tchr. Southwestern Consol. Schs., Hanover, Ind., 1971-73; asst. prin. Whitewater Consol. Sch., Lyons, Ind., 1978-80; assoc. prof., dir. secondary edn. Birmingham (Ala.)-So. Coll., 1980-86, chmn. freshman seminar, 1984-86; 1988-95 Ga. Dept. Edn., Atlanta, 1988-95; evaluator So. Assn. Schs. and Colls., 1988—; ednl. cons. Ga. Dept. Edn., Atlanta, 1988-95; chmn. Effective Sch. Rsch. Program, 1991; adj. prof. Ind. U., Bloomington, 1975-80, Samford U., 1980-84, Auburn U., 1987, U. Ala., Gadsen, 1984-85, Brenau U., Gainesville, Ga., 1988-96, Reinhardt Coll./Brenau Coll. Collaboration, 1995—, Ala. A&M U., 1999, univ. supr., 1996—; cons. Intervarsity Beach Project, 1982—, Ford Ednl. Found., Parker H.S., Birmingham, Ala., 1981-85, Christian Acad., Cornerstone, Baton Rouge, 1983-84, FCA, 1983, Happy Valley Elem., Fairview Elem. Schoolwide Project, 1995, Walker County Curriculum Specialist, 1995-96, Nicholas Soc., 1997—; tech. advisor Polk County Schoolwide Projects, 1995; ednl. cons. Ga. Dept. Edn., Atlanta, 1988-95; coord. 9th Dist. Schs. of Excellence, Ga., 1988-92; ednl. cons. Effective Schs. Rsch./Authentic Ins.; team leader sch. improvement teams Ga. Dept. Edn., Calhoun, 1995; numerous ESEA Instrnl. Confs., Ga., 1993-94; presenter ESEA Instrnl. Conf., Statesboro, 1994, Carrolton, Ga., 1995; dir. 1st State Remedial Edn. Conf., Lafayette, Ga., 1994; dir. 1st statewide instrnl. conf. ESEA, 1995-96, Lone Oak Edn. Svcs., 1998; participant Inst. for Comm. Seminars, Birmingham So. Coll., 1983-86; tech. advisor Floyd County Schoolwide Project, 1995—, Dade County Schoolwide Project, 1996; student tchr. supr. Covenant Coll., Chattanooga, 1996—; dir. Title I Northwest Ga. Instrnl. Conf., 1996; ednl. cons. Attention Deficit Disorder/HD, 1995—; dir. Lone Oak Edn. Svcs. 1999—. Author: (with Don Manlove) Classroom Climate Teacher-Student Relations, Expectancy Effects, 1976; rsch. asst. (with Floyd Coppedge) Binford Middle School Project, Bloomington, Ind., 1976, Individual Instrn. Project, 1975, Lebanon High Sch. Project, 1975-76, Katherine Hamilton Rsch. Project, New Albany, Ind., 1974 (with Carol Lewis). Bd. dirs. Boys Club of Am., Paducah, Ky., 1963-65; tech. adv. Polk County Consolidated Schs., 1995-96, Dade County Consolidated Schs., 1995. Basketball scholar, 1965, attention deficit rsch. scholar univ. supr., Ala. A&M U., 1997—; Spenser grantee, 1981, Mellon grantee, 1985; grad fellow Okla. State Sch. Supt.,1975-77, Nat. Study Sch. Evaluation fellow Ind. U., 1977. Mem. Ga. Com. Leaders Assn., Internat. Platform Assn., Phi Delta Kappa. Avocations: jogging, basketball, camping. Home: 406 N Malone St Athens AL 35611-1567

HAWN, GOLDIE, actress; b. Washington, Nov. 21, 1945; d. Edward Rutledge and Laura (Steinhoff) H.; m. Gus Trinkonis, May 16, 1969 (div.); m. Bill Hudson (div.); children: Oliver, Kate Garry, Wyatt Russell. Student, Am. U. Profl. dancer, 1965; profl. acting debut in Good Morning, World, 1967-68; mem. company TV series Laugh-In, 1968-70; appeared in TV spl. Pure Goldie, 1971; films include: The One and Only Genuine Original Family Band, 1968, Cactus Flower, 1969 (Acad. award best supporting actress 1969), There's A Girl In My Soup, 1970, $, 1971, Butterflies Are Free, 1971, The Sugarland Express, 1974, The Girl from Petrovka, 1974, Shampoo, 1975, The Duchess and the Dirtwater Fox, 1976, Travels with Anita, 1978, Foul Play, 1978, Seems Like Old Times, 1980, Lovers and Liars, 1981, Best Friends, 1982, Swingshift, 1984, Overboard, 1987, Bird on a Wire, 1989, Deceived, 1991, Housesitter, 1992, Death Becomes Her, 1992, Crisscross, 1992, The First Wives Club, 1996, Everyone Says I Love You, 1996; exec. producer and star films Private Benjamin, 1980, Protocol, 1984, Wildcats, 1986, My Blue Heaven (co-exec. prodr. only), 1990, Something to Talk About, 1995 (exec. prodr. only), The Out of Towners, 1999, Town and Country, 1999; host TV spl. Pure Goldie, 1970, Goldie Hawn Special, 1978, Goldie and Liza Together, 1980, Goldie and Kids: Listen to Us!, 1982. Office: care ICM Ed Limato & S Dontanville 8942 Wilshire Blvd Beverly Hills CA 90211-1934

HAWRYLYSHYN, BOHDAN, business educator; b. Koropec, Ukraine, Oct. 19, 1926; s. Dmytro and Teodosia (Sadowska) H.; m. Leonida Hayowsky, June 10, 1950; children: Leslie, Patricia, Christine. MASc in mech. Engring., U. Toronto, 1954; Diploma in Indsl. Mgmt., Internat. Mgmt. Inst., Geneva, 1958; PhD in Econs., U. Geneva, 1975; hon. degree, York U., Alta. U., Ternopil Acad. Carpathian U. Officer UNRRA, Germany, 1946-47; positions in rsch., engring. and mgmt. Can., 1954-60; mem. faculty Internat. Mgmt. Inst., Geneva, 1960-68, dir., 1968-86, scholar in residence, 1986-89; chmn. bd. IMI Kiev, 1989—, Renaissance Found., 1990-98; chmn. coun. advisors Ukraine, 1991-98; advisor to the Pres., Ukraine, 1992-94; dir. Internat. Acd. Environment, Geneva, 1995-96; lectr.

in more than 60 countries; advisor to chmn. Parliament and prime minister Ukraine, 2000—; cons. to govts., internat. orgns. and bds. of transnat. corps. Author: Road Maps to the Future, in 8 lang. edits., other books; contbr. more than 100 articles to publs.; mem. editl. bds. several jours. Recipient Gold medal Pres. of Italian Republic, Medal of merit, Pres. of Ukraine, various scholarships and awards. Fellow World Acad. Art and Sci., Internat. Acad. Mgmt., Acad. of Scis. Ukraine, Club of Rome. Ukrainian Catholic. Home: 5 chemin du Reposoir, Veyrier, CH 1255 Geneva Switzerland Office: CP 5/Conches, CH 1231 Geneva Switzerland

HAWS, E. THOMAS, civil engineer, consultant; b. Southend-on-Sea, Eng., Jan. 19, 1927; s. Edward and Phyllis A. (Thomas) H.; m. Moira J. Forbes, Aug. 26, 1950; children: Gordon F., Linda J., Tony D. (dec.). Degree, St. John's Coll., Cambridge U., 1947. Sr. engr. Sir A. Gibb & Ptnrs., London, 1947-63; dir. Soil Mechanics Ltd., London, 1963-78; mng. dir. Engring. & Resources Consultants, Bracknell, Eng., 1969-78; dir. Rendel Palmer & Tritton, London, 1978-92; mng. dir. Rendel Parkman, London, 1979-92; Parsons lectr. Royal Soc. London, 1996. Contbr. articles to profl. jours. Chmn. environment com. Internat. Commn. on Large Dams, Paris, 1979-93, Brit. Dam Soc., London, 1986-89, Brit. Hydromechanics Rsch. Assn., Cranfield, Eng., 1975-78; v.p. Internat. Commn. on Large Dams, Paris, 1993-96. Fellow Royal Acad. Engring., Instn. Civil Engrs., Instn. Profl. Engrs. (New Zealand). Avocations: photography, golf, hill walking, music. Home and Office: E T Haws Consulting Engrs, 7 Southview Rd, Marlow Bucks SL7 3JR, England

HAWTHORNE, MARION FREDERICK, chemistry educator; b. Ft. Scott, Kans., Aug. 24, 1928; s. Fred Elmer and Colleen (Webb) H.; m. Beverly Dawn Rempe, Oct. 30, 1951 (div. 1976); children: Cynthia Lee, Candace Lee; m. Diana Baker Razzaia, Aug. 14, 1977. BA, Pomona Coll., 1949; PhD (AEC fellow), U. Calif. at Los Angeles, 1953; DSc (hon.), Pomona Coll., 1974; PhD (hon.), Uppsala U., 1992. Rsch. assoc. Iowa State Coll., 1953-54; rsch. chemist Rohm & Haas Co., Huntsville, Ala., 1954-56, group leader, 1956-60; lab. head Rohm & Haas Co., Phila., 1961; prof. chemistry U. Calif., Riverside, 1962-68, UCLA, 1968—, U. Calif., 1998—; vis. lectr. Harvard U., 1960, Queen Mary Coll., U. London, 1963; vis. prof. U. Tex., Austin, 1974, Harvard, 1968; mem. sci. adv. bd. USAF, 1980-86, NRC Bd. Army Sci. and Tech., 1986-90; disting. vis. prof. Ohio State U., 1990; mem. dir.'s external adv. bd. divsn. M, Los Alamos (N.Mex.) Nat. Lab., 1991-94; lectr. in field. Editor-in-chief: Inorganic Chemistry, 1969-00. Decorated Meritorious Svc. medal USAF, 1986; recipient Chancellors Research award, 1968, Herbert Newby McCoy award, 1972, Am. Chem. Soc. award in Inorganic Chemistry, 1973, Glenn T. Seaborg medal, 1997, Tolman Medal award, 1986, Nebr. sect. Am. Chem. Soc. award, 1979, Disting. Service in the Advancement of Inorganic Chemistry award Am. Chem. Soc., 1988, Disting. Achievements in Boron Sci. award, 1988, Bailar medal, 1991, Polyhedron Medal and prize, 1993, Chem. Pioneer award Am. Inst. Chemists, 1994, Willard Gibbs medal Am. Chem. Soc., 1994, Internat. award in Polyhedral Borane Chemistry, Internat. Com. on Boron Chemistry, 1996, Basolo medal, 2000; named sr. scientist Alexander von Humboldt Found., Inst. Inorganic Chemistry U. Munich, 1990-96, Centenary lectr. Royal Soc. Chemistry, London, 1998; Sloan Found. fellow, 1963-65, Japan Soc. Promotion Sci. fellow, 1986; named Col. Confederate Air Force, 1984. Fellow AAAS; mem. U.S. Nat. Acad. Scis. (award in chem. scis. 1997), Am. Acad. Arts and Scis., Göttingen Acad. Scis. (corr. mem.), Aircraft Owners and Pilots Assn., Cosmos Club, The Internat. Soc. for Neutron Capture Therapy for Cancer (mem. exec. com. 1992-00, pres. 1996-98), Sigma Xi, Alpha Chi Sigma, Sigma Nu. Home: 3415 Green Vista Dr Encino CA 91436-4011

HAWTHORNE, NAN LOUISE, internet resources consultant, web designer, writer, editor; b. Hawthorne, Nev., Jan. 3, 1952; d. Louis Frederick Haas Jr. and Merle Forrest (Ohlhausen) Ritter; m. James Denver Tedford, Dec. 20, 1981. BS, No. Mich. U., 1981. Mng. dir. CyberVPM.com, Seattle, 1997—; pres., dir. Vols. in Agys. of King County, 1997-98; webmaster Purrfect Pals, 1997—; mem. media team Points of Light Found., 1997—; writer, editor The Associated Blind Inc. Internet Initiative, 1999—; web content editor/trainer Networks, Assn. for Vol. Admin., 2000. Author: CyberVPM.com Resources for Vol. Programs, 1995—; Building Better Relationships with Volunteers, 1997, Managing Volunteers in Record Time, 1997, Recognizing Volunteers Right From the Start, 1998. Mem. Wash. State Coun. on Volunteerism and Citizen Svcs., 1992-94; trainer United Way of King County Vol. Ctr., 1993-99; bd. dirs. Dovia of King County, 1992, 96-98; mem. adv. bd. Retired Sr. Vol. Program, 1995-98; bd. dirs. Cmty. Vol. Svcs.; pres., 1996-97. Mem. Assn. Vol. Adminstrs. (tech. com. 1998—). E-mail: hawthorne@cybervpm.com.

HAWTHORNE, STEPHANIE JOSEFA JANE, editor; b. Guildford, Surrey, Eng.; d. James Francis and Ivy Ellen Jennie (Crawley) H. LLB with honors, King's Coll., London, 1977. Dep. editor Fin. Times Bus. Info., London, 1985-89; editor Pensions World, Butterworths Tolley, London, 1989—; mng. editor Charity World/Butterworths Tolley, London, 1993-95; editor PW On Line (Url:www.pensionsworld.co.uk), London, 1997—, Counsel, Butterworths Tolley, London, 1997—; freelance journalist, broadcaster, conf. spkr. Recipient several journalism awards. Avocations: tennis, opera, drama, rambling, sailing. Office: Butterworths Trolley, 2 Addiscombe Rd, Croydon CR9 5AF, England

HAY, DAVID RUSSELL, retired cardiologist; b. Christchurch, Canterbury, New Zealand, Dec. 8, 1927; s. James Lawrence and Davidina (Gunn) H.; m. Jocelyn Valerie Bell, Feb. 22, 1958; children: Nicola Mary, Lesley Natasha. MB, ChB, U. New Zealand, Otago, 1951, MD, 1960. Resident Postgrad. Med. Sch., London, 1952, Brompton Hosp., London, 1953-54, Nat. Heart Hosp., London, 1954-55, Christchurch Hosp., 1957-59; physician North Canterbury Hosp. Bd., Christchurch, 1959-64, head dept. medicine, chmn. med. svcs., 1978-85; med. dir. Nat. Heart Found., Christchurch, New Zealand, 1977-92, pres., 1996-99; mem. found. coun., sec., mem. various coms., 1968-99; clin. reader U. Otago Christchurch Clin. Sch., 1980-88; mem. expert adv. panel on smoking and health WHO, 1977—; mem. adv. com. on smoking and health New Zealand Ministry Health, 1974-88, adv. com. on prevention of cardiovascular disease, 1985-87; mem. resuscitation com. New Zealand Emergency Care Com., 1979-87. Editor: Coronary Heart Disease: Prevention and Control, 1983; contbr. numerous articles, mainly on smoking and health and preventive cardiology, to profl. jours. Decorated Comdr. Order Brit. Empire, 1981; recipient Tobacco or Health medal WHO, 1995, N.Z. Commemoration medal, 1990; named Knight Bachelor, 1991. Fellow Royal Australasian Coll. Physicians (councillor 1964-66, censor 1975-79, mem. specialist adv. com. cardiology 1980-87, v.p. 1988-92, Coll. medal 1993), Royal Coll. Physicians (London); mem. New Zealand Med. Assn. (pres. Canterbury divsn. 1972), Australia and New Zealand Cardiac Soc. (New Zealand chmn. 1977-82), Christchurch Hosps. Med. Staff Assn. (chmn. 1983-85), Christchurch Golf Club. Home: 20 Greers Rd,, Christchurch 4, Canterbury, New Zealand

HAY, ELIZABETH DEXTER, embryology researcher, educator; b. St. Augustine, Fla., Apr. 2, 1927; d. Isaac Morris and Lucille (Lynn) H. AB, Smith Coll., 1948; MA (hon.), Harvard U., 1964; ScD (hon.), Smith Coll., 1973, Trinity Coll., 1989; MD, Johns Hopkins U., 1952, LHD (hon.), 1990. Intern in internal medicine Johns Hopkins Hosp., Balt., 1952-53; instr. anatomy Johns Hopkins U. Med. Sch., Balt., 1953-56, asst. prof., 1956-57; asst. prof. Cornell U. Med. Sch., N.Y.C., 1957-60; asst. prof. Harvard Med. Sch., Boston, 1960-64, Louise Foote Pfeiffer assoc. prof., 1964-69, Louise Foote Pfeiffer prof. embryology, 1969—, chmn. dept. anatomy and cellular biology, 1975-93; prof. dept. cell biology, 1993—; cons. cell biology sect. NIH, 1965-69; mem. adv. coun. Nat. Inst. Gen. Med. Sci., NIH, 1978-81; mem. sci. adv. bd. Whitney Marine Lab., U. Fla., 1982-86; mem. adv. coun. Johns Hopkins Sch. Medicine, 1982-96; chairperson bd. sci. counselors Nat. Inst. Dental Rsch., NIH, 1984-86; mem. bd. sci. counselors Nat. Inst. Environ. Health Sci., NIH, 1990-93. Author: Regeneration, 1966; (with J.P. Revel) Fine Structure of the Developing Avian Cornea, 1969; editor: Cell Biology of Extracellular Matrix, 1981, 2d edit., 1991; editor-in-chief Developmental Biology Jour., 1971-75; contbr. articles to profl. jours. Mem. Scientists Task Force of Congressman Barney Frank, Massach, 1982-92. Recipient Disting. Achievement award N.Y. Hosp.-Cornell Med. Ctrl. Alumni Coun., 1985, award for vision rsch. Alcon, 1988, Excellence in Sci. award Fedn. Am. Socs. Exptl. Biology. Mem. Soc. Devel. Biology (pres. 1973-74, E.G. Conklin award 1997), Am. Soc. Cell Biology (pres. 1976-77, legis. alert com. 1982—, E.B. Wilson award 1989, chair 40th anniversary 2000), Am. Assn. Anatomists (pres. 1981-82, legis. alert com. 1982—, Centennial award 1987, Henry Gray award 1992), Am. Acad. Arts and Scis., Johns Hopkins Soc. Scholars, Nat. Acad. Sci., Inst. Medicine, Internat. Soc. Devel. Biologists (exec. bd. 1977), Boston Mycol. Club. Home: 14 Aberdeen Rd Weston MA 02493-1733 Office: Harvard Med Sch Dept Cell Biology 220 Longwood Ave Boston MA 02115-5701

HAY, GEORGE AUSTIN, actor, producer, director, musician, artist; b. Johnstown, Pa., Dec. 25, 1915; s. George and Mary Louise (Austin) H. BS, U. Pitts., 1938; postgrad., U. Rochester, 1939; MLitt, U. Pitts., 1948; MA, Columbia U., 1948. dir. Jr. League hosp. shows, N.Y.C., 1948-53. Producer, dir. off-Broadway prodns., 1953-55; motion picture casting dir. for Dept. Def. films, Astoria Studios, N.Y., 1955-70, motion picture producer-dir., U.S. Dept. Transp., Washington, 1973—, Office Presdl. Personnel, The White House, 1993—; group exhbns. of paintings and sculpture include, Lincoln Ctr., N.Y.C., 1965, Parrish Art Mus., Southampton, N.Y., 1969, Carnegie Inst., 1972, Duncan Galleries, N.Y.C., 1973, Bicentennial Exhbn. Am. Painters, Paris, 1976, Chevy Chase Gallery, 1979, Watergate Gallery, 1981, Le Salon des Nations a Paris, 1983; rep. permanent collections, Met. Mus. Art, N.Y.C., Library Congress, also, pvt. collections; bibliog. reference to works pub. in History of Internat. Art, 1982; author, illustrator: Seven Hops to Australia, 1945, The Moving Image, A Career in Pictures, 1990; Dir.: Bicentennial documentary Highways of History, 1976; dir.: film World Painting in Museum of Modern Art, 1972; Composer: Rhapsody in E Flat for piano and strings, 1950; writer: TV program Nat. Council Chs., 1965; Broadway appearances include: What Every Woman Knows, 1954; original Broadway run of Inherit the Wind, 1955-57; created role of Prof. Fiveash in premiere of The Acrobats, White Barn Theater, Westport, Conn., 1961; feature films include: Murder, Inc., 1960, Pretty Boy Floyd, 1960, The Landlord, 1970, Child's Play, 1971, Chekhov's The Bet, 1978, Being There, 1980, No Way Out, 1986, Her Alibi, 1988, Air Force One, 1997, Guarding Tess, 1994, Contact The Contender, 1997; TV appearances include Am. Heritage, 1961, Americans-A Portrait in Verses, 1962, Naked City, 1962, U.S. Steel Hour, 1963, Another World, 1965, Edge of Night, 1968, As the World Turns, 1969, Love Is a Many-Splendored Thing, 1972, The Adams Chronicles, 1976, A Woman Named Jackie, 1991; piano soloist in concerts and recitals, 1937; performer Cruise Ship, Europe, 1938; author, illustrator: The Arts Scene; contbr. articles to periodicals. Apptd. time adv. panel, pres.'s coun. Coll. William and Mary; mem. World Affairs Coun., Am. Archtl. Found.; bd. govs., trustee Hist. Home of Pres. James Monroe; mus. donor Am. doctor's office turn-of-century period preservation; bd. dirs. Washington Film Coun. With AUS, 1942-46, PTO. Recipient Loyal Svc. award Jr. League, 1953, St. Bartholomew's Silver Leadership award, 1966, Gold medal Accademia Italia, 1980, Smithsonian Instn. Pictorial award, 1982; Fed. Govt. Honor award in recognition 45 yrs. dedicated svc., 2000; subject of biog. work: Austin Hay, Adventures of a Christmas Child, 1970. Mem. NATAS, AFTRA, SAG, Am. Artists Profl. League, Allied Artists Am., Internat. Bach Soc., Beethoven Soc. (bd. dirs.), Nat. Soc. Arts and Letters (bd. dirs.), Music Libr. Assn., Nat. Symphony Orch. Assn., Actors Equity Assn., Nat. Trust Hist. Preservation, SAR, Nat. Parks and Conservation Assn., Shakespeare Oxford Soc., St. Andrew's Soc., Victorian Soc. (bd. dirs.), Cambria County Hist. Soc., Am. Philatelic Soc., Am. Mus. Moving Image, Jimmy Stewart Mus. (Indiana, Pa.), English Speaking Union (bd. dirs.), Nat. Arts Club (N.Y.C.), Players Club (N.Y.C.), Nat. Travel Club, Columbia U. Club, Nat. Press Club, Arts Club of Washington, Classic Car Club Am., Nat. Naval Med. Command, Sigma Chi, Phi Mu Alpha.

HAY, IAIN MILL, geographer, educator; b. Wanganui, New Zealand, Jan. 28, 1960; s. William Mill and Christina Gilmour (Carruthers) H. BSc with honors, U. Canterbury, Christchurch, New Zealand, 1982; MA, Massey U., Palmerston North, New Zealand, 1985; PhD, U. Wash., 1989; grad. cert. tert. edn., Flinders U., Adelaide, Australia, 1996. Jr. lectr. Massey U., 1983-85; lectr. U. Wollongong, Australia, 1990-91; lectr. Flinders U., 1992, sr. lectr., 1993-96, reader, 1997-2000, prof., 2000—; mem. Australian Nat. Com. for Geography. Author: The Caring Commodity, 1989, Money, Medicine and Malpractice in American Society, 1992, Communicating in Geography and the Environmental Sciences, 1996, Making the Grade, 1997; editor: Qualitative Research Methods in Human Geography, 2000. Active South Australian Gov.'s Leadership Found. Flying officer, Royal New Zealand Air Force, 1978-81. Recipient Fulbright-Hayes award, U.S., 1985; Brit. Acad. Vis. fellow, U.K., 1994. Mem. Assn. Am. Geographers, Inst. Australian Geographers, Royal Geog. Soc. South Australia, New Zealand Geographical Soc. Avocations: cycling, reading, swimming, rogaining. Home: 22 Mitchell St, Hyde Park SA 5061, Australia Office: Flinders U Dept Geography, GPO Box 2100, Adelaide SA 5001, Australia

HAY, JOHN A., academic administrator; m. Barbara Hay; children: Christopher, Katherine, Timothy, Benjamin. BA with honrs., We. Australia; MA, Cambridge U.; PhD, We. Australia; LittD hon., Deakin U. Lectr. in English U. We. Australia, 1967-72, sr. lectr., 1972-78, head of dept., 1978-80, prof. English, 1980-85, deputy chair acad. bd., 1985-87; dean of arts Monash U., Australia, 1987-88, sr. deputy vice-chancellor, 1988-92; vice-chancellor, pres. Deakin U., Victoria, Australia, 1992-95; vice-chancellor U. Queensland, Brisbane, 1996—; chair Com. for Univ. Tchg. and Staff Devel.; mem. Conf. of Queensland Vice-Chancellors. Author numerous books in field and contbr. articles to profl. jours. Trustee Queensland Performing Arts Trust; bd. dirs. Open Learning Agy. of Australia. Received on behalf of Univ. Queensland: Australia's 1998 Univ. of the Yr. award Good Univs. Guides. Office: Univ Queensland, Brisbane Qld 4072, Australia*

HAY, JULIE, training company executive; b. Edgware, Eng., July 15, 1942; div.; children: Terry Clark, Steven Clark. Diploma in mgmt. studies, Ealing Coll., Eng., 1975; MPhil, Henley Mgmt. Coll., Eng., 1989. Cert. tchg. and supervising transactional analyst; master practitioner and trainer in neuro-linguistic programming. Sci. asst. Civil Svc., Dept. Sci. and Indsl. Rsch., Eng., 1958-61; cost clk. Kodak, Harrow, Eng., 1961-64; supr. sales support Dexion, Wembley, Eng., 1964-67; asst. to acct. Amoco, Wembley, 1967; co. tng. officer Glacier Metal Co., Alperton, Eng., 1967-71; adminstrv. officer London Borough of Harrow, Eng., 1971-74; cons., trainer, mgr. Brit. Airways, London, 1974-86; CEO A.D. Internat., Watford, Eng., 1986—. Author: Transactional Analysis for Trainers, 1992, 96, Working it Out at Work: Understanding Attitudes and Building Relationships, 1993, Transformational Mentoring-Creating Developmental Alliances for Changing Organizational Cultures, 1995, The Gower Assessment and Development Centre, 1997, Action Mentoring, 1997, 99. Fellow Inst. Pers. Devel.; mem. Inst. of Mgmt., Internat. Transactional Analysis Assn. (tchg., pres. 1990-91), European Transactional Analysis Assn. (tchg., pres. 1987-89), Chartered Inst. Transport. Avocations: riding horses, travel. Office: A D Internat, Sherwood House 7 Oxhey Rd, Watford WD1 4QF, England

HAY, KENNETH GORDON, artist, art educator; b. Inverness, Scotland, June 15, 1955; s. Ian Gordon McHattie and Ishbel Jean (Mackenzie) H. BFA, Leeds U., 1977; dipl. belle anti, Florence Acad., 1980; MA in Visual Arts, U. Wales, 1982, PhD of Aesthetics, 1990. Asst. editor Dictionary of Art, London, 1987-88; lectr. West Surrey Coll. Art and Design, Farnham, U.K., 1988-89; lectr., studio coord. Dept. Fine Arts, Leeds U., Eng., 1989-95; lectr., dept. head Leeds U., 1995—, Head Sub-Faculty of Arts, 1999—; vis. lectr. Newport Gwent Coll., Caerleon, Gwent, U.K., 1983-89, U. Wales, Aberystwytn, Wales, 1982-86, North East London Polytech., 1987-89; rschr. Crafts Coun. Dept. Edn. and Sci., London, 1986-87. Exhibited at Venice Biennale, Transculture Pavilion, 1995, Vancouver, London, Houston, Scotland, Berlin, Leeds, Reykjavik, Melbourne exhibits, 1995-2000; contbr. articles to profl. jours. Mem. NEAB (com., univ. rep.), AUT, European League Insts. Art (dept. rep.). Avocations: art, music, cooking, reading, cycling. Office: Univ Leeds Dept Fine Art, Woodhouse Ln, W Yorks Leeds LS2 9JT, United Kingdom

HAY, LAURETTE, research director, psychologist, researcher; b. Nice, Provence, France, June 1, 1947; d. Jacques and Suzanne (Buffet) H.; 1 child, Célia. Psychology Degree, U. Aix-Marseille, France, 1968; specialized studies cert., U. Aix-Marseille, 1970, Psychology Mastership, 1972, D in Behavioral Scis., 1979, Nat. Doctoral Dissertation Neuroscis., 1987. Rsch. tech. asst. CNRS, Marseille, 1968-71, trainee rschr., 1972, rsch. attaché, 1972-79, sr. rschr., 1979-91, rsch. dir., 1991—; guest lectr. for grad. students U. Bourgogne, Dijon, France, 1987, U. Montpellier, France, 1987, 88, U. Aix-Marseille II, 1989. Editor: Development of Eye-hand Coordination Across the Lifespan, 1990; contbr. chpt. to book. Grantee European Tng. Program, 1978, 81, CNRS, 1982, Naturalia and Biologia, 1984, 85. Mem. European Brain and Behavior Soc., European Neurosci. Assn., Assn. Rschrs. in Phys. and Sport Activity, Nat. Union Sci. Rschrs., Peace Movement. Avocations: music, reading, gardening, woodworking, stonework. Office: CNRS-Univ Aix Marseille I, Av Escadrille Normandie, 13397 Marseille Cedex 20, France

HAYAKAWA, KAN-ICHI, retired food science educator; b. Shibukawa, Gumma, Japan, Aug. 12, 1931; came to U.S., 1961, naturalized, 1974; s. Chyogoro and Kin (Hayakawa) H.; m. Setsuko Maekawa, Feb. 18, 1967. BS, Tokyo U. Fisheries, 1955; PhD, Rutgers U., 1964. Rsch. fellow Canners' Assn. Japan, 1955-60; asst. prof. food sci. Rutgers U., New Brunswick, N.J., 1964-70; assoc. prof. food sci. Rutgers U., 1970-77, prof. food engring., 1977-82, Disting. prof. food engring., 1982-99, prof. emeritus, 1999—, ret., 1999; OAS vis. prof. U. Campinas, Brazil, summers 1972, 73, vis. prof., 1994; cons. to food processing cos.; organizer, chmn., participant NSF sponsored U.S.-Japan Coop. Conf., Tokyo, 1979; lectr. Industry R&D Inst. and Nat. Taiwan U., 1982, Wuxi Inst. Light Industry, China, 1986, Tokyo U. of Fisheries, 1992. Co-editor: Heat Sterilization of Food, 1983. Contbr. articles to books, profl. jours. and encys.; developer new math methods for predicting safety of food processes; found theoretical and exptl. theorems on heat and mass transfer in biol. material with or without strain-stress formation. Rsch. grantee USPHS, 1966-73, Nabisco Found., 1975-76, NSF, 1981-82, travel grantee NSF, 1972, Rutgers Rsch. Found., 1977, rsch. grantee Advanced Food Tech. Ctr., 1985-89, John von Neumann Nat. Supercomputer Ctr., 1989-90, Pitts. Nat. Supercomputer Ctrs., NSF, 1990-97, Cray Rsch. Inc., 1993-95, U.S. Army Natick R&D Ctr., 1992-94, USDA, 1994-98. Fellow Inst. Food Technologists; mem. ASHRAE (life, chmn. tech. com. on thermophys. property values of food 1981-85, mem. com. 1981-96), Sigma Xi. Home: 631 Lake Dr Princeton NJ 08540-5634

HAYAKAWA, TATSUJI, economist; b. Asahikawa, Hokkaido, Japan, Sept. 11, 1963; came to U.S., 1989; s. Shinichi and Michiko Hayakawa. BA in Econs., Hitotsubashi U., Tokyo, 1986, MA in Econs., 1989; PhD in Econs., U. Pa., 1994. Economist Internat. Devel. Ctr. of Japan, Tokyo, 1994-95, Inter-Am. Devel. Bank, Washington, 1995—. Contbr. articles to profl. jours.; contbr. Yuhikaku Dictionary of Econ. Terms, 1998. Mem. Am. Econ. Assn., Japanese Econ. Assn., Japan Soc. Monetary Econs. Avocation: baseball. Office: Inter-Am Devel Bank 1300 New York Ave NW Washington DC 20577-0001

HAYASHI, HIDETAKA, engineering and marketing electronic products executive; b. Fukuoka, Japan, Dec. 5, 1943; s. Fujimaru and Michiko Hayashi; m. Michiko Kawashima, May 15, 1974; children: Mariko, Hanako. B of Elec. Engring., Shibaura Inst. Tech., Tokyo, 1964; M of Elec. Engring., Tokyo Met. U., 1966. Engr. R&D telecomm. cables Fujikura Ltd., Tokyo, 1968-69, project mem. mgmt. info. sys., 1969-79, asst. mgr. R&D telecomms. cables, 1979-81, mgr. R&D electronic materials and components, 1981-87, gen. mgr. Flexible Printed Circuits engring., 1987-94, gen. mgr. engring. and mktg. electronic products, 1994—; part-time lectr. Chiba (Japan) U., 1995-98; presenter Procs. Printed Cir. World Conv. 4, 1987; chmn. steering com. Ecodesign 99 Japan Symposium, 1999. Co-author: (book) Printed Circuit Handbook, 1987. Mem. Japan Printed Cir. Assn. (standardization com. 1984-92, Standardization Work award 1996), Japan Inst. Printed Cirs. (mem. editl. com. 1986-94, coun. mem. 1988-91, mem. prodn. tech. com. 1994-98), Japan Inst. Electronic Packaging (dir. 1998—). Avocations: traveling, history, ham radio, social dancing, Go. Home: 355-7 Kami-Iwahashi Shisui, 285-0905 Imba-Gun Chiba-Ken Japan Office: Fukikura Ltd, 1-5-1 Kiba Koto-ku, 135-8512 Tokyo Japan

HAYASHI, KOYA, chemistry educator; b. Furano, Japan, Aug. 2, 1947; s. Shinichi and Fumi (Komatsuda) H.; m. Seiko Kitahara, May 15, 1970 (div. 1981); children: Takuya, Nobuya; m. Keiko Mori, June 11, 1986; children: Takehiro, Moe. PhD, Tokyo Inst. Tech., 1975; D of Univ. (hon.), U. Bordeaux (France) I, 1983. Asst. prof. chemistry Okayama (Japan) U. Sci., 1976-90, prof. chemistry, 1990—, head planning office, 1996—. Rsch. grantee Kashima Found., Tokyo, 1998. Avocations: skiing, tennis, kayaking, travel. Home: 11-3 7 chome, Sakuragaokanishi, Sanyo-cho 709-0802, Japan Office: Okayama U Sci, 1-1 Ridai-cho, Okayama 700-0005, Japan

HAYASHI, KOZABURO, virologist, ophthalmologist; b. Kyoto City, Japan, Oct. 14, 1937; s. Izumi and Ikuko (Yoshimi) H.; m. Masuko Yamada, Jan. 23, 1969; children: Ayato, Keiko, Naomi. MD, Tokushima U., Japan, 1961; PhD, Tokyo U., 1975. Asst. prof. Inst. Med. Sci., Tokyo U., 1965-71, 75-82, assoc. prof., 1982; lab. chief Koriyama Inst. Med. Immunology, Japan, 1982-89; dir. Kobe Inst. Health, Japan, 1989—; vis. scientist NIDR, NIH, Bethesda, Md., 1971-75. Author: Immunofluorescence in Medical Science, 1983, Eye and Herpes Viruses, 1990, Herpes Virus Infections, 1996, Powerful English for Medical Research, 1998, Medical and Pharmaceutical Virology, 1998. Mem. Japanese Virologist Soc., Japanese Ophthalmologist Soc., Japanese Immunologist Soc., N.Y. Acad. Scis., Japanese Clin. Virologist Soc. E-mail: kih-info-1@mse.biglobe.ne.jp. Home: 1-26-8 Chofugaoka, Chofu City, Tokyo 182-0021, Japan Office: Kobe Inst Health, 4-6 Minatojima-Nakamachi, Chuo-Ku Kobe 650-0046, Japan

HAYASHI, KYOZO, neurobiochemist, researcher; b. Hashima, Gifu, Japan, Oct. 6, 1930; s. Shunjiro and Kazue (Kunieda) H.; m. Motoko Nakamura, Apr. 27, 1964. BS, Gifu Pharm. U., 1954; MS, Kyoto U., 1956, PhD, 1959. Postdoctoral fellow U. Tex., Austin, 1959-61; assoc. Kyoto U., 1961-63, assoc. prof., 1968-82; assoc. prof. Osaka U., 1963-68; prof. Gifu Pharm. U., 1982-94, prof. emeritus, 1994; invited prof. Kyoto Pharm. U., 1994—, Osaka U. Pharm. Scis., 1995—. Recipient awards Pharm. Soc. Japan, 1967, 95, Senji Miyata Found., 1978, Gifu News Paper, 1988. Mem. Gifu Biosci. Assn. (pres. 1994—), Neurochem. Soc. Japan (councilor 1985—), Japanese Biochem. Soc. (pres. 1994, Chubu area, 1995-96), Japan Found. for Applied Inst. (councilor 1988—), Japan Snake Inst. (councilor 1988—), Japan Salivary Gland Soc. (councilor 1985—), Japanese Soc. for Neuroimmunol. (councilor 1995—), Gifu Int. Bio-Inst. (trustee 1996—). Avocations: fishing, hiking. Home: 38-18 Shimogamo, Izumigawa-cho Sakyo-ku, Kyoto 606-0807, Japan Office: Osaka U Pharm Sci, Nasahara, Takatsuki 569-11, Japan

HAYASHI, MITSUHIKO, retired physics educator; b. Okazaki, Aichi Pref, Japan, Sept. 3, 1930; s. Katsuzo and Rakuko (Morita) H.; m. Etsuko Ito, Oct. 18, 1964; children: Mayura, Nao. BS, Nagoya (Japan) U., 1958, MS, 1960; PhD, Tokyo Inst. Tech., 1971. Rsch. assoc. Nagoya U., 1960-70, asst. prof., 1970-75, assoc. prof., 1975-76; prof. Toyama (Japan) Med. and Pharm. U., 1976-96, prof. emeritus, 1996—; lectr. Kinjo Women's Coll., Nagoya, 1962-73, Toyama U., 1985-90; cons. Noritake China Co., Nagoya, 1973-76; vis. scientist U. Wash., Seattle, 1980-81, 82, Tech. U. Denmark, Lyngby, 1986; guest prof. Delft U. Tech., The Netherlands, 1987. Author: Introductory Physics, 1966, Ultrafine Particles 1984; contbr. articles to profl. jours. Supporting mem. Asia Health Inst., Nisshin, Japan, 1978—, Yamabato Home for Disabled, Makinohara, Japan, 1980—. Mem. Phys. Soc. Japan, Am. Phys. Soc. Presbyterian. Avocation: concerts. Home: 831-2758 Kitayama Obata, Moriyama-ku Nagoya 463-0011, Japan

HAYASHI, TAKEMI, physics educator; b. Nagoya, Aichi, Japan, Oct. 8, 1938; s. Katsuzo and Rakuko (Morita) H.; m. Mariko Tsurumi, Sept. 24, 1978; children: Akiko, Kazutaka. BS, Nagoya (Japan) U., 1961, MS, 1963, DSc, 1966. Rsch. fellow Hiroshima (Japan) U., 1966-83, lectr., 1983; assoc. prof. Kure Nat. Coll. Tech., Kure-Hiroshima, Japan, 1983-85, prof., 1985-91; prof. Kogakkan U., Ise, Japan, 1991—. Contbr. articles to profl. jours. Mem. AAAS, Phys. Soc. Japan, Am. Phys. Soc., Am. Assn. Physics Tchrs. Office: Kogakkan U, 1704 Kodakujimoto-cho, Ise Mie 516-8555, Japan

HAYASHI, YOSHIHIKO, dental educator, researcher; b. Moji, Fukuoka, Japan, Jan. 11, 1952; s. Morio and Sachiko (Kunizawa) H.; m. Ryoko Kinoshita, Oct. 14, 1979; children: Mitsuhiko, Yoko. DDS, Tokyo Med. and Dental U., 1976; PhD, Kyushu U., Fukuoka, 1982. Instr. Showa U., Tokyo, 1976-77; instr. Kyushu U., 1981-86, asst. prof., 1986-92, assoc. prof., 1992-95; prof. Nagasaki U., 1995—; chief Nagasaki U. Dental Hosp., 1995—; lectr. Japan Internat. Cooperation Agy., Fukuoka, 1994—; organizer Scanning Microscopy 1996 meeting, Bethesda, Md., 1997 meeting, Chgo.

Contbr. articles to profl. jours. Italian Govt. scholar, 1983-84; fellow Japanese Min. of Edn., 1991, 95, 97. Fellow Japanese Assn. for Conservative Dentistry (dir. 1996—), Japanese Assn. Clin. Endodontics (bd. dirs. 2000—); mem. AAAS, Japanese Assn. for Oral Biology. Office: Nagasaki U Sch Dentistry, Sakamoto 1-7-1, Nagasaki 852-8588, Japan

HAYASHI, YOSHIHIRO, architect; b. Hikone, Japan, Sept. 29, 1940; s. Genzo Odachi and Koshie (Yoshida) H.; m. Ikuko Koyama, Dec. 29, 1996. B of Engring., Kogakuin U., Tokyo, 1965; MA, U. Mich., 1975. Supt. Sato Hide Komuten Co. Ltd., Tokyo, 1965-72; dir. Yoshihiro Hayashi Architects and Assoc., Tokyo, 1975—. Author: Zosaku, 1981. Recipient Nika-Ten award Nika Orgn., Japan, 1981, 83. Fellow Archtl. Inst. Japan, Japan Inst. Architects, Tokyo Soc. Architects and Bldg. Engrs. Roman Catholic. Avocations: sculpture, oil painting. Home: 2-58-5 Kikunodai, Chiyofu-Shi Tokyo 182, Japan Office: 2-58-5 Kikunodai, Choufu-shi Tokyo 182-0007, Japan

HAYASHI, YOSHIKO, economist, educator; b. Kyoto City, Kyoto, Japan, May 11, 1969. BA, Doshisha U., Kyoto, 1992; MA, Osaka City U., 1994. Lectr. Osaka U. Econs., 1998—. Home: 1-16-17 Minaminakaburi, 573 Hirakata Osaka, Japan

HAYASHIDA, MOTOI, psychiatrist, educator; b. Tokyo, Feb. 6, 1932; came to U.S., 1959; MD, Keio U., Tokyo, 1958, ScD, 1967. Diplomate Am. Bd. Psychiatry and Neurology. Chief alcoholism treatment unit VA Med. Ctr., Phila., 1982-86, sr. psychiatrist addictions treatment unit, 1986-93; dir. Nat. Inst. Alcoholism, Japan, 1993-97; med. dir. Yokohama Maioka Hosp., Kanagawa, Japan, 1997—; adj. prof. dept. psychiatry U. Pa., Phila., 1993—; hon. prof. dept. neuropsychiatry Keio U., Tokyo, 1993—; cons., speaker on alcoholism. Contbr. articles on alcoholism profl. jours. and gen. mags. Recipient Meritorious Svc. award VA, 1987; Fulbright scholar, Tokyo, 1959-62. Mem. Am. Psychiat. Assn. (corresponding), Am. Soc. Addiction Medicine (cert.), Japanese Med. Soc. Am. (bd. dirs.), Japanese Med. Soc. Alcohol Related Problems (chmn. bd. dirs. 1995-97), Japanese Med. Soc. Alcohol Studeies, Japanese Psychiatric Soc. Alcoholism (mem. coun., bd. dirs.). Office: 3482 Maioka, Totsuka-ku Yokohama-shi, Kanagawa 244-0813, Japan

HAYCOCK, CHRISTINE ELIZABETH, medical educator emeritus, health educator; b. Mt. Vernon, N.Y., Jan. 7, 1924; d. John B. and Madeline (Sears) H.; m. Sam Moskowitz, July 6, 1958 (dec. Apr. 1997). SB, U. Chgo., 1948; MD, SUNY, Bklyn., 1952; MA in Polit. Sci., Rutgers U., 1981. RN, N.J.; diplomate Am. Bd. Surgery. Intern Walter Reed Army Med. Ctr., Washington, 1952-53; resident in surgery St. Barnabas Med. Ctr., Newark, 1954-58, St. John's Episcopal Hosp., Bklyn., 1958-59; pvt. practice Newark, 1959-68; asst. prof. surgery, N.J. Med. Sch. U. Med. and Dentistry N.J.-N.J. Med. Sch., Newark, 1968-75; assoc. prof. surgery, N.J. Med. Sch. UMDNJ, Newark, 1975-89, prof. clin. surgery, 1989-92; prof. emeritus, 1992—; chief GYN Svc., VA Hosp., East Orange, N.J. Trauma Soc.; pres. Med. Amature Radio Coun., 1981, bd. dirs. (Coun. award 1978); editorial bd. Jour. N.J. Med. Soc., 1979-95, The Physician and Sports Medicine, 1975—, The Main Event, 1987; adv. com. N.J. Phys. Conditioning of the Police Tng. Commn., 1984-96. Editor: Trauma and Pregnancy, 1985, Sports Medicine for the Athletic Female, 1980; contbr. articles to profl. jours. Chmn. bd. Essex County chpt. Am. Cancer Soc., West Orange, N.J., 1978-79, bd. mgrs., Livingston, N.J., 1962—, hon. life mem., 1992. With U.S. Army, 1947-86, col. Res. ret. Recipient Outstanding Alumnae award Bloomfield Coll., 1971, Res. Forces Achievement award, 1974, Distinguished Lecturer award Downstate Med. Ctr., 1976, Dr. Frank L. Babbott Meml. award SUNY Alumni Assn., 1982, Pres. Honor citation, N.J. Assn. Phys. Edn. and Health Tchrs., 1982, Presdl. Citation, N.J. Assn. for Health, Phys. Edn. and Recreation, 1984, Med. Bd. Svc. award Newark City Hosp., 1986, Bertha Van Hoosen award Am. Med. Women's Assn., 1997; grantee Abbott Labs, 1981-82. Fellow ACS (hon., life, N.J. com. on trauma 1970-91), Am. Coll. Sports Medicine (trustee 1978-80), Photog. Soc. Am. (chmn. video/motion picture divsn. 1993-95; Silver medal jour. award 2000); mem. AMA, Am. Med. Women's Assn. (bd. dirs. 1976-86, pres. 1980, hosp. assn. com. 1985—, Silver Medallion award 1980), Zonta Internat., Assn. Women Surgeons (treas. 1989-91, chair found. com. 1991-95, sec. 1995-99, Disting. Surgeon award 1990), N.J. Women's Assn. (pres. 1976, treas. 1989-92, Woman of Yr. 1987), Amateur Radio Relay League. Republican. Avocations: photography, dog training, sports, collecting elephants, amateur radio. Home: 361 Roseville Ave Newark NJ 07107-1721

HAYDEN, ALBERT A., retired historian, educator; b. Cape Girardeau County, Mo., Sept. 18, 1923; s. Howard Ebren and Clara Anna (Rust) H.; m. Priscilla Anne Hayden, Sept. 11, 1954; children: Keith A., Anne M. BA in History with honors, U. Ill., 1950; MA, Bucknell U., 1952; PhD, U. Wis., 1959. Instr. to prof. history Wittenberg U., Springfield, Ohio, 1959-94, ret., 1994; vis. assoc. prof. history Kent (Ohio) State U., summer 1964. Mng. editor: Studies in Brit. History and Culture, 1976-94; author: New South Wales Immigration Policy, 1971; contbr. numerous articles to profl. jours. With USAAF, 1943-46. Recipient Disting. Svc. award Ohio Acad. History, 1994; Fulbright grantee, 1954-55. Fellow Internat. Biog. Assn., Am. Biog. Inst.; mem. Am. Hist. Assn., Midwest Conf. on Brit. Studies, N.Am. Conf. Brit. Studies, Ohio Acad. History (exec. coun. 1982-85). Home: 1329 Eastgate Rd Springfield OH 45503-2423

HAYDEN, HARROLD HARRISON, information company executive; b. Cin., Jan. 16, 1942; s. Harold Richard and Blanche Marie (Sargent) H. BA, Millikin U., Decatur, Ill., 1964; MA, DePaul U., Chgo., 1970. Dir. mktg. tng. Automatic Electric, Northlake, Ill., 1968-70; dir. Universal Tng. Co., Wilmette, Ill., 1970-80; pres. Performance Achievement Group, Chgo., 1980-85; v.p. Lead Mgmt. Service, Chgo., 1985-90, Qualified Lead Systems, Chicago Heights, Ill., 1990—; pres. Intramark, Chicago Heights, Ill., 1992-94, chmn., 1995-97; pres. Pace Airline Svcs. USA, Chgo., 1994-97; exec dir. Internat. Meetings Inst., 1997—. Author: (multimedia package) Successful Telephone Selling, 1979, Santa Fe Railroad Data, 1975, Best Ill. award, 1975; editor Secrets of Successful Telemarketing, 1985. Mem. Ohlmstead Hist. Soc., Riverside, Ill., 1985; bd. dirs. 44th Ward Bus. Com., Chgo., 1985-86; exec. mgr. British Consortium, 1989-91; bd. dirs. North Park Village, 1993-96; bd. dirs. Ill. Acad. Criminology, 1996-2000; vols. v.p. Am. Police Ctr. & Mus., 1996—. Recipient award Best Condo Bldg., Northside Real Estate Bd., Chgo., 1985. Mem. Am. Mgmt. Assn. (spkr. 1979-85), Pine Point Ski Club, Simply Singles (CEO). Avocations: sailing, skiing. Office: Intramark One World Trade Ctr 2400 Merchandise Mart Chicago IL 60654

HAYDEN, JOHN CARLETON, priest, history educator; b. Bowling Green, Ky., Dec. 30, 1933; s. Otis Roosevelt and Gladys (Gatewood) H.; m. Jacqueline Green, Apr. 8, 1972; children: Jonathan Christopher Janani, Johanna Christina Jamila. BA, Wayne State U., 1955; MA, U. Detroit, 1962; LTh with honors, Coll. Emmanuel and St. Chad, Saskatoon, Sask., Can., 1963, MDiv, 1991; PhD, Howard U., 1972. Ordained deacon Episc. Ch., 1963, priest, 1964. Tchr. St. Mary's Sch. for Indian Girls, Springfield, S.D., 1955-56, Detroit Pub. Schs., 1956-59; instr. St. Chad's Secondary Sch., Regina, Sask., 1962-64; Anglican chaplain U. Sask., Regina, 1963-67, instr. history, 1965-68; asst. prof. history Howard U., Washington, 1972-78; scholar in ch. history Howard U., 1978-79; chmn. dept. history Morgan State U., Balt., 1979-86; prof. history Frostburg (Md.) State U., 1986-87; assoc. dean Sch. Theology, U. of South, Sewanee, Tenn., 1987-92; lectr. ch. history Howard U., 1992—; priest-in-charge St. Michael and All Angels Ch., Adelphi, Md., 1992-94; instr. history Montgomery C.C., 1992-94; Episcopal/Anglican chaplain, lectr. history Howard U., Washington, 1994—; reader Gen. Ordination Exams., 1990-92, Evangelical Edn. Soc., 1987-99, dir.; assoc. priest All Sts. Chapel, Sewanee, 1987-92; priest assoc. sisterhood St. John the Divine, Toronto, 1978—; rector Holy Comforter Ch., Washington, 1982-86; coord., cons. steering com. Afro-Anglican Conf., 1992-95; confrater St. Gregory's Abbey, 1954—; assoc. Sisters of St. Mary, Sewanee Province, 1992—. Contbr. articles to profl. jours. Bd. dirs. Washington Urban League, 1983-87; life mem. NAACP, Nat. Urban League; pres. Sask. Assn. for Retarded Children, Regina, 1966-68; sec. bd. dirs. St. Mary's Episcopal Ctr., 1988-92; bd. dirs. Nat. Coun. Chs., 1988-95; mem. program com. Kanuga Conf. Ctr., 1989-94, mem. diversity com. bd. advisors, 1994-2000, bd. dirs., 2000—; mem. bd. advisors St. Andrew's/Sewanee Sch., 1990-99; convenor, steering com. Episc. Coun. on Global Mission. 1989-90; trustee Washington Episcopal Sch., 1992—. Recipient rsch. award Am. Philos. Soc., 1976, Absalom Jones award Washington Nat. Cathedral, 1987, Univ. svc. award Grambling (La.) State U., 1990, Disting. Svc. award Kanuga Conf. Ctr., 1991; Angus Dunn fellow Washington Diocese, 1973, 74, 78, 95, 96, 98, 99, 2000, rsch. grantee Spencer Found., 1975; Robert B. Moton scholar, 1978; Coolidge fellow Columbia U. Assn. for Religion and Intellectual Life, summer 1998. Mem. Union Black Episcopalians (life, trainer, parliamentarian). Democrat. Avocations: reading, swimming, meditation, travel. Office: Howard U Episcopal/Anglican Ministry Msc 590517 2400 6th St NW Washington DC 20059-0001

HAYDEN, WILLIAM GEORGE (BILL HAYDEN), former Australian governor general; b. Brisbane, Queensland, Australia, Jan. 23, 1933; m. Dallas Broadfoot, May 7, 1960; 3 children. B in Econs., U. Queensland; D. (hon.), Griffith U., 1990; LLD (hon.), U. Queensland, 1990; D. (hon.), U. Ctrl. Queensland, 1992; adj. prof. (hon.), Queensland U. Tech., 1996; LittD (hon.), U. Southern Queensland, 1997. With Queensland State Pub. Svc., 1950-52, Queensland Police Force, 1953-61; mem. for Fed. div. Oxley Ho. of Reps., Australian Nat. Parliament, 1961-88; adj. prof. Queensland U. Tech., 1996; opposition spokesman on health and social welfare Australian Labor Party, 1967-72, minister for social security, 1972-75, treas., 1975, opposition spokesman on def., 1975, opposition spokesman for econ. affairs and econ. devel., 1977, min. fgn. affairs, 1983-87, min. for fgn. affairs and trade, 1987-88, gov. gen., 1989-96. Named Companion of the Order of Australia, Prior of the Order of St. John, Australian Humanist of the Yr., 1996; recipient Gwanghwa Medal of the Korean Order of Diplomatic Merit. Fellow Royal Australasian Coll. Physicians (honoris causa). Avocations: music, golf, horse riding, cross country skiing. Address: PO Box 7829 Waterfront Pl, Brisbane QLD4000, Australia

HAYDEN, WILLIAM TAYLOR, lawyer; b. Cin., Feb. 14, 1954; s. Joseph Page Jr. and Lois Elaine (Taylor) H.; m. Debbie Jane Kraus, Nov. 27, 1976; children: Page Ann, William Taylor, Michael Joseph, Amy Weber. BA in Econs., Denison U., 1976; JD, U. Cin., 1979. Bar: Ohio 1979, U.S. Dist. Ct. (so. dist.) Ohio 1979. Assoc. Cohen, Todd, Kite & Stanford, Cin., 1979-85, ptnr., 1986-96, mng. ptnr., mem. mgmt. com., 1988-96; sec. to bd. dirs. The Midland Co., 1988—, also bd. dirs.; trustee Fernald Litigation Settlement Fund, 1990—. Bd. dirs., mem. exec. com. Cin. Restoration, Inc., 1989-98, chair bd. dirs., 1995-96; dir. Clermont Bank, 1998-99, Ctr. Bank, 2000—; mem. audit com. Ctr. Bank, 2000—. Mem. ABA (corp. sect., tort and ins. law sect., tax sect., real estate and trust sect.), Ohio State Bar Assn., Queen City Club, Coldstream Country Club, Met. Club. Republican. Methodist. Home: 7266 Nottinghill Ln Cincinnati OH 45255-3964 Office: PO Box 1104 Cincinnati OH 45201-1104

HAYDON, JOHN RALPH, physician, retired military officer; b. Rochester, Kent, Eng., Mar. 8, 1942; s. John Richard and Mary Helen (Hancocks) H.; m. Christine Isabel Craig, oct. 19, 1973; children: Richard James Spencer, David John Chevalier. MRCS, LRCP, Middlesex Hosp., London, 1969; MRCGP, Glasgow U., 1976; MSc, London Sch. Hygiene/Tropical, Medicine, 1979; MFOM, Faculy Occupl. Medicine, 1982; DObstRCOG, Middlesex Hosp., 1970; DIH, Sch. Hygiene and Tropical, Medicine, 1979. Med. opers., staff of surgeon gen. Min. of Def., 1990-93; DACOS med. staff CINCFLEET, 1993-95; health and rsch. staff of surgeon gen. Min. of Def., 1995-96. Contbr. articles to profl. jours. Fellow Faculty of Occupl. Medicine, Royal Coll. Physicians, Royal Soc. Medicine; mem. Soc. Occupl. Medicine, Med. Soc. of London, Royal Coll. Physicians (lic.), Royal Coll. Surgeons, Brit. Med. Assn. Clubs, Nat. Maritime Mus. Friends. Avocations: antiquarian books, maritime watercolors, antiques. Home: Field House South Ln, Clanfield Hampshire Great Britain PO8 0RB Office: BM1 Hlth Svcs Murray Hsc, 5 Vander St, London SW1H OA2, England

HAYES, CHARLES AUSTIN, economic development executive, consultant; b. Norlina, N.C., Nov. 4, 1946; s. Clarence Holt and Eleanor Mitchell (Spain) H.; m. Janet McDougald Perkinson, Mar. 7, 1998; 1 child, Elizabeth Warren; stepchildren: Grant Levi Perkinson, Anna Stewart Perkinson. BSBA, East Carolina U., 1972, MA in Edn., 1974. Cert. econ. developer. Instr. in bus. Isothermal Community Coll., Forest City, N.C., 1972-73, Wilson (N.C.) Tech. Coll., 1973-74; county mgr., indsl. developer Warren County, Warrenton, N.C., 1974-78; prin. Warrenton Ins. & Real Estate, 1978-86; pres. Moore County Econ. Devel. Corp., Pinehurst, N.C., 1986-96; pres., CEO Rsch. Triangle Regional Partnership, N.C., 1996—; adj. faculty mem. Sandhills Community Coll., 1987-96. Author: Managing Financial and Marketing Rural Economic Development. Adv. bd. Cape Fear Area Consortium of Small Bus. Tech. and Devel. Ctr.; mem. friends of children com. Bapt. Children's Home, 1986-96; ex officio dir. Pinehurst Area Conv. and Vis. Bur., 1988-96. With U.S. Army, 1968-69, Vietnam. Recipient Disting. Svc. award, Warren County, N.C., 1977. Mem. Internat. Devel. Rsch. Coun., N.C. Indsl. Assn. (pres. 1978-79), Am. Econ. Devel. Coun., So. Indsl. Devel Coun., Sandhills C. of C. (ex officio), Pinehurst Country Club, Rotary (Sandhills, N.C.) (bd. dirs. 1989-96. Avocations: golf, reading, traveling. E-Mail: chayes@researchtriangle.org. Office: Research Triangle Regional Partnership PO Box 80756 Raleigh NC 27623-0756

HAYES, CYNTHIA ANN, administrative assistant, writer; b. L.A., Sept. 11, 1954; d. Lafayette and Verna (O'Gee) H.; 1 child, LaLaunie Charisse. Student, U. Calif., L.A., 1972-75. Clerk underwriting unit Great Am. Insurance Co., L.A., 1978-79; administrv. asst. Bill Dodd Real Estate Co., L.A., 1979-80, L.A. Dept. Water and Power, 1980—; v.p. Images By Haze, Laguna Niguel, Calif., 1990-91. Author: The My Family Collection, 1985, That Lovely Piece of Art, 1997, The Death of Lillie Maroe, 1998, The Night Aunt Ives Went to Sleep, 1999. Donor The Brotherhood Crusade, The Donor's Welfare Plan. Mem. U. Calif. L.A., The Duvall Found. Democrat. Baptist. Avocations: sewing, creating graphic designs, sailing, cycling, attending concerts and theater.

HAYES, DURRIE ALLAN, economic development coordinator; b. Easton, Md., Dec. 7, 1949; s. Louis Ernest Jr. and Ruth Evelyn Hayes; m. Kathren Ann Meredith, Feb. 4, 1989 (div. Sept. 1999). BA in Geography, Salisbury State U., 1974. Econ. devel. coord. Talbot County Office Econ. Devel., Easton, Md. Bd. dirs. Chesapeake Bay Regional Tech. Ctr. of Excellence, Wye Mills, Md., 1998—, Chesapeake Country, Easton, Md., 1994-97; commr. Oxford (Md.) Town Commn., 1989-94; campaign mgr. Md. State Sen. Fichard F. Colburn, Cambridge, Md., 1994; head coach varsity girls softball Easton H.S. Republican. Episcopalian. E-mail: dhayes@talbgov.org. Office: Talbot County Office Econ Devel 29137 Newman Rd Ste 1 Easton MD 21601-7075

HAYES, ERIC JAMES, consulting company executive; b. Airdrie, Scotland, Aug. 28, 1941; s. David and Ellen (O'Donnell) H.; m. Eva Mary Smith, Apr. 4, 1970; children: Anthony David, Stephen James. BSc, Strathclyde U., 1963; MSc, McMaster U., 1965; PhD, U. Ill., 1970. Chartered engr. Industry analyst Rowe & Pitman, London, 1973-75; mgr. Inco Europe, London, 1975-97; dir. Abacus Consultancy, Chelmsford, U.K., 1997—; chmn. World Bur. of Metal Statistics, Ware, U.K., 1995-97. Editor: World Stainless Steel, 1982-95; contbr. articles to profl. jours. Home: 6 Linroping Ave, Canvey Island SS8 8NE, England Office: Abacus Consultancy, 59 New Street, Chelmsford CM1 1NE, England

HAYES, JOHN TREVOR, art historian, writer, exhibition organizer, retired museum administrator; b. Jan. 21, 1929; s. Leslie Thomas and Gwendoline (Griffiths) H. Attended (hon. fellow), Keble Coll., Oxford (Eng.) U., Courtauld Inst. Art, London, Inst. Fine Arts, N.Y.; MA, Oxford U.; PhD, London U. Asst. keeper London Mus., 1954-70, dir., 1970-74; dir. Nat. Portrait Gallery, London, 1974-94; Commonwealth Fund fellow NYU, 1958-59; vis. prof. history of art Yale U., 1969; chmn. Walpole Soc., 1981-96. Author: London: a pictorial history, 1969, The Drawings of Thomas Gainsborough, 1970, Catalogue of Oil Paintings in the London Museum, 1970, 2nd edit. (with Mireille Galinou), 1996, Gainsborough as Printmaker, 1971, Rowlandson: Watercolours and Drawings, 1972, Gainsborough: Paintings and Drawings, 1975, The Art of Graham Sutherland, 1980, (catalogue) Gainsborough Exhbns., Tate Gallery, London, Grand Palais, Paris, 1980-81, The Landscape Paintings of Thomas Gainsborough, 1982, (with Lindsay Stainton) Gainsborough Drawings, 1983, The Art of Thomas Rowlandson, 1990, The Portrait in British Art, 1991, Brit. Paintings, Nat. Gallery Art Washington Systematic Catalogue, 1992, Gainsborough and Rowlandson: A New York Private Collection, 1998, Gainsborough Exhbn., Ferrara, Italy, 1998; various London Mus. and Nat. Portrait Gallery publs.; contbr. numerous articles to Burlington Mag., Apollo, and other jours. Decorated Comdr. Order of Brit. Empire. Fellow Soc. Antiquaries, Garrick Club. Office: 61 Grantham Rd, Chiswick, London W4 2RT, England

HAYES, MARY ESHBAUGH, editor, writer; b. Rochester, N.Y., Sept. 27, 1928; d. William Paul and Eleanor Maude (Seivert) Eshbaugh; m. James Leon Hayes, Apr. 18, 1953; children: Pauli, Eli, Lauri Le June, Clayton, Merri Jess Bates. BA in English and Journalism, Syracuse U., 1950. With Livingston County Republican, Geneseo, N.Y., summers, 1947-50, mng. editor, 1949-50; reporter Aurora Advocate, Colo., 1950-52; reporter-photographer Aspen Times, Colo., 1952-53, columnist, 1956—, reporter, 1972-77, assoc. editor, 1977-89, editor-in-chief, 1989-92, contbg. editor, 1992—; tchr. Colo. Mountain Coll., 1979, Aspen corr. Reuters, 1997—. Author, editor: The Story of Aspen, 1996; contbg. editor: Destinations Mag., 1994-97, Aspen Mag., 1996—; editor: Aspen Potpurri, 1968, rev. edit., 1990. Mem. Nat. Fedn. Press Women (1st prizes in writing and editing 1976-80, 1st prize Aspen Potpourri rev. 1990, 1st prize Story of Aspen 1996, 1st prize in adv. photography 1998), Colo. Press Women's Assn. (writing award, 1974, 75, 78-85, sweepstakes award for writing 1977, 78, 84, 85, 91-93, 2d place award 1976, 79, 82, 83, 94, 95, Woman of Achivement 1986). Home: PO Box 497 Aspen CO 81612-0497 Office: Box E Aspen CO 81612

HAYES, STEPHEN KURTZ, writer; b. Wilmington, Del., Sept. 9, 1949; s. Ira Maurice and Carolyn (Kurtz) H.; m. Rumiko Urata, Apr. 14, 1980; children: Reina Emily, Marissa Christine. BA, Miami U., Oxford, Ohio, 1971. Ordained Tendai sect Japanese Esoteric Buddhist priest, 1991. Author: The Ninja and Their Secret Fighting Art, 1981, Ninjutsu: Art of the Invisible Warrior, 1984, The Mystic Arts of the Ninja, 1985; Ninja: Spirit of the Shadow Warrior, Vol. I, 1980, Warrior Ways of Enlightment, Vol. II, 1981, Warrior Path of Togakure, Vol. III, 1983, Legacy of the Night Warrior, Vol. IV, 1984, Wisdom from the Ninja Village of the Cold Moon, 1984, Ninja Realms of Power, 1986, Tulku, 1985, Ancient Art of Ninja Warfare, 1988, Lore of the Shinobi Warrior, 1989, Action Meditation, 1992, Enlightened Self-Protection, 1992. Bd. mem. Tibetan Cultural Ctr.; founder Stephen K. Hayes' Quest Ctr. for Martial Arts Tng., 1996. Named to Black Belt Hall of Fame, Black Belt. mag., 1985. Mem. Tibetan Med. Inst. (life), Togakure Ryu Ninjutsu (10th degree black belt), To-Shin Do (founder, 1997). Home: PO Box 326 Bellbrook OH 45305-0326 Office: PO Box 291947 Dayton OH 45429-0947

HAYES, WILLIAM, academic administrator; b. Killorglin, Ireland, Nov. 12, 1930; s. Robert and Eileen (Tobin) H.; m. Joan Mary Ferriss, Aug. 28, 1962 (dec. 1996); children: Julia, Robert, Stephen. MSc, PhD, U. Coll., Dublin, Ireland, 1955; MA, PhD, U. Oxford, Eng., 1957; DSc (hon.), Nat. U. Ireland, 1988, Purdue U., Ind., 1996. Lectr. U. Oxford, 1961-87; pres. St. Johns Coll., Oxford, 1987—; vis. prof. U. Ill., 1971; head Clarendon Lab., Oxford, 1985-87; hedomadal coun. Oxford U., 1989—, pro vice-chancellor, 1990—; del. Oxford U. press, 1991—; chmn. curators Oxford U. Chest, 1992—. Co-author: (with R. Loudon) Scattering of Light by Crystals, 1978; (with A.M. Stoneham) Defects and Defect Processes in Non-Metallic Solids, 1985. Sr. fellow Am. Nat. Sci. Found., 1963-64, St. Johns Coll. fellow, 1960-87. Mem. Royal Irish Acad. (hon.). Avocations: walking, reading, music. Home and Office: St Johns Coll, Presidents Lodgings, OX1 3JP Oxford England

HAYES-GILL, BARRIE ROBERT, electronic systems educator, consultant; b. West Kirby, Cheshire, Eng., Feb. 27, 1953; s. Robert Reynolds and Joan (Farrow) Gill; m. Mary Bridget Doherty; children: Charlotte, Jessica. BSEE, Nottingham U., Eng., 1975, PhD in Elec. Engring., 1978. Chartered engr., Eng. Product engr. Tex. Instruments, Bedford, Eng., 1978-79, Amalgamated Elec. Industries Semiconductors, Lincoln, Eng., 1979-80; sr. engr. Marconi Electronic Devices, Ltd., Lincoln, 1980-81, Nottingham Trent U., 1981-86; sr. lectr. Nottingham U., 1986—; project monitoring officer Dept. of Trade and Industry, Eng., 1992-95; invited lectr. Semiconductor Gen. Systems Thomson, Malta, 1996, U. Kebangsaan Malaysia, Kuala Lumpur, Malaysia, 1989; cons., expert witness, Nottingham, 1997; cons. in telemetric monitoring, integrated circuit design, med. electronics, electronic sys. design. Co-author: (with Edward Arnold) Introduction to Digital Electronics, 1998; contbr. articles to profl. jours.; patentee in field. Dep. warden Nightingale Hall, Nottingham U., 1995. Mem. IEEE, Instn. Elec. Engrs., Fedn. Engrs. and Nat. Ingenieurs. Anglican. Avocations: tennis, hockey, squash. E-mail: barrie.hayes-gill@nottingham.ac.uk. Office: U Nottingham Dept Elec Engr, University Pk, Nottingham NG7 2RD, England

HAYEZ, JEAN-YVES, child and adolescent psychiatrist, psychologist; b. Elouges, Belgium, May 7, 1946; s. Henry and Edyle (Bustin) H.; m. Jacqueline Gauthy, Aug. 22, 1970; children: Marie-Agnès, Cécile, Jérôme, Jean-François, Astrid. Universitary I, Cath. U. Louvain, Belgium, 1970, universitary II, 1974, D in Psychology, 1982. Med. specialization in child and adolescent psychiatry. Intern Clin. St. Pierre, Leuven, Belgium, 1970-74; resident Centre Chapelle-aux-champs, Brussels, 1975-79; dir. dept. child psychiatry Cath. U. Louvain, 1980—, prof. child psychiatry, 1988—; exec. mgr. coop. network REBLASAM (scientific exchs. in field of mental health between Belgium and S.Am.), Cath. U. Louvain, 1987-95. Author: La Guidance Parentale, 1978 (Henry Jaspar prize 1980), L'éduquer, 1982, Le psychiatre a l'hopital d'enfants, 1991, L'enfant victime d'abus sexuel et sa famille, 1997, others; contbr. articles to profl. jours. Recipient chevalier de l'Ordre de Leopold. Mem. French Soc. Child and Adolescent Psychiatry, Belgian Soc. Child and Adolescent Psychiatry, European Assn. Mental Health--Children, Adolescents, Family (v.p. commn. permanente enforce maltraiter). E-mail: jean-yves.hayez@pscl.ucl.ac.be. Home: Ave du Guéret 13, 1300 Limal Belgium Office: Cliniques St-Luc, Ave Hippocrate 10, 1200 Brussels Belgium

HAYMAN, JAMES LESLIE BADDOCK, executive search consultant; b. Melbourne, Victoria, Australia, June 17, 1947; s. Eric Roland and Jean Leslie (Baddock) H.; m. Kerri Leigh Timms, Dec. 1, 1973; children: Nicholas James, Lachlan Curtis. B in Econs., Monash U., Melbourne, 1970; MBA, U. Melbourne, 1975. Corp. planner Philip Morris, Melbourne, 1970-73; economist GM, Melbourne, 1974-75; gen. mgr. spl. projects Tomasetti & Son, Melbourne, 1975-79, fin. dir., 1979-81; dir. Sacs Consulting Group, Melbourne, 1981-85; mng. dir. Slade Consulting Group, Ltd., London, 1985-88, Horton Internat., Melbourne, 1988-98; ptnr. Heidrick & Struggles, Melbourne, 1998—. Fellow Australian Inst. Co. Dirs., Royal Melbourne Golf Club, Melbourne Cricket Club, Athenaeum Club. Avocations: golf, running. Office: Heidrick & Struggles, 140 William St Level 33, Melbourne 3000, Australia

HAYMAN, JEFFREY L., insurance company executive; b. St. Paul, Jan. 18, 1960; m. Deborah L. Slocum, Mar. 30, 1985; children: Brian, Rebecca, Stephen. BA in Econs. and Polit. Sci. cum laude, St. Olaf Coll., 1982; MBA in Fin., U. Hartford, 1991. CLU, ChFC. Bus. analyst The Travelers Property-Casualty Claim Dept., Hartford, Conn., 1986-86; mng. cons. The Travelers Agy. Consulting and Fin. Svcs., Hartford, 1986-90; asst. dir. field ops. The Travelers Personal Lines, Hartford, 1990-91; regional fin. officer personal lines The Travelers Corp., Hartford, 1991-93; v.p. Travelers SECURE, Direct Response Mktg. Travelers Property Casualty, Hartford, 1994-97; v.p., CFO specialty auto divsn. Travelers Property Casualty Corp., Hartford, 1997-98; regional v.p. Am. Internat. Group Cos. Japan & Korea, Tokyo, 1998-99; chmn. Am. Home Assurance Co.-Japan Am. Internat. Group, Tokyo, 1999—; mem. R.I. Auto Ins. Plan Bd., Johnstown, 1990-91. Mem. Japan Fgn. Non-Life Ins. Assn. (rep. 1998—), Am. C. of C. Avocation: music. E-mail: hayman@aig.co.jp. Fax: 81-3-5619-2538.

HAYMES, JERRY LYNN, entertainment industry executive; b. Verron, Tex., Aug. 30, 1940; s. Arthur L. and Georgia H.; m. Brenda Dee, Aug. 1, 1962 (div. June 1981); children: Tracy, Darren. BS, Abilene Christian Univ., 1975; AS, Kilgore Coll., 1988; D in music, London Conservitory of Music, London, 1969. Drummer/singer Norman Petty Studio, Clovis, N.Mex., 1955-57; performer, 1955—; drummer/singer Sun Records, Memphis, 1957; CEO various radio stations., Longview, Tex., 1955-77, Umpire Entertainment, Longview, Tex., 1980—; performer, 1960—; bd. dirs. Country Music Assn., Nashville, 1960's, Internat. Talent Buyer Assn., 1970's; adv. bd., bd. dirs. Texas County Music Assn., 1995—. Record promotor It's A Heart

Ache, 1978 (Gold Record 1978); songwriter What Then?, 1956 (Gospel music award 1967), So Fine, 1959 (Triple Gold Record 1981); drummer Party Doll, 1957 (Gold Record 1957). Umpire Southwest Conf. Baseball Umpire Assn., Tex., 1968-98; adv. Vernon Reg. Jr. Coll. Fine Arts Dept., 1997—. With U.S. Army, 1960-62, ETO, 1964-68, Vietnam. Recipient Sun Legends Group Rock-a-Billy Artist award Rock-n-Roll Hall of Fame, 1996, Top Ten Record Artist for the Past 45 Years award Bill Board Mag., 1999. Mem. Sons of Confederate Vet., Am. Fed. of Musicians, Baseball Umpire Assn. (pres. 1979-84). Avocations: collecting music memorbilia, sports officiating. Office: Umpire Entertainment 4608 Leonard St Vernon TX 76384-4931

HAYNER, JEANNETTE CLARE, former state legislator; b. Jan. 22, 1919; m. Herman H. Hayner, 1942; children: Stephen A., James K., Judith A. BA, U. Oreg., 1940, JD, 1942, PhD (hon), Whitman Coll., 1992. Atty. Bonneville Power Co., Portland, Oreg., 1943-47; mem. Wash. Ho. of Reps., 1972-76, Wash. Senate from Dist. 16, 1977-92, minority leader, 1979-80, 83-86, majority leader, 1981-82, 87-92; dist. chmn. White House Conf. on Children and Youth, 1970; dir. Standard Ins. Co. Portland, 1974-90. Mem. Walla Walla Dist. 140 Sch. Bd., 1956-63, chmn. bd., 1959-61; mem. adv. bd. Walla Walla Youth and Family Svc. Assn., 1968-72; active YWCA, 1968-72; chmn. Walla Walla County Mental Health Bd., 1970-72; former mem. Wash. Coun. on Crime and Delinquency, Nuclear Energy Coun., Bonneville Power Regional Adv. Coun., State Wash. Organized Crime Intelligence Adv. Bd.; mem. Coun. State Govts. Governing Bd.; former asst. whip Republican Caucus. Mem. Wash. State Centennial Commn.; bd. dir. Washington Inst. for Policy Studies, 1992—; bd. dir. chmn. bd. TV Washington. Recipient Merit award Walla Walla C. of C., Pres's. award Pacific Luth. Univ., 1982, Pioneer award U. Oreg., 1988, Lifetime Achievement award Wash. State Ind. Colls., 1991, Washington Inst. Columbia, 1991; named Legislator of Yr. Nat. Rep. Legislators' Assn., 1986, Chairman's award, 1989, Wash. Young Rep. Citizen of Yr., 1987, Legislator of Yr. Nat. Rep. Legislators Assn., 1989. Mem. Oreg. Bar Assn., Delta Kappa Gamma (hon.), Kappa Kappa Gamma. Lutheran. Home: PO Box 454 Walla Walla WA 99362-0013*

HAYNES, BARBARA JUDITH, language educator; b. Trenton, N.J., Apr. 6, 1942; d. Harry G. and Doris M. (Leigh) Horne; m. Joseph A. Haynes, Dec. 11, 1965; children: Joseph III, Jennifer, Charles R. III. Student, Douglass Coll., 1960-62; diploma propeudétique, U. Paris, 1965; MAT, Fairleigh Dickinson U., 1979. Cert French, ESL, elem. tchr., supervision, N.J. ESL tchr. Magnet Ctr., Orange, N.J., 1979-86; ESL tchr. River Edge (N.J.) Bd. Edn., 1986—, world lang. facilitator, 1999—; ESL/bilingual stds. com. Nat. Bd. for Profl. Teaching Stds., 1994-99; presenter in field; cons. in field. Author: Prentice Hall Regents ESL, Newcomer Program Grades K-2, 1996; co-author: Classroom Teacher's E.S.L. Survival Kit 1, 1994, Classroom Teacher's E.S.L. Survival Kit 2, 1995, Newcomer Program Grades 3-6, 1997; content editor everything esl.net., 1998—. Pres. Bergan County ESL/Bilingual Tchrs., Paramus, N.J., 1990-93. N.J. Govs. Tchr. grant, 1989. Mem. TESOL (elem. spl. interest group sec. 1994-96, nominations com. 1996, assoc. chair elem. interest sect. 2000, Newbury House award for excellence in tchg. 1994), N.J. TESOL-BE (bd. dirs., chmn. elem. spl. interest group rep. 1994-96, rep.-at-large 1996-98, editor newsletter 1997—, ESL Tchr. of Yr. award 1993). Avocations: reading, travel. Home: 18 Oakwood Rd Allendale NJ 07401-2117 Office: River Edge Bd Edn 410 Bogert Rd River Edge NJ 07661-1813

HAYNES, JAMES ALMAND, media studies educator; b. Haynesville, La., Nov. 10, 1933; s. James Elmer and Mary Ann (Almand) H.; m. Eva Clara Viveka Reuterskiöld (div.); 1 child, James Jesper. Student, La. State U., 1952-55, Tulane U., 1955, U. Edinburgh, 1957-59, U. Paris, 1969-72. Founder Paperback Bookshop, Edinburgh, 1959-64; artistic dir., founder Traverse Theatre, Edinburgh, 1962-66; co-dir. London Traverse Theatre Co., 1965-66, London Arts Lab., 1967-69; co-dir., co-editor London Internat. Times Co., 1966-69; co-dir. Videoheads, Amsterdam and Paris, 1967—; prof. media studies U. Paris, 1969—; editor Handshake Editions, Paris, 1981—; co-editor Cassette Gazette, Paris, 1969—; co-dir. Edinburgh Writers Conf., 1962, co-dir. Edinburgh Drama Conf., 1963; dir. Edinburgh Poetry Conf., 1964. Author: Thanks for Coming! An Autobiography, 1984; editor: Traverse Plays, 1965; and over 10 others. Recipient Winner Best Ideas and Projects of 1992 Inst. for Social Inventions, 1992, The Whitbread Prize, 1965. Avocations: helping friends in Eastern Europe and Russia. Home: 83 rue de la Tombe Issoire, 75014 Paris France

HAYNES, JANICE JAQUES ELIZABETH, educator, editor; b. Casper, Wyo., May 31, 1924; d. George Havelock and Grace Mary (O'Keefe) Jaques; m. David Clark Haynes, Dec. 16, 1951; children: Judith J., David C. AB, Stanford Univ., 1945; MA, Claremont Grad. Sch., 1947. Tchr. Girls Collegiate Sch., Claremont, Calif., 1945-47, Fullerton (Calif.) Jr. Coll. H.S., 1947-48, Stanley Clark Sch., South Bend, Ind., 1963-69, Wis. Sch. for Deaf, Delavan, 1971-73; editor Gila Bend Herald, Gila Bend, Ariz., 1974-79; migrant coord. La. Paloma (Ariz.) Elem.; mid. sch. tchr. Humboldt (Ariz.) Jr. High., 1984-87; coord. Yavapai Indian Reservation, Prescott, Ariz., 1988-92. Editor: Prescott Symphony Guild, 1997-98. Mem. Alpha Delta Kappa (pres. 1985-86), Philanthropic Ednl. Orgn., Phi Beta Kappa. Avocations: short story writing. Home: 831 Bertrand Ave Prescott AZ 86303-4011

HAYNES, JEAN REED, lawyer; b. Miami, Fla., Apr. 6, 1949; d. Oswald Birnam and Arleen (Wiedman) Dow. AB with honors, Pembroke Coll., 1971; MA, Brown U., 1971; JD, U. Chgo., 1981. Bar: Ill. 1981, U.S. Ct. Appeals (7th cir.) 1982, U.S. Dist. Ct. (no. dist.) Ill. 1983, U.S. Dist. Ct. (cen. dist.) Ill., 1988, N.Y. 1991, U.S. Dist. Ct. (so. dist.) N.Y. 1991, U.S. Dist. Ct. (no. and ea. dists.) N.Y. 1992, U.S. Ct. Appeals (10th cir.) 1993, U.S. Ct. Appeals (11th cir.) 1995. Tchr. grades 1-4 Abbie Tuller Sch., Providence, 1971-72; tchr., facilitator St. Mary's Acad., Riverside, R.I., 1972-74; tchr., head lower sch. St. Francis Sch., Goshen, Ky., 1974-78; law clk. U.S. Ct. Appeals (7th cir.), Chgo., 1981-83; assoc. Kirkland & Ellis, Chgo., 1983-87, ptnr., 1987—; assoc. editor Litigation Mag., 1997-99. Assoc. editor: Litigation Mag., 1997-99. Governing mem. Art Inst. Chgo., 1982-90, mem. aux. bd., 1986-90, membership com. aux. bd., 1987-90, v.p. for devel., 1988-90; vis. com. U. Chgo. Law Sch., 1990-92; pres. com. All Stars Project, Inc., 1997—; adv. com. Youth Devel. Ct, 1997—, bd. dirs. 1999—. Mem. ABA (com. on affordable justice litigation sect. 1988—), Ill. Bar Assn. (life), Assn. Bar City N.Y., Internat. Bar Assn., Am. Judicature Soc. (life, chmn. membership com. 1991-97, treas. 1997-99, chmn. fin. com. 1997-99, v.p. 1994-97, exec. com. 1992—, pres. 1999—, bd. dirs. 1991—, chair adminstrv. com. 1997—), Three Lincoln Ctr. Condominium Assn. (pres. 1995-99, v.p. 1999—), Law Club Chgo., Mid-Am. Club. Office: Kirkland & Ellis Citicorp Ctr 153 E 53rd St New York NY 10022-4611

HAYOUN, MAURICE-RUBEN, educator; b. Paris, Sept. 22, 1950; s. Isaac and Gracia (Benarroch) H. Doctorat d'Etat es Lettres, U. Paris Sorbonne, 1985. Prof. U. Strasbourg, France, 1979—; assoc. prof. U. Heidelberg, Fed. Republic Germany, 1984, U. W. Berlin, 1985; vis. prof. Hochschule Judische Studien Heidelberg, 1983—. Author: Mosché Narboni, 1986, Maïmonide, 1987, La philosophie et la théologie de Moïse de Narbonne, 1989, Le judaïsme moderne, 1989, La littérature rabbinique, 1990, La philosophie mediévale juive, 1991, Averroés et L'averroïsme, 1991, Les mémoires de Jacob Emden ou l'anti-Sabbataï Zewi, 1992, Maïmonide, 1994, Maïmonide et la Pensée juive, 1994, La liturgie juive, 1996, Des Lumières de Cordove aux Lumières de Berlin: Une histoire intellectuelle du judaïsme, vol. I, 1996, vol. II, 1998, La science du judaïsme, 1997; (with Gershom Scholem) Le nom et les symboles Dieu dans la mystiBque juive, vol. I 1983, vol. II 1989, La Kabbale, les thèmes fondamentaux, 1985, De la création du monde jusqu'à Varsovie, 1990, Un Juif allemand à Jérusalem, 2000; (with Salomon Maïmon) Histoire de ma vie, 1984, Commentateur du Guide des égarés de Moïse Maïmonide, 1999; (with Samson-Raphaël Hirsch) Les dix-neuf épîtres sur le judaïsme, 1987, (with Franz Rosenzweig) Le livret de l'entendement sain et malsain, 1988, (with Georg M. Langer) L'érotique de la Kabbale, 1990, (with Theodor Lessing) La haine de soi: le refus d'être juif, 1991, (with Heinrich Grätz) La construction de l'Histoire juive, suivi de Gnosticisme et judaïsme, 1992, (with Léo Baeck) L'Essence du judaïsme, 1993, (with Hermann Cohen) L'éthique du judaïsme, 1994, Moïse Mendelssohn, Que sais-je?, 1997, (with D. Jarrassé) Synagogues, Que sais-je?, 1999, Le Zohar. Aux origines de la mystique juive, 1999. Fellow Meml. Found. for Jewish Culture, N.Y., 1979085, Alexander Von Von Humboldt Stiftung, Bonn, Fed. Republic Germany, 1984-85. Mem. Soc. des Etudes Juives, Soc. Asiatique. Avocation: tennis. Home: 51bis Rte de la reine, 3 rue Florence Blumenthal, F-75016 Paris France Office: Inst Etudes Hebraiques, Inst Etudes Hebraiques, Strasbourg France

HÄYRYNEN, YRJO-PAAVO, psychologist; b. Viburg, Karelia, Finland, Nov. 14, 1933; s. Yrjö and Aune Matilda (Huunonen) H.; m. Liisa Melkas, June 3, 1957; children: Autti, Maunu, Simo, Hanna. PhD, Helsinki (Finland) U., 1970. Rsch. asst. dept. psychology Helsinki U., 1962-65, assoc. prof., 1969-71; jr. rschr. Acad. Finland, 1966-68, sr. rschr., 1972-73; prof., chmn. psychology U. Joensuu, Finland, 1973-98, prof. emeritus, 1998; chmn. Com. on U. Degree Reform, Finland, 1969-72, Commn. Finnish-Soviet Coop. in Psychology, 1975-87. Author: Educability of People and Education Policy, 1976, Creativity in Community, 1993; editor Finnish Jour. Psychology, 1970-78. With Finnish Mariners, 1956-57. Mem. Westermarck Soc., Am. Psychol. Assn. (affiliate). Avocation: Normandy culture. Office: Univ Joensuu Dept Psychol, PO Box 111, 80101 Joensuu Finland

HAYS, DIANA JOYCE WATKINS, consumer products company executive; b. Riverside, Calif., Aug. 29, 1945; d. Donald Richard and Evelyn Christine (Kolvoord) Watkins; m. Gerald N. Hays, Jan 30, 1964 (div. Jan. 1970), 1 child, Tad Damon. BA, U. Minn., 1975, MBA, 1982; BS in Computer Sci. cum laude, Nat. U., 1997, MS in Software Engring. magna cum laude, 1998. Microsoft cert. sys. engr.; cert. in C/C programming. Dir. environ./phys. sci. Sci. Mus. Minn., St. Paul, 1972-76; dir. mktg. rsch. No. Natural Gas Co., Omaha, 1977-78; mktg. asst., asst. product mgr. Gen. Mills, Inc., Mpls., 1978-81; product mgr. ortho pharms. Consumer Products div. Johnson & Johnson, Raritan, N.J., 1981-82, product dir. home diagnostics, 1982-86; mktg. dir. new market devel. Consumer Products div. Becton Dickinson & Co., Franklin Lakes, N.J., 1986-90; dir. home diagnostics worldwide program Becton Dickinson Advanced Diagnostics Div. Becton Dickinson & Co., Balt., 1990-93; founder, pres. Exec. Computing Solutions, Inc., Vista, Calif., 1991—; product mktg. mgr. Jostens Learning Corp., San Diego, 1994-95; mgr. MIS Circus Distbn., Inc., Vista, Calif., 1995-96; product mktg. mgr. St. Bernard Software, San Diego, Calif., 1997; software engr. NCR Corp., San Diego, 1997—; chmn. energy exhibit com. Assn. Sci.-Tech. Ctrs., Washington, 1974-75. Producer Ecologenie, 1975. Recipient Tribute to Women and Industry award YWCA, 1989. Mem. Am. Mktg. Assn., NAFE, Twin Mgmt. Forum, Am. Assn. of Health Svcs. Mktg., Capital PC User Group, Beta Gamma Sigma (life). Republican. Mem. Disciples of Christ Ch. Avocations: photography, travel. Office: NCR Corp 17095 Via del Campo San Diego CA 92127-1711

HAYS, HERSCHEL MARTIN, electrical engineer; b. Neillsville, Wis., Mar. 2, 1920; s. Myron E. and Esther (Marquardt) H.; E.E., U. Minn., 1942; grad. student U. So. Calif., 1947; children: Howard Martin, Holly Mary, Diane Esther, Willet Martin Hays II. Elec. engr. City of Los Angeles, 1947-60; pres. Li-Bonn Corp. Served as radio officer, 810th Signal Service Bn., U.S. Army, 1942-43; asst. signal constrn. officer, E.T.O., 1943-45, tech. supr. Japanese radio sys., U.S. Army of Occupation, 1945-46; mem. tech. staff, Signal Corps Engring. Labs., U.S. Army, 1946; col. U.S. Army, ret. Signal Officer Calif. N.G. 1947-50. Registered profl. engr. Calif. Mem. Eta Kappa Nu, Pi Tau Pi Sigma, Kappa Eta Kappa. Republican. Episcopalian. Home: 603 Alhambra Rd Venice FL 34285-2502

HAYS, MARY KATHERINE JACKSON, civic worker; b. Flora, Miss.; d. Rufus Lafayette and Ada (Collum) Jackson; m. Halbert Puffer Oliver, Aug. 9 1927 (dec. 1934); m. Donlad Osborne Hays, Aug. 30, 1937. Student, U. Miss., 1925-26, Millsaps Coll., 1926-27, 43-44; grad., Clark Bus. Sch., 1934; student, Columbia U., 1935; stuent, Strayer Bus. Coll., 1951. Sec. to pres. McCullough Box and Crate Co., Pharr, Tex., 1934-36; sec. to field supr. Miss. Unemployment Compensation Commn., 1936-37; rep. Homes of Tomorrow, 1940 N.Y. World's Fair; sec. to head interior design Lord & Taylor, N.Y.C., 1940; sales dept. Knabe Piano Co., N.Y.C., 1941-43. Active, Little Theatre, Wilkes Barre, Pa., 1937-39; charter mem., incoroporator Conf. State Socs., Washington, 1952; vol. worker Am. Cancer Soc., Washington, 1957; mem. Center City Residnets Assn., Phila., 1956; mem. women's com. Nat. Symphony Assn., vol. worker USO, 1945-48, mem. symphony sustaining com. drives, 1957; mem. women's com. Corcoran Gallery Art, Wasington, 1957-62; mem. Pierce-Warwick Adoption Assn. of Washington Home for Foundlings; vol. Washington Heart Assn., 1959-66; mem. Nat. Capital Area chpt. United Ch. Women, 1957-72; mem. D.C. Episcopal Home for Children, 1961-86, D.C. Salvation Army Aux., 1962—. Mem. Miss. State Soc. D.C. (sec. 1950-53), Miss. Women's Club D.C., DAR (chpt. regent 1972-74, vice chair D.C. com. celebration Washington's birthday 1972-76, state libr. 1974-76, state officers club 1976—), UDC (chpt. historian 1982-84, 86—, chaplain 1984-86), Johnstone Clan Am. (exec. coun. 1976-81, nat. chair membership com. 1976-81), First Families of Miss., Women's Club of Flora, Miss., The Washington Club. Episcopalian. Home: 200 Dominican Dr Apt M201 Madison MS 39110-8630

HAYS, ROBERT WILLIAM, communications consultant, educator, writer; b. Atlanta, Oct. 17, 1925; s. Calvin Samuel and Elizabeth (Green) H.; m. Rebecca Copeland, June 15, 1950; children: Michael, David, William. Student, Duke U., 1943-44; AB summa cum laude, Presbyn. Coll. S.C., 1947; MEd, Emory U., 1957. Comml. mgr. Sta. WSFT-AM, Thomaston, Ga., 1947-48, Sta. WLBG, Clinton, S.C., 1948; co-owner Clinton Plastic Co., 1948-49; instr. English So. Tech. Inst. (now So. Polytechnic State U.), Chamblee, Ga., 1950-51; supr. of tng. course devel. Lockheed Aircraft Corp., Marietta, Ga., 1951-52; asst. prof. So. Tech. Inst. (now So. Polytechnic State U.), Chamblee, Ga., 1952-57; head English dept. So. Tech. Inst. (now So. Polytechnic State U.), Marietta, 1953-73, assoc. prof., 1958-60, prof., 1960-85, prof. emeritus, 1985—; cons. in communications, Marietta, 1965—, Mid. East, summer 1968-70. Author: Pacific Parodies, 1947, Principles of Technical Writing, 1965, Practically Speaking in Business, Industry and Government, 1969, Guide to Technical Writing, 1970, (with others) Getting Your Message Across, 1981; published many poems; contbr. numerous articles to profl. jours. Mem. adv. bd. Salvation Army, Marietta, 1996—; program dir., Marietta History Mus./Kiwanis Culture Capsule, 1999. Served to lt. (j.g.) USNR, 1943-46. Hixson fellow Kiwanis, 1996; recipient Arthur Williston award, 1967, Internat. Tech. Communications Conf. Honor, 1980, 83, Cmty. Svc. award King Ctr., 1994, 95. Fellow Soc. for Tech. Comm. (life, Disting. award 1993); mem. Assn. for Bus. Comm., Ga. Poetry Soc. (program dir. "Culture Capsule" 1999), Kiwanis. Home: 3360 Trickum Rd Marietta GA 30066-4683

HAYS, WILLIAM GRADY, JR., corporate financial and bank consultant; b. Covington, Ga., July 9, 1927; s. William Grady and Ella Maude (Wofford) H.; m. Emily Ann Holcombe, Aug. 1, 1954; children: Woodfrin Grady, Steven Gregory, William Danfield. BS, U. Ga., 1949; M.Litt., U. Pitts., 1950. Pres. First So. Corp., Atlanta, 1955-57; v.p. Comml. Trust Co., 1957-59; pres., CEO Comml. Acceptance Corp., 1959-74; fin. cons. William G. Hays & Assocs., Inc., 1974—; cons., CEO N.Am. Acceptance Corp., 1974—; cons. Kaleidoscope, Inc., 1979—, Speir Ins. Agy., Inc., 1982—; CEO United Am. Fin. Corp., Knoxville, Tenn., 1983—; cons. Banque Nationale De Paris, Nat. Westminister Bank, PLC, United Bank of Kuwait, PLC, Security Pacific Nat. Bank, First Nat. Bank of Boston; trustee Beacon Fin. Group, Inc., 1986; cons. Micro Mart, Inc., 1987; examiner World Bazzar Franchise Corp., 1992; spl. master Hannover Corp. Am., 1991; spl. agt. Diversified Growth Corp., 1989; trustee Internat. Trading Inc., 1993, Aledo Fin. Svcs., Inc., 1985, Flexel, Inc., RDM Sports Inc. Contbr. articles to profl. jours. Mem. Kappa Delta Pi. Republican. Presbyterian. Clubs: Cherokee Town and Country, Univ. Yacht. Home: 2755 Normandy Dr NW Atlanta GA 30305-2822 Office: 1442 W Peachtree St NW Ste 218 Atlanta GA 30309-2955

HAYTHORNTHWAITE, ROBERT MORPHET, civil engineer, educator; b. Whitley Bay, Eng., May 5, 1922; came to U.S., 1953, naturalized, 1964; s. William and Doris (Morphet) H.; m. Beatrice Mary Swift, Mar. 29, 1952; children: Richard Swift, Jennifer Anne, Susan Mary, Sheila Margaret. BSc, Durham U., 1942, London U., 1945; PhD, London U., 1952; MS, Brown U., 1953, MA, 1957. Registered profl. civil engr., Pa. Sci. officer Bldg. Rsch. Sta., Watford, Eng., 1942-47; lectr. Sheffield U., 1947-53; instr. to assoc. prof. Brown U., 1953-59; prof. engring. sci. U. Mich., 1959-67; prof. engring. mechanics Pa. State U., 1967-79, head dept., 1967-74; dean Coll. Engring. Tech., Temple U., Phila., 1979-81, prof. engring. sci., 1979-96, prof. emeritus, 1996—; vis. prof. Cambridge U., 1961, Manchester U., 1965-66, Lehigh U., 1974-75; cons. to Coun. Grad. Schs. U.S., Detroit Tank Arsenal, Engrs. Coun. for Profl. Devel., NASA, NSF. Editor Proc. of the 3d U.S. Nat. Congress Applied Mechanics, 1958, Mechanics, 1972, 73, 88-97; contbr. articles to profl. jours. Commonwealth Fund fellow, 1950. Fellow ASCE (tech. editor jour. engring. mechanics divsn. 1967-70, chmn. engring. mechanics divsn. 1966-67, rsch. prize 1963), Am. Acad. Mechanics (pres. 1969-71, Disting. Svc. to Theoretical and Applied Mechanics medal 1996, pub. Mechanics jour. 1997—, conf. procs., 1999); mem. ASME, Am. Soc. Engring. Edn. (chmn. mechanics div. 1966-67), Sigma Xi, Tau Beta Pi (faculty adviser Pa. Beta chpt. 1968-79). Home: 313 Wellington Ter Jenkintown PA 19046-3831

HAYTON, BERNARD QUENTIN, JR., library media specialist; b. Effingham, Ill., July 8, 1942; s. Bernard Q. and Sarah Elizabeth (Mann) H.; m. Susan K. Harmeson, Aug. 19, 1967; children: Raymond Todd, Katherine Ann. BS in Edn., Ill. State U., 1967; MS in Edn. Media, Ind. U., 1970. Cert. libr. media specialist, Ill., Mont. Media dir. Rich Cen. High Sch., Olympia Fields, Ill., 1967-70; audio-visual dir. Niles North High Sch., Skokie, Ill., 1970-71; audio-visual specialist New Trier High Sch., Winnetka, Ill., 1971-75; libr. Busby (Mont.) Sch., 1975-76; dir. libr. and media Morris (Ill.) Community High Sch., 1976-98; retired, 1998; media instr. Northeastern Ill. U., Chgo., 1970-75; chmn. Festival of Christmas Crafts, Morris, 1980-94; mem. edn1. adv. com. Chgo. Tribune, 1991-97. Scoutmaster Boy Scouts Am., 1963; mem. Presbyn. Ch., 1988. Mem. SAR. Avocations: crafts, avid reading, traveling, camping. E-mail:BHayton@aol.com. Home: 1248 Park Blvd Morris IL 60450-1247

HAYTON, DAVID JOHN, barrister, educator; b. Sunderland, England, July 13, 1944; s. Arthur and Beatrice (Thompson) H.; m. Linda Patricia Rae, Mar. 17, 1979; 1 child, John James. LLB, U. Newcastle-Upon-Tyne, 1966, LLD, 1980; MA, U. Cambridge, 1973. Cert. barrister, 1968. Lectr. Sheffield U., U.K., 1966-69; barrister Lincoln's Inn, U.K., 1970—; lectr. London U., 1970-73, Cambridge U., 1973-87; fellow Jesus Coll., Cambridge, 1973-87; prof. law King's Coll., London U., 1987—, dean law faculty, 1988-90, head U.K. Delegation to The Hague Confs. on Pvt. Internat. Law on Trusts, 1984, on Succession, 1988; recorder County Ct. S.E. Cir. England, 1984-2000, hon. reader Inns Ct. Sch. Law, 1984-96; chmn. London U. Bd. Studies in Law, 1992-95, dept. chair Trust Law Com., 1994—; vis. rsch. prof. Nijmegen U., 1995-97; acting justice Bahamas' Supreme Ct., 2000. Author: Law of Trusts, 1989, 3d edit., 1998, Registered Land, 1973, 3d edit., 1981, I.M.R.O. Report on Trusts and Financial Services Law, 1990; editor: Commentary & Cases on Law of Trusts, 6th through 10th edits., 1975-96, Underhill's Law of Trusts & Trustees, 13th through 15th edits., 1979-95, European Succession Laws, 1991, 2d edit., 1998, Modern International Developments in Trust Law, 1999. Mem. Internat. Acad. Estate and Trust Law, Marylebone Cricket Club, Commonwealth Trust, Cambridge Rugby Club, Soc. Pub. Tchrs. Law (hon. sec. 1996—), The Atheneum. Avocations: squash, tennis, cricket, winetasting, theatre-going. Office: Kings Coll Law Sch, Strand, London WC2R 2LS, England

HAYWARD, FREDRIC MARK, social reformer; b. N.Y.C., July 10, 1946; s. Irving Michael and Mildred (Feingold) H.; m. Ingeborg Beck, Aug. 18, 1971 (div. 1974); 1 child, KJ. BA, Brandeis U., Waltham, Mass., 1967; MA, Fletcher Sch. Law & Diplomacy, Medford, Mass., 1968, MALD, 1969. Exec. dir. Men's Rights, Inc., Boston, 1977—; vis. lectr. Tufts U., Medford, Mass., 1979; lectr. in field; conductor workshops in field; mem. adv. bd. Ctr. for Men's Studies, 1988-93; host, prodr. The SacraMENshow; founder Nat. Coalition Just Draft; co-founder Free Men Boston; co-founder, v.p. Children's Rights Coun. Sacramento, SAFE (Stop Abuse for Everyone); co-founder, exec. dir. The Fathers' Symposium, 1996—. Author 3 published anthologies; contbg. editor: The Liberator, Forest Lake, Minn., 1988-89; contbg. writer Spectator, Berkeley, Calif., 1988—; contbr. articles to profl. jours. V.p. Stop Abuse for Everyone. Farrell fellowship on Men, 1989; Fletcher Sch. Law and Diplomacy fellow, 1967-69; recipient award of Excellence Nat. Coalition of Free Men, 1993, award Western Access Video Excellence, 1995. Mem. Nat. Congress for Men (bd. dirs. 1981-90), Am. Fedn. TV and Radio Artists, Men. Internat. (bd. dirs. 1982-86). Office: Mr Inc PO Box 163180 Sacramento CA 95816-9180

HAYWARD, MARY MAVIS, retired chemist; b. Johannesburg, South Africa, June 23, 1928; d. George Atherstone and Alma Beatrice (Laschinger) Webb; m. Ian Norrie Hayward, Oct. 4, 1952; children: Keith, Martin, Patrick. BSc, Witwatersrand U., Johannesburg, 1948. Factory chemist IXL Co., Johannesburg, 1949; indsl. chemist Johannesburg Municipality, 1949-51, Coun. Indsl. and Sci. Rsch., 1951-52. Author: Anglican Women's Fellowship Handbook, 1965, Anglican Women's Fellowship Vestments, 1967, Anglican Women's Fellowship Funeral Booklet, 1967; editor Nat. Coun. Women Newsletter, 1994. Mem. nat. exec. com., past pres. Johannesburg Br., past sec. Nat. Coun. Women South Africa, 1955—; mem. nat. exec. com, past pres. Johannesburg Diocese, treas., past sec. Anglican Women's Fellowship, 1966-99. Mem. South African Assn. Women Grads., Rand Women Pioneers. Avocations: amateur philately, bridge playing. Home: 5 The Spur, St Georges Village, Bedfordview Gauteng, South Africa

HAYWARD-WILLIAMS, CAROLYN ROSE, management and technology consultant; b. Phila., Oct. 10, 1963; d. William L. and Elizabeth F. (Fogg) Hayward; m. Terence Gary Williams, Feb. 17, 1996. B in Engring., Vanderbilt U., 1987; MS, Johns Hopkins U., 1991; MBA, U. Md., 1993. Student engr. Gen. Motors, Ypsilanti, Mich., summers 1985-86; sr. systems engr. Westinghouse Electric, Balt., 1987-91; assoc. Booz-Allen & Hamilton, Balt., 1992; sr. assoc. Booz-Allen & Hamilton, London, 1993—; presenter numerous tech. and bus. analyses, presentations in field. Mem. IEEE. Avocations: skiing, horseback riding, travel, reading. Office: Booz Allen & Hamilton, 7 Savoy Ct Strand, London WC2R 0EZ, England

HAYWOOD, JOHN WILLIAM, JR., manufacturing engineering consultant; b. Savannah, Ga., Mar. 10, 1955; s. John William Sr. and Elizabeth (Williams) H.; m. Carol Johnice Staton, Jan. 15, 1976 (div. 1985); children: Venus Roshone, Maurice Antonio. BS in Mech. Engring. Tech. cum laude, Savannah State Coll., 1979; MS in Tech. summa cum laude, Pitts. State U., 1980. Aircraft foreman Grumman Aircraft Corp., Savannah, 1977-80; sr. mfg. engr. Superior Accessories Co., Parsons, Kans., 1980-81; sr. mech. engr. Martin Marietta Aerospace, Orlando, Fla., 1981-85; mem. tech. staff Rockwell Internat., Duluth, Ga., 1985-86; sr. mfg. engr. Boeing Airplane Co., Wichita, Kans., 1986-87; engring. cons. Sverdrup Tech. Inc., Elgin FB, Fla., 1987-90; pvt. practice engring. cons. Raritan, N.J., 1990-92; pvt. practice contract engring. Savannah, Ga., 1992—; cons. TP Cons., Oakland, N.J., 1990-91; mgr. environ. and indsl. engring. N.J. Inst. Tech., Newark, 1991-92; safety cons. N.Am. Contract Engring. Svcs., Tigard, Oreg., 1993-94; environ. mgr. Chatham County Dept. of Pub. Health, Savannah, Ga., 1995-96; cons. engr. HCI, Savannah, 1996—. Contbr. numerous articles to profl. jours. Teacher Macedonia Bapt. Ch., Savannah, 1991—; mentor Ramah Jr. Acad., Savannah, 1991—. With USAF, 1973-77. Mem. AIAA, Am. Soc. Safety Engrs., Inst. Indsl. Engrs., Soc. Mfg. Engrs. Republican. Home and Office: 18 Vermont View Dr # 2 Watervliet NY 12189-1037

HAYWOOD, ROGER, communications executive; b. London, July 24, 1939; s. George and Ethel (Reynolds) H.; m. Sandra Yenson, June 30, 1962; children: Sarah, Ian, Mark, Laura. CAM diploma in advt., Comm., Adv., & Mktg. Ed. Found., London, 1974; CAM diploma in pub. rels., Coll. for Distributive Trades, London, 1974. Press officer Dunlop Internat., London, 1965-69; dir. pub. rels. Air Products Ltd., London, 1969-74; mng. dir. Tibbenham Group, Norwich, UK, 1974-82, RHA Ltd., London, 1982-92; chmn. Kestrel Comm Ltd., London, 1992—; chmn. Worldcom Group Inc., N.Y., 1990-92, Worldcom Europe, 1997-98; chmn. Pub. Rels. Stds. Coun., 1998—. Author: All About Public Relations, 1984, 2nd edit., 1992, Managing Your Reputation, 1994, Public Relations for Marketing Professionals, 1997. Strategy adviser UK Govt., London, 1986-97; chmn. Children First Charity, London, 1992-96; dir. Childrens Wish Found., Atlanta, 1992-95. Fellow Inst. Pub. Rels. (pres. 1990-91, Sword of Excellence 1984), Chartered Inst. Mktg. (chmn. 1991-92), Inst. Dirs., Royal Soc. Arts. Avocations: history, media, music, politics, writing. E-mail: r.haywood@kestrelcomms.co.uk. Home: Broadway House-The Broadway, London SW 191RL, England Office: Kestrel Comm Ltd, Broadway House The Broadway, London SW19 1RL, England

HAZAMA, FUMIO, mathematician researcher; b. Fukuoka, Japan, Jan. 16, 1954; s. Shizuomi and Hatsuko H. MS, U. Tokyo, 1978, PhD, 1984. Asst. Tokyo Denki U., Saitama, Japan, 1982-86, lectr., 1986-90, assoc. prof., 1990-96, prof., 1996—. Editor: Algebraic Cycles and Related Topics, 1995. Avocations: piano playing, timpani playing. Home: 408-1434 Kasse, Fujimi Saitama 354-0031, Japan Office: Tokyo Denki Univ Dept of Natural Scis, Hiki-Gun, Saitama 350-0394, Japan

HAZARD, CHRISTOPHER WEDVIK, international business executive; b. N.Y.C., Aug. 9, 1943; s. Herbert Ray and Ellen Clausine (Wedvik) H.; m. Sally Grace Woodruff, Sept. 1, 1966; children: Mark Alexander, Julie Lynne. BA, Ohio State U., 1965; MPA, U. Colo., 1973; postgrad., U. Pa., The Wharton Sch. Officer USAF, 1965-86; near east region dir. ops. Def. Security Assistance Agy., Washington, 1982-86; exec dir. internat. mktg. United Def. Ltd. Partnership, Arlington, Va., 1986—. Pres. M. Vernon Citizens Assn., Alexandria, Va., 1984-85; mem., 1982—. Recipient Def. Superior Svc., Sec. of Def., 1986, Joint Svc. Achievement, Dept. of Def., 1984; decorated Air Force Meritorious Svc. medal. Avocations: international affairs, historic preservation, sailing, gardening, woodworking. Home: 9399 Mt Vernon Cir Alexandria VA 22309-3218

HAZARD, HEATHER ALISON, economist, educator; b. Trenton, N.J., May 5, 1957; d. Harry Williams and Erna Helena (Rainio) H.; m. Christian Erik Kampmann, June 21, 1986; children: Alexandra, Henrik. BCE, MIT, 1978; M in Engring., U. Toronto, 1979; M in Pub. Affairs, Applied Econs., Princeton U., 1984; PhD in Pub. Policy, Harvard U., 1988. Profl. cons. engr. Cambridge (Mass.) Systematics, Inc., 1980-82; rsch. asst. Princeton (N.J.) U., 1983; indsl. econ. Unilever PLC, London, 1984-85; postdoctoral fellow Harvard U., Boston, 1988-90; lectr., vis. scholar Sloan Sch. Mgmt. MIT, 1990-91; assoc. prof. Copenhagen Bus. Sch., 1991—. o-editor: International Competitiveness, 1988; contbr. articles to profl. jours. and chpts. to books. nternat. Affairs fellow Coun. Fgn. Rels., Nat. Inst. Dispute Resolution fellow, 1987-88, Dively fellow, 1986-87, Kennedy fellow, 1985-88, Prickett fellow, 1982-84, 1907 Found. fellow, 1979, Canadian Open fellow, 1978-79; Gen. Motors scholar, 1976-78; recipient Masters award Canadian Transp. Rsch. Forum, 1979, Statoil Prize for Rsch. in Applied Econs., 1993. emocrat. Unitarian. Office: Copenhagen Bus Sch, Howitzves 60, 8840 Rødkaersbro DK-1366, Denmark

HAZARD, JEAN, endocrinologist, educator; b. Paris, Jan. 1, 1921; s. René and Yvonne (Chevalier) H.; m. Janine Hugot, July 10, 1953; children: Martine, Marielle, Jean-René. MD, U. Paris, 1953. Intern various hosps., Paris, 1949-53; clinic chief U. Paris Faculty Medicine, 1953—, fellow prof., 1963-69, prof., 1969-90, hon. prof., 1990—; chief med. svc. Hosp. Broussais, Paris, 1963-69, Hosp. Henri Mondor, Créteil, France, 1969-90. Author: Abrégé d'Endocrinologie, 2000, L'homme hormonal une histoire illustrée, 1995 (Medec prize 1995). Decorated chevalier Legion of Honor. Avocation: art history. Home: 84 rue de Longchamp, 75116 Paris France

HAZARD, MARIE-JO ZIMMERMANN, journalist; b. Nancy, France, Feb. 24, 1938; d. Jean and Marie-Alice (Fevre) Zimmermann; m. Jean-Marie Hazard; children: Emmanuel, Christophe, Etienne, Damien, Domitille. BA, U. Nancy, 1963. Tchr. Nat. Edn., Briey, France, 1961-67; editor Vie Nouvelle, Paris, 1971-76; freelance journalist France, 1976-79, 85-91; editor Cimade, Paris, 1979-85, Pontifical Mission Socs., Paris, 1991—. Author: Printemps d'Eglise, 1986, Un seul Dieu, plusieurs Eglises, 1988, Entrée de Service, 1991, Une écharpe rouge, 1992. Mem. AJIR Profl. Assn. Journalists (gen. sec. 1990-92, pres. 1992-94). Roman Catholic. Avocations: music (harp and piano), travel. Home: 9 rue de la Liane, 78310 Maurepas France

HAZAS, JOSE LUIS, media specialist company executive; b. Valencia, Spain, Nov. 30, 1959; m. Maria Isabel Fernandez-Cid; 3 children. Grad. in law, U. Complutense, Madrid, 1982; MBA, Sch. Indsl. Orgn., Madrid, 1985. Asst. human resources dept. Union Explosivos Rio Tinto, Madrid, 1986-87; comml. dir. Media Control, Madrid, 1990-92, Sofres Audiencia de Medios, Madrid, 1992-94; dir. client svc. Initiative Media Spain, Madrid, 1987-90, dep. mng. dir., 1994-97, mng. dir., 1997-99, 1999—. Avocations: golf, canoeing, reading, cinema. Office: Initiative Media Spain, Plz Manuel Gomez Moreno s/n, 28020 Madrid Spain

HAZEL, MARY BELLE, university administrator; b. Orange, N.J., May 30, 1932; d. Morris M. Sr. and Robena (Brinkley) Thomas; m. James H. Hazel, Sept. 28, 1958 (div. Sept. 1976); children: Sharon Marie Hazel-Griggs, James Thomas. BS in Bus. Adminstrn., Seton Hall U., South Orange, N.J., 1992, MA in Edn. cum laude, 1998. Publs. asst. advt. and pub. rels. dept. Foster Wheeler Corp., N.Y.C., 1969-87; ind. contractor, 1987-92; adminstrv coord. dean's office U. Medicine & Dentistry N.J. Sch. Health Related Professions, Newark, 1992—. Elder Elmwood United Presbyn. Ch. Mem. AAUW, NAFE, Smithsonian Nat. Assn., Soc. Allied Health Professions N.J., Spinal Cord Injured-Family Support Group-Kessler Inst. Rehab.

HAZELL, ROBERT JOHN DAVIDGE, policy institute director; b. Apr. 30, 1948; s. Peter Hazell and Elizabeth Complin Fowler; m. Alison Sophia Mordaunt, 1981; 2 children. MA with honors, Wadham Coll., Oxford. Bar, 1973. Barrister England, 1973-75; with immigration dept., policy planning unit, gaming bd., race rels., broadcasting, prison and police depts. Home Office, 1975-89; dir. Nuffield Found., London, 1989-95; dir. constn. unit Sch. Pub. Policy Univ. Coll. London, 1995—, prof. govt. and the Constn., 1998—. Author Conspiracy and Civil Liberties, 1974; editor The Bar on Trial, 1978, Constitutional Futures, 1999; contbr. to profl. jours. Recipient Haldane medal RIPA, 1978; CS Travelling fellow, 1986-87. Avocations: opera, canoeing. Office: Sch Pub Pol U Coll London, 29 Tavistock Sq, London WC1H 9EZ, England*

HAZELTON, PENNY ANN, law librarian, educator; b. Yakima, Wash., Sept. 24, 1947; d. Fred Robert and Margaret (McLeod) Pease; m. Norris J. Hazelton, Sept. 12, 1971; 1 child, Victoria MacLeod. BA cum laude, Linfield Coll., 1969; JD, Lewis and Clark Law Sch., 1975; M in Law Librarianship, U. Wash., 1976. Bar: Wash. 1976, U.S. Supreme Ct. 1982. Assoc. law libr., assoc. prof. U. Maine, 1976-78, law libr., assoc. prof., 1978-81; asst. libr. for rsch. svcs. U.S. Supreme Ct., Washington, 1981-85, law libr., 1985; law libr. U. Wash., Seattle, 1985—; prof. law U. Wash., Seattle, 1985—; tchr. legal rsch., law librarianship, Indian law; cons. Maine Adv. Com. on County Law Librs., Nat. U. Sch. Law, San Diego, 1985-88, Lawyers Cooperative Pub., 1993-94. Author: Computer Assisted Legal Research: The Basics, 1993; contbr. articles to legal jours. Recipient Disting. Alumni award U. Wash., 1992. Mem. ABA (sect. legal edn. and admissions to bar, chair com. on librs. 1993-94, vice chair 1992-93, 94-95, com. on law sch. facilities 1998—), Am. Assn. Law Schs. (com. law librs. 1991-94), Law Librs. New Eng. (sec. 1977-79, pres. 1979-81), Am. Assn. Law Librs. (program chmn. ann. meeting 1984, exec. bd. 1984-87, v.p. 1989-90, pres. 1990-91, program co-chair Insts. 1983, 95), Law Librs. Soc. Washington (exec. bd. 1983-84, v.p., pres. elect 1984-85), Law Librs. Puget Sound, Wash. State Bar Assn. (chair editl. adv. bd.), Wash. Adv. Coun. on Librs., Westpac. Office: U Wash Marian Gould Gallagher Law Libr 1100 NE Campus Pkwy Seattle WA 98105-6605

HAZUDA, HELEN PAULINE, sociologist, educator; b. San Francisco, Oct. 20, 1943; d. Alexander William and Dolores Underwood (Green) H.; children: Ann Elizabeth Richter, Sean. BA in Sociology and Philosophy, Incarnate Word Coll., 1965, MA in Edn. and History, 1968; PhD in Sociology, U. Tex., 1975. Asst. prin. Incarnate Word H.S., San Antonio, 1967-71; discipline head for curriculum, instrn., dir. bilingual edn. Our Lady the Lake U., San Antonio, 1976-79; asst. prof. clin. medicine in medicine and psychiatry U. Tex. Health Sci. Ctr., San Antonio, 1980-88, assoc. prof. medicine dept. medicine and psychiatry, 1988-96, prof. medicine dept. medicine and psychiatry, 1996—; del. Gov's White House Conf. Children and Youth, Austin, 1970; admissions com. med. sch. U. Tex. Health Sci. Ctr., San Antonio, 1986-91, med. humanities curriculum planning com., 1989-91, tech. adv. panel for clin. and epidemiological rsch., 1991—; faculty mem. Ctr. Ethics and the Humanities in Health Care, 1992—, assoc. dir. Med. Humanities Course, 1997-98, Instnl. Rev. Bd., 1998—, dep. chair, 1999—; doctoral dissertation com. Sch. Nursing, 1992-93, adj. asst. prof. medicine and psychiatry, 1979-80; lectr. Incarnate Word Coll., San Antonio, 1971-72; cons. San Luis Valley Health and Aging Study/U. Colo. Health Sci. Ctr., Denver, 1992—; mem. nat. adv. panel RMC Rsch. Corp., 1977-81; mem. ad hoc study section NIH, 1988, mem. clin. applications and prevention adv. com. divsn. epidemiology and clin. applications Nat. Heart, Lung and Blood Inst., 1991-94, chair behavioral medicine working group, 1993-94, task force on rsch. in epidemiology and prevention cardiovascular disease, 1993-94; reviewer grants and proposals; mem. working group on epidemiology of hypertension in Hispanic-Ams., Native Ams., and Asian/Pacific Islanders-Ams., 1993-94; co-chair NHLBI Conf. socioeconomic status and cardiovascular health and disease, 1995, data and safety monitoring bd. multi-ethnic study atherosclerosis, 1999—, mem. external adv. group study of women's health issues, 1999—; cons. McDonnell-Douglas Automation Co., St. Louis, 1969-78, Devel. Assocs., 1975-77; spkr. and presenter in field. Contbr. articles to profl. jours. Panelist San Antonio Cmty. Symposium on the Changing Role Women in Personal and Profl. Life, 1976; resource person Leadership San Antonio, 1976; co-chair Working Women in Am.: Where Are They and Why are They There?, 1976-77; judge Hobby Middle Sch. Sci. Fair, San Antonio, 1984, John Jay H.S. Sci. Fair, San Antonio, 1987, Alamo Area Regional Sci. Fair, San Antonio, 1987; alumnae bd. dirs. Incarnate Word H.S., San Antonio, 1986-89; pledge vol. Womens Faculty Assn., San Antonio, 1991. U.S. Seminar on the Epidemiology and Prevention Cardiovascular Disease fellow, Lake Tahoe, Calif., 1983; instl. rsch. grantee U. Tex. Health Scis. Ctr./Hogg Found. for Mental Health, Austin, 1981-82; grantee Am. Heart Assn., 1983-84, Morrison Trust Found., 1986-87, NIH, 1979—, Nat. Cancer Inst., 1985-89. Mem. Sociol. Assn., Soc. for Behavioral Medicine, Am. Diabetes Assn., Soc. for Epidemiol. Rsch., Am. Heart Assn. (mem. coun. on cardiovasc. epidemiology), Am. Soc. Bioethics and Humanities, Gerontol. Soc. Am., Acad. Behavioral Medicine Rsch., Gerontol. Soc. Am., Phi Kappa Phi, Kappa Gamma Phi, Alpha Chi, Alpha Lambda Delta. Avocations: hiking, horseback riding, reading, travel, music. Office: U Tex Health Sci Ctr Dept Medicine/Epidemiology MC 7873 7703 Floyd Curl Dr San Antonio TX 78229-3900

HE, BAOGANG, political scientist, educator; b. Baotou, China, Oct. 15, 1957; s. Ming and Aicong (Yang) H.; m. Suxing Mao; 1 child, Xing. BA, Hangzhou U., China, 1981; MA, People's U. of China, Beijing, 1986; PhD, Australian Nat. U., Canberra, 1994. Lectr. U. Tasmania, Hobart, Australia, 1993-96, sr. lectr., 1997-98, assoc. prof. polit. sci., 1999—. Author: The Democratization of China, 1996, The Democratic Implication of Chinese Civil Society, 1997, Nationalism, National Identity, Democratization in China (with Yingjie Guo), 1999. Recipient H. Mayer prize Australian Polit. Sci. Assn., 1994; Australian Rsch. Coun. grantee, 1997. Office: Univ of tasmania, Sandy Bay GPO Box 252-22, Hobart TAS, Australia

HE, BIN, biomedical engineer, educator; b. Zhejiang, China, Aug. 14, 1957; s. Liangjin Zhu and Suqing He; m. Wenjing Ye, July 30, 1986; children: Eric J., Jefferey. BS, Zhejiang U., 1982; PhD, Tokyo Inst. Tech., 1988; postgrad., Harvard U./MIT, 1989-91. Rsch. scientist Harvard U./MIT, Cambridge, Mass., 1991-94; dir. biomed. functional imaging and computation lab. U. Ill., Chgo., 1994—. Guest editor IEEE Transactions on Info. Tech. in Biomedicine, 1998—, Critical Revs. in Biomed. Engring., 1998—, Methods of Information in Medicine, 1998—, IEEE Engring. in Medicine and Biology Mag., 1997-98; gen. chair 3d Internat. Workshop on Biosignal Interpretation; reviewer NSF, Arlington, Va., 1998—, Med. Rsch. Coun. Can., Ottawa, 1998—; contbr. articles to profl. jours. Bd. dirs. Am. Zhu Kezhen Edn. Found., Calif., 1998—; pres. Japan Zhejiang U. Alumni Assn., Tokyo, 1988-89; mem. exec. com. Higher Inst. Biomed. Engring., Hangzhou, China, 1998. Recipient Biomed. Engring. Rsch. award Whitaker Found., 1992, Young Investigator 2d Pl. award N.Am. Soc. Pacing and Clin. Electrophysiology, 1992, Rsch. Fellowship award Am. Heart Assn., 1990, Tejima prize, 1989, NSF Career award, 1999, univ. scholar award U. Ill., 1999. Mem. IEEE (sr., local arrangement chair internat. sci. meeting on electromagnetics in medicine 1996-97, theme co-chair internat. conf. engring. in medicine and biology 1997-98, vice chmn. EMB Chgo. chpt. 1997-98, tech. program chair Asia-Pacific conf. on Biomed. Engring. 2000, EMBS regional conf. com. 2000—), N.Y. Acad. Sci., Biomed. Engring. Soc., Am. Soc. for Engring. Edn. Achievements include development of laplacian electrocardiography and rsch. on brain electric source imaging. Fax: 312-413-0024. E-mail: bhe@uic.edu. Office: U Ill MC-154 851 S Morgan St Chicago IL 60607-7042

HE, CHAOLAI, meterologist, researcher; b. Lipu, Guangxi, Peoples Republic of China, Oct. 18, 1938; s. Fangjun He and Yuying Wu; m. Dachun Pan, Feb. 11, 1969; children: Jing, Yue. Stidemt, South Ctrl. Inst. Tech., Peoples Republic of China, 1963, Beijing Lang. Inst., 1974-75. Mem. staff Nat. Inst. Metrology, Beijing, 1963-80; engr. Elec. divsn. NIM, Peoples Republic of China, 1981-86; assoc. prof. Electromagnetic divsn. NIM, Peoples Republic of China, 1987-94, prof., 1995—; vis. scientist NIST, U.S., 1981-83. Mem. editl. bd. Jour. Astronautic Metrology and Measurement, 1990-94; contbr. articles to profl. jours. Mem. N.Y. Acad. Scis. Office: NIM Electromagnetic Divsn, No 18 Bei San Huan Dong Lu, 100013 Beijing Peoples Republic of China

HE, CHUANQI, science educator; b. Wuhan, Hubei, China, Feb. 20, 1962; s. Hanshan He and Shoazhen Yan. BS in Biology, Wuhan (China) U., 1983; MS, Chinese Acad. Scis., Beijing, 1988. Asst. rschr. Genetics Inst. Chinese Acad. Scis., 1983-88, asst. prof. Bur. Biology, 1988-92, dep. dir. biology, 1992-93, dir. planning Bur. Planning Fin., 1995-99, rsch. prof. Bur. Planning, 1998—; 2d sec. sci. office Chinese Embassy, Washington, 1993-95; dep. dir. World Sci. and Tech. R&D, Chengdu, China, 1996—; sr. cons. Bush-Xinhua Fin. Svc. Ltd., Beijing, 1999—. Author: Benefit Effect Management, 1992, Second Modernization, 1999, National Innovation System, 1999, Management: Modernization of Business Management, 1999, Knowledge Innovation, 2000, Distribution Revolution, 2000. Dep. dir. Diplomat Club of Chinese Embassy, Washington, 1994. Mem. N.Y. Acad. Scis., Sci. & Tech. Policy and Mgmt. Assn. (vice chmn. 1996—), Modernization Club (bd. dirs. 1999—). Office: Chinese Acad Scis Bur Plan, 52 Sanlihe, 100864 Beijing China

HE, DONGQI, mathematician, researcher, educator; b. Xuchang, Henan, China, Nov. 5, 1958; s. Lianji He and Jinghe Luo; m. Qing Li, Nov. 22, 1996; chldren: He Li, Li He. BEngring., Beijing Inst. Aeronautics, 1982; MSc, Beijing Inst. Tech., 1990; PhD, Inst. Sys. Sci. Sinica, Beijing, 1996. Engr. Min. Aviation Industry, China, 1982-88; asst. prof. Beijing Med. U., 1990-95, prof., 1996-99, dir. dept. biomath. and biostats., 1997-2000; dir. dept. biomath. and biostats. Med. Sch. Peking U., 2000—. Editor-in-chief: Calculus and Its Applications in Biomedicine, 1998; mem. editl. bd. Jour. Biomathematics, 1998—; contbr. articles to profl. jours. Mem. Soc. Biomathematics China (sec. gen. 1998—), Chinese Maths. Soc. Office: Med Sch Peking U, Dept Biomaths and Biostats, 100083 Beijing China

HE, GUO-WEI, medical educator, cardiovascular scientist/surgeon; b. Wuhan, Hubei, China, May 8, 1947; s. Tong He and Su-Yun Chen; m. Cheng-Qin Yang, 1975; 1 child, Yang-Hui He. MD, Anhui Med. U., Hefei, China, 1969; M of Med. Scis., Peking Union Med. Coll., Beijing, 1982; PhD, Monash U., Melbourne, Australia, 1989. Dir. cardiovascular rsch. Starr Acad. Ctr., St. Vincent Hosp., Portland, Oreg., 1994; prof. cardiothoracic surgery U. Hong Kong Hosp. Authority, 1995—, chair prof., 1995-2000; vis. prof. cardiac surgery Gt. Wall Hosp., Beijing, 1996; hon. prof. Anhui Med. U., 1999. Editor: Arterial Grafts for Coronary Artery Bypass Surgery: A Textbook for Cardiovascular Clinicians and Researchers, 1999; contbr. over 350 articles to sci. publs. Bd. dirs. Xiamen (China) Med. Coll., 1997. Rsch. grantee Hong Kong Govt. Rsch. Coun., 1997, 99, St. Vincent Found., Portland, 1994—. Mem. Am. Assn. Thoracic Surgery, Soc. Thoracic Surgeons, Am. Physiol. Soc., Hong Kong Med. Rev. Coun. Avocations: classical music, Chinese ancient literature, mathematics, physics. Fax: 852-2645 1762. E-mail: gwhe@cuhk.edu.hk. Office: 5A Block B, Prince of Wales Hosp, Shatin, Hong Kong SAR, China

HE, JI-FAN, mechanics educator, researcher; b. Shanghai, China, June 30, 1937; s. Ji-Mei He and Lian-Ying Sun; m. Bang-An Ma, Feb. 14, 1972. MSc, Tsinghua U., Beijing, 1959. Asst. Tsinghua U., Beijing, 1959-79, lectr., 1979-86, assoc. prof., 1986-96, prof., 1996—. Contbr. articles to profl. jours. Mem. Chinese Soc. Theoretical & Applied Mechanics, Chinese Soc. Composite Materials, Chinese Soc. Vibration Engrs. Home: Tsinghua U, Apt House 17, Beijing 100084, China Office: Tsinghua U, Dept Engring Mechanics, Beijing 100084, China

HE, LI, aerospace engineer; b. Xian, Shaanxi, China, Apr. 6, 1956; s. Qinhan and Guigin (Zhang) H.; m. Yan Liu, Dec. 30, 1984; children: Jenny, Bobby. BSc, Beijing U. of Aero. & Astro., China, 1982, MSc, 1984; PhD, Cambridge U., 1990. Trainee Gaoqao Village, Xian, China, 1974-76; apprentice 3d Constrn. Firm, Xian, China, 1976-77; rsch. assoc. Cambridge U., 1990-91, sr. rsch. fellow, 1991-93; lectr. Durham U., 1993-98, reader, 1998-2000, prof., 2000—; vis. prof. Beijing U. Aero. and Astro., 1996—, Northwestern Polytech. U., 1996—; tech. cons. European Gas Turbines, Lincoln, 1993—; engring cons. Rolls-Royce, Derby, 1993-98; cons. GEC Alsthom, Rugby, 1994—, Parsons, Newcastle, 1995-97. Contbr. articles to sci. jours. Recipient ORS award Com. of the Vice-Chancellor, 1988, Edward Boyle award, 1988; EPSRC grantee Engring. Rsch. Coun., Swindon, 1994, 99. Mem. ASME, Internat. Gas Turbine Inst. Avocations: classical music, playing violin and piano. Office: Sch Engring, South Rd, DH1 3LE Durham England

HE, LIN, dermatologist, medical educator, researcher; b. Shenyang, China, Oct. 1, 1936; s. Zhenqiang and Shuguang (Zhang) H.; m. Yuzhi Liu; children: Aizhong, Lizhong. BMed, Beijing Med. Coll., 1960. Resident physician Ya Ang Hosp., Ya Ang City, China, 1960-62; resident physician Tie Xi Dist. Hosp., Shenyang, 1962-80, physician in charge, 1980-84; physician in charge Inst. Med. Info., Shenyang, 1984-87, vice chief physician, 1987-90; chief physician, prof. dermatology Liaoning Med. Staff Coll., Shenyang, 1990—; cons. venereal disease health-edn., Shenyang, 1988-89; cons. venereal disease infor., Shenyang, 1989-93. Author: Dermatologic Signs and Internal Illness, 1987, Modern Sexually Transmitted Disease, 1988, Signs of Bodily Surface Recognized and Diagnosis and Therapy, 1992, Practical Manual of Diagnosis and Therapy of Dermatologic and Venereal Diseases, 2000; editor China Med. Abstract Pediatrics, 1985-93. Lectr. China Dem. Party of Farmer-Workers, Shenyang, 1988. Avocations: playing violin, boxing. Home: 32, 6-431 Jigung Yi St, Tie Xi, 110023 Shenyang China Office: Liaoning Med Staff Coll, 79 Jixian St, Heping Dist, 110005 Shenyang China

HE, QINGPING, environment researcher; b. Nanchong, Sichuan, People's Republic of China, May 12, 1960; s. Zhongsun He and Suqing Xian; m. Yu Wu, July 17, 1984; 1 child, Jingzhou. BSc, Lanzhou U., People's Republic of China, 1982; MSc, Liaoning U., Shenyang, People's Republic of China, 1984; PhD, Exeter (U.K.) U., 1993. Lectr. U. of Electronic Sci. and Tech. of China, Chengdu, 1985-89; rsch. fellow U. Exeter, 1989-90, 1993—; rschr. Internat. Atomic Energy Agy., Vienna, 1996—. Contbr. articles to profl. publs. Rsch. grant Internat. Atomic Energy Agy., 1998, 99. Mem. British Hydrologica Soc., Internat. Assn. of Hydrological Scis. Home: 8 Castle Mount, Exeter EX4 4JW, United Kingdom Office: U Exeter Dept Geog, Amory Bldg Rennes Dr, Exeter EX4 4RJ, United Kingdom

HE, QIUSHUI, microbiologist; b. Shenyang, China, Nov. 8, 1962; s. Yongshan and Yuqin (Li) H.; m. Dexian Shi, June 27, 1989; 1 child, Beiou. MD, China Med. U., Shenyang, 1985; PhD, Turku (Finland) U., 1994. Asst. editor Chinese Med. Jour., Beijing, 1985-87; project officer Ministry of Pub. Health, Beijing, 1987-91; postdoctoral rsch. fellow Vienna Biocenter, 1994-95; rsch. asst. Nat. Pub. Health Inst., Turku, 1991-94; rsch. fellow Nat. Pub. Health Inst., 1995—; docent in molecular microbiology Turku U., 1998—. Office: Nat Pub Health Inst, Kiinamyllynkatu 13, 20520 Turku Finland

HE, QUN, research scientist; b. Changsha, Hunan, China, Jan. 30, 1957; s. Yao Nan He and Jun Yu Shi; m. Guang Yuan Wang, June 16, 1988; 1 child, He Yang. BS, Shanghai Med. U., 1982; MSc, China Pharm. U., Nanjing, 1987; MD/PhD, Hunan Med. U., 1994; Doctor, Huangpu English Coll., Changsha, 1996; DSc, Changsha Pharm. Sch., 1998. Medical diplomate China. Pharmacist Natural Medicine Hosp., Changsha, 1975-77; engr. Hunan Pharm. Co., Changsha, 1982-84; instr. Hunan Med. U., Changsha, 1988-93, assoc. prof., 1994-98; prof. Biomedicine Ctr., Changsha, 1998—; sec. gen. Hunan Pharm. Co., Changsha, China, 1982-84; dir. grad. studies, Changsha, 1998—; cons. Guangian Pharms., 1998—; advisor Huangpu English Coll., 1996—; vis. prof. Wayne State U., Detroit, 1996-98. Author: (book) Physiology, 1990 (Excellent Textbook award 1995), Role of Histamics in Hemopoiesis, 1994 (Young Scientist award 1994), Leukemia Research, 1999 (Natural Sci. award 1999); editor: (book) Blood Physiology, 1997. Recipient awards Min. of Edn., Beijing, 1998, scientific rsch. award NSF, Beijing, 1999, biomed. rsch. award Biomedicine Ctr., Changsha, 1999. Mem. China Pathophysiology (Young Scientist medal 1994), N.Y. Acad. Scis. Avocations: reading, basketball, swimming. Office: Letter Box 24 Hunan Med U, 88 Xiangya Rd, 410078 Changsha/Hunan China

HE, SHANGKUAN, anatomist, educator; b. Liuzhou, People's Republic of China, Oct. 1, 1942; s. Chaoqing He and Suxiu Deng; m. Fengying Cui, 1966; children: Yimei, Yibing. Residential physician Guangxi Region, Liuzhou, 1964-72; asst. lectr. The First Mil. Med. Coll., Guangzhou, 1972-74; lectr. Guangzhou Med. Sch., PLA, 1974-93; asst. prof. Guangzhou Jr. Med. Coll., 1993-98, prof., 1998—. Editor: Anatomical Basis of Microsurgery, 1995, Clinical Applied Anatomy, 1997; vice editor-in-chief Surgical Anatomy for Functional Reconstruction of the Hand, 1996, Basic and Clinical Research on Glossoscopy, 1998, Chinese Juor. of Clin. Anatomy, 1998—; contbr. articles to profl. publs. Fellow Chinese Assn. of Anatomy. Office: 13 Shiliugang Rd, Chigang, Guangzhou 510315, People's Republic of China

HE, SHIPING, molecular biologist, researcher; b. Xiwen County, Guang dong, China, Mar. 11, 1958; arrived in Eng., 1989; s. Yongyan He and Xiuzhen Chen He; m. Ya-Ling Lin, Dec. 20, 1993; 1 child, Shao Jian. BS, U. South China, Guangzhou, 1978; MS, Beijing Agrl. U., 1983; PhD, U. Cambridge, Eng., 1993. Asst. lectr. U. South China, 1979-80; asst. lectr. Beijing Agrl. U., 1983-84, lectr., 1984-89; rsch. assoc. Leicester (Eng.) U., 1993-96; lectr. Birmingham (Eng.) U., 1996—; asst. sec. Assn. Genetics, Beijing, 1986-88; pres. Assn. Life Scis., Cambridge, 1991-92. Inventor in field. Sino-Brit. scholar Brit. Coun., Cambridge, 1989; rsch. grantee Wellcome Trust, 1993. Mem. AAAS, Biochem. Soc. U.K., N.Y. Acad. Scis. Avocations: chess, table tennis, badminton. Home: 100 Poole Crescent Harborne, Birmingham B17 OPD, England Office: Birmingham U Sch Medicine, Dept Medicine, Birmingham B15 2TT, England

HE, SUSAN LI, business development executive; b. Kunming, Yunnan, China, Apr. 10, 1963; d. Qi Chang He and He Chu Yan; m. Hans Baekgaard; 1 child, Adam. BA, Yunnan U., Kunming, China, 1984; BSc, Australian Nat. U., Canberra, 1989. Interpreter Bur. Fgn. Trade, Kunming, 1984-85; rsch. asst. U. NSW, Canberra, 1987-89; grad. trainee Commonwealth Bank of Australia, Sydney, 1989-90; rsch. officer Nat. Ctr. for Social and Econ. Mktg., Canberra, 1991-95; mgr. Asia programs Economist Intelligence Unit, Sydney, 1995-98; internat. bus. devel. mgr. NRMA Ins. Ltd., Sydney, 1998—. Office: NRMA Ins Ltd, 388 George St, 2000 Sydney NSW, Australia

HE, XIAO YAN CLARA, scientist, physician; b. Feng Cheng, Liaoning, China, Dec. 13, 1957; s. Xi and Yan Jie (Zhou) X. BMed, Med. U. Shanghai, 1982, M of Medicine, 1988; PhD in Medicine, U. New South Wales, 1995. Cert. in med. rsch. Hosp. physician Jinan Centre Hosp., 1983-85, Shanghai First People's Hosp., 1988-90; rsch. asst. dept. medicine U. New South Wales, Sydney, 1993; postdoctoral rsch. fellow St. Vincent's, 1994-96; sr. rsch. fellow, lab. mgr. medicine Liverpool Hosp., Sydney, 1996—; Post doctoral rsch. fell., St. Vincent's Hosp., Sydney. Contbr. articles to Transplantation, Pathology, Jour. Immunology, others. Recipient Young Investigator award Internat. Transplantation soc., 1998; Transplantation soc. Australia and New Zealand travel grantee, 1998; Ingham Med. Rsch. grantee, 1998; Nat. Health and Med. Rsch. Coun. grantee, 1999, 2000. Mem. Transplantation Soc. Australia and New Zealand, Australian Soc. for Med. Rsch., Amer. Assn. for the Advancement of Sci. Avocations: classical music, arts, dancing. Home: 93 Bellinger Rd, Ruse NSW 2560, Australia Office: Liverpool Hosp Dept Medicine, Crnr Campbell/Goulburn Sts, Sydney Australia 2170

HE, XIAOHONG, finance educator; b. Beijing, May 15, 1953; came to the U.S., 1984; d. DongChang He and Zhuobao Li; m. Ping Su, June 29, 1949; 1 child, Xiaowei Su. MA in Internat. Bus., U. Tex., Dallas, 1986, MS in Fin., 1989, PhD in Internat. Mgmt., 1991. Engr., rschr. China's Nat. Acad. Agr. Mechanization Scis., Beijing, 1977-84; rsch. assoc. Hass Bus. Sch. U. Calif., Berkeley, 1984-85; mgmt. cons. Greyhound Lines & China Auto Import Co., Dallas, 1985-89; v.p. China Auto Import Co., Dallas, 1989-91; dir. Far East Econ. Devel. Greyhound Lines, Dallas, 1989-91; dir. Internat. Bus. ExchangeProg. Quinnipiac U., 1991-93; prof., chair internat. bus. and mktg. dept. Quinnipiac U., Hamden, Conn., 1997—; dir. Internat. Bus. Rsch. Quinnipiac U., 1993-94. Contbr. numerous articles to profl. jours., chpts. to books. Outstanding R&D Award, China's Machine Building Min., 2d Prize, 1993, 3rd Prize 1979-81, Citation of Excellence, Highest Quality Rating by ANBAR Electronic Intelligence (U.K.), 1998, Literati Club award for excellence, MCB Univ. Press (U.K.), 1999. Mem. Internat. Mgmt. Devel. Assn., Nat. Assn. Purchasing Mgmt., Assn. Global Bus., Assn. Internat. Trade and Fin., Acad. Internat. Bus. (Best Paper award N.E. chpt. 1992), Soc. Global Bus. Edn. (pres.). Office: Quinnipiac U Sch Bus 275 Mount Carmel Ave Hamden CT 06518-1961

HE, XINYU, mathematician, educator; b. Beijing, Apr. 29, 1970; d. Wentao He and Lieyan Li. PhD in Math., U. Warwick, Eng., 1996. Rschr. dept. math. U. Warwick, 1996—. Contbr. articles to profl. jours., including Applied Math. Letters, Physics of Fuids. Mem. London Math. Soc., Soil Assn. Avocations: music, mushrooms. Home: Shenzhen China Office: U Warwick, Math Dept, Warwick CV4 7AL, England

HE, XU-CHANG, chemist; b. Shanghai, China, Nov. 12, 1941; s. Long-Sun and Chuan-qi (Pan) H.; m. Xing Chen, May 1, 1969; 1 child, Gang. Grad., Fudan U., Shanghai, 1964. Rsch. assoc. dept. natural products Shanghai Inst. Organic Chemistry, Academia Sinica, 1964-85; rsch. assoc. prof. dept. synthetic drugs Shanghai Inst. of Materia Medica, Academia Sinica, 1998-96; rsch. prof. Shanghai Inst. Materia Medica, Academia Sinica, 1996—; postdoctoral rsch. assoc. dept. chemistry U. N.C., Chapel Hill, 1985-88; postdoctoral chemist chemistry and life scis. dept. Research Triangle Inst., N.C., 1988-89. Mem. Am. Chem. Soc., Chinese Chem. Soc. Avocations: traveling, volleyball. Home: 94/913 Lane, Yan An Zhong Lu, Shanghai 200040, China Office: Shanghai Inst Materia Medica, 294 Tai-Yuan Rd, Shanghai 200031, China

HE, YAPING, safety engineer, researcher; b. Tangshan, Hebei, China, Apr. 14, 1957; arrived in Australia, 1993; s. Guanghui He and Xiuying Zhang; m. Xue Yang. BE, Beijing U. Sci. and Tech., 1982; MEngSci, U. Queensland, Brisbane, Australia, 1987, PhD, 1991. Rsch. asst. Tianjin (China) U., 1982-83, Australian Def. Force Acad., Canberra, 1986-87, Australian Nat. U., Canberra, 1987-92; rsch. assoc. Victoria U., Melbourne, Australia, 1994-98; sr. profl. officer Scientific Svcs. Lab., Melbourne, 1998—. Contbr. articles to profl. jours. Recipient Australia Day award Dept. Industry, Sci. and Resources, 1994. Mem. Fire Safety Soc., Risk Engring. Soc. Avocations: tennis, swimming, volleyball.

HEAD, BEN THOMAS, lawyer; b. Oklahoma City, Nov. 1, 1920; s. Ben Thomas Head and Virginia (Broados) Pine; m. Mary C. Johnston, Feb. 28, 1930 (div. June 1983); children: Marcy, Paul, Eric; m. June Leftwich, Mar. 22, 1986. BBA, U. Okla., 1942, LLB, 1948, JD, 1970. Bar: Okla., Tex. Pres., chmn., chief exec. officer RepublicBank, Austin, Tex., 1978-84; sr. lectr. banking U. Tex., Austin, 1984-88; U.S. trustee U.S. Dist. Ct. (so. and we. dists.) Tex., Houston, 1988-93; pres., CEO United Va. Bank (now Crestar), Newport News, Va., 1975-78; chmn. City Savs., San Angelo, Tex., 1986-87. V.p. Oklahoma City C. of C., 1973, chmn. Austin C. of C., 1983; pres. progress com. Newport News., Va., 1978; bd. dirs., chmn. fin. com. Austin Presbyn. Sem., 1982-90; bd. dirs. fin. com. Tex. Presbyn. Found., 1988—; trustee, vice chmn. bd., Hampton U., 1980—. Col. U.S. Army, 1942-46, India. Named Exec. of Yr. Austin C. of C., 1983. Mem. Rotary. Avocations: golf, walking. Home: 3234 Tarryhollow Dr Austin TX 78703-1639 Office: 816 Congress Ave Ste 1200 Austin TX 78701-2442

HEAD, MARK D., insurance and employee benefit broker; b. Dallas, Apr. 24, 1958; s. Claude D. III and Mariam Joyce H. Student, Richland Coll., 1979, 80, 83. Assoc. Baldwin Fin. Group, 1981-88; owner Mark D. Head Ins., 1989-91; pres. MDH Benefits Corp., 1992—; sr. cons. Ins. Ptnrs. S.W. Corp., 1998—. Mem steering com. Anita N. Martinez Ballet Forklorico, 1995; mem. steering com. Positive Parents Dallas, 1982-87; mem. adv. com. DISD Bus. and Mgmt. Ctr., 1982-87; mem. edn. com. Goals for Dallas, 1985-87; campaign treas. David Childs, 1995. Mem. Nat. Assn. Life Underwriters, Nat. Assn. Health Underwriters, Tex. Assn. Health Underwriters, Tex. Assn. Life Underwriters (bd. dirs. Dallas assn. 1986-87, chair LUPAC, bd. dirs. 1994-96, chair health and employee benefits, chair pub. rels. 1995-96), Dallas Assn. Health Underwriters, Dallas Jaycees (bd. dirs. 1982-84, mem. fin. com. 1984, dir. comm. 1984), World Future Soc., Internat. Platform Assn. Office: Ins Ptnrs S W Corp 4131 N Central Expy Ste 500 Dallas TX 75204-2175

HEAD, WILLIAM IVERSON, SR., retired chemical company executive; b. Tallapposa, Ga., Apr. 4, 1925; s. Iverson and Ruth Britain (Hubbard) H.; m. Mary Helen Ware, June 12, 1947; children: William Iverson, Connie Suzanne Head Toohey, Alan David. BS, Ga. Inst. Tech., 1949; D of Textile Engring. (hon.), World U., 1983; PhD in Indsl. Mgmt., Columbia Pacific U., 1988. Textile engr. Tenn. Eastman Co., Kingsport, 1949-56, quality control-mfg. sr. textile engr., 1957-67, dept. supt., 1968-74; supt. acetate yarn dept., bus. team, chem. divsn. Eastman Kodak Co., Kingsport, 1975-85; info. officer U.S. Naval Acad., 1983-97; adv. bd., rsch. assoc. Point One Adv. Group, Inc., 1988—. Patentee textured yarns tech. in U.S. Great Britain, Fed. Republic of Germany, Japan and France. Capt. USNR, 1943-83. Decorated Navy Commendation medal, Selective Svc. Sys. Meritorious Svc. medal. Mem. Internat. Soc. Philos. Enquiry (pers. coms. 1978-79, v.p. 1979-80, sr. rsch. fellow and internat. pres. 1980-85, diplomate, trustee 1986—, chmn. bd. trustees 1987—, Whiting Meml. award 1993), Prometheus Soc., Naval Res. Assn., Assn. Naval Aviation, Mil. Order World Wars, Res. Officers Assn. (pres. Tenn. dept. 1981-82, nat. councilman 1991-98, nat. coun. steering com. 1993-97), Ret. Officers Assn., VFW, Mensa (pres. Upper East Tenn. 1976-79), Sons of Revolution, Internat. Legion of Intelligence. Unitarian. Home: 4035 Lakewood Dr Kingsport TN 37663-3374

HEAD, WILLIS STANFORD, music educator, performer; b. Memphis, June 21, 1953; s. Willis Lockhart and Mildred (Garrard) H. B in Music Edn., Ark. State U., 1975, M in Music Edn., 1980. Percussion instr. Dixie Music Camp, Jonesboro, Ark., 1972-81; timpanist Tupelo (Miss.) Symphony Orch., 1973-74, N.E. Ark. Symphony, Jonesboro, 1974-81; band dir. Mammoth Spring (Ark.) High Sch., 1975-77; percussionist Memphis Symphony and Little Symphony, 1981—, "Artists in Schs.", Memphis, 1985—; bd. dirs. Lindenwood Percussion Studio, Memphis, 1980—; lectr. Mid-South Bible Coll., Memphis, 1982—; percussion instr. Shelby State Community Coll. Memphis, 1984—; percussion cons. Harding Acad., Memphis, 1985—, Osceola (Ark.) High Sch., 1986—, Millington (Tenn.) High Sch., 1987—; timpanist Jackson (Tenn.) Symphony Orch. Mem. Percussive Arts Soc. (sec. treas. 1977-78), Nat. Assn. Recording Arts and Scis., Phi Mu Alpha Sinfonia Frat., Kappa Delta Pi. Home: 652 S Prescott St Memphis TN 38111-4325 Office: Lindenwood Percussion Studio 2400 Union Ave Memphis TN 38112-4318

HEADINGS, RENEÉ, artist, sculptor; b. West Palm Beach, Fla., Oct. 25, 1958; d. Philip Oscar and Myrna Lichtblau; m. Donald Headings Jr., Feb. 14, 1979. Grad. h.s., West Palm Beach. Sculpture bronze monument Returning on the Wings of Peace, 1995, Makin Tracks, 1999 (medal of honor), Yesterday, Today, Tomorrow, 1998, pub. art pieces. Fellow Am. Artist Profl. League; mem. Soc. Animal Artists (treas. 1997—), Catherine Lorillad Wolfe Art Club, Am. Soc. Maine Artists, Nat. Sculpture Soc. Avocation: golf. Home: PO Box 73 Skytop PA 18357-0073

HEADY, EUGENE JOSEPH, lawyer; b. Poughkeepsie, N.Y., Jan. 25, 1958; s. William and Margaret Patricia Heady; m. Susan Leigh Snead, July 31, 1987; children: Anthony Ray, Emily Rene, Katie Shanell. BS in Engring., U. Hartford, 1981; JD cum laude, Tex. Tech. U., 1996. Bar: Tex. 1996, Ga. 1997, Colo. 1997, Fla. 1998, Supreme Ct. Ga. 1997, U.S. Dist. Ct. (no. dist.) Ga. 1997, Ct. Appeals Ga. 1997. V.p. Heady Electric Co., Inc., Poughkeepsie, 1980-83; project mgr. ANECO, Inc., West Palm Beach, Fla., 1987-93; assoc. Smith, Currie & Hancock LLP, Atlanta, 1996—. Editor-in-chief: Tex. Tech Law Rev. vol. 27, 1995-96; student editor: Tex. County Ct. Bench Manual, 1996, Bench Book for the Tex. Jud., 1996; editor: Tex. Tech Legal Rsch. Bd., 1995-96; co-author: Ga. Suppl. to Fifty State Construction Lien and Bond Law, 1996, 97, 98, Ga. chpt. Fifty State Construction Lien and Bond Law, 2000; author: chpts. in Alternative Clauses to Standard Construction Contracts, 1998, 99, 2000; contbr. numerous articles to profl. jours. Mem. ABA (forum on the constrn. industry, vice-chmn. region IV sect. of pub. contract law), Scribes-The Am. Soc. Writers on Legal Subjects. Avocations: writing, reading. E-mail: gjheady@smithcurrie.com. Fax: 404-688-0671. Home: 2412 Waterscape Trl Snellville GA 30078-7740 Office: Smith Currie & Hancock LLP 2600 Harris Tower 233 Peachtree St NE Ste 2600 Atlanta GA 30303-1530

HEADY, FERREL, retired political science educator; b. Ferrelview, Mo., Feb. 14, 1916; s. Chester Ferrel and Loren (Wightman) H.; m. Charlotte Audrey McDougall, Feb. 12, 1942; children—Judith Lillian, Richard Ferrel, Margaret Loren, Thomas McDougall. A.B., Washington U., St. Louis, 1937, A.M., 1938, Ph.D., 1940; hon. degrees, Park Coll., 1973, John F. Kennedy U., 1974, U. N.Mex., 1993. Jr. adminstrv. technician, also adminstrv. asst. Office Dir. Personnel, Dept. Agr., 1941-42; vis. lectr. polit. sci. U. Kansas City, 1946; faculty U. Mich., 1946-67, prof. polit. sci., 1957-67; dir. Inst. Pub. Adminstrn., 1960-67; acad. v.p. U. N.Mex., Albuquerque, 1967-68; pres. U. N.Mex., 1968-75, prof. pub. adminstrn. and polit. sci., 1975-81, prof. emeritus, 1981—; Asst. to commr. Com. Orgn. Exec. Br. of Govt., 1947-49; dir., chief adviser Inst. Pub. Adminstrn., U. Philippines, 1953-54; mem. U.S. del. Internat. Congress Adminstrn. Scis., Spain, 1956, 80, Germany, 1959, Austria, 1962, Poland, 1964, Mexico, 1974; exec. bd. Inter-Univ. Case Program, 1956-67; sr. specialist in residence East-West Center, U. Hawaii, 1965; mem. Conf. on Pub. Service, 1965-70; chmn. bd. Assoc. Western Univs., 1970-71; commr. Western Interstate Commn. Higher Edn., 1972-77; mem. commns. on bus. professions and water resources, mem. exec. com. Nat. Assn. State Univs. and Land Grant Colls., 1968-75. Author: Administrative Procedure Legislation in the States, 1952, (with Robert H. Pealy) The Michigan Department of Administration, 1956, (with Sybil L. Stokes) Comparative Public Administration: A Selective Annotated Bibliography, 1960, Papers in Comparative Public Administration, 1962, State Constitutions: The Structure of Administration, 1961, Public Administration: A Comparative Perspective, 1966, rev. edit., 1979, 6th edit., 2000, One Time Around, 1999; contbr. profl. jours. Chmn. state affairs com. Ann Arbor Citizens Coun., Mich., 1949-52; mem. exec. com. Mich. Meml.-Phoenix Project and Inst. Social Rsch., 1960-66; mem. Gov. Mich. Constl. Revision Study Commn., 1960-62; schs. and univs. adv. bd. Citizens Com. for Hoover Report, 1949-52, 54-58; cons. to Ford Found., 1962; chmn. Coun. on Grad. Edn. in Pub. Adminstrn., 1966; mem., vice chmn. N.Mex. Gov.'s Com. on Reorgn. of State Govt., 1967-70; mem. N.Mex. Am. Revolution Bicentennial Commn., 1970-73, N.Mex. Gov.'s Com. on Tech. Excellence, 1969-75, Nat. Acad. Pub. Adminstrn.; mem., vice chmn. N.Mex. Constl. Revision Commn., 1994-95. Served to lt. USNR, 1942-46. Recipient Faculty Disting. Achievement award U. Mich., 1964, N.Mex. Disting. Pub. service award, 1973, award of distinction U. N.Mex. Alumni Assn., 1975, Outstanding Grad. Tchr. award U. N.Mex., 1981-82, Fulbright sr. lectureship, Colombia, 1992, Waldo award for career contbns. to lit. and leadership of pub. adminstrn., 1994. Mem. Am. Polit. Sci. Assn., Am. Soc. Pub. Adminstrn. (pres. 1969-70), AAUP (chmn. com. T 1957-61), Am. Council Edn. (mem. commn. on fed. relations 1969-72), Phi Beta Kappa, Phi Kappa Phi. Presbyterian. Home: 2901 Cutler Ave NE Albuquerque NM 87106-1714

HEAL, GEOFFREY MARTIN, economics educator; b. Bangor, Wales, Apr. 9, 1944; s. Thomas John and Gwen Margaret (Owen) H.; m. Felicity Chandler, 1967 (div. 1979); m. Ann Marie Biafore, 2000; children: Bridget, Natasha, Marie. BA first class, Cambridge U., 1966, PhD, 1969. Dir. studies Christs Coll., Cambridge U., 1967-73; prof. econs. Sussex U., Brighton, Eng., 1973-81, head dept. econs., 1976-81; mng. editor Rev. Econ. Studies, London, 1973-78; dir. Economists Adv. Group, London, 1975-80; prof. Essex U., Colchester, Eng., 1981-83; exec. dir. Fin. Telecommunications, London, 1984-89; prof. Grad. Sch. Bus., Columbia U., N.Y.C., 1983—; sr. vice dean Grad. Sch. Bus. Columbia U., 1991-94; Fulbright prof. U. Siena, Italy, 1997; Paul Garret prof. pub. policy and corp. responsibility Columbia U., N.Y.C., 1995—; cons. U.K. Dept. Energy, London, 1973-76, U.S. Dept. Energy, Washington, 1976-78, OPEC Sec. Gen., Vienna, Austria, 1979-81, OECD, Paris, 1994, Global Environ. Facility, World Bank, 1994, Internat. Brotherhood of Teamsters, 1995-2000, United Mineworkers of Am., 1990-98; mem. Pew Oceans Commn. Author: The Theory of Economic Planning, 1973, Public Policy and the Tax System, 1976, Economic Theory and Exhaustible Resources, 1979, Linear Algebra and Linear Economics, 1980, The Evolving International Economy, 1987, Oil in the International Economy, 1991, The Economics of Exhaustible Resources, 1993, Sustainability: Dynamics and Uncertainty, 1998, Valuing the Future, 1998, Topological Methods in Social Choice, 1998, The Economics of Increasing Returns, 1999, Environmental Markets, 2000, Nature and the Marketplace, 2000. Grantee NSF, NOAA, Sloan Found. Fellow Econometric Soc., Royal Soc. Arts. Home: 800 W End Ave # 13E New York NY 10025-5467 Office: Columbia Univ Bus Sch Uris Hall New York NY 10027

HEALD, BRUCE DAY, English and music educator, historian; b. Boston, June 5, 1935; s. Henry M. and Muriel D. (Day) H. m. Helen Peaslee, May 21, 1960; children: William Forristall III, Craig, Eric Bentley, Allyson Kaye. A.A., Boston U., 1956; B.S. in Music Edn., Lowell State U., 1959; M.A., Columbia Pacific U., 1984, Ph.D., 1985. Supr. music Ashland-Meredith Union 2, Meredith, N.H., 1959-64; dir. music, lectr. fine arts Belknap Coll., Center Harbor, N.H., 1963-65; dir. bands Plattsburgh (N.Y.) City Schs., 1969-70; supr. music Inter-Lakes Sch. Dist., Meredith, 1965-69, dir. music edn., 1970-77; dir. instrumental music Kennebunk (Maine) High Sch., 1977-79; prodn. mgr. Annalee Mobilitee Dolls, Meredith, 1979-81; lectr. English and journalism Moultonborough Acad., 1981-86; dir. music Congl. Ch., Laconia, N.H., 1985-86; chair English dept. Holy Trinity Sch., Laconia, 1987—; mentor Columbia Pacific U., 1986—; instr. music N.H. Coll., Manchester, 1988—; historian Weirstimes Pub. Co., 1992—; lectr. English lit. Plymouth State Coll., 1995-97, lectr. U.S. history, 1998—. Author: Follow the Mount, 1968, 70, 93, 97, Postmaster of the Lake, 1971, Mail Service on the Lake, 1980, Steamboats in Motion, 1984, New Hampshire Learnin' Days, 1987, Boats 'n Ports I and II, 1989, Landmarks and Legacy, 1990, The Boston See Party, 1991, Reminisce the Valley, 1992, Shadows in the Window, 1995, Images of America: Meredith, 1996, Images of America: The Lakes Region of New Hampshire, 1996, vol. I and II, 1998, Images of America: The Upper Merrimack to Winnipesaukee by Rail, 1997, Images of America: Boats and Ports in Lake Winnipesaukee, vol. I and II, 1998, Images of America: The White Mountains Region by Rail, 1999, Image of America: Plymouth State College, 1999, Images of America: Stereoptic Memories of the White Mountains, 2000, Images of America: Lakes and Ponds of the Granite State, 2000; composer: Kennebunk Concert March, The Hills of Old N.H., Moultonboro Concert March, Cascades, Trilogy. Commr. Parks and Playgrounds, Meredith, 1966-69; selectman Town of Meredith, 1971-76; pres. Lake Winnipesaukee Hist. Soc. Served with USMC, 1954-62. Mem. Nat. Catholic Edn. Assn., Masons. Republican. Home: PO Box 1052 Meredith NH 03253-1052 Office: Holy Trinity Sch Laconia NH 03246

HEALD, DAVID JAMES, aerospace executive; b. Bryn Mawr, Pa., Mar. 11, 1960; s. George Benton Heald III and Linda Louise (Dutcher) Urie; m. Jennifer Alene John, Mar. 20, 1993. BS in Petroleum Engring., Pa. State U., 1982; MBA in Internat. Mktg., St. Joseph's U., 1994. Regional sales mgr. Eutectic Castolin, L.A., 1983-85; legal account specialist Harris Lanier, L.A., 1985-87; product specialist Sys. Monitoring divsn. Vickers Inc., Glenolden, Pa., 1988-89, internat. product specialist, 1989-90, internat. product mgr., 1990-91, internat. sales mgr., 1991-93, applications engring. mgr., 1993-96, sales mgr., 1997—; divsn. sales mgr. Eaton Sterer Engring., L.A., 1997—; industry advisor Pa. State Applied Rsch., University Park, 1994—. Mem. World Affairs Coun., Phila., 1994; cons. Jr. Achievement, Phila., 1994—; elder Aston Presbyn. Ch., 1995. Mem. Am. Helicopter Soc., Vibration Inst. Am., Army Aviation Assn. Am., Mensa, Phi Mu Delta, Phi Theta Kappa (Acad. Achievement award 1991). Republican. Avocations: rock climbing, bicycling, running, home beer brewing, reading. Office: 4690 Colorado Blvd Los Angeles CA 90039-1106 Address: 4341 Marion Ave Cypress CA 90630-4254

HEALEY, LORD DENIS WINSTON, politician, writer; b. Mottingham, Kent, Eng., Aug. 30, 1917; s. William and Winifred Mary (Powell) H.; m. Edna May Edmunds, Dec. 21, 1945; children: Jenifer, Timothy, Cressida. MA, Oxford (Eng.) U., 1940; DLitt (hon.), Bradford U., 1983; LLD (hon.), Leeds U., 1991. Internat. sec. Labour Party, 1945-52; sec. for def., 1964-70, chancellor of exchequer, 1974-79, m.p., 1952-92, Lord Healey of Riddlesden, 1992—; chmn. interim com. IMF, 1977-79; pres. Birkbeck Coll., London, 1993-99; mem. Coun. Global Energy Studies, London, 1981—. Author: Healey's Eye, 1980, The Time of My Life, 1989, When Shrimps Learn to Whistle, My Secret Planet, 1992. Maj. Royal Engrs., 1940-45, North Africa, Italy. Decorated M.B.E., Queen Elizabeth, 1945, Privy Councillor, 1964, Companion of Honour, 1979. Fellow Royal Soc. Lit. Avocations: music, painting, walking. Office: 8 House of Lords, London SW1, England

HEALEY, THOMAS J., former government official, brokerage house executive; b. Balt., Sept. 14, 1942; m. Margaret Sachs Healey; children—Megan, Jeremiah. A.B., Georgetown U., 1964; M.B.A., Harvard U., 1966. Chartered fin. analyst, real estate counselor. Mgr. project fin. group Dean Witter, 1975-82; mng. dir., mgr. corp. fin. Dean Witter Reynolds Capital Markets, 1982-83; asst. sec. domestic fin. Dept. of Treasury, Washington, 1983-85; v.p. real estate Goldman Sachs & Co, N.Y.C., 1985-88, mng. dir. pension svcs. group, 1988-99, mng. dir. institutional sales and mktg., 1999—, mem. partnership com. Home: Van Bureun Rd New Vernon NJ 07976 Office: Goldman Sachs & Co 32 Old Slip Fl 18 New York NY 10005-3504 also: 85 Broad St New York NY 10004*

HEALEY, TIM, retired radiologist; b. Reading, Berkshire, Eng., Apr. 23, 1935; s. Thomas Henry and Evelyn (Hamilton) H.; m. Ruth Stagg, Aug. 18, 1958; children: Clifford Trevor, Janet Vivienne, Sandra Caroline. MBChB, Sheffield U., Eng., 1959; DMRD, RCS/RCP, Eng., 1963; FFRRCS, RCS, Eng., 1966; FRCR, RCR, Eng., 1975. House phys. Sheffield Royal Inf., 1959-60, house surgeon, 1960, sr. house officer, 1960, sr. house officer radiology, 1960-61, registrar, 1961-63; sr. registrar Leicester Inf., 1963-65, Sheffield Inf., 1965-66; cons. radiologist Barnsley, 1966—; BSI coord. BIR/RCR, 1990—; mem. numerous health coms. of BSI, others. Contbr. articles to profl. jours. Recipient Boots Drummond Meml. prize Sheffield U., 1958, BIR Travel scholarship, Scandinavia, 1964. Fellow Inst. Diagnostic Engring., Brit. Inst. Radiology (sec. No. Eng. br. 1980-85, pres. 1985-90, Disting. Svc. medal 1995), Sheffield U. Assn. (pres. 1989-90). Avocations: reading, writing. E-mail: tim.healey@virgin.net. Home: Northfield, Salisbury St, Barnsley S Yorkshire S75 2TL, England

HEALY, JAMES CASEY, lawyer; b. Washington, Feb. 19, 1956; s. Joseph Francis Jr. and Patricia Ann (Casey) H.; m. Kelly Anne Quinn, Nov. 4, 1995; 1 child, Caitlin Quinn. BS, Spring Hill Coll., 1978; JD, Emory U., 1982. Bar: Ga. 1983, Conn. 1983, U.S. Dist. Ct. Conn. 1984, U.S. Tax Ct. 1984, U.S. Supreme Ct. 1987. Assoc. Gregory and Adams PC, Wilton, Conn., 1982-87, ptnr., 1988-89, mng. ptnr., 1990-94; v.p. Gregory and Adams PC, Wilton, 1995—; spl. counsel Wilton Police Commn., 1986-98; mem. Parks and Recreation Commn., 1991—, sec., 1991-93, chmn., 1997—; corporator Ridgefield Bank, 1997—. Bd. dirs. Mark Lavin Meml. Offshore Med. and Safety Found., Empire, Mich., 1987-97, Village Market Inc., 1988-90; chmn. leadership giving program United Way, 1991; bd. mgrs. Wilton Childrens. Ctr., 1996-98; mem. athletic fields subcom. of bldg. com. Wilton H.S., 1998-99; mem. steering com. Wilton Family Recreation and Activity Ctr., 2000—; active various charity and athletic orgns. Mem. ABA, State Bar Ga., State Bar Conn. (exec. com., planning and zoning sect. 1992-94, 98—), Am. Planning Assn., Stamford/Norwalk Regional Bar Assn. (law office mgmt. com. 1994-96, co-chmn. land use com. 1996—, real estate broker's contract com. 1997-98), Wilton C. of C. (bd. dirs. 1994-96), Silver Spring Country Club. Republican. Roman Catholic. E-mail: jhealy@gregoryandadams.com. Office: Gregory and Adams 190 Old Ridgefield Rd Wilton CT 06897-4023

HEALY, JOANNE P., accounting educator; b. Corning, N.Y., Sept. 8, 1949; d. Clayton Arthur and Beverly Jean Palmer; children: Samuel A., Clayton J., Joseph A. BA in Math., SUNY, Geneseo, 1971; PhD, SUNY, Buffalo, 1994; MBA, Rochester Inst. Tech., 1980. CPA, N.Y.; CMA; CFP. Payroll supr. Voplex Corp., Pittsford, N.Y., 1972-74; acct. Davenport Machine Tool divsn. Dover Corp., Rochester, N.Y., 1974-78; staff acct. Bonadio, Insero & Co., Rochester, 1979-80; asst. prof. SUNY, Geneseo, 1982-87, 91-93; tchg. asst. SUNY, Buffalo, 1987-91; asst. prof. Kent (Ohio) State U., 1993—. Contbr. articles to profl. jours. Mem. AICPA, Am. Acctg. Assn., Inst. Mgmt. Accts. (dir. manuscripts 1984-85, 94-98, v.p. adminstrn. and fin. 1996-98), Ohio Soc. CPAs. Avocations: sewing, fishing. E-mail: jhealy@bsa3.kent.edu. Office: Dept Acctg Kent State Univ Kent OH

HEALY, JOSEPH FRANCIS, JR., lawyer, arbitrator, retired airline executive; b. N.Y.C., Aug. 11, 1930; s. Joseph Francis and Agnes (Kett) H.; m. Patricia A. Casey, Apr. 23, 1955; children: James C., Timothy, Kevin, Cathleen M., Mary, Terence. BS, Fordham U., 1952; JD, Georgetown U., 1959. Bar: D.C. 1959. With gen. traffic dept. Eastman-Kodak Co., Rochester, N.Y., 1954-55; air transp. examiner CAB, Washington, 1955-59; practiced in Washington, 1959-70, 80-81; asst. gen. counsel Air Transport Assn. Am., 1966-70; v.p. legal Eastern Air Lines, Inc., N.Y.C. and Miami, Fla., 1970-80; ptnr. Ford, Farquhar, Kornblut & O'Neill, Washington, 1980-81; v.p. legal affairs Piedmont Aviation, Inc., Winston Salem, N.C., 1981-84, sr. v.p., gen counsel, 1984-89, ret., 1989; sr. v.p., gen. counsel Trans World Airlines Inc., Mt. Kisco, N.Y., 1993-94. Mem. bd. visitors Sch. Law Wake Forest U., 1988-96. 1st lt. USAF, 1952-54. Mem. FBA, Am. Arbitration Assn. (mem. nat. panel arbitrators 1989—), Nat. Aero. Assn., Internat. Aviation Club (Washington), Univ. Club (Washington), Beta Gamma Sigma, Phi Delta Phi. Home: 104 Overlink Ct Lynchburg VA 24503-3200

HEALY, MICHAEL PATRICK, lawyer; b. Sioux Falls, S.D., Apr. 27, 1962; s. Patrick Joseph and Carolyn Cathrine (Billion) H.; m. Sarah E. Recker, Dec. 30, 1989 (div. Nov. 19, 1992); m. Sonya R. Dollar, Sept. 27, 1997. Bar: Mo. 1987, Kans. 1989, U.S. Dist. Ct. (we. dist.) Mo. 1987, U.S. Ct. Appeals (8th cir.), U.S. Ct. Appeals (10th cir.), U.S. Dist. Ct. Kans. 1989, U.S. Supreme Ct. 1995. Assoc. Stites McIntosh Knepper & Hopkins, Kansas City, Mo., 1987-94; ptnr. McIntosh Knepper Hobson & Healy, Kansas City, 1994-2000; gen. coun., bd. dirs. D.M.I., Inc., Sioux Falls, 1994—; mem. The Healy Law Firm, LLC, 2000—; v.p., gen. counsel J.L. Healy Constrn. Co., Sioux Falls, 1993-95. Mem. Am. Trial Lawyers Assn., Mo. Assn. Trial Lawyers, Mo. Bar Assn. Republican. Methodist. Office: The Healy Law Firm LLC 1201 Walnut St #2200 Kansas City MO 64106-2506

HEALY, NICHOLAS JOSEPH, lawyer, educator; b. N.Y.C., Jan. 4, 1910; s. Nicholas Joseph and Frances Cecilia (McCarthy) H.; m. Margaret Marie Ferry, Mar. 29, 1937; children: Nicholas, Margaret Healy Parker, Rosemary Healy Bell, Mary Louise Healy White, Donall, Kathleen Healy Hamon. AB, Holy Cross Coll., 1931; JD, Harvard U., 1934. Bar: N.Y. 1935, U.S. Supreme Ct. 1949. Pvt. practice N.Y.C., 1935-42, 48—; mem. Healy & Baillie (and predecessor law firms), 1948—; spl. asst. to atty. gen. U.S., 1945-48; tchr. admiralty law NYU Sch. Law, 1947-86, adj. prof., 1960—; Niels F. Johnsen vis. prof. maritime law Tulane Maritime Law Ctr., 1986; vis. prof. maritime law Shanghai Maritime Inst. (now Shanghai Maritime U.), 1981, 86, 88. Contbr. chpts. on admiralty to Ann. Survey Am. Law, 1948-87; author: (with Sprague) Cases on Admiralty, 1950, (with Currie) Cases and Materials on Admiralty, 1965, (with Sharpe) Cases and Materials on Admiralty, 1974, 3rd edit., 1998, (with Sweeney) The Law of Marine Collision, 1998; editor: Jour. Maritime Law and Commerce, 1980-90, mem. bd. editors, 1969-79, 91—; assoc. editor: American Maritime Cases; mem. scientific bd. Il Diritto Marittimo; contbr. to Ency. Brit. Chmn. USCG Adv. Panel on Rules of the Road, 1966-72; mem. permanent adv. bd. Tulane Admiralty Law Inst. Lt. (s.g.) USNR, 1942-45. Fellow Am. Coll. Trial Lawyers; mem. ABA (ho. of dels. 1964-66), N.Y. State Bar Assn., Assn. of Bar of City of N.Y., N.Y. County Lawyers Assn., Maritime Law Assn. U.S. (pres. 1964-66), Assn. Average Adjusters U.S. (chmn. 1959-60), Com. Maritime Internat. (exec. coun. 1972-79, v.p. 1985-91, hon. v.p. 1991—), Ibero-Am. Inst. Maritime Law (hon.). Home: 132 Tullamore Rd Garden City NY 11530-1139 Office: Healy & Baillie 29 Broadway Fl 27 New York NY 10006-3201

HEALY, TOM, stock exchange executive; b. Dublin, Ireland, Feb. 25, 1950; s. Henry and Mary (Reilly) H.; m. Marie O'Grady, Sept. 1, 1979; children: Aoife, Aisling, Fiona, Sean. BA, Trinity Coll., Dublin, 1974. Various mgmt. positions Indsl. Devel. Authority, Ireland, 1975-80; comms. mgr. Irish Trade Bd., 1980-87; chief exec. Irish Stock Exch., Dublin, 1987—. Office: The Irish Stock Exchange, 24-28 Anglesea St, Dublin Ireland*

HEANEY, SEAMUS JUSTIN, poet, educator; b. Mossbawn, County Derry, No. Ireland, Apr. 13, 1939; s. Patrick and Margaret H.; m. Marie Devlin, 1965; children: Michael, Christopher, Catherine. B.A., Queen's U., Belfast, 1961; postgrad., St. Joseph's Coll., Belfast, 1961-62; Ph.D. (hon.), Queen's U., Belfast. Tchr. St. Thomas's Secondary Sch., Belfast, No. Ireland, 1962-63; lectr. St. Joseph's Coll. Edn., Belfast, 1963-66, Queen's U., Belfast, 1966-72; free-lance writer, 1972-75; lectr. Carysfort Coll., 1975-81; Boylston visiting prof. rhetoric and oratory Harvard U., 1982—; prof. poetry Oxford U., 1989-94. Author: Eleven Poems, 1965, Door into the Dark, 1969, Death of a Naturalist, 1966 (Somerset Maugham award 1967, Cholmondeley award 1968), Wintering Out, 1972, North, 1975 (W.H. Smith award, Duff Copper prize), Stations, 1975, Bog Poems, 1975, Field Work, 1979, Poems: 1965-75, 1980, Preoccupations: Selected Prose 1968-78, 1980, Sweeney Astray: A Version from the Irish, 1984, Station Island, 1984, The Haw Lantern, 1987 (Whitbead award), The Government of the Tongue, 1988, The Place of Writing, 1990, New Selected Poems, 1966-78, 1990, (play) The Cure at Troy (A Version of Sophocles' Philoctetes), 1991, Seeing Things, 1991, (Oxford lectures) The Redress of Poetry, 1995, The Spint Level, 1996; ed. poetry anthologies. Recipient Eric Gregory award, 1966, Faber Meml. prize, 1968, Irish Acad. Letters award, 1971, Denis Devlin Meml. award, 1973, Am.-Irish Found. award, 1975, E.M.Forster award Nat. Inst. Arts and Letters, 1975, Bennett Award, 1982, Premio Mondello (Internat. Poetry prize) Mondello Found., Palermo, Sicily, 1993, Nobel Prize for Literature, 1995. Mem. Royal Dublin Soc. (hon. life), Am. Acad. Arts and Letters (fgn. hon.), Am. Acad. Arts and Scis. (hon. life), Irish Acad. Letters. Office: Harvard U Dept English Cambridge MA 02138*

HEANUE, ANNE ALLEN, retired librarian; b. Ft. Oglethorpe, Ga., Feb. 7, 1940; d. James Edward and Mary (Dennean) Allen; m. Kevin E. Heanue, July 20, 1963; children: Mary, Brian, Patricia. BA cum laude, Dunbarton Coll., 1962; MA, Georgetown U., 1966; MS in Libr. Sci., Cath. U. Am., 1976. Libr. Deloitte Haskins and Sells, Washington, 1977-79; asst. to dir. Am. Libr. Assn., Washington, 1979-81, asst. dir., 1981-84, assoc. dir., 1984-98; ret., 1998. Bd. dirs. Alexandria (Va.) LWV, 1967-78; chmn. Alexandria Spl. Edn. adv. com., 1978-79; mem. Alexandria Gypsy Moth Control Commn., 1991-96. Recipient Fed. Librs. Round Table Achievement award, 1988. Mem. ALA, Hist. Soc. Washington, D.C., Va. Hist. Soc., Rappahannock Hist. Soc., D.C. Libr. Assn. (bd. dirs. 1994-97), Beta Phi Mu, Pi Gamma Mu. Roman Catholic. Avocations: reading, traveling, theater.

HEAP, SIR PETER (WILLIAM), consultant, retired diplomat; b. Dunchurch, Eng., Apr. 13, 1935; s. Roger and Dora (Hosier) H.; m. Ann Lind Johnson, Sept. 18, 1986; children: Alan, Derek (dec.), Angela, Jane; stepchildren: Christopher, Sabrina. BA in Politics, Philosophy and Econs., Oxford (Eng.) U., 1959; MA, Merton Coll., Oxford. With Brit. Embassy, Dublin, Ireland, 1959-60; with Brit. High Commn., Ottawa, Can., 1960-63, Colombo, Sri Lanka, 1963-66; with Ministry of Def., London, 1966-68, Fgn. Office, London, 1968-71; dep. dir. gen. Brit. Info. Svcs., N.Y.C., 1971-76; with Brit. Embassy, Caracas, Venezuela, 1976-80; head energy, sci. and space dept. Fgn. Office, London, 1980-83, Brit. High Commr., Nassau, The Bahamas, 1983-86; minister Brit. High Commn., Lagos, Nigeria, 1986-89; sr. trade commr. Hong Kong, 1989-92; Brit. amb. to Brazil, 1992-95; adviser to bd. HSBC Investment Bank Ltd., London, 1995-98; non-exec. dir. D.S. Wolf Internat., 1998-99; cons. Amerada Hess Ltd.; adviser to bd. BOC Group; chmn. Britain/Brazil Trade Adv. Forum; mem. internat. com. Confedn. Brit. Industries. 2d lt. Brit. Army, 1954-56. Mem. Brazilian C. of C. in Great Britain (chmn. 1995—), Reform Club London.

HEAP, SYLVIA STUBER, civic worker; b. Clifton Springs, N.Y., Sept. 25, 1929; d. Stanley Irving and Helen (Hill) Stuber; m. Walker Ratcliffe Heap, June 9, 1951; children: Heidi Anne, Cynthia Joan, Walker Ratcliffe III. BA cum laude, Bates Coll., 1950; postgrad., U. Conn. Sch. Social Work, 1952-54, Boston U. Sch. Social Work, 1953-54, SUNY, Brockport, 1979, SUNY, Potsdam, 1980; MS in Adult Edn., Syracuse U., 1989. Dir. Y-Teens YWCA, Holyoke, Mass., 1950-51; social group worker West Haven (Conn.) Cmty. House, 1951-54; program dir. YWCA, Ann Arbor, 1954-55, part-time, 1955-59; mem. adv. bd. divsn. continuing edn. Jefferson C.C., 1965—, chmn. adv. bd., 1968-98; pres. Jefferson County Med. Soc. Aux., 1971-72; bd. dirs. St. Lawrence Valley Ednl. TV, 1973-83, sec., 1976-80, treas., 1980-82; v.p., 1982-83, dir. Chem. People Project, 1983; bd. dirs. Watertown Lyric Theatre, 1973-83; bd. dirs. N.Y. State Med. Soc. Aux., 1974-85, 2d v.p. bd., 1979-80; fitness instr. Jefferson Community Coll., Watertown, 1977-86; chmn. health projects N.Y. State Med. Soc. Aux., 1981-85. Named Citizen of Yr., Greater Watertown C. of C., 1975, Friend of C.C., N.Y. State Bd. Trustees, 1988. Mem. AAUW, Bates Key, Alliance with the Jefferson County Med. Soc., Phi Beta Kappa. Unitarian Universalist (UN office envoy 1978—, St. Lawrence dist. envoy 1992—).

HEARD, RONALD ROY, motion picture producer; b. Denver, Oct. 3, 1947; s. John Arthur and Louise Marie (Smith) H.; m. Kim Widing Aug. 12, 1967 (div. 1969). BS, Colo. State U., 1969; postgrad., U. Colo., 1969-72, U. Paris/Sorbonne, 1964-65. Prodn. design/stage mgr. The Rolling Stones, London, 1969-99; property/set dresser Universal Studios, Universal City, Calif., 1978-79, Warner Bros. Studios, Burbank, Calif., 1979-80; producer stage plays Hollywood, 1980-85; music video cons. L.A., 1984—; corres. CBS Network News, Chgo., 1971-72; writer/photographer UPI/Nat. Geographic/Denver Post, 1969-73; ptnr. Silver Screen Ptnrs. II and III, L.A., 1986—; CEO, pres. Radio Safari, 1991—; pres. Brightstar Entertainment dba Liberty Tree Studios, 1994—; owner Yankee Pride Ent., North Hollywood, Calif., 1986—, LAPD Police Cmty. rep. 1995-95, LAPD Citizen Tagger Task Force, 1995. Exec. com. Dem. Party, Larimer County, Colo., 1972-79; Dem. candidate for Ho. of Rep., 1972, 76. Named honorary citizen of S.D. by Gov. Richard Kneip, 1972. Mem. Am. Film Inst., Smithsonian Instn., Statue of Liberty/Ellis Island Cen. Commn., Rock and Roll Hall of Fame (founding mem.). Democrat.

HEARN, CHARLES LEE, petroleum reservoir engineer; b. Nashville, May 22, 1935; s. Charles Aubrey and Florence Rebecca (Conner) H.; m. Lerma Loula Engberg, July 21, 1962; children: Robert Aubrey, Lerma Rebecca. B in Engring., Vanderbilt U., 1957; PhDChemE, Rice U., 1963. Registered profl. engr., Okla. Rsch. engr. Cities Svc. Oil Co., Tulsa, 1963-67, rsch. mgr., 1967-73, chief reservoir engr., 1973-81, engring. cons., 1981-85; tech. coord. Occidental de Colombia, Bogota, 1985-88; sr. engring. cons. Occidental Petroleum, Bakersfield, Calif., 1988-95; sr. staff engr. Occidental of Qatar, Doha, 1995-97, ret., 1997; petroleum reservoir engring. cons., 1997—. Contbr. more than 15 articles to profl. jours. Patentee in field. Mem. Soc. Petroleum Engrs. Achievements include contributions to petroleum reservoir description and numerical reservoir simulation.

HEARN, JOHN PATRICK, biologist, educator; b. Limbdi, India, Feb. 24, 1943; s. Hugh Patrick and Cynthia Ellen (Nicholson) H.; m. Margaret Ruth McNair, Sept. 30, 1967; children: Shaun, Karina, Bruce, Adrian, Nicholas. BS, Univ. Coll., Dublin, Ireland, 1966, MSc, 1968; PhD, Australian Nat. U., Canberra, 1972. Lectr. in zoology Strathmore Coll., Nairobi, Kenya, 1967-69, head biology dept., dean sci., 1968-69; rsch. scholar zoology dept. Australian Nat. U., 1969-72; scientist med. rsch. coun. reproductive biology unit U. Edinburgh, Scotland, 1972-79; prof. in reproductive biology Univ. Coll., London, 1979-95; dir. Wellcome Labs. of Comparative Physiology, Inst. Zoology Zool. Soc. London, 1979-80, dir. sci., 1980-87; prof. dept. physiology Med. Sch. U. Wis., Madison, 1990-96; dir. Wis. Regional Primate Rsch. Ctr., 1990-96; prof., sr. cons. scientist WHO, Geneva, Switzerland, 1997—; dir., research school of bio. science Australian Nat. Univ., Canberra, Australia; cons. scientist WHO, Geneva, 1978-79; mem. coun. NIH Nat. Ctr. Rsch. Resources, 1995—, NAS Inst. for Lab. Animal Resources, 1991—; mem. tech. adv. com. Contraceptive Devel. Orgn., 1990—. Author, editor: Reproduction in New World Primates, 1983, Advances in Animal Conservation, 1985, Reproduction and Disease in Captive and Wild Animals, 1988, Conservation of Primates Studies in Biomedical Research, 1995. Recipient Bolliger award Australian Mammal Soc., 1972; fellow Inst. Biology, 1980. Fellow Zool. Soc. London (sci. medal 1983); mem. Am. Soc. Primatology, Soc. for Study of Reproduction, Soc. for Study of Fertility, Primate Soc. Gt. Britain (Osman-Hill medal 1986), Internat. Primatol. Soc. (pres. 1984-88). Avocations: gymnasium, running, conservation. Office: The Research School of Biological Sciences, The Australian National University, GP0475 Canberra City ACT 2601, Australia*

HEARNE, GEORGE ARCHER, academic administrator; b. Tampa, Fla., Oct. 31, 1934; s. William Duncan and Marguerite Estelle (Archer) H.; m. Jean May Helmstadter, June 9, 1956; children: Diana Leslie, George Harrison. BA, Bethany Coll., 1955; MDiv, Yale U., 1958; MA, Ill. State U., 1968; HHD (hon.), Culver-Stockton Coll., 1986; LLD, Bethany Coll., 1997. Min. Arlington Christian Ch., Jacksonville, Fla., 1958-59; dir. admissions Eureka (Ill.) Coll., 1960-70, v.p. student devel., 1970-73, dean admissions and student devel., 1973-77, dean admissions and coll. rels., 1977-82, v.p. coll. rels., 1982-84, exec. v.p., 1984-85, pres., 1985—. Bd. dirs. Christian Ch., Ill., Wis. and Ind., 1985—, Higher Edn. divsn. Christian Ch., St. Louis, 1985—; pres. Eureka Bd. Edn., 1967-76; active various cmty. drives. Mem. Assoc. Colls. Ill. (bd. dirs. 1985—), Fedn. Ill. Ind. Colls. and Univs. (bd. dirs. 1985—), Coun. for Advancement and Support of Edn., Coun. Ind. Colls., Coun. of Pres. (higher edn. div.). Lodge: Rotary. Avocations: reading, music, antiques, golf. Office: Eureka Coll 300 E College Ave Eureka IL 61530-1562

HEARNE, JOHN Q., media and telecommunications executive; b. San Francisco, June 10, 1948; s. John P. and Genevieve (Carolan) H.; m. Elizabeth Michaels, 1977; children: Jennifer, Brendan, Megan. BA in Math. summa cum laude, UCLA, 1970; JD, Stanford U., 1973. Bar: Calif. 1974, D.C. 1977. Assoc. Fisher, Wayland, Cooper & Leader, Washington, 1977-82, ptnr., 1983-89, of counsel, 1990-98; chmn., CEO Point Telesys., Inc. (formerly Point Comms. Co.), 1988—; chmn., pres. Point Broadcasting Co., 1994—; chmn. Gold Coast Broadcasting Co., 1994—, High Desert Broadcasting Co., 1996—, CyberFirst, Inc., 1997—, Expedite.com. LLC, 2000—, ExpediteMedia.com LLC, 2000—; chmn., pres. Point BTA cos., 1998—, Point Capital Group, 1999—; bd. dirs. SpinWare, Inc., STPCS, Inc. Mem. bd. visitors Stanford Law Sch., 1998—. Woodrow Wilson Nat. fellow, 1970. Mem. Fed. Comm. Bar Assn. (chmn. common carrier practice com. 1984-87, chmn. access com. 1987-88), Cellular Telecomm. Industries Assn. (bd. dirs. 1990-94), Surfrider Found., U.S. Surfing Fedn., Nat. Scholastic Surfing Assn., Malibu Surfing Assn., Rotary (chmn. environ. com. 1994-95), Phi Beta Kappa. Office: 715 Broadway Ste 320 Santa Monica CA 90401-2640

HEARTT, CHARLOTTE BEEBE, university official; b. N.Y.C., Nov. 12, 1933; d. Stacey Kile and Charlotte Beebe; m. William Hollis Peirce, 1954 (div. 1960); children: Daniel Converse, William Kile; m. Stephen Heartt, 1962 (div. 1968); children: Thomas Beebe, Sarah Lincoln. BA, Wellesley Coll., 1954. Intern Office of V.p. Richard Nixon, Washington, 1953; asst. Computing Numerical Analysis Lab. U. Wis., Madison, 1954-56; dir. fund raising Boston Arts Festival, 1961; asst. to dean coll. rels. Radcliffe Coll., Cambridge, Mass., 1961-62; sec. to chmn. dept. city planning Harvard U., Cambridge, 1962; Fulbright program adviser, study abroad adviser Brandeis U., 1966-71, dir. office internat. programs, 1971-76, dir. found. and corp. rels., 1976-79; dir. corp. rels., asst. dir. devel. Smith Coll., Northampton, Mass., 1979-81; dir. devel. Smith Coll., Northampton, 1981-95, dir. prin. gifts, 1995-98; ind. cons., 1999—. Mem. Commonwealth Task Force on the Open Univ., 1973; bd. dirs. Coun. on Internat. Ednl. Exch., 1973-77, mem. exec. com., 1975-77; bd. dirs. Boston Area Seminar for Internat. Students, 1973-76; mem. adv. com. New England Colls. Fund, 1981-95; trustee Berkshire Sch., 1989-98, trustee emerita, 1999—; bd. dirs. Hampshire Cmty. United Way, 1996—; mem. devel. com. Belmont Day Sch., Belmont, Mass. Mem. Sect. on U.S. Study Abroad (nat. sec., regional rep. 1972-74), Nat. Assn. Fgn. Student Affairs (nat. commr. liaison), Nat. Assn. Women Deans, Adminstrs. and Counselors (internat. students and programs com. 1974-76), Nat. Soc. Fund Raisers, Coun. for Advancement and Support Edn. E-mail: heartt@mediaone.net. Home: 11 Carver Rd Wellesley MA 02481-5351

HEATH, BERTHANN JONES, education administrator; b. Dallas, May 4, 1938; d. James Lafayette and Allie Mae (Hudson) Jones; m. John Willie Heath, Jr., July 14, 1963 (div. 1975); 1 child, John William, III. BS cum laude, Pepperdine U., 1959; MS, UCLA, 1960. Nat. cert. family and consumer scientist. Tchr., dept. chair L.A. Unified Sch. Dist., 1960-69, dist. resource tchr., 1972-75; counselor L.A. H.S., 1968-72; regional supr., home econs. edn. L.A. Regional Office, Calif. State Dept. Edn., 1975-85; program mgr., sch.-to-career transition San Diego City Schs., 1985—; trustee Consumer Credit Counselors of San Diego and Imperial Counties, Calif., 19865; mem. adv. com. Calif. State Dept. Edn. Home Econs. and Health Careers, Sacramento, 1985-98; mem. articulation team SDUSD and San Diego C.C.s, 19875. Author, contbr. to curriculum guides, pamphlets and leaflets. V.p. San Diego chpt. The Links, Inc., 1995-97; presenter TV-8 Looks at Learning and Inside San Diego, 1985-95. Recipient Appreciation/Commendation award Calif. Dept. Edn., 1987, Nat. Gourmet Cook award Nat. Assembly, Links, Inc., 1996, Fin. Literacy Program Svc. award Consumer Credit Counselors of San Diego and Imperial Counties, 1996, Am. Assn. Family and Consumer Scis. Nat. Leader of Yr. award, 1998; named Woman of Distinction, Women, Inc., 1999. Mem. Am. Vocat. Assn. (bylaws chair family and consumer scis. edn. divsn. 1993-97), Nat. Assn. Local Suprs. of Family and Consumer Scis. (pres. 1992-93), Am. Vocat. Assn. (mem. policy and planning com. 1991-97), Calif. Assn. Family and Consumer Scis. (mem. San Diego chpt., chair secondary edn. 1985-95, state chair edn. com. 1989-90, ex-officio mem. articulation com. 1989-96), So. Calif. Biotech. Consortium (charter 1994-96), Alpha Rho Tau, Delta Sigma Theta, Kappa Omicron Nu, Phi Delta Kappa. Avocations: food design and recipe experimentation, writing, elder care research and development. Office: San Diego Unified Sch Dist Revere Ctr 6735 Gifford Way San Diego CA 92111-6509

HEATH, DONALD WAYNE, securities wholesale executive, financial planner; b. Wendover, Utah, July 2, 1942; s. Earl Charles and Violet (Susich) H.; m. Barbara Lyn Beesley, Aug. 11, 1963 (div. Nov. 1979); children: Jeffrey Earl, Christian Edward, Jill Elena; m. Laurie Jean Lichter, Feb. 28, 1981; children: Michele Samuel, Adam Ryan, Jason Charles. BBA, U. Nev., 1964, postgrad., 1980-81. CLU, chartered fin. cons. Agt., tng. supr., sales mgr. N.Y. Life Ins. Co., Reno, 1969-79; sales mgr. N.Y. Life Ins. Co., Stockton, Calif., 1981-83; commr. of ins. State of Nev., Carson City, 1979-81; field v.p. Integrated Resources, N.Y., 1983-84; securities wholesaler Angeles Corp., L.A., 1984-85; v.p. sales Ins. Office of Am., El Torro, Calif., 1985-87; regional v.p. Capstone Fin. Svcs., Inc., Houston, 1987-88; regional mktg. dir. Ameritas Variable Life Ins. Co., Lincoln, Nebr., 1988—; estate planning and bus. ins. specialist Merrill Lynch Life Agy., Inc., San Diego, 1992—; pres. Heath Fin. Dynamics Corp., Stockton, 1985-92; instr. U. Nev., 1974-80, U. of the Pacific Sch. of Bus. and Pub. Adminstrn., 1986-87. Recipient Paul Hammel Meml. Trophy Nev. Assn. Life Underwriters, 1972; fellow Life Underwriter Tng. Coun. Mem. Internat. Assn. Fin. Planning, Nat. Assn. Security Dealers, Nat. Assn. Ins. Commrs. (chmn. 1979-81, western zone exec. com. 1979-81), Am. Soc. CLU's and Charter Fin. Cons. (Stockton chpt., exec. com. 1979-81), U. Nev. Alumni Assn. (pres. 1976), No. Nev. Assn. Life Underwriters (pres. 1975), Calif. Assn. of Life Underwriters (chmn. ethics com. 1987-88), Masons, Mornging Star, Shriners, Passé Club, Million Dollar Round Table. Avocations: fishing, traveling. Home: 18252 Smokesignal Dr San Diego CA 92127-3123

HEATH, ERNIE THOMAS, tourism management educator; b. Fort Beaufort, Cape Province, South Africa, Jan. 22, 1952; s. Willem Adries and Vera Magdalene (Moss) H.; m. Elize Steyn, Dec. 3, 1977; children: Johan, Eric, Erwil. BCom, U. Stellenbosch, 1975, BCom with honors, 1977; MCom with honors, U. Fort Hare, Alice, 1981; DCom, U. Port Elizabeth, 1987. Bus. econs. lectr. U. Fort Hare, 1977-83; sr. lectr. U. Port Elizabeth, 1983-89, chief rschr. Inst. for Planning Rsch., 1988-89, prof., dir., 1990; chief dir., dep. exec. dir. South African Tourism Bd., 1990-95; prof., head dept. tourism mgmt. U. Pretoria, 1996—, dir. Ctr. for Afrikatourism, 1999—; mem. tech. rev. team WTTC, 1998; presenter in field. Author: (with others) Tourism Destination Marketing: A Strategic Planning Approach, 1992, Managing Tourism Services, 1994; contbr. more than 60 articles to profl. publs. Founding trustee Open Africa Initiative, Cape Town, 1983. Fellow Inst. for Mktg. Mgmt. (hon. v.p. 1999); mem. Indian Ocean Tourism Orgn. (specialist strategic advisor 1999—, exec. bd. dirs. 1994-99, Chmn.'s Merit award 1999), Tourism Soc. Britain, Travel and Tourism Rsch. Assn. Avocations: cycling, hiking, golfing. Office: U Pretoria, Duxburry Rd/Dept Tour Mgmt, 0002 Pretoria Gauteng, South Africa

HEATH, MARIWYN DWYER, writer, legislative issues consultant; b. Chgo., May 1, 1935; d. Thomas Leo and Winifred (Brennan) Dwyer; m. Eugene R. Heath, Sept. 3, 1956; chilren: Philip Clayton, Jeffrey Thomas. BJ, U. Mo., 1956. Mng. editor Chemung Valley Reporter, Horseheads, N.Y., 1956-57; freelance writer, platform spkr., editor Tech. Transls., Dayton, Ohio, 1966—; cons. Internat. Women's Commn., 1975-76; ERA coord. Nat. Fedn. Bus. and Profl. Women's Clubs, 1974-82, 92—; polit. and mgmt. coms. ERAmerica, 1976-82, exec. dir., 1982-88; pres. Miami Valley Regional Transit Authority, 1986-88; chair Regional Transit Coalition, 1991-94. Author: 75 Years and Beyond-BPW/USA, 1994. Active Gov. Ohio Task Force Credit for Women, 1973, Ohio Womens Commn., 1990-98, vice-chair, 1993-96, chair, 1996-98; midwest regional adv. com. SBA, 1976-82; task force Women Ohio Bicentennial Commn., 1999—; pres. Dayton Pres. Club, 1973-74; chmn. Ohio Coalition ERA Implementation, 1974-75; appt. joint civilian orientation conf. U.S. Dept. Def., 1988. Recipient Legion of Honor award Dayton Pres. Club, 1987, Keeper of Flame award Ohio Sec. of State, 1990; named one of 10 Outstanding Women of World Soroptimist Internat., 1982; named to Ohio Womens Hall of Fame. Mem. AAUW (dir. Dayton 1965-72, Woman of Yr. award Dayton 1974), Nat. Fedn. Bus. and Profl. Womens Clubs (pres. Dayton 1967-69, Ohio 1976-77, nat. polit. action com. 1985-98, chmn. 1988-98), Miami Valley Mil. Affairs Assn. (bd. dirs.), Ohio Women (v.p. 1983-86, bd. dirs. 1977-89), Assn. Women Execs., Women in Comm. Republican. Roman Catholic. Address: 10 Wisteria Dr Dayton OH 45419-3451

HEATH, RICHARD ALBERT, psychology educator; b. Newcastle, NSW, Australia, Aug. 15, 1946; s. Robert C. and Esther Heath; m. Susan Mary Marjorie Heer, Mar. 29, 1975; 1 child, David. BSc with honors, U. Newcastle, 1970; PhD, McMaster U., Hamilton, Ont., Can., 1976. Lectr. U. Newcastle, 1975-83, sr. lectr., 1984-90, assoc. prof., 1991—. Author: Mathematical and Theoretical Systems: Proceedings in the 24th International Congress of Psychology, 1989. Scholar McMaster U., 1970; Rsch. grantee Australian Rsch. Grants Com., 1978-95, Rsch. grantee Worksafe Australia, 1986. Avocations: bassoon, computing. Fax: 61-2-49216980. Office: U Newcastle Dept Psychology, University Dr, Callaghan NSW 2308, Australia

HEATH-STUBBS, JOHN (FRANCIS ALEXANDER), poet; b. London, July 9, 1918; s. Francis and Edith (Marr) H-S. BA with first class honors, Queen's Coll., Oxford (Eng.) U., 1943, MA, 1972. English master Hall Sch., Hampstead, Eng., 1945; editl. asst. Hutchinson's Illus. Encyclopedia, 1945-46; Gregory fellow in poetry Leeds (Eng.) U., 1953-55; vis. prof. English U. Alexandria, Egypt, 1955-58, U. Mich., Ann Arbor, 1960-61; part-time lectr. in English Coll. St. Mark and St. John, London, until 1973. Writings include: (poetry) Wounded Thammuz, 1942, Beauty and the Beast, 1943, The Divided Ways, 1946, The Swarming of the Bees, 1950, The Triumph of the Muse, 1958, The Blue Fly in His Head, 1962, Selected Poems, 1965 (Arts Coun. Gt. Britain award 1965), Satires & Epigrams, 1968, Artorius, Book One, 1970, (with S. Spender, F.T. Prince) Penguin Modern Poets No. 20, 1972, Four Poems in Measure, 1973, Twelve Labours of Hercules, 1974, Parliament of Birds, 1975, The Watchman's Flute, 1978, The Mouse, The Bird, The Sausage, 1978, Birds Reconvened, 1980, Buzz Buzz, 1981, This Is Your Poem, 1981, Naming the Beats, 1982, The Immolation of Alepi, 1985, Cats Parnassus, 1987, Time Pieces, 1988, Collected Poems, 1988, A Partridge in a Pear Tree, 1988, A Ninefold of Charms, 1989, The Game of Love & Death, 1990, Parson Cat, 1991, Chimeras, 1992, Sweet Apple Earth, 1993, Galileo's Salad, 1996, Torriano Sequences, 1997, The Sound of Light, 1999, (autobiography) Hindsights, 1993; (translations) Poems from Giacomo Leopardi, 1947, Aphrodite's Garland, 1952, (with P. Avery) Hafiz of Shiraz, Thirty Poems, 1955, Selected Prose & Poetry of Giacomo Leopardi, 1966, The Horn (A. V. Vigny), 1969, (with P. Avery) The Ruba'iyat of Omar Khayyam, 1979, Eight Poems of Sulpicia, 2000; (criticism) The Darling Plain, 1950, Charles Williams, 1955, The Ode, 1969, The Verse Satire, 1969, The Pastoral, 1969, Literary Essays, 1998; editor: Selected Poems of Shelley, 1947, Selected Poems of Tennyson, 1947, Selected Poems of Swift, 1947, (with D. Wright) The Forsaken Garden, 1950, Images of Tomorrow, 1953, (with Wright) The Faber Book of 20th Century Verse, 1954, rev. 1965, Selected Poems of Alexander Pope, 1965, Poems of Science, 1984 (P. Salman); author: (autobiography) Hindsights, 1993. Recipient Queen's Gold medal for poetry, 1973, Cross of St. Augustine, 1999, Order of Brit. Empire. Fellow Royal Soc. Lit., Charles Williams Soc. (pres. 1999—). Mem. Ch. of Eng. Home: 22 Artesian Rd, London W2 5AR, England also: David Higham Assocs, 5-8 Lower John St, London W1, England

HEATON, CHARLES HUDDLESTON, retired church musician; b. Centralia, Ill., Nov. 1928; s. Wilbur Estel Heaton and Nina Huddleston; m. Jane Pugh, Apr. 17, 1954 (dec. Sept. 1999); children: Rebecca Lynn Turner, Charles Jr., Matthew Aaron. BMus, DePauw U., 1950; M of Sacred Music, Union Theol. Sem., N.Y.C., 1952, D of Sacred Music, 1957. Min. of music 2d Presbyn. Ch., St. Louis, 1956-72; organ tchr. So. Ill. U., Carbondale, 1962-64; dir. music Temple Israel, St. Louis, 1959-70; lectr. music Pitts. Theol. Sem., 1973-76; organist, dir. East Liberty Presbyn. Ch., Pitts., 1972-93; ret.; interim organist, choirmaster Calvary Epis. Ch., Pitts., 1996-97; organist in residence Trinity Cathedral, Pitts., 1993-96, 97—; cons. organ design various chs. and schs. Author: How to Build a Church Choir, 1958, Worship Services of Sacred Music, 1962. Fellow Am. Guild Organists (nat. councillor 1967-70, regional chmn. 1970-72); mem. Organ Hist. Soc. Avocations: reading, walking. E-mail: charles.h.heaton@gte.net. Home: 5932 Elgin St Pittsburgh PA 15206-1644

HEATON, LARRY CADWALDER, securities company executive; b. St. Louis, Aug. 19, 1934; s. John Raymond and Martha Elizabeth (Simpson) H.; m. Dorothy Mueller, Dec. 10, 1953; children: Tannice Jo, Larry C. II, Kent M., Eric S., Elmo D.J., David J. II. Student, So. Ill. U., 1959; BSBA, U. Tampa, 1962; postgrad., Chgo. Kent Coll. Law, 1962-65. Registered investment advisor. Adjuster N.Y. Ctrl. R.R., Chgo., 1962-65; salesman/sales mgr. SCM Inc., Chgo., 1965-68; agt., gen. agt. Thomas Jefferson Life Ins., Champaign, Ill., 1969-75; gen. agt. Ctrl. Nat. Life Ins., Jacksonville, Ill., 1975-80; pres., co-founder Nurses Guaranteed Retirement Life Ins., Jacksonville, Fla., 1980-85; gen. agt., mgr. Nat. Old Line Ins., Little Rock, 1985-95; pres., owner Larry C. Heaton & Assocs., Jacksonville, Fla., 1996—; chmn. PFL Agts. Adv. Bd., Little Rock, 1992. Co-author state manual: Illinois Young Republicans, 1965 (Nat. Young Republican award). Adminstrv. asst., speech writer Ill. Young Republicans, 1962-68; precinct capt. Cook County Rep. Orgn., Oak Park, Ill., 1965-68; mem. Rep. Presdl. Task Force, Washington, 1982—; mem. House/Senate Adv. Bd., Washington, 1985—. Sgt. U.S. Army, 1953-56. Recipient Bronze plaque Nat. Assn. Life Underwriters, 1973, Nat. Performance award Nat. Assn. Life Underwriters, 1973, Nat. Quality award Nat. Assn. Life Underwriters, 1974, Million Dollar Round Table award Nat. Assn. Life Underwriters, 1970-85. Mem. Inst. CFPs, Internat. Assn. Fin. Planning, Masons (32d degree). Republican. Episcopalian. Avocations: family, golf, painting, sailing. Office: Larry C Heaton & Assocs 287 Edgewater Branch Dr Jacksonville FL 32259-4493

HEATON, THOMAS PETER STARKE, broadcast editor; b. Celle, Germany, Nov. 16, 1928; s. Traugott Heinrich Oskar Starke and Ella Helene Meyerowitz Heaton; m. Pamela June Stevenson, June 1, 1957 (div.); m. Jackie Noble, Dec. 20, 1972; 1 child, Stephen. BA with honors, Sch. Oriental and African Studies, London, 1955, MA with distinction, 1960; postgrad. cert. in edn., Inst. of Edn., London, 1957. Persian monitor BBC Monitoring Svc., Caversham, Eng., 1955-56; edn. officer Brit. Overseas Civil Svc., Aden, South Arabia, 1957-61, vice prin. govt. secondary sch., 1961-64, chief insp. of schs., 1964-66, dep. permanent sec. of Ministry of Supreme Coun. Affairs, 1966-68; h.s. English tchr., dept. head Ministry of Edn., Nairobi, Kenya, 1968-70; Arabic monitor BBC Monitoring Svc., 1970-73, editor Mid. East/African Summary of World Broadcasts, 1973-76, sr. asst. in East African Unit, 1976-81, Arabic monitor, editor East African Unit, 1983—. Author: In Teleki's Footsteps: A Walk Across East Africa, 1990. 2nd lt. Brit. Army, Royal Lincolnshire Regiment, 1948-50.

HEATTER, JOSEPH JOHN, material handler; b. Allentown, Pa., Feb. 20, 1978; s. Herman John and Ruth Marie (Dunkelberger) H. Cert. operation on automatic CAD, Berks Career and Tech. Ctr., Oley, Pa., 1997. Computer

designer Nothstien Car & Truck Ctr., Fleetwood, Pa., 1991-93. Achievements include patent for electrolosis powered engine. Avocations: drwing, creative ideas, inventing.

HEBEBRAND, JOHANNES, psychiatrist, geneticist; b. Erlangen, Germany, Apr. 16, 1957; s. Karl and Agathe (Lexis) H.; m. Kathrin Moeller, Dec. 27, 1983; children: Jan, Lena, Moritz, Franziska. MD, U. Heidelberg (Germany), 1983; Prof. Medicine, U. Marburg (Germany), 1995. Rsch. asst. dept. human genetics U. Bonn (Germany), 1984-89; splst. child and adolescent psychiatry Philipp's U. Marburg (Germany), 1990-95, head clin. rsch. group dept. child and adolescent psychiatry, 1995—; cons. Obesity Treatment Ctr. Insula, Berchtesgaden, Germany, 1996—. Recipient Christina Barz Stiftung award, 1995. Office: Philipp's U Marburg Dept, Child & Adolescent Psychiat, 35033 Marburg Hessia, Germany

HEBERLING, TIMOTHY ALAN, information scientist; b. Portsmouth, Va., Sept. 3, 1955; s. Donald Anthony and Phyllis Elaine (McMillan) H.; m. Judith Ann Tohill, June 13, 1992; children: Ellen, Ben, Hanna. Student, James Madison U., 1973-74; BS in Computer Sci., Va. Tech., 1986. Commd. 2nd lt. USAF, 1986, advanced through grades to capt., 1990; law enforcement specialist USAF, Hampton, Va., 1975-79; entry controller USAF, Chievres, Belgium, 1979-82; security police flight chief USAF, Enid, Okla., 1982-83; comms.-computer officer Air Force Hdqts., Washington, 1987-91; info. systems officer Def. Info. Systems, Reston, Va., 1991-94; sr. systems adminstr. The White House, Washington, 1994-96; ret. USAF, 1995; sr. info. systems engr. Mitretek Systems, McLean, Va., 1996-97; tech. mgr. AOL Internet Svcs., Sterling, Va., 1997—; cons. WebVisor, Leesburg, Va., 1996—. Blood drive coord. Def. Info. System Agy., Reston, 1991-94, United Way vol. Decorated various Air Force medals. Mem. Air Force Security Police Assn. Home: 19553 Herndon Ct Leesburg VA 20175-6759 Office: Am Online Internet Svcs 22080 Pacific Blvd Sterling VA 20166-9304

HEBERT, MICHEL, mathematics educator; b. Longueuil, Que., Can., Oct. 18, 1951; s. Isaac Hebert and Gertrude Jomphe; m. Louise Saint-Laurent, Apr. 6, 1974. BSc in Math., Laval U., Que., 1979, MSc. in Math., 1981, PhD in Math., 1984. Asst. prof. math. U. Zambia, Lusaka, 1984-86; postdoctoral fellow McGill U., Montreal, Que., 1986-88; maitre de conf. U. Scis. and Techs. Masuku, Franceville, Gabon, 1988-90; rschr., adj. prof. math. Laval U., 1990-93; asst. prof. math. Am. U., Cairo, 1993-95, assoc. prof. math., 1995—, math. unit head, 1995-98. Contbr. articles to math. jours. Mem. Am. Math. Soc. Home: 8 Ibrahim Naguib, 1003 Garden City Cairo, Egypt Office: Am U in Cairo Dept Sci/Math, 113 Kasr El-Aini POB 2511, 11511 Cairo Egypt

HEBEY, PIERRE, lawyer; b. Algiers, Algeria, Aug. 7, 1926; s. Jacques Hebey and Odette Hebey-Bensaid; m. Isabelle Marry (div.); 1 child, Emmanuel; m. Geneviève Prim, Nov. 9, 1973. Diplômé d'Etudes Supérieures in Pvt. Law and Econ. Politics, U. Paris. Pvt. practice Paris, 1946—. Author: L'Esprit Nouvelle Revue Francaise: 1908-194, 1981, La Nouvelle Revue Française des Années Sombres, 1992 (Chateaubriand prize), Les Passions Moderees, 1995, Deux amis de toujours, 1997, Alger 1898, 1996, Le Gout de L'inactuel, 1998, Une Seule Femme, 1999, others. Named Comdr. Légion d'Honneur French Dept. Cultural Affairs, Officer Ordre de Mérite French Dept. Justice. Avocations: collecting contemporary and art deco art. Home and Office: 10 Blvd Suchet, 75016 Paris France

HEBLING, JANOS, physicist, educator; b. Zirc, Hungary, May 9, 1954; s. Laszlo and Maria (Soss) H.; m. Dora Takacs, Apr. 23, 1976; children: Eszter, Anna, Dora. D, Attila Jozsef Univ., Szeged, Hungary, 1982; candidate of scis., Hungarian Acad. Scis., Budapest, 1992. Postgrad. rsch. fellow Hungarian Acad. Scis., Szeged, 1978-80; asst. prof. dept. exptl. physics Attila Fozsef, Szeged, 1981-89, asst. prof. dept. optics and quantum electronics, 1989-99; prof. dept. exptl. phys. U. Pecs, 1999—; vis. scientist Max Planck Inst., Stuttgart, Germany, 1988-89, 93-95, 98. Contbr. articles to profl. jours. Mem. Roland Evtvos Phys. Soc. (Pal Selinyi award 1991), N.Y. Acad. Scis. Fax: 36-72-501571. E-mail: hebling@fizika.jpte.hu. Home: Hsbiart basa 6, H-6723 Szeged Hungary Office: U Pecs Dept Exp Phys, Ifjusag u 6, H-7624 Pecs Hungary

HÉBRAUD, MICHEL YVES, microbiologist; b. Romans Sur Isère, France, Oct. 9, 1960; m. Ermelinda De Sousa, Sept. 7, 1985; children: Jérémy, Sophie, Alice. D Biology et Physiologie Vegetales, U. Lyon I, Villeurbanne, France, 1988. Head of rsch. 2d class Nat. Inst. for Rsch. in Agronomy, Clermont-Ferrand, France, 1989-94; head of rsch. 1st class Clermont-Ferrand, France, 1995—. Mem. French Soc. for Microbiology, Am. Soc. for Microbiology, Société Française D'Électrophorèse. Office: Nat Inst Rsch Agronomy, SRV-Microbiologie, 63122 Saint Genes-Champanelle France

HECHAÏMÉ, CAMILLE ISKANDAR, publishing executive; b. Bikfaya, Lebanon, Aug. 1, 1933; s. Iskandar Hechaïmé and Rose Labaki. MA in Philosophy, Jesuit Philosoph Coll., Paris, 1957; MA in Arabic Lit., State U., Lyon, France, 1961, PhD in Arabic Lit., 1966; BA in Theology, Jesuit Theol. Coll., Lyon, 1964. Prof. State U., Aleppo, Syria, 1974-81; vis. prof. St. Joseph U., Beirut, 1987—; mng. dir. Dar al-Machreq Pub., Beirut, 1988—. Author, translator some 25 books on Arab lit., history, edn. and theology; editor Al Machriq Jour., Beirut, 1991—; contbr. articles to profl. jours. Avocations: reading, jogging. Office: Dar el-Machreq, Rue Universite St Joseph, PO Box 166778 Beirut Lebanon

HECHT, ANDREAS, biologist; b. Kempten, Germany, Oct. 31, 1961; s. Josef Anton and Anna (Walburga) H.; m. Ulrike Veronika Lohnert, Sept. 14, 1984; children: Julia, Timm. Degree, U. Heidelberg, 1987, PhD, 1990. Rsch. assoc. Ctr. for Molecular Biology U. Heidelberg, Heidelberg, Germany, 1987-90; post-doctoral rsch. scientist U. Freiburg, Freiburg, Germany, 1990-92, UCLA, 1992-95; sr. scientist Max-Planck Inst. Immunobiology, Freiburg, 1996—; instr. U. Freiburg, 1996—. Contbr. articles to profl. jours. Recipient Fellowship for Gifted Students, State of Bavaria, 1982-85, Fellowship Studienstiftung des Deutschen Volkes, 1986-87, Young Scientist award Soc. for the Promotion of Rsch. in Sci., Heidelberg, 1988, Rsch. Fellowship Deutsche Forschungsgemeinschaft, 1992-94. E-mail: hecht@immunbio.mpg.de. Office: Max Planck Inst Immunobiol, Stuebeweg 51, Freiburg D-79108, Germany

HECHT, DONN, songwriter, screenwriter, agent; b. Pitts., Apr. 18, 1930; s. Matthew J. and Valeria H.; m. Rosana Aguirre Acevedo, Feb. 21, 1975; children: Donn Jr., Beverly. Creative works include: (compositions) Walking After Midnight, Snowbound, Night Train, La Mirada, Cry Not for Me, The Touch of His Hand, The Sermon On The Mount, Rock Bottom, So Dear to My Heart, Never No More, Spring is Gone, Without Your Love, Theme for Billie, I Took the Blues Out of Tomorrow, In the Country, The Battle of Chavez Ravine, Downgrade, I'm Satisfied, Poet's Love Letter, Philosophy, One-By-One, Fingerprints, Who Am I?, Ballad of the M.I.A., Old Candles, I Used to Know Her, No Matter What, Mr. Blue Jay, If I Were Your Pillow, It's Not Enough, Nothing But Love, Half Past Midnight, The Theme from the Raisin Tree, Once Upon a Star, Save a Place in Your Heart for Me, I Was Only Teasing You, Who Knows, As Long As I Have You, I Never Got Over You, More and More and More, I'll Still Be in Love with You, All Those Teardrops, I've Cried, Until, With Love Everything Will be Right, It's Funny What Love Can Do, Because I Just Can't Take It, That's What Love Means to Me, I Don't Want No Heartaches, It All Depends on You, Pills, Pills, Pills, Why Are You Leaving Me, Well That's Love, Day By Day, Zombie Woman, One Short of Living, Together, Too Much Month for the Money Blues, Sho Ya' Right, Misery, (recs.) The Patsy Cline Story, 1977, I Remember Patsy, 1978, All My Best, 1979, Unstoppable, 1982, Come Down from the Hills, 1984, The Trinity Session, 1989, The Chase, Garth Brooks, 1992-94 (No. 1 Best Seller Billboard Top Country Albums Chart), Greatest Hits (Patsy Cline), 1992-93 (No. 1 Best Seller Billboard Top Country Catalogue Albums), (motion picture soundtracks) Coalminer's Daughter, 1980, Sweet Dreams, 1986, (TV series) Wise Guy, 1989-99, Diamonds and Chicken Soup, Clear and Present Danger, Your Ring is Off My Finger (but Still Around My Heart), (song) Hawaii Five-O, Alice in Wonderland, Millenuim II, The Pretenders, Women O the Night, Theme for Celine Dion, Theme for Holiday in Spain, Hello Bed, I Guess I'll Just Be Moving On, Looking for Mr. Right; Debut album box set Prodrs. Showcase, Platinum 2000 series with co-writer Sylvia Sue Blackard: Beyond This Time and Day, Love Everlasting (And True), Take a Chance On Me, At Last I Belong, Here Comes Fun and Games, The Mystery of Love, How Did We Get Here, Heart Whispers, Desert Heart, Candle of Love, Vision of Dreams, She Has My Heart and the Key, Your First Love Will Be My Last, On the Wings of Love, Love Keeps on Singing, Two Hearts-One Love, Sweet September, She Is My Texas Star, Destiny, Sunset in Santa Fe, I Can't Get Over You ('Till I'm Out From Under Him), Let's Drink to What If, Your Heart Was Home to Me, Letter to My Heart, Pages of the Past, Light in the Window, Soulmate; contbr. articles to profl. jours. Recipient Billboard Gold Medallion (three-time recipient, two top ten, one #1), 2000, Broadcast Music Inc. Spl. Citation of Achievement award, 2000. Achievements include having a collective career sales of approximately 21 million. Address: ASCAP Bldg One Lincoln Plaza New York NY 10023

HECK, DEBRA UPCHURCH, information technology, procurement professional; b. Valparaiso, Fla., Nov. 4, 1956; d. Robert P. and Sallaine S. (Sledge) Upchurch; m. Robert J. Heck, May 31, 1980; children: Andrew W., Jennifer A. BS in Math., Purdue U., 1978, MS in Mgmt., 1980. Analyst mgmt. sci. Monsanto Corp. Mgmt. Sci., St. Louis, 1980-81; sys. analyst Monsanto Agr. Group, St. Louis, 1981-82, sr. sys. analyst, 1982-84; sr. analyst mgmt. sci. Monsanto Polymer Products Group, St. Louis, 1984-86; project total quality fundamentals instr. Monsanto Co., St. Louis, 1985-86; project mgr. Monsanto Chem. Co., St. Louis, 1986-88; group leader Monsanto Corp. MIS, St. Louis, 1988-92, sr. group leader, 1992-95; info. tech. dir. Monsanto Bus. Svcs.-Fin., St. Louis, 1995-96; info. tech. dir. Monsanto Bus. Svcs.-Fin. & Procurement, St. Louis, 1996, dir. strategic sourcing, procurement strategic initiatives, 1997-2000, pharmacia exec. dir. non-supply procurement, 2000—. Trustee, chair fall gathering, doubles, social com. Ethical Soc., St. Louis, 1982—; mem. sci. adv. com., PTO bd. Parkway Sch. Dist., St. Louis, 1992—; vol. St. Louis Assn. for Retarded Citizens, 1978-85. Mem. Nat. Assn. Purchasing Mgmt., Human Resource Sys. Profls., Leadership Am. Alumni (award 1994). Avocations: travel, sports, friends, family. Office: Monsanto Co 800 N Lindbergh Blvd Saint Louis MO 63167-0001

HECK, JOHN KEVIN, construction manager; b. Houston, Oct. 8, 1957; s. John William and Marilyn Ruth Heck; m. Diane Johns Heck, Feb. 11, 1995; children: John Jr., Nicole, Laura. Master carpenter Carpenters Union, Gloucester, N.J., 1981-86; ops. mgr. West Enterprises, Williamstown, N.J., 1986-88; c.o. officer Segal Assocs., Belmawr, N.J., 1987-89; pres., owner R & K Ent. & Katri Constrn., Woodbury, N.J., 1988-92; project mgr. Emcee Constrn., Mt. Laurel, N.J., 1993-95, Rangelini, Inc., Sewell, N.J., 1996-98, Eagle Constrn. Svcs., Inc., Burlington, N.J., 1999—; blueprint and drafting instr. Atlantic County Vo-Tech Sch., 1983-87; cons. to planning bd. Medford Lakes Borough, N.J., 1998-99; cons., estimator Ragan Design Group, Medford, N.J., 1998—; pres. South Jersey Resdl. Builders Assn., Williamstown, 1986-90; chief labor negotiator South Jersey Contractors Assn., Williamstown, 1986-89. Arbitrator Juvenile Justice Com., Woodbury, 1989-92; pres. Woodbury Football Assn., 1994, coach, 1990-95; float builder Medford Lakes Canoe Carnival, 1995—. Mem. Medford Lakes Country Club, Colony Club (Medford Lakes), KC (4th degree). Roman Catholic. Avocations: antique collecting, canoeing, collecting classic cars, travel, buying and renovating properties. Home: 164 Chippewa Trl Medford Lakes NJ 08055-1842

HECKEL, RICHARD WAYNE, metallurgical engineering educator; b. Pitts., Jan. 25, 1934; s. Ralph Clyde and Esther Vera (Zoerb) H.; m. Peggy Ann Simmons, Jan. 3, 1959 (dec. Apr. 1998); children: Scott Alan, Laura Ann Rowe. BS in Metall. Engring., Carnegie Mellon, 1955, MS, 1958, PhD, 1959. Sr. research metallurgist E.I. duPont de Nemours & Co., Wilmington, Del., 1959-63; prof. metall. engring. Drexel U., Phila., 1963-71; head dept. materials sci. and engring. Carnegie Mellon, Pitts., 1971-76; pres., prof. emeritus dept. materials sci. and engring. Mich. Tech. U., Houghton, 1976—; commr. at large Engring. Workforce Commn., 1997—. Contbr. articles to profl. jours. Served as 1st lt. Ordnance Corps, U.S. Army, 1959-60. Recipient Lindback Teaching award Drexel U., 1968; Research award Mich. Tech. U., 1985. Fellow ASM Internat. (life; Bradley Stoughton Young Tchr. of Metallurgy award 1969, Phila. Ednl. Achievement award 1967); mem. The Metals, Minerals and Materials Soc., Am. Welding Soc. (Adams Meml. mem. 1966), Am. Soc. Engring. Edn., Sigma Xi, Omicron Delta Kappa, Tau Beta Pi, Phi Kappa Phi, Alpha Sigma Mu. Address: 1281 Hickory Ln Houghton MI 49931-1609 Office: Mich Tech U Dept Metall & Materials Engring Houghton MI 49931

HECKENKAMP, ROBERT GLENN, lawyer; b. Quincy, Ill., June 29, 1923; s. Joseph Edward and Ethel E. (Requet) H.; m. Jean E. Duker, June 22, 1946 (dec. 1983); children: Gae Kelly, Joy Heckenkamp-Roate; m. Wilma E. Dobbs, Nov. 15, 1985. BS, Quincy Coll., 1947; JD, DePaul U., 1949. Bar: Ill. 1949, U.S. Dist. Ct. (cen. and so. dists.) Ill. 1949, U.S. Ct. Appeals (7th cir.) 1952, U.S. Supreme Ct. 1965. Sr. ptnr. Heckenkamp, Simhauser, Ward & Zerkle, Springfield, Ill. Fellow Am. Coll. Trial Lawyers (com. chmn. 1983-86), Internat. Acad. Trial Lawyers; mem. ABA, Ill. State Bar Assn. (pres. 1980-81), Sangamon County Bar Assn., Assn. Trial Lawyers Am., Ill. Trial Lawyers Assn. (pres. 1977-78). Soc. Trial Lawyers. Avocations: hunting, fishing. Home: 60 Yacht Club Rd Springfield IL 62707-9525 Office: Heckenkamp Simhauser Ward & Zerkle 700 E Adams St Ste 202 Springfield IL 62701-1953

HECKER, JUTTA, writer; b. Weimar, Germany, Oct. 13, 1904; d. Max and Lili (Kaiser) H. DPhil, Realgymnasium, Weimar, Germany; student, U. Munich, U. Jena. Student asst. Hamburg (Germany) Gymnasium, 1937-39; lectr. German Hochschule for Lehrerbildung, 1939-40; headmistress Lehrerbildung Anstalt, Honnef, Germany, 1940-45; writer, novelist Weimar, 1945—. Author: Die Altenburg, 1955, Wieland, 1958, Eckermann, 1960, Schiller, 1965, Winckelmann, 1965, Corona, 1970, Als ich zu Goethe Kam, 1974, Bernhard Suphan, 1983, Max Hecker, 1984. Mem. Deutscher Schriftstellerverbund. Home: Jenaerstrasse 3,, Hellerweg 18, D-99425 Weimar Germany

HECKLER, WALTER TIM, association executive; b. Kimberley, Republic South Africa, Jan. 30, 1942; s. Walter Martin and Mavis Joyce (Cardinal) H.; m. Renée Anne Tamborello, Dec. 16, 1984; children: Cindy, Mark, Timothy, David, Chelsea, Mia. BS in Biology, Lamar U., Beaumont, Tex., 1963. Chief rsch. technician M.D. Anderson Cancer Inst., Houston, 1963-69; rsch. asst. Salk Inst. Biol. Studies, La Jolla, Calif., 1969-70; dir. tennis Westwood Country Club, Houston, 1970-75; gen. mgr. Chancellors Racquet Club, Houston, 1975-82; chief exec. officer U.S. Pro Tennis Assn., Houston, 1982—. Mem. Am. Soc. Assn. Execs., U.S. Profl. Tennis Assn. (pres. 1980-82), Profl. Assn. Diving Instrs. Avocations: tennis, diving, boating, skiing. Office: US Profl Tennis Assn World Hdqrs 1 USPTA Centre 3535 Briarpark Dr Houston TX 77042-5245

HECKLINGER, RICHARD E., ambassador; b. Syracuse, N.Y.; m. Carol Pratt. Grad., St. Lawrence U.; JD, Harvard U.; grad. in advanced internat. studies, Johns Hopkins U. Joined Fgn. Svc., Dept. State, Washington, 1967—, prin. dep. asst. sec. for econ. and bus. affairs, sr. advisor and exec. asst. to under sec. for econ. affairs; dep. chief mission U.S. Mission to OECD; dep. asst. sec. for European and Can. affairs Dept. State, sr. insp. Office Insp. Gen., advisor to under sec. for polit. affairs, dir. Internat. Energy Policy Office; acting dep. asst. sec. for internat. affairs Dept. Energy, Washington; amb. to Thailand, Am. Embassy, Bangkok. Office: APO AP 96546 Am Ambassador To Thailand Washington DC 20521-0001

HECKMAN, CHARLES WILLIAM, biologist, ecologist, limnologist; b. Bklyn., Aug. 23, 1941; s. Charles Gerard and Ruth (Horie) H.; m. Wai-Yuen Sylvia Woo, Aug. 31, 1974; children: Charles, Sylvia, Francis. BS, Manhattan Coll., Riverdale, 1963; MS, St. John's U., Jamaica, 1973; D, Univ. Hamburg, Germany, 1979, Habilitation, 1988. Rsch. scientist Institut fur Hydrobiologie & Fischereiwissenschaft, Hamburg, 1978-81, researcher, 1981-87; self employed, 1987-90; mem. Projeto Ecologia do Pantanal U. Federal de Mato Grosso, 1990-95; pvt. dozent inst. do rsch., 1995-98; mem. rsch. project on salmon migration U.S. Forest Svc., 1998—; mem. editl. staff Studies on Neotropical Fauna and Environment, 1995—, Life Scis. Advances, 1983-90; lector for the book series: Freshwater Fishes of Europe; supr. Brazilian degree candidates (MS, PhD), 1991—. Author: (book) Rice Field Ecology in Northeast Thailand, 1979, Phnom Pehn Airlift, 1990, The Pantanal of Pocone, 1998; contbr. numerous articles to sci. jours. Capt. USAF, S.E. Asia, 1964-68. Scholar N.Y. State Regents, Manahattan Coll., 1959-63, St. John's U., 1969-70, 72-73, Arnold Air Soc. scholar Manahattan Coll., 1962. Mem. Sociedade Brasileira de Limnologia, Freshwater Biological Assn., Vietnam Vets. of Am. (life). Avocations: numismatics, veterans rights, translations, judo. Home: Moorwisch 10, D-22547 Hamburg Germany Office: Inst. Hydrobiology & Fisch., Zeiseweg 9, D-22765 Hamburg Germany

HECKMAN, JAMES JOSEPH, economist, econometrician, educator; b. Chgo., Apr. 19, 1944; s. John Jacob and Bernice Irene (Medley) H.; m. Lynne Pettler, 1979; children: Jonathan Jacob, Alma Rachel. AB in Math. summa cum laude (Woodrow Wilson fellow), Colo. Coll., 1965; MA in Econs., Princeton U., 1968, PhD in Econs. (Harold Willis Dodds fellow), 1971; MA, Yale U., 1989. Lectr. Columbia U., 1970-71, asst. prof. econs., 1971-73, assoc. prof., 1973-74; assoc. prof. econs. U. Chgo., 1973-76, prof., 1976—, Henry Schultz prof. of econ., 1985-95, Henry Schultz Disting. Svc. prof., 1995—, prof. econs. Harris Sch. Pub. Policy, 1990—, dir. Ctr. for Program Evaluation Harris Sch. Pub. Policy, 1991—, dir. Econs. Rsch. Ctr. Dept. Econs., 1997—; A. Whitney Griswold prof. econs. Yale U., New Haven, 1988-90, Sterling prof., 1990, prof., dept. stats., 1990; dir. Ctr. for Program Evaluation Harris Sch. Pub. Policy U. Chgo., 1991—, dir. Econs. Rsch. Ctr. Dept. Econs., 1997—; rsch. assoc. Nat. Bur. Econs. Rsch., 1970-77, sr. rsch. assoc., 1977-85, 87—; Irving Fisher prof. econs. Yale U., 1984; Ben Porath lectr. Hebrew U., 2000; disting. lectr. So. Econ. Assn., 2000; treas. Chgo. Econ. Rsch. Assocs.; rsch. assoc. Econs. Rsch. Ctr.-NORC, 1985—; cons. in field; cons. Chgo. Urban League, 1978-86; mem. status Black Ams. com. NRC; JAE lectr. Yale U., 1997; Marschak lectr. Econometric Soc., 1997; Woytinsky lectr. U. Mich., 1999, Harris lectr. Harvard U., 1995, Wildavsky lectr. U. Calif. (Berkeley), 1999; Fisher Schultz lectr. Econ. Soc., 2000; Ruth and Seymour Harris lectr. Kennedy Sch., 1995; hon. prof. U. Tucuman, Argentina, 1998. Editor Jour. Polit. Economy, 1981-87, Evaluating a Job Training Program: Empirical and Methodological Lessons, 1997, Evaluation Social Programs, 1997; assoc. editor Jour. Econometrics, 1977-83, Jour. Labor Econs., 1983—, Econs. Revs., 1987—, Rev. of Econs. and Statistics, 1994—, Jour. Econ. Perspectives, 1989-96, Labor Econs., 1992—; author (with B. Singer and G. Tsiang) Lecture Notes on Longitudinal Analysis, 1994; editor: (with B. Singer), Longitudinal Analysis of Labor Market Data, 1985, (with E. Leamer) Handbook of Econometrics, Vol. 5, Incentives in Govt. Bureaucracies: A Study of Performance Standards And Their Effects, The Economic Approach to Program Evaluation; Am. editor Rev. Econ. Studies, 1982-85; contbr. articles to profl. jours. Founding faculty and curriculum com. U. Chgo. Harris Sch. Pub. Policy. Recipient L. Benezet Alumni prize Colo. Coll., 1985, Nobel Prize Economics, 2000; fellow J.S. Guggenheim Found., 1978-79, Social Sci. Rsch. Coun., 1977-78, Ctr. for Advanced Study in Behavioral Scis., 1978-79. Fellow Am. Bar Found. (sr., rsch. affiliate 1989-91, sr. rsch. fellow 1991—), Econometric Soc., Am. Acad. Arts and Scis. (elected), Nat. Acad. Scis.; mem. Am. Econ. Assn. (mem. exec. com. 2000—)John Bates Clark medal 1983), Midwest Econs. Assn. (pres.-elect 1996-97, pres. 1997-98), Am. Statis. Assn., Indsl. Rels. Rsch. Assn., Econ. Sci. Assn. (founder), Phi Beta Kappa. Home: 4807 S Greenwood Ave Chicago IL 60615-1913 Office: U Chgo Dept Econs 1126 E 59th St Chicago IL 60637-1580

HECTOR, VIVIAN CLEAVE, social worker; b. Newport, Isle Wight, U.K., June 30, 1952; s. Malcolm Basil Vivian Fellender and Marjorie Clara (Cleave) H.; m. June Hilton, Dec. 9, 1972; children: Toby, Louise, Luke, Tamsyn. MA in Child Protection Studies, Leicester U., 1996; diploma in Social Work, Sunderland Poly., 1989. Cert. qualification in child protective family social work, cert. qualification in social work. Inspector NSPCC, London, 1980-81, Manchester, Eng., 1981-82; inspector, team mem., project leader NSPCC, Wrexham, Wales, 1982-95; coord. therapeutic svcs. Prospects Ctr. for Young People, Wrexham, 1996-98; ops. mgr. FSS Midlands, Bridgnorth, 1998-99; dir. FSS Etrucia, Newcastle Under Lyme, 2000—; originator, trustee Stepping Stones, Wrexham, 1983-96, chair mgmt. com., 1996—; cons. Prospects Tng. Svcs., Wrexham, 1996-99. Author: The Significance of Practitioner Gender in Work With Survivors of Sexual Abuse, 1997. Recipient advanced award in social work. Mem. Brit. Assn. for Study and Prevention of Child Abuse and Neglect. Office: FSS Midlands, Horsehay House Bridge Rd, Horsehay Telford TF4 3PY, Wales

HEDAR, PER ANDERS, engineering educator; b. Stockholm, Sept. 4, 1923; s. Sam F. and Elna T. (Magner) H.; m. Birgit Johansson, Aug. 26, 1950 (dec. Sept. 1986); children: Margareta, Karin, Mikael. Civil Engr., Royal Inst. Tech., 1948; MS, Chalmers U. Tech., 1954, D of Tech., 1960. First engr. than road engr. Royal Bd. Rds and Waterways, 1952-61; acting prof. hydraulics and soil mechanics Chalmers U. Tech., 1958-60, 62-64; cons. engr., owner P.A. Hedar A B, Gothenburg, Sweden, 1961-99; assoc. prof. Royal Inst. Tech., Stockholm, 1986-88. Author: Stability of Rock-Fill Breakwaters, 1960; contbr. articles to profl. jours. bd. dirs. AB Armerad Betong, 1961-77. Mem. ASCE (life), Permanent Internat. Assn. of Navigation Congresses (Swedish del. working groups on breakwaters 1981—). Home: Storuddens Gard, SE 63517 Näshulta Sweden

HEDBERG, JOHN CHARLES, investor; b. St. Paul, Minn., June 27, 1933; s. William Rueben and Esther Mathilda (Jenson) H.; m. Sarah Cornelia McLouth, Sept. 10, 1954 (div. Sept. 1981); children: John, Theodore, Lisa, Benjamin; m. Carrie Ann Walker, Sept. 19, 1986; children: Patrick, Holly, Emily. BS with distinction, U. Minn., 1955, JD, 1960. Sec.-treas. Chateau Co-Op Restaurant, 1951-54; acctg. intern Gen. Mills, Kankakee, Ill., 1955-56; law clk. Judge Laurens L. Henderson, Phoenix, 1960-61; law ptnr. Cox & Hedberg, Phoenix, 1961-71; pvt. practice Phoenix, 1971-73; ptr. Hedberg & Kirschbaum, Phoenix, 1973-78; legal counsel Sea Ray Boats, Phoenix, 1970-78, v.p., legal counsel, 1978-87; dir. Sea Ray Credit Corp., 1980-87; dir. Sea Ray Boats, Inc., 1982-89, pres., 1988-89; pres. Sea Ray Boats Europe BV, 1988-89; bd. dirs. Healthwaves Corp., Phoenix; trustee Ray Employees' Stock Ownership Trust and Ray Employees Retirement Plan, 1979-89; advocate before Ariz. and appellate cts., U.S. Dist. Ct., Ariz., 9th Cir. Fed. Ct. Appeals. Chmn. U. Minn. Rep. Club, Mpls., 1954-55; chancellor's assoc. U. Tenn., Knoxville, 1987-89; treas./dir. Esperanza, 1989—. Mem. Beta Gamma Sigma. Avocations: tennis, reading. Home: 12636 S Honah Lee Ct Phoenix AZ 85044-3510

HEDELIUS, TOM CHRISTER, banker; b. Lund, Sweden, Oct. 3, 1939; s. Curt H. and Brita (Påhlsson) H.; m. Ulla Marianne Ericsson, 1964; children: Henrik, Stefan, Peter. MBA, U. Lund, 1965; Dr. Econ. (hon.), U. Umeå, 1989. Indsl. expert Svenska Handelsbanken, Stockholm, 1967-69, credit mgr., 1969-74, head regional unit, 1974-76, head ctrl. credit dept., 1976-78, pres., 1978-91, chmn. bd. dirs., 1991—; chmn. bd. dirs. Bergman & Beving AB, Stockholm, Svenska Le Carbone AB, Sundbyberg, Sweden; vice chmn. bd. dirs. AB Industrivärden, Stockholm, Telefon AB LM Ericsson, Stockholm; bd. dirs. Svenska Cellulosa Aktiebolaget SCA, Stockholm, AB Volvo, Göteborg; mem. SAS Assembly of Reps., Stockholm. Office: Svenska Handelsbanken, Kungsträdgårdsgatan 2, S-106 70 Stockholm Sweden

HEDER, MATS OLOF, mechanical engineer, educator, automotive historian; b. Degerfors, Sweden, July 1, 1960; s. Henry Stig and Maja Ingegerd (Almen) H.; m. Rikako Fujita. MSc, Chalmers U., 1985, PhD, 1992. Postdoctoral fellow U. Tokyo, 1992-93; lectr. U. Karlstad, Sweden, 1993—; structural analysis cons., 1997—. Cpl. Swedish Army Res., 1980—. Mem. Soc. Automotive Historians, Vet. Car Club (Gt. Britain). Avocations: automotive literature, automotive history, restoring cars, construction. Home: Snarstadtorp Ovre Falla, S-655 93 Karlstad Sweden Office: U Karlstad, Universitetsgatan 1, S-651 88 Karlstad Sweden

HEDGER, CECIL RAYMOND, lawyer; b. Tracy, Minn., Feb. 28, 1947; s. Raymond O. and Willie (Weems) H.; m. Jane E. Scott, June 6, 1970 (div. 1987); 1 child, Anne Kathryn. BA, U.S.D., 1969; JD, U. Nebr., 1972. Bar: Calif. 1972, U.S. Ct. Appeals (9th cir.) 1972, Nebr. 1973, U.S. Ct. Appeals (8th cir.) 1973, U.S. Ct. Appeals (5th cir.) 1973, Utah 1978, U.S. Dist. Ct. Utah 1978, U.S. Ct. Appeals (10th cir.) 1978, Colo. 1981, U.S. Dist. Ct. Colo. 1981. Assoc. Nelson & Harding, Lincoln, Nebr., 1972-74, ptnr., 1974-77; ptnr. Nelson & Harding, Salt Lake City, 1977-79, Denver, 1979-81, 84-88; ptnr. Musick, Peeler & Garnett, L.A. and Denver, 1981-84, Harding & Ogborn (successor firm of Nelson & Harding), Denver, 1990-98; of counsel VanCott, Bagely, Cornwall & McCarthy, Salt Lake City, 1998—; Contbr. chpts. to legal book. Mem. ABA (practice and procedure under the nat. labor rels. act, labor law sect.). Avocations: golf, rocketry, hiking, reading.

Office: VanCott Bagely Cornwall & McCarthy PO Box 45340 Salt Lake City UT 84145-0340*

HEDGES, DONALD WALTON, lawyer; b. Kansas City, Mo., May 24, 1921; s. Byron C. and Irma (McCleary) H.; m. Mary Elizabeth Mancill, Jan. 29, 1944 (div.); children: Judith Elizabeth, Donna Louise, Byron C. III, Steven M.; m. Diane Scheid, Jan. 15, 1965; children: Scott Andrew, Hillary Carson. Student, Principia Coll., 1939-40; BS, U. Pa., 1943, LLB, 1947; D. Bus. Sci. (hon.), Webber Coll., 1947. Bar: Pa. 1949, U.S. Ct. Appeals (3d cir.) 1979, U.S. Dist. Ct. (ea. dist.) Pa. 1949. Law clk. to Chief Justice Horace Stern Pa. Supreme Ct., 1948-49; mem. firm Mancill, Cooney, Semans & Hedges, 1949-64; ptnr. Wolf, Block, Schorr & Solis Cohen, Phila., 1965-82, Obermayer, Rebmann, Maxwell & Hippel, Wayne, Pa., 1986-88; pvt. practice law Wayne, Pa., 1989—; dir. Servotronics, Inc. Trustee Atwater Kent Mus. Served as lt. (j.g.) Air Force, USNR, 1943-46. Decorated Distinguished Flying Cross, Air medal. Mem. ABA, Pa. Bar Assn., Phila. Bar Assn., Juristic Soc. Phila., Beta Theta Pi. Episcopalian. Clubs: Union League (Phila.); Sharswood Law (U. Pa.), Merion Cricket. Home: 538 Whitford Hills Rd Exton PA 19341-2050

HEDGES, MARK STEPHEN, clinical psychologist; b. Chgo., Feb. 15, 1950; s. Norman T. and Doris Mae (Walters) H.; BS, Purdue U., 1972; MA, U. S.D., 1974, PhD, 1977; m. Janice Finnie, Aug. 16, 1975; children: Anna, Miriam. Psychology intern Western Mo. Mental Health Ctr., Kansas City, 1975-76; dir. children and adolescent svcs., psychologist Northeastern Mental Health Ctr., Aberdeen, S.D., 1977—; chmn. Northeastern Area Local Interagency Team. Mem. adv. bd. S.D. Mental Health Planning and Coord. Adv. Coun. Mem. APA, S.D. Assn. Sch. Psychologists, CASSP (co-chairperson Aberdeen area), Phi Beta Kappa, Psi Chi, Phi Kappa Phi. Methodist. Office: Northeastern Mental Health Ctr 703 3rd Ave SE Aberdeen SD 57401-4508

HEDIN, LARS TORE, physicist, researcher; b. Oerebro, Sweden, Feb. 6, 1930; s. Tore Knut Albert and Ingrid Anna Augusta (Fosselius) H.; m. Hillevi Ingar Gudrun Nilehn, May 23, 1953; children: Ylva, Goerel, Astrid. Civil Engr., Royal Inst. Tech., Stockholm, 1955, Tech. Licentiat, 1960; PhD, Chalmers U. Tech., Goteborg, 1965. Rsch. asst. Royal Inst. Tech., Stockholm, 1955-60, U. Uppsala, Sweden, 1960-62; resident rsch. asst. Argonne (Ill.) Nat. Lab., 1962-64; rsch. asst. to asst. prof. Chalmers U., Göteborg, 1964-70; prof. Linköping U., 1970-71, Lund U., 1971-95; physicist Max-Planck Inst., Stuttgart, 1995-98; dir. for Theory II, Max-Planck Inst., Stuttgart. Author: Solid State Theory, vol. 23, 1969, X-Ray Spectroscopy, 1973, Handbook on Synchrotron Radiation, 1983; editor Solid State Commn., 1971-90. Avocations: history, tennis, hiking. Office: U Lund Dept Theoret Physics, SÖlvegatan 14 A, 22362 Lund Sweden

HEDLEY-WHYTE, JOHN, anesthesiologist, educator; b. Newcastle-upon-Tyne, Eng., Nov. 25, 1933; came to U.S., 1960, naturalized, 1965; s. Angus and Nancy (Nettleton) H.-W.; m. Elizabeth Tessa Waller, Sept. 19, 1959. Student, Harrow Sch., 1947-52; BA (Rothschild scholar Clare Coll.), Cambridge U., 1955, MB, 1958, MA, 1959, MD, 1972; AM (hon.), Harvard U., 1967. House surgeon St. Bartholomew's Hosp., London, 1958-59; resident in anesthesia Mass. Gen. Hosp., 1960-62, hon. anesthetist, 1977—; clin. asst. anesthesia Harvard U., 1961-63, instr., 1963-65, clin. assoc., 1965-67, assoc. prof., 1967-69, prof., 1969-76, 1st David S. Sheridan prof. anaesthesia and respiratory therapy, 1976—; prof. dept. health policy and mgmt. Harvard U. Sch. Pub. Health, 1988-2000; chmn. faculty seminar in health and medicine Harvard U., 1975-76; anesthetist-in-chief Beth Israel Hosp., Boston, 1967-88; chmn. com. on rsch. Beth Israel Hosp., 1976-82; cons. in field; mem. tech. adv. bd. on med. devices tech. Am. Nat. Standards Inst., 1973-83; U.S. del. Internat. Electrotech. Commn., 1989-91, 92—; leader U.S. del. Internat. Orgn. Standardization, Geneva, 1973-89, chmn. com. TC 121, SC 3 on anaesthetic and respiratory equipment, 1978—. Author: Respiratory Care, 1965, Applied Physiology of Respiratory Care, 1976, Continuous Anesthesia Vapor Monitoring, 1990, Operating room and Intensive Care Alarms and Information Transfer, 1992; contbr. articles to profl. jours. Recipient Hichens prize St. Bartholomew's Hosp., London, 1957. Fellow ACP (life), German Soc. Anaesthesia and Intensive Care Medicine (hon., life), Am. Soc. Testing and Materials (hon., chmn. com. F29 1983-89, Merit award 1994, user vice chmn. 2000—); mem. Am. Physiol. Soc., Abernethian Soc. (past pres.), Am. Soc. Anesthesiologists (chmn. com. mech. equipment 1977-82, chmn. com. on equipment and standards 1982-84), Mass. Soc. Anesthesiologists (pres. 1973-74), Am. Soc. Pharmacology and Exptl. Therapeutics, Roxbury Soc. Med. Improvement (libr. 1970-88, sec.-treas. 1988—), Mass. Med. Soc. (coun. 1975-78), Fairhaven Preservation Assn. (chmn. 1990—), Boodle's Club, The Country Club, Somerset Club, Harvard Club of Boston, Vicarage Club. Democrat. Episcopalian. Achievements include discovery that human blood has a constant relative solubility for oxygen. Office: VA Med Ctr 1400 Vfw Pkwy Boston MA 02132-4927

HEDLUND, CHARLES JOHN, oil company executive, conservationist; b. Appleton, Minn., Nov. 3, 1917; s. William Martin and Sophia Stickney Hedlund; m. Helen Marie Thorstenson, Aug. 30, 1940; children: Susan Louise, Patricia Jo, Ann Elizabeth, Christopher Charles. B Chem. Engring., B Bus. Adminstrn., U. Minn., 1940; LLD (hon.), Am. U., Cairo, 1993. Refinery engr. Std. Oil Co. La., Baton Rouge, 1940-46; with coord. and econs. dept. Std. Oil Co. (N.J.) (now Exxon), N.Y.C., 1947-52; dir. program Petroleum Adminstrn. for Def., Washington, 1952-53; mgr. coord. and econ. dept. Std. Oil Co. (N.J.), N.Y., 1954-59; exec. v.p. Esso Std. Italia, Genoa, Italy, 1960-61; pres. Svenska Esso AB, Stockholm, Sweden, 1962-66; v.p. mktg. Esso Europe, London, 1967; v.p. Exxon, pres. Esso Mid. East, N.Y., 1968-80; mem. exec. com. Arabian Am. Oil Co., Dhahran, Saudi Arabia, 1968-80; chmn. petroleum working group NATO, Paris, 1952-53. Chmn. Anglo Am. Sch.-Stockholm, 1962-66; trustee The Nature Conservancy, 1978-87(chmn. 1984-85), N.Y. adv. bd. Salvation Army, 1970-80, Am. Mus. Natural History, 1979-89, Conservation Internat., 1987— (founding chmn. 1987-95), Am. U. Cairo, 1976— (chmn. 1980-92). Named to Order of Arts and Scis. 1st Class, Govt. Egypt, 1993. Mem. Baltrusol Golf Club (N.J.), Country Club Fla., Ocean Club Fla. (trustee 1997—), The Little Club, Century Assn. (N.Y.), Lansdowne Club (London), Tau Beta Pi, Beta Gamma Sigma, Phi Lambda Upsilon. Republican. Episcopalian. Avocations: conservation, education, golf, tennis, birding. Home: 58 Country Rd S Vlg Of Golf FL 33436-5612 Office: Conservation Internat 2501 M St Washington DC 20037

HEDLUND, PAUL JAMES, lawyer; b. Abington, Pa., June 26, 1946; s. Frank Xavier and Eva Ruth (Hoffman) H.; m. Marta Louise Brewer, Dec. 7, 1985; children: Annemarie Kirsten, Brooke Ashley, Tess Kara. BSME, U. Mich., 1968; JD, UCLA, 1973. Bar: Calif. 1973, D.C. 1994, U.S. Dist. Ct. (ctrl. dist.) Calif. 1977, U.S. Dist. Ct. (ea. dist.) Calif. 1991, U.S. Dist. Ct. (no. dist.) N.Y. 1994, U.S. Patent and Trademark Office 1978, U.S. Ct. Appeals (9th cir.) 1994, U.S. Supreme Ct. 1997. Staff engr. So. Calif. Edison, L.A., 1968-70; ptnr. Hedlund & Samuels, L.A., 1974-88, Kananack, Murgatroyd Baum & Hedlund (and predecessor firms), L.A., 1988-92; shareholder Baum, Hedlund, Aristei, Guilford & Downey (and predecessor firms), L.A., 1993—; lectr. in field. Mem. Bar. Assn. D.C., Consumer Attys. of L.A. County Bar Assn. Office: Baum Hedlund Aristei Guilford & Downey 12100 Wilshire Blvd Ste 950 Los Angeles CA 90025-7107

HEDRICK, MARC HAMILTON, plastic surgeon; b. Durant, Okla., Aug. 13, 1962; m. Tracey Gibson, Mar. 8, 1991; children: Catherine, Marc II. BA in biology and Chemistry, Soo. Meth. U., 1984; MD, U. Tex., Dallas, 1988. Diplomate Am. Bd. Surgery; lic. physician Okla., Calif., Pa. Rsch. asst. polymer chemistry So. Meth. U., Dallas, 1982-83; intern/resident in gen. surgery U. Okla., Oklahoma City, 1988-91, 93-95; rsch. fellow fetal surgery Fetal Treatment Ctr., U. Calif., San Francisco, 1991-93; resident in plastic and reconstructive surgery UCLA, 1995-97; craniomaxillofacial and pediat. plastic surgery fellow U. Pitts., 1997-98; asst. prof. divsn. plastic and reconstrv. surgery dept. surgery, UCLA, 1998—; asst. prof. divsn. genetics dept. pediats. UCLA, 1998—; co-dir. Regenerative Bioengring. and Repair Lab., UCLA, 1998—, co-dir. Gonda (Goldschmied) Wound Treatment and Clin. Tissue Engring. Ctr., 1998—, co-dir. Cosmetic Surgery Ctr., 1998—; clin. instr. surgery U. Calif.-San Francisco, 1991-93; staff plastic surgeon Summit Med. Ctr., Oakland, Calif., 1991-93, Calif. Pacific Med. Ctr., San Francisco, 1992-93, Forbes Regional Hosp., Monroeville, Pa., 1997-98, Harbor-UCLA Med. Ctr., Torrance, Calif., 1995-97, 98—, Olive View-UCLA Med. Ctr., Sylmar, Calif., 1995-97, 98—, UCLA Med. Ctr., 1995-97, 98—, West L.A. (Wadsworth) VA Med. Ctr., Santa Monica, Calif., 1998—; vis. prof. U. de Carabobo, Valencia, Venezuela, 1998; lectr. in field. Contbr. numerous articles and abstracts to profl. jours.; assoc. editor Revista de Cirugia Infantil, 1993; reviewer Plastic and Reconstructive Surgery, 1999; patentee in field. Recipient Univ. Surg. Soc. award, 1994, Oklahoma City Surg. Soc. award 1995, James Barrett Brown award, 1996; H. Dale Collins scholar, 1991-92, 92-93, tabas scholar, 1998; rsch. grantee U. Calif.-San Francisco/REAC, 1992-93, Am. Soc. Aesthetic Plastic Surgery, 1997-98, Plastic Surgery Ednl. Found., 1999-2000, Frontiers of sci., 1999-2000, Kinetic Concepts, Inc., 2000—. Mem. AMA, ACS (assoc.), Am. Soc. of Plastic and Reconstructive Surgeons (cand. mem.), Plastic Surgery Rsch. Coun., Wound Healing Soc., Tissue Engring. Soc., UCLA Dental Rsch. Inst. (assoc.), Phi Delta Theta, Alpha Lambda Delta, Phi Eta Sigma. Office: UCLA Dept Surgery 10833 Leconte Chs 64 140 Dept S Los Angeles CA 90095-0001

HEDRICK, WYATT SMITH, pharmacist; b. Roswell, N.Mex., Sept. 28, 1951; s. Wyatt Smith and Roberta Walker (Stuart) H. BS in Pharmacy, U. N.Mex., 1974; MS in Hosp. Pharmacy, U. Houston, 1978. Registered pharmacist, N.Mex., Tex. Pharmacy intern St. Mary's Hosp., Roswell, N.Mex., 1973, Ea. N.Mex. Med. Ctr., Roswell, 1973-74, U-SAVE Drug, Roswell, 1974-75; pharmacy resident U. Tex. Med. Br. Hosps., Galveston, 1977-78; staff pharmacist Meml. Gen. Hosp., Las Cruces, N.Mex., 1978, Columbia Med. Ctr. West, El Paso, Tex., 1978—. Mem. Am. Soc. Health-Sys. Pharmacists, Tex. Soc. Health-Sys. Pharmacists, El Paso Area Soc. Health-Sys. Pharmacists. Avocations: reading, traveling, physical fitness. Home: 1028 Quinault Dr El Paso TX 79912-1223

HEDSTROM, SUSAN LYNNE, maternal women's health nurse; b. Dowagiac, Mich., Jan. 17, 1958; d. Clinton J. and Gloria Anna (Hyink) Moore. ADN, Southwestern Mich. Coll., 1978. RN cert. maternal-newborn, Mich., Ind., Calif., Ga., Fla. Staff nurse obstetrics unit Lee Meml. Hosp., Dowagiac, Mich., 1979-81, Meml. Hosp., South Bend, Ind., 1981-90; with MRA Staffing Systems, Inc., Ft. Lauderdale, Fla., 1990-93; staff nurse traveler MUSC, Charleston, S.C., 1990-91; nurse Desert Hosp., Palm Springs, Calif., 1991, Ind. U. Hosp., Indpls., 1992, Valley Med Ctr., Fresno, Calif., 1992; staff nurse post partum/nursery Tallahassee Meml. Regional Med. Ctr., 1993-95, asst. head nurse post partum, 1995—. Mem. Am. Women's Health, Obstetrics and Neonatal Nurses. Office: Tallahassee Meml Reg Hosp Magnolia Dr & Miccosukee Rd Tallahassee FL 32308

HEEB, HANS-RUDOLF, software company executive; b. Zurich, Switzerland, Apr. 29, 1957; s. Hans and Emmi (Schmid) H.; m. Karin Freudenreich, Sept. 2, 1988; children: Felix, Alice. PhD, ETH Zurich, 1988. Rsch. staff mem. IBM Rsch., Yorktown Heights, N.Y., 1988-94; v.p. R&D, Diagonal Systems, Zurich, 1994-98; CEO esmertec inc., Zurich, 1999—. Mem. IEEE (sr.), Assn. Computing Machinery.

HEEFNER, REGINALD LEE, linguist, entertainer, author; b. Chambersburg, Pa., Feb. 17; s. Theodore Charles and Doris Elinor (Byers) H. BA in Russian Lang. and Lit., U. Md., 1978, BA in Chinese, 1982; diploma, U.S. State Dept. Japanese lang. and Area Studies Rsch. Inst., 1986. Judo/ju-jitsu instr. Chambersburg YMCA, 1968-74; self def. instr. Wilson Coll. Women, Chambersburg, 1970; Chinese linguist U.S. Army Security Agy., Monterey, Calif., 1974-78; unarmed combat instr. Ft. Meade, 1978—; multi-linguist Nat. Security Agy., Ft. Meade, Md., 1979-89; cons. U.S. State Dept., Tokyo, 1989; entertainer Hollywood, Calif., 1990—; film actor Balt., 1991—; humanities instr. Ctrl. Mich. U., Ft. Meade, 1983-84; Russian instr. Ctrl. Tex. Coll., Ft. Meade, 1985; multi-linguist svc. operator Visa Corp., Owings Mill, md., 1991-92; fgn. lang. tng. design and devel. cons. Nat. Cryptologic Sch., 1998-99. Actor: (film) Major League II, 1992; (stage) A Christmas Carol, 1967. Counselor YMCA, Chambersburg, 1968-74; self-def. instr. Bryn Mawr (Pa.) Coll., 1994-95. With U.S. Army, 1973-78. Recipinet Yonkyu 4th class Aikido Aikido Internat. Hdqrs., 1989. Mem. Screen Actors Guild, Am. Guild Variety Artists, U.S. Judo Assn. (life, Godan), Youth Hostels Internat. (life), U.S. Chess Fedn. (life), Assn. U.S. Army. Avocations: martial arts (judo/ju-jujitsu sr. nat. examiner/coach, classical budo dojo 1996—), swimming, chess, travel, drama. Home and Office: Japanese Lang & Area Specialists 25 Hazel St Chambersburg PA 17201-1138

HEEGER, ALAN JAY, physicist; b. Sioux City, Iowa, Jan. 22, 1936; s. Peter J. and Alice (Minkin) H.; m. Ruthann Chudacoff, Aug. 11, 1957; children: Peter S., David J. BA, U. Nebr., 1957; PhD, U. Calif., Berkeley, 1961; hon. degree, U. Mons, Belgium, 1993; D in Tech. honoris causa, Linköping (Sweden) U., 1996; PhD honoris causa, Abo Akademie, Turku, Finland, 1998; DHL honoris causa, U. Mass., 1999; DS honoris causa, U. Nebr., 1999. Asst. prof. U. Pa., Phila., 1962-64; asso. prof. U. Pa., 1964-66, prof. physics, 1966-82; prof. physics U. Calif., Santa Barbara, 1982—, dir. Inst. for Polymers and Organic Solids, 1983-2000; pres. UNIAX Corp., Santa Barbara, 1990-94, chmn. bd., 1990-99, chief tech. officer, 1999—; dir. Lab. for Rsch. on Structure of Matter, U. Pa., 1974-81, acting vice provost for rsch., 1981-82; Morris Loeb lectr. Harvard U., 1973. Editor-in-chief Synthetic Metals jour., 1983-2000; contbr. sci. articles to profl. jours. Recipient John Scott medal City of Phila., 1989, Oliver P. Buckley prize; Alfred P. Sloan fellow, Guggenheim fellow, Balzan prize for the sci. of new materials Balzan Found., Italy and Switzerland, 1995, Nobel Prize in Chemistry, 2000; govt. grantee. Fellow Am. Physics Soc. (Buckley prize for solid stae physics 1983). Achievements include patents in field. Office: U Calif Dept Physics Santa Barbara CA 93103 also: UNIAX Corp 6780 Cortona Dr Santa Barbara CA 93117-3022

HEEMSKERK, FRANK MARTINUS JOHANNES, neurobiologist, pharmacologist; b. son, N Brabant, The Netherlands, Dec. 21, 1961; arrived in Belgium, 1995; s. Frederik Jan and Hendrica Everdina Johanna (Laméris) H.; m. Johanna Petronella Maria Van Sloten, May 7, 1987; 1 child, Maurits Frederik Willem. DSc, U. Utrecht, The Netherlands, 1986, PhD, 1989. Rsch. asst. Rudolf Magnus Inst. Pharmacology U. Utrecht, The Netherlands, 1986-89; Fogarty vis. fellow Nat. Inst. Child Health and Human Devel. NIH, Bethesda, Md., 1990-91; sr. guest rschr. Nat. Inst. Mental Health, Bethesda, Md., 1992-94; vis. scientist Pasteur U., Strasbourg, France, 1995-98; dir. sci. coordination Tibotec NV, Mechelen, Belgium, 1999—. Contbr. over 47 articles to profl. jours. Bd. dirs. Found. for Bach Cantata Performances, 1982-85; coun mem. Evangelical Luth. Ch., Bethesda, Md., 1993-94,. recipient Vis. fellowship Fogarty Ctr., 1990, Clin Medicine fellowship Am. Philos. Soc., 1992; grantee Dutch Epilepsy Found., 1986, 88. Mem. Soc. for Neurosci. Avocations: violin, choir singing, history, cultural diversity.

HEER, EDWIN LEROY, insurance company executive; b. American Falls, Idaho, Aug. 19, 1938; s. Edwin Frederick and Kathryn Irene (Franks) H; m. Jacqulin S. Jefford, May 23, 1960 (div. Mar. 1978); 1 child, Kevin Jack; m. Judith Lee Overton-Jones, Jan. 2, 1980. BS, U. Alaska, 1963; MBA, St. Mary's U. Tex., San Antonio, 1976. Asst. actuary Aetna Life & Casualty Co., Hartford, Conn., 1963-68; assoc. actuary Ins. Co. of N.Am., Phila., 1968-72; asst. v.p. USAA, San Antonio, 1972-78; v.p., corp. actuary W.R. Berkley Corp., Greenwich, Conn., 1978-91; sr. v.p., chief corp. actuary W.R. Berkley Corp., Conn., 1991—; bd. dirs. Union Std. Ins. Co., Dallas, Carolina Casualty Ins. Co., Jacksonville, Fla., Great Divide Ins. Co., Scottsdale, Ariz., Nautilus Ins. Co., Scottsdale, Ariz., ACADIA Ins. Co., Portland, Maine, Berkley Risk Mgrs., Inc., Rasmussen Agy., Inc., Somerset, N.J., FICO Ins. Co., Bethesda, Md., Berkley Regional Ins. Co., St. Louis, Chesapeake Bay Property and Casualty Ins. Co., Richmond, Va. Fellow Casualty Actuarial soc.; mem. Am. Acad. Actuaries, Soc. Chartered Property Casualty Underwriters (cert.). Republican. Lutheran. Avocations: fishing, travel, birding. Home: 44 Strawberry Hill Ave Stamford CT 06902-2632 Office: W R Berkley Corp 165 Mason St Greenwich CT 06830-6608

HEER, EWALD, engineer; b. Friedensfeld, Germany, July 28, 1930; s. Johannes and Lilli Friedericke (Jauch) H.; came to U.S., 1956. Diploma Archtl. Engring., Sch. Hamburg, 1953; B.S., CUNY, 1959; M.S., Columbia U., 1960, C.E., 1962; Dr Engring. Sc. magna cum laude, Tech. U., Hanover, Fed. Republic Germany., 1964; m. Hannelore M. Oehlers, Jan. 26, 1952; children: Thomas Ewald, Eric Martin. Engr. Hinz Architects, Hamburg, Fed. Republic Germany, 1952-55; design engr. Hewitt Robins Co., N.Y.C., 1956-59; rsch. engr. Weidlinger Cons., N.Y.C., 1959-62, McDonnell Douglas, St. Louis, 1964-65; rsch. mgr. GE, Phila., 1965-66; rsch. mgr. Jet Propulsion Lab., Pasadena, Calif., 1966-70, program mgr. advanced studies, 1971-76, dir. rsch. program autonomous systems and space mechanics, 1976-84, pres. Heer Assocs., Inc., 1984—; program mgr. Lunar exploration office NASA, Washington, 1970-71; adj. prof. U. So. Calif., 1973-84, dir. Inst. Technoecon. Studies, 1978-84. Author: Operation Systems-Humans-Intelligence-Machines, 1998. Fellow ASME; assoc. fellow AIAA; mem. ASCE, IEEE, Am. Mgmt. Assn., Internat. Fedn. Theory Machines and Mechanisms, Sigma Xi. Editor: Remotely Manned Systems, 1973, Robots and Manipulator Systems I & II, 1977, Machine Intelligence and Autonomy for Aerospace Systems, 1988, Mechanism and Machine Theory; contbr. articles to profl. jours. Home: 5329 Crown Ave La Canada Flintridge CA 91011-2807 Office: 4800 Oak Grove Dr Pasadena CA 91109-8001

HEFFER, JEAN, historian, educator; b. Paris, Oct. 1, 1933; s. Ernest and Marguerite (Labarre) H.; m. Yvette Marty, July 27, 1961; children: Patrick, Gabriel. Agregation, Sorbonne, 1957; D 3d cycle, U. Toulouse, 1967; D, U. Paris I, 1984. Asst. prof. history Sorbonne, Paris, 1969-70, U. Paris 1, 1970-84; prof. history Ecole Hautes Etudes en Sciences Sociales, Paris, 1985—. Author: The Port of New York and the American Foreign Trade, 1860-1900, 1986. Mem. French Assn. Econ. Historians (pres. 1987-90), French Assn. Am. Studies (v.p. 1987—). Avocations: music, piano, violin. Home: 42 bis ave Carnot, 94500 Champigny sur Marne France Office: Ecole Hautes Etudes Social Sci, 11 rue Pierre et Marie Curie, 75005 Paris France

HEFFERNAN, JOHN WILLIAM, retired journalist; b. Stockbridge, Hants., Eng., Oct. 21, 1910; came to U.S., 1946; s. John and Alice Ann (Edwards) H.; m. Edith Curry, Dec. 10, 1948 (dec. Aug. 1990); 1 stepchild, Anthony Edward; m. Martha Powell Hensley, Apr. 25, 1992. Student, Clarks Coll., Eng., 1924-26. Sub-editor Central News, London, 1929-34; sub-editor Press Assn., London, 1934-36, sports reporter, 1936-39; fgn. corr. Reuters, N.Y.C., 1946; fgn. corr. at UN, N.Y.C., 1946-57; chief corr. Reuters, Washington, 1957-76; ret., 1976. Pres. Gasparilla Island Conservation and Improvement Assn., Boca Grande, Fla., 1994; bd. dirs. Gasparilla Island Bridge Com., 1996-97. With Brit. Army, 1941-46, promoted maj. 1945. Decorated Comdr. Order of Brit. Empire, 1969. Mem. Nat. Press Club (pres. 1969), UN Corr. Assn. (pres. 1956), Overseas Press Club. Avocations: golf, swimming. Home: PO Box 687 Boca Grande FL 33921-0687

HEFFERNAN, THOMAS CARROLL, English literature and American studies educator; b. Hyannis, Mass., Aug. 19, 1939; arrived in Japan, 1984; s. Thomas (Hugh) Carroll and Mary Elizabeth (Sullivan) H.; m. Nancy Elizabeth Iler, 1972 (div. 1977). BA in English, Boston Coll., 1961; MA in English Lit., Victoria U. Manchester, Eng., 1963; PhD in English Lit., Sophia U., 1990. Asst. lectr. in English U. Manchester, Eng., 1964-65, U. Bristol, Eng., 1965-66; instr. English U. Hartford, West Hartford, Conn., 1967-70, N.C. State U., Raleigh, 1971-73; poet in the schs. N.C. Dept. Pub. Instrn. and Arts Coun., Raleigh, 1973-77; lectr. in English and humanities Program for Afloat Coll. Edn., USN, Norfolk (Va.) & San Diego, Calif., 1982-84; lectr. in English, history and philosophy U. Md., Asian Divsn., Tokyo, 1984-92; vis. prof. English U. Kagoshima, Japan, 1992-94; prof. English and Am. studies Kagoshima Prefectural Coll., Japan, 1994—; editor, pub., dir. Yorick Books, Boston and Hartford, 1967-71; dir., poetry instr. Martha's Vineyard Writers Workshop, Vineyard Haven, Mass., 1973-77; vis. artist in poetry N.C. Arts Coun., N.C. Dept. C.Cs., Raleigh, 1977-81; vis. artist in poetry S.C. Arts Commn., Columbia, 1981-82; editor, pub. Plover/Chidori, Okinawa, Japan, 1987-92; lectr. in field. Author: The Liam Poems, 1981 (Roanoke-Chowan 1982), Art and Emblem: Early 17th Century English Poetry of Devotion, 1991, Gathering In Ireland, 1996; editor (Celtic issue) Internat. Poetry Rev., 1979; contbr. chpts. to books and articles to profl. jours. Recipient Mainichi award Internat. Haiku in English, Mainichi Daily News, Japan, 1985, 87, 88, 89, 90, 91, 92, 93, 97, Portfolio Poetry award Poetry Ctr.-Guilford Coll., Greensboro, N.C., 1983, Mainichi Culture Seminar Haiku award Mainichi Daily News/Japan Air Lines, Tokyo, 1986, Internat. Haiku award Itoen Co., Tokyo, 1990, 1995. Mem. MLA, Internat. Comparative Lit. Assn., Renaissance Inst. (Tokyo), Internat. Ezra Pound Conf., Japan Emily Dickinson Soc., English Literary Soc. Japan, Japan Shakespeare Soc., Japan Am. Lit. Soc., Japan Assn. Lang. Tchrs. (local chpt. v.p. 1992-94). Avocations: singing, walking, traveling. Office: Kagoshima Prefectural Coll, 1-52-1 Shimo-Ishiki-Cho, Kagoshima 890-0005, Japan

HEFFNER, DANIEL JASON, film producer; b. N.Y.C., Mar. 30, 1956; s. Richard Douglas and Elaine Peggy (Segal) H.; m. Beth Klein, May 26, 1991; children: Jeremy Aaron, Zachary David. BS in Comm., Ithaca Coll., 1978. Prodn. exec. Columbia Pictures, L.A., 1982-85; prodn. exec., prodr. Walt Disney Pictures, L.A., 1985-88; v.p. prodn. Buena Vista Pictures Distbn. divsn. Walt Disney Co., L.A., 1988-91; pres. Poo Bear Prodns. Inc., 1991—. Asst. dir. (film) The Big Chill, 1982; co-prodr. (film) Cocktail, 1988; exec. prodr. (film) The Good Mother, 1988; co-exec. prodr. (film) Holy Matrimony, 1993; asst. dir., 2d unit dir. (film) The Seventh Veil, 1999; line prodr., 1st asst. dir. Highway 395, 1999. Mem. Dirs. Guild Am. Democrat. Jewish. E-mail: danheffner@earthlink.net. Fax: 818-789-0213. Home: 4119 Woodman Ave Sherman Oaks CA 91423-4331

HEFFNER, KRYSTIAN MARIA, economic geographer educator, urban planner; b. Rybnik, Poland, Oct. 10, 1951; s. Jan and Felicja (Łyczko) H.; m. Zofia Morawska; children: Marcin, Michael, Jakub. Masters Degree, Wroclaw (Poland) U., 1974; PhD, Wroclaw Tech. U., 1978; prof., Geog. Inst., Warsaw, Poland, 1992. Asst. prof. Silesian Inst., Opole, Poland, 1978-80, sr. prof. asst., 1980-91, prof., 1992—; prof. Lodź (Poland) U., 1994—; dir. Silesian Inst., Opole, 1991-96; prof. Sch. Econ., Katowice, Poland. Author: Oppelner Schlesien der Bevölkerungs-und Raum umgestaltungsverlauf des Dorfbesiedlungssystems, 1993; editor: Small Regions in United Europe, 1997, Region and Regionalism, 1999. Recipient Maciej Rataj Found., Warsaw, 1993. Mem. Polish Geog. Soc. (regional pres. 1986-94), Polish Urban Soc. (regional pres. 1990-96). Avocations: map collection, internat. tourism, beer glasses collection. Home: Sciegiennego 13/7, 45-709 Opole Poland Office: Silesian Inst, Piastowska 17, 45-081 Opole Poland

HEFNER, WILLIAM JOHNSON, JR. (W. JOHN HEFNER, JR.), oil and gas industry executive; b. Oklahoma City, July 29, 1952; s. William Johnson and Eloise (Wallace) H.; m. Deborah Seyan Raulston, Nov. 23, 1979; children: Margaret Leigh, Virginia Lynn. BA in Journalism, U. Okla., 1980; MBA, Oklahoma City U., 1983. Reporter city desk The Daily Oklahoman, Oklahoma City, 1978-79; field landman Gerald D. Whitfield, Oklahoma City, 1980, W.W. Blair, Oklahoma City, 1980-81; field landman, in-house landman T.S. Dudley Land Co., Oklahoma City, 1981-82; landman, part owner Arbuckle Enterprises, Inc., Oklahoma City, 1984-88; mng. ptnr. Hefner Co., Oklahoma City, 1986-93, Hefner Prodn. Co., Oklahoma City, 1986-93; leasing agt. First Resource Realty, Inc., Oklahoma City, 1987; leasing agt., property mgr. Alquest Property Corp., Oklahoma City, 1987-88; pres. Hefner Corp., Oklahoma City, 1988-93, Hefner Co., Inc., Oklahoma City, 1994—. Bd. dirs. Hist. Preservation, Inc., 1982—, mem. trees, parks and beautification com., 1983-85, 88-89, 95, chmn. trees, parks and beautification com., 1986, mem. projects com., 1986, 89, 91, 94-99, mem. enforcement com., 1984-85, 88, mem. long range planning com., 1988-89, mem. oil and gas com., 1991, mem. fin. and budget com., 1989, 1st v.p., 1988, 2d v.p., 1989, mem. assoc. bd., 1992, chmn. pub. rels. com., 1992, mem. real estate com., 1998-99; reporter, editor The Heritage Hills Herald, 1987-89, vice-chmn., 1993-97; participant Heritage Hills Housetour, 1982, 87, 93; pres. Hist. Preservation Inc., 2000—; pres. Midtown Redevel. Corp., 2000; assoc. bd. dirs. Okla. Med. Rsch. Found., 1988-92, mem. fin. and investment com., 1991, exec. com., 1991—, bd. dirs., 1992—; bd. dirs. Lyric Theatre, 1990-92, adv. bd. dirs., 1992-95; bd. dirs. Deaconess Hosp., 1991—, mem. exec. com., 1993-95, 2d v.p., 1994-95; bd. dirs. Deaconess Health Care Corp., 1994—; mem. devel. com. Casady Sch., 1994, co-chair leadership circle, 1994; active Leadership Oklahoma City Class XI, 1993; vestry mem. St. Paul's Cathedral, 1990-92, mem. Usher's Guild, 1988-97, 99—; bd. dirs. Children's Med. Rsch., 1992-94; bd. dirs. Okla. Heritage Assn., 1994-99; active Downtown Now, 1989—, Oklahoma City Art Mus., 1985—, U. Okla. Found., Norman, 1990—, YMCA, 1988-94, Com. of 100, 1993—, bd. dirs. 1996-97; mem. com. Leadership Ctr. Casady Sch., 1999—. Mem. Ind. Petroleum Assn. Am., Okla. Ind. Petroleum Assn., Chafing Dish Soc., Okla. Hist. Soc., Petroleum Club, Oklahoma City Golf and Country Club (stockholder 1986—), Magna Charta Barons (Somerset chpt.), Lotus Club, Kiwanis Club

Oklahoma City (bd. dirs. 1993-94, co-chmn. interclub com. 1993). Republican. Episcopalian. Avocation: historical preservation. Office: Hefner Co Inc PO Box 2177 Oklahoma City OK 73101-2177

HEFTER, LAURENCE ROY, lawyer; b. N.Y.C., Oct. 13, 1935; s. Charles S. and Rose (Postal) H.; m. Jacqulyn Maureen Miller, June 13, 1957; children: Jeffrey Scott, Sue-Anne. B.M.E., Rensselaer Poly. Inst., 1957, M.S. in Mech. Engring., 1960; J.D. with honors, George Washington U., 1964. Bar: Va. 1964, N.Y. 1967, D.C. 1973. Instr. Rensselaer Poly. Inst., Troy, N.Y., 1957-59; patent engr. Gen. Electric Co., Washington, 1959-63; sr. patent atty. Atlantic Research Corp., Alexandria, Va., 1963-66; assoc. firm Davis, Hoxie, Faithfull & Hapgood, N.Y.C., 1966-69; mem. firm Ryder, McAulay & Hefter, N.Y.C., 1970-73, Finnegan, Henderson, Farabow, Garrett & Dunner, LLP, Washington, 1973—; professorial lectr. trademark law George Washington U., 1981-90; mem. adv. com. U.S. Patent and Trademark Office, 1988-92, Trademark Rev. Commn., 1986-89. Named in Best Lawyers in Am., Best Lawyers in Washington. Mem. ABA (chmn. patent office affairs com. patent, trademark and copyright sect. 1976-80, unfair competition com. 1980-81, governing com. franchise forum 1994-97), N.Y. State Bar Assn., D.C. Bar Assn., Va. Bar Assn. (dir. patent, trademark and copyright sect. 1976-78), Internat. Bar Assn. (chmn. trademark com. 1986-90), Am. Patent Law Assn. (chmn. trademark com. 1979-81, dir. 1981-84), U.S. Trademark Assn. (dir. 1982-84, elected Guide to World's Leading Experts in Trademark Law, Guide to World's Leading Experts in Patent Law), Order of Coif, Alpha Epsilon Pi. Home: 6904 Loch Lomond Dr Bethesda MD 20817-4756 Office: 1300 I St NW Washington DC 20005-3314

HEGARTY, MARY FRANCES, lawyer; b. Chgo., Dec. 19, 1950; d. James E. and Frances M. (King) H. BA, DePaul U., 1972, JD, 1975. Bar: Ill. 1975, U.S. Dist. Ct. (no. dist.) Ill. 1976, U.S. Supreme Ct. 1980. Ptnr. Lannon & Hegarty, Park Ridge, Ill., 1975-80; pvt. practice, Park Ridge, 1980—; dir. Legal Assistance Found. Chgo., 1983—. Mem. revenue study com. Chgo. City Coun. Fin. Com., 1983; mem. Sole Source Rev. Panel, City of Chgo., 1984; pres. Hist. Pullman Found., Inc., 1984-85; apptd. Park Ridge Zoning Bd., 1993-94. Mem. Ill. State Bar Assn. (real estate coun. 1980-84), Chgo. Bar Assn., Women's Bar Assn. Ill. (pres. 1983-84), NW Suburban Bar Assn., Park Ridge Women Entrepreneurs, Chgo. Athletic Assn. (pres. 1992-93). Democrat. Roman Catholic. Office: 301 W Touhy Ave Park Ridge IL 60068-4204

HEGAZI, HESHAM AHMED, mechanical engineer, educator; b. Cairo, Feb. 11, 1970; s. Ahmed Mahmoud Hegazi and Nahda Hanafy Abdel-Hamid; m. Shaimaa A. Badawy; 1 child, Ahmed. BSc with honors, Cairo U., 1992, MSc, 1997. Tchg. asst. Cairo U., 1992-97, asst. lectr., 1997—; design engr. Pantech. Design Office, Cairo, 1992-94; tchg. asst. Am. U. Cairo, 1996—; maintinance engr. various factories, 10th Ramadan, Egypt, 1996—. Contbr. articles to profl. pubs. Editor NASR Automotive Mag., 1995-96. Mem. ASME (Best Paper award 1999, Student Travel award 1999), Egyptian Syndicate Engrs. Home: 1/12 Zahraa El-Maadi, Cairo Egypt Office: Mech Design Prdn Dept, Cairo U Faculty Engring, 12316 Cairo Egypt

HEGAZY, AHMAD KAMEL, plant ecology educator; b. Belbis, El Sharkia, Egypt, Feb. 22, 1953; s. Kamel Ahmad Hegazy and Inaam Hassan Eed; m. Eman Abdel Raouf Abdel Aziz, Oct. 25, 1962; children: Neisma, Nouran, Housam. BSc, U. Cairo, Giza, Egypt, 1976, MSc, 1980; PhD, U. Alta., Edmonton, Can., 1987. Demonstrator Cairo U., Giza, 1976-80, asst. lectr., 1980-87, lectr., 1987-92, assoc. prof., 1992-98, prof., 1998—; land resources cons. Ctr. for Environment and Devel. for the Arab Region and Europe, Conv. on Internat. Trade in Endangered Species, others. Editor: Environment 2000 and Beyond, 1999; co-editor: Reviews in Ecology, 1997; co-author: Encyclopedia of Deserts, 1999, Allelopathy, Vol. II, Basic and Applied Aspects, 1999; contbr. articles to profl. jours. Mem. local and regional coms. on environmental issues. Recipient prize for environ. protection Acad. Sci. Rsch. and Tech., Egypt, 1997, Internat. Jury of Slow Food Internat. award. Fellow World Acad. Art and Sci.; mem. Internat. Allelopathy Soc. (regional coord. 1996—), Internat. Assn. Ecology, Devel. Sci. and Tech. Awareness Soc. (founder). Avocations: camping, swimming, jogging, mountaineering, reading. E-mail: akhegazy@main-scc.cairo.eun.eg. Office: Dept Botany Faculty Sci, Univ Cairo, 12613 Giza Egypt

HEGAZY, IBRAHIM ABD-ELAZIZ, marketing educator, consultant; b. Cairo, Mar. 8, 1962; s. Abdelaziz Mohamed Hegazy and Esmat Ibrahim Allam; m. Jasmine-Sarah Mohamed Taha-Zaky, Sept. 1, 1989; 1 child, Alya. BA, Am. U., Cairo, 1984, MBA, 1987; PhD, George Washington U., 1990. Pres. ETIDCO, Cairo, 1988-94; prof. mktg., pub. rels. and sales mgmt. Am. U. in Cairo, 1990—, lectr. Inst. Mgmt. Devel., 1991—, dir. Inst. Mgmt. Devel., 1995—; ptnr. Dr. A.M. Hegazy & Co., Cairo, 1988—; lectr. German C. of C., Cairo, 1990—; bd. mem. Nat. Plastic Co., Cairo, 1993-96; pres. Vidi Ad, Cairo, 1994—. Editor: Marketing Privatization in Egypt, 1996. Mem. econ. com. Nat. Dem. Party, 1996. Mem. Am. Mktg. Assn., Internat. Advt. Assn. (mktg. diploma), Egyptian Am. C. of C. Avocations: music, travel, watch collecting, boating. Office: Am Univ in Cairo Mgmt Dept, 113 Kasr-Eleini St, Cairo Egypt

HEGDE, BELLE MONAPPA, academic administrator; b. India, Aug. 18, 1938; s. Vorvady Shanker and Belle Chandravathi (Shetty) H.; m. Hebri Malathi, May 5, 1960; children: Meenakshi, Maina, Manjunath. MBBS, Stanley Med. Coll., Madras, India, 1960; MD, King George Med. Coll., Lucknow, India, 1964. Reader Kasturba Med. Coll., 1964, assoc. prof., 1969-72, prof., 1972-88, dir. prof., 1988-90, prin., 1990-92, dean, 1990-98; pro vice chancellor Manipal (India) Acad. Higher Edn. Deemed U., 1998-2000; vice-chancellor, 2000—. Author: books; contbr. 132 articles to profl. jours., articles to newspapers. Chmn. Bharathiya Vidya Bhavan (Indian Inst. Culture). Commonwealth fellow Common Univs. Assn., fellow Heart and Chest Assn.; recipient Disting. Physician award Assn. Physicians India, 1995, Best Oration award IMA, 1995, Best Pub. Paper award Jour. Indian Med. Assn., 1996. Fellow Royal Coll. Physicians (London, Edinburgh, Glasgow, Dublin), Am. Coll. Cardiology; mem. Lions Club (gov.). Avocations: reading, writing, swimming. Home: Belle Monappa Hegde, Mahe House, Karnataka 575 004 Manipal 576119, India Office: Mahe Univ, Vice Chancellor s Office, Karnataka 575 001 Manipal 576 119, India

HEGDE, MIJAR RADHAKRISHNA, brewery company official, researcher; b. Mijar, Karnataka, India, Apr. 30, 1939; arrived in Eng., 1968; s. Jarkala Sheshappa and Jarkala Kamala (Shetty) H.; m. Rita Teresa Lobo, Oct. 26, 1976; children: Nakul, Natasha. BSc, Bombay U., 1964; MSc, London U., 1974; diploma, Inst. Packaging, 1986. Cert. chemist, packaging technologist. Shift mgr. Star Metal Refinery, Bombay, 1964-66; med. rep. Reptakos, Brett, Bombay, 1966-68; analyst Benskins Brewery, Watford, Eng., 1968-70; chief analyst Ind Coope Brewery, Romford, Eng., 1970-75; rsch. scientist Allied Breweries, Burton-on-Trent, Eng., 1975-85; packaging technologist Carlsberg Tetley Burton Brewery, Burton-on-Trent, 1985-97; packaging tech. authority Bass Brewers Burton Brewery, Burton-on-Trent, 1997—. Mem. Inst. Quality Assurance, Inst. Brewing. Avocations: tennis, cricket, golf. Office: Bass Brewers Burton Brewery, 137 High St, Burton upon Trent DE14 1JZ, England

HEGDE, SUBHASCHANDRA NINJOOR, zoologist, educator; b. Ninjoor, Karnataka, India, July 5, 1942; s. Sadashiva Anjar and Padmavathi (Shetty) H.; m. Bharathi Narsu Shetty, June 10, 1973; 2 children. BSc, Mahatma Gandhi Meml. Coll., Karnatak, India, 1963; MSc, Karnatak U., Dharwad, 1967, PhD, 1974. Demonstrator Karnatak U., 1970-74, lectr. zoology, 1976-80; postdoctoral fellow Nat. Inst. Rsch. in Dairying, Shinfield, Eng., 1974-76; reader Mangalore (India) U., 1980-87, prof., 1987—; vis. prof. U. Ariz., Tucson, 1992-93; vice chancellor U. Mysore, India, 1997—; head physiology divsn. dept. bioscis. Mangalore U., 1980-88, chmn. dept. applied zoology, 1988—; vis. fellow Indian Coun. Med. Rsch., New Delhi, 1978, Indian Nat. Sci. Acad., New Delhi, 1995. Contbr. over 60 articles to sci. publs. Mem. Indian Soc. for Comparative Aminal Physiology, Inst. Biologists (U.K.), Soc. Biol. Chemists, Press Club (Mangalore), Lions (Mangalagangotri, India). Avocations: public speaking, gardening, general science reading. Home: Vidvath, Dakshina Kannada, Karnatak Assaigoli 574199, India Office: Univ Mysore, Mysore 570005, India

HEGEDÜS, MIHÁLY, nutritionist; b. Oroszka, Hungary, May 24, 1943; s. Lajos and Anna (Kellessy) H. BS, MS in Chem. Engring., Tech. U. Budapest, 1967, D Tech. Biochemistry, 1973; PhD, Hungarian Acad. Sci., 1986, habil. vet. medicine, 1997. Rsch. scientist Nat. Inst. Human Nutrition, Budapest, 1967-72; from rsch. scientist to prof. Univ. Vet. Sci., Budapest, 1972—. Author: Evaluation of Feed Proteins, 1981; contbr. more than 200 articles to profl. jours. Recipient Niveau prize Pro Agroferm et Biotechnologia; Szèchenyi Prof. scholar. Mem. European Soc. Comparative and Vet. Nutrition, Internat. Soc. Animal Hygiene, Hungarian Sci. Soc. Food Industry, German Soc. Nutritional Physiology, Pub. Body of Hungarian Acad. Scis. Avocation: winter sports. Office: U Vet Sci Dept Animal Breed, and Nutri Rottenbiller 50, 1077 Budapest Hungary

HEGEDÜS, TIBOR, astronomer; b. Szeged, Hungary, June 18, 1961; s. József and Józsefné Terézia (Szvoboda) H.; m. Márta Garab, Aug. 23, 1984; children: Anett, Rita, Bálint. MS, Jate U., Szeged, 1985; D Univ., Elte U., Budapest, 1996, PhD, 1997. Cert. physicist. Tech. asst. Baja Astron Obs, Hungary, 1984-85, asst. rschr., 1985-88, rschr., 1988-93, dir. in charge, 1994—, dir., 1995—; guest lectr. Jpte U., Pécs, Hungary, 1993. Mem. editl. bd. Earth and Sky, 1987-90, Meteor, 1990-92; co-editor IAPPP '95 Symposium, 1996. Mem. curatory Baja Obs. Found., 1993—; mem. presidency T.I.T. Bacskai Orgn., Baja, 1991; mem. sci. adv. corp. Bacs-Kiskun, Hungary, 1994—. Mem. Internat. Astron. Union, Internat. Amateur-Profl. Photoelectric Photometry Orgn. (leader Hungarian wing 1992—), Hungarian Astron. Assn. (pres. 2000—), Hungarian Astronautical Assn., Assn. Popularization of Natural Scis. (Hungary) Sci. Pop. Corp. Avocations: amateur photography, travel, electronic and classical music, computer hardware. Office: Baja Astron Obs, Szegediut PF 766, H-6500 Baja Hungary

HEGGIE, ANDREW ALISTAIR CROMIE, surgeon; b. Melbourne, Victoria, Australia, July 16, 1955; s. Leslie Featherstone and Edna Mabel (Cromie) H.; m. Denise Maree Lawry, Oct. 6, 1979; children: Katrina, Andrew, Caroline. BDSc, U. Melbourne, 1977, MDSc, 1980, MBBS, 1991. Cert. medicine, dentistry. Resident Royal Melbourne Hosp., 1979-81; chief resident U. Wash., Seattle, 1983; cons. surgeon Royal Melbourne Hosp., 1984—; intern Austin Hosp., Melbourne, 1992; head oral and maxillofacial surgery, craniofacial unit Royal Children's Hosp. Melbourne, 1994—; dir. rsch. unit for facial disorders Univ. Melbourne. Contbr. articles to profl. jours. Fellow Royal Australasian Coll. Dental Surgeons (OMS); mem. Australian and New Zealand Assn. Oral and Maxillofacial Surgeons, Am. Assn. Oral and Maxillofacial Surgeons, Australian Med. Assn., Australian Dental Assn. Avocations: skiing. Office: Royal Childrens Hosp, Flemington Rd Parkville, Melbourne 3052 Vic, Australia

HEGGLAND, ROAR ASBJØRN, geophysicist, researcher; b. Vikebygd, Norway, May 25, 1954; s. Knut and Ruth Ellinor (Owe) H.; m. Lindis Åslid; children: Sunniva, Julia. BSc, U. Bergen, Norway, 1978, MSc, 1982. Geophysicist Statoil, Stavanger, Norway, 1984-85; sr. geophysicist Statoil, Stavanger, 1985-95, staff geophysicist, 1995—. Contbr. articles to profl. jours. Office: Statoil Den Norske Stats, Oljeselskap AS, N-4035 Stavanger Norway

HEIBERG, JENS GERHARD, retired company executive; b. Oslo, Apr. 20, 1939; s. Gerhard H. and Johanne Marie Baumann (Nielsen) H.; m. Else Cathrine Matheson. Grad., Copenhagen Sch. Econs./Bus.; student, Calif. State U., 1964. Mkt. analyst Norsk Hydro, 1965; head dept. and sales dir. Borregaard, Austria, 1966-72; asst. mng. dir. Norcem, 1972-73; pres. A/S Norcem, Aker Norcem A/S, Aker a.s., 1973-89; chmn. bd. Aker A/S, Oslo, 1989-96; pres., CEO Lillehammer Winter Olympics, 1994; ptnr. Norscan Ptnrs. AS, 1994—; ret.; chmn. bd. Den Norske Banka ASA, Norwegian Trade Coun.; bd. dirs. Petroleum Geo-Svcs. A/S, Nefinsa, S.A., Valencia, IESE, Barcelona; sr. ptnr. Scandinavian Equity Ptnrs. Ltd., Sweden; mem. Internat. Olympic Com., 1994—.

HEICK, ALEX, physician, neurologist; b. Copenhagen, Denmark, Jan. 25, 1949; s. Bent Heick and Ruth Preisler (Jensen) Hansen; m. Annelise Dal, Feb. 2, 1978; children: Lykke, Frederikke, Esben. M in Psychology, U. Copenhagen, 1978, MD, 1979. Cert. specialist of neurology. Intern dept. orthopedic surgery Kommune Hosp., Copenhagen, 1980-81; intern dept. medicine Bispebjerg Hosp., Copenhagen, 1981-82; intern dept. anaesthesiology Rønne Sygehus, Denmark, 1982-83; resident dept. neurosurgery Rigs Hosp., Copenhagen, 1983-85; resident dept. neurology Roskilde (Denmark) Hosp., 1986-93; with dept. neurology Glostrup U. Hosp., Denmark, 1994-99; cons. dept. neurology Holbaek Hosp.; chmn. polit. adv. group Minister of Health, Copenhagen, 1994-96; chmn. bd. Gladsaxe Gymnasium, Denmark, 1994-96, 98—; chmn. BL-TV, Copenhagen, 1998—. Author: (book) Sundhedens Pris (about Health Politics), 1995; contbr. articles to profl. jours. Ctr. Dem. Party candidate for European Parliament, Denmark, 1994; chmn. Dist. City Coun. of Bispebjerg, Denmark, 1998—. Maj., Royal Danish Med. Corps. Decorated UN medal for mil. svc. Mem. AAAS, Danish Neurol. Soc., Masons. Lutheran. Avocations: music, painting, basketball. Home: Tonemestervej 9, Copenhagen NV 2400, Denmark Office: Dept Neurology, Glostrup U Hosp, Glostrup 2600, Denmark

HEICK, LEON JOSEPH, data processing executive; b. New England, N.D., May 14, 1944; s. Joseph Philiph and Frances (Bosepflug) H.; m. Alicia Marie Finneman, July 13, 1968; children: Brent, Royce, Travis. BS in Bus. Adminstrn., U. Mary, Bismarck, N.D., 1991, BS in Acctg., 1998. Computer operator North Ctrl. Data Corp., Mandan, N.D., 1968-69, computer programmer, 1970-71, programming mgr., 1972-78, sys. mgr., 1979-83, asst. gen. mgr., 1984—, mgr. multi million dollar offshore software devel. projects, 1991—; dir. Project Back Home Coop, Mandan, 1994—, Rural Electric and Telephone Credit Union, Bismarck, N.D., 1993—. Singer No. Lights Barbershop Chorus, Bismarck, 1991-93; active ch. choir. With U.S. Army, 1965-67, Vietnam. Mem. Am. Legion, KC, Elks, Amvets. Avocations: singing, guitar playing, golf, hunting, fishing. Office: North Ctrl Data Corp PO Box 728 Mandan ND 58554-0728

HEIDE, JOHN WESLEY, engineering executive; b. Chgo., Sept. 14, 1946; s. Frederick Bernard Heiner-Heide and Eleanor Francis (Tuttle) Heide; m. Patricia Ann Lynn, A g. 5, 1967 (div. Jan. 1973); children: John Wesley, Joseph Edward. AA, Phoenix Jr. Coll., 1972; BS, Ariz. State U., 1975. Quality assurance engr. Tex. Instruments, Dallas, 1969-70, ITT Courier, Tempe, Ariz., 1975-79; sr. project engr. GTE Comms., El Paso, 1979-83, Telxon Corp., Houston, 1983-87; engring. mgr. United Techs., Niles, Mich., 1987-91, Automotive Industries, Midland, Tex., 1991-94; divsn. quality assurance mgr. Pec Golden Triangle Plastics, El Paso, Tex., 1994-95; indsl. engring. mgr. Elcom, Inc., El Paso, Tex., 1995-97; quality assurance mgr. United for Excellence Inc., El Paso, 1997-99; TQM mgr. Dayco Inc., El Paso, 1999—; instr. engring. Houston C.C., 1984-85. Author: Reflections, 1990, Scan-It, 1991, A Step Beyond the Fog, 1992, How Cheap Is Cheap, 1993. Candidate for mayor, El Paso, 1980, 82, 84; candidate for State Rep., Berrien Springs, Mich., 1990. With USMC, 1965-69, Vietnam. Mem. NSPE, Soc. Plastics Engrs. (pres.), Inst. Indsl. Engring. (v.p. 1982-83), Soc. Mfg. Engrs. (v.p.), Am. Soc. Quality Control (v.p.). Republican. Lutheran. Avocations: European travel, genealogy, stamp and coin collecting. Fax: 915-860-2116. Home: 10732 Chert St El Paso TX 79924-1647 Office: Dayco Industrial Divsn 12134 Esther Lama Dr Ste 200 El Paso TX 79936-7727

HEIDEMAN, NIKOLAAS JOHANNES HENDRIK, mathematics educator; b. Weesp, Holland, June 2, 1939; arrived in South Africa, 1950; s. Simon Heideman and Annie (Ebmeijer) Van Luyt; m. Anne Felicity Garrett, Sept. 25, 1963 (div. June 1978); children: Kerry, Patrick, Lucienne; m. Linda Lee Stephens, Jan. 20, 1979; children: Paul, Vicky. BSc, U. Cape Town, South Africa, 1959, BSc with honors, 1962; MA, Washington U., 1967, PhD, 1970. Lectr. U. Witwatersrand, Johannesburg, South Africa, 1963-65; assoc. prof. Rhodes U., Grahamstown, South Africa, 1970—; vis. assoc. prof. U. Waterloo, Can., 1995. Author: Invitation to the South African Math Olympiad, 1995. Vice chmn. South African Math Olympiad, 1992—, chmn. 1997—. Mem. South African Math Soc. (sec. 1972-76, treas. 1979-81), Assn. Math Edn. South Africa (chmn., vice-chmn. Grahamstown br.). Avocations: wind surfing, hiking, gardening. Office: Rhodes U, PO Box 94, Grahamstown 6140, South Africa

HEIDENDAL, GUIDO ALFONS, nuclear medicine physician; b. Rykevorsel, Antwerp, Belgium, Feb. 15, 1936; s. Felix Heidendal and Emerance Pauwels; m. Martine Jeune, May 6, 1970; children: Carine, Barbara, Philip. MD, U. Louvain, Belgium, 1962; specialist in nuclear medicine, Mayo Clinic, 1972. Bd. cert. nuclear medicine, U.S. Internist City-Hosp., Maaseik, Belgium, 1970, U. Louvain; U. Lyon, France; U. Amsterdam, The Netherlands, 1970; dir. dept. nuclear medicine Free U., Amsterdam, 1972-85, Acad. Hosp., Maastricht, The Netherlands, 1985—; mem. Dutch Bd. Nuclear Medicine, 1972-80; vis. prof. nuclear medicine Georgetown U., Washington, 1983; prof. nuc. medicine U. Maastricht, 1997. Referent: Biologie et Pathologie, 1982, Adrenal Scintigraphy, 1978, Preoperative Pulmonary in Extensive Lung Resection, 1986. Capt. Belgian Army, 1967-68. Fellow Am. Coll. Nuclear Medicine, Royal Soc. Medicine; mem. European Union Med. Specialists, Am. Soc. Nuclear Medicine, Belgian Soc. Nuclear Medicine, Netherland's Soc. Nuclear Medicine. Avocations: philosophy, music, science. Home: Graaf Van Waldeckstraat 20, 6212 AP Maastricht The Netherlands Office: Acad Hosp, P DeByelaan 25, 6202 AZ Maastricht The Netherlands

HEIDER, SUELI, music director; b. Sao Paulo, Dec. 28, 1953; d. Antonio and Ermelinda (do Rego) Bispo. MusB, Faculty Music, Sao Paulo, 1976, Musikhochschule Köln, Germany, 1982. Tchr. Conservatorie Music Ernesto Nazareth, Sao Paulo, 1974-77; repetiteur Internat. Curse Teresopolis, Rio de Janeiro, 1975-76; repititeur Internat. Curse Curitiba, Parana, Brazil, 1977; lectr. music Faculty Music, Sao Paulo, 1976-77; dir. Musikschule Stadt, Leichlingen, Germany, 1984-86; pres. Inst. Study Music, Leichlingen, Germany, 1985-91; cons. Inst. Brasileiro Estudos Music., Sao Paulo, 1993—; dir. Bergische Krammermusikvereinigung, Solingen, Germany, 1990—. Mem. Brazil Soc. Music, Acad. Brasil-Europa, Acad. Paulista history. Home: Dingshauser Str, 42655 Solingen Germany Office: Acad Brasil-Europa, An der Muenze 1, 50668 Cologne Germany

HEIDKAMP, MARY LOUISE, leadership management consultant; b. Chgo., Feb. 5, 1949; d. Herbert John and Mary Anne (Dunsheath) Heidkamp; m. James R. Lund, Aug. 19, 1978; children: Maura, Matthew. BA in Sociology, Clarke Coll., 1971; D in Ministry, McCormick Theol. Sem., 1993. Tchr. Kyoto and Tokyo, Japan, 1971, 74-75; coord. Social Ministry Diocese Providence, 1977-80; dir. Office Peace and Justice Diocese Rochester, N.Y., 1980-86; cons. Louisville, 1986-1989; co-dir. Office Peace and Justice Archdiocese Chgo., 1989-1999; cons. Oak Park, Ill., 1999—; vis. asst. prof. U. Ill., Chgo., 2000—. Author: (with Jim Lund) Moving Faith into Action, 1990; columnist New World Newspaper, 1997—. Mem. adv. bd. Chgo. Project Violence Prevention, 1996—. Recipient Disting. Alumnae award for humanitarian svc. Clarke Coll., Dubuque, Iowa, 1996, Cardinal Bernardin award Assn. Chgo. Priests, 1997. Mem. Assn. Cons. Non-Profits, Nat. Assn. Social Action Dirs. of The ROUNDTABLE (founding mem., bd. dirs. 1982-86, 93-99, co-recipient with J. Lund Harry A. Fagan ROUNDTABLE award 1996), Nat. Interfaith Com. Worker Justice (bd. dirs. 1996—), Internat. Grail. Roman Catholic. Avocations: running marathons, travel. Fax: 708-386-8375. E-mail: heidkampml@aol.com. Office: Cons Svcs 1160 S Kenilworth Ave Oak Park IL 60304-1945

HEIDT, FRANK DIETRICH, physicist, educator; b. Rastatt, Germany, June 9, 1944. Diploma of Physics, U. Karlsruhe, Germany, 1969, PhD in Civil Engring., 1975. Rsch. engr. Engring. Office, Karlsruhe, 1969-71, U. Karlsruhe, 1971-76, Dornier GmbH, Friedrichshaven, 1976-80; prof. physics U. Siegen, 1980—. Contbr. over 125 articles to profl. jours. Home: Bürgerstr 66, 57234 Wilnsdorf Germany Office: Univ-GH Siegen, Walter-Flex-Str 3, 57068 Siegen Germany

HEIDUSCHKA, PETER, bioelectrochemist, researcher; b. Bautzen, Saxonia, Germany, Oct. 23, 1960; s. Pawoł Hejduška and Ilse (Müller) Richter; m. Anke Teuber, July 30, 1993; children: Julia, Sonja. Diploma in tchg., Tchrs. Tng. Coll., Halle, Germany, 1985, D in Natural Scis., 1988. Sci. asst. Tchrs. Tng. Coll., Halle, 1988-92; sci. asst. in phys. chemistry U. Tübingen, 1992-95, sci. asst. in ophthalmology, 1995—. Contbr. articles to profl. jours. including Bioelectrochem. Bioenergy, Electroanalysis, Electrochim. Acta, Chem. European Jour., Neuropharmacology. Dep. Town Coun., Bautzen, 1979-84. Served with Anti-Aircraft Def., German Mil., 1979-81. Grantee Deutsche Forschungs-Gemeinschaft, 1992. Mem. Gesellschaft Deutscher Chemiker, Neurowissenschaftliche Gesellschaft. Avocation: ballroom dancing. Office: U Muenster Exptl Ophthal, Domagkstr 15, D-48149 Münster Germany

HEIFETS, LEONID, microbiologist, educator; b. Russia, Jan. 5, 1926; came to U.S., 1979; s. Boris and Luba Heifets; m. Seraphima Apsit, Jan. 1955 (div. July 1978); children: Michael, Herman. MD, Med. Inst., Moscow, 1947, PhD, 1953; DSc, Acad. Med. Scis., Moscow. Asst. prof. Med. Inst., Arkhangelsk, Russia, 1950-54, assoc. prof., 1954-57; lab. dir. Mechnikov Rsch. Inst., Moscow, 1957-69; sr. rschr. Inst. for Tb, Moscow, 1969-78; rsch. fellow Nat. Jewish Hosp., Denver, 1979-80; lab. dir. Nat. Jewish Ctr., Denver, 1980—; asst. prof. Colo. U., Denver, 1980-86, assoc. prof., 1986-92, prof. microbiology, 1992—; mem. com. on bacteriology Internat. Union Against Tb, Paris, 1986—. Author: Effectiveness of Vaccination, 1968, Clinical Mycobacteriology (Clinics in Laboratory Medicine), 1996; author, editor: Drug Susceptibility, 1991; assoc. editor Internat. Jour. Tuberculosis; contbr. articles to profl. jours. Mem. Am. Soc. Microbiology. Avocations: hiking, snowshoeing, photography, history. Office: Nat Jewish Med Rsch Ctr 1400 Jackson St Denver CO 80206-2761

HEIKKINEN, JARI OLAVI, medical physicist, researcher; b. Kuopio, Finland, July 24, 1965; s. Voitto Antero and Hanna Kyllikki Heikkinen; m. Jenni Julia Hiltunen, Nov. 15, 1999. MSc, Kuopio U., 1991, cert. in med. physicist, 1996, PhD, 1999. Med. physicist Kuopio U. Hosp., 1989-90, asst. physicist, 1993-95; med. physicist Kotka (Finland) Ctrl. Hosp., 1990, Mikkeli (Finland) Ctrl. Hosp., 1990-93, 96—, Mid.-Finland Ctrl. Hosp., Jyvdskyld, 1995, S. Karelia Ctrl. Hosp., Lappeenranta, Finland, 1996; cons. Labquality Ltd., Helsinki, 1995—; radiation expert Mikkeli Provincial Govt. Contbr. articles to profl. jours. Lt. Air Force Signal Corps, 1986—. Mem. European Assn. Nuc. Medicine, Finnish Soc. Nuc. Medicine, Finnish Soc. Med. Physics and Med. Engring., Finnish Assn. Physicist Medicine. Fax: 358155512406. Office: Mikkeli Ctrl Hosp, Porrassalmenkatu 35-37, 50100 Mikkeli Finland

HEIL, ALAN LEWIS, JR., retired radio broadcast executive; b. Louisville, Ky., Oct. 21, 1935; s. Alan Lewis and Edna Mae Welch Heil; m. Dorothy Finnegan Heil, Aug. 23, 1959; children: Wendy Heil Packer, Susan Heil Cheatham, Nancy Heil Knor. BA in English, Duke U., 1957. Reporter Newark Evening News, 1957-58, 60-62; chief Mid. East bur., corr. Voice of Am., Beirut, Cairo, Athens, 1965-71; chief N.Y. bur. Voice of Am., 1972-73; chief news and current affairs Voice of Am., Washington, 1973-81; dir. broadcast ops. Washington, 1983-87, dep. dir. programs, 1987-95, dep. dir., 1996-98. Contbr. chpts. to books, articles to mags. Recipient Meritorious Honor award USIA, Washington, 1972, Disting. Honor award, 1987, Disting. Honor award VOA, 1998. Mem. Sr. Execs. Assn., USIA Alumni Assn. Presbyterian. Home: 8401 Porter Ln Alexandria VA 22308-2140

HEIL, MARY RUTH, former counselor; b. Westerville, Ohio, June 8, 1921; d. George Walter and Bertha Ellen (Shrodes) H. BS in Edn., Ohio State U., 1944; MEd, Wayne State U., 1956; cert. advanced study, Western Carolina U., 1987; cert. theol. edn., U. South, 1987. Cert. counselor, tchr., Ohio, Ky., Mich., Fla., N.C. Tchr. 7th grade Cheshire (Ohio) Sch., 1942-43; tchr. biology, English Ohio Soldiers' and Sailors' Orphans' Home, Xenia, 1943-47; tchr. 7th grade Lakeview High Schs., Winter Garden, Fla., 1947-48; tchr. English, journalism Pine Mountain (Ky.) Settlement Sch., 1948-49; field and established camp dir. Columbus (Ohio) and Franklin County Girl Scouts, 1949-50; tchr. Mary Lyon Jr. High Sch., Royal Oak, Mich., 1950-56, 57-62, Coston Secondary Modern Girls' Sch., Greenford, Middlesex, Eng., 1956-57; tchr. English West Henderson High Sch., Hendersonville, N.C., 1962-65, guidance counselor, 1965-86. Chmn. Mayor's Com. Employment of Handicapped, Hendersonville, 1972-74; v.p. Mountain Ramparts Health Planning Bd., Asheville, N.C., 1972-76, Western Carolina Health Systems Agy. Bd., Morganton, N.C., 1976-82; bd. dirs., sec., com. chmn., Henderson County Dispute Settlement Bd., 1989-95; exec. com., bd. dirs. Western Carolina Presbyn. Retirement Com., 1987-94; active Henderson County Coun. Women, Hendersonville, 1994-96, treas.; mem.-at-large Pisgah coun. Girl Scouts U.S., 1994-98, chair fund devel. com., 1995-98, exec. com., 1997-98; bd. dirs. Henderson County Coun. on Aging, 1998—, chair nom. com., 1999.

Named Woman of Achievement, Hendersonville Bus. and Profl. Women's Club, 1978, Civitan Citizen of Yr., Civitan Club, Hendersonville, 1986, Order Ky. Cols., 1988 ; recipient award Galludent U., Washington, 1986, Thanks Badge, Pisgah Coun., Girl Scouts U.S., 1998, state degree of Style, Dignity, Title and Honor of Dame, Baron of Shalford, Eng., 2000. Mem. NEA, ACA, Royal Oak Edn. Assn. (pres. 1954-56), N.C. Assn. Educators (pres. dist. 1970-72), Henderson County Mental Health Assn. (bd. dirs. 1965-74), Alpha Delta Kappa (N.C. 1st v.p. 1978-80, state pres. 1980-82, S.E. region grand v.p. 1987-89), Kappa Delta Pi. Democrat. Episcopalian. Avocations: golf, bowling, raising Irish Setters, classical music. Home: RR 6 Box 137 Hendersonville NC 28792-9428

HEILBORN, GEORGE HEINZ, investor; b. Cologne, Germany, Feb. 27, 1935; came to U.S., 1941; s. Walter and Christine (Spiegel) H.; m. Phyllis Dorothy Ehrhardt, Sept. 30, 1972; children: Stephanie, Allison. BA, Northwestern U., 1956; AM, Harvard U., 1958. With Thompson Ramo Wooldridge Products Co., El Segundo, Calif., 1958-60; project mgr. Electronics div. Gen. Mills, Mpls., 1960-61, Philco Corp., Willow Grove, Pa., 1961-63; pres., chmn. Info. Processing Systems, Inc., Hackensack, N.J., 1963-92; pres. G.H. Heilborn & Co., Inc., 1992—; bd. dirs. Continental Info. Sys. Corp. Mem. bd. vis. Coll. Arts and Scis., Northwestern U., 1992—, alumni regent, 1997—; mem. grad. sch. alumni coun. Harvard U., 1993—, chmn., 1996-98; trustee Family Counseling Svc., Ridgewood, N.J., 1992-95; mem. fin. and investment com. Children's Aid and Family Counseling, N.J., 1996—. Mem. Computer Dealers and Lessors Assn. (founding mem. 1971, pres. 1980-82, chmn. 1982-84), Equipment Leasing Assn. Am., U.S.-USSR Trade and Econ. Coun., N.Y. Acad. Scis., Harvard Club of N.Y. Home: 385 Knollwood Rd Ridgewood NJ 07450-4814 Office: G H Heilborn & Co Inc One University Plz Hackensack NJ 07601

HEILBRON, JOHN L., historian; b. San Francisco, Mar. 17, 1934; s. Louis Henry and Delphine A. (Rosenblatt) H.; m. Patricia Ann Lucero, Mar. 25, 1959 (dec. Dec. 1993); m. Alison Margaret Browning, May 28, 1995. AB, U. Calif., Berkeley, 1955, MA, 1958, PhD, 1964; Laurea in Philosophy honoris causa, U. Bologna, 1988; PhD (hon.), U. Pavia, 2000, U. Uppsala, 2000. Asst. dir. Sources for History of Quantum Physics, Berkeley and Copenhagen, 1961-64; asst. prof. history, philosophy of sci. U. Pa., Phila., 1964-67; asst. prof. history U. Calif., Berkeley, 1967-71, assoc. prof., 1971-73, prof., 1973-94, dir. Office for History of Sci. and Tech., 1973-94, class of 1936 prof. history and history of sci., 1985-94, editor Hist. Studies in Phys. Scis., 1980—, vice chancellor, 1991-94, prof. emeritus, 1994; Andrew Dickson White prof. at large Cornell U., 1984-90; chmn. Acad. Senate Berkeley div. U. Calif., 1988-90; sr. rsch. fellow Worcester Coll., Oxford and Oxford Mus. for the History of Sci., 1997—. Author: H.G.J. Moseley, The Life and Letters of an English Physicist, 1887-1915, 1974, (with P. Forman and S. Weart) Physics circa 1900: Personnel, Funding and Productivity of the Academic Establishments, 1975, (with W. Shumaker) John Dee on Astronomy, 1978, Electricity in the 17th and 18th Centuries: A Study of Early Modern Physics, 1979, 99; Historical Studies in the Theory of Atomic Structure, 1981, Elements of Early Modern Physics, 1981, (with R.W. Seidel and B.R. Wheaton) Lawrence and his Laboratory: Nuclear Science in Berkeley, 1931-61, 1981, (with B.R. Wheaton) Literature on the History of Physics in the 20th Century, 1981, (with Wheaton) An Inventory of Published Letters to and from Physicists, 1982, Physics at the Royal Society during Newton's Presidency, 1983, The Dilemmas of an Upright Man: Max Planck as Spokesman for German Science, 1986, 2000, (with E. Crawford and R. Ullrich) The Nobel Population, 1901-1937: A Census of Nominees and Nominators for the Prizes in Physics and Chemistry, 1987, (with Seidel) A History of the Lawrence Berkeley Laboratory, vol. 1: Lawrence and His Laboratory, 1990, Weighing Imponderables and Other Quantitative Science Around 1800, 1993, Geometry Civilized: History, Culture, Technique, 1998, The Sun in the Church: Cathedrals as Solar Observatories, 1999; editor: Benjamin Franklin's Briefe von der Elektrizität, 1983, (with T. Frängsmyr and R. Rider) The Quantifying Spirit in the 18th Century, 1990. Mem. Internat. Acad. History of Sci., History of Sci. Soc. (Sarton medalist), Brit. Soc. History of Sci., Am. Acad. Arts and Scis., Am. Philos. Soc., Royal Swedish Acad. Scis. (fgn.). Home: April House, Shilton near Burford OX18 4AB, England Office: Oxford Mus History of Sci, Broad St, Oxford OX1 3A2, England

HEILER, SIEGFRIED, statistician; b. Wangen, Allgaeu, Germany, Oct. 20, 1938; s. August and Lotte (Fleischer) H.; m. Ilse Hoptner, Mar. 21, 1963 (div. Mar. 1976); 1 child, Eva; m. Hildegard Rausch-Heiler, June 16, 1977; children: Mark, Patrick. Verwaltungs-inspektor, Staatl Verwaltungs Schule, Stuttgart, Bad-Wuertt, 1959; Diplom, Volkswirt, U. Tubingen/Hamburg/Munchen, 1963; Dr.rer.pol., U. Tubingen, 1966. Asst. prof. Tech. U., Berlin, 1969-71, prof., 1971-72; prof. stats. U. Dortmund, Fed. Republic Germany, 1972-87; dean dept. stats. U. Dortmund, 1974-75, 79-80, 1989-90, pres. European Courses in Advanced Stats., 1993-97; pres. Deutsche Statische Gesellschaft, 1988-92. Author: Einfuhrung in die Statistik, 1971, Wirtschaftprognosen, 1973, Deskriptive und Explorative Datenanalyse, 1994; co-author: (with P. Michels) A Course in Time Series Analysis, 2000; editor: Recent Trends in Statistics, 1983; contbr. articles to sci. jours. Mem. Internat. Statis. Inst., Deutsche Statistische Gesellschaft. Home: Mozartstrasse 8, Konstanz, 78464 Baden-Wurttemberg Federal Republic of Germany Office: Fak Wirtschaftswiss U Dept Maths & Stats, Fach D 129, 78457 Konstanz Federal Republic of Germany

HEILIG, MARGARET CRAMER, nurse, educator; b. Lancaster, Pa., Jan. 17, 1914; d. William stuart and Margaret White (Snader) Cramer; m. David Heilig, June 1, 1942 (dec. 1998); children: Judith, Bonnie, Barbara. BA in Psychology, Wilson Coll., 1935; MSW, U. Pa., 1940; AAS in Nursing, Delaware County C.C., 1970. RN. Caseworker Children's Bur., Lancaster, Pa., 1935-37, Phila., 1939-42; group worker Ho. of Industry Settlement Ho., Phila., 1937-39; curriculum chmn. Upper Darby (Pa.) Adult Sch., 1958-68; health asst., camp mother Paradise Farm Camp, Downington, Pa., 1960-70; camp nurse Paradise Farm Camp, Downington, 1970-78, infirmary dir., 1978-86; med. surg. nurse Crozer-Chester Med. Ctr., Chester, Pa., 1970; outpatient nurse Maternal Infant Care, Chester, 1971; coll. nurse Delaward County C.C., Media, Pa., 1971-76; dir. health svcs., 1976-84, health cons., 1984—; writer bi-weekly health newsletter Life Lines, 1973—, Health Svcs., 1988—; mem. spkrs. bur., 1975-93; cons. Coll. Health svc. for Middle States Evaln., 1988; nurse for health screening children's program Tyler Arboretum, Media, 1982-93, Update on Personal Helth, Broadmeadows Women's Prison, 1973, 82. Author: First Aid Booklet, 1976; contbr. articles and columns in health field. Former leader Delaware County coun. Girl Scouts U.S.A.; clk. Lansdowne Friends Meeting, 1987-91, active newsletter, 1990-94; mem. Upper Darby Recreation Bd., 1956-58, Upper Darby Adult Sch. Bd., 1956-68, curriculum chmn., 1958-68; provider host home for fgn. exch. studens, 1965-75; participant Audubon Ann. Bird Count, 1970—; coord., dir. Bi-Ann. Soc. Friends Ch. Retreat, 1970-92; ARC Spkrs.'s Bur.-AIDS; tchr. beginning birding course Del. County C.C.; bd. dirs. Ret. Sr. Vol. Progam Del. County, 1991-97. Recipient Ollie B. Moten award Am. Coll. Health Assn., 1987, Disting. Nursing Alumni award Del. County C.C., 1995; inducted inot Legion of Honor Chapel of Four Chaplains, 1980; honored by dedication Park Area on Campus Del. county C.C.; team leader homeless advocacy Upper Darby, Pa., 1990-98; vol. Coun. Bd. Tyler Arboretum, 1989-94. Mem. ANA, Pa. Nurses Assn., Delaware County Nurses Assn. (membership chmn. 1977-78), Southeastern Pa. Coll. Health Nurses Assn. (co-founder, pres. 1983-85), Middle Atlantic Coll. Health Assn., Delaware Valley Soc. Adolescent Health, Family Svc. Assn. Delaware county (bd. dirs. 1989-91), LWV, women's Internat. League for Peace and Freedom (bd. dirs. Del. county group. 1998—), Brandywine Conservance, Tour Guide, Phila., Historic Area, Arch St. Friends. Quaker. Avocations: birding, piano, choral music, nature walking, handicrafts (craft participant Pa. Renaissance Faire 1985—, writer health and safety column in Shire Chronicle for participants 1993-96). Home and Office: 605 Mason Ave Drexel Hill PA 19026-2429

HEILIG, UWE JENS GERHARD, physicist; b. Tübingen, Germany, Sept. 29, 1964; s. Hans-Dieter and Ute (Freundt) H.; m. Monika Ida Nussbaum, Dec. 13, 1991; children: Malte, Carolin. PhD, U. Tübingen, 1993. Cons. PMB Logistikberatung, Essen, Germany, 1994-97; logistics mgr. Metabowerke GmbH & Co., Nurtingen, Germany, 1997—. Mem. German Physics Soc., N.Y. Acad. Scis. Home: Ziegelhuette 4, 72555 Metzingen Germany

HEILMAN, CARL EDWIN, lawyer; b. Elizabethville, Pa., Feb. 3, 1911; s. Edgar James and Mary Alice (Bechtold) H.; m. Grace Emily Greene, Nov. 29, 1934 (div. 1952); children: John Greene, Elizabeth Greene; m. Claire Virginia Phelps, Oct. 10, 1952 (dec. June 1990); m. Marie Wilmot Russ, Nov. 23, 1990. BA, Lafayette Coll., Easton, Pa., 1932, MA, 1933; JD magna cum laude, U. Pa., 1939. Bar: N.Y. 1940, Pa. 1940, Mass. 1973, U.S. Supreme Ct. 1960. Tchr. English Easton High Sch., 1934-36; assoc. Dwight, Harris, Koegel & Caskey, N.Y.C., 1939-42; atty. OPA, Washington, 1942-43, N.Y. Gov.'s Commn. to Investigate Workmen's Compensation Law, N.Y.C., 1943-44; assoc. Dewey, Ballantine, Bushby, Palmer & Wood, N.Y.C., 1944-59, ptnr., 1959-73; counsel to firm Csaplar & Bok, Boston and San Francisco, 1973-90; trustee Upsala Coll., East Orange, N.J., 1970-73. Fellow Am. Bar Found., mem. ABA, Nat. Trust for Hist. Preservation, Order of Coif. Republican. Episcopalian. Home: 5850 Meridian Rd Apt 508A Gibsonia PA 15044-9683

HEILMANN, CHRISTIAN FLEMMING, corporate executive; b. Apr. 26, 1936; s. Poul Bent and Hedvig Buchwald (Miller) H.; m. Marilyn Mildred Harter, July 9, 1959 (div. 1973); children: Christian Philip, Nicholas John, Claire Marie; m. 2d, Judith Lucy Tucker, Sept. 15, 1973; children: Per Flemming, Niels Henrik. MA, Cambridge (Eng.) U., 1957. Mng. dir., CEO Metal Box South Africa Ltd., Johannesburg, 1970-77; trustee Nat. Devel. and Mgmt. Found., South Africa, 1970-75; v.p. Continental Can Co., Stamford, Conn., 1977-78; pres. Continental Group Europe, Brussels, Belgium, 1978-80, Continental Diversified Industries, Stamford, Conn., 1980-81; exec. v.p., chief administrative officer Continental Group, Inc., Stamford, Conn., 1982-84; dir., pres, CEO Am. Can Can, Inc. (name changed to Onex Packaging Inc. 1986), Rexdale, Ont., 1984-89; N.Y. rep. Dansk Samvirke, 1996; chmn., CEO Brockway Standard, Inc., Atlanta, 1989-94; dir., bd. dirs. Whitlock Packaging Co., Okla., 1998—; mem. adv. coun. U. Toronto Bus. Sch., 1985-92; bd. dirs. Porter Chadburn, Inc., Omaha, Porter Chadburn PLC, London, OShaughnessy Funds, Inc. U.S. rep. Nat. Olympic Com. Denmark, 1994-96; attachè Danish Sports Orgn. for the Disabled 1996 Paralympic Games in Atlanta; bd. dirs. Am. Friends of Cambridge U., 1996—; mem. Cornell U. Coun., 1996-2000; bd. dirs. Jacob Riis Settlement House, N.Y.C., 1996—, v.p., 1999; trustee Am. Scandinavian Found., 1997, Paul Smith's Coll., St. Regis, N.Y., 1997—. Apptd. Knight of the Order of Dannebrog, Denmark, 1998. Mem. Danish-Am. Soc. (bd. dirs. 1990—, pres. 1996-2000), Danish Am. C. of C. (bd. dirs. 1995—), Greenwich Country Club.

HEILMANN, GERHARD MAX, retired physicist, educator; b. Limbach, Sachsen, Germany, July 30, 1926; s. Otto Karl and Martha Hulda (Nollau) H.; m. Ursula Katharina Pehl; children: Judith, Johannes. Diploma in physics, U. Frankfurt, Germany, 1953, PhD, 1958. Rsch. asst. U. Frankfurt, 1953-63; dozent Tech. Sch., Friedberg, Germany, 1963; sr. rsch. assoc. U. Newcastle-upon-Tyne, Eng., 1963-66; lectr. U. Eichstätt, Germany, 1969-72, chmn. physics, 1972-91, ret., 1991. Contbr. articles to sci. publs. Roman Catholic. Avocations: astronometry on pocket computers. Home: Obernhofer Str 15, 56377 Seelbach Germany

HEILMAN-SOBIE, KIMBERLY MARIE, lawyer; b. Bakersfield, Calif., Mar. 14, 1971; d. Robert Fred and Susan Ellen Heilman; m. Edward Alexander Sobie, Nov. 11, 1995. BS in Polit. Sci. and Psychology, U. Oreg., 1993, JD, 1996; LLM in Taxation, U. Wash., 1997. Bar: Wash., 1996. Assoc. Preston, Gates & Ellis, Seattle, 1997-98; sr. assoc. Arthur, Andersen, LLP, Seattle, 1998—. Legal rschr.: (book) Public and Media Relations for the Fire Service, 1998. Mem. ABA, Wash. State Young Lawyers Assn., Mensa. Avocations: pianist, painting, photography. Office: Arthur Andersen LLP 801 2nd Ave Ste 800 Seattle WA 98104-1573

HEIM, BRUNO BERNARD, archbishop; b. Olten, Switzerland, Mar. 5, 1911; s. Bernhard and Elizabeth Heim-Studer. Student, Benedictine Coll., Engelberg, Switzerland, 1926-31; Drphil, Thomas Aquinas U., Rome, 1934; BD, Fribourg U., Switzerland, 1937; DCL, Gregorian U., Rome, 1946; grad., Pontificial Diplomatic Acad., Rome, 1947. Ordained priest Roman Cath. Ch., 1938, consecrated bishop, 1961. Curate in parishes Arbon and Basel Switzerland, 1938-42; chief chaplain for Italian and Polish mil. internees in Switzerland, 1943-45; sec. Nuncio Roncalli (Pope John XXII) in Paris, 1947-51; auditor Nunciature, Vienna, Austria, 1951-54; councillor Nunciature, Bonn, Fed. Republic of Germany, 1954-61; apostolic del. Scandanavia, 1961-69; nuncio Finland, 1966-69; nuncio Egypt, pres. of Caritas, 1969-73; apostolic del. Great Britain, 1973-82, nuncio, 1982-85. Author: Coutumes et droit héraldiques de l'Eglise, 1950; Heraldry in the Catholic Church, 1978, 82; Liber amicorum, 1982, Or & Argent, 1994. Decorated officer Acad. Légion d'honneur France, 1951, knight of honour Teutonic Order, 1961; Cross of Merit with star (Germany), 1961; gt. cross Order of Malta, 1962; Golden Cross with star (Austria), 1962; gt. officer of Merit, Italy, 1965; gt. cross of Finnish Lion, 1969; gt. cross Order of St. Maurice and Lazarus, Savoy, 1973; Gt. Cordon first class Order of Republique, Egypt, 1974; gt. cross Order of St. John, Britain, 1979; Order of Isabel la Catolica, Spain, 1982; gt. prior and bailiff gt. cross justice, decorated with the Collar of Constantinian Order of St. George, 1989; gt. officer Order of Polonia Restituta, 1985; Collar of the Illustrious Royal Order of St. Januarius. Mem. Internat. Heraldic Acad., Soc. Suisse d'Hèraldique, Accademia del Collegio Araldico, Real Acad. de la Historia Madrid, Accad. Archeologica Italiana, Socita' Italiana di studi Araldici, French Heraldic and Geneal. Soc., Soc. Suisse Heraldique (hon.), Adler Vienna (hon.), Herold Berlin (hon.), Heraldry Soc. Scotland (hon.), Socs. Heraldica Scandinavica (v.p. inst. heraldic and geneal. studies Canterbury), Cambridge U. Heraldic and Geneal. Soc. (patron). Club: Atheneum (London). Avocations: heraldic painting, gardening, cooking. Address: Zehnderweg 31, CH 4600 Olten Switzerland

HEIM, THOMAS GEORGE, lawyer; b. Phila., Feb. 5, 1945; s. Joseph E. and Lillian H.; m. Anne Mary Fatkin, Aug. 23, 1969; children: Thomas George, Susan, James, Christopher. AB, Seton Hall U., 1967; JD, Rutgers U., 1971. Bar: N.J. 1971, U.S. Dist. Ct. N.J. 1971, U.S. Ct. Mil. Appeals 1971, U.S. Ct. Appeals (3d cir.) 1976, U.S. Supreme Ct. 1992. Ptnr. Granite & Heim, Woodbury Hts., N.J., 1979—; mcpl. prosecutor Borough of Woodbury Heights, 1979-81, solicitor Woodbury Heights Planning Bd., 1983-87; mcpl. ct. judge Borough of Woodbury Hts., 1998—. Pres. St. Margeret Regional Sch .Bd., 1978-87; lector St. Margaret Ch., Woodbury Hts.; chmn. local adv. com. probation dept. Gloucester County, chmn. Human Rels. Commn., 1994-96. Capt. JAGC, U.S. Army, 1971-74. Named Profl. Lawyer of Yr., N.J. Commn. on Professionalism in Law, 1998. Mem. ABA, N.J. State Bar Assn., Gloucester County Bar Assn. Democrat. Roman Catholic. Home: 228 Cherry Ave Woodbury Hgts NJ 08097-1111 Office: PO Box 69 Woodbury Heights NJ 08097-0069

HEIMANN, JOHN GAINES, investment banker; b. N.Y.C., Apr. 1, 1929; s. Sidney M. and Dorothy V.B. (Gainesburg) H.; m. Margaret E. Fechheimer, Dec. 2, 1956 (div.); children: Joshua Gaines, Eliza Faith; m. Maria Cristina Anzola, Oct. 17, 1989. BA in Econs., Syracuse (N.Y.) U., 1950; LLD (hon.), St. Michael's Coll., 1979. V.p. Smith, Barney & Co., N.Y.C., 1955-66; sr. v.p., dir. E.M. Warburg, Pincus & Co., Inc., N.Y.C., 1967-75; N.Y. State supt. banks, 1975-76, N.Y. State commr. housing and community renewal, 1976-77; compt. of the currency Washington, 1977-81; co-chmn. exec. com. Warburg, Paribas, Becker, N.Y.C., 1981-82; dep. chmn. A.G. Becker Paribas Inc., Paribas Internat., 1982-84; vice chmn. Merrill Lynch Capital Markets, N.Y.C., 1984-91; chmn. Europe/Middle East Merrill Lynch, London, 1988-90; chmn. global fin. instns. group office of chmn. Merrill Lynch & Co. Inc., N.Y.C., 1991-99; chmn. Fin. Stability Inst. of the Bank for Internat. Settlements, N.Y.C., 1999—; chmn. Merrill Lynch Internat. Bank; chmn. Fin. Svcs. Coun.; mem. exec. com. Inst. Internat. Fin.; chmn. Fed. Fin. Instns. Exam. Coun., 1979-81, Comml. Reinvestment Task Force, 1978-81, 20th Century Task Force on Internat. Debt Crisis; lectr. Harvard U., Yale U., Columbia U., U. Calif., NYU; mem. adv. bd. sch. mgmt. Fishman-Davidson Ctr. for Study of Svc. Sector; chmn. Brit-N.Am. com.; trustee Nat. PolicyAssn.; vice chmn., chmn. securities subcom. Am. Banking and Securities Assn. of London; chmn. N.Y. State Supt.'s Adv. Com. on Transnat. Banking Instns., 1981; co-chmn. Derivatives Policy Group; mem. Fed. Res. Bank of N.Y.'s Internat. Capital Markets Adv. Com.; mem. adv. com. on fin. svcs. Dept. U.S. Treasury; mem. Prep for Prep; mem. governing coun. Ctr. for Study of Fin. Instns. Bd. dirs., treas. Group of Thirty; bd. dirs. Am. Ditchley Found., Citizens Com. for N.Y.C.; mem. N.Y.C. Housing Partnership, Citizens Com. for Affordable Housing; trustee Hampshire Coll., mem. strategic com. France Tresor; mem. Citizens Com. for N.Y. C., bd. dirs., Inst. Internat. Fin.; mem. adv. coun. Ctr. for Econ. Policy Rsch.; mem. Coun. Fgn. Rels. Named Housing Man of Yr. Nat. Housing Conf., 1976; recipient Bank Adminstrn. Key for Disting. Svc., 1980, Alexander Hamilton award Treasury Dept., 1981, Brotherhood award NCCJ, 1986, Pacesetter award Nat. Assn. Bank Women, Inc., 1986. Mem. Nat. Policy Assn. (vice chmn.), Fgn. Rels. Coun. Democrat. Office: Fin Stability Inst 33 Liberty St New York NY 10045-1003

HEIMBOLD, CHARLES ANDREAS, JR., pharmaceutical company executive; b. Newark, May 27, 1933; s. Charles Andreas and Mary Joseph (Corrigan) H.; m. Monika Astrid Barkvall, Sept. 22, 1962; children: Joanna, Eric, Leif, Peter. B.A. cum Laude, Villanova U., 1954; LL.B. cum laude, U. Pa., 1960; LL.M., NYU, 1966; postgrad., Hague Acad. Internat. Law, 1959. Bar: N.Y. 1962. Assoc. Milbank, Tweed, Hadley & Mc Cloy, 1960-63; staff atty. Bristol-Myers Squibb Co., N.Y.C., 1963-70, dir. corp. devel., 1970-73, v.p. planning and devel., 1981-84, sr. planning and devel., 1981-84; pres., health care group, 1984-88, pres., health care group and sr. v.p. planning and devel., 1988-89, dir., 1989; exec. v.p. Bristol-Myers Squibb Co., N.Y.C., 1989-92, pres., 1992—, pres. and CEO, 1994—; chmn., CEO, 1995—; bd. dirs. Mobil Corp. Trustee U. Pa., Am. Mus. Natural History; bd. dirs. Phoenix House; chmn. bd. overseers U. Pa. Law Sch. With USN, 1954-57. Mem. Assn. Bar of City of N.Y., Riverside Yacht Club, River Club, Causeway Club. Home: Leeward Ln Riverside CT 06878-2409 Office: Bristol Myers Squibb Co 345 Park Ave Fl 44 New York NY 10154-0004

HEIMBUCH, SUSANNE SEBESTA, public relations, marketing executive; b. Denver, Aug. 12, 1945; d. Benjamin C. and Patricia C. (Clancy) Sebesta; divorced, 1985; 1 child, John. BSBA, U. Minn., 1981; postgrad., U. St. Thomas, Mpls., 1988-91; student, Clemson U., 1994, Alliance Française, Mpls., 1996-97, UCLA, 1999. Ind. real estate broker, 1974-84, pub. rels. cons., writer, 1981-85; stock, bond and mut. fund broker Summit Investment Corp., Mpls., 1985-87; sr. investor rels. account exec. Edwin Neuger & Assocs., Mpls., 1987-90; corp. and investor rels. mgr. Met. Fin. Corp., Mpls., 1990-94; investor rels. cons. Cellex Bioscis., Inc., Mpls., 1995-98; dir. investor and pub. rels. Mercury Air Group, Inc., L.A., 1998—; writer bylaws, mem. steering com. Textile Ctr. Minn., 1993-94. Fund raiser Fiber/Metal Arts Show, 1994-96, Flight Path Learning Ctr. So. Calif., 1998—; cmty. liaison Mercury Air Group, Inc., 1998-99. Recipient AMC Poetry award, 1999, Evaluator awards Toastmasters Internat., 1985. Mem. Nat. Assn. Investors Corp. (regional, nat. bd. dirs. 1982-90), Nat. Investor Rels. Inst. (bd. dirs. Twin Cities chpt. 1992-94), Aero Club So. Calif. (acting sec. 1999). Avocations: poetry, writing travelogues, skiing, in-line skating, dancing. Office: Mercury Air Group Inc 5456 Mcconnell Ave Los Angeles CA 90066-7062

HEIMBURGER, IRVIN LEROY, retired surgeon; b. Tsinan, China, Sept. 28, 1931; came to U.S., 1934; s. LeRoy Francis and Margaret Coleman (Smith) H.; m. Marcia Jean Enlow, June 30, 1963; children: Angela R., Jeffrey L., Christian I., Jenny E. BA, Drury Coll., 1953; MD, Vanderbilt U., 1957. Diplomate Am. Bd. Surgery, Am. Bd. Thoracic Surgery. Intern Vanderbilt U. Hosp., Nashville, 1957-58; resident in surgery Ind. U. Hosp., Indpls., 1958-63; thoracic fellow Leeds (Eng.) U. Hosp., 1963-64; from instr. to clin. assoc. prof. Ind. U. Med. Ctr., Indpls., 1964-80; med. staff St. Mary Med. Ctr., Evansville, Ind., 1966—, Deaconess Hosp., Evansville, Ind., 1966—. Contbr. articles to profl. jours. Pres. Vanderburgh County Med. Soc., Evansville, Ind., 1977-78. Fellow ACS (pres. Ind. chpt. 1977-78); mem. Cen. Surg. Assn., Internat. Cardiovascular Soc., Soc. Thoracic Surgeons, Midwest Surg. Soc. Home: 7700 Newburgh Rd Evansville IN 47715-4530

HEIMER, HANS, electric power engineering executive, consultant; b. Vienna, Austria, Mar. 11, 1927; arrived in Eng., 1939; s. Alfred and Ida (Schwarz) H.; m. Brenda Jean Porter, Dec. 26, 1952. Intermediate BSc, U. London, 1945; Higher Nat. Cert. in Elec. Engring., Stockport Coll. Further Edn., Eng., 1950, 56. Registered engring. European Fedn. Nat. Engring. Assns., 1990. Project engr. Kennedy & Donkin Cons. Engrs., Manchester, Eng., 1956-61, chief elec. design, 1961-65, dep. head generation dept., 1965-78, head generation dept. (chief engr.), 1978-82, mktg. cons., 1982-85; chief elec. engring. Toshiba Internat. Co., London, 1985-91; quality assurance cons., Siemens, Manchester, 1991-93; ret., 1994. Contbr. articles to profl. jours. Fellow Instn. Elec. Engrs. London (chmn. N.W. Ctr. 1985-86), Inst. Mgmt. Vedantin. Avocations: music, gardening, home maintenance, philosophy. Home: 27 Reading Dr, Sale M33 5DJ, England

HEIN, ROBERT ELDOR, electrical engineer; b. Portland, Oreg., Oct. 31, 1943; s. Eldor William and Beulah Gertrude (Billeter) H.; m. Bernice Alfreda Naessens, June 19, 1965; 1 child, Trent Robert. BSEE, U. Colo., 1966. Registered profl. engr., photographer. Design engr. Woodward Gov., Ft. Collins, Colo., 1970-71; dir. design engring. Coors Container Co. div. Coors Corp., Golden, Colo., 1971-81; mgr. advanced tech. Martin Marietta Corp., Denver, 1981-85; dir. research support Solar Energy Research Inst., Golden, 1985-88; dir. telecommunications network and distrubuted computing Martin Marietta Astronautics Group, Denver, 1988—. Vestry coun. St. John Chrysostum Episcopal Ch.; mem. adv. bd. Red Rock Community Coll., Denver, 1976-80; bd. mgrs. N.W. YMCA, Arvada, Colo., 1978-81. Served to Capt. USAF, 1966-70, Vietnam. Mem. IEEE (sr., pres. IAS-GLASS com. 1982), Profl. Photographers Am., Denver Apple Users Group (pres. 1984-85), Am. Mgmt. Assn. Lodge: Elks. Avocations: photography, microcomputers, communications, swimming. Home: 11735 W 72nd Pl Arvada CO 80005-3204 Office: Lockheed Martin Corp Astronautics Group Space Launch Sys PO Box 179 Denver CO 80201-0179

HEINAMANN, PAUL LINDSAY, non-executive director of companies; b. Cape Town, South Africa, Dec. 7, 1941; s. Alwyn Paul and Lucy Amelia (Parker) H.; m. Melanie Mary Weis, May 1, 1965; children: Nicholas Paul, Jonathan Josef. AMP, INSEAD, Fontainebleu, France, 1985. Trainer, mgr. Willis Faber Dumas & Rowand, Cape Town, 1960-66; asst. mgr. Stenhouse, Cape Town, 1966-69; exec. dir. Instnl. Ins. Brokers, Cape Town, Johannesburg, South Africa, 1969-75; chief exec. Rand Bank Ins. Brokers, Johannesburg, 1975-76; exec. dir. Alexander Forbes Ltd., Johannesburg, 1976-89, chief exec., 1989-98, non-exec. chmn., 1998-2000. Chmn. adv. bd. The Salvation Army, Johannesburg, 1994—. Fellow Soc. Risk Mgrs.; mem. South African Ins. Brokers Assn. (pres. 1991-92), Ins. Inst. South Africa (pres. 1992), Rand Club, Inanda Club, Bryanston Country Club. Anglican. Avocations: genealogy, golf, tennis, walking. Home: PO Box 68562, Bryanston Johannesbg 2021, South Africa

HEINDEL, NED DUANE, chemistry educator; b. Red Lion, Pa., Sept. 4, 1937; s. Penrose Horace and Dorothy May (Strayer) H.; m. Linda Clarella Heefner, Aug. 26, 1959. B.S., Lebanon Valley Coll., Annville, Pa., 1959; D.Sc. (hon.), Lebanon Valley Coll., 1985; M.S., U. Del., 1961, Ph.D., 1963; postdoctoral studies, Princeton U., 1964; DSc (hon.), Albright Coll., 1993. Instr. chemistry U. Del., 1962-63; asst. prof. chemistry Ohio U., Ironton, 1964-65, Marshall U., Huntington, W. Va., 1964-66; asst. prof. to assoc. prof. chemistry Lehigh U., Bethlehem, Pa., 1966-73, H.S. Bunn prof., 1973—, dir. Ctr. Health Scis., 1980-88; prof. nuclear medicine Hahnemann Med. U., Phila., 1971—; cons. Pa. State Police Crime Lab., Bethlehem, 1975-88; cons. safety program J.T. Baker Chem. Co., Phillipsburg, N.J., 1978-83; regional lectr. Mid. Atlantic region Sigma Xi. Author: Iron, Armor and Adolescents, 1982; editor: Chemistry of Radiopharmaceuticals, 1978; contbr. numerous articles to profl. jours. Trustee Keystone Jr. Coll., LaPlume, Pa., 1975-90, Ctr. for History of Chemistry, Phila., 1982—, Nat. Found. for History of Chemistry, Phila., 1988—. Recipient Alumni Assn. award Lebanon Valley Coll., 1971; fellow NSF, 1963-64; recipient numerous rsch. grants. Mem. Am. Chem. Soc. (councilor, bd. dirs., pres. 1994, Harry and Carol Mosher award 1995), Royal Soc., Soc. Nuclear Medicine, Am. Assn. Pharm. Scientists, Sigma Xi. Republican. Methodist. Home: 200 Hexenkopf Rd Easton PA 18042-9570 Office: Dept Chem Lehigh U Bethlehem PA 18015

HEINE, ACHIM, industrial designer, educator; b. Bischofsheim, Germany, June 11, 1955; s. Joachim and Gisela (Braun) H. Diploma, Hochschule Gestaltung, Offenbach, Germany, 1984. Co-founder Ginbande Design, Frankfurt, Germany, 1985-95; mng. dir. Heine/Lenz/Zizka, Frankfurt, 1989—; prof. Hochschule der Künste, Berlin, 1993—; founder Heine Assocs., Berlin, 1995—; jury mem. Fed. Award Product Design, 1996.

Designer pullout table/bench system, table system (Furniture of Yr. award 1988), extendable lamp (Innovative Design 1994). Bd. trustees German Design Coun., 1997—. Recipient Fed. Award for Product Design, Frankfurt, 1996. Office: Heine/Lenz/Zizka, Niddastrasse 84, D-60329 Frankfurt Germany

HEINE, LEONARD M., JR., investment executive; b. N.Y.C., Nov. 14, 1924; s. Leonard Max and Elise (Frey) H.; m. Sandra Fleming, Oct. 14, 1966; children: Michael Kenneth, Nancy Ellen, Thomas Charles, Christopher Altman. BS in Econs., U. Pa., 1948. Salesman Lehman Bros., N.Y.C., 1952-58; sales mgr. Rothschild, N.Y.C., 1958-62; gen. ptnr. R.J. Buck & Co., N.Y.C., 1962-70; pres., founder, chmn. Mgmt. Asset Corp., Westport, Conn., 1970-90; investment mgr., chmn., pres. LMH Fund Ltd., 1983—; pres. Heine Mgmt. Group, Inc., 1983—; chmn., pub. Weston (Conn.) Voice. Treas. Weston Pub. Libr., 1980-81; trustee Preservation Found., Palm Beach, Fla.; bd. dirs. Fairfield Home Elderly; nat. commr. Anti-Defamation League; bd. dirs. Intracoastal Health Sys., West Palm Beach, Fla.; trustee Albert Einstein Coll. Medicine's Soc. Founders. With U.S. Army, 1943-46. Decorated Purple Heart. Mem. Am. Soc. Profl. Cons., Birchwood Country Club (Westport), U. Pa. Club (N.Y.C.), Palm Beach Country Club (Fla.). Republican.

HEINE, PETER JOHANNES, jounalist; b. Oldenburg, Fed. Republic Germany, Oct. 23, 1955; s. Johannes N. and Hilde (Thieken) H.; children: David, Cornelia. Student, U. Gottingen, Fed. Republic of Germany, 1973-79. Documentarist Wirtschaftswoche Weekly Mag., Dusseldorf, W.Ger., 1980-81; gen. editor Heinrich Bauer Verlag, Verlag, W.Ger., 1982-83, Bild-Zeitung, Stuttgart, Fed. Republic of Germany, 1983-87; dep. editor-in-chief Rotenburger (Fed. Republic of Germany) Kreiszeitung, 1987; mng. editor Trendletter newsletter Spiegel-Verlag, Hamburg, Fed. Republic of Germany, 1988-89; PRS Oberreifenberg, Fed. Republic of Germany, 1989-90; news editor VWD, Eschborn, Fed. Republic of Germany, 1990-94, desk editor, 1990-91, N.Y. corr., 1991-93, desk mgr., 1993-94; editor Börse Online Fin. Newsweekly, Cologne, Frankfurt, 1994-95; exec. editor, PR, comm. dept. Siemens AG. Power Generation Group (KWU) Standpunkt Mag., Erlangen, 1996-98; editor-in-chief Euro-Wirtschaftsmagazin monthly, Weiterstadt, 1998-99; founder, editor Dragon News, Singapore, Stetten, 1999—. Corr. Steelweek, Germany, 1995-97. Mem. Verein des JohannisbeerKasekuchens (2d chmn. 1975-77, 1st chmn. 1983-87, pres. 1987—0. Conservative. Jewish. Fax: 0711-794 33 99.

HEINE, SUSANNE, religious studies educator; b. Prague, Jan. 17, 1942; arrived in Austria, 1945; Degree, U. Vienna, 1966, ThD, 1973, habilitation, 1979. Ordained to ministry Luth. Ch., 1968. Vicar Luth. Ch., Vienna, 1966-68; asst. New Testament studies U. Vienna, 1968-79, lectr., 1979-82, prof. religious edn., 1982-90; prof. pastoral theology and psychology of religion U. Zurich, 1990-96, U. Vienna, 1996—; cons. JCCS/InterEuropean Commn. on Ch. and Sch., 1982-91; head project study Islam in Textbooks, Vienna, 1988-95; cons. com. for questions concerning Islam KWR, 1996—; mem. working group Friends of Abraham, 1996—. Author: (TV series) A House in Jerusalem, 1990-91, 94-95. Mem. Internat. Soc. Psychology of Religion and Sci. of Religion (bd. dirs. 1998—), European Assn. for World Religions in Edn. (vice chair 1990-94), Working Group on Christian-Jewish Rels. in Switzerland (bd. dirs. 1995-96), Sigmund Freud Soc. (scientific bd. 1995—), World Coun. Chs. (faith and order plenary commn. 1995-98), Scientific Soc. of Theology (vice chair 1996—), World Conf. Religions for Peace (rsch. group on social ethics). Home: Buchfeldgasse 9, A-1080 Vienna Austria Office: U Vienna Theol Faculty, Rooseveltplatz 10, A-1090 Vienna Austria

HEINEMANN, LOTHAR ALFRED, epidemiologist; b. Berlin, Aug. 19, 1941; s. Gerhard and Edith (Kunert) H.; m. Gisela Wick, Sept. 30, 1972; children: Klaas, Antje. MSc in Medicine, Humboldt Univ, 1966, MD, 1968, MSc in Psychology, 1972, DSc, 1977. Rsch. asst. med. faculty Humboldt Univ., Berlin, 1967-76; head dept. epidemiology Acad. of Sci., Berlin, 1977-83, head dept. preventive cardiology, 1984-90; dir. inst. Center Epidemiology and Health Rsch., Berlin, 1990—; sec., gen. Med. Rsch. Coun., Berlin, 1984-88; cons. WHO, Geneva, 1986, Alexandria, Egypt, 1986, 87. Author: Handbook for Epidemiology, 1994; contbr. over 350 articles to profl. jours. Mem. European Soc. for Cardiology (scientific com. 1988-94), Coun. Epidemiology and Prevention ISFC, N.Y. Acad. Sci. Home: Bahnhofstr 33, 16341 Zepernick Germany Office: ZEG Ctr Epidemiology, Invalidenstr 115, 10115 Berlin Germany

HEINICKE, JOACHIM WERNER, chemistry educator, researcher; b. Aue, Sachsen, Germany, May 4, 1947; s. Helmut and Ingeborg (Brandes) H.; m. Elisabeth Günther, 1969; children: Cornelia, Matthias. Diploma in chemistry, U. Halle, Germany, 1970, PhD, 1974. Docent in inorganic chemistry U. Greifswald, Germany, 1990, prof. inorganic chemistry, 1992; dir. Inst. Inorganic Chemistry, U. Greifswald, 1992-98; rschr. in silicon and phosphorous organic chemistry. Co-author: Arsenheterocyclen, 1978; contbr. 90 articles to profl. jours. Mem. Soc. German Chemists, Internat. Coun. on Main Group Chemistry. Office: Dept Chemistry, Soldtmannstr 16, D-17487 Greifswald Germany

HEINIG, NORMAN THOMAS, consulting company executive; b. Chgo., Feb. 20, 1928; s. Oscar William and Agnes Kerchville (Lamar) H.; BS, Northwestern U., 1955; MS, San Francisco U., 1982; children: Norman, William, Mary, Barbara, Tanya, Randy. Apprentice, Sanger Plumbing, 1945-50; engr., project mgr. Commonwealth Plumbing Co., Chgo., 1957-65; cons. engr. Architects Mech. Design Svc. Corp., Chgo., 1965-73; owner Heinig Cons. Plumbing Engring. Co., Mission Viejo, Calif., 1974—. Bd. dirs. Chgo. Boys Club, 1961; pres. PTA, 1967; leader Boy Scouts Am., 1955-65. Mem. Am. Soc. Plumbing Engrs. Republican. Roman Catholic. Clubs: Chgo. Athletic, Royal League, Elks. Home and office: PO Box 2777 Mission Viejo CA 92690-0777

HEININEN, LASSI KALEVI, political scientist; b. Pori, Satakunta, Finland, Apr. 8, 1952; s. Matti Aimo and Kaino Annikki (Moisalo) H.; m. Marja Leena Blomroos; children: Helmi Ilona, Tarmo Alarik. Licenciate degree, U. Tampere, Finland, 1991, MA, 1987; PhD, U. Lapland, 1999. Gen. sec. disarmament week com. UN, Finland, 1985-87; from project rschr. to rschr. Tampere Peace Rsch. Inst., Finland, 1988-91; coord. study program Arctic Ctr., Rovaniemi, Finland, 1991-95, sr. scientist, 1995—; coord. Kuhmo Summer Acad., Finland, 1987-97, Calotte Acad., Finland, 1991—; dir. Inst. Summer Sch., U. Lapland, 1996; chair steering com. No. Rsch. Forum. Editor: Arctic Environmental Problems, 1990, The Changing Circumpolar North: Opportunities for Academic Development, 1994, Europe's Northern Dimension, 1997, The New North of Europe, 1998; author: (with others) Expanding the Northern Dimension, 1995, European Pohjoinen 1990-luvulla, 1999. Exec. com. Finlands Peace Com., 1982-90. 2d lt. Finnish mil., 1972-73. Mem. Northern Policy Assn. Finland (sec. 1994—). Avocations: literature, movies, biking.

HEININGER, ULRICH FRANZ, pediatrician, researcher; b. Munich, Bavaria, Germany, Aug. 21, 1961; s. Hansfritz and Erika (Biberacher) H.; m. Heike Daniela Koerner, Apr. 30, 1993; children: Anna Sophia, Lukas Thomas. MD, Ludwig-Maximilians U., Munich, 1988; PhD, Friedrich-Alexander U., Erlangen, Germany, 1995. Pediat. trainee Friedrich-Alexander U., Erlangen, 1987-93, attending physician, 1993-98, asst. prof. pediat., 1995-98; asst. prof. pediat. U Klinik Kinder/Jugendliche, Basel, Switzerland, 1998—; vis. prof. UCLA, 1996-97. Author: Die Neubewertung von Pertussis und Parapertussis, 1995, Impfratgeber Pädiatrie, 1999; contbr. chpts. to books and articles to profl. jours. Fellow European Soc. for Pediat. Infectious Diseases, 1996-98. Roman Catholic. Avocations: nature, family activities, books, bicycling. Fax: (41) 61-685-6012. Office: U Klinik Kinder/Jugendliche, PO Box, CH-4005 Basel Switzerland

HEINISCH, GOTTFRIED, pharmaceutical chemistry educator; b. St. Pö, Austria, Oct. 27, 1938; s. Anton and Maria Heinisch; m. Heidemarie Krögler, Apr. 3, 1961; children: Vivika, Stefan. PharmM, U. Vienna, Austria, 1962, PhD, 1968. Asst. prof. U. Vienna, 1961-75, reader pharm. chemistry, 1975-78, assoc. prof., 1978-91; prof. U. Innsbruck, Austria, 1991—; bd. dirs. Inst. Pharm. Chemistry, U. Innsbruck, 1993. Author: Arzneimittelschnellerkennung, 1984 (rev. yrly.), Arneistoffidentifizierung, 1986, Identifizierung offizineller Arzneistoffe, 1993; contbr. numerous articles to profl. jours. Recipient Forschungsförderungspreis, City of Vienna, 1977. Mem.Austrian Pharm. Soc. (v.p. 1980-90, pres. 1990-96), German Pharm. Soc., Austrian Chem. Soc., Internat. Soc. Heterocyclic Chemistry, Internat. Soc. Antiviral Res. Avocations: photography, tennis, mountaineering, chess, multi media shows. Office: Inst Pharmacy, Innrain 52a, Innsbruck Austria A-6020

HEINLE, RICHARD ALAN, lawyer; b. New Kensington, Pa., May 13, 1959; s. Robert Alan and Barbara Jane Heinle; m. Sharon Eileen Farrell, Oct. 20, 1990; children: Kelly, Kyra, Casey. AB with highest honors, U. Chgo., 1981; JD cum laude, Georgetown U., 1984. Bar: Ill. 1984, Fla. 1994. Assoc. Arnstein & Lehr, Chgo., 1984-89, Foley & Lardner, Chgo., 1989-93; ptnr. Foley & Lardner, Orlando, Fla., 1994—; counsel Better Bus. Bur. Ctrl. Fla., Orlando, 1996—. Mem. Mfrs. Assn. Ctrl. Fla. (bd. dirs. 1995—), Fla. C. of C. (bd. dirs. 1999—), Phi Beta Kappa. Roman Catholic. Avocations: golf, running. Home: 8100 Vineland Oaks Blvd Orlando FL 32835-8215 Office: Foley & Lardner 111 N Orange Ave Ste 1800 Orlando FL 32801-2386

HEINLE, ROBERT ALAN, physician; b. Tarentum, Pa., Oct. 26, 1933; s. Edward William and Mary Alice (Purvis) H.; B.S., U. Pitts., 1955, M.D., 1959; m. Barbara Klimeck, Aug. 23, 1958; children: Richard, Jeffrey, Ronald, Robert, Thomas, Timothy. Intern, U. Pitts. Health Center, 1959-60, resident, 1962-65; research fellow in medicine Peter Bent Brigham Hosp., 1965-67; research asso. in medicine Harvard Med. Sch., 1967-68; asst. prof. medicine U. Rochester (N.Y.) Med. Sch., 1968-71, asso. prof., 1971-75, clin. assoc. prof., 1975-98; dir. cardiovascular lab. Genesee Hosp., Rochester, 1975-98; sr. assoc. physician Strong Meml. Hosp., Rochester, 1975-98; cons. Am. Heart Jour., 1973—; NIH research fellow, 1965-68. Bd. dirs. Blue Cross in Rochester, Blue Shield in Rochester. Served with U.S. Army, 1960-62. Fellow ACP, Am. Coll. Cardiology; mem. Am. Heart Assn., AMA, Am. Fedn. Clin. Research, Rochester Individual Practice Assn. (dir.), Phi Beta Kappa, Omicron Delta Kappa, Alpha Omega Alpha. Republican. Roman Catholic. Home: 415 Warren Ave Rochester NY 14618-4319 Office: 224 Alexander St Rochester NY 14607-4002

HEINONEN, JOUKO ENSIO, investment advisor, trading company executive, strategic advisor; b. Tervakoski, Janakkala, Finland, Apr. 14, 1948; s. Esko Ensio and Kerttu Inkeri (Laitila) H.; m. Ulla-Riitta Snellman, Dec. 2, 1972; children: Kristian, Tommi, Pia Marianne. BSc in Econs., Helsinki Sch. Econs. and Bus. Adm, 1972. Mgmt. course sec. Finnish Inst. Mgmt., Helsinki, 1971-72; chmn., CEO Multitrade Cons. Ltd., Helsinki, 1972-80, M-Cons. Ltd. (Metra Group), Helsinki, 1974-82, JHI Project Mgmt., Ltd., London, 1979-84; chmn TSC Ltd., Helsinki, 1988—. Advisor/mem. Tartu Peace Movement, Helsinki, 1991—; advisor/expert Karelian Fedn., Helsinki, 1994—. 2d lt. Finnish Army, 1969. Mem. Intra-Global Fin. Inst. (fin. expert 1995—), The Highlander Club (life), The Oxford Club (life). Avocations: music, swimming, jogging, gym exercise, political/economic literature. Home: Santakatu 2 E 76, FIN00180 Helsinki Finland Office: TSC Ltd, Kaivokatu 8 7th Fl, FIN00180 Helsinki Finland

HEINONEN, OLAVI ENSIO, judge; b. Kuopio, Finland, Sept. 12, 1938; s. Eino Ensio and Aili Edith (Vesa) H.; m. Marjatta Rahikainen, 1962; children: Heikki, Hanna, Hilkka, Hannu. LLD, U. Helsinki, 1967; LLD (hon.), U. Turku, 1995. Asst. prof. law U. Helsinki, 1969-70; justice Supreme Ct., 1970-86, chief justice, 1989—; parliamentary ombudsman, 1986-89; chmn., mem. law coms. Govt. of Finland. Author books on criminal justice and policy; contbr. articles to profl. jours. Office: Supreme Ct, Pohjoisesplanadi 3, 00170 Helsinki Finland

HEINRICH, CHRISTOPH ANDREAS, geochemistry and economic geology educator; b. Thalwil, Zürich, Switzerland, Sept. 8, 1953; s. Fritz and Margrit (Hanhart) H.; m. Angela R. M. Beda, Sept. 26, 1980; children: Michael, Benjamin, Sarah. MSc in Geology, Swiss Fed. Inst. of Tech. ETH, Zurich, Switzerland, 1978, Dr.sc.nat., 1983. Jr. exploration geologist Comalco, Australia, 1978; postdoctoral scientist Australian Commonwealth Sci. and Indsl. Rsch. Orgn., Sydney, Australia, 1984-86; prin. rsch. scientist Australisian Geol. Survey Orgn., 1986-94; prof. Swiss Fed. Inst. of Tech., Zurich, 1994—. Editl. bd. Economic Geology, 1992—; contbr. numerous articles to profl. publs. With Swiss Army, 1975-83. Recipient Paul Niggli medal Swiss Mineralogic and Petrologic Soc., 1992. Mem. Soc. Econ. Geologists (bd. dirs. 1999—), Soc. Geology Applied to Ore Deposits (bd. dirs. 1997—), Swiss Geotech. Commn. (bd. dirs. 1995—). Office: ETH Zurich Dept Earth Sci, ETH Zentrum No, 8092 Zurich Switzerland

HEINRICH, MICHAEL ERNST, biologist, anthropologist; b. Karlsruhe, Germany, July 4, 1957; s. Horst E. Heinrich and Marga H. Guenther; m. Susann Hammacher, May 16, 1991; children: Liliana, Viola. MA, Wayne State U., 1982; diploma in biology, U. Freiburg, Germany, 1985, Dr.rer.nat, 1989. Rschr. U. Freiburg, 1989-93, lectr., 1993-99; prof., head Ctr. of Pharmacognosy and Phytotherapy The Sch. of Pharmacy, U. London, 1999—. Mem. editl. bd. Jour. Ethnopharmacology, Zeitschrift für Phytotherapie; contbr. articles to profl. jours. Fellow Linnean Soc. (London); mem. Am. Anthropol. Assn., Internat. Soc. Ethnopharmacology (bd. dirs. 1992—, pres. 2000-02). Avocations: books, biking. Office: Sch Pharmacy, 29-39 Brunswick Sq, London WC1N 1AX, England

HEINRICH, RANDALL WAYNE, lawyer; b. Houston, Nov. 29, 1958; s. Albert Joseph Sr. and Beverly June Earles; m. Linda Carol Cheek, June 6, 1993; children: Angela Leigh, Conrad Randall. BA, Baylor U., 1980, postgrad., 1981; postgrad., Rice U., 1981-82; JD, U. Tex., 1985. Bar: Tex. 1985. Assoc. Baker & Botts, Houston, 1985-87, Chamberlain, Hrdlicka, White, Williams & Martin, Houston, 1987-91, Norton & Blair, Houston, 1991-92; of counsel Gillis & Slogar, Houston, 1992—; mng. dir. Baytree Investors, Houston, 1993-97. Mem. dirs.' circle Houston Grand Opera, 1991, The Arts Symposium, 1991, Center Stage, Alley Theater, Houston, 1992-93, Houston Entrepreneurs' Forum, 1990-91; bd. dirs. The Cadre, 1991-92; pres. Exchange Club of Bayou City, 1992-93. Mem. ABA (YLD securities law com. 1993-95, vice chmn. 1994-95), NASD Pool Securities Arbitrators, Am. Arbitration Assn. (mem. nat. panel neutrals), Houston Bar Assn., Forum Club Houston, Phi Delta Theta. Republican. Baptist. Home: 4318 Saint Michaels Ct Sugar Land TX 77479-2986 Office: Gillis & Slogar 1000 Louisiana St Ste 6905 Houston TX 77002-5014

HEINTZ, CAROLINEA CABANISS, retired home economics educator; b. Roanoke, Va., Jan. 19, 1920; d. Luther Bertie and Emblyn Bird (Jennings) Cabaniss; m. Howard Elmer Smith, Dec. 19, 1942 (div. Aug. 1975); children: Emblyn Davis, Cynthia Shannon, Cheryl Peterson, Melyssa Sexton; m. Raymond Walter Heintz, May 21, 1977; 1 stepchild, James. BS in Home Econ. Edn., U. Ala., Tuscaloosa, 1941; vocat. home econ. degree, Montevallo Coll., 1941. Cert. vocat. home econs. tchr. Swimming instr. Camp Mudjekeewis, Centerlovel, Maine, summer 1940; home econs. tchr. Roanoke Pub. Schs., 1941-43; dietitian U. Va., Charlottesville, 1943; nutrition edn. specialist Liberty Health Ctr. Svcs., Liberty Center, Ohio, 1974-80; home economist Dayton Hudson Dept. Store, Toledo, 1980-84; splty . food instr., continuing edn. U. Toledo, 1984-85; pres., mem. Greater Toledo Nutrition Coun., 1966-98; bd. dirs. Sunset House Aux., pres. 1999-2000. Spkr. United Way, Toledo, 1965-90; founder, pres. Mobile Meals Toledo, Inc., 1968-71, mem. adv. bd., 1988-95, 2000, bd. dirs., chmn. pub. rels., 1997-99, nominating com., 2000, Spirit of Mobile Meals award, 1998; affiliate mem. Arts Commn., Toledo, 1976-77; chmn. Saphire Ball, Toledo Symphony Orch., Toledo Opera, 1978; adminstrv. coord. Feed Your Neighbor program Met. Chs. United, Toledo, 1979-86; deacon Collingwood Presbyn. Ch., 1969-71, elder, 1972-74, 77-79, trustee, 1984-86, elder, clk. of session, 1991-94, elder, 1997-99, stewardship chmn., 1996-97, del. to Maumee Valley Presbytery, 1991-99; mem. steering com. Interfiath Hospitality Network, 1992-94, bd. dirs., 1993-94; alt. del. Gen. Assembly Presbyn. Ch. U.S.A., 1993, del.-commr., 1994. Recipient Woman of Toledo award St. Vincent Hosp. and Med. Ctr. Guild, 1967, 80, Outstanding Community Svc. award United Way, 1987, Henry Morse vol. award, Greater Toledo award United Way, 1998, runner-up Nat. Vol. of the Year award Project Meal Found., Reynolds Metal Co., 1998. Mem. AAUW (bd. dirs. 1974-76, 94-96, 97-98, chmn. mem. gourmet group 1966-99, 2000, edn. found. chmn. 1994-96, book sale chmn. 1998, nominating com. chmn.), Ohio Med. Aux. (1st v.p. 1973-74), Aux. Acad. Medicine (pres. 1967-68, chmn. edn. gourmet group 1966-99, 2000, Health Care award 1974), Indian Trails Garden Club (pres. 1997-98), Sigma Kappa (various alumni offices). Republican. Avocations: volunteering, gourmet cooking, traveling, entertaining, bridge. Home: 3407 Bentley Blvd Toledo OH 43606-2860

HEINZ, ANDREAS, psychiatrist, neurologist; b. Stuttgart, Germany, Feb. 4, 1960; s. Dieter and Annemarie Dorothea (Rübartsch) Heinz; m. Jacqueline Juliet Jones. MD, Ruhr U., Bochum, Germany, 1988; MA, Freie U., Berlin, 1994. Cert. med. bd. German Soc. of Physicians in Neurology, Psychiatry, Psychotherapy, Neurophysiology. Scientific asst. Ruhr U. Dept. Neurology, 1988-91, Freie U. Dept. Psychiatry, 1991-95; spl. vol. NIMH Clin. Brain Disorders Br., Washington, 1995-97; sr. supr. dept. neurology Ruhr U., 1997-99; asst. dir. dept. add. med. Ctr. Inst. of Mental Health, Mannheim, 1999—; tchr. Bochum Physiotherapists' Sch., St. Josef's Hosp., Germany, 1989-91, Nurses' Sch. of U. Clinic Virchow, Berlin, 1994-95. Contbr. articles to profl. jours. Counsellor Soc. for Threatened Minorities, Bochum, 1988-91; vol. Initiative for Immigrant Children, Bochum, 1982-84, Fair Trade with the Third World Club, Ludwigsburg, Germany, 1976-80. Civil Svc. physician St. Josef's Hosp., Bochum, 1988-90. Recipient W. Feueslein award for alcoholism rsch., 2000; German Rsch. Found. scholar for professorship, Bonn, 1995. Mem. Soc. for Neurosci., German Soc. for Clin. Neurophysiology, Berlin Soc. Philosophy and the Scis. of Psychiatry. Protestant. Avocations: history, urban development, Zen, Aikido. Office: Ctrl Inst Mental Health, J-5 Mannheim B-W, Germany

HEINZ, RONEY ALLEN, civil engineering consultant; b. Shawano, Wis., Dec. 29, 1946; s. Orville Willard and Elva Ida (Allen) H.; m. Judy Evonne Olney, Oct. 30, 1965. BSCE, Mont. State U., 1973. Surveyor U.S. Army Corps Engrs., Seattle, 1966-73; civil engr. Hoffman, Fiske, & Wyatt, Lewiston, Idaho, 1973-74, Tippetts-Abbott-McCarthy-Stratton, Seattle, 1977-79; asst. editor Civil Engring. Mag. ASCE, N.Y.C., 1974-77; constrn. mgr. Boeing Co., Seattle, 1979-83; owner, gen. mgr. Armwavers Ltd., South Bend, Wash., 1983—; pres. Great Walls Internat. Inc., 1993-95, 99—, Heinz Internat., Inc., 1995—, Interocean Mgmt. Svcs., Inc., Republic of Panama, 1998—; mem. dams and tunnels del. to China, People to People Internat., Spokane, 1987; mem. U.S. com. on Large Dams. Asst. editor Commemorative Book Internat. Congress on Large Dams, 1987; contbr. articles to profl. publs., including Civil Engring. Mag., Excavator Mag., Internat. Assn. for Bridge and Structural Engring., Japan Concrete Inst., others. Internat. dir. Canaan Christians Fund, Aberdeen, 1993—; bd. dirs. Seaman's Ctr., Aberdeen, Wash., 1990—. Recipient First Quality award Asphalt Paving Assn. Wash., 1991. Mem. ASCE (sec. met. sect. 1975-76, assoc. mem. forum), ASTM (Student award 1973)., USCOLD. Republican. Lutheran. Achievements include management of first commercial installation worldwide of sediment control by water jets, of development of first private harbor and container terminal in Panama in Manzanillo Bay, Colon. Office: Armwavers Ltd PO Box 782 South Bend WA 98586-0782

HEINZ, ULRICH WALTER, theoretical physics educator; b. Ludwigshafen/Rhein, Fed. Republic Germany, Apr. 25, 1955; s. Walter Jakob and Ortrud (Goepelt) H.; divorced; children: Jutta Franziska, Richard Stefan, Juergen Andreas; m. Christiane Heinz-Neidhart, Sept. 17, 1994; children: Matthias Claus, Michael Neidhart. Dipl.-Phys., J. W. Goethe U., Frankfurt, Fed. Republic of Germany, 1978, Dr. phil. nat., 1980, Habilitation, 1984. Rsch. asst. J. W. Goethe U., Frankfurt, Fed. Republic of Germany, 1978-80, rsch. assoc., 1982-84; postdoctoral fellow Yale U., New Haven, 1980-82; vis. asst. prof. Vanderbilt U., Nashville, 1983-84; asst. physicist Brookhaven Nat. Lab., Upton, N.Y., 1984-86, assoc. physicist, 1986-87; prof. U. Regensburg, Fed. Republic Germany, 1987-2000; staff mem. CERN, Geneva, Switzerland, 1998-2000; prof. Ohio State U., Columbus, 2000—; cons. Oak Ridge (Tenn.) Nat. Lab., 1983-84; guest scientist Brookhaven Nat. Lab., Upton, N.Y., 1987—; PAC mem. CERN, Geneva, 1988-91, 98—. Contbr. over 160 scientific articles to profl. jours. Vertrauensdozent Studienstiftung des Deutschen Volkes, Bonn, Fed. Republic of Germany, 1991-2000. NATO Foreign Exchange fellow, 1981; DFG Habilitation fellow, 1981; BMFT Rsch. grantee, 1988-2000, GSI Rsch. grantee, 1991-2000; recipient Hess Prize, 1988. Mem. Am. Phys. Soc., German Phys. Assn. E-mail: heinz@mps.ohio-state.edu. Office: Ohio State U Dept Physics 174 W 18th Ave Columbus OH 43210

HEISER, ROLLAND VALENTINE, former army officer, foundation executive; b. Columbus, Ohio, Apr. 25, 1925; s. Rudolph and Helen Cecile H.; m. Gwenne Kathleen Duquemin, Feb. 26, 1949; children: Helen Heiser Sanford, Charlene Heiser Wolff. BS, U.S. Mil. Acad., 1947; MS in Internat. Affairs, George Washington U., 1965. Commd. 2d lt. U.S. Army, 1947; advanced through grades to lt. gen., 1976; army planner Washington, 1973-74; comdr. 1st Armored divsn. Germany, 1974-75; chief of staff U.S. Army Europe, 1975-76; chief of staff U.S. European Comd., 1976-78, ret., 1978; pres. New Coll. Found., Sarasota, Fla., 1979—. Decorated D.S.M. with oak leaf cluster, Def. Superior Svc. medal, Legion of Merit (3), Bronze Star, others. Mem. Sarasota Com. 100, Retired Officers Assn., Sarasota County C. of C., Ret. Officers Sarasota (past pres., dir.), Masons. Republican. Episcopalian. Home: 4104 Las Palmas Way Sarasota FL 34238-4532 Office: New Coll Found 5700 N Tamiami Trl Sarasota FL 34243-2146

HEISKANEN, TOMI PENTTI, chemical company executive; b. Helsinki, Dec. 6, 1954; s. Pentti Heiskanen and Anna (Piipponen) Heino; m. Anette Alice Avellan, Dec. 9, 1961; children: Tomas, Charlotta. MSc in Engring., U. Tech., Espoo, Finland, 1978, PhD in Engring., 1985; MSc in Mgmt., MIT, 1988. Rsch. asst. U. Tech., 1979-81, lectr., 1979-85; rsch. engr. Neste Oy, Porvoo, Finland, 1983-85, prodn. supt., 1985-86, mgr. planning, 1986-87, mgr. bus. devel., 1988-90, v.p. R & D, 1990-92, corp. v.p., 1992-95; pres. Optatech OY, Espoo, Finland, 1995—; chmn. bd. Technosphere OY, TACT Holding OY, DEGT OY, DESDE OY; dir. various coms. Contbr. articles to profl. jours.; patentee in field. Sublt. Finnish Navy, 1981-82. Grantee Neste Found., various dates. Mem. Tech. Soc. Finland. Avocations: tennis, downhill skiing, golf. Home: Tikasniityntkuja 7 B, 02200 Espoo Finland Office: Optatech OY, Luomannotko 4, FIN02200 Espoo Finland

HEISLER, NORMA BOODMAN, psychotherapist; b. N.Y.C., Nov. 11, 1933; d. David Louis and Belle (hochstein) Boodman; m. Arthur Heisler, Aug. 9, 1952; children: Miriam, Daniel. Cert., Pratt Inst., 1956; BA in Psychology, Bklyn. Coll., 1972; MSW, NYU, 1977; postgrad., N.Y. Sch. for Study of Psychoanalytic Psychotherapy, 1979-83, Karen Horney Inst. Study Psychoanalysis, 1984-86, Erickson Inst., 1992-93; PhD, Nat. Inst. Expressive Therapy, 1996. Cert. clin. social worker, art therapist, clin. hypnotherapist; cert. Am. Acad. Bereavement. Personnel asst. R.H. Miller, N.Y.C., 1952-56; freelance comml. artist Wolf Studios and Lowenstein Studios, 1957-69; tchr. Yeshivab Onel Moshe, N.Y.C., 1971-72; family counselor, art therapist Lillian Sklar Filler Day Care Ctr., N.Y.C., 1973-76; therapy intern L.I. Coll. Hosp., N.Y.C., 1976-77; tchr. adult edn. Kingsborough C.C., N.Y.C., 1978-79; psychotherapist N.Y. Psychotherapy and Counseling Ctr., 1978-89; part-time pvt. practice, 1981—; field instr., supr. social work C.I.H., 1989-92; pvt. practice, 1992—. One-woman shows include Jewish Cmty. House, N.Y.C., 1960; 2 person shows include Ahda Artzt Gallery, 1969; group shows include Caravan Art Gallery, 1953, 54, 55, Bklyn. Mus., 1956, 57 (award), Duncan Gallery, 1958, Art U.S.A., 1958, Kottler Gallery, 1958, Directions Gallery, 1959, Boston Art Festival, 1960, Pa. Acad. Fine Arts, Phila., 1961, St. Louis U., 1962, Ruth Sherman Gallery, 1965, N.Y. World's Fair, Ahda Artz Group, 1970, 71, Abra Gallery, 1999, Monserrat Gallery, 1999, Gallery Alexia, 1999, Stephen Gary Gallery, Monterral Gallery, 1999, 2000, Monserrat Gallery, 2000. Recipient Latham award for brotherhood, 1954, 55, 56, 57, 59, Grumbacher award of merit, 1960; art awards. Fellow Soc. Clin. Social Workers; mem. Nat. Assn. Social Workers (diplomate), Nat. Expressive Therapy Assn., Soc. Advancement of Psychoanalytic Devel. Psychology, Am. Orthopsychiat. Assn., N.Y. Artists Equity Assn. Jewish. Home: 2373 E 7th St Brooklyn NY 11223-5434

HEISS, MANFRED STEPHAN, computer scientist; b. Munich, May 15, 1965; s. Stephan and Helga (Tolkowsky) H. M Computer Sci., Tech. U. Munich, 1991. Pvt. practice cons., trainer Munich, 1990-92; software devel. mgr. IXOS AG, Munich, 1992—; cons. Siemens, Munich, 1991-95; mem. supervisory bd. IXDS AG, Munich, 1999—. Author: Static Analysis of Parallel Lisp, 1991. Home: Josephsburgstrasse 129, 81673 Munich Germany

HEISS, MARKUS MARIA, surgeon, educator, researcher; b. Frankfurt on the Main, Germany, Dec. 11, 1956; s. Lorenz and Paula (Zimmerer) H.; m. Simone Antonia Weissauer, June 5, 1993; children: Antonia, Constan-

tin. Student, Tech. U., Darmstadt, Germany, 1975-76; student in medicine, U. Antwerp, Belgium, 1977; med. diploma, U. Bochum, Frankfurt, Munich, Germany, 1983; postgrad., Jesuitical U., Munich, 1984-85. Bd. cert. surgeon; med. bd. cert.; Visa qualifying exam. of Ednl. Commn. for Fgn. Med. Grads.; bd. cert. vascular surgeon; European bd. cert. vascular surgeon. Fellow scientist Inst. Immunology Soc. for Radiation and Environ. Rsch., Munich, 1984-85; resident dept. surgery Klinikum Grosshadern, Munich, 1985-96, attending surgeon, 1996-98, head clin. rsch., 1996-98, asst. prof. surgery, 1998—; vice project leader working group Gastrointestinal Cancer Tumor Ctr., Munich, 1996-98, Malignant Melanoma Tumor Ctr., Munich, 1996-98; presenter in field. Contbr. articles to profl. publs.; reviewer profl. jours. Mem. Friedrich Naumann Found., Gummersbach, 1981, Young Leaders Conf. at Atlantik Brücke and Am. Coun. on Germany, Nashville, 1993. Recipient Best Abstract award Am. Soc. Clin. Oncology, 1992; scholar U. Antwerp, 1977, Friedrich Naumann Found., 1981, Friedrich Bauer Found., 1987; sci. grantee Dr. Mildred Scheel Found., 1992, Munich Med. Heptomato Coun., 1998. Mem. Internat. Soc. Endovascular Surgery, German Soc. Immunology, German Soc. Surgeons (Heinrich-Bauer prize for cancer rsch. 1995, prize for sci. exhbn. 1997, scholar 1991), Bavarian Assn. Surgeons (Otto-Goetze prize 1990, Nepomuk-von-Nussbaum prize 1995). Roman Catholic. Avocations: tennis, skiing, sailing, philosophy, evolution theories. Home: Ferdinand-von-Miller Str 21, 82343 Niederpöcking Bavaria, Germany Office: LMU U Klin Grosshadern, Marchioninistr 15, 81377 Munich Bavaria, Germany

HEISSMEYER, HANNES HINRICH, physician; b. Templin, Brandenburg, Germany, Aug. 12, 1939; s. Kurt and Eva (Schneider) H.; m. Elisabeth Pretzien, Mar. 17, 1943; children: Hendrik, Niels. Dr. Med., Med., Marburg, Germany, 1963, Priv. Dozent, 1973, Prof., 1979. Intern U. Marburg, 1963-65; asst. Max-Planck-Inst., Tuebingen, Germany, 1965-68; sr. physician U. Freiburg (Germany), 1968-78; head physician Diakonie Krankenhaus, Schwaeb-Hall, Germany, 1978—; dir. Diakonie Krankenhaus, Schwaeb-Hall, 1999. Author: Naturwissenschafte, 1971; contbr. articles to profl. jours. Recipient Byk-Gulden Forschungspreis, 1971. Mem. Deutsch Ges. Verdauungsrheiten, Heilmeyer Ge. Innere Medizin. Office: Diakoniekrankenhaus, Diakoniestr, 74523 Schwaebisch Hall Baden-Wuert, Germany

HEISTARO, SAMI MIKAEL, medical researcher; b. Helsinki, Finland, May 27, 1971; s. Paavo Sakari and Eivor Marita (Bergstrom) H. MD, U. Helsinki, 1998. Rschr. Nat. Pub. Health Inst., Helsinki, 1994—; mem. exec. bd. Kandidaattikustannus, Helsinki, 1994-97. Editor: (book) Therapia Fennica 97, 1997. Vice-chmn. exec. bd. Student Union of the U. Helsinki, 1996, mem. Consistorium, U. Helsinki, 1995-98; chmn. Helsinki Med. Students' Assn., 1998. Mem. Finnish Med. Assn. (del. com. 1997—), Jr. Drs. Assn. Finland (exec. bd. 2000—). Lutheran. Avocations: classical singing, male choir singing, organizational activities. Office: Nat Pub Health Inst, Mannerheimintie 166, 00300 Helsinki Finland

HEITMANN, BERIT LILIENTHAL, scientist; b. Copenhagen, Denmark, Nov. 21, 1962; d. Heinrich Lilieuthal and Nina Elly (Melchiorsen) H.; m. Morten Wulff, May 12, 1990; children: Inez, Mathias. Grad., Royal Dental Coll., Copenhagen, Denmark, 1987; PhD in Nutrition, Inst. Human Nutrition, Copenhagen, Denmark, 1992. Sr. rschr. Inst. Human Nutrition, Copenhagen, 1990-92; sr. rschr. Inst. Preventive Medicine, Copenhagen, 1992-94, rsch. assoc. prof., 1994-98; head sect. Ctr. for Preventive Medicine, Glostrup, Denmark, 1998—. Pres. Danish Assn. Study Obesity, 1996—. Office: Glostrup Univ Hosp, Ctr Preventive Medicine, 2600 Glostrup Denmark

HEITNER, JOHN A. (JACK HEITNER), English language educator, writer; b. Bklyn., May 7, 1931; s. Samuel and Constance (Stannage) H.; m. Susanne James, 1956 (div. 1985); children: Randall, Steven, Wendi. BA cum laude, Hofstra U., 1959; MA, Cornell U., 1960; PhD, U. Rochester, 1968. Instr. SUNY, Albany, 1962-65; assoc. prof. Ctrl. Conn. State U., New Britain, 1965—; lectr. Am. lit. N.W. U., Lanzhou, China, summer 1990, Chingdao (China) U., summer 1990; presenter in field. Author: The Search for the Real Self, 1978, At the Edge of Consciousness, 1987, rev. edit., 1996; contbr. articles and poems to profl. jours. Chmn. Caucus of Local Party Presdl. Nominations, New Britain, 1976; del. Dem. Congl. Caucus, New Britain, 1976, Dem. State Caucus, Southington, Conn., 1972; founder, coord. Ctrl. Literary Soc., 1983—, Humanistic Edn. Support Group, 1973. 1st lt. USMC, 1951-54. N.Y. State Coll. tchg. fellow N.Y. State Regents, 1959-61. Mem. AAUP, Melville Soc., Hawthorne Soc., Mark Twain Circle, John Gardner Soc. (paper presenter 2000), Kappa Delta Pi. Mem. Eckankar Ch. Avocations: world travel, rock climbing, hiking, mountain climbing. Office: Ctrl Conn State U Stanley St New Britain CT 06053

HEITSCH, LEONA MASON, artist, writer; b. Pontiac, Mich., Jan. 6, 1931; d. Russell Leonard and Margaret M. (Arnold) Mason; m. Charles Weyand Heitsch, July 5, 1952; children: Russell, Carrie, Grace, Charles, Irene. BA in chemistry, U. Mich., 1952. Ednl. asst. Spl. Sch. Dist., St. Louis County, Mo., 1969-81; commentator Sta. KUMR, Rolla, Mo., 1996—. Author: (pvt. printing) Echoes of the Ridge, 1985, Get Him to St. Louis, 1983; contbg. author: (poem anthology) Seasons of the Ozarks, 1998; contbr. poetry, articles to various publs. Sec., activist Mo. Assn. Children with Learning Disabilities, St. Louis, 1973-75; fundraising, writing Friends of Foster-Dolbeer Farm, Walled Lake, Mich., 1996—; contbg. poet Wis. Breastfeeding Coalition, Lac du Flambeau, 1996—. Recipient honorable mention Mo. Writers Week award for poetry, 1992, 94, grand prize Artists Embassy Internat., San Francisco, 1997, Editors Challenge award Internat. Soc. Authors and Artists, Abilene, Tex., 1997, included in Memories and Memories, Anthology of Mo. authors, 2000. Mem. St. Louis Poetry Soc., Rolla Area Writers Guild. Avocations: fruit growing, nature study, genealogy, swimming. Home and Office: Ridge Orchards HC 1 Box 66 Bourbon MO 65441-9305

HEITZ, EDWARD FRED, freight traffic consultant; b. Chgo., May 18, 1930; s. Fredo and Hildur (Olson) H.; m. Gaymae Woodrow Heitz, Apr. 28, 1960; children: Merry, Ted. Student, Northwestern U., Chgo., 1950-55. Registered I.C.C. practitioner. Supr. transp. rsch. Internat. Minerals and Chem. Corp., Chgo., 1946-58; asst. freight traffic mgr.-rate rsch. C.&N.W.Ry., Chgo., 1958-64; traffic mgr. U.S. Dept. Agriculture, Washington, 1964-78; agriculture transp. analyst Fed. R.R. Adminstrn., Washington, 1978-82; freight traffic cons. Falls Church, Va., 1982-96; ret., 1996; participant with Am. Arbitration Assn. in program applying arbitration techniques to settlement of class action insur. claims for first time, 1998-2000. Commr. Boy Scouts Am., Fairfax County, Va., 1974-77; chmn. Community Action Agy. County of Fairfax, 1975-77; v.p. Coun. of Fairfax PTAs, 1975; deacon Arlington Ch. of Christ, Falls Ch. Ch. of Christ; mem. Fairfax Com. of 100.

HEIZER, EDGAR FRANCIS, JR., venture capitalist; b. Detroit, Sept. 23, 1929; s. Edgar Francis and Grace Adelia (Smith) H.; m. Molly Bradley Hunt, June 17, 1952; children: Linda Heizer Seaman, Molly Hunt, Edgar Francis III. BS, Northwestern U., 1951; JD, Yale U., 1954. Bar: Ill. 1954; CPA, Ill. Mem. audit and tax staff Arthur Andersen & Co., Chgo., 1954-56; fin. analyst Kidder, Peabody & Co., Chgo., 1956-58; mgmt. cons. Booz, Allen & Hamilton, Chgo., 1958-62; asst. treas., mgr. venture capital divsn. Allstate Ins. Co., Northbrook, Ill., 1962-69; chmn., founder, CEO Heizer Corp., a venture capital & bus. devel. co., Chgo., 1969-85; venture capitalist Tucker's Town, Bermuda, 1985—; bd. dirs. Needham & Co., N.Y., Material Sci. Corp., Elk Grove Village, Ill., Manus Health Systems Inc., Lake Forest, Ill., Chesapeake Energy Corp., Oklahoma City, Okla.; mem. adv. bd. Kellogg Sch. Mgmt., Northwestern U.; chmn. Heizer Ctr. for Entrepreneurship at Kellogg Sch. Mgmt. Mem. Nat. Venture Capital Assn. (founder, 1st pres., chmn.), Nat. Assn. Small Bus. Investment Cos., Delta Upsilon (chmn. bd. dirs. 1985-88, chmn. ednl. found. 1990-98). Republican. Presbyterian. Clubs: Chgo. Curling, Shoreacres, Econ. of Chgo., Coral Beach and Tennis, Mid-Ocean; Riddells Bay Golf (Bermuda). Home: 28 S Shore Rd, Tuckers Town HS 02, Bermuda also: 261 Bluffs Edge Dr Lake Forest IL 60045-3301

HEIZER, RUTH BRADFUTE, philosophy educator; b. Knoxville, Tenn., Oct. 8, 1933; d. George Archibald and Margaret Eleanor (Smith) Bradfute; m. James Lee Heizer, Aug. 3, 1956; children: John Philip, Mark Russell, Virginia Ruth. BA, Baylor U., 1954; MRE, So. Baptist Theol. Sem., 1957; MA, U. Ky., 1965; PhD, Ind. U., 1971; postgrad., Oxford (Eng.) U., 1980-81, 89. Tchr. Jefferson County Pub. Schs., Louisville, 1956-58; secondary tchr. Gallatin County Pub. Schs., Warsaw, Ky., 1959-60, 61; teaching assoc. dept. philosophy Ind. U., Bloomington, 1965-67; from instr. to assoc. prof. Georgetown (Ky.) Coll., 1967-83, prof., 1983-95, prof. emeritus, 1996—, chair dept. philosophy, 1981-93; vis. prof. philosophy Baylor U., Waco, Tex., 1979, 84; tchr. oral English Jiangnan U., Wuxi, China, summers 1990, 91, Yantai U., China, summer 1994, Inst. for Advanced Qualification of Workers of Edn., Kazan, Russia, summer, 1995; prof. Moscow Bapt. Theol. Sem., 1996-98. Author: Bradfute Beginnings, 1988; co-author: Women, Philosophy, & Sport, 1983, Contemporary Essays on Greek Ideas, 1987. Deacon Faith Bapt. Ch., Georgetown. Recipient NEH summer stipend, 1973. Mem. AAUW, Am. Philos. Assn., So. Soc. Philosophy and Psychology, Ky. Philos. Assn. (pres. 1973-74), Bapt. Assn. Philosophy Tchrs. (pres. 1988-89), Omicron Delta Kappa (Baylor Woman of Merit award 1980). Republican. Avocations: photography, fgn. travel, teaching ESL. Home: 7231 Wellswood Ln Knoxville TN 37909-2436

HEJAZI, NEDAL ABDALLAH, physician, consultant; b. Gaza, Palestine, July 4, 1966; s. Abdallah Kh. and Myriam Ibrahim Hejazi. MD, U. Heidelberg, Germany, 1991. Cert. German Bd. Neuol. Surgery, 1997. Intern, resident in gen. surgery and neurosurgery Kopfklinikum of the U. of Heidelberg, Germany, 1990-91; resident in neuol. surgery U. Münster, Germany, 1992-95; resident in neurol. surgery U. Bochum, Duisburg, Germany, 1995-97, cons. neurosurgeon dept. of neurosurgery, 1997-98; cons. neurosurgeon Acad. Ctr. of U. Innsbruck, Feldkirch, Austria, 1999—; mem. German project group Cerebral Cystic Tumors, 1997—. Avocations: diving, swimming, bicycling, reading. Office: Dept Neurosurgery, Carinagasse 9, A-6800 Feldkirch Austria

HÉJJAS, ISTVÁN, optoelectronics researcher; b. Kecskemét, Hungary, Feb. 24, 1938; s. István and Magdolna (Sándorfi) H.; m. Andrea Tokes; children: Miklós, Emese, Marianna. MSME, Tech. U., Miskolc, Hungary, 1961; MSEE, Tech U., Budapest, 1970, PhD, 1973. Cert. mech. engr. and elec. engr. Prof.'s asst. Tech. U., Miskolc, 1961-62; head of dept. Vilati Co., Budapest, 1962-77; sc. prin. co-worker HIKI Inst., Budapest, 1977-78; chief engr. MIKI Engring. Inc., Budapest, 1978—; cons. Nat. Com. R&D, Budapest, 1977-96. Contbr. tech. articles to profl. jours.; patentee in field. Recipient Excellent Inventor Golden degree Nat. Office of Inventions, 1984, 89. Mem. Lorand Eötvös Soc. Physics, Sc. Assn. Automation, Hungarian Assn. Indsl. Property. Ind. Farmer's Party. Buddhist. Avocations: ancient Oriental philosophies, cycling, gardening. Office: MIKI Engring Inc, MIKI Engring Inc, Erzsebet Str 2-4, H-1045 Budapest Hungary

HEJZLAR, JOSEF, limnologist, educator; b. Liberec, Czech Republic, Sept. 7, 1956; s. Josef and Lydie Rozalie (Podracká) H.; m. Vladimira Chroustova, Jan. 25, 1980; children: Iva, Jan, Stepan. MS, Inst. Chem. Tech., Prague, Czech Republic, 1980, PhD, 1985. Rsch. scientist Hydrobiol. Inst. Czech Acad. Scis., Ceske Budejovice, Czech Republic, 1985—; lectr. U. South Bohemia, Ceske Budejovice, 1994—. Contbr. articles to profl. jours. Mem. Czech Chem. Soc. Office: Czech Acad Hydrobiol In, Na Sadkach 7, 37005 Ceske Budejovice Czech Republic

HELALI, HAKIM, science association administrator. Pres. Afghanistan Acad. Scis., Inst. Social Scis., Kabul, Afghanistan. Office: Inst Social Scis, Sher Alikhan St, Kabul Afghanistan*

HELANDER, HERBERT D.F., anatomist; b. Lund, Sweden, Dec. 7, 1935; s. Dick A.V. and Maria A.E. H.; m. Kerstin G. Lindblom, Mar. 29, 1961; children: Carl, Per, Nils. MD, U. Goteborg, Sweden, 1963, PhD in Anatomy, 1962. Lic. physician, Sweden. Prof. anatomy U. Umea, Sweden, 1966-84; sr. rsch. adviser Astra Hassle AB, Molndal, Sweden, 1984—; vis. asst. prof., dept. medicine U. Okla., 1964-65, vis. prof. physiology, U. Ala., Birmingham, 1970-82, vis. prof. dept. medicine, UCLA, 1983—; adj. prof. anatomy U. Goteborg, 1985—. Contbr. articles to profl. jours. Fulbright scholar to U.S., 1964-65; sr. vis. scientist NSF, 1970-71. Mem. European Gastro Club, Am. Gastroenterol. Assn., Am. Soc. Cell Biology. Office: Astra Zeneca AB, 43183 Mölndal Sweden

HELAS, GÜNTER, chemist; b. Hainsberg, Germany, June 27, 1946; m. Angelika; children: Martin, Silvia, Christian. Dr.rer.nat., Tech. U. Darmstadt (Germany), 1976. Rsch. asst. Tech. U. Darmstadt (Germany), 1972-76; scientist MPI Chemistry, Mainz, Germany, 1977-87, sr. scientist, 1987—, temp. acting dir. dept biogeochemistry, 1993, 94, 96; hon. prof. chemistry dept. U. Witwatersrand, South Africa, 1997-2000. Contbr. articles to profl. jours. Ablett fellow SRCNS, Witwatersrand U., Johannesburg, South Africa, 1995-96. Mem. Am. Geophys. Union, European Geophys. Soc., Gesellschaft Deutscher Chem. Office: Max-Planck Inst Chem, POB 3060, 55020 Mainz Germany

HELBERG, SHIRLEY ADELAIDE HOLDEN, artist, educator; b. Solvay, N.Y.; d. Isaac Edgar and Gladys Evelyn (Tucker) Holden; m. Burton Edward Helberg; children: Keir Holm, Kristin Vaughan, Kecia Tucker Lau, Kandace Holden Mead, Kraig Brownlee. BE, Johns Hopkins U., 1969; MFA, Md. Inst. Art, 1975. Tchr. various schs., N.J. and Pa., Manchester (Pa.) Pub. Schs., 1965-84, Balt. City Schs., 1988-92; demonstration tchr. Balt. City Schs., O'Donnell Heights Sch., 1992. One-woman shows include U. Va. Charlottesville, 1974, Cayuga Mus. Art and History, Auburn, N.Y., 1974, Hist. Soc. York Mus., Pa., 1977, York Coll., 1984, Country Club York; represented in permanent collections Pres. Richard Nixon; author: (poetry book) Chosen Few; author, illustrator: The Kitty Cat Who Wanted to Fly, 1999, The Jumping Frog of Calaveras County, 1999. Bd. dirs. York (Pa.) Arts Coun., 1964-66. Named Outstanding Tchr. Northeastern Sch. Dist. Bd. Edn. Mem. NEA, Nat. League Am. Pen Women (Pa. State art chmn. 1972-74, pres. Pa. orgn. 1974-76, nat. scholarship chair 1976-98, registrar 1986-88, 5th v.p. 1988-90, 1990. Disting. Svc. award 1978, 80, 82, 84, 86, 88, 90, 92, Disting. Achievement award 1988, 94), Pa. State Edn. Assn., Internat. Platform Assn., Harrisburg Art Assn., York Art Assn., Pa. Watercolor Soc., Johns Hopkins Faculty Club. Republican. Methodist. Home: 5433 Pigeon Hill Rd Spring Grove PA 17362-8854 also: 727 S Ann St Baltimore MD 21231-3402

HELBRECHT, ILSE, geographer, educator; b. Stuttgart, Germany, Feb. 27, 1964. BA, U. Muenster, 1985, MA, 1990; PhD, Tech. U. Munich, 1993; habilitation, Tech. U., Munich, 1999. Lectr. Tech. U. Munich, Germany, 1990-94; postdoctoral fellow U. B.C., Can., 1994-96; lectr. Tech. U. Munich, 1996—. Author: Crisis Region Ruhr Area, 1989, Planning's Ending, 1991, Urban Marketing, 1994; editor: Social Geography, 1998. Grantee German Rsch. Found., 1997-99. Office: Dept Geography, Tech Univ Munich, 80290 Munich Germany

HELD, GERHARD, environmental consultant, meteorologist; b. Vienna, Austria, Mar. 5, 1944; arrived in South Africa, 1970; s. Herbert and Hilde Maria (Willigens) H.; m. Diane Phyllis Eastham, Feb. 23, 1974 (div. Nov. 1984); children: Brendon, Mark, Michelle (twins). PhD in Meteorology and Physics, U. Vienna, 1968. Part-time climatologist Austrian Weather Bur., Vienna, 1965-67, meteorologist, 1969-70; radar meteorologist specialist rschr. Coun. Sci. and Indsl. Rsch., Pretoria, South Africa, 1970-92; air pollution meteorologist specialist rschr. Coun. Sci. and Indsl. Rsch., Pretoria, 1981-92; sr. environ. cons. ESKOM T-R-I, Johannesburg, South Africa, 1992-99; chief cons., 1999-2000; prof. radar meteorology Inst. Pesquisas Meteorols. U. Estadual Paulista, Bauru, São Paulo, 2000—; external supr. grad. students, South Africa; organizer of sci. confs. Contbr. articles to profl. jours., chpts. to books; asst. editor Wetter & Leben jour., Vienna, 1965-70; referee profl. jours in field. Convenor, organizer art exhbn. Pretoria Art Mus., 1996. Served with Austrian Air Force, 1968. Mem. South African Soc. Atmospheric Scis. (founding, coun., treas., pres. 1998-2000), Environ. Sci. Assn. (founding, chmn. 1997-2000), Nat. Assn. for Clean Air. Roman Catholic. Avocations: photography, travel, wildlife, skiing, hiking. Home: Apto 81, Rua São Gonçalo 6-73, 17012170 Bauru, São Paulo Brazil Office: IMPMet/UNESP, cx Postal 281, 17033360 Bauru, São Paulo Brazil

HÉLEIN, FRÉDÉRIC, mathematics educator; b. Versailles, France, Apr. 22, 1963; s. Jean and Renée (Lottier) H. PhD in Math., Poly. Sch., Palaiseau, France, 1989; Habilitation in Math., U. Paris 11, Orsay, France, 1991. Armament engr. Armament Adminstrn., Paris, 1986-91; prof. math. Superior Normal Sch. Cachan, France, 1991—; prof. Inst. Univ. de France, 1997—. Author: (with F. Bethuel and H. Brezis) Ginzburg-Landau Vortices, 1994; Applications harmoniques, lois de conservation et repères mobiles, 1996; co-editor: Nematics, 1990. Recipient Prix Verdaguer, Acad. Scis., Paris, 1991, Cours Peccot, Coll. France, Paris, 1994, Prix Fermat rsch. math. U. Toulouse, 1999. Avocations: piano, church organ. Home: Tour Jade, 16 rue Vandrezanne, 75013 Paris France Office: ENS de Cachan Dept Math, ENS de Cachan Dept Math, 61 av du Pré Wilson, 94235 Cachan Cedex, France

HELENE, CLAUDE MICHEL, professor of biophysics; b. Chauvigny, Vienne, France, Jan. 29, 1938; s. Roger and Jeanne (Bideau) H. Agrégation de physique, Ecole Normale Supérieure, Paris, 1962; PhD, U. Paris, 1966; Dr. honoris causa, Liege U., Belgium, 1989; Katholicke U Leuven, Belgium, 1997. Researcher Centre Nat. de la Recherche Scientifique, Paris, 1962-67; dir. research CNRS, Orléans, France, 1967-76; prof. Mus. Nat. D'Histoire Naturelle, Paris, 1976—; dir. Ctr. Biophysique Moléculaire, Orléans, 1974-82, Inserm Rsch. Unit 201, Paris, 1980—; sci. dir. Rhône-Poulenc, 1990-99. Editor Trends in Photobiology, 1982, Structure and Function of Biological Macromolecules, 1983; contbr. over 400 articles to profl. jours.. Decorated Ordre Nat. du Mérite (France), Légion D'Honneur (France). Mem. French Acad. Scis.; fellow AAAS. Office: Mus Nat D'Histoire, 43 Rue Cuvier, 75005 Paris France

HELFMAN, CAROLYN RAE, middle school educator; b. Dallas, July 15, 1941; d. Alfred Sallinger and Hermine Rita Morgenstern; m. Kenneth Harvey Helfman, Aug. 10, 1963 (div. June 1980); children: Theresa, Daniel, Kory. BA, Washington U., St. Louis, 1963; MEd in Counseling, U. North Tex., 1992. Tchr. Richardson (Tex.) Ind. Sch. Dist., 1963-64; homebound tchr. Garland (Tex.) Ind. Sch. Dist., 1970-71; tchr. Hockaday Sch., Dallas, 1971-84, 88-99, asst. head mid. sch., 1993-96, head mid. sch., 1996-99, assoc. head of sch., 1999—; mktg. mgr. Omniplan Architects, Dallas, 1984-88; assoc. head sch. Bryn Mawr Sch., Balt., 1999—. Mem. bd. dirs. devel. com. Temple Emanu-El, Dallas, 1998-99; bd. dirs. Anti Defamation League, Dallas, 1996-98. Mem. AAUW, ASCD, Nat. Mid. Sch. Assn., Ind. Schs. Assn. of S.W. (mem. adv. planning com. 1995—, mem. evaluation team 1998), Phi Delta Kappa. Jewish. E-mail: helfmanc@brynmawr.pvt.k12.md.us. Home: 4100 N Charles St Apt 714 Baltimore MD 21218-1030 Office: Bryn Mawr Sch 109 W Melrose Ave Baltimore MD 21210-1397

HELGASON, PALL BERGSSON, physician; b. Stockholm, June 22, 1938; s. Helgi Bergsson and Liney (Johannesdottir) H.; m. Sigurlaug R. Karlsdottir, Apr. 7, 1962 (dec. Apr. 1996); children: Arna, Gunnlaug, Ragnheidur Liney, Snorri Karl. MD, U. Iceland, 1967. Cert. physical medicine and rehab. Rot intern Landspitalinn, St. Josephs, City Hosp., Reykjavik, Iceland, 1967-68; resident City Hosp., Reykjavik, 1968-70; resident physical medicine and rehab. Mayo Clinic, Rochester, Minn., 1970-74; asst. prof. anatomy U. Iceland, Reykjavik, 1974-84, lectr. phys. medicine and rehab., 1975-93; cons. phys. medicine and rehab. Landspitalinn, St. Josephs, Reykjavik, 1974-81, head dept. phys. medicine and rehab., 1981-93; cons phys. medicine and rehab. dept. pulmonary medicine Vitisstadir Hosp. Geriatric Med. Landspitalinn, 1993-96; cons. geriatric medicine Sundsvall, Sweden, 1997; med. officer Olafsfjordur, Iceland, 1998; chief phys. medicine and rehab. FSA Hosp., Iceland, 1998-99; cons. Icelandic Sports Union for the Handicapped, Reykjavik, 1976—, Icelandic Red Cross, Reykjavik, 1976-95. Recipient sci. award NATO, Iceland, 1970, 73, sci. award Icelandic Govt., 1972. Fellow Am. Acad. Physical Medicine and Rehab.; mem. Am. Congress Rehab. Medicine, Internat. Soc. Paraplegia, European League Against Raeum. Mem. Nat. Ch. of Iceland. Home: Graenatun 8, IS-200 Kodavogue Iceland Mailing Address: PO Box 182, IS-212 Gardabae Iceland

HELIAS, CATHERINE ANNIE, biologist, researcher; b. Pont L'Abbé, France, Sept. 8, 1966; d. Jean-Claude and Anne-Marie (Goraguer) H. PhD, U. Brest, France. Rschr. Hosp., Brest, 1993-97, tchr., rschr., 1997-99; engr. Hosp. Strasbourg, France, 1999—. Mem. European Cytogeneticists Assn. Office: CHU Hautepierre, 67000 Strasbourg France

HELIOFF, ANNE GRAILE, painter; b. Liverpool, Eng.; d. Max and Frances Elizabeth (Beilenson) H.; m. Benjamin Michael Hirschberg. Student, Columbia U., Art Students League, N.Y.C. mem. U.S. del. 5th Congress Internat. Assn. Art, Tokyo, 1966, invitation Woodstock Artists Assn., 1994; dir. exhbns. including 50 Yrs. of Woodstock Art (N.Y.), N.Y. State Tri-Centennial, 1959, dir. N.Y. State dedication show Lighthouse for Blind, N.Y.C. One-woman shows include Capricorn Gallery, N.Y.C., 1966-69, Phoenix Gallery, N.Y.C., 1972, 74, 76, 82, 85, Woodstock (N.Y.) Artists Assn., 1988; group exhbns. include Milch Gallery, N.Y.C., 1939-40 (Paintings of Yr. 1946), Pepsi-Cola Nat. travelling shows to major mus., U.S., 1947, Nat. Gallery Art, Washington, Pa. Acad. Ann, Art U.S.A., also bicentennial exhbn., 6 Americans in France traveling show, 1976, Mus. in Florence and Naples, Italy; slide show Am. Art 6th Congress Internat. Assn. Art, Helsinki, finland. Recipient Silver medal Albany (N.Y.) Mus. Art and Sci., 1957; Homer Boss scholar, 1939, Y. Kuniyoshi scholar and asst., 1940-45. Mem. Arista, Woodstock Artists Assn. (life, past dir.), Art Students League (past dir.), Am. Soc. Contemporary Artists (past dir., awards in oil, watercolor and acrylic), Nat. Assn. Women Artists, N.Y. Soc. Women Artists (past dir.), Archives of Am. Art, Smithsonian Mus. Address: 340 W 28th St New York NY 10001-4732

HELL, JUDIT, philosophy educator; b. Miskolc, Hungary, Apr. 1, 1954; d. Istvan Hell and Anna Sikora; m. Barnabas Gönczy, Aug. 6, 1977 (div. 1980); m. Peter Andrik, July 6, 1985; 1 child, Judit Gönczy. MA, Kossuth U., Debrecen, Hungary, 1977, Kossuth U., Debrecen, Hungary, 1985; postgrad., Eötvös U., Budapest, Hungary, 1990; PhD, Hungarian Acad. Scis., Budapest, 1993. Tchr. Bathori Second Sch., Nyirbator, Hungary, 1978-80, Kilian Second Sch., Miskolc, 1980-86; asst. U. Miskolc, 1986-89, lectr., 1989-94, sr. lectr., 1994—. Author: Frigyes Medveczky, 1995; editor: Socialethics, 1996, Multiculturalism Studies, 1998; contbr. articles to profl. jours. Pres. European Condorcet-Circle, No. Hungary, Miskolc, 1996. Grantee Collegium Hungaricum, Vienna, 1992, 94, 99, Ministry of Culture, Saxony, 1996. Fellow Hungarian Assn. Applied Philosophy; mem. Hungarian Philos. Assn., Internat. Assn. Tchrs. Philosophy, Internat. Lukacs Assn. Roman Catholic. Avocations: travel, television, books, journals. Home: Kiraly St 7, H-3530 Miskolc Hungary Office: U Miskolc, Egyetemvaros, 3515 Miskolc Hungary

HELLAND, SHERMAN M., writer; b. Racine, Wis., Nov. 16, 1913; s. Severin and Marie Kutinka (Fyhrie) H.; m. Rose Martha Steuck, Aug. 12, 1939; children: Mary, Sandra, Karen, Harold. Mgr. retail meats C&W Haummersen, Racine, Wis., 1933-35; sales area developer George A. Hormel Co., Austin, Minn., 1936-51; mgr. bus. analysis U.S. Govt., Richmond, Va., 1951-53; sales mgr., beef grader Donner Packing Co., Milw., 1953-54; supr. chain store meat Godfrey Co., Waukesha, Wis., 1954-55, purchaser, merchandiser select beef and lamb, 1956-57, with, 1958-76; cons. agr., livestock, breeding feeding, merchandising retail meat, 1991—. Author: Hoofs, Amen, 1978, E. Coli Kills--Wake Up or Die, 1997. Pres. Old Jr. Club of Milw. County, 1980. With USN, 1945. Mem. Am. Legion (chpt. pres. 1981-82). Republican. Lutheran. Avocations: flying, hunting, golf, fishing, philosophy. Home and Office: 5020 S 55th St Apt 303 Greenfield WI 53220-5370

HELLEBO, OLAV, business executive; b. Norway, July 16, 1965; s. Rolf and Alice Hellebo; m. Marlene Hellebo, May 15, 1993; 1 child, Jan Olav. Student, Norwegian Sch. Mgmt., 1988; BBA summa cum laude, Hofstra U., 1990; MBA, IESE, Barcelona, Spain, 1992. Bus. devel. mgr. Schering-Plough Internat., Kenilworth, N.J., 1994-96; product dir. Claritin, Schering Labs., Kenilworth, 1996-98; dir. Schering-Plough, Paris, 1998—. V.p. AIESEC, Hempstead, N.Y., 1989-90. Cpl., inf. Norwegian Army, 1984-85. E-mail: olav.hellebo@spcorp.com. Office: Schering-Plough 2000 Galloping Hill Rd Kenilworth NJ 07033-1328

HELLER, FREDERICK KEACH, JR., lawyer; b. Lynchburg, Va., June 9, 1947; s. Frederick Keach Sr. and Evelyn (Leftwich) H.; m. Andrea Mancuso, Dec. 27, 1969; 1 child, Jenny Evelyn. BA, Yale U., 1969, JD, 1973. Bar: Ga. 1973. Assoc. Kilpatrick, Cody, Rogers, McClatchey & Regenstern,

Atlanta, 1973-79; ptnr. Kilpatrick & Cody, Atlanta, 1979-91; ptnr. Kilpatrick & Cody, Brussels, 1992-95, mng. ptnr., 1995-97; chmn. European offices Kilpatrick Stockton, London, 1997—; dir. Bellsouth Internat. Ltd., Bellsouth Ltd., Bellsouth Personal Comm. Ltd., Kilpatrick Stockton Ltd. Mem. ABA, Internat. Bar Assn., Yale Club N.Y. Roman Catholic. Avocations: running, reader. Home: 20 Grosvenor Crescent Mews, London SW1X 7EX, England Office: Kilpatrick Stockton, 68 Pall Mall, London SW1Y 5ES, England

HELLER, FRIEDRICH OTTO, science educator; b. Wiesbaden, Germany, Aug. 10, 1939; s. Friedrich Georg (Fritz) and Marie Anna (Paul) H.; m. Elly Stutzel, Oct. 29, 1971; children: Bodo Friedrich Georg, Constance Annette. Dr.rer.nat., Tech. U., Darmstadt, Germany, 1979. Scientist Optical Industry Carl Zeiss, Baden-Wurttemberg, Germany, 1960, 66, 70-71; scientist in med. tech. Geraeteentwicklung Phywe AG, Goettingen, Germany, 1972, Inst. for Water, Soil and Air Hygiene, Berlin, 1973-78; tchr. biology, physics, math. and chemistry Gymnasien, Germany, 1969-70, 79-81; bus. mgmt. and computer staff Bonn-Alfter, Wiesbaden and Cologne, Germany, 1980, 82, 83, Stadtverwaltung Bad Honnef, Nord, Germany, 1985-87; biotope mgr. Nettersheim/Eifel, 1987; tchr. Deutsch Ausländische Arbeitsgemeinschaft, Bonn, 1991—. Contbr. articles to profl. jours. Mem. AAAS, Acad. Scis., Deutsche Botanische Gesellschaft, Naturschutzbund Deutschland, Assn. Ornithologists Bayerns, German Ornithol. Soc., Internat. Assn. Gideons Germany, N.Y. Acad. Sci. Avocations: ornithology, viola, reading. Office: Deutsche Ausländische Arbeitgemeinschaft, Siegburger Strasse 9, D-53229 Bonn Germany

HELLER, JAN, physiologist, researcher; b. Prague, Czechoslovakia, June 19, 1952; s. Jan and Danuše (Vondrušková) H.; m. Jana Matunová, Sept. 14, 1974; children: Jan, Michaela. Med. diploma, Prague U., 1976, PhD, 1981. Rschr. faculty phys. edn. and sports Charles U., Prague, 1981-83; rschr. Faculty of Medicine, Paris, 1983-84; head lab. exercise physiology Rsch. Inst. Physiol. Culture, Prague, 1984-90; head biomed. lab. faculty phys. edn. and sport Charles U., Prague, 1991—; invited prof. med. faculty U. Antioquia, Medellin, Colombia, 1993; cons. Czech Olympic Com., Prague, 1997—, Grant Agy. for Univ. Devel., Prague, 1995—. Author: (textbook) Exercise Physiology, 1996; contbr. articles to profl. jours. Mem. Czech Soc. Kinanthropology (exec. com. 1994—), Soc. Physiology (France), N.Y. Acad. Scis., Czech. Soc. Sports Medicine (mem. exec. com. 1999—). Avocations: literature, arts, recreational sports, gardening. Home: Terronská 811/27, 160 00 Prague Czech Republic Office: Charles U Biomed Lab, J Martího 31, 162 52 Prague Czech Republic

HELLER, JIRI, physiologist; b. Prague, Sept. 4, 1931; s. Frantisek and Ruzena (Sachova) H.; m. Vera Fulinova, Nov. 14, 1958 (div. Dec. 1987); children: Vera, Jiri; m. Sona Kamaradova, June 24, 1988; 1 child, Stepan. MD, Charles U., Prague, 1956, PhD, 1963. Asst. prof. Charles U., Prague, 1956-62; sr. rschr. Inst. Profl. Diseases, Prague, 1962-66, Inst. Cardiovascular Diseases, Prague, 1966-71; sr. rschr. Inst. Clin. Exptl. Medicine, Prague, 1971—, head dept. exptl. medicine, 1992—; prof. 2d Med. Sch., Charles U., Prague, 1990—. Author: Conditioned Reflex Diuresis, 1959. Capt. Czech Army, 1956-57. Mem. Academia Europea (hon.), Czech Nephrology Soc. (hon.). Avocations: music, gardening. Home: Stechovicka 13, CZ-10000 Prague 10, Czech Republic Office: Inst Clin Exptl Medicine, Videnska 800, CZ-14000 Prague 4, Czech Republic

HELLER, KURT ALOIS, psychology educator; b. Külsheim, Baden, Germany, Aug. 22, 1931; s. Arthur and Theresia (Schwind) H.; m. Irmgard E. Holz, July 20, 1957; children: Christian M., Susanne I. MA in Psychology, U. Heidelberg, Germany, 1964, PhD, 1968. Qualification as tchr. of deaf, as speech therapist. Rsch. asst. U. Heidelberg Tchrs. Coll., 1965-66; dir. Baden-Württemberg State Ednl. Guidance & Counseling Ctr., Stuttgart, 1966-68; asst. prof. psychology dept. spl. edn. Tchrs. Coll., U. Heidelberg, 1969-70; prof. psychology, dir. Inst. Ednl. Psychology U. Bonn, 1971-75; prof. ednl. psychology U. Cologne, 1976-81; prof. psychology, dir. Inst. Ednl. Psychology U. Munich, München, 1982—, coord. internat. MA study program PSYCHOLOGY EXCELLENCE dept. psychology and edn., 1998—; dir. Rsch. Ctr. for Psychol. Tests, U. Bonn, 1971-76, Ctr. for Study of Excellence, 1998—; advisor German Acad. Exch. Svc., Bonn, 1994-2001; German project leader Amérique Latine Formation Acad./European Union, Brussels, 1995-98. 1st editor International Handbook of Research and Development of Giftedness and Talent, 1993—, 2d edit., 2000; editor: High Ability Studies, 1996—, Behavioral and Brain Scis. Assoc., 1995—; mem. editl. bd. 8 nat. and internat. jours. and book series; contbr. articles to profl. jours, chpts. to over 350 books. Acad. scholar Volkswagen Found., 1989-90. Fellow Humboldt Soc. Sci. and Arts, German Soc. Psychology (exec. com. sect. ednl. psychology 1985-91, editor in chief jour. 1978-96), N.Y. Acad. Scis. (psychology sect.). Fax: 49-89-2180-5250. Office: U Munich Dept Psychology, Leopoldstr 13, D-80802 Munich Germany

HELLER, LUCY, publishing company executive; b. London, Feb. 8, 1959; d. Lukas Heller and Caroline (Carter) Garnham; m. Charles Elton, Mar. 3, 1990; children: Lotte, Abraham. Degree in politics, philosophy, econs., Oxford (Eng.) U., 1977. Asst. v.p. Bankers Trust, N.Y.C., 1981-87; mng. dir. Mfrs. Hanover, London, 1987-90; treas. Booker, London, 1990-95; chmn. Verso, London, 1995-97; gen. mgr. The Observer, London, 1998-99; mng. dir. Times Supplements, Ltd., 2000—; commr. Inst. Pub. Policy Rsch. Commn. on Pub. Policy & Bus., 1995-97; chmn. Bank of Eng./Brit. Bankers Assn. Comml. Paper com., 1987; non-exec. dir. Bush Theatre, London, 1993—, Prospect Mag., 1997—. Author, editor: Eurocommercial Paper, 1988; contbr.: Guide to Capital Markets, 1989, 90. Home: 24 Maida Ave, London W2 1ST, England Office: The Observer, 119 Farringdon Rd, London EC1R 3ER, England

HELLER, PETER SETON, composer; b. N.Y.C., Aug. 4, 1926; s. M.J. and Rose Backer H.; m. Mary Wellington Wheeler, June 30, 1956; 1 child: Kate Lawrence Heller O'Reilly. AB, Harvard U., 1949, LLB, 1952. Bar: N.Y. Assoc. Webster & Sheffield, N.Y.C., 1952-60, ptnr., 1960-86, mng. ptnr., 1986-90, retired, 1990—; composer. Hon. dir. Philharm. Symphony Soc. N.Y.; vice-chmn. St. Lukes-Roosevelt Hosp. Ctr.; trustee The Brearley Sch., 1965-80, Radcliffe Coll., 1977-83, William Matheus Sullivan Musical Found.; dir. Am. Composers Orch., Am. Assn. for Internat. Comm. Free Jurists; v.p. Associated Harvard Alumni, 1977-80; overseer Harvard Coll., 1983-90; dir. Equitable Life Assurance Soc., 1986-90; pres. Harvard Club N.Y.C., 1996-99. Staff sgt. U.S. Army, 1944-46. Mem. Cambridge Boat Club, Century Assn., Harvard Club N.Y.C., Nantucket Yacht Club, Shimmo Rowing Club, Siasconset Casino Assn., Sankaty Head Golf Club. Avocations: rowing, archaeology, painting, golf, tennis.

HELLER, RONALD IAN, lawyer; b. Cleve., Sept. 4, 1956; s. Grant L. and Audrey P. (Lecth) H.; m. Shirley Ann Stringer, Mar. 23, 1986; 1 child, David Grant. AB with high honors, U. Mich., 1976, MBA, 1979, JD, 1980. Bar: Hawaii 1980, U.S. Ct. Claims 1982, U.S. Tax Ct. 1981, U.S. Ct. Appeals (9th cir.) 1981, U.S. Supreme Ct. 1992; Trust Ter. Pacific Islands 1982, Rep. Marshall Islands 1982; CPA, Hawaii. Assoc. Hoddick, Reinwald, O'Connor & Marrack, Honolulu, 1980-84; ptnr. Reinwald, O'Connor & Marrack, Honolulu, 1984-87; stockholder, bd. dirs. Torkildson, Katz, Fonseca, Jaffe & Moore, Honolulu, 1988—; adj. prof. U. Hawaii Sch. Law, 1981; arbitrator ct.-annexed arbitration program First Cir. Ct., State of Hawaii; author, instr. Hawaii Taxes. Bd. dirs. Hawaii Women Lawyers Found., Honolulu, 1984-86, Hawaii Performing Arts Co., Honolulu, 1984-93; panel of arbitrators Am. Arbitration Assn., 1987-99; actor, stage mgr. Honolulu Cmty. Theatre, 1983-87, Hawaii Performing Arts Co., Honolulu, 1982-87. Named NFIB Hawaii outstanding sm. bus. vol. 1998. Fellow Am. Coll. Tax Counsel; mem. AICPAs (coun. 1994-96), ABA, Hawaii State Bar Assn. (chair tax sect. 1997-98, chair state and local tax com. 1994-95), Hawaii Soc. CPAs (chmn. tax com. 1985-86, legis. com. 1987-88, bd. dirs. 1988-98, pres. 1994-95), Hawaii Women Lawyers. Office: Torkildson Katz Fonseca Jaffe & Moore 700 Bishop St Fl 15 Honolulu HI 96813-4187

HELLERQVIST, CARL GUSTAF, biochemist, educator; b. Sundsvall, Sweden, Oct. 30, 1940; s. Rune Gustaf Hellerqvist and Ingeborg Hidur Olson; m. Charlotte Carin-Ulla Strandberg, June 1, 1963; children: Monica, Anna-Carin. Filosophie kandidate: chemistry, math., Stockholms Univ., Sweden, 1967; filosohie licentiat: chemistry, Stockholms Univ., 1968, filosophie doktor: chemistry, 1971. Instr. dept. organic chemistry Stockholms U., Sweden, 1967-78; asst. prof. Stockholms U., 1969-71; rsch. scientist dept. biology Johns Hopkins U., Baltimore, 1973-74; asst. prof. dept. biochemistry Vanderbilt U., Nashville, 1974-81; assoc. prof. Vanderbilt U., 1982-99; founder, cons. CarboMed., Inc., Brentwood, Tenn., 1991—; assoc. prof. Vanderbilt U., 1995-99; prof. biochemistry and medicine Nashville, 1999—; docent faculty scis., Stockholms U., Sweden, 1971—. Mem. Soc. Neurosci., Am. Assn. Cancer Rsch., Am. Soc. Clin. Oncology, Soc. for Glycobiology (sec. 1987-93), Brentwood Country Club, Percy Priest Yacht Club, U.S. Sail. Avocations: sailing. Fax: 615-322-6354. E-mail: carl.g.hellerqvist@vanderbilt.edu. Office: Vanderbilt U 23rd Pierce 634 Mrb 1 Nashville TN 37232-0001

HELLING, CLAUDIA KRISTINE, geologist; b. Freiberg, Germany, Mar. 6, 1970; d. S. Udo Wilbrecht and C. Hildeposd (Poppitz) H. Diploma in hydrology, Freiberg U., 1994, postgrad., 1994-98. Geologist BIUG, Freiberg, 1997—; conf. mgr. uranium mining & hydrogeology Freiberg U., 1997-98. Contbr. articles to profl. jours. Mem. Assn. for Environ. Geoscis. (pub. rels. 1998), Internat. Assn. Hydrogeologist, German Geol. Assn. Avocations: mountain climbing, walking, volleyball, reading. Office: Freiberg Univ, G Leuires Str 12, 09596 Freiberg Germany

HELLINGWERF, ROBERT HENDRICUS, geology educator; b. Amsterdam, Nov. 23, 1954; s. Arie Hendricus and Florida Johanna (Hutzezon) H.; m. Karin Gunilla Bjoerkqvist, Aug. 25, 1990; children: Amanda Maria, William Hendricus. BS in Geology, U. Amsterdam, 1976, MS in Geology with distinction, 1982, PhD in Geology, 1986. Assoc. prof. U. Goteborg, Sweden, 1989-2000; univ. lectr. geochemistry U. Goteborg, 1993-94, lectr. mineralogy, ore geology, econ. geology, 1995—; pres., dir. H.G.R. Ltd., Goteborg, 1991—; lectr. Sch. Mining Metallurgy, Filipstad, Sweden, 2000—; adj. prof. applied geology Lulee U. Technology, Sweden, 1996-99; dir. Rock Rsch., Amsterdam, 1990-95; cons. Raw Materials Group, Stockholm, 1994-96. Contbr. articles to profl. jours. Mem. Soc. Econ. Geologists. Avocations: collecting rocks and minerals, outdoor activities. Office: Sch Mining Metallurgy, Box 173, SE-68224 Filipstad Sweden

HELLMAN, F(REDERICK) WARREN, investment advisor; b. N.Y.C., July 25, 1934; s. Marco F. and Ruth (Koshl) H.; m. Patricia Christina Sander, Oct. 5, 1955; children: Frances, Patricia H., Marco Warren, Judith. BA, U. Calif., Berkeley, 1955; MBA, Harvard U., 1959. With Lehman Bros., N.Y.C., 1959-84, ptnr., 1963-84; exec. mng. dir. Lehman Bros., Inc., N.Y.C., 1970-73; pres. Lehman Bros., Inc., 1973-75; ptnr. Hellman Ferri Investment Assocs., 1981-89, Matrix Ptnrs., 1981—; chmn. Hellman & Friedman LLC, San Francisco; bd. dirs. DN & E Walter, Levi Strauss & Co., Il Fornaio (Am.) Corp., Sugar Bowl Corp., Young & Rubicam Holdings, Inc.; chmn. Hellman & Friedman, LLC; hon. trustee The Brookings Inst.; chmn. Voice of Dance. Chmn. bd. trustees The San Francisco Found. Mem. Bond Club, Piping Rock Club, Century Country Club, Pacific Union Club. Office: Hellman & Friedman LLC 1 Maritime Plz Fl 12 San Francisco CA 94111-3404

HELLMAN, PER INGVAR, metal products executive; b. Kalmar, Sweden, Jan. 27, 1936; s. Svante Olof Alexander and Ingegerd Maria (Hoflund) H.; m. Wivi-Anne Maria Rosell, Apr. 2, 1960; children: Pernilla Maria, Annika Amelie. M in Tech., Royal Inst. Tech., Stockholm, 1962; D in Tech., Royal Inst. Tech., 1966. Rsch. engr. Söderfors (Sweden) Specialty Steel Works, 1965-72, rsch. dir., 1972-79, divsn. mgr., 1979-82, exec. v.p., 1982-86; divsn. mgr. ABB Powdermet, Surahammar, Sweden, 1987-95, Böhler Edelstahl, Kapfenberg, Austria, 1995—; chmn. Swedish Powder Metallurgy Rsch., 1983-86. Contbr. articles to profl. jours. Recipient The Wallquist Gold medal Royal Inst. Tech., Stockholm, 1983, Europe Achievement award Am. Soc. Metals, 1988. Fellow Royal Acad. Engring. Scis. Achievements include inventor, developer and market introducer of powder metallurgy high speed steels; developer, market introducer of as-hip powder metallurgy high speed steels; patentee in field. Home: Södra Långgatan 5, S-39232 Kalmar Sweden Office: Böhler Edelstahl, PO Box 96, A-8605 Kapfenberg Austria

HELLSING, ANNA-LISA, ergonomist; b. Uppsala, Sweden, May 19, 1936; d. Seved and Gun (Tideström) Ribbing; m. Krister Hellsing, May 1963 (div. 1990); three children. Registered Phys. Therapist, Karolinska U., Stockholm, 1958; MSc in Biology, Uppsala U., 1969, M in Medicine, 1987. Physiotherapist LokaSpa, 1958; physiotherapist Uppsala U. Hosp., 1959-60, physiotherapist in charge, 1974-75, tchr. physiotherapy, instr., 1975-87; physiotherapist Uppsala County Coun., 1962-74; ergonomist Öebro (Sweden) Dept. Occupl. Medicine, 1987—; presenter in field. Contbr. articles to profl. jours. Liberal Party del. Örebro Cmty., 1989-93, Tech. Dept., 1993-97, Örebro County Coun., 1993—. Recipient Golden Helix award Hewlett Packard, Stockholm, 1993. Mem. Swedish Liberal Party. Avocations: scuba diving, gliding, environmental inform and activity. Home: Järle 297, 71391 Nora Sweden Office: Örebro Med Ctr Hosp, SE-70185 Örebro Sweden

HELLSING, BO, physics educator; b. Lund, Sweden, July 20, 1952; s. Gustaf and Chris (Wennström) H.; children: Mikko, David, Rut, Ida. MSc in Physics, Chalmers U. Tech., Göteborg, Sweden, 1978, PhD in Theoretical Physics, 1984. Rsch. asst. Chalmers U. Tech., Göteborg, Sweden, 1978-94; assoc. prof. in theoretical physics Chalmers U. Tech., Göteborg, 1991, lectr. in physics, 1994—, assoc. prof. Named Hon. Rsch. Assoc. U. Tech., Chalmers, 1991. E-mail: hellsing@fy.chalmers.se. Home: Hábergsstigen 5, S-41319 Göteborg Sweden Office: Chalmers U Tech, Dept Physics, S-41296 Göteborg Sweden

HELLSPONG, MATS, ethnologist, educator; b. Stockholm, Sweden, Oct. 15, 1940; s. Gustaf Malte and Gertrud Augusta (Wedin) H.; m. Eva Helena Svanfeldt, Dec. 4, 1970; children: Sara, Maja. BA, Stockholm U., 1965, PhD, 1982. Lectr. ethnology Stockholm U., 1976—, dir. studies Inst. Ethnology, 1973-83, head dept., 1983-95. Author: (with O. Löfgren) Country and Town, 1972, The Sport of Boxing in Sweden, 1982, Swedish Officers' Messes, 1998, The Popular Sports, 2000. Avocations: tennis, golf, bird watching. Home: Riddargatan 51, 11457 Stockholm Sweden Office: Inst Ethnology, Lusthusporten 10, 10691 Stockholm Sweden

HELLSTRÖM, MATS, Swedish government official; b. Stockholm, Jan. 12, 1942; s. Gunnar and Kajsa (Johansson) H.; m. Elisabeth Hellström; children: Johan, Katarina. Grad., Stockholm U. Lectr. econs. Stockholm U., 1965-69; mem. Swedish Parliament, 1969-96, mem. fgn. affairs parliamentary com., 1969-82, chmn. childcare svc. com., 1970-75, chmn. fin. com., 1982-83, vice chmn. EU del., 1991-93; adv. Ministry of Labour, Stockholm, 1974-76; chmn. The Riksdag Com. on Fin., 1982-83; min. fgn. trade Govt. of Sweden, Stockholm, 1983-86, min. agr. and Nordic affairs, 1986-91. Bd. mem. Social Democratic Party, 1969-96, mem. exec. com. youth league, 1968-72, vice chmn. parliamentary EU-com., 1992-94; min. fgn. trade and European Union affairs, 1994-96; Sweden's amb. to Germany, 1996—. Home: Nytorgsgaten 19A, Stockholm Sweden

HELLSTROM, THOMAS GERT, environmental scientist; b. Lund, Sweden, Apr. 3, 1948; s. Gosta Valdemar and Hillevi Rut (Andersson) H. MSc, Lund Inst. Tech., 1973, PhD, 1980; MSc, U. Calif., Davis, 1975. Rsch. engr. Lund Inst. Tech., 1974-77; scientist Swedish Water and Air Rsch. Inst., Stockholm, 1977-85; assoc. prof. Uppsala U., 1985-90; cons. Malva AB, Stockholm, 1985—; sec. Internat. Assn. for Water Quality, Stockholm, 1996—. Contbr. articles to profl. jours. Avocations: sailing, cooking, fishing. Home: Ostgotagatan 42, Stockholm S-11664, Sweden Office: Swed Water Wastewater Assn, Stockholm S-10153, Sweden

HELLYER, TIMOTHY MICHAEL, protective services officer; b. Chgo., Nov. 30, 1954; s. William Al and Dotha Helen (Bucknum) H.; m. Nancy Ruth O'Donnell, Nov. 29, 1986; children: Jennifer Lynn, Allyson Jean. Student, So. Ill. U., 1985-86. Cert. firefighter III; cert. paramedic. Firefighter/paramedic Palatine (Ill.) Fire Dept., 1980—; instr. CPR, Chgo. Heart Assn., 1976—; pres. N.W. Assn. Provider Emergency Med. Svcs. Sys., 1989-92; mem. No. Ill. Critical Stress Debriefing Team. Deacon Palatine Presbyn. Ch., 1989-92; mem. comm. coun. Sch. Dist. 300, 1993—, mem. Year Round Sch. com., 1998-99; mem. improvement team Westfield Cmty. Sch., 1993—. Named Firefighter of the Yr., Jaycees of Palatine, 1987. Mem. Prehosp. Care Providers Ill. (bd. dirs. 1990), St. Francis Hook and Ladder Soc., Ill. Profl. Firefighters Assn., Smithsonian Instn., Nat. Trust Historic Preservation, Nat. Geographic Soc., U.S. Naval Inst., Nat. Space Soc. Republican. Presbyterian. Avocations: collecting Disney memorabilia, gardening, model railroading. Home: 1600 Kensington Dr Algonquin IL 60102-5104 Office: Palatine Fire Dept 39 E Colfax St Palatine IL 60067-5297

HELM, JOHN LESLIE, mechanical engineer, company executive; b. Red Wing, Apr. 10, 1921; s. Leslie Cornell and Dora (Mcguigan) H.; m. Nancy Ellen Molle, May 15, 1954; children: John Leslie, Juli-Ann, Catherine Marie. BSME, Columbia, 1943, MS, 1944; postgrad. in nuclear engring., U. Conn., 1956-57. Registered profl. engr., N.Y. Asst. in mech. engring. Columbia U., 1943-44; process engr. Metals Disintegrating Co. unit of Manhattan Project, Elizabeth, N.J., 1944-45; project engr. Aero Manuscripts Inc., 1945-46; staff engr. ctrl. engring. dept. Gen. Foods Corp., White Plains, N.Y., 1946-52; with Gen. Dynamics Corp., Groton, Conn., 1952-74; supervisory engr. USS Nautilus Propulsion Plant; dep. project mgr., chief engr. S5W Skipjack Submarine Nuc. Propulsion Project; project mgr., chief engr. S5G Narwal Submarine Nuc. Propulsion Project; spl. tech. asst. Office of Pres. Electric Boat divsn. Gen. Dynamics Corp., 1965-72; gen. mgr. Gen. Dynamics Energy Sys., 1972-74; founder, pres., CEO Proto-Power Mgmt. Corp., Groton, 1974-82; also dir.; pres., CEO Proto-Power corp. subs. of Killmorgen Corp., 1982-89; dir. Electronic Assocs., Inc., West Long Branch, N.J., 1983-89; founder, pres., CEO Transplex Inc., 1990—. Mem. Groton Bd. Edn., 1967-77, chmn., 1976-77; mem. State of Conn. Nuclear Adv. Coun., 1996—. Recipient citation for work on Manhattan Project, War Dept., 1945. Mem. ASME, Shonnecosset Yacht Club, Off Soundings Club, Princeton Club, Thames Club, N.Y. Yacht Club, Theta Tau. Republican. Roman Catholic. Home: 116 Tyler Ave Groton CT 06340-5923 Office: North Stonington Profl Ctr Routes 2 & 184 North Stonington CT 06359

HELMER, DAVID ALAN, lawyer; b. Colorado Springs, May 19, 1946; s. Horton James and Alice Ruth (Cooley) H.; m. Jean Marie Lamping, May 23, 1987. BA, U. Colo., 1968, JD, 1973. Bar: Colo. 1973, U.S. Dist. Ct. Colo. 1973, U.S. Ct. Appeals (10th cir.) 1993, U.S. Ct. Claims 1990, U.S. Supreme Ct. 1991. Assoc. Neil C. King, Boulder, Colo., 1973-76; mgr. labor rels., mine regulations Climax Molybdenum Co., Inc. divsn. AMAX, Inc., Climax, Colo., 1976-83; prin. Law Offices David A. Helmer, Frisco, Colo., 1983—; sec., bd. dirs. Z Comm. Corp., Frisco, 1983-90; cmty. bd. dirs. Wells Fargo Bank, N.A., Frisco, 1996—. Editor U. Colo. Law Rev., 1972-73; contbr. articles to legal jours. Bd. dirs. Summit County Coun. Arts and Humanities, Dillon, Colo., 1980-85; advisor Advocates for Victims of Assault, Frisco, 1984—; legal counsel Summit County United Way, 1983-95, v.p., bd. dirs., 1983-88; bd. dirs., legal counsel Summit county Alcohol and Drug Task Force, Inc., Summit Prevention Alliance, 1984—, Pumpkin Bowl Inc./Children's Hosp. Burn Ctr., 1989—; chmn. Summit County Reps., 1982-89; chmn. 5th Jud. Dist. (Colo.) Rep. Com., 1982-89; chmn. resolutions com. Colo. Rep. Conv., 1984, del. Rep. Nat. Com., 1984; chmn. reaccreditation com. Colo. Mountain Coll., Breckenridge, 1983, mem. steering com., 1997-99; founder, bd. dirs. Dillon Bus. Assn., 1983-87, Frisco Arts Coun., 1989—; atty. N.W. Colo. Legal Svcs. Project, Summit County, 1983—; mcpl. judge Town of Dillon, 1982—, Town of Silverthorne, Colo., 1982—; dir. Snake River Water Dist., 1998—. Sgt. USAR, 1968-74. Mem. ABA, Colo. Bar Assn., (bd. govs. 1991-93, mem. exec. com. 1995-97), Continental Divide Bar Assn. (prs. 1991-95, v.p. 1995-97), Summit County Bar Assn. (pres. 1990-99), Dillon Corinthian Yacht Club (commodore local club 1987-88, 95-97, vice commodore 1994, club champion 1989-91, 94, 95, 97, 98, winner Colo. Cup, Colo. State Sailing Championships 1991), Phi Gamma Delta. Lutheran. Home: PO Box 300 352 Snake River Dr Dillon CO 80435-0300 Office: PO Box 868 611 Main St Frisco CO 80443-0868

HELMES, GÜNTER, German educator, researcher; b. Siegen, Westfalia, Germany, July 19, 1954; s. Wilhelm and Inge (Sieberkrob) H.; m. Sabine Meyer, Sept. 13, 1996; children: Carla Cathrin, Mattea Sophie, Camilla Elisa. PhD, U. Siegen, 1985; Habilitation, U. Paderborn, 1995. Fgn. lang. asst. U. London, 1984-86; asst. prof. U. Paderborn, 1986-95; lectr. U. Auckland, New Zealand, 1991, U. Dresden, 1995; assoc. prof. U. Siegen, 1996-97, U. Kassel, Germany, 1998-2000, U. Siegen, Germany, 2000—; lectr. U. Guangzhou, China, 1998, U. Szeged, Hungary, 1999; expert Studienstiftung, Bonn, Germany, 1990—. Author: Robert Müller, Studien zu seinem Werk, 1986; editor: Works of Robert Müller, 12 vols., 1990-96, Works of Richard Beer-Hofmann, 6 vols., 1993-96, Don Juan Anthology, 1994, Kindermedien-Medienkinder, 1997, Works of Gabriele Reuter, Hermann Bahr and Johannes Schlaf, 1997. Mem. Assn. German Scholars. Home: Birlenbacher Strasse 199, 57078 Siegen Germany Office: U Siegen, Adolf-Reichwein-Str, D-57068 Siegen Germany

HELMI, DAHLI, accounting educator and administrator; b. Grand Junction, Colo., Dec. 28, 1948; d. Forrest Walter and Mary (Crockett) G.; 1 child, Kimberly. BS, Ea. Oreg. State U., 1971; MBA, Portland (Oreg.) State U., 1976; D of Bus. Adminstrn., George Washington U., 1984. Instr. acctg. Portland State U., 1976-79, George Mason U., Fairfax, Va., 1980, George Washington U., Washington, 1981-82; asst. prof. Oreg. State U., Corvallis, 1983-86; rsch. fellow U. Notre Dame, South Bend, Ind., 1986-88; assoc. prof. Am. U., Washington, 1988-90; chair, Walpert, Smullian & Blumenthal prof. Towson (Md.) State U., 1990-92; chair Morgan State U., Balt., 1992-97, prof. acctg., 1997-2000; prof. acctg. Wilson Coll., Chambersberg, Pa., 2000—. Contbr. articles to profl. jours. Named Tchr. of Yr., Alpha Lambda Delta, 1986; Peat Marwick Mitchell & Co. fellow, 1986-88. Mem. Internat. Assn. Acctg. Research and Edn., Am. Inst. CPA's, Nat. Assn. Accts. (Andrew Barr award 1982, 84, Cert. Merit 1982), Am. Acctg. Assn., Inst. Cert. Mgmt. Accts. Democrat. Home: 3308 Walnut Ave Owings Mills MD 21117-1118 Office: Wilson Coll 1015 Philadelphia Ave Chambersburg PA 17201-1279

HELMICK, RAYMOND GLEN, priest, educator; b. Arlington, Mass., Sept. 7, 1931; s. Raymond Glen and Alice Cecilia (Clancy) H. BA, Boston Coll., 1956, MA in philosphy, 1957; lic. philosphy, Weston Coll., 1957; lic. theol., Hochschule St. Georgen, Frankfurt, 1964. Joined Jesuit Order, 1949, ordained priest Roman Cath. Ch., 1963. Assoc. dir. Ctr. for Human Rights & Responsibilities, London, 1973-79, Inst. Soc. Rsch., London, 1973-79; found., co-dir. Ctr. of Concern for Human Dignity, London, 1979-81; sr. assoc. Conflict Analysis Ctr., Washington, 1982—; prof. of conflict resolution Boston Coll., 1984—; sr. assoc. Ctr. Strategic & Internat. Studies, Washington, 2000—; exec. comm. U.S. Interreligious Comm. for Peace in the Middle East, Seattle, 1987—, adv. bd. Organ. for Human Rights in Iraq, Boston, 1992—. Author: (with Richard Hauser) A Social Option, 1975, La Question Libanaise Selon Raymond Edde, 1990. Mediation No. Irish conflict, 1972-81, 92—, Kurdish conflict, 1973-81, 87—, Lebanese conflict, 1982—, Israeli-Palestinian conflict, 1986—, Balkan conflict, 1995—. Democrat. Roman Catholic. Office: Boston Coll Chestnut Hill MA 02467

HELMUTH, REINER FRANZ BERNHARD, molecular biologist, educator, scientist; b. Andernach, Germany, Aug. 16, 1950; s. Franz and Lotte (Strutz) H.; m. Giovanna Biagina Morelli, June 9, 1977; 1 child, Maria Cristina. Diploma in biology, Free U., Berlin, 1974, PhD in Natural Scis., 1977. Cert. pub. health servant, Min. of Health. Rsch. assoc. Max Planck inst. for Molecular Genetics, Berlin, 1977-78; rsch. assoc. Fed. Health Inst., Berlin, 1978-91, head of lab., 1992—; head Nat. Reference Lab., Berlin, 1996—; pvt. expert WHO, Geneva, 1985—, European Union, Brussels, 1982—. Editor: Safety of Growth Promoters, 1984. Avocations: jogging, amateur radio, saxophone. Home: Hochsitzweg 49, 14169 Berlin Germany Office: BgVV, Diedersdorfer Weg 1, 12277 Berlin Germany

HELPPIE, CHARLES EVERETT, III, financial consultant; b. Highland Park, Mich., Feb. 1, 1952; s. Charles Everett and Patricia Elizabeth (Cote) H.; m. Vali Renée Terhune, July 29, 1972. Student, Ea. Mich. U., 1970-73. Sales rep., sales mgr. Mich. Autosonics, Inc., Ann Arbor, 1972-74; mgr. World Wide Movers, Inc., Ypsilanti, Mich., 1973; sales rep. Godfrey Moving & Storage Co., Ann Arbor, 1974-78; account exec. Merrill Lynch Pierce Fenner & Smith, Detroit, 1978-83, E. F. Hutton, Ann Arbor, 1983-87; asst. br. mgr. Shearson Lehman Hutton, Ann Arbor, 1987-90; fin. cons. Shearson Lehman Bros., Detroit, 1991-92; investment exec. Paine Webber, Inc., Farmington Hills, Mich., 1992-99, br. office ins. coord., 1993—; accounts v.p. Paine Webber, Inc., Farmington Hills, 1999-2000; v.p. investments, divisional life ins. cons. Paine Webber, Inc., Birmingham, Mich., 2000—. Artist and engr. auto. models including MPC World Champion, 1977 (1st Pl. 1977). Campaign worker Dem. Com., Ypsilanti, 1965-71; organizer Anti-

War Workshops, Ypsilanti, 1968-70; pres., organizer Fin. Svcs. Softball League, Detroit, 1979-83; mem. Colonial Leadership Coun., Boston. Mem. Am. Funds Group (All-Am. Team), Nameless Nat. Luminaries (founder, chartered), Detroit Tigers Fantasy Camp (chartered), Key and Kite Club, Aim Summit Club (chmns. coun. 1992—), Franklin Group of Funds, Paine Webber Premium Producers Guild, Paine Webber Preservation Planning Inst. (cons. forum "Top 75" mem. managed and retirement accounts svcs.), Paine Webber Pacesetter Club. Avocations: model car building and collecting, automobile and auto racing photography, baseball. Office: Paine Webber Inc 210 S Old Woodward Ave Ste 250 Birmingham MI 48009-6114

HELSEN, LIEVE, chemical engineer, researcher; b. Herentals, Belgium, Apr. 24, 1970; d. Marcel and Maria (Laureys) H. Grad. in Chem. Engring., K.U. Leuven, Belgium, 1993, postgrad., 1993-2000. Contbr. articles to profl. jours. Mem. Leefmilieu Antwerpen. Avocations: travel, mountain bike, volley, tramping, nature. Office: KU Leuven, Celestijnenlaan 300A, 3001 Heverlee Belgium

HELSINGIUS, MIKA PETRI, optical engineer; b. Nastola, Finland, Feb. 24, 1966; s. Orvo Veikko and Leila Tuula Laakso. Diploma in engring., Tampere U. of Tech., 1992, Lic. of Tech., 1998, D of Tech., 1998. Rsch. asst. Signal Processing Lab., Tampere, 1990-93; rschr. Digital Media Inst., Tampere, 1995-99, project mgr., 1999-2000; rsch. mgr. Rsch. Ctr. for Info. Tech., Lahti, Finland, 2000—; vis. scientist Kobe (Japan) U., 1993-95, Boston U., 1998. Contbr. articles to sci. and profl. jours. With Finnish Army, 1985-86. Mem. Tekniikan Akateemiset, Lahden seudun diplomi insinöörit ja arkkitehdit. Avocations: gardening, aquarium, literature, Japanese culture. Home: Papinpolku 7, Nastola 15560, Finland Office: Rsch Ctr for Info Tech, Saimaankatu 11, Lahti 15140, Finland

HELSLEY, ALEXIA JONES, archivist; b. Louisville, Ky., Sept. 9, 1945; d. George Alexander and Evelyn (Masden) J.; m. Terry Lynn Helsley, Oct. 11, 1969; children: Cassandra Keiser, Jacob Henry. BA in History, Furman U., 1967; MA in History, U. S.C., 1974; cert., Modern Archives Inst., Washington, 1978, S.C. Exec. Inst., Columbia, 1995. Archival asst. S.C. Dept. Archives and History, Columbia, 1968-69, archivist I, 1969-72, asst. reference archivist, 1972-76, supr. reference and rsch., 1976-88, dir. pub. programs divsn., 1988-96, dir. edn., 1996-99; dir. spl. projects, editor Biograph. Directory S.C. House of Reps., 1999—; historian Am. Lodging Resources, Inc. Author: Harbison: an Historical Sketch, 1986, First Baptist Church of Irmo: Historical Overview, 1992, Researching Family History: A Workbook, 1992, 96, The 1840 Revolutionary Pensioners of Henderson County, North Carolina, 1996, Unsung Heroines of the Carolina Frontier, 1997, Silent Cities: Cemeteries and Classrooms, 1997, South Carolina's African American Confederate Pensioners, 1923-1925, 1998, Voices of Revolutions: South Carolinians in the War for American Independence, 2000; co-author: The Many Faces of Slavery-Documents from S.C. Dept. of Archives and History, 1999, S.C. Court Records, 1993, The Changing Face of S.C. Politics, 1993, African American Genealogical Research, 1997; contbr. articles to profl. jours. Chair social and recreation com. Harbison Cmty. Assn., Columbia, S.C., 1984-89; trustee S.C. Hall of Fame, Myrtle Beach, 1988-96; vice-chair Columbia Quincentennial Commn. S.C., 1989-93; pres. Richland Sertoma, Columbia, 1998-99. Recipient Willie Parker Peace History Book award, 1997; named to Hon. Order of Ky. Cols., Richland Sertoman of Yr., 2000. Mem. Henderson County Geneal. and Hist. Soc. (charter, v.p. 1998-2000), Pace Soc. Am. (trustee), Joseph McDowell Nat. Soc. DAR, Soc. Am. Archivists (chair reference, access, outreac sect. 1981-83), S.C. Hist. Assn. Baptist. Home: 1 Northpine Ct Columbia SC 29212-2911 Office: SC Dept Archives History 8301 Parklane Rd Columbia SC 29223-4905

HELSTEIN, IVY RAE, communications executive, psychotherapist, writer; d. Harold and Celia Weintraub Markowitz; children: Hilary, Eden, Flyn. BA, Queens Coll., 1958; MA in Human Behavior, Goddard Coll., Plainfield, Vt., 1979. Founder, pres. Comm. Dynamics, Great Neck, N.Y., 1973—; creator Practical Spiritualism; instr., lectr. classroom mgmt. skills various sch. dists., N.Y., 1976; instr. assertiveness tng., conflict mgmt., adult continuing edn. Hofstra U., Hempstead, N.Y., 1976, C.W. Post U., Brookville, N.Y., 1979; adj. faculty Nassau C.C., Garden City, 1977—. Author: Great Persuaders: Sales Training, 1984, Great Communicators II, 1987, Infinite Abilities: Living Your Life on Purpose, 1999. Trainer N.Y. State Child Protective Svcs., 1995—, Suffolk County (N.Y.) Dept. Labor, 1997. Mem. Nat. Spkr. Assn. (profl., past pres., Chpt. Mem. of the Yr. award 1986), Tri-State Nat. Spkrs. Assn. (pres. 1985-86), Authors Guild, Inc. Avocation: world travel. E-mail: IHelstein@aol.com. Home and Office: 27 Georgian Ln Great Neck NY 11024-1615

HELTON, ARTHUR CLEVELAND, advocate, lawyer, scholar, writer; b. St. Louis, Jan. 24, 1949; s. Arthur Cleveland Sr. and Marjorie Jane (Russell) H.; m. Jacqueline Dean Gilbert, May 14, 1982. AB, Columbia Coll., 1971; JD, NYU, 1976. Bar: N.Y. 1977, U.S. Dist. Ct. (so. and ea. dists.) N.Y. 1977, U.S. Ct. Appeals (2d cir.) 1978, U.S. Ct. Appeals (1st cir.) 1980, U.S. Ct. Appeals (4th and 9th cir.) 1988, U.S. Ct. Appeals (5th, 7th and 11th cir.) 1989, U.S. Ct. Appeals (3d cir.) 1994, U.S. Supreme Ct. 1980. Assoc. appellate counsel Legal Aid Soc., N.Y.C., 1976-79; assoc. Mailman & Rutheizer, N.Y.C., 1979-82; dir. refugee project Lawyers Com. Human Rights, N.Y.C., 1982-94; dir. migration programs, forced migration projects Open Soc. Inst., N.Y.C., 1994-99; vis. prof. internat. rels. Ctrl. European U., 1997-2000; course co-dir. Sommer U. Ctrl. European U., 1999-2000; adj. prof. law NYU, 1986-99; sr. fellow Coun. Fgn. Rels., 1999—; chair Internat. Social Svcs., USA br. Author: (with others) Forced Displacement and Human Security in the Former Soviet Union: Law and Policy, 2000, The Rights of Aliens and Refugees: The Basic ACLU GUide to Alien and Refugees Rights, 1990; contbr. articles to profl. jours. Recipient Pub. Svc. award Law Alumni Assn. NYU, 1987; grantee The German Marshall Fund, The Ford Found. Fellow Am. Bar Found.; mem. Coun. Fgn. Rels., ABA (co-chmn. immigration and nationality law com. sect. internat. law and practice 1997—, coord. com. on immigration law 1997-2000, adv. com. immigration pro bono devel. and bar activation project 2000—), Internat. Bar Assn., Assn. Bar N.Y.C. (chmn. com. on immigration and nationality law 1982-85, legal assistance com. 1985-88, civil rights com. 1988-91, internat. human rights com. 1991-94, internat. law com. 1995-98, adminstrv. law com. 1999—), Pub. internatl. imm., naturalization, and customs. Home: 245 7th Ave Apt 10B New York NY 10001-7301 Office: Coun Fgn Rels 58 E 68th St New York NY 10021-5953

HELVE, HELENA MARKETTA, religious studies educator; b. Salo, Finland; d. Erkki and Kaarina (Linna) Toivonen; m. Lauri Kaarle Olavi; 1 child, Tuuli. MA, U. Helsinki, Finland, 1977, Lic. Phil., 1984, PhD, 1987. From sr. lectr. to prof. dept. comparative religion U. Helsinki, Finland, 1987-89; prof. dept. folklore & comparative religion U. Turku, Finland, 1990; rschr. Acad. Finland, Helsinki, 1991-94, rsch. dir., 1995-97; Editl. bd. Internat. Review for the History of Religions, 1995—; intern Bull. Youth Rsch., 1998—. Author: The World View of Young People, 1993, Nuoret Humanistit, Traditionalistit ja Individualistit, 1993; editor: Arvot Maailmankuvat Sukupuoli, 1997, Unification and Marginalistion of Young People, 1998, Rural Young People in Changing Europe, 2000; co-editor: Youth and Life Management-Research Perspectives, 1996; mem. editl. bd. Internat. Review for the History Religions, 1995—, Youth Studies, 1998, Internat. Bulletin Youth Rsch., 1998—, Jour. Identity Jour. Theory and Rsch., 2000—; contbr. articles to profl. jours. Pres. Finnish Youth Rsch. Soc., 1992—; dir. Finnish Youth Rsch. Programme 2000, 1994-99, Nordic rsch. coord., 1998—; rsch. dir. Nat. Youth Policy Rev., Coun. Europe, 1996. Mem. Finnish Soc. Study of Comparative Religion (sec., v.p. 1989-96), Internat. Assn. History of Religions (exec. mem. 1995-2000), European Assn. and Study of Religions (v.p. 2000). Office: Dept Comparative Religion, PO Box 59, 00014 Helsinki Finland

HEMACHUDHA, THIRAVAT, neurologist, educator; b. Bangkok, Thailand, Dec. 22, 1954; s. Chitt and Pairoj Hemachudha; m. Aphirudee Poshakrishna, Nov. 1983; children: Ramon, Pasin. BS, Chulalongkorn U., 1974; MD, Chulalongkorn Hosp., 1976. Bd. cert. Medicine, Neurology. Intern, resident Chulalongkorn Hosp., Bangkok, Thailand, 1977-82; asst. prof. neurology Chulalongkorn Hosp., Bangkok, 1983-88, prof. neurology, 1989—; dir. rsch. rabies WHO, Bangkok, 1990-93, expert adv. panel rabies, 1990—; fellow neurology and neuroimmunology Johns Hopkins U., Balt., 1985-86; guest lectr. Am. Soc. Tropical Medicine and Hygiene, 1993, Inst. Pasteur, Paris, 1997, Internat. Rabies Meeting in the Ams., 1999. Contbr. chpts. in books and articles to profl. jours. Disting. rschr. Nat. Rsch. Coun., 1992, 94, Mahidol U., 1993. Mem. AAAS, Thai Neurol. Soc. (sci. pres. 1997-98, bd. dirs.), N.Y. Acad. Scis., Am. Neurol. Assn. Avocations: tennis, swimming. E-mail: fmedthc@md2.md.chula.ac.th. Fax: (662) 256-4513. Home: 144 Sukhumvit 39, 10110 Bangkok Thailand Office: Chulalongkorn U Hosp, Rama 4 Rd Dept Medicine, Bangkok 10330, Thailand

HEMANN, RAYMOND GLENN, research company executive; b. Cleve., Jan. 24, 1933; s. Walter Harold and Marsha Mae (Colbert) H.; m. Lucile Tinnin Turnage, Feb. 1, 1958; children: James Edward, Carolyn Frances; m. Pamela Schaap Lehr, Dec. 18, 1987. BS, Fla. State U., 1957; postgrad., U.S. Naval Postgrad. Sch., 1963-64, U. Calif., Los Angeles, 1960-62; MS in Systems Engring., Calif. State U., Fullerton, 1970; MA in Econs., Calif. State U., 1972; cert. in tech. mgmt., Calif. Inst. Tech., 1990. Comml., glider and pvt. pilot. Aero. engring. aide U.S. Navy, David Taylor Model Basin, Carderock, Md., 1956; analyst Fairchild Aerial Surveys, Tallahassee, 1957; research analyst Fla. Rd. Dept., Tallahassee, 1957-59; chief Autonetics divsn. N.Am. Rockwell Corp., Anaheim, Calif., 1959-69; v.p., dir. R.E. Manns Co., Wilmington, Calif., 1969-70; mgr. Avionics Design and Analysis Dept. Lockheed-Calif. Co., Burbank, 1970-72; mgr. Advanced Concepts divsn. Lockheed-Calif. Co., 1976-82; gen. mgr. Western divsn. Arinc Research Corp., Santa Ana, 1972-76; dir. Future Requirements Rockwell Internat., 1982-85, dir. Threat Analysis, Corp. Offices, 1985-89; pres., CEO Advanced Systems Rsch., Inc., 1989—; adj. sr. fellow Ctr. Strategic and Internat. Studies, Washington, 1987—; bd. dirs., mem. exec. com. Fla. State U. Rsch. Found., 1995—; bd. dirs. Assn. Mgmt. Svc. Inc.; bd. dirs., pres. Associated Aviation, Inc., 1980-96, Am. Heart Assn., Sau Gabriel Valley; chmn. adv. coun. Coll. Engring. Fla. State U./Fla. A&M U., 1995; cons. to dir. Ctrl. Intelligence, Nat. Intelligence Coun., Nat. Air Intelligence Ctr., Inst. Def. Analyses, Battelle Meml. Inst., Ctr. Strategic and Internat. Studies; sec., bd. dirs. Calif State U., Fullerton, Econs. Found.; mem. naval studies bd. panels NAS, 1985—, Arms Control Working Group; chmn. indsl. panel Nat. Labs. Infrastructure Study, Office Sec. Def., 1995; chmn. indsl. panel Future Dirs. Mil. Aeronautics Study, 1996; asst. prof. ops. analysis dept. U.S. Naval Postgrad. Sch., Monterey, Calif., 1963-64, Monterey Peninsula Coll., 1963; instr. ops. analysis Calif. State U., Fullerton, 1963, instr. quantitative methods, 1969-72; program developer, instr. systems engring. indsl. rels. ctr. Calif. Inst. Tech., 1992-96; lectr. Brazilian Navy, 1980, U. Calif., Santa Barbara, 1980, Yale U., 1985, Princeton U., 1986, U.S. Naval Postgrad. Sch., 1986, Ministry of Def., Taiwan, Republic of China, 1990; Calif. Inst. Tech. Assocs., 1992—; mem. exec. forum Calif. Inst. Tech., 1991—. Contbr articles to profl. jours. and new media. Chmn. comdr.'s adv. bd. CAP, Calif. Wing; reader Recording for the Blind, 1989—. With AUS, 1950-53, Operation Blue Jay. Syde P. Deeb scholar, 1956; recipient honor awards Nat. Assn. Remotely Piloted Vehicles, 1975, 76; named to Hon. Order Ky. Cols., 1985. Fellow AAAS Sr. Scientists and Engrs., AIAA (assoc.); mem. IEEE (life), Ops. Rsch. Soc. Am., Air Force Assn., N.Y. Acad. Scis., Assn. Old Crows., L.A. World Affairs Coun., Phi Kappa Tau (past pres.). Episcopalian. Office: Advanced Sys Rsch Inc 33 S Catalina Ave Ste 202 Pasadena CA 91106-2426

HEMBERG, ESKIL, music director, composer; b. Stockholm, Jan. 19, 1938; s. Bengt E. E. and Ingeborg R. (Thelander) H.; m. Birgit S. Ohlsson , July 8, 1962; children: Anna Maria, Johan, Love. Degree in music teaching, Royal Coll. Music, Stockholm, 1961, higher cantor's degree, 1961, higher organist's degree, 1964. Exec. producer Swedish Radio, Stockholm, 1963-70; planning mgr., dir. fgn. rels. Nat. Inst. Concerts, Stockholm, 1970-83; managing and artistic dir. Gothenburg (Sweden) Opera and Symphony, 1984-87; gen. dir. Royal Opera, Stockholm, 1987-96; prof. Swedish studies, artist in residence Bethany Coll., Lindsburg, Kans., 2000—; condr. Stockholm U. Chorus, 1959-84, Grammophone Records. Composer operas, choral works, chamber music. Sweden state grantee, 1972, 73, 75, 81; recipient Johannes Norrby medal Royal Acad. Music, 1978, Zoltan Kodaly medal Hungary, 1982, Pro Arte et Scientia medal U. Gothenburg, 1987, His Majesty the King's Own medal, 1993, Gold medal Royal Opera, Stockholm, 1996, Kurt Atterberg prize, 1997; decorated comdr. Order of Merit (Portugal) 1991, Grosses Bundes-Verdienstkreuz (Germany), 1995. Mem. Royal Swedish Acad. Music, Assn. Internat. Dirs. de l'Opera, Swedish Composers Assn. (pres. 1971-83), Internat. Fedn. for Choral Music (advisor, bd. dirs. 1984-90, pres. 1999—), Swedish Choral Dirs. Assn., Swedish Composers Rights Assn. (v.p. 1972-83), Internat. Music Coun. UNESCO (pres. 1991-93). Home: Floravägen 3, 13141 Nacka Sweden

HEMBERGER, GLEN JAMES, university band director, music educator; b. Boulder, Colo., Jan. 18, 1962; s. James Frank and Jacqueline Ann (Kent) H.; m. Linda Dawn Thomas, June 3, 1989. BME, U. Colo., 1985, MMus, 1989. Dir. bands Thornton (Colo.) Sr. High Sch., 1985-87; grad. asst. U. Colo. Bands, Boulder, 1987-89; assoc. dir. bands, mem. music edn. faculty U. R.I., Kingston, 1989-92; assoc. dir. bands Okla. State U., Stillwater, 1992-97; doctoral conducting assoc. U. North Tex., 1997-99; dir. bands Southeastern La. U., 1999—; clinician R.I. Music Educators' State Conv., 1992, summer music camp U. Wis., 1993, 99, Chinese Armed Police Band, Beijing, 1996, 97, Melbourne, Brisbane & Sydney, Australia, 1997, Nat. Taiwan U. Wind Orch., Taipei and Hong Kong, 1996, Beijing Band Dirs. Assn., 1996, 97, U. S.D. Band Festival, 1996; guest condr. high schs., honor bands, clinics, 1984—, USCG Band, Okla. Mozart Internat. Music Festival, 1995, 96, Norwegian Band Championships, Hamar, 1999, Trondheim, 2000; founder So. New Eng. H.S. Honor Band, 1991. Contbr. articles to profl. jours.; presenter in field. Mem. Olympic All-Am. Marching Band, L.A., 1984. Mem. Coll. Band Dirs. Nat. Assn. (mem. jour. staff, nat. athletic band adv. coun., clinician nat. conv. 1995, 97), Internat. Assn. Jazz Educators, Music Educators Nat. Conf., World Assn. for Symphonic Bands and Ensembles, Okla. Music Educators Assn. (clinician state conv. 1995, jazz ensemble performance 1997), Phi Mu Alpha Sinfonia, Kappa Kappa Psi, Tau Beta Sigma, Pi Kappa Lambda. Home: 46305 Charles Dr Hammond LA 70401-4028 Office: Southeastern La Univ PO Box 815 Hammond LA 70402-0001

HEMBY, JAMES B., JR., college president; b. Ayden, N.C., Mar. 1, 1934; m. Joan Edwards Hemby; children: James B. III, Scott Edwards, Thomas Simmen. BA, Barton Coll., 1955; BD, Vanderbilt U., 1958; MA, Tex. Christian U., 1964, PhD, 1965. Grad. teaching fellow Tex. Christian U., Ft. Worth, 1962-64; instr. Memphis State U., 1964-65; dir. admissions Barton Coll., Wilson, N.C., 1959-62, assoc. prof. English, 1965-68, prof., 1968-73, chmn. English dept., 1973-79, Am. Coun. Edn. fellow in acad. adminstrn., 1979-80, provost, 1980-83, pres., 1983—; dir. N.C. Writing Project, 1980-85; pres. N.C. Lit. and Hist. Assn., 1983-84; chmn. N.C. Writer's Conf., 1982-83; pres. Carolinas Intercollegiate Athletic Conf., 1989-91, N.C. Assn. Colls. and Univs., 1993-94, pres. N.C. Assn. Ind. Colls. and Univs., 1995-99. Editor: Crucible, 1973-83. Bd. dirs. Wilson County chpt. ARC, 1985-96, Flynn Home, 1998—, Budget & Comm. United Way, 1997—, Novopharm, 1998—; mem. Wilson County Bd. Edn., 1974-86, N.C. Humanities Coun., 1988-91; exec. com. Triangle East, 1985-91; bd. dirs. The Lost Colony, 1998-99. Lilly Found. vis. scholar, Duke U., 1977; Fulbright grantee, 1990; recipient Disting. Svc. award N.C. High Sch. Athletic Assn., 1993. Mem. MLA, Am. Coun. Edn., Nat. Assn. Ind. Colls. and Univs. (pres. N.C. chpt. 1995-99), N.C. Assn. Colls. and Univs (pres. 1993-94), Internat. Assn. Univ. Pres., Coun. for Ind. Colls., Am. Assn. Higher Edn., Nat. Assn. Intercollegiate Athletics (coun. of pres. 1991-93), Rotary Club. Democrat. Avocations: tennis, bicycling, chess, creative writing. Home: 800 W Nash St Wilson NC 27893 Office: Barton Coll Off of Pres PO Box 5000 Wilson NC 27893-7000

HEMELÍKOVÁ, BLANKA, literary history researcher; b. Praha, Czech Republic, May 14, 1953; d. Václav and Tekla Hemelík. PhD, Charles U., Prague, Czech Republic, 1983. Rschr. Inst. for Czech Lit., Prague, 1981—. Violinist Ensemble of Folk Music Josef Vycpálek, Prague, 1978—. Avocation: violin. Home: Ostrovske'ho 253/3, 15000 Praha 5 Czech Republic

HEMILÄ, HARRI OLAVI, biochemist, epidemiologist, researcher; b. Valkeakoski, Finland, June 16, 1958; s. Simo Olavi and Anja Heleena (Innala) H.; life ptnr. Teija Tuulikki Koivula; children: Joonas, Mikko, Antti. MSc, U. Helsinki, Finland, 1983, PhD, 1993, MD, 1999. Rsch. assoc. U. Helsinki, 1986-90, 95—, docent in biochemistry, 1996. Contbr. articles to profl. jours. Achievements include research on the role of vitamin C on infectious diseases. E-mail: harri.hemila@helsinki.fi. Office: U Helsinki Dept Pub Health, Mannerheimintie 172, 00014 Helsinki Finland

HEMINGWAY, J. E. (JULIE ELAINE HEMINGWAY-REID), lyricist; b. Phoenix, Sept. 27, 1960; d. Robert Lee and Mary Jane Jones; m. Stan Lee Hemingway, Jan. 1, 1985 (div. Dec. 1991); m. Jerry Rayman Reid, Nov. 21, 1992; 1 child, Lindel Marie; stepchildren: Casey, Tatum. AA, Nat. Edn. Ctr., Phoenix, 1989; BFA, U. Phoenix, 1997. Lic. realtor, Ariz. Technician, tchr. Phoenix Piano, 1978-88; realtor Cambio Property Mgmt., Scottsdale, 1988-92, Devon Properties Inc., Long Beach, Calif., 1992-93; office products mgr. Long Beach, 1993-95; contemporary imagist Librans Studio One, Carlsbad, Calif., 1995—. Contbr. to various poetry anthologies including The Best Poets of '90s, 1997, The Garden of Life, 1995, The Best Poems of 1997, 1998, The Sounds of Laughter, 1998. Active The Am. Liver Found., advocate Coalition against Hepatitis. Mem. The Internat. Soc. Poets, Nat. Libr. Poetry (Editors Choice award 1996, 97, 98). Avocations: piano, interior design. E-mail: libran1@home.com.

HEMLEY, EUGENE ADAMS, trade association executive; b. Bklyn., Feb. 20, 1918; s. Benjamin and Fannie (Gottlieb) H.; m. Charlotte McClure, Dec. 22, 1948; children: Philip, Paul, Anne, Margaret. BEE, U.S. Naval Acad., 1940; MS in Internat. Affairs, George Washington U., 1968. Served as midshipman USN, 1936-40, commd. ensign, 1940, advanced through grades to capt., 1959, ret., 1970; elec. officer USS Nashville, 1940-43; engring. officer USS Seadragon, 1944; exec. officer USS Greenling, 1945, USS Becuna, 1949-1950; comdg. officer USS Bang, 1951, USS Volador, 1952; ops. officer Sur As Dev Det Surface Anti-Submarine Devel. Detachment, Fla., 1953-55; comdg. officer USS Bristol, 1956-1957, USS Taconic, 1961-62, USS Northampton, 1965-66; dir. fleet comm. divsn. Office Chief of Naval Ops., 1958-61, dep. dir. info. systems divsn., 1968-70; comdg. officer U.S. Naval Comm. Sta., Japan, 1962-65; War Gaming dept. head U.S. Naval War Coll., 1967-68; dir. mgmt. info. systems Nat. Girl Scout Orgn., N.Y.C., 1970-74; computerization mgr. Nat. Coun. on Internat. Trade Documentation (name changed to The Internat. Trade Facilitation Coun.), N.Y.C., 1974-84, assoc. dir., 1984-85, exec. dir., 1985-92, hon. dir., 1992—; pres. Feda Realty Corp., 1993—; U.S. bus. adviser meetings UN Econ. Commn. for Europe, 1982-92, cos., 1992. Editor: Cardis Stds. Manual, 1981. Mem. Citizens nominating com. Town of Scarsdale, 1982-83. Decorated Silver Star. Mem. U.S. Naval Inst., Naval Acad. Alumni Assn. (v.p. N.Y. chpt. 1982-83, pres. 1984-85, trustee 1985—), Naval Order U.S. (vice cmdr. N.Y. chpt. 1997-2000, comdr. 2000—), Internat. C. of C. (electronic data interchange working group and incoterms panel of experts 1991-92), Squadron A Assn. (Naval Officers' Club). Clubs: N.Y. Yacht, Scarsdale Town, West Point, Westchester County Tennis (v.p. 1983-84, pres. 1985-87). Home and Office: 20 Cohawney Rd Scarsdale NY 10583-2227

HEMMA, SHERIF MOHAMED FATHY, pharmaceutical executive; b. Alexandria, Egypt, Dec. 27, 1959; s. Mohamed Fathy Ahmed Hemma and Nawal Ahmed Zaki El Adawy; m. Kamilia Ayad, Jan. 11, 1982. BS in Commerce, Ain Shams U., Cairo, 1980; MBA, U.S. Internat. U., San Diego, 1984. Cert. acct., Egypt. Staff auditor Coopers & Lybrand, Cairo, 1981-83; semi-sr. auditor Coopers & Lybrand, San Francisco, 1985-86; audit mgr. Coopers & Lybrand, Cairo, 1986-92; fin. and control mgr. Xerox, Cairo, 1992-93; fin. mgr. Bristol Meyers Squibb, Cairo, 1993-94; dep. fin. dir. Hoechst Marion Roussel, Cairo, 1995-99; fin. dir. mid. ea. region Pfizer, Cairo, 1999—; dir. rep. Can. Exec. Svc. Orgn., Cairo, 1990-92. Lit. critic Rosa El Youssef Mag., 1987-91. Mem. Egyptian Jr. Businessmen, Egyptian Fin. Forum. Home: 100 Osman Ebn Afan St, Heliopolis Egypt

HEMMENT, PETER LAYTON, microelectronics educator and researcher; b. Dereham, Norfolk, Eng., Apr. 9, 1936; s. Harold Charles and Margaret (Pashley) H.; m. Pamela Elliott Smith; children: Julie Dawn, Andrew Layton. BSc, City U., London, 1964, DSc, 1993; PhD, Reading (Eng.) U., 1970. Rschr. UKAEA, 1960-70, U. Surrey, Guildford, Eng., 1970—. Contbr. more than 300 articles to profl. jours. including Jour. Applied Physics, Nuclear Instruments and Method, IEEE Electron Device Letters. Avocations: travel, squash, badminton, photography, family activities. Office: Sch Electronic Engring, Info Tech & Maths U Surrey, Guildford Surrey GU2 7XH, England

HEMMERSAM, FLEMMING PETER, Danish folklorist, researcher; b. Sønderborg, Denmark, May 3, 1940; s. Christian Wilhelm and Rita Rosa (Kristensen) H.; m. Kirsten Wegge Nordahl, Dec. 2, 1961 (div. Feb. 1970); 1 child, Jon Sebastian; m. Lis Olsen, July 5, 1975; children: Mikkel, Rasmus. MA in Nordic Folklore, U. Copenhagen, 1985. With U. Copenhagen, 1985-88, 98—; free-lance rschr., 1988—; chmn., organizer Nordic Working Group for rsch. in workers culture with confs. in Copenhagen, 1983, 92, Norrköping, Sweden, 1986, Tampere, Finland, 1989. Editor: To Work, to Life or to Death--Studies in Working Class Lore, 1996; mem. editl. adv. bd. Folklore in Use: Applications in the Real World, 1993—; contbr. articles to profl. jours. Recipient Workers Cultural Found. prize, Denmark, 1995. Mem. Soc. for Folklore in Germany, Folklore Fellows (assoc.). Socialist. Home: Fiskerhusene 110, 2620 Albertslund Denmark

HEMMERSBACH, PETER, chemist; b. Ruppichteroth, Germany, July 25, 1950; s. Peter and Maria (Putz H.; m. Hiltrud Krolla, May 25, 1979; children: Sarah, Anna. Diploma in Chemistry, U. Muenster, Germany, 1975, PhD, 1981; Staatsprjfung Lehramt, Muenster, 1980. Tchr. Herder-Gymnasium, Koeln, Germany, 1980-84; lab. mgr. Hormone Lab., Aker Hosp., Oslo, Norway, 1985-91, scientific dir., 1991—; prof. Inst. of Pharmacy/ U. Oslo, Norway, 2000—; mem. IOC Med. Commn., Lausanne, Switzerland, 1998. Editor: (book) Blood Samples in Doping Control, 1994. Mem. Gesellschaft fur Toxikologische und Forensische Chemie. Avocations: marathon, golf, opera. Office: Hormone Lab, Aker Hosp, N-0514 Oslo Norway

HEMMES, MARCIA KAY, special education educator; b. Grand Rapids, Mich., May 17, 1963; d. Max Lloyd and Marian Ruth (Kitler) Pettit; m. Patrick Thomas Hemmes, Oct. 15, 1988 (div.); 1 child, Whitney Sarah. AA, Grand Rapids Jur. Coll., 1991; BS, Grand Valley State U., 1994, M in Learning Disabilities, 1998. Tchr. spl. edn. Kelloggsville Pub. Schs., Grand Rapids, 1994—. Avocations: softball, spirit squad coaching. Home: 2952 Sharon Ave SW Wyoming MI 49509-2521

HEMMILA, HEIKKI MATIAS, physician, researcher; b. Brisbane, Queensland, Australia, Feb. 5, 1955; s. Kaarlo Matias and Helvi Rakel (Alahautala) H.; m. Rea Irene Veki, Nov. 29, 1979 (div. Aug. 1995); children: Joonas Mikael, Aleksi Matias; m. Maarit Hannele Polso, Feb. 3, 1996; 1 child, Hanna Maria. MD, Oulu U., 1980. Pathologist Oulu U., 1978-80, asst. physician, 1980; gen. practitioner Perhonjokilaakso Health Ctr., 1980—; rschr., lectr. Folk Medicine Ctr., Kaustinen, 1993—. Councillor Mcpl. Coun., Kaustinen, 1992-96. Mem. Finnish Med. Assn., Finnish Assn. Manual Medicine, Lions. Conservative Party. Avocations: photography, folk arts. Home: Ketuntie 20, 69600 Kaustinen Finland Office: Folk Medicine Ctr, Pajalantie 24, 69600 Kaustinen Finland

HEMMINGS, PETER WILLIAM, orchestra and opera administrator; b. London, Apr. 10, 1934; s. William and Rosalind (Jones) H.; m. Jane Frances Kearnes, May 19, 1962; children: William, Lucy, Emma, Rupert, Sophie. Grad., Gonville and Caius Coll., Cambridge, England, 1957; LLD (hon.), Strathclyude U., Glasgow, 1978; DFA, Calif. State U., 2000. Clk. Harold Holt Ltd., London, 1958-59; planning mgr. Sadlers Wells Opera, London, 1959-65; gen. adminstr. Scottish Opera, Glasgow, 1962-77; gen. mgr. Australian Opera, Sydney, 1977-79; gen. dir. L.A. Music Ctr. Opera, 1984-2000; gen. mgr. New Opera Co., London, 1956-65; dir. Royal Acad. Music; gen. cons. Compton Verney Opera Project. Lt. Brit. Signal Corps, 1952-54. Decorated Order Brit. Empire. Fellow Royal Scottish Acad. Music, Royal Acad. Music (hon.); mem. Am. Friends of Sadlers Wells (pres. 1994-99), Opera Am. (bd. dirs.), Garrick Club (London), Royal Opera House Covent Garden (bd. dirs. 1999—). Anglican. Home: 775 S Madison Ave Pasadena CA 91106-3831 Office: 51 Queens Gate Gardens, London SW7 5NF, England

HEMOND, DAVID LAURENCE, lawyer; b. Holyoke, Mass., May 10, 1950; s. Harold Crean and Frances (Field) H.; m. Jacquelyn Ives, Aug. 22, 1987. BA, U. Conn., 1972; MA in Tchg., Conn. Coll., New London, 1973; JD, U. Conn., 1976. Bar: Conn. 1976; U.S. Dist. Ct. Conn. 1978. Assoc. Morgan, Moukawsher and Willetts, New London, 1976-79; legis. atty. Conn. Law Revision Commn., Hartford, 1979-89, chief atty., 1989—; reporter drafting com. Nat. Conf. Commrs. on Uniform State Laws, Chgo., 1999—. Named 1988 Citizen of Yr. Conn. Probate Assembly. Mem. Conn. Bar Assn. Avocations: amateur radio operator. E-mail: davidhemond@worldnet.att.net. Home: 637 Hopmeadow St Simsbury CT 06070-2451

HEMPEL-JØRGENSEN, ANNE, medical researcher; b. Sonderborg, Denmark, Nov. 6, 1963; d. IB and Karen (Elbrønd) H-J. MD, Århus U., Denmark, 1992, PhD, 1998. Rsch. asst. Århus U., Denmark, 1992-94, 95—; MD Sjlkeborg Hosp., Denmark, 1994-95. Home: Schleppeorellsgade 71, 8000 Århus C Denmark Office: U Århus, Dept Environ & Occup Med, Århus Denmark

HEMPELMANN, ALEXANDER MICHAEL, astrophysicist, researcher; b. Kirchmoeser, Brandenburg, Germany, Oct. 26, 1950; s. Josef and Jutta (Kospoth) H.; m. Cornelia Fuhrmann, May 20, 1974 (div.); children: Kati, Wulf, Stefan; m. Barbara Neuendorf, Apr. 21, 1997; 1 child, Uta. Diploma in Physics, U. Jena, Germany, 1976; PhD, Acad. Scis., Berlin, 1986. Collaborator Acad Scis. GDR, Potsdam, Germany, 1976-89; head dept., mem. supervisory bd. Astrophysics Inst. Potsdam, 1990-91, sr. collaborator, 1992-98; project mgr. dept. astrophysics U. Hamburg, 1998—. Contbr. articles to profl. jours. Polit. activist Neues Forum, Potsdam, 1989; mem. Buendnis 90, 1990, Bü90/Grüne, 1991—. Avocations: historical studies, politics, literature, gardening. Home: Otto-Nagel Str 15, D-14467 Potsdam Germany Office: Hamburger Sternwarte, Gojenbergsweg 112, D-21029 Hamburg Germany

HEMPELMANN, (CARL) ERNST, biochemist; b. Damme, Germany, June 26, 1946; s. Ernst and Anni (Holthaus) H.; m. Trude Werner, Apr. 7, 1972; children: Anne, Nils, Jörn. MSc in Biochemistry, U. Tübingen, Germany, 1974, PhD in Biochemistry, 1977. Rsch. fellow Nat. Inst. Med. Rsch., London, 1978-80; rsch. assoc. U. Göttingen, Germany, 1981-82; rsch. asst. U. Heidelberg, Germany, 1983-88; vis. scientist Hebrew U., Jerusalem, 1989; sr. lectr. U. Witwatesrand, Johannesburg, South Africa, 1990-92; sr. rsch. fellow U. Munich, 1995-96; vis. scientist U. London, 1998—. Contbr. articles to profl. jours. Roman Catholic. E-mail: ehempelman@aol.com. Office: Guys Hosp Med Sch, London SE1 9RT, United Kingdom

HEMPHILL, WILLIAM ALFRED, III, marketing executive; b. Pitts., Mar. 3, 1949; s. William Alfred II and Virgie Mae (Fisher) H.; m. Sandra Lynn von Lohen, Feb. 17, 1973; 1 child, Michelle Elise. BS, USAF Acad., 1972; postgrad., Air Force Squadron Officer's Sch., 1977, Ariz. State U., 1981-85; Exec. Masters in Bus. Admin., Claremont Grad. U., 1992; postgrad., Air Force Command and Staff Coll., 1997. Commd. 2d lt. USAF, 1972, advanced through grades to capt., 1976; radar navigator SAC USAF, Blytheville AFB, Ark., 1974-77; B-52 radar navigator SAC USAF, Rapid City, S.D., 1977-79; resigned regular USAF, 1979; maj. USAFR, 1988, area res. liaison officer, 1988-96; wings res. coord., 1996-97; retired USAFR, 1998; mktg. rep. Sperry Def. Systems, Phoenix, 1979-82, Sperry Space Div., Phoenix, 1982-83; product devel. mgr. Motorola Govt. Electronics Group, Tempe, Ariz., 1983-84; mktg. dir. Conrac SCD Div., Duarte, Calif., 1984-88; cons. Upland, Calif., 1988; nat. sales mgr. TEAC Am., Inc., Montebello, Calif., 1989-92; mktg. mgr. Mekel Engring, Walnut, Calif., 1992-94; venture devel. mgr. Thermo Tech. Ventures, Idaho Falls, 1994-96; deputy program mgr. TTV, Idaho Falls, 1996-99; program mgr. LockLeed Martin Logistic Svcs., Greenville, S.C., 1999—. Author: (with other); A Programmable Display Generator System, 1982. Position paper writer Rep. Nat. Com., 1980; pres. bd., performer Concert Dance Theater, 1988-92; mem. West End Rep. Club, Ontario, Calif., Idaho State U. Coll. Bus. Advisory Panel, 1996-99; vestry mem. St. Mark's Episc. Ch., Upland, Calif., 1988-91, dir. Homeless Shelter, 1988-91; dir. Rocky Mountain Venture Group, 1995-99.. Mem. Am. Mgmt. Assn., Nat. Contract Mgmt. Assn. (treas. 2000), Tech. Mktg. Soc. Am., Air Force Assn., USAF Acad. Grad. Assn. Episcopalian. Lodge: Elks. Avocations: golf, tennis, jogging.

HEMPLEMAN, WARWICK, small business owner; b. Durham, N.C., Apr. 23, 1959; arrived in Germany, 1988; s. David William and Barbara Florence (Hampe) H.; m. Dagmar P.E. Ross, June 8, 1989 (separated). BA magna cum laude, Adelphi U., 1980. Salesman Gingiss Formalwear, Atlanta, 1977, 79; warehouse worker Feature Sys., N.Y.C., 1980-81; prodn. asst. Giraldi Prodns., N.Y.C., 1981-82; self-employed prodn. asst. and prodn. coord. N.Y.C., 1981-86; self-employed grip/technician U.S. and Germany, 1985—; owner, founder Applied Film Theory, Munich and Cologne, Germany, 1992—; cons. mem. Arbeitsgruppe Kran Sichecheit, Berlin, 1999—; lectr., instr. Industrie und Handelskammer, Cologue, 1998—; jury mem. CINEC awards, Munich, 1998—. Mem. Internat. Assn. Theatrical and Stage Employees, Bundesverband von Beleuchter (local 52). Office: Applied Film Theory, Emil-Hoffmann-St 55, 50996 Cologne Germany

HEMPSTONE, SMITH, JR., diplomat, journalist; b. Washington, Feb. 1, 1929; s. Smith and Elizabeth (Noyes) H.; m. Kathaleen Fishback, Jan. 30, 1954; 1 dau. Student, George Washington U., 1946-47; BA with honors, U. of South, 1950, LittD (hon.), 1969; Nieman fellow, Harvard U., 1964-65. Rewrite man AP, Charlotte, N.C., 1952; with Nat. Geog. mag., Washington, 1954; reporter Louisville Times, 1953, Evening Star, Washington, 1955-56; fgn. corr. Africa, Asia, Europe and Latin Am. for Chgo. Daily News, 1960-66; fgn. corr. Washington Evening Star, 1966-69, assoc. editor, 1970-75; exec. editor Washington Times, 1982-84, editor-in-chief, 1984-85; nationally syndicated newspaper columnist, 1970-89, ambassador to Kenya, 1989-93; diplomat in residence U. of the South, Sewanee, Tenn., 1993, Va. Mil. Inst., Lexington, 1994; Fellow Inst. Current World Affairs, 1956-60. Author: Africa, Angry Young Giant, 1961, Rebels, Mercenaries and Dividends-The Katanga Story, 1962, Rogue Ambassador, 1997; (novel) A Tract of Time, 1966, In the Midst of Lions, 1968; editorial bd.: Nieman Reports, 1965-73. Alumni trustee U. South, 1974-78; bd. govs. Inst. Current World Affairs, 1974-78. Recipient Fgn. Corr. award Sigma Delta Chi and Overseas Press Club. Mem. Chevy Chase Club (Md.), Met. Club (Washington), Explorers Club (N.Y.C.). Episcopalian. Home and Office: 7611 Fairfax Rd Bethesda MD 20814-1313

HEMSING, JOSEPHINE CLAUDIA, public relations professional for performing arts; b. Paris, France, June 5, 1953; d. Albert E. and Esther (Davidson) H.; m. Daniel F. Cameron, Sept. 22, 1990. Student, Sorbonne U. de Paris, 1972-73; BA, Sarah Lawrence Coll., 1974; postgrad., CUNY, 1982-93. Dep. dir. distbn. ASCAP, N.Y.C., 1975-81; assoc. dramaturg and festival coordinator Städtische Bühnen Freiburg, Fed. Republic Germany, 1981-82; publicity asst. Audrey Michaels Pub. Relations, N.Y.C., 1983; publicity assoc. N.Y. Philharmonic, N.Y.C., 1984-85; publicist The Carson Office, N.Y.C., 1985-89; founder, dir. Hemsing Assocs., Inc., N.Y.C., 1989—. Mem. prodn. staff for New Russian Chamber Orch., N.Y.C., 1976-79, Encompass Music Theatre, N.Y.C., 1978-79, Wallgraben Theater on Tour, U.S.A., 1980, Rodger Hess Prodns., N.Y.C., 1982, John Hart Assoc., N.Y.C., 1982, Peter Witt Players Prodns., N.Y.C., 1982-83, numerous Broadway and off-Broadway shows including How I Got That Story, 1982, Twice Around the Park, 1983, Diary of a Madman, 1989; NBC-TV documentary Missiles Go Home, 1981; numerous published translations. Democrat. Home: 401 E 80th St Apt 29K New York NY 10021-0654 Office: 401 E 80th St Apt 14H New York NY 10021-0650 also: Hemsing Int c/o A Forgeron, 21 rue Chevert, 75007 Paris France

HEMSLEY, THOMAS JEFFREY, retired vocalist; b. Coalville, Great Britain, Apr. 12, 1927; s. Sydney William and Kathleen Annie (Deacon) H.; m. Gwenllian Ellen James, Nov. 9, 1960; children: William T.J., Matthew W.D., Michael R. MA, U. Oxford, 1948. Prof. singing Guildhall Sch. Music & Drama, London, 1987-97; ret., 1997; guest prof. Royal Danish Acad. Music, 1990-91; dir. Opera Dartington Internat. Music Summer Sch., 1987—. Appeared in maj. opera houses and concert halls throughout world; author: Singing & Imagination, 1998. Vicar choral St. Pauls Cathedral, 1950-51. Named hon. mem. Royal Acad. Music, 1974, hon. fellow Trinity Coll. Music, 1988, Guildhall Sch. Music fellow, London, 1996. Fellow Royal Soc. Arts; mem. Royal Philharmonic Soc. (life), Garrick Club, British Actors Equity (life). Avocations: gardening, mountain walking. Fax: 0181 348 3397. Home: 10 Denewood Rd. London N6 4AJ, England

HENCKAERTS, JEAN-MARIE ROBERT ADRIAAN, legal advisor; b. Hasselt, Limburg, Belgium, Aug. 24, 1966; s. François Henckaerts and Annette Hindrikx; m. Mei-Hui Wei, Jan. 13, 1994; 1 child, Pauline. LLB, U. Brussels, 1989; LLM, U. Ga., 1990; D Juridical Sci., George Washington U., 1994. Assoc. Troutman Sanders, Atlanta, 1990-91; rsch. asst. Law Sch. George Washington U., Washington, 1991-93; postdoctoral rsch. fellow U. Brussels, 1993-96; legal advisor Internat. Com. of Red Cross, Geneva, 1996—; lectr. Boston U. Brussels, 1994-96, Webster U., Geneva, 1998. Author: Mass Expulsion in Modern International Law and Practice, 1995; editor: The International Status of Taiwan in the New World Order, 1996; co-editor: Eastern Europe in Europe, 1996; corr. editor Internat. Legal Materials, 1995—; mem. editl. com. Ministry Justice, State Report to Human Rights Com., 1996; mem. editl. bd. Belgian Red Cross, 1996—. Fellow Inter-Am. Inst. Human Rights, 1992, Harvard Human Rights Program, 1993, Human Rights fellow Coun. Europe, 1992-93. Mem. Internat. Law Assn. (mem. internat. com. on internally displaced persons 1995—), Am. Soc. Internat. Law, Acad. Coun. UN Sys. Office: Internat Com of Red Cross, 19 Ave de la Paix, 1202 Geneva Switzerland

HENCKE, PAUL GERARD, editor, writer, broadcaster; b. St. Louis, Oct. 4, 1927; s. Richard and Louise (Dierkes) H.; widowed, 1975; children: Thomas, John, Christopher, Mary, Andrew, Joseph, James; m. Jeannye Thornton, Sept., 1976; children: Matthew, Maximillian. BS, St. Louis U., 1950. Mag. and newspaper writer, freelancer St. Louis Globe-Dem., Nation's Bus. mag., Washington, St. Louis, 1947-53; assoc. editor Kiplinger Washington Letter, 1966-74; editor weekly newsletter U.S. News & World Report, Washington, 1974-85; editor newsletters Nat. Inst. Bus Mgmt., N.Y.C., Alexandria, Va., 1985-94; editor Phillips Pub. Internat., 1994-96. Broadcaster: NBC, 1977-79, Nat. Pub. Radio, 1979-80; broadcaster, commentator CBS, 1981—; co-editor: Dear NASA: Please Send Me A Rocket; contbr. numerous mag. and newspsper features. With USCG, 1945-47. Mem. AFTRA, Nat. Press Club. Roman Catholic. Home: 6315 Naval Ave Lanham Seabrook MD 20706

HENDERSON, D. AUSTIN, computer scientist; b. London, Ont., Can., Jan. 25, 1943; came to U.S., 1966; s. Dugald Austin and Nancy (Gilbert) H.; m. Lynne Ellen McHugh, Aug. 29, 1981; children: Kimberly, Mark, Brooke. Honors BSc in Math. and Sci., Queen's U., Kingston, Ont., 1965; MS in Computer Sci., U. Ill., 1967; PhD in Elec. Engring., MIT, 1975. Rsch. asst. computation structures and programming MIT, Cambridge, 1967-75; cons. on computer graphics and networks MIT Lincoln Lab., Lexington, 1968-75; cons. computer graphics and applications programmin Bolt Beranek and Newman Inc., Cambridge, 1970-75, computer scientist, 1975-78; mem. rsch. staff Xerox Palo Alto (Calif.) Rsch. Ctr., 1978-86; PARC-EuroPARC liaison Rank Xerox Cambridge (Eng.) EuroPARC, 1987-89; v.p. Fitch Richardson Smith, Worthington, Ohio, 1989; area mgr. design, use and shared spaces Sys. Scis. Lab., Xerox Palo Alto Rsch. Ctr., 1989-90; mgr. user interface architecture Xerox Corp., Palo Alto, 1990-94; user experience architect advanced tech. group Apple Computer, Inc., Cupertino, Calif, 1994-95, mgr. user experience lab., 1995-96, mgr. discourse architecture lab. Apple Rsch. Labs., 1996-97; prin. Pliant Rsch., Berkeley, Calif., 1997—, Rivendel Consulting & Design, Inc., La Honda, Calif., , 1997—. ontbr. articles to profl. jours.; patentee in field. em. Assn. Computer Machinery Spl. Interest Group on Computer Human Interaction (vice chair 1988-89, co-chair 1989-91, 91-93, past chair 1994-95, conf. chair 1985, disting. svc. award 1995). Avocations: kayaking, tennis, hiking, canoeing, photography. Home and Office: 8115 La Honda Rd PO Box 334 La Honda CA 94020-0334

HENDERSON, SIR DENYS HARTLEY, business executive; b. Oct. 11, 1932; s. John Hartley and Nellie (Gordon) H.; m. Doreen Mathewson Glashan; children: Nicola Mary, Fiona Elizabeth. MA, LLB, U. Aberdeen, U.K.; LLD (hon.), U. Aberdeen, 1987; DUniv. (hon.), U. Brunel, 1987, U. Strathclyde, 1993; LLD (hon.), U. Nottingham, 1990, U. Manchester, 1991, U. Bath, 1993; DSc (hon.), Cranfield Inst. Tech., 1989, U. Teesside, 1993. Non-exec. dir. Barclays Bank plc, 1983-97, The RTZ Corp. plc, 1990-96, Schlumberger, Ltd., 1995—, Market & Opinion Rsch. Internat., Ltd., 1995—; non-exec. dir. Rank Group plc, London, 1994—, chmn., 1995—; non-exec. dir. Dalgety plc, 1996-98, chmn., 1997-98; chmn. Stock Exch. Listed Co., 1987-91; mem. N.Y. Stock Exch. Listed Co. Adv. Com., 1988-90; chmn. adv. bd. Spencer Stuart & Assocs., Ltd., 1995—; mem. bd. dirs. Imperial Chem. Industries plc, London, 1957-95, dep. chmn., 1986-87, chmn., 1987-95; chmn. Zeneca Group plc, 1993-95; 1st commr. and chmn. The Crown Estate, 1995—. Trustee Nat. History Mus., 1989-98; mem. presdl. com. CBI, 1987-96; mem. adv. coun. Prince's Youth Bus. Trust, 1986-99; chancellor Bath (U.K.) U., 1993-98; mem. ct. of govs. Henley Mgmt. Coll., 1986-96, chmn., 1989-96. Mem. Law Soc. Scotland, Athenaeum Club, Royal Automobile Club. Avocations: swimming, reading, travelling, gardening, golf. Office: The Rank Group PLC, 6 Connaught Pl, London W2 2EZ, England

HENDERSON, GEORGE POLAND, publisher; b. London, Apr. 24, 1920; s. George James and Emma Rouse (Wilson) H.; m. Shirley Prudence Cotton, Apr. 27, 1953; children: Crispin Alastair Poland, Antony James Willis. Student, U. London, 1938-40. Comml. ref. libr. Guildhall Libr., London, 1938-63; dir. Kellys' Directories Ltd., Kingston-upon-Thames, 1963-66; dir., chmn. bd. CBD Rsch., Ltd., Beckenham, 1966—. Compiler, editor: Current British Directories, 6 edits., 1953-71, European Companies: Guide to Sources of Information, 3 edit., 1961-72, Directory of British Associations, 11 edit., 1965-92. Capt. Royal Artillery, Eng., 1940-46. Fellow Inst. of Dirs., Royal Philatelic Soc.; mem. Royal Instn. of Gt. Britain, European Assn. Directory Pubs. (pres. 1976-78), Assn. Brit. Directory Pubs. (pres. 1974-75). Avocations: travel, gardening, postal history. Office: CBD Research Ltd, 15 Wickham Rd, Beckenham BR3 5JS, England

HENDERSON, IAN RAMSAY, investment company executive; b. London, Jan. 6, 1949; s. David Hope and Eleanora Anderson (Borrie) H.; m. Virginia Theresa Freeman, Oct. 28, 1978; children: Alexander Storm David Hope, Charles John Bernard Hope, George Ian Henry Hope. MA, Edinburgh U., 1970, LLB, 1972. Chartered acct., Eng., Wales. Articled clk. Peat Marwick Mitchell, London, 1972-75; acct. Peat Marwick Mitchell, Calgary, Can., 1975-77; mgr. investments Morgan Grenfell & Co., London, 1977-82; dir., mng. dir. Wardley Marine Ltd., London, 1982-86; bd. dirs. Fleming Investment Mgmt. Ltd., London. Mem. Brooks St. James, West Sussex Golf Club, Inst. Chartered Accts. Eng. and Wales, Securities Inst. Avocations: golf, tennis, theatre, squash. Home: 20 Westbourne Park Rd, London W25 PH, England Office: Fleming Investment Mgmt Ltd, 25 Copthall Ave, London W25 PH, England

HENDERSON, JAMES GARY, marketing executive; b. Plainfield, N.J., Jan. 27, 1954; s. Douglas Ploughman and Eileen (Burke) H.; m. Luellen Marie Schmeelk, June 18, 1977; children: James Burke, Taylor Walter, Farrell Eileen. BS in Mktg., Pace Univ., 1976. Account exec. Ossining Citizen Register (N.Y.), 1976-77; reporter Dispatch, White Plains, NY, 1977-79; group account exec. Westchester Rockland Newspaper, White Plains, NY, 1977-79; fin. advt. mgr. Gannett Westchester Rockland Newspapers, Westchester, NY, 1979-81; group dir. spl. projects Gannett Westchester Rockland Newspapers, Westchester, 1980-81, mag. advt. mgr., 1981-82; sales exec. Actmedia Inc. Mktg. Corp. of N.Y.C., 1982-86; exec. v.p. mktg. and sales Point of Purchase Radio, 1986-91; pres., CEO St. Ives Devel. Group, 1991-93; pres. Muzak In-store Mktg. Grp., 1993-97; CEO CDUniverse.com, 1998-99; sr. v.p. Floorgraphics, Inc., 1999—. Advt. and pub. rels. dir. Bedford Town Rep. Campaign, N.Y., 1977; bd. dirs. Ridgefield Pub. Libr., 1985-92, Ridgefield Pub. Libr., 1985-91, Bedford Hills Fire Dept., 1977, capt. H&L Co., 1977; chmn. Ridgefield Firehouse Firehouse Study Com.; bd. dirs. Ridgefield Basketball Assn.; founder, bd. dirs. Tri-County Basketball League, 1996—; founder Ridgefield Basketball Club. Recipient Outstanding Salesmanship awds. Westchester Ann. Commerce and Industry sects., 1977-80. Mem. Westchester Advt. Club, Sales Mktg. Club of Westchester. Roman Catholic. Home: 50 S Ridge Ct Ridgefield CT 06877-5420

HENDERSON, JAMES STUART, dean, medical educator, retired; b. Dundee, Scotland, May 26, 1928; arrived in St. Vincent & The Grenadines, 1993.; s. James Duncan and Caroline Stuart (Fowlie) H.; m. Ursula Offenbacher, Mar. 16, 1956; children: Benjamin Duncan, Adam Stuart. M.B.Ch.B., St. Andrews (Scotland) U., 1951. Instr. Duke U., Durham, N.C., 1955-57; rsch. assoc. The Rockefeller Inst., N.Y.C., 1957-60, asst. prof., 1960-70; prof. pathology U. Man., Winnipeg, Can., 1970-93; dean Kingstown (St. Vincent) Coll. Medicine, 1993-95; dean Kigezi Internat. Sch. Medicine, Cambridge, Eng., 1998-99, ret., 1999; cons. Deer Lodge Vets. Hosp., Winnipeg, 1970-83, Winnipeg Gen. Hosp., 1970-93, St. Boniface Hosp., Winnipeg, 1985-93; author computer-assisted interactive ednl. programs in pathology. Contbr. articles to profl. jours. Capt. Royal Army Med. Corps, 1952-54. Fellow Royal Soc. Medicine; mem. Brit. Med. Assn., Am. Soc. for Investicative Pathology, Rotary (sgt.-at-arms 1996-97). E-mail: jhenders@caribsurf.com. Home: Villa Calliaqua PO, Saint Vincent West Indies

HENDERSON, JOHN, electronics executive; b. Tacoma, Apr. 30, 1960. BA, U. Wash., 1982, MBA, 1984. Assoc. sales dir. Radio Shack, Seattle, 1985-90; asst. v.p. Werik Electronics, Seattle, 1990-95, v.p., 1995—; assoc. liaison subs. Werik Electronics, Berlin, Tokyo, Tel Aviv. Office: Werik Electronics Ste 110B 2445 4th Ave S Seattle WA 98134-1939

HENDERSON, KENNETH ATWOOD, investment counseling executive; b. Watertown, Mass., Oct. 18, 1905; s. Charles William and Anna Lyons (Atwood) H.; m. Elizabeth Berry Marshall, June 10, 1944 (dec. Mar. 1994); 1 child, Caroline Marshall. BS, Harvard U., 1926. With fgn. dept. Brown Bros. & Co., Boston, 1926-30; analyst Weil McKey & Co., Boston, 1931; analyst, editor Poor's, Babson Park, Wellesley, Mass., 1937; investment counsellor Cromwell & Cabot, Inc., Boston, 1937-42, 46-50; sr. v.p. John P. Chase, Inc., Boston, 1950-74; pvt. practice investment counselling Waban, Mass., 1975—, Etna, N.H., 1975—; dir., treas. Henniker Crutch Co. Author: Handbook of American Mountaineering, 1942, New England Canoeing Guiide, 1965, 68, 71; editor: Appalachia, 1947-55; contbr. articles Am. Alpine Jour., Appalachia, Alpine Jour., others. Active investment, fin. coms. 2d Ch., Newton, Mass. Comdr. USNR, 1942-46. Fellow Harvard Travellers Club (hon., trustee of permanent funds); mem. Boston Security Analysts Soc., Bond Analysts Soc. Boston, Pub. Utility Analysis Boston, Am. Alpine Club (hon., hon. treas., Angelo Heilprin award 1982), Can. Alpine Club, London Alpine Club, Harvard Mountaineering Club, Explorers Club (medalist New England chpt.), Appalachian Mountain Club (hon.), Mountain Guides Assn. (hon.), Res. Officers Assn., Ret. Officers Assn., Mil. Order of the World Wars (perpetual mem.), 10th Mountain Divsn. Assn. (hon.). Home: 373 Center Hanover Rd Etna NH 03750

HENDERSON, LESLEY, botanist; b. Benoni, South Africa, June 30, 1956; d. Brian and Dinah Hilda (Hoffman) H. BSc in Botany with honors, U. Witwatersrand, Johannesburg, South Africa, 1979. Rschr. Botanical Rsch. Inst., Pretoria, 1979-85; rschr., project leader agrl. rsch. coun. Plant Protection Rsch. Inst., Pretoria, South Africa, 1985—, project leader, co-coord. agrl. rsch. coun., 1990—, database mgr. agrl. rsch. coun., 1990—; mgr. computerized database So. African Plant Invaders Atlas, 1993-99. Author: Barrier Plants of Southern Africa, 1987, Plant Invaders of Southern Africa, 1995; co-author (chpt. in book) The Ecology and Management of Biological Invasions in Southern Africa, 1986, Vegetation of Southern Africa, 1997, (books) Declared Weeds and Alien Invader Plants in South Africa, 1987, Plant Invaders of the Transvaal, 1987; contbr. numerous articles to profl. jours. Mem. So. African Weed Sci. Soc. (Davd Annecke rsch. award 1998), South African Assn. Botanists, Assn. Taxonomic Study of the Flora of Tropical Africa. Avocation: gardening with indigenous plants. Office: Plant Protection Rsch Inst, Nat Botan Inst Pvt Bag X101, 0001 Pretoria South Africa

HENDERSON, MARY LOUISE, civic worker; b. Windsor, Ont., Can., Apr. 24, 1928; came to U.S., 1932; d. Kenneth Charles and Florence McGie (Morton) Campbell; m. Ernest Flagg Henderson III, Dec. 31, 1953; children: Ernest Flagg IV, Roberta C. BA, Bard Coll., 1950. V.p. Ruse & Urban, Inc., advt., Detroit, 1950-53; v.p., bd. dirs. Henderson House Am., Sudbury, Mass., 1969—. Pres. Wellesley (Mass.) Friendly Aid Assn., 1970-75, Newton (Mass.) Wellesley Hosp. Aid, 1980-82, 88-89; co-founder, exec. com. mem. Wellesley Community Ctr., 1972—, pres., 1983-85; bd. dirs., mem. exec. com. Norumbega Coun. Boy Scouts Am., 1974-95, pres., 1989-91; mem. exec. com. Knox Coun. Boy Scouts Am., 1995—; trustee Newton-Wellesley Hosp., 1982—, mem. exec. com., 1990-96; bd. dirs., mem. exec. com. Greater Boston adv. bd. Salvation Army, 1985—; mem. nat. adv. bd. Officers Tng. Sch. Salvation Army, 1994—; bd. dirs. Newton-Wellesley Vis. Nurse Assn., 1974—; corporator Boston Bio-Med. Inst., 1990—; mem. corp. Ptnrs. Healthcare Sys., 1999—, also others. Mem. Mensa, Am. Needlepoint Guild (founder, pres. Mass. chpt. 1974-77, bd. dirs. 1974—, nat. historian 1989-97). Republican. Episcopalian. Avocations: travel, reading, needlepoint. Home: 171 Edmunds Rd Wellesley MA 02481-1331

HENDERSON, MICHAEL L., engineering executive; b. Shawnee, Okla., Feb. 23, 1947; s. Zacr L. and Betty J. Henderson; m. Irma Henderson, May 14, 1999; children: Michelle L., Marla A. BS in Engring., Tex. A&I U., 1970. Registered profl. engr., Tex. Various supervisory/mgmt. positions Ctrl. Power & Light Co., Corpus Christi, Tex., 1970-92; dir. ops. Ctrl. and S.W. Energy, Inc., Dallas, 1992-94; cons. Power Energy Cons., Atlanta, 1994-95; ops. mgr. Dominion Energy Inc., 1995-99; gen. mgr. Egenor, dir. Duke Energy INternat., 1999—; physics prof. Victoria Jr. Coll., 1983-88. Address: PO Box 25434 Miami FL 33102-5434

HENDERSON, PAUL LLOYD, electrical engineer; b. Sydney, Australia, May 2, 1961; s. Lloyd Muriel (Archinal) H.; m. Lindy Louise Gell, Oct. 7, 1989; children: Daniel, Lachlan. Elec. engring. degree, U. New South Wales, Australia, 1983; postgrad. in diploma mgmt., Deakin, Australia, 1993. Cert. expert on structured cabling systems, MIEEE. Design gnr. STC-Alcatel, Sydney, 1983-86; sr. design engr. Plessey, Sydney, 1986-88; sr. project mgr. Honeywell, Sydney, 1990-92; sr. tech. cons. Wang, Sydney, 1992-94; sr. project mgr. Digital, Sydney, 1994—; dir. Synergetic Comm., Sydney, 1992—; mem. Standards Australia, Sydney, 1993—; rep. Australian Telecomm. Users Group, 1993—. Co-author: Australian Telecommunications Cabling Standards A53080, 1996; chief engr. numerous telecomm. inventions, patentee in field, 1983-86. V.p. Rotoract, Sydney, 1986. Mem. IEEE (cert. expert structured cabling systems), Project Mgmt. Inst., PMP. Avocations: sailing, mountain biking, swimming. Home: 39 Marlow Ave, Sydney Denistone NSW 2114, Australia Office: Compaq, 410 Concord Rd, Rhodes NSW 2138, Australia

HENDERSON, RICHARD, molecular biologist, researcher; b. Edinburgh, Scotland, July 19, 1945; s. John Wastle and Grace Simpson (Goldie) H.; m. Penelope Fitzgerald, 1969 (div. 1988); children: Jennifer, Alastair; m. Jade Li, 1995. BS in Physics first class, Edinburgh U., 1966; PhD, Cambridge U., Eng., 1970. Mem. rsch. staff MRC Lab. Molecular Biology, Cambridge, 1969-70, 73-79, sr. rsch. staff, 1979-84, spl. appts. grade rsch. staff, 1984-86, joint head divsn. structural studies, 1986-2000, dep. dir., 1995-96, dir., 1996—; postdoct. fellow Yale U., New Haven, Conn., 1970-73; lectr. in field. Contbr. numerous articles to profl. jours. Helen Hay Whitney postdoct. fellow 1970-73; recipient William Bate Hardy prize Cambridge Philosph. Soc., 1978, Ernst-Ruska prize for electron microscopy, 1980, Rosenstiel award, 1991, Louis Jeantet award, 1993, Gregori Aminoff prize for christallography Royal Swedish Acad., 1999. Fellow Darwin Coll., Royal Soc., Acad. Med. Scis. (London); mem. European Molecular Biology Orgn., Nat. Acad. Scis. (fgn. assoc.). Office: MRC Lab Molecular Biology, Hills Rd, Cambridge CB2 2QH, England

HENDERSON, THOMAS HORATIO, retired agronomist educator; b. Grand Bay, Dominica, Aug. 17, 1927; s. Evan Alfred and Seranie Helen (Thomas) H.; m. Malachi Sylvestine Eugene (dec. 1975); children: Thelma, Carl, Ian, Geoffrey, Charlene, James; m. Claudia Nonna Mitchel, Feb. 17, 1980; 1 child, Triona. Diploma in agr., East Caribbean Farm Inst., Trinidad, 1955, Imperial Coll. Tropical Agr., Trinidad, 1959; MSc, Cornell U., 1962; PhD, U. Wis., 1969. Farm mgr. Imperial Coll. Tropical Agr., Trinidad, 1959-62; assoc. dean faculty agr. U. W.I., Trinidad, 1971-73; lectr., prof., dept. head faculty agr. U. W.I., Trinidad, 1962-88; agr. ext. expert FAO (Food and Agrl. Orgn.) of UN, Grenada, 1974-75; dir. Caribbean agrl. ext. project U. W.I./MUCIA (Midwest Univs. Consortium for Internatl. Activities, Inc., USA), 1980-88; pvt. cons. Dominica, 1989—; agr. ext. cons.

FAO (Food and Agrl. Orgn.) of UN, Western Somoa, Africa, Caribbean, South Am., 1970, 79, 80, 91, 94, 97, 98; cons. World Bank, Caribbean region, 1991, 92, 93; dir. Banana Mktg. Bd., Dominica, 1984-94; chmn., dep. chmn. Agrl. and Indsl. Devel. Bank, Dominica, 1988-95. Author: Fifty Years of Research in Tropical Agriculture, 1975; editor Ext. newsletter, 1970-76; contbr. chpt. to book and articles to profl. jours. Scout master Dominica Grammar Sch. Scout Troop, 1950-53; pres. PTA, Trinidad, 1963-67; musical dir. various ch. choirs, Dominica, 1992—; v.p. Coun. on Aging, Dominica, 1998—. Recipient Gold medal for outstanding contbn. to Caribbean agr. Midwest Univs. Consortium for Internat. Activities, 1987. Mem. Agrl. Soc. Trinidad and Tobago, Jamaica Agrl. Soc., Assn. Agrl. Ext. Workers. Roman Catholic. Avocations: choral music, Caribbean literature, gardening. Home: Morne Daniel, PO Box 418, Roseau Dominica

HENDERSON, WILLIAM DAVID, mechanical engineer; b. El Paso, Tex., May 1, 1950; s. Weldon Oliver and Betty Joyce (Woodson) H.; m. Karen Sue George, July 22, 1972; children: Carrie Ann, Heather Marie. BSME, U. Tex., El Paso, 1974. Registered profl. engr., Tex. Engr. trainee Otis Engring. Corp., Corpus Christi, Tex., 1974-75; design engr. Otis Engring. Corp., Dallas, 1975-81, design mgr., 1981-88, staff engr., 1988-91; engring. projects mgr. Baker Oil Tools, Houston, 1991-97; mgr. design engring. OSCA, Houston, TX., 1997-99; tech. profl. leader sand control team Halliburton Energy Svcs., Carrollton, Tex., 1999—. Mem. ASME. Republican. Baptist. Achievements include 12 patents in methods and apparatus for downhole tools for oil and gas wells. Home: 1207 Vaughan Ln Tioga TX 76271-2933 Office: Halliburton Energy Svcs 2601 E Belt Line Rd Carrollton TX 75006-5401

HENDERSON, WILLIAM J., association executive; b. Paris, Ill., July 24, 1925; s. William M. and Lena (Johnson) H.; m. Mary Ann Ferguson, July 15, 1950 (dec. Oct. 1985); children: Beth Grafton, Mark W.; m. Virginia Skram, Dec. 24, 1986; children: John Skran, Peggy Skran, Salli Skran. BA, Aurora U., 1950; postgrad. U. Ill. 1951. Adminstrv. asst. Assoc. Industries, Rock Island, Ill., 1951-54; pers. dir. George Evans Corp., Moline, Ill., 1954-58; dir. econ. edn. & pub. rels. Assoc. Industries of Mo., 1958-62; exec. v.p., Assoc. Credit Bureau of Midwest, 1962-72; v.p., Houston, 1972-78; pres. Internat. Credit Assn., St. Louis, 1978-91; ret., 1991; pres., chief exec. officer Henderson Enterprises, 1991. With USN, 1943-46. Recipient Freedom Found. award, Valley Forge, 1956. Mem. U.S. Chamber Am. Soc. Assoc. Execs. (v.p., bd. dirs. 1981-84, mem. exec. com.), Ind. Soc. Assn. Execs. (past pres. 1971-72), Mo. Soc. Assn. Execs., St. Louis Meeting Planners (bd. dirs. 1983—), St. Louis Assn. Execs. (v.p. 1984-85, pres. 1985—), U.S. C. of C. (com. of 100), Running and Fitness Assn. (dir. 1987—), Aurora U. Alumni Assn. (chmn. Gateway chpt.), Masons, Shriners. Home and Office: 14172 Woods Mill Cove Dr Chesterfield MO 63017-3436

HENDERSON, WILLIAM J., postmaster general; b. June 16, 1947; 2 children. Grad., U. N.C. With U.S. Postal Svc.; postmaster, divsn. gen. mgr. U.S. Postal Svc., Greensboro, N.C.; v.p. employee rels. U.S. Postal Svc., chief mktg. officer, sr. v.p., chief operating officer, 1994-98, postmaster gen., CEO, 1998—. With U.S. Army. Recipient Roger W. Jones award for Exec. Leadership Am. U., 1998, John Wanamaker award U.S. Postal Svc., 1997. Office: US Postal Svc L'Enfant Plz SW Rm 10022 Washington DC 20260-0010*

HENDERSON-SELLERS, BRIAN, computer scientist, educator; b. Blackburn, Lancashire, Eng., Jan. 25, 1951; arrived in Australia, 1988; s. Ronald Henderson and Mary (Crossley) Sellers; m. Ann Futtit, Sept. 22, 1974. BS, London U., 1972; MS, Reading U., 1973; PhD, Leicester U., 1976. Lectr. Salford (Eng.) U., 1976-88; sr. lectr., assoc. prof. U. NSW, Sydney, Australia, 1988-93; prof. U. Tech., Sydney, 1993-96, Swinburne U. Tech., Melbourne, Australia, 1996-99, U. Tech., Sydney, 1999—; dir. Ctr. Object Tech. Applications and Rsch., Sydney, Melbourne, 1994—. Author: Engineering Limnology, 1984, Book of Object-Oriented Knowledge, 1997, Object-Oriented Metrics, 1996, The OPEN Process Specification, 1997, The OPEN Toolbox of Techniques, 1998. Fellow Australian Computer Soc., Australian Instn. Engrs., Inst. Math. and Its Application. Avocations: classical music, computer music, ballroom dancing. Office: Univ Tech Sydney, Broadway NSW, Australia

HENDLER, ROSEMARY NIELSEN, business owner, digital artist; b. Sydney, Australia, Oct. 18, 1946; came to U.S., 1954, naturalized, 1970; d. Robert Stanley McFarlane and Joyce Elizabeth (Annetts) Nielsen; m. Joel Arnold Hendler, June 1, 1977; 1 child, Stewart Maxwell. BA, U. Calif., Berkeley, 1968; postgrad., Acad. Art San Francisco, 1974-76, UCLA, 1985-87. Buyer linens Breuners Home Furnishings, Oakland, Calif., 1969-71; buyer textiles Liberty House, San Francisco, 1971-73, Bullock's, Palo Alto, 1973-75; graphic artist Montclarion Pubs., Oakland, 1975-77; pres., owner Cordeaux River Trading Co., L.A., 1986-93; owner, prnr. Hendler Graphics, Orinda, Calif., 1995—. Advisor (CD-ROM) Visionary Stampede, Multimedia Project, San Francisco; exhibited computer art in numerous one-woman shows, 1994, 95, 96, 97, 98, 99. Bd. dirs. docent coun. L.A. County Mus. Art, 1981—; VIP hostess Olympic Games, L.A., 1984; bd. dirs. Young Audiences, L.A., 1985-87; exec. bd. Orinda Arts Coun., 1991—, pres., 1993-94; mem. art guild Oakland Mus., 1991—; mem. task force Arts and Cultural Coun. of Contra Costa County, 1994—; mem. pilot Arts Docent Program touring art in all stas. for pub. and schs.; mem. Arts Coun. of Big Bear Valley. Recipient Design award Levi Strauss, 1975, Honorable Mention award Manhattan Arts Internat., 1996, Merit award Paperworks, Conn., 1997. Mem. NAFE, AAUW (bd. dirs. Big Bear Valley chpt. 1999—), Nat. Assn. Local Arts Agys., Arts Coun. of Big Bear Valley, Nat. Assn. Desktop Pubs., Calif. Assn. Local Arts Agys., Jr. League L.A., Costume Coun., L.A. County Mus. Art, Lamorinda Arts Alliance, Artists in Tech. Republican. Office: PO Box 2922 Big Bear Lake CA 92315-2922

HENDLEY, COIT TAYLOR, III, chemistry educator; b. Washington, Apr. 29, 1952; s. Coit Taylor Jr. and Barbara (Davidson) H.; m. Mary Wilson, July 8, 1985; children: Coit Taylor IV, Kevin Patrick. BA in Chemistry, Cornell U., 1975; MA in Sci. Edn., U. Md., 1990. Cert. advanced tchg., Md. Sci. tchr. South River H.S., Davidsonville, Md., 1976-77, Old Mill (Md.) H.S., Davidsonville, Md., 1978-87, Eleanor Roosevelt H.S., Greenbelt, Md., 1987-92, 97—, Frederick Douglass H.S., Upper Marlboro, Md., 1993-97; mem. U. Md. Balt. County Engring. Adv. Bd., 1996—, Eleanor Roosevelt H.S. Tech. Acad. Faculty Adv. Bd., 1997—, Eleanor Roosevelt H.S. Sci. and Tech. Faculty Adv. Bd., 1997—. Recipient Leo Schubert Meml. award Chem. Soc. Washington, 1997, Md. Presdl. awar for excellence in math. and sci. tchg., 1998, Radioshack Nat. Tchr. award, 2000; Growth Initiatives for Tchrs. fellow GTE, 1996-97. Mem. NEA, Am. Chem. Soc. (educators divsn.), Am. Assn. Physics Tchrs., Nat. Sci. Tchrs. Assn., Md. Assn. Sci. Tchrs., Prince Georgs County Tchrs. Assn. Office: Eleanor Roosevelt HS 7601 Hanover Pkwy Greenbelt MD 20770-2099

HENDOLIN, MINNA LEENA, biochemist; b. Eno, N. Carelia, Finland, Feb. 16, 1965; d. Pekka Kalervo and Maija Hilve Elisa (Tolvanen) Turunen; m. Panu Henrik Hendolin, Nov. 2, 1996; children: Noora Sofia, Rasmus Panu Eemeli. MS, U. Kuopio, Finland, 1991; PhD, U. Kuopio, 1998. Rsch. assoc. U. Kuopio, 1990-94, instr. of biotechnology, 1994-95; scientist embryology Pharming Oy, Kuopio, 1995—, mgr. quality assurance, 1999—. Author: Rats, Researchers and Results, 1996. Grantee Olvi Found., Kuopio, 1991. Mem. SSF/Cambridge. Lutheran. Avocation: volleyball. Office: Pharming Oy, Neulaniementie 2, 70210 Kuopio Finland

HENDREN, ROBERT LEE, JR., academic administrator; b. Reno, Oct. 10, 1925; s. Robert Lee and Aleen (Hill) H.; m. Merlyn Churchill, June 14, 1947; children: Robert Lee IV, Anne Aleen. BA magna cum laude, Coll. Idaho, LLD (hon.); postgrad., Army Univ. Ctr., Oahu, Hawaii. Owner, pres. Hendren's Inc., 1947—; pres. Albertson Coll. Idaho, Caldwell, 1987—; bd. dirs. 1st Interstate Bank Idaho. Trustee Boise (Idaho) Ind. Sch. Dist., chmn. bd. trustees, 1966; chmn. bd. trustees Coll. Idaho, 1980-84; bd. dirs. Mountain View coun. Boy Scouts Am., Boise Retail Merchants, Boise Valley Indsl. Found., Boise Redevel. Agy., Ada County Marriage Counseling, Ada County Planning and Zoning Com.; chmn. bd. Blue Cross Idaho. Recipient Silver and Gold award U. Idaho, Nat. award Sigma Chi. Mem. Boise C. of C. (pres., bd. dirs.), Idaho Sch. Trustees Assn., Masons, KT, Shriners, Rotary (Paul Harris fellow). Home: 3504 Hillcrest Dr Boise ID 83705-4503 Office: Albertson Coll Idaho 2112 Cleveland Blvd Caldwell ID 83605-4432

HENDRICKS, EDWARD DAVID, speaker, educator, consultant; b. Bridgeport, Conn., July 29, 1946; s. James Lyons and Dorothy (James) H.; m. Elizabeth Mary Jessop, Sept. 14, 1968; children: Maureen, David. BS, BA, U. N.C., Charlotte, 1975; MA, SUNY, Albany, 1976. Cert. assn. exec. Contracts adminstr. Eutectic Corp., Flushing, N.Y., 1969-70; contracts adminstr. Interroyal Corp., N.Y.C., 1970-71, regional sales mgr., 1971-72; dir. tech. assistance project Conn. Justice Commn., Hartford, 1976-78; dir. Fairfield County Criminal Justice Planning Commn., Stratford, Conn., 1978-79; dir. adminstrn. ACME, Inc., N.Y.C., 1979-81, v.p., 1981-88, pres., 1988-96; pres. Inst. of Mgmt. Cons., N.Y.C., 1990-92, Coun. Consulting Orgns., N.Y.C., 1989-92, Found. for Excel in Cons. and Mgmt., N.Y.C., 1989-92, Edward D. Hendricks & Assocs., 1995—; dir. ctr. corp. edn. Sacred Heart U., 1999—; bd. dirs. Profl. Svcs. Coun., Washington, N. Am. Mgmt. Coun., N.Y.C.; steering com. UNDP/ILO Ea. Europe Project, Geneva, 1990-95; keynote speaker Escort Internat. Conf., Sofia, Bulgaria, 1990; faculty mem. Leadership Studies Program, Sacred Heart U., 1998—. Author: Student Rights and Responsibilities, 1973, An Insider's Guide To Consulting Success, 1997, Successful Business Networking, 1998, Back on the Right Track, 1999; contbg. author: A History of Consulting, 1987, The Role of Associations, 1990. Campaign coord. James Martin for Congress, Charlotte, 1973; internat. adv. com. mem. U.S. Dept. Commerce, 1994—; treas. Big Bros./Sisters of Fairfield County, Bridgeport, Conn., 1976-78; bd. dirs. United Way of Fairfield County, 1978; permanent deacon Roman Cath. Ch. With USCG, 1965-69. Elected Student Body Pres. U.N.C., Charlotte, 1975; recipient Hon. Mention award NSF, 1972, Acad. Fellowship SUNY, Albany, 1975-76. Fellow Am. Soc. Assn. Execs. (dir. 1991-96); mem. Tri-State Profl. Spkrs. Assn. (treas. 1995-96), N.Y. Soc. Assn. Execs. (pres., bd. dirs. 1986-92, Outstanding Assn. Exec. 1995), Disabled Am. Vets., Mensa, Inst. Mgmt. Cons. (bd. dirs. N.Y. chpt. 1996—). Avocations: speaking, counselling, various sports. Office: 354 Anton St Bridgeport CT 06606-2119

HENDRICKS, GILBERT L., III, physiologist, researcher; b. Richmond, Va., 1959; s. Gilbert L. Jr. and Ina Mae Hendricks. BS in Biology, Pa. State U., 1981, BS in Microbiology, 1984, MS in Physiology, 1989, PhD in Physiology, 1994. Surg. technician Lewistown (Pa.) Hosp., 1982-85; grad. rsch. asst. Pa. State U., University Park, 1987-94; postdoctoral rsch. scientist Biotech. Inst., University Park, 1995-96; instr., rsch. assoc. Pa. State U., University Park, 1998—; advisor to MS candidates Pa. State U., 1993-94, instr. U.S.-AID Egypt project, 1994. Contbr. articles to profl. jours. Mem. SAR, Sons of Confederate Vets., Gamma Sigma Delta. Methodist. Achievements include development of assay to measure hormone production by leukocytes; determined corticotropin releasing factor (CRF) stimulates adrenocorticotropic hormone by chicken leukocytes, identified macrophage as primary leukocyte responsible for immune adrenocorticotropic hormone production. Avocation: basketball.

HENDRICKS, LEONARD D., emergency medicine physician, consultant; b. Chgo., Feb. 29, 1952; s. Leonard D. and Edith V. (Elliott) H.; m. Gail Williams, Aug. 26, 1989. BS in Engring., U. Ill., 1974; MD, U. Wis., 1979. Diplomate Am. Bd. Emergency Medicine, Am. Bd. Forensic Examiners, Am. Bd. Forensic Medicine, Am. Bd. Psychol. Specialties, Am. Acad. Experts in Traumatic Stress subsplty. cert. in forensic traumatology, Am. Bd. Quality Assurance and Utilization Review Physicians with subsplty. cert. in risk mgmt., Am. Bd. Managed Care Medicine. Med. dir. Cuyahoga County Corrections Facility; emergency physician Meridia Huron Hosp., East Cleveland, Ohio; asst. dir. emergency medicine Kaiser Permanente Hosp., Parma, Ohio; emergency physician Western Res. Care System, Youngstown, Ohio; dir. emergency medicine St. Joseph Riverside Hosp., Warren, Ohio; med. dir. emergency medicine Allen Meml. Hosp., Oberlin, Ohio; pres., CEO Avatar Healthcare Svcs.; med dir. urgent care/emergency dept. Peoples Hosp., Mansfield, Ohio; med. dir. emergency dept. Lodi Cmty. Hosp.; cons. Friedman, Domiano and Smith Law Firm, Cleve., Newman & Boyer Law Firm, Chgo., Jaffe & Hough Law Firm, Phila.; regional physician mgr. Birman & Assocs.; instr. emergency medicine Case Western Res. U., Cleve., Northeastern Ohio U., Rootstown; instr. ACLS, Am. Heart Assn.; instr. advanced trauma life support ACS; instr. pediatric ALS, neonatal resuscitation, Am. Acad. Pediatrics. Fellow Am. Bd. Forensic Examiners, Am. Coll. Medicine, Am. Coll. Emergency Physicians, Am. Acad. Experts in Traumatic Stress; mem. Am. Coll. Physician Execs., Soc. Acad. Emergency Medicine.

HENDRICKS, NATHAN VANMETER, III, lawyer; b. Decatur, Ga., Dec. 16, 1943; s. Nathan VanMeter and Ella L. (Ward) H.; m. kathryn A. Barnes, Aug. 19, 1972; children: Nathan VanMeter, Seaton Grantland. BA, Washington and Lee U., 1966, LLB, 1969. Bar: Ga., 1970. Practiced in Swift, Currie, McGhee and Hiers, Atlanta, 1969—, assoc., 1969-70; assoc. Henning, Chambers and Mabry, Atlanta, 1970-71; assoc. Redfern, Butler and Morgan, Atlanta, 1971-73, ptnr., 1973-77; ptnr. Cobb, Hyre, Hendricks & Ferguson, Atlanta, 1978-91; pvt. practice Atlanta, 1991—. Contbr. numerous articles to profl. jours. and publs. Chmn. Younger Lawyers Com. Campaign for mayor, Atlanta, 1972, re-election campaign for chmn. of Fulton County Bd. Commnrs., 1986; active host com. 1988 Dem. Nat. Conv.; mem. High Mus. of Art, group leader ann. fund-raising campaign, 1973-75, chmn. young careers group, 1972-73, sec. young men's round table, 1974-75; active ann. fund-raising campaign Atlanta Symphony Orch. Assn., 1977-78, Atlanta Arts Alliance, 1977-79, Atlanta Botanical Garden, 1986-88; bd. dirs. Atlanta Hunter-Jumper Classic, 1978-79, pres., 1979; bd. dirs. Save America's Vital Environment, sec. 1971-74; bd. dirs. Merrie-Woode Found., v.p., 1978-79, chmn., pres., 1981-93, exec. com. Give Wildlife a Chance fund, Ga. Dept. Natural Resources, 1988. Mem. Am., Atlanta (mem. real estate sect. 1972—, com. 1978) bar assns., State Bar of Ga. (mem. real estate sect. 1972—), Lawyers Club Atlanta, Washington and Lee U. Alumni Assn. (dri. 1972-82, pres. Atlanta chpt. 1973-75, Law Sch. Class agt. 1999—), , Ansley Golf Club, Piedmont Driving Club, Wildcat Cliffs Country, The Nine O'Clocks Club, N.C. Soc. of the Cin., Beta Theta Pi, Phi Delta Phi. Home: 230 The Prado NE Atlanta GA 30309-3336 Office: 6085 Lake Forrest Dr NW Ste 200 Atlanta GA 30328-3846

HENDRICKS, SUSAN COSTINETT, transportation planner; b. North Shields, Eng., Oct. 5, 1969; came to U.S., 1974; d. Patrick Joseph Costinett and Joyce Elaine Johnstone; m. Gary Linn Hendricks, Mar. 17, 1990; children: Caitlin Danielle, Jessica Morgan, Emily Mozina. BS in Math. and Econs., U. Wash., 1995. Technician Barton-Aschman Assocs., Pasadena, Calif., 1988-90, KJS Assocs., Inc., Bellevue, Wash., 1990-95; assoc. KJS Assocs., Inc., Bellevue, 1995-97; sr. assoc. KJS Assocs., Inc., 5, 1998-99, prin. assoc., 2000—; software developer Fed. Hwys. Adminstrn., Washington, 1996-2000; cons. Municipality of Anchorage, 1997-2000; spkr. in field. Contbr. articles to profl. jours. Troop leader Girls Scouts USA, South King County, Wash., 1999-2000. Mem. PTA, Transp. Rsch. Bd., Inst. Transp. Engrs., Women's Transp. Seminar. Roman Catholic. Avocations: crafts, gardening, cooking, teaching children. E-mail: susan@kjsa.com. Fax: 425-746-6611. Home: 14051 SE 195th Pl Renton WA 98058-9418 Office: KJS Assocs Inc 914 140th Ave NE Bellevue WA 98005-3482

HENDRICKSE, RALPH GEORGE, medical educator; b. Cape Town, South Africa, Nov. 5, 1926; s. William George and Johanna Theresa (Dennis) H.; m. Begum Abdurahman; 5 children. MB, BChir, U. Cape Town, South Africa, 1948, MD, 1957, DSc in Medicine (hon.), 1998. Staff mem. McCord Zulu Hosp., Durban, South Africa, 1949-54; sr. registrar Univ. Coll. Hosp., Ibadan, Nigeria, 1955-57; lectr., sr. lectr. U. Ibadan, 1957-62, prof., head dept. pediat., 1962-69, dir. Inst. Child Health, 1964-69; prof. tropical pediat. and internat. child health U. Liverpool, Eng., 1969-91, dean Sch. of Tropical Medicine, 1988-91, ret., prof. emeritus, 1991—; cons. to Fed. Ministry Health, Nigeria, 1965-69; founder, life mem., former v.p. Paediatric Assn. of Nigeria, 1969—; mem. Tropical Medicine Bd. of the MRC of U.K., 1977-81. Founder, editor-in-chief Annals of Tropical Pediat., 1981—; editor-in-chief, author: (textbook) Pediatrics in the Tropics, 1991; prodr. (film) Sickle Cell Anemia in Nigerian Children, 1964. Rockefeller fellow, 1961-62, Heinz (sr.) fellow Brit. Ped. Assn., 1961. Fellow Royal Soc. Tropical Medicine and Hygiene (mem. coun. 1978-80, 85-87), Royal Coll. Physicians (Edinburgh, London, Frederick Murgatroyd Meml. prize 1970), Royal Coll. Pediat. and Child Health (hon. founder 1996); mem. Brit. Pediat. Assn. (mem. acad. bd. 1983-86, Heinz fellow 1961, hon. membership in Recognition of Outstanding Contbns. to Pediat. and Child Health award 1995), Internat. Pediat. Assn. (adv. expert on tropical pediat. 1986—). Avocations: photography, sketching, cycling, swimming, theatre. Home: 25 Riverbank Rd, Heswall Wirral Liverpool L60 4SQ, England

HENDRICKSON, ALAN BRYCE, commercial banker; b. Glen Cove, N.Y., Dec. 9, 1945; s. Charles John and Adela Bromfield (Gunthel) H.; m. Jean Edith Peschenski, Nov. 25, 1967 (div. 1985); m. Stella M. Sarasy, Mar. 2, 1991; children—Michael A., Laura J. Student Wake Forest U., 1963-66; B.A. in Econs., C.W. Post Coll., 1966-67. Asst. v.p. Franklin Nat. Bank and European Am. Bank, N.Y.C., 1967-74; v.p. Mfrs. Hanover Trust Co., N.Y.C., 1974-85. Pres. Lynbrook chpt. Am. Cancer Soc., 1972-73, mem. theater com. Melville chpt. (N.Y.), 1975-80; coach Syosset Soccer Club (N.Y.), 1985-87; 1st v.p. Bank Leumi, 1985-87; exec. v.p., COO, CFO Canover, 1987-96,treas, 1978; coach Syosset Little League, 1978-80; mem. adv. com. Mineola chpt. Am. Heart Assn., 1978-80. Mem. N.Y. State Soc. C.P.A.s, Syosset C. of C. (bd. dirs. 1975-78, treas. 1976-77). Republican. Episcopalian; sr. v.p., dir. purchasing & contracts, Salomon Smith Barney, 1996-99, purchasing & operations consultant, 2000—Home: 19 Wilshire Dr Syosset NY 11791-2923 Address: Canover Ind Inc 25 Hickory Rd Woodmere NY 11598-1829

HENDRICKSON, CHRIS THOMPSON, civil and environmental engineering educator, researcher; b. Oakland, Calif., Mar. 31, 1950; s. Harold Thompson and E. Jean (Loomis) H.; m. Kathleen Devine, May 28, 1977; children: Andrew, Thomas, Peter. BS, MS, Stanford U., 1973; PhB, Oxford U., 1975; PhD, MIT, 1978. Asst. prof. Carnegie-Mellon U., Pitts., 1978-83, assoc. prof., 1983-87, prof., 1987—; assoc. dean Carnegie Inst. Tech., 1991-96, Duquesne Light Co. prof. Engring., 1996—, head dept., 1996—. Author: (with others) Transportation Investment and Pricing Principles, 1984, Project Management for Construction, 1989, Knowledge-based Process Planning for Construction and Manufacturing, 1989, Computer Integrated Building Design, 1993; editor Jour. Transp. Engring.; contbr. articles to profl. publs. Bd. mem. St. Edmund's Acad., Pitts. Recipient C.E. Ladd Rsch. award Carnegie Inst. Tech., 1979; Rhodes scholar, 1973. Mem. ASCE (com. chmn. 1983—, chmn. urban transp. divsn. 1989-90, dept. heads exec. com. 2000-2002, Huber Rsch. award 1989, Masters Transp. Engring. award 1994), Am. Econ. Assn., Transp. Rsch. Bd. (com. chmn. 1989-96), Phi Beta Kappa, Tau Beta Pi. Home: 6933 Rosewood St Pittsburgh PA 15208-2638 Office: Carnegie Mellon U Pittsburgh PA 15213-3890

HENDRICKSON, WILLIAM GEORGE, business executive; b. Plainview, Minn., May 31, 1918; s. Clarence and Hildegarde (Heaser) H.; m. Virginia M. Price, Sept. 1, 1942; children: Robert, Thomas, Donald, Julie Ann. BS, St. Mary's Coll., Winona, Minn., 1939; MS, U. Detroit, 1941; PhD, U. Wis., 1946; D Humanities, St. Mary's U., Winona, Minn., 1991. Scientist Wis. Alumni Research Found., Madison, 1946-54, dir. devel., 1954-61; v.p. Ayerst Labs. div. Am. Home Products Corp., N.Y.C., 1961-67, exec. v.p., 1967-69; group v.p. Am. Home Products Corp., N.Y.C., 1969-80; chmn. emeritus bd. St. Jude Med., Inc., St. Paul; bd. dirs. emeritus Rsch. Corp. Techs., Tucson, chmn. bd. dirs. IntelliNet, Naples, Fla. Mem. Am. Chem. Soc., N.Y. Acad. Scis., Country Club N.C., Royal Poinciana Golf Club, Sigma Xi. Republican. Roman Catholic.

HENDRIKSE, FREDERIK, ophthalmologist, educator; b. Singapore, Sept. 1, 1947; s. Willem Eduard H.; m. Hilda Dykstra, Jan. 9, 1973; children: Karin, Jeroen, Madzy. MD, Erasmus U., 1973; PhD of Ophthamology, U. Nymegen, 1981. Diplomate European Bd. Ophthalmology. Asst. prof., prof. ophthalmology U. Nymegen, The Netherlands, 1986-93; prof. ophthalmology, dept. chair U. Maastricht, The Netherlands, 1993—, chmn. Eye Rsch. Inst., 1997—. Contbr. more than 130 articles to profl. jours. Mem. European Assn. Vision Rsch., The Vitreous Soc., Am. Acad. Ophthalmology, French Soc. Ophthalmology, Club Jules gonin, Internat. Xerophthalmia Club, South African Vitreoretinal Soc. (hon.). Avocations: music, sailing, rowing. Home: Leystenstraat 24, 6325 AR Berg en Terblyt The Netherlands Office: Univ Maastricht Eye Clinic, PO Box 5800, 6202 AZ Maastricht The Netherlands

HENDRIKSE, GEORGE W., educator; b. The Netherlands, Nov. 1, 1958; s. Aegidius and Cor (Holtackers) H. BA, Tilburg U., 1981; MA, U. Pitts., 1983, PhD, 1988. Research asst. Tilburg U., The Netherlands, 1980-81; teaching asst. U. Pitts., 1981-83, teaching fellow, 1983-86; visiting prof. U. Limburg, The Netherlands, 1986-88; asst. prof. Tilburg U., The Netherlands, 1988-91, assoc. prof., 1992-96; prof. Erasmus U., Rotterdam, 1996—. Contbr. articles to profl. jours. Recipient EARIE Essay Competition Prize European Assn. for Research in Indsl. Econs., 1989, Owens Fellowship Owens Found., 1986. Mem. Owens Found., European Assn. for Research in Indsl. Econs., Am. Econ. Assn., Rand Jour. Econs. Home: Anna Paulownahof 202, Heikantstraat 73, 9290 Overmer Belgium Office: EUR, PO Box 1738 Office F3-51, 3000DR Rotterdam The Netherlands

HENDRIKS-JANSEN, HORST JURGEN, author; b. Surabaja, Indonesia, Sept. 13, 1938; s. Jan Hendrik and Margaret Sophy (Sewig) H.; m. Fotini Kafiri, Feb. 29, 1967. BSc, MIT, 1961; MA, Sussex U., Falmer, U.K., 1991, PhD, 1995. Freelance author/lectr. Spain, 1961-67, Greece, 1967-71, U.K., 1991—; lectr./rschr. London, 1971-79; dir. Michael Jansen Ltd., Surrey, 1979-91. Author: Environmental Design for Handicapped Children, 1976, Catching Ourselves in the Act, 1996; contbr. articles to profl. jours. Avocations: reading, listening to music.

HENDRY, JEAN SHARON, psychopharmacologist; b. Hanover, Pa., June 2, 1947; d. Clarence Richard and Frances Lee (Manger) Shaver; 1 child, Robert Andrew. BA, Hunter Coll., 1976; MA, Princeton U., 1978; PhD, 1980. Rsch. asst. Hunter Coll., N.Y.C., 1974-75; asst. instr. Princeton U., Princeton, N.J., 1976-78; post doctoral fellow Med. Coll. Va., Richmond, 1979-82; psychology instr. U. Richmond, 1985-86, Pa. State U., Media, Pa., 1987-88; guest reviewer various psychological and pharmacological jours. Contbr. numerous articles to profl. jours. Active Nat. Trust for Historic Preservation, Arts Coun. of Moore County, Colonial Williamsburg Found., World Wildlife Assn., The Humane Soc. of the U.S. Mem. APA, U.S Equestrian Team, Am. Psychol. Soc., Nat. Wildlife Fedn., Assn. Princeton Grad. Alumni, Am. Horseshow Assn., Nature Conservancy, Nat. Audubon Soc., Sigma Xi. Avocations: horse breeding, training, and showing, working out, reading, photography.

HENEMAN, ROBERT LLOYD, management educator; b. Mpls., Jan. 17, 1955; s. Herbert G. Jr. and Jane R. Heneman; m. Renee Brausch, Sept. 9, 1989. BA, Lake Forest Coll., 1977; MA, U. Ill., 1979; PhD, Mich. State U., 1984. Personnel specialist Pacific Gas & Electric Co., San Francisco, 1979-80; assoc. prof. Mgmt. Ohio State U., Columbus, 1984—, dir. grad. programs in labor and human resources. Author: Merit Pay, 1992, Staffing Organizations, 1994, 3d edit., 2000, Business-Driven Compensation Policies, 2000. Mem. ch. coun. Holy Trinity Luth. Ch., Columbus. Mem. Acad. of Mgmt. (exec. com. human resource divsn. 1988-93, program chair 1992-93, divsn. chair 1994-95), Am. Compensation Assn. (rsch. com. 1992-93, edn. com. 1993-94, acad. ptnr. network, 1997—, cert. program fac., 1992—), Phi Kappa Phi, Sigma Iota Epsilon, Psi Chi. Home: 4815 Lytfield Dr Dublin OH 43017-2174

HENES, SAMUEL ERNST, lawyer; b. Oberlin, Ohio, Jan. 28, 1937; s. Ernst Louis and Martha Hannah (Artz) H. A.B. with honors, Cornell U., 1959; LL.B., Harvard U., 1962. Bar: Ohio, 1962. Assoc. Arter & Hadden, Cleve., 1962-70, ptnr., 1971-89. Trustee Musart Soc., Cleve., 1980—, pres. 1985-94; trustee Young Audiences Greater Cleve., Inc., 1982-85, George P. Bickford Found., 1981-90; hon. trustee So. Lorain County Hist. Soc., Wellington, Ohio, 1988—. Served to 1st lt. U.S. Army, 1963-65. Mem. ABA, Cleve. Bar Assn., Ohio State Bar Assn. Republican. Methodist. Club: Rowfant (Cleve.) (sec. 1985-89). Avocations: book collecting; amateur harpsichordist; swimming; travel;. Home: 13605 Shaker Blvd Apt 2B Cleveland OH 44120-1503

HENG, DONALD JAMES, JR., lawyer; b. Mpls., July 12, 1944; s. Donald James and Catharine Amelia (Strom) H.; m. Kathleen Ann Bailey, Sept. 2, 1967; 1 child, Francesca Remy. BA cum laude, Yale U., 1967; JD magna cum laude, Minn., 1971. Bar: Calif. 1971, U.S. Dist. Ct. (no. dist.) Calif. 1971, U.S. Ct. Appeals (9th cir.) 1971. Assoc. Brobeck, Phleger & Harrison, San Francisco, 1971-73, ptnr., 1978-90; atty.-adviser Office Internat. Tax Counsel, Dept. Treasury, Washington, 1973-75; pvt. practice law San Francisco, 1990—; lectr., writer on tax-related subjects. Note and comment editor Minn. Law Rev., 1970-71. Co-recipient award for outstanding performance Am. Lawyer Mag., 1981; Fulbright scholar, Italy, 1967-68.

Mem. ABA, Calif. Bar Assn., Oakland Mus. Assn. (pres. 1985-87, bd. dirs. 1983-89), Mus. Soc. San Francisco, Fine Arts Mus. (bd. dirs. 1989-90), Order Coif. Republican. Congregationalist. Office: 388 Market St Ste 500 San Francisco CA 94111-5313

HENG, LEE-KWANG, opthalmologist; b. Singapore, July 27, 1957; parents Siak-Kwang Heng and Wee-Chee Lee. MB, BS, Nat. U. Singapore, 1981. Intern Singapore Gen. Hosp., 1981-82; med. officer Singapore Armed Forces, 1982-84; resident in ophthalmology Singapore Gen. Hosp., 1985-86; professorial fellow Moorfields Eye Hosp., U.K., 1986-87; registrar Singapore Gen. Hosp., 1987-89; sr. registrar Nat. U. Hosp., Singapore, 1989-91; vitreoretinal fellow UCLA, 1992; cons. Singapore Nat. Eye Cen., 1993-94, Mt. Elizabeth/Gleneagles Hosp., Singapore, 1994—; vis. cons. Singapore Nat. Eye Cen., 1994—; dir. Specialist Eye Cons., Singapore, 1994—; lectr. Nat. U. Singapore, 1989-93. Edtl. bd. Asia Pacific Jour. Ophthalmology., 1990-94. Physician Home for the Aged, Singapore, 1991—. Cpt. Singapore Armed Forces, 1982-84. Fellow Am. Acad. Ophthalmology, Royal Coll. Surgeons, Royal Coll. Ophthalmologists. Avocations: music, tennis, history. Home: 34 Keris Dr, 1545 Singapore Singapore Office: Mt Elizabeth Hosp, 3 Mt Elizabeth, 0922 Singapore Singapore

HENGARTNER, HANS, immunologist, educator; b. Zuchenriet, Switzerland, Feb. 26, 1944; s. Hans and Paula (Schlauri) H.; m. Marlies Haag, July 23, 1971; children: Daniela, Stefan, Corinne. Diploma in Biology, Fed. Inst. Tech. ETH, Zurich, Switzerland, 1968, PhD, 1973. With Swiss Army, 1967-91; postdoc. fellow Cambridge (Eng.) U., 1973-75; mem. Basel (Switzerland) Inst. Immunology, 1975-80, Inst. Exptl. Immunology, U. Hosp., Zurich, 1980—; prof. immunology U. and ETH Zurich, 1989—; mem. Swiss Rsch. Coun., 1996—; chmn. dept. Biol. ETH, Zurich, 2000. Contbr. articles to profl. jours. Recipient Cloetta prize Cloetta Found., Zurich, 1988, Ernst Jung prize Jung Stiftung, Hamburg, Germany, 1997, Otto Nägeli prize Bonizzi-Theiler Found., Bern, Switzerland, 1998. mem. Am. Soc. Immunology, Swiss Soc. Immunology, German Soc. Immunology, Rotary. Avocations: jogging, skiing, golfing. Home: Oberrenggstrasse 15, 8135 Langnau Switzerland Office: Inst Exp Immunology U Hosp, Schmelzbergstr 12, 8091 Zurich Switzerland

HENGELS, CHARLES FRANCIS, management consultant, educator; b. Oak Park, Ill., Sept. 4, 1948; s. Charles Leo and Vivian Marguerite (Brust) H. BS in Econs. with distinction and honors, Purdue U., 1970; BA in Polit. Sci. with distinction and honors, 1970, MS in Edn., 1976, MS in Sociology, 1978. Cert. secondary tchr. Staff resident, tchg. asst. Purdue U., West Lafayette, Ind., 1975-78; dir., exec. v.p. Am. Med. Bldgs., Milw., 1978-80; exec. v.p. Sys. Planning Corp., Arlington, 1980—; bd. dirs. Print Services Group, Reston, Va.; cons. Ind. Council for Econ. Edn., West Lafayette, 1976-77. Author: (poetry) America, 1971 (Freedom Found. award 1971). Regional dir. Com. for Responsible Health Care, Washington, 1978-80; dep. campaign mgr. Virginians for Zummalt U.S. Sen. campaing, Richmond, 1976. Lt. spl duty (intelligence) USN, 1970-74. Decorated Navy Achievement medal with Combat V (2), Combat Action ribbon; recipient Gen. Dynamics award Gen. Dynamics Corp., 1970, chgo. tribune award, 1970; named Disting. Naval Grad., 1970. Mem. Purdue Alumni Assn., Mensa, Kappa Delta Pi, Alpha Kappa Delta, Pi Sigma Alpha, Phi Kappa Phi, delta Rho Kappa, Phi Eta Sigma. Republican. Roman Catholic. Avocations: athletics, writing, teaching. Home: 6135 Wellington Commons Dr Alexandria VA 22310-5307 Office: System Planning Corp 1000 Wilson Blvd Arlington VA 22209-3901

HENGEVELD, MICHIEL WILLEM, psychiatrist; b. Ede, The Netherlands, Feb. 8, 1945; s. Barthold Hengeveld and Elisabeth Soeters; m. Janny Hess, Dec. 15, 1975 (div. 1990); children: Willemyn, Eva; m. Liesbeth Van Londen, Mar. 20, 1992; children: Paul Johan, Hans Maurits, Simon Benjamin, Naomi Joan. MD, U. Amsterdam, The Netherlands, 1971; PhD, Leiden (The Netherlands) U., 1983. Chief psychiat. cons. liaison svc. Leiden U. Hosp., 1979-96; prof. med. sexology U. Med. Ctr., Utrecht, The Netherlands, 1988—; chief psychiat. inpatient unit Leiden U. Med. Ctr., 1981-85, chief psychiat. outpatient svc., 1988—. Author: Self-help for erectile problems, 1989, 2d edit., 1994, Medicine and love, 1989, Management of Suicide Attempters Presented to General Hospitals, 1994, The Psychiatric Evaluation, 1997; editor: The psychiatrist in the general hospital, 1984, Psychiatry in somatic practice, 1997. Mem. Netherlands Consortium Cons. Liaison Psychiatry (chmn. 1983-96), Netherlands Assn. Impotence Rsch. (sec. 1986-91), Netherlands Assn. Psychiatry (mem. com. rsch. quality 1991-96, chmn. sect. sexology 1991—), Internat. Acad. Sex Rsch. Office: Leiden U Med Ctr Dept Psych, PO Box 9600, 2300 RC Leiden The Netherlands

HENGGE-ARONIS, REGINE, biology educator; b. Trossingen, Germany, Nov. 2, 1956; d. Felix and Elisabeth (Mayer) Hengge; m. Dimitris Aronis; children: Elisabeth-Maria, Emmanuel. Diploma in biology, U. Konstanz, Germany, 1981, D of Natural Scis., 1986, privat dozent, 1994. Cert. in biology. Postdoctoral fellow Princeton U., 1987-88; from asst. prof. to assoc. prof. U. Konstanz, 1988-98; prof. Free U. Berlin, 1998—. Invited reviewer: (sci. jours.) Genes and Devel., Jour. Molecular Biology, Embo Jour., Molecular Microbiology; mem. editl. bd. Jour. Bacteriology, 1995—, reviewer. Student fellow Studienstiftung des Deutschen Volkes, 1976-81, grad. student fellow, 1984-85, postgrad. fellow Boehringer Ingelheim Fonds, 1985-87; recipient dozenten-stipendium Fonds der Chemischen Industrie, 1995, Landesforschungspreis, State of Baden-Württemberg, 1996, Gottfried-Wilhelm-Leibniz prize Deutsche Forschungsgemeinschaft, 1998, rsch. stipend, 1987-88. Mem. AAAS, German Soc. for Hygiene and Microbiology (Förderpreis 1993), Am. Soc. for Microbiology, Vereinigung für Allgemeine und Angewandte Mikrobiologie, Gesellschaft Deutscher Naturforscher und Arzte, German Soc. Genetics. Fax: (49)-30-838-3118. Office: Free U Berlin, Konigin-Luise-Str 12-16a, 14195 Berlin Germany

HENGSTLER, JAN GEORG, toxicologist, researcher; b. Heidelberg, Germany, July 5, 1965; s. Klaus and Brigitte (Wagner) H. Dr.rer.pol., U. Mainz, Germany, 1991, Habilitation, 1998. Rsch. project mgr. Inst. Toxicology, Mainz, 1990—, study dir. test facility mutagenicity in vitro and in vivo, 1994—. Pub., editor: Control Mechanisms of Carcinogenesis, 1996; contbr. articles to profl. jours. Recipient Innovation prize Rheinland Pfalz, 1999. Home: Dominikanerstr 8, 55131 Mainz Germany Office: Inst Toxicology U Mainz, Obere Zahlbacher Str 67, 55131 Mainz Germany

HENIGSON, ANN PEARL, freelance writer, songwriter, lyricist; b. N.Y.C., Jan. 20, 1946; d. Leo and Lillian Shires; m. David Henigson, Oct. 23, 1988 (dec. July 1993); stepchildren: Helaine, Kenneth, Keith. Student, U. Miami, Fla., 1964-68, Miami-Dade Jr. Coll. Author: (song/poem) American Flag, 1986, pub. in Congressional Record, 1990, Dreamin' Reality, 1986, Parents, 1986, Miss Liberty, 1986, Eternal Love, 1986, (Looking at You) Face of Love, 1986, Book Without a Cover, 1986, 8 Days of Hanukkah, 1986, Songwriter, 1986, Hanukkah Sing Along, 1988, Oh Baby, Oh Baby, 1991, Hold Me Tight, 1995, Democracy, Democracy, (Freedom, Freedom) 1995, and numerous others; (cartoons/drawings) Ducks/Birds, 1988. Activist, lobbyist; candidate bd. govs. State of Fla., (non-attorney) 1993; 1st female usherette Temple Israel of Greater Miami High Holy Day Svcs.; mem. Civic League Miami Beach, 1976-89; patron Temple Emanu-El Cultural Series, 1989-90; mem. Friends of Bass Mus., 1991; del. nat. Dem. party, 1970s. Mem. ASCAP, Soc. Profl. Journalists, Quill and Scroll, Toastmasters International (named competent toastmaster), Tiger Bay Club, 1974-91, Sigma Delta Chi. Avocations: football, baseball, stamp collecting, travel, designing jewelry.

HENINGTON, DAVID MEAD, library director; b. El Dorado, Ark., Aug. 16, 1929; s. Bud Henry and Lucile Check (Scranton) H.; m. Barbara Jean Gibson, June 2, 1956; children—Mark David, Gibson Mead, Paul Billins. BA, U. Houston, 1951; MS in L.S., Columbia U., 1956. Young adult libr. Bklyn. Pub. Libr., 1956-58; head lit. and history dept. Dallas Pub. Libr., 1958, asst. dir., 1962-67; dir. Waco (Tex.) Pub. Libr., 1958-62, Houston Pub. Libr., 1967-95. Served with USAF, 1951-55. Council on Library Resources fellow, 1970-71; recipient Liberty Bell award Houston Bar Assn., 1976. Mem. ALA, AIA (hon. mem. Tex. chpt.), Am. Mgmt. Assn., Tex. Libr. Assn. (Libr. of Yr. 1976, Disting. Svc. award 1993), Philos. Soc. Methodist. Home: 6225 San Felipe St Houston TX 77057-2809

HENKE, JÜRGEN, institute administrator, forensic consultant; b. Lauenburg, Germany, Nov. 17, 1948; s. Fritz and Kate (Borkenhagen) H.; m. Lotte Hansen, June 16, 1975. PhD, U. Kiel, Germany, 1974. Asst. Red Cross BTS, Baden-Baden, Germany, 1974-79; asst., serologist Inst. Forensic Medicine U. Düsseldorf, Germany, 1978-84; head of lab. Inst. Blood Group Rsch., Düsseldorf, 1985—, Institut fuer Blutgruppenforschung, Cologne, Germany, 1990—; mem. commn. for parentage testing guidelines Robert-Koch-Inst., Berlin, 1995, Fed. Chamber Physicians, 1999; v.p. Internat. Congress Med. Toxicology and Legal Medicine Experts, 1999. Author: Neue Ergebnisse in der forensischen Serologie, 1984; editor: DNA-Polymorphisms in Forensics and Medicine, 1990, Genome Research, 1990, Molecular Biology in Tumor Research, 1991, Humanbiologische Spuren, 1995. Served with German Army, 1967-68. Office: Inst Blutgruppenforschung, 50501 Cologne Germany

HENKE, ROBERT JOHN, lawyer; b. Hammond, Ind., Mar. 25, 1958; s. Robert L. and Lucille Adeana (Wright) H.; m. Jo Ellen Hurst, Mar. 24, 1979; children: Emily Jo, Robert James. Student, Ind. U., 1982-84; BA cum laude, Trinity Coll., 1986; JD with high distinction, Valparaiso U., 1990. Bar: Ind. 1990, Ill. 1990, U.S. Dist. Ct. (no. and so. dists.) Ind. 1990, U.S. Dist. Ct. (no. dist.) Ill. 1990. Assoc. atty. Schlyer & Assoc., Griffith, Ind., 1990-92; judicial clk. Lake County Ind. Criminal Divsn., Crown Point, Ind., 1992 ; atty. Carr & Henke, Portage, Ind., 1993-95; pvt. practice Portage, Ind., 1995—. Contbr. chpts. to books on trial practice and discovery. Sr. pastor Chapel of the Dunes, Gary, Ind., 1986-98; sub-deacon Holy Resurrection Orthodox Ch., Hobart, Ind., 1998-99; priest St. John Chrysostom Orthodox Ch., Ft. Wayne, Ind., 1999 . Hoosier State scholar State of Ind., 1976, Law scholar, Valparaiso U. Sch. Law, 1989-90. Mem. ABA, Ill. Bar Assn., Ind. Bar Assn., Lake County Bar Assn., Federalist Soc., Jus Vitia, Delta Theta Phi. Republican. Orthodox. Avocations: woodworking, church history researcher, hunting, fishing, power lifting. Office: 5955 Central Ave Portage IN 46368-2945

HENKE, SHAUNA NICOLE, police dispatcher, small business owner; b. San Bernardino, Calif., Oct. 25, 1966; d. Gary Duane and Pamela Denyne (Duke) H. BA, U. San Francisco, 1988. Cert. police officer std. and tng. dispatcher, Calif.; internat. telecommunicator instr. tng. cert. Assn. Pub. Safety Comm. Ofcls. Pub. rels. dir. Sta. KUSF Radio, San Francisco, 1986; theater and recreational asst. Hamilton Field Recreation, Novato, Calif., 1986-89; morning asst., newswriter Sta. KTID Radio, San Rafael, Calif., 1987-88; dispatcher Warren Security, San Rafael, Calif., 1988-89; pub. safety dispatcher Twin Cities Police Dept., Larkspur/Corte Madera, Calif., 1989-94; family svc. worker Head Start, Bogalusa, La., 1994-95; police dispatcher Mandeville (La.) Police Dept., 1995-96, Bogalusa (La.) Police Dept., 1996—; EMS Dispatcher Lifeline EMS, Bogalusa, 1998-2000; co-owner Time After Time Designs. Mem. St. Matthew's Episcopal Churchwomen, Washington Parish. Mem. Assn. Pub. Safety Ofcls. Internat., La. Indian Heritage Assn., Medicine Wheel Intertribal Soc. (sec., co-treas., newsletter editor, genealogy chair). E-mail: rosedown66@yahoo.com. Office: Bogalusa Police Dept 214 Arkansas Ave Bogalusa LA 70427-3810

HENKEL, ANDREAS WOLFRAM, biochemist, researcher; b. Sinn, Hessen, Germany, Feb. 20, 1961; s. Horst and Gerda Lieselotte (Bartel) H.; m. Maria Kerstin Hartmann, Oct. 6, 1990; 1 child, Julia. Diploma in biology, U. Frankfurt, Germany, 1987, PhD in Biochemistry, 1991. Cert. radiation safety officer. Postdoctorate U. Hosp., Marburg, Germany, 1991-92, U. Colo. Health Scis. Ctr., Denver, 1992-95; group leader Max-Planck-Inst. for Med. Rsch., Heidelberg, 1995—; sci. cons. U. Colo., Denver, 1995; lectr. in field. Contbr. articles to sci. jours. PhD stipendee German Scholarship Found., 1989-90; fellowship grantee Human Frontier Sci. Program Orgn., Strasbourg, France, 1993-95. Mem. Internat. Soc. Neurochemistry, German Soc. Biochemistry, Am. Biophys. Soc. Avocations: computer programming, arachnology, astronomy, traveling, chaos theory. Home: Hauheckenweg 17, 69123 Heidelberg Germany Office: Max-Planck-Inst Med Rsch, Jahnstrasse 29, 69120 Heidelberg Germany

HENKEL, ARTHUR JOHN, investment banker; b. Bklyn., Aug. 27, 1945; s. Arthur John and Catherine Rita (Burns) H.; m. Coralee S. Olicker, Sept. 27, 1981; children: Andrea Rae, Austin Olicker, Reid Baras, Kyra Leigh. USPHS trainee U. Chgo. Hosps., Clinics, 1969-71, adminstrv. asst. fiscal affairs, 1971; cons. Booz, Allen Hamilton, Inc., N.Y.C., 1972-74; dir. ambulatory ops. New Eng. Med. Ctr. Hosp., Boston, 1974-75, dir. ambulatory care, 1975-77; assoc. mcpl. fin. dept. Kidder, Peabody and Co., Inc., N.Y.C., 1977-78, asst. v.p., 1978-79, v.p., 1979-80, mng. officer health fin. group, 1980-87, dir., 1984-87, mng. dir., 1986-87; v.p. mcpl. fin. dept. Goldman, Sachs & Co., N.Y.C., 1987-95; v.p. Shattuck Hammond Ptnrs., Inc., N.Y.C., 1995-96, mng. dir., 1996-98; mng. dir. Bear, Stearns & Co., Inc., N.Y.C., 1998—; instr. cmty. health Tufts Sch. Medicine; mem. exec. com. alumni coun. U. Chgo. Program Hosp. Adminstrn., 1972-76; spl. teaching cons. fin. evaluation hosp. capital projects HEW, 1973. Chmn. investments com. Better Boys Found./ NFL Players Assn. awards banquet, 1979, 80—. Recipient Mary Bachmeyer award U. Chgo., 1971, citation Commonwealth Mass., 1976.

HENKEL, MALTE, physics educator; b. Oberhausen, Germany, Jan. 2, 1960; s. Rudolf Georg Walter and Ilse (Hedemann) H.; m. Maria do Rosário de Lima Catalão Henkel. Diploma in physics, U. Bonn (Germany), 1984, D of Physics, 1987. Asst. Saclay, France, 1988-89, U. Geneva (Switzerland), 1989-93; chargé de cours U. Fribourg (Switzerland), 1993; rsch. assoc. U. Oxford (Eng.), 1993-95; prof. physics U. Nancy (France), 1995—. Author: Introduction to Conformal Invariance, 1993, Conformal Invariance and Critical Phenomena, 1999. Mem. Student Mission Germany, Marburg, 1986-88. Recipient Ann. prize of German/Israeli Minerva Found., 1987. Mem. German Phys. Soc., Swiss Phys. Soc., French Phys. Soc. Avocations: history, writing, walking, tennis, arts. Office: Lab Physique Matériaux, U Nancy I BP 239, F 54506 Nancy France

HENKEN, BERNARD SAMUEL, clinical psychologist, speech pathologist; b. Everett, Mass., May 30, 1919; s. Issac Edward and Sarah B. (Shatzman) H.; m. Charlotte Popovsky, Dec. 20, 1953; children: Karen Beth, Donna Michele. Student, Boston Coll., 1938-41; BS, Harvard U., 1947; MS, Purdue U., 1950; D. Sci. in Psychology, Calvin Coolidge Coll., 1955. Lic. psychologist, cert. sch. psychologist, cert. rehab. counselor, lic. speech pathologist, Mass.; diplomate Am. Assn. Clin. Counselors. Psychologist Carney Hosp., Boston, 1950-51; dir. speech pathology, psychologist Audiology Ctr., Lynn, Mass., 1951-56; psychologist, chief clin. counseling svcs. Brusch Med. Ctr., Cambridge, Mass., 1956-80; speech pathologist Mass. Gen. Hosp., Boston, 1951-52; speech pathologist, sch. psychologist Everett Pub. Schs., 1955-85; psychologist Rescue Inc., 1959-71, v.p., 1972-74; psychologist, clin. counselor North Shore Children's Hosp., Salem, Mass., 1966-74; psychologist Medford (Mass.) Pediatric Assocs., 1974-94; prof. psychology Calvin Collidge Coll., Boston, 1958-69; lectr. psychology Lawrence Meml. Hosp., Medford, Mass., 1975-77, univ. extension courses Harvard U., 1960-68; psychologist Alfano Med. Inst., Melrose, Mass., 1956-64; guest lectr. Duke U. Med. Ctr., 1965, 72; co-chair symposium on clin. counseling and medicine Tufts U., 1974. Contbr. articles to profl. jours.; creator Henken Operator Safety Evaluation Technique; editor Clin. Counseling Bulletin, 1970-84. Cpl. M.C. U.S. Army, 1942-45, PTO. Cpl. M.C., U.S. Army, 1942-45, PTO. Mem. APA (charter mem. divsn. of psychotherapy), Am. Coll. Counselors (cert. forensic psychology), Nat. Assn. Sch. Psychologist Assn. (nat. cert. in sch. psychology), Am. Coll. Counselors, Mass. Speech and Hearing Assn. (treas. 1957-59), Am. Assn. Clin. Counselors (pres. 1959-63), Mass. Sch. Psychologists Assn. (pres. 1972-74). Republican. Jewish. Avocations: sports, music. Home and Office: 118 Waverly Ave Melrose MA 02176-4217

HENKES, EVERT, oil company executive; b. Mene Grande, Venezuela, Dec. 4, 1943; m. Penny, June 28, 1968; three children. BSc, Cornell U. With Norcros Ltd., England, 1970-73, Shell Internat. Chem. Co., 1973; mktg. mgr. Temana Internat., England, 1974-81; v.p. internat. marine Shell Internat. Trading Co., England, 1981-83; supplies and trading dir. Shell Eastern Petroleum, Singapore, 1983-86; area coord. Shell Internat. Petroleum Co., England, 1986-89; mng. dir. Shell Chems. UK Ltd. England, 1989-92; metals coord. Billiton, The Hague, The Netherlands, 1992-95; chems. coord. Shell Internatl Chem. Co. Ltd., 1995-97; CEO Shell Chems. Ltd., London, 1998—. Office: Shell Chems Ltd, Shell Ctr, London SE1 7NA, England

HENKIND-JOSLOW, JANICE VERONICA, family nurse practitioner; b. N.Y.C., Feb. 3, 1951; d. William I. and Veronica A. Benjamin; BA, Mercy Coll., 1972; MS, U. Bridgeport, 1977; BSN U. Mass., 1993, MSN, 1995; postgrad. Yale U., 1995—; m. Paul Henkind, May 22, 1977 (dec. 1986); 1 child, Aaron Samuel; m. David L. Joslow, May 6, 1988 (dec. 1995); 1 child, Sarah Edith. Electron microscopist Boyce Thompson Inst. for Plant Rsch., 1972-74, dept. ophthalmology Montefiore Hosp. and Med. Ctr., 1974-76; exec. adminstr. Assn. for Rsch. in Vision and Ophthalmology, New Rochelle, N.Y., 1977-87, mng. editor Ophthalmology, Jour. Am. Acad. Ophthalmology, 1979-87, also XXIV Internat. Congress Opthalmology; pres. Med. Dialogues, Inc., N.H. Inn Mgmt. Co., Inc.; corporator Inn at Amherst Corp. Trustee Old Sturbridge Village, Mass., 1988-93, mem. fin. com., 1987-88, mem. long range planning com. 1988-93, bd. overseers, 1984—; mem. corp. N.Y. Bot. Garden, 1984—. Winner Martha Stone award in floriculture, 1983, 84. Mem. Assn. Women in Sci., Nat. Assn. Female Execs. Am., Assn. for Rsch. in Vision and Ophthalmology (hon.), Sigma Theta Tau, Alpha Sigma Lambda. Author: (with Keith Zinn) chpt. The Retinal Pigment Epithelium, 1979, Biomedical Foundations of Ophthalmology; contbr. articles to profl. jours. Address: 58 Sunset Ave Amherst MA 01002-2018

HENLEY, JOSEPH OLIVER, manufacturing company executive; b. Sikeston, Mo., June 25, 1949; s. Fred Louis and Bernice (Chilton) H. m. Jane Ann Rhodes, Aug. 21, 1971. BSBA, U. Mo., 1972; MBA, Mich. State U., 1973. Ops. analyst Midland-Ross, Inc., Cleve., 1974, prodn. control mgr., 1974-75; engring. systems mgr. Cameron-Waldron div., Somerset, N.J., 1989-95, prodn. control mgr., 1976-77; prodn. planning and mfg. systems mgr. ICM div. Massey Ferguson, Inc., Akron, Ohio, 1977-78; sr. audit specialist mfg. United Techs. Corp., Hartford, Conn., 1978-82; mfg. control systems mgr. UT Diesel Systems div., Hartford, Conn., 1983-84, materials mgr., 1983-84, internal cons., 1984-86; inventory mgr. Pratt & Whitney Aircraft div., Hartford, Conn., 1986-89, mgr. sychronous mfg., 1989-95; dir. mfg. Case Corp., Racine, Wis., 1996—. With Army N.G., 1970-72. Mem. Nat. Assn. Purchasing Mgmt., Am. Prodn. and Inventory Control Soc., Assn. for Mfg. Excellence (N.E. region bd. dirs.), Beta Gamma Sigma, Sigma Iota Epsilon, Omicron Delta Epsilon. Presbyterian. Home: 2400 SW Winterfield Ct Lees Summit MO 64081-4098 Office: Case Corporation 700 State St Racine WI 53404-3392

HENLEY, TERRY LEW, computer company executive; b. Seymour, Ind., Nov. 10, 1940; s. Ray C. and Barbara Marie (Cockerham) H.; children: Barron Keith, Troy Grayson, Walker Reed; m. Jennifer L. Baldwin, Sept., 1991. BS, Tri-State U., 1961; MBA, Loyola U., 1980, D of Psychology, 1982. R & D engr. Halogens Rsch. Lab. Dow Chem. Co., Midland, Mich., 1961-63; lead process engr., polymer plant Dow Chem. Co., Bay City, Mich., 1964; supt. bromide-bromate plants Dow Chem. Co., Midland, 1964-68; nat. sales mgr. Ryan Industries, Louisville, 1968-70; internat. sales mgr. Chemineer, Inc., Dayton, Ohio, 1970-77; cons. mktg. Xenia, Ohio, 1977-78; pres. Med-Systems Mgmt., Inc., Dayton, 1978-99, Medconnect Ltd., 1994—, Statis. Outcome Rsch. Corp., 1994-99; chmn. United Telemgmt. Inc., Dayton, 1991—; pres. MedStrategy Consultants, 1997—, HealthServe, LLC, 2000—. Author: Chemical Engineering, 1976; contbr. articles to profl. jours.; patentee in field. Mem. ASTM (com.), AIChE, Am. Hosp. Assn., Computer Based Patient Record Inst., Internat. Graphoanalysis Soc., Radiology Bus. Mgmt. Assn., Am. Nat. Std. Inst. (X12 health ins. com.), Am. Med. Peer Rev. Assn., Am. Mgmt. Assn., Med. Group Mgmt. Assn., Ohio Handwriting Analysts Assn., Ohio Ambulance Assn., Ohio Fire Chiefs Assn. Inc., Ohio Firefighters Assn., Healthcare Fin. Mgmt. Assn., Assn. Electronic Healthcare Transactions, Data Interchange Stds. Assn., Inc., U.S. C. of C. (telecomm. infrastructure rsch. task force, health and benefits policy com., Civic award 1990), Am. Med. Info. Assn., Freedom in Medicine Found. Home: 278 N Childrens Home Rd Troy OH 45373-8653 Office: HealthServe LLC 7812 Mcewen Rd Dayton OH 45459-3910

HENMAN, TIM, professional tennis player; b. Sept. 6, 1974. Profl. tennis player, mem. Davis Cup squad, 1994. Recipient Silver medal at Olympics with Neil Broad, 1996; winner Syndney Task Kent, 1997; winner Under 18 singles and doubles Nat. Titles, 1992; winner doubles title Guardian Direct Cup, 1999. Office: Internat Mgmt Group 1 Erieview Plz Ste 1300 Cleveland OH 44114-1715*

HENNAGAN, MONIQUE, Olympic athlete; b. Columbia, S.C., May 26, 1976. Degree in psychology, U. N.C., 1998. Co-winner 4X400 meter relay U.S.A. Track and Field Team, Sydney, 2000. Office: USA Track and Field Team One RCA Dome Ste 140 Indianapolis IN 46225*

HENNE, ANDREA RUDNITSKY, business educator; b. Phila., Sept. 11, 1952; d. Isadore and Florence (Sanders) Rudnitsky; m. Lawrence Michael Henne, May 27, 1984; children: Laura Joy, Michael Andrew. BS, Temple U., 1974; MA in Edn., UCLA, 1975, EdD, 1983. Prof. L.A. City Coll., 1975-90; dir. curriculum devel. Bridges Learning Ctr., Solana Beach, Calif., 1992-94; instr. San Diego Mesa Coll., 1995-98; web mgr./on-line edn. coord. Calif. Sch. Profl. Psychology, 1999—; bus. cons., San Diego, 1994—. Author: Intensive Records Management, 4th edit., 1998. Vol. Solana Beach Elem. Sch., San Diego, 1990—, Girl Scouts U.S.A., San Diego, 1995—. Edn. Professions Devel. Act fellow UCLA, 1975; named Outstanding Young Careerist, Bus. and Profl. Women, L.A., 1979. Mem. ASCD, Assn. Records Mgmt. and Adminstrn., Inc., Nat. Bus. Edn. Assn., Calif. Bus. Edn. Assn. (sec., v.p. and pres. 1976-79), Delta Pi Epsilon. Avocations: studying piano, computers, aerobics.

HENNEBERG, ALEXANDRA EHRENGARD, neuropsychiatrist, neuroimmunologist; b. Braunschweig, Germany, Oct. 28, 1956; d. Baron Horst-Henning Hans and Baroness Margarete Hildegard (Küpper) Kirchbach; m. Hans-Joachim Heinrich Henneberg, Oct. 27, 1988; children: Felix Karl Viktor, Julius Horst Friedrich, Sophia Ingeborg Amalie. 2d med. exam, U. Tübingen, Germany, 1977; 3d med. exam., U. Bonn, Germany, 1982; habilitation in neurology, U. Ulm, Germany, 1993. Guest worker Med. Rsch. Ctr., London, 1979-80; asst. physician dept. psychiatry Hosp. of Psychiatry, Cologne, Germany, 1987-88; asst. physician dept. neurology U. Ulm, Germany, 1982-87, 89-92, asst. med. dir. dept. neurology, 1992-95; med. dir. Hosp. for Parkinson's Disease, Bad Nauheim, Germany, 1995—; prof. U. Giessen, Germany, 1999—; mem. Neurology Rsch. LLab., Ulm, 1982-87; head Neuroimmunology Rsch. Group, Ulm, 1989-95, Epileplology, 1998, Physical Therapy, 1999; del. German Soc. Med. Dirs., 2000—, Dist. Med. Soc., 2000—. Author: Immunological Alterations in Psychiatric Diseases, 1997, Parkinson—zu neuern Gleichgewicht finden, 1997, (with J. Komm and K. Prokein) Parkinson und?, 1998, (with L. Johner) Parkinson-Lexikon fur Patieuteu.; contbr. articles to med. jours. Recipient award Winter Workshop on Schizophrenia, London, 1992, Poster prize German Soc. Neurology, 1999; scholar Studienstiftung Deutschen Volkes, Bonn, 1974-82; grantee Hertiestiftung, Frankfurt, Germany, 1987, Stanley Found., Arlington, Va., 1993. Mem. Internat. Soc. for Pathophysiology, Internat. Soc. for Neuroimmunomodulation, German Soc. Neurology, German Soc. Immunology, German Soc. Psychiatry, German Soc. Neurochemistry, German Soc. Neuropathology, German Soc. Neurogenetics, N.Y. Acad. Scis., German Soc. Electrotherapy (sci. com.). Avocations: playing violin, dancing, riding, reading. Fax: 06008/930849. Office: Hosp for Parkinsons Disease, F Groedel Str 6, D-61231 Bad Nauheim Germany

HENNEKAM, BERNARDUS MARTINUS JOHANNES, government official; b. Princenhage, The Netherlands, Oct. 31, 1941; m. Dingena Gommers; children: Michiel, Bernardus, Adriana. Student of Law, Cath. U. Brabant, Tilburg, The Netherlands. Educator; mem., then alderman Mcpl. Coun. Urban Dist. Breda; mem. exec. com. Urban Dist. Breda; mem. Dutch Lower House, 1978—; mem. Benelux Parliament, Brussels, chmn., 1987-88; sec. sec. Benelux Econ. Union, Brussels, 1990—; 1st spokesman for traffic and circulation; chmn. for internal affairs and 1st spokesman for his party Permanent Commn. Office: Benelux Econ Union, rue de la Régence 39, 1000 Brussels Belgium

HENNEMAN, STEPHEN CHARLES, psychotherapist; b. Chgo., June 17, 1949; s. Charles Philip Jr. and Marion Louise (Eichberger) H.; m. Patrica Ann York, Feb. 14, 1975 (div. Sept. 1980); 1 child Charles Philip III; m. Marion Jean McDermand, Oct. 4, 1980; stepchildren: Ervin F. Schrock Jr., Lisa Ann Schrock, Thomas M. Schrock. BA in Journalism, Colo. State U., 1971; MA in Counseling, U. N.D., 1987. Commd. 2d lt. USAF, 1971,

advanced through grades to maj., 1984; missile launch officer 570th Strategic Missile Squadron, Davis Monthan AFB, Ariz., 1972-76; info. officer 321st Strategic Missile Wing, Grand Forks AFB, N.D., 1976-79; missile combat crew flight comdr. 446th Strategic Missile Squadron, Grand Forks AFB, 1980-82; missile combat crew comdr. evaluator 321st Strategic Missile Wing, Grand Forks AFB, 1982, wing nuclear surety officer, 1982-83, chief weapon safety branch, 1983-85; asst. ops. officer 320th Strategic Missile Squadron, F E Warren AFB, Wyo., 1985-86; dep. wing inspector 90th Strategic Missile Wing, F E Warren AFB, 1986-88; ops. officer 319th Strategic Missile Squadron, F E Warren AFB, 1988-89; dep. chief war res. materiel div. Hdqrs. U.S. Air Forces in Europe, Ramstein Air Base, Fed. Republic Germany, 1989-92; vol. and outreach coord. Safe House/Sexual Assault Svcs., Inc., Cheyenne, Wyo., 1992-93; quality control investigator Dept. Employment State of Wyoming, Cheyenne, 1993-95; counselor Wyo. State Penitentiary, Rawlins, 1995-96, counseling team leader, 1996-97; residential counselor Aurora (Colo.) Cmty. Mental Health Ctr., 1997-99, mental health clinician, 1999—. Advocate, counselor Safehouse/Sexual Assault Svcs., Inc., Cheyenne, 1985-89; sec., bd. dirs. Carbon County Citizens Organized to See Violence Ended, 1996-97. Mem. ACA, Am. Mental Health Counselors Assn., Colo. Counselors Assn. Avocations: photography, popular music recordings collecting, reading.

HENNESSEY, WILLIAM JOSEPH, physician; b. Troy, N.Y., Mar. 8, 1947; s. Joseph William and Loretta (Brooks) H.; m. Patricia McMahon, Jan. 23, 1983; children: Bridget Marie, Jason William, Matthew Brian, Mark Andrew. BS, Rensselaer Poly. Inst., 1969; MD, Albany Med. Coll., 1973. Cert. Am. Bd. of Ob/Gyn. Resident in ob-gyn Albany (N.Y.) Med. Ctr. Hosp., 1973-76; pvt. practice specializing in ob-gyn. Troy, N.Y., 1976—; mng. ptnr. Ob-Gyn Health Ctr. Assocs., 1985; attending physician Albany Med. Ctr. Hosp., Samaritan Hosp., St. Peters Hosp.; treas. med. staff Samaritan Hosp., 1988, sec. med. staff, 1989, v.p. med. staff, 1990, pres., 1991; clin. asst. dept. ob-gyn Albany Med. Ctr. and Albany Med. Coll., 1976—, clin. instr.; chmn. dept. ob-gyn Samaritan Hosp., 1991-95; bd. dirs. PSRO, 1981-85, PRO, 1985-86. Fellow Am. Coll. Ob-Gyn, Am. Fertility Assn.; mem. Am. Chem. Honor Soc., AMA, N.Y. State Med. Soc., Rensselaer County Med. Soc., Northeast Ob-Gyn Consortium, Am. Assn. Gynecol. Laporoscopists, Sampson Soc. (pres.). E-mail: whennessey@aol.com.

HENNICOT-SCHOEPGES, ERNA, government executive; b. Dudelange, July 24, 1941; married; three children. Student, Royal Acad. Music, Brussels, 1960-67. Spkr. Luxembougish Program of Radio Luxembourg, 1963-79; piano tchr. Acad. of Music, Luxembourg, 1976-87; mem. Local Coun. of Walferdange, 1976-87; mem. Parliament, chmn. Parliamentary Commn. for Edn. and Culture, 1979-89; nat. chmn. Christian-Social Women, 1979-88; mem. Parliamentary Assembly of the Coun. of Europe, Parliamentary sec. of Christian-Dem. Group, mem. Commn. for Edn. and Culture, mem. Commn. for Migrants and Refugees, 1984-89; mayor Walferdange, 1988-95; mem. Congress for Cmtys. and Regions, mem. parliamentary assembly of the O.S.C.E.; pres. Internat. Found. for the Dialogue between Christians, Jews and Moslems, 1989-95; pres. of the Parliament, 1989-95; mem. Prime Min. Jean-Claude Junccker's Govt., Min. of Edn. and Vocat. Tng., Min. of Culture, Min. of Cults, 1995; nat. chmn. Christian-Social Party, 1995—; Min. of Culture, Govt. of Luxembourg. Office: Ministry of Culture/Rel Aff, 20 Montee de la Petrusse, L-2912 Luxembourg Luxembourg*

HENNIG, EWALD MAX, biomechanics researcher; b. Bocholt, Germany, Apr. 7, 1950; s. Ewald and Gerda (Nedetzky) H.; m. Sieglinde H. Opitz, May 22, 1975. Diploma in Physics, J.W. Goethe U., Frankfurt, Germany, 1975; PhD, Pa. State U., State College, 1984. Acad. rschr. U. Konstanz, Germany, 1984-87; prof. U. Essen, Germany, 1987—; cons. Stiftung Warentest, Berlin, 1990—. Patentee in field. Mem. Internat. Soc. Biomechanics. Avocations: sport activities, running, skiing, tennis. Office: U Essen, Biomechanik Labor FB 2, 45141 Essen Germany

HENNIGAR, DAVID JOHN, investment broker; b. Windsor, N.S., Can., July 5, 1939; s. Dean S. and Jean B. (Jodrey) H.; m. Carolyn Hiltz, June 8, 1964; children: Brian, Jan. B of Commerce, Mt. Allison U., 1960; MBA, Queen's U., 1962. Investment analyst Burns Fry Ltd. and predecessor co., Toronto, Ont., Can., 1963-66; br. mgr. Burns Fry Ltd. and predecessor co., Halifax, N.S., Can., 1966-71, Atlantic regional dir., 1971-93; chmn. bd. dirs. Annapolis Basin Inc., Landmark Global Fin. Inc.; chmn. Extendicare Inc., Acadian Securities Inc., Aquarius Coatings Inc., Cougar Aviation Inc., High Liner Foods, Inc., Tomanet Inc.; bd. dirs. Crown Life Ins. Co., Minas Basin Pulp & Power Co. Ltd., Scotia Investment Ltd., Cobi Foods Inc., Atlantic Shopping Ctrs. Ltd., Maritime Paper Products Ltd., Sentex Systems Ltd., Alternative Fin. Corp., CentrSource Corp. Bd. dirs., treas. Izaak Walton Killam Hosp. for Children, Halifax, 1976-82; bd. dirs. Inst. for Rsch. on Pub. Policy, 1983-89; chmn. Oceans Inst. Can.; mem. Trilateral Commn., 1988-94; bd. govs. Dalhousie U., 1983-90; dir. Hope Air Inc. Mem. Investment Dealers Assn. Can. (nat. bd. dirs. 1985-87), Internat. Oceans Inst., Halifax Club. Home: 51 Forest Ln, Bedford, NS Canada B4A 1H8 Office: 3 Bedford Hills Rd, Bedford, NS Canada B4A 1J5 also: Extendicare, 3000 Steeles Ave E, Ontario, ON Canada L3R 9W2

HENNING, WILLIAM CLIFFORD, cemetery consulting company executive; b. Kalamazoo, Oct. 21, 1918; s. Russell and Dott Lois (Stauffer) H.; m. Charlotte Conrad, Sept. 14, 1946; children: Peggy Henning Berlin, Helen L. Henning Boddy. BA, Albion Coll. (Mich.), 1940; postgrad., Northwestern U. Law Sch., 1940-42, U. Mich. Law Sch., summer 1941. Sec. Sycamore (Ill.) C. of C., 1945-46; exec. sec. Allegheny County Funeral Dirs. Assn., Pitts., 1946-48, Am. Cemetery Assn., Columbus, Ohio, 1948-56; owner, pres. Am. Cemetery Cons., Inc., Springfield, Ohio, 1961-89; cons., 1989—; sec., treas., gen. mgr. Rose Hill Burial Park, Springfield, Ohio, 1956-76. Contbr. articles to profl. jours. County chmn. United Appeals Fund, 1962; bd. dirs., 1964-67; moderator Snowhill United Ch. Christ, Springfield, 1958-60. Served to 1st lt. USAAF, 1943-45; PTO. Decorated Air medal with 2 oak leaf clusters. Mem. Am., Central Ohio (pres. 1958), cemetery assns., Ohio Assn. Cemetery Supts. and Ofcls. (pres. 1960), Am. Soc. Profl. Cons. Republican. Club: Springfield Lit. (pres. 1984). Lodges: Eagles, Kiwanis (pres. Springfield 1963), Masons. Home: 2714 Rockford Dr Springfield OH 45503-1931

HENNINOT, JEAN-PIERRE, information systems specialist; b. Lille, France, May 11, 1948; s. Jean-Baptiste and Suzanne (Decuyper) H.; m. Maria Micinic, Sept. 15, 1973; children: Michel, Nicolas, Elisabeth. Dipl.engring., Ecole Polytech., France, 1967, Ecole NAt. Superior Telecomm., France, 1972. Dir. line & transmission Amiens, 1972-77; dir. ops. Intenat. Directorate, France, 1977-84; dir. network engring. Sofrecom, France, 1984-90; dir. telecomm. Railway Telecomm. Agy. - SNCF, France, 1990-97; dep. dir. info. sys. and tel. SNCF, France, 1997—. Mem. IRSE. Roman Catholic. Avocations: philately, German, Russian, windsurfing. Home: 27 rue de Fontarabie, 75020 Paris France Office: SNCF, 34 rue du Commandant Mouchotte, 75699 Paris Cedex, France

HENNION, CAROLYN LAIRD (LYN HENNION), investment executive; b. Orange, Calif., July 27, 1943; d. George James and Jane (Porter) Laird; m. Reeve L. Hennion, Sept. 12, 1964; children: Jeffrey Reeve, Douglas Laird. BA, Stanford U., 1965; grad. Securities Industry Inst., U. Pa., 1992. CFP, fund specialist; lic. ins. agt.; registered gen. securities prin. Portfolio analyst Schwabacher & Co., San Francisco, 1965-66; adminstrv. coord. Bicentennial Commn., San Mateo County, Calif., 1972-73; dir. devel. Crystal Springs Uplands Sch., Hillsborough, Calif., 1973-84; tax preparer Household Fin. Corp., Foster City, Calif., 1982; freelance, 1983-87; sales promotion mgr. Franklin Distbrs., Inc., San Mateo, 1984-86, v.p. and regional sales mgr. of N.W., 1986-91, v.p. Mid-Atlantic, 1991-94; v.p. Viatech, Inc., 1986-92; propr. Buncom Ranch, 1990—; v.p. Keypoint Svcs. Internat., 1992—; pres. Brock Rd. Corp., 1993—; v.p. Strand, Atkinson, Williams & York, Medford, Oreg., 1994—. Editor: Lest We Forget, 1975. Pres. South Hillsborough Sch. Parents' Group, 1974-75; sec. Vol. Bur. of San Mateo County, Burlingame, Calif., 1975; chmn. Cmty. Info. Com., Town of Hillsborough, 1984-86, mem., subcom. chmn. fin. adv. com., 1984-86; mem. adv. com. Jackson County Airport, 1996—, vice chair, 1999—; mem. coun. Town of Buncom, Oreg., 1990—; bd. dirs. Pacific N.W. Mus. Natural History, 1995-96; chmn. Jackson County Applegate Trail Sesquicentennial Celebration, 1995-97; treas. Sesquicentennial Wagon Train, 1995-97; founding dir. So. Oreg. Hist. Soc. Found., v.p., sec., 1995-98, pres., 1998—; trustee Oreg. Shakespeare Festival Endowment Fund, 1996-2000, sec., treas., 1997-98, pres., 1998-2000; bd. dirs. Providence Cmty. Health Found., 1996—, chmn. planned giving com., 1997-2000, sec., 1998-2000, v.p. 2000—; dir. Rogue Valley Manor Cmty. Svcs., 1996—, vice-chair, 1997—; dir. Craterian Performances Co., 1997—, chmn. mem. com., 1998—; dir. So. Oreg. Estate Planning Coun., 1997—, pres., 1998-99, Oreg. Cmty. Found. leadership coun., 2000—. Recipient awards Coun. for Advancement and Support of Edn., 1981, Exemplary Direct Mail Appeals Fund Raising Inst., 1982, Golden Mic award Frederic Gilbert Assocs., 1993; named Wholesaler of Yr., Shearson Lehman Hutton N.W. Region, 1989, among Top 300 Fin. Advisors, Worth Mag., 1998, Top 250 Fin. Advisors, 1999, Among 10 Outstanding Brokers Registered Rep. Mag., 2000. Mem. So. Oreg. Estate Planning Coun., Buncom Hist. Soc., Oreg. Shakespeare Festival, Britt Festivals, So. Oreg. Hist. Soc., Jr. League, Medford Rogue Rotary. Republican. Home: 3232 Little Applegate Rd Jacksonville OR 97530-9303 Office: Strand Atkinson Williams & York 611 Medford Ctr Medford OR 97504-6002

HENNO, JAAK, computer scientist, educator; b. Võru, Estonia, Aug. 16, 1941; s. Alo and Alice (Matsin) H.; m. Mare Hallikmaa; 1 child, Katrin. PhD in Math., U. Tartu, Estonia, 1976. Asst. prof. Tallinn (Estonia) Tech. U., 1964—; vis. asst. prof. U. Tech., Tampere, Finland, 1986-87, Tech. U., Budapest, Hungary, 1987, Vaasa, Finland, 1990-92, 93-94; bd. dirs. Hypermedia Co., Tallinn, Estonia, 1995—. Author: (book) Prolog and Olympian Gods, 1991; editor: Hypermedia in Tallinn, 1996; contbr. about 60 articles to profl. jours. Mem. European Assn. Theoretical Computer Scientists, Assn. Computing Machinery. Avocations: record collecting, music. E-mail: jaak@ce.ttu.ee. Office: Tallinn Tech U, Ehitajate Tee 5, EE-0108 Tallinn Estonia

HENRARD, JACQUES, mathematics educator; b. Kinshasa, Congo, July 4, 1940; s. Jean and Renee (Fraeys) H.; m. Françoise Liegeois, July 25, 1965; children: Jean, Marc, Luc, Anne. PhD in Math., Cath. U. Louvain, Belgium, 1966. Rschr. Nat. Sci. Found., Belgium, 1963-66; staff mem. Boeing Sci. Rsch. Lab., Seattle, 1966-70; rsch. assoc. Yale U., New Haven, 1971; prof. math. U. Namur, Belgium, 1971—, chmn. dept., 1976-79; pres. Nat. Belgian Com. on Astronomy, 1996-99. Editor: Longterm Evolution of Planetary Systems, 1988, Interactions between Physics and Dynamics of Solar System Bodies, 1993, Chaos in Gravitational N-Body Systems, 1996, The Dynamical Behaviour of Our Planetary System, 1997, Dynamics of Comets and Asteroids and Their Role in Earth History, 1998; editor-in-chief Celestial Mechanics, 1989—. Recipient Agathon de Potter prize Acad. Belgium, 1985. Mem. Internat. Astron. Union (pres. commn. 7 1988-91), European Astron. Soc. (founding), Belgian Soc. Astronomy. Home: 4 Rue Decelle, B-5100 Namur Belgium Office: U Namur Dept Math FUNDP, 8 Rempart de la Vierge, B-5000 Namur Belgium

HENRICH, RAINER, theologian, researcher; b. Thusis, Grisons, Switzerland, May 8, 1955; s. Paul and Ruth (Pfändler) H. Lic. Theol., U. Zurich, Switzerland, 1985. Rschr. Bullinger-Briefwechseledition, Zurich, 1986—. Contbr. articles to profl. jours. Recipient Conrad Ferdinand Meyer prize, 1994. Mem. Zwingliverein. Office: Bullinger Briefwechseledit, Kirchgasse 9, CH 8001 Zurich Switzerland

HENRICSON, BETH ELLEN, microbiologist; b. Johnson City, N.Y., Apr. 22, 1947; d. Clifford Lyle and Margaret Addison (Moore) Hevenor; m. Lawrence Karl Henricson, Aug. 9, 1969; children: Erik Karl, Karen Jeanette. BS in Microbiology, Pa. State U., 1969; postgrad., U. Rochester, 1969-70; MEd Overseas Grad. program, Boston U., Sechenheim, Germany, 1987; PhD in Biomed. Sci., Uniformed Svcs. U. Hlth. Scis., 1992. Registered clin. pub. health microbiologist Am. Acad. Microbiologists. Med. technologist Dept. of Army, Ft. Hood, Tex., 1981-84; microbiologist, med. technician Dept. of Army 5th Gen. Hosp., Stuttgart, Germany, 1986-87; predoctoral rsch. fellow USUHS, Bethesda, Md., 1987-92; NRC fellow FDA Ctr. Biol. Evaluation & Rsch., NIH, Bethesda, Md., 1992-93; postdoctoral rsch. fellow Henry M. Jackson Found., Bethesda, Md., 1993-95; microbiologist supr., quality assurance coord. Va. Dept. Agrl. and Consumer Svcs., Warrenton, Va., 1995—. Contbg. author Endotoxin Research, 1990, Bacterial Endotoxins, 1995; author, editor VDACS Office of Animal Industry Lab. Svcs. Quality Assurance Guidance Manual; contbr. articles to profl. jours. including Infection & Immunity, Molecular Medicine, Jour. Endotoxin Rsch., Jour. Vet. Diagnostic Investigation. Leader Boy Scouts Am., Hawaii, Tex., Germany, 1978-85, Girl Scouts Am., Tex., Germany, 1982-87; vol. Washington AIDS Ride, 1996—; mem. ACLU. N.Y. State Regents scholar, 1965. Mem. AAAW, LWV, ACLU, AAUW, N.Y. Acad. Scis., Assn. Vet. Microbiologists (v.p. Colonial States chpt. 1996-98, pres. 1999—), Am. Assn. Vet. Lab. Diagnosticians (Bacteriology, Mycoplasmology, Mycology steering com.), Am. Soc. Microbiology, Internat. Endotoxin Soc., Nat. Environ. Health Assn., Iota Sigma Pi, Phi Sigma, Phi Beta Kappa, Phi Kappa Phi. Achievements include research in endotoxin analogs, LPS (lipopolysaccharide)-inducible gene expression, acyloxyacyl hydrolase contbn. to LPS detoxification, LPS and Taxol activation of Lyn Kinase autophosphorylation and LPS-induced cytokine production; contribution of C. diphtheriae to wound infection in an equine. Office: Va Dept Agrl Warrenton Regional Lab 272 Academy Hill Rd Warrenton VA 20186-4305

HENRIKSEN, JENS HENRIK, physician, educator, scientist; b. Copenhagen, Aug. 23, 1945; s. Jens Einar and Christa Marie Louise (Sahl) H.; m. Karin Højer-Pedersen Dahi. Degree in Medicine, U. Copenhagen, 1972, D in Med. Sci., 1982. Bd. cert. clin. physiology and nuclear medicine. Registrar Kommunehospitalet/Bispebjerg Hosp., Denmark, 1973-76; registrar/sr. registrar clin. physiology Hvidovre Hosp., 1976-80, registrar/sr. registrar internal medicine, 1980-82, chief physician dept. clin. physiology, 1984; sr. registrar/cons. Bispebjerg Hosp./Rigshospitalet, Denmark, 1982-84; prof. clin. physiology U. Copenhagen, 1994—; pres. Soc. of Theoretical and Applied Therapy, Copenhagen, 1989-90, Danish Soc. Clin. Physiology and Nuclear Medicine, Copenhagen, 1991-93. Author: Pathogenesis of Ascites in Cirrhosis, 1982, Ernest Henry Starling (1866-1927), Physician and Physiologist-A Short Biography, 2000; author, editor: Degradation of Bioactive Substances, 1991; assoc. editor Liver, 1986-91; editor Scandinavian Jour. of Clin. and Lab. Investigation, 1988—; rev. editor Clin. Physiology, 1991-97; contbr. articles to profl. jours. Recipient Kommunitetet, U. Copenhagen, 1968-72, Tode award Danish Soc. Medicine, 1995, Klein award Copenhagen Soc. Medicine, 1997; Rsch. grantee The John and Birthe Meyer Found., 1990, 92, 94, 97. Fellow Internat. Coll. Angiology; mem. Internat. Assn. Study Liver, European Assn. for the Study of Liver, Internat. Union Physiol. Scis. (bd. mem. coun. clin. physiology 1993—), N.Y. Acad. Scis. Home: Fasanhaven 16, DK-2820 Gentofte Denmark Office: Hvidovre Hosp U Copenhagen, Dept Clin Physiology 239, DK-2650 Hvidovre Denmark

HENRIKSSON, ANDERS STEN, geologist; b. Hofors, Sweden, Jan. 18, 1962; s. Sten and Anna (Eriksson) H.; m. Ann-Kristin Juntti, June 19, 1990. MSc, Uppsala U., 1990, PhD, 1994. Scientist, educator Uppsala U., Sweden, 1990-95; scientist U. Salamanca, Spain, 1995-96, U. Kiel, Germany, 1997-99, U. Lulea, Sweden, 1999—. Author: Late Cretaceous Calcareous Nannoplankton and the Extinctions at the Cretaceous/Tertiary Boundary, 1995; contbr. articles to profl. jours. Home: Kopmanvagen 28, 950 40 Tore Sweden

HENROTIN, YVES EDGARD, medical educator; b. Marche, Belgium, Nov. 5, 1964; s. Jean and Elise (Jourdevant) H.; m. Annick Roderbourg, Nov. 20, 1962; children: Charlotte, Pierre. Bachelor, U. Liege, PhD, 1994, cert. in pedagogy, 1996. Asst. U. Liege, 1987-90, leading scientist, 1994-95, profl. lectr., 1996-99; dept. mgr. Hosp., Marche, 1991—; adj. prof. U. Liege, 1999—; cons. Pharm. Co., Belgium, 1995—. Contbr. articles to profl. jours. Tech. cons. Sports Assn., 1993. Mem. Osteoarthritis rsch. Soc., Am. Coll. Rheumatology, N.Y. Acad. Scis., Bone and Joint Surgery Assn., Rotary. Avocations: football, walking, music, skiing, golf. Fax: 04-366-47-34. E-mail: yhenrotin@ulg.ac.be. Home: Aux Grands Champs 63, 4052 Beaufays Belgium Office: Bone and Cartilage Metab, CHU Sart-tilman Path Inst, 4020 Liège Belgium

HENRY, CARL NOLAN, lawyer; b. Washington, Sept. 30, 1965; s. Robert Benjamin Covington III and Inola Francis Henry. BA in Polit. Sci., U. Calif., Berkeley, 1987, JD, 1993. Bar: Calif. 1993, U.S. Supreme Ct. 1997, U.S. Ct. Appeal (9th cir.) 1993, U.S. Dist. Ct. (no., ctrl. dists.) Calif. 1993. Dep. atty. gen. Calif. Dept. Justice, L.A., 1994-99, 99—; staff atty. to Hon. Janice Rogers Brown Calif. Supreme Ct., San Francisco, 1999. Career Awareness Acad. scholar Home Savings Am., 1983; Liberal Arts award Bank Am., 1983. Mem. L.A. Angel City Links Assn. (O. J. Simpson Acad. scholar 1983), L.A. Ephebian Honor Soc. Democrat. Methodist. Avocations: sports, politics, music, history, education. Office: Calif Dept Justice 300 S Spring St Ste 5000 Los Angeles CA 90013-1230

HENRY, CATHERINE, financial communications executive; b. N.Y.C., Oct. 12, 1966; d. Lowell Albert Henry and Joan Logue Kinder. BA, Wheaton Coll., 1989; MA, Sais Johns Hopkins U., Bologna, Italy, 1992; MBA, SDA Bocconi Sch. Mgmt., Milan, Italy, 1993. Asst. product mgr. Etee Lauder, Milan, 1990-92; mktg. associate Nestle, Milan, 1993; asst. project mgr. World Bank IFC, Washington, 1994-97; dir. mktg. Stern Stewart & Co., N.Y.C., 1997-99; dir. corp. practice Burson Marsteller, Paris, 1999—. Mem. Financial Women's Assn., The Whitney Mus. (jr. bd. mem.), Mus. Modern Art, Cooper Hewitt Mus. (design league). Avocations: tennis, literature, modern art. E-mail: catherine henry@bm.com. Office: Burson Marsteller France, 6 rue Escudier, 92772 Boulogne Billancourt France

HENRY, CHARLES HOWARD, non-commissioned officer; b. Aurora, Ill., Oct. 14, 1966; s. Howard Hufford and Barbara Jeanne (Keller) H.; m. Trisha Barnhisel, May 8, 1999. Personnelman 3d class, USS Guardfish USN, San Diego, 1986-89, yeoman 2d class, cmdr. submarine group 5, 1989-92; yeoman 2d class, USS Alabama USN, Silverdale, Wash., 1993-96; pers. officer, cmdr. submarine squadron 22 USN, La Maddalena, Sardinia, Italy, 1996-98; yeoman divsn. leading petty officer USS Jefferson City USN, San Diego, 1998—; mem. U.S. Naval Inst., 1991-98. Named Sr. Sailor of Yr., Cmdr. Submarine Squadron 22, USN, 1997. Mem. Non-Commissioned Officers Assn. Republican. Lutheran. Avocations: investing, current events, reading, music. Office: US Navy Uss Jefferson City # 759 FPO AP 96669-2415

HENRY, DAVID HOWE, II, retired diplomat; b. Geneva, N.Y., May 19, 1918; s. David Max and Dorothy (Buley) H.; m. Margaret Beard, Nov. 16, 1946; children: David Beard, Peter York, Michael Max, Susan. Student, Hobart Coll., 1935-37, Sorbonne, 1937-38; A.B., Columbia U., 1939; student, Russian Inst., 1948-49, Harvard U., 1944-45, Nat. War Coll., 1957-58. Ins. agt., 1939-41; mem. fgn. service Dept. State, 1941-71; assigned Dept. State, Montreal, 1941-42, Beirut, 1942-44, Washington, 1944-45, 48-52, 57-66, 70, Moscow, 1945-48, 52-54, Vladivostok, 1945-46, Berlin, 1955-57; acting dir. Office Research and Intelligence Sino-Soviet bloc, 1958-59; dir. dept. polit. affairs Nat. War Coll., 1959-61; dep. dir. Office Soviet Affairs, 1961-64, dir., 1964-65; mem. Policy Planning Council, 1965-66; dep. chief of mission Am. embassy, Reykjavik, Iceland, 1966-69; information systems specialist, 1970; polit. and security council affairs UN, N.Y.C., 1971-78. Mem. Kappa Alpha. Presbyterian. Club: Rotarian. Home: 2551 SW Brookwood Ln Palm City FL 34990-4752

HENRY, GEOFFREY ARAMA, prime minister of Cook Islands; b. Reureu, Aitutaki, Cook Islands, Nov. 16, 1940; s. Arama and Mata Uritaua (Cameron) H.; m. Louisa Olga Hoff, June 1965; children: Walter Tetautua, Ewen Tapukura, Alexander Tama, Marise Olga, Geoffrey Marouna (dec.), Heidirose Matangaro. BA in English and Edn., Victoria U., Wellington, New Zealand, 1959. Tchr. Jr. High Sch., Aitutaki, Cook Island, 1965-66; ind. M.P. Cook Islands, 1965-68; tchr. Avarua Primary Sch., Rarotonga, Cook Island, 1966-67; rsch. officer Premier's Dept., Rarotonga, 1970-71; pvt. practice land owner's agt., high ct. counsel Rarotonga, 1971-80; cabinet min. Cook Islands, 1972-78; pvt. practice law clk. Rarotonga, 1980-82; dep. prime min. Govt. of Cook Islands, 1983-89, prime min., 1989-99; atty. gen., min. police, min. fin., min. cultural devel., leader of opposition New Zealand Film Unit. Trans., interpreter, commentator documentaries on Cook Islands, info. booklets and ednl. jours, 1959-68. M.P., Cook Islands, 1965-68; min. edn., justice and lands, 1972-73; min. fin., edn., planning and stats., 1973-78; postmaster gen., 1973-78; min. fin., tourism, police, immigration, external affairs, justice, and survey, 1983; min. tourism, arts and culture, edn., pub. works, 1984-85; min. fin. fgn. affairs, tourism, crown law, pub. works, legisl. svc., arts, and culture, 1989-94, min. fin., min. police, atty. gen., 1994—; prime min., min. fin., econ. devel., environ. svcs. C.I. Investment Corp., 1995-98. Recipient silver Jubilee medal from Her Majesty Queen Elizabeth II, 1977, new Zealand Commemoration medal, 1990, Knight Comdr. of British Empire, 1992, Samoan Matai title Afionga Tui Saua, 1993. Mem. Lions Club (found. mem.). Mem. Cook Islands Party. Mem. Cook Islands Christian Ch. Avocations: golf, tennis, cricket. Home: Takkuvaine, Rarotonga Cook Islands

HENRY, LOIS HOLLENDER, psychologist; b. Phila., Jan. 19, 1941; d. Edward Hubert and Frances Lois (Nesler) Hollender; m. Charles L. Henry, Oct. 24, 1964 (div. 1971); children: Deborah Lee, Randell Huitt, Andrew Edward. BA, Thomas A. Edison Coll., 1979; MSW, Fordham U., 1981; PhD in Indsl. Psychology, City U. L.A., 1992. Diplomate cert. neurofeedback provider; cert. social worker, Ariz., N.Y., N.J., EEG Biofeedback Practitioners; lic. svc. profl., career counselor, Ariz. Pers. asst., sec. IBM, Paterson, N.J. and St. Louis, 1964-66; min.'s asst. Grace Luth. Ch., St. Cloud, Fla., 1966-68; adminstr./tchr. Fla. Finishing Acad., St. Cloud, 1968-70; adminstrv. asst. Newark Book Ctr., 1972-77; intern, med. social worker Jersey City Med. Ctr., 1979-80; intern, psychiatric/med. social worker VA Med. Ctr., Lyons, N.J., 1980-81; sch. social worker Lakeview Learning Ctr., Budd Lake, N.J., 1981-82; mgr. human resources Terak Corp., Scottsdale, Ariz., 1982-85; v.p. counseling and bus. devel. Murro & Assocs., Phoenix, 1985-88, exec. v.p. cons., 1988-91; prin. career cons. Henry & Assocs., Scottsdale, 1982—; staff psychologist Nelson O'Connor & Assocs., Phoenix, 1993-97; v.p. dir. profl. svcs. Lee Hecht Harrison, Phoenix, 1997-98; cert. neurotherapist Forensic Psychol. Svcs., Phoenix, 1995-96; career cons., individual/family counselor/psychotherapist/neurotherapist, spkr., Henry & Assocs., Scottsdale, 1982—; adj. prof. Ottawa U.; mem. employers com. Ariz. Dept. Econ. Security; cons. in field. Coordinator-vol. Job-A-Thon, Phoenix, 1983. Fellow Am. Orthopsychiat. Assn., Internat. Assn. Outplacement Profls. (treas. Ariz. region 1992-95, assoc. editor Internation Jour. Neuronal Regulation), Nat. Registry of Soc. Neuronal Regulation (diplomate, charter mem.); mem. NASW, Soc. Human Resource Mgmt., Am. Assn. Psychophysiology. Office: 8628 E Granada Rd Scottsdale AZ 85257-2943

HENRY, NICHOLAS LLEWELLYN, college president, political science educator; b. Seattle, May 22, 1943; s. Samuel Houston and Ann (Connor) H.; m. Muriel Bunney; children: Adrienne Richardson, Miles Houston. B.A., Centre Coll. Ky., 1965; M.A., Pa. State U., 1967; M.P.A., Ind. U., 1970, Ph.D., 1971. Asst. to dean Coll. Arts and Scis.; instr. Ind. State U., 1967-69; vis. asst. prof. U. N.Mex., 1971-72; asst. prof. polit. sci. U. Ga., 1972-75, assoc. prof., 1975-78, prof., 1978-87, dir. Ctr. Pub. Affairs, 1975-80, dean Coll. Pub. Programs, 1980-87; prof., pres. Ga. So. U., Statesboro, 1987-98; prof. polit. sci. Ga. So. U., 1998—. Author or editor 12 books; contbr. numerous articles to profl. jours. Recipient Author of Yr. award Assn. Sci. Jours.; named One of 100 Most Influential People in Ga., Ga. Trend, 1994. Fellow Nat. Acad. Pub. Adminstrn.; mem. Cosmos Club (Washington). Office: Ga So U PO Box 8101 Statesboro GA 30460-1000

HENRY, OLGA ELAINE, nursing educator, health care trainer; b. London, Ont., Can., Aug. 29, 1943; came to U.S., 1979; d. Andrej and Agafia (Schur) Olejar; m. Ronald John Chapchuk, June 4, 1965 (div. July 1980); children: Timothy Jon, Robin Anne Marie; m. Gilbert Armstrong Henry, Dec. 18, 1984; children: Douglas Richard, Valerie Jean, Pauline Michelle. RN, Atkinson Sch. Nursing, Toronto, Ont., 1965; BSN, U. Western Ont., London, 1966; MBA, cert. health svcs. adminstrn., Nova Southeastern U., Ft. Lauderdale, Fla., 1988. Cert. home health nurse, cert. corp. trainer, cert. continuing edn. provider. Dir. edn. Mississauga (Ont.) Hosp., 1974-79, North Ridge Hosp., Ft. Lauderdale, Fla., 1980-84; adminstr. Barna Inst., Inc., Ft. Lauderdale, 1984-85; coord. health care City of Ft. Lauderdale, 1985; supr. nursing Maxicare Home Health, Ft. Lauderdale, 1985-88; dir. nursing All-Care Health Svcs., Lauderhill, Fla., 1988-90, Enteral & Parenteral Support Svc., Sunrise, Fla., 1990; supr. nursing Mederi of Broward County, Inc., Coral Springs, Fla., 1991-93; coord. staff edn. Mederi of Broward County, Inc., 1993-98; adj. prof. Broward C.C., Ft. Lauderdale, 1993—; cons., corp. trainer Profl. Edn. Enterprises, Inc., Coral Springs, 1984—. Mem. South Fla. Dem. Club, Hollywood, 1996. Mem. ANA, NAFE, The Profl. Woman Spkrs. Bur., Fla. Nurses Assn., Women Health-

care Execs. Network, Nova Southeastern U. Sch. Bus. Alumni Assn. (bd. dirs. Broward County chpt. 1995—). Avocations: gardening, photography, needlework.

HENRY, PHILIP LAWRENCE, marketing professional; b. Los Angeles, Dec. 1, 1940; s. Lawrence Langworthy and Ella Hanna (Martens) H.; m. Claudia Antonia Huff, Aug. 9, 1965 (div. 1980); children: Carolyn Marie, Susan Michelle; m. Carrie Katherine Hoover, Aug. 23, 1985. BS in Marine Engring., Calif. Maritime Acad., 1961. Design engr. Pacific Telephone Co., San Diego, 1963-73; service engr. Worthington Service Corp., San Diego, 1973-78; pres. Realmart Corp., San Diego, 1978-81; dir. mktg. Orbit Inn Hotel and Casino, Las Vegas, 1981-84; pres. Comml. Consultants, Las Vegas, 1984—, Gray Electronics Co., Las Vegas, 1986—; chmn. bd. dirs. Las Vegas Accomodations Unltd., 1997—; mng. mem. G/Tracker Techs., LLC, 1998, Strobe Detector Techs., LLC, 1998; bd. dirs. Silver State Classic Challenge, Inc. Inventor electronic detection devices, 1986—. Served to lt. (j.g.) USNR, 1961-67. Republican. Avocation: amateur radio, open road auto racing, storm chasing. Home: 1843 Somersby Way Henderson NV 89014-3876

HENRY, RICHARD CHARLES, communications executive; b. Reading, Eng., Feb. 26, 1941; s. John Richard and Blanche Catherine (Barrett) H.; m. Judith Ann Massey, Apr. 16, 1976; children: Charles, Belinda, Jane, Margaret. Chartered acct., U.K. Capt. Territorial Army, 1961-76; mng. cons. Coopers and Lybrand, London, 1978-84; dir. fin., sec. The Press Assn. Ltd., London, 1984-96; group fin. dir. Nation Media Group Ltd., Nairobi, Kenya, 1996—. Treas. Hon. Arty. Co., London, 1990-93, v.p., 1994-96. Decorated Territorial Decoration. Fellow Inst. Chartered Accts., Army and Navy Club, Muithaga Club (Nairobi, Kenya).

HENRY, RICHARD JOSEPH, JR., nursing home management executive; b. Melrose, Mass., Sept. 1, 1954; s. Richard Joseph and Janet Louise (Behrle) H.; m. Diane Marrianne Rael, June 20, 1987; children: Aliandra, Joseph. ThB, So. Coll., Collegedale, Tenn., 1980; postgrad., George Washington U., 1980-81. Cert. nursing home adminstr. Asst. adminstr. Care More, Inc., Chattanooga, 1980-81; dir. devel./adminstrn. Macon (Ga.) Health Care Ctr., 1981-82; adminstr. Sierra Health Care Ctr., Truth or Consequence, N.Mex., 1982-84, Belen (N.Mex.) Health Care Ctr., 1984-85; asst. dir. ops./adminstrn. West Mesa Health Care Ctr., Albuquerque, 1985-86; adminstr. Hobbs (N.Mex.) Health Care Ctr., 1986-87; dir. adminstrv. svcs. Care More, Inc., Macon, 1987-88; adminstr., exec. dir. Aloha Health Care Ctr., Kaneohe, Hawaii, 1988-90; sr. v.p. Aloha Mgmt. Co., Kaneohe, Hawaii, 1990-96, 1993-96; exec. dir., v.p. Health Quality Mgmt. Group The Rehab. Ctr. of Beverly Hills, 1996-97; pres. The Heaton Group, Albuquerque, 1997-2000, LTC Alliance Nursing Home Consultanting Firm, Albuquerque, 2000—; registered preceptor Hawaii Adminstr.-in-Tng. Program, 1989-93. With USAF, 1972-78, USNG, 1974-78. Named Adminstr. of the Yr. Care More, Inc., 1985. Fellow Am. Coll. Health Care Adminstrs. (pres., sec. 1989-91), Hawaii Long Term Care Assn. (pres. 1992-94), Rotary (pres.-elect Windward Oahu chpt., dir. cmty. svcs. 1988-90, Rotarian of Yr. award 1990, Disting. Svc. award 1995). Republican. Avocations: soccer, web page design, computer systems. Home: 6621 Barber Pl NE Albuquerque NM 87109-2747

HENRY, ROY MONROE, financial planner; b. Oct. 27, 1939; s. Roy Monroe and Nancy Lowe (Morse) H.; m. Meredith Elaine Hjelmstad, Aug. 20, 1961; children: Robin E., Roy M. III. BBA, Kennedy-Western, 1990. Registered prin., rep.-NASD; LUTCF. Airman 1st class USAF, Turkey, 1957-61; estimator Con P. Curran Printing Co., St. Louis, 1961-64; sales mgr. Prudential Ins. Co., St. Louis, 1964-72; pres. Roy M. Henry & Assocs., Chesterfield, Mo., 1972-76, St. Louis Fin. Planners, Chesterfield, Mo., 1976-83, First Fin. Planners, Chesterfield, Mo., 1983—; guest spkr. Purdue U., Yale U., Stanford U. Appeared on (TV show) 20/20, 1991; contbr. articles to profl. jours. Named Fin. Planner of Yr., 1987; commd. mem. Hon. Order of Ky. Cols. Fellow Life Underwriting Tng. Counsel; mem. Internat. Assn. Fin. Planners (bd. dirs. 1984-86), Mo. Athletic Club, Internat. Assn. of Registered Fin. Cons. (emeritus). Republican. Lutheran. Avocations: travel, model trains, cars, video and career. Home: 2031 Kehrsboro Dr Chesterfield MO 63005-6512

HENRYSSON, HARALDUR, judge; b. Feb. 17, 1938; m. Elisabet Kristinsdottir; 1 child. Cand. juris, U. Iceland, 1964. Asst. judge Criminal Ct., Kopavogu, Iceland, 1964-73; judge Criminal Ct., Reykjavik, 1973-88; judge Supreme Ct., Reykjavik, 1988—, chief justice, 1996-97; chmn. com. investigating accidents at sea, 1973-83. Mem. Grand Cross Icelandic Falcon. Fax: 562-3995. Office: Domhusid v Arnarhol, 150 Reykjavik Iceland

HENSCHKE, CLAUDIA INGRID, physician, radiologist; b. Berlin, Mar. 3, 1941; d. Ulrich Konrad and Gisela Franziska H. BA in French, So. Meth. U., 1962, MS in Math. Stats., 1966; PhD in Stats., U. Ga., 1969; MD, Howard U., 1977; Radiologist, Harvard U., 1981. Diplomate Am. Bd. Radiology. Internship, residency dept. radiology Harvard Med. Sch./Brigham and Women's Hosp., 1977-81, clin. fellow in radiology, 1977-81; rsch. fellow in radiology Brigham and Women's Hosp., 1981-82, Harvard Med. Sch., Boston, 1981-82; rsch. fellow in epidemiology Harvard Sch. of Pub. Health, 1981-82; assoc. radiologist Brigham and Women's Hosp., 1982-83, co-dir. Thoracic Divsn., 1983; asst. attending radiology to assoc. radiologist The N.Y. Hosp. - Cornell Med. Ctr., 1983-87, 87-92, sect. chief, chest imaging to chief of divsn., 1988-92, 92-95, attending radiologist, 1992—, chief, Divsn. of Health Care Policy and Tech. Assessment, 1995—, chief, Divsn. of Chest Imaging, 1995—; various acad. positions to prof. radiology, Cornell U. Med. Coll., 1992—; cons. Rockefeller U., 1986—, Med. Billing Program Devel. and Med. Computer Systems Planning, 1986—; lectr. in field; mem. numerous coms. in field; vis. prof. numerous univs., including Columbia U., 1999, Roy Castle Internat. Ctr. for Lung Cancer Rsch., Liverpool, Eng., 1999, Washington U., 1999, Clinica U., Pamplona, Spain, 1999, U. Rochester, N.Y., 1999, others. Mem. editl. bd. Complications in Surgery, 1995—, Investigative Radiology, 1990-94, Clin. Imaging, 1988—, Acad. Radiology, 1994—, others; reviewer Am. Jour. Cardiology, 1982—, Chest, 1992—, Radiology, 1993—, Jour. of Computed Assisted Tomography, 1995—, Am. Jour. of Radiology, 1995—, others; contbr. numerous books, including: Women's Complete Handbook, 1994, Introduction to Statistics and Computer Programming, 1975, Instructions for General Purpose Program Package, 1971, First and Second Biomedical Computing Symposium 1965 and 1966, 1967; contbr. numerous articles to profl. jours. and publs. Named Ky. Col. by Gov. of Ky., 1963; grantee in field. Mem. Am. Statis. Soc., Am. Assn. Women Radiologists (Marie Curie award/2d place 1994), Radiol. Soc. N.Am., Am. Coll. Radiology, Soc. Thoracic Radiology, Sigma Xi, Phi Kappa Phi. Office: New York Hosp/Dept Radiol Cornell Med Ctr New York NY 10021

HENSE, DONALD LANGFORD, educational association administrator; b. St. Louis, July 4, 1942; s. Fred Hense and Lillie Ivy H.; 1 child, Dana. AB, Morehouse Coll., 1970; postgrad., Stanford U., 1973. Dir. govtl. rels. Howard U., Washington, 1973-79, Boston U., 1979-81, Dartmouth Coll., Hanover, N.H., 1984-86; v.p. for devel. and univ. rels. Prairie View (Tex.) A&M U., 1986-88; v.p. for devel. Nat. Urban League, N.Y.C., 1988-90; dir. Nat. Fedn. of Interfaith Vol. Caregivers, Kansas City, Mo., 21st Century Found., N.Y. Merrill scholar Charles E. Merrill Trust, U. Ghana, 1969, Rockefeller Intern in Econs., Rockefeller Found., Cornell U., 1968, Ford Found. Dissertation fellow, Stanford U., 1973, NDEA fellow, 1970-72. Mem. Nat. Soc. Fundraising Exec. (DC chpt. bd. dirs. 1993-96, Fundraising Exec. of Yr. 1999), Kappa Alpha Psi. Baptist. E-mail: dhense@friendshiphouse.net. Office: Friendship House Assn 619 D St SE Washington DC 20003

HENSEL, ANDREAS, pharmacist; b. Dahn, Pfalz, Germany, June 8, 1962; s. Robert Hensel and Hildegard Maurer; m. Sabine Inge Cartellieri, Nov. 28, 1988. BS in Pharmacy, U. Regensburg, Germany, 1985; PhD, U. Regensburg, 1988. Postdoctoral fellow McGill U., Montreal, Canada, 1988-89; group leader R&D ASTA Medica AG, Frankfurt, Germany, 1990-94; asst. prof. U. Erlangen, Germany, 1995-98, habilitator, 1998-99; assoc. prof. biosci. U. Würzburg, Germany, 1999—; pres. Glycopharmacy Group, Erlangen. Author: Memofix Pharmazie, 1995; contbr. articles to profl. jours. Achievements include patent for polysaccharides, 1998. Avocations: mountain climbing, classical music. Office: U Erlangen, Staudtstr 5, 91058 Erlangen Germany

HENSEL, ROBIN ANN MORGAN, mathematics and computer science educator; b. Buffalo, Dec. 1, 1960; d. Robert R. and Vivian J. (Kline) Morgan; m. John Peter Max Hensel; 1 child, Jonathan Peter. BS in Math., Wheaton Coll., 1981; MA in Math., SUNY, Buffalo, 1983; EdD in Higher Edn. Tchg., W.Va. U., 1988. Mathematician Morgantown (W.Va.) Energy Tech. Ctr. U.S. Dept. Energy, 1983-88; computer sys. analyst Morgantown (W.Va.) Energy Tech. Ctr., U.S. Dept. Energy, 1988-90; asst. prof. math. and computer sci. Salem-Teikyo U., Salem, W.Va., 1990-95, assoc. prof., 1995—. Violinist Morgantown Cmty. Arts Orch., 1984-89, Amherst Symphony, N.Y., 1981-83, Morgantown Christian and Missionary Alliance Ch. Orch., 1992—; instr. ARC, 1982; mem. Christian and Missionary Alliance; trustee Alliance Christian Sch., 1995—, pres. bd. trustees, 1997—. N.Y. State Regents scholar, 1978. Mem. Am. Math. Soc., Nat. Coun. Tchrs. Mathematics, Cum Laude Soc., Assn. Women in Math., Math. Assn. Am., Phi Delta Kappa. Republican. Avocations: swimming, music, camping. Home: 163 Scenery Dr Morgantown WV 26505-2534 Office: Salem-Teikyo U Dept Maths and Tech Studies Salem WV 26426

HENSEL, WITOLD, archaeologist; b. Poznan, Poland, Mar. 29, 1917; s. Maksymilian and Maria (Formanowicz) H.; m. Maria Chmielewska, June 5, 1941; children: Wojciech (dec. 1997), Zdzislaw, Leszek, Barbara. M in Philosophy, U. Poznan, 1938, Docent, 1948; PhD, Cath. U. Lublin, Poland, 1945; D (hon.), U. Poznan, 1987. Lectr. Cath. U. Lublin, 1944-45; prof. extraordinary, head chair archaeology U. Poznan, 1951-55, dean history and philosophy dept., 1951-53; vice dir. Inst. History Material Culture Polish Acad. Scis., Warsaw, 1953-54, dir., 1954-89; prof. extraordinary U. Warsaw, 1954-56, prof. ordinary, 1956-87, head chair Slavonic archaeology dept., 1956-65, head chair prehistoric and early medieval archaeology, 1968-70, prof. emeritus, 1987—; prof. emeritus Polish Acad. Scis., 1989—; leader expdns. Poland, Yugoslavia, France, Italy, Algeria. Author: Studia i materiały do osadnictwa Wielkopolski wczesnohistorycznej, vol. I-VIII, 1948-95, vol. V-VIII (with Zofia Kurnatowska), Słowiańszczyzna wczesnosredniowieczna, 1952, 56, 65, 87, Polska przed tysiacem lat, 1960, 64, 67, La naissance de la Pologne, 1966, The Beginnings of the Polish State, 1960, Najdawniejsze stolice Polski, 1960, Archeologia o poczatkach miast slowianskich, 1963, Anfänge der Städte bei der Ost and Westslawen, 1967, Ziemie polskie w pradziejach, 1969, Archeologia i prahistoria, 1971, Polska starozytna, 1973, 80, 88, Ur-und Frühgeschichte Polens, 1974, Odkakadojdeni Slovenite, 1983, Skadpryszli Srowianie, 1984, Le origini della Polonia, 1986; editor: Slavia Antigua vol. I, 1948, (with Zofia Kurnatogyka), vol. XXVII, 1989—. Decorated comdrs. cross with star Polonia Restituta; comdr. Cross al Merito della Republica Italiana; recipient State prize, 1955, 66, Copernicus medal Polish Acad. Scis., 1977, Gold medal Czechoslavak Acad. Scis., 1975, Polish Parliament award, 1965-69. Mem. Polish Acad. Scis. (mem. presidency 1984-89), Mak, Acad. Scis. and Arts, Sâchsische Acad. Scis., Deutschen Archäol. Instituts (O.M.-Berlin), Istituto Italiano Preist, Protost (Firenze), Union Pre and Protohist. Scis. (internat. coun. 1956-91, hon. com. 1991—), Union Studies Origin Towns (chmn. internat. com. 1962-94), Internat. Congress Slavists (v.p. 1971-92), Internat. Slav. Archaeol. (pres. 1966, v.p. 1966-92), Internat. Union Anthropol. and Ethnographic Studies (hon., chmn. nat. com. 1986-89), Polish Archaeol. and Numismatic Soc. (hon., chmn. 1969-70), Jugoslavian Archaeol. Socs., Polish Anthropol. Soc., Soc. of Scis. of Plock, Instytut Zachodni, Soc. Wojciech Kętrzyński, Olsztyn. Home: m 109, Marszalkowska 84/92, 00-514 Warsaw Poland

HENSHAW, BEVERLY ANN HARSH, women's health nurse, consultant; b. Jasper, Mich., Aug. 26, 1937; d. Arthur Estol and Doris Ione (Lindsay) Harsh; m. Robert E. Henshaw, Aug. 30, 1958; children: Kit, Kim, Brad; m. Kenneth P. Wilkinson, Apr. 8, 1978; children: Jeff, Brian, David. BSN, U. Mich., 1960; cert. ob-gyn. nurse practitioner, Johns Hopkin's U., 1973; MSN, Pa. State U., 1983. RN, Pa.; cert. nurse practitioner. Instr. Sch. Nursing Pa. State U., University Park, NP women's health; NP, clinic mgr. Family Health Svcs., Inc., State College, Pa.; pvt. practice cons. 5; care coord. Health Beginnings Plus Project; cons. in field. Mem. Am. Acad. Nurse Practitioners, Assn. Women's Health, Ob. and Neonatal Nurses, ANA, NANPRH, Jacobs Inst. of Women's Health, Assn. Reproductive Health Profls., Lamaze Internat. E-mail: bevhenshaw@aol.com. Home: RD 1 Box 340 Port Matilda PA 16870-9426

HENSLOWE, PHILIP FRANCIS, public relations and training consultant; b. Liverpool, Lancashire, Eng., Apr. 27, 1934; s. Francis Arthur and Mercy Eleanor (Robertson) H.; m. Elizabeth Moira Allely, Sept. 24, 1960; children: Anyon, James, Peter. Ed., RMA Sandhurst, 1952-53. Commd. officer Royal Arty., 1954, advanced through grades to maj., 1967, served in Korea, Japan, Hong Kong, Malaya, and Germany,, 1954-57; adj. and troop comdr., Royal Arty., Germany, Borneo, Eng., 1957-67; gunnery instr., battery comdr., ops. staff officer NATO, 1967-73; ret., 1973; mgr. Celtic Cross Ltd., Devon-Cornwell Counties, Eng., 1973-75, RB& A Rickaby, St. Austell, Eng., 1975-79; cmty. officer Bournville Village Trust, Birmingham, Eng., 1979-87, pub. rels. officer, 1987-89; exec. dir. Bournville Pub. Rels. Svcs., Birmingham, 1989-92; dir. pub. affairs BVT Group, Birmingham, 1992-97; ret., 1997; ptnr. Moyclare Enterprise Group, Birmingham; ptnr. Moyclare Enterprise Group, Liskeard, Comwall. Author: Public Relations for Housing Associations, 1983, 90 Years On, 1984, 91. Chmn. consultative com. W. Midlands Police, Birmingham, 1983-86; chmn. governing body Kings Norton Girls Sch., 1989-94; chmn. Crimestoppers Bd., Birmingham, 1989-94, Zillwood Edn. Trust U.K., 1989-92, Mktg. Stds. Bd., 1990-97; bd. govs. Liskeard Sch. and C.C., 1999—; mem. Devon & Cornwall Crimestoppers, 1999—. Fellow Comm., Advt. and Mktg. Found., Inst. Pub. Rels. (chmn. West Midlands region 1986-88); mem. Inst. Mgmt., Internat. Pub. Rels. Assn., Worshipful Co. of Marketors. Anglican. Avocations: music, performing arts, reading, gardening. Home: Moyclare Liskeard, Cornwall PL 144EH, England Office: Moyclare Enterprise Group, PO Box 48 Liskeard, Cornwall PL14 4YP, England

HENTER, JAN-INGE, pediatrician; b. Gothenborg, Sweden, Aug. 28, 1953; s. Edgar and Berit (Larsson) H.; m. Maria Axelsson, Oct. 5, 1979; children: Gustav, Viking. MD, Uppsala (Sweden) U., 1980; PhD, Karolinska Inst., Stockholm, 1990. Med. diplomate. Intern various hosps., Uppsala and Enköping, 1980-82; resident St. Göran's Children's Hosp., Stockholm, 1982-86, staff physician, 1987-90; chief hematology dept. pediatric hematology and oncology Karolinska Hosp., Stockholm, 1990—; assoc. prof. pediatrics Karolinska Inst., 1993—; chmn. Internat. Familial Hemophagocytic Lymphohistiocytosis Study Group, N.J., 1993—. Author: Familial Hemophagocytic Lymphohistiocytosis, 1990; contbr. numerous articles to profl. jours. Bd. dirs. Swedish Drs. for the Environment, 1991-95. Mem. Swedish Med. Assn., Nordic Orgn. Pediatric Hematology/Oncology, Am. Soc. Pediatric Hematology/Oncology, Internat. Soc. Pediatric Oncology, Internat. Histiocyte Soc. (sci. com. 1992-98), Histiocyte Soc. (bd. dirs. 1995—). Avocations: tennis, skiing, out-door activities, journeys. Office: Karolinska Hosp, Dept Pediatrics, S 171 76 Stockholm Sweden

HENTGES, DAVID JOHN, microbiology educator; b. LeMars, Iowa, Sept. 18, 1928; s. Romaine Francis and Geneva Mae (Kruger) H.; m. Kathleen Edwina Mullan, Dec. 28, 1957; children: Stephen Edward, Kathleen Marie, Margaret Ann. BS, U. Notre Dame, 1953; MS, Loyola U., Chgo., 1958, PhD, 1961. Asst. prof. Creighton U. Sch. Medicine, Omaha, 1964-67, assoc. prof., 1967-68; assoc. prof. U. of Mo. Sch. of Medicine, Columbia, 1968-72, prof., 1972-81, interim chmn., 1976-79; prof., chmn. Tex. Tech. U. Sch. Medicine, Lubbock, 1981-96, vice provost for rsch., dean grad. sch. biomed. scis., 1996-98, assoc. dean basic scis., 1996-98, dean emeritus, 1998—. Editor: Human Intestinal Microflora, 1983, Medical Microbiology, 1986, Microbiology and Immunology, 2d edit., 1995; regional editor Microbial Ecology in Health and Disease, 1987-96; mem. editl. bd. Infection and Immunity, 1983-92, Anaerobe, 1998—; contbr. chpts. to books and articles to profl. jours. Lay gen. chmn. Diocesan Cath. Appeal, Lubbock, 1989, 97; coexec. dir. Cath. Found. Diocese of Lubbock, 1998—. Named Knight Comdr. with star Order of the Holy Sepulchre, 2000, Knight of Merit with star Constantinian Order of St. George, 2000. Fellow Am. Acad. of Microbiology (emeritus); mem. Cath. Acad. of Scis., Soc. for Microbial Ecology and Disease (pres. 1987-89), Serra Internat. (dist. gov. 1987-88), Sigma Xi. Republican. Roman Catholic. Avocations: gardening, fly fishing. Home: 4601 88th St Lubbock TX 79424-4107

HENTSCHEL, EBERHARDT CEDRIC, cultural relations administrator; b. Willesden, England, Dec. 6, 1912; s. William Moritz and Martha Maria (Janitzka) H.; m. Eva Clara Bolgar, Jan. 29, 1946; children: George, Christopher, Anthony, Barbara. BA, U. Coll. London, 1934, MA, 1937; PhD, U. London, 1961. Reader English Uppsala U., Sweden, 1941-46; dir. British Coun., Amsterdam, 1946-48, Israel, 1950-54, Mex., 1954-58, Finland, 1958-60, Jamaica, 1960-66, Bavaria, 1966-74. Author: Alexander von Humboldt's Synthesis of Literature and Science, 1969, The Byronic Teuton, 1978; editor: Lord Byron, A Self-Portrait, 1979, Powys to Eric the Red, 1983, Powys on Keats, 1993; translator: (3 vols.) German Short Stories, 1975, 77, 82; contbr. articles to profl. jours. Fellow Royal Geographical Soc.; mem. Powys Soc., Inst. Germanic Studies. Avocation: architectural history. Home: Millpool Cottage, Suffolk, Ellingham NR35 2EP, England

HENTSCHEL, KLAUS, science historian; b. Bad Nauheim, Hessen, Germany, Apr. 4, 1961; s. Hans Dieter and Ruth (Schmidt-Stockhausen) H.; m. Ann Marie Lehar, Jan. 3, 1992. MA in Philosophy, U. Hamburg, Germany, 1985, diploma in physics, 1987, PhD in History of Sci. summa cum laude, 1989, Habilitation, 1995. Vis. rschr. Einstein papers project Boston U., 1987; Rathenau fellow Verbund Wissenschaftsgeschichte, U. Berlin, 1989-90; rschr. DFG project U. Hamburg, 1990-91; resident fellow Dibner Inst. for History of Sci. and Tech., Cambridge, Mass., 1996-97; asst. prof. U. Göttingen, Germany, 1991-96, 97—. Author: Interpretations and Misinterpretations of Relativity Theory by Einstein's Contemporaries, 1990 (Kurt Hartwig Siemers prize Hamburg Wissenschaftliche Stiftung 1990), Der Einstein Turm, Erwin F. Freundlich und die Relativitatstheorie, 1992, English transl., 1997; contbg. editor: The Collected Papers of Albert Einstein, Vol. 5; editor (anthology of primary sources) Physics and National Socialism, 1996; co-editor: Carl Runge-Max Planck Letter Diary, 1999. Studienstiftung des Deutschen Volkes fellow, 1980-87; recipient Heinz-Maier-Leibnitz prize German Fed. Minstry Sci. and Edn., 1992, Paul Bunge prize for study on history of instrumentation, 1993, Marc-Auguste-Pictet prize, Geneva Acad., 1998, Leopoldina prize in history of sci., 1999. Mem. History of Sci. Soc., Philosophy of Sci. Assn., Deutsche Gesellschaft Geschichte der Medizin, Naturwissenschaften, Math. Tech., Agricola-Gesellschaft, German Phys. Soc. (bd. mem. history of physics sect. 1999—). Avocations: photography, bicycling, listening to music. Office: Univ Göttingen, Humboldtallee 11, Inst Wiss, D-37073 Göttingen Germany

HENTSELL, DAVID, management consultant; b. U.K., Sept. 30, 1955. Contracts negotiator Bacchus Internat., London, 1974-78; regional dir. sales and mktg. Le Meridien Hotels, Middle East, 1978-84; regional dir. U.K. and France CFCI, Paris, 1984-92; group co-chmn. Instore Images, U.K., 1997—; performance coach Interaction Internat., 1992—; cons. over 1200 managers, owners, dirs. Author: Negotiating Tactics, 1998, 24 Key Characteristics of Great Leaders, 1998; contbr. articles to profl. publs. Fellow Inst. Sales and Mktg. Mgmt. Avocations: health and gym fitness, golf, reading, creating new material, giving back. E-mail: david hentsell@compuserve.com.

HENTZE, JOACHIM, economist, educator; b. Rechlin, Germany, June 23, 1940; s. Wilhelm and Erna (Klage) H.; m. Ursula Klippel, Aug. 28, 1971; children: Michael, Kirsten. GCE, Leibnizschule, Hanover, 1961; M, Univ. Göttingen, 1966; PhD, U. Hanover, 1969; D (hon.), U. Sofia, 1998. Head of dept. mgmt. U. Braunschweig, 1980; guest lectr. U. Nebr., 1985, Beijing (China) U., 1987, Tech. U., Sofia, 1992; mng. dir. Inst. of Econs., Braunschweig, 1988-92; chmn. Comm. of Econs., Braunschweig, 1989-92. Author: Personalwirtschaftslehre, 1995, Unternehmungsplanung, 1992, Personalführungslehre, 1997, Personalcontrolling, 1993. Avocations: skiing, mountain climbing, literature. Office: Technische U, Abt-Jerusalem Str 4, 38106 Braunschweig Germany

HENTZE, MATTHIAS WERNER, scientist; b. Rheda-Wiedenbrueck, Germany, Jan. 25, 1960; s. Werner and Maria Hentze; m. Sabine B.C. Schoenfeld, Aug. 3, 1984; children: Eva Kathrin, Stephanie Ellen, Carolin Heike. MD, cert. physician, U. Muenster, Germany, 1984. Physician Vinzenz Hosp., Rheda-Wiedenbrueck, 1985; postdoctoral rschr. NIH, Bethesda, Md., 1985-87; vis. assoc. NIH, Bethesda, 1987-89; group leader European Molecular Biology Lab., Heidelberg, Germany, 1989—; dean grad. studies European Molecular Biology Lab., Heidelberg, 1996—, sr. scientist, 1998—. Mem. editl. bd. Trends in Biochem. Scis., 1996—, Embo Jour., 1999—; contbr. articles to profl. jours. Recipient Gottfried Wilhelm Leibniz prize, 2000. Mem. RNA Soc. (mem. editl. bd. 1996—), European Molecular Biology Orgn., German Soc. for Biochemistry and Molecular Biology. Avocations: history, arts, enology, sports. E-mail: hentze@embl-heidelberg.de. Office: European Molecular Biol Lab, Meyerhofstrasse 1, D-69117 Heidelberg Germany

HENYCH, IVO, metal processing consultant; b. Skvorec, Prague, Czechoslovakia, Jan. 12, 1935; s. Rudolf and Vera (Stadelmann) H.; m. Alexandra Spada; 1 child, Blanka Cartier. MS in Engring., State U. Mining and Metallurgy, Ostrava, Czechoslovakia, 1962. Metallurgist, mgr. Kralodv Zelezarny, Kraluvdvur, Czechoslovakia, 1961-68; metall. researcher Georg Fischer, Ltd., Schaffhausen, Switzerland, 1968-80, br. mgr., 1980-95; gen. mgr. licensing Georg Fischer Disa Engring., Schaffhausen, Switzerland, 1996-2000; foundry industry cons. Schaffhausen, 2000—; mgr. Foundry Tech. Transfer. Contbr. articles to profl. jours.; patentee in field. Named to Ductile Iron Hall of Fame, 1998. Mem. Verein Deutsche Giessereifachleute, Am. Foundrymen Assn., Lic. Exec. Soc. Avocations: photography, computers. Home: IM Buel 21, 8234 Stetten Switzerland

HENZE, HANS WERNER, composer, conductor; b. Gütersloh, Ger., July 1, 1926; s. Franz and Margarete (Geldmacher) H.; Mus D U. Edinburgh, 1971. Artistic dir. Ballet of the Hessian State Theatre, Wiesbaden, from 1950; prof. composition Mozarteum, Salzburg, 1962-67, Hochschule für Musik, Cologne, 1980-91; dir. Accademia Filarmonica Romana, Rome, 1981—, Munich Biennale, 1988, 90, 92, 94, 96; pres. Contemporary Opera Studio English Nat. Opera, 1996—; compositions include: operas: Das Wundertheater, 1948-64, Blvd. Solitude, 1951, König Hirsch, 1953-56, Der Prinz von Homburg, 1958-59, rev. 1991, Elegy for Young Lovers, 1961, rev. 1987, Der Junge Lord, 1964, The Judgement of Calliope, 1964, 91, Die Bassariden, 1964-65, rev. 1992, La Cubana, 1973, Don Chisciotte, 1976, We Come To The River, 1974-76, Il Ritorno d'Ulisse in Patria, 1981, The English Cat, 1980-83, Das verratene Meer, 1986-89, IL Re Teodoro in Venezia, 1991-92, Venus and Adonis, 1993-95; radio operas: Ein Landarzt, 1951, 94, Das Ende einer Welt, 1953, 93; music for films including Muriel The Young Törless, numerous ballets, 9 symphonies, chamber music, vocal music and orchestra works. Recipient Robert Schumann prize, 1951, Prix d'Italia, 1953, Sibelius Gold medal London, 1956, North Rhine Westphalia Art prize, 1957, Music Critics prize Buenos Aires, 1958, Great Arts award Berlin, 1959, Arts award Lower Saxony, Hannover, 1961, Bach prize of Free Hanseatic City of Hamburg, 1983, Ludwig Spohr Preis, 1976, Ernst-von-Siemens-Preis, 1990, Apollo d'Oro Bilbao, 1990, Grand Cross Disting. Svc. of the Order of Merit of Fed. Rep. Germany, 1991, Music award of Duisburg, 1995, Annette-von-Droste-Hülshoff prize, 1996, Spl. Cultural award City of Munich, 1996, Hans von Bülow medal Berlin Philharmonic Orch., 1997, Bavarian Order of Maximilian for Sci. and Art, 1998; Hon. fellow Royal Northern Coll. Music, 1998. Author: Undine, Diary of a Ballet, 1958; Essays, 1964; (with H. Enzenberger) El Cimmarron-A Work Report, 1971; Musik und Politik, 1976; The English Cat - A Work Report, 1982; New Aspects of Musical Aesthetics I-IV, 1979-1990, Reiselieder mit böhmischen Quinten Autobiography, 1996, Bohemian Fifths: An Autobiography (translated by Stewart Spencer 1998), Komponieren in der Schule, 1998. Office: Schott Musik Internat, Weihergarten 5, 55116 Mainz Germany also: Schott Musik Internat, Postfach 36 40, D-55026 Mainz Germany

HEO, MANE, international politics educator; b. Pajoo, Kyong-gi, South Korea, Feb. 23, 1939; m. Eun-Hee Park; 1 child, Seung-jyung. B, Hankuk U. Fgn. Studies, Seoul, Korea, 1963; M in Internat. Polit. Sci., Korea U., Seoul, 1970; PhD, U. Paris I, 1979. Asst. prof. Pusan (Korea) Nat. U., 1980-82, assoc. prof., 1984-90, prof. internat. politics, 1989—, dir. Unification Rsch. Inst., 1986-88; adv. prof. Ministry of Justice, Seoul, 1989—; vice-dir. Korean Soc. of Contemporary European Studies, 1994—; dir. Ctr. for

European Studies, 1997—; dir. Yong-Nam br. Korean Assn. Internat. Studies, Kyong-Nam, Korea, 1987-88; presenter, lectr. in field. Author: Marxism and the Contemporary World, 1984, Korean Peninsula and Foreign Policy, 1988, Peace and Security in Northeast Asia, 1997 (English edit.), Foreign Policy of De Gaulle, 1997, New International Politics, 1997, Europe's Integration Politics--Grand Design for Greater Unity, 1999. 1st lt. Korean Army, 1964-67. Mem. Korea Soc. Contemporary European Studies (pres.), Internat. Polit. Sci. Assn. (dir. 1997-99). Avocations: tennis, golf. Office: Coll Edn Pusan Nat U, 30 Changjeon-dong, 609-735 Pusan Korea

HEPBURN, KATHARINE HOUGHTON, actress; b. Hartford, Conn., May 12, 1907; d. Thomas N. and Katharine (Houghton) H.; m. Ludlow Ogden Smith (div.). AB, Bryn Mawr Coll., 1928; LHD (hon.), Columbia U., 1992. Actress: (films) A Bill of Divorcement, 1932, Christopher Strong, 1933, Morning Glory, 1933 (Acad. award for best performance by actress 1934), Little Women, 1933, Spitfire, 1934, The Little Minister, 1934, Alice Adams, 1935, Break of Hearts, 1935, Sylvia Scarlett, 1936, Mary of Scotland, 1936, A Woman Rebels, 1936, Quality Street, 1937, Stage Door, 1937, Bringing up Baby, 1938, Holiday, 1938, The Philadelphia Story, 1940 (N.Y. Critic's award 1940), Woman of the Year, 1941, Keeper of the Flame, 1942, Stage Door Canteen, 1943, Dragon Seed, 1944, Without Love, 1945, Undercurrent, 1946, Sea of Grass, 1946, Song of Love, 1947, State of the Union, 1948, Adam's Rib, 1949, The African Queen, 1951, Pat and Mike, 1952, Summertime, 1955, The Rainmaker, 1956, The Iron Petticoat, 1956, The Desk Set, 1957, Suddenly Last Summer, 1959, Long Day's Journey into Night, 1962 (Best Actress, Cannes Internat. Film Festival), Guess Who's Coming to Dinner, 1967, (Acad. award for best actress 1968),The Lion in Winter, 1968 (Acad. award for best actress 1969), Madwoman of Chaillot, 1969, Trojan Women, 1971, A Delicate Balance, 1973, Rooster Cogburn, 1975, Olly, Olly, Oxen Free, 1978, On Golden Pond, 1981 (Acad. award for best actress 1981), George Stevens: A Filmmaker's Journey, 1984, The Ultimate Solution of Grace Quigley, 1985, Love Affair, 1994; (plays) The Czarina, 1928, The Big Pond, 1928, Night Hostess, 1928, These Days, 1928, Death Takes a Holiday, 1929, A Month in the Country, 1930, Art and Mrs. Bottle, 1930, The Warrior's Husband, 1932, Lysistrata, 1932, The Lake, 1933, Jane Eyre, 1937, The Philadelphia Story, 1939, Without Love, 1942, As You Like It, 1950, The Millionairess, Eng. and U.S.A., 1952, The Taming of the Shrew, The Merchant of Venice, Measure for Measure,, Eng. and Australia, 1955, Merchant of Venice, Much Ado about Nothing, Am. Shakespeare Festival, 1957, toured later, 1958, Twelfth Night, Antony and Cleopatra, Am. Shakespeare Festival, 1960, Coco, 1969-70, toured, 1971, The Taming of the Shrew, 1970, A Matter of Gravity, 1976-78, West Side Waltz, 1981, (TV movies) The Glass Menagerie, 1973, Love among the Ruins, 1975, The Corn Is Green, 1979, Mrs. Delafield Wants to Marry, 1986; Laura Lansing Slept Here, 1988, The Man Upstairs, 1992, This Can't Be Love, 1994, One Christmas, 1994; narrator, co-writer documentary Katharine Hepburn: All About Me, 1993; author: The Making of the African Queen, 1987, (autobiography) Me, 1991. Recipient gold medal as world's best motion picture actress Internat. Motion Picture Expn., Venice, Italy, 1934, ann. award Shakespeare Club, N.Y.C., 1950, award Whistler Soc., 1957, Woman of Yr. award Hasty Pudding Club, 1958, outstanding achievement award for fostering finest ideals of acting profession, 1980, lifetime achievement award Coun. Fashion Designers Am., 1986, award Kennedy Ctr. Awards, 1990. Office: James D Miller Ltd 350 5th Ave Ste 5019 New York NY 10118-0080

HEPPELL, (THOMAS) STRACHAN, government agency administrator; b. Teesside, Eng., Aug. 15, 1935; s. Leslie Heppell and Doris Potts; m. Felicity Rice, 1963; 2 children. Degree, Queen's Coll., Oxford, Eng., 1058. Asst. prin. Nat. Assistance Bd., 1958-63, prin. Cabinet Office Dept. Health and Social Security, 1963-71; asst. dir. social welfare Hong Kong, 1971-73; asst. sec. Dept. Health and Social Security, 1973-79, undersec., 1979-83, dep. sec. Dept. of Health, 1983-94; chair mgmt. bd. European Agy. for the Evaluation of Medicinal Products, 1994—; cons. Dept. of Health, 1995—; mem. Broadcasting Standards Commn., U.K., 1996—; vis. fellow London Sch. Econs., 1997—; chair Family Fund Trust, 1997—. Contbr. articles to profl. jours. Fax: 020-7418 8409. Office: European Agy Evaluation Medicinal Products, 7 Westferry Circus, Canary Wharf London E14 4HB, England

HEPPER, DIETMAR, electronics engineer; b. Hamburg, Germany, June 17, 1957; s. Heinz and Godula (Bötefür) H. Diploma of engring., U. Hannover, Germany, 1983. Sci. rsch. asst. U. Hannover, 1984-87; devel. engr. Deutsche Thomson-Brandt GmbH, Hannover, 1988-95, sr. devel. engr., 1996—. Contbr. articles to profl. jours. and confs.; patentee in field. Office: Deutsche Thomson-Brandt, Deutsche Thomson-Brandt, Karl-Wiechert-Allee 74, 30625 Hannover Germany

HEPTINSTALL, DEBRA LOU, marketing professional; b. Tacoma, Mar. 5, 1952; d. Fred Bernard and June Isabella (Carter) H.; m. Michael Emory Smith, Sept. 26, 1980. Cert., Ctrl. Va. C.C., 1970, AAS cum laude, 1973. Advt. mgr. Times Record/Roane County Reporter, Spencer, W.Va., 1976-78; advt. clk., sales asst. The Washington Post, 1978-79; advt. mgr. The Reston (Va.) Times, 1979-80; ind. sales contractor The Washington Post, 1980-81, advt. sales rep., 1981-85, mktg. analyst pricing, 1985-87; advt. mgr. The Springfield (Va.) Connection Newspaper, 1988; mktg. promotional mgr. Def. News, Springfield, 1988; asst. rsch. dir. The Times Jour. Co., Springfield, 1988-91; mktg. analyst B&W Nuclear Environ. Svcs., Inc., Lynchburg, Va., 1993-94; adminstr., receptionist Indsl. Products, Co., Lynchburg, Va., 1994—. Methodist. Avocations: playing classical piano, Tae Kwon Do karate. Home: 404 College Park Dr Lynchburg VA 24502-2410

HEPWORTH, JOHN LEONARD, chemist, researcher; b. Salt Lake City, Nov. 2, 1927; s. Peter Leonard and Flora Victoria (Burningham) H.; m. Caryl Peterson, Mar. 19, 1951; children: Dale, Diana, Vicki, Joseph, James, John T. BS, U. Utah, 1952; MS, U. Idaho, 1958. Chemist GE Co., Richland, Wash., 1953-57, Am. Potash and Chem. Corp., Henderson, Nev., 1957-58; sr. chemist Thiokol Corp., Brigham City, Utah, 1958-90; supr. propellant devel. sect. Thiokol Corp., Brigham City, 1960, sr. scientist, 1967, dept. mgr. asst., 1970; instr. propellant chemistry Utah State U., Logan, 1962; cons. Battelle Inst., Hanford, Wash., 1965-68, McGraw-Hill, Inc., 1968-90; vol. substitute tchr. math., chemistry, physics, religion Box Elder H.S., Brigham City, Utah, 1998—; vol. tchr. for young adults with spl. needs, 1999—. Author: A Review of Hydrazinium Diperchlorate, 1967; contbr. articles to profl. publs. Missionary LDS Ch., 1948-50, 90-93; instr. Early Morning Seminary, 1954-57; officer PTA, 1960-62; coach Little League Sports, 1964-75; H.S. athletic officiator, 1972-92. With USN, 1946-48. Republican. Achievements include patents for development of separation process of Uranium and Plutonium from fission products, separation of radioactive Cesium from fission products, development of first stage propellant for Minuteman, C-4 and C-5 Trident, and Peacekeeper missiles, supervision of space shuttle development, development of delayed quick-cure catalyst employed in all three stages of Trident missiles. Avocations: playing the flute, reading, travel, athletics. E-mail: jhepworth@favorites.com. Home: 560 Holiday Dr Brigham City UT 84302-2387

HERAGU, SUNDERESH SESHARANGA, industrial engineering educator, consultant; b. Hassan, Karnataka, India, June 28, 1959; came to U.S. 1988; s. Heragu Ramanuja Sesharanga and Seethamma Sesharanga Iyengar; m. Rita Sunderesh Narasimhan, June 18, 1989. BEng, U. Mysore, India, 1982; MBA, U. Sask., 1985; PhD, U. Man., 1988. Lectr. Adichunchanagiri Inst. Tech., Chikmagalur, India, 1982-83; asst. prof. SUNY, Plattsburgh, 1988-91; assoc. prof. indsl. engring. Rensselaer Poly. Inst., Troy, N.Y., 1991—; adj. prof. U. Man., 1989-92; lectr. in field; presenter seminars, N.Am., Europe and India. Guest editor European Jour. Ops. Rsch.; author textbook: IIE Transactions (Gold award of Excellence in facilities planning); contbr. articles to profl. jours. U. Man. grad. fellow, 1987-88. Mem. Inst. Mgmt. Sci., Inst. Indsl. Engrs., Prodn. and Ops. Mgmt. Soc., Ops. Rsch. Soc. Am., Soc. Mfg. Engrs. Hindu. Avocations: exercise, swimming, jogging. Home: 4009 Windsor Dr Troy NY 12180-3522 Office: Rensselaer Poly Inst Decision Sci & Engring Troy NY 12180-3590

HERAK, JANKO N., biophysics educator; b. Brašljevica, Croatia, Feb. 5, 1937; s. Nikola and Dragica (Car) H.; m. Ana Skrbin; children: Carol Mirna, Maja. BSc, U. Zagreb, Croatia, 1960, MSc, 1964, PhD, 1967. Rsch. asst. Rudjer Bošković Inst., Zagreb, 1960-64; rsch. assoc. Duke U., Durham, N.C., 1964-66; rsch. assoc. Rudjer Bošković Inst., 1966-67, head magnetic resonance lab., 1967-76; prof. physics and biophysics, dept. pharmacy/biochemistry U. Zagreb, 1976—, head biophysics divsn., 1976—; vis. prof. U. B.C., Vancouver, 1973-74. Author: (textbook) Physics, (in Croatian) 1990; editor: Magnetic Resonance in Chemistry and Biology, 1975, Biological Supramolecular Structure and Function, 1983, Distinguished Croatian Scientists in America, 1998, Vol. II, 2000; contbr. over 100 articles to profl. publs. (in English). Fellow Soc. Free Radical Rsch.; mem. European Phys. Soc. (coun. mem. 1975-76), Yugoslav Biophys. Soc. (pres. 1982-84), Croatian-Am. Soc. (v.p. 1998). Avocations: mushrooms, tennis. Home: Siget 8/VIII, 10020 Zagreb Croatia Office: U Zagreb Dept Pharmacy, A Kovacica 1, 10001 Zagreb Croatia

HERAK, JURE, chemical engineer; b. Brasljevica, Croatia, June 17, 1940; s. Nikola and Dragica (Car) M.; m. Slavica Loncar, Sept. 16, 1967; children: Dean, Daniel. M, Faculty Tech. U. Zagreb, Croatia, 1973, D, 1977. Chem. technologist Pliva, Zagreb, Croatia, 1964-70, rsch. scientist, 1971; asst. Faculty Tech. U. Zagreb, 1972, rsch. assoc., 1988—. Contbr. articles to profl. jours. Mem. Croatian Chem. Soc., N.Y. Acad. Scis. Roman Catholic. Avocations: mountain climbing, cycling. Office: Pliva Rsch Inst, Prilaz Baruna Filipovica 25, 10000 Zagreb Croatia

HERALD, GEORGE WILLIAM, foreign correspondent; b. Berlin, Jan. 3, 1911; came to U.S., 1941; s. Bruno H. and Paula J. (Levy) H.; m. Martha A. Dubois, Mar. 24, 1948; children: Steve Anderew, Patricia Claudia. LLD cum laude, Basle (Switzerland) U., 1934; postgrad., Columbia U., 1950-52. Staff corr. UBS, B.Y.C., London, Paris, 1945-46; bus. chief UBS, Berlin and Vienna, 1946-49; spl. writer United Features, N.Y.C., 1949-52; assoc. editor UN World mag., N.Y.C. and Europe, 1952-55; head bur. Vision, Inc., Paris, 1955—. Author: My Favorite Assassin, 1943, (with others) Off the Record, 1952, Tatiana, 1955 (adapted for TV movie), (with Soraya Esfandiary) My Life as an Empress, 1962, The Big Wheel, 1963, Art and Money, 1977; contbg. editor Am. Peoples Ency., 1952-62; contbr. numerous articles to mags., including Reader's Digest, Harper's, McCall's. Capt. U.S. Army, 1942-45. Recipient Best Spl. Reporting from Abroad award Mex. Press, 1989. Mem. Authors League Am., Internat. Press Inst., Internat. Arts Coun., Overseas Press Club Am., Anglo-Am. Press Club. Office: Vision Inc Vision Bldg 310 Madison Ave Rm 1412 New York NY 10017-6006

HERAULT, YANN, embryologist, researcher; b. Nantes, Bretagne, France, Jan. 21, 1966; s. Rene and Jeannine (Danet) H. Lic., U. Paris XI, 1987, Maitrise, 1988, Magistere, 1989; Diplome d'Etude Approfondie, U. Lyon I, France, 1989; PhD, U. Lyon I, 1993; postgrad., Ecole Normale Superieure, St. Cloud, 1993. Postdoctorate U. Geneva, Switzerland, 1993-99; ATIPE group leader Genetic and Devel. Pathology CNRS UPR 9074, 1999—. Contbr. articles to med. and sci. jours. Fellow Assn. Recherche contre Cancer, 1993, European Molecular Biology Orgn., 1994-96. Fax: 33 238 257979. E-mail: herault@cnrs-orleans.fr. Office: CNRS UPR 9074, 3B Rue de la Ferollerie, 45071 Orleans Cedex 2, France

HERBER, STEVEN CARLTON, physician; b. L.A., Aug. 25, 1960; s. Raymond and Marilyn Joyce (Dart) H.; m. Katherine Carol Jones, Apr. 23, 1989. BS, Pacific Union Coll., 1982; Dr.med., Loma Linda U., 1986. Diplomate Nat. Bd. Med. Examiners, Am. Bd. Plastic Surgery. Resident surgeon Med. Ctr. Loma Linda (Calif.) U., 1986-90; resident plastic surgery Yale U., New Haven, Conn., 1990-92; asst. prof. surgery Loma Linda (Calif.) U., 1993-98; med. dir. Ctr. for Plastic Surgery at St. Helena Hosp., 1998—. Contbr. articles to profl. jours. NIH grantee, 1988, MacPherson Soc. Clin. Sci. fellow, 1992; recipient Leadership award, AMA, 1991, 98. Fellow ACS; mem. Am. Soc. Plastic Surgeons (bd. dirs.), Am. Cleft Palate, Craniofacial Assn., Calif. Med. Assn., San Bernardino County Med. Soc., Yale Plastic Surgery Soc. Republican. Adventist. Avocations: travel, collections of watches, books. E-mail: sch@napanet.net. Office: 1030 Main St Ste 206 Saint Helena CA 94574-2056

HERBERS, KLAUS, historian, educator; b. Wuppertal, Germany, Jan. 5, 1951; s. Theodor and Marga (Finkeldey) H.; m. Gertrud Ehrat; children: Philipp, Judith, Leonie, Hanna. Chmn. medieval history dept. U. Erlangen-Nurnberg, Germany, 1998—; dir., pres. Wiss. Beirat der Deutschen St. Jakobusgesellschaft, 1987-2000; pres. Ak Hagiographie, Stuttgart, 1994-2000. Author: Deutsche Jakobspilger und ihre Berichte, Liber Sancti Jacobi, Papstregesten Series: Jakobus-studien Hagiographie im Kontext, Leo IV und das Papsttum in der Mitte des 9. Office: U Erlangen-Nurnberg, Inst Geschichte Kochstr 4, D 91054 Erlangen Germany

HERBERT, ANTHONY JAMES, lawyer; b. Cambridge, Eng., Mar. 28, 1940; s. Kenneth Faulkner and Kathleen Ellis (Robertson) H.; m. Lowell Pelton, May 4, 1968 (div.); children: Dominic James, Daniel Mark, Julia Lowell; m. Mary Gosling, Mar. 11, 1998. BA, King's Coll., Cambridge, 1962, MA, 1965. Cert. solicitor of Supreme Ct., Eng. Assoc. Allen & Overy, London, 1965-70, ptnr., 1970-2000; cons., 2000—. Mem. Law Soc. Avocation: painting. Home: 12 Perrymead St, London SW6 3SP, England Office: Allen & Overy, One New Change, London EC4M 9QQ, England

HERBERT, CATHERINE DEMING, English educator; b. Charlottesville, Va., July 30, 1968; d. Robert Beverley and Jennette (Campbell) H. BA, U. Va., Charlottesville, 1990; MA, James Madison U., 1994; postgrad., U. Paul Valéry, Montpellier, France, 1999—. Sec. sr. dept. urology U. Va., Charlottesville, 1990-92; tchg. asst. dept. English, James Madison U., Harrisonburg, Va., 1993-94, instr., 1994-95; vol., English tchr./trainer Peace Corps, Madagascar, 1995-98. EMT, Western Albemarle Rescue Squad, Crozet, Va., 1989-95; incident comdr. for search and rescue Appalachian Search and Rescue Conf., Va., 1986-95. Episcopalian. Avocations: reading, cooking, hiking. Home: 7 rue du Generale Rene, 34000 Montpellier France

HERBERT, JAMES ALAN, writer; b. Burlington, Vt., July 29, 1945; s. Alan Wells and Rose Marion H.; m. Martha Lebedzinski, June 20, 1976 (div. 1983); children: Denise M., Jeni Ayn; m. Margaret Harris, Oct. 20, 1992; 1 child: Alicia Ayn. Student, Wittenberg U., Springfield, Ohio, 1963-65, SUNY, Buffalo, 1986, Niagara U., 1991. McLean Trucking Co., 1969-86; Author, 1986—. Author: The Third Testament, 1988, Rock and Roll Politics, 1992. Committeeman Conservative Party, N.Y., 1971; pub. rels. Vietnam Vets. of Am., 1989-91. Served to cpl. USMC, 1966-69, Vietnam. Recipient conspicuous svc. award State of N.Y., 1991. Mem. Toastmasters Internat. (treas. Buffalo chpt. 1988-90), Niagara Falls Transp. Club, Buffalo Transp. Club. Avocations: boating, golf, swimming. Office: PO Box 83 North Boston NY 14110-0083

HERBERT, JEFFREY WILLIAM, investment company executive; b. July 21, 1942; s. Alexander William John and Amy (Whitwell) H.; m. Sheila Heane, 1965; 3 children. B in Mech. Engring., Loughborough U.; MIEE, 1968. Mng. dir. Rover-Triumph Cars Ltd., 1976-81, GEC Diesels Ltd., 1981-85; exec. dir. industry Charter Consolidated PLC, 1985-89; chmn. Cape, 1985—; CEO Charter Plc, 1990—, chmn., 1996—; chmn. Anderson Group, 1987-95, Esab AB, 1994—; non-exec. dir. Vickers, 1991—, M&G Investment of London, 1993; liveryman Wheelwrights Co., 1993. Avocations: shooting, jogging, tennis, cars. Office: Charter Plc, 7 Hobart Pl, London SW1W OHH, England*

HERBERT, JOHNNY PAUL, race car driver; b. Brentwood, Essex, Eng., June 25, 1964; arrived in Monaco, 1996; m. Becky Cross; children: Chloe, Aimelia. Profl. race car driver Formula One, 1989—. 1st pl. finisher Le Mans 24 Hours, 1991, 1st pl. Grand Prix, Silverstone, Eng., 1995, 3d pl., Monaco, 1996, 3d pl. Hongaroring, 1997. Office: The Johnny Herbert Fan Club, The Nutshell Swan Ln, Margaretting Tye Essex CM4 9JU, England Address: PP Sauber AG, Wildbachstr 9, CH-8340 Hinwil Switzerland*

HERBERT, KEVIN BARRY JOHN, classics educator; b. Chgo., Nov. 18, 1921; s. William Patrick and Margaret (Lomasney) H.; m. Margaret Frances Lambin, Dec. 28, 1946; children: John Barry (dec.), Catherine Ann (Mrs. John Reilly). BA, Loyola U., Chgo., 1946; MA, Harvard U., 1949, PhD, 1954. Instr. classics Marquette U., Milw., 1948-52; instr. Ind. U., Bloomington, 1952-54; master St. Paul's Sch., Concord, N.H., 1954-55; asst. prof. Bowdoin Coll., Brunswick, Maine, 1955-62; asso. prof., prof. Washington U., St. Louis, 1962-92, chmn. dept., 1982-92, prof. emeritus, 1992—, curator emeritus, 1994—; reader Advanced Placement Latin, 1962-68, chief reader, 1969-73; mem. Latin test com. Coll. Entrance Exam. Bd., 1968-73; dir. tours to Europe and Middle East, 1973-96; referee Am. Coun. of Learned Socs., 1990-94; mem. editorial and adv. bd. Internat. Jour. of the Classical Tradition, 1993—. Author: Hugh of St. Victor: Soliloquy on the Earnest Money of the Soul, 1956, Ancient Art in Bowdoin College, 1964, Greek and Latin Inscriptions in the Brooklyn Museum, 1972; co-editor: Ancient Collections in Washington University, 1973; contbr. to: Great Events from History, 2 vols., 1972, Greek Coins in the Wulfing Collection of Washington University, 1994, Maximum Effort The B-29s Against Japan, 1983, Roman Republican Coins in the Wulfing Collection of Washington University, 1987, Roman Imperial Coins in the Wulfing Collection of Washington U.: 31BC-AD180, 1996; prodr. exhbns. and descriptive catalogs Washington U. Gallery of Art: Greek Coins, Fall term, 1989, Roman Republican Coins, Fall term, 1990, Goddesses, Queens and Women of Achievement: 550 B.C.-A.D. 1979, Spring Term, 1993; guest editor Classical Bull., 1998, 99; translator (Greek and Latin commentaries) St. Paul Epistle to the Romans, 1999—; contbr. articles and revs. to profl. jours. With USAAF, 1942-45. Decorated DFC, Air medal with two silver oak leaf clusters, others; recipient dean's award for outstanding teaching Univ. Coll., Washington U., 1985, Mentoring award, Grad. Sch., Wash. U., 2000; Wilbour fellow Bklyn. Mus., 1967. Fellow Am. Numis. Soc.; mem. Am. Philol. Assn., Classical Assn. Middle West and South. Home: 1124 Basswood Ln Saint Louis MO 63132-3008

HERBERT, MARILYNNE, public relations executive, freelance photographer; b. Columbus, Ga., Aug. 12, 1944; d. Herbert Paul and Victoria (Raskin) Gruber; m. Victor Daniel Herbert, June 23, 1968 (div. 1990); children: Alissa, Laura. BA, Colo. Woman's Coll., 1966. Adminstrv. asst. pub. rels. dept. Mt. Sinai Med. Ctr., N.Y.C., 1966-68; freelance photographer N.Y.C., 1977—; sr. account exec. Ruder-Finn, Inc., N.Y.C., 1986-93; dir. pub. rels. Iona Coll., New Rochelle, N.Y., 1993-94; sr. account exec. Coll. Connections Inc., N.Y.C., 1994-96; sr. mgr. media rels. Halstead Comm., N.Y.C., 1997—; cmty. rels. coord. Osborn Retirement Cmty., 1995—. Bd. dirs. Women of Westchester, White Plains, N.Y., 1977—, Byrdcliffe Performing Arts Orgn., New Rochelle, 1987-91, Nat. Women's Polit. Caucus, Westchester County, 1988—, Sr. Pers. Placement Bur., Inc., 1989-92; bd. dirs., sec. New Rochelle Cmty. Fund, 1986-91. Recipient Spl. Recognition award Nat. Women's Polit. Caucus, 1989. Mem. Am. Soc. Mag. Photographers, Assn. for Women in Comm., Lake Katonah Club (bd. govs. 1995-98). Jewish. Home: 77 Upper Lake Shore Dr Katonah NY 10536-2646

HERBERT, SALLY MARY, accountant; b. Grenada, Miss., Oct. 8, 1948; d. William Archie and Gladys Marie (Vance) H.; m. Gil Lewis Turchin, Jan. 1, 1981. B.B.A., U. Miss., 1973. C.P.A., Miss., Tex. Staff acct. Deloitte Haskins & Sells, Memphis, Tenn., 1974-79, supr., 1979-80, mgr., 1980-82, mgr., New Orleans, 1982-83, mgr., Dallas, 1983-84; pres. Pro Cons., Inc., 1984-88; pvt. practice acctg., 1988-90; sr. mgr. Deloitte & Touche, Dallas, 1990-92; ptnr. Deloitte & Touche, 1992-96, Deloitte Consulting, 1996—. Mem. cast pub. TV film How to Reconcile Your Bank Account, 1977-79; mem. editorial bd. The Woman C.P.A., 1979-81. Chmn. coms. Provida; vol. Girls Clubs of Memphis, 1977-80; mem. budget coms. United Way, Memphis, 1976-78. Recipient Gold medal Miss. State Bd. Pub. Accountancy, Jackson, 1974. Mem. Am. Soc. Women Accts. (bd. dirs. 1977-81, v.p. 1978-79, pres. 1979-80), Am. Woman's Soc. C.P.A.s (nat. bd. dirs. 1980-81), Tenn. Soc. C.P.A.s (state council 1980-81), Bus. Adminstrn. and Acctg. Alumni Assn. U. Miss. (bd. dirs. 1983-91). Office: Deloitte Consulting 2200 Ross Ave Ste 1600 Dallas TX 75201-6778

HERBITS, STEPHEN EDWARD, strategic consultant; b. Pittsfield, Mass., Mar. 13, 1942; s. Nathaniel R. and Esther (Levin) H. AB, Tufts U., 1964; JD, Georgetown U., 1972. Adminstrv. asst. for rsch. U.S. Senator Edward W. Brooke of Mass., 1966; staff asst., staff dir. Wednesday Group, U.S. Ho. of Reps., 1967-68; commr. President's Commn. All-Vol. Armed Forces, 1969-70; cons. Bailey, Deardourff & Assocs., Inc., Washington, 1969, 73, 74, 77; v.p. fin. devel. Sabre Found., Fond-du-Lac, Wis., 1970; legis. asst. to U.S. Senator Robert T. Stafford of Vt., 1971-73; spl. asst. to asst. sec. def. manpower and res. affairs Dept. of Def., 1973-74; spl. asst. to dir. Presdl. Pers. Office, White House, Washington, 1974-75; counsel U.S. del. Multilateral Trade Negotiations Office Spl. Rep. for Trade Negotiations, 1975-76; spl. asst. to sec. and dep. secs. def. Dept. Def., 1976-77; v.p. Seagram Overseas Sales Co., 1977-79; mng. dir. Kirin-Seagram, Japan, 1977-79; v.p. Seagram Europe, 1979-80; pres. Browne Vintners, Joseph E. Seagram & Sons, Inc., N.Y.C., 1980-82; mng. dir. Seagram Far East, 1982-83; v.p. corp. devel. Seagram Co. Ltd., 1983-86; exec. v.p. external affairs and. corp. policy Seagram Co. Ltd., 1977-86. Contbr. articles to profl. publs. Bd. dirs. The Century Coun., 1993-94. Mem. D.C. Bar Assn. Home and Office: 1000 Venetian Way Apt 904 Miami FL 33139-1008

HERBO, PREBEN, real estate agent; b. Copenhagen, Denmark, May 8, 1923; s. Anders Rasmussen and Else Herbo; m. Anne Dorph Brouger, Oct. 20, 1962; children: Anders, Lise. Grad., Mil. Officer's Acad., 1948-50, The Armoured Sch., 1955. From commd. officer to maj. Dsnish Royal Guard Hussars, Naestved, Denmark, 1946-70; real estate agt. Copenhagen, 1956—; landowner Sonnerup Manor Estate, Hvalsoe, Denmark, 1985-96; owner Tadre Forests, 1996—; chmn. bd. Herbo Property Cos., Copenhagen. Mem. Internat. Real Estate Fedn., Danish Real Estate Orgn. Avocation: hunting. Home: Tadre Moellevej 22, Frederiksberg Alle 18-20, 4330 Hvalsoe Denmark

HERBOLD, JOACHIM ROLF, insurance company executive; b. Bretten, Germany, Sept. 22, 1959; s. Werner and Ruth (Goetz) H.; m. Juliane Helene Bopp-Herbold, Dec. 22, 1990; 1 child, Theresa. Diploma in Agr., Hohenheim U., Stuttgart, Germany, 1985, PhD in Agr., 1995. Agr. mgr. Evangelisches Bauernwerk, Waldenburg, Germany, 1986-87; asst. mgr. Retratechnik, Munich, 1987-89; rschr. Hohenheim U., 1989-92; asst. mgr. Munich Reins. Co., 1993—. Author: Bodenunabhaengige Kulturverfahren im Gemuesebau, 1995; contbr. articles to profl. jours. Mem. U. Hohenheim, Verein Deutscher Landwirte. Roman Catholic. Home: Rosenstr 20, D-86856 Hiltenfingen Germany Office: Munich Reinsurance Co, Koeniginstr 107, D-80791 Munich Germany

HERBST, ABBE ILENE, lawyer; b. N.Y.C., June 19, 1955; d. Seymour and Charlotte (Wolper) H. BA summa cum laude, Fordham U., 1976, JD, 1979. Bar: N.Y. 1980, N.J. 1980, U.S. Supreme Ct. 1986. Law clk. Keenan, Powers & Andrews, N.Y.C., 1978-79, assoc., 1980-83; assoc. DeForest & Duer, N.Y.C., 1983-90, ptnr., 1991—. Editor: Fordham Urban Law Journal, 1978-79. Recipient Outstanding Presentation award Cmty. Svc. Soc., N.Y.C., 1986. Mem. ABA, N.Y. State Bar Assn., N.J. State Bar Assn., N.Y. County Lawyers Assn., Fin. Women's Assn. N.Y., Riverdale Mental Health Assn., Phi Beta Kappa. Avocations: travel, collecting miniature cat figurines. Office: DeForest & Duer 90 Broad St Fl 18 New York NY 10004-2276

HERBST, MICHAEL CASPER, editor, consultant; b. Johannesburg, South Africa, Sept. 29, 1944; s. Christiaan F. Beyers and Angeline (Greeff) H.; m. Johanna Susanna Thirion, Feb. 8, 1965; children: Christiaan, Lydia, Michael. Diploma in Nursing Edn., Wits U., Johannesburg, 1978; diploma in Occupl. Health, Potchefstroom U., South Africa, 1983; BA, U. South Africa, 1986; M of Arts and Scis., Potchefstroom U., 1987. Hosp. supt. Anglo Am. Corp., South Africa, 1967-72; head edn. and tng. Iron and Steel Corp. of South Africa, Vandersbiilpark, South Africa, 1972-82; lectr. Potchefstroom U., 1982-87; prof. U. Venda, Republic of Venda, 1988-91; mgr. edn. South African Pharmacy Coun., Pretoria, 1991-94; dir. Ind. Exams. Bd., Johannesburg, 1994-96; editor Dem. Nursing Orgn. of South Africa, Pretoria, 1996—; specialist cons. Messrs McClintock and Skinner, Johannesburg, 1988-90; health cons. Anglo Am. Corp., 1990; ednl. cons. Toyota South Africa, Johannesburg, 1994-96; mng. dir. Phoenix Found. for Specialised Edn., Pretoria, 1996—; dir. MEVK Adult Examinations, Pretoria, 1998—. Co-author: Pharmacotherapy: A Guide to Clinical Pharmacy, 1993; author: Publishing Your Research: Pain or Pleasure?, 2000; editor (monthly profl. mag.) Nursing Update, 1996—, (quar. rsch. jour.) Curationis, 1997—. Mem. exec. com. Soc. for Disabled, Potchefstroom, 1985-87, Soc. for Mental Health, Potchefstroom, 1986-87; chairperson Rsch. and Publs. Com., Thohoyandon, Venda, 1989-91. Named Emeritus prof. U. Venda, 1991.

Mem. Internat. Chemical Indusrty Clin. Forum (chair 1984-87), South Africa Nursing Assn. (chair 1986-87), Dem. Nursing Orgn. South Africa, 1996—). Presbyterian. Avocations: music, birdwatching, hiking, botany. Home: 615 Duniet St Elardus Pk, 0181 Pretoria South Africa Office: Dem Nursing Orgn S Africa, 605 Church St, 0083 Arcadia Pretoria South Africa

HERBST, TODD L., lawyer; b. N.Y.C., July 15, 1952; s. Seymour and Charlotte (Wolper) H.; m. Robyn Beth Kellman, June 3, 1979; children: Scott Marshall, Carly Nicole. BA, CUNY, 1974; JD, John Marshall Law Sch., 1977. Bar: N.Y. 1978. Assoc. Max E. Greenberg, Cantor & Reiss, N.Y.C., 1977-83, mng. ptnr., 1984-87; sr. ptnr. Max E. Greenberg, Trager, Toplitz & Herbst, N.Y.C., 1988—; bus. cons. Shimizu Corp., U.S., 1983—, NTT Internat. Corp., Japan and U.S., 1996—, Dillingham Constrn. Holdings, Inc., San Francisco, 1987—, Gottlieb Skanska, Inc., N.Y.C., 1980—, Jolly Hotels, Italy, 1993—, Legal Commentary UPN News, N.Y.; lectr. Nat. Assn. Corp. Real Estate Execs. Exec. editor John Marshall Law Rev. Mem. ABA, Am. Inst. Archs., N.Y. State Bar Assn., Am. Corp. Counsel Assn., N.Y. County Lawyers Assn. Avocations: writing poetry, automobiles. Home: 7 Brookwood Ln New City NY 10956-2203 Office: Max E Greenberg Trager Toplitz & Herbst 100 Church St New York NY 10007-2601

HERCZEGH, GÉZA, judge. Judge Internat. Ct. Justice, The Hague, The Netherlands. Office: Peace Palace, Carnegieplein 2, 2517KJ The Hague The Netherlands

HERDENDORF, CHARLES EDWARD, III, retired oceanographer, limnologist, consultant; b. Lorain, Ohio, Oct. 2, 1939; s. Charles Edward, Jr. and Esther Kathryne Herdendorf; m. Ricki Sue Crowl, May 22, 1993. BS, Ohio U., 1961, MS, 1963; PhD, Ohio State U., 1970. Cert. profl. geologist, Am. Inst. Profl. Geologists. Geologist, section head Ohio Dept. Natural Resources, Sandusky, Ohio, 1960-71; assoc. prof. geol. scis. and zoology Ohio State U., 1971-76, prof., 1976-88, prof. emeritus, 1988—; dir. Franz Theodore Stone Lab. and Ctr. for Lake Erie Area Rsch., Put-in-Bay, Ohio, 1971-88; dir. Ohio Sea Grant Coll. program Ohio State U., Columbus, 1978-88; sci. dir. Columbus-Am. Discovery Group, Columbus, 1988-95; apptd. by Ohio Gov. to Acid Rain Forest Task Force, 1984, Ohio Maritime Adv. Coun., 1999. Author: Ohio's Natural Heritage, 1979 (Ohioana Book Award 1980), Journal of Great Lakes Research, 1997; Author/Editor: Large Lakes of the World, 1990, Lake Erie Handbook, 1993, Science on a Deep-Ocean Shipwreck, 1995. Vol. naturalist Ohio Divsn. Nat. Areas and Preserves, Huron, Ohio, 1988—; pres. Beachwood Villas Assn., Huron, 1989-90; advisor Nat. Maritime Hist. Soc., Peekskill, N.Y., 1989—; trustee Ohio Hist. Soc., Columbus, 1995-96, Great Lakes Hist. Soc., Vermilion, Ohio, 1999—. With ROTC, USAF, 1957-58. Recipient Citizenship medal SAR, 1990; named to Hall of Fame F. T. Stone Lab., Ohio State U., 1996, Diver of Year Bay Area Divers, 1998. Fellow Geol. Soc. Am., Explorers Club; mem. Ohio Acad. Sci. (pres. 1995-96, Centennial Honoree 1991), Internat. Assoc. for Great Lakes Rsch. (bd. dirs. 1977-80, v.p. 1979-80, Best Paper of Yr. 1998), Am. Fisheries Soc. (cert. fisheries scientist, cert. underwater archaeologist), NSPE, Ohio Office Hist. Preservation, U.S. Nat. Park Svc. Republican. Methodist. Avocations: photography, scuba diving, boating, aircraft piloting, hiking. E-Mail: herdendorf.1@osu.edu. Home: 585 West Shore Blvd Put-in-Bay OH 43456 Office: Ohio State U Ste 410 1507 Cleveland Rd E Apt 410 Huron OH 44839-9503

HERDMAN, JOHN MARK AMBROSE, retired British government official; b. Rhu, Scotland, Apr. 26, 1932; m. Elizabeth Anne Dillon, 1963; 3 children. B.A., U. Dublin, 1954, M.A., 1962. Joined Brit. Overseas Civil Service, 1954; served as dist. officer and dist. commr. in Kenya; joined Her Majesty's Diplomatic Service, 1964, serving in Lebanon, Jordan, Zambia, Saudi Arabia and Malawi; dep. gov. Bermuda, 1983-86; gov. Brit. Virgin Islands, 1986-91. Avocations: philately, gardening, fishing. Address: Tullywhisker House, Berry Ln Worplesdon, Surrey England*

HERDSON, PETER BARRIE, forensic pathologist, educator; b. Auckland, New Zealand, Dec. 29, 1932; s. Cecil Hastings and Florence Mavis (O'Connor) H.; m. Mary Louise Harvey, Apr. 26, 1960 (div. 1985); children: Peter, Sarn, Caroline; m. Caroline Sarah Reid, May 23, 1986; stepchildren: Christopher, Reid, Rachel Reid. B Med. Sci., Otago (New Zealand) U., 1956, B Medicine, B Surgery, 1959; PhD, Northwestern U., Chgo., 1965. Lic. physician, New Zealand, U.K., Australian Capital Ter., N.S.W. Lectr. dept. anatomy U. Otago Med. Sch., Dunedin, New Zealand, 1956-68; resident med. officer Mater Misericordiae Hosp., Auckland, New Zealand, 1959; resident house officer Auckland Pub. Hosp., 1960; New Zealand scholar Bland-Sutton Inst. Pathology, Middlesex Hosp., London, 1961-63, asst. pathologist, 1962-63; Am. cardiovascular rsch. fellow dept. pathology Northwestern U. Med. Sch., Chgo., 1963-65, asst. prof. pathology, 1965-67, assoc. prof. pathology, 1967-69; asst. pathologist Henrotin Hosp., Chgo., 1964-69; found. prof., chmn. dept. pathology U. Auckland Sch. Medicine, 1969-85; prof., chmn. dept. pathology and lab. medicine King Faisal Specialist Hosp. & Rsch. Ctr., Riyadh, Saudi Arabia, 1985-91; prof., dir. ACT pathology Canberra Hosp., Woden, Australia, 1991-2000; prof. pathology U. Sydney, Canberra Clin. Sch., 1994—; vis. prof. pathology Duke U. Med. Sch., Durham, N.C., 1977; external examiner acad. promotions King Saud U., Riyadh, 1992—; med. adviser May and Baker New Zealand Ltd., 1972-85, May and Baker Australia Ltd., 1983-85, Rhone-Poulenc Sante, Paris, 1986-90; mem. Nat. Pathology Accreditation Adv. Coun., 1991-2000; mem. Drug Assessment Adv. Com., New Zealand, 1970-85; mem. Maternal Mortality Rsch. Com., New Zealand, 1969-80; chmn. rsch. adv. com. Cancer Soc. New Zealand, 1970-82; mem. joint rels. com. Univ.-Hosp. Bd., Auckland, 1969-85; mem. Postgrad. Com. in Medicine, Canberra, 1991-2000; mem. Internat. Liaison Com. of Pres. of Pathology Colls., 1972-99; coroner's pathologist, Auckland, 1969-85; New Zealand aviation aircraft investigator, 1972-85; pathologist Mt. Erebus Disaster, 1979-80; coroner's pathologist, Canberra, 1991—. Mem. editl. bds. Pathology, 1972—, Adis Press, 1972-92, Histopathology, 1976—, Bull. Saudi Heart Assn., 198—, Internat. Jour. Immunorehab., 1995—; mem. editor-in-chief Annals of Saudi Medicine; editor ACT Pathology Newsletter, 1991-2000. Fellow Royal Coll. Pathologists Australasia (New Zealand concillor 1972-78, v.p. 1979-83, pres. 1983-85), Royal Australasian Coll. Radiologists (hon.); mem. World Assn. Socs. Pathology (dir.-at-large 1985-89, v.p. 1989-93, pres. 1993-95, Gold Headed Cane award 1997), Canberra Medico-Legal Soc. (found. pres. 1992-94), Pharm. Soc. New Zealand, Am. Assn. Pathologists, Am. Soc. Clin. Pathologists., Am. Soc. Exptl. Pathology, Am. Soc. Nephrology, Australian Capital Ter. Med. Officer's Assn., Australian Med. Assn. (pres. ACT branch, m 1999-00), Am. Soc. Clin. and Exptl. Pharmacologists, Australian Soc. Exptl. Pathology, Australasian Soc. Nephrology, Brit. Soc. Forensic Scis., Internat. Acad. Pathology, Internat. Soc. Nephrology, New Zealand Med. Assn., New Zealand Soc. Pathologists (pres. 1974, standing com. on tng. of pathologists 1971-83), Pathological Soc. Gt. Britain and Ireland, Auckland Medico-Legal Soc. (exec. com. 1974-85), Riyadh Pathology Club, Phi Rho Sigma (hon.). Avocations: gardening, washing cars. Home: 18/51 Musgrave St, Yarralumla, Canberra ACT 2600, Australia Office: PO Box 9585, Deakin Canberra ACT 2600, Australia

HERENDEEN, DAVID WARREN, baritone, director, music educator; b. Rochester, N.Y., Nov. 23, 1956; s. Robert Wood and Elsie Arthur (Smith) H.; m. Sara Bunn (div. 1986); 1 child, Fletcher Wood; m. Mary Louise Kemp, Nov. 24, 1988; 1 child, Elizabeth Grace. MusB, Oberlin Coll., 1978, M Music Theater, 1979; D in Musical Arts, U. Ariz., 1993. Apprentice Santa Fe Opera, 1979; resident baritone Mich. Opera, Detroit, 1979-80; teaching fellow Hartt Sch. Music, Hartford, Conn., 1980-81; resident Deutsche Oper Berlin, 1988-89; asst. prof. music Edinboro (Pa.) U., 1989-96; assoc. prof., 1996, dir. cultural affairs, 1995-97; assoc. prof., dir. opera/music theater Oklahoma City U., 1997—; performer, asst. to dir. in The Yellow Sound, Guggenheim Found., N.Y.C., 1981; stage dir., resident artist Brevard (N.C.) Music Ctr., 1996-97. Created role of Roderick Usher in world premier of Fall of the House of Usher, Hartt Opera Theater, 1980. Recipient German-Am. award German-Am. Soc., N.Y.C., 1988. Mem. Nat. Assn. Tchrs. Singing, Phi Mu Alpha (adviser 1990—). Presbyterian. Home: 2004 NW 21st St Oklahoma City OK 73106-1614 Office: Oklahoma City U Petree Sch Music and Performing Arts 2501 N Blackwelder Ave Oklahoma City OK 73106-1402

HERES DIDDENS, JOHANNA GEURTINA, translator; b. Heerlen, The Netherlands, Dec. 11, 1920; d. Cornelis and Geertina Alida (Boonstra) Wischmeyer; m. Gezinus Heres Diddens, Feb. 22, 1952; children: Kitty, Tineke, Bea, Corinne, Gerhard, Fenna. Diploma, U. Amsterdam, 1975; M in Lit., U. Groningen, 1998. Exec. sec. various firms, The Netherlands, 1939-52; owner, dir. Trainingschool, Amsterdam, 1959-72; freelance translator, conf. and legal interpreter Amsterdam, 1957—. Mem. Dutch Translators Assn. (v.p. Utrecht), Mensa. Avocations: music, painting, fancy work. Home: Scheeneweg 25, NL-8488 BG Nijeholtwolde Fryslan, The Netherlands

HERFKENS, EVELINE, government official; b. The Hague, The Netherlands, Jan. 9, 1952. Grad., U. Leoden, 1975. With policy office Ministry Fgn. Affairs, 1976-81; mem. Lower House, 1981-90; exec. dir. World Bank, 1990-96; ambassador Internat Orgns., Geneva, 1996-98; min. Ministry Devel. Coop., The Hague, The Netherlands, 1998—; lectr. econs., 1965-71; mem. Brandt commn. Internat. Devel. Issues, 1977-82; prof. internat. devel. Inst. Social Scis., The Hague, 1979-80; deputy sec. gen. UN Conf. Trade & Devel., 1980-85; Den Uyl prof. U. Amsterdam. Office: Ministry Devel Coop, Bezuidenhoutsweg 30, 2594 AC The Hague The Netherlands*

HERFORD, MARK JOHN, communications executive; b. Sydney, NSW, Australia, Nov. 3, 1953; s. John Rogers Herford and Helen May (Lambert) McLeod; m. Stephanie Kay Wilkes, July 1988; children: Christopher, Amy. BA, U. Sydney, 1972; BL, U. New Eng., Australia, 1977. Dir. Herford Cox Cons., Brisbane, Australia, 1985-86; dep. mng. dir. The Macro Group, Sydney, 1986-91; acct. dir. Shandwick, London, 1992-94; regional dir. Europe, Shandwick, Geneva, 1997-99; mng. dir. Switzerland, Shandwick Internat., Geneva, 1999—; chmn. Bus. Software Alliance, Sydney, 1987-90. Recipient Crisis Comm. award Pub. Rels. Inst. Australia, 1985. Avocations: music, skiing, golf, literature, sailing.

HERGENC, GULAY, science educator; b. Akhisar, Turkey, July 23, 1951; d. Orhan Kaya and Necla Sen (Ozbay) Cetinkaya; m. Sabri Memet Hergenc, July 17, 1977; 1 child, Doga. BSc, Bogazici U., Istanbul, Turkey, 1974, MA, 1976; MSc, Marmara Med. Faculty, Istanbul, 1987, specialization in clin. biochemistry, 1990, PhD in Biochemistry, 1994. Cert. chem. engr., clin. biochemist, asst. prof. biochemistry, 1996. Market rsch. chief Rhone-Poulenc, Istanbul, 1976; rsch. asst. Marmara Med. Faculty, Istanbul, 1984-90; clin. lab. mgr. Hipokrat, Istanbul, 1995-99; head biochemistry dept. Kocaeli (Turkey) Med. Faculty, 1998; biochemistry lectr. Bogazici U., 1999; biochemistry lectr. dept. biochemistry Yeditepe Med. Faculty, Istanbul, 1999—; cons. Yildiz TU Medikosoyal Clin. Lab., Istanbul, 2000. Contbr. articles to sci. jours. Recipient Poster award Turkish Biochem. Soc.; Scientist Raising scholar TUBITAK, 1968-72. Mem. AACC (travel grantee 1998), EAS (travel grantee 1998), IAS, Am. Assn. of Clin. Chemistry, Internat. Atherosclerosis Soc., European Atherosclerosis Soc., Turkish Soc. Cardiology, Turkish Soc. Biochemistry, Turkish Soc. Hematology, Turkish Soc. Free Radical Rsch., World Heart Fedn. Coun. Cardiovasc. Disease Epidemiology and Prevention, English Biochem. Soc., Trombosis Soc., Atherosclerosis Edn. and Rsch. Group, Turkish Soc. and Clin. Lab., Turkish Sci. and Tech. Rsch. Found. Avocations: sculpture making, dancing. Fax: 90 212 5880277.

HERGENHAN, JOYCE, public relations executive; b. Mt. Kisco, N.Y., Dec. 30, 1941; d. John Christopher and Goldie (Wago) H. BA, Syracuse U., 1963; MBA, Columbia U., 1978. Reporter White Plains Reporter Dispatch, 1963-64; asst. to Rep. Ogden R. Reid Washington, 1964-68; reporter Gannett Newspapers, 1968-72; with Consol. Edison Co. of N.Y., Inc., N.Y.C., 1972-82, v.p., 1977-79, sr. v.p. pub. affairs, 1979-82; v.p. corp. pub. relations General Electric Co., Fairfield, Conn., 1982-98; pres. GE Fund, 1998—. Office: GE 3135 Easton Tpke Fairfield CT 06431-0002

HERGERT, HERBERT LAWRENCE, consultant; b. Portland, Oreg., Feb. 20, 1927; s. John Edward and Elizabeth (Blahm) H.; m. Lois Marion Lilly, Dec. 20, 1949; children: Lawrence A., Gregory K., David E., Daniel W. BA, Reed Coll., 1948; MS, Oreg. State U., 1951, PhD, 1954. Asst. prof. Oreg. State U., Corvallis, 1952-54; rsch. chemist Rayonier Inc., Shelton, Wash., 1954-70; asst. dir. R&D ITT Rayonier Inc., N.Y.C., 1970-72, v.p., dir. R&D, 1972-80, dir. quality, 1971-79, v.p., dir. tech. mktg., 1980-87; sr. scientist Repap Techs. Inc., Valley Forge, Pa., 1987-97; trustee Textile Rsch. Inst., Princeton, N.J., 1976-82, Tech. Assn. Pulp & Paper Industries, Atlanta, 1980-83; forest products con., Pottstown, Pa., 1987-97; adj. prof. N.C. State U., 1998—. Contbr. over 90 papers to profl. jours. and 7 chpts. to books. Chmn., bd. dirs. Shelton (Wash.) Gen. Hosp., 1962-66, Shelton Sch. Dirs., 1966-70; adv. bd. Cons. Bapt. Theol. Seminary, Denver, 1968-79. Corp. USAAF, 1945-46. Fellow Internat. Acad. Wood Sci.; mem. Am. Botanical Soc., Internat. Paleobotanical Soc., Soc. Wood Sci. and Tech., Am. Chem. Soc., Tech. Assn. Pulp and Paper Industry. Republican. Baptist. Achievements include 6 U.S. patents and 36 foreign patents. Home: 901 Burdan Dr Pottstown PA 19464-4475

HERING, EKBERT, physics/management educator, university president; b. Stuttgart, Germany, May 9, 1943; s. Wilhelm and Gertrud (Barth) H.; m. Christiane Festing; children: Stefan, Martina. MSc in Physics, U. Stuttgart, 1969, PhD in Physics, 1971, MSc, 1975, PhD in Econ., 1984. Prof. U. Aalen, Germany, 1971-97, pres., 1997; cons. in field. Author: Physics for Engineers, 7th edit., 1999, Electronic for Engineers, 3d edit., 1998, Informatics for Engineers, 1995, Management and Leadership, 3d edit., 1999, others; contbr. articles to profl. jours. Mem. Aalen Symphonic Orch. Mem. Lions Club. Avocations: active violing playing, writing, walking, theatre. Home: Im Buerglesbuehl 41, D-73540 Heubach Germany Office: Aalen Univ, Beethovenstr 1, D-73430 Aalen Germany

HERING, SOLANGE, training business consultant; b. Jan. 6, 1966; d. Oscar Eugenio Hering and Margarita Chambeaux; married, Nov. 7, 1998; 1 child. BA n Psychology, Mexico City. bus. adminstrn. diplomate. Bus. tng., 1994-97; import/export cons. Chile, 1995-98; bus. tng. cons., 1999—; acad. mgr. San Felipe, Chile, 1999—; psychologist, San Felipe, Chile, 1995-96, 98. Mem. APA. Home: Casima 175, San Felipe Region V, Chile Office: Hadm Inst, San Felipe Region V, Chile

HERISANU, NICOLAE HORATIU, engineering educator; b. Cisnadie, Sibiu, Romania, Nov. 22, 1965; s. Nicolae and Eugenia Herisanu; m. Nicoleta Mioara Marginean, Aug. 24, 1997. MSc, Poly. Inst. Traian Vuia, Timisoara, Romania, 1990; PhD, U. Poly., Timisoara, 1999. Cert. in engring. Asst. Poly. U., Timisoara, 1990-95, lectr., 1996—; hon. rschr. Timisoara br. Romanian Acad., 1999. Author: (books) Vibrations. Themes and Examples of Calculus-Design, 1992, Elements of Machine-Tool Vibrations, 1999, Dynamics of Structures, 1999. Mem. Romanian Soc. Theoretical and Applied Mechanics, Romanian Soc. Acoustics. Avocations: sports, computers, reading books. E-mail: herisanu@mec.utt.ro. Office: Poly U Timisoara, Bd Mihai Viteazu # 1, Timisoara 1900, Romania

HÉRITIER, MICHEL, physicist; b. Hanoi, Vietnam, Aug. 31, 1945; s. Hugues Henri Héritier and France Michon; m. Anny Aguilar, Aug. 17, 1972; children: Valerie, Nathalie, Pascal, Guillaume, Anne. MS, Ecole Normale Supérieure, Paris, 1969; PhD, U. Parix XI, Orsay, 1975. Asst. U. Parix VII, 1968-71; maitre-asst. U. Paris XI, Orsay, 1971-84, maitre de vonf., 1984-85, prof. 2d class, 1985-88, prof. 1st class, 1988-93, prof. exceptional, 1993—; dir. Orsay Solid State Physics Inst., 1989-98, Solid State Physics Doctoral Sch., Paris area, 1989—. Contbr. articles to profl. jours. Mem. Am. Phys. Soc., Phys. Soc. Japan, Soc. Française Physique, Conseil Nat. Univs. Fax: 33-1-59-15-69-36. E-mail: Heritier@lps.u-psud.fr. Home: 44 rue de Garches, F-92210 Saint-Cloud France Office: U Paris XI, Ctr Sci d'Orsay Bat 510, F-91405 Orsay France

HERKSTRÖTER, CORNELIUS, retired oil industry executive. Pres. Royal Dutch Petroleum Co., The Hague, The Netherlands, to 1998; also chmn. com. mng. dirs. Royal Dutch/Shell Group Cos., to 1998, ret., 1998. Office: Royal Dutch/Shell Group Cos, 30 Carel van Bylandtlaan, 2596 HR The Hague The Netherlands

HERLITZ, GUNTER, company executive; b. Berlin, Feb. 9, 1913; m. Edith Mallwitz. With Herlitz AG, Berlin, 1935—, exec. chmn., 1972—, chmn. supervisory bd., hon. chmn. supervisory bd., 2000—; chmn. supervisory bds. Herlitz AG, Berlin, Herlitz Internat. Trading Aktiengesellschaft, Ismaning. Office: Herlitz AG, AM Borsigturm 100, D-13507 Berlin Germany*

HERMAN, ALEXIS M., federal official; b. Mobile, Ala., July 16, 1947. Grad., Xavier U., 1969. Founder, CEO A.M. Herman & Assocs., Washington; nat. dir. Minority Women's Employment Program, Washington, until 1977; dir. Women's Bur. Dept. Labor, Washington, 1977-81; chief staff, then dep. chair Dem. Nat. Conv. Com., Washington, until 1991, CEO, 1991-92; dep. dir. Clinton-Gore Presdl. Transition Office, Washington, 1992-93; asst. to President U.S., Pub. Liaison dir. White House, Washington, 1993-96; sec. labor U.S. Dept. Labor, Washington, 1997—. Recipient Sara Lee Front Runner award, 1999. Mem. Nat. Coun. Negro Women, Delta Sigma Theta. Office: US Dept Labor Office Sec Washington DC 20210-0001

HERMAN, BARRY MARTIN, international economist; b. Bklyn., June 27, 1943; s. Aaron and Fannie Herman; m. Martha Feldman, Mar. 19, 1967; children: Alicia, Mark. AB, Columbia U., 1965; MBA, U. Chgo., 1967; PhD, U. Mich., 1974. Mgmt. analyst U.S. Bur. of the Budget, Washington, 1967; lectr. in econs. U. Mich., Dearborn, 1972-73; asst. prof. Dickinson Coll., Carlisle, Pa., 1973-75; instr. Lehman Coll., CUNY, Bronx, 1975-76; econs. affairs officer UN, N.Y.C., 1976-89, chief developed economies sect., 1989-95, chief internat. econ. rels. br., 1995-99, chief fin. and devel. br., 1999—. Editor, author: International Finance and Developing Countries in a Year of Crisis, 1998, Financial Turmoil and Reform, 1999; contbr. articles to profl. jours. Mem., rev. panel, children in a globalizing world UNICEF, N.Y.C., 1997—; resource person, expert group on capital market volatility Commonwealth Secretariat, London, 1998; mem. conf. planning com. Global Interdependence Ctr., Phila., 1995-98. Mem. Am. Econs. Assn. E-mail: herman@un.org. Office: Dept Econs and Social Affairs UN New York NY 10017

HERMAN, ELVIN E., retired consulting electronic engineer; b. Mar. 17, 1921; s. John Lawrence and Martha Elizabeth (Conner) H.; m. Grace Winifred Eklund, Sept. 29, 1945; 1 child, Jane Ann Herman Fischer. BSEE, State U. Iowa, 1942. Engr., sect. head Naval Rsch. Lab., Washington, 1942-51; sect. head Corona (Calif.) Labs., Nat. Bur. Stds., 1951-53; sect. head, lab. mgr., tech. dir. radar sys. group Hughes Aircraft Co., El Segundo, Calif., 1953-83; cons. electronic engr., Pacific Palisades, Calif., 1983-88; ret., 1988. Recipient Meritorious Civilian Svc. award Naval Rsch. Lab., 1946. Fellow IEEE. Achievements include 24 patents in field. Home: 1200 Lachman Ln Pacific Palisades CA 90272-2228

HERMAN, JOSH SETH, actor, clown, magician; b. Passaic, N.J., Aug. 13, 1957; s. George and H. Lillian (Lissak) H. BS, U. Houston, 1980; student, HB Studio, 1984. Corp., radio, TV spokesman, symbol Rockaway's Playland, Rockaway Beach, N.Y., 1984; actor Royal Ct. Repertory Co., N.Y.C., 1984-85; clown Herriott Circus at Kid's World, Longbranch, N.J., 1985; illusionist, magician's asst. John Bundy Prodns., Woodbridge, N.J., 1985; magic demonstrator Mecca Magic, Bloomfield, N.J., 1985—; corp. symbol Little Jake Welsh Farms, Long Valley, N.J., 1985—; creator of clown team (with Dawn Spaven) Smilin Josh and Miss Silly Bubbles, 1985; local advance publicity clown Great Am. Circus, Allan C. Hill Entertainment Corp., Sarasota, Fla., 1986; clown in TV comml., performer Powerplant Entertainment Ctr., Six Flags Corp., Balt., 1986; prin. nat. TV comml. Dial Soap, 1987; performer Macy's TV comml., 1989; co-producer TV show (with Dawn Spaven) The Neighborhood Playground, 1990. Appeared in TV commls. Great Adventure Amusement Park, 1991, Wendy's Internat., 1992, Delta Airlines, 1997, 98; performer Good Living Exposition Home Shows, 1992-97. Mem. Nutley (N.J.) Little Theatre, 1984—, Studio Players Essex County, Montclair, N.J., 1985-86; bd. dirs. New Theatre North Jersey, Pompton Plains, N.J., 1984-86. Mem. Screen Actors Guild, World Clown Assn., Clowns Am. Internat., Merri Makers Clown Alley, Internat. Brotherhood Magicians. Office: PO Box 553 Clifton NJ 07012-0553

HERMAN, LARRY MARVIN, psychotherapist; b. Pitts., Feb. 15, 1951; s. Albert Sanford and Miriam (Pearl) H.; m. Sandy Lee Checkler, Apr. 28, 1988; 1 child, Barry Craig, 1 stepchild, Mark. BA, W.Va. U., 1973, MS, 1974. Lic. profl. counselor; lic. mental health counselor, Fla. Career counselor Community Coll. Allegheny County, Monroeville, Pa., 1975; job devel. specialist Ohio State Rehab. Svcs. Commn., Steubenville, Ohio, 1975-77; mental health therapist St. John Med. Ctr., Steubenville, 1977-88; pvt. practitioner Stream, Inc., Steubenville, 1985-88; sr. therapist The Cloisters of Pine Island, Pineland, Fla., 1988-90; pvt. practice Ft. Myers, Fla., 1990-92; program dir. adult psychiat. svcs. Deering Hosp., Miami, Fla., 1992-94; dir. adult svcs. Grant Ctr., 1992; pvt. practice San Jose, Costa Rica, 1992-97; dir. profl. svcs. Deering Hosp., Miami, 1994-97; CEO, owner Clin. Neurosci. Inst., Inc., Coral Gables, Fla., 1997—, CNS Labs., Inc., Coral Gables, 1997—; cons. Stream, Inc., Steubenville, 1985-88. Author relaxation and self-motivation program: Power From Within, 1990. Mem. Am. Mgmt. Assn. Avocations: reading, golf, target shooting, computer applications. E-mail: lherman@cnsinstitute.com. Office: 1516 Venera Ave Coral Gables FL 33146-3011

HERMAN, LESZEK, electronics engineer; b. Cieszyn, Poland, May 25, 1950; s. Wladyslaw and Cecylia (Rygiel) H.; m. Ewa Szpikowska, Oct. 24, 1980; children: Ewelina, Wojciech. Degree in engring., Tech. U. Silesia, 1975, MSc, 1980. Engr. ZNSM, Szczecin, Poland, 1977-79; mgr. Polish TV, Szczecin, 1979-80; engr. Meratronik, Szczecin, 1980-83, 109 Mil. Hosp., Szczecin, 1983-85; designer Meramont, Szczecin, 1985-87; engr. Warski/Szczecin Shipyard, 1987-90; co-owner Baltic Elec. S.C. Neurocomputing Div., Szczecin, 1992-2000; pres. Sm@art, Inc., 2000—. Mem. Assn. Logic Programming. Avocations: photography, climbing. E-mail: lherman@klub.chip.pl. Home: ul Okulickiego 75B, PL-71-035 Szczecin Poland

HERMAN, MAJA See HERMAN-SEKULICH, MAYA B.

HERMAN, MARIAN AUGUSTYN, institute director, physicist, researcher; b. Poznan, Poland, Nov. 28, 1936; s. Alojzy and Małgorzata Herman; m. Anna Pytlewicz, Apr. 6, 1963 (div. 1988); children: Krzysztof, Robert; m. Jolanta Senator, June 7, 1994. MSc, U. Tech., Gdańsk, Poland, 1960; PhD, U. Tech., Warsaw, 1968, DSc, 1987. Cert. prof. tech. studies, 1997. Rsch. asst. U. Tech., Warsaw, 1961-69; asst. prof. Inst. Electron Tech., Warsaw, 1969-71; asst. prof. Inst. Physics, Polish Acad. Scis., Warsaw, 1971-87, assoc. prof., 1988-96, prof., 1997, dept. head, 1974-80; dep. dir. Inst. Vacuum Tech., Warsaw, 1990, prof., 1992. Author: Semiconductor Heterojunctions-Physics, Technology, Applications, 1987, Semiconductor Superlattices, 1986, 2nd edit., 1989, Physical Problems of Epitaxy, 1986; co-author: Molecular Beam Epitaxy-Fundamentals and Current Status, 1989, 2nd edit., 1996. Ruling bd. mem. Polish Trade Union Educators, Warsaw, 1980. Lt. Polish Res., 1960. Mem. Polish Crystal Growth Soc. (ruling bd. mem., pres. 1995-98), Polish Vacuum Soc. (ruling bd. mem., pres. 1998—), Polish Phys. Soc. Roman Catholic. Avocations: classical music, tourism, theatre. Home: Fl 15, 117 Miedzyborska St, PL-04013 Warsaw Poland Office: Inst Physics Polish Acad Scis, 32/46 Lotnikov Av, PL-02-668 Warsaw Poland

HERMAN, MARY MARGARET, neuropathologist; b. Plymouth, Wis., July 26, 1935; d. Elmer Fredolein and Esther Lydia (Bross) H.; m. Lucien Jules Rubinstein, Jan. 31, 1969. BS in Med. Sci., U. Wis., 1957, MD, 1960. Diplomate Nat. Bd. Med. Examiners, Am. Bd. Anatomic Pathology, Am. Bd. Neuropathology. Intern Mary Hitchcock Meml. Hosp., Hanover, N.H., 1960-61; resident in neurology U. Wis. Hosps., 1961-62; intern in pathology Yale U., New Haven, 1962-63, asst. resident in pathology, 1963-64, fellow neuropathology, 1964-65, rsch. assoc. pathology, 1967-68; fellow neuropathology Stanford U., Palo Alto, Calif., 1965-66, fellow, acting instr. neuropathology, 1966-67, asst. prof. pathology, 1967-74, assoc. prof., 1974-81; prof., co-dir. divsn. neuropathology U. Va. Sch. Medicine, Charlottesville, 1981-91, prof. clin. pathology, 1991-92; spl. expert neuropathology in clin. brain disorders br. NIMH, Washington, 1991-96, sr. staff scientist, 1996—; neuropathologist NIMH Brain Collection, 1992—, Stanley Fund Brain Collection, 1992—; vis. asst. prof. Albert Einstein Coll. Medicine, Bronx, N.Y., 1971-72; mem. program project rev. com. Nat. Inst. Neurol. and Communicative Diseases, NIH, 1973-77; cons. lab. svc. VA Hosp., Salem, Va., Ctrl. Va. Tng. Ctr., Lynchburg, 1982-92, ad hoc mem. pathology A study sect., 1986-91; cons. neuropathologist D.C. Med. Examiner's Office, Washington, 1992—, D.C. Gen. Hosp., 1992—; mentor scientist NIH In-

tramural Rsch. Tng. award, Fogarty Fellows, Howard Hughes Med. Inst./ MCPS/NIH student and tchr. internships program, Stanley Found. scholar's program. Mem. edit. bd. Jour. Neuropathology and Exptl. Neurology, 1989-93; contbr. over 150 articles to profl. jours. Recipient Rsch. Career Devel. award NIH, 1967-72, Faculty Devel. award Merck Found., 1969. Mem. AAAS, AMA, Am. Assn. Anatomists (trust fund com.), Soc. Biol. Psychiatry, Am. Assn. Neuropathologists (Weil award 1974), Am. Soc. for Investigative Pathology, Soc. for Devel. Biology, Internat. Soc. Neuropathology, Am. Soc. Cell Biology (rsch. fellowship program, mentor scientist summer tchr. 1994), Internat. Acad. Pathology, Soc. In Vitro Biology, Soc. Neurosci. Achievements include work on neuropathology of serious mental disorders, aluminum neurotoxicity, and embryonal tumors of the CNS. Avocations: gardening, music, tennis. E-mail: mh230t@nih.gov. Home: 10008 Stedwick Rd Apt 304 Montgomery Village MD 20886-3718 Office: Clin Brain Disorders Br Nimh Nih Msc 4091 Bethesda MD 20892-0001

HEŘMAN, MIROSLAV, radiologist, educator; b. Olomouc, Czech Republic, Oct. 13, 1959; s. Jaroslav and Eva Heřman; m. Zuzana Hermanova, Dec. 30, 1983; children: Jan, Zuzana. MD, Palacky U., 1985, PhD, 1997. Cert. radiologist. Radiologist Regional Inst. Nat. Health, Ostrava, Czech Republic, 1985-86, Univ. Hosp. Olomouc, 1986-94; sec. dept. radiology Palacky U., Olomouc, 1995-2000, assoc. prof., 1998—, vice dean faculty medicine, 2000—; external tchr. Secondary Health Sch., Olomouc, 1992-97; vis. fellow U. Hosp. Trieste, Italy, 1994. Contbr. articles to profl. jours. Grantee Czech Ministry of Health, 1995-97. Mem. European Assn. Radiology, Czech Radiol. Soc., Radiol. Soc. N.Am. (corr.). Avocations: sports, computers. Home: Trnkova 28, 77900 Olomouc Czech Republic Office: Univ Hosp Dept Radiology, IP Pavlova 6, 77520 Olomouc Czech Republic

HERMAN, ROBERT LEWIS, cork company executive; b. N.Y.C., July 16, 1927; s. Nat W. and Ruth (Stockton) H.; m. Susan Marie Volper, Dec. 10, 1966; children: Candia Ruth, William Neal. AB, Columbia U., 1948, BS, 1949. V.p. Joseph Samuels & Sons, Inc., Whippany, N.J, 1953-62; pres. Dependable Cork Co., Inc., Morristown, N.J, 1962—; sr. chmn. Amorim Indsl. Solutions, Inc., Trevor, Wis., 1999—; bd. dirs. Concorco LDA, Lisbon, Portugal, Oporto, Portugal, Amorim Indsl. Solutions, LDA, Oporto, Portugal. Inventor Corticiera natural cork wallcovering. Comdr. C.E. Corps, USNR, 1949-53. Mem. N.J. Mfrs. Assn., Naval Res. Assn., U.S.C. of C., Navy League Club, Columbia U. Club, Princeton Club (N.Y.C.). Home: PO Box 1023 Morristown NJ 07962-1023 Office: PO Box 1102 Morristown NJ 07962-1102

HERMAN, STEVEN L, broadcast executive, journalist, author; b. Cin., Nov. 20, 1959; arrived in Japan, 1990; s. Kenneth and Hazel (Jaeger) H.; m. Erika Hidaka Onosaka, 1981 (div. 1985); m. Rie Sasaki, 1998; 1 child, Ian-Benjamin. Student, U. Nevada, 1975-79, Am. U., 1988-90; BA, Thomas Edison State Coll., 1993; postgrad. cert. creative writing, Bath Coll. U., Eng., 1999. Licensed FCC first class radiotelephone. Reporter Associated Press, Washington and Tokyo, 1990-96; producer PBS-NHK Asia Now, Tokyo, 1990-94; assignment editor KVBC-TV, Las Vegas, 1983-84, KTIE-TV, Ventura, Calif., 1984-86; pres. Globe Net Prodns. K.K., Tokyo, 1994-97; dir. Japan, Discovery Channel, Tokyo, 1997-2000; sr. v.p. Pacific Century Cyber Works-Japan, 2000—. Author: Sunset 2020, 1996, Last Assignment, 1999. Recipient Asia Media Leader award World Econ. Forum, 1997. Mem. Fgn. Press in Japan (chmn.), Fgn. Corr. Club Japan, Am. C. of C. (Japan chpt.). Avocations: amateur radio, backgammon, horseback riding, photography. Office: Yebisv Garden Pl Twr 32 Fl, 4-20-3 Ebisu Shibuya-ku, Tokyo 150-6032, Japan

HERMAN, WILLIAM CHARLES, lawyer; b. N.Y.C., Nov. 6, 1935; s. Milton and Hortense (Rosenthal) H.; m. Elizabeth Leitner; children: Howard, Sarah Jane (dec.). BA, CCNY, 1958; LLB, Columbia U., 1959. Bar: N.Y. 1960, U.S. Dist. Ct. (so. and ea. dists.) 1964, U.S. Ct. Appeals (2d cir.) 1964, U.S. Supreme Ct. 1964. Assoc. Howard H. Spellman, N.Y.C., 1960-61; pvt. practice law N.Y.C., 1962-65; assoc. Gilbert S. Rosenthal, N.Y.C., 1965-70; ptnr. Rosenthal & Herman, N.Y.C., 1970-82, Rosenthal, Herman & Mantel, P.C., N.Y.C., 1982-94, Rosenthal & Herman, P.C., N.Y.C., 1994—. Bd. dirs., Camphill Spl. Schs., Inc., Glenmoore, Pa., 1980—; bd. dirs. Camphill Found., Kimberton, Pa., 1987—; trustee Camphill Assn., N.Am., Copake, N.Y., 1982—. With U.S. Army, 1959-60. Fellow Am. Acad. Matrimonial Lawyers (chmn. matrimonial law com. 1982-84); mem. ABA, N.Y. State Bar Assn., N.Y. County Lawyers Assn. (bd. dirs. 1979-85), Am. Coll. Family Trial Lawyers (diplomate). Avocations: charitable activities, fishing, platform tennis. E-Mail: rhpc8911@aol.com. Home: 95 Lord Kitchner Rd New Rochelle NY 10804-2230 Office: 60 E 42nd St New York NY 10165-0006

HERMAN-GIDDENS, GREGORY, lawyer; b. Birmingham, Ala., Aug. 8, 1961. BA, U. N.C., 1984; JD, Tulane U., 1988; LLM in Estate Planning, U. Miami, 1993. Bar: N.C. 1988, U.S. Dist. Ct. (mid. dist.) N.C. 1988, Fla. 1992, U.S. Supreme Ct. 1998; cert. specialist in estate planning and probate law, N.C. State Bar Bd. Legal Specialization; grad. leadership triangle program 1996. Assoc. N. Joanne Foil, Atty. at Law, Durham, N.C., 1988-92, Catalano, Fisher, Gregory & Crown, Chartered, Naples, Fla., 1993, Northen, Blue, Rooks, Thibaut, Anderson & Woods, L.L.P., Chapel Hill, N.C., 1994-96; pvt. practice Chapel Hill, 1996—; profl. adv. com. Triangle Cmty. Found., 1999—. Mem. Chapel Hill Bd. Adjustment, 1989-92; bd. dirs. Friends of Chapel Hill Sr. Ctr., 1994-97; mem. Orange County Adv. Bd. on Aging, 1994-97, vice-chair, 1996-97; treas., bd. dirs. Orange County Literacy coun., Carrboro, N.C., 1994-98; mem. nat. com. on planned giving N.C. Planned Giving Coun. Mem. ABA (coms. on stds. of tax practice and tax practice mgmt. of tax sect., coms. on lifetime and testamentary charitable gift planning and planning for execs. and profls. of real property, probate and trust sect. 1996—), N.C. Bar Assn. (law and aging com. young lawyers divsn. 1994-98, elder law sect. coun. 1998—, career devel. com. young lawyers divsn. 1990-91, dir. young lawyers divsn. 1997-98, endowment com. 1997—, estate adminstrn. manual com. estate planing & fiduciary law sect. 1997—), Nat. Acad. Elder Law Attys., Durham/Orange Estate Planning Coun., Kiwanis Club Orange County (pres. 1998-99), Phi Beta Kappa, Psi Chi. Office: 1829 E Franklin St Ste 700D Chapel Hill NC 27514-5867

HERMANN, DONALD HAROLD JAMES, lawyer, educator; b. Southgate, Ky., Apr. 6, 1943; s. Albert Joseph and Helen Marie (Snow) H. AB (George E. Gamble Honors scholar), Stanford U., 1965; JD, Columbia U., 1968; LLM, Harvard U., 1974; MA, Northwestern U., 1979, Ph.D., 1981; MA in Art History, Sch. Art Inst. Chgo., 1993; postgrad., U. Chgo., 1998—. Bar: Ariz. 1968, Wash. 1969, Ky. 1971, Ill. 1972, U.S. Supreme Ct. 1974. Mem. staff, directorate devel. plans U.S. Dept. Def., 1964-65; With Legis. Drafting Research Fund, Columbia U., 1966-68; asst. dean Columbia Coll., 1967-68; mem. faculty U. Wash., Seattle, 1968-71, U. Ky., Lexington, 1971-72; mem. faculty DePaul U., 1972—, prof. law and philosophy, 1978—, dir. acad. programs and interdisciplinary study, 1975-76, assoc. dean, 1975-78, dir. Health Law Inst., 1985—; lectr. dept. philosophy Northwestern U., 1979-81; counsel DeWolfe, Poynton & Stevens, 1984-89; vis. prof. Washington U., St. Louis, 1974, U. Brazilia, 1976, U. P.R. Sch. Law, 1993; lectr. law Am. Soc. Found., 1975-78, Sch. Edn. Northwestern U., 1974-76, Christ Coll. Cambridge (Eng.) U., 1977, U. Athens, 1980; vis. scholar U. N.D., 1983; mem. NEH seminar on property and rights Stanford U., 1981; participant law and econs. program U. Rochester, 1974; mem. faculty summer seminar in law and humanities UCLA, 1978; Bicentennial Fellow of U.S. Constitution Claremont Coll., 1986; Law and Medicine fellow Cleve. Clinic., 1990; bd. dirs. Coun. Legal Edn. Opportunity, Ohio Valley Consortium, 1972, Ill. Bar Automated Rsch. Corp., 1975-81, Criminal Law Consortium Cook County, Ill., 1977-80; cons. Adminstrv. Office Ill. Cts., 1975-90; reporter cons. Ill. Jud. Conf., 1972-90; mem. Ctr. for Law Focused Edn., Chgo., 1977-81; faculty Instituto Superiore Internazionale Di Science Criminali, Siracusa, Italy, 1978-82; cons. Commerce Fedn., State of São Paulo, Brazil, 1975; residential scholar Christ Ch., Oxford, 1999. Editor: Jour. of Health and Hosp. Law, 1986-96, DePaul Jour. Healthcare Law, 1996—, AIDS Monograph Series, 1987—. Bd. dirs. Ctr. for Ch.-State Studies, 1982—, Horizons Cmty. Svcs., 1985-88, Chgo. Area AIDS Task Force, 1987-90, Howard Brown Health Ctr., 1994—; dir., v.p. Inst. for Genetics, Law and Ethics, Ill. Masonic Hosp., 1993—; trustee 860 N. Lakeshore Trust, Chgo., Ill., 1993-95; bd. visitors Oriental Inst., U. Chgo., 1995—, bd. dirs. Renaissance Soc., 1995—; mem. Cook County States Atty. Task Force on Drugs, 1985-90, Cook County States Atty. Task Force on Gay and Lesbian Issues, 1990—; mem. Ill. HIV Prevention Cmty. Planning Group, Ill. Dept. Pub. Health. John Noble fellow Columbia U., 1968, Internat. fellow, NEH fellow, Law and Humanities fellow U. Chgo, 1975-76, Law and Humanities fellow Harvard U., 1973-74, Northwestern U., 1978-82, Criticism and Theory fellow Stanford U. 1981, NEH fellow Cornell U., 1982, Judicial fellow U.S. Supreme Ct., 1983-84, U. Ill. fellow med. ethids rsch. group; Dean's scholar Columbia U., 1968, Univ. scholar Northwestern U., 1979. Mem. ABA, Ill. Bar Assn., Chgo. Bar Assn., Am. Acad. Polit. and Social Sci., Am. Law Inst., Am. Soc. Law, Medicine and Ethics, Am. Soc. Polit. and Legal Philosophy, Nat. Health Lawyers Assn., Am. Judicature Soc., Am. Philos. Assn., Soc. for Bus. Ethics, Soc. for Phenomenology and Existential Philosophy, Internat. Assn. Philosophy of Law and Soc., Soc. Writers on Legal Subjects, Internat. Penal Law Soc., Soc. Am. Law Tchrs., Am. Assn. Law Schs. (del., sect. chmn., chmn. sect. on jurisprudence), Am. Acad. Healthcare Attys., Ill. Assn. Hosp. Attys., Chgo. Coun. Fgn. Rels., Evanston Hist. Soc., Northwestern U. Alumni Assn., Signet Soc. of Harvard, Quadrangle Players, Hasty Pudding Club, University Club, Quadrangle Club, Tavern Club, Cliff Dwellers Club, Arts Club Chgo., Legal Club Chgo., Law Club Chgo. Episcopalian. Home: 1243 Forest Ave Evanston IL 60202-1451 Office: DePaul U Coll Law 25 E Jackson Blvd Chicago IL 60604-2287 also: 880 N Lake Shore Dr Chicago IL 60611-1761 also: 21 Nando-Machi Shinjukuko, Tokyo 162, Japan

HERMANN, RAPHAEL PIERRE, secondary education educator; b. Waimes, Belgium, Mar. 27, 1973; s. Hermann Pierre and Agnhs Velz; m. Katrien Sevrin, Sept. 11, 1999. Physics grad., U. Lihge, Belgium, 1995, philosophy grad., 1998. Tchr. informatics Social Promotion Sch. StVith, Butgenbach, 1994-98; rsch. asst. ednl. rsch. dept. U. Lihge, 1998-99, asst. gen. physics dept., 1999—; h.s. tchr. sys. theory Social Promotion Sch. for Educators, Lihge, 1999—. Author: (books) Le Concept de Temps en Physique, 1995, Elaboration de la Definition Aristotilicien du temps, 1998. Avocations: Go, yoga, role-playing. E-mail: r.hermann@ulg.ac.be. Home: Bld E de Laveleye 75, Lihge 4000, Belgium Office: U Lihge, Bat B5 Gen Physics, Lihge 4000, Belgium

HERMANN, ROBERT BELL, physical chemist, consultant; b. Bellevue, Pa., Dec. 12, 1930; s. Gustave Adolph and Alida Mae (Bell) H.; m. Phyllis Ann Halley, Aug. 7, 1958 (div. Feb. 1982); children: Deborah, David, Stephen; m. Carol Sue Lester, June 12, 1985. BS in Chemistry, U. Mich., 1953; MS, Wayne State U., 1960, PhD, 1962. Organic chemist Parke-Davis & Co., Detroit, 1953-58; NSF postdoctoral fellow U. Wis., Madison, 1962-63; postdoctoral fellow Ill. Inst. Tech., Chgo., 1963-64; computational chemist Eli Lilly & Co., Indpls., 1964-93; vis. prof. Ind. U.-Purdue U. Ind., Indpls., 1994—; cons. Eli Lilly & Co., 1994—. Contbr. articles to profl. jours. Presbyterian. Achievements include research of relationship between molecular surface area and solubility especially with regard to hyrdophobic interactions; patent for inhibitors of phospholipase A2. Office: Ind U Purdue U Indpls Dept Chemistry 402 N Blackford St Indianapolis IN 46202-3217

HERMANN, ROBERT EWALD, surgeon; b. Highland, Ill., Jan. 28, 1929; s. Ewald E. and Erna (Pabst) H.; m. Barbara Bower, Aug. 23, 1952 (dec. Aug. 1980); m. Polly Dreher, Mar. 8, 1986; childrn: Robert Jr., Barry, Monty. AB cum laude, Harvard U., 1950; MD, Washington U., St. Louis, 1954. Diplomate Am. Bd. Surgery. Intern, resident Univ. Hosps., Cleve., 1954-61; chmn. gen. surgery Cleve. Clinic, 1969-94, emeritus cons. dept. gen. surgery, 1994—; clin. prof. surgery Case Western Res. Sch. Medicine, Cleve., 1970—; dir. Am. Bd. Surgery, Phila., 1975-81; mem. Residency Rev. Com., Chgo., 1975-81. Author: Surgery of Gallbladder, Bile Ducts, Pancreas, 1979, Surgical Practice of Cleveland Clinic, 1985; contbr. over 180 articles to med. jours., 53 chpts. to books. Trustee Cleve. Clinic Found., 1976-77. Capt. M.C. U.S. Army, 1956-57. Recipient Roswell Park Gold medal Buffalo Surg. Soc., 1993. Mem. ACS (gov. 1981-87, v.p. 1996-97, Disting. Svc. award 1994), Am. Surg. Soc., German Surg. Soc. (hon.), Internat. Surg. Soc., Internat. Coll. Surgeons (hon.), Soc. Surg. Oncology, Soc. Surgery Alimenatary Tract (pres. 1988-89), Assn. Program Dirs. Surgery (pres. 1979-81), Ea. Surg. Soc. (pres. 1985-86), Pan-Pacific Surg. Assn. (v.p. 1991-93), Joint Commn. on Accreditation of Healthcare Orgns. (bd. commrs. 1997—). Republican. Avocations: tennis, golf, sailing, music. Home: 1 Bratenahl Pl Apt 1403 Bratenahl OH 44108-1156 Office: Cleve Clinic A-80 9500 Euclid Ave Cleveland OH 44195-0001

HERMANNSSON, STEINGRIMUR, former prime minister of Iceland; b. Reykjavik, Iceland, June 22, 1928; s. Hermann Jonasson and Vigdis (Steingrimsdottir) H.; m. Gudlaug Edda Gudmundsdottir; children: Hermann, Hlif, Gudmundur; children by previous marriage: John Bryan, Ellen Herdis, Neil. BSc in Elec. Engring., Ill. Inst. Tech., 1951; MSc, Calif. Inst. Tech., 1952. Engr. City of Reykjavik Elec. Power Works, 1952-53, State Fertilizer Plant, 1953-54, So. Calif. Edison Co., L.A., 1955-56; ptnr., engr. Bldg. Contractors Ltd., Reykjavik, 1957; bd. dirs. State and City of Reykjavik Geothermal Drilling Enterprise, 1957-78; dir. Nat. Rsch. Coun. of Iceland, 1957-78; mem. Icelandic Parliament, 1971-94, minister of justice and ecclesiastical affairs and of agr., 1978-79, minister fisheries and comms., 1980-83, prime minister, 1983-87, 88-91, minister fgn. affairs, 1987-88; gov. Ctrl. Bank of Iceland, 1994-98; mem. Icelandic del. to UN, 1956-57, 91; mem. com. on higher end. and rsch. Coun. of Europe, 1959-74; mem. sci. com. OECD, 1962-78; chmn. Icelandic Environ. Protection Assn., Millennium Inst., Arlington, Va. Author numerous articles on electrification, econ. and indsl. devel. and politics. Sec. Proressive Party, 1971-79, chmn., 1979-94. Recipient Disting. Svc. award Calif. Inst. Tech., 1986, Profl. Achievement award Ill. Inst. Tech., 1991, Gold medal Icelandic Athletics Assn., others; Paul Harris fellow. Mem. Rotary Club, Icelandic Engring. Soc., Icelandic Environ. Protection Soc. (chmn.), Surbey Rsch. Soc. (chmn.).

HERMANS, JOHANNES JOZEF ROBERTUS, pharmacology researcher; b. Amby, Limburg, The Netherlands, Aug. 10, 1966; s. J.M.G. Wiel and Berty (Decker) H. DSc, U. Maastricht, The Netherlands, 1988, PhD, 1992. Postdoctoral fellow Philipps U., Marburg, Germany, 1994-95; postdoctoral fell in cardiovascular rsch. U. Maastricht, The Netherlands, 1996—. Contbr. articles to profl. jours. Recipient Postdoctoral fellowship grant Alexander von Humboldt Stiftung, Marburg, Germany, 1994, 95, Grant for rsch. project Dutch Kidney Found., 1996-99. Roman Catholic. Avocations: angling, billiard. Home: Oranjeplein 1, 6333 BD Schimmert-Nuth The Netherlands Office: U Maastricht Cardiovas Rsch Inst, Dept Pharm Tox PO Box 616, 6200 MD Maastricht The Netherlands

HERMANS, LOEK, government official; b. Heerlen, The Netherlands, Apr. 23, 1951. Degree in politics, Cath. U., Nijmegen, 1976. Mem. Nijmegen Coun., 1974-78, Lower House, 1977-90; burgomaster of Zwolle, 1990-94, Queen's Commr. in the Province of Friesland, 1994-98; min. Ministry Edn., Cultural Affairs & Sci., Zoetermeer, The Netherlands, 1998—; lectr. Gelderland Coll. Pub. Adminstrn., 1972-76. Office: Ministry Edn, Europaweg 4 PO Box 25000, 2711 AH Zoetermeer 2700 LZ Zoetermeer, The Netherlands also: PO Box 25000, 2700LZ Zoetermeer The Netherlands*

HERMAN-SEKULICH, MAYA B. (MAJA HERMAN), poet, essayist, editor; b. Belgrade, Serbia, Yugoslavia, Feb. 17, 1959; came to U.S., 1980, naturalized, 1992; d. Bogomir Herman and Lily (Strauss) Tišma; m. Milosh Sekulich. MA, Belgrade U., 1977; PhD in Comparative Lit., Princeton U., 1986. Fulbright lectr. Rutgers U., New Brunswick, N.J., 1982-84; cons. Novo Arts, N.Y.C., 1988-90; vis. lectr. Princeton (N.J.) U., 1985, 88; lectr., reader in field. Author: (poems) Camerography, 1990, Cartography, 1992, Out of the Museum of Wanderings, 1997, Out of the Waste Land, 1998 (English/Serbian edit.); (essays) Sketches for Portraits, 1992, (essays) Literature of Transgression, 1986, rev. edit., 1994, The Jade Window: Images from Southeast Asia, 1994, English lang. edit., 1998; editor/translator: Anxiety of Influence (Harold Bloom), 1981, Cathedral (Raymond Carver), 1991, Myth and Structure (Northrop Frye), 1991, Poems of Our Climate (Wallace Stevens), 1995; contbg. editor Night, 1990-91; edited and translated intros. to 10 books; contbr. to scholarly jours.; correspondant (weekly) VREME, Belgrade, 1995—. Princeton U. fellow, 1980-85, Fulbright fellow, 1982-84. Fellow AAUW; mem. PEN (Am. chpt., Serbian chpt.), Poetry Soc. Am. Avocations: swimming, skating, world travel. Home: 69 5th Ave Apt 11A New York NY 10003-3008

HERMANSSON, STURE, legal administrator; b. Trollhätten, Sweden, June 13, 1944; s. Herbert and Elna Hermansson; m. Birgitta Hermansson; children: Maria, Emma. Named Hon. Lt. Col. State of Ala., 1983; recipient Dist. Svc. award Rotary Internat., 1991-92, Meritorious Svc. citation Rotary Internat., 1995. Mem. Värmland Athletic Fedn., Värmland Horse Sport Fedn. (pres.). Office: County Adminstrn of, Värmland, S-65186 Karlstad Sweden

HERMANT, PIERRE CLAUDE, equipment company executive; b. Canteleu, France, May 20, 1940; s. Pierre Alphonse and Bernadette (Senechal) H.; m. Michele Henriette Moyse, Apr. 28, 1967; children: Patrick, Isabelle. Degree in engring., Arts et Metiers, France, 1963; MSc, Stanford (Calif.) U., 1964. Quality assurance supr., safety engr., then tng. mgr. Caterpillar France, S.A., Grenoble, 1966-73; asst. buyer Caterpillar Tractor Co., Aurora, Ill., 1973-74; buyer Caterpillar France, S.A., Grenoble, 1974-79; quality mgr. Caterpillar France, S.A., 1979-85, purchasing mgr., 1985-90, unit mgr., 1990-93, quality mgr., 1993-99; cons. quality mgmt., 1999—. City counselor, City of Echirolles, Isere, France, 1983-89. 2d lt. French Army, 1964-66; liaison officer U.S. Army Depot, France, 1965-66. Mem. Engrs. Assn., Stanford Club France, France-U.S.A., Lions. Roman Catholic. Avocation: travel. Home: 7 Allee Maurice Ravel, 38130 Echirolles France

HERMES, KATHERINE ANN, historian, history educator; b. Cin., 1959; d. William Anthony and Rose Helen Hermes. BA cum laude, U. Calif., Irvine, 1985; JD, Duke U., 1992; PhD, Yale U., 1995. Adj. prof. N.C. Ctrl. U., Durham, 1989-90; lectr. U. Otago, Dunedin, New Zealand, 1992-97; assoc. prof. Ctrl. Conn. State U., New Britain, 1997—. Editor: Australasian Jour. Am. Studies, 1995 (Fulbright Issue), (articles) Conn. History, 1999—; exhibn. sculpture Moray Place Gallery, 1995. Election judge State of Calif., Orange County, 1984. Mem. Am. Hist. Assn., Conn. Hist. Soc., Orgn. Am. Historians, Inst. Am. Indian Studies (mem. Deer clan). Office: Ctrl Conn State U 1615 Stanley St New Britain CT 06053-2439

HERMET, JEAN-PIERRE, HENRY, healthcare company executive; b. Biarritz, France, Sept. 5, 1943; s. Maurice Gabriel and Cornelie (Van Den-Dries) de Courson; divorced; children: Stephane, Isabelle, Sebastien; m. Evelyne Madeleine Valentin, Nov. 4, 1982; 1 child, Virginie. MBA, Ecole Superieure de Commerce, Bordeaux, France, 1968; Lic. in Scis. Econs., Droit U., Bordeaux, 1969; MBA, Inst. Adminstr. Enterprises, Bordeaux, 1969. Mgr. mktg. Schering, Plough, France, 1974-79; mng. dir. Whitehall, Paris, 1979-86; v.p. Jouveinal, Paris, 1986-89; dir. Allergan, Mougins, France, 1989-90; pres. Europe Belmac, Valbonne, France, 1991-92; pres. Joint Ptnrs. for Healthcare, Paris, 1993—; CEO, chmn. Hemopharm, Gardanne, France, 1995-98, Peptide Immunne Ligands Pil, Paris, France, 1997-98, Hybrigenics, Paris, 1997-98, Hemosystem, Marseilles, France, 1999—; assoc. prof. Inst. Adminstrn. Enterprises, 1971-83. Contbr. articles to profl. jours. Home: 4 Ter Ave Charles de Gaulle, 92100 Boulogna France Office: 26 Rue JM Keynes, 13013 Marseille France

HERMISSON, HANS-JÜRGEN, theologian, scientist; b. Falkenstein, Neumark, Germany, May 17, 1933; ž; s. Karl-Friedrich and Gertrud (Lueder) H.; m. Susanne Heinle, Mar. 8, 1968; children: Joachim, Ulrich, Mirjam. PhD, Kirchliche Hochschule, Berlin, 1962. Asst. Theol. Faculty U., Heidelberg, Germany, 1963-67; asst. prof. Theol. Faculty U., Heidelberg, 1967-77; prof. Theol. Faculty U., Bonn, Germany, 1977-82, Tuebingen, Germany, 1982-98; dean Theol. Faculty U., Bonn, 1980-81, Tuebingen, 1987-88, 95-96. Author: Language and Rite in Ancient Israelite Cult, 1965, Studies in Ancient Israelite Proverbial Wisdom, 1968, Studies in Prophecy and Wisdom, 1998, Old Testament Theology and History of Israelite Religion, 2000; co-author: Faith, 1978, Deuterojesaja, 1987—. Lutheran. Home: Stauffenbergstr 11, D 72074 Tübingen Germany

HERMSTEINER, MARKUS GERARD JOSEF, obstetrician-gynecologist, researcher; b. Herbern, N.R.Westph, Germany, Nov. 15, 1961; s. Siegfried Rudolf, and Gisela Ottilia (Limbach) H.; m. Almut Wendt, July 17, 1992; 1 child, Astrid. MD, Justus-Liebig U., Giessen, Germany. Rschr. dept. physiology U. Giessen, Germany, 1990; resident Giessen Dist. Hosp., Lich, Germany, 1991-93; resident dept. Ob-Gyn. Univ Giessen, 1994-95, rsch. fellow, 1996—; dir. microvessel rsch. lab. U. Giessen, Germany, 1996. Spokesman regional bd. for human rights edn., Amnesty Internat. German sect., 1985-86, mem. working group on human rights in medicine and psychology, 1986-92. Grantee German Acad. Exchange Svc., Bristol, Eng., 1986; recipient award for young scientists German Coll. Ob-Gyn, 1996. Mem. German Soc. Ob.-Gyn. (scholar 1996), Internat. Soc. for Study of Hypertension in Pregnancy. Roman Catholic. Avocations: photography, art history, cycling. Office: Univ Giessen Hosps Ob-Gyn, Kliniktrasse 32, D-35392 Giessen Germany

HERNADI, ANDRAS, economist; b. Budapest, Hungary, July 25, 1946; s. Lajos Hernadi; m. Eva Maroti, July 14, 1979; 1 child, Julia. PhD, U. Econs., Budapest, 1972; Candidate D., Hungarian Acad. Scis., 1979. From rsch. fellow to dep. dir.-gen. Inst. World Econs., Hungarian Acad. Scis., Budapest, 1971-90, dir. Japan east and s.e. Asia rsch. ctr., 1990—; vis. scholar Hitotsubashi U., Tokyo, 1975-76; vis. prof. Kyoto (Japan) U., 1984-85. Author: New Stage of Development of the Japanese Economy in the 1970s, 1980, The Asia-Pacific Region, 1982, The Far Eastern Challenge, 1985, Consumption and Development, 1992, others; contbr. over 80 articles to profl. jours. Mem. European Assn. Japanese Studies (v.p. 1988-96). Avocations: jazz, tennis, swimming. E-mail: ahernadi@vki3.vki.hu. Home: 18 Vasarhelyi, 2092 Budakeszi Hungary Office: Inst World Econs, PO Box 936, 1535 Budapest Hungary

HERNANDEZ, ALEJANDRO, financial analyst; b. Tegucigalpa, Honduras, Sept. 7, 1977; s. Jorge Hernandez-Alcerro and Mariza Hernandez-Veiga. Student, London Sch. Econs., 1998; BA in Econs. cum laude, Rice U., 1999. Cons. Banco del Pais, San Pedro Sula, Honduras, 1997, Ralph Lauren, San Pedro Sula, 1998, RDA Cons., Houston, 1999; fin. analyst Enron Corp., Houston, 1999—; bd. dirs. Catrachos Online, Houston. Author website Honduras Resources, 1995, editor, 1996 (Best Webpage award 1997). Candidate for coll. presidency, Houston, 1997; campaign participant Nat. Party, Honduras, 2000. Mem. Golden Key Nat. Honor Soc. Avocations: politics, web design, travel, sports. Fax: (713) 345-6209. E-mail: alejandro.hernandez@enron.com. Office: Enron 333 Clay St Ste 1663 Houston TX 77002-4000

HERNANDEZ, EULOGIO JOSE, electrical engineer; b. Puerto la Cruz, Venezuela, Mar. 4, 1968; s. Eulogio and Maria del Valle (Malave) H.; m. Agustina Gutierrez, Dec. 9, 1995; 1 child, Maria Gabriela. Degree in elec. engring., U. de Oriente, Venezuela, 1993; degree in engring. mgmt., U. Santa Maria, Venezuela, 1996. Telecomm. technician CANTV, Barcelona, Venezuela, 1992-93; elec. engr. CANTV, Puerto la Cruz, Venezuela, 1993-95, maintenance supr., 1995-97, fitness supr., 1997-99, zone supr., 1999—; prof.'s chair U. Oriente, Barcelona, 1997; prof. IUPSM, Barcelona, 1994. Recipient Best Young Rschr. of Yr., Coun. Puerto La Cruz, 1994. Mem. IEEE, CIV. Avocations: softball, baseball, basketball. Office: CANTV, C/Arismendi Piso 5 Ofic 79, 6023 Puerto La Cruz Venezuela

HERNANDEZ, HECTOR MANUEL, consulting engineer, engineering educator; b. Bogotá, Colombia, Dec. 15, 1938; s. Pedro and Josefina (Ramirez) H.; m. Nohora Patricia Segura, Feb. 22, 1975; children: Claudia Liliana, Maria Paula, Andrea. Civil engr. degree, Nat. U., 1963; MSEE, Kans. U., 1966. Elec. engr. prof. Nat. U., Bogotá, 1966-69; head planning sect. Interconexion Electrica I.S.A., Bogotá, 1969-77; head elec. sector study ISA, Bogotá, 1978-79; head planning office ISA, Medellin, Colombia, 1980-92; cons. engr. Inter-Am. Devel. Bank, Washington, 1993; project mgr. AENE Cons., Bogotá, 1994-97; elec. engr. prof. Colombian Sch. Engring., Bogotá, 1994—, Nat. U., Bogotá, 1969-78. Recipient Julio Garavito Merit Order Colombian Govt., 1996. Mem. IEEE, Asociacion Colombiana de Ingenieros Electricos y Mecanicos, Colombian Soc. of Engring. (Lorenzo Codazzi award 1980, Enrique Morales award 1973). Roman Catholic. Achievements include development of the computer model to perform the long term, least cost, power generation expansion planning for the Colombian power generation system. Home: Calle 97 No 22-80 Apto 304, Santa Fe de Bogotá Colombia Office: Colombian Sch Engring, Autopista Norte Km 13, Santa Fe de Bogotá Colombia

HERNÁNDEZ, JEHÚ, food products executive; b. Reynosa, Mexico, Aug. 26, 1975; s. Raúl and Jovita (Morón) H. Grad., Flores Magón H.S., Matamoros, Mex. Parasitologist, bacteriologist, chemist Gamesa, Monterey, Mex., 1993-98; rschr. in field. Mem. Am. Soc. Microbiology. Fax: 88-13-31-77. E-mail: jehu43@hotmail.com. Home: Paris 13, Matamoros Tamaulipas Mexico Office: Gamesa, Ave Republic Mexicana, Monterrey Nuevo Leon, Mexico

HERNANDEZ, MACK RAY, lawyer; b. Austin, Tex., Sept. 8, 1944; s. Mack and Mary (Prado) H.; m. Mary Lynn McGuire, May 11, 1979 (div. Sept. 1988); 1 child, John Christopher. BA, U. Tex., 1967, JD, 1970. Bar: Tex. 1970, U.S. Dist. Ct. (we. dist.) Tex. 1972. Staff atty. Travis County Legal Aid Soc, Austin, 1970-71; pvt. practice Austin, 1971—. Bd. dirs. Austin C. of C., 1983-86, Meals on Wheels, Austin, 1972-76; trustee Austin C.C., 1988—; vice-chair, 1990-92, chair, 1992-94; chmn. bd. dirs. Am. Cancer Soc., Austin, 1988-95. Mem. Tex. Bar Assn., Travis County Bar Assn., Coll. of State Bar, Tex. Bar Found. Avocations: travel, jogging, hiking, backpacking. E-mail: mrhernandez@hernandezlaw.com. Office: 524 N Lamar Blvd Ste 202 Austin TX 78703-5422

HERNANDEZ, RAMON, medical products company executive; b. La Baneza, Leon, Spain, Oct. 24, 1961; s. Atilano Hernandez and Maria Asuncion Vecino; m. Celestina Canteli; children: Hernandez, Rodrigo. MD, Oviero, Spain, 1980; PhD, Madrid U., 1992; MSc in Health Svcs. Mgmt., U. London, 1994. Prin. in health planning Cartelayleon Regional Govt., Vallaroud, Spain, 1987-92; assoc. tchr. in pub. health Madrid U., 1994; outcomes rsch. mgr. Merck Sharp and Dohme, Madrid, 1995-97, health benefit mgr., 1998, med. affairs head, 1999—; tchr. Politecnics U., Valencia, 1995-98. Author: Health Management, 1996. Office: Marck Sharp Dohme Spain, C/Josefa Valcarler 38, 28027 Madrid Spain

HERNANDEZ, RAMON POMES, physics educator; b. Palma Soriano, Cuba, Dec. 5, 1947. BSc in Physics, U. Oriente, Santiago de Cuba, 1970; PhD in Physics in Math., U. St. Petersburg, 1976; DSc, Nat. Commn. of Acad. Degrees, 1982. Tchr., 1961-64, Militar Sch., 1964-66; prof. to sr. prof. U. Santiago de Cuba, 1970-82; v.p. Acad. of Scis. of Cuba, 1982-91; prof., head of divsn. NCSR, 1991-94, head of x-ray lab., 1995—. Editl. com. 5 jours.; contbr. numerous articles to profl. jours. Mem. NCSR (scientific coun.), Nat. Scientific Coun. of the Acad. of Scis. of Cuba, Cuban Physics Soc. Achievements include research in crystallography, crystal-physics, and crystal-chemistry using X-ray diffraction. Home: Ave Camaguey No 11238, Cerro, Havana Cuba

HERNANDEZ GRESS, NEIL, engineering researcher; b. Mexico City, July 28, 1970; s. Pedro Hernandez Skewes and Mercedes Gress de Hernandez; m. Teresa Osorio, Mar. 7, 1994; 1 child, Catherine Aimee. Engr., ITESM, Mexico City, 1993; M, Nat. Poly. Inst. Toulouse, France, 1995, PhD, 1998. Sys. adminstr. SEDESOL, Mexico City, 1993-94; diagnosis mgr. SAVE European programme, Brussels, 1995-98; jr. rsch. LAAS/CNRS, Toulouse, 1999—; cons. AMADEUS European Project, Brussels, 1999—; chmn. Fusion 99, Las Vegas, 1998. Contbr. articles to profl. jours. French Govt. scholar, 1994. Avocations: squash, karting, reading. E-mail: hdez@laas.fr. Office: LAAS/CNRS, 7 Av du Col Roche, Toulouse France 31077

HERNANDEZ-ILESCAS, JUAN HOMERO, epidemiologist, educator; b. Papantla, Veracruz, Mexico, Jan. 4, 1935; s. Juan Bartolo Hernandez-Garcia and Emma Illescas; m. Gloria Tena, Sept. 12, 1964; children: Gloria Andrea, Juan Homero, Emma Juliana. UNAM, Mexico City, 1958; Diploma tropical medicine, Sorbonne, Paris, 1961; diploma hosp. adminstrn., Mexico City, 1972. Dir. Nat. Med. Edn., Mexico City, 1972-79, October Hosp. Issste, Mexico City, 1979-80; dir. hosp. norms Ministry Health, Mexico City, 1984-98; head infectology unit Clinica Londres, Mexico City, 1998—; prof. medicine UNAM, Mexico City, 1965-93, LaSalle U., Mexico City, 1981; prof. infectory Nursery Sch., Panamerican U., Mexico City, 1998—; med. dir. Durango Hosp., Mexico City, 1990-92; head Atlantic Bank Med. Svcs., Mexico City, 1993-96. Contbr. articles to profl. jours. Mem. APHA, Med. Assn. Physicians with Scholarships in France (founder, sec., treas., v.p., pres.), Internal Medicine Mexico Assn. (founder, sec. 1982-83), Soc. Mexican de Salud Publica, Assn. Fronteriza Mexicana Estadounidense de Salud Publica, Soc. Mexicana de Infectologia, Assn. Mexican de Hosps., Inst. Mexicano de Cultura Academia de Ciencias Medicas, Found. UNAM (founder), Assn. des Members des Palmes Academiques, Alianza Francesa de Mexico, N.Y. Acad. Scis. Roman Catholic. Avocations: astronomy, collecting art and antiques, books, music, writing monographs. Fax: 523 2518. E-mail: hillescas@infosel.net.mx. Home: Anaxagoras 848 Bis, 03100 Mexico City DF, Mexico

HERNANDEZ MOLLAR, JORGE SALVADOR, foreign diplomat; b. Melilla, Spain, Sept. 3, 1945. Mem. European Parliament, 1999—, mem. com. citizens' freedoms/rights, justice/home affairs, substitute com. on employment and social affairs, substitute com. on fisheries; mem. Group of the European People's Party (Christian Democrats) and European Democrats; vice-chmn. delegation for relations with the Maghreb countries and the Arab Maghreb Union. People's Party. *

HERNDON, JAMES HENRY, orthopedic surgeon, educator; b. L.A., Oct. 31, 1938; s. James Greene and Kathleen Theresa (Murphy) H.; m. Geraldine Grace Armiger, Feb. 26, 1971; children: Jennifer, Jonathan. BS, Loyola U., L.A., 1961; MD, UCLA, 1965; MA, Brown U., 1979; MBA, Boston U., 1990; MA (hon.), Harvard U., 1999. Diplomate Am. Bd. Orthopaedic Surgery (bd. dirs., pres. 1991-92). Intern Hosp. of U. Pa., Phila., 1965-66, resident in surgery, 1966-67; resident in orthopaedics Mass. Gen. Hosp., Boston, 1970, chief resident in orthopaedics, 1967-70; asst. clin. prof. orthopaedic surgery Mich. State U., Grand Rapids, 1974-77, assoc. clin. prof., 1977-78; prof., chmn. dept. orthopaedics Brown U., Providence, 1979-88; surgeon-in-chief dept. orthopaedic surgery R.I. Hosp., Providence, 1979-88; Silver prof., chmn. dept. orthopaedic surgery U. Pitts., Pitts.; chief orthopaedics, 1988-98; chief dept. orthopaedics and rehab. Presbyn. U. Hosp., Pitts., 1988-98; assoc. sr. vice chancellor Health Svcs. U. Pitts. Med. Ctr., 1995-98, v.p. med. svcs., 1995-98; chmn. ptnrs. dept. orthopaedic surgery Mass. Gen. Hosp., 1998—, Brigham Women's Hosp., 1998—; examiner Am. Bd. Orthopaedic Surgery, Chgo., 1977—, pres., 1990-91; ptnrs. healthcare prof. Harvard Med. Sch., 1998—. Reviewer Jour. Bone and Joint Surgery, 1975—; contbr. articles to profl. jours., chpts. to books; author books in field. Trustee Meeting St. Sch., Providence, 1984-88, Harmarville Rehab. Hosp., Pitts., 1989-95; mem. bd. govs. Arthritis Found., Providence, 1984-88, Pitts., 1989—; bd. dirs. Make A Wish Found., chmn., 1998-99. Recipient Edith and Carl Lasky Meml. award UCLA Med. Sch., 1965, Bronze award Am. Congress Rehab. Medicine, 1972, Clin. Rsch. award N.Y. Med. Soc., 1974. Fellow ACS, Am. Acad. Orthopaedic Surgeons (treas. 1994-97); mem. Am. Orthopaedic Assn. (pres. 1999-00), Orthopaedic Rsch. Soc., Residence Rev. Com. Orthopaedic Surgery (past chmn.), Am. Soc. Surgery of Hand, Agawam Hunt Club, Hope Club, Longue Vue Club. Office: Massachusetts Gen Hosp Gray 624 55 Fruit St Boston MA 02114-2696

HERNDON, JOHN LAIRD, consulting firm executive; b. Shreveport, La., 1958; s. Jack and Irene Herndon. BS Econs., Millsaps Coll., Jackson, Miss., 1981; MBA, U. Miss., Oxford, 1997. Cons. Jackson, Miss., 1981-84; fin. analyst Coldwell Banker, L.A., 1984-86; sr. fin. analyst Kenneth Leventhal & Co., L.A., 1986-87; asst. contr. E&Y Real Estate Group, L.A., 1987-89, contr., 1989-95; dir. Ernst & Young LLP, N.Y., 1996—. Author numerous articles; speaker in field. John Palmer scholar U. Miss., Oxford, 1996-97. Mensa Internat. Episcopalian. Avocation: tennis. Office: Ernst & Young LLP 125 Chubb Ave Lyndhurst NJ 07071-3504

HERNDON, VENABLE, screenwriter, educator; b. Phila., Oct. 19, 1927; s. Hunter Venable and Isabelle Kearney (Flaig) H.; m. Ursule Molinaro (div. 1973); m. Sharon Anson, 1985. Diploma, Lawrenceville Sch., 1945; BA, Princeton U., 1949; MA, Harvard U., 1951. Copywriter Gimbels, N.Y.C., 1951-53, Bambergers, Newark, 1953-56; copywriter, account exec. Hicks and Greist Advt., N.Y.C., 1956-67; screenwriter with studios United Artists, Paramount, Columbia, Los Angeles, N.Y.C., 1967-74; freelance screenwriter N.Y.C., 1974—; instr. dramatic writing program NYU, N.Y.C., 1977—; cons. Films in Progress, Inc., Hoboken, N.Y., 1984—; adj. prof. dramatic writing Tisch sch. arts NYU, 1975-88; asst. prof. dramatic writing, 1989-96; assoc. prof. dramatic writing, 1996—. Editor, co-founder The Chelsea Rev., 1958-66; playwright Until the Monkey Comes, 1968; author: (film script with Arthur Penn) Alice's Restaurant, 1970, (biography) James Dean, A Short Life, 1974. Served to cpl. U.S. Army, 1946-48. Grantee N.Y. Creative Artists Pub. Service Program, 1980-81. Mem. ASCAP, Dramatists Guild, Writers Guild Am. West. Democrat. Avocation: playing piano. Home: 238 W 22nd St New York NY 10011-2701

HERNE, VIIVE, biologist; b. Polva, Estonia, Mar. 19, 1957; d. Aavo and Õie (Tenno) H. Biol., U. Tartu, 1980. Rschr. Inst. Exptl. and Clin. Medicine, Tallinn, Estonia, 1980-87; biol. Biotechnol. Enterprise Acad. Scis., Tallinn, 1987-92; lab. doctor Tallinn Diagnostic Ctr., 1992—. Contbr. articles to profl. jours. Scholarship Nordic Coun. Ministries, 1997. Home: Paasiku 22-202, 13916 Tallinn Estonia Office: Tallinn Diagnostic Ctr, Suur Ameerika 18, 10122 Tallinn Estonia

HEROLD, IVAN, anesthesiologist, educator; b. Prague, Czechoslovakia, Jan. 18, 1953; s. Erich and Iva (Jachym) H.; m. Jana Kraumann, May 13, 1977; children: Tomáš, Štěpán, Martin. MD, Charles U., Prague, 1977, PhD, 1998. Resident in anesthesia/intensive care Klaudian's Hosp., Mlada Boleslav, Czech Republic, 1977-86, fellow in anesthesia and intensive care medicine, 1986, vice chmn. dept. anesthesia and ICU, 1986-91; chmn. dept. anesthesia and ICU Klaudian's Hosp., Mlada Boleslav, 1992—. Author: Textbook of Regional Anaesthesia, 1998; editor: (books) Proceedings in Mechanical Ventilation, 1997, 99, Treatment of Ventilation Failure, 1995; contbr. abstracts to profl. jours. Mem. Czech Soc. Anesthesia and Intensive Care Medicine (1st v.p. 1995—), European Soc. Anesthesiologists, European Soc. Regional Anesthesia, European Soc. Intensive and Critical Care Medicine, N.Y. Acad. Scis. Office: Klaudian's Hosp, V Klementa 147, 293 50 Mlada Boleslav Czech Republic

HEROLD, JEFFREY ROY MARTIN, retired library director; b. Chgo., Aug. 9, 1941; s. Roy George and Anne (Polacek) H.; m. Carol Ann Courtial, June 20, 1964; children: Kristin Ann, Timothy Scott. MEd, SUNY, Buffalo, 1966; PhD, Ohio State U., 1969; MLS, Kent State U., 1986. Teaching assoc. Ohio State U., Columbus, 1965-69; asst. prof. edn. SUNY, Cortland, 1969-74, Ind. U. Pa., 1974-75; lectr. in edn. Kelvin Grove Coll., Brisbane, Australia, 1976-78; assoc. dir. office continuing edn. Ohio State U., Columbus, 1979-84; extension libr. Columbus Pub. Libr., 1985-87; dir. Bucyrus (Ohio) Pub. Libr., 1987-2000, Bucyrus Libr. Consortium, 1989-2000; bd. dirs. North Ctrl. Libr. Cooperative, Mansfield, Ohio, 1991-93; adv. coun. Classical WOSB-FM, The Ohio State U., Marion, 1998-2000. Book reviewer: Libr. Jour., 1988-97. Chair McGovern for Pres. Com., Cortland County, N.Y., 1972; founder and pres. SUNY Founds. of Edn. Assn., 1971-72. Grantee Timken Found., 1989, 96, Ohio Humanities Coun., 1994, 95, 97, Libr. Svcs. and Tech. Act, 1998. Mem. ACLU, ALA, Pub. Libr. Assn. (Univ. Press books for pub. librs. com. 1990-93), Ohio Libr. Coun. Avocations: reading, walking.

HERON, FRANCES DUNLAP, author, educator; b. Fulton, Mo., Dec. 26, 1906; d. Elijah Scott and Emma Susan (Owen) Dunlap; m. Laurence Tunstall, June 17, 1931 (dec.); children: Susan Heron Wollam, Alfred, Frances E. (dec.), Donald (dec.). AA, William Woods Coll., Fulton, 1925; BJ, U. Mo., 1927. Mem. editl. staff Christian Bd. Publ., St. Louis, 1927-31, Christian Advocate, Chgo., 1944-56; book reviewer Chgo. sunday Tribune, 1943-56; dir. edn. Grace United Protestant Ch., Park Forest, Ill., 1959-60; pub. sch. tchr. Dist. 147, Harvey, Ill., 1966-85; vol. preserving history Flossmoor (Ill.) Cmty. Ch., 1940—; lectr., writer Spiritual Frontiers Fellowship, Evanston, Ill., 1962-68. Author: Betty Ann, Beginner, 1930, With My Whole Heart, 1950, The Busy Berrys, 1950, Kathy Ann, Kindergartner, 1955, Here Comes Elijah, 1959, Jay Bain, Junior Boy, 1963; writer articles for Nat. Coun. Chs. Elections judge, 1950-68; neighborhood solicitor Am. Cancer Soc., 1997. Recipient Spl. Distinction prize Sch. Journalism, Columbia, Mo., 1927. Mem. PEO Sisterhood (historian 1949-67, 71—), Callaway County Hist. Soc., Perry County Historians. Democrat. Avocations: travel, genealogy, antiques, parapsychology. Home: 18520 Stewart Ave Homewood IL 60430-3036

HEROUIN, FRANÇOISE, finance executive; b. Enghien Les-Bains, Vald'oise, France, Aug. 6, 1962; arrived in Switzerland, 1997; d. Claude and G. (Rouland) H. Diploma, HEC-Paris, 1984, ESCP, 1993; IMD, Luasanne U., 2000. Corp. acct. Hewlett Packard, Evry, France, 1984-86; budget contr. SITA, Paris, 1986-87, billing mgr., 1987-90, mgmt. control dir., 1990-97, v.p. bus. fin., 1997-2000, v.p. fin. network svcs., 2000—. Contbr. articles to profl. jours. Mem. HEC. Office: SITA, Ch de Joinville 26, 1216 Cointrin Geneve, Switzerland

HEROUX, ERICK J., languages educator; b. Ft. Myers, Fla.. BA, U. Calif., Santa Cruz, 1989; PhD, U. Oreg., 1997. Asst. prof. Tamsui Oxford Univ. Coll., Tanshui, Taiwan, 1998-99, Nat. Chengchi U., Taipei, Taiwan, 1999—. Mem. MLA, Am. Studies Assn. Office: Nat Chenghci U, Dept English, Taipei Taiwan, ROC 116

HERPE, GEORGES, astronomy engineer, researcher; b. Plouedern, Finistere, France, June 9, 1943; s. Louis and Marie (Grall) H. Degree, Ecole Supérieure Techniques Aéronautiques et Constrn. Automobile, Paris, 1966; D degree, U. Paris, 1969. Fluid mechanics engr. Lab. Aerothermique, Meudon, 1966-69; aerodynamics tchr. Ecole Aviation Civile Alger, 1969-72; astronomy engr., rschr. Observatory of Meudon CNRS, 1972—. Mem. Ctr. Nat. Recherche Scientifique. Avocation: soccer. Office: CNRS, Observatoire de Meudon, 92195 Meudon France

HERPST, ROBERT DIX, lawyer, optics and materials technology executive; b. Teaneck, N.J., Jan. 23, 1947; s. Harold Dix and Anita Augusta (Adams) H.; children: Katherine Elizabeth, Lauren Gabrielle, Sarah Elizabeth; m. Theresa M. Jacobini, Oct. 24, 1987. BS, NYU, 1969; JD, Rutgers U., 1972. Bar: N.J., U.S. Supreme Ct. Assoc. Pitney, Hardin & Kipp, Morristown, N.J., 1972-77, BOC Group, Inc., Montvale, N.J., 1977-89; div. counsel BOC Group, Inc., Montvale, 1978-82, corp. counsel, asst. sec., 1982-88; pres. Internat. Crystal Labs., Garfield, N.J., 1982-88, mng. dir., chmn. bd. dirs., 1988—. Patentee in field. Avocations: golf, politics, stock market, graphic arts. Office: Internat Crystal Labs 11 Erie St Garfield NJ 07026-2307

HERR, WERNER FRIEDRICH, physicist, researcher; b. Schottenstein, Germany, Feb. 22, 1955; s. Heinz and Waltraud (Schimek) H. Diploma in Physics, Ruprecht-Karls-Univ., Heidelberg, Germany, 1980; PhD in Natural Sci., Ruprecht-Karls-Univ., 1985. Physicist U. Heidelberg (Germany), 1981-85; rsch. fellow European Orgn. Particle Physics, Geneva, 1986-87, sr. physicist, 1988—. contbr. articles to profl. jours. Mem. German Physics Soc., European Physics Soc. Avocations: mountaineering. Office: European Orgn Particle Phys, CERN, 1211 Geneva Switzerland

HERRAIZ, TOMAS, food chemist; b. Casasana, Spain, Aug. 22, 1961; s. Macario and Angela (Tomico) H.; m. Nadine Jagerovic, Aug. 6, 1994; 1 child, Victor. BS in Chemistry, U. Complutense, Madrid, 1984, PhD, 1989. Predoctoral fellow Govt. of Spain, 1986-90; NATO scholar U. Calif., Davis, 1991-92; rschr. CSIC, Madrid, 1993—. Contbr. articles to profl. jours., chpts. to books. Mem. Am. Soc. for Enology and Viticulture, Spanish Royal Soc. Chemistry. Avocations: travel, outdoor adventures, sports. Office: Inst Fermentaciones Indsl, Juan de la Cierva 3, 28006 Madrid Spain

HERRANEN, KATHY, artist, graphic designer; b. Zelienople, Pa., Dec. 22, 1943; d. John and Helen Elizabeth (Sayti) D'Biagio; m. John Warma Herranen, Dec. 31, 1974 (div. Feb. 1994); 1 child, Michael John. Student, Scottsdale (Ariz.) C.C., 1990—. Cert. tchr. art, State Bd. Dirs. for Cmty. Coll. of Ariz. Horseback riding instr. Black Saddle Riding Acad., Lancaster, Calif., early 1960's; tel. company supr. Bell Tel., Bishop, Calif., 1965; reporter, part-time photographer Ellwood City (Pa.) Ledger, 1967-70; backcountry guide and cook Mammoth Lakes (Calif.) Pack Outfit, 1970; motel mgr. Mountain Property Mgmt., Mammoth Lakes, 1970-72; reporter, bookkeeper Hungry Horse (Mont.) News, 1973-74; pig farmer Columbia Falls, Mont., 1973-75; fine artist, illustrator, graphic designer Mont., Calif., and Ariz., 1980—; fine arts cons. Collector's Gallery, Galleri II, Yuma, Ariz., 1983-84; wind chime designer, creator Phoenix, 1995—; represented by Marcella's Ariz. Collection, Phoenix, 1995—, Backstreet Furniture and Art, Phoenix, 1995—, Hohn Gallery Fine Arts, Ltd., Scottsdale, 1997—; guest lectr. Paradise Valley Tchrs Acad., Phoenix, 1993, Sr. Adult Edn. Program, Scottsdale (Ariz.) Cmty. Coll., 1994, pastel painting instr., 1996; guest demonstrator Binder's Art Ctr., Scottsdale, 1995, Backstreet Furniture and Art, Phoenix, 1995-96; guest lectr., demonstrator Summer Edn. Program Paradise Valley Sch. Dist., 1996, 99, 2000; guest demonstrator Phoenix Artists Guild, 2000, Paradise Valley Artists, 2000. Solo shows include Pinnacle, Phoenix, 1993, Villas of Sedona, Ariz., 1995. Sec. Young Dems., Ellwood City, late 1960's, Vistas Home Owners Assn., Phoenix, 1995—; troubleshooter Maricopa County Elections Dept., Phoenix, 1994-96, 2000. Recipient 1st place award Potpourri Artists, Yuma, Ariz., 1981, Subscriber award Butte (Mont.) Arts Coun., 1981, 2nd place award Desert Artists, Yuma, 1982, honorable mention Yuma County Fair, Yuma, 1983, Wildlife Painting Exhibit, Scottsdale, 1993, honorable mention Scottsdale Studio 13, 1991, 92, Fountain Festival Juried Competitive Exhbn. Fine Arts, 1993, Special award, 1993, Merit award, 1993, 94 (2). Mem. Nat. Assn. Sr. Friends Fine Artists (chair 1995—, honorable mention 1993, People's Choice award 1996), Women's Caucus for Art, Phoenix Artists Guild, Ariz. Pastel Artists Assn. (charter. membership chair 1995-96, 2d v.p., show chair 1996, guest demonstrator 1995, guest lectr. 1998, Merit award 1995), Ariz. Art Alliance (publicity chmn. 2000—), Artists and Craftsmen of Flathead Valley (founder, charter mem., pres. 1981-82), Phi Theta Kappa. Republican. Lutheran. Avocations: public speaking and acting, dancing, stamp collecting, photography, interior decorating. Office: 4114 E Union Hills Dr Unit 1011 Phoenix AZ 85050-3355

HERRANZ CASADO, JULIÁN, archbishop; b. Baena, Spain, Mar. 31, 1930. Dr.Canon Law, Pontifical U. St. Thomas, 1956; MD, U. Barcelona, 1953. Ordained priest, Roman Cath. Ch., 1955; bishop, 1991, archbishop, 1994. Sec. Pontifical Coun. for Interpretation of Laws, Rome, 1984; pres. Disciplinary Commn. of Roman Curia, Rome, 1999—; advisor Congregation for Bishops, 1984; judge Supreme Tribunal of Apostolic Signature, Holy See, 1991—; pres. Pontifical Coun. for Laws, 1994—; mem. Congregation for Clergy, 1999—; mem. Pontifical Commn. for Latin Am., 1999—. Author: Le statut juridique des Laics, 1983, La nuova legislazione della Chiesa, 1990. Home: Borgo Santo Spirito 16, 00193 Rome Italy Office: Palazzo delle Congregazioni, Piazza Pio XII 10, I-00193 Rome Italy

HERREGAT, GUY-GEORGES JACQUES, banker; b. Oostende, West Flanders, Belgium, July 22, 1939; came to U.S., 1966; s. Georges-Albert Maurice and Marie-Gerard S. (Elleboudt) H. Licence en philosophie, U. Louvain, 1961, licence en philosophie et lettres, 1964; postgrad., Yale U., 1966-67, PhD in Econs., 1972. Rsch. asst. U. Louvain (Belgium), 1964-66; rsch. assoc. Nat. Bur. Econ. Rsch., N.Y.C., 1967-72; internat. economist Brown Bros. Harriman & Co., N.Y.C., 1973-74; asst. v.p. Chem. Bank, N.Y.C., 1974-76; dep. chief economist European Am. Bank, N.Y.C., 1977-80; sr. advisor, sr. v.p. Societe Generale de Banque, N.Y.C., 1980-85; mgr. Banque Worms, N.Y.C., 1985-86; sr. v.p., dep. gen. mgr. Credit du Nord, N.Y.C., 1986-93; sr. v.p. Banque Paribas, N.Y.C., 1993-2000; sr. credit officer for N.Am. BNP-Paribas, N.Y.C., 2000—; cons. Am. Bankers Assn., N.Y.C., 1971, SEIDEIS-Futuribles, Paris, 1967-80, Ford Found., N.Y.C., 1972-73. Author: Managerial Profiles and Investment Patterns, 1972, (with others) The Diffusion of New Industrial Processes, 1974, THe Finances of the Performing Arts, 1974; contbr. articles to profl. jours. Yale U. fellow, 1966-67, Nat. Bur. Econ. Rsch. fellow, 1971-72; named Aspirant de Recherches Fonds National Belge de la Recherche Scientifique, 1967-72. Mem. Am. Econ. Assn., Acad. Polit. Sci., Yale Alumni Assn., Japan Soc., Inst. Internat. Bankers, Belgian-Am. C. of C. (bd. dirs. 1986—). Home: 30 E 81st St New York NY 10028-0222 also: 253 Atlantic Fire Island Pines NY 11782 also: 800 West Ave Miami Beach FL 33139-5542 Office: BNP-Paribas 787 7th Ave 31st Fl New York NY 10019-6018

HERREN, MICHAEL WAYNE, classical studies educator; b. Santa Ana, Calif.; s. Cecil Ray Herren and Carol Jean McCollum; m. Dana Tenny, Aug. 28, 1962 (div. Feb. 1975); m. Shirley Ann Brown, Apr. 12, 1975; children: Sarah, Michael Aidan. BA, Claremont McKenna Coll., 1962; MSL, Pontif. Inst. Mediaeval Studies, Toronto, Can., 1967; PhD, U. Toronto, 1969. Asst. prof. classics York U., Toronto, 1969-74, assoc. prof. classics, 1974-78, prof. classics, 1978-98, disting. rsch. prof. classics, 1998—; adj. prof. medieval studies U. Toronto, 1990—; cons. Royal Irish Acad. Latin Texts, Dublin, 1995—. Editor, translator: The Hisperica Famina, 2 vols., 1974, 87, Social Sciences and Humanities Research Coun., 1974, 87, Iohannis Scotti Eriugenae Carmina, 1993, Latin Letters in Early Christian Ireland, 1996; editor Jour. Medieval Latin, 1991-96, gen. editor, pub., 1996—; mem. adv. bd. Filologia Mediolatina Spoleto It jour., 1994—. Bd. dirs. Mozart Soc., Toronto, 1990—. Fellow Alexander von Humboldt, 1981-82, 88-89, Killam Rsch. Can. Coun., 1995-97, Guggenheim Rsch., 1998—. Fellow Royal Soc. Can.; mem. Medieval Acad. Am., Classical Assn. Can., Soc. for Promotion of Eriuenian Studies. Avocations: classical music vocalist, opera and lieder. Office: Atkinson Coll, York U, Toronto, ON Canada M3J 1P3

HERRERA, ALBERTO LUCAS, microbiologist, educator; b. Havana, Cuba, Oct. 18, 1943; s. Agustín Regino Herrera and Isaura Guirola; m. Mayra Enma Virgos, Aug. 6, 1972; children: Carlos Alberto, Irina Maria. B in Biol. Scis., Havanna U., 1970, D in Biol. Scis., 1982; MS, Liverpool (Eng.) U., 1976. Instr. Havana U., 1971-76, asst. prof., 1976-83, auxiliar prof., 1983—, titular rschr., 1992—; mem. rsch. coun. Havana U., 1983-86, mem. com. for tchg. category, 1985—, mem. com. for rschr. category, 1992—, chmn. com. for postgrad. programs valuations of master and doctorate, 1995—; vis. prof. U. S.M. Tucumán, Argentina, 1988—; mem. Biology Faculty Rsch. Coun., Havana, 1988—, Permanent Bd. for Doctoral Degree in Biol. Scis., Havana, 1988—, Com. for Doctoral Program, Havana, 1995—. Author: Methodological Orientations about Industrial Microbiology, 1982, Manual of Laborator for Industrial Microbiology, 1983, 88, Manual of Culture Media for Microorganisms, 1985, Notions About Numerical Taxonomy, 1988; contbr. chpt. to book and articles to profl. jours.; patentee in field. Mem. Cuban Microbial Soc., Cuban Microbial Collection Cultures, Internat. Orgn. Biotechnology and Bioengring. Roman Catholic. Avocations: watching movies, going to the beach, fishing, camping. Home: Pocito 61, e/ San Luis y Delicias, 10700 Havanna Cuba Office: U Havana Faculty Biology, Calle 25 e/JeI Vedado, 10400 Havanna Cuba

HERRERA, SANDRA JOHNSON, school system administrator; b. Riverside, Calif., June 21, 1944; d. William Emory Johnson and Mildred Alice (Alford) Wimer; m. Wynn Neal Huffman, Feb. 19, 1962 (div. May 1967); 1 child, Kristen Lee; m. Steven Jack Herrera, June 21, 1985 (div. Dec. 1997). AA in Purchasing Mgmt., Fullerton Coll., 1983; BSBA, U. Redlands, 1985, MA in Mgmt., 1988. Sr. purchasing clk Fullerton (Calif.) Union High Sch. Dist., 1969-77, buyer, 1977-79, coord. budgets and fiscal affairs, 1979-83; asst. dir. fin. svcs. Downey (Calif.) Unified Sch. Dist., 1983-85; dir. acctg. Whittier (Calif.) Union High Sch. Dist., 1985-89; asst. supt. bus. Whittier City Sch. Dist., 1989-91, Oxnard Elem. Sch. Dist., 1991—; cons. Heritage Dental Lab., El Toro, Calif, 1981-97. Spl. dep. sheriff Santa Barbara (Calif.) County Sheriff's Mounted Posse, 1986-90; spl. dep. marshal U.S. Marshals Posse, Los Angeles, 1987-95. Mem. Calif. Assn. Sch. Bus. Ofcls. (treas. S.E. sect. 1985, mem. acct. R & D com. 1983-89, mem. chief bus. officials com. 1989—), So. Calif. Paraders Assn. (exec. sec. 1976-97), Calif. State Horsemens Assn. (regional v.p. 1986-87, sec. 1988), Alpha Gamma Sigma. Avocations: horseback riding, golf, reading, micro-computers, model trains. Home: 1720 Ironbark Ct Oxnard CA 93030-3410 Office: Oxnard Elem Sch Dist 1051 S A St Oxnard CA 93030-7442

HERRERA-LLERANDI, RODOLFO EDUARDO, surgeon, educator; b. Guatemala City, Guatemala, Aug. 6, 1915; s. Carlos and Chusita (Llerandi) H.; m. Odette Lefebre, June, 1954 (div. 1961). BA, Paris U., 1931-32, BA, BPh, 1934; BS, MIT, 1938; MD, Harvard U., 1942; D Honoris Causa, Francisco Marroquin U., Guatemala, 1995. Diplomate Am. Bd. Surgery. Resident and fellow in surgery Mass. Gen. Hosp., Boston, 1942-47; instr. in surgery Harvard Med. Sch., Boston, 1945-47; chief of surgery Hosp. San Vincente, Guatemala City, Guatemala, 1948-58; hon. prof. surgery U. De San Carlos, Guatemala City, 1955-67, Hosp. Mil., Guatemala City, 1955-67; dean and prof. surgery U Francisco Marroquin Sch. of Medicine, Guatemala City, 1978—; surgeon in chief U. Hosp. Esperanza, 1963—; pres. Nat. Congress Medicine, 1956-57, Nat. Anti-TB Assn., Guatemala, 1960-62, Fund. Chusita Llerandi de Herrara, Guatemala, 1972—. Contbr. articles to profl.

jours, sci. mags. Cons. Nat. Anti-TB Assn., Guatemala, Child Welfare Assn., Guatemala. Capt. Guatemalan Army. Decorated Legion of Honor, France Chevalier Order St. Fortunat; Order Rodolfo Robles, Orden del Quetzal; recipient Gold medal Mass. Gen. Hosp., 1961, U. San Carlos, 1967; Disting. Citizen diploma Municipality de Guate, Guatemala, 1980, Banco Indsl., S.A., 1989, Rotary Club Guatemala, 1989. Mem. Internat. Soc. Surgery (nat. del. 1977-91), Am. Assn. Thoracic Surgeons (hon.), Coll. of Physicians and Surgeons of Guatemala. Avocations: helicopter pilot, collector Mayan relics. Office: F Marroquin U Med Sch Med, 6a Ave 7-55 Zona 10, 01010 Guatemala City Guatemala

HERRERIAS, CARLA TREVETTE, epidemiologist, health policy analyst; b. Chgo., Apr. 8, 1964; d. Ludvik Frank and Carlotta Trevette (Walker) Koci; m. Jesus Herrerias, Feb. 25, 1989; children: Elena Mikele, Coco Trevette. BS in Med.Tech., Ea. Mich. U., 1987; MPH in Molecular and Hosp. Epidemiology, U. Mich., 1991. Med. clk. hydramatic divsn. GM, Ypsilanti, Mich., 1983-86; researcher, support staff dept. human genetics U. Mich., Ann Arbor, 1987-91; program mgr. Am. Acad. Pediatrics, Elk Grove Village, Ill., 1991-99; sr. health policy analyst Am. Acad. Pediats., Elk Grove Village, Ill., 1999—. Project mgr., contbr.: Clinical Practice Guideline: Otitis Media with Effusion in Young Children, 1994. Mem. APHA, Ill. Pub. Health Assn., Assn. for Health Svcs. Rsch., U. Mich. Alumni Soc., U. Mich. Club Chgo. Avocations: reading, biking, needlework, horseback riding. Office: Am Acad Pediatrics 141 NW Point Blvd Elk Grove Village IL 60007-1019

HERRERO, HENAR, mathematician, educator; b. Megeces, Valladolid, Spain, Apr. 26, 1966; d. Justo and Victoria (Sanz) H. Mathematician, U. Valladolid, 1989; D of Physics, U. Navarra, 1994. Asst. prof. U. Navarra, Pamplona, Spain, 1989-94, U. Complutense, Madrid, Spain, 1994-95; prof. U. Castilla-La Mancha, Ciudad Real, Spain, 1995—. Contbr. articles to profl. jours. V.p. Assn. Cultural Oretana, Ciudad Real, 1996—. Grantee Spanish Govt., 1980-94, 90-94, FBP Paris, 1996-97. Roman Catholic. Office: U De Castilla-La Mancha, Campus Universitario, 13071 Ciudad Real Spain

HERREROS, CARLOS, accountant, consultant; b. Torrelavega, Cantabria, Spain, July 26, 1941; s. Carlos Herreros and Josefa de las Cuevas. Grad., U. Madrid, 1962; MSc in Bus. Adminstrn., London Bus. Sch., London, 1996. CPA. Ptnr. Herreros de la Fuente Cifrian Cons., Santander, 1986—; tutor Euroforum, Madrid, 1996; mgmt. prof. Escuela de Orgn. Indsl., Madrid, 1996. Fellow Am. Seminar in Salzburg; mem. Real Golf de Pedreña. Avocations: golf, reading, swimming. Office: Herreros Fuente Cifrian, Calvo Sotelo 11, 39002 Santander Spain

HERRICK, ELBERT CHARLES, chemist, consultant; b. Joliet, Mont., Oct. 16, 1919; s. Charles Albert and Marie (Johnson) H.; m. Doris Christine Brock, June 1, 1962; children: David, Dennis, Douglas, Donna. BSChemE, Mont. State U., 1941; degree of ChemE, Princeton U., 1942; PhD in Organic Chemistry, MIT, 1949. Rsch. chemist Cen. Rsch. Dept. E.I. duPont de Nemours, 1949-54; assoc. rsch. chemist Houdry Process Corp., 1955-58; supr. chem. rsch. Climax Molybdenum Co., Mich., 1958-59; sr. rsch. chemist R&D div. Sun Oil Co., 1959-61; sr. rsch. chemist Textile Fibers div. Dow Chem. Co., 1962-64; pvt. practice cons. chemist and chem. engr., 1964-65; organic sect. head Great Lakes Rsch. Corp., 1965-67; dir. chem. rsch. Escambia Chem. Corp., 1967-69; sr. rsch. chemist Air Products and Chems., Inc., 1969-77; sr. chem. engr., scientist Tracor Jitco, Inc., 1977; environ. systems scientist The MITRE Corp., 1977-88; sr. staff specialist Dynamac Corp., 1988-89; pvt. practice Woodbine, Md., 1989—. Patentee in field; contbr. articles to profl. jours. Lt. USAF, 1942-45, ETO. Fellow Am. Inst. Chemists; mem. Am. Inst. Chem. Engrs., Am. Chem. Soc., N.Y. Acad. Scis., Sigma Xi, Tau Beta Pi, Phi Kappa Phi. Democrat. Adventist. Avocations: gardening, reading. Home and Office: Sunset Summit 2403 Vine Cir Rocklin CA 95765-4716

HERRIDGE, ALISTAIR FREDERICK, retired engineer; b. Rangiora, Canterbury, New Zealand, Nov. 10, 1937; s. Frederick George and Rita Irene (Claridge) H.; m. Julianne Lois Jaine, Dec. 31, 1960; children: Shirley Jean Herridge Watson, Iain George. Diploma in tractor equipment, Engring. Tech. Tng. Internat., Australia, 1968; DSc in Engring., Albert Einstein Internat. Acad. Found., 1991. Trade cert. New Zealand Cert. Bd. Carpentry apprentice Hanrahan & Watson Builders, Ashburton, New Zealand, 1954-59; carpentry foreman Lynn's Hardware & Joinery, Ashburton, 1959-61; carpentry foreman and engr. Burnetts' Motors, New Zealand, 1961-70; operator, owner Ashburton, 1971-73, pvt. practice engring., 1973-96; ret.; chmn. Lynn Hist. Woodworking Trust and Mus. Ornamental Turning, Ashburton. Contbr.: Turning and Woodwork, 1991. Bd. dirs. Ashburton Enterprise Agy., 1996—. Recipient Acad. Found. cross of merit award Albert Einstein Internat. Acad. Found., 1992. Mem. NRA, Soc. Mfg. Engrs. (com. mem. South Island chpt. 1986-93, Pres. award 1992), New Zealand Crippled Childrens Soc., Disabled Persons Assn., New Zealand Spinal Trust. National Party New Zealand. Presbyterian. Avocations: collecting fine porcelain, shooting firearms, cars, reading, family history. Home: 123-B Kermode St, Ashburton 8300, New Zealand

HERRIN, STEPHANIE ANN, retired aerospace engineer, yachtsman; b. Oakland, Calif., May 13, 1950; d. Thomas Edgar Herrin and Mary Teresa Silva; m. Este Stovall, May 20, 1989. BSc, U. Pacific, 1976; MSc, Columbia Pacific U., 1978; PhD in Engring. & Applied Scis., U. Bradford, West Yorkshire, U.K., 1994. Reliability engr. Applied Tech. Litton Industries, Sunnyvale, Calif., 1979-80; sr. reliability engr., reliability project mgr. ESL, Inc., Sunnyvale, 1980-84; sr. reliability and quality assurance engr. Martin Marietta, Balt., 1984-85; lead, sr. reliability engr. Los Alamos Tech. Assn., Albuquerque, 1985-86; sr. reliability engr. Boeing, Houston, 1987-89; sr. sys. engr., knowledge capture engr. Astrobiology Inst. NASA-Ames Rsch. Ctr., Moffett Field, Calif., 1988-99; marine capt. pvt. personal yacht, 1999—; cons. Lawrence Livermore Labs., Livermore, Calif., 1985-87; failure analysis engring. radiographer, analyst Ford Aerospace & Comm. Corp., Palo Alto, Calif., 1973-79; owner, analyst Fail Safe Radiography, Palo Alto, 1975-81. Contbr. articles to profl. jours. Recipient U.S. govt. Manned Flight Awareness award, 1994, 96-97; NASA grantee, 1987-89, 90-93, 94-95; recipient numerous fellowships and lifetime awards. Mem. IEEE (reliability & maintainability soc., engring. in medicine & biology computer soc., info. theory, sys., man & cybernetics, oceanic engring. soc.), AAUW. Achievements include patent for real-time automated diagnosis and intelligent utility for maintainability. Home: 343 Center St Redwood City CA 94061-3883

HERRING, GROVER CLEVELAND, lawyer; b. Nocatee, Fla., Dec. 9, 1925; s. Joseph I. and Martha (Selph) H.; m. Dorothy L. Blinn, Apr. 17, 1947; children: Stanley T., Kenneth Lee. JD, U. Fla., 1950. Bar: Fla. 1950. Assoc. Haskins & Bryant, 1950-52; sole practice West Palm Beach, Fla., 1952-60, 64—; ptnr. Blakeslee, Herring & Bie and predecessor firm, 1953-60, Warwick, Paul & Herring, 1964-70, Herring & Evans now Arnstein & Lehr, 1970-95, Baldwin & Herring, West Palm Beach, Fla., 1995-96; atty. City of Atlantis, Fla., City of West Palm Beach, 1960-63, Town of Ocean Ridge, Fla., 1953-61, 64-66, Village of Royal Palm Beach, Fla., 1964-72, Town of South Palm Beach, Fla., 1966-72; spl. master-in-chancery 15th Jud. Cir. Palm Beach County, 1953-54; judge ad litem Mcpl. Ct., West Palm Beach, 1954-55; bd. dirs. Lawyers Title Services Inc., West Palm Beach. Contbr. legal articles to profl. revs. Active PTA, Family Service Agy., Palm Beach County Mental Health Assn.; chmn. profl. sect. ARC, 1960; mem. Charter Revision Com. West Palm Beach, 1960-65, Palm Beach County Resources Devel. Bd., 1959-64, Dem. Exec. Com., 1965-70; apptd. mem. Govtl. Study Commn. by Fla. Legis.; bd. dirs. Community Chest. Served with USNR, 1944-46. Mem. ABA, Palm Beach County Bar Assn. (treas. 1960), John Marshall Bar Assn., Fla. Bar Assn., Am. Judicature Soc., Lawyers Title Guaranty Fund (field rep. 1955-60, 64-74), East Coast Estate Planning Council, Nat. Inst. Mcpl. Law Officers, Law-Sci. Acad., Assn. Trial Lawyers Am. (assoc. editor 1960-92), Lawyers Lit. Club, Nat. Mcpl. League, U. Fla. Law Ctr. Assn., World Peace Through Law Ctr., Fla. Sheriff's Assn. (hon.), U. Fla. Alumni Assn., VFW, Am. Legion, West Palm Beach C. of C., Civic Music Assn., Palm Beach County Hist. Soc. (pres. 1969-72), New Eng. Hist. Geneal. Soc. Boston. Clubs: West Palm Beach Country (hon.); Airways (N.Y.C.). Lodges: Eight Oaks River, Masons (32 deg.), Elks, Moose. Home: 3507 N Australian Ave West Palm Beach FL 33407-4511

HERRING, JACKSON REA, physicist; b. Ashland, Ky., Oct. 2, 1931; s. Ralph Alderman and Willeen (Tull) H.; m. Betty Jean Pegram, Jan. 31, 1959; children: Peter, Christopher. BS in Physics, Wake Forest U., 1953; MS in Physics, U. N.C., 1956, PhD in Physics, 1959. Theoretical physicist theoretical divsn. Goddard Space Flight Ctr., NASA, Washington, 1959-61; theoretical physicist Goddard Inst. for Space Studies NASA, N.Y.C., 1961-64; theoretical physicist Goddard Space Flight Ctr. NASA, Greenbelt, Md., 1964-72; sr. scientist Nat. Ctr. Atmospheric Rsch., Boulder, Colo., 1972-98, sr. scientist emeritus, 1998—; mem. adv. com. NASA Ames-Stanford Ctr. for Turbulence Rsch., 1988-89; sr. postdoctoral fellow Nat. Ctr. for Atmospheric Rsch., Advanced Study Program, Boulder, 1972; invited prof. U. Pierre-Marie Currie, Paris, 1995. Editor: (with McWilliams) Lecture Notes on Turbulence, 1989. Green scholar U. Calif. San Diego Inst. of Geophysics and Planetary Physics, 1978. Fellow Am. Phys. Soc. (fellowship com. 1996). Home: 2581 Briarwood Dr Boulder CO 80305-6803 Office: Nat Ctr Atmospheric Rsch PO Box 3000 Boulder CO 80307-3000

HERRINGER, FRANK CASPER, diversified financial services company executive; b. N.Y.C., Nov. 12, 1942; s. Casper Frank and Alice Virginia (McMullen) H.; m. Maryellen B. Cattani; children: William, Sarah, Julia. AB magna cum laude, Dartmouth, 1964, MBA with highest distinction, 1965. Prin. Cresap, McCormick & Paget, Inc. (mgmt. cons.), N.Y.C., 1965-71; staff asst. to Pres., Washington, 1971-73; adminstr. U.S. Urban Mass Transp. Adminstrn., Washington, 1973-75; gen. mgr. San Francisco Bay Area Rapid Transit Dist., 1975-78; exec. v.p. Transam. Corp., San Francisco, 1979-86, pres., dir., 1986-99, CEO, 1991-99, chmn., 1996—; mem. exec. bd. AEGON N.V., 1999-2000; chmn. AEGON USA, 1999-2000; bd. dirs. Unocal Corp., Charles Schwab & Co., Mirapoint, Inc., Fluid Ventures, Inc. Mem. Cypress Point Club, San Francisco Golf Club, Olympic Club, Pacific Union Club, Stock Farm Club, Phi Beta Kappa. Office: Transam Corp 600 Montgomery St San Francisco CA 94111-2702

HERRMANN, DIETER BERNHARD, astronomer; b. Jan. 3, 1939; s. Arthur and Elsbeth (Tiesler) H.; m. Ingrid Sender, Dec. 23, 1978. Student, Humboldt U., 1957-63; diploma physics, 1963, D natural sci., 1969, D sci., 1986, prof. (hon.), 1986. Scientific asst. Inst. for Radiation Protection, Berlin, 1963-69; head dept. for history of astronomy Archenhold-Sternwarte, Berlin, 1970-76, dir. observatory, 1976—; dir. Zeiss-Grossplanetarium Berlin, 1987—; presenter in field. Author 24 books on history of astronomy and other fields, 1975—; contbr. articles to profl. jours.; narrator (sci. TV show) Aha, 1977-90. Mem. Internat. Astron. Union, Astronomische Gesellschaft, Gesellschaft zur Wissenschaftlichen Untersuchung von Parawissenschaften (v.p.), Leibniz-Societät, 1996. Office: Archenhold-Sternwarte, Alt Treptow 1, 12435 Berlin Germany

HERRMANN, FRANK (HENRY), painter, educator; b. Westmont, N.J., Mar. 1, 1945; s. Francis H. and Carolyn (Vance) C.; m. Stephanie Karanzalis, Feb. 2, 1969; children: Jason Thomas, Zachary Francis. BA, Western Ky. U., 1969; MFA, U. Cin., 1972. Instr. Western Mich. U., Kalamazoo, 1972-73; prof. fine art U. Cin., 1973—. One-man shows include Western Ky. U., 1968, U. Cin., 1971, 72, 82, 83, 92, U. Akron, 1974, Colo. State U., 1979, Ga. Southwestern State U., Americus, 1980, First Inst. Art and Design, Hong Kong, 1980, Toni Birckhead Gallery, Cin., 1983, 89, Centre Coll., Danville, Ky., 1983, U. Ky., 1985, Ohio U., Athens, 1990, Henri Gallery, Washington, 1984, 86, 91, Taylor's Contemtoraea, Hot Springs, Ark., 1993; exhibited in group shows at Miami U., Oxford, Ohio, 1970, 71, Findlay Coll., 1978, Dayton Art Inst., 1979, Murray State U., Ky., 1980, Toni Birckhead Gallery, Cin., 1981, 83, 90, 91, Nornberg Gallery Contemporary Art, St. Louis, 1983, Henri Gallery, Washington, 1983, 84, 85, 87, 89, Contemporary Arts Ctr., Cin., 1991, Ruschman Gallery, Indpls, 1998, Closson's Art Gallery, Cin., 1996, 98, Frank Herrmann Aronoff Ctr. Gallery, Cin., 1998, 99, many others; represented in numerous pub. and pvt. collections. Bd. dirs. Contemporary Arts Ctr., CIn., 1990-91. Fellow Ohio Arts Coun., 1983, Cin. Summer Fair Inc., 1983-84, Arts Midwest Nat. Endowment Arts, Mpls., 1990; grantee Ohio Arts Coun., Columbus, 1983, 86, Summer Fair Inc., Cin., 1990, U. Cin. Rsch. Coun., 1982, 91. E-mail: fherrman@fuse.net. Office: U Cin Sch Art Daap Ml0016 Cincinnati OH 45221-0001

HERRMANN, GUENTER, surgeon; b. Berlin, June 13, 1945; s. Ferdinand Hirschter and Ursula Herrmann Clauer; m. Annegret Dies, Aug. 28, 1971; children: Frank, Bettina. Med.. Approbation, Free U. Berlin, 1972, Promotion, 1975; Arzt fuer Chirurgie, Bezirksärztekammer, Mainz, 1978. Med. asst. Univ.-Hosp., Mainz, 1971, Paulinenstift-hosp., Wiesbaden, 1971-72; asst. physician St. Josefs Hosp., Wiesbaden, 1972-73; wissenschaftlicher asst. chir. Univ.-Hosp., Mainz, 1973-78; physician St. Hildegardis Hosp., Mainz, 1978-88; med. supt. Dist.-Hosp., Gruenstadt, 1988—. Mem. Berufsverband der Deutschen Chirurgen, Deutsche Gesellschaft fuer Unfallchirurgie, Verband der leitenden Krankenhausärzte Deutschlands, Lions. Avocations: old medical books. Office: Kreiskrankenhaus Gruenstadt, Westring 55, D-67269 Gruenstadt Germany

HERRMANN, HANS JÜRGEN, scientist, administrator; b. LaHabana, Cuba, Jan. 1, 1954; s. Hans Georg and Ruth (Behnke) H.; children: Moritz, Max, Philipp. B and Abitur, Colegio Andino, 1972; diploma in physics, U. Cologne, PhD. CTE CEA Saclay, Paris, 1982-84; chargé de recherches CNRS, Paris, 1984-90, dir., 1991—; dir. PVG KFA, Jülich, Germany, 1990-94; chair nat. sci. ESPCI, Paris, 1994—; prof. U. Stuttgart, 1995; dir. HLRZ, Jülich, 1990-94, PMMH, ESPCI, 1994—; sci. review com. Dowell Schlumberger, Ridgefield, 1993—; W.F. James prof. St. Francis Xavier U., 1994. Author: Computational Physics and Cellular Automata, 1989, Statistical Models for the Fracture of Disordered Media, 1990, Fermion Algorithmes, 1991, Dynamics of First Order Transitions, 1992; mng. editor Internat. Jour. Mod. Physics C, 1990—; mem. editorial bd. Jour. Physics A, U.K., 1987-90, Physica A., Holland, 1991—, Fractals, Singapore, 1992—, The European Phys. Jour. E. Guggenheim fellow, 1986. Avocations: sports, painting. Home: 70 rue J P Timbaud, 75011 Paris France Office: PMMH ESPCI, 10 rue Vauquelin, 75231 Paris France

HERRMANN, KARLHEINZ SIEGFRIED, cardiologist; b. Dresden, Germany, 1953; s. Siegfried and Christa H.; m. Ulrike Beierlein; 1 child, Philipp. MD, U. Heinrich-Hein-U., Dusseldorf, Germany, 1980. Founder, head microcirculatory rsch. dept. Bayer AG, Germany, 1980-82; clin. & scientific asst. dept. cardiology U. Gottingen, Germany, 1982-86, head microcirculatory labs. dept. cardiology, 1986-87; head rsch. projects Stuttgart, Germany, 1987—; lectr. in field. Contbr. articles to profl. jours. Mem. German Soc. Cardiology, German Soc. Microcirculation, European Soc. Microcirculation, Deutsche Herzstiftung. Avocations: literature, arts, wine, gourmet cooking, music. Office: Konigstr 2, 70173 Stuttgart Germany

HERRMANN, LACY BUNNELL, investment company executive, financial entrepreneur, venture capitalist; b. New Haven, May 12, 1929; s. James Joseph and Helen Georgia (Bunnell) H.; m. Elizabeth Ocumpaugh Beadle, May 23, 1953; children: Diana Parsons, Conrad Beadle. AB, Brown U., 1950; postgrad., London Sch. Econs., 1953-54; MBA, Harvard U., 1956. Asst. to purchasing mgr. and buyer Westinghouse Elec. Corp., Metuchen, N.J., 1956-60; asst. v.p. Douglas T. Johnston & Co., Inc., N.Y.C., 1960-66; v.p. Johnston Mut. Fund, Inc., N.Y.C., 1964-66; gen. ptnr. Tamarack Assocs., N.Y.C., 1966-84; chmn. bd., pres. Family Home Products, Inc., N.Y.C., 1972-84, Buxton's Country Shops, Jamesburg, N.J., 1973-86; founder, pres. STCM Corp., moneymarket fund, N.Y.C., 1974-76; vice chmn. bd. trustees, v.p. Centennial Capital Cash Mgmt. Trust, N.Y.C. successor to STCM Corp., 1976-81; chmn. bd. trustees, pres. successor fund Capital Cash Mgmt. Trust, 1981—; founder, chmn. bd. trustees, pres. Trinity Liquid Assets Trust, 1982-85, Oxford Cash Mgmt. Fund, 1982-88, Prime Cash Fund, 1982—; chmn., CEO, Aquila Mgmt. Corp., 1983—; founder, sponsor, mgr. Pacific Capital Cash Assets Trusts, 1984—, Hawaiian Tax-Free Trust, 1985—, Churchill Cash Reserves Trust, 1985—, Tax-Free Trust Ariz., 1986—, Tax-Free Trust Oreg., 1986—, Tax-Free Fund Colo., 1987—, Churchill Tax-Free Fund of Ky., 1987—, Pacific Capital Tax-Free Cash Assets Trusts, 1988—, Pacific Capital U.S. Govt. Securities Cash Assets Trust, 1988—, Narragansett Insured Tax-Free Income Fund, 1992—, Tax-Free Fund for Utah, 1992—, Aquila Rocky Mountain Equity Fund, 1994—, Aquila Cascadia Equity Fund, 1996—, VP Aquila Distributors, Inc.; bd. dirs. Quest for Value Fund Investment Trust, Quest for Value Accumulation Trust, Quest Cash Res., Inc.; trustee Oppenheimer/Quest group funds global Value Fund, 1994—, Oppenheimer Rochester Funds; organizer, bd. dirs. and/or cons. to numerous sml. to medium sized-corps. and orgns.; founding dir. mgmt. cons. firm merged with Towers, Perrin, Forster & Crosby; instr. Rutgers U., 1958-59; chmn., pres. bd. dirs. In-Cap Mgmt. Corp, 1984-98; speaker various profl. investment orgns. Contbr. articles to profl. jours. Organizer, trustee endowed award Internat. div. Grad. Sch. Journalism, Columbia U., 1962—; trustee Meml. and Endowment Trust of St. Paul's Ch., Westfield, N.J., 1968-96; mem. capital devel. com. St. Luke's Ch., Darien, Conn., 1978-85, mem. coll. scholarship fund com., 1976-85; trustee Brown U., 1990-96, trustee emeritus, 1996—, Hopkins Sch., New Haven, 1993—. Lt. (j.g.) USN, 1951-54, Korea; lt. USNR ret. Mem. N.Y. Soc. Security Analysts, Harvard Bus. Sch. Club N.Y. (bd. dirs., officer, 1958-71), Assoc. Alumni Brown U. (bd. dirs. 1978-87, exec. com. 1980-85, pres. 1983-85), Harvard Club, N.Y. Athletic Club, Brown U. Club, N.Y.C. Club (bd. dirs. 1981-88), Brown U. of Fairfield Country Club (pres. 1977-82, bd. dirs. 1977—), Univ. Club (R.I.), Faculty Club Brown U., Stratton Mountain Country Club, Orleans Yacht Club, Ariz. club, Outrigger Canoe Club (Honolulu), Lahaina Yacht Club (Maui). Republican. Episcopalian. Home: 6 Whaling Rd Darien CT 06820-5930 Office: 380 Madison Ave New York NY 10017-2513

HERRON, JOHN, administrator; b. Home Hill, Australia, Sept. 4, 1932; married; 10 children. B of Medicine, U. Queensland, Australia. Resident Rugby, England, 1963; sr. surgeon Mater Pub. Hosp., Brisbane, Australia, 1974-90; v.p. Queensland Liberal Party, Australia, 1976-79, pres., 1980-84; elected Queensland Senate, Australia, 1990, chmn. cmty. affairs com., 1994-95; shadow min. Dept. Health & Dept. Health & Human Svcs., Australia, 1994-95; min. Ministry Aboriginal and Torres Strait Islander Affairs, Australia, 1996—. Office: Min Aboriginal Affairs, Parliament House Ste MF 44, Canberra ACT 2600, Australia*

HERRON, TIMOTHY DANIEL, professional golfer; b. Mpls., Feb. 16, 1970; s. Carson H. Student, U. N.Mex. Profl. golfer, 1993—; mem. U.S. Walker Cup Team, 1993; finished top 10 NIKE Miss. Gulf Coast Classic, 1995, Bay Hill Invitational, Greater Vancouver Open, Kemper Open, Meml. Tournament, CVS Charity Classic, Buick Classic, 1996, LaCantera Tex. Open, 1996; winner Honda Classic, 1996, LaCantera Tex. Open, 1997; finished top ten Tucson Chrysler Classic, Meml. Tournament, Doral-Ryder Open, 1998, GTE Byron Nelson Classic, 1998; winner Bay Hill Invitational, 1999; mem. PGA Tour charity team BellSouth Classic, 1999. Avocations: fishing, pool, snow skiing. Office: SW Sect of PGA Am 5040 E Shea Blvd Ste 250 Scottsdale AZ 85254-4687*

HERSCHBACH, DUDLEY ROBERT, chemistry educator; b. San Jose, Calif., June 18, 1932; s. Robert Dudley and Dorothy Edith (Beer) H.; m. Georgene Lee Botyos, Dec. 26, 1964; children: Lisa Marie, Brenda Michele. BS in Math., Stanford U., 1954, MS in Chemistry, 1955; AM in Physics, Harvard U., 1956, PhD in Chem. Physics, 1958; DSc (hon.), U. Toronto, 1977, Cornell Coll., 1988, Framingham State Coll., 1989, Adelphi U., 1990, Dartmouth Coll., 1992, Charles U., Prague, 1993, U. Ill., Chgo., 1994, Wheaton Coll., 1995, Franklin & Marshall Coll., 1998. Jr. fellow Harvard U., Cambridge, Mass., 1957-59, prof. chemistry, 1963-76, Frank B. Baird prof. sci., 1976—, mem. faculty council, 1980-83, master Currier House, 1981-86; asst. prof. U. Calif., Berkeley, 1959-61, assoc. prof., 1961-63; cons. editor W.H. Freeman lectr. Haverford Coll., 1962; Falk-Plaut lectr. Columbia U., 1963; vis. prof. Gottingen (Germany) U., summer 1963, U. Calif., Santa Curz, 1972; Harvard lectr. Yale U., 1964; Debye lectr. Cornell U., 1966; Rollefson lectr. U. Calif., Berkeley, 1969; Reilly lectr. U. Notre Dame, 1979; Phillips lectr. U. Pitts., 1971; disting. vis. prof. U. Ariz., 1971, U. Tex., 1977, U. Utah, 1978; Gordon lectr. U. Toronto, 1971; Clark lectr. San Jose State U., 1979; Hill lectr. Duke U., 1988; Priestly lectr. Pa. State U., 1990; Kaufman lectr. U. Pa., 1990; Polanyi lectr. U. N.C., 1991; Dreyfus lectr. Dartmouth Coll., 1992; Paulins lectr. Calif. Inst. Tech., 1993; Bernstein lectr. UCLA, 1994; Brown lectr. Rutgers U., 1995. Assoc. editor: Jour Phys. Chemistry, 1980-88.. Guggenheim fellow U. Freiburg, Germany, 1968; vis. fellow Joint Inst. for Lab. Astrophysics U. Colo., 1969; Fairchild Disting. scholar Calif. Inst. Tech., 1976; Sloan fellow, 1959-63, Exxon Faculty fellow, 1980-96, Miller fellow U. Calif. Berkeley, 1997; recipient pure chemistry award Am. Chem. Soc., 1965, Centenary medal, 1977, Pauling medal, 1978; Spiers medal Faraday Soc., 1976, Polanyi medal, 1981, Langmuir prize, 1983, Nobel Prize in Chemistry, 1986, Nat. Medal of Sci. NSF, 1991, Heyrovsky medal 1992, Sierra Nevada Disting. Chemist award, 1993, Kosolapoff medal, 1994, William Walker prize, 1994; named to Calif. Pub. Edn. Hall of Fame, 1987. Fellow Am. Phys Soc. (chmn. chem. physics div. 1971-72), Am. Acad. Arts and Scis.; mem. AAAS, Am. Chem. Soc., Nat. Acad. Scis., Royal Soc. Chemistry (fgn. hon. mem.), Am. Philos. Soc., Phi Beta Kappa (orator Harvard U. 1992), Sigma Xi. Office: Harvard U Dept Chemistry Mallickrodt Lab B9-34 12 Oxford St Cambridge MA 02138-2902

HERSH, BURTON DAVID, author; b. Chgo., Sept. 18, 1933; s. Maurice Henry and Florence Nita Hersh; m. Ellen Eiseman, Aug. 3, 1957; children: Leo Joseph, Margery Clara. BA, Harvard Coll., 1955. Cons. Sundance Inst., Park City, Utah, 1991; elected to Acad. Sr. Profls. at Eckerd Coll., St. Petersburg, Fla., 1993. Author: (novel) The Ski People, 1968, (nonfiction books) The Education of Edward Kennedy 1972 (Book Find Club award 1972), The Mellon Family (Fortune Club award 1978, Book of the Month Club award), The Old Boys, 1992, The Shadow President: Ted Kennedy in Opposition, 1997. Dir. N.H. Civil Liberties Union, Concord, 1983-86; founding chmn. Bradford Conservation Com., N.H., 1970s; fin. com. N.H. Dem. Party, 1970s. With U.S. Army, 1957-59, Germany. Fulbright scholar U.S. Govt., 1955-56; Bread Loaf fellow Bread Loaf Writer's Workshop, Middlebury, Vt., 1964, others. Mem. Authors Guild Am., Am. Soc. Journalists and Authors, Assn. Former Intelligence Officers (bd. dirs. New Eng. br. 1992—), Internat. Soc. for Comparative Lit. and Theatre, PEN, Phi Beta Kappa. Democrat. Jewish. Avocations: print collecting, skiing, tennis, investing.

HERSH, IRA PAUL, tax and financial planning consultant; b. Bklyn., July 14, 1948; s. Saul and Mildred (Leibowitz) Hershkowitz; m. Jan Bennett; children: Marcy Fay, Gregory Alexander, Carrie Elizabeth. BA, Queens Coll., 1969. Tax mgr. Wiss and Co., N.Y.C., 1970-77; contr. Assets Adminstrn. and Mgmt., Stamford, Conn., 1978-79; tax mgr. Exec. Monetary Mgmt., Inc., N.Y.C., 1980-84; pvt. practice tax and fin. planning, 1985—; pres. MacArthur Equities Ltd., 1985—. Mem. Rolling Hills Country Club. Home and Office: 20 Branch Brook Rd Wilton CT 06897-1520

HERSH, ROBERT MICHAEL, lawyer, insurance company executive; b. N.Y.C., Feb. 12, 1940; s. Isaac and Esther (Cohen) H.; m. Louise Hersh, Sept. 23, 1984; 1 child, Lauren. BA, Columbia U., 1960; JD, Harvard U. Bar: N.Y. 1964. Assoc. Malcolm A. Hoffmann, N.Y.C., 1964-66, Valicenti, Leighton, Reid & Pine, N.Y.C., 1966-68; atty. Kraftco Corp., N.Y.C., 1968-74; assoc. counsel Equitable Life Assurance Soc. U.S., N.Y.C., 1974-76, asst. gen. counsel, 1976-78, v.p., counsel, 1978-83, v.p., assoc. gen. counsel, 1983-88; v.p., gen. counsel Integrity Life Ins. Co., N.Y.C., 1988-93; assoc. gen. counsel Met. Life ins. Co., N.Y.C., 1994—; dir. Ideal Mut. Ins. Co., 1972-74; chief announcer Madison Sq. Garden Track Meets, 1974—; chief Eng. lang. athletics announcer Olympic Games, 1984, 88, 92, 96 World Championships, 1991, 93, 95, 97, 99 World Indoor Championships, 1987, 99, World Jr. Championships, 1994, 98. Columnist: Track & Field News, 1973-84, sr. editor, 1974—; contbg. editor Runner Mag., 1980-87; contbr. articles to profl. jours. With USAR, 1963-69. Mem. Assn. of Bar of City of N.Y. (com. profl. and jud. ethics 1978-81, consumer affairs com. 1984-85, ins. com. 1985-88), USA Track & Field (dir. 1979—, chmn. records com. 1979-88, chmn. rules com. 1989—, gen. counsel 1989-98, chmn. grand prix 1982-96, Robert Giegengack award for outstanding svc. 1997), Internat. Amateur Athletic Fedn. (tech. com. 1984-99, coun. 1999—, competition commn. 1999—, mktg. commn. 1999—), Assn. Track & Field Statisticians, Fedn. Am. Statisticians of Track. Home: 92 Club Dr Roslyn Heights NY 11577-2732 Office: MetLife 1 Madison Ave New York NY 10010-3603

HERSHATTER, RICHARD LAWRENCE, lawyer, writer; b. New Haven, Sept. 20, 1923; s. Alexander Charles and Belle (Blenner) H.; m. Mary Jane McNulty, Aug. 16, 1980; children by previous marriage: Gail Brook, Nancy Jill, Bruce Warren; 1 stepdau., Kimberly Ann Matlock Kleiman. BA, Yale U., 1948; JD, U. Mich., 1951. Bar: Conn. 1951, Mich. 1951, U.S. Supreme Ct. 1959. Pvt. practice New Haven, 1951-85, Clinton, Conn., 1985—; state

trial referee, 1984—. Author: The Spy Who Hated Licorice, 1966, Fallout For a Spy, 1968; The Spy Who Hated Fudge, 1970, Hung Jury, 1999. Mem. Clinton Rep. Town Com., Conn., 1982-2000, chmn., 1984-88; mem. Branford (Conn.) Bd. Edn., 1963-71. With Air Corps, U.S. Army, 1942-44, AUS, 1944-46. Mem. Conn. Sch. Attys. Coun. (pres. 1977), Middlesex County Bar Assn., Mystery Writers Am., Masons. Office: 41 West Rd Clinton CT 06413-2316 also: 166 Route 81 Killingworth CT 06419-1469

HERSHBERGER, RUDY CRIST, real estate agent; b. Ohio, Aug. 11, 1946; s. Crist and Emma Hershberger; m. Vicki Lynn Hershberger, Dec. 19, 1970; 1 child, Brett. Grad. elem. sch., Burton, Ohio, 1960. Splicer Ohio Bell Tel., Cleve., 1969-76, Pacific Bell Tel., Hanford, Calif., 1976-94; real estate agt. Coldwell Banker, Mountain Home, Ark., 1997—; treas. North Ctrl. Bd. Realtors, Mountain Home, 1998—. Sgt. USMC, 1965-69. Recipient Presdl. Unit Citation. Mem. VFW (life), NRA (life), Bass Anglers Sportsmans Soc. (life), Baxter County Republicans. Avocations: fishing, hunting, fishing lure manufacturing. Home: 60 Forest Hills Dr Mountain Home AR 72653-9174 Office: Coldwell Banker Colonial Real Estate 420 S Main St Ste 6 Mountain Home AR 72653-3896

HERSHENSON, MIRIAM HANNAH RATNER, librarian; b. Springfield, Mass., July 23, 1944; d. David and Thelma (Wasserman) Ratner; m. Frank J. Hershenson, July 7, 1968; children: Trent M., Scott D. AB, Syracuse U., 1966; MS, Simmons Coll., 1967; postgrad., Nova U., 1987-89. Cert. tchr./librarian, Mass. Media specialist Quincy (Mass.) Pub. Schs., 1967-71, Virginia Beach (Va.) Pub. Schs., 1982-84, Portsmouth (Va.) Pub. Schs., 1984; regional children's coord. Broward County Libr., Ft. Lauderdale, Fla., 1985-88, br. liaison, 1988-89, br. librarian, 1989-93, regional br. supr., 1993—. Mem. ALA, Pub. Libr. Assn., Fla. Libr. Assn. (caucus chair 1990-91), Broward County Libr. Assn. (pres. 1994-95), Hadassah (life, chpt. pres. 1983-84), Nat. Coun. Jewish Women (life), Jewish Women Internat. (life), Brandeis Univ. Women (life). Office: 100 S Andrews Ave Fort Lauderdale FL 33301-1830

HERSHEY, BARBARA (BARBARA HERZSTEIN), actress; b. Hollywood, Calif., Feb. 5, 1948; d. William H. Herzstein; 1 child, Tom; m. Stephen Douglas, Aug. 8, 1992 (div. 1995). Student public schs., Hollywood. Appearences include (TV series) The Monroes, 1966-67, From Here to Eternity, 1979, (mini-series) A Man Called Intrepid, 1979, Return to Lonesome Dove, 1993, Abraham, 1994; other TV appearances include Gidget, 1965, The Invaders, 1967, Daniel Boone, 1967, Love Story, 1973, Bob Hope Chrysler Theatre, 1967, High Chaparral, 1967, Kung Fu, 1973, CBS Playhouse, 1967, (TV movies) Flood, 1976, In the Glitter Palace, 1977, Just a Little Inconvenience, 1977, Sunshine Christmas, 1977, Angel on My Shoulder, 1980, The Nightingale, 1985, My Wicked, Wicked Ways... The Legend of Errol Flynn, 1985, Passion Flower, 1986, Killing in a Small Town, 1990 (Emmy award 1990, Golden Globe award 1991), Paris Trout, 1991 (Emmy award nomination), Stay the Night, 1992, Abraham, 1994, (films) With Six You Get Egg Roll, 1968, Last Summer, 1969, Heaven with a Gun, 1969, The Liberation of L.B. Jones, 1970, The Baby Maker, 1970, The Pursuit of Happiness, 1971, Dealing, 1971, Boxcar Bertha, 1972, Angela (Love Comes Quietly), 1974, The Crazy World of Julius Vrooder, 1974, Diamonds, 1975, You and Me, 1975, Dirty Night's Work, 1976, The Stunt Man, 1980, Take This Job and Shove It, 1981, The Entity, 1982, The Right Stuff, 1983, Americana, 1983, The Natural, 1984, Hoosiers, 1986, Hannah and Her Sisters, 1986, Tin Men, 1987, Shy People, 1987 (Best Actress Cannes Film Festival, 1987), A World Apart, 1988 (Best Actress Cannes Film Festival, 1988), The Last Temptation of Christ, 1988, Beaches, 1988, Tune in Tomorrow, 1989, Defenseless, 1991, The Public Eye, 1992, Falling Down, 1993, Swing Kids, 1993, Splitting Heirs, 1993, A Dangerous Woman, 1993, Last of the Dogmen, 1995, Portrait of a Lady, 1996 (nominated Golden Globe Best Supporting Actress, nominated Academy award Best Supporting Actress), The Pallbearer, 1996, A Soldier's Daughter Never Cries, 1998, Frogs for Snakes, 1998, The Staircase, 1998, Breakfast of Champions, 1999, Passion, 1999; (theatre, Broadway) Einstein and the Polar Bear, 1981. Recipient Golden Palm award for best actress Cannes Film Festival, 1987, 1988. Office: CAA care Jenny Rawlings 9830 Wilshire Blvd Beverly Hills CA 90212-1804 also: Bymel O'Neill Mgmt care Suzan Bymel N Vista Los Angeles CA 90046

HERSHEY, COLIN HARRY, management consultant; b. Everett, Pa., Aug. 31, 1935; s. Harry and Marjorie (Nycum) H.; m. Jacqueline Anderson, June 14, 1974; children: Barclay Harry, Marjorie Anderson. BSCE, Lehigh U., 1957; MBA, U. Pitts., 1967, postgrad., 1968. Registered profl. engr., Pa. Civil engr. contracting divsn. Dravo Corp., Pitts., 1957-59, cost engr., 1961-63; field engr. Army Corps Engrs., Pitts., 1958-61; mgr. mgmt. info. systems, atomic power divsn. Westinghouse Electric Co., Pitts., 1964-67; counselor Planning Dynamics, Inc., Pitts., 1968-70, v.p., 1970-72, pres., 1972-77, pres., chmn., 1977—. Author, editor: Strategic Planning Concepts, 1985; contbr. articles to profl. jours. Mem. Am. Mgmt. Assn. (adv. com. Strategic Mgmt. Program), Strategic Leadership Forum, Duquesne Club, Alpha Tau Omega, Chi Epsilon. Office: Planning Dynamics Inc 135 Industry Dr Pittsburgh PA 15275-1035

HERSHEY, LINDA ANN, neurology and pharmacology educator; b. Marion, Ind., Jan. 15, 1947; d. Matthew John and Janice Elaine Kwolek; m. Charles Owen Hershey, May 1, 1976; children: Edward, William, Erin. BS, Purdue U., 1968; PhD, Washington U., St. Louis, 1973, MD, 1975. Diplomate Am. Bd. Psychiatry and Neurology. Resident in neurology Barnes Hosp., St. Louis, 1976-78; fellow in clin. pharmacology Strong Meml. Hosp., Rochester, N.Y., 1978-80; asst. prof. neurology Case Western Res. U., Cleve., 1980-86; assoc. prof.neurology and pharmacology SUNY, Buffalo, 1986-94, prof. neurology and pharmacology, 1994—; chief neurology svc. Buffalo VA Med. Ctr., 1986—; mem. neurology adv. group VA, Washington, 1994—; sr. examiner ABPN, 1997—. Co-author: Handbook of Dementing Illnesses, 1994, Essentials of Pharmacology, 1995, Practice of Geriatrics, 1998, Hypertension Primer, 1999, Management of Ischemic Stroke, 2000; mem. editl. bd. Clin. Pharmacology and Therapeutics, 1993—, Stroke, 1995—. Co-dir. Alzheimers Disease Assistance Ctr., Buffalo, 1994-99; elder Univ. Presbyn. Ch., Buffalo, 1995-99. Grantee Sterling-Winthrop Co., 1992-96, Lorex Pharms., 1995-96, Parke-Davis, 1990-92, 96-98, Nat. Inst. Neurol. and Communicative Disorders and Stroke, 1994-98, Bayer Pharms., 1998-99, Ortho-McNeil Pharms., 1999-2000, Novartis Pharms., 2000—. Fellow Am. Acad. Neurology, Am. Neurol. Assn.; mem. Am. Soc. Clin. Pharmacology and Therapeutics, Am. Heart Assn. (mem. exec. com. stroke coun. 1993-97, chmn. program com. stroke coun. 1993-97). Achievements include evaluating use of MRI in patients with vascular dementia, describing natural history of vascular and mixed dementia, validating cognitive and functional screening instruments in patients with vascular dementia, reviewing stroke types and prevention strategies in women, comparing various presenile dementias, assessing the role of hypertension in the development of dementia and preparing VA practice guidelines for treatment of Alzheimer's disease. E-mail: hershey.linda@buffalo.va.gov. Fax: (716) 862-3140. Office: VA WNH Healthcare Sys 3495 Bailey Ave Buffalo NY 14215-1129

HERSLEY, DENNIS CHARLES, environmentalist, software systems consultant; b. Idaho Falls, Idaho, July 11, 1947; s. Cyril R. and Bardella (Webb) H.; m. Jane Anne Lilly, Jan. 16, 1993; children: Cary Connolly, Laura Lilly, Claire Lilly. Student, U. So. Calif., 1964-65; electronics tech. cert., Idaho State U., 1970; postgrad., U. Santa Clara, 1979. Cert. FCC 1st class radio engr. with TV and radar endorsements.;. Ptnr. Intensive Care Tech. Svcs., Pocatello, Idaho, 1972-74; test engring. mgr. Nat. Semiconductor, Sunnyvale, Calif., 1975-76; test ops. mgr. Amdahl Ireland, Ltd., Dublin, 1978; engr., planner, analyst Amdahl Corp., Sunnyvale, 1979-85; CFO, chmn. Provista Software Internat., San Jose, Calif., 1985-86; pres. Almaden Consulting, Santa Cruz, Calif., 1985—; co-founder, pres., dir. non profit sci. rsch. Citizens United for Responsible Environmentalism, Inc., Santa Cruz, Calif., 1994—; CFO Rsch. Consultation, Inc., Santa Cruz, Calif., 1998—; planner, sponsor Fusewest Regional Tech. Conf., Scottsdale, Ariz., 1988-89; tech. curriculum advisor Idaho State U., 1970-75; participant 3d Internat. Conf. on bioaerosols, Fungi and Mycotoxins, 1998. Inventor calculator design, 1975; featured on BBC documentary, 1998. Recipient Outstanding Alumnus award, Idaho State U., 1975, Honored Donor award Monterey Bay Aquarium, 1996. Mem. Calif. Assn. Non-Profits, No. Calif. Focus Users Group (asst. editor 1988-90), Santa Cruz Tech. Alliance. Office: CURE 2375 Benson Ave Santa Cruz CA 95065-1674

HERSMAN, FERNANDO WILLIAM (FERD HERSMAN), retired engineering executive; b. Cin., Apr. 27, 1922; s. Fernando William and Eliza Ann (Garforth) H.; m. Jill Ann Becker, June 30, 1951; children: Michael S., John A., F. William, Christopher B., Jan (dec.). BSChemE, U. Cin., 1949. Registered profl. engr., Ohio. Process engr. Frigidaire div. Gen. Motors, Dayton, Ohio, 1949-51; project engr. Vulcan-Cin., 1951-57; R&D engr. U.S. Indsl. Chems. div., Cin., 1957-61; v.p. Fischer Indsl. Equipment, Inc., Cin., 1961-83, pres., owner, 1983-89. Mem. Mayor's Fin. Com., Greenhills, Ohio, 1983, Charter Commn., Greenhills, 1988-89; elder Blue Ash. Presbyn. Ch., 1996-98. Staff sgt. U.S. Army, 1942-45, PTO; lt. USNR, 1950-67. Decorated Bronze Star with one oak leaf cluster. Mem. AIChE (chmn. Ohio Valley chpt. 1966-67), Ret. Engrs. and Scientists Cin., SAR, Am. Legion. Republican. Presbyterian. Avocations: golf, photography, travel. Home: 46 Carpenter's Ridge Rd Cincinnati OH 45241-3274

HERSON, ARLENE RITA, producer, journalist, television program host, radio commentator and panelist; b. N.Y.C.; d. Sam and Mollie (Friedman) Hornreich; m. Milton Herson, June 16, 1963; children: Michael, Karen. Student, Queens Coll., 1957, New Sch. for Social Rsch., N.Y.C., 1960. Exec. sec. Tex McCrary, Inc., N.Y.C., 1958-60; asst. to William L. Safire, Safire Pub. Rels., N.Y.C., 1960-62; columnist The Advisor, Inc., Middletown, N.J., 1974-78; prodr., host The Arlene Herson Show, N.Y.C., 1978—; syndicated nationally on Tempo TV, 1988, Channel Am., 1989-93; spokesperson Storer Cable TV, Monmouth County, 1989-91, Nutri/Systems, Monmouth and Ocean Counties, 1989-90; news anchor Nostalgia Cable TV Network at Rep. Nat. Conv., 1993; cons., talent coord. Super Annuities, 1993-94; moderator debate on capital punishment, 1998; guest lectr. Polo Plus Lecutre Series, 1997; moderator panel on assisted suicide, 1999; panelist The Am. Sr. Side-WXEL-Nat. Pub. Radio, 1999—; guest lectr. Brandeis U. Libr. Fund, 2000, Lynn U. Excalibur Soc. Columnist Boomer Times & Sr. Life, 2000—; contbg. writer The Washington/Hampton Connection Dan's Papers, 1993-98, The Hill Newspaper, 1994-98; exec. producer The Magic Flute, conductor Victor Borge, DAR Constitution Hall, Washington, 1995, 1776, 1997; exec. producer, casting dir. (musical) 1776, DAR Constitution Hall, Washington, 1996, encore prodn., 1998; prodr. 1776 (featuring current mems. of Congress), 1998; interviewer Steven Spielberg's Shoah Found., 1997-99; co-host radio program Changing Times, 1999; host WXEL-TV Pledge Drive, 2000. Bd. dirs. women's activities campaign for Sen. Jacob J. Javits, N.Y.C., 1968, Monmouth (N.J.) Mus., 1982-86, Will Rogers Inst., 1992—, Washington Symphony Orch., 1994-98, v.p., 1994; mem. 92d St. Y Benefit com., Variety-The Children's Charity; mem. Women's Project and Prodns., 1992; com. mem. Children's Psychiat. Ctr., 1971-90, Monmouth Park Charity Fund, 1980-90; mem. corp. exec. bd. Family and Childrens' Svcs., 1985-90, Ctrl. Park Conservancy, Women of Washington, also mentor program Women's Econ. Devel. Coun.; life mem. N.Y. chpt. Brandeis U. Libr. Fund; mem. dir.'s resource coun. Nat. Women's Econ. Alliance; mem. social com. Westbridge Condominium; fin. chmn. Mike Herson for Congress, 1994, fin. com. March of Dimes, 1995; mem. profl. women's coun. Nat. Mus. of Women in the Arts, 1994; com. mem. Vincent T. Lombardi Cancer Rsch. Ctr., 1994-98, Parkinson's Action Network, 1996; publicity chmn. exhbn. for Israel Tennis Ctrs. Excalibur Soc. of Lyn U., 1996—; mem. adv. coun. to co-chmn. Rep. Nat. Com., 1997—; mem. Power of Women Effecting Renewal, 1997; mem. 2d decade coun. Am. Film Inst., 1998; bd. dirs. A Healing Among Nations, 1999; mem. Soc. of 100, Fla. Philharm. Orch., 1999; mem. benefit com. Caldwell Theatre, 1999; bd. dirs. Miami City Ballet, 1999, honors bd., 2000; founder Israel Children's Ctrs., 2000. Recipient CAPE award for best talk show on Cable TV Network, 1984-93, Woman of Achievement in Comm. award Adv. Commn. on Status of Women, 1986, Pub. and Leased Access (PAL) award for best talk show Paragon Cable TV, N.Y.C., 1988, spl. resolution N.J. Assembly, 1988, Willie award for outstanding svc. Will Rogers Inst., 1992; named Disting. Alumni mem. Waldorf Astoria, 1998; nominee Cable ACE award for best talk show series nationwide. Mem. NAFE, NATAS, Nat. Acad. Cable Programming, Nat. Assn. Profl. Women, Women in Commn., Women in Cable, Women in Film and Video, Am. Women in Radio and TV, Power Women Effecting Renewal, Internat. Radio and TV Soc., Internat. Newswoman's Assn., Rep. Gov's. Assn., Nat. Press Club, Friends for Life, Friars Club (house com. 1993, admissions com. 1994—), Bethesda Country Club, Lotos Club, East River Tennis Club, Excalibur Soc. of Lynn U., Seagate Beach Club, Polo Club (cmty. rels. com. 1998-99, social com. 2000), Profl. Bus. Forum, Boca Raton Roundtable. Avocations: tennis, swimming, reading. E-mail: aherson123@aol.com. Fax: 561-998-4776.

HERTELEER, WILLY MAURITS, career officer; b. Assenede, Belgium, Jan. 10, 1941; s. Philemon and Margaretha (Kesbeke) H.; m. Jacqueline Liekens; children: Herman, Ingrid, Astrid, Iris. Commd. Belgian Navy, 1962, advanced through grades to rear-adm., 1992, chief of naval staff, 1993-95, vice admiral, chief def. staff, 1995-99, aide to the king, 1999—. Office: Belgian Navy, Rue D'Evere, 1140 Brussels Belgium

HERTSCH, BODO WOLFHARD, veterinarian, educator; b. Potsdam, Germany, June 27, 1943; s. Kurt Hans and Elfriede Mathilda (Thaermann) H.; m. Ingrid Banning, Mar. 14, 1971; children: Claudia, Florian. MS, Free U., Berlin, 1968, PhD, 1970. Asst. vet. clinic for horses Vet. U., Hannover, Germany, 1969-74, head asst. clinic for horses, 1974-82, asst. vet. prof., 1982-94; prof. clinic for horses, surgery, radiology Free Univ., Berlin, 1994—. Author: (books) Anatomy of Horses, 1983, Angiographic Examinations of Equine Extremities, 1983, The Hoof, 1996; editor Equine Abstracts, (award 1984). Cons. Soc. for Prevention of Cruelty to Animals, German Equine Fedn., 1989—. Mem. German Vet. Soc., Soc. Equine Medicine (pres. 1992—), Soc. Berlin Student Riders (pres. 1994—). Home: Hohenzollernstr 7, 14109 Berlin Germany Office: Equine Clinic Free U Berlin, Oertzenweg 19B, 14163 Berlin Germany

HERTWIG, MANFRED HANS FRIEDBERT, physicist, researcher; b. Wattwil, Switzerland, July 21, 1957; s. Hans and Frieda (Bleiker) H.; divorced; 1 child, Pascal. MSC, U. Zurich, Switzerland, 1989, diploma in Exptl. Physics, 1989; PhD, Swiss Fed. Inst. Tech., Zurich, 1997. Rsch. scientist, physicist U. Zurich, 1990-91, Swiss Fed. Inst. Tech., 1992—; info. specialist, analyst, sys. engr. Computer Industry, 1991-92; rschr. project mgmt. Industry/Univ., 1992—; rschr. EC, 1992—; presenter in field. Reviewer rsch. pubs. Sci. Jours. Internat., 1994—; contbr. articles to profl. jours. Cpl. Atomic & Chem. Weapons Def. Svc., Switzerland, 1977—. Mem. European Phys. Soc., Swiss Phys. Soc., Swiss Acad. Sci., Phys. Soc. Zurich, European Optical Soc., Internat. Soc. for Optical Engring., N.Y. Acad. scis. Avocations: astrophysics, astronomy, literature, music, sports. Home: Brunaustrasse 60, CH-8002 Zurich Switzerland Office: Swiss Fed Inst Tech, Tannenstrasse 3 IKB E 16 2, CH-8092 Zurich Switzerland

HERTZBERG, HENRY, radiologist, educator; b. Bklyn., Oct. 21, 1933; s. Louis and Bessie (Eisman) H.; m. Dori Balter, June 10, 1962; children: Richard, Lisa. BS, CCNY, 1955; MD, SUNY, Bklyn., 1959. Diplomate Am. Bd. Radiology. Intern Kings County Med. Ctr., Bklyn., 1959-60; resident Roosevelt Hosp., N.Y.C., 1960-63; dir. radiology Fort Gordon (Ga.) Army Hosp., 1963-65; pvt. practice Green Brook, N.J.; assoc. dir. dept. radiology Somerset Med. Ctr., Somerville, N.J., 1975-85; dir. dept. radiology Muhlenberg Med. Ctr., Plainfield, N.J., 1985-92; attending radiologist Muhlenberg Med. Ctr., 1992—; clin. asst. prof. radiology Rutgers U. Med. Ctr., 1985—. Capt. M.C., U.S. Army, 1963-65. Mem. AMA. Avocation: travel. Home: 182 Deer Run Watchung NJ 07069-6222 Office: Assoc Radiologists PA 239 Us Highway 22 Green Brook NJ 08812-1916

HERTZBERGER, HERMAN, architect, educator; b. Amsterdam, The Netherlands, July 6, 1932; s. Herman and Margaretha Johanna (Prins) H.; m. Johanna C. van Seters, 1957; children: Akelei, Veroon, Titus. Grad., Tech. U. Delft, The Netherlands, 1958. Practice architecture Amsterdam, 1958—; prof. archtl. design Tech. U. Delft, 1970—, U. Geneva, 1986-93; chmn. Berlage Inst. Amsterdam, 1990-95. Archtl. designs include Centraal Beheer, Apeldoorn, Netherlands, 1972, De Drie Hoven, Amsterdam, 1974, Music Ctr. Vredenburg (A.J. v. Eck award 1980), Utrecht, netherlands, 1979, 2 schs., Amsterdam, 1983, Lima housing complex, West Berlin, 1986, office bldg. Ministry of Social Welfare, The Hague, 1990, Chassé Theatre, Breda, 1995, Theater Markant, Uden, 1996; co-editor (Dutch) Forum, 1959-63. Recipient Archtl. awrd Town of Amsterdam, 1968, Eternit award, 1974, Fritz Schumacher award, 1974, award Town of Amsterdam, 1985, Premio Europa award, 1991. Office: Architectuurstudio Herman Hertzberger, Gerard Doustraat 220 PO Box 74665, 1070 BR Amsterdam The Netherlands*

HERTZOG, JAMES HENRY, pediatrician, educator; b. Elmira, N.Y., Aug. 8, 1959; s. Frank Vernooy and Doreen Bridges Hertzog. AB, Cornell U., 1981; MS, SUNY, Buffalo, 1982; MD, SUNY, Syracuse, 1986. Diplomate Nat. Bd. Med. Examiners, Am. Bd. Pediat., Am. Bd. Pediat. subboard Pediat. Critical Care Medicine. Resident in pediat. SUNY Health Sci. Ctr., Syracuse, 1986-89, chief resident pediat., 1989-90; fellow pediat. critical care Children's Hosp. Phila., 1990-93; asst. prof. pediat. Georgetown U. Med. Ctr., Washington, 1993-99; assoc. prof. pediat. A.I. duPont Hosp. for Children, Wilmington, Del., 1999—. Fellow Am. Acad. Pediat.; mem. Soc. Critical Care Medicine. Avocations: distance running, skiing. Office: AI duPont Hosp for Children 1600 Rockland Rd Wilmington DE 19803-3607

HERTZ PICCIOTTO, I., epidemiologist, educator; b. N.Y.C., Aug. 29, 1948; d. Theodore M. Hertz and Edith Ida Ravis; m. Henri Picciotto; children: Sally, Neil. BA in Math., U. Calif., Berkeley, 1970, M in Pub. Health, 1984, MA in Bio-Statistics, 1985, PhD in Epidemiology, 1989. Tchr. math. and computer sci. Urban Sch. of San Francisco, 1979-82; staff rsch. assoc. U. Calif., Davis, 1985-87; epidemiologist State of Calif. Dept. Health Svcs., Berkeley, 1988-89; asst. prof. U. N.C., Chapel Hill, 1990-95, assoc. prof., 1995-98, prof., 1999—; vis. scientist Nat. Inst. of Environ. Health Scis., Rsch. Triangle Park, N.C., 1989-90. Contbr. articles to profl. jours. Grantee NIH. Fellow Carolina Population Ctr.; mem. Internat. Soc. Environ. Epidemiology (councillor 1996-99, pres.-elect 2000—), soc. for Epidemiologic Rsch., soc. for Pediat. and Perinatal Epidemiology Rsch., Am. Pub. Health Assn. Avocations: choreography, dance. Office: U NC Dept Epidemiology McGavran-Greenberg Cb 7400 Pittsboro & Vance Chapel Hill NC 27599-0001

HERVE, THIERRY JEAN, physicist, researcher; b. Vitré, France, Dec. 22, 1959; s. Roger Victor and Odette Victorine (Bouvet) H.; m. Valérie Jacqueline Bonnétat, Mar. 23, 1996; 1 child, Ismaël. Engr. in Physics and Electronics, Inst. Chimie/Physique Ind., Lyon, France, 1982; DEA in Info. Processing, Inst. Nat. Poly. Grenoble, France, 1984, PhD in Electronics, 1987; habil., Faculty Medicine Grenoble, 1999. Assoc. prof. ENSERG/Inst. Nat. Poly. of Grenoble, 1986-88; postdoctoral fellow NTT Basic Rsch. Labs., Tokyo, 1988-89; attaché scientifique Univ. Hosp. Grenoble, 1996—; sr. rschr. INSERM, Grenoble, 1989—; cons. Thomson LCR, Orsay, France, 1988, MXM, Antibes, France, 1991-93; invited rschr. NTT Basic Rsch. Labs., Tokyo, 1990, Tokyo Med. and Dental U., 1999, Tokyo U., 1999—; group leader rsch. team Microsystems and Interpretation of Functional Signals of Livings, 1998. Co-author: Artificial Intelligence and Cognitive Science, 1987; contbr. articles to profl. jours. With French Mil., 1982-83. Mem. Neurosci. Soc. France, N.Y. Acad. Sci. Roman Catholic. Avocations: judo, skiing, tennis, mountain climbing. Office: TIMC Faculty of Medicine, CNRS UMR 5525, 38706 La Tronche France

HERXHEIMER, ANDREW, clinical pharmacologist; b. Berlin, Nov. 4, 1925; s. Herbert G.J. and Ilse M. (König) H.; m. Susan Jane Collier, 1961 (div. 1974); children: Charlotte Jane, Sophie Mary; m. Christine Bernecker, 1983. MB BS, U. London, 1949. Jr. med. posts Nat. Health Svc., U.K., 1949-50; lectr. in therapeutics St. Thomas' Hosp. Med. Sch., London, 1953-58; Nuffield med. fellow U. Utah, Salt Lake City, 1958-59; from lectr. to sr. lectr. in pharmacology London Hosp. Med. Coll., 1960-76; sr. lectr. in clin. pharmacology Charing Cross & Westminster Med. Sch., London, 1976-91; cons. U.K. Cochrane Ctr., Oxford, 1992-95, emeritus fellow, 1996—; bd. dirs. Ethical Investment Rsch. Svc.; founding mem. DIPEx project, Oxford U.; clin. effectiveness adviser Barnet Health Authority, London; chmn. health com. Consumers Internat., 1983-96; chmn. Internat. Soc. Drug Bulls., 1986-96; adviser La Revue Prescrire, Paris, 1997-99. Editor Drug & Therapeutics Bull., 1962-92; co-editor: Pharmaceuticals and Health Policy, 1981, Nausea and Vomiting, 2000; contbr. articles, reports to profl. publs. Mem. Working Party on Chem. and Biol. Weapons, U.K., Health Action Internat.-Europe, The Netherlands. Fellow Royal Coll. Physicians; mem. Brit. Pharmacol. Soc., European Assn. Sci. Editors, Healthwatch, U.K. Drug Utilisation Rsch. Group. Avocations: travel, reading. Home: 9 Park Crescent, London N3 2NL, England

HERZ, WERNER, chemist, educator; b. Stuttgart, Germany, Feb. 12, 1921; came to U.S., 1937, naturalized, 1944; s. Alfred and Hedwig (Loewenstein) H.; m. Marcia Lucile King, Feb. 22, 1945; children—Michael John, Patrick Werner, Monica Lucile, Andrea Lauren. B.A., U. Colo., 1943, M.A., 1945, Ph.D., 1947. Instr. math. U. Colo., 1946-47; Am. Cyanamid fellow U. Ill., 1947-49; with Fla. State U., Tallahassee, 1949—; prof. chemistry Fla. State U., 1959—, Robert O. Lawton disting. prof., 1987—; mem. chemistry panel Cancer Chemotherapy Nat. Service Center, 1959-62, NSF, 1961-64; cons. Nat. Cancer Inst., 1962-65; mem. cancer chemotherapy study sect. NIH, 1962-66, mem. medicinal chemistry study sect., 1970-74. Author: The Shape of Molecules, 1963; editorial bd.: Jour. Organic Chemistry, 1962-63, sr. editor, 1963-89; editor: Fortschritte der Chemie Organischer Naturstoffe, 1969—; bd. editors: Planta Medica, 1978—, Phytochemistry, 1981—. Mem. Am. Chem. Soc. (councilor Fla. sect. 1960-79, adv. bd. Petroleum Research Fund 1970-72), Chem. Soc. London, Phi Beta Kappa, Sigma Xi, Sigma Pi Sigma, Alpha Chi Sigma, Pi Mu Epsilon, Phi Lambda Upsilon. Research and numerous publs. on isolation and structure determination of plant products with emphasis on possible applications to chemotaxonomy and cancer chemotherapy, structure synthesis and transformations of terpenoid substances; studies of molecular rearrangements in chemistry. Home: 314 Saratoga Dr Tallahassee FL 32312-2041

HERZBERG, DOROTHY CREWS, secondary education educator; b. N.Y.C., July 8, 1935; d. Floyd Houston and Julia (Lesser) Crews; m. Hershel Zelig Herzberg, May 22, 1962 (div. Apr. 1988); children: Samuel Floyd, Laura Jill, Daniel Crews. AB, Brown U., 1957; MA, Stanford U., 1964; JD, San Francisco Law Sch., 1976. Legal sec. various law firms, San Francisco, 1976-78; tchr. Mission Adult Sch., San Francisco, 1965-66; tchr. secondary and univ. levels Peace Corps, Nigeria, 1961-63; investigator Office of Dist. Atty., San Francisco, 1978-80; sr. adminstr. Dean Witter Reynolds Co., San Francisco, 1980-83; registered rep. Waddell and Reed, 1983-84; fin. services rep. United Resourceds, Hayward, Calif., 1984-86; tax preparer H&R Block, 1987; revenue officer IRS, 1987-89; now tchr. ESL West Contra Costa Sch. Dist., El Cerrito, Calif., 1989—, tchg. citizenship Richmond adult edn., 1994-96; chair social justice coun. Unitarian Universalist Ch. of Berkeley. Editor: (newsletters) Coop. Nursery Sch. Council, 1969-71, Miraloma Life, 1976-82. Bd. dirs. LWV, San Francisco, 1967-69, mem. speakers bur., 1967-80; pres. Council Coop. Nursery Schs., San Francisco, 1969-71; bd. dirs. Miraloma (Calif.) Improvement Club, 1977-88, pres., 1980-81; alt. for supr. San Francisco Mayor's Commn. on Criminal Justice, 1978; chairperson social justice coun. Unitarian Universalist Ch. Berkeley, 1997—. Democrat. Home: 1006 Richmond St El Cerrito CA 94530-2616

HERZEL, FRANK, research physicist; b. Guestrow, Germany, May 17, 1963; s. Alois and Helgard (Bohnsack) H. Diploma in physics, Humboldt U., Berlin, 1989; PhD in Nat. Scis., U. Rostock, Germany, 1993. Asst. U. Rostock, 1989-93; rschr. IHP, Frankfurt (Oder), Germany, 1993—. Contbr. articles to profl. jours. Recipient Gustav-Magnus award Humboldt U., 1989. Office: IHP, Im Technologiepark 25, 15236 Frankfurt (Oder) Germany

HERZFELD, CHARLES MARIA, physicist; b. Vienna, Austria, June 29, 1925; came to U.S., 1942, naturalized, 1949; s. August Alfred and Frieda Auguste (Poehlman) H.; children: Charles Christopher, Christine Augustine, Paul Vincent; m. Shannon Stock Shuman, June 9, 1990. BS in Chem. Engring. cum laude, Cath. U. Am., 1945; PhD (Carnegie Found. fellow), U. Chgo., 1951. Lectr. chemistry Cath. U. Am., 1946; lectr. gen. sci. Coll. U. Chgo., 1946-47; lectr. physics DePaul U., Chgo., 1948-50; physicist Ballistic Research Lab., Aberdeen, Md., 1951-53, Naval Research Lab., Washington, 1953-55; lectr. physics U. Md., 1953-57, prof. physics, 1957-61; cons. chief heat and power div. Nat. Bur. Standards, 1955-56, acting asst. chief, 1956-57, chief heat div., 1957-61, asso. dir. bur., 1961; asst. dir. Advanced Research Project Agy., Dept. Def., 1961-63, dir. ballistic missile def., 1963; dep. dir. Advanced Research Projects Agy., 1963-65, dir., 1965-67; tech. dir. def. space group ITT, Nutley, N.J., 1967-74; tech. dir. aerospace-electronics-components-energy group ITT, 1974-76, tech. dir. telecommunications and

electronics group N.Am., 1978-79; v.p., dir. research ITT Corp., 1979-83, v.p., dir. research and tech., 1983-85; vice chmn. Aetna, Jacobs and Ramo, N.Y.C., 1985-90; dir. def. rsch. and engring. Dept. Def., Washington, 1990-91; cons. to Office Sci. and Tech. Policy, Exec. Office Pres. of U.S., Washington, 1991; chmn. bd. Westronix Co., Midvale, Utah, 1985-88; mem. Def. Sci. bd., 1968-83, Def. Policy Bd., 1985-90, Nat. Commn. on Space, 1985-86; cons. in field; fellow Hudson Inst., 1970-90; mem. Brookings Inst. 5th Conf. for Career Execs. in Fed. Govt., 1958, mem. chief of Naval Ops. exec. panel, 1970—; mem. Tech. Review Bd. Hong Kong, 1993-94, Nat. Security Advisory Bd., Los Alamos Nat. Lab.; adj. fellow Ctr. Strategic and Internat. Studies, Washington, 1995—. Editor: Temperature, Its Control in Science and Industry, vol. III, 1962; contbr. articles to profl. jours. Recipient Flemming award, 1963; Meritorious Civilian Service medal Dept. Def., 1967. Fellow AAAS, Am. Phys. Soc., Conf. on Sci., Philosophy and Religion, Coun. Fgn. Rels., Ctr. for Strategic and Internat. Studies (Washington); mem. Explorers Club, Inst. for Strategic Studies (London), Cath. Assn. Internat. Peace (pres. 1959-61), Cosmos Club (Washington).

HERZMANN, JAN, statistician; b. Prague, Czech Republic, Mar. 26, 1953; s. Jiří and Ludmila (Krausová) H.; m. Věra Řehořová, July 28, 1977; children: Petr, Eva. D Natural Scis., Charles U., Prague, 1978; PhD, High Sch. Econs., Prague, 1984. Cert. math. stats., mktg. rsch. Statistician Pub. Opinion Rsch. Inst., Prague, 1977-85, project mgr., 1986-92; project mgr. Factum, Prague, 1992-94, mng. dir., 1994—; vis. prof. Econ. U., Prague, 1988—. Co-author: Sondy do Verejného Mínění, 1990, Sociologieky Slovník, 1997. Pres.. founding bd. Found. Pangea, Prague, 1996—; bd. mem. J. Pavlík Found., Prague, 1996—. Recipient jr. fellows award Acad. Scis., Prague, 1978,. Mem. European Soc. for Opinion and Mktg. Rsch., Czech Mktg. Assn. (v.p. 1997). Avocation: voluntary work with children. Office: Sofres-Factum Ltd, Vysehradská 53, 128 00 Prague 2, Czech Republic

HERZOG, ANDREAS, soccer player; b. Vienna, Austria, Sept. 10, 1968. Midfielder Werder Bremen (Germany) Football Club, Nat. Team Austria. Winner Two World Cups, 1990, 98. Address: Ernst-Happel Stadion A/F, Meierelstrasse 7, 1020 Wien Austria*

HERZOG, BRIGITTE, lawyer; b. St. Sauveur, France, Jan. 11, 1943; came to the U.S., 1970, naturalized, 1976; d. Roger and Berthe (Niobey) Ecolivet; m. Peter E. Herzog, June 29, 1970; children: Paul Roger, Elizabeth Ann. Licence en Droit, Law Sch. Pantheon, Paris, 1967; diploma d'Etudes Superieures in internat. and criminal law, Law Sch. Pantheon, 1968; diploma, Acad. Internat. Law, The Hague, The Netherlands, 1969; JD, Syracuse Coll. Law, 1975. Bar: Paris 1968, N.Y. 1976. Assoc. Chardenon Law Firm, Paris, 1968-70, Cleary, Gottlieb et al, Paris, 1976-77; staff atty. Carrier Corp., Syracuse, N.Y., 1977-83; sr. atty. Carrier Corp., Syracuse, 1983-84, asst. gen. counsel, 1984-86; counsel European and Transcontinental Ops. Carrier Corp., Surrey, Eng., 1986-89; assoc. gen. counsel Carrier Corp., Syracuse, 1990; dir. legal affairs Otis, Paris, 1990-92; v.p. legal affairs European and Transcontinental Ops. Otis Internat., Inc., 1992-97; dep. gen. counsel Otis Elevator Co.-Europe; v.p. legal affairs Otis Elevator North European Area, 1998—. Contbr. to Harmonization of Laws in EEC Fifth Sokol Colloquium, 1983; contbr. articles on French and internat. law to profl. jours. Bd. dirs. Syracuse Stage Guild, 1974-77; chair legal com. European Elevator Assn. Mem. ABA, Am. Fgn. Law Assn. Roman Catholic. Home: 112 Erregger Rd Syracuse NY 13224-2220 Office: Otis, 4 Place Victor Hugo, Courbevoie France

HERZOG, ROMAN, German government official; b. Landshut, Germany, Apr. 5, 1934. Attended, U. Munich, Freje U Berlin and Hochschule für Verwaltungswissenshaft, Speyer. Mem. bd. evangelische kirche in Deutschland Chamber for Pub. Accountability, 1971-80; rep. Rhineland-Palatinate in Bundestag, 1973-78; chair Evangelical Working Party CDU/CSU, 1978-83; min. culture and sport Baden-Württemberg, 1978-80, min. interior, 1980-83; mem. fed. com. CDU, 1979-83; v.p. Fed. Constl. Ct., 1983-87, pres., 1987-94; cand. of CDU for Pres. of Rep., 1994; hon. prof. Hochschule für Verwaltungswissenschaft, Speyer U. Tübingen; pres. Fed. Republic Germany, 1994-99; chmn., Conv. on European Union Charter of Fundamental Rights European Union, Brussels, 1999—. Co-author: Kommentar zur Grundgesetz, 1968, Staaten der Frühzeit: Ursprünge und Herrschaftsformen, 1988. Office: Conv on EU Charter of Fundamental Rights, rue Wiertz 60, B-1047 Brussel Belgium*

HERZSTEIN, BARBARA See **HERSHEY, BARBARA**

HERZSTEIN, ROBERT EDWIN, history educator, author; b. N.Y.C., Sept. 26, 1940. BA, NYU, 1961, MA, 1963, PhD, 1964. Asst. prof. Carnegie-Mellon U., Pitts., 1964-65, MIT, Cambridge, Mass., 1966-72; assoc. to prof. U. S.C., Columbia, 1972—, Carolina disting. prof., 1990—; spl. aide to gov. Conn., Hartford. Author: Waldheim: The Missing Years, 1988, Roosevelt & Hitler: Prelude to War, 1980, Henry R. Luce: A Political Portrait, 1994, The War that Hitler Won, 1978. Advisor, witness Govt. Reform subcom. U.S. Ho. of Reps., 1994-98; co-organizer Conf. on the legacy of Nuremberg trials, Columbia, 1997. Recipient Founders Day award NYU, 1965, Russell award U. S.C., 1978, Signing pen by Pres. Clinton upon signing Nazi War Crimes Disclosure Act, 1998. Mem. German Studies Assn., WWII Studies Assn., Soc. for Historians of Am. Fgn. Rels. Jewish. Fax: 803 777-4494.

HESELTINE, MICHAEL RAY DIBDIN, retired government minister; b. Swansea, Wales, Mar. 21, 1933; s. Rupert and Eileen Ray H.; m. Anne Edna Harding Williams, 1962; 3 children. Educated, Pembroke Coll., Oxford U.; hon. degree, Liverpool U., 1988. Dir. Bow Publs., 1961-65; chmn. Haymarket Press, 1965-70; M.P. for Tavistock, 1966-74, M.P. for Henley, 1974—; parliamentary sec. Ministry of Transport, 1970; parliamentary under-sec. of state Dept. Environment, 1970-72; minister aerospace and shipping, 1972-74; opposition spokesman for industry, 1974-76, for environment, 1976-79; sec. of state for environment, 1979-83; sec. of state for def., 1983-86, sec. of state for environment, 1990-92, pres. bd. trade, 1992-95; dep. prime min., 1st sec. of state, London, 1995-97; chmn. Haymarket Pub. Group Ltd., Conservative Mainstream, 1997, Anglo-China Forum, 1998. Author: Reviving the Inner Cities, 1983, Where There's a Will, 1986, The Challenge of Europe, 1989, Life in the Jungle, 2000. Hon. fellow RIBA, Inst. of Mktg. Mem. Carlton Club. Office: House of Commons, London SW1P 3NP, England

HESHIKI, ATSUKO S., physician; b. Chiba, Japan, Dec. 17, 1938; d. Yasuyuki and Naoko (Shiomoya) Shishikura; m. Yoshitada Heshiki; children: Ine, Kana. MD, Tokyo Women's Med. U., 1964. Diplomate Am. Bd. Radiology, Japan Bd. Radiology. Intern. USAF Hosp., Tachi Kawa, 1964-65, Evanston (Ill.) Hosp., 1965-66; resident Johns Hopkins Hosp., 1966-70; asst. prof. Johns Hopkins Hosp., Balt., 1972-74; assoc. prof. Gunma U. Hosp., Maebashi, Japan, 1974-87; prof., chmn. Saitama Med. Sch., Moro, Japan, 1987—. Mem. editl. bd. Digital Imaging periodical; invited editor: Magnetic Resonance Jour. Mem. Internat. Soc. Magnetic Resonance Medicine (bd. dirs.), Soc. Computer Applications Radiology (bd. dirs.), Med. Women's Internat. Assn. (nat. coord.). Office: Saitama Med Sch, Iruma gun, Saitama 350-0495, Japan

HESKIN, KENNETH JOSEPH, psychology educator; b. Belfast, No. Ireland, Sept. 28, 1945; arrived in Australia, 1988; s. John and Ethel Louise (Livingston) H.; m. Susan Elaine Hartley, Mar. 11, 1967; children: Victoria Siobhan, David Alan, Matthew Kenneth. BA with honors, Queens U., Belfast, 1968; PhD, Durham (Eng.) U., 1975; MA, Trinity Coll., Dublin, 1979. Rsch. asst. Durham (Eng.) U., 1968-72; lectr. New U. of Ulster, Coleraine, No. Ireland, 1972-76; lectr. Trinity Coll., Dublin, 1976-85, sr. lectr., 1985-87, head dept., 1987-88; head dept. Swinburne U., Melbourne, 1988-94, head Sch. Social and Behavioral Scis., 1994-2000; dep. vice-chancellor, CEO Swinburne Sarawak Inst. Tech., Kuching, East Malaysia, 2000—; vis. Fulbright fellow U. Calif., Davis, 1977-78. Author: Northern Ireland: A Psychological Analysis, 1980; contbr. articles to profl. jours. Recipient Fulbright fellowship Fulbright Found., 1977-78. Fellow British Psychol. Soc. (assoc.); mem. APA (internat. affiliate), Australian Psychol. Soc., Reversal Theory Soc. (pres. 1995-97). Avocation: golf. Office: Swinburne Sarawak Inst Tech, Jalan Simpang Tiga, 93576 Kuching Sarawak

HESLOT, HENRI, molecular and cell biologist; b. Paris, Apr. 27, 1921; s. François and Henriette (Guérin) H.; m. Jeanne chambon, Sept. 11, 1950; children: André, Sylvie, François, Jean. Ingenieur Agronome, Inst. Nat. Agronomique, Paris, 1945; Lic. en Scis., U. Paris, 1948; PhD, Inst. Nat. Agronomique, 1957. Rschr. CNRS, Paris, 1946-48; fellow Brit. Coun., Cambridge, Eng., 1948-49; dir. lab. INRA, Paris, 1961—; maitre de conf. de génétique Inst. Nat. Agronomique, Paris, 1961—, prof. genetic and molecular biology, 1970—; cons. to beverage industries. Author: Molecular Biology and Genetic Engineering of Yeast, 1992, ; contbr. numberous articles to profl. jours.; patentee in field. Recipient Mérite Agricole Min. of Agr., 1976, Palmes Académiques Min. of Edn., 1976. Mem. Acad. Agr. of France, Soc. of Microbiology, Soc. Biochemistry, Conseil des Applications de L'Academie des Scis. Avocations: Islamic and far eastern art, travel, photography. Home: 29 Rue Rousselet, 75007 Paris France

HESS, BARRY JOEL, small business owner; b. Jan. 29, 1957. B in English and History, Fordham U., 1978. Pres. Empirico Internat. Trading Co., Glendale, 1985—, DCI Network Mktg. Co., Island Falls, Maine, 1997-98. Polit. spkr. Libertarian Party, 1998—. Address: PO Box 6011 Glendale AZ 85312-6011

HESS, DARLA BAKERSMITH, cardiologist, educator; b. Valparaiso, Fla., June 4, 1953; d. James Barry and Irma Marie (Baker) Bakersmith; m. Leonard Wayne Hess, July 20, 1988; 1 child, Ever Marie. BS, Birmingham So. Coll., 1975; MD, Tulane U., 1979. Diplomate Am. Bd. Internal Medicine, Am. Bd. Cardiovascular Disease. Commd. ensign USN, 1979, advanced through grades to lt. comdr., 1988; resident in internal medicine Portsmouth (Va.) Naval Hosp., 1979-82, cardiologist, head non-invasive cardiology, 1986-88; fellow in cardiology San Diego Naval Hosp., 1982-84; cardiologist, head med. officer in charge ICU Camp Lejeune (N.C.) Naval Hosp., 1984-85; asst. prof. medicine U. Miss. Med. Ctr., Jackson, 1988-91, asst. prof. ob/gyn., 1990-91; dir. noninvasive sect. cardiology, dir. fetal echocardiograp U. Mo., Columbia, 1991—, co-dir. Adult Cogenital Heart Disease Clinic, 1991—, assoc. prof. medicine, assoc. prof. ob/gyn., 1998—. Author: (with others) Obstetrics and Gynecology Clinics, 1992, Clinical Problems in Obstetrics & Gynecology, 1993, General Medical Disorders During, 1991; co-editor: Fetal Echocardiography, 1999; contbr. articles to So. Med. Jour., Ob/Gyn. Clinics N.Am., So. Med. Assn. Annual Meeting, Soc. Perinatal Obs., Jour. Reproductive Medicine, Am. Soc. Endocardiography. Fellow Am. Coll. Cardiology; mem. Am. Heart Assn. (fellow stroke coun.), Am. Soc. Echocardiography, Am. Assn. Nuclear Cardiology, Phi Beta Kappa, Alpha Omega Alpha. Republican. Episcopalian. Home: 21021 N Ponderosa Rd Clark MO 65243-9531 Office: U Mo Health Sci Ctr 1 Hospital Dr Columbia MO 65201-5276

HESS, DONALD MARC, holding company executive; b. Bern, Switzerland, Aug. 3, 1936; s. Hector Albert and Louise (McNeir) H.; divorced; 1 child, Alexandra. Ecole Superieure De Commerce, Neuchatel U.; brewmaster, Doemens, Munich, 1957. Pres. Steinholzli Brewery, Bern, 1957-68; chmn. Hess Holding, Bern, 1968—; chmn. Valser Mineral Water, Ltd., Vals, CH, Hess Ltd., Bern, Blue Lake, Ltd., Blausee, CH, Hess Internat., V.V., Rotterdam, The Netherlands; CEO The Hess Collection Winery, Napa, Calif.; bd. dirs. Kambly Bisquits, Ltd., Trubschachen, CH, 1988—, Hess Art Collection Ltd., Bern, CH, 1998—; founder Hess Collection Contemporary Art Mus., Napa, Calif., 1989—, Hess Collection Art Exbhn. Space at Vinopolis-City of Wine, 1 Bank End, London, 1999—. Editor: Hess Collection, 1989 (named one of best books in Switzerland 1989), Hess Collection New Works, 1998, Franz Gertsch, Hess Collection, 1999. Co-founder Kunst Heute Found., Bern, 1982; pres., mem exec. com. International Green Cross Switzerland, 1994-96. Office: Hess Holding Steinholzli, CH-3097 Bern Switzerland

HESS, DOROTHY HALDEMAN, college official; b. Bareville, Pa., July 2, 1941; d. Titus Myer and Anna Mae (Haldeman) H. BA, Elizabethtown Coll., 1965. Tchr. French and German, Millville (N.J.) Jr. High Sch., 1965-67; tchr., dir. Full Day Head Start, Lancaster, Pa., 1967-72; ednl. cons. and trainer Day Care Ctrs. Inc., Harrisburg, Pa., 1972-74; supr. database Architectron Ltd., Newport Beach, Calif., 1980-83; info. specialist Woodbury U., L.A., 1983-85; asst. dir. adminstrv. computing Scripps Coll., Claremont, Calif., 1985-87, dir. info. systems and computing, 1987-97; cons. info. systems analysis and planning Dorothy Hess & Assocs., Claremont, 1997—. Contbg. author: CWIS and Networks, 1992, Administrative Systems, 1993. Mem. Internat. POISE Users Group Inc. (founding, bd. dirs. 1987-91, pres.-elect 1992-93, pres. 1993-94), Assn. for Mgmt. of Info. in Higher Edn. (speaker 1991), Inst. for Ednl. Computing. Avocations: making pottery, travel, choral singing.

HESS, GEORGE FRANKLIN, II, lawyer; b. Oak Park, Ill., May 13, 1939; s. Franklin Edward and Carol (Hackman) H.; m. Diane Ricci, Aug. 9, 1974; 1 child, Franklin Edward. BS in Bus., Colo. State U., 1962; JD, Suffolk U., 1970; LLM, Boston U., 1973. Bar: Pa. 1971, Fla. 1973, U.S. Tax Ct. 1974, U.S. Dist. Ct. (so. dist.) Fla. 1975. Assoc. Hart, Childs, Hepburn, Ross & Putnam, Phila., 1970-72; instr. Suffolk U. Law Sch., Boston, 1973-74; ptnr. Henry, Hess & Hoines, Ft. Lauderdale, Fla., 1974-79; with Mousaw, Vigdor, Reeves & Hess, Ft. Lauderdale, Fla., 1979-94; pvt. practice Ft. Lauderdale, Fla., 1995—. Bd. dirs. Childrens Home Soc., Ft. Lauderdale, 1985-89, Nadeau Charitable Found., 1985—. Lt. USNR, 1963-66. Mem. ABA, SAR, Fla. Bar Assn., Broward County Bar Assn., Lauderdale Yacht Club, USN League, Phi Alpha Delta. Episcopalian. Home: 2524 Castilla Is Fort Lauderdale FL 33301-1505 Office: 333 N New River Dr E Fort Lauderdale FL 33301-2241

HESS, HEINZ-JUERGEN, science historian; b. Rheinbach, Bonn, Germany, Sept. 20, 1941; s. Anton and Katharina (Kraywinkel) H.; m. Ute Hantke, July 4, 1967; children: Rainer, Christa. Stateexamination, U. Bonn, 1965, PhD, 1970. Editor Leibniz Archive, Hannover, Germany, 1970-72, head dept., 1973—. Author: Kant's Supreme Principles, 1970; editor vols. of edition: Leibniz' Mathematical Correspondence, 1986, 95; contbr. articles to profl. jours. Mem. Kant Gesellschaft ev Bonn, Internat. Acad. Hist. of Sci. Avocation: computer science. Office: Leibniz-Archiv, Waterloostr 8, D-30169 Hannover Germany

HESS, JÜRGEN, immunologist; b. Huenfeld, Hessen, Germany, May 6, 1960; s. Hans and Anni (Kemler) H.; m. Manuela Welzel, May 20, 1995; children: Alina, Steven. Biologist, U. Würzburg, Germany, 1986, Dr. rer. nat., 1990. Postdoctoral fellow Sandoz/SFI, Vienna, Austria, 1990-92; rsch. asst. U. Ulm, Germany, 1992-97, Max Planck Inst for Infection Biology, Berlin, 1997-2000, November AG, Erlangen, Germany, 2000—. Guest editor: Behring Inst. Mitteilung, 1994; mem. editl. bd. Infection and Immunity. With German Air Force, 1979-80. Avocations: cinema, sports, reading. Office: November AG, Josef Schalk Strasse 3, D-91056 Erlangen Germany

HESS, MARILYN ANN, state legislator; m. Dennis J. Hess; children: Christine, Craig. AA, NYU, 1977; BBA in Mgmt. cum laude, Pace U., 1980. Assoc. Merrill Lynch, N.Y.C., 1972-77; home improvement contractor Conn., 1982-90; mem. Conn. Ho. of Reps., 1993—; state rep. 150th Assembly Dist., Conn., 1993—; chmn. Conn. Internat. Trade Coun., 1995—; mem. Rep. Roundtable of Greenwich, 1993—, Amb. Roundtable, 1994—, Conn. Reps. for Choice, 1992—; dir. Rep. Town Com., 1989—. Organizer pack 516 Boy Scouts Am., N.Y.C., 1976; fund raiser, chmn. Lewisboro Neighbor's Club, South Salem, 1979; sec. Ridgefield HIst. Dist. Commn., 1984-85, Greenwich Hist. Dist. Commn., 1988-90, Friends of the Byram Shubert Libr. Bd., 1989-93; del. Parents Together, 1980; underwriting com. Bruce Mus. Ball, 1990-91; alternate Greenwich Planning and Zoning Commn., 1990-93; founding trustee Byram Scholarship fund, 1991—; co-founder Byram River Watershed Alliance, 1995—; bd. dirs. YMCA, Greenwich, 1997—. Named Mother of Yr., Town and Village Newspaper, 1974. Home: 29 Field Point Dr Greenwich CT 06830-7013 Office: Ho of Reps State Capitol Hartford CT 06106

HESS, WALTER OTTO, surgeon; b. Zurich, Switzerland, July 26, 1918; s. Walter and Hermine (Schäublin) H.; m. Charlotte Schmidlin, May 17, 1947 (dec. Feb. 1974); children: Gerhard Walter, Claudia Renate. MD, U. Zurich, 1944. Lic. MD, Switzerland. Resident pathology Swiss Rsch. Inst., Davos, Switzerland, 1945-46; resident Surgical Clinic U. Basle, Switzerland, 1946-49, first resident, 1950-57; resident Surgical Clinic U. Heidelberg, Fed. Republic of Germany, 1949-50; prof. surgery Alexandria (Egypt) U., 1957-59; pvt. practice Zurich, Switzerland, 1960-81; prof. Surgery U. Basle, Switzerland, 1964-85; leading physician Inst. Med. Experts, Zurich, 1988-93. Author: Chirurgie des Pankreas, 1950, Operative Cholangiographie, 1954, Erkrankungen der Gallenwege und des Pankreas, 1959, 1986-93 (prize 1960), 2d edit. in English, French and Spanish, 1996, Textbook of Bilio-pancreatic Diseases, 4 vols., 1997. Dep. Cantonal Parliament, Zurich, 1968-81; del. Internat. Red Cross, Geneva, 1969-72; Counsellor Community Coun., Kilchberg, Switzerland, 1975-79. Capt. Swiss Army, 1951-54. Named Hon. Mem. Italian Soc. Surgery, Rome, 1972, Acad. Lancisiana, Rome, 1973, Surgical Assn. Cuba, Havana, 1974, Acad. Peruana de Cirugua, 1975, Colegio Brasiliero de Cirugioes, 1975, Acad. de Ciencias Medicas de Cordoba, 1977, Hon. Prof. U. Ica, Peru, 1978. Mem. Swiss Med. Assn., Swiss Soc. Surgery, Swiss Soc. Gastroenterology, Internat. Hepato-Pancreato-Biliary Assn. (hon.), Masons (W. master 1984-90 In Labore Virtus, Grand Officer Swiss Grand Lodge). Mem. Liberal Party. Avocation: history. Home: Chalberweidstrasse 47, Canton Zurich, CH-8127 Forch Switzerland

HESSE, CHRISTIAN HERMANN, mathematics and economics educator; b. Oberkirchen, Germany, Aug. 2, 1960; s. Robert and Renate H. MA, Ind. U., 1984; MS, Harvard U., 1986, PhD, 1987. Vis. rsch. fellow Australian Nat. U., 1985-86, 1986-87; prof. U. Stuttgart, 1991—; rsch. fellow Harvard U., 1984-87; asst. prof. U. Calif., Berkeley, 1987-91; vis. prof. U Concepcion, Chile, 95-95; cons. DG-Bank, Frankfurt, 1995; adviser U.S. Dept. Def., 1988. Author: Limit Theorems for Linear Processes and Applications, 1987; contbr. articles to profl. jours. including Econometric Theory, Annals of Statistics and Jour. Multivariate Analysis. Recipient Alan Abrams meml. award Stanford U., 1984. Mem. Internat. Statis. Inst., Studienstiftung des Dt Volkes, Gesellschaft fuer Angewandte Math. and Mechanik (GAMM), Inst. Math. Stats. (IMS) Deutsche Mathemat Vereing (DMV), Harvard Club. Home: Wiesenaeckerstr 19, 70619 Stuttgart Germany Office: U Stuttgart, Pfaffenwaldring 57, 70569 Stuttgart Germany

HESSE, MICHAEL, chemist; b. Tel-Aviv, Israel, Mar. 22, 1954; s. Ernest and Lily (Stern) H.; m. Riveka Newman, Sept. 2, 1975; children: Alon, Vered, Erez. BS, U. Beer-Sheva, Israel, 1979; degree in contamination control, U. Utha, Israel, 1985; degree in engring., Technion Inst., Israel, 1991. Rsch. chemist Min. Def., Israel, 1972-82; group leader quality assurance lab. Dor Chems. Ltd., Haifa, Israel, 1982-83; group leader polymer rsch. lab. Frutarom, Israel, 1983-84; quality assurance, contamination lab. mgr. Nat. Semiconductor, Migdal Haemek, Israel, 1984-91; quality assurance, quality control mgr. Unidress Industries Ltd., Haifa, 1991-95; gen. mgr. Uniclean, Haifa, 1996—. Sgt. maj. Israeli Def. Force, 1972-75. Mem. Am. Soc. Quality, Inst. Environ. Scis. Office: Uniclean, PO Box 10335, 26111 Haifa Bay Israel

HESSE, VOLKER, pediatrician; b. Röbel, Müritz, Germany, Aug. 18, 1942; s. Werner Walter and Marianne (Gross) H.; m. Gertraud Daniel, May 25, 1974; children: Lydia-Kathrin, Juliana. Med. degree summa cum laude, Friederich Schiller U., Jena, Germany, 1968, MD, 1969, Dr.sc.med., 1979. Head dept. pediatric endocrinology Univ. Children's Hosp., Jena, 1979-89; med. dir. Children's Hosp. Berlin-Lichtenberg, Germany, 1989-91; vice med. dir., chmn. dept. pediatrics Hosp. Berlin-Lichtenberg, 1991, head dept. social pediatrics, 1997—; prof. pediatrics Friedrich Schiller U., 1988; hon. prof. Humboldt U., Berlin, 1989. Editor: (textbook) Endocrinology in Childhood and Adolescence, 1982; author: Iodine and Rickets Proplylaxis 1976-1989, 1990 (Finkelstein prize, Schlossman prize 1981); contbr. articles to profl. jours. Silbert scholar UCLA, 1984. Mem. European Soc. Pediatric Endocrinology (pres. 1990-91), Lawson Wilkins Pediatric Endocrine Soc., European Soc. for Pediatric Rsch., N.Y. Acad. Scis., North German Pediatric Soc. (pres. 1996-97), Berlin Goethe Soc. (coun. mem.). Avocations: medical history, history of endocrinology, German classic literature, publications on the poets Goethe and Schiller. Office: Hosp Berlin Dept Pediatrics, Gotlindestrasse 2-20, D-10365 Berlin Germany

HESSELBEIN, FRANCES RICHARDS, foundation executive, consultant, editor; b. South Fork, Pa.; d. Burgess Harmon and Anne Luke (Wicks) Richards; widowed, 1978; 1 child, John Richards. DHL (hon.), Buena Vista Coll., 1987, Juniata Coll., 1990, Hood Coll., 1991; D Mgmt. (hon.), GM Inst., 1990; LLD (hon.), Wilson Coll., 1991; LHD (hon.), Marymount-Tarrytown Coll., 1993; DHL (hon.), Boston Coll., 1994, U. Nebr., Kearney, 1994, Lafayette Coll., 1995, Carroll Coll., 1996, Fairleigh Dickinson U., 1996, Muhlenburg Coll., 1996; LLD (hon.), Moravian Coll., 2000. CEO Talus Rock Girl Scout Coun., Johnstown, 1970-74, Penn Laurel Girl Scout Coun., York, Pa., 1974-76, Girl Scouts U.S., N.Y.C., 1976-90; pres., CEO Peter F. Drucker Found. Nonprofit Mgmt., N.Y.C., 1990-99, chmn., 1999—; bd. dirs. Mut. of Am. Ins. Co., N.Y.C.; mem. nat. bd. visitors Peter F. Drucker Grad. Mgmt. Sch. Claremont (Calif.) Grad. Sch., 1987—; chmn. bd. govs. Josephson Ethics Inst.; mem. adv. com. to bd. dirs. N.Y. Stock Exch., 1988-91; bd. govs. Ctr. for Creative Leadership, Greensboro, N.C., 1992-98; mem. adv. bd. Harvard Bus. Sch.'s Initiative on Social Enterprise, Harvard's Kennedy Sch. Govt. Nonprofit Policy and Leadership Program. Editor-in-chief Leader to Leader; co-editor The Leader of the Future, The Organization of the Future, The Community of the Future, Drucker Found. Future Series, Leader to Leader Book, 1999, Leading Beyond the Walls, 1999. Trustee Juniata Coll., Huntingdon, Pa., 1988—, Allentown (Pa.) Coll., 1988-97; mem. Pres.'s Adv. Com. on Points of Light Initiative Found., 1989; bd. dirs. Nat. Exec. Svc. Corps., N.Y., Commn. on Nat. and Cmty. Svc., 1991-94, Village Found., also vice-chmn.; mem. adv. bd. The Leadership Inst., U. So. Calif., 1991, Harvard Bus. Sch.'s Initiative on Social Enterprise, Harvard U.'s John F. Kennedy Sch. Govt. Nonprofit Policy and Leadership Program. Recipient Outstanding Achievement award Inter-Svc. Club Coun., Johnstown, 1976, Entrepreneurial Woman award Women Bus. Owners of N.Y., 1984, Nat. Leadership award United Way of Am., Washington, 1985, Disting. Cmty. Svc. award Mut. of Am. Ins. Co., 1985, Dir.'s Choice award Nat. Women's Econ. Alliance, 1989, Pa. Soc. Disting. Citizen award, 1991, Wilbur M. McFeeley award Internat. Mgmt. Coun. YMCA, 1993; inducted into the Bus. Hall of Fame, Johnstown, 1995; named Outstanding Exec., Savvy Mag., 1985; on cover BusinessWeek, 1990, Presdl. Medal of Freedom, 1998; featured in Chief Exec. mag., 1995, Fortune, 1995, 96, Chapel of Four Chaplaing Gold Legion of Hon. medal, 1999; named Disting. Alumni Fellow U. Pitts., 1999, Disting. Dau. of Pa., Gov. Ridge, 1999, Woman of Yr., Boy Scouts of Greater N.Y. Mem. Sky Club, Pa. Soc. Office: Peter F Drucker Found Nonprofit Mgmt 320 Park Ave 3d Fl New York NY 10022-6815

HESTER, EDWARD JOHN, industrial psychologist, researcher; b. Chgo., Jan. 23, 1938; s. Edward J. and Irene M. (Kalteux) H.; m. Sanda A. Waljeski, June 22, 1961 (div. May 1985); children: Katrina, Lisa, Gretchen, Ingrid, Edward, Heidi; m. Mary L. Derum, May 23, 1985; children: Jane, Glynnis, James, Neill. BS in psychology, Loyola U., Chgo., 1960, MA in social and indsl. psychology, 1965, PhD in indsl. psychology, 1969. Registered psychologist, Ill. Dir. rehab. Goodwill Industries, Chgo., 1962-76; rehab. specialist Goodwill Industries of Am., Dallas, 1976-78; dir. human svcs. Goodwill Industries, Kalamazoo, 1978-80; pvt. practice Cary, Ill., 1980-81; dir. ctr. for handicapped City Colls., Chgo., 1981-83; dir. rsch. Menninger Return to Work Ctrs., Topeka, 1983-93; instr. Loyola U., Chgo., 1966-73; pres. Hester Evaluation Systems, Chgo., 1984—. Author: Menninger RTW Scale, 1986 (JPD Rsch. award 1987, 1990), Worker Compensation Rehabilitation, 1989. Mary E. Switzer scholar Switzer Found., 1986, 95. Mem. Nat. Rehab. Assn., Nat. Assn. Rehab. Profls. in Pvt. Sector, Assn. Test Pubs., Am. Psychol. Assn. Avocations: fishing, gardening. Office: Hester Evaluation Systems Inc 2410 SW Granthurst Ave Topeka KS 66611-1274

HESTER, KARLTON EDWARD, composer, performer, music educator; b. El Paso, Tex., Feb. 11, 1949; s. Webb and Clara (Briggs) H.; m. Bette Jean Hered; 1 child, Karlton William. MusB, U. Tex., El Paso, 1971; MusM, San Francisco State U., 1978; PhD in Composition, CUNY, 1990. Music dir. Eisenhower H.S., Rialto, Calif., 1971-74, San Francisco and Oakland (Calif.) Pub. Schs., 1977-82, Contempory Jazz Art Movement, San Francisco and N.Y.C., 1977-82; pres. Hesteria Records & Pub. Co., San Francisco and N.Y.C., 1981—; asst. prof. Coll. of S.I., N.Y., 1990-91; artist in residence N.Y. Found. for Arts, N.Y.C., 1984-88, N.Y. Found. for the Arts, N.Y.C., 1984-91; composer in residence Western Edition Cultural Ctr., San Francisco, 1980-81; asst. prof. Coll. S.I., N.Y., 1990-91; Herbert Gussman

dir. jazz studies Cornell U., Ithaca, N.Y., 1991-2000; dir. jazz studies U. Calif., Santa Cruz, 2000—; pres. Interdisciplinary Artists Aggregation, Inc., Ithaca, N.Y.; adj. prof. Bronx (N.Y.) C.C., 1985-88, Coll. S.I., N.Y., 1988-91; composer in residence, music dir. Cazadero Music Camp, Berkeley, Calif., 1982. Author: The Melodic and Polyrhythmic Development of John Coltrane's Spontaneous Composition in a Racist Society, 1997, From Africa to Afrocentric Innovations Some Call Jazz, 2000; editor Juba Jour.; producer, composer record albums. Mem. Rosicrucian Order, San Jose, Calif., 1980—. Recipient S.I. Cmty. TV NOVA video award for A Children's Jazz Video; grantee NEA, 1985, 89, New Engl. Coun. for Arts, 1986, S.I. Coun. for Arts, 1987, 90, 91, Fund for U.S. Artists at Internat. Festival & Exhbns., 1994-95, Howard Found. merit award in composition, 1996; fellow Mellon Found., 1991-92. Mem. ASCAP (popular and standard awards), Nat. Flute Assn., Am. Fedn. Musicians. Avocation: sports. Office: U Calif Santa Cruz Music Dept Santa Cruz CA 95064

HESTER, LINDA HUNT, university dean, counselor; b. Winston-Salem, N.C., June 16, 1938; d. Hanselle Lindsay and Jennie Sarepta (Hunt) H. BS with honors, U. Wis., 1960, MS, 1964; PhD, Mich. State U., 1971. Lic. ednl. counselor, Wis. Instr. health and phys. edn. for women U. Tex., Austin, 1960-62; asst. dean women U. Ill., Urbana, 1964-66; dean of women, asst. prof. sociology and phys. edn. Tex. Woman's U., Denton, 1971-73; rsch. assoc. bur. higher edn. Mich. Dept. Edn., Lansing, 1969-70; counselor Dallas Challenge and Dallas Ind. Sch. Dist., 1989-90. Bd. dirs. Dallas Opera, 1986—; Stradivarious mem. Dallas Symphony, 1991—; assoc. mem. Dallas Mus. Art, 1991—; friend of Kimbell Art Mus., Philharmonic Ctr. for Arts, Naples, Fla., Naples Mus. Art. Fellow coll. edn. Mich. State U., 1968. Mem. Am. Counseling Assn., Am. Coll. Pers. Assn., Nat. Assn. Women in Edn., Brookhaven Country Club, Wyndemere Country Club, Delta Kappa Gamma, Alpha Lambda Delta. Republican. Presbyterian. Avocations: golf, reading, sailing, cooking, travel. Home and Office: 7606 Wellcrest Dr Dallas TX 75230-4857

HESTER, PAUL V., career officer. BSBA in Accountancy, U. Miss., 1969, MBA in Accountancy, 1970; student pilot tng., Columbus AFB, Miss., 1971; student, Squadron Officer Sch., 1974, Air Command and Staff Coll., 1979; M in Mil. Arts and Scis., U.S. Army Command and Gen. Staff Coll., 1980; student, Nat. War Coll., 1990, Harvard U., 1992; sr. def. fellow, Harvard U., 1993. Commd. 2d lt. USAF, 1970, advanced through grades to maj. gen., 1998; stationed at Davis-Monthan AFB, Ariz., 1972, 73-74; aircraft comdr. 354th Tactical Fighter Squadron, Korat Royal Thai AFB, Thailand, 1973; various positions Luke AFB, Ariz., 1974-76; F-15 instr., flight examiner 525th Tactical Fighter Squadron, Bitburg Air Base, W. Germany, 1977-79; stationed at Langley AFB, Va., 1980-86; chief Ho. of Reps. liaison, sec. Air Force legis. liaison Hdqs. USAF, Washington, 1986-89; stationed at Kadena Air Base, Japan, 1990-92; div. chief weapons tech. control div. Joint Chiefs of Staff, Washington, 1993-94; Joint Chiefs of Staff rep. Com. Security and Cooperation Europe, Vienna, Austria, 1994-95; comdr. 35th Fighter Wing, Misawa Air Base, Japan, 1995-97, 53rd Wing, Eglin AFB, Fla., 1997; dir., legis. liaison Office Sec. Air Force, Washington, 1997-99; comdr. U.S. Forces in Japan, 5th Air Force, Yokota Air Base, Japan, 1999—. Decorated Legion of Merit with oak leaf cluster, Air medal with four oak leaf clusters; Vietnam Gallantry Cross with palm. Office: 374 CS/SCBBSS, Tijita Air Base Japan

HESTHAMMER, JONNY, geologist; b. Bergen, Norway, Mar. 7, 1965; s. Jan Gerhard and Solfrid Johanne Saele Hesthammer; m. Hilde Anita Larsen, Aug. 24, 1996; 1 child, Jostein Larsen. Cand. Magisterii, U. Bergen, 1988, PhD, 1999; MS, U. B.C., Vancouver, Can., 1991. Field geologist Geol. Survey of Can., Vancouver, 1988-90; geologist Husky Oil, Calgary, Can., 1991; sr. geologist Statoil, Bergen, Norway, 1991—; PhD rschr. U. Bergen, 1995-99. Contbr. numerous articles to profl. jours. Mem. Norsk Geologisk Forening (Reusch award 2000), European Assn. of Geoscientists and Engrs. (Disting. Lectr. award 1997). Home: Veslefrikkveien 26, 5142 Fyllingsdalen Norway

HESTHOLM, STIG OTTAR, scientist, consultant; b. Bergen, Hordaland, Norway, May 15, 1962; s. Norvald Artur and Grace Kirsten Johanna (Skiftesvik) H.; m. Elisabeth Mosby Irgens (div. 1997); 1 child, Maja; m. Wenche Listhaug; 1 child, Eystein. BSc in Applied Math., U. Bergen, Norway, 1985, MSc in Applied Math., 1987; PhD in Geophysics, U. Bergen, 1999, Rice U., 1999. Scientist Scientific Ctr. IBM, Bergen, 1987-94; rschr. U. Bergen, 1995, cons., 1999—; rschr. Norsk Hydro, Bergen, 1985; tchr. AOF, Norway, Bergen, 1990-91; group leader, rsch. asst. U. Bergen, 1985-86, seismologist, 1995-97. Contbr. articles to profl. publs. Corporal The Norwegian Army, 1981-82. Mem. Soc. for Exploration Geophysicists, European Assn. of Geoscientists and Engrs., European Geophys. Soc., Am. Geophys. Union, Seismol. Soc. of Am. Avocations: classical music, skiing, choirs. Home: Johan Hjorts Vei 65, 5081 Bergen Norway Office: U Bergen Solid Earth Phys, Allégaten 41, 5007 Bergen Norway

HESTON, RENATE, nursing administrator; b. Gross-Strehlitz, Germany; came to U.S., 1960; d. Guenter and Elisabeth (Englich) Paetzold; m. Leonard Lancaster Heston; children: Barbara and Ardis (twins). BSN; BS in Human Svcs., U. Minn., 1987. RN, Minn., Iowa, Oreg.; cert. nursing supr.-adminstr.; bd. cert. gerontolog. nurse. Staff nurse, asst. head nurse; head nurse psychiat. unit Oreg. State Hosp., U. Oreg., U. Iowa Med. Sch.; nurse supr. The Wilder Found., New Brighton, Minn.; cons. in field. Co-author: The Medical Casebook of Adolf Hitler. Bd. dirs., dir. vol. svcs. U. N.A. Minn., 1973-88. Mem. AAUW, U. Minn. Alumni Assn. Avocations: classical music, reading, gardening, visual arts, gourmet cooking. E-mail: clinic-s.eben-po:rhestont@fairview.org. Home: 128 Windsor Ct New Brighton MN 55112-3372 Office: Ebenezer Social Ministry 2545 Portland Ave Minneapolis MN 55404-4406

HETFLEJŠ, JIŘÍ, chemist, researcher; b. Trutnov, E. Bohemia, Czech Republic, Jan. 10, 1936; s. František and Marie (Bieglova) H.; m. Blanka Podolská, June 30, 1965; children: Silvie, Martin. Engr., U. Pardubice, Czech Republic, 1961; PhD, Inst. Chem. Proc. ASCZ, Prague, 1964; DSc, Czech Acad. Sci., 1980. Rsch. assoc. MIT, Boston, 1966-67; head rsch. group Inst. Chem. Proc. Fundamentals/Acad. Sci. Czech Republic, Prague, 1969-85, dep.to dir., 1985-90, head dept., 1985-96. Editor Collection Czech Chem. Soc., 1969-99; contbr. articles to profl. jours. Recipient Sci. awards Czech Acad. Sci., 1979, 82, 84, Chemistry award Czech Acad. Sci./GDR, Prague/Berlin, 1980. Mem. Czech Chem. Soc. Roman Catholic. Office: Inst Chem Proc Fundamentals Czech Acad Scis, Rozvojová 135, 165 02 Prague Czech Republic

HETHERWICK, GILBERT LEWIS, lawyer; b. Winnsboro, La., Oct. 30, 1920; s. Septimus and Addie Louise (Gilbert) H.; m. Joan Friend Gibbons, May 31, 1945 (dec. Aug. 1964); children: Janet Hetherwick Pumphrey, Ann Hetherwick Lyons Winegeart, Gilbert, Carol Hetherwick Sutton, Katherine Hetherwick Hummell; m. Mertis Elizabeth Cook, June 6, 1967. BA summa cum laude, Centenary Coll., 1942; JD, Tulane U., 1949. BAr: La. 1949. With legal dept. NorAm Energy Corp., Shreveprot, La., 1949-53; dir. Blanchard, Walker, O'Quin and Roberts, PLC, Shreveport, 1953-99, of counsel, 2000—. Mem. Shreveport City Charter Revision Com., 1955; mem. Shreveport Mcpl. Fire and Police Civil Svc. Bd., 1956-92, vice chmn., 1957-78, chmn., 1978-88. Served with AUS, 1942-46. Recipient Tulane U. Law Faculty medal, 1949. Mem. ABA, La. Bar Assn., Shreveport Bar Assn. (pres. 1987), Energy Bar Assn., Order of Coif, Phi Delta Phi, Omicron Delta Kappa. Episcopalian. Home: 4604 Fairfield Ave Shreveport LA 71106-1432 Office: Bank One Tower Shreveport LA 71101

HETLAGE, ROBERT OWEN, lawyer; b. St. Louis, Jan. 9, 1931; s. George C. and Doris M. (Talbot) H.; m. Anne R. Willis, Sept. 24, 1960; children: Mary T., James C., Thomas K. AB, Washington U., St. Louis, 1952, LLB, 1954; LLM, George Washington U., 1957. Bar: Mo. 1954, U.S. Dist. Ct. (ea. dist.) Mo. 1954, U.S. Supreme Ct. 1957. Ptnr. Hetlage & Hetlage, 1958-65; ptnr. Peper, Martin, Jensen, Maichel & Hetlage, St. Louis, 1966-97, chmn., 1994-97; of counsel Blackwell Sanders Peper Martin LLP, St. Louis, 1998—. 1st lt. U.S. Army, 1954-58. Fellow Am. Bar Found. (life, bd. trustees 1996—); mem. ABA (chmn. real property, probate and trust law sect. 1981-82), Bar Assn. Met. St. Louis (pres. 1967-68), Mo. Bar (pres. 1976-77), Am. Coll. Real Estate Lawyers (pres. 1985-86), Am. Judicature Soc., Anglo-Am. Real Property Inst. (chmn. 1991). Office: Blackwell Sanders Peper Martin LLP 720 Olive St Saint Louis MO 63101-2338

HETLELID, KJELL BIRGER, pharmacist; b. Hjelmeland, Norway, Jan. 26, 1938; s. Mikkel and Thea (Roren) H.; m. Solveig Norunn Rodde, Aug. 10, 1963; children: Knud, Bodill, Siri. Degree in pharmacy, U. Oslo, 1963; cert. specialist in hosp. pharmacy, Norwegian Govt., 1992. Chief mgr. Svane-apoteket, Stavanger, Norway, 1963-67; govt. appointee to establish a hosp. pharmacy Govt. of Nordlis, Stavanger, 1969-79, Govt. of Brundtlands, Forde, Norway, 1979-92; apptd. to own/operate a pharmacy group Govt. of Brundtlands, Volda, Norway, 1992—. Mem. city coun. of Stavanger, 1971-75; cons. in social affairs for Govt. of Norway; mem. of jury at Gulating Lagmanns Rett, Stavanger; elected mem. for Labor Party for Harlem-Brundtland Prime Minister Campaign. Capt. Norwegian Army, 1965-81. Fellow Fedn. Internat. Pharm., Internat. Aviation Passenger Assn., Norsk Framasoytisk Forening, European Assn. of Hosp. Pharmacists, Norges/Apoteker/Forening. Achievements include being first pharmacist in Europe to design and engineer the home parenteral nutrition for patients with short bowel syndrome in childhood. Avocations: botanical herbs, tropical orchis and birds, gardening, photography. Home: Solakrossvegen 13D, 4050 Sola Norway Office: Sola Apotek Pb 16, N-4050 Sola Norway

HETTLICH, FRANK WILHELM HORST, mathematician, researcher; b. Osnabrück, Germany, Apr. 21, 1963; s. Johannes and Lieselott (Ackermann) H.; m. Christine Steiner, Aug. 15, 1989 (div. June 1991); m. Regina Grosch, Oct. 20, 1995; children: Benjamin, Rebecca. Diploma, U. Göttingen, Germany, 1989; Doctorate, U. Erlangen, Germany, 1992; habil., U. Erlangen, 1999. Rsch. asst. U. Göttingen, 1989-90, U. Erlangen, 1992-00, U. Karlsruhe, 2000—. Contbr. articles to profl. jours. Grantee U. Erlangen, Germany, 1990-92, Deutsche Forschungsgemeinschaft, 1995. Avocations: family activities, playing violin, jogging. Office: U Karlsruhe, Englerstr 2, 76128 Karlsruhe Bavaria, Germany

HETZEL, ALICE M., statistician, researcher; b. Guthrie, Okla., Feb. 9, 1922; d. Eugene Tilden and Ina (Pence) H. BS, Okla. State U., 1942; post-grad., Georgetown U., 1945. Economist Navy Dept., Washington, 1943-46; statistician USPHS, Washington, 1946-50, U.S. Navy Dept., Washington, 1950-61; spl. asst. to chief Nat. Office Vital Stats., Washington, 1961-68, chief marriage and divorce stats., 1968-74; dep. dir. divsn. vital stats. NCHS, Washington, 1974-83; rschr. self employed, Silver Spring, Md., 1983—. Author: U.S. Vital Statistics System 1950-1995, 1997, Marriage and Divorce Statistics and the Health Department, 1971, Health Survey of the Trust Territory of the Pacific Islands, 1959; co-author: Vital Statistics Rates in the U.S. 1940-1960, 1968. Recipient Exemplary Svc. award Nat. Vital Statistics Program, 1983. Mem. Argyle Country Club. Home: 1300 Ednor Rd Silver Spring MD 20905-5110

HETZEL, PATRICK LOUIS, marketing educator; b. Phalsbourg, France, July 2, 1964; s. Rodolphe and Irene (Mertz) H.; m. Fabienne Nina Maennlein, Sept. 1, 1990; 2 children. MBA, Robert Schuman U., 1986; PhD, Inst. Adminstrn. Enterprises, Lyon, France, 1993. Mktg. asst. K-Way, Pirmasens, Germany, 1986-87; asst. prof. ESC, Lyon, 1988; from asst. prof. to assoc. prof. Jean Noulin U., Lyon, France, 1989-97; prof. Robert Shuman U., Strasbourg, France, 1997-99, U. Pantheon-Assas, Paris, 1999—; vis. prof. Carlson Sch., Mpls., 1996, Terry Coll., Athens, Ga., 1997, U. Bern, Switzerland, 1997-98. Office: CIFFOP, 83 bis rue Notre Dame Champ, 75006 Paris France

HETZHEIM, ANNEMARIE MAGDALENA, organic chemistry educator; b. Hof, Bavaria, Germany, Aug. 3, 1935; d. Kurt Franz and Charlotte (Wiedemann) H. Diploma in chemistry, U. Greifswald (Germany), 1960, PhD, 1963, habilitation, 1968. Sci. asst. Inst. Organic Chemistry, Greifswald, 1960-64, asst. prof. organic chemistry, rschr., 1964-68; dir. rsch. group heterocyclic chemistry Acad. Sci., Riga, Latvia, 1970-72; assoc. prof. organic chemistry Inst. Organic Chemistry, Greifswald, 1972-90; vis. prof. Inst. Organic Chemistry, Würzburg, Germany, 1991; prof. organic chemistry, prin. Inst. Organic Chemistry, Greifswald, 1992-98; dir. dept. organic chemistry Inst. Chemistry and Biochemistry, Greifswald, 1999—. Contbr. numerous articles to profl. jours. Mem. German Chem. Soc. Avocations: mountain hiking, classical music, painting, travelling. Home: Friedrich-Krüger, Str 17, 17489 Greifswald Germany Office: Inst Organic Chemistry, Univ Soldtmannstr 16, 17487 Greifswald Germany

HETZNER, MARC A., lawyer; b. Logansort, Ind., Apr. 24, 1953; s. John R. and Nelma L. (Byrt) H.; m. Rosalie M.; children: Collette N., Christopher R., Kimberly A. BA, Ind. U., 1975, MBA, 1983, JD, 1983. Bar: Ind. 1983, U.S. Dist. Ct. (so. dist.) Ind. 1983, U.S. Tax Ct. 1983, U.S. Ct. Appeals (7th cir.) 1988. Ptnr. Krieg Devault Alexander & Capehart, Indpls., 1989—. Contbr. articles to profl. jours. 1st lt. U.S. Army, 1975-79. Fellow Am. Coll. Trust & Estate Counsel; mem. Ind. State Bar Found., Indpls. Estate Planning Coun. Office: Krieg DeVault Alexander & Capehart 1 Indiana Sq Ste 2800 Indianapolis IN 46204-2079

HEUDIER, JEAN-LOUIS FERNAND, astronomer, educator; b. Paris, July 3, 1944; s. Jean Francois and Andree Helene (Dargnat) H.; m. France Michel, July 12, 1968; children: Claire, Laure. M in Physics, 1968, diploma in Astrophysics, 1970. Head Schmidt Telescope, France, 1973-89; chmn. I.A.U. on Photography, 1978-81, Astrorama, France, 1987-96; chmn. Animation Scientifique Sud Est Mediterranée, France, 1979-82, Assn. Niçoise Animation Info. Scientifique, France, 1982-86, PARSEC, France, 1986—. Author: La Photographie Astronomique A Grand Champ, 1992, Objectif Cosmos, 1992, Le Livre du Ciel, 1995, Le Livre de la Lune, 1996, Abedaire du Suleil, 1994; editor: Astronomical Photography, 1976, 78, 91, 92. E. Girard award Soc. Astronomique de France, 1977, Jean Perrin award Soc. Française de Physique, 1982, Flamarion award Soc. Astronomique de France, 1991. Home: 93 Quai des Etats Unis, 06300 Nice France Office: PARSEC, 18 Avenue Maréchal Foch, 06000 Nice France

HEUER, BRURIA, plant physiologist, researcher; b. Piatra Neamtz, Romania, Apr. 12, 1949; arrived in Israel, 1961; d. Theodor and Sally (Rosenfeld) H. BSc, Bar-Ilan U., Ramat Gan, Israel, 1971; MSc, Hebrew U., Rehovot, Israel, 1973, PhD, 1979. Rsch. asst. ARO, Bet Dagan, Israel, 1971-79, scientist, 1978—; lectr. internat. courses, Bet Dagan, 1987-98; bd. dirs. Capital Com., Israel, 1987-89; examiner GITT, Israel, 1990—; rsch. assoc. U. Ill., Chgo., 1981; assoc. prof. U. Ill., Urbana-Champaign, 1995-96; cons. Chief Scientist of Ministry of Agr., Israel, 1987-89; instr. Rupin Coll., Israel, 1990—; cons. Dept. Agr., Israel, 1991-94. Mem. Am. Soc. Plant Physiology, Scandinavian Soc. Plant Physiology, Am. Soc. Soil Sci. Mem. Labor Party. Avocations: books, movies, bridge. Office: ARO, Volcani Ctr, POB 6, Inst Soil Water Environ Scs, Bet Dagan 50250, Israel

HEUER, MARTIN, temporary services executive; b. Algoma, Wis., Oct. 16, 1934; s. Orland Fred and Gertrude Mayme (Zimmerman) H.; m. Rita Mae Prokash, Oct. 27; children: Martin Joseph, Ronald James. AA, SUNY, 1973, AS, 1975. Commd. 2d lt. C.E. U.S. Army, 1954, advanced through grades to lt. col., 1968; flight comdr., adminstrv. and maintenance officer 1st Aviation Co., Ft. Riley, 1958-61; with 937th Engr. Aviation Co. 937th Engr. Aviation Co., Panama, Lima, Peru, Panama and Lima, Peru, 1961-65; maintenance officer 174th Aviation Co. 174th Aviation Co., Vietnam, 1966; adj. 14th Combat Aviation Bn. 14th Combat Aviation Bn., 1966-67; dir. sys., curriculum and spl. projects divsn. Army Primary Helecopter Sch., Ft. Wolters, Tex., 1967-69; aviation advisor Wis. Army N.G. Wis. Army N.G., West Bend, 1969-70; airfield comdr. Cu Chi Army Airfield, Cu Chi Army Airfield, Vietnam, 1970-71; engr. advisor Wis. N.G., Eau Claire, Vietnam, 1971-73; mgr., area mgr. Manpower Temp. Svcs., Eau Claire, 1973-76; exec. v.p. Aide Svcs. Inc., KARI Svcs. Inc., Tampa, 1976-80; pres., chmn. Aide Svcs. Inc., KARI Svcs. Inc., Tampa, Fla., 1980—; pres., chmn. bd. Aide Svcs. Inc. and KARI Svcs., Inc., Tampa, Fla., 1980—; pres., chmn. Capitol Svcs. Inc., Tallahassee, 1982-86; pres., chmn. AIDE 2000 Inc., 1998—, pres. bd. dirs. Ft. Wolters Fed. Credit Union, 1967-69; chmn. bd. Digital Control Corp., Seminole, Fla., 1981-98. Pres. Seminole H.S. Band Boosters, 1974-79; v.p. Pinellas County Band Boosters, 1977-78; bd. dirs. Seminole H.S. Booster Assn., 1975-79, pres., 1978-79. Decorated Legionof merit with 1 oak leaf cluster, Bronze star medal with 3 oak leaf clusters, Air medal with 3 oak leaf clusters; recipient First Band Booster Pres. award Seminole H.S., 1979, Svc. to Mankind award Sertoma, 1980. Mem. Assn. Manpower Franchise Owners (dir. 1980-82, 83-86, treas. 1981-82, chmn. 1984-86), Assn. U.S. Army (chmn. bd. govs. 1981-82, asst. state v.p. Suncoast chpt. and Fla., 1981-82, state v.p. 1982-84, chmn. chpt. comms. com. nat. adv. bd. 1982-86, mem. corp. adv. coun. 1985-90, bd. dirs. Sun Coast chpt. 1994—), Army Aviation Assn. Am., Air Force Assn., Soc. Am. Mil. Engrs., Res. Officers Assn., Ret. Officers Assn., Future Farmers Am. Alumni Assn., Nat. Assn. Temp. Svcs. (treas./sec. Fla. chpt. 1991-94), Vietnam Helicopter Pilots Assn. (bd. dirs. Fla. chpt. 1993—, v.p. 1996-98, pres. 1998-2000, chmn. bd. dirs. 2000—). Republican. Office: Ste 102 5402 Beaumont Center Blvd Tampa FL 33634-5202

HEUER, SAM TATE, lawyer; b. Batesville, Ark., July 11, 1952; s. Albert A. and Mary (Baker) H.; children: Noal Tate, Polly Anna, Charles Albert; m. Max Parker. BBA in Banking and Fin., U. Miss., 1974; JD, U. Ark., 1978. Bar: Ark. 1979, U.S. Dist. Ct. (ea. and we. dist.) Ark. 1979, U.S. Ct. Appeals (8th cir.) 1980. Dep. pros. atty. 4th Jud. Dist., Fayetteville, Ark., 1979-80; assoc. Davis Bracey & Heuer, Springdale, Ark., 1980-81; pvt. practice, Batesville, 1981-86; pros. atty. 16th Jud. Dist., Batesville, 1983-86; assoc., salesman Crews & Assocs., Little Rock, 1987-88; assoc. John Wesley Hall P.C., Little Rock, 1988-93; ptnr. Heuer Law Firm, Little Rock, 2000—. Mem. ATLA, Ark. Prosecutor's Assn. (bd. dirs. 1984-86, v.p. 1985-86), Ark. Trial Lawyers Assn., Am. Trial Lawyers Assn., Pulaski County Attys. Assn. Democrat. Episcopalian. Office: Heuer Law Firm 124 W Capitol Ave Ste 1650 Little Rock AR 72201-3758

HEUISLER, CHARLES WILLIAM, lawyer; b. Phila., May 24, 1941; s. Isaac Kilner and Mary Gertrude (Smith) H.; m. Judith Ann Hargadon, June 26, 1965; children: Karen L. Heuisler Murphy, Susan M. Heuisler McCabe, Charles W. Jr. BA in Modern Lang., Coll. of Holy Cross, 1963; JD, Villanova U., 1966. Bar: N.J. 1966, U.S. Dist. Ct. N.J. 1966, U.S. Ct. Appeals (3d cir.) 1970, U.S. Supreme Ct. 1972; cert. civil trial atty. Am. Bd. Trial Advs. Law clk. to Hon. John B. Wick, Superior Ct. of N.J., Chancery Divsn., Camden, 1966-67; shareholder Archer & Greiner, Haddonfield, N.J., 1972—. Counsel, mem. adv. bd. Haddonfield Symphony Soc., 1980—; chmn. South Jersey Performing Arts Ctr., 1992-98. Mem. FBA, N.J. Bar Assn. (trustee from Camden County 1989-93), Camden County Bar Assn. (pres. 1985-86, trustee, Peter J. Devine award 1991), Rotary (pres. Camden 1987-88). Avocations: tennis, sailing. Home: 1236 Folkestone Way Cherry Hill NJ 08034-3021 Office: Archer & Greiner PC One Centennial Sq Haddonfield NJ 08033

HEUMAN, DONNA RENA, lawyer; b. Seattle, May 27, 1949; d. Russell George and Edna Inez (Armstrong) H. BA in Psychology, UCLA, 1972; JD, U. Calif., San Francisco, 1985. Cert. shorthand reporter, Calif. Owner Heuman & Assocs., San Francisco, 1978-86; lic. real estate briker Calif., 1990—; co-founder, chair, CFO Atherton Park Foods, Inc., Menlo Park, Calif., 1996—; Mem. Hastings Internat. and Comparative Law Rev., 1984-85; bd. dirs. Saddleback, 1987-89. Jessup Internat. Moot Ct. Competition, 1985, bBd. dirs. N. Fair Oaks Adv. Coun., vice chair, sec. 1993-95. Mem. ABA, NAFE, ATLA, AOPA, Nat. Shorthand Reporters Assn., Women Entrepreneurs, Mensa, Calif. State Bar Assn., Nat. Mus. of Women in the Arts, Calif. Lawyers for the Arts, San Francisco Bar Assn., Commonwealth Club, World Affairs Coun., Zonta (bd. dirs.). Home: 750 18th Ave Menlo Park CA 94025-2018 Office: Superior Ct Calif Hall Of Justice Redwood City CA 94063

HEUMANN, KLEMENS RICHARD, electrical engineering educator, researcher; b. Lünen, Germany, May 15, 1931; s. Aloys and Anna Maria (Frank) H.; m. Renati Heumann. Diploma in engring., Rheinisch-Westfälische Technische Hochschule, Aachen, Fed. Republic Germany, 1956; DEng, Tech. U. Berlin, 1961. Rsch. engr. AEG Rsch. Inst., Berlin, 1956-68, gen. mgr., 1969-78; prof. power electronics U. Hannover, Fed. Republic Germany, 1978-83, Tech. U. Berlin, 1983—; cons. in field. Co-author: Characteristics and Applications, 1968; author: Fundamentals of Power Electronics, 1974, Converter Techniques, 1978; contbr. numerous articles to profl. jours. Recipient William E. Newell award IEEE Power Electronics Soc., 1985. Mem. Verband Deutscher Elektrotechniker, IEEE. Roman Catholic. Avocations: history, bicycling, gardening. Office: Tech U Berlin Electrotech, Einsteinufer 19, D-10587 Berlin 10, Federal Republic of Germany

HEUN, WERNER, law educator; b. Frankfurt, Germany, Sept. 25, 1953; s. Gerhard and Helga (Schunck) H.; m. Sarah Jay Weaver, Feb. 14, 1986; children: James Erik, Julian Gerrit Heun-Weaver. Degree in Law, U. Würzburg, Germany, 1977, Dr.iur.utr., 1983; Habil., U. Bonn, 1988. Rsch. asst. U. Bonn, 1980-83, asst., 1983-88; counselor-at-law Bonn, 1980-83; substitute prof. U. Cologne, Germany, 1988-89, U. Bielefeld, Germany, 1989, U. Hamburg, Germany, 1989-90; prof. law U. Göttingen, Germany, 1990—. Author: Das Mehrheitsprinzip in der Demokratie, 1983, Staatshaushalt und Staatsleitung, 1989, Das Budgetrecht im Regierungssystem der USA, 1989, Funktionell-rechtliche Schranken der Verfassungsgerichtsbarkeit, 1992; co-author: Grundgesetz-Kommentos, 3 vols., 1996-2000. Mem. Vereinigung der deutschen Staatsrechtslehrer, Deutsche Gesellschaft zur Erforschung des Politischen Denkens, Gesellschaft für Rechtsvergleichung, Deutsche Vereinigung für Parlamentsfragen. Office: Inst Allgemeine Staatslehre, Gosslerstrasse 11, D-37073 Göttingen Germany

HEURLIN, BERTEL, political scientist, eductor; b. Copenhagen, Oct. 18, 1935; s. Paul and Kirsten (Bruhn) H.; m. Kirsten Riemer Jørgensen, 1957 (div. 1979); children: Thomas, Anne, Martin. BA, U. Copenhagen, 1956, MA, 1961, PhD, 1962. Sec. Ministry Fgn. Affairs, Copenhagen, 1962-64; assoc. prof. polit. sci. U. Copenhagen, 1964-91, prof. Jean Monnet prof., 1991—; rsch. dir. Danish Inst. Internat. Affairs, Copenhagen, 1996—; vis. rsch. prof. Stanford U., 1973-74, U. Calif., Berkeley, 1985-86; cons. Ministries Edn., Def. and Fgn. Affairs; TV and radio commentator; co-chmn. Nat. Danish Com. on Security and Disarmament, 1981-84, 87-95; mem., sec. Nat. Danish Def. Commn. of 1988, 1997. Author 40 books including The Politics of Disarmament, 1971, Nuclear Weapons Control, 1986, NATO, Europe, Denmark, 1990, Peace and Conflict, 1991, Denmark and the European Union, 1994, Problems of European Security, 1995, Germany in Europe in the 90s, 1996, The World 2000, 1996, The Baltic States in World Politics, 1997, German and Danish Security Policy, 1998, The New World Order, 2000, Global, Regional and National Security, 2000 ; contbr. articles on internat. politics, polit. theory, strategy and arms control to profl. jours. Jean Monnet fellow European Univ. Inst., Florence, 1990-91. Home: 16 Duevej, DK-2000 Frederiksberg Denmark Office: U Copenhagen Inst Pol Science, 15 Rosenborggade, DK-1130 Copenhagen Denmark also: Danish Inst Internat Affairs, 5 Nytorv, DK-1450 Copenhagen Denmark

HEUSENER, MICHAEL, mathematician; b. Kempten, Germany, Apr. 14, 1961; s. Norbert and Helga (Bock) H. Diploma in math., U. Frankfurt, Germany, 1986, PhD, 1992. Vis. prof. U. Toronto, Ont., Can., 1992; asst. U. Siegen, Germany, 1992-97; Tng. and Mobility of Rschrs. fellow U. Toulouse, France, 1997-99; prof. U. Blaise Pascal, Clermont-Ferrand, France, 1999—. Marie Curie Rsch. grantee U. Paul Sabatier, Toulouse, France, 1997-99. Office: U Blaise Pascal, Lab Math Pures Complex des Cézeaux, F-63177 Aubière Cedex, France

HEUSER, GERD, technical inspection company researcher, educator; b. Bensberg, Germany, June 16, 1946; s. Wilhelm and Katharina (Nebel) H.; m. Zita Griess, Jan. 6, 1977; children: Susanne, Christian. Grad. engr., Tech. U. Aachen, Germany, 1973, DEng, 1979, Habilitation, 1994. Sci. asst. Tech. U. Aachen, 1973-79, lectr., 1987-94, univ. lectr., 1994—; ofcl.-in-charge Fed. Bur., Bonn, Germany, 1980-81; sci. collaborator TÜV Rheinland, Cologne, Germany, 1981-87; head R & D dept. TÜV Kraftfahrt GmbH, Cologne, Germany, 1988-93, head R & D and lab., 1994—. Contbr. articles to profl. publs., including Automobiltechnische Zeitschrift, Forschung im Ingenieurwesen; patentee in field, including 6 components force torque transducer, crash test facility, cone and plate viscometers. Recipient prize Friedrich-Wilhelm-Stiftung, Aachen, 1994. Home: Von der Leyenstrasse 20, D-51069 Cologne Germany

HEUSKEL, DIETER, consulting company executive; b. Daun, Germany, Dec. 22, 1950; s. Heinz and Brunhilde (Hommes) H.; m. Heidi Marks, July 21, 1978; children: Christian, Sabine. Diplom volkswirt, U. Bonn, Germany, 1976, Dr.rer.pol, 1979. Geschaftsfuhrer Inst. Bus. and Traffic Rsch., Bonn, 1976-79; cons. The Boston Consulting Group, Munich and Düsseldorf, Germany, 1980-86; ptnr. The Boston Consulting Group, Munich and

Düsseldorf, 1986—. Office: Boston Consulting Group, Stadttor 1, 40219 Düsseldorf Germany

HEUSSER, DANIEL, editor; b. Zurich, Switzerland, July 6, 1948. Sales/mktg. mgr. Electric Ltd., Zürich, 1973-84; info. ctr. mgr. ELVIA Versicherungen, Zürich, 1984-89; profit-ctr. mgr. Eurotax (Schweiz) AG, Freienbach, 1989-92; coord. ea. Europe activities Eurotax (Internat.) AG, Freienbach, 1992-94; editor Daniel Heusser Unternehmer, Herrliberg, 1994—; gen. mgr. HW-Vertriebs GmbH, Haar/Munich, 1999—; with Found. of DaKaeLag, pub. co., Herrliberg, Switzerland, 1998—. Avocations: oldtimer boats, singing, sailing, journalism. Office: Daniel Heusser/Unternehmer, Bergstrasse 51, CH 8704 Herrliberg Switzerland also: DaKaeLag, Bergstrasse 51, CH-8704 Herrliberg Switzerland also: HW-Vertriebs GmbH, Hans Pinsel Strasse 1, D-85540 Haar/Munich Germany

HEUTS, BOUDEWIJN ADRIAAN, ethologist; b. Leuven, Belgium, Jan. 23, 1943; s. Maria-Joseph Cornelis and Mariette Melanie (Knops) H.; m. Frida Irena Roggen, Oct. 21, 1967; 1 child, Liesbeth. Diploma, U. Leuven, Belgium, 1966; PhD in Social Scis., U. Amsterdam, 1979. Lctr. in ethology U. Louvain, Leuven, Belgium, 1966-68; lctr. in ethology U. Amsterdam, 1968-99, lectr. in anatomy, 1988—; mem. editl. bd. Jour. Behavioural Processes, Louvain-la-Neuve, 1970—. Contbr. articles to profl. jours. Office: U Amsterdam, Kruislaan 320, 1098SM Amsterdam The Netherlands

HEW, DAVID SIN TECK, lawyer; b. Singapore, Mar. 1, 1952; s. Fook Loong and Kim Heok (Poh) H.; m. Yue-Lin Phay, Dec. 2, 1978; children: David, Chin-Kean. LLB with honors, U. Singapore, 1977; LLM, Nat. U. Singapore, 1989; postgrad. course in law, Bd. Legal Edn., Singapore, 1977; MBA, U. Strathclyde, 1991. Notary pub. Advocate, solicitor Supreme Ct.; commr. for oaths Singapore, 1978—; apptd. expert, chmn. experts meeting Commn. on Trade in Goods and Svcs. and Commodities UN Conf. on Trade and Devel., Geneva, 1999; apptd. cons. Asia Pacific Perspective on Financing for Devel. meeting UN Econ. and Social Commn. for Asia and the Pacific. Lt. Singapore Armed Forces, 1971-73. Recipient Lifeteime Achievement award World News Hall of Fame, Countertrade and Offset, 1996. Mem. Singapore Law Soc., Asian Pacific Countertrade Assn. (creator, founder 1994, sec. gen. 1994—), Acad. Law. Home: No 10 Buckley Rd, Singapore 309766, Singapore

HEWEL, HORST FERDINAND, retired electronics engineer; b. Berlin, Apr. 25, 1908; s. Ferdinand and Margarete (Büttner) H. TV engr. Telefunken, Berlin, 1933-45; film engr. Mosaik-Film, Berlin, 1945-49; sr. engr. NWDR/SenderFreies, Berlin, 1950-73; ret., 1973; ofcl. TV cons. Senate of West Berlin, 1952-82. Recipient Hans-Bredow medal ARD German Broadcasting Authorities, 1973. Achievements include development of 625-line TV camera unit, portable and complete in 4 boxes; development of cheap receivers, roving microphone for radio. Avocation: biology. Home: Scheelestr 58, 12209 Berlin Germany

HEWES, ROBERT CHARLES, radiologist; b. Balt., Feb. 14, 1953; s. Gordon Cecil and Gladys Dorothy (Barringham) H.; m. Judith Renee Lacy, Mar. 23, 1975; children: Christy, Amy, Jeremy. Student, Columbia Union Coll., 1973, Kettering Coll. of Med. Arts, 1971; BS, Loma Linda U., 1976, MD. Diplomate Am. Bd. Med. Examiners, Am. Bd. Radiology with subspecialty in vascular and internat. radiology. Resident in radiology Loma Linda (Calif.) U., 1978-81, asst. prof. radiology, 1983-84; fellow in orthopedic radiology Hosp. for Spl. Surgery Cornell U. Med. Ctr., N.Y.C., 1981-82; fellow in interventional radiology Johns Hopkins U. Hosp., Balt., 1982-83; assoc. prof. Wright State U.; mem. staff Kettering (Ohio) Med. Ctr., vice chmn. dept. radiology, 1985-87, chmn., 1988-95; pres. Patient First Imaging Network, 1994-95, med. dir., 1996-98; pres. Kettering Radiologists, Inc., 1987-95, 97-99; bd. dirs. Spring Valley Acad., chmn. fin. mgmt. com., 1998-99; pres. Alumni Assn. Spring Valley Acad., 1987-89. Contbr. articles on radiology to profl. jours. Bd. mem. Seventh Day Adventist Ch., Kettering, Ohio. Recipient Cert. of merit Am. Roentgen Ray Soc., 1983, Disting. Alumnus award Kettering Coll. of Med. Arts, 1990. Mem. AMA, Radiol. Soc. N.Am., Soc. Cardiovascular and Interventional Radiology, Miami Valley Radiol. Soc. (pres. 1994), Alpha Omega Alpha (award). Republican. Adventist. Avocations: radio-controlled airplanes, ham radio, woodworking, sports. Office: Hilton Head Hosp Dept Radiology PO Box 21117 Hilton Head Island SC 29925-1117

HEWETT, KEVIN BRIAN, environmental chemist; b. Long Beach, Calif., May 6, 1967; s. Harvey Jackson Jr. and Theresa M. Hewett. BS, N.C. State U., 1989; MS, Cornell U., 1992, PhD, 1994. Postdoctoral rsch. Tex. A&M U., College Station, 1994-96, Kans. State U., Manhattan, 1996-98; chemist II County Sanitation Dist. L.A. County, Carson, Calif., 1998-99; sr. chemist County Sanitation Dist. L.A. County, Carson, 1999—. Contbr. articles to profl. jours. Mem. AAAS, Am. Chem. Soc., Air and Waste Mgmt. Assn., N.Y. Acad. Scis. E-mail: hewett@gus.net. Office: County Sanitation Dist LA County 24501 Figueroa St Carson CA 90745-6311

HEWITSON, WILLIAM CRAIG, physician, career officer; b. Park City, Utah, July 4, 1961; s. William Glenn and Darlene Marie Hewitson; m. Deanne Gomm, July 15, 1983; children: William Brent, Staci Anne. BA with honors, U. Utah, 1986; MD, USUHS, 1991; MPH, Johns Hopkins U., 1995. Diplomate Am. Bd. Preventive Medicine. Officer U.S. Army, advanced through grades to maj., 1986; transitional intern Fitzsimons Army Med. Ctr., Aurora, Colo., 1991-92; 2d brigade surgeon 7th Inf. Divsn., Ft. Ord, Calif., 1992-93; divsn. surgeon 7th Inf. Divsn., Ft. Lewis, Wash., 1993-94; resident in general preventive medicine Walter Reed Army Inst. Rsch., Washington, 1994-96; chief injuries and occupation illnesses U.S. Army Ctr. for Health Promotion and Preventive Medicine, Aberdeen Proving Grounds, Md., 1996-98; chief preventive medicine divsn. Gen. Leonard Wood Army Cmty. Hosp., Ft. Leonard Wood, Mo., 1998—; dir. The Preventive Health Care Mgmt. Group, Salt Lake City, 1996-97; cons. Med. Adv. Sys., Owings, Md., 1995-98. Contbr. articles to profl. jours. Advancement chmn. Big Piney dist., Boy Scouts Am., Waynesville, Mo., 1999, Four Rivers dist. health and safety com., 1998, Pack # 1036 com. chmn., Ft. George G. Meade, 1995-97; missionary LDS Ch. Sch., Argentina, 1980-82. Mem. AMA (Physician Recognition award 1997), Assn. Mil. Surgeons U.S., Masons. Avocations: running, fitness, flying, golf, tennis. Office: Gen Leonard Wood Army Cmty Hosp 126 Missouri Ave Fort Leonard Wood MO 65473-8952

HEWITT, JAMES WATT, lawyer; b. Hastings, Nebr., Dec. 25, 1932; s. Roscoe Stanley and Willa Manners (Watt) H.; m. Marjorie Ruth Barrett, Aug. 8, 1954; children: Mary Janet, William Edward, John Charles, Martha Ann. Student, Hastings Coll., 1950-52; BS, U. Nebr., 1954, JD, 1956, MA, 1994. Bar: Nebr. 1956. Practice Hastings, 1956-57, Lincoln, Nebr., 1960—; v.p., gen. counsel Nebco, Inc., Lincoln, 1961—; vis. lectr. U. Nebr. Coll. Law, 1970-71. Mem. state exec. com. Rep. Party, 1967-70, mem. state ctrl. com., 1967-70, legis chmn., 1968-70; bd. dirs. Lincoln Child Guidance Ctr., 1969-72, pres., 1972; bd. dirs. Lincoln Cmty. Playhouse, 1967-73, pres., 1972-73; trustee Bryan Meml. Hosp., Lincoln, 1968-74, 76-82, chmn., 1972-74; bd. dirs. Lincoln Libr., 1990-97; trustee U. Nebr. Found., 1979—; dir. Bryan Meml. Hosp. Found., Lincoln, 1994—; pres, dir. Nebr. State Hist. Soc. Found., Lincoln, 1994—; dir. Nebr. state chpt. The Nature Conservancy, 1993-97. Capt. USAF, 1957-60. Fellow Am. Bar Found. (Nebr. state chmn. 1988-92, 99—, chmn. 1994-95); mem. ABA (Nebr. state del. 1972-80, bd. govts. 1981-83), Nebr. State Bar (chmn. ins. com. 1972-76, chmn. pub. rels. com. 1982-84, pres. 1985-86), Fed. Bar Assn., Lincoln Bar Assn., Newcomen Soc. (Nebr. chair 1995—), Am. Rose Soc., Nebr. Rose Soc., Lincoln Rose Soc., Nebr. Club, Country of Lincoln Club, Round Table, Beta Theta Pi, Phi Delta Phi. Congregationalist. Home: 2990 Sheridan Blvd Lincoln NE 68502-4241 Office: PO Box 80268 1815 Y St Lincoln NE 68508-1233

HEWITT, PAUL DEANE, headmaster; b. Belfast, No. Ireland, Jan. 5, 1947; s. Victor and Edith (McWhinney) H.; m. Christine Mary Burns, July 11, 1974; children: Colin, Cathy, Gillian. BA, Queen's U. Belfast, 1970, MA, 1979; edn. diploma, U. London, 1973. Asst. master Belfast Royal Acad., 1970-84; headmaster The Royal Sch. Dungannon, Northern Ireland, 1984—. Mem. Admiralty Interview Bd., Royal Navy, 1988—; bd. visitors Her Majestys Prison, Maghaberry, Northern Ireland, 1991—. Fellow Royal Soc. Arts, Inst. Mgmt.; mem. Youth Coun. No. Ireland. Avocations: rugby football, golf, ancient and modern church music, piano. Home: Headmasters Residence, Royal Sch, Dungannon BT71 6AP, Northern Ireland Office: The Royal Sch Dungannon, Dungannon BT71 6AP, Northern Ireland

HEWITT, WILLIAM HARLEY, investment and marketing executive; b. Ithaca, N.Y., June 29, 1954; s. William Leonard and Myrtie Mae (Van Etten) H. Student, Cornell U., 1972-74, Syracuse U., 1974-77. Broker First Jersey Securities, Peabody, Mass., 1979-80; rep. Garrett Arthur Assoc., Cambridge, Mass., 1980-82; pres. Wealth Adv. Group, Boston, 1982-85; cons. The New Eng., Boston, 1985-89; mng. prin. Century Cos. of Am., Waverly, Iowa, 1989-93; regional dir. Nationwide Life/Variable Products, 1993—; cons. Ednl. Tng. Systems, Boston, 1990-91. Author: (reference) Investment Product Selling System, 1989, Market Secrets, 1991. Mem. Nat. Trust for Hist. Preservation, Washington, 1989-92. Mem. Investment Tng. Assn. (mng. ptnr.), Aircraft Owners and Pilot Assn., Internat. Platform Assn., Ducks Unltd. Avocations: skiing, sailing, flying, golf, cooking, jazz. Home: 2031 Hummingbird Dr Jackson WI 53037 Office: Nationwide Life Ins Columbus OH 50677-9202

HEWSON, DONNA WALTERS, financial consultant; b. Columbia, S.C., Mar. 28, 1947; d. Jerry William and Rosa (Bryant) Walters; 1 child, Robert Alton Smith Jr.; m. James Robert Hewson, Oct. 1983 (div. 1986). Student, Hollins Coll., 1971-72, Va. Western Coll., 1972, Va. Polytech. and State U., 1972-73, U. S.C., 1978-79, 84, 85. Lic. fin. cons.; lic. U.S. SEC; lic. gen. securities Am. Stock Exch., Chgo. Bd. Options Exch., Pacific Stock Exch., Phila. Stock Exch.; lic. securities rep. Nat. Assn. Securities Dealers, S.C., N.C., Pa., Mont., Tex.; lic. life, accident and variables, S.C.; cert. investment advisor rep., S.C. Sales rep. Russell-Jeffcoat Realtors, Columbia, S.C., 1969-71; broker Russell-Jeffcoat Realtors, Columbia, 1971-72; adminstrv. asst. Roanoke (Va.) Valley Psych. Ctr., 1975-76; sales rep. Moore Bus. Forms, Columbia, 1976-79; project sales mgr. Continental Mortgage Investors, Columbia, 1979-80; broker, project sales mgr. Tom Jenkins Realty, Columbia, 1980-81; sales mgr., broker in charge RELM, Inc., Columbia, 1982-83; sales mgr. So. U.S. Realty/U.S. Shelter, Columbia, 1983-84; pres. WaltersHewson Co., Inc., Columbia, 1984-92; v.p. Realm, Inc., Columbia, 1988-89, pres., 1989—; fin. cons. Merrill Lynch, 1992—. Pub. rels. chmn., bd. dirs. Women's Symphony Assn., 1988; pres. S.C. Philharm. Chorus, Columbia Choral Soc.; mem. Trinity Episcopal Cathedral, Unitarian Universalist Fellowship, Hist. Columbia Found.; com. chmn. Vol. Profls. Cultural Coun. Mem. NOW, MENSA, Columbia C. of C. (com. chmn. 1987—), Nat. Assn. Real Estate Appraisers (sr. mem., cert., treas. 1990—), Columbia Bd. Realtors (mem. Million Dollar Club 1981, 84, 86, Grievance com. mem. 1986-88), S.C. Assn. Realtors (Profl. Stds. Com. 1986, polit. affairs com. 1987), Palmetto Real Estate Educators, S.C. Assn. Securities Dealers, Greater Columbia C. of C. Area Couns. Episcopalian. Avocations: piano, historic preservation, voice, fine arts.

HEY, RICHARD NOBLE, marine geophysicist; b. Lebanon, Tenn., June 2, 1947; s. Richard and Miriam (Jennings) H. BS, Calif. Inst. Technology, 1969; PhD, Princeton U., 1975. Rsch. assoc. U. Tex., Galveston, 1974-75; from asst. to geophysicist Hawaii Inst. Geophysics, Honolulu, 1975-80; from asst. to assoc. rsch. geophysicist Scripps Inst. Oceanography, La Jolla, Calif., 1981-86; prof. U. Hawaii, Honolulu, 1986—; adj. lectr. Scripps Inst. Oceanography, La Jolla, 1983-90. Fellow Geol. Soc. Am., Am. Geophys. Union; mem. AAAS. Office: U Hawaii at Manoa Inst Geophysics Planetology Honolulu HI 96822

HEYCK, THEODORE DALY, lawyer; b. Houston, Apr. 17, 1941; s. Theodore and Richard and Gertrude Paine (Daly) H. BA, Brown U., 1963; postgrad., Georgetown U., 1963-65, 71-72; JD, N.Y. Law Sch., 1979. Bar: N.Y. 1980, Calif. 1984, U.S. Ct. Appeals (2d cir.) 1984, U.S. Supreme Ct. 1984, U.S. Dist. Ct. (so. and ea. dists.) N.Y. 1980, U.S. Dist. Ct. (we. and no. dists.) N.Y. 1984, U.S. Dist. Ct. (cen. and so. dists.) Calif. 1984, U.S. Ct. Appeals (9th cir.) 1986. Paralegal dist. atty. Bklyn., 1975-79; asst. dist. atty. Bklyn. dist., Kings County, N.Y., 1979-85; dep. city atty. L.A., 1985—; bd. dirs. Screen Actors Guild, N.Y.C., 1977-78. Mem. ABA, ATLA, AFTRA, NATAS, SAG, Bklyn. Bar Assn., N.Y. Trial Lawyers Assn., N.Y. State Bar Assn., Calif. Bar Assn., Fed. Bar Coun., L.A. Coun. Bar Assn., Actors Equity Assn. Home: 2106 E Live Oak Dr Los Angeles CA 90068-3639 Office: Office City Atty City Hall E 200 N Main St Los Angeles CA 90012-4110

HEYD, BRUNO, surgeon; b. Ingwiller, France, July 16, 1960; s. Alfred and Georgette (Hamm) H.; m. Patricia Champreux; m. Julien P. Ysaline. Med. Cursus, Strasbourg U. Med. Sch., 1986; PhD in Health Sci., Strasbourg U. Med. Sch., Besancon, France, 1997; MD in Digestive Surgery, Besancon (France) U. Med. Sch., 1991. Resident Ctr. Hosp. & Univ., Besancon, France, 1986-91, chief resident, 1992-94; rsch. resident Ctr. Hosp. & Univ., Lausanne, Switzerland, 1994-95; surgeon U. Ctr. Hosp. & Univ., 1995-98, prof. gen. surgery, 1998—. Mem. Assn. Univ. Rsch. Chirurgie, Assn. French Chirurgie Hepato Biliaire Transplantation, Assn. French Surgery. Office: CHU Svc Chirurgie Digestive, Blvd Fleming, 25030 Besançon France

HEYDEN, ANDERS, mathematics educator, computer researcher; b. Malmö, Sweden, May 5, 1965; s. Knut and Karin Persson; m. Susanne Heyden, June 13, 1992; children: Martin, Malin, Linnea. MSc in Engring., Lund (Sweden) U., 1989, PhD in Engring. Math., 1995, DSc in Math., 1999. Rsch. asst. Lund U., 1995-98, assoc. prof., 1998—; sr. rschr. CellaVision AV, Lund, 1998—; cons. C Techs. AB, Lund, 1999—. Contbr. articles to profl. jours.; patentee in field. Mem. IEEE Computer Soc. Avocations: family activities, outdoor activities, travel, bicycling. Fax: 46 46 2224010. E-mail: heyden@maths.lth.se. Office: Ctr for Math Scis, Box 118, SE-22100 Lund Sweden

HEYDRICK, LINDA CAROL, consulting company executive, editor; b. Pomona, Calif., July 25, 1947; d. Robert Bruce and Wanda Georgine (Wellman) Middough; m. Stephen R. Bova, Jan. 20, 1968 (div. May 1981); children: Karen E., Lori L.; m. Allen L. Heydrick, Mar. 15, 1995. Student, El Camino Coll., Gardena, Calif., 1965-66. Sec. TRW, Inc., Manhattan Beach, Calif., 1967-68, USAF NCO Clubs, Mildenhall, Eng., 1968-70; adminstrv. asst. Prudential-Bache Securities, N.Y.C., 1970-73, Tex. Instruments, Inc., Dallas, 1980-83; asst. to pres. Acclivus Corp., Dallas, 1983-85, mgr. design and prodn., 1985-88, mgr. ops., 1988-89, v.p. ops., 1989—; cons. Digital Equipment Corp., Boston, 1984-89, coord. internat. translations of books, audiotapes and videotapes, 1993—. Editor: (books and videotapes) BASE for Sales Performance, 1984, Acclivus Sales Negotiation, 1985, The New BASE for Sales Excellence, 1989, Major Account Planning and Strategy, 1993, rev., 1996, Building on the BASE (award for best new tng. products Human Resource Exec.), 1993, R3 Service, (award for best new tng. product Human Resource Exec. 1998) 1997. Organizer Meals on Wheels, Denton, Tex., 1977; editor, pub Denton Bible Ch., 1993—. Mem. ASTD, Instructional Systems Assn., Nat. Soc. for Performance and Instrn., Soc. for Aplied Learning Tech., Soc. for Accelerative Learning and Tchg., Internat. Listening Assn. Republican. Avocations: Christian studies, fine arts, design, performing arts. Office: Acclivus Corp 14500 Midway Rd Dallas TX 75244-3109

HEYER, CAROL ANN, illustrator; b. Cuero, Tex., Feb. 2, 1950; d. William Jerome and Merlyn Mary (Hutson) H. BA, Calif. Lutheran U., 1974. Freelance artist various cos., Thousand Oaks, Calif., 1974-79; computer artist Image Resource, Westlake Village, Calif., 1979-81; staff writer, artist Lynn-Davis Prodns., Westlake Village, Calif., 1981-87; art dir. Northwind Studios Internat., Camarillo, Calif., 1988-89; illustrator Touchmark, Thousand Oaks, 1989—; cons. art dir., writer Lynn-Wenger Prodns., 1987-89; guest spkr. Ariz. Kidney Found. Children's Art and Lit. luncheon 2000, Thousand Oaks Libr., Author's Faire, Calif. Luth. U., Soc. Children's Book Writers and Illustrators, Illustrators Day, Ventura County Reading Assn.'s Author's Faire; guest artist/spkr. Oxnard Libr.; booksignings/appearances Anaheim Conv. Ctr., L.A. Conv. Ctr., Am. Booksellers Assn.; guest 1996 Readout, grand opening Barnes and Noble, Thousand Oaks; represented by Art Works, N.Y.C.; invited artist Ann. Art Show, Chemers Gallery; spkr. in field. Illustrator (children's books) A Star in the Pasture, 1988, The Dream Stealer, 1989, The Golden Easter Egg, 1989, All Things Bright and Beautiful, 1992, Rapunzel, 1992, The Christmas Carol, 1995, Prancer, Gift of the Magi, Black Beauty, Dinosaurs Strange and Wonderful, Down the Great Unknown, 1999, Flame and Clay (teachers' big book) 1998, 3 Repeat Jobs for Hampton/Brown (teacher's big book), (illustrator) Night Journey, 1999, Here Come the Brides, (adult book) The Artist's Market, also L.A. Times, Daily News, The Artist's Mag., News Chronicle; also cover art for Troll Assoc., Top Secret, The Loveless Cafe (cookbook), Ellery Queen's Mystery Mag., Frontispiece Collectors Leather Bound Edition, Crippen and Landru Mystery Covers, Dragon mag., Dungeon mag., Aboriginal Sci. Fiction mag., Wizards of the Coast, (game covers) F.X. Schmid - Puzzle Wizards of the Coast (fantasy collector cards, Dune and Hobbit) and various novels, books and games; illustrator Bugs Bunny Coloring Book, Candyland Work Book, The Dragon Sleeps Step Ahead Workbook, City of Sorcers, CD-ROM cover for Memorex/Roaring Mouse Prodns.; interior art for various publs. including (mags.) Amazing Stories two covers, Interzone, Aboriginal Sci. Fiction Mag., Alfred Hitchcocks Mystery Mag., Ideals mag., Ellery Queen's Mystery mag. two covers, Realms of Fantasy mag., Sci. Fiction Age mag., Tomorrow mag., (book) Tome of Magic, (book) Top Secret, (book, interiors) Star Trek Next Generation, (also art for game cards), (repeat covers) Crippen and Landru, (game book cover) Wizards of the Coast; writer (screenplay) Thunder Run, 1986; illustrator, writer (children's books) Black Beauty, Beauty and the Beast, 1989, The Easter Story, 1989, Excalibur, Robin Hood, 1993, Sleeping Beauty in the Wood, 1996, The Christmas Story, 1996, Down the Great Unknown, 1999, Flame and Clay, 1998, Black Beauty; paintings for line of Fantasy Art Prints, Scafa/Tornabene, religious art prints; rep. by Every Picture Tells a Story Gallery, Worlds of Wonder; cover art/bookmark for Antioch Pub.; new cover for Baen Books; art for Maruri USA Corp.; 2 covers for young adults Hyperion/Disney Press; one-woman show Adventures for Kids Gallery; illustrator poster for motion picture and TV fund; writer Disney ednl. prodns., others; freelance artist Disney Interactive. Guest spkr. Ariz. Kidney Found. Recipient Lit. award City of Oxnard Cultural Arts Commn. and Carnegie Art Inst., 1992, Best Cover Art Boomerang award, 1989, Cert. of Merit, Career Achievement award Calif. Luth. U., 1993, Cert. of Excellence Alumni Career Achievement award, 1993, Print's Regional Design Ann. award, 1992, Best Paper Backs award Internat. Reading Assn./Children's Book Coun. Joint Com., 1994, Spectrum Internat. Competition for Best in Contemporary Fantastic Art. Mem. Soc. Children's Book Writers (judge 1990, Mag. Merit award 1988, Keynote spkr.), Assn. Sci. Fiction and Fantasy Artists (nominated for Chelsey award), Soc. Illustrators (Cert. of Merit 1990-92, winner Ann. Illustration West show, award L.A. chpt. 1998). Achievements include being featured in articles. Home and Office: Touchmark 925 Ave Arboles Thousand Oaks CA 91360

HEYER, JOHN HENRY, II, lawyer; b. Rochester, N.Y., May 4, 1946; s. Joseph Lester and Margaret Mary (Darcy) H.; m. Charla Ann Prewitt (dec.); children: Thomas, William, John III, Richard, Mary. BA, U. Colo., 1969; JD, U. Denver, 1972. Bar: Colo. 1973, U.S. Dist. Ct. Colo. 1973, N.Y. 1976, Pa. 1979, U.S. Dist. Ct. (we. dist.) N.Y. 1980, U.S. Supreme Ct. 1982. Atty. Texaco, Inc., Denver, 1973-75; sole practice Olean, N.Y., 1975—; pres. Northeastern Land Svcs., Inc., Olean, N.Y., 1982—; v.p. Vector Capital Corp., Rochester, N.Y., 1985-87; chpt. 7 trustee U.S. Bankruptcy Ct., we. dist. N.Y., 1986—. Editor: New York Oil and Gas Statutes, 1985. Asst. dist. atty. Cattaraugus County, Olean, 1978-81; bd. dirs. Olean YMCA, 1989—, v.p. 1993-94, pres., 1994-99, pres. bd. trustees, 1999—; bd. dirs. Buffalo Philharm. Symphony Cir., v.p., 1993, pres., 1994-95; bd. dirs. Friends of Good Music, pres. 1994-95. Mem. N.Y. State Bar Assn. (real property sect., real property devel. com.), Erie County Bar Assn., Cattaraugus County Bar Assn. (sec.-treas. 1997, v.p. 1998, pres. 1999), Eastern Mineral Law Found. (trustee 1984—, exec. com. 1994-95), Ind. Oil and Gas Assn. N.Y. (bd. dirs. 1986—, sec. 1986-87, v.p. 1988—), SAR, Selden Soc. Roman Catholic. Office: PO Box 588 201 N Union St Olean NY 14760-2738

HEYERDAHL, JENS P., business executive; b. Oslo, Feb. 17, 1943; s. Jens and Sessan (Lyche) H.; widowed; 2 children. Student, Cavalry Officers Sch., 1961-63; degree in law, Oslo U., 1968; MBA, European Inst. Adminstrn. Affairs, Fontainebleau, France, 1970. Atty. Thommessen, Karlsrud, Heyerdahl & Brunsvig, Oslo, 1968; mem. staff Directorate for Legal Harmonization, EEC, Brussels, 1969; legal cons. Insp. of Taxes, Oslo, 1970-71; dep. judge of Lier Røyken and Hurum Magistrate, 1971-72; co. sec. Dyno Industrier A.S., Oslo, 1972-75; v.p. indsl. devel. and investments Orkla Industrier A/S, 1975-79, mng. dir., 1979-85; group chief exec. Orkla Borregaard A.S. (merger), 1986-91, Orkla ASA (merger), Oslo, 1991—; bd. dirs. BASF Norge, Hafslund ASA, Oslo, several subs. cos. Orkla ASA. Avocation: riding (internat. awards in Grand Prix show-jumping events). Office: Orkla ASA, PO Box 423 Skøyen, N-0213 Oslo Norway

HEYLIGHEN, FRANCIS PAUL, cybernetician, researcher; b. Vilvoorde, Belgium, Sept. 27, 1960; s. Jaak Constant and Suzanne Gabriele (Delsupehe) H.; m. Zlatka Naydenova, June 15, 1991. MSc, Free U. Brussels, 1982, PhD, 1987. Rschr. Internat. Solvay Insts. for Physics and Chemistry, Brussels, 1982-83; rsch. asst. Nat. Fund for Sci. Rsch., Brussels, 1983-87, postdoctoral fellow, 1989-94; rsch. asst. Rsch. Coun. Free U. Brussels, 1987-88; rsch. assoc. Fund for Sci. Rsch.-Flanders, Brussels, 1994—. Author: Representation and Change, 1990; editor: Self-Steering and Cognition in Complex Systems, 1990, The Evolution of Complexity, 1999; mem. editl. bd. Principia Cybernetica, 1990—, Informatica, 1993—, Jour. Memetics, 1995—, Entropy, 1999—; contbr. more than 70 articles to profl. jours. Office: Free Univ Brussels, Krijgskundestraat 33, B-1160 Brussels Belgium

HEYMAN, GENE MORRIS, research psychologist, educator; b. Fayetville, N.C., June 26, 1945; s. Philip and Florence Ehrlich Heyman; m. Martha Lynn Pott, May 11, 1987; 1 child, Phoebe Lily Ehrlich Pott-Heyman. BA, U. Calif., Riverside, 1966; PhD, Harvard U., 1977. Postdoctoral fellow U. Chgo., 1981-83; rsch. scientist Lederle Labs., Pearl River, N.Y., 1983-88; assoc. prof. psychology Harvard U., Cambridge, Mass., 1989-98; rsch. psychologist McLean Hosp., Belmont, Mass., 1998—; lectr. Harvard U. Med. Sch., Boston, 1998—; cons., 1998—. Bd. editors, Jour. Exptl. Analysis of Behavior, 1978-83, 95-98; contbr. articles to profl. jours. and ency. Grantee NSF, 1995-98, Nat. Inst. Drug Abuse, 1998—, Nat. Inst. Alcoholism and Alcohol Abuse, 1995-98, Russell Sage Found., 1995-98. Mem. Am. Psychol. Soc., Behavioral Pharmacol. Soc., Soc. Quantitative Analysis of Behavior. Avocations: tennis, skiing. Office: McLean Hosp 115 Mill St Belmont MA 02478-1048

HEYMAN, IRA MICHAEL, federal agency administrator, museum executive, law educator; b. N.Y.C., May 30, 1930; s. Harold Albert and Judith (Sobel) H.; m. Therese Helene Thau, Dec. 17, 1950; children: Stephen Thomas (dec.), James Nathaniel. AB in Govt., Dartmouth Coll., 1951; JD, Yale U., 1956; LLD (hon.), U. Pacific, 1981, Hebrew Union Coll., 1984, U. Md., 1986, SUNY, Buffalo, 1990. Bar: N.Y. 1956, Calif. 1961. Legis. asst. to U.S. Senator Ives, 1950-51; assoc. Carter, Ledyard & Milburn, N.Y.C., 1956-57; law clk. to presiding justice U.S. Ct. Appeals (2d cir.), New Haven, 1957-58; chief law clk. to Supreme Ct. Justice Earl Warren, 1958-59; acting assoc. prof. law U. Calif., Berkeley, 1959-61, prof. law, 1961-66, prof. city and regional planning, 1966-93, prof. emeritus, 1993—, vice chancellor, 1974-80, chancellor, 1980-90, chancellor emeritus, 1990—; counselor to Sec. of Interior Dept. Interior, Washington, 1993-94; sec. Smithsonian Inst., Washington, 1994-99, sec. emeritus, 2000—; vis. prof. Yale Law Sch., 1963-64, Stanford Law Sch., 1971-72. Editor Yale Law Jour.; contbr. articles to profl. jours. Sec. Calif. adv. com. U.S. Commn. Civil Rights, 1962-67; trustee Dartmouth Coll., 1982-93, chmn., 1991-93; mem. Lawyers' Com. for Civil Rights under Law, 1977-95; chmn. exec. com. Nat. Assn. State Univs. and Land Grant Colls., 1986; bd. regents Smithsonian Instn., 1990-94; bd. dirs. Presidio Trust, 2000—. 1st lt. USMC, 1951-53, capt. Res. ret. Decorated chevalier Legion of Honor (France). Mem. Am. Acad. Arts and Sci.

HEYN, ARNO HARRY ALBERT, retired chemistry educator; b. Breslau, Germany, Oct. 6, 1918; s. Myron and Margarete M.E.C. (Cierpinski) H.; m. Helen A. Pielemeier, Mar. 14, 1942; children: Evan A., Margaret L., Robert E. BS, U. Mich., 1940, MS, 1941, PhD in Analytical Chemistry, 1944. Exptl. chemist Sun Oil Co., Norwood, Pa., 1944-47; from instr. to prof. chemistry Boston U., 1947-84, prof. emeritus, 1984; vis. scientist Brookhaven Nat. Lab., summers 1954-56; acad. guest Eidg. Techn. Hochschule, Zurich, 1965, Gesellschaft F. Kernforschung, Karlsruhe, 1973, 80, 81, 82, Landesanst. F. Wasserbiologie, Vienna, 1973; sci. adviser Boston Dist. U.S. FDA, 1967-72. Contbr. articles to profl. jours. Fellow AAAS; mem. Am. Chem. Soc. (councilor 1967-97, alt. councilor 1998—, chmn. coun. com. on

constn. and bylaws 1983-85, coun. policy com. 1986-91, vice-chmn. 1987-88, com. on coms. 1992-94, Henry Hill award N.E. sect. 1986, editor Nucleus 1989—), AAUP (treas. Boston U. chpt. 1979-83), Sigma Xi, Phi Lambda Upsilon, Sub Sig Outing Club (Boston). Avocation: locksmithing. Home: 21 Alexander Rd Newton MA 02461-1830

HEYN, WILLIAM BURRIS, investment banker; b. Nov. 6, 1971. BA, Yale U., 1994. Fin. analyst Morgan Stanley, N.Y.C., 1994-96; assoc. CIBC Oppenheimer, N.Y.C., 1997-99, J.P. Morgan, N.Y.C., 1999—.

HEYNEN, HILDE MARIA, architecture educator; b. Antwerp, Belgium. Engr.-arch., U. Leuven, Belgium, 1981, MPH, 1982, PhD in Applied Scis. in Arch., 1988. Asst. U. Leuven, 1982-95, lectr., 1995—, assoc. prof., 1999—; vis. asst. prof. MIT Sch. Arch., Cambridge, Mass., 1991, 92. Author: (book) Architecture and Modernity: A Critique, 1999; editor: (book) Wonen tussen gemeenplaats en poëzie, 1993; mem. editl. bd. Archis, 1996, Yearbook Arch. Flanders, 1992-98. Postdoctoral fellow The Getty Grant Program, 1993-94. Fax: 32-16-32-19-84. E-mail: hilde:heynen@asro.kuleuven.ac.be. Office: U Leuven Dept ASRO, Kasteel van Arenberg, 3001 Heverlee Belgium

HEYNINCK, JEAN-MARIE, personnel executive; b. Familleureux, Hainaut, Belgium, Dec. 18, 1944; s. Isidore Heyninck and Anna-Marie Hennau; m. Patricia De Cooman; children: Stephane, Xavier, Alexis. Grad. in Psychology, U. Louvain, Belgium, 1969, grad. in Safety and Health, 1982. Sci. researcher U. Louvain, 1969-70; pers. supr. Don Internat., Manage, Belgium, 1970-71; mgr. human rels. Stewart Warner Corp., Ghlin, Belgium, 1971-77, cons. in human resources, 1989—; psychologist Cen. PMS, Bersilles L'Abbaye, Belgium, 1977-78; human relations mgr. S.A. Signode N.V., Carnieres, Belgium, 1978-87; pers. mgr. S.A. Match, Fleurus, Belgium, 1987-89, cons. in human resources, 1989—. Social judge Work Ct., Charleroi, Belgium, 1979-89. 1st sgt. Belgian Mil., 1964-66. Mem. Compagnie des Dirigeants de Service du Personnel. Home: Rue Saint Pierre 61, Besonrieux (La Louviere), Hainaut B7100, Belgium Office: CERC, Rue Saint Pierre 61, B 7100 La Louviere Belgium

HEYSTEK, KRISTEN MARGARET, librarian; b. Toledo, Sept. 9, 1949; d. James Lewis and Mary Esther (McQuire) Sacksteder; m. William Vreeland Jr., May 23, 1969 (div. 1975); 1 child, William III; m. Larry Heystek, 1981 (div. 1998). B in Gen Studies, U. Mich., 1975, MLS, 1979. Activity dir., social svc. designee Friendship Village Retirement Ctr., Kalamazoo, 1978-80; night circulation libr. supr. Ednl. Resource Ctr. We. Mich. U., Kalamazoo, 1980-81; substitute tchr. Montgomery Pub. Schs., Clarskville, Tenn., 1981-82; lbir. Robert F. Sink Libr., Ft. Campbell, Ky., 1982-83; vol. libr. Blanchfield Army Community hosp., Ft. Campbell, Ky., 1983-84; med. cir. libr. Mercy Hosp., Watertown, N.Y., 1986; subsitute tchr. Jefferson County BOCES, Watertown, N.Y., 1986-87; libr. Phillips Coll., Atlanta, 1988—; substitute tchr. Clayton County Pub. Schs., Joesnboro, Ga., substitute para/profl. Kalamazoo Pub. Schs., 1993-97; sales assoc. Trugreen, 1998, ret., 1999. Mem. U. Mich. Alumni Assn. in Libr. Sci. Avocations: family cooking, travel.

HEYWANG-KOEBRUNNER, SYLVIA H., radiologist, educator; b. Karlsruhe, Germany, July 31, 1956; d. Walter and Ditha (Bierwag) H.; m. Gerhard Köbrunner, Mar. 11, 1989; children: Sandra, Petra. MD, Ludwig-Maximilians U., Munich, Germany, 1981, Dr. med. habil, 1992. Bd. cert. physician, 1982, radiologist, 1990. Resident radiology Ludwig-Maximilians U., Munich, Germany, 1983-90, mem. staff, 1990-92, asst. prof., 1991-92; asst. prof. U. Leipzig (Germany), 1993; asst. prof., vice dir. diagnostic radiology Martin Luther U., Halle, Germany, 1994-96, assoc. prof., vice dir. diagnostic radiology, 1996—. Author: Contrast-enhanced MRI of the breast, 1990, 2d edit., 1996, Breast Imaging, 1996; mem. editl. bd. European Radiology, Diagnostic Imaging, Roe Fo, der Radiologe, Roentgenpraxis; sect. editor Eurorad; reviewer Radiology, Jour. Computer Assisted Tomography, JMRI, European Radiology, Acta Radiologica, Roe Fo.; contbr. articles to profl. jours.; patents for breast biopsy coil, substance for interstitial marker solution, inauguration of contrast enhanced breast MRI 1985, first MR-guided vacuum breast biopsy, 1997, fixation device for MRI of the breast. Scholar breast imaging German Cancer Assn., 1982; recipient MR prize Internat. MR-Symposium, 1991, 1st prize on tchg. film Congress Soc. for cont. med. edn., 1994, medal Inst. Internat. d'Imagerie Med. Monaco, 1995, Ann. Editor's excellence award Jour. Computer Assisted Tomography, 1997, Yvette Mayent prize Institut Curie, 1999. Mem. German Radiol. Soc. (head breast imaging com., Holthusenring award 1992), German Senology Soc. (bd. mem. 1995—), Radiol. Soc. N.Am., European Assn. Radiology, European Soc. Magnetic Resonance Medicine, European Congress Radiology (head breast com. 2000—), N.Y. Acad. Sci. Avocations: music, science. Office: U Halle Diagnostic Radiolog, Magdeburger strasse 16, 06112 Halle Germany

HEYWOOD, ANNE, artist, educator, writer; b. Newport, R.I., Sept. 15, 1951; d. Albert Paul and Eileen Frances (Laforest) Boretti; m. Ciro DiGiovanni, May 24, 1969 (div. 1980); 1 child, Carlo; m. Henry Robert Heywood, Nov. 9, 1985. BA in Art summa cum laude, Bridgewater (Mass.) State Coll. Tchr. drawing and pastels Silver Lake Reg. H.S. Adult Edn., Kingston, Mass., 1991-95; art educator pastels, drawing South Shore Art Ctr., Cohasset, Mass., 1996—; art educator pastels Fuller Mus. Art, Brockton, Mass., 1996—, Pastel Painters Soc. Cape Cod, Barnstable, Mass., 1997—; art educator drawing Swinburne Sch., Newport, R.I., 1995, Round Top Ctr. for Arts, Damariscotta, Maine, 1996; pastel demonstrator spkr. numerous art orgns., Weymouth, Milton, Mass. and Conn., 1995—. Contbg. artist: (included in books) Best of Pastel, 1996, Landscape Inspirations, 1997, Best of Sketching and Drawing 1999; one-woman shows include East Bridgewater (Mass.) Pub. Libr., 1992, 95, Mass. Audubon Soc., Marshfield, 1992, South Shore Natural Sci. Ctr., Norwell, Mass., 1993, Marion (Mass.) Art Ctr., 1994, Fuller Art Mus., Brockton, Mass., 1995, 2000, Passage Gallery, South Shore Art Ctr., Cohasset, Mass., 1996, 98, Sparrow House, Plymouth, Mass., 1997, 2000, Landmark Bldg., Boston, 1999; exhibited in group shows at Pembroke (Mass.) Art Festival, 1991, Earth Kingdom Gallery, Hanover, Mass., 1992, Duxbury Art Assn., Mass., 1993, Trenton (N.J.) State Coll., 1994, Bridgewater State Coll., 1994, Audubon Soc., Marshfield, Mass., 1994-97, Zullo Gallery, Medfield, Mass., 1995-99, Maine Art Gallery, Wiscasset, 1995, Pastel Soc. Am., N.Y.C., 1995, 97, Internat. Assn. Pastel Socs., 1997, 99, East Bridgewater Pub. Libr., 1996, 97, Joseph A. Driscoll Gallery, Brockton, 1996, Left Bank Gallery, Wellfleet, Mass., 1997, Gallery at C3TV, South Yarmouth, Mass., 1997, 20th Ann. Salmagundi Club, N.Y., 7th Nat. Biennial Exhbn. Degas Soc., La. (La. Watercolor Soc. award of merit), Colo. History Mus. Exhbn., 16th Ann. Fla. Pastel Soc. Exhbn., 48th Nat. Exhbn. Contemporary Realism in Art, Mass., Soc. Western Artists, 1999; also corp. collections; contbr. articles to profl. jours.; editor Pastel Painter's Soc. of Cape Cod newsletter, 1998-99, mem. bd. dirs., 1999—. Sec. East Bridgewater Arts Coun., 1992-97, Artists Cir. at Fuller Mus., Brockton, Mass., 1995-97. Recipient 1st pl. drawing East Bridgewater Art Festival, 1991, 1st pl. awards Wickford (R.I.) Art Assn., 1992, Taunton (Mass.) Art Assn., 1993, South Shore Art Ctr. Blue Ribbon Members Show, Cohasset, 1994, Fuller Art Mus., Brockton, 1994, 1st pl. pastels Plymouth Guild May Members Show, 1994, award Providence Art Club, 1996, award of distinction All New Eng. Color Show, Cohasset, 1996, convention image award Internat. Assn. Pastel Socs., 1997, George Inness Jr. Meml. award for pastel Salmagundi Club, 1999; Vt. Studio Ctr. Residency fellow, 1999. Mem. Internat. Assn. of Pastel Socs., Am. Artists Profl. League, Associated Pastelists on Web (signature mem.), Salmagundi Club, Allied Artists of Am., Pastel Painters Soc. Cape Cod (signature mem., Canson-Talens award 1997), Conn. Pastel Soc., Pastel Soc. Am. (Holbein award 1995), Oil Pastel Assn./United Pastellists Am., Nat. Assn. Women Artists (D.Wu and Elsie Ject-Key Meml. award 2000), Salmagundi Club. Roman Catholic. Avocations: reading, walking, biking, choir. Home and Studio: 85 Ashley Dr East Bridgewater MA 02333-1703

HEZEL, FRANCIS XAVIER, clergy member, educator; b. Buffalo, N.Y., Jan. 29, 1939; arrived in Micronesia, 1963; s. Francis Xavier Hezel and Patricia Mary Kolb. BA, Fordham U., N.Y.C., 1962; MA, Fordham U., 1963, HHD (hon.), 1994; MDiv, Woodstock (Md.) Coll., Md., 1969; MST, Woodstock Coll., 1970; HHD (hon.), U. Guam, 1986, Fordham U., 1995. Ordained priest Roman Cath. Ch., 1969;. Tchr. Xavier H.S., Chuuk, Micronsia, 1963-66, 69-73; prin. Xavier H.S., Chuuk, 1973-75, dir., 1976-82; dir. Micronesian Seminar, 1972—; regional superior Jesuits of Micronesia, 1992-98; dir. Med. Grad. Support Program, Micronesia, 1996—; mem. com. evaluate health svcs. in Pacific Inst. Medicine, Washington, 1996-97; assoc. Micronesia Area Rsch. Ctr. Author: First Taint of Civilization, 1983, Strangers in Their Own Land, 1995; prodr. (TV documentaries) Island Topics, 1994-98; corr. Jour. Pacific History; contbr. arricles to profl. jours. Mem. Chuuk State Bd. Edn., 1987-90, Com. Primary Health Care, Chuuk, 1987-88, Pohnpei (Micronesia) Econ. Coun., 1996—. Mem. Pacific Islands Assn. Libr. Archives, Assn. Social Anthropologists Oceania. Roman Catholic. Avocations: basketball, tennis, writing. Home & Office: Micronesian Seminar PO Box 160 Pohnpei FM 96941-0160

HEZIR, JOSEPH S., energy and environmental company executive; b. Pitts., Aug. 27, 1950; s. Joseph F. and Elizabeth G. H.; m. Joyce Ann Martincic, May 12, 1979; children: Alexandra M., Damjan S. BS, Carnegie-Mellon U., 1972, MS, 1974. Rsch. engr. St. Joe Minerals Corp., Monaca, Pa., 1971, Carnegie-Mellon U., Pitts., 1972; planning analyst City of N.Y., 1973; budget examiner U.S. Office Mgmt. and Budget, Washington, 1974-82, dep. assoc. dir., 1986-92; sr. corp. analyst Exxon Rsch. and Engring. Corp., Florham Park, N.J., 1982; mng. ptnr. The EOP Group, Inc., Washington, 1992—; mem. adv. bd. Competitiveness Policy Coun., Washington, 1992-94, NASA Adv. Coun., Washington, 1992-93. Dir. nat. capital chpt. ARC, Washington, 1987-90. Fellow Coun. Excellence in Govt.; mem. NAS (mem. study bds.), Croatian Fraternal Union Am. Roman Catholic. E-mail: jshezir@819eagle.com. Home: 1509 Pennycress Ln Vienna VA 22182-1473 Office: EOP Group Inc 819 7th St NW Washington DC 20001-3762

HIBI, HIDEHARU, oral and maxillofacial surgeon, researcher; b. Nagoya, Aichi, Japan, Mar. 7, 1963; s. Hideo and Chieko (Kondo) H.; m. Yuko Shiina, Mar. 29, 1992; children: Hanae, Haruka, Taichi. B Dentistry, Tokyo Med. and Dental U., 1987, PhD, 1991. Dental diplomate, Japan, specialty in prosthodontics.. Staff dentist Tokyo Med. and Dental U. Dental Hosp, 1991-92, Nagoya (Japan) U. Med. Hosp.., 1992-95; dir. dept. oral and maxillofacial surgery Holy Spirit Hosp., Nagoya, 1995—; vis. lectr. Nagoya U. Sch. Medicine, 1995—. Author: Oral and Maxillofacial Implant, 1995. Rsch. grantee Rsch. Found. Electrotech. of Chubu, Nagoya, 1994, Ministry Edn., Tokyo, 1995. Fellow Internat. Assn. Oral and Maxillofacial Surgeons; mem. AAAS, Acad. Osseointegration, Japan Prosthodontic Soc., N.Y. Acad. Scis. Avocations: meditation, skiing, swimming. Home: 19-1 nanzan-cho, Mizuho-ku, Nagoya 467-0023, Japan Office: Holy Spirit Hosp, 56 kawanayama-cho, Showa-ku, Nagoya 466-8633, Japan

HIBI, NOZOMU, biochemist, researcher; b. Nagoya, Japan, Sept. 21, 1950; s. Yoshio and Kura (Muramatsu) H. BAgr, Hokkaido U., Sapporo, Japan, 1973, MAgr, 1975, MD, 1979. Rsch. asst. Hokkaido U., 1981-84; postdoctoral fellow Roswell Park Meml. Inst., Buffalo, 1984-86; sect. chief Shinotest Inc., Sagamihara, Japan, 1986-89, SRL, Inc., Hachioji, Japan, 1989—. Contbr. articles to Neurol. Sci., Biochem. Jour., Internat. Jour. Oncology, others. Mem. Japanese Biochem. Soc., Japanese Cancer Assn. Office: SRL Inc, 153 Komiya, Hachioji, Tokyo 192-0031, Japan

HIBINO, HIROYUKI, virologist; b. Tokushima, Japan, Nov. 19, 1938; s. Masao and Sadako (Niwa) H.; m. Mitsuko Inoue, Apr. 2, 1969; 4 children. BS, Nagoya (Japan) U., 1961, D of Agrl. Sci., 1966. Technical offcl. Inst. for Plant Virus Rsch., Chiba, Japan, 1966-82; plant virologist Internat. Rice Rsch. Inst., The Philippines, 1982-88; tech. offcl. Nat. Agrl. Rsch. Ctr., Tsukua, Japan, 1988-95, Chugoku Nat. Agrl. Expl. Sta., Fukuyama, Japan, 1995-97, Nat. Inst. Agro-Environ. Sci., Tsukuba, Japan, 1997-99; vis. sci. U. Calif., Riverside, 1969-70; Japan internat. coop. agy. expert Cen. Rsch. Inst. Agrl., Bogor, Indonesia, 1975-78. Contbr. articles to profl. jours. Recipient Sci. Merit Award Sci. and Tech. Agy., Japan, 1991. Mem. Phytopath. Soc. Japan (councilor 1994—, award 1990), Soc. Japanese Virologist, Am. Phytopath. Soc. Home: Shimohara 448-8, 305-0063 Tsukuba Japan Office: IRRI Japan Office, Owashi 1-2, Tsukuba 305-8686, Japan

HIBINO, KEN, chemist, researcher; b. Kitakyusyu City, Fukuoka, Japan, Nov. 29, 1949; s. Osamu and Kazuko Inoue; m. Satoko Yamada, Apr. 29, 1986; children: Ryo, Yutaka, Taku. Bachelor's degree, U. Tokyo, 1975, MD, 1977, PhD, 1982. Rschr. Nitto Denko Corp., Ibaraki, 1981-82, asst. chief rschr., 1985-93, chief rschr., 1994—; rschr. Membrane Tech. and Rsch., Menlo Park, 1983-84. Author: (books) Handbook of Membrane Reactor, 1990, Plant Cell and Tissue Culture for the Production of Food Ingredients, 1999. Mem. Am. Chem. Soc., Japan Soc. for Biosci., Biotech., and Agrochemistry. Avocations: baseball, golf, personal computer. Fax: 81 726 21 0309. E-mail: ken hibino@gg.nitto.co.jp. Office: Nitto Denko Corp, Shimohozumi 1-1-2, Osaka Ibaraki City 567-8680, Japan

HICHENS, ANTONY PEVERELL, building and mining products company executive; b. Cornwall, Eng., Sept. 10, 1936; s. Robert Peverell and Catherine Gilbert (Enys) H.; m. Sczerina Neomi Hobday, Aug. 9, 1963; 1 child, Tamsin. MA in Jurisprudence, Oxford (Eng.) U., 1959; MBA, U. Pa., 1965. Called to the bar, 1960. Planner Rio Tinto-Zinc Corp., London, 1960-69; mgr. corp. planning Rio Algom, Toronto, Can., 1969-72; fin. dir. Redland Plc., Eng., 1972-81; mng. dir. fin. Consolidated Gold Fields Plc., Eng., 1981-89; chmn. Caradon Plc., Eng., 1985-98; dep. chmn. Candover Investments Plc., London, 1990—, Courtaulds Textiles Plc., London, 1991-2000, LASMO plc, 1995-2000, chmn., 2000—; chmn. David S. Smith (Holdings), PLC, 1999—. Served to lt. comdr. Royal Naval Res., 1954-69. Named to Oxford Ct. of Benefactors, Oxford U., 1992, Waynflete Fell. of Magdalen Coll., Oxford, 1997. Mem. Brooks' Club. Avocations: shooting, wine, travel.

HICK, KENNETH WILLIAM, marketing company executive; b. New Westminster, B.C., Can., Oct. 17, 1946; s. Les Walter and Mary Isabelle (Warner) H. BA in Bus., Eastern Wash. State Coll., 1971; MBA (fellow), U. Wash., 1973, PhD, 1975. Regional sales mgr. Hilti, Inc., San Leandro, Calif., 1976-79; gen. sales mgr. Moore Internat., Inc., Portland, 1979-80; v.p. sales and mktg. Phillips Corp., Anaheim, Calif., 1980-81; owner, pres., chief exec. officer K.C. Metals, San Jose, Calif., 1981-87; owner, pres., chief exec. officer Losli Internat. Inc., Portland, Oreg., 1987-89; pres. Resources N.W. Inc., 1989—; communications cons. Asso. Pub. Safety Communication Officers, Inc., State of Oreg., 1975-93; numerous cons. assignments, also seminars, 1976-98. Contbr. articles to numerous publs. Mem. Oreg. Gov.'s Tax Bd., 1975-76; pres. Portland chpt. Oreg. Jaycees, 1976; bd. fellows U. Santa Clara, 1983-90. Served with USAF, 1966-69. Decorated Commendation medal. Mem. Am. Mgmt. Assn., Am. Mktg. Assn., Assn. M.B.A. Execs., Assn. Gen. Contractors, Soc. Advancement Mgmt., Home Builders Assn. Roman Catholic. Home: 25659 Cheryl Dr West Linn OR 97068-4589 Office: Resources NW Inc 19727 Highway 99E Hubbard OR 97032-9716

HICKCOX, LESLIE KAY, health educator, consultant, counselor; b. Berkeley, Calif., May 12, 1951; d. Ralph Thomas and Marilyn Irene (Stump) H. BA, U. Redlands, 1973; MA in Exercise Physiology, U. of the Pacific, 1975; MEd, Columbia U., 1979; MEd in Health Edn., Oreg. State U., 1987, MEd in Guidance & Counseling, 1988, EdD in Edn., 1991. Cert. state C.C. instr. (life), Calif. Phys. edn. instr., dir. intramurals SUNY, Stony Brook, 1981-83; instr. health edn. Linn-Benton C.C., Oreg., 1985-94; health and phys. edn. instr. Portland C.C., 1994-95; edn. supr., instr. Oreg. State U., Corvallis, 1988-90; instr. human studies and comm. Marylhurst Coll., Portland, Oreg., 1987-96; instr. health edn. U. (New Zealand) Auckland, 1991; instr. health curriculum and supervision Concordia Coll., Portland, Oreg., 1992; instr., coord. dept. health, phys. edn. and recreation Rogue C.C., Grants Pass, Oreg., 1995-97; assoc. prof., coord. health and phys. edn. Western Mont. Coll., Dillon, 1997-99; asst. prof. health edn. Northeastern Ill. U., Chgo., IL, 1999—; founder Experiential Learning Inst., 1992—, found., Lilly N.W. High Edn. Tchg. Conf., 1996; founding v.p. Home Health Diagnostics, Portland, Oreg., 1996. Contbr. articles to profl. jours. Mem. ASCD, Am. Pub. Health Assn., Am. Sch. Health Assn., Assn. for Advancement of Health Edn., Higher Edn. R & D Soc. Australasia, Coun. for Adult and Exptl. Learning, Kappa Delta Phi, Phi Delta Kappa. Home: 1110 Dewey Ave Evanston IL 60202-1121 Office: Dept Health Phys Edn Recreation and Athletics Northeastern Ill Univ 5500 N Saint Louis Ave Chicago IL 60625-4679

HICKEL, WALTER JOSEPH, investment firm executive, forum administrator; b. nr. Claflin, Kans., Aug. 18, 1919; s. Robert A. and Emma (Zecha) H.; m. Janice Cannon, Sept. 22, 1941 (dec. Aug. 1943); 1 child, Theodore; m. Ermalee Strutz, Nov. 22, 1945; children: Robert, Walter Jr., Jack, Joseph, Karl. Student pub. schs., Claflin; D.Eng. (hon.), Stevens Inst. Tech., 1970, Mich. Tech. U., 1973; LL.D. (hon.), St. Mary of Plains Coll., St. Martin's Coll., U. Md., Adelphi U., U. San Diego, Rensselaer Poly. Inst., 1973, U. Alaska, 1976, Alaska Pacific U., 1991; D.Pub. Adminstrn. (hon.), Willamette U. Founder Hickel Investment Co., Anchorage, 1947—; gov. State of Alaska, 1966-69, 90-94; sec. U.S. Dept. Interior, 1969-70; sec. gen. The Northern Forum, 1994—; former mem. world adv. council Internat. Design Sci. Inst.; former mem. com. on sci. freedom and responsibility AAAS; nominated for pres. at 1968 Republican Nat. Convention; co-founder Yukon Pacific Corp.; founder Inst. of the North, 1996—. Author: Who Owns America?, 1971; contbr. articles to newspapers. Mem. Republican Nat. Com., 1954-64; bd. regents Gonzaga U.; bd. dirs. Salk Inst., 1972-79, NASA Adv. Coun. Exploration Task Force, 1989-91; mem. Governor's Econ. Com. on North Slope Natural Gas, Alaska, 1982. Named Alaskan of Year, 1969, Man of Yr. Ripon Soc., 1970; recipient DeSmet medal Gonzaga U., 1969, Horatio Alger award, 1972, Grand Cordon of the Order of Sacred Treasure award His Imperial Majesty the Emperor of Japan, 1988. Mem. Pioneers of Alaska, Alaska C. of C. (former chmn. econ. devel. com.), Equestrian Order Holy Sepulchre, Knights Malta, KC. Achievements include leading the first Alaska Chamber economic trade mission to Japan. Home: 1905 Loussac Dr Anchorage AK 99517-1225 Office: PO Box 101700 Anchorage AK 99510-1700

HICKEN, RUSSELL BRADFORD, art dealer, appraiser; b. Jacksonville, Fla., Dec. 24, 1926; s. Leslie Adames and Nettie Bradford (Frazee) H.; m. Margot Louise Ward, Apr. 14, 1978. BS, Fla. State U., 1951. Tchr. Fletcher H.S., Jacksonville, 1951-57; dir. Jacksonville Art Mus., 1957-64, 69-75, Tampa (Fla.) Art Inst., 1964-67, Mint Mus. Art, Charlotte, 1967-69, Hollywood (Fla.) Art & Culture Ctr., 1975-77; art dealer Russel B. Hicken, Fine Arts Ltd., Tampa, Miami, 1977—; sr. cons. Koger Gallery and Gardens, Jacksonville, 1999—. Mem. Bakehouse Art Ctr., Miami, 1996—, Sesquicentennial Commn., Jacksonville, 1972. With U.S. Army, 1944-46, ETO. Mem. Am. Assn. Mus., S.E. Mus. Conf. (pres. 1969-70, AAM rep. 1970-76). Democrat. Avocations: chess, backgammon, travel. Fax: 850-907-0066. Home and Office: 5403 Widefield Rd Tallahassee FL 32308-6454

HICKEY, BARRY JAMES, archbishop; b. Leonora, Australia, Apr. 16, 1936; s. Gregory Maurice and Freda (Kruse) H. Lic. Sacred Theology, Urbaniana U., Rome, 1959; BA, U. West Australia, Perth, Australia, 1971, MSW, 1973; DD (hon.), 1984. Ordained priest Roman Cath. Ch., 1958, ordained bishop, 1984. Dir. Centrecare, Perth, 1973-83, Cath. Immigration, Perth, 1976-83; parish priest Sacred Heart Ch., Highgate, Australia, 1983-84; bishop of Geraldton (West Australia) Roman Cath. Ch., 1984-91; archbishop of Perth St. Mary's Cathedral, 1991—; chair Nat. Cath. Liturgy Commn., Sydney, Australia, 1993—; sec. Bishops' Com. for Migrant Affairs, Sydney, 1992—. Author: Preparing Couples for Marriage, 1982. Capt. Australian Army Res., 1962-67. Named to Order of Australia, 1980. Avocations: tennis, reading, walking, music. Office: St Mary's Cathedral, Victoria Sq, Perth WA 6000, Australia*

HICKEY, BOBBY RAY, underwriting assistant; b. Louisville, Apr. 13, 1960; s. Virgle Ray and Doris Jean (Adams) H. Student, U. Louisville, 1990. Various positions Kroger, Louisville, 1980-87; student asst. U. Louisville, 1987-91, libr. asst. I, 1991-95; mail courier Ky. Farm Bur. Ins., Louisville, 1995, underwriting asst., 1995—; auto underwriting dept. rep. to safety com. Ky. Farm Bur., 1996. Neighborhood rep. Environ. Health Task Force, Louisville, 1996; neighborhood rep. Family Health Ctrs., Louisville, 1986—, vice chmn., 1991—, chairperson nominating com., 1994—, mem. mktg. com., 1997. Recipient Berney H. Kroger Cert. Merit Cmty. Svc., 1982, William O. Cowger award Jefferson County Rep. Com., Louisville, 1986, Mayor's citation City of Louisville, 1990, 96, cert. of recognition Jefferson County Commr., 1996. Mem. Toastmasters (v.p. pub. rels. Ky. Farm Bur. chpt. 1996). Roman Catholic. Avocations: reading, community service, theatre, travel, music. E-mail: BRH6078@bellsouth.net. Office: Ky Farm Bur Ins 9201 Bunsen Pkwy Louisville KY 40220-3793

HICKEY, DAVID PATRICK, telecommunications executive, electronic engineer; b. Cork, Ireland, June 21, 1960; s. Patrick Damian and Una Winifred (Brennan) H. BEngring., Univ. Coll., Dublin, 1981. Student engr. Dept. Posts and Telegraphs, Dublin, 1979-81; telecomms. engr. Telecom Ireland, Dublin, 1981-86; telecomms. cons. Datanet Ltd., Dublin, 1986-98; gen. mgr. Europe WorldPort Comm., Dublin, 1998—; bd. dirs. Datanet, Datenet Internat., WorldPort Comm. Ltd., WorldPort Europe. Mem. IEE (assoc. mem., sec. 1986-87, chmn. 1987-88), Instn. of Engrs. of Ireland, Chartered Inst. Arbitrators. Roman Catholic. Avocations: golf, squash, flying. Office: WorldPort Comms Inc, Blanchardstown Corp Park, Dublin 15, Ireland

HICKEY, ELIZABETH LOUISE, advertising agency executive, limousine company executive; b. N.Y.C., Nov. 6, 1958; d. Louise Anthony and Josephine Morgan (Stancisko) Piccoli; m. Mark Hickey, Oct. 15, 1983; children: Caitlin, John, Alanna, Shannon. BA, U. Rochester, 1979; Cert. in Graphic Design, Mass. Coll. Art, 1984. Art and recreation therapist Fernald State Sch., Waltham, Mass., 1979-82; art dir. Wizard of Adz, Dedham, Mass., 1984-89; graphic designer Imageworks, Waltham, 1984-92; pres., mktg. dir. Limo Dreams, Inc., Waltham, 1985-90; creative dir. Wizard of Adz, Dedham, Mass., 1989; art dir. Emerson Lane Fortuna, Boston, 1989—; faculty mem. Mass. Coll. Art, 1987—, mem. portfolio rev. com.; art dir. Arnold Fortuna Lane, Boston, 1991-93; sr. art dir. Hill Hollidays, 1993-94; creative dir. Holland Mark Martin, 1994-96, Heater Advt. 1997-98; v.p. assoc. creative dir. Arnold Advt., 1996-97; CEO, creative dir. Veloctiy Inc., 1999—. Recipient Alcoholism and Communications Mktg. Achievement award Nat. Found. for Alcoholism Communication, 1986, New Eng. Best of Broadcast award, 1991, 93, 97, Francis J. Hatch award, 1991, 93, 94, 96, Cannes Internat. advt. award, 1994, Clio Nat. Advt. award, 1994. Mem. Advt. Club of Greater Boston. Democrat. Roman Catholic. Avocations: white water rafting, mountain climbing. Home and Office: Velocity Inc 46 Shirley Rd Waltham MA 02452-8031

HICKEY, JAMES ALOYSIUS CARDINAL, archbishop; b. Midland, Mich., Oct. 11, 1920; s. James P. and Agnes (Ryan) H. J.C.D., Lateran U., Italy, 1950; S.T.D., Angelicum U., Italy, 1951; M.A., Mich. State U., 1962. Ordained priest Roman Catholic Ch., 1946; sec. to Bishop of Saginaw, 1951-60; rector St. Paul Sem., Saginaw, Mich., 1960-68; aux. bishop Saginaw, 1967-69; chmn. bishops' com. on Priestly Formation, 1968-69; rector N.Am. Coll., Rome, 1969-74; bishop of Cleve., 1974-80, archbishop of Washington, 1980—; chancellor Cath. U. Am., 1980—; elevated to cardinal, 1988; mem. Ctrl. Com. for 1975 Holy Year, 1973-75; chmn. Bishop's Com. Pastoral Rsch. and Practices, 1974-77, Bishop's Com. for Doctrine, 1979-82; chmn. bd. trustees Basilica of the Nat. Shrine of Immaculate Conception, 1980—; chmn. Bishops' Com. Human Values, 1984-87; chmn. Bishop's Com. on N.Am. Coll., 1988-92, 94-97. Episc. advisor to Serra Internat., 1981-88; Episc. moderator Holy Childhood Assn., 1984-93; elected mem. Secretariat Synod of Bishops, 1991-94. Address: Archdiocese Washington Archdiocesan Pastoral Ctr PO Box 29260 Washington DC 20017-0260

HICKEY, JEROME EDWARD, investment company executive; b. Chgo., June 25, 1937; s. Matthew Joseph and Naomi (Pope) H.; m. Denise Coakley, May 20, 1967; children: J. Graham, Matthew, Elizabeth, George, Peter. BS in Econs., Coll. of the Holy Cross, 1959; MA in Philosophy, Boston Coll., 1964. Instr. Cranwell Sch., Lenox, Mass., 1964-66; acct. exec. Paine Webber, N.Y.C., 1966-68; v.p. Hickey & Co., Chgo., 1968-72, Ralph W. Davis, Chgo., 1972-75, Weeden & Co., Chgo., 1975-78; founder, pres. Jerome Hickey Assocs., Chgo., 1979-84; pres. No. Trust Brokerage, Chgo., 1984-87; sr. v.p. Stein Roe & Farnham, Chgo., 1988-93; sr. v.p., mng. dir. SEI Corp., Chgo., 1993-96; founder, mng. dir. Dearborn Ptnrs., Chgo., 1997—. Dir. Western Golf Assn., Golf, Ill., 1979—, chmn. exec. com., 1991-96; trustee St. Ignatius Coll. Prep., Chgo., 1988-93, chmn., 1990-93. Named Outstanding Young Man in Am., 1971. Mem. Knollwood Club (Lake Forest, Ill., dir. 1976-79), Bond Club Chgo. (dir. 1974-75), Econ. Club Chgo., Desert Forest Golf Club, The Boulders. Roman Catholic. Home: 1923 N Fremont St Chicago IL 60614-5016 Office: Dearborn Ptnrs 200 W Madison St Chicago IL 60606-3414

HICKEY, JOHN KING, lawyer, career officer; b. Mt. Sterling, Ky.; s. John Andrew and Anna Christine H.; m. Elizabeth Jane Pattavina, Nov. 23, 1944; children: Roger Dennis, John King, Patricia Elizabeth Corsini. JD, U. Ky., 1948; M in Internat. Affairs, George Washington U., 1974. Bar: Ky. 1949, Colo. 1958, U.S. Ct. Military Appeals 1959, U.S. Supreme Ct. 1959. Commd. 2d. lt. U.S. Army Air Forces, 1942; advanced through grades to col. USAF, 1964, ret., 1970; dir. legal judicial adminstrn. Council State Govts., Lexington, Ky., 1971-73; dir. continuing legal edn. U. Ky. Coll. Law, Lexington, Ky., 1973-86; pvt. practice Lexington, Ky., 1986—. Mem. Nat. Assn. Attorneys Gen. (outstanding contributions award 1973, sec.), U. Ky. Law Alumni Assn. (sec., treas. 1973-76, appreciation award 1976), Ctrl. Ky. Knife Club (plaque 1997). Democrat. Roman Catholic. Avocations: machairologist, reading, walking, swimming. Office: 3340 Nantucket Dr Lexington KY 40502-3205

HICKEY, MAURICE ROBERT, pharmacist; b. Endiburgh, Scotland, Mar. 14, 1959; s. Maurice and Florence (Findlay) H.; m. Margaret Fitzpatrick, May 28, 1984; children: Roisin Ann, Andrea. BSc in Pharmacy with honors, U. Strathclyde, 1981, MBA, 1989. Pharmacist Grampian Health Authority, U.K., 1982-84; mgr. Plymouth & South Devon Coop. Soc. Ltd., U.K., 1985-88; pharmacist MHR Ltd., Plymouth, 1991-94; mng. dir. Fernley Wallis Pharmacy Ltd., Forres, Morayshire, 1994—. Fellow Royal Soc. Arts; mem. China Philatelic Soc., Nepal & Tibet Philatelic Cir. Avocations: wine, philately, cycling. Office: Maurice Hickey Pharmacy, 99 High Sch, Forres 1V36 1AA, Scotland

HICKEY, ROBERT JAMES, III, geologist, geographer, educator; b. Media, Pa., June 12, 1965; s. Robert and Kate H. BS in Geology, Edinboro U. of Pa., 1987; MS in Geology, Wash. State U., 1990; PhD in Geography, U. Idaho, 1994. Tchg. asst. dept. geology Washington State U., Pullman, 1988-90; tchg. asst. dept. geography U. of Idaho, Moscow, 1991-94; asst. prof. dept. geology State U. of W. Ga., Carrollton, 1994-96; sr. lectr. Sch. of Spatial Scis., Curtin U. Tech., Perth, Australia, 1997-2000; asst. prof. dept. geography Ctrl. Wash. U., 2000—; cons. various mining cos., govt. agys. and environ. groups, U.S. and Australia, 1990—. Presenter papers at sci. confs. Recipient Dean's medallion for Excellence in Tchng., Curtin U., 1998, 99, Grad. Student Assn. Tchg. Excellence award, U. Idaho, 1994; grantee Crown Resources Corp., Buckhorn Mt., Wash., 1989, Australian Rsch. Coun., 1997, Curtin U. Tech., 1997,. Mem. Am. Assn. Geographers (finalist for Warren Nystrom award 1995), Australasian Surveying and Mapping Lectrs. Assn. (sec. 1997-99), Australian Urban and Regional Info. Systems Assn. (Best Presented Paper ann. conf. 1997), Mapping Scis. Inst. of Australia (councillor WA Australia chpt. 1999-2000, web editor 1997-2000). Avocations: reading, travel, karate, weightlifting. E-mail: rhickey@cwu.edu. Home: 1402 Cora #2 Ellensburg WA 98926 Office: Curtin U Tech Sch Spat Scis, GPO Box U 1987, Perth WA 6845, Australia Office: Ctrl Wash U Dept Geography/Land Studies Ellensburg WA 98926

HICKISH, GORDON WALTER, physician; b. London, Oct. 7, 1925; s. James Richard and Hilda Nellie (Boryer) H.; m. Aileen Key, July 8, 1949; children: Mary, Angus, Joseph, Tamas, Dinah, Annie. MBChB, Edinburgh U., 1948; dipl. child health, London U., 1954. Physician Leith Hosp., Edinburgh, Scotland, 1948-49, 51-52; resident, pediatric registrar Odstock Hosp., Salisbury, Eng., 1952-54; gen. practitioner London, 1954-70, Christchurch, Eng., 1970—; med. registrar Princess Beatrice Hosp., London, 1956-60; practitioner St. Bartholomew's Hosp., London, 1960-90; aviation med. examiner, FAA, 1976—; diving med. examiner Health and Safety Exec., U.K., 1978—. Author: Disorders of the Ear, Nose and Throat, 1985, New Tools for General Practitioners, 1992, 93, 94; translator Ten Years that Changed the Face of Mental Illness, 1999; contbr. articles to profl. jours. Pres. Bransgore Cmty. Care Group, 1972—. Surgeon lt. comdr. Royal Navy, 1949-51, res. 1951-74. Fellow Royal Soc. Medicine, Med. Soc. Edinburgh; mem. Royal Coll. Gen. Practitioners (provost), Hearing Concern Trustee. Mem. Ch. of Eng. Avocations: cycling, cross-country skiing, sailing, beekeeping, reading. Home: Heather Cottage, Burnt House Ln, Bransgore, Christchurch Dorset BH23 8AL, England Office: New Med Centre, Ringwood Rd Bransgore, Dorset Christchurch BH23 8AD, England

HICKMAN, CHARLES WALLACE, Internet executive; b. Des Moines, Sept. 19, 1952; s. James Charles and Margaret Wallace (McKee) H.; m. Rebecca Ann Nyman, July 31, 1993; children: Matthew, Heidi. BBA, U. Iowa, 1974, MA, 1975. Economist U.S. Dept. Labor, Washington, 1976; project coord. Ind. U., Bloomington, 1977; dir. mem. rels. Am. Assembly Collegiate Schs. Bus./Internat. Assn. Mgmt. Ed., St. Louis, 1978-99; v.p. for acad. affairs Quisic, L.A., 1999—. Office: Quisic 6255 W Sunset Blvd Ste 801 Los Angeles CA 90028-7409

HICKMAN, ROSEMARY, surgeon, researcher; b. Durban, Natal, South Africa, Mar. 22, 1940; d. Michael Hoste and Dorothy Kathlee (Margrie) H.; m. Wopke Van Hoorn (div. 1985); children: Dorothy Rosemary, Aaltje Rosemary. MB ChB, U. Cape Town, South Africa, 1964, MD, 1968, ChM, 1972. Prin. surgeon U. Cape Town, 1976—, assoc. prof., 1975—; asst. to mgr. vol. svcs. St. Luke's Hospice, Cape Town, 1999—. Contbr. some 140 articles to profl. jours. Med. Rsch. Coun. South Africa grantee, 1970-95. Mem. Women in Medicine Group, South African Assn. Med. Women. Anglican. Avocation: lawn bowls, knitting, walking, gardening. Home: 25 Strubens Rd, Mowbray 7705, South Africa

HICKS, ANDREW CHARLES, surgeon, consultant; b. Longreach, Queensland, Australia, Nov. 25, 1918; arrived in Kenya, 1952; s. Charles Maurice and Elizabeth (Smith) H.; m. Sheila Una O'Toole, Aug. 31, 1946 (dec.); children: Anthony, Brian, Alison Rosemary, Amanda Christine; m. Regina Kalile Ipopo, Aug. 4, 1975 (dec. Apr. 1984); children: Arune Salma, Alan Ambokile; m. Bilha Nakhanu Siambi, Aug. 16, 1986. Lic., Royal Coll. Physicians, London, 1942; student, Middlesex Hosp. Med. Sch., London, 1937-42. House surgeon, registrar Middlesex Hosp., London, 1947-50; sr. surg. registrar Stoke Mandeville Hosp., Aylesbury, Eng., 1950-52; cons. gen. surgeon Nairobi (Kenya) Hosp., 1952—, casualty supr., 1975-82; external examiner in surgery U. Nairobi, 1977; Chmn. joint adv. com. Provision Pvt. Healthcare Kenya, 1997—. Contbr. numerous articles to profl. jours. Bd. dirs. Nairobi Hospice, 1996—; sr. steward Lavington United Ch., Nairobi, 1984-85, chapel steward, 1992—, elder. Capt. Royal Army Med. Corps. Britain, 1943-46. Decorated officer brother Order of St. John, 1968. Fellow Royal Coll. Surgeons (Eng.), Assn. Surgeons East Africa, Internat. Coll. Surgeons, Brit. Med. Assn. (hon. sec. Kenya br. 1954-66); mem. Med. Assn. Kenya (1st pres. 1963, Privileged Silver Mem. award 1987, 88, chmn. Kenya Med. Assn. Trust 1988, ethics and stds. com. 1994), Lions Club (chmn., pres. 1962, Nairobi host). Avocations: photography, gardening, studying nature, camping safaris, defining and writing on early local medical history. Office: Nairobi Hosp, Argwings Khodek Rd PO Box 30026, Nairobi Kenya

HICKS, CELIA RACHEL, ophthalmology researcher; b. Penzance, England, Feb. 21, 1965; arrived in Australia, 1995; d. John Michael and June Rhodes (Binns) H.; m. Carlos Eduardo Elissegaray, Sept. 15, 1996; children: Grace Lilian, Juan Sebastian. BA, U. Cambridge, England, 1987, MBBCh, 1989, MA, 1990. House officer Middlesborough and Norfolk Hosps., England, 1990-91; sr. house officer U. Hosp. Wales, 1991; demonstrator in anatomy U. Cambridge, England, 1991-92; sr. house officer ophthalmology Moorfields Eye Hosp., England, 1992-95; rsch. surgeon Lions Eye Inst., Nedlands, Australia, 1995-98, clin. trial coord., 1998—. Contbr. articles to profl. jours.; patentee in field. U. Cambridge scholar, 1985, 87. Fellow Royal Coll. Ophthalmologists. Office: Lions Eye Inst, 2 Verdun St, Nedlands 6009, Australia

HICKS, DOLORES KATHLEEN (DE DE HICKS), foundation director; b. Mount Vernon, Iowa, Sept. 22, 1932; d. Edward M. and Olga Marie (Hekl) Staskal; m. Roswell Allen Hicks, Sept. 5, 1952; children: Thomas, Gregory, Bryan, Kevin. Student, Colo. Coll., 1950-52. Exec. women's wardrobe cons. Bullock's, Torrance, Calif., 1985-86; exec. dir. The Vol. Ctr., Torrance, 1986—; pres. Vol. Ctrs. So. Calif., 1988; coord. First Lady of Calif. Outstanding Vol. Awards, Sacramento, 1993; nat. bd. dirs. Vol. Ctrs.-Points of Light Found., Washington, 1993-96. Pres. LWV, Palos Verdes Peninsula, Calif., 1981-83; chair Year of the Coast, Calif. LWV, Sacramento, 1984; active in state and local polit. campaigns. Named YWCA Woman of the Yr., YWCA, Torrance, 1986, Woman of Distinction, Soroptomist, Torrance, 1988. Mem. Pvt. Industry Coun. (bd. mem. 1994-97), Cmty. Assn. of the Peninsula (life, pres. 1984-87, Palos Verdes Peninsula Citizen of Yr. 1987, Outstanding Vol. award 1988), So. Bay Prodrs. Guild (Outstanding Interviewer 1995), Vol. Ctrs. of Calif. (bd. mem. 1988—, Founders award 1991), Gamma Phi Beta (alumni mem., Internat. Carnation award 1992, Achievement award 1993). Democrat. Roman Catholic. Avocations: gourmet cooking, home decorating, entertaining, reading, traveling.

HICKS, GERALD, artist; b. London, Dec. 6, 1927; s. Algernon Joseph Hicks and Annie Elizabeth Newell; m. Anne Marguerite Christine Hayward, Apr. 8, 1952; children: Simon Richard William, Miranda Kim Marguerite. Diploma in Fine Art, Slade Sch., London, 1950; Art Tchr.'s Diploma, London U., 1951. Head of art Cotham Grammar Sch., Bristol, 1951-81, sch. gov., 1975-81; vis. lectr. Bristol U., 1970s, 80s; artists chmn. Royal West of Eng. Acad., Bristol, 1970s, v.p. 1997—; chair S.W. Sports Orgns., 1980s, Bristol Civic Soc., 1988-90; chmn. coaching Brit. Judo Assn., 1970s. Oneman shows include Royal West of Eng., King St. Gallery, London. Chmn. Bristol Sports Assn., 1980s, Bristol Arts Cons. Ctr., 1970s; vice-chmn. S.W. coun. Sport and Recreation; coun. mem. S.S. Gt. Britain Project, 1970s, 80s, 90s. Recipient Mem. British Empire award HM The Queen, 1994, Queen's Silver Jubilee award for painting, 1977, others; Judo 7th Dan, 1997. Home: Goldrush Great George St, B 51 5QT Bristol England

HICKS, HAROLD EUGENE, chemical engineer; b. Mpls., Jan. 20, 1919; s. Julius and Della (Beebe) H.; m. Ruth Esther Nelson, Oct. 4, 1941 (dec. Mar. 1989); children: Barbara H. Young, Charlotte H. Silvia, David H., Douglas E.; m. Virginia C. Hobson, Mar. 31, 1990. B Chem. Engring., U. Minn., 1941; postgrad., U. Del., 1946-47. Chemist Hercules Powder Co., Wilmington, Del., 1941, rsch. chemist, 1941, 46-50; prodn. supr. Hercules Powder Co., Hattiesburg, Miss., 1950-64; plant mgr. Hercules Powder Co., Chicopee, Mass., 1964-66; plant mgr. Hercules Inc., Franklin, Va., 1966-68, Brunswick, Ga., 1968-76, Louisiana, Mo., 1978-80; tech. advisor Dawood-Hercules, Lahore, Pakistan, 1976-78; vol. exec. Internat. Exec. Svc. Corp., 1986-94; pres. The Book Shop, Inc., Brunswick, 1991—; bd. dirs. Downtown Devel. Authority, Brunswick. Mem. county cos. Glynn County; dir. St. Mark's Towers, Glynn-Brunswick Navy League of the U.S., Pine Belt Savings & Loan Assn, Hattiesburg, Miss., 1958-64, dir., 1st Nat. Bank of Brunswick, Ga., 1969-76. Maj. U.S. Army, 1941-46, ETO. Mem. AIChE (emeritus), Am. Chem. Soc. (emeritus), Rotary. Methodist. Avocations: computers, photography, travel, reading, gardening. Home: 262 Sutherland Bluff Dr Sutherland Bluff GA 31331-9239

HICKS, J. ROBERT, industrial packaging executive, retired; b. Chgo., July 7, 1930; s. Robert David and Ada Medora (Yoder) H.; m. Gloria D. Brown, Feb. 14, 1956 (divorced); 1 child, Michael Patrick; m. Jeannine E.G. Weyns, Dec. 23, 1972; 1 child, Stefanie Maria. BA in Bus. Adminstrn., Knox Coll., Galesburg, Ill., 1952; student, Am. Inst. Banking, 1955. Mgr. tech. svcs. ITW Signode, Glenview, Ill., 1956-68; mgr. sales engring. Europe ITW Signode, Dinslaken, Germany, 1968-76; mng. dir. ITW Signode, Zaventem, Belgium, 1976-81; mgr. application rev. Europe ITW Signode, Newbury, Eng., 1981-87; European sales mgr. ITW Shippers, Carnières, Belgium, 1987-95; ret. Ill. Tool Works, Glenview, Ill., 1995; pres. Hicks Cons., Hever, Belgium, 1995—. Sgt. U.S. Army, 1952-54, Korea. Mem. Am. Belgian Assn. (1st Am. pres. 1992-97). Fax: 32-15-616-520.

HICKS, JAMES THOMAS, lawyer, physician; b. Brownsville, Pa.; s. Thomas A. and Florence Julia (O'Donnell) H. AB, BS, MS, U. Pitts.; PhD, George Washington U.; MD, U. Ark.; JD, DePaul U.; LLM in Health Law, Loyola U., 1989. Bar: Ill. 1977, Pa. 1977, U.S. Supreme Ct. 1980, N.Y. 1988, D.C. 1988, U.S. Dist. Ct. D.C. 1988, U.S. Ct. Appeals (7th cir.) 1977, U.S. Ct. Appeals (D.C. and Ill. cirs.) 1988; lic. airline transport flight instr. Tchr. DePaul U. Coll. Law, Chgo., 1990—; intern USPHS Hosp., Balt.; resident VA Hosp., Pitts.; pvt. practice River Forest, Ill., Oak Brook Terrace, Ill. Contbr. editor Hosp. Mgmt. mag. Asst. surgeon USPHS. Recipient Outstanding Alumnus award De Paul U., 1980. Fellow ACP, Am. Coll. Pathologists, Am. Acad. Forensic Scientists, Am. Soc. Clin. Pathologists; mem. ABA (com. on professionalism and ethics, vice-chmn. health law com. gen. practice sect.), Royal Coll Physicians (Eng.), Assn. Trial Lawyers Am., Pa. Bar Asns., Ill. Bar Assn., Chgo. Bar Assn. (health law com., ethics com.), Ill. Trial Lawyers Assn., D.C. Bar Assn., Pa. Trial Lawyers Assn., N.Y. Bar Assn., Univ. Club, Carlton Club, Elks, Moose, Oak Park Country Club. Office: Ste 218 17 W 706 Butterfield Rd Oakbrook Terrace IL 60181

HICKS, PETER ALASTAIR, agroindustry specialist; b. Kampala, Uganda, Aug. 20, 1945; s. Peter Henry and Annie Harper (Gavin) H.; m. Constance Lilian Skinner, Sept. 16, 1967; children: Tara Anne, Adrian John. BS with honors, U. Reading, Eng., 1968; Cert., U. Ill., 1980; M of Engring. Sci., U. Sydney, Australia, 1983; PhD in Agrl. Scis., Pacific Western U., 2000. Mngmt. trainee H.J. Heinz Co., Ltd., London, 1964-68; food engr. IFRPD Kasetsart U., Bangkok, 1977-78; vis. fellow U. South Pacific, Apia, West Samoa, 1981; lectr. I U. Western Sydney, Australia, 1970-83; food industries officer FAO/UN, Rome, 1984-86; sr. regional agroindustries and posharvest officer FAO/UN, Bangkok, 1987—; dir. Hawkaid R&D Co., Richmond, Australia, 1982-90; tech. advisor Asia-Pacific Food Industry Jour., 1991—; advisor Acad. Consortium of Thai Univs. in Agro Industry Curriculum, 1995—; hon. assc. Food Tech. Assn. NSW, 1974-84; spkr. in field. Contbr. over 160 articles to profl. jours., chpts. to books. Chmn. Orchid Garden Condominium, Thailand, 1995-97, Food Engring. Group, Australian Inst. of Food Sci. and Tech., 1972-74, Coun. for Edn. in World Citizenship U.K., 1964; bd. govs. Bangkok Patana Sch., 1977-78; mem. found. com. UN-related Internat. Sch., Bangkok. Fellow Australian Inst. Food Sci. and Tech.; mem. Asian Assn. Agrl. Engrs. (life, founding, v.p.), Thai Assn. Food Sci. and Tech. (life). Avocation: numismatics, swimming. Office: Food and Agr Orgn UN, 39 Phra Atit Rd, Bangkok 10200, Thailand

HICKS, ROGER GEORGE, information systems consultant, educator; b. Gloucester, Gloucestershire, England, Nov. 28, 1945; arrived in New Zealand, 1977; s. Alfred James and Gladys (Sale) H.; m. Glenis Evelyn Gibson, Dec. 13, 1969; children: Richard, Joanne, Lynette. BSc with honors, U. Bath, England, 1968. chartered engr. Sr. sys. engr. Rolls Royce Engines, Bristol, England, 1969-72; sr. software engr. Digital Equiptment Corp., Reading, England, 1972-77; supervising sys. programmer New Zealand Dept Health, Auckland, 1977-78; systems mgr. AHI Computer Svcs., Auckland, 1978-81; tech. mgr. Paxus, Auckland, 1981-86; ind. software mgr. Rakon Computers, Auckland, 1986-88; open systems unit mgr. Digital Equipment Corp., Auckland, 1988-90; prin. RNG Consulting, Auckland, 1990-95; lectr. U. Auckland, 1991-96; sys. architect Clear Comms., 1995-99; prin. cons. Price Waterhouse Coopers, 1999—; founder, pres. UNIFORUM New Zealand, 1985-97; chmn. New Zealand Software Standards Com., 1991-94; nat. focal point rep. UNESCO Reg. Info. Network for SE Asia & Pacific, New Zealand, 1994—; leader UNESCO Reg. Info. and Informatics Network for Pacific Island Nations, 1999—. Mem. New Zealand Computer Soc., British Computer Soc., Assn. Computing Machinery, Internet Soc. of New Zealand (chair 1995-96), Asia Pacific Internet Assn. (bd. dirs. 1997-99). Avocations: computers, reading, poetry, movies, family life. Office: PriceWaterhouseCoopers, Pvt Bag 92162, Auckland New Zealand

HICKS, SUSAN LYNN BOWMAN, small business owner; b. Flint, Mich., Mar. 24, 1952; d. Richard and Carol Joanne (Haney) Bowman; m. Duane James Hicks, Aug. 6, 1977. BA, U. Mich., Flint, 1975; MA, Cen. Mich. U., 1981. Med. social worker Flint Osteo. Hosp., 1974-77; dir. med. social work and patient rels. Crittenton Hosp., Rochester, Mich., 1978-89; coord. geriatric social work Genesys Regional Med. Ctr., 1990—; owner, Susan Hicks Enterprises, 1988—; mgmt. tng. and devel. cons. Buick, Oldsmobile, Cadillac div. GM, Grand Blanc, Mich., 1985. Bd. dirs., chmn. com. Rochester Area Youth Guidance, Mich., 1986, chmn., 1988; bd. dirs. E. ctrl. Mich. chpt. Alzheimer's Assn., 1994. Mem. Soc. for Hosp. Social Work Dirs. (Recognition award 1984, 85, pres.-elect 1985-86, pres. 1986-87, chmn. polit. and social action com. 1988—), Nat. Assn. Social Workers, NAFE, Soc. Patient Representatives. Methodist. Avocations: tap dancing, writing. Home and Office: 8201 Sawgrass Trl Grand Blanc MI 48439-1874

HICKS, WILLIAM HAMPTON, pianist, conductor, voice coach; b. Lexington, Ky., Nov. 30, 1956; s. Billy and Betty (Clark) H. Student, U. Cin. Asst. condr. opera cos. including The Cin. Opera, The Omaha Opera, N.Y.C. Opera, The Friends of French Opera, The Met. Opera, Santa Fe Opera, Can. Opera., 1975-91; free-lance voice coach N.Y.C., 1977—; assoc. condr. to John McGlinn, N.Y.C., 1983—; assoc. condr., pianist Am. Mus. Theatre Series Library of Congress, Washington, 1984-88; condr. Opera Uptown, N.Y.C., 1984; assoc. condr. New Amsterdam Theatre Co., N.Y.C., 1984-86, Jerome Kern Festival, Carnegie Hall, N.Y.C., 1985; assoc. dir. Natchez Opera Festival, 1991; asst. condr. The Met. Opera, N.Y.C., 1995—; asst. chorus master The Met. Opera, 1999—; performed with Roberta Peters, The White House, 1991; voice coach to Luciano Pavarotti, Teresa Stratas, Thomas Hampson, Harolyn Blackwell, Angelina Reaux, Judy Kaye, Israel Vocal Arts Inst., Juilliard Opera Ctr., The Richard Tucker Found.; music dir. The Singers Devel. Found., 1994—; ofcl. pianist The George London Found., 1998—, The Licia Albanese/Puccini Found., 1989—, Opera Index, 1993—; creative dir. OperaMCY; cons. mcy.com. Stage debut in Giordano's Fedora, Met. Opera, 1996; pianist various recordings including The Films of Léonide Massine, 1979-81, Songs of New York, 1984, Kiri Sings Gershwin, 1987, Gershwin Overtures, 1987, Blackwell Sings Bernstein: A Simple Song, 1996; condr. opera Monteverdi's Il Ritorno d'Ulisse in Patria, 1988-89; soloist PBS telecast Evening at the Pops, 1990; appeared with Luciano Pavarotti on The David Letterman Show, 1993. Mem. Am. Lyric Theater Assn., Inc. (co-founder, 1st v.p. 1999—), Omega Investment Club (founder, presiding ptnr. 1996—).

HICKSON, GARY WAYNE, communications executive; b. Tamworth, NSW, Australia, Dec. 5, 1959; s. Robert Raymond Hickson and Florence Daphne Kilpatrick; m. Michelle Anne Nugent, Sept. 9, 1989; children: Zachary James, Samuel Peter. Grad. h.s., Tamworth, 1977. Race broadcaster Radio 2TM, Tamworth, 1977-86, Sky Channel, Sydney, Australia, 1988-92; sports editor News Corp., Tamworth, 1984-86; editor News Corp., Sydney, 1986-95, publ., 1995—. Broadcaster NSW Best Race Description, 1989, 90. Mem. NSW Alzheimers' Assn. (dir.). Office: News Corp, 2 Holt St Surry Hills, Sydney NSW 2010, Australia

HIDA, TOYOAKI, physician, researcher; b. Tsushima, Aichi, Japan, Oct. 20, 1955; s. Yutaka and Yukiko (Mizuno) H.; m. Mineko Ukai, June 5, 1988; children: Chie, Keiichiro. MD, Nagoya (Japan) City U., 1980. Clin. fellow Sch. Medicine Nagoya City U., 1980-82; clin. staff mem. Enshu Gen. Hosp., Hamamatsu, Japan, 1982-86; clin. and rsch. fellow Aichi Cancer Ctr., Nagoya, 1986-88; clin. staff mem. Aichi Cancer Ctr., 1988-93, head internal medicine, 1996—; rsch. fellow Nat. Cancer Inst., Rockville, Md., 1994-96. Office: Aichi Cancer Ctr, 1-1- Kanokoden Chikusa-ku, Nagoya Aichi 464-8681, Japan

HIDAI, HIDEO, hospital administrator, educator; b. Yokohama, Kangawa, Japan, Feb. 8, 1934; s. Toraji and Yuki (Nakajima) H.; m. Yoshiko Kato, Nov. 25, 1971; children: Takeo, Yasuo. MD, Yokohama City U., Japan, 1959, PhD, 1966. Intern USAF Hosp., Tachiwaka, 1959-60; asst. Yokohama City U., 1960-69, asst. prof., 1970-82; dir. Yokohama Dai-ichi Hosp., 1983—; vis. prof. St. Mariannna U., Kawasaki, Japan, 1994—. Contbr. articles to Jour. of Urology, Surgery Today, Trans. Am. Soc. Artificial Internal Organs. Mem. Kanagawa Social Welfare Com., 1990—; trustee Japanese Soc. for Dialysis Therapy, Tokyo, 1991—, pres. elect 43d gen. congress, Yokohama, 1998. Recipient Sakaguchi prize Japanese Urolog. Assn., Nagoya, 1967. Avocation: surf fishing. Home: 5-13-4 Hon-Fujisewa, Fujisawa Kanagawa 251-0875, Japan Office: Yokohama Dai-ichi Hosp, 6-20 Kinko-cho, Kanagawa Yokohama 221-0056, Japan

HIDAI, HOICHI, Asian studies educator; b. Kobe, Japan, June 17, 1919; s. Toraji and Yuki (Nakajima) H.; m. Matsuko Nakamura, Mar. 30, 1956; children: Masako Sato, Atsuko Iwata. B in Commerce, Tokyo U. Commerce, 1947. Asst. prof. Aoyamagakuin U., Tokyo, 1950-52; asst. prof. Osaka (Japan) City U., 1953-71, prof., 1971-83; prof. Osaka Keizai Hoka U., Yao (Osaka), Japan, 1983—, v.p., 1985-89, dir. Inst. Asian Studies, 1987-91; vice-chmn. Internat. Conf. Korean Studies, Peking, China and Osaka, Japan, 1988-90; trustee Osaka Info. and Computer Coll., 1993—; dir. O.I.C. Internat. Rsch. Ctr., Osaka, 1994—. Editor: Kanto Shiryo, 1994. Named prof. emeritus Osaka City U., 1983. Mem. Hist. Soc. Japan, Assn. Studies of Chinese Soc. and Culture, Josuikai (Alumni Assn. Hitotsubashi U.). Avocations: philately, European railway traveling, collection of foreign railway timetable. Home: Satakedai 5-9-1, Suita Osaka 565-0855, Japan Office: Osaka Keizai Hoka Univ, Gakuonji 6-10, Yao Osaka 581-8511, Japan

HIDAKA, MUTSUO, superconductive electronics researcher; b. Miyazaki, Japan, Aug. 30, 1956; s. Fujio and Nobuko (Tokou) H.; m. Keiko Kobayashi, Nov. 18, 1984; 1 child, Eitaro. BS, Kyushu U., Fukuoka, Japan, 1980, MS, 1982; PhD, Tokyo U., 1998. Rschr. NEC Corp., Kawasaki, Japan, 1982-88, supr., 1988-90, 91-95, prin. rschr.st, 1995—; vis. scientist Ariz. State U., Tempe, 1990-91. Recipient Best Presentation award R & D Assn. for Future Electron Devices, Tokyo, 1997. Recipient Best Poster award 6th Internat. Superconductive Electronics Conf., 1997. Mem. Japan Soc. Applied Physics, Inst. Electronics, Info. and Comm. Engrs. Avocations: jogging, history. Home: 907-303, 1-8-14 Takezono, Tsukuba 305, Japan Office: NEC Corp Fund Rsch Labs, 34 Miyukigaoka, Tsukuba 305-8501, Japan

HIDALGO, FRANCISCO JAVIER, chemist, biochemist, researcher; b. Sevilla, Spain, Nov. 8, 1959; s. Francisco and Victoria (Garcia) H.; m. Rosario Zamora, Apr. 21, 1990. BSc, U. Sevilla, 1981, PhD, 1985. Rsch. assoc. Consejo Superior de Investigaciones Cientificas, Sevilla, 1986-87, rsch. scientist, 1990—, vice dir. Inst. Grasa, 1994—; rsch. assoc. Cornell U., Ithaca, N.Y., 1987-88, U. Calif., Davis, 1988-89. Contbr. articles to profl. jours. Fulbright awardee, 1987. Mem. Real Soc. Española de Quimica, Am. Oil Chemists Soc. Office: CSIC Inst de la Grasa, Avda Padre Garcia Tejero 4, 41012 Sevilla Spain

HIDALGO-QUEHL, GUILLERMO, investment executive; b. San Salvador, El Salvador, Dec. 22, 1923; s. Jose Alberto and Albina (Quehl) H.; m. Isabelle Widmer, Aug. 17, 1959; 2 children, Cristina and Beatrice. LLD, Nat. U. El Salvador, 1951. Legal advisor Ministry of Justice, San Salvador, El Salvador, 1958-60; deputy minister fin. Ministry of Finance, San Salvador, El Salvador, 1961; deputy gov. Ctrl. Res. Bank, San Salvador, El Salvador, 1961-73; minister Ministry of Econs., San Salvador, El Salvador, 1973-75; gov. Ctrl. Res. Bank, San Salvador, El Salvador, 1975-77; atty. Sr. Counsellor Pvt. Office, San Salvador, El Salvador, 1978-89; pres. Salvadorean Stock Exch., San Salvador, El Salvador, 1989—; deputy gov. Interamerican Devel. Bank, El Salvador, 1962-73, gov., 1973-75; gov. Ctrl. Am. Bank Econ. Integration, El Salvador, 1973-77, Internat. Monetary Fund, El Salvador, 1975-77; lectr. Nat. U. El Salvador, 1959-60, Ctrl. Am. Cath. U., 1985-87. Co-author: Role of the Central Reserve Bank on the Anniversary of the Central Economic Development of El Salvador, 1984. Office: Mercado de Valores El Salvador, Salvadorean Stock Exch, Edif Centroam Alameda Roosevelt 3107, San Salvador El Salvador also: Blvd y Condominio, Los Heroer 8 Piso Local D, San Salvador El Salvador*

HIDEG, JÁNOS, surgeon; b. Kalazno, Hungary, Jan. 25, 1933; s. János and Katalin (Meilinger) H.; m. Zsuzsanna Kulcsár, Aug. 18, 1962 (dec. 1989); 1 child, János. MD, Med. U., Budapest, Hungary, 1959; flight surgeon cert., Postgrad. Med. Sch., Budapest, Hungary, 1970; PhD, Hungarian Acad. Scis., Budapest, 1983, DSc, 1984. Lic. med. doctor, surgeon, flight surgeon. Flight surgeon Hungarian Aeromedical Rshc. Inst., Budapest, 1959-60, head surgeon, 1960-67, comdt., 1967-70; dir. Rsch. Inst. Mil. Medicine, Budapest, 1991-93, sci. advisor, 1993—. Author: (procs. of 28th internat. congress of physiol. sci.) Gravitation Physiology, 1980; editor Jour. Hungarian Mil. Medicine; patentee in field. Maj. gen. Med. Corps of Hungarian Army, 1983-91, Budapest. Named merited doctor, Hungarian People's Rep., 1972, Golden Order of Labour, 1980, Order of Star, 1984. Mem. Internat. Acad. Astronautics, Internat. Astronautical Fedn., Intercosmos Coun.

HIDEN, ROBERT BATTAILE, JR., lawyer; b. Boston, May 8, 1933; s. Robert Battaile Sr. and Clotilda (Waddell) H.; m. Ann Eliza McCracken, Mar. 27, 1956; children: Robert B. III, Elizabeth Patterson, John Hughes. BA, Princeton U., 1955; LLB, U. Va., 1960. Bar: N.Y. 1961, U.S. Ct. Appeals (2d cir.) 1974, U.S. Dist. Ct. (so. dist.) N.Y. 1975. Assoc. Sullivan & Cromwell, N.Y.C., 1960-67, ptnr., 1968-98, of counsel, 1999—. Articles editor and contbr. U. Va. Law Rev., 1959-60; contbr., mem. bd. editors Futures Internat. Law Letter, 1987-92. Trustee Hampton (Va.) U. and Hampton Inst., 1984—; commr. Larchmont Little League, N.Y., 1964-68; chmn. Larchmont Jr. Sailing Program, 1977-78; vestry, jr. warden St.

John's Episc. Ch., Larchmont, 1982-86, 99—. Served to lt. (j.g.) USNR, 1955-57. Mem. ABA, N.Y. State Bar Assn., Assn. of Bar of City of N.Y., N.Y. County Bar Assn., Am. Judicature Soc., Raven Soc., Order of Coif, Omicron Delta Kappa. Democrat. Clubs: Larchmont U. (pres. 1976-77), Larchmont Yacht (trustee 1979-85, sec. 1990—); N.Y. Yacht (N.Y.C.); Scarsdale Golf (N.Y.). Avocations: skiing, golf, sailing, tennis. Home: 2 Walnut Ave Larchmont NY 10538-4232 Office: Sullivan & Cromwell 125 Broad St Fl 28 New York NY 10004-2489

HIEBEL, HANS HELMUT, German studies educator; b. Reichenberg, Germany, May 18, 1941; m. Ursula Elvira Schmeller; children: Holger, Hannah. D, U. Erlangen, Germany, 1972, Phd Habilitation, 1982. Prof. U. Erlangen and Giessen, 1983-85; prof. German U. Graz, Austria, 1985—. Author: Die Zeichen des Gesetzes - Franz Kafka, 1983, Henrik Ibsens psycho-analytische Dramen, 1990, Frauz Kalka: Form, 1999; editor: Medien und Maschinen, 1991, Kleine Medienchronik, 1997, Grosse Medienchronik, 1999. Office: Karl Franzens U, Universitätsplatz 3, 8010 Graz Austria

HIEKATA, TOMIZO, surgery educator; b. Izumozaki, Niigata, Japan, May 26, 1934; s. Kohki and Etsu H.; m. Mizuko Matsuda, Feb. 27, 1968; 1 child. MD, Tokyo U., 1959, PhD, 1964. Asst. Tokyo U., Japan, 1964--66; postdoctoral fellow Yale U., 1966-67, rsch. assoc., 1968-69; instr. Tokyo Women's Med. Coll., Japan, 1970-73; assoc. prof. St. Marianna U., Japan, 1974-87, prof., 1987—; councilor Japanese Assn. for Thoracic Surgery, 1975—, Japanese Soc. for Cardiovascular Surgery, Japan, 1988—, Internat. Soc. Cardio-Thoracic Surgeons, 1990—. Avocations: classical music, pictures, tennis, swimming. Office: St Marianna Med U Yokohama Seibu Hosp, 1197-1 Yasashi-Cho, Asahi-Ku Yokohama Japan

HIEKEN, CHARLES, lawyer; b. Granite City, Ill., Aug. 15, 1928; s. Samuel and Margaret (Isaacs) H.; m. Donna Jane Clanin, Jan. 6, 1961; children: Tina Jane, Seth Paul. SBEE, MIT, 1952, SMEE, 1952; LLB, Harvard U., 1957. Bar: Ill. 1957, Mass. 1958, U.S. Supreme Ct. 1960, U.S. Ct. Customs and Patent Appeals 1961, U.S. Ct. Claims 1963, U.S. Ct. Appeals (fed. cir.) 1982. Patent asst. Lab. Electronics, Boston, 1954-56, Fish, Richardson & Neave, Boston, 1956-57; assoc. Hill, Sherman, Meroni & Simpson, Chgo., 1957, Joseph Weingarten, Boston, 1957-58; assoc. Wolf, Greenfield & Hieken, Boston, 1958-61, ptnr., 1961-70; prin. Charles Hieken Law Offices, Waltham, Mass., 1970-87; ptnr. Fish & Richardson, Boston, 1987-94, prin., 1995—; mem. Pres. Carter's adv. com. on indsl. innovation, 1979. Mem. pres.'s adv. coun. Bentley Coll., 1993—; mem. coun. Harvard Law Sch. Assn., 1998—. Served with U.S. Merchant Marine, 1944-47, U.S. Army, 1952-54. Mem. Boston Bar Assn. (mem. civil procedure com. 1959—), Mass. Bar Assn. (chmn. intellectual property com. 1977-80), Ill. State Bar Assn., Boston Patent Law Assn. (chmn. pub. rels. com. 1965-66, chmn. antitrust law com. 1966-70, 78-80, treas. 1970-71, v.p. 1971-72, pres.-elect 1972-73, pres. 1973-74), IEEE (sr. life), Down Town Club (bd. govs.), Tau Beta Pi, Eta Kappa Nu. Home: 193 Wilshire Dr Sharon MA 02067-1561 Office: Fish & Richardson PC 225 Franklin St 31st Fl Boston MA 02110-2804

HIELM, BORJE GUSTAV, airline captain, historian, journalist; b. Helsinki, Finland, June 24, 1927; s. Ejnar Olof and Alfa Maria Viola (Ahrenberg) H.; m. Sirkka Anna Liisa Peltola Hielm, Jan, 1950 (div. Sept. 1, 1954); m. Christina Margareta Laxen Hielm, Feb. 26, 1955; children: Maria Christina, Anna Katrina, Margit Charlotta, Finn Gustav Sebastian. Navigator's lic., Air Svc. Tng., Hamble Hants, Eng., 1949; airline transport pilot's lic., 1949. Glider pilot Finnish Aeronautical Assn., Jamjarvi, Finland, 1945, 47; pilot tng. Finnish Air Force Air Acad., Kauhava, Finland, 1946; fighter pilot Finnish Airforce, Utti, Finland, 1947-48; first officer Finnair, Helsinki, Finland, 1951-55, capt., 1955-82; dir. Finnish Aviation Mus., Vantaa, Finland, 1983-92; editor-in-chief Feeniks Mag., Vantaa, Finland, 1983—; chmn. Finnish DX Club, Helsinki, Finland, 1954-58; commentator YLE Finnish Broadcasting and TV on Space and Aviation, 1958—; founder, chmn, IPMS Finland, Helsinki, 1968-72. Prodr., author: Series of 7 1/2 hour programs on history on the Space Age, Finnish TV; Space News, 1963-78; editor-in-chief Feeniks, 1983—; contbr. articles to profl. jours. Pres. Nylands Constitutionals, Espoo, Finland, 1976-88, South Espoo Constnl. Soc., Finland, 1977-88; v.p. Constnl. Party, Helsinki, Finland, 1982-86; mem. Espoo City Coun., 1977-84, Electoral mem. in Presdl. Elections, 1978. Mem. Sydkustens Soldatgossar (sec.), Finnish Aviation Mus. Soc. (editor-in-chief quarterly, Feeniks mag., 1983—), Aviation Mus. Support Fund. Lutheran. Avocations: aviation history, clippings, model building, painting, photography. Home: Fredriksgatan 77 A8, FIN00100 Helsinki Finland

HIELM, SEBASTIAN, food microbiologist; b. Espoo, Finland, Feb. 9, 1967; s. Borje and Christina H.; m. Sara Christina Ehnholm, July 3, 1993; three children. DVM, U. Helsinki, 1994, PhD, 1999. From rschr. to asst. prof. Dept. Food & Environ. Hygiene, Helsinki, 1994—. Chmn. bd. Helsinki Zoo, 1997—. Office: Dept Food & Environ Hygiene, Hameentie 57, Helsinki 00580, Finland

HIEMKE, CHRISTOPH, biologist; b. Augsburg, Germany, Sept. 9, 1948; s. Bruno and Irmgard (Geiger) H.; m. Marianne Nagel, Jan. 8, 1980. Diploma, U. Bonn. (Germany), 1973, PhD, 1977. Prof. neurochemistry U. Mainz (Germany) Med. Sch., 1988—; head lab. neurochemistry dept. psychiatry U. Mainz, 1988—. Postdoctoral rsch. fellow U. Essen (Germany), 1977-88. Office: U Mainz Dept Psychiatry, Untere Zahlbached Str 8, D-55101 Mainz Germany

HIER, MARSHALL DAVID, lawyer; b. Bay City, Mich., Aug. 24, 1945; s. Marshall George and Helen May (Copeland) H.; m. Nancy Speed Brown, June 26, 1970; children: John, Susan, Ann. BA, Mich. State U., 1966; JD, U. Mich., 1969. Bar: Mo. 1969. Assoc. Peper, Martin, Jensen, Maichel and Hetlage, St. Louis, 1969-76, ptnr., 1976-95; prin. Bertram, Peper and Hier, P.C., St. Louis, 1996—; bd. dirs. Gateway Ctr. Met. St. Louis, Mercantile Libr. Assn., St. Louis Soc. Blind and Visually Impaired. Contbr. articles to profl. jours. Mem. St. Louis Bar Assn. (editor jour. 1988—), St. Louis Civil Round Table (former pres.). Baptist. Home: 17141 Chaise Ridge Rd Chesterfield MO 63005-4457*

HIERGESELL, DAVID HENRY, association executive; b. Hackensack, N.J., Nov. 4, 1963; s. Richard Mason and Doris Marie Hiergesell; m. Patricia Lynn Hiergesell, Dec. 30, 1995; 1 child, Blake. BA in Psychology, U. Nebr., 1990; MBA, Averett Coll., Danville, Va., 1999. Exec. dir. Conservative Ednl. Found., Lincoln, Nebr., 1987-90; membership mgr. Nat. Assn. of Mfrs., Washington, 1990-95; dir. bus. devel. T.I. Group, Washington, 1995-99; dir. membership, assn. devel. dept. Internat. Dairy Foods Assn., Washington, 1999—; cons. Annapolis Ctr., Md., 1999—. Adv. bd. Inst. for the Environment, Washington, 1997-99. Mem. Am. Soc. Assn. Execs. Republican. Avocations: current events, internet, skiing, reading. Home: 5104 Doyle Ln Centreville VA 20120-1705

HIERHOLZER, CHRISTIAN E., surgery educator; b. Bochum, Germany, Jan. 22, 1964; s. Gunther and Elisabeth (Birth) H. MD, Ludwig-Maximilians-U., Munich, 1990. Bd. cert. surgery, Germany. Intern dept. surgery Ludwig-Maximilians-U., 1990-91; resident dept. surgery Tech. U. Munich, 1992-95, 2000; rsch. fellow dept. surgery U. Pitts., 1995-98; asst. prof. surgery Tech. U. Munich, 2000—. Contbr. articles to profl. jours. Recipient Young Investigators Rsch. award Assn. Acad. Surgery, 1998, Young Investigators Rsch. award Shock Soc., 1998, E.K. Frey Rsch. award German Soc. Critical Care, 1998; rsch. fellow German Rsch. Found., 1995-97, NIH, U. Pitts., 1997-98. Fellow German Soc. Surgery. Home: Arabella St 5, 81925 Munich Germany Office: Tech U Munich Dept Surgery, Ismaningestr, 81675 Munich Germany

HIERSEMANN, CHARLES GERD, publisher; b. Leipzig, Germany, June 23, 1938; s. Anton Martin and Erica (Praetorius) H.; m. Oda Marie von Breitenbuch, Oct. 21, 1971; children: Kathrin, Florian Martin, Martina, Sabine. Student, U. Stuttgart, Germany, 1961-62, U. Hamburg, Germany, 1963-64. With C.H. Beck'sche Pubs., Munich, 1961-63; prodn. mgr. Blackwell and Mott Pubs., Oxford, Eng., 1964-65; prodn. specialist, lectr. Latin, Presses Universitaires de France, Paris, 1965-66; pres. Stuttgart Litterary Assn. of 1839, 1970—; chmn. Anton Hiersemann, Pub., Ltd., Stuttgart, 1969—, E. Hauswedell and Co., Pubs., Ltd., Stuttgart, 1983—. Author: Export im Zwielicht, 1991; co-editor: Lexikon des gesamten Buchwesens, 1987—. Justice of Commerce, Stuttgart Ct., 1986—. Lt. col. German Army, 1959. Avocations: travel, sports, history, Latin language. Office: Hiersemann Hauswedell Pubs, Halden Str 30, 70376 Stuttgart Germany

HIETAHARJU, AKI JUHANI, neurologist, researcher; b. Ähtäri, Finland, May 8, 1959; s. Antti Juhani and Anneli Tuulikki (Villgren) H.; m. Helinä Laholuoma, June 27, 1987; children: Heidi Suvi Maaria, Maria Anna Adeline. MD, U. Tampere (Finland), 1985, PhD, 1993. Cert. specialist in neurology, 1991. Intern/asst. neurologist Tampere U. Hosp., 1987-91; neurologist Kankaanpää (Finland) Rehab. Ctr., 1991-93, asst. head physician, 1996-97; sr. officer dept. neurology Tampere Univ. Hosp., 1997—; rschr. U. Tampere, 1987-93; field dir. Internat. Leprosy Mission, Dinajpur, Bangladesh, 1994-95, mem. Leprosy Coordinating Com., Bangladesh, 1994-95. Author: Nervous System Involvement in Systemic Rheumatic Diseases, 1993; contbr. articles to med. jours. Mem. Finnish Med. Assn., Duodecim Med. Soc. (Best Med. Case Study of Yr. 1991). Evangelical Lutheran. Avocations: mission work, science fiction, literature, Bengali language. Office: Tampere University Hospital, PO Box 2000, 33521 Tampere Finland

HIGASHI, TOSHIAKI, occupational health educator; b. Suzuka City, Mie, Japan, Jan. 28, 1954. MD, Keio U., Tokyo, 1978, PhD, 1985. Asst. prof. Sch. Medicine Keio U., 1986-88; assoc. prof. U. Occupational and Environ. Health, Kitakyushu, Japan, 1988-92, dir. dept. work sys. and health, prof., 1992—; chmn., 1988; vis. assoc. prof. McGill U., Montreal, Que., Can., 1989; cons. Japan Asbestos Assn., Tokyo, 1982—, Kurosaki Ref. Co., Kitakyushu, 1990—, Fukuoka (Japan) Prefecture Health Promotion Ctr., 1993—; indsl. physician Densoh Co., Kitakyushu, 1993—; councilor Human Medica Creation Centre, 1996—. Author: International Asbestos Medical Research, 1995; editor: Health Risks from Exposure to Mineral Fibres, 1993; patentee personal exposure monitor. Organizer Devel. of New Industry, Kitakyushu, 1993—. Mem. Am. Conf. Govtl. Indsl. Hygienists, Japan-Korea Sci. Com. on Occupational Health (organizing mem.). Home: 2-8-8 Asakawa Gakuendai, Yahatanishi Kitakyushu 807-0871, Japan Office: U Occpl & Environ Health Dept Work Sys & Health, 1-1 Iseidgaoka Yahatanishi-ward, Kitakyushu 807-8555, Japan

HIGASHINO, KAZUYA, internist, educator; b. Osaka, Japan, Sept. 20, 1930; s. Toshimasa Oue and Aiko H.; m. Tamiko Okuda, Feb. 27, 1962; children: Koji, Mayuko. MD, Osaka U., 1954, postgrad., 1960, PhD, 1960. Diplomate Japanese Bd. Internal Medicine. Intern Osaka U. Hosp., 1954-55, staff dept. medicine, 1960-72, lectr., 1972-74, asst. prof., 1974-78, assoc. prof., 1978-81; rsch. assoc. U. Pitts., 1964-65; v.p. Kinki Cen. Hosp., Itami, Hyogo, 1981-82; prof. medicine Hyogo Coll. Medicine, Nishinomiya, 1983-99, prof. emeritus, 1999—; hosp. dir. Rsch. Found. for Gout, Shinjuku, Tokyo, 1983—; dir. Japanese Found. Applied Enzymology, Osaka, 1991—; dir. Osaka Found. Promotion of Clin. Immunology, 1991—. Author: Purine Metabolism, 1982, Alkaline Phosphatase in Cancer, 1983; editor: Metabolism, 1974-89, Hyperuricemia and Gout, 1994—. Recipient Kurokawa prize Kanae Found. New Remedies, Tokyo, 1977. Mem. Japanese Soc. Internal Medicine (councilor 1979-96, disting. mem.), Japanese Soc. Gastroenterology (councilor 1987-96), Japan Soc. Clin. Biochemistry and Metabolism (councilor 1984—, dir. 1990—), Japanese Cancer Assn. (councilor 1984—), Japanese Soc. Uric Acid, Purine and Pyrimidine Disorders (councilor, dir. 1976—), Japanese Soc. Respiratory Disease, Japanese Geriatric Soc. (councilor 1989—), Japanese Assn. Gout and Nucleic Acid Metabolism (chmn. bd. dirs. 1999—), Liver Cancer Study Group Japan (sec. 1990—96), N.Y. Acad. Sci., Rotary. Buddhist. Home: 1-3 Inaba, 3-Chome Higashi-osaka-shi, Osaka 578, Japan Office: Third Dept Internal Medicine, 1-1 Mukogawa-Cho Nishinomiya-Shi, Hyogo 663, Japan

HIGASHIYAMA, ATSUKI, psychologist; b. Kasai, Japan, Aug. 20, 1951; s. Sadao and Chizu (Uchiyama) H.; m. Kiyomi Miyake, Dec. 16, 1979; children: Aigo, Hiroko, Seigo. BA, Osaka City U., 1974, MA, 1976, PhD, 1983. Asst. Osaka Prefectural U., Japan, 1978-81, lectr., 1981-88, assoc. prof., 1988-96, prof., 1996—; vis. lectr. U. Western Ont., Can., 1985-86; postdoctoral fellow York U., Can., 1986. Author: Role of Convergence in Binocular Visual Space (in Japanese), 1987; contbr. articles to profl. jours. Mem. AAAS, Japanese Psychol. Assn., Psychonomic Soc. Home: 7-6 Kakinokizaka, Hashimoto 648-0097, Japan Office: Faculty Letters, Ritsumeikan U Kita-ku, Kyoto 603-8577, Japan

HIGATSBERGER, MICHAEL JOSEF, physics educator emeritus; b. Unterbergern, Austria, June 8, 1924; s. Michael and Berta (Schmidt) H.; m. Lucia Sartori, Dec. 1955; 1 child, Michael Richard. PhD in Physics, Math. and Chemistry, U. Vienna, Austria, 1949; D h.c., Tel Aviv U., 1992. Univ. asst. U. Vienna, 1949-61, assoc. prof. exptl. physics, 1965-69, prof., 1969-2000, prof. emeritus, 2000—; mem. faculty U. Minn., Mpls., 1952-53; cons. U.S. Army, Ft. Belvoir, Va., 1954-55; sci. and tech. dir. Austrian Rsch. Ctr., Seibersdorf, 1956-71; numerous invited lectrs. in Austria and other countries; bd. dirs. Bank Gutmann. Author 5 books; contbr. more than 200 articles to sci. publs.; holder more than 70 Austrian and fgn. patents. Mem. internat. bd. govs. Weizmann Inst. Sci., Israel, 1993—; bd. govs. Tel Aviv U., 1993—. Mem. N.Y. Acad. Scis., Rotary (pres. Vienna 1979-80). Office: U Vienna Inst Exptl Physics, Boltzmanngasse 5, A-1090 Vienna Austria

HIGBY, EDWARD JULIAN, safety engineer; b. Milw., June 9, 1939; s. Richard L. Higby and Julie Ann (Bruins) O'Kelly; m. Frances Ann Knoodle, 1959 (div. 1962); 1 child, Melinda Ann Mozader. BS in Criminal Justice, Southwestern U., Tucson, 1984. Tactical officer Miami Police Dept., Fla., 1967-68; intelligence officer Fla. Divsn. Beverages, 1968-72; licensing coord. Lums Restaurant Corp., Miami, 1972-73; legal asst. Walt Disney World, Lake Buena Vista, Fla., 1973-78; loss control cons. R.P. Hewitt & Assocs., Orlando, Fla., 1978-79; safety coord. City of Lakeland, Fla., 1979-94. Author: Safety Guide for Health Care, 1979. Councilman City of Bay Lake, 1974-76, mayor, 1975-76; active Fla. League of Cities, 1974-76, Tri-County League of Cities, 1974-76, Orange County Criminal Justice Coun., 1974-78, Ctrl. Fla. Safety Coun., 1978-79; bd. dirs. Greater Lakeland chpt. ARC, 1980-86, chmn. bd. dirs., 1983-84, 85-86, chmn. health svcs., 1980-86; mem. budget com. United Way Ctrl. Fla., 1983-85; bd. dirs. Tampa Area Safety Coun., 1983-92, pres., 1990-91; bd. dirs. Imperial Traffic Safety Coun., 1983-89; mem. Polk County Disaster Coordination Com., bd. dirs., 1984-92; bd. dirs. Employers Health Care Group Polk County, 1987-89, Parent Resources and Info. on Drug Edn., 1989-92; bd. dirs. ARC Polk County chpt., 1990-92, 94-96, coord. Mass Care, 1994-95, chmn. Health and Safety, 1994-95, chmn. Risk Mgmt., 1995-96; active ARC Disaster Svcs. Human Resources Sys., 1994-99; mem. Fla. Adv. Com. Arson Prevention, Local Emergency Planing Com., State of Fla., 1987-92, 94—, Fla. Disaster Mortuary Team, 1995—; mem. adv. panel Polk County Industry Cmty., 1997—; mem. adv com. Charlotte Harbor Nat. Estuary, 1997. With U.S. Army, 1963-64. Named Vol. of Yr., Greater Lakeland chpt. ARC, 1983-84. Mem. NRA (life), World Safety Orgn., Fla. Sheriffs Assn. (hon. life), Internat. Assn. Identification (life, Fla. divsn., Russian divsn.), Nat. Found. Mortuary Care, Automatic Fire Alarm Assn., Disaster Emergency Response Assn. (life), Environ. Assessment Assn., U. Fla. Nat. Alumni Assn. (life), Fla. Pub. Health Assn., Fla. Fedn. Safety, Am. Soc. Safety Engrs. (mem. regional oper. com. 1983-85, 88-90, profl. devel. com. 1983, 85, chpt. bd. dirs. 1983-87, chpt. pres. 1984-85, v.p. profl. devel. region VIII 1988-90, Safety Profl. of Yr. 1984-85, Albert G. Mowson award 1995-96), Heartland Safety Soc. (life, pres. 1982-83, 94-95), Fla. Citrus Safety Assn. (pres. 1981-83), Nat. Fire Protection Assn., Am. Indsl. Hygiene Assn. (Fla. chpt.), Fire Marshals Assn. N.Am., Soc. Fire Protection Engrs. (bd. dirs. Fla. chpt. 1994-99), So. Health Assn., Fla. Affiliation of Ins. Safety Reps., Internat. Critical Incident Stress Found., Critical Incident Stress Debriefers Fla., Nat. Assn. Search and Rescue, Fla. Funeral Dirs. Assn., Fla. Emergency Preparedness Assn., Fla. Assn. Code Enforcement, Internat. Assn. Arson Investigators, Fla. Cracker Cattle Assn. (life), Harley Owners Group (life), Am. Motorcycle Assn. (life), Lakeland Rifle and Pistol Club. Republican. Avocations: hunting, fishing.

HIGBY, WAYNE (DONALD HIGBY), artist, educator; b. Colorado Springs, Colo., May 12, 1943; s. Donald W. and Betty (Bates) H.; m. Donna Claire Bennett, Mar. 12, 1966; children: Austin Myles, Sarah Lark. BFA, U. Colo., 1966; MFA, U. Mich., 1968. Prof. art N.Y. State Coll. Ceramics, Alfred U., 1973—; chair divsn. ceramic art, 1983-91; panelist Task Force for Individual Artists N.Y. State Coun. Arts, 1980-82, chair, 1978, mem. visual arts panel, 1976, 77; mem. NEA Visual Artists Fellowship/Crafts, 1986, NEA Visual Arts Overview Panel, 1989-90; hon. prof. art Hubei Acad. Fine Arts, Wuhan, People's Republic of China, 1992, ceramic art Jingdezhen Ceramic Inst, People's Republic of China, 1994. One-man exhbns. include Helen Drutt Gallery, 1988, 90, Mus. of Art and Design, Helsinki, Finland, 1999; invitational exhbns. include 8th and 13th Chunichi Internat. Exhbn. Ceramic Art, Nagoya, Japan, 1980, 85, respectively, Everson Mus. Art, Syracuse, N.Y., 1981, 87, 89, Am. Craft Mus., N.Y.C., 1982, 89, Jacksonville (Fla.) Mus. Art, 1982, Nelson-Atkins Mus. Art, Kansas City, 1983, Boston Mus. Fine Arts, 1984, Victoria and Albert Mus., London, 1986, Seoul Olympics Arts Festival, 1988, Nat. Mus. Ceramic Art, Balt., 1989, Kanazawa, Ishibkawa Pref, Japan, 1991, Nat. Mus. Modern Art, Tokyo, 1992-93, Met. Mus. Art, N.Y.C., 1999; public collections include Met. Mus. Art, N.Y.C., Mpls. Mus. Art, Phila. Mus. Art, Everson Mus. Art, Joslyn Mus. Art, Omaha, Am. Craft Mus., Victoria and Albert Mus., Boston Mus. Fine Arts, Bklyn. Mus. Art, L.A. County Mus. Art. Bd. dirs. Haystack Mountain Sch. Crafts, Deer Isle, Maine, 1983—, pres., 1989-92. Howard Found. fellow, 1985-86, 89-90; recipient Master Tchr. award U. Hartford, 1990, Chancellor's award SUNY, 1993; named visionary of Am. craft Am. Craft Mus., 1995. Mem. Coll. of Fellows Am. Craft Coun. Office: N Y State Coll Ceramics Alfred U Alfred NY 14802

HIGGENS, WILLIAM JOHN, III (TREY HIGGENS), sales executive; b. Evanston, Ill., May 26, 1951; s. William John Jr. and Delores May (Fuller) H.; m. Melanie Ann Mayer (div.); children: Melissa Lee, Tracy Ann; m. Barbara Carrie Simcoe, July 8, 1989. BS in Mktg. Mgmt., Miami U., Oxford, Ohio, 1973. Sales rep. A.B. Dick Co., Chgo., 1973-76; dist. sales mgr. McGraw-Hill Pub. Co., Chgo., 1976-85, CMP Publ., Inc., Chgo., 1985-91, McGraw-Hill Pub. Co., Chgo., 1991-96; dir. sales and mktg. Lightwave Mag., Integrated Comms. Design Mag., Oak Brook, Ill., 1996—. Mem. Bus. Mktg. Assn. (bd. dirs. 1984—, cert. bus. communicator 1989). Republican. Episcopalian. Avocations: flying, golf, reading, travel, computers. Home: Peregrine Lake Estates 873 W Lukas Ave Palatine IL 60067-2381 Office: PennWell Pub Co 2625 Butterfield Rd Ste 138S Oak Brook IL 60523-1244

HIGGINBOTHAM, CAROL A., chemistry educator; b. Pella, Iowa, Nov. 2, 1967; d. Larry E. and Dorothy N. Toom; m. David N. Higginbotham, Aug. 1987; 1 child, John Patrick. BA in Chemistry, Ctrl. Coll., Pella, 1992; PhD in Biochemistry, Mont. State U., 1996. Asst. prof. chemistry Barat Coll., Lake Forest, Ill., 1996-99, Ctrl. Oreg. C.C., College Bend, 1999—. Mem. Am. Chem. Soc., Sigma Xi, Iota Sigma Pi. E-mail: chiggingbotham@cocc.edu.

HIGGINBOTHAM, EVE JULIET, ophthalmologist, educator; b. New Orleans, Nov. 4, 1953; d. Luther Aldrich and Ruby Edith (Clark) H.; m. Frank Christopher Williams, June 7, 1986. BSChE, MS in Engring., MIT, 1975; MD, Harvard U., 1979. Intern Pacific Med. Ctr., San Francisco, 1979-80; resident La. State U. Eye Ctr., 1980-83; fellow Mass. Eye and Ear Infirmary, Boston, 1983-85; asst. prof. U. Ill., Chgo., 1985-90; assoc. prof. U. Mich., Ann Arbor, 1990-94; prof., chair dept. ophthalmology U. Md., Balt., 1994—. Co-editor: Management of Difficult Glaucoma, 1994, Clinician's Guide to Comprehensive Ophtholomology, 1998; contbr. articles to profl. jours; mem. editl. bd. Jour. of Glaucoma, 1990-93, Archives of Ophthalmology, 1994—; sect. editor: Glaucoma in Principles and Practice of Ophthalmology. Bd. dirs. Prevent Blindness Am., Schaumburg, Ill., 1990-97, chair publs. com., 1990-95, chair scientific adv. com., 1995—. Fellow Am. Acad. Ophthalmology (trustee 1992-95); mem. Women in Ophthalmology (bd. dirs. 1990-99), Assn. Univ. Profs. Ophthalmology, Assn. in Rsch. in Vision and Ophthalmology, Md. Soc. Eye Physicians and Surgeons (v.p. 1997-99, pres. 2000—), Balt. City Med. Soc. (treas. 1999-00, v.p. 2000—). Avocations: golf, piano. Office: U Md 419 W Redwood St Baltimore MD 21201-1734

HIGGINBOTHAM, JOHN TAYLOR, lawyer; b. St. Louis, Feb. 10, 1947; s. Richard Cann and Jocelyn (Taylor) H.; m. Lauren Flint Totty, Aug. 9, 1975 (div. 1979). BA, UCLA, 1969; JD, Columbia U., 1972. Bar: N.Y. 1975, Calif. 1976. Assoc. Kirlin, Campbell & Keating, N.Y.C., 1972-74; atty. Nat. Bank of N.Am., N.Y.C., 1974-76, Bank of Am., 1977; assoc. Barger & Wolen, L.A., 1977-78, Halperin, Shivitz, Scholer, Schneider & Eisenberg, 1978-79; atty., dir. real estate Korvettes, Inc., N.Y.C., 1979-82; assoc. Leon Katz, Bklyn., 1983-84, Finley, Kumble, Wagner, Heine, Underberg, Manley & Casey, N.Y.C., 1984-86; assoc. regional counsel HUD, N.Y.C., 1986-88, Sterling Securities, Inc., Manhasset, N.Y., 1989-93, Willkie, Farr & Gallagher, N.Y.C., 1993. Editor: Safe Deposit Decisions and Practice, 1977—. Mem. NARAS, NATAS, Acad. Motion Picture Arts and Scis., League Am. Theatres and Prodrs. Inc.

HIGGINBOTHAM, KENNETH JAMES, financial services executive; b. Phila., Aug. 3, 1942; s. James V. and Elizabeth R. (Roebus) H.; m. Ruth M. Schaffer, Apr. 12, 1969; children: Jennifer K., Scott G. BA, Rutgers U., 1971; MBA, Drexel U., 1973. Fin. analyst, discount window Fed. Res. Bank of Phila., 1972-77; corp. cash mgmt. cons. First Pa. Bank NA, Phila., 1977-79; EFT cons. Control Data Corp., Mpls., 1979-84; dist. rep. Aid Assn. for Lutherans, Appleton, Wis., 1984-94; reg. rep. Lincoln Fin. Advisors, Richboro, Pa., 1994-00; independent fin. planner, 2000—; adj. faculty LaSalle U., Phila., 1977—. With USN, 1963-67. Mem. Am. Assn. U. Profs., Soc. Fin. Svc. Profls., Fin. Planning Assn., Bucks County Estate Planning Coun. (officer, sec.). Office: Ind Fin Planners 21 Holly Hill Rd Richboro PA 18954-1917

HIGGINS, ERIC CRAIG, science writer; b. Liberal, Kans., Nov. 23, 1960; s. Harbert Heath and Ruth Eileen H.; m. Ginger Yang, Jan. 2, 1986 (div. 1990). BA, Hawaii Loa Coll., 1984; graduate, U.S. Army Acad. Health Scis., 1985. Cert. nurses aid, Okla. Computer operator Continental Oil Co., Ponca City, Okla., 1980, 82; tractor driver Golden View Farms, Tonkawa, Okla., 1983; med. specialist U.S. Army, Fort Bragg, N.C., 1985-87; nurse tech. I St. Joseph Med. Ctr., Ponca City, 1989, 91; marine biological aide Nat. Marine Fisheries Svc., Galveston, Tex., 1990; cert. nurses aide Okla. Dept. Human Svcs., Ponca City, 1997; freelance sci. writer Monument, Colo., 1998—. Contbr. articles to profl. jours. Patrol leader Boy Scouts Am., Tripoli, Libya, 1970-73; scribe DeMolay, Ponca City, 1978-79; lt. in safety patrol Oil Co. Sch. AAA, Tripoli, Libya, 1972-73; spl. duty emergency rm. Womack Army Hosp., Fort Bragg, N.C., 1986. Recipient Biology award No. Okla. Coll., Tonkawa, 1978, Gen. Sci. award Okla. State U., Stillwater, 1979. Mem. Am. Cancer Soc., Nature Conservancy, Reef Environ. Edn. Found. (fish surveyor 1998-99), Coral Reef Alliance, Divers Alert Network. Republican. Presbyn. Avocations: seashells, painting, scuba diving, writing, hiking. E-mail: higglwrlk@aol.com. Home: 18643 Lower Lake Rd Monument CO 80132-9042

HIGGINS, HUNTLY GORDON, research scientist; b. Perth, Australia, Jan. 18, 1917; s. Harold Darwin and Cora Frances (Moore) H.; m. Irena Higgins; children: Peter, Barbara, Matthew. BSc with honors, U. Western Australia, Perth, 1939; D Applied Sci., U. Melbourne, Australia, 1962. Geologist oil and mining cos. and Western Australia Sch. Mines, Australia and New Guinea, 1938-40; rsch. scientist, sr. prin. rsch. scientist CSIRO Divsn. Forest Products, Melbourne, 1945-73; asst. chief CSIRO Divsn. Chem. Tech., Melbourne, 1973-79, chief, 1979-82; hon. rsch. fellow CSIRO Forestry and Forest Products, Melbourne, 1982—; contbr. to confs. in field. Editor, author: A Commpnplace Book, 1996; contbr. over 180 articles to profl. jours. Pres. Internat. Assn. Sci. Papermakers, 1970-72, Australian Pugwash Com., 1967, chair S.E. regional conf., 1967. With RAAF, 1941-45. Mem. Tech. Assn. Australian and New Zealand Pulp and Paper Industry (pres. 1966-67, hon. life mem.). Avocations: bridge, chess, golf, history. Home: 59 Fellows St, Kew Melbourne Victoria 3101, Australia Office: CSIRO, Div Forestry & Forest Prod, Clayton VIC 3169, Australia

HIGGINS, IAN KEVIN, English educator; b. Brisbane, Queensland, Australia, Jan. 29, 1959; s. Kevin Stanley and Marie Elaine (Pyne) H. BA in English with 1st class honors, U. Queensland, 1981, MA in English, 1982; PhD in English, U. Warwick, 1990. Tutor U. Queensland, 1981-82; tutor, rsch. asst. U. Warwick, Eng., 1983-84; sr. tutor in English La Trobe U., Melbourne, Australia, 1985-91; lectr. in English Australian Nat. U., Canberra, 1991-97, sr. lectr. in English, 1997—. Author: Swift's Politics: A Study in Disaffection, 1994; contbr. to book: Jonathan Swift: A Collectio of Critical Essays, 1995. Office: Australian Nat U, Canberra ACT 0200, Australia

HIGGINS, JOHN RONAN JOSEPH, obstetrical and gynecological educator; b. Dungannon, Ireland, May 15, 1964; arrived in Australia, 1996; s. Patrick J. and Mary T. (Curry) H.; m. Ann M. McCaul, July 1990; children: Patrick, Sarah, John, David. BA, Trinity Coll. Dublin, Ireland, 1986, MB, BChir, B in Art of Obstetrics, 1988, MA, MD, 1996. Specialist in obstetrics Irish Med. Coun. Resident Federated Dublin Voluntary Hosps., Dublin, 1988-91; resident Rotunda Hosp., Dublin, 1991-92, rschr., registrar, 1993-96; fellow Royal Womens Hosp., Melbourne, Australia, 1997-99; sr. lectr. U. Melbourne, 2000—; med. advisor Australian Action on Pre-Eclampsia, 1999—. Author: (chpt.) Year Book of Obstetrics and Gynaecology, 1997, (chpt.) Contributions To Obstetrics and Gynaecology, 1999. Mem. Royal Coll. Physicians Ireland, Royal Coll. Obstetricians/Gynecologists (Blair-Beil Meml. lectureship 1999), Australasian Soc. Study of Hypertension in Pregnancy (exec. com. 1998—, Andrew Phippard Young Investigator award 1998), Jr. Ob/gyn. Soc. (chairperson 1995-96). Mem. Social Dem. and Labour Party. Roman Catholic. Avocations: golf, soccer, squash, swimming. Office: U Melbourn Mercy Hosp, Dept Ob/gyn Clarendon St, East Melbourne Australia

HIGGINS, MARIKA O'BAIRE, nurse, philosopher, educator, writer, entrepreneur; b. Manila, The Philippines, Oct. 3, 1947; d. Gerald John and Giovanna (BelForti) Barry; children: Matthew, Alexei, Rita, D. Patrick. Student, U. Conn., 1964-65; diploma, Ellis Hosp. Sch. Nursing, 1977; BSN, Russell Sage Coll., 1980, postgrad., 1983, 94; grad. ontological design, Logonet Inc. ODC-J, 1993; postgrad. in humanities, Calif. State U., Dominguez Hills, 1995—; postgrad., Univ. Dundee, 2000—. RN, N.Y.; lic. Avatar Master/Wizard. English tchr. Lang. Inst., Taipei, Taiwan, 1971-73; team leader, staff nurse in acute psychiatry Samaritan Hosp., Troy, N.Y., 1978-80; staff nurse, pediatric ICU Albany (N.Y.) Med. Ctr., 1980-84, 97—; rsch. nurse Commn. on Quality Care for Mentally Disabled, Albany, 1984; staff nurse Columbia-Greene Med. Ctr., Catskill, N.Y., 1984-89; night charge nurse Conifer Park, Scotia, N.Y., 1991-92; nursing educator St. Clare's Hosp., Schenectady, N.Y., 1992-96; founder Create What You Prefer, 1995—; nurse Pediat. High Tech Home Care, 1996—; adjunct clin. educator Albany Med. Ctr. So. Vt. Coll., Bennington, 1997—; philosophy coaching Cmty. Hospice Saratoga, N.Y., 1998—; founder Future Design and Create What You Prefer. Publ. poet, lit. writer; comml. artist Echo Mag. Vol. curriculum designer in gifted and talented programs; mem. Red Cross Disaster Team. Mem. Amnesty Internat. Childreach Plan Internat., Upstate Independent Filmakers/Screenwriters, Thorobred Toastmasters (pres.). Home and Office: PO Box 5102 221 Caroline St Saratoga Springs NY 12866-3505

HIGGINS, MARY CELESTE, lawyer, researcher; b. Chgo., Feb. 9, 1943; d. Maurice James and Helen Marie (Egan) H. AB, St. Mary-of-the-Woods Coll., Ind., 1965; JD, DePaul U., 1970; LLM, John Marshall Law Sch., Chgo., 1976; postgrad., Harvard U., 1981, 82, MPA, 1982; MPhil, U. Cambridge (Eng.), 1983. Bar: Ill., 1970, U.S. Dist. Ct. (no. dist.) Ill. 1970. Sole practice Chgo., 1970-72, 79-80; atty. corp. counsel dept. Continental Bank, Chgo., 1972-76; asst. sec., asst. counsel Marshall Field & Co., Chgo., 1976-79; sr. atty. Mattel, Inc., Hawthorne, Calif., 1980-81; rch. in revitalization and adjustment of U.S. Industries in U.S. and world markets, 1981-83; legal cons., 1983-85; Midwest regional officer Legal Svcs. Corp., 1985-87, assoc. dir., 1986, acting dir. office of field svcs., 1986-87, dir., 1987-89; dir. Meridian One Corp., Alexandria, Va., 1990—. Recipient Am. Jurisprudence awards for acad. excellence, 1966-70. Mem. Ill. Bar Assn. Home: 203 Yoakum Pkwy Apt 508 Alexandria VA 22304-3711

HIGGINS, DAME ROSALYN, judge of international court of justice; b. June 2, 1937; d. Lewis Cohenand F. Inberg; m. Terence L. Higgins, 1961; 2 children. Student, Cambridge U., Yale U. Intern Office Legal Affairs UN, 1958; commonwealth fund fellow, 1959; vis. fellow Brookings Inst., Washington, 1960; jr. fellow internat. studies L.S.E., 1961-63, vis. fellow, 1974-78; staff specialist internat. law Royal Inst. Internat. Affairs, 1963-74; prof. internat. law U. Kent, Canterbury, Eng., 1978-81, L.S.E., 1981-95; judge Internat. Ct. Justice, The Hague, The Netherlands, 1995—; mem. com. human rights UN, 1985-95; vis prof. Stanford U., 1975, Yale U., 1977; v.p. Am. Soc. Internat. Law, 1972-74. Author: The Development of International Law through the Political Organs of the United Nations, 1963, Conflict of Interests, 1965, The Administration of the United Kingdom Foreign Policy through the United Nations, 1966, UN Peacekeeping: Documents and Commentary; editor: (with James Fawcett) Law in Movement—Essays in Memory of John McMahon, 1974, Problems & Process, 1994, Terrorism & International Law, 1997; contbr. articles to profl. jours. Mem. Ordre Palmes Academiques. Avocations: sports, cooking. Office: Internat Ct Justice, Peace Palace, 2517KJ The Hague The Netherlands

HIGGINS, THOMAS LEO, physician; b. Everett, Mass., Feb. 27, 1955; s. Louis Joseph and Mary Ann (Marino) H.; m. Suzanne Marguerite Furlong, July 11, 1981; children: Amy, Matthew, William. BA, Boston U., 1978, MD, 1978. Diplomate Am. Bd. Internal Medicine, Am. Bd. Anesthesiology; cert. critical care. Staff physician Whidden Hosp., Everett, Mass., 1983-84; resident Mass. Gen. Hosp., Boston, 1984-86, chief resident, 1986-87; dir. cardiothoracic ICU Cleve. Clinic, 1987-94, dir. outcomes rsch., 1994-95; pres. Med. Strat Rsch., Bratenahl, Ohio, 1995-96; dir. adult critical care Baystate Med. Ctr., Springfield, Mass., 1996—; cons. in field. Editor: The High Risk Patient, 1995; contbr. articles to profl. jours. Lt. USPHS, 1981-83. Fellow ACP, Am. Coll. Cardiology, Am. Coll. Critical Care Medicine.

HIGGS, ROGER HUBERT, physician, educator; b. Aldershot, Eng., Dec. 10, 1943; m. Susan Hewer, Jan. 9, 1971; children: Benjamin, Jessie. BA, Cambridge (Eng.) U., 1966, MB BChir, 1969, MA, 1970. Gen. practitioner South London, 1975—; sr. lectr., chair dept. gen. practice and primary care Kings Coll. Sch. Medicine, London, 1981-89, prof., 1989—; dep. head divsn. primary care/pub. health GKT Sch. Medicine Kings Coll. Sch. Medicine, 1998—; chair Med. Audit in Gen. Practice, South London, 1991-99; bd. dirs. Centre of Med. Law and Ethics, Kings Coll., 1983—. Author books on devel. in gen. practice and on med. ethics. Decorated mem. Brit. Empire. Fellow Royal Coll. Physicians (London), Royal Coll. Gen. Practitioners. Avocations: planting trees, playing oboe. E-mail: roger.higgs@kcl.ac.uk. Office: Weston Edn Ctr, Cutcombe Rd Bessemer Rd, London SE5 9PJ, England

HIGH, DAVID ROYCE, lawyer; b. Oklahoma City, Aug. 28, 1950; s. Jack Eugene and Harriett Ann High; m. Charlotte Anne Bonsteel, Dec. 28, 1975; 1 child, Katie McKenzie. BA, U. Okla., 1973; JD, Oklahoma City U., 1978. Bar: Okla. 1978, U.S. Dist. Ct. (we. dist.) Okla. 1978, U.S. Ct. Appeals (10th cir.) 1990. Assoc. Tomerlin & High, Oklahoma City, 1978-80; ptnr. Tomerlin, High & High, Oklahoma City, 1980-92, pvt. practice law, 1992—. Legal counsel The Children's Ctr., Bethany, Okla., 1978—, Oklahoma City Beautiful Inc., 1982-89. Mem. ABA, Okla. Bar Assn. (gov. 1988-91), Oklahoma County Bar Assn. (bd. dirs. 1981-91, v.p. 1984-85, Outstanding Oklahoma County Young Lawyer award 1981). Avocation: tennis. Office: Tomerlin High & High 3601 N Classen Blvd Ste 203 Oklahoma City OK 73118-3269

HIGHAM, JOHN ARTHUR, Queen's counsel, solicitor advocate; b. Liverpool, U.K., Aug. 11, 1952; s. Frank Greenhouse and Muriel (King) H.; m. Francesca Mary Antonietta Ronan (dec.); children: Miranda Elizabeth Francesca, Charlotte Daisy Emilia, John Christian Alexander; m. Catherine Mary Ennis, Dec. 10, 1988; children: Patrick Rupert James, Edmund George Christopher, Cecily Mary Catherine. MA, Churchill Coll., Cambridge, Eng., 1974, LLM, 1975. Called to the Bar Lincoln's Inn, 1976, Gray's Inn, 1989; appointed Queen's Coun., 1992, solicitor adv., 1999, recorder, 2000—; ptnr. Stephenson Harwood, 2000—. Joint editor: Loose on Liquidations, 1981, The Law and Practice of Corporate Adminstrations, 1994; contbr. A Practitioner's Guide to Corporate Insolvency, 1991. Mem. Lancashire County Cricket Club. Avocations: opera, gardening, cricket. Office: Stephenson Harwood, One St Paul Churchyard, London EC4M 8FH, United Kingdom

HIGHSMITH, ANNA BIZZELL, executive secretary; b. Richmond, Va., May 31, 1947; d. John Lee and Jacquelyn Frances (Miller) Bizzell; m. Jack Francis Starkey, Jan. 25, 1970 (div. Apr. 1972); 1 child, Mary Cathereine; m. Lemuel Martin Highsmith, May 25, 1974; 1 child, Lemuel Tayloe. Student, N. Fla. Jr. Coll., 1965-66, Armstrong State Coll., 1966-71. Sec. Seaboard Coastline RR, Savannah, Ga., 1966-76; sec., bookkeeper Highsmith Enterprises, Savannah, 1976—; Centennial Olympic vol. Yachting-Sports Info. Desk, Olympic Village, Savannah, Ga., 1996. Pres., chmn. of bd. Ballet South, Inc., Savannah, 1982-89, bd. dirs., advisor to pres., 1989-97, pres., 1997-98. Mem. Nat. Assn. Women in Constrn. (bd. dirs. 1982-87, 90-92, v.p. 1987-88, pres. 1989-90, 90-91, 94-95), Rinky Dink Sailing Club (sec., editor newsletter 1990-93, liaison 1989-93, prin. race officer 1993, cert. club race officer 1994), Geechee Sailing Club (editor newsletter 1990-91, sec. 1993), Savannah Yacht Club.. Republican. Episcopalian. Avocations: reading, sailing, ballet. Home: 519-A Whitfield Ave Savannah GA 31406-8207

HIGI, WILLIAM L., bishop; b. Anderson, Ind., Aug. 29, 1933. Student, Mt. St. Mary of the West Sem., Xavier U. Ordained priest Roman Cath. Ch., 1959. Bishop Roman Cath. Diocese of Lafayette, Lafayette, Ind., 1984—. Home: 610 Lingle Ave Lafayette IN 47901-1740 Office: Bishops Office PO Box 260 Lafayette IN 47902-0260

HIGINBOTHAM, HARLOW NILES, economist; b. Joliet, Ill., Nov. 25, 1946; s. Harlow Niles and Eleanor (Dickson); m. Linda Anne Hutton, Dec. 12, 1970 (div. July 1985); m. Susan Ellen Spika, Apr. 27, 1991. BA, Harvard U., 1968; MA, U. Chgo., 1972, PhD, 1976. CFA. Statistician Uniroyal Inc., Joliet, 1969-71; assoc. A.T. Kearney Inc., Chgo., 1976-79, mgr., 1979-88, prin., 1989-93, v.p., 1993—. Mem. Union League Club, Casino. Republican. Episcopalian. Avocations: gardening, skiing. Home: RR 2 Joliet IL 60432-9802 Office: AT Kearney Inc 222 W Adams St Ste 2393 Chicago IL 60606-5307

HIGINBOTHAM, JACQUELYN JOAN, lawyer; b. Dec. 15, 1951; d. Ivan Lyle and Ruth Harriet (La Point) H.; m. Robert Redditt; children: Altara Roxana, Rigel Rowena. AA, Northeastern Jr. Coll., Sterling, Colo., 1972; BA, U. No. Colo., 1974; JD, U. Colo., 1978. Bar: Colo. 1978, U.S. Dist. Ct. Colo. 1978, U.S. Ct. Appeals (10th cir.) 1983. Staff, mng. atty. Colo. Legal Svcs., Ft. Morgan, 1979—. Mem. adv. bd. Caring Ministries Morgan County, 1986-87. Mem. Colo. Bar Assn., Christian Legal Soc., Order of Coif. Democrat. Episcopalian. Avocations: astronomy, music, skating. Home: 702 Sherman St # 1123 Fort Morgan CO 80701-3540 Office: Colo Legal Svcs 209 State St Fort Morgan CO 80701-2115

HIHARA, KATSUJI, accounting educator; b. Taka-gun, Hyogo, Japan, Feb. 16, 1949; s. Takeo and Shigeko (Shimoyama) H.; m. Masami Yoshida, Nov. 13, 1988; 1 child, Keita. B Comml. Sci., Kwansei Gakuin U., Nishinomiya, Japan, 1971; MBA, Kobe U., 1973, D of Bus. Administrn., 1996. Asst. Toyama U., Japan, 1975-76, asst. prof., 1976-79, assoc. prof., 1979-88, prof., 1988-89; prof. Kobe U. of Commerce, Japan, 1989—; head grad. sch. bus. adminstrn., head dept. bus. adminstrn. Kobe U. of Commerce, 1992-93. Author: (books) Inflation Accounting (in Japanese), 1984, Income Concepts in Inflation Accounting (in Japanese), 1995; contbr. articles to profl. jours. Mem. Am. Acctg. Assn., Japan Acctg. Assn. Avocation: skiing. Home: 2-30-22 Yokoo, Suma-ku Kobe 654-0131, Japan Office: Kobe U of Commerce, 8-2-1 Gakuennishi-machi, Nishi-ku Kobe 651-2197, Japan

HIHARA, YUKAKO, research scientist; b. Tokyo, May 10, 1970; Yukitaka and Michiko (Kusuhara) H.; m. Kintake Sonoike, Apr. 14, 1995; 1 child, Sanekata. BS, U. Tokyo, 1993, MS, 1995, DSc, 1998. Rsch. fellow Japan Soc. for the Promotion of Sci., Tokyo, 1997-2000; rsch. assoc. dept. biochemistry and molecular biology Saitama (Japan) U., 2000—. Mem. Japanese Soc. Plant Physiologist, Botanical Soc. Japan. Avocations: viola, classical music. Home: Shinjuku-ku, c/o Shinanomachi 29, 160-0016 Tokyo Japan Office: Saitama Univ, 255 Shimo-Ohkubo, Urawa Saitama 338-8570, Japan

HIJLKEMA, SJOUKE LAMBERTUS ANNA, drilling manager; b. Eindhoven, The Netherlands, July 7, 1956; Three children. Engring. degree in Chem. Tech., Leeuwarden U., 1978. Tng. driller Shell Internat., Holland, 1978-80; asst. driller Shell Internat., Brunei, 1980-82, driller, 1982-84; toolpusher Shell Internat., 1984; toolpusher, sr. toolpusher Shell Expro, Aberdeen, 1984-86, 88-89, prodn. chemist, fluid engr., 1987-88; sr. toolpusher, engr. Shell Can., 1989-91; sr. toolpusher Shell Internat., Holland, 1991-92, sr. toolpusher, engring. supt., 1992-94; supt. Occidental Netherlands, 1994-96, drilling mgr., 1996-98; head well engring. ops. Shell Internat., Nigeria, 1998—; dir. Consulting Agy. in Design and Execution of Projects in Oil and Gas Industries, The Netherlands, 1994—. Avocations: golf, fishing. Office: Shell Internat-DWW-WARRI, PO Box 245, 2501 CE The Hague The Netherlands

HILA, ANTONIO CALLEJA, historian, educator, researcher, writer; b. Casiguran, Sorsogon, Philippines, Oct. 14, 1947; s. Mateo Hicarte and Carolina Roco (Calleja) H.; m. Maria Corazon Jose Alejo, Apr. 2, 1977; children: Hiyas, Lakan Emmanuel, Ani, Aya Fatima. AB in History, U. the Philippines, Quezon City, 1967; MA in History, U. Santo Tomas, Manila, 1990, PhD in History summa cum laude, 1998. Instr. Lyceum the Philippines, Manila, 1968-71; instr. De La Salle U., Manila, 1971-72, 76-77, asst. prof., 1978-79, assoc. prof., 1986—, chair dept. history, 1993—; head dept. Allied Svcs. & Pub. Rels. Office Philippine Heart Ctr. Asia, 1976-81; planning officer Metro Manila Commn., 1983-85; rschr., writer Cultural Ctr. the Philippines, Manila, 1986—. Columnist, music critic Metro Manila newspapers, 1973—, Philippines Daily Inquirer, 1986—; co-author: Metro Manila, Towards the City of Man: Total Human Resource Development, 1985, Selected Readings on J.P. Rizal, 1989; issue editor Anuario/Annales, 1987. Mgr. Philippine Philharm. Orch., 1985-86; mem. Philippine Nat. Hist. Soc., 1989—, Manila Studies Program, 1996—; mem. exec. com. Nat. Com. Hist. Rsch., 1998—, Nat. Commn. Culture and Arts, 1998—. Avocations: choral conducting, singing, vocal coaching, concert directing, stamp collecting. Home: Teacher's Village, 67 A-1 Matahimik St, Diliman Quezon City 1101, Philippines Office: De La Salle U, Dept History, Taft Ave, Manila 1104, Philippines

HILBERG, RAUL, political science educator; b. Vienna, Austria, 1926; came to U.S., 1939.; PhD in Pub. Law and Govt., Columbia U., 1955. Prof. polit. sci. U. Vt., Burlington, now prof. emeritus, 1991. Author: The Destruction of European Jews 1961, in German, 1982, 2nd expansion in English, 1985, third expansion in French, 1988, German, 1990, Italian, 4th expansion in Japanese, 1997, Romanian, 1997, Italian, 1999, Perpetrators Victims Bystanders, 1992, German, Dutch, French, Italian edits., 1992-99, The Politics of Memory, 1996, German, French, Japanese edits., 1994-98; editor: Documents of Destruction, 1971. Served with U.S. Army, 1944-46. Office: 236 Prospect Pkwy Burlington VT 05401-4148

HILBERG, WOLFGANG, technology educator; b. Giessen, Hessen, Germany, Feb. 7, 1932; s. Jakob P. W. and Katharina E. (Ruhl) H.; m. Birgitt Weimann; children: Annette, Steffi, Katja, Sebastian, Eva, Moritz. Diploma in engring., U. Darmstadt, Germany, 1958, D of Engring., 1963. Cert. in elec. engring. Rschr. Telefunken, Ulm, Germany, 1958-72; Digital Tech. chair, prof. U. Darmstadt, 1972—. Author 12 books; contbr. articles to profl. jours.; patentee in field; inventor radio controlled watch. Recipient NTG Rsch. award, 1964. Mem. IEEE (sr.), Informationstechnische Gesellschaft, Gesellschaft fuer Informatik. Avocations: walking, skiing, climbing, paragliding, windsurfing. E-mail: hil@dtro.tu-darmstadt.de. Fax: 06151-163331. Home: Im Geisner 11, D-64401 Bieberau Germany Office: U of Tech, D-64283 Darmstadt Germany

HILBERN, SANDRA J., social sciences educator, retired counselor; b. Vallejo, Calif., July 2, 1945; d. Curtis Tom Sr. and Pauline Stout (Daniels) Hamilton; m. James W. Hilbern Sr., Nov. 27, 1970 (div. Aug. 1993); 1 child, James William Jr. BSE, Northeastern Okla. State U., 1970, MS, 1973; postgrad., U. Tex., Dallas, 1977, So. Ill. U., 1978, Northeastern Okla. State U., 1976-89. Cert. tchr., Okla. Elem. tchr. Okay (Okla.) Pub. Schs., 1970-75; sr. vocat. rehab. counselor State Okla. Dept. Rehab., Muskogee, 1975-98; prof. Connors State Coll., Muskogee, 1989—, mem. gerontol. consumer adv. com., 1999—. Unit commr. Boy Scouts Am., Muskogee, 1984-86; coach, team mother Green County Soccer League, Muskogee, 1979-81; publicity dir. single living bd. Christ Ch., Tulsa, 1998—, Phoenix Singles pres., v.p., 1996-99. Sgt. U.S. Army, 1966-69. Recipient Outstanding Recognition award for Outstanding Svc., U.S. Ho. of Reps., 1998, Pres.'s award for Outstanding Svc. Okla. Rehab. Counselors Assn., 1984. Mem. Okla. Rehab. Soc. (sec. 1978-84), Okla. Assn. Developmental Educators, Okla. Assn. C.C.'s. Democrat. Avocations: silk and dried floral arranging, organizing fine arts and cultural tours. Office: Connors State Coll 201 Court St Muskogee OK 74401-6324

HILBERT, OTTO KARL, II, lawyer; b. Colorado Springs, Colo., Feb. 9, 1962; s. Otto Karl and Mary Rachel (Shine) H.; m. Lucille Megan O'Shaughnessy, Apr. 21, 1995. BA, U. Notre Dame, 1984, postgrad., 1985; JD, U. Colo., 1988. Bar: Colo. 1989, Ariz. 1989, Wis. 1998, U.S. Dist. Ct. (no. dist.) Calif, U.S. Ct. Appeals (9th cir.) 1991, U.S. Tax Ct. 1992, U.S. Ct. Appeals (10th cir.) 1993, U.S. Supreme Ct. 1995. Assoc. Kelly, Stansfield & O'Donnell, Denver, 1988-89, 92-93, Russell Piccoli, Ltd., Phoenix, 1989-92, LeBoeuf, Lamb, Greene & MacRae LLP, Denver, 1993-96; shareholder Reinhart, Boerner, Van Deuren, Norris & Rieselbach PC, Denver, 1996—; arbitrator Nat. Assn. Securities Dealers, Inc., 1993—, Nat. Futures Assn., 1993—, Nat. Arbitration and Mediator's Internat. div. bds. arbitration. Mem. law sch. adv. coun. U. Notre Dame, 1989-92; cons. Ariz. Spl. Olympics, Phoenix, 1989-92; mem. Edward Frederick Sorin Soc., Notre Dame, Ind., 1989—; bd. dirs. Denver Athletic Club, 2000—. Mem. ABA, Colo. Bar Assn., Denver Bar Assn., Ariz. Bar Assn., Wis. Bar Assn., Notre Dame Club of Phoenix (1st v.p. 1991-92, bd. dirs. 1989-92, Award of the Yr. 1992), Notre Dame Club of Denver (bd. dirs. 1995-97), Lakewood Country Club (v.p., bd. dirs. 1998—). Republican. Roman Catholic. Avocations: piano, guitar, golf. Address: Reinhart Boerner Van Deuren 1775 Sherman St Ste 2100 Denver CO 80203-4320

HILBRECHT, NORMAN TY, lawyer; b. San Diego, Feb. 11, 1933; s. Norman Titus and Elizabeth (Lair) H.; m. Mercedes L. Sharratt, Oct. 24, 1980. B.A., Northwestern U., 1956; J.D., Yale U., 1959. Bar: Nev. 1959, U.S. Supreme Ct. 1963. Assoc. counsel Union Pacific R.R., Las Vegas, 1962; ptnr. Hilbrecht & Jones, Las Vegas, 1962-69; pres. Hilbrecht, Jones, Schreck & Bernhard, 1969-83, Hilbrecht & Assocs, 1983—, Mobil Transport Corp., 1970-72; gen. counsel Bell United Ins. Co., 1986-94; mem. Nev. Assembly, 1966-72, minority leader, 1971-72; mem. Nev. Senate, 1974-78; legis. commn., 1977-78; asst. lectr. bus. law U. Nev., Las Vegas.; oper. mem. Corp. Svcs. Group, 1998—; pres. Corp. Svcs. Co., 1998—, Nev. Incorporating Co., 1998—; mng. mem. Amcorp, LLC., 1999—. Author: Nevada Motor Carrier Compendium, 1990, Nevada Corporation Handbook, 1999. Mem. labor mgmt. com. NCCJ, 1963; mem. Clark County (Nev.) Dem. Ctrl. Com., 1959-80, 1st vice chmn., 1965-66; del. Western Regional Assembly on Ombudsman; chmn. Clark County Dem. Conv., 1966, Nev. Dem. Conv., 1966; pres. Clark County Legal Aid Soc., 1964, Nev. Legal Aid and Defender Assn., 1965-83; assoc. for justice Nat. Jud. Coll., 1993, 94, 95, 96. Capt. AUS, 1952-67. Named Outstanding State Legislator Eagleton Inst. Politics, Rutgers U., 1969, Best Lawyers in Am., Bar of Nev., 1993. Mem. ABA, ATLA, Am. Judicature Soc., Am. Acad. Polit. and Social Sci., State Bar Nev. (chmn. adminstrv. law 1991-94, chmn. sect. on adminstrv. law 1996), Nev. Trial Lawyers (state v.p. 1966), Am. Assn. Ret. Persons (state legis. com. 1991-94), Rotary, Elks, Phi Beta Kappa, Delta Phi Epsilon, Theta Chi, Phi Delta Phi. Lutheran. Office: 723 S Casino Center Blvd Las Vegas NV 89101-6716

HILDEBRAND, THEODOR LORENZ, software and service company executive, consultant; b. Berlin, Sept. 27, 1946; s. Theodor Bernhard and Hildegard Charlotte (Besser) H.; m. Patricia Victoria Schnabel, Apr. 18, 1976; children: Theodore, Laetitia, Hadrien. Diploma in math. and physics, Free U. Berlin, 1969; diploma in computer sci. and econs., U. Bonn, Germany, 1972. Asst. Inst. for Computer Sci. (GMD), St. Augustin, Germany, 1969-72; rsch. asst. U. Bonn, 1973-76; sys. engr. Nat. Textile Inst., Boulogne, France, 1977-79; cons. Credit Lyonnais Bank, Paris, 1991-93; head telecom & R&D dept. Sligos (Svcs. Bancaires), Puteaux, France, 1979-91; project dir. European Payment Svcs. Sligos, Paris, 1993-96; IT dir. B&S Card Service, Frankfurt, Germany, 1996-98, Atos Processing Svcs., Frankfurt, 1998—; expert in Esprit program Commn. European Comtys., Brussels, 1989-92; tech. dir. European Info. On-Line Svcs., Paris, 1991-93. Co-author: Introduction to Informatics, 1973; inventor computer for schs. Mem. Assn. for Computing Machinery, Gesellschaft für Informatik, Petri Nets Working Group. Lutheran. Avocations: swimming, travel. Office: Atos Processing Svcs, D-60303 Frankfurt Germany

HILDEBRANDT, FREDERICK DEAN, JR., management consultant; b. Upper Darby, Pa.; m. Marjorie Louise Smith, July 27, 1968; children: Frederick Dean III, Elizabeth Florence. AB magna cum laude, Dartmouth Coll., 1954, MS, 1955. Engr. Eastman Kodak Co., Rochester, N.Y., 1957-60; systems mgr. J.T. Baker Chem. Co., Phillipsburg, N.J., 1960-63; assoc. Booz, Allen & Hamilton Inc., N.Y.C., 1963-72, v.p., 1972-78; sr. v.p. Am. Ins. Assn., N.Y.C., 1978-81; v.p. Travelers Ins. Cos., Hartford, Conn., 1981-89; pres. Dean Hildebrandt & Assocs., Simsbury, Conn., 1989—; adminstr. Ins. Rsch. Coun., 1979, bd. dirs., 1982-88; vice chmn. bd. dirs. Workers Compensation Rsch. Inst., 1987-88. With U.S. Army, 1955-57. Mem. Inst. Mgmt. Cons. (cert. mgmt. cons.), Phi Beta Kappa.

HILDEBRANDT, JANELLE DINER, sales executive; b. Little Rock, Dec. 16, 1957; d. Jack and Wilma Canada Diner; m. Kendall C. Russell, May 24, 1981 (div. Dec. 1994); children: K. Clinton, Jr., Adam A.; m. Larry Paul Hildebrandt, July 19, 1997. BEE, Vanderbilt U., 1979, BS in Math., 1979; MBA, City Univ., 1982. Engr. Martin Marietta Aerospace, Orlando, Fla., 1979-81; sr. engr. Beoing Aerospace Co., Kent, Wash., 1981-83; dir. Advanced Technology Labs, Bothell, Wash., 1983-92; bus. devel. mgr. 3M, St. Paul, 1992-97; internat. bus. devel. 3M, St. Paul, Minn., 1997—; cons. Custom Interfaces, Bothell, Wash., 1983-87. Patentee in field. Mem. Rotary, Soroptimist, AAUW. Avocations: swimming, cooking. Office: 3M 512 Crater Lake Ave # 3M Medford OR 97504-6810

HILDMANN, ECKART, environmentalist; b. Bitterfeld, Germany, Dec. 31, 1935; s. Otto and Charlotte (Gotze) H.; m. Renate Muller; children: Birgit, Dirk. Dipl.ing., Mining Acad., Freiberg, Germany, 1960; Dipl.oec., U. Halle, Germany, 1972, Dr.oec., 1988. Head environ. affairs Mining Industry, Bitterfeld, Germany, 1973-84; planning reclamation Ministry of Coal, Leipzig, Germany, 1984-90; head environ. affairs MIBRAG, Bitterfeld, Germany, 1990-94, LMBV, Berlin, 1994-98. Author: (periodical) Water, Air and Soil Pollution, 1996, Journal of Rural Engineering and Development, 1996, Surface Mining, 1997; co-author: Brown Coal Surface Mining and Reclamation, 1997. Avocations: classical music, orinthology, botany, mineralogy, wandering. Home: Eichbergstr 7A, D 36039 Fulda Germany Office: LMBV, Brehnaer Str 41-43, D 06749 Bitterfeld Germany

HILDRETH, ETHAN JOE DAVID, school principal, communications consultant; b. Atlanta, July 6, 1967; s. Joe Fred and Virginia Ruth Hildreth; m. Crystal Lee Hildreth, Aug. 18, 1990; children: Kemble August, Jonathan Dane, Laura Faye. BS, USAF Acad., 1989; MA, U. Tenn., 1992; PhD, Ga. State U., 1997. Cert. tchr., Ga. Tchr. English Eagle's Landing H.S., McDonough, Ga., 1991-98; sch. adminstr. Pate's Creek Elem. Sch., Stockbridge, Ga., 1998—; instr. Clayton State Coll., Morrow, Ga., 1998—; comm. cons. Word3 Comm., McDonough, 1999—. Author: Writing An Imperial Narrative, 1997, Word3: Effective Communication for Professionals, 2000; editor: Marriage: A Biblical Perspective, 1994; editor/founder (lit. mag.) The Gyre, 1992-98. Newsletter editor Henry Heritage Reading Coun., Henry County, Ga., 1997; soccer coach Henry County Soccer Assn., 1997—. With USAF, 1985-89. Recipient Fulbright Meml. Fund scholar Japanese Nat. Govt., 1999. Mem. Ga. Assn. Ednl. Leaders, Profl. Assn. Ga. Educators, Sigma Tau Delta. Baptist. Avocations: writing, chess, beekeeping.

HILFIKER, KARL FRANZ, thermodynamics educator; b. Boswil, Switzerland, June 4, 1941; s. Karl and Anna (Jochum) H. MS in Mech. Engring., Swiss Inst. Tech., Zurich, Switzerland, 1967, PhD, 1975. Process engr. Swiss Aluminium, Zurich, 1967-68; design engr. Nabalco, Sydney, Australia, 1969-72; head process engring. Swiss Aluminium, 1975-80; prof. UPM, Dhahran, Saudi Arabia, 1980-83; cons., 1983-86; prof. U. Applied Sci., Lucerne, Switzerland, 1987—. Avocations: mountaineering, philosophy, religions. Home: Sonnenbergstrasse 39, 6060 Sarnen Obwalden Switzerland Office: U Applied Sci Lucerne, Tecknikumstrasse, 6048 Horw Lucerne Switzerland

HILFSTEIN, ERNA, science historian, educator; b. Krakow, Poland; came to U.S., 1949, naturalized, 1954; d. Leon and Anna (Schornstein) Kluger; m. Max Hilfstein; children: Leon, Simone Juliana. BA, CCNY, 1967, MA,

1971; PhD, CUNY, 1978. Tchr. secondary schs. N.Y.C., 1968-84, 86-92; collaborator Polish Acad. Scis., 1968-85; vis. prof. Queens Coll., 1973; affiliate Grad. Sch./Univ. Ctr., CUNY. Author: Starowolski's Biographies of Copernicus, 1980; collaborator English version of Nicholas Copernicus Complete Works, vol. 1, 1972, vol. 2, 1978, vol. 3, 1985, vols. 2 and 3, 2d edit., 1992; co-translator: The Leviathan in the State Theory of Thomas Hobbes: Meaning and Failure of a Political Symbol, 1996; editor: Science and History, 1978, Copernicus and His Successors, 1995, Sebastian Petrycy, A Polish Renaissance Scholar, 1997; contbr. articles and revs. to profl. jours. NEH grantee, 1984-85; recipient Rector's medal Univ. M. Kopernik, Torun, 1989, Order of Merit Silver medal Rep. of Poland, 1991. Mem. History Sci. Soc., Polish Inst. Arts and Scis. in Am., CUNY Acad. for the Humanities and Scis., N.Y. Acad. Scis., Kosciuszko Found., United Fedn. Tchrs. (chpt. chmn. 1978-84, 86-92, del. 1980-92), Am. Mus. Nat. History, Libr. Congress, Nat. Commn. Am. Fgn. Policy, New Craow Friendship Soc. (bd. dirs. 1998—). Home: 1523 Dwight Pl Bronx NY 10465-1121 Summer Address: Woodheaven Estate 375 Westwood Dr Hurleyville NY 12747-5506

HILGENBERG, JOHN CHRISTIAN, financial executive, corporate director, consultant; b. Balt., Sept. 6, 1941; s. Carl R. and Elizabeth (Rianhard) H.; m. Evelyn Brantley Handy, Apr. 1, 1971; children: Rodney, Crady. BA, Yale U., 1963; MBA, U. Va., 1965. With internat. lending divsn. Md. Nat. Bank, Balt., 1970-75; v.p., dir. fin. svcs. S.M. Hyman Co., Balt., 1975-78; v.p. fin. Eastmet Corp., Balt., 1978-85; trustee Harbor Hosp. Ctr., 1975—; v.p., treas., dir. Sky Alland Rsch. Corp., 1986, 89-90; pres., bd. dirs. Ski Tech. Holdings, Inc. and CADS USA, Inc., 1987-89; pres. The Eager St. Group, Inc., Balt., 1991—; cons., investor in early-stage cos., 1986—; bd. dirs. Synthecell Corp., pres. 1992-95; bd. dirs. Genetic MediSyn Corp., The Tech. Group, 1991-95, U. Pharmaceuticals Md., 1996-99, L. Gordon Packaging Corp., 1996-99, Simulation Interactive Online, Inc., 1999—. Lt. USNR, 1965-70. Mem. Elkridge Club, Maryland Club, Balt. Choral Arts Soc. (dir. 1975—). Republican. Episcopalian. Home: 2705 Greenspring Valley Rd Owings Mills MD 21117-4306 Other: 392 Cole Hill Rd Standish ME 04084-5646

HILGENFELDT, ULRICH, pharmacologist, scientist, educator; b. Wolfen, Germany, Feb. 16, 1942; s. Bruno and Eleonore (Roessler) H.; m. Gabriele Georgi, Aug. 22, 1968; children: Beate, Britta, Fabian, Tobias; m. Gabriela Kienapfel, June 16, 1989; 1 child, Verena. MS, U. Heidelberg, 1969, PhD, 1972, habil., 1980. Prof. pharmacology Ruprecht Karls U., Heidelberg, Germany, 1988—, head dept. pharm. pharmacology, 1996—. Mem. Dt. Ges. Biol. Chem., Dt. Ges. Naturforsch. and Arzte, Dt. Ges. Pharm. Tocicology, N.Y. Acad. Sci. Home: Boehacker 1, 69253 Heiligkreuzsteinach Germany

HILGER, HANS HERMANN, cardiologist; b. Remscheid, Germany, Mar. 16, 1928; s. Robert and Elisabeth (Schaefer) H.; m. Dorothee Graf, Aug. 1, 1956 (dec. 1981; children: Karin, Renate; m. Renate Kullmann Bracht, Aug. 23, 1984; children: Sigrid, Detlef. MD, U. Bonn, Germany, 1955. Intern Univ. Hosp., Heidelberg, Germany, 1955-56; fellow Inst. Physiology U. Göttingen, Germany, 1956-58; resident in internal medicine Univ. Hosp., Bonn, 1958-64, from sr. registrar to prof., 1964-71; chairperson internal medicine Univ. Hosp., Cologne, 1971-93; dean med. faculty U. Cologne, Germany, 1978-79. Author: Internal Medicine in Praxis and Clinic, 1973-91; author, editor: The Medical Profession in the Course of Time, 1990; editor: Signal Averaging Technique in Clinical Cardiology, 1981, Holter Monitoring Technique, 1985, Invasive Cardiovascular Therapy, 1987, Electrocardiography and Cardiac-Drug Therapy, 1989. Chmn. bd. dirs. Hufeland Prize Found., Cologne, 1988—. Mem. German Soc. Cardiology, German Austrian Soc. Internal Intensive Care Medicine, German Soc. Internal Medicine, Rotary Internat. Home: Rheingoldstr 19, 50354 Huerth Cologne, Germany Office: U Cologne Med Faculty, Joseph Stelzmann Str 9, 50924 Cologne Germany

HILGERS, MICHA, psychoanalyst, consultant; b. Aachen, Germany, Aug. 15, 1954; s. Peter Paul Michael and Philippine (Weishaupt) H. Diploma in psychology, U. Marburg, Germany, 1982; grad. in psychoanalysis, Alfred-Adler-Inst.-Aachen-Cologne, Aachen, 1990. Psychologist various hosps., Bad Wildungen, Germany, 1978-82; pvt. practice,, Aachen, 1982—; supr. Alfred Adler Inst., Aachen-Cologne, 1997—; supr. forensic and psychiat. hosps., Aachen and Düren, 1990—; cons. ecol. orgns., Germany, 1992—, Luxemburg, 1996; cons. Dept. Environ. Aachen, also others; expert German Bundestag Town Coun., 1993, 94, 97; publicist Frankfurter Rundschau, 1994—, Die Tageszeitung, Berlin, 1994—, also others. Author: Psychoanalysis of Car Driving, 1992, Shame Aspects of an Emotion, 1996, Motivational Research for Ecopolicy, 1997, The Monstrogity in Culture, 1999; also articles. Expert Deutscher Naturschutzring, Bonn, 1998. Mem. German Soc. for Individual Psychology, German Soc. for Psychoanalysis, Psychotherapy, Psychosomatics and Depth Psychologie. Avocations: sports, music, literature, cooking, art. Fax: 49 241 503695. Office: Oppenhoffallee 7, D-52066 Aachen Germany

HILGERTOVÁ, JIRINA, biochemist; b. Praha, Czech Republic, Oct. 18, 1936; d. Octavian and Amalie (Novakova) Hiebel; m. Ivan Hilgert, Jan. 24, 1959; children: Jan, Tomás. MS, Charles U., 1959, PhD, 1967, RNDr, 1968. Rsch. asst. Lab. for Endocrinology and Metabolism Charles U., Praha, 1959-67, rsch. scientist, 1967-83, sr. staff scientist, 1983—; rsch. asst. Jackson Lab., Bar Harbor, Maine, 1967; vis. scientist dept. physiologie INSERM, Paris, 1983, Inst. Biochemistry U. Griefswald, Germany, 1987. Contbr. articles to profl. jours. Mem. Fedn. European Biochem. Soc., Czech Med. Soc., Zonta Internat (pres. Praha-Bohemia club 1997-99). Avocations: photography, literature, skiing, canoeing. Home: U dubu 26, 147 00 Praha 4-Branik, Czech Republic Office: Charles U Dept Internal Med, U nemocnice 1, 128 21 Praha 2, Czech Republic

HILKEMEYER, RENILDA ESTELLA, nurse; b. Martinsburg, Mo., July 29, 1915; d. Henry Gerard and Anna Marie (Bertels) Hilkemeyer. Diploma in nursing, St. Mary's Hosp., St. Louis U., 1936; B.S. in Nursing Edn., George Peabody Coll. for Tchrs., Nashville, 1947; postgrad., U. Minn., 1950, U. Tex. Sch. Nursing, 1981; D of Pub. Svc. (hon.), St. Louis U., 1988. Staff nurse oper. rm. St. Mary's Hosp., Jefferson City, Mo., 1936-37; dist. pub. health nurse Mo. Div. Health, Jefferson City, 1937-40, cons. nursing edn., Mo., 1950-55; asst. dir. nursing Gen. Hosp. No. 1, Kansas City, Mo., 1947-49; asst. exec. sec. Mo. Nurses Assn., Jefferson City, 1949-50; dir. nursing U. Tex. System Cancer Ctr., Houston, 1955-77, asst. to pres. nursing resources, 1977-79, staff asst. to pres., prof. oncology nursing, 1979-84; mem. grant rev. com. NIH Nat. Cancer Inst, 1979-83, program rev. com., 1975-77, cons., 1982—; cons. NIH Nat. Heart, Blood and Lung Inst., 1983—, Worker's Inst. Safety, Health, 1983—; chmn., mem. scholarship and professorship com. Cancer Soc., 1980—, mem. nursing adv. com., 1963-80, 85—, profl. edn. com., 1984—, emeritus mem. 1996—; chmn. nursing adv. com., mem. adminstrv. bd. Renilda Hilkemeyer Child Care Ctr., U. Tex. Med. Ctr., 1969—. Book reviewer Am. Jour. Nursing, 1982; contbr. articles to profl. jours, chpts. to books. Pres. Braes Interfaith Ministries, 1991, 94, 95, 98. Recipient Outstanding Profl. Women's award Tex. Fedn. Houston Profl. Women, 1983, outstanding contbns. Award, Nat. Cancer Inst., 1983, Disting. Svc. award Am. Cancer Soc., 1981, Nurse of Yr. Award, Houston Area League Nursing, 1973, Matrix Award, Theta Sigma Phi, Houston, 1963, Disting. Merit award Internat. Soc. Nurses in Cancer Care, 1986, Vol. of the Yr. award Braes Interfaith Ministries, 1997; new child care ctr. at U. Tex. Med. Ctr. Houston, named in her honor, 1981 (1st ctr. established 1969); grantee HEW, 1974-77, Am. Cancer Soc., 1974-75, Tex. Fedn. and Profl. Women's Club, 1977-83, Am. Cancer Soc. 1st Nat. Nursing Leadership award, 1989. Achievement: pioneer in cancer nursing. Mem. ANA, Oncology Nursing Soc. (founding mem. 1991), Tex. Nurses Assn. (pres. 1962-64, bd. dir. 1964-66, 71-75, Nurse of Yr. award 1979, dist. 9 svc. award 1970), Am. Med. Writers Assn. (Houston-Galveston sect. 1983-84), Sigma Theta Tau, Altrusa Club (pres. 1983-84, Houston). Home: 3707 Murworth Dr Houston TX 77025-3531

HILL, ALFRED DEWAYNE, religious studies educator; b. Chattanooga, Dec. 7, 1947; s. Elsie and Frances H.; m. Nov. 24, 1984; 1 child, Alfred DeWayne II. BA, Am. Bapt. Coll., Nashville, 1970; MDiv, Memphis Theol. Sem., 1979; D Ministry, Louisville Presbyn. Sem., 1989. Pastor Mt. Calvary Bapt. Ch., Knoxville, Tenn., 1971-76; staff writer Nannie Helen Bourroughs Sch., Washington, 1972-76; writer "The Informer" Sunday Sch. Pub. Bd., Nashville, 1980-89; dean Memphis S.S. & B.T.U. Congress, 1990-96; prof. LeMoyne-Owen Coll., Memphis, 1990—; funeral dir. R.S. Lewis & Sons Funeral Home, Memphis, 1995—; lectr. Nat. Congress of Christian Edn., 1989. Mem. Shelby County Interfaith, Memphis, 1990, Progressive Nat. Convention, Washington, 1970, Nat. Conf. Black Churchmen, Washington, 1976. Mem. Tenn. Funeral Dirs. and Embalmers, Memphis Bapt. Minister's Assn., Operation PUSH, Masons. E-mail: p491@aol.com. Office: Pilgrim Rest Bapt Ch 491 E Mclemore Ave Memphis TN 38106-3007

HILL, BARRY MORTON, lawyer; b. Wheeling, W.Va., Sept. 13, 1946; m. Jacqueline Sue Jackson, Aug. 12, 1967 (div. Mar. 1988); children: Jackson Duff, Brandy; m. Lisa C. Wien, Jan. 7, 1989; 1 child, Gabriel Hunter. BS in Journalism, W.Va. U., 1968, JD, 1977. Bar: W.Va. 1977, U.S Dist. Ct. (no. and so. dists.) W.Va. 1977, Ohio 1978, U.S. Dist. Ct. (no. dist.) Ohio 1978, U.S. Ct. Appeals (3d, 4th, 6th and D.C. cirs.) 1984, U.S. Supreme Ct. 1984, U.S. Ct. Appeals (2d and 11th cirs.) 1986, Pa. 1986, U.S. Ct. Appeals (5th, 7th and 10th cirs.) 1988; cert. civil trial specialist Nat. Bd. Trial Adv., med. profl. liability trial splst. Am. Bd. Profl. Liability Attys. Ptnr. Parsons Thompson & Hill, Wheeling, W.Va.; mem. W.Va. Pattern Jury Instrn. Panel, 1986; mem. exec. com. for rev. jury selection U.S. Dist. Ct. (no. dist.) W.Va.; mem. W.Va. Bar Civil Procedure Rules Rev. com., 1987; chmn. W.Va. std. med. malpractice jury instrn. com., 2000; draftsman Interprofl. Code for Attys. and Physicians W.Va., 1987-88; adj. prof. Saba U. Sch. of Medicine, 1994—. Founding sponsor Civil Justice Found. Served to 1st lt. U.S. Army, 1969-71. Mem. Assn. Trial Lawyers Am. (sec. Pres.' coun. 1987-88, key person com., 1987-88, Pres.' coun. study com. 1988—, ins. practices com. 1988—), Am. Bd. Profl. Liability Attys. (diplomate), Ohio Acad. Trial Lawyers, Pa. Trial Lawyers Assn., W.Va. Trial Lawyers Assn. (pres. 1987-88, Outstanding mem. 1984), So. Trial Lawyers Assn. (bd. govs. 1988—). Democrat. Avocations: SCUBA, tennis, travel, writing, golf. Office: Parsons Thomson & Hill 1325 National Rd Wheeling WV 26003-5705

HILL, BEVERLY ELLEN, health sciences educator; b. Albany, Calif., May 20, 1937; d. Bert E. and Catherine (Doyle) H. BA, Coll. Holy Names, 1960; MS in Edn., Dominican Coll., 1969; EdD, U. So. Calif., 1978. Producer, dir. Health Scis TV U. Calif., Davis, 1966-69, coordinator Health Scis. TV, 1969-73; asst. dir. IMS U. So. Calif., Los Angeles, 1973-76, asst. dir. continuing edn., 1976-80, dir. biocommunications, 1976-80; dir. Med. Ednl. Resources Program Ind. U. Sch. Medicine, Indpls., 1980—; acting asst. dean continuing med. edn. Ind. U. Sch. Medicine, 1991-95; Presenter Cath. U. Nijmegen, Netherlands, 1980, 81, European Symposium on Clin. Pharmacy, Brussels, 1982, Barcelona, Spain, 1983. Contbr. articles to profl. jours. Pres. Indpls. Shakespeare Festival, 1982-83; mem. subcom. Ind. Film Commn., Indpls., 1984—. Recipient first place in rehab. category 4th Biannual J. Muir Med. Film Fest., 1980. Mem. Assn. Biomed. Communications (bd. dirs. 1985—), Health Scis. Com. Assn. (bd. dirs. 1976-79, First Place Video Festival, 1979), Assn. for Edn. Communications and Tech. Avocations: painting, travel, archeology, music, tennis, swimming. Home: 5249 W 59th St Indianapolis IN 46254-1109 Office: Med Ednl Resources Program BR 156 1226 W Michigan St Indianapolis IN 46202-5212

HILL, BRIAN HERBERT WILLIAM, publisher; b. Victoria, B.C., Sept. 20, 1949; s. George William and Clarice Rosalie (Ashbee) H.; m. Penelope Dinard Yerby, Apr. 24, 1976; children: Stephen, Rebecca. BA, U. Victoria, Can., 1971; MA, U. B.C., Vancouver, 1975; PhD, U. London, 1982. U.K. dir. Oceana Publs., Inc., U.K., 1982-92; CEO Simmonds & Hill Pub., U.K., 1992—, Primrose Hill Press, U.K., 1997—; cons. Wildy & Sons, London, 1994—. Editor: (book) Consolidated Treaty Series Index, 1984-86, 10 vols.; author: (books) Law and Practice Under the Gatt, 1988, International Commercial Arbitration, 1990, Canada: Chronology and Fact Book, 1973. Recipient Commonwealth fellowship Commonwealth Secretariat, U.K., 1976-82. Mem. Theydon Bois Golf Club, Am. Soc. Internat. Law. Avocation: golf. Office: Primrose Hill Press Ltd, 58 Carey St, WC2A2JB London England

HILL, CAROL KOELLING, library director. BS, Mo. Western State, 1974; MLS, Emporia State U., 1980. Libr. dir. City of Fort Walton Beach, Fla., 1995—. E-mail: fwblibr@fwb.org. Office: 105 Miracle Strip Pkwy SW Fort Walton Beach FL 32548-6614

HILL, CATHERINE STANTON, freelance artist. BA, UCLA. Creator musical notes posters, 1980-97; illustrator Engring. and Sci. mag., newspapers CALTECH, 1985-96. Author, artist: (comics) Mad Raccoons, 1-7, 1991-97, (book) The Mad Raccoons Collection, 1995; illustrator (book) The Three Palladins, 1977, Beware of the Mouse, 1978, Quest of Excalibur, 1979, The Blue World, 1979; prodn. designer Clash of the Titans, 1979; contbr. (comics) The Dreamery, 1987-90; creator poster Stephen J. Gould lecture, press kit Screamin' Jay Hawkins, 1988, paintings Harlan Ellison; caricaturist (book) Martin Scorsese—A Journey, 1991; exhibns. include The Poulsen Galleries, 1998-99, Tirage Gallery, 1999, Pasadena Hist. Mus., 1999, Glendale Art Assn., 1999. Recipient First prize (2) Glendale Art Assn., 1999. Mem. San Gabriel Art Assn. (1st prize and mem. award 1997). Avocation: plein air oil painting around California and the Southwest.

HILL, CHARLES LESTER, drama educator, poet, playwright; b. Albemarle, N.C., June 26, 1954; s. Thomas Dwight and Carolyn Jane (Curlee) H. BS in English/Drama, Pfeiffer Coll., 1975; Cert. of Completion Korean Lang. Course, Yonsei U., Seoul, 1982; MA in Korean Lit., Seoul Nat. U., 1986. Dormitory house counselor, English tutor Louisburg (N.C.) Coll., 1975-78; vis. lectr. Han Nam U., Taejon, South Korea, 1978-86; vis. instr. Stanly C.C., Albemarle, 1987-88; interim pastor Oakboro (N.C.) Presbyn. Ch., 1988; artist-in-residence, interim pastor Madison (Wis.) Campus Ministry, U. Wis., 1993-94; asst. prof. Han Nam U., Taejon, 1992—; performer, presenter U. of the Philippines, Quezon City, 1995-96; lectr. Presbyn. Ch., Louisville, 1987-98; guest vis. prof. Colo. Coll., Colorado Springs, 1998; asst. dir. Korean Studies Han Nam U., Taejon, 1994-96; adj. prof. Hawaii Tokai Internat. Coll., 1999-00; instr., Honolulu, 1999—. Playwright, performer: Cross Dialogue, 1975, Second Sunrise, 1996; performer Picasso at The Lapin Agile, 1999; transl., author papers; contbr. poetry to mags. Ednl. missionary Presbyn. Ch., Louisville, 1978—; founder, mgr., bd. dirs. Solomon's Porch Coffeehouse, Oakboro, 1973-77; dir., performer Youth Camp and Drama Workshop, Oakboro, 1974-75; human rights advocate Presbyn. Ch., Taejon, 1978-87; interpreter, transl., educator Han Nam U., Taejon, 1989-92. Mem. English Lang. and Lit. Soc. of Taejon, ASIANetwork (presenter, panel participant, com. mem., performer 1993-98), Rho Alpha (Best Actor awards 1973). Democrat. Avocations: hiking, guitar, international traveling, tennis, piano. Home and Office: 1463A Kealia Dr Honolulu HI 96817-1957

HILL, DAVID, poet, translator; b. Portsmouth, Hampshire, Eng., Nov. 11, 1971; s. Bryan and Marjorie Irene (Sivyour) H. BA in Modern Langs. with 1st class honors, Oxford (Eng.) U., 1995, MA, 1998; diploma in translation, Inst. Linguists, London, 1999. Author: (poetry) Angels and Astronauts, 1999, Bald Ambition, 2000; contbr. poems to numerous mags. and anthologies throughout world; prodr. monthly poetry pamphlet Lyriklife. Mem. Inst. Linguists (assoc., London). Avocations: Eastern European and international travel, musical performance. E-mail: lyriker@hotmail.com. Home: PO Box 133, 1255 Budapest Hungary

HILL, DEBORA ELIZABETH, writer, journalist, screenwriter; b. San Francisco, July 10, 1961; d. Henry Peter and Madge Lillian (Ridgeway-Aarons) H. BA, Sonoma State U., 1983. Talk show host Rock Jour. Viacom, San Francisco, 1980-81; interviewer, biographer Harrap Ltd., London, 1986-87; editor North Bay Mag., Cotati, Calif., 1988; guest feature writer Argus Courier, Petaluma, Calif., 1993-95; concept developer BiblioBytes, Hoboken, N.J., 1994-95, White Tiger Films, San Francisco, 1995—; feature writer The Econs. Press, 1996-97; literary agt. The Thornton Agy., Portland, Oreg., 1998—; assoc. prodr. White Tiger Films, 1995—; concept developer Star Trek: Voyager and Star Trek: Deep Space Nine, 1997-98, 99—; mem. Writers Net The Online Wordbiz Directory, Writers for Hire, The Hollywood Direct Access Directory. Author: The San Francisco Rock Experience, 1979, CUTS from a San Francisco Rock Journal, 1982, Punk Retro, 1988, Gale Research-Resourceful Woman, 1994, St. James Guide to Fantasy Writers, 1996, St. James Guide to Famous Gays and Lesbians, 1997, SuperGirls: The Co-Ed Murders, 1999; co-author: Rumour Has a Memory, 1999, The Land of the WAND, 1999, The Lost Myths Saga, vol. 1, The Crystal Chalice, vol. 2, 1999, The Sword and the Scabbard, vol. 3, 2000, The Pentacular, Volume 4, 2000; co-writer, cons. producer The Danger Club, Danger Club II; elderly care columnist www.accesslife.com., 2000—; contbr. stories and articles to profl. jours. No. Calif. corr. Neighborhood Am. Democrat. Avocations: clothing design, cooking, internet, reading, interior design. E-mail: debora.hill@lycos.com; debhll@aol.com. Home: 8312 Windmill Farms Dr Cotati CA 94931-4570 Address: Roxy Books 4110 Pacific Ave Ste 102 Forest Grove OR 97116-2275

HILL, EDWARD WILLIAM, economics educator, urban and regional planner; b. Derby, Conn., Jan. 4, 1952; s. John B. and Marie Louise (Wierdo) H.; mm. Karen Louise Upton, June 7, 1975; 1 child, Emma Rose. BA, U. Pa., 1973; M City Planning, MIT, 1976, PhD, 1981. Lectr. Boston U., 1978-79; v.p. Country Stores Inc., Seymour, Conn., 1980-84; asst. prof. urban studies and pub. adminstrn. Cleve. State U., 1985-90, assoc. prof., 1990-93, prof., 1993—; prin. Otter Rock Econs., 1980—; mem. adv. bd. Ctr. for Policy Alternatives, Washington, 1990-94; cons. to Hungarian and Russian municipalities USIA, 1991-95; non-resident sr. fellow Brookings Instn., Washington, 2000—; mem. adv. bd. Reinvestment Fund, Phila., 2000—. Co-author: Banking on the Brink, 1992; co-editor: Financing Economic Development, 1990, Metropolis in Black and White, 1992, Global Perspectives on Economic Development, 1997; assoc. editor Econ. Devel. Quar., 1989-94, editor, 1994—. Chmn. Oxford (Conn.) Planning Commn., 1983-85; mem. exec. bd. Cuyahoga County Planning Commn., Cleve., 1987-89; active Leadership Cleve., 1997, Gov.'s Urban Revitalization Task Force, 1999. Recipient comprehensive planning award Mo. chpt. Am. Planning Assn., 1986, Robertson prize Urban Studies editors, 1994; Catherine Bauer Wurster fellow Joint Ctr. for Urban Studies, MIT, 1979-81. Office: Coll Urban Affairs Cleve State U Cleveland OH 44115

HILL, GEORGE ARTHUR, physicist; b. Swinton, England, Nov. 6, 1947; s. Leslie and Edith (Fewster) H.; m. Barbara Carol Stringfellow, Sept. 23, 1967; 1 child, Simon Andrew. BS, Hull U., England, 1970, DPhil, 1976. Lectr. Physics Inst. Malta, 1976-78; rsch. asst. Theoretical Chem., Cambridge, England, 1981-82; rsch. engr. Standard Telephone Labs., 1982-85; prin. rsch. physicist Coherent Ltd., Harlow, 1985-91; technician Caedmon Sch., Whitby, England, 1991—; dir. Evolution Towards Higher Order Structures, 1982—. Author: The Cybernetic Student, 1980. With Royal Air Force, 1968-70. Rsch. fellow Hull U., 1978-81. Mem. Inst. Phys. Avocations: music, outdoor activities. Office: Caedmon sch, Airy Hill, Whitby YO21 1QA, England

HILL, GEORGE JAMES, physician, educator; b. Cedar Rapids, Iowa, Oct. 7, 1932; s. Gerald Leslie and Essie Mae (Thompson) H.; m. Helene Zimmermann, July 16, 1960; children: James Warren, David Hedgcock, Sarah, Helena Rundall. AB, Yale U., 1953; MD, Harvard U., 1957; MA, Rutgers U., 1999. Intern N.Y. Hosp., 1957-58; fellow and resident in surgery Peter Bent Brigham hosp. and Harvard Med. Sch., 1958-61, 63-66; clin. assoc. NIH, Bethesda, Md., 1961-63; instr. surgery U. Colo., 1966-67, asst. prof., 1967-72, asso. prof., 1972-73; prof. Washington U., 1973-76; prof., chmn. Marshall U., 1976-81; prof., dir. surg. oncology U. of Medicine and Dentistry of N.J.-N.J. Med. Sch., Newark, 1981-96; prof. emeritus U. of Medicine and Dentistry of N.J. - N.J. Med. Sch., Newark, 1997—; Am. Cancer Soc. prof. clin. oncology U. Medicine and Dentistry N.J.-N.J. Med. Sch., Newark, 1989-92; pres. faculty N.J. Med. Sch., Newark, 1991-92; clin. prof. surgery Uniformed Svcs. U. of the Health Scis., Bethesda, Md., 1989—, Mt. Sinai Sch. Medicine, N.Y.C., 1999—; acting pres. Sterling Coll., Craftsbury Common, Vt., 1996; rsch. coord. St. Barnabas Med. Ctr., Livingston, N.J., 1997-99; hon. mem. med. sch. staff St. Barnabas Med. Ctr., 1999—, chmn. clin. cancer edn. com. Nat. Cancer Inst., 1978-80; vis. fellow in molecular biology Princton U., 1988. Author: Leprosy in Five Young Men, 1970, paperback edit., 1979, Outpatient Surgery, 1973, 3d edit., 1988, Clinical Oncology, 1977; contbr. articles to med. jours. Pres. Tri-State Area coun. Boy Scouts Am., Huntington, W.Va., 1980-82, v.p. Essex coun., 1983-89, commr., 1998, commr. No. N.J. Coun., 1998-00, v.p., 2000—, chmn. nat. health careers exploring com., 1987-92; pres. W.Va. divsn. Am. Cancer Soc., 1980-81, pres. N.J. divsn., 1987-89; pres. Am. Assn. Cancer Edn., 1985-86; mem. N. J. State Commn. on Cancer Rsch., 1983-84; trustee Frost Valley YMCA, 1986—, Sterling Coll., Craftsbury Common, Vt., 1990—; nat. dir.-at-large Am. Cancer Soc., 1989-96, mem. nat. exec. com., 1990-91, hon. life mem., 1996—; vestry Ch. of the Holy Innocents, 1994-96. Capt. M.C., USNR; active duty USN, 1990-91, ret., 1992. Recipient Civic Actions medal Republic South Vietnam, 1972, Lederle Med. Faculty award, 1970, Silver Beaver award Boy Scouts Am., 1981, Silver Antelope award, 1998, Am. Cancer Soc. Nat. Divisional award, St. George medal, 1992, Gorgas medal Assn. Mil. Surgeons U.S., 1991, Outstanding Svc. medal Uniformed Svcs. U. Health Scis., 1992, Meritorious Svc. medal USN, 1993, Nat. William Spurgeon III award Boy Scouts Am., 1994; named Jerseyan of Week, Newark-Star Ledger, 1987, 93; Damon Runyon fellow, 1973-76. Mem. ACS (mem. com. on cancer 1987-93), Acad. Medicine N.J. (pres. 1992-93), Soc. Univ. Surgeons, Soc. Surg. Oncology (exec. coun. 1985-88), Ctrl. Surg. Assn., Am. Assn. Cancer Edn. (pres. 1985-86, Edwards medal 1994), Am. Assn. Cancer Rsch., Med. HistorySoc. N.J. (v.p. 2000-02), Essex County Med. Soc. (pres. 1995-96), Med. Soc. N.J. (chmn. com. cancer control 1985-94, sec. 1995-96), Oncology Nursing Soc. (hon.), AAUP (pres. chpt. 1988-89), SAR (chpt. sec. 1999—, v.p. N.J. state soc. 2000—), N.J. Med. Club (pres. 1999-2000), Harvard Club (N.Y.C. and Boston), Univ. Club (Denver), Army and Navy Club, Explorers Club, Soc. Mayflower Descs., Order Founders and Patriots of Am. (coun. N.J. state soc. 1999—), Soc. of Colonial Wars (coun. N.J. state soc. 2000—), Yale Club Ctrl. N.J. (pres. 1991-93), Sigma Xi (chpt. pres. 1986-87), Alpha Omega Alpha. Republican. Episcopalian. Address: 3 Silver Spring Rd West Orange NJ 07052-4317 also: PO Box 313 South Orange NJ 07079-0313

HILL, GEORGE ROY, film director; b. Mpls., Dec. 20; s. George Roy and Helen Frances (Owens) H.; m. Louisa Horton, Apr. 7, 1951. B.A., Yale U.; B of Lit., Trinity Coll., Dublin, Ireland. Acting debut: (play) The Devil's Disciple, Dublin, 1948; other stage appearances include The Creditors, 1950; toured with Margaret Webster's Shakespeare Repertory Co.; writer, actor: (teleplay) My Brother's Keeper, 1953; writer, producer, dir.: (teleplay) Judgement at Nuremberg, 1957; dir.: (Broadway plays) Look Homeward, Angel, 1957, The Gang's All Here, Period of Adjustment, Greenwillow, 1960, Henry, Sweet Henry, 1967, (off-Broadway show) Moon on a Rainbow Shawl, 1962, (films) Period of Adjustment, 1962, Toys in the Attic, 1963, The World of Henry Orient, 1964, Hawaii, 1966, Thoroughly Modern Millie, 1967, Butch Cassidy and the Sundance Kid, 1969, Slaughterhouse-Five, 1972, The Sting, 1973, The Great Waldo Pepper, 1975, Slap Shot, 1977, A Little Romance, 1979, The World According to Garp, 1982, The Little Drummer Girl, 1984, Funny Farm, 1988. Served as pilot USMC, World War II and Korean War. Recipient Acad. award for best dir. of The Sting, 1973; Emmy award nominations for A Night to Remember, The Helen Morgan Story, Child of Our Time; Acad. award nomination for Butch Cassidy and the Sundance Kid, 1969; Cannes Internat. Film Festival Jury Prize for Slaughterhouse Five, 1972. Office: Pan Arts Prodns 59 E 54th St Rm 73 New York NY 10022-4211

HILL, GRANT, professional basketball player; b. Dallas, Oct. 5, 1972; s. Calvin and Janet Hill. BA in History, Duke U., 1994. Forward Detroit Pistons, 1994-99, Orlando Magic, 2000—. Named to Dream Team III U.S. Olympic Team, 1996, Co-rookie of Yr., 1994. Office: Orlando Magic PO Box 76 Orlando FL 32802-0076

HILL, HOWARD DARNELL, education educator, dean; b. May 4, 1942; s. Howard Jr. and Della Mae (Williams) H.; m. Clemmie Faye Coulter, Dec. 24, 1963; children: Ray Darnell, Edith Renee (dec.). BA in Social Studies, Philander Smith Coll., 1964; MSE in Secondary Sch. Adminstrn., Ark. State U., 1968; PhD in Curriculum and Instrn., Kans. State U., 1973; postdoctoral study in ednl. adminstrn., U. S.C., 1983-85. Secondary tchr. Jonesboro Pub. Sch., Ark., 1964-66; supr. instrn. Marion Sch., Ark., 1966-69; asst. prin. West Memphis (Ark.) Schs., 1969-70; secondary tchr. Tunica Pub. Sch., Miss., 1970-71; asst. prof. edn. U. Houston, 1973-77; assoc. prof. Miss. Valley State U., Itta Bena, 1977-78; prof., chmn., program coord. dept. edn. S.C. State U., Orangeburg, 1978-87; dir. chpt. programs Phi Delta Kappa Hdqs., Bloomington, Ind., 1987-97; dean Sch. Grad. Studies S.C. State U., 1997-98, dir. doctoral program, chair ednl. leadership/counselor edn., 1998—; cons. Nat. Ednl. Svc., Bloomington, Ind. Contbr. articles to profl.

jours. and books. Named Tchr. of Yr., S.C. State U. Sch. Edn., 1983. Contbr. articles to profl. jours. and books. Named Tchr. of Yr., S.C. State U. Sch. Edn., 1983. Mem. ASCD, John Dewey Soc., Am. Assn. Colls. Tchr. Edn., Nat. Coun. Social Studies, Nat. Alliance Black Sch. Educators, Coun. of Grad. Sch. Deans, Assn. Tchrs. of Edn., Nat. Assn. Secondary Sch. Prins., Rotary Internat., Phi Delta Kappa. Home: 1186 Pruitt Dr NW Orangeburg SC 29118-4024 Office: SC State U PO Box 7607 Orangeburg SC 29117-0001

HILL, JEFFERSON BORDEN, regulatory oversight officer, lawyer; b. Wilmington, Del., Nov. 5, 1941; s. Julian Werner and Mary Louisa (Butcher) H.; m. Gabrielle Marie Tourville, Mar. 19, 1976; children: Corinna Borden Hill, Lydia Richards Hill. BA, Harvard U., 1963, LLB, 1967. Bar: Del. 1967, D.C. 1972. Legis. asst. Congressman William V. Roth, Jr., Washington, 1967-70; attorney Antitrust div. U.S. Dept. Justice, Washington, 1970-76; asst. dir. Office of Policy Planning and Legis., Antitrust Div., U.S. Dept. Justice, Washington, 1976-77; br. chief Office Info. and Regulatory Affairs, Office Mgmt. Budget, Washington, 1977—; adj. prof. Georgetown U., Washington, 1987-96. Mem. Met. Club. Republican. Home: 639 E Capitol St SE Washington DC 20003-1234 Office: Office Mgmt and Budget 17th And Pennsylvania Ave NW Washington DC 20503-0001

HILL, SIR JOHN MCGREGOR, physicist, corporate executive; b. Feb. 21, 1921; s. John Campbell and Margaret Elizabeth (Park) H.; m. Nora Eileen Hellett, 1947; 3 children. BS, King's Coll., London; PhD, St. John's Coll., Cambridge U. Research physicist Cavendish Lab., Cambridge, Eng., 1946-48; lectr. London U., 1948-50; formerly with U.K. Atomic Energy Authority, London, from 1950, mem. for prodn., 1964-67, chmn., 1967-81; chmn. Brit. Nuclear Fuels, Ltd., 1971-83, Amersham Internat., 1975-88, Rea Bros. PLC, London, 1987-95; chmn. Aurora PLC, 1984-88. Mem. Adv. Council on Tech., 1968-81. Served to flight lt. RAF, World War II. Decorated knight Queen Elizabeth II, Legion of Honor (France). Fellow Royal Soc., Inst. Physics, Royal Acad. Engring.; mem. U.S. NAE (fgn. assoc.). Club: East India. Home: Dominic Ho, Sudbrook Ln, Richmond TW10 7AT, England*

HILL, LA JOYCE CARMICHAEL, marketing professional; b. Tifton, Ga., Nov. 14, 1952; d. Ralph Eugene and Vista Eloise (Dooley) Carmichael; m. Bobby Wayne Hill, Jan. 1, 1972. AS, Abraham Baldwin Agrl. Coll., Tifton, 1971. With R.E. Carmichael Co. Inc., 1970-89, sec./treas., 1978-88, pres., chmn. bd., 1988-89; gen. mgr. J & B Power Equipment, Inc., 1989-95; v.p. J&B Power, 1995—; pres. JBH Investments, Inc., 1999—. Fund drive chair United Way, 1999, pres., 2000; mem. Downtown Devel. Authority, 1997—. Mem. Chula Charge United Meth. Women (sec.-treas. 1986—), Tifton Exch. Club (pres. 1994-95, treas. 1996—). Methodist. Avocations: Needlework, reading, collecting antiques. Home: PO Box 947 Tifton GA 31793-0947

HILL, LARKIN PAYNE, real estate company data processing executive; b. Oct. 30, 1954; d. Max Lloyd and Jane Olivia (Evatt) H. Student, Coll. Charleston, 1972-73, U. N.C., 1973. Lic. real estate broker, N.C. Sec., property mgr. Max L. Hill Co., Inc., Charleston, S.C., 1973-75, sec., data processor, 1979-82, v.p. adminstrn., 1982—; resident mgr. Carolina Apts., Carrboro, N.C., 1975-77; sales assoc., Realtor, Southland Assocs., Chapel Hill, N.C., 1977-78; cons. specifications com. Charleston Trident Multiple Listing Service, 1985. Bd. dirs. Charleston Area Arts Coun., 1992-93; co-chair Beaux Arts Ball, Sch. Arts. Mem. Royal Oak Found., Scottish Soc. Charleston (bd. dirs. 1989-91), Preservation Soc., Charleston Computer Users Group, N.C. Assn. Realtors, Spoleto Festival USA (chmn. auction catalog com. 1990-92). Republican. Methodist. Avocations: reading, crossword puzzles, American Staffordshire Terriers. Home: 7 Riverside Dr Charleston SC 29403-3217 Office: Max L Hill Co Inc Re/max Realty Svcs 824 Johnnie Dodds Blvd Mount Pleasant SC 29464-3103

HILL, LAWRENCE SIDNEY, management educator; b. Gary, Ind., Nov. 10, 1923; m. Evelyn Honig, Mar. 22, 1964; 1 child, Robert J. BSE, Purdue U., 1947, MBA, U. So. Calif., L.A., 1960; MSIE, U. So. Calif., 1962, Engr. I.E., 1965, PhD, 1968. Registered profl. engr., Calif. Asst. indsl. engr. USX Corp., Gary, Ind., 1947; indsl. hygiene engr. Ill. Dept. Pub. Health, Chgo., 1948-51; indsl. engr. USX Corp., Gary, 1951-52; sr. engr. Nat. Safety Coun., Chgo., 1953; sr. indsl. engr. Martin Marietta Co., Balt., 1953-55; group head McDonnell Douglas Co., Santa Monica, Calif., 1955-57; sr. mem. staff The Rand Corp., Santa Monica, 1957-71; prof. mgmt. Calif. State U., L.A., 1969—; cons., prin. engr. Ralph M. Parsons Co., Pasadena, 1973-82; cons., sr. mem. tech. staff TRW Inc., Redondo Beach, Calif., 1982-90; cons., environ. mgr. USN, Long Beach, Calif., 1991-94; vis. lectr. Ops. Rsch. Soc. Am./ Inst. Mgmt. Scis., 1973-95, expert witness in safety, mgmt., 1986—. Contbr. articles to profl. jours., books. Mem. Alpha Pi Mu, Alpha Iota Delta. Avocations: profl. and coll. sports. Home: 3653 Oceanhill Way Malibu CA 90265-5637

HILL, LEDA KATHERINE, librarian; b. Bklyn., Feb. 16, 1952; d. David and Leda Louise (Jones) H. BA, Bklyn. Coll., 1974, MS in Edn., 1989; MLS, Queens (N.Y.) Coll., 1995. New bus. coord. INAC Corp., Cranford, N.J., 1974-80; paralegal Orgn. Women for Legal Awareness, Inc., East Orange, N.J., 1980-83; tchr. Roselle (N.J.) Bd. Edn., 1983-84; libr., tchr. N.Y.C. Bd. Edn., Bklyn., 1985—. Mem. Bklyn. Reading Coun., N.Y.C. Sch. Librs. Assn., Am. Libr. Assn., Am. Assn. Sch. Librs. Office: Middle School 2 655 Parkside Ave Brooklyn NY 11226-1505

HILL, MICHAEL WILLIAM, library director; b. Ross on Wye, Eng., July 27, 1928; s. Geoffrey William and Dorothy (Ursell) H.; m. Elma Jack Forrest, 1957 (dec. 1967); children: Sally Ann, Alastair Geoffrey Frank; m. Barbara Joy Youngman, 1969. MA, Oxford (Eng.) U., 1953, MS, 1954. Chartered chemist. Rsch. chemist Laporte Chems., U.K., 1953-56; head of chem. rsch. Morgan Crucible Co., U.K., 1956-59, process control mgr., 1959-63, tech. pub. rels. mgr., 1963-64; asst. keeper Brit. Mus., U.K., 1964-68, keeper, 1968-73; dir. Sci. Reference Libr. Brit. Libr., U.K., 1986-86; pres. Internat. Fedn. of Information and Documentation, 1985-90; v.p. Internat. Assn. Tech. Univ. Librs., 1976-81; chmn. coun. ASLIB, U.K., 1979-81; chmn. Circle of State Librs., U.K., 1977-79, hon. mem., 1990. Co-editor: Bowker-Saur Guides to Information Sources; author: Michael Hill on Science, Invention and Information, 1988, National Information Policies and Strategies, 1994, National Information Policies, 1996, the Impact of Information on Society, 1998; co-author: Patent Documentation, 1978. Fellow Inst. Info. Scientists, Royal Soc. Arts, Mfrs. and Commerce; mem. Royal Soc. Chemistry, Sutton & Cheam. Soc. (vice chmn. exec. bd.), United Oxford and Cambridge Univ. Club, Oxford Soc., Libr. Assn. Avocation: charitable work, enjoying the pleasures of life.

HILL, MIROSLAV, molecular biologist; b. Ostrava, Czechoslovakia, Dec. 25, 1929; arrived in France, 1968; s. Karel and Hildegarda (Kručinská) H.; m. Jana Filipová, Feb. 12, 1965; 1 child, Ivan. MD, Faculty of Medicine, Brno, Czechoslovakia, 1953; PhD, Inst. Biophysics, Brno, 1958; D honoris causa, Masaryk U., Brno, 1999. Asst. prof. Faculty of Medicine, 1953-58; jr. researcher Inst. Biophysics, 1959-62, sr. researcher, 1963-66, head lab. cytogenetics, 1966-68; rsch. fellow dept. molecular biology Faculty of Sci., Brussels, 1962-63; sr. researcher Inst. Gustave-Roussy, Villejuif, France, 1968-72; head lab. cellular and molecular biology Inst. Cancer Immunogenetics, Villejuif, 1973-84; dir. rsch. Centre Nat. Recherche Sci., Paris, 1973-97; vis. scientist sch. medicine U. Miami, Fla., 1985-86; vis. prof. Keio U., Tokyo, 1985. Co-author: Autoradiography, 1966; contbr. articles and revs. to profl. jours. Mem. Am. Assn. Cancer Rsch., Tissue Culture Assn., N.Y. Acad. Scis., Nat. Geographic Soc. Roman Catholic. Avocations: tennis, skiing. Office: Bioinfor Unit Ctr Nat Recherche Sci, 7 rue Guy Moquet, F-94801 Villejuif France

HILL, NORMA LOUISE, librarian; b. Somerville, Mass., Oct. 27; d. Southern G. and Marguerite M. (Smith) Smallwood; m. George Forris Hill, Dec. 30, 1954; children: Gregory Harrison, Jonathan Smallwood. AB, Wheaton Coll., 1952; MS in Libr. Sci., Our Lady of the Lake Coll., 1975; postgrad., Harvard U., 1994. Grad. asst. Our Lady of the Lake Coll., San Antonio, 1974-75; libr. Cmty. Guidance Ctr., San Antonio, 1975; 86th tactical fighter wing 86th Tactical Fighter Wing, Ramstein, Fed. Republic Germany, 1976-79; info. mgmt. specialist Exec. Office of the Pres., Washington, 1980; dept. head Howard County (Md.) Libr., 1980-81, asst. dir., 1981-86, dir., 1996—; del. Gov's. Conf. on Libr. and Info. Sci., 1991. Mem. Friends of the Howard County Libr., Howard County Literacy Coalition, 1984, Md. Adv. Coun. on Librs., 1987-88; adv. bd. State Libr. Resource Ctr., 1986-88, network planning and resource sharing task force, 1988-89; bd. dirs. Columbia Found., 1992-98, sec. 1994-98, Howard County Housing Alliance, 1992-93; mem. adv. bd. Johns Hopkins U. Columbia Ctr., 1994—; mem. cmty. rels. coun. Howard County Gen. Hosp., 1995—; mem. bd. Equal Bus. Opportunity Commn., 1996—; mem. leadership Howard Co. Bd. Health Improvement, 1996—. Recipient Insp. Gen. Spl. Achievement award USAF, 1977, 78. Mem. Md. Assn. Pub. Libr. Adminstrs., Md. Libr. Assn. (chair nominations com. 1984-85, co-chmn. fed. rels. subcom. 1985-86, 1st v.p., pres.-elect 1986-87, pres. 1987-88, exec. bd. 1988-89, chair awards com. 1991, legis. com. 1997—, award 1993), ALA (pub. libr. divsn., nominations com. 1989-90), Pub. Libr. Assn., NAFE, Leadership Howard County, Nat. Coun. of Negro Women, Alpha Kappa Alpha. Democrat. Office: Howard County Libr 6600 Cradlerock Way Columbia MD 21045-4912

HILL, PAUL WINDWOOD, geophysicist; b. Tipton, W.Midlands, U.K., Oct. 21, 1952; s. Job Henry and Matilda (Whitehouse) H.; m. Sandra Pearl Tierney, July 29, 1989 (div. Oct. 1991); m. Marli Aparecida Monteiro de Barros, Dec. 19, 1991. BSc in Geology with honors, U. Wales, Swansea, U.K., 1984. Sr. engring. inspector Fordath Ltd., West Bromwich, U.K., 1969-81; geophysicist Seismograph Svc. Ltd., Bromley, U.K., 1984-91; sr. geophysicist Haliburton geophys., Bedford, U.K., 1991-95, Geco-Prakla Schlumberger, Gatwick, U.K., 1995-96, Compagnie Générale de Géophysique, Massey, France, 1996-97, Geco-Prakla Schlumberger, Gatwick, U.K., 1997—. Mem. AAAS, N.Y. Acad. Sci., Planetary Soc. Avocations: geology, astronomy, archaeology, computing, model engineering. Home: Condominio Lagoa Azul, Rua C # 8-Q 08 Lote 115, Itepeba Maricá RJ, Brazil

HILL, PETER WILLIAM, university official, educator; b. Ipswich, Suffolk, Eng., June 3, 1966; s. George Thomas and Joyce Ethel (Harvey) H.; m. Margaret Clare Attlee, May 24, 1969 (div. 1998); children: Joanna, Rebecca, David, Andrew, Rachel. BA with honors, U. London, 1973; Diploma in Edn., Murdoch U., 1977, PhD, 1982. Supt. edn. Edn. Dept. Western Australia, 1982-85, asst. dir., 1985-86; chmn. Victorian Curriculum Assessment Bd., 1986-89; chief gen. mgr. Dept. Sch. Edn., Victoria, Victoria, Australia, 1989-92; prof. edn. U. Melbourne, Australia, 1994—, dep. dean, 1995—; chair bd. dirs. Australian Prins. Ctr., Ltd. Trustee Nat. Ctr. on Edn. and the Economy. Fellow Australian Coll. Edn.

HILL, PHILIP, retired lawyer; b. East Saint Louis, Ill., Mar. 13, 1917; s. Nehemiah William and Lulu Myrtle (Johnson) H.; m. Betty Jean Stone, July 4, 1942; children: William Stone, Thomas Chapman, Nancy Layton, Mary Anne. AB in Chemistry, U. Ill., 1937; PhD in Chemistry, Ohio State U., 1941; JD, John Marshall Law Sch., Chgo., 1968. Bar: Ill. 1968, U.S. Patent Office 1969, U.S. Ct. Appeals (fed. cir.) 1982. With Standard Oil Co. Ind., 1941-78, patent atty., 1969-73, dir. petroleum and corp. patents and licensing, 1973-78; ptnr. Hill & Hill, Lansing, Ill., 1978-86, pvt. practice law Philip Hill, P.C., 1987-96; ret., 1996; cons. Univ. Patents, Inc., Norwalk, Conn., 1980-89; treas. Am. Waste Reduction Corp., 1992-96. Mem. ABA, AAAS, Ill. State Bar Assn., Am. Intellectual Property Law Assn., Chgo. Patent Law Assn., Am. Chem. Soc., Phi Beta Kappa, Sigma Xi, Phi Kappa Phi. Methodist. Clubs: Kiwanis (Lansing, pres. 1959, 84). Contbr. articles to profl. jours.; patentee in field. Home: 17946 Chicago Ave Lansing IL 60438-2261 Office: PO Box 187 Lansing IL 60438-0187

HILL, RICHARD INGLIS, retired civil engineer; b. Callander, Perthshire, Scotland, May 8, 1933; s. John Imrie and Margaret Logan (Inglis) H.; m. Margaret McEwen, June 3, 1959; children: John Douglas, Richard Graham. BSc in Civil Engring., U. Strathclyde, 1954. Grad. asst., asst. engr., sr. engr., asst. county surveyor Perth and Kinross County Coun., 1954-72; county surveyor, engr. Selkirk County Coun., 1972-75; dir. roads engring., dir. roads and transp. Borders Regional Coun., 1974-95; dir. tech. svcs. Scottish Borders Coun., 1995-98; ret., 1998; presenter numerous tech. papers; former advisor to conv. Scottish local authorities on roads and transp. matters. Past sec., chmn. Perth Round Table; clk. ch. congl. bd., Ch. of Scotland, elder. Decorated Order Brit. Empire. Fellow Instn. Civil Engrs., Instn. Hwy. and Transp. Chartered Engrs. (past sec. chmn.); mem. Assn. Mcpl. Engrs. (past chmn. Edinburgh and East of Scotland divsn.). Avocations: walking, music, golf, country dancing. Home: Silverdale Ormiston Grove, Melrose Roxburghshire TD6 9SR, Scotland

HILL, ROBERT, administrator; b. Adeliade, Australia, Sept. 25, 1946; married; 4 children. B of Law, U. Adelaide; M of Law, U. Laws, London. Elected Senate of South Australia, 1980; shadow min. Dept. Justice, the ACT and Status of Women, Australia, 1988-89, Dept. Fgn. Affairs, Australia, 1989-93, Dept. Defense & Dept. Pub. Adminstrn., Australia, 1993-94, Dept. Edn., Sci. & Tech., Australia, 1994-96; leader of opposition Australian Senate, 1990-96, leader of govt., 1996—; min. Dept. Environment, Australia, 1996—. Office: Dept Environment, Parliament House Ste MG68, Canberra ACT 2600, Australia*

HILL, ROBERT ARTHUR, ballet dancer; b. Copiague, N.Y., Feb. 5, 1961; s. Richard Louis and Margaret Theresa (Krantz) H. Dancer Atlantic Contemporary Ballet Theatre, Atlantic City, 1980-82; joined Am. Ballet Theatre, N.Y.C., 1982, soloist, 1986-89; principal dancer Am. Ballet theatre, N.Y.C., 1993—, N.Y.C. Ballet, 1989-90; pres. Roalda Ltd., London, 1990—; prin. dancer Royal Ballet, London, 1991-93; guest artist Scottish Ballet, 1988, San Francisco Ballet, 1989, La Scala, Milan, 1989—, Royal Ballet, London, 1990—, Am. Ballet Theatre, 1990, Teatro Colon, Buenos Aires, 1990—. Appearances include Kennedy Ctr. Honors, 1986, Columbia pictures Little Nikita, 1987, Internat. Ballet Festival, Havana, Cuba, 1988, Japan Ballet Festival, 1989, 90, T.O. Hotshoe Show, 1988, 89, Toronto, Can., Spoleto Festival, Italy, 1988,Monterrey, Mex., 1989; performed in Etudes, Giselle, Les Liasons Dangereuses, Manon, Romeo and Juliet, The Sleeping Beauty, The Nutcracker, Swan Lake, Theme and Variations, Enough Said, Requiem, Symphonie Concertante, Americans We, Enought Said, States of Grace, Cruel World. Avocations: travel, foreign languages, outdoors. Home and Office: 1202 Lexington Ave # 231 New York NY 10028-1425 also: American Ballet Theatre 890 Broadway Fl 3 New York NY 10003-1211*

HILL, ROBERT MARTIN, retired protective services official, forensic document examiner, consultant, writer, lecturer; b. Hammond, Ind., Dec. 10, 1949; s. Donald Edwin and Norma Jeanne (Beal) H.; m. Connie Carolina Nordquist, Dec. 19, 1970. BA, U. Minn., 1974; postgrad., U. Phoenix; cert. in fin. fraud, IRS, Glynco, Ga., 1984; cert. in questioned documents, U.S. Secret Service, Glynco, Ga., 1986. Cert. police officer, Ill., Minn., Ariz.; cert. fraud examiner. Police officer Rolling Meadows (Ill.) Police Dept., 1970-72, St. Paul Police Dept., 1972-79; police officer Scottsdale (Ariz.) Police Dept., 1980-81, police fraud detective, 1981—; com. mem. Fraud Ariz. Banker's Assn., 1985-86; lectr. various colls. and orgns.; pres. Assoc. Document Labs., Inc.; forensic document examiner. Contbr. articles to profl. publs. Recipient Dirs. Commendation U.S. Secret Svc., Washington, 1986, Commendation, Dept. Defense, 1993; named Investigator of Yr. Econ. Crime Investigators, 1991. em. Internat. Assn. Credit Card Investigators (v.p. 1985-86, pres., bd. dirs. 1 986-88, Internat. Law Enforcement Officer of the Yr. award 1986, Ariz. chpt. Police Officer of the Yr. 1984, 86, 93), Internat. Assn. Auto Theft Investigators, Am. Acad. Forensic Scis., Internat. Police Assn., Assn. Cert. Fraud Examiners, Southwest Assn. Forensic Document Examiners, Internat. Assn. for Identification. Republican. Baptist. Avocations: travel, photography, weightlifting. Office: 9065 E Via Linda Scottsdale AZ 85258-5400

HILL, RONALD JAMES, political science educator; b. Braunston, Eng., July 4, 1943; arrived in Ireland, 1969; s. Richard and Elsie Irene (Wilson) H.; m. Ethna Josephine Frayne, July 11, 1986; m. Jacqueline Rhoda Thomas, July 23, 1971 (div. May 1984); 1 child, Jennifer Elizabeth. BA, Leeds (Eng.) U., 1965; MA, Essex (Eng.) U., 1968, PhD, 1974. Jr. lectr. Trinity Coll., Dublin, 1969-72, lectr., 1972-80, assoc. prof., 1980-91, prof., 1991—. Author: Soviet Political Elites, 1977, Soviet Politics, Political Science and Reform, 1980, Soviet Union: Politics, Economics and Society, 1985, 89; co-author: The Soviet Communist Party, 1981, 83, 86; gen. editor Economies and Societies in Transition, 1988—; editor Irish Slavonic Studies, 1989—. Mem. Irish Assn. for Russian and Ea. European Studies (pres. 1994-97), Brit. Assn. for Slavonic and Ea. European Studies, Am. Assn. for the Advancement of Slavic Studies. Avocations: music, languages. Office: Polit Sci Dept, Trinity Coll, Dublin 2, Ireland

HILL, THOMAS CLARKE, IX, accountant, systems specialist, entrepreneur; b. Chgo., July 5, 1969; s. Thomas Clarke VIII and Arlene Mae (Wertz) H. BA in Polit. Economy and Politics, Lake Forest Coll., 1992; postgrad., DePaul U., 1998-2000. Legis. asst. State Rep. William E. Peterson, Prairie View, Ill., 1989-92, State Sen. William E. Peterson, Prairie View, 1992-94; project mgr. Vernon Twp., Prairie View, 1992-94; cons. Resource Tech. Assocs., Des Plaines, Ill., 1994-95; acct., systems specialist Green Acres Country Club, Northbrook, Ill., 1995—; owner IX Designs, 1997—. Precinct com. Lake County (Ill.) Rep. Ctrl. Com., 1990—; chmn. Lake County Young Reps., 1993; del. state conv. Rep. Ctrl. Com., Peoria, Ill., 1992; election judge Office of County Clk., Lake County, 1988-90; treas. Medinah Investment Club. Frances Beidler scholar Lake Forest Coll., 1990-91, 91-92. Mem. Nat. Eagle Scout Assn., Club Accts. Assn. Am. (assoc.), Shriners, Masons, Mensa, KT, Phi Beta Kappa, Pi Sigma Alpha. Avocations: camping, trapshooting, woodworking. Home: 64 Berkshire Ln Lincolnshire IL 60069-3203 Office: Green Acres Country Club 916 Dundee Rd Northbrook IL 60062-2798

HILL, THOMAS WILLIAM, JR., lawyer, educator; b. N.Y.C., Dec. 25, 1924; s. Thomas William Sr. and Marion (Bond) H.; m. Elizabeth Rowe, June 18, 1949; children: Gretchen P., Catharine B., Thomas William III. BS, U. Pa., 1948; MBA, NYU, 1950; JD, Columbia U., 1953. Bar: N.Y. 1953, D.C. 1954, U.S. Supreme Ct. 1958, Fla. 1989; CPA, N.Y. Sr. tax acct. Hurdman & Cranstoun, 1949-50; asst. U.S. atty. So. Dist. N.Y., 1953-54; assoc. Cahill, Gordon, Reindel & Ohl, 1954-58; sr. ptnr. Spear & Hill, 1958-75; ptnr. Sidley & Austin, 1981-86; pres. Belco Petroleum Co., N.Y.C., 1962-63; legal adviser Sultanate of Oman, 1972-76; adj. prof. law U. Miami, 1986-97. Contbr. articles to profl. jours. Vice chmn., pres., trustee Internat. Coll., Beirut, Lebanon, 1978-91. 1st lt. AUS, 1943-46. Decorated Bronze Star, Purple Heart, Medal of Oman (Sultanate of Oman), Order of Homayun (Iran). Mem. ABA, Assn. of Bar of City of N.Y., IBA, Racquet and Tennis Club (N.Y.C.), Mayacoo Golf Club, Taconic Golf Club, Phi Delta Phi, Kappa Sigma. Home: 2627 Muirfield Ct West Palm Beach FL 33414-7019

HILL, VIRGIL LUSK, JR., academic administrator, naval officer; b. Shelby, N.C., Apr. 2, 1938; s. Virgil Lusk and Ellen (Dilling) H.; m. Mary Kimberly Jordan, Jan. 11, 1964; children: James S., Katherine E. BS in Naval Sci., U.S. Naval Acad., 1961. Commd. ensign USN, 1961, advanced through grades to rear adm. (upper half), 1989; served on USS Thomas Jefferson, Groton, Conn., 1966-70; material officer COMSUBRON 18, Charleston, S.C., 1970-73; exec. officer USS L. Mendel Rivers, Charleston, 1973-75; comdg. officer USS Hammerhead, Norfolk, Va., 1976-80; dir. spl. projects Office Chief Naval Ops., Washington, 1980-83; comdr. Submarine Devel. Squadron 12, Groton, 1983-85; dir. attack submarine divsn. Office of Chief Naval Ops., Washington, 1985-87; comdr. Submarine Group 5, San Diego, 1987-88; supt. U.S. Naval Acad., Annapolis, Md., 1988-91; comdr. operational test and evaluation forces USN, Norfolk, 1991-93; pres. Valley Forge (Pa.) Military Acad. and Coll., 1993—. Bd. dirs. Commn. of Ind. Colls. and Univs. of Pa.; bd. dirs. Greater Main Line br. ARC, Southeastern Pa. chpt. Decorated Distinguished Svc. medal with gold star, Legion of Merit with 3 gold stars, Meritorious Service medal with 3 gold stars, Navy Commendation medal with 1 gold star; recipient Admiral David Glasgow Farragut award Naval Order of U.S. 1996, Robert Morris award Boy Scouts Am., 1996, Order of Magna Charta, 1996. Mem. Assn. Mil. Colls. and Schs. of the U.S. (former pres.), United Svcs. Orgn. of Phila. (bd. dirs.), Assn. Ind. Colls. and Univs. Pa. (bd. dirs.), Nat. Assn. Ind. Colls. and Univs. (pub. rels. commn.), Pa. Assn. Colls. and Univs., Pa. Assn. Ind. Schs., Nat. Assn. Ind. Schs., U.S. Naval Inst., Naval Order of the U.S., Mil. Order of Fgn. Wars, U.S. Navy League, Naval Submarine League, World Affairs Coun. of Phila., Sunday Breakfast Club of Phila., Penn Club of Phila., Union League of Phila. (bd. dirs.), St. David's Golf Club (Wayne, Pa.), others. Office: Valley Forge Mil Acad and Coll 1001 Eagle Rd Wayne PA 19087-3613

HILL, WALLACE HARRY, sports television consultant; b. Chgo., Oct. 14, 1935; s. Wallace George and Evelyn Teresa (O'Connor) H.; m. Mary Helen Du Beau, Oct. 21, 1956 (div. Jan. 1970); children: Scott, Amy, Molly, Betsi; m. Judith Ellen Swigost, May 16, 1982;. BA in Comm., Am. U., 1960. TV prodn. mgr. NBC Sports, N.Y.C., 1973-92; pvt. practice sports TV cons. N.Y.C., 1992—; mem. broadcast adv. bd. NBA, N.Y.C., 1992-98. Prodr. (film) Skills That Last A Lifetime, 1972 (Silver award), In Search of Spring, 1973 (Silver award), Internat. Film & TV Festival N.Y. With U.S. Army, 1954-56. Mem. Internat. TV Assn., Nat. Assn. Broadcasters (assoc.). Avocation: golfer. Home and Office: 155 E 34th St Apt 12C New York NY 10016-4751

HILLABY, JOSEPH GORDON, research scientist; b. Leeds, Yorks, Eng., Mar. 21, 1933; s. Albert Ewart and Mabel (Colyer) H. Rsch. fellow, U. Bristol. Rsch. scientist U. Leeds, 1950-53, 54-56, Mil. Intelligence, 1957-61; prin. lectr. history Hereford Coll. Higher Edn., 1961-77, U. Bristol, 1977-93; pres. Herefordshire County Archaeol. Soc., 1969, 80; vice chmn. Worcestershire Archaeol. Soc., 1995-97, chmn., 1997-2000; coun. mem. Jewish Hist. Soc. Eng., 1997—. Chmn. Coun. Protection of Rural Eng., 1992-98. Home: The Roughs, Hollybush, Ledbury Hertfordshire HR8 1EU, England

HILLERT, RICHARD WALTER, composer, educator, author; b. Granton, Wis., Mar. 14, 1923; s. Richard Henry and Amelia Matilde (Trimberger) H.; m. Gloria Rose Bonnin, Aug. 20, 1960; children: Kathryn, Virginia, Jonathan. BS in Edn., Concordia U., 1951; MusM, Northwestern U., Evanston, Ill., 1955, MusD, 1968; DHL (hon.), Concordia U., Nebr., 2000. Tchr., dir. music Bethlehem Luth. Ch., St. Louis, 1951-53, Trinity Luth. Ch., Wausau, Wis., 1953-59; prof. music Concordia U., River Forest, Ill., 1959-91, distn. prof. music, 1987, prof. emeritus, 1991—. Music editor: Inter Lutheran Commission on Worship, 1966-78, Lutheran Church-Missouri Synod, 1968-69, Chrismas Annual, 1985-89; assoc. editor Ch. Music, 1966-81; contbr. articles to profl. jours.; composer: Sonata for Violin and Piano, 1953, Sonata for Flute and Piano, 1954, Symphony in Three Movements, 1955, Prelude and Toccata for Organ, 1956, Alternations Number One for 7 Instruments, 1966, Divertimento for 5 Instruments, 1967, Angus Dei for 3 Choirs and Percussion, 1974, Partita for Organ: Picardy, 1978, Divertimento Number Two for 11 Players, 1983, Evening Prayer for Cantor, Congregation, and Organ, 1984, The Pillars for Wind Symphony, 1989, Fantasia on The Nunc Dimittis for Chamber Orch., 1990, Sine Nomini for Symphonic Band, 1995, Suite for Strings, 1996, Sonata for Flute and Harpsichord, 1997, Seven Psalms of Grace for Baritone Solo, Choirs and Orch., 1998. Recipient 1st prize Internat. Soc. Contemporary Music, 1961-62. Mem. Assn. Luth. Ch. Musicians (life), Pi Kappa Lambda, Sigma Alpha Iota. Avocations: traveling, American popular music before 1950, political and music biography. Home: 1620 Clay Ct Melrose Park IL 60160-2419

HILLERY, MARY JANE LARATO, columnist, producer, television host, reserve army officer; b. Boston, Sept. 15, 1931; d. Donato and Porzia (Avellis) Larato; m. Thomas H. Hillery, Feb. 25, 1961; 1 son, Thomas H. Assoc. Sci. (scholar), Northeastern U., 1950; BS, U. Mass. Harvard Extension, 1962; grad., Command and Gen. Staff Coll., 1982. Sales agt., linguist Pan Am. Airways, Boston, 1955-61; interpreter Internat. Conf. Fire Chiefs, Boston, 1966; tchr. Spanish YWCA, Natick, Mass., 1966-67; cmty. rels. cons., adv. bd. dirs., lectr. for migrant edn. project div., Mass. Dept. Cmty. Affairs, Boston, 1967-69; editor-in-chief Sudbury (Mass.) Citizen, 1967-76; assoc. editor The Beacon, 1976-79, contbg. editor, 1979-83; area editl. adviser Beacon Pub. Co., Acton, Mass., 1970-80, editor, 1976-80; columnist Town Crier (now Sudbury TAB), 1987—; contbg. editor Towne Talk, 1975-79, Citizens' Forum, 1975-81; editor Spl. Forces Ann. History, 1989-90; dir. pub. affairs Mass. Dept. Environ Quality Engring., 1981-83; prodr., host TV interview show For the Record, 1985—; pub. affairs officer Fed. Emergency Mgmt. Agy., 1995—; women vets. spkr. State House Mass. ofcl. Vets. Day observances, ceremonies, 1999. Editor Hansconian, 1983-85. Mem. Bus. Adv. Com., 1972-77, Sudbury Sch. Com., 1976-77; mem. Meml. Day Celebration Com., 1972—, master of ceremonies, 1973—; chmn. Sudbury WWII Commemorativ e Cmty., 1992-96; chmn. Sudbury Korean War 50th Anniversary Commemorative Com., 2000—; mem. Sudbury Town Report, 1967-72, 85-88, chmn., 1969-72; chmn. Sudbury Vets. Adv. Com., 1986-92; panelist Internat. Women's Year Symposium, 1975, Women in Politics, 1987, Women in Mil., 1987; mem. congl. 5th dist. Mass. nomination bd. West

Point, apptd. mil. aide-de-camp to Mass. Gov. Wm. Weld, 1992—; Veterans' agent Town of Sudbury, 1992—. Served with USN, 1950-54; lt. col. USAR; Persian Gulf, 1991-92; liaison officer U.S. Mil. Acad. West Point, 1976-89, 93—; pub. affairs officer 94th USAR Command, 1982-83, Office of Sec. of Def., The Pentagon, Washington, 1989-93. Decorated Meritorious Svc. medal, 1985, Joint Svc. Achievement medal, 1991, Nat. Def. medal-Bronze Stars, 1991, Outstanding Svc. award Sec. Def. Pub. Affairs, 1992, Joint Meritorious unit award, 1992, Def. Superior Svc. medal, 1993; named Editor of Yr., Beacon Pub. Co., 1970; recipient medal of appreciation Internat. Order DeMolay, 1969, certificates of appreciation U.S. Def. Civil Preparedness Agy., 1975, Mass. Bicentennial Commn., 1976, Appreciation award U.S. Mil. Acad., 1976-86, citations Mass. State Senate, 1979, 82, Newswriting award Media Contest Air Force Sys. Command, 1984, Outstanding Svc. award Sec. Def. Pub. Affairs, 1991, Cmty. Citizen award Citizen of Yr., Sudbury Grange, 1996, Cmty. Svc. award DAR, 2000, George Washington Honor medal Bay State chpt. Freedoms Found. at Valley Forge, 1998. Mem. LWV (dir. 1964-68), Nat. Editl. Assn., Nat. Newspaper Assn., Nat. Press Club, Rotary Internat. (mem. Sudbury chpt. scholarship chmn. 1993—, bd. dirs. 1994-95, 96-97, 97—, pub. rels. chmn. 1995-97, assoc. editor The Bulletin, 1996-97, Found. Chmn. 1997-99, pres.-elect 2000—), New Eng. Press Assn., Internat. Platform Assn. (Silver Bowl award for poetry 1997), Bus. and Profl. Women's Club (Sudbury 1st v.p. 1973, pres. 1973-76, parliamentarian 1978-88, 90-92, legis. chair 1990-92, state bylaws com. 1977-78, 79-81, 86-88, state legis. chmn. 1979-81, 86-88, state polit. action com. chmn. 1988-89, Woman of Yr. 1979, Woman of Achievement 1982), Nat. League Am. Pen Women (exec. bd. Boston 1974-76, 78-88, pres. Boston chpt. 1976-78, 94-98, 2000—, state exec. bd. 1994-1998, publicity chmn. 1979-80, chmn. bylaws com. 1979-80, 86-88, parliamentarian 1978-80, 82-88, auditor 1980-82, 84-88, 1st v.p. 1988-92, nat. editor Achievements, The Pen Woman 1992-94, nat. protocol chairperson 1998, nat. scholarship chmn. 1998—, nat. 4th v.p. 2000—), Res. Officers Assn. (life, dept. sec. 1978-79, dept. army v.p. 1992-95, pres. Boston chpt. 1986-88, dept. pres.-elect 1995-96, dept. pres. 1996-97, army v.p. 1995-96, army coun. rep. 1989-92, budget com., 1990-91, dept. publicity chmn. 1988-92, editor Advisor 1991-95, Outstanding Svc. award 1978-79, co-chair Nat. Conv. 1995-98), Spl. Forces Assn. (Green Berets, asst. to chmn. nat. conv. 1999-2000), Korean War Vets. Mass. (life). Omega Sigma. Home: 66 Willow Rd Sudbury MA 01776-2663

HILLERY, PATRICK JOHN, former president of Ireland; b. Miltown-Malbay, Ireland, May 2, 1923; s. Michael Joseph and Ellen (McMahon) H.; m. Mary Beatrice Finnegan, Oct. 27, 1955; children: John, Vivienne (dec.). Ed., Rockwell Coll., Cashel, Ireland, Univ. Coll., Dublin, Ireland; BSc, Univ. Coll., Dublin, Ireland, 1943, MB, BCh, BAO, 1947; DPH with honors, 1952; LLD (hon.), Nat. U. Ireland, 1962, U. Dublin, 1977, U. Melbourne, Australia, 1985, Limerick U., Ireland, 1990; PhD (hon.), Pontifical U. Maynooth, 1988. Mem. Health Coun., Ireland, 1955-57; med. officer Miltown-Malbay, Ireland, 1957-59; coroner, West Clare, Ireland; minister for edn. Govt. of Ireland, 1959-65, minister for industry and commerce, 1965-66, minister for labour, 1966-69, minister fgn. affairs, 1969-72; v.p. Commn. European Communities, Brussels, 1973-76; pres. Ireland, 1976-90. Hon. freeman City of Dublin. Fellow Royal Coll. Surgeons Ireland (hon.), All-India Inst. Med. Scis. (hon.), Royal Coll. Gen. Practitioners (hon.), Royal Coll. Physicians Ireland (hon.), Pharm. Soc. Ireland, Irish Mgmt. Inst. (life); mem. Royal Irish Acad., Irish Med. Assn. (hon. life). Office: Greenfield Rd, Sutton Dublin 13, Ireland

HILLERY, ROBERT CHARLES, naval engineer, management consultant; b. Waltham, Mass., May 3, 1953; s. Robert Parker Hillery; m. Diane Christine Kelly, Aug. 5, 1989; children: Kathleen, Kristen, Matthew. BA in Marine Transp., Mass. Maritime Acad., Buzzards Bay, 1975; MA in Internat. Rels., Salve Regina Coll., Newport, R.I., 1988; MA in Strategic Studies, Naval War Coll., Newport, 1991. Commd. ensign U.S. Navy, 1977, advanced through grades to comdr., 1990; exec. officer USS Charles F. Adams, Mayport, Fla., 1988-90; head enlisted engring. assignments U.S. Navy Bur. of Pers., Washington, 1990-92, head sea spl. programs, 1992-95; tech. advisor Navy Pers. R & D Ctr., San Diego, 1990-95; mem. membership bd. Surface Navy Assn., Arlington, Va., 1990-95; comdg. officer Fleet Surveillance Support Command, 1995-97; ret. USN, 1998; prof. computer techs. N.H. Cmty. Tech. Coll., 1998—; mgmt. info. sys. cons. Pers. Sys. Ctr. Naval Analysis, 1991; prin. rschr. Navy Enlisted Pers. Assignment model, 1990-95. Contbr. articles to profl. jours. Recipient George Washington Honor medal Freedoms Found. at Valley Forge, 1979; MIT fellow, 1991. Mem. U.S. Naval Inst. Home: 5 Whittaker Dr Stratham NH 03885-2278

HILLERY, THOMAS HUNGIVILLE, journalist, financial consultant; b. Boston, Dec. 15, 1962; s. Thomas Hungiville and Mary Jane (Larato) H.; m. Patricia Hillery. BA, Clark U., 1985; Magistri in Artibus Liberalibus, Harvard U., 1997. Accredited assessor # 666, Mass. Promotions dept. WCRB-FM, Waltham, Mass., 1990-92; journalist Dorchester News, Boston, 1992—. Author: "Make Advertising Work! Use Demographics, Psychographics and Purchasing Data." Bd. assessors Town of Sudbury, 1987-96. Thomas H. Hillery fellowship. Mem. Internat. Assn. Assessing Officers, Mass. Assn. Assessing Officers, U.S. Libr. Congress, Jonas Clark Fellows, Clark U. Alumni Coun., Clark Legacy Soc., Harvard Club Boston, Harvard Investment Assn., Nat. Press Club, Nat. Trust for Hist. Preservation, Internat. Platform Assn., New Eng. Hist. Geneaol. Soc., Sons Union Vets. Civil War, KC, Masons (past master Charles A. Welch Lodge, past high priest Houghton Royal Arch, Grand Royal Arch chpt. exemplification degree team 1992-93, dist. dep. grand treas. 1992-93), Scottish Rite, Order Eastern Star, Shriners, Mil. Order Loyal Legion U.S., Sons of Am. Legion Post 191 (chaplain), Ancient and Honorable Artillery Co. (Hillery pedigree registered Coll. of Arms London, armorial bearings granted), Freedom's Found. at Valley Forge (Bay State chpt.). Home: 66 Willow Rd Sudbury MA 01776-2663 Office: 299 Savin Hill Ave Ste 1 Boston MA 02125-1055

HILLIARD, DAVID CRAIG, lawyer, educator; b. Framingham, Mass., May 22, 1937; s. Walter David and Dorothy (Shortiss) H.; m. Celia Schmid, Feb. 16, 1974. BS, Tufts U., 1959; JD, U. Chgo., 1962. Bar: Ill. 1962, U.S. Supreme Ct. 1966. Mng. ptnr. Pattishall, McAuliffe, Newbury, Hilliard & Geraldson, Chgo., 1984—; adj. prof. law Northwestern U., 1971—, chmn. Symposium Intellectual Property Law and the Corp. Client, 1987—; lectr. in advanced trademark law U. Chgo. Law Sch., 1999—. Author: Unfair Competition and Unfair Trade Practices, 1985, Trademarks, 1987, Trademarks and Unfair Competition, 1994, 4th edit., 2000, Trademarks and Unfair Competition Deskbook, 2000; editor-in-chief Chgo. Bar Record, 1978-81. Trustee Art Inst. Chgo., 1980—, vice chmn., 1999—, mem. exec. com., 1995—, chmn. sustaining fellows, 1981-85, chmn. adv. com. dept. architecture, 1981—, pres. aux. bd., 1977-79, chmn. exhbns. com., 1993—, chmn. bd. govs. of the sch., 1997—; trustee Newberry Libr., 1983—, exec. com., 1987—; pres. Lawyers Trust Fund Ill., 1985-88; mem. vis. com. DePaul U. Law Sch., U. Chgo. Sch. of Law, chmn., 1987-88, Northwestern U. Assocs., 1985—; mem. profl. adv. bd. Atty. Gen. Ill., 1982-84; mem. Ill. Commn. on Rights of Women, 1983-85; bd. dirs. Ill. Inst. Continuing Legal Edn., 1980-82; pres. Planned Parenthood Assn. Chgo., 1975-77. Lt. JAGC, USN, 1962-66. Recipient Maurice Weigle award, 1974, Chgo. Coun. Lawyers award for jud. reform, 1983. Fellow Am. Coll. Trial Lawyers (chmn. courageous adv. com. 1995-97); mem. ABA (chmn. trademark divsn. 1986-87, mem. coun. 1991-95, intellectual property law sect.), Ill. Bar Assn., Chgo. Bar Assn. (pres. 1982-83, founding chmn. young lawyers sect. 1971-72), Internat. Trademark Assn. (bd. dirs. 1989-91, ADR panel of neutrals 1994—), Arts Club, Chgo. Club, Econ. Club, Grolier Club, Lawyers Club, Legal Club (pres. 1989-90), Univ. Club, Casino, Wayfarers Club (pres. 1994-95). Home: 1320 N State Pkwy Chicago IL 60610-2118 Office: Pattishall McAuliffe Newbury Hilliard & Geraldson 311 S Wacker Dr Ste 5000 Chicago IL 60606-6631

HILLINGER, CHARLES, journalist, writer; b. Evanston, Ill., Apr. 1, 1926; s. William Agidious H. and Caroline Bruning; m. Arlene Otis, June 22, 1948; children: Brad, Tori. BS in Polit. Sci., UCLA, 1951; degree (hon.), Marymount Coll., Palos Verder, 1997. Circulation mgr., columnist Park Ridge (Ill.) Advocate, 1938-41; copy boy, libr., feature writer Chgo. Tribune, 1941-43; reporter, feature writer, syndicated columnist L.A. Times, 1946-92, ret., 1992. Author: California Islands, 1957, Bel-Air Country Club, A Living Legend, 1993, Charles Hillinger's America, 1996, Charles Hillinger's Channel Islands, 1998, Hillinger's California, 1997, (audiobook) Charles Hillinger's America, 1999, California Characters, 2000. Mem. adv. bd. Santa Cruz Is. Found., Santa Barbara, Calif., 1992—; treas. 8-Ball Welfare Found. Greater L.A. Press Club, 1992—. With USN, 1943-46. Mem. Greater L.A. Press Club (sec. 1978-88, v.p. 1988-90, pres. 1990-92), Dutch Treat Club W. Avocations: tennis, golf, hearts. Home: 3131 Dianora Dr Rncho Pls Vrd CA 90275-6200

HILLION, HERVE PIERRE, supply chain consultant; b. Paris, Feb. 17, 1962; s. Pierre Theodore and Jeanine Henriette (Garde) H.; m. Martine Anne Giblin, Nov. 12, 1988; children: Helene, Roland, Marc. Diploma, Ecole Polytechnique, Paris, 1983, Ecole Nat. Ponts et Chaussees, 1985; MS, MIT, 1986; PhD, U. Paris VI, 1988. Rschr. INRIA (Institut Natl. De Recherche En Informatique Et Automatique), Paris, 1986-89; mgr. Soc. Etudes Rsch. & Tech., Paris, 1989-92; mng. ptnr. P.E.A. (Productive Edge Associates), 1992—. Author: Production Management, 1988. E-mail: Herve.Hillion@pea.fr. Home: 15 Rue Gay Lussac, 75005 Paris France

HILLION, PIERRE THÉODORE MARIE, mathematical physicist; b. Saint-Brieuc, France, Jan. 31, 1926; s. Pierre Auguste Alexandre and Olive Jane (Marion) H.; m. Jane Garde, July 9, 1955 (dec.); children: Catherine, Pierre, Joëlle, Hervé. Licencie es Scis., Engr. Ecole, 1950; Docteur es Sciences, 1957. Engr. Le Matèriel Electrique Schneider-Westinghouse, 1950-55; math. physicist Sect. Technique de L'Armèe, 1955-64; head math. phys. dept. Laboratoire Ctrl. de L'Armement, 1964-83; sci. cons. Ctr. D'Analyse de Dèfense, 1983-91; maitre de confs. Ecole Nationale Supérieure des Techniques Avancées, 1976-88; mem. Electromagnetic Acad. MIT. Contbr. articles on high energy physics, math. physics and numerical analysis to profl. jours. Mem. du bur. Assn. de Parents d'Éléves, 1965-76. With French Army, 1950. Recipient Mèrite pour la Recherche et l'Invention, 1965, Palmes Acadèmiques, 1970, Ordre Nat. pour le Mèrite, 1978, Legion d'Honneur, 1988. Mem. Societé Mathématique de France, Societé Française de Radioprotection, Syndicat de la Presse Scientifique, Internat. Assn. Math. Physics. Roman Catholic. Home: 86 bis Rt de Croissy, 78110 Le Vésinet Yvelines, France

HILLIS, RICHARD RALPH, geology and geophysics educator; b. Glasgow, Scotland, Nov. 18, 1964; arrived in Australia, 1992; s. Ralph Agnew and Elizabeth Margaret (Mitchell) H.; m. Belinda Mary Ingleton, Apr. 3, 1994; children: James Ingleton, Lachlan Ralph. BSc with honors, U. London, 1985; PhD, Edinburgh (Scotland) U., 1989. Lectr. to sr. lectr. geophysics Adelaide (Australia) U., 1992-99; prof. petroleum reservoir properties Adelaide U., Nat. Ctr. Petroleum Geology & Geophysics, 1999—; cons. Shell U.K., London, 1992, Oil Co. Australia, Brisbane, 1993, Santos, Adelaide, 1994—, Magellan Petroleum, Brisbane, 1994, Phillips Oil Co. Australia, Perth, 1994, 99, Petrocorp NZ, 1995, Chevron U.K., London, 1995, Arco U.K., London, 1995, Enterprise Oil, Perth, 1995, Fletcher Challenge Petroleum, Brunei, 1996, Conoco U.K., Aberdeen, Scotland, 1997. Contbr. numerous articles to profl. jours. Fellow Geol. Soc. London; mem. Am. Assn. Petroleum Geologists, Am. Geophys. Union, Australian Soc. Exploration Geophysicists (South Australian com. 1994—, South Australian pres. 2000), Petroleum Exploration Soc. Australia, Geol. Soc. Australia, European Assn. Geoscientists & Engrs., Soc. Exploration Geophysicists, Adelaide Football Club, South Australian Cricket Assn. Avocations: sports, travel, gardening, house renovation. Office: U Adelaide, NCPEG, Adelaide SA 5005, Australia

HILLIS, WILLIAM DANIEL, biology educator; b. Paris, Ark., June 12, 1933; s. Charles Raymond Hillis and Carra Elizabeth (Daniel) Coffee; m. Argye Idell Briggs, Dec. 23, 1952; children: William Daniel Jr., David Mark, Argye Elizabeth Trupe. BS, Baylor U., 1953; MD, Johns Hopkins U., 1957. Lic. in medicine and surgery, Md., Tex. Asst. prof. pathobiology Johns Hopkins U. and Sch. Hygiene and Pub. Health, Balt., 1965-68, assoc. prof., 1968-72; asst. prof. Johns Hopkins U. Sch. Medicine, Balt., 1972-76, assoc. prof., 1976-82; prof., chmn. dept. biology Baylor U., Waco, Tex., 1982-85, Cornelia Marshall Smith prof. biology, 1985-98; disting. prof. biology Baylor U., Waco, 1995—; exec. v.p. Baylor U., Waco, Tex., 1985-89, v.p. student affairs, 1989-98; cons. Nat. Cancer Inst., Bethesda, Md., 1965-68, Nat. Heart and Lung Inst., Bethesda, 1977-82; dir. Health Professions Rsch. Tng. Program, Balt., 1979-82, Out-Patient Clin. Rsch. Ctr., Balt., 1975-82. Contbr. articles to profl. jours. Pres. Bapt. Home Md., Balt., 1972-81; Md. rep. exec. com. So. Bapt. Conv., NAshville, 1977-82; bd. dirs. Food for Hungry, Glendale, Calif., 1972-82, Caritas, Waco, Tex., chair, 1989-95. Col. USAF, 1960-65, USAFR, 1965-85. Recipient Louis Livingston Seaman award Assn. Mil. Surgeons U.S., 1978, Disting. Alumnus award Baylor U., 1998; named Outstanding Prof. Baylor U., 1985. Mem. Am. Assn. Immunologists, Soc. for Exptl. Biology and Medicine, Am. Soc. for Microbiology, N.Y. Acad. Sci., McLennan County Med. Soc., Waco C. of C. (bd. dirs. 1987), Johns Hopkins Soc. of Scholars, Mortar Bd., Phi Beta Kappa, Alpha Omega Alpha, Omicron Delta Kappa. Democrat. Clubs: Brazos (Waco); Johns Hopkins (Balt.). Avocations: vocal music, drama, gardening, carpentry, philately. Home: 3640 Alta Vista Dr Waco TX 76706-3741 Office: Baylor Univ PO Box 97388 Waco TX 76798-7388

HILLIS, WILLIAM EDWIN, forester; b. Geelong, Victoria, Australia, Feb. 9, 1921; s. William Herbert and Emily (Burville) H.; m. Marjorie Maureen Moore, Nov. 15, 1952; children: Rosemary, David, Margaret. Diploma in Applied Chemistry, Gordon Inst. Tech., Geelong, 1942; BSc, Melbourne (Australia) U., 1947, MSc, 1951, DSc, 1966. Control chemist Coal Gas Industry, Melbourne, 1939-42; chemist CSIR, Melbourne, 1942-47; wood scientist, chief rsch. scientist CSIRO, Melbourne, 1947-86; vis. fellow Australian Nat. U., Canberra, 1973-85; vis. lectr. Monash U., Melbourne, 1990—; coord. forest products divsn. Internat. Union Forestry Rsch. Orgns., 1976-83, exec. bd. mem., 1976-83. Editor: Wood Extratives, 1962; co-editor: (with A.G. Brown) Eucalypts for Wood Production, 1978, 84; author: Heartwood and Tree Exudates, 1987; contbr. articles to profl. jours., chpts. to books. Fellow Internat. Acad. Wood Sci. (pres. 1978-82), Inst. Wood Sci. (chmn. Australian br. 1973-77, mem. com. 1977—, Stanley A. Clarke meml. medal 1986), Australian Acad. Tech. Scis. and Engring.; mem. Internat. Assn. Wood Anatomists (hon.), Australian Inst. Foresters. Avocations: music, international affairs. Home: 12 Lindsay St, McKinnon VIC 3204, Australia

HILLMAN, ARYE LAIB, economics educator, consultant; b. Bad Wörishofen, Germany, Jan. 13, 1947; s. Joshua and Rushka (Borenstein) H.; m. Jeannette Mann, 1967; children: Tamara, Ilana, Nachman Eliyahu, Benjamin. BA with 1st class honors in Econs., U. Newcastle, Australia, 1967; M in Econs. with honors, Macquarie U., Sydney, Australia, 1970; PhD, U. Pa., 1973. Rsch. fellow U. Pa., Phila., 1970-73; lectr. econs. Tel Aviv U., 1974-79; sr. lectr. Bar-Ilan U., Ramat Gan, Israel, 1980-82, assoc. prof., 1982-84, prof., 1984—, William Gittes chair in internat. econs., 1990—; vis. fellow Australian Nat. U., Canberra, 1979; vis. prof. dept. econs. UCLA, 1985-87, Woodrow Wilson Sch. Princeton U., 1989; cons. World Bank, Washington, Econ. Commn., Brussels, GATT, Geneva, Office of Prime Min., Govt. Israel; vis. scholar Internat. Monetary Fund, 2000; vis. prof. U. Catania, 2000; Albert Winsemius prof. Nanyang Technol. U., Singapore, 2000. Author: The Political Economy of Protection, 1989; contbg. editor: Markets and Politicians, 1991, The Perspective From Israel, Europe 92, 1991, The Transition from Socialism in Eastern Europe: Domestic Restructuring and Foreign Trade, 1992, Financing Government in Transition: Bulgaria, The Political Economy of Tax Policies, Tax Bases, and Tax Evasion, 1995; editor European Jour. Polit. Econ., 1994—; contbr. articles to numerous profl. jours. Recipient Max Planck prize in Econs., 1994. Fellow Japanese Soc. Promotion Sci.; mem. European Econ. Assn., Israel Econ. Assn., Am. Econ. Assn., Royal Econ. Soc., Mont Pelerin Soc., European Pub. Choice Soc. (pres. 1996-97). Jewish. Home: Ha'Arava 5, 43575 Ra'anana Israel Office: Bar-Ilan U, 52900 Ramat Gan Israel

HILLMAN, HAROLD HYRAN, retired physiologist; b. London, U.K., Aug. 16, 1930; s. David and Annie H.; m. Elizabeth Holland, Oct. 23, 1973; children: Alexander, Rachel, Benedict, Sophia. MB/BChir, Middlesex Hosp., London, 1956, MRCS, 1956; BS in Physiology, U. Coll., London, 1958; PhD in Biochemistry, Inst. Psychiatry, London, 1963. Rsch. asst., lectr. Inst. Psychiatry, London, 1958-62; rsch. fellow, docent Inst. Neurobiology, Goteborg, Sweden, 1962-64; lectr. Inst. Neurology, London, 1964-65; sr. lectr. Battersea Coll., London, 1965-68; reader in physiology U. Surrey, Guildford, Eng., 1968-95, dir. unity lab., 1970-95; med. adviser Inst. Biol. Psychiatry, Bangor, Wales, 1990-93; sec. London Med. Postgrad., 1985-2000; vis. prof. Mahidol Univ., Thailand, 1995. Author: Certainty and Uncertainty in Biochemical Techniques, 1972, Living Cell, 1980, Cellular Structure Mammalian Brain, 1986, Atlas of Cellular Structure Human Nervous System, 1991, The Case for New Paradigms in Cell Biology and Neurobiology, 1991. Exec. mem. Brit. Amnesty, London, 1970-80; senator U. Surrey, Guildford, 1979-89; chmn. Surrey Assn. Univ. Tchrs., Guildford, 1978-89; chmn. Freedom to Care, 1997—; sec. Physicians for Human Rights, U.K., 1997—. Recipient medal Free U. Brussls, 1975. Fellow Royal Soc. Medicine; mem. Physiol. Soc., Brit. Med. Assn. (chmn. Guildford divsn. 1995-99). Avocations: writing short stories, amnesty work, reading. Home: 3 Merrow Dene, 76 Epsom Rd, Guildford GU12BX, England

HILLMAN, JOHN RICHARD, agricultural and biotechnological studies educator, researcher; b. Farnborough, Kent, U.K., July 21, 1944; s. Robert and Emily Irene (Barrett) H.; m. Sandra Kathleen Palmer, Sept. 23, 1967; children: Robert George, Edmund John. BSc, Univ. Coll. of Wales, Aberystwyth, 1965, PhD, 1968; ScD (hon.), U. Strathclyde, Glasgow, 1994; DSc (hon.), U. Abertay Dundee, 1996. Lectr. in plant physiology U. Nottingham, U.K., 1968-71; lectr. in botany U. Glasgow, 1971-77, sr. lectr., 1977-80, reader, 1980-82, prof. botany, 1982-86; dir. Scottish Crop Rsch. Inst., Dundee, 1986—; vis. prof. U. Dundee, U. Edinburgh, U. Glasgow, U. Strathclyde; cons. in field; founder, dep. chmn. Mylnefield Rsch. Svcs., Ltd.; chmn. U.K. Tech. Foresight Panel for Agr., Natural Resources and Environment, 1994, Agr., Horticulture and Forestry, 1995-97. Author/editor various books in plant physiology, biochemistry and biotech.; contbr. over 150 articles to profl. jours. Recipient U.K. Rsch. Coun. award, 1968—, Brit. Potato Industry award, 1999; named Bawden lectr., 1993, Courtauld lectr., 1995. Fellow Linnean Soc., Royal Soc. Edinburgh, Inst. of Biology, Brit. Inst. Mgmt., Royal Soc. for Encouragement of Arts, Manufactures and Commerce, BioIndustry Assn. (bd. dirs.), Inst. Horticulture. Avocations: landscaping, building renovations, horology. Office: Scottish Crop Rsch Inst, Mylnefield Invergowie, Dundee DD2 5DA, Scotland

HILLMAN, RITA, investor; b. N.Y.C., May 16, 1912; d. Rudolf and Bertha (Goodman) Kanarek; m. Alex L. Hillman, Aug. 23, 1932 (dec. 1968); children: Richard Alan (dec.), Alex L. Student NYU, 1929-32. Mem. Met. Mus. Art (mem. vis. com. 20th century art dept.), Am. Friends Israel Mus. (exec. com.), Bklyn. Acad. Music (mem. exec. com.), Internat. Ctr. Photography (hon. chmn.), Alex Hillman Family Found. (pres.). Home: 895 Park Ave New York NY 10021-0327 Office: 630 5th Ave New York NY 10111-0100

HILLOCKS, GEORGE, education educator, researcher, consultant; b. Cleve., June 15, 1934; s. George and Ina Ternan Hillocks; m. Jo Anne Bruce, 1957 (div. 1998); children: Marjorie Anne, George McInnes. BA, Coll. of Wooster, 1956; MA, Case Western Res. U., 1958, PhD, 1970. English tchr. Euclid (Ohio) Pub. Schs., 1956-58, 59-65; English instr. Bowling Green (Ohio) State U., 1965-70, asst. prof. English, 1970-71; asst. prof. Edn. U. Chgo., 1971-75, assoc. prof. Edn., 1975-85, prof. Edn. and English, 1985—; dir. MA program in tchg. English U. Chgo., 1971—; vis. Thomas R. Watson disting. prof. U. Louisville, 2000. Author: Research on Written Composition: New Directions for Teaching, 1986, Teaching Writing as Reflective Practice, 1995 (David H. Russel award 1997), Ways of Thinking, Ways of Teaching, 1999; co-author: The Dynamics of English Instruction, 1971. Fellowship Ctr. for Advanced Study in Behavioral Scis., 2000—. Fellow Nat. Conf. on Rsch. on Lang. and Literacy (pres. 2000—); mem. Nat. Coun. of Tchrs. of English (Assembly for Rsch. 1986), Am. Edn!. Rsch. Assn. Avocations: reading, writing, bagpipes. Home: 1524 E 59th St # 3B Chicago IL 60637-2009 Office: U Chgo 5835 S Kimbark Ave Chicago IL 60637-1635

HILLS, CARLA ANDERSON, lawyer, former federal official; b. Los Angeles, Jan. 3, 1934; d. Carl H. and Edith (Hume) Anderson; m. Roderick Maltman Hills, Sept. 27, 1958; children: Laura Hume, Roderick Maltman, Megan Elizabeth, Alison Macbeth. AB cum laude, Stanford U., 1955; student, St. Hilda's Coll., Oxford (Eng.) U., 1954; LLB, Yale U., 1958; hon. degrees, Pepperdine U., 1975, Washington U., 1977, Mills Coll., 1977, Lake Forest Coll., 1978, Williams Coll., 1981, Notre Dame U., 1993, Wabash Coll., 1997. Bar: Calif. 1959, DC 1974, U.S. Supreme Ct. 1965. Asst. U.S. atty. civil divsn. L.A., 1958-61; ptnr. Munger, Tolles, Hills & Rickershauser, L.A., 1962-74; asst. atty. gen. civil divsn. Justice Dept., Washington, 1974-75; sec. HUD, 1975-77; ptnr. Latham, Watkins & Hills, Washington, 1978-86, Weil, Gotshal & Manges, Washington, 1986-88; U.S. trade rep. Exec. Office of the Pres., 1989-93; chmn., CEO Hills & Co. Internat. Cons., 1993—; vice chair bd. dirs. Inter-Am. Dialogue, U.S. China Bus. Coun.; bd. dirs. Am. Internat. Group, Time-Warner, Lucent Techs., Inc., Bechtel Enterprises Holdings, Chevron Corp., TCW Group, Inc.; adj. prof. Sch. Law, UCLA, 1972; mem. Trilateral Commn., 1977-82, 93—, Am. Com. on East-West Accord, 1977-79, Internat. Found. for Cultural Cooperation and Devel., 1977-89, Fed. Acctg. Standards Adv. Council, 1978-80; mem. corrections task force L.A. County Sub-Regional; adv. bd. Calif. Council on Criminal Justice, 1969-71; standing com. discipline U.S. Dist. Ct. for Central Calif., 1970-73; mem. Adminstrv. Conf. U.S., 1972-74; exec. com. law and free soc. State Bar Calif., 1973; bd. councillors U. So. Calif. Law Center, 1972-74; trustee Pomona Coll., 1974-79; trustee Brookings Instn., 1985; mem. at large exec. com. Yale Law Sch., 1973-78; mem. com. on Law Sch. Yale U. Council; Gordon Grand fellow Yale U., 1978; mem. Sloan Commn. on Govt. and Higher Edn., 1977-79; advisory com. Princeton U., Woodrow Wilson Sch. of Pub. and Internat. Affairs, 1977-80; trustee Am. Productivity and Quality Ctr., 1988; council mem. Calif. Gov. Coun. Econ. Policy Adv., 1993-98, Coun. on Fgn. Rels., 1993—; vice-chair Nat. Com. on U.S.-China Rels., 1993—, bd. dirs., U.S.-China Bus. Coun., vice-chair, 1995—. Co-author: Federal Civil Practice, 1961; co-author, editor: Antitrust Adviser, 1971, 3d edit., 1985; contbg. editor: Legal Times, 1978-88; mem. editorial bd. Nat. Law Jour., 1978-88. Trustee U. So. Calif., 1977-79, Norton Simon Mus. Art, Pasadena, Calif., 1976-80; trustee Urban Inst., 1978-89, chmn., 1983-89; co-chmn. Alliance to Save Energy, 1977-89; vice chmn. adv. coun. on legal policy Am. Enterprise Inst., 1977-84; bd. visitors, exec. com. Stanford U. Law Sch., 1978-81; bd. dirs. Am. Coun. for Capital Formation, 1978-82; mem. exec. com. Inst. for Internat. Econs., 1993—; mem. adv. com. MIT-Harvard U. Joint Ctr. for Urban Studies, 1978-82. Fellow Am. Bar Found.; mem. Am.'s Soc. (bd. dirs.), L.A. Women Lawyers Assn. (pres. 1964), ABA (chair publs. com. antitrust sect. 1972-74, council 1974, 77-84, chair 1982-83), Fed. Bar Assn. (pres. L.A. chpt. 1963), L.A. County Bar Assn. (fed. rules and practice com. 1963-72, chair issues and survey 1963-72, chair sub-com. revision local rules for fed. cts. 1966-72, jud. qualifications com. 1971-72), Am. Law Inst., Am. China Soc. (bd. dirs. 1995—), Yale of So. Calif. Club (bd. dirs. 1972-74), Yale Club. Clubs: Yale of So. Calif. (dir. 1972-74); Yale (Washington). Office: Hills & Co 1200 19th St NW Ste 201 Washington DC 20036-2429

HILLS, ROBERT O., retired pharmaceutical company executive; b. Bklyn., Apr. 13, 1946; s. Harry Stith and Elaine H.; m. Charlene Rose Cummins, Dec. 31, 1998; children: Alexander Winston, Jonathan Harry. AB, Princeton U., 1967; JD, U. Pa., 1971. Atty. Kelly Drye & Warren, N.Y.C., 1971-74, Merck Rsch. Labs., Rahway, N.J., 1974-76; sr. atty., dir. licensing, exec. dir. strategic planning Merck Sharpe & Dohme, West Point, Pa., 1976-90; v.p. mktg. human health divsn. Merck & Co., Whitehouse Station, N.J., 1991-93; sr. v.p. Merck-Medco divsn. Merck & Co., Mahwah, N.J., 1994. Co-author: Price Controls and the Auto Industry, 1973. Bd. dirs. Planned Parenthood Assn. Bucks County, Solebury Hist. Soc.

HILLSTROM, THOMAS PETER, engineering executive; b. Lakewood, Ohio, Apr. 20, 1943; s. Harry Edward and Mary Pauline (Mauss) H.; m. Jean Elizabeth Greenfield; children: Edward, Mary. BS in Mech. Engring., Northwestern U., Evanston, 1966; MBA, Northwestern U., Chgo., 1977. Design engr. Internat. Harvester, Hinsdale, Ill., 1966-74, project engr., 1974-78, product safety engr., 1978-82; mgr. engring. Fire Apparatus Div., FMC, Tipton, Ind., 1982-85; mgr. contract engring. FMC Naval Systems Div., Mpls., 1985-87, program mgr., 1987-90, mgr. splty. engring., 1990-91; program mgr. United Def., L.P., Mpls., 1985—. Patentee in field. Mem. Soc. Automotive Engrs., Am. Soc. Agrl. Engrs., System Safety Soc., Boy Scouts Am. Order of the Arrow. Republican. Home: 4340 Hackley Point Ln Muskegon MI 49441-4818 Office: United Def LP 4800 E River Rd Minneapolis MN 55421-1402

HILSABECK, ROBIN C., neuropsychologist; b. Sept. 4, 1968. MA, La. State U., 1996, PhD, 1999. Case mgr. Lees-Haley Psychol. Corp., Encino, Calif., 1991-94; neuropsychology extern La. State U., Baton Rouge, 1994-98; neuropsychology intern U. Okla. Health Scis. Ctr., Oklahoma City, 1998—. Office: La State U 236 Audubon Hl Baton Rouge LA 70803-0001

HILSCHER, HELMUT, physics educator; b. Kauffung, Germany, Dec. 19, 1940; s. Martin and Selma (Finger) H.; m. Ursula Thomas, Aug. 28, 1968; children: Rainer, Peter. Diploma, U. Heidelberg, 1966, PhD in Physics, 1969. Scientific asst. U. Heidelberg, 1969-70; engr. for theoretical calculations MAN, Munich, 1970-71; scientific asst. U. Munich, 1971-75; postdoctoral rschr. CERN, Geneva, Switzerland, 1971-75; tchr. Germany, 1975-82; lectr. physics edn. U. Regensburg, Germany, 1982-92; univ. prof. physics edn. U. Augsburg, Germany, 1992—. Author: Elementarteilchen, 1980, Kernphysik, 1996, Elementare Teilchenphysik, 1996; co-author: Handbuch der Experimentellen Physik, 1996, (CD-ROM) Physikalische Freihandexperimente, 1998, 99. Mem. Deutsche Physikalische Gesellschaft, Am. Assn. of Physics Tchrs., Verein Mathematisch-Naturwissenschaftlicher Unterricht. Office: U Augsburg, Universitätsstrasse, D-86135 Augsburg Germany

HILT, MARY LOUISE, artist; b. Muskegon, Mich., May 17, 1947; d. Jack Lyle and Martha Campbell (Van Epps) H.; m. Randolph Allen Austill, March 3, 2000. Student, Layton Sch. Art (now Milw., Inst. Design and Art), 1966-68. art tchr. for spl. needs adults Kelliher Ctr., Arlington, Mass., 1994-96. One-woman show Harvard Law Sch., Cambridge, 1987, Armenian Genocide Collection, Mass. State House, Boston, 1995, Armenian Libr. and Mus. of America, Watertown, Mass., 1995-96, 99; two-person show Fruenthal Ctr. for Performing Arts, Muskegon, 1989; exhibited in group shows at Bravos Gallery, Georgetown, Mass., 1987, 90-92, 94, 96, Nat. Arts Club, N.Y.C., 1997, Fed. Res. Bank, Boston, 1998, Art and Cultural Ctr., Fallbrook, Calif., 2000, others. Mem. Copley Soc. Boston, Cambridge C. of C. Episcopalian. Office: Hilt Studio 33 Richdale Ave Cambridge MA 02140-2627

HILT, THOMAS HARRY, minister; b. Phila., May 19, 1947; s. Francis Joseph and Alice Elizabeth (Flanagan) H.; m. Carolyn Louise Poulsen, Aug. 23, 1969; 1 child, Tamara Leah. BA, Tusculum Coll., Greeneville, Tenn., 1969; grad., Missionary Tng. Sch., Long Beach, Calif., 1974; M Ministry, Internat. Sem., Plymouth, Fla., 1983, D Ministry, 1984; PhD, Carolina U. of Theology, 1992. Ordained min. of Gospel, Okinawa, Japan, 1979. Mem. staff Christians in Action, Long Beach, 1974-77; missionary Christians in Action, Okinawa, Japan, 1977-79; founder Christians in Action Evang. Ch., Guam, 1979-81; founder, dir. Micronesian Evang. Mission, Barrigada, Guam, 1981—; founder, adminstr. Evang. Christian Acad., Chalan Pago, Guam, 1982—; founder, dir. Family Counseling Ministries, 1990—; mem. Nat. Bible Week-Guam Com., 1988-92; advisor Guam chpt. Women's Aglow Fellowship Internat., 1987-90; chaplain Guam Fire Dept., 1992-2000; chmn. bd. Guam Critical Incident Stress Mgmt. team, 1997-2000. Mem. Guam Gov.'s Social Svcs. Adv. Bd., 1981-83; mem. standards of licensing com. child welfare task force Guam Dept. Pub. Health and Social Svcs., 1982-83; mem. Blue Ribbon Commn. on Edn., 1991-93. With U.S. Army, 1970-73. Recipient award Ancient Order of Chamorri, 1983, 1st place award Guam Press Club, 1985. Mem. Am. Acad. Experts in Traumatic Stress, Guam Ministerial Assn. (sec.-treas. 1980-81, pres. 1983-84, 86-88, v.p. 1991-92), Bible Soc. Micronesia (pres. bd. dirs. 1989-90, v.p. bd. 1991-92, 99-2000). Home: 211 Clara St Toto GU 96927 Office: PO Box 23998 Barrigada GU 96921-3998

HILTON, RICHARD PAUL, geology educator, paleontological consultant; b. Ross, Calif., Jan. 22, 1944; s. Francis Edward and Phyllis Ann Hilton; m. Judith Ann Couk, Mar. 22, 1970 (div. 1984); children: Brandon Kent, Jakob Evert; m. Kristin Anne Buhl, May 29, 1995. AS, Marin Jr. Coll., Kentfield, Calif., 1966; BA in Geology, Chico State Coll., 1972; MA in Phys. Sci., Calif. State U., Chico, 1975. Instr. geology Napa (Calif.) Coll., 1973, Lassen Coll., Susanville, Calif., 1975, Saddleback Coll., Mission Viejo, Calif., 1977-80; instr. geology, biology and astronomy Butte Coll., Durham, Pentz, Calif., 1974-75; instr. geology and astronomy Calif. State U., 1975; instr. geology and earth sci. Modesto (Calif.) Jr. Coll., 1975-77; prof. geology Sierra Coll., Rocklin, Calif., 1981—, chmn. Nat. History Mus., 1997—; paleontol. cons., Meadow Vista, Calif., 1997—; mem. adv. bd. in geosci. Calif. State U., 1997—. Author, editor field guies Nat. Assn. Geology Tchrs., 1994; contbr. articles to sci. jours., including Jour. Vertebrate Paleontology, Paleobios, Calif. Geology. Staff sgt. USAF, 1966-69. Grantee NSF, 1980, Sierra Coll., 1988, 90. Mem. Soc. Vertebrate Paleontology, Assn. for Women Geologists, Nev. Paleontol. Soc. (bd. dirs. 1998—), Volcanological Soc. Sacramento. Avocations: paleontology, photography, collecting art and antiques, travel. E-mail: rhilton@scmail.sierra.cc.ca.us. Office: Sierra Coll 5000 Rocklin Rd Rocklin CA 95677-3337

HILTON, ROBERT PARKER, SR., national security affairs consultant, retired naval officer; b. Atlanta, Mar. 17, 1927; s. William Linwood and Elizabeth Shumate (Parker) H.; m. Joan Maxine Mader, Sept. 3, 1955; children: Robert Parker, Wendy Hilton-Jones. B.A., U. Miss., 1948; postgrad., Naval War Coll., 1961, Nat. War Coll., 1968; M.A. in Russian Affairs, Georgetown U., 1964; postgrad., Sino-Soviet Inst. George Washington U., 1964-68. Commd. ensign U.S. Navy, 1948, advanced through grades to rear adm., 1972; svc. all operational fleets cruisers/destroyers Korea, Japan, Vietnam, Italy, Belgium; asst. chief staff logistics CINCSOUTH, Naples, Italy, 1972-74; dep. dir. force devel. and strategic plans Office Joint Chiefs Staff, 1974-76; dir. East Asia and Pacific region Office Sec. Def., Washington, 1976-77; dir. strategy plans and policy div. OPNAV (OP60), 1977-78; asst. dep. CNO, Plans and Policy, 1979; dep. asst. chief staff Plans and Policy SHAPE, 1979-81; vice dir. ops. Office Joint Chiefs Staff, 1981-83; retired USN, 1983; sole proprietor Hilton Assocs., Alexandria, Va., 1984-98; cons. nat. security affairs, also nat. security and def. matters Inst. Def. Analyses, Alexandria, Va., 1984-94, mem. rsch. staff, 1994—. Decorated Def. D.S.M., Navy D.S.M., Def. Superior Svc. medal, Legion of Merit, Bronze Star, Joint Service Commendation medal. Mem. Coun. Fgn. Rels., Councillor Atlantic Coun. (sr.), U.S. Naval Inst., Nat. Trust Historic Preservation, Pi Sigma Alpha, Pi Kappa Phi, Phi Delta Theta. Episcopalian. Clubs: Masons, Army Navy Country. Home: 3628 Orlando Pl Alexandria VA 22305-1147 Office: Inst Def Analyses 1801 N Beauregard St Alexandria VA 22311-1701

HILTON, STANLEY GOUMAS, lawyer, educator, writer; b. San Francisco, June 16, 1949; s. Loucas Stylianos and Effie (Glafkides) Goumas; m. Raquel Estrella Villalba, Feb. 25, 1996. BA with honors, U. Chgo., 1971; JD, Duke U., 1975; MBA, Harvard U., 1979. Bar: Calif. 1975, U.S. Dist. Ct. Calif. 1975, U.S. Ct. Appeals (9th cir.) 1983, U.S. Supreme Ct. 1985. Libr. asst. Duke U. Libr., Durham, N.C., 1972-75, Harvard U. Libr., Cambridge, Mass., 1977-79; minority counsel U.S. Senator Bob Dole, Washington, 1979-80; adminstrv. asst. Calif. State Senate, Sacramento, 1980-81; pvt. practice San Francisco, 1981—; adj. assoc. prof. Golden Gate U., San Francisco, 1991—. Author: Bob Dole: American Political Phoenix, 1988, Senator for Sale, 1995, Glass Houses, 1998 (best writer 1998). Pres. Com. to Stick With Candlestick Park, San Francisco, 1992-96, Value Added Tax Now, San Francisco, 1994—, Save the 4th Amendment, San Francisco, 1995—; pres., CEO Animalism, Inc.; CEO Fountain of Youth. Mem. Calif. State Bar, Abolish the Fed. Res. Bank Assn. (pres. 1999—), Hellenic Law Soc., Bechtel Toastmasters Club (pres.), Rhinoceros Toastmasters Club (CTM 1998). Democrat. Avocations: philately, photography, classical music, ancient Greek and Roman history. Office: 580 California St Ste 500 San Francisco CA 94104-1000

HILTON, THEODORE CRAIG, computer scientist, computer executive; b. Oakland, Calif., June 14, 1949; s. Theodore Caldwell and Maxine (Donnelly) H.; m. Peggy Estes, May 21, 1990; children: Christopher, Kelly, Clark, Lisa, Trey. BS in Internat. Rels., Occidental Coll., 1972; BS, Calif. Inst. Tech., 1972; MS in Computer Sci., N.Y. Inst. Tech., 1980. Ptnr., founder Cen. Data Corp., L.A., 1971—, CEO, 1988—; engr. RSK, L.A., 1972-73; prof. Lake (Fla.) Coll., 1981-85, dept. chmn., 1983-85; prin. rsch. invest. U.S. Dept. Def., L.A., 1985-88; chmn. Access LLC, 1996—; chmn., CEO E-City Corp., 1996—; chmn. WEB Holdings Corp., 1998; bd. dirs. TBS S.A., Versailles, France, Carolina Access LLC, S.E. Data Comms.; adv. bd. Accurate Rsch. Corp., 2000; U.S. presenter SOLE Internat. Conv., 1991, CALS presenter, 1995; chmn. Web Holdings Corp., 1996—; chmn., CEO E-City LLC, 1996—. Author: Web Databases & PHP3, 1999, Data-Base Development, 1999; creator: (computer systems) E-City, 1956 Broadcast Management System, 1972, ICSS, 1974, EBook, 1993, Quality Assurance System, 1994; patentee Autonomous Network Smart Labels, filterable ditigal advertising, Internet database mgmt. sys.; contbr. over 59 articles to profl. jours. Named Wall St. Bus. Man of Yr., 2000, S.C. Bus. Man of Yr., 1999. Mem. IEEE, IEEE Computer Soc., Am. Mgmt. Assn., Logistics Engrs. Soc., Data Processing Mgmt. Assn., N.Y. Acad. Scis., Rotary (Paul Harris fellow). Achievements include patents on image system and public network exchange systems. Office: Cen Data Corp 145 N Church St Ste 402 Spartanburg SC 29306-5163

HILTUNEN, JUKKA KALERVO, biochemist, educator; b. Suomussalmi, Finland, Apr. 10, 1949; s. Ville and Elsa (Anneli) H.; m. Pirkko Marketta Pietilainen, June 29, 1974; children: Matti Pellervo, Jussi Antero, Anni Katriina. Grad., Suomussalmen Lukio, Suomussalmi, 1969; Lic. Medicine, U. Oulu, Finland, 1974, MD, 1977, PhD, 1977. Diplomate Bd. Clin. Chemistry, Finland. Postdoctoral fellow Ind. U., 1979-80; rsch. assoc. forensic medicine U. Oulu, Finland, 1981-82; asst. physician Oulu U. Ctrl. Hosp., Finland, 1983-84, specialist physician, 1984-86; jr. rsch. fellow Acad. Finland, 1990-94; prof. Med. Biochemistry U. Kuopio, Finland, 1994-96; prof. Biochemistry U. Oulu, Finland, 1996—; project leader Biocenter Oulu U., 1989—. Contbr. articles to profl. jours. Recipient Poul Astrup prize Poul Astrup Found., Trondheim, Norway, 1990. Mem. Finnish Coll. Physicians (chmn. Oulu subdivsn. 1993-94), Am. Soc. Cell Biology, Soc. Biochemistry, Biophysics, Microbiology Fenniae. Avocations: orienteering, cross country skiing, letters. Fax: 358-553-1141. E-mail: kalervo.hiltunen@oulu.fi. Home: Kirkkokatu 73 A 9, Oulu FIN-90120, Finland Office: U Oulu Dept Biochemistry, Linnanmaa, Oulu FIN-90540, Finland

HIMANKA, ERKKI SAKARI, radiologist, oncologist; b. Helsinki, Finland, Jan. 2, 1910; s. Kyosti Albert and Selma (Narhinen) H.; m. Maija Liisa Aaltonen, Dec. 23, 1970. MD, Helsinki U., 1940. Chief dist. physician Finnish Lappland, 1944-46; asst. physician Tiurinniemi Tuburcul, Finland, 1946-48; asst. radiologist Falun Hosp., Sweden, 1948-50; asst. chief physician Radiol. Clinic Orebro Ctr. Hosp., Sweden, 1950-52; radiologist, oncologist Soder Hosp., Stockholm, 1952-53, Radiumhemmet, Karolinska Hosp., Stockholm, 1953-55; physician in chief Southeast Finland's X-Ray Clinic, Lappeenranta, 1955-62, Dist. Hosp., Porvoo, Finland, 1962-70; radiologist, chief oncologist Tampere Ctrl. Hosp., Finland, 1970-73; cons. x-ray diagnostics Sweden, Finland, Norway, 1973-90. Physician Finnish Mil., 1939-44. Evangelic Lutheran. Avocations: chamber music, playing violin, literature.

HIMBERT, MARC EMILE, metrologist, educator; b. Paris, Dec. 11, 1957; s. Jean Gustave and Andree (Soulier) H.; m. Sylvie Sade Albertus, Apr. 7, 1978 (div. Dec. 1987); children: Anne-Laure, Marie-Alice; m. Catherine Veronique Pons, May 6, 1994; children: Marion, Luce. M in Physics, U. Paris VI, 1977; PhD, Ecole Normale Superieure, Paris, 1980; Final Diploma, Sciences-Politiques, Paris, 1981; Doctorat d'Etat es Sciences, U. Paris VI, 1987. Jr. prof. Ecole Normale Superieure ULM, Paris, 1976-80; jr. scientist CNRS, 1980-83, sr. scientist, 1983-88; prof. Conservatoire Arts et Metiers, Paris, 1989-92, full prof., 1992—, dep. dir. lab. metrology, 1991-94; mem. exec. bd. B.N. Metrology France, 1993—, dir. lab. metrology, 1996—; dir. Lab. Laser Physics, Paris 13, 1994-98. Contbr. articles to profl. jours.; patentee in field. Recipient Laureate Concours Gen., Ministry of Edn., France, 1974, Chevalier, Palmes Academiques, 1994. Mem. French Soc. Physics, TEFA S.A. (chmn. 1994—), Ecole Normale Superieure Fellows Assn. (pres. 1978). Roman Catholic. Avocation: French country songs. Home: 47 Rue General Leclerc, F95500 Gonesse France Office: Conservatoire Arts Metiers, 292 Rue Saint Martin, F-75003 Paris France

HIMBURG, SUSAN PHILLIPS, dietitian, educator; b. Norfolk, Va., May 17, 1946; d. Claude Ralph Jr. and Sarah Ann (Gilbert) Phillips; m. James Donald Himburg, Feb. 9, 1968; 1 child, Karlene Susan. BS, Fla. State U., 1968; M in Med. Sci., Emory U., 1972; PhD, U. Miami, Fla., 1979. Dietetic intern Emory U., Atlanta, 1971; clin. dietitian Emory U. Hosp., Atlanta, 1972-73; from instr. to prof. Fla. Internat. U., Miami, 1973—, dir. coordinated program in dietetics, 1979-99, dir. health scis. recruitment and retention program, 1985—, chmn. dietetics and nutrition, 1992-97, self-study dir., 1997-2000; grant reviewer disadvantaged assistance program HHS, Rockville, Md., 1989—; site visitor So. Assn. Colls. and Schs., Atlanta, 1987—. Author: (tng. manual) ADA Self-Study, 1988, 91, 95; contbr. articles to profl. jours. Fellow Am. Dietetic Assn. (site visitor 1985—, chairperson commn. on accreditation 1992-93, medallion 1996); mem. Soc. Nutrition Edn., Fla. Dietetic Assn. (del. 1990-2000, Disting. Dietitian 1995), Miami Dietetic Assn. (mem. nominating com. 1989, Disting. Dietitian 1994), Phi Kappa Phi, Kappa Omicron Nu. Office: Fla Internat Univ Ch 201 Coll Health Scis Miami FL 33199-0001

HIMES, DIANE ADELE, buyer, fundraiser, actress, lobbyist; b. San Francisco, Aug. 11, 1942; d. L. John and Mary Louise (Young) H. BA, San Francisco State U., 1964. Rep. west coast home furnishings Allied Stores, nationwide; gift buyer Jordan Marsh, Miami; buyer The Broadway Stores; west coast sales mgr. Xmas divsn. Vincent-Lippe, L.A.; midwest sales mgr. Vincent-Lippe, Chgo.; bd. dirs. L.A. Womens' Shakespeare Group, 1992-93. Actress Nine 'O Clock Players, 1995, short film The Traveling Companion, 1998. Co-chair Californians Against Initiative No On #64, 1988—; founding co-chair Life AIDS Lobby, 1985-88; Beverly Hills rent control bd., 1984; co-chair Californians Against Proposition #64, 1986, co-chair mcpl. elections com., L.A. Named Woman of Yr. for L.A. ACLU, 1987, Christopher Street West, 1988, Woman of the Yr. of L.A. Avocations: acting, appearing in short films.

HIMMELSTRAND, J. ULF I., sociology educator, writer; b. Tirupattur, India, Aug. 26, 1924; arrived in Sweden, 1935; s. John Sebastian and Elsa (Nygren) H.; m. Karin Birgitta Hagberg, Dec. 3, 1949; children: Jonas, Annika, Nina. BA, U. Uppsala, Sweden, 1948, Fil.lic., 1955, DSc, 1960. Rockefeller postdoctoral fellow U. Calif., Berkeley, 1960-61, U. Chgo., 1960-61, Columbia U., 1960-61; docent in sociology U. Uppsala, 1960-69, prof. sociology, 1969-89, prof. emeritus, 1989—; vis. prof. sociology U. Nairobi, Kenya, 1987-91; prof. sociology U. Ibadan, Nigeria, 1964-67; fellow Coll. for Advanced Behaviorial Sci., Palo Alto, Calif., 1968-69. Author: (in Swedish) The Civil War Nigeria-Biafra, 1969; editor, co-author: Africa Reports on the Nigerian Crisis, 1978, Beyond Welfare Capitalism, 1981, Interfaces in Economic and Social Analysis, 1992; co-editor, co-author: African Perspectives on Development, 1994, How to Become and Remain a Marxicizing Sociologist, 1998, Three Faces in Russian Sociology—Surviving Intellectually in a Totalitarian Society, 2000, The Twinkling of an Eye—Memoirs, 2000; newspaper columnist Dagens Nyheter, Stockholm, 1988-90, local newspapers, Härnösand and Uppsala, 1994—; writer, commentator newspaper Aftonbladet, 1992-95; contbr. articles to profl. jours. Chmn. Swedish Sociol. Assn., 1972-74; v.p. Internat. Sociol. Assn., 1974-78, pres., 1978-82; v.p. Internat. Social Sci. Coun., Paris, 1981-86. Grantee Bank of Sweden Tercentenary Found., Swedish Coun. for Humanities and Social Scis., 1955-86. Mem. Internat. Sociol. Assn. (life), Swedish Sociol. Assn., Soc. for Advancement of Socio-Econs. Mem. Swedish Social Dem. Party. Avocations: reading and writing poetry, classical music, long distance bicycling. Home: Hamnesplanaden 4B, S-753 19 Uppsala Sweden Office: Inst Sociology, PO Box 821, S-75108 Uppsala Sweden

HIMPSEL, FRANZ JOSEF, physicist, educator; b. Rosenheim, Germany, 1949; came to U.S., 1977; Diploma in physics, U. Munich, 1973, PhD in Physics, 1977. With IBM Rsch., Yorktown Heights, N.Y., 1977-95, 1st level mgr., 1982-85, 2nd level mgr., 1985-95; prof. physics U. Wis., Madison, 1995—, co-dir. sci. Synchrotron Radiation Ctr., 1997—. Contbr., co-contbr. articles to profl. jours. Fellow Am. Phys. Soc., Am. Vacuum Soc. (Peter Mark award 1985); mem. N.Y. Acad. Scis., German Phys. Soc. Fax: 608-265-2334. E-mail: fhimpsel@facstaff.wisc.edu. Office: Univ Wis Dept Physics 1150 University Ave Madison WI 53706-1302

HIN, LIN YEE, obstetrician; b. Ipoh, Malaysia, Apr. 26, 1969; parents Tian Chin Hin and Kah Heng Loh; m. Mei Ki Maggie Tsang, June 13, 1997. MBBCh, Queen's U. Belfast, 1994. Physician Royal Victoria Hosp., Belfast, Ireland, 1994-95, Prince of Wales Hosp., Hong Kong, 1996-99, Human Health Assoc., Hong Kong, 1999—. Fellow Royal Statis. Soc. Home: 7H Block 48, Shatin NT Hong Kong Office: Beverly Med Ctr, 1 Tong Ming St, Tweung Kwan O Kowloon, Hong Kong

HINCH, EDWARD JOHN, fluid dynamics engineer, researcher; b. Peterborough, England, Mar. 4, 1947; s. Joseph Edward and Mary Grace (Chandler) H.; m. Christine Bridges, June 28, 1969; children: Clare, Robert. BA, Cambridge U., England, 1968, PhD, 1973. Fellow Trinity Coll., Cambridge, 1971—; asst. lectr. Cambridge U., 1972-75, lectr., 1975-94, reader, 1994-98, prof., 1998—. Author: Perturbation Methods, 1991; contbr. articles to profl. jours. Decorated chevalier Nat. Order Merit (France). Fellow Royal Soc. Office: Trinity Coll, Cambridge CB2 1TQ, England

HINCHEY, JOHN WILLIAM, lawyer; b. Knoxville, Tenn., June 18, 1941; s. Roy William and Ruth (Owenby) H.; m. Sherie Paulette Archer, May 12, 1968; children: Paul William, Meredith Marie, John Oliver. AB, Emory U., 1964, LLB, 1965; LLM, Harvard U., 1966; MLitt., Oxford U., 1980. Bar: Ga. 1965, U.S. Dist. Ct. (no., mid. and so. dists.) Ga. 1968, U.S. Ct. Appeals (11th cir.) 1968, U.S. Supreme Ct. 1969. Asst. atty. gen. State of Ga., Atlanta, 1968-72; ptnr. McConaughey & Hinchey, Decatur, Ga., 1972-76, Phillips & Mozley, Atlanta, 1976-84, Phillips, Hinchey & Reid, Atlanta, 1984-92, King and Spalding, Atlanta, 1992—. Contbr. to profl. jours. and treatises. Mem. ABA (chair Forum on Constrn. Industry), Am. Coll. Construction Lawyers, Am. Arbitration Assn., Ga. Bar Assn., Atlanta Bar Assn. (chair constrn. law sect. 1999—), London Ct. of Internat. Arbitration, Druid Hills Golf Club. Republican. Methodist. Office: King & Spalding 191 Peachtree St SW Atlanta GA 30303-3637

HIND, HARRY WILLIAM, pharmaceutical company executive; b. Berkeley, Calif., June 2, 1915; s. Harry Wyndham and B.J. (O'Connor) H.; m. Diana Vernon Miesse, Dec. 12, 1940; children—Leslie Vernon Hind Daniels, Gregory William. BS, U. Calif., Berkeley, 1939; LLD, U. Calif.-Berkeley, 1968; DSc (hon.), U. Scis. Phila., 1982. Founder Barnes-Hind Pharms., Inc., Sunnyvale, Calif., 1939—; pres. Hind Health Care, Inc. Contbr. articles to profl. jours.; designer ph meter and developer of ophthamic solutions. Mem. chancellor's assocs. U. Calif.; trustee emeritus U. Calif.-San Francisco Found. Recipient Ebert award for pharm. research, 1948, Eye Research Found. award, 1958, Helmholtz Ophthalmology award for research, 1968, Carbert award for sight conservation, 1973, Alumnus of Yr. award U. Calif. Sch. Pharmacy, 1965, Disting. Service award U. Calif. Proctor Found., 1985, Commendation by Resolution State of Calif., 1987, Pharmaceutical Achievements commendation State of Calif. Assembly, Hon. Recognition award Contact Lens Mfrs. Assn., 1990. Fellow AAAS; mem. Am. Pharm. Assn. (Man of Yr. Pharmacist's Planning Svc. 1987), Am. Optometric Assn. (Man of Yr. award, 1987), Contact Lens Soc. Am. (Hall of Fame 1989), Am. Assn. Pharm. Scientists, Am. Chem. Soc., Calif. Pharm. Assn., N.Y. Acad. Scis., Los Altos Country Club, Sigma Xi, Rho Chi, Phi Delta Chi.

HINDERLICH, HORST KLAUS, health facility administrator; b. Langewahl, Germany, Dec. 17, 1942; s. Herbert Heinz and Else Frieda (Liepe) H.; m. Hilde Johanne Scharf, June 14, 1969; 1 child, Hauke. BBA, U. Bremen, 1971; D (hon.), Univ. San Tomas, Bolivia, 1996; Senator (hon.), U. Applied Scis., Bremen, Germany, 2000. Bd. mem. HAG Gen. Foods, Bremen, Germany, 1969-86; cons. John Stark & Ptnr., Frankfurt, Germany, 1986-87; mng. dir. R&B Food Handels GmbH, Bremen, 1988-89, Rotes-Kreuz-Krankenhaus, Bremen, 1990—; instr. Bus. Acad. Bremen, 1969—; bd. dirs. Bremen Hosp. Assn., Hosp. Dirs. Assn. Author: the red Cross Hospital Writes History, 1999; contbr. articles to profl. jours. Chmn. C. of C. Bremen, 1970—; hon. judge Labor Ctr., Bremen, 1972—. Col. German Air Force, 1963—. Recipient Life Saving medal City of Berlin, 1956, Hon. Cross in Gold Ministry Def., 1991, Gold Cross KNBLO, 1996, Bolivian Navy Merit medal, 1996, Bolivian Air Force Merit medal, 1997, Peruvian Nat. Police Grand Officer Cross, 1999. Mem. German Pers. Assn., German Mil. Res. Assn., Press Club Bremen, Golf Club Worpswede. Lutheran. Avocations: golf, reading, travel, walking, power walking. Home: Birkenheide 14, 27711 Osterholz Scharmbeck Germany Office: Red Cross Hosp, St Pauli Deich 24, 28199 Bremen Germany

HINDERLITER, RICHARD GLENN, electrical engineer; b. Tulsa, Apr. 9, 1936; s. Robert Verl and Aileen (Burton) H.; m. Leila Ratzlaff, June 8, 1958; children: Daniel Scott, Susan Paige, Alison Ann, Matthew Glenn. BSEE with honors, U. Kans., 1958; MSEE, NYU, 1960, PhD in Ops. Rsch., 1973. Staff mem. Bell Labs., Murray Hill, N.J., 1958-62; dept. head Bell Labs., Holmdel, N.J., 1962-72, Whippany, N.J., 1972-82; divsn. mgr. AT&T, N.Y.C., 1982-83, Bellcore, Morristown, N.J., 1984-91. Contbr. articles to Internat. Conf. on Communications, Computer Mag., Internat. Symposium on Subscriber Loops, Internat. Teletraffic Conf. Chmn. Zoning Bd. of Adjustment, Chatham Twp., N.J., 1992-99; scoutmaster Boy Scouts Am., Chatham Twp., Red Bank, N.J., Wichita, Kans., 1958-2000. Recipient Silver Beaver award Morris-Sussex coun. Boy Scouts Am., 1988, Eagle Scout Hall of Fame, 1998, Outstanding Vol. award with spl. recognition Vols. of Morris County; James E. West fellow Boy Scouts Am. Fellow AAAS; mem. IEEE (sr.), N.Y. Acad. Scis., Inst. for Ops. Rsch. and the Mgmt. Scis., Meth. Friday Niters Fellowship Soc. (pres.), Kiwanis (treas. Chatham, George F. Hixon fellow), Tau Beta Pi, Theta Tau (vice regent), Eta Kappa Nu (pres.). Methodist. Achievements include application of ops. rsch. techniques to large software systems.

HINDS, EDWARD DEE, insurance and investment professional, financial planner; b. Madera, Calif., May 13, 1949; s. Edward Dee Jr. and Donna (Parker) H.; m. Olga P. Hinds; children: Sarah, Stephen, Rebekah. Grad., Life Underwriting Tng. Coun. CLU; registered fin. cons. Sr. acct. agt. Allstate, Lemoore, Calif., 1983-90; gen. agt. various, Paso Robles, Calif, 1990—; gen. ptnr. Edward D. Hinds, Ins. and Fortress Fin. Strategies, Paso Robles, 1990—, Edward D. Hinds, Ins., 1995—; founder, gen. ptnr. Fortress Fin. Strategies, A Registered Investment Adviser, 1995-97; founder, gen. mgr. Hinds Fin. Group, LLC, 1998—; benefits cons. U-Haul Dealers, Cen. Calif., 1992—, KOA, Calif., 1997. Mem. Soc. Fin. Svc. Profls., Nat. Assn. Ins. and Fin. Advisors, Nat. Assn. Health Underwriters, Nat. Assn. of Alternative Benefit Cons.

HINDS, GLESTER SAMUEL, financier, program specialist, tax consultant; b. N.Y.C., July 4, 1951; s. Glester Samuel and Kathryne Elizabeth (Ellison) H. BBA, Bernard M. Baruch Coll., 1973; MBA in Fin., Columbia U., 1975. Cert. Stock broker, ins. broker, financier, notary pub. Staff acct. Peat Marwick Mitchell, N.Y.C., 1975-77; fin. analyst Citicorp, N.Y.C., 1977-79; sr. fin. analyst Am. Express, N.Y.C., 1979-80; owner, cons. Hinds Fin. Svcs., Long Island, N.Y., 1980-87; owner, founder, pres. Emerald Advt. Co., 1985—; program specialist Calif. FTB, Manhasset, N.Y., 1987—; founder, dir., pres. New Alliance Inc., 1999—; founder, dir. Worldstar Enterprises, Inc., 1999—; dir., ptnr. D.H. Holdings, Inc.; cons. Am. Entrepreneur's Assn., L.A., 1980-89, Mildred Burke Prodns., 1982-84, Worldwide Diamonds Assn., 1983-85, Acad. Fin. Aid Matching Svcs., 1983-87; licensee Creative Capital Pubs., Inc., 1983; with Mail Order Assocs., Inc., 1984—; holder minority interest Carlton Blues Football Team, Australia. Editor: Financial Newsletter the H-Club, 1978-82; actor: On Camera TV Acting, 1986; contbr. articles to profl. jours., to Passport For Travel newsletter. Funder U.S. Olympic Com. Team Ptnr. Program, 1999; mem. Presdl. Nat. Steering Com., Rep. Presdl. Task Force; founder Heritage Found., Washington, 1981, Ronald Reagan Rep. Ctr., 1989; founding mem. FDR Meml. Constrn. Project, 1996; mem. chmn.'s com. U.S. Senatorial Bus. Adv. Bd., 1981, 82; mem. Nassau-Suffolk Neighborhood Network; mem. Jim Valvano Found. for Cancer Rsch., Am. Heart Assn., The Children's Charity Fund, N.Y. Sportscene Children's Found. Recipient Edward M. Paster Meml. award, Sigma Alpha award, Beta Gamma Sigma award, Beta Alpha Psi award, Bernard M. Baruch Coll., 1973, Distinction award Am. Express, 1993, 97, Humanitarian Gold Record of Achievement ABI, 1994, Leader in sci. award, 1995, Presdl. Seal of Honor, 1996, Internat. Man of the Yr. award in Sci., 1993, Internat. Cultural Diploma of Honor Am. Biog. Inst., 1994, name permanently enshrined on Nat. Rep. Victory Monument, Ronald Reagan Rep. Ctr., Rep. medal of merit, 1995, task force cert. of merit; named Toronto Sports Club Athlete of Yr., 1987, Nat. Wrestling Hall of Fame, 1991. Mem. Am. Mgmt. Assn., USA Amateur Athletes, Interval Internat., Am. Mus. Natural History (assoc.), Am. Soc. Notaries (life), U.S. Olympic Soc. (life), N.Y. Pub. Interest Rsch. Group, 24K Club, USA Wrestling, Franklin Mint Collectors Soc., Pro-Wrestling Hall of Fame

(chmn. until 1994), U.S. Tennis Assn., Nat. Amateur Wrestling Hall of Fame (ptnr., fundraiser), Insiders Money Club, Internat. Platform Assn., Am. Cancer Soc., Am. Inst. Cancer Rsch., Troy Aikman Found., Carter Ctr., Environ. Def. Fund, Internat. Soc. Financiers (cert. 1985), Coram Civic Assn. (acting pres.), Oxford Club (life), Carlton Blues Football Team (Australia), World Trade Ctr. Club. Methodist. Home: PO Box 971 Coram NY 11727-0971 Office: California Franchise Tax Bd 1325 Franklin Ave Fl 5 Garden City NY 11530-1666

HINDS, SAMUEL ARCHIBALD ANTHONY, president of Guyana; b. Mahaicony, E. Coast Demerara, Dec. 27, 1943; married; 3 children. Attended, Queen's Coll., Georgetown, U. New Brunswick. Various pos. Bauxite Co., Linden, Guyana, 1967-92; mem. sci. and ind. com. Nat. Sci. Rsch. Coun., 1973-76; former chair Guyanese Action for Reform and Democracy; prime minister Guyana, 1992—. Office: care Office of Prime Minister, Kingston Wight's Lane, Georgetown Guyana*

HINDUJA, SRICHAND PARMANAND, association executive; b. Shikarpour, Sindh, India, Nov. 28, 1935; s. Hinduja Parmanand Deepchand and Jamuna Parmanand (Bajaj) H.; m. Madhu Srichand Menda, May 28, 1963; children: Shanu, Vinoo. Grad., Davar Coll. Commerce, Mumbai, India; LLD (hon.), U. Westminster, London, 1996; D in Econs. (hon.), Richmond Coll., London. Chmn. Hinduja Group Cos., London, 1962, Hinduja Found., London, 1962—; global coord. IndusInd, 1993—; pres. IndusInd Internat. Fedn., 1996—; chmn. trustees Hinduja Cambridge Trust, 1991; mem. adv. coun. Dharam Hinduja Indic Rsch. Ctr., Columbia U., N.Y.C., 1994; chmn. Amas Bank (Switzerland) Ltd.; mem. adv. bd. Centre for Internat. Bus. and Mgmt., Judge Inst. Mgmt. Studies, Cambridge U. Author: Indic Research and Contemporary Crisis, 1995, The Essence of Vedic Marriage for Success and Happiness, 1996; conceptualizer series of paintings Theorama, 1995. Mem. Duke of Edinburgh's Award Fellowship, London, Corp. of Mass. Gen. Hosp.; chmn. Hinduja Nat. Hosp., Hinduja Commerce Coll. Mem. Les Ambassadeurs, Ritz Club, Royal Overseas League. Avocations: volleyball, cricket, tennis, Indian classical and folk music, research and study of Indic philosophy. Office: Hinduja Group of Companies, 80 Haymarket, London SW1Y 4TE, England

HINE, SCOTT TERRENCE, business executive; b. Wellington, New Zealand, Apr. 27, 1972; s. Wayne Terrence and Marilyn Joy (Everette) H. B in Commerce, U. Canterbury, Christchurch, New Zealand, 1993; cert. in acctg., Inst. Chartered Accts., New Zealand, 1996; cert., Inst. Mgmt., Auckland, New Zealand, 1999. Mgmt. acct. Carter Holt Harvey, Auckland, 1994-95, bus. analyst, 1995-97, project mgr., 1997-98, project leader, 1998-99, strategy leader, 1999; bus. devel. mgr. Motherwell, Auckland, 1999—; bus. mgr. Mi-Servicer, Sydney, Australia, 2000; co. dir., founder Sapphire; fin. controller Project Crimson Trust, Auckland, 1994-96. Treas., sec. Project Crismon Trust, 1994; leader J&J New Leaders Award, Auckland, 1998 (New Leaders award, 1998). Recipient Youth Leadership award Auckland Rotary, 1994. Mem. New Zealand Inst. Mgmt., Inst. Chartered Accts. New Zealand. Avocation: ironman triathalon. Office: Mi-Services Group, 22a Lismore St, New Plymouth New Zealand

HINER, GLADYS WEBBER, psychologist; b. Mt. Park, Okla., Mar. 10, 1907; d. Santford and Erie Emma (Rose) Webber; m. Wayman Hiner, Aug. 11, 1927 (dec. Mar. 1967); children: Waynel Cook, Sandra Homer. BS, U. Okla., 1934, MS, 1955, PhD, 1962; HHD (hon.), Wagon Wheel Found., McCloud, Okla., 1973. Bd. cert. devel. psychologist. Tchr. Okla. City Pub. Schs., 1953-61; dir. Dale Rogers Tng. Ctr., Okla. City, 1962-63; prof. Okla. City U., 1963-72, Rose State Coll., Okla. City, 1972-86; cons. Wagon Wheel Sch. McLoud, Okla., 1962-82, pvt. practice, Okla. City, 1986—. Supr. Sunday Sch. Trinity Baptist Ch., Okla. City, 1940-72; bd. dirs. Okla. State Assn. for Mentally Retarded Children, 1963-67, Youth and Child Coun. Okla. U. Med. Sch., 1966-69, Bridge Builders, Okla. City; Dem. state del., 1986. Fellow Okla. Psychol. Assn., Am. Assn. on Mental Deficiency; mem. The Acad. Ret. Profls., Okla. Hist. Soc., DAR, Colonial Dames, Psi Chi, Phi Theta Kappa. Avocations: reading, swimming, bridge. Home: 800 S Canadian Trails Dr Norman OK 73072-7627

HINES, EDWARD FRANCIS, JR., lawyer; b. Norfolk, Va., Sept. 5, 1945; s. Edward Francis and Jeanne Miriam (Caulfield) H.; m. Elaine Geneva Carroll, Aug. 21, 1971; children: Jonathan Edward, Carolyn Adele. AB, Boston Coll., 1966; JD, Harvard U., 1969. Bar: Mass. 1969. Assoc. Choate Hall & Stewart, Boston, 1969-77, ptnr., 1977—; bd. dirs. Univ. Hosp., Boston, 1990-96, vice-chmn., 1994-96. With USAR, 1969-75. Recipient Boston Coll. High Sch. St. Ignatius award, 1998. Mem. Boston Bar Assn. (pres. 1988-89), Boston Bar Found. (pres. 1995-97), Mass. CLE (pres. 1985-87), Carroll Ctr. for Blind (bd. dirs. 1983-89, 90-96, chmn. 1994-96), Mass. Taxpayers Found. (bd. dirs. 1987—), Am. Heart Assn. (bd. dirs. Dallas 1984-86, 91-2000, chmn. 1998-99, award of merit 1983), Assoc. Industries Mass. (bd. dirs. 1990—, chmn. 1996-98), Am. Coll. Greece (Athens, bd. dirs., vice chmn. 1988-97), Fed. Tax Inst. New Eng. (treas. 1994—), Social Law Libr. (trustee 1993-98), Supreme Jud. Ct. Hist. Soc. (trustee 1989-96), Accion Internat. (bd. dirs. 1999—), North Andover Country Club, Boston Coll. Club, Bay Club. Office: Choate Hall & Stewart Exchange Pl 53 State St Boston MA 02109-2804

HINES, JOHN DAVID, research scientist; b. Chester, England, Aug. 8, 1970; s. John Thomas and Virginia Rose (Wilde) H. BS in Chemistry, U. Liverpool, England, 1993; DPhil in Phys. Chemistry, U. Oxford, England, 1996. Rsch. scientist Unilever Rsch., England, 1996—; mem. tech. adv. com. U. Minn., Mpls., 1998—. Contbr. articles to profl. jours. Mem. Am. Chem. Soc., Royal Soc. Chemistry. Office: Unilever Rsch Ltd, Olivier Van Noortlan 120, 3BO AC Vlaardingen The Netherlands

HINESCU, MIHAIL EUGEN, physician, researcher; b. Sighisoara, Mures, Romania, Dec. 24, 1959; s. Mihai and Cornelia (Covesan) H.; m. Lavinia Georgeta Stefan, Sept. 12, 1992; children: Alina, Ioana. MD, U. Medicine, Bucharest, Romania, 1985, PhD, 1998. Asst. prof. U. Medicine, Bucharest, 1992-99, sr. lectr., 1999—; rschr. Army Ctr. for Med. Rsch., Bucharest, 1991—. Contbr. articles to profl. jours. Recipient Victor Babes prize Romanian Acad., 1985. Home: 2 Ionita Cegan Str BL P11, SC 2 AP 41, Bucharest Romania Office: Carol Davila U Med & Pharm, PO Box 12-128, Bucharest Romania

HING, PETER, materials scientist; b. Rose Hill, Mauritius, Sept. 6, 1941; s. Roger Ng Yau Hing and Anne Marie Li Yun Lan; m. Angeline Pit Lan Ng Yau Ching, Dec. 26, 1965 (wid.). BS in Physics, Baroda, India, 1964; Diploma, Materials Sci. and Engring., Oxford, U.K., 1967; PhD, Metallurgy of Materials, Oxford, U.K., 1971; Rsch. Fellow, Warwick U., 1973. Fellow Inst. of Materials, Inst. Ceramics; chartered engr., physicist. Materials scientist Thorn Lighting, Ltd., Leicester, U.K., 1973-76, sr. materials scientist, 1976-79, prin. materials scientist, 1980-87; prin. materials rsch. engr. Thorn Emi Cen. Rsch. Lab., London, 1987-91; assoc. prof. Materials Engring/Nanyang Tech. U., Singapore, 1991—; dir. Advanced Materials Rsch. Ctr., Singapore, 1999—; pres. Inst. of Materials of East Asia, Singapore, 1993-96; v.p. Inst. of Materials, Singapore, 1996-99. Editor conf. proceedings in field; inventor in field. Fellow Inst. Materials U.K., Inst. of Ceramics, Inst. of Materials (East Asia) (pres. 1993-96). Roman Catholic. Avocations: golf, reading, travel, dancing, wine tasting. Home: 39A Nahyang View, 639538 Singapore Singapore Office: Nanyang Technol Univ, Nanyang Ave, 639798 Singapore Singapore

HINGHOFER-SZALKAY, HELMUT G., physiologist, educator; b. Graz, Styria, Austria, Jan. 22, 1948; s. Günther and Hermine (Kundigraber) Hinghofer-S.; m. Irma Leber, Apr. 6, 1979; children: Dagmar, Stephan. MD, U. Graz, 1974, Dozent, 1981. Rsch. asst. Physiol. Inst., Graz, 1970-74, asst. prof., 1974-82, assoc. prof., 1982-84; rsch. scientist NASA/Ames Rsch. Ctr., Moffett Field, Calif., 1984-85; assoc. prof. physiology U. Graz, 1985-95, prof., 1995—, chmn., 2000—; sci. cons. European Space Agy., Paris, 1980—; mem. Austrian-Soviet mission Austromir, 1989-91, RLF, 1993-97; sec. IUPS Sat. Cardiovasc. Symposium, Budapest and Graz, 1980; local organizer 3rd European Symposium on Life Sci. Space, Graz, 1987, Space for Life Symposium, Vienna, 1992; head Inst. for Adaptive and SpacefligPhysiology, ASM Graz, 1994—. Mem. Am. Physiol. Soc., Aerospace Med. Assn., Internat. Acad. Astronautics, German Physiol. Soc., Austrian Physiol. Soc. (sec. 1979-83, 97—), Sci. Soc. Styrian Physicians (sec. Graz chpt. 1976—), Austrian Soc. for Space Medicine (Vienna, v.p. 1991-96, sec. gen. 1997—), Internat. Soc. Gravitational Physiology (trustee 1998—). Avocations: sauna, music, traveling. Office: U Graz Dept Physiology, Harrachgasse 21, A-8010 Graz Austria

HINGIS, MARTINA, tennis player; b. Kocise, Slovenia, Sept. 30, 1980. Profl. tennis player, 1994—; winner Australian Open Tokyo, 1999, Doubles winner Australian Open, 1999. Winner Australian Open, Wimbledon and U.S. Open, 1997, all grand slam double titles, Australian Open, Roland Garros, Wimbledon, U.S. Open, 1998. Office: c/o WTA Tour 133 1st St NE Saint Petersburg FL 33701-3352*

HINGSTON, ANDREW BRIAN, ecologist; b. Launceston, Tasmania, Australia, Aug. 3, 1963; s. Brian William and Marie Vivian (Mann) H.; m. Pakinee Limwathanagura, Mar. 24, 1999. BS, U. Tasmania, Hobart, Australia, 1995, degree in forest ecology, 1997. Farm labourer Chudleigh, Australia, 1980-88; share farmer Eric Richardson, Chudleigh, Australia, 1984-85; nursery hand Elizabeth Town (Australia) Nursery, 1989; timber yard hand Timberworld Pty. Ltd., Meander, Australia, 1989-92; tech. officer CRC for Temperate Hardwood Forestry, Hobart, 1996, U. Tasmania, 1997-99; cons. Queen Victoria Mus., Launceston, Australia, 1995-96, Forestry Tasmania, Hobart, 1998. Contbr. articles to profl. jours. Vol. Quamby Landcare Group, Jackey's Marsh, Australia, 1991-92, 98, Cmty. Aid Abroad, Hobart, 1993-99, Nat. Parks & Wildlife Svc., Coles Bay, Australia, 1994-98, Lambert Park Bushcare Group, Hobart, 1998-99. Recipient Ralston Trust zoology prize U. Tasmania, 1993; Tasmania honours scholar U. Tasmania, 1996-97, APA scholar, 1998—. Mem. Ecol. Soc. Australia, Australasian Pollination Ecologists Soc., Deloraine Field Naturalist's (v.p. 1992-93). Avocations: planting trees, bushwalking, weight training, gardening, bike riding. Office: U Tasmania Dept Geog & Env, GPO Box 252 78, Hobart, Tasmania 7001, Australia

HINITZ, BLYTHE SIMONE FARB, early childhood and elementary school educator; b. N.Y.C., Apr. 10, 1944; d. Max S. and Gertrude A. (Nachitowitz) Farb; m. Herman J. Hinitz, June 27, 1965. BA, Bklyn. Coll., 1965, MS, 1970; EdD, Temple U., 1977. Master tchr., tchr. N.Y. Bd. Edn., 1965-71; assoc. instr. child devel. C.C. of Phila., 1977-78; prof. early childhood edn. Coll. N.J., Trenton, 1978—; bd. dirs. Mercer County Child Devel. Program, Inc., 1980—; H-Edn. (on-line hist. of edn. list), (mem. adv. bd. dirs.) 1999—. Author: Teaching Social Studies to the Young Child, 1992; co-author: History of Early Childhood Education, 2000; co-editor: bibliography of Selected Resources for the International Year of the Child, 1979; editor book rev. Jour. of Early Childhood Tchr. Edn., 1988-97; contbr. chpts. to books including Early Childhood Education for Peace in Nuba, Resources for Early Childhood, Creating An Inclusive College Curriculum: A Teaching Sourcebook From the New Jersey Project; contbr. to Eisenmann Historical Dictionary of Women's Education in the U.S., 1998, Peace Education: Contexts and Values, 1999; contbr. articles to profl. jours. Mem. human svc. degree com. Thomas Edison State Coll., N.J., 1992-98; mem. Delaware Valley Child Care Coun. Mem. Am. Ednl. Rsch. Assn. (chmn. program SIG Peace Edn. 1996—), Ea. Ednl. Rsch. Assn., Nat. Assn. Edn. Young Children (tchr. edn. panel 1991-94), Nat. Assn. Early Childhood Tchr. Educators (nat. treas. 1989-93, bd. dirs.), Assn. Childhood Edn. Internat., World Orgn. Early Childhood Edn., History Edn. Soc. (internat. standing conf. on history of edn. working group on early childhood edn.), Nat. Coun. for History Edn. (focus group on nat. history stds. 1994), N.J. Coun. for History Edn. (state adv. bd. 1995—), N.J. Assn. Early Childhood Tchr. Educators (pres. 1994-97, bd. dirs. 1997—), N.J. Prof. Devel. Ctr. for Early Care and Edn. (Adv. bd.), Kappa Delta Pi (bd. dirs. Trenton alumni chpt., pres. 1997-99, counselor 1999—), Phi Delta Kappa (greater Trenton area chpt., editor newsletter 1994-98), Phi Kappa Phi. Avocations: music, dance, gardening. Home: PO Box 348 Feasterville PA 19053-0348 Office: Coll NJ Elem/Early Childhood Edn Dept Ewing NJ 08628-0718

HINKLE, DOUGLAS PADDOCK, retired languages educator; b. Stamford, Conn., June 9, 1923; s. Frank Leslie and Kathryn B. Paddock Hinkle; m. Rose-Marie Hecker, Apr. 14, 1966; children: Anthony Barton, Monica Kathryn. BA, U. Va., 1952, MA, 1954. Lic. law enforcement officer, Ohio. Tchr. English Va. Pub. Schs., Nelson County, 1948-49; dir. binat. ctr. U.S. Info. Svc., La Paz, Bolivia, 1955-57, Caracas, Venezuela, 1958; asst. prof. Spanish and French Sweet Briar Coll., Amherst, Va., 1958-62, Southwestern U., Memphis, 1962-63; coll. editor modern langs. D.C. Heath & Co., Boston, 1963-65; assoc. prof. modern langs. Ea. Ky. U., Richmond, 1965-67; sr. lectr. modern langs. Ohio U., Athens, 1967-93, prof. emeritus modern langs., 1994—; forensic artist LETN-TV, Dallas, 1990-91; program evaluator NEH, Washington, 1975-78. Author: (books) Faces of Crime, 1989, Mug Shots, 1990, (book of poetry) Poetry Is You, 1977, (slideshow/video program) Remembering Faces, 1990; mem. editl. bd. NAMES, 1968-74. Chmn. drug abuse com. Kiwanis Club, Athens, Ohio, 1983-87; cert. aux. Athens Police Dept., 1982-87, forensic artist, 1981-87; bd. dirs. Cen. Va. Crime Clinic, Richmond, 1994-97. Cpl. U.S. Army, 1943-46. Recipient Caballero, Order of Condor award Republic of Bolivia, 1957. Mem. Athens Bar Assn. (Citizenship award 1983), Portrait Soc. Am., Ctrl. Va. Crime Clinic (bd. dirs. 1995-98), Va. Mus. Fine Arts, Fraternal Order of Police (hon. permanent mem.), Raven Soc., Phi Beta Kappa. Republican. Roman Catholic. Avocations: painting, writing, historical linguistics, marksmanship. E-mail: dphrmh@cs.com. Home: 9305 Cason Rd Glen Allen VA 23060-3513

HINKLE, MURIEL RUTH NELSON, naval warfare analysis company executive; b. Bayonne, N.J., Mar. 17, 1929; d. Andrew and Florence Martha Ida (Nuber) Nelson; m. David Randall Hinkle, June 5, 1954; children: Valerie Nelson, Janet Lee, Sally Ann. Student, Md. Coll. for Women, 1947-49; BA, U. Md., 1951. Mgr. Wildacres Thoroughbred Horse Farm, Waterford, Conn., 1960-70; illustrator naval warfare predictions/computer simulated naval engagements Analysis & Tech., Inc., North Stonington, Conn., 1970-73; pres. Sonalysts, Inc., Waterford, Conn., 1973-88, 94-98, CEO, 1973—; also founder, past dir. Command Engring. & Tech. Svcs. Co.; pres., CEO, chmn. Stonington Farms Inc. (now Mystic Valley Hunt Club), 1983; adv. bd. Conn. Nat. Bank, 1988-92; chmn., CEO Angiers Assocs., 1989-96, S.I. Devel. Corp., 1989—; cons. Def. Nuclear Agy. for Tactical Nuclear Effects in anti-submarine warfare, 1974-75; spl. edn. substitute tchr. Waterford Pub. Schs., 1968-74. Co-author: Scope of Acoustic Communications Systems in Naval Tactical Warfare, 1974, Non-Acoustic Anti Submarine Warfare, 1974, Nuclear Weapons Effects in Anti Submarine Warfare, 1974, Measures of Effectiveness, Naval Tactical Communications, 1975, Destroyer ASW Barrier, 1977. Bd. trustees Thames Sci. Ctr., 1979-82. Recipient commendation for svcs. to submarine force Comdr. Submarine Squadron Ten, 1973, SBA New Eng. Contractor of Yr. award, 1986, SBA Adminstr.'s award for excellence, 1985, 86, bus. assoc. of yr. award Naval Inst., 1999. Mem. Am. Horse Shows Assn., Nat. Audubon Soc., Submarine Devel. Group Two Wives Club (pres. 1968), Sigma Kappa (pres. Senesk chpt. 1987-89), Navy Wives Club. Republican. Baptist. Home: 9 Cove Rd Stonington CT 06378-2304 Office: Sonalysts Inc PO Box 280 215 Parkway N Waterford CT 06385-1209

HINKSON, GREGORY EVELYN, bank executive; b. Bridgetown, Barbados, Dec. 26, 1964; s. Evelyn F. and Karma G. (Butcher) H.; m. Neila K. Lav Harper, July 21, 1990; 1 child, Neysa K.L. BSc in Computer Sci. with honors, U. W.I., Barbados, 1986. Acct. Price Waterhouse, Barbados, 1987-90; fin. analyst London Life & Casualty Reins. Corp., Barbados, 1990-92; v.p. investments London Life Bank Corp., Barbados, 1992-95; mgr. CIBC Caribbean Ltd., St. Michael, Barbados, 1995-96; gen. mgr. CIBC West Indies Offshore Banking Corp., St. Michael, Barbados, 1996—. Mem. Kiwanis. Avocations: coin collecting, travel. Office: CIBC West Indies Holdings Ltd, CIBC West Indies Holdings, CIBC Centre Warrens, Saint Michael Barbados

HINLOOPEN, JEROEN, economist, educator, researcher; b. Grypskerk, Groningen, The Netherlands, Nov. 6, 1968; s. Bob and Nellie (Claasen) H. M Econometrics, Erasmus U. Rotterdam, The Netherlands, 1993; PhD in Econs., European U. Inst., Florence, Italy, 1997. Asst. rsch. prof. U. Copenhagen, 1997; asst. prof. indsl. econs. Delft (The Netherlands) U. Tech., 1997-98, 99—; rsch. economist Dutch Ctrl. Bank, Amsterdam, The Netherlands, 1998-99; sr. rsch. economist Ministry Econ. Affairs, The Hague, The Netherlands, 1999—; external cons. for Dujat (Dutch-Japanese Trade Assn.), Sassenheim, The Netherlands, 1995—; rsch. ptnr. Ace project European Commn., Brussels, 1996-99. Contbr. articles to profl. jours., including Internat. Jour. Indsl. Orgns., Jour. Econs., Jour. Indsl. Econs. Recipient young economist essay award European Assn. for Rsch. in Indsl. Econs., Copenhagen, 1998. Mem. European Econ. Assn., Royal Econ. Soc. Mem. Gereformeerd Ch. Avocations: playing the piano, playing tennis. Office: Ministry Econ Affairs, Econ Policy Dir, PO Box 201, 2500 EC The Hague The Netherlands

HINNER, PAUL GEORG, sales executive; b. Vienna, Austria, May 8, 1967. M, U. Econs. & Bus. Adminstrn., Vienna, 1995. Adminstr. possystems Shell Austria, Vienna, 1996; sales rep. cards Shell Austria, Innsbruck, Austria, 1997-98; sales rep. lubricants Shell Austria, Vienna, 1998-99, asst. sales team leader, 1999—. Mem. Lions Club Tyrol. Home: Schoenburgstrasse 25/18, A-1040 Vienna Austria

HINO, TARO, engineering educator; b. Ina, Nagano, Japan, May 31, 1927; s. Kazuma and Miyuki (Nozawa) H.; m. Mariko Nakanishi, Oct. 15, 1961; children: Yuhichi, Kohji, Kenzaburoh. B Engring., Tohoku U., Japan, 1953; M Engring., Tokyo Inst. Tech., 1957, PhD, 1960. Cert. elec. engr. Asst. prof. Tokyo Inst. Tech., 1960-62, assoc. prof., 1962-73, prof. engring., 1973-88, prof. emeritus, 1988—; prof. Kanagawa U., Japan, 1988-98, lectr., 1998—; vis. prof. Nanjin Inst. Tech., China, 1985. Author: Basic Theory of Electrical Measurements, 1983; patentee in field; inventor new elec. source. Mem. IEEE (life), Inst. Elec. Engring. Japan (life, head domestic com. 1985-96, paper award 1975. Home: 37-18 Shinoharanishicho, Kohokuku, Yokohama 222-0025, Japan Office: Kanagawa U, 3-27-1 Rokkakubashi, Kanagawaku, Yokohama 221-8686, Japan

HINOJOSA, FEDERICO GUSTAVO, JR., judge; b. Edinburg, Tex., Apr. 16, 1947; s. Federico Gustavo and Zulema (Trevino) H.; m. Yolanda Silva, 1970 (div. 1977); 1 child, Cynthia; m. Magdalena Garza, Oct. 30, 1992. BA, Pan Am. U., 1969; JD, U. Houston, 1977. Bar: Tex. 1977, U.S. Dist. Ct. (so. dist.) Tex. 1977, U.S. Ct. Appeals (5th cir.) 1980, U.S. Supreme Ct. 1980. Assoc. Clark, Lowes & Carrithers, Houston, 1977-79; ptnr. Clark & Hinojosa, Houston, 1979-81; child support atty. Tex. Dept. Human Resources, McAllen, 1981-83; asst. dist. atty. Hidalgo County, Edinburg, 1983-84; assoc. Atlas & Hall, McAllen, 1984-87; ptnr. Lewis, Pettitt & Hinojosa, McAllen, 1987-91; justice Tex. Ct. Appeals for 13th Dist., Corpus Christi, 1991—. Sgt. USAF, 1970-74. Mem. State Bar Tex., Mexican-Am. Bar Tex., Mexican-Am. Bar Assn. Coastal Bend (dir. 1993-94), Hidalgo County Bar Assn. (dir. 1986-90). Democrat. Office: 13th Ct Appeals 100 E Cano St Edinburg TX 78539-4548

HINOJOSA, RAUL, physician, ear pathology researcher, educator; b. Tampico, Tamulipas, Mexico, June 18, 1928; came to U.S., 1962, naturalized, 1968; s. Raul Hinojosa-Flores and Melida (Prieto) Hinojosa; m. Berta Ojeda, Sept. 25, 1953; children—Berta Elena, Raul Andres, Jorge Alberto, Maria de Lourdes. B.S. in Biology, Inst. Sci. and Tech., Tampico, 1946; M.D., Nat. Autonomous U. Mexico, Mexico City, 1954. Asst. prof. U. Chgo, 1962-68, assoc. prof., 1968-97, assoc. prof. emeritus, 1998—, dir. temporal bone program for ear rsch., 1962—, rsch. assoc., 1968-88; rsch. fellow biophysics Harvard U., Boston, 1963; rsch. assoc. in neuropathology, Harvard U., 1964, rsch. fellow in anatomy, 1965. Editor temporal bone histopathology update Am. Jour. of Otolaryngology, 1989-94. Recipient Rsch. Career Devel. award NIH, 1962-65, rsch. grantee, 1962—, hearing rsch. study sect. grantee, 1988-92. Mem. AAAS, Internat. Otopathology Soc., Microscopy Soc. Am., Midwest Soc. Electron Microscopists, Assn. Rsch. in Otolaryngology, Am. Otological Soc., N.Y. Acad. Scis. Home: 5316 S Hyde Park Blvd Chicago IL 60615-5706 Office: U Chgo 5841 S Maryland Ave Chicago IL 60637-1463

HINOSHITA, FUMIHIKO, nephrologist; b. Kyoto, Japan, Nov. 21, 1955; s. Junichi and Akiko (Nagata) H. MD, Tokyo Med. and Dental U., 1981, PhD, 1986. Med. staff Tokyo Med. and Dental U., 1986-87; expert clinician Toride (Japan) Kyodo Hosp., 1987-91; rsch. assoc. Harvard Med. Sch., Boston, 1991-92; nephrologist Toranomon Hosp., Tokyo, 1992-97; chief nephrologist Hiratsuka (Japan) Kyosai Hosp., 1997-98; assoc. prof. Internat. U. Health and Welfare, Japan, 1998—; asst. prof. Sci. U. Tokyo, 1996-97. Contbr. articles to profl. jours. Del. 32d Japan and Am. Student Conf., 1980. Winner 1st prize Seven Univs.' English Oratorical Contest, 1978; grantee Okinaka Meml. Inst. for Med. Rsch., 1995-96, Shimabara Sci. Promotion Found., 1997, grants-in-aid for sci. rsch. Ministry of Edn., Sci. and Culture Japan, 1993-97, 99—; IgA Nephropathy fellow, 1993. Mem. Internat. Soc. Nephrology, Japanese Soc. Internal Medicine, Am. Soc. Nephrology. Avocations: classical music, travel, English conversation. Home: 5-2-2-605 Fuda, Chofu Tokyo 182-0024, Japan Office: Internat U Health & Welfare Organized Ctr Clin Medicine, 2600-1 Kita-Kanemaru, Otawara Tochigi 324-0011, Japan

HINRICHS, TODD AARON, securities executive; b. Windom, Minn., July 8, 1969; s. Theodore Lynn and Shirley Ann (Hughes) H.; m. Sonja Anne Warinner, June 26, 1999. AB, U. Chgo., 1993. V.p. Kemper Securities, Chgo., 1992-97; v.p., sr. analyst ABN-AMRO Inc., Chgo., 1997—; Adv. bd. One team One Bank rep. ABN-AMRO, 1999; adv. asset divestiture Govt. of N.S., Halifax, 1999. Contbr. articles to profl. jours. Presbyterian. Avocations: travel, running, biking, gardening, playing piano. Office: ABN-AMRO Inc 208 S Lasalle St Lbby 2D Chicago IL 60604-1004

HINRICHSEN, NEIL ROY, information scientist; b. Durban, South Africa, Aug. 31, 1959; s. Stanley William and Mary Elizabeth (Melck) H. B of Comm. in Info. Systems with honors, U. Cape Town, South Africa, 1990. From mgr. to tech. dir. Realtime, Cape Town, 1980-96; mng. dir. Netscape SA, Cape Town, South Africa, 1995-96; founder Worldshift Seminars, Knysna, South Africa, 1997—; co-founder Fundamo, 1999—. With South African Army, 1983-85. Mem. Computer Soc. South Africa, Mensa. Avocations: water sports, marathon running, music, reading. Office: Worldshift, PO Box 1400, Knysna 6570, South Africa

HINRIKUS, HIIE, physicist, physics educator; b. Tallinn, Estonia, Nov. 2, 1934; d. Voldemar and Elfriede H.; m. Osvald Pehlak; 1 child, Hannes. MS in Physics, Moscow M.V. Lomonssov State U., 1960; PhD, All Union Rsch. Inst., Moscow, 1967; DS, Acad. Sci., Moscow, 1989. Engr. Radio Engring. Factory, Tallinn, Estonia, 1960-62; rschr. All Union Rsch. Inst., Moscow, 1962-66; sr. rschr. ARIPREM, Moscow, 1966-68; sr. lectr. Tallinn (Estonia) Tech. U., 1968-71, assoc. prof., 1971-89, prof., 1989—. Author: Parameters of Masers, 1968, Noise in Laser Systems, 1987; editor, co-author: Laser Rangemeters, 1995; contbr. articles to profl. jours. Recipient Silver medal USSR Ctrl. Exhbn., 1988; grantee Estonian Sci. Found., 1992—. Mem. IEEE (EMBS 1996—), Estonian Soc. Biomed. Engring. (pres. 1994—), IFMBE (working group for European Aet. 1998—), Estonian Union of Scientists (bd. dirs. 1988-98), EFOMP (sci. com. 1996—), ESEM. Home: Kaare 9A, 11618 Tallinn Estonia Office: Tallin Tech U, Ehitajate Rd 5, 19086 Tallinn Estonia

HINSHAW, ERNEST THEODORE, JR., private investor, former Olympics executive, former financial executive; b. San Rafael, Calif., Aug. 26, 1928; s. Ernest Theodore and Ina (Johnson) H.; m. Nell Marie Schildmeyer, June 24, 1952; children: Marc Christopher, Lisa Anne, Jennifer, Amy Lynn. AB, Stanford U., 1951, MBA, 1957. Staff asst. to pres. Capital Research and Mgmt. Co., Los Angeles, 1957-58; dir. planning Capital Research and Mgmt. Co., 1967-68; fin. analyst Capital Research Co., Los Angeles, N.Y.C., 1958-68; v.p. Capital Research Co., 1962-71, mgr. N.Y.C. office, 1962-66; dir., exec. v.p. Am. Funds Service Co., Los Angeles, 1968-69; pres. Am. Funds Service Co., 1969-72, chmn. bd., 1972-82; dir. pres. Capital Data Systems, Inc., Los Angeles, 1971-73; chmn. Capital Data Systems, Inc., 1973-79; v.p. Capital Group, Inc., Los Angeles, 1973-83; sr. v.p. Growth Fund Am., 1973-74, pres., 1974-76, chmn. bd., 1976-82, dir., 1974-96; sr. v.p. Income Fund Am., 1973-74, pres., dir., 1974-76, chmn. bd., 1976-82, dir., 1974-96; commr. yachting 1984 Olympic games Los Angeles Olympic Organizing Com., 1980-84; dir. Capital Research & Mgmt. Co., 1972-83; mem. guest faculty Northwestern U. Transp. Center, 1965-66; mem. ops. com. Investment Co. Inst., 1970-74. Bd. dirs. Newport Harbor Nautical Mus., 1989-92, Girl Scout Coun. Orange County, 1993—, chair fin. com., 1996-97, treas., 1998—; trustee Friends of Girl Scouts Trust; mem. investment com. Hoag Hosp. Found., 1992-97. Served to 1st lt. USMC, 1951-53. Mem. Soc. Airline Analysts (sec. 1965-66), Los Angeles Soc. Fin. Analysts,

N.Y. Soc. Security Analysts, Am. Statis. Assn., Town Hall Calif., Nat. Kite Class (pres. 1968-69), Lido 14 Internat. Class Assn. (pres. 1978-79), Assn. Orange Coast Yacht Clubs (commodore 1976), So. Calif. Yachting Assn. (commodore 1979), B.O.A.T., Inc. (dir. 1977-81), Pacific Coast Yachting Assn. (dir. 1979-80), U.S. Yacht Racing Union (dir. 1980-81), U.S. Sailing Ctr. Long Beach, Calif. (adv. coun. mem.). Democrat. Clubs: Wall Street (N.Y.C.); University (Los Angeles); Lido Isle Yacht (Newport Beach, Calif.) (commodore 1973); Stanford U. Sailing (trustee 1984-96); St. Francis Yacht (San Francisco); Ft. Worth Boat. Home: 729 Via Lido Soud Newport Beach CA 92663-5530

HINSHAW, ROBERT, psychotherapist, publishing executive. BA, Northwestern U., 1969; lizentiat, U. Zürich, Switzerland, 1979, PhD, 1983. Diploma C.G. Jung Inst., Zurich, 1981. Psychotherapist Sanatorium Bellevue, Kreuzlingen, Switzerland, 1973-75; pvt. practice Jungian analyst Zürich, 1973—; book pub. Daimon Verlag, Einsiedeln, Switzerland, 1978—; editor, translator and cons. in field. Editor, pub.: A Testament to the Wilderness, 1985, (collection of essays) The Rock Rabbit and the Rainbow: Laurens v.d. Post Among Friends, 1998. Mem. Internat. Assn. for Analytical Psychology (bd. dirs., co-v.p.), Schweizerische Gesellschaft für Analytische Psychologie (bd. dirs. 1988-91), C.G. Jung Inst. (curatorium mem. 1991—, v.p. 1997—). Avocations: reading, film, photography, outdoors, sports. E-mail: info@daimon.ch.

HINSON, ROBERT WILLIAM, advertising executive, consultant; b. Neptune, N.J., Nov. 30, 1944; s. Herbert William and Bernice (Stadelhofer) H. AB in Econs. and Sociology, Boston Coll., 1966. Media planner Benton & Bowles, Inc., N.Y.C., 1968-70; v.p., assoc. media dir. SSC&B: Lintas Worldwide, N.Y.C., 1970-74, sr. v.p., dir. media ops., 1976-80; v.p., assoc. media dir. Foote Cone & Belding, Inc., L.A., 1974-76; exec. v.p., chmn. mgmt. com., chmn. ops. com., dir. media svcs. Rosenfeld, Sirowitz & Lawson, Inc., N.Y.C., 1980-85, exec. v.p., dir. mktg. and media svcs., chief adminstrv. officer, 1986-87; pres., chief exec. officer Hinson and Assocs., Inc., N.Y.C., N.J., 1987-91; cons. in field, 1991—. Author: Media Leverage, 1985. Media dir. Tuesday Team, Reagan-Bush '84 campaign, 1984; sustaining mem. Rep. Nat. Com.; mem. Ronald Reagan Presdl. Libr. Found., Monmouth County (N.J.) Rep. Orgn.; bd. dirs. Monmouth (N.J.) Symphony Orch.; mem. nat. campaign com. Boston Coll. Mem. NATAS, Internat. Assn. TV, Arts and Scis., Internat. Radio and TV Soc., Media Dirs. Industry Coun., Am. Assn. Advt. Agys. (media policy com. 1980-87), Am. Rsch. Found. (media com. coun. 1983-86), Boston Coll. Alumni Assn., Wagner Soc. N.Y., Monmouth County Hist. Soc., Alliance Francaise of Monmouth County (N.J.), Alliance Francaise of Ft. Lauderdale, Nature Conservancy, Nat. Trust for Hist. Preservation, Vieux Carre Property Owners Assn., N.Y. Athletic Club, Deal (N.J.) Golf and Country Club, Allenhurst (N.J.) Beach Club, Coral Ridge (Fla.) Country Club. Roman Catholic. Home: PO Box 182 Allenhurst NJ 07711-0182 also: 133 N Pompano Beach Blvd Pompano Beach FL 33062-5720 also: 921 Chartres St New Orleans LA 70116-3227

HINTERAUER, LORENZ KURT, radiologist; b. Dornbirn, Austria, July 12, 1952; s. Kurt Johann and Silvia H.; children: Robert Alexander, Rudolf Maximilian. MD, U. Innsbruck, 1976; FA, U. Zurich, 1984. Radiologist-in-chief LKH Lienz, Austria, 1985-92, KH Bludenz, Austria, 1992—. Office: KH Bludenz/Rontgen, Spitalgasse 13, A-6700 Bludenz Austria

HINTERBERGER, FRIEDRICH, economist; b. Schwanenstadt, Austria, Dec. 16, 1959; s. Fritz and Erika (Henning) H.; m. Bärbel Nowitzki, Oct. 8, 1996; 1 child, Christian. M of Econ. and Social Sci., U. Linz, Austria, 1985; D of Polit. Sci., U. Giessen, Germany, 1990. Asst. U. Giessen, 1985-91; fellow German Sci. Found., Bonn, 1991-93; economist Wuppertal Inst., Germany, 1993—; pres. Sustainable Europe Rsch. Inst., Vienna, 1999—; officer-in-charge Wuppertal Inst., Germany, 1997-99. Author: (book) Ökologische Wirtschaftspolitik, 1996, Ecological Economic Policy; contbr. articles to profl. jours. Fellow Verein für Social Politik; mem. European Soc. Ecol. Econs. (v.p. 1998—). Avocation: family. Office: Seri, Schwarzspanier str 4/8, 1090 Vienna Austria

HINTERBERGER, WOLFGANG ALEXANDER, physician; b. Vienna, Austria, July 24, 1949; s. Alexander and Gertrude (Wolfgang) H.; m. Margareta Fischer; children: Alexander, Barbara, Christoph, Lorenz. MD, U. Vienna, Austria, 1972, dozent, 1981. MD U. Vienna, Austria, 1972; Fred Hutchinson Cancer Ctr., Seattle, 1978; sec. Austrian Acad. of Scis., 1980-86; prof. medicine U. Vienna, Austria, 1989; sec. European Soc. for Bone Marrow Transplantation, 1989-92; head 2d dept. medicine Donauspital, Vienna, Austria, 1992—; head Ludwig Boltzmann Inst. for Stem Cell Transplantation, Vienna, 1993; head, 2d dept. medicine Donauspital, Vienna, Austria, 1992. Contbr. over 270 articles to profl. jours. Avocations: classical music, biking. Office: Donauspital, Vienna Austria

HINTERHUBER, HANS HARTMANN, management educator, researcher; b. Bruneck, Italy, Aug. 20, 1938; s. Hans Hinterhuber and Elsa Beikircher; m. Barbara Maria Prugger; children: Andreas, Monika, Lukas, Katharina. Diploma in engring., Leoben Mining U., 1960, Dr Habilitation, 1969; Dr, U. Venice, Italy, 1963; Dr Habilitation, Ministry of Edn., Rome, 1967. Mgmt. asst. Agip SpA, Milan, Italy, 1963-68; supply mgr. Aral Italiana SpA, Milan, 1969-70; head dept. math. Tech. U., Graz, 1970-74, U. Innsbruck, Austria, 1974—; vis. prof. U. Bocconi, Milan, 1994; head faculty I.I.M.T., Milan, 1971-73; mem. sci. adv. bd. Progros AG, Basel, Switzerland, 1990—; v.p. Agip Austria AG, Vienna, 1983—; co-dir. internat. working seminars on prodn. econs., Innsbruck. Author, editor 30 books on strategic mgmt. and related subjects; assoc. editor thunderbird Internat. Bus. Rev.; contbr. over 300 articles to profl. jours. Mem. Alb Dei Dottori Commercialisti, Rotary, Innsbruck Goldenes Dachl, Tyrolean-Arabian Soc. (pres.). Office: U Innsbruck, Dept Mgmt, A-6020 Innsbruck Austria

HINTON, SUSAN FRAZIER, secondary education educator; b. Lebanon, Tenn., Dec. 13, 1951; d. Henry Edward and Frances (Fuston) Frazier; m. Jerry Lee Hinton, 1993; children: Troy E. Hinton, David L. Hinton, Rance Kelly Jr. BS, Belmont U., Nashville, 1972; Master's degree, Ala. A&M U., 1974, EdS, 1976. Cert. elem. tchr., Ala.; reading specialist, Ala.; cert. adminstrn. supr. schs. Dir. migrant edn. Morgan County Sch. Sys., Decatur, Ala., 1986-89, elem. tchr., 1972-86, 1989-98; lang. arts tchr. DeKalb Mid. Sch., Smithville, Tenn., 1998-2000; dir., tchr. Dekalb County H.S., 2000—; cons., chmn. So. Assn. Colls. and Univs., 1993—. Vol. Hospice of Am., Huntsville, Ala., 1992—, 4-H Clubs of U.S., Morgan County, 1989-96; organist Smithville (Tenn.) First Bapt. Ch., 1995-96, asst. choir dir., pianist Kingdom Kids; active DeKalb Art League, 1998—; mem. Southern Gospel Singing Group-The Harmoneers, 1998—; mem., asst. pianist DeKalb Cmty. Chorus. Mem. NEA (del. 1986, mem. pub. rels. com., Ala. Educator of Yr. 1986, Morgan County Tchr. of Yr. 1996), Nat. Coun. Tchrs. English, Ala. Edn. Assn. (del., mem. various commns.), Morgan County Edn. Assn. (pres. 1972, 76), Profl. Bus. and Profl. Womens' Club, Smithville Study Club. Democrat. E-mail: hinton@dtccom.net. Home: PO Box 622 Smithville TN 37166-0622

HINZ, SHIRLEY SORENSEN, administrative secretary; b. Denver, Sept. 28, 1942; m. Dale Edward Hinz, Sept. 3, 1966; children: Andrew Christian, Tammy Lynn Dahl. Student, Ft. Lewis Coll., 1961, Barnes Bus. Coll., 1982; spl. publishing diploma, Inst. Children's Lit., 1994. Adminstrv. asst. USDA, Ft. Collins, Colo., 1989; divsn. sec. U.S. Dept. Energy, Golden, Colo., 1991; sect. sec. U.S. Dept. Interior, Ft. Collins, 1992—; mem. labor mgmt. partnership coun. U.S. Dept. Interior, 1994-95. Author numerous poems and short stories; writer/songwriter. Active Ault (Colo.) Sr. Ctr., 1989—. Recipient Editor's Choice award Nat. Libr. Congress, Nat. Libr. Poetry, 1995-96, Accomplishment of Merit award Creative Arts & Sci. Enterprises, 1996, Nat. Merit Award cert. Larimer County Fed. Exec. Assn., 1996, awards Poetry Guild, 1996-97; named to Internat. Poetry Hall of Fame, Nat. Libr. Congress, 1997. Mem. Internat. Soc. Poets (disting.), Famous Poets Soc. (Diamond Homer award 1996), Acad. of Am. Poets. Lutheran. Avocations: gardening, studying and working in bonsai, song writing. Home: PO Box 1063 304 Cherry Ln Ault CO 80610 Office: US Dept Interior 4512 Mcmurry Ave Fort Collins CO 80525-3400

HIPONA, CESAR DUMPIT, civil engineer; b. Cagayan de Oro City, Philippines, Apr. 12, 1926; s. Vicente Calusa Hipona and Gorgonia Dumpit; m. Eva Marfori, Sept. 25, 1924; children: Mipona Zimmerman, Francisco Marfori Hipona, Cesar Marfori Hipona, Jr. BSCE, Far Ea. U., Manila. Instrument man City Engrs. Office, Cagayan de Oro City, Philippines, 1951-53; bldg. inspector city engring. Cagayan de Oro City, Philippines, 1953-55, asst. civil engr., 1955-58; pvt. practice civil engring. Philippines, 1958—, contractor, pvt., 1961-87, real estate appraiser, pvt., 1992-99. Mem. Chamber of Real Estate and Builders Assn. (pres. 1989-93, v.p. 1994-99), Cagayan de Oro Contractor Assn. (pres. 1980-85), KC, Rotary, Philippine Real Estate Appraiser Assn. (v.p., bd. dirs.), others. Office: 27 Pabayo St, Cayan de Oro City 9000, Philippines

HIPPE, ZDZISLAW STANISLAW, computer chemistry educator; b. Cracow, Poland, Jan. 9, 1930; m. Monika P. Kornicka; children: Arthur, Paulina. MSc, U. Tech., Gdánsk, Poland, 1955; PhD, U. Tech., Gliwice, Poland, 1965; habilitation, U. Tech., Lódź, Poland, 1968. Rsch. asst. U. Tech., Gdánsk, 1953-56; sr. rsch. officer Paint & Varnish Inst., Gliwice, 1956-69, rsch. dir., 1960-63; head dept. U. Tech., Rzeszow, 1969—; dean faculty of chem. U. Tech., Rzeszow, Poland, 1970-72; v.p. U. Tech., Rzeszow, 1973-81; cons. artificial intelligence task group CODATA, Paris, 1991-99. Author: Data Processing in Chemistry, 1981, Artificial Intelligence in Chemistry: Structure Identification and Simulation of Organic Reactions, 1991, Artificial Intelligence in Chemistry, 1993. Chmn. Coun. East-So. Macro Region Poland, Cracow, 1973-81. Recipient State Award in Sci. and Tech., State Coun., Warsaw, Poland, 1964, Rsch. award Mayor of Rzeszow, 1995. Mem. Polish Chem. Soc. (rep. to Fedn. European Chem. Socs. 1989—), Polish Acad. Scis. (bd. chemometrics, com. analytical chemistry 1989—). Avocations: sailing, swimming. Home: 5 Ossolińskich St, 35-328 Rzeszów Poland Office: U Tech Dept Computer Chem, 6 Powstańców Warszawy, 35-041 Rzeszów Poland

HIRABAYASHI, ATSUMU, physicist, researcher; b. Kobe, Japan, Nov. 3, 1958; s. Keizo and Etsuko (Kishimoto) H.; m. Hiroko Furuyama, June 11, 1995; children: Itsuko, Tatsuo. BS, Kyoto (Japan) U., 1982, MS, 1984, PhD, 1987. Researcher Hitachi, Ltd., Tokyo, 1987—. Office: Hitachi Ltd, Central Rsch Lab, Kokubunji Tokyo 185-8601, Japan

HIRAGA, MASAHARU, heating and cooling products company advisor; b. Maebashi, Gunma-ken, Japan, Apr. 13, 1939; s. Minoru and Fusa (Kanai) H.; m. Keiko Sunaga, Oct. 29, 1975; children: Tomoko, Fumiko. BS, Tohoku U., Sendai, Japan, 1963; MS, Tohoku U., 1969, D of Engring., 1972. Electronic engr. OKI Electric Co., Takasaki, Japan, 1963-65; asst. to prof. Tohoku U., 1965-67; mech. engr. Sanden Corp., Isesaki, Japan, 1972-74; mgr. sales engring. Sanden Internat. Inc., Dallas, 1975-77; mgr. automotive products devel. Sanden Corp., Isesaki, 1977-78, gen. mgr., chief engr. automotive products devel., 1979-87, sr. gen. mgr. product devel., 1989-91, dir. R&D dept., 1991-97, exec. officer corp. R&D, 1998-2000, R&D advisor, 2000—. Author tech. papers and articles on wobbleplate type, scroll type compressors and other products; patentee in field. Recipient Nat. Invention award Japan Inst. Invention and Innovation, Tokyo, 1986. Mem. Soc. Automotive Engrs., Soc. Refrigeration of Japan. Avocations: square dance calling, dancing. Home: 4-8-34 Honjo Honjo-shi, Saitama-ken 367, Japan Office: Tech Head Office, 20 Kotobuki-cho Isesaki-shi, Isesaki-shi, Gunma-ken 372, Japan

HIRAHARA, PATTI, public relations executive; b. Lynwood, Calif., May 10, 1955; d. Frank C. and Mary K. Hirahara; m. Terry K. Takeda, Sept. 1995. AA, Cypress Coll., 1975; BA, Calif. State U., Fullerton, 1977. Pub. affairs dir. United TV, L.A., 1977-80; v.p. Asian Internat. Broadcasting Co., L.A., 1980-81; mktg. cons. Disneyland, Anaheim, Calif., 1982; pub. rels. agt. Japan External Trade Orgn., L.A., 1982-86, 87-92; owner, pres. Prodns. By Hirahara, Anaheim, 1982—; comml. photographer Hirahara Photography, Anaheim, 1977-83; publicist Tokyo Met. Govt., 1981, World Trade Week So. Calif., 1997, 98, 99; advisor State Colo. Trade Mission to Japan, 1986, State Ariz. Trade/Investment Mission to Japan, 1987, County Riverside, Calif. for Japanese trade, investment, tourism, 1986-88; coord. JETRO's bus. Study Series, L.A., 1988; advisor Japan External Trade Orgn., 1987-88, TV Prodr./Host: Images, 1980, Expressions, 1994. Mem. reader panel Golf for Women Mag. Bd. dirs. Nisei Week Japanese Festival, L.A., 1980-81; mem. Anaheim H.S. 20 Yr. Reunion Com., 1993. Nat. scholar Seventeen Mag. Youth Adv. Coun., 1973; named Orange County Nisei Queen, Suburban Optimist Club, Buena Park, Calif., 1974, nat. semi-finalist Outstanding Working Women Competition Glamour Mag., 1975; recipient svc. award Suburban Optimist Club of Buena Park, 1975. Mem. NAFE, Soc. Profl. Journalists (bd. dirs. 1980-81), World Trade Ctr. Assn. Orange County, Japanese Am. Citizens League, Am. Women in Radio and TV (bd. dirs. So. Calif. chpt. 1980-82, vice-chair western conf. 1981), So. Calif. Golf Assn., No. Calif. Golf Assn., Pub. Rels. Soc. Am. (Orange County chpt. 1990), Adelaide Price Elem. Sch. (30 yr. reunion chair 1997), Suburban Optimist Club of Buena Park (bd. dirs. 1993-96, chairperson 30th Anniversary Celebration 1996, Optimist of Yr. 1995-96), Hunter Ranch Golf Club, Alpha Gamma Sigma.

HIRAI, DENITSU, surgeon; b. Yokkaichi, Mie, Japan, July 27, 1943; came to U.S. 1969; s. Denyomu and Shizuo (Tanaka) H.; m. Fumiko Hada, June 14, 1969; 1 child, R. Lisa. MD, U. Tokyo, 1968. Diplomate Am. Bd. Surgery, Am. Bd. Quality Assurance and Utilization Rev. Physicians, Am. Bd. Surg. Critical Care; cert. nutrition support physician; cert. wound care specialist. Intern and residency Waterbury (Conn.) Hosp., 1969-74; fellow Mt. Sinai Hosp., 1974-75; asst. chief surgery VA Med. Ctr., Lincoln, Nebr., 1975-80; chief surgery VA Med. Ctr., Lincoln, 1981-2000; asst. clin. prof. surgery Creighton U., Omaha, 1982-84, asst. prof. surgery, 1984-2000; clin. instr. U. Nebr., Omaha, 1986-88, clin. asst. prof. surgery, 1988-2000; assoc. prof. clin. surgery, mem. surgery staff Sch. Medicine U. So. Calif., L.A., 2000—. Author: Brain Ticklers (Japanese), 1983. Fellow ACS, Am. Coll. Critical Care Medicine; mem. AAAS, AMA, ACS, Am. Soc. Parenteral and Enteral Nutrition, Soc. Am. Gastrointestinal Endoscopic Surgeons, Southwestern Surg. Congress, Soc. Critical Care Medicine, Assn. VA Surgeons. Avocations: photography, Braille transcription, karate (Okinawa Koburyu Nidan). Office: Dept Surgery USC Sch Medicine 1510 San Pablo St # St514 Los Angeles CA 90033-4586

HIRAI, MICHIHIRO, computer engineer, translator, educator; b. Tokyo, Mar. 28, 1943; s. Yoshimichi and Katsuyo (Ohnuki) H.; m. Jadwiga Teresa Los, Aug. 12, 1978; children: Anna Mari, Natalia Emi, Sylvia Naomi. BEng, U. Tokyo, 1965; MSE, U. Pa., 1973. Registered profl./cons. engr., Japan; nat. lic. interpreter guide in English and German, Japan. With Hitachi Ltd., Yokohama, Japan, 1965-72; engr. Hitachi Ltd., Hadano, Japan, 1972-79, sr. engr., 1979-86, chief engr., 1986-98; dir. Hitachi Inst. Fgn. Langs., Yokohama, Japan, 1998—. Contbr. to book; patentee logic tracer. Mem. Info. Processing Soc. Japan (head working group 6 of spl. com. 1, 1987—), Japan Cons. Engrs. Assn., Soc. Writers, Editors and Translators. Home: 530-9 Ojiri, Hadano-shi, Kanagawa-ken 257-0011, Japan Office: Hitachi Inst Fgn Langs, 850 Maioka-cho Totsuka-ku, Tokohama 244-0813, Japan

HIRAI, TOSHIRO, battery research engineer; b. Iwami-cho, Japan, Aug. 14, 1952; s. Fumiko and Michio (Takagaki) H.; m. Miwako Tachibana, Nov. 21, 1976; children: Miho, Rina, Yumi. B of Engring., Kyoto U., 1976, M of Engring., 1978, D of Engring., 1985. Rsch. scientist Advanced Energy Tech., Burnaby, Can., 1989-92; sr. rsch. engr. NTT, Tokai, Japan, 1985-89; group leader NTT, Musashino, Japan, 1995—. Contbr. articles to Jour. Electrochem. Soc., others; patentee in field. Mem. Inst. Elec., Info. and Comm. Engrs., Electrochem. Soc. Japan, Electrochem. Soc. Avocations: reading and writing detective novels, baseball, cooking. Home: 2-27-3-101 Koenji-kita, Suginami-ku, Tokyo 166-0002, Japan Office: NTT Integrated Info & Energy Sys Labs, Atsugi, Kanagawa 243 0198, Japan

HIRAMATSU, KENICHIRO, neurosurgeon; b. Kyoto, Japan, Sept. 15, 1953; s. Saburo and Kazue (Ochi) H.; m. Miharu Minamitani, Mar. 30, 1981; 2 children. MD, Nara Med. U., 1978, D of Med. Scis., 1990. Intern Nara Med. U., Kashihara, Japan, 1978-79; resident Osaka (Japan) Prefectural Hosp., 1979-80; instr. Nara Med. U., 1985-90, asst. prof., 1993-96; chief sect. neurosurgery Nabari (Japan) City Hosp., 1997—. Contbr. articles to profl. jours. Clin. fellow Osaka Minami Nat. Hosp., 1981-83, Osaka Police Hosp., 1983-85, Rsch. fellow U. Va., Charlottesville, 1991-92; grantee Ministry Edn. Sci. & Culture, Tokyo, 1993, Chiyoda Mut. Life Found. AID, Tokyo, 1994. Mem. Japanese Neurosurg. Soc. (trustee 1984—), Japanese Soc. Stroke, Japanese Soc. CBF and Metab, Soc. Neurosci. Avocations: sailing, skiing, music, travel, reading. Home: 4-12 Jingu 1-chome, Nara 631, Japan Office: Nabari City Hosp Dept Neurosurgery, 178 Yurigaoka Nishi, 1-bancho Nabari 518-04, Japan

HIRAMATSU, MITSUO, engineering researcher; b. Hamamatsu, Shizuoka, Japan, 1955; s. Yoshio and Masa (Fujiwara) Hiramatsu. B in Engring., Shizuoka U., Hamamatsu, 1977, M in Engring., 1979, D in Engring., 1982. Rschr. Hamamatsu Photonics K.K., 1982-83, 85-91, sr. rschr., 1991-94; vis. scientist Inst. for Molecular Sci., Okazaki, Japan, 1983-85; group leader Lab. Molecular Biophotonics, Hamakita, Japan, 1994—. Author: Biophotons, 1998; U.S. patentee in field. Mem. Am. Chem. Soc. Office: Lab Molecular Biophotonics, 5000 Hirakuchi, Hamakita 434-8555, Japan

HIRAMATSU, TAKESHI, cardiovascular surgeon; b. Nerima-ku, Japan, Dec. 16, 1959; m. Hideko Hiramatsu, Mar. 29, 1986; 1 child, Chisa. MD, Chiba (Japan) U., 1984; PhD, Tokyo Women's Med. U., 1992. Cert. tchg. dr. Japanese Assn. Thoracic Surgery, Japanese Assn. Surgery. Resident in cardiac surgery Tokyo Women's U., Heart Inst. of Japan, 1984-85, clin. fellow, 1986-90, asst. in pediat. cardiac surgery, 1990—; rsch. fellow cardiac surgery Boston Children's Hosp./Harvard Med. Sch., 1992-94. Contbr. articles to profl. jours. Avocations: golf, skiing, movies. E-mail: shira-mat@hij.twmu.ac.jp. Office: Tokyo Women's Med U, Kawada-cho 8-1, Shinjuku-ku 261-8666, Japan

HIRAMATSU, YUJI, surgeon, educator; b. Ichinomiya, Japan, June 21, 1961; s. Hitoshi and Tome (Fujieda) H ; m. Yuko Ishi, Oct. 25, 1987; 1 child, Yuta. MD, U. Tsukuba, Japan, 1986, PhD, 1997. Resident U. Tsukuba, Japan, 1986-92; staff surgeon Hitachi Gen. Hosp., Japan, 1992-94, Tsukuba Meml. Hosp., Japan, 1996-98; asst. prof. surgery U. Tsukuba, Japan, 1998—. Medtronic Japan fellow Young Japanese Investigator, Tokyo, 1994-95. Mem. Japanese Assn. Thoracic Surgery, Japan Surg. Soc., Japanese Soc. Cardiovascular Surgery. Avocations: baseball, golf, running. Home: 281-73 Shimo-yokoba, Tsukuba 305-0075, Japan Office: U Tsukuba, 1-1-1 Tennoh-dai, Tsukuba 305-8575, Japan

HIRANO, KO, store automation, import/export company executive; b. Osaka, Japan, Aug. 20, 1953; s. Noboru and Mayumi (Hitomi) H.; m. Etsuko Fujimoto, Nov. 7, 1981; 1 child, Soma. LLB, Tokyo U., 1976. Task force leader Mitsubishi Corp., Tokyo, 1976-91; pres., CEO Den Corp., Tokyo, 1991-93; pres., CEO Ace Rsch. Inst., Tokyo, 1993-96, chmn., CEO, 1996—; exec. v.p., COO Ace-Denken Co., Ltd., Tokyo, 1996—. Mem. City Club of Tokyo. Avocations: the way of tea, hiking, swimming, photography. Office: Ace-Denken Co Ltd, 3-12-9 Higashi-Ueno Taitoku, Tokyo 110, Japan

HIRANO, MASAMI, medical educator, researcher, hematologist; b. Kuwana, Mie, Japan, July 13, 1936; s. Yasuo and Teru Hirano; m. Sachiyo Sekiya, May 20, 1961; children: Naoto, Yoshio. MD, Nagoya U., 1961, Dr.Med.Sci., 1968. Asst. prof. medicine Nagoya U. Sch. Medicine, 1969-72; assoc. prof. medicine Fujita-Gakuen U. Sch. Medicine, Toyoake, 1972-81; prof. medicine Fujita Health U. Sch. Medicine, 1981—; dean Sch. Medicine Fujita-Gakuen U., 1998—. Mem. Am. Soc. Hematology, N.Y. Acad. Sci., Internat. Soc. Hematology, Japan Soc. Clin. Hematology, Japanese Cancer Assn. Avocations: swimming, golf. E-mail: mhirano@fujita-hu.ac.jp. Office: Fujita Health U, Toyoake 470-1192, Japan

HIRANO, TADASHI, cell biologist, educator; b. Tado, Mie, Japan, Nov. 15, 1922; s. Tunehichi and Mitue (Kusanagi) H.; m. Rieko Iizuka, Oct. 19, 1956; children: Naoko, Atsushi. BS, Sci. U. Tokyo, 1954; D in Med. Sci., U. Tokyo, 1959; D (hon.), Debrecen U. Sch. Medicine, Hungary, 1994. Lectr. Japan Women's U., Tokyo, 1954-59; vis. assoc. prof. So. Ill. U., Carbondale, 1959-63; sr. scientist Tokyo Met. Isotope Rsch. Ctr., 1963-67, dir., 1969-80; assoc. prof. U. Ottawa, Canada, 1967-69; prof., dir. rsch. ctr. Jikei U. Sch. Medicine, Tokyo, 1980-88, vis. prof., 1988—; vis. prof. Debrecen (Hungary) U. Sch. Medicine, 1990-94, hon. prof., 1994—; hon. advisor Mendel World Found., 1992. Editor: Biotechnology of Yeast, 1988; contbr. articles to profl. jours. including Jour. Bacteriology, Jour. Ultrast. Rsch., European Jour. Cell Biology, Antonie van Leevwenhoek, N.Y. Acad. Sci., Experientia, Cytologia, Japanese Jour. Genetics. Recipient Mendel medal Mendelianum, Brno, 1992. Mem. Japanese Soc. Electron Microscopy (emeritus, disting. scientist award 1989), Japan Soc. for Cell Biology, Japan Mendel Soc. (exec. dir. 1980-99, pres. 1999—), Internat. Com. Yeast IUMS, Microscopy Soc. Am. (emeritus). Avocations: music, poetry, travel. Home: 2-13-22 Honcho, Koganei, Tokyo 184, Japan Office: Jikei U Sch Medicine, 3-25-8 Nishi-Shinbash Minatoku, Tokyo 105, Japan

HIRANO, TOSHIO, medical educator; b. Osaka, Japan, Apr. 17, 1947; s. masami and Kaoru (Kubota) H.; m. Chiyoko Koyanagi, Dec. 8, 1974; 2 children. MD, Osaka U., 1972, PhD, 1979. Vis. fellow NIH, Balt., 1973-76; assoc. prof. Kumamoto (Japan) U., 1980-84; assoc. prof. Osaka U., 1984-89, prof., 1989—. Author: Nature, 1986, Handbook of Experimental Pharmacology, 1990, The Cytokine Handbook, 1991, 2d edit., 1994; contbr. articles to profl. jours.; mem. editl. bd. Cytokine, London, 1989—, Jour. Molecular Medicine, Berlin, 1994—. Recipient Erwin von Balz prize Boehringer, 1986, Rheumatism prize Japan Ciba-Geigy, 1990, prize for immunology Sandoz, Basel, Switzerland, 1992. Mem. Japanese Soc. for Immunology (bd. dirs. 1992—), Internat. Soc. Immunopharmacology (mem. coun. 1991—). Home: 2-7-6 Anryu Suminoe-ku, Osaka 559-0003, Japan Office: Osaka U Grad Sch Medicine, 2-2 Yamada-Oka, Suita Osaka 565-0871, Japan

HIRANO, YORIO, English language and literature educator; b. Itoigawa, Niigata, Japan, Nov. 5, 1952; s. Junei and Takako Hirano; m. Naomi Mori. BA, Kyoto (Japan) Prefectural U., 1975; MA, Osaka City (Japan) U., 1977. Tchr. Sano H.S., 1981-82; part-time instr. Kansai Fgn. Lang. Jr. Coll., 1982-83; lectr. English, Sugiyama Jogakuen U., Nagoya, Japan, 1987-92, assoc. prof., 1992-97, prof., 1997—. Mem. MLA, oc. English Studies (Japan), Japan Ezra Pound Soc. Avocations: theater, listening to music. Home: 1-806 Moritaka Nishi Jutaku, 2-814 Moritaka Higashi, Moriyama-ku, Nagoya 463-0033, Japan Office: Sugiyama Jogakuen U Sch, Human Sci 47-234 Takenoyama, Aichi Nisshin-Shi 470-0131, Japan

HIRAOKA, MASAYASU, cardiologist; b. Oita City, Japan, Apr. 1, 1940; s. Saburo and Masuko (Ooki) H.; m. Mari Katoh, May 14, 1965; children: Miki, Miina, Rika. MD, Tokyo Med. & Dental U., 1964, PhD, 1969. Vis. instr., then asst. prof. U. Chgo., 1969-72; from instr. to prof. Tokyo Med. & Dental U., 1973—. Editor: Electropharmacological Control of Cardiac Arrhythmias, 1993; contbr. articles to profl. jours. Grantee Japanese Heart Found., Tokyo, 1976, Inoue Sci. Found., Tokyo, 1991. Fellow Am. Coll. Cardiology; mem. Am. Heart Assn. (coun.), Internat. Soc. Electrocardiology, Internat. Soc. Heart Rsch. (coun.). Office: Dept Cardiovasc Disease, Med Rsch Inst Tokyo U, 1-5-45 Yushima 113-8510, Japan

HIRASAWA, EIJI, biochemist, researcher; b. Tonami, Toyama, Japan, Aug. 22, 1950; s. Shuji and Mikiko (Matsui) H.; m. Mariko Nomura, Sept. 28, 1974; 3 children. BS, Toyama U., 1973; MAgr, Kyoto U., 1977, DAgr (hon.), 1981; DSc (hon.), Osaka City U., 1985. Cert. supr. radiohandling. Rsch. assoc. Osaka City U., 1979-88, instr., 1988-94, assoc. prof., 1994-96, prof., 1996—; supr. radiohandling Osaka City U., 1984—. Contbr. articles to profl. jours. Alexander von Humboldt fellow, Germany, 1984-86. Mem. Botanical Soc. of Japan, Japanese Soc. Plant Physiologists, Am. Soc. Plant Physiologists. Avocation: history. Home: Yamasaka 3 3 14, Higashisumiyoshi ku, 546-0035 Osaka Japan Office: Osaka City U, Sugimoto 3 3 138, Sumiyoshi-ku Osaka 558-8585, Japan

HIRASAWA, YASUSUKE, orthopedic surgeon; b. Japan, Sept. 20, 1937; married; 2 children. MD, Kyoto Prefectural U., 1963, PhD, 1969. Rsch. fellow UCLA Med. Ctr., 1965-67; clin. fellow Harvard Med. Sch., R.B. Brigham Hosp., Boston, 1972; vis. prof. U. Würzburg, König-Ludwig-Haus, Germany, 1980-81; prof., chmn. dept. orthop. surgery Kyoto Prefectural U. Medicine, 1989—; dir. rehab. divsn. Kyoto Prefectural U. Medicine. Contbr. articles to profl. jours.; mem. editl. bd. Jour. Orthop. Surgery, Hong Kong, Operative Orthopädie u Truamatologie.; mem. editl. adv. bd. Jour. Orthop. Rsch. Mem. Internat. Coll. Surgeons (gov. 1998—), Internat. Soc. Orthop. and Traumatology, N.Y. Acad. Scis., Internat. Soc. Plastic and Reconstructive Surgery, Japanese Assn. Rehab. Medicine (exec. bd. dirs. 1998—),

Japanese Soc. for Surg. of the Hand (exec. bd. dirs. 1998—). Office: Kyoto Prefectural U, Dept Orthop Surg, Kyoto 602-8566, Japan

HIRASHIMA, HIROSHI, chemistry educator; b. Tokyo, Mar. 9, 1944; s. Susumu and Noriko (Yanase) H.; m. Kozue Terashima, Mar. 1, 1975; children: Kaoru, Mayumi. B Engring., Keio U., Tokyo, 1966, M Engring., 1968, D Engring., 1974. Asst. Keio U., 1969-76, asst. prof., 1976-83, assoc. prof., 1983-90, prof. applied chemistry, 1990—; rschr. Techniche Hochschule Aachen, Germany, 1977-79. Author: (in Japanese) Preparation of Functional Thin Films by Sol-Gel Method, 1992; contbr. more than 80 articles to profl. jours. Mem. Ceramic Soc. of Japan (Advances in Ceramics award 1978, editor jour. 1979-81), Chem. Soc. of Japan, Am. Ceramic Soc., Materials Rsch. Soc., New Glass Forum. Home: 3-16-10 Nishihara, Shibuya-ku, Tokyo 151-0066, Japan Office: Keio U Faculty Sci & Tech, 3-14-1 Hiyoshi, Kohoku-ku Yokohama 223-8522, Japan

HIRATA, MASAHIKO, agricultural scientist; b. Kobe, Hyogo, Japan, Mar. 15, 1955; s. Masahisa and Fumie (Fujimori) H.; m. Rumiko Fujiwara, June 19, 1982. BSc, U. Tokyo, 1979, MSc, 1982, PhD, 1989. Asst. prof. Miyazaki (Japan) U., 1982-92, assoc. prof., 1992—. Author: (with T. Okubo et al): Introduction to Animal Production, 1996; contbr. articles to profl. jours. Mem. Japanese Soc. of Grassland Sci. (editor 1995—, planning com. 1995—, terminology com. mem. 1997—, Rsch. Encouragement award 1989, councillor 1999—, Award of the Soc. 2000). Office: Faculty of Agrl, Miyazaki Univ, Miyazaki 889-2192, Japan

HIRATA, TOMIO, engineering educator; b. Sendai, Japan, Oct. 13, 1949; s. Kunizo and Yaeko (Matsune) H.; m. Nobuko Abematsu, May 6, 1984; children: Reiko, Kouichi. BSc, Tohoku U., Sendai, 1976, MSc, 1978, PhD in Engring., 1981. Asst. prof. Toyohashi (Japan) U. Tech., 1981-86; lectr. Nagoya (Japan) U., 1986-89, assoc. prof., 1989-93, prof. Faculty of Engring., 1993—. Author: Algorithms and Data Structures, 1990; mem. editorial bd. Transactions of Info. Processing Soc. Japan, 1994—. Mem. Inst. Electronics, Info. and Comm. Engrs., Info. Processing Soc. Japan, Assn. for Computing Machinery. Office: Nagoya U, Faculty of Engring, Nagoya 464-8603, Japan

HIRATSUKA, MAKOTO, lawyer; b. Tokyo, Dec. 22, 1939; s. Ryozo and Aiko (Funao) H.; m. Reiko Ariizumi, Mar. 9, 1968; children: Mihoko, Yoichi, Koji. LLB pvt. law course, Tokyo U., 1963, LLB pub. law course, 1964; diploma in shipping law, U. Coll., London, 1972. Atty. Graham James & Ralph, Tokyo, 1966-71, Ince & Co. Solicitors, London, 1972-73, Braun Moriya Hoashi & Kubota, Tokyo, 1973-76; sr. ptnr. Hiratsuka & Ptnrs., Tokyo, 1976—. Fellow Internat. Acad. Trial Lawyers; mem. First Tokyo Bar Assn., Japanese Maritime Law Assn., Tokyo South Rotary Club (sec. 1992-93). Office: Hiratsuka & Ptnrs 1104 Kioi, TBR Bldg 5-7 Kojimachi, Tokyo 102-0083, Japan

HIRAYAMA, EIJI, psychologist, educator; b. Tokyo, Sept. 13, 1955; s. Gosai and Shizuko Hirayama; m. Atsuko Hanaoka; three children. BA, Aoyamagakuin U., Tokyo, 1979, Rikkyo U., Tokyo, 1981; MA, Kyushu U., Fukuoka, Japan, 1986, PhD, 1996. Cert. clin. psychologist. Chief Psychol. Clinic, Kyushu U., Fukuoka, 1989-90; counselor Student Counseling Ctr., Fukuoka U., 1990-96; assoc. prof. Matsuyama (Japan) Shinonome Coll., 1996-99, Aoyamagakuin U., Tokyo, 1999—. Author: Clinical Psychology Today: On Mental Health, 1994, Encounter Group and the Process of Personal Growth, 1998; contbr. articles to profl. jours. Mem. APA, Japan Psychoanalytical Assn., Assn. Japanese Clin. Psychology (The Most Disting. Sci. award 1999). Home: 6-77-1-501 Takinogawa, Kita-ku, Tokyo 114-0023, Japan Office: Aoyamagakuin U Faculty Lit, Shibuya 4-4-25 Shibuya-ku, Tokyo 150-8366, Japan

HIRAYAMA, MASAHIRO, electronics executive; b. Obihiro, Hokkaido, Japan, Sept. 4, 1942; s. Masaaki and Shigeno Hirayama; m. Mitsuko Umemura, Oct. 4, 1969; children: Hiroshi, Keiko. BS, Hokkaido U., Sapporo, Japan, 1966; MS, Hokkaido U., 1968. From supr. to project leader NTT LSI Lab., Atsugi-shi, Japan, 1984-92; gen. mgr. NTT Electronics Tech. Corp., Atsugi-shi, 1992-97, exec. dir., 1996—, also bd. dirs. Author: Ultra-High Speed ICs, 1990, Compound and Josephson High Speed Devices, 1993. Mem. IEEE Electron Devices Soc. (Overseas advisor Symposium 1989-92), Inst. Electronics, Info. and Comm. Engrs. (sec. 1977-78, exec. officer 1990-92), Japan Applied Physics Soc. Avocations: tennis, skiing, skating, hiking. Home: 4328-7 Oyama-cho, Machida-shi 194-0212, Japan Office: NTT Electronics Corp, 1-12-1 Dogenzaka Shibuyaku, Tokyo 150-0043, Japan

HIREMATH, SHOBHA RANI R., pharmaceutics educator; b. June 24, 1964; married; children: Anirudh, Atul. BPharm, Bangalore (India) U., 1984, MPharm, 1986; PhD, U. Hyderabad, India, 1995. Registered pharmacist, Karnataka, India. Lectr. dept. pharmaceutics Al-Ameen Coll. Pharmacy, Bangalore, India, 1986-92, asst. prof., 1992-97, prof., head dept., 1997—; pharmacy insp. Karnataka State Pharm. Coun., Pharmacy Coun. India; mem. local inspection com. Rajiv Gandhi U. Health Scis., Karnataka; guide for several MPharm and PhD students Bangalore U. and Rajiv Gandhi U. Health Scis.; examiner, paper valuator ednl. instns.; lectr., presenter profl. confs. and symposia; cons. in field. Referee Indian Jour. Pharm. Scis.; contbr. articles to profl. publs., including Indian Jour. Pharm. Scis., Indian Drugs, Die Pharmazie, Ea. Pharmacist. Rsch. grantee All India Coun. Tech. Edn., Govt. of India, 1999. Mem. Am. Assn. Pharm. Scientists, Controlled Release Soc. (India chpt.), Indian Soc. Tech. Edn. (life), Indian Membrane Soc. (life), India Pharm. Assn., Assn. Pharmacy Tchrs. India (life), Pharm. Scis. Group (Eng.). Fax: 080-2278464. E-mail: shobha24@yahoo.com. Home: II Main, II Stage, Rajajngr, 749 Gurudatta, E Block, Karnatak Bangalore 560 010, India Office: Al-Ameen Coll Pharmacy, Hosur Rd, Nr Lalbagh Main G, Bangalore 560 027, India

HIRNING, FREDRIC CARL, pharmacist; b. Lodi, Calif., Aug. 20, 1947; s. Clarence Christian Reuben and Gertrude (Hoff) H.; m. Marilyn Kay Truitt, Aug. 31, 1968; children: Lindsay Ann, Katherine Erin, John Michael. BS in Pharmacy cum laude, U. of the Pacific, 1970, PharmD cum laude, 1972; cert. pharmacy mgmt., U. N.C., 1989; cert. health care mgmt., U. So. Calif., 1991. Registered pharmacist, Calif. From pharmacist to dir. pharmacy Mercy Hosp., Sacramento, 1970-76; dir. pharmacy St. Josephs Med. Ctr., Stockton, 1976-80, pharmacist, 1980-82; dir. pharmacy svcs. Sutter Davis (Calif.) Hosp., 1983-85; pharmacist Relief Pharmacy Svc., Stockton, 1985-87; dir. pharmacy svcs. Drs. Hosp. Manteca, Calif., 1987—; adj. prof. U. of the Pacific Sch. Pharmacy, Stockton, 1987-89, new dean search com., 1994-95; instr. chemical dependency studies Calif. State U., Sacramento, 1991-95; instr. drug & alcohol counselor cert. program U. of the Pacific, Stockton, 1993-95, bd. dirs. pharmacy assoc., 1990—; field monitor Occupl. Healthcare Svcs., Larkspur, Calif., 1988-93; chmn. Calif. Vet. Diversion Com., 1993-95; vice-chmn. Calif. Nursing Diversion Com., 1992-94; cons. and presenter in field. Co-author: Purchasing and Inventory Control, 1992, Points of Light, A Guide for Helping..., 1996; contbr. articles to profl. jours. Active Bishops Adv. Com. on Drug and Alcohol, Fresno, 1987—, Partners in Prevention/Parents Who Care, Stockton, 1987-95, Pharmacists Against Drug Abuse, 1986—, Calaveras County Drug Abuse Task Force, San Andreas, Calif., 1986-87, Leadership, Manteca, 1989-90; asst. scoutmaster Boy Scouts Am., Stockton, 1991—; bd. dirs. PALS-Drug Treatment Program, Stockton, 1993-95; coun. mem. Lincoln H.S., Stockton, 1991-93. Recipient Geigy Leadership award Sacramento Valley Soc. Hosp. Pharmacists, 1976, Commendation award San Joaquin County Sheriff, 1982, Appreciation award Boy Scouts Am., 1990, Nat. Cmty. Svc. award U.S. Pharmacist jour., 1993; named Disting. Pharmacist, Roerig Pharmaceuticals, 1989, Disting. Alumni, U. of the Pacific Alumni Assn., 1997; named to Lodi Union H.S. Sports Hall of Fame, 1994. Mem. Internat. Pharmacy Fedn., Am. Pharm. Assn. (del. 1990-95), Acad. Pharmacy and Practice & Mgmt. of Am. Pharm. Assn. (edn. standing com. 1993-94, vice-chmn. awards standing com., sect. chmn. 1994-95, Merit award 1999), Am. Soc. Health-Sys. Pharmacists, Calif. Pharmacists Assn. (editl. rev. com. 1993—, ednl. found. adv. com. 1997—, Bowl of Hygeia award 1991), Am. Inst. for the History of Pharmacy, Christian Pharmacists Fellowship Internat., Internat. Pharmacists Anonymous, Am. Pharm. Assn. Found., Am. Soc. Health-Sys. Pharmacists Found., Internat. Coalition Addiction Studies Educators, Acad. Hosp. Pharmacists (bd. dirs. 1994-96, Quality Commitment award 1995), San Joaquin Pharmacists Assn. (bd. dirs. 1989-94, pres. 1993), Cen. Valley Soc. Hosp. Pharmacists (bd. dirs. 1988-93, pres. 1992, Pharmacist of Yr. 1992), San Francisco Zool. Soc., U.S. Holocaust Meml. Mus. Assn., Nat. Eagle Scout Assn., Rho Chi. Republican. Episcopalian. Avocation: travel. Home: 1707 Lakeshore Dr Lodi CA 95242-4223

HIRNLE, PETER, gynecologist, obstetrician, radiation oncologist, cancer researcher; b. Aug. 29, 1953; 1 child, Christoph. MD, Bonn (Germany) U., 1983; PhD, Tübingen (Germany) U., 1991. Cert. Med. Sci. Project leader U. Bonn Konrad-Adenauer Grant, 1982-83, U. Tübingen Mildred Scheel Grant, 1983-88; head lymphol. lab. U. Tübingen, prof. gynecology, 1991—. Author: (with others) Lymph Stasis, 1991; chief editor: Our Opinion, Wroclaw, 1981; co-editor: Lymphology, European Jour. Lymphology and Related Problems; contbr. articles to profl. jours. German Rsch. Soc. grantee Tübingen, 1985, Erwin Riesch grantee Tübingen, 1988. Mem. AAAS, Am. Assn. Cancer Rsch., European Soc. Therapeutic Radiology and Oncology, Internat. Soc. Lymphology, N.Y. Acad. Scis., others. Roman Catholic. Achievements include determination of basic conditions for local treatment of lymph node metastases and lymphomas; use of liposomes as drug carriers for endolymphatic diagnosis and therapy. Home: Ursrainer Ring 104, 72076 Tübingen Germany Office: Dept Gynecology, U Schleichstrasse 4, 72076 Tübingen Germany

HIROKAWA, SHOJI, chemistry educator; b. Asahikawa, Hokkaido, Japan, Feb. 18, 1942; s. Masao and Misako (Yamamoto) H.; m. Yoshiko Konno, June 6, 1971; children: Mio, Mahito. BS, Kyoto U., 1965, MS, 1967, ScD, 1976. Rsch. fellow Kyoto (Japan) U., 1970-82; assoc. prof. Kyushu Inst. Design, Fukuoka, 1982-88, prof., 1988—. Contbr. articles to profl. jours. Mem. AAAS, Am. Phys. Soc., N.Y. Acad. Scis, Chem. Soc. Japan, Phys. Soc. Japan. Avocation: reading. Office: Kyushu Inst Design Dept Environ Design, 4-9-1 Shiobaru Minami-ku, Fukuoka 815-8540, Japan

HIROSE, CHIAKI, chemist, physicist, educator; b. Tokyo, Oct. 15, 1940; s. Norimichi and Kazue (Tshinaka) H.; m. Michiko Kawamata, Oct. 1968; children: Naoko, Ichiro, Tomoko. BSc, U. Tokyo, 1963, MSc, 1965, PhD, 1969. Rsch. assoc. Tokyo Inst. Tech., 1966-79, assoc. prof., 1979-89, prof., 1989—; rsch. fellow Rice U., Houston, 1969-71. Author: Advances in Multi-Photon Processes and Spectroscopy, 1995. Mem. Chem. Soc. Japan, Phys. Soc. Japan, The Spectroscopical Soc. Japan. Home: 3-15-15 Mukaibara Asao-ku, Kawasaki 215-0007, Japan Office: Tokyo Inst Tech, 4259 Nagatsuta-cho Midori, Yokohama Kanagawa 226-8503, Uapan

HIROSE, EIKO IKEDA, psychologist, educator; b. Urawa, Saitama, Japan, June 4, 1968; d. Hiroshi and Fusako (Matsumoto) Ikeda; m. Kazusada Hirose, Mar. 3, 1996. BA, U. Tokyo, 1991, MA, 1993. Lic. h.s. English tchr. Rsch. scientist Tokyo Met. Inst. Gerontology, 1994-96, Found. of Children's Future, Tokyo, 1999-2000; lectr. psychology Tamagawa U., Tokyo, 1999-2000; asst. prof. Tokyo Woman's Christian U., 2000—. Contbr. articles to profl. jours. Mem. APA, Japanese Psychol. Assn., Japanese Assn. Ednl. Psychology. Home: 5-18-17 Kugayama Apt 334, Suginami Tokyo 168-0082, Japan

HIROSE, GENJIRO, neurology educator; b. Shizuoka, Japan, Aug. 11, 1939; s. Ichiro and Setsu (Niwa) H.; m. Yuko Tokikuni, Nov. 13, 1942; children: Jun, Rie. MD, Kyoto (Japan) Prefectural U. Medicine, 1966; PhD, Kanazawa (Japan) U., 1974. Chief resident U. Va. Dept. Neurology, 1970-71; rsch. fellow dept. neurology Harvard Med. Sch., 1971-72; asst. prof. internal medicine Kanazawa Med. U., 1973-74, assoc. prof. internal medicine, 1974-86, prof. dept. neurology, 1986—, chmn. dept. neurology, 1986—; cons. neurologist Asanogawa Gen. Hosp., Kanazawa, 1973—. Mem. Am. Neurol. Assn. (corr.), Am. Acad. Neurology (corr.). Avocations: photography, classical music, fishing. Home: Akasia 1-46 Uchinada-cho, Kahoku-gun, Ishikawa 920-02, Japan Office: Kanazawa Med Univ, Uchinada-cho Kahoku-gun, Ishikawa 920-02, Japan

HIROSE, MASAAKI, biochemist, educator; b. Kyoto, Japan, Nov. 12, 1941; s. Chojiro and Yae (Nakai) H.; m. Fumiko Amagi, Mar. 30, 1968; 2 children. BA, Kyoto U., 1965, MA, 1967, PhD, 1973. Asst. prof. Kyoto U., 1968-75; assoc. prof. Kyoto U., Uji, Japan, 1984-89, prof. biochemistry, 1989—; assoc. prof. Nara (Japan) Women's U., 1975-84. Contbr. articles to profl. jours. Trustee The Fujisawa Found., Osaka, Japan, 1996—. Fellow Japan Soc. Biosci., Biotech. and Agrochemistry (councilor 1998—), Japanese Biochem. Soc. (councilor 1990—); mem. Biophys. Soc. Japan, 1972. Avocations: listening to classic music, playing tennis, gardening. Home: Terada Fukatani 64-239, Jyoyo 610-0121, Japan Office: Kyoto U, Gokasho, Uji 611-0011, Japan

HIROSE, MUNETAKA, anesthesiologist; b. Kyoto, Japan, Mar. 9, 1962. MD, Kyoto Prefectural U. Medicine, 1987, PhD, 1993. Diplomate Japanese Bd. Anesthesiology. Resident Kyoto Prefectural U. Medicine, 1987-88, Kyoto 1st Red Cross Hosp., 1988-89; chief anesthesiologist Maizuru Nat. Hosp., Kyoto, 1993-95; asst. prof. Kyoto Prefectural U. Medicine, 1995—, chief anesthesiologist, 1996-98; rsch. fellow Mass. Gen. Hosp., Boston, 1992-93, 98-99. Contbr. articles to med. jours. Mem. Japan Soc. Pain Clinicians (diplomate), Japan Soc. Anesthesiologists (diplomate), Am. Soc. Anesthesiologists. Avocation: tennis. Office: Kyoto Prefectural U Med, Dept Anesthesiology, Kamigyoku Kyoto 602-8566, Japan

HIROSE, TERUO TERRY, surgeon, educator; b. Tokyo, Jan. 20, 1926; s. Yohei and Seiko (Ogushi) H.; m. Tomiko Kodama, June 1, 1976; 1 son, George Philamore. BS, Tokyo Coll., 1944; MD, Chiba U., Japan, 1948, PhD, 1958. Diplomate Am. Bd. Surgery, Am. Bd. Thoracic Surgery. Intern Chiba U. Hosp., 1948-49, resident in surgery, 1949-52; resident in surgery Am. Hosp., Chgo., 1954; resident in thoracic surgery Hahnemann Med. Coll., Phila., 1955-56, N.Y. Med. Coll., N.Y.C., 1961-62; practice medicine specializing in surgery Chiba, Japan, 1952-53; chief of surgery Tsushimi Hosp., Hagi, Japan, 1958-59; asst. prof. surgery Chiba U., 1959; research fellow advanced cardiovascular surgery Hahnemann Hosp., Phila., 1959; teaching fellow surgery N.Y. Med. Coll., 1959-60, instr., 1961-62; pvt. practice N.Y.C., 1965-89, N.J., 1965-89; dir. cardiovascular lab. St. Barnabas Hosp., N.Y.C., 1975-84; sr. attending surgeon St. Barnabas Hosp., 1965-81; chief vascular surgery Union Hosp., Bronx, N.Y., 1966-67; attending surgeon Flower and Fifth Ave Hosp., N.Y.C., 1973-80, Jewish Hosp. Med. Center, Bklyn., 1976-80, St. Vincent Hosp., N.Y.C., 1976-88, Mamonides Hosp., Bklyn., 1976-78, Passaic Gen. Hosp., 1977-88, Westchester (N.Y.) County Hosp., 1977-78, Yonkers (N.Y.) Profl. Hosp., 1978-79, Westchester Sq. Hosp., 1978-84, Yonkers Gen. Hosp., 1980-89, St. Joseph Hosp., Yonkers, 1980-89; clin. prof. surgery N.Y. Med. Coll., 1974-89; dir. KPMG Health Care, Japan, 1997—; chmn., prof. dept. health care adminstrn. Shumei U., Tokyo, $D, 1999—. Author: (in Japanese) A Chaos of American Medicine, 1987, Japanese Doctor, 1987, Where American Medicine Is Going, 1988, Major Surgery Without Blood Transfusion, 1990, Problems and Solutions of American Medicine, 1991, Warning for Modern Medical Science (New Medical Ethics), 1992, Comparative Studies of Medical System in the World, 1992, The Changing Face of Geriatrics, 1994, Monologue of Japanese American Physician, 1995, Environmental Medicine, 1998, Japan! Do Not Follow American Health Care System, 1998, Quality of Life in Modern Medicine, 1998, Medicine About Life and Death, 1998, 99, Why AIDS Can Not Be Conquered, 1999, Mechanism of Human Body, 2000; author 10 med. monograms, 1968-80; editor Japanese Med. Planner Ltd.; contbr. over 700 articles to profl. jours. Recipient Hektoen Bronze medal AMA, 1965, Gold medal, 1971. Fellow Am. Coll. Angiology, Am. Coll. Chest Physicians, Am. Coll. Cardiology, Internat. Coll. Surgeons, N.Y. Acad. Medicine; mem. Am. Assn. Thoracic Surgery, N.Y. Soc. Thoracic Surgery, Pan-Pacific Surg. Assn., Internat. Cardiovascular Soc., Am. Geriatric Soc., Am. Fedn. Clin. Rsch., Am. Writers Assn. Achievements include invention of single pass low prime oxygenator; pioneer aortocoronary direct bypass surgery, open heart surgery without blood transfusion.

HIROTA, SHIGERU, medical educator; b. Tokyo, Aug. 7, 1960; s. Minoru and Kimie (Fukamachi) H. MD, Gunma U., Maebashi, Japan, 1986; PhD, Niigata (Japan) U., 1995. Fellow Gunma U., Maebashi, 1986-87, Niigata U., 1987-92; vice-chmn. Akita (Japan) Red Cross Hosp., 1992-95, 96—; vis. prof. So. Ill. U., Springfield, 1995-96. Contbr. articles to profl. jours.; reviewer Gastroenterology, U.S., 1994—, The Cancer Jour., Europe, 1995—. Mem. AAAS, Am. Assn. Cancer Rsch, Anticancer Therapeutics and Oncology. Avocations: tennis, golf. Home: 1-8-9 Chuuou, Warabi Saitama 335, Japan Office: Akita Red Cross Hosp/Gastro, 222-1 Nawashirosawa Saruta, Kamikitade Akita 010-1495, Japan

HIROYASU, SHUNGO, surgeon; b. Onomichi, Hiroshima, Japan, Dec. 14, 1962; s. Misao and Mutsue Okamoto; m. Wakaba Miyake, Aug. 2, 1993; 1 child, Ryu. MD, Nat. Def. Med. Coll., Tokorozawa, Saitama, Japan, 1987; PhD, Ryukyu U., Nishihara, Okinawa, Japan, 1999. Cert. in medicine. Resident Nat. Def. Med. Coll., 1987-89, clin. fellow, 1989-93; postdoctoral fellow Ryukyu U., Nishihara, 1993-97, asst. lectr., 1997—. Contbr. articles to profl. jours. Mem. Japan Surg. Soc., Japanese Soc. Gastroenterology. Avocations: golf, diving, gardening, skiing. Fax: 098-895-5993. E-mail: hiroyasu@med.u-ryukyu.ac.jp. Office: U Ryukyu Sch Medicine, 207 Uehara Nishihara cho, Okinawa 903-0125, Japan

HIROYUKI, HASHIMOTO, engineering educator; b. Yubari, Hokkaido, Japan, Aug. 27, 1938; s. Masaji and Teruko Hashimoto; m. Noriko Hashimoto, Apr. 29, 1966. BSc, Tohoku U., Japan, 1961, MC, 1963; PhD, Tohoku U., 1966. Lectr. Tohoku U., 1968-70, assoc. prof., 1970-78, prof., 1978-96; sr. mng. dir. Ebara Rsch. Co., Fujisawa, Japan, 1996-2000, v.p., 2000—. Mem. ASME, AIAA, Japan Soc. Mech. Engring., Japan Soc. Multiphase Flow, Inst. Liquid Atomization Spray Sys. Buddhist. Achievements include patents for vibration pumps (Japan). Office: Ebara Rsch Co, Honfujisawa 4-2-1, Fujisawa Japan

HIRSCH, ERHARD, educator; b. Leipzig, Germany, Apr. 24, 1928; s. Walter and Elisabeth (Otto) H.; m. Irmgard Ewert, Jul. 27, 1957; children: Annette, Wolfgang. Diploma, Martin Luther Univ., Halle, Germany, 1953. Lectr. of classical languages Univ. Halle, 1954-93, professorship, 1993; prof. emeritus, 1994. Author: Dessau Woerlitz: Englightment & Early Classic, 1985, 2nd edit., 1987, Dessau im Gartenreich, 1994; editor: Carl August Boettiger: Reise nach Woerlitz 1797, Jour. for Woerlitz, 1971, Dessau Woerlitz Beitraege, 1988—. V.p., pres. Dessau Woerlitz Commn., U. Halle, 1967—. Recipient Monuments Culivation prize Gov. of Saxony-Anhalt, 1997, Leibniz prize Acad. of Sci. of Berlin, 1983. Home: Fischer von Erlach Str 11, G 06114 Halle Germany

HIRSCH, ETIENNE CHARLES, neurobiologist; b. Paris, Mar. 18, 1958; s. Henri and Maria (Fischer) H.; m. Agathe Naline, Oct. 3, 1981; children: Julien, Laure, Anne-Flore. Biochemistry master, U. Paris, 1983, PhD, 1988. Rschr. French Rsch. Ministry, Paris, 1983-87; first class rschr. CNRS, Paris, 1988-93, rsch. dir., 1993—; cons. Biocom, Les Ulis, France, 1987-93; mem. bd. Scientific Bd. of Hosp. Salpetriere, Paris, 1993—, Scientific Bd. Forneurobiology at Inserm, Paris, 1995—. Contbr. articles to profl. jours. Mem. Soc. for Neurosci. (Washington), Soc. of Neuroscis. (Paris), Soc. Neuropathology. Avocations: golf, travel. Home: 10 Rue D'Anjou, 78000 Versailles France

HIRSCH, MARTIN ALAN, dentist; b. N.Y.C., Mar. 26, 1947; s. Arthur Morris and Lillian (Brachfeld) H.; m. Noreen Ellen Hirsch, July 20, 1980; children: Jennifer, Kimberly. BS, CUNY, 1968; DMD, U. Pa., 1972; splty. in prosthondontics, U. Iowa, 1975; splty. in maxillofacial prosthetics, U. Chgo., 1976. Dental extern The Coatsville (Pa.) Hosp., 1971-72; dental intern Mt. Sinai Hosp., N.Y.C., 1972-73; resident VA Hosp., Iowa City, 1973-75, U. Chgo. Hosp. and Clinics, 1975-76; asst. prof. dept. otolaryngology Abraham Lincoln Sch. of Medicine U. Ill. Med. Ctr., Chgo., 1976-77; dir. maxillofacial prosthetics clinic Ctr. for Craniofacial Anamolies U. Ill. Med. Ctr., Chgo., 1976-77; asst. prof. U. Ill. Coll. Dentistry, Chgo., 1977-93; staff dept. dentistry U. Ill. Hosp. Med. Ctr., Chgo, 1979-83; staff dept. surgery dental section Cuneo Hosp., Chgo., 1979-87, Cabrini Hosp., Chgo., 1979-92; staff dept. dentistry Ill. Masonic Med. Ctr., Chgo., 1979—, mem. head and neck treatment ctr., 1981—; sr. staff Columbus Hosp. dept. surgery dental sect., Chgo., 1979-98; pvt. practice gen., cosmetic and prosthetic dentistry Chgo., 1979—; attending Cath. Health Ptnrs., Chgo., 1998—; adj. instr. U. Chgo. Hosps. and Clinics, 1975-76; spkr. dental confs., symposiums, seminars; made presentations to lay audiences on radio and TV. Spkr. Am. Cancer Soc., Chgo. divsn., 1981-87, chmn. profl. edn. com., 1981-85, mem. oral cancer com., 1982-86. Mem. ADA, Ill. Dental Soc., Chgo. Dental Soc. Avocations: swimming, reading. Home: 1578 Hazel Ln Winnetka IL 60093-1313 Office: 2800 N Sheridan Rd Chicago IL 60657-6156

HIRSCH, MICHAEL LEE, social studies educator, mayor; b. Mar. 22, 1957; s. Ronald Raymond and Rosemary Hirsch; Carol Jane Moczygemba, Sept. 5, 1987. BA, U. Wis., Milw., 1980, MA, 1984; PhD, U. Tex., 1990. Lectr. U. Wis., Milw., 1986-88; instr. Lawrence U., Appleton, Wis., 1988-90; vis. asst. prof. St. Norbert Coll., DePere, Wis., 1990-92; assoc. prof. sociology Ctrl. Meth. Coll., Fayette, Mo., 1992-98, prof., 1999—, Barker-Oakes disting. prof. social scis., 1998—; facilitator City Vote Electoral Democracy Conf., 1997. Contbr. chpts. to books, articles to profl. jours.; presenter papers in field. Mem. City Coun., Fayette, 1994-98, mayor of Fayette, 1998—; bd. dirs. Fox Valley Fair Housing Coun., Appleton, 1990-92, Sr. Ctr., Fayette, 1994-99; mem. ethics bd. Lenoir Retirement Cmty., Columbia, Mo., 1992-99; mem. Fayette Area Heritage Assn.; mem. Soc. for Better Fayette Cmty.; mem. Fayette Area Betterment Group; mem. Howard County Tourism Coun., Mid-Mo. Solid Waste Dist. Recipient Congl. citation, 1994. Mem. Am. Sociol. Assn., Soc. for Study of Symbolic Interaction, Midwest Sociol. Soc., Soc. Study Applied Sociology, Mo. Sociol. Assn., Rotary Internat. Avocations: reading, weight lifting, travel, community service. E-mail: mhirsch@cmc2.cmc.edu. Home: 200 N Vine St Fayette MO 65248-1180 Office: Ctrl Meth Coll 411 Central Methodist Sq Fayette MO 65248-1129

HIRSCH, PAUL J., orthopedic surgeon, medical executive, educator; b. Bklyn., Oct. 12, 1937; s. Morris M. and Dorothy (Wolitzer) H.; 1 child, Jeremy S. BA in English, Roanoke Coll., 1957; MD, U. Va., 1961. Diplomate Am. Bd. Orthopedic Surgery. Intern NYU-Bellevue Med. Ctr., N.Y.C., 1961-62, resident, 1964-68; chief orthopedic surgery Raritan Valley Hosp., Green Brook, N.J., 1969-71; pvt. practice orthopedic surgery Bridgewater, N.J., 1971—; clin. prof. orthopaedic surgery Seton Hall Sch. Grad. Med. Edn.; vice chmn., bd. dirs. MIIX Group, Inc.; pres., med. dir. InterMedix, Lawrenceville, N.J.; emeritus staff, orthopaedic svc. Somerset (N.J.) Med. Ctr.; courtesy staff Robert Wood Johnson U. Hosp., New Brunswick, N.J.; clin. asst. prof. orthopedic surgery Rutgers Med. Sch., 1971-79; clin. instr. orthopedic surgery NYU-Bellevue Med. Ctr., 1969-79; clin. assoc. prof. orthopedic surgery N.J. Med. Sch., 1980—; clin. prof. orthopedic surgery Seton Hall Sch. Postgrad. Medicine; chmn., bd. trustees Jour. Bone and Joint Surgery, 1999; mem. practicing physicians adv. group Nat. Com. Quality Assurance, 1996-98. Chmn. publs. com. Jour. Med. Soc. N.J., 1980-85; contbr. articles, editor profl. jours.,; mem. editorial bd. N.J. Medicine; editor-in-chief N.J. Medicine. Trustee Rutgers Prep. Sch., pres. bd. trustees, 1983-86; trustee Raritan Valley C.C.; bd. dirs. N.J. Med. Polit. Action Com., 1983—, chmn. N.J. Com. for Quality Orthopedic Care; bd. trustees Orthopaedic Rsch. and Edn. Found., 1989-94. Mem. ACS, AMA, Am. Orthopaedic Assn., Am. Acad. Orthopaedic Surgeons (bd. councilors 1982-88), Am. Coll. Physician Execs., Eastern Orthopaedic Assn. (trustee 1981-84), N.J. Orthopaedic Soc. (pres. 1979-80), Med. Soc. N.J. (chmn. orthopaedic sect. 1977-78, ho. of dels. 1976—, treas. 1982-86, 2d v.p. 1986-87, 1st v.p. 1987-88, pres. elect 1988-89, pres. 1989-90, trustee 1982-91), Somerset County Med. Soc., Acad. Medicine of N.J. (chmn. orthopaedic sect. 1975-78, trustee 1978-91, 95—, pres. elect 1982-83, pres. 1983-84), Am. Trauma Soc. (pres. ctrl. Jersey unit 1977-81), Internat. Soc. Orthopaedic Surgery and Traumatology, N.J. Health Scis. Group (treas. 1982-83), N.J. Hosp. Assn. (trustee 1986-89), N.J. Assn. Med. Splty. Socs. (pres. 1979-80, dir. 1981-85), Ind. Sch. Chmn. Assn., Med. Inter-Ins. Exch. N.J. (bd. govs. 1987-90), N.J. State Med. Underwriters, Inc. (bd. dirs. 1990-99, vice chmn. bd. dirs. 1991-99). Office: Green Knoll Profl Park US Hwy 202-206 Bridgewater NJ 08807-1746

HIRSCH, PETER BERNHARD, metallurgist; b. Berlin, Jan. 16, 1925; arrived in Eng., 1939, naturalized, 1946.; s. Ismar and Regina (Less) H.; m. Mabel Anne Kellar Stephens, July 22, 1959; stepchildren: Janet Susan Caldwell, Paul Roderick Noel Kellar. BA, Cambridge (Eng.) U., 1946, MA, 1950, PhD, 1951; DSc (hon.), Newcastle U., 1979, City U., 1979, Northwestern U., 1982; ScD, East Anglia U., 1983; D Eng., Liverpool U., 1991, Birmingham U., 1993. Rschr. on structure of coal Cavendish Lab. Cambridge U., 1950-53, ICI fellow, 1953-55, rschr. on plastic deformation of metals, 1955-58, asst. dir. rsch. on physics, 1957-58, univ. lectr. physics, 1958-64, univ. reader physics, 1964-66, fellow Christ's Coll., 1960-66, hon. fellow Christ's Coll., 1978; hon. fellow Imperial Coll., London, 1988, St.

Catharine's Coll., 1982; mem. U.K. Atomic Energy Authority, 1982-94, chmn., 1982-84; Isaac Wolfson prof. metallurgy, head dept. metallurgy and sci. Oxford U., 1966-92, prof. emeritus, 1992—; fellow St. Edmund Hall, 1966—; hon. prof. Beijing U. of Sci. and Tech., 1986—; chmn. metallurgy and materials com., mem. engring. bd. Sci. Rsch. Coun., 1970-73; mem. Coun. Sci. Policy, Electricity Supply Rsch. Coun., 1969-82, Adv. Com. Safety of Nuclear Installations, 1977-82; mem. equipment subcom. U. Grants Com., 1977-83; mem. tech. adv. bd. Monsanto Electronic Materials Co., 1985-88; mem. tech. adv. com. Advent, 1982-91; dir. Cogent Ltd., 1985-89; chmn. Isis Innovation Ltd., 1988-96; chmn. tech. adv. group Structural Integrity, 1993—; chmn. materials processes adv. bd. Rolls Royce, plc, 1996-2000; non-exec. dir. Rolls Royce Assocs. Ltd., 1994-97; dir. Oxford Med. Image Analysis Ltd., 2000—. Co-author: Electron Microscopy of Thin Crystals, rev. edit., 1977; editor: The Physics of Metals II-Defects, 1975, Topics in Electron Diffraction and Microscopy of Materials, 1999; co-editor: Progress in Materials Science, vol. 36, 1992, Fracture, Plastic Flow and Structural Integrity, 2000; contbr. articles to profl. jours. Created knight bachelor, 1975; recipient C.V. Boys prize Inst. Physics and Phys. Soc., 1962, Wihuri (Finland) Internat. prize, 1971, Arthur von Hippel award Materials Rsch. Soc., 1983, Wolf prize in physics Wolf Found., 1983-84, Disting. Scientist award Electron Microscopy Soc. Am., 1986, Holweck prize Inst. Physics and French Phys. Soc., 1988, Gold medal Japan Inst. Metals, 1989, Acta Metallurgica Gold medal, 1997. Fellow Royal Soc. (Hughes medal 1973, Royal medal 1977, coun. 1977-79), Inst. Physics (coun. 1968-72), Franklin Inst. (life, Clamer medal 1970), Royal Microscop. Soc. (hon.); mem. Royal Acad. Scis., Letters and Fine Arts of Belgium (assoc.), Inst. Metals (coun. 1968-73, Rosenhain medal 1961), Metals Soc. (coun. 1076-82, Platinum medal 1976), Materials Sci. Club (A.A. Griffith medal 1979), Academia Europaea, Materials Rsch. Soc. India (hon.), Japanese Soc. Electron Microscopy (hon.), Chinese Electron Microscopy Soc. (hon.). Jewish. E-mail: peter.hirsch@materials.ox.ac. Home: 104A Lonsdale Rd, Oxford OX2 7ET, England Office: U Oxford Dept Materials, Parks Rd, Oxford OX1 3PH, England

HIRSCH, RICHARD GARY, lawyer; b. L.A., June 15, 1940; s. Charles and Sylvia (Leopold) H.; m. Claire Renee Recsei, Mar. 25, 1967; 1 child, Nicole Denise. BA, UCLA, 1961; JD, U. Calif., Berkeley, 1965. Bar: Calif. 1967, U.S. Dist. Ct. (ctrl. dist.) Calif. 1967, U.S. Supreme Ct. 1972, U.S. Ct. Appeals (9th cir.) 1989, U.S. Dist. Ct. (ea. dist.) Calif. 1991. Dep. dist. atty. L.A. Dist. Atty.'s Office, 1967-71; ptnr. Nasatir, Hirsch & Podberesky, Santa Monica, Calif., 1971—; commr. Calif. Coun. Criminal Justice, 1977-81; mem. Spl. Com. on Cts. in the Media/Judicial Coun. Calif., 1979. Co-author: California Criminal Law Proceedings/Practice, 1st edit., 2d edit., 3rd edit., 4th edit. Pres. bd. trustees Santa Monica Mus. Art, 1984-91; chmn. Greek Theatre Adv. Com., L.A., 1976-79; mem. L.A. Olympic Organizing Com., 1981-84; bd. dirs. Ocean Park Cmty. Ctr., 1995—, bd. chair, 1997—. Recipient Spl. Merit Resolution, L.A. City Coun., 1984, Criminal Def. Atty. of Yr. award Century City Bar Assn., 1996. Fellow Am. Bd. Criminal Lawyers (bd. dirs., v.p. 1998—); mem. Calif. Attys. Criminal Justice (pres. 1987, bd. trustees), Criminal Cts. Bar Assn. (pres. 1981, Spl. Merit award 1988), L.A. County Bar Assn. (Criminal Def. Atty. of Yr. 1999), Santa Monica C. of C. (bd. dirs. 1995-97). Avocations: cooking, reading, community service. Office: Nasatir Hirsch Podberesky 2115 Main St Santa Monica CA 90405-2215

HIRSCH, STUART, orthopaedic surgeon; b. N.Y.C., June 7, 1941; m. Lisa; children: Todd, Scott. MD, U. Va., 1966. Diplomate Am. Bd. Orthopaedic Surgeons. Intern Downstate Med. Ctr., N.Y.C., 1966-67, resident in surgery and trauma, 1967-68; resident in orthopedic specialty tng. Downstate Med. Ctr., 1970-73; A-O fellowship Basel, Switzerland, 1973; chmn. dept. orthopaedics Somerset Med. Ctr., Somerville, N.J.; cons. in field. Capt. USAF, 1968-70. Fellow Am. Coll. Surgeons; mem. Am. Orthopaedic Assn. (exec. com.), Am. Acad. Orthopedics (treas., bd. dirs. 1997—, fin. com. chmn., resolutions com.), N.J. Orthopedic Soc. (exec. com. 1979—, pres. 1986, chair/ethics com. 1984, program com. chmn. 1982), Somerset Med. Ctr. (chmn. dept. orthopaedics 1997—, chmn. emergency dept. 1995—, mem. exec. com. 1986-95), Somerset County Med. Soc. (exec. com. 1990—, county del., ethics com. chair), SICOT, N.J. Acad. Medicine, Arthroscopy Assn. of N.Am.

HIRSCHBERG, JENÖ, otolaryngologist; b. Miskolc, Borsod, Hungary, May 11, 1928; s. Jenö and Gizella (Schmeisz) H.; m. Clara Safáry, July 20, 1954; children: Andor, Henrik. MD, Semmelweis Med. U., Budapest, Hungary, 1952, otorhinolaryngologist, 1957, phoniatrician, 1979, pediat. otorhinolaryngology, 1980, audiologist, 1996; DSc, Hungarian Acad. Scis., 1985. MD Hosp. for Aviation Medicine, 1956; specialist in otorhinolaryngology Heim Pál Children's Hosp., Budapest, 1956-67; chmn., prof. ENT dept. Heim Pál Hosp. for Sick Children, Budapest, 1975-93; chief phys. ENT dept. Madarász Children's Hosp., Budapest, 1967-75, sci. cons. Phoniatrics and Cleft Palate Ctr., 1993—. Author: Hearing Impairment in Children, 1978, Velopharyngeal Insufficiency, 1986; co-author: (with T. Szende) Pathological Cry, Stridor and Cough in Infants, 1982, Pathologische Schreistimme, Stridor und Hustenton im Säuglingsalter, 1985; editor: Cleft Lip and Cleft Palate, 1996, Cleft Palate and Velopharyngeal Insufficiency, 1997; co-editor: (with Gy. Szépe and E. Vass-Kovács) Papers in Interdisciplinary Speech Research, 1972, (with Z. Lábas) Pediatric Oto-rhino-laryngology, 1988; mem. various editl. bds.; co-author 10 more books; contbr. over 260 articles to sci. pubs.; patentee in field. Capt., air physician Hungarian Army Air Force, 1952-56. Mem. Hungarian Soc. Oto-rhino-laryngologists (bd. dirs., Cseresnyés medal 1996), Hungarian Assn. Phonetics, Phoniatrics and Logopedics (hon. pres. 1994—, Kempelen medal 1968, bd. dirs.), Union of European Phonatricians (pres. 1978-79, mem. Gen. Sec. 1983-91, Gutzmann medal 1980, bd. dirs.), European Soc. Pediat. Oto-rhino-laryngology (pres. 1982-86, bd. dirs.), Internat. Assn. Logopedics and Phoniatrics (chmn. cleft palate com. 1986—, bd. dirs. 1974-80, 89-95), Internat. Assn. Phonosurgeons (bd. dirs. 1990—), Internat. Fedn. Oto-rhino-laryngology Socs. (mem. standing com. phoniatrics and voice care 1995—), Schweizerische Gesellschaft für Phoniatrie, Logopädie und Audiologie (hon.), Osterreichische Gesellschaft für Logopädie, Phoniatrie und Pädaudiologie (hon.), others. Office: Childrens Hosp ENT Cleft Pl, Madarasz u 22/24, 1131 Budapest Hungary

HIRSCHBERG, WOLFGANG HARRY GEORG, physician, researcher; b. Gelsenkirchen, Germany, Feb. 22, 1954; s. Rudolf and Irmgard (Leites) H.; m. Annette Luise Anschütz, May 13, 1988; children: Mairena, Valerian, Leander. Med. Diplomate, U. Frankfurt, Germany, 1980, MD magna cum laude, 1982. Staff psychiatrist Psychiat. Hosp., Kiedrich, Germany, 1982-83; sci. fellow Univ. Hosp., Frankfurt, 1983-84; staff neurologist Neurologic Hosp., Bad Homburg, GErmany, 1984-85; staff psychiatrist Ctrl. Inst., Mannheim, Germany, 1985-87; staff child and adolescent psychiatrist Pfalzinstitut, Klingenmunster, Germany, 1987-93, head physician, 1993-98; pvt. practice Karlsruhe, Germany, 1998—. Contbr. articles to profl. jours. Office: Amalienstrasse 23, D-76133 Karlsruhe Germany

HIRSCHFIELD, ALAN JAMES, entrepreneur. BS, U. Okla.; MBA, Harvard U. V.p. Allen & Co., Inc., 1959-67; v.p. fin., dir. Warner Bros. Seven Arts, Inc., 1967-68; with Am. Diversified Enterprises, Inc., 1968-73; pres., CEO Columbia Pictures Industries, N.Y.C., 1973-78; vice chmn., COO 20th Century-Fox Film Corp., L.A., 1979-81, chmn. bd., CEO, 1981-85; cons., investor entertainment industries, L.A., 1985-89; mng. dir. Wertheim Schroder & Co., L.A., 1990-92; co-CEO, co-chair Data Broadcasting Corp., 1990-2000, dir., 2000—; bd. dirs. Cantel Internat., Inc., Chyron Inc.; dir. CBSmarketwatch.com, Jackpot, Inc., 1998—; vice-chair JNet Enterprises, 2000—. V.p. bd. dirs. Cure for Lymphoma Found., 1998; bd. dirs. Nat. Mus. Am. Indian George Gustav Heye Ctr., 1997—; trustee Grand Teton Music Festival, 1998—. Office: PO Box 7443 Jackson WY 83002-7443

HIRSCHHORN, BERNARD, educator, historian, researcher, writer; b. N.Y.C., Aug. 23, 1922; s. Benjamin and Pauline (Schechner) H. BSS cum laude, City Coll. N.Y., 1943; MA in History, Columbia U., 1944, PhD in History, 1981. Licensed tchr., chmn. Bd. Examiners of Bd. Edn. N.Y. High sch. social studies tchr. Bd. Edn., N.Y.C., 1952-65, high sch. chmn., 1965-91; rschr., writer N.Y.C., 1991—; adj. asst. prof. history Bd. Higher Edn., N.Y.C., 1947-76; dir. N.Y.C. Coun. on Economic Edn., 1980's; asst. examiner Bd. Examiners of City of N.Y., 1965-1980s; assoc. Seminar on The City Columbia U., 1976—. Author: The Perilous Presidency, 1979, Words and Issues: From 'Slivers' to Missiles, 1985 (N.Y. Times paperback), Democracy Reformed: Richard Spencer Childs and His Fight For Better Government, 1997; author: (with others) The Encyclopedia of New York City, 1995, Dictionary of American Biography, 1995, Walt Whitman: An Encyclopedia, 1998, A Global Encyclopedia of Historical Writing, 1998, Scribner's Encyclopedia of American Lives, 1999, Historical Dictionary of the Gilded Age, 2000, Encyclopedia of the American Civil War, 2000; bibliographer: Richard Spencer Childs, The Urban History Newsletter, 1996, 97; guest editor Urban History (Mag. History issue), 1990; reviewer: Social Education, The New American Poverty, 1985, Boston's Wayward Children: Social Services for Homeless Children, 1830-1930, (Mag. History issue) 1990, Good-bye Machiavelli: Government and American Life, (History issue) 1998, The History Tchr., The Great Depression, 1999; contbr. articles to profl. jours. and newspaper. pvt. U.S. Army, 1946-47. Recipient NEH award Harvard U., 1983, Tufts U., 1984, Brandeis U., 1985, Brown U., 1986, Princeton U. and St. Andrews (Scotland) U., 1987; Fulbright scholar Institut d'Etutes Politiques, Paris, 1963, English-Speaking Union scholar Oxford (Eng.) U., 1982. Mem. Nat. Coun. History Edn., Org. Am. Historians, Urban History Assn., Soc. Historians of the Gilded Age and Progressive Era, Nat. Civic League, New Eng. Historical Assn. Democrat. Jewish. Avocations: attending cultural events (including films), nature walks, beach walking, swimming. Home: 301 E 21st St New York NY 10010-6534

HIRSCHKLAU, MORTON, lawyer; b. N.Y.C., Mar. 9, 1932; s. Joseph I. and Sylvia (Kleiner) H.; m. Martha R. Silverstein, June 21, 1953; children: Mitchell L., Deborah E. Hirschklau Loeber, Susan I. AB, Syracuse U., 1953, JD, 1959. Bar: N.Y. 1959, N.J. 1960, U.S. Supreme Ct. 1963, U.S. Ct. Appeals (3d cir.) 1982. Law sec. Superior Ct. N.J., Paterson, 1959-60; assoc. Theodore D. Rosenberg, Esquire, Paterson, 1960-63; ptnr. Hirschklau, Wasserman & Welch, Oakland, N.J., 1963-73; pvt. practice Fair Lawn, N.J., 1973-76; ptnr. Hirschklau, Feitlin & Trawinski, Fair Lawn, 1976-84, Muscarella, Hirschklau, Bochet, Feitlin, Trawinski & Edwards, Fair Lawn, 1984-90, Karas, Kilstein, Hirschklau, Feitlin & Youngman, Fair Lawn, 1990-99, Morton Hirschklau, Esq. and Assocs., 1999—; planning bd. atty. Borough of Fair Lawn, 1961-65, Borough atty., 1965, 81-83; planning bd. atty., Borough of Emerson, 1967-71, zoning bd. atty., 1971-83; zoning bd. atty. Village of Ridgewood, 1977—, Borough of Saddle River, 1996—; spl. counsel Bergen County Park Commn., Paramus, N.J., 1987-88; chmn. N.J. Supreme Ct. Com. on Ethics, 1987-88. Bd. dirs., atty. Fair Lawn Mental Health Ctr., 1965—; bd. dirs., past pres. Opportunity Ctr., Inc., Fair Lawn; pres. Fair Lawn Clean Govt. Assn., 1968-70. Lt. USNR, 1953-56. Mem. N.J. Bar Assn., Bergen County Bar Assn. (chmn. real estate com.), Fair Lawn Rotary Club (past pres.). Avocations: golf, tennis, collecting porcelains. Office: 9-10 Saddle River Rd Fair Lawn NJ 07410-5721

HIRSCHMANN, FRANZ GOTTFRIED, aerospace executive; b. Kempten, Germany, Oct. 4, 1945; came to U.S., 1973; s. Kurt Rudolf G. and Linda (Krieger) H.; m. Cindy Villarica, Nov. 27, 1992; children: Dillon G., Michael A. BS, FWG Coll., Cologne, Germany, 1965; MA, U. Bonn, Germany, 1973; MBA, Pepperdine U., 1981. Mktg. mgr. Western U.S. and S. Am. regions United Techs./Ambac, L.A., 1978-80; mktg. mgr. Western U.S. and Pacific regions Buehler Inc., L.A. and N.C., 1981-83; mgr. internat. mktg. Gen. Dynamics, Pomona, Calif., 1983-84, mgr. info. svcs., 1984-88, mgr. spl. projects, 1988-89; mgr. bus. devel. and market rsch. Hughes Aircraft Co., Canoga park, Calif., 1989-93, mgr. strategic planning, 1993-98; mgr. bus. analysis Boeing, Anaheim, Calif., 1999—; owner Hirschmann Industries (Entertainment Co.), 1992—. Author: Mandaic Inscription, 1970; inventor deciphering lang. computer. Vol. Lincoln Club, L.A., 1981; co-founder Retinitis Pigmentosa Found. Mem. Nat. Mgmt. Assn., Pepperdine U. Alumni Assn. (exec. bd.), Sierra Club (leader, vice chmn. coun. 1990-93). Democrat. Lutheran. Avocations: photography, hiking, sailing, yoga, ancient languages. Home: PO Box 5251 Fullerton CA 92838-0251 Office: Boeing ICS 3370 E Miraloma Ave Anaheim CA 92806-1911

HIRSCHY, JAMES CONRAD, radiologist; b. Kalaupapa, Hawaii, July 6, 1938; s. Ira Dwight and Florence (Moeller) H.; m. Jill Spiller, Oct. 5, 1965; children: Philip, Julia, Thomas. AB, Princeton U., 1960; MD, Jefferson Med. Coll., 1964. Diplomate Am. Bd. Radiology. Intern Pa. Hosp., Phila., 1965; resident N.Y. Hosp., N.Y.C., 1965-68, asst. radiologist, 1968-97; radiologist, out-patient dept. Hosp. for Spl. Surgery, N.Y.C., 1968-99; ptnr., pvt. practice N.Y.C., 1968-94; univ. diagnostic med. imaging radiologist Doshi Diagnostics, 1994-98; mem. cons. staff radiology Calvary Hosp., Bronx, 1997-99; with Doshi Diagnostics, 1999—; cons. Squibb Corp., Union Carbide, N.Y.C., 1968-88, Exxon Corp., N.Y.C., 1968-90, N.Y. Telephone Co., N.Y.C., 1970-94, Life Extension Inst., 1992-94. Author: (with others) Computed Tomography of Spine, 1983; contbr. articles to profl. jours. Capt. USAR, 1965-72. Fellow N.Y. Acad. Medicine, Am. Coll. Chest Physicians; mem. N.Y. State Radiol. Soc. (del.), Met. Opera Club (pres. 1990-92), N.Y. Roentgen Soc. Republican. Roman Catholic. Achievements include research on imaging lumbrosacral spine. Address: 333 E 57th St # 2A New York NY 10022-2950

HIRSH, BERNARD, supply company executive, consultant; b. Seguin, Tex., July 18, 1916; s. Samuel and Sarah (Marks) H.; m. Johanna Charlotte Cristol, Feb. 14, 1941 (dec. Jan. 1977); children: Richard, Robert, Terry, Cristy; m. Beatrice Castelle, Feb. 11, 1978. BA, U. Tex., 1939, LLB, JD, 1939. Bar: Tex. 1939. Claims rep. Handley Claim Svc., Dallas, 1939-41; spl. agt. War Food Adminstrn., U.S. Govt., Dallas, 1941-44; pres. Milliners Supply Co., Dallas, 1945-82, chmn. bd., 1982-85, chmn., owner, 1985—. Pres. Temple Emanu-El Brotherhood, Dallas, 1960-62, Temple Emanu-El, Dallas, 1970-72, Nat. Fedn. Temple Brotherhoods, N.Y.C., 1974-76; chancellor Jewish Chautauqua Soc., N.Y., 1970-72. Mem. Dallas Bar Assn., State Bar Tex., Columbian Country Club. Avocations: travel, reading. Office: Milliners Supply Co 911 Elm St Dallas TX 75202-3112

HIRSHMAN, CAROL ANN, anesthesiology educator; b. Mont., Que., Can., Aug. 12, 1944; came to U.S., 1969; d. Philip and Susan (Lubert) Ditkofsky; m. John A. Hirshman, Jan. 31, 1970; 1 child, David. BSc, McGill U., Mont., 1965, MD, 1969. Instr. U. Colo. Med. Ctr., Denver, 1974, asst. prof., 1974-75; asst. prof. U. Oregn. Health Sci. Ctr., Portland, 1976-80, assoc. prof., 1980-84, prof., 1984-86; prof. Johns Hopkins Hosp., Balt., 1986-98; H. Bendixen prof. anesthesiology, vice chair rsch., prof. pharmacology Columbia U., N.Y.C., 1998—. Editor: Anesthesiology, 1986-95; contbr. numerous articles to profl. jours. Recipient numerous NIH grants. Office: Columbia U Coll P&S P&S Box 4C 630 W 168th St New York NY 10032-3702

HIRST, PAUL HEYWOOD, retired education educator; b. Huddersfield, Yorkshire, Eng., Nov. 10, 1927; s. Herbert and Winifred (Michelbacher) H. BA in Math., Cambridge U., 1948, MA, 1951; MA, Oxford U., 1955; DEd (hon.), Coun. Nat. Academic Awards, Eng., 1992. postgrad. cert. in edn., Cambridge U., 1952; academic diploma in edn., U. London, 1954. H.S. tchr. in Math. various schs., Eng., 1948-55; lectr., tutor, Dept. Edn. Oxford U., 1955-59; lectr. in Philosophy of Edn. U. London Inst. Edn., 1959-65; prof. Edn. U. London Kings Coll., 1965-71; prof. Edn., fellow Wolfson Coll., Cambridge U., 1971-88, emeritus prof. Edn., emeritus fellow, 1988—; vis. prof. U. London Inst. Edn., 1991—, U. B.C., 1964, 67, U. Malawi, 1969, U. Edmonton, Alta., 1988, Sydney, 1988; mem. govt. inquiry into edn. of ethnic minority children, 1981-85; dir. govt. rsch. project on tchr. tng., 1982-86; mem., chmn. Univs. Coun. for the Edn. of Tchrs., 1970-88. Author: Knowledge and the Curriculum, 1974, Moral Education in a Secular Society, 1974, (with R.S. Peters) The Logic of Education, 1970; editor, contbr.: Educational Theory and Its Foundation Disciplines, 1983; co-editor, contbr.: Philosophy of Education: The Analytic Tradition, 1998; mem. editl. bd. Jour. Philosophy Edn., 1968—, Brit. Jour. Tchr. Edn., 1980—, McGill Jour. Edn., 1984—. De Carle lectr. U. Otago (New Zealand), 1976; Fink lectr. U. Melbourne, 1976. Mem. Royal Norwegian Soc. Scis. and Letters (overseas), Philosophy of Edn. Soc. (honorary v.p.), Royal Inst. Philosophy Coun., Athenaeum. Avocation: music (especially opera). Home: Flat 3, 6 Royal Crescent, Brighton BN2 1AL, England

HIRTLE, STEPHEN C., information sciences educator; b. Oak Park, Ill., Nov. 6, 1954; s. Russell C. and Janet L. (Bolles) H. BA, Grinnell Coll., 1976; MA, U. Mich., 1978, 80, PhD, 1982. Asst. prof. SUNY, Albany, 1982-87; asst. prof. U. Pitts., 1987-89, assoc. prof., 1989-99, prof., 1999—; chair dept. info. sci., U. Pitts., 1992—. Co-editor Spatial Cognition & Computation, 1998—. Mem. Classification Soc. N.Am. (pres. 1998-99). Office: Dept Info Sci U Pitts Pittsburgh PA 15260

HIRVELÄ, ANTTI JUHANI (JUSSI HIRVELÄ), marketing professional; b. Helsinki, Finland, June 16, 1962; s. Jouko Paavo and Aija Leena (Aartela) H.; m. Jutta Kaisa Nieminen, July 13, 1991; 1 child, Jesse. Grad., Comml. Coll., Hameenlinna, Finland, 1983; MTT, Inst. Mktg., Helsinki, 1985; MBA, Turku (Finland) Sch. Econs., 1998. Mng. dir. MRes H & N, Hml, Finland, 1981-84; mktg. informer Raisio Group, Helsinki, 1984-88, market rsch. mgr., 1988-91; product mgr. Raisio Margarine, Raisio, Finland, 1991-94; mktg. mgr., dir. Raisio Margarine, Raisio, 1996—; project mgr. Benecol, Raisio, 1994-96; tchr. Mktg. Inst., Helsinki, 1986-91; mem. creative advtsg. team. Actor The Noble Man Turku City Theatre, 1996. Pres. Round Table, Naantali, 1996—. Lt. Finnish Army, 1983-84. Mem. Jr. C. of C., Margarine Assn. (v.p. 1997—). Avocations: theatre, golf, race driving, playing trumpet. Office: Raision Margarine, Ph 101, 21201 Raisio Finland

HISAMA, TOSIAKI, special education psychologist, educator; b. Imari, Saga-Ken, Japan, May 8, 1930; came to U.S., 1963; s. G.T. and Mika (Tashiro) K.; m. Kay K. Hisama, Apr. 8, 1960; children: Fuki Marie, Ellie M. BS, Keio U., Tokyo, 1954, U. Tokyo, Tokyo, 1956; MS, Western Reserve U., Cleve., 1965; PhD, U. Oreg., Eugene, 1971. Chief psychologist Musashi Mental Hosp., Tokyo, Japan, 1956-63; staff psychologist Eastern State Hosp., Williamsburg, Va., 1965-67; assoc. dir. Experienced Tchr. Edn. Program/So. Ill. U., Carbondale, Ill., 1971-94; from asst. to assoc. So. Ill. U., Carbondale, Ill., 1971-94; prof. Kansai Gaidai U., Osaka, Japan, 1994—; prof. Kansai Gaidai U., 1994—; presenter in field. Contbr. over 50 academic articles to profl. jours. Recipient Fullbright Scholarship, U.S. Govt., Washington, 1963. Home: 38-19 Ogura-higashi-machi, Osaka 573-1174, Japan Office: Kansai Guidai U, 16-1 Kita-Katahoko-cho, Osaka 517 1101, Japan

HISCOCK, SIMON JOHN, botanist, researcher, educator, artist; b. Newbury, Berkshire, Eng., June 11, 1963; s. Lesley John Peter and June Rose (Penny) H. BA with honors in Botany, Oxford U., 1985, MA in Botany, 1991, DPhil Plant Scis., 1993. Schoolmaster biology Mary Hare Grammar Sch., Newbury, Eng., 1986-87, St. Bartholomews Sch., Newbury, 1988-90; BBSRC David Phillips Rsch. fellow dept. plant scis. Oxford U., 1997—; jr. rsch. fellow Worcester Coll., Oxford, 1994-96, sr. rsch. fellow, 1997—; lectr. St. Hildas Coll., Oxford, 1996—, Worcester Coll., Oxford, 1996—; tutor biol. sics. Corpus Christi Coll., Oxford, 1998—. Contbr. articles to profl. jours.; artist over 200 bot. paintings. Fellow Linnean Soc. London. Avocations: water color artist, plant photography, botanical illustration, cricket, orchid hunting. Home: Minnibrook Cottage, Winterbourne, Newbury RG16 8BA, England Office: U Oxford Dept Plant Scis, South Parks Rd, Oxford OX1 3RB, England

HISE, MARK ALLEN, dentist; b. Chgo., Jan. 17, 1950; s. Clyde and Rose T. (Partipilo) H. AA, Mt. San Antonio Coll., Walnut, Calif., 1972; BA with highest honors, U. Calif., Riverside, 1974; MS, U. Utah, 1978; DDS, UCLA, 1983. Instr. sci. NW Acad., Houston, 1978-79; chmn. curriculum med. coll. prep program UCLA, 1980-85; instr. dentistry Coll. of Redwoods, Eureka, Calif., 1983; practice dentistry Arcata, Calif., 1983—; participant numerous radio and TV appearances. Editor: Preparing for the MCAT, 1983-85; contbr. articles to profl. jours.; speaker in field. Recipient awards for underwater photography; Henry Carter scholar U. Calif., 1973, Calif. State scholar 1973, 74, Regents scholar U. Calif., 1973; Calif. State fellow, 1975, NIH fellow, 1975-79. Mem. AAAS, ADA, Calif. Dental Assn., Acad. Gen. Dentistry, Nat. Soc. for Med. Rsch., North Coast Scuba Club. Roman Catholic. Avocation: underwater photography. Home and Office: 1225 B St Arcata CA 95521-5936

HISERT, GEORGE A., lawyer; b. Schenectady, N.Y., Sept. 18, 1944. BS summa cum laude, Brown U., 1966, MS, 1966; JD cum laude, U. Chgo., 1970. Bar: Calif. 1971. Law clk. to Hon. Sterry R. Waterman U.S. Ct. Appeals (2nd cir.), 1970-71; ptnr. McCutchen, Doyle, Brown & Enersen, San Francisco, 1977-93; now ptnr. Brobeck, Phleger & Harrison. Mem. editl. bd. Chgo. Law Rev., 1969-70; ABA sect. on bus. law liaison to UCC Permanent Editl. Bd. Mem. ABA (subcom. letter of credit, subcom. secured trans. of uniform comml. code com. bus. law sect., subcom. on syndications and loan participations of comml fin. svc. com., bus. law sect.), Internat. Bar Assn. (banking law com., bus. law sect.), State Bar Calif. (uniform comml. code com. bus. law sect., vice-chair 1992-93, chair 1993-94), Am. Coll.Comml. Fin. Lawyers, Order of Coif, Sigma Xi. Office: Brobeck Phleger & Harrison Spear St Tower One Market Plz San Francisco CA 94105

HISHIDA, ATSUYUKI, researcher; b. Higashiosakashi, Osaka, Japan, June 20, 1970; s. Koji and Shizue (Sato) H. BS in Forestry, Tokyo U. Agr., 1994, MS in Forestry, 1996, PhD in Forestry, 1999. Tchr. h.s. Kaisei Gakuen, Tokyo, 1996-99; rsch. Nat. Inst. Health Scis., Ibaraki, Japan, 1999—. Mem. Japan Wood Rsch. Soc., Mycological Soc. Japan, Japanese Soc. Horticultural Sci., Japanese Soc. Pharmacognosy. Avocations: coffee making, sightseeing, classical music, old Japanese literature, mushroom hunting. Office: Nat Inst Health Scis Tsukuba Medicinal Plant Rsch Sta, 1 Hachimandai Tsukuba Science City, Ibaraki 305-0843, Japan

HISHINUMA, SHIGERU, molecular pharmacologist; b. Japan, Nov. 18, 1960; s. Toku and Kaneko (Sano) H.; m. Kuniko Matsuo, May 7, 1988; children: Ryo, Yu. BSc, Meiji Pharm. U., 1983, MSc, 1985, PhD, 1988. Vis. scholar in pharmacology U. Cambridge, Eng., 1994-95; asst. prof. pharmacodynamics Meiji Pharm. U., Tokyo, 1988—. Author: Receptor desensitization and Ca2+-signaling, 1996; contbr. articles to profl. jours. including British Jour. of Pharmacology, Jour. Neurochemistry, Japanese Jour. Pharmacology, Folia Pharmacologica Japonica and Biochem. Biophys. Rsch. Comm. Grants-in-aid for scientific rsch. Ministry of Edn., Sci., Sports and Culture of Japan, 1992, 95-98, 2000-2001. Mem. Japanese Pharmacol. Soc. (councilor 1993—), Japanese Biochem. Soc., Pharm. Soc. of Japan. Achievements include research on internalization of histamine H1 receptor, receptor resensitization inhibiting development of its desensitization. Office: Meiji Pharm U Pharmacodynam, Noshio 2-522-1, Kiyose Tokyo 204-8588, Japan

HISKES, DOLORES G., educator; b. Chgo.; d. Leslie R. and Dagmar (Brown) Grant; m. John R. Hiskes; children: Robin Caproni, Grant. Student, U. Ill., Chgo. Presenter workshops in devel. and implementation of tutoring programs and ednl. materials. Author/illustrator: Phonics Pathways, Pyramid, The Short-Vowel Dictionary; developer ednl. games: The Train Game, Blendit!, Wordwatch, The Long and the Short of It. Mem. Assn. Am. Educators, Assn. Ednl. Therapists, Calif. Assn. of Res. Specilaists, Orton Dyslexia Soc., Learning Disabilities Assn., Nat. Right to Read Found., The Calif. Reading Assn., Pubs. Mktg. Assn., Pacific Ednl. Mktg. Assn., Calif. Watercolor Soc., Commonwealth Club of Calif., Bay Area Ind. Pubs. Assn. Avocations: watercolors, travel, reading, exercise. E-mail: dor@dorbooks.com. Office: Dorbooks PO Box 2588 Livermore CA 94551-2588

HITE, CATHARINE LEAVEY, orchestra manager; b. Boston, Oct. 1, 1924; d. Edmond Harrison and Ruth Farrington Leavey; m. Robert Atkinson Hite, Aug. 28, 1948; children: Charles Harrison, Patricia Hite Barton, Catharine Hite Dunn. BA, Coll. William and Mary, 1945. Restoration guide Williamsburg Restoration, 1944-45; asst. edn. dept. Honolulu Acad. Arts, 1945-46; sec., tour guide edn. dept. office chief curator Nat. Gallery Art, 1946-48; opera liason/coord. Honolulu Symphony, 1972-73, asst. to gen. mgr., 1973-75, community devel. dir./opera coord., 1975-77, dir. ops./opera prodn. coord., 1977-79, orch. mgr., 1979-84, mem. exec. com., 1965-69, pres. women's assn., 1965-66; com. chmn., opera assn. chmn. Hawaii Opera Theatre, 1966-69. Mem. W. R. Farrington Scholarship Com., 1977—, chmn., 1982-94; mem. community arts panel State Found. Culture and the Arts, 1982, State Found. Music and Opera, 1984; docent Iolani Palace, 1990—; docent Honolulu Acad. Arts, 1996—. Mem. Jr. League, Alliance Française, Hawaii Watercolor Soc. Mem. Phi Beta Kappa. Episcopalian.

HITES, BECKY E., financial executive; b. Oceanport, N.J., Sept. 24, 1964; d. Robert William and Beatrice Everitt (Beck) H. BBA in Econs., West Ga. Coll., 1986; MBA in Fin., Ga. State U., 1992. Pers. asst. The Robinson-

Humphrey Co., Inc., Atlanta, 1986-88, rsch. asst., 1988-89, analyst asst., 1989-92, sr. analyst asst., 1992-95, fin. analyst, 1995-96; mergers and acquisitions Kurt Salmon Assocs., Atlanta, 1996-98; corp. fin. BT Alex Brown, 1998-99; v.p. M. Hecht & Assocs., N.Y.C., 1999—; guest lectr. MBA program Ga. State U., 1995, State U. West Ga., 1998, 99, 2000. Patron Ga. Shakespeare Festival, 1986—; vol. Com. to Elect Paul Coverdell, 1992. Mem. Assn. for Investment Mgmt. and Rsch. (program com. ann. conf. 1996), Inst. Chartered Fin. Analysts (Cert. of Achievement 1993-95), Assn. of Women in Metal Industries (Atlanta chpt. program chair 1995-96, treas. 1997-98, co-chair conf. 1998,), N.Y.C. Soc. Fin. Analysis, Beta Gamma Sigma, Omicron Delta Kappa. Baptist.

HITOTUMATU, SIN, mathematics educator; b. Tokyo, Mar. 6, 1926; s. Mitosi and Yayoi (Nakayama) H.; m. Mutuko Chikasue, May 30, 1964; children: Akira, Takesi. BS, U. Tokyo, 1947, ScD, 1954. Assoc. prof. St. Paul's U., Tokyo, 1952-55; prof. St. Paul's U., 1962-69; assoc. prof. U. Tokyo, 1955-62; prof. math. Kyoto (Japan) U., 1969-89, prof. emeritus, 1989—; prof. dept. computer scis. Tokyo Denki U., Hatoyama, Japan, 1989-2000. Mem. Math. Soc. Japan (exec. 1970-75), Info. Processing Soc. (chmn. numerical analysis sect. 1984-88), Japan Assn. math. Edn. (adviser 1987). Office: Tokyo Denki U, Hatoyama Town Ishisaka, Hatoyama 350-03, Japan

HITTLE, JAMES DONALD, writer, business consultant; b. Bear Lake, Mich., June 10, 1915; s. Harry F. and Margaret Jane (McArthur) H.; m. Edna Jane Smith, Dec. 9, 1939 (dec. 1969); children: Harry McArthur, James Richard; m. Patricia Ann Herring, Sept. 5, 1970. B.A., Mich. State U., 1937; M.S. in Oriental History and Geography, U. Utah, 1952. Commd. 2nd lt. USAR cav., 1937; resigned USAR, 1937; directly commd. 2nd lt. USMC, 1937, advanced through grades to brig. gen., 1958, legis. asst. to comdt., 1952-58; asst. to sec. def. legis. affairs, 1958-60, ret., 1960; dir. nat. security and fgn. affairs VFW, 1960-67; syndicated columnist Copley News Service, 1964-69; mil. commentator MBS, 1964-69; dir. DISC, Inc., 1960-67; spl. counsel Senate Armed Services Com., 1968-69; cons. House Armed Services Com., 1968-69; founder, dir. D.C. Nat. Bank, 1965-69; asst. sec. navy for manpower and res. affairs, 1969-71; sr. v.p. govt. affairs Pan Am. World Airways, Washington, 1971-73; cons. to adminstr. VA, 1973-77; cons. to pres. Overseas Pvt. Investment Corp., 1974-75; participant comml. air mgmt. survey S.E. Asian Transp. and Communications Commn., 1975; cons. Gleason Assocs. Inc., 1974-90, LTV Aerospace and Def. Corp., 1975-88, Marriott Corp., 1975—, KMS Industries, Inc., 1985-90; comdt. U.S. Marine Corps, 1979-81; sec. U.S. Navy, 1981-82; counselor to Sec. of Navy, 1982-87; mem. adv. com. USN Postgrad. Sch. 1983-87, 89-94. Author: History of the Military Staff, 1949; also articles; editor: Jomini's Art of War, 1945; columnist: Navy Times, 1974-95, N.Y. Times Regional Newspapers, 1993—. Bd. dirs. Stafford County (Va.) Indsl. Devel. Authority, 1974-88, 90-96, vice chmn., 1993-96; vice chmn. Belleau Woods U.S. Mil. Cemetery Meml. Day Svcs., 1978—. Decorated Legion of Merit with combat V, Purple Heart, Medal of Combat Merit France, Cross of Chevalier, Mil. Order European Vets.; recipient Alfred Thayer Mahan award Navy League U.S., 1960, Scroll of Honor, 1967, silver medal City of Paris, 1961, gold medal, 1972, George Washington award Freedom Found., 1967, 69, Selective Svc. Sys. Disting. Svc. award, 1971, U.S. Navy Civilian Disting. Svc. award, 1971, 87, Meritorious Pub. Svc. citation U.S. Marine Corps, 1981, Outstanding Alumnus award Mich. State U., 1987, Disting. Alumni award Coll. Arts and Letters, 1994, Commemorative medal China duty, Republic of China, Commemorative medal Murmansk convoy svcs., Russian Fedn. Mem. VFW, Am. Legion, Brit. Legion (hon.), La. State Hist. Soc. (hon. life), Mil. Order World Wars, Clan MacArthur Soc. Am., Navy League, U.S. Marine Corps League (legis. com. 1980-82), Battleship Assn. U.S., 1st Marine Div. Assn. (life), 3d Marine Div. Assn. (life), Co. Mil. Historians, Mil. Order of Carabao, China-Burma-India Vets. Assn., China Marine Assn., Sons of Union Vets. of Civil War, Sons of the Revolution, Naval and Maritime Correspondents Circle, USS Washington Reunion Group, Army-Navy Club of Washington (pres. 1983-87, pres. emeritus 1988—), Phi Kappa Phi, Phi Kappa Delta. Address: 3137 14th St S Arlington VA 22204-4330

HITTMAIR, OTTO HEINRICH, physics educator; b. Innsbruck, Austria, Mar. 16, 1924; s. Rudolf and Margarete (Schumacher) H.; m. Anni Rauch, Dec. 3, 1956; children: Christine, Elisabeth, Georg, Margarete. PhD, U. Innsbruck, 1949, dozent, 1953; DTech (hon.), Tech. U. Budapest, 1982. Vis. scientist Inst. Advanced Studies, Dublin, 1951, MIT, Cambridge, Mass., 1951-52; attache CNRS, Paris, 1952-54; sr. fellow U. Sydney (Australia), 1954-56; vis. scientist Comision Nacional de Energia Atomica, Buenos Aires, 1957; scientist Atomic Inst. Austrian Us, 1958-60; prof. physics Tech. U. Vienna, 1960-92, prof. emeritus, 1992—, dean Faculty Scis., 1968-89, rector, 1977-79. Author: (with S.T. Butler) Nuclear Stripping Reactions, 1957, Quantum Theory, 1972, (with G. Adam) Theory of Heat, 1971, 4th edit., (with H. Weber) Superconductivity, 1979, (with H. Hunger) Academy of Sciences—Development of an Austrian Research Institution, 1997. Recipient Jubilee medal U. Innsbruck, 1970, prize for sci. and tech. City of Vienna, 1982, Wilhelm Exner medal Austrian Trade Assn., 1980, Prechtl medal Tech. U. Vienna, 1996. Mem. Austrian Acad. Scis. (sec. 1983-87, pres. 1987-91, v.p. 1991-97, Erwin Schrödinger prize 1974), Internat. Soc. Engring. Edn. (v.p. 1973-97, Ring of Honor 1997), Royal Soc. Scis. Uppsala, Austrian Phys. Soc., European Sci. Found. (exec. coun. 1983-89). Roman Catholic. Office: Tech U, Karlspatz 13, A-1040 Vienna Austria

HITZIOS, GEORGIOS, chemical engineer; b. Serres, Makedonia, Greece, Nov. 3, 1964; s. Aemilios and Vasiliki (Stamtsi) H. MSc in Chem. Engring., Royal Inst. Tech., Stockholm, 1987. Admission to Tech. Chamber of Greece, 1988. Rschr. dept. chem. tech. Royal Inst. Tech., Stockholm, 1988; lab chemist Castrol AB, Stockholm, 1990-94, Hellenic Sugar Industry SA, Serres, 1994; prodn. supr. liquid detergents divsn. Flos SA, Serres, 1995-99; plant mgr. XPS prodn. Fibran SA, Nigrita, 1999—. Chmn., exec. officer Hellenic Cmty., Uppsala, Sweden, 1993-94; rep. of party orgn. in Sweden to 2d and 3d Congress of Nea Democratia, 1986, 94; mem. Town Coun., Sidirokastro, 1995-98. Mem. Hellenic Soc. Chem. Engrs., Swedish Soc. Chem. Engrs., Planetary Soc. Christian Orthodox. Home: Sahtouri 14, GR-62300 Sidirokastro Greece Office: Fibran SA, GR-62200 Nigrita Greece

HIWAKI, KENSEI, economics educator; b. Ashikita, Kumamoto, Japan, Jan. 21, 1940; s. Tsuneyoshi and Hatsune (Tomizaki) H.; m. Yukiko Aida, Jan. 8, 1982; children: Yoh-Ichi, Yumi, Aimi. BA, Drew U., 1970; MA, Duke U., 1972; PhD, CUNY, 1980. Lectr. Tokyo Internat. U., Kawagoe, Japan, 1980-81, asst. prof., 1982-83, assoc. prof., 1984-85, prof., 1986—; lectr., grad. fellow CUNY, 1975-79; exch. prof. Willamette U., Oreg., 1984; guest prof. Coll. of Europe, Brugge, Belgium, 1990-91. Author, editor Human Systems Management 1989—; contbr. articles to profl. jours. Japanese nat. leader Ship for South-East Asian Youth, 1980; chmn. Campaign for Bldg. Tomorrow's City Tsurugashima, 1994-95. Recipient 20th Century Achievement award Internat. Inst. for Advanced Studies in Sys. Rsch. and Cybernetics, 1999. Mem. Japanese Econ. Assn., Human Systems Mgmt. (editl. bd. 1987—), Internat. Conf. on Systems Rsch., Informatics and Cybernetics (bd. dirs. 1994—). Home: 4-8-3 Isehara, Kawagoe Saitama 350-1108, Japan Office: Tokyo Internat U, 2509 Matoba, Kawagoe Saitama 350-1198, Japan

HIWAKI, OSAMU, information scientist, educator; b. Kitakyushu, Fukuoka, Japan, Sept. 6, 1963. B.Engring., Osaka (Japan) U., 1987, M.Med. Sci., 1989; PhD, Kyushu U., Fukuoka, 1992. Postdoctoral fellow Japanese Soc. for Promotion of Sci., 1992-94; vis. assoc. Calif. Inst. Tech., Pasadena, 1993-94; assoc. prof. dept. info. sci. Hiroshima City (Japan) U., 1994—. Recipient Sakamoto award Japanese Soc. Med. Electronics and Biol. Engring., 1992. Mem. IEEE, Bioelectromagnetics Soc. Office: Hiroshima City U, 3-4-1 Ozuka-Higashi, Hiroshima 731-3194, Japan

HIXON, ROBIN RAY, food service executive, writer; b. Vancouver, Wash., May 4, 1954; s. Charles Donovan and Leona Margaret (Teske) Hixson. Exec. chef, Am. Culinary Fedn., 1972-77; BA in Bus., Purdue U., 1992. Cert. Am. Restaurant Assn., 1992. Apprentice Redlion Inns, Vancouver, 1972-77, exec. chef, 1977-80; exec. chef Hilton Hotel, Baton Rouge, 1981; chief steward Delta Queen Steamboat Co., New Orleans, 1981-86, gen. mgr., 1986-88; exec. chef Icicle Seafoods Inc., Seattle, 1989-92, Sea Spirit Cruise Lines, Inc., 1992-93, Petersburg Fisheries, Inc., Alaska, 1993-96; dir. ops. The Calzone-Co. Inc., Duncan & Ptnrs., Pete's Pizza Inc., Spokane, Wash., 1996-97; writer, layout coord. Dream Works, Seattle, 1997—; cons. RSVP Travel Prodns., Inc., Mlps., 1992—, Arctic Storm, Inc., Seattle, 1998—. Author: American Regional Cuisines, 1987; contbr. articles to profl. jours. Mem. Nat. Trust for Hist. Preservation, 1982-92, Wash. Hist. Preservation, 1990-92, Oreg. Pub. Broadcasting, 1990-92, N.Y. Met. Opera, 1973-80; performer Peruvian Singers, 1972-74, A Chorus-Line, 1975-76, Spokane's Mens Chorus, 1996-97. Mem. Am. Culinary Fedn. (writer 1985-91), Chefs De Cuisine Soc. Oreg. (sgt. at arms 1974-80), N.Y.C. Acad. Theatre and Dance, Am. Film Inst. Democrat. Home: 1701 Broadway St # 262 Vancouver WA 98663-3436

HIYAMA, KEIICHIRO, biochemical engineer, researcher; b. Ibaraki, Osaka, Japan, Nov. 5, 1942; s. Hachiro and Sumie (Harada) H.; m. Miyoko Yakura, May 14, 1972; children: Takeshi, Kayo, Takuya. B of Engring., Doshisha U., Kyoto, Japan, 1965, M of Engring., 1967; DEng, Kyoto (Japan) U., 1977. Rsch. Osaka (Japan) Mcpl. Tech. Rsch. Inst., 1967-78, sr. rsch. staff, 1978-87, assoc. sr. rsch., 1987-91, sr. rsch., 1991—; rsch. assoc. dept. chemistry U. Chgo., 1978-79. Co-author: Biochemical Engineering for 2001, 1992, Better Living through Innovative Biochemical Engineering, 1994. Mem. Am. Chem. Soc., Chem. Soc. Japan (Technol. Devel. award 1999), Soc. Biosci. and Bioengring. Japan, Japanese Biochem. Soc., Biophys. Soc. Japan, Japan Soc. Biosci., Biotech. and Agrochemistry, Kinki Chem. Soc. Avocations: exec. tchr. of Shakuhachi. Office: Osaka Mcpl Tech Rsch Inst, 1-6-50 Morinomiya Joto-ku, Osaka 536-8553, Japan

HIYAMA, TAMEJIRO, research chemist, chemistry educator; b. Ibaraki, Osaka, Japan, Aug. 24, 1946; s. Hachiro and Sumie Hiyama; m. Hisako Tsujimoto, Feb. 15, 1975; children—Kazuko, Taichi, Hitoshi. B., Kyoto U., 1969, M.Eng., 1971; D. Eng., Kyoto U., 1975. Lectr. Kyoto U., Japan, 1972-81; research fellow Sagami Chem. Research Ctr., Sagamihara, Kanagawa, Japan, 1981-83, sr. research fellow, 1983-88, exec. research fellow, 1988-92; prof. rsch. lab. resources utilization, Tokyo Inst. Tech., 1992-97; prof. grad. sch. Kyoto U., 1997—. Co-author: (in Japanese) Highly Selective Synthesis in Organic Chemistry, 1982, Organic Synthesis, 1997. Contbr. articles to profl. jours. Harvard U. fellow 1975-76. Mem. AAAS, Chem. Soc. Japan (Progress award 1980), Kinki Chem. Soc., Assn. Synthetic Organic Chemistry Japan, Am. Chem. Soc., Royal Soc. Chemistry. Home: 8-47 Nishichujo-cho Irabaki, Osaka 567-0887, Japan Office: Divsn Material Chemistry, Grad Sch Kyoto U Yoshida, Sakyo-ku Kyoto 606-8501, Japan

HJÄRPE, JAN ÖSTEN, religion and history educator; b. Göteborg, Sweden, July 13, 1942; s. Eric Georg and Gertrud Elisabet (Persson) H.; m. Marianne Sjöberg, Aug. 16, 1969; children: Erik Mattias, Helena Elisabet, Katarina Maria. BTh, Uppsala (Sweden) U., 1965, BA History of Religions/Semitical Langs., 1967, DTh in History of Religions, 1972. Lectr. history of religions Uppsala U., Umeå U., 1972-76, Åbo Akademi, Finland, 1976; assoc. prof. U. Lund, Sweden, 1976-82, prof. Islamology, 1984—; rsch. officer Nat. Bd. Rsch., Sweden, 1982-84; counselor Fgn. Ministry, Stockholm, 1983-84. Author: Analyse Critique des Traditions Arabes sur les Sabéens Harraniens, 1972, Islam, Lära och Livsmönster, 1979, 85, Politisk Islam, Studier i Muslimsk Fundamentalism, 1983, 90, Islams Värld, 1987, 90, 93, Araber Och Arabism, 1994; contbr. over 300 articles to profl. jours. Com. mem. Global Processes Swedish Coun. for Planning and Coord. of Rsch. Mem. Royal Acad. Letters, History and Antiquities, The Nathan Söderblom Soc., The Royal Soc. of Letters Lund, The New Soc. Letters Lund, Academia Europea, Collegium of Rsch., Swedish Rsch. Inst. Istanbul. Avocations: music, literature. Home: Virvelvindsvägen 4 f, S-222 27 Lund Sweden Office: Dept History Religions, Allhelgona Kyrkogata 8, S-223 62 Lund Sweden

HJELMFELT, DAVID CHARLES, lawyer; b. Chgo., Nov. 25, 1940; s. Allen T. and Doris (Hauber) H.; m. Kendall L. Lawrence, Aug. 17, 1969; children: Trevor Christian, Rebecca Kirstan. AB cum laude, Kans. State U., Manhattan, 1962; LLB, Duke U., 1965. Bar: Kans. 1965, Colo. 1965, D.C. 1973, U.S. Supreme Ct. 1978, U.S. Ct. Appeals (D.C. cir.) 1973, U.S. Ct. Appeals (5th and 11th cirs.) 1981, U.S. Ct. Appeals (10th cir.) 1982. Vis. prof. Sch. Law U. Okla., Norman, 1970-71; staff atty. U.S. AEC, Albuquerque, 1971-73; ptnr. Goldberg, Fieldman & Hjelmfelt, Washington, Colo., 1973-78; sole practice Fort Collins, Colo., 1978-81; ptnr. Hjelmfelt & Larson, Fort Collins, Colo., 1981-90; sole practice Fort Collins, Denver, Colo., 1990-95, Denver, 1995—. Author: Antitrust and Regulated Industries, 1985, Executive's Guide to Marketing, Sales & Advertising Law, 1990; contbr. articles to profl. jours. Mem. coun. liberal edn. Kans. State U.; bd. dirs. Heritage Christian Sch., 1988; bd. dirs. Christian Conciliation Svc., Fort Collins. Lt. JAGC USNR, 1965-68. Mem. ABA (essential facilities monograph com. antitrust sect.), Colo. Bar Assn., Rep. Sen. Inside Circle Club. Office: 1600 Stout St # 1905 Denver CO 80202-3160

HJELM-WALLÉN, LENA, Swedish government official; b. Sala, Sweden, Jan. 14, 1943; m. Ingvar Wallén; 1 child. Attended, U. Uppsala, Sweden. Tchr. Sala, Sweden, 1966-69; M.P. Parliament of Sweden, 1968—; min. without portfolio Govt. of Sweden, 1974-76, min. edn. and cultural affairs, 1982-85, min. internat. devel. cooperation, 1985-91, min. fgn. affairs, 1994-98, dep. prime minister, 1998—; mem. exec. com. Social Dem. Labor Party, 1968, mem. parliament exec., 1976-82, spokeswoman on schs., 1978-87, spokeswoman on edn., 1991-94. Office: Prime Ministers Office, Rosenbad 4, 103 33 Stockholm Sweden

HJERTÉN, STELLAN VILHELM EINAR, biochemist; b. Forshem, Sweden, Apr. 2, 1928; s. Vilhelm Gustav Florentin and Judith Kristina (Johansson) H.; m. Laila Elisabet Woxström, July 24, 1965; 1 child, Marie-Christine. PhD, Uppsala U., Sweden, 1967. Asst. prof. Uppsala U., 1967-69, prof. in biochemistry, 1969—. Mem. editl. bd. several sci. jours.; contbr. numerous articles to profl. jours. and publs.; patentee in field. Recipient The Björkén prize Uppsala U., 1985, Electrophoresis Soc. Founder's award, 1988, Frederick Conf. award, 1993, The Hirai prize, Japan, 1994, Am. Chem. Soc. award 1996, The Torbern Bergman medal The Swedish Chem. Soc., 1996. Office: Uppsala Biomed Ctr, Inst Biochem/Box 576, S-751 23 Uppsala Sweden

HJØRLAND, BIRGER, information scientist; b. Naerum, Denmark, Jan. 1, 1947; s. Helge Benjamin and Hilma (Samberg) H.; m. Ida Rabes, Aug. 22, 1981; children: Jesper, Peter. MA in Psychology, U. Copenhagen, 1974; PhD in Libr. & Info. Sci., U. Gothenburg, Sweden, 1993. Rsch. librarian, coord. computer-based info. scis. Royal Libr., Copenhagen, Denmark, 1968-90; head dept. Royal Sch. Libr. & Info. Sci., Copenhagen, 1990—; prof. Coll. of Boraas, Sweden, 2000—; lectr. Royal Sch. Libr. & Info. Sci., 1973-78; external lectr., U. Copenhagen, 1983-86. Author: Information Seeking and Subject Representation: An Activity-Theoretic Approach to Information Science, 1997; contbr. articles to profl. jours.; mem. editl. bd. Online Info. Rev., Internat. Yearbook of Libr. and Info. Mgmt.; referee Jour. Am. Soc. Info. Sci. Served in Danish Army, 1965-66. Home: Tordisvej 16, DK-2880 Bagsvaerd Denmark Office: Ryal Sch Libr Info Sci, 6 Birketinget, DK-2300 Copenhagen Denmark also: Coll of Boraas, S-501 90 Boraas Sweden

HJORTDAL, OLAV, retired oral surgeon; b. Sykkylven, Sunmøre, Norway, Sept. 26, 1929; s. Ole and Karoline (Straumsheim) H.; m. Ragnhild Drabløs, 1955; children: Kristin, Ole Johan. Diploma, Norges Tannlegehøgskole, Olso, 1954, U. Oslo, 1966. Asst. dept. oral surgery and oral medicine U. Oslo, 1964-67, lectr., 1968; asst. Rudolf Virchof KH, Berlin, 1969-70; oral surgeon dept. oral surgery Lillehammer County Hosp., Norway, 1978-97, retired, 1997. Contbr. articles to profl. jours. Avocations: salmon fishing, hunting, music. Home: Kirkegt. 12, 2609 Lillehammer Norway

HJORTH, JAN E., retired entrepreneur, small business consultant; b. Stockholm; arrived in France, 1998; s. Sven E.G. and Solbritt E. (Djurling) H.; m. Christina Eywor Treu, Sept. 9, 1963 (dec. 1982); children: Peter, Charlotte; m. Christina B. af Klercker. MSc, Royal Tech. U., Stockholm, 1962; grad. advanced mgmt. program, Harvard U., 1972. Commd. officer Royal War Sch., Stockholm, 1954; head dept. A. Johnson & Co., Stockholm, 1962-71, head tech. mktg. function, 1971-77; pres., owner Newtech AB, Stockholm, 1977-82; mng. dir. Newtech Devel. AB, Stockholm, 1982-86; head Swedish Eureka Secretariat NUTEK, Stockholm, 1986-93; pres., owner EuroAdvice AB, Stockholm, 1993-96; chmn. bd. dirs. Nordtech GmbH, Hamburg, Germany, 1978-82, SME Bus. Support AB, Lidingö, 1993-96; bd. dirs., owner, Newtech Far East Pty., Singapore, 1979-82; komanditeur Proscan GmbH, Salzburg, Austria, 1995-99; Swedish del. East-West Trade Seminar, UN Econ. Coun., Geneva, 1975; expert on com. for tech. trade Swedish Ministry of Trade, 1979-81. Contbg. author: UN Licensing Manual, 1977; initiator, editor: The Eureka SME Guide, 1991-92. Auditor Licensing Exec. Soc., Sweden, 1976-77. Fellow St.Örjans Gille. Avocations: sailing, golf, history, literature. Home: La Grande Gazagne, FR-30360 Cruviers Lascours France Office: Nordtech KEG, S:t Julien strasse 31/5st, A 5020 Salzburg Austria

HJORTH, NIELS, environmental service company executive; b. Frederiksberg, Copenhagen, Denmark, Oct. 31, 1934; s. Otto Martin and Lilly Astrid Marie Johanne (Lyng) H.; m. Bitten Ida Clemens Pedersen, Mar. 2, 1957; children: Gerd, Malene, Ole. MSc in Chem. Engring., Tech. U. Denmark, 1959; diploma, European Coll., Bruge, Belgium, 1973, Danish Sch. Pub. Adminstrn., 1985. Rsch. fellow Roskilde Slagteriernes Forsknings Inst., 1961-63; head chem. lab. N. Foss Electric, Hilleroed, Denmark, 1963-65; insp. factories Danish Working Environ. Svc., Copenhagen, 1965-73, prin. adminstr., 1975-77; dep. area dir. Danish Working Environ. Svc., Slagelse, Denmark, 1977-85; area dir. Danish Working Environ. Svc., Copenhagen, 1985-94; prin. adminstr. European Union Commn., Luxembourg, 1973-75; chief tech. adviser Nat. Working Environ. Authority, Copenhagen, 1994—; councellor European Union Commn., World Bank, Danida, 1973-96; pres. FEANI, 1987-94; pres. com. on risk assessment Danish Acad. Tech. Scis., 1985-92. Contbr. articles to profl. jours., project documents, proposals, and appraisals. Lt. Royal C.E., 1959-60. Mem. Soc. Danish Engrs. (pres. 1981-85), Danish Soc. for Working Environ. (pres. 1977-79). Avocations: photography, sailing, hiking, jazz music. Home: Pile Allé 31 Noedebo, DK-3480 Fredensborg Denmark Office: Nat Working Environ, Authority Landskronagade 33, DK-2100 Copenhagen Denmark

HLA, SEIN WAI, microbiologist, researcher; b. Yangon, Myanmar, Apr. 28, 1955; arrived in New Zealand, 1997; d. Maung Maung and Sein (Bwint) H.; m. Kyaw Zeya, Nov. 29, 1985; children: Pwint, Wai, Kyaw. MBBS, Inst. Medicine, Yangon, Myanmar, 1980; D Bacteriology, Inst. Medicine, 1986; MS, Nat. U. Singapore, 1998. Civil asst. surgeon Ministry of Health, Yangon, 1982-83; microbiologist Inst. Medicine, Yangon, 1983-91; rsch. student microbiology and medicine Nat. U. Singapore, 1992-95; rsch. fellow dept. of medicine Wellington Sch. of Medicine, U. Otago, 1998—. Recipient Myanmar Outstanding Student scholarship, 1972, Nat. U. Singapore Rsch. scholarship, 1992. Mem. Singapore Soc. Microbiology, Microscopy Soc. Singapore. Buddhist. Avocations: swimming, cooking. E-mail: well.sleep@xtra.co.nz. Fax: 04-479-2069. Home: 38 Lincoln Ave, Tawa Wellington New Zealand

HLAVÁČEK, IVAN, mathematician, researcher; b. Náchod, Czech Republic, Mar. 27, 1933; s. Miloslav and Marie (Sakařová) H.; m. Helena Kybicová, Dec. 28, 1961; 1 child, Lucie. CE, Czech Tech U., Prague, 1956, CandSc, 1960; DSc, Acad. Scis. Czech Republic, Prague, 1987. Asst. prof. Czech Tech. U., 1958-63; rsch. worker Inst. Math., Acad. Scis., Prague, 1963-80; sr. rsch. worker Acad. Sci., Prague, 1980—; expert UNESCO, Warangal, India, 1968-69; vis. prof. univs. Rome, Paris, Göteborg, Sweden, London, Jyväskylä, Finland, 1977-89; mem. com. for math. Grant Agy. Czech Republic, Prague, 1993-97. Co-author: Mathematical Theory of Elastic and Elasto-plastic Bodies: An Introduction, 1981, Solution of Variational Inequalities in Mechanics, 1988, Numerical Methods for Unilateral Problems in Solid Mechanics, 1996; contbr. over 100 articles to internat. math. jours. Recipient Bolzano medal Acad. Scis. Czech Republic, 1995. Home phone: 74 778577. Avocation: amateur violinist in a symphonic orchestra. Home: Na Vysluní 19, CZ-10000 Prague 10, Czech Republic Office: Acad Scis Czech Republic, Inst Math, Žitná 25, CZ-11567 Prague 1, Czech Republic

HLAVIČKA, JAN, electrical engineering educator; b. Prague, Czech Republic, Feb. 18, 1942; s. František and Božena (Jägerová) H.; m. Vlasta Mrázová, June 20, 1966; 1 child, Zuzana. Engr., Czech Tech. U., Prague, 1964, DSc, 1987. Rschr. Rsch. Inst. Math. Machines, Prague, 1964-84; asst. prof. Czech Tech. U., Prague, 1984-91, full prof., 1991—, dean faculty elec. engring., 1990-94, vice rector, 1994-97. Author: Diagnostics of Electronic Digital Circuits, 1982. Fellow Instn. Electrical Engrs.; mem. IEEE (sr. mem.), N.Y. Acad. Scis. Avocations: history, music. Office: Czech Tech Univ, Fac of EE Technicka 2, 166 27 Prague 6, Czech Republic

HLENGWA, MSAWAKHE ALMON, educational administrator; b. Umzinto/Dumisa, South Africa, Dec. 3, 1940; s. Alfred Mdipheni and Homlova Malta (Maphumulo) H.; m. Homusa Lillian Mthethwa, June 25, 1977; children: Bongeka Buhle, Thuthuka. BA, U. Zululand, South Africa, 1970; BEd, U. Natal, South Africa, 1974, BA with honors, 1982. Asst. tchr. Dlangewa H.S., 1971-77; prin. Luther H.S., 1978; lectr. U. Natal, 1979-92, sr. lectr., 1993-95, head dept., 1996-99; asst. dir. Yale/Ohio Univs., 1999—; mem. Usibe Rsch. Sub Com., 1995—, KZM Provincial Lang. Com., 1999—; chief examiner Sr. Exam. KZM, 1992-99; mem. Province/Zulu Subject Com. KZN, 1996-99; coord. Usha B.W. Vilaliga award, 1995—. Author: Amazoma, 1992, Amagempe, 1995, Inoeke, 1993, Isi Zulu Samanje, 1995. Co-foounder Udondolo Lwesizwe, Dumisa, 1978—; chairperson Anti Rent Com., Sobantu, 1982-85, Edn. Devel. Com., Dumisa, 1995—. Named Best English, Damelin, 1972. Mem. Usiba Writers Guild, Isi Zulu Subject Com., Provincial Lang. Com. Avocations: tennis, music, reading books. Home: PO Box 101037, Scottsville 3209, South Africa Office: U Natal, PO Box X01, Pietermaritzburg South Africa

HLOZEK, CAROLE DIANE QUAST, business executive; b. Dallas, Apr. 17, 1959; d. Robert E. and Bonnie (Wootton) Quast. BS, BBA, Tex. A&M U., 1982. CPA, Tex. Internal auditor Brown & Root Inc., Houston, 1982-84; asst. contr. Wilson Supply Co., Houston, 1984-86; sr. acctg. supr. Hydro Conduit Corp., Houston, 1986-87; fin. analyst Am. Capital, Houston, 1989-94; dir. adminstrn., CFO, Am. Gen. Securities, Inc., Houston, 1994-98; CFO 1st Fin. Group Am., Houston, 1998-2000; controller, CFO Clearworks, 2000—. Chmn. bd. dirs. On Our Own Inc., 1987-91. Mem. Tex. Soc. CPA's, Mensa, Houston Zool Soc., Houston Livestock Show and Rodeo, CPA's Helping Schs., Houston Mus. Natural History. Home: 13527 Greenwood Manor Cypress TX 77429-4840 Office: Clearworks Net 2450 Fondren Rd Ste 200 Houston TX 77063-2323

HLUPIĆ-VIDJAK, VLATKA, economist educator; b. Zagreb, Croatia, 1965; s. Vladimir and Helena (Muić) H.; m. Hrvoje Dominik, July 16, 1994; 1 child, Tomislav. Diploma in Econs., U. Zagreb, Croatia, 1988; MSc, U%, Croatia, 1990; PhD, London Sch. Econs., 1993. Chartered European engr. Tchg. asst. Faculty of Econs. U. Zagreb, Croatia, 1988-91; rsch. asst. London Sch. Econs., 1992; lectr. dept. info. sys. and computing Brunel U., London, 1993-98, sr. lectr. dept. info. sys. and computing, 1998—; cons. more than a dozen cos.; cons. U. Zagreb, 1996—. Contbr. numerous articles to profl. jours. and papers to confs. Recipient scholarship Croatian Ministry of Sci., Zagreb, 1990, rsch. grant Brunel U., 1994, 97. Mem. IEEE, Brit. Computer Soc., Croatian Simulation Soc., Operational Rsch. Soc. of Gt. Britain, Ednl. Kinesiology Found. Roman Catholic. Avocations: travel, fashion design, singing, reading, painting. Office: Brunel U, Info Sys & Computing Dept, Uxbridge UB8 3PH, England

HO, ANDREW CHUNG-YIN, obstetrician, gynecologist; b. Hong Kong, June 21, 1947; s. Cheung Fai and Pok Man (Wong) H.; m. June Lo-Lin Liau, Sept. 3, 1976; children: Natasha, Cassandra, Vanessa, Desiree, Stanton. MBBS, U. Hong Kong, 1972. Sr. med. and health officer Govt of Hong Kong, 1980-81; pvt. practice ob-gyn., Hong Kong, 1981—; hon. clin. lectr. U. Hong Kong, 1980-81; hon. cons. gynecologist Buddhist Hosp., Hong Kong Hosp. Authority, 1985—. Pres. Hong Kong Youth for Christ, 1989-93; dir. Internat. Christian Assembly Hong Kong, 1980-96. Fellow Royal Coll. Ob-Gyn., Hong Kong Coll. Ob-Gyn., Hong Kong Acad. Medicine; mem. Hong Kong Med. Assn., Singapore Med. Assn., Royal Hong Kong Jockey Club. Avocations: tennis, swimming. Office: Rm 705 Argyle Ctr, 688 Nathan Rd, Kowloon Hong Kong China

HO, ANTHONY MING-HEI, anesthesiology educator; b. Hong Kong, Nov. 26, 1954; s. Wai Hin Ho and Mui Lee; m. LeeAnne Hope Contardi, Sept. 26, 1986; 1 child, Adrienne. BS, Union Coll., Schenectady, N.Y., 1976; MS, Stanford U., 1978; MD, McMaster U., Hamilton, Ont., Can., 1983. Design engr. Nat. Semicondr. Corp., Santa Clara, Calif., 1978-79, Bell-No. Rsch. Ltd, Ottawa, Ont., 1979-80; intern U. Toronto, Can., 1983-84; anes-

thesiology resident McMaster U., Hamilton, Can., 1984-87; cons., pvt. practice Catharines Gen. Hosp. and Hotel Dieu Hosp., St. Catharines, Can., 1987-89, Hamilton (Can.) Health Scis. Corp., 1989-2000; asst. clin. prof. McMaster U., 1989-96, assoc. clin. prof., 1996-99; assoc. prof. anesthesiology Chinese U. Hong Kong, 1999—; staff anesthesiologist Prince of Wales Hosp., Hong Kong; Home phone: 852 2563 6830. Office phone: 852 2632 2735. Please give details of your internship and residencies, give beginning date of any private practice, and give your position at Prince of Wales Hosp. and beginning date. Contbr. articles to med. jours., including Anesthesiology, Jour. Trauma, Can. Jour. Anesthesia, Chest. Recipient faculty citation Vincennese U., 1995. Fellow Royal Coll. Physicians Can.; mem. Internat. Anesthesia Rsch. Soc., Internat. Trauma Anesthesia and Critical Care Soc. (Prospective award 2000). Avocations: swimming, music, gardening. Fax: 852 2637 2422. E-mail: hoamh@cuhk.edu.hk. Home: 1702 A Westlands Gardens, Westlands Rd, Hong Kong China Office: Prince of Wales Hosp, Dept Anes-Intensive Care, Shatin Hong Kong NT, China

HO, CHIH-MING, physicist, educator; b. Chung King, China, Aug. 16, 1945; came to U.S., 1968; s. Shao-Nan and I-Chu Ho; m. Shirley T.S. Ho, Mar. 4, 1972; 1 child, Dean. BSME, Nat. Taiwan U., 1967; PhD, Johns Hopkins U., 1974. Assoc. rsch. scientist Johns Hopkins U., Balt., 1974-75; asst. prof. U. So. Calif., L.A., 1976-81, assoc. prof., 1981-85, prof., 1985-91; prof. UCLA, 1991—, Ben Rich-Lockheed Martin prof., 1996-99; dir. Ctr. for Micro Systems, 1993-2000; cons. Flow Industries, Kent, 1982, Dynamics Tech., Torrance, Calif., 1977, Rockwell Internat., Canoga Park, Calif., 1980-83. Contbr. articles to profl. jours.; patentee in field. Fellow AIAA, Am. Phys. Soc.; mem. Nat. Acad. Engring., Academia Sinica, Phi Beta Kappa. Achievements include research in micro-electro-mechanical systems, biomedical engineering, turbulence, aerodynamics, nois.

HO, CHU EU, civil engineer; b. Singapore, Aug. 26, 1959; s. Ching Yu and Mei Foon (Lim) H.; m. Pee She Patsy Chen; children: Ivan, Vivianne. B in Civil Engring. with hons., Nat. U. Singapore, 1984; MSc, U. London, 1985; DIC, Imperial Coll. London, 1985. Reg. profl. engr., Singapore. Civil engr. Housing Devel. Bd., Singapore, 1984; assoc. Ove Arup & Ptnrs., Singapore, 1986-95; gen. mgr. Presscrete Engring., Singapore, 1995-99; grad. tchg. asst. MIT, 1999—; mem. examining panel Profl. Engrs. Bd., Singapore, 1996—. Recipient Lee Found. award, 1984. Mem. ASCE (mem. protem com. 1996—), Inst. Engrs. Singapore. E-mail: chueuho@mit.edu.

HO, CHUNG-RU, oceanographer, educator; b. Taichung, Taiwan, Nov. 16, 1961. Grad., Nat. Taiwan Ocean U., 1984; PhD, U. Del., 1994. Assoc. engr. EBASCO-CTCI, Taipei, 1988-90; assoc. prof. Nat. Taiwan Ocean U., Keelung, 1994—; cons. EBASCO-CTCI, Taipei, 1996-97. Lt. Taiwan Army, 1986-88. Mem. AGU. Office: Nat Taiwan Ocean Univ, 2 Pei-Ning Rd, Keelung 20243, Taiwan

HO, GEK MUI, chemicals executive; b. Singapore, Singapore, Sept. 26, 1970; d. Nam Seng and Ah (Heng) H.; m. Ming Jie Cai, Jan. 9, 1999. Diploma, Singapore Polytech., 1990, advanced diploma, 1997; grad. diploma, Singapore Inst. Mgmt., 1999; MBA, U. Hull, Singapore, 2000. Lab. technician Union Carbide, Singapore, 1990-92; chemist Union Carbide Asia Pacific Inc., Singapore, 1992-94, application specialist, 1994-98, tech. mgr., 1999—. Mem. NACE, Singapore Soc. Biotech. and Microbiology. Avocations: reading, outdoor activities, bowling, swimming.

HO, HSIU-HWANG, philosophy educator; b. Lo-tung, I-lan, Taiwan, Aug. 29, 1938; s. Yu-lan Ho; m. Fung-oi Lui; children: Tien-Hsiu, Tien-Yin, Jo-Shao. AB, Nat. Taiwan U., Taipei, Taiwan, 1962, MA, 1965; PhD, Mich. State U., 1969. Asst. prof. Calif. State U., Stanislaus, 1969-72; asst. prof. to assoc. prof. to prof. The Chinese U. of Hong Kong, 1972—. Author 29 books; contbr. numerous articles to profl. publs. 2d lt. Taiwan-Republic of China Army, 1962-63. Recipient numerous scholarship and fellowships. Mem. Am. Philos. Assn. Avocations: reading, writing, Chinese calligraphy, star watching, music listening. Home: 22E Blk 5, Laguna City 4150, Hong Kong

HO, HWA-SHAN, engineering executive, civil engineer, consultant, drilling engineer; b. Hualien, Taiwan, Sept. 10, 1941; came to U.S., 1964; s. Tung-Mu and Mien (Lin) H.; m. Rita Ying-Huei Chau, Aug. 24, 1969 (dec. Dec. 1993); m. Jenny Shijin Wang, Oct. 24, 1994; children: Yvonne Y.F., Isaac Y.J., Yvette Y.F. BSCE, Nat. Taiwan U., 1963; MS in Engring., Brown U., 1966, PhD in Engring., 1969. Assoc. in rsch. Brown U., Providence, R.I., 1968-69; asst. prof. civil engring. Univ. So. Calif., L.A., 1969-74; sr. engring. technologist Ralph M. Parsons Co., Pasadena, Calif., 1974-76; assoc. prof. civil engring. U. Utah, Salt Lake City, 1976-81; sr. rsch. specialist Exxon Production Rsch. Co., Houston, 1981-84; cons. scientist Sperry-Sun Drilling Svcs., Houston, 1984-92; pres. Tapong RTI, Inc., Spring-Klein, Tex., 1992—; cons. Diamant Boart Stratabit, Brussels, 1991-95, Geothermal Energy Rsch. & Devel. Co., Tokyo, 1994-96. Mem. Orgn. of Chinese Americans, Houston, 1990—, Chinese Profl. Club (officer 1993), Houston, 1992-94. 2nd lt. USAF, 1963-64, Taiwan. Mem. ASCE, Soc. Petroleum Engrs. Achievements include 10 U.S. patents on directional drilling tech.; first to use software program to correct error in MWD Survey due to drillstring deformations enabling elimination of gyro wireline re-survey; first to devel. comprehensive rock-bit interaction model in drilling trajectory prediction; first to propose designed PDC Bits with specific walk tendencies and anti-walk bits; first to study the effect of drillstring stiffness in torque-drag monitoring calculations; first to propose "compliance-based" torque-drag monitoring; improved self-consistent forward stepping algorithm in trajectory prediction; first to infer formation dip and strike from directional drilling data; rsch. on a new gen. variational method to solve boundary value problems in linear sys. with interfaces, multiple connectivities. E-mail: HwashanHo@aol.com. Home: 5411 Mineral Creek Ct Spring TX 77379-8869 Office: TAPONG RTI INC PO Box 11170 Spring TX 77391-1170

HO, KC, electrical engineering educator; b. Hong Kong, July 28, 1965; Keng Wai Ho and Po Mei Chan. BSc in Engring., Chinese U. Hong Kong, 1983-88, PhD in Electronic Engring., 1988-91. Rsch. assoc. Royal Mil. Coll. Can., Kingston, Ont., 1991-94; mem. sci. staff Nortel Networks (formerly BNR), Montreal, 1995-96; assoc. prof. U. Saskatchewan, Saskatoon, Can., 1996-97; asst. prof. U. Mo., Columbia, 1997—; cons. Nortel Networks, Montreal, 1996—. Contbr. articles to profl. jours.; patentee in field. Mem. IEEE (sr.). Avocation: reading. Office: Dept Electrical Engring Univ Mo Columbia Columbia MO 65211-0001

HO, KEANG-PO, information engineering educator; b. Guangdong, China, Dec. 15, 1968. BS, Nat. Taiwan U., Taipei, 1991; MS, U. Calif., Berkeley, 1993, PhD, 1995. Rschr. Bellcore (now Telcordia Techs.), Red Bank, N.J., 1995-97; prof. dept. info. engring. Chinese U. Hong Kong, Shatin, 1997—. Contbr. articles to profl. jours. HKSAR grantee, 1999. Mem. IEEE. E-mail: kpho@ie.cuhk.edu.hk. Office: Chinese U Hong Kond, Dept Info Engring, Shatin Hong Kong

HO, KHEK YU, gastroenterologist, educator; b. Taiping, Perak, Malaysia, Dec. 9, 1960; s. Lien See and Ah Moy (Yong) H.; m. Margaret Chee-Peng Lim; 1 child, Shin Chang. M.B.B.S. (honours class I), Sydney (Australia) U., 1986; MD, Nat. U. Singapore, 1999. Professorial intern Concord Hosp., Sydney, 1986-87; house physician Waikato Hosp., Hamilton, N.Z., 1987-88; med. registrar Auckland (N.Z.) Hosp., 1988-93; rsch. fellow Nat. U. Singapore, 1993-95, lectr., 1995-97, asst. prof., 1997-2000, assoc. prof., 2000—, elected mem. med. faculty bd., 1999—; sec. Nat. Found. for Digestive Diseases, Singapore, 1995-98; sci. chmn. 2d Nat. Nurses Endoscopy Workshop, Singapore, 1999—; invited faculty Endoscopic Ultrasound Workshop, India, 1999. Assoc. editor Gut issues Nat. Found. for Digestive Diseases, 1995—. Med. advisor Hepatitis Support Group, Singapore, 1997—. Recipient Jan Coppleson Meml. prize for cancer medicine U. Sydney, 1986; China Med. Bd. fellow Nat. U. Singapore, 1997. Mem. ACP, Am. Coll. Gastroenterology, N.Y. Acad. Scis. Avocations: Chinese martial arts, jogging, swimming. Home: Block 54, Toh Tuck Rd #09-01, Singapore 596745, Singapore Office: Nat Univ Hosp Dept Med, 5 Lower Kent Ridge Rd, Singapore 119074, Singapore

HO, KWOK CHIANG, transportation engineer; b. Singapore, Singapore, June 5, 1968; parents Wee Ho and Tong Kiaw Ng; m. Tang Heng Lim, Feb. 14, 1996. BS with honors, Nat. U. Singapore, 1993. Rsch. analyst Def. Sci. Org., Singapore, 1993-96; project officer Ctr. Signal Processing, Nanyang Technol. U., Singapore, 1996-2000; asst. chief tech. officer Addest Technovation Pvt. Ltd., Singapore, 2000—; presentor Internat. Conf. Acoustics, Speech and Signal Processing, 1995, 96, 98. Contbr. articles to profl. jours. Avocations: playing chess, jogging, reading. Office: 20 Ayer Rajah Crescent, 09-19 Technopreneur Ctr, 139964 Singapore Singapore

HO, MAN KAY, solicitor; b. Hong Kong, Aug. 29, 1962; d. Nga Ming and Yuk Mei (Li) Ho; m. Ho Ming Herbert Hui, Aug. 29, 1987; children: Colin Hui King Jeung, Clarice Hui Kar Yee. LLB, Hong Kong U., 1984; MBA, York U., Can., 1987. Bar: Supreme Ct. Hong Kong 1991, Supreme Ct. Eng. and Wales 1991, Australian Capital Ter. 1991, Supreme Ct. Singapore 1995, Supreme Cts. Queensland, NSW and Victoria 1996. Articled clk. Deacons, Hong Kong, 1987-89; solicitor Gallant Y.T. Ho & Co., Hong Kong, 1990-92, Victor Chu & Co., Hong Kong, 1992-95; ptnr. Siao, Wen, Liu & Leung, Hong Kong, 1995-2000; dir. Kinsway Capital Ltd., Hong Kong, 2000—; non-exec. bd. dirs. Rising Devel. Holdings Ltd., Hong Kong. Roman Catholic. Office: Kingsway Capital Ltd, 5/F Hutchison House Central, Hong Kong Hong Kong

HO, PATRICK CHI-PING, ophthalmologist, educator, eye surgeon; b. Hong Kong, July 24, 1949; s. Thomas Shi-yuen and Chan-ha (Cheung) H.; m. Sibella Hu Hui Chung, 1997; children: Jacque Lyn, Patrick Jason. BS, Stetson U., 1972; MD, Vanderbilt U., 1976. Diplomate Am. Bd. Ophthalmology. Rsch. assoc. Eye Rsch. Inst., Boston, 1980-86; clin. fellow Harvard Med. Sch., Boston, 1980-83; clin. asst. prof. dept. ophthalmology U. Calif., San Francisco, 1983-86; sr. lectr. Chinese U. of Hong Kong, 1984-86, reader, 1986-88, prof. ophthalmology, 1988-94; vis. and/or hon. prof. 15 univs. and hosps. in China, 1985—; sr. scientist Hong Kong Biotech. Inst., 1988-94; med. dir. Hong Kong Eye Bank and Rsch. Found., 1985—; mem. exec. com. Hong Kong Eye Bank, 1986—, bd. dirs., chmn. eye tissue lab. com., 1991—, vice-chmn. 1997—; chmn. Hong Kong Eye Found., 1994—; subdean faculty of ophthalmology Hong Kong Coll. Surgeons, 1993-96; mem. preparatory com. Hong Kong Spl. Adminstrv. Region of China, mem. selection com. of first govt., 1996—; vice chmn. Policy Rsch. Inst. of Hong Kong, 1996—; advisor Hong Kong Inst. for Promotion of Chinese Culture, 1995—; hon. dir. Internat. Health Exch. Ctr. of Ministry Health, China, 1995—; mem. Hong Kong Arts Devel. Coun. Contbr. 7 chpts. to books, more than 80 articles and abstracts to sci. publs.; mem. editl. bds. numerous jours. including Jour. AMA, 1984-95, Afro-Asian Jour. Ophthalmology, 1987—, Asia-Pacific Jour. Ophthalmology, 1989—, Jour. Hong Kong Med. Assn., 1991-95, Ocular Surgery News Internat. Edit., 1995—, Fundus of CMA, 1995—. Rep. Chinese People's Polit. Consultative Conv., People's Republic of China, 1993—; mem. Hong Kong Acad. Medicine Found. Fund, 1991—; mem. optometry bd. Supplementary Med. Profession Coun., Hong Kong, 1988-98, chmn. preliminary disciplinary investigation com., 1996-98; mem. human organ transplant bd. Dept. of Health, Hong Kong, 1995—; mem. Preparatory Com. on Chinese Medicine, 1995—; mem. working group on laser safety Com. Sci. and Tech. Hong Kong Govt., 1989-91; mem. Hong Kong Fire Svc. Dept., 1987-90; mem. preparatory com. Hong Kong Spl. Adminstrv. Zone, 1995—; vice chm. Hong Kong Policy Rsch. Inst., 1996—; adviser Hong Kong Inst. Promotion of Chinese Culture, 1995—; hon. adviser Hong Kong Mems. Fedn. Chinese Med. Assn., 1995—; cons. Hong Kong Optometric Assn., 1994—; dir., chief clin. adviser LifeTech Enterprises Hong Kong, 1995—; tech. adviser Sigh First Project, Lions Club Internat. Found., 1993—; bd. dirs. Highlights Internat., 1992—; co-editor Highlights Internat. Chinese edit., 1995—; mem. adv. panel Internat. Ophthalmic Exch. Soc., 1994—; hon. dir. Internat. Health Exchg. Ctr. U. Health, People's Rep. of China, 1993—; co-chmn. We. Pacific Region Internat. Agy. for Prevention of Blindness, 1995—; mem. provisional urban coun. Hong Kong Spl. Adminstrv. Govt., 1997-99, mem. standing com., culture select com., 1997-99; chmn. gen. com. Hong Kong Philharm. Soc., 1997—; mem. Hong Kong Arts Devel. Coun., 1998; chmn. strategic and devel. bd. Hong Kong Arts Devel. Coun., 1998. James P. Miller scholar, 1972-74, The Seeing Eye Inc. scholar, 1974-75, Merck Sharpe and Dohme travel fellow, 1982; numerous lectureships. Fellow ACS, Am. Acad. Ophthalmology; mem. Hong Kong Ophthal. Soc. (chmn. 1986-91, coun. 1985-86), Hong Kong Surg. Laser Assn. (convernor of interim coun. 1989-90, pres. 1990-93), Hong Kong Coll. Surgeons (coun. 1990-93, edn. com. 1991-93), Hong Kong Med. Assn. (coun. 1988-92, chmn. profl. affairs 1990-91, chmn. sci. subcom. 1988-91, dep. hon. sec. 1986-88), Asia Pacific Acad. Ophthalmology (coun. 1985-89, v.p. 1989—), Internat. Intraocular Implant Club, Asia-Pacific Intraocular Implant Assn., Myopia Internat. Rsch. Found., Club Jule's Gonin, others. Fax: 882-25010666. E-mail: cpho724@hkstar.com. Office: 8th Fl Kailey Tower, 16 Stanley St, Central Hong Kong China

HO, ROBERT EN MING, neurosurgeon, educator; b. Honolulu, Nov. 13, 1942; s. Donald Tet En Ho and Violette (Weeks) Gould; m. Edie Olsen, June 27, 1964; children: Lisa, Amy. BS cum laude, Mich. State U., 1964; MD, Wayne State U., 1968. Diplomate Am. Bd. Neurol. Surgery. Surg. intern Detroit Gen. Hosp., 1968-69, surg. resident, 1969-70, neurosurg. resident, 1972-76; microsurg. fellow Neurochirurgische Universtatskilinik, Zurich, Switzerland, 1976; instr. dept. neurosurgery Wayne State U., Detroit, 1977-79; dir. dept. neurosurgery Gertrude Levin Pain Clinic, 1977-80; asst. prof., 1979-84; chief neurosurg. svcs. Health Care Inst., 1979-84; clin. asst. prof., 1984—; founder, dir. Microneurosurg. Lab., 1977-89, dir. spine and spine reconstruction dept. neurosurgery med. sch., 1992-97; dir. neuroscis. intensive care unit Harper Hosp., Detroit, 1980-84, spine and spine reconstruction fellowship Wayne State Med. Sch., 1992-97; mem. audit com. Detroit Gen. Hosp., 1977-80, mem. med. device com., 1977-80, mem. credentials com, 1978-84; sec., treas. Detroit Neurosurg. Acad. Program Com., 1978-84; mem. emergency room com. Harper Hosp., 1980-84, neuroscis. intensive care unit com., 1980-84; dir. Oakland-Macomb PPO; chief neurol. sect. William Beaumont Hosp., Troy, Mich., mem. adv. bd., 1986-90; chmn. adv. com. traumatic brain injury/spinal cord injury, State Mich., 1993-96; presenter of numerous exhibits, profl. papers; organizer numerous med. meetings; lectr. in field. Contbr. articles to profl. jours. Served with U.S. Army, 1970-72, Vietnam. Recipient Intern of Yr. award Detroit Gen. Hosp., 1969. Mem. AMA, ACS, Congress Neurol. Surgeons, Detroit Neurosurg. Acad., Mich. Assn. Neurol. Surgeons (sec.-treas. 1979-82, v.p. 1982-84, pres. 1984-86, bd. dirs. 1986-90), Mich. State Med. Soc., Oakland County Med. Soc., Wayne County Med. Soc., Internat. Coll. Surgeons (U.S. sect.), Am. Assn. Neurol Surgeons (spinal disorders sec. 1981, cerebrovascular surgery sect.). Fax: 810-263-3819. Office: 15520 19 Mile Rd Ste 450 Clinton Township MI 48038-6332

HO, SA VAN, chemical engineer, researcher; b. Gia Dinh, Vietnam, Feb. 15, 1951; came to US, 1970; s. Duong Van Ho and Nguyet Thi Nguyen; m. Huong Mai Hoang, Aug. 1974; 1 child Mai-Lan. BS, U. Calif. Poly., 1974; MS, Cornell U., 1976, PhD, 1978. Engring. assoc. Merck Sharp & Dohme, Rahway, N.J., 1978-80; sr. rsch. engr. Monsanto Co., St. Louis, 1980-82, rsch. splst., 1982-84, sr. rsch. specialist, 1984-86, assoc. fellow, 1986-88; sci. fellow, 1990-95, sr. fellow, dir., 1995—; product devel. mgr. Eastman Kodak, Rochester, N.Y., 1988-90. Recipient award for environ. sustainability Nat. Awards Coun. Environ. Sustainability, 1996-98, for Lasagna tech., 1997. Mem. AIChE, ACS. Achievements include patents for protein purification, 1987, soil remediation, 1995, membrane separation, 1996; development of novel protein precipitation method combining neutral and charged polymers, Lasaga TM technology, an in situ remediation technology, new class of supported polymeric liquid membranes for organics, salts, water separations with applications in wastewater treatment and food processing. Avocations: classical music, philosophy, nature, cultures, travel. Home: 11231 Mosley Farm Ct Saint Louis MO 63141-7663 Office: Monsanto Co 800 N Lindbergh Blvd Saint Louis MO 63167-0001

HO, SHIU FAI, marine design consultant; b. Hong Kong, July 15, 1952; s. Pui and Kit Ming (Mak) H.; m. Ching Lin Chui, Nov. 4, 1981; 1 child, Gilbert Pak Yan. BS in Nautical Studies with Honors, Plymouth (Eng.) Polytech., 1976; MS in Internat. Mktg., U. Strathclyde, Eng., 1990; MBA in Tech. Mgmt., Deakin U., Australia, 1996. Chartered engr. U.K., chartered profl. engr. Australia. Naval architect Hong Kong & Yaumati Ferry Co., Ltd., Hong Kong, 1970-83; owner, prin. HOSF Marine Design Consultant, Hong Kong, 1983—; bd. dirs. Fasinla Ltd., Hong Kong. Author: (case study) Diagnostic Engineering, (Inst. Diagnostic Engrs. 1st prize 1991). Pres. Hong Kong Jaycees 1982. Fellow Inst. Diagnostic Engrs. (U.K.), Inst. Mgmt. (U.K.), Australian Inst. Mgmt.; mem. Soc. Naval Architects and Marine Engrs. (U.S.), Royal Inst. Naval Architects (U.K.), Instn. of Engrs. (Australia), Inst. Measurement and Control (U.K.), Chartered Inst. of Transport (U.K.). Avocation: tennis. Office: HOSF Marine Design Cons, PO Box 98454, Tsimshatsui Hong Kong Hong Kong

HO, THOANG SI, oil and gas executive; b. Dongha, Quangtri, Vietnam, Apr. 10, 1938; d. On Cong and Khec Thi (Ngo) H.; m. Cam Nhung Thi Tran, Feb. 1, 1968; children: Ho Thi Cam Hoai, Ho Hieu Giang. BS in Chemistry, Hanoi (Vietnam) U., 1959; MS in Chemistry, Moscow State U., 1962, PhD in Chemistry, 1967, DSc in Chemistry, 1974; Dr.h.c., Russian Acad. Scis., Moscow, 1992. Asst. prof. Hanoi U., 1962-64; dir. Inst. of Chemistry, Hanoi, 1978-87; v.p. Nat. Ctr. for Sci. Rsch. of Vietnam, 1977-92, pres. Ho Chi Minh City br., 1983-92; pres., CEO Petrovietnam, Hanoi, 1992-96, chmn. bd., 1996—; mem. State Com. for Sci. & Tech. Policy, 1992—; dep. Nat. Assembly of Vietnam, 1997—. Co-author: Modern Problems of Physical Chemistry, 1972; co-author: Activity and Physico-Chemical Properties of High Silica Zeolites and Zeolite Containing Catalysts, 1976; editor-in-chief Jour. of Chemistry, 1978-93; contbr. over 180 articles to profl. jours. Hon. mayor City of Oklahoma City, 1994; decorated Order of Friendship, Russian Fedn., 1997. Mem. Chem. Soc. of Vietnam (pres. 1995—), Am. Chem. Soc. Mem. Vietnam Communist Party. Avocations: ping-pong, tennis, piano, guitar. Home: 710/1 Nguyen Kiem Str, Ho Chi Minh City Vietnam Office: Vietnam Oil and Gas Corp, 69 Nguyen Du/22 Ngo Quyen, Hanoi Vietnam

HO, YAN-KI RICHARD, economics and finance educator; b. Hong Kong, Feb. 9, 1952; s. Yue-Chip and Pui-Luen (Chung) H.; m. Liza Lai-To Poon, July 19, 1984. BS, U. Hawaii, 1975; MS, U. Wis., 1977, PhD, 1979. Rsch. asst. U. Wis., Madison, 1975-79; lectr. Chinese U. Hong Kong, 1979-87; prin. lectr. Hong Kong Bapt. Coll., 1987-88, reader/head of fin., 1988-90, assoc. dir. Bus. Rsch. Ctr., 1988-90; head econs. and fin. City Univ. of Hong Kong, 1990-95; prof. fin., aq. dir. Asia Asia Pacific Fin. Markets Rsch. Ctr. Editor: The Hong Kong Financial System, 1991, The Hong Kong Financial Institutions and Markets, 1986, Hong Kong Economic Papers, 1991; contbr. articles to profl. jours. Mem. Banking Tng. Bd., Vocat. Tng. Coun., 1982—; subject specialist Hong Kong Coun. for Acad. Accreditation, 1988—; part-time mem. Ctrl. Policy unit Hong Kong SAR Govt., 1998—; vice chmn. Hong Kong Policy Rsch. Inst., 1997—. Named Most Outstanding Grad. in Agrl. Econs. in State of Hawaii Western Agrl. Econ. Assn., 1975. Mem. Hong Kong Econ. Assn. (sec. 1983-84), Am. Fin. Assn., Am. Econ. Assn.; assoc. mem. Centre for Pacific Basin Monetary and Econ. Studies. Office: City Poly of Hong Kong, Fac of Bus, Kowloon Hong Kong

HO, YIK HONG, colon and rectal surgeon; b. Singapore, Apr. 21, 1956; s. Peng Yoke Ho and Mei Yiu (Lucy) Fung; m. Chui Wah Ludmilla Tung, Sept. 13, 1984; 1 child, Elaine Jo-Lan. MBBS with honors, U. Queensland, 1980. Intern Princess Alexandra Hosp., Brisbane, Australia, 1980-81, resident, 1981-82; med. officer Sai Ying Pun Hosp./Tang Shiu Kin Hosp., Hong Kong, 1982-83; registrar U. Surg. Unit Queen Mary Hosp., Tung Wah Hosp., Hong Kong, 1983-89; sr. registrar Singapore Gen. Hosp., 1989-93, cons., 1993-98, dir. Pelvic Floor Lab., 1996—, sr. cons., 1998—; vis. staff sr. cons. surg. oncology Nat. Cancer Centre, 1999—; rsch. fellow U. Hosp., U. Nottingham, U.K., 1989; part-time clin. lectr. Nat. U. Singapore, 1990—; dep. chmn. Electronics Med. Records Workgroup, Singapore Gen. Hosp., 1994—; vis. staff, sr. cons. surg. oncologg Nat. Cancer Ctr., Singapore, 1999—. Mem. editl. rev. com. Annals of Acad. of Medicine, 1994—, mem. editl. com., 2000—; mem. editl. com. Singapore Gen. Hosp. Procs., 1995-99, assoc. editor, 1995-98, editor, 1999—; contbr. articles to profl. jours. Scholarship Australian Kidney Found., 1977. Fellow Royal Australasian Coll. Surgeons, Royal Coll. Surgeons (Edinburgh), Royal Coll Physicians and Surgeons (Glasgow), Internat. Coll. Surgeons (Singapore sect. com. mem. 1994-96, 98-99, treas. 97-99, sec. 1999, pres. 2000); mem. Singapore Soc. Continence (v.p. 1993—), Biomed. Rsch. and Exptl. Therapeutics Soc. Singapore (hon. sec. 1993-95, pres. 1995-97), Internat. Soc. Surgery (nat. rep. 1999), Am. Soc. Colon-Rectal Surgeons (mem. internat. adv. com. 2000). Avocations: fitness, computer, photography, swimming, tai-chi. Office: Dept Colorectal Surgery, Singapore Gen Hosp Outram Rd, Singapore 16908, Singapore

HOADLEY, WALTER EVANS, economist, financial executive, lay worker; b. San Francisco, Aug. 16, 1916; s. Walter Evans Sr. and Marie Howland (Preece) H.; m. Virginia Alm, May 20, 1939; children: Richard Alm, Jean Elizabeth (Mrs. Donald A. Peterson). AB, U. Calif., 1938, MA, 1940, PhD, 1946; D in Comml. Sci., Franklin and Marshall Coll., 1963; LLD (hon.), Golden Gate U., 1968, U. Pacific, 1979; hon. degree, El Instituto Technologico Autonomo de Mexico, 1974. Collaborator U.S. Bur. Agrl. Econs., 1938-39; rsch. economist Calif. Gov.'s Reemployment Commn., 1939, Calif. Gov.'s State Planning Bd., 1941; rsch. economist, teaching fellow U. Calif., 1938-41, supr. indsl. mgmt. war tng. office, 1941-42; econ. adviser U. Chgo. Civil Affairs Tng. Sch., 1945; sr. economist Fed. Res. Bank Chgo., 1942-49; economist Armstrong World Industries, Lancaster, Pa., 1949-54, treas., 1954-60, v.p., treas., 1960-66, dir., 1962-87; sr. v.p., chief economist, mem. mng. com. Bank of Am. NT & SA, San Francisco, 1966-68, exec. v.p., chief economist, mem. mng. com., mem. mgmt. adv. council, chmn. subs., 1968-81; ret., 1981; sr. research fellow Hoover Inst., Stanford U., 1981—; dep. chmn. Fed. Res. Bank, Phila., 1960-61, chmn., 1962-66; chmn. Conf. Fed. Res. Chmn., 1966; faculty Sch. Banking U. Wis., 1945-49, 55, 58-66; adviser various U.S. Govt. Agys.; Wright Internat. Bd. Econ. and Investment Advisors, 1987—; spl. adviser U.S. Congl. Budget Office, 1975-87; mem. pub. adv. bd. U.S. Dept. Commerce, 1970-74; mem. White House Rev. Com. for Balance Payment Stats., 1963-65, Presdl. Task Force on Growth, 1969-70, Presdl. Task Force on Land Utilization, Presdl. Conf. on Inflation, 1974; gov. Com. on Developing Am. Capitalism, 1977—, chmn., 1987-88; dir. PLM Internat., 1989-97, Transisco Industries, Inc., 1981-95, Davis/Selected/Venture Advisors, 1981-96. Mem. Meth. Ch. Commn. on World Svc. and Fin. Phila. conf., 1957-64, chmn. investment com., 1964-66; bd. dirs., exec. com. Internat. Mgmt. and Devel. Inst., 1976-97; trustee Pacific Sch. Religion, 1968-89; adviser Nat. Commn. to Study Nursing and Nursing Edn., 1968-73; trustee Duke U., 1968-73, pres.'s assoc., 1973-80; trustee Golden Gate U., 1974-94, chmn. investment com., 1977-93; trustee World Wildlife U.S. Fund The Conservation Found., 1987-90; mem. periodic chmn. adminstrv. bd. Trinity United Meth. Ch., Berkeley, Calif., 1966-84; mem. adminstrv. bd., advisor Lafayette (Calif.) United Meth. Ch., 1984—; mem. bd. overseers vis. com. Harvard Coll. Econs., 1969-74; chmn. investment com. Calif.-Nev. Meth. Found., 1968-75, mem., 1976-91; mem. Calif. Gov.'s Coun. Econ. and Bus. Devel., 1978-82, chmn., 1980-82; trustee Hudson Inst., 1979-84; co-chmn. San Francisco Mayor's Fiscal Adv. Com., 1978-81, mem. 1981-96; chmn. Bay Area Econ. Advisers, 1982—; spl . adviser Presdl. Cabinet Com. Innovation, 1978-79; mem. Calif. State Internat. Adv. Com., 1986-94; regent U. Calif., 1990-91; mem. adv. coun. Calif. Environ. Tech. Ptnrship., 1993-94; mem. econ. adv. coun. Calif. Inst. Fed. Policy Rsch., 1994—; trustee Internat. Ho. U. Calif., 1991—, Devel. Com., 1994—, chmn., 1995-97. Fellow Am. Statis. Assn. (v.p., bd. dirs. 1952-54, pres. 1958), Nat. Assn. Bus. Economists (San Francisco chpt. exec. com. 1989—), Am. Fin. Assn. (bd. dirs. 1955-56, pres. 1969); mem. Conf. Bus. Economists (chmn. 1962), Atlantic Coun. of U.S. (bd. dirs. 1985—), Internat. Acad. Mgmt., 1980—; U.S. Coun. for Internat. Bus. (sr. trustee 1992—), Commonwealth Club of Calif. (pres. 1987, chmn. pub. affairs-comm. com. 1995—), Am. Econ. Assn., Am. Mktg. Assn., Am. Bankers Assn. (chmn. urban and cmty. affairs com. 1972-73, mem. econ. adv. coun. 1976-78), Nat. Bur. Econ. Rsch. (bd. dirs. 1965-81), Western Econ. Assn. (bd. dirs., mem. steering com. 1966-94, 97—), U. Calif. Alumni Assn. (pres. 1989-91, pres. class of 1938 1988—, chmn. investment com. 1983-89, 94-96, Alumnus of Yr. 1993, Chancellor's Highest award 1999), U.S. Nat. Com. on Pacific Econ. Coop. (vice chmn. 1984-89, mem. exec. com. 1989-94), Caux Internat. Roundtable (chmn. steering com. 1993-97), St. Francis Yacht Club, Commonwealth Club, Pacific Union Club, Bankers Club, Silverado Country Club, Phi Beta Kappa Assocs. (bd. dirs. 1986-95), Kappa Alpha. Office: Bank of AmRet Execs CA5-705-11-01 555 California St San Francisco CA 94104-1502

HOAN, PHAM HUY, editor-in-chief; b. Hanoi, Vietnam, Mar. 7, 1941; s. Pham Huy Nhiem and Hong Thi Bich; m. Nguyen Thi Hong Ha, Jan., 1975; children: Tuan Anh, Pham. Student, Tech. Coll., Hanoi, 1969, Dimitrov Inst., Bulgaria, 1986, Sch. Journalism, Germany, 1989. Cert. mech. engr. Engr. automobile factory Hanoi, 1969-79; journalist Lao Dong newspaper, Hanoi, 1980-86, dep. chief, chief internat. dept., 1986-92, dep. editor, 1993-95, editor-in-chief, 1995—. Mem. Assn. Journalists Vietnam, Confedn.

Trade Union Vietnam, Vietnam Forum Environ. Journalists (chmn. 1998—). Avocation: classical music. Home: 49 Bach Mai St, Hanoi Vietnam Office: Bao Lao Dong, 51 Hang Bo St, Hanoi Vietnam

HOANG, LOC BAO, electrical engineer; b. Saigon, Vietnam, Feb. 26, 1964; came to U.S., 1980; s. Chau Van Hoang and Quy Thi Bui; m. Tracy Phuong-Nga Doan, Dec. 7, 1990; children: Kimberly Bao, Christopher Dang-Khoa. BSEE, U. Calif., Berkeley, 1988; MSEE, San Jose State U., 1993. Design engr. Xicor, Inc., Milpitas, Calif., 1989-90; sr. design engr. Nat. Semiconductor Corp., Santa Clara, Calif., 1991-93, Silicon Storage Tech., Inc., Sunnyvale, Calif., 1993-94; design mgr. Winbond Memory Lab., San Jose, Calif., 1994-97; dir. design Winbond Electronics Corp. Amer., San Jose, Calif., 1997—; presenter Internat. Symposium on VLSI Tech., 1993. Mem. IEEE. Achievements include patent for Row Decoder and Driver with Switched-Bias Bulk Regions; semiconductor mem. device with dataline undershoot detection and reduced read access time, electrically byte selectable and byte alterable mem. arrays, flash cell having self-timed progamming memory device and method of operation, semiconductor memory device with reduced read disturbance, semiconductor memory array with buried drain lines and method therefore, semiconductor memory array partitioned into memory blocks and sub-blocks and method of addressing, and other patents; patent pending for notable findings of methods and design techniques to improve performance and/or reliability of non-volatile semiconductor memories. Avocations: music, movies, swimming, table tennis. Office: Winbond Electronics Corp Am 2727 N 1st St San Jose CA 95134-2029

HOANG, NGOC CAM, physicist; b. Quangbinh, Vietnam, Oct. 3, 1953; d. Hoanh and Thanh Lich (Tran) H. BS in Physics, Kishinev STate U., Russia, 1975; PhD, Inst. Physics, Hanoi, Vietnam, 1987; D of Phys. Math. Scis., Lebedev Phys. Inst., Moscow, 1999. Instr. Hanoi State U., Vietnam, 1975-77, lectr., 1978-83; rsch. scientist Inst Physics, Hanoi, 1983-91; sr. rsch. scientist Pebedev Phys. Inst., Moscow, 1993—; vis. scientist Inst. Applied Phys., Kishinev, Moldova, 1993. Contbr. articles to profl. jours. Mem. TWOWS, N.Y. Acad. Scis. Avocation: writing. Office: Lebedev Phys Lab Dept Optic, 53 Lehinsky Prospect, 117924 Moscow Russia also: Inst Physics Nat Ctr Natural Scis & Tech, PO Box 429 BOHO, Hannoi 10000, Vietnam

HOANG, THU-ANH, diagnostic radiologist; b. Dalat, Vietnam, Oct. 22, 1956. MD, U Iowa Coll. Med., 1983. Diplomate Am. Bd. of Radiology. Intern Strong Meml. Genesee Hosp., Rochester, N.Y., 1983-84; resident in diagnostic radiology Allegheny Gen. Hosp., Pitts., 1985-89; fellow U. Calif. Irvine Med. Ctr., Orange, 1989-90; fellow in neuroradiology Loma Linda (Calif.) U. Med. Ctr., 1991-93; chief neuroradiology Jerry L. Pettis Vets. Meml. Hosp., Loma Linda, 1993-98; staff radiologist Lima (Ohio) Meml. Hosp., 1999—; asst. prof. radiologist, Loma Linda, CA, 1992-98. Mem. Am. Coll. Radiology, Radiol. Soc. N. Am. Office: Good Samaritan Hosp 1225 Wilshire Blvd Los Angeles CA 90017-1901

HOAR, JERE RICHMOND, journalism educator, writer; b. Dyersburg, Tenn., Oct. 23, 1929; s. Eldon Jesse and Lula Mae Zimmerman (Parks) H.; m. Betty Jane Smith, May 12, 1954 (div. Sept. 1977); children: Lu Ann Smith, Thomas Jonathan, Benjamin Jere. BS, Auburn U., 1951; MA, U. Miss., Oxford, 1954; PhD, U. Iowa, 1960. Bar: Miss. 1971. Reporter Troy (Ala.) Messenger, 1947-49, Troy Herald; news editor The Oxford (Miss.) Eagle, 1953-54, Jour. So. Commerce, Oxford, 1953-54; editor Iowa Pub. Mag., Iowa City, 1954-56; grad. asst. U. Iowa, Iowa City, 1954-56; asst. prof. journalism U. Miss., University, 1956-59, assoc. prof. journalism, 1959-67, prof. journalism, 1967-86, emeritus prof. journalism, 1986—; preceptorship in law Freeland & Gafford Law Offices, Oxford, 1966-67, 69-71; lawyer, Oxford, 1971—; prof. journalism Ctr. for Cooperative Study in Britain, King's Coll., London, summer 1988, 90; advisor Miss. Poll; reference person Miss. Press; expert witness in field. Author: Comprehensive Construction Planning, 1975, Body Parts, 1997; editor: Erosion Control, 1962, Mississippi Newspapers and the Law, 1965, 69; co-editor: Lawyer in the Classroom Directory, 1978, Media Law Handbook, 1981; author of short stories; contbr. articles to profl. jours. Local in polit. campaigns. With USAF, 1951-53. Recipient first place internat. lit. competition Writers Unlimited, Pascagoula, Miss., 1973, Kansas Arts Coun./KQ award, 1989-90, Ione Burden Novel award Deep South Writers Competition, U. Southwestern La., 1994, Silver Em for Contbns. to Journalism, Miss. Scholastic and the Dept. Journalism, University, 1995; Fulbright fellow Costa Rica, 1979. Mem. ABA (governing com. forum on comm. law), Assn. for Edn. in Journalism and Mass Comm. (chair tchg. com. law divsn.), Miss. Bar Assn., Sigma Delta Chi, Kappa Tau Alpha. Republican. Methodist. Avocations: reading, raising and training English Setters, shooting, riding. E-mail: jrhoar@watervalley.net. Home: 71 County Road 215 Oxford MS 38655-8858

HOBBS, F.D. RICHARD, physician, researcher, educator; b. Welwyn Garden City, U.K., Nov. 2, 1953; s. Frederick Derek and Nancy Elizabeth (Wilde) H.; m. Jane Marilyn Porter, June 18, 1977; children: Rebecca Charlotte Elizabeth, Frederick Charles Edward. MB ChB, U. Bristol, Eng., 1977. Prin. gen. practice Bellevue Med. Ctr., Birmingham, Eng., 1981—; assoc. regional advisor in gen. practice West Midlands RHA, Eng., 1986-92; sr. lectr. U. Birmingham, 1986-92, prof. primary care and gen. practice, 1992—, asst. dean faculty medicine, 1993-96, head divsn. primary care, pub. health and occupl. health, 1999—; mem. European Soc. Cardiovascular Working Group on Heart Failure, Med. Rsch. Coun. Med. Adv. Bd.; Nat. Ctr. for Health Tech. Assessment program chair Primary Care Cardiovascular Soc.; bd. dirs. European Soc. Primary Care Gastroenterology. Editor (with V. Drury) Treatment and Prognosis in General Practice, 1990, Towards Quality Care: A Management and Audit Programme in Upper GI Disorders, 1995; author: (with A Harris, T. Wykes and T. Brisby), Aggression and Violence in General Practice, 1995, (with C. Bradley) Prescribing in Primary Care, 1998; contbr. over 300 articles to profl. jours., 18 chpts. to books. Fellow Royal Coll. Gen. Practitioners; mem. Med. Protection Soc. (coun., bd. dirs. 1996—). Avocations: travel, gardening, architecture, music. Office: U Birmingham Med Sch, Divsn Primary Care, Edgbaston Birmingham B15 2TT, England

HOBBS, GUY STEPHEN, financial executive; b. Lynwood, Calif., Feb. 23, 1955; s. Franklin Dean and Bette Jane (Little) H.; m. Laura Elena Lopez, Jan. 6, 1984; 1 child, Mariah Amanda. BA, U. Calif., Santa Barbara, 1976; MBA, U. Nev., 1978. Sr. rsch. assoc. Ctr. for Bus. and Econ. Rsch., Las Vegas, Nev., 1978-80; pvt. practice mgmt. cons. Las Vegas, 1979-82; mgmt. analyst Clark County, Las Vegas, 1980-81, sr. mgmt. analyst, 1981-82, dir. budget and fin. planning, 1982-84, comptroller, dir. fin., chief fin. officer, 1984-96; pres. Hobbs, Ong & Assocs., Inc., 1996—; lectr. in mgmt. Coll. Bus. and Econs., U. Nev., Las Vegas, 1977-88; pres. Pacific Blue Ent., 1991—; mem. Interim Legis. Com. Infrastructure Fin., 1993-94; mem. Interim Legis. Com. Studying Laws Relating to the Distbn. of Taxes in Nev., 1995-96, 97—. Author publs. in field. Mem. exec. bd. Miss Nevada USA and Miss NEVADA Teen USA, 1996—; instr. Las Vegas Baseball Acad., 1998—; head coach, Silver State Girls Soccer League, 1998—. Mem. Am. Soc. Pub. Adminstrn. (Pub. Adminstr. of Yr. 1987), Govt. Fin. Officers Assn. (Fin. Reporting Achievement award 1984-95, Disting. Budget Presentation, award 1993-96), Nev. Taxpayers Assn. Republican. Avocations: sports, photography, travel. Office: Hobbs Ong & Assocs Inc 3900 Paradise Rd Ste 152 Las Vegas NV 89109-0928

HOBBS, HORTON HOLCOMBE, III, biology educator; b. Gainesville, Fla., Dec. 17, 1944; s. Horton Holcombe Jr. and Georgia Cates (Blount) H.; m. Susan Claire Krantz, Oct. 12, 1967; children: Heather H. Killion, Horton Holcombe IV. BA, U. Richmond, 1967; MS, Miss. State U., 1969; PhD, Ind. U., 1973. Instr. Christopher Newport Coll., Newport News, Va., 1973-75; asst. prof. George Mason U., Fairfax, Va., 1975-76; prof. biology Wittenberg U., Springfield, Ohio, 1976—; com. mem. Nongame Wildlife Tech. Adv. Com., Columbus, Ohio, 1989-95; trustee Island Cave Rsch. Ctr., 1987—. Author: The Crayfishes and Shrimp of Wisconsin, 1988; life scis. editor: Nat. Speleological Soc. Bull., Huntsville, Ala., 1985-96; contbr. over 150 articles to profl. jours. Campaign co-chair County Park Dist., Springfield, 1980. Fellow Nat. Speleological Soc. (bd. govs. 1985-88, hon. life mem.), The Explorers Club, Ohio Acad. Sci.; mem. Crustacean Soc. (coun. mem. 1980-83), Biol. Soc. Wash. (exec. coun. 1976-77), Am. Cave Conservation Assn. (bd. dirs. 1993—), Karst Waters Inst. (bd. dirs. 1999—), Cave Conservancy of the Virginias (bd. dirs. 1988—). Achievements include development of Ohio's Cave Protection Law; participation in International Speleological Expeditions to Costa Rica. Office: Wittenberg U Dept Biol Springfield OH 45501

HOBBS, MARCUS EDWIN, chemistry educator; b. Chadbourn, N.C., Aug. 11, 1909; s. Julius Charles and Maude Elizabeth (Player) H.; m. Sarah Ferguson Blanchard, July 3, 1937; children—Sarah Lillian, Joan Elizabeth. A.B., Duke U., 1932, M.A., 1934, Ph.D., 1936. Indsl. research fellow tobacco Duke, 1931-33, instr. chemistry, 1936, asst. prof., 1942, asso. prof., 1945, prof., 1950—, univ. disting. service prof. emeritus, 1978—, chmn. dept. chemistry, 1951-54; dean Duke (Grad. Sch. Arts and Scis.), 1954-58, dean of univ., 1958-64, vice provost, 1960-64, provost, 1969-71, charge spl. courses in chemistry of explosives, 1941-42; research assoc. Nat. Def. Research Com., George Washington U., 1942-45; civilian cons. Nat. Def. Research Com., George Washington U. (div. 2), 1942-44, Nat. Def. Research Com., George Washington U. (div. 3), 1943-45; adviser Office Ordnance Research, 1951-61, chief scientist, acting, 1951-52; Dir. N.C. Blue Cross and Blue Shield, Inc., 1967-81, chmn. exec. com., 1978-81; mem. adv. coun. Army Research Office, 1970-76; mem. adv. com. jr. sci. and humanities symposia Dept. Army, 1974-77, adviser, 1980-85 ; mem. NSF adv. panel U.S.-Japan Coop. Service Program, 1963-65; adv. com. utilization R & D, USDR, 1964-70; mem. N.C. Bd. Sci. and Tech., 1963-75; chmn. exec. com. Research Triangle Inst., 1958-68, 71-98. Contbr. articles to profl. jours. Recipient Army-Navy Certificate of Merit for sci. work with OSRD during World War II, 1945; Outstanding Civilian Svc. medal Dept. Army, 1959; Cigar Industry Rsch. award, 1959, Univ. medal for Disting. Meritous Svc. Duke U., 1989, Archie K. Davis award, 1999. Fellow AAAS; mem. Am. Chem. Soc. (chmn. N.C. sect. 1946), AAUP, Rotary (pres. Durham 1978-79), Phi Beta Kappa, Sigma Xi, Phi Lambda Upsilon, Sigma Pi Sigma, Sigma Chi. Home: 2701 Pickett Rd Apt 4009 Durham NC 27705-5652

HOBBS, PETER THOMAS GODDARD, trust administrator; b. Gloucester, Eng., Mar. 19, 1938; s. Reginald Stanley and Phyllis Gwendoline (Goddard) H.; m. Victoria Christabel Matheson, Apr. 4, 1964; 1 child, Katharine Emily. MA, Exeter Coll., Oxford, Eng., 1962. Mgr. Imperial Chem. Industries, Eng., 1962-79; bd. dirs. Wellcome Found. Ltd., Wellcome Plc, Eng., 1979-92; Her Majesty's Inspector of Constabulary, Eng., 1993-98; chmn. Learning from Experience Trust, 1998—; mem., chmn. Employment Affairs Bd. and Coun., Chem. Industries Assn., Eng., 1979-93; dep. chmn. Pharms. and Fine Chems. Joint Indsl. Coun., Eng., 1979-89; mem. edn. and tng. com. Confedn. Brit. Industry, London, 1989-94; chmn. Edcn. Ctr., U. York, Eng., 1992-94. Contbr. articles to profl. jours. Mem., chmn. Learning From Experience Trust, London, 1988—; dep. chmn. Roffey Park Inst., Horsham, Eng., 1989-93; founder, chmn. Employer's Forum on Disability, London, 1990-93; mem. Edexcel Found., London, 1995-98; bd. dir. Forensic Sci. Svcs. U.K., 1996—; past coun. mem. Mgmt. Ctr. Europe, Brussels. Capt. Royal Logistics Corps., Territorial Army, 1957-68. Decorated companion Royal Inst. Pers. and Devel. Fellow Royal Soc. Arts U.K., Inst. Dirs. U.K. (mem. employment affairs com. 1989-93); mem. United Oxford and Cambridge Club. Avocations: history, topography, opera, theatre.

HOBER, DIDIER, virologist; b. Bruay-en-Artois, France, Sept. 16, 1961; s. Jean and Juliette (Guilluy) H.; m. Christine Vandenberghe, Dec. 27, 1986; children: Loanah, Candice, Blandine. MD, Sch. of Medecine, Lille, France, 1991, PhD, 1994; habilitation, 1996. Resident Univ. Hosp., Lille, France, 1986-91; asst. Ctr. Hospitalier Territorial, Papeete, Tahiti, 1989-90; postdoctoral scholar UCLA Sch. of Medicine, 1991-92; asst. Univ. Hosp., Lille, 1992-96, univ. lectr., staff physician, 1996—; tchr. CNAM Pacific U., Papeete, 1989-90; mem. sci. bd. Sch. of Medicine, Lille, 1993—. Mem. editl. bd. Annales de Biologie Clinique, 1996—; contbr. numerous articles to profl. jours. Capt. Officer of the Reserve, 1995. Named prizewinner Univ. Hosp., 1991, Sch. of Medicine, 1994; recipient prize Roger Bellon Lab., Lille, 1990, scholarship INSERM Rels. Internat., UCLA, 1990-91, prize Shering Lab., Lille, 1994. Mem. Am. Soc. for Microbiology, French Soc. Microbiology, Internat. Cytokine Soc. Home: 17 rue du Moulin, 59133 Camphin-on-Carembaut France Office: Laboratoire de Virologie U Hosp Ctr, Bat IRFPPS Place Verdun, 59037 Lille France

HOBERG, EIKE, cardiologist; b. Dortmund, Germany, Oct. 20, 1951; s. Giesbert and Christel (Heese) H.; m. Ulrike Stüben, Apr. 24, 1981; children: Kathrin, Inger, Hanne. MD, U. Wurzburg, 1976. Intern/resident U. Würzburg, 1976-78; fellow Cmty. Hosp., Dortmund, 1979-82; fellow and sr. attending Med. Univ. Clinic, Heidelberg, Germany, 1982-89, assoc. prof., 1989-92, prof. medicine, 1995—; med. dir. Compass-Reha-Centrum, Kiel, Germany, 1992—. Author: ST-Segment-Analysis of Holter Monitoring, 1990. With German Marines, 1978-79. Fellow Internat. Soc. Holter Monitoring; mem. German Soc. Cardiology, German Soc. Internal Medicine, German Soc. Prevention and Rehab. of Cardiac Disorders. Avocations: contemporary arts, tennis. Office: Compass-Reha-Centrum, Heikendorfer Weg 9-27, D-24149 Kiel Germany

HOBSON, ART S., physicist; b. Phila., Nov. 27, 1934; s. Leland S. and Marjorie P. (Breitweg) H.; m. Dodie Frances Kech, June 1959 (div. 1971); children: Ziva, David; m. Marie Riley, 1997. B in Music, U. North Tex., 1955; BSc, Kans. State U., 1960, PhD, 1964. From asst. prof. physics to prof. physics U. Ark., Fayetteville, 1964-99, prof. emeritus, 1999—. Author: Concepts in Statistical Mechanics, 1971, Physics & Human Affairs, 1982, Physics: Concepts & Connections, 1994, 2d edit., 1998. Served in U.S. Army, 1955-57, Germany. Mem. AAAS, Nat. Sci. Tchrs. Assn., Am. Assn. Physics Tchrs., Union Concerned Scientists, Fedn. Am. Scientists (coun. 1987-91), Am. Phys. Soc. (newsletter editor 1986-96, exec. com. 1997-99). Democrat. Avocations: writing, jazz, skiing, travel, reading. E-mail: ahobson@mail.uark.edu. Office: Dept Physics U Arkansas Fayetteville AR 72701

HOBSON, BURTON HAROLD, publishing company executive; b. Galesburg, Ill., Apr. 16, 1933; s. Burt and Geneva (Sornberger) H.; m. Maxine C. Meyer, Aug. 9, 1953; children: Alice L., Andrew J., Mark R. BA, U. Chgo., 1953. Mgr. collector's coin dept. Marshall Field & Co., Chgo., 1953-61; sales mgr. Sterling Pub. Co., Inc., N.Y.C., 1961-66; v.p. sales Sterling Pub. Co., Inc., 1966-72, exec. v.p., 1972-79, pres., 1979-95, chmn., 1995—, dir., 1966—. Author: (with Fred Reinfeld) Manual for Coin Collectors and Investors, 1963, Picture Book of Ancient Coins, 1963, U.S. Commemorative Coins and Stamps, 1964, Catalogue of the World's Most Popular Coins, 1965, What You Should Know about Coins and Coin Collecting, 1965, Hidden Values in Coins, 1965, International Guide to Coin Collecting, 1966, Coins You Can Collect, 1966, Coin Identifier, 1966, Coin Collecting As a Hobby, 1967, (with Robert Obojski) Illustrated Encyclopedia of World Coins, 1970, Catalogue of Scandinavian Coins, 1970, Historic Gold Coins of the World, 1971, Coin Collecting for Beginners, 1970, Stamp Collecting for Beginners, 1970, Coins and Coin Collecting, 1971; editor: The Benenson Restaurant Guide, 1985; pub. Gastronome mag., 1993—. Recipient Robert Friedberg award for numismatic lit., 1972. Mem. Am. Numismatic Soc., Confrérie des Chevaliers du Tastevin, Confrérie de la Chaine des Rôtisseurs (nat. pres.), Culinary Inst. Am. (trustee), Am. Acad. Chefs (trustee), Univ. Club of N.Y., Delta Upsilon. Home: 600 Harbor Blvd Unit 833 Weehawken NJ 07087-6748 Office: Sterling Pub Co 387 Park Ave S New York NY 10016-8810

HOC, JEAN-MICHEL, psychology researcher; b. Flers-Lez-Lille, Nord, France, June 22, 1948; s. Pierre and Simone (Bonnamy) H.; m. Ginette Larvor, Feb. 8, 1952; children: Tristan, Tanguy. PhD in Psychology, U. Paris V, 1978. Rschr. Centre. Nat. de la Recherche Scientifique, Paris, 1973-86, St. Denis, France, 1986-93, Valenciennes, France, 1993—; head Centre Nat. de la Recherche Scientifique Rsch. Team, St. Denis, 1990-93, Valenciennes, France, 1993-99. Author: Cognitive Psychology of Planning, 1988; editor: Expertise and Technology, 1995, others; editor Le Travail Humain, 1989—. Mem. European Assn. of Cognitive Ergonomics, Soc. Francaise de Psychologie, Association pour la recherche Cognitive. E-mail: Jean-Michel.Hoc@univ-valenciennes.fr. Office: CNRS-U Valenciennes, Lamih Percotec Le Mont Houy, F-59313 Valenciennes Cedex 9, France

HOCANIN, AYKUT, science educator; b. Kalkanli, Cyprus, Aug. 14, 1970; parents Yusuf Ziya and Seval Hocanin. BSEE, Rice U., 1992; MSEE, Tex. A&M U., 1993; postgrad., Bogazici U., Istanbul, Turkey, 1994—. Computer programmer Ea. Mediterranean U., Magosa, Cyprus, summer 1992; tchg. asst. Tex. A&M U., College Station, 1992-93, Koc U., Istanbul, 1995-98, Isik U., Istanbul, 1999—. Contbr. articles to profl. jours. and conf. procs. Casp scholar Amideast, 1988, Fahir Ilkel PhD scholar Bogazici U., 1999. Mem. Inst. Elec. and Electronics, Comm. Soc., N.Y. Acad. Scis. Avocations: soccer, basketball. E-mail: hocanin@busim.ee.boun.edu.tr. Office: Bogazici U, Bebek, Istanbul 80815, Turkey

HOCH, IVO, library director; b. Slany, Czech Republic, Aug. 14, 1950; s. Antonín Hoch and Helena (Šlapáková) Hochová; m. Eva Šelová, June 20, 1975; 1 child, Dana. PhD, Charles U., Prague, Czech Republic, 1979. Libr. Czech Nat. Libr., Prague, 1969-71; info. specialist Teplotechna, 1971-90; libr. dir. CAFL, Prague, 1990—. Contbr. articles to profl. jours. Mem. IAALD, Sdružení knihovníku a inf. pracovníku. Avocations: cultural activities, travel. Office: Ctrl Agrl & Forestry Libr, Slezska 7, Prague 120 56, Czech Republic

HOCH, SCOTT MABON, professional golfer; b. Raleigh, N.C., Nov. 24, 1955; m. Sally Hoch; children: Cameron, Katie. B in Comm., Wake Forest U., 1978. Profl. golfer PGA, 1978—. Named All-Am., 1977-78; mem. NCAA Championship Team, 1975; mem. (nat. teams) World Amateur Team Championships, 1978, Walker Cup, 1979, Pres.'s Cup, 1994, 96, Ryder Cup, 1997; mem. PGA Tour Charity Team, Deposit Guaranty Golf Classic, 1999; won Walker Cup, 1979, Quad Cities Open, 1980, Pacific Masters (Japan), 1982, Casio World Open (Japan), 1982, USF&G Classic, 1982, Lite Quad Cities Open, 1984, Vardon Trophy, 1986, Casio World Open (Japan), 1986, Las Vegas Invitational, 1989, Korea Open, 1990, Bob Hope Chrysler Classic, 1994, Pres.'s Cup, 1994, Heineken Dutch Open, 1995, Greater Milw. Open, 1995, 97, Michelob Championship, 1996. Avocations: sports.

HOCHBAUM, MARTIN, trade association administrator; b. N.Y.C., Nov. 7, 1941; s. Issie and Lena H.; m. Victoria Eiger, June 15, 1982; children: Eden, Lee, David. PhD, CUNY, 1974. Nat. affairs dir. Am. Jewish Congress, N.Y.C., 1972-97; mng. dir. Diamond Dealers Club, N.Y.C., 1997—; dir. Ctr. Applied Rsch., N.Y.C., 1975-85. Editor: Poor Jews, 1974; contbr. op-eds to newspapers. Avocations: jogging, reading. Home: 89 Essex Ave Montclair NJ 07042-4124 Office: Diamond Dealers Club 580 5th Ave Fl 10 New York NY 10036-4781

HOCHBERG, MARK STEFAN, foundation president, cardiac surgeon; b. Providence, Nov. 26, 1947; s. Robert and Gertrude (Meth) H.; m. Faith Shapiro, June 6, 1976; children: Alyssa T., Asher R. BA, Brown U., 1969; MD, Harvard U., 1973; MD (Honoris Causa), Chongqing Sch. Med. Sci., China, 1987. Diplomate Am. Bd. Thoracic Surgery, Am. Bd. Surgery. Chief resident cardiothoracic surgery Mass. Gen. Hosp., Boston, 1980; clin. fellow in surgery Harvard Med. Sch., Boston, 1980; attending cardiac surgeon Newark Beth Israel Med. Ctr., 1981-93, dir. cardiac surgery, 1988-93; cons. cardiac surgeon Overlook Hosp., Summit, N.J., 1983-93; asst. prof. surgery U. Medicine and Dentistry of N.J., Newark, 1981-87, assoc. prof. surgery, 1987-93; spl. asst. to pres., vis. prof. surgery George Washington U., Washington, 1993-94, dean of univ. affairs, prof. surgery, 1994-95; sr. scholar Assn. Acad. Health Ctrs., 1995-96; pres. Healthcare Found. N.J., Roseland, 1996—; chmn. grant rev. com. N.J. affiliate Am. Heart Assn., New Brunswick, 1986-88, bd. dirs., 1986-93; bd. dirs., mem. com. on med. affairs Corp. of Brown U., Providence, 1987—. V.p. Temple B'nai Jeshurun, Short Hills, 1988-92; trustee Coun. N.J. Grantmakers, 1997—, pres. 2000—; mem. vis. com. Northeastern U. Sch. of Law. Lt. comdr. USPHS, 1975-77. Fellow ACS, Am. Coun. Edn.; mem. Soc. Thoracic Surgery, Am. Assn. Thoracic Surgery, Alpha Omega Alpha. Office: Healthcare Found NJ 75 Livingston Ave Roseland NJ 07068-3701

HOCHBERG, MICHAEL EDWARD, population biologist; b. L.A., Calif., Sept. 15, 1960; arrived in France; 1991; s. Howard Edmond Hochberg and Dorothy Gwen (Kaplan) Harper; m. Joelle Janine Chimbert, May 30, 1987; children: Kevin, Julien. BSc, Univ. Calif., 1982, MSc, 1985; PhD, Imperial Coll., London, 1989. Researcher Imperial Coll., 1989-91, Cen. Nat. de la Recherche Scientific, Paris, 1991-95; rsch. dir. CNRS, Paris, 1995—; editor-in-chief Ecology Letters, Paris, 1998—. Editor: Aspects in the Genesis and Maintenance of Biological Diversity, 1996; programmer ednl. software, Popdyn, 1989. Recipient Bourse Chateaubriand award French Gov., 1985-86, Silver medal CNRS, 1997, Overseas Rsch. award Vice Principals and Chancellors of the U.K., 1986; hon. fellow U. Wis., 1998. Mem. British Ecological Soc. Avocation: wine tasting. Office: CNRS, 7 Quai St Bernard CC237, 75252 Paris France

HOCHHALTER, GORDON RAY, advertising communications executive; b. Jerome, Idaho, Oct. 3, 1946; s. Ralph R. and Evelyn (McClellan) H. BA, Brigham Young U., 1972. Asst. promotion supr. Armstrong World Industries, Lancaster, Pa., 1972-74, promotion supr., 1974-76, sr. promotion supr., 1976; asst. advt. mgr. R.R. Donnelley & Sons Co., Chgo., 1976-79, asst. mgr. advt., sales promotion, 1979-81, advt. mgr., 1981-84, group mgr. mktg. com., creative devel., 1984-86, dir. mktg. com., creative dir., 1986-91; v.p., gen. mgr., creative dir. Mobium Corp. Design & Communications, Chgo., 1991-96, v.p., creative dir. design and conceptual devel., 1996-97; chief creative officer Mobium Creative Group, Chgo., 1998-99, mng. ptnr./creativitystrategytechnology, 2000—; v.p., creative cons. Caviale Fashions, N.Y.C., 1987—. Author: Strategies for a New Age of Business Communications, New Media in a New Age of Business Communications, Creative Leverage in a New Age of Business Communications, Integrating Communications in a New Age of Business Marketing; monthly columnist Integrated Mktg. and Promotion Mag.; contbr. to profl. jours. and Libr. of Congress. Recipient London Internat. Advt. awards, 1987, One Show, Type Dirs. Club, Clio awrds, Art Dirs. Club awards, Andy awards, Addy awards, Internat. Advt. Festival AIGA awards, ProCom awards, Ace awards, Chgo. Tower awards, 1987-2000, Am. Bus. Press Objective and Results award, 1992, Cresta Internat. Advt. award, 1993, Sawyer award Bus. Mktg. Mag., 1993, High-Tech. Advt. award MARCOM, 1994-96, Pinnacle award MARCOM, 1994, Icon award Bus. Week Mag., 1994-95, 98-2000. Mem. Am. Ctr. for Design, Am. Advt. Fedn., Am. Inst. Graphic Arts, Chgo. Advt. Fedn., Bus. Mktg. Assn., N.Y. Art Dirs. Club. Office: Mobium Creative Group The Merchandise Mart 200 World Trade Ctr Ste 2000 Chicago IL 60654

HOCHMAN, JUDITH L., executive recruiter; b. N.Y.C.; d. Jules and Beatrice Hochman. BA, Pa. State U., 1964; MA, Columbia U., 1965; MSW, NYU, 1971. Psychotherapist, tchr., cons. L.A. and N.Y.C., 1971-81; v.p. Search Internat., L.A., 1981-88; sr. cons. Korn Ferry Internat., L.A., 1988; pres. Hochman & Assocs., Inc., L.A., 1989—. Avocations: tennis, hiking, photography, antiques. Office: 1801 Avenue Of The Stars Los Angeles CA 90067-5902

HOCHMAN, JUDITH S., cardiologist; b. N.Y., Feb. 20, 1951; m. Richard Fuchs, June 28, 1981; children: Michael, Daniel, Benjamin. BA magna cum laude, Brandeis Univ., 1972; MA, Harvard Univ., 1974, MD, 1977. Dir. cardiac rsch. St. Lukes Roosevelt Hosp., N.Y., 1997—, sr. attending in medicine, 1997—, dir. cardiac stepdown, 1992—, dir. cardiac care unit, 1983—; assoc. prof. medicine Columbia Univ., N.Y., 1996—; com mem. Progarm Project Review Com., Bethesda, 1996—; adv. bd. Cardio Tech., Pine Brook, N.Y., 1997—. Co-author: (chpt. in book) Textbook of Cardiovascular Medicine, 1998, Atlas of Heart Disease, 1996; contbr. articles to profl. jours. Fellow Am. Coll. Cardiology, AHA (chair acute cardiac care ctr.); mem. Am. Fedn. Clinical Rsch. (chair), N.Y. Heart Assn., Am. Assn. Advancement of Sci., AMA, Phi Beta Kappa. Avocations: skiing, tennis, sailing. E-mail: jsha@columbia.edu. Office: St Lukes Roosevelt Hosp Ctr 1111 Amsterdam Ave New York NY 10025-1716

HOCHREITER, JOHN ALLEN, computer company owner, firefighter; b. Buffalo, Mar. 5, 1949; s. Robert Allen and Dorothy Eileen (Scully) H.; m. Shelley Cunningham, July 30, 1977; children: Sean Scully, Mark Andrew. BA, Niagara U., 1971; MEd, Boston Coll., Chestnut Hill, Mass., 1975. Mid. sch. tchr. sci. St. Rose of Lima Sch., Buffalo, 1971-73; mgr., dir. Snowflake Ventures, Ellicottsville, N.Y., 1973-74; itinerant tchr. for blind and visually impaired Buffalo Pub. Schs., 1975-77, itinerant tchr. coord., 1977-79; dept. mgr. Computac, Inc., West Lebanon, N.H., 1979-87, exec. v.p., 1987-92, pres., CEO,, 1992—; bd. dirs. Mascoma Savs. Bank, Lebanon, N.H. Baseball coach Sr. Babe Ruth League; mem. Hanover (N.H.) Improvement Soc., 1996—, bd. dirs., 1997-99, v.p. bd. dirs., 1999—; chmn. Dresden Sch. Bd., Hanover, 1988-89, Hanover Sch. Bd., 1987; lt. Hanover Dept.-Etna Sta., 1983—. Mem. Conn. and Passumpsic Rivers R.R. Assn.,

Hanover Country Club, Rotary (pres. 1996, presdl. citation 1996, Paul Harris fellow 1998). Republican. Roman Catholic. Avocation: golf. Fax: 603-298-6189. E-mail: john@computac.com.

HOCHSTEIN, MARTIN ALAN, endocrinologist; b. Bklyn., Mar. 24, 1943; s. Isaac Leib and Ann Hochstein; m. Rachel Hochstein, June 15, 1969; children: David, Rosalyn. BA, Yeshiva U., 1964; MD, U. Louisville, 1969. Straight med. intern Maimonides Med. Ctr., Bklyn., 1966-70, med. resident, 1970-71; 2nd yr. med. resident Albert Einstein Coll. Medicine, Bronx, 1971-72; asst. chief med., lt. comdr. USPHS Hosp., Staten Island, N.Y., 1972-74; fellow John's Hopkins Sch. Medicine, Balt., 1974-75; dir. medicine Bergen Pines County Hosp., Paramus, N.J., 1976-81; clin. assoc. prof. medicine U. Medicine and Dentistry N.J., Newark, 1976—; pvt. practice endocrinology and metabolism Paramus, 1981—. Author: (with others) The Practice of Medicine: A Self-Assessment Guide, 1976. Fellow ACP, Am. Assn. Clin. Endocrinology, N.J. Acad. Medicine; mem. The Endocrine Soc., Johns Hopkins Med. and Surg. Assn. Jewish. Avocations: scuba diving, cycling, swimming. Office: One Sears Dr Paramus NJ 07652

HOCHSTRASSER, BARBARA, health facility administrator, consultant; b. Bern, Switzerland, Mar. 21, 1954; d. Giselher Paul and Doris Martha (Angst) H. MD, U. Bern, 1979, Dr.med.Sci, 1980; MPH, Harvard U., 1983. Diplomate Am. Bd. Psychiatry, Am. Bd. Neurology; cert. specialist psychiatry and psychotherapy, Switzerland. Resident Inst. Sozial- und Präventivmedizin der Med. Fakultät, Bern, 1980-81, Chirurgische Klinik des Bürgerspitals, Solothurn, 1981-82; resident in psychiatry Mass. Gen. Hosp., Boston, 1984-87, clin. fellow psychiatry, 1988-89, clin. assoc. dept. psychiatry, 1989-90; intern in internal medicine Mt. Auburn Hosp., Boston, 1987-88; asst. dir. pain rehab. programs Spaulding Rehab. Hosp., Boston, 1989-90; sr. attending rsch. dept. U. Psychiat. Hosp., Zürich, 1990-96; med. dir., psychiatrist in chief Privatklinik Meiringen, Switzerland, 1996—; instr. psychiatry Harvard U., Boston, 1989-90; com. for control AIDS rsch., Swiss Fed., 1997—. Contbr. articles to profl. jours. Mem. Swiss Soc. Biol. Psychiatry (sec. 1996—), Swiss Soc. Psychiat. Epidemiology (com. mem. 1993—), Swiss Med. Assn., Swiss Soc. Psychiatry, Internat. Assn. Quality of Life Rsch., Am. Psychiat. Assn., Mass. Psychiat. Assn., Internat. Assn. for Study of Pain. Roman Catholic. Office: Privatklinik Meiringen, CH-3860 Meiringen Switzerland

HOCK, CHRISTIAN, information scientist; b. Munich, May 25, 1960; m. Kristina Kerner, July 28, 1995; 1 child, Maximilian. Diploma in engring., Technische U. Munich, 1988; D in Engring., U. Bundeswehr, Neubiberg, Germany, 1994. Sys. engr. U. Armed Forces, Neubiberg, 1988-94; team leader Integrated Kinematic Measurement, Neubiberg, 1994-95; project mgr. Kayser-Threde GmbH, Munich, 1996-98, head dept., 1998—. Avocations: sports, electronics. E-mail: Christian.Hock@t-online.de and hc@kayser-threde.de. Fax: 00498972495433. Home: Taulerstr 10, 81739 Munich Germany Office: Kayser-Threde GmbH, Perchtingerstr 3, 81379 Munich Germany

HOCK, MORTON, entertainment advertising executive; b. N.Y.C., June 24, 1929; s. Louis and Grace Dora (Solomon) H.; m. Anita Zagerman, Nov. 8, 1959; children—Jennifer, Jonathan. With Blaine Thompson Co., N.Y.C.; acct. supr. David Merrick Productions, 1954-60; advt. mgr. Paramount Pictures, N.Y.C., 1960-63, v.p., 1967-71; dir. advt. United Artists Corp., N.Y.C., 1963-67; exec. v.p. Charles Schlaifer & Co., Inc., N.Y.C., 1972-83; exec. v.p. entertainment div. DDB Needham Worldwide, N.Y.C., 1983—; mgmt. supr. Universal Pictures Account, United Artists Theatres Account, Gramercy Pictures Account. Contbr. articles to Variety. Mem. adv. com., bd. dirs. Will Rogers Found., 1983—. Named Showman of Yr. Nat. Assn. Theatre Owners; recipient Nat. Screen Svc. award for best theatre trailer. Mem. Acad. Motion Picture Arts and Scis. (bd. dirs.), Motion Picture Pioneers. Clubs: Variety of N.Y. (pres. 1979-80); Friars (admission com.). Lodge: B'nai Brith (trustee cinema unit 1980—). Avocations: sports; music; reading; travel.

HOCKEIMER, HENRY ERIC, business executive; b. Winzig, Germany, Apr. 3, 1920; came to U.S., 1946, naturalized, 1951; s. Erich and Gertrude (Masur) H.; m. Margaret Feeny, May 26, 1956; children: Ellen Patricia, Henry Eric. Student, RCA Insts., 1946-47; electronics and bus. mgmt., N.Y.U., 1948-51. With Philco-Ford Corp., Phila., 1947—, gen. mgr. communications and tech. services div., 1962-63, corp. v.p., 1963-72; v.p., gen. mgr. refrigeration products div. Connorsville, Ind., 1972-75; pres. Ford Aerospace & Communications Corp., Dearborn, Mich., 1975-85; v.p. Ford Motor Co., 1981-85; cons. USIA, Washington, 1985, dep. dir. TV and film service, 1985-87, asst. dir., 1987-88, assoc. dir. for mgmt., 1988-91, cons., 1991—; commr. RIAS, 1991—; exec. adv. bd. mem. Starmountain Inc., 1995—. Mem. Assn. Former Intelligence Officers (bd. dirs.), Engring. Soc. Detroit, Smithsonian, University Club Washington, Washington Arts Soc.

HOCKEY, PHILIP ANTHONY RICHARD, ornithologist, researcher; b. Bournemouth, Dorset, Eng., Mar. 8, 1956; arrived in South Africa, 1979; s. Bryan John and Jill (Boucher) H.; m. Carole Theresa De Rome (div. 1984). BSc with honors, U. Edinburgh, Scotland, 1977; PhD, U. Cape Town, South Africa, 1983. Rschr. Nature Conservancy Coun., Scotland, 1978-79; sr. rsch. officer U. Cape Town, 1986, lectr., 1987-89, sr. lectr., 1990-95, assoc. prof., 1996—; cons. Dept. Water Affairs and Forestry, South Africa, 1993—, Seychelles Island Found., 1999-00; bird tour leader Felix Unite Tours, Namibia, 1992—. Author: (book) Waders of Southern Africa, 1995; co-author: (book) Sasol: Birds of Southern Africa, 1993; contbr. sci. papers to profl. jours.; mem. editl. bd. Jour. Biol. Conservation, 1998—. Rsch. grantee Total Found., 1998-00, World Conservation Union, 1999-00, Nat. Rsch. Found., 1984-00. Mem. Brit. Ecol. Soc., Brit. Ornithologists Union, Royal Soc. South Africa. Avocations: photography, squash, gardening, traveling. Office: U Cape Town, Percy FitzPatrick Inst, 7701 Rondebosch South Africa

HOCKEY, STUART WILLIAM, retired headmaster; b. Sherborne, Dorset, Eng., Oct. 3, 1935; s. Clifford William and Dorothy Winifred (Smith) H.; m. Marjorie Mary Forbes, Mar. 31, 1970; 1 child, Susan. BA, Cambridge (Eng.) U., 1957, MA, 1961. Asst. tchr. physics Marlborough Coll., Wiltshire, 1957-61, head of physics, 1962-66, 70-71, housemaster, 1971-82; rsch. fellow United Steels, Sheffield, 1961; rsch. fellow Sch. Coun., Nuffield Sci. Tchg. Project Southampton (Eng.) U., 1965-69; headmaster Christ Coll., Brecon, 1982-96; inspector Headmasters' Conf., 1993-97; A level chief examiner Nuffield Sci. Tchg. Project, Cambridge, 1968-89; gov. St. John's-on-the-Hill Prep. Sch., Chepstow, 1987-96, Sidbury Ch. of Eng. Primary Sch., 1999—; mem. Curriculum Coun. for Wales, Curriculum and Assessment Authority, Wales, 1992-95; bd. dirs. Ind. Schs. Joint Coun. Common Entrance Exam., 1991-96; chmn. Health Edn. Com., Curriculum Coun. Wales, 1994-95. Author: Introduction to Calculus, 1969, Fundamental electrostatics, 1972; co-author: Physics by Experiment, 1973; contbr. to books: Schools' Mathematics Project Advanced Mathematics, 1963, Nuffield Advanced Physical Science, 1972; contbr. articles to profl. jours. including Nature, Brit. Jour. Edn. Psychology, among others. Chmn. Ind. Schs. Info. Svcs., Cardiff, Wales, 1984-87, 95-96, local Conservative Policy Forum, 1998—; program sec. local Nat. Assn. Decorative and Fine Arts Socs., 1999—; asst. Nat. Youth Orch. of Gt. Britain, London, 1967-68. Recipient Open scholarship Clare Coll., Cambridge, 1953. Fellow Inst. Dirs., Royal Soc. Arts; mem., Pub. Schs. East India Club. Anglican. Avocations: reading, music, chess, photography, decorative arts.

HOCKING, CLARE SHELLEY, occupational therapist, educator; b. Lower Hutt, New Zealand, Dec. 15, 1956; d. Walter Raymond and Rachel Muriel (Shelley) H. Diploma in occupl. therapy, Ctrl. Inst. Tech., Trentham, New Zealand, 1982, advanced diploma in occupl. therapy, 1989; MHSc in Occupl. Therapy, U. South Australia, Adelaide, 1997. Registered occupl. therapist. Occupl. therapist Canterbury Area Health Bd., Christchurch, New Zealand, 1982-84; sr. occupl. therapist Auckland (New Zealand) Area Health Bd., 1984-90; sr. lectr. Auckland Inst. Tech., 1990-96; prin. lectr. Auckland U. Tech., 1997—; lectr. U. South Australia, 1996; monitor ongoing profl. competence program for occupl. therapists, 1997—; rep. World Fedn. Occupl. therapists, 1998—. Author: (with w. Becker, A. Cornell, A. Henderson, C. Higgins) Cornerstone: A Professional Development Programme for Occupational Therapists, 1996, (with M. Wallen) Australian Occupational Therapy Journal Manual for Referees, 1999; contbr. numerous articles to profl. jours.; editor Jour. Occupl. Sci., 1996—, New Zealand Jour. Occupl. Therapy, 1990-97; mem. editl. bd. Occupl. Therapy Internat., 1994—. Mem. World Fedn. Occupl. Therapists, New Zealand Assn. Occupl. Therapists. Office: Auckland U Tech, Akoranga Dr Pvt Bag 92 006, 1020 Northcote Auckland, New Zealand

HOCKNEY, DAVID, artist; b. Bradford, Yorkshire, Eng., July 9, 1937; s. Kenneth and Laura H. Attended, Bradford Coll. Art, 1953-57, Royal Coll. Art, London, 1959-62; D (hon.), U. Aberdeen, 1988; hon. degree, Royal Coll. Art, London, 1992. Lectr. U. Iowa, 1964, U. Colo., 1965, U. Calif. Berkeley, 1967; lectr. UCLA, 1966, hon. chair of drawing, 1980. One-man shows include Kasmin Gallery, 1963-89, Mus. Modern Art, N.Y.C., 1964, 68, Stedelijk Mus., Amsterdam, Netherlands, 1966, Whitechapel Gallery, London, 1970, Andre Emmerich Gallery, N.Y.C., 1972-96, Musee des Arts Decoratifs, Paris, 1974, Museo Tamayo, Mexico City, 1984, L.A. Louver, Calif., 1986, 89—, Nishimura Gallery, Tokyo, 1986, 89, 90, 94, Met. Mus. Art, 1988, L.A. County Mus. Art, 1988, 96, Tate Gallery, London, 1988, 92, Royal Acad. Arts, London, 1995, Hamburger Kunsthalle, 1995, Nat. Mus. Am. Art, Washington, 1997, 98, Mus. Ludwig, Cologne, 1997, MFA, Boston, 1998, Centre Georges Pompidou, Paris, 1999, Musee Picasso, Paris, 1999, others; designer: Rake's Progress, Glyndebourne, Eng., 1975; sets for Magic Flute, Glyndebourne, 1978, Parade Triple Bill, Stravinsky Triple Bill, Met. Opera House, 1980-81, Tristan und Isolde, Los Angeles Music Ctr. Opera, 1987; Turandot Lyric Opera, Chgo., 1992—, San Francisco Opera, 1993, Die Frau Ohne Schatten, Covent Garden, London, 1992, L.A. Music Ctr.Opera, 1993; author: David Hockney by David Hockney, 1976, David Hockney: Travels with Pen, Pencil and Ink, 1978, Paper Pools, 1980, David Hockney Photographs, 1982, Cameraworks, 1983, David Hockney: A Retrospective, 1988, Hockney Paints the Stage, 1983, That's the Way I See It, 1993, David Hockney's Dog Days, 1998, Hockney on Art, 1999; illustrator: Six Fairy Tales of the Brothers Grimm, 1969, The Blue Guitar, 1977, Hockney's Alphabet, 1991. Recipient Guinness award and 1st prize for etching, 1961, Gold medal Royal Coll. Art, 1962, Graphic prize Paris Biennale, 1963, 1st prize 8th Internat. Exhbn. Drawings Lugano, Italy, 1964, 1st prize John Moores Exhbn. Liverpool, Eng., 1967, German award of Excellence 1983, 1st prize Internat. Ctr. of Photography, N.Y., 1985, Kodak photography book award for Cameraworks, 1984, Praemium Imperiale Japan Art Assn., 1989, 5th Ann. Gov. Calif. Visual Arts award, 1994; named Companion of Honour, Her Majesty, the Queen of Eng., 1997. Office: 7508 Santa Monica Blvd Los Angeles CA 90046-6407

HOCQUELLET, PIERRE, chemist, researcher; b. Bordeaux, France, Sept. 11, 1936; s. Pierre Guy Hocquellet and Jeanne Farmer; m. Anne-Marie Bret, Sept. 6, 1958; children: Brigitte, Richard, Agnès. BS, Faculty Scis., Bordeaux, 1959. Engr. Mcpl. Lab. Bordeaux, 1960-91, European Inst. Environment, Bordeaux, 1991-97; vis. prof. atomic spectroscopy U. Bordeaux I, 1979-93, U. Bordeaux II, 1982-96. Contbr. articles to profl. jours. Recipient Analytical Chemistry award French Indsl. Chem. Soc., 1979. Mem. N.Y. Acad. Scis. Avocations: heraldry, sigillography.

HODAKIEVIC, JAMES JOSEPH, secondary education educator; b. Cleve., Aug. 21, 1947; s. Joseph Edward and Genevieve Sophie (Chodakowski) H.; m. Johanna Rita Dolphin, Feb. 15, 1969; children: Peter James, Bethany Nanette. BS in Edn., Bowling Green State U., 1969, MEd, 1972; postgrad., Kent State U., 1980-82. Cert. edn., Ohio. Driver edn. tchr. Lakota Local Schs., Kansas, Ohio, 1969; tchr., coach Western Res. H.S., Warren, Ohio, 1969-71; instr., football coach Bowling Green (Ohio) State U., 1971-72; tchr., head football coach West Holmes H.S., Millersburg, Ohio, 1972-75, Defiance (Ohio) H.S., 1975-79, Bedford (Ohio) H.S., 1979—; guest lectr. Bowling Green State U. Athletics, 1975-77; summer sch. tchr. Maple Heights (Ohio) H.S., 1981; staff dir. Ozzie Newsome Football Camp, Cleve., 1987; spkr. Youngstown (Ohio) State U. Athletics, 1994; staff Ohio State Summer Football Camp, 1997, Pa. State Summer Football Camp, 1997, 2000. Recipient Dr. Lee Tressel Meml. Coaching award Cleve. Touchdown Club, 1994; named Coach of Yr., Coshocton (Ohio) Tribune, 1974, Greater Cleve. Conf., 1993, Lake Erie League Erie Divsn., 1998, 99. Mem. NEA, Nat. Fedn. Interscholastic Coach, Am. Football Coaches Assn. (assoc.), Ohio H.S. Football Coaches Assn., Greater Cleve. Football Coaches Assn. (pres., league dir., Golden Deeds award 1997). Avocation: golf. Home: 907 School Ave Cuyahoga Falls OH 44221-4113 Office: Bedford City Schs Bedford HS 481 Northfield Rd Bedford OH 44146-2201

HODAPP, SHIRLEY JEANIENE, curriculum administrator; b. Uniontown, Pa., July 10, 1934; d. James Sylvester and Nellie Mae (Kennedy) Amos; children: Holly Hodapp Vining, Curtis, David, Gordon. BS in Elem. Edn., Otterbein Coll., 1956; MEd, Wright State U., 1973; EdS, U. Toledo, 1990. Cert. elem. tchr., local supt., Ohio. Tchr. 3rd grade Elyria (Ohio) City Schs., 1955-56; tchr. 2nd grade Beavercreek Local Schs., Xenia, Ohio, 1956-57; tchr. elem. Xenia City Schs., 1965-73; ednl. facilitator Wright State U., Dayton, Ohio, 1973-74; adminstr. Marion S. Kinsey PreSch., Xenia, 1974-79; adminstr. elem. Northea. Local Schs., Defiance, Ohio, 1979-85; supr. elem. Defiance County Bd. Edn., 1985-92, dir. curriculum and related svcs., 1992-94; nat. cons. ITE Ednl. Cons., 1995—; dir. Little Gnat Early Childhood, Babson Park, Fla., 1998—; adj. prof. Defiance Coll., 1985-93, U. Toledo, 1989, N.W. Tech. Coll., Archbold, Ohio, 1989-90, Bowling Green State U., 1994; dir. Little Gnat Kindergarten Readiness program, Babson Park Elem. Sch., 1996—, Little Gnat Early Childhood Program, Babson Park, 1998—; cons. in field. Author: Learning About Our World-Germany, 1993, Integrated Thematic Experiences, Implementation Guide, 1994; author and editor: Solving The Puzzles of Early Childhood, 1986, Integrated Thematic Experiences, Vol. I, 1993; contbr. articles to profl. jours. Chmn. Tng. Ohio's Parents for Success Program, Defiance County, 1989-92; mem. Early Childhood Intervention Collaborative, Defiance County, 1988-92, Four County Early Childhood Adv. Coun., Archbold, 1986-90; host Ohio Coop. Ext. Svc. Internat. Exch. Program, Defiance, 1990; chmn. Defiance 2000 Sch. Readiness Fair, 1994; coord. Lake Wales Pub. Libr. Time to Rhyme Presch. Summer Program, 1995; bd. dirs. Lake Wales Cmty. Theatre, 1995—; presch. planning com. Babson Park Elem. Sch., 1995—; corr. sec. Fla. Fedn. Music Clubs, 1995—; vol. dir. Little Gnat Program, Babson Park Elem. Sch.; mem. adv. bd. Renaissance Abbey Acad., Lakeland, Fla.; mem. Polk County Success by Six Com., 1999. Martha Holden Jennings grantee 1993; named Early Childhood Advocate of Yr., Defiance Assn. for Edn. Young Children, 1988, Leader of Lang. Arts Support Groups in Ohio, Ohio Dept. Edn., 1990, Outstanding Fla. Sch. Vol., Fla. Dept. Edn., 1997, Polk County Sch. Vol. of Yr., 1997, Nat. Points of Light award, 1998. Mem. ASCD, AAUW, Nat. Coun. Tchrs. Social Studies, Nat. Coun. Tchrs. Math., Nat. Assn. for Edn. of Young Children, Polk Coun. for Edn. of Young Children, Assn. Childhood Edn. Internat., Nat. Fedn. Music Clubs. Avocations: music, theatre, reading, travel. Home: 493 N Crooked Lake Dr Babson Park FL 33827-9710

HODARA, RALPH LEON, consulting company executive; b. Buenos Aires, Aug. 30, 1921; s. Isaac and Fortunée (Levy) H.; m. Dolly D. Azicri, Oct. 1, 1948; children: Christian Yves, Alain Didier, Carole Anne. Student, Facultad de Ingenieria, Buenos Aires, 1941; BS, Columbia U., 1944; MS, MIT, 1945. Asst. researcher MIT, Cambridge, Mass., 1945-46; field engr. Barnes Textiles Assocs., Boston, 1946-47; mng. dir. BTCI, Paris, 1948-89; also bd. dirs. BTCI, London; mng. dir. Alec., 1990-98. Contbr. articles to profl. jours. Mem. Textile Inst. Home: 34 rue du Docteur Blanche, 75016 Paris France Office: Alec, 34 Rue du Docteur Blanche, 75781 Paris Cedex 16 France

HODBOD, LUDEK, career officer, engineering educator; b. Michalovce, East Slovakia, Slovak Republic, July 25, 1949; arrived in Czech Republic, 1949; s. Vladimir Hodbod and Milada (Samkova) Hodbodova; m. Marie Ledvinkova, Nov. 24, 1972; children: Martin, Pavel, Michal, Zuzan. Grad. engr., Mil. Acad., Vyskov, Czech Republic, 1971, Mil. Acad., Brno, Czech Republic, 1975; PhD, Mil. Acad., Brno, Czech Republic, 1993, assoc. prof., 1995. Commd. Czech Armed Forces, advanced through grades to lt. col., 1985; co. comdr. Czech Armed Forces, Hodonin, Czech Republic, 1971-72, intelligence officer, 1972-73, regiment staff comdr., 1975-77, dep. regiment comdr., 1977-80; civil def. regiment staff comdr. Czech Armed Forces, Kutna Hora, Czech Republic, 1980-82; civil def. regiment comdr. Czech Armed Forces, Varnsdorf, Czech Republic, 1982-86; tchr. Mil. Acad., Brno, Czech Republic, 1986-94, head subject group, 1994—, cons., 1995—, doctoral adviser, 1996—. Contbr. articles to profl. jours. Mem. local bd. reps. Brno, 1992-94. Avocations: computer, music, reading, sport activities, gardening. E-mail: ludek.hodbod@vabo.cz. Home: Bzenecka 16, 628 00 Brno Czech Republic Office: Mil Acad, Kounicova 65, 612 00 Brno Czech Republic

HODEK, IVO, biologist, researcher; b. Prague, Czech Republic, June 3, 1931; s. Jiri and Marie (Maresova) H.; m. Jarmila Hofmanova, June 2, 1958 (div. Aug. 1964); 1 child, Petr; m. Magdalena Eisenhutova, Apr. 28, 1967. MSc in Biology, Charles U., Prague, 1954, DSc, 1966; Cand. Sci., Acad. Scis., Prague, 1957. Sr. Entomology Inst., Acad. Scis., 1957-78, leading scientist, 1979-85; sr. leading scientist Acad. Scis., Budejovice, Czech Republic, 1986—; external reader Charles U., Prague, 1989—. U. South Bohemia, Ceske Budejovice, 1995—. Author: Biology of Coccinellidae (Ladybirds), 1973, Diapause and Life Strategies in Insects, 1983, (with A. Honek) Ecology of Coccinellidae (Ladybirds), 1996; editor: Ecology of Aphidophaga, 1986, European Jour. Entomology, 1984—; mem. editl. bd. Polish Jour. Ecology, Biocontrol Sci. and Tech., U.K. Fellow Royal Entomol. Soc. (London), Brit. Ecol. Soc.; mem. Internat. Union Biol. Scis. (pres. Czech com. 1995-99), Italian Acad. Entomology. Achievements include discovery of prey specificity in Coccinellidae (ladybirds), multiple pathways of development of dormancy (hibernation, estivation), and role of temperature during this process, recurrent photoperiodic response. Office: Acad Scis Entomology Inst, BraniŠovská 31, 370 05 České Budějovice Czech Republic

HODGE, ANN LINTON, artist; b. Long Beach, Calif., Aug. 24, 1934; d. Mills Schuyler and Irma Jean (Linn) Hodge; m. Quentin Conitz Becker, Dec. 19, 1968 (dec. May 1978); children: Susan Jean Becker Pedersen, Kathryn Ann Becker Michlitsch, Deborah Rena Becker Lippert, Naomi Ruth, David Mills, Sharon Elizabeth Becker Glutting. Student, U. So. Calif., Long Beach, Carroll N. Jones Jr.'s Sch. Fine Arts, Stowe, Vt., 1990-92. Fine arts portrait artist individual commns. Whittier and Long Beach, Calif., 1958-68; mural artist for local businesses Whittier and Long Beach, 1958-68; fine arts portrait artist individual commns. Mandan & Bismarck, N.D., 1968—; instr. basic drawing and advanced portraiture The Renaissance Palette Sch. Fine Arts, Mandan, 1970—; adj. prof. basic drawing Bismarck State Coll., Mandan, 1996; ofcl. state portrait artist Rough Rider Hall of Fame, N.D. State Capital, Bismarck, 1994—; judge art show Glen Ullin (N.D.) Art Assn., 1995; guest lectr. art Shiloh Christian Sch., Bismarck, 1988, Hughes Jr. H.S., Bismarck, 1996. Portraits on display on Internet, 1995—; two-woman show at Bismarck Arts and Gallery, late 1960's - early 1970's. Bible tchr., Bismarck, 1980's. Avocations: building furniture, Bible teaching, writing poetry, reading, making Christmas decorations. Address: The Renaissance Palette 1008 6th Ave NW Mandan ND 58554-2407

HODGE, BOBBY LYNN, mechanical engineer, manufacturing executive; b. Yadkinville, N.C., Oct. 14, 1956; s. Robert Henry and Betty Jean (Martin) H.; m. Robin Mayhue Renegar, June 8, 1979; children: Andrew, Adam. AAS with honors, Forsyth Tech. Inst., Winston-Salem, N.C., 1976; BS in Engring. Tech., U. N.C., Charlotte, 1978. Design engr. Clark/Gravely Corp., Clemmons, N.C., 1978-79; project engr. Clark/Gravely Corp., 1979-80; design engr. Ingersoll-Rand, Davidson, N.C., 1980-83, devel. engr., 1983-85; sr. applications engr. INA Bearing Co., Ft. Mill, S.C., 1985-87, mgr. automotive driveline engring. group, 1987-88, mgr. automotive applications engring., 1988-89, dir. automotive applications engring., 1989-96, dir. automotive engring., 1996-99; v.p. engring./product devel. The Setco Group, Cin., 1999—; internat. spkr. on design and application of anti-friction bearings. Contbr. articles to profl. jours.; inventor, 9 patents in field. Mem. adv. coun. U. N.C.-Charlotte Coll. Engring. Mem. ASME, SAE (mem. manual transmission com., mem. automatic transmission com., mem. clutch stds. com.), Soc. Tribologists and Lubrication Engrs., Am. Soc. Metals. Republican. Baptist. Avocations: golf, hunting, woodworking. Home: 1518 Jolee Dr Hebron KY 41048-9514 Office: The Setco Group 5880 Hillside Ave Cincinnati OH 45233-1599

HODGE, GREGORY LIONEL, medical scientist, researcher; b. Adelaide, Australia, July 7, 1952; s. Lionel William and Rita May (Kruger) H.; m. Sandra Joy Duncan, Feb. 24, 1979; children: Elke, Alex, Chelsea, Sam. B in Applied Sci. Med. Tech., U. South Australia, 1976. Sr. med. scientist NCH, Adelaide, Australia, 1976—. Contbr. articles to profl. jours. Pres. Australasian Flow Cyr. Group, 1999—. Mem. Australian Soc. Blood Transfusion. Home: 29 Snows Rd Stirling, Adelaide 5152, Australia Office: Womens and Childrens Hosp, 72 King William Rd, North Adelaide 5006, Australia Address: Adelaide Womens/Chldns Hosp, Dept Haematol, 72 King WmRd, Adelaide SA 5006, Australia

HODGES, CARROLL BROADUS, retired army officer; b. Tulsa, Okla., Jan. 3, 1914; m. Harriet Eloise; children: Keith, Howard. BA, Okla. Bapt. U., Shawnee, 1935; MS, U. Okla., 1936; postgrad., Duke U., 1937-38, U. Edinburgh, Scotland, 1938-39; PhD, U. Munich, Germany, 1948; LLD (hon.), Chosun U., Korea, 1973; ScD (hon.), Chung-Ang U., Korea, 1974. Instr./dean of men Anatolia Coll., Salonika, Greece, 1939-40; asst. to pres./instr. Judson Coll., Marion, Ala., 1940-41; commd. 2d lt. U.S. Army, 1942, advanced through grades to col.; instr. OCS, U. Fla. U.S. Army, Gainesville, 1942-43; adminstr. Economic Divsn., Mil. Govt. Hdqs., U.S. Forces U.S. Army, Frankfort, Germany, 1945-46; ops. officer U.S. Army/USAF CIC U.S. Army, Munich, 1947-50; chief pers. rsch. U.S. Army Rsch. & Devel. Command U.S. Army, Washington, 1951-56; asst. chief, staff pers., Hdqs. UN Command/U.S. Forces Japan U.S. Army, Tokyo, 1956-60; chief Pers. Mgmt. & Systems Devel. Group, R&D Command U.S. Army, Washington, 1960-62; dir. pers. tng. & adminstrn., U.S. Combat Devels. Command U.S. Army, Ft. Belvoir, Va., 1962-64; chief of staff, Korea Mil. Adv. Group U.S. Army, Seoul, 1964-69; ret. U.S. Army, 1969; mgmt. cons. Kelly & Assocs., Ft. Pierce, Fla., 1969-72; dir. Am.-Korean Found., Seoul, 1972-79; internat. rels. advisor to comdr. U.S. Forces, Seoul, 1979-85. Mem. exec. com. USO Coun. of Korea; dir. Korean-Am. Assn.; com. chmn. Seoul Internat. Rotary Club; spl. mem. Am. C. of C., Korea Advisor to Pres., Korea Vet.'s Assn.; dep. dir. Open Heart Surgery program, Korea; advisor Pearl S. Buck Found. for Amerasian Children. Awarded Legion of Merit medals, 1962, 1964; apptd. Am. spl. advisor to Japanese Olympic Planning Com., 1957-60; awarded prime min.'s citation as one of 50 Ams. making the most significant contributions to U.S.-Korea rels. during past 100 yrs.; recipient Korea Presdl. medal for disting. svc. to veterans of Korea and Vietnam; apptd. hon. col., U.S. Army Mil. Adv. Group, upon 100th anniversary of U.S.-Korea rels.; featured in book A Degree of Difference, 1983, as one of 10 most disting. grads. of Okla. Bapt. U. since its founding in 1912; honored by erection of bronze statue by Girls' Comml. H.S. for major contributions to Korea-wide edn.; nominated by Hdqs. U.S. Forces Command, for the Assn. of the U.S. Army's Exceptional Svc. award for contributions to the Command's mission, the cmty. and U.S.-Korea rels., 1994. Mem. Assn. of the U.S. Army. Fax: 321-259-6809. E-mail: chodges@castlegate.net. Home: 972 Fostoria Dr Melbourne FL 32940-1512

HODGES, RAYMOND GREGG, county official; b. New Hope, Ala., Nov. 15, 1942; s. Raymond Edward and Leota Gregg Hodges; m. Marie Therese Hodges, Feb. 28, 1967; children: Tracy Hodges Thompson, David, Aimee. BS, Miss. State U., Starksville, 1971, MA, 1974; EdD, U. Ala., Tuscaloosa, 1982. County agt. Ala. Coop. Ext. Sys., Russellville, 1975-77, Gadsen, 1977-81; county coord. Ala. Coop. Ext. Sys., Cullman, 1981—. Bd. dirs. Jr. Beef Expn., Montgomery, 1981—, Cullman C. of C., 1983-86; bd. dirs. Farm City, Montgomery, Ala., 1985—, pres., Cullman City, 1989; pres. United Way, Cullman, 1985; active USAD Poliski-Am. Project, 1991. Staff sgt. USAF, 1966-70. Named Top 100 Citizen 1900 Hist. Soc., 2000. Mem. Cullman County Cattlemen Assn., Cullman County Poultry & Egg Assn. Baptist. Avocations: walking, landscaping, wood working, music, world news. Office: Cullman Ext Office 402 Arnold St NE Ste G1 Cullman AL 35055-1952

HODGES-ROBINSON, CHETTINA M., nursing administrator; b. Roosevelt, N.Y., Mar. 12, 1963; d. Clifford and Janice (Revis) Hodges-Jones; m. Darrell K. Robinson, Mar. 17, 1991. BSN, NYU, 1986; postgrad., C.W. Post U. Cert. med.-surg. nurse basic life support and advanced cardiac life support. Staff nurse NYU Med. ctr., N.Y.C., 1986-87, Christ Hosp., Jersey City, 1986-87; cardiothoracic recovery rm. and post-anesthesia nurse, staff nurse Lenox Hill Hosp., N.Y.C., 1987-94; asst. nurse mgr. critical care/intensive/coronary care unit Good Samaritan Hosp., West Islip, L.I., N.Y., 1994—; staff nurse cardiovasc. ICU U. Hosp. at Stony Brook, N.Y., 1995—;

field nurse Staff Builders, Medford, N.Y., 1995—; asst. head nurse, subacute, rehab. unit Jewish Home and Hosp., Bronx, N.Y., 1996—. Mem. Luth. Ch. of the Good Shepherd, Roosevelt, N.Y. Mem. ANA, N.Y. State Nurses Assn., N.J. Nurses Assn., Black Nurses Assn. (L.I. chpt.), Zeta Alpha Beta (bd. election Suffolk County inspector). Home: 119 S 28th St Wyandanch NY 11798-2813

HODGSON, CLAGUE PITMAN, molecular biologist; b. Rochester, Minn, July 6, 1946; s. Corrin Haley and Florence Mary (Pitman) H.; m. Kristi Kay Lauruhn; children: Corrin William, Riley Clague. BS, U. Minn., 1976, PhD in Cell and Devel. Biology, 1983. Teaching asst. U. Minn., Mpls., 1976-78; predoctoral fellow Mayo Grad. Sch. Medicine, Rochester, 1978-83; postdoctoral fellow Baylor Coll. Medicine, Houston, 1983-85; asst. prof. molecular and devel. biology Ohio State U., 1985-91; assoc. prof., chief divsn. cancer biology, gene therapy lab. Creighton U. Sch. Medicine, Omaha, Nebr., 1991—; reviewer grants and contracts NIH, 1986—; chief exec. officer Nature Tech. Corp., Omaha, 1988—; cons. NIH, various cos., 1985—. Author: Retro-Vectors for Human Gene Therapy, 1996; sect. editor: Current Sci., 1993-95, Expert Opinion in Therapeutic Patents; contbr. numerous articles to profl. jours. Recipient Nat. Rsch. Svc. award NIH, 1983-85, fellow, 1983-85, First Ind. Rsch. and Transition award NIH, 1989-93, NIH Shannon Dirs. award, 1995, Inventor's Network Trialon award, 1991, John C. Kenefick award, 1991. Mem. AAAS, Am. Soc. for Cell Biology, Am. Soc. Microbiology, Human Genome Orgn. Achievements include invention of retrotransposon gene transfer sys., synthetic sapphire ultramicrotone knife, virosomes, self-assembling genes. Home: 109 S 54th St Omaha NE 68132-3401 Office: Nature Tech Corp 4701 Innovation Dr Lincoln NE 68521-5330

HODGSON, HUMPHREY JULIAN, medical educator; b. Sheffield, England, Apr. 5, 1945; s. Harold Robinson and Celia Frances H.; m. Shirley Victoria Penrose, Apr. 3, 1971; children: Julian Lionel, Anna Bryony. BA, Oxon, England, 1966, BS, 1969, MS BCh, 1970, DM, 1974. Cons. physician Hammersmith Hosp., London, 1978-99; vice dean Royal Postgrad. Med. Sch., London, 1986-97, prof. gastroenterology, 1992-95, prof. medicine, 1995-97; prof. medicine Imperial coll. of Sci. Tech. and Medicine, London, 1997-99, Royal Free & Univ. Coll. Sch. Medicine, London, 1999—; cons. physician Royal Free Hosp., London, 1999—. Author: Textbook of Gastroenterology, 1984, Gastroenterology Science Practice, 1994; contbr. articles to profl. jours. Rsch. fellow Royal Free Hosp., London, 1974-76, Travel fellow Mass. Gen. Hosp., Boston, 1976-77. Fellow Royal Coll. Physicians (acad. registrar 1992-96); mem. British Soc. Gastroenterology (chmn. edn. 1988-92), Assn. Physicians. Home: 40 Onslow Gardens, London N10 3JU, England Office: Royal Postgrad Med Sch, Royal Free Campus/Dept Med, Royal Free Univ Coll SOM, London NW3 2PF, England

HODGSON, JOHN, agricultural educator; b. Askrigg, U.K., Mar. 1, 1937; s. Richard Mason and Beatrice Alice (Holden) H.; m. Margaret Ruth Watkinson, Aug. 2, 1960; children: Michael Andrew, Caroline Ruth, Katherine Anne, Richard John, David James. BSc in Agriculture, Leeds, U.K., 1960; PhD in Agricluture, Leeds, 1968, DSc in Agricluture, 1987. Cert. Practising Agriculturalist. Scientific officer Grassland Rsch. Inst., U.K., 1960-62; lectr. Dept. Agriculture, U. Leeds, 1962-68; SSO-PSO Grassland Rsch. Inst., U.K., 1969-74; PSO Hill Farming Rsch. Orgn., U.K., 1974-86; prof. agronomy Massey U., New Zealand, 1986-91, prof. pastoral sci., 1992—; head sch. for environ. Massey U., 1995—; hon. vis. prof., Beijing Agrl. U., 1993—, Gansu Grassland Ecol. Rsch. Inst., 1996—. Author: (book) Grazing Mgmt. and Sci. Into Practice, 1990; Co-editor: (books) Sward Measurement Handbook, 1981, The Ecology and Mgmt. of Grazing Systems, 1996, New Zealand Pasture and Crop Sci., 2000. Recipient Sir John Hammond Meml. prize, British Soc. Animal Production, 1981, British Grassland Soc. award, 1991. Fellow Royal Soc. New Zealand; mem. British Grassland Soc., New Zealand Grassland Assn., New Zealand Inst. Agricultural Sci. Office: Inst of Natural Resources, Massey U, Palmerston North 11 222, New Zealand

HODGSON, THOMAS RICHARD, retired healthcare company executive; b. Lakewood, Ohio, Dec. 17, 1941; s. Thomas Julian and Dallas Louise (Livesay) H.; m. Susan Jane Cawrse, Aug. 10, 1963; children: Michael, Laura, Anne. BSChemE, Purdue U., 1963, DEng. (hon.), 1993; MSE, U. Mich., 1964; MBA, Harvard U., 1969. Devel. engr. E.I. Dupont, 1964; assoc. Booz-Allen & Hamilton, 1969-72; with Abbott Labs., North Chicago, Ill., 1972—, gen. mgr. Faultless div., 1976-78, v.p. gen. mgr. hosp. div., 1978-80, pres. hosp. div., 1980-83, group v.p., pres. Abbott Internat. Ltd., 1983-84; also bd. dirs. Abbott Internat. Ltd.; exec. v.p. parent co., pres. Abbott Internat. Inc. Abbott Labs., North Chicago, Ill., 1985-90; pres., chief oper. officer Abbott Labs., Abbott Park, 1990-99; mem. engring. vis. com. Purdue U., 1996—; bd. dirs. St. Paul Cos. Mem. Lake Forest (Ill.) Bd. Edn., 1986-90; trustee and mem. exec. com. Rush-Presbyn. St. Luke's Med. Ctr. Chgo., 1992—; overseer Harvard Bus. Sch. Club Chgo., 1993—. Baker scholar; NSF fellow; recipient Disting. Engring. Alumni award Purdue U., 1985. Mem. Chgo. Coun. Fgn. Rels., Econ. Club, Knollwood Club, Shoreacres Club, Chgo. Club, Phi Eta Sigma, Tau Beta Pi. Home: 1015 Ashley Rd Lake Forest IL 60045-3379 Office: Abbott Labs 100 Abbott Park Rd Abbott Park IL 60064-3502

HODIS, HOWARD NEIL, medical educator. BS, U. So. Calif., L.A., 1980, MD, 1984. Asst. prof. U. So. Calif., L.A., 1990-96, asst. prof. molecular pharmacology and toxicology, 1996—, assoc. prof. medicine and preventive medicine, 1996—. Office: U So Calif 2250 Alcazar St # St132 Los Angeles CA 90033-1004

HODNICAK, VICTORIA CHRISTINE, pediatric nurse; b. Detroit, Dec. 29, 1960; d. Roderick Lewis and Beverly Caroline (Backus) Turner; m. Mark Michael Hodnicak, Sept. 20, 1986; children: Christopher Alan and Matthew Lewis (twins). ADN, Henry Ford C.C., Dearborn, Mich., 1982. RN, Mich., Tenn. Charge nurse, surg. nurse Harper Grace Hosp., Detroit, 1982-86; neonatal nurse St. John Hosp., Detroit, 1986; home care nurse, coord. med. mgmt. Bloomfield Nursing Svcs., Clawson, Mich., 1986-88; coord. pediatric endocrine growth study So. Health Sys., Memphis, 1988-92; nurse specialist, growth study coord. U. Tenn. Med. Group/St. Jude Children's Rsch. Hosp., Memphis, 1992-98; care coord., educator Pediatric Svcs. Am., Memphis, 1998-99; home care pediatric nurse Personal Pediatric Nursing Profls., Pontiac, Mich., 1987-88; staff nurse Nancy Kissick's Profl. Nursing Svc., Mt. Clemens, Mich., 1988. Inventor Growth Hormone new dose form, 1991, Hydrocortisone dose and stress dosing card, 1990; contbr. articles to profl. jours.; inventor equipment cart for vent. patients. Mem. Pediatric Endocrinology Nursing Soc. (membership com. 1992), Endocrine Nursing Soc., Human Growth Found., Neurofibromatosis Found., Turner Syndrome Soc., MAGIC Found., Alexander Graham Bell Assn. for Deaf. Lutheran. Avocations: crafts, doll collecting, travel.

HODOBA, DANILO DANIEL, psychiatrist; b. Sr. Mitrovica, Vojvodina, Yugoslavia, Feb. 15, 1951; arrived in Croatia, 1970; s. Stjepan and Magdalena (Perković) H.; m. Nevenka Čakić, Feb. 28, 1976; 1 child, Ivan. MD, U. Zagreb (Croatia), 1975, MSc, 1983, DSc, 1985. Physician in gen. practice Croatia, 1975-78; psychiatrist Psychiat. Hosp. Vrapče, Zagreb, 1978-91, head dept. psychiat. rsch., 1991—, head psychophysiology dept., 1992—, pres. coun. experts, 1993-95, pres. bd. dirs., 1995-97; pres. bd. dirs. Helios Ins. Co., Zagreb, 1992-94. lectr. on sleep, epilepsy, aging; contbr. articles to profl. jours. Mem. Croatian Med. Assn., Internat. Psychogeriatric Assn., European Sleep Rsch. Soc., Croatian Sleep Rsch. Soc. (pres. 1994—), Acad. Med. Scis. Avocations: history of ancient civilizations, bicycling. Office: Psychiat Hosp Vrapče, Bolnička 32, 10090 Zagreb Croatia

HODSOLL, FRANCIS SAMUEL MONAISE, government official; b. Los Angeles, May 1, 1938; s. Frank and Adelaide (Monaise) H.; m. Margaret Mimi McEwen, Aug. 18, 1963; children—Lisa-Monaise, Francis Hamill McEwen. BA, Yale U., 1959; MA, LLB, Cambridge U., 1963; JD, Stanford U., 1964; Fgn. Svcs. econ. course, Washington, 1972; DFA (hon.), Pratt Inst., 1983, U. Mass., 1986. Assoc. Sullivan & Cromwell, N.Y.C., 1965-66; fgn. service officer Adminstrv. Office Am. embassy, Belgium, 1966-68; asst. polit. advisor SHAPE, Belgium, 1968-69; controlling dir. Warner, Barnes & Co., Manila, 1964-71; oceans policy officer State Dept., Washington, 1969-71; spl. asst. chmn. Council on Environ. Quality, Washington, 1972-73; spl. asst. adminstr. EPA, Washington, 1973-74; dir. energy conservation div. Commerce Dept., Washington, 1974, staff dir. cabinet work edn. task force, 1974, exec. asst. to undersec., 1974-76, dept. asst. sec. commerce for energy and strategic resources, 1976-77; dir. Office of Law of Sea Negotiation State Dept., Washington, 1977, dep. U.S. spl. rep. for nonproliferation, 1978-80; mem. White House transition team Exec. Office Pres., Washington, 1980-81; dep. asst. to Pres. and dep. to chief of staff White House, Washington, 1981; chmn. Nat. Endowment for Arts, Washington, 1981-89; exec. assoc. dir., chief fin. officer U.S. Govt. Office Mgmt. and Budget, Exec. Office of Pres., Washington, 1989-91; dep. dir. for mgmt. Office Mgmt. and Budget, Exec. Office of Pres., Washington, 1991-93; bd. dirs. Ctr. for Arts and Culture; co-chmn. Sally Mae Edn. Svcs. Coun., 1995-96, Am. Assembly Arts and the Pub. Purpose, 1996-97; CEO Southwest Colo. Data Ctr., 1994-97; cons. in field. Chmn. Ouray County (Colo.) Rep. com., 1995-96; commr. Ouray County, 1997— (chmn. bd. 2000—); dir. Colo. River Water Conservation Dist., 1997—; v. chair Nat. Assn. Counties Geospatial Data com., 1998-99; mem. Gen. Govt. Transition Team Colo. Gov. elect Bill Owens, 1998-99; mem. review com. New Century Colo., 1999—; mem. New Century Colo. Com., 1999—, Nat. Assn. Counties Rural Leadership Caucus and Telecom. Task Force, 1999—. Lt. U.S. Army, 1959-60. Mem. N.Y. State Bar Assn., Stanford U. Alumni Assn., Yale Club, Met. Club, Zeta Psi. Republican. Episcopalian.

HODSON, ROY GOODE, JR., retired logistician; b. Enon, Ala., July 22, 1927; s. Roy Goode and Ilda Fern (Jinks) H.; m. Mildred Bernice Parlier, Dec. 3, 1966 (dec. July 1992); children: Joan Hodson Bash, Scott Daniel, Jayne Clymer. Student, San Diego Jr. Coll., 1947-49, San Diego Vocational, 1947-49, San Diego State Coll., 1949-50. Security officer US Naval CB Ctr. (Civil Service), Port Hueneme, Calif., 1950-52; logistician Gen. Dynamics, San Diego, 1952-64, GTE Govt. Systems, Inc., Mt. View, Calif., 1964-89. Bd. dirs. San Jose Civic Light Opera Assn., 1988-95; advisor San Jose Children's Musical Theater, 1995—; mem. Yu-Ai Kai Japanese Am. Cmty. Sr. Svc., Sta. WNIT-TV PBS, WFWA-TV. With U.S. Army, 1945-47. Recipient Bravo award Silhoutte mag., 1988, Ginny award, 1989. Mem. AMVETS, Am. Assn. Ret. Persons, Am. Film Inst., Humane Soc. U.S., Am. Legion, Nat. Arbor Day Found., Easter Seals Found., Nat. Svc. Found., Nature Conservancy, Internat. Freelance Photographers Orgn., Internat. Platform Assn., Am. Philatelic Soc., Nat. Pks. and Conservation Assn., Calif. State Pks. Found., Spiceland Hist. and Tourism Soc., Am. Image Press Club, Nat. Humane Edn. Soc., Ind. Sheriffs Assn., Humane Soc. Noble County, Noble County Hist. Soc., Albion C. of C., Am. Indian Edn. Found., Am. Indian Relief Coun., Nat. Audubon Soc., Cornell Lab. of Ornithology, Wildlife Land Trust. Democrat. Mem. Church of Christ. Avocations: photography, lapidary, geneaology, music. Home: 4611 W 300 S Albion IN 46701-9449

HOECKMANN, OLAF OTTOMAR, archeology; b. Barth, Germany, July 10, 1935; s. Heinrich and Hedwig-Elisabeth (Gutzmann) H.; m. Ursula Haefner, Aug. 29, 1967. DrPhil, U. Muenster, Germany, 1962. Asst. Univ., Muenster, Germany, 1963-65, Roemisch-Germanisches Zentral Mus., Mainz, Germany, 1965-74; konservator Roemisch-Germanisches Zentral Mus., Mainz, 1974-77, oberkonservator, 1977-97, ret., 1997. Author: Anthropomorphic Sculpture of the Neolithic, 1965, Ancient Navigation, 1985; contbr. over 100 articles to profl. jours. Grantee Deutsche Forschungsgemeinschaft, 1963, Stiftung Archaeologie in Koeln, 1998. Evangelical. Home: Taunusstr 39, D 55118 Mainz Germany

HOEDL, HEINZ, banking executive; b. Vienna, Austria, June 23, 1941. Grad., U. Econ. and Bus. Adminstrn., Vienna, 1963. Asst. v.p. Raiffeisen Zentralbank, Vienna, 1969-74, sr. v.p., gen. mgr. internat. divsn., 1974-2000, exec. v.p., head internat. bus. units, 2000—; mem. supr. bd. OOO Raiffeisenbank Austria, Moscow, Raiffeisenbank (Romania) S.A., Bucharest, Raifeisenbank (Bulgaria) AD, Sofia, Joint Stock Comml Bank Raiffeisenbank Ukraine, Kiev. Office: Raiffeisen Zentralbank AG, A-1030 Vienna Austria

HOEFFE, OTFRIED GERHARD, philosophy educator; b. Leobschuetz, Germany, Sept. 12, 1943; s. Wilhelm Lucian and Susanne (Pawelke) H.; m. Evelyn Brigitte Anetsberger, Dec. 18, 1970; children: Moritz, Julia, Teresa. PhD, U. Munich, 1970, habilitation, 1975. Vis. scholar Columbia U., N.Y.C., 1970-71; sci. asst. U. Munich, 1971-76; prof. philosophy U. Duisburg, 1976-78; prof. moral and polit. philosophy U. Freiburg, Switzerland, 1978-92; prof. philosophy U. Tuebingen, Germany, 1992—; dean, vice-dean faculty U. Tuebingen, 1995—; dir. Internat. inst. for Social Philosophy and Politics, U. Freiburg, 1978-92, dean faculty, 1983-85; fellow Inst. Advanced Studies, Wissenschaftskolleg, Berlin, 1985-86; vis. prof. many European univs. Author: Immanuel Kant, 1983, 4th edit., 1996, English edit., 1994, Political Justice, 1987, English edit., 1995, Morals as Price of Modernity, 1992, 3d edit., 1995, Aristotle, 1996, 2d edit., 1999, Reason and Law, 1996, Is There an Intercultural Criminal Law?, 1999, Democracy in the Age of Globalization, 1999; editor Zeitschrift fuer Philosophische Forschung, 1976—. Lt. German Artillery, 1962-64. Recipient prize Egnér Found., Zürich, 1992. Mem. German Soc. for Philosophy, Adv. Coun. Goerres Soc., Rotary Internat. Roman Catholic. Home: 13 Schwabstrasse, 72074 Tübingen Germany Office: Philosophical Seminar, 1 Bursagasse, 72070 Tübingen Germany

HOEFFEL, JEAN-CLAUDE EDMOND, radiology educator; b. Pnom Penh, Cambodia, Mar. 10, 1933; arrived in France, 1945; s. Ernest Hoeffel and Renée Caplan; m. Françoise Rose Boutet; children: Christine, Olivier. MD, U. Paris, 1965; prof. faculty, U. Nancy, France, 1967. Chief radiology svc. Hosp. Jeanne d'Arc, Toul, 1970; chief radiol. pediat. svc. Children's Hosp., Nancy, 1978. Office: Children's Hosp, 5 rue Morvan, 54511 Vandoeuvre-Les-Nancy France

HOEFKENS, ERWIN A., information systems executive; b. Lier, Belgium, Dec. 7, 1962; s. Augustijn and Jeann (Ven den Bruel) H.; m. Constantia Verstrepen, Sept. 24, 1988; children: Jeffrey, Lennert. Grad. in engring., Cath. U. Louvain, 1984. Sys. analyst CMB NV, Antwerp, Belgium, 1985-87; project mgr. CMB Transport NV, Antwerp, 1988-89, info. sys. devel. mgr., 1990-94; info. sys. mgr. Aseco Internat., Antwerp, 1994-95; info. sys. exec. for agys. SCL, Antwerp, 1996-97; info. sys. exec. Aseco Internat., 1997-98; info. sys. exec. European region Safmarine, Antwerp, 1999—.

HOEFLIN, RONALD KENT, philosopher, intelligence test designer, newsletter publisher; b. Richmond Heights, Mo., Feb. 23, 1944; s. William Eugene and Mary Elizabeth (Dell) H. Student, Calif. Inst. Tech., 1962-63, U. Calif., Berkeley, 1966-67, U. N.C., 1970-71; BA, U. Minn., 1968, Shimer Coll., 1974; MLS, Ind. U., 1970; MA, New Sch. Social Rsch., 1979, PhD, 1987. With various librs., 1969-85; publisher, editor Triple Nine Soc., N.Y.C., 1979-81, 85-89; publisher, editor, founder Top One Percent Soc., N.Y.C., 1989—, One-in-a-Thousand Soc., N.Y.C., 1992—. Designer (intelligence tests) Mega Test, 1985, Titan Test, 1990, Ultra Test, 1995, Hoeflin Power Test, 1996. Mem. Am. Philos. Assn. (Fifth Ann. Rockefeller prize 1988), Mensa, Mega Soc. (founder 1982), Prometheus Soc. (founder 1982). Office: PO Box 539 New York NY 10101-0539

HOEFLING, RONALD WALTER, physicist; b. Chemnitz, Saxony, Germany, June 7, 1954; s. Johannes and Hanni H.; m. Gudrun Eckardt, Aug. 2, 1975; children: Felix, Christian. Diploma in Physics, Dresden U. Tech., Germany, 1979; Dr. rer. nat., Chemnitz U. Tech., Germany, 1988. Phys. engring.; optics. Software developer Robotron, Chemnitz, 1979-84; scientist Acad. Scis., Chemnitz, 1984-91; head group Franhofer Inst. for Machine Tools and Forming Tech., Chemnitz, 1991-98; head Ctr. Micro Fabrication Franhofer Inst. for Machine Tools and Forming Tech., 1999—; head holography work group VDI-GESA, Germany, 1997—. Author: VDI Berichte, 1988; contbr. articles to profl. jours. Mem. Internat. Soc. for Optical Engring., Euspen. Avocations: outdoor activities. Office: Frahnofer Inst IWU, Reichenhainer Str 88, D-09126 Chemnitz Saxony, Germny

HOEHER, MARTIN, cardiologist, researcher; b. Cologne, Germany, Oct. 6, 1957; s. Karl-Heinz and Annemarie (Mauel) H.; m. Dagmar Klatt, Apr. 8, 1989. MD, U. Cologne, 1983. Fellow in cardiology U. Cologne, 1983-84, 87-88, fellow in physiology, 1984-87; fellow in cardiology U. Ulm, Germany, 1988-92; asst. dir. cardiology U. Ulm, 1993—. Contbr. articles to profl. jours. Mem. European Soc. Cardiology, German Soc. Cardiology, Am. Heart Assn. Roman Catholic. Avocations: piano, organ, computers. E-mail: martin@hoeher.de. Home: Klosterhof 18/2, 89077 Ulm Germany Office: U Ulm, Robert-Koch-Str 8, 89081 Ulm Germany

HOEKL, JAN KAREL, immunologist; b. Brno, Moravia, Czech Republic, Oct. 24, 1939; s. Jan and Ruzena (Kasparova) H.; m. Jirina Budarova, Dec. 20, 1969; children: Jana, Marketa. MS, Faculty Life Sci., Brno, 1962; PhD, Acad. Sci., Prague, Czech Republic, 1972. Rschr. Acad. Sci., Prague, 1964-71, Teaching Hosp., Brno, 1971-84, Transplant Surgery, Brno, 1985—. Coauthor: Cyclosporine A, 1994. Mem. Transplantation Soc., European Transplantation Soc. Avocations: basketball, tennis. Office: Transplant Surgery, Pekarska 53, 656 91 Brno Moravia, Czech Republic

HOEL, ROBERT FREDRICK, JR., construction executive, civil engineer; b. St. Louis, Apr. 14, 1949; s. Robert F. Sr. and LaVerne (Schaller) M. BSCE, U. Mo., 1971. Registered profl. engr., Mo., Fla. Project mgr. Hoel-Steffen Constrn. Co., St. Louis, 1971-79; project dir. Sverdrup Corp., St. Louis, 1979-82; regional mgr. Vector Constrn. Co., Orlando, Fla., 1982-84; sr. project mgr. Fed. Constrn. Co., St. Petersburg, Fla., 1984-87; v.p. dir. ops., regional mgr. Brown & Root Bldg. Co., Clearwater, Fla., 1987-99; v.p. Centex-Rooney Constrn. Co., Fort Lauderdale, Fla., 1999—. Mem. Mo. Soc. Profl. Engrs., Fla. Engring. Soc., Mo. Athletic Club. Roman Catholic. Home: 4909 SW 5th Pl Cape Coral FL 33914-6501 Office: Centex-Rooney Constrn Co 6300 NW 5th Way Fort Lauderdale FL 33309-6136

HOEL, TERJE, physician, consultant, microbiologist; b. Oslo, Norway, Jan. 25, 1958; m. Tryggve and Ase (Nordback) H.; m. Anne Svendsen, Dec. 29, 1984; children: Henrik, Silje, Hedda. Degree in preclin. medicine, Justus-Liebig U., Giessen, Germany, 1980; degree in clin. medicine, U. Oslo, 1984. Sr. registrar Telemark Ctrl. Hosp., 1985-86, Nat. Inst. Pub. Health, 1987-91; dir. medicine Oslo City Dept. Health and Environment, 1991-93; chief physician cons. Dept. Med. Microbiology, 1993-94, Ulleval U. Hosp. Vaccination, 1996—; physician control communicable diseases Oslo, 1997—; cons. physician Ulleval U. Hosp. Author: Medical Microbiology and Infectious Diseases. Capt. Inst. Microbiology, Armed Forces Med. Svcs., Norwegian Army, 1985-90. Mem. Norwegian Microbiology Soc. (pres. 1996-98), Norwegian Med. Assn., Norwegian Soc. for Infectious Diseases. Home: Idrettsveien 9E, N-1358 Oslo Norway Office: Ulleval U Hosp, N-0407 Oslo Norway

HOELDERICH, WOLFGANG FRIEDRICH, chemistry engineering educator; b. Mannheim, Baden, Germany, July 10, 1946. Master degree, U. Karlsruhe, Germany, 1972, doctor degree, 1975; postdoctoral, MIT, 1976-77. Rsch. chemist Badische Anilin und Soda Fabrik Aktiengesellschaft, Ludwigshafen, Germany, 1978-83, group leader, 1983-92, rsch. rep. in catalysis divsn., various leading positions, 1987-92; univ. prof. RWTH, Aachen, Germany, 1992—, dir. rsch. inst., 1992—; cons. in field, 1992—. Co-editor: (books) Zeolites and Related Microporous Materials: State of the Art, 1994, Guidelines for Mastering the Properties of Molecular Sieves, NATO ASI Series B: Physics, Volume 221, 1989; contbr. articles to profl. jours.; patentee in field. Scholarship NATO, 1976; fellowship Japanese Chem. Soc., 1997. Mem. German Zeolite Assn., German Catalysis Assn. Avocations: skiing, swimming, tennis, reading. Office: U Tech RWTH Aachen, Worringerweg 1, 52074 Aachen Germany

HOELTGEN, KARL JOSEF, English literature educator; b. Haan, Rhineland, Germany, Nov. 2, 1927; s. Karl and Maria (Conrads) H.; m. Freda Morley, Sept. 23, 1958; 1 child, Daniel. Dr phil, U. Bonn, Germany, 1955, Habilitation in English Philology, 1968. Cert. high sch. tchr., Germany. Instr. English, U. Bonn., 1956-58, asst. English dept., 1959-68, lectr., 1968; lectr. U. Leicester, Eng., 1958-59; prof., chmn. dept. English, U. Erlangen-Nuernberg (Germanyú, 1968-96, prof. emeritus, 1996—, dean philos. faculty, 1972-73; tchr. pub. schs., Bonn and Bruehl, Germany, 1956-58; chmn. acad. studies com. Standing Conf. Philos. Faculties in Germany, 1972-96; vis. fellow, assoc. Clare Hall, Cambridge (Eng.) U., 1972—, Linacre Coll., Oxford (Eng.) U., 1981—. Author: Francis Quarles (1592-1644), 1978, Aspects of the Emblem, 1986, also other books and edits. in English lit., especially 16th-17th centuries; contbr. more than 80 articles to profl. jours., including Anglia, Rev. English Studies, Notes and Queries, The Libr., Emblematica, English Lit. Renaissance, English Manuscript Studies, Explorations in Renaissance Culture. Founding mem. German-Brit. Soc., Nuernberg, 1971, v.p., 1978-99; active in establishing Erlangen and Stoke-on-Trent, Eng., becoming twin cities, 1988. Decorated hon. officer Order Brit. Empire; recipient Cecil Oldman silver medal for disting. contbns. in bibliography U. Leeds, Eng., 1974, Acad. award Volkswagen Found., 1984; festschrift The Art of the Emblem in Honor of K.J. Hoeltgen, 1993. Mem. Renaissance Soc. Am., Soc. for Emblem Studies (bd. dirs. 1990—), South Ctrl. Renaissance Conf. (hon.), Prince Albert Soc. (founding), Internat. Assn. Univ. Profs. English (exec. com. 1995-98). Office: U Erlangen-Nuernberg, English Dept, Bismarckstr 1, D-91054 Erlangen Germany

HOENIG, JOHANNES FRANZ, plastic surgeon, educator; b. Dülmen, Germany, July 15, 1956; s. Johann Josef and Emy Bernadette (Gelshefarth) H. MD, U. Ulm, Germany, 1986; DMD, U. Ulm, 1988; PhD, U. Goettingen, Germany, 1995. Diplomate German Bd. Plastic and Reconstructive Surgery. Resident U. Ulm, 1985-86, U. Würzburg, Germany, 1986-88; sr. resident U. Goettingen, 1989-93, instr. in plastic and reconstructive surgery, 1992, cons. in plastic and reconstructive surgery, 1993, prof. in plastic and reconstructive surgery, 1995; lectr. craniofacial and plastic surgery U. Med. Sch. Goettingen, 1993-94; gen. mgr. Medline Pub., 1992. Author numerous books and more than 200 articles; editor, author: Plastic Surgery, 1994, Aesthetic Surgery, 2000; inventor multi-point contact osteosynthesis plate; patentee in field. Mem. Art Collection, Goettingen, 1991; founder Bernhard Rosevelt Gelschefarth Soc., Germany 1996. Mem. German Soc. Plastic and Reconstructive Surgery, Am. Soc. Plastic and Reconstructive Surgery, N.Y. Acad. Sci., German Soc. Craniofacial Osteology (chmn. 1994-97), European Assn. Aesthetic Plastic Facial Surgeons (pres. 1997-2000). Avocations: painting, music, skydiving, horseback riding. Office: Univ Hosp Med Sch, Robert Koch Str 40, 37075 Göttingen Germany

HOENIG, THOMAS M., bank executive; b. Fort Madison, Iowa, Sept. 6, 1946. BA in Econs., St. Benedict's Coll., 1968; MA, PhD, Iowa State U. of Sci. & Tech., Ames, 1974. Economist banking supervision area Fed. Reserve Bank of Kansas City, Mo., 1973; v.p. Fed. Reserve Bank of Kansas City, 1981, sr. v.p., 1986, CEO, 1991, pres., CEO, 1991—; mem. Free Open Market Com.; bd. dirs., mem. banking adv. bd. U. Mo., Kansas City; mem. banking adv. bd. U. Mo., Columbia. Trustee Benedictine Coll., Atchison, Kans., Midwest Rsch. Inst. Office: Fed Res Bank of Kans City 925 Grand Blvd Kansas City MO 64106-2006 Home: 615 W Meyer Blvd Kansas City MO 64113-1543*

HOENIGSWALD, HENRY MAX, linguist, educator; b. Breslau, Germany, Apr. 17, 1915; s. Richard and Gertrud (Grunwald) H.; m. Gabriele Schoepflich, Dec. 26, 1944; children: Frances Gertrude, Susan Ann. Student, U. Munich, 1932-33, U. Zurich, 1933-34, U. Padua, 1934-36; DLitt, U. Florence, 1936, Perfezionamento, 1937; LHD (hon.), Swarthmore Coll., 1981, U. Pa., 1988; MA (hon.), U. Pa., 1971. Staff mem. Istituto Studi Etruschi, Florence, 1936-38; lectr., rsch. asst., instr. Yale U., 1939-42, 44-45; lectr., instr. Hartford Sem. Found., 1942-43, 45-46; lectr. Hunter Coll., 1942-43, 46; lectr. charge Army specialized tng. U. Pa., Phila., 1943-44, assoc. prof., 1948-59, prof. linguistics, 1959-85, prof. emeritus, 1985—, chmn. dept. linguistics, 1963-70, co-chmn., 1978-79, cn. Caldwell Prize com., 1989-91; P-4 Fgn. Service Inst., Dept. State, 1946-47; asso. prof. U. Tex., 1947-48; sr. linguist Deccan Coll., India, 1955; Fulbright lectr., Kiel, summer 1968, Oxford U., 1976-77; corp. vis. com. fgn. lits. and linguistics MIT, 1968-74; chmn. overseers com. to visit dept. linguistics Harvard U., 1978-84; vis. assoc. prof. U. Mich., 1946, 52, Princeton U., 1959-60; vis. assoc. prof. Georgetown U., 1952-53, 54, Collitz prof., 1955; vis. prof. Yale U., 1961-62, U. Mich., 1968; mem. Seminar, Columbia U., 1965—; vis. staff mem., Leuven, 1986; fellow St. John's Coll., Oxford U., 1976-77; del. Comparative Linguistics Internat. Rsch. and Exchs. Bd., 1986; cons. Etymological Dictionary of Old High German, 1980—; Poultney lectr. Johns Hopkins U., 1991; co-promotor, Leuven, 1992; mem. acad. com. Yarmouk U., 1997. Author: Spoken Hindustani, 1946-47, Language Change and Linguistic Reconstruction, 1960, Studies in Formal Historical Linguistics, 1973; editor: Am. Oriental Series, 1954-58, The European Background of American Linguistics, 1979, (with L. Wiener) Biological Metaphor and Cladistic Clas-

sification, 1987, (with M.R. Key) General and American Ethnolinguistics, 1989; assoc. editor Indian Jour. Linguistics, 1977—; cons. editor Jour. History of Ideas, 1978—; adv. bd. Lang. and Style, 1968—, Jour. Indo-European Studies, 1973—, Diachronica, 1984-94, Lynx, 1988—; csr. internat. adviser, cons. editor Internat. Ency. Linguistics, 1986-91; editl. cons. Biographical Dictionary of Western Linguistics, 1994—. Am. Council Learned Socs. fellow, 1942-43, 44, Guggenheim fellow, 1950-51, Newberry Library fellow, 1956, NSF and Center Advanced Study Behavioral Scis. fellow, 1962-63, Faculty fellow Modern Langs. Coll. House, 1990-91; Festschrift in his honor, 1987. Fellow British Acad. (corr.), Am. Acad. Arts and Scis.; mem. NAS, Am. Philos. Soc. (rsch. com. 1984, libr. com. 1984-94, chmn. 1988-94, membership com. class IV 1984-90, chmn. 1987-90, exec. com. 1988-94, publs. com. 1994—, Henry Allen Moe prize 1991), N.Y. Acad. Scis., Linguistic Soc. Am. (pres. 1958), Am. Oriental Soc. (editor 1954-58, pres. 1966-67), Philol. Soc. (London), Linguistic Soc. India, Societas Linguistica Europaea, Linguistics Assn. Gt. Britain, Internat. Soc. Hist. Linguistics, Indogermanische Gesellschaft, Am. Philol. Assn., Classical Assn. Atlantic State, Soc. Linguistica Italiana, Henry Sweet Soc., Studienkreis Geschichte der Sprachwissenschaft, N.Am. Assn. History of Lang. Scis., Fulbright Assn., Internat. Soc. Friends of Wroclaw U., Fedn. Am. Scientists. Home: 908 Westdale Ave Swarthmore PA 19081-1804 Office: U Pa 618 Williams Hall Philadelphia PA 19104-6305

HOEPTNER, NORBERT, engineering educator; b. Aschaffeuburg, Bayern, Germany, Dec. 7, 1952; s. Erich and Ursula K. (Kothe) H.; m. Gertraud E. Flickenscher, Sept. 23, 1978; children: Birgit, Christiane. Diplom-Ingenieur, Tech. Hochschule, Darmstadt, 1976; Dr.-Ingenieur, TU, Karlsruhe, 1982. Engr. Tekade, Nuernberg, 1977; wiss.asst. TU, Karlsruhe, 1977-82; akad. oberrat TU, Hamburg-Harburg, 1982-89; prof. U. Applied Scis., Pforzheim, 1989-91, dekan, 1991-97, rector, 1997—; cons. Polytechnic, Singapore, 1992; head Stewbeis-Stiftung, Stuttgart, 1992—. Patentee in field. Organist Cath. Ch., Karlsbad, leader ch. choir. Mem. IEEE, VDI. Roman Catholic. Home: Fliederstrasse 16, D-76307 Karlsbad Germany Office: Univ Pforzheim, Tiefenbronnerstr 65, D-75175 Pforzheim Germany

HOERAUF, KLAUS HEINRICH, anesthetist, researcher, anesthesiology educator; b. Ludwigshafen, Germany, Feb. 1, 1962; s. Emil and Ursula M. (Gotz) H. Student, U. Heidelberg, U. Mainz; DrMed, U. Muenster, 1989; Univ. Prof., U. Vienna, 1999. Rsch. fellow Univ. Hosp., Muenster, Germany, 1986-92; rsch. fellow Univ. Hosp., Regensburg, Germany, 1992-94, cons., rschr., 1994-96; cons. Univ. Hosp. Vienna, Austria, 1996—; lectr. in field. Contbr. numerous articles to profl. jours. Mem. several internat. sci. socs. Avocations: sports, music, leterature, history. E-mail: klaus.hoerauf@univie.ac.at.

HOERNER, JOHN LEE, retail store executive; b. Lincoln, Nebr., Sept. 23, 1939; s. Robert L. and Lulu (Stone) H.; m. Susan Kay Morgan, Nov. 12, 1959 (div. Nov. 1971); m. Anna Lea Thomas, Feb. 16, 1973; children: John Scott, Joanne Lynne. BSBA, U. Nebr., 1961. Sr. buying and mktg. positions Hovland-Swanson Co., Lincoln, Nebr., 1959-68; gen. mdse. mgr. Woolf Bros., Kansas City, Mo., 1968-72; sr. v.p. Hahne's, Newark, 1972-81; pres., chief exec. officer H & S Pogue Co., Cin., 1981; pres., CEO L.S. Ayres & Co., Indpls., 1982-85, chmn., CEO, 1985-87; chmn., pres., CEO Debenhams divsn. Burton Group plc, London, 1987-92; chmn. Harvey Nichols, 1988—; CEO Arcadia Group plc, London, 1992-98, dir., 1998—; non-exec. dir. BAA plc; chmn. Brit. Fashion Coun., 1997-2000. Author: Ayres Adages, 1983. Vice chmn. Dogs' Home, Battersea, Eng., 1995—. Office: Arcadia Group PLC, Colegrave Hse 70 Berners St, London W1T 3NL, England

HOERNER, WOLFGANG PETER, educator; b. Kalisz, Poland, Nov. 24, 1944; s. Wilhelm and Lydia (Kind) H.; m. Anais Bailly, Dec. 19, 1969; children: Fernand, Clara. Licence es lettres, Univ., Toulouse, France, 1969; Dr. phil, Univ., Bochum, Germany, 1977; Dr. phil. habil, Univ., Oldenburg, Germany, 1991. Asst. Univ. Bochum, 1972-74; deputy prof. Univ. Hamburg, Hamburg, Germany, 1978-79; rsch. fellow Univ. Bochum, 1979-93; prof. Univ. Leipzig, Germany, 1993—. Author: Curriculumentwicklung in Frankreich, 1979, Ecole et culture technique Experiences Europeennes, 1987, Technische Bildung und Schule, 1993; co-author: Bildungssysteme in Europa, 1996; co-editor: Bildungseinheit und Systemtransformation, 1999, Transformation im Bildungswesen und europäische Perspektiven, 1999. Recipient rsch. scholarship Univ. Bochum, 1975-77. Mem. Comparative and Internat. Edn. Soc. (pres. German sect. 1998-2000), Assn. Tchr. Edn. In Europe. Avocation: choir. Home: Hustadtring 35, D-44801 Bochum Germany Office: Univ Leipzig, Karl-Heine Str 22B, D-04229 Leipzig Germany

HOEY, HILARY MARIE CONSTANCE VICTORIA, pediatrics educator; b. Dublin, Apr. 29, 1946; d. Raphael John and Gladys Cynthia (Breen) Hoey; m. Peter Harris, Jan. 20, 1982; children: Raphline Gladys, Peter Raphael. MB, BCh, BAO, Univ. Coll., Dublin, 1971, diploma in child health, 1974; MRCPI, Royal Coll. Physicians, Dublin, 1979, FRCPI (hon.), 1992; MD, Trinity Coll., Dublin, 1988, MA (hon.), 1992, FTCD, 1994. Cert. med. pediatrician, pediatric endocrinologist. Sr. house officer Rotunda Hosp., Dublin, 1974; sr. registrar Hosp. for Sick Children, London, 1980-82; fellow in pediatric endocrinology U. Calif., San Francisco, 1982; lectr. in pediatrics Trinity Coll., 1983-87, prof. pediatrics, 1991—; cons. pediatrician Nat. Children's Hosp., Dublin, 1991—, also bd. govs.; pediatric endocrinologist Our Lady's Hosp. Crumlin, Dublin, 1991—; mem. gov. bd. and coun. Trinity Coll., 1992—; mem. Postgrad. Med. and Dental Bd., 1992—, Tallaght Regional Hosp. Bd., 1993—; med. dir. Adelaide and Meath Hosp. Dublin, 1996—. Author, editor: Paediatric Nephro-Urology, 1989; contbr. articles to med. jours., booklets. Recipient Irish Dir. Euro Growth Study award EEC, 1991—, Best Rsch. Paper award (edn. sect.) Brit. Diabetic Assn. 1992. Fellow Royal Coll. Physicians Ireland (guest lectr. 1992), Royal Coll. Medicine, Royal Acad. Medicine (coun. mem. 1994—); mem. Brit. Pediatric Assn. (regional advisor 1991—), European Soc. for Pediatric Endocrinology, Irish Paediatric Assn. (pres. 1995—). Avocations: tennis, gardening, old masters, music, golf. Home: Ivy House, Main St, Leixlip Co Kildare, Ireland Office: Trinity Coll Dublin Dept Pediatrics, Harcourt St, Dublin 2, Ireland

HOFACKER, LUDWIG GEORG, chemistry educator; b. Ansbach, Bavaria, Germany, Jan. 12, 1930; s. Georg and Maria (Irg) H.; m. Ursula Anna Hellweg, 1959; children: Sunna, Ivo. PhD, U. Goettingen, Federal Republic of Germany, 1958. Vis. prof. chemistry U. Fla., Gainesville, 1963, ETH, Zurich, Switzerland, 1964; assoc. prof. chemistry Northwestern U., Evanston, Ill., 1964-68; prof. chemistry Tech. U. Munich, 1969-99, prof. emeritus, 1999—. Editor: (jour.) Chem. Physics, 1972—. Mem. German Chem. Soc., German Phys. Soc., Am. Phys. Soc.

HOFER, ERHARD F., science educator; b. Klagenfurt, Austria, June 29, 1949; s. Rafael and Ernestine (Krammer) H.; m. Renate Warbinek, June 10, 1977; children: Matthias, Fabian. PhD in Biochemistry, U. Graz, Austria, 1975; dozent in molecular biology, U. Vienna, 1988, prof. degree, 1997. Postdoctoral fellow Rockefeller U., N.Y.C., 1978-81; lab. head Sandoz Ltd., Vienna, Basel, Switzerland, 1984-91; rsch. group leader U. Vienna, 1991-95, prof., 1996—. Contbr. articles to profl. jours.; patentee in field. Recipient Coord. grant European Commn. 1995, 98. Avocations: travelling, mountaineering, skiing. Office: Dept Vasc Bio U Vienna, Brunnerstr 59, A-1230 Vienna Austria

HOFER, FERNANDA MARIA, geneticist; b. Lucerne, Switzerland, May 23, 1929; d. Josef Otto and Anna-Maria (Isenschmid) H. PhD, U. Berne, 1969. Teaching asst. dept. microbiology U. Berne, Switzerland, 1965-69; rschr. blood transfusion svc. ctrl. lab. Swiss Red Cross, Berne, 1970-71; rschr. in bacteriology Swiss Fed. Dairy Rsch. Inst., Berne, 1972-81, scientific asst., 1982-84; ret., 1985—. Contbr. articles to profl. jours. Mem. Am. Soc. for Microbiology, Swiss Soc. for Microbiology, Swiss Acad. Scis., Soc. Scientific Rsch., Swiss Assn. Univ. Women. Roman Catholic. Achievements include discovery of antisuppressors in schizosaccharomyces pombe; lactose-plasmids in lactobacillus casei; gene transfer system in a lactobacillus species. Avocations: philosophy, music, skiing. Home: Obergutschstrasse 18, CH-6003 Lucerne Switzerland

HOFER, MICHAL, biomedical researcher; b. Brno, Czech Republic, Dec. 4, 1957; s. Jaroslav and Eva (Kadlčíková) H; m. Zuzana Sedlakova, Nov. 13, 1999. MD, Masaryk U., 1983, PhD, 1988. Scientist Inst. of Biophysics, Acad. of Scis. of the Czech Republic, Brno, 1988-93, scientist, project leader, 1993—; vice chmn. Grant Agy. of the Acad. of Scis. of the Czech Republic, Praha, 1995-98. Contbr. articles to profl. jours. including Jour. of Leukocyte Biology, Radiation Rsch., Internat. Jour. of Immunopharmacology, Blood, European Jour. Haematology. Grantee Grant Agy. of the Czech Republic, 1993-95, 96-98, 99—. Mem. European Soc. for Radiation Biology (coun. mem. 1996—), Czech Radiobiological Soc. Achievements include research in the field of experimental radiation hematology and pharmacological radiation protection. Home: Kroftova 66, 61600 Brno Czech Republic Office: Inst Biophy Acad Scis, Královopolská 135, 61265 Brno Czech Republic

HOFER, MYRON A(RMS), psychiatrist, researcher; b. N.Y.C., Dec. 20, 1931; s. Philip and Frances Louise (Heckscher) H.; m. Lynne Hofer, June 12, 1954; children: Timothy Philip, Adeline Van Nostrand; Andrew Paul. AB, Harvard U., 1954, MD, 1958. Diplomate Am. Bd. Psychiatry and Neurology. Resident in medicine Mass. Gen. Hosp., Boston, 1958-60; rsch. assoc. N.Y. Hosp. - Cornell, N.Y.C., 1960-62, Nat. Inst. Mental Health, Bethesda, Md., 1962-64; resident in psychiatry N.Y. State Psychiat. Inst., N.Y.C., 1964-66; asst. prof. to prof. psychiatry & neurosci. Albert Einstein Coll. Medicine, Bronx, N.Y., 1966-84; prof. psychiatry Coll. Physicians and Surgeons Columbia U., N.Y.C., 1984—; dir., Dept. Devel. Psychobiology, N.Y. State Psychiatric Inst., 1984—; Thomas William Salmon lectr., 1996. Author: Roots of Human Behavior, 1981; editor jours. Psychosomatic Medicine, 1972-99, Devel. Psychobiology, 1981—, Behavioral Neurosci., 1993-97, Perinatal Devel., 1987. Mem. adv. bd. Soc. for the Right to Die, N.Y.C., 1979; trustee Dalton Sch., N.Y.C., 1970-71. Lt. comdr. USPHS, 1962-64, Washington. Recipient Rsch. Scientist award, NIMH, Bethesda, 1993, Merit award, 1986-96. Mem. Am. Psychosomatic Soc. (pres. 1982-83), Internat. Soc. Devel. Psychobiology (pres. 1980-81), Psychiatric Rsch. Soc., Acad. Behavior Medicine Rsch., Century Club. Avocations: sailing, gardening, squash, prints, drawings. Office: NY State Psychiat Inst 722 W 168th St Unit 40 New York NY 10032-2603

HOFEREK, MARY JUDITH, database administrator; b. East Orange, N.J., Nov. 1, 1943; d. George William and Jessie (Rucki) H. BA, Trenton State Coll., 1965; MA, U. Mich., 1969; PhD, U. Wis., 1978; MS, Am. U., 2000. Sys. analyst Fed. Govt., Kansas City (Mo.), Washington, 1984-88; sr. sys. engr. CDSI, Rockville, Md., 1988-90; sr. database adminstr. IBM/Loral/Lockheed Martin, Reston, Va., 1990—; adj. prof. U. Md. Univ. Coll., College Park, 1988—. Author: Going Forth: Leadership Issues for Women in Sport, 1978; co-editor: Women and Leadership, 1978; contbr. articles to profl. jours. Mem. Women's Polit. Caucus, Washington, Polish Am. Arts Assn., Washington. Mem. IEEE. Avocation: tennis. Home: 218 Rabbitt Rd Gaithersburg MD 20878-1135

HOFERT, JACK, consulting company executive, lawyer; b. Phila., Apr. 6, 1930; s. David and Beatrice (Schatz) H.; m. Marilyn Tukeman, Sept. 4, 1960; children: Dina, Bruce. BS, UCLA, 1952, MBA, 1954, JD, 1957. Bar: Calif. 1957; CPA, Calif. Tax supr. Peat, Marwick Mitchell & Co., L.A., 1959-62, tax mgr., 1974-77; v.p. fin. Pacific Theaters Corp., L.A., 1962-68; freelance cons. L.A., 1969-74; tax mgr. Lewis Homes, Upland, Calif., 1977-80; pres. Di-Bru, Inc., L.A., 1981-87, Scolyn, Inc., L.A., 1988-95; bus. cons., 1995—; dir. Valley Fed. Savs. and Loan Assn., 1989-92. Mem. UCLA Law Rev., 1956-57; contbr. articles to tax, fin. mags. Served with USN, 1948-49. Avocation: tennis. Home and Office: 2479 Roscomare Rd Los Angeles CA 90077-1812

HOFF, JONATHAN M(ORIND), lawyer; b. Chgo., July 4, 1955; s. Irwin S. and Ida (Indritz) H. AB, U. Calif., Berkeley, 1978; JD, UCLA, 1981. Bar: Calif. 1981, U.S. Dist. Ct. (no. and cen. dists.) Calif. 1981, N.Y. 1982, U.S. Dist. Ct. (so. dist.) N.Y. 1982, U.S. Ct. Appeals (4th, 5th, 7th, 8th, 9th, 10th cirs.) 1982. Ptnr. Weil, Gotshal & Manges, N.Y.C., 1981-98, Cadwalader, Wickersham & Taft, N.Y.C., 1998—. Comment editor UCLA Law Rev., 1980-81; contbr. articles to law jours. Mem. ABA, Calif. Bar Assn. Office: Cadwalader Wickersham & Taft 100 Maiden Ln New York NY 10038-4818

HOFF, PAUL, psychiatrist, educator; b. Ulmen, Eifel, Germany, May 16, 1956; m. Christine Hoff, July 4, 1986; 1 child, Sophia. MD, U. Mainz, Germany, 1980; PhD, U. Munich, 1988, univ. lectr., 1994. With depts. psychiatry, neurology, forensic psychiatry U. Munich, 1981-96; prof. Rheinisch-Westfalische Technische Hochschule, Aachen, Germany, 1997—. Contbr. articles to profl. jours. Office: U Hosp Dept Psychiatry, Pauwels Str 30, D 52074 Aachen Germany

HOFFBRAND, ALLAN VICTOR, hematology educator; b. Bradford, Eng., Oct. 14, 1935; s. Philip and Minnie (Freedman) H.; m. Irene Jill Mellows, Nov. 3, 1963; children: Caroline Ruth, Philip, David. MA, Queen's Coll., Oxford U., Eng., 1957, DM, 1972; BM, BChir, London Hosp., 1959. House physician and surgeon, registrar London Hosp., 1960-62; rsch. fellow, hon. sr. registrar Royal Postgrad. Med. Sch., London, 1962-67; rsch. fellow New Eng. Med. Ctr., Boston, 1967-68; lectr. Royal Postgrad. Med. Sch., 1968-73; prof hematology Royal Free Hosp. and Sch. Medicine, London, 1974-96, prof. emeritus, 1996—; systems bd. Med. Research Council, London, 1983-86. Author: Essential Haematology, 1980, 84, 93; editor: Recent Advances in Haematology, vol. 2, 1978, vol. 7, 1993; Postgraduate Haematology, 1981, 98, Atlas of Clinical Haematology, 1988, 94, 2000, Hematology at a Glance, 2000; contbr. articles to profl. jours. Grantee Med. Rsch. Coun., Leukemia Rsch. Fund, Wellcome Trust, Cancer Rsch. Campaign. Fellow Royal Coll. of Physicians (London and Edinburgh), Royal Coll. of Pathologists, Acad. Med. Sci.; mem. Brit. Soc. for Haematology (pres. 1990), Am. Soc. for Hematology. Office: Dept of Hematology, Royal Free Hosp Pond St, London NW3 2QG, England

HOFFENBLUM, ALLAN ERNEST, political consultant; b. Vallejo, Calif., Aug. 10, 1940; s. Albert A. and Pearl Estelle (Clarke) H. BA, U. So. Calif., 1962. Mem. staff L.A. County Rep. Com., 1967-71; staff dir. Rep. Assembly Caucus Calif. legislature, Sacramento, 1973-75; polit. dir. Rep. Party of Calif., L.A., 1977-78; owner Allan Hoffenblum & Assocs., L.A., 1979—. Pub. Calif. Target Book, 1994—. Capt. USAF, 1962-67, Vietnam. Decorated Bronze Star medal. Mem. Internat. Assn. Polit. Cons., Am. Assn. Polit. Cons. Jewish. Office: 9000 W Sunset Blvd Ste 707 West Hollywood CA 90069-5807

HOFFER, PETER, publisher, journalist; b. Vienna, Austria, May 30, 1932; s. Josef and Julia (Schindler) H.; m. Monika Wareka, Apr. 15, 1987. MCom, Vienna (Austria) U. Econs., 1957. Editor Associated Press, Vienna, 1955-62; mgr. comm. IBM, Austria, 1962-68; corr. Austrian Radio & TV, Prague, Austria, 1968-69; dir. Pressebureau PR, Vienna, 1969—, Austrian Journalists Index, Vienna, 1983—. Editor Austrian Journalists Index, Austrian Politicians Index. Mem. Fgn. Press Club. Home and Office: Indexdatenverlag, Frimmelgasse 41, A-1190 Vienna Austria

HOFFER, ROY DANIEL, forensic electrical engineer, fire investigator; b. Lancaster, Pa., Jan. 1, 1957; s. Earl C. and Pearl H. BS in Physics magna cum laude, Millersville U., 1979; MSEE, U. Pa., 1981. Lic. profl. engr., Pa. Lighting and switching power supply design engr. Armstrong World Industries, Lancaster, Pa., 1981-86; motor drive and switching power supply design engr. York (Pa.) Internat. Corp., 1986-91; supr. instrument engring./design engr., Datcon Instrument divsn. High Voltage Engring. Corp., Boston, 1991-93; tech. rep., applications engr. Consulting Engrs., Lancaster, 1993; calibration engr. Warner-Lambert Co., Morris Plains, N.J., 1994-96; forensic engr., expert witness, fire origin and cause determination, accident analysis, safety engr., elec. and electronics design cons. Hoffer Engring., Lancaster, 1994—; mech. engring., physics, fire origin and cause investigation and environ. sci. prof. Stevens Coll. of Tech., Lancaster, 1998-2000. Com. mem., vol. Redeemer Luth. Ch., Lancaster, 1986—, bd. dirs., 1992-2000; mem. Leadership Lancaster, 1992. Recipient Sojourners award USAR, 1976; Ashton fellow, 1979-81. Mem. IEEE, Instrument Soc. Am. (sr.), Nat. Fire Protection Assn., Internat. Assn. Arson Investigators, Pa. Assn. Arson Investigators, Lancaster Lebanon Sci. and Tech. Alliance (bd. dirs., treas.). Achievements include 27 patents for slow acting photocell lamp dimming control, power ltd. fluorescent lighting system, variable speed single and 3 phase AC motor drive systems.

HOFFHEIMER, DANIEL JOSEPH, lawyer; b. Cin., Dec. 28, 1950; s. Harry Max and Charlotte (O'Brien) H.; children: Rebecca, Rachel, Leah. Grad., Phillips Exeter Acad., 1969; AB cum laude, Harvard Coll., 1973; JD, U. Va., 1976. Bar: Ohio 1976, U.S. Dist. Ct. (so. dist.) Ohio 1976, U.S. Ct. Appeals (6th crct.) 1977, U.S. Ct. Appeals (D.C. and fed. crcts.) 1986, U.S. Ct. Internat. Trade 1986, U.S. Tax Ct. 1992, U.S. Supreme Ct. 1980, U.S. Tax Ct. 1992. Assoc. Taft, Stettinius & Hollister, Cin., 1976-84, ptnr., 1984—; lectr. law Coll. Law, U. Cin., 1981-83; trustee Judges Hogan & Porter Meml. Trust; mem. adv. bd. Ohio Dist. Ct. Rev. Editor-in-chief U. Va. Jour. Internat. Law, 1975-76; co-author: Practitioners' Handbook Ohio First District Court Appeals, 1984, 2d edit., 1991, Federal Practice Manual, U.S. 6th Circuit Court of Appeals, 1999, Manual on Labor Law, 1988; mem. editl. bd. Probate Law Jour. Ohio, 2000—; contbr. articles to profl. jours. Mem. Cin. Symphony Bus. Rels. Com., 1977-86, Cin. Composers Guild, 1988-93, Ohio Supreme Ct. Com. Racial Fairness, 1993—; trustee Underground R.R. Freedom Mus., 1995—; mem. adv. bd. for Consumer Protection, Cin., 1978-80, Hoxworth Blood Ctr. Univ. Cin. Hosp., 1994-99; mem. bd. Hebrew Union Coll. Jewish Inst. Religion, 1994—, WGUC-FM Pub. Radio, 1988—, vice chmn., 1993-96, chmn., 1996-98; trustee Cin. Chamber Orch., 1977-80, Seven Hills Sch., Cin., 1980-86, Internat. Visitors Ctr., Cin., 1980-84, Friends Coll. Conservatory of Music, Cin., 1985-86, Cin. Symphony Orch., 1988-94, 96—, sec., 1996-99, vice chair 1999—, Children's Psychiat. Ctr., Cin., 1986-89, treas., 1987-89; vice chmn. Jewish Hosp., Cin., 1989-92; Leadership Cin., 1989-90; sec., trustee Cin. Symphony Musicians Pension Fund, 1989-99, Jewish Cmty. Rels. Coun., 1990-98, v.p., 1996-98; sec. Nat. Conf. Commn. Justice, 1992-99, treas. 1999—; counsel Cin. AIDS Commn., 1991—, Cin. Inst. Fine Arts Govt. Affairs Com., 1993-94, B'nai B'rith Nat. Coun. Legacy Devel., 1996-97. Named Outstanding Young Man, U.S. Jaycees, 1984, 98. Life fellow Am. Bar Found., Ohio Bar Found.; fellow Am. Coll. of Trust & Estate Counsel; mem. ABA, Internat. Bar Assn., Internat. Trade Bar Assn., Internat. Arbitration Assn. (comml. arbitrator 1991-95), Fed. Bar Assn. (treas. 1984, sec. 1985, v.p. 1986-87, pres. 1987-88), Ohio State Bar Assn., Cin. Bar Assn. (trustee 1988-93, v.p. 1990-91, pres. 1992-93, chair Cin. Acad. Leadership for Lawyers 1998—), Harvard Club of Cin. (bd. dirs. 1980-88, v.p. 1983-86, pres. 1986-87). Democrat. Avocations: music, tennis, Chinese and Japanese art. Home: 1 Forest Hill Dr Cincinnati OH 45208-1953 Office: 1800 Firstar Tower 425 Walnut St Cincinnati OH 45202-3923

HOFFHEIMER, MICHAEL HARRY, law educator; b. Cin., Dec. 21, 1954; s. Harry Max and Charlotte (O'Brien) H.; m. Luanne Buchanan; children: Joseph Allen, Jean Sarah. BA with gen. honors, Johns Hopkins U., 1977; MA, U. Chgo., 1978, PhD in History, 1981; JD cum laude, U. Mich., 1984. Bar: Ohio 1984, U.S. Dist. Ct. (ea. dist.) Ky. 1984, U.S. Ct. Appeals (6th cir.) 1984, U.S. Dist. Ct. (so. dist.) Ohio 1985, D. C. Ct. Appeals 1985, U.S. Supreme Ct. 1987, U.S. Ct. Appeals (5th cir.) 1987. Intern Office of State Appellate Defender, Ottawa, Ill., summer-fall 1982; summer assoc. Frost & Jacobs, Cin., 1983, assoc., 1984-87; asst. prof. law U. Miss., Oxford, 1987-90, assoc. prof. law, 1990-97, prof. law, 1997—, Miss. Def. Lawyers Assn. Disting. lectr., 1998—; adj. faculty U. Cin. Coll. Law, 1985-87; panel mem. Hamilton County Pub. Defender, Cin., 1985-87. Author: Justice Holmes and the Natural Law, 1992, Eduard Gans and the Hegelian Philosophy of Law, 1995, Directory of Law Reviews, 4th edit., 1999, Fiddling for Viola, 2000; articles editor U. Mich. Jour. Law Reform, 1983; contbr. articles to profl. jours. Kunstader fellow U. Chgo., 1978-79. Office: U Miss Law Ctr Oxford MS 38677

HOFFHEIMER, MINETTE GOLDSMITH, community service volunteer; b. Cin., May 1, 1927; d. Philip Hess and Cecile (Crager) Goldsmith; m. Arthur Hoffheimer Jr., June 16, 1948; children: Craig R., Roger Steven, James Martin, Mark Todd. Student, Conn. Coll. for Women, New London, 1945-48. Editor, prodr. (book in braille) Lilias Yoga and You, 1974, (poems) Marjorie's Book, 1974; editor: Lilias Yoga and Your Life, 1981; contbr. short story: (anthology) Cincinnati Short Story Winners, 1985. Trustee, sec. Cin. chpt. Nat. Coun. Jewish Women, 1966-73, chmn. and developer Large Type Program of Aid to Visually Handicapped, 1964-75, chmn. Angel Ball, 1968, on Angel Ball com. 1964-69, treas. thrift shop, 1965-67, auditor, mem. budget, ways and means, survey and evaluation coms., 1971; trustee Clovernook Home and Sch. for Blind, Cin., 1980-87; founder, 1st pres. Clovernook Assocs., Cin., 1981-85; trustee, chmn. edn. com., Boca Raton (Fla.) Mus. Art, 1996—; program developer, tchr. of Yoga to Blind, Cin., 1973-87;. Named Vol. of Yr. Clovernook Home and Sch. for Blind, 1976, Woman of Yr. Cin. Enquirer, 1983. Mem. Brandeis, Nat. Braille Assn. (After 4000 hours svc. award 1971, 15 yr. cert. svc. 1986), Cin. Yoga Tchrs. Assn., Life Long Learning Soc. Fla. Atlantic U., Friends of Boca Raton Mus. Art., others.

HOFFMAN, BRUCE ROBERT, international relations educator, consultant; b. N.Y.C., July 17, 1954; s. David Hoffman and Audrey Francine Mont. AB in Govt. and History with honors, Conn. Coll., New London, 1976; BPhil in Internat. Rels., Oxford (Eng.) U., 1978, PhD, 1986. Social scientist The RAND Corp., Santa Monica, Calif., 1983-90, sr. social scientist, 1990-94, dir. strategy and doctrine program, 1993-94, cons., 1994-98; dir. Ctr. for Study of Terrorism and Polit. Violence, St. Andrews (Scotland) U., 1994-98, chmn. dept. internat. rels., 1994-98, reader internat. rels., 1995-98; dir. Rand Corp., Washington, 1998—. Author: The Failure of Britain's Military Strategy in Palestine, 1983, Inside Terrorism, 1998; contbr. articles to profl. jours.; editor-in-chief Studies in Conflict and Terrorism, 1997—. Pres. Joshua Lipschitz Soc., Oxford, 1979, 81, 83. Recipient Intelligence Cmty. Seal medallion, CIA, Washington, 1994, Santiago Grisolia prize for excellence in the study of violence also awarded vis. chair Queen Sofia Ctr. for Study of Violence, 1998; rsch. grantee Nat. Inst. Justice, 1992, Airy Neave Meml. Trust, London, 1997. Mem. The Army and Navy Club. Avocations: fly fishing, bicycling, hiking, collecting antiques. Office: Rand 1200 S Hayes St Arlington VA 22202-5050

HOFFMAN, CARL H(ENRY), lawyer; b. St. Louis, May 28, 1936; s. Carl Henry and Anna Marie (Remlinger) H.; m. Pamela L. Polk, May 8, 1971 (div. Novl 1982); children: Kurt M., Jennifer K. BS, St. Louis U., 1958; postgrad., U. Mex., Mexico City, 1958, U. Nev., 1960-61, Tex. Technol. Coll., 1961-62; JD, Washington U., St. Louis, 1966. Bar: Mo. 1966, Fla. 1969, U.S. Supreme Ct. 1970; cert. civil trial adv. Nat. Bd. Trial Advocacy. Pilot Eastern. Airlines, Inc., Miami, Fla.; assoc. Spencer & Taylor, Miami, Fla., 1969-70; pvt. practice, Miami, 1970-80; ptnr. Hoffman & Hertzig, P.A., Coral Gables, Fla., 1980—. Capt. USAF, 1958-63. Mem. ABA, ATLA, Fla. Bar (cert. civil trial lawyer, cert. bus. litigation lawyer, civil procedure rules com., chmn. aviation law com. 1997-98), Fla. Acad. Trial Lawyers, Am. Jurisprudence Soc., Greater Miami C. of C. (trustee). Office: Hoffman & Hertzig PA 241 Sevilla Ave Ste 900 Coral Gables FL 33134-6600

HOFFMAN, DARNAY ROBERT, management consultant; b. N.Y.C., Nov. 25, 1947; s. Bill and Toni (Darnay) H.; m. Jennifer Lea Sheppard, Aug. 20, 1984; children by previous marriage: Brandon, Brett; m. Sydney Biddle Barrows, May 14, 1994. BA, SUNY, 1977; MBA, CUNY, 1980; JD, Yeshiva U., 1982. Pres., mgmt. cons. Darnay Hoffman Assocs., Inc., 1969—; mgmt. cons. Hoffman Rsch. Group Inc., N.Y.C., 1977—; rsch. assoc. Baruch Coll., 1977-79; bd. dirs. Hobton Realty Corp.; dir. Nat. Conf. Law Historians Am., 1987—. Author: Murder in the Wilderness, 1989, Allen Contact, 1989, (pamphlet) Products in Decline, 1980. Mem. ABA, Am. Mgmt. Assn., Am. Mktg. Assn., Acad. Mgmt. Scis., Player's, Beta Gamma Sigma, Alpha Delta Sigma.

HOFFMAN, DAVID ALLEN, mathematician; b. Far Rockaway, N.Y., July 21, 1944; s. Seymour Hoffman and Dorothy Task; m. Joan Ellen Sarnat, June 8, 1974; children: Joseph, Michael. BA, U. Rochester, 1966; Phd, Stanford U., 1973. Asst. prof. U. Mich., 1972-73, U. Mass., 1973-77; vis. prof. Stanford U., Calif., 1977-78; assoc. prof. U. Mass., 1978-84, prof., 1984-95; vis. prof. U. Paris, 1989; vis. rsch. prof. Ecole Polytechnique, 1990; co-dir. Ctr. Geometry, Analysis, Numerics & Graphics, 1987-92; rschr. MSRI, Berkeley, Calif., 1993-96; assoc. dir. MSRI, Berkeley, 1996—; sr. scientist NERSC, 1997—. Mem. Am. Math. Soc., Math. Assn. Am. (Chauvenet prize 1990), Soc. Indsl. and Applied Maths. Office: MSRI 1000 Centennial Dr Berkeley CA 94720-5070

HOFFMAN, DAVID NATHANIEL, lawyer; b. N.Y.C., Aug. 10, 1960; s. Martin J. and Edith D. Hoffman; m. Joan Lynne Fiden, Feb. 18, 1990;

children: Benjamin, Emily. JD, SUNY, Buffalo, 1986; cert. in bio-ethics, Columbia U., 1996. Bar: N.Y. 1997, U.S. Dist. Ct. (ea. dist.) N.Y. 1997, U.S. Dist. Ct. (so. dist.) N.Y. 1997. Litigation assoc. Martin, Clearwater & Bell, N.Y.C., 1986-88; assoc., then ptnr. Kanterman, Taub & Breitner, N.Y.C., 1988-94; founding ptnr. Breitner & Hoffman, N.Y.C., 1994-99, Hoffman & Arshak P.C., N.Y.C., 1999—; guest lectr. Columbia U. Sch. Psychology, Wycoff Heights Med. Ctr., Flushing Hosp. Med. Ctr., N.Y. County Lawyers Assn. Mem. Am. Soc. Law Medicine and Ethics, Nature Conservancy, Amnesty Internat., Habitat for Humanity, Assn. of Bar of City of N.Y. (legis. liaison com. on med. malpractice 1988-96, chmn. 2000—, com. on bio-ethics). Avocations: sailing, SCUBA diving, woodworking, bicycling, philosophy. Office: 233 E 69th St New York NY 10021-5414

HOFFMAN, FRANKLIN THOMAS, artist, printmaker, retired army officer; b. El Paso, Sept. 10, 1953; s. Franklin A. and Evelyn M. (Parker) H. BA in Art cum laude, U. Alaska, 1982. Enlisted U.S. Army, 1972, commd. 2d lt., 1982, advanced through grades to capt., 1985; comdr. HHB 1st Cavalry, Ft. Hood, Tex., 1988-90; asst. prof. mil. sci. Mont. State U., Bozeman, 1990-95. designer-craftsman U.S. Army Europe, Germany, 1984. Decorated Meritorious Svc. medal. Mem. Soc. N.Am. Goldsmiths, Am. Legion, Mont. Orienteering (founder). Office: Hoffman Originals PO Box 365 Ellettsville IN 47429-0365

HOFFMAN, FRED L., human resources professional; b. Wauseon, Ohio, Mar. 13, 1953; s. Lowell Max and Annabell (Whitmire) H.; m. Diane Patricia Pope, Sept. 19, 1975; Brandon C. BSBA, Bowling Green U., 1975. Asst. mgr. indsl. rels. Colonial Press div. Sheller-Globe Corp., Clinton, Mass., 1975-76; dir. human resources Leece-Neville div. Sheller-Globe Corp., Gainesville, Ga., 1976-88; v.p. human resources, staff ops. Golder Assocs., Atlanta, 1988—; bd. dirs. Hoffman-Rettig Foods, Inc., Maquoketa, Iowa, Golder Assocs. Inc., Atlanta. Guest columnist BG News, 1971-75. State dir. pub. rels. Ohio League of Coll. Reps., Columbus, 1974, 75; lt. col. aide-de-camp gov.'s staff Gov. Joe Frank Harris, Atlanta, 1983-91. Recipient disting. svc. award Bowling Green State U., 1975. Mem. Atlanta C. of C., Soc. Human Resources Mgmt., Antaen Soc. (pres. 1974-75), Pres.'s Club Bowling Green State U., Omicron Delta Kappa, Phi Delta Theta. Home: 235 Parian Run Duluth GA 30097-2418 Office: Golder Assocs Corp 3730 Chamblee Tucker Rd Atlanta GA 30341-4414

HOFFMAN, GARY RODGER, state government official; b. Pitts., May 11, 1942; s. Harold and Rose M. (Lewis) H.; m. Betty Schwartz, Oct. 30, 1977; 1 child, Brooke Sara. BA magna cum laude, U. Pitts., 1964, LLB, 1967. Bar: U.S. Supreme Ct., Pa. 1967, Fed. Ct. (we. dist.) Pa. 1967. Dir. Pa. code and bull. Legis. Reference Bur., Harrisburg, Pa., 1969—; sec. Jt. Com. on Documents, Harrisburg, 1992—. Bd. dirs. Ctrl. Pa. Friends of Jazz; past. bd. dirs., officer Juvenile Diabetes Found., Harrisburg, 1981-93; bd. dirs. Swatara Twp. Authority, Harrisburg, 1986-91. Mem. Nat. Assn. Secs. of State (pres. adminstrv. codes and registers 1994-97). Office: Pa Code and Bull Legis Reference Bur 641 Main Capitol Building Harrisburg PA 17120-0022

HOFFMAN, IRA ELIOT, lawyer; b. Highland Park, Mich., Jan. 3, 1952; s. Maxwell Mordecai and Leah (Silverman) H.; m. Ruth Felsen, Aug. 19, 1975 (div. 1981); 1 child, Daniel Gideon; m. Meredith Lippman, Dec. 17, 1988; 1 child, Lauren Samantha. BA, U. Mich., 1973; MSc in Econs., London Sch. Econs., 1975; JD cum laude, U. Miami, 1983. Bar: Fla. 1983, U.S. Ct. Appeals (D.C. cir.) 1984, D.C. 1985, Md. 1991, U.S. Ct. Appeals (10th cir., 4th cir) 1992, U.S. Dist. Ct. (D.C. dist.) 1992, U.S. Dist. Ct. Md., 1992, U.S. Ct. Appeals (fed. cir.) 1994, U.S. Ct. Fed. Claims, 1998. Tchr. London Sch. Econs., 1975-77; rsch. assoc. Shiloah Ctr. Mid. East Studies, Tel Aviv U., 1978-80; staff atty. FTC, Washington, 1983; law clk. U.S. Ct. Appeals (D.C. cir.), Washington, 1983-84; assoc. Fried, Frank, Harris, Shriver & Jacobson, Washington, 1984-86, 87-88; counsel Ministry of Def. Mission to the U.S., Govt. of Israel, N.Y.C., 1986-87; counsel to vice chmn. U.S. Internat. Trade Commn., Washington, 1988-89; assoc. Howrey & Simon, Washington, 1989-91; pres. Israel Housing Investors, Inc., Rockville, Md., 1990-92; v.p. H.P.F. Prefab Constrn., Ltd., Givatayim, Israel, 1991-92; of counsel Savage & Schwartzman, Balt., 1992-94, McAleese & Assocs., P.C., McLean, Va., 1995-98, Grayson & Kubli, P.C., McLean, 1998—; pres. Smart Planet, LLC, Rockville, Md., 1998—. Translator: The Emergence of Pan-Arabism in Egypt, 1980; contbr. articles to profl. jours. Spl. counsel Nat. Sudden Infant Death Syndrome Found., Landover, Md., 1984-86; hon. counsel to chmn. Nat. Holocaust Meml. Coun., Washington, 1985. Mem. ABA. Jewish. Avocations: travel, sports, history. E-mail: hoffmani@cais.com.

HOFFMAN, IRWIN, orchestra conductor; b. N.Y.C., Nov. 26, 1924; s. Harry and Augusta (Cohen) H.; m. Esther Glazer, Feb. 21, 1946 (div. 1990); children: Joel H., Gary, Toby, Deborah; m. Maria Lourdes Lobo, 1990. Student, Juilliard Sch. Music, 1942-43, 45-48; MusD (hon.), U. Tampa, 1984. dir. music Orquesta Sinfonica de Chile, 1994-97. Condr. Phila. Orch. at Robin Hood Dell, summer 1942, Bronx (N.Y.) Symphony, 1948-52, Yonkers (N.Y.) Philharm., 1950-52, Westchester (N.Y.) Chamber Orch., 1950-52, for Martha Graham Dance Co., 1949-50; condr., mus. dir. Vancouver (B.C., Can.) Symphony Orch., 1952-64; assoc. condr. Chgo. Symphony Orch., 1964-68, acting music dir., 1968-69, condr., 1969-70, prin. condr. Grant Park, Chgo., 1965-73; permanent condr. Belgian Radio and TV Symphony Orch., 1973-76; music dir. Fla. Orch., 1968-87, music dir. laureate, 1987-95; music dir. Flagstaff (Ariz.) Festival of Arts, 1983-95; condr. St. Louis Little Symphony, summers 1959-64, lectr., condr., U. B.C., State Coll. Wash., 1958, guest condr. Toronto, Vancouver, Chgo., Israel Philharm., 1960, Dallas Symphony, 1962, Brazil, 1962, 78, St. Louis Symphony Orch., 1963, Miami and Tampa symphonies, 1967, protege of Serge Koussevitzky, Tanglewood, 1948-50, guest condr. BBC Symphony, Manchester, Eng., 1968, Brussels (Belgium), Radio Orch., 1968, Strasbourg (France) Radio Orch., 1968, BBC Welsh, 1969-82, BBC Scottish, 1971-82, BBC No. Orch., 1971-82, Orch. Nat., France, 1970, Orch. Philharmonique, France, 1970, Orch. Nat., Peru, 1970, Philharmonia Orch., Eng., 1971, Chgo., Vancouver symphonies, 1971, N.J., Denver, Costa Rica, 1977-78, Chgo., 1977, Montevideo (Uruguay) Nat., 1979, Buffalo symphonies, 1980-81, New Orleans Philharm., 1981, Winnipeg Symphony, 1985, Pitts. Symphony, 1986, Colorado Springs Symphony, 1989, Kitchener-Waterloo Symphony, 1989, music dir. Nat. Symphony Orch. of Costa Rica, 1987—; guest condr. Israel Chamber Orch., 1990, Jalapa Symphony, Mex., 1990, Phoenix Symphony, 1991, UNAM Mex., 1991, Orch. Symphonique Francaise, 1991, Orquesta Sinfonica, Caracas, 1992, 93, 94, Orquesta Sinfonica De Chile, 1992, 93, 94, music dir. 1995-97; guest condr. Orquesta Sinfonica de San Luis, Argentina, 1994, Orquesta de Sodre, Montevideo, Uruguay, 1994, Orquesta de Concepcion, Chile, 1995, Orquesta Sinfonica de Buenos Aires, 1996, 98, Taipei Symphony Orch., 1997, 98, 99, 2000, Orquesta Sinfonica de Bogotá, 1998, 99, Fla. Orch., 1999, Nat. Symphony Guatemala, 1998, Orquesta Sintonica Panama, 1999; music dir. Orquesia Sinfonica-De Bogota, Colombia, 2000—; composer two string quartets, violin sonata, Orquesta Filarmónica of Bogotá, Columbia, 1997, 98, others; collector autography music manuscripts, mus. memorabilia. Served with AUS, 1943-45. Juilliard fellow, 1948. Home and Office: Orquesta Sinfonica Nacional, PO Box 1035-1000, San Jose Costa Rica

HOFFMAN, JAMES PAUL, lawyer, hypnotist; b. Waterloo, Iowa, Sept. 7, 1943; s. James A. and Luella M. (Prokosch) H.; 1 child, Tiffany K. B.A., U. No. Iowa, 1965, J.D. U. Iowa, 1967. Bar: Iowa 1967, U.S. Dist. Ct. (no. dist.) Iowa 1981, U.S. Dist. Ct. (so. dist.) Iowa 1968, U.S. Dist. Ct. (so. dist.) Ill, U.S. Tax Ct. 1971, U.S. Ct. Appeals (8th cir.) 1970, U.S. Supreme Ct. 1974. Sr. mem. James P. Hoffman, Law Offices, Keokuk, Iowa, 1967—; chmn. bd. Iowa Inst. Hypnosis. Fellow Am. Inst. Hypnosis; mem. ABA, Iowa Bar Assn., Lee County Bar Assn., Assn. Trial Lawyers Am., Ill. Trial Lawyers Assn., Iowa Trial Lawyers Assn. Democrat. Roman Catholic. Author: The Iowa Trial Lawyers and the Use of Hypnosis, 1980. Home and Office: PO Box 1087 Middle Rd Keokuk IA 52632-1087

HOFFMAN, JANET N., psychic counselor; b. New Somerset, Ohio, Dec. 16, 1936; d. Charles Kennith and Jenny (Douds) Speedy; m. A. William Anderson, May 19, 1956: children: William, Robert, James; m. Sherwin Joseph Hoffman, Nov. 30, 1985. Student, Asbury Coll., 1953-54, Harvard U., 1971. Clk. Higbee Co., Cleve., 1955-56; adminstrv. asst. GE, Cleve., 1956-58, Hardware Mut., Boston, 1958-60; owner, operator Pantry Rest Motel, Toronto, Ohio, 1975-80; pvt. practice psychic counselor Toronto, 1980—; guest talk show Sta. WEIR, Weirton, W.Va., 1980-81, Sta. WLIT, Steubenville, Ohio, 1980-81, Sta. WSTV, 1988-90, 92, 96; lectr. various women's clubs, Steubenville. Avocations: writing, lyrics writing. Home: 1303 N 4th St Toronto OH 43964-1807

HOFFMAN, LORRE C., fine art educator, sculptor; b. Heber, Utah, Mar. 30, 1959; d. Darrel C. and Sue B. Hoffman; m. Andy Anderson, Aug. 21, 1985 (div.); m. Scott M. Greenig, Sept. 5, 1992; 1 child, Ben M. BA, Mont. State U., 1986; MFA, Cranbrook Acad. Art & Arch., 1988. Prof. fine art Gustavus Adolfus Coll., St. Peter, Minn., 1989-90; vis. prof. fine art Cen. Conn. State U., New Britain, 1990-91; assoc. prof. fine art U. Colo., Denver, 1991—. Exhibited sculpture at San Diego Art Inst., 1999, U. Hawaii; contbr. bibiliography/rev. to Art W America, 1998. Com. mem. mus./gallery com. Arvada Ctr., 1992-00; sub-com. mem. Denver Mayor's Office of Art Culture & Film, 1993-00. Save Outdoor Sculpture grantee Smithsonian Instn. & Nat. Inst. for Conservation of Cultural Property, 1992-95. Mem. Internat. Sculpture Ctr. Democrat. Avocations: skiing, back packing, gardening, racquetball, reading. E-mail: lhoffman@carbon.cudenver.edu. Home: 1860 Race St Denver CO 80206-1116 Office: U of Colo-Denver Campus Box 177 PO Box 173364 Denver CO 80217-3364

HOFFMAN, MICHAEL BERNARD, import, export company executive; b. Newton, Mass., May 20, 1953; s. Bernard G. and Anne L. Hoffman; m. Evelyn Jean Klinner, Apr. 27, 1974; children: Joshua N., Elisabeth M., Benjamin V. Sr. buyer Franklin, Mass., 1978-92; prin. buyer Liberty, S.C., 1993-95; bus. mgr. Global Supply Mgmt., N. Siuox City, S.D., 1995-99; dir. Global Supply Mgmt., Newark, Calif., 1999—; bus. mgr. Memory Team Lead, N. Sioux City, 1999—; dir. global Commodity Mgr. Mem. Nat. Assn. Purchasing Mgrs. (chair, bd. dirs. 1998-99). Avocation: international travel. Home: 558 Maar Pl Fremont CA 94536-4462

HOFFMAN, PAUL JEROME, psychologist, statistician; b. San Francisco, June 25, 1923; s. Louis and Bessie (Brodofsky) H.; m. Elaine Stroll, Mar. 18, 1944; children: Valerie, Elizabeth, Jonathan. BA in Exptl. Psychology, Stanford U., 1949, PhD in Psychology and Statistics, 1954. Diplomate Am. Coll. Forensic Examiners, Am. Bd. Psychol. Specialties; lic. psychologist, Oreg., Calif. Asst. prof. Wash. State U., Pullman, 1953-57; asst. prof. U. Oreg., Eugene, 1957-60, adj. prof., 1967-76; prin. Paul J. Hoffman Assocs., San Carlos, Calif., 1985—; pres. Magic7 Software Co., Los Altos, Calif., 1985-98, Paul J. Hoffman Psychometrics, Inc., Los Altos, Calif., 1978-83; cons. Am. Airlines, Dallas, 1990, 91, Nat. Heart, Lung and Blood Inst. NIH, Bethesda, Md., 1978, Am. Assn. State Psychol. Bds. Nat. Exam. Com., N.Y.C., 1972-78; prof. dept. adminstrv. scis. U.S. Naval Postgrad. Sch., Monterey, Calif., 1981-84; consulting psychologist Hewlett Packard Co., Palo Alto, Calif., 1981-83; vis. disting. prof. psychology U. Hawaii, Honolulu, 1978; testing cons. Nat. Bd. Med. Examiners and Am. Bd. Internal Medicine, Phila., 1971-72; pres., founder Oreg. Rsch. Inst., Eugene, 1960-77. Author: (with others) Decision Processes, 1954, Formal Representation of Human Judgement, 1968, Computer Aided Decision Analysis, 1993, Expert Evidence: A Practitioner's Guide to Law, Science and the FJC Manual, 1997; contbr. 53 articles to profl. jours. Chair fgn. policy Dem. Ctrl. Com., Oreg., 1960-72; advisor Sen. Wayne Morse, Oreg., 1964-70; chmn. Bob Straub for Gov. Com., Oreg., 1974. Lt. USAF, 1942-46. Grantee NIH, 1958-72, NSF, 1961-63. Fellow AAAS, APA, Psychonomic Soc., Psychometric Soc., Human Factors Soc.; mem. Am. Statis. Assn., Oreg. Psychol. Assn. (pres. 1962-63), Oreg. Inventor's Coun. Achievements include copyrights for expert systems software, consensus building software. Home: 1120 Royal Ln San Carlos CA 94070-4277

HOFFMAN, PHILIP GUTHRIE, former university president; b. Kobe, Japan, Aug. 6, 1915; s. Benjamin Philip and Florence (Guthrie) H. (Am. citizens); m. Mary Elizabeth Harding, Aug. 31, 1939; children: Philip Guthrie, Mary Victoria Hoffman Forsyth, Ruth Ann Hoffman Cabler, Jeanne Hoffman Camp. Student, George Washington U., 1936-37; A.B., Pacific Union Coll., 1938; M.A., U. So. Calif., 1942; Ph.D., Ohio State U., 1948; H.H.D. (hon.), Jacksonville U.; LL.D. (hon.), U. Americas, U. Akron; L.H.D. (hon.), Pikeville Coll., Marshall U., U. Houston, 1987; D.L. (hon.), Kyung Hee U., Korea; D.H.C. (hon.), Autonomous U., Guadalajara (Mex.); Litt.D. (hon.), U. St. Thomas, 1979. Credit mgr. Harding Sanitarium, Worthington, Ohio, 1938-40; instr. history Ohio State U. Columbus, 1946-49; asst. prof. history U. Ala., Tuscaloosa, 1949-51, assoc. prof., 1951-53, dir. arts and scis. extension services, 1949-53; dean, assoc. prof. history gen. extension div. Oreg. System Higher Edn., Portland, 1953-55; prof. history Portland State Coll., Oreg., 1955-57, dean faculty, 1955-57; v.p., dean faculties, prof. history U. Houston, 1957-61, pres., 1961-79, pres. emeritus, 1979—; cons. Mitchell Energy and Devel. Corp., Houston, 1980-81; pres. Tex. Med. Ctr. Inc., Houston, 1981-85; dir. Fed. Res. Bank Dallas. Mem. Nat. Commn. on Accrediting; mem. Am. Council on Edn., Coll. Entrance Exam. Bd. Lt. (j.g.) USNR, 1943-45. Recipient Centennial Achievement award Ohio State U., 1970, Merit award U. So. Calif., 1975. Mem. Tex. Hist. Assn., Gulf Hist. Assn., Am. Hist. Assn., Assn. Tex. Coll. and Univs. (pres.), Assn. Urban Univs. (pres. 1965-66), Nat. Assn. State Univs. and Land-Grant Colls. (dir. 1971-75), So. Univ. Conf. (pres. 1976-77), Phi Kappa Phi, Phi Alpha Theta (nat. pres. 1952-54), Omicron Delta Kappa. Clubs: Petroleum (Houston), Torch (Houston); Houston; River Oaks (Houston). Lodge: Rotary. Home: 2929 Buffalo Speedway Unit 2208 Houston TX 77098-1711

HOFFMAN, ROBERT DEAN, JR., lawyer; b. New Orleans, Dec. 15, 1954; s. Robert Dean Sr. and Ruth Ann (Wheelahan) H.; m. Katherine Bel Thielen, 1987; children: Taylor Ann, R. Dean III. BS, Auburn U., 1975; JD, Loyola U., New Orleans, 1978; LLM in Taxation, Emory U., 1980. Bar: La. 1978, U.S. Dist. Ct. (ea. dist.) La. 1978, U.S. Ct. Appeals (5th cir.) 1979, U.S. Tax. Ct. 1981, U.S. Ct. Appeals (11th cir.) 1981, U.S. Dist. Ct. (mid. dist.) La. 1982, U.S. Dist. Ct. (we. dist.) La. 1995. Ptnr. Ballin & Hoffman, New Orleans, 1978-90; shareholder Burke & Mayer, 1994—; hearing com. mem. La. Atty. Disciplinary Bd., 1999—. Lanaza-Greco Meml scholar Loyola U., 1978. Fellow La. Bar Found.; mem. ABA, La. Bar Assn., La. State Bar Assn. (asst. bar examiner 1990—). Club: Over the Mountain Athletic (commr. 1985—, sportsmanship award 1986), Krewe of Olympia. Home: 12 Oaklawn Dr Covington LA 70433-4510 Office: 1100 Poydras St Ste 2000 New Orleans LA 70163-1121

HOFFMAN, RONALD BRUCE, biophysicist, life scientist, human factors consultant; b. Balt., Mar. 29, 1939; s. Marvin Lionel and Edna Mildred (Fillman) H.; m. Carolyn Jean Phillips, July 6, 1969; children: Christine B., David A., Matthew T. BS in Physics, U. Md., 1962; MA in Psychology, U. Houston, 1971, PhD in Biophys. Sci., 1974. Cert. human factors engring. profl. Assoc. engr. Douglas Aircraft Co., Inc., Santa Monica, Calif., 1962-64; aerospace engr. NASA Johnson Space Ctr., Houston, 1964-67, 68; sr. rsch. analyst Northrop Svcs., Inc., Houston, 1974; NRC-NASA rsch. assoc. NRC, Washington, 1975-77; rsch. scientist, mgr. life scis. GE/MATSCO, Houston and Moffett Field, Calif., 1977-80; site mgr. Tech. Inc., Washington, 1980-82; sr. project mgr. GE, Washington, 1982-85; mgr. biotech. Advanced Tech. Inc., Reston, Va., 1985-87; lead scientist MITRE Corp., McLean, Va., 1987-95, sr. human factors engr., 1995-96; lead human factors engr. Mitretek Systems (formerly with MITRE Corp.), McLean, 1996—; co-investigator Apollo-Soyuz Test Project exptl. team NASA, Houston, 1974-75; mem. govt. industry adv. group for man systems integrated standards, Houston, 1988; life sci. cons. Mitsui and Co., Ltd., Biosystems Internat., Tokyo, 1985-86. Fellow AIAA (assoc., USAF space ops. workshop Colorado Springs, Colo. 1984-85, chmn. life scis. and sys. tech. com. 1989-91, chmn. human factors engring. working group 1991-96, dep. group dir. space and missiles group 1993-96), Aerospace Med. Assn., Aerospace Factors Assn.; mem. Soc. for Neurosci., Human Factors and Ergonomics Soc. (pres. Potomac chpt. 1997), Southwestern Psychology Assn., Am. Soc. Gravitational and Space Biology, Sigma Xi (rsch. fellow 1974), Phi Kappa Phi. Avocations: photography, scuba diving. Office: Mitretek Systems Inc M/S Z-410 7525 Colshire Dr Mc Lean VA 22102-7400

HOFFMAN, ROY EMANUEL, chemist, researcher; b. London, May 24, 1963; arrived in Israel, 1990; s. David and Patricia Ada (Rose) H.; m. Channa Froukje Bachrach, Oct. 27, 1992; children: Jonathan, Rina, Akiva, Sara. BSc, Imperial Coll., London, 1984; PhD, Birkbeck Coll., London, 1987. Postdoctoral fellow Syracuse (N.Y.) U., 1987-90; postdoctoral Lady Davies fellow Hebrew U., Jerusalem, 1990, lab. mgr., 1990—. Mem. Israel Chem. Soc., Royal Soc. Chem., Israeli New Moon Soc. (chmn.). Jewish. Avocations: videography, astronomy. Home: 59/5 Mitspe Nevo, 98410 Maale Adumim Israel Office: Hebrew Univ Dept Organ Chem, Givat Ram, 91904 Jerusalem Israel

HOFFMAN, WILLIAM KENNETH, retired obstetrician, gynecologist; b. Milw., Jan. 18, 1924; s. William Richard and Marian (Riegler) H.; m. Peggy Folsom, July 28, 1952; children: Janet Susan, Ann Elizabeth. Student, U. Wis., 1942-43, U. Pa., 1943-44; postgrad., U. Pa., 1954-55; MD, Marquette U., 1947. Diplomate Am. Bd. Ob-gyn. Intern Columbia Hosp., 1947-48, resident ob-gyn., 1948-49, mem. staff, 1949-91; ret., 1991; preceptor R.E. McDonald, MD, Milw., 1949-50; resident in ob-gyn U. Chgo., 1950-51; practice medicine specializing in ob-gyn, Milw., 1955-74; mem. staff, Columbia Hosp.; dir. health service U. Wis.-Milw., 1974-91, cons. Sch. Nursing, 1976-77, clin. assoc. prof., 1979-91, vice chmn., mem. instl. rev. bd., 1976-91, mem. instl. safety and health com., 1981-91, chmn., 1984-88. Recipient, Spaights Plaza Awd., U. Wisconsin-Milwaukee, 1998. Mem. ACOG, Am. Coll. Health Assn., Am. Coll. Sports Medicine, Royal Soc. Medicine, Am. Cancer Soc. (bd. dirs. Wis. divsn. 1983-88, pub. edn. com. Milw. divsn.). Home: 2023 E Trolley Ct Boise ID 83712-8445

HOFFMANN, ACHIM ALBERT, humanities educator; b. Brandenburg, Germany, Oct. 24, 1930; s. Otto Eduard and Lida Bertha (Gruneberg) H.; m. Gisela Hannelore Bechstedt, July 28, 1956; children: Christine, Ralph. PhD in English Studies, 1970, PhD habilitatus, 1977. English lang. tutor Coll. Higher Edn., Potsdam, Germany, 1957-64, head English lang. and linguistics dept., 1964-72, head English linguistics dept., 1972-90; head modern English dept. Potsdam U., 1990-93, head English and Am. studies dept., 1993-95, prof. emeritus, 1995—; elected mem. acad. senate Potsdam Coll. Higher Edn., 1979-91; mem. English and Am. studies adv. com. Min. Higher Edn., Berlin, 1975-90; mem., dep. head univ. coun. Potsdam U., 1994-96; mem. selecting com. for appointment of new profs. various univs., Potsdam, Rostock, Magdeburg, Germany, 1993-95. Author, editor: English Grammar: A University Handbook, 1977 (Humboldt medal 1976); editor: Modern English for Teacher Students, 4 vols., 1977-80 (Neubauer medal 1980). Active Tchr. Parent Assn., 1964-82. Mem. Deutscher Hochschulverband, Deutscher Anglistenverband, Deutsch-Englische Gesellschaft. Avocations: reading books and periodicals in English, traditional jazz, photography. Office: U Potsdam Inst Anglistik, Postfach 60 15 53, D-14415 Potsdam Germany

HOFFMANN, ACHIM GUNTER, computer scientist, educator, researcher; b. Backnang, Baden, Germany, Feb. 24, 1962; s. Hans Karl and Helga (Pieper) H.; m. Andrea Kniest, Mar. 28, 1997. MS, Tech. U., Berlin, 1985, PhD in Computer Sci., 1992, PhD in Philosophy, 1993, DSc, 1997. Tchg. and rsch. asst. Tech. U., Berlin, 1986-91; lectr. U. NSW, Sydney, 1993-96, sr. lectr., 1996—; cons. Daimler Benz Rsch., Berlin, 1992-93, 95. Author: Paradigms of Artificial Intelligence, 1998; contbr. articles to profl. jours. including Neurocomputing and Connection Sci. Mem. IEEE, Gesellschaft fü Informatik (Germany). Avocation: chess. Office: U NSW, Sch Computer Sci & Engring, Sydney NSW 2052, Australia

HOFFMANN, BERND, veterinarian, educator; b. Neudek, Sudetenland, Dec. 12, 1940; s. Anton and Gertrud Pauline (Menzl) H.; m. Irene Eichstadt, Mar. 19, 1965; children: Andrea, Ulrich, Juergen. DVM, U. Munich, 1965, habilitation, 1972. Lectr. in physiology Colo. State U., Fort Collins, 1965-67; scientific asst. Tech. U. Munich, 1967-72, sr. rsch. asst., 1972-77; vis. prof. U. Ill., Urbana, 1977-78; dir., prof. Fed. Health Inst., Berlin, 1978-84; prof. Justus-Liebig-U., Giessen, Germany, 1984—; v.p. Justus-Liebig-U., Giessen, 1997-99; dean coll. vet. medicine U. Giessen, 1989-90, 93-94, acting dept. head, 1987-88, 91-92, 96-97, 99—; pres. Acad. Animal Health, Bonn, 1990—; mem., vice chmn. Vet. Products Com., Berlin, 1985—; vice chmn. adv. panel Bgvv, Berlin, 1998—; vis. prof. Olsztyn U., Poland, 1999—. Contbr. articles to profl. jours. and chpts. to books. Grantee German Rsch. Found., 1985—. Mem. various nat. and internat. profl. socs. including German Soc. Endocrinology (task force hormone toxicology). Roman Catholic. Office: Justus Liebig U, Frankfurter Str 106, 35392 Giessen Germany

HOFFMANN, BEVERLY L'HOTE, computer systems manager; b. New Orleans, Apr. 30, 1946; d. Theodore August and Dorothy Elizabeth (Ferchaud) H.; m. James Paul Comola, Aug. 31, 1985; 1 stepchild, Jon Ronald Comola. BA summa cum laude, North Tex. U., 1968; postgrad., U. Dallas, Irving, Tex., 1970-72. Cert. integrated resource mgmt.; capital area master naturalist. Systems engr. Internat. Bus. Machines, Dallas, 1968-69; math. instr. Dallas Ind. Sch. Dist., 1970-71; math. instr. Richardson (Tex.) Ind. Sch. Dist., 1971-77, chmn. math. dept., 1976-77; systems analyst Tex. Instruments, Dallas, 1977-89, Nice, France, 1989-91; systems mgr. Tex. Instruments, Plano, 1992-95, Austin, 1996—; cons. in field. Vol. Heard Nature Ctr., McKinney, Tex., 1992-94; lectr. St. Rita Ch., Dallas, 1981-88; monitoring Avian productivity and survivorship. Mem. Travis Audubon Soc., Sun City Georgetown Nature club (founder, pres. 1997-98), Lady Bird Johnson Wildflower Ctr. (docent), Austin Herb Soc., The Nature Conservancy. Avocations: birding, native plants, basketweaving. Home: 115 Blue Sky Ct Georgetown TX 78628-4522

HOFFMANN, BIRGIT SUSANNE, physician, researcher; b. Berlin, Jan. 5, 1967; d. Gerhard Max and Ute Anna (Niedergesaess) H. Med. Diplomate, Free U., Berlin, 1992, MD, 1995. House officer anesthesia DRK Hosp. Westend, Berlin, 1993-94; fellow in internal medicine/intensive care U. Magdeburg (Germany), 1994—. Contbr. articles to profl. jours. Office: Otto-von-Guericke U Intensive Care, Leipziger Str 44, 39120 Magdeburg Germany

HOFFMANN, CARLO JEAN, business executive; b. Luxembourg, Luxembourg, Sept. 21, 1948. Officer holding cos. Internat. Bank at Luxembourg, 1974-79; credit officer Dresdner Bank, Luxembourg, 1979; sec. gen. Quilvest and Quinsa Groups, Luxembourg, 1981—. Address: Quilvest SA, 84 Grand Rue BP 154, 2011 Luxembourg Luxembourg

HOFFMANN, CHRISTIAN WALTER U., mathematician; b. Geislingen, Germany, Nov. 28, 1945; s. Dietrich Ferdinand F. and Hildegard Paula M. (Hilliges) H.; m. Elisabeth Kaeser, Aug. 28, 1973; children: Rafael S., Florian S., Jael C. Diploma in math., Swiss Fed. Inst. Tech., Zurich, 1971, DS in Math., 1976. Tchr. mechanics Technikum, Biel, Switzerland, 1971; teaching asst. mechanics Swiss Fed. Inst. Tech., Zurich, 1971-74, teaching asst. math., 1974-76; rschr. Fed. Inst. Forest, Snow, Landscape Rsch., Birmensdorf, Switzerland, 1977—. Coun. mem. Salem Bapt. Ch., Zurich, 1972-76, Bapt. Fedn. Switzerland, 1975-79. Mem. AMS, Internat. Biometric Soc. (newsletter editor 1987—), Gesellschaft Angew Math. & Mechanics. Avocations: choir singing, astronomy, languages, religion, hiking. Office: Fed Inst Forest Forest Snow Landscape, Zuericherstrasse 111, CH-8903 Birmensdorf Switzerland

HOFFMANN, FRANK WILLIAM, library science educator, writer; b. Geneva, N.Y., May 2, 1949; s. Frank Anton and Lydia Mae (Mayer) H.; m. Lee Ann Black, Jan. 5, 1980. BA, Ind. U., 1971, MLS, 1972; PhD, U. Pitts., 1977. Libr. Memphis Pub. Libr., 1972-74; grad. asst. Grad. sch. Libr. & Info. Sci. U. Pitts., 1974-77; libr. Woodville State Hosp., Carnegie, Pa., 1976-78; prof. Sam Houston State U., Huntsville, Tex., 1979—; part-time reference libr. Carlow Coll., Pitts., 1974-76, Northland Pub. Libr., Pitts., 1976-78; adj. prof. La. State U., 1980, U. Houston, 1985-88, U. Tex., Brownsville, 1996-97; editor Haworth Press, Binghamton, N.Y., 1990—, ABC-Clio, 1997. Author: The Literature of Rock, vol. 1, 1981 (Best Acad. Book, Choice Mag. N.Y.C. 1981), vol. 2, 1986, vol. 3, 1995, Popular Culture and Libraries, 1984, Intellectual Freedom & Censorship, 1988 (Best Acad. Book, Choice Mag. N.Y.C. 1988), Encyclopedia of Fads, vol. 1, 1990, vol. 2, 1991, vol. 3, 1992, vol. 4, 1993, American Popular Culture, 1995, Library Collection Development Policies, 1996, Guide to Popular U.S. Government Publication, 5th edit., 1998, Grantmanship for Schools and Public Libraries, 1998, Intellectual Freedom Bibliography, 1998; editor: Popular Culture in Libraries, 1993-96, Popular Culture Sourcebooks, 1990—; reviewer jours. in field; editor (book series) Popular Culture, 1977—; contbr. articles to profl. jours. Bd. trustees Montgomery County Pub. Libr. Sys., Conroe, Tex., 1990—; lay rep. Houston Area Librs., 1990—; automation consortium mem. North Harris C.C.- Montgomery Librs., Houston, 1994—. Mem. ALA, Spl. Libr. Assn.

(Tex. chpt. bd. dirs. 1979-89), Popular Culture Assn., Beta Phi Mu. Democrat. Avocations: record collecting, weightlifting, cycling, reading. Home: 30 E Shadowpoint Cir The Woodlands TX 77381-5142 Office: Sam Houston State U Dept Libr Sci PO Box 2236 Huntsville TX 77341-2236

HOFFMANN, GEORG FRIEDRICH, pediatrics educator, consultant researcher; b. Goslar, Germany, Nov. 29, 1957; s. Robert Friedrich and Maria (Andrietz) H.; m. Ellen Renate Blum-Hoffmann, June 1, 1984; children: Christine Wenona, Johanna Elisabeth, Maria Charlotte, Matthias Friedrich. MD, Staatsexamen, U. Göttingen, Germany, 1984; Habilitation, U. Heidelberg, Germany, 1992. Cert. pediatrician. Postdoctoral fellow U. Calif., San Diego, 1984-86, sr. scientist, 1992; tng. in pediat. Univ. Children's Hosp., Göttingen, 1986-90; tng. in pediat. Univ. Children's Hosp., Heidelberg, 1990-91, assoc. prof., 1992-94; prof. pediat. Univ. Children's Hosp., Marburg, Germany, 1994-99; prof. pediats. Univ. Children's Hosp., Heidelberg, Germany, 1999—. Author: Die Mevalonazidurie, 1994, Vademecum Metabolicum: Manual of Metabolic Pediatrics, 1999; editor, author supplement European Jour. Pediat., 1994; editor Neuropediatrics, 1996—, Jour. Inherited Metabolic Disease, 1997—; contbr. articles to med. jours., including Jour. Inherited Metabolic Disease. Mem. European Soc. Pediat. Rsch. (coun. 1992-95, hon. awx. 1995-98), Soc. Pediatric Rsch., Vorsitzender Arbeitsgemeinschaft pädiatrische Stoffwechselstörungen. Avocation: water sports. Home: Rosenstrasse 4, D-35096 Weimar Germany Office: Univ Children's Hosp, Univ Childrens Hosp, INF 150, D-69120 Heidelberg Germany

HOFFMANN, GÜNTER GEORG, chemist; b. Oberhausen, Germany, July 21, 1954; s. Adolf and Maria (Hitschfel) H.; m. Heike Hoffmann, Mar. 23, 1978; children: Marcel Oliver, Vanessa Ina, David Gerrit. Diplom Chemie, Ruhruniversitaet, 1978, Dr.rer.nat., 1983. Wissenschaftl. hilfskraft Ruhruniversitaet, Bochum, 1978-82, wissenschaftl. mitarbeiter, 1982-83; postdoctoral fellow Universitaet - GHS, Essen, 1983-85, Max-Planck-Institut fuer Strahlenchemie, Muelheim, 1985-86; wissenschaftlicher mitarbeiter Ruhruniversitaet, Bochum, 1986-87; researcher in chemistry Universitaet - GHS, Essen, 1988-96, Celanese GmbH Werk Ruhrchemie, Oberhausen, 1997-98, Hoffmann Datentechnik HHD, Oberhausen, 1998—; Exerptor Beilstein-Institut, Frankfurt, 1978-89. Contbr. numerous articles to profl. jours. Recipient Bennigsen-Foerder award Ministerin fuer Wissenschaft und Forschung des Landes NRW, 1989. Mem. Am. Chem. Soc., Soc. for Applied Spectroscopy, Gesellschaft Deutscher Chemiker, Deutscher Arbeitskreis fur Angewandte Spektroskopie, Coblentz Soc., Internat. Union Pure and Applied Chemistry, Liebig-Vereinigung für Organische Chemie, Coleo e.V. Avocations: biology, physics, astronomy, medicine, music, electronics. E-mail: hoffmann-oberhausen@t-online.de. Home: Wachstrasse 29, D-46045 Oberhausen Germany Office: Hoffmann Datentechnik HHD, Postfach 10 06 31, D-46006 Oberhausen Germany

HOFFMANN, HANS JUERGEN, physicist; b. Lobnitz, Germany, Sept. 22, 1943; s. Johann and Sofie H.; m. Sigrid Loercher, Aug. 27, 1971; children: Regina Christiane, Anne Birgit. Diploma in Physics, Tech. U. Karlsruhe, 1969, Dr.rer.nat., 1972, Dr.rer.nat.habil., 1979. Asst. Tech. U. Karlsruhe, 1971-81; vis. scientist IBM, Yorktown Heights, N.Y., 1980; research physicist Schott Glaswerke, Mainz, 1981-84; mng. scientist Schott Glaswerke, 1985-92; prof. physics and tech. optics Fachhochschule, Goettingen, 1992-96; prof. vitreous materials U. Tech., Berlin, 1996—. Contbr. articles to profl. jours.; patentee in field. Mem. German Phys. Soc., German Glass-Tech. Soc., Soc. Glass Technology Great Britain. Office: Technische U Berlin, Englische Strasse 20, 10587 Berlin Germany

HOFFMANN, JÖRG CARL, physician; b. Hannover, Germany, Aug. 10, 1964; s. Karl and Ingeborg (Basse) H.; m. Elisabeth Kronenbitter, May 16, 1992; children: Hannah, Sarah. MD, U. Heidelberg, Germany, 1990. Bd. cert. for internal medicine. Applied Immunology rsch. fellow German Cancer Rsch. Ctr., Heidelberg, 1990-92; resident in internal medicine Hannover Med. Sch., 1992-96, U. Tübingen, Germany, 1996, U. Saarland, Homburg, Germany, 1997—; head core facility IBD in vivo models and sec. German med. network on inflammatory bowel disease. Contbr. articles to profl. jours. Recipient grant DAAD (German Acad. Exch. Svc.), 1986-87, 89-90, Rheumatology Rsch. award Kurt-Eberhard Bode, Germany, 1994, IBD Rsch. award Ludwig Demling, Germany, 2000. Mem. Anglo-German Med. Soc., German Soc. Immunology, German Soc. Digestive and Metabolic Disorders, Working Group Adhesion Molecules, German Soc. Internal Medicine. Avocations: mountain skiing, squash, playing cello. Office: U Saarland Med Klinik, Innere Medizin II, D-66421 Homburg Germany

HOFFMANN, KATHRYN ANN, humanities educator; b. Rockville Centre, N.Y., Oct. 26, 1954; d. Manfred and Catherine (Nanko) H.; m. Brook Ellis, Nov. 25, 1987. BA summa cum laude, SUNY Buffalo, 1975; MA, The Johns Hopkins U., 1979, PhD, 1981. Asst. prof. French lit. and lang. U. Wis., Madison, 1981-88; asst. prof. French lit. and lang. U. Hawaii-Manoa, Honolulu, 1992-97, assoc. prof., 1997—; mng. ptnr. Yuval Design Partnership, Chgo., 1988-92. Author: Society of Pleasures: Interdisciplinary Readings in Pleasure in Power during the Reign of Louis XIV, 1997 (Aldo and Jeanne Scaglione prize for French and Francophone Studies 1998); assoc. editor Substance, 1982-87; contbr. articles to profl. jours.; designer clothing accessories. Grantee NEH, 1993, 95; fellow Inst. Rsch. in Humanities, 1984-85, Am. Coun. Learned Socs., 1984-85, Camargo Found., 1998; recipient Aldo and Jeanne Scaglione prize for French and Francophone studies MLA, 1998, Regents' medal for excellence in tchg., 1998. Mem. MLA, Internat. Soc. for the Study of European Ideas, Am. Soc. for 18th Century Studies, Hawaii Assn. Lang. Tchrs., N.Am. Soc. for 17th Century French Lit., Soc. for Interdisciplinary French 17th Century Studies (exec. com. 1994-96), Soc. for Interdisciplinary Study Social Imagery, Phi Beta Kappa. Home: 3029 Lowrey Ave # K3203 Honolulu HI 96822-1800 Office: U Hawaii Manoa Langs & Lits Europe Ams 1890 East West Rd Rm 483 Honolulu HI 96822-2318

HOFFMANN, LUTZ, economics educator; b. Flensburg, Germany, May 15, 1934; s. Walther Gustav and Cornelia (Rooseboom) H.; m. Helga Ena Petersen; children: Tobias, Ilka, Daniel. Student, U. Münster, Kiel, Fed. Republic Germany, 1954-59; PhD in Econs., Kiel U., 1962; habilitation, Saarbrücken U., 1969. Rschr. The Netherlands Econ. Inst., Rotterdam, 1959-60; staff investment planning divsn. Glanzstoff AG, Wuppertal, 1962-63; acad. counselor Inst. European Econ. Policy, 1963-69; prof. econs. U. Regensburg, Fed. Republic of Germany, 1969-89; pres. German Inst. Econ. Rsch., Berlin, Fed. Republic of Germany, 1989-99; prof. econs. U. Berlin; econ. advisor Econ. Planning unit Prime Minister's Dept., Kuala Lumpur, Malaysia, 1971-73; cons. World Bank, Washington, 1977-78; dir. UN Conf. on Trade and Devel., Geneva, 1985-89; prof. econs. Free U. Berlin, 1989-99. Contbr. articles to profl. jours. Office: German Inst Econ Rsch, German Inst Econ Rsch, Königin-Luise-Strasse 5, D-14195 Berlin Germany

HOFFMANN, ROALD, chemist, educator; b. Zloczow, Poland, July 18, 1937; came to U.S., 1949, naturalized, 1955; s. Hillel and Clara (Rosen) Safran (stepson Paul Hoffmann); m. Eva Börjesson, Apr. 30, 1960; children: Hillel Jan, Ingrid Helena. BA, Columbia U., 1958; MA, Harvard U., 1960, PhD, 1962; D Tech. (hon.), Royal Inst. Tech., Stockholm, 1977; D.Sc. (hon.), Yale U., 1980, Columbia U., 1982, Hartford U., 1982, CUNY, 1983, U. P.R., 1983, U. Uruguay, 1984, U. La Plata, SUNY, Binghamton, 1985, Colgate U., Lehigh U., 1989, Carleton Coll., 1989; DSc (hon.), Ben Gurion U. of the Negev, 1989, U. Md., 1990, U. Athens, 1991; D.Sc. (hon.), U. Thessaloniki, Greece, 1991, U. Ariz., 1991, U. Cen. Fla., 1991, Bar Ilan U., 1991; DSc (hon.), U. St. Petersburg, Russia, 1991, U. Barcelona, 1992, Ohio State U., 1993; others. Jr. fellow Soc. Fellows Harvard, 1962-65; assoc. prof. Cornell U., Ithaca, N.Y., 1965-68; prof. Cornell U., 1968-74, John A. Newman prof. phys. sci., 1974-96, F.T. Rhodes prof. humane letters, 1996—. Author: (with R.B. Woodward) Conservation of Orbital Symmetry, 1970, Solids and Surfaces, 1988, (with V. Torrence) Chemistry Imagined; author: The Metamict State, 1987, Gaps and Verges, 1990, The Same and Not the Same, 1995, (with S. Leibowitz Schmidt) Old Wine, New Flasks, 1997, Memory Effects, 1999, (drama) (with C. Djerassi) Oxygen, 2000. Recipient award in pure chemistry Am. Chem. Soc., 1969, Arthur C. Cope award, 1973, Fresenius award Phi Lambda Upsilon, 1969, Harrison Howe award Rochester sect. Am. Chem. Soc., 1970; ann. award Internat. Acad. Quantum Molecular Scis., 1970, Pauling award, 1974, Nobel prize in chemistry, 1981, inorganic chemistry award; Am. Chem. Soc., 1982, Nat. Medal of sci., 1983, Priestley medal, 1990, Centennial medal Harvard U., 1994, Jawarharlal Nehru Birth Centenary award, 1998. Mem. NAS (award in chem. scis. 1986), Am. Acad. Arts and Scis., Russian Acad. Scis. (N.N. Semenov Gold medal), Internat. Acad. Quantum Molecular Scis., Royal Soc. (fgn.), Indian Nat. Sci. Acad., Royal Swedish Acad. Scis., Finnish Acad. Arts and Letters. Office: Cornell U Dept Chemistry Ithaca NY 14853

HOFFMANN-PETERSEN, ERIK, civil engineer; b. Skive, Denmark, July 8, 1950. MSc, Tech. U. Denmark, 1974; BS, Bus. U. Copenhagen, 1976. Cons. engr. R&H, Denmark, 1974-79; dept. mgr. East Asiatic Co., Denmark, 1979-84; sr. cons. PA Internat., Denmark, 1984-85; v.p. F.L. Smith & Co., Denmark, 1985-88; pres., CEO FLS Miljo, Denmark, 1988—. Office: FLS Miljo, FLS miljo a/s, Ramsingvej 30, DK 2500 Valby Denmark

HOFFMEYER, ERIK, former bank executive; b. Dec. 25, 1924; s. Skat and Aase (Thejll) H.; m. Eva Kemp, Jan. 6, 1949 (dec. 1989); m. Ninna Fisker, Sept. 14, 1990 (dec. 1992); m. Lise Rafaelsen, Sept. 3, 1994. DSc, U. Copenhagen, 1958. With Danmarks Nationalbank, 1951-59; Rockefeller fellow, 1954-55; lectr. econs. U. Copenhagen, 1956, prof., 1959-64; econ. counsellor Danmarks Nationalbank, 1959-62; gen. mgr. Bikuben Savs. Bank, 1962-64; chmn. bd. govs. Danmarks Nationalbank, 1965-94; gov. for Denmark to IMF, 1965-94; pres. Assn. Polit. Economy, 1951-53; bd. dirs. Danish Acad. Tech. Scis.; chmn. C.L. David Collection, 1977—; dep. chmn. Danmarks Nationalbank Anniversary Found., 1968, chmn., 1977-95, Housing Mortgage Fund, 1969-72, European Investment Bank, 1973-77; com. govs. Cen. Banks EEC-Countries, 1973-93, chmn., 1975-76, 79-81, 91-92, Coun. European Monetary Inst., 1994; dep. chmn. Danish Export Fin. Corp., 1975-94. Author: Dollar Shortage and the Structure of U.S. Foreign Trade, 1958, Price Stability and Full Employment, 1960, Structural Changes on the Money and Capital Markets, 1960, The Theory of Economic Welfare and the Welfare State, 1962, Industrial Growth, 1963, Monetary History of Denmark, 1968, The International Monetary System, 1992, Monetary Policy Issues, 1993, Decision Making for European Economic and Monetary Union, 2000; contbr. to Nationaløkonomisk Tidsskrift and internat. econ. jours. Chmn. Found. for Trees and Environment Protection, 1979—, Danish Securities Coun., 1996—, Politikens Fund, 1996—; pres. Psychiat. Found., 1996—, Laurits Andersen Found., 1982-90, Group of Thirty, 1984—, King Frederik VII Found., 1985, chmn., 1987—; chmn. adv. com. Environ. Support Fund for Ea. European Countries, 1995—. Office: c/o Group of Thirty Danmarks Nationalbank, Havnegade 5, 1093 Copenhagen Denmark

HOFFMEYER, WILLIAM FREDERICK, lawyer, educator; b. York, Pa., Dec. 20, 1936; s. Frederick W. and Mary B. (Stremmel) H.; m. Betty J. Hoffmeyer, Feb. 6, 1960 (div.); 1 child, Loise C.; m. Karen L. Semmelman, 1985. AB, Franklin and Marshall Coll., 1958; JD, Dickinson Sch. Law, 1961. Bar: Pa. 1962, U.S. Dist Ct. (mid. dist.) Pa. 1981, U.S. Supreme Ct. 1983. Pvt. practice law, 1962-81; sr. ptnr. Hoffmeyer & Semmelman, 1982—; adj. prof. real estate law York Coll. Pa., 1980-92, real estate law, paral legal program Pa. State U., 1978—. Autor: Abstractor's Bible, 1981, Pennsylvania Real Estate Installment Sales Contract Manual, 1981, Real Estate Settlement Procedures, 1982, Contracts of Sale, 1984, How to Plot a Deed Description, 1985; author, lectr., moderator and course planner numerous Pa. Bar Inst. CLE Programs. Recipient Disting. Svc. award Gen. Alumni Assn. Dickinson Sch. Law, 1993, Pa. Bar medal, 1997. Mem. ABA, Pa. Bar Assn. (chmn. unauthorized practice of law com.), York County Bar Assn. (chmn. continuing legal edn. com. 1992-96), Am. Coll. Real Estate Lawyers, Lions (past pres. East York club), Masons (past pres. York County Shrine club), York Area C. of C. (chair small bus. support network 1997-99). Address: 30 N George St York PA 17401-1214

HOFFSTAETTER, GEORG HEINZ, research physicist; b. Mannheim, Germany, July 21, 1968; s. Heinz Friedrich and Elisabeth Christiane (Sterr) H.; m. Anke Maria Angelika Roemer; children: Samuel, Lydia, Tabea, Prisca, Silas. Diploma in physics, Darmstadt (Germany) U. Tech., 1991; MS, Mich. State U., 1992, PhD, 1994, habilitation, 2000. Rsch. fellow Nat. Superconducting Cyclotron Lab., East Lansing, Mich., 1991-94; rsch. assoc. Deutsches Elektronen-Synchrotron, Hamburg, Germany, 1994-96; faculty Darmstadt U. Tech., 1996-98; accelerator physicist Deutsches Elektronen-Synchrotron, Hamburg, 1998—; mem. internat. adv. com. Workshop on Polarized Protons at High Energies, Hamburg, 1999. Contbr. sci. articles to profl. jours. Recipient Heraeus prize Heraeus Holding, 1991; Quadrille Ball fellow, 1994. Mem. German Merit Found., Phi Kappa Phi. Fax: 49 40 8998 4305. E-mail: georg.hoffstaetter.desy.de. Office: DESY, Notkestrasse 85, 22607 Hamburg Germany

HOFIUS, OTFRIED, theologian; b. Siegen, Germany, July 22, 1937; s. Karl and Helene (Hauser) H.; m. Elisabeth Bock, May 14, 1965; children: Christoph, Antje. D in Theology, U. Gottingen, Germany, 1969. Parish priest Siegen, Germany, 1965-72; prof. U. Paderborn, Germany, 1972-80, U. Tuebingen, 1980—. Office: Liebermeisterstrasse 12, 72076 Tuebingen Germany

HÖFLING, BURKHARD KONRAD, mathematician; b. Koblenz, Germany, Dec. 4, 1966; s. Edgar Burkhard and Erika Katherina (Bilz) H. Diploma in math., Johannes-Gutenberg U., Mainz, Germany, 1993, Dr.rer.nat., 1996. Wissenschaftlicher Angestellter U. Mainz, 1995-96; postdoctoral fellow Ctr. for Math. and its Applications Australian Nat. U., Canberra, 1996-98; vis. assoc. prof. dept. math. Bilkent U., Ankara, Turkey, 1998; wissenschaftlicher Mitarbeiter U. Jena, Germany, 1999—. Contbr. articles to profl. jours. Office: Math Inst, Friedrich Schiller U, D-07740 Jena Germany

HOFLUND, DAN MAGNUS OLOF, corporate lawyer; b. Uppsala, Sweden, Nov. 1, 1957; s. Olle and Annalisa H.; m. Catharina Wretlind, Sept. 16, 1995 (div. Jan. 1999); 1 child, Anna. Grad., U. Uppsala, Sweden, 1982. Law clk. Dist. Ct. of Gotland, Visby, Sweden, 1983-85; reporting clk. Svea Ct. of Appeal, Stockholm, 1985-90, assoc. judge, 1991; legal counsel Skandia Ins. Co. Ltd., Stockholm, 1991-95; corp. counsel, head corp. law dept. Sweden Post, Stockholm, 1995-97; gen. counsel, head of staff legal affairs and security Postgirot Bank AB, Stockholm, 1997—. Avocation: golf. Office: Postgirot Bank AB, Master Samuelsgatan 70, 10500 Stockholm Sweden

HOFMEYR, JAN HENDRIK, marketing professional; b. Beaufort West, South Africa, Feb. 2, 1953; s. Willem Arend and Ursula Joan (Heneke) H.; m. Sheila Cameron Griffiths, Sept. 14, 1974; children: Lauren, Justin, Lyndall, Megan. BA with honors, U. Cape Town, South Africa, 1975, MA, 1977, PhD, 1979. Lectr. U. Durban-Westville, South Africa, 1978-80; sr. lectr. U. Cape Town, 1981-92; dir., Rsch. Surveys Pty. Ltd., Cape Town, 1993—; cons. Rsch. Surveys Pty. Ltd., Cape Town, 1988-92, Progressive Fed. Party, South Africa, 1986-87; election rsch. dir. African Nat. Congress, South Africa, 1994—. Author: The Cynic's Guide to the Stock Exchange, 1988; co-author: Religion, Intergroup Relations & Social Change in South Africa, 1988; inventor the conversion model. Coun. mem. Progressive Fed. Party, South Africa, 1986-88, Nat. Dem. Movement, South Africa, 1988-89, Dem. Party, South Africa, 1989-90. Recipient John Player Spl. award South African Mktg. Rsch. Assn., 1990; rsch. grantee Human Scis. Rsch. Coun., South Africa, 1973-76, 78-85; Jamieson scholar U. Cape Town, 1977. Avocations: music, golf. Office: Rsch Surveys Pty Ltd, 99 Kloof St, Cape Town 8001, South Africa

HOFNUNG, MAURICE JACKY, microbiologist, educator; b. Arles, France, Feb. 3, 1942; s. Salomon Nathan and Rose (Korn) H.; m. Michèle Guillaume, Dec. 14, 1979; children: Clovis, Virgile, France. Degree in engring., Poly. U., Paris, 1963; PhD, U. Paris, 1972. Rsch. dir. CNRS, Paris, 1988—; prof. Inst. Pasteur, Paris, 1988—; unit dir. CNRS, 1979, Inst. Pasteur, 1980. Contbr. articles to sci. publs. Lt. French armed forces, 1962-65. Recipient Sci. prize League Against Cancer, Paris, 1978, 84; decorated Chevalier, Ordre du Mérite, Paris, 1989. Mem. French Acad. Sci. (corr.), French Genetic Toxicology Soc. (pres. 1985-88). Avocations: recorder, windsurfing. Home: 5 place d'Alleray, 75015 Paris 75015, France Office: Inst Pasteur, 25 rue du Dr Roux, 75015 Paris France

HOFRICHTER, DAVID ALAN, management consultant; b. Lakewood, Ohio, July 10, 1948; s. David Christian and Virginia Amelia (Rickley) H.; m. Carol Ann Rybak, May 15, 1971; children: Kristin Ann., Matthew David. BA, Baldwin-Wallace Coll., 1970; MA, Duquesne U., 1972, PhD, 1976. Assoc. Hat Group, Inc., Pitts., 1977-78, prin., 1978-80, dir. orgn. and manpower svc., 1980-81; gen. mgr. Hat Group, Inc., Cin., 1981—, ptnr., gen. mgr., 1983-85, v.p., gen. mgr., 1985-86; sr. v.p., gen. mgr. Hat Group, Inc., Chgo., 1986-89, v.p., regional mgr., 1989-90, v.p., mng. dir., 1990-94, v.p., mng. dir. global account mgmt. and midwest ops., 1994-98; sr. v.p., mng. dir. U.S. Bus. Devel., 1998-99, global mng. dir. e-bus., 1999; ptnr. in charge midwest consulting Pricewaterhouse Coopers, Chgo., 1999—; mem. ptnrs. mgmt. com. Hay Group, Inc., 1990—, also bd. dirs.; bd. dirs. Nat. Health Care Practice, Chgo.; lectr. Hay Compensation Confs.; spkr. Conf. Bd. Fortune Mag. Conf., 1996. Author: Executive Compensation in Health Care, 1986, Selecting People Who Can Implement Strategy, 1989, Reinforcing Organizational and Individual Competencies Through Compensation, 1992, Broad Banding: Fit or Fad, 1993, The Changing Nature of Work and Organization, 1993, People, Performance, and Pay, 1996, Secrets of the Rich and Famous, 1999. Mem. Am. Psychol. Assn., Am. Soc. Cons. Mgmt. Engrs., Fin. Planning Assn. for City Chgo., Pa. Psychol. Assn., Nat. Register Health Svc. Providers in Psychology, Chgo. Exec. Club, Ruth Lake Country Club (Hindsdale, Ill.), Oak Brook (Ill.) Polo Club. Republican. Roman Catholic. Avocations: golf, swimming, flying, tennis, shooting. Home: 60 Derby Ct Oak Brook IL 60523-2650 Office: Pricewaterhouse Coopers LLP 203 N LaSalle St Chicago IL 60601-1210

HOGAN, DANIEL JOHN, financial executive; b. Binghamton, N.Y., Dec. 28, 1951; s. Donald William and Theresa Francis (Kofira) H.; m. Nora D. Hogan, Dec. 6, 1980 (div. Jan. 1997); children: David, Kevin; m. M. Kathleen Hogan, Sept. 20, 1997; 1 child, Daniel. BA in Govt. and Law, Lafayette Coll., Easton, Pa., 1974; MBA in Fin., SUNY, Binghamton, 1976. Acct. Crown Zellerbach, Carthage, N.Y., 1976-80; contr. Crown Zellerbach, Glens Falls, N.Y., 1980-83, Port Angeles, Wash., 1983-86; bus. contr. James River Corp., Norwalk, Conn., 1986-89, gen. mgr. pvt. label, 1989-94, v.p. systems, 1994-97; v.p. productivity James River Corp., Chgo., 1997-98; v.p. info. tech. James River Corp., Norwalk, 1998, v.p. fin., 1999—; Mem. Danbury (Conn.) Sch. Bd., 1994-96; mem. Danbury Rep. Town Com., 1994-97. Home: 23 Kent Rd Newtown CT 06470-1784 Office: Fort James Corp 800 Connecticut Ave Ste 6 Norwalk CT 06854-1628

HOGAN, JOHN DONALD, college dean, finance educator; b. Binghamton, N.Y., July 16, 1927; s. John D. and Edith J. (Hennessy) H.; m. Anna Craig, Nov. 26, 1976; children—Thomas P., James E. A.B., Syracuse U., 1949, M.A., 1950, Ph.D., 1952. Registered prin. Nat. Assn. Securities Dealers. Prof. econs., chmn. dept. Bates Coll., Lewiston, Maine, 1953-58; dir. edn. fin. research State of N.Y., 1959, chief mcpl. fin., 1960; staff economist, dir. research Northwestern Mut. Life Ins. Co., Milw., 1960-68; v.p. Nationwide Ins. Cos., Columbus, Ohio, 1968-76; dean Sch. Bus. Adminstrn. Central Mich. U., Mt. Pleasant, 1976-79; v.p. Am. Productivity Ctr., Houston, 1979-80; pres., chmn., chief exec. officer Variable Annuity Life Ins. Co., Houston, 1980-83; sr. v.p. Am. Gen. Corp., Houston, 1983-86; dean, prof. fin. Coll. Commerce U. Ill., Champaign, 1986-91; dean, prof. fin. and econs. Coll. Bus. Adminstrn. Ga. State U., Atlanta, 1991-97, prof. fin. and econs., 1998—; bd. dirs. Covenant Med. Ct., Champaign, 1986-92, Sinfonia da Camera, Champaign, Ga. Coun. on Econ. Edn., Pvt. Industry Coun., World Trade Ctr., Atlanta. Author: American Social Legislation, 1965, U.S. Balance of Payments and Capital Flows, 1967, School Revenue Studies, 1959, Fiscal Capacity of the State of Maine, 1958, American Social Legislation, 1973; editor: Dimensions of Productivity Research (2 vols.), 1981; contbr. articles to jours., abstracts to profl. meetings. Bd. dirs. Goodwill Industries, Columbus, 1972-76, chmn. capital fund drive, 1974-75; mem. Houston Com. on Fgn. Rels., 1980—, Chgo. Coun. on Fgn. Rels., 1986—, Chgo. com., 1987—. Served with U.S. Army, 1944-46, ETO; capt. (ret.) USAR. Maxwell fellow Syracuse U., 1950-52; recipient Best Article award Jur. Risk and Ins., Alumni Appreciation award U. Ill., 1991, 1964, Medal of Merit Poznan U., Poand, 1999; Maxwell Centennial lectr. Maxwell Grad. Sch., Syracuse U., 1970. Mem. Acad. Mgmt., Am. Econ. Assn., Inst. Mgmt. Scis., Nat. Assn. Bus. Economists, Nat. Tax Assn. (dir. 1981-85, treas., exec. com. 1988—), Inst. Rsch. in Econs. of Taxation (dir. 1984—), Columbus C. of C. (chmn. econ. policy com. 1972-76), Phi Kappa Phi, Beta Gamma Sigma, Columbus Athletic Club, Heritage Club (Houston), Univ. Club (Chgo.), Lincolnshire Fields Country Club (Champaign), Commerce Club (Atlanta), World Trade Club (Atlanta, bd. dirs. 1993—). Clubs: Columbus Athletic; Heritage (Houston); University (Chgo.), Lincolnshire Fields Country (Champaign); Commerce Club (Atlanta). Office: Ga State U Coll Bus Adminstrn University Pl Atlanta GA 30303

HOGAN, KENNETH JAMES, lawyer; b. Chgo., Apr. 22, 1970; s. James Kenneth and Marlene Ann (Beaman) H.; m. Melanie Sue Niles. BA, U. Ill., Urbana, 1992; JD, U. Ill., Champaign, 1995. Bar: Ill. 1995, U.S. Dist. Ct. (no. dist.) Ill. 1995. Legal advisor, hearing officer dept. adminstrv. hearings Office of Ill. Sec. of State, Joliet, Ill., 1996-98; staff atty. rsch. dept. Appellate Ct. of Ill. 3d Dist., Ottawa, Ill., 1998-99; appellate law clk. Justice Kent Slater Appellate Ct. of Ill. 3d Dist., Macomb, Ill., 1999—. Asst. to committeeman Orland Twp. Rep. Orgn., Orland Park, Ill., 1996-98; chmn. Ind. Leadership 2000, Orland Park, 1997. Republican. Roman Catholic. Home: 723 N Campbell St Apt A Macomb IL 61455-1543 Office: Appellate Ct Ill 3d Dist 219 N Randolph St Macomb IL 61455-2217

HOGAN, MARK JAMES, clinical pharmacist, pharmaceutical firm executive; b. Bloomington, Ill., July 2, 1956; s. James F. and Evelyn H.; m. Denise M. Deluca, May 4, 1984. BS in Pharmacy, St. Louis Coll. Pharmacy, 1979; PharmD, U. Cin., 1981. Registered pharmacist, Ohio, Mich., Mo. Resident Univ. Cin. Hosps., 1979-81; clin. coord. Harper-Grace Hosps., Detroit, 1981-82, asst. corp. dir., 1982-84; mgr. research and devel. Profl. Drug Systems, St. Louis, 1984-89, v.p., gen. mgr., 1989—; adj. asst. prof. Wayne State U. 1982-84; computer cons. MegaSource, Detroit, 1983-84; staff cons. dept. medicine Faith Hosp., St. Louis, 1984—. Assoc. editor: Evaluations of Drug Interactions, 1985; author, editor company and hosp. publs. Contbr. chpts. in books, columns to profl. publs. Instr. basic life support Am. Heart Assn., 1978-82. Recipient Upjohn Pharmacy Achievement award St. Louis Coll. Pharmacy, 1979, Mckesson Robbins award, 1979; cert. of recognition Student Am. Pharm. Assn., 1979. Mem. Am. Pharm. Assn., Am. Soc. Hosp. Pharmacists, Mensa, Rho Chi. Office: Profl Drug Systems 530 Maryville Centre Dr Ste 25 Saint Louis MO 63141-5825

HOGAN, PAULINE ADINA, entrepreneur; b. N.Y.C., June 12, 1935; 1 child, Laurence D. Hogan, Jr. Cert. in Gerontology, U. Mass., Boston, 1997. Owner Boston Camera Sales, 1963-75; Notary Pub. Mass., 1971—; owner Designs By Pauline's, Boston and Littleton, Colo., 1975—. Fin. sec. Women's Svc. Club, Boston, 1971—; mem. coordinating com. Older Women's League, Cambridge, Mass., 1993—; chair com. Gray Pathersop Mass., Cambridge, 1993—; soprano gospel choir. Recipient Bus. Woman of Yr. award Nat. Assn. Bus. and Profl. Women, 1981, Cmty. award Action for Boston Cmty. Devel., 1999. Mem. Nat. Assn. Colored Women's Club, Inc. (Mass. state pres. 1991-95), Nat. Com. Household Employment (Mass. state pres.). Avocations: dancing, singing, travel, baking, meeting new people.

HOGAN, STEPHEN JOHN, electrical engineer; b. Columbia, Mo., July 10, 1951; s. Joseph C. and Mary E. (Carrere) H.; m. Ann M. Blicher, Apr. 5, 1975; children: Emily, Meghan, Courtney. BSEE, U. Notre Dame, 1973; MSEE, U. Colo., 1978. Registered profl. engr., Colo., Mass. Rsch. engr. Whirlpool Corp., Benton Harbor, Mich., 1974-77; scientist Solar Energy Rsch. Inst., Golden, Colo., 1978-84; v.p., gen. mgr. Spire Corp., Bedford, Mass., 1984—; invited participant 1st ann. Frontiers of Engring. Symposium NAE. Contbr. articles to profl. publs. Bd. dirs. Colo.-Sierra Fire Protection Dist., Gilpin County, 1980-84; chief Colo.-Sierra Vol. Fire Dept., 1982-84. Mem. IEEE (sr.), ASTM (E-44 vice chmn.), Sigma Xi, Eta Kappa Nu. Achievements include patents for novel control circuitry and advance materials developments; establishment of solar cell production facilities in China and India. E-mail: shogan@spirecorp.com. Home: 21 Natalie Rd Chelmsford MA 01824-4240 Office: Spire Corp 1 Patriots Park Bedford MA 01730-2396

HOGARTH, CYRIL ALFRED, physicist, consultant; b. London, Jan. 22, 1924; s. Alfred and Florence May (Farrow) H.; m. Audrey Jones, Sept. 4, 1951; children: Celia Joy, Yvonne Mary (dec.), Adrian John. BSc, U. London, 1943, PhD, 1948, DSc, 1977. Chartered physicist, Inst. Physics, U.K.; chartered engr. Inst. Elec. Engrs., U.K. Lectr. Chelsea Poly., London, 1948-49; rsch. fellow U. Reading, Eng., 1949-51; sr. scientific officer Royal

Radar Establishment, Malvern, Eng., 1951-58; head dept. physics Brunel U., Acton, Eng., 1958-64; pro-vice chancellor Brunel U., Uxbridge, Eng., 1978-80, prof. physics, 1964-89; head dept. physics Brunel U., Uxbridge, 1964-82, 84-85, prof. emeritus physics, 1989—; cons. Westcode Semiconductors, Ltd., Chippenham, Eng., 1958-98, others; expert witness patent litigation; vis. prof. univs. Braunschweig, West Indies, Morocco, Malaysia, Budapest, phys. electronics South Bank U., 1987—. Author, editor: Materials used in Semiconductor Devices, 1965; co-author, co-editor: (with J. Blitz) Techniques of Non-destructive Testing, 1960; editl. bd. Internat. Jour. Electronics, 1964-96, Vacuum, 1996—; contbr. over 400 articles to profl. jours. Mem. Parish coun., Gerrards Cross, Eng., 1974—; mem. S. Buckinghamshire Dist. Coun., Eng., 1983—, chmn., 1993-95; chmn. Local Authorities M25 Consortium, 1991—. Lt. Royal Naval Vol. Res., 1944-46. Fellow Inst. Physics (coun. 1967-73, v.p. 1969-73), Inst. Elec. Engrs., Royal Soc. Arts; mem. Royal Overseas League, Physical Soc. Club. Anglican. Avocations: gardening, travel, theater, bridge. Home: Shepherds Hey Orchehill Ave, Gerrards Cross SL9 8QG, England Office: Dept Elec and Computer Engr, Brunel Univ, Uxbridge UB8 3PH, England

HÖGBERG, LARS GUSTAF, physics researcher, administrator; b. Örebro, Sweden, Dec. 24, 1936; m. Monica Johansson, July 23, 1936; children: Daniel, Gudrun, Torun. MSc in Plasma Physics, Uppsala U., Sweden, 1961. Rschr./faculty Uppsala U., 1958-65; with Nat. Def. Rsch. Inst., Stockholm, 1965-80; dir. office regulation and rsch. Swedish Nuclear Power Inspectorate, Stockholm, 1980-89, dir. gen., 1989-99; dir. gen. Ministry of Environment, Stockholm, 2000—; gov. for Sweden Internat. Atomic Energy Agy., Vienna, Austria, 1992-94, 97—; chmn. steering com. Nuclear Energy Agy., Orgn. Econ. and Coop. Devel., Paris, 1998—; bd. dirs. Nat. Inst. of Radiation Protection, Stockholm, 1989-99, Swedish Plant Inspectorate, Stockholm, 1989-94. Fellow Royal Swedish Acad. Engring. Scis. Office: Ministry of Environment, 10333 Stockholm Sweden

HOGBERG, THOMAS, oncologist, researcher; b. Mariestad, Sweden, Mar. 5, 1947; s. Folke and Astrid (Lundgren) H.; m. Marina Skalin; children: Nils, Jeanna. MD, Uppsala (Sweden) U., 1978; PhD, Linkoping (Sweden) U., 1992. Sr. cons. dept. gynecologic oncology Univ. Hosp. Linkoping, 1990-92, head dept. gynecologic oncology, 1992-97, sr. cons.; assoc. prof. oncology U. Lund, Sweden, 1997; sr. cons. dept. gynecologic oncology The Norwegian Radium Hosp., Oslo, 1997-99; sr. cons. Linkoping, 1999—; assoc. prof. oncology U. Lund, Sweden, 1997. Author: Ovarian Cancer: Treatment Results, Prognostic Factors and Tumor Surveillance, 1992. Mem. Am. Soc. Clin. Oncology, Internat. Soc. Gynecologic Oncology, European Soc. Therapeutic Radiol. Oncology. Office: Dept Gynecologic Oncology, University Hospital, SE 58185 Linkoping Sweden

HOGELAND, RICHARD WRIGHT, executive, lawyer; b. Huntington Valley, Pa., Aug. 28, 1929; s. Elias Wright and Dorothy (McDonald) H.; m. Virginia Lea Claiborne, Dec. 21, 1952 (wid.); children: Ahna Elisabeth Claiborne Hogeland, Richard Claiborne Wright Hogeland; m. Sheila Richardson, Oct. 8, 1983. BA, U. Okla., 1952; JD, So. Meth. U., 1957, LLM in Comp. Law, 1958; Diploma Comp. Law, Faculty Internat. Droit, Luxembourg, 1958; LLM in Internat. Law, Harvard U., 1959. Bar: Tex., Pa., D.C.; U.S. Customs Ct., U.S. Supreme Ct. Gen. atty. Internat. Aluminium Co. of Am., 1959-64; gen. counsel Warner Lambert, 1964-67; dir. Alco Standard; pres., CEO World Res. Co. (divsn. of Alco Standard); dir., chmn., CEO Barnes & Tucker Co., 1967-73; dir., chmn. fin. com. Nat. Coal Assn., 1967-73; chmn., CEO The Natural Resource Group of Gulf and Western Inc., N.J. Zinc Co.; dir. Marquette Cement, Quebec Iron and Titanium Corp., Flying Diamond Oil Corp.; dir., chmn., CEO Jersey Miniere Zinc Co.; dir. Asturienne New Jersey, S.A.; chmn. Zinc Inst. of N. Am., 1973-78; vice-chmn. Artemis Corp.; chmn., CEO Remington Bus. Sys., 1978-80, RHS Venture Assocs. Inc., T.J. Cope Inc., 1980-97; chmn. Mavil S.A., 1984-97. Contbr. papers for pub. to internat. orgns. 1st lt. U.S. Army, 1952-54, Korea. Mem. numerous profl. orgns., socs., and clubs. Avocations: cross/country skiing, horseback riding, landscape gardening, theater, gourmet cooking. Home: Stonely Woods Manor, Fadmoor, North Yorkshire YO62 7JH, England

HÖGEMANN, BERNHARD GERHARD, gastroenterologist, educator; b. Oelde, Germany, Nov. 26, 1952; s. Werner and Luzie (Böckenförde) H.; m. Helma Bublitz, Apr. 22, 1992; 1 child, Maximilian. Med. diplomate, Westfälische Wilhelms U., 1977, PhD, 1984. Intern Army Mil. Hosp., Hamm, Germany, 1978-79; resident St. Josephs Hosp., Wuppertal, Germany, 1979-80, Herz-Jesu Hosp., Münster, Germany, 1980-81; resident Westfälische Wilhelms U., Münster, 1981-85, chief cons., 1985-93; chief dept. medicine II Klinikum Osnabrück, Germany, 1993—; assoc. prof. Westfälische Wilhelms U., Münster, 1987-93, prof. medicine, 1993. Author: Diagnostic and Therapeutic ERCP, 1990; contbr. articles to profl. jours. Mem. Norddeutsche Gesellschaft für Gastroenterologie Hannover (sec. 1996). Roman Catholic. Avocations: music, skiing, sailing. Office: Klinikum Osnabrück, Am Finkenhügel 1, D-49076 Osnabrück Germany

HOGENAUER, GREGOR, microbiology educator; b. Vienna, Austria, Dec. 14, 1933; m. Ellen. PhD, U. Vienna, Austria, 1960. Rsch. asst. Fla. State U., Tallahassee, 1960-61, Cornell U., Ithaca, N.Y., 1962; univ. asst. U. Vienna, Austria, 1963-70; lab. head Sandoz Rsch. Inst., Vienna, 1970-78; dept. head Sandox Rsch. Inst., Vienna, 1978-82, divsn. head, 1982-84; prof. microbiology U. Graz, Austria, 1984—; reviewer Austrian Sci. Found., Vienna, 1991-97. Mem. Austrian Acad. Scis. Office: U Graz Inst Microbiology, Universitaetsplatz 2, A-8010 Graz Austria

HOGENSEN, MARGARET HINER, librarian, consultant; b. Ottawa, Kans., Oct. 11, 1920; d. Hebron Henry and Nellie Evelyn (Godard) Hiner; widowed. BA, U. Wichita, 1942; BS in Library Sci., U. Denver, 1945. Circulation librarian Boise (Idaho) Pub. Library, 1945-49, Pomona (Calif.) Pub. Library, 1950-51; reference librarian WFIL-TV, Phila., 1963-69; rsch. dir. Concept Films, Washington, 1969-72; ind. researcher, cons. Greenbelt, Md., 1973-80. Bd. dirs. Greenbelt Homes, Inc., 1977-93, 98-2000, pres., 1983-88, treas. 1998-2000; past mem. bd. dirs. Greenbelt Consumer Coop., Nat. Coop. Bank, Nat. Coop. Bus. Assn.; pres. Ea. Coop. Housing Orgn., 1992-95. Mem. Nat. Assn. Housing Coops (bd. dirs. 1986-87, 1990-94). Democrat. Christian Scientist. Avocation: travel. Home: PO Box 218 Greenbelt MD 20768-0218

HÔGER, HARALD ERICH WILHELM, animal scientist; b. Vienna, Austria, July 16, 1954; s. Erich Rudolf and Helga (Bubendorfer) H.; m. Brigitte Anna Blasch, Oct. 25, 1979; children: Astrid, Ulrich, Joachim. M.Vet. Medicine, DVM, U. Vet. Medicine, Vienna, 1979. Asst. U. Vienna, 1980-94, asst. prof. med. faculty, 1994—; cons. in field; assoc. Biotox KEG; lectr. U. Veterinary Medicine, Vienna. Contbr. articles to profl. jours. Chmn. Scripture Union Austria, Bad Ischl, 1989—; coun. mem. Luth. Mission, Baden, Austria, 1992—. Mem. Soc. for Lab. Animal Sci. Lutheran. Avocations: music, organizing concerts, pets, mountain climbing. Office: Inst Lab Animal Sci and Genetics, Brauhausgasse 34, A-2325 Himberg Austria

HOGG, DOUGLAS MARTIN, British government official; b. Feb. 5, 1945; m. Sarah Boyd-Carpenter, 1968; 2 children. Student, Christ Ch., Oxford; law degree, Kennedy Law Sch., 1968. Mem. Ho. Commons, Eng., 1979—, mem. agrl. select coms., 1979-82, PPS to chief sec., HM treasury, 1982-83, asst. govt. whip, 1983-84, parly under-sec. state, 1986-89, min. state, min. for industry and enterprise, 1989-90, min. State, Fgn. and Commonwealth Office, 1990-95, min. agri., fisheries and food, 1995-97. Office: House of Commons, London SW1A 0AA, England*

HØGLEND, PER ANDREAS, psychiatry educator, researcher, psychotherapist; b. Oslo, Jan. 12, 1946; s. Trygve and Hilda Johanne (Hansen) H.; m. Ellebeth Saetre, Apr. 17, 1978 (div. 1988); children: Hanne Elise, Stina Charlotte; m. Gabriele Katharina Juliane Mayerhofer, Apr. 6, 1991; children: Paul Mathias, Morten Andreas. MD, PhD, U. Oslo, 1995. Med. diplomate 1972; bd. specialist in psychiatry, 1981. Pvt. practice gen. practitioner Skien, Norway, 1972-75; resident psychiatrist Telemark Psychiat. Hosp., Skien, 1975-78, Ulleval Psychiat. Clinic, Oslo, 1978-81; sr. psychiatrist Psychiat. Clinic, Vinderen-U. Oslo, 1982-88, chief psychiatrist, 1989; assoc. prof. U. Oslo, 1990-96, prof., 1997—; med. officer of health, Finnmark, Norway, 1979; advisor Nat. Dir. of Health, Norway, 1982-84, Nat. Coun. for Sci. and the Humanities, Norway, 1994-96; dir. Network Psychotherapy Rsch., Norway, 1988-96. Advisory editor Psychotherapy Rsch., 1996—; assoc. editor Jour. Psychotherapy Practice and Rsch., 1996—; contbr. articles to profl. jours. Rsch. grantee Am. Psychoanalytic Assn., 1992, Nat. Coun. for Sci. and the Humanities, 1995-96, Norwegian Coun. for Mental Health, 1996-97. Mem. Soc. for Psychotherapy Rsch. (Internat. Early Career Rsch. award 1999), Norwegian Med. Assn., Norwegian Psychiat. Assn. Avocations: jazz trumpet playing in comboes and big bands. Home: Skjoldveien 5, 0881 Oslo Norway Office: U Oslo Dept Psychiatry, PO Box 85 Vinderen, 0319 Oslo Norway

HOGREFE, HENNING, physicist; b. Benefeld, Germany, Sept. 22, 1953; m. Gundula Smagon, Nov. 23, 1990; children: Ulla, Bianca, Ines. M in Physics, Tech. U. Hannover, Germany, 1979; Dr. rer. nat. in physics, U. Hamburg, Germany, 1985. Staff scientist U. Hamburg, 1979-84, German Electron Synchrotron, Hamburg, 1984, Lawrence Berkeley Lab., U. Calif., Berkeley, 1985-87; physicist Robert Bosch GmbH, Reutlingen, Germany, 1987-98, Automotive Lighting Reutlingen GmbH, Reutlingen, 1999—. Patentee in field of illumination optics; contbr. articles to profl. jours. With German Marines, 1972-73. Office: Robert Bosch GmbH, D 72703 Reutlingen Germany

HOGWOOD, CHRISTOPHER JARVIS HALEY, music director, educator; b. Nottingham, Eng., Sept. 10, 1941; s. Haley Evelyn and Marion Constance (Higgott) H. BA, Cambridge U., 1964, MA, 1969; postgrad., Charles U., Prague, Czechoslovakia, 1964-65; DMus (hon.), U. Keele, 1991. Founding mem. Early Music Consort of London, 1967-76; dir. The Acad. Ancient Music, London, 1973—; music faculty U. Cambridge, 1975—; artistic dir. Handel & Haydn Soc., Boston, 1986—; dir. music St. Paul Chamber Orch., 1987-92; prin. guest condr. St. Paul Chamber Orch., 1992-98, Kammerorchester Basel, 2000—; artistic dir. Summer Mozart Festival Nat. Symphony Orch. USA, 1993—; assoc. dir. Beethoven Academie, Antwerp, 1998—; hon. prof. music Keele (Eng.) U., 1986-89; internat. prof. early music performance Royal Acad. Music, London, 1992—; vis. prof. dept. music King's Coll., London, 1992-96. Author: Music at Court, 1977, The Trio Sonata, 1979, Haydn's Visits to England, 1980, Handel, 1984; editor Music in Eighteenth Century England, 1983, Holmes' Life of Mozart, 1991. Decorated comdr. Order of the Brit. Empire, 1989; recipient Willson Cobbett Medal Worshipful Co. Musicians, London, 1986, named Freeman, Worshipful Co., 1989, Disting. Musician award Inc. Soc. Musicians, 1997, Martinu medal Bohuslav Martinu Found., Prague, 1999; hon. fellow Jesus Coll., Cambridge, 1989, Pembroke Coll., Cambridge, 1992. Home and Office: 10 Brookside, Cambridge CB2 1JE, England

HOHLS, TREVOR, geneticist; b. Port Shepstone, Natal, South Africa, May 24, 1969; s. Alwin Johan and Jean (Geldenhuys) H.; m. Jeanette Bird, May 8, 1993. BSc in Agriculture, U. Natal, Pietermaritzburg, South Africa, 1991, PhD, 1995. Lectr. U. Natal, Pietermaritzburg, S. Africa, 1994-96, sr. lectr., 1997-98; trait integration mgr. Monsanto, Petit, S. Africa, 1998—. Contbr. articles to profl. jours. Recipient A.R. Saunders medal Faculty of Agriculture, 1991, PhD scholarship for scis. U. Natal, 1993-96. Mem. S. African Genetics Soc., S. African Soc. Crop Prodn., Internat. Biometric Soc. Home: PO Box 60, Hurlingham, Sandton 2070, South Africa Office: Monsanto, PO Box 7424, Petit 1512, South Africa

HOHMAN, SHAROLYN ANN, chamber administrator; b. Wayne, Nebr., Sept. 7, 1945; d. Frederick August and Anna Marie Thun; m. William John Hohman, Aug. 21, 1965 (div. Aug. 13, 1983). BA, Grand Canyon U., 1979; MA, No. Ariz. U., 1986. Owner, pres. Curtmen's Office Supply, Goodyean, Ariz., 1980-84; exec. sec. Avondale (Ariz.), Goodyear, Litchfield Park C. of C., Avondale, 1984-88; pres., CEO Tri-City West C. of C., Avondale, 1988—; dir. Ariz. C. of C., 1998. Pres. Southwest Cmty. Network, Avondale, 1997; v.p. New Life Shelter, Litchfield Park, 1997; gov. appointed Ariz. Vocat. Tech. Adv. Bd., Phoenix, 1997—. Named Trendsetter by Today's Ariz. Woman, 1998. Mem. Assn. C. of C., Ariz. Chamber Execs. (pres. 1998), Jaycees (Jaycee of Yr. 1987). Avocations: teaching american sign language, playing bridge. Office: Tri-City West C of C 501 W Van Buren St Ste K Avondale AZ 85323-1307

HOHMEYER, OLAV HANS, economist, educator; b. Minden, Germany, Nov. 23, 1953; s. Karl-Heinz and Ingeborg (Artus) H.; m. Ulrike M. Wehking, Mar. 22, 1985. Grad., U. Bremen, Fed. Republic Germany, 1980, PhD, 1989. Researcher Hochschule für Wirtschaft, Bremen, 1980, U. Oldenburg, Fed. Republic Germany, 1980-82; sr. researcher Frannhofer Inst. für Systemtechnik und Innovationsforschung, Karlsruhe, Fed. Republic Germany, 1982-89; dept. head on tech. change Frannhofer Inst. für Systemtechnik und Innovationsforschung, Karlsruhe, Germany, 1989-92, dept. head energy and environ., 1993-94; dir. dept. environ. econs. Ctr. European Econs. Rsch., Mannheim, Germany, 1994-98; chair energy and resource econs. U. Fleusburg, Germany, 1998—; cons. Commn. of the European Communities, Luxemburg, 1990-91. Author: Employment Effects of Energy Conservation Investments, 1985, Technometrie, 1987, Social Costs of Energy Consumption, 1988, Soziale Kosten des Energieverbrauchs, 1988, 89, External Environmental Costs of Electric Power, 1991. Recipient Fraunhoferpreis Fraunhofer-Gesellschaft, Munich, 1988, 91, Deutscher Engiepreis, Deutsche Energie Gesellschaft, Munich, 1989. Mem. Internat. Input Output Assn., Internat. Soc. Ecol. Econs., European Assn. Environ. and Resource Economists. Lutheran. Achievements include development of new methodology for measuring the comparative levels of technological achievements of nations; of new model integrating branch specific emission coefficients into official input-output tables for Germany; first to analyze the difference in external costs of electricity generation between conventional electric power production and renewables.

HOHN, BARBARA LEONORE, research scientist; b. Klagenfurt, Austria, Sept. 15, 1939; d. Walter and Liesl (Wohlfarth) Freiinger; m. Thomas Hohn, Nov. 17, 1962; children: Andreas, Michael. Diploma, U. Vienna, Austria, 1962; postgrad., Max Planck Inst., Tübingen, 1962-67; PhD, U. Tübingen, 1967; postgrad., Yale U., 1967-68, Stanford U., 1968-70, Basel (Switzerland) U., 1971-77, Friedrich Miescher Inst., Basel, 1978-85. Cert. in plant molecular biology. Group leader Friedrich Miescher Inst., Basel, 1985—; lectr. U. Basel, 1989, prof., 1996; lectr. in field. Editor: Plant Gene Research, Basic Knowledge and Application, 1987—; patentee in field. Recipient Sci. prize Town of Basel, 1992. Mem. Internat. Soc. Plant Molecular Biology (bd. dirs. 1993-96), European Molecular Biology Orgn., Academia Europaea (founding mem.), Swiss Nat. Rsch. Coun. Avocations: hiking, skiing, kayaking, traveling, theater. Home: Hangstrasse 35, CH 4144 Arlesheim Switzerland Office: Friedrich-Miescher-Inst, PO Box 2543, CH 4002 Basel Switzerland

HOHN, HAZEL MARJORIE, author; b. Bklyn.; d. Hamilton Alan Stamper and Hazel P. (Walker) Sprague; m. Werner Aloysius Hohn, July 26, 1960 (div. 1984); children: Carol, Susan; children from previous marriage: James, John. AA, Western Nev. C.C., 1981. Aircraft welder Piper Aircraft, Lock Haven, 1942-43; freelance writer, 1950—; sec. Nat. Air Transport Coord. Com., N.Y.C., 1959; spkr. on aviation history, 1984—. Author: The King Who Could Not Smile, 1963; contbr. story to textbook: The New Tall Tales 4th Grade Reader, 1964, Open Windows, 1957; contbr. articles to newspapers, stories to textbooks, juvenile mags., including Child Life, Scholastic mag., Highlights for Children. Active People for the Ethical Treatment of Animals, Reno, Nev., 1996—. Pilot Women Air Force Svc. Pilot, 1943-45. Mem. Exptl. Air Force Assn. (bd. dirs. 1972—), Air Force Assn. (mem. coun. 1988—), Women Airforce Svc. Pilots WWII, Women Mil. Aviators, Women in Mil. Svc. to Am. (charter mem., recruiter), Ninety Nines, B-26 Marauder Club, B-24 Club (liberator). Democrat. Christian Scientist. Avocations: music, reading, pets, community activities, sports. Home: 2750 Dickerson Rd Apt D Reno NV 89503-4912

HOHNEN, STUART ALEXANDER, resources and energy consultant; b. Sydney, Australia, Mar. 1, 1944; s. Ross Ainsworth and Phyllis Adele (Whitten) H.; m. Wibbina Jacoba Klompker, Mar. 29, 1987; children: Angela, Jeb, Isabel, Meiske, Anna. BE with hons., Adelaide U., Australia, 1966; MBA, Stanford U., 1970. Bus. devel. mgr. Dillingham Devel. Co., San Francisco, 1970-71; various positions Dept. Resources Devel., Perth, Australia, 1973-82, chief exec., 1982-87; exec. dir. Anglo Pacific Resources, Perth, 1987-90; mng. dir. Cockburn Corp., Perth, 1992-93; prin. Ventnor Cons., Perth, 1994—; mem. Energy Bd. of Review, Perth, 1992-93; mem. Energy Implementation Group, Perth, 1994-95; dept. chmn. Gas Corp. of West Australia, Perth, 1995-98; coun. Nat. Competition Council, Melbourne, 1995-98; dir. Carnarvon Petroleum, Perth, 1994—. Mem. Fellow Australian Inst. Company Dirs.; mem. Weld Club. Office: 2/5 Ventnor Avenue, 6005 West Perth Australia

HØIE, TORE A., management consultant; b. Øystese, Norway, Feb. 11, 1942; s. Jens W. and Gerd M. (Watvedt) H.; m. Marit F. Fossan; 1 child, Siri Synnøve. Assoc., Heriot-Watt U., Scotland, 1965, Higher Nat. Diploma, 1966; PhD, Tech. U. Denmark, 1980. Rschr. Norwegian Computing Ctr., Oslo, 1966-67; project planner Christiani & Nielsen, Copenhagen, 1967-68; sys. engr. IBM, Denmark and U.S., 1968-83; tech. mgr. EDB, Oslo, 1983-86; tech. dir. Norstar, Oslo, 1986-87; owner mgmt. cons. co. Fringilla, Fjellhamar, Norway, 1987—. Author: Central Systems Architecture, 1979, Performance Control, 1982, Service-Methods and Management, 1999. Avocations: squash, internet role playing. Home and Office: Bragesvei 7C, 1472 Fjellhamar Norway

HØIER, RENÉ, reproductive physiology educator, researcher; b. Copenhagen, Mar. 7, 1948; s. André and Kirsten (Schäfer) H.; children: Thor, Mikkel. MS, U. Copenhagen, 1979; PhD, Royal Vet. and Agrl. U., Frederiksberg, Denmark, 1992. Rsch. scientist in molecular biology Tech. U., Denmark, 1979-80, U. Copenhagen, 1980-81; rsch. scientist in reproductive endocrinology and physiology Royal Vet. and Agrl. U., 1985-92, postdoctoral fellow in reproductive endocrinology, 1993-96, assoc. prof. reproductive physiology, 1996-99; vis. prof. Pa. State U., State Coll., 1996, 97; spkr. nat. and internat. sci. congresses. Coauthor: Studies of White Whales (Delphinapterus leucas) and Narwhals (Monodon monoceros) in Greenland, 1994; contbr. numerous articles to internat. sci. jours., including Acta Agr. Scandinavia, Acta Vet. Scandinavia, Comparative Biochem. Biophysics, European Jour. Clin. Chemistry and Clin. Biochemistry, Jour. Comparative Pathology, Jour. Small Animal Practice, Jour. Vet. Medicine, Lab. Robotic Automation, Reprodn. Domestic Animals, Theriogenology, Vet. Clin. Pathology. With Danish Civil Def., 1975. Grantee State Agrl. and Vet. Rsch. Coun., 1992, 93, Henriksens Mindefond, 1993. Mem. Soc. for Study Fertility. Avocations: literature, music, sports. Office: Royal Vet and Agrl U, Dyrlegevej 68, DK-1870 Frederiksberg C, Denmark

HOJO, JUNICHI, chemistry educator; b. Kitakyushu-shi, Fukuoka, Japan, Jan. 10, 1949; s. Asaichi and Tokie H.; m. Fumiko (Furukawa) H., May 5, 1974; children: Takuma, Yuko. BS in Engring., Kyushu U., Fukuoka, Japan, 1971; MS in Engring., Kyushu U., 1973, PhD, 1980. Rsch. asst. Kyushu U., Fukuoka, Japan, 1973-80; lectr. Kyushu U., 1980-81, assoc. prof., 1981-94, prof., 1994—. Mem. Ceramic Soc. Japan, Am. Ceramic Soc. Home: 2 60 13 Miwadai, Fukuoka-Shi 811-0212, Japan Office: Kyushu U Grad Sch Engring, 6 10 1 Hakozaki Higashi Ku, Fukuoka shi 812-8581, Japan

HOJO, MASASHI, chemistry educator; b. Uchiumi-mura, Ehime-ken, Japan, Feb. 17, 1952; s. Tsugio and Toshiko (Kuroda) H.; m. Mari Hashimoto, Dec. 1, 1987; children: Ken-ichi, Shigefumi. BS, Kobe (Japan) U., 1974; MS, Kyoto (Japan) U., 1976, PhD, 1981. Instr. Kochi U., 1979-87, lectr., 1987-89, assoc. prof., 1989—; rsch. assoc. U. Calgary, Alta., Can., 1982-84, Tex. A&M U., College Station, 1987-88; vis. rschr. Monash U., Clayton, Victoria, Australia, 1997. Contbr. articles to profl. jours. Mem. Am. Chem. Soc., Royal Soc. Chemistry, N.Y. Acad. Scis., Chem. Soc. Japan, Japan Soc. for Analytical Chemistry, Polarographic Soc. Japan, Internat. Soc. Electrochemistry. Avocation: classical music. Home: 399-13 Mama, Kochi 780-0973, Japan Office: Kochi U Dept Chemistry, 5-1 Akebono-cho 2 Cho-me, Kochi 780-8520, Japan

HOJS, RADOVAN, nephrologist, consultant; b. Maribor, Slovenia, July 20, 1959; s. Jože and Marija (Blatnik) H.; m. Tanja Fabjan, Mar. 20, 1985; 1 child, Nina. MD, U. Ljubljana, Slovenia, 1984, PhD, 1996. Physician Tchg. Hosp. Maribor, 1984—, internist, nephrologist, cons., 1990—; lectr. Med. Sch., Maribor, 1993—, head Dept. Nephrology, 1998, head Clin. Dept. Internal Medicine, 1999; asst. tchr. Med. Faculty, Ljubljana, Slovenia, 1995—, asst. prof., 1997—; pres. Med. Meeting Maribor, 1995—. Contbr. articles to profl. jours. Mem. European Dialysis and Transplant Assn./European Renal Assn., Am. Inst. Ultrasound in Medicine, N.Y. Acad. Sci. Home: Pot K Mlinu 15, 2000 Maribor Slovenia Office: Tchg Hosp Maribor/Nephrol, Ljubljanska 5, 2000 Maribor Slovenia

HOKA, SUMIO, anesthesiologist, educator; b. Kagoshima, Japan, July 9, 1952; s. Shigeru and Nobuko (oohori) H.; m. Kimiko Matsuo, Mar. 11, 1979; children: Tomomi, Naomi, Yutaro. MD, Kyushu U., Fukuoka, Japan, 1978. Cert. Japanese Bd. Anesthesiology. Instr. Kyushu U. Hosp., 1981-85, asst. prof., 1991-97; vis. prof. Med. Coll. of Wis., Milw., 1985-87; lectr. Kyushu U., 1987-89; chief in anesthesiology St. Mary's Hosp., Kurume, Japan, 1989-90; prof., chmn. dept. anesthesiology Kitasato (Japan) U., 1997—; adv. bd. Jour. of Anesthesia, Tokyo, 1994—. Mem. Am. Soc. Anesthesiologists. Avocations: mountain climbing, jogging, fishing, playing "Go". Home: 1-19-4 Naruse, Machida Tokyo 194, Japan Office: Kitasato U Hosp/Dept Anesthesiology, 1-5-5 Kitasato, Sagamihara 228-8555, Japan

HOKAMOTO, KAZUYUKI, materials scientist, educator; b. Kumamoto, Japan, Oct. 20, 1959; s. Kazuhiro and Seiko (Shimoda) H.; m. Yoko Oda, May 13, 1995; children: Hikaru, Yuki. B in Engring., Kumamoto U., Japan, 1982, M in Engring., 1984; D in Engring., Kyushu U., Fukuoka, Japan, 1988. Rsch. assoc. Kumamoto U., Japan, 1987-91, asst. prof., 1991-93, assoc. prof., 1993—; vis. scholar U. Calif., San Diego, La Jolla, 1990-91, Ga. Tech.. Atlanta. 1996; sec. internat. workshop on explosion, shockwave and high pressure phenomena, Kumamoto, Japan, 1997. Contbr. articles to profl. jours., chpts. to books. Recipient Rsch. grantee Heiwa-Nakajima Fedn., 1999, Mazda Fdn., 1997-98, Iketani Fdn., 1995-96, Amada Fdn., 1995. Mem. Japan Inst. Metals, Japan Soc. Technol. Plasticity, Japan Welding Soc. Home: 5-9-11 Oiyama, Kumamoto 862-0924, Japan Office: Kumamoto U Shockwave Rsch, 2-39-1 Kurokami, Kumamoto 860-8555, Japan

HOKBORG, SVEN-OLOF, military officer; b. Karlstad, Sweden, May 24, 1941; came to U.S., 1969; m. Ingalill Hokborg. M Aero. Engring., Royal Inst. Tech., Stockholm, 1965; MBA, U. Stockholm, 1969; M Sys. Mgmt., U. So. Calif., 1972. Commd. lt. Swedish Air Force, 1965, advanced through grades to maj. gen., 1988; lectr. aeronautics Air Force Acad. Swedish Air Force, Uppsala, Sweden, 1965; vice tech. dir. fighter wing F12 Swedish Air Force, Kalmar, Sweden, 1965-69; with sys. planning divsn. Air Materiel Dept., Stockholm, 1969; asst. air attaché Royal Swedish Embassy, Washington, 1970-73; chief flight safety materiel sect. Air Materiel Dept., Stockholm, 1973-74, dir. planning directorate, 1979-80, comdr. Air Force Material Command, 1989-93; chief project mgmt. group New Attack A/C for Air Force, 1974-79; dir. Aircraft Directorate, 1980-89; def. and air attaché Def. Coop. Sweden-U.S. Embassy, Sweden, 1994-98; chmn. SAAB Nyge Aero Corp, 2000—; expert Def. Dept. Commn. for Accident Investigations. Author tech. textbooks in field; contbr. articles to profl. jours. Bd. dirs. Swedish Aviation History. Hon. fellow Am.-Scandinavian Found., N.Y., 1969-70; recipient Thulin Gold medal for Aero. Achievement, 1995, Program Mgr. of Yr., Swedish Acad. Projects, 1998, Legion of Merit, 1999. Mem. Royal Acad. Mil. Scis., Aero. Rsch. Inst. Sweden (former vice chmn. bd. dirs.), Swedish Soc. Aero. and Astronautics (pres. 1983-86). Office: 8151 Silverberry Way Vienna VA 22182-5300

HOKE, RUDOLF, legal history educator; b. Duisburg, Germany, Aug. 15, 1929; s. Ralph and Hermine Hoke. JD, U. Vienna, Austria, 1953; Dr.rerum politicarum, U. Vienna, 1956. Lectr. in legal history U. Saarbrücken, Germany, 1966-71, assoc., 1971; prof. legal history U. Vienna, 1971—, dir. Inst. Austrian and German Legal History, 1971-97, dean faculty of law, 1979-81. Author: Die Reichsstaatsrechtslehre des Johannes Limnaeus, 1968, Österreichische und Deutsche Rechtsgeschichte, 1992; contbr. articles to profl. jours., and to book. Recipient Grand Silver Badge of Honor, Pres. of Republic of Austria, 1982. Mem. Austrian Soc. Canon Law (pres. 1975, 92), Soc. Legal History (pres. 1977-78, 89-90, 96-97). Home: Hofzeile 10-12, A-1190 Vienna Austria Office: U Vienna, Schottenbastei 10-16, A-1010 Vienna Austria

HOKENSTAD, MERL CLIFFORD, JR., social work educator; b. Norfolk, Nebr., July 21, 1936; s. Merl Clifford and Flora Diane (Christian) H.; m. Dorothy Jean Tarrell, June 24, 1962; children: Alene Ann, Laura Rae, Marta Lynn. B.A. summa cum laude, Augustana Coll., 1958; Rotary Found. fellow, Durham (Eng.) U., 1958-59; M.S.W., Columbia U., 1962; Ph.D., Brandeis U., 1969, Inst. Ednl. Mgmt., Harvard U., 1977. With Lower East Side Neighborhood Assn., N.Y.C., 1962-64; community planning assoc. United Community Services, Sioux Falls, S.D., 1964-66; instr. Augustana Coll., Sioux Falls, 1964-66; research assoc. Ford Found. Project on Community Planning for Elderly, Brandeis U., Waltham, Mass., 1966-67; prof., dir. Sch. Social Work, Western Mich. U., Kalamazoo, 1968-74; prof., dean Sch. Applied Social Scis., Case Western Res. U., Cleve., 1974-83; Ralph and Dorothy Schmitt prof. Sch. Applied Social Scis., Case Western Res. U., 1983—, chmn. PhD program, 1990-94; prof. internat. health Sch. of Medicine, 1994—; vis. prof. Inst. Sociology, Stockholm U., 1978, Fulbright lectr., 1980; vis. prof. Nat. Inst. Social Work, London, 1981, Sch. Social Work, Stockholm U., 1982-86, Eotvos Lorand U., Budapest, Hungary, 1992, 95, 96, London Sch. Econs., 1994; Fulbright rsch. scholar Inst. Applied Social Rsch., Oslo, 1989; fellow U. Canterbury, Christchurch, New Zealand, 1994; mem. UN tech. com. World Assembly on Aging, 2000—. Author: Participation in Teaching and Learning: An Idea Book for Social Work Educators; editor: Meeting Human Needs: An International Annual, Vol. V, Linking Health Care and Social Services: International Perspectives; editor-in-chief Internat. Social Work Jour., 1985-87; co-editor: Profiles in Internat. Social Work, 1992, Issues in International Social Work, 1997, (internat. issue) Jour. Gerontol. Social Work, 1988, (internat. mental health issue) Jour. Sociology and Social Welfare, 1990, Jour. Social Policy and Administration, 1993, Jour. Aging Internat., 1994, Jour. Applied Social Scis., 1996; contbr. articles to profl. jours., chpts. to books. Mem. alcohol tng. rev. com. Nat. Inst. Alcoholism and Alcohol Abuse, 1974-78; workshop leader Am. Assn. State Colls. and Univs., 1974; chmn. U.S. com. XVIII Internat. Congress Schs. Social Work, 1976; chmn. Kalamazoo County Cmty. Mental Health Svcs. Bd., 1971, vice chmn., 1972; mem. edn. and tng. task force Mich. Office Drug Abuse and Alcoholism, 1972-73; mem. Mich. Assn. Mental Health Bds., 1972; bd. dirs. Cleve. United Way Svcs., 1982-84, del. assembly, 1974-82, mem. periodic rev. oversight com., 1982, mem. leadership devel. com., 1978, cmty. resources com., 1988—; bd. dirs. Kalamazoo United Way, 1968-72; trustee Cleve. Internat. Program for Youth Workers and Social Workers, chmn. program com., 1985-87; mem. program devel. com. Cleve. Center on Alcoholism, 1976; trustee Alcoholism Services Cleve., Inc., 1977-86, v.p., 1982-85; trustee Cmty. Info./Vol. Action Ctr., 1982-88, chmn. leadership devel. com., 1984-86, chmn. unmet needs com., 1986-88, exec. com., 1985-88, v.p., 1986-88; exec. com. Western Reserve Geriatric Edn. Ctr., 1995—; mem. adv. com. Coun. for Internat. Exch. Scholars, 1991-93, Fedn. for Cmty. Planning Coun. on Older Persons, 1991—, chmn. caregiver support program initiative, 1995-96; mem. task force of social transition in Soviet Union, U.S. State Dept. Bur. Human Rights and Humanitarian Affairs; mem. UN NGO Com. on Aging, 1996—; mem. adv. coun. Cuyahoga County Dept. Adult and Sr. Svcs., 1998—; co-chmn. U.S. Com. for Internat. Yr. of Older Persons, 1999. Named Outstanding Alumnus, Augustana Coll., 1980, Ohio Soc. Worker of the Yr., 1992; Fulbright Research fellow; NIMH trainee, 1960-62; Vocat. Rehab. trainee, 1966; Gerontology trainee, 1967; Rotary Found. fellow, 1958-59. Mem. NASW (internat. com. 1989-93, chmn. 1992-93), Acad. Cert. Social Workers, Internat. Assn. Schs. Social Work (exec. bd. 1978-92, 98—, treas. 1978-86, v.p. N.Am. 1988-92, membership sec. 1996—), Internat. Coun. on Social Welfare (dir. U.S. com. 1982-92), Coun. on Social Work Edn. (del. 1972-75, 77-83, chmn. ann. program meeting 1973, chmn. com. on nat. legis. and adminstrv. policy 1975-79, mem. nominating com. 1978-81, internat. com. 1980-86, 96—, chmn. com. 1982-84, dir. 1979-82, exec. com. 1986-89, pres. 1986-89), Nat. Conf. on Social Welfare (bd. dirs. 1978-80, chmn. sect. V program com. 1977-78), World Future Soc. (area coord. 1972-74), Fulbright Assn. (v.p. N.E. Ohio chpt. 1990-91), Nat. Coun. on Aging (bd. dirs. 1991-97, internat. com. 1991-97, pub. policy com. 1992-97). Democrat. Episcopalian. Home: 2917 Weymouth Rd Cleveland OH 44120-2234 Office: Case Western Res U 10900 Euclid Ave Cleveland OH 44106-1712

HOKIN, LOWELL EDWARD, biochemist, educator; b. Chgo., Sept. 20, 1924; s. Oscar E. and Helen (Manfield) H.; m. Mabel Neaverson, Dec. 1, 1952 (div. Dec. 1973); children: Linda Ann, Catherine Esther (dec.), Samuel Arthur; m. Barbara M. Gallagher, Mar. 23, 1978 (div. July 1998); 1 child, Ian Oscar. Student, U. Chgo., 1942-43, Dartmouth Coll., 1943-44, U. Louisville Sch. Medicine, 1944-46, U. Ill. Sch. Medicine, 1946-47; MD, U. Louisville, 1948; PhD, U. Sheffield, Eng., 1952. Postdoctoral fellow dept. biochemistry McGill U., 1952-54, faculty, 1954-57, asst. prof., 1955-57; mem. faculty U. Wis., Madison, 1957—, prof. physiol. chemistry, 1961-68, prof. pharmacology, 1968-99, prof., chmn. pharmacology, 1968-93, prof. emeritus, 1999—. Contbr. numerous articles to tech. jours., chpts. to numerous books on phosphoinositides, biol. transport, the pancreas, the brain and lithium in manic-depression. With USNR, 1943-45. Mem. AAAS, Am. Soc. Biochemistry and Molecular Biology, Biochem. Soc. (U.K.), Am. Soc. Pharmacology and Exptl. Therapeutics, N.Y. Acad. Scis. Home: 5 Nokomis Ct Madison WI 53711-2710 Office: U Wis Med Sch Dept Pharm 1300 University Ave Madison WI 53706-1510

HOKL, JAN KAREL, immunologist; b. Brno, Czech Republic, Oct. 24, 1939; s. Jan. and Ruzena (Kasparova) H.; m. Jirina Budarova, Dec. 20, 1969; children: Jana, Marketa. MS, Faculty Life Sci., Brno, 1962; PhD, Acad. Sci., Prague, Czech Republic, 1972. Rschr. Acad. Sci., Prague, 1964-71, Tchg. Hosp., Brno, 1971-84, Ctr. Cardiovascular and Transplant Surgery, Brno, 1985—. Co-author: Cyclosporine A, 1994; contbr. articles to profl. jours. Mem. Transplant Soc., European Transplant Soc. Avocations: basketball, tennis. Office: Ctr Cardiovascular and, Transplant Surgery, Pekarska 53, 656 91 Brno Czech Republic

HOLBROOKE, RICHARD CHARLES ALBERT, ambassador, government official; b. N.Y.C., Apr. 24, 1941; s. Dan and Trudi (Moos) H.; children: David Dan, Anthony Andrew. B.A., Brown U., 1962; postgrad., Princeton, 1969-70. Joined Fgn. Service, 1962; served in Vietnam, 1963-66; mem. White House staff, 1966-67; assigned State Dept.; staff Paris (France) peace talks on Vietnam, 1968-69; dir. Peace Corps, Morocco, 1970-72; mng. editor Fgn. Policy mag., 1972-77; dir. publs. Carnegie Endowment for Internat. Peace, 1973-76; cons. Commn. Orgn. Govt. for Conduct of Fgn., 1974-75; contbg. editor Newsweek Internat., 1976; asst. sec. for East Asian and Pacific affairs Dept. State, Washington, 1977-81; v.p. Public Strategies, Washington, 1981-85; sr. advisor Lehman Bros., 1981-84; mng. dir. Shearson Lehman Bros., 1985-93; U.S. amb. Federal Republic of Germany, 1993-94; asst. sec. state European and Can. affairs Dept. State, Washington, 1994-96; vice chmn. Credit Suisse First Boston, N.Y.C., 1996-99; U.S. amb. to U.N. N.Y.C., 1999—; chief negotiator Dayton Peace Accords, 1995; spl. presdl. emissary to Cyprus; etrustee Internat. Voluntary Services; mem. Trilateral Commn. Author: vol. The Pentagon Papers, 1967; Contbr. numerous articles to, N.Y. Times, Washington Post, Wall St. Jour., Atlantic, other mags. and jours. Bd. dirs. Internat. Rescue Com.; chmn. Refugees Internat. Mem. Am. Acad. Berlin, Council Fgn. Relations, Inst. Strategic Studies. Office: US Mission to the UN 799 United Nations Plz New York NY 10017-3589

HOLCEPL, JAMES ROBERT, sales professional; b. Cleve., Sept. 23, 1947; s. Robert J. and Julia M. Holcepl; m. Julie M. Holcepl, Sept. 18, 1971; children: Christopher J., Andrew J. AA, Cuyahoga C.C., Cleve., 1971; BA, Baldwin-Wallace Coll., 1979; MBA, Cleve. State U., 1999. Trade/text buyer Metro Campus Book Ctr./Cuyahoga C.C., Cleve., 1974-77; dist. sales mgr. Bantam Books, Inc., N.Y.C., 1977-81, regional sales mgr., 1981-90; divsn. sales mgr. Bantam-Doubleday-Dell, N.Y.C., 1990-92, retail chain sales mgr., 1992-99; ea. region sales mgr. McGraw-Hill Profl. Book Group, N.Y.C., 1999—, nat. field sales mgr., 2000—. Pres. of church consistory Ch. of the Redeemer UCC, Westlake, Ohio, 1995-96. Tech. sgt. Ohio ANG/USAF, 1967-76. Recipient Event Mktg. Achievement award Michiana News Svc., Niles, Mich., 1995. Mem. Sales and Mktg. Execs. of Cleve., U.S. Power Squadron (chmn. elective courses 1995-97, Jim Crane Meml. Elective Course award 1997-98), Beta Gamma Sigma. Mem. United Ch. of Christ. Avocations: musician/banjo and guitar, collecting old musical instruments, power boating.

HOLCOMB, BRADLEY J., procurement and supply management executive. BS in Engring. Sci., Ariz. State U., 1974, MS in Indsl. Engring., 1975; MS in Chem. Engring., U. Rochester, 1984; postgrad., U. Mich., 1995. Indsl. engr. ops. rsch. Mgmt. Svcs. Divsn. Eastman Kodak Co., Rochester, N.Y., 1976-78; supr. production control Film Mfg. Divsn. Eastman Kodak Co., Rochester, N.Y., 1979-82, devel. engr. coating technology, 1983-84; dir. bus. devel. electronic technologies Corp. Comml. Affairs Eastman Kodak Co., Rochester, N.Y., 1985-87; mgr. mfg. color printing materials Electronic Photography Divsn. Eastman Kodak Co., Rochester, N.Y., 1988-90, gen. mgr. internat. mktg. and sales, 1991-92; gen. mgr. product devel and manufacture partnerships Digital Imaging Platform Ctr. Eastman Kodak, Rochester, N.Y., 1993-94; dir. supplier relationship mgmt. corp. puchasing Eastman Kodak Co., Rochester, N.Y., 1994-96; v.p., chief procurement officer Global Procurement and Materials Mgmt. Praxair, Inc., Danbury, Conn., 1996-98; v.p. Supply Chain Mgmt., chief procurement officer Amer. Precision Industries, Inc., Buffalo, N.Y., 1998-2000; v.p., chief procurement officer Waste Mgmt., Inc., Houston, 2000—; guest lectr. Ariz. State U., Mich. State U., Rochester Inst. Technology. With USAF, 1967-71. Mem. Nat. Assn. Purchasing Mgrs., Ctr. for Advanced Purchasing Studies Purchasing Execs. Roundtable. E-mail: bjholcomb@msn.com. Home: 9217 Beech Meadow Ct Clarence Center NY 14032-9332

HOLCOMB, CARAMINE KELLAM, volunteer worker; b. Painter, Va., Jan. 23, 1941; d. Emerson Polk and Amine (Cosby) Kellam; m. Isaac Somers White, Nov. 25, 1961 (div. 1975); children: Kellam White Griffin, Caramine White, Virginia Somers White; m. Harry Sherman Holcomb III, May 12, 1979. AA, St. Mary's Coll., Raleigh, 1960; Cert., Richmond Bus. Coll., Va., 1961. Bd. dirs. Kellam Energy, Inc., Belle Haven. Va., 1980—, AUto Plus, Inc., Belle Haven, 1980-89, Shore Stop, Inc., Bele Haven, 1981-89. Contbr. articles to profl. jours. Trustee Northampton-Accomack Meml. Hosp., Nassawadox, Va., 1986-98, v.p. aux., 1986-88, pres., 1988-90, sec. bd. trustees, 1989-91, vice chmn., 1991-94, chair, 1994-96; bd. dirs. Ea. Shore Hist. Soc., Onancock, Va., 1987-92, Shore Life Svcs., 1998—, Eastern Shore C.C. Found., 1998—; bd. dirs. Med. Soc. Va. Alliance, Richmond, 1984-94, v.p., 1989-91, pres., 1992-93; treas. E. Polk Kellam Found., 1991—; mem. session Belle Haven Presbyn. Ch., 1999—. Mem. AMA Alliance Bd. (ERF com. 1994, AMA-ERF com. chmn. 1994-95, field dir. 1995-98, bylaws chmn. 1999-2000), Med. Soc. Va. Trust, Garden Club Ea. Shore (pres. 1973-75). Avocations: tennis, sailing, travel, reading, flower arranging. Home: PO Box 38 Franktown VA 23354-0038

HOLCOMB, LYLE DONALD, JR., retired lawyer; b. Miami, Fla., Feb. 3, 1929; s. Lyle Donald and Hazel Irene (Watson) H.; m. Barbara Jean Roth, July 12, 1952; children: Susan Holcomb Davis, Douglas J., Mark E. BA, U. Mich., 1951; JD, U. Fla., 1954. Bar: U.S. Ct. Appeals (5th and 11th cirs.) 1981, U.S. Supreme Ct. 1966. Ptnr. Holcomb & Holcomb, Miami, 1955-72; assoc. Copeland, Therrel, Baisden & Peterson, Miami Beach, Fla., 1972-75; ptnr. Therrel, Baisden, Stanton, Wood & Setlin, Miami Beach, Fla., 1976-85, Therrel, Baisden & Meyer Weiss, Miami Beach, Fla., 1985-93; pvt. practice Tallahassee, Fla., 1993-95; organizing pres. So. Fla. Migrant Legal Svcs. Program (now Fla. Rural Legal Svcs.), 1966-68. Mem. exec. coun. So. Fla. coun. Boy Scouts Am., 1958-93; past pres., past counselor Miami chpt. Huguenot Soc. Fla. Served with USNR, 1947-53. Recipient Silver Beaver award So. Fla. coun. Boy Scouts Am., 1966. Fellow Am. Coll. Trust and Estate Counsel, 1980-94, Acad. Fla. Probate and Trust Litigation Attys., 1980-95; mem. Dade County Bar Assn. (dir. 1960-71, sec. 1963-71), Miami Beach Bar Assn. (pres. 1980), Estate Planning Coun. Greater Miami, Soc. Mayflower Descs. (past pres. Miami club, past counselor soc.), SAR (past pres. Miami chpt.), Univ. Yacht Club. Republican. Mem. Ch. of Christ. Home: 3538 Killarney Plaza Dr Tallahassee FL 32308-3491

HOLCOMBE, HOMER WAYNE, nuclear quality assurance professional; b. Winston-Salem, N.C., Oct. 7, 1949; s. Calvin Littleberry Holcombe and Mary Elizabeth (Fisher) Portwood; m. Kathleen Lorraine Sheldon; children: Matthew Michael Dickson, Meghan Elizabeth Holcombe, Adam Wayne Holcombe. AAS in Quality Assurance, Metropolitan State Coll., Denver, 1980; BS in Bus. Adminstrn., City U., Seattle, 1982. Cert. nuclear insp. Engring. assoc. Stone & Webster Engring. Corp., Boston, 1974-76; authorized nuclear insp. Hartford Steam Boiler Inspection & Ins. Co., Denver, 1976-80; project quality dir. Morrison-Knudsen Co., Elma, Wash., 1980-84; asst. project mgr. Pullman/Kenith-Fortson Co., Waynesboro, Ga., 1984-87; project quality mgr. MK-Ferguson Co., U.S. DOE Savannah River Site, Aiken, S.C., 1987-90; quality dir. MK-Ferguson of Oak Ridge Co., U.S. DOE Oak Ridge Site, Oak Ridge, Tenn., 1990-92; dep. gen. mgr. MK-Ferguson of Idaho Co., U.S. DOE Idaho Nat. Engring. Lab., Idaho Falls, 1992-94, gen. mgr., 1994-95; project mgr., naval facilities environ. restoration Morrison-Knudsen Co., Charleston, S.C., 1995-96; project mgr. ICBM Neutralization Facility Rep. of Ukraine Morrison-Knudsen Co., Cleve., 1996—; lectr. Aiken (S.C.) Tech. Coll., 1987; program mgr. cooperative threat reduction program Republic of Ukraine Morrison Knudsen Co., Cleve., 1998—. With U.S. Navy, 1968-74. Mem. Am. Nuclear Soc., Am. Soc. for Quality Control, Am. Welding Soc. Republican. Office: Morrison-Knudsen Co 1500 W 3rd St Cleveland OH 44113-1422

HOLDEN, BARRY BARFIELD, political science educator; b. London, July 14, 1936; s. Kenneth Esmond and Isobel Mary (Barclay) H.; m. Barbara Lyn Davies, Mar. 30, 1963; children: Karen, Robert. BA, U. Keele, Eng., 1959. Asst. lectr. U. Southampton, Eng., 1962-63; lectr. dept. politics U. Reading, Eng., 1963-71, sr. lectr., 1971—. Author: The Nature of Democracy, 1974, Understanding Liberal Democracy, 1988, 2d edit., 1993; editor, contbr.: The Ethical Dimensions of Global Change, 1996; editor: Global Democracy, 2000. Mem. Polit. Studies Assn. Avocations: tennis, badminton, concerts. Home: Threeways Croft Rd, Spencers Wood, RG7 1DR Reading England Office: U Reading Dept Politics, Whitenights PO Box 218, RG6 2AA Reading England

HOLDER, HOWARD RANDOLPH, SR., broadcasting company executive; b. Moline, Ill., Nov. 14, 1916; s. James William and Charlotte (Brega) H.; m. Clementi Lacey-Baker, Feb. 21, 1942; children: Janice Clementi Black, Susan Charlotte Holder, Marjory Estelle Holder, Howard Randolph Jr. BA, Augustana Coll., 1939. With radio stas. WHBF, Rock Island, Ill., 1939-41, WOC, Davenport, Iowa, 1945-47, WINN, Louisville, 1947, WRFC, Athens, Ga., 1948-56; pres. Clarke Broadcasting Corp., 1956-91, chmn., 1991—; chmn. WGAU and WNGC, Athens, 1956—, KVML and KZSQ, Sonora, Calif., 1987—, KJMQ, Atwater, Calif., 1995—, KTFN and KLOQ, Merced, Calif., 1996—; mem. adv. bd. U. Ga. Coll. Journalism and Mass Comm., 1973-78, sec., 1973-74; pres. Mid-West Ga. Broadcasting, Inc., 1965-68; bd. dirs. AP Broadcasters, Inc., 1983-91, C&S Nat. Bank (now Bank of Am.), 1965-68. Author: Escape to Russia, 1995. Chmn. adv. bd. Salvation Army, 1962-63, life mem., 1952—; chmn. Athens Parks and Recreatoin Bd., 1952-62; chmn. Cherokee dist. Boy Scouts Am., 1966-67, bd. N.E. Ga. Eagle Scout Assn., 1989; mem. adv. bd. Clarke County Juvenile Ct., 1960-72, Athens-Clarke ARC, 1950-70; chmn. region IV Ga. divsn. Am. Cancer Soc., 1968; bd. dirs. Athens Crime Prevention Com., 1960-70; mem. Georgians for Safer Hwys., 1970; trustee Ga. Rotary Student Fund, Inc., 1969-90, trustee emeritus, 1990—; mem. Model Cities Policy Bd., 1970-71, Ga. Criminal Justice Coord. Com.; mem. Ga. Productivity Bd., 1984-85, hon. chmn. N.E. Ga. March of Dimes, 1996, 97, Walk Am., 1997; mem. bicentennial alumni activities com. U. Ga., 1982; co-pres. Friends U. Ga. Mus. Art, 1973-75; state bd. advisors Ga. Mus. Art, 1984—, life mem., 1997—; sec. adv. bd. Henry W. Grady Coll. Journalism and Mass Comm., U. Ga. adv. coun., 1990-92; mem. adv. group views for the nineties U. Ga., 1989-92; mem. fine arts task force, adv. com. for evaluation v.p. for svcs., U. Ga., 1989; mem. adv. com. Ga. Commn. for Nat. Bicentennial, 1976; bd. dirs. Rec. for the Blind, 1977-83, Athens Symphony, 1981-85, Quality Growth Task Force N.E. Ga., 1989-91; mem. Ga. Gov.'s Jail/Prison Overcrowding Com., 1982; mem. svcs. adv. coun. UGA, 1990—; mem. WWII Commemorative Com., 1993-95; trustee Clementi and Randolph Holder Girl Scout Trust, 1997—; bd. dirs. Lyndon House Arts Ctr. Found., 1995-97. With AUS, 1941-46, ETO, maj. USAR ret.; hon. adm. Navy Supply Corps, 1997; col. R.I. Militia, 1997. Decorated Bronze Star with valor in battle insignia; named Boss of Yr., Athens Jr. C. ofC., 1959, Broadcaster-Citizen of Yr., Ga. Assn. Broadcasters, 1962, Ga. Assn. Broadcasters Hall of Fame, 1993, Employer of Yr., Bus. and Profl. Women's Club, 1969, Athens Citizen of Yr., Rotary Club, 1971, Athens Woman's Club, 1971; recipient Silver Beaver award Boy Scouts Am., 1973, James E. West Fellowship award, Inspiration award Athens Cmty. Coun. on Aging, 1990, Advt. Silver medal Am. Advt. Fedn., Liberty Bell award Athens Bar Assn., 1977, Robert Stolz medaille, 1973, Nat. DAR medal of Hon., 1983, Cert. of Merit United Daus. of the Confederacy, 1983, Disting. Citizen award Ga. Dept. Labor, 1994, George Washington Patriotic Achievement award Soc. of Cin. in the State of Ga., 1996, Outstanding Ga. Citizen Sec. of State, 1997, Gov.'s Outstanding Svc. award, 1997, Key to City, Athens/Clarke County, 1997, Disting. Eagle award and Regent for life Nat. Eagle Scout Assn.; Paul Harris fellow, 1978, Will Watt fellow, 1984, Hue Thomas fellow, 1989, James E. West fellow, 1999; H. Randolph Holder Day proclaimed by the City of Athens, 1989, 98; named hon. admiral Navy Supply Corps, 1998, Key to Athens/Clarke, 1998, hon. col. R.I. Militia, 1998, NSCS Goodwill Ambassador award, 1999. Mem. Res. Officers Assn. (life, pres. Athens chpt. 1962), Am. Ex-Prisoners War (life), Ga. Assn. Broadcaster (pres. 1961), Athens Area C. of C. (pres. 1970), Ga. AP Broadcasters (pres. 1963), Augustana Coll. Alumni Assn. (bd. dirs. 1973-76, Outstanding Achievement award 1973), Golden Quill, Gridiron, Sigma Delta Chi, Alpha Psi Omega, Alpha Delta Sigma, Gamma Kappa (Ga. Pioneer Broadcaster of Yr. award 1971, 91, Lamplighter award 1993), Phi Omega Phi (pres. 1938-39), Touchdown Club (pres. Athens club 1963-64), Rotary (pres. Athens club 1957-58, govt. dist. 692 1969-70, Rotary internat. pub. rels. com. 1987-90, W. Lee Arrandale Vocat. Excellence award 1992). Office: Clarke Broadcasting Corp 383 Westview Dr Athens GA 30606-4635

HOLDER, NEVILLE LEWIS, chemist; b. St. Joseph, Barbados, May 28, 1940; came to U.S., 1968, permanent resident, 1982; s. Cardon Elliot and Viola (Brathwaite) Tudor; m. Hyacinth Isoline Swaby, Sept. 4, 1965; children: Louis, Nadine, Nicole. BS with honors, U. West Indies, 1965, MS, 1969; PhD, U. Waterloo, 1973. Chemist Gillette Rsch. Inst., Rockville, Md., 1968-69, rsch. chemist, 1973-78; assoc. sr. investigator SmithKline Beecham Pharms., King of Prussia, Pa., 1978-92; sr. rsch. scientist Rhone-Poulenc Rorer Pharms., Collegeville, Pa., 1992-98; rsch. fellow Aventis Pharms. (formerly Rhone-Poulenc Rorer Pharms.), Collegeville, Pa., 1998—. Mem. editl. bd. Jour. Organic Chemistry, Carbohydrate Chemistry; contbr. numerous articles to profl. jours.; patentee in field. Mem. com. Boy Scouts Am., Cherry Hill, N.J., 1980-90. Recipient Barbadian Am. Alliance Accomplishment award, 1991; grad. scholar U. W.I., 1968-68, Ministry Edn. Bursary, Barbados Govt., 1961-64. Mem. Am. Chem. Soc., Nat. Orgn. Profl. Advancement Black Chemists & Chem. Engrs. (facilities chair Sci. Bowl Del. Valley chpt. 1990-98, scholarship & edn. coms. 1995—, v.p. 1996, v.p. Delaware Valley chpt. 1997-98, pres. Del. Valley chpt. 1998—, Corp. Liason award 1991), Phila. Organic Chemist Club, Toastmasters Internat. (charter, sergeant at arms 1990-91, treas. 1991-92, v.p. membership 1992, Compotent Toastmaster award 1989, Able Toastmaster award 1997). Episcopalian. Achievements include research in isolation and structure elucidation of natural products from the Jamaican cedar plant, synthesis of carbohydrate enones and their photochemical transformation to branched-chain monosaccharides, organic synthesis of drug substances, intermediates, isomers and potential impurities, chromatographic isolation and structure elucidation of impurities and decomposition products of drug substances and their synthetic intermediates, application of preparative HPLC using chiral and achiral stationary phases. Home: 13 Clemson Rd Cherry Hill NJ 08034-1213 Office: Aventis Pharms 500 Arcola Rd Collegeville PA 19426-3930

HOLDERFIELD, MARILYN IDA, jazz vocalist; b. Cleve., May 16, 1937; d. Edward F. and Geraldine Genevieve (Patek) Koblenzer; m. Dennis Holderfield, July 22, 1961 (div.); children: Michael Lee, Lisa Geraldine; m. Lloyd W. Frueh II, Feb. 21, 1986. Student, Cuyahoga C.C., Cleve., 1975. Jazz vocalist; vocal jazz clinician Lakewood High Sch., 1990-92. Long term engagements as jazz vocalist Keyboard Lounge, Fairview Park, Ohio, 1979-81, The Cabin, Willoughby, Ohio, 1981-86, Sammy's in the Flats, Cleve., 1983-92; featured performer Pub. Radio WKSU-FM Live at Cain Park, 1984, Pub. TV WEAO-TV Marilyn Holderfield in Concert, 1985; featured performer sound rec. An Evening with Marilyn and Chick, 1986, Marilyn Holderfield and Friends, 1992; jazz vocalist for spl. events, concerts and pvt. parties. Performer, Jerimiah's Jazz Jam Benefit for Multiple Sclerosis, Cleve., 1980-91, Literacy Spl. WVIZ-TV, Cleve., 1988; tutor Project Learn, Cleve., 1992-93, ESL Project, Lakewood, 1992. Mem. NOW, Internat. Assn. Jazz Educators, No. Ohio Jazz Soc., Am. Fedn. Musicians (bd. dirs. Local 4 1992—), Planned Parenthood Assn., The Hermit Club. Avocations: reading, walking, gardening, fly fishing, pool. Home: 19000 Lake Rd Apt 2109 Cleveland OH 44116-1760

HOLDSCLAW, CHAMIQUE SHAUNTA, professional basketball player; b. Flushing, N.Y., Aug. 9, 1977. Grad., U. Tenn., 1999. Basketball player Washington Mystics, 1999—. Named to Kodak 25th Anniversary Team, Women's Basketball Jour., Sports Illustrated and Sporting News Nat. Women's Player of Yr., 1999; Naismith finalist, winner Sullivan award, named AP Women's Basketball Player of Yr., 1997-98, 1998-99; recipient Gold medal 1998 World Championships, 1997 World Qualifying Tournament, 1995 Olympic Festival, USA Basketball Player of Yr. award, 1997, ESPY's for Female Athlete of Yr. award, second consecutive Women's Basketball Player of Yr., 1999, Naismith award Atlanta's Tip-Off Club, 1995; honored as one of 12 female athletes selected as inspirational role models by Women's Sports and Fitness magazine, 1998; named to Street & Smith All-American, three-time USA Today All-American, N.Y.C. Player of Yr; named Rawlings/WBCA Player of Yr., Player of Yr. Columbus, Ohio Touchdown Club, 1995. Office: Washington Mystics MCI Center 601 F St NW Washington DC 20004-1605

HOLDWAY, DOUGLAS ALAN, toxicologist, consultant; b. Montreal, Que., Can., Jan. 23, 1954; arrived in Australia, 1986; s. Charles Edward and Jeanette (Menzie) H.; m. Tracey Ann Monkhouse, June 11, 1983; children: Nathanial Edward, Jazmin Adryanna Hedy, Morgan Alexander Douglas. BSc with honors, U. Guelph, Ont., Can., 1976, MSc, 1978, PhD, 1983. Rsch. asst., tutor U. Guelph, 1976-78, 80-83; sci. subvention researcher Fed. Fisheries Rsch. Sta., St. Andrews, New Brunswick, 197880; NRC/Can. rsch. assoc. U. Waterloo, Ont., Can., 1983-85; Can. Govt. Lab. vis. fellow Environment Can., Burlington, Ont., 1985-86; rsch. scientist, head aquatic toxicology dept. Office of the Supervising Scientist, Jabiru, N.T., 1986-88, sr. rsch. scientist, head aquatic toxicology dept., 1988-89; chief environ. toxicologist Royal Melbourne (Victoria, Australia) Inst. Tech., 1989—, assoc. prof., 1993-97, prof. ecotoxicology, 1997—; head Oil Spill Rsch. Group, 1995—; mem. auditor rev. panel EPA, Melbourne, 1990-92; head environ. effects group, mem. rev. task force Jaakko Poyry Oy/Alberta Rsch. Coun., Helsinki, Finland, 1990; Australian expert aquatic toxicology OECD Test Guidelines Program, Canberra, 1991—. Author numerous book chpts. and sci. papers; assoc. editor Jour. of Ecosystem Stress and Recovery; editl. bd. Sci. Total Environment, 1999—; regional editor Spill Sci. & Tech. Bull., 1996-99, mem. editl. bd., 1999—. Govt. of Ont. scholar, 1972, 77-79; EPA grantee, 1990—, Commonwealth Pulp and Paper Rsch. Adv. Bd. grantee, 1991—, Australian Rsch. Coun. grantee, 1991—. Mem. ASTM, Nat. Geog. Soc., Soc. Environ. Toxicology and Chemistry (editl. bd. 1988-90), Australian Soc. Ecotoxical (v.p. 1999—), Australian Inst. Biology, Australasian Soc. Limnology. Avocations: guitar, bush walking, scuba diving, gardening, rugby. Office: RMIT Univ, Dept Appl Biol Biotechnol, Melbourne Vic 3001, Australia

HOLDYCH, THOMAS J., law educator; b. Rockford, Ill., Dec. 17, 1944; s. Ervin Charles and Beverly Jean (Vernell) H.; m. Carolyn Jean Holdych; children: Stephen Thomas, David James. BA, Rockford Coll., 1966; JD, U. Ill., 1970. Law clk. Calif. Supreme Ct., San Francisco, 1970-71; assoc. O'Melveny & Meyers, L.A., 1970-71, 71-72; asst. prof. law U. Puget Sound, Tacoma, Wash., 1972-74, assoc. prof. law, 1974-80, prof. law, 1980-94; prof. law Seattle U., 1994—. Contbr. articles to profl. jours. including Cambrian Law Rev., DePaul Law Rev., and Med. Malpractice Law and Strategy. Chmn. Harbor Covenant Ch., Gig Harvor, Wash., 1980-85, 96-98; sec. Pacific N.W. Conf., Evangl. Covenant Ch., Bellevue, Wash., 1987-89. Mem. Christian Legal Soc. Republican. Avocations: fishing, photography. Office: Seattle U 900 Broadway Seattle WA 98122-4340

HOLÉ, STÉPHANE JEAN-FRANCOIS, researcher, educator; b. Pontoise, France, Jan. 18, 1968; s. Jean-Francois Holé and Annie Pouget Gaudeaux; m. Christelle Courrègelongue; 1 child, Clément. Maitrise, U. Pierre et Marie Curie, Paris, 1990, DEA, 1991, PhD, 1996. Moniteur U. Paris 12, 1991-95; ATER U. Pierre et Marie Curie, 1995-97, maitre de conférences, 1997—. Contbr. articles to profl. jours. Engr. 1st class Train, 1993-94. Avocations: wood-carving, neurology. Office: UMPC-LIS, 10 Rue Vauquelin, 75005 Paris France

HOLENDER, IOAN, opera director; b. Temesvar, Romania, July 18, 1935; arrived in Austria, 1959; s. Anton and Magda Holender; m. Angelika Holender, Aug. 13, 1991; 3 children. Dir. Staatsoper, Vienna, Austria, 1992—. Office: Wiener Staatsoper, Opernring 2, 1010 Vienna Austria

HOLFELD, DONALD RAE, railroad consultant; b. Lestock, Sask., Can., Apr. 10, 1947; came to the U.S., 1994; s. Alexander R. and Edith (Schwab) H.; m. Patricia Elizabeth Sewell, July 16, 1994. BS, U. Alta., 1973. Registered profl. engr. Assn. Profl. Engrs. B.C. Maintenance engr. CN Rail, Kamloops, B.C., 1977-80; track and roadway engr. CN Rail, Kamloops, 1980-81; planning engr. CN Rail, Montreal, 1981-82, track rsch. engr., 1982-83, sys. engr. tech., 1983-89, sys. dir. ops. tng., 1989-94; dir. tng. and engring. Zeta-Tech. Assocs., Inc., Cherry Hill, N.J., 1994—; aux. prof. McGill U., Montreal, 1988-94; lectr. in field. Inventor in field. Recipient Golden Spike awards Internat. Rwy. Tng. Assn., 1989-94. Mem. ASTD, Am. Rlwy. Engring. and Maintenance of Way Assn. Avocations: singing, jogging, travelling, reading, cooking. Office: Zeta-Tech Assocs Inc 900 Kings Hwy N Ste 208 Cherry Hill NJ 08034-1516

HOLFORD-STREVENS, LEOFRANC ADRIAN, university press official; b. London, May 19, 1946; s. Adrian Theodore and Bertha Matilda (Curry) H.-S.; m. Bonnie Jean Blackburn, Jan. 6, 1990. BA, Oxford (Eng.) U., 1967, MA, 1970, DPhil, 1971. Proofreader Oxford U. Press, 1971-84, copy editor, 1984—. Author: Aulus Gellius, 1988, (with Bonnie J. Blackburn) Oxford Companion to the Year, 1999; editor, translator: (with Blackburn) The Perfect Musician, 1995; editor, trans. chpt. in Fauvel Studies, 1997; contbr. articles to classical, musicological and English lit. jours., also to reference works, including Oxford Classical Dictionary, 3d edit., 1990. Mem. Oxford Philol. Soc. (pres. 1999-2000), Royal Mus. Assn., Am. Musicological Soc., Plainsong and Medieval Music Soc., Renaissance Soc. Am. Avocations: languages, literature, history, music, reading about politics. Home: 67 St Bernards Rd, Oxford OX2 6EJ, England Office: Oxford U Press, Great Clarendon St, Oxford OX2 6DP, England

HOLGATE, STEPHEN TOWNLEY, physician, medical educator, researcher; b. Heywood, U.K., May 2, 1947; s. William Townley and Helen Margaret (Lancaster) H.; m. Elizabeth Karen Malkinson, Oct. 28, 1972; children: Matthew, Edmund, Katharine, Michael. BSc in Biochemistry, U. London, 1968, MB, BChir, 1971, MD, 1979; DSc, U. Southampton, Eng., 1991; MD (hon.)ú, U. Ferrara, Italy, 1997; PhD (hon.), Jallegonian U., Kracow, Poland, 1999. Ho. physician and surgeon Charing Cross Hosp., London, 1971-72; sr. ho. physician Nat. Hosp. Nervous Disease & Brompton Hosps., 1972-74; registrar in gen. and respiratory Medicine Southampton & Salisbury Hosps., 1974-75; lectr., hon. sr. registrar Southampton Gen. Hosp., 1975-80; sr. lectr., reader, prof. U. Southampton/Southampton Gen. Hosp., 1980-87, Med. Rsch. Coun. clin. prof., 1987—; post-doctoral rsch. fellow Harvard Med. Sch., Boston, 1978-80; mem. sys. bd. Med. Rsch. Coun., 1991-95; chmn. Com. on the Med. Effects of Air Pollutants, Dept. Health, 1992—; mem. expert panel Dept. Environment, Transport Air Quality Stds. and Regions, 1992—; mem. Merck Bd. Sci. Advisers, Merck Rsch. Labs., 1998—. Co-editor: (with W. Busse) Asthma and Rhinitis, 1995; lead editor: (with J.M. Samet, H.S. Korren, R.L. Maynard) Air Pollution and Health, 1999, (with H. Boushey, L. Fabbri) Difficult Asthma, 1999; co-editor Clin. and Exptl. Allergy, 1991—. Chmn. Asthma, Allergy and Inflammation Rsch. Trust, Southampton, 1990; mem. Mason Family Rsch. Trust, London, chmn., 1999—; mem. Pharm. and Biotechnology Task Force of the S.E. Eng., Guildford, 1999—. Recipient World Health award Rhone Poulenc Rorer Found., London, 1995, Internat. prize for medicien King Faisal Found., Saudi Arabia, 1999. Fellow Royal Coll. Physicians (London and Edinburgh, Graham Bull prize for med. rsch. 1993), Acad. Medicine U.K., Inst. Biology, Royal Coll. Pathologists. Avocations: gardening, running, cricket. Office: Resp Cell & Moleular Biology Divsn, Southampton Gen Hosp, Southampton SO16 6YD, United Kingdom

HOLICS, KLARA MARIA, pediatrician, educator; b. Salgotarjan, Hungary, Apr. 7, 1934; d. Endre and Iren (Szathmary) H.; m. Tamas Kolos, Apr. 27, 1968; children: Peter, Judit. MD, Semmelweis Med. U., Budapest, 1958, cert. pathology, 1961, cert. pediats., 1964. Pathologist Haynal Imre Postgrad. Med. U., Budapest, 1958-64; pediatrician Heim Pal Hosp. for Children, Budapest, 1964—, chief Ctr. of Cystic Fibrosis, 1977—; 1st sec. of Hungarian group Cystic Fibrosis Assn., Budapest, 1977—; pres. Hungarian Cystic Fibrosis Assn., Budapest, 1995—; Hungarian rep. Internat. Cystic Fibrosis Assn., Budapest, 1991—. Author: Mucoviscidosis for Doctors, 1986, Mucoviscidosis for Parents, 1981, Me and Cystic Fibrosis, 1997; gen. editor Esszencia, 1994. Recipient award Ministry of Health, 1988, Championship Volleyball award Hungarian Nat. Sport Club, 1953. Avocations: literature, music, travel, writing. E-mail: holicscf@mail.matav.hu. Home: Burok u 15, 1124 Budapest Hungary Office: Heim Pal Hosp for Children, Ulloi ut 86, 1089 Budapest Hungary

HOLIK, BOBBY, professional hockey player; b. Jihlava, Czech Republic, Jan. 1, 1971. Left wing Hartford Whalers, 1989-92, New Jersey Devils, 1992—. Winner bronze medal with Czech Nat. Jr. team in 1990 World Championships; played in 1991 world Championships. Office: New Jersey Devils Continental Airlines Arena PO Box 504 East Rutherford NJ 07073-0504

HOLIK, JOSEF FRIEDRICH, retired diplomat, consultant; b. Tetschen, Bohemia, Czech Republic, Apr. 20, 1931; s. Josef J. and Hermine (Luksch) H.; m. Wiltrud Magis, Apr. 6, 1937; children: Viola, Peter, Olivia. JD, U. Wuerzburg, Germany, 1960. Amb. German Fgn. Office, Somalia, 1971-74; head of del. Mutual Balanced Force Reductions, Vienna, 1984-87; commr. for arms control and disarmament German Govt., Bonn, 1987-95; mem. UN Sec. Gen. Adv. Bd. for Disarmament, N.Y.C., 1991-99; mem., trustee UN Inst. for Disarmament Rsch., Geneva, 1991-99, Bonn Internat. Inst. on Conversion, 1994—; bd. chmn. Saint Barbara Found., Munster.

HOLL, HELMUT J., engineering educator; b. Wels, Austria, Apr. 30, 1963; s. Helmut E. and Katharina Holl; m. Barbara G. Roithmayr, Sept. 5, 1987; children: Eva, Katrin, Christina. Diploma in mech. engring., Tech. U. Vienna, Austria, 1987; PhD, Univ. Linz, Austria, 1995. Cert. in mech. engring. Engr. Voest Alpine Industriean, Lagenbau, Austria, 1987-91; asst. prof. Univ. Linz, 1991—. Inventor in field. Mem. Gesellschaft fur angewandte Mathematik und Mechanik, Soc. Exptl. Mechanics. Office: U Linz, Altenbergerstr 69, A-4040 Linz Austria

HOLL, JAMES ANDREW, prehospital care administrator; b. Jersey City, Sept. 15, 1961; s. Charles J. Jr. and Alice M. (Kearney) H. Cert. paramedic, N.J. Coll. Dentistry/Medicine, 1981; AS in Nursing, Atlantic C.C., 1986; BA in Nursing Mgmt., Stockton State Coll., 1991; postgrad. flight nurse prog., USAF Sch. Aerospace Medicine, 1993. Cert. emergency nurse, flight nurse. Firefighter, EMT instr., med. coord. Brigantine (N.J.) Fire Dept., 1979—, firefighter, instr. dep. coord emergency mgmt., 1987—; paramedic mobile intensive care West Jersey Health System, 1982-83, Underwood Meml. Hosp. 1980—; forensic med. investigator Atlantic County Med. Examiners Office, 1982-86; nurse dept. intensive care, emergency Shore Meml. Hosp., 1986-97. Mem. 714th Aeromed. Squad USAF, 1991—. Decorated USAF Commendation medal, 1997; recipient citation Senator Dan Dalton. Mem. Nat. Flight Nurses Assn., Nat. Registry Emergency Med. Technicians, N.J. State Emergency Med. Technician Instrs., Emergency Nurses Assn., Emergency Med. Svcs. Physicians Assn. (assoc.), Internat. Assn. Firefighters, Atlantic County Firefighters Assn. Office: 1417 W Brigantine Ave Brigantine NJ 08203-2147 Address: PO Box 164 Brigantine NJ 08203-0164

HOLLADAY, CARL R., New Testament educator; b. Huntingdon, Tenn., Oct. 18, 1943; s. Ben R. and Inus R. Holladay; m. Donna H. Holladay, Aug. 28, 1964; children: John Krister, Ben Hardeman, Andrew Patrick. BA, Abilene Christian U., 1965, MDiv, 1969; ThM, Princeton Theol. Sem., 1970; PhD, U. Cambridge, Eng., 1975. Asst. prof. New Testament, Yale Div. Sch., New Haven, Conn., 1975-78, assoc. prof. New Testament, 1978-80; assoc. prof. New Testament Candler Sch. Theology, Emory U., Atlanta, Ga., 1980-90, prof. New Testament,, 1990—, assoc. dean, 1983-91, dean faculty and acad. affairs, 1992-94. Author: Theios Aner in Hellenistic Judaism, 1977, First Letter of Paul to the Corinthians, 1979, (with J. Hayes) Biblical Exegesis, 1982, Fragments From Hellenistic Jewish Authors, 4 vols., 1983-96. Exec. dir. Christian Scholarship Found., Atlanta, 1983—; pres. North Ga. chpt. Fulbright Assn., Atlanta, 1998-99, 2000-01. Fulbright Sr. scholar, 1994-95; recipient Henry T. Luce Fellow in Theology award Assn. Theol. Schs., 1999-2000. Home: 668 Clifton Rd NE Atlanta GA 30307-1789 Office: Emory Univ Candler Sch Theology Atlanta GA 30322-0001

HOLL-ALLEN, ROBERT THOMAS JAMES, surgeon; b. Leamington Spa, U.K., Dec. 3, 1934; s. Robert Thomas James and Florence Janet Rachel (Wimbush) Allen; m. Julia Anne Gollanche, Sept. 2, 1992 (div. 1992); children: Jonathan, Robert G., Amanda; stepchildren: Daniel, Maxine, Sarah, Robin. BSc with honors, Univ. Coll., London, 1956, B Medicine B Surgery with honors, 1959; MS, London U., 1971, MD, 1972. Various intern and residency posts U.K., 1959-64; resident in surgery Radcliffe Infirmary/Oxford (Eng.) U., 1964-66; chief resident in surgery West Midland Hosps., U.K., 1966-73; rsch. fellow dept. surgery Harvard U., 1968-69; hon. sr. lectr. surgery U. Birmingham, Eng., 1980—; pvt. practice surgeon Birmingham and London, 1973—. Contbr. articles to profl. publs. Mayor's consort, Solihull, 1987-88. Recipient Wessex Rsch. award, 1965. Fellow ACS, Royal Coll. Surgeons, Royal Soc. Medicine; mem. N.Y. Acad. Scis., Squire Club. Avocations: golf, reading, travel, gourmet dining. Home: 1 Avenbury Dr, Solihull B91 2QZ, England Office: 681A Warwick Rd, Solihull B91 3DA, England also: 144 Harley St, London W1N 1AH, England

HOLLÁN, SUSAN R., hematologist, educator; b. Budapest, Hungary, Oct. 26, 1920; d. Henrik and Malvina (Hornik) Hollán; m. Gyorgy Révész, 1944; children: Thomas, Mary Christine. MD, U. Budapest, 1947, PhD, 1956; DSc, U. Budapest Med. Sch. and Hungarian Acad. Sci., 1972. Sci. advisor Inst. Exptl. Medicine, Budapest, 1954-91; dir. Nat. Inst. Hematology & Blood Transfusion, Budapest, 1959-85, dir. gen., 1985-90; prof. hematology Postgrad. Med. Sch., 1970-90. Author: Basic Problems of Transfusion, 1965, Haemoglobins and Haemoglobinopathies, 1972; author numerous prof. papers; editor: Hungarian Medical Encyclopedia, 1967-72, Advances in Physiological Science, vol. 6 of Genetics, Structure, Function of Blood Cells, 1981, Management of Blood Transfusion Services, 1990; editor-in-chief Haemotologia, 1967—, Management of Blood Transfusion Services, 1990. Recipient Hungarian Acad. award, 1970, Hungarian Nat. prize, 1974; rsch. fellow I dept. medicine U. Budapest, 1950-54. Mem. Hungarian Acad. Sci. (pres. 1976-85), Soc. Bologie, College de France (corr.); hon. mem. Am. Soc. Hematology, Purkinje Soc., Turkish Soc. Haematology, German Soc. Haematology, Soviet Soc. Haematology, Polish Soc. Haematology, Romanian Soc. Haematology, Hungarian Soc. Genetics (hon. (pres.). Office: Nat Inst Hamatology/Immunol, Daroczi ut 24, 1113 Budapest Hungary

HOLLAND, AGNIESZKA, film director, screenwriter; b. Warsaw, Poland, 1948; m. Laco Adamik. Editor FAMU Film Sch., Prague, Czechoslovakia; asst. to Krzysztof Zanussi X, Warsaw, 1973. Works include: (co-dir. with Jerzy Domaradzki and Pawel Kedzierski) Screen Test, 1977; (co-screenwriter) Rough Treatment, 1978; (worked on films) A Love in Germany, Man of Marble, Man of Iron, The Orchestra Conductor, Korczak, Danton, 1982; (screenwriter) Anna; (dir.) Provincial Actors, 1979, The Fever, 1980, The Lonely Woman, 1981, Angry Harvest, 1985, To Kill a Priest, 1988, Europa Europa, 1992, Oliver, Oliver, 1993, (tv series) Fallen Angels, 1993, The Secret Garden, 1993, Total Eclipse, 1995, Washington Square, 1997, The Third Miracle, 1999; and numerous documentaries for French TV. Office: Creative Artists Agency 9830 Wilshire Blvd Beverly Hills CA 90212-1825

HOLLAND, ANN LIVINGSTON, emergency medicine physician; b. Montgomery, Ala., Jan. 13, 1946; d. Wendell Howell and Ramona Tripp Livingston; m. Carroll H. Faulkner, June 13, 1981; child from previous marriage: Emilie. BA, U. Pa., 1968; MD, Temple U., 1978. Diplomate Am. Bd. Family Physicians. Pvt. practice family medicine Bangor, Maine, 1981-88; commd. officer USPHS-Indian Health Svc., Okla., 1989-92; emergency physician Maine, Pa., 1992—; adv. bd. Bangor City Nursing Facility. Cmty. rels. coun. Penobscot Job Corps Ctr., Bangor, 1981—. Fellow Am. Acad. Family Physicians; mem. Internat. Physicians for Prevention of Nuclear War, Al-Anon Family Groups. Episcopalian. Avocations: church choir, European travel, gardening. e-mail: moomadoc@hotmail.com.

HOLLAND, GEORGE FRANK, II, investment company executive; b. N.Y.C., Jan. 19, 1931; m. Elizabeth R. Hardy, Aug. 31, 1957; children: Steven Todd, William Eric, Roger Hardy, Ellen. AB, Ind. U., 1953, MBA, 1957. Asst. v.p. Am. Fletcher Nat. Bank, Indpls., 1957-70; exec. v.p., dir., sec. Traub Co. Inc., Indpls., 1970-97; v.p. investment David A. Noyes & Co., Indpls., 1998—. Contbr. articles to profl. jours. Lt. col. USAFR, 1953-77. Mem. Indpls. Soc. Fin. Analysts (past pres.), Res. Officers Assn., Ret. Officers Assn., Ind. U. Alumni Assn., Carmel Breakfast Sertoma Club (past pres.), Indpls. Stock & Bond Club, Am. Legion, Sigma Chi Alumni Assn. Republican. Episcopalian. Home: 20 Wildwood Dr Carmel IN 46032-1416 Office: David A Noyes & Co 111 Monument Cir Ste 300 Indianapolis IN 46204-5110

HOLLAND, JAMES R., real estate corporation executive; b. St. Louis, Feb. 20, 1944; s. Randolph and Thelma (Robinson) H.; m. Helen M. Devine, Feb. 18, 1972; children: Danielle, James Randolph, Eric Marc. Student, Principia Coll., 1962-64; BFA, Ohio U., 1966; postgrad., U. Mo. Sch. Journalism, 1966. Photog. intern Nat. Geog. Soc., Washington, 1966, contract photographer for mag., 1967-68; film prodr. Christian Sci. Ctr., Boston, 1969-74; real estate developer, pres. Brownstone Properties, Inc., Boston, 1975-77; real estate broker Street & Co., Inc., Boston, 1978-82; pres. A Bit of Boston Real Estate, Inc., Boston, 1982—. Author: The Amazon, 1971, Mr. Pops-Arthur Fiedler, 1972, Tanglewood (foreward Michael Tilson Thomas), 1973; illustrator-photographer Continental and Colonial Currency of Colonial America; contbr. Photojournalism-Principles and Practice (Clifton Edom), 2d edit., 1980; articles, photographs contbd. to various nat., internat. newspapers, mags., encys., video games, numerous textbooks; writer documentary film scripts; film work has appeared on NBC, ABC, CBS, PBS, BBC; prodr. limited edit. karate video tapes Twinkle Toes Videos; photographs and films in permanent collections Truman Libr., JFK Libr., Boston Pub. Libr., Ohio, Mo. univs., others. Active Neighborhood Assn. Back Bay, 1972—, Boston Home and Property Owners Assn.; assoc. Boston Pub. Libr.; lifetime Friend of Beverly Hills (Calif.) Pub. Libr., Dickerson Park Zoo, Mus. Ozarks History; mem. 10th Anniversary com. Boston U.'s Photographic Resource Ctr.; sponsor Babe Ruth Baseball League Team, 1992—; league sponsor Back Bay, Beacon Hill and North End Little League Teams, 1999—. Recipient World Press Competition award, 1967, Newsweek/Bolex documentary film awrad, 1969, Indsl. Photography Film Competition award, 1970, Internat. Film and TV Festival of N.Y. bronze medal, 1971; named AAU Nat. Karate Champion, 1989; ranked 6th nationally in weapon's forms Reeves Sport Karate Ratings, 1989. Mem. Am. Soc. Mag. Photographers, Nat. Press Photographers (awards 1966, 67, 68), N.Am. Sport Karate Assn. (various awards). Office: A Bit of Boston Real Estate Inc 5 Brimmer St Boston MA 02108-1001

HOLLAND, JIMMIE C., psychiatrist, educator; b. Forney, Tex., Apr. 9, 1928; m. James F. Holland; 5 children. BA, Baylor U., 1948, MD, 1952. Diplomate Am. Bd. Psychiatry, Am. Bd. Neurology. Instr. to prof. SUNY, Buffalo, 1956-73; assoc. prof., assoc. attending physician to asst. dir. cons.-liaison psychiatry Albert Einstein Coll. Medicine and Montefiore Med. Ctr., Bronx, N.Y., 1973-77; chair dept. psychiatry and behavioral Scis., Wayne E. Chapman prof. in psychiat. oncology Meml. Sloan Kettering Cancer Ctr., N.Y.C., 1977—; prof. dept. psychiatry Cornell U. Med. Coll., N.Y.C., 1977—; asst. attending physician to dir. dept. psychiatry E.J. Meyer Meml. Hosp./Erie County Med. Ctr., Buffalo, 1956-73; cons. NIMH-USSR joint schizophrenia study Psychiat. Rsch. Inst., Moscow, 1972-73, Nat. Inst. Drug Abuse and Alcoholism, Rockville, Md., 1973-75; chmn. psychiatry com. Cancer and Leukemia Group B Clin. Trials, Brookline, Mass., 1976—; cons. nat. adv. com. on hospice Robert Wood Johnson Found. and NIH, New Brunswick, N.J., 1980-84; mem. cancer control grant rev. com. Nat. Cancer Inst., Bethesda, Md., 1981-85; mem. com. study health consequences of stress of bereavement, Inst. of Medicine, Washington, 1983-84; chmn. task force on psychosocial oncology European Sch. Oncology, Venice, Italy, 1988-89; mem. Commn. on AIDS in N.Y. State Prisons, 1989. Editor: Handbook of Psycho-oncology: Psychological Care of the Patient with Cancer, 1989; editorial bd. Cancer Nursing Jour., 1977—, Oncology jour., 1980—; author, co-author 142 jour. articles, book chpts., monographs; cons., commentator film The DNR Dilemma, 1987. Bd. dirs. Cancer Care, Inc., 1979-81. Recipient Disting. Alumna award Baylor U., Waco, Tex., 1982; Am. Cancer Soc. Medal of Honor, 1994;. Fellow Am. Coll. Psychiatrists, Am. Psychiat. Assn., Acad. Psychosomatic Medicine (founding); mem. Am. Soc. Psychiat. Oncology/AIDS (pres. 1988—), Am. Cancer Soc. (nat. div. com. on rehab. 1979—, chair workshop psychol., social and behavioral medicine aspects of cancer, 1981, chair nat. com. psychosocial edn. and rsch., 1986—, del.-at-large 1986—), Am. Psychosomatic Soc., Soc. for Liaison Psychiatry (Spl. citation 1989), Am. Soc. Clin. Oncology, Internat. Psycho-oncology Soc. (founder, chair exec. com. 1984—). Office: Meml Sloan-Kettering Cancer Ctr 1275 York Ave New York NY 10021-6094

HOLLAND, JOHN BEN, clothing manufacturing company executive; b. Scottsville, Ky., Mar. 26, 1932; s. Elbridge Winfred and Lou May (Whitney) H.; m. Margaret Irene Pecor, Jan. 31, 1954; children: John Sandra, Robert. BS in Acctg., Bowling Green U., 1959. With Union Underwear Co., Inc., Bowling Green, Ky., 1961—, v.p. adminstrn., 1972-74, vice chmn., 1975, chmn., chief exec. officer, 1976-96; ret., 1996, cons., 1996—; bd. dirs. Dollar Gen. Corp., Farmers Nat. Bank, Fruit of Loom. Bd. dirs. Ky. Coun. Econ. Edn., Louisville, 1981-90, Ky. Advocates for Higher Edn. Inc., 1985-93, Ky. C. of C., 1987-88, Camping World Inc., 1985-97, Associated Industries of Ky., Ireland-Am. Econ. Adv. Bd., Tech. Corp. Inc.; chmn. corp. coun. Western Ky. U., devel. steering com., 1985-96; vice-chmn. West Point Pepperial, Inc., 1989-92; chmn. Intermodal Transp. Authority, 1998-2000. Mem. Bowling Green-Warren County C. of C. (bd. dirs. 1981-85), Am. Arbitration Assn. (panel 1985-93). Office: Fruit of the Loom Inc PO Box 90015 Bowling Green KY 42102-9015

HOLLAND, JOSEPH JOHN, financial manager; b. New Brunswick, N.J., Nov. 7, 1927; s. Thomas Clifford and Ruth Elizabeth (Feaster) H.; m. Bernice T. Kearns, Jul. 1, 1984; B.S. magna cum laude, Mount St. Mary's Coll., 1952; M.B.A., Rutgers U., 1955; 1 son, Wayne Joseph. Sr. acct. Peat, Marwick, Mitchell & Co., Newark, 1952-61; plant controller, ops. auditor Crane Co., N.Y.C., 1961-65; fin. controller Ingersoll-Rand Co., U.K., 1965-68; v.p., controller PPD Corp., Newark, 1968-73; v.p. fin., treas. Edgcomb Steel & Aluminum Corp., Hillside, N.J., 1973-76; cons. in field, North Brunswick, N.J., 1978; v.p. fin., dir. Berry Solar Products, Edison, N.J., 1978-86; dir. fin. control Berger Industries, Maspeth, N.Y., 1986-88; cons. in field Milltown, N.J., 1988-96; ret. CPA, N.J., N.Mex.; Tex. Served with USN, 1946-48. Mem. Am. Inst. C.P.A.s. Clubs: Sales Execs. of N.J. (chmn. disting. salesman award 1978), Elks, Exchange (New Brunswick, N.J.). Home: 29 Highland Dr Milltown NJ 08850-1012

HOLLAND, LESLIE ARTHUR, physicist, editor, educator; b. London, June 14, 1921; s. Charles Arthur and Kate Ellen (Mines) H.; m. Doris Elsie Rider, May 20, 1944; children: John, Jennifer, Peter. D.Tech., U. West London Brunel, 1967; DSc, Rouen U., France, 1970. With Scophony Electronics, 1938-39, Simmonds Aerocessaries, 1939-44; dir. thin film deposition lab. Edwards High Vacuum Ltd., Crawley, Eng., 1944-65; dir. R&D and cen. rsch. lab. Edwards High Vacuum Internat., Crawley, 1966-73; assoc. reader physics dept. Brunel U., London, 1962-76; Whitworth fellow U. Sussex (Eng.) Sch. Math. and Physics, 1974-75, prof. Sch. Engring./Applied Sci., 1976-85; vis. lectr. prodn. tech. Cranfield Inst. Tech., 1972-75; cons. engr., physicist, inaugural chmn. Inst. Physics "Vacuum Group", England, 1965-71; non-exec. dir. SIRA Inst., England, 1973-81; pres. Internat. Union of Vacuum Sci. Tech. & Application, 1977-80. Author: The Vacuum Deposition of Thin Films, 1956, The Properties of Glass Surfaces, 1965; co-author: Vacuum Manual, 1974; editor, co-author: Thin Film Microelectronics, 1965; editor: High Vacuum Series, 1965-70; adv. editor Thin Solid Films, 1963-76; editor Jour. Vacuum, 1993-99, Plasma Tech. series, 1979—; patentee; numerous papers in field. Recipient Silver medal Plastics Inst., 1955, Welch medal Am. Vacuum Soc./Am. Inst. Physics, 1976, Whitworth medal Dept. Edn. Sci., 1976; Whitworth fellow. Fellow Am. Optical Soc. (emeritus), Am. Vacuum Soc. (emeritus), Indian Vacuum Soc. (hon.), Inst. of Physics (chartered physicist), Inst. Elec. Engrs. (chartered engr.), Soc. Glass Tech. Office and Home: Hazelwood, Balcombe Rd, Crawley RH10 3NZ, England

HOLLAND, NEILA ANCHIETA, business educator, consultant; b. Rio de Janeiro; came to U.S., 1978; d. Marsio and Taimyrse Trindade Anchieta; m. John Eric Holland, Aug. 29, 1981; 1 child: Heather. BBA, Fed. U. Rio de Janeiro, Brazil, 1976; MBA, Sul Ross State U., 1979; PhD in Mgmt., 1995. Prof. mgmt. Dallas Bapt. U., 1993—; prof. bus. Northwood U., Dallas, 1993-96; owner Internat. Quality Mgmt., Dallas, Rio de Janeiro, 1993—; exec. dir. Richland Coll., Dallas, 1996-97; prof., acad. coord. Paul Quinn Coll., Dallas, 1999; cons. Proderf, Rio de Janeiro, 1998, SESCON-MA, San Luiz, Brazil, 1998-99, TELEPAR, Curitiba, Brazil, 1996; vis. prof. Ecole Europeenne des Affaires, Paris, 1999, Richmond Am. U., London, 2000. Author: Internacionalizacao dos Negocios, 1999, The POQ Model, 1995, Modelo POQ, 1994; contbr. articles to profl. jours. Mem. Acad. Internat. Bus., Am. Soc. for Quality, Ft. Worth Hispanic C. of C. Avocations: classical ballet, international travel, research. Office: Paul Quinn Coll 3837 Simpson Stuart Rd Dallas TX 75241-4331

HOLLAND, PHILLIP KENT, aerospace engineer; b. Wichita, Kans., Oct. 10, 1959; s. Phillip Norman and Lafreda Louise (Davenport) H.; m. Linda Kay Rosenbaum, June 27, 1980 (div. Dec. 1987); m. Delaine Marie Thompson, Mar. 17, 1989. BS in Aerospace Engring., Wichita State U., 1993. Seating engr. Raytheon Aircraft, Wichita, 1979-93; R&D group engr. Interiors and Seating Group Bombardier Learjet Inc., Wichita, 1993-99; pres. Millennium Concepts Inc., Wichita, 1999—. Mem. AIAA, Soc. Aerospace Engrs., (mem. AS8049 ad hoc com. 1990-97, vice chmn. SAE seat com. 1997—), GAMA (seat working group 1994—), Aviation Rulemaking Adv. Com. (AC25.562-1 seat working group 1994-96). Republican. Greek Orthodox. Achievements include design and certification engr. on aircraft seats and interiors. Home: 4206 Spyglass Cir Wichita KS 67226-3354 Office: Millennium Concepts Inc 1999 Amidon St Ste 230 Wichita KS 67203-2123

HOLLAND, ROSEMARY SHERIDAN, program evaluation consultant; b. Detroit, Oct. 15, 1939; d. Geoffrey Francis and Mary Ann (Beirne) Sheridan; m. Neal Holland, Sept. 1961 (div. Apr. 1968); 1 child, Daniel Holland; m. Fred Fechheimer, Nov. 29, 1974; 1 child, Steve Fechheimer. PhB, U. Detroit, 1961; MSW, U. Mich., 1969, MA, 1984, PhD, 1984. Tchr. Prince Georges County Bd. Edn., Seat Pleasant, Md., 1961-63; adminstrv. asst. Neighborhood Svc. Orgn., Detroit, 1969-73; dir. mental health planning Cmty. Health Planning Coun. S.E. Mich., Detroit, 1971-73; coord. adult mental health svcs. Detroit/Wayne County Comty. Mental Health Bd., 1973-76; asst. prof. U. Detroit, 1984-89. Mem. NASW, APHA, APA. Avocations: walking, travel, reading.

HOLLAND, ROY WILLIAM HENRY, retired liberal studies educator; b. Birmingham, Eng., Feb. 8, 1927; s. William Henry and Elizabeth Lucetta (Bennett) H.; m. Beatrice Pockett, Aug. 26, 1949, Vincenza Roselli, Sept. 7, 1966; children: Lynda, Susan, Jane, Maria, Neil, Rachel, Tessa; m. Melanie Susan Steyn, Mar. 8, 1986; children: Kurt, Julian, Philip. BA, U. Cambridge, 1957, MA, 1961; M in Philosophy, U. Sussex, 1981. Nat. cert. in mech. engring., 1946; teaching cert., 1950. Lectr. in English U. Botswana, Lesotho, Swaziland, 1966-70; sr. lectr. in English U. Botswana, 1971-74, U. Rhodesia, 1977-81; assoc. prof. English U. of the North, 1983-85; prof. English, head of dept. U. Venda, 1985-89, dean, faculty of arts, 1987-89; ret., 1989. Author: (poems) Twelve Poems, 1973, Insights and Outsights, 1989, (short stories) News from Parched Mountain, 1999, Pivot of Violence, 1999, Flakes of Dark and Light, 1999, Just a Bit Touched,, 1999; co-editor: (with Donald Stuart) The Will to Die (Can Themba), 1970; co-author (with Charles Muller) Study Guide for English Skills, Explorations in the Novel, Practical English Handbook, Workbook of Practical English. Recipient bursary Bd. of Extra-Mural Studies, Cambridge U., 1954-57. Mem. Soc. of Authors. Address: Cyril Wood Court Flat Number 2, 89 West Street Bere Regis, BH20 7HH Dorset England

HOLLAND, RUBY MAE, social welfare administrator. BA in Sociology, Shaw Coll., 1976, MA in Comparative Lit., 1978; DD, Wayne Theol. Sem., 1992; D of Psychology, Western Mich. U., 1982. Adminstr. Terrell Day Care Ctr., 1980-83; instr. Reborn Acad., 1984-87; English instr. Ctrl. H.S., 1987-92; enabler Maplegrove children's program U. Mich., Dearborn, 1992—; adminstr., guidance counselor, tchr. Mothers Love, Oak Park, Mich., 1992—. Assoc. min. Unity Cathedral of Faith Ministries; mem. For My People; CEO Forums in Christ Ministries.

HOLLAND, TRISTAM KEITH, friar, liturgist; b. Nottinghamshire, Eng., Mar. 20, 1946; s. George and Eva (Pinion-Clark) H. MA, Cambridge (Eng.) U., 1988. Entered Soc. of St. Francis, Anglican Ch., 1967—. mem. liturgical commn. Ch. of Eng., 1992—, mem. gen. synod, 1994—. Editor: Celebrating Common Prayer, 1992, Exciting Holiness, 1997, The Word of the Lord, 4 vols., 1998-2000, The Gospel of the Load, 1999. Mem. Labour Party. Avocations: music, travel, history. Home and Office: Soc of St Francis, Hilfield Friary, Dorchester Dorset DT2 7BE, England

HOLLANDER, LAWRENCE JAY, marketing executive; b. Chgo., Feb. 15, 1940; s. Harry and Ann Blanche Hollander; m. Sallie Sue Mines, June 21, 1964 (div. Aug. 1999); children: Marla, Amy, Rebecca. BSBA, Roosevelt U., 1963. Dir. Far East ops. Indsl. & Sci. Conf. Mgmt., Chgo., 1972-77; dir. mktg. Far East ops. Clapp & Poliak, Inc., N.Y.C., 1978-81; pres. Expoconsul Internat. Inc., Princeton, N.J., 1981-95, EI Mktg., Inc., Princeton, 1987-94, Ctr. for Tech. Concepts, Inc., Princeton, 1988-92, Expoconsul Mktg. Group, Inc., Princeton, 1992-94; dir. corp. fin. J.S. Holdings Group, Inc., Bay Head, N.J., 1996; shareholder, investment banker J.S. Securities, Inc., Bayhead, N.J., 1995-96; pres. Entrepreneurial Mgmt. Group, Inc., Princeton, N.J., 1996—. Bd. dirs. Congregation Beth Chaim, West Windsor, N.J., 1984, Jewish Cmty. Ctr., of Delaware Valley, Ewing, N.J., 1987-96, v.p. 1990-92, pres. 1993-94; bd. dirs. Jewish Fedn. Mercer and Buck Counties, N.J., Pa., 1988-95, v.p., 1989-90; mem. planning bd. West Windsor Twp., N.J., 1997—. Mem. Rotary Club of the Princeton Corridor (charter mem. 1986—, sec. 1990-91, sgt.-at-arms 1991-92, 97-98, bd. dirs. 1992-93, 96—). Republican. Jewish. Avocations: weight-lifting, walking, tennis. Office: Entrepreneurial Mgmt Grp Inc PO Box 2231 Princeton NJ 08543-2231

HOLLANDER, LEWIS E., JR., physicist, consultant; b. Woodmere, N.Y., June 6, 1930; s. Lewis E. and Alice E. (Clark) H.; m. Hanne Weise Olesen, Oct. 8, 1967; children: James W., Scott L., Heather A., Lexa, Ellen H., Lewis E. III. BA, Adelphi U., 1951; postgrad., Case Western Res. U., 1955-57; PhD, Lincoln U., 1965. Sr. scientist Victoreen Instruments, Cleve., 1955-57; rsch. scientist Lockheed Missiles & Space, Palo Alto, Calif., 1957-61; dir. Endevco Solid State Lab., Los Altos, Calif., 1961-65; dir. rsch., sec., treas. Integrated Transducers, Guynabo, P.R., 1965-68; pres., CEO Green Mansions, Inc., Redmond, Oreg., 1954—. Author: Successful Endurance Riding, 1981, Endurance Riding from Beginning to Winnnig, 1989, 4th edit., 1996; contbr. articles to profl. jours. Lt. (j.g.) USNR, 1951-55. Recipient World Champion Long Course 65-69 Age Group award 1998. Fellow Am. Soc. for Psychical Rsch., Soc. for Sci. Exploration; mem. Am. Aging Assn. (dir.), Am. Phys. Soc. Achievements include 22 patents in semiconductors, acoustics, and instrumentation. Avocation: triathlon. Office: Green Mansions Inc PO Box 100 Redmond OR 97756-0009

HOLLANDS-ROBINSON, PHYLLIS, artist; b. Chgo., Jan. 10, 1925; d. Augustus Thurston Hollands and Catherine Una Gilmer; m. Marvin John Robinson, Sept. 18, 1948; children: Catherine Hollands Robinson Bufkin, Anne Hollands Robinson Howard. Student, Fairmont Jr. Coll., Washington, Chgo. Acad. Fine Arts, Acad. de la Grande Chaumiere, Paris; studied with, Pierre Bertrand, Paris. Exhibited in more than 75 one-person shows, including Royal Acad., London, Bernheim Jeune, Paris, Musee Galleria, Les Peintres Temoins de leur Temps, Paris; represented in French museums, also pvt. and corp. collections, U.S. and abroad. Co-founder Lyric Opera, Chgo., 1940s; active Humane Soc. Recipient Caritas award Kennedy Found. for Retarded Children, 1952-72, Am. Cancer Soc. award Collier Co. Unit, 1992-93; named one of Outstanding Artists of World, Jahn & Ollier Engraving Co. Avocations: art, music, environment, literature, science. Home: 1827 Princess Ct Naples FL 34110-1001

HOLLAR, JEFFREY ALLEN, foreign language educator, biologist; b. Ft. Belvoir, Va., Aug. 18, 1960; arrived in Japan, 1990; s. Benjamin Chalmers and Betty Lou (Reger) H. BS, James Madison U., 1987, MS, 1990. Cert. in tchg. English to Children/David English House, Hiroshima, Japan, 1994. Student tchg. asst. chemistry dept. James Madison U., Harrisonburg, Va., 1985-87; grad. tchg. asst. biology dept., 1987-88; rsch. asst. biology dept. James Madison U., Harrisonburg, 1988-90; fgn. lang. instr. Kaminaka Town Bd. Edn., Tokushima, Japan, 1990-92; fgn. lang. instr. advisor Tokushima (Japan) Prefectural Bd. Edn., 1992-93; fgn. lang. instr. Matsushige Town Bd. Edn., Tokushima, 1993-97, Kisawa Village Bd. Edn., Tokushima, 1997—. Hosp. corpsman with USN, 1980-84, USNR, 1984-90. Mem. Am. Soc. for Microbiology, Japan Assn. for Lang. Tchg. (pres. Tokushima chpt. 1995-97, membership chair tchg. children spl. interest group 1997-99), Phi Kappa Phi. Avocations: scuba diving, trekking, volunteering at community activities, reading. Office: Kisawa Village Bd Edn, 43-1 Maeda Kisawa-son, Tokushima-ken 771-6105, Japan

HOLLAR, MICHAEL JOHN, customer service representative; b. Stevens Point, Wis., Dec. 8, 1963; s. John B. and Norita Hollar. BS in Bus. Edn., U. Wis., Eau Claire, 1987. Data entry staff ANCO Cons., Milw., 1987-88, customer svc. rep., 1988-95; office mgr. Tech. Resources, Inc., Milw., 1995-97; legis. asst. Trustmark Ins., Lake Forest, Ill., 1997-98, customer svc. supr., 1999-2000, compliance analyst, 2000—. Adv. bd. FBLA/PBL Bus. Edn., Madison, 1990-97; pres. St. Pius X Parish Coun., Appleton, Wis., 1992-93. Mem. Wis. Assn. of Parliamentarians (v.p., corr. sec., recording sec. 1990—). Republican. Roman Catholic. Avocations: running, beach, working out. Home: 5757 N Sheridan Rd Apt 20F Chicago IL 60660-8713

HOLLARD, DIDIER, pediatrician; b. Digne, France, Jan. 19, 1939; s. René and Raymonde (Caussel) H.; m. Danielle Pontvianne, Feb. 17, 1962; children: Pierre, Marc, Stephanie. MD, U. Lyon, France, 1969. Pvt. practice Rillieux. City rep. Rillieux, 1971-77, 89—. Avocation: horseback riding. Home: 120 route de Geneve, 69140 Rillieux France Office: 58 avenue de L'Europe, 69140 Rillieux France

HOLLAWAY, LEONARD CHARLES, engineering educator; b. Dover, Kent, Eng.; s. Reginald George and Beatrice Louise (Carlton) H.; m. Patricia Mary Tacey, Sept. 1967; 1 child, Suzanne Louise. BSc in Engring., U. London, 1958, MSc in Engring., 1965, PhD, 1970. Chartered engr., U.K. Engr. Thurrock (U.K.) Borough Coun., 1958-60; rsch. engr. John Laing R&D, London, 1960-62; lectr. U. Surrey, Guildford, U.K., 1962-76, sr. lectr., 1976-84, reader, 1984-88, prof., 1988—; warden U. Surrey, London, 1964-67. Author: Polymer Composites for Civil and Structural Engineers, 1993; editor: Polymers and Polymer Composites in Construction, 1990, Handbook of Polymer Composites for Engineers, 1994, Strengthening of Reinforced Concrete Structures Using Externally-bonded FRP Composites in Structural and Civil Engineering, 1999. Recipient Sims Gold medal Soc. Engrs., 1972. Fellow Inst. Civil Engring.; mem. Inst. Structural Engring. Avocations: playing the violin, opera, walking, swimming. Office: U Surrey Dept Civil Engring, Stag Hill, Guildford GU2 7XH, England

HÖLLDOBLER, BERTHOLD KARL, zoologist, educator; b. Erling-Andechs, Germany, June 25, 1936; came to U.S., 1973; s. Karl and Maria (Russmann) H.; m. Friederike Probst, Feb. 9, 1980; children: Jakob, Stefan, Sebastian. Dr. rer. nat., U. Wurzburg, 1965; Dr. habil., U. Frankfurt a.M., 1969; Doctorate (hon.), U. Konstanz, 2000. Prof. zoology U. Frankfurt a.M., 1971-72; prof. biology Harvard U., Cambridge, Mass., 1973-90, Alexander Agassiz prof. zoology, 1982-90; prof. U. Wurzburg, Germany, 1989—; adj. prof. U. Ariz., Tucson; rsch. assoc. Harvard U. Author: (with Edward O. Wilson) The Ants, 1990 (Pulitzer Prize for gen. non-fiction 1991), (with E.O. Wilson) Journey to the Arts, (Shortlisted for the Rhone-Poulenc Sci. Book prize, 1995, Phi Beta Kappa prize, 1995). John Simon Guggenheim fellow, 1980; recipient Sr. Scientist award Alexander von Humboldt Found., 1986-87, Gottfried Wilhelm Leibniz prize, 1989, Phi Beta Kappa prize (with E.O. Wilson) 1995, Karl Ritter von Frisch medal and Sci. prize, German Zool. Soc., 1996, Körber-prize for European Sci., 1996, Benjamin Franklin, Wilhelm v. Humboldt Prize of the German Amer. Acad. Counc. (GAAC), 1999. Fellow AAAS, Am. Animal Behavior Soc.; mem. Nat. Acad. of Sci. (fgn. mem.), Am. Acad. Sci., German Acad. der Naturforscher Leopoldina, Bayerische Acad. der Wissenschaften, Acad. Europaea, Berlin-Brandenburgische Acad., Am. Philos. Soc. (fgn. mem.). Office: Biozentrum Am Hubland, D-97074 Würzburg Germany

HOLLEAUX, JEAN-MARC MAURICE, business executive; b. Limoges, France, Oct. 14, 1932; s. Georges and Marguerite (Coquelin) H.; m. Alice Gueyffier, Jan. 18, 1958; children: Georges, Didier, Louis. Diploma, Inst. Etudes Politiques, Paris, 1954; Lic. en droit, U. paris, 1955. Fin. exec. Cie Pechiney, Paris, 1958-67, Scal G.P., Paris, 1967-71, Cegedur, Paris, 1971-78; pres. Manufacture Marocaine d'Aluminum, Casablanca, Morocco, 1972-85, Alliages frittes Metafram, Paris, 1982-89, Compagnie Generale D'Electrolyse Du Palais, 1990-95. Author: La crise des paiements allemands, 1955; Les delais de paiement en France, 1977. Served to lt. inf., French Army, 1955-58. Home: rue Saint Senoch 9, 75017 Paris 17eme, France

HOLLENDER, LARS GÖSTA, dental educator; b. Veinge, Sweden, Oct. 22, 1933; came to U.S., 1984; s. Gunnar Yngve and Astrid Margareta (Andersson) H.; m. Gunnel Charlotta Bergdahl, May 19, 1956 (div. 1975); children: Peter, Marie, Lena, Stefan; m. Sheridan Ellen Houston, Apr. 8, 1989; 1 child, Ashley Ellen. DDS, Sch. Dentistry, Malmö, Sweden, 1958, PhD, 1964. Diplomate Am. Bd. Oral and Maxillofacial Radiology. Assoc. prof. Sch. Dentistry, Malmö, 1964-68; prof., chair Sch. Dentistry, Göteborg, Sweden, 1969-87; prof., dir. U. Wash. Sch. Dentistry, Seattle, 1988—; sec. gen. Internat. Assn. Dentomaxillofacial Radiology, 1974-85; vis. prof. UCLA Sch. Dentistry, 1980-82, U. Wash. Sch. Dentistry, 1984-87; sec./treas. Am. Bd. Oral and Maxillofacial Radiology, 1992-94, pres., 1995, councillor, 1996—. Editor-in-chief Odontologist Revy, 1964-69; contbr. over 100 chpts. to books and articles to profl. jours. Recipient Rsch. prize South Swedish Dental Soc., 1964, Rsch. prize Swedish Dental Assn., 1965, Elander Rsch. prize Gothenburg Dental Soc., 1976. Mem. ADA, Am. Acad. Oral and Maxillofacial Radiology (pres. 1997-98), Internat. Assn. Dental and Maxillofacial Radiology (hon.), Australian Maxillofacial Radiology Soc. (hon.), Wash. State Dental Assn., King County Dental Assn. Avocations: reading, golf, cooking, travel, music. Office: Univ Wash Sch Dentistry PO Box 356370 Seattle WA 98195-6370

HOLLENWEGER, WALTER JACOB, religious studies educator; b. Antwerp, Belgium, June 1, 1927; Swiss citizen; s. Walter Otto and Anna (Spörri) H.; m. Erica Busslinger. Verbi Divini Min., U. Zürich, Switzerland, 1961, ThD, 1966. Ordained Swiss Reform Ch., 1961. Banker various orgns., Switzerland, 1947-50; rsch. asst. U. Zürich, 1961-65; exec. sec. World Coun. Chs., Geneva, 1965-71; prof. mission U. Birmingham, Eng., 1971-89; free-lance author and educator Switzerland and Germany, 1989—. Author: Interkulturelle Theologie, 3 vols., 1979-88, The Pentecostals, 1988, Pentecostalism, 1997; editor: Studies in the Intercultural History of Christianity, 1975; author of numerous plays. Recipient award for theology, Germany, 1995, Life Achievement award Soc. for Pentecostal Studies, 1999; hon. fellow Selly Oak Colls., Birmingham, 1996. Home: Im Grueb, CH 3704 Krattigen Switzerland

HOLLIDAY, CHARLES O., JR., chemical company executive; b. Nashville, Tenn., Mar. 9, 1948; s. Charles O. Sr. and Ann (Hunter) H.; m. Ann Blair, June 27, 1970; children: Scot, Chad. BS in Indsl. Engring., U. Tenn., 1970. Registered profl. engr., Tenn. Engr. DuPont, Nashville, 1970-72, mfg. supr., 1972-74; mfg. supr. DuPont, Wilmington, Del., 1974-77; various mfg. assignments in fibers dept. DuPont, Charleston, S.C., Martinsville, Va., Seaford, Del., 1978-84; corp. plans mgr. DuPont, Wilmington, 1984-86, global bus. dir. Nomex, 1986-87, global bus. dir. Kevlar, 1987-88, dir. mktg. chems. & pigments, 1988-90; v.p., then pres. Asia Pacific DuPont, Tokyo, 1990-92, sr. v.p., 1992-95, chmn. Asia Pacific, 1995, exec. v.p., mem. office chief exec., 1995-97; CEO DuPont, Wilmington, 1998, chmn., 1999—. Vice chmn. John F. Kennedy Ctr. Performing Arts; active Alliance Global Sustainability, Del. Bus./Pub. Edn. Coun., U. Tenn., Winterthur Mus. Mem. World Bus. Coun. Sustainable Devel. (vice chmn.), Asia Pacific Coun., Bus. Coun., Bus. Roundtable, Catalyst, Del. Bus. Roundtable, Japan Am. Soc. Del., Pioneer Hi-Bred Internat. Inc., Singapore-U.S. Bus. Coun., Soc. Chem. Industry. Office: E I Du Pont de Nemours 1007 Market St Wilmington DE 19801-1227*

HOLLINBECK, ETHEL LINDELL, sculptor; b. Kewanee, Ill., Feb. 1, 1910; d. Gustav (Lindstrom) and Hilda Louise (Gustafson) Lindell; m. Richard Oftebro Hollinbeck, Mar. 27, 1928; children: Marilyn, David, Richard Jr. Grad., Mpls. Sch. of Arts, 1948. Exhibited in group shows at Met. Mus., N.Y.C., Walker, Mpls. on Com., Minn. First Outdoor Sculpture Show, Woman's Club of Mpls., Swedish Mus. of Art, St. Paul Gallery of Arts, Mpls. Inst. of Arts; works include many portraits. Recipient many awards. Mem. Soc. of Minn. Sculptors, Profl. Artists' Equity Assn. Home: 3330 Edinborough Way Apt 1407 Edina MN 55435-5955

HOLLINGER, CHARLOTTE ELIZABETH, medical technologist, tree farmer; b. Meadville, Miss., June 29, 1951; d. John Fielding and Irene Elizabeth (Mullins) H. BS in Biology, U. So. Miss., 1973. Cert. med. Technologist ASCP. Staff med. technologist U. Miss. Med. Ctr., Jackson, 1974-76, Grady Hosp., Atlanta, 1976, Atlanta ARC, 1976-78; staff med. technologist I Emory U. Hosp., Atlanta, 1978-85, staff med. technologist II, 1985-88, asst. chief technologist, 1988-94; del. Blood Bank Del. to People's Republic China, People-to-People, Seattle, 1988. Supporter numerous civic orgns. including World Wildlife Fund, AmFAR, HSUS, Open Hand Project, Atlanta Humane Soc. Mem. Am. Assn. Blood Banks, Am. Soc. Clin. Pathologists, NOW, Forest Farmers Assn., Habitat for Humanity, People for Ethical Treatment Animals, People-to-People, Miss. Forestry Assn., Cousteau Soc., Ga. Pub. TV, U. So. Miss. Alumni Assn., Atlanta Zool. Soc., Delta Zeta, Pi Tau Chi. Roman Catholic. Avocations: reading, needlework, traveling, swimming, camping. Home: 2490 Silver King Dr Grayson GA 30017-1470

HOLLINGSWORTH, ABNER THOMAS, university dean; b. Wilmington, Del., Mar. 19, 1939; s. Abner and Dorothy Elizabeth (Dunn) H.; m. Jacqueline Manning, Mar. 19, 1966; 1 child, Alexander Thomas. BSin BA, U. Del., Newark, 1964; MBA, Mich. State U., 1966, PhD, 1969. Asst. prof. mgmt. So. Ill. U., Carbondale, 1969-71, Fla. Atlantic U., 1971-73; assoc. prof. mgmt. U. S.C., 1973-77, prof. mgmt., 1977-80; prof. mgmt. U. Petroleum and Minerals, Dhahran, Saudi Arabia, 1980-82; prof. mgmt., chmn. mgmt. dept. U. N.C., Asheville, 1983-87; dean Sch. Bus. Adminstrn. Monmouth Coll., 1987-88, prof. mgmt., 1988; prof. mgmt. and dir. Bus. Rsch. Inst. St. John's U., 1988-90; prof. mgmt. and dean Sch. Bus. Fla. Inst. Tech., Melbourne, 1990—; cons. in field; conductor numerous tng. programs. Author: (with Richard Hodgetts) Readings in Basic Management, 1975, (with H. H. hand) A Practical Approach to the Management of Small Business, 1979, Readings in Small business Management, 1979, Supervisory Behavior, 1974, (with R. Howell and R. Hodgetts) A Reader, Study Guide in Basic Management, 1979, others; assoc. editor Jur. Bus. Rsch., 1984-87; editorial bd. Jour. Mgmt., 1977-79, book reviewer for Acad. Press, Bus. Pubs., Inc., Wiley/Hamilton, many others; contbr. articles to profl. jours. Bd. dirs. Holmes Regional Med. Ctr. & Health First, Inc., Melbourne, Jr. Achievement of Ea. Ctrl. Fla., United Way. Rsch. grantee, Inst. Pub. Utilities, Mich. State U., 1967, Fla. Atlantic U., 1972, U. S.C., 1975, Social Security Adminstrn., 1977, others. Avocations: scuba diving, sailing, reading. Office: Fla Inst Tech Sch Bus 150 W University Blvd Melbourne FL 32901-6982

HOLLINGSWORTH, JOHN ARTHUR, business education educator; b. Martins Ferry, Ohio, Oct. 12, 1952; s. William Arvine and Lillian Theo (Dean) H. AAB in Retail Mktg. cum laude, Belmont Tech. Col., 1975; BSBA in Helth and Hosp. Admin., Wheeling Jesuit U., 1979, MBA, 1984; PhD in Bus. Admin., U. Miss., 1993. Cert. secondary edn. tchr., Ohio. Computer operator Stone & Thomas Co., Wheeling, W. Va., 1971-76; mgr. carpet dept. L.S. Good & Co., Wheeling, 1976-78; store mgr. Rite Aid Corp., Harrisburg, Pa., 1978-79; lectr. Belmont Tech. Col., St. Clairsville, Ohio, 1981-83; rsch. and teaching asst. U. Miss., Oxford, 1984-88; bus. admin. instr. St. John's U., N.Y.C., 1989-94; asst. prof. bus. dept. Coll. Staten Island/CUNY, 1994-98; asst. prof. mgmt. info. sys. No. State U., Aberdeen, S.D., 1998—; statis. cons. Reidenbach, Grubbs & Assoc., Jackson, Miss., 1986-87; session chair and discussant Internat. Bus. Schs. User Group, Omaha, Nebr., 1990. Poll election judge, Shadyside, Ohio, 1975-80. Selected for Group Projects Abroad to Turkey, Fulbright Program and Am. Forum Global Edn., N.Y.C., 1996. Mem. Inst. Mgmt. Sci., Acad. Mgmt., Assn. Info. Sys., Info. Resources Mgmt. Assn., Nat. Decision Scis. Inst. (session chair, discussant 1993-95, selected for New Faculty Consortium, 1993). Republican. Avocations: travel, photography, ethnography. Office: No State Univ Box 713 1200 S Jay St Aberdeen SD 57401-7155

HOLLINSHEAD, ALAN GEORGE, company executive, financial advisor; b. Littleborough, Lancashire, Eng., May 18, 1940; m. Joseph Johnson and Lottie (Jones) H.; m. Pamela Geraldine Cheesley, Feb. 14, 1991; children: Zoë, Timothy. Registered Soc. Fin. Advisors. Prodn. mgr. OSRAM (GEC) Ltd., U.K. and India, 1957-79; sr. assoc. Abbey Life, U.K., 1979-2000; sr. fin. advisor Allied Dunbar, 2000—; chmn., mng. dir. A&P Bus. Fin. (Merseyside) Ltd., U.K., 1987—; chmn. Daylight Trust, U.K., 1995—; web page designer Proprietor AP4 Internet, 1997—. Trustee Davenham Christian Healing Trust, 1999. Fellow Instn. Electronics (hon.; chmn. gen. coun. 1993—), Inst. Dirs.; mem. Inst. Mgmt., Life Assurance Assn. E-mail: alan@aandp.co.uk. Home: 34 Colmore Ave, Wirral Merseyside CH63 9NL, England

HOLLIS, JULIA ANN ROSHTO, critical care and medical/surgical nurse; b. Monroe, La., June 25, 1945; d. Joseph Edward Roshto and Eleanor Cloverdale Larsen; m. William Davis Hollis, Mar. 2, 1964; children: David Terrel, Julia Allison. BSN, N.E. La. U., 1976. RN, La., Ala., Miss.; cert. BCLS, ACLS. Staff nurse to head nurse E.A. Conway Hosp., Monroe, 1977-84; staff nurse, charge nurse ICU, critical care North Monroe Community Hosp., Monroe, 1984-87; staff nurse neurotrama surg. ICU U. South Ala. Med. Ctr., Mobile, 1988-89; staff nurse, charge nurse Norrell Health Care, Mobile, 1990—, Medforce Internat., New Orleans; owner Resource Mgmt., 1997. Mem. AACN, AAUW, Ala. Nurses Assn., Met. Writer's Guild. Home: 5073 Dawes Lane Ext Theodore AL 36582-9627

HOLLIS, LINDA EARDLEY, urban planning consultant; b. Washington, Feb. 1, 1948; d. Edward Pixton and Margy (Anderson) Eardley; m. Daryl Joseph Hollis, July 18, 1970. BA, Pa. State U., University Park, 1968; M in Regional Planning, U. N.C., 1979. Planning analyst First-Citizens Bank, Raleigh, N.C., 1973-76; rsch. assoc. ctr. for urban regional studies U. N.C., Chapel Hill, 1978-79; rsch. assoc. The Osprey Co., Tallahassee, 1980-81, Patrick H. Hare Planning and Design, Washington, 1982-83; cons. Tischler & Assocs., Inc., Bethesda, Md., 1983-97; analyst dept. fiscal svcs. Md. Gen. Assembly, Annapolis, 1988-89; dir. devel. policy Urban Land Inst., Washington, 1997-99; ind. cons., 1997, 99—; sr. rsch. assoc. Solimar Rsch. Group, 2000—. Rep. Mason dist. Fairfax County Commn. on Organ and Tissue Donation and Transplantation, 1995-97, vice chmn., 1996-97. Mem. Am. Planning Assn. (nat. bd. dirs., regional rep. 1986-88, chmn. nat. state policy coordinating com. 1987-88, rep. citizens adv. com. met. devel. Met. Washington Coun. of Govts. 2000—). Democrat. Avocations: music, reading, traveling. Home and Office: 4002 Rose Ln Annandale VA 22003-1943

HOLLIS, SHEILA SLOCUM, lawyer; b. Denver, July 15, 1948; d. Theodore Doremus and Emily M. (Caplis) Slocum (dec.); m. John Hollis; 1 child, Windsong Emily Lanford. BS in Journalism with honors, U. Colo., 1971, BS in Gen. Studies cum laude, 1971; JD, U. Denver, 1973. Bar: Colo. 1974, D.C. 1975, U.S. Supreme Ct. 1980. Trial atty. Fed. Power Commn., Washington, 1974-75; assoc. firm Wilner & Scheiner, Washington, 1975-77; dir. office enforcement Fed. Energy Regulatory Commn., Washington, 1977-80; pvt. practice, 1980-87; ptnr. Vinson & Elkins, Washington, 1987-92; sr. ptnr. Metzger, Hollis, Gordon & Alprin, Washington, 1992-97; mng. ptnr. D.C., chair energy practice Duane, Morris & Heckscher, LLP, Washington, 1997—; professorial lectr. in energy law George Washington U., 1980—. Co-author: Energy Decision Making, 1983, Energy Law and Policy, 1989; mem. editl. bd. Oil and Gas Reporter, Pub. Utility Fortnightly; contbr. articles to profl. publs. Established and developed enforcement program Fed. Energy Regulatory Commn.; mem. adv. bd. Pub. Utility Ctr., N.Mex. State U., 1986-94, Gas Industry Stds. Bd., 1998—; pres. Women's Coun. Energy and Environ., 1997—; mem. bd. dirs. Nat. Assn. Vets. Health Care. U. Denver scholar, 1972-73. Fellow ABA (mem. ho. of dels., chair elect sect. environ., energy and resources, chair coord. group energy law 1989-92, 95-97, chair standing com. environ. law 1997-2000, mem. nominating com.); mem. Internat. Bar Assn., Am. Law Inst., Nat. Gas Inst. (chmn. 1983-90), Fed. Energy Bar Assn. (pres. 1991-92), Oil and Gas Ednl. Inst. (v.p.), Southwestern Legal Found. (trustee), Colo. Bar Assn., D.C. Bar Assn., Women's Bar Assn. D.C., John Carroll Soc., Nat. Press Club, Cosmos Club, George Washington U. Club. Roman Catholic. Office: Duane Morris & Heckscher LLP 1667 K St NW Ste 700 Washington DC 20006-1608

HOLLIS, TIMOTHY MARTIN, bank executive; b. Marietta, Ga., Nov. 13, 1962; s. Milton Joel and Mary Syvila (Skanner) H. BSBA in Mgmt., Shorter Coll., 1986. Desk supr. front desk Wyndham Hotel Co., Atlanta, 1986-87; personal banker C&S/Sovran Corp., Atlanta, 1987-90, sr. personal banker, 1990-91; asst. br. mgr., banking officer NationsBank of Ga., N.A., Atlanta, 1991-92, banking ctr. mgr., 1992-95; sales mgr. First Union Nat. Bank Ga., Atlanta, 1995-97; fin. specialist AVP, 1997—. Treas., mktg. chairperson, fin. com., bd. trustees Choral Guild of Atlanta, 1991; mem. Buckhead Young Reps., Atlanta, 1989-92; bd. dirs. Artcare, Inc., Atlanta, 1991-94; docent, vol., mem. Friends of Zoo Atlanta; mem. steering com. First Night Atlanta, 1993-99, 1994 class Atlanta Midtown Leadership Program, Atlanta Midtown Alliance, 1992—, Human Rights Campaign Fund, 1992—, GAPAC, 1993-95; mem. adv. bd. Atlanta Exec. Network, 1993-96, Joining Hearts, Inc., 1994-99; steering com. Aids Walk Atlanta, 1995-97; bd. dirs. Positive Impact, 1996-97, Pets are Lovin Support, Inc., 1997-99; co-chair Young Profls. of Atlanta Exec. Network, 1996-98; conf. chair First Night Internat., 1998—; bd. dirs. AIDS Treatment Initiatives, 1997—, pres., 1998—. Mem. Atlanta Track Club (vol.). Methodist. Avocations: running, singing, working-out, volunteering. Home: 28 Finch Trail NE Atlanta GA 30308-2418 Office: First Union Nat Bank Ga 1605 Monroe Dr NE Atlanta GA 30324-5003

HOLLMANN, WILDOR, physician; b. Menden/Westfalen, Germany, Jan. 30, 1925; s. Albert and Hetty (Bomnueter) H.; m. Inge Cuesters; children: Helmut, Ulrike. MD, U. Cologne, Germany, 1954; MD (hon.), Free U., Brussels, 1986. Founder Inst. Cardiology and Sports Medicine, Cologne, 1958, chmn. cardiology and sport medicine, 1965; rector German Sport U., Cologne, 1969-71; pres. German Fedn. Sports Medicine, 1984-98, World Fedn. Sports Medicine, 1986-94, German Olympic Soc., 1994-97; hon. prof. U. Thessaloniki, Greece, 1994; sci. com. German Def. Ministry, 1969-94. Recipient Carl-Diem award, 1961, HuFeland award, 1963, Max-Buerger award 1969, Gold medal German Med. Assn., 1976, Sir-Philip-Noel-Baker award UNESCO, 1976. Office: German Sport U, 50933 Cologne NRW, Germany

HOLLMEN, ARNO ILMARI, anesthesiology educator; b. Helsinki, Nov. 19, 1930; s. Aarne Johannes and Wilma Maria (Karlstrom) H.; m. Ulla Margareta Kiuru, May 24, 1953; children: Laura Margareta, Lauri Juhani, Satu Margareta. MD, U. Turku, 1956; PhD, U. Helsinki, 1968. Resident anesthesiology U. Copenhagen, 1959-60; chmn. dept. anesthesiology Kuopio Cen. Hosp., Finland, 1963-65, Oulu County Hosp., Finland, 1965-72; prof., chmn. dept. Oulu U., 1974-92, sr. lectr. dept. anesthesiology, 1993—; vis. prof. Stanford (Calif.) U., 1970-71, UCLA, 1975-76, Columbia U., N.Y.C., 1983, 85, U. Tex., San Antonio, 1985-86, clin. prof., 1986-94; exec. mem. European Com. Allied Spl. Maternal and Neonatal Care, 1979—. Edtl. Bd. Acta Anesthesiology Scandinavia, Current Opinions in Anesthesiology, Regional Anesthesia, Internat. Jour. Obstetrical Anesthesia. Dep. chmn. sect. med. scis. Coun. for Higher Edn., Helsinki, 1990; mem. coun. Finnish Red Cross, 1987-90; chmn. med. sci. com. Nat. Def., Helsinki, 1990-92. Decorated knight 1st class Order of White Rose, 1982. Fellow Royal Coll. Anaesthetists (U.K.); mem. European Acad. Anesthesiologists, Eur. Soc. Regional Anesthesia (bd. dirs.), N.Y. Acad. Sci., Assn. Researchers and Members of Parliament, Finnish Soc. Future Studies. Avocations: gardening, golf. Home: Yrjonk 25C17, 00100 Helsinki Finland

HOLLO, GABOR, ophthalmologist; b. Budapest, Dec. 19, 1960; s. Istvan and Friderika (Hollitscher) H.; m. Marta Varga, Feb. 24, 1990; children: Hollo, Balazs. MD, Semmelweis U. Med. Sch., 1985, PhD, 1996. Resident in ophthalmology Semmelweis U. Med. Sch., Budapest, 1985-89, prof.'s asst., 1990-97; dir. glaucoma svc. Semmelweis U. Med. Sch., 1997—. Author: Practical Ophthalmology, 1995, Glaucoma: Pathophysiology and Clinics, 1997; contbr. articles to profl. jours. Mem. Soc. for Sci. Edn., Hungarian Soc. for Natural Scis., Hungarian Ophthal. Soc., European Glaucoma Soc. (travel and rsch. subcom. 1992—), Assn. for Eye Rsch., ARVO. Office: Semmelweis U Med Sch, 1st Dept Ophthalmology Tomo Str 25/29, 1083 Budapest Hungary

HOLLO, ILKKA PENTTI, Finnish military officer; b. Tampere, Finland, Nov. 10, 1944; s. Jorma Olavi and Anna (Tirkkonen) H.; m. Riitta Sassi, 1967 (div. 1970); 1 child, Tommi; m. Pirjo Tuulikki Iskanius, 1971; children: Mikko, Kaisa. Student, Mil. Acad., Helsinki, 1964-67, War Coll., Helsinki, 1975-77. Comdr. Karelia Jaeger Bn., Finland, 1988-90, North Karelia Brigade, Finland, 1990, Res. Officer Sch., Finland, 1991-92, Lapland Mil. Province, Finland, 1993-94; head def. policy dept. MoD, Finland, 1994-98; chief of ops. Finnish Def. Forces, Finland, 1998-99, chief of def. staff, 2000—. Dep. chair ctrl. coun. Finnish Ice Hockey Fedn., 1990—. Mem. Internat. Ice Hockey Fedn. (in-line com. 1998-99). Avocations: ice hockey, golf, hunting.

HOLLÒ, ISTVÁN, medical educator, endocrinology researcher; b. Budapest, Hungary, Mar. 25, 1926; s. Kálmán and Julia (Bender) H.; m. Friderika Hollitscher, Jan. 21, 1960; 1 child, Gábor. MD, Semmelweis Sch. Medicine, Budapest, Hungary, 1951, PhD, 1963. Prof. 1st dept. medicine Semmelweis Sch. Medicine, Budapest, 1975-96, head 1st dept. medicine, 1981-93, vice dean, 1978-84, vice rector, 1984-88; cons. Inst. Gerontology, Budapest, 1971-81. Author 4 books; contbr. articles to profl. jours. Mem. Hungarian Endocrinology Soc. (coms. 1960-94), Hungarian Med. Soc. (coms. 1970—), Hungarian Rheumatology Soc., Hungarian Osteoporosis Soc. (pres. 1993, hon. pres. 1993—), Korányi Sándor Soc. (pres. 1984-90). Avocations: gardening, botanics, paleontology. Home: Katona József 26, Budapest Hungary Office: 1st Dept Medicine, Korányi Sándor u 2/a, 1083 Budapest Hungary

HOLLÓ, JÁNOS, chemical engineer, educator, research director; b. Szentes, Hungary, Aug. 20, 1919; s. Gyula and Margit (Mandl) H.; m. Hermina Milch, May 2, 1944 (div. July, 1956); children: Andrew, Nick; m. Veronika Novák, Dec. 27, 1956; 1 child, Dorottya. Diploma in Chem. Engring., Tech. U., Budapest, Hungary, 1941, PhD, 1947; D honoris causa, Tech. U., Budapest, 1990, Tech. U., Vienna, 1973, Tech U., Berlin, 1983, U. Horticulture, 1991. Engr. Various industries, Budapest, 1941-46; head of quality control lab. Brewery, Budapest, 1946-48, tech. dir., 1948-52; prof. Tech. U., Budapest, 1952-90, prof. emeritus, 1990—; dir. Ctrl. Rsch. Inst. for Chemistry Hungarian Acad. Sci., Budapest, 1972-91, rsch. prof., 1991—; dean of faculty chem. engring. Tech. U., Budapest, 1955-57, 1963-72. Author: (books) (with others) Food Industries I, II, Malting and Brewing, Automatization in Food Industry, Die Saure Hydrolyse der Stärke, Raw Materials of Malting and Brewing, Technology of Malting and Brewing, Plant Alfa-1, 4-glucan Phosphorylase, Some Problems of the Up-to-Date Fermentation Research, The Application of Molecular Distillation, Fat Sciences, Food Industries and Environment, Biotechnology and Food Industry, Application de La Spectrometry de Masse (SM) et de la Resonance Magnétique, Nuclaire (RMN) dans les Industries Alimentaires, Natürliche und Synthetische Zusatzstoffe in der Nahrung der Menschen, NIR-Infrared Diffuse Reflectance/Transmittance Spectroscopy, Biotechnology of Food and Feed Prodn., The Bioconversion of Starch, Aliments Non-conventionels a Destination Humaine; Interpretation Dictionay of Food Science; also (with co-authors) approx 600 articles contbr. to profl. jours.; head ediotrial bds. of Acta Alimentaria, Internat. Jour. of Food Scis., Food Investigations, Biotech. and Environ. Protection Today and Tomorrow; mem. editorial bds. 4 German, a French, a Polish, a Spanish, a Bulgarian and Hungarian jours. Recipient Sigmond Elek prize, 1959, Török Gábor prize, 1969, Hungarian State prize, 1975, prix Acad. Internat. de Lutece, 1978, Hungarian Sci. Socs. prize, 1979, Ferenc Tangl prize, 1987, and many others; decorated commdr. de l'Ordre du Mérite pour la Recherche et l'Invention, 1962, Chevalier de L'Ordre des Palmes Académiques, 1968; medal of the French Starch Syndicate, 1960, Chevreul medal, 1986, Saare medal, 1974, Normann medal, 1986, Interpetrol medal, 1973. Mem. Hungarian Acad. Scis. (pres. complex com. food sci., com. tech. scis. and biotech. scis.), Polish Acad. Scis. (fgn., Copernicus medal 1974), German Acad. Scis. (fgn.), N.Y. Acad. Scis. (fgn.), Finnish Acad. Tech. Sci. (fgn.), Internat. Acad. Food Sci. Tech., Austrian Sci. Soc. of Food Industries (hon.), Polish Sci. Soc. Food Industries (hon.), Internat. Soc. Fat Rsch. (founder, past pres.), Hungarian Sci. Soc. for Food Industries (founding sec.-gen., past pres., hon. pres., pres. ISO cereals and pulses com. 1960-99, diploma hon. of ISO, Internat. Coun. Agr. and Food Industry (pres.). Avocations: classical music, books, museums. Office: Hungarian Acad Scis Ctrl Rsch Inst Chemistry, Pusztaszeri ut 59/67, 1025 Budapest Hungary

HOLLOWAY, DONALD PHILLIP, lawyer; b. Akron, Ohio, Feb. 18, 1928; s. Harold Shane and Dorothy Gayle (Ryder) H. BS in Commerce, Ohio U., Athens, 1950; JD, U. Akron, 1955; MA, Kent State U., 1962. Bar: Ohio 1955. Title examiner Bankers Guarantee Title & Trust Co., Akron, 1950-54; acct. Robinson Clay Product Co., Akron, 1955-60; libr. Akron-Summit Pub. Libr., 1962-69, head fine arts and music divsn., 1969-71, sr. libr., 1978-82; pvt. practice law Akron, 1982—. Payroll treas. Akron Symphony Orch., 1947-61; treas. Friends Libr. Akron and Summit County, 1970-72. Mem. AMA, ALA, Ohio Bar Assn., Akron Bar Assn., Ohio Libr. Assn., Nat. Trust Hist. Preservation, Music Libr. Assn., Soc. Archtl. Historians, Coll. Art Assn., Art Librs. N.Am., Akron City Club, North Coast Soc. Republican. Episcopalian. Avocations: art and architecture, music, travel. Home: 601 Nome Ave Akron OH 44320-1682

HOLLOWAY, GORDON ARTHUR, lawyer; b. Wichita, Kans., July 27, 1938; s. George Arthur and Margurite (Bondurant) H.; m. Carol H. Criss, Sept. 1, 1960; children: Gregory Arthur, Suzanne Criss, Garrett Austin. BBA, U. Tex., 1960, JD, 1963. Bar: Tex. 1963, Colo. 1993. Assoc. McGregor, Sewell, Junell & Riggs, Houston, 1963-71; ptnr. Sewell and Riggs, Houston, 1971-93, Holloway & Rowley, 1994—. Staff sgt. Air N.G., 1964-71. Mem. Am. Bd. Trial Advocates (diplomate), Nat. Assn. Railroad Trial Counsel, Internat. Assn. Defense Counsel, Tex. Bd. Legal Specialization (cert. personal injury, civil trial law), Houston Club, Intertel. Office: Holloway & Rowley P C 1415 Louisiana St Ste 2550 Houston TX 77002-7378

HOLLOWAY, JACQUELINE, county commissioner; b. Knoxville, Tenn., Mar. 16, 1935; d. Clyde Herbert and Ernestine Cooper; m. George Rudolph Holloway, July 21, 1951; children: Lynda, George Jr., Michelle, Cheryl, Ingrid. AA in Bus., Cooper Inst., Knoxville, 1961; cert., U. Tenn. Ctr. Govt. Tng., 1990. Biol. technician Oak Ridge (Tenn.) Nat. Lab., 1963-96; county commr. Anderson County, Clinton, Tenn., 1990—. Mem. exec. com. Anderson County Dems.; pres. Dem. Women, Tenn., 1996-98; v.p. Dem. Fedn., Tenn., 1996-98; chmn. Families First Coun., 1997—; vice chair Am.'s Promise, 1999—; bd. dirs. Anderson County Health Coun., 2000—. Mem. Tenn. County Commn. Assn. (bd. dirs. 1991-2000), Tenn. County Svcs. Assn. Methodist. Home and Office: 102 Artesia Dr Oak Ridge TN 37830-7817

HOLLOWAY, JAMES LEMUEL, III, foundation executive, retired naval officer; b. Charleston, S.C., Feb. 23, 1922; s. James Lemuel and Jean Gordon (Hagood) H.; m. Dabney Hix Rawlings, Dec. 14, 1942; children: Lucy Dabney Lyon, Jane Meredith. BSEE, Naval Acad., Annapolis, 1942. Cert. naval aviator, naval nuclear reactor operator. Commd. ensign USN, 1942; served in destroyers USN, Atlantic, Pacific World War II, 1942-45; carrier jet fighter pilot USN, Korea, 1951-53; comdr. 1st nuclear carrier Enterprise USN, Vietnam, 1965-67; advanced through grades to adm. USN, 1973; comdr. carrier striking force U.S. 6th fleet, Ea. Mediterranean, 1970; comdr. U.S. 7th fleet USN, Vietnam, 1971-73; vice chief naval ops. USN, 1973-74, mem. Joint Chiefs of Staff, Dept. Def., 1974-78, chief naval ops., 1974-78, ret., 1978; pres. Coun. Am.-Flag Ship Operators, Washington, 1981-88; pres. Naval Hist. Found., Washington, 1982-98, chmn., 1998—; def. and fgn. policy cons. Paine Weber, Inc., 1980-88; bd. dirs. Statia Terminals Inc., Deerfield, Fla.; chmn. Dept. of Def. Spl. Rev. Group investigating Iranian hostage rescue, 1981; exec. dir. Presdl. Task Force on Combatting Terrorism, 1985; spl. envoy V.P. Bush to Middle East, 1986; commr. Predl. Blue Ribbon Commn. on Def. Mgmt., 1985, congl. Commn. on Mcht. Marine and Def., 1987-88, Presdl. Commn. on Long Term Integrated Strategy, 1987-88; U.S. rep. to South Pacific Commn., 1990-94. Tech. advisor: (film) Top Gun, 1985; contbr. articles to mags. Trustee St. James Sch., Md., 1962—, pres., 1989—, chmn. 1996; bd. dirs. Olmsted Found., Washington, 1978—, mem. bd. advisors The Citadel, 1981-86; chmn. adv. bd. U.S. Naval Acad., 1983-91; chmn. Hist. Annapolis Found., Inc., 1986-96, chmn. emeritus, 1996—; pres., chmn. Naval Acad. Found., 1994—; trustee George Marshall Found., 1988-96; dir. Atlantic Coun., 1987-96; bd. visitors and govs. St. John's Coll., 1995, Bd. Mariners Mus., Newport News, Va., 1995—. Decorated Bronze Star, Air medals (3), Legion of Merit (2), DFC, Def. DSM with 2 oak leaf cluster, Navy DSM with 4 oak leaf clusters, Order of Rising Sun (Japan), Grand Cross (Fed. republic Germany), Legion of Honor (France), Rank of Commandeur, 31 others; recipient Triennial Modern Patriot award SAR, 1994, Disting. Patriot award, 1999, Disting. Pub. Svc. award Navy League, 1996, Disting. Patriot award SAR, 1999, Disting. Grad. award U.S. Naval Acad., 1999, 2000; elected Nat. Wrestling Hall of Fame, 1998. Mem. Assn. Naval Aviation (chmn. 1985-91), Met. Club (Washington gov. 1988—, pres. 1992), Golden Eagles, Brook Club (N.Y.C.), N.Y. Yacht Club (N.Y.C.), Md. Club (Balt.), Annapolis Yacht Club, Soc. Cin., Alfalfa Club (Washington). Republican. Episcopalian. Avocation: sailing. Home: 1694 Epping Farms Rd Annapolis MD 21401-6672

HOLLOWED, ANNE BABCOCK, biologist; b. Mpls., June 14, 1956; d. Edmund Page and Madolyn (Youse) Babcock; m. John James Hollowed, June 13, 1981; children: John James Jr., Madolyn Maureen, Thomas Garrity. BA in Biology and Geology, Lawrence U., 1978; MS in Biological Oceanography, Old Dominion U., 1981; PhD in Fisheries, U. Wash., Seattle, 1990. Rsch. biologist U. Wash., Seattle, 1982; fisheries rsch. biologist Nat. Marine Fisheries Svc., Seattle, 1982-95, task leader, 1995-98, program leader, 1998—. Mem. Am. Inst. Fishery Rsch. Biologists, Am. Assn. Advancement Sci. Meth. Fax: 206-526-6723. E-mail: anne.hollowed@noaa.gov.

HOLLOWELL, MONTE J., engineer, operations research analyst; b. Helena, Ark., Dec. 30, 1949; s. Jerry B. and Imogene Hollowell; m. Jan Bennett, Nov. 19, 1972; children: J. Brett, Matt J. BS in Math., BA in Physics, Ouachita Baptist Univ., 1972; MS in Indsl. Engring., U. Tex., El Paso, 1978. Air def. officer U.S. Army, 1972-80; industrial engr. PPG Industries, Wichita Falls, Tex., 1980-82; industrial engr. U.S. Army Missile Command, Redstone Arsenal, Ala., 1982-85, gen. engr., 1985-98; gen. engr. U.S. Army Aviation and Missile command, Redstone Arsenal, 1998—. Mem. Nat. Mil. Intelligence Assn. (Tennessee Valley chpt.), U.S. Army Space and Missile Def. Assn., Redstone Arsenal Military Ops. Rsch. Soc., Air Def. Artillery Assn., Assn. Old Crows. Home: 12038 Chicamauga Trl SE Huntsville AL 35803-1546 Office: Advanced Systems Concepts Redstone Arsenal AL 35898-5242

HOLM, SIR IAN, actor; b. Sept. 12, 1931; s. James Harvey and Jean (Wilson) Cuthbert; m. Lynn Mary Shaw, 1955 (div. 1965); m. Sophie Baker, 1982 (div. 1986); m. Penelope Wilton, 1991. Student, Royal Acad. Dramatic Art, 1950-53; LittD (hon.), U. Sussex, 1999. Actor with Shakespeare Mem. Theatre, 1954-55; in repertory, 1956; toured in Titus Andronicus, 1957; numerous roles Royal Shakespeare Co. including Henry V, Romeo and Richard III, 1958-67; plays include Moonlight, 1993, Landscape, 1994, King Lear, 1997 (Evening Std. award for Best Actor, Olivier award Best Actor and Critics Cir. award, 1998); film appearances include Young Winston, Alien, Chariots of Fire (named Best Supporting Actor, Cannes Film Festival, 1981, Brit. Acad. Film and TV Arts, 1982, Acad. Award nomination Best Supporting Actor, 1982), Greystoke, Brazil, Dance With A Stranger, 1985, Wetherby, 1985, Dreamchild, 1985, Another Woman, 1988, Henry V, 1990, Hamlet, 1990, Kafka, 1991, The Naked Lunch, 1992, Blue Ice, 1992, Hour of The Pig, 1993, The Madness of King George, 1994, Lochness, 1994, Mary Shelley's Frankenstein, 1995, Big Night, 1995, Night Falls on Manhattan, 1995, The 5th Element, 1996, A Life Less Ordinary, 1996, The Sweet Hereafter, 1996 (Genie Best Actor award), Existenz, 1998, Simon Magus, 1998, The Match, 1998, Esther Kahn, 1999, Joe Gould's Secret, 1999, Beautiful Joe, 1999, Lord of the Rings, 2000; others; TV appearances include The Lost Boys (Best Actor award Royal TV Soc., 1979), Strike, 1981, (miniseries) Game, Set and Match, 1988, The Last Romantics, 1991, (series) The Borrowers, 1992-93, others; TV appearances include Landscape, BBC, 1995, King Lear, BBC, 1997, Alice Through the Looking Glass, Channel 4, 1998, The Last of the Blonde Bombshells, 2000; Films include Esther Kahn, 1999, Joe Gould's Secret, 1999, Beautiful Joe, 1999, Lord of the Rings, 2000, From Hell, 2000. Awarded Knighthood by Queen of Eng., 1998; recipient Tony award for Best Supporting Actor, 1967, Evening Std. award, 1967, 93, 97, Genie award, 1997, Olivier award, 1998.

HOLM, JOY ALICE, psychology educator, art educator, artist, goldsmith; b. Chgo., May 21, 1929; d. Alvin Herbert and Willette Eugenia (Miller) H. BFA, U. Ill., 1952; MS in Art Edn. Inst. Design, Ill. Inst. Tech., 1956; PhD in Edn., U. Minn., 1967. Tchr. art, Eng. West Chgo. H.S., 1952-54; instr., tchr. art J.S. Morton H.S. & Jr. Coll., Cicero, Ill., 1954-65; asst. prof. art & design Mankato (Minn.) State U., 1965-66; asst. prof. art Ill. State U., Normal, 1966-69; assoc. prof. art & design So. Ill. U., Edwardsville, 1969-71; assoc. prof. art edn. Winona (Minn.) State U., 1971-75; assoc. prof., chmn. dept. art St. Mary's Coll. of Notre Dame, Ind., 1975-76; assoc. prof. art & design, secondary, continuing edn. U. Wis., Eau Claire, 1976-78; assoc. prof. art & design Sch. Art & Design Kent (Ohio) State U., 1978-80; lectr. Jungian studies C.G. Jung Inst., Chgo., 1980-82; adj. assoc. prof. art edn. Sch. Art and Design, Sch. Edn. U. Ill., Chgo., 1981-82; lectr. U. Calif. Ext., Santa Cruz, 1983—; adj. prof. art edn., design San Jose (Calif.) State U., 1983-84; owner bus. designer-goldsmith Oak Park, Ill., 1980-82, Carmel, Calif., 1982-87; owner bus. designer-goldsmith Atelier XII, Winona, 1988—; curriculum cons. North Ctrl. Assn. Accreditation Team State of Ill., Edwardsville, 1970; regional cons. Supt. Pub. Instrn., Springfield, Ill., 1970; juror exhbns.; panelist, spkr., presenter confs., meetings. Contbr., cons. Alternative Medicine: A Definitive Guide, 1994; contbr. articles to profl. jours; one-woman shows: J. Sterling Morton H.S. & Jr. Coll., 1963, Russell Art Gallery, Bloomington, 1968, Owatonna (Minn.) Art Ctr., 1980, 86; exhbns. include La Grange (Ill.) Art League (Best of Show, 1st Place award prints), 1963, 64, Minn. Mus. Art, 1974, 75, Craft & Folk Art Mus., L.A., 1978, The Gallery Kent State U., 1978, 79, Saenger Nat. Small Sculpture and Jewelry Exhibit, 1978, Diamonds Internat., N.Y., 1978, Inst. Design Alumni, 1988, Internat. Biographical Ctr. Congress Exhbn., Edinburgh, Scotland, 1994, others. Fellow World Lit. Acad.; mem. AAUP, Nat. Art Edn. Assn. (rep. Wis. Women's Caucus Houston Conf. 1978, higher edn. divsn. 1961—), Am. Assn. Higher Edn., Coll. Art Assn., Soc. N.Am. Goldsmiths, Internat. Sculpture Ctr., Gemological Inst. Am., C.G. Jung Inst. (Chgo.), Hon. Soc. Illustrators (hon.), Internat. Soc. Study of Subtle Energies and Energy Medicine, Inst. Noetic Scis., Alpha Lambda Delta (hon.), Phi Kappa Phi (hon.). Methodist. Office: Atelier XII PO Box 183 Winona MN 55987-0183

HOLM, NILS GUSTAV, comparative religion educator; b. Mariehamn, Finland, Apr. 9, 1943; s. Gustaf Adolf and Hjördis Ida Elisabeth (Hollfast) H.; m. Marita Signhild Michaelsen, Dec. 30, 1967; 1 child, Fredrik Gustaf Nilsson. M in Theology, Åbo (Finland) Acad. U., 1970, Lic. Phil., 1973; D in Theology, Uppsala (Sweden) U., 1976. Sr. lectr. Uppsala U., 1980—; prof. comparative religion Åbo Acad. U., 1981—; sr. lectr. Helsinki (Finland) U., 1984—; 1st vice rector Åbo Acad. U., 1991-94. Author: Scandinavian Psychology of Religion, 1987 (also in German), History of Religions, 1993; editor: Religious Ecstasy, 1982; editor, author: World Views in Modern Society, 1986, Archiv für Religionspsychologie, 1997; editor (series) Religionsvetenskapliga skrifter, 1981—. Mem. Internat. Assn. Psychology and Religion (pres. 1995—), Finnish Soc. Scis. and Letters. Avocations: music, singing. E-mail: nholm@abo.fi. Office: Åbo Acad Univ, Biskopsgatan 10, FIN20500 Åbo Finland

HOLMAN, JAMES LEWIS, financial and management consultant; b. Chgo., Oct. 27, 1926; s. James Louis and Lillian Marie (Walton) H.; m. Elizabeth Ann Owens, June 18, 1948 (div. 1982); children: Craig Stewart, Tracy Lynn, Mark Andrew; m. Geraldine Ann Wilson, Dec. 26, 1982. BS in Econs. and Mgmt., U. Ill., Urbana, 1950, postgrad., 1950; postgrad. Northwestern U., 1954-55. Traveling auditor, then statistician, asst. controller parent buying dept. Sears, Roebuck & Co., Chgo., 1951-54; asst. to sec.-treas. Hanover Securities Co., Chgo., 1954-65; asst. to controller chem. ops. div. Montgomery Ward & Co. Inc., Chgo., 1966-68; controller Henrotin Hosp., Chgo., 1968; bus. mgr. Julian, Dye, Javid, Hunter & Najafi, Associated, Chgo., 1969-81, cons. 1981-84; vol. cons., adminstrv. asst. Fiji Sch. Medicine, Suva, 1984-86, cons., 1987-89; vol. bus. cons. U.S. Peace Corps Honduras, 1989, cons., 1989—; cons., dir., sec.-treas. Comprehensive Resources Ltd., Glenview (Ill.), Wheaton (Ill.) and Walnut Creek, Calif., 1982; bd. dirs., sec.-treas. Medtran, Inc., 1980-83; sec. James C. Valenta, P.C., 1979-82; sponsored project adminstr. Northwestern U., Evanston, Ill., 1984. Sec., B.R. Ryall YMCA, Glen Ellyn, Ill., 1974-76, bd. dirs., 1968-78; trustee Gary Meml. United Meth. Ch., Wheaton, 1961-69, 74-77; bd. dirs. Goodwill Industries Chgo., 1978-79, DuPage (Ill.) Symphony, 1954-58, treas., 1955-58. Served with USN, 1944-46. Baha'i. Mem. Kiwanis (bd. dirs. Chgo. 1956-60, bd. dirs. youth found. 1957-60, pres. 1958-60). Home and Office: 1571 Burr Oak Ct # B Wheaton IL 60187-2709

HOLMAN, J(OHN) LEONARD, retired manufacturing corporation executive; b. Moose Jaw, Sask., Can., Aug. 30, 1929; s. Charles Claude and Lillian Kathleen (Haw) H.; m. Julia Pauline Benfield, July 18, 1953; children: Nancy Jane, Sally Joan. B.S. in Civil Engring., U. Alta., 1953. Pres. Consolidated Concrete Ltd., Calgary, Alta., Can., 1969-72; dir., pres. BACM Industries Ltd., Calgary, 1972-76; exec. v.p. Genstar Corp., Calgary, 1976-79, San Francisco, 1980-87; dir. several subs. cos. Genstar Corp.; pres., chief exec. officer CBR Cement Corp., San Mateo, Calif., 1986-88, chmn. bd., 1988-89, ret., 1990; bd. dirs., officer several nat. trade assns. Mem. Assn. Profl. Engr. Alta. (life), Calgary Exhbn. and Stampede (hon. life., dir.), Calgary Golf and Country Club, Bernardo Heights Country Club. Home: 111 Country Club Estates, 111-5555 Elbow Dr SW, Calgary, AB Canada T2V 1H7

HOLMAN, JOHN RICHARD, magazine editor; b. Dartford, England, Feb. 4, 1950; s. John and Florence H. BSc, U. Bristol, 1971. Civil servant Dept. Health & Social Security, London, 1975-79; from asst. to catalogue editor to editor Gibbons Stamp Mo. Stanley Gibbons Ltd., London, 1980-88; editor Royal Mail, London, 1988—; lectr. in econ. history Brunel Tech. Coll., Bristol, 1972-73; dep. warden Univ. Residence Hall, Bristol, 1972-75. Author: Stamp Collecting: A Guide to Modern Philately, 1983, The Stanley Gibbons Guide to Stamp Collecting, 1989. Fellow Royal Philatelic Soc.; mem. Nat. Philatelic Soc. London, Econ. History Soc. Avocations: Jacobite history, travel, reading biographies. Office: Royal Mail, 2-14 Bunhill Row, London EC1Y 8HQ, England

HOLMDAHL, LENA E., surgeon, educator; b. Lerum, Sweden, Aug. 15, 1954; d. Tord O. and Maj-Britt E. (Wimby) Norin; m. Magnus S.B. Holmdahl, June 9, 1979; children: Per, Anders. MD, U. Göteborg, Sweden, 1979, PhD, 1994. Resident Alingsas (Sweden) Hosp., 1979-86; staff surgeon Ostra Hosp., Göteborg, 1987-94, 1996, asst. prof., 1994-95; vis. prof. U. Fla., Gainesville, 1995-96, assoc. prof., 1996; colorectal surgeon Sahlgrenska U. Hosp., Göteborg, 1996—. Editor Trauma News, Göteborg, 1992-95; guest editor supplement European Jour. Surgery, 1997. Recipient Best Exptl. Work award Scandinavian Surg. Soc., 1993. Mem. N.Y. Acad. Scis. Achievements include understanding of the pathophysiology of peritoneal tissue repair. Avocations: outdoor activities, music, literature. Office: Sahlgrenska U Hosp/Ostra, Colorectal Unit, 41685 Göteborg Sweden

HOLMDAHL, SVANTE MARTIN, university president, anesthesiology educator; b. Gothenburg, Sweden, June 10, 1923; s. Henrik and Ingrid (Dahlgren) H.; m. Karin Barbro Jehander, Mar. 24, 1949; children: Maria, Henrik, Rikard, Gundela, Joakim, Andreas. MD, Uppsala (Sweden) U., 1950, PhD in Medicine, 1956; PhD, U. Miami, Fla., 1972. Asst. Surg. Clinic/Uppsala U., 1950-55, asst. prof., 1956; asst. lectr. dept. anesthesiology Postgrad. Med. Sch., London, 1956-57; head dept. anesthesiology Uppsala U., 1957-80, prof., 1965-89, vice-dean faculty medicine, 1966-69, dean faculty medicine, 1969-70, v.p., 1970-78, pres., 1978-89; vis. prof. Columbia U., N.Y.C., 1960-61; advisor anesthesiology WHO, 1963, 68, 70; sci. advisor anesthesiology nat. Bd. Health, Sweden, 1967-86, Swedish Nat. Bd. Univs. and Colls., 1979. Author: Pulmonary Uptake of Oxygen in Prolonged Apnea, 1956; contbr. over 180 articles to profl. jours. Chmn. com. on genetic engring. Swedish Parliament, 1990-92. Fellow Royal Coll. Anesthetists (London, hon.); mem. Am. Soc. Univ. Anesthesiologists (hon.), German Soc. Anesthesiologists (hon.), Scandinavian Soc. Anesthesiologists (hon.), Swedish Soc. Anesthesia and Intensive Care (hon.). Home: Dobelnsgatan 26 a, Uppsala S-752 37, Sweden Office: Uppsala U, PO Box 256, Uppsala S-75105, Sweden

HOLME, BØRGE, materials scientist; b. Voss, Hordaland, Norway, Mar. 24, 1968; s. Jørund Asle and Grete (Osnes) H. BS, U. Oslo, 1991, MS, 1992, PhD, 1996. Avocations: inventions, skiing, vol. Christian work. Postdoctoral scientist Norsk Hydro, Oslo, 1997, Norwegian Rsch. Coun., Oslo and Grenoble, France, 1998; rsch. scientist Sintef, Oslo, Norway, 1999—. Contbr. articles to profl. jours. Leader Christian Union Oslo, 1993-95. Cpl. Norwegian Army, 1987-88. Recipient award Thor Eriksen's Meml. Fund, Oslo, 1987, award for Best Poster for Materials Sci., Kuopio, Finland, 1994, HM King Harald's Gold medal U. Oslo, 1997. Mem. Oslo Student Christian Fellowship (hon.). Lutheran. Office: SINTEF Materials Technology, PO Box 124 Blindern, N-0314 Oslo Norway

HOLMEFJORD, IVAR, aquaculturist, consultant; b. Bergen, Hordaland, Norway, Apr. 11, 1958; s. Reidar and Kristina (Havsgård) H.; m. Lillian Eikeland, Oct. 1, 1983; children: Reidar, Magnus, Kristian, Amalie. Cand. Magistratus, U. Bergen (Norway), 1984, M, 1986, PhD, 1996. Fish farmer Bolaks Ltd., Eikelandsosen, Norway, 1981-83; rsch. asst. Inst. Aquaculture Rsch., Sunndalsøra, Norway, 1984-87; rsch. fellow Inst. Aquaculture Rsch., Sunndalsøra, 1987-90, scientist, 1991-98, head of mariculture divsn., 1998-2000; dir. Real Fjord Ltd., Eikelandsosen, Norway, 2000—; bd. dirs. Norway Marine Culture Ltd., Aure, Norwegian Halibut Ltd., Rørvik; dir. bd. Real Fjord Ltd. Contbr. articles to profl. jours. Sgt. infantry Army, 1978. Mem. Norwegian Assn. Aquaculture, Internat. Coun. Exploration of the Sea (mem. working group on marine fish culture). Avocations: piano playing, soccer, mountain walking. Home: Hagen, N-5640 Eikelandsosen Norway Office: Real Fjord Ltd, Sjølseng Møre and Romsdal, N-5640 Eikelandsosen Norway

HOLMÉN, HANS GUNNAR, geographer, educator; b. Örebro, Sweden, Oct. 9, 1948; s. Gunnar and Märta (Westerberg) H.; m. Kerstin Elisabeth Nilsson, Jan. 14, 1989 (div. Aug. 1994); children: Jesper, Anders. BA, Lund (Sweden) U., 1983, Lic. of Social Scis., 1989, PhD, 1991. Assoc. prof. social and econ. geography Lund U., 1996—; cons. Swedish Coop. Ctr., 1990, Swedish Internat. Devel. Coop. Agy., Sida, 1995-96, UNSO/UNDP, 1996-98. Award: The Thorild Dahlgren Price for Social Science, 1994. Office: U Linköping, Dept Geography, 581 83 Linköping Sweden

HOLMES, BARRY, microbiologist; b. London, Mar. 26, 1947; s. Frank George Henry and Annie H.; m. Jennifer Lillian Taylor, Nov. 4, 1972; children: Deborah, Ian, Emma, William. BSc, U. Wales, 1969; MSc, U. London, 1970, PhD, 1985, DSc, 1994. Head Nat. Collection of Type Cultures Pub. Health Lab. Svc., London, 1971—. Recipient Bergey award Bergey's Manual Trust, 1998. Fellow Inst. Biology, Am. Acad. Microbiology. Home: 54 The Highway, Stanmore Middlesex HA7 3PN, England Office: Nat Collection Type Cultures, 61 Colindale Ave Ctrl Pub Health Lab, London NW9 5HT, England

HOLMES, DOUGLAS QUIRK, investment banker; b. Cleve., Mar. 21, 1956; s. Allen C. and Mary Elizabeth (Quirk) H.; m. Melinda Baldwin Palmer, Oct. 25, 1980; children: Alison Morgan, Sarah Baldwin. BA, Kenyon Coll., Gambier, Ohio, 1978; MBA, Dartmouth Coll., Hanover, N.H., 1984. Assoc. Lazard Freres & Co., N.Y.C., 1984-86, First Boston, Chgo., 1986-88; sr. v.p. Kidder, Peabody & Co., Chgo., 1988-92; exec. mng. dir. Carleton, McCreary, Holmes & Co., 1992-99; ptnr. Full Circle Investments, Cleve., 1999—. Mem. Union Club Cleve., Kirkland Country Club (Cleve.), Tavern Club (Clev.), Chagrin Valley Hunt Club, Dusquene Club (Pitts.). Republican. Office: Full Circle Investments 1100 Superior Ave E Ste 1400 Cleveland OH 44114-2518

HOLMES, ELIZABETH, psychologist; b. Boston, Sept. 2, 1951; d. Charles R. and Evelyn M. (Bedia) Holmes; m. John Mateczun; children: Erin Kathleen, Adam Michael, Laura Kathleen. BS in Psychology and Urban Studies, U. Bridgeport, 1974, MS in Sch. Psychology, 1976; PhD in Clin. Psychology, Calif. Sch. Profl. Psychology, 1979. Diplomate Am. Bd. Profl. Psychology. Dir. hall U. Bridgeport (Conn.), 1974-76; counselor Crisis Ho., San Diego, 1976-77, Tech. Rsch., Inc., San Diego, 1977-78; psychology intern County Mental Health, San Diego, 1978-79; commd. lt (j.g) Med. Sch. Corps USN, 1979; intern Nat. Navel Med. Ctr., Bethesda, Md., 1979-80, chmn. dept. behavioral psychology, 1980-84; cons., faculty psychology intern, head HIV/AIDS program U.S. Naval Hosp., Bethesda, Md., 1983-87; psychologist, program developer Trasher Faber Assocs., Norfolk, Va., 1987-91; rsch. dir. MAFORPAC, Campt H.S. Smith, Hawaii, 1991-94; asst. prof. dept. psychiatry and med. psychology Uniformed Svcs. U. Health Scis.,

1984—; prof. dept. lead, ethics and law U.S. Naval Acad., Annapolis, Md., 1994-99; clin. psychologist U.S. Naval Hosp., Rota, Spain, 1999—; lectr. Georgetown U. Sch. Dentistry, 1983-87; adj. asst. prof. Eastern Va. Med. Sch., 1989—; psychol. cons. to dental div. Bur. Medicine and Surgery; cons. in field. Trustee Calif. Sch. Profl. Psychology, 1977-79, Tidewater AIDS Crisis Task Force. Mem. Am. Psychol. Assn., Am. Assn. Dental Schs., Womens Network Hampton Rds., Antarctican Soc., Soc. Women Geographers. Office: Psc 819 Box 18 FPO AE 09645-2500

HOLMES, GENTA HAWKINS, diplomat; b. Anadarko, Okla., Sept. 3, 1940. BA, U. So. Calif., 1962. Jr. officer U.S. Embassy, Abidjan, Ivory Coast, 1964-66; with office spl. assistance to Sec. of State for Refugee Affairs, 1966-68; spl. asst., youth officer U.S. Embassy, Paris, 1968-71; with N.Y. regional office OEO, 1972-73; with office devel. fin., econ. bur. U.S. Dept. State, 1973-74; chief econ. and commercial sect. U.S. Embassy, Bahamas, 1974-77; congl. fellow Am. Polit. Sci. Assn., 1977-78; with bur. congl. rels. U.S. Dept. State, 1978-79; asst. adminstr. legis. affairs AID, 1979-82; mem. 25th Exec. Seminar in Nat. and Internat. Affairs, 1982-83; mem. bd. examiners, 1983-84; dep. chief of mission U.S. Embassy, Lilongwe, Malawi, 1984-86, Port-au-Prince, Haiti, 1986-88, Pretoria, South Africa, 1988-90; U.S. amb. to Namibia, 1990-92; dir. gen. fgn. svc., dir. pers. U.S. Dept. State, Washington, 1992-95; diplomat in residence U. Calif., Davis, 1995-97; U.S. amb. to Australia, 1997—. Office: US Embassy Canberra APO AP 96549

HOLMES, HARRY DADISMAN, health facility administrator; b. Houston, Aug. 8, 1944; s. Harry Newton and Ruth Eleanor (Dadisman) H.; m. Patricia Ann Hunt, Aug. 23, 1969; children: Hillary Hunt, Ashley Elizabeth. BA, Rice U., 1966; MA, La. State U., 1968; PhD, U. Mo., 1973. Asst. prof. urban devel. U. Tenn., Knoxville, 1973-76; asst. to exec. v.p. Tex. Med. Ctr., Inc., Houston, 1976-80; dir. govt. affairs, orgnl. liaison U. Tex. System Cancer Ctr., Houston, 1980-90, asst. to pres., 1981-90; assoc. v.p. gvtl. rels. U. Tex. M.D. Anderson Cancer Ctr., Houston, 1990—; mem. Cancer Ctrs. Adminstrs. Forum, 1994—; mem. select com. on pub. issues Greater Houston Hosp. Coun., 1983-94; mem. exec. adv. bd. White, Petrov and McHone, 1987-95; mem. pub. rels. adv. coun. Tex. Med. Ctr., 1985—; chair South Tex. Legis Conf., 1985, 87; founder Biotech. Assn., 1986; mem. exec. com. Nat. Cancer Ctr. Networks, 1998—. Mem. adminstrv. bd. St. Luke's Meth. Ch.; mem. Mayor's Task Force on Pvt. Sector Initiatives for Houston, 1981-82, Houston C.C. Found. Bd., 1992—, Greater Houston Partnership State and Fed. Com., 1989—; mem. U. Tex. Tex./Mex. Border Health Task Force, 1989—, exec. com., 1989—; pres. Houston Higher Edn. Fin. Corp., 1989—; mem. Rice U. Fund Coun., 1991-94, Nat. Cancer Ctrs. Task Force, 1991—; mem. exec. bd. Leadership Houston, 1983-86, Houston Ctr. for Humanities, 1983-86; mem. govt. rels. com. Greater Houston Hosp. Coun., 1985-95; mem. com. Instnl. Task Force on Oncology in Chile, 1986-87; exec. com. Instnl. Strategic Planning Com., 1986-95; divsn. chmn. United Way of Houston, 1983; com. to evaluate the status of minority and women faculty, faculty adminstrs. and adminstrv. staff U. Tex., M.D. Anderson Cancer Ctr., 1990. White fellow U. Mo., 1972. Mem. Am. Assn. Cancer Insts. (mem. govt. rels. com. 1998—, chair 1999-2000), Houston C. of C. (cochmn. govt. rels. com. 1982-83), Rice U. Alumni Assn. (exec. bd., chmn. publs. com. 1982-83), Phi Alpha Theta. Home: 5642 Cedar Creek Dr Houston TX 77056-2310 Office: U Tex MD Anderson Cancer Ctr 1515 Holcombe Blvd Houston TX 77030-4009

HOLMES, IAN HAMILTON, microbiologist; b. Melbourne, Australia, June 30, 1935; s. Philip Edward and Edith Margaret (Smith) H.;; m. Jenifer Lucy Tonkin, May 21, 1960; children: Lucy Hamilton, Julia Carolyn, Melissa Louise. BSc with honors, U. Melbourne, 1958; PhD, Australian Nat. U., 1961. Lectr. in microbiology U. Melbourne, 1964-68, sr. lectr., 1969-74, assoc. prof. microbiology, 1975—; chmn. study groups Internat. Com. Taxonomy of Viruses, 1973-96; edit. bd. Jour. Virology, U.S., 1980-86; advisor, edit. bd. Archives of Virology, Australia, 1985-94, editor, 1995—. Patentee in field; contbr. over 100 articles to profl. jours. Recipient Nat. Sci. and Tech. award Clunies Ross Meml. Found., 1998. Anglican. Avocations: orchid growing, viticulture. Office: Dept Microbiology, and Immunology U Melbourne, Parkville VIC 3052, Australia

HOLMES, PAUL ARTHUR, polymer scientist, researcher; b. Sheffield, Yorkshire, Eng., July 9, 1951; s. Arthur Holmes and Minnie May; m. Julie Lesley Benjamin; children: Benjamin Marc, Thomas Paul. BSc in Chemistry with 1st class honours, U. Manchester, Eng., 1972, PhD in Polymer Sci., 1976. Sr. rsch. scientist ICI plc, Runcorn, Eng., 1976-89; chief rsch. scientist Pilkington plc, St. Helens, Eng., 1989—; panel mem. Engring. and Phys. Scis. Rsch. Coun., Swindon, Eng., 1990—; dir. Ctr. for Adhesive Tech., Cambridge, End., 1991-94. Contbg. author: Developments in Crystaline Polymers, 1988, Development in Polymer Degradation, 1987. Mem. Royal Soc. Chemistry (chartered). Achievements include patents for manufacture and use of biodegradable thermoplastic polyhydroxybutyrate, vehicle windows with enhanced intruder resistance. Office: Pilkinkton Tech Ctr, Hall Lane, Lathom, Ormskirk L40 5UF, England

HOLMES, RICHARD BALE, county manager; b. Cambridge, Mass., Nov. 2, 1948; s. Joseph Alexander and Jane (Krug) H.; m. Martha Whemann, Aug. 28, 1971; children: Christine Jones, Rebecca Ann. BS in Civil Engring., Union Coll., 1971, BS in Indsl. Econs., 1971; MS in Urban Planning, U. Ariz., 1973. Cert. Am. Inst. Cert. Planners. Urban planner Louisville & Jefferson County Planning Commn., 1973-75; environ. planner Berkshire County Regional Planning Commn., Pittsfield, Mass., 1975-79; from environ. planner to dir. Clark County Dept. Comprehensive Planning, Las Vegas, 1979-99; asst. county mgr. Clark County, Las Vegas, 1999—; mem. State Land Use Planning Advisory Coun., Carson City, Nev.; chair adv. bd. on water resources planning and devel., Carson City. Office: Clark County Mgr's Office 500 S Grand Central Pkwy Las Vegas NV 89155-0001

HOLMES, RICHARD BROOKS, mathematical physicist; b. Milw., Jan. 7, 1959; s. Emerson Brooks Holmes and Nancy Anne Schaffter; m. Sandra Lynn Wong, June 27, 1998. BS, Calif. Inst. Tech., 1981; MS, Stanford (Calif.) U., 1983. Sr. sys. analyst Comptek Rsch., Vallejo, Calif., 1982-83; staff scientist Western Rsch., Arlington, Va., 1983-85; sr. scientist AVCO Everett (Mass.) Rsch. Lab., 1985-88; prin. rsch. scientist North East Rsch. Assocs., Woburn, Mass., 1988-90; sr. mem. tech. staff Rocketdyne divsn. Rockwell Internat., Canoga Park, Calif., 1990-95; sr. staff scientist Lockheed Martin Rsch. Labs., Palo Alto, Calif., 1995-98; pres. Nutronics, Inc., Carson City, Nev., 1998—; cons. North East Rsch. Assocs., 1990. Contbr. Matched Asymptotic Expansions, 1988; contbr. articles to Phys. Rev. Letters, Phys. Rev., Jour. of the Optical Soc. Am. and IEEE Jour. of Quantum Electronics. Mem. No. Calif. Scholarship Founds., Oakland, 1977; mem. Wilderness Soc., Washington, 1989. Stanford fellow Stanford U., 1982; fellow MIT, 1990; recipient Presdl. Medal of Merit, 1992. Mem. AAAS, SPIE (conf. organizer 1995—), Am. Phys. Soc., Optical Soc. Am. Achievements include patents for means for photonic communication, computation, and distortion compensation; discovery of spin-two phonons. Office: Nutronics Inc 1668 E Clearview Dr Carson City NV 89701-6572

HOLMES, ROBERT WAYNE, service executive, consultant, biological historian; b. Brush, Colo., July 16, 1950; s. George William Jr. and Reba Mary (Sandel) H. BA, Western State Coll., 1972. Exec. Rose Exterminator Co., San Francisco, 1986-92; founder, owner BFE Cons., 1992—. Author: The Killing River, Countdown. Mem. Smithsonian Instn., Washington, 1986, Sta. KRMA-TV-PBS, Denver, 1987, Ft. Morgan (Colo.) Heritage Found., 1988, Ctr. for Study of Presidency, Wilson Ctr., Nat. Mus. Am. Indian, Nat. Trust for Hist. Preservation, 1994-95. Mem. AAAS, N.Y. Acad. Scis., Acad. Polit. Sci., Wilson Ctr. Assoc. Ctr. for Study of the Presidency, Am. Mus. Natural History, Nat. Trust for Hist. Preservation, Denver Mus. Natural History, Nat. Mus. Am. Indian, Nature Conservancy, FPCN, SoAm. Explorers Club.

HOLMES, SETH MCELWEE, medical researcher; b. Balt.; s. Edwin Ruthven III and Carolyn McElwee H. BS, U. Wash., 1997; postgrad., U. Calif., San Francisco, 1997—, San Francisco Theol. Sem., San Anselmo, Calif., 1998—. Health coord. Camp Spalding, Newport, Wash., 1997; rschr. spiritual care in medicine U. Calif., San Francisco, 1999—. Vol. med. asst. Hosp. Vozandes, Quito, Ecuador, 1995-96; constrn. mission leader 1st Presbyn. Ch. Spokane, Tijuana, Mex., 1990-97, Habitat for Humanity, Oakland, Calif., 1999; svc. learning project leader Ptnrs. in Hope, Mexico City, 1999. Mem. Christian Med. and Dental Soc. (leader 1997—), Phi Beta Kappa, Golden Key. Presbyterian. Avocations: back packing, telemark skiing, biking, reading, swing dancing. E-mail: smholm@itsa.ucsf.edu.

HOLMES, SUE ELLEN, library director; b. Lawrence, Mass., Oct. 4, 1950; d. Francis Augustine and Katherine Elizabeth (Gallagher) H. MLS, U. R.I., 1977. Dir. children's svcs. Stevens Meml. Libr., North Andover, Mass., 1977-90; libr. dir. Stevens Meml. Libr., North Andover, 1990—. Mem. ALA, New Eng. Libr. Assn., Mass. Libr. Assn. Roman Catholic. Office: Stevens Meml Libr 345 Main St North Andover MA 01845-2636

HOLMES, SVEN ERIK, federal judge, educator; b. Grand Junction, Colo., Feb. 13, 1951; s. Clifford Newton and Ruth (Bradley) H.; m. Lois Romano, Oct. 31, 1983; children: Kristen Elizabeth Romano, Virginia Morgan Romano. AB, Harvard U., 1973; JD, U. Va., 1980; LLM, Georgetown U., 1987. Bar: Okla. 1980, D.C. 1985, U.S. Dist. Ct. D.C. 1985, U.S. Dist. Ct. (no., ea. and we. dists.) Okla. 1985, U.S. Ct. Appeals (10th and D.C. cirs.) 1985, U.S. Tax Ct. 1985, U.S. Ct. Claims 1985, U.S. Supreme Ct., 1994. Campaign coord. David L. Boren for Gov., Oklahoma City, 1975; adminstrv. asst. to gov. State of Okla., Oklahoma City, 1975-77; law clk. to judge U.S. Dist. Ct. (no. dist.) Okla., Tulsa, 1980-81; assoc. Doerner, Stuart, Saunders, Daniel & Anderson, Tulsa, 1981-83; exec. dir. Dems. for "80's", Washington, 1983-85; from assoc. to ptnr. Williams & Connolly, Washington, 1985-87, 89-95; designated liaison staff mem. Senate Select Com. on Secret Mil. Assistance to Iran, Washington, 1987; gen. counsel, staff dir. Senate Select Com. on Intelligence, Washington, 1987-89; U.S. dist. judge U.S. Dist. Ct.for No. Dist. Okla., Tulsa, 1995—; v.p. Balt. Orioles, 1989-93; adj. prof. constl. law U. Tulsa Sch. Law. Mem. Okla. Bar Assn., D.C. Bar Assn. Lutheran. Avocations: reading, tennis. Office: US Dist Ct 411 US Courthouse 333 W 4th St Tulsa OK 74103-3839

HOLMES, TIMOTHY ALASTAIR, mortgage banker; b. Perth, Australia, May 5, 1947; s. Robert and Joan Lucille (MacLeod) H.; m. Carol Mary Milne; children: Joanna, Tiffany, Lucy. Trainee mgr. JB Were & Son, Perth, 1967-69; trainee operator Wedd Durlacher & Mordaunt, London, 1970-72; mgr. Town & Country Bldg. Soc., Perth, 1972-74, investments mgr., 1974-78; gen. mgr. Permanent Investment Bldg. Soc., Perth, 1978-85; mng. dir. Internat. Fin. and Investment Pty. Ltd., Perth, 1985—; bd. dirs. Cape Hotels Ltd., Perth, Paladian Securities Pty., Ltd., IF&I Securities Pty., Ltd., chmn. Internat. Fin., Perth. Austrian consul, 1983—; commr. Child Health Rsch. Found., Perth, 1990—, Anglican Edn. Commn., 1987-94. Pilot/officer Australian Air Force, 1967-70. Decorated Knights Cross 1st Class, Austrian Govt. Fellow Australian Inst. Directors, Fin. Industry Assn., Australian Inst. of Directors, Australian Inst. of Mktg.; mem. Young Pres.'s Orgn. (internat. pres. 1995-96), Weld Club, Western Australian Club, West Australian C. of C. (v.p. 1983-84). Episcopalian. Avocations: golf, fishing, walking, tennis, skiing. Office: Internat Fin/Invest Pty Ltd, 250 St Georges TCE/QV1 Bldg, 6000 Perth Australia

HOLMGREN, JAN ROLAND, microbiology and immunology educator, biomedical researcher; b. Borås, Sweden, Mar. 25, 1944; s. Roland A. and Ingrid E. H.; m. Ann-Mari Svennerholm; children: Anders, Anna, Cecilia. MB, Univ. Göteborg, Sweden, 1965; PhD in Sci., Univ. Göteborg, 1969, MD, 1973. Docent and asst. prof., dept. bacteriology U. Göteborg, Sweden, 1969-71; rschr., asst. prof. Swedish Med. Rsch. Coun., 1971-74, special rsch. position, assoc. prof. immunology, infectious diseases, 1974-80; prof. medical microbiology, head dept. med. microbiology, immunology U. Göteborg, 1980—; bd. dirs. Internat. Ctr. Diarrhoeal Disease Rsch., Bangladesh, Swedish Agy. Rsch. Cooperation with Devel. Countries, Swedish Med. Rsch. Coun., Wallenberg Found., Sweden, Astra Rsch. Ctr., India, Diarrhoeal Disease Ctr. Program World Health Orgn., 1986-91; mem. global vaccine program WHO, 1989-99; chair sci. adv. bd. Internat. Vaccine Inst., Seoul, 1999—. Author: Cholera And Related Diarrheal Disease, 1980, Acute Enteric Infectious, 1981, Tumor Marker Antigens, 1985, Development of Vaccines and Drugs Against Diarrhea, 1986; editorships: Medical Biology 1974-86, Current Microbiology 1979-80, International Journal Diarrhoeal Diseases 1983—, Microbial Pathogenesis 1986—, Vaccine 1991—, Infection and Immunity 1992-96, Jour. Clin. Microbiology, 1998—, Jour. Health, Nutrition and Population, 2000—; contbr. over 400 articles to profl. jours.; developer of vaccines against cholera and other mucosal lining infections. Recipient Hilda and Alfred Erikssons Sci. prize Royal Swedish Acad. Sci., 1977, Anders Jahre prize II Norway, 1982, Louis Jeantet Prix de Medecine, Louis Jeantet Foundation, Geneva Switzerland, 1994, Söderberg prize Swedish Med. Assn., 1994. Achievements include development of vaccines against infections -- esp. cholera -- that attack mucosal linings, such as those in the respiratory and digestive tracts. His vaccines have immunized over 1 million people worldwide. Office: Inst Med Microbiology, Box 435, 40530 Göteborg Sweden

HOLMGREN, MYRON ROGER, social sciences educator; b. Willmar, Minn., Mar. 19, 1933; s. Alfred and Cleora Victora (Scott) H.; m. Ellen Mary Shaheen, June 9, 1957; children: Brian, Mary Jo Haas. BA, Mankato State U., 1958; MA, No. Colo. State U., 1959. Instr. Grinnell (Iowa) H.S., 1959-62, Joliet (Ill.) Jr. Coll., 1962-66; instr., fin. advisor Am. Express Fin. Advisors, Joliet, 1966-72; instr. Benedictine Coll., Atchison, Kans., 1973, Moraine Valley C.C., Palos Hills, Ill., 1974-75, Minooka (Ill.) H.S., 1974-93; dept. chmn. Minooka H.S., 1984-87, lcal dir. Xerox Award in Humanities, 1988-93, dir., coach Scholastic Bowl Team, 1976-93, chmn. philosophy & goals North Etrl. Accreditation, 1987-88. Author: Profitable Pricing Techniques, 1973; contbr. articles to profl. jours. Block chmn. March of Dimes, Am. Cancer Soc., 1989, 92-93; treas. bd. dirs. The Family Counseling Agy. of Will and Grundy Counties, 1996-99. Asian Found. grant, 1962. Mem. NEA, Ill. Edn. Assn., Ill. Assn. Econ. Tchrs., Ill. Consumer Edn. Assn., Internat. Platform Assn. Republican. Episcopalian. Avocations: reading, writing, travel, gourmet cooking, market analysis. Home: 1314 Douglas St Joliet IL 60435-5814

HOLMGREN HÄGG, ANNA MARIA, chemical engineer; b. Stenungsund, Bohuslan, Sweden, Sept. 19, 1969; d. Bo Verner and Berit (Byquist) Holmgren; m. Anders Hägg, July 31, 1999. MSc, Chalmers U. Tech., Sweden, 1993, Lic. Engring., 1997, PhD, 1998. Cons., specialist in catalysis, CFD Caran Automotive, Gothenburg, Sweden, 1998-2000; car exhaust specialist Volvo Car Corp., Torslanda, Sweden, 2000—; cons. EcoCat, Sweden, 1996-99. Mem. Cat Women Congress, Volvo Cars. Avocations: sailing, wine tasting, floor-ball, art.

HOLMGREN ÖHMAN, PEGGY MARIA, study and career counselor, educator, researcher; b. Stockholm, Apr. 4, 1946; d. Yngve Johan Fredrik and Carin Maria Wilhelmina (Lindh) H.; m. Christer Öhman, Jan. 16, 1971; children: Mattias Fredrik, Pär Niklas, Maria Therese Olivia. Diploma in Edn. and Career Counselling, Stockholm Inst. Edn., 1978; BS in Social Psychology, U. Stockholm, 1983; MS in Edn., Stockholm Inst. Edn., 1995. Chief sec. Swedish Air Force, Stockholm, 1970-74, Swedish Navy, Stockholm, 1974-78; study and career counselor, educator Huddinge-gymnasiet, Huddinge, Sweden, 1979, Solbergaskolan, Stockholm, 1979-83, Kvarnbergsskolan, Huddinge, 1983—, Sjödalsgymnasiet, Huddinge, 1996—. Mem. Internat. Assn. for Ednl. and Vocat. Guidance, Assn. of Fredrika Bremer. Home: Blacksvampsvagen 47, 141 60 Huddinge Sweden Office: Kvarnbergsskolan, Gymnasievagen 6, 141 38 Huddinge Sweden

HOLM-HADULLA, RAINER MATTHIAS, psychiatrist, psychotherapist, psychoanalyst; b. Peine, Germany, Sept. 22, 1951; s. Gottfried and Margarethe (Partusch) H.; m. Christel Fahrig, July 1, 1977; children: Moritz-Nicolas, Fédéric. MD, U. Heidelberg, 1976, Habil., 1996. Ward physician Psychiat. Clinic, Wiesloch, Germany, 1977-78; physician, lectr. Psychiat. Clinic, U. Heidelberg, 1978-86; chief Psychotherapeutic Counseling Svc., Heidelberg, 1986—; tng. therapist, supr. Psychotherapeutic Tng. Inst., Heidelberg, 1990—; assoc. prof. U. Heidelberg, 1996—; cons. coaching in pvt. practice, 1996—; vis. prof. Santiago de Chile, 1987, 89. Author: The Art of Psychotherapy, 1997, Creativity, 2000; contbr. articles to profl. jours. Avocations: classical music, opera, singing. Office: Neue Schlosstr 42, D-69117 Heidelberg Germany

HOLMQUIST, JEFFERY R., retail executive; b. Park Ridge, Ill., June 12, 1961; s. Gene Edward and Virginia Lucille H.; m. Lisa Sena, Mar. 21, 1987; children: Benjamin, Christine. BS in Accountancy, U. Ill., 1985, BS in Orgnl. Behavior, 1985. Sys. analyst Sears Roebuck and Co., Chgo., 1985—, sr. sys. programmer, 1990; sys. cons. Sears Roebuck and Co., Hoffman Estates, Ill., 1991-92, quality mgr., 1993-94, strategic initiative mgr., 1995-97, strategic initiative dir., 1997-2000, dir. volunteerism, 1998. Bd. dirs. Vol. Ctr., Barrington, Ill., 1999—. Mem. Mensa. Avocations: travel, Tae Kwon do. E-mail: jeffrholmquist@juno.com.

HOLOHAN, WILLIAM FINBARR, solicitor, arbitrator; b. Limerick, Munster, Limerick, Jan. 28, 1960; s. Gerard Laurence and Mary (Neenan) H.; m. Miriam Murphy, Jan. 2, 1995; 1 child. BCL, Nat. U. Ireland, Cork, 1980, LLB, 1982; Diploma in Internat. Law, Acad. Internat. Law, The Hague, The Netherlands, 1982. Solicitor/attorney, Ireland, 1983, trademark agt. Irish Patents Office, 1986, commr. for oaths, High Ct., 1986; chartered arbitrator, Eng.; Fellow Ctr. Internat. Legal Studies, Salzburg, Austria. Apprentice Coakley, Moloney & Flynn, Cork, 1980-83, asst. solicitor, 1983-86; jr. ptnr. Hughes & MacEvilly, Cork, 1986-89; equity ptnr. G.J. Moloney & Co., Cork and Dublin, Ireland, 1989-98; principal Bill Holohan and Assocs., 1998—; reg. european trademark practitioner, European Office for Harmonisation of the Internal Market, Alicante, Spain, 1996. Co-author: Bankruptcy Law and Practice, 1991, Leasing-Ireland, 1993; International Civil Procedures, 1995, International Rescue Of Companies, 1997; author: Limitation of Liability Under the Merchant Shipping Acts, 1893-1981, 1982; (booklet) An Overview of Franchising in Ireland, 1996. Nat. sec. Cath. Boy Scouts Ireland, 1993-99; chmn. Fedn. Irish Scout Assns., 1995, 96, Scout Found. No. Ireland, 1993-99, Scout Found. Repubic of Ireland, 1993—. Fellow Centre Internat. Legal Studies, Salzburg, Austria, 1995. Mem. Law Soc. Ireland, European Cmtys. Trade Mark Practitioners Assn., Chartered Inst. Arbitrators, Assn. Internat. de Jeunes Avocats, Irish Maritime Law Assn. (coun. mem. 1984—, sec. 1998—), Irish Franchise Assn. (legal advisor 1988—, dir. 1997), Solicitors Apprentices Debating Soc. Ireland (pres., auditor 1982, 83). E-mail: holohanb@indigo.ie. Avocations: scouting, swimming, music, reading. Office: 88 Ranelagh Rd, Dublin 6, Ireland also: Courthouse Chambers, Washington St, Cork Ireland also: 38 Sunday Well Rd, Cork Ireland

HOLONYAK, NICK, JR., electrical engineering educator; b. Zeigler, Ill., Nov. 3, 1928; s. Nick and Anna (Rosoha) H.; m. Katherine R.A. Jerger, Oct. 8, 1955. BS, U. Ill., 1950, MS, 1951, PhD (Tex. Instruments fellow), 1954; DSc (hon.), Northwestern U., 1992; DEng. (hon.), Notre Dame U., 1994. Mem. tech. staff Bell Telephone Labs., Murray Hill, N.J., 1954-55; physicist, unit mgr., mgr. advanced semiconductor lab. Gen. Electric Co., Syracuse, N.Y., 1957-63; prof. elec. engring. and materials research lab. U. Ill., Urbana, 1963—, John Bardeen chair prof. elec. & computer engring. & physics, 1993—; mem. Center Advanced Study, 1977—; series editor Prentice-Hall, Inc., 1962—; cons. Monsanto Co., 1964-89, Nat. Electronics Co., 1963-70, Skil Corp., 1967, GTE Labs. Tech. Adv. Council, 1973, Xerox, 1983-87, Ameritech, 1985-86. Author: (with others) Semiconductor Controlled Rectifiers, 1964, Physical Properties of Semiconductors, 1989. Served with U.S. Army, 1955-57. Recipient Cordiner award GE, 1962, John Scott medal City of Phila., 1975, GaAs Conf. award with Welker medal 1976, Monie A. Ferst award Sigma Xi, 1988, Nat. Medal Sci. NSF, 1990, NAS award Indsl. Application Sci., 1993, ASEE Centennial medal, 1993, 50th Ann. award Am. Elec. Assn., 1993, Japan Prize, 1995. Fellow IEEE (life, Morris Liebmann award 1973, Jack A. Morton award 1981, Edison medal 1989, Third Millennium medal), Am. Acad. Arts and Scis., Am. Phys. Soc., Am. Optical Soc. (Charles H. Townes award 1992), Internat. Engring. Consortium; mem. AAAS, NAE, NAS (Indsl Application of Sci. award 1993), Electrochem. Soc. (Solid State Sci. and Tech. award 1983), Math. Assn. Am., Ioffe Inst. (hon. 1992), Minerals, Metals and Materials Soc. (John Bardeen award 1995), Russian Acad. Scis. (fgn. mem.), Eta Kappa Nu (Karapetoff Eminent Mems. award 1994, eminent mem. 1998), Tau Beta Pi (Outstanding Alumnus award 1999). Home: 2212 Fletcher St Urbana IL 61801-6915 Office: U Ill Dept Elec/Computer Engring 1406 W Green St Urbana IL 61801-2918

HOLOVKO, MYROSLAV, physicist, educator; b. Chernijv, Ukraine, Oct. 29, 1943; s. Fedir and Anastasija Holovko; m. Natalija Havryliv, June 1, 1974; 1 child, Kateryna. BSc, Pedagogical Inst., Ivano-Frankivsk, Ukraine, 1965; PhD, U. Lviv, Ukraine, 1970; DSc, Inst. for Theoretical Physics, Kyiv, 1980. Cert. tchr. Sci. rschr. dept. statis. physics Inst. for Theoretical Physics, Lviv, 1969-80, head. dept. for theory of solutions, 1980-90; head. dept. for theory of solutions Inst. for Condensed Matter Physics, Lviv, 1990—; prof. dept. theoretical physics Lviv State U., 1991—; vis. scientist U. Regensburg, Germany, 1997, 98, 99, Instituto de Quimica de UNAM, Mex., 1996, U. P. et M. Curie, Paris, Max-Planck Inst. Chemie, Mainz, Germany, U., Utah, Salt Lake City. Author: (with I.R. Yukhnovskii) The Statistical Theory of Classical Equilibrium Systems, 1980; mem. editl. bd. Ukrainian Jour. Physics, 1988-94, Condensed Matter Physics, 1992—; contbr. chpt. to book, more than 150 articles to profl. jours. ISF grantee, 1994-96; INTAS-Ukraine grantee, 1998-99. Mem. Sci. Coun. of Electrochemistry and Corrosion of Russian Acad., Ukrainian Phys. Soc. (coordination coun. 1990—, cochmn. Sci. Coun. liquid state Ukrainian Acad.).

HOLOWACZ, ERIC VAUGHN, non-profit executive director; b. Princeton, N.J., May 23, 1968; s. Edward Franklin and Linda (Michaels) H. BA in Art History and English Lit., U. S.C., 1990. Clk. Fed. Res. Bank of Richmond, Columbia, S.C., 1987-89; project coord. S.C. Arts Commn., Columbia, 1990-92; ops. mgr. Spoleto Festival U.S.A., Charleston, S.C., 1993-95; exec. dir. Arts Coun. Beaufort (S.C.) County, 1996—; vice chmn. S.C. Presenters Network, Rock Hill; devel. chmn., bd. mem. S.C. Artisans Ctr., Walterboro, S.C. Editor: South Carolina Writers Directory, 1990-92; contbr. articles to profl. jours.; writer, host (weekly TV news segment) WJWJ-TV Art News, 1997—. Vol. Joe Riley for Gov., Charleston, 1994; officer Mazyck-Wraggboro Neighborhood Assn., Charleston, 1994-95; panel moderator S.C. Book Festival, Columbia, 1997; county bd. mem. Hist. Preservation Rev. Bd., Beaufort County, S.C., 1997—. Mem. Society of Friends. Avocations: writing, sailing, painting, music. Home: PO Box 2575 Beaufort SC 29901-2575 Office: Arts Coun Beaufort County PO Box 482 Beaufort SC 29901-0482

HOLOWINSKY, IVAN ZENOVE, psychologist, educator; b. Zarvanytsia, Ukraine, Apr. 25, 1927; came to U.S., 1949; s. Wasyl and Maria H.; m. Natalie Petrowsky, Nov. 22, 1952; children: Yuri, Mary. B of Philosophy, Salzburg (Austria) U., 1948; MEd in Psychology, Temple U., 1954, EdD in Ednl. Psychology, 1961. Diplomate Am. Bd. Psychology. Sch. psychologist Camden (N.J.) Bd. Edn., 1954-59; clin. psychologist The Vineland (N.J.) Tng. Sch., 1959-66; asst. prof. psychology Rutgers U., New Brunswick, N.J., 1966-70, assoc. prof., 1970-74, prof., 1974—, assoc. dean Grad. Sch. Edn., 1990-96; mem. adv. bd. Ency. of Spl. Edn., 1985-87; mem. N.J. Spl. Edn. Study Commn., 1982-85; mem. N.J. Adv. Commn. Handicapped, 1981-87. Author: Psychology of Exceptional Children, 1983; co-editor: Teacher Education in Industrialized Nations, 1995. Mem. exec. bd. Ukrainian Congress Com. U.S., 1990—. With U.S. Army, 1950-52, Korea. Fulbright scholar, 1995. Fellow APA, Am. Acad. Sch. Psychology. Office: Rutgers U Dept Ednl Psychology New Brunswick NJ 08901

HOLSGROVE, GARETH JOHN, consultant; b. London, U.K., Jan. 27, 1946; s. Howard Ernest and Margaret Adelaide (Gadau) H.; m. Linda Susan Barnes, Aug. 19, 1970; children: Claire Louise Ann, Gareth Paul Rhys. B in Edn., Sussex U., Brighton, U.K., 1969; MSc, Salford U., Salford, U.K., 1979; PhD, U. E. Anglia, Norwich, U.K., 1987. Cert. tcrh., tchr. deaf, paediatric audiologist. Tchr. partial-hearing unit Co. Avon, Bath, U.K., 1975-76; ednl. audiologist Thomasson Sch., Bolton, U.K., 1976-79; sr. adv. tchr. Hertfordshire Co. Coun., Hertford, U.K., 1979-90; dir. med. edn. St. Bartholomew's Med. Sch., London, 1990-96; cons. Cambridge Med. Edn. Cons., St. Neots, 1998—; academic dean Coll. Osteopaths, London, 1998-2000; ednl. cons. Royal Coll. Gen. Practitioners, London, 1991-95, Aga Khan U., Karachi, Pakistan, 1997—, Coll. Physicians and Surgeons Pakistan, 1999—; cons. med. edn. Australian Govt., Canberra, 1995-96; nat. facilitator curriculum change, Nat. Health Svc. Exec., Leeds, U.K., 1993-96. Contbr. Author: (books) Teaching Medicine in General Practice, 1997, The Certification and Recertification of Doctors, 1994. Mem. Rotary Internat., 1989—. Recipient 1st prize Nat. Film & Video Competition, Round Table, U.K., 1986; certificate Ednl. Merit, British Med. Assn., 1992, 94. Avocations: cooking, photography, travel, music. Home: 95 St Neots Rd, Saint Neots PE19 7AL, U.K.

HOLSHEK, CHRISTOPHER JOHN, civil-military relations consultant; b. Cornwall, N.Y., Nov. 4, 1960; s. John G. and Audrey M. Holshek. AA in Liberal Arts and Mil. Sci., N.Mex. Mil. Inst., 1980; BA in Internat. Affairs with honors, George Washington U., 1982, BA in German Lang., Lit. and History, 1983; MA in Internat. Rels. with distinction, Boston U., 1990. Author: East Asia and the Pacific: The Military and Strategic Balance, 1982; contbr. articles to profl. jours. With USNG, 1980-84, USAR, 1984—. Recipient UN medal, 1996. Mem. Am. Inst. Contemporary German Studies, Am. Coun. on Germany, Civil Affairs Assn. (life), Res. Officers Assn./ Interallied Confedn. Res. Officers, UN Assn. of U.S.A. (mem. spkr.'s bur. 1998—), Phi Theta Kappa. Address: 1704 Rosewood Ct Highland Mills NY 10930-5221

HOLSTEIN, PER EVALD, surgeon; b. Copenhagen, July 14, 1939; s. Evald Theodor Olsen ne Lise H.; m. Lene Ilsoe Hansen, June 7, 1965; children: Peter, Lea, Adam, Julie. MD, U. Copenhagen, 1985. Chief vascular surgeon Bispebjerg Hosp., Copenhagen, 1985-95; chief vascular surgeon Rigs Hosp., U. Copenhagen, 1996, chief surgeon, wound healing ctr., 1996—; cons. in field; cons. surgeon Steno Diabetes Ctr., Copenhagen, 1980—. Contbr. articles to profl. jours. Fellow Internat. Soc. Prosthetics and Orthotics (pres. Denmark chpt. 1993-96); mem. European Soc. Vascular Surgery, Danish Soc. Vascular Surgeons (pres. 1991-93). Avocation: classical art. Home: Osterbrogade 54A, DK-2100 Copenhagen Denmark Office: U Hosp Rigs Hosp, Bispebjerg Hosp DP S, DK-2400 Copenhagen NV, Denmark

HOLSTEIN, VAGN, oil and gas consultant; b. Aarhus, Denmark, June 22, 1949; s. Viggo and Annelise (Lerbaek) H.; m. Ingelise Johansen, Apr. 10, 1982; children: Jakob Viggo, Anne-Kathrine. M of Engring., Danish Tech. U., Lyngby, 1975; postgrad., Heriot Watt U., Edinburgh, Scotland, 1979-80. Sr. field engr. Schlumberger, 1975-79; petroleum engr. Burmah Oil, Swindon, Eng., 1980-84; reservoir engr. Maersk Oil & Gas, Copenhagen, 1984-88; sr. petroleum engr. DANOP, Horsholm, Denmark, 1988-94; sr. cons. Holstein Cons., Holte, Denmark, 1994—. Mem. Soc. Profl. Well Log Analysts, Soc. Petroleum Engrs., Ferrari Club Denmark. Avocations: tennis, golf, sailing, vintage cars, model railroads. Home and office: Skovmindevei 14, DK 2840 Holte Denmark

HOLST-JENSEN, OLE, engineer, consultant; b. Svenborg, Denmark, Jan. 12, 1949; s. Erik and Else (Toft-Nielsen) H.-J.; m. Anni Vestergaard Buhl Mikkelsen; children: Nikolaj, Anders, Louise. MSc, Tech. U. Denmark, 1974; grad., U. Toronto, 1977. R&D engr. Danfoss, Nordborg, 1977-83; cons. Jydsk Teknologisk, Aarhus, Denmark, 1983-86; R&D train noise Ascan Scandia A/S, Randers, Denmark, 1986-89; mgr. dep. environ. Abrahamsen & Nielsen A/S, Aarhus, Denmark, 1989-93; gen. mgr. Odegaard & Danneskiold-Samsoe, Samsoe, Jylland, Arhus, Denmark, 1993-99; dep. mgr. Ingemansson Tech., Aarhus, 1999—; working group mem. ISO/ TC43/SC1/WG-34, 1988-99; convener working group ISO/TC43/SCI/ WG41, 1993-99; lectr. in field. Author: Noise Reduction in Metal Working Industry, 1999; contbr. articles to profl. jours. Bd. leader Youth Club, Beder, Denmark, 1997-98. Mem. Acoustic Soc. Am., Inst. Noise Control Engring., Danish Acoustic Soc. Avocations: classic cars, hydrofoil ships, kayak rowing, skiing. Home: Stokrosevej 29, DK 8330 Beder Denmark

HOLT, MAVIS MURIAL, parents group executive; b. Sturgis, S.D., Apr. 30, 1932; d. Walter Raleigh and Mabel Henrietta (Krauser) Egnew; m. Howard Ray, Dec. 7, 1951; children: David Ray, Roberta Grace, Timothy Mark, Elizabeth Linda. Cert. in counseling, family issues, Multnomah Sch. of Bible, Portland, Oreg.; cert. youth at risk program, Portland State Coll.; student, North Portland Bible Coll., Long Ridge Writers Group, 1993—, Stratford Career Inst., 1999—. Mgr. The Press, Portland, 1970-71; with McDonald's Corp., Portland, 1970s; exec. dir., founder PAPYAC-Peers and Parents, Inc., Portland, 1991-97. Chairperson Neighbor Watch, Portland; block home chmn., Portland; neighborhood treas., vice chair Mill Park Neighborhood Assn., Portland, land use chair, 1993-98; vice chairperson adv. bd. David Douglas H.S., Portland; activist Neighborhood Involvement, Mill Park, City of Portland, 1985—; mem. Mid County Caring Cmty., David Douglas H.S., 1998; worker various polit. campaigns, 1995-98. Named Neighbor of Yr., Mid County Memo, Portland, 1994, Citizen of Month, 1997; recipient Neighborhood Plan award Mill Park Neighborhood Assn., 1995; grantee Mill Park Nature Scape, 1997. Avocations: gardening, hiking, walking, local park development. Home and Office: 1235 SE 115th Ave Portland OR 97216-3567

HOLT, MICHAEL KENNETH, management and finance educator, consultant, city councilman; b. Jackson, Tenn., Apr. 13, 1961; s. Kenneth Harvey and Dorothy (Price) H.; m. Carol Lynn Walls, Aug. 13, 1983; children: Mitchell Harris, Marleigh Allison. BS, Union U., 1983; MS, La. State U., 1985; PhD, U. Memphis, 2000. CPM. Broker First Nat. Bank of Commerce, New Orleans, 1985-86; mgr. Invest at Jackson (Tenn.) Nat. Bank, 1986-87; stock broker Merrill Lynch, Jackson, Tenn., 1987-89; prof. Union U., Jackson, Tenn., 1989—; chmn. bd. Leaders Credit Union, Jackson, Tenn.; dir. Ctr. Bus. and Econ. Devel., 1999—; cons. Best Home Ctr., Jackson, Tenn., 1994-97, mem. regional planning commn., 1996—; cons. Quaker Oats, Jackson, 1991, Memphis Cablevision, Memphis, 1990; nominee bd. dirs. Fed. Res. Bank St Louis, 1997. Editor: Jour. Industry and Commerce, 1993-94, Update, 1990—; contbr. articles to profl. jours. City councilman Jackson, Tenn., 1999—. Recipient Instrnl. Innovation award Union U., 1995. Office: Union U 1050 Union University Dr Jackson TN 38305-3697

HOLT, PHILETUS HAVENS, III, architect; b. Summit, N.J., Aug. 19, 1928; s. Robert Sherman and Alice Kathleen (Gallwey) H.; m. Nancy deFreest Brownley, June 16, 1950; children—Alexandra Foster, Robert Stephen. A.B. with honors, Princeton U., 1950, M.F.A., 1952. Registered architect, N.J., N.Y., Conn., Mass., Maine, Vt., Pa., Md., Calif.; lic. profl. planner, N.J. Designer W.F.R. Ballard, Architect, N.Y.C., 1952-55; designer, assoc. C.K. Agle, Architect, Princeton, N.J., 1955-65; ptnr. Holt & Morgan, Princeton, 1965-72; prin. Holt Morgan Russell Architects, P.A., Princeton, 1972—; v.p. Architects Housing Co., Trenton, N.J., 1976-90; mem. State Rev. Bd. for Historic Sites, N.J., 1983—, vice chmn., 1989-97, chmn. 1997—; guest lectr. U. Pa., Phila., 1972—. Architect Douglass & Cook Colls. (hon. mention Am. Inst. Steel Constrn. 1979), 1977, Batsto Visitors Ctr., 1982, (restoration and preservation) Drumthwacket Gardens, 1983; illustrator book: Gardens of Illusion (Alice Davis Hitchcock award 1982), 1982. Trustee, Arts Council of Princeton, 1970-82, pres., 1972; mem. Mayor's Adv. Com. for Downtown, Princeton, 1971-72. Recipient Design awards N.J. Soc. Architects/AIA, 1970, 71, 73, 75, N.J. Hist. Preservation award, 1995. Mem. AIA (medal 1952), Hist. Soc. of Princeton (former trustee, pres. 1980-82), Soc. Archtl. Historians. Club: Corinthians (N.Y.C.). Home: 3472 Lawrenceville Rd Princeton NJ 08540-4718 Office: Holt Morgan Russell Architects 350 Alexander St Princeton NJ 08540-7106

HOLT, SIDNEY JOSEPH, marine biologist, environmental consultant; b. London, Feb. 28, 1926; s. Sidney and Ethel Maud (Fryatt) H.; children: Timothy Sidney, Nicholas William, David George. BSc with 1st class honours, U. Reading, Eng., 1947, DSc, 1958. Naturalist Ministry of Agr., Fisheries and Food, Lowestoft, Eng., 1947-50; scientist Nature Conservancy, Edinburgh, Scotland, 1950-53; various staff positions including dir. fisheries resources FAO of UN, Rome, 1953-70, 74-80; sec. Internat. Oceanographic Commn. UNESCO, Paris, 1970-72; founder, exec. dir. Internat. Ocean Inst., Malta, 1972-74; spl. asst. to asst. dir. gen. for fisheries FAO of UN, 1975-78; prof. environ. studies U. Calif., Santa Cruz, 1978-80; sr. Overseas fellow St. John's Coll., Cambridge (Eng.) U., 1980-81; prof. internat. ocean affairs U. Malta, 1972-74; sr. advisor on Mediterranean marine affairs UN, 1972-74; cons. Internat. Fund for Animal Welfare, Yarmouth, Mass., 1980—; cons. to UNEP, World Conservation Union, Worldwide Fund for Nature, Greenpeace, Italian, French, Seychelles, Chilean, others. Contbr. over 200 articles to profl. jours. Sr. advisor Marine Stewardship Coun. Recipient Gold medal World Wildlife Fund 1979, Golden Ark, Royal Ct. of Netherlands, 1980, Planet Earth award Internat. Fund for Animal Welfare, 1995; named Global 500 Laureate, UN Environ. Programme, 1990. Mem. Internat. League for the Protection of Cetaceans (founder, CEO 1981—), Ind. World Commn. Oceans (Soares commn.). Avocation: welfare of wild and domestic animals, sustainable living. Home and Office: Hornbeam House, 4 Upper House Farm Crickhowell, Powys NP8 1BP, Wales

HOLT, WILLIAM HENRY, physicist, researcher; b. San Antonio, Aug. 5, 1939; s. Joseph Marion and Mildred Louise (Ragsdale) H.; m. Margaret Ann Harrell, June 21, 1963; children: Benjamin, Andrew. BS cum laude, St. Mary's U., San Antonio, 1960; MA, U. Tex., 1962, PhD, 1967. Postdoctoral fellow, lectr. U. Man., Winnipeg, Can., 1966-69; rsch. physicist Naval Surface Warfare Ctr., Dahlgren, Va., 1969—. Patentee; contbr. articles and papers to numerous sci. jours. and revs. Past tchr. Sunday sch. St. Matthias United Meth. Ch., Fredericksburg, Va.; past co-chmn. edn., past lay leader, past mem. pastor-parish rels. com., past chmn. coun. on ministries. Mem. Am. Phys. Soc., Can. Assn. Physicists, Materials Rsch. Soc., Sigma Xi, Sigma Pi Sigma, Lions. Office: Naval Surface Warfare Ctr Dahlgren VA 22448-5000

HOLTAPPELS, PETER, chemist, research scientist; b. Bonn, Germany, Apr. 1, 1966; s. Wilhelm and Margarete (Becker) H.; m. Regina Pieger, June 4, 1993; children: Timo, Ronja. Chem. Diplomate, U. Bonn, 1993, D of Natural Sci., 1997; postgrad., Risø Nat. Lab., Roskilde, Denmark, 1997-2000. Staff scientist Tech. U. Munich, 2000—. Contbr. articles to profl. jours. Mem. Internat. Soc. for Solid State Ionics, German Chem. Soc.

HOLTEDAHL, KNUT ARNE, medical educator; b. Bergen, Norway, Mar. 13, 1944. Prof. gen. medicine U. Tromso, Norway. Achievements include research in clinical medicine, clinical epidemiology, clinical skills. Office: U Tromsø, Inst Cmty Medicine, 9037 Tromsø Norway

HOLTER, KNUT, religious studies educator; b. Drobak, Norway, Oct. 12, 1958; s. Finn and Ingrid (Jensen) H.; m. Berly Gilje, June 28, 1980; children: Anne, Kjersti, Morten. MTheol, Sch. of Mission and Theology, Stavanger, Norway, 1985; ThD, U. Oslo, 1993. Ordained minister Ch. of Norway, 1986. Army chaplain Norwegian Army, Norway, 1986-87; rsch. fellow Sch. of Mission and Theology, Stavanger, 1987-93, assoc. prof., 1993—. Author: Second Isaiah's Idol-Fabrication Passages, 1995, Tropical Africa and the Old Testament, 1996, Yahweh in Africa: Essays on Africa and the Old Testament, 2000; editor: Bulletin for Old Testament Studies in Africa, 1996—; contbr. articles to profl. jours. Lt. Norwegian Army, 1984-94. Office: Sch Mission/Theology, Misjonsvegen 34, N-4024 Stavanger Norway

HÖLTERMANN, WALTER, anesthesiologist; b. Damme, Germany, Feb. 27, 1952; s. Hans and Edith (Adelmeyer) H.; m. Anna Elisabeth Krieg, Oct. 10, 1980; children: Annelen, Friederike, Clara. Dipl.Ing., U. Osnabrück, Germany, 1972; MD, U. Marburg, Germany, 1981. Resident in pathology U. Dusseldorf, 1980-82; resident in anesthesiology St. Marien Hosp., Hagen, Germany, 1982-85; cons. anesthesiologist U. Marburg, 1985-98; med. supr. St. Bonifatius Hosp., Lingen, Germany, 1998—; chmn. Konvent of the U. Marburg, 1992-98, mem. senate, 1991-92. Contbr. articles to profl. jours. Vice pres. Korporationsring, Marburg, 1985-98. Co-recipient Edens prize Heinlich-Heine U., 1981. Mem. European Soc. Anaesthesiology, European Soc. Intensive Care Medicine. Mem. Free Democracy Part of Germany. Roman Catholic. Avocations: gardening, history of 19th and 20th century in Europe. Home: Birkhuhnstr 2, D-49808 Lingen Germany Office: St Bonifatius Hosp, Postfach 2040, D-49803 Lingen Emsland, Germany

HOLTHOUSE, DAVID JOHN, surgeon, reseacher; b. Adelaide, Australia, Feb. 23, 1970; s. Ian and Shirley (Daniels) H.; m. Anthea Marie Fitzgerald, Feb. 20, 1993; 1 child, Pholin. B Med Sci., U. Western Australia, Perth, 1991, MB BS with honors, 1994; Diploma of Child Health, PMH, Perth, 1999. Intern SCGN, Perth, 1995; resident MO SCGN/PMH, Perth, 1996-97; gen. surg. registrar RPH, SCGH, Perth, 1998—; gen. practitioner Dogswamp Med. Ctr., Perth, 1996—; mem. Hepatitis C Coun. Western Australia, 1998—, Tropical Medicine Group, Perth, 1994—; clin. rschr. SCGN PMH, Perth, 1997—. Contbr. articles to profl. jours. Mem. RACS, AAGP, AMA, N.Y. Acad. Scis., Young Liberals Assn. (treas. 1988). Avocations: astronomy, Egyptology, valve radio restoration, old books, restoration vintage vehicles. Home and Office: 39 Doney St, Alfred Cove 6154, Australia

HOLTHUIS, LIPKE BIJDELEY, curator; b. Probolinggo, Indonesia, Apr. 21, 1921; s. Bernard Jan and Neeltje (bij de Ley) H. PhD, Nat. U., Leiden, The Netherlands, 1946; PhD (hon.), U. Trondheim, Norway, 1972. Asst. curator Nat. Mus. Natural History, Leiden, 1941-47, curator, 1947-59, sr. curator, 1959-86, emeritus curator, 1986—; mem. Internat. Commn. Zool. Nomenclature, 1953-96, v.p., 1964-77, acting pres., 1965-72, sec. gen., 1977-89. Contbr. over 500 articles to profl. jours. Recipient Spl. Recognition award U.S. Nat. Mus. Natural History, 1986; named Officer Order of Orange-Nassau, Queen of the Netherlands, 1986. Mem. Zool. Soc. London (corr. mem. 1951—), Carcinologica Soc. Japan (hon.), Sociedade Brasileira de Carcinologia (hon.), Soc. Bibliography Natural History (hon.). Avocations: history of biology, bibliophyly. Home: Schouwenhove 180, 2332 DT Leiden The Netherlands Office: Nat Mus Natural History, Darwinweg 2 PO Box 9517, 2300 RA Leiden The Netherlands

HOLTMANN, EVERHARD, political science educator; b. Kamen, Germany, June 11, 1946. MA, Bochúm U., 1971, PhD, 1975; PhD Habilitation, Erlanger U., 1986. From asst. to prof. Erlanger U., 1974-92; prof. Martin Luther U., Halle, 1992—. Editor: Politik-Lexikon, 3d edit., 2000; co-editor: Handbúch Politisches System der Búndersrepublic Deutschland, 1999. Mem. German Assn. Polit. Sci. Office: Martin Lúther Univ, Postfach, D-06099 Halle Germany

HOLTON, J(ERRY) THOMAS, concrete company executive; b. Middletown, Ohio, June 7, 1932; s. Joseph Walton and Elizabeth (Fagaly) H.; m. Annie Lou Dearborn, Sept. 26, 1958; children: Elizabeth, Luanne, Ruth, Catherine, J. Thomas Jr. BSE, Princeton U., 1954; MBA, Harvard U., 1959. V.p. Sherman Concrete Pipe Co., Birmingham, Ala., 1959-66, pres., 1966-74; pres. Sherman Industries, Birmingham, 1974-84; pres., chmn. Sherman Internat. Corp., Birmingham, 1984—; bd. dirs. Fed. Res. Bank Atlanta, Robin-Morton Corp., KSA, Inc., Sciotoville, Ohio, The Shaw Group Ltd., Halifax, N.S., Stockham Valve & Fittings Co. Inc. Pres. coun. U. Ala. Birmingham, 1984-92; mem. exec. bd. Boy Scouts Am., Birmingham, 1985—; chmn., Salvation Army, Birmingham; elder Briarwood Presbyn. Ch., Birmingham, 1968—. Lt. comdr. Civil Engring. Corp. USN, 1954-57. Mem. Birmingham Country Club, Shoal Creek, The Club, Summit Club. Home: 10 Ridge Dr Birmingham AL 35213-3632 Office: Sherman International Inc 402 Office Park Dr Ste 100 Birmingham AL 35223-2435

HOLTON, SAMUEL MELANCHTHON, education educator emeritus, consultant; b. Durham, N.C., May 29, 1922; s. Holland and Lela Daisy (Young) H.; m. B. Margaret Umberger, June 21, 1952; children: Robert Wilson, Margaret Dwyer, Grace Holland, Elizabeth Brooke. AB magna cum laude, Duke U., 1942, MEd, 1947; BS, NYU, 1943; MA, Yale U., 1947, PhD, 1948. Prin. Bartlet Yancey High Sch., Yanceyville, N.C., 1953-55; instr. U. N.C., Chapel Hill, 1948-49, asst. prof., 1949-53, assoc. prof., 1953-58, prof. edn., 1958-87, prof. emeritus, 1987—; chmn. Com. on Preparation Secondary Tchrs., N.C., 1960-63. Author: Understanding the American Public High School, 1969; co-author: Readings in American Education, 1963; editor The High Sch. Jour., Chapel Hill, 1950-53, 55-64; mem. editorial bd. N.C. Tchr. Edn., 1986-92; cons. editor Encyclopedia of World Biography, 1987—; editor Secondary Education Encyclopedia Americana. 1996; contbr. numerous articles to scholarly and profl. jours. Mem. Chapel Hill-Carrboro Sch. Bd., 1969-75, Charter Commn. Town of Chapel Hill, 1974-75; bd. dirs. Goodwill East Cen. N.C., 1978—; trustee N.C. Wesleyan Coll. 1986—, chmn. com. on edn. Capt. USAAF, 1942-46, CBI. Recipient Silver Beaver award Boy Scouts Am., 1960. Fellow Philosophy of Edn. Soc.; mem. South Atlantic Philosophy of Edn. Soc. (bd. dirs.), N.C. Assn. Colls. of Tchr. Edn. (bd. dirs. 1980-95), Ret. Faculty Assn. U. N.C. Chapel Hill (pres. 1991-93), Kiwanis (bd. dirs. Chapel Hill Club 1956-58, 91-93), Phi Beta Kappa, Omega Delta Kappa. Democrat. Methodist. Avocations: scouting, gardening, property mgmt., bridge, family geneology. Home: 411 Holly Ln Chapel Hill NC 27514-3020

HOLTROP, JAN FOKKE, petroleum engineering educator, consultant; b. Sungei Gerong, Sumatra, Indonesia, Oct. 4, 1935; arrived in The Netherlands, 1939; s. Fokke Jan Holtrop and Mathilde Van Dijk; m. Josepha Anthonia Hulsing, Apr. 6, 1959 (div.); children: Marijke, Sefke Jan, Paul, Tjeerd; m. Dirkje Cornelia De Jong, Jan. 5, 1983. MSc cum laude, Tech. U., Delft, The Netherlands, 1958, PhD cum laude, 1962. Lt. cavalry The Netherlands, 1962-65; petroleum engr. Brunei Shell, 1965-67, ops. mgr., 1978-80; petroleum engr. Shell Pakistan, Bangladesh, 1967-68; mining mgr. Shell Delfstoffen, The Netherlands, 1968-73; exptl. mgr. Shell Coal, Indonesia, 1974; ops. mgr. Sarawak Shell, East Malaysia, 1975-78; with Shell Ctrl. Office, The Netherlands, 1980-86, rsch. mgr. well tech., 1986-90; prof. petroleum engring. Tech. U., Delft, 1982-85, prof. prodn. tech., 1990-99; pres. Horizontal Ventures Inc., Tulsa, Okla., 1996. Bd. dirs. Petro Union, Evansville, Ind., 1997, Greka Energy Corp., Santa Maria, Calif., 1999. Mem. Soc. Petroleum Engrs. Avocation: biology.

HOLTUG, NILS, philosophy and ethics educator; b. Copenhagen, Aug. 19, 1964; s. Benth and Inge Holtug. MA, U. Copenhagen, 1990, PhD, 1995. Rsch. fellow U. Copenhagen, 1992-97, prof., 1997—; cons. Danish Coun. of Ethics, Copenhagen, also advisor. Contbr. chpts. to books, articles to profl. jours. Grantee Danish Rsch. Acad., 1993, Danish Rsch. Couns., 1992-95, 96-97. Mem. Ethics Rsch. Group, Internat. Assn. Bioethics. Home: Krugersgade 1 4tv, Copenhagen DK-2200N, Denmark Office: U Copenhagen Dept Philosoph, Njalsgade 80, Copenhagen DK-2300S, Denmark

HOLTZ, E. M. CATARINA, judge; b. Lund, Sweden, July 20, 1942; d. N. Lage and Greta I. M. (Johansson) Billing; m. Arne K. Holtz, Feb. 12, 1936; children: Agneta, Aina, Elisabeth. Student, U. Oreg., 1961-62; English degree, U. Uppsala, Sweden, 1963, LLM, 1970; postgrad., Rutgers U., 1979-81, Somerset County Coll., 1979-81. Asst. prosecutor Uppsala, 1970; asst. judge Dist. Ct., Sala, Sweden, 1970-72; asst. judge Srea Ct. of Appeal, Stockholm, 1972-73, asst. justice, 1973-75; judge Dist. Ct. Uppsala, 1975-83; assoc. justice Svea Ct. of Appeal, 1983—, permanent justice, 1989; legal adviser Ministry of Justice, Sweden, 1983-89; judge Bds. of Appeal, European Patent Office, Munich, Germany, 1989—. Contr. articles to profl. jours.

HOLTZ, GILBERT JOSEPH, steel company executive; b. N.Y.C., Jan. 23, 1924; s. Al S. and Carrie (Schindler) H.; m. Carla Kahn, July 18, 1848; children: Steven J., Robert A. Student, NYU, 1940-42. V.p. Hanger Svc. Co., Yonkers, N.Y., 1946-48; owner Economy Sales Co., Yonkers, 1948-50; v.p. Belvedere Space Saving Products, Inc., 1951-72; pres. Walnut Metal Industries, Inc., Yonkers, 1955-72, Belvedere Home Products Inc. (formerly 411 Walnut St. Corp.), 1962—, Holtz Realty Corp., 1962—, Walnut Assn. Inc., 1961—, Belvedere Internat. Ltd., 1970—. Patentee in field. Ward leader 2d Ward Republican County Com., Yonkers. Served with AUS, 1943-46. Decorated Bronze Star; recipient Conspicuous Svc. Cross, N.Y. State. Mem. Rotary. Home: 182 Tibbetts Rd Yonkers NY 10705-2646 Office: 937 Saw Mill River Rd Yonkers NY 10710-3230

HOLTZ, JOHN WILLIAM, property management executive; b. Fremont, Nebr., Nov. 16, 1950; s. John Lee and Lavon Darlene Holtz. BA, U. Denver, 1973; MBA, U. Colo., 1985. Gen. mgr. Paralegal Assocs., Denver, 1976-82; claims investigation mgr. City and County of Denver, 1982-89; mgmt. cons. Veri-Fax, Littleton, Colo., 1989-91; mgr. fin. svcs. U. Denver, 1991-94; regional mgr. 1st Am. Real Estate Info. Svcs., Denver, 1994-98, Affordable Residential Cmtys., Denver, 1998—.

HOLTZ, LAURENCE, artisan, photographer; b. Spangler, Pa., Jan. 9, 1949; s. Paul Omer and Helen Zita (McCombie) H.; m. Priscilla Suzanne Adsit, May 17, 1981; 1 child, Samara Adsit. BA, LaSalle Coll., Phila., 1974. Hand weaver Hardwick, Vt., 1987—. Contbr. short story and poetry to Coldspot, 1998. Mem. Ctrl. Vt. Regional Planning Commn., Montpelier, 1982, Plainfield (Vt.) Planning Commn., 1982; vol. Vt. Dept. Corrections Northeast Regional Correctional Facility, St. Johnsbury, 1998—; mem. Reparative Probation Bd., Barre Office, 1998—. Mem. New England Antiquities Rsch. Assocs., Vt. Weaver's Guild, Hardwick Area Writer's Group. Zen Buddhist. Avocations: instrumental music, creative writing. Office: PO Box 51 Hardwick VT 05843-0051

HOLTZMAN, ARNOLD HAROLD, chemical company executive; b. Phila., May 11, 1932; s. William and Rae (Shapiro) H.; m. Phyllis Raskow, June 26, 1955; children: Rosalind Ann, Linda Susan, William Lewis. BS, Drexel Inst., 1954; MS, Lehigh U., 1956, PhD, 1957. Asst. metallurgist J. Bishop & Co., Malvern, Pa., 1954; with duPont Co., various locations, 1957-89; rsch. mgr., dist. sales mgr. polymer intermediates dept. duPont Co., Wilmington, Del., 1973-76; mgr. new bus. programs, ctrl. R&D dept. duPont Co., Wilmington, 1976-78, mgr. health products, 1980-81, dir. devel. divsn. ctrl. R&D dept., 1982-89, cons., 1989—; pres. Action Games, Inc., 1988; rsch. assoc. Elwyn, Inc, 1997—; bd. dirs. Perceptive Sys. Inc. Bd. dirs. Alzheimer's Assn. (Del. chpt.), 1992-97, pres., 1992-95, Foxfire Printing Inc. Recipient John Price Wetherill medal Franklin Inst., 1969. Fellow Am. Soc. Metals; mem. Sigma Xi. Achievements include patentee in processing of metals and non metals. Home and Office: 208 Stonecrop Rd Wilmington DE 19810-1320

HOLTZMAN, JOAN KING, musician, composer; b. Aberdeen, S.D., Aug. 14, 1925; d. James Wilfred and Miriam Hughes (Evans) K.; m. Wayne Harold Holtzman, Aug. 23, 1947; children: Wayne Jr., James, Scott, Karl. B in Music Edn., Northwestern U., 1947; EdMA, Stanford U., 1948. Pres. Jojo's Prodns., Austin, Tex., 1991—. Author: (with Leslie Holtzman) The Fat Rat and This and That, 1997, (with Rosario Ahumada de Diaz) Happy Times with English, 1987; composer, pianist, singer children's cassettes Jo Jo's Songs for Growing Up, 1991, Beasts, Veggies and Sospetigious Things, 1993; composer melodies song book and cassette Symphony for Simple Simon, 1984 (award of excellence Am. Symphony Orch. League, 1984); composer numerous songs. Active Save Children Fedn., 1954—, pres. 1958; vol. Austin Cerebral Palsy Ctr., 1955-59; mem. Pan Am. Round Table, 1958—, sec. 1965-66; co-founder Internat. Hospitality Com. Austin, 1960—, chmn. host families, 1960-62; pres. PTA Austin H.S., 1972; mem. Austin Arts Commn., 1977-83; mem. nat. adv. coun. Nat. Sch. Vol. Program, Washington, 1976-91; mem. adv. com. Austin Ind. Sch. Dist., 1983-91, forming future com., 1982; mem. arts plan task force City of Austin, 1985; docent, gov. mansion, 1983—; nat. class rep. Northwestern U. Sch. Music, 1977-91; mus. vol. Austin State Hosp., 1967-83; sec. bd. dirs. Austin Symphony Orch. Soc., 1968—; state bd. dirs. Very Special Arts - Tex., 1987-91; bd. dirs, chmn. coms. Child and Family Svcs., Austin, 1965-82. Named Outstanding Fundraiser Austin Symphony Devel. fund drive, 1981; Festival Favorite New Tex. Choral Music Festival, Austin, 1995, Yellow Rose Tex., Tex. Gov., 1995, Vol. of Yr., 1995. Mem. Women's Symphony League Austin (pres. 1958-59, charter mem., Woman of Yr. award 1991), Austin Jr. League (Vol. Extraordinaire award 1985), Mortar Bd. U. Tex. Austin (Citation award 1976), Playhouse Singers, Settlement Club, Austin Woman's Club, Univ. Ladies Club (pres. 1971-72), Sigma Alpha Iota (charter mem., pres. 1972-73, Rose of Honor award 1976). Office: Jojo's Prodns 3300 Foothill Dr Austin TX 78731-5823

HOLTZMAN, WAYNE HAROLD, psychologist, educator; b. Chgo., Jan. 16, 1923; s. Harold Hoover and Lillian (Manny) H.; m. Joan King, Aug. 23, 1947; children: Wayne Harold, James K., Scott E., Karl H. BS, Northwestern U., 1944, MS, 1947; PhD, Stanford U., 1950; LHD (hon.), Southwestern U., 1980. Asst. prof. psychology U. Tex., Austin, 1949-53, assoc. prof., 1953-59, prof., 1959—, dean Coll. Edn., 1964-70, Hogg prof. psychology and edn., 1964—; assoc. dir. Hogg Found. Mental Health, 1955-64, pres., 1970-93, spl. counsel, 1993—; dir. Social Sci. Rsch. Coun., 1957-63, Centro de Investigationes Sociales, Mex., 1960-70; cons. USAF, also mem. sci. adv. bd., 1969-71; mem. com. basic rsch. com. NRC, 1968-71; mem. behavioral sci. study sect. USPHS, 1957-59, mem. mental health study sect., 1960, chmn. personality and cognition rsch. rev. com., 1968-72; mem. rsch. adv. panel Soc. Security Adminstrn., 1961-62; mem. L.Am. adv. bd. IBM, 1985-89; dir. WHO Collaborating Ctr. in Mental Health for Tex. and Mex., 1993—. Author: (with B.M. Moore) Tomorrow's Parents, 1964, Computer Assisted Instruction Testing and Guidance, 1971, (with R. Diaz-Guerrero and J. Swartz) Personality Development in Two Cultures, 1975, Introduction to Psychology, 1978; (with K.A. Heller and S. Messick) Placing Children in Special Education, 1982, (with T. Bornemann) Mental Health of Immigrants and Refugees, 1990, School of the Future, 1992, Holtzman Inkblot Technique Research Guide, 1999, (with M.R. Rozenweig, Michel Sabourin and David Belauger) History of the International Union of Psychological Science, 2000; editor: Jour. Ednl. Psychology, 1966-72. Trustee Ednl.

Testing Service, Princeton, 1972-74, 77-80, 83-86, J.W. and Cornelia Scarborough Found., 1977-82, Ctr. for Applied Linguistics, 1978-80, Salado Inst. Humanities, 1980-85, Population Inst., 1979-85, Menninger Found., 1982—, Population Resource Ctr., 1980—, chmn. bd. dirs.; dir. Sci. Rsch. Assocs., 1975-88; pres., bd. dirs. S.W. Ednl. Devel. Lab., 1974-75; mem. adv. com. computing activities NSF, 1970-73; mem. computer sci. and engring. bd. NAS, 1971-73, chmn. panel on selection and placement of mentally retarded students, 1979-82; chmn. interdisciplinary cluster on social and behavioral devel. Pres.'s Biomed. Research Panel, 1975-76; bd. dirs. Found.'s Fund for Rsch. in Psychiatry, 1973-77, chmn., 1976-77; dir. Conf. of S.W. Found., 1976-84, pres., 1978-79; mem. nat. adv. mental health coun. Alcohol, Drug Abuse, and Mental Health Adminstrn., 1978-81; mem. acad. info. sys. adv. coun. IBM, 1982-85; chmn. bd. dirs. The Menninger Clinic, 1993-97, The Learning Initiative, 1995—. Lt. (j.g.) USNR, 1944-46. Faculty Research fellow Social Sci. Research Council, 1953-54; Faculty Research fellow Center Advanced Study Behavioral Scis., 1962-63. Fellow APA, AAAS; mem. Tex. Psychol. Assn. (pres. 1957), S.W. Psychol. Assn. (pres. 1958), Am. Statis. Assn., InterAm. Soc. Psychology (pres. 1966-67), Am. Ednl. Rsch. Assn., Internat. Union Psychol. Scis. (sec.-gen. 1972-84, pres. 1984-88, exec. com. 1972-92), Philos. Soc. Tex. (pres. 1982-83), Sigma Xi. Methodist. Home: 3300 Foothill Dr Austin TX 78731-5823

HOLTZMANN, HOWARD MARSHALL, lawyer, judge; b. N.Y.C., Dec. 10, 1921; s. Jacob L. And Lillian (Plotz) H.; m. Anne Fisher, Jan. 14, 1945 (dec. Aug. 1967); children: Susan Holtzmann Richardson, Betsey; m. Carol Ebenstein Van Berg, Dec. 23, 1972. AB, Yale Coll., 1942, JD, 1947; LittD (hon.), St. Bonaventure U., 1952; LLD (hon.), Jewish Theol. Sem., N.Y.C., 1990. Bar: N.Y. 1947. Atty. Colorado Fuel & Iron Corp., Buffalo, N.Y., 1947-49; ptnr. Holtzmann, Wise & Shepard, N.Y.C., 1949-95; judge Iran-U.S. Claims Tribunal, The Hague, Netherlands, 1981-94; arbitrator and dispute resolution cons., 1994—; arbitrator Claims Resolution Tribunal for Dormant Accounts, Zurich, Switzerland, 1998—; U.S. del. UN Commn. on Internat. Trade Law, 1975—, Hague Conf. on Pvt. Internat. Law, 1985; advisor U.S.A. Arbitration agreements with USSR, Russian Fedn., China, Hungary, Bulgaria, Czechoslovakia, Poland and German Dem. Republic. Author, editor: A New Look at Legal Aspects of Doing Business with China, 1979; co-author: A Guide to the Unicitral Model Law on International Commercial Arbitration—Legislative History and Commentary, 1988 (cert. of merit Am. Soc. Internat. Law 1991); contbr. chpts. to books and articles to law jours. Mem. governing coun. Downstate Med. Sch. SUNY, Bklyn., 1961-78; trustee St. Bonaventure U., Olean, N.Y., 1968-90, trustee emeritus, 1990—; chmn. bd. Jewish Theol. Sem., N.Y.C., 1983-85, hon. chmn., 1985—; trustee Inst. Internat. Law, Pace U. Sch. Law, 1992—. Mem. ABA (chmn. com. code ethics comml. arbitrators 1973-77), Internat. Council for Comml. Arbitration (hon. vice chmn., chmn.), Am. Arbitration Assn. (hon. chmn., adv. bd. Stockholm arbitration Inst., Gotshal Internat. Arbitration award 1980), Internat. C. of C. (vice chmn. arbitration commn. 1979—), Am. Bar Found., N.Y. County Lawyers Assn., Internat. Law Assn., Am. Fgn. Law Assn. (v.p. 1995—), Internat. Bar Assn., N.Y. State Bar Assn., Assn. of Bar of City of N.Y., Am. Soc. Internat. Law (cert. merit 1991), Soc. Profls. in Dispute Resolution, Indsl. Rels. Rsch. Assn., N.Y. Law Inst., Am. Judicature Soc., Am. Assn. for Internat. Commn. of Jurists.

HOLUB, JAN HUBERT, radioactive waste company executive; b. Blatna, Czech Republic, Nov. 3, 1936; s. Jan Radr and Marie (Ziegelhainova) Holubova; m. Hedvika Sterova, Dec. 30, 1967; children: Jan, Petr. MSc, Tech. U., Brno, Czech Republic, 1959; PhD, Tech. U., Praha, Czech Republic, 1970; diploma, Econ. U., Praha, 1987, Charles U., Praha, 1988. Divsn. head Inst. for Rsch., Prodn. and Application of Radioisotopes, Praha, 1959-71; subject specialist Internat. Atomic Energy Agy., Vienna, Austria, 1971-76; secretariat head Czechoslovak Commn. for Atomic Energy, Praha, 1977-84; dept.head Inst. for Nuclear Info., Praha, 1984-86; divsn. dep. dir. NYCOM, Praha, 1986-96; sci. specialist cons. nuclear wastes and trasp. materials ARAO, Praha, 1997-99; cons. Radioactive Waste Agy., 1998—; cons. Uranium Industry, Ostrov, 1987-90; asst. prof. Tech. U., Plzen, 1987-88; cons. IAEA, Vienna, 1991-95, expert, 1987-95. Co-author Inis Atomindex, 1971-76; inventor in field. Recipient grants IAEA, Vienna, 1991-95, hon. diplomas CSKAE, Praha, 1980, UVVVR, Praha, 1979. Mem. Ecol. Soc., Sci.-Tech. Soc. (medal 1980), Med. Soc. Roman Catholic. Avocations: chess, tennis, history. Home: Na Trebesine 68, CZ-10000 Prague 10, Czech Republic

HOLUB, KAREL, seismologist, researcher; b. Prague, Czech Republic, Nov. 9, 1933; s. Karel and Anna (Dubská) H.; m. Marie Dupáková, Apr. 24, 1954 (div. 1982); children: Karel, Michal, Marek; m. Olga Cabová, Aug. 18, 1984; 1 child, Kateřina. Diploma in applied geophysics, Charles U., Prague, 1959, Dr.rer.nat., 1982, PhD, 1991. Rsch. technician Geophys. Inst. Czechoslovak Acad. Scis., Prague, 1953-59, rschr., 1960-78; project leader Rsch. Mining Inst., Ostrava, Czech Republic, 1979-93; prin. rschr. Inst. Geonics Acad. Scis., Ostrava, 1994—; cons. Tech. U., Ostrava, 1994. Patentee in field. Recipient Award Czechoslovak Acad. Scis., 1963; grantee Grant Agy. Czech Republic, 1996-97, 98-2000. Mem. Czech Soc. for Mechanics, Czech Assn. Applied Geophysicists, N.Y. Acad. Scis. Roman Catholic. Avocations: philatelist, travel. Home: Zelená 47, CZ 70200 Ostrava 1, Czech Republic Office: Inst Geonics Acad Scis, Studentská 1768, CZ 70800 Ostrava Poruba, Czech Republic

HOLUBAR, KARL H., medical educator, physician; b. Vienna, Austria, June 3, 1936; s. Gottlieb and Therese (Kugler) H.; m. Christine Bodenstein, Nov. 24, 1960; children: Karl, Leopold. MD, U. Vienna, 1960. Assoc. prof. U. Vienna, 1970-77, prof. dermatology, 1977-83, assoc. prof. history of medicine, 1986-89, prof., chmn. history of medicine dept., 1989—; prof., chmn. dermatology dept. Hebrew U., Jerusalem, 1983-86. Author: Challenge Dermatology, 1993, Sun and Skin, 1994, Medical Technology and Doctors' Speech, 1997. Recipient Hoechst award, 1969, May Ritter award, 1975, Unilever award, 1979. Fellow Royal Coll. Physicians; mem. Academia Galileiana di Scienze Lettere ed Arti, European Soc. Dermatology (pres. 1999), European Soc. History of Dermatology and Venerology (pres.). Avocations: linguistics, cycling, calligraphy, poetry. Office: U Vienna Inst History of Medicine, Wahringerstrasse 25, A-1090 Vienna Austria

HOLUBARSH, CHRISTIAN J.F., cardiologist; b. Torgau, Germany, Aug. 22, 1949; s. Johannes and Margarete (Korsinek) H.; m. Monika Welhäuser, May 14, 1976; children: Cornelia, Markus, Raphael, Janek. Approbation, Univ. Tübingen, 1975, MD, 1975. Diplomate Am. Bd. Internal Medicine, Diplomate Cardiology. Asst. doctor in pathology Univ. Ulm, Germany, 1975-77; asst. doctor in physiology Univ. Tübingen, 1978-83; asst. doctor in internal medicine Univ. Freiburg, Germany, 1983-90; prof. internal medicine, 1993-2000; venia legendi in physiology Univ. Tübingen, 1981, venia legendi in internal medicine Univ. Freiburg, 1989. Editor: Cardiac Energetics, 1987, Inotropic Stimulation and Myocardial Energetics, 1989, Molecular and Functional Alterations of the Failing Human Myocardium, 1992; contbr. over 100 articles to profl. jours. Recipient Fraenkel award of Germany Soc., 1988, Young Investigators award Internat. Soc. Cardiovascular Pharmacology, 1987. Avocation: sports. Home: Starenweg 1, 79211 Denzlingen Germany Office: Medizinische University, Hugstetterstr 55, 79106 Freiburg Germany

HOŁUBOWICZ, TADEUSZ, horticulture educator, researcher; b. Czabarówka, Poland (now Ukraine), Apr. 4, 1929; s. Jan and Julia (Podgóreczna) H.; m. Janina Rupinska, Feb. 14, 1952; children: Roman, Witold. MSc in Horticulture, Agrl. U. Poznan, Poland, 1954, PhD in Horticulture, 1963, asst. prof. in horticulture, 1970, full prof. horticulture, 1976. Dir. Inst. Hort. Prodn. Agrl. U. Poznan, 1970-78, dean faculty horticulture, 1972-81, head pomology dept, 1978-97, univ. tchr., 1953-99. Author: (textbook) Pomology, 1993, 2d edit., 1999; co-author: Physiology of Fruit Trees, 1979, 2d edit., 1984, Soil Management and Fertilization of Horticultural Plants, 1983, 3d edit., 1997; contbr. over 100 articles to sci. publs. Recipient Golden Cross of Merit, Pres. Poland, 1973, Cross of Liberty, 1977, Hon. Distinction City of Poznan, 1979. Mem. Internat. Soc. Horticultural Sci. (chmn. working group 1976-91), Polish Soc. Horticultural Soc. (v.p. 1988-92), Com. Horticultural Sci. (v.p. 1986-96). Avocations: gardening, bridge, travel. Home: Husarska 4 m 7, 60-331 Poznan Poland Office: Agrl Univ PoznaN, Dabrowskiego 159, 60-594 Poznan Poland

HOLWELL, PETER, management consultant; b. Mar. 28, 1936; s. Frank and Helen (Howe) H.; m. Jean Patricia Ashman, 1959; 1 son, 1 dau. BSc in Econ., London Sch. Econs. Articled clk. Arthur Andersen & Co., 1958-61, mgmt. cons., 1961-64; head univ. computing O & M unit U. London, 1967-77, sec. for acctg. & adminstrv. computing, 1977-82; clk. of the ct., 1982-85; prin. U. London, 1985-97, dir. sch. exams coun., 1988-97; mgmt. cons. Prince of Wales' Inst. Architecture, 1998-99, Chatham Hist. Dockyard Trust, 1999—; mem. U. London Exams and Assessments Coun., 1991-96. Mem. Samuel Courtauld Adv. Bd., 1985-98; non-exec. mem. N.E. Thames Regional Health Authority, 1990-94; chmn. City of East London Family Health Svcs. Authority, 1994-96; chmn. St. Marks Rsch. Found. and Ednl. Trust, 1995-2000; vice chmn. coun. Wye Coll., U. London, 1995-2000, mem. coun. Sch. Pharmacy, 1996—, Edexcel Found. Coun., 1996-97. ACA Ltd. (dir.), 1998—. Office: Hookers Green, Bishopsbourne, Canterbury Kent CT4 5JB, England

HOLY, JIRI, literature educator; b. Novy Jicin, Moravia, Czech Republic, Apr. 28, 1953; s. Karel and Vera (Hubenakova) H.; m. Lida Anna Petrikova, July 9, 1982; children: Anna, Magdalena, Katerina. PhD, Charles U., Prague, Czech Republic, 1977; postgrad., Inst. for Czech Lit., Prague, 1982-85. Editor Cesky Spisovatel, Prague, 1978-82; sci. worker Inst. for Czech Lit., Prague, 1985-93, head theory dept., 1993-96; lectr. Czech lit. U. Saarbrucken, Germany, 1993-94; asst. in Czech lit. U. Regensburg, Germany, 1994-95; docent in Czech lit. Charles U., 1994—; guest prof. in Slavic lit., Humboldt U., Berlin, 1999-2000. Author: Prace a Basnivost, 1990, Ceska Literatura 1910-1945, 1991, Nova Ceska Epika, 1995, Ceska Literatura Od Roku 1945 Do Soucasnosti, 1996; co-author, editor: Cesky Parnas. Literatura 1970-1990, 1993, Ceska Lit. Od Pocasku K Dnesku, 1998; mem. editorial bd. Kriticky Sbornik, 1990—, Balagan, 1994—, Literarni Noviny, 1996-99. Mem. Czech Fraternal Hussite Ch. Avocation: sports. Home: Renoirova 13, 152 00 Prague Czech Republic

HOLZ, DIETMAR ALEXANDER, materials engineer, process development engineer; b. Hamburg, Germany, Nov. 2, 1962; s. Karl Robert and Eva Brigitte (Fieltz) H.;p m. Annette Schomberg, May 18, 1990; children: Maximilian, Jannik, Frederik, Lennart. Diploma in Engring., Tech. U. Hamburg, 1990, PhD, 1994. Cert. auditor. Asst. Tech. U. Hamburg, 1990-95; devel. engr. Philips Bus. Group Advanced Ceramics and Modules, Hamburg, 1995-2000. Author: Characterization of Reaction-bonded Al2O3 ceramics, 1994. Obergefreiter German Navy, 1981-83. Avocations: material science, family, sports. Home: Schulstrasse 11a, 24640 Schmalfeld Germany Office: Ferroxcube Deutschland GmbH, Essener Strasse 4, 22419 Hamburg Germany

HOLZ, DIETRICH ADOLF, materials scientist; b. Görlitz, Germany, Apr. 12, 1931; s. Adolf and Johanna Frieda (Gerber) H.; m. Hannelore Glass, Dec. 12, 1963; children: Holz, Kristina. Diploma in forestry, Tech. U., Dresden, Germany, 1953, D in Forestry, 1959, DSc in Tech., 1972. Scientific asst. Tech. U., Dresden, 1953-58; scientist Staatliches Holzkontor, Berlin, 1958-60; scientist Inst. for Musikinstrumentenbau, Zwota, 1960-76, leading scientist in material rsch. musical instruments, 1976-96; lectr. Westsächsische Hochschule Zwickau, 1988—; cons. in field. Contbr. articles to profl. jours. Mem. Deutsche Physikalische Gesellschaft, Deutsche Ges. für Holzforschung, German Soc. of Mycology. Lutheran. Avocations: mycology, environmental protection in forestry, playing piano. Home: Schulstrasse 4, 08258 Markneukirchen Germany

HOLZ, GEORGE G., IV, research scientist, medicine educator; b. Santa Monica, Calif., May 8, 1953; s. George G. and Mignon M. (Kiproff) H. BS, Cornell U., 1975; PhD, U. Ill., 1984. Rsch. fellow Tufts U. Med. Sch., Boston, 1984-89; rsch. assoc. Howard Hughes Med. Inst., Boston, 1990-93; instr. medicine Mass. Gen. Hosp.-Harvard Med. Sch., Boston, 1990-93, asst. prof. medicine, 1994-98; assoc. prof. physiology and neurosci. NYU Med. Sch., N.Y.C., 1998—. Corp. mem. Marine Biol. Lab., Woods Hole, Mass. Recipient Rsch. award Am. Diabetes Assn., 1996, 2000; N.Y. State Regents scholar Cornell U., 1971-75; rsch. grantee NIH. Mem. AAAS, Soc. for Neurosci., Endocrine Soc., Soc. Gen. Physiologists, Am. Diabetes Assn. Home: PO Box 288 West Falmouth MA 02574-0288

HOLZ, HANS HEINZ, philosophy educator; b. Frankfurt, Germany, Feb. 26, 1927; s. Friedrich and Martha Dorothea Berta (Kreiss) H.; m. Brigitte Klara Scheben (div. 1959); m. Silvia Elisabeth Markun, Apr. 20, 1979. Dr phil, U. Leipzig, 1969. Freelance journalist Frankfurt, 1945-56, Zurich, Switzerland, 1960-70; mem. editorial staff Deutsche Woche, Munich, 1957-59; chief dept. Abendstudio Hessischer Rundfunk, Frankfurt, 1962-64; prof. philosophy U. Marburg, Fed. Republic Germany, 1971-79, U. Groningen, The Netherlands, 1979-97; prof. emeritus U. Groningen, 1997—; founder, pres. Found. Ctr. for Philos. Studies, Sant' Abbondio. Author numerous books including Philosophische Theorie der bildenden Künste, vol. 3, 1996, Problemgeschichte der Dialektik, vol. 3, 1997; editor: Selected Works of Leibniz, 1959-65; co-editor: Studien zur Dialektik, 33 vols., 1978-89, Dialektik, 24 vols., 1980-92, Topos, 1993—; contbr. articles to profl. jours. Recipient medal of honor Verein Deutscher Ingenieure, 1986. Mem. Internat. Assn. for Dialectical Philosophy (pres. 1981-88, hon. pres. 1992—), Internat. Assn. for Legal and Social Philosophy (sec. 1951-54), Leibniz-Sozietaet Berlin. Home: PO Box 76, CH-6577 S Abbondio Switzerland Office: U Groningen Faculty Philosophy, A-Weg 30, NL 9718 Groningen CW, The Netherlands

HOLZAPFEL, WILFRIED BERND, physics educator; b. Magdeburg, Germany, Feb. 17, 1938; s. Adolf and Elisabeth (Scheibe) H.; m. Waltraud Boehringer; children: Bernd, Anne. Diploma in physics, Tech. U., Karlsruhe, 1963, PhD, 1966. Rsch. assoc. Tech. U., Karlsruhe, 1966-67; rsch. asst. U. Ill., Urbana, 1967-69, Tech. U., Munich, 1969-71; head high pressure lab. MPI, Stuttgart, 1971-78; prof. exptl. physics U. Paderborn, 1978—; chmn. European High Pressure Rsch. Group, Europe, 1979-81; mem., chmn. bd. dirs. HASYLAB, Hamburg, 1991. Editor: High Pressure Science and Technology, 1990; co-editor, co-author: High Pressure Techniques in Chemistry and Physics, 1997; co-editor Jour. Superhard Materials; contbr. more than 200 articles to profl. jours. including Phys. Rev. B.

HOLZAPFEL, WOLFGANG, physicist, industrial researcher; b. Seeon, Bavaria, Germany, May 8, 1960; s. Karl Maria and Waltraud (Baumgartner) H. Physics diploma, Tech. U., Munich, 1986, PhD, 1989. Indsl. rschr. Dr. Johannes Heidenhain GmbH, Traunreut, Germany, 1989-95, mgr. fundamental rsch., 1995—. Office: Dr Johannes Heidenhain GmbH, Dr J Heidenhain Strasse 5, D-83301 Traunreut Bavaria, Germany

HOLZER, PETER, pharmacologist; b. Vorau, Austria, Feb. 26, 1951; s. Peter and Maria (Wetzelberger) H.; m. Ulrike Petsche, Oct. 8, 1983; children: Veronika, Judith. MS, U. Graz, 1976, PhD, 1978. Postdoctoral fellow U. Cambridge, U.K., 1980; vis. scientist UCLA, 1989; from assoc. prof. to prof. U. Graz, 1990-93; from univ. asst. to univ. docent U. Graz, Austria, 1977-85; from univ. docent to assoc. prof. U. Graz, 1985-90. Editor: Calcitonin Gene-Related Peptide, 1992, Neurogenic Inflammation, 1996, Problems of Gastrointestinal Tract in Anesthesia, 1999; contbr. more than 200 articles to profl. publs. Recipient rsch. prize Austrian Soc. Pathology, 1990, C.A. Ewald prize German Soc. Gastroenterology, 1988, prize Sandoz Found., Vienna, Austria, 1988. Mem. European Neuropeptide Club (chmn. 1994), Austrian Neurosci. Assn. (sec. 1993), Br. Pharmacol. Soc., Internat. Union Pharmacology (sec. gastrointestinal pharmacology sect. 1994), Am. Gastroenterological Assn., German Soc. Pharmacology and Toxicology, Austrian Neuroscience Assn. (vice-chmn. 2000). Avocations: foresting, mushrooms, classical music, history. Office: Dept Exptl Clin Pharmacol, U Graz Universitatsplatz 4, A-8010 Graz Austria

HOLZER, RICHARD, architect, educator, consultant; b. Vienna, Austria, 1923; s. Steve and Nora (Turcsan) H.; m. Leticia L. Pallete, Feb. 9, 1958; 1 child, Lynn T. BA in Arch., U. Panama, 1951; MA in Arch., U. Calif., Berkeley, 1957. Registered architect, Panama, Tex., Va. Ptnr. Schay & Holzer, Panama, 1957-70; pres. Holzer, Narbona, Bond, Panama, 1971-89, Holzer & Narbona, Panama, 1990—, R. Holzer Archtl. Cons., Inc., Panama, 1991—; prof. design and archtl. theory U. Panama, 1965-79. Mem. AIA, Panama Soc. Engrs. and Architects (bd. dirs.), Instituto P. De Arquitectura and Urbanisho (founding pres. 1996), Rotary (pres. 1985-86). Home: Apdo 833-0019, Calle 50 # 120, Panama City Panama

HOLZER, WERNER, editor; b. Zweibruecken, Palatinate, Germany, Oct. 21, 1926; s. Robert and Barbara H.; m. Monika Aschke, 1962; children: Katharina, Philip. Editor Frankfurter Rundschau, Germany, 1973-92. Author: Das nackte Antlitz Afrikas, 1961; 26mal Afrika, 1967; Vietnam oder die Freiheit zu sterben, 1968; Bei den Erben Ho Tschi Minhs, 1971; 20mal Europa, 1972, Was Kostet Die Welt Europe and the U.S., 1998. Decorated commendatore Italian Order Merit, Grand Cross Order of Merit, Fed. Republic Germany; recipient European prize Cortina Ulisse, 1962, Theodor-Wolff prize, 1964, Nat. Journalism award, 1968. Mem. PEN. Home: 20 Am Zollstock, Bad Homburg, Hesse Federal Republic Germany

HOLZINGER, ANDREAS, cell biologist, researcher; b. Zell Am See, Salzburg, Austria, Aug. 1, 1969; s. Karl Preining and Rosemarie H.; m. Ingrid Hocheneder, Oct. 3, 1992; 1 child, Julia. MA, U. Salzburg, Austria, 1992, PhD, 1995. Rsch. asst. Univ. Salzburg, 1995—. Office: Salzburg Univ, Hellbrunnerstr 34, A 5020 Salzburg Austria

HOLZKAN, SILVIA JORGELINA, accountant; b. Buenos Aires, Oct. 7, 1948; d. Samuel Holzkan and Berta Barenstein; m. Joaquin Abramowitz, Feb. 1, 1969; children: Damian, Lara. Grad., Harvard U., 1990, 97, Stanford U., 1994. Cost and budget analysis Ford Co., Argentina, 1969-70; advisor Tire Co., Argentina, 1970-79; advisor pvt. company Argentina, 1979-84, advisor family cos., 1984-89; adminstrv. mgr. Clinica Bessone, Argentina, 1988-97; gen. mgr. Clinica Bessone, 1997—. Avocation: stained glass. Office: Clinica Bessone, Pauneero 1648, 1663 San Miguel de Tucuman Argentina

HOLZMAN, FRANKLYN DUNN, economics educator; b. Bklyn., Dec. 31, 1918; s. Abraham and Mollie (Mandel) H.; m. Mathilda Sara Wiesman, Dec. 14, 1946; children—Thomas Ludwig, David Carl, Miriam Alexandra. B.A., U. N.C., 1940; M.A., Harvard, 1948, Ph.D., 1952. Economist Dept. Treasury, 1947-48, cons., 1949-52; research fellow Russian Research Center, Harvard, 1949-52, research asso., 1961—; prof. econs. U. Wash., 1952-61; prof. econs. Tufts U., mem. faculty Fletcher Sch. Law and Diplomacy, 1961-92; vis. prof. UCLA, 1956, Stanford U., 1957, Columbia U., 1961, MIT, 1963; cons. U.S. Dept. Treasury, 1950, 51, UN, 1963-64, 89, ACDA, 1964-73, Joint Econ. Com., U.S. Congress, 1959, 73, 81, U.S. Commn. on Trade and Investment Policy, 1971, U.S. Dept. Commerce, 1972, 75-78, Stockholm Internat. Peace Rsch. Inst., 1978, Brookings Instn., 1978; Am. co-dir. Joint U.S.-Hungarian Ann. Econ. Confs. and Rsch. Effort, 1973-86. Author: Soviet Taxation: The Fiscal and Monetary Problems of a Planned Economy, 1955, Foreign Trade under Central Planning, 1974, Financial Checks on Soviet Defense Expenditures, 1975, International Trade Under Communism-Politics and Economics, 1976, Soviet Economy: Past, Present and Future, 1982, Economics of Soviet Bloc Trade and Finance, 1987; contbr. 125 articles to scholarly jours. Served to staff sgt. USAAF, 1942-45. Co-winner Furth Internat. Ruble Convertibility competition, 1990; honored by publ. Econ. Adjustment and Reform in Ea. Europe and the Soviet Union: Essays in Honor of Franklyn D. Holzman, edited by Josef C. Brada, Ed A. Hewett and Thomas Wolf, 1988. Mem. Am. Econ. Assn. (chmn. com. on US-USSR Confs., 1985-87), Am. Assn. Advancement of Slavic Studies (exec. com. 1964-65), Am. Assn. Study of Soviet-Type Economies (exec. com. 1966-67), Econometric Soc., Assn. for Comparative Econ. Studies (pres. 1976-77). Home: 33 Peacock Farm Rd Lexington MA 02421-6341

HOLZMAN, PHILIP SEIDMAN, psychologist, educator; b. N.Y.C., May 2, 1922; s. Barnet and Natalie (Seidman) H.; m. Hannah Abarbanell, Sept. 18, 1946; children: Natalie Kay, Carl David, Paul Benjamin. BA, CCNY, 1943; PhD, U. Kans., 1952. Diplomate: Am. Bd. Examiners Profl. Psychology. Psychology intern Topeka VA Hosp., 1946-49; psychologist Topeka State Hosp., 1949-51, cons., 1951-58; psychologist Menninger Found., Topeka, 1949-68; dir. research tng. Menninger Found., 1963-68; prof. psychiatry and psychology U. Chgo., 1968-77; prof. psychology dept. psychology Harvard U., 1977-92; prof. dept. psychiatry Med. Sch., 1977-92; Esther and Sidney R. Rabb prof. psychology Harvard U., 1984-92, prof. emeritus, 1992; chief Lab. of Psychology McLean Hosp., Belmont, Mass., 1977—; tng. and supervising psychoanalyst Boston Psychoanalytic Soc. and Inst., 1977—; vis. prof. U. Minn., 1965, U. Kans., 1966, Boston U., 1973, Jefferson Med. Coll., 1981, U. Pa., 1987; Thomas William Salmon lectr. N.Y. Acad. Medicine, 1994; mem. small grants com. NIMH, 1960-64, clin. projects research rev. com., 1964-68, clin. program projects research rev. com., 1970-74, treatment devel. and assessment rev. com., 1982-86; cons. Ill. State Psychiat. Inst., 1970-77; mem. adv. coms. classification of mental disorders WHO. Author: (with others) Cognitive Control, 1959, Psychoanalysis and Psychopathology, 1970, (with Karl Menninger) The Theory of Psychoanalytic Technique, rev. edit, 1973; editor: (with Merton M. Gill) Psychology Versus Metapsychology, 1975, (with Mary Hollis Johnston) Assessing Schizophrenic Thinking, 1979; bd. editors: Psychol. Issues, 1968—, Contemporary Psychology, 1969-76, Bull. of Menninger Clinic, 1961—, also Psychoanalysis and Contemporary Thought, Jour. Psychiat. Rsch., 1980-92; assoc. editor Schizophrenia Bulletin, Schizophrenia Rsch., Harvard Review of Psychiatry, Harvard Mental Health Letter; contbr. articles to profl. jours. Mem. Topeka Mayor's Com. on Human Rels., 1963-68; chmn. bd. dirs. Founds.' Fund for Rsch. in Psychiatry; mem. program adv. com. MacArthur Found., sci. adv. bd. NIMH, 1986-92; bd. trustees Menninger Found., 1978—; mem. sci. coun. Nat. Alliance Rsch. Schizophrenia and Depression, 1989—. With AUS, 1943-46. Recipient Career Scientist award NIMH, 1974-77, 92—; Stanley Dean award Am. Coll. Psychiatrists, 1984, Lieber prize Nat. Alliance for Rsch. in Schizophrenia and Depression, 1988, Joseph Zubin award Soc. Rsch. in Psychopathology, 1994; Townsend Harris medal CCNY, Gold medal for lifetime achievement APA, 1997, William K. Warren award Internat. Congress on Schizophrenia Rsch., 1997. Fellow APA, AAAS, Am. Acad. Arts and Scis., Am. Coll. Neuropsychopharmacology, Soc. Neurosci.; mem. Am. Psychoanalytic Assn., Boston Psychoanalytic Soc., Am. Psychopath. Assn., Inst. Medicine of NAS, Soc. for Rsch. in Psychopathology (pres. 1997-98). E-mail: psh@wjh.harvard.edu. Office: Harvard U William James Hall Cambridge MA 02138 also: McLean Hosp Lab Belmont MA 02178

HOLZNER, BURKART, sociologist, educator; b. Tilsit, Germany, Apr. 28, 1931; came to U.S., 1957, naturalized, 1965; s. Hans Otto and Brigitte (Prenzel) H.; children by previous marriage: Steven, Daniel, Claire; m. Leslie Salmon-Cox; stepchildren: Sara Ruth Salmon-Cox, Weir Becket Strange. Student, U. Munich, 1949-52, 53-54, U. Wis., 1952-53; postgrad., U. Wis., 1957-59; Diplom Psychologe, U. Bonn, 1957, Dr.Phil., 1958. Grad. asst., acting instr. U. Wis., 1958-60; asst. prof. U. Pitts., 1960-63, assoc. prof., 1963-65, prof., chmn. sociology dept., 1966-80, dir. bd. visitors field staff Learning Research and Devel. Center, 1964-66, 71-78, dir. Univ. Ctr. for Internat. Studies, 1980-2000, prof. Univ. Ctr. for Internat. Studies, 1998—, disting. svc. prof. internat. studies, 1999—, also sr. rsch. assoc.; assoc. sociologist, assoc. dir. Social Sci. Rsch. Inst., U. Hawaii, 1965-66; vis. prof. sociology, dir. Social Rsch. Centre, Chinese U. of Hong Kong, 1969-70, external examiner in sociology, 1995-98; vis. prof. U. Augsburg, 1977, Chinese Acad. Social Scis., Beijing, 1979, 80; cons. Nat. Inst. Edn., Westinghouse Electric Corp.; mem. exec. com. Pa. Coun. for Internat. Edn., 1980-89, chmn., 1980-83, 88-89. Author: Amerikanische und deutsche Psychologie, 1958, Völkerpsychologie, 1960, Reality Construction in Society, rev. edit, 1972, (with John Marx) Knowledge Application: The Knowledge System in Society, 1979; editor: (with Roland Robertson) Identity and Authority, Explorations in the Theory of Society, 1980, (with Jiri Nehnevajsa) Organizing for Social Research, 1981, (with Zdenek Suda) Directions of Change: Modernization Theory, Research and Reality, 1981, (with Andrew Dinniman) Education for International Competence in Pennsylvania, 1988; co-editor Knowledge: Creation, Diffusion, Utilization, 1985, Knowledge in Society, 1987-89. Mem. dist. export council U.S. Dept. Commerce. Recipient Philip R.A. May award for internat. svc., 1991; named hon. citizen of Johnstown, Pa., hon. mem. U. Augsburg, 1990. Mem. Am. Sociol. Assn., North Central Sociol. Assn., Pa. Sociol. Assn., Sociol. Rsch. Assn., Sozialwissenschaftlicher Studienkreis für Internationale Probleme, Internat. Soc. for Comparative Study of Civilizations (mem. U.S. coun., v.p. 1977-79), Assn. Internat. Edn. Adminstrs. (exec. com. 1986—, pres. 1990-91, Charles Klasek award for career achievement in internat. edn. 2000), World Federalist Assn. Pitts. (pres. 1996—). Home: 1700 Grandview Ave Apt 801 Pittsburgh PA 15211-1006 Office: U Pitts Dept Sociology U Ctr Internat Studies 2N26 Posvar Hall Pittsburgh PA 15260

HOLZNER, JOHANN, educator; b. Innsbruck, Austria, Sept. 16, 1948; s. Karl and Luise (Stolz) H.; m. Gisela Rieder, Aug. 27, 1971; children: Birgit, Julia. D, U. Innsbruck, 1972. Lectr. U. Innsbruck (Austria), 1971-79, 80—, U. Wroclaw (Poland), 1980, U. Salzburg (Austria), 1987, U. Calif., Santa Barbara, 1994, 96. Author: Franz Kranewitter, 1985; editor: Innsbrucker Beitraege zur Kulturwissenschaft, Die Bibel im Verstaendnis der Gegenwartsliteratur, 1988, Aesthetik der Geschichte, 1995, Literatur in Suedtirol, 1997, Literatur der Inneren Emigration aus Oesterreich, 1998. Chmn. Theodor Kramer Gesellschaft, Wien, 1994-96; mem. exec. bd. Oesterreichische Gesellschaft Germanistik, Wien, 1994-95; chmn. Literarisches Forum, Wien, 1985-97. Mem. Internat. Vereinigung Germanische Sprach and Literaturwissenschaft, Gesellschaft Exilforschung. Roman Catholic. Home: Hoehenstrasse 133, A-6020 Innsbruck Austria Office: U Innsbruck, Innrain 52, A-6020 Innsbruck Austria

HOLZNER, JOHANN HEINRICH, pathologist, educator; b. Bregenz, Austria, Dec. 3, 1924; s. Hans Georg and Franziska (Lenz) H.; m. Elfriede Schweighofer, Aug. 30, 1953; children: Michael, Ursula. MD, U. Med. Sch., Vienna, 1951, Univ. dozent, 1966, prof. pathology, 1969. Resident dept. pathology U. Vienna, 1951-58, asst. prof., 1959-63, head labs. dept. gynecol. pathology, 1963-69, chmn., dir. dept. pathology, 1969-93; rsch. fellow USPHS, N.Y.C., 1958-59; head pathology Hosp. Rudolfinerhaus, Vienna, 1988—; v.p. Supreme Ct. Pub. Health, Vienna, 1988-95; cons. Ctrl. Office Statistics, Vienna, 1980—. Editor, author: Pathology-Arbeitsbuch. Fellow Royal Coll. Pathologists, Internat. Acad. Cytology (v.p. 1986-95); mem. German Soc. Pathology (pres. 1981-82), Austrian Soc. Pathology (hon. pres. 1970-72), European Soc. Pathology (hon., pres. 1991-93), European Soc. Cytology (hon., pres. 1992-93), Austrian Cancer Soc. (pres. 1980-90), Akad. d.Naturforscher Leopoldina (adj.), Hungarian Soc. Pathology (hon.). Office: Ctrl Lab Pathology Histolog, Billrothstrasse 78, A-1190 Vienna Austria

HOMBROUCKX, REMI OCTAVE, nephrologist; b. Landen, Belgium, June 7, 1945; s. Jean Joseph and Julie Cecile (Vanhoebrouck) H.; m. Carine Jeanne Verhegge, June 24, 1972; children: Michel, Nathalie. MD with great distinction, Ghent State U., 1970; specialization in nephrology, Univ. Hosp., Ghent, 1976. Specialization in internal medicine U. Hosp., Ghent, 1975, specialization in nephrology, 1976; head dept. nephrology-dialysis Werken Glorieux, Ronse, Belgium, 1976—; ad interim head internal medicine Butare Nat. U., Rwanda, 1974; sci. adv. bd. Aksys Ltd., 1995—. Contbr. articles to profl. jours.; patentee in field. Recipient 1st prize Assn. Flemish Nephrologists, 1992, European Soc. Artificial Organs AKZO award, 1993. Mem. Am. Soc. for Artificial Internal Organs (chmn. conf., Lippincott Raven award 1996), Internat. Soc. Nephrology (chmn. conf.), Internat. Soc. for Artificial Organs (chmn. conf.), European Dialysis and Transplant Assn., Soc. Francophone Dialyse, Nederlandstalige Belgische Vereniging voor Nefrologie, Orgn. van het Paramedisch Pers. der Dialyse en Transplantatiecentra (hon.). Roman Catholic. Avocations: music, wine, bicycling. Fax: 32-55-9337 47. Office: VZW Werken Glorieux, Hogerlucht 6, 9600 Ronse Oost VL, Belgium

HOMEIER, HERBERT HANS HEINRICH, chemistry educator, computer software researcher; b. Hannover, Germany, Aug. 7, 1957; s. Willi Heinrich Günther and Brigitte (Bachmann) H.; m. Silke Arndt, July 19, 1985; children: Anne Brigitte, Gesa Marie. Diploma in physics, U. Heidelberg, Germany, 1986; D in Natural Scis., U. Regensburg, Germany, 1990, Habilitation in Theoretical Chemistry, 1996. Rsch. asst. U. Regensburg, 1986-90, sci. asst., 1990-96, sr. sci. asst., 1996-2000, lectr., 1996—; with sci. and computing industry, Munich, 2000—; vis. rschr. Acad. Scis., Rez, Czech Republic, 1994, Fribourg (Switzerland) U., 1992-93, U. Autonoma Madrid, 1996-97, U. Louvain, Belgium, 1999; webmaster dept. chemistry U. Regensburg, 1995—; sci. adv. bd. Electronic Computational Chemistry Confs., 1996-98, organizer, 1999. Author: Integraltransformationsmethoden und Quadraturverfahren für Molekülintegrale mit B-Funktionen, 1990, Extrapolationsverfahren für Zahlen-, Vektor- und Matrizenfolgen und ihre Anwendung in der Theoretischen und Physikalischen Chemie, 1996. Served with German mil., 1976-78. Grantee Studienstiftung des Deutschen Volkes, 1978-85, Fgn. Study grant, 1981-82. Mem. German Phys. Soc., Bunsengesellschaft. Avocations: music, badminton, cycling. Home: Niefangweg 3, D-93049 Regensburg Germany Office: Inst Physikalische Theoretische Chemie, Universitätsstrasse 31, D-93053 Regensburg Germany

HOMENTCOVSCHI, DOREL, researcher, educator; b. Dondosani, Moldova, Oct. 22, 1942; s. Teodor and Victoria (Coban) H.; Polixenia Valeria Belgun, Apr. 5, 1966 (div. Sept. 1989); children: Razvan, Corina Simona. BS, Univ. Bucharest, Romania, 1965, PhD, 1970. Asst. prof. Polytech. Inst. of Iasi, 1966-67; asst. prof., lectr. Polytech. Inst. of Bucharest, 1970-80, assoc. prof., 1980-87, chmn. of math., 1987-88; analyst milk factory Bucharest, 1988-89; prof. Polytech. Univ. Bucharest, 1990—; dir. Inst. of Applied Math. of Romanian Acad., 1995—. Author: Complex Variable Functions with Applications, 1986; contbr. articles to profl. jours. Recipient rsch. grant Tempus Project Polytech. Torino, 1993, Cost Project Polytech. Grenoble, 1993, Duke Univ., 1994, SUNY, 1993, 95, 96, 97. Mem. IEEE. Avocations: hiking, skiing. Office: Inst Applied Math, PO Box 1-24, Ro70 700 Bucharest Romania

HOMER, THOMAS KEITH, transportation consultant; b. Middlesbrough, Teesside, England, May 7, 1967; s. Thomas Joseph Terrence and Marjorie (Bell) H. Degree in Transport Mgmt., Aston U., Birmingham, Eng., 1989. Mktg. asst. Brit. Rlwy. Bd., Birmingham, 1987-88; cons. Transp. Planning Assocs., Birmingham, 1989-93, Oscar Faber, Birmingham, 1993—. Mem. Chartered Inst. of Transport. Office: Oscar Faber, Beaufort House, 94/96 Newhall St, Birmingham B3 1PB, England

HOMMA, TEIICHI, applied physics researcher; b. Minato ku, Tokyo, Japan, Apr. 22, 1931; s. Toshihito and Toshiko (Inaba) H.; m. Etsuko Suda, June 7, 1963. BEng, Chiba (Japan) Inst. Tech., 1958; MEng, U. Tokyo, 1961, DEng, 1965. Rsch. asst. U. Tokyo, 1961-65, lectr., 1965-66, assoc. prof., 1966-86, prof., 1986-92, prof. emeritus, 1992—; prof. Chiba Inst. Tech., 1992—; vis. rschr. McMaster U., Hamilton, Ont., Can., 1968-69. Contbr. articles to profl. jours. Mem. Japan Soc. Corrosion Engring. (v.p. 1992-93). Avocation: painting. Home: Shirokane 4-9-9, 108-0072 Minato ku Tokyo Japan Office: Chiba Inst Tech, Tsudanuma 2-17-1, 275 Narashino, Chiba Japan

HOMMA, TOSHIAKI, respiratory physiologist; b. Tokyo, Oct. 2, 1954; s. Tetsuo and Yohko (Uchimura) H.; m. Fumiko Tange, June 6, 1980; children: Yuichi, Yuki, Sachi. BS, U. Tsukuba, Japan, 1980; MD, U. Tsukuba, 1984, PhD, 1984. Cert. in internal and thoracic medicine, Japan Soc. Chest Diseases. Resident trainee Gakuen Hosp., Tsukuba, 1984-85, Kekken Hosp., Tokyo, 1985-86; chief instr. Seiranso Hosp., Tohkai, Japan, 1986-88; asst. prof. Tsukuba Univ., 1988-93, 1996—, ward dir., 1989-93; rsch. assoc. Nat. Jewish Ctr., Denver, 1993-96. Author: Sports Medicine Guide, 1994, Laboratory Medicine, 1996, Geriatric Medicine, 1997, Practice of Internal Medicine, 1997. Exec. Onogawa Coun., Tsukuba, 1997; committeeman Prevention Disasters, Tsukuba Univ., 1997. Grantee in respiratory physiology, Chest Co., 1997, in physiol. technique, Teijin Co., 1997. Mem. Japanese Soc. Respiratory Care, Japanese Thoracic Soc., Japanese Internal Medicine. Avocations: model aircraft. Home: 14-25 Onogawa, Tsukuba Ibaraki 305, Japan Office: Univ Tsukuba Clin Medicine, 1-1-1 Tennoudai, Tsukuba Ibaraki 305, Japan

HOMMEL, BERNHARD, psychologist, researcher; b. Niederstotzingen, Germany, Mar. 19, 1958; s. Hans Bernhard and Margarete Erna Paula (Steinkamp) H. Diploma in Psychology, U. Bielefeld, 1987, PhD, 1990; Dr.habil., Ludwig-Maximilian U. Munich, 1997. Rsch. asst. U. Bielefeld, 1987-90; sr. rschr. Max-Planck Inst. for Psychol. Rsch., 1990-99; prof. gen. psychology U. Leiden, The Netherlands, 1999—. Editor: Theoretical Issues in Stimulus-Response Compatibility, 1997; contbr. articles to profl. jours. Mem. Scientific Coun. Max-Planck Soc., 1988-90. Mem. Deutsche Gesellschaft for Psychology, European Soc. for Cognitive Psychology, Psychonomic Soc. Office: U Leiden Sect Exp/Theo Psyc, Wassenaarseweg 52, 2300 RB Leiden The Netherlands

HOMMEL, MANFRED RAINER WOLFGANG, geography educator; b. Oberhof, Germany, Sept. 13, 1944; s. Heinz and Emmi (Walch) H.; m. Marianne Schmidt, July 30, 1970; children: Kerstin, Britta. D of Natural Scis., Ruhr-U., Bochum, Germany, 1972, Habilitation, 1980. Wiss. asst. Ruhr-U., Bochum, 1970-81; prof. U. Duisburg, Germany, 1982-83; privatdozent Ruhr-U., Bochum, 1983-85, apl. prof., 1985—; vice-dean Ruhr-U., Bochum, 1984-85, 87-90, head of dept., 1992-93. Author: Central place preferences in multi-centered conurbations: the case of Rhine-Ruhr, 1974, Industrial estates in old industrialized regions: the case of Scotland, 1983; co-editor: Stadt und Kulturraum, 1989, Vor Ort im Ruhrgebiet, 1993. Office: Ruhr-U Bochum, Geographisches Inst, D-44780 Bochum Germany

HOMOLKA, JIRI, administrator; b. Prague, Czech Republic, Aug. 3, 1950; s. Jiri and Jirina (Jancikova) H.; m. Jaroslava Kortusova, Oct. 5, 1978; children: Jiri Jr., Petra. MD, Charles U., Prague, Czech Republic, 1974, PhD, 1984. Physician 1st Med. Faculty, Prague, Czech Republic, 1974-81; asst. prof. 1st Med. Faculty, Prague, 5, Czech Republic, 1981-93, assoc. prof., 1993-98, chief dept., 1998—; assoc. prof. Charles U., 1993. Author: Interstitial Lung Diseases, 1999. Grantee Immunopathogenesis IPF and Sarcoidosis Ministry Health, 1994-98. Fellow ACCP; mem. ERS, Czech Pneumological and Phthisiological Soc. (pres. 1994-98, com. mem. 1981—). Avocations: tennis, fishing, cycling. Office: Charles U 1st Lung Dept, Katerinska 19, 120 00 Prague Czech Republic

HOMSY, CHRISTIAN CHERIF, medical devices company executive; b. Cairo, Dec. 27, 1958; arrived in Belgium, 1981; s. Roland Y. and Marie-Louise A. (Antonius) H.; m. Sylvia G. Hollander, July 18, 1987; children: Karim, Bastian, Benjamin. M of Med. Scis., U. Cath., 1983, MD, 1987; MBA, Inst. for Mgmt. Devel., 1991. Resident in orthop. surgery Free U., Brussels, 1987-90; resident in surgery Harvard Med. Sch., Boston, 1987; mktg. assoc. Eli Lilly/CPI, London, 1992-93; country mgr. France Guidant/CPI, Paris, 1993-95; dir. clin. affairs Europe Guidant Hdqs., Brussels, 1995-97; mng. dir. Europe Guidant/CPI, 1997-99; dir. clin. affairs Europe, European tng. Guidant Hdqrs., Brussels, 1999—. Mem. Royal Belgian Acad. of Surgeons. Avocations: competitive sailing, skiing, classical and jazz music. Office: Guidant European Hdqrs, Culliganlaam 2B, 1831 Diegem Belgium

HON, GIORA, philosopher of science; b. Afula, Israel, Dec. 20, 1950; s. Mordechei Honigwachs and Ruth (Merenlander) H. BSc, Tel-Aviv U., 1975; MSc, London U., 1977, PhD, 1984. Postdoct. Hebrew U., Jerusalem, 1986-87; lectr. Haifa (Israel) U., 1987—. Author: Studies in History and Philosophy of Science, 1987, 89, Annals of Science, 1987, Historical Studies in the Physical and Biological Sciences, 1989, Review of Metaphysics, 1995, Foundations of Physics, 1996. Humboldt fellow Konstanz U., Germany, 1989-90, rsch. fellow DAAD, 1995, vis. fellow, CNRS, Paris, 1993, Ctr. Philosophy of Sci., Pitts., 1996-97. Office: U Haifa, Dept Philosophy Mt Carmel, 31905 Haifa Israel

HON, JOHNNY SEI-HOE, banker; b. Hong Kong, Dec. 22, 1971; arrived in U.K., 1986; s. Frank Tak Sun Hon and Betty Ling Wong. BSc with honors, King's Coll., London, 1983; PhD, U. Cambridge, Eng., 1998; DLitt (hon.), Augsburg Evang. Theol. Sem., 1996. Pres. Pacific Investments, U.K., 1995-97; mng. dir. Global Fin. Solutions Ltd., U.K., 1997-98, Global Underwriting Plc, U.K., 1998—; pres. Jolly First Capital Ltd., Hong Kong, 1998—, ABN Amro Bank, Hong Kong, 1998-2000; mktg. dir. Heyner Investment (U.K.) Ltd., 2000—. Contbr. articles to profl. jours. With Brit. armed forces, 1987-89. Fellow Am. Biog. Inst.; mem. Brit. Psychol. Soc., Oxford and Cambridge Club. Avocations: reading, music, theater, wine tasting, golf. Office: Flat 188, 2 Lansdowne Row Berkeley Sq, London W1X 2LL, England Home: 60 Shelford Rd, Fulbourn Cambridge CB1 5HJ, England

HONAKER, CHARLES RAY, health facility administrator; b. Charleston, W.Va., Jan. 13, 1947; s. Charles Frederick and Avis Linda (McCarthy) H.; m. Sarah Powers, Aug. 30, 1969; children: Charles Erik, Cara Powers, Katherine Powers, Erin Powers. BA, U. Del., 1977; M in Health Sci., Johns Hopkins U., 1981. Cert. nursing home adminstr., healthcare exec.; diplomate Am. Coll. Healthcare Execs. Dir. residential treatment Gov. Bacon Health Ctr.-State of Del., Delaware City, 1975-80; sr. health planner State of W.Va., Charleston, 1980-83; assoc. hosp. adminstr. Pinecrest State Hosp., Beckley, W.Va., 1983-84; nursing home adminstr. Arthur B. Hodges Ctr., Charleston, W.Va., 1984-86, Carondelet Holy Family Ctr., Tucson, 1986-89; hosp. adminstr. Carondelet Holy Cross Hosp., Nogales, Ariz., 1989-96; CEO St. Thomas More Health Sys., Canon City, Colo., 1996—; bd. mem., v.p. So. Ariz., Am. Cancer Soc., 1989-94; chair, bd. mem. Office of Rural Health, U. Ariz., Tucson, 1990—; chmn. bd. Ariz. Rural Health Assn., Phoenix. Bd. dirs. Sahuarita (Ariz.) Unified Sch. Dist., 1987-91, C. of C., Nogales, 1995, St. Scholastica Acad., Canon City, 1998—, Fremont County, Colo. Econ. Devel. Coun., 1998—. Fellow Am. Acad. Med. Adminstrs., Am. Coll. Health Care Adminstrs.; mem. U.S.-Mex. Border Health Assn., Ariz.-Mex. Commn. (pub. health coms.). Republican. Roman Catholic. Avocations: dog breeding and showing, Arabian horse breeding, shooting, hunting. Home: PO Box 2136 Canon City CO 81215-2136 Office: St Thomas More Health Sys 1338 Phay Ave Canon City CO 81212-2302

HONAKER, JIMMIE JOE, lawyer, ecologist; b. Oklahoma City, Jan. 21, 1939; s. Joe Jack and Ruby Lee (Bowen) H.; children: Jay Jimmie, Kerri Ruth. BA, Colo. Coll., 1963; MA, U. No. Colo., 1991; JD, U. Wyo., 1966, MS, 1995; postgrad., Utah State U., 1995—. Bar: Colo. 1966, U.S. Dist. Ct. Colo., U.S. Ct. Appeals (10th cir.), Ute Indian Tribal Ct. Utah. Pvt. practice Longmont, Colo., 1966-91. Incorporator Longmont Boys Baseball, 1969; chmn. Longmont City Charter Commn., 1973; chmn. ch. bd. 1st Christian Ch., Longmont, 1975, 76; chmn. North Boulder County unit Am. Cancer Soc., 1978, 79. Recipient Disting. Svc. award Longmont Centennial Yr., 1971; named Outstanding Young Man, Longmont Jaycees, 1973. Mem. ABA, Colo. Bar Assn. (interprofl. com. 1972-91, environ. law sect. 1999—), Denver Bar Assn., Christian Legal Soc., Internat. Assn. Approved Basketball Ofcls. (cert.), Nat. Eagle Scout Assn., Ecol. Soc. Am., Colo. Mountain Club, Uintah Mtn. Club, Phi Alpha Delta, Alpha Kappa Psi, Xi Sigma Pi, Alpha Tau Omega. Avocations: private pilot, mountain climbing. Address: Utah State U PO Box 1320 Logan UT 84322-0001

HONDA, BAKU, linguist; b. Mar. 13, 1930; s. Tsunezo and Yoshiko (Yoshida) H.; m. Hiroko Ishimaru; 1 child, Ko Honda. BA, Hiroshima U., 1953, MA, 1955. Assoc. prof. Fukuoka Kyoiku U., Munakata, Japan, 1966-72, prof., 1972-92, prof. emeritus, 1992—; vis. scholar Harvard U., 1988, 90; prof. Kyushu Sangyo U., Fukuoka, Japan, 1992-2000; vis. scholar UCLA, 1963, 69, 80, Harvard U., 1988, 90. Author: Categorical Grammar with English and Mathematical Expressions, 1997, Categorial Grammar, 1981, Translator and Compiler: Lado's Language Testing, 1971; contbr. articles to profl. jours. Home: 2-34-6 Kashii Higashi Ku, Fukuoka 813-0011, Japan

HONDA, KEIZOH, research engineering executive; b. Kobe, Japan, Jan. 11, 1955; s. Mamoru and Teruko (Awada) H.; m. Masako Miki Honda, Sept. 20, 1981. EdB, Osaka (Japan) U., 1977, MEE, 1980, DEng, 1996. Rschr. Heavy Apparatus Eng. Lab., Toshiba Corp., Yokohama, Japan, 1980—, specialist, 1987—, sr. specialist, 1994-98, mgr. energy sys. intellectual property dept., 1998-99; chief specialist tech. coordination dept. Toshiba Corp., Tokyo, 2000—; vis. prof. Kagawa U., 2000—. Patentee: Remote maintenance apparatus, 1993; contbr. articles to profl. jours. Recipient Tech. award Japan Welding engring. Soc., 1988. Mem. Japan Welding Soc. (patent award 1998). Avocation: music. Office: Power Systems Toshiba Corp, 1-1 Shibaura 1 chome, Minato-ku, Tokyo 105-8001, Japan

HONDA, MASAKI, oral surgeon; b. Obushi, Aichi, Japan, Sept. 29, 1964; p. Tsutomu and Eiko (Ishida) H. DDS, Aichi Gakuin, Japan, 1988; PhD, Nagoya U., Japan, 1999. Resident Sekizenkai, Japan, 1989-91, Nagoya U., Japan, 1992-94. Contbr. articles to profl. jours. Mem. Japanese Soc. of Oral and Maxilofacial Surgeons. Avocations: driving, photography, touring. Home: 5-55 Toshin-Cho Obu-Shi, Obu-shi 474-0073, Japan Office: Nayoya U Sch Medicine, 65 Tsuruma-cho Showa-ku, Aichi-ken 466-8550, Japan

HONDA, MASAO, neurologist, hospital administrator; b. Tokyo, Dec. 23, 1933; s. Jiro and Misuko (Kumamoto) H.; m. Namiko Hosoya, Nov. 2, 1963. MD, Keio U., Tokyo, 1958, PhD, 1969. Intern USAF Hosp., Tachikawa, Japan, 1958-59; resident Balt. City Hosp., 1959-60, Sinai Hosp., Balt., 1960-62, Johns Hopkins Hosp., Balt., 1962-65; neurologist Yokohama (Japan) City Hosp., 1965-99, dir., 1993-99; dir. Yokohama Stroke and Brain Ctr., 1999—; prof. Tokai U., Japan, 1993—. Author: Neurological Examination, 1970, Management of Stroke and Neuromuscular Diseases, 1989, Approach to Neurological Diseases, 1996. Mem. Johns Hopkins Med. and Surg. Assn., Tokyo Gariou/Fulbright Alumni Assn., Internat. Stroke Assn. Home: 3-5-8 Higashi-Gotanda, Tokyo 141, Japan Office: Yokohama City Hosp, 56 Okazawacho, Yokohama 240, Japan

HONDA, TAKUYA, engineering educator; b. Shimizu, Japan, July 17, 1945; s. Chiyuki and Michiko (Sando) H.; m. Kuniko Yamada, Mar. 27, 1977; three children. BS, Tokyo Inst. Tech., 1968, MS, 1970, D in Engring., 1978. Asst. prof. Tokyo Inst. Tech., 1971-85, assoc. prof., 1985-92; prof. JAIST, Tatsunokuchi, Japan, 1992—; senator JAIST, 1993-95, 98-2000, dean, 1995-97. Author: Surface Science, 1973, Catalytic Chemistry, 1987; contbr. articles to profl. jours. Buddhism. Avocations: reading, music, tennis, skiing, walking. Home: 6-59 Yamajimadai, Matto 924-0836, Japan Office: Japan Adv Inst Sci Tech, 1-1 Asahidai Tatsunokuchi, Ishikawa 923-1292, Japan

HONE, GEOFFREY WILLIAM, lawyer; b. Sydney, NSW, Australia, Nov. 20, 1943; s. Brian William and Althea Enid (Boyce) H.; m. Anthea Alicia Milne, Feb. 24, 1973; children: Imogen, Tamsin, Michael. LLB with honors, U. Melbourne, Australia, 1967. Cert. barrister and solicitor. Articled clk. Blake & Riggall, Melbourne, 1967-68; assoc. Cravath, Swaine & Moore, N.Y., 1968-69; asst. mgr. J. Henry Schroder Wagg & Co. Ltd., London, 1969-70; assoc. Blake & Riggall, Melbourne, 1971-74; ptnr. Blake Dawson Waldron, Melbourne, 1975—; bd. dirs. Securities Exchs. Guarantee Corp. Ltd., Australia, The Queen's Trust for Young Australians; mem. legal com. Cos. and Securities Adv. Com., Australia, 1989—. Mem. Internat. Bar Assn., Law Coun. Australia (dep. chmn. corps. com. 1985-88), Melbourne Club. Avocations: tennis, opera, bridge. Home: 20 Millicent Ave, Toorak 3142, Australia Office: Blake Dawson Waldron, 101 Collins St 39th Fl, Melbourne 3000, Australia

HONEGGER, CLAUDIA, sociology educator; b. Zurich, Nov. 13, 1947; d. Otto and Ada (Kaufmann) H.; m. Ulf Matthiesen, Sept. 1984 (div. 1996); children: Toby, Kai. PhD, U. Bremen, Germany, 1979. Rsch. asst. Germany, 1981-82, asst. U. Frankfurt, Germany, 1983-89; prof. U. Berne, Switzerland, 1990—. Author: Die Hexen der Neuzeit, 1978, Die Ordnung der Geschlechter, 1991; editor: Das Ende der Gemütlichkeit, 1998; co-editor: Frauen in der Soziologie, 1998. Mem. Swiss Sociol. Assn. (pres. 1995-97). Office: U Bern, Lerchenweg 36, 3000 Bern Switzerland

HONEGGER, FEDERICO, artist; b. Milan, Italy, Sept. 11, 1926; s. Carlo and Maria Antonia (Casiraghi) H.; m. Lucia Serafina Carminati, Apr. 30, 1959; children: Carlo, Marco, Andrea, Anna. Baccalaureat, Coll. St. Michel, 1945; law degree, Cath. U., 1952. Textile practice Vereinigte Seidenwebereien AG, Krefeld, Germany, 1950-51; with Gaspare Honegger, Milan, Italy, 1946-59; buying mgr. Carminati Industrie Tessili SpA, Milan, 1960-82. Author: The Digital Outlook, 1984, (art project) The Ke'nosis Project, 1986 (award), Jacobs Ladder, 1989, The Eye of the Needle, 1992, Portraits, 1992, Cromatic Alphabets, 1993, Constellations, 1993, Adam's Rib, 1994, Metaphysical Alphabets, 1994, The Signs-Number of Image, 1996, The Universe of Fragments, 1996, The Profecy of Ezechiele, 1998, God All in Everybody, 1999, Soul and Body, 1999, El Shadday-The Primary Numbers, 1999, The Background, Place of Dialogue Between Thou (two) and Innumerable, 2000. Recipient Silver Palette City of Milan, 1979, Top 70 Winner Art '95 N.Y. Internat. Competition, 1995. Mem. Symbolicum Art Group (co-founder). Fax: 0039-2-6590687. Home and Office: Via Annunciata 23/2, 20121 Milan Italy

HONEK, ALOIS, entomology researcher; b. Prague, Czech Republic, May 3, 1945; s. Alois and Hana (Smidrkalóva) H. D of Natural Scis., Charles U., Prague, 1969; PhD, Agr. U., Prague, 1983. Rsch. worker Entomology Inst. Acad. Sci., Prague, 1968-72, Rsch. Inst. Plant Prodn., Prague, 1972—. Author: Ecology of Coccinellidae, 1996. Roman Catholic. Avocation: hiking. Office: Rsch Inst of Plant Prodn, Drnovská 507, 16106 Prague Czech Republic

HÖNERLAGE, BERND, physicist, educator; b. Castrop-Rauxel, Germany, Aug. 8, 1946; s. Heinrich and Ruth (Lichtenfeld) H.; m. Marja Zdimerova, Aug. 27, 1970. Diploma in physics, Marburg (Germany) U., 1970; PhD, Frankfurt (Germany) U., 1973; habilitation, Strasbourg (France) U., 1985. Asst. prof. physics Regensburg (Germany) U., 1973-79; scholar German Rsch. Found., Regensburg, 1979-80; asst. prof. physics Essen (Germany) U., 1980-81; rschr. CNRS, Strasbourg, 1982-88, dir. rsch., 1988-93; prof. physics Strasbourg U., 1993—; assoc. prof., Strasbourg U., 1980, 81. Contbr. chpts. to books, articles to profl. jours. Mem. German Physics Soc., French Optical Soc. Avocation: hiking. Office: IPCMS/Gonlo, 23 rue du Loess, F-67037 Strasbourg France

HONEYCOMBE, GORDON, writer; b. Karachi, British India, Sept. 27, 1936; arrived in Australia, 1993; s. Gordon Samuel and Dorothy Louise Reid (Fraser) H. MA (hons.), Oxford Univ., 1961. Announcer Radio Hong Kong, Hong Kong, 1956-57, BBC Scottish Home Svc., Glasgow, 1958; actor Tommorow's Audience, Eng., 1961-62, Royal Shakespeare Co., Eng., 1962-63; newscaster ITN, London, 1965-77, TV-am, London, 1984-89. Author: Neither the Sea nor the Sand, 1969, Dragon Under the Hill, 1972, Adam's Tale, 1974, Red Watch, 1976, The Edge of Heaven, 1981, Nagasaki 1945, 1981, Royal Wedding, 1981, The Murders of the Black Museum, 1982, The Year of the Princess, 1982, Selfridges, 1984, TV-am's Official Celebration of the Royal Wedding, 1986, Siren Song, 1992, More Murders of the Black Museum, 1993, The Complete Murders of the Black Museum, 1995; writer TV plays: The Golden Vision, 1968, Time and Again, 1974, The Thirteenth Day of Christmas, 1986; writer stage plays and musicals: The Miracles, 1960, The Redemption, 1963, Paradise Lost, 1975, The Princess and the Goblins, 1976, A King Shall Have A Kingdom, 1977, Lancelot and Guinevere, 1980, Waltz of My Heart, 1980; actor: Suspects, 1989, Aladdin, 1989, Run For Your Wife!, 1990, The Taming of the Shrew, 1998, Princess Ida, 1997, The Mikado, 1999; acted in several TV shows, series, plays; voice-over for numerous TV documentaries, commercials and cinema shorts. Named Newscaster of Yr., TRIC, 1989. Mem. Ambrosians. Avocations: crosswords, jigsaws, walking. Address: c/o ACE, 436 Albany Hwy Victoria Pk, Perth WA 6100, Australia

HONEYMAN, JOHN RAYMOND, account manager, consultant; b. Norfolk, Va., Nov. 6, 1966; s. Franklin Charles and Dorothy Irene (Schultz) Leonard. BA in Internat. Bus., Japanese, No. Ctrl. Coll., Naperville, Ill., 1992; certificate, Kansai Gaidai U., Osaka, Japan, 1991. English tchr. Aeon, Inc., Osaka, Japan, 1993-94; mgr. liaison office Gemstar Japan, Tokyo, 1994-97; product planner Canon, Inc., Tokyo, 1997-98; strategic account mgr. IMR Global, Tokyo, 1998—. Scholar Kansai Gaidai U., Kirakata, Osaka, Japan, 1991. Mem. Survive! in Asia, Am. C. of C. (Japan chpt. com. sec. 1998—). Avocations: aikido, scuba diving, fitness, cooking, technology. Office: IMRglobal Corp Ltd Daiwa Nakameguro Bldg 6th Fl, 4-6-1 Nakameguro, Meguro-ku Tokyo 153-0061, Japan

HONG, CHANG YONG, chemist; b. Seoul, May 22, 1958; s. Won Il and Young Ae (Kim) H.; m. Woo Kyung Kang, Mar. 24, 1985; children: Hong Eun Young, Hong Sung Min. BS summa cum laude, Seoul Nat. U., 1981; MS, KAIST, 1983; PhD, Harvard U., 1991. Sr. rsch. scientist LG R&D Ctr., Tae-Jon, Korea, 1993-94, prin. rsch. scientist, 1995-99; v.p., rsch. fellow LG Chem. Rsch. Pk., Tae-Jon, 2000—; scientific cons. LG Chem. Rsch. Pk., Tae-Jon, 1992-93. Contbr. articles to profl. jours.; patentee in field; inventor Factive (Gemifloxacin). Mem. Am. Chem. Soc., Korean Chem. Soc., Korean Chem. Soc. (councilor). Avocations: music, history. Home: 6-205 LG Apt 381-42, Doryong Dong Yusung Gu, Tae-Jon 305-340, Korea Office: LG Chem Rsch Pk, PO Box 61 Yusung, Tae-Jon 305-380, Korea

HONG, CHU-WAN, materials scientist, researcher; b. Kang-Shan, Taiwan, Sept. 20, 1959; arrived in Germany, 1984; s. Shin-Lie Hong and Min-Show Wang. BS, Tech. U. Hamburg-Harburg, Germany, 1987; MS, Tech. U. Hamburg-Harburg, 1991, PhD, 1995. Rsch. scientist Mercedes-Benz AG, Stuttgart, Germany, 1991; vis. rschr. Nippon Steel Corp., Kawasaki, Japan, 1992; rsch. scientist Tech. U. Hamburg-Harburg, 1992-94; head of lab. U.

Erlangen-Nuernberg, Germany, 1994-98; with Siemens Matsushita Components OHG, Deutschlandsberg, Austria, 1998—; guest lectr. U. Erlangen-Nuernberg, Germany, 1999—. Author: Computer-Aided Process Modeling of Colloidal Powder Forming, 1996; contbr. articles to profl. jours.; inventor in field. Served with Taiwanese army, 1981-83. Recipient Best Paper award Max-Planck-Soc., Stuttgart, 1993. Mem. Am. Ceramic Soc., German Soc. Materials Sci. Home: Am Müehlgarten 47, D-91080 Spardorf Germany Office: Siemens Matsushita Comp OHG, Siemensstrasse 43, A-8530 Deutschlandsberg Austria

HONG, FENG-LEI, physicist; b. Shanghai, China, June 8, 1963; parents Feng-Hua and Ling-Xia (Wei) H.; m. Katsumi Taniguchi, Feb. 22, 1992; 1 child, Takeaki. BS, U. Tokyo, 1987, MS, 1989, PhD, 1992. Spl. researcher basic sci. program Inst. Phys. and Chem. Rsch., Saitama, Japan, 1992-94; rsch. scientist Nat. Rsch. Lab. Metrology, Tsukuba, Japan, 1994-99; sr. rsch. scientist Nat. Rsch. Lab. Metrology, Tsukuba, 1999—; guest tchr. Sophia U., Tokyo, 1992; vis. mem. JILA Nat. Inst. Stds. and Tech. U. Colo., 1997-99. Translator: Longman Dictionary of Physics, 1996; editor: New Mainland, 1989-90; contbr. articles to profl. jours. Recipient The Forum prize Fgn. Min., Japan, 1987. Mem. Optical Soc. Am., Phys. Soc. Japan, Japan Soc. Applied Physics. Avocations: swimming, tennis, running, photography, TV. Home: 1-102-504 Kashuga, 305 Tsukuba Japan Office: Nat Rsch Lab Metrology, 1-1-4 Umezono, 305 Tsukuba Japan

HONG, FRANK DAE UN, research scientist; b. Kwang-Joo, South Korea, Nov. 16, 1958; came to U.S., 1974; s. Dong Gun and Myung Soon (Oh) H. BS, Baylor U., 1981; postgrad., Johns Hopkins U., 1981-82; PhD, U. Calif., San Diego, 1992. Postdoctoral rsch. fellow Fred Hutchinson Cancer Rsch. Ctr., Seattle, 1993, Salk Inst., LaJolla, Calif., 1994-95, U. Tex. Southwestern Med. Ctr., Dallas, 1996-97, U. Tex./M.D. Anderson Cancer Ctr., Houston, 1998—; rsch. scientist Biosynthesis Inc., Dallas, 1996. Mem. Gamma Beta Phi. Achievements include discovery that genetic mutations can be exploited to develop a tumor-specific therapy by triggering genomic instability. Office: Univ of Texas Dept Head & Neck Surgery M D Anderson Cancer Ctr Houston TX 77030

HONG, GUANG, mechanical engineer, educator; b. Ji'an, Jiang Xi, China, July 1, 1950; arrived in Australia, 1990; d. Zhi and Yi-jun (Liu) H.; m. Ji-gen Xia, Jan. 22, 1977; 1 child, Hong Xia. M in Engring., Huazhong U. Sch. and Tech., Wuhan, China, 1982; PhD, Cambridge (Eng.) U., 1989. Lectr. Huazhong U. Sci. and Tech., 1976-85; rsch. assoc. Rutherford Appleton Lab., Oxfordshire, Eng., 1989-90; rsch. fellow U. Tech., Sydney, Australia, 1990-91, lectr. engring., 1992-97, sr. lectr., 1997—, head mech. engring. group, 1999—. Contbr. articles to profl. jours. Recipient Schlumberger studentship Commonwealth Trust, Trinity Coll., Cambridge U., 1986-87. Mem. ASME, Soc. Automotive Engrs. Avocations: reading, music, table tennis, shopping. Office: Univ Tech Sch Mech Engring, PO Box 123, Broadway, Sydney NSW 2007, Australia

HONG, GUOWEI, computer engineer; b. Zhongshan, China, Aug. 14, 1969; p. Rongmao and Gan Hong; m. Ying Shen, Jan. 12, 1993; children: Daniel, Joshua. BSc, Shenzhen U., 1991; PHD, U. Ctrl. Preston, 1995. From rsch. fellow to sr. rsch. fellow Colour & Imaging Inst. U. Derby, UK, 1996—. Office: U Derby Colour Imaging Inst, Kingsway House Kingsway, Derby UK DE223HL

HONG, JAE-DONG, engineering educator; b. Daegu, South Korea, Mar. 20, 1954; came to U.S., 1981; s. Hyun-Tae and Kyung-Hee (Kim) H.; m. Bong-Sun Lee, Sept. 25, 1981; children: Thomas, Christina, James. BS, Korea U., Seoul, 1979; MS, Pa. State U., 1985, PhD, 1988. Quality and process engr. Daewoo Heavy Indsl., Anyang, South Korea, 1979-81; asst. prof. to assoc. prof. S.C. State U., Orangeburg, 1988-97, prof., 1997—. Contbr. articles to prof. jours. Named Dist. Prof. by Gov. S.C., 1993. E-mail: zfújdhong@scsu.edu. Home: 106 Fox Run Ct Orangeburg SC 29118-9791 Office: S C State Univ 102 Lewis Lab Orangeburg SC 29117-0001

HONG, JEESUN, interpreter, educator; b. Seoul, Republic of Korea, July 1, 1969; d. Soon Young and Dong Yon (Chang) H.; m. Chulki Kim, Oct. 19, 1996. Bachelor in English Lit. and Lang., Yonsei U., Republic of Korea, 1992; master, Hankuk U. Fgn. Studies, Republic of Korea, 1996. Interpretation diplomate. Coord. video div. Columbia Tristar Films Korea, Seoul, 1992-93; freelance interpreter various internat. cos., 1995—; instr. English Korea Broadcasting Sta., Seoul, 1993-94; lectr., prof. Brain Korea 21 grad. sch. interpretation and transl. Hankuk U. Fgn. Studies, 1997—; freelance interpreter Hansol PCS, 1998. Freelance interpreter Korea Food and Sci. Assn., Korea Nat. Tourism Orgn. (featuring Pres. Kim Dae-jung), Conf. Hewlett Packard's Inkjet Printer and Imaging Sys., numerous others. Mem. Interpretation and Transl. Rsch. Inst. (head publs. 1996—). Methodist. Avocations: jogging, reading. Fax: 82-2-796-9117. Home: 1-1001 Shindongah Apt, Sobinggodong Yongsanku, Seoul 140-751, Republic of Korea

HONG, JIAHE, medical educator, researcher; b. Shanghai, China, Oct. 22, 1939; m. Liqing Sun, Feb. 14, 1969; 1 child, Jun. MD in Traditional Chinese Medicine, Shanghai U., 1964. Physician Longhua Hosp., Shanghai, 1965-86, chief physician, 1986-91; prof., rschr., acad. adviser for doctoral candidates Shanghai U. Traditional Chinese Medicine, Shanghai, 1991—, pres. Pub. House, 1986—, dean Hepatic Disease Inst., 1993—; mem. drug approval com. Shanghai Health Adminstrn., 1997—, Drug Approval Com. of China Health Ministry, Beijing, 1992—; acad. advisor Australian Nat. T.C.M. and Acupuncture Assn., Melbourne, 1997—; fellow Experts Consulting Com. of Shanghai Chinese Drug Co., 1992—. Author: Sex Education, 1987; chief editor: Practical Hepatopathy Treatment, 1995; vice chief editor: China Ency. Sexualogy, 1997; contbr. articles to profl. jours. Recipient Outstanding Contbn. prize State Coun. Peoples Republic of China, 1996, Excellence Paper prize Internat. Acad. Conf. Traditional Chinese Medicine, 1997, Sci. and Tech. 2 prize China Nat. Traditional Chinese Med. Adminstrn., 1996. Mem. Shanghai Sex Edn. Soc. (chmn. 1992-98, hon. chmn. 1998—), Shanghai Xuhui Dist. Sci. and Tech. Assn. (vice chmn. 1990—), Shanghai S.T.P. and AIDS Prevention and Treatment Assn. (standing com. 1995), Shanghai Geriat. Soc. (vice chmn. 1992—), Shanghai Internat. GiGong Rehab. Tng. Inst. (pres. 1998—), Shanghai GiGong Rehab. Assn. (vice chmn. 1986—). Avocations: music, arts. Home: Rm 602 No 230/37, Guan Shen Yun Rd, Shanghai 200233, China Office: Shanghai U Trad Chinese Med, 530 LingLing Rd, Shanghai 200032, China

HONG, JIN-LONG, engineering educator; b. Taipei, Taiwan, Republic of China, Sept. 7, 1955; s. Jen-Ying and Tsan-Shuang (Wu) H.; m. Chi-Fung Chu; children: Min-Chun, Shu-Kai. BS, Nat. Taiwan U., 1979; PhD, U. Mass., 1987. Postdoctoral U. Conn., Storrs, 1987-89; assoc. prof. Nat. Sun Yat-Sen U., Kaohsiung, Taiwan, 1989-98, prof., 1998—. With Army Republic of China, 1979-81. Mem. The Polymer Sci. Avocations: singing, swimming, basketball, TV watching, music. Office: Inst Materials Sci/Engring, Nat Sun Yat Sen U, Kaohsiung 80424, Repulic of China

HONG, KEUM-SHIK, engineer educator; b. Moonkyung, Korea, Aug. 25, 1957; s. Saejae and Saryun (Kang) H.; m. Eunhee Kang, Dec. 9, 1984; children: Brian Sungmin, Melissa Jiyeon. BS, Seoul Nat. Univ., Seoul, Korea, 1979; MS, Columbia Univ., 1987, Univ. Ill., 1991; PhD, Univ. Ill., 1991. Rschr. Daewoo Heavy Industries, Incheon, Korea, 1982-85; rsch. assoc. Univ. Ill., Urbana, Ill., 1991-92; rschr. Inst. of Precision Machinery Design, Seoul, 1992-93; asst. prof. Pusan Nat. Univ., Pusan, Korea, 1993—, chmn. dept. control and mech. engring., 1995-97; assoc. editor: The Inst. of Control, Automation and Systems Engrs., Seoul, 1996—. Contbr. articles to profl. jours. With Army, 1979-82, Taegu. Recipient fellowship Kim Chuman, 1972-75, Kyungbook Nat. Univ., 1975-78, Cert. of award Army, 1981. Mem. IEEE, Am. Soc. Mech. Engrs., Inst. of Control Automation and Systems Engrs., Korean Soc. Mech. Engrs. (divsn. assoc. editor 1996—). Avocations: mountain climbing, tennis. Office: Pusan Nat Univ, Kumjeong-ku, 609 735 Pusan Korea

HONG, MIN, biochemistry and molecular biology educator; b. Shang Liao, Jilin, China, Aug. 25, 1945; s. Hengan Hong and Shuqin Cao; m. Ruiyun Zhang, Oct. 4, 1975. B in Medicine, Beijing Med. U., 1969; M, Norman Bethune Med. U., 1981; postdoct., Laval, Quebec, 1993. Physician, lectr. Ctrl. Hosp., Si Ping, China, 1970-78; tchg. asst., postgrad. Norman Bethune Med. U., Chang Chun, China, 1978-81, lectr., 1981-90, tutor for Master degree students, 1991-96, assoc. prof., 1990-94, prof., 1994—, head biochemistry dept., 1994-96, vice dean Coll. Basic Medicine, 1995—, tutor for Doctor degree students, 1996; vis. scholar Laval, Quebec, 1985. Editor: Jour Norman Bethune University Med. Sci., 1992. Recipient Scientific Advancement Jilin Province of People's Republic of China, State Edn. Com. People's Republic of China, 1996. Mem. Acad. Biochemistry and Molecular Biology of China. Avocations: music, photography. Office: Norman Bethune Med U, Coll Basic Medicine, PC130021 Changchun Jilin, China

HONG, SEOK HYUN, publishing executive; b. Seoul, Korea; s. Jin Ki and Yun Nam (Kim) H.; m. Yun Gyun Shin; children: Jeong Do, Jeong Hyun, Jeong In. BS, Seoul Nat. U., 1972; MS, Stanford U., 1978, PhD, 1980. Economist World Bank, Washington, 1977-82; chief asst. The Minister of Fin., Seoul, 1983; chief asst. to chief of the staff to the Pres. of Korea, Seoul, 1983-85; sr. fellow Korea Devel. Inst., Seoul, 1985-86; sr. exec. v.p. Samsung Corning Co., Ltd., Seoul, 1986-94; publ., pres., CEO Joongang Ilbo, Seoul, 1994—. Recipient Official Commendation award Pres. Korea, 1984, 97, Letter of Appreciation Minister of Environ., 1996. Mem. Korea CALS/EC Assn. (chmn. 1996—), Korean Newspaper Assn. (vice-chmn. 1994—), World Assn. Newspaper (bd. dirs. 1999—), Stanford U. Alumni Seoul Assn. (chmn. 1997—), KAIST, Korean Fedn. Sci. and Tech. Soc. (v.p. 1999—). Korea Baduk. Office: Joongang Ilbo, 7 Soonwha-dong Chung-ku, 100-759 Seoul Korea

HONG, SOON-YOUNG, federal official; b. Jan. 30, 1937; married; four children. Degree in Law, Seoul (Korea) Nat. U., 1961; postgrad., Columbia U., 1970. Joined Ministry Fgn. Affairs, 1962; vice-consul Korean Consulate Gen. Ministry Fgn. Affairs, Hong Kong, 1965; second sec. Korean Embassy Ministry Fgn. Affairs, Santiago, Chile, 1967; dir. legal affairs Office Planning and Mgmt. Ministry Fgn. Affairs, 1971; first sec. Korean Embassy Ministry Fgn. Affairs, Washington, 1971; dir. N.Am. divsn. I Am. Affairs Bur. Ministry Fgn. Affairs, 1974; counsellor Korean Permanent Observer Mission to UNS Ministry Fgn. Affairs, N.Y., 1977; min. Korean Embassy Ministry Fgn. Affairs, Lagos, Nigeria, 1980; dir.-gen. African Affairs Bur. Ministry Fgn. Affairs, 1981, sec. to the Pres. for Polit. Affairs, 1983, amb. extraordinary, plenipotentiary Islamic Rep. Pakistan, 1984, dep. min. for econ. affairs, 1987, amb. extraordinary, plenipotentiary to Malaysia, 1990, amb. extraordinary, plenipotentiary to Russian Fedn., 1992, vice min. fgn. affairs, 1993, amb. extraordinary, plenipotentiary to Fed. Republic of Germany, 1995; amb. to China Republic of Korea. Pvt. Republic of Korea Army, 1958. *

HONG, SUNG CHICK, sociology educator; b. Chonan, Korea, June 28, 1929; s. In Sun and Seung Soon (Park) H.; m. Jae Eun Song, Jan. 15, 1946; children: Sook-Hwa, Wook-Hwa, Eun-Hwa, Koo-Hwa, Dae-Hwa, Joon-Hwa, Yung-Hwa. BA, U. Wash., 1955, MA, 1957, PhD, 1959. Ast. prof. Korea U., Seoul, 1960-61, assoc. prof., 1961-66, prof., 1966-94, prof. emeritus, 1994—; chmn. bd. dirs. Asian Social Sci. Rsch. Inst., Seoul, 1991—; mem. Dem. Peaceful Unification Adv. Coun., Seoul, 1992—. Author: A Study of Korean Values, 1969, Intellectuals and Modernization, 1970, Conditions of Social Development, 1985, Social Development and Problems of Values, 1994. Decorated Nat. Order of Merit (Korea). Mem. Korean Sociol. Assn. (pres. 1967-68), Korean Social Sci. Rsch. Coun. (prs. 1984-88), Assn. Asian Social Sci. Rsch. Couns. (pres. 1985-88), Rep. of Korea Acad. Scis., Baekwoon Archery Club. Methodist. Avocations: archery, golf, tennis, mountain climbing. Home: 294-1 Jeongnung-4Dong, Sungbuk-ku, 136-104 Seoul Korea Office: Asian Social Sci Rsch Inst, 278-40 Hongje-3Dong, 120-093 Seoul Korea

HONG, TZUNG-PEI, computer scientist, educator; b. Kaohsiung City, Taiwan, June 24, 1963; s. Wan-Sheng and Hsiu-Lien (Chen) H.; m. Yueh-Lung Huang, Jan. 12, 1991; children: Ching-Tang, Ching-Chin. Bachelor's, Nat. Taiwan U., Taipei, 1985; PhD, Nat. Chiao-Tung U., Hsin-Chu, Taiwan, 1992. Lectr. Nat. Chiao-Tung U., 1991-92; assoc. prof. Chung-Hua Poly. Inst., Hsin-chu, Taiwan, 1992-94, Kaohsiung Poly. Inst., 1994-97; assoc. prof. I-Shou U., Kaohsiung, 1997-99, prof., 1999—; cons. Vulcan Indsl. Corp., Kaohsiung, 1994—, Wan-Sheng Metal Corp., Kaohsiung, 1994—; assoc. rschr. Nat. U. Kaohsiung, 1997-2000, prof. and dir. of libr. and info. ctr., 2000—. Contbr. articles to profl. jours. 2d lt. Chinese Army, 1985-87. Recipient Nat. Sci. Coun. rsch. award, 1992, 93, 95, 96, 97, 98, 99, 2000. Mem. IEEE, Inst. Info. and Computing Machinery, Assn. Computing Machinery. Avocations: sports, reading, music. Home: 184 Hsin-Hsing St, Kaohsiung City 800, Taiwan Office: I-Shou U 1 Sect 1, Hsueh-Cheng Rd, Kaohsiung 84008, Taiwan

HONG, YANG-PYO, political ethics educator; b. Taegu, Korea, Sept. 27, 1936; s. Soon-Kyu and Jung-Hwa (Jeon) H.; m. Deung-Ja Hwang Hong, Nov. 12, 1966; children: Seong-Hun, Seong-Yeon. BA, Dong-Ah U., Pusan, Korea, 1970; MA, Grad. Sch. Kyungpook Nat. U., Taegu, Korea, 1975, PhD, 1984. Instr. Taegu (Korea) U., Kyungpook Nat. U., 1975-76; asst. Peace Rsch. Inst. Kyungpook Nat. U., Taegu, Korea, 1976-77; instr. Kyungpook Nat. U., Taegu, Korea, 1977-80, asst. prof., 1980-84, assoc. prof., 1984-90; fullbright sr. vis. scholar Hoover Inst. Stanford U., Stanford, Calif., 1985; prof. Kyungpook Nat. U., Taegu, Korea, 1985—; dir. Korean Polit. Sci. Assn., Seoul, Korea, 1997—; v.p. Korean Ethics Assn., Seoul, Korea, 1993, 98—. Author: Causes of War, 1984, Understanding of Ideologies, 1985, Democratic Principles and Community, 1999; contbr. papers in field. Bd. mem. Taegu (Korea) YMCA, 1996; standing com. Taegu Citizens Activity for Economy Justice, 1990; dir. Peace House for Runaway Adolescence, Taegu, Korea, 1997. Capt. Ordnance, 1960-73, Korea. Recipient award for 20 Yrs. Svc. Kyungpook Nat. U., Taegu, Korea, 1996, award of Spl. Contbn. for Taegu (Korea) YMCA. Mem. Internat. Polit. Assn. Presbyterian. Avocations: vocal music, mountain climbing. E-mail: yphong@bh.kyungpook.ac.kr. Fax: 82-53-950-5947. Home: 257-23 Sinamdong Dong-ku, Taegu 701-014, Republic of Korea

HONG, YING-YI BRADY, educator; b. Kaohsung, Taiwan, Dec. 15, 1961; s. Yuan-Ming and Pau-Hsow (Hsiao) H.; m. Tsuei-Li Shelly Shen, Aug. 30, 1964; 2 children. B, Chung Yuan Christian Univ., Chung-Li, Taiwan, 1984; M, Nat. Chen-Kung Univ., Tainan, Taiwan, 1986; PhD, Nat. Tsing-Hua Univ., Hsin-Chu, Taiwan, 1990. Instr. Nat. Tsing-Hua Univ., 1988-89; assoc. prof. Chung Yuan Christian Univ., Chung-Li, 1991-95, prof., 1995—, exec. asst., 1997—, chair dept. E.E., 1999—; cons. Taiwan Power Co., 1993-95; paper review chmn. Elec. Power Symposium, 1993; cons. Tao-Yuan Cmty. Coll., 1998. Contbr. articles to profl. jours. Sec. Kou-Ming party, Taipei, 1980-84. With Army, 1980. Recipient Excellence Rsch. award Nat. Sci. Coun., 1992-99; rsch. award Min. Edn., 1988; rsch. grant Nat. Sci. Coun., 1991-99. Mem. IEEE, Chinese Incubation Soc. Avocations: reading, painting, sightseeing. Office: Chung Yuan Christian Univ, 320 Chung-Li Taiwan

HONG, YI-REN, medical educator; b. Chang-Hua, Taiwan, Nov. 5, 1954; s. Kuan Hong and Sueu Lian; m. Yen-Chin Wang, Aug. 12, 1989; 1 child, Geraldine. BS, Chung-Shin U., Taichun, Taiwan, 1977; MS, Nat. Chung-Shin U., Taichun, Taiwan, 1979; PhD, U. Md., 1994. Cert. biochemistry and molecular biology. Rsch. assoc. Union Chem. Labs., Indsl. Tech. Rsch. Inst., Hsinchu, Taiwan, 1981-87; post-doctoral staff U. Md., Balt., 1993-94; assoc. prof. Kaohsiung (Taiwan) Med. U., 1995—; advisor dept. neurosurgery Kaohsiung Med. U., 1995—. Scholar Ministry Edn., Taiwan, 1978, Govt. Abroad scholar Nat. Sci. Coun., Taiwan, 1987, Indsl. Tech. Rsch. Inst. scholar, Hsinchu, 1990. Democrat. Avocations: history, writing. E-mail: yiren@mail.nsysu.edu.tw. Fax: 886-7-3218309. Office: Kaohsiung Med U, 100 Shih-Chuan 1st Rd, Kaohsiung Taiwan

HONG, YONG-KIL, neurosurgeon, educator; b. Seoul, Korea, June 22, 1955; child Sung-Seong and Soon-Bun Park; m. Jung-Kyung Kim, June 17, 1984; children: Kyung-Eui, Joon-Eui. BS in Medicine, Cath. U., Seoul, 1980, MS in Medicine, 1985, PhD in Medicine, 1992. Diplomate Korean Bd. Neurosurgery. Intern St. Mary's Hosp. Cath. U., Seoul, 1980-81, resident in neurosurgery Kangnam St. Mary's Hosp., 1981-85, from instr. to asst. prof., 1988-96, assoc. prof., 1997—; exec. sec. Cath. Cancer Ctr., Cath. Med. Ctr., Seoul, 1997-99; acad. adviser Cath. U., Seoul, 1998-99. Contbr. articles to profl. jours. Capt. Korean Army, 1985-88. Grantee Ministry Sci. and Tech., 1998, 99. Mem. Korean Brain Tumor Soc. (mem. exec. com., award 1999), Korean Neurosurgical Soc., Korean Cancer Assn., Joint Sect. Am. Assn. Neurosurgeons and Congress Neurosurgeons. Avocations: golf, travel, music. Fax: 82-2-504-4248. Home: Hanshin Seorae Apt 4-502, 137-040 Seoul Korea Office: Cath U Sch Medicine, Banpo-dong 505, 137-040 Seoul Korea

HONG, YU-CHING, dental educator, researcher; b. Chung-Hua, Tai-Chung, Taiwan, May 30, 1926; s. Sui-Liu and Pih (Liu) H.; m. Hsiu-Hua Ko, Aug. 1, 1957; children: Chi-Yuang, Chi-Horng. MPH, U. Mich., 1958; D Med. Sci., Med. Sch., Osaka, Japan, 1960; DDS, Kyushu Dental Coll., Kokura, Japan, 1984. Rsch. fellow Royal Dental Coll., Copenhagen, 1966, Havard Sch. Dental Medicine, Boston, 1966-68, Nat. Bur. of Stds., Washington, 1979; health specialist Provincial Taipei Pub. Health Ctr., Taiwan, 1950-56, dir. Sch. of Health, 1956; lectr. Nat. Taiwan U. Sch. Dentistry, Taipei, 1958-62, assoc. prof., 1963-65, prof., 1965-96, dean, 1972-78, hon. prof., 1996—. Recipient Outstanding Educators award Dept. of Interior, Taiwan, 1986. Mem. Assn. for Dental Sci. (Taiwan), Taiwan Dental Assn. (Outstanding Dental Profession award 1990, 98). Avocations: stamp collecting, coin collecting, gardening. Home: 333 Pa-Teh Rd 2d Sect, Taipei Taiwan Office: Nat Taiwan U Sch Dentistry, 1 Chang-Te St, Taipei Taiwan

HONG, ZUU-CHANG, engineering educator; b. Bei-Kun, Yuan-Lin, Taiwan, Apr. 25, 1942; s. San-Lin and Fei-Rien (Jih) H.; m. Sue-Jane Chen, Jan. 15, 1974 (div. Apr. 1979); children: Grace Shau-Wei Hong, Chao-I Hong; m. Hsiu-Ching Chen, Apr. 14, 1982; children: Chao-Tien Hong, Chao-Hun Hong, Chao-Min Hong. BS, Nat. Taiwan U., 1968; MS, U. Calif., Davis, 1971; PhD, U. Ill., 1975. Assoc. to full prof. dept. mech. engring. Nat. Taiwan U., Taipei, 1975-80, prof., 1982-85; prof. and head dept. mech. engring. Nat. Taiwan Inst. Tech., Taipei, 1980-82; prof., dean Coll. Engring., Nat. Cen. U., Chungli, Taiwan, 1985-88, prof., 1988—; cons. Chun-San Inst. Sci. and Tech., Lung-Tan, Tao-Yuan, 1981-93, 95—, Taiwan Inst. Econ. Rsch., Taipei, 1989-94; prof.-in-charge Automatic Control Lab., Taiwan U., 1976, Computational Fluid Dynamic Lab. Cen. U., 1985, Satellite Engring. Lab., 1995; mem. indsl. devel. adv. coun. Min. Econs., Taiwan, 1983—; dir. Office Com. Precision Machinery Industry Devel., Min. Econ. Affairs, Taiwan, 1997-98; mem. adv. sci. and tech. group Ministry of Def., Taiwan, 1998—. Editor-in-chief Jour. of Chinese Soc. of Mech. Engring., 1979-89, Trans. of Aero. and Astronautical Soc. of Republic of China, 1994-99; editor-in-chief: (book) Experiments for Mechanical Engineering, 1983; contbr. articles to profl. jours., publs. With Chinese Navy, ROTC, 1968-69. Recipient Disting. Rsch. award Nat. Sci. Coun., Taipei, 1991-92; Disting. Prof., Nat. Cen. U., Chung-Li, 1989, Disting. Paper of Yr. Soc. of Theoretical and Applied Mechanics, Tainan, 1982. Mem. AIAA (assoc. fellow), AASRC (chmn. orgn. com. 2d nat. conf. computational fluid dynamics 1993, chmn. tech. com. 2d and 3d global Chinese conf. astronautical sci. technol. 1994, 1997), Chinese Inst. Engrs. (Disting. Paper of Yr. 1979), Chinese Soc. Mech. Engrs. (bd. dirs. 1980-85, 97—, Disting. Paper of Yr. 1984, 86, chmn. orgn. com. 3d nat. conf. mech. engring. 1986), Chinese Soc. Aeros. and Astronautics (bd. dirs. 1986-93, 95—), Welding Soc. of Rep. of China (bd. dirs. 1986-95), Chinese Soc. of Automation (bd. dirs. 1992—, vice chmn. 1994-98), Soc. Mfg. Engrs. (chmn. Taipei chpt. # 242 1993-94, 96, bd. dirs. 1985—), Am. Inst. Aeronautics and Astronautics (assoc. fellow), 1997, others. Achievements include patent in field. Home: Lane-16 Wen-Chou St 5th Fl # 11, 10616 Taipei Taiwan Office: Nat Ctrl Univ, Dept Mech Engring, 32054 Chung-Li Taiwan

HONGCHOY, GEORGE M., investment banker; b. Hong Kong, Feb. 7, 1962; s. George William and May M.L. (Seah) H.; m. Dannie C.H. Ling, Feb. 14, 1987. B Commerce, U. Canterbury, New Zealand, 1985; MBA, U. Pa., 1991. CPA, Hong Kong. Sr. auditor Arthur Young, New Zealand, 1985-87; capital markets exec. Security Pacific Bank, New Zealand, 1987-89; sr. cons. Arthur Andersen & Co., Hong Kong, 1991-92; dir. Jardine Fleming Securities Ltd., Hong Kong, 1992—. Contbr. articles to various publs. Mem. fin. and fund raising coms. Hong Kong Physically Handicapped and Able-Bodied Assn., 1994 . Mem. New Zealand Soc. Accts. (assoc.), Hong Kong Soc. Accts., Chartered Inst. Arbitrators, Inst. Chartered Secs. and Adminstrs., Bankers Inst. New Zealand, U. Pa. Club of Hong Kong (pres. 1995-96), Diocesan Sch. Old Boys Assn. (hon. treas.), Wharton Club of Hong Kong (v.p. 1999). Avocations: golf, tennis, photography. Home: Flat 6C, 35-37 MacDonnell Rd, Hong Kong Hong Kong Office: Jardine Fleming Securities, Jardine Fleming Securities, Jardine House Ctrl 45th Fl, Hong Kong Hong Kong

HONGLADAROM, SORAJ, philosopher, educator; b. Bangkok, Thailand, Feb. 15, 1962; s. Tongchan and Manassawasd (Wararangsri) H.; m. Krisadawan Metavikul, July 25, 1988; 1 child, Pariwat. BA, Chulalongkorn U., 1983; MA, Ind. U., 1986, PhD, 1991. Asst. prof. Chulalongkorn U., Bangkok, 1991—. Author: Horizons of Philosophy, 1998, Buddhism and Human Rights in the Thoughts of Sulak Sivaraksa and Phra Dhammapidok, 1998; contbr. articles to profl. jours. Mem. Am. Philos. Assn., Soc. for Philosophy and Religions of Thailand. Buddhist. Avocation: piano. Home: 695 Ladprao 11, Bangkok 10900, Thailand Office: Dept Philosophy Fac Arts, Chulalongkorn U, Bangkok 10330, Thailand

HONGO, KOHEI, engineering educator; b. Sendai, Japan, June 2, 1939; s. Unkoh and Miyono Hongo; m. Atsuko Nishiyama, Oct. 15, 1968; children: Hiroo, Kohta, Michita. BEE, Tohoku U., 1962, MEE, 1964, Dr. Elec. Engring., 1967. Rsch. assoc. Tohoku U., Sendai, 1967-68; lectr. Shizuoka U., Hamamatsu, Japan, 1968-69; asst. prof. Shizuoka U., 1969-79, prof. engring., 1979-91; cons., 1991—; cons. engring., 1991, prof. sci., Toho U., 1991. Author: Introduction to A-C Circuit, 1978, EM Wave, 1983, Theory of Fundamental EM Field, 1990, Applied Mathematics, 1992, Antenna Theory and Design, 1992. Mem. Inst. Electronics, Info. and Communication Engrs., IEEE. Home: Nakashizu 3-34-24, Sakura, Chiba Japan Office: Hongo Cons, 2-2-1 Miyama Funabashi, Chiba Japan

HONGUH, YOSHINORI, research scientist, engineer; b. Fujisawa-shi, Japan, Oct. 16, 1956; s. Naoki and Kayoko (Takemura) H.; m. Akemi Mitani, Feb. 22, 1989; 1 child, Satoko. BS, U. Tokyo, 1979, MS, 1981, PhD, 1984. Rschr. R & D Ctr. Toshiba Corp., Kawasaki, 1984-89, rsch. scientist R & D Ctr., 1989-95, sr. rsch. scientist R & D Ctr., 1995—. Contbr. articles to profl. jours. including Optical Rev., Applied Optics, and Japanese Jour. Applied Physics. Mem. Optical Soc. Am., Phys. Soc. Japan, Japan Soc. Applied Physics (Optics prize for excellent paper award 1995). Avocations: jogging, swimming. Home: 3-11-21-A201 Nakahara, Isogo Yokohama 235-0036, Japan Office: Toshiba Corp R & D Ctr MSL, 1 Komukai Toshiba-cho, Saiwaiku Kawasaki 212-8582, Japan

HONG-YI, LEE, chemistry educator; b. Shanghai, Nov. 25, 1952; s. Lee Yan-Biao and Lu Yun-Zheng; m. Qiu Wen-Ying, Nov. 28, 1983; 1 child, Lee Han-Ling. BS, Shanghai Tchr.'s U., 1982. Asst. Shanghai Second Poly. U., 1982-87, lectr., 1987-94, prof., 1994—. Contbr. articles to profl. publs. Mem. AAAS, Nat. Geog. Soc., Planetary Soc., N.Y. Acad. Scis. Mem. Democratic Party. Avocation: music. Home: 320 Ln No 53 Fu Xing R(C), Shanghai 200021, China Office: Shanghai Second Poly Univ, No 80 Shan Xi R(N), Shanghai 200041, China

HONIG, WILLIAM MARTIN, electronics/physics/math/bioengineering researcher; b. N.Y.C., May 30, 1933; arrived in Australia, 1972; s. Saul S. and Jeanette J. (Stahl) H.; m. Frances Mary Good, June 4, 1981; 1 child, Bryony. BEE, Cooper Union, 1954; MEE, Poly. U. N.Y., 1956; PhD, U. Western Australia, Perth, 1976. Rsch. assoc. Microwave Rsch. Inst., N.Y.C., 1955-57; rsch. assoc. radiation lab. Johns Hopkins U., Balt., 1957-59; dir. rsch. Loral Corp., N.Y.C., 1959-65; pres. Honig Labs., Inc., Westbury, N.Y., 1965-68; dir. rsch. Cavitron Corp., N.Y.C., 1968-72; asst. prof. U. Western Australia, Perth, 1972-73; assoc. prof. Curtin U., Perth, 1973-80, prof. (reader), 1980—. Mem. editorial bd. Behavioral and Brain Scis., 1980—, Physics Essays, 1988—, Speculations in Sci. and Tech., 1977—, Biomed. Engring. Jour., 1980-86; founder, pub., editor-in-chief Speculations in Sci. and Tech., 1977-84; contbr. 98 articles to profl. jours.; U.S. patents (11) for electronic devices and bioengring.; author 5 books in quantum mechanics and relativity. Leader radio and TV campaign for successful reduction of Perth Mains voltage, 1979-90; TV and radio commentator on sci. and tech. on nat. networks, Australia, 1976-87. Recipient Eminent Engr. award Tau Beta Pi, 1970, 1st prize for best TV sci. docu-

mentary European Film Festival, 1983. Fellow Australian Inst. Elec. and Electronics Engrs.; mem. IEEE (sr.), Am. Phys. Soc.

HONIGSBERGER, LEO MAX, neurophysiologist, consultant; b. Birmingham, Eng., Dec. 20, 1928; s. Max and Lorna (Mayell) H.; m. Johanna De Kock, Jan. 21, 1954; children: Laura, Julia. MB, ChB, U. Cape Town, South Africa, 1957. Cons. clin. neurophysiologist Midland Ctr. for Neurosurgery and Neurology, Birmingham, 1964-71, United Birmingham Hosps., 1971-93, Worcester (Eng.) Royal Infirmary, 1993—; chmn. Bromsgrove and Redditch Health Authority, 1982-86. Mem. Bromsgrove Dist. Coun., 1980-82. Fellow Royal Coll. of Psychiatrists. Avocation: wine. Home: Sch Ln Alvechurch, Worcestershire B48 75A, England Office: HMP Birmingham, Winson Green Rd, Birmingham B18 4AS, England

HONJO, TASUKU, biochemist, educator; b. Kyoto, Japan, Jan. 27, 1942; s. Shoichi and Ryu-ko (Yoneda) H.; m. Shigeko Kodani, Feb. 4, 1969; children: Hajime, Yasuko. MD, Kyoto U., 1966, PhD, 1971. Asst. prof. Dept. Physiol. Chemistry Tokyo U., 1974-79; prof. Dept. Genetics Osaka (Japan) U., 1979-84; prof. Dept. Med. Chemistry Kyoto (Japan) U., 1984—, dean Faculty of Medicine, 1996-2000; dir. Inst. Molecular Biology and Genetics Kyoto U., 1988-97. Editor: Immunogloblin Genes, 1993, (jour.) Current Biology, 1993, Jour. Exptl. Medicine, 1992, Sci., 1995. Recipient award Asahi Shinbun, 1981, Kihara award Japanese Soc. Genetics, 1984, Behring-Kitasato prize Hoechst Chem., 1992, Japan Acad. prize, 1996; Fogarty scholar NIH, 1992-96. Mem. Am. Assn. Immunologists (hon.), Human Genome Orgn. Avocations: golf, art. Home: 19-4 Iwakura Ohsagi-cho, Kyoto 606-0001, Japan Office: Kyoto U, Dept Med Chemistry, Kyoto 606-8501, Japan

HONJOL, NADER MOHAMMED, physician; b. Nablus, Jordan, Oct. 5, 1954; s. Mohammed Hafiz Honjol and Fatima Shukri Sharif; m. Rima Dawoud Sharif, Dec. 6, 1984; children: Haytham, Yazan, Miras. MD, Ain Shams Med. Sch., Cairo, 1978; diploma in anesthetics, Royal Coll. Anesthesia, London, 1987. Diplomate Jordanian Bd. in Anaesthesia. Rotating intern Ain Shams U. Hosps., Cairo, 1979-80; resident in anaesthesia U. Hosp. of Jordan, Amman, 1980-83; lectr. in anesthesia U. Jordan, Amman, 1983-85; registrar anaesthesia U. Hosp. of Wales, Cardiff, U.K., 1985-88; sr. registrar anaesthesia Riyadh Armed Forces Hosp., Saudi Arabia, 1988-94, cons. anaesthetist and chronic pain mgmt., 1994—; coord. Arab/Saudi Bd. Examination in Anaesthesia, Riyadh Armed Forces Hosp., 1995—; chmn. of equipment and new drug com., Riyadh Armed Forces Hosp., 1994—, supr. residency tng. programme in anaesthesia, 1995—, mem. enquiry com., 1989—; spkr. in field. Reviewer Saudi Med. Jour.; contbr. articles to profl. jours. and publs.; co-author CPR, shock mgmt. book and series of basic med. problems and mgmt. for sch. students in Arabic. Mem. Royal Coll. Anaesthetists U.K., European Soc. Anaesthesiologists, Jordanian Med. Assn., Jordanian Assn. Anaesthesia, Gen. Med. Coun./London. Avocations: swimming, jogging, reading. Office: Riyadh Armed Forces Hosp, PO Box 7897, Riyadh 11159, Saudi Arabia

HONKALA, EINO JUHANI, dental educator; b. Elimaki, Kymi, Finland, Oct. 18, 1945; s. Mikko Frans and Mirja Serafina (Kotiranta) H.; children: Otto, Nora. LDS, U. Helsinki, 1974; D in Odontology, U. Kuopio, Finland, 1984, Docent in Preventive Dentistry, 1985; MSc, London Hosp. Med. Coll., 1986; Docent in Cariology, U. Helsinki, 1993; DDPH, Royal Coll. Surgeons Eng. Specialist in dental pub. health, Nat. Bd. Health. Prof. in preventive cmty. dentistry U. Dar es Salaam, Tanzania, 1986-88; assoc. prof. in cariology U. Kuopio, 1986-95; assoc. prof. in health edn. U. Jyvaskyla, Finland, 1990-91; prof. in cariology U. Helsinki, 1995-96, assoc. prof. in dental infectious diseases, 1996-98; prof. dental pub. health Kuwait U., 1999—, vice-dean rsch. and student affairs, 1999—; vis. prof. in pediat. dentistry U. Minn., 1994; mem. senate U. Dar es Salaam, 1987-88; mem. coun. U. Kuopio, 1992-94; dir. Helsinki Internat. Inst. for Oral Health. Editor: Pedodontics, 1984; mem. editl. bd. Tanzanian Dental Jour., 1995—, Med. Prins. and Practice, 1999—. Active Health Authority Bd., Kuopio, 1981-84, Finnish Bd. of Univs., Finland, 1975-80; mem. Coun. of Union of Univ. Rschrs., 1981. Rsch. grantee Acad. of Finland, 1985, 97. Office: Fac Dentistry Kuwait Univ, PO Box 24923, Safat 13110, Kuwait

HONKAPOHJA, SEPPO MIKKO SAKARI, economics educator; b. Helsinki, Finland, Mar. 7, 1951; s. Helge Uolevi Albin and Eila (Pulkkinen) H.; m. Sirkku Anna-Maija Halme, 1973; children: Alpo, Aino-Marja. Grad. A-levels, United World Coll. of Atlantic, U.K., 1970; M of Social Scis., U. Helsinki, 1972, Licentiate of Social Scis., 1974, D of Social Scis., 1979. Sci. dir. Yrjö Jahnsson Found., Helsinki, 1975-87; prof. econs. Turku (Finland) Sch. Econs. and Bus. Adminstrn., 1987-91, prof.-at-large of econs., 1992—; prof.-at-large of econs. U. Helsinki, 1981-91, acting prof. econs., 1985-87, prof. econs., 1992—; vis. lectr., scholar Harvard U., 1978-79; vis. assoc. prof. econs. Stanford U., 1982-83; sr. fellow Acad. Finland, Helsinki, 1982-83, acad. prof., 1989-95, 2000—. Assoc. editor: Scandinavian Jour. Econs., 1980-83, 89—, chief editor, 1984-88; assoc. editor: European Econ. Rev., 1991-93, chief editor, 1993-98; mem. adv. bd.: Jour. Econ. Surveys, 1994—, Internat. Jour. Devel. Planning Lit., 1984—, Macroecon. Dynamics, 1997—, German Econ. Rev., 1999—; editor: (books) Information and Incentives in Organizations, 1989, The State of Macroeconomics, 1990, (with others) Frontiers of Economics, 1985, Macroeconomic Modelling and Policy Implications, 1993; contbr. numerous articles to profl. jours. and textbooks. Vice-chmn. Kansallis Found. for Fin. Rsch., Helsinki, 1989-96; mem. supervisory bd. Okopankki Ltd., Helsinki, 1996-97, chair, 1997—; mem. gov. body Finnish Cultural Found., Helsinki, 1994—, chmn., 1997—. Fellow Econometric Soc.; mem. Academia Europaea, Finnish Econ. Assn. (bd. dirs. 1989-91), European Econ. Assn. (mem. coun. 1985-86, 89-94, fellow 1999—), Internat. Econ. Assn. (exec. com. 1995—), Finnish Acad. Sci. and Letters, Jan Tinbergen Inst. for Devel. Planning (mem. internat. adv. bd. 1984—). Avocation: fishing. Office: U Helsinki Dept Econs, PO Box 54 Unioninkatu 37, FIN00014 Helsinki Finland

HONMA, KOICHI, pathologist, researcher; b. Shiroishi, Miyagi, Japan, Mar. 28, 1955; s. Tsuneo and Mieko (Isago) H.; m. Kiyomi Fukuda, Nov. 27, 1986; children: Shiko, Seiji, Shino. BM, Tohoku U. Sch. Medicine, 1979; MD, Dokkyo U. Sch. Medicine, 1986. Instr. Dokkyo U. Sch. Medicine, Tochigi, Japan, 1981-84, asst. prof., 1984-92, assoc. prof., 1992—; mem. sci. com. No. 9 ILO Conf., Kyoto, Japan, 1995-97. Contbr. articles to profl. jours. Founder, diplomatic counselor London Diplomatic Acad., 2000—. Mem. Deutsche Gesellschaft für Pathologie, European Respiratory Soc., Am. Thoracic Soc., Pulmonary Pathology Soc., European Soc. Pathology. Avocations: music, sports. Fax: 81-28-625-6075. Home: Tomatsuri 3-6-45, Utsunomiya Tochigi 320-0056, Japan Office: Dokkyo U Sch Medicine Dept Pathology, Kitakobayashi 880, Mibu Tochigi 321-0293, Japan

HONOUR, OSUWE, drilling engineer; b. Freetown, Sierra Leone, Jan. 18, 1970; s. Frank Oshonogo Osuwe and Jannet Onyeachom. Ordinary diploma, Opencast Poly., Benin City, Nigeria, 1992, higher tech. diploma petroleum engring., 1998; postgrad. Internat. Well Ccontrol Forum driller's level. Floorman, derrickman Lonestar Drilling Co., Sapele, Nigeria, 1994—; asst. driller Lonestar Drilling Co., Sapele. Mem. Geosci. Student Fellowship, World Pen Pal Club. Mem. Ministry of God. Avocations: reading, travel, sports. Home: PO Box 7342, PMB 1718 Benin City Nigeria Office: Lonestar Drilling Co, PMB 4104 Sapele Delta, Nigeria

HONSA, VLASTA, retired librarian; b. Žilina, Czechoslovakia, Sept. 1, 1924; came to U.S., 1951; d. František Petr and Marie (Širkova) Petrova; m. Vladimir Honsa, June 26, 1948; children: Patricia, Eva Honsa-Hogg. BA, Charles U., Prague, 1947; MLS, Ind. U., 1968. Gifts libr. Ind. U. Libr., Bloomington, 1968-70; head reference dept. Clark County Libr., Las Vegas, Nev., 1970-80; asst. adminstr. Clark County Libr., Las Vegas, 1980-94; ret., 1994; coord. Found. Collection, part of the Found. Ctr.'s Cooperating Collections network, Clark County Libr., 1979-94. Author: Nevada Foundation Directory, 1984, 2d edit., 1989, 3rd edit., 1994. Bd. dirs. So. Nev. Musical Arts Soc., Las Vegas, 1989-92; organized and presented fundraising workshops for cmty. fund raisers sponsored by Las Vegas-Clark County Libr. Dist., 1979-94. Recipient Ind. U. grant-in-aid to conduct rsch. of publs. in cen. Am. univs. and nat. librs., 1970, Champion award Las Vegas-Clark County Libr. Dist., 1985. Mem. ALA, AAUW, Nev. Libr. Assn., Univ. Nevada Las Vegas Faculty Club. Roman Catholic. Avocations: reading, music, arts, travel. E-Mail: honsa@worldnet.att.net. Home: 2680 Congress Ave Las Vegas NV 89121-1316

HOO, SIM WANG, electronics executive. Diploma in elec. and electronics engring, Ngee Ann Tech. Coll., Singapore. Electronics engr. Neutron Corp., Well Seis Internat. Ptd. Ltd.; chmn., CEO, co-founder Creative Tech. Ltd., 1981—. Fax: 65-773-0353. Office: 31 International Bus Park, Singapore 609921, Republic of Singapore*

HOOD, ALASTAIR SHERIDAN, product manager; b. Carrickfergus, No. Ireland, Apr. 16, 1970. BEng in Comm. Engring. with honors, U. Plymouth, 1993, PhD in Optical Engring., 1997. Rsch. asst. U. Plymouth, 1993-96; design/devel. engr. Renishaw Plc, Eng., 1997-98, product mgr., 1998—. Avocations: skiing, climbing, mountain biking, walking. Fax: 01453 524219. E-mail: alastair.hood@renishaw.com. Home: 71 Redland Rd, Redland Bristol BS6 6AQ, England Office: Renishaw Plc, New Mills Wotton-under-Edge, Gloucester GL12 8JR, England

HOOD, JAMES MICHAEL, lawyer; b. Des Moines, Mar. 27, 1945; s. James Vincent and Maybl (Rayburn) H.; m. Sherrie Elaine Lazar, Apr. 16, 1973; children—James Michael, Grace. B.A., Drake U., 1967, J.D., 1970. Bar: Iowa 1970, U.S. Dist. Ct. (so. dist) Iowa 1970, U.S. Dist. Ct. (no. dist.) Iowa 1972, U.S. Dist. Ct. (so. dist.) Ill. 1978, U.S. Supreme Ct. 1978. Sole practice, Davenport, Iowa, 1970—. Served with USN, 1970-72. Mem. ABA, Iowa Bar Assn., Scott County Bar Assn., Assn. Trial Lawyers Iowa, Assn. Trial Lawyers Am., Iowa Assn. Worker Compensation Lawyers. Home: 2213 Fairhaven Rd Davenport IA 52803-2334 Office: 302 Union Arcade Bldg Davenport IA 52801

HOOD, ROBERT HOLMES, lawyer; b. Charleston, S.C., Oct. 5, 1944; s. James Albert and Ruth (Henderson) H.; m. Mary Agnes Burnham, Aug. 5, 1967; children: Mary Agnes, Elizabeth, Robert Holmes Jr., James Bernard. BA, U. of the South, 1966; JD, U. S.C., 1969. Bar: U.S. Supreme Ct. 1969, S.C. 1969, U.S. Dist. Ct. S.C. 1969, U.S. Ct. Appeals (4th cir.) 1969. Asst. atty. gen. State of S.C., Columbia, 1969-70; ptnr. Sinkler, Gibbs & Simons, Charleston, 1970-85; prin. Hood Law Firm, Charleston, 1985—. Mem. Assn. Def. Trial Attys. (pres. 1985-86), Am. Bd. Trial Advs. (diplomate, pres. Charleston chpt. 1997), Internat. Assn. Def. Counsel, Def. Rsch. and Trial Inst. (bd. dirs. 1987-90), Fedn. Ins. and Corp. Counsel, S.C. Def. Trial Attys. Assn. (pres. 1980-81), Network of Trial Law Firms. Episcopalian. Office: 172 Meeting St Charleston SC 29401-3126

HOOD, ROGER GRAHAME, criminologist, educator; b. Bristol, Eng., June 12, 1936; s. Ronald Hugo and Phyllis Eileen (Murphy) H.; m. Barbara Blaine Smith, June 15, 1963 (div. July 1985); 1 child, Catharine Rachael; m. Nancy Colquitt Lynah, Oct. 5, 1985; stepchildren: Clare, Zoe. BSc in Sociology, U. London, 1957; PhD, U. Cambridge, Eng., 1963; D of Civil Law, U. Oxford, 1999. Rsch. officer London Sch. Econs. U. London, 1957-58, 61-63; lectr. social adminstrn. U. Durham, Eng., 1963-67; asst. dir. rsch. Inst. Criminology U. Cambridge, 1967-73, reader in criminology, 1973-95; prof. criminology U. Oxford, Eng., 1995—; dir. Ctr. Criminol. Rsch., 1973—; parole bd., Eng., Wales, 1972-73, judicial std. bd. Eng., Wales, 1979-85; mem. dept. com. Rev. Parole Sys., 1987-88; expert cons. on death penalty UN, Vienna, 1988, 95, 2000; gen. editor Clarendon Studies in Criminology, 1993-98 mem. editl. bd. The British Jour. Criminology, 1973-88, Crime and Justice, an Annual Review of Research, 1988-96, European Jour. of Crime, Criminal Law and Criminal Justice, 1993—. Author: Sentencing in Magistrates' Courts, 1962, Borstal Re-Assessed, 1965, Sentencing the Motoring Offender, 1972; (with Leon Radzinowicz) Criminology and the Administration of Criminal Justice: A Bibliography, 1976 (Joseph L. Andrews award Am. Assn. Law Librs. 1976), A History of English Criminal Law and its Administration, vol. 5, The Emergence of Penal Policy, 1986, 2d edit., 1990, The Death Penalty: A World-Wide Perspective, 1989, 2d edit., 1996, Race and Sentencing: A Study in the Crown Court, 1992; (with Richard Sparks) Key Issues in Criminology, 1970; (with Stephen Shute) The Parole System at Work, 2000; editor: Crime, Criminology and Public Policy, 1974; contbr. articles to profl. jours. Pres. British Soc. Criminology, 1986-89. Fellow Brit. Acad., 1992—, Clare Hall, 1969-73, All Souls Coll., 1973—; apptd. Comdr. of Order of Brit. Empire, 1995, Queen's Counsel (honoris causa), 2000; recipient Sellin-Glueck award Am. Soc. Criminology, 1986. Avocations: touring, cooking. Home: 63 Iffley Rd, Oxford OX4 1EF, England Office: All Souls Coll, U Oxford, Oxford OX1 4AL, England

HOOD, RONALD CHALMERS, III, historian, writer; b. Florence, Ala., Apr. 2, 1947; s. Ronald Chalmers II and Elizabeth Woods (Craig) H.; m. Lucile O'Connor, Dec. 20, 1969; children: Ronald Chalmers IV, Reed Cathleen. BS, U.S. Naval Acad., 1969; MA, U. Maine, Orono, 1972; PhD, U. Md., 1979. Commd. 2d lt. USMC, 1969, advanced through grades to capt., 1973, resigned, 1982; historian, writer Johns Hopkins U., Balt., 1982—, George Mason U., Fairfax, Va., 1982—, U. Md., College Park, 1982—; lectr. Smithsonian Instn., Washington, 1988; speaker Conf. on Strategic Studies, Washington, 1985; co-chair Muscle Shoals Revisited Conf. on Future of Tenn. Valley, 1993; theatre and arts critic The Daily Jour. Author: (history monograph) Royal Republicans, 1985; co-author: (mil. history) Military Effectiveness, 1987, Body, Mind, Spirit: 75 Years of Camp Hazen YMCA, 1995; contbr. editorial columns to Washington Post, Richmond Times-Dispatch, Potomac News, articles to profl. jours. Asst. scoutmaster Boy Scouts Am., Woodbridge, Va., 1989—; advisor County Sch. Bd., Prince William County, Va., 1991; instr. ARC, Prince William County, 1982—. Samuel Eliot Morison fellow U. Maine, Orono, 1971-72, Grad. Sch. fellow U. Md., 1975, fellow Am. Philos. Soc., 1998, sr. fellow to France Am. Coun. Learned Societies, 2000-2001. Mem. AAUP, Writers' Ctr., Smithsonian Instn., Nat. Geographic Soc. Avocations: travel, acting, bike riding, aquatic activities, cross-country skiing. Fax: (703) 497-9578. Home and Office: 12317 Oakwood Dr Woodbridge VA 22192-1911

HOOD, THOMAS GREGORY, minister; b. Stamford, Conn., Mar. 26, 1948; s. George E. and Shirley W. (Brundage) H.; m. Esther A. Whitcomb, July 1, 1967; children: Thomas G., Sarah D. BA, Johnson State Coll., 1984; MDiv, Covington Sem., Rossville, Ga., 1986, PhD in Counseling, 1988. Ordained to ministry Fellowship of Christian Assemblies, 1969, Am. Bapt. Chs. in U.S.A., 1984. Asst. pastor Bethel Full Gospel Ch., Barton, Vt., 1968-71; pastor Lyndonville (Vt.) Full Gospel Ch., 1969-71, Sheffield (Vt.) Fed. Ch., 1971-74, Sutton (Vt.) Bapt. Ch., 1972-84, Adams Center (N.Y.) Bapt. Ch., 1984—; del. Am. Bapt. Conv., N.Y., 1984—. Author: The Lord's Prayer, 1986, A Theology of Victory, 1987, Biblical Principles, 1988; composer religious songs. Mem. Am. Bapt.Mins. Coun. Republican. Home: 13463 US Rt 11 Adams Center NY 13606

HOODBHOY, PERVEZ AMIRALI, physicist, educator; b. Karachi, Pakistan, July 11, 1950; s. Amirali and Malek Hoodbhoy; m. Hajra Ahmed, Dec. 22, 1974; children: Asha, Alia. BS, MIT, 1973, MS, 1973, PhD, 1978. Prof. physics Quaid-e-Azam U., Islamabad, Pakistan, 1973—; vis. prof. MIT, Carnegie Mellon, U. Wash., U. Md. Author: Islam and Science-Religious Orthodoxy and the Battle for Rationality, 1991 (Best Book of Yr. award Pakistan); editor: Baqi Beg Memorial Volume, 1989, Education and the State: Fifty Years of Pakistan; prodr. popular sci. TV serials; contbr. some 60 articles to profl. jours.; prodr. 19 sci. edn. documentaries. Recipient Abdus Salam award for math., 1984, Faiz Ahmed Faiz award for edn., 1991, Baker award for electronics, 1968. E-mail: hoodbhoy@isb.pol.com.pk. Office: Quaid-e-Azam U, Physics Dept, Islamabad 45320, Pakistan

HOOGENRAAD, JOHANNES HERMAN, physicist; b. Utrecht, The Netherlands, July 9, 1968; s. Willem Jan and Hendrika Margaretha (Van Steijn) H. MSc, U. Utrecht, The Netherlands, 1992; PhD, U. Amsterdam, The Netherlands, 1996. Tutor Nijenrode U., Breukelen, The Netherlands, 1987; founder Hoogenraad Interface Svcs., Utrecht, The Netherlands, 1988—; rschr. Fom-Amolf, Amsterdam, The Netherlands, 1992-96, Philips Rsch. Labs., Eindhoven, The Netherlands, 1996-98; devel. mgr. Software ASM Lithography, 1998—; sci. guest U. Fla., Gainesville, Fla., 1990-91; vis. fellow Ctr. for Ultrafast Optical Scis., Ann Arbor, Mich., 1994. Contbr. articles to profl. jours. Mem. Am. Phys. Soc., Inst. Physics (London). E-mail: Jan.Hoogenraad@asml.nl. Avocations: chamber choir, ham radio, travel. Home: Schapenhoeve 11, 3992 PL Houten The Netherlands Office: ASML, De Run 110, 5503 LA Veldhoven The Netherlands

HOOGENRAAD, NICHOLAS J., biochemist, researcher, educator; b. The Hague, The Netherlands, Feb. 17, 1942; s. Martinus E. and Cornelia A. (Haremaker) H.; m. Joan M. Fleming, Feb. 20, 1965; children: Andrew, Kirsten. B Agrl. Sci., U. Melbourne, Australia, 1965, PhD in Biochemistry, 1969. Asst. prof. pediats. Stanford (Calif.) U., 1971-74, vis. prof. biochemistry, 1979; lectr. in biochemistry La Trobe U., Bundoora, Victoria, Australia, 1974-75, sr. lectr. biochemistry, 1976-83, reader in biochemistry, 1984-91, prof., head dept. biochemistry, 1992—; vis. scientist Imperial Cancer Rsch. Fund, London, 1986. Mem. editl. bd. Today's Life Scis., 1989—; contbr. over 100 articles to sci. jours. Mem. Australian Soc. Biochemistry and Molecular Biology (Amrad-Pharmacia Biotech. medal 1994, pres. 1997-98), Australian Acad. Scis. (chair nat. com. for biochemistry and molecular biology 1997—). Avocations: growing grapes, winemaking. Office: La Trobe U, Dept Biochemistry, 3083 Bundoora Victoria, Australia

HOOGERWERF, ANDRIES, political scientist; b. Delft, The Netherlands, Mar. 11, 1931; s. Andries and Gepkina (Mulder) H.; m. Dini Leppink; children: Maaike, Hanneke, Petra. MA in Polit. Sci., Free U. Amsterdam, 1960, Dr. Social Scis., 1964. Asst. prof. Free U. Amsterdam, 1960-69; full prof. polit. sci. U. Nijmegen, 1969-75; full prof. polit. sci. U. Twente, Enschede, 1975-93, prof. emeritus, 1993—. Author: The Balance of Politics, 1995, Violence in the Netherlands, 1996, Elites in Democracy, 1997, Christian Thinkers on Politics, 1999. Knight Order of the Dutch Lion, 1993. Mem. Royal Netherlands Acad. Arts and Scis. Home: Schumannlaan 30, 7522 KE Enschede The Netherlands

HOOGMARTENS, MICHAEL JAMES, orthopedic surgeon, medical educator; b. Tongeren, Belgium, May 18, 1937; s. John H. and Gertrude Boonen. MD cum laude, U. Leuven (Belgium), 1962, Orthopedic Surgery, 1967, D in Med. Scis., 1986. Lectr. U. Leuven (Belgium), 1971-87, assoc. prof., 1987—; mem. Belgian Bd. Orthopedic Surgery, 1974—, coun. Verbond der Belgische Beroepsverenigingen van Geneesheren-specialisten, 1979—. Capt. Belgian Army, 1967-68. World Health fellow 1261, 1972, NIH fellow, 1972. Mem. Belgische Vereniging Orthopedie en Traumatologie (mem. coun. 1971—), Union Européenne Médecins Spécialistes (Belgian co-del. 1981—). Roman Catholic. Avocations: history. Home: Lindelaan 5, B-3001 Leuven Belgium Office: U Hosp, Weligerveld 1, B-3212 Pellenberg Belgium

HOOGWERF, BYRON JAMES, physician; b. Sioux Falls, S.D., Feb. 8, 1945; s. Henry (dec.) Hoogwerf and Nellie (Verbrugge) Hoogwerf-Christians; m. Judith Anne Barrett, Aug. 16, 1966 (div. 1985); children: Jennifer Anne, Byron James II; m. Heidi Ellen Gaenslen, Dec. 21, 1985; 1 child, Rebecca Alexandra. BA, Calvin Coll., 1967; MD, U. Minn., 1971. Intern Hennepin County Med. Ctr., Mpls., 1971-72, resident internal medicine, 1976-78; fellow, endocrinology Univ. Minn., Mpls., 1978-81, asst. prof., 1981-85; staff physician Cleve. Clinic Found., 1985—, chmn., endocrinology, 1988-91, program dir. internal medicine residency, 1997—. Contbr. chpts. to books and over 85 articles to profl. jours. Bd. dirs. Diabetes Assn. Greater Cleve., 1986-95, pres. bd. dirs., 1992-93; bd. dirs. Camp Ho Mito Koda, Cleve., 1986—. Recipient Tng. grant NIH, U. Minn., 1978-79, Nat. Rsch. Svc. award NIH, U. Minn., 1979-81, Spl. Emphasis Rsch. Career award NIH-Nat. Inst. Aging, U. Minn., 1982-85, NIH Post CABG Trial award, 1987-95. Fellow ACP (cert. diabetes edn.), Am. Assn. Clin. Endocrinologists; mem. AAAS, Endocrine Soc., Am. Diabetes Assn. (chmn. publs. com. coun. on nutritional scis. and metabolism 1988-91, profl. practice com. 1992-94, chmn. coun. on nutritional scis. and metabolism 1996-98, bd. dirs. 1998—, pub. com. 1998—), Endocrine Soc., Soc. for Clin. Trials. Presbyterian. Home: 2237 Demington Dr Cleveland OH 44106-3320 Office: The Cleveland Clinic Found 9500 Euclid Ave Cleveland OH 44195-0002

HOOK, MICHAEL JOHN, advertising executive; b. London, July 3, 1934; s. Frederick John Hook and Eileen Naomi-Louisa (Cox) Robinson; m. Hazel Rowling, Aug. 23, 1958; children: Philip, Christine. Messenger Spottiswoode Dixon & Hunting, London, 1950-52, overseas media buyer, 1954-62; internat. media exec. CPV Internat., London, 1962-66; head internat. media Ogilvy & Mather, London, 1966-79; mng. dir. Ogilvy & Mather Internat. Media, London, 1979-87; internat. dir. Yershon Media, London, 1987-89, chmn., founder Media Mondiale, Andover, Eng., 1989—. Mem. Hampshire (Eng.) Ambs., 1995—. Bombadier Royal Arty., 1952-54. Fellow Inst. Practitioners in Advt. (chmn. 1967-69), Internat. Advt. Assn. (activities chmn. 1974-76, membership chmn. 1976-78). Avocation: bowls. Office: Media Mondiale Ltd, 82A High St, Andover SP10 1NG, England

HOOKER, JAMES TODD, manufacturing executive; b. Ashland, Ohio, Dec. 21, 1946; s. Melvin Todd and Harriett (Lutz) H.; m. Sallie Foulkrod Utz, Feb. 22, 1975; 1 child, Stephanie Rae. BSBA magna cum laude, Ashland U., 1973. Advt. mgr. The Gorman-Rupp Co., Mansfield, Ohio, 1974-76, mfg. engr., 1976-79; asst. service mgr. The Gorman-Rupp Co., Mansfield, 1979-80, gen. service mgr., 1980-86, asst. sales mgr., 1986-90; mgr. mfg. The Gorman-Rupp Co., Mansfield, Ohio, 1990-95, dir. mfg., 1995-98, v.p. mfg. and facilities, 1998—. Solicitor United Way, Mansfield; moderator, bd. deacons Presbyn. Ch., 1988-89, elder, mem. Session; chmn. bd. Trustees Richland County Leadership Unltd.; mem. Heritage Found.; plank owner USN Meml. Found.; chmn. bd. Mansfield Richland County Chamber Edn. Found. Decorated Vietnamese Gallantry Cross. Republican. Home: 1090 Trout Dr Mansfield OH 44903-9144 Office: The Gorman-Rupp Co 305 Bowman St Mansfield OH 44903-1600

HOON, GEOFFREY, federal official; b. Derby, Dec. 6, 1953; married; 3 children. Grad., Jesus Coll., Cambridge U. Lectr. in law Leeds U., 1976-82; vis. prof. law U. Louisville, 1979-80; barrister, 1982-84; mem. European Parliament, 1984-94; elected MP, 1992—; opposition whip, 1994-95, opposition spokesman on trade and industry, 1995; parliamentary sec. Lord Chancellor's Dept., 1997-98, min. of state, 1998-99; min. state for Asia, the Pacific and the Middle East Fgn. and Commonwealth Office, 1999, min. State for Europe, 1999; sec. State of Def., 1999—. Office: Ministry of Def, Main Bldg Whitehall, London SW1A 2HB, England*

HOOPER, ANNE DODGE, pathologist, educator; b. Groton, Mass., July 16, 1926; d. Carroll William and Bertha Sanford (Wiener) Dodge; m. William Dale Hooper, June 17, 1952; children: Elizabeth Anne, Joan Elaine, Caroline Mae. AB, Washington U., St. Louis, 1947, MD, 1952. Diplomate in pathologic anatomy, clin. pathology and forensic pathology Am. Bd. Pathology. Rotating intern Virginia Mason Hosp., Seattle, 1952-53; resident in internal medicine St. Francis Hosp., Hartford, Conn., 1953-54; resident in pathologic anatomy and clin. pathology New Britain (Conn.) Gen. Hosp., 1954-57, Presbyn. Hosp., Phila., 1957-58; resident in forensic pathology Office Med. Examiner, Phila., 1958-60; from pathologist to acting chief lab svc. VA Hosp., Coatesville, Pa., 1960-66; dir. lab. St. Albans (Vt.) Hosp., 1966-69, Kerbs Hosp., St. Albans, 1966-71, Williamson Appalachian Regional Hosp., South Williamson, Ky., 1971-73, Beckley (W.Va.) Appalachian Regional Hosp., 1974-76; asst. prof. pathology W.Va. Sch. Osteo. Medicine, Lewisburg, 1977, assoc. prof. pathology, 1978-97, cons. in pathology, 1997—; lab. accreditation insp. CAP, 1992—, Am. Osteo. Assn., 1986-99; assoc. med. examiner State of W.Va., 1999—; med. missionary Kijabe Hosp., Kenya, 1998, SALFA lab., Madagascar, 2000. Contbr. articles to profl. jours. Pres. local elem. sch. PTA, St. Albans, 1967-68; pres. Greenbrier unit Am. Cancer Soc., Lewisburg, 1989-93, bd. dirs. W.Va. div., Charleston, 1987-94, profl. edn. com. W.Va. div., 1982-94. Fellow Coll. Am. Pathologists, Am. Acad. Forensic Scis.; mem. AMA, W.Va. Med. Soc., Raleigh County Med. Soc., Am. Soc. Clin. Pathologists, Internat. Acad. Pathologists, Nat. Assn. Med. Examiners, Am. Osteo. Coll. Pathologists (assoc.). Avocation: playing violin and viola. Office: 63 Cedar Knoll Ronceverte WV 24970-9700

HOOPER, KELLEY RAE, delivery service executive; b. Tulsa, Aug. 24, 1960; d. Kenneth Roe Sharp and Beverly Jane (Phillips) Jenkins; m. John Patrick Hooper, Apr. 30, 1988 (dec. Oct. 1990). BS, Okla. State U., 1982; postgrad., So. Nazarene U., 1991—. Ter. mgr. Am. Fidelity Ins. Co., Oklahoma City, 1982-87; account exec. United Parcel Svc., Inc., Oklahoma City, 1987-89, customer svc. office supr., 1991, next day air letter ctr. coord., 1990, dist. office mgr., 1991-92, dist. area mgr.; dist. sales mgr. ctrl. Ohio United Parcel Svc., Inc., Columbus, 1994-96; v.p. mktg. and sales Premier Courier, Columbus, 1997-98; human resources dir. Mobile Instruments, Bellefontaine, Ohio, 1998—. Dist. region grant com. United Parcel Svc. Found., Oklahoma City, 1992; mem., donor Omniplex Sci. Mus., Oklahoma City,

1990—, Ballet Okla., Oklahoma City, 1992—, Oklahoma City Arts Mus., 1992—; mem. Wexner Ctr. for Arts, 1996—, COH Builders Exch., Greater Columbus Conv. and Visitor Bur., Leadership Columbus, 1997-98, Columbus Arts Mus.; active Columbus Arts Mus., Spl. Wish Found. Mem. NAFE, Mail Systems Mgmt. Assn., Am. Mgmt. Assn., Advt. Fedn., Nat. Trust for Hist. Preservation, Soc. for Human Resources Mgmt., Art Inst. Chgo., Sierra, Internat. Wine Club, Smithsonian Assocs., Okla. State U. Alumni Assn., Sales Execs. Club, Rotary, Pi Sigma Alpha. Democrat. Avocations: competitive volleyball, antique collecting, traveling, reading. Home: 9484 Toms Ln Belle Center OH 43310-9755 Office: 333 Water Ave Bellefontaine OH 43311-1733

HOOPIS, HARRY PETER, insurance executive, entrepreneur; b. Providence, May 14, 1947; s. Peter Harry and Angela Rose (Taraborelli) H.; m. Demetra Psilopoulos, Feb. 20, 1972; children: Krina Angela, Peter Harry. BS in Acctg., U. R.I., 1969. CLU; chartered fin. cons. Coll. agt. Northwestern Mut. Life Ins. Co., Kingston, R.I., 1968-69; spl. agt. Northwestern Mut. Life Ins. Co., Providence, 1969-71; dist. agt. Northwestern Mut. Life Ins. Co., Wakefield, R.I., 1971-74; asst. supt. manpower devel. Northwestern Mut. Life Ins. Co., Milw., 1974-77; gen. agt. Northwestern Mut. Life Ins. Co., Evanston, Ill., 1977—; cons., speaker ins. industry, U.S. and Can., 1977—, Purdue Mgmt. Inst., Lafayette, Ind., 1987-88; pres. Gama Internat., 1996-97. Author: (with others) Sales Focus Workbook, 1985, Fixed Activity Commitment, 1980, Managing Sales Professionals, 1993, Essentials of Management Development, 1999. Mem. Nat. Gen. Agts. and Mgrs. Assn. (pres. 1989-90, Yates Meml. award 1988, named Master Agy. Builder, 1983-97, sec., bd. dirs. 1989—), Am. Soc. CLUs, Chgo. Assn. CLUs (bd. dirs. 1978-81), Gama Internat. (pres. 1997). Republican. Avocations: skiing, golf, jogging. Office: Hoopis Fin Group 790 W Frontage Rd Northfield IL 60093-1210

HOOTMAN, HARRY EDWARD, retired nuclear engineer, consultant; b. Oak Park, Ill., June 5, 1933; s. Merle Albert and Rachel Edith (Atkinson) H.; m. Linda P. Smith, Nov. 23, 1963; children: David, Holly, John. BS in Chemistry, Mich. Technol. U., 1959, MS in Nuc. Engring., 1962; LLB, LaSalle Ext. U., 1971, MA in English Lit., U. S.C., 1999. Registered profl. engr., S.C. Rsch. assoc. Argonne (Ill.) Nat. Lab., 1959-62; process engr. Savannah River Plant, Aiken, S.C., 1962-65; rsch. assoc. reactor physics group, nuclear engring. div. Savannah River Lab., Aiken, 1965-87; with New Reactor Devel. Group, 1987-92, adv. engr. Planning, Studies and Analysis, 1992-95; ret., 1995; cons. transuranic waste disposal and incineration, radioisotope prodn., separation and shielding; instr. Math. and Engring. Dept. U. S.C., Aiken, 1979-80, 90-94. Inventor alpha waste incinerator. Bd. dirs. Central Savannah River Area Sci. and Engring. Fair, Inc., Augusta, Ga., 1972-91. Served to sgt. USAF, 1953-57. Mem. Am. Acad. Environ. Engrs., Nat. Soc. Profl. Engrs. (local chmn. 1978-79), Am. Nuclear Soc. (local chmn. 1979-80), Am. Phys. Soc., Sigma Xi. Baptist. Home: 820 Brandy Rd SE Aiken SC 29801-7281

HOOVER, LOLA MAE, retired communications company executive; b. Monticello, Ark., Apr. 1, 1947; d. Victor Arthur and Essie (Humphries) Piper; divorced; 1 child, Larry Wayne. With prodn. dept. AT&T, West Chicago, Ill., 1965-78, 1st level shop mgr., 1978-83, warehouse mgr., 1983-84, office mgr., 1984-86, with Mfg. Resource Planning Project, 1986-87, leader Mfg. Resource Planning project, 1987-88, mgr. script planning and prodn. control, 1988-91, 2d level mgr. custome svcs. and prodn. shop, 1992-96; mem. pres.'s coun., staff mgr. AT&T, Bedminster, N.J., 1993-94; mfg. mgr. Dallas Works, Mesquite, Tex., 1994-97; ret. AT&T (Lucent Techs.), 1996. Baptist. Home: 207 Briar Ln North Aurora IL 60542-1211

HOPE, DAVID MICHAEL, bishop; b. Apr. 14, 1940. Student, Nottingham U., Linacre Coll. Oxford. Curate St. John's Tuebrook, Liverpool, Eng., 1965-70; chaplain Ch. of Resurrection, Bucharest, Romania, 1967-68; vicar St. Andrew's, Warrington, Eng., 1970-74; prin. St. Stephen's House, Oxford, Eng., 1974-82; warden Cmty. St. Mary the Virgin, Wantage, Eng., 1980-87; vicar All Saints' Margaret St., London, 1982-85; bishop of Wakefield (Eng.), 1985-91, bishop of London, 1991-95, archbishop of York (Eng.), 1995—. Author: The Leonine Sacramentary, 1971, Living the Gospel, 1993. Named prelate Order of Brit. Empire, 1991-95, dean Chapels Royal, 1991-95, KCVO, 1995. Office: Bishopthorpe, York Y023 2GE, England

HOPE, GERRI DANETTE, telecommunications management executive; b. Sacramento, Feb. 28, 1956; d. Albert Gerald and Beulah Rae (Bane) Hope. AS, Sierra Coll., Calif., 1977; postgrad. Okla. State U., 1977-79. Instructional asst. II San Juan Sch. Dist., Carmichael, Calif., 1979-82; telecomm. supr. Delta Dental Svc. of Calif., San Francisco, 1982-85; telecomm. coordinator Farmers Savs. Bank, Davis, Calif., 1985-87; telecomm. officer Sacramento Savs. Bank, 1987-95; owner GDH Enterprises, 1993-97; telecomm. analyst II contractor dept. ins. State Calif., 1995—; sr. telecomms. engr. Access Health, Inc., Rancho Cordova, Calif., 1996-97, Any Time Access, Sacramento, 1997-98, GDH Enterprises, North Highlands, 1993-97; employment devel. dept. assoc., info. systems analyst specialist State of Calif., 1998—; founder Custom Label Designer, Sacramento, 1993-96; mem. telecomm. adv. panel Golden Gate U., Sacramento; lectr. in toll fraud prevention and network security. Mem. Telecomm. Assn. (v.p. membership com. Sacramento Valley chpt., 1993, v.p. dir. programs 1997-98, corp. conf. com. programs bd. 1997-99, v.p. pub. rels. bd.), Am. Philatelic Soc., Sacramento Philatelic Assn., Errors, Freaks and Oddities Club, Philatelic Collectors. Republican. Avocations: writing, computers, philately, animal behavior, participating in Christian ministry. Home: 3025 U St Antelope CA 95843-2513 Office: State Calif EDDI DPDI Telecom 800 Capital Mall MIC58-25 Sacramento CA 95814

HOPE, JAMES ARTHUR DAVID See HOPE OF CRAIGHEAD, LORD

HOPE, MARGARET LAUTEN, civic worker; b. N.Y.C.; 1 son, Frederick H., III. Privately educated. Ball com. various charity fund raising events. Mem. Jr. League N.Y.C., Everglades Club, Women's Nat. Rep. Club (N.Y.C.), St. James Club (London). Address: PO Box 601 Palm Beach FL 33480-0601

HOPE OF CRAIGHEAD, LORD (JAMES ARTHUR DAVID HOPE), lord of appeal in ordinary, life peer of Bamff; b. June 27, 1938; s. Arthur Henry Cecil and Muriel Ann Neilson (Collie) H.; m. Katharine Mary Kerr, 1966; 3 children. BA, St. John's Coll., Cambridge, 1962; LLB, Edinburgh U., 1965; MA, St. John's Coll., Cambridge, 1978; LLD (hon.), Aberdeen U., 1991, Strathclyde U., 1993, Edinburgh U., 1995; chancellor, Strathclyde U., 1998. Admitted Faculty of Advocates, 1965; standing jr. Coun. in Scotland to Bd. Inland Revenue, 1974-78; advocate dep., 1978-82; Queens Counsel, Scotland, 1978; dean Faculty of Advocates, 1986-89; lord justice gen. Scotland, 1989-96; lord pres. Court of Session, Scotland, 1989-96; chmn. Med. Appeal Tribunal, 1985-86; legal chmn. Pensions Appeal Tribunal, 1985-86. Co-editor: Gloag & Henderson's Introduction to the Law of Scotland, 1968, asst. editor, 1980, 1987; co-editor Armour on Valuation for Rating, 1971, 85; (with A.G. M. Duncan) The Rent Scotland Act 1984, 1986. Chmn. subcom. on law and instns. House of Lords Select Com. on European Union, 1998—. Lt. Nat. Svc. Seaforth Highlanders, 1957-59. Fellow Am. Coll. Trial Lawyers (hon.); mem. Can. Bar Assn., Stair Soc. (pres. 1993—). Avocations: walking, music, ornithology. Home: 34 India St, Edinburgh EH3 6HB, Scotland

HOPF, FRANK RUDOLPH, dentist; b. N.Y.C., Sept. 1, 1920; s. Rudolph Aldridge and Jennie Victoria (Fusco) H.; B.S., Purdue U., 1942; postgrad. Middlesex U. Sch. Medicine, 1943-44; D.D.S., N.Y. U., 1953, postgrad., 1957-61; M.A., Columbia, 1953, M.P.H., 1955; m. Elsie Hedlund, Sept. 10, 1949; children—Christine, Frank, Victoria, William, Robert. Asst. dir. Bur. Dental Health, N.Y. State Dept. Health, Albany, 1956-57, regional dental dir., White Plains, 1967-90; pvt. practice dentistry specializing in periodontics, Rye, 1957—. Research asso. dept. periodontics, N.Y. U. Coll. Dentistry, 1958-61; clin. asst. prof. dept. periodontics N.J. Coll. Medicine and Dentistry, Jersey City, 1962-67; adj. asst. prof. dept. community dentistry Columbia Sch. Dental and Oral Surgery, N.Y.C., 1971-76; vis. prof. dept. preventive dentistry, Pitts. U. Sch. Dentistry, 1967-72. Pres., Country Ridge Home Owners Assn., Rye Brook, N.Y., 1960-62. Served with USNR, 1944-46. NIH grantee, 1957. Fellow Am. Public Health Assn., Am. Sch. Health Assn., N.Y. Acad. Dentistry, Am. Coll. Dentists; mem. ADA, N.Y. State Public Health Assn. (pres. 1970-72), Westchester Shore Dental Study Club (pres. 1960-61), Royal Soc. Health, North Eastern Soc. Periodontics, AAAS, Westchester Acad. Medicine, Am. Soc. Dentistry for Children, Federation Dentaire Internationale. Roman Catholic. KC (4 deg.). Club: Westchester Country (Rye, N.Y.). Contbr. articles to profl. publs. Home: 42 Rockinghorse Trl Rye Brook NY 10573-1038 Office: 33 Cedar St Rye NY 10580-2031

HOPF, GÜNTER HERBERT, pharmacologist, toxicologist; b. Landau, Pfalz, Germany, Mar. 27, 1944; s. Günter Paul and Anna Maria (Brombacher) H. Lic. Pharmacist, U. Erlangen-Nürnberg, Germany, 1973, Lic. Physician, 1980, MD, 1982. Specialist in pharmacology and toxicology, 1993. Sci. postgrad. fellow U. Erlangen-Nürnberg, Germany, 1980-88; sci. fellow Drug Commn. of German Med. Profession, Cologne, Germany, 1988-90, commissionary exec. dir., 1990-91, vice exec. dir., 1991-93; pharmacological advisor German Med. Assn., Düsseldorf, Germany, 1994—; cons. Nat. Com. Physicians and Health Ins., Cologne, 1989-93, Med. Women's Internat. Assn., 1990—, WHO: Internat. Drug Monitoring Program, Geneva, 1990-93, Nat. Health Authority, Berlin, Germany, 1990-93 and other commns. and adv. groups. Mem. ad hoc commn. Ann. Report on Drug Prescriptions, 1990, 91, 92, 93, 95—; coord.: Price Comparison List, 1992; author, coord.: Drug Prescriptions, 17th edit., 1992; contbr. articles to profl. jours. Mem. Student's Parliament, Erlangen, 1968, Frat. Corps Baruthia, Erlangen, 1968—; editorial com. sch. jour. Pupille, 1963-65. Capt. Mil. Hosp., German Navy, 1973-75. Mem. Soc. German Pharmacologists and Toxicologists, German Soc. Drug Use and Pharmacoepidemiology, European Soc. Pharmacovigilance, Internat. Soc. Pharmacoepidemiology. Avocations: paramedicine, windsurfing, sailing, diving, mountain hiking. Home: Robert-Koch Str 42, 50931 Cologne Germany

HOPF, SIGRID, retired psychologist, researcher, educator; b. Bremen, Germany, May 22, 1935; d. Henrich and Louise (Meyer) Focke; m. Uto E. Hopf, Aug. 24, 1961. Diploma, U. Marburg, Germany, 1961, D degree, 1972. Programmer Heinkel Aeroplanes, Munich, 1962-64; rsch. asst. Max-Planck Inst. for Psychiatry, Munich, 1964-90; lectr. U. Regensburg, 1979-85, U. Vienna, Austria, 1985-89; rsch. assoc. Rsch. Unit for Human Ethology MPG, Andechs, 1990-96, U. Munich, 1996-98; ret.; mem. steering com. Confs. for a More Dem. UN, London, 1991; UN rep. Internat. Coun. Psychologists, 1987—; mem. NGO Com. on the Family, Vienna, 1994—; mem. Austrian Assn. for Interdisciplinary Family Rsch., Vienna, 1988—, Assn. for Anthropology, Berlin, 1992—. Contbr. articles to profl. jours. including Internat. Jour. Primatology, Internat. Jour. Behavioral Devel., among others. Travel grantee European Tng. Program in Brain and Behaviour Rsch. (Brussels), 1974. Mem. Psychologists Profl. Union (women's issues rep. 1993—), Assn. for Ecology and Politics, Psychologists for Social Responsibility, Womens Internat. League for Peace and Freedom (adviser 1988). Avocations: observing nature, human-environment interaction, psychological implications of globalisation. Home: Begonien Str 10, D-80939 Munich Germany

HOPFE, HAROLD HERBERT, retired chemical engineer; b. Ware, Mass., Apr. 21, 1936; s. Herbert Henry and Lottie Maud (Senecal) H.; m. Winifred Ann Dorsey, June 29, 1957; children: Peter Harold, William David, Susan Elizabeth Haryasz. BSChemE, U. Mass., 1958, MSChemE, 1970. Registered profl. engr., N.Y. Devel. engr. Monsanto Co., Indian Orchard, Mass., 1961-82, corp. fellow, 1982-98; ret., 1998; CEO U.S. Wave Energy, Inc., Longmeadow, Mass., 1995—; pres. Polystress Co., Longmeadow, 1988—. Author: (software), tech. editor: Stress/Strain in Polymers, 1993; patentee ocean wave power generators, polymer processing systems. Children's story author/reader Pub. Libr., Longmeadow, 1989, Shriners Hosp., Springfield, Mass., 1989. Recipient Centennial award Boston Edison, 1986. Mem. Soc. Am. Inventors. Avocation: computer software devel. Home: 65 Pioneer Dr Longmeadow MA 01106-2805

HOPFER, ANDRZEJ JERZY, surveying educator; b. Warsaw, Poland, Aug. 6, 1933; s. Jerzy Edward and Halina Janina (Jacobson) H.; m. Izabela Anna Madej, June 15, 1958; children: Jacek, Joanna. MSc, Polytechnic U., Warsaw, Poland, 1957, PhD, 1964; Dr. Honoris Causa, Sopron, Hungary, 1994, Agrl. U. Cracow, 1997. Asst. Polytechnic U., Warsaw, Poland, 1958-60; dir. Dept. Regional Planning, Olsztyn, Poland, 1970—; prof. U. Agriculture and Tech., Olsztyn, Poland, 1974, dean Faculty of Surveying, 1975-77, rector, 1975-81, 90-96; vis. prof. U. Tech., Delft, The Netherlands, 1982-83. Author: (book) Rural Land Management, 1984, others. Fellow Royal Inst. Chartered Surveyors; mem. Internat. Soc. City and Regional Planners, Assn. Polish Valuers (pres. 1992—), European Real Estate Soc., Polish Acad. Scis. Avocation: jogger. Office: Olsztyn Univ, 15 Prawocheńskiego St, 10-724 Olsztyn Poland

HÖPKER, WILHELM-WOLFGANG, physician, educator; b. Frankfurt, Main, Germany, July 15, 1942; s. Wilhelm and Ruth (Gätjens) H.; m. Doris Herfel, July 18, 1970; children: Tilo Martin, Katja Anne. MD, U. Heidelberg, Germany, 1970; dr. honoris causa, Tongji Med. U., 1996. Pvt. dozent U. Heidelberg, 1976-78, prof., 1979-87; prof. U. Münster, 1978; chief Inst. Pathology Allgemeines Krnkenhaus Barmbek, Hamburg, 1987—. Author: Informatik in der Pathologie, 1970, Spätfolgen extremer Lebensverhältnisse, 1974, 2d edit., 1983, Obduktionsgut, 1976, Problem der Diagnose, 1977, Gelenkzwischenscheiben, 1984, Lungenkarzinom, 1987 (Chinese edit., 1991). Col. physician Oberstarzt Sanitätstruppe der Bundeswehr, 1990. Recipient Friendship award People's Republic of China, 1997. Mem. Deutsch-Chinesische Gesellschaft für Medizin (pres. 1991-99). Office: Allgem Krankenhaus Barmbek, Rübenkamp 148, D-22291 Hamburg Germany

HOPKINS, SIR ANTHONY (PHILIP), actor; b. Port Talbot, South Wales, U.K., Dec. 31, 1937; s. Richard Arthur and Muriel Annie (Yeates) H.; m. Petronella Barker, 1967 (div. 1972); 1 child, Abigail; m. Jennifer Ann Lynton, Jan. 13, 1973. Student, Welsh Coll. Music and Drama, Cardiff, Wales, 1954-56, Royal Acad. Dramatic Art, London, 1961-63; DLitt (hon.), Wales, 1988; Fellow (hon.), St. David's Coll., Lampeter, Wales, 1992. Ind. stage, screen, TV actor, 1963—. Made London stage debut in Julius Caesar, 1964; mem. Nat. Theatre Co., 1966-73; appeared in Juno and the Paycock, 1966, A Flea in Her Ear, 1966, Three Sisters, 1967, The Dance of Death, 1967, As You Like It, 1967, The Architect and the Emperor of Assyria, 1971, A Woman Killed with Kindness, 1971, Coriolanus, 1971, The Taming of the Shrew, 1972, Macbeth, 1972, Equus (Best Actor award N.Y. Drama Desk, Best Actor award Outer Critics Circle, Best Actor award Am. Authors Celebrities Forum), N.Y.C., 1974-75, (L.A. Drama Critics award), L.A., 1977, The Tempest, L.A., 1979, Old Times, N.Y.C., 1983, The Lonely Road, London, 1985, Pravda, Nat. Theatre, London, 1985-86 (Olivier award 1985, Stage Actor award Variety Club), King Lear, Nat. Theatre, London, 1986-87, Anthony & Cleopatra, Nat. Theatre, London, 1987, M Butterfly, Shaftesbury Theatre, London, 1989, (also dir.) August, 1994; films include (debut) The Lion in Winter, 1968, Hamlet, 1969, The Looking Glass War, 1970, When Eight Bells Toll, 1971, Young Winston, 1972, A Doll's House, 1973, The Girl from Petrovka, 1974, Juggernaut, 1974, A Bridge Too Far, 1977, Audrey Rose, 1977, International Velvet, 1977, Magic, 1978, The Elephant Man, 1979, A Change of Seasons, 1980, The Bounty, 1984 (Film Actor award Variety Club), The Good Father, 1985, 84 Charing Cross Road, 1986 (Best Actor award Moscow Film Festival 1987), The Dawning Lambs, 1991 (Acad. award for Best Actor 1992, Best Actor award Chgo. Film Critics 1992, Best Actor award Boston Film Critics 1992, Best Actor award N.Y. Film Critics 1992, Film Actor award Variety Club 1992, Best Film Actor award BAFTA 1992), Freejack, One Man's War, 1990, Spotswood/The Efficiency Expert, 1990, Howard's End, 1991, Bram Stoker's Dracula, 1992, Chaplin, 1992, Remains of the Day, 1993 (Acad. award nominee for Best Actor 1994, Best Actor award L.A. Film Critics Assn. 1993, Best Actor award Nat. Soc. film Critics (U.S.A.) 1993, BAFTA UK best film actor award, Guild of Regional Film Writers UK Best Actor award, Variety Club UK Film Actor award 1993, Japan Critics Best Actor in a Fgn. Film award), Shadowlands, 1993 (Best Actor award Nat. Bd. Rev. 1993, Best Actor award L.A. Film Critics Assn. 1993, Best Actor award Nat. Soc. Film Critics (U.S.A.) 1993), the Trial, 1993, The Road to Welville, 1993, Legends of the Fall, 1994, The Innocent, 1995, Nixon, 1995 (Acad. award nominee for Best Actor 1996), August, 1996, Surviving Picasso, 1996, The Edge, 1997, Amistad, 1997, The Mask of Zorro, 1998, Meet Joe Black, 1998, Instinct, 1999, Titus, 1999, Mission Impossible II, 2000; BBC-TV series War and Peace (Best TV Actor award Soc. Film and TV Arts), 1972; TV shows include A Heritage and Its History, 1968, Vanya, Hearts and Flowers, Three Sisters, The Peasant's Revolt, Dickens, Danton, The Poet Game, Decision to Burn, War and Peace, Cuculus Canorus, Lloyd George, Q.B. VII, 1971, Find Me, A Childhood Friend, Possessions, All Creatures Great and Small, 1975, The Lindbergh Kidnapping Case, 1976 (Emmy award), Victory at Entebbe, 1976, Dark Victory, Mayflower: The Pilgrim's Adventure, 1979, The Bunker, 1980 (Emmy award), Peter and Paul, 1980, Othello, BBC, 1981, Little Eyolf, BBC, 1981, The Hunchback of Notre Dame, 1982, A Married Man, 1984, The Arch of Triumph, CBS, 1984, Hollywood Wives, ABC, 1984, Guilty Conscience, CBS, 1984, Blunt, BBC, 1985, the Tenth Man, CBS, 1988, Across the Lake, BBC, Heartland, BBC, Great Expectations, 1989, Disney Primetime, To Be The Best, 1990, others. Decorated Comdr. of Order of Brit. Empire, 1987, Knights Bachelor, 1993, Comdr. of Order of Arts & Letters, France, 1996. Office: CAA 9830 Wilshire Blvd Beverly Hills CA 90212-1804

HOPKINS, ARLENE MARIE, retired insurance company executive; b. Redwing, Minn., Feb. 22, 1945; d. Arnold Clarence and Margaret (Hammarstrand) Budenski; m. Ernest Richard Hopkins, Sept. 14, 1974. Student, Mpls. Bus. Coll., 1965; A in Mgmt., Ins. Inst. Am., 1993. Clk. typist Northwestern Nat. Ins. Co., Mpls., 1965-66; file clk. typist Crum and Forster, Mpls., 1966-67, jr. claims examiner, 1967; office adminstr. Crum and Forster, Rochester, Minn., 1967-70; loss coding specialist Crum and Forster, San Francisco, 1970; multiline claim rep. Crum and Forster, Sacramento, 1970-72; workers compensation claims rep. Crum and Forster Indsl. Indemnity, Stockton, Calif., 1972-77; examiner workers compensation div. Crum and Forster Indsl. Indemnity, Sacramento, 1977-82; workers compensation claims supr. Kemper, Sacramento, 1982-87; div. claims examiner Kemper, Overland Park, Kans., 1987-88; sr. claims supr. Kemper, City of Industry, Calif., 1989, Sacramento, Calif., 1989-90; with div. claims exam. Kemper, Folsom, Calif., 1990-97; best practice claims auditor Kemper, Long Grove, Ill., 1997-99; ret., 1999. Mem. VFW (pres. ladies aux. 1983-84). Democrat. Lutheran. Home: 162 Hopfield Dr Folsom CA 95630-8064

HOPKINS, CATHY, sculptor, educator; b. East Orange, N.J., Sept. 24, 1947; d. Walter and Dorothy Jean (Levin) Pottow; m. Samuel G. Hopkins, Aug. 5, 1967 (div. 1979); 1 child, Augusta Anne. BA, Bryn Mawr Coll., 1969; cert., Pa. Acad. Fine Arts, 1973. Sculptor to mus. Maltbie Assocs., Mt. Laurel, N.J., 1975—; sculptor to mummers string bands and fancy brigades Phila. New Year's Assn., 1985—; tchr. sculpture Fleisher Art Meml., Phila., 1977—, faculty rep. to bd. dirs., 1986-89; tchr. sculpture Wayne (Pa.) Art Ctr., 1989-93, Perkins Art Ctr., Mooretown, N.J., 1999—; instr. karate World Tang Soo Do Assn., Phila., 1989—. Works include Twitty Bird, Twitty City, Nashville, 1982, life size relief to full round figures Sports Sprites, Phila, 1985, bronze figure with child Tribute to Nursing, Presbyn. Med. Ctr., Phila., 1989, plankton marquee Nautilus, Norfolk, Va., 1993; commd. Lloyd Hall sculpture City of Phila. Fairmont Park Commn., 1994, Re-devel. Authority City of Phila., Firemen's Union Hall, Phila., 1980. Rceipient best outdoor mural award O.I.C., Phila., 1981; grantee CETA, 1977-79. ellow Pa. Acad. Fine Arts (v.p. 1991-92, Bertha M. Goldberg 1975); mem. Artists Equity (cert. of appreciation for work in pub. places 1982), Internat. Sculpture Ctr. Democrat. Avocations: karate, squash, tennis, skiing. Home and Studio: 1220 S 6th St Philadelphia PA 19147-4828

HOPKINS, CHRISTOPHER EDWARD, engineer; b. Manchester, Eng., Feb. 15, 1957; s. Patrick Adrian and Sheila (Berry) H.; m. Catharine Ann McLean, Oct. 16, 1987; children: Nicholas Christopher, Robert Adrian. BSc, Manchester Polytech., 1980; MSc, U. Manchester Inst. Sci./Tech., 1984. Engr. British Aerospace Plc, Warton, Eng., 1980-83; sr. systems analyst Normalair-Garrett Ltd., Yeovil, Eng., 1984-87; prin. rsch. engr. Sundstrand Corp., Rockford, Ill., 1987-96; mng. dir. Abacus Engring. Systems Ltd., Out Rawcliffe, Eng., 1996—. Inventor in field. Mem. IEEE. Avocation: competitive running. E-mail: chrish@aes-ltd.demon.co.uk. Home: Bowland Ho Lancaster Rd, Out Rawcliff PR3 6BL, England Office: Abacus Engring Systems Ltd, Bowland House Lancaster Rd, Out Rawcliffe PR3 6BL, England

HOPKINS, COLIN, bank executive; b. Sarn, Wales, Aug. 7, 1933; s. Wyndham and Frances Mary (John) H. MBA, Century U., 1981, PhD, 1982; MS, Pacific Western U., 1983; BA, Columbia Pacific U., 1984, MA, 1985; D in Mgmt., Calif. U. for Advanced Studies, 1987. Adminstrv. asst. Nat. Coal Bd., Wales, 1948-53; internat. exec. The Brit. Bank of the Middle East, 1954-85; group rep. The Hong Kong and Shanghai Banking Corp., Zürich, Switzerland, 1986-87; pres., CEO Internat. Adminstrv. Svcs., Inc., Rancho Mirage, Calif., 1992-99; mem. Port Mgmt. Com., Djibouti, Republic Djibouti, 1975-80, Nat. Monetary Authority, Djibouti, 1977-80, Refugee Com., Djibouti, 1977-80; pres. Djibouti Bankers Assn., 1974-80; dir. Oman Devel. Bank, Muscat, 1982-85; founding com. Oman Inst. Bankers, 1982-85. Trustee Ch. of Eng., Tunis, Tunisia, 1967-71; hon. Brit. consul Brit. Fgn. Office, Djibouti, Republic of Djibouti, 1977-80. Named Comdr., Royal Jordanian Order of Independence, Jordan, 1967, Officer, Order of the Brit. Empire, 1979. Fellow Chartered Inst. Bankers, Inst. Adminstrv. Mgmt., Inst. Mgmt. Specialists, Brit. Inst. Mgmt.; mem. Jordan Lodge (life). Avocations: bridge, ancient history, classical music, French cuisine, baking. E-mail: bridgend@aol.com. Fax: 44 1656 728158.

HOPKINS, DAVID LEE, medical manufacturing executive; b. Marietta, Ohio, Nov. 5, 1937; s. David Russel and Bonnie Grace (Adams) H.; m. Marcia Loretta Hopkins, Oct. 12, 1957; children: Tamara, Theresa, Tracey, David, Heidi, Wendy, Jeremy. Student, U. Dayton, 1955-57, Lorain (Ohio) C.C., 1959; BS, Ohio State U., 1960. Sales mgr. Am. Hosp. Supply, Columbus, Ohio, 1957-75; divsn. mgr. Baxter Healthcare, Stone Mountain, Ga., 1975-80; owner Hosp. Sterile Products, Stone Mountain, Ga., 1980-84; owner Angio Systems, Inc., Ducktown, Tenn., 1984—, also chmn. bd.; bd. dirs. Dalore, Inc., Ducktown, Ashfield Med., Cumbernauld, Scotland, First Nat. Bank of Polk County. Elder World Harvest Ch., Ellijay, Ga. Mem. Rotary (pres. 1968-87, bd. dirs. 1990-91, Presdl. Citation 1987, Paul Harris fellow 1988), Copper Basin Area C. of C. (bd. dirs., pres.). Avocations: reading, fishing, shooting, coaching, hiking. Office: Angio Systems Inc PO Box 760 7 Hopkins Pl Ducktown TN 37326

HOPKINS, HERBERT ZIEGLER (ZEKE), retired aerospace engineering company executive; b. Atlanta; s. Herbert Ziegler and Winifred (Bird) H.; m. Barbara Hester, Nov. 25, 1949 (div. 1971); children: Marian H. Nishi, Margaret H. Volk, Michael Ziegler H.; m. Patricia Irene Hopkins, Sept. 1, 1985. BS in Mil. Art and Engring., U.S. Mil. Acad., 1946; MS in Aerospace Engring., Princeton U., 1949. Commd. lt. USAF, 1946, advanced through grades to capt., 1952; resigned, 1955; fighter pilot 20th Fighter Group, Shaw AFB, S.C., 1946-48; engring. flight test officer Flight Test Divsn., Wright-Patterson AFB, Ohio, 1949-51, USAF Flight Test Ctr., Edwards AFB, Calif., 1951-55; engring. test pilot N.Am. Aviation, L.A., 1955-62; COO XB-70 N.Am. Aviation, Palmdale, Edwards AFB, 1962-66, project engr. DC-10 govt. applications, 1968-82; program mgr. DC-10/KC-10 McDonnell Douglas, Long Beach, Calif., 1983-88, program mgr. T-45, 1988-89; ret., 1990; cons. McDonnell Douglas, 1992-95. Docent Palm Springs Air Mus., 2000—. Fellow Soc. Exptl. Test Pilots (charter mem., pres. 1966-67, James H. Doolittle award 1983); mem. Nat. Right to Work Legal Def. Found., Citizens Against Govt. Waste (pres.'s club), Young Am.'s Found. (charter mem. Reagan Ranch Trust). Republican. Avocations: tandem bicycling, physical fitness. E-mail: zekepat@aol.com. Home: 21 Scarborough Way Rancho Mirage CA 92270-1625

HOPKINS, JOHN FREDERICK, performance artist, producer; b. Dallas, June 30, 1960; s. Joseph F. and Allene William Hopkins; 1 child, Gavin. Performer, mgr. Six Flags Over Tex. Amusement Pks., Dallas, 1977-87; performer Childrens TV Workshop, N.Y.C., 1987-89; assoc. show prodr. Sid & Marty Kroft TV, Hollywood, Calif., 1989-92; owner Le Theatre de Marionette, Dallas, 1992—. Prodr. (stage prodn.) BLAST, 1990; performer Art of Puppetry, 1995-99; creator, prodr. Roswell Anniversary Interactive Walkthrough, 1997. Avocations: sculpting, woodworking, scuba diving, animation. E-mail: jhopkinz@airmail.net. Home: 1004 Belvedere Dr Arlington TX 76010-2926 Office: Le Theatre de Marionette 462 Northpark Ctr Dallas TX 75225-2207

HOPKINS, LAURIE BOYLE, academic administrator; b. Columbia, S.C., Apr. 12, 1951; p. E.C. McGregor and Nancy Ruff Boyle; m. Christie Benet Hopkins, May 25, 1979; children: Alice Benet Hopkins, Thomas Ruff Hopkins; 1 child from previous marriage, Earle Sligh McElveen. BS, U. S.C., 1976, PhD in Math., 1981. Adj. prof. U. S.C., Columbia, 1981-82; asst. prof. Columbia Coll., 1984-89, assoc. prof., 1989-92, prof. math., chmn. dept. math., 1992-98, dir. faculty devel., 1997-98, provost, 1998—. Contbr. articles to profl. jours. Recipient Twin Tribute to Women and Industry Diamond award YWCA, Columbia, 1995, Excellence and Innovation with the use of tech. in collegiate math. award Internat. Conf. on Tech., 1998. Mem. Am. Math. Soc., Math. Assn. Am., Nat. Coun. Tchrs. Math., S.C. Coun. Tchrs. Math. E-mail: lhopkins@colacoll.edu. Office: Columbia Coll 1301 Columbia College Dr Columbia SC 29203-5949

HOPKINS, PHILIP JOSEPH, journalist, information technology professional; b. Orange, Calif., Dec. 10, 1954; s. Philip Joseph and Marie Elizabeth Hopkins; m. Susan Lisa Ingman, Oct. 5, 1991; 1 child, Robin Genevieve Hopkins. BA in Journalism, San Diego State U., 1977; cert. tissue therapist, Ctr. for Decubitis Ulcer Rsch., 1981. Reporter La Jolla (Calif.) Light & Jour., 1973; editl. cons. San Diego Union, 1974; asst. prodr. Southwestern Cable TV, San Diego, 1974; corr. Mission Cable TV, San Diego, 1975; photojournalist United Press Internat., San Diego, 1976; editor Rx Home Care mag., L.A., 1981, Hosp. Info. Mgmt. mag., 1981; editor, assoc. pub. Arcade mag., 1982; mng. editor Personal Computer Age, L.A., 1983-84; bur. chief Newsbytes syndicated column, 1985-86; v.p. Humbird Hopkins Inc., L.A., 1978-89; writer, editor, rschr. Ind. Rsch. and Info. Svc., 1988-90; writer, analyst Geneva Bus. Rsch., 1990; sci. writer The Cousteau Soc., 1990; pub. cons. U. So. Calif., 1989-90; sr. web devel. mgr. KP-IT Kaiser Permanente, 1991—. Co-author: The Students' Survival Guide, 1977, 78; photographs have appeared in Time and Omni mags., The Mythology of Middle Earth, Parenting Your Aging Parents, Beginners Guide to the SLR, NBC-TV's Saturday Night Live. Pres. Ind. Writers of So. Calif., 1988. Recipient 1st and 4th place awards Nikon, Inc., Photo Contest, 1974, 3rd prize Minolta Camera Co. Creative Photography awards, 1975, Best Feature Photo award Sigma Delta Chi Mark of Excellence contest, 1977. Mem. Healthcare Info. and Mgmt. Sys. Soc., Computer Press Assn. (life, hon.). Office: Kaiser Permanente 393 E Walnut St IT 992 Pasadena CA 91188-0001

HOPKINS, ROBERT ARTHUR, retired industrial engineer; b. Youngstown, Ohio, Dec. 14, 1920; s. Arthur George and Margaret Viola (Brush) H.; m. Mary Madelaine Bailey, Apr. 6, 1946; 1 child, Marlaine Hopkins Kaiser. BBA, Case Western Reserve U., 1949; cert. loss control engr., U. Calif., Berkeley, 1969. Ins. agt. Nat. Life and Accident Ins. Co., Lorain, Akron, Ohio, 1951-56, San Mateo, Calif., 1951-56; ins. agt., engr. Am. Hardware Mt. Ins. Co., San Jose, Fresno, Calif., 1956-60; loss control engr. Manhattan Guarantee-Continental Ins. Co., Calif., 1967-77. Organizer Operation Alert DC, Lorain, 1951-52; prin. spkr. DC, Fresno, 1957; active Pleasant Hill (Calif.) Civil Action Com., 1981-83; civilian coord. Office Emergency Svcs., Pleasant Hill, 1983-85; advisor, coord. airshows and warbird aircraft, 1980—; chmn. bd. Western Aerospace Mus., Oakland, Calif., 1988; ops. asst. for tower and ops. 50th Anniversary Golden Gate Bridge, San Francisco, 1987; advisor, coord. Travis AFB Air Expo '90, 1990; advisor Air Expo '96, NAS Alameda (Calif.) 50th Anniversary, 1990; advisor NAS Moffett Field Air Show, 1990, 92, Calif. Coast Air Show, Half Moon Bay, 1993-94, Dixon May Fair honoring WWII 50th anniversary, 1995; warbird coord. Port of Oakland Airshow, 1987; warbird advisor/coord. Beale AFB, 1993—; mem. Smithsonian Mus, Smithsonian Air & Space Mus; charter mem. Nat. Mus. of Am. Indian, Am. Air Mus. Britain; life mem. Western Aerospace Mus. Served with USAAC, 1942-46. Recipient Letter of Appreciation Fresno DC, 1957, cert. of appreciation City of Pleasant Hill, 1986, cert. of recognition and spl. citizenship award Calif. State Senate, 1995. Mem. No. Calif. Safety Engrs. Assn. (v.p., pres., chmn. 1974-77), Confederate Air Force (mem. staff, leader Pacific wing 1980—), Nat. Aero. Assn., Aero. Club No. Calif., Hamilton Field Assn. (dir. ops. Wings of Victory Air Show 1987, coord. 1988, 89—, asst. to pres. 1989—, advisor contr. 1990—), VFW (life, state civil disaster chmn. Area 5 Calif. 1991), Air Force Assn., Kiwanis (chpt. sec.-treas.), Am. Air Mus. in Britain, Nat. Trusst Hist. Preservation. Republican. Roman Catholic. Avocations: fishing, reading, writing, aircraft restoration. Home: 48 Mazie Dr Pleasant Hill CA 94523-3310

HOPKINS, TOM, artist; b. Summerside, P.E.I., Can., Dec. 9, 1944; s. Archibald Sherard and Frances May (McCulloch) H.; m. Rita Markovits, Dec. 13, 1986; children: Jacob, Anna. BFA, Mt. Allison U., 1970; MBA, Concordia U., 1987. Prof. painting and drawing McGill U., 1980-83, Dawson Coll., 1982-87, Concordia U., 1983—; v.p. Can. Inst. for Psychosynthesis, 1973-78. Exhibited in shows at Mira Godard Gallery, Toronto, U. Toronto Hart House, Equinox Gallery, Vancouver, Virginia Miller Gallery, Miami, Art Gallery of N.S., Galerie Michel Guimont, Que., Concordia U. Art Gallery, Grunwald Gallery, Toronto, others; represented in collections at Alcan, Art Gallery of Lethbridge, Alta., Art Gallery of Windsor, Art Gallery of N.S., Mt. Allison U., Royal Bank of Can., Mus. Que., Microsoft Corp., Seattle, Bank N.S., others. Grantee Can. Coun., 1980, 81, 85, Ministry Cultural Affairs Que., 1988, 90. Avocation: music. Office: Studio 999, rue du College # 30, Montreal, PQ Canada H4C 2S3

HOPKINSON, BRIAN ERIC, engineering executive, consultant; b. Ault Hucknall, Derbyshire, England, Mar. 4, 1931; came to U.S., 1957; arrived in Venezuela, 1968; s. Albert and Ellen (Wass) H.; m. Margaret Anne Clough, Dec. 22, 1954; children: Faye Elizabeth, Lisa Jane, Ian Robert, Patrick Brian. BS, London U., 1953, Loughborough (Eng.) U., 1953. Corrosion splst. Nat. Assn. Corrosion Engrs. Exptl. officer U.K. Atomic Energy Authority, Harwell, Eng., 1953-57; rsch. scientist Internat. Nickel Co., Bayonne, N.J., 1957-63; sr. engr. Exxon Engring., Florham Park, N.J., 1963-68, Creole Petroleum Corp., Amuay Refinery, Venezuela, 1968-76, Exxon Svcs. Venezuela, Amuay Refinery, 1976-97; cons. P.C.I. Ingenieros, Amuay Refinery, 1997-98; mem. refining tech. com. Exxon USA, Baytown, 1972-81; cons. Petroleos de Venezuela. Contbr. articles to profl. jours.; patentee in field. Decorated Order of Merit for work in petroleum industry Govt. of Venezuela, 1990. Fellow Instn. of Metallurgists; mem. Staten Island Cricket Club, Marylebone Cricket Club. Avocation: cricket. Office: 27 Queens Gate, Stoke Bishop, Bristol BS9 1TZ, England

HOPKINSON, SHIRLEY LOIS, library and information science educator; b. Boone, Iowa, Aug 25, 1924; d. Arthur Perry and Zora (Smith) Hopkinson; student Coe Coll., 1942-43; AB cum laude (Phi Beta Kappa scholar 1944), U. Colo., 1945; BLS, U. Calif., 1949; MA (Honnold Honor scholar 1945-46), Claremont Grad. Sch., 1951; EdM, U. Okla., 1952, EdD, 1957 Tchr. pub. sch. Stigler, Okla., 1946-47, Palo Verde High Sch., Jr. Coll., Blythe, Calif., 1947-48; asst. librarian Modesto (Calif.) Jr. Coll., 1949-51; tchr., librarian Fresno, Calif., 1951-52, La Mesa, Cal., 1953-55; asst. prof. librarianship, instructional materials dir. Chaffey Coll., Ontario, Calif., 1955-59; asst. prof. librarian ship, San Jose (Calif.) State Coll., 1959-64; assoc. prof., 1964-69, prof., 1969—; bd. dirs. NDEA Inst. Sch. Librs., summer 1966; mem. Santa Clara County Civil Service Bd. Examiners. Recipient Master Gardner cert. Oreg. State U. Extension Svc. Book reviewer for jours. Mem. ALA, Calif. Library Assn., Audio-Visual Assn. Calif., NEA, AAUP, AAUW (dir. 1957-58), Bus. Profl. Women's Club, Sch. Librs. Assn. Calif. (com. mem., treas. No. sect. 1951-52), San Diego County Sch. Librs. Assn. (sec. 1945-55), Calif. Tchrs. Assn., LWV (bd. dirs. 1950-51, publs. chmn.), Phi Beta Kappa, Alpha Lambda Delta, Alpha Beta Alpha, Kappa Delta Pi, Phi Kappa Phi (disting. acad. achievement award 1981), Delta Kappa Gamma (sec. 1994-96, legis. liaison, 1996—). Author: Descriptive Cataloging of Library Materials; Instructional Materials for Teaching the Use of the Library. Contbr. to profl. publs. Editor: Calif. Sch. Libraries, 1963-64; asst. editor: Sch. Library Assn. of Calif. Bull., 1961-63; book reviewer profl. jours. Office: 1340 Pomeroy Ave Apt 408 Santa Clara CA 95051-3658

HOPMANN, PHILIP TERRENCE, political science educator; b. St. Louis, June 25, 1942; s. Irvin Herman and Loretta (Gerlach) H.; m. Marita Raubitschek, Aug. 24, 1968; children: Alexander Irvin, Nicholas Erich. AB, Princeton U., 1964; MA, Stanford U., 1965, PhD, 1969. Rsch. asst. Stanford (Calif.) U., 1965-67, instr., 1967-68; prof. polit. sci. U. Minn., Mpls., 1968-85; prof. polit. sci. Brown U., Providence, 1985—, dir. program on global security Watson Inst. Internat. Study, 1993—, dir. Internat. Rels. program, 1985-94; cons. U.S. Inst. of Peace, 1998—; chmn. faculty exec. com. Brown U., Providence, 1994-95. Author: Unity and Disintergration in International Alliances, 1973, 84, The Negotiation Process and the Resolution of International Conflicts, 1996. Fulbright-Hays fellow Coun. Internat. Ednl. Exch., Belgium, 1975-76, 82-83, Jennings Randolph sr. fellow U.S. Inst. Peace, 1997-98; grantee Orgn. Security and Cooperation in Europe, Austria, 1997-98. Mem. Internat. Studies Assn. (editor 1980-85, v.p. 1991-92), Internat. Polit. Sci. Assn., Arms Control Assn., Am. Polit. Sci. Assn. Democrat. Home: 76 Humboldt Ave Providence RI 02906-4533 Office: Brown U Watson Inst/Internat Studie PO Box 1970 Providence RI 02912-1970

HOPP, MICHAEL, medical educator, researcher; b. Jerusalem, Oct. 22, 1941; s. Hans and Rebecca (Rachman) H.; m. Doreet Shapiro, 1967; children: Illona, Johnathan. BSc, Hebrew U., 1965, CRP, 1970, MPH, 1979; MA, Cornell U., 1981, PhD, 1983. Lectr. Cornell U., Ithaca, N.Y., 1979-83; dir. HOP Rsch., Tel-Aviv, 1989-98; sr. lectr. Hebrew U., Rehovot, 1984-98, dir. dept. med. edn., 1994-97; head acad. studies Tadmor, Israel, 1996-99; chair Rupin Inst., Hefer, Israel, 1998—. Contbr. articles to profl. jours. Mem. CHRIE, Am. Sociol. Assn., Am. Evolutionary Assn. Home: 6 Hana Senesh, Herzliyya Israel Office: Rupin Inst, 40250 Emek Hefer Israel

HOPPE, ANDREAS, geologist, administrator; b. Guben, Germany, Aug. 4, 1948; s. Heinz and Margarete (Nathke) H.; m. Dorothee Fischer-Defoy; children: Robert, Richard. Diploma in Geology, U. Heidelberg, Germany, 1975; Doctor, U. Freiburg, Germany, 1979, Habilitation, 1991. Asst. prof. U. Freiburg, 1979-86, assoc. prof., 1986-93; dir. Geol. Survey, Hesse, Germany, 1993—; guest lectr. U. Belo Horizonte and Salvador da Bahia, Brazil, 1983, 85. Editor: Amazonia: an Interdisciplinary Approach, 1990 (in German; Freiburg; Br.); editor sci. serials in geology; contbr. articles to profl. jours. Mem. German Geol. Soc. (Hermann-Credner prize 1985), Geol. Soc. Am. Avocations: reading, classical music. E-mail: ahoppe@hlug.de. Office: Hessisches Landesamt, Leberberg 9, D-65193 Wiesbaden fuer Umwelt und Geologie Germany

HOPPE, ULF-PETER JÜRGEN, atmosphere physicist; b. Schlüchtern, Germany, Jan. 10, 1955; s. Kurt and Christa (Giesler) H.; m. Ulrike Back, May 3, 1985; two children. Diploma in physics, U. Bonn, 1982, DSc, 1985. Rsch. asst. U. Bonn, Germany, 1981-85; postdoctoral fellow Royal Norwegian Coun. Scientific & Indsl. Rsch., Kjeller, Norway, 1985-86; from sr. scientist to prin. scientist Norwegian Def. Rsch. Establishment, Kjeller, 1986—. Chmn. bd. dirs. ALOMAR, 2000—. Mem. Norwegian Geophys. Soc., European Geophys. Soc., Optical Soc. Am. Office: Norwegian Def Rsch Establishment, PO Box 25, N-2027 Kjeller Norway

HOPPEN, KARL THEODORE, history educator; b. Monchengladbach, Fed. Republic Germany, Nov. 27, 1941; came to Ireland, 1947, came to Britain, 1966; s. Paul Theodore and Edith Margareta (Van Brussel) H.; m. Alison Mary Buchan, Aug. 8, 1970; children: Martha, Katherine, Theodore. BA with honors, U. Coll., Dublin, Ireland, 1961, MA with honors, 1963; PhD, Trinity Coll., Cambridge, Eng., 1967. Lectr. U. Hull, Eng., 1966-75, sr. lectr., 1974-86, reader, 1986, prof., 1997, 1998—; vis. fellow Nat. Humanities Ctr. Research Triangle Park, N.C., 1985-86, Sidney Sussex Coll. Cambridge, 1988. Author: The Common Scientist in 17th Century, 1970; Elections, Politics and Society in Ireland 1832-1885, 1984; editor: Edition: Papers of the Dublin Philosphical Society 1683-1709, 1982; contbr. articles to profl. jours. Rsch. grantee Brit. Social Sci. Rsch. Coun., 1973-75, Sir Philip Reckitt Trust, 1976. Fellow Royal Hist. Soc.; mem. Irish Hist. Soc., Agrl. History Soc., Brit. Soc. for History Sci. Avocations: music, wine. Office: U Hull,, Dept History, Hull HU6 7RX, England

HOPPENSTEADT, JON KIRK, law librarian; b. Milw., Feb. 24, 1959; s. George Arthur and Sheila Ann (Doyle) H. BA, U. Nev., 1980, '81; MA, Denver U., 1984; JD, U. Minn., 1989; postgrad., Coll. San Mateo, 1985. Asst. mgr. Farwell & Mikkelson, Reno, 1977-83; rschr., abstractor Trend-Track, Boulder, Colo., 1983; reference libr. intern Denver U., Englewood (Colo.) Pub. Libr., 1984; indexer, abstractor Info. Access Co., Foster City, Calif., 1984-86; pub. libr. intern Mpls. Pub. Libr., 1987-88; student dir. Legal Assistance to Minn. Prisoners, Mpls., 1988-89; reference libr. U. Minn. Law Libr., Mpls., 1988-91; victims' rights advocate Rohnert Park, Calif., 1992-96, Palm Harbor, Fla., 1996—; with Wear Its At, Palm Harbor, Fla., 1997-98; elderly aid, Reno, 1976-83, Itasca, Ill., 1994, Palm Harbor, Fla., 1997—. Cataloger Westlaw Legal Database Catalog, 1991. Mem. Nat. Orgn. for Victim Assistance, Washington, 1992; founder Profls. for Access, Santa Rosa, Calif., 1993; mem. Nat. Victim Ctr., Ft. Worth, 1993—; vol., cataloger Palm Harbor Libr., Palm Harbor, Fla., 2000—; vol. East Lake Cmty. Libr., Palm Harbor, 2000—. Democrat. Lutheran. Avocations: photography, drawing, hiking. Home and Office: 2890 Spring Oak Ct Palm Harbor FL 34684-1662

HOPPER, WALTER EVERETT, lawyer; b. Houghton, Mich., Oct. 29, 1915; s. Walter E. and Maude (Crum) H.; m. Jeannette Ross, Aug. 23, 1941 (dec. 1947); dau., Nancy Cameron Hopper Marcovici; m. Diana Kerensky, Sept. 24, 1958. A.B., Cornell U., 1937, J.D., 1939; grad., Command and Gen. Staff Sch., Indsl. Coll. Armed Forces. Bar: N.Y. 1939, U.S. Supreme Ct. 1946, D.C. 1959. Practice in Ithaca, 1939-42, N.Y.C., 1946—; mobilization designee, office dep. chief of staff mil. ops. Dept. of Army, 1952-67; chmn., chief exec. officer Fort Amsterdam Corp., 1973-81; dir. Davis Brake Beam Co. Chmn. trustees Loyal Legion Found.; trustee Inst. on Man and Sci., 1969-71, Signal Hill Ednl. Ctr.; bd. dirs. U.S. Flag Found. Lt. col., inf. ETO, col. AUS (ret.). Decorated Army Commendation medal with oak leaf cluster; N.Y. State Conspicious Service Cross with Maltese Cross; Order Ruben Dario Nicaragua; comdr. Order Orange-Nassau, Netherlands; Order St. John of Jerusalem. Mem. Internat. Assn. Protection Indsl. Property (exec. com. Am. group 1958-71), Internat. Fiscal Assn., British Fifth Army Old Comrades Assn., Nat. Fgn. Trade Council (mem. coms.), Internat. C. of C. (rep. internat. conf. revision internat. conv. protection indsl. property 1958, U.S. council 1949-71, mem. coms.), Am. Arbitration Assn. (panelist), U.S. Trademark Assn. (past v.p., dir., chmn. internat. com.), UN Assn. (dir. N.Y. chpt. 1964-66), Holland Soc. (pres. 1966-71), Loyal Legion (comdr.-in-chief 1964-67), Assn. Bar City N.Y., N.Y. State Criminal Bar Assn., Res. Officers Assn. (pres. N.Y. State 1949), Confrerie des Chevaliers du Tastevin, Pilgrims, Soc. War 1812, Founders and Patriots of Am., Mayflower Descs., Soc. Colonial Wars, St. Nicholas Soc. (pres. 1982-84), S.R., Huguenot Soc. Am. (pres. 1972-75), Mil. Order Fgn. Wars, Soc. of Cin., St. Andrews Soc., Explorers Club (N.Y.C.), Univ. Club (N.Y.C.), Met. Club (Washington), Army-Navy Club (Washington). Home: 715 Park Ave New York NY 10021-5047

HOPPS, RAYMOND, JR., lawyer, film producer; b. Balt., July 26, 1949; s. Raymond Hopps Sr. and Ella Louise Dixon. BA cum laude, Howard U., 1971; JD, Loyola U., Chgo., 1974. Bar: Ill. 1975. CEO, art atty. Cmty. Legal Counsel, Chgo., 1972; staff and adminstr. Chgo. Vol. Legal Svcs., 1972-74; assoc. Archie B. Weston Sr. Ltd., Chgo., 1975-77; pvt. practice Chgo., 1977-78, film prodr., 1978; prodr. N.Y. Film Colony, 1979; with svc. work Internat. Econs.; owner, prodr., artist Am. Oriental Internat. Ltd., Balt., 1980—; staff rschr. Task Force for Cmty. Broadcasting, Chgo., 1973-78; atty. cons. Assn. of AudioVisual Prodrs., Chgo., 1978; coord. N.Y. Film Colony, 1979; staff atty. Ebony Talent Assocs., Chgo. Composer: Concerto Impossible, 1987, For Your Eyes Only, 1981, Victory for the Free Planet, 1991; author: (prose) Master E, 1986; composer, author: Free Planet, 1991; writer, film prodr. for screen. Staff artist Eubie Blake Cultural Ctr., Balt., 1990—; assoc. Nat. Football League and Balt. Ravens. With USAF, 1968-91, brig. gen. Res. Mem. NAACP, Internat. Mid. East Assn., Am. Mgmt. Assn., Equal Opportunity Found., Jim Straw Heritage Exch., WFI Corp. Democrat. Avocations: music, dancing, films, walking. Address: Garrison Bldg 2806 Ste 1 South Baltimore MD 21216 Office: AMI Ltd Motion Pictures PO Box 67585 Baltimore MD 21215-0016 also: 3704 Ferndale Ave Baltimore MD 21207-7163

HOQUE, ENAMUL, botanist, environmental scientist, educator; b. Gaibandha, Bangladesh, Jan. 1, 1956; s. Ismail Hossain and Abeda Khatoon; m. Angelika Hennig, Apr. 29, 1981; children: Jasmin, Gitta. HSc, Dacca Govt. Coll., Bangladesh, 1972; MSc in forestry, Tech. U. Dresden, Germany, 1980, PhD in Forest Botany, 1981, DSc in Plant Physiology, 2000. Forest botany scientist Munich U., 1981-86; applied optics scientist GSF-Nat. Rsch. Ctr. Environment & Health, Oberschleissheim, Germany, 1987-88, optical info. processing scientist, 1989-90, xenobiotics in plants scientist, 1991-97, microbiology and biogeochemistry scientist, 1998—; session chmn. Ecoinforma, Bayreuth, 1990, 92, mem. program com., Fla., 1996; external PhD examiner TU Dresden, 1992—, Mangalore U., India, 1995—. Author: Biochemie und Physiologie erkrankter Fichten, 1990; contbr. articles to profl. jours. V.p. Bangladesh Studien-und Entwicklungszentrum, Germany, 1996. GDR scholar Min. Edn., Dhaka, 1974; talent scholar Bd. Intermediate and Secondary Edn., Dhaka, 1972. Mem. Am. Soc. Photobiology. Avocations: wandering, swimming, touring, gymnastics. Office: GSF Nat Rsch Ctr Envir-Hlt, Ingolstädter Landstr 1, 85758 Oberschleissheim Germany

HORA, HEINRICH, physicist; b. Bodenbach-Elbe, Romania, July 1, 1931; s. Otto and Elisabeth (Schneider) H.; m. Rosemarie Weiler, July 1, 1956; children: Michael, Ulrike McCluskey, Maria Carmody, Beate Steller, Dorle Minikin, Regina Law. Dipl. Phys., U. Halle-Wittenberg, Germany, 1956; Dr.rer.nat., U. Jena, 1960; DSc, U. New South Wales, 1981. Rsch. asst. to dir. R & D Ziess, Jena, 1956-60, Oberkochen, 1960-61; rsch. scientist IBM Lab., Boblingen, Germany, 1961-62; rsch. scientist Max-Planck-Inst. Plasmaphysik, Garching, Germany, 1962-67, prin. rsch. scientist, 1969-75; sr. rsch. scientist Westinghouse Rsch. Ctr., Pitts., 1967-68; assoc. prof. Rensselaer poly. Inst. - Hartford Grad. Ctr., 1969-75; prof. theoretical physics, head dept. theoretical physics U. New South Wales, Sydney, 1975-82, prof. emeritus, 1982—; adj. prof. U. Western Sydney, 1999—; vis. prof. U. Rochester, 1973-74, U. Bern, 1978-79, U. Tokyo, Weizmann Inst., 1984, U. Iowa, U. Giessen, 1985, 89, U. Osaka, 1990; sci. assoc. CERN, Geneva, Switzerland, 1990-962; Konrad-Zuse prof. elec. engring. Regensburg, 1993-95; guest prof. Osaka U., 1996; mem. convenor Dirac Funds for Theoreticla Physics, U. New South Wales, 1979-92; lectr. Nuclear Club Wall St., 1978; cons. Rhombic Corp., Vancouver, 1990—, C&C Reston, Va., 1999—. Author: Laser Plasmas and Nuclear Energy, 1975, Nonlinear plasma Dynamics at Laser Irradiation, 1979, Physics of Laser Driven Plasmas, 1981, Plasmas at high Temperature and Density, 1991, Elektrodynamik, 1994, Nonlinear Force and Ponderomotion, 1996, Innovation & Technology, 1998, Laser Plasma Physics: Forces and the Nonlinearity Principle, 2000, (with others) Equation of State, 1986, Plasmas at High Temperature and Density, 2d edit., 2000, Laser Plasma Physics: Forces and the Nonlinearity Principle, 2000, others; editor-in-chief Laser and Particle Beams; Physics of High Energy Density, 1982-91, emeritus, 1991—; co-editor: Laser Interaction and Related Plasma Phenomena 12 vols., 1971-93, Directions in Physics by P.A.M. Dirac, 1977; editl. bd. Chinese Laser Jour., 1988-95, Cechosl Jour. Physics, 1992—; contbr. articles to profl. jours.; patentee in field. Mem. bd. City Coun. Ottobrunn, Bavaria, 1972-75. Recipient medal Lebedev Inst. Acad. Sci., USSR, 1978, Ritter-von-Gerstner medal, 1985, German Sprots Gold medal, 1982, H & E Heraeus award, 1989, Edward Teller medal, 1991; USAF grantee, 1972; vis. fellow Australian Nat. U., Canberra, 1994-98. Fellow Inst. Physics (London), Australian Inst. Physics (dir. New South Wales 1979-85); mem. Am. Phys. Soc., German Phys. Soc., Soc. Advance Fusion Energy (N.Y. dir. 1979—), Internat. Soc. for Applied Optics, Rotary. Roman Catholic. Home: PO Box 343, Connels Point 2221, Australia Office: U New South Wales, Dept Theoretical Physics, Sydney 2052, Australia

HORÁČEK, JAROMÍR, mechanical engineer, researcher, educator; b. Prague, Czech Republic, Oct. 17, 1946; s. Miroslav and Jarmila (Boušková) H.; m. Jana Semotánová, July 16, 1971; children: Štěpán, Šárka. Ing., Czech Tech. U., Prague, 1970; CSc in Thermomechanics, Czechoslovak Acad. Scis., Prague, 1977, DSc (hon.), 1990. Rschr. Aero. Rsch. and Test Inst., Prague, 1970-72; leading rschr. Inst. Thermomechanics Acad. Scis., Prague, 1977-90, head dept., dep. dir. R & D, 1990—; lectr. Czech Tech. U., 1993—. Mem. editl. bd. Mech. Engring., 1991—, Machine Vibration, 1995; editor-in-chief Engring. Mechanics, 1994—; contbr. articles to sci. jours., including Jour. Fluids and Structure, Engring. Structures, Jour. Sound and Vibration. Grantee Commn. European Cmtys., 1993. Mem. Czech Soc. for Mechanics. Avocations: football, skiing, hillwalking. Office: Acad Scis Inst Thermomech, Dolejškova 5, 182 00 Prague 8, Czech Republic

HORACEK, VIT, lawyer; b. Kladno, Czech Republic, Oct. 6, 1967; s. Frantisek and Vera (Bazikova) H.; m. Petra Loulova, June 21, 1991; children: Anna, Alzbeta. Magister, JD, Charles U., Prague, 1991, PhD, 1994; postgrad., U. Birmingham, Eng., 1993. Lawyer Kovo a.s., Prague, 1990-91, law offices, Prague, 1991-92; trainee lawyer Glatzova & Co., 1994, ptnr., 1995—; dir. real estate cos. and subs. of banks; arbitrator Prague Stock Exch. Arbitration Ct., 1998—. Author: Arbitration and Civil Process Systems, 1998, also legal and legal bus. articles. Avocations: tennis, classical music. Office: Glatzova & Co, Husova 5, 1100 00 Prague 1, Czech Republic

HORAK, JAROMIR, chemistry educator; b. Jimramov, Czech Republic, Jan. 7, 1927; s. Alois and Anna (Matejkova) H.; m. Jaroslava Moravkova, Aug. 21, 1963; children: Jaromir, Jan, Vit. MSc, Tech. U. Brno, 1950; PhD, Inst. Chem. Tech., Czech Republic, 1961; DSc, Charles U., 1981. From asst. prof. to prof. inorganic chemistry Inst. Chem. Tech., Pardubice, 1952-92; rsch. worker Acad. Sci. Czech. Rep., Prague, 1993—. Mem. Deutsche Bunsengesellschaft. Avocations: volleyball, tennis, cross-country skiing. Home: Brozikova 429, 53009 Pardubice Czech Republic Office: U Pardubice, Nam cs legii 565, 53210 Pardubice Czech Republic

HORAK, JIRI JAN FRANTISEK, medical educator; b. Hradec Kralove, Czech Republic, Oct. 20, 1945; s. Jiri Horak and Vera (Pitrova) Horakova; m. Libuse Duskova, Oct. 31, 1974; children: Eliska, Jiri. MD, Charles U., Prague, 1972; PhD, Inst. Clin. Exptl. Medicine, Prague, 1979. Bd. cert. in internal medicine, gastroenterology. Jr. doctor City Hosp., Turnov, Czech Republic, 1972-73, Nachod, Czech Republic, 1973-74; asst. prof. Third Faculty Medicine/Charles U., Prague, 1979-86, assoc. prof., 1986-92, prof., 1992—; head dept. internal medicine, Third Faculty Medicine, Charles U., 1990—, vice-dean, 1990-97; dep. dir. Faculty Hosp. Kralovske Vinohrady, Prague, 1990-96. Patentee in field; contbr. articles to profl. jours. Mem. Kan/Club of Engaged Citizens, Hradec, 1968. Sgt. Czech Army, 1963-65. Mem. CM Club (founding mem.), Czech Soc. of Hepatology (vice-chmn. 1997—). Roman Catholic. Avocations: swimming, sailing, hiking. Office: Dept Medicine I/Third Fac, Charles U/Ruska 87, CZ-10000 Prague 10 Czech Republic

HORÁK, PETR, philosophy educator, journal editor; b. Brno, Czech Republic, Sept. 5, 1935; s. Alois and Felicitas (Jellinková) H.; m. Hana Přileská, June 3, 1977. PhD, Masaryk U., Brno, 1966; CSc, Acad. Scis., Prague, Czech Republic, 1966. Archivist Dist. of Brno Archives, 1960-61; postgrad. rschr. Acad. Scis., Prague, 1962-66, rschr., 1967-89; asst. prof. philosophy Masaryk U., Brno, 1990-93, prof. philosophy, 1993—; vis. prof. U. Paul Valéry, Montpellier, France, 1995-97. Editor, translator, contbr. (jour.) Filosofický časopis (Philos. Rev.), 1990—. Office: Filosofický časopis, Jilská 1, CZ-11000 Prague Czech Republic

HORÁLEK, VRATISLAV, mathematician, consultant; b. Roudnice upon Elbe, Czech Republic, Aug. 16, 1926; s. František and Štěpánka (Dyk) H.; m. Tatána Haralík, Aug. 2, 1980. Degree in engring., Tech. U., Prague, Czech Republic, 1950; PhD, Charles U., Prague, Czech Republic, 1961; DSc, Czech Acad. Scis., Brno, Czech Republic, 1969. Rsch. worker Nat. Rsch. Inst. for Machine Design, Prague, 1950-61, sr. rsch. worker, 1961-69, head of rsch. group on stochastic analysis, 1969-81, head divsn. applied math. statistics, 1981-91; cons. in applied math. statistics Prague, 1991—; chmn. tech. com. for applied statistics in standardization Czech Inst. for Standardization, Prague, 1969—. Author: (book) Progress in Statistics, 1974, (monographs) Foundations of Stereology, 1974, Sampling Inspection Schemes in Industry, 1979, Statistical Process Control and Applied Statistics, 1991; contbr. papers to jours. in field; patentee in field; regional editor Exec. Scis. Inst., U.S., 1965-92, Statis. Theory and Methods Abstracts, The Netherlands, 1985—. Recipient Nat. prize for devel. in applied math. Czech Acad. Scis., 1964, Tech. Progress prize Fed. Ministry of Heavy Industry, Czech Republic, 1978, Bernard Bolzano Golden medal Acad. of Scis. of Czech Republic, 1993. Fellow Czech Cybernetic Soc. (staff 1974—, chmn. stereological sect. 1976-91, award 1992), Czech Soc. for Quality (staff 1990—, award 1995); mem. Internat. Soc. Stereology (staff 1974—, Czech rep. 1976-91). Avocations: plastic arts and painting, theater, concerts, mountain touring, sports. Home: Měchenická 14/2558, 141 00 Prague Czech Republic

HORAN, MARY ANN THERESA, nurse; b. Denver, July 4, 1936; d. John Paul and Lucille (Somma) Perito; m. Stephen F. Horan, Sr., Dec. 28, 1957; children: Seanna, Dana, Michelle, Annette, Stephen Jr., Christine,

David. BSN, Loretto Heights Coll., Denver, 1958; postgrad, Pima Community Coll., 1982. RN, Ala. Staff nurse Med. Ctr. Hosp., Huntsville, Ala., 1978-79, Crestwood Hosp., Huntsville, 1980-81, St. Joseph Hosp. Eye Surgery, Tucson, 1981—; v.p. Success Achievement Ctr., Tucson, 1987—; Shaklee distbr., 1996—. Contbr. articles to nursing jours., poetry to lit. jours. Republican. Roman Catholic. Home: 8311 E 3rd St Tucson AZ 85710-2550

HORÁNYI, GYÖRGY, chemist, researcher; b. Budapest, Hungary, July 18, 1934; s. Sándor and Lilli (Göllei) Hechtl; m. Annabella Kun, June 20, 1959; children: Gábor, Tamás, András. MS, Eötvös Loránd U., Budapest, 1958, PhD, 1962; Candidate of Sci., Hungarian Acad. Scis., Budapest, 1967, DSc, 1976; prof., Eötvös Loránd U., Budapest, 1981, Dr. Habil, 1996. Cert. in chemistry, phys. chemistry. Asst. prof. Eötvös Loránd U., Budapest, 1958-61; rsch. scientist Cen. Rsch. Inst. for Chemistry, Budapest, 1961-69, sr. rsch. scientist, 1969-77, sci. advisor, 1977—; vis. prof. U. Ill., Urbana, 1990, Abo Akademi, Turku, Finland, 1994. Author: Electrocatalysis, 1990, (book chpt.) A Specialist Periodical Report, Catalysis, Vol. 12, 1996, Interfacial Electrochemistry, 1999; contbr. articles to profl. jours., chpts. to books. Spokesman Dem. Charter, Hungary, 1991-93. Mem. Internat. Soc. Electrochemistry (nat. sec. 1980-86), Hungarian Chem. Soc., Commn. on Electrochemistry (chmn. 1990-93), Hungarian Acad. Scis. Home: Kükülló u 12, 1026 Budapest Hungary Office: Hungarian Acad Scis Cen Rsch Inst Chemistry, Inst Chem/Chem Rsch Ctr, Pusztaszeri ut 59-67, 1025 Budapest Hungary

HORCHLER, FRIGYES (FRED) S., automotive executive; b. Budapest, Hungary, Oct. 2, 1928; s. Frigyes M. Horchler and Maria J. Szilágyi; m. Angela M. Bartholy, Aug. 11, 1951; 1 child, Gabor. BSc in Econs., Higher Inst. Econs., Budapest, 1953; MSc in Engring., Budapest Tech. U., 1957; postgrad., Northwestern U., 1972. Cert. mech. engr. Budapest Tech. U.; cert. economist Higher Inst. Econs., Budapest. Sr. spl. advisor Office Prime Min., Govt. Hungary, Budapest, 1969-79; v.p. internat. ops. Rába Hungarian Rlwy. Carriage and Machine Works, Győr, 1979-89; trade commr., comml. attaché of Hungary Govt. Hungary, Chgo., 1984-89; sr. spl. advisor to the chmn. Hungarian Credit Bank, Budapest, 1989-91; sr. v.p. Cohfin Co. Hongroise Financielle S.A., Paris, Budapest, 1991-93; chief comml. officer Petőfi Printing and Pkg. Co., Kecskemét, Hungary, 1993-95; sr. spl. advisor Hungarian-Am. Enterprise Fund, Washington, Budapest, 1995-96; dir. strategic planning N.Am. Bus. Industries, Budapest, 1996—; sr. spl. advisor agrl. machinery UN Indsl. Devel. Orgn., Vienna, Austria, 1970—; sr. spl. advisor heavy duty automotives UN European Econ. Commn., Geneva, 1975—. Author: Austro-Hungarian Trade, 1975. Recipient Lipot Aschner award, 1999. Mem. Internat. Union Pub. Transport, Am. Pub. Transit Assn. Achievements include patents for auger conveyors. Avocations: hiking, swimming, rowing. E-mail: horchler@nabi.hu. Fax: 36-1-407-2931. Home: Stromfeld Aurél utca 32, H-1124 Budapest Hungary Office: NABI-NAm Bus Industries, Újszász utca 45, H-1165 Budapest Hungary

HOŘEC, JAROMÍR, poet; b. Chust, Czechoslovakia, Dec. 18, 1921; s. Karel Habr and Ludmila (Zemanová) Habrová; m. Věra Tauchmanová, Jan. 31, 1948; 1 child, Dospívová Blanka. Grad. philology, U. Charles, Prague, Czech Republic, 1953, PhD, 1968. Editor in chief Mladá Fronta, 1945-50, MÍR, 1950-53, Hlas Revoluce, 1953-65, Magnet, 1965-70, 90-93; editor-in-chief UK, tchr. social scis. and journalism U. Charles, Prague, 1965-69; editor in chief Čas Periodical, 1992-2000. Author: (poetry) Jasina, Květen 1, 1946, Na časy, 1947, Hněv trávy, 1966, Aneška Česká, 1990, Bohemus, 1991, Ne, 1995, Vnitrozemí, 1996, Pulnoční jam session, 1996, Pozdvihování Slov, 1996, Přísezné Svedectrí, 1997, Chleb na sole, 1998, Dilna Hölderlinova, 1999, Testamenty, 1999, Úpadek hverd, 2000; (hist. books) i děti šly na smrt, 1960, Kronika české synkopy I-II, 1975, 1990, Doba Ortelu, 1992, Halasové, 1992, Podkarpatská Rus-země neznámá, 1994, Země naděje, 1995, v blásě sn'289s, 1999, První kroky svobody, 2000. Active Movement Democratic of T.G. Masaryk, v.p., 1992-2000. Mem. Soc. of Friends of Subcarpatian Rus (pres. 1991-2000), Soc. Writers (pres. revision com.), Soc. Journalists. Avocation: philately. E-mail: gold@altis.cz. Home: Jihozápadní III no 14, 141 00 Prague Sporilov, Czech Republic

HOŘEJŠÍ, JAN, obstetrician-gynecologist; b. Prague, Czech Republic, May 6, 1940; s. Jaroslav and Marie (Musilová) H.; m. Anděla Hamouzová, Apr. 6, 1967; children: Jakub, Barbora. MD, Charles U., 1963. Diplomate Gynecology and Obstetrics, Pediatric Gynecology. Lectr. Inst. Normal Anatomy Charles U., Prague, Czech Republic, 1963-66; physician Ob-Gyn. Dept., Kutna Hora, Czech Republic, 1966; physician Ob-Gyn. Dept. Tchg. Hosp. Charles U., Prague, 1966-72, cons. Dept. Ob-Gyn., 1973-89, head dept. obstetrics and adult and pediat. gynecology, 1990-95, 99—, prof. Ob-Gyn. Dept., 1995—, head of chair pediat. gynecology postgrad. med. sch., 1997—; cons. Ministry of Health, Prague, 1993. Author: Pediatric Gynecology, 1990. Mem. Internat. Fedn. Pediatric and Adolescent Gynecology (exec. bd., treas.), Czech. Ob-Gyn. Soc. (pres.), Czech Soc. Pediatric and Adolescent Gynecology (pres.), Fothergill Club Gt. Britain, Hungarian Ob-Gyn Soc. (hon.), Slovak Ob-Gyn. Soc. (hon.). Avocations: music, cycling. Home: Vapencova 10, CZ147 00 Prague Czech Republic Office: Charles U Prague 2d Med Faculty, V uvalu 84, CZ 150 06 Prague Czech Republic

HOŘEJŠÍ, JIŘÍ, physicist; b. Straškov, Czech Republic, Aug. 21, 1951; s. Václav and Blažena (Sekyrová) H.; m. Ivana Mezteková, Sept. 5, 1974; children: Kateřina, Michaela. D Natural Scis., Charles U., Prague, Czech Republic, 1975, PhD, 1980, DSc, 1995. Rsch. scientist Inst. Nuclear Rsch., Řež, Czech Republic, 1979-80; rsch. scientist Nuclear Centre Charles U., Prague, 1980-81, sr. scientist, 1986-92, assoc. prof. physics, 1992-98, head theory divsn., dep. dir., 1990-99, prof., 1998—; dir. Inst. Particle Nuclear Physics, Charles U., Prague, 1999—; rsch. scientist Joint Inst. Nuclear Rsch., Dubna, Russia, 1981-84, sr. scientist, 1984-86. Author: Introduction to Electroweak Unification, 1994; contbr. articles to sci. jours. Home: U Smaltovny 25, 170 00 Prague 7, Czech Republic Office: Charles U Nuclear Ctr, Faculty Math & Physics, 180 00 Prague 8, Czech Republic

HORHOIANU, GRIGORE, physicist, researcher; b. Balanesti, Gonj, Romania, Feb. 17, 1948; s. Grigore and Lucretia Horhoianu; m. Valeria-Elena Sendruc, Mar. 2, 1975; children: Ion, Mihai. MSc, U. Bucharest, Romania, 1971; PhD, Inst. Atomic Physics, Bucharest, 1987. Cert. physicist. Sci. rschr. Inst. Nuc. Rsch., Pitesti, Romania, 1971-85, sr. rschr., 1985—, head lab., 1989—. Contbr. articles to profl. jours. Mem. European Nuc. Soc. E-mail: ghor@easynet.ro. Home: trivale bl 40/D/9, Pitesti Arges, Romania Office: Inst Nuc Rsch, Mioveni Pitesti Arges 0300, Romania

HORI, AKIHIRO, television station researcher; b. Tokyo, Mar. 21, 1953; s. Shigeo and Setsuko (Mitani) H. B of Engring., U. Electro-Comms., 1975, M of Engring., 1977. Rschr. Hitachi Ctrl. Rsch. Lab., Tokyo, 1982-86; engr. project divsn. Hitachi Fiber Optics, Yokohama, Japan, 1986-90; chief rschr. Nippon TV Network Corp., Tokyo, 1990—. Holder over 50 patents in field; contbr. articles to profl. jours.; editor Jour. of the Inst. of Image Info. and TV Engrs. Mem. Assn. Radio Industries and Bus. (chmn. compression tech. working group and XML working). Avocations: flying, scuba diving, skiing, golf. Home: 2-18-10 Seijo Setagaya, Tokyo 157-0066, Japan Office: NTV, 14 Nibancho Chiyoda, Tokyo 102-8004, Japan

HORI, ARIYUKI, neurologist, researcher; b. Toyama, Japan, Mar. 15, 1958; s. Nobuyuki and Tami (Ichii) H. MD, Kanazawa Med. U., Kohoku, Japan, 1982; PhD, Toyama Med. and Pharm. U., 1986. Diplomate Japanese Bd. Psychiatry of Welfare Ministry, Japanese Bd. Clin. Neurology, Japanese Bd. Internal Medicine, Japanese Bd. Rehab. Medicine. Instr. Toyama Med. U., 1986-87; clin. fellow Chiba (Japan) U., 1987-88; instr. Kanazawa Med. U., 1988-92, asst. prof., 1992-95, 1997—; rsch. fellow Harvard Med. Sch., Boston, 1995-97; asst. prof. neurology Kanazawa Med. U., 1997—; dir. Joganji Hosp., Tyoama, 1997—, neurology, 1997—, neurophysiology lab. Kanazawa Med. U., 1999—; assoc. dir. med. info. ctr. Kanazawa Med. U., 1999—, assoc. prof. med. info. ctr., 2000—. Contbr. articles to profl. jours. Rsch. grantee Japanese Welfare Ministry, 1991-93, Nat. Epifellows Found., Am. Epilepsy Soc., 1995, Epilepsy Rsch. Found., Japanese Epilepsy Soc., 1998, Japanese Welfare Ministry, 2000-2001. Mem. World Fedn. Sleep Rsch. Soc. (rev. editor sleep rsch. online 1997—), Soc. for Patients with ALS in Kanazawa (bd. dirs. 1995—), Vis. Nurse Orgn. (bd. dirs. 1997—). Avocations: twin study, composing, collecting analogue records, tennis, skiing. E-mail: hori-a@kanazawa-med.ac.jp. Fax: 81 76-286-2187. Home: Hamansu 2-chome 53, Uchinada Ishikawa 920-0268, Japan Office: Kanazawa Med U Dept Neurol, Daigaku 1-1 Uchinada-machi, Kahoku-gun Ishikawa 920-0293, Japan

HORI, KEIKO, English literature educator; b. Himeji, Hyogo, Japan, Jan. 18, 1954; d. Takeshi Nishiyama and Fumiko Hori; 1 child, Grace. BA summa cum laude, Osaka (Japan) U., 1976, MA, 1978; postgrad., U. N.H., 1979-80, Osaka (Japan) U., 1978-82. Instr. Osaka Kyoiku U., 1981-82, tenured asst. prof., 1982-87, assoc. prof., 1987-2000, prof., 2000—; instr. Osaka U., Toyonaka, Japan, 1988-90, 92-95; vis. prof. U. Wyo., Laramie, 1986-87. Co-author: Imeji to shite no Toshi: Gakusaiteki Toshi Bunkaron, 1996; annotator: (textbook) American Businessman: Lessons from Life, 1994; co-annotator: (textbook) American and English Ideals, 1991. Recipient Kusumoto award, 1976. Mem. Modern Lang. Assn., English Literary Soc. Japan, Japan Assn. English Romanticism, Japan Assn. Coll. English Tchrs. Home: 7-4-1-3 Umamikita, Koryocho Kitakatsuragigun, Nara 635-0831, Japan Office: Osaka Kyoiku U, 4-698-1 Asahigaoka, 582-8582 Kashiwara Osaka, Japan

HORI, YASUSHI, pharmacist, analytical chemist, toxicologist; b. Niigata, Japan, Nov. 19, 1965; s. Masuro and Chieko (Kuwano) H.; m. Sonomi Ishimoto, Apr. 5, 1992; 1 child, Midori. BS, Niigata Coll. Pharmacy, 1988. Clin. pharmacist Shinrakuene Hosp., Niigata, 1989-93; clin. pharmacist Niigata City Gen. Hosp., 1993—, head, sect. analytical toxicology, 1999—; assoc. rschr. dept. hygiene and preventive medicine, Niigata U. Sch. Medicine, 1994—, dept. analytical chemistry, Niigata Coll. Pharmacy, 1999—. Contbr. articles to profl. jours. Mem. Japanese Soc. Clin. Toxicology, Japan Soc. Analytical Chemistry. Avocation: fly fishing. Office: Niigata City Gen Hosp, 2-6-1 Shichikuyama, Niigata 950-8739, Japan

HORIGOME, HITOSHI, pediatric cardiologist; b. Ina, Nagano, Japan, July 28, 1956; s. Setsuo Hiraide and Rokuko Horigome; m. Yumi Sakamoto, Apr. 7, 1985; 2 children. MB, U. Tsukuba, Japan, 1982, MD, 1991. Clin. trainee Tsukuba Univ. Hosp., 1982-83; med. staff Kanagawa Children's Med. Ctr., Yokohama, Japan, 1984-85, Ibaraki Children's Hosp., Mito, Japan, 1985-92; asst. prof. U. Tsukuba, 1992—. Author: (book) Magnetocardiography, 1997; contbr. articles to profl. jours. Mem., foster parent Plan Internat. Japan, Tokyo, 1995. Avocation: swimming. Home: 2-5-20 Umezono, 305-0045 Tsukuba Ibaraki, Japan Office: U Tsukuba Dept Pediats, 1-1-1 Tennodai, 305-8575 Tsukuba Ibaraki, Japan

HORIGUCHI, SUSUMU, information science educator; b. Kouga, Shiga, Japan, July 10, 1952; d. Tadao and Saku (Hatakeyama) H.; m. Etsuko Horiuchi, Jan. 24, 1954; 1 child, Miki. Degree in engring., Tohoku U., Sendai, Japan, 1976, masters degree, 1978, DEng, 1981. Rsch. assoc. Tohoku U., 1981-85, 86-89; vis. scientist IBM Watson Rsch. Ctr., N.Y.C., 1985-86; assoc. prof. Tohoku U., 1989-92; prof. Grad. Sch. Info. Sci., JAIST, Ishikawa, Japan, 1992—; senator Grad. Sch. Info. Sci., JAIST, Ishikawa, 1999—; IBM Fellowship rschr. IBM Japan, Tokyo, 1989-90. Internat. advisor Jour. Microelectronics, 1992—. RCA fellow, 1981. Mem. IEEE (sr., program chairperson ISPAN '96 1994, Student Paper award 1986, ISPAN Contbn. award 1996), IEICE (guest editor 1995, 97), IPS. Avocations: fishing, tennis, Indian ink drawing. Office: JAIST, Grad Sch Info Sci, Tatsunok Ishikawa 923-1292, Japan

HORIGUCHI, TOYOTA, environmental design educator; b. Tokyo, Oct. 22, 1955; parents Minoru and Reiko (Okumura) H. BA, Yale Coll., 1979, MArch, 1981. Chief arch. Studio 80, Tokyo, 1986-89; prin. SDA, Tokyo, 1989-95; assoc. prof. Kyoto (Japan) City U. of Arts, 1995—. Photographer: (book) Shishosetsu from Left to Right, 1995; exhibited photography Kyoto Culture Mus., 1997, 98, 99. Recipient Urban Design award Nagoya City, 1995, Arch. award Nara City, 1998, Kitakyushu City, 1998. Mem. Japan Inst. Archs. Home: 1-10-23-310 Sumiyoshi, Yamate Higashinadaku, Kobe 658-0063, Japan Office: 186-908 Rokkaku, Higashinotoin Higashi, Kyoto Nakagyoku 604-8133, Japan

HORII, KIYOSHI, mechanical engineer, educator; b. Kamimeguro Tokyo, Japan, Sept. 16, 1943; s. Minazo and Tamano Horii; m. Yoshi Seo, May 5, 1978; children: Yuka, Miho. D in Engring., Waseda U., 1973. Asst. Waseda U., Tokyo, 1973-76; lectr. Okinawa (Japan) U., 1976-77; assoc. prof. Shirayuri Women's Coll., Tokyo, 1977-85, prof., 1985—; cons. JRDC, Tokyo, 1985-95; organizer forum ASME, 1991—; com. mem. Ministry Agr., 1999-2000. Recipient Ichimura award, 1995, Min. award Sci. and Tech. Agy., 1995. Mem. Jet Soc. Aero. Space Sci., Japan Soc. Multiphase Flow (bd. dirs. 1998—), Japanese Soc. Mech. Engrs. (tech. com. 1998, info. com. 1999). Home: 5-8-15-107 Kamimeguro, Tokyo 153-0051, Japan Office: Shirayuri Women's Coll, 1-25 Midorigaoka, Chofu-shi Tokyo 182-8525, Japan

HORII, REIICHI, foreign language educator, library director; b. Kyoto, Japan, Nov. 5, 1925; s. Jiro and Mitsu Horii; m. Kazuko Ohashi, Feb. 13, 1960; 2 children. BA, Kyoto U., 1949. Lectr. Tokai U., Shimizu, Shizuoka, Japan, 1951-53, Kansai U., Suita, Osaka, Japan, 1952-57; asst. prof. Aichi (Japan) U., Toyohashi, 1957-64, prof., 1964-71; prof. Nanzan U., Nagoya, Aichi, 1971-78; prof. Kansai Gaidai U., Hirakata, Osaka, 1978—, dir. libr., 1988—; mem. com. XIII Internat. Congress of Linguists, Tokyo, 1982. Author: Dictionary of Japanese Etymology, 1983, Language and Community, 1988, Language of Kyoto, 1988, Women's Languages, 1990, Dictionary of Foreign Origin's Words, 1994, Dictionary of Osaka Dialect, 1995, Empathic Linguistics, 1996, Comparative Linguistics, 1997, Dictionary of Stereotyped Phrase, 1997, Wonder of Language, 1998, Etymological Dictionary of Kansai Dialect, 1999. Recipient Ordre des Palmes Acad., Govt. of France, 1974, Nat. Order of Merit, 1976. Mem. Linguistic Soc. of Japan (editor 1981-82), Phonetic Soc. of Japan, Soc. French Lang. and Lit., Japan Soc. of Stylistics, Soc. of Expression-Formation Studies, Soc. of Mediterranean Studies, Shinmura Found. (mem. jury Shinmura prize 1982—). Avocation: music. Home: 43-3 Kuzuha-Nakamachi, Hirakata Osaka 573-1107, Japan Office: Kansai Gaidai U, 16-1 Kitakatahoko-cho, Hirakata Osaka 573-1158, Japan

HORIUCHI, ATSUSHI, physician, educator; b. Tsuru, Yamanashi, Japan, Nov. 12, 1929; s. Masashige and Suzuyo Horiuchi; m. Dec. 1, 1961 (dec. June 1977); 1 child, Tadashi; m. Mar. 30, 1981. MD, Nihon U., Tokyo, 1956, D in Med. Sch., 1961. Clin. fellow Sch. Medicine Nihon U., 1957-62; rsch. fellow Sch. Medicine Yale U., New Haven, 1962-64; instr. Sch. Medicine Nihon U., 1964-73, assoc. prof., 1973-74; prof. Sch. Medicine Kinki U., Osaka, Japan, 1974-97; dir. Sakai Hosp./Kinki U. Sch. Medicine, 1999&. Office: Kinki U Sch Medicine Sakai Hosp, 2-7-1 Harayamadai, Sakai 590-132, Japan

HORIUCHI, NOBORU, biochemist, educator; b. Ikoma, Japan, Aug. 11, 1947; s. Shigekazu Matsubara and Akiko Horiuchi; m. Mariko Tobe, July 8, 1980; children: Hanna, Isaku. DDSc, Tokyo Dental Coll., 1972; PhD, Tokyo Med. and Dental U., 1976. Rsch. assoc. Tokyo Med. and Dental U., Tokyo, 1976-77; lectr., assoc. prof. Showa U., Tokyo, 1977-86; rsch. fellow in medicine Harvard Med. Sch., Boston, 1980-83; staff scientist Helen Hayes Hosp., West Harverstraw, N.Y., 1986-89; rsch. scientist II Cedars-Sinai Med. Ctr., L.A., 1989; prof. biochemistry Ohu U., Koriyama, Japan, 1990—. Contbr. articles to profl. jours. Grantee NIH/Nat. Cancer Inst. Cedars Sinai Med. Ctr., 1989-92, Ministry of Edn. Sci. and Culture Japan Ohu U., 1993-95, 98-2000. Mem. The Endocrine Soc., The Am. Soc. for Bone and Mineral Rsch., The Japanese Biochem. Soc. (councilor 1995—). Avocations: reading, swimming, gardening. Home: 1-65 Yatsuyamada, Koriyama 963-8052, Japan Office: Ohu U Sch Dentistry, Tomita-machi, Koriyama 963-8611, Japan

HORIUCHI, TOHRU, orthopaedist; b. Sapporo, Hokkaido, Japan, Dec. 23, 1934. Grad., Hokkaido U., 1961; MD, Hokkaido U., Sapporo, 1968. Faculty medicine Hokkaido U., 1962-68, Nayoro (Japan) City Hosp., 1968, Ohji Gen. Hosp., Tomakomai, Japan, 1970; pvt. practice Horiuchi Orthopedic Clinic, Tomakomai, Japan, 1971—. Contbr. articles to profl. jours. Mem. AAAS, N.Y. Acad. Scis., Japanese Orthopaedic Assn. Office: Horiuchi Orthopedic Clinic, 1-1 Shintomi Cho 2 Chome, Tomakomai Hokkaido 053-0805, Japan

HORKÁ, MARIE, analytical chemist; b. Znojmo, Morava, Czech Republic, Dec. 16, 1957; d. Jaroslav and Antonie (Kašparová) H. BS, U. Chem. and Tech., Praha, Czech Republic, 1979, MS, 1982; PhD, Czech Acad. Sci., Brno, 1992. Worker, specialist Inst. Analytical Chemistry, Czech Acad. Sci., Brno, 1982-88, ind. worker, specialist, 1988-92, scientist, 1992—. Contbr. articles to profl. jours. Mem. Czech Sci.-Tech. Soc. E-mail: horka@iach.cz. Office: UIACH, AV ČR Veveří 97, 611 42 Brno Czech Republic

HORMESS, HARALD ANDREAS, economist, business executive; b. Erlanger, Bavaria, Germany, Feb. 24, 1958; s. Heinrich and Sophie Dorothee (Hemmeter) H.; m. Ruth Kleinwachter, Dec. 22, 1997; children: Chiara, Alicija, Maxine. Student, Fachhochschule, Frankfurt, Germany, 1982. Jr. media planner Saahehi & Saatehi, Frankfurt, 1983-86; media planner DMB&B, Frankfurt, 1986-89; media supr. Young & Rubicam, Frankfurt, 1989-92; head of media planning Publicis, Frankfurt, 1992-96; gen. mgr. Optimedia, Frankfurt, 1996-2000; mng. dir. Zenith Media, Frankfurt, 2000—. Mem. Kommunikationsverband (bd. dirs. 1998). Avocations: soccer, chess, reading. Office: Zenith Media GmbH, Rohmerplatz 35, 60486 Frankfurt Germany

HORN, GYULA, former prime minister of Hungary; b. Budapest, Hungary, July 5, 1932; s. Géza and Anna (Csornyei) H.; m. Anna Király; children: Anna, Gyula. MA, Rostow Inst. Econs., USSR, 1954; BA, Polit. Acad. of the Hungarian Socialist Workers Party, 1972, PhD, 1976. Ofcl. Ministry of Fin., Budapest, 1954-59; desk officer Ministry of Fgn. Affairs, Budapest, 1959-61; embassy sec. Diplomatic Mission, Sofia, 1961-63, Belgrade, 1963-69; from staff mem. to head Internat. Dept. Hungarian Socialist Workers Party Cen. Com., Budapest, 1969-85; state sec. Ministry of Fgn. Affairs, Budapest, 1985-89; minister fgn. affairs Govt. of Hungary, Budapest, 1989-90; mem. Parliament, Budapest, 1990—, chmn. Fgn. Affairs Com., 1990-93; Prime Minister Hungary, Budapest, 1994-98; founding mem. Hungarian Socialist Party, 1989, pres., 1990-98; v.p. Socialist Internat., N.Y.C., 1996. Author: Jugosalavia, Our Neighbour, Social and Political Changes in Albania since World War II, Development of the East-West Relations in the 70s, Piles 1991, Those Were the 90s, 1999; co-author more than 100 articles in tech. periodicals. Decorated Golden Labor Order of Merit, grand cross Fed. Republic of Germany; recipient Sharp Blade award, Solingen, 1991, Karl prize Aachen, 1991, Humanitarian award German Freemasons, 1992, Gold Europe award, 1994, Kassel: Glass of Understanding award, 1995, prize of Ludwig Wünsche, 1998. Mem. Hungarian Soc. Polit. Scis., European Hon. Senate. Office: Köztarsasag ter 26, 1081 Budapest Hungary

HORN, LEE SHAWN, photojournalist; b. Miami, Fla., Feb. 21, 1977; s. Andrew Warren and Melinda F. (Fink) H. Grad. h.s., Miami, 1995. Ind. filmmaker Miami, 1993—; newsroom worker ABC, Miami, 1996; v.p. Fla. Internat. U., 1999; pres. Sports Ltd. Edits. & Memorabilia, 1996—; v.p. Fla. Internat. U., 1999; asst. head coach football team Gulliver Prep., 1997—; asst. dir. Super Bowl halftime show, 1999. Vol. Atlanta Com. Olympic Games, 1996. Democrat. Avocations: football, skiing, fishing, traveling.

HORN, MICHIEL STEVEN DANIEL, history educator; b. Baarn, The Netherlands, Sept. 3, 1939; arrived in Can., 1952, naturalized, 1957; s. Daniel and Antje Elisabeth (Reitsma) H.; m. Cornelia Schuh, Dec. 29, 1984; children: Daniel André, Patrick Benjamin. BA, U. B.C., 1963; MA, U. Toronto, 1965, PhD, 1969. Jr. officer Bank of Montreal, Victoria, B.C., Can., 1956-58; lectr. history Glendon Coll., York U., Toronto, Ont., Can., 1968-69, asst. prof., 1969-73, assoc. prof., 1973-82; prof. York U., Toronto, Ont., Can., 1982—, chmn. dept., 1973-78, 82-93; assoc. prin. Coll., 1978-81, dir. Can. Studies, 1986-89; acad. cons.-coord. Living and Learning in Retirement, 19765. Editor, author: The Dirty Thirties, 1972; author: The League for Social Reconstruction, 1980, The Great Depression of the 1930s in Canada, 1984, Years of Despair, 1986, Becoming Canadian, 1997, Academic Freedom in Canada, 1999; co-author: A Liberation Album, 1980, Canada, A Political and Social History, 1982; editor: A New Endeavor, 1986, Academic Freedom, 1987, The Depression in Canada, 1988; co-editor: Studies in Canadian Social History, 1974. Mem. North York Hist. Bd. and Local Archtl. Conservancy Adv. Com., 1977-80. Woodrow Wilson fellow 1963-64, Can. Coun. fellow/grantee, 1974-75, Social Sci. and Humanities Rsch. Coun. grantee, 1986-89, 90-91, Glendon Coll. rsch. leave fellowship, 1993-94. Mem. York U. Faculty Assn. (chmn. 1972-73), Can. Assn. Univ. Tchrs. (exec. com. 1973-75, acad. freedom and tenure com. 1984-90), Ont. Confedn. Univ. Faculty Assns. (chmn. 1976-77), Massey Coll. Common Room Club, Glendon Squash Club (Toronto). Office: York U, 2275 Bayview Ave, Toronto, ON Canada M4N 3M6

HORN, PETR JAN, electrical engineer; b. Kamenny Privoz, Czechoslovakia, July 31, 1946; arrived in Switzerland, 1968; s. Stanislav Vaclav and Zdenka Marie (Borovickova) H.; 1 child from previous marriage, Barbara; m. Zuzana Bubrjakova, Aug. 28, 1999. MS, Swiss Fed. Inst. Tech., Zurich, 1972; PhD, Swiss Fed. Inst. Tech., 1978. Sci. co-worker Swiss Fed. Inst. Tech., Zurich, 1972-78; patent engr. E. Blum & Co., Zurich, 1979-80; rsch. engr. Novasina AG, Zurich, 1980-89; head devel. Knobel AG, Ennenda, Switzerland, 1989-95, Horsch Elektronik AG, Gams, Switzerland, 1995—. Co-author: Active Filter Design Handbook, 1981, CRC Handbook of Electrical Filter, 1997; contbr. articles to profl. jours.; patentee in field. Mem. IEEE. Avocations: skiing, tennis, mountain-hiking, biking, swimming. Home: Muehlestr 2, 9470 Buchs SG Switzerland Office: Horsch Elektronik AG, Haagerstr, 9473 Gams Switzerland

HORN, SUSAN DADAKIS, statistics educator; b. Cleve., Aug. 30, 1943; d. James Sophocles and Demeter (Zessis) Dadakis; m. Roger Alan Horn, July 24, 1965; children: Ceres, Corinne, Howard. BA, Cornell U., 1964; MS, Stanford U., 1966, PhD, 1968. Asst. prof. Johns Hopkins U., Balt., 1968-76, assoc. prof., 1976-86, prof. stats. and health svcs. rsch. methods, 1986-92; sr. scientist Intermountain Health Care, Salt Lake City, 1992-95; prof. dept. med. informatics Sch. Medicine U. Utah, Salt Lake City, 1992-99; rsch. prof. U. Tex.-Houston Sch. Nursing, 1999—; sr. scientist Inst. for Clin. Outcomes Rsch., Salt Lake City. Fellow Am. Statist. Assn., Assn. for Health Svcs. Rsch.; mem. APHA, Biometric Soc., Assn. for Health Svcs. Research, Sigma Xi, Phi Beta Kappa, Phi Kappa Phi. Presbyterian. Avocations: tennis, swimming. Home: 1793 Fort Douglas Cir Salt Lake City UT 84103-4451 Office: Inst Clin Outcomes Rsch 2681 Parleys Way Ste 201 Salt Lake City UT 84109-1630

HORNABROOK, RICHARD WILLIAM, neurologist; b. Wellinston, New Zealand, Dec. 1, 1925; s. Sidney Roland and Kate (Philipps) H.; m. Fay Marshall, June 1960; children: Charles William, Richard Sidney, Sarah Kit. MB, BChir, U. Otago, New Zealand, 1949, MD, 1955. Demonstrator anatomy U. Otaso, 1952, rsch. asst., 1953-54; acad. registrar nervous diseases Nat. Hosp. Queen Sq., London, 1954-55, house physician, 1955-58, resident med. officer, 1958-59; asst. prof. neurology Cornell Svc. Bellevue Hosp., N.Y.C., 1959-60; staff neurologist Wellinston Hosp., 1961-63, 66-68, 76-92; med. officer Kuru rsch. Okapa, Papua New Guinea, 1964-66; dir. Papua New Guinea Inst. Human Biology and Med. Rsch., 1968-75; clin. reader Wellinston Med. Sch., 1976-92. Mem. editl. bd. Topics in Tropical Neurology, 1974, Essays on Kuru, 1975, Handbook of Beetes of New Guinea, 1973. Fellow Royal Australian Coll. Physicians. Avocation: natural history. Home and Office: 27 Orchard St, Wadestwn Wellington New Zealand

HORNBLOW, ANDREW REED, academic administrator, psychologist; b. Wellington, New Zealand, June 25, 1942; s. Maxwell H. and Patricia (Gooch) H.; m. Daphne Tui Skeels, May 7, 1966; children: Linda Joy, Michael Andrew, Douglas Arthur. BA, Victoria U., 1967; MA, U. Canterbury, 1970, diploma in clin. psychology, 1971; PhD, Monash U., 1978. Psychologist Sunnyside Hosp., Christchurch, New Zealand, 1967-71; student counselor U. Canterbury, Christchurch, 1971-74; sr. tchg. fellow, lectr. Monash U., Melbourne, Australia, 1974-78; from sr. lectr. to prof. Christchurch Sch. Medicine U. Otago, 1978-94, dean, 1994—; dep. chmn. Health Rsch. Coun. New Zealand, 1996—; bd. dirs. Pub. Health Commn., New Zealand, 1993-95; chmn. Alcohol Adv. Coun., 1999—; adj. prof. U. Canterbury, 1999—. Recipient New Zealand commemorative medal, 1990. Fellow New Zealand Psychol. Soc. (pres. 1980-81); mem. Mental Health Found. (chmn. 1981-86), Pub. Health Assn. (pres. 1986-91). Avocations: walking, gardening, camping, travel. Home: 32 Puriri St Riccarton, Christchurch New Zealand Office: Christchurch Sch Medicine, Riccarton Ave PO Box 4345, Christchurch New Zealand

HORNE, DAVID JAMES, clinical psychologist, educator; b. Belfast, Northern Ireland, Mar. 7, 1942; arrived in Australia, 1958; s. Colin James and Margaret Elizabeth (Parsons) H.; m. Linda Olive King, June 29, 1968 (div. 1986); children: Katherine Elizabeth, Rebecca Louise; m. Sue Catherine Morgan, July 11, 1998. BA with honors, U. Adelaide, Australia, 1964; MPhil, U. London, 1968; PhD, U. Melbourne, Australia, 1974. Registered psychologist, Victoria; chartered psychologist Brit. Psychol. Soc. Sr. clin. psychologist Guys Hosp., London, 1966-68; lectr. U. Melbourne, 1969-74, sr. lectr., 1974-88, reader, assoc. prof., 1988—; cons. clin. psychologist Royal Melbourne Hosp., 1969—; mem. Psychologists Registration Bd., Victoria, 1988-99; cons. Victorian Workcover Authority, Australia, 1993-95. Co-editor: Coping With Trauma: The Victim and the Helper, 1994; editor: (video program) Psychiatric Art: An Illustrated Talk By Dr. E.C. Dax, 1982; contbr. chpt. to book. Rsch. grantee Victorian Health Promotion Found., Australia, 1989-91, Nat. Health and Med. Rsch. Coun., Australia, 1994-95. Fellow Australian Psychol. Soc. (chair Coll. Clin. Psychologists 1979-84, chair Victorian br. 1990-93); mem. Australian Assn. Cognitive and Behaviour Therapy (pres. 1980-81). Avocations: Australian and European art, railway travel. E-mail: d.horne@psych.unimelb.edu.an. Office: U Melbourne Royal Melbourne Hosp, Dept Psych Charles Connibere Bldg, Melbourne VIC 3050, Australia

HORNE, FRANCIS PHILIP, English literature educator; b. Inverness, Scotland, Mar. 6, 1958; s. Frank Andrew and Jocelyn Elizabeth (McLaurin) H.; m. Judith Victoria Hawley, July 28, 1990; 1 child, Olivia. MA in English, Jesus Coll., Cambridge, Eng., 1979, PhD in English, 1984. Jr. rsch. fellow Christ's Coll., Cambridge, 1983-84; lectr. in English U. Coll., London, 1984-95, reader in English, 1996-2000, prof. English, 2000—; vis. scholar Harry Ransom Humanities Rsch. Ctr., 1999. Author: Henry James and Revision: A Study of the New York Edition, 1990; editor: Henry James: A Life in Letters, 1999, The Tragic Muse by Henry James, 1995, A London Life and the Reverberator, 1989. Mem. Henry James Soc. (sec.-treas.). Office: U Coll London, Gower St, London WC1E 6BT, England

HORNE, MARILYN, mezzo-soprano; b. Bradford, Pa., Jan. 16, 1934; d. Bentz and Berneice H.; m. Henry Lewis (div.); 1 child. Ed., U. So. Calif.; MusD (hon.), Rutgers U., 1970, Jersey City State Coll., 1973, Brown U., 1984, Juillard Sch. Music, 1994; DLitt (hon.), St. Peter's Coll.; LHD (hon.), Kean Coll., 1977. Operatic debut as Hata in The Bartered Bride, Los Angeles Guild Opera, 1954; La Scala debut in Oepidus Rex, 1969; Met. Opera debut as Adalgisa in Norma, 1970; other roles include Rosina in Barber of Seville, Cleonte in The Siege of Corinth, Isabella in L'Italiana in Algieri, Carmen at Met. Opera, 1972-73, Laura in Harvest, Chgo. Lyric Opera, Marie in Wozzeck, San Francisco Opera; also appeared in Phigenie en Tauride, Semiramide, Samson et Dalila at Met. Opera, 1987, The Ghost of Versailles, 1991, Pelléas et Mélisande, 1995; other appearances include Venice Festival by invitation of Igor Stravinsky, Am. Opera Soc., N.Y.C., for several seasons, Vancouver Opera, Philharm. Hall, N.Y.C., Paris, Dallas, Houston, Covent Garden, London, roles at La Scala, Italy, Rossini Opera Festival, Pesaro, Italy, Met. Opera, 1987; recital debuts in Madrid, Dresden, East Berlin, 1987, performed at inauguration of U.S. President Clinton, 1993; ann. recital at Carnegie Hall, European tour with husband for Dept. State, 1963; rec. artist for London, Columbia, Deutsche Grammaphon and RCA records; recs. include sountrack Carmen Jones. Founder Marilyn Horne Found. Recipient Grammy awards, 1964, 81, 83, 94., Handel medallion, 1980, Premio d'Oro, Italian Govt., 1982, Commendatore al merito della Repubblica Italiana, 1983, Gold Merit medal Nat. Soc. Arts and Letters, 1987, Fidelio Gold medal, 1988, George Peabody award, 1989, Silver medal Covent Garden Royal Opera House, 1989, Disting. Dau. of Pa. Silver medal San Francisco Opera, 1990, Nat. Arts medal, 1992; named to Harold C. Schonberg's N.Y. Times' list of 9 All-Time, All-Star Singers in Met. Opera's 100 Years, 1984, Musician of Yr. Musical Am., 1995. Achievements includes having the leading exponent florid vocal style, music of Rossini, Handel, Vivaldi. Office: care Columbia Artists Mgmt Inc Wilford Divsn 165 W 57th St New York NY 10019-2201 also: care Met Opera Assoc Attention: Artistic Dept Lincoln Ctr New York NY 10023 also: BMG Classics/RCA 1540 Broadway New York NY 10036-4039

HORNER, ALTHEA JANE, psychologist; b. Hartford, Conn., Jan. 13, 1926; d. Louis and Celia (Newmark) Greenwald; children: Martha Horner Hartley, Anne Horner Benck, David, Kenneth. BS in Psychology, U. Chgo., 1952; PhD in Clin. Psychology, U. So. Calif., 1965. Lic. psychologist, N.Y., Calif. Tchr. Pasadena (Calif.) City Coll., 1965-67; from asst. to assoc. prof. Los Angeles Coll. Optometry, 1967-70; supr. Psychology interns Pasadena Child Guidance Clinic, 1969-70; pvt. practice specializing in psychoanalysis and psychoanalytic psychotherapy. N.Y.C., 1970-83; supervising psychologist dept. psychiatry Beth Israel Med. Ctr., N.Y.C., 1972-83, coordinator group therapy tng., 1976-82, clinician in charge Brief Adaptation-Oriented Psychotherapy Research Group, 1982-83; assoc. clin. prof. Mt. Sinai Sch. Medicine, N.Y.C., 1977-91, adj. assoc. prof., 1991—; mem. faculty Nat. Psychol. Assn. for Psychoanalysis, N.Y.C., 1982-83; sr. mem. faculty Wright Inst. Los Angeles Postgrad. Inst., 1983-85; pvt. practice L.A., 1983—; clin. prof. dept. Psychology UCLA, 1985-95. Author: (with others) Treating the Neurotic Patient in Brief Psychotherapy, 1985, Object Relations and the Developing Ego in Therapy, 1979, rev. edit., 1984, Little Big Girl, 1982, Being and Loving, 1978, 3d edit. 1990, Psychology for Living (with G. Forehand), 4th edit., 1977, The Wish for Power and the Fear of Having It, 1989, The Primacy of Structure, 1990, Psychoanalytic Object Relations Therapy, 1991, Working With the Core Relationship Problem in Psychotherapy, 1998, Chrysalis, 1999, Get Over It! Untie Your Relationship Knots and Move On, 2000; mem. editorial bd. Jour. of Humanistic Psychology, 1986—, Jour. of the Am. Acad. of Psychoanalysis; contbr. articles to profl. jours. Mem. AAAS, APA, Calif. State Psychol. Assn., Am. Acad. Psychoanalysis (sci. assoc.), So. Calif. Psychoanalytic Soc. and Inst. (hon.). Office: PMB 256 3579 E Foothill Blvd Pasadena CA 91107-3119

HORNER, CARL MATTHEW, chemistry educator; b. Cicero, N.Y., June 4, 1930; s. Oscar Wendell and Gladys Cecilia (Horner) H. BS, LeMoyne Coll., 1952; MS, Syracuse U., 1958, PhD, 1965. Asst. prof. analytical chemistry SUNY-Oneonta, 1958-61, assoc. prof., 1961-64, prof., 1964-67, prof. emeritus, 1998—; coord. ann. instrumental chemistry workshops, 1986-95. NSF CAUSE grantee, 1979-82; NSF CSIP grantee, 1986-88; Walter B. Ford Found. grantee, 1980, 83. Mem. AAAS, Am. Chem. Soc., N.Y. Acad. Scis. Avocations: scuba diving, underwater photography. Achievements include: research in infrared spectroscopy and laboratory robotics. Home: 24 Suncrest Ter Oneonta NY 13820-4632

HORNER, HARRY CHARLES, JR., sales executive, theatrical and film consultant; b. Pitts., Oct. 30, 1937; s. Harry Charles and Sara Marie (Hysong) H.; m. Patricia Ann Hagarty, June 15, 1965 (div. 1981); m. Sharon Kae Wyatt, Dec. 30, 1983; children: Jeffrey Brian, Jennifer Leigh, Mark Gregory. BFA, U. Cin., 1963; postgrad., Xavier U., Cin., 1963-64. Mgr. Retail Credit Co., Atlanta, 1964-68; ops. mgr. Firestone Tire and Rubber Co., L.A., 1968-80; exec. v.p. Romney/Ford Enterprises Inc., Scottsdale, Ariz., 1980-85; sales mgr. Environ. Care Inc., Calabassas, Calif., 1985-93; ops. v.p. Albuquerque (N.Mex.) Grounds Maintenance, Inc., 1993—; pres., chief exec. officer The Cons. Group Cos. Ltd., Palm Desert, Calif., 1984—; pres. E. Valley Theatre Co., Chandler, Ariz., 1984-86. Cons. Ariz. Commn. on Arts, Phoenix, 1983-84. Republican. Mem. LDS Ch. Avocations: flying, model railroads. Office: Environmental Care Inc 2920 E Illini St Phoenix AZ 85040

HORNER, JEFFREY THOMAS, public policy researcher; b. Groton, Conn., May 21, 1961; s. David and Nancy (Northwood) H. BA, Adrian Coll., 1984; M in Urban Planning, Wayne State U., 1993. Sales rep. Saturn & Assocs., Detroit, 1986-88, Designer Vertical Blind Co., Dearborn Heights, Mich., 1988-90; cmty. devel. block grant adminstr. City of Oak Park, Mich., 1990-91; rsch. technician Wayne State U., Detroit, 1993-94; downtown devel. auth. cons. City of Hazel Park, Mich., 1994-95; rsch. asst. Wayne State U., 1995-97; rsch. assoc. Citizens Rsch. Coun. Mich., Livonia, Mich., 1997—; lectr. Wayne State U., 2000—, bd. mem. State Policy Ctr. Mem. Mensa, Am. Planning Assn., Am. Inst. of Cert. Planners, Internat. Soc. Philos. Inquiry. Home: 27155 Hoover Rd Warren MI 48093-4553

HORNER, MATINA SOURETIS, retired college president, corporate executive; b. Boston, July 28, 1939; d. Demetre John and Christine (Antonopoulos) Souretis; m. Joseph L. Horner, June 25, 1961; children: Tia Andrea, John, Christopher. AB cum laude, Bryn Mawr Coll., 1961; MS, U. Mich., 1963, PhD, 1968; LLD (hon.), Dickinson Coll., 1973; LLD, Mt. Holyoke Coll., 1973; LLD (hon.), U. Pa., 1975, Smith Coll., 1979, Wheaton Coll., 1979, U. Mich., 1989; LHD (hon.), U. Mass., 1973, Tufts U., 1976, U. Hartford, 1980, U. New Eng., 1987, Bentley Coll., 1989, New Eng. Coll., 1989, Pine Manor Coll., 1989, Am. Coll. Greece, 1990; DLitt (hon.), Claremont U. Ctr. and Grad Sch., 1988, Hellenic Coll., 1990; LHD (hon.), Colby Sawyer Coll., 1991. Teaching fellow U. Mich., Ann Arbor, 1962-66, lectr. motivation personality, 1968-69; lectr. social relations Harvard U., Cambridge, Mass., 1969-70, asst. prof. clin. psychology, 1970-72, assoc. prof. psychology, 1972-89, cons. univ. health svcs., 1971-89; pres. Radcliffe Coll., Cambridge, 1972-89, pres. emerita, 1989—; exec. v.p. TIAA-CREF, N.Y.C., 1989—; bd. dirs. Neiman Marcus Group, Boston Edison Co.-NSTAR. Co-author: The Challenge of Change, 1983; contbr. psychol. articles on motivation to profl. jours. and chpts. to books. Mem. adv. coun. NSF, 1977-87, chair, 1980-86; bd. trustees Twentieth Century Fund, The Century Found., 1973—, Am. Coll. of Greece, 1983-90, Mass. Eye and Ear Infirmary, 1986-90, Com. for Econ. Devel., 1988—, vice-chmn., 1992-98; bd. trustees Mass. Gen. Hosp., Inst. Health Professions, 1988—, vice chmn., 1994, chair, 1995; bd. dirs. Coun. for Fin. Aid to Edn., 1985-89, Beth Israel Hosp., 1989-95; bd. dirs. Revson Found., 1986-92, chmn., 1992-97; bd. dirs. Women's Rsch. and Edn. Inst., 1979—, chair rsch. com., 1982—; mem. Coun. on Fgn. Rels., 1984—; exec. com. ACE Bus. Higher Edn. Forum, 1984-86; exec. com. New Eng. Colls. Fund, 1980—, 2d v.p., 1984-85, 1st v.p., 1985-88, pres., 1988-89; mem. nat. panel to study declining test scores Coll. Entrance Exam. Bd., 1976-77; exec. com., chair task force Pres.'s Commn. for Nat. Agenda for 1980s, 1979-80; adv. com. Women's Leadership Conf. on Nat. Security, 1982—; exec. com. Coun. on Competitiveness, 1986-89; chair task force on health care Challenge to Leadership Conf., 1987-89; bd. dirs. Greenwall Found., 1997, Fund for City of N.Y., chair, 1997. Recipient Roger Baldwin award Mass. Civil Liberties Union Found., 1982, citation of merit Northeast Region NCCJ, 1982, Career Contbn. award Mass. Psychol. Assn., 1987, Disting. Bostonian award, 1990, Ellis Island medal, 1990. Mem. NOW (nat. corp. adv. bd. of legal def. and edn. fund 1984—), Am. Laryngol. Voice Rsch. and Edn. Found. (pres.), Nat. Inst. Social Scis. (medal for outstanding svc. 1973), Phi Beta Kappa, Phi Delta Kappa, Phi Kappa Phi.

HORNICK, SUSAN FLORENCE STEGMULLER, secondary education educator, fine arts educator; b. Aug. 29, 1947; d. August George and Florence Maybell (Meisinger) Stegmuller; m. Jesse Allan Hornick, July 20, 1974. BA, Queens Coll., 1969, MS in Art Edn., 1973; permanent N.Y. state reading profl. diploma, Hunter Coll., 1984, advanced cert. ednl. supervn./adminstrn. summa cum laude, 1996. Lic. tchr. fine arts, N.Y.C.; permanent cert. tchr. art, N.Y.; cert. in ednl. adminstrn. and supervision, N.Y.; permanent cert. sch. dist. adminstr., N.Y. Fine arts tchr. Hillcrest H.S., Jamaica, N.Y., 1973-74, Ea. Dist. H.S., Bklyn., 1974-75, Tottenville H.S., S.I., N.Y., 1975-76; fine arts tchr., title 1 reading tchr. Prospect Heights H.S., Bklyn., 1976-78; fine arts tchr. Grover Cleveland H.S., Ridgewood, N.Y., 1978—; dept. coord. Grover Cleveland H.S., Ridgewood, 1996-98; tchr. reading, English and reading improvement through art; yearbook advisor, 1979; cooperating tchr., trainer art Queens Coll., Flushing, N.Y., 1991, 2000; tchr. "bridge" ESL and math. Newcomers H.S. Summer Sch., L.I., N.Y. Exhbns. include U.S. Capitol, Washington, Lever House Exhibit, 1984-97, N.Y.C. Transit Mus., 1987-99, Sotheby's, 1992, Internat. Arrivals bldg. JFK Kennedy Airport (award winning mural by Joanna Kadlubowska, 1992), Queens Theater in the Park, Flushing, N.Y., 1993, 97, Nat. Mus. Am. Indian, Smithsonian Inst., 1992, 93, Mus. of City of N.Y., 1998, U.S. Capitol, Washington, 1982, 86, 88. Recipient Medal for Superior Performance, N.Y.C. Transit Authority, 1996, Cert. Apprecation for Outstanding Performance as Art Educator in N.Y.C. Pub. Schs., 1985. Home: 46-05 Hanford St Douglaston NY 11362

HORNIG, CLAUS RUEDIGER, neurologist, educator; b. Giessen, Germany, May 14, 1954; s. Herbert and Martha Hornig; m. Sabine Obermeier, Sept. 1, 1983; children: Claudia, Thorsten. MD, Justus Liebig U., Giessen, 1981. Med. diplomate, 1979. Rsch. fellow Rodenwald Inst. Virology, Koblenz, Germany, 1979-80; rsch. fellow U. Giessen Dept. Neurology, 1981-85, cons., 1986-88, sr. lectr., 1988-94, prof. neurology, 1994—, dept. head, 1996—. Mem. European Neurol. Soc., European Stroke Coun., Am. Heart Assn. (stroke coun.). Office: Krankenhaus Weilmünster, Weilstrasse 10, 35789 Weilmünster Germany

HORNIK, JOSEPH WILLIAM, civil engineer; b. N.Y.C., May 7, 1929; s. Joseph and Josephine (Nemecek) H.; m. Barbara Joan Simko, Nov. 16, 1957; children: Heidi Josepha, Joseph Jared, Jason William, Heather Justine. B.C.E., Cooper Union, 1952; grad. studies, Columbia U., 1955-61. Lic. profl. engr., N.Y., Conn., Fla., P.R.; lic. land surveyor, N.Y. Field engr. Stone & Webster Enging. Corp., Roanoke Rapids, N.C., and Portsmouth, Va., 1952-54; sr. engr. Howard, Needles, Tammen & Bergendoff, Jersey City, 1954-56; resident engr. Edwards & Kelcey, Bridgeport, Conn., 1956-59; project engr., project supt. The Austin Co., Bklyn. and San Juan, P.R., 1959-62; resident engr. Seelye, Stevenson, Value & Knecht, Whitehall, N.Y., 1962-65; county engr., county supt. hwys. County of Rockland, New City, N.Y., 1965-90; cons. engr. West Nyack, N.Y., 1967—; village engr. Village of Sloatsburg, N.Y., 1972-81, 85-88, Village of Haverstraw, N.Y., 1982-83, Village of Monroe, N.Y., 1984-92, Village of New Hempstead, N.Y., 1988-90, Village of Nyack, N.Y., 1988-94. Mem. Rockland County Planning bd., 1972-90, Rockland County Drainage Agy., 1972-90, Rockland County Soil and Water Conservation Agy., 1972-90, Rockland County Traffic Safety Bd., 1979-90, Nat. Com. on Uniform Traffic Control Devices, 1985—. Fellow ASCE; mem. NSPE, N.Y. State County Hwy Supts. Assn. (dir. 1975-87, v.p. 1980-81, pres. 1982), N.Y. State Soc. Profl. Engrs., Nat. Assn. County Engrs. (dir. 1984-90), Nat. Assn. Counties, Am. Rd. and Transp. Builders Assn., Rockland County Assn. Hwy. Supts. (pres. 1979), Inst. Engrs., Architects and Surveyors of P.R., Soil and Water Conservation Soc. Am., Omega Delta Phi. Clubs: West Nyack Swim and Tennis, West Rock Tennis. Home and Office: 2 Dearborn Rd West Nyack NY 10994-1104

HORNIK, KURT OTTO, mathematics and statistics educator; b. Vienna, Austria, Aug. 16, 1963; s. Kurt and Helen (Hofbauer) H. MS, Tech. U. Vienna, 1985, PhD, 1987. Asst. prof. Tech. U. Vienna, 1986-87, U. Calif., San Diego, 1987-88; asst. prof. Tech. U. Vienna, 1988-90, assoc. prof., 1990—. Mem. IEEE (letters editor 1993—). Roman Catholic. Home: Seebensteiner Str 59, Sautern A-2823, Austria Office: Tech Univ Vienna, Wiedner Hauptstr 8-10/1071, Wien A-1040, Austria

HÖRNING, BERNHARD, science educator; b. Moers, Germany, Aug. 29, 1961; s. Wilhelm and Margareta Hörning. MS, U. Kassel, Witzenhausen, Germany, 1991, PhD, 1997. Mng. dir. Advice Ctr. for Proper Animal Housing, Witzenhausen, Germany, 1989-93; sci. collaborator U. Kassel, 1993-98, asst. prof., 1998—; mem. com. Advice Ctr. for Proper Animal Housing, 1994—. Author: Status of the European Brown Bear, 1992, Proper Pig Housing (in German), 1992, 4th edit., 1999, Russian and Finnish edits., 1997; co-author: Proper Cattle Housing (in German), 1992, Italian edit., 1995, Finnish edit., 1996, Proper Poultry Housing (in German), 1992, 4th edit., 1998; editor: Ecological Pig Husbandry (in German), 1993, Ecological Poultry Husbandry (in German), 1995, Rare Pig Breeds and Alternatives in Pig Breeding (in German), 1997; co-editor: Ecological Cattle Husbandry (in German), 1997, (series) Animal Management, 1996—. Recipient Rsch. award for animal-friendly husbandry Schweisfurth Found., 1994. Mem. German Soc. for Rare Breeds (coord. for rare pig breeds), Internat. Soc. for Applied Ethology, Internat. Soc. for Animal Husbandry, Soc. for Ecol. Animal Husbandry. Avocation: animal observation. Fax: 0049-5542-981588. E-mail: hoerning@wiz.uni-kassel.de. Office: U Kassel, Nordbahnhofstr 1 a, D-37213 Witzenhausen Germany

HORNING, MARKUS, marine biologist, educator; b. Braunschweig, Germany, Feb. 14, 1960; came to U.S., 1992; s. Hans M. and Ursula Horning. MS, Freiburg (Germany) U., 1988; PhD summa cum laude, Bielefeld (Germany) U., 1992. Biologist Max-Planck-Inst., Seewiesen, Germany, 1989-92; postdoctoral rsch. physiologist Scripps Instn. Oceanography, San Diego, 1992-96; asst. rsch. scientist Tex. A&M U., Galveston, 1996-98, assoc. rsch. scientist, 1998—, dir. Lab. Applied Biotelemetry and Biotech., 2000—; assoc. prof. marine scis., U. Alaska, Fairbanks, 1999—; sole propr. Ultramarine Instruments, Galveston, 1997—; scientific program com. 1st World Marine Mammal Sci. Conf., Monaco, 1998. Contbr. articles to profl. jours.; inventor in field; assoc. editor Marine Mammal Sci., 1996-98. Recipient U.S. Antarctica medal, NSF, 1981. Mem. AAAS, Ecol. Soc. Am., Am. Physiol. Soc., Animal Behavior Soc., Soc. Marine Mammalogy, Am. Soc. Photogrammetry and Remote Sensing, N.Y. Acad. Sci. E-mail: horningm@tamug.tamu.edu. Office: Tex A&M U 5007 Avenue U Galveston TX 77551-5926

HORNING, ROBERT ALAN, securities broker; b. Bristol, Tenn., Jan. 8, 1954; s. Sanford Lee and Pauline Stern (Marks) H.; m. Phyllis Ann Bockian, Apr. 12, 1981; children: Aaron Marks, Rachel Michelle. BA, U. Tenn., 1976, MA, 1979. Edn. specialist Knoxville (Tenn.) Police Dept., 1979-80; security cons. Sonitrol of Knoxville, 1980-81; sales rep. Guardsmark, Inc., Charleston, W.Va., 1981-84; mgr. in charge Guardsmark, Inc., L.A., 1984-88; v.p. mktg.-western region Fed. Armored Express, L.A., 1988-92; ptnr. Upton Affiliates, L.A., 1993—; sch. improvement chairperson Orville Wright Math Sci. Magnet. Bd. dirs. B'Nai Tikvah Congregation, L.A., 1989—, v.p. membership, 1991, v.p. ritual com., treas.; governance coun. Paseo Del Rey Natural Sci. Magnet Sch., 1996—; chmn. sch. improvement coun. Orville Wright Sci. and Math Magnet Sch., 2000. Mem. Am. Soc. Indsl. Security (chmn. L.A. chpt. 1990), Internat. Platform Assn., Phi Beta Kappa, Omicron Delta Kappa. Democrat. Jewish. Avocation: reading. Home: 7911 Denrock Ave Los Angeles CA 90045-1112

HORNING, ROSS CHARLES, JR., historian, educator; b. Watertown, S.D., Oct. 10, 1920; s. Ross Charles and Harriett (Meaghan) H. BA, Augustana Coll., 1948; MA, George Washington U., 1952; PhD (Sanders fellow), 1958; postgrad. Russian, Inst. Langs. and Linguistics, Georgetown U., 1952-53. Instr. Wis. State U., Eau Claire, 1958-59; asst. prof. St. John's U., Collegeville, Minn., 1959-64; assoc. prof. Russian history and internat. affairs Creighton U., Omaha, 1964-68, prof., 1968—; pres. faculty Creighton U., 1984-86, chmn. athletic bd., Athletic Hall of Fame com., 1987-88, mem. athletic bd., 1992—, mem. pub. honors com., 1984-90, 93-96, 97—. Bd. advisors Red Cloud Indian Sch., Pine Ridge, S.C.; bd. govs. Irish Am. Partnership, Boston. Recipient Disting. Faculty Service award Creighton U., 1982; Fulbright scholar India, summer 1967. Mem. AAAS, Am. Assn. Advancement Slavic Studies, Am. Hist. Assn., Am. Soc. Internat. Law, AAUP, Orgn. Am. Historians, Conf. Slavic and European Studies, Am. Com. for Irish Studies, Midwest Conf. on Asian Affairs, Que. Studies Assn., Joslyn Liberal Arts Soc., S.W. Am. Assn. Advancement Slavic Studies, Western Social Sci. Assn., Am. Fgn. Service Assn., Canadian History Assn., Assn. Canadian Studies in U.S., Assn. Asian Studies, Omaha Symphony Assn., Atlanta Econ. Soc., Assn. Canadienne de Sci. Politique, Internat. Law Assn. (Am. br.), World Peace Through Law Center, Fgn. Service Club (Washington), Asia Soc., Opera-Omaha, Assn. Profl. Baseball Players (life), Fulbright Alumni Assn. (life), Omaha Press Club, Alpha Sigma Nu. Home: 4955 Cuming St Omaha NE 68132-1549

HORNOK, LÁSZLÓ, microbiologist, educator; b. Újpest, Hungary, Aug. 13, 1947; s. Elek and Katalin (Szeberényi) H.; m. Borbála Tóth; 1 child, Kinga. MSc, Gödöll Agrl. Scis., 1970; PhD, Com. Sci. Qualification, Budapest, 1980; DSc, Hungarian Acad. Scis., 1994. Rschr. Plant Protection Inst., Hungarian Acad. Scis., Budapest, 1971-89, assoc. dir., 1987-88; rschr. Agrl. Biotech. Ctr., Gödöllo, 1990-94; sci. advisor Agrl. Biotech. Ctr., Godollo, 1995—; prof., head dept. microbiology Godollo U. Agrl. Scis., 1995—; mem. editl. bd. Acta Phytopathologica et Entomologica Hungarica, Budapest, 1992—; mem. mgmt. com. COST Action 835, Brussels, 1998—. Editor: (with T. Érsek) Pathogens and the Infected Plant, 1985; contbr. numerous articles to profl. jours. Sgt. maj. People's Army of Hungary, 1965-66. Recipient Acad. prize Hungarian Acad. Scis., 1998. Mem. Microbiol. Soc. Hungary (mem. exec. bd. 1990—, Manninger medal 1997). Office: Agrl Biotech Ctr, Szent-Györgyi A u 4, 2101 Gödöll Hungary

HORNSBY, BRUCE RANDALL, composer, musician; b. Richmond, Va., Nov. 23, 1954; s. Robert Stanley and Lois (Saunier) H.; m. Kathy Yankovich, Dec. 31, 1983. BA, U. Miami, Coral Gables, Fla., 1977. Recording artist; albums include The Way It Is, 1986 (double platinum award, gold award Eng., Platinum award Can., gold award Germany, gold award Australia), Scenes from the Southside, 1988 (platinum award, gold award Eng., platinum award Can.), A Night on the Town, 1990 (gold award Can., silver award Eng.), Harbor Lights, 1993 (gold award), Hot House, 1995, Spirit Trail, 1998; composer numerous songs including The Way It Is (Song of Yr. ASCAP 1987), Mandolin Rain, Jacob's Ladder, Every Little Kiss, Valley Road, Look Out Any Window, Defenders of the Flag, On the Western Skyline, The End of Innocence, Across the River, Lost Soul, Fields of Gray, Rainbow's Cadillac, Walk in the Sun, Spider Fingers, (with E-40) Things'll Never Change, 1997; performed on records by Bob Dylan, The Grateful Dead, Rock and Roll Hall of Fame Concert Album, 1996, Tin Cup soundtrack, Bonnie Raitt, Bob Seger, Squeeze, Cowboy Junkies, Huey Lewis, Nitty Gritty Dirt Band, Chaka Khan, others; performed the Nat. Anthem, World Series Game 5, 1997. Recipient Best New Artist Grammy award, 1986, Best Bluegrass Rec. Grammy award, 1989, Best Pianist Keyboard Mag., 1987, 88, 89, 90, 91, 93; Best Song of Yr. Grammy nomination, 1989, Record of Yr. Grammy nomination, 1989, Best Performance by a Duo or Group Grammy nomination, 1990, Best Original Score Emmy award, 1987, Best Pop Instrumental Grammy award for "Barcelona Mona" with Branford Marsalis, 1994, Best Pop Instrumental Grammy nomination for "Star Spangled Banner" with Branford Marsalis, 1995, Best Pop Instrumental Grammy nomination for "Song B", 1995, Best Song Written for a Motion Picture "Love Me Still" with Chaka Khan Grammy nomination, 1995; winner Best Beyond album Downbeat Reader's Poll, 1994. Home: 311 Indian Springs Rd Williamsburg VA 23185-3942

HORNSTEIN, FLORIAN FREIHERR VON, advertising executive; b. Munich, Bavaria, Germany, May 28, 1956; s. Wolfgang Freiherr and Elga (Jarolimek) von H.; m. Brigitte Herrmann, Nov. 4, 1987; children: Carina, Benita. Grad. h.s., Munich; apprenticeship as banker, 1978. CEO Serviceplan Holding, Munich, 1996—, Serviceplan Advt. Agy., Munich, 1994—; mng. dir. Mediaplus Svc. Plc, Munich, 1998—, Plannet Multimedia Plc, Munich, 1997—, Serviceplan Vital Plc, Munich, 1997—, HCCS Plus Plc, Munich, 1999—, Brandeveut plc, 2000—. Recipient London Internat. Advt. award, 1994, Internat. Advt. Film and TV Festival N.Y. Bronze medal, 1990, Finalist award, 1993, Merit award Internat. Exhbn. Art Dirs. Club, 1991. Mem. Internat. Munich Yacht Club. Office: Serviceplan Advt Group, Briennerstr 45a-d, 80333 Munich Bavaria, Germany

HORNSTEIN, MARK, financial executive; b. N.Y.C., Dec. 7, 1947; s. Joseph and Anne (Fox) H.; BBA, Pace U., 1969; postgrad. N.Y.U., 1973. Staff acct. Peat, Marwick, Mitchell & Co., N.Y.C., 1969-70; sr. acct. Robert J. Cofini & Co., N.Y.C., 1972-74; asst. v.p. United Va. Factors Corp., N.Y.C., 1974-77; asst. v.p., adminstrv. head mortgage loan div. James Talcott, Inc., N.Y.C., 1977-78; loan adminstrn. officer Aetna Bus. Credit, Inc., East Hartford, Conn., 1978-79; asst. v.p. A.J. Armstrong Co. Inc. (now Bankamerica Bus. Credit, Inc.), N.Y.C., 1979-83; v.p. Leucadia Nat. Corp., N.Y.C., 1983—; treas. Am. Investment Co., St. Louis, 1984—; asst. v.p. Cardiff Equities Corp. (merger Leucadia Nat. Corp.), La Jolla, 1984-86; v.p. Charter Nat. Life Ins. Co., St. Louis, 1985-93, PHLCORP, Inc. (formerly Baldwin United Corp.), Phila., 1987—; sec. Bolivian Power Co., Ltd., LaPaz, Bolivia, 1988-94; v.p. Transp. Capital Corp., N.Y.C., 1992-94, chmn., pres., 1994-96. Served with USNR, 1970-72. Home: 25 Sutton Pl S New York NY 10022-2441 Office: 315 Park Ave S New York NY 10010-3607

HORNUNG, VOLKER, chemist, management consultant; b. Stuttgart, Germany, Oct. 15, 1940; s. Alois and Luise (Riffel) H.; m. Beate Klau; children: Dagmar Daniela, Raoul Robin. Diploma in Chemistry, Tech. H.S., Stuttgart, Germany, 1966; PhD, U. Basel (Switzerland), 1970. Product line mgr. Varian, Zug, Switzerland, 1971-75; sales mgr. Fisher Scientific, Zürich, Switzerland, 1975-78; dept. head Dr. C. Otto, Bochum, Germany, 1978-82; subsidiary co. mgr. Greiner Electronics, Langenthal, Switzerland, 1982-84; mgmt. cons. Dortmund, Germany, 1984—; group leader devel. photoelectron spectrometry, 1967-71; devel. engr. analytical instrument for cement industry, 1985-87. Contbr. over 30 articles to profl. jours. Mem. N.Y. Acad. Scis. Avocations: teaching, skiing, sailing. Home: Jasminstr 21, 44289 Dortmund Germany Office: Dr Hornung Mgmt Consulting, PO Box 420133, 44275 Dortmund Germany

HORNYCH, ANTONIN FRANÇOIS, physician, researcher; b. Prague, Czechoslovakia, Sept. 8, 1930; arrived in France, 1970.; s. Antonin and Anna (Faltusova) H.; m. Helena Jarosova, July 1959 (dec. March 1983); 1 child, Pierre; m. Yvetta Zlatovsky, April 4, 1986. MD, Charles U. Med. Sch., Prague, 1956, Marie Curie Med. Sch., Paris, 1974. cert. internal med. 1st, 2nd degrees; cardiology, nephrology Inst. for postgrad. Edn., Czechoslovakia. Intern in internal medicine Prague, 1955-56; intern dept. internal medicine Most Regional Hosp., Czechoslovakia, 1956-57; resident Inst. for Cardiovascular Research, Prague, 1958-59, staff mem. cardiology dept., 1958-65; staff mem., lectr., 1969-70; assoc. dir. hemodial and transplant programs Inst. for Cardiovascular Research, 1965-67; rsch. fellow U. Paris Coll. of Med., 1967-68; asst. prof. exptl. med. dept. U. Paris Med. Sch., 1970-74; staff mem., researcher Inst. Nat. Santé Recherche Med., Paris, 1970—; visiting prof. Munich Med. Sch. TUM, 1986, dir. hypertension lab. U-28 INSERM, Paris, 1980-94. Contbr. over 100 articles to numerous profl. jours. Mem. Internat. Acad. Human Rights, Paris, 1986-87. Served with the French Med. Reserves. Mem. Order of Med., Internat. Soc. of Nephrology, French Soc. of Nephrology, Internat. Soc. of Hypertension, French Soc. of Cardiology, Hypertension Br., Czechoslovakian Soc. Arts and Scis., Czechoslovakian Sportive Orgn. Roman Catholic. Avocations: opera, tennis, windsurfing, skiing, horseback riding. Office: Hosp Broussais European Hosp George, Pompidou 20 Rue Leblanc, 75908 Paris Cedex 15, France

HOROI, REX STEPHEN, ambassador. Permanent rep. of Solomon Islands UN, N.Y.C. Office: Perm Mission of Solomon Isl 800 2nd Ave Ste 400L New York NY 10017-4709*

HOROSZEWICZ, JULIUSZ STANISLAW, oncologist, cancer researcher, laboratory administrator; b. Warsaw, Poland, Jan. 4, 1931; came to U.S., 1961; s. Tytus Michal and Stefania (Domanska) H.; children: Nike Joanna, Peter Juliusz. D of Medicine summa cum laude, Acad. of Medicine, Lodz, Poland, 1954, DMSc, 1960. Teaching asst. dept. bacteriology Acad. of Medicine, Lodz, 1950-55, asst. prof., 1955-59, assoc. prof., 1959-61; cancer rsch. scientist Roswell Park Meml. Inst., Buffalo, 1962-64, sr. cancer rsch. scientist, 1964-67, assoc. cancer rsch. scientist, 1967-76, prin. cancer rsch. scientist, 1976-86; assoc. chief oncological urology rsch. N.Y. State Dept. Health, Roswell Park Meml. Inst. Div., Buffalo, 1986-88; dir. exptl. cancer ctr. Millard Fillmore Hosp., Buffalo, 1988-98; dir. UICC-Internat. Union against Cancer, 1988-98; dir. electron microscopy lab. viral oncology, 1963-66, dir. human fibroblast interferon program Roswell Park Meml. Inst., 1976-82; chmn. Pleuro-Pneumonia Like Organisms subcom. human cancer virus task force Nat. Cancer Inst., Bethesda, Md., 1963-64, mem. Nat. Prostatic Cancer Project working cadre, 1972-74; assoc. rsch. prof. microbiology SUNY, Buffalo, 1966-96; rsch. prof. biology Canisius Coll., Buffalo, 1968-96, Niagara U., Niagara Falls, N.Y., 1968-96; sci. cons. Cytogen Corp., Princeton, N.J., 1990-92, Pacific NW Rsch. Found., Seattle, 1993-97. Mem. editl. bd. The Prostate, 1994—; contbr. more than 100 articles to profl. jours.; patentee on specific monoclonal antibody for diagnosis and treatment of human prostate cancer. Rockefeller Found. fellow, 1961-62; Rsch. grantee Nat. Cancer Inst., 1979-82, Phi Beta Psi, 1987-96; named Citizen of Yr. Am.-Polish Eagle, Buffalo, 1967. Mem. AAAS, Am. Assn. Cancer Rsch., Am. Soc. Microbiology, Polish Soc. for Bacteriology, Am. Cancer Soc., Am. Assn. for Clin. Rsch., N.Y. Acad. Scis., Lodz Sci. Soc. Roman Catholic. Achievements include 4 patents on specific monoclonal antibody for diagnosis and treatment of human prostate cancer. Avocations: fishing, bridge, classical music, chess. Home: PO Box 92, 60 Arrow Dr, Barry's Bay, ON Canada K0J 1B0

HOROWITZ, BEN, health facility administrator; b. Bklyn., Mar. 19, 1914; s. Saul and Sonia (Meringoff) H.; m. Beverly Lichtman, Feb. 14, 1952; children: Zachary, Jody. BA, Bklyn. Coll., 1940; LLB, St. Lawrence U., 1940; postgrad., New Sch. Social Rsch., 1942. Bar: N.Y. 1941. Dir. N.Y. Fedn. Jewish Philanthropies, 1940-45; assoc., ea. regional dir. City of Hope, 1945-50, nat. exec. sec., 1950-53, exec. dir., 1953-85, gen. v.p., bd. dirs., 1985—, bd. dirs. nat. med. ctr., 1980—; bd. dirs. Beckman Rsch. Inst., 1980—. Mem. Gov.'s Task Force on Flood Relief, 1969-74; bd. dirs., v.p. Hope for Hearing Found., UCLA, 1972-96; bd. dirs. Forte Found., 1987-92, Ch. Temple Housing Corp., 1988-93, Leo Baeck Temple, 1964-67, 86-89, Westwood Property Owners Assn., 1991—. Recipient Spirit of Life award, 1970, Gallery of Achievement award, 1974, Profl. of Yr. award So. Calif. chpt. Nat. Sco. Fundraisers, 1977; Ben Horowitz chair in rsch. established at City of Hope, 1981; city street named in his honor, 1986. Jewish. Formulated the role of City of Hope as pilot center in medicine, science and humanitarianism, 1959. Home: 221 Conway Ave Los Angeles CA 90024-2601 Office: City of Hope 11645 Wilshire Blvd Los Angeles CA 90025-1708

HOROWITZ, IRA R., gynecologic oncologist; b. Bklyn., Dec. 17, 1954; s. Benjamin and Frieda Horowitz; m. Julie A. Wood; children: Andrea, Rebecah. BA in Biology, U. Rochester, 1976; MD, Baylor U., 1980. Diplomate Am. Bd. Ob/Gyn. Resident to chief resident Baylor Coll. Medicine, Houston, 1980-84; gynecologic oncology fellow Johns Hopkins Med. Inst., Balt., 1985-87; clin. instr. ob-gyn. Baylor Coll. Medicine, 1984-85; instr. ob-gyn. Johns Hopkins U. Sch. Med., 1985-87, asst. prof. ob-gyn., oncology, 1987-92; prof. ob-gyn. Emory U. Sch. Medicine, Atlanta, 1992-99, Emory U. Sch. Med., Atlanta, 1999—; assoc. prof. ob-gyn. Emory U. Sch. Medicine, Winship Cancer Ctr., Atlanta, 1993-99; asst. prof. Emory U. Sch. Medicine, Atlanta, 1995-99—; mem. Winship Cancer Inst., 1999—. Co-editor: Plantao em ginecologia e obstetricia, 1995, Obstetrics & Gynecology On Call, 1st edit., 1993, Advances in Obstetrics and Gynecology, vol. 3, 1996, Advances in Obstetrics & Gynecology, vol. 4, 1997. Fellow ACOG, ACS, Internat. Soc. Study Vulvovaginal Disease; mem. Soc. Gynecologic Oncologists, Soc. Gynecologic Surgeons, Soc. Surg. Oncology. Avocations: camping, travel. Office: Emory U Sch Medicine GYN/OB 1639 Pierce Dr Atlanta GA 30322-0001

HOROWITZ, JOSEPH, marketing professional; b. Haifa, Israel, Feb. 12, 1954; s. Mayer and Hana Ester (Kestenberg) H.; m. Rivka Statman, Apr. 2, 1955; children: Einav, Dolev. BA, Tel Aviv U., Israel, 1986; MA, Tel Aviv U., 1988, MBA in Mktg., 1991; MA, Haifa U., 1988. Commd. Israeli Def. Force/Israeli Air Force, 1973, advanced through grades to col.; 1992; ret., 1995; pres. Lahav, Tel Aviv, 1995-97, Ashrot, Tel Aviv, 1997-99; mktg. dir. Rafael, Haifa, 1999—. Avocations: photography, computers. Home: 10 Khilat Budapest, 64701 Tel Aviv Israel

HOROWITZ, KENNETH P., lawyer; b. N.Y.C.; s. Philip and Roslyn Horowitz. BA, SUNY, Brockport, 1977; MA in Internat. Rels., Georgetown U., 1984; JD, Bklyn. Law Sch., 1987. pres. 130 Hicks St. Owners Corp., Bklyn., 1987—. Mem. firm Goldberg Weprin & Ustin LLP, N.Y.C. Mem. ABA, Assn. Bar of City of N.Y. E-mail: kphorowitz@gwulaw.com. Home: 123 Pierrepont St Brooklyn NY 11201-2759 Office: Goldberg Weprin & Ustin LLP 1501 Broadway Fl 22 New York NY 10036-5686

HORRIDGE, GEORGE ADRIAN (ADRIAN HORRIDGE), biologist, author, researcher; b. 1927; m. Audrey Lightburne, June 26, 1954; children: Mark, Alison, Naomi, Rebecca. Student, St. John's Coll., Cambridge, Eng., 1946; First Class Honours in Natural Scis., Tripos, Cambridge, Eng., 1950. From scientific officer to sr. scientific officer dept. of structures Royal Aircraft Establishment, Farnborough, Eng., 1953-54; rsch. fellow St. John's Coll., Cambridge, Eng., 1954-56; from lectr. to reader in zoology St. Andrews U., Eng., 1956-69; dir. marine lab. St. Andrews U., 1960-69; prof. behavioral biology Australian Nat. U., Canberra, 1969, exec. dir. Ctr. Visual Scis., 1987-90; university fellow Australian Nat. U., 1994-97, rschr. emeritus, 1997—; examiner in biology U. Sains and U. Malaya, Sains and Kuala Lumpur, Malaysia, 1972-76, 80-84; chief scientist U.S. Rsch. Ship Alpha Helix Moluccas and Banda, 1975; vis. assoc. prof. UCLA, 1959-60; fellow Ctr. for Advanced Study in the Behavioral Scis., Stanford, Calif., 1959-60; vis. prof. Yale U., New Haven, Conn., 1965, U. St. Andrews, Scotland, 1992; vis. fellow Churchill Coll., Cambridge, Eng., 1993-94; mem. German amb. com. for exchange fellowships with Australia, 1975-80, min. of sci.'s com. for Queen's fellowships in marine scis., 1977-80; lectr. in field. Author: (with T. H. Bullock) The Structure and Function of the Nervous Systems of Invertebrates, 2 vols., 1965, Interneurons, 1968, The Compound Eye of Insects, 1975, The Prahum Traditional Sailing Boat of Indonesia, 1981, 2nd edit., 1986, Sailing Craft of Indonesia, 1986, Outrigger Canoes of Bali and Madura, Indonesia, 1987, Natural and low-level seeing systems, 1993; contbr. 220 articles to profl. jours. Fellow Royal Soc. London, Australian Acad. Scis. (mem. industry forum 1990, chmn. sect. 7 com. 1991-93), Royal Soc. Eng.; Cambridge Philosophical Soc., Physiol. Soc., Soc. Exptl. Biology, Soc. Nautical Rsch. Avocations: biological sciences in S.E. Asia, languages, photography, drawing. Fax: (61)-(2)-6249-3808. E-mail: horridge@rsbs.anu.edu.au. Home: 76 Mueller St, Yarralumla ACT 2600, Australia Address: Australian Nat U Rsch Sch Biol Scis, PO Box 475, Canberra ACT 2601, Australia

HORSKY, JAN JOSEF, theoretical physics educator, scientist; b. Špinov/Nížkov, Czechoslovakia, Apr. 13, 1940; s. Josef and Františka Ann (Hrůzová) H.; m. Marie Eleonora Štusová, Aug. 10, 1963; children: Jiří, Pavel. CSc, Charles U., 1970, DSc, 1980. Asst. theoretical physics U. Brno, Czech, 1962-73, docent of theoretical physics, 1973-81, prof. theoretical physics, 1981—; mem. com. for dr. degree in theoretical physics Masaryk U., Brno, 1992; mem. com. for CSc degree in theoretical physics Charles U., 1975; mem. conf. com. Czech U., 1988. Author: Introduction to the Theory of Relativity in Czech, 1975, A. Einstein in Czech, 1998; author/co-author: Space, Time, Gravitation in English, 1987, Relativistic Universe in Czech, 1997, Theoretical Mechanics in Czech, 1998, Albert Einstein in Czech, 1998; mem. editl. bd. Masaryk U. of Jour. Univs., 1995; contbr. sci. articles to profl. jours. Fireman Village of Spinov, 1973. Mem. Am. Physical Soc. (mem. topical group on gravitation), N.Y. Acad. Scis., Internat. Astron. Union, Internat. Soc. for Gen. Relativity and Gravitation, European Astron. Soc., Sisyfos Club. Avocations: popularization of modern physics, philosophy, photography, life of people in our countryside. Home: Psenik 13, 639 00 Brno Czech Republic Office: Masaryk Univ Faculty Scis, Dept Theoretical Physics Kotlarska 2, 61137 Brno Czech Republic

HORSLEY, JACK EVERETT, lawyer, writer; b. Sioux City, Iowa, Dec. 12, 1915; s. Charles E. and Edith V. (Timms) H.; m. Sallie Kelley, June 12, 1939 (dec.); children: Pamela, Charles Edward; m. Bertha J. Newland, Feb. 24, 1950 (dec.); m. Mary Jane Moran, Jan. 20, 1973; 1 child, Sharon. AB, U. Ill., 1937, JD, 1939. Bar: Ill. 1939. temporary prof. law NYU, N.Y.C., 1974; mem. Harlan Moore Heart Rsch. Found., 1968—, asst. treas., 1996—; mem. lawyers adv. coun. U. Ill. Law Forum, 1960-63; lectr. Practicing Law Inst., N.Y.C., 1967-73, U. Ill., Champaign, 1974, Ct. Practice Inst., Chgo., 1974—, Coll. Law Inst. Continuing Legal Edn. U. Mich., 1967, Bankers' Seminar, 1992; vis. lectr. Orange County (Fla.) Med. Soc., 1985, San Diego Med. Soc., 1970, U. S.C., 1976, Duquesne Coll., 1970, U. Ill. Law Forum, 1972, alumni adv. com., 1991—; vis lectr. trial practice NYU Coll. Law, 1972; faculty banker seminar Wis. Med. Assn., Lake Geneva, 1997; lectr. med./legal seminars on tour Chgo., Cleve., Pa., Orlando, 1995; chmn. rev. bd. Ill. Supreme Ct. Disciplinary Comm., 1973-76, adv. cons., 1976—; lectr. Cleve. Hosp., Shelby, N.C., 1976; adv. dir. First Nat. Bank of Mattoon, 2000—; vis. prof. trial practice Fordham Law Sch., N.Y.C., 1969; vis. prof. U. Berkeley Coll. Law, 1999; legal advisor 1st Nat. Bank Mattoon, 1999—; vis. lectr. John Marshall Sch. Law, Chgo., 1999-2000. Narrator Poetry Interludes, Sta. WLBH-FM, 1977-91; author: Trial Lawyer's Manual, 1967, Voir Dire Examinations and Opening Statements, 1968, Current Development in Products Liability Law, 1969, Illinois Civil Practice and Procedure, 1970, The Medical Expert Witness, 1973, Testifying in Court, 1973, 5th edit., 1992, supplement 4th edit., 1993, The Doctor and the Law, 1975, The Doctor and Family Law, 1975, The Doctor and Business Law, 1976, The Doctor and Medical Law, 1977, Anatomy of a Medical Malpractice Case, 1984, 3d edit., 1993, History of Craig & Craig, Attorneys, 1968-89, 1990, supplement, 1993, 2d edit., 1994, Trilogy: The Frivolous Law Suit, 2000, Municipals: G.O. of Revenue, 1992, World War II, D-Day, 1st edit., 1994, 2d edit., 1998, World War II Air Mus., Duxford, Eng., 1999, Trial Techniques, 1995, Legal Liability Exposure of Trust Co., 1996, 2d edit., 1999, On Trust Dept. Guide-lines and Risks, 1996, On Federal Evidence and Examination, 1995, 96, 97, Memories of World War II In the European Theater, 1997, 2d edit., 1999, History of the Bar in East Central Illinois, 1997, Remembrances: An Autobiography, 1998, 2d edit., 2000, Views of Christianity: Origin of Man, 1999, (pamphlet) A Doctor's Duty: Prescription Care, 1999; co-author: RN Legally Speaking, 1998, Matthew Bender Forensic Sciences, 1988, 2d edit., 2000; editor Med. Econs., 1969—, Fifty Eight Years as Attorney, 1997, 2nd edit., 1998, update edit., 2000; legal cons. Mast-Head, 1972; contbr. A.L.L. Life, Stafford, Va., 1988—, Eagle Forum (On Pro-Life, Alton, Ill., 1999), Fed. Evidence Rules, 1996, Cross-Exam. Techniques and Potential Traps, 1996, Forensic Scis. on Texts and Treatises, 1981, 2d edit. 1999, Christianity: The Origin of Man Creationism vs. Darwinism, 1999, supplement, 1999; cons., reviewer Civil Practice State and Fed. Cts., 1998-99; contbr., cons. editor Eagle Forum; contbr. U. Ill. Law Review, 2000; contbr. articles to profl. jours. Alt. del. to Rep. Platform Com., 2000; active Senatorial Reelection Com., 1993; mem. exec. com. Ill. Rep. Election Campaign, 1997; founding mem. U.S. Air Mus., Am. Air Mus., U.S. Supreme Ct. Hist. Soc.; pres. bd. edn. sch. dist. 100, 1946-48; bd. dirs. Harlan Moore Heart Rsch. Found., 1968-91, hon. dir., 1991—; vol. reader in rec. texts Am. Assn. for Blind, 1970-72; chmn. exec. com. U. Ill. Law Forum, 1990-91; founding mem. Home for Law Alumni Found., Chgo., 1999; pres. Res. Officers Assn. East Cen. Ill., 1988-89, 99-2000, chair, bd. dirs., 2000—; founder Bertha Newland Horsley award St. John's Coll. Nursing, Springfield, Mary Jane Horsley award trophy Mattoon (Ill.) H.S.; mem. exec. com. Ill. Rep. Election Campaign, 1997. Lt. col. U.S. Army, 1942-46, ETO, USA JAGD (hon., ret., promoted hon. full col., 1997). Recipient Disting. Svc. award U. Ill., 1995. Fellow Am. Coll. Trial Lawyers (co-chair membership commn. 1998); mem. ABA, Ill. Bar Assn. (exec. coun. ins. law 1961-63, com. chmn. banking law 1972, lectr. law course for attys. 1962, 64-65, sr. counsellor 1989—, Disting. Svc. award 1982-83), Assn. of Bar of City of N.Y. (non-resident), Coles-Cumberland Bar Assn. (v.p. 1968-2000, pres. 1969-70, chmn. com. jud. inquiry 1976-80, chair meml. com. 1989-2000, mem. exec. com. 1998, sr. counsellor 1989, co-author Forensic Scis. Jour. 1991, 2d edit. 1999), Am. Arbitration Assn. (nat. panel arbitrators, counsel advisor hearing officers in Ill. 1996-97), U. Ill. Law Alumni Assn. (life mem., pres. 1966-67, Alumni of Month Sept. 1974, exec. com. 1990-91), Ill. Appellate Lawyers Assn., Soc. Legal Scribes (chair emeritus 1995—), Ill. Def. Counsel Assn. (pres. 1967-88), Soc. Trial Lawyers (chmn. profl. activities 1960-61, bd. dirs. 1966-67), Fed. Ct. Hist. Soc. (co-chmn.), Adelphic Debating Soc., Assn. Ins. Attys., Internat. Assn. Ins. Counsel, Am. Judicature Soc., Res. Officers Assn. (pres. 1997-98, chair exec. com., pres. emeritus 1999), U. Ill. Alumni Assn. (exec. com. 1990-91), Soc. Legal Scribes, Masons (lectr. ceremonial 32 degree Scottish Rite 2000, Sr. Master award 1992), Delta Phi (exec. com. alumni assn. 1960-61, 67-68), Sigma Delta Kappa. Lutheran. Home: 913 N 31st St Mattoon IL 61938-2271

HORST, SAMUEL LEVI, history educator, researcher, writer; b. Lancaster, Pa., July 18, 1919; s. Elmer Kuhns and Katie (Buckwalter) H.; m. Sarah Elizabeth Good, July 19, 1948 (dec. Aug. 1991); children: Kenneth, Hannah, Sylvia, Barbara, Mary, Carol; m. Mary Ellen Stutzman, Mar. 18, 1995. BA in Social Scis., Goshen Coll., 1949; MA in History, Am. U., 1962; PhD in History, U. Va., 1977. H.s. tchr. Eastern Mennonite H.S., Harrisonburg, Va., 1949-50, 50-51, 54-55, 60-61; tchr. Eastern Mennonite Coll., Harrisonburg, Va., 1962-84, prof. emeritus history, 1984-99. Author: Mennonites in the Confederacy, 1967, Education for Manhood, 1987; editor: The Fire of Liberty in their Hearts, 1996; co-editor: Conscience in Crisis, 1979. Mem. Harrisonburg/Rockingham Bicentennial Commn., Harrisonburg/Rockingham Coun. on Human Rels. Grantee NEH, 1979; fellow Johns Hopkins U., 1969, Inst. for Editing of History, Nat. Hist. Publs., 1981. Mem. Va. Hist. Soc., So. Hist. Assn., Peace History Soc., Harrisonburg/Rockingham Hist. Soc., Mennonite Hist. Soc., Shenandoah Valley Mennonite Historians. Home: 857 Old Furnace Rd Harrisonburg VA 22802-6004 Office: Eastern Mennonite U Harrisonburg VA 22802

HORTA, JOSÉ CARLOS DE OLIVEIRA SOUSA, civil engineering consultant; b. Homoine, Mozambique, Dec. 16, 1935; s. José Maria de Sousa Horta and Maria do Carmo de Oliveira; children: Viriato, Soahanta Vololona, Maria Carmen, José Daniel. Candidate in Civil Engring., U. Liege, Belgium, 1957; DSc in Earth Scis., U. Algiers, Algeria, 1972, cert. in applied geophysics, 1973. Polit. adviser Movimento Popular de Libertação de Angola, 1959-61; geotech. and hwy. engr. Ministry Pub. Works, Algiers, 1966-73; acting dir. Civil Engring. Lab., SONATRACH, Beni Mered, Algeria, 1978-80; sr. hwy. and geotech. engr. Louis Berger Internat. Inc., Paris and East Orange, N.J., 1980-91; project mgr., regional rep. DMJM Internat., Washington, 1991-92; civil engring. cons., Lisbon, 1992—; participant internat. confs. on soils, constrn. materials, road design, constrn. and maintenance, including 5th Internat. Conf. on Low-Volume Roads, Raleigh, N.C., 1991, 2d Internat. Conf. on Roads and Road Transport Problems, New Delhi, 1995. Contbr. articles to profl. jours. and confs., including Engring. Geology, Geotechnique. Mem. ASTM, Indian Roads Congress (life). Avocations: gymnastics, swimming, dancing, music, reading. Fax: 351-21-4103515. E-mail: soushort.joyc@mail.telepac.pt. Home: Apt 3F, Av Bombeiros Voluntarios 42, 1495-020 Algés Lisboa, Portugal

HORTA, MARCIO LEAL, anesthesiologist; b. Belo Horizonte, Brazil, Dec. 3, 1938; s. Pedro Jardim and Carmelita (Souza) H. Grad. in medicine, Fed. U. Minas Gerais, Brazil, 1962. Asst. prof. Fed. U. Minas Gerais, Brazil, 1963-67; prof. Cath. U. Pelotas, Brazil, 1968—; dir. Ctr. Biol. & Health Scis. Catholic U. Pelotas, Brazil, 1976-79; clin. dir. U. Hosp., Pelotas, 1997-99. Mem. Am. Soc. Regional Anesthesia, Latino-Am. Soc. Regional Anesthesia, Brazilian Soc. Anesthesiology (superior qualification), Rotary. Roman Catholic. Avocation: popular music. E-mail: marciolhorta@uol.com.br.

HORTALEZA, ROLANDO BONIFACIO, manufacturing company executive; b. Santa Mesa, Manila, The Philippines, May 2, 1959; s. Cresencio Hernandez and Cecilia (Bonifacio) H.; m. Rosalinda Ang; children: Allue Krisanne, Alfonso Inigo, Alexone Rolando Jr., Allenjan Rosanne. BS in Pre-Medicine, U. of the East, The Philippines, 1979; MD, Fatima Med. Sch., The Philippines, 1985. Cert. MD Philippine Regulations Commn. Chmn., CEO Splash Mfg. Corp., 1985—, Splash Properties, Inc., 1995-99, Splash Rsch. Inst., 1997—, Splash Holdings, Inc., 1998—; vice-chmn. HBC, Inc., The Philippines, 1993—, Splash Found., Inc., The Philippines, 1997—, World Ptnrs. Fin. Corp., The Philippines, 1998—. Active Couples for Christ Quezon City Chpt. Recipient Agora award for outstanding achievement in entrepreneurship Philippine Mktg. Assn., 1997. Mem. Makati Bus. Club, Philippine C. of C. Avocations: tennis, golf, weight training, basketball. Office: Splash Holdings Inc, 548 Mindanao Ave, Quezon City 1116, The Philippines

HORTON, DAVID ROBERT, writer, consultant; b. Perth, W.A., Australia, Apr. 4, 1945; m. Vicki Elizabeth Horton; children: Vanessa Joan, Tanya Elizabeth. BSc with honors, U. Western Australia, Perth, 1966; MSc, U. New Eng., Armidale, Australia, 1969, BA, 1973, PhD, 1976, DLitt, 1997. Tchg. fellow U. Melbourne, Australia, 1966, U. New Eng., Armidale, Australia, 1967-73; postdoctoral fellow U. York, Eng., 1973-74; palaeoecologist Australian Inst. Aboriginal and Torres Strait Studies, Canberra, Australia, 1974-84, acting dep. prin., 1984-85; dir. publishing Aboriginal Studies Press, 1985-98; mem. Australian Inst. Aboriginal and Torres Strait Studies, 1978-98; mem. edit. bd. Aboriginal History, 1984-87; mem. adv. bd. Australian Culture, Canberra, 1994-97; mem. adv. panel NSW Premier history awards, Sydney, Australia, 1997. Major works include Recovering the Tracks, 1991, Encyclopaedia of Aboriginal Australia, 1994 (NSW Premier Lit. Awards Book of Yr. 1995), Aboriginal Australia map, 1996, The Pure State of Nature, 1999. Avocations: writing, editing, stud sheep farming.

HORTON, GRAHAM ARTHUR, computer scientist; b. Hitchin, Eng., July 16, 1962; s. Arthur Frederick and Margaret Hilda (Brown) H.; m. Gabriele Erika Übelacker, July 10, 1993. MS, Erlangen (Germany) U., 1989, DEng, 1991, Habilitation, 1998. Asst. prof. computer sci. Erlangen U., 1991—, U. Denver, 1996. Contbr. chpt. to: High Performance Computing, 1994, Parallel Scientific Computing, 1994; contbr. articles to sci. publs. Undergrad. scholar German Acad. Exch. Svc., 1983; recipient Wolfgang Finkelnburg prize, 1998. Office: Erlangen Univ, Cauerstrasse 6, 91058 Erlangen Germany

HORTON, JEANETTE, municipal government official; b. Paterson, N.J., Dec. 1, 1938; d. David and Mary (Carpenter) Potash; m. Troy Horton, Oct. 31, 1958 (dec. May 1990); m. Christos Prousalis, June 29, 1991. Student, Broward C. C., 1970-72, Barry U., 1982, Fla. Atlantic U., 1983-84, Fla. State U., 1985. Cert. mcpl. clk., Fla. Bookkeeper Fla. Housewares, Miami, Fla., 1961-65; asst. to comptroller Gulf Stream Press, Miami, 1965-70; comptroller Chrysler Plymouth, Miami, Fla., 1970-75; mcpl. clk., fin. dir. Village of Biscayne Park, Fla., 1975-91, Bal Harbour (Fla.) Village, 1991—. Commr. Cooper City, Fla., 1971-73. Mem. Fla. Assn. City Clks. (scholarship 1985-87, scholarship chmn. 1988-89), Am. Bus. Woman of Yr. award 1985, pres., v.p. 1985-87), Dade/Broward City Clks. and Fin. Dirs. (pres. 1992-93), Fla. City and County Mgrs. Assn., Bus. and Profl. Women (pres. 1981), Internat. Mcpl. Clks. Assn., Pers. Mgmt. Assn., Acad. for Advanced Edn. of Mcpl. Clk. Cert. Lic. Ofcl. Democrat. Roman Catholic. Avocation: reading. Home: 4219 Pierce St Hollywood FL 33021-5946 Office: Village of Bal Harbour 655 96th St Bal Harbour FL 33154-2428

HORTON, JOSEPH JULIAN, JR., academic dean, educator; b. Memphis, Tenn., Nov. 7, 1936; s. Joseph Julian and Nina (Williams) H.; m. Linda Anne Langley, May 30, 1964; children: Joseph Julian, Anne Adele, David Douglas. AA, Lon Morris Jr. Coll., 1955; BA, N.Mex. State U., 1958; MA, So. Meth. U., 1965, PhD, 1968; postgrad., Harvard U., 1970-71. Claims examiner Social Security Adminstrn., Kansas City, Mo., 1958-60; claims authorizer Social Security Adminstrn., Kansas City, 1960-61; with FDIC, Washington, 1967-71; fin. economist FDIC, 1967-69, coord. merger analysis, 1969-71; prof., chmn. dept. econs. and bus. Slippery Rock (Pa.) State Coll., 1971-81; vis. fin. economist Fed. Home Loan Bank Bd., Washington, 1978-79; prof., chmn. commerce divsn. Bellarmine (Ky.) Coll., 1981-82, dean W. Fielding Rubel Sch. Bus., 1982-86; dean Sch. Mgmt. U. Scranton, Pa., 1986-96; dean Coll. Bus. Adminstrn. U. Ctrl. Ark., Conway, 1996—; asst. prof. George Washington U., Washington, 1968-69, U. Md., College Park, 1969-70; pres. Pa. Conf. Economists, Internat. Acad. Bus. Disciplines, Congress of Polit. Economists, U.S.A. Bd. editors Ea. Econ. Jour.; contbr. articles to profl. jours. Recipient Cokesbury award So. Meth. U., 1965; NSF Grad. fellow, 1964-66, Ford Found. Dissertation fellow, 1966-67, Harvard U. Rsch. fellow, 1970-71, Bank Adminstrn. Inst. Clarence Lichtfeldt fellow, 1981, Burk fellow. Mem. Am. Econ. Assn., Am. Fin. Assn., Internat. Acad. Bus. Disciplines (pres.), N.Am. Econs. and Fin. Assn. (bd. dirs., v.p., pres.), Ea. Econ. Assn. (v.p.). Office: U Cen Ark Office of Dean Coll Bus Adminstrn Conway AR 72035-0001

HORTON, KENNETH, investor; b. Newport, Nebr., May 11, 1921; s. Fred and Clara E. (Cottrel) H.; m. Evelyn H. Shafer, Dec. 29, 1939 (div. 1961); children: Kenneth Eugene, Helen Clara Catherine; m. Arlene J. Mitchell, July 23, 1962. AA, Valley Coll., San Bernardino, Calif., 1951; grad., Law Enforcement Officers Tng. Sch., San Bernardino, Calif., 1957. Crew leader 1st suppression fire crew Civilian Conservation Corp, Glendora, Calif., 1937-39; journeyman R.R. Car Shop/Santa Fe R.R., San Bernardino, 1940-44; boy's counselor San Bernardino County Juvenile Hall, 1948-53; supr. state champion drill team Calif. Youth Authority, Whittier, 1954; layout carpenter Bectal Constrn. Co., Oro grande, Calif., 1954-55; patrolman, vice officer Police Dept., San Bernardino, 1956-66; ind. investor Thousand Oaks, Calif., 1950—. Sustaining mem. Rep. Nat. Com., Washington, 1978—. With U.S. Army, 1944-45. Decorated Combat Infantryman medal, Bronze Star medal; recipient Letter of Appreciation for apprehending holdup man Security Pacific Bank, 1974. Lutheran. Avocations: maker of fine furniture, 1st edition book collection, antique automobiles. Address: PO Box 1432 Thousand Oaks CA 91358-0432

HORTON, MICHAEL L., mortgage company executive, publishing executive; b. Pasadena, Calif., Oct. 19, 1961; s. Jerry S. and Mary L. Horton. BA in Bus. Econs., Claremont McKenna Coll., 1983. Lic. real estate broker. Gen. mgr. I.W.S., Pasadena, 1976-80; proprietor NBB Svcs. Orgn., Upland, Calif., 1980-85; regional mgr. Sycamore Fin. Group Inc., Rancho Cucamonga, Calif., 1984-87; CEO, pres. Boulder Fin. Corp., Rancho Cucamonga, 19875, M.C.M. Pub. Corp., Rancho Cucamonga, 19925; pres., CEO Sandstone Realty Group, Inc., 19955; chm. C.H.A.M.P. Inc., 1996—. Author: A Real Estate Professional's Guide to Mortgage Finance, 1985; author Mortgage Fin. Newsletter, 19845; author fin. workshop. Mem. Rep. State Ctrl. Com., Calif., 1980—, Bldg. and Industry Assn., Rancho Cucamonga, 1988—, Res Publica Soc., Claremont, Calif., 1986—; donor mem. L.A. World Affairs Coun., 1988—. Claremont McKenna Coll. scholar, 1981-83; recipient Dons D. Lepper Meml. award Exec. Women Internat., 1981, So. Calif. Edison Bus. Competition award, 1979, 81. Mem. Nat. Assn. Realtors, Inland Empire West Bd. Realtors. Avocations: basketball, racquet sports, water sports. Office: Boulder Fin Corp 494 N Mountain Ave Upland CA 91786-9302

HORTON, PATRICIA MATHEWS, musician, violist and violinist; b. Bklyn., Mar. 6, 1932; d. Edward Joseph and Margaret (Briggs) Mathews; m. Ernest H. Horton Jr., Mar. 6, 1982; 1 stepchild, Carol Horton Tremblay. Student in viola, William Primrose Master Class, 1980; student, Glendale (Calif.) C.C., 1981-90, 93, 99, 2000, Art Ctr. Coll. Design, Pasadena, Calif., 1988-93; student in painting composition, Peter Liashkov, L.A., 1993-97. Profl. musician on violin and viola, 1951-86; musician on tour U.S., Can., Cuba, 1952-57. Played with New Orleans Philharm., 1959-61, U.S. Tour of San Francisco Ballet, 1965, L.A. Civic Light Opera, 1974-80; played L.A. engagements of Bolshoi Ballet Co., 1975, Am. Ballet Theatre, 1974-80, N.Y.C. Opera, 1974-80, Royal Ballet of London, 1978, Alicia Alonzo's Cuban Ballet, 1979, Harlem Ballet, 1984, Deutsche Oper Berlin, 1985; played on motion picture and TV soundtrack recs., through 1986; one-woman shows include Claremont (Calif.) Sch. Theology, 1997, Pasadena First United Meth. Ch., 1997, 99, La Canada Flintridge Libr., 1999. Active Dem. Nat. Com., Women's Caucus for Art. Mem. Am. Fedn. Musicians (life). Avocations: hiking local mountains, desert and beaches, studying classical guitar.

HORTON, PAUL CHESTER, psychiatrist; b. Cin., Jan. 29, 1942; s. Paul Chester Sr. and Elizabeth Pauline (Rice) H.; m. JoAnn Alice Baker, Aug. 30; children: Paul Andrey, Alexander Robert. BA, U. Minn., 1964; MD, & 1968. Diplomate Am. Bd. Psychiatry and Neurology. Rotating intern U. Cin., 1969; resident in psychiatry Yale U., New Haven, 1972; staff psychiatrist Guidance Clinic of Camden County, West Collingswood, N.J., 1972-74, Milford (Conn.) Family and Child Guidance Clinic, 1974-77; mem. faculty Sch. Medicine Yale U., New Haven, 1974-76; pvt. practice Meriden, 1974—; cons. psychiatrist Child Guidance Clinic Cen. Conn., Meriden, 1980—; med. dir., 1994-99; psychiat. cons. to Meriden Pub. Sch. System, 1999—; mem. faculty U. Conn. Sch. Medicine, Farmington, 1978-79; cons. Caring for Children, San Francisco, 1989—; psychiat. cons. Meriden Pub. Schs., 1999—; reviewer Am. Jour. Psychiatry, 1980—, and others. Author: Solace, 1981, Solace, paperback edit. 1983, Solace, Japanese edit., 1985; sr. editor: The Solace Paradigm, 1988; contbr. articles to profl. jours. Big Brother Big Bros. Orgn., Mpls., 1964-68. Lt. comdr. USN, 1972-74. Mem. Am. Psychiat. Assn., Meriden Wallingford Med. Assn., Gridiron Club. Home: 18 Metacomet Dr Meriden CT 06450-3568 Office: 234 Hobart St Meriden CT 06450-4380

HORTON, THOMAS ROSCOE, business advisor; b. Fort Pierce, Fla., Nov. 17, 1926; s. Charles Montraville Horton and Ruby Mae (Swain) Warren; m. Marilou Deeming, Dec. 19, 1947; children—Susan, Jean, Marilyn. BS, Stetson U., 1949, LHD (hon.), 1982; MS, U. Fla., 1950, PhD, 1954; LLD (hon.), Pace U., 1976; DLitt (hon.), U. Charleston, 1980. Instr., asst. headmaster Bolles Sch., Jacksonville, Fla., 1950-52; with IBM Corp., Armonk, N.Y., 1954-82; pres., chief exec. officer Am. Mgmt. Assn., N.Y.C., 1982-89, chmn., chief exec. officer, 1989-91, chmn., 1991-92; advisor Stetson U., DeLand, Fla., 1992-96; bd. dirs. The Comml. Bank; mem. adv. bd. Who's Who in Fin. and Industry, 1988—, Who's Who in Am., 1999—; vis. disting. scholar Corp. Governance Ctr., Kennesaw State U., 1999—; panelist White House Conf. on Productivity, 1981; co-chair White House Conf. on Critical Infrastructure Assurance, 2000. Author: What Works for Me, 1986, Beyond the Trust Gap, 1990, The CEO Paradox, 1992; editor: Traffic Control - Theory and Implementation, 1965; columnist Mgmt. Rev., 1982-92, Dirs. & Bds., 1998—; assoc. prodr. SHO Entertainment, Inc., 1997—. Life mem. Salvation Army; trustee Bethune-Cookman Coll., Daytona Beach, Fla., 1971-82, hon., 1982—; trustee Pace U., N.Y.C., 1975-92, emeritus trustee, 1992—; trustee Am. Grad. Sch. Internat. Mgmt., Glendale, Ariz., 1982-92, Stetson U. Bus. Sch. Found., 1992—; mem. econ. devel. com. City of DeLand (Fla.), 1992-98; trustee emeritus Stetson U., 1996—; bd. dirs. Kids Voting USA, 1991-2000, chair, 1992-98; adv. bd. Am. C. of C. of Cuba in U.S., 1996—; bd. dirs. Ctr. for Bd. Leadership. Washington, 1999—; bd. visitors The Bolles Sch., Jacksonville, Fla., 1998—; panelist White House Conf. on Critical Infrastructure Assurance, 2000. Fellow Acad. Mgmt., Internat. Acad. Mgmt. (vice chancellor); mem. European Found. for Mgmt. Devel., Japan Mgmt. Assn. (hon.), Korean Mgmt. Assn. (hon.), Pres.' Assn. N.Y.C. (chmn. 1982-91), Nat. Assn. Corp. Dirs. (faculty mem., bd. dirs. 1996—, chair 1999—), Internat. Coun. for Innovation in Higher Edn., Assn. Internat. des Etudiants en Scis. Econs. et Commls. (hon. dir. 1990—), Russian Econs. Soc. (hon.), Mgmt. Exec. Soc., Conf. Bd. (sr.), Sigma Phi Epsilon (co-founder Fla. Beta chpt 1949—), DeLand Country Club, Lake Beresford Yacht Club. Methodist. Office: Stetson U PO Box 8395 Deland FL 32720

HORTON, WILFRED HENRY, mathematics educator; b. Newark, Nottingham, Eng., May 27, 1918; s. Henry and Alice M. (Spence) H.; m. Margaret E. Haskard; children: Richard, Sheila, David, Jennifer. BSc in Math. with honors, U. Coll., Nottingham, 1940; Engr., Stanford U., 1959. With De Havilland Aircraft Co., Hatfield, Eng., 1940-45, Percival Aircraft, Luton, Eng., 1945-50; sr. sci. officer Royal Aircraft Establishment, Farnborough, Eng., 1950-54, prin. sci. officer, 1954-57; assoc. prof. Stanford (Calif.) U., 1959-67; prof. Ga. Inst. Tech., Atlanta, 1967-84; prof. emeritus U. System Ga., 1985—; cons. various orgns. Contbr. articles to profl. jours. and encys. Achievements include design of test facilities for supersonic aircraft, hypersonic wind tunnel.

HORVAT, BRANKA, immunologist, educator; b. Belgrade, Yugoslavia, June 21, 1960; came to France, 1991; s. Branko Horvat and Ranka Peasinovic; m. Siniša Lohinski, June 22, 1985; children: Artur, Nikola. MD, U. Belgrade, 1983; MSc, U. Zagreb, Croatia, 1985, PhD, 1989. Intern Zagreb Med. Ctr., 1984-85; rsch. affiliate Yale U. Sch. Medicine, New Haven, Conn., 1985-88; asst. prof. U. Zagreb Sch. Medicine, 1989-91; post vert Inserm Ctr. Immunology, Marseille, France, 1991-93; asst. prof. Ecole Normale Superieure, Lyon, France, 1993—. Co-author: (paper) Transgenesis and Targeted Mutagenesis in Immunology, 1994; contbr. articles to profl. jours. Recipient Youth Travel award Fedn. European Biochem. Socs., 1990, Rsch. grant Fond. Med. Rsch., Paris, 1992. Mem. Croatian Assn. Immunologists, European Assn. Cancer Rsch., French Assn. Immunologists. Office: Ecole Normale Superieure, de Lyon 46 Allee D'Italie, 69364 Lyon France

HORVATH, ARPAD, engineering educator; b. Subotica, Yugoslavia, Jan. 28, 1969; came to U.S., 1993; s. Matyas and Katalin H.; m. Tunde Balvanyos, July 23, 1993. Diploma in Engring., Tech. U. of Budapest, 1993; MS, Carnegie Mellon U., 1995, PhD, 1997. Postdoctoral rschr. Carnegie Mellon U., Pitts., 1997; rsch. faculty Carnegie Mellon U., 1998-99; asst. prof. U. Calif., Berkeley, 1999—; program co-chair IEEE Internat. Symposium on Electronics and the Environment, Danvers, Mass., 1999; conf. co-chair, San Francisco, 2000; co-dir. NATO Advanced Rsch. Workshop, Budapest, 2000. Co-developer: (model and software) Economic Input-Output Analysis Life-Cycle Assessment (EIO-LCA), 1996-99; contbr. over 39 articles to profl. jours. Recipient AT&T Found. Indsl. Ecology Faculty fellowship, 1998-99, NSF/Lucent Techs. Indsl. Ecology fellowship, 1998-2000. Mem. Internat. Input-Output Assn.; assoc. mem. ASCE. E-mail: horvath@ce.berkeley.edu. Office: Dept Civil Engring & Environ Engring U Calif 215 Mclaughlin Hall Berkeley CA 94720-1712

HORVÁTH, CSABA, chemical engineering educator, researcher; b. Szolnok, Hungary, Jan. 25, 1930; came to U.S., 1963; s. Gyula and Róza (Lányi) H.; children: Donatella, Katalin. Diploma in Chem. Engring., U. Tech. Scis., Budapest, Hungary, 1952, Dr. (hon.), 1986; PhD, J.W. Goethe U., Frankfurt-Main, Germany, 1963; MA (hon.), Yale U., 1979. Asst. in chem. tech. U. Tech. Scis., Budapest, 1952-56; chem. engr. Hoechst AG, Frankfurt am Main, 1956-61; research fellow Harvard U., Cambridge, Mass., 1963-64; research assoc. Yale U. Sch. Medicine, New Haven, 1964-69, assoc. prof., 1970-79, prof. chem. engring., 1979—, chmn. dept. chem. engring., 1987-93; prof. chem. engring. Llewellyn West Jones Jr., 1993-98, Roberto C. Goizueta, 1998—; cons. various govt. and indsl. orgns. Co-author: Introduction to Separation Science, 1973; assoc. editor: Encyclopedia of Bioprocess Technology, 1999; editor: Series High Performance Liquid Chromatography, 1981—, Capillary Electrochromatography (spl. issue of Jour. of Chromatography), 2000; mem. editl. bd. 9 sci. periodicals; contbr. more than 290 rsch. papers and articles to sci. publs. Recipient S. Dal Nogare award Delaware Valley Chromatography Forum, 1978, Tswett medal 15th Internat. Symposium on Advances in Chromatography, 1979, Humboldt sr. U.S. scientist award Humboldt Found., Fed. Republic of Germany, 1982, EAS Chromatography award, 1986, Van Slyke award N.Y. Metro Sect. Am. Assn. Clin. Chemists, 1992, A.J.P. Martin award Chromatography Soc. U.K., 1994, Disting. Contbn. in Separation Sci. award Calif. Separation Sci. Soc., 1995, Nat. award N.E. Region Chromatography Discussion Group, 1997, Halász medal award Hungarian Soc. for Separation Sci., 1997, Golay award 21st Internat. Symposium on Capillary Chromatography and Electrophoresis, 1999, M. Widmer award The New Swiss Chem. Soc., 2000, medal Conn. Separation Sci. Coun., 2000. Fellow AIChE, Am. Inst. Med. and Biomed. Engrs. (founding); mem. AAAS, Deutsche Gesellschaft fuer Chemisches Apparatewesen, Chemische Technik und Biotechnologie e.v., Am. Chem. Soc. (nat. chromatography award 1983), Am. Ceramic Soc., Hungarian Chem. Soc. (hon.), Hungarian Acad. Scis. (external), Hungarian Soc. Separation Sci. (hon.), Conn. Acad. Sci. and Engring., Conn. Acad. Arts and Scis., Inst. Food Technologists, Sigma Xi. Home: PO Box 605 41 Temple Ct New Haven CT 06511-6820 Office: Yale U PO Box 208286 9 Hillhouse Ave New Haven CT 06511-6815

HORVÁTH, FERENC, geophysics educator, researcher, consultant; b. Párkány, Hungary, Mar. 24, 1944; s. Ferenc Máté and Aloisia (Pilsinger) H.; m. Mariann Domján; children: Örs, Marcell, Lilla. Diploma Geophysics, Eotvos U., Budapest, Hungary, 1967; PhD, Eotvos U., 1970; candidate, Hungarian Acad. Scis., 1988. Asst. Eotvos U., Budapest, Hungary, 1967-73, lectr., 1973-74; assoc. prof., 1994—; rsch. fellow Hungarian Acad. Sci., Budapest, Hungary, 1974-88, sr. rsch. fellow, 1988-94; prof., head Eotvos U., Budapest, 1999—. Co-editor: American Association Petroleum Geology Memoir, 1988, Tectonophysics Jour., 1993, 95. Recipient Spl. Commendation award Am. Assn. Petroleum Geologists, 1997. Fellow European Union Geoscis. (hon.), Geol. Soc. Am. (hon.); mem. Acad. Europaea. Roman Catholic. Office: Geophysics Dept Eotvos Univ, Ludovika Tér 2, H-1083 Budapest Hungary

HORVATH, MIHALY, physician; b. Pécs, Hungary, Apr. 7, 1924; s. János Horvath and Erzsébet Malmosi; m. Etelka Szieberth, Aug. 12, 1951; 1 child, Judith. MD, Elisabeth U., Pécs, 1948; cert. clin. chemistry, Med. U., Pécs, 1954; diploma (hon.), U. Pasteur, Strasbourg, 1997. Asst. prof. Med. U., Pécs, 1958; clin. chemist State Hosp. Cardiology, Balatonfüred, Hungary, 1958-91; asst. prof. Chem. U., Veszrémi, Hungary, 1972-91; titular prof. Med. U., Budapest, Hungary, 1984; mem. radiol. com. Hungarian Acad. Scis., Budapest, 1990-94; ret., 1994; mem. adv. bd. World Nuc. Cardiology. Author: (with G. Hoffmann) Nuclear Stethoscope-like Probe Systems, 1987, Myocardial Viability, 1994. Recipient G. Hevesy medal Hungarian Nuc. Med. Soc., 1988, J. Neumann medal, 1988, Z. Bay medal Z. Bay Sci. Found., 1988, medal of honor U. Pasteur, 1997. Achievements include: ECG Gated Averaging in the Cardiology computed Radiocardiocyclography. Avocations: history, technical development, tennis. Home: Liliom u.4, H-8230 Balatonfüred Hungary Office: Gyógytér 2, H-8230 Balatonfüred Hungary

HORVATH, SUZANNE KORN, historian; b. Budapest, Hungary, July 5, 1936; arrived in France, 1956; d. Jozsef and Ilona (Goldstein) Kovacsi; m. Ervin Horvath, 1961 (div. 1971); 1 child, Sophie. Degree in engring., U. Nancy, 1960; diploma, U. Paris, 1974, D in History, 1983. Engr. CNRS, Paris, 1968-98. Co-author: Les Noms de Naissance en Afrique Noire, 1972; contbr. articles to profl. jours.

HORVATH, WERNER, radiologist, artist; b. Linz, Austria, Nov. 13, 1949; s. Stefan and Maria (Pichler) H.; m. Ilse Beham, June 21, 1975; children: Patrick, Nina. MD, U. Vienna, 1975; Radiologist, KH Barmh. Bruder, Linz, Austria, 1983. Turnusarzt several hosps., Linz, Austria, 1975-78; asst. radiology KH Barmh. Br., Linz, Austria, 1978-82, oberarzt, 1983-88, primarius, 1988—, authorized rep. radiation protection, 1988—, authorized rep. cont. edn., 1988—. Contbr. numerous articles to profl. jours.; exhbns. include Galerie du Temple, Paris, 1994, Raika, Linz, Austria, 1994, 95, Galerie Zlaty Kriz, Budweis, 1995, 96, 97, Embassy of Czech Republic, Vienna, 1997, Virtual Mus. of Political Art, internet, 1997, City Mus. Krumau, Czech Republic, Castle of Puchenau, Castle of Hagenberg, 1998. Mem. German Soc. Phlebology (Senator Putter prize 1982), Med. Soc. Upper Austria (auditor 1994-97). Avocations: philosophy, constructivism in art and medicine. Office: Krankenhaus der Barmherzigen Bruder, Seilerstatte 2, A-4020 Linz Upper-Austria, Austria

HORWATH, CAROLINE CHRISTINE, nutritionist; b. Liverpool, Eng., Dec. 30, 1961; arrived in New Zealand, 1987; d. Anton and Lilian Christina Horwath. BSc with honors, U. Adelaide, Australia, 1983; postgrad. diploma nutrition & dietetics, Flinders U., Adelaide, 1984; PhD, U. Adelaide, 1988. Lic. dietitian. Lectr. dept. human nutrition St. Bartholomew's Hosp. Med. Coll., London, 1992-93; lectr. dept. human nutrition U. Otago, Dunedin, New Zealand, 1987-95, sr. lectr. dept. human nutrition, 1995—; vis. assoc. prof. Pub. Health Sch., U. Minn., Mpls., 1998-99; vis. rsch. fellow nutrition dept. Wageningen (The Netherlands) Agrl. U., 1993; prin. investigator New Zealand Nat. Nutrition Surveys, 1989-91, 97-99; mem. Internat. Union Nutritional Scis. Com. II/4, 1995—. Contbr. numerous articles to profl. jours. Recipient CSR Chems. Ltd. prize in chemistry, 1982; David Murray scholar in sci. Adelaide U., 1982; staff traveling fellow U. Otago, 1988. Mem. Am. Soc. Behavioral Medicine, Nutrition Soc. New Zealand. Avocations: Latin-Am. dancing, watercolor painting, yoga. Fax: 64 3 479 7959. E-mail: caroline.horwath@stonebow.otago.ac.nz. Office: U Otago Dept Human Nutrit, Union St, Dunedin New Zealand

HORWELL, DAVID CHRISTOPHER, pharmaceutical company executive; b. Exeter, Eng., June 6, 1945; s. Leonard Reginald and Gladys Winifred (Walling) H.; m. Gillian Cornelia Ockford, Aug. 29, 1970; children: Andrew Jonathan, Sarah Louise. BS with honors, London U., 1967; PhD, Leicester (Eng.) U., 1970. Lab. asst. ICI Pharm., Welwyn, Eng., 1962-63, Cheshire, Eng., 1963-64; rsch. postdoctoral sci. Nat. Rsch. Ctr. Can., Ottawa, Ont., 1970-71, U. Gainesville, Fla., 1971-72, Imperial Coll., London, 1972; rsch. sci. Eli Lilly, Windlesham, Eng., 1973-82; dir. chemistry Parke-Davis, Cambridge, Eng., 1982—, sr. dir., 1992—, disting. rsch. fellow, 1996; vis. prof. U. East Anglia, Norwich, Eng., 1987-98, U. Hertforshire, 1993—; spkr. in field. Cons. editor Bioorganic and Medicinal Chemistry Letters, 1991—, Bioorganic and Medicinal Chemistry, 1992—; mem. editl. bd. Jour. Peptide Rsch., 1997; contbr. articles to sci. jours. Recipient Chmn. Disting. Sci. Achievement award Warner-Lambert, 1990, award for medicinal chemistry Royal Soc. Chemistry, 1998; Disting. Rsch. fellow Warner-Lambert, 1996. Fellow Royal Soc. Chemistry, N.Y. Acad. Scis. Avocations: travel, skiing, golf, music, science, food and wine. Office: Parke Davis Neurosci Rsch, The Forvie Site Robinson Wy, Cambridge CB2 2QB, England

HORWILL, FRANK MERRICK, retired psychologist; b. Edinburgh, Scotland, May 11, 1936; arrived in Australia, 1951; s. Lionel Clifford and Vera Merrick (Walker) H.; m. Dawn Alison Kimber, Aug. 14, 1965; children: Alison Louise, Glenda Susan. Diploma of divinity, Melbourne Coll. Divinity, 1959; diploma, Bapt. Coll. Victoria, Australia, 1960; BA, U. Melbourne, 1965. Ordained minister Bapt. Union Victoria; registered psychologist, Victoria. Pastor Bapt. Union Victoria, 1957-67; psychologist Australian Dept. Labour, Melbourne, 1967-76; ret. Melbourne suburbs, Cohuna and Stawell, 1967-76; dir. ct. counseling Family Ct. Australia, Melbourne, 1976-78, prof. asst. to prin. dir. ct. counselling, 1978-90, mgr. statis. analysis, 1990-95, ct. counsellor, 1996-97; ret., 1997. Com. mem. Victorian Family Coun., 1976-78; mem. pub. questions com. Bapt. Union Victoria, 1976-77; com. mem. Justice in Broadcasting, 1977-84; convenor and member of working parties of psychologists on several issues of polit. and civic importance. Mem. Australian Psychol. Soc. (Victorian state com. 1984-87), Christian Counsellors Assn. (pres. 1986-90). Baptist. Avocations: church activities, reading, genealogy. Home: 48 Essex Rd, Surrey Hills VIC 3127, Australia

HORWING, JOAKIM DAVID OLOF, financial consultant; b. Karlskoga, Sweden, Jan. 9, 1965; s. Bjorn Ingmar and Monica (Berglund) H.; m. Eva Katarina Persson, June 6, 1992; children: Martina, Hanna. BSBA, U. Lund, Sweden, 1988. With Tetra Pak, Lund, 1988-90; project leader Vestos/Custos, Helsingborg, Sweden, 1990-91; asst. treas. Ratos, Stockholm, 1991-97; fin. mgr. Fabege, Stockholm, 1997-98; v.p. ABB Fin. Consulting, Stockholm, 1998—. Mem. Lunds Acad. Sailing Assn. (sec. 1988). Avocations: golf, sailing. E-mail: joakim.horwing@se.abb.com. Office: ABB Fin Consulting, 113 96 Stockholm Sweden

HORWITZ, DAVID LARRY, pharmaceuticals company executive, researcher, educator; b. Chgo., July 13, 1942; s. Milton Woodrow and Dorothy (Glass) H.; m. Gloria Jean Madian, June 20, 1965; children: Karen, Laura. BA, Harvard U., 1963; MD, U. Chgo., 1967; Phd, 1968; MBA, Lake Forest Grad. Sch. Mgmt., 1991. Diplomate Am. Bd. Internal Medicine. Resident in internal medicine U. Chgo. Hosp., 1971-72; fellow in endocrinology U. Chgo., 1972-74; asst. prof., 1974-79; assoc. prof. U. Ill., Chgo., 1979-90; clin. prof. medicine, 1990-92; med. dir. Baxter Healthcare Corp., Deerfield, Ill., 1982-91; v.p. med. and profl. affairs, 1991-92; v.p. med. and regulatory affairs SciClone Pharms., San Mateo, Calif., 1992-95; exec. v.p., 1995-97; sr. v.p. Tech. Advanced Tissue Scis., La Jolla, Calif., 1998—. Contbr. articles to profl. jours. Comdr. USNR, 1969-71. Recipient Outstanding Young Citizen of Chgo. award Chgo. Jr. C. of C., 1976, Outstanding Young Citizen Ill. award Jaycees, 1977. Fellow ACP; mem. Am. Diabetes Assn. (bd. dirs. No. Ill. affil. 1976-92, pres. 1987-89, R & D award 1974-76), Am. Assn. Clin. Nutrition, Endocrine Soc. Achievements include pharmaceutical and medical device research and regulatory strategic planning.

HORWITZ, ELEANOR CATHERINE, information and education official; b. N.Y.C., Dec. 21, 1941; d. Fritz and Hedwig E.F. (Kramer) Jahoda; m. Paul Horwitz, Aug. 15, 1964; children: Gregory Douglas, Catherine Helen, Laura Elizabeth. BA, Swarthmore Coll., 1962; MA, NYU, 1967; MS, Cornell U., 1969; postgrad., Oreg. State U., 1969-70. Sci. tchr. New Lincoln Sch., N.Y.C., 1962-67; coordinator outdoor edn. Lane County Int. Edn. Dist., Eugene, Oreg., 1969-70; staff writer Billerica (Mass.) Banner, 1971-72; instr., writer Mass. Audubon Soc., Lincoln, 1972-75; pub. use specialist U.S. Fish and Wildlife Service, Concord, Mass., 1975; staff writer Soc. Am. Foresters, Washington, 1975-76; chief info. and edn. Mass. Div. Fisheries and Wildlife, Westborough, 1977—; mem. Mass. Gov.'s Forestry Rev. Bd., Boston, 1976-77; mem. steering com. Sec.'s Adv. Group on Environ. Edn. Exec. Office of Environ. Affairs, Commonwealth of Mass., 1990—, co-chair, 1992-97, chair, 1997-98; bd. dirs. Mass. Wildlife Fedn., 1986—, v.p., 1989-95, 97—, pres., 1995-97. Author: Clearcutting, A View from the Top, 1974; author, editor: Ways of Wildlife, 1977 (ACI Book award 1978); editor: (mag.) Massachusetts Wildlife, 1977—; contbr. articles to popular mags. Active Concord Natural Resources Commn., 1976-82, chmn. 1979-80; trustee Concord Land Conservation Trust, 1988—, trustee Holbrook Island Trust, 1995-2000; MBA rep. West Conn. Union Ch., 1998—. Recipient R.E. Dimmick award Oreg. Wildlife Soc., 1970, citation Worcester County League Sportsmen's Clubs, 1987, citation Minutemen chpt. Ducks Unltd., 1987, Conservation award Mahar Fish & Game Assn., 1991, Woman of Yr. award N.E. County Quabbin Anglers Assn., 1991, Sportsman of Yr. New England Outdoor Writers, 1998. Mem. Outdoor Writers Assn. Am., Outdoor Writers Assn., New Eng. Outdoor Writers Assn. (membership sec. 1987-90, bd. dirs. 1987—, sec. 1990-93, v.p. 1993-94, 99-2000, pres. 1994-95), Am. Forestry Assn. (life), New Eng. Conservation Info. and Edn. Assn. (chmn. 1986-87, 90-91, Conservation Communicator of Yr. 1999), Mass. Wildlife Fedn. (Conservationist of Yr. 1999), Wildlife Soc. (profl. cert., chmn. edn. com. 1974-76, 84-87, nominating com. 1990-91, Leopold award com. 1996-98, cert. of recognition 1978), Nashoba Sportsmen's Club, Concord Rod and Gun Club, Maynard Rod and Gun Club (hon.). Mem. United Ch. of Christ. Office: Mass Divsn Fisheries and Wildlife Westborough MA 01581

HORWITZ, KATHRYN BLOCH, molecular biologist; b. Sosua, Dominican Republic, Feb. 20, 1941; came to U.S., 1952; d. Werner Meyerstein and Olga (Schlesinger) Bloch; m. Lawrence David Horwitz, June 14, 1964; children: Phillip Andrew, Carolyn Anita. BA, Barnard Coll., 1962; MS, NYU, 1966; PhD, U. Tex. Southwestern Med. Sch., Dallas, 1975; postdoctoral, U. Tex. Sch. Medicine, San Antonio, 1978. Instr. U. Tex. Sch. Medicine, San Antonio, 1978-79; asst. prof. U. Colo. Med. Sch., Denver, 1979-84, assoc. prof., 1984-89, prof. of medicine, pathology and molecular biology, 1989—; cellular physiology panel NSF, 1985-88; biochem. endocrinology study sect. NIH, 1989-93; mem. Pres.'s Cancer Panel Spl. Commn. on Breast Cancer, 1992, Breast Cancer Task Force, NIH, 1981-84. Author over 150 breast cancer and steroid receptors research papers, books; assoc. editor, editl. bd. for several scientific jours. Chair, sci. adv. bd. Cancer League of Colo., 1987-91; organizer Keystone Symposia on Steroid Receptors, 1996, 98, 2000. Recipient Nat. Bd. award Med. Coll. Pa., 1986, Wilson Stone award M.D. Anderson Hosp. and Tumor Inst., 1976, Rsch. Career Devel. award Nat. Cancer Inst., 1981-86, MERIT award NIH, 1992, The U. Helsinki medal and Second Siltavouri lectr. Finland, 1993, William L. McGuire Meml. lectr., 1997, Bicenntenial lectr. U. Louisville, 1998, Disting. Sci. award Clin. Ligand Assay Soc., 2000; grantee NSF, Am. Cancer Soc., Nat. Found. Cancer Rsch. Dept. of the Army, NIH. Mem. Endocrine Soc. (program com. 1989-91, nominating com. 1989-91, chair 1991, coun. 1992-95, pres.-elect 1997-98, pres. 1998-99, immediate past pres. 1999-2000, mem. devel. com. 2000—), Am. Fedn. Clin. Rsch., Am. Soc. Cell Biology, Am. Assn. Cancer Rsch. (program com. 1994-95, state legis. com. 1993—), Western Soc. Clin. Investigation, AAAS, Am. Soc. Biochemistry and Molecular Biology. Democrat. Jewish. Avocations: skiing, reading, gardening, traveling. Office: U Colo Dept Medicine PO Box B151 Denver CO 80201-0151

HORWITZ, MARCUS AARON, microbiologist, immunologist; b. Elmira, N.Y., May 3, 1946; s. Abraham and Rose (Hirsch) H.; m. Helene L. DesRuisseaux, Nov. 27, 1981; children: Joshua, Daniel. AB in Physics, Cornell U., 1968; MD, Columbia U., 1972. Diplomate Am. Bd. Internal Medicine, Am. Bd. Infectious Diseases. Resident in medicine Albert Einstein Coll. Medicine, Bronx, N.Y., 1972-74; fellow in infectious diseases Albert Einstein Coll. Medicine, 1976-77; epidemic intelligence svc. officer Ctrs. for Disease Control and Prevention, Atlanta, 1974-76; NIH postdoctoral fellow The Rockefeller U., N.Y.C., 1977-80, asst. prof., 1980-84, assoc. physician, 1980-84; chief infectious diseases UCLA Sch. Medicine, L.A., 1985-92, prof. medicine and microbiology, immunology, 1985—; chmn. scientific adv. bd. Am. Leprosy Found., Rockville, Md., 1990—; trustee Trudeau Inst., Saranac Lake, N.Y., 1994-97; mem. tuberculosis panel U.S. - Japan Coop. Med. Scis. Program, 1991-95. Mem. editl. bd., guest editor: Jour. of Clin. Investigation, 1989-96; editor: (book) Bacteria - Host Cell Interaction, 1988; patentee vaccine for Legionnaires' Disease, vaccine for tuberculosis, Exochelins. Cmdr. USPHS 1974-76. Recipient Alexander Langmuir award Ctrs. for Disease Control, Atlanta, 1976, Faculty Rsch. award Am. Cancer Soc., 1985. Fellow AAAS, Infectious Diseases Soc. Am. (Squibb award for Outstanding Rsch. 1991). Office: UCLA/Dept Medicine CHS 37-121 10833 Le Conte Ave Los Angeles CA 90095-3075

HOSAGOUDAR, VIRUPAKSHAGOUDA BHIMANAGOUDA, research scientist; b. Bilgi, Bijapur, India, June 1, 1953; s. Bhimanagouda Yoganagouda and Gangamma Patil; m. Sharada Parvatagouda Patil, May 22, 1985; children: Rajeshwari, Mahantesh, Ishwaragouda. MSc, Shivaji U., India, 1976, DBM, 1978; PhD, Bharathiar U., India, 1987, DSc, 2000. Rsch. fellow Bot. Survey India, Coimbatore, 1981-89, rsch. assoc., 1989-92, pool officer, 1992-95; scientist Tropical Bot. Garden & Rsch. Inst., Kerala, India, 1995—; disting. standing mem. rsch. bd. advisors Am. Biog. Inst. Author: Meliolales of India, 1996; co-author: Fungi of Kerala, 1996, The Meliolineae, A Supplement, 1997; contbr. articles to profl. jours. Mem. FPSI, Indian Phyt. Pathology, N.Y. Acad. Sci. Office: Microbiology Divsn, Tropical Bot Garden & Rsch, Palode Thiruvananthapuram 695 562, India

HOSAKA, YASUHIRO, biomedical researcher; b. Kyoto, Japan, Jan. 8, 1931; s. Minoru and Sawa (Tsukada) H.; m. Tomoko Ogawa, Nov. 2, 1958; children: Yuki, Naoki, Taisuke. MD, Nagoya (Japan) U., 1955; Dr.Med.Sci., Osaka (Japan) U., 1960. Rsch. assoc. Rsch. Inst. Microbiol. Diseases, Osaka U., 1960-74, assoc. prof., 1974-88; prof. Osaka U. Pharm. Scis., 1988-98; mem. bd. Hosaka Pediats., Hirakata, 1998—; vis. scientist Wistar Inst., Phila., 1974-76; adv. com. Internat. Congress of Virology, 1990, 93, 96, 99. Co-author: Medical and Pharmacological Virology, 1990, Illustration of Viruses, 1979. Mem. Japanese Soc. of Electron Microscopy (pres. 1994-95, Seto prize 1967), Japanese Soc. Virology, Japanese Soc. Immunology, Japanese Soc. Pharmacology, Am. Soc. Microbiology. Home: 9-6 Miyanoshita, Hirakata 573-0046, Japan Office: Hosaka Pediatrics 3-12-1, Kouriga-oka, Hirakata 573-0084, Japan

HOSAKO-NAITO, YUKI, surgeon; b. Hino, Japan, Oct. 28, 1964; d. Shinichiro and Taeko (Kamata) H.; m. Walter Ray Naito, Apr. 29, 1995; 1 child, Sato. MD, Tokyo Women's Med. Coll., 1990. Surgeon Tokyo Met. Fuchu Hosp., 1994-93, Tokyo U. Sch. Medicine, 1994-95; filiate rschr. Yale U., New Haven, Conn., 1995-96; surgeon Tokyo U. Sch. Medicine, 1996-97, Japanese Red Cross Med. Ctr., Tokyo, 1997-98; surgeon musashino Red

Cross Hosp., 1998-99. Mem. Japanese Assn. Otolaryngology, Japanese Assn. Logopedics Phoniatrics, Japanese Assn. Study Taste and Smell. Office: Musashino Red Cross Hosp, 1-26-1 Kyounann Cho, musashino-shi, Tokyo 180-8610, Japan

HOSCHL, CYRIL, mechanical engineer, educator; b. Klatovy, Czech Republic, Apr. 6, 1925; s. Cyril and Vilma (Kobrova) H.; m. Helena Grimmerova, Jul. 17, 1948; children: Cyril, Viktor. Eng., Tech. Univ., Praha, Czech Republic, 1949; assoc. prof., TU Liberec, Liberec, Czech Republic, 1956, prof., 1966; DrSc., Acad. Scis., Praha, 1990. Asst. TU, Praha, 1949-50; researcher CKD Machine Works, Praha, 1951-56; educator TU, Liberec, 1956-70, prorector, 1960-65, dean, 1966-70; scientist Acad. Scis., Praha, 1971-93; emeritus scientist, 1994—. Author: Strength of Materials, 1971; co-author: Advanced Comp. Methods, 1975, Strength of Materials, 1989; contbr. articles to profl. jours. Recipient Gold medal Acad. Scis., 1990. Mem. Czech Soc. Mechanics, IFToMM. Home: Vyzlovska 52, 100 00 Praha Czech Republic Office: Inst of Thermomechanics, AV CR Dolejskova 5, 182 00 Praha Czech Republic

HOSHI, HAJIME, research scientist; b. Tokyo, June 10, 1961; s. Yoshio and Chieko H.; m. Kyoko, Oct. 29, 1995. BS, Tokyo Inst. Tech., 1984, MS, 1986, PhD, 1992. Tech. assoc. Inst. Molecular Sci., Aichi, Japan, 1986-93; rsch. assoc. Tokyo Inst. Tech., 1993—. Contbr. articles to profl. jours.; mem. editl. staff Molecular Elecs. & Bioelecs., 1996-98. Mem. Japan Soc. Applied Physics. Office: Tokyo Inst Tech, O-okayama, Tokyo 152-8552, Japan

HOSHI, TSUTAO, science and technology research institute director; b. Iwaki-shi, Japan, Apr. 25, 1939; s. Mitsuo and Gen (Suzuki) H.; m. Teruko Kato, Nov. 3, 1966; children:Shinich, Yukie, Yuji. BS in Elec. Engring., Ibaraki U., Hitachi-shi, Japan, 1962; D Engring., U. Tokyo, 1982. Head reactor accident rsch. lab. Japan Atomic Energy Rsch. Inst., Tokai-mura, 1980-83, gen. mgr. reactor decommissioning, 1985-91, dep. dir. rsch. reactor dept., 1991-93, dir. nuclear ship rsch. and devel., 1993-98; dir. Rsch. Orgn. Info. Sci. and Tech., 1998—; dir. nuclear safety bur. Sci. and Tech. Agy. Japan, 1983-85. Mem. Atomic Energy Soc. Japan. Avocations: I-go, fishing, painting. Home: 131-36 Yanokura, Nakayama, Taira, Iwaki-shi 970-8031, Japan Office: RIST, Tokai-mura, Ibaraki 319-1106, Japan

HOSHIDE, TOSHIHIKO, mechanical engineering educator; b. Yanai, Japan, Sept. 27, 1954; s. Shuichi and Miwako (Katano) H.; m. Hiromi Sato, Sept. 22, 1985; children: Takafumi, Ayaka. BS, Kyoto (Japan) U., 1977, MS, 1979, PhD, 1984. Cert. mech. engring. Rsch. assoc. Kyoto U., 1980-86; vis. rsch. assoc. U. Ill., Urbana, 1986-87; rsch. assoc. Kyoto U., 1987-89, assoc. prof., 1989—. Recipient ESIS award, 1998. Office: Grad Sch Energy Sci Kyoto U, Yoshida-honmachi Sakyo-ku, Kyoto 606-8501, Japan

HOSHINO, SADAO, physicist; b. Tokyo, Sept. 7, 1926; s. Shuichi and Eiko (Godai) H.; m. Toki Kusaka, Nov. 14, 1954; children: Moriyuki, Hiroshi, Takashi. Rsch. asst. Osaka (Japan) U., 1948; rsch. asst. Tokyo Inst. Tech., 1948-49, rsch. assoc., 1949-59, assoc. prof., 1959-60; rsch. assoc. Pa. State U., State College, 1956-59; asst. physicist Brookhaven Nat. Lab., Upton, N.Y., 1958-59; assoc. prof. U. Tokyo, 1960-66, prof., 1967-87, prof. emeritus, 1987; prof. Tsukuba (Japan) U., 1987-90; Tele & Fax 045-331-4752. Author: Neutron Diffraction, 1961; editor, author: Neutron Diffraction, 1976; contbr. over 100 papers to profl. jours. Mem. Am. Phys. Soc., N.Y. Acad. Scis., Phys. Soc. Japan (pres. 1984-85), Crystallog. Soc. Japan (pres. 1986). Avocations: Japanese fencing, music, reading, gardening. Home: 41-5 Kamaya-cho Hodogaya-ku, Yokohama 240-0063, Japan

HOSHINO, YOSHIRO, industrial technology critic; b. Tokyo-Shi, Tokyo-Hu, Japan, Jan. 13, 1922; s. Teruoki and Matsue Hoshino; m. Kumiko Serizawa, July 7, 1954; children: Syuichiro, Kenjiro, Chieko, Tetsuro. B, Tokyo Inst. Tech., 1944, Dr., 1980. Asst. tech. staff Agy. of Tech., Tokyo, 1944-45, critic, 1945-62; prof. Ritsumeikan U., Kyoto, 1962-68, cirtic, 1968-81; prof. indsl. tech. Teikyo U., Tokyo, 1981-97, critic, 1997—; hon. prof. N.E. U., Shenyang, Republic of China, 1985—. Author: Collected Works of Yoshiro Hoshino, 1977-79, Future of Civilization, 1980, Fundamental Problems on Latest Technology, 1986, Technology, Economy and Politics—Japan and China, 1945-1991, 1993. Bd. dirs. Japanese Soong Chingling Meml. Found., Tokyo, 1988—. Avocation: driving. Home: 9-8-19 Chiyogaoka Asao-ku, Kawasaki-shi, Kanagawa-ken 215-0005, Japan

HOSHIYAMA, TADAFUMI, optoelectronics executive, researcher; b. Tokyo, July 9, 1945; s. Chutaro and Shizuyo (Shono) H.; m. Yaeko Hasao, Dec. 15, 1975; 1 child, Akana. BSc, Kyoto (Japan) U., 1968. Engr. NEC Corp., Tokyo, 1968-83, mgr., 1984-95, chief engr., 1996-98; v.p. Showa Optronics Co. Ltd., Yokohama, Japan, 1999—; cons. tech. com. Nat. Spatial Data Infrastructure Promoting Assn., Tokyo, 1996-99; mem. Geog. Info. Sys. Tech. Com. of Min. Postal Svcs., Tokyo, 1997-98. Contbr. articles to profl. jours.; inventor in field. Recipient prize Def. Munition Found., Tokyo, 1980. Mem. Assn. Comm., Electronics, Intelligence and Info. Systems, Internat. Soc. Optical Engring. Home: 3-6-4-1303 Hisamoto Takatsu-ku, Kawasaki 213-0011, Japan Office: Showa Optronics Co Ltd, 1-22-1 Hakusan Midori-ku, Yokohama 226-0006, Japan

HOSIER, LINDA G., educator; b. Somerville, N.J., Mar. 15, 1948; d. Louis S. and Linda Julia (Braun) Grube; m. David Keith Short, Aug. 1, 1970 (div. Apr. 1986); children: Kristi Elizabeth, Andrew Alan; m. Robb R. Hosier, July 25, 1998; children: Robb R. Jr., Scott J., Timothy I., James E., Sherry H. BA, Pfeiffer Coll., 1970; MEd, U. N.C., 1973. Ordained min. of gospel Impact Worship Ctr., High Point, N.C., 1999. Tchr. English Lexington (N.C.) City Schs., 1970-71; tchr. lang. arts, social studies Kannapolis (N.C.) City Schs., 1971-73; tchr. English, history Franklinton (N.C.) City Schs., 1973-74; tchr. English Bristol (Tenn.) City Schs., 1976-77; tchr. lang. arts, social studies High Point (N.C.) City Schs., 1983; tchr. acad. gifted lit., math. Stokes County Schs., Danbury, N.C., 1983-95; tchr. lang. arts and social studies Guilford County Schs., 1995-99, tchr. academically gifted, 1999—; coord. childrens ministries Cathedral of Praise Ch., Greensboro, N.C., 1993-99; missionary to Haiti, the Sioux Indian Nation, Mex.; min. Gospel Impact Worship Ctr., HIgh Point, N.C. Mem. NEA, N.C. Edn. Assn., N.C. Assn. of Gifted, N.C. Tchrs. of English. Avocations: reading, travel, writing, gardening, singing. Home: 9027 Ambridge Ln Kernersville NC 27284-9267

HOSKIE, LORRAINE, consumer products representative, poet; b. Nansemond County, Va., Aug. 26, 1953; m. Eddie Lewis Hoskie, July 7, 1972 (div. Oct. 1980); children: Jacqueline Marie, Quinton Lewis. BS, Va. Commonwealth U., 1977. Clk. Christian Children's Fund, Richmond, 1977-79, corr. rsch. clk., 1979-80; eligibility worker City of Richmond, 1982-83; substitute tchr. Sch. Bd., Richmond, 1983-86; telemarketer Energy Savs. Exterior, Richmond, 1995-96; CRT operator Snelling Pers. Svcs., Richmond, 1996; mail clk. Abacus, Richmond, 1997; office worker Kelly Svcs., Richmond, 1997; remittance processor Calipher, Inc., Richmond, 1997—; substitute tchr. Sch. Bd. of Franklin, Va., 1987; ch. sec. SDA-Ephesus, Richmond, 1981-82; vol. worker Bapt. Student Union Va. Commonwealth U., Richmond, 1971-72, math. tutor Spl. Svcs. Program, 1972. Sec. Ephesus Prison Ministry, 1996—; team sec. Ephesus Va. Dept. Correction, 1993-94. Named Golden Poet, World of Poetry, Sacramento, 1990, recipient award of merit cert., 1990; recipient Poet of Merit award Am. Poetry Assn., 1988, Appreciation award VA Dept. Corrections, 1994, Pres. award for literary excellence Nat. Authors Registry, 1994. Democrat. 7th Day Adventist. Avocations: crocheting, creative writing, music, poetry writing. Home: 3912 Chamberlayne Ave Apt D-17 Richmond VA 23227-4261

HOSKING, GEOFFREY ALAN, history educator, literary critic; b. Troon, Scotland, Apr. 28, 1942; s. Stuart William Steggall and Jean Ross (Smillie) H.; m. Anne Lloyd Hirst, Dec. 19, 1970; children: Katherine, Janet. BA, Kings Coll. Cambridge, 1963, MA, 1967; postgrad., Moscow U., 1964-65, Oxford (Eng.) U., 1965-66; PhD, Kings Coll., Cambridge, Eng., 1970. Lectr. U. Essex, Colchester, Eng., 1966-76; vis. lectr. U. Wis., Madison, 1971-72; sr. lectr., reader U. Essex, 1976-84; prof. Russian history U. London, 1984-99, Leverhulme pers. rsch. lectr., 1999—; Reith lectr. BBC, 1988; Gast prof. Stanisches Inst., 1980-81; expert Coun. of Moscow Sch. Polit. Studies, 1992; mem. overseas policy com. Brit. Acad., 1995-2000; mem. Coun. Writers' and Scholars' Ednl. Trust, 1985. Author: The Russian Constitutional Experiment: Government and Duma, 1907-1914, 1973, Beyond Socialist Realism: Soviet Fiction since Ivan Denisovich, 1980, History of the Soviet Union, 1985, 3d edit., 1992, Russian edit., 1994 (L.A. Times History Book prize 1986), The Awakening of the Soviet Union, 1990, (with Jonathan Aves and Peter Duncan) The Road to Post-Communism: Independent Political Movements in the USSR, 1985-1991, 1992, Russia: People and Empire, 1552-1917, 1997; editl. bd. Nations and Nationalism, Nationalities Papers, Revs. in History. Mem. internat. acad. coun. Mus. Contemporary History, Moscow, 1995. Fellow Brit. Acad.; mem. Nat. Assn. Soviet & East European Studies, Br. Univs. Assn. Slavists. Office: Sch Slavonic & E European Studies,, U London Senate House Male St, London WCIE 7H WCIE 7H, England

HOSKING, RICHARD FRANK, English language educator; b. Sydney, NSW, Australia, Mar. 31, 1933; s. Frank and Marjorie (Abbott) H. BA, Sydney U., 1955, Cambridge (Eng.) U., 1960; MA, Cambridge (Eng.) U., 1964. Asst. keeper oriental manuscripts and printed books Brit. Mus., London, 1961-71; prof. English, Hiroshima (Japan) Shudo U., 1973-98, prof. anthropology, 1993-98, emeritus prof., 1998—; writer, lectr. on food culture. Author: A Dictionary of Japanese Food, 1996, At the Japanese Table, 2000; editor: Asian Scripts, 1966; translator: (from German) Churches in Rock, 1970; also articles, chpt. to book. Travel fellow John Goodenday Trust, Hebrew U. Jerusalem, 1960-61. Fellow Royal Asiatic Soc., Athenaeum (London), Guild Food Writers. Anglican. Avocations: harpsichord, cooking. Address: The Athenaeum, Pall Mall, SW1 London England

HOSKINS, BARBARA R(UTH) WILLIAMS, elementary educator, elementary principal; b. Pineville, Ky., June 7, 1945; d. John and Patsy Ann (Buell) Williams; m. Teddy Michael Hoskins, Dec. 12, 1961; children: Susan Ann Hoskins Brown, Shelia Marie Hoskins Key. BS, Union Coll., 1977, MA, 1978, postgrad., 1980-89; postgrad., U. Ky., 1990. Cert. elem. edn., elem./secondary principalship, elem./secondary supervision, dir. pupil pers., Ky. Tchr. Bell County Bd. Edn., Pineville, 1977—, prin., 1997—; edn. instr. S.E. C.C., Middlesboro, Ky., 1987—; BLS instr. Am. Heart Assn., Corbin, Ky., 1990—. Co-author: History of Bell County, 1994. Active Bell County Hist. Soc., 1992—, Laubach Literary Action Agy., Bell County, 1991—, Nat. Arbor Day Found., Nebr., 1995. Mem. Bell County Edn. Assn., Upper Cumberland Edn. Assn., Ky. Edn. Assn., NEA, Nat. Alliance Tchrs. Math. and Sci., Bell County Extension Coun., Iota Sigma Nu. Republican. Baptist. Avocations: walking, jogging, science and math activities, local history research. Home: RR 1 Box 69 Pineville KY 40977-9712 Office: Arjay Elem Sch HC 69 Arjay KY 40902-9802

HOSKINS, BOB (ROBERT WILLIAM HOSKINS), actor; b. Bury St. Edmunds, Suffolk, Eng., Oct. 26, 1942; s. Robert and Elsie Lillian Hoskins; m. Jane Livesey (div.); 2 children: Alex, Sarah; m. Linda Banwell, 1984; 2 children: Jack, Rosa. Student, Stroud Green Sch. Stage debut in Romeo and Juliet, Victoria Theatre, Stoke-on-Trent, 1968; joined Royal Shakespeare Co., 1976; stage appearances include Pygmalion, Albery, Eng., 1974, Aldwych, 1976, The World Has Turned Upside Down, 1978, Has Washington Legs?, 1978, True West, 1989, Guys and Dolls, 1981, Old Wicked Songs, 1996-97, Stage, 1996-97; TV appearances include On The Move, 1976, Pennies From Heaven, 1978, (miniseries) Flickers, 1980, Othello, 1981, The Dunera Boys, 1986, The Changeling, 1993, World War II: When The Lions Roared, 1994; film appearances include Zulu Dawn, 1980, The Long Good Friday, 1981, Cotton Club, 1984, Mona Lisa (Best Actor award Cannes Festival, Nat. Soc. Film Critics, 1987), Who Framed Roger Rabbit?, 1988, Mermaids, 1990, Heart Condition, 1990, Shattered, 1990, The Favor the Watch, 1990, The Projectionist, 1990, Hook, 1991, Passed Away, 1991, Super Mario Bros., 1992, Nixon, 1995, Michael, 1996, Cousin Bette, 1996, Twenty-Four/Seven, 1997, 1 Inch Over the Horizon, 1997, Felicias Journey, 1999, David Copperfield TV, 1999, others; (films) actor, writer, director The Raggedy Rawney, 1988; actor, director The Rainbow, 1994; actor, prodr. The Secret Agent, 1995. Avocations: photography, gardening, playgoing. Office: Internat Creative Mgmt Ltd, Oxford House 76 Oxford St, London W1N 0AX, England

HOSKINS, IFFATH ABBASI, obstetrician-gynecologist; b. Karachi, Pakistan, June 18, 1951; came to U.S., 1977; d. Mohd Ahson and Mehru Kazi Abbasi; m. William John Hoskins, Nov. 9, 1985 (dec. June 1984); children: Ahad Jamie, Mariya Aisha. MD, Dow Med. Coll., Karachi, 1975. Fellow high risk obstetrics Walter Reed Army Hosp., Washington, 1983-85, attending high risk obstetrics, 1985-87; dir. rsch. Bellevue Hosp., N.Y.C., 1987-90, chief obstetrics, 1990-97; assoc. prof. NYU Sch. Medicine, N.Y.C., 1994—; residency program dir., chief dept. ob-gyn. NYU Downtown Hosp., N.Y.C., 1997—; attending NYU Downtown Hosp., N.Y.C. Contbr. over 75 articles to profl. jours. Capt. USN, 1979—. Mem. ACOG (sec. 1999—, Cmty. Svc. award 1999). Republican. Muslim. Avocation: reading. E-mail: iffath.hoskins@med.nyu.edu. Home: 343 E 74th St Ph 4C New York NY 10021-3777 Office: NYU Downtown Hosp Dept Ob-Gyn 170 William St New York NY 10038-2649

HOSKINS, WILLIAM ANDREW, aerospace engineer; b. Cincinnati, July 31, 1962; s. William K. and Elizabeth G. H.; m. Megan Elizabeth Hyde, Sept. 10,1988; 1 child, Christa Meiyan. BS in physics (summa cun laude), Yale Univ., 1984; MSE in mech. and aerospace engring., Princeton Univ., 1990. Physics tchr. Crossroads Sch., Santa Monica, Calif., 1984-86; prin. devel. engr. Primex Aerospace Co., Redmond, Wash., 1989—; ptnr. Hoskins LP, 1997—. Recipient Schultz Prize in physics Yale Univ., 1984, Guggenheim fellowship Princeton Univ., 1986. Mem. AIAA. Avocations: soccer, running, hiking. E-mail: wah@rocket.com. Home: 7025 137th Ave NE Redmond WA 98052-9411 Office: Primex Aerospace Co PO Box 97009 Redmond WA 98073-9709

HOSKISON, GEORGE ARTHUR, farming executive; b. Durban, Natal, South Africa, Sept. 13, 1934; s. George and Florence Olive (Graham) H.; m. Maria Elizabeth Drexer, June 30, 1965; children: Trudy, Cindy. Mgr. Fine Wool Products, South Africa, 1957-67; dir. Rainbow Chicken, South Africa, 1967-70; mng. dir. Earlybird Farms, South Africa, 1970-84, Hosgro Farms, South Africa, 1984—; dir. Sunbird Flowers, South Africa, 1997—, Sacca Ltd., South Africa, 1980-82; chmn. South African Broiler Orgn., 1980-89. Recipient Export Achievement award, 1989. Office: Hosgro Farms, Northlands, Gauteng 2116, South Africa

HOSKOVEC, JIRI, psychologist, researcher; b. Usti nad Labem, Czechoslovakia, Feb. 19, 1933; s. Vaclav and Marie Hoskovec; m. Edith Pantucek, Dec. 12, 1970; children: Simona, David, Vitus. PromPsych, Charles U., Prague, 1956, CSc, 1965, PhD, 1966. Diagnostician Diagnostic Ctr. for Children, Dobrichovice, Czechoslovakia, 1956; rschr. Occupational Safety Rsch. Inst., Prague, 1956-60; scientist Inst. of Psychology Charles U., Prague, 1960-68; scientist Traffic Safety Inst. Kuratorium fürVerkehrssicherheit, Vienna, 1968-69; scientist dept. psychology Charles U., Prague, 1969-95, prof. dept. psychology, 1995—; scientist Lehigh U., Bethlehem, Pa., 1965, 71, Stanford U., 1966, Akron (Ohio) U., 1983. Author: Hypnosis and Suggestion, 4th edit., 1998, Theory of Hypnosis, 1970, History of Experimental Psychology, 1992, (with J. Brozek) T.G. Masaryk on Psychology, 1995, Psychological Ideas and Society, 1997, (with S. Hoskovcova) A Brief History of Czech and Central European Psychology, 2000. Mem. coordination com. Civic Forum of Psychologists in Czech Republic, Prague, 1989; chmn. Acad. Coun. Philos. Faculty, Charles U., 1990. Fellow Am. Soc. Clin. Hypnosis (hon.); mem. Czech-Moravian Psychol. Soc., Czech Med. Soc. J.E. Purkyne. Mem. Hussite Ch. Home: Moskevska 32, 101 00 Prague 10, Czech Republic Office: Charles U Dept Psychology, Celetna 20, 110 00 Prague Czech Republic

HOSMAN, SHARON LEE, music educator; b. Bisbee, Ariz., Nov. 2, 1943; d. Roy Lee and Virginia Baldwin (Bandel) H. BA, Loretto Heights Coll., 1965; MA, U. No. Colo., 1979. Tchr. Livermore (Calif.) Sch. Dist., 1965-66, Jefferson County Pub. Schs., Golden, Colo., 1966-97; faculty rep. North Area Citizens Adv. Com., Arvada, Colo., 1979-81, S.I.P.C., Arvada, 1982-83, North Area Sch. Improvement Process Com., Arvada, 1984-91, North Area Accountability com., 1991-92. Piano accompanist for sch. groups, 1965-97. Mem. NEA, DAR, Jefferson County Edn. Assn., Colo. Edn. Assn., Music Tchrs. Nat. Assn., Colo. State Music Tchrs. Assn., Denver Area Music Tchrs. Assn., Musicians' Soc. Denver, Am. Guild Organists, Hereditary Order of First Families of Mass., Smithsonian, Denver Rescue Mission, Denver Dumb Friends League, St. Luke's Hosp. Aux. (life). Republican. Episcopalian. Avocations: art, music, drama, reading, gardening.

HOSNI, FAROUQ ABDELAZIZ, Egyptian government official, sculptor; b. Alexandria, Egypt, 1938. Grad. in arts, U. Alexandria. Worked in Cultural Palace, Alexandria, 1967-82; dir. Egyptian Acad. Arts, Rome, 1982-85; min. culture Govt. of Egypt, Cairo, 1987—. Office: Ministry of Culture, 2 Shagaret al-Dorr Zamalek, Cairo Egypt*

HOSNY, EHAB AHMED, pharmacist, educator; b. Alexandria, Egypt, Apr. 6, 1954; s. Ahmed H.; m. Haifaa Ahmed El-Essawry, Apr. 6, 1981; children: Ahmed, Mohamed, Heba. BS, Cairo U., 1976; M, Al-Azhar U., Cairo, 1981; PhD, U. Wis., 1988. Demonstrator Al-Azhar U., Cairo, 1978-81, teaching asst., 1981-84; rsch. asst., teaching asst. U. Wis., Madison, 1984-88; lectr. Al-Azhar U., 1988-91; asst. prof. King Saud U., Riyadh, Saudi Arabia, 1991-95, assoc. prof., 1995-99, prof., 1999—. Author: Peptide and Protein Drug Delivery, 1990. Peace fellow Purdue U., West Lafayette, Ind., 1983-84; U. Wis. scholar, 1984-88. Mem. AAAS, Arab Pharmacists Union, Pharm. Soc. Egypt, N.Y. Acad. Scis. Moslem. Office: King Saud U Coll Pharmacy, PO Box 2457, Riyadh 11451, Saudi Arabia

HOSOE, EIKOH (TOSHIHIRO HOSOE), photographer, educator; b. Yonezawa, Japan, Mar. 18, 1933; s. Yonejiro and Mitsuko (Nakagawa) H.; m. Misako Imai, Apr. 2, 1962; children—Kenji, Kanako, Kumiko. BA, Tokyo Coll. Photography, 1954; DLitt (hon.), Patent U. Am., 1999. Prof. Tokyo Inst. Poly., 1975—; dir. Kiyosato Mus. Photographic Arts, Japan. One-man shows include Konishiroku Gallery, Ginza Tokyo, 1956, 60, Nikon Salon, Ginza, 1969, Smithsonian Instn., Washington, 1969, Light Gallery, N.Y.C., 1973, 75, 83, Nikon Salon, 1977, Photographers' Gallery, Melbourne, Australia, 1979, Silver Image Gallery, Ohio State Univ., Columbus, 1979; FNAC Forum, Paris, 1980, Galerij Paule Pia, Antwerp, Belgium, 1981, Internat. Mus. Photography, Rochester, N.Y., 1982-92, Ctr. for Creative Photography, Tucson, U. Ariz., 1990, Internat. Ctr. Photography, N.Y., 1991, Japanese Am. Cultural and Comm. Ctr., L.A., Mus. Photographic Arts, San Diego, 1992, ICAC Weston Gallery, Tokyo, 1993, De Beyerd Mus., Breda, The Netherlands, 1993, Mus. of Arts, Wash. State U., U.S.A., 1994; public collections include Shadai Gallery, Tokyo, Nihon Univ., Tokyo, Mus. Modern Art, N.Y.C., Internat. Mus. Photography, George Eastman House, Rochester, N.Y., Smithsonian Instn., Washington, Nat. Gallery of Can., Ottawa, Victoria and Albert Mus., London, Bibliotheque Nationale, Paris, Musee d'Art de Ville de Paris, Nat. Gallery of Australia, Canberra. Recipient Photographer of Yr. award Japan Photo Critics Assn., 1963, Art award Ministry of Edn., 1970, Ville de Paris, 1982, Toyo award Soc. Photographic Sci. and Engring., 1995, Purple Ribbon medal Govt. of Japan, 1998. Mem. Photographers Soc. of Japan (photographer of the yr., 1993), Japan Soc. Art and History of Photography (v.p.), Japan Profl. Photographers Soc. (v.p.).

HOSOE, TOSHIHIRO See **HOSOE, EIKOH**

HOSOJIMA, HIROYUKI, diabetologist, educator; b. Inami, Toyama, Japan, Apr. 29, 1945; s. Chohjiroh and Miyo Hosojima; m. Etsuko Numata, Mar. 3, 1974; children: Michihiro, Shohko, Masako. MD, Kanazawa (Japan) U., 1970, PhD, 1981. Coun. in medicine, diabetology, endocrinology. Vis. asst. prof. U. Mo., Columbia, 1979-80; asst. prof. Kanazawa Med. U., 1993—; dir. Japan Diabetic Com., 1972—. Author: Diabetes Care, 1989, Current Concepts of Aldose Reductase and its Inhibitors, 1990, Recent Advances in Insulin Therapy, 1990, Current Status of Prevention and Treatment of Diabetic Complication, 1990. Mem. N.Y. Acad. Sci. Buddhist. Avocation: golf. Home: Ishikawa-Kahokugun, Daigaku 2-54, Uchinada 920-02, Japan Office: Kanazawa Med Univ, Daigaku 1-1 Ishikawa-Kahok, Uchinada 920-02, Japan

HOSOMI, TAKASHI, economist; b. Miyazu, Kyoto, Japan, Apr. 24, 1920. B.Econs., Tokyo Imperial U., 1942. Dir. gen. taxation bur. Min. Fin., Tokyo, 1969-71, vice minister fin. internat. affairs, 1971-72, spl. advisor to Min. of Fin., 1972-74; advisor The Indsl. Bank of Japan, Tokyo, 1974-81; chmn. The Overseas Econ. Coop. Fund, Tokyo, 1981-87, NLI Rsch. Inst., Tokyo, 1988—; mem. Japan-Gt. Britain Commn., 1985—; Japanese mem. Japan-U.S.-Europe Trilateral Commn., 1978—. Decorated The Grand Cordon of the Order of the Sacred Treasure, Japanese Govt., 1992. Avocations: golf, swimming. Office: NLI Research Inst, 1-1-1 Yuraku-cho Chiyoda-ku, Tokyo 100-0006, Japan

HOSONO, TOSHIO, electronics educator; b. Tokyo, Mar. 31, 1922; s. Nobujirou and Eiko Hosono; m. Chisako Hosono, May 30, 1959; children: Shigeharu Hiroyuki, Hanayo Hirakawa. B in Engring., Nihon U., Tokyo, 1943; M in Engring., Tokyo U., 1946, D in Engring., 1957. Tutor Tokyo U., 1946-54; instr. Nihon U., 1954-56, asst. prof., 1956-61, prof., 1961-92, prof. emeritus, 1992—; vis. researcher U. Ill., Champaign-Urbana, 1961-62; vis. prof. Kwait U., 1982; advisor Honda Inst. Electronics, Inc., Tokyo, 1979-99. Author: Fundamentals of Electromagnetic Waves, 1973, Fast Inversion of Laplace Transform, 1984, Science of Entropy, 1991, Metaelectrodynamics, 1999, Fundamentals of Information Science, 1999; inventor helical coaxial cable. U. Tokyo fellow, 1945, 46; recipient 5-dan degree of Japanese Go Game award Nihon-Ki-In, 1997, Third Class Order award Sacred Treasure from the Emperor, 1998. Fellow IEEE (life, sr., sci. and tech. promoting prize Japan chpt. 1978), Inst. Electronics, Info. and Comm. Engrs. Japan; mem. Inst. Elec. Engrs. Japan (chmn. electromagnetics com. 1970-73), Electromagnetics Acad. Avocations: gardening, classical music, Go. E-mail: thosono@ele.cst.nihon.u.ac.jp. Home: Narashinodai 2-4-20, Funabashi 274-0063, Japan Office: Nihon U Coll & Tech, Kanda-Surugadai 1-8, Chiyodaku 101-0062, Japan

HOSOYA, NORIYASU, endodontist, educator; b. Yokohama, Kanagawa, Japan, June 26, 1956; s. Toranosuke and Sadako (Ueno) H.; m. Mutsumi Tamura, May 24, 1987; children: Kana, Meri. DMD, Tsurumi U., Yokohama, 1982, PhD, 1991. Instr. Tsurumi U., Yokohama, 1982—, asst. prof., 2000—; vis. prof. Northwestern U., Chgo., 1993-94. Contbr. articles to profl. jours. Mem. Am. Assn. Endodontists, Japanese Soc. Conservative Dentistry, Japan Endodontic Assn. Home: 16-7 Otomo Kanazawa, Yokohama Kanagawa 236-0024, Japan Office: Tsurumi U Sch Dental Med, 2-1-3 Tsurumi, Tsurumi-ku Yokohama 230-8501, Japan

HOSOYA, YASUO, management consultant; b. Kobe, Japan, Oct. 29, 1922; s. Teruzo and Kane (Kuwabuchi) H.; m. Misae Furukawa (div.); children: Sadako Takamatsu, Terufumi Hosoya; m. Ayako Mori, Jan. 5, 1956; children: Yasuaki Hosoya, Yoko Ara. Student, Kwansei Gakuin U., 1944-47. Tchr. langs. Riseisha H.S., Osaka, Japan, 1943-44; asst. sec. Kawanishi Machine Mfg. Co., Osaka, 1945; interpreter various units U.S. Army, Japan, 1946-56; mgmt. tng. dir. U.S. Army, Kanagawa, Japan, 1956-65; asst. to pers. mgr. Mitsubishi Oil Co. Ltd., Tokyo, 1965-72; advisor mgmt. devel. All Nippn Airways, Tokyo, 1965-72; pres., chief cons. Mgmt. Inst., Yokohama, Japan, 1965—; cons. ptnr. Japan Productivity Ctr., Tokyo, 1960-94. Author: Introduction to Management, 1960, 3d edit., 1990; contbg. author: Handbook of Management Education, 1968; editor, annotator, translator: Behavioral Science Concepts in Case Analysis, 1970, Systems Analysis-A Diagnostic Approach, 1976. With Japanese Army, 1944-45. Mem. Japan Acad. Orgnl. Scis.

HOSRI, FERNAND ANTOINE, corporate executive; b. Beirut, Lebanon, Jan. 20, 1942; s. Antoine C. and Matilde R. (Arrigoni) H.; m. Eugenie V. Saad, June 7, 1969; children: Joumana, Riccardo, Carine. Proficiency in Italian, Dante Alighieri Inst., Rome, 1959; French Baccalaureate, Coll. de La Salle, Beirut, 1961; Proficiency in English, Mich. U., 1963; BA Internat. Law, Am. U. of Beirut, 1967. Founder, mng. dir. Ets. F.A. Hosri, Beirut, 1966, Mobilier Confort, Beirut, 1971; co-founder, exec. dir. Sacotel Sarl, Beirut, 1978; founder, mng. dir. Jorica Traders (Overseas) Ltd., Limassol, Cyprus, 1990, Jorica Hoteliere (France), Agen, 1990; founder, gen. mgr., CEO Makas Est. for Safety Equipment, Jeddah, Saudi Arabia, 1992—; founder, managing dir., CEO IMFAH Real Estate Co., Beirut, Lebanon, 1997. Contbr. articles to profl. jours.; editor, co-author: (booklet) Lebanese Pound Crisis in Lebanon, 1986. Founder, pres. Phoenicia Sporting and

Cultural Club, Ghebaleh, Lebanon, 1964, Hosri Family Assn., Beirut, 1993, chmn. St. Nohra Charitable Trust Ghebaleh, Lebanon, 1994. Recipient medal and diploma of honor Terra Santa Mission, Jerusalem, 1959, Apostolic Benediction from Pope Paul VI, 1969, from Pope John Paul II, 1996, Golden Athena Internat. Econ. Performance Award, Athens, 1998. Mem. Beirut Businessmen's Assn., Lebanese Ins. Brokers Assn., Nat. Fire Protection Assn., Lebanese Political Assn., 1997, The Oxford Club, Lions (honour roll cert., 1983, Pres.'s plaque of appreciation 1984, medal of merit 1986, highest plaque of appreciation 199e, pres., dist. chmn. Beirut chpt. 1985-87), Internat. Grand Prix to Commercial Prestige Europe, Monaco, 1997. Avocations: car rallies, jogging, Bibliophile, classical music. Home: Pasteur St F Hosri Bldg, PO Box 11-565, Beirut Lebanon Office: Makas Establishment Safety Equipment, PO Box 8605, Jeddah 21492, Saudi Arabia

HOSSACK, IRENE ANN, writer, researcher; b. Melrose, Scotland, Oct. 6, 1958; d. Donald Brown and Mary (McDermott) H.; children: Jenny Ann, Katie Grace. Higher nat. diploma, The Queen's Coll., Glasgow, Scotland, 1979; BA, Deakin U., Geelong, Australia, 1990; MA, Monash U., Melbourne, 1993, PhD, 1998; MSc in Pub. Rels., U. Stirling, 1999. Tutor Glasgow U., 1995-96; vis. rsch. scholar U. Strathclyde, Glasgow, 1996-97; freelance writer, rschr. Crieff, Scotland, 1997—. Contbr. poems to profl. publs. Mem. MLA, Soc. Authors, Poetry Soc., British Comparative Lit. Assn., Australian & South Pacific Assn. Comparative Lit., Inst. Pub. Rels. Avocations: golf, cooking, music. Home: Hollybank Murrayfield Loan, Perthshr Crieff PH73EE, Scotland

HOSSAIN, AKM MOSHARROF, pharmacologist, medical educator; b. Lakshmipur, Bangladesh, June 25, 1958; s. Mohammed Wazi Ullah and Mobashera Begum; m. Nazma Ara, Nov. 4, 1989; 1 child, Shafayat Mosharrof Mutaki. B of Medicine, Sofia (Bulgaria) Med. Acad., 1984; PhD, Bulgarian Acad. Scis., Sofia, 1988; MD, Sofia Med. Acad., 1988. Rsch. physician Bulgarian Acad. Scis., 1988; sr. scientific officer Bangladesh Inst. Rsch. and Rehab. in Diabetes, Endocrine and Metabolic Disorders, Dhaka, Bangladesh, 1989-91; asst. prof. Sylhet (Bangladesh) Osmani Med. Coll., 1991-97, assoc. prof., 1997—. Prin. investigator inventions in field; co-editor: Introduction to Neuropharmacology, 1994; contbr. papers to confs., articles to profl. jours., chpt. to book. Recipient scholarship Bulgarian Ministry Edn., 1977-88. Mem. European Brain and Behaviour Soc., European Behavioural Pharmacology Soc. Moslem. Avocations: travel, reading, public service. Home: 48 Dilu Rd New Eskaton, Dhaka 1000, Bangladesh Office: Sylhet Osmani Med Coll, Dept Pharmacology, Sylhet 3100, Bangladesh

HOSSAIN, M. IQBAL, pediatrician; b. Sirajganj, Rajshahi, Bangladesh, Jan. 1, 1961; s. Elius Uddin and Mosammot Hamida (Begum) Talukder; m. Rehana Yasmin, Oct. 9, 1986; children: M. Rezoan, Ibnat Aniqa. Higher secondary sch. cert., Sirajganj Coll., 1979; MB, BChir, Rajshahi Med. Coll., Bangladesh, 1985; diploma in child health, Inst. Child Health, Bangladesh, 1990; postgrad., U. Calif., Davis, 2000. Intern Rajshahi Med. Coll. Hosp., Bangladesh, 1985-86; med. officer Sirajganj Children Hosp., Bangladesh, 1986-91, jr. cons., chief physician, 1991-93; med. officer Internat. Ctr. for Diarrhoeal-Diseases Rsch., Bangladesh, 1993-99, asst. scientist, 1999—. Contbr. articles to profl. jours. Joint sec. Chandpal Polli Chikitsa Kendro, Srirajganj, 1990—. Grantee Bangladesh Integrated Nutrition Project, 1998; Travel scholar Internat. Congress on Coop. Rsch. with Devel. Countries, Basel, Switzerland, 1999; Fogarty fellow U. Calif., Davis, 2000. Mem. Bangladesh Med. Assn., Bangladesh Pediat. Assn., Bangladesh Pvt. Med. Practitioner Assn. Islam. Avocations: reading, indoor games, music. Home: 949/3/C East Shewrapana, 1216 Dhaka Bangladesh Office: ICDDR B, Mohakhali, 1212 Dhaka Bangladesh Address: Apt II 14H 300 Solano Park Cir Davis CA 95616

HOSSAIN, M. MOZAFFOR, education educator; b. Joypurhat, Bangladesh, July 19, 1954; s. Osman Ali and Shabizan Begam Mondal; m. Jinat Rehana, Dec. 24, 1982; children: Mafruha Mowrin, Mashiat Mowsin. BSc with honors, U. Rajshahi, Bangladesh, 1974, MSc, 1975; PhD, Leningrad Poly. Inst., USSR, 1987. From lectr. to assoc. prof. Rajshahi U., 1979-94, prof., 1994—; vis. prof. U. Salahuddin, Iraq, 1989-90; provost Rajshahi U. Syeed Amir Ali Hall, 1994-97. Author: Electronics, 1997; co-author: (with Saidur Rahman Khan) Pulse and Switching Circuit, vol. I & II, 1994; contbr. articles to profl. jours. Gen. sec. Rajhahi U. Tchrs. Assn., 1998; exec. com. Bangladesh U. Tchrs. Fedn., 1998-99; sec. Rajshahi U. Club, 1994. Fellow N.Y. Acad. Sci.; mem. Bangladesh Phys. Soc. (life), Bangladesh Elect. Soc. (life), Univ. Housing Soc. Ltd. (chmn. 1990—). Avocations: reading, writing, gardening, travel, fishing. Office: Univ Rajshahi, Dept Applied Physics Electr, Rajshahi Bangladesh

HOSSAIN, MOHAMMAD MUJAFFAR, animal science educator, researcher; b. Comilla, Bangladesh, Jan. 20, 1955; s. Zinnot Ali Fakir and Khadeza Begum; m. Shajeda Akhter, July 1, 1983; children: Tamanna, Towfiah. BSc in Animal Husbandry, Bangladesh Agrl. U., 1978, MSc in Poultry Sci., 1979, MSc in Animal Sci., 1983; PhD, Reading (Eng.) U., 1993. Asst. instr. BARD, Bangladesh, 1982-83; lectr. Bangladesh Agrl. U., 1983-86, from asst. prof. to assoc. prof., 1986-99, prof., 1999—. Mng. editor Bangladesh Jour. Animal Sci.; contbr. articles to profl. jours. Commonwealth scholar, 1988. Mem. Bangladesh Animal Husbandry Assn. (joint sec. 1996-98), World Poultry Sci. Assn. Islamic. Avocation: meditation. Home: Luxmipur, Elliotgonj Bazar, Comilla Bangladesh Office: Bangladesh Agrl U, Dept Animal Sci, Mymensingh 2202, Bangladesh

HOSSAIN, MOHAMMAD SHAKHOWAT, computer programmer; b. Tangail, Bangladesh, Nov. 11, 1964; s. Mohammad Munsur Rahman and Tambia Akhtar Begum; m. Umma Sufia Salma Hossain, Oct. 16, 1992; children: Shakip, Shamit. BS in Physics with honors, Chittagong U., Bangladesh, 1985, MS in Physics, 1986. Computer programmer and instr. RCRS, Dhaka, Bangladesh, 1989-90, Elite Trading Ltd., Dhaka, 1990, MSI, Dhaka, 1990-92; lectr. computer dept. Sayed Abul Hossain Coll., Bangladesh, 1992; data mgmt. asst. BRAC, Dhaka, 1992-93; computer programmer Ministry of Def., Kuwait, 1993-98, Nahar Mansion, Dhaka, Bangladesh, 1997-99; dir. sales and computer divsn. D.M. Corp., Dhaka, 1998—, AiPath Bangladesh Ltd., Dhaka, 2000—; software cons., Minhaz Group, Dhaka, 1991-92. Author: (manuals) Wordstar Manual, 1990, Lotus 123 Manual, 1990, DBase III Plus Manual, 1990, Wordperfect 5.1, 1990. Student leader Chittagong U., 1982. With Bangladesh Army, 1992-93. Mem. IEEE Computer Soc., Bangladesh Computer Soc. Avocations: travel, reading sci. jours., software devel. and collection, nature. Home: c/o Engr Forhad Ali, 26 Nabab Katara 1st Flr Ea, Dhaka 1000, Bangladesh Office: AiPath Bangladesh Ltd, 69/L Panthapath, Dhaka 1205, Bangladesh

HOSSAIN, MOHAMMED MUSHARAF, business management educator; b. Comilla, Bangladesh, Feb. 1, 1946; s. Mohammed Amir and Maksuda Khatun (Masu) H.; m. Begum Syeda Delware, Dec. 3, 1970; children: Ferdousi, Mahmuda, Khadeza, Tareque. B in Commerce, Victoria Coll., 1966; M in Commerce, Dhaka U., 1972, PhD, 1989; grad. in coop. edn. and mgmt., U. Wis., 1984. Lectr. Hajigonj Degree Coll., Chandpur, Bangladesh, 1974-75; prin. Nasirkote Coll., Chandpur, 1975-77; lectr. Govt. Coll., Bangladesh, 1977-90; chmn. dept. mgmt. Islamic U., Kushtia, Bangladesh, 1990-96, dean faculty bus. adminstrn., 1997-99; warden Islamic U. Hall, Kushtia, 1990-91, provost, 1991-92. Author: Management Theory and Practice, 1983. Office: Islamic U, Kushtia Bangladesh

HOSSAIN, MOHAMMED ZAKER, lawyer; b. Murshidabad, India, Apr. 30, 1940; arrived in Bangladesh, 1963; s. Shaikh Jamiruddin and Rabia Begum; m. Hosne Ara Daud, June 12, 1964; children: Ashraf Hossain Siddiky, Sajjad Hossain Siddiky, Masud Rana Siddiky, Sadia Afreen. BA with honors, Calcutta U., 1963; MA in Philosophy, Dhaka (Bangladesh U.), 1966, LLB, 1967; postgrad., Calif. U., 1990. Coun. appelate divsn. Supreme Ct., Bangladesh, 1972—. Contbr. article to profl. jour. Pres. City Corp. Tax Rev. Bd., Dhaka, Bangladesh, 1983-85; patron Child's Hosp., Dhaka, 1978—; trustee Anjuman M. Islam, Dhaka, 1979—. Fellow Ctr. Legal Studies (Austria); mem. Environ. Def. Assn. (pres. 1992—), Internat. Bar Assn., State Bar Calif., Law Asia, Asia-Pacific Forum, Red Cross Soc. (life), Dechara Club (sec. relief distbn.), Stratford Gala Club. Address: 27, Gandaria Keshab Banerjee Rd, Dhaka Bangladesh

HOSSFELD, CHRISTOPHER, financial educator, researcher; b. Saarbrücken, Germany, Oct. 29, 1965; s. Ekkehard Hossfeld and Anna-Luise (Weber) Hossfeld-Umlauf; m. Danielle Loinard, July 11, 1992. BS, Willi-Graf Gymnasium, Saarbrücken, 1984; MBA, U. Saarland, Saarbrücken, 1990, PhD in Bus. Adminstrn., 1995. Asst., chair banking and fin. U. Saarland, 1989-97; freelance collaborator Coopers & Lybrand, Saarbrücken, 1990—; lectr. Acad. for Advanced Edn. of Bank Employees, Kaiserlautern and Saarbrücken, 1990-97, Acad. for Advanced Edn. of Employees, Idar-Oberstein, Germany, 1993-95, Profl. Sch. for Tech. Sci. and Bus. Adminstrn., Saarbrücken, 1994-95, U. Paris 3. Author: Comparison of Financial Statements of German and French Banks, 1996; contbr. articles to profl. jours. Home: 7 Allee de L'Oseraie, 78630 Orgeval France Office: U Saarland Lehrstuhl Bankbetriebslehre, Nouvelle 94 Ave Gresillons, 92600 Asnieres France

HØSTAKER, ROAR, political science educator; b. Dale, Norway, Sept. 17, 1962; s. Torfinn and Gudveig (Nesse) H.; divorced; children: Aslak, Mira. Cand. Polit., U. Bergen, Norway, 1992, Dr.Polit., 1997. Rsch. assoc. Los-Ctr. Norwegian Ctr. for Study of Mgnt. and Orgn., Bergen, 1992-96, rschr., 1996-98; assoc. prof. polit. sci. Lillehammer (Norway) Coll., 1998—. Co-author: Policy and Practice in Higher Education: Reforming Norwegian Universities, 2000. Office: Lillehammer Coll, Storhove, 2626 Lillehammer Norway

HØSTGAARD-JENSEN, PETER, power station executive; b. Balling, Denmark, June 30, 1945; s. Johan Magnus and Astrid Gudrun Høstgaard (Møller) Jensen; m. Helle Kjaer, Jan. 24, 1970; children: Jesper, Per, Kirsten. MSChemE, Tech. U. Denmark, Copenhagen, 1970. Chem. engr. Carlsberg Breweries, Copenhagen, 1971, Faelleskemikerne I/S Nordkraft, Aalborg, Denmark, 1971-83; prodn. mgr. I/S NEFO, Vodskov, Denmark, 1983-90; CEO, I/S Nordkraft, Aalborg, 1990-94, I/S Nordjyllandsvaerket, Vodskov, 1995-99, NV Kraft A/S, 1999-2000, Elsam A/S, 2000—; chmn. Environ. Com. of the Danish Power Stas., 1985-89; mem. rsch. com. Danish Ministry of Energy, 1988-94. Sgt. Danish Armed Forces, 1970-71. Mem. Internat. Union Producers and Distbrs. of Elec. Energy (mem. environ. com. 1991—). Office: Elsam A/S Overgade 45, 7000 Fredericia Denmark

HOSTLER, CHARLES WARREN, former ambassador, international affairs consultant; b. Chgo., Dec. 12, 1919; s. Sidney Marvin and Catherine (Marshall) H.; 1 son, Charles Warren, Jr. B.A., U. Calif. at Los Angeles, 1942; M.A., Am. U., Beirut, Lebanon, 1955, Georgetown U., 1950; Ph.D., Georgetown U., 1956. Commd. 2d lt. U.S. Air Force, 1942, advanced through grades to col., 1955; ret., 1963; dir. internat. ops. McDonnell Douglas Corp., Middle East, N.Africa, Beirut, 1965-67; mgr. internat. ops. McDonnell Douglas Corp., Paris, 1963-65; mgr. internat. mktg., missiles and space McDonnell Douglas Corp., 1967-69; pres. Hostler Investment Co., Newport Beach, Calif., 1969-74; chmn. bd. Irvine (Calif.) Nat. Bank, 1972-74; dir. Wynn's Internat., Inc., Fullerton, Calif., 1971-74; dep. asst. sec. for internat. commerce, dir. Bur. Internat. Commerce, U.S. Dept. Commerce, Washington, 1974-76; regional v.p. Mid-East and Africa, E-Systems Inc., Cairo, Egypt, 1976-77; pres. Pacific SW Capital Corp., San Diego, 1977-89; ambassador U.S. Govt., Bahrain, 1989-93; hon. consul gen. State of Bahrain, 1993—; adj. prof. Sch. Internat. Svc., Am. U., Washington, 1955-63, adj. prof. political sci., San Diego State U., 1999—; pres. San Diego Consular Corps. Author: Turkism and the Soviets, 1957, The Turks of Central Asia, 1993; contbr. articles to econ., comml. and mil. jours. Chmn. Calif. Contractors State Lic. Bd., 1973-79, San Diego County Local Agy. Formation Commn., 1979-89; chmn. Calif. State Park and Recreation Commn., 1983-89; pres. San Diego Consular Corps, 1996-98; vice-chmn., bd. dirs. People-to-People Internat. Decorated Legion of Merit; recipient Fgn. Affairs award for pub. svc. U.S. State Dept. Mem. Middle East Inst. (bd. govs. 1962-80, 93—), VFW, Ret. Officers Assn., Coun. Am. Ambs., Vets. Office Strategic Svcs. Office: 1101 First St # 302 Coronado CA 92118-1474

HOTALING, BROCK ELLIOT, software development leader; b. Libertyville, Ill., Dec. 5, 1947; s. Robert Bachman and Janet Marion (Kelley) H.; m. Elizabeth Quadi Darbeh, Dec. 31, 1976 (div. Aug. 1985); children: Kesely, Michael, Robert. BSc, Mich. State U., 1969. High sch. tchr. Tubman H.S., Monrovia, Liberia, West Africa, 1970-72; sys. mgr. J.F. Kennedy Med. Ctr., Monrovia, Liberia, West Africa, 1973-75; sys. mgr., acct. Lone Star Shipping Lines, Monrovia, Liberia, West Africa, 1975-77; data processing mgr. Firestone/U.S. Trading Co., Monrovia, Liberia, 1977-80; software engr. Wang Labs., Lowell, Mass., 1980-85, mgr. R&D, 1985-91; dir. software engring. Marcam Corp., Newton, Mass., 1991-93, dir. applied tech., 1994—; software arch. PSW Technologies, N.Y.C., 1995-96; pres. InterNova Corp., Westport, Conn., 1996—. Patentee networked time mgmt. device. Organizer, coach Nat. Up-Country Basketball Tourney, Gbarnga, Liberia, 1970-71; capt., organizer, player, dir. Liberian Nat. Duplicate Bridge Assn., Monrovia, 1974-80; coach Youth Soccer Assn., Lowell, 1985-88. Named Nat. Pairs Champion, Liberian Duplicate Bridge Assn., 1976, 78. Avocations: modeling human behavior patterns, duplicate bridge, sports, parenting, reading. Home: 278 Saugatuck Ave Westport CT 06880-6431 Office: Inter Nova Corp 15 Franklin St Westport CT 06880-5903

HOTOKKA, MATTI, chemist, educator; b. Poytya, Finland, May 26, 1950; s. Martti and Aili (Viertokangas) H.; m. Terhi Salmio, Oct. 20, 1973. MSc, U. Turku, 1975; PhD, Abo Acad. U., 1982. Rschr. Finnish Acad. Scis., Turku, 1975-86; prof. Abo Acad. U., Turku, 1986—. Mem. Am. Chem. Soc. Home: Sirkkalenkatu 34 R 26, F-20700 Turku Finland Office: Abo Acad U, Dept Chemistry, F-20500 Abo Finland

HO TRIEU, LUAN NGOC, energy economist, researcher; b. Saigon, Vietnam, June 20, 1952; s. Gia Van Ho and Tong Thanh Trieu; m. Anne Elizabeth Allsop, May 6, 1978 (dec. 1988); m. Dao Thi Xuan Nguyen, Oct. 5, 1990; 1 child, Hung Nam. BEcons., U. Western Australia, Perth, 1975, BA in Math., 1979; Grad. Diploma in Econometrics and Stats., Australian Nat. U., Canberra, 1985, Grad. Diploma in Econs., 1991, M Econs. of Devel., 1994. Rsch. officer Dept. Productivity, Canberra, 1979-81; sr. rsch. officer Dept. Employment, Edn. and Tng., Canberra, 1981-86; prin. rsch. officer Australian Bur. Agr. and Resource Econs., Canberra, 1986—. Author: A Model of the World Uranium Market, 1992, Energy Efficience Trends in Australia, 1993, Australian Energy Consumption and Production, 1993, 95, Elasticity of Energy Demand in Australia, 1996, Net Economic Benefits of the Oil Industry in Australia, 1996; contbr. articles to profl. jours. Mem. AAAS, Australia and New Zealand Econ. Soc., Australian Agrl. and Resource Econs. Soc., Vietnamese Profls. Soc. (sec. Canberra chpt. 1991-96). Achievements include designing the first economic model of the world uranium market, the first model to decompose energy efficiency trends in Australia, the first model to decompose CO2 emission by economic activities in Australia.

HOTTA, HAK, microbiology educator; b. Ibaraki, Osaka, Japan, Oct. 21, 1949; s. Susumu and Toshiko (Oh-hata) H.; m. Tomoko Tsukiji, May 18, 1974; children: Ken, Gou, Makiko. MD, Osaka U., 1974; Dr. Med. Sci., Kobe (Japan) U., 1985. Physician Osaka U. Hosp., 1974-75, Prefectural Nishinomiya (Japan) Hosp., 1975-77; rsch. assoc. Kobe U. Sch. Medicine, 1977-87, asst. prof., 1987-88, assoc. prof., 1988-94, prof., 1994—. Author: Viral Hepatitis and Liver Disease, 1994; contbr. articles to profl. jours. Mem. AAAS, Am. Soc. Microbiology, Soc. Japanese Virologists, Japanese Soc. for Immunology, Japanese Soc. for Bacteriology, Japanese Cancer Assn., Japanese Soc. for Investigative Dermatology. Home: 2-2-12 Makami-cho, Osaka Takatsuki 569-1121, Japan Office: Kobe Univ Sch Medicine, 7-5-1 Kusunoki-cho Chuo-ku, Kobe Hyogo 650-0017, Japan

HOTTA, MASASHI, electronics engineer and educator; b. Niihama, Ehime, Japan, Aug. 19, 1965; s. Kazumasa and Katsuko (Kamada) H. B.Engring., Ehime U., 1988, M.Engring., 1990; D.Engring., Osaka Prefecture U., 1995. Cert. electromagnetic theory/opto-electronics engr. Asst. prof. elec. and electronic engring. Ehime U., Matsuyama, 1990-99; lectr. elec. and electronic engring. Yamaguchi U., Ube, 1999—; vis. scholar in elec. engring. UCLA, 1997-98. Contbr. articles to profl. jours. Mem. IEEE, AAAS, Optical Soc. Am., Inst. Electronics, Info. and Comm. Engrs. JP, Internat. Soc. Optical Engring., Planetary Soc. Office: Yamaguchi U E & E Eng Dept, 2-16-1 Tokiwadai, Ube 755-8611, Japan

HOTTA, MASATO, dental educator; b. Unomachi, Ehime, Japan, Jan. 18, 1954; s. Shigeo and Miyoko (Yamaguchi) H.; m. Mayumi Takada, May 12, 1985; 1 child, Akiyuki. DDS, Gifu Dental Coll., 1982; PhD of Dental Sci., Asahi U., 1988. Instr. Gifu Dental Coll., Hozumi, Japan, 1982-85; instr. Asahi Univ., Hozumi, 1985-90, asst. prof., 1990—; vis. scientist Baylor Coll. Dentistry, 1995-96. Author: New Functionality Materials, 1993; contbr. articles to profl. jours. Grantee Japanese Ministry Edn., 1993, 94, 95. Mem. AAAS, Internat. Assn. Dental Rsch., Internat. Acad. Periodontology (cert. of achievement 1995), Japanese Soc. Conservative Dentistry (dir. 1991—), Japan Acad. Color for Dentistry (cons. 1995-98, dir. 1999—), Japanese Soc. Dental Materials and Devices. Avocations: golf, tennis, baseball. Home: 566-9 Kamijuku, Sunomata-cho 503-0103, Japan Office: Asahi Univ Sch Dentistry, 1851 Hozumi, Hozumi-cho 501-0296, Japan

HOTTENROTH, DAWN CATHLEEN, city official; b. San Diego, Aug. 20, 1966; d. Jerry Lloyd and Claudia Louise Hildreth; m. Daniel Hottenroth, Feb. 20, 1994. BS in Environ. Health, San Diego State U., 1988; postgrad., Portland State U., 1990-91. Cert. environ. health specialist, Calif.; cert. sanitarian, Oreg.; CPESC. Environ. health specialist San Diego County, 1988-90; sanitarian Multnomah County, Portland, Oreg., 1990-92; environ. specialist City of Portland, 1992—. Active Girl Scouts U.S. Recipient Girl Scout Gold award Imperial County Coun., San Diego, 1984. Mem. City of Portland Profl. Employees Assn. (pres. 1997—, rep. 1993-97), Internat. Erosion Control Assn. Democrat. Avocations: hiking, reading, crafts. Office: City of Portland Bur of Environ 1120 SW 5th Ave Rm 1000 Portland OR 97204-1912

HOU, CHUN-KAN, materials scientist; b. Yunlin, Taiwan, Sept. 19, 1951; s. Sun-Yuan and Chi-yi (Lee) H.; m. Yueh-Hua Cheng, Jan. 14, 1979; children: Tzu-Hui, Ju-Lin. BS, Chung Yuan Christian U., Taiwan, 1974; MS, Nat. Tsing Hua U., Taiwan, 1976, PhD, 1990; postgrad., Ill. Inst. Tech., Chgo., 1981-83. Engr. Govt. Arsenal, Kaohsiung, Taiwan, 1977-78; rsch. scientist China Steel Corp., Kaohsiung, 1978-92; assoc. prof. Nat. Yunlin Inst. Tech., 1992-95, chmn. mech. engring. dept., 1994-96, prof., dean technol. coop., 1996-97, dean acad. affairs, 1997—; cons. China Steel Corp., Kaohsiung, 1992-94, Gloria Heavy Indsl. Corp., Tainan, 1993-96. Contbr. articles to profl. jours. Recipient Nat. Disting. Applied Scientist award Taiwan Govt., 1989, Nat. Disting. Rsch. award, 1990. Avocations: reading, table tennis, mountain climbing. Office: Nat Yunlin U of Sci & Tech, 123 University Rd Sec 3, Touliu 640, Taiwan

HOU, HO-SHONG, transportation engineer; b. Chia-Yi, China, Apr. 3, 1944; s. Charng-Lih and Yu-Chieu (Lee) H.; m. Pai-Ho Chen; children: Su-I, Cheng-Yi, Peng-Hsi, Peng-Huei. B, Nat. Cheng King U., Tainan, Taiwan, 1967, MSCE, 1969; PhD, U. Fla., 1976. Chief Taichung Harbor Hydraulic Lab., Muchi, Taiwan, 1969-73; grad. asst., assoc. U. Fla., Gainesville, 1973-76; dir. Taichung Harbor Lab., Wachi, Taiwan, 1976-78, Grad. Inst. Harbor & Ocean Engring., Keelung, Taiwan, 1978-81; deputy dir. Inst. Harbor & Marine, Wuchi, Taiwan, 1981-85; dir. engring. divsn. Inst. Transp., Taipei, China, 1985-96, dep. dir. gen., 1996-97; dir. gen. dept. rail, hwy. and tourism Ministry of Transp. and Comm., Taipei, 1998-99; dep. mayor Kaohsiung City Govt., China, 1999—; prof. air transport adminstrn. Inst. Aeronautics and Astronautics, Nat. Cheng Kung U., Tainan, 1996—; vice chmn. Ocean Engring. Rsch. Com., Taipei, 1980-94, Internat. Rel. Coun., Chinese Underwater Tech. Assn., 1990-94; exec. sec. organizing com. 20th Internat. Conf. Coastal Engring, Taipei, 1986; del. Chinese Taipei APE TPT WG Port Expert Group, 1996—. Contbr. articles to profl. jours. Fellow CICHE; mem. ASCE, Chinese Port & Harbor Assn. (exec.dir. 1988-96), Chinese Oceanic Sci. & Tech. Assn. (exec. dir. 1986-96), Assn. Hydraulic Engring. (pres. 1966), Chinese Oceanic Engring. Assn. (exec. dir. 1998—). Achievements include research on new design and notable findings for metal investigation, on harbor and coastal engineering. E-mail: hs hou@keg.gov.tw. Home: PO Box 47-89, Taichung 40089, Taiwan Office: No 2 Su-Wei 3d Rd, Kaohsiung Taiwan China

HOU, JIAN-CUN, medical educator; b. Hwai-yuan, An-hwei, China, June 16, 1923; s. Pao-Chang Hou and Wen-Ying Liao; m. Dong-Sen Liu, Dec. 24, 1952; two children. BS in Chemistry, Nanking U., Chengtu, China, 1946; postgrad., West China Union U., Chengtu, 1946; MB, BChir, MD, Hong Kong U., 1951; PhD in Pathology, London U., 1960. Demonstrator physiology and biochemistry Hong Kong U., 1951-52, jr. lectr. pathology, 1956-57; rsch. assoc. Chinese Acad. Med. Scis., Beijing, 1953-56; univ. demonstrator pathology London U., 1958-60; postdoctoral rschr. Karolinska Inst. Cell Rsch., Stockholm; sr. lectr. Chinese U. Coll. Medicine, Beijing, 196-77; prof. assoc. Peking Union Med. Coll., Chinese Acad. Med. Sci., Beijing, 1978-85, prof., 1985—; dep. dir. WHO Collaborating Ctr. for Rsch. in Immunology, Chinese Acad. Med. Scis., Beijing, 1978-90; rsch. fellow Inst. Basic Med. Sci., Chinese Acad. Med. Scis., Beijing, 1985—. Author: Theory and Practice of Immunofluorescent Technique, 1978, Cellular and Molecular Basis of Immunopathology, 1984, Newer Concept in the Mechanism of Complement mediated Inflammatory Tissue Injury and the Modulation of the Inflammatory Response, 1998. Mem. nat. com. Chinese People's Polit. Consultative Conf., 1988-98. Graham scholar Univ. Coll. Hosp. Med. Sch., London U., 1958-60. Mem. China Assn. Social Econ. Cultural Exchange (v.p. 1993—), N.Y. Acad. Scis. Avocations: photography, antique studies, traveling. Home: 31 Da Shui Che Hutung, Beijing 100034, China Office: Inst Basic Med Sci CAMS, Dongdan Santiao, Beijing 100005, China

HOU, TUNG-HSU, industrial engineering educator, researcher; b. Chai-Yi, Taiwan, June 17, 1959; s. Huo-Yen Hou and Chin-Ying Lin; m. Mei-Hsiang Chiu, Jan. 17, 1987; 1 child, Justin Tony. BS, Nat. Chiao-Tung U., Hsin-Chu, Taiwan, 1982, MBA, 1984; MS, SUNY, Buffalo, 1990, PhD, 1992. Chief prodn. control sect. Yeh-Long Co., Kaohsiung, Taiwan, 1986-87; software engr. Chinese Petroleum Co., Kaohsiung, 1987-88; tchg. asst. SUNY, 1990-92; assoc. prof. indsl. engring. Nat. Yunlin U. Sci. and Tech., Touliu, Taiwan, 1992—, chief R & D, 1997—; cons. Dah San Elec. Cable Co., Touliu, 1996-97, Chong Cheng Bridge Works Co., Yunlin, Taiwan, 1997-98, Provincial Nan-Tou (Taiwan) Hosp., 1997—, Provincial Po-Tzu (Taiwan) Hosp., 1997—. Contbr. articles to sci. jours., including Internat. Jour. Prodn. Rsch., Internat. Jour. Human Factors in Mfg., Internat. Jour. Pattern Recognition and Artifical Intelligence, Internat. Jour. Advanced Mfg. Tech., also chpt. to book. Recipient A grade rsch. award Nat. Sci. Coun., Taipei, Taiwan, 1995=98; scholar Soc. Mfg. Engrs., Buffalo, 1992. Mem. Human Factors and Ergonomic Soc., Chinese Indsl. Engrs. Soc., Ergonomics Soc. Taiwan. Avocations: reading, music, meditation. Office: Nat Yunlin U Sci and Tech, 123 University Rd Sec 3, Touliu 640, Taiwan

HOU, ZONE YUAN, cardiologist, clinical pharmacologist; b. Chia-Yi, Taiwan, Sept. 6, 1953; s. Shen and Liao-Chao Hou; m. Mei-Hui Mar. 14, 1982; two children. MD, Taipei Med Coll., 1979. From resident to attending physician Vet. Gen. Hosp., Taipei, 1981-95; chief God's Help Hosp., Chia-Yi, 1995-96, vice supt. for med. svc., 1996-99; cardiologist Schmidt Group Practice Clinic, Kaohsiung, Taiwan, 1999—; assoc. prof. Nat. Yang-Ming U. Sch. Medicine, 1993—. Merck Co. Found. Internat. Clin. Pharmacology fellow, 1989-91, Dept. Pharmacology, Georgetown U. Med. Ctr. Rsch. fellow, 1988-90. Fellow European Heart Assn., Am. Coll. Cardiology; mem. Am. Heart Assn., Am. Soc. Clin. Pharmacology & Therapeutics. Avocations: tennis, music, jogging. Home: 13 Fl 79 Woh Long Rd, 807 Kaohsiung Taiwan

HOUBRECHTS, STEPHAN, research scientist; b. Genk, Limburg, Belgium, Feb. 10, 1971; s. Werner Houbrechts and Ilona Borocz; m. Kristel De Beuckeleer. Lic. Chemistry, Cath. U. Leuven, Belgium, 1993, DSc, 1998. Rsch. asst. Fund for Sci. Rsch. Flanders, Leuven, 1994-98; jr. rschr. Deutsche Forschungsgemeinschaft, Hamburg, Germany, 1996-97; frontier rschr. Inst. for Phys. and Chem. Rsch., Wako-shi, Saitama, Japan, 1998-99; sr. rschr. F.W.O.-Flanders, Leuven, 1998—; conf. sec. Franqui-Workshop on Plastic Electronics and Photonicson, Bruges, Belgium, 1999; HRS advisor Tohoku U., Sendai, Japan, 1997. Contbr. articles to profl. jours. Avocations: traveling, soccer, snooker. Fax: 32 0 16 327982. E-mail: stephan.houbrechts@fys.kuleuven.ac.be. Office: Cath U Leuven, Celestijnenlaan 200D, 3001 Leuven Belgium

HOUCK, JOHN DUDLEY, investment adviser, educator; b. Detroit, May 5, 1939; s. Horace Alonzo and Mae Edward (Snyder) H.; m. Carol Kay Houck, July 13, 1958; children: Sallie Mae Williams, Cheryl Ann Richard, Jonathan Matthew, Rebecca Cyrene Myers, James Timothy. AA, L.A. Valley Coll., 1964; BS in Bus. Econs., Pacific Western U., 1982; MS in

Mgmt., Am. Coll. for Fin. Scis., 1994; MA in History, Gulf So. U., 1993. Pres., CFO Western Pacific Fin. Svcs., Inc., L.A., 1976—; adj. prof., U. Phoenix, Webster U., and Antelope Valley Coll. Mem. LDS Ch. Avocations: golf, fishing, history. Office: Western Pacific Fin Svcs Inc 1036 E Avenue J # 212 Lancaster CA 93535-3840

HOUE, HANS, veterinarian, research center administrator; b. Humlum, Struer, Denmark, June 21, 1961; s. Laurids and Lis (Sørensen) H. DVM, Royal Vet. and Agrl. U., Copenhagen, 1986, PhD, 1991, DVSc, 1996. Pvt. practice, Struer, 1986-88; asst. prof. Royal Vet. and Agrl. U., 1991-95, assoc. prof., 1995-97; dir. Rsch. Ctr. for Mgmt. Animal Prodn., Danish Inst. Agrl. Scis., Tjele, Denmark, 1997—; vis. scientist Mich. State U., East Lansing, 1993-94. Co-editor: The Veterinary Clinics of North America, 1995. Grantee C.O. Jensen Meml. Found., 1993, Aage and Edith Dyssegaards Found., 1993, Ellen and Hans Hermers Found., 1995. Mem. Danish Vet. Assn., Danish Boologic Soc. (bd. dirs. 1997—). Avocations: tennis, philosophy, buildings. Home: Thagaardvej 14, 7600 Struer Denmark Office: Rsch Ctr Mgmt Animal Prodn, and Health, PO Box 50, 8800 Tjele Denmark

HOUEL, ALAIN, training company executive; b. Rabat, Morocco, Apr. 11, 1946; s. Guy and Nicole (Ducousso) H.; m. Brigitte Moreau, Feb. 4, 1986; children: Simon, Florent. MA in Sociology, Sorbonne U., 1970. Dir. Nat. Open Univ., Caracas, Venezuela, 1979-82; cons. Fid, Bogotá, Colombia, 1982-84; tng. mgr. Matra, Paris, 1984-85; cons. Paris, 1986-91; pres. PEP-Formation, Paris, 1991-94; assoc. Demerara Cons. Systems, Amsterdam, The Netherlands, 1994-97; pres. Formateurs & Cons. Assocs., Paris, 1997—. Author: Devil's Road, 1995, How to Cope with Difficult People, 1994; inventor in field. Mem. Future's Memory Assn. (pres. 1995). Home: 23 Rue Lecourbe, 75015 Paris France Office: Demerara Cons Systems, 204 rue de Vaugirard, 75015 Paris France

HOUENIPWELA, RICK, banker. Gov. Ctrl. Bank of Solomon Islands, 1996—. Office: Ctrl Bank of Solomon Islands, PO Box 634, Honiara Solomon Islands*

HOUGH, JACK VAN DOREN, otologist; b. Lone Wolf, Okla., Sept. 12, 1920; s. Chapman Ernest and Hazel (Van Doren) H.; m. Joan Ingle, Dec. 29, 1943; children: Ted Chapman, Jack Van Doren Jr., Timothy Ingle, David Alliston. BS, Southeastern State U., 1939; MD, U. Okla., 1943. Diplomate Am. Bd. Otorhinolaryngology. Intern USN Hosp., Farragut, Idaho, 1944; resident, then fellow in otolaryngology U. Okla. Hosps., Oklahoma City, 1946-50; clin. instr. otorhinolaryngology U. Okla. Health Scis. Ctr., Oklahoma City, 1950-51; now clin. prof. otorhinolaryngology, head and neck surgery U. Okla. Health Scis. Ctr.; pvt. practice Oklahoma City, 1951—; bd. dirs. MAP Internat., Inc.; developer surg. techniques and instruments for hearing restoration and middle ear reconstrn., electromagnetic hearing devices, cochlear implants. Contbr. sci. articles and textbook chpts. to med. publs. Past ruling elder, Cen. Presbyn. Ch., Oklahoma City; founder, Covenant Community Ch. Oklahoma City, 1980, now session moderator. Decorated Bronze Star, recipient Presdl. Unit citation, Navy Dept. citation for heroism; recipient Harris P. Mosher award Triologic Soc., numerous awards from profl. orgns.; inducted into Okla. Hall of Fame, 1991. Mem. AMA, Am. Bd. Otolaryngology, Am. Acad. Otolaryngology-Head and Neck Surgery, Am. Otological Soc. (past pres., award of merit), Head and Neck Surgery of Am., Am. Triological Soc., Oklahoma County Med. Assn., Okla. Med. Assn., Okla. Acad. Medicine, Osler Soc., Am. Acad. Ophthalmologic and Otolaryngologic Allergy, Christian Med. Soc., Christian Soc. Otolaryngology-Head and Neck Surgeons (founder, past pres.), MAP Internat. (founder), Otosclerosis Study Group (past pres.), Audiology Soc., Von Bekesy Soc. (past pres.), Pan-Am. Assn. Otorhinolaryngology and Bronchoesophagology, Politzer Soc., Am. Sci. Affiliation, numerous other profl. orgns. Home: 9117 SW 22nd St Oklahoma City OK 73128-4918 Office: Hough Ear Inst 3400 NW 56th St Oklahoma City OK 73112-4404

HOUGH, JANET GERDA CAMPBELL, research scientist; b. Glen Ridge, N.J., Dec. 22, 1948; d. Ralph William and Gerda Lydia (Baarck) Campbell; m. John Harrison Hough, Oct. 1, 1966 (div.); 1 child, Laura Leigh. Student Temple U. and Tyler Sch. Art, Phila., 1970-72, Pa. Acad. Fine Arts, 1972, Camden County Coll., Blackwood, N.J., 1973-75; B.S., Thomas Jefferson U., 1977. Lab. animal technician Inst. Med. Rsch., Camden, N.J., 1972-75; rsch. technician dept. biochemistry Thomas Jefferson U., Phila., 1976, phlebotomist, hematology technician, 1976-78, med. technologist spl. hematology, 1978-79, rsch. technician dept. med. genetics, 1979-80; with micromedic systems Rohm & Haas, Horsham, Pa., 1981-85; micromedic Internat. Clin. Nuclear Inc., Costa Mesa, Calif., and Horsham, 1985-91. Collaborator, editor textbook Hematology for Medical Technologists, 1983; poet, illustrator Thought Progressions, 1984. Charter mem. Nat. Rep. Presdl. Task Force, 1984—, Nat. Rep. Senatorial Com., 1984—, Rep. Presdl. Citizen's Adv. Commn., 1989-91, Nat. Rep. Congl. Com., 1992—. Mem. Internat. Soc. Poets, Am. Poetry Assn. (pub. anthologies 1986-90), Nat. Libr. Poetry (pub. anthology 1992). Roman Catholic. Avocations: drawing, painting, long-distance walking.

HOUGH, LAWRENCE A., former financial organization executive. In engring., Stanford U.; grad., Sloan Sch. of Mgmt., MIT. Fin. analyst Stanford U.; with Student Loan Mktg. Assn., Washington, D.C., 1973-77, 79-96, exec. v.p., mktg. svcs. and systems, pres., chief exec. officer, 1990-96; pres., CEO Albert Lord, 1996—; CEO, co-chmn. Sato Travel, Washington, 1999—. Chmn. bd. Shakespeare Theater, Washington. Address: Shakespeare Theatre 516 8th St SE Washington DC 20003-2834 Office: Sato Travel 1005 N Glebe Rd Ste 300 Arlington VA 22201-5713

HOUGH, MELISSA ELLEN, curator, museum director; b. Phila., July 24, 1951; d. William Howard Hough and Charlotte Dolores DeHaven. BA, Beaver Coll., 1973; MA, U. Pa., 1980. Asst. curator INA Corp. Mus., Phila., 1980-82; curator CIGNA Mus. and Art Collection, Phila., 1982-84, chief curator, mgr., 1984—. Editor: The Centennial Book, 1975; author (exhbn. catalogues) CIGNA Mus. Exhbn. Catalogues, 1981-91; curator, author (exhibit and catalogue) Ships and the Sea, 1988. Mem. Am. Assn. Mus., Nat. Assn. Corp. Art Mgrs. (adv. bd. 1990-97), Mus. Coun. Greater Delaware Valley (program chair 1987-91), Fireman's Hall Mus. (exec. bd. mem., v.p. 1994-99), Slate Belt Heritage Ctr. (collection com. chair 1999—). E-mail: melissa.hough@cigna.com. Office: CIGNA Mus and Art Collection TL07E 1601 Chestnut St Philadelphia PA 19192-0003

HOUGH, ROBERT ALAN, civil engineer; b. East Orange, N.J., Aug. 6, 1959; s. Robert Elmer and Margaret (Dean) H. AB in Civil Engring., Lafayette Coll., 1981; MBA in Mgmt., Fairleigh Dickinson U., 1995. Registered profl. engr., N.J. Project mgr. water/wastewater engring. dept. Van Note-Harvey Assocs., Princeton, 1981—, head dept., 1994—; twp. engr. Twp. of Woolwich, Gloucester County, N.J., 1993—. Class rep. Pingry Sch. Alumni Assn., 1977—, bd. dirs., 1981—; bd. dirs., pony league dir., mgr., coach Springfield Jr. Baseball League, Inc., 1985—, pres., 1989-90; mem. bd. Union County Regional H.S. Dist. No. 1, 1997, Springfield Twp. Planning Bd., 2000—. Mem. NSPE, ASCE, Am. Water Works Assn., N.J. Soc. Profl. Engrs., Water Environ. Fedn., N.J. Assn. Environ. Authorities, N.J. Soc. Mcpl. Engrs. Roman Catholic. Avocations: softball, golf. Home: 38 Tudor Ct Springfield NJ 07081-3023 Office: Van Note-Harvey Assocs 777 Alexander Rd Princeton NJ 08540-6300

HOUGHTON, ANDREW JULIAN NICOLAS, scientific administrator; b. Fareham, Hampshire, U.K., Oct. 16, 1951; s. Roy William and Phyllis Mary (Woodman) H.; m. Linda Shirley Dickson, May 19, 1979; 1 child, James. BSc, U. Sussex, 1973; PhD, U. Nottingham, 1979. Chartered physicist. Exec. engr. British Telecom, Ipswich, U.K., 1979-84; engring. mgr. STC/Nortel, Paignton, U.K., 1984-92; scientific officer European Commn., Brussels, 1992—. Contbr. articles to profl. jours.; patentee in field. Recipient Electronics Letters Premium award Instn. Elec. Engrg., U.K., 1985. Mem. Inst. of Physics. Avocations: sports, football, horse-racing, book collecting. Home: Rue Copernic 103, 1180 Brussels Belgium Office: European Commn, Rue de la Loi 200, 1049 Brussels Belgium

HOUGHTON, ERNEST LESLIE, economics educator; b. Sydney, NSW, Australia, Aug. 2, 1943; s. Leslie Henry and Daphne Annie (Swadling) H.; m. Janice Margaret Davis (div. 1994); 1 child, Christopher Ernest; m. Karen Insuk Yim, Jan. 8, 1995. B of Econs., U. Sydney, Australia, 1965, PhD, 1972. Lectr. U. Sydney, 1972-95, sr. lectr., 1995—, head econometrics and bus. stats., 1999—; cons. Environ. Protection Authority, Melbourne, Australia, 1972, BP Coal, Sydney, 1978, Australian Tourist Commn., Melbourne, 1980, McKinsey & Co., Sydney, 1989, Goodman Fielder, Sydney, 1992, Reark Rsch., Sydney, 1992. Contbr. articles to profl. jours. Australian Rsch. Coun. grantee, 1997, 99. Mem. Australian Soc. for Ops. Rsch. (com. mem. 1993—), Inst. for Ops. Rsch. and Mgmt. Sci., Australian and New Zealand Acad. Mgmt., Econ. Soc. of Australia and New Zealand, Statis. Soc. of Australia. Avocations: sailing, boatbuilding. Office: U Sydney, Parramatta Rd, Sydney NSW 2006, Australia

HOUGHTON, GRAHAM WHITFIELD, religious studies educator; b. Palmerston N., New Zealand, Sept. 22, 1937; s. Clarence Noel and Francis Winnifred (Pratt) H.; m. Carol Ann McDearmid, Aug. 24, 1968; 1 child, Dilkusha Nichole. BA, Azusa Pacific U., 1970; MA, UCLA, 1970, PhD, 1981; BDiv, United Theol. Coll., Bangalore, India, 1978. Ordained to ministry Evang. Ch. India, 1973. Diary farmer, agricultural contractor Manawatu, New Zealand, 1952-60; missionary OMS Internat., Madras, India, 1965-67; misionary, prin. Madras Bible Sem., 1971-82; co-founder, prin. S. Asia Inst. Advanced Christian Studies, Bangalore, India, 1983—; cons. Overseas Coun. Internat., Indpls. Contbr. articles to profl. jours. Mem. Assn. Evang. Theol. Edn. India (founding). Avocations: gardening, hiking, walking, swimming.

HOUGHTON, JAMES RICHARDSON, retired glass manufacturing company executive; b. Corning, N.Y., Apr. 6, 1936; s. Amory and Laura (Richardson) H.; m. May Tuckerman Kinnicutt, June 30, 1962; children: James DeKay, Nina Bayard. AB, Harvard U., 1958, MBA, 1962. With Goldman, Sachs & Co., N.Y.C., 1959-61; with Corning Glass Works (name changed to Corning Inc. 1989), 1962-96; European area mgr. Corning Glass Works, Zurich, Switzerland, 1964-68; v.p., gen. mgr. consumer products divsn. Corning Glass Works, 1968-71, vice chmn. bd., dir., chmn. exec. com., 1971-83, chmn. bd., CEO, 1983-96; bd. dirs. Met. Life Ins. Co., J.P. Morgan Co., Inc.; mem. Harvard Corp. Trustee Corning Inc. Found., Corning Mus. Glass, Pierpont Morgan Libr., N.Y.C., Met. Mus. Art; mem. Trilateral Commn., Bus. Coun. With U.S. Army, 1959-60. Episcopalian. Clubs: Corning Country; River, Harvard, Univ., Links (N.Y.C.); Brookline (Mass.) Country; Tarratine (Dark Harbor, Maine); Augusta (Ga.) Nat. Golf; Rolling Rock, Laurel Valley Golf (Ligonier, Pa.). Office: Corning Inc 80 E Market St Ste 201 Corning NY 14830-2722

HOUGHTON, JOHN THEODORE, former meterological agency director; b. Dyserth, Wales, Dec. 30, 1931; s. Sidney Maurice and Miriam (Yarwood) H.; m. Margaret Edith Broughton, Apr. 7, 1962 (dec. July 1986); children: Janet Margaret, Peter John; m. Sheila Thompson, Feb. 27, 1988. BA in Physics with honors, Jesus Coll., Oxford, Eng., 1951, MA, DPhil, 1955; DSc (hon.), U. Wales, 1991, U. Stirling, 1992, U. East Anglia, 1993, U. Leeds, 1995, Heriot-Watt U., 1997, U. Greenwich, 1997, U. Glamorgan, 1998, U. Reading, 1999. Rsch. fellow Royal Aircraft Establishment, Farnborough, 1954-57; lectr. atmospheric physics Oxford U., 1958-62, reader, 1962-76, prof., 1976-83; dir. Appleton Lab. Sci. Engring. Rsch. Coun., 1979-83; dep. dir. Rutherford Appleton Lab. Sci. Engring. Rsch. Coun., Didcot, Oxfordshire, 1981-83; chief exec., dir. gen. U.K. Meteorol. Office, Bracknell, 1983-91; Mem. Bd. Brit. Nat. Space Ctr., 1986-91; chmn. Joint Sci. Com. World Climate Rsch. Program, 1976-84; chmn. earth observation adv. com. European Space Agy., 1982-92; co-chmn. working group 1 Intergovtl. Panel on Climate Change, 1988—, U.K. Royal Commn. on Eviron. Pollution, 1992-98; mem. U.K. Govt. Panel on Sustainable Devel., 1994-2000. Author: Physics of Atmospheres, 1977, 2d edit., 1986, Does God Play Dice?, 1988, Global Warming: The Complete Briefing, 1994, 2d edit., 1997, The Search for God: Can Science Help, 1995 ; co-author: Infra-red Physics, 1966, Remote Sounding of Atmospheres, 1984. Decorated comdr. Brit. Empire, knight bachelor; recipient Rank prize for opto-electronics Rank Orgn., 1988, Gold medal Royal Astron. Soc., 1995, Internat. Meteorol. Orgn. prize, 1998; fellow Jesus Coll., 1973, hon. fellow, 1983. Fellow Royal Soc., Royal Meteorol. Soc. (pres. 1976-78, Darton prize 1954, Buchan prize 1966, Symans Gold medal 1991, hon.), Inst. Physics (Charles Cree medal and prize 1979, GLazebrook medal and prize 1989), Optical Soc. Am.; mem. Am. Meterol. Soc. (hon.), World Meteorol. Orgn. (v.p. 1987-91). Office: IPCC Unit, Hadley Ctr Meteorological Office, Bracknell RG12 2SZ, England

HOU HSIAO-HSIEN, film director, producer, writer; b. Kwantung, China, Apr. 8, 1946. Student film and drama dept., Taipei Nat. Acad. Arts. Dir. Cute Girl, 1981, Cheerful Wind, 1982, Green Green Grass of Home, 1982, The Sandwich Man, 1983, The Boys from Fengkuei, 1983, A Summer at Grandpa's, 1984, Dust in the Wind, 1986, Daughter of the Nile, 1987, A City of Sadness, 1989 (Golden Lion award Venice Film Festival), The Puppetmaster, 1993 (Cannes Jury prize 1993), Goodbye South, Goodbye, 1996; prodr., writer Heartbreak Island, 1995; author (screenplay), prodr. Growing Up, 1982; author (screenplay), dir. A Time to Live and a Time to Die, 1985; author (screenplay), actor Taipei Story, 1985; prodr. A Borrowed Life, 1994; prodr., dir. Good Men, Good Women, 1995, Goodbye South, Goodbye, 1996, Flowers of Shanghai, 1998. Office: HHH Films, 2d F No 5 Alley 23 Wan Ning St, Taipei Taiwan also: Dept of Motion Picture Affairs, 2 Tienstin St, Taipei Taiwan China*

HOULE, JEFFREY ROBERT, lawyer; b. Biddeford, Maine, July 27, 1965; s. Marcel Paul and Lois Marie (Jackson) H.; m. Lorren Johnston Houle, Oct. 11, 1997; children: Grace Morgan, Hunter Jackson. AB, Boston Coll., Chestnut Hill, Mass., 1987; JD, Western New Eng. Coll., Springfield, Mass., 1991; LLM in Taxation, Cert. in Employee Benefits Law, Georgetown U., Washington, 1992, LLM in Securities Regulation, 1995. Bar: D.C., N.Y., Conn., Mass., Maine. Pres. A.F.I. Investments, Springfield, Mass., 1988-91, Washington Capital Ventures, LP, Washington, 1995-98; law clk. Stones Solicitors, Exeter, Devon, Eng., 1989; jud. intern to the Hon. Joan Glazer Margolis U.S. Magistrate Judge, New Haven, Conn., 1990; legal intern Office of Atty. Gen. Robert Abrams, N.Y.C., 1990; analyst The Bur. of Nat. Affairs, Inc., Washington, 1992; assoc. Andros, Floyd & Miller PC, Hartford, Conn., 1992-94, Elias, Matz, Tiernan & Herrick LLP, Washington, 1994-98; founding ptnr. Greenberg Traurig LLP, McLean, Va., 1998—. Contbr. articles to profl. jours. With U.S. Army, 1984-86. Mem. ABA, The Army and Navy Club, The Federalist Soc.,The Tower Club, Phi Alpha Delta. Republican. Roman Catholic. Avocations: hiking, swimming, horseback riding, international travel. Home: 710 Parrish Farm Ln Great Falls VA 22066-1003 Office: Greenberg Traurig LLP 1750 Tysons Blvd Ste 1200 Mc Lean VA 22102-4211

HOULE, JOSEPH ADRIEN, orthopedic surgeon; b. Ft. Saskatchewan, Alta., Can., Nov. 3, 1928; came to U.S., 1978; s. Adelard Houle and Bertha (Durocher) Guay; divorced; children: Valerie, Diane, Lorraine, Louis, Doreen, Ludmilla, Virginia; m. Marjorie Elizabeth Tuhy. BSc, cert. in premed., U. Ottawa, 1955; MD, Laval U., 1960, Licentiate Med. Council of Can., 1960. Cert. specialist orthopaedic surgery, Quebec, Can. Intern Hotel Dieu Hosp., Quebec City, Can., 1959-60; resident in gen. surgery St. Vincent de Paul Hosp., Sherbrooke, Que., Can., 1960-61, St. Vincent's Hosp., Bridgeport, Conn., 1961-62; resident in orthopaedic surgery Montreal Children's Hosp., Montreal Gen. Hosp. and Queen Mary's Vet. Hosp., 1962-65; practice medicine specializing in orthopaedic surgery Montreal, Can., 1965-78; chief of orthopaedic surgery Thomas Davis Med. Ctr., Tucson, 1978-95, ret., 1995. Produced film Mechanical Knee, 1969. Mem. Bd. Med. Examiners of Ariz., 1978. Served to capt. Royal Can. Forces, 1956-67. Mem. AMA, Can. Orthopaedic Assn., Ariz. Orthopaedic Assn., Pima County Med. Soc. Roman Catholic. Avocations: photography, flying, woodworking. Home: PO Box 11225 Casa Grande AZ 85230-1225 Office: Thomas Davis Med Ctrs 1789 E Hatfield Rd Casa Grande AZ 85222-1225

HOULIHAN, GAIL LANIER, child advocate, educator; b. Mt. Vernon, N.Y., Sept. 15, 1936; d. Fred K. Cordes and Burniece Ruth Oliver Phillips; m. Raymond D'Arsey Houlihan, Jr., May 16, 1959 (div. July 1997); children: Jeffrey John, Raymond D'Arsey III, Michael William, Pamela Lanier, Sean Patrick. BA in English, Douglass Coll., New Brunswick, N.J., 1958. With exec. mgmt. trainee program Doubledy Pub. Co., N.Y.C., 1958-59; elem. sch. tchr. Pennsauken (N.J.) Sch. Dist., 1959; conf. coord. for nat. conf. Nat. Assn. Foster Care Reviewers, 1991-92. Mem. Gov.'s Com. for Children, Youth and Families, 1978-82; mem. township com. Bordentown (N.J.) Twp. Govt., 1982-88, dep. mayor, 1985, 87, mayor, 1986; mem. Bordentown Twp. Planning Bd., 1986-88; founding mem. Bordentown Sewerage Authority, 1986, vice chmn., 1986, chmn., 1987, 91, bd. dirs., 1986-92; coord. Bordentown Twp. Emergency Mgmt., 1987-91; mem. State Health Planning Bd., 1994—; active N.J. State Adv. Coun., Trenton, 1979—, mem. exec. com., 1979-86; trustee Assn. for Children of N.J., Newark, 1980—, treas., 1989-91, adminstrv. v.p., 1995-97; bd. dirs. Comty. Concerts of Bordentown, 1980-91, pres., 1986-88; bd. dirs. Prevention Edn., Inc., Lawrence Twp., N.J., 1990-92; vice chmn. Children's Interagy. Coordinating Coun., Mt. Holly, N.J., 1993-97, chmn., 1997—; bd. dirs. Morris Hall St. Lawrence Rehab. Ctr., 1993—; chair cmty. svc. bd. MH/StL, 1998—. Home: 119 Chatsworth Ave Beach Haven NJ 08008-1538

HOUNKONNOU, MAHOUTON NORBERT, physics educator; b. Adjohoun, Benin, June 7, 1956; s. Kounoudji F. and Laly (Megnon) H.; m. Lidwine Arlette Elisha, Oct. 7, 1988; children: Cornelia Priscile Ayessi, Doriane Norlyce Senami, Mehdi Noudehou Amaury. MS, Polytech. U., 1984; DSc, Catholic U., 1992. Asst. lectr. Nat. U., Cotonou, Benin, 1984-92; sr. researcher Catholic U., Louvain, Belgium, 1992-93; dir. Theoretical Physics Rsch. Unit, Porto-Novo, Benin, 1993—; researcher Free U., Brussels, 1990-93; prof. Inst. Math. & Physics, Porto-Novo, Benin, 1994—. Author: Dynamics and Orientational Order of Elongated Molecules in Solution Subjected to External Fields, 1992, Exact Non-Relativistic Quantum-Mechanical Body-Fixed Hyperspherical Parametrization of the N-Atom Problem is Attainable, 1992, Contemporary Problems in Mathematical Physics, 2000; assoc. editor Jour. Analysis Geometry and Math. Physics. Mem. League of Human Rights, Cotonou, 1989. Grantee Free U., Brussels, 1993; winner Third World Acad. Scis. in Theoretical Physics, 1996. Mem. N.Y. Acad. Scis., Am. Phys. Soc. Avocations: sports, reading, theatre. Home: Atlantique, 07-0196 Cotonou Benin Office: Inst Math & Physics, 613 Porto Novo Oueme, Benin

HOUNSFIELD, GODFREY NEWBOLD, radiation scientist; b. Aug. 28, 1919; s. Thomas H. Ed., City and Guilds Coll., London; diploma, Faraday House Elec. Engring. Coll., London; MD (hon.), U. Basel, 1975; DSc (hon.), City U., 1976, U. London, 1976; DTech (hon.), U. Loughborough, 1976; D honoris causa, Cambridge U., 1992. Joined EMI Ltd., Hayes, Middlesex, Eng., 1951, head med. systems sect., cen. research labs., 1972-76, sr. staff scientist, 1977—; professional fellow in imaging scis. Manchester U., 1978-86. Contbr. articles to sci. jours. Recipient Nobel prize in Physiology or Medicine, 1979; MacRobert award, 1972; Wilhelm-Exner medal Austrian Indsl. Assn., 1974; Ziedses des Plantes medal Physikalishe Medizinische Gesellschaft, Würzburg, 1974; Prince Philip Medal award CGLI, 1975; ANS Radiation Industry award Ga. Inst. Tech., 1975; Lasker award Lasker Found., 1975; Duddell Bronze medal Inst. Physics, 1976; Golden Plate award Am. Acad. Achievement, 1976; Reginald Mitchell Gold medal Stoke-on-Trent Assn. Engrs., 1976; Churchill Gold medal, 1976; Gairdner Found. award, 1976; decorated comdr. Order Brit. Empire, 1976, knight, 1981. Fellow Royal Soc. Achievements include leading design team for 1st large all-transistor computer to be built in Gt. Britain; invented EMI-scanner computerized transverse axial tomography system for X-ray exam.; developed new X-ray technique (EMI-scanner system). Office: Ctrl Research Labs EMI Group, Dawley Rd, Hayes Middlesex UB3 1HH, England

HOUPERT, LUC GABRIEL, engineer, educator; b. Forbach, Lorraine, France, Apr. 16, 1953; s. Louis and Marie-Louise (Streiff) H.; m. Dominique Pillant; children: Sylvain, Nathalie, Isabelle. DEA, Inst. Nat. des Scis. Appliquees, Lyon, France, 1977, PhD, 1980. Rschr., tchr. Inst. Nat. des Scis. Appliquees, Lyon, 1977-80; tribologist, analyst Svenska Kullager Fabriken Rsch., Nieuwerein, 1981-84; NRC-NASA rsch. assoc. NASA, Cleve., 1984-85; sr. rsch. engr. Svenska Kullager Fabriken Rsch., 1985-86; rsch. engr. Soc. d'Applications Generales d'Electricite et de Mecanique, Argenteuil, 1987-90; scientist Timken Rsch., Colmar, 1991—. Contbr. more than 25 articles to profl. jours. Pres. Ctr. d'Initiation a la Musique, Wettolsheim, 1996—. Recipient Innovation award NASA, 1985. Mem. European Indsl. Rsch. Mgmt. Assn., Soc. des Ingenieurs de l'Automobile. Avocations: jogging, chess, hiking. Home: 1 rue de Fleurie, 68920 Wettolsheim France Office: Timken France, BP 89, 68002 Colmar France

HOURANI, LAUREL LOCKWOOD, epidemiologist; b. Carmel, Calif., Sept. 10, 1950; d. Eugene Franklin and Katherine Ruth (Miller) Betz; m. Ghazi Fayez Hourani, Feb. 28, 1984; children: Nathan, Danna, Lisa. BA, Chico State U., 1977; MPH, Am. Univ. Beirut, 1983; PhD, U. Pitts., 1990. Prog. evaluator Community Hosp. Monterey Peninsula, Carmel, Calif., 1978-81; instr./researcher Am. Univ. Beirut, 1981-85; predoctoral fellow U. Pitts., 1985-89; researcher, cons. V.A. Med. Ctr., Pitts., 1988-90; dir., tumor registry Med. Ctr. U. Calif. Irvine, Orange, 1990-92; epidemiologist Naval Health Rsch. Ctr., San Diego, 1993-95; head divsn. health scis., 1995—; cons. Nat. Devel. Commn. South Lebanon, 1981-83. Author: No Water, No Peace, 1985; contbr. articles to profl. jours. Bd. dirs. Am. for Justice in Middle East, Beirut, 1982-85, Nat. Devel. Com., South Lebanon, 1983-85. Recipient grant V.A., Pitts., 1989, rsch. grant U. Rsch. Bd., Beirut, 1985. Mem. Am. Psychol. Assn., Am. Pub. Health Assn., Soc. for Epidemiologic Rsch. Office: Naval Health Rsch Ctr Divsn Epidemiology PO Box 85122 San Diego CA 92186-5122

HOUSE, ANN, home health nurse, administrator; b. Wharton, Tex., Apr. 14, 1952; d. Ardell William and Mary Elizabeth (Thomas) Staggs; children: Candice Ann Petersen, Amy House. BSN cum laude, N.E. La. U., 1989. RN, La.; cert. med.-surg. nurse, home health nurse, ANA. Staff nurse/charge nurse med.-surg. diabetes unit Glenwood Regional Med. Ctr., West Monroe, 1989-90, charge nurse med.-surg., diabetes unit, 1990-93; case mgr., asst. clin. dir. AlphaCare Home Health Inc., Monroe, 1993-94; DON Med-Care Home Health Inc., Ruston, La., 1994-96; asst. DON Today's Home Health, Inc., Monroe, 1994-97; DON Aging Care Home Health, Monroe, 1997; patient care coordinator Hospice Care Fdn., Rayville, La., 1998-99; with Delhi (La.) Hosp. Home Health, 1999—. Flutist Twin City Concert Band; vol. ARC, Monroe, 1994-95. Mem. ANA, La. State Nurses Assn., Nat. Assn. Health Care Quality, Monroe Dist. Nurses Assn. ARC, Am. Diabetes Assn., Med.-Surg. Nurses Assn., Sigma Theta Tau (Lambda Mu chpt.). Avocations: music, needlework, gardening, flutist. Home: 6022 Highway 17 Delhi LA 71232-2016

HOUSOVA, JIRINA, food service executive, researcher; b. Zlin, Czechoslovakia, June 25, 1938; d. Ladislav and Jirina (Knedlova) Pucherna; m. Jaromir Housa, Aug. 13, 1963. MS, Czech Tech. U., Praha, 1961; PhD, Czech Tech. U., 1968. Rschr. Rsch. Inst. Food Industry, Praha, Czechoslovakia, 1961-63, Tech. U., Praha, 1963-68; scientist Food Rsch. Inst., Praha, 1968-75, head dept., 1975—; mem. editl. bd. Czech Jour. of Food Scis., Praha, 1982—, Jour. Food Engring., London, 1987—; mem. com. Czech Grant Agy., Praha, Czech Republic, 1993-98; lectr. Chem. U., Praha, Czech Republic, 1995—. Co-author: Catering for Tomorrow, 1990; contbr. articles to profl. jours. Recipient Food Sci. Results award Czechoslovak Agr. Acad., Praha, 1973, 87, Honors Rsch. Activity award Min. Agr. and Nutrition, Praha, 1975. Fellow Czech Acad. Agr. Scis., Czech Nutrition Soc. Avocations: recreational touring, culture, history. Office: Food Research Inst, Radiova 7, 10231 Praha Czech Republic

HOUSSOU, CONSTANT PLACIDE, psychiatrist; b. Parakou, Borgou, Benin, Oct. 5, 1958; arrived in France, 1991; s. Casimir and Félicienne (Houngbo) H. MD, UNB, Benin, 1985; postgrad. cert. clin. psychology, Paris 13, 1993; qualification epidemiology, Paris 6, 1993; qualification in clin. psychiat. trials, FUAG, France, 1992-94; behavior and cognitive therapist, AFTC, France, 1991-94; postgrad., Paris 8. Registrar Dist. Health Ctr., Benin, 1985-86, sr. cons., 1986-88; psychiatrist UNB, Benin, 1988-91, Lille 2, 1991-94; registrar in psychiatry Pub. Health Hosp., France, 1995-98; interim chief med. info. and rsch. dept. Interdepartmental Psychiat. Pub. Hosp., France, 1998-99; cons. Pub. Health Hosp., France, 1999—; with Dist. Health Ctr., Benin, 1985-86, 86-88; acad. rschr. Nat. U. Hosp., Benin, 1988-91, Pub. Health Hosp., France, 1991—. Contbr. articles to profl. jours. Mem. dist. mgmt. com., Benin, 1986-88. 2nd class Benin Nat. Svc., 1980. Mem. Soc. Medico Psychologique, Assn. Francaise d'alcoologie, Assn. Francaise Therapie Comportementale et Cognitive. Avocations: sport, music, dance. Office: Ctr Hosp Interdeptl, 2 rue des finets, 60607 Clermont France Address:

Ctr Hosp Interdept Clermont, Secteur 60G02 2 rue finets, 60607 Clermont France

HOUSTON, ALLAN WADE, professional basketball player; b. Louisville, Apr. 4, 1971; married. BA in African-Am. Studies, U. Tenn., 1993. Guard Detroit Pistons, 1993-96, New York Knicks, 1996—. Achievements include NBA Draft first round eleventh pick, 1993. Office: New York Knicks Madison Square Garden 2 Penn Plz New York NY 10121-0101

HOUSTON, CAROLINE MARGARET, editor; b. Harrogate, Eng., May 8, 1964; came to U.S., 1975; d. William H. and Sylvia (Fineron) H. BA in Internat. Studies and Mid East Studies, George Mason U., 1989, postgrad., 1990—. Cert. fluency in Farsi and French; cert. diamontologist and gemologist Diamond Coun. Am.; lic. pvt. pilot. Editor Maxim Techs., Vienna, Va., 1988-89; sec. Am. Near East Refugee Aid, Washington and Israel, 1989-90; asst. sec., treas. World Resources Inst., Washington, 1990-91; asst. dir. client svcs. Britches of Georgetowne, McLean, Va., 1991-92; reference copyright sr. clk., preservation technician Libr. Congress, Washington, 1992-95, copyright office automation asst., 1995-99; devel. cons. Legacy Internat., Jerusalem, 1990-91. Violinist with semi-profl. orchs., 1972-84. Mem. NOW, Amnesty Internat.; chmn., treas. Episcopal Ch. of Va., No. Va. Chpt. Holy Land Com. Mem. NAFE, Internat. Studies Assn., Mid. East Inst., Libr. Congress Profl. Assn. (chair membership com., co-chair pub. affairs com.), Atlantic Coun. U.S. Avocations: study of languages, piloting, martial arts, computer programs. Home: 8174 Peakwood Ct Apt 6 Manassas VA 20111-2143

HOUSTON, ELIZABETH REECE MANASCO, correctional education consultant; b. Birmingham, Ala., June 19, 1935; d. Reuben Cleveland and Beulah Elizabeth (Reece) Manasco; m. Joseph Brantley Houston; 1 child, Joseph Brantley Houston III. BS, U. Tex., 1956; MEd, Boston Coll., 1969. Cert. elem. tchr., Calif., cert. spl. edn. tchr., Calif., cert. community coll. instr., Calif.; cert. adminstr., Calif. Tchr., elem. Ridgefield (Conn.) Schs., 1962-63; staff, spl. edn Sudbury (Mass.) Schs., 1965-68; staff intern Wayland (Mass.) High Sch., 1972; tchr., home bound Northampton (Mass.) Schs., 1972-73; program dir. Jack Douglas Ctr., San Jose, Calif., 1974-76; tchr. specialist spl. edn., coord. classroom svcs., dir. alternative schs. Santa Clara County Office Edn., San Jose, Calif., 1976-94; instr. San Jose State U., 1980-86, U. Calif., Santa Cruz, 1982-85, Santa Clara U., 1991-94; cons. Houston Rsch. Assocs., Saratoga, Calif., 1981—. Author: (manual) Behavior Management for School Bus Drivers, 1980, Classroom Management, 1984, Synergistic Learning, 1986, Learning Disabilities in Psychology for Correctional Education, 1992. Recipient President's award Soc. Photo-Optical Instrumentation Engrs., 1979, Classroom Mgmt. Program award Sch. Bds. Assn., 1984, Svc. to Youth award, Juvenile Ct. Sch. Adminstrs. of Calif., 1989-94; grantee Santa Clara County Office Edn. Tchr. Advisor Program U.S. Sec. Edn., 1983-84. Home: 12150 Country Squire Ln Saratoga CA 95070-3444

HOUSTON, THOMAS P., family physician, medical association official; b. Starkville, Miss., Aug. 27, 1951; s. P.D. Jr. and Jean Porter (Benison) H.; m. Cheryn Elizabeth Alten, July 1983; 1 child, Stephen. BA in Biology and Chemistry, U. Miss., Oxford, 1973; MD, U. Miss., Jackson, 1977. Diplomate Am. Bd. Family Practice. Resident in family practice U. Miss., Jackson, 1977-80, chief resident, 1979-80; asst. prof. family medicine Ohio State U., Columbus, 1981-83; assoc. dir. family practice residency program Floyd Med. Ctr., Rome, Ga., 1983-86; assoc. prof. family medicine, dir. family practice residency U. Kans. Sch. Med., Wichita, 1986-90; dir. dept. preventive medicine and pub. health AMA, Chgo., 1990-96, dir. sci. and pub. health adv. programs, 1996—; dir. SmokeLess States Nat. Tobacco Prevention and Control Program, 1993—; cons. tobacco prevention and control for state, fed. and internat. govts. and agys. Author, editor: AMA Guideline for Diagnosis and Treatment of Nicotine Dependence, 1994; assoc. editor: Guides to the Evaluation of Permanent Impairment, 1994; mem. editl. adv. bd. Tobacco Control: Internat. Jour., 1993—; contbr. articles to med. jours. Bd. dirs. Ill. divsn. Am. Cancer Soc., Chgo., 1994—. Recipient The Surgeon Gen.'s medallion, 1988, awrd for disting. svc. on behalf of Am.'s Youth, 1990; Carrier scholar U. Miss., 1969-73; grantee Robert Wood Johnson Found., 1993—. Fellow Am. Coll. Preventive Medicine (chmn. program planning com. ann. meeting 1997); mem. Am. Acad. Family Physicians (health edn. com.). Methodist. Avocations: gardening, cooking, travel, music (singing classical music, trumpet). Fax: 312-464-4111. E-mail: thomas houston@ama-assn.org. Home: 817 Brighton Dr Wheaton IL 60187-8109 Office: Am Med Assn 515 N State St Chicago IL 60610-4325

HOUTZAGER, MARIANNE JOHANNA (MARIAN DE BOYEN), writer, artist, photographer; b. The Hague, Aug. 31, 1953; d. Joseph Houtzager and Gisèle Van Boeyen. HAVO, NTI, Rotterdam, Holland, 1972. Author: (booklet) The Winterwren, 1994, The Orca, 1995, (book) Action Skoatter in the Lead, 2000; one-person shows include (gouaches) Town Hall Krimpen a/d Yssel, 1976, (photographs) Wolvega Racecourse, 1996; exhibited group shows (gouaches) Gallery Los, Krimpen a/d Yssel, 1977. Avocations: drawing, photographing, private flying, co-owner trotting horse. Home: PO Box 143, 2920 AC Krimpen a/d Yssel The Netherlands

HOUTZAGERS, GYS, business consultant; b. Amsterdam, The Netherlands, June 4, 1953; s. J. H. Houtzagers and A.G. Wiersinga; m. D.N. Siouverman, Oct. 18, 1990; 1 child, Mayliss. B Mgmt., JVABO, The Netherlands, 1987; MBA, JBO, The Netherlands, 1991; postgrad., U. Amsterdam, The Netherlands, 1995. Project mgr. JCT GSD, The Netherlands, 1987-89; mgr. ICT ALV, The Netherlands, 1989-95; sr. cons. Vroon, The Netherlands, 1995-97; dir. human resources mgmt. Baan, The Netherlands, 1997-98; prin. bus. cons. Ward Cambell, The Netherlands, 1999—. Author: Developments in JCT, 1999; contbr. articles to profl. jours. Mem. JHRIM, NVP. Home: Herenmarkt 20, 1013 ED Amsterdam The Netherlands Office: Ward Cambell Int, Steenwerweg 3, 5708 Helmad The Netherlands

HOUZE, HERBERT GEORGE, writer; b. Brockville, Ont., Can., Apr. 18, 1947; s. McLean and Grace Lynham (Sayce) H.; m. Carolyn Pierce Johnson, July 8, 1972 (div. May 1990); children: Jennifer E., Alexander J. M., Andrew W.; m. Christine Mary Reinhard, Sept. 13, 1996. BA, McMaster U., Hamilton, Ont., 1969; MA, Vanderbilt U., 1971. Curator of mil. history Chgo. Hist. Soc., 1973-76; curator Winchester Mus. Buffalo Bill Hist. Ctr., Cody, Wyo., 1983-91; advisor Royal Mil. Coll. Can. Mus., Kingston, Ont., 1979—; dir. John McLaren & Sons Distillers Ltd., London and Perth, 1990—. Author: (books) Knightly Musings, 1988, The Sumptuous Flaske, 1989, To the Dreams of Youth, 1992, Winchester History, 1994, Colt Rifles & Muskets, 1996, Winchester Model 52, 1997, Winchester Bolt Action Rifles, 1998, Winchester Model 1876 Centennial, 2000, Arming the West, 2000. Mem. Arms and Armour Soc. London, Armor & Arms Club N.Y., Les Amis du Musee de Liege.

HOUZIAUX, MUTIEN-OMER, linguistics educator; b. Rochefort, Belgium, Jan. 29, 1935; s. Joseph and Josephine (Wenin) H.; m. Marlene Lavalle; children: Anne, Patrick, Pascal, Estelle. Degree, U. Notre Dame de la Paix, Namur, Belgium, 1954; Philology Agr., U. Liege, Belgium, 1956. Titular tchr. Ecole Normale, Verviers, Belgium, 1956-61; prof. U. Sherbrooke, Que., Can., 1965-66, U. Rosario, Argentina, 1982; asst. U. Liege, 1961-67, lectr. linguistics, 1967-78, asst. prof., 1968—, project dir. Faculty Medicine, 1986-95; project dir. Sci. Med. Rsch. Found., Brussels, 1971-80; cons. in field. Author: Enquête Dialectale A Celles-Lez-Dinant, 1959, Vers L'Enseignement Assisté Par Ordinateur, 1972, Education Du Patient Et Ordinateur Le Didacticiel David, 1995, À la recherche des Requiem de Fauré ou l'Authenticité Musicale en questions, 2000. Organist St. Paul's Cathedral, Liege, 1975-99. Mem. Belgian Soc. Authors, Composers and Editors. Home: 10 Rue Meloye, B-4130 Esneux Belgium Office: U Liege, Siam Doceo Lab Rue Stevart, B-4000 Liege Belgium

HOVANESSIAN, ARA GIRAGOS, biochemist; b. Aleppo, Syria, May 21, 1948; s. Arakel and Dirouhi (Kojakian) H. BS, Am. Univ. of Beirut, 1972, MS, 1974; PhD, King's Coll., London, 1978. Rschr. Nat. Inst. for Med. Rsch., Mill Hill, Eng., 1975-78, EMBO/Inst. Pasteur, Paris, 1978-80; rschr. CNRS/Inst. Pasteur, Paris, 1981-85, dir. rsch., 1985—, head of unit, 1990—; cons. CNRS, Paris, 1986-91, ANRS, Paris, 1993, Jour. of Interferon Cytokine Rsch., 1991—, Apoptosis, Eng., 1996—. Inventor in field. Recipient European award for interferon rsch., Hanovre, 1990, Milstein award Interferon Soc., San Francisco, 1990; decorated Knight, French Govt., 1994. Mem. AAAS, Internat. Soc. for Interferon Rsch. (bd. dirs. 1991-96), Am. Soc. Virology. Avocations: classical music, piano, swimming, sightseeing. Office: Inst Pasteur, 28 rue du Dr Roux, 75724 Paris France

HOVDE, LEIF ARNE, primary education educator; b. Ålesund, Norway, Apr. 24, 1943; s. Johan and Signe Elise (Thunem) H. Tchr., Volda Tchr. Tng. Coll., Norway, 1964. Tchr. Larsgården Sch., Ålesund, 1964—. Editor: (scouting mag.) Avleggeren, Larsgårdsposten, 1968—. Mem. nat. bd. YMCA Scouts of Norway, 1966-68, 76-82, 95-99; dist. leader, bd. dirs. Sunnmøre Dist. YMCA Scouts of Norway, 1962-95; local group leader YMCA Scouts, Ålesund, 1964—; mem. Town Coun., Ålesund, 1971-79, 87—; chmn. Health and Social, Ålesund, 1995-99; chmn. Outreach Com., Ålesund, 1991—; mem. cen. com. Christian Dems., Ålesund, 1971—. With Civil Def., 1964-85. Recipient White award Norwegian Scout Orgn., 1976, Golden award YMCA Scouts of Norway, 1982. Christian Democrat. Lutheran. Avocations: scouting, hill walking, classical music, literature, correspondence. Home: Steinvågvegen 5, 6005 Ålesund Norway Office: Larsgården Primary Sch, Husafjellet 11, 6009 Ålesund Norway

HOVDESTAD, WAYNE ROY, petroleum engineer; b. Kyle, Can., Feb. 8, 1958; s. Roy Osmond and Joann Shirley (Hanscam) H.; m. Michelle Diane Trew, May 17, 1980 (div. Mar. 1996); 1 child, William Roy Patrick; m. Maria Anatolievna Sinkova, Aug. 17, 1997; 1 child, Stephanie Maria. BE, U. Saskatchewan, Can., 1979; ME, U. Calgary, Can., 1989. Engr. Texaco Can., Calgary, 1979-82, supr. engr., 1983-89; bus. engr. Texaco Inc., Houston, 1982-83; bus. devel. ESSO Can., Calgary, 1990-91; sr. engr. Petronas, Kuala Lumpar, Malaysia, 1991-94; pvt. practice Calgary, 1994-95; sr. planner Qatar Gen. Petroleum Corp., Doha, 1996-2000; sr. mgmt. Eurogas Corp., Calgary, 2000—. Contbr. articles to profl. jours. Grantee Govt. Alberta, Can., 1986. Orthodox Christian. Avocations: Aikido, karate, languages. E-mail: wrhovdestad@home.com. Office: Eurogas Corp, Ste 440 333-5th Ave SW, Calgary, AB Canada T2P 3B6

HOVE, LEIV MAGNE, orthopaedic surgery educator, consultant; b. Bergen, Norway, Aug. 14, 1948; s. Peter and Frøydis (Ullahammer) H.; m. Vibeke Kaartvedt, June 30, 1973; children: Morten, Eirik, Elisabeth, Marianne. MD, U. Copenhagen, 1974; DMS, U. Bergen, 1994. Diplomate in gen. surgery, plastic surgery, orthopedic surgery, hand surgery. Resident in gen., orthopedic, plastic and hand surgery, Norway, 1974-83; fellow in hand surgery Bergen, 1983-85, cons. in hand surgery,, 1985-90, cons. in orthopedic surgery,, 1990-92; assoc. prof. orthopedic surgery Haukeland U., Bergen, 1992-97; prof. U. Bergen, 1998—; cons. in hand and upper limb surgery, 1995—. Author: Distal Radius Fracture. A Study of Occurence, Treatment and Complication, 1994; contbr. articles to internat. orthopedic jours. Lt. Royal Norwegian Navy, 1977-78. Fellow Nordic Orthopedic Fedn.; mem. Scandinavian Hand Soc., European Fedn. for Surgery of Hand (del. 1995-99), European Rheumatoid Arthritis Surg. Soc., Norwegian Soc. for Surgery of Hand (pres. 1995-99), Norwegian Orthopedic Soc., Norwegian Surg. Soc., Norwegian Rheumatoid Arthritis Surg. Soc., Brit. Soc. Surgery Hand. Home: Storheia 25, N-5046 Rådal Bergen, Norway Office: Haukeland U Hosp, Orthopedic Dept, N-5021 Bergen Norway

HOVELL, SIMON ALEXANDER, systems consultant; b. London, Sept. 5, 1967; s. John Herbert H. and Jennifer (Kijkadt) Robson. B of Engring., U. Edinburgh, Scotland, 1990, PhD, 1994. Rsch. engr. BT, Ipswich, England, 1994-96, sr. rsch. engr., 1996-98; sr. devel. engr., devel. quality mgr. Brand Comm., Huntingdon, England, 1998-99; head devel. Brand Comm., 1999-2000; info. tech. cons. Albera Networks, Cambridge, Eng., 2000—; cons. in field. Contbr. articles to profl. jours.; patentee in field. Mem. IEEE. E-mail: simon@hovell.com. Avocations: skiing, pool, music, reading, technology. Home: 75 Rampton Rd, Willingham CB4 5JQ, England Office: Albera Networks, Cowley Rd, Cowley Cambridge CB4 0WS, England

HOVENGA, EVELYN JOHANNA, health administration executive; b. Koog a/d Zaan, The Netherlands, Aug. 12, 1945; arrived in Australia, 1958; d. John and Guurtje (Koopman) Vroom; m. Kenneth Hovenga, June 20, 1964 (div. 1977); two children. B Applied Sci., Latrobe U., 1982; M in Health Adminstrn., U. New South Wales, 1990, PhD, 1995. Nursing rsch. officer Health Dept. Victoria, Melbourne, 1983-85, nursing advisor, 1985-86; rsch. asoc. Monash Med. Ctr., Clayton, Australia, 1987-88; asst. dir. nursing Goulburn Valley Base Hosp., Shepparton, Australia, 1989; dir. Evelyn J.S. Hovenga & Assocs., Melbourne, 1989-93; assoc. prof. Ctrl. Queensland U., Rockhampton, 1993—. Editor: Health Informatics: An Overview, 1996. Fellow Australian Coll. Health Svc. Execs., Royal Coll. of Nursing Australia; mem. Internat. Med. Informatics Assn. (pres.), Nursing Informatics Spl. Interest Group, Am. Med. Informatics Assn., Health Informatics Soc. of Australia (bd. dirs.). Office: Ctrl Queensland U/Info&Comm, Yaamba Rd, 4702 Rockhampton Australia

HOVETTE, PHILIPPE CHARLES, military physician, researcher; b. Hanoi, Tonkin, Vietnam, July 10, 1953; s. Pierre Ernest Hovette and Marie Jeanne Farez; m. Lydia Germaine Lerolle; children: Christophe, Maxime. MD, U. Bordeaux, France, 1980. With French Mil. Med. Svc., 1972, advanced thourgh ranks to med. chief; asst. dept. tropical medicine Mil. Hosp. Marseille, France, 1987-94; head dept. internal medicine Mil. Hosp. Djibouti, 1994-97; head dept. internal medicine & infectious disease Mil. Hosp. Dakar, Senégal, 1997—. Mem. Soc. Internal Medicine, Soc. Tropical Medicine. Office: Hopital Principal, BP 3006 Dakar Senegal

HOVING, JOHN HANNES FORESTER, consulting firm executive; b. N.Y.C., July 18, 1923; s. Hannes and Mary Alma (Gilbert) H.; m. Anne Fisher Spiers, Feb. 1, 1958; children: Christopher, Karen Anne, Katherine Jean. BA in History, U. Chgo., 1947. Radio news editor, reporter Milw. Jour., Capital Times, Madison, Wis., 1947-51; asst. to chmn. Democratic Nat. Com., 1952-54; exec. positions Kefauver, Stevenson, Johnson, Humphrey, Sanford presdl. campaigns; asst. to presdl. asst. for trade policy 1962; v.p. exec. action Air Transp. Assn. Am., Washington, 1956-64; propr. cons. firm Washington, 1964-72; sr. v.p. Federated Dept. Stores, Inc., Cin., 1972-82; pres. The Hoving Group (cons. firm), Washington, 1982—. Chmn. Washington Theol. Consortium, 1993-96; mem. adv. bd. Fashion Inst. Design Merchandising; past dep. chmn. planning Dem. Nat. Com. With AUS, 1943-46. Decorated Purple Heart, Bronze Star. Mem. Am. Assn. Polit. Cons., Met. Club, Nat. Press Club, Nat. Capital Dem., Queen City Club (Cin.), Lotos Club (N.Y.C.). Home: 4831 Albemarle St NW Washington DC 20016-4346

HOVLAND, MARTIN TORVALD, marine geologist, engineer, researcher, educator; b. London, June 6, 1945; arrived in Norway, 1947; s. Arvid and Phyllis Mary (Toogood) H.; m. Målfrid Østerbø, Feb. 3, 1969; children: Morten, Øyvind, Ingrid. MSc, U. Bergen, Norway, 1969; PhD, U. Tromsø, Norway, 1992. Tchr. Sola (Norway) Ungdomsskole, 1969-73, Nchelenge (Zambia) Secondary Sch., 1973-76; engr. Statoil Rsch., Stavanger, Norway, 1976-80, Statoil Engring., Stavanger, 1980-92; rschr. Statoil Engring., Trondheim and Baku, Azerbaijan, 1992-95; specialist Statoil Engring., Stavanger, 1995—; tutor, lectr. marine geology and geophysics U. Trondheim, 1993—; panel mem. Ocean Drilling Program, College Station, Tex., 1986—, invited scientist, 1992-93, specialist, 1994, mem. program planning group for gas hydrates, 1998-99, chmn. artic program planning group, 2000—; conf. organizer Shallow Gas Group, Edinburg, Scotland, 1989-90; vis. prof. Sunderland U., U.K., 2000—. Author: Seabed Pockmarks and Seepages, 1988, Discovery of Norwegian Coral Reefs, 1999; contbr. articles to sci. jours., including Marine Geology, Terra Nova, Marine and Petroleum Geology; patentee for gas drainage pipe (U.S.) and for articulated tunnel (Norway). Football coach, trainer Sola Idrettslag Children's Football, 1976-83; chmn. Sola Folk U., 1976-80; mem. com. Nature Conservation, Stavanger, 1970-73. With Norwegian Royal Air Force, 1968-69. Environ. rsch. grantee Stavanger Aftenblad, 1971. Mem. Norwegian Geol. Assn. Avocations: cycling, kayak paddling, mountain climbing, skiing. Office: Statoil, Forusbeen 50, N-4035 Stavanger Norway

HOVMAND, MADS FREDERIK, biologist; b. Hellerup, Denmark, Aug. 5, 1945; s. Henrik and Annelise (Reffs) H.; m. Estrella Nielsen, 1972 (div. 1982); children: Ivalo, Peter; m. Lene Hartmann, 1997; children: Jorgen, Bodil. MSc, U. Copenhagen, 1974, PhD, 1978. Rschr. Tech. U., Lyngby, Denmark, 1978-82; project mgr. air pollution lab. EPA, Riso, Denmark, 1983—; sr. scientist Nat. Environ. Rsch. Inst., Roskilde, Denmark, 1998—; expert in field. Mem. Soc. Environ. Engring., Danish Assn. Masters & PhDs, Royal Soc. No. Antiquaries. E-mail: MFH@DMV.dk. Office: Nat Environ Rsch Inst, 399 Frederiksborgvej, DK-4000 Roskilde Denmark

HOVSEPYAN, YURIY IVANOVICH, physicist; b. Baku, Russia, July 13, 1932; s. Ivan Pavlovich and Helen Sergeevna (Ter-Azaryan) Osipov.; m. Aleksandra Pavlovna Tretyakova, Nov. 5, 1961 (div. Nov. 1989); 1 child, Karen; m. Rimma Kuzminichna Malyshkina; children: Karina, Bagrat. Diploma of physicist, M.V. Lomonosov-Moscow State U., 1954; PhD, P.N. Lebedev Physics Inst., 1978. Sr. scientist P.N. Legedev Physics Inst., Moscow, 1965—. Contbr. articles to profl. jours. Recipient 1st prize Acad. Scis., Moscow, 1966, 10th All-Moscow Math. Olympiad, 1947. Avocations: math., cosmology, mountain skiing, swimming, horses. Office: PN Lebedev Physics Inst, Leninskiy Prospekt 53, 117924 Moscow Russia

HOWALD, JOHN WILLIAM, lawyer; b. St. Louis, Dec. 21, 1935; s. Herbert John and Irene Dorothy (Weber) H.; m. Nina M. Zierenderg, June 15, 1957 (div. 1970); children: Deborah A., Catherine A., Laura A., John William; m. Betty L. Curtis, Feb. 14, 1971 (div. 1999); 1 stepchild, Tracy L. BS, U. Mo., 1957; JD, St. Louis U., 1962. Bar: Mo. 1962, U.S. Dist. Ct. (ea. dist.) Mo. 1962, U.S. Ct. Appeals (8th cir.) 1965, U.S. Supreme Ct. 1985. V.p. sales Eureka Svc. and Equip. Co., Eureka, Mo., 1959-62; ptnr. Sheehan, Furtaw & Howald, Hillsboro, Mo., 1963-64, Thurman, Nixon, Smith & Howald, Hillsboro, 1964-70, Thurman, Nixon, Smith, Howald, Weber & Bowles, Hillsboro, 1970-80, Thurman, Smith, Howald, Weber & Bowles, Hillsboro, 1989-91, Thurman, Howald, Weber, Bowles & Senkel, Hillsboro, 1991-95, Thurman, Howald, Weber, Senkel & Norrick, L.L.C., Hillsboro, 1995—; bd. dirs. LaBarque Ent. of Jefferson County, Hillsboro, 1965—, Rustic Hills Resort Ltd., Hillsboro, 1968—. Mem. Mo. Ethics Commn., 1994-98, vice-chmn., 1995-96, chmn., 1996-98. Lt. (j.g.) USN, 1957-59. Recipient Spl. award, Meramec Basin Assn., 1967, 69. Fellow Am. Bar Found., Am. Coll. Trust and Estate Counsel (Mo. chmn. 1987-92); mem. ABA, Estate Planning Coun. St. Louis (pres. 1990-91), Mo. Bar Assn. (bd. govs. 1975-87, Pres. Spl. award 1979), Jefferson County Bar Assn. (pres. 1963-64). Avocations: travel, golf. Home: 9662 W Vista Dr Hillsboro MO 63050-3112 Office: Thurman Howald Weber Senkel & Norrick LLC PO Box 800 One Thurman Ct Hillsboro MO 63050

HOWARD, ANTHONY JOHN, medical microbiologist; b. London, Apr. 14, 1949; s. Richard James and Elsie Grace Evelyn (Wright) H.; m. Christine Murphy, Feb. 24, 1973; children: Joanna Elizabeth, Thomas James. MB BS, London U., 1972, MSc, 1977, Assoc. Kings Coll., 1972. House physician St. George's Hosp., London, 1972-73, house surgeon, 1973, sr. house officer in pathology, 1973-74, registrar in med. microbiology, 1974-76; lectr. in med. microbiology London Hosp. Med. Coll., 1976-79, sr. lectr. in med. microbiology, 1979-81; cons. in med. microbiology Gwynedd Health Authority, Bangor, North Wales, 1981-93; dir. Bangor Pub. Health Lab., 1993-95; dir. Pub. Health Lab. Wales Univ. Hosp. Wales, Cardiff, 1995—. Author, editor sci. articles and papers in med. jours. and books. Fellow Royal Coll. Pathologists (mem. coun. 1993—); mem. Welsh Microbiol. Assn. (pres. 1990-93), Hosp. Infection Soc. (sec. 1986-89), Brit. Soc. for Antimicrobial Chemotherapy (mem. coun. 1992-94), Brit. Soc. for Study of Infection (mem. coun. 1989-91), Marylebone Cricket Club. Avocations: cricket, music, history of medicine.

HOWARD, BART, songwriter; b. Burlington, Iowa, June 1, 1915. Accompanist to Mabel Mercer, 1946-50; pianist, compere, master of ceremonies Blue Angel Cabaret, 1952-60. Composer, lyricist Fly Me To The Moon, numerous other pop songs, 1952—; appeared on albums (Portia Nelson) Let Me Love You, (KT Sullivan) In Other Words. Sgt. U.S. Army, 1941-45. Recipient award Japanese Soc. for Rights of Authors, Composers and Publishers, 1996; inducted into Songwriters Hall of Fame, 1999. Mem. ASCAP, Dramatist Guild, The Actors Fund. Home: PO Box 333 North Salem NY 10560-0333

HOWARD, BERNARD EUFINGER, mathematics and computer science educator; b. Ludlow, Vt., Sept. 22, 1920; s. Charles Rawson and Ethel (Kearney) H.; m. Ruth Belknap, Mar. 29, 1942. Student Middlebury Coll., 1938-40; B.S., MIT, 1944; M.S., U. Ill., 1947, Ph.D., 1951. Staff mem. Radiation Lab, MIT, Cambridge, 1942-45; asst. math. U. Ill., Champaign-Urbana, 1945-49; sr. mathematician Inst. Air Weapons Rsch., U. Chgo., 1951, asst. to dir. Inst. for Systems Rsch., 1952-56, assoc. dir., 1956-60, assoc. dir. Labs. for Applied Sci., 1958-60; dir. Sci. Computing Ctr. U. Miami, Coral Gables, Fla., 1960-64, prof. math. and computer sci., 1960-91, prof. emeritus, 1991—, assoc. faculty Grad. Sch. of Internat. Studies, 1996—; chmn. bd. dirs. Sociocybernetics, Inc.; exec. sec. Air Force Adv. Bd. Simulation, 1951-54; cons. Systems Rsch. Labs, Inc., Dayton, Ohio, 1963-67, acting dir. math. scis. div., 1965; cons. Variety Children's Rsch. Found., Miami, 1964-66, Fla. Power & Light Co., Miami, 1968, Shaw & Assocs., 1964-75; vis. fellow Dartmouth Coll., Hanover, N.H., 1976; co-investigator Positron Emission Tomography Ctr., U. Miami Dept. Neurology/Mt. Sinai Med. Ctr., 1981-84. Creator Parabolic-Earth Radar Coverage Chart, 1944; co-creator: (with Henry W. Kunce) Sociocybernetics, 1971, Optimum Curvature, 1964, Optimum Torsion, 1974, (with J.F.B. Shaw) Principles in Highway Routing, (with James M. Syck) Twisted Splines, 1992. Chmn. bd. dirs. Blue Lake Assn., Inc., Miami, 1969-96, chmn. emeritus 1996—. Am. Soc. Engring. Edn.-Office of Naval Research fellow Naval Underwater Systems Ctr., 1981, 82. Mem. Am. Math. Soc., Soc. Indsl. and Applied Math. (treas. S.E. sect. 1964), Am. Phys. Soc., Assn. Computing Machinery (chpt. chmn. 1969-70), IEEE, AAUP (chpt. sec. 1974-91), Sigma Xi, Phi Kappa Phi, Pi Mu Epsilon, Alpha Sigma Phi, Alpha Epsilon Lambda. Home: 7320 Miller Dr Miami FL 33155-5504 Office: U Miami Sci Computing Ctr Coral Gables FL 33124

HOWARD, BLAIR DUNCAN, lawyer; b. Alexandria, Va.; s. T. Brooke and Elizabeth Duncan H.; m. Catherine Cremins; children: Thomas Brooke II, Caitlin Margaret. BA, U. Va., 1960; LLB, American U., 1963. Ptnr. Howard, Leino & Howard, Alexandria, Va., 1966—. Capt. USA, 1963-65. Named One in Best Lawyers of America (book), 1989—, Superstar Ohio Assn. Criminal Defense Lawyers, Columbus, 1994, One of Top Lawyers in Met. Washington, Washingtonian Mag. article, 1997. Fellow Am. Coll. Trial Lawyers; mem. ABA, ATLA, Alexandria Bar Assn., Va. State Bar Assn. (faculty professionalism course 1990-93). Office: Howard Leino & Howard 19 Culpeper St Warrenton VA 20186-3319

HOWARD, CHRISTOPHER JOHN, research scientist; b. Narrandera, Australia, June 23, 1942; s. Herbert Oliver and Vera Millicent (Pausey) H.; m. Susanne Margaret Allison, July 22, 1972; children: Andrew James, Alexandra Louise. BA in Math. with honors, U. Melbourne, 1966, DSc in Physics, 1995; PhD in Physics, U. Nottingham, 1970. Rsch. scientist Australian Nuclear Sci. and Tech. Orgn., Lucas Heights, 1970—; sr. vis. fellow Cavendish Lab., Cambridge, Eng., 1975-76; vis. scientist Centre d'Etudes Nucleaires de Grenoble, France, 1978; sr. vis. fellow dept. physics U. Edinburgh, 1984, 88; vis. prof. dept. chemistry U. Sydney, 1998; vis. fellow Australian Nat. U., 1998-99; mem. Australian Nat. Com. for Crystallography, Canberra, 1990-98. Co-editor Jour. Applied Crystallography, 1990—; contbr. numerous articles to profl. jours. Mem. Asian Crystallographic Assn. (v.p. 1996-99). Avocations: sailing, walking, wine appreciation. E-Mail: cjh@ansto.gov.au.

HOWARD, CLIVE JONATHAN, protective services official, consultant; b. Knutsford, Cheshire, Eng., Sept. 17, 1957; s. John Sidney H. and Iris Katherine (Finnegan) Patrick; m. Susan Carol Green, Oct. 21, 1985; children: Thomas G., Rebecca K., William J. Arch., Kingston Poly.; 3-D Design, Leeds Poly., 1981. Firearms instr.; rangemaster; defensive tactics instr., drill instr. Inspector Hong Kong Police, 1985-88, inspector police tactical unit, 1988-90, officer 1/C ranges, weapon tng. police tactical unit, 1990-96, chief drill and musketry instr., 1996—; Instr., trainer Pressure Point Control Tactics, 1997—; dir. Hereward Restaurant Devel., Ltd., Eng., 1980—. Mgr. Hong Kong Nat. Cricket Team, 1998—. Lt. Brit. Territorial Army, 1979-82; lt. Brit. Army, 1983-85. Mem. Internat. Assn. Law Enforcement Firearms Instructors, Kowloon Cricket Club, Police Cricket Club (chmn. 1998—). Avocations: cricket, rugby, squash, skiing. Home: Flat 10 8 Mansfield Rd, The Peak Hong Kong HKSAR, China Office: Kowloon City Police Sta, Argyle St, Hong Kong HKSAR, China

HOWARD, EARL MICHAEL, composer; b. L.A., Jan. 12, 1951; s. Alvin F. and Estelle (Seid) H.; m. Liz Phillips, Sept. 27, 1980; 1 child, Heidi. BFA, Calif. Inst. of Arts, 1974. Music dir. Parabola Arts Found., N.Y.C., 1985-99; Fromm Found. fellow Harvard, Boston, 1998—. Composer numerous compositions. Recipient grants N.Y. State Coun. of the Arts, Nat. Endowment for the Arts, 1978-79, N.Y. Found. for the Arts. Democrat. Avocations: cooking, walking, collecting CDs, fine bourbons. E-mail: sculpsound@unidial.com

HOWARD, ERIC SEVAN, conservationist, environmental manager; b. Washington, Dec. 8, 1964; m. Maya Vanderbilt; children: Graham, Tristram, Cecilia. BA, Wesleyan U., 1986; M in Environ. Mgmt., Duke U., 1989. Instr. Great Hollow Wilderness Sch., New Fairfield, Conn., 1986-87; info. officer IUCN Environ. Law Ctr., Bonn, Germany, 1990-92; Conservation fellow World Wildlife Fund, Washington, 1993-94; assoc. Benchmark Environ. Cons., Portland, Maine, 1995-97; mng. dir. Goshen Assocs., 1997-98; exec. dir. Maine Wood Products Assn., Newport, Maine, 1998—; exec. adminstr. Nat. Assn. Environ. Profls., 2000—; cons. UNEP, UN FAO., Maine Ctr. for Innovation in Biotechnology, U.N. Biodiversity and Climate Convention Secretariats, U.S. Agy. Internat. Devel. Co-author: Self Regulation of Environmental Management: An evaluation of international industry association guidelines, 1996, ISO 14001: International Environmental Management systems, 1996; editor: Sourcebook for Conservation and Biological Diversity Information, 1995, Teaching International Environmental Law, 1994; editor ICEL References, 1990-92; contbr. to Yearbook of Internat. Environ. Law, 1990-97; contbr. articles to European Cmty. on Internat. Environ. Law, mem. editl. bd., 1997—; author articles. Chair Eagle Feather award com. Maine Businesses for Social Responsibility, 1996-99. McKenna Fund grantee, 1985; Policy Studies fellow US EPA, 1988; Fulbright scholar, W. Germany, 1989-90. Mem. Soc. Internat. Devel., Fulbright Assn. (bd. dirs., chair task force on sci. and environment), Appalachian Mountain Club. Avocations: mountain climber, sailing. Home: 98 Summit St South Portland ME 04106-2257 Office: Maine Wood Products Assn PO Box 370 Newport ME 04953-0370

HOWARD, GERALD KENNETH, minister; b. Cleve., May 25, 1938; s. Fred Joseph and Thelma Josephine (Johnson) H.; m. Donna Ashmore, Nov. 26, 1977 (div. Dec. 1990); children: Charles (dec.), Tyrone Mayo-Howard, Keisha Mayo-Howard, Nakesha. BS in Sociology, Southeastern U., 1978; MDiv, Nat. Theol. Sem., Balt., 1982; DD, Nat. Theol. Sem., 1982; PhD, Cornestone Sem., Jerusalem, Israel, 1991; DD (hon.), Kashi Dharma Peetha, Varanasi, Calcutta, India, 1981; DHL (hon.), Teamer Sch. Religion, 1983; MS in Pastoral Counseling, Evang. Theol. Sem., Dixon, Mo., 1993; DD (hon.), Martha's Vineyard Theol. Sem., Oak Bluffs, Mass., 1995; M in Social Work, Hamilton U., 1995, PhD in Sociology, 1997. Lic. to ministry Bapt. Ch., 1970, ordained, 1972; lic. pastoral counselor. Diplomate Am. Bd. Examiners Psychotherapy. Asst. pastor Abyssinian Bapt. Ch., Phila., 1973-77, 1980-89; new pastor Gibson Temple Bapt. Ch., Phila., 1977-80; pastor Unity Bapt. Ch., Chester, Pa., 1989-92, Pinkett Tab. Meth. Ch., Phila., 1993-98; casework supr. Commonwealth Pa. Dept. Pub. Welfare, Phila., 1971-98; assoc. pastor Ebenezer Bapt. Ch., 1991-98; asst. pastor Cana Galilee Bapt. Ch., 1999—; program coord. Sulzberger Personal Examination Ctr., Phila., 1999—; casework supr. Commonwealth Pa. Dept. Pub. Welfare, Phila., 1971—; del. Nat. Bapt. Conv. USA, Inc., Baton Rouge, 1969—; commd. chaplain, Nat. Chaplain's Assn., Gatlinburg, Tenn., 1975—; corr. sec. New Hope Bapt. Assn., Chester, 1989-92; clergy to police, 35th Dist., Broad St., Phila. Police Dept., 1974; v.p., rep. Cornerstone U. and Sem., Jerusalem, 1990; mem. Bibl. Life Found., 1995. With U.S. Army, 1961-64, Korea. Recipient Outstanding Svc. award Nat. Chaplain's Assn., Gatlinburg, 1976, Legion of Honor The Chapel of Four Chaplains, Phila., 1978, 83, Martin Luther King award Defense Pers. Support Ctr., Phila., 1987, Dedicated Christian Svc. award, Pa. Bapt. State Conv., Phila., 1990, Disting. Person and Outstanding Citizen awards Phila. City Coun., 1991. Fellow Am. Coll. Clinic Adminstrs.; mem. Am. Assn. Christian Counselors, Bibl. Life Found., Masons. Democrat. Home: 1552 E Upsal St Philadelphia PA 19150-1423 Office: Pinkett Tab Friendly Meth Church 1913 N 21st St Philadelphia PA 19121-2108

HOWARD, JOHN WAYNE, lawyer; b. Dec. 17, 1948; s. Joseph Leon and Irene Elizabeth (Silver) H.; m. Kathleen Amanda Busby, Oct. 7, 1978. BA, U. Calif., San Diego, 1971; JD, Calif. Western Sch. Law, 1976; postgrad., San Diego Inn of Ct., 1979, Hastings Coll. Advocacy, 1981; grad. Program of Instrns. for Lawyers, Harvard Law Sch., 1992. Bar: Calif. 1978, U.S. Dist. Ct. (so. dist.) Calif. 1978, U.S. Supreme Ct. 1989, Colo. 1989, U.S. Dist. Ct. (no. dist.) Calif., U.S. Dist. Ct. (ea. dist.) Calif., U.S. Ct. Appeals (9th cir.) 1995, U.S. Ct. Appeals (D.C. cir.) 1996, U.S. Ct. of Claims 1996. Assoc. Robert T. Dierdorff, San Diego, 1978-79; pvt. practice San Diego, 1979-82; ptnr. Howard & Neeb, San Diego, 1982-84; prin. John W. Howard and Assocs., San Diego, 1984-86; gen. counsel Ace Parking, Inc., 1986-89, CCCA Inc., 1989-93; pres. Individual Rights Found. Inc., 1993-95, Inst. for Constitutional Rights, Inc., 1995—, John W. Howard and Assoc., 1995—; jud. arbitrator Superior Ct. Calif., 1983—. Chmn. San Diego County Indigent Def. Adv. Bd., 1981-84, mem. subcom. on def. monitoring and budget for Office Defender Svcs. of San Diego County; mem. select com. on small bus. Calif. State Assembly, 1983-90; chmn. San Diego Pub. Arts Adv. Bd.; mem. San Diego County Coun. of Com. Chairs; chmn. precinct orgn. Roger Hedgecock for Supt. Campaign Com., 1976, mem. steering com., 1976; chmn. steering com. Hedgecock for Mayor, 1982, Cleator for Mayor, 1986; chmn. Muscular Dystrophy Telethon, San Diego, 1983; vice chmn. San Diego Festival of Arts, 1983-84; pres. Bowery Theatre, San Diego, 1984-89; pres., bd. dirs. La Jolla Stage Co.; founder, bd. dirs. San Diego Theatre League; 1st v.p., bd. dirs. Muscular Dystrophy Assn.; bd. dirs. Patrick Henry Meml. Found., Brookneal, Va., The Poe Mus., Richmond, Va., San Diego Med. Oncology Rsch. Found., Ilan-Lael Found., Multiple Sclerosis Soc., Am. Ballet Found., Wellness Cmty., Teatro Macara Magica; bd. dirs., chmn. legal affairs subcom. Calif. Motion Picture Coun.; mem. adv. bd. dirs. San Diego Motion Picture Bur.; mem. pub. edn. com. Am. Cancer Soc.; founder, bd. dirs. San Diego Theatre Found., 1984—; mem. 44th Congl. Dist. Adv. Com.; mem. Com. to Re-Elect Congressman Bill Lowery; mem. San Diego County 4th Dist. Adv. Com. Mem. ABA, ATLA, Calif. State Bar Assn., Am. Corp. Counsel Assn., U. Calif.-San Diego Alumni Assn. (past v.p., bd. dirs.), Calif. Western Sch. Law Alumni Assn., Friendly Sons of St. Patrick, Delta Kappa Epsilon, Phi Alpha Delta, Kiwanis, Enright Inn of Ct., Am. Inns of Ct. Republican.

HOWARD, JOHN WINSTON, Australian politician; b. Sydney, Australia, July 26, 1939; s. Lyall Falconer and Mona Jane Howard; m. Alison Janette Parker, 1971; 3 chidlrren. LLB, U. Sydney. Solicitor Supreme Ct., NSW, Australia, 1962; ptnr. solicitors' firm, 1968-74; M.P. for Bennelong, NSW, Fed. Parliament, 1974—; min. for bus. and consumer affairs, 1975-77, min. assisting prime minister,, 1977, fed. treas.,, 1977-83, dep. leader opposition,, 1983-85, leader opposition, 1985—; leader Liberal Party, 1985-89; Prime Minister Govt of Australia, 1996—. Mem. state exec. NSW Liberal Party, 1963-74; v.p. NSW div. Liberal Party, 1972-74. Office: St MG8, Parliament House, Canberra ACT 2600, Australia

HOWARD, JOSEPH HARVEY, retired librarian; b. Olustee, Okla., Jan. 15, 1931; s. William Lester and Letitia Browder (Dickey) H.; m. Patricia Shaughnessy Schiebel, Apr. 10, 1980. B in Mus. Edn., U. Okla., 1952, MLS, 1957. Assoc. dir. pub. svcs. U. Colo. Libr., Boulder, 1960-63; vol. Peace Corps, Kuala Lumpur, Malaysia, 1963-65; head catalog dept. Washington U., St. Louis, 1956-67; asst. chief descriptive cataloging divsn. Libr. of Congress, Washington, 1967-68; chief descriptive cataloging divsn. Libr. of Congress, 1968-72, chief serial record divsn., 1972-75, asst. dir. (cataloging) processing dept., 1975-76, asst. libr. for processing svcs., 1976-83; dir. Nat. Agrl. Libr., Beltsville, Md., 1983-94, ret., 1994. Author: Malay Manuscripts—A Bibliographical Guide, 1966. Served with AUS, 1952-54. Recipient Outstanding Svc. to Librarianship award U. Okla., 1979. Mem. ALA (Melvil Dewey medal 1985).

HOWARD, LILLIE PEARL, English language educator, academic administrator; b. Gadsden, Ala., Oct. 4, 1949; d. Zola Mae H.; children: Kimberly Denise Kendricks, Benjamin Richard Kendricks. BA, U. South Ala., 1971; MA, U. N.Mex., 1972, PhD, 1975; cert. Inst. Ednl. Mgmt., Harvard U., 1988. Asst. prof., assoc. prof., now prof. English Wright State U., Dayton, Ohio, 1975—, asst. dean, then assoc. dean Coll. Liberal Arts, 1982-87, asst. v.p. acad. affairs, 1987-88, assoc. v.p. acad. affairs, 1988-99, assoc. provost, dean acad. affairs, 1999—. Author: Zora Neale Hurston, 1980; editor: Alice Walker and Zora Neale Hurston: The Common Bond, 1993; co-editor: Dad, I Served: The Autobiography of C.J. McLin, Jr., 1998; contbr. articles to Dictionary of Literary Biography, various other publs. Ford Found. fellow, 1971-75. Mem. Am. Assn. Higher Edn., Zora Neale Hurston Soc., Nat. Assn. Acad. Affairs Adminstrs., Acad. Assemby of Coll. Bd.; NCA cons.-evaluator, mem. of NCA Review Coun. Avocations: reading mysteries, singing, dance, gardening. Office: Wright State Univ Colonel Glenn Hwy Dayton OH 45435

HOWARD, MELVIN, financial executive; b. Boston, Jan. 5, 1935; s. John M. and Molly (Sagar) H.; m. Beverly Ruth Kahan, June 9, 1957; children: Brian David, Marjorie Lyn. BA, U. Mass., 1957; MS, Columbia U., 1959. Fin. exec. Ford Motor Co., Dearborn, Mich., 1959-67; v.p. adminstrn. Shoe Corps. of Am., Columbus, Ohio, 1967-70; contr., sr. v.p. fin., chief fin. officer Xerox Corp., 1970-84, exec. v.p., chmn. fin. svcs., 1984-86, vice chmn. of bd., 1986-90, bd. dirs., 1982-90; pres., CEO Ehrlich Bober Fin. Corp., 1990-92; mng. dir. Taurus Adv. Group, 1993-94; bd. dirs. Gould Pumps, Inc., Sector Mgmt., Inc. Trustee Nursing and Home Care, Commonwealth Coll. 1st lt. AUS, 1957. Mem. Birchwood Country Club, Frenchman's Creek Country Club, Beta Gamma Sigma. Home: 3139 Miro Dr S Palm Beach Gardens FL 33410-1285

HOWARD, MICHAEL, British government official; b. July 4, 1941; s. Bernard and Hilda Howard; m. Sandra Clare Paul; 2 children; 1 stepchild. MA, LLB, Cambridge (Eng.) U. Called to bar Inner Temple, 1964, created Queen's counsel. Jr. counsel to Crown, 1980-82, recorder,, 1986—, contested Liverpool and Edge Hill,, 1966, 70; chmn. Bow Group, 1970-71; M.P. from Folkestone and Hythe Ho. of Commons, London, 1983—; Parliamentary under sec. of state Dept. Trade and Industry, London, 1985-87; min. of state Dept. Environ., London, 1987-90; sec. of state for employment, London, 1990-92, sec. of state for environ., 1992-93; sec. of state Home Dept., London, 1993-97; bencher, 1992; joint vice chmn. Conservative Employment Com., 1983-94; PPS to solicitor gen., 1984-85. Major scholar Inner Temple, 1962. Mem. Soc. Conservative Lawyers (vice chmn. 1985), Carlton Club (Coningsby, Eng.). Avocations: watching football (Swansea and Liverpool), watching baseball (N.Y. Mets). Office: House of Commons, London SW1A 0AA, England*

HOWARD, MICHAEL ELIOT, historian, educator; b. London, Nov. 29, 1922; s. Geoffrey Eliot and Edith Julia Emma (Edinger) H. MA, U. Oxford, 1948, LittD, 1976; LittD, Leeds (Eng.) U.; DLitt, U. London, 1988. Asst. lectr. history Kings Coll. U. London, 1947-53, lectr. war studies, 1953-62; prof. war studies U. London, 1963-68; fellow higher defence studies All Souls Coll., Oxford, 1968-77; prof. history of war U. Oxford, 1977-80, regius prof. modern history, 1980-89; prof. history Yale U., New Haven, 1989-93; pres. Internat. Inst. Strategic Studies, London. Author: The Franco Prussian War, 1961 (Duff Cooper Prize, 1962), Grand Strategy, vol. IV, 1971 (Wolfson award for history); many others. Served to capt. Brit. Army, 1942-45. Decorated Mil. Cross His Majesty King George VI, 1943; named Knight Bachelor Her Majesty Queen Elizabeth II, 1986, Commdr. of the Brit. Empire, 1987; recipient Atlantic award NATO, 1989. Fellow Brit. Acad., U.S. Acad. Arts and Scis., Athenaeum Club, Garrick Club (London). Anglican.

HOWARD, MICHAEL MCGREGOR, economist, educator, school administrator; b. Bridgetown, Barbados, Sept. 26, 1949; s. Evans McGregor and Ruby (Brian) H.; m. June Patricia Alkins, Oct. 5, 1974; children: Cherita Lyn, Steve Allan. BA, U. West Indies, 1971, MS, 1974, PhD, 1985. Sr. economist Cen. Bank Barbados, 1974-79; rsch. fellow U. of the W-I, Barbados, 1979-81, lectr., 1981-90, sr. lectr., 1990—, dean, 1993-94, head dept. econ., 1994—; bd. dirs. Barbados Nat. Bank. Author: The Fiscal System of Barbados, 1979, Dependence and Development in Barbados, 1945-85, 1989, Public Finance in Small Open Economies, The Caribbean Experience, 1992. Named Economist of Year, Barbados Econ. Soc., 1993. Mem. Nat. Econ. Coun. Avocations: tennis, Spanish, travelling, hiking. Home: No 20 Oxnards, Saint James Barbados

HOWARD, O.M. ZACK, biomedical researcher; b. Altus, Okla., Dec. 17, 1961; d. K.C. and Vernie V. (Roach) H.; m. James A. Turpin, June 9, 1990. BS, U. Okla., 1983; PhD, U. S.C., 1987. Rsch. asst. dept. chemistry U. Okla., Norman, 1981-83; teaching asst. dept. chemistry U. S.C., Columbia, 1983-84, grad. rsch. asst., 1984-87; postdoctoral fellow M.D. Anderson Cancer Ctr., Houston, 1987, project investigator, 1987-89; scientist I, Nat. Cancer Inst.-Frederick Cancer R&D Ctr. PRI/Dynacorp Co., Frederick, Md., 1989-92, scientist, group leader, 1992-99, scientist II, 1999-2000; staff scientist Nat. Cancer Inst., Frederick, Md., 2000—. Contbr. articles to profl. jours.; inventor in field. Fellow M.D. Anderson Cancer Ctr., 1987. Mem. AAAS, ACS, Am. Assn. Cancer Rsch., Golden Key, Phi Beta Kappa. Avocations: reading, bicycling, cats. Office: NCI-FCRDC PO Box B Frederick MD 21702-1124

HOWARD, RON, director, actor; b. Duncan, Okla., Mar. 1, 1954; s. Rance and Jean Howard; m. Cheryl Alley, June 7, 1975; 4 children: Bryce, Jocelyn and Paige (twins), Reed. Student, U. So. Calif., Los Angeles Valley Coll. Co-chmn. Imagine Films Entertainment, L.A. Actor: (theatre) The Seven Year Itch, 1956, Hole in the Head, 1963; (films) The Journey, 1959, Five Minutes to Live, 1959, Music Man, 1962, The Courtship of Eddie's Father, 1963, Village of the Giants, 1965, Wild Country, 1971, Happy Mother's Day... Love George, 1973, American Graffiti, 1973, The Spikes Gang, 1974, The First Nudie Musical, 1976, Eat My Dust, 1976, The Shootist, 1976, Grand Theft Auto (also dir.), 1977, More American Graffiti, 1979, The Magical World of Chuck Jones, 1992; (TV, host/narrator) Frank Capra's American Dream, 1997; dir.: Night Shift, 1982, Splash, 1984, Cocoon, 1985, Gung Ho, (also exec. prodr.) 1986, No Man's Land, (also exec. prodr.) 1987, Willow, 1988, Parenthood (also co-author) 1989, Backdraft, 1991, Far and Away (also co-prodr., co-author) 1992, The Paper, 1994, Apollo 13, 1995 (Outstanding Directorial Achievement in Motion Picture award Dirs. Guild Am. 1996), Ransom, 1996, Edtv, 1999; exec. prodr.: Clean and Sober, 1988, Vibes, 1988, Closet Land, 1991, Inventing the Abbotts, 1997, Hiller and Diller (TV, exec.), 1997, From the Earth to the Moon (mini series), 1998, Sports Night (TV series, exec.), 1998, Felicity (TV series, exec.), 1998, Student Affairs (TV), 1999, How to Eat Fried Worms, 1999, Detox, 1999, The PJs (TV series, exec.), Edtv, 1999; regular TV series: The Andy Griffith Show, 1960-68, The Smith Family, 1971-72, Happy Days, 1974-80; other TV appearances include New Breed, Wonderful World of Disney, Gentle Ben, Laverne and Shirley, Twilight Zone, Danny Kaye Show, Fugitive, Dennis the Menace, Bonanza, Five Fingers, Gunsmoke, The F.B.I., 11th Hour, (TV movies) The Migrants, 1974, Locusts, 1974, Huckleberry Finn, 1975, Cotton Candy (co-writer, dir.) 1978, Act of Love, 1980, Bitter Harvest, 1981, Fire On the Mountain, 1981, Skyward (dir., co-exec. prodr.) 1981, Through the Magic Pyramid (dir., exec. prodr.) 1981, When Your Lover Leaves (co-exec./prodr.) 1983, Return to Mayberry, 1986, (actor) Osmosis Jones, 2000 (animation). Mem. AFTRA, SAG, Acad. Motion Picture Arts and Scis. Office: care of Peter Dekom Bloom DeKom & Hergott 150 S Rodeo Dr Beverly Hills CA 90212-2408 also: Imagine Entertainment 9465 Wilshire Blvd Fl 7 Beverly Hills CA 90212-2606

HOWARD, SAMSON, computer consultant, middle school educator, publishing executive; b. Bethlehem, Pa., June 14, 1955; s. Howard Theodore and Kathryn Longfellow (Heaton) MacF. BS in Math. cum laude, Yale U., 1977; MS in Computer Sci., Boston U., 1987. Owner, cons. Trinity Cons., Boston, 1984—; ESL tchr. Cath. Charitable Bur., Boston, 1992; substitute tchr. Boston Sch. Dept., 1993—; owner, pub. Trinity Pub., Boston, 1994-97, pres., treas., 1997-99, exec. treas., 1999—; rschr., developer, 1999—; tchr. pvt. students, 1993-95. Author, editor: Voices, 1994. Campaign worker Bob Dole Campaign, Boston, 1987; asst. bookkeeper Jewish Nat. Fund, 1996-97; office asst. Ruby Rogers Advocacy & Drop-In, 1997-99. Republican. Avocations: chess, recorder, acoustic guitar. Home and Office: 658 1/2 E 6th St Fl 1 Boston MA 02127-3132

HOWARTH, GORDON STANLEY, gastroenterological histologist; b. Liverpool, Eng., Mar. 29, 1955; s. Stanley and Edna (Baker) H.; m. Catherine Ann Walker, Nov. 5, 1983; children: Christian Gordon, Scott Ashley. BSc, U. Adelaide, 1976, BSc with honors, 1977. Hosp. scientist Inst. of Med. and Vet. Sci., Adelaide, 1977-87; rsch. officer U. Adelaide, 1988-89; rsch. scientist Child Health Rsch. Inst., Adelaide, 1990—; radiation safety officer Child Health Rsch. Inst., North Adelaide, 1990—, occupl. health and safety officer, 1990—; biosafety com. mem. Women's and Children's Hosp., North Adelaide, 1994—; vis. rsch. fellow physiology U. Adelaide, 1999. Contbr. articles to profl. jours.; patentee in field. Sch. coun. mem. Salisbury Park Primary Sch., 1994—, chmn., 1999-2000; pres. Elizabeth H.S. Old Scholars Assn., 2000—. Recipient Travel award Inst. of Med. and Vet. Sci., 1982, Best Presentation award Australian Soc. of Parenteral and Enteral Nutrition, 1993. Mem. Am. Gastroenterol. Assn., Gastroenterol. Soc. of Australia, Endocrine Soc. of Australia (Travel award 1996). Mem. Ch. of Eng. Avocations: collecting records, collecting Beatle's memorabilia, music. Home: 7 Winston Crescent, Hillbank 5112, South Australia Office: Child Health Rsch Inst, 72 King William Rd, North Adelaide 5006, Australia

HOWARTH, GRAHAM ALISTAIR, research chemist; b. Chester, Cheshire, U.K., Apr. 17, 1957; s. George Raymond and Dorothy May (Berry) H.; m. Bernice Williamson, Oct. 11, 1980; children: Emma Louise, Andrea Collette, Janine Caroline. Grad., U. Ctrl. Lancashire, 1984; MS with distinction, Imperial Coll., London, 1996, Diploma, 1997. Chartered chemist. Sr. shift chemist Courtaulds, Preston, U.K., 1975-80; polymer technician Akzo Nobel Coatings, Darwen, U.K., 1980-84, chem. buyer, 1984-87; polymer chemist Indsl. Copolymers, Darwen, 1987-90, chief chemist, 1990-94, tech. mgr., 1994—; specialist lectr. Imperial Coll. London, 1997—. Contbr. articles to profl. jours. Recipient Paper of Yr. award Surface Coatings Internat., 1999. Fellow Royal Soc. Chemistry; mem. Inst. of Materials, Inst. Corrosion, Nat. Assn. Corrosion Engrs., Tech. of Surface Coatings (assoc.), Oil and Color Chemists Assn. (program officer 1996—, coun. mem. 1996—). Avocations: travel by train, gardening, photography. Home: 4 Normandy Rd, Preston PR4 0AY, England

HOWAT, KEVIN JOHN, publishing executive; b. Turtle Creek, Pa., May 22, 1953; s. Jack William and Julia (Green) H.; m. Jane Elizabeth Townsend, Sept. 30, 1984; children: Lucy, Sophia Jane. BA cum laude, Franklin & Marshall Coll., 1975. Exec. editor, pub. Internat. Thomson, Wadsworth, Belmont, Calif., 1979-88; new products mgr. The Learning Co., Fremont, Calif., 1988-90; sr. acquisitions editor Addison-Wesley Edn. Software, Redwood City, Calif., 1990-92; dir. strategic mktg., bus. devel. Macromedia Inc., San Francisco, 1992-94; v.p. product devel., pub. Simon & Schuster Pub., N.Y.C., 1994-98; v.p., bus. devel., brand mgmt. Time Inc. New Media, N.Y.C., 1998-2000, sr. v.p. bus. devel. and sales, 2000—; founder, adv. bd. New Media Ctrs., San Francisco, 1993-94;. Pub. numerous CD-ROM software (various awards). Program com. EDUCOM (Educational Comp. Conf.), Washington, 1990-93. Recipient Ednl. Software Product award Softward Pub. Assn., 1990. Avocations: music, mountain biking, theater, running. Home: 51 Crow Hill Crest Mount Kisco NY 10549-3804 Office: Time Inc New Media 1271 Ave Americas New York NY 10020

HOWDEN, FRANK NEWTON, Episcopal priest, humanities educator; b. Phila., Mar. 23, 1916; s. John George and Sarah Harvey (McFarlane) H.; m. Cornelia Jane Fenton, Oct. 7, 1943 (dec. Aug. 1981); children: Robert Newton, William John McFarlane, Susan Catherine Victoria Howden Blanchard, Sarah Jane Fenton; m. Mary Valerie Clark, Apr. 23, 1983. AB, U. of the South, 1940; STB, Gen. Theol. Sem., N.Y.C., 1943; MS, Ctrl. Conn. U., 1968; postgrad., McGill U., Montreal, Can., 1953-56. Ordained priest Episcopal Ch.; cert. tchr., Conn. Curate St. Peter's Ch., Auburn, N.Y., 1943-44, All Angels Ch., N.Y.C., 1944-45; priest in charge (vicar) St. John's Ch., Sewaren and Fords, N.J., 1945-48; rector St. Luke's Ch., St. Albans, Vt., 1951-56, Trinity Ch., Waterbury, Conn., 1956-66; history tchr. Woodbury (Conn.) H.S., 1966-69; prof. humanities Waterbury State Tech. Coll., 1970-82; rector Trinity Ch., Lime Rock, Conn., 1969-85, elected rector emeritus, 1985—; pres. Priests' Fellowship, Conn., 1958-59; archdeacon New Haven County, Diocese of Conn., 1963-66, dean Litchfield Deanery, 1984-85. Author: A Rule of Life, 1954, Life Here and Hereafter, 1992. 1st lt. Chaplain Corps, U.S. Army, 1948-51, chaplain Vt. Nat. Guard, 1952-56. Mem. St. Margaret's Soc. (assoc.), Over-Seas League (London), English-Speaking Union. Democrat. Avocations: photography, audio-visual presentations, preaching and taking services in Anglican churches. Home: 9 Argyle Rd Southborough, Tunbridge Wells TN4 0SU, England

HOWE, BRIAN LESLIE, government official; b. Melbourne, Australia, Jan. 1, 1936; m. Renate Morris, May 8, 1962; children: John, Abbey, Sarah. B.A., Melbourne U., Diploma in Criminology; postgrad., McCormick Theol. Sem., Chgo. Mem. faculty Swinburne Inst. Tech., Melbourne, sr. lectr. in sociology, until 1977, also chmn. dept. social and polit. studies; now minister housing and regional devel. Govt. of Australia, Canberra; mem. Australian Labor Party, 1961—, Australian Ho. of Reps., Canberra, 1977-96, mem. standing com. on environment, 1978—, mem. joint com. on publs., 1978—, minister for def. support, 1983-84, minister social security, 1984-90, min. for community svcs. and health, 1990-93; founder, first dir. Centre for Urban Research and Action, Melbourne, dep. prime min., 1991-96; prof. assoc. dept. soc. work Ctr. Pub. Policy U. Melbourne, 1996—. Mem. various nat. policy coms. Australian Labour Party, chmn. caucus econs. com., mem. caucus resources com., mem. urban and regional affairs com. Office: The University of Melbourne, School of Social Work, Victoria ACT 3010, Australia

HOWE, DRAYTON FORD, JR., lawyer; b. Seattle, Nov. 17, 1931; s. Drayton Ford and Virginia (Wester) H.; m. Joyce Arnold, June 21, 1952; 1 son, James Drayton. AB, U. Calif., Berkeley, 1953; LLB, U. Calif., San Francisco, 1957. Bar: Calif. 1958. CPA Calif. Atty. IRS, 1958-61; tax dept. supr. Ernst & Ernst, San Francisco, 1962-67; ptnr. Bishop, Barry, Howe, Haney & Ryder, San Francisco, 1968—; lectr. on tax matters U. Calif. extension, 1966-76. Mem. Calif. Bar Assn., San Francisco Bar Assn. (chmn. client relations com. 1977), Calif. Soc. CPA's. Office: Bishop Barry Howe Haney & Ryder Watergate Tower III 2000 Powell St Ste 1425 Emeryville CA 94608

HOWE, JAMES EVERETT, investment company executive; b. N.Y.C., Mar. 30, 1930; s. Ernest Joseph and Gladys Montgomery (Sills) H.; m. Judith DePuy Keating, May 9, 1959; children: James E. Jr., David K. BA, Williams Coll., 1952; MBA, Columbia U., 1954. Chartered fin. analyst. Statistician J.P. Morgan & Co., N.Y.C., 1956-59; investment research officer Morgan Guaranty Trust Co., N.Y.C., 1959-65; sr. analyst Tri-Continental Corp., N.Y.C., 1965-80; asst. v.p., voting shareholder J&W Seligman & Co., N.Y.C., 1980-81; chmn. investment com. Charles Edison Fund, Newark, 1981—. Trustee Brook Found., N.Y.C., 1966-72, Charles Edison Fund, 1972—; bd. deacons Brick Presbyn. Ch., N.Y.C., 1963-66. 1st lt. USAF, 1954-56, ETO. Recipient fin. award Wall Street Journal, 1954. Mem. N.Y. Soc. Security Analysts, Assn. for Investment Mgmt. and Rsch., Machinery Analysts N.Y. (charter, pres. 1967-68), Environ. Control Analysts N.Y. (charter, pres. 1975), Jamestowne Soc., Princeton Co. (charter, gov. 1993-94), Genesee Valley Club, Short Hills Club, Alpha Kappa Psi. Republican. Presbyterian. Avocation: photography. Home: 33 Keats Rd Short Hills NJ 07078-2913 Office: One Riverfront Plz Newark NJ 07102-5401

HOWE, JOHN KINGMAN, manufacturing, sales and marketing executive; b. Everett, Wash., Nov. 7, 1945; s. John Cutler and Nancy Carpenter (Kingmanú) H.; m. Loretta Kerr, aug. 27, 1966; children: Steven Cutler, Nancy Kingman. Student, Ohio State U., 1963-65. Field technician Data Corp., Dayton, Ohio, 1965-66; letter carrier U.S. Postal Svc., Dayton, 1966; sales rep. E.S. Klosterman Co., Dayton, 1966-71; v.p., 1971-72; v.p. sales, dir. Springfield Binder Corp., Ohio, 1981-84; dir., pres., CEO, 1984-95; dir., pres., The John K. Howe Co., Inc., Dayton, 1972-87, chmn., CEO, 1987—; dir., pres. The John K. Howe Co., Inc., Dayton, Ohio, 1972-87, chmn., chief exec. officer, dir. 1987—; pres. Cutler-Kingman, Inc. div. Thump Properties, Cin., 1979-86, owner, 1986—; gen. ptnr. H&B Enterprises, Dayton, 1977-86, Design Investment Properties, Dayton, 1979-86, BMR Properties, Ltd., Dayton, 1979-82; adminstr. John K. Howe Co./Profit Sharing, Cin., 1973—, John K. Howe Co./Pension Plan, 1976—; owner Androscoggin Designs, Dayton, 1979-86. Pres. South Dixie Bus. Assn., 1989-91, chmn., 1992-94, chmn., 1992-94; pres. woods of Lincoln Park Homeowners's Assn., 1992-94; mem. Fraze Pavilion fund raising com., 1991-92; mem. Confrerie de la Chaines de Rotisseurs Bailliage de Cin., 1993—; chmn. ops. com. Adams Place Condominium Owners Assn., Inc., 1996-98, v.p., bd. mgrs., 1998-99,

pres. bd. mgrs., 1999—. Republican. Presbyterian. Office: The John K Howe Co Inc 400 Pike St Fl 6 Cincinnati OH 45202-4237

HOWE, JOHN PRENTICE, III, health science center executive, physician; b. Jackson, Tenn., Mar. 7, 1943; s. John Prentice and Phyllis (MacDonald) H.; children: Lindsey Warren, Brooke Olmsted, John Prentice IV. BA, Amherst Coll., 1965; MD, Boston U., 1969. Diplomate Am. Bd. Internal Medicine, internal medicine and cardiovascular disease. Research assoc. cellular physiology Amherst Coll., 1963-64; research assoc. cardiovascular physiology Boston U. Sch. of Medicine, 1966-67, lectr. medicine, 1972-73; intern Boston City Hosp., 1969-70, asst. resident, 1970-71; research fellow in medicine Harvard U., 1971-73, Peter Bent Brigham Hosp., 1971-73; survey physician Framingham Cardiovascular Disease Study, Nat. Heart and Lung Inst., 1971; asst. clin. prof. medicine U. Hawaii, 1973-75; asst. prof. medicine U. Mass., 1975-77, assoc. prof., 1977-85, vice chmn. dept. medicine, 1975-78, asst. dean continuing edn. for physicians, 1976-78, assoc. dean profl. affairs and continuing edn., 1978-80, acad. dean, 1980-85, vice chancellor, 1980-85, acting chmn. dept. anatomy, 1982-85; pres., prof. medicine U. Tex. Health Scis. Ctr., San Antonio, 1985—; assoc. chief div. medicine U. Mass. Hosp., 1975-78, dir. patient care studies dept., 1975-80, chief of staff, 1978-80. Mem. editorial bd. Archives Internal Medicine, 1991—; contbr. numerous articles to profl. jours., chpts. to books. Trustee S.W. Found. for Biomed. Rsch., San Antonio Med. Found., S.W. Rsch. Inst. Maj. M.C, U.S. Army, 1973-75. Alfred P. Sloan scholar Amherst Coll., 1962-65; recipient Ruth Hunter Johnson award Boston U. Sch. of Medicine, 1969. Fellow ACP, Am. Coll. Cardiology, Am. Coll. Chest Physicians; mem. AMA (del. ho. of dels. 1995—, coun. on sci. affairs 1993—), Am. Heart Assn. (fellow coun. clin. cardiology), Tex. Med. Soc. (coun. med. edn. 1986—, ho. of dels. 1989—, pres.-elect 1997—), Tex. Soc. Biomed. Rsch. (past pres.), Bexar County Med. Soc. (exec. com. 1985—, pres. 1996), Alpha Omega Alpha, Omicron Kappa Epsilon. Avocations: tennis; skiing.

HOWE, JONATHAN TRUMBULL, naval officer; b. San Diego, Aug. 24, 1935; s. Hamilton Wilcox and Margaret (Backus) H.; m. Harriet Mangrum, June 21, 1957; children: Richard, Jonathan, David, Katharine, Paul, Margaret. BS, U.S. Naval Acad., 1957; MA, Tufts U., 1968, MALD, PhD, 1969. Commd. ensign USN, 1957, advanced through grades to adm.; chief of staff 7th Fleet USN, Yokosuka, Japan, 1979-80; dir. polit. mil. plans div. OpNAv USN, Washington, 1980-81; mil. asst. Dep. Sec. Def., Washington, 1982-83; dir. polit. mil. bur. Dept. of State, Washington, 1983-84; comdr. cruiser-destroyer group 3 San Diego, 1985-86; dep. chmn. mil. com. NATO, Brussels, 1986-87; asst. to chmn. Joint Chiefs of Staff, Washington, 1987-89; comdr. Allied forces So. Europe NATO, Naples, Italy, 1989-91; comdr. U.S. Naval Forces Europe USN, London, 1989-91; dep. asst. to Pres. of U.S. for nat. security affairs Washington, 1991-93; ret. USN, 1992; spl. rep. of sec. gen. UN, Somalia, 1993-94; exec. dir. Arthur Vining Davis Found., Jacksonville, 1994—. Author: Multi-Crises: Seapower and Diplomacy in the Missile Age, 1971; contbr. articles to jours. in field. Decorated (6) Def. D.S.M., (2) Navy D.S.M., (3) Legion of Merit, Def. Superior Svc. medal, Nat. Security medal (civilian). Office: 111 Riverside Ave Ste 130 Jacksonville FL 32202-4921*

HOWE, KAREN LOUISE, lawyer; b. Corning, N.Y., Jan. 2, 1964; d. George R. Cleveland and Alberta B. Rhoda; m. William Earl Howe, May 1, 1993. BS, Keuka Coll., 1986; JD, Syracuse Coll., 1989. Bar: N.Y. 1990. Pub. defender Cortland (N.Y.) County Pub. Defender's Office, 1990-99. Mem. N.Y. State Bar Assn., Cortland County Bar Assn. Office: Howe Law Office PO Box 5462 55 Main St Cortland NY 13045-2609

HOWE, KATHY ELEANOR, geography educator, massage therapist; b. Murton, Eng., July 11, 1948; d. George and Laura (Young) Shovlin; m. David William Howe, June 21, 1969. Cert. edn., U. Wales, Swansea, 1969. Qualified tchr., Eng. and Wales; cert. massage therapist. Asst. tchr. geography The Nelson Thomlinson Sch., Wigton, Eng., 1969-88, acting head geography dept., 1988-89, asst. tchr., 1989—; exch. tchr. geography, social studies, economic studies Onslow Coll., Wellington, New Zealand, 1986; tchr. sports massage (part-time) Carlisle Coll., Eng., 1996-97; co-prin. Carlisle Massage Sch., 1990—. Recipient Duke Edinburgh's Gold award, Swansea, 1969; finalist Cumbria Women Yr., Eng., 1995; marathon champion women age 40-44 Brit. Amateur Athletics Fedn., London, 1989. Fellow Royal Geog. Soc.; mem. Assn. Tchrs. and Lectrs., Carlisle Aviation, No. Vets. Athletic Club (Women's 10km Road Champion 1992, 93, 94, 95, 97). Avocations: distance running, private aviation (pvt. pilot's license 1995, 96), travel, music, countryside. Home: 176 Lansdowne Crescent, Carlisle CA3 9ER, England

HOWE, LYMAN HAROLD, III, chemist; b. Wilkes-Barre, Pa., Nov. 5, 1938; s. Lyman Harold and Esther Madeline (Smith) H.; m. Mary Louise Reinhart, June 16, 1962; 1 child, Jennifer. B.S., Duke U., 1960; M.S., Emory U., 1961; Ph.D., U. Tenn., 1966. Rsch. assoc. Emory U., 1960-61; rsch. and teaching assoc. U. Tenn., 1962-66; rsch. chemist water mgmt. TVA, Chattanooga, 1966-97. Co-author publs. in field. Fellow ASTM (water com. results advisor 1976-97, Max Hecht award 1985, Award of Merit 1993); mem. Am. Chem. Soc., Am. Contact Bridge League (Ace of Clubs award, third place Chattanooga Club Master of Yr. award 1989, reviewer environ. sci. and tech. 1989), U.S. Chess Fedn. Clubs: Torch (1st v.p. chpt. 1981, pres. 1982-83, 2d v.p. 1984-88). Presbyterian. Home: 1241 Mountain Brook Cir Signal Mountain TN 37377-2127

HOWE, LORD RICHARD EDWARD GEOFFREY (BARON HOWE OF ABERAVON), former British government official; b. Dec. 20, 1926; s. B.E. Howe and E.F. (Thomson) H.; m. Elspeth Rosamund Morton Shand; 1 son, 2 daus. M.A., 1950, LL.B. (scholar), 1951, Trinity Hall, Cambridge; LLD (hon.) U. Wales, 1988; DCL (hon.) City U., 1993. Chmn., Cambridge U. Conservative Assn., 1951, Bow Group, 1955; mng. dir. Crossbow, 1957-60; editor, 1960-62; called to bar Middle Temple, 1952, created Queen's counsel, 1965, bencher, 1969; M.P. for Bebington, 1964-66, Reigate, 1970-74, East Surrey, 1974-92; Solicitor-Gen., 1970-72; Min. for Trade and Consumer Affairs, 1972-74; M.P., mem. Conservative Shadow cabinet, 1974-79, Chief Front Bench Spokesman on Treasury and Econ. Affairs, 1975-79; Chancellor of Exchequer, 1979-83; Chmn. Interim Com. IMF, 1982-83; Sec. State for Fgn. and Commonwealth Affairs, 1983-89; Dep. Prime Minister, 1989-90, Leader House of Commons, Lord Pres. of Coun., 1989-90; dep. chmn. Glamorgan Quarter Sessions, 1966-70; chmn. Framington Russian Investment Fund, 1994—; patron Enterprise Europe, 1990—; v.p. Royal United Svcs. Inst. for Def. Studies, 1991—; spl. adv. European and internat. affairs Jones, Day, Reavis and Pogue, 1991—; the visitor Sch. of Oriental and African Studies U. London, 1991—. Author: Conflict of Loyalty, 1994. Mem. Gen. Council of the Bar, 1957-61, Council of Justice, 1963-70; sec. Conservative Parliamentary Health and Social Com., 1964-65; patron Enterprise Europe, 1990—; mem. adv. coun. Presidium of Supreme Rada of Ukraine, 1991-97. Mem. Interdepartmental Com. on Age of Majority, 1965-67; chmn. bd. Ely Hosp. Inquiry, Cardiff, 1969; mem. council mgmt. Pvt. Patients' Plan, 1969-70; mem. internat adv. coun. Inst. Internat. Studies Stanford (Calif.) U., J.P. Morgan and Co., 1993—. Decorated Knight, privy councillor, 1972, Life Baron, 1992; recipient Grand Order of Merit Fed. Republic of Germany, 1992, Joseph Bech prize, 1993, Companion of Honor award, 1996. Office: House of Lords, London SW1A 0PW, England

HOWE, VIRGINIA HOFFMAN, nurse administrator; b. Buffalo, Apr. 14, 1940; d. George C. Jr. and Mabel (Parrish) Hoffman; m. Lawrence T. Howe, Apr. 11, 1970; children: Daniel George, Timothy Kelly. AAS, Trocaire, 1977; BS in Community Health Nursing, SUNY, Buffalo, 1986. RN, N.Y. Assoc. coord. oper. rm. Buffalo Gen. Hosp., head nurse oper. rm. gen. surgery, oper. rm. staff nurse, nurse clinician otolaryngology and ear, nose, throat dept., nurse clinician divsn. plastic and reconstructive surgery, nursing instr., educator, discharge planning nurse, cmty. health nurse, nurse paralegal. Mem. Assn. Operating Rm. Nurses.

HOWELL, ALVIN HAROLD, engineer, company executive, educator; b. Sedgwick, Kans., Feb. 5, 1908; s. George Alfred and Gertie (Johnson) H.; m. Helen Whitney, Sept. 7, 1934; children—Elizabeth, Alvin Harold, John Arthur, Gordon Howard. B.S., U. Kans., 1929; student, Union Coll., Schenectady, 1929-30; M.S., Mich. Coll. Mining and Tech., 1934; Sc.D., Mass. Inst. Tech., 1938. Registered profl. engr., Mass. Test engr. Gen. Electric Co., Schenectady, 1929-30; instr. Mich. Coll. Mining and Tech., 1931-34, research geophys. prospecting methods, summers 1931-34; research assoc. MIT, Cambridge, 1939-40; vis. prof., adminstrv. officer Radar Sch., 1942-43; asst. prof. elec. engring. Tufts U., Medford, Mass., 1940-41, assoc. prof., head dept. elec. engring., 1941-43, prof., head dept. elec. engring., dir. research, 1943-70, prof., dir. Balloon Astronomy Lab., 1970-78, emeritus prof., 1978—; devel. rocket and balloon type instrumentation; dir. Doble Engring. Co., 1960—, v.p., 1961-63, chmn. exec. com., 1969—, chmn. bd., 1979—; Mem. NRC; cons. on tethered and free floating balloon systems Air Force Geophysics Lab. Author: (with others) Principles of Radar, 1944; Contbr. (with others) articles to profl. publs. Recipient Exceptional Service award USAF, 1955; Distinguished Service award Tufts U., 1973; Tufts Service citation Tufts U. Alumni Assn., 1974; lab. named in his honor Tufts U., 1984. Mem. IEEE, Am. Phys. Soc., AAAS, AAUP, Sci. Ballooning Assn. (v.p. 1975-78), Am. Soc. Engring. Edn., Sigma Xi, Eta Kappa Nu, Tau Beta Pi. Baptist. Achievements include development of balloon-borne telescope for tracking planets and stars and balloon-borne payload for precisely pointing at ground targets to permit radiometric and interferometric measurements at IR wave lengths. Home: 990 Massachusetts Ave Arlington MA 02476-4532 Office: Tufts U Dept Elec Engring Medford MA 02155

HOWELL, BRUCE INMAN, academic administrator; b. Roanoke Rapids, N.C., Mar. 12, 1942; s. Leroy Inman and Pauline (Massey) H.; m. Mable Lea Smith, Aug. 22, 1965; children: Bruce Inman Jr., Virginia Lea. BS in English and History, East Carolina U., 1964, MA in History and Sch. Adminstrn., 1965; postgrad., N.C. State U., 1971, 84, Mich. State U., 1971, Duke U., 1976, N.C. Bank Dirs. Coll., 1999. Cert. grad. tchr., prin., supr., N.C., investment banker, stock exchange and brokerage office procedures. Instr., grad. asst. East Carolina U., Greenville, N.C., 1964-65; stockbroker Interstate Securities Corp., Charlotte, N.C., 1968-70; dean continuing edn. Lenoir C.C., Kinston, N.C., 1970-75; pres. Sampson Tech. Coll., Clinton, N.C., 1975-80, Wake Tech. C.C., Raleigh, N.C., 1980—; adj. prof. dept. adult and C.C. edn. N.C. State U., 1982—, gen. adv. com., 1982; mem. Wake County-Raleigh Pvt. Industry Coun., 1983-94, Raleigh Econ. Devel. Roundtable, 1984—, exec. com.; adv. N.C. govt. agys., Wake Co. Communities in Schs., 1990—; adv. Cen. Carolina Consortium, 1993-97, pres., 1996-97; mem. numerous ednl. commns. and task forces. Author: Debasement: A Problem of Imperial Rome, 1966, The Lenoir County Story, 1968; editorial bd. Community Coll. Review, N.C. State U., 1982-93; contbr. articles to profl. jours. Mem. Lenoir County Schs. Vocat. Adv. com., 1972-75, Econ. Devel. Com., Fuguay-Varina; bd. dirs. Lenoir County Heart Fund, 1972, Lenoir County Fair Assn., 1970, Branch Banking & Trust Co., Cary, N.C., 1980-98; chmn. bd. dirs. Crescent State Bank, 1998—; mem. Wake County Interagy. Coord. Coun., 1981; membership com. N.C. Lit. and Hist. Assn., 1978; mem. adminstrv. bd. Westminster United Meth. Ch., 1973-76; active First United Meth. Ch., Clinton, 1977-81, chmn. adminstrv. bd., 1978-80, White Plains, 1981—, trustee, 1997—. Grad. fellow East Carolina U., 1964-65; Kellogg Community Svcs. fellow, Lenoir Community Coll., 1971; named one of Outstanding Young Men Am., 1975, 77, 78, Jacyee of Yr., 1967, Outstanding Old Jaycee of Yr., 1971; recipient Chief Exec. Officer award So. Region Assn. Community Colls., 1989. Mem. Am. Coun. on Edn., Nat. Coun. Cmty. Svcs. Continuing Edn., Nat. Coun. Resource Devel., So. Assn. Colls. and Schs. (evaluation com. 1982, 90, 92-94), N.C. Assn. Colls. and Univs. (mem. govtl. agys. liaison com. 1983-90, pres. 1993), N.C. C.C. Adult Edn. Assn., N.C. Assn. Pub. C.C. Pres. (numerous com. assignments, pres. 1986-87), N.C. Employees Assn., Nat. Geneal. Soc. (N.C. chpt.), Am. Numismatic Assn., Greater Raleigh C. of C. (mem. adv. com. manpower resource devel. program 1980, leadership round table 1983—, higher edn. roundtable 1986—), Cary C. of C. (econ. devel. com. 1983—, edn. task force com. 1987—), Fuquay-Varina C. of C. (bd. dirs. 1987-90), Execs. Club of Raleigh (pres. 1996-98), Cary Rotary (pres. 1999-2000), Phi Delta Kappa, Kappa Delta Pi. Avocations: antiques, furniture refinishing, gardening, numismatics. Home: 1105 Queensferry Rd Cary NC 27511-6426 Office: Wake Tech Community Coll 9101 Fayetteville Rd Raleigh NC 27603-5655

HOWELL, CHARLES MAITLAND, dermatologist; b. Thomasville, N.C., Apr. 14, 1914; s. Cyrus Maitl and Lilly Mae (Ammons) H.; m. Betty Jane Myers, Feb. 12, 1949; children—Elizabeth Myers, Pamela Jane. B.S., Wake Forest U., Winston-Salem, N.C., 1935; M.D., U. Pa., 1937. Intern Charity Hosp., New Orleans, 1937-38; resident in medicine Burlington County Hosp., Mt. Holley, N.J., 1938-39; sch. physician Lawrenceville (N.J.) Sch., 1939-42; resident in pathology N.C. Baptist Hosp., Winston-Salem, 1947-48; resident in dermatology Columbia-Presbyn. Med. Ctr., N.Y.C., 1948-50; resident in allergy Roosevelt Hosp., N.Y.C., 1950-51; practice medicine specializing in dermatology Winston-Salem, 1951—; mem. staff N.C. Bapt., Forsyth Meml. hosps.; mem. faculty Bowman Gray Sch. Medicine, Wake Forest U., 1951-86, head. sect., 1984-86, prof. dermatology, 1967-84, prof. emeritus, 1984, head sect., 1961-86, acting head sect., 1984-86. Served as officer M.C. AUS, 1942-46. Fellow Am. Acad. Dermatology, Am. Acad. Allergy; mem. N. Am. Clin. Dermatol. Soc., N.Y. Acad. Scis. Democrat. Baptist. Clubs: Old Town (Winston-Salem); Bermuda Run Country (Clemmons, N.C.). Home: 1100 E Kent Rd Winston Salem NC 27104-1116 Office: 340 Pershing Ave Winston Salem NC 27103-2513

HOWELL, DONALD LEE, lawyer; b. Waco, Tex., Jan. 31, 1935; s. Hilton Emory and Louise (Hatchett) H.; m. Gwendolyn Avera, June 13, 1957; children: Daniel Liege, Alison Avera, Anne Turner. BA cum laude, Baylor U., 1956; JD with honors, U. Tex., 1963. Bar: Tex. 1963. Assoc. Vinson & Elkins, Houston, 1963-70, ptnr., 1970—, mem. mgmt. com., 1980-99. Capt. USAFR, 1956-59. Fellow Am. Bar Found., Tex. Bar Found., Houston Bar Found., Am. Law Inst.; mem. ABA, Am. Coll. Bond Counsel, Houston Bar Assn., Nat. Assn. Bond Lawyers (pres. 1981-82, bd. dirs. 1979-83), Attys. Liability Assurance Soc. (Bermuda bd. dirs. 1992—, chmn. 2000—, U.S. bd. dirs. 1992—, chmn. 2000—), Houston Club, Houston Ctr. Club, Order of Coif, Phi Delta Phi. Democrat. Episcopalian.

HOWELL, FRANK EDWARD, artist; b. Fargo, N.D., Dec. 27, 1940; s. Edward Austin Scott and Joyce Peterson H.; m. Judy Lohrey, Sept. 14, 1963 (div.); children: Dan, Amanda; m. Catherine Carroll Hubbard, July 20, 1990. BFA, U. Ariz., 1963; MFA, U. Oreg., 1965. Cert. tchr., Calif. Ceramics tchr., chmn. art dept. L.A. City Sch. Sys., 1966-71; founder, owner, tchr. Mud In Your Eye Pottery, Los Gatos, Calif., 1971-89, San Francisco, 1980-88; owner, potter Mud In Your Eye Pottery, Belllingham, Wash., 1996—. Author: The Craft of Pottery, 1975; prin. works include City of South Pasadena Playground sculpture. Founder, bd. dirs. Los Gatos Parking Commn., 1982-93; coach Am. Youth Soccer Orgn., Los Gatos, 1973-83; bd. dirs. Los Gatos C. of C., 1980-82, 86-88; v.p. Old Fairhaven Assn., Bellingham, 1996—. Named Member of Yr. Los Gatos C. of C., 1984; recipient Svc. Commendation award Town of Los Gatos, 1994. Mem. Washington Potters Assn., Lions. Avocations: golf, travel. E-mail: howells@az.com. Office: Mud In Your Eye Pottery 911 Harris Ave Bellingham WA 98225-7032

HOWELL, GEORGE BEDELL, equity investing and managing executive; b. Schenectady, Sept. 19, 1919; s. Jesse M. and Grace (Gerhaeusser) H.; m. Mary Barbara Crohurst, July 10, 1944; children: Raymond Gary, Terry Barbara, Janice Patricia, Nancy Jo, George Bedell Jr. BS in Adminstrv. Engring., Cornell U., 1942. With GE, 1946-59; v.p. mfg. Leece Neville Co., Cleve., 1959-61, Royal Electric Co., Pawtucket, R.I., 1961-62; dir. ops. packaging equipment and product devel. Acme Steel Co. (merged with Interlake Steel Corp. 1965), 1962-64; v.p. adminstrv. svc. Interlake Steel Corp., Chgo., 1964-66; v.p. internat. divsn., v.p. Acme Products divsn. Interlake Steel Corp., 1966-70; CEO Golconda Corp., Chgo., 1970-72; v.p. devel. Internat. Minerals & Chems. Corp., 1972-73, sr. v.p., pres. industry group, 1974-77, exec. v.p., 1977-81; pres., CEO Wurlitzer Co., 1982-86, chmn., pres., CEO, 1986-87, vice chmn., 1987-88; prin. Mid West Ptnrs., Chgo., 1988-89; gen. ptnr. Pfingsten Ptnrs., Chgo., 1989-94, ptnr., 1994—; chmn. Hallcrest Holding Corp., 1992-97, dir. exec. com., 1998—. Chmn. bd. trustees Village of Oak Brook, Ill., 1965-73, pres., 1973-79; trustee Christ Ch., Oak Brook, vice chmn., 1992-97, trustee emeritus, 1998. N.Y. State and Univ. scholar Cornell U., 1942. Mem. McGraw Wildlife Found., Chgo. Athletic Assn., Medinah Country Club, Econ. Club (Chgo.), Ocean Reef Club (Fla.). Home: 5 Brighton Ln Oak Brook IL 60523-2323 Office: 520 Lake Cook Rd Ste 375 Deerfield IL 60015-5632

HOWELL, JAMES BURT, III, agricultural products company sales consultant; b. Dec. 11, 1933; s. James Burt and Catharine Stanger (Sparks) H.; m. Lorraine Marie Chanatry, Feb. 18, 1995. BS with honors, Rutgers U., 1956; MBA, U. Del., 1980. Agrl. sales rep. Allied Chem. Corp., Phila., 1957-59; sales cons. Asgrow Seed Co. subs. Upjohn Co., Vineland, N.J., 1960—; bd. dirs. Advance Weight Systems, Inc., LaGrange, Ohio. Mem. ofcl. bd. (session) 1st Presbyn. Ch. of Cedarville, 1960—; admissions liaison officer U.S. Mil. Acad., West Point, N.Y., 1973—; chmn. Lawrence Twp. Zoning Bd. Adjustment. With U.S. Army, 1957, col. USAR. Recipient Burpee Hort. award Rutgers U., 1955. Mem. Am. Def Preparedness Assn., Vegetable Growers Assn. N.J., Pesticide Assn. N.J. (bd. dirs.), Res. Officers Assn. U.S., Phi Beta Kappa, Alpha Gamma Rho, Alpha Zeta (Centennial Honor Roll 1997). Home: 589 Sayres Neck Rd Cedarville NJ 08311-2311 Office: Asgrow Seed Co 1740 E Oak Rd Vineland NJ 08361-2504

HOWELL, LLEWELLYN DONALD, management educator; b. Oct. 12, 1940; m. Susana G. Lacayo; 1 child, Joseph L. BS in Sci. Edn. cum laude, SUNY, Brockport, 1963; MA in Govt., Internat. Affairs, Fla. State U., 1967; PhD in Internat. Rels., Syracuse U., 1973. Rsch. and teaching asst. dept. govt. Fla. State U., 1965-66; instr. Peace Corps tng. ctr. U. Hawaii, 1966; instr. polit. sci. Onondaga C.C., Syracuse, 1969; vis. rschr. Inst. S.E. Asian Studies, Singapore, 1970-71; asst. prof. polit. sci. U. Hawaii, Hilo, 1971-74; from asst. prof. to prof. internat. rels. Am. U., Washington, 1974-91, interim chair dept. comparative and regional studies, 1990-91; prof. internat. mgmt. Am. Grad. Sch. Internat. Mgmt., Glendale, Ariz., 1991—, prof., dept. chair, internat. studies, 1991-95, assoc. v.p. overseas programs, 1995-97; lectr. Fgn. Svc. Inst., 1980-91; adj. prof. nat. security affairs Naval Postgrad. Sch., Monterey, Calif., 1987; sr. rsch. assoc. Third Point Systems, Monterey, 1984-86; adj. prof. Monterey Inst. Internat. Studies, 1986; dir. Washington Summer Inst. in Quantitative Polit. Rsch., 1981-83; vis. asst. prof. polit. sci. U. Hawaii, Manoa, 1974, vis. prof. mgmt., 1998, 2000. Editor: Handbook of Country and Political Risk Analysis, 2d edit., 1998; editor Internat. Studies Notes, 1991-2000; co-editor: International Education: An Agenda for the Future, 1984, Malaysian Foreign Policy, 1990; contbr. articles to profl. jours. and chpts. to books. Coach boys' baseball and basketball, 1986-99. Recipient Fulbright-Hayes award, 1987-88, Summer Rsch. Initiation award NSF, 1974; NSF grant, 1991-94; Shell Internat. Studies fellow, 1970-71. Mem. Internat. Studies Assn., Acad. Internat. Bus., Am. Polit. Sci. Assn., Assn. for Asian Studies, Am. Fgn. Svc. Assn. (assoc.), Malaysia-Am. Soc. (pres. 1981-84, 86-87), Coun. Internat. Bus. Risk Mgmt. Office: Am Grad Sch Internat Mgmt Dept Internat Studies 15249 N 59th Ave Glendale AZ 85306-3236

HOWELL, WILLIAM PAGE, real estate executive; b. Carnegie, Okla., July 27, 1952; s. Herman Glen and Muriel Joyce (Raby) H.; 1 child, Blake Alexander Sewell-Howell. BS, Southwestern U., Weatherford, Okla., 1975; MS, U. Okla., 1976. Chief exec. officer, pres. Howell Assocs., Norman, Okla., 1976-84; dir. Saudi Arabian Investment Corp., Dallas, London, 1984-87; dir. acquisitions Mitsui Fudosan (N.Y.) Inc., N.Y.C., 1987-93; prin., ptnr. Peninsula Mgmt. Corp., N.Y.C., 1993—; pres. Howell Assocs. of N.Y., N.Y.C., 1993—; mng. ptnr. Cushman Peninsula Asset Mgmt. Group, N.Y.C., 1993—; chmn., pres. Boutique Hotels and Resorts, N.Y.C., 1998—; chmn., CEO, H.A.I. Investment Advisors, N.Y.C., 1999—; dir. adv. bd. Comml. Property News, N.Y.C., 1990—. Demographics coord. Dem. Nat. Com., Atlanta, 1976-77. Mem. Urban Land Inst., Assn. Fgn. Investors in U.S. Real Estate, Fedn. Internat. Adminstrs. de Bein Conseils Immobiliers, Japan Soc., N.Y. Real Estate Club, Internat. Devel. Rsch. Coun. Avocations: flying, skiing, skydiving, fishing, golf. Home: 111 E 30th St Apt 10A New York NY 10016-7352

HOWELL, WILLIAM ROBERT, retail company executive; b. Claremore, Okla., Jan. 3, 1936; s. William Roosevelt and Opal Theo (Swan) H.; m. Judy Howell; children: Ann Elizabeth, Teresa Lynn. BBA, U. Okla., 1958. With J.C. Penney Co., Inc., 1958—; store mgr. J.C. Penney Co., Inc., Tulsa, 1968-69; dist. mgr., dir. Treasury Stores subs., Dallas, 1969-71; div. v.p., dir. domestic devel. Treasury Stores subs., N.Y.C., 1973-76, regional v.p., western regional mgr., 1976-79, sr. v.p., dir. merchandising, mktg. and catalog, 1979-81, exec. v.p., 1981-82, vice chmn. bd. dirs, 1982-83, chmn., chief exec. officer, 1983-97; chmn. emeritus J.C. Penney Co., Inc., Plano, Tex., 1997—; bd. dirs. Exxon-Mobil Corp., Pfizer Corp., Bankers Trust Co., Halliburton Co., The Williams Cos., Am. Electric Power. Mem. Bus. Coun., Dirs.' Table, Delta Sigma Pi, Beta Gamma Sigma.

HOWELLS, GWYN, general practice physician; s. Isaac Cecil and Evelyn (Phillips) H.; m. Enid Blewett, Oct. 20, 1956; children: David, Jonathan. BSc, U. Wales, 1951; MB BCh, Welsh Nat. Sch. Medicine, 1954. House physician Cardiff Royal Infirmary, 1954; house surgeon Swansea Gen. Hosp., 1955, med. registrar, 1957; pvt. practice Swansea, 1959—; primary care physician Swansea, 1957—; lectr. U. Wales Coll. of Medicine, 1980—; vis. rsch. fellow U. Melbourne, 1994—; adviser Bd. of Health, Guernsey, 1997. Author: Adults with Learning Disabilities: A Practical Approach for Health Professionals, 1997; contbr. articles to profl. jours. Mem. Glantawe Hosp. Mgmt. Com., 1973, West Glamorean Health Authority, 1974-94; adv. com. Devel. of Svcs. Comdr. Royal Navy, 1955-57, Res., 1955-75. Fellow Royal Soc. of Medicine; mem. Submarine Officers Assn., Bristol Channel Yacht Club, Internat. Fellowship of Flying Rotarians. Avocations: flying, sailing, practical philosophy. Home: 15 Marine Walk, Swansea SA1 1Y2, United Kingdom Office: St Helen's Med Ctr, St Helen's Rd, Swansea Wales

HOWELLS, JOHN GWILYM, medical scientist; b. Anglesey, Wales, June 24, 1918; s. Richard David and Mary (Hughes) H.; m. Ola Margaret Harrison, Dec. 12, 1943; children: David, Richard, Cheryl, Roger. MBBS, London U., 1943, MD, 1950. House physician Charing Cross Hosp., London, 1943; trainee Gottingen (Germany) U., 1946; registrar Maudsley Hosp., London, 1947-49, Inst. Neurology, London, 1948; dir., rsch. dir. Inst. Family Psychiatry, Ipswich, Eng., 1949-83; tchr. U. Cambridge, Eng., 1974-83; mem. East Anglian Regional Hosp. Bd., Cambridge, 1965-74; mem. faculty bd. clin. medicine U. Cambridge, 1974-77. Author: Family Psychiatry, 1963, Theory and Practice of Family Psychiatry, 1967, Nosology of Psychiatry, 1970, The Royal College of Psychiatry, Remember Mania, 1974, Principles of Family Psychiatry, 1975, Integral Clinical Investigation, 1982, Reference Companion to the History of Abnormal Psychology, 1983 (Acad. Book of Yr. 1985), Concept of Schizophrenia, 1990; editor: Modern Perspectives in Psychiary, 12 vols., 1965-85, World History of Psychiatry, 1974; co-author: Family Relations Indicator, 1967, Family and Schizophrenia, 1985, Family Diagnosis, 1985, Clematis, 1990, Guide to Clematis, 1990, Growing Clematis, 1994, The Rose and The Clematis, 1996, The Viticellas, 1998. Capt. Royal Army Med. Corps, 1944-46. Disting. fellow Am. Psychiat. Assn., 1968; fellow WHO, 1961. Fellow Royal Coll. Psychiatrists (founder), Royal Soc. Medicine (life); mem. World Psychiat. Assn. (chmn. history of psychiatry), Brit. Med. Assn. (life). Avocations: research on Genus Clematis, history, opera, walking, traveling. Fax: 01206-337-333.

HOWELLS, MURIEL GURDON SEABURY (MRS. WILLIAM WHITE HOWELLS), volunteer; b. White Plains, N.Y., May 3, 1910; d. William Marston and Katharine Emerson (Hovey) Seabury; m. William White Howells, June 15, 1929; children: Muriel Gurdon Howells Metz, William Dean. Founder Brit. War Relief Soc., Madison, Wis., 1941, pres., 1941-43; apptd. visitor dept. decorative arts and sculpture Boston Mus. Fine Arts, 1955-72, dept. Am. decorative arts, 1972-97; mem. ladies com. Inst. Contemporary Art, Boston, 1955-68; co-founder, trustee Strawbery Banke Mus., Inc., Portsmouth, N.H., 1958-75, overseer, 1975-81, hon. overseer, 1981—; co-founder, steering com. Guild, 1959-91. Bd. dirs. Garden Club Am., 1959-62, nat. chmn. medal award com., 1962-65, judge flower arrangements; pres. Piscataqua Garden Club, 1952-54; mem. Harvard Solomon Islands Expdn., Malaita, 1968; 1st chmn. Boston chpt. Venice Com., Internat. Fund for Monuments (now Save Venice Inc.), 1970-71, vice chmn. Boston chmn., 1971-77, mem. exec. com., 1971-89, hon. chmn., 1989—. Recipient King's medal for Svc. in the Cause of Freedom, 1946, Hist. Preservation award zone 1 Garden Club Am., 1976. Mem. Nat. Soc. Colonial Dames N.H., Soc. Preservation of New England Antiquities, Mayflower Soc., Women's Travel Club (pres. 1967-69), Chilton Club, Colony Club. Address: 11 Lawrence Ln Kittery Point ME 03905-5104

HOWE OF ABERAVON, BARON See HOWE, LORD RICHARD EDWARD GEOFFREY

HOWER, JEANNE LOUISE, landscape designer; b. Mpls., Apr. 24, 1948; d. Archie Edward and Joyce Loucille (Cleve.) Hower; divorced; 1 child, Angela Marie. Student in landscape design, Olympic Coll., 1983-85; student in interior design, Life Time Career, Grand Rapids, Minn., 1975-77. Receptionist Bradfords, Inc., Anoka, Minn., 1966-67; inspector quality Pioneer Plating Co., Mpls., 1967-68, Honeywell County, Mpls., 1968-72; owner Jeanne's Profl. Finishing, Brementon, Wash., 1976-79; interior designer Office Interiors of Seattle, 1979-82; landscape designer, owner Horizon's Landscape Design, Bremerton, Wash., 1986-97; art dir. fairgrounds, Bremerton, 1978-81; crafts artist Artist Club, Bremerton, 1981-88; profl. gardener Gardener's Club, 1988-97. Floral, landscape and interior design projects. Affil. mem. Epilepsy Assn., Seattle, 1987-97, Nature Conservaory, 1990-97, Save the Whales, 1985-90. Mem. Am. Soc. Landscape Designer (affill.). Avocations: reading, gardening, collecting, crafts, saving the earth. Home and Office: 1733 Winfield Ave Bremerton WA 98310-4438

HOWES, ALFRED S., business and insurance consultant; b. Troy, N.Y.; s. Alfred G. and Frances (Youngs) H.; m. Elizabeth Hoffner, Oct. 10, 1942; children: Wendy, Mary Lee, Constance Ellen. Student, Brown U., 1934-35, U. Ala., 1935-36, Syracuse U., 1943-44. Cert. agt., advanced underwriting cons., N.Y., Vt. With Mass. Mut. Life Ins. Co. (formerly Conn. Mut. Life Ins. Co.); owner bus. cons. co., 1946; pres. Employee Incentive Plans of Am., Inc.; bd. dirs. Bering Trading Corp., Employee Incentive Plans, Inc., Killip Svcs., Inc., SVM Inc., EAH (Del.), Inc., Emerson Plastics Corp., Insulating Shapes Inc., Scotsmoor Co. Inc., Smiley Bros., Inc., Pub. Gray Letter, Century Planning Co., Inc., Hurd Shoe Co., Wood & Hyde Co., ApMew, Inc., Am. Paper Machinery, Inc., Broad St. Realty Corp., Mech. Tech. Inc., Mohonk Vly Oil Co., Inc., Utica Bulk Terminals, Inc.; purchasing agent for Neutral Nations. Contbr. articles to profl. jours. Active N.Y. State Temporary Commn. on Banking, Ins. and Fin. Svcs., 1983-84. Served with U.S. Army, 1943-46, ETO. Mem. Nat. Assn. Life Underwriters (pres. N.Y. chpt. 1965-66, life, pub. rels. chmn.), N.Y. State Assn. Life Underwriters (chmn. com. to revise laws concerning decedents and their estates, pres. 1966-67), N.Y.C. Assn. Life Underwriters (bd. dirs., pres.), Am. Philatelic Soc., Assn. for Advanced Life Underwriting (pres. 1970-71), Million Dollar Roundtable, Collectors Club, Brown Club (N.Y.C.), Fort Schuyler Club (Utica), Princeton Club (N.Y.C.), Ft. Orange Club (Albany). Home: 42 Fenimore Rd Scarsdale NY 10583-2252 Office: 530 5th Ave 12th Floor New York NY 10036-5101

HOWES, THEODORE CLARK, claims examiner; b. Ridgefield, Conn., Dec. 25, 1929; s. Robert Clark and Phyllis Evelyn (Greene) H.; m. Anne Christine Tourgee, Sept. 28, 1968. BS, Springfield (Mass.) Coll., 1956. Cert. tchr., Mass. Claims examiner Geico, Chevy Chase, Md., 1967-78, U.S. Dept. Labor, Washington, 1978—. Innovator in use of laser for mil. application. Sgt. USAF, 1948-52. Mem. VFW, Soc. Mayflower Descendants, Alden Kindred Am., Am. Legion. Republican. Congregationalist. Avocations: hunting, fishing, gardening, horseback riding, antiques. Home: Fox Meadow Farm 17110 Bollinger School Rd Emmitsburg MD 21727-8721 Office: US Dept Labor 200 Constitution Ave NW Washington DC 20210-0001

HOWIE, JOHN ROBERT, lawyer; b. June 29, 1946; s. Robert H. and Sarah Francis (Caldwell) H.; children: John Robert, Ashley Elizabeth, Lindsey Leigh. BBA, North Tex. State U., 1968; JD, So. Meth. U., 1976. Bar: Tex. 1976, U.S. Dist. Ct. (no. dist.) Tex. 1977, U.S. Ct. Appeals (5th, 9th, 10th and 11th cirs.), U.S. Supreme Ct. 1985, U.S. Dist. Ct. (so., ea. and we. dists.) Tex. 1987; cert. in personal injury trial law Tex. Bd. Legal Specialization, 1982. With Law Offices of Windle Turley, Dallas, 1976-88, Misko & Howie, 1988-95; ptnr. Howie & Sweeney, LLP, 1995—; adj. prof. trial advocacy So. Meth. U. Sch. Law, 1988-89, 92—, So. Meth. Sch. Law exec. bd.; rsch. fellow Southwestern Legal Found. Lt. comdr. USN, 1968-73. Recipient Disting. Alumnus U. of North Tex. Fellow So. Trial Lawyers Assn., Roscoe Pound Found. Civil Trial Adv.-Nat. Bd. Trial Adv. (cert. civil trial law), Internat. Acad. Trial Lawyers, Tex. Bar Found., Internat. Soc. Air Safety Investigators (contbr. Million Dollar Argument series 1989); mem. ABA (vice chmn. aviation law sect. 1986-91, chair 1992), Tex. Trial Lawyers Assn. (bd. dirs. 1983—), Dallas Trial Lawyers Assn. (sec.-treas. 1984, v.p. 1985, pres. 1986), Assn. Trial Lawyers Am. (vice chmn. aviation sect. 1984-85, chmn. 1986), Am. Bd. Trial Advocates (sec. Dallas chpt. 1988, pres. 1989), State Bar Tex. (aviation law sect. coun. 1994—, personal injury trial specialist), Lawyer/Pilots Bar Assn., Flight Safety Found., Million Dollar Advs. Forum, Trial Lawyers for Pub. Justice Found., Ark. Trial Lawyers Assn., Ga. Trial Lawyers Assn., N.Mex. Trial Lawyers Assn., Ind. Trial Lawyers Assn., So. Meth. U. Jour. Air Law and Commerce (bd. advs.), Pres.'s Coun. U. North Tex., Internat. Soc. of Barristers. Home: 6508 Turtle Creek Blvd Dallas TX 75205-1244 Office: Howie & Sweeney LLP 2911 Turtle Creek Blvd Ste 1400 Dallas TX 75219-6258

HOWITT, PAMELA TESLER, development and philanthropy consultant, association administrator; b. Providence, Apr. 10, 1955; d. Marvin Gerald and Marilyn (Schaffer) Tesler; m. Steven Samuel Howitt, Apr. 7, 1990. BFA, U. R.I., 1977; M in Profl. Studies magna cum laude, Pratt Inst., 1979. Dir. youth devel. programs Pratt Inst., Bklyn., 1979-80, dir. alumni resources, 1980-85; major gifts devel. officer Columbia U., N.Y.C., 1985-87; dir. devel. Columbia U./Columbia Presbyn. Med. Ctr., N.Y.C., 1987-89; asst. dean for devel. and external rels. Grad. Sch. Design Harvard U., Cambridge, Mass., 1989-93; exec. dir. Charitable Found., 1993—, pres. devel. and philanthropy, 1993—; cons., fundraiser for various civic, polit., religious orgns. in N.Y., Mass. and R.I., 1979—; cons., pres. Devel. & Philanthropy. Author: (documentary) Coping with Death and Dying with Adolescents through Art Therapy. Mem. Nat. Soc. Fundraising Execs., Coun. for the Advancement and Support of Edn., Assn. Small Founds., Univ. Club R.I. Home: 425 Pine St Seekonk MA 02771-2601

HOWLETT, CAMERON ROLFE, pathologist, educator; b. Rotorua, New Zealand, June 3, 1940; s. Henry William and Beatrice Mary (Keane) H.; m. Annette Elizabeth Thomas, June 25, 1971; children: Andrew Cameron, Angus James. B Vet. Sci., U. Sydney, Australia, 1963, PhD, 1973. Comparative pathologist; registered specialist histopathologist Bd. Vet. Surgeons NSW. Pvt. practice vet. surgeon Sydney, 1963-65, Eng., 1965-66; postgrad. scholar U. Sydney, 1967-71; lectr. Sch. Pathology U. NSW, Sydney, 1972-76, sr. lectr., 1976-86, assoc. prof., 1987-94, prof., 1995—; postgrad. scholar U. Sydney, 1967-71; vis. fellow Oxford (Eng.) U., 1987-88; Australian del. Internat. Liaison Com. World Biomaterial Socs., 1993—; fellow biomaterials sci. and engring. Internat. Com. World Biomaterial Socs., 1996; hon. assoc. faculty vet. sci. U. Sydney, 1981—; cons. pathologist HCOA Profls., Sydney, 1987—; cons. numerous cos. on biocompatibility med. devices; assessor rsch. groups issued by Australian Rsch. Coun. and Nat. Health & Med. Rsch., 1982—. Contbr. articles to profl. jours.; editl. bd. Jour. of Biomed. Materials Rsch., Vet. and Comparative Orthopaedics and Traumatology Jour., Clin. Implant Dentistry and Related Rsch. Mem. therapeutic devices evaluation com., Fed. Govt., Canberra, 1989—, chmn. biomaterials panel, 1989—, mem. cardiovascular device panel, 1992—, mem. tracking device panel, 1995—. Recipient travel grant Brit. Coun., Oxford U., 1979, 81. Mem. Royal Coll. Vet. Surgeons, Coll. Vet. Scientists Australia, Australian Soc. Exptl. Pathology (treas., coun. mem. 1985-89), Australian Soc. Biomaterials (found. mem., pres., v.p., coun. mem. 1989—). Mem. Democratic Labour party. Avocations: dixieland jazz, reading, fishing, surfing. Office: U New South Wales, Sch Pathology, Sydney 2052 NSW, Australia

HOWLETT, STEPHANIE ANN, home care equipment sales representative, nurse; b. Kansas City, Kans., Dec. 23, 1957; d. Wayne Stewart and Anna Marie (Barancik) H. AA, Kansas City Community Coll., 1979; student, Colo. Ctr. for The Blind, 1995-96. RN. Critical care nurse Providence-St. Margarets Health Ctr., Kansas City, Kans., 1979-82; primary pvt. duty nurse Quality Care In, Kansas City, Mo., 1980-81; dir. nursing Profl. Nursing Service, Kansas City, Mo., 1981-86; med. services cons. Crawford Health and Rehab. Services, Kansas City, Mo., 1986; sales rep. HOMEDCO, Lenexa, Kans., 1986-92, mem. presidents adv. coun., 1986-92; mem. adv. bd. Olsten Health Care Svcs., Kansas City, Mo., 1986-92, utilization rev. com., 1986-92, budget com., 1987-92. Mem. Jr. League, Wyandotte and Johnson County, 1988-91; vol. Vis. Nurses Assn., 1997-98, Network Rehab. Svcs., 1998-2000; vol. coord. Catch A Ride of Johnson County, Kans., 1999—. Named one of Outstanding Young Women Am., 1987. Mem. NAFE, Nat. Rehab. Assn., Assn. Rehab. Nurses, Support Hospice Oncology Profls., Kansas City Met. Discharge Coords., Kansas City Regional Homecare Assn. (edn. com., infusion therapy com.), Kiwanis Club of Lenexa (bd. dirs.), Bi Partisian. Avocations: travel, reading, exercise, learning adaptability to blinded skills. Home: 9416 W 125th St Overland Park KS 66213-4731

HOWORTH, DAVID, producer, director; b. N.Y.C., Aug. 30, 1941; s. Marion Beckett and Dorothy Huldah (Cowing) H.; m. Bea Borges, May 6, 1967. AA, Santa Barbara (Calif.) C.C., 1970; student, UCLA, 1977, Am. Film Inst., L.A., 1982. V.p., co-owner Golden Coast Films, Santa Barbara, 1971-82, owner, prodr., dir., 1982—. Software developer, prodr. Internet Career Vision, Wildlife/Nature series, 1993; prodr., dir. Careers: Nursing, 1993; co-prodr., co-writer (ednl. picture) Just Beer, 1983. With USMCR, 1960-65. Recipient awards Columbus Internat. Film/Video Festival, 1993, Nat. Mental Health Assn., 1981, Excellence-Suitable for Family Viewing, No. Calif. Motion Picture and TV Coun., 1975. Mem. NATAS, AMA (acad. med. films), Internat. Interactive Comms. Soc., Greater Santa Barbara Advt. Club (pres. 1972). Avocations: historical films, records, swimming, boating. E-mail: gcf@silcom.com. Office: Golden Coast Films H102 2020 Alameda Padre Serra # H102 Santa Barbara CA 93103-1756

HOXIE, RALPH GORDON, educational administrator, author; b. Waterloo, Iowa, Mar. 18, 1919; s. Charles Ray and Ada May (Little) H.; m. Louise Lobitz, Dec. 23, 1953 (dec. 1992); m. Ada B. Edgerton, June 21, 1997. BA, U. No. Iowa, 1940; MA, U. Wis., 1941; PhD, Columbia, 1950; LLD (hon.), Chung-ang U., 1965; LittD (hon.), D'Youville Coll., 1966; grad., Air War Coll., 1971; LHD (hon.), Gannon U., 1988, Wesley Coll., 1989, U. No. Iowa, 1990, Shepherd Coll., 1992, Teikyo Post U., 1994, Long Island U., 1995, Fitchburg State Coll., 1997. Roberts fellow Columbia, 1946-47, Roberts travelling fellow, 1947-48, asst. to provost, 1948-49; asst. prof. history, gen. editor Social Sci. Found.; asst. to chancellor U. Denver, 1950-53; project asso. Columbia Bicentennial History, 1953-54; dean Coll. Liberal Arts and Scis., L.I. U., 1954-55; acting dean C. W. Post Coll., 1954-55, dean, 1955-60, provost, 1960-62, pres., 1962-68; chancellor L.I. U., 1964-68, cons., 1968-69; pres. Center for Study of Presidency, 1969-95; chmn. Ctr. for Study of Presidency, 1995-96, pres., chmn. emeritus, 1997—; pub. mem. Fgn. Svc. officer selection bd. U.S. Dept. State; vis. lectr. U. Ala., U. Calif., Irvine, Columbia U., U. Colo., Colo. State U., U. Wyo., Chapman Coll., U. No. Colo., Colo. Coll., Gannon U., Gettysburg Coll., Heidelberg Coll., U. Kans., Kans. State U., Muskingum Coll., Post Coll., St. Francis Coll. N.Y., USAF Acad., Naval War Coll., Nat. Archives, Nat. War Coll., Oglethorpe U., U. Genoa, Italy, U. Pitts., U. Tex., El Paso, U Wis., Northwestern U., U. No. Iowa; bd. govs. Banque Continentale br. Franklin Nat. Bank. Author: John W. Burgess, American Scholar, 1950, Command Decision and the Presidency, 1977, (with others) A History of The Faculty of Political Science, Columbia University, 1955, Organizing and Staffing the Presidency, 1980; editor: Frontiers for Freedom, 1952, The White House: Organization and Operations, 1971, The Presidency of the 1970's, 1973, The Presidency and Information Policy, 1981, The Presidency and National Security Policy, 1984; editor Presdl. Studies Quar., 1970-95; contbg. author: (with others) Freedom and Authority in Our Time, 1953, The Coattailless Landslide, 1974, Power and the Presidency, 1976, Classics of the American Presidency, 1980, The Blessings of Liberty, 1987, Popular Images of American Presidents, 1988, Rating Game in American Politics, 1988, Science and Technology Advice to the President, Congress, and Judiciary, 1988, The American Presidency: Historical and Contemporary Perspectives, 1988, Points of View, 1988, The Presidency in Transition, 1989, Dictionary of American History, 1996, Points of View, 1998, Moral Authority of Government, 1999; contbr. articles to profl. jours. and encys. Bd. dirs. United Fund L.I., Bklyn. Inst. Arts and Scis., Tibetan Found., L.I. Coun. Alcoholism, Bklyn. chpt. ARC Greater N.Y.; chmn., pres. bd. dirs. Am. Friends Chung-ang U.; pres. Pub. Mems. Assn. Fgn. Svc.; trustee Air Force Hist. Found., U. No. Iowa Found., Nat. Inst. Social Scis., Kosciuszko Found. N.Y., Mackinac Coll., North Shore chpt. Am. Assn. UN, Downtown Bklyn. Assn., Coun. Higher Ednl. Instns. N.Y.C.; mem. adv. bd. L.I. Air res. Ctr.; co-founder, mem. adv. coun. Robert A. Taft Inst. Govt.; sec. Nassau County Commn. on Govt. Revision; co-chmn. Nassau-Suffolk Conf. Christians and Jews; dir., pres. Great-N.Y. Coun. Fgn. Students; bd. govs. Human Resources Ctr., N.Y. Korean Vets. Meml. Commn. Served to capt. USAAF, 1942-46; brig. gen. USAF ret. Decorated Meritorious Svc. medal, Legion of Merit, Korean Cultural medal, numerous other medals; recipient Disting. Svc. medal City N.Y., 1965, Alumni Achievement award U. No. Iowa, 1965, Alumni Achievement award Columbia U., 1997, Columbia award for Disting. Achievment, 1997; named Man of Yr. Paderewski Found., 1966, Man of Yr. Eloy Alfaro Found., 1966. Fellow Am. Studies Assn. Met. N.Y.; mem. Am. Hist. Assn., Internat. Assn. Univ. Pres., Am. Polit. Sci. Assn., Acad. of Polit. Sci., Navy League, Air Force Assn., Res. Officers Assn. (pres. Mitchel chpt.), V.F.W., Am. Legion, L.I. Assn. (dir.), Am. Polar Soc., Kappa Delta Pi, Pi Gamma Mu, Alpha Sigma Lambda, Delta Sigma Pi, Gamma Theta Upsilon. Episcopalian. Clubs: Century Assn., Met., Columbia Univ. Faculty House (N.Y.C.); Met. (Washington); Bklyn., Montauk (Bklyn.); Old Westbury Golf and Country and Mill River (hon.). Home: PO Box 248 Oyster Bay NY 11771-0248 Office: 208 E 75th St New York NY 10021-2925

HOXTER, CURTIS JOSEPH, international economic adviser, public relations and public affairs counselor; b. July 20, 1922; s. Jacob and Hanna (Katzenstein) H.; m. Grace Lewis, Feb. 4, 1945 (dec.); children: Ronald Alan, Victoria Ann, Audrey Theresa; m. Allegra Branson, Jan. 2, 1981. AB, NYU, 1948, MA, 1950. Staff contbr. AUFBAU-Reconstn., N.Y.C., 1939-40; feature writer, reporter L.I. (N.Y.) Daily Press, 1940-42; editor, writer, analyst Office War Info., N.Y.C., 1943-45; pub. info. officer Dept. State, 1945-47; dir. pub. rels. Internat. C. of C., 1948-53; info. cons. Econ. Cooperation Agy., Washington, 1950-55; exec. v.p. George Peabody and Assocs., Inc., 1953-56; pvt. practice, 1956—; pub. rels. cons. various cos. and govt. agys.; columnist Scripps-Howard Newspapers; adviser U.S. Com. for UN Day, Internat. Economy mag., on internat. econ. and fin. problems to govt. agys., U.S. Del. Disarmament Conf., London; mem. internat. adv. bd. Bus. Week Chief Exec. Roundtable; exec. dir. adv. com. to Chancellor of Austria; mem. adv. com. Grad. Sch. Internat. Rels., U. Calif., San Diego; spl. advisor to pres. European Commn. Contbr. and commentator articles to nat. mags. and newspapers. With AUS, World War II. Decorated Order of Merit of the Republic of Austria, 1991. Mem. Met. (N.Y.C.), Econ. Club N.Y., Leewood Country Club, Coral Beach and Racquet (Bermuda), Univ. Club (Washington). Office: 380 Lexington Ave New York NY 10168-0002

HÖXTERMANN, EKKEHARD, biologist, educator; b. Sondershausen, Germany, May 19, 1953; s. Josef and Ruth (Bock) H.; m. Jutta (Karge) May 13, 1983; children: Julia, Martin. Diploma, Humboldt U., Berlin, 1978, D of Natural Scis., 1985; Habilitation, Friedrich Schiller U., Jena, Germany, 1994. From rsch. aspirant to asst. dept. gen. botany Humboldt U., Berlin, 1982-85; biology historian Pub. Peace Rsch. Group, Berlin, 1985-90; asst. Inst. for Biochemistry U. Cologne, Germany, 1990-93; lectr. history of biochemistry Friedrich Schiller U., Jena, 1994-96; lectr. history of biology Free U. Berlin, 1996—; freelancer Hist. Working Group of Mus. for Natural History, Berlin, 1998—; vis. scientist Lomonosov State U., Moscow, 1983. Author: (books) Otto Warburg (1883-1970) An Architect of Science, 1984, On the History of Photosynthesis and Metabolism Research at Berlin University, 1991, On the History of Plant Physiology and Biochemistry, 1998. Recipient Leopoldina award German Acad. Naturalists, 1994, Haberlandt prize Humboldt U., Berlin, 1978; Goethe scholar City Coun. Berlin, 1975. Home: Märkische Allee 326, D-12689 Berlin Germany Office: Mus for Natural History, Invalidenstr 43, D-10115 Berlin Germany

HOY, FRANCIS STOWE, management educator; b. Abington, Pa., Sept. 27, 1946; s. Richard Carlyle and Kathleen Helen H.; m. Patricia Margarita Echegaray; children: Jessica H. Boutte, Morris N., Erika H. Lane, Ashlee K. BBA, U. Tex., El Paso, 1967; MBA, U. North Tex., 1970; PhD, Tex. A&M U., 1979. Supr. acctg. office Southwestern Bell Tel. Co., Houston, 1971; mgr. Travel, Inc., El Paso, 1972-73; instr. mktg. Tarleton State U., Stephenville, Tex., 1973-75; lectr. mgmt. Tex. A&M U., College Station, 1975-78; asst. prof. mgmt. U. Ga., Athens, 1978-83, state dir. Ga. small bus. devel. ctr., 1984-88, Carl R. Zwerner prof., 1988-91; dean coll. bus. adminstrn. U. Tex., El Paso, 1991—; Chair worker transition pilot training project Tex. Workforce Commn., El Paso, 1997, Ctrl. European Small Bus. Enterprise Devel. Commn., Czech Republic, Hungary, Poland, 1991-95. Author: Employee Development Programs, 1985; editor: Moving to Sustainabilitiy, 1995; editor Entrepreneurship Theory Practice, 1991-94; spl. issues editor Jour. Bus. Venturing, 1996-98. Mem. Gov.'s Interagy. Coun. Small Minority Bus., Atlanta, 1984-88; bd. dirs. edn. rsch. found. Family Firm Inst., 1998—; vice chair, bd. dirs. Rio Vista Rehab. Ctr., El Paso, 1996—; vice chair United Way, El Paso, 1998—. Recipient Leavey award Freedoms Found., 1998. Fellow U.S. Assn. Small Bus. Entrepreneurship (v.p. 1990—); mem. Internat. Coun. Small Bus. (sr. v.p. 1990—, Wilford White fellow 1997), Acad. Mgmt. (chair entrepreneurship divsn., editor, Mentorship award 1991, Innovation award 1997), Greater El Paso C. of C. (chair bus. resources coun. 1991—). Avocations: traveling, reading, writing, hiking. Fax: 915-747-5147. E-mail: fhoy@utep.edu. Home: 504 Sandbar Ct El Paso TX 79922-2236 Office: Coll Bus Adminstrn U Tex El Paso TX 79968-0001

HOY, GEORGE PHILIP, clergyman, food bank executive; b. Indpls., Feb. 5, 1937; s. Clarence Augustus Hoy and Margaret Louise (Etter) Wooley; m. Barbara J. Turpen, Aug. 11, 1957 (dec. Feb. 1987); children: Rene Hoy Riegle, Sherri Hoy Haas, Matthew Philip; 1 foster child, Richard H. Johnson; m. Sandra L. Knipe, July 30, 1999. BA, Ky. Wesleyan Coll., 1958; MDiv, So. Bapt. Theol. Sem., Louisville, 1962. Ordained to ministry United Ch. of Christ, 1962, Nat. Bapt. Conv. 1997. Pastor Union United Ch. of Christ, Evansville, Ind., 1962-72, Faith United Ch. of Christ, Ft. Wayne, Ind., 1975-80, St. Matthew's United Ch. of Christ, Evansville, 1981-87; dir. Youth Svc. Bur., Evansville, 1972-75; pastor St. Peter's United Ch. of Christ, Evansville, 1987-94; mem. faculty Brescia U., Owensboro, Ky., 1970-72; chaplain Evansville State Hosp., 1966-72, Fraternal Order Police, Evansville, 1982-92, chaplain, life mem.; dir. Tri-State Food Bank, Evansville, 1987-2000, ret. 2000; del. gen. synod Ind.-Ky. Conf., United Ch. of Christ, 1978-81. Religion columnist Evansville Press, 1983-93. Vol. Habitat for Humanity, Americus, Ga., 1980-81; mem. City-County Human Rels. Commn., Evansville, 1984-93; bd. dirs. Leadership Evansville, 1987-92, Outreach Ministries, Evansville, 1987-93; mem. regional bd. advisors Ch. World Svc., 1987—; mem. Ill. and Ind. Hunger Coalitions; mem. Bread for the World, Amnesty Internat., Food Rsch. and Action, Police Athletic League; mem. Vanderburgh County Coun., 1992—, pres., 1994-95, v.p., 1997; v.p. Vanderburgh County Coun., 1997; bd. dirs. Repertory People of Evansville, St. Anthony Ctr. for Family Life, Vanderburgh County Coun. on Aging; mem. cmty. adv. coun. Evansville Ctr. for Med. Edn.; mem. Local Emergency Planning Com.; supr. Vanderburgh County Soil and Water conservation Dist.; chair fin. Pigeon Creek Greenway; assoc. pastor First Ebenezer Bapt. Ch.; chmn. hunger walk CROP; bd. mem. Southwestern Ind. Disaster Resistance Cmty. Corp.; walk coord., com. mem. Evansville Stand for Children. Recipient ecumenical award Evansville Area Coun. of Chs., 1987, Native Am. award Coun. of Bear, Evansville, 1988, Individual Achievement award Leadership Evansville, 1998, Martin Luther King Jr. Cmty. Svc. award Black Leadership Conf., 2000, Starfish award Tri-State Food Bank, 2000, award for outstanding svc. to foster parents, others; named to CROP Honor Roll, 1997, Hon. Order Ky. Cols. Mem. NAACP, ACLU, Internat. Brotherhood Magicians, Ind. Psychol. Assn., Tri-State Pastors Circle (pres. 1984-85), Northside Ministerial Assn., Evansville Tri-State Assn. (pres. 1972-75), Isaac Walton League, Greenpeace, Silent Singers (hon.). Democrat. Avocations: music, art, drama, dance performing, model railroading. Home: 217 Cherry St Evansville IN 47713-1242

HOYER, HANS, law educator; b. Vienna, Austria, Apr. 29, 1936; s. Hans and Margaretha (Plefka) H.; m. Dorothea Kretz, Mar. 29, 1936; children: Evelyn (dec.), Barbara, Elizabeth, Hans Xaver, Hans Lukas. Dr iur, Vienna U., Austria, 1958; Universitätsdozent, Vienna U., 1970. Asst. U. Vienna, 1958-59; candidate for judicial office Vienna Apellate Ct., 1959-61; judge at various dist. cts. near and in Vienna, 1962-66; judge Comml. Ct. Vienna, 1966-69; asst. U. Vienna, 1966-71, assoc. prof., 1971-86, full prof. civil and comparative law, 1986—; bd. dirs. 6 companies. Editor: (series of law books) Wiener Rechtswissenschaftliche Studien; author: (law book) Die Simultanhypothek, 1973, 77; editor and author: Das Einheitliche Wiener Kaufrecht, 1992; co-editor (jours) Zeitschrift für Rechtsvergleichung, Österr. Notariatszeitung. Recipient Grosses Ehrenzeichen Republik Österreich, 1983. Mem. Österreichische Gesellschaft für Rechtsvergleichung (pres.). Alt-Katholisch. Home and Office: Schottenbastei 10-16, A 1010 Wien Austria

HOYOS, ARTURO, lawyer, educator, consultant, researcher; b. Panama City, Panama, Dec. 9, 1948; s. Arturo and Maria (Phillips) H.; m. Victoria Romero, Jan. 10, 1976 (div. Apr. 1984); 1 child, Maria Eugenia; m. Ginny Boyd, Dec. 28, 1985; children: Carlos Arturo, Alejandro Antonio. Diploma in labor law, U. Javeriana, Colombia, 1971; JSD, U. Javeriana, 1972; MA in Devel. Econs., U. Sussex (Eng.), 1974; postgrad., Cambridge (Eng.) U., 1974, U. Bologna, Italy, 1988. Bar: Panama 1972. Gen. dir. labor Ministry Labor and Social Welfare, Panama City, 1972-73, gen. dir. employment, 1974-76; prof. tax law U. Panama Law Sch., Panama City, 1975-90, prof. labor law, 1984-92; assoc. Arias, Fabrega and Fabrega, Panama City, 1976-89; Supreme Ct. justice Panama City, Republic of Panama, 1990—; Supreme Ct. chief justice, 1994—; external cons. ILO, Geneva, 1976-77; vis. scholar Mexican Ministry Labor and Social Welfare, 1977, 81; vis. prof. U. Amazones, Manaus, Brazil, 1983, Inst. Legal Studies, Nat. U. Mex. and U. Iberoamericana, Mexico City, 1986, 92, U. Seville, Spain, 1992. Author: Derecho Pannameño del Trabajo, 1982; contbr. articles on labor, constl., tax, and procedural law to legal jours. Scholar Brit. Coun., 1973-74, ILO, Turin, Italy, Geneva, Madrid, 1983. Mem. Panama Bar Assn. (dir. Lex law rev. 1985—), Panamanian Acad. Law, Ibero-Am. Acad. Labor Law and Social Security. Home: PO Box 657, Panama Zone 9-A, Panama Office: Corto Surpema, Edif 236, Ancon, Calle Culebra, Apdo 1770 Panama Panama

HOYT, EARL EDWARD, JR., industrial designer; b. Binghamton, N.Y., July 16, 1936; s. Earl Edward and Lea (LaRue) H.; m. Bernice Phillips Maseritz, Aug. 20, 1960; children: Earl Edward III, Justin Phillips. B with honors in Indsl. Design, Pratt Inst., 1960. Designer Donald Deskey Assocs., N.Y.C., 1960-65; pres. The Hoyt Group Inc., Franklin Lakes, N.J., 1965—; instr. Sch. Visual Arts, N.Y.C., Pratt Inst., Rutgers Sch. Package Engring.; lectr. in field. Awarded more than 85 patents in field. Served with U.S. Army, 1954-56. Recipient awards archtl. design concept Am. Inst. Architects, 1964, Package Yr. Package Design Mag., 1970, Grand/Excellence in Design and Quality Soc. Plastic Industy, 1972, design Am. Inst. Graphic Artists Competition, 1st prize splty. design innovation-1st prize household products-1st prize communication excellence N.J. chpt. Packaging Inst. USA, 1979, package yr. Food and Drug Packaging Mag., 1978, 80, Jupiter Engring. excellence in design Western Plastics Exposition, 1980, package design excellence Clio, 1978, 81, 87, outstanding packaging achievement N.J. Packaging Execs. Club, 1982, 83, 86 (best of show/package yr.). Mem. Indsl. Designers Soc. Am. Republican. Avocations: watercolor artist, skiing, fishing, outdoor activities, guitar. Home: 24 Woodland Rd Stone Ridge NY 12484-5514 Office: The Hoyt Group Inc PO Box 928 Woodstock NY 12498-0928

HOYT, JOHN ARTHUR, humane society executive; b. Marietta, Ohio, Mar. 30, 1932; s. Claremont Earl and Margaret Adeline (Hawkins) H.; m. Gertrude Ellen Mohnkern, June 7, 1957; children: Margaret Rose, Karen Elizabeth, Anne Christine, Julie Kay. BA, Rio Grande Coll., 1954, DD, 1968; MDiv, Colgate Rochester Div. Sch., 1958; Dr honoris causa, U. Bucharest, Romania, 1995; LHD (hon.), St. Thomas U., Miami, Fla., 1998, U. St. Petersburg, Russia, 1997. Ordained to ministry Baptist Ch., 1957; pastor Allen Park (Mich.) Bapt. Ch., 1958-60, First Presbyn. Ch., Leroy, N.Y., 1960-64; sr. minister Drayton Ave. Presbyn. Ch., Ferndale, Mich., 1964-68, First Presbyn. Ch., Fort Wayne, Ind., 1968-70; pres. Humane Soc. U.S., Washington, 1970-91, chief exec., 1992-97; pres. emeritus, 1997—; pres. Humane Soc. Internat., Washington, 1991-94; pres., dir. Humane Soc. of Can., Toronto, 1994-98; vice chmn. bd. dirs. EarthKind Internat., Washington, London, 1991-98; pres. Earthkind, U.S., Washington, 1994-97. Author: Animals in Peril: How "Sustainable Use" is Wiping Out the World's Wildlife, 1994. Pres. Nat. Assn. for Humane and Environ. Edn., East Haddam, Conn., 1970-94, chmn. bd. dirs. 1973-95; trustee Rio Grande (Ohio) Coll., 1979-86, Lake Erie Coll., Painesville, Ohio, 1986-88; bd. dirs. The Am. Fondouk, Boston, 1986-97, Earth Day 1990, 1989-90, Global Tomorrow Coalition, 1989-94; pres. World Soc. for Protection of Animals, London, 1986-90, v.p., 1990-98; pres. dir. Ctr. for Respect Life and Environment, Washington, 1986-98; pres., dir. Internat. Ctr. Earth Concerns, Calif., 1994-98; dir. Grupo de los Cien, Mex., 1994-98, Counterpart International., Washington, 1997—; mem. Earth Charter Commn.; v.p. Internat. Devel. Conf., Washington, 1997-99; pres., dir. East Restoration Corps., Washington, 1999—. Recipient Disting. Alumnus award Rio Grande Coll., Founders award for Humane Excellence ASPCA, 1991, George T. Angell

Humanitarian award Mass. SPCA, 1992, Pres.'s Disting. Ministry award Sch. of Theology at Claremont, Calif., 1995, Reverence for Life Commendation Albert Schwertzer Inst. for the Humanities, 1998. Home: 320 Bear Castle Dr Bumpass VA 23024-4925 Office: Humane Soc US 2100 L St NW Ste 500 Washington DC 20037-1596

HOYT, LUPÉ ANN GONZÁLEZ, small business owner; b. San Pedro, Calif., Jan. 6, 1952; d. Pedro Meléndez and Nellie (Baldonado) González; m. Robert Alan Hoyt, Oct. 8, 1977; children: Karen Elena, David Elijah, Sylvia Carol. A in Bibl. Studies, Bethany Bible Coll.; BA in Psychology and Counseling, La. Bapt. U. Christian counselor Ashland Christian Counseling Svcs., Cin., 1999—; instr. Temple Baptist Coll., Cin., 2000. Vol. Fernside Ctr. for Grieving Children, Am. Cancer Soc. Mem. Am. Assn. Christian Counseling, Nat. Alliance Hispanic Health. Republican. Baptist. Avocations: botany, ancient history, loom weaving, Navajo language and culture, herb gardens. Home: 4525 Floral Ave Cincinnati OH 45212-3251 Office: Ashland Christian Counseling Svcs PO Box 12687 Cincinnati OH 45212-0687

HOZ, SHMARYAHU, chemist, researcher, educator; b. Jerusalem, Feb. 12, 1945; s. Jacob and Pnina H.; m. Tova Fostick, Feb. 25, 1971; children: Bilha, Penina, Benaya. BSc, Hebrew U., 1967, MSc, 1969; PhD, Bar-Ilan U., Ramat-Gan, Israel, 1973. Head dept. chemistry Bar-Ilan U., Ramat-Gan, 1985-87, prof., 1990—, v.p. rsch., 1996—; bd. dirs. Bar-Ilan Rsch. Devel. Co., Ltd.; mem. com. Standard Bur., Tel-Aviv. Contbr. articles to profl. jours.; patentee in field. Served Israeli Def. Force, 1962-65. Recipient Landau Rsch. award, 1991. Mem. Israel Chem. Soc., Am. Chem. Soc. Office: Bar Ilan U, 52900 Ramat Gan Israel

HOZAK, PAVEL, cell/molecular biologist, researcher; b. Turnov, Czechoslovakia, June 26, 1958; s. Bretislav and Eva (Svatonova) H. MSc, Lomonosov State U., Moscow, 1982; PhD, Charles U., Prague, 1987. Rsch. scientist Inst. Exptl. Medicine, Prague, Czechoslovakia, 1987-90; rsch. fellow Sir William Dunn Sch. Pathology, U. Oxford, Eng., 1991-94; head lab. Inst. Exptl. Medicine, Prague, Czech Republic, 1995—; head dept. cell and molecular biology 3d Med. Faculty Charles U., Prague, 2000—; biomed. rsch. fellow The Wellcome Trust, London, 1995-98; pres. Internat. Workshop Cell Nucleus, 1999-2000. Contbr. chpt. to book; organizer confs. Rsch. grantee The Brit. Coun., 1991-98, The Royal Soc., London, 1992, NSF, 1998—. Mem. Electron Microscopy Soc. Avocations: classical music, hiking, painting, art. Office: Inst Exptl Medicine, Videnska 1083, 14220 Prague 4, Czech Republic

HOZAYEN, HOZAYEN A., engineering educator, consultant, researcher; b. Giza, Egypt, Nov. 2, 1961. BS, Cairo U., Egypt, 1984, MS, 1987; PhD, U. of Waterloo, Ontario, 1992. Demonstrator Cairo U., Egypt, 1984-88; rsch. asst. U. of Waterloo, Ont., Can., 1988-91; asst. rsch. officer Nat. Rsch. Counc., Ottawa, Can., 1992-96; adj. prof. U. of Saskatchewan, Can., 1993-97; asst. prof. Cairo U., Cairo, Egypt, 1996—. Recipient award Can. Tech. Asphalt Assoc., 1992. Office: Cairo Univ, Faculty of Engring Pub Wks, 12613 Cairo Egypt

HOZUMI, MOTOO, medical educator, medical researcher; b. Fukushima, Japan, Mar. 12, 1933; s. Akiine and Fumi Hozumi; m. Sakiko Wakabayashi, May 4, 1963; children: Yuko, Masamichi, Ayako. BSc, Tokyo U. Edn., 1956, MSc, 1958, Dsc, 1961. Rsch. mem. Nat. Cancer Ctr. Rsch. Inst., Tokyo, 1962-64, chief ctrl. lab., 1964-75; dir. dept. chemotherapy Saitama (Japan) Cancer Ctr. Rsch. Inst., 1975-93, dir., 1990-93; spl. rsch. Saitama (Japan) Cancer Ctr., 1993-96; rsch. mem. Roswell Park Meml. Inst., Buffalo, N.Y., 1965-67; vis. prof. Showa U. Med. Sch., Tokyo, 1988—; cons. Japan Immunoresearch Inst., Takasaki, Japan, 1993-98. Author: Advances in Cancer Research, 1983, Ciba Foundation Symposium, 1990, Status of Differentiation Therapy, 1991, (rev. jour.) CRC Critical Rev. Oncol./Hematol., 1985. Recipient Princess Takamatsu Cancer Rsch. Found. prize, 1974. Mem. AAAS, Japanese Cancer Assn. (councilor 1973-98, meritorious mem. 1999—), Japan Hematol. Soc. (councilor 1992-98, meritorious mem. 1999—), Am. Assn. for Cancer Rsch., N.Y. Acad. Scis. Avocation: music. Home: 12-288 Fukasaku, Omiya Saitama 330, Japan

HRABAL, ANTONIN, physician, medical educator; b. Prilepy, Kromeriz, Czech Republic, May 21, 1957; s. Bedrich and Stepanka (Mizia) H. MD, Charles U., Prague, Czech Republic, 1982, PhD, 1986, 92; DSc, U. San Jose, Costa Rica, 1998. Med. diplomate. Rschr. Charles U., Prague, 1976-88, physician, tchr., 1985-92; physician, rschr. Inst. Hippokrates, 1992-99; tchr. Palacki U., Olomouc, Czech Republic, 1989-97, 99, U. Ctr. Inst. Hippokrates, 1997—; chmn. Inst. Hippokrates, 1992-99; head physician U. Hosp., 1995-99; founder Found. Nadace Hippokrates, 1997-99; head rsch. Univ. Ctr., 1998-99. Mem. N.Y. Acad. Scis. Achievements include inventor of regeneration of tissues by deep stimulation through interference of electric and magnetic fields; deep brain stimulation; special immunomodulation diagnostic and therapeutic methodology therapy of autoimmune diseases, antiaging methodology/telomeraza and hormone replacement. Avocations: high technology computers, theoretical physics, cosmology. Home: Hruba Voda 59, 78361 Hlubocky Czech Republic

HRABOVSKY, MILAN, physicst; b. Bratislava, Czechoslovakia, Jan. 20, 1944; s. Josef and Eva (Vrbova) H.; m. Jarmila Maskova, June 7, 1968; children: Jana, Milan. MS, Charles U., Prague, Czech Republic, 1967, PhD, 1973. Rsch. asst. Inst. Elec. Engring., Prague, Czech Republic, 1967-73, rsch. scientist, 1973-90; rsch. scientist Inst. Plasma Physics, Prague, Czech Republic, 1990—. Contbr. articles to profl. jours.; patentee in field. Mem. IUPAC, CIGRE, European Soc. High Temperature Materials Process. Avocations: sports, music. Home: Vasatkova 1019/2, 198 00 Prague 9, Czech Republic Office: Inst Plasma Physics, Za Slovankou 3, 182 21 Prague 8, Czech Republic

HRADIL, STEFAN KLAUS, sociologist, educator; b. Frankenthal, Pfalz, Germany, July 19, 1946; s. Stefan and Ria (von Dungen) H.; children: Katharina, Johanna. MA, U. Munich, 1974, PhD, 1980, habilitation, 1985; DSc (hon.), U. Econ. Scis., Budapest, Hungary, 1994. Asst. U. Munich, 1974-86, sr. asst., 1986-89; prof. U. Bamberg, Germany, 1990-91, U. Mainz, Germany, 1991—; dean faculty of social sci. U. Mainz, 1997-98; mem. Fed. Commn. of Rsch. on the Social and Polit. Change in Eastern Germany, 1990-96. Author: Social Structure Analysis in an Advanced Society, 1987, The Single-Society, 1995, Social Inequality in Germany, 7th edit., 1999; editor: (with P. A. Berger) Life Locations, Life Careers, Life Styles, 1990, (with U. Gerhardt, D. Lucke, B. Nauck) The Family In Future, (with S. Immerfall) The Western European Countries in Comparative Perspective, 1997; contbr. profl. jours. Mem. Internat. Sociol. Assn., European Sociol. Assn., German Sociol. Assn. (treas. 1993-94, pres. 1995-98). Avocations: reading books on history and art, bicycling, classical music. Office: Johannes Gutenberg Univ, Kleinmann Weg 2, D-55099 Mainz Germany

HRAZDIRA, IVO, medical educator; b. Stity, Czechoslovakia, Oct. 3, 1930; s. Eduard and Marie (Luzna) H.; m. Antonie Pacnerova, Aug. 17, 1957; children: Iva, Zuzana. MD cum laude, Masaryk U., Brno, Czechoslovakia, 1956; PhD, Comenius U., Bratislava, Slovakia, 1963; D Sc, Charles U., Prague, Czechoslovakia, 1981. Asst. prof. Faculty of Medicine, Brno, 1956-66, sr. lectr., 1966-69, assoc. prof., 1972-81, prof., 1981—; vis. prof. Sch. Medicine, Oran, Algeria, 1969-72; vice dean Faculty of Medicine, Brno, 1985-91; head dept. biophysics, Brno, 1975-96; head Ctr. for Diagnostic Ultrasound, Brno, 1990-97. Editor, co-author: (textbook) Biophysics, 1983-90; co-author: Ultrasound in Diagnostics and Therapy, 1982, Biophysics for Physicians, 1982; editor: Introduction to Color Duplex Ultrasonography, 1998; co-editor: (scientific jour.) Scripta Medica, 1985-99. Recipient Pioneer award Am. Inst. Ultrasound in Medicine, Washington, 1988, G.J. Mendel gold medal Czech Acad. Scis., Prague, 1991. Mem. European Fedn. Societies for Ultrasound in Medicine and Biology (bd. dirs. 1984-90), European Com. for Ultrasound Radiation Safety, Czech Soc. for Ultrasound in Medicine (bd. dirs.). Avocations: gardening, hiking, skiing. Home: Gorkeho 58, Brno 602 00, Czech Republic Office: Faculty of Medicine, Masaryk U, Jostova 10, Brno 662 43, Czech Republic

HRBÁČEK, JAROSLAV, hydrobiologist, consultant; b. Brno, Morava, Czech Republic, May 12, 1921; s. Jaroslav and Františka (Vránová) H.; m. Marta Esslová, June 16, 1959 (dec. Oct. 1996); children: Jan, Marta. RNDr, Charles U., Prague, 1948; CSc, Charlés U., Prague, 1958; DrSc, Czechoslovak Acad. Sci., Prague, 1985. From asst. to assoc. prof. Faculty of Natural Sci. Charlés U., 1948-58; head lab. hydrobiology Czechoslovak Acad. Sci., 1958-86; cons. Bot. Inst. and Hydrobiol. Inst. Czechoslovak Acad. Sci., České Budějovice, 1987—; mem. Sci. Collegium Biology of Organisms and Populations Czechoslovak Acad. Sci., Prague, 1954-92; sci. sec. Czechoslovak Nat. Com. of Internat. Biol. Programme Internat. Com. Sci. Unions, Prague, 1961-71, Czechoslovak Nat. Com. of Man and Biosphere UNESCO, Prague, 1972-87. Co-author: Lakes and Reservoirs, 1984; editor, contbr.: Hydrobiological Studies, 1966, 2 vols., 1973; contbr. over 50 articles to profl. jours. Recipient D'Ancona medal U. Padua, Italy, 1954, Thienemann-Naumann medal Soc. Internat. Limnologiae, 1983, Silver and Golden Gregor Mendel medal of Czech Acad. Sci., 1971, 86, Golden Meml., Faculty Natural Sci. Charles U., 1995. Mem. Am. Soc. Limnology and Oceanography, Ecol. Soc. Am. (hon.), Československá Zoologická Společnost, Československá Limnologická Společnost (pres. 1973-76, hon. 1997—), Zool. Soc. London (corres.). Roman Catholic. Achievements include discovery that the change in fish stock influences the zooplankton composition not quantitatively, by changing the biomass of the prey, but qualitatively, by changing the species composition. Home: Hekrova 820, CZ 149 00 Prague Czech Republic

HRDLIČKA, MICHAL, psychiatrist, researcher; b. Brno, S. Moravia, Czechoslovakia, Mar. 28, 1965; s. Michal H. and Nina (Vyskočilová) Hejlová; m. Darina Novotná, Mar. 15, 1996. MD, Masaryk U., Brno, Czechoslovakia, 1989; PhD, Charles U., Prague, 1996. 1st, 2nd degree Cert. Psychiatry, Cert. Psychotherapy. Psychiatrist Psychiatric Hosp., Brno, Czech Republic, 1989-94, dep. head dept., 1994-95, head dept., 1996; asst. prof. dept. psychiatry 2nd Med. Sch. Charles U., Prague, 1996-99; assoc. prof., chmn. dept. psychiatry 2nd Med. Sch. Charles U., 5, 1999—. Author: (with D. Hrdlickova) Dementia and Memory Disorders, 1999, Electroconvulsive Therapy, 1999; contbr. articles to profl. jours. Mem. mng. bd. Pangea Found., Prague, 1997—. Mem. Czech Psychiatric Assn., Czech Chamber Physicians (mem. scientific bd. 1999—). Avocations: literature, theatre, history. Office: Dept Psychiatry 2nd Med Sch, V Uvalu 84, 150 18 Prague Czech Republic

HRDY, JAROMÍR, physicist, researcher, consultant; b. Jičín, Czech Republic, Sept. 4, 1938; s. Jaroslav and Ludmila (Tomášu) H.; m. Drahomíra Chládková, Jan. 24, 1976; children: Jaromíra, Martin. Diploma in physics, Charles U., Prague, Czech Republic, 1962; D in Natural Scis., Charles U., 1966; DSc, Czechoslovak Acad. Scis., Prague, 1988. Postgrad. fellow Czechoslovak Acad. Scis., 1962-66, scientist, 1966-69, sr. scientist Inst. Physics, 1970—; postdoctoral fellow Johns Hopkins U., Balt., 1969-70; cons. Sincrotrone Trieste, Italy, 1990-91; external tchr. Charles U. faculty math. and physics, Prague, 1994—; mem. rev. com. European Synchrotron Radiation Facility, 1999—, chmn., 2000—. Contbr. over 50 articles to profl. jours. Mem. European Synchrotron Radiation Soc. (exec. com. 1991-92), Czech Synchrotron Radiation Soc. (head 1992—), Internat. Union Crystallography (synchrotron radiation com. 1993-96). Home: Kahovská 1706/2, 14900 Prague 4, Czech Republic Office: Inst Physics Czech Acad Scis, Na Slovance 2, 18040 Prague 8, Czech Republic

HREIDARSSON-DOWNEY, ROBERT ARNI, lawyer, consultant; b. Reykjavik, Iceland, May 16, 1946; s. William Gerald Jr. and Laufey (Arnadottir) Downey; m. Hildur Thorlaksdottir (div. 1973); children: Arni, Robert; children: Tomas, Richard, William. Student, Menntaskolinn Jr. Coll., Reykjavik, 1967, U. Iceland, Reykjavik, 1975; LLD, U. Iceland, Reykjavik, 1976. Bar: Icelandic Advs. 1979. Tchr. English High Sch. Vesturbaejarskoli, Reykjavik, 1968-70, Coll. Night Sch. of Reykjavik, 1970-73, High Sch. Laugalaekjarskoli, 1970-74; various positions, 1973—; dir., founder Estate Agy., 1976, Eurocard Iceland, 1979-82, Kort Ltd.-Holding Co., 1982-91, Interactive Electronics Ltd., Washington, Eng., 1987-92, Matchwork Ltd., Washington and Eng., 1987-92; dir. Goldfeder Scandinavia, Ltd., Copenhagen, 1988-92; pvt. practice, 1976—; bd. dirs., chmn. The Weekend Post, Reykjavik, 1985-88; atty. to all dist. cts. in Iceland; law rep. Euorcard, Iceland, 1978-94; founder, pres. Fofnir Investment Co., 1991—; founder, chmn. Icelandic TV Co. Ltd., 1998-99, Popptini, Fridi Fjilundrun Ltd., 1999-2000; chancellor, chmn. Radio Mothikler Ltd., 2000—. Founder United World Found., London, Peace 2000 Inst., Iceland, 1995, guardian, 1995—; dir. Football Support Club to the Falcons, 1995, Hlidarendi Ltd. Mem. Assn. Icelandic Advocates, Patron Internat. Bar Assn., Order of Oddfellows. Office: Hafnarstraeti 20, 101 Reykjavik Iceland

HŘIB, JIŘÍ EMIL, plant physiologist; b. Frydek-Místek, Czech Republic, Sept. 16, 1942; s. Jiří and Antonie (Zelená) H.; m. Marie Malá, Jan. 16, 1970; 1 child, Martina. Diploma in agrl. engring., U. Agr., Brno, Czech Republic, 1966, PhD, 1973. Scientist Lab. of Sci. Film Czechoslovak Acad. Scis., Brno, 1967-73, scientist Inst. Vertebrate Zoology, 1973-74, scientist Inst. Botany, 1974-83, scientist Inst. of Exptl. Phytotechnics, 1984-87, scientist Inst. of Systematic and Ecol. Biology, 1987-91; scientist Inst. Plant Genetics SAS, Nitra, 1991-97; sr. scientist Inst. Plant Genetics and Biotech. SAS, Nitra, 1997-98. Author (rsch. film) Ontogeny of the Alga Scenedesmus quadricauda, 1973 (monograph) The Co-Cultivation of Wood-Rotting Fungi with Tissue Cultures of Forest Tree Species, 1990; co-author (rsch. film) Regeneration of the Cap in the Alga Acetabularia mediterranea, 1980; contbr. articles to profl. jours. Mem. N.Y. Acad. Scis., Internat. Assn. Plant Tissue Culture and Biotech., Czech Botanical Soc., Czech Soc. Sci. Cinematography. Roman Catholic. Home: Ukrajinská 17, 625 00 Brno Czech Republic

HRINAK, DONNA JEAN, ambassador; b. Sewickley, Pa., Mar. 28, 1951; d. John and Mary (Pukach) H.; m. Gabino (Lou) Flores, July 15, 1977; 1 child, Wyatt A. Flores. BA, Mich. State U., 1972. State dept. officer Am. Embassy, Bogota, Colombia, 1979-81; former dep. prin. officer Am. Embassy, Warsaw, Poland, 1977-79, Mexico City, 1974-81; former min. counselor Am. Embassy, Teguciagalpa, Honduras, 1989-91; regional affairs officer for C.Am. Dept. State, Washington, 1982-84, dep. asst. sec. for inter-Am. affairs, 1991-93; dep. prin. officer U.S. Consultate Gen., Sao Paulo, Brazil, 1984-87; coord. Policy for Summit of Ams. 1994, 1993-94; amb. to Dominican Republic Santo Domingo, 1994-97; amb. to Bolivia-La Paz, 1998—. Named one of Ams. Ten Outstanding Young Working Women, Glamour mag., 1985. Mem. Am. Fgn. Svc. Assn., Exec. Women in Govt., Inter-Am. Dialogue Fgn. Policy Assn. Avocations: reading mysteries, playing tennis, watching baseball. Office: US Embassy La paz US Dept State Washington DC 20521-0001

HRITZ, GEORGE F., lawyer; b. Hyde Park, N.Y., Aug. 28, 1948; s. George F. and Margaret M. (Callahan) H.; m. Mary Elizabeth Noonan; 1 child, Amelia C. Hritz. AB, Princeton U., 1969; JD, Columbia U., 1973. Bar: N.Y. 1974, D.C. 1978, U.S. Supreme Ct. 1979. Law clk. U.S. Dist. Ct. (ea. dist.) N.Y., N.Y.C., 1973; assoc. Cravath, Swaine & Moore, N.Y.C., 1974-77; counsel U.S. Senate Select Com. Ethics Korean Inquiry, Washington, 1977-78; ptnr. Moore & Foster, Washington, 1978-80, Davis, Weber & Edwards, N.Y.C., 1980-2000; assoc. ind. counsel Washington, 1986-89; ptnr. Hogan & Hartson, LLP, N.Y.C., 2000—; mem. adv. com. U.S. Dist. Ct. (ea. dist.) N.Y., 1990—. Trustee Fed. Bar Found., 1998—; bd. dirs. gen. counsel exec. com. Internat. Rescue Com., 1982—; chmn. planning bd. Village of Sleepy Hollow, N.Y., 1993-97; bd. dirs. exec. com. Princeton in Africa, 2000—. Mem. Fed. Bar Coun., D.C. Bar Assn. Home: 505 Cognewaugh Rd Greenwich CT 06807-1110 Office: Hogan & Hartson LLP 100 Park Ave Rm 3200 New York NY 10017-5516

HROCH, JAROSLAV, philosophy educator; b. Brno, Czech Republic, May 6, 1947; s. Jaroslav and Frantiska (Pribylova) H.; m. Zdenka Broncova, July 14, 1973; 1 child, Jan. MA, Charles U., Prague, 1976, PhD, 1977; MA, Masaryk U., Brno, 1971, CSc, 1984, Docent, 1995. Secondary sch. tchr. several schs., 1971-77; lectr. Tech. U., Brno, 1977-80; rschr. Czechoslovak Acad. Scis., Brno, 1981-90; sr. lectr. Faculty of Law Masaryk U., 1990-92, sr. lectr. Faculty of Arts, 1993-95, docent, 1995—; chmn. sci. bd. Inst. Religious Studies, Czechoslovak Acad. Scis., 1990-91; mem. sci. bd. Faculty of Law, Masaryk U., 1991-92, head dept. langs., 1991-92, mem. acad. senate, 1996—; vis. scholar IREX, Washington, 1994, Jan Hus Found., Cambridge, 1995, 97, Cath. U. Am., Washington, 1997. Author: Practice and Tradition, 1989, The Problem of Understanding and Post-Analytic Philosophy, 1996, Philosophical Hermeneutics in the History and Present, 1997, 98; co-author, editor: Czech Philosophy in Twentieth Century, 1995; co-author: Principles of Philosophy, 1992, 93, 95; contbr. articles to profl. jours. Lt. Mil. Acad., 1972-73. Jan Hus. Found. grantee, 1995, 97. Mem. Philos. Soc., Philos. Union (mem. Brno com. 1990—). Avocations: symphony music, theatre. Home: Rezkova 20, 602 00 Brno Czech Republic

HRONES, STEPHEN BAYLIS, lawyer, educator; b. Boston, Jan. 20, 1942; s. John Anthony and Margaret (Baylis) H.; m. Anneliese Zion, Sept. 11, 1970; children: Christopher, Katja. BA cum laude, Harvard U., 1964; postgrad., U. Sorbonne, Paris, 1964-65; JD, U. Mich., 1968. Bar: Iowa 1969, Mass. 1972, U.S. Dist. Ct. Mass. 1973, U.S. Ct. Appeals (1st cir.) 1979, U.S. Tax Ct. 1985, U.S. Supreme Ct. 1991. Pvt. practice Heidelberg, Germany, 1970-72, Boston, 1973-86; ptnr. Hrones and Harwood, Boston, 1986-90, Hrones and Garrity, Boston, 1990—; clin. assoc. Suffolk U. Law Sch., Boston, 1979-82; faculty advisor Harvard Law Sch., 1988—; instr. Northeastern Law Sch., 1998; Mass. Continuing Legal Edn. Programs, 1988—. Author: How To Try a Criminal Case, 1982, Criminal Practice Handbook, 1995, 2d edit., 1999, Massachusetts Jury (Criminal) Instructions, 2d edit., 1999; contbr. articles to profl. jours. Trustee Orgn. for Assabet River, 1990-99; mem. schs. and scholarship com. Harvard U.; fundraiser Harvard Coll. Fund, 1985—. Recipient Edward J. Duggan Pvt. Counsel award for zealous advocacy and outstanding legal svcs. to the poor Com. for Pub. Counsel Svcs., 2000; Fulbright scholar, 1968-69. Mem. ACLU, Nat. Assn. Criminal Def. Lawyers, Mass. Assn. Criminal Def. Lawyers, Mass. Bar Assn., Boston Bar Assn., Nat. Lawyers Guild. Democrat. Avocations: squash, skiing, wind-surfing, vegetable gardening, yard sales. Fax: (617) 227-3908. E-mail: azhroe@aol.com. Home: 39 Winslow St Concord MA 01742-3817 Office: Hrones and Garrity Lewis Wharf Bay 232 Boston MA 02110

HRUBY, JAN, agronomist, researcher; b. Uherské Hradiště, Czech Republic, Dec. 28, 1943; s. Vilém and Alice (Bílková) H.; m. Jiřina Kočičková, Dec. 22, 1979; 1 child, Alice. Diploma in engring., Agrl. U., Brno, Czech Republic, 1966, PhD, 1990. Head of dept. State Testing Inst. Quality Agrl. Products, Brno, 1966-82; dep. dir. sci. Rsch. Inst. Soil Mgmt., Hrušovany, 1982-84; sci. sec. Rsch. Inst. Crop Prodn., Hrušovany, Czech Republic, 1985-90; dir. Rsch. Inst. Agroecology, Hrušovany, 1991-92; dep. dirs. Rsch. Inst. Animal Nutrition, Pohořelice, 1993-94; prin. rsch. scientist Rsch. Inst. Fodder Plants, Troubsko, Czech Republic, 1995—. Editor: Ekologické a ekonomické systémy hospodareni na pudě, 1996, Nové pohledy na jakost produktu rostlinného puvodu, 1997; contbr. over 250 articles to profl. pubs. Mem. Czech Acad. Agrl. Scis., Internat. Soil Tillage Rsch. Orgn. Home: Veveří 34, 602 00 Brno Czech Republic

HRUSAK, ONDREJ, physician; b. Praha, Czech, Oct. 20, 1965; s. Zdenek and Slavka H.; m. Sarka Hrozinkova, Feb. 11, 1991; children: Kristian, Jachym. MD, Charles Univ., Praha, 1990, PhD, 1999. Head cell immunology unit Inst. Immunology, Praha, Czech, Republic, 1996—. Contbr. articles to profl. jours. Recipient Josef Hlavka's award Josef Hlavka's Found., 1994. Mem. European Haematology Orgn., Internat. Soc. Haematology. E-mail: ondrej.Hrusak@lfmotol.cuni.cz. Office: Inst Immunology, 150 06, Praha 5 Czech Republic

HRYCEK, ANTONI JAN, physician, medical educator; b. Przeworsk, Przemysl, Poland, Jan. 13, 1948; s. Eugeniusz Wincenty and Janina Stanisława (Mikluszka) H.; m. Bogdana Joanna Moczarska, Aug. 25, 1985; children: Eugeniusz, Maria. Physician diploma with distinction, Silesian Med. Acad., Katowice, Poland, 1971; MD, Silesian Med. Acad., 1976, PhD, 1986. 1st degree splst. in internal diseases, 2nd degree splst. in internal diseases, splst. in ultrasonographic diagnostic. Asst. Dept. Internal and Occupl. Diseases, Zabrze, Poland, 1972-74; sr. asst. Second Dept. Internal Diseases, Katowice, Poland, 1975-79; tutor Second Dept. Internal Diseases, Katowice, 1979-86, chief of staff, 1983, asst. prof., 1986-94, prof., 1995; vice dean med. faculty Silesian Med. Acad., Katowice, 1990-93, 93-96; prof. II Dept Internatl Medicine, Katowice, 1996—; cons. med. physics Silesian U., Katowice, Poland, 1996, supr. student scientific groups. Contbr. 105 articles to profl. jours. Cooperator Friends of Polish U. Abroad, London and Zurich. Grantee Italian Govt., 1981, Silesian Med. Acad., 1983; recipient spl. award Jury of T. Chałubiński Contest, 1979, awards for scientific and didactic achievements Silesian Med. Acad. Mem. Polish Med. Soc., Polish Soc. Internal Medicine (exec. bd. 1998), N.Y. Acad. Scis. Avocations: literature, classical music. Home: ul Tysi—clecia 86a/34, 40-871 Katowice Poland

HSEE, CHRISTOPHER K., business educator; b. Shanghai, Oct. 20, 1963; s. Adam C.T. and Christina Hsee; m. Jingjing Hsee; 1 child, Emily. BA, U. Hawaii, 1989; PhD, Yale U., 1993. Mem. faculty grad. sch. bus. U. Chgo., 1993—. Contbr. articles to profl. jours. Grantee NSF, 1995-96, 97-98, 99—; recipient Best Paper award Assn. for Consumer Rsch., 1999. Office: Grad Sch Bus U Chgo 1101 E 58th St Chicago IL 60637-1561

HSI, MORRIS YU, mechanical engineer, applied researcher; b. Taipei, Taiwan, Aug. 23, 1951; s. En Sui and I Hsian (Wang) H.; m. Linda Syau Lin Chang, Aug. 28, 1982. BSME with honors, Nat. Cheng Kung U., Tainan, Taiwan, 1974; MSME, Iowa State U., 1979; PhD in Applied Mechanics, U. Mich., 1987. Registered prof. engr., Mich. Mech. engr. Taiwan Power Co., Keelung, 1976-77; product design engr. Ford Motor Co., Dearborn, Mich., 1987-92, tech. specialist, 1992-97; tech. specialist Ford Visteon Automotive Sys., Plymouth, Mich., 1997—; reviewer, evaluator of tech. pubs. profl. socs. Contbr. articles to profl. jours. 2d lt. Taiwanese Army, 1974-76. Recipient Henry Ford Technol. award Ford Motor Co., 1990, Mich. Outstanding Engr. in Industry Am. Consulting Engrs. Coun. Mich. and Mich. Soc. Profl. Engrs., 1999. Mem. NSPE, Soc. Automotive Engrs. (noise and vibration gen. com.), Mich. Soc. Profl. Engrs. (dir. Detroit Metro chpt. 1999—). Achievements include pioneering in application of computational aeroacoustics to automotive projects; pioneering in application of computational fluid dynamics to analyze and design vehicle's underhood thermal environment; patents pending on noise control of automotive climate control systems. Avocations: painting, swimming. Home: 46922 Elmsmere Dr Northville MI 48167-1034 Office: Ford Visteon Automotive Sys 45000 Helm St Plymouth MI 48170-6046

HSIAO, MING-YUAN, nuclear engineer, researcher; b. Kaohsiung, Taiwan, Feb. 23, 1954; came to U.S., 1978; s. Fei and Hwang-Fang H.; m. Shwu Chuen Lee. MS, U. Ill., 1980, PhD, 1983. Postdoctoral fellow Los Alamos (N.Mex.) Nat. Lab., 1983-84; asst. prof. Pa. State U., University Park, 1984-90; sr. engr. Commonwealth Edison Co., Chgo., 1990—. Author, reviewer jour. publs.; contbr. articles to profl. jours. including Physics of Fluids, Nuclear Fusion, Nuclear Tech., Fusion Tech., Computer Physics Comm., Nuclear Engring. and Design. Univ. fellow U. Ill., 1981-83, Profl. Devel. fellow U.S. Dept. Energy, 1987; recipient Faculty Summer Rsch. award Argonne (Ill.) Nat Lab., 1986-89. Mem. Am. Nuclear Soc. (Mark Mills award 1984), Sigma Xi, Phi Tau Phi. Achievements include identification of and studies on velocity space particle loss mechanism in field reversed configurations; research in fusion plasma theory and engineering, computational physics and engineering, and nuclear fuel management. Office: Commonwealth Edison Co 1400 Opus Pl Ste 400 Downers Grove IL 60515-1198

HSIEH, BOR-SHEN, dean, medical educator; b. Chang-Hwa, Taiwan, Nov. 18, 1942. BS, Nat. Taiwan U., 1967; DMSc, Tokyo Med. Sch., 1975. Prof. internal medicine Nat. Taiwan U. Coll. Medicine, Taipei, 1983—, dean, 1995—; trustee Nat. Health Rsch. Inst., Republic of China; mem. com. for med. edn. Ministry Edn., Republic of China; mem. com. for sci. edn. Nat. Sci. Coun., Republic of China. Author of 5 books; contbr. articles to profl. jours. Mem. Formosan Med. Assn. (pres. 1998—). Achievements include research on hypertension, electrolyte physiology and medical education. Fax: 886-2-23224793. Office: Nat Taiwan U, 1 Jenai Rd Sec 1, Taipei Taiwan

HSIEH, SHOU-SHING, mechanical engineering educator, researcher; b. Hsin-Chu, Taiwan, Dec. 8, 1950; s. Yuan-Wei and Chiu-Jue (Liao) H.; m. Cho-Yin, Nov. 24, 1984; children: Pei-Chun, Kao-Han, Pei-Mon, Pei-Chin, Pei-Nan. BSME, Tatung Inst. Tech., Taipei, Taiwan, 1973; MSME, Nat. Taiwan U., 1978, Drexel U., Phila., 1980; MSc, Ohio State U., 1981, PhD, 1983. Rsch. assoc. Inst. Nuclear Enrgy Rsch., Lung-Tan, Tao-Yuan, Taiwan, 1975-76; postdoctoral rschr. dept. mech. engring. Ohio State U., Columbus, 1983-84; assoc. prof. dept. mech. engring. Nat. Sun Yat-Sen U., Kaohsiung, Taiwan, 1984-89, prof. dept. mech. engring., 1989—; Sun Yat-

Sen prof. Nat. Sun Yat-Sen U., Kaohsiung, 1987—; dir. Energy Rsch. Ctr. Nat. Sun Yat-Sen U., Kaohsiung, Taiwan, 1987-90, chmn. dept. mech. engring., 1990-96; dean Coll. Engring. Nat. Sun Yat-Sen U., Kaohsiung, 1996—, Sun Yat-Sen chair, 1997—; Disting. prof. Nat. Scis. Coun., Taiwan, 1996—. Contbr. over 60 articles to profl. jours.; patentee in field. Recipient Def. Rsch. Project Outstanding Performance award Dept. Mil. Def., Taiwan, 1987, Nat. Sci. Coun. Outstanding Rsch. award, Taiwan, 1990, 92, 94, Chung-shan Acad. award, Taiwan, 1995, Nat. Acad. award, Taiwan, 1996. Fellow ASME; mem. AIAA, Chinese Soc. Mech. Engring. Avocations: listening to radio, reading, sports (basketball and table tennis). Office: Nat Sun Yat-Sen U, Kaohsiung 80424, Taiwan

HSIEH, SHU-SEN See XIE, SHU-SEN

HSIEH, SHYU-HSIEN, physics educator; b. Guang Chow, China, July 20, 1946; s. Chao-Fen and Mu-Hsien (Wu) H.; m. Rosalind Jane Wu; children: Andrew, Christina. MS, MIT, 1968; PhD, Columbia U., 1975. Postdoctoral dept. of physics Brandeis U., Waltham, 1975-76; NRC fellow Goddard Inst. of Space Studies, N.Y.C., 1976-82; postdoctoral Pitts. U., 1983-90; prof. dept. physics Soochow U., Taipei, Taiwan, Republic of China, 1996—. Overseas mem. of legis. Legislative Yumen of the Republic of China, 1980-86; CEO Yang China Party, Taipei, 1990-93. Mem. AAAS, N.Y. Acad. Sci. Office: Dept Physics Soochow U, Shihlin Wai Shuangshi, Taipei Taiwan

HSIEH, SUNG-TSANG, medical educator, researcher, neurologist; b. Tainan, Taiwan, Sept. 30, 1957; s. Guo-Jen Hsieh and Su-Sui Chen; m. Whei-Min Lin, Jan. 29, 1985; children: Paul-Chen Hsieh, Christine Yi-Chen Hsieh. MD, Nat. Taiwan U., Taipei, 1983; MPH, Harvard U., 1989; PhD, Johns Hopkins U., 1993. Resident in neurology Nat. Taiwan U. Hosp., Taipei, 1983-88; fellow in neurosci. Johns Hopkins U., 1993-95; attending physician Nat. Taiwan U. Hosp., Taipei, 1995—, dir. divsn. neuromuscular disorders, dept. neurology, 1995—. Contbr. articles to med. jours.; reviewer Acta Neurol. Taiwanica, 1995—. Recipient Peter Lamper Young Investigator award Soc. Exptl. Neuropathology, Washington, 1995. Mem. Am. Acad. Neurology, Soc. Neurosci. Avocations: jogging, baseball. Home: 4 Fl 4-1 Aly 3 Ln 183, Ho Ping E Rd Sec 1, Taipei 106, Taiwan Office: Nat Taiwan U Coll Medicine, 1 Jen-Ai St Sec 1 Rm 638, Taipei 10018, Taiwan

HSING, YUE CHENG, aeronautical engineer; b. Chung Hau, Taiwan, June 5, 1958; s. Hong Chien and Lily Y. (Yang) H.; m. Ling Wei, June 16, 1985; children: Hsiang Chun, Hsiang Wen. BS, Chung Yuan Christian U., Chung Li, Taiwan, 1980, MS, 1982; PhD, Carnegie Mellon U., Pitts., 1997. Asst. scientist Chung Shan Inst. Sci. and Tech., Tau Yuan, Taiwan, 1982-86, assoc. scientist, 1987—. Contbr. articles to profl. jours. Recipient honor of outstanding achievement Republic of China, Taiwan, 1998. Mem. Soc. Explosives and Propellants, Aero. and Astronautical Soc. Republic of China (life), Sigma Xi (life). Mem. Kuomintang (Chinese Nat. Party). Avocations: reading, hiking. Home: 14-6 Garden 2nd Rd 2nd Sec, Hsien Tien 231, Taiwan

HSIUNG, LUKE LIEH-MING, metallurgist, electron microscopist; b. Tainan, Taiwan, Nov. 11, 1953; came to U.S., 1983; s. Ping-Lin and Pao-Hsu Hsiung; m. Ching-Hsin Hsuing, July 25, 1982; children: Amy, David, Jessica. BS, Nat. Taipei Inst. Tech., 1976; MS, N.Mex. Inst. Mining and Tech., Socorro, 1985; PhD, Rensselaer Poly. Inst., 1989. Metall. engr. China Steel Corp., Kaohsiung, Taiwan, 1978-83; rsch. asst. N.Mex. Tecg., Socorro, 1983-85, Rensselaer Poly. Inst., Troy, N.Y., 1986-89; rsch. assoc. U. Va., Charlottesville, 1989-93, sr. scientist, 1993-95; metallurgist Lawrence Livermore Lab., Livermore, Calif., 1995—. Mem. Tri-Valley Chinese Bible Ch., Pleasanton, Calif., 1996—, deacon, 2000. Mem. The Metall. Soc., Materials Rsch. Soc. Christian. Avocations: music, reading, basketball, church. Office: Lawrence Livermore Lab 7000 East Ave # L369 Livermore CA 94550-9516

HSIUNG, TAI-PING JACOB, avionics executive, researcher; b. Pingtung, Taiwan, China, July 1, 1949; s. Yu-Chen and Shu-Fang (Wang) H.; m. Ying-Ying Lily Tseng, Oct. 31, 1977; children: Bor-Kai, Wei-Wei. BSEE, Chung-Cheng Inst. Tech., Taoyuan, Taiwan, 1970; MS, UCLA, 1976; degree in engring., U. So. Calif., 1981, PhD, 1983. Tchg. asst. Chung Cheng Inst. Tech., Taoyuan, 1970-74; instr. Chinese Air Force Acad., Kangshan, 1976-80; dep. dir. Aero. Rsch. Lab., Taichung, 1983-92; mgr. Ctr. for Aviation and Space Tech. Indsl. Tech. Rsch. Inst., Hsinchu, 1992-97; cons. Ministry of Econ. Affairs, Taipei, 1995-96, gen. mgr. Wavetrend Tech. Co. Ltd., 1997—. Col. Taiwan mil., 1983-92. Recipient Bea Liang-A medal Ministry of Nat. Def., 1988. Mem. IEEE, Aero. and Astronautical Soc. of the Republic of China (exec. editor 1991-94, Svc. medal 1991). Avocations: golfing, planting, fishing. Home: 97 Yung Ting 2nd St, Taichung Taiwan

HSU, BAYSUNG, physics educator; b. Shanghai, People's Republic China, Feb. 2, 1929; s. Yong-yee and Ming-hya (Yang) H.; m. Sophie Marian Yang, Sept. 1, 1960; children: Van Bing, Kay Lynn. BSc Tech. with 1st class honors, Victoria U., Manchester, Eng., 1954, PhD, 1958. Rsch. physicist PIRA Internat., Leatherhead, Surrey, Eng., 1958-64; prof. physics Chinese U. of Hong Kong, Shatin, Hong Kong, 1964-94, dean sci. faculty, 1966-67, 69-71, 1977-79, pro-vice-chancellor, 1979-93, council mem., 1977-93. Contbr. articles to profl. publs. Dep. chmn. Joint Com. on Student Fin., Hong Kong, 1969-87; mem. Com. for Sci. Coord., Hong Kong, 1969-81, Coun. of Hong Kong Poly., 1975-83. Named Hon. Officer Brit. Empire, Queen of England. Mem. Phys. Soc. Hong Kong (founder, chmn. 1966-67). Avocations: reading, music. Home: 65 Sheung Shing St 2d fl, Kowloon Hong Kong Office: Chinese U of Hong Kong, Dept Physics, Shatin Hong Kong

HSU, BILIN SPRING, orthodontic educator; b. Taipei, Taiwan, Dec. 12, 1953; s. Chung-Ming and Show-Hwa (Hu) H.; m. Ai-Jen Alice Chang, Nov. 23, 1953; 1 child, Hank Li-Hen. B Dental Surgery, Nat. Def. Med. Ctr., Taipei, 1979; MPH, Columbia U., 1986, orthodontic diploma, 1986. Orthodontic diplomate, U.S.A., Taiwan. Teaching asst. Nat. Def. Med. Ctr., Taipei, 1979-86, asst. prof., 1986-90; resident Tri-Svc. Gen. Hosp., Taipei, 1979-83, attending physician, orthodontist, 1986-87; assoc. prof. Nat. Yang-Ming U., Taipei, 1990—; sect. dir. Vets. Gen. Hosp., Taipei, 1987—. Maj. Nat. Def. Med. Ctr., 1979-87. Recipient Plaques Navy Gen. Hosp. Kao-Hsion, 1988, Taipei County Dental Assn., 1991, Hqrs. Taiwan Dental Assn., 1995. Mem. Taiwan Assn. Orthodontists (dir. 1988—, editor-in-chief 1992-94), Chinese Dental Assn. (dir. 1991—), Taipei Dental Assn. (dir. 1992-95), Alumni Assn. Nat. Def. Med. Ctr. (sec. gen. 1992-94). Avocations: golf, badminton, baseball follower, mountain hiking, bridge. Office: Dr Hsu's Orthodontic Clinic, 99 An-Ho Rd Sect 1 # 2F-1, Taipei 106, Taiwan

HSU, CHAO TIEN, pathologist, researcher; b. Chiayi, Taiwan, Republic of China, Jan. 7, 1959; s. Jung Chou and Chiang Li-Yu (Chiang) H.; m. Su Man Lin, June 6, 1988; children: Herng Shouh, Shao Chen. MD, China Med. Coll., Taichung, 1985; PhD, Nagasaki (Japan) Med. Sch., 1992. Asst. prof. Nagasaki U., 1992; assoc. prof. China Med. Coll., Taiwan, 1992—; chief cytopathology CMCH, Taiwan, 1996; chief pathology God's Help Hosp., Taiwan, 1996—; med. examiner Taichung, Chung-Hwa, Yun-Lin, Chiayi, Taiwan, 1992—; cytology cons. Taiwan Provincial Inst., Taiwan, 1994—; dir. med. rsch. God's Help Hosp., Taiwan, 1996—; chmn. dept. of pathology China Med. Coll. Hosp., 1998—, dean Sch. of Medicine, China Med. Coll., 1999—. Contbr. articles to profl. jours. including Acta Med. Nagasaki, Japanese Heart Jour., Jour. Japanese Assn. Chest Surgery, among others. 2d lt. Taiwanese Mil., 1985-87. Recipient numerous grants. Fellow Yoneyama Rotary Club; mem. AAAS, Pathology Soc. (Japan), Pathology Soc. (Taiwan), Cell and Molecular Soc. (Taiwan), Clin. Cytology Soc. (Taiwan), Neurosci. Soc. (Taiwan), Clin. Pathology Soc. (Taiwan), Internat. Acad. Cytology (Germany). Avocations: music, tennis, golf. Office: China Medical Coll Dept Path, 91 Hsueh Shih Rd Sch med, T'aichung Taiwan

HSU, CHAO-CHIN, obstetrician, gynecologist, educator; b. Chia-Yi, Taiwan, Nov. 24, 1956; s. Jung-Chou and Li-Yu (Chiang) H.; m. Tsui-Chen Chang; children: Isabel, Leonard, Rosie. MD, Nat. Taiwan U., Taipei, 1982; PhD, U. Cambridge, Eng., 1992. Cert. specialist Bd. Ob-Gyn., Taiwan. Resident Nat. Taiwan U., 1984-88; attending staff Nat. Cheng Kung U. Hosp., Tainan, Taiwan, 1988-98, dir. dept. ob-gyn., 1992-98; assoc. prof. Nat. Cheng Kung U., Tainan, Taiwan, 1993-98, chmn. dept. ob-gyn., 1994—; med. dir. Taiwan United Birth-promoting Experts ART Clinic, Tainan, 1998—; rsch. fellow U. Cambridge, 1989-92. Editor: New Aspects in Obstetrics and Gynecology, 1994; contbr. articles to profl. jours. 2d lt. Taiwan Air Force, 1982-84. Eng. Govt. scholar, 1990-92; Wolfson Bursary fellow, 1991-92; Nat. Sci. Coun. grantee, 1992—. Mem. Am. Soc. Reproductive Medicine, European Soc. Human Reproduction and Embryology, Chinese Fertility Soc. (supervisory mem. exec. coun. 1996—), Taiwanese Menopause Soc. (sec.-in-gen. 1995—), Chinese Osteoporosis Soc. (supervisory mem. exec. coun. 1997—), Assn. Ob-Gyn. R.O.C. (dep. gen. sec. 1996—), Rotary (exec. com. soc. svc. 1994—). Avocations: classical music, golfing, swimming. Home and Office: TUBE Art Clinic, 226 Sect 2 Chung-Yi Rd, Tainan 700, Taiwan

HSU, CHENG, decision sciences and engineering systems educator; b. Taipei, Republic of China, May 11, 1951; came to U.S., 1976; s. Chung-Yu and Te-Zeng (Yeh) H.; 1 child, Diana. BS in Indsl. Engring., Tunghai U., Taichung, Republic of China, 1973; MS, Ohio State U., 1978, PhD, 1983. Info. engr. China Tech. Cons., Inc., Taipei, 1975-76; grad. rsch. asst. Ohio State U., Columbus, 1977-80, grad. teaching assoc., 1980-82; asst. prof. decision scis. and engring. systems Rensselaer Poly. Inst., Troy, N.Y., 1982-88, assoc. prof., 1988-96, dir. undergrad. programs, 1989-91, dir. doctoral program, 1994—, prof., 1996—; cons. Coopers & Lybrand, Albany, N.Y., 1988, Digital Equipment Corp., Nashua, N.H., 1991, Gen. Electric R&D, Schenectady, N.Y., 1995—; co-founder, bd. dirs. EnterNet, 2000—; patentee in field. Author: Enterprise Integration and Modeling: The Metadatabase Approach, 1996, Innovative Planning for Electronic Commerce and Enterprises: A Reference Model, 2000. Grantee GM, CED, Johnson & Johnson, 1986-89, Aluminum Co. Am., Digital Equipment Corp., 1992-95, GM, IBM, 1986-95, AT&T, 1987, NATO, 1988, State of N.Y., 1988, NSF, 1991-96, Samsung, 1995-98, U.S. Army, 1995-96, N.Y. State Dept. Transp., 1997-99. Mem. IEEE (sr.), ACM, Soc. Mfg. Engrs. (sr.), Prodn. and Ops. Mgmt. Soc., N. Am. Chinese Bus. Educators Assn. (bd. dirs. 1988-90). Republican. Home: 168 Maxwell Rd Newtonville NY 12110-4949 Office: Rensselaer Poly Inst 5219 CII Troy NY 12180-3590

HSU, CHIEH-LIN, dean, law educator. Dean coll. law Nat. Taiwan U., Taipei. Fax: (886-2) 2394-8914. Office: Nat Taiwan U Coll Law, 21 Hsuchow Rd, Taipei Taiwan*

HSU, CHUNG YI, neurologist; b. Taipei, Taiwan, China, Oct. 14, 1944; s. Huo and Jane (Wu) H.; m. Amy Yang, Sept. 27, 1974; children: Alice L., Virginia, Charles Y. MD, Nat. Taiwan U., Taipei, 1970; PhD, U. Va., 1975. Diplomate Am. Bd. Psychiatry and Neurology. NIH fellow Diabetes Rsch. Ctr., U. Va., Charlottesville, 1975-77; fellow dept. pharmacology Med. U. S.C., Charleston, 1977, intern dept. medicine, 1977-78, resident dept. neurology, 1978-80, chief resident dept. neurology, 1980-81, fellow clin. neuropharmacology, 1981, dir. neuropharmacology dept. neurology, 1981-89; dir. neuropharmacology div. restorative neurology Baylor Coll. Medicine, Houston, 1989-93; head cerebrovascular disease sect., dept. neurology Washington U. Sch. Medicine, St. Louis, 1993—; mem. adv. panel on drug info. U.S. Pharmacopeial Conv., Rockville, Md., 1985-90; mem. Nat. Inst. Neurol. Disease and Stroke, NIH, 1988-97, mem. nat. adv. bd. on med. rehab. rsch. Nat. Inst. Child Health and Human Devel., NIH, 1997—. Mem. editl. bd. Stroke, Jour. Cerebral Blood Flow and Metabolism, Jour. Neurotrauma, Clin. Neuropharmacology; mem. guest editl. bd. Jour. Formosan Med. Assn.; editor 4 monographs; contbr. articles to profl. jours. Mem. rsch. and program evaluation com. Am. Heart Assn., 1998—; chair Bugher Found. award rev. com., 1999, 2000. 2d lt. Taiwan Navy, 1970-71. Grad fellow U.Va. Sch. Medicine, Charlottesville, 1971-75; recipient Nat. Rsch. Svc. award USPHS, 1977, 81, NIH Tchr. Investigator Devel. award 1983-88, NIH Javits Neurosci. Investigator award, 1991—, Disting. Rschr. award Vivian L. Smith Found., 1993-94, Taiwanese Am. Found. award, 1997. Fellow Am. Acad. Neurology; mem. Am. Heart Assn. (fellow stroke coun., chair brain rev. com. 1996-97, rsch. program and devel. com. 1998—), Am. Neurol. Assn., Taiwan Stroke Soc., Taiwan Neurol. Soc., Internat. Soc. Cerebral Blood Flow and Metabolism, Neurotrauma Soc. (pres. 1992-93), N.Am. Taiwanese Prof. Assn. (pres. 1995-96), Taiwanese Assn., Charleston (pres. 1984-85), Dana Alliance for Brain Initiatives. Avocation: literature. Home: 538 Conway Village Dr Saint Louis MO 63141-5807 Office: Washington U Sch Medicine Dept Neurology Box 8111 660 S Euclid Ave Saint Louis MO 63110-1010

HSU, CHUNG-PING, surgeon; b. Keelung, Taiwan, Republic of China, Jan. 21, 1955; s. Ming-Kao and Pi-Chu (Lin) H.; m. Yao-Hua Kuan; children: Yu-Liang, Yeu-Torng, Yu-Chern. MD, Nat. Def. Med. Ctr., Taipei, Taiwan, 1980. Diplomate Bd. Surgery, Bd. Digestive Surgery, Bd. Chest & Critical Care Medicine, B.d Thoracic and Cardiovascular Surgery, B.d. Emerg. Med. Resident, chief resident Vets. Gen. Hosp., Taipei, Taiwan, 1981-86; attending surgeon 804 Gen. Hosp., Taoyuan, Taiwan, 1986-89, chief, 1989-90; attending surgeon Vets. Gen. Hosp., Taichung, Taiwan, 1990—, chief surg. emergency, 1997—; tutor Nat. Yang-Ming U., 1998—; Rsch. fellow Duke U. Med. Ctr., Durham, N.C., 1993-94; coord. nutrition support team Vets. Gen. Hosp., Taichung, Taiwan, 1996—. Co-author: Atlas of Cardiothoracic Surgery, 1995; contbr. numerous articles to profl. jours. Major Army of Taiwan, 1980-90. Fellow Coll. Chest Physicians; mem. Surg. Assn. (Taipei), Thoracic and Cardiovascular Assn. (Taipei), Chest and Critical Care Medicine (Taipei). Avocations: reading, classical music, golf. Home: 8F-2 #60 Sec 2, 2nd Rd Chorng-Der, Taichung Taiwan, Taiwan Office: Vets Gen Hosp Dept Surgery, # 160 Sect 3 Taichung-Kang Rd, T'aichung Taiwan

HSU, FRANK FU-CHANG, computer engineer; b. Taipei, Taiwan, Sept. 19, 1969; s. I-Hsung and Ying-Jing Hwang H.; m. Yun Li, July 12, 1997. BS in Elec. Engring., U. Ill. Urbana-Champaign, 1992, MS in Elec. Engring., 1994, PhD in Elec. Engring., 1998. Product engr. Intel Corp., Santa Clara, Calif., 1996; design-for-test engr. Texas Instruments, Dallas, 1998—. Sunday sch. instr., 1999—. Mem. IEEE. Christian and Missionary Alliance. Avocations: reading, hiking, skiing, drawing. Fax: 214-480-2356. E-mail: f-hsu2@ti.com.

HSU, GUANG-HUI, mathematician, educator; b. Shanghai, China, Apr. 13, 1935; m. Jia-Ling Lu, Sept. 30, 1966; 1 child, Junke. Grad., Beijing U., 1957. From asst. to assoc. prof. Inst. Math. Chinese Acad. Scis., Beijing, 1957-80; rsch. fellow Hohenheim U., Bonn U., Germany, 1980-82; vis. prof. Tech. U. Denmark, Lyngby, Denmark, 1982, Free U. Math. Ctr., Amsterdam, The Netherlands, 1984; from assoc. prof. to prof. Inst. Applied Math. Chinese Acad. Scis., Beijing, 1980—, chmn. acad. degree com., 1984-98; chair acad. com. Asian-Pacific Ops. Rsch. Ctr., Beijing, 1995—. Author: Stochastic Service Systems, 1980, 2d edit., 1988; editor: Handbook of Operations Research Fundamentals, 1999; contbr. articles to profl. jours. Mem. Ops. Rsch. Soc. China (pres. 1988-96, hon. pres. 1997—), Assn. Asian-Pacific Ops. Rsch. Socs. (pres. 1989-91), Internat. Fedn. Ops. Rsch. Socs. (v.p. 1992-94). Office: Inst Applied Math, PO Box 2734, 100080 Beijing China

HSU, JOHN WEN-CHAIN, family medicine educator, consultant; b. Tainan, Taiwan, June 30, 1960; s. Tien-Shaw Hsu and Pau (Chuan) H.; m. Pei-Ling Tsai; children: Elizabeth, Paul. MD, Kaohsiung (Taiwan) Med. U., 1986, PhD, 1991; MPH, Johns Hopkins U., 1993. Diplomate in family medicine, critical care and emergency medicine. Intern Kaohsiung Med. Univ. Hosp., 1985-86, resident, 1986-90; attending physician Kaohsiung Med. U., 1989—, assoc. prof. family medicine, 1991; prof. T-Jen Inst. Tech., Taiwan, 1999—. Contbr. articles to profl. jours., including Forensic Sci. Internat., Australian Dental Soc., Jour. Adolescent Health. Bd. dirs. Zanchuan Assn., Taiwan, 1995-99, Chuanyoung Assn., Taiwan, 1998. Rsch. grantee Academia Sinica, Taiwan, 1990. Mem. Am. Acad. Family Physicians, WONCA, N.Y. Acad. Scis. Avocations: tennis, golf. Home: PO Box 307, Kaohsiung Taiwan Office: Kaoshiung Med Univ Hosp FM, 100 Shih Chuan 1st Rd, Kaohsiung Taiwan

HSU, KYLIE, language and linguistics educator, researcher. BA, U. Mich., 1980; MA, Calif. State U., Northridge, 1994; PhD, UCLA, 1996. Lang. and math. instr. U. Mich., Ann Arbor, 1976-80; asst. to pres. Am. GNC Corp., Chatsworth, Calif., 1980-86, exec. v.p., 1986-93; instr. in Chinese UCLA, 1994-95; dir. lang. inst. Pacific States U., L.A., 1996-97; asst. prof. Calif. State U., L.A., 1997—; assoc. dir. Chinese Studies Ctr., Calif. State U., L.A., 1999—; manuscript evaluator Edwin Mellen Press, Lewiston, N.Y., 1998—; editor-in-chief Pacific States U. Newsletter, 1997; judge Chinese Poetry Recital Contest, L.A., 1997; conf. chair Eng. Lang. Tchg. Conf., L.A., 1996; com. chair Major Tsai Scholarship in Chinese Studies, 1999. Author: Discourse Analysis, 1998; contbr. articles to profl. jours. Presdl. fellow/rsch. grantee U. Calif., Berkeley, 1996-97; fellow State of Calif., 1996-97; Vieta Vogt Woodlock scholar, 1976-80, Olive M. Roosenraad Meml. scholar 1976-80, scholar W.K. Kellogg Found., 1977-80, James B. Angell scholar, 1979-80; recipient lit., sci. and arts scholarship U. Mich., 1977-80, Martin Luther King scholarship, 1977-80, W.K. Kellogg Found. scholarship, 1977-78, Olive M. Roosenraad Meml. scholarship, 1976-80, Vieta Vogt Woodlock scholarship, 1976-80, Alumnae Coun. scholarship U. Mich., 1976-80, Regents-Alumni scholarship, 1976-77, Bausch & Lomb Hon. Sci. award, 1976, Innovative Instrnl. award Calif. State U., L.A., 1998; State of Calif. fellow, 1996-97; named One of 2000 Outstnading Scholars of 20th Century, 2000. Mem. IEEE (exhibits chair 1993), Linguistic Assn. of the Southwest (organizer 31st ann. mtg.), Modern Langs. and Lits. (curriculum com. chair 1998), Am. Coun. on Tchg. of Fgn. Langs. (panel chair 1997), Am. Assn. for Applied Linguistics (session chair 1995), Assn. for Linguistic Typology (scholar 1995), Phi Beta Kappa. E-mail: kyliehsu@msn.com. Office: Calif State U LA 5151 State University Dr Los Angeles CA 90032-4226

HSU, MING-YU, engineering educator; b. Kweiyang, Kweichow, China, Dec. 4, 1925; s. Pei-Kung and Wan-Ju (Hsiao) H.; m. Chih-Ju Yao, Jan. 1, 1952; children: Chi-Hsing, Chi-Yun, Chi-En, Chi-Che, Chi-Cheng. BE, Nat. Kweichow U., 1948; Dipl.Engr., Delft Tech. U., The Netherlands, 1959. Registered profl. engr., Ill., Ga., Fla., S.C. Prof. Cheng-Kung U., Tainan, Taiwan, 1960-68; dir. Land Devel. Commn., Taipei, 1960-68; engring. cons. Ministry of Housing & Utilities, Sehba, Libya, 1968-71; sr. engr. Philipp Holzmann Ag., Hamburg, Fed. Republic of Germany, 1971-74, Weber, Griffith & Mellican, Galesburg, Ill., 1974-80; chief engr. Chatham Engring. Co., Savannah, Ga., 1980-82; sr. cons. Hussey, Gay, Bell & DeYoung, Inc., Savannah, 1982—; prof. Savannah Coll. of Art and Design, 1986—; designed and constructed numerous indsl. office, apt. and comml. bldgs., marine structures including docks, loading platforms, marinas, shipyards and water and waste water treatment structures. Contbr. articles on structural engring. to profl. jours. Mem. Nat. Soc. Profl. Engrs., ASCE. Home: 1115 Wilmington Island Rd Savannah GA 31410-4508 Office: Hussey Gay Bell & DeYoung 329 Commercial Dr Savannah GA 31406-3630

HSU, NAN-YUNG, chest surgeon; b. Kaohsiung, Taiwan, May 6, 1955; d. Lien-Tin Hsu and Kin-Shau Haung; m. Chao-Shin Li, Sept. 19, 1984; children: Chih-Chei, Su-Tien. MD, U. Yung Ming, Taipei, Taiwan, 1982. Cert. in medicine. Attending dr. chest surgery Taichung Vet. Gen. Hosp., 1989-96, Kaohsiung Chung Gang Meml. Hosp., 1996-97; chief chest surgery China Med. Coll. Hosp., Taichung, 1997—. Contbr. articles to med. jours. Fellow Am. Coll. Chest Physicians; mem. Am. Assn. for Cancer Rsch. (corr. mem.). Avocations: golf, music, traveling, reading. Office: China Med Coll Hosp, # 2 Yuh-Der St, Taichung 405, Taiwan

HSU, PAO-CHIU, water treatment engineer, educator; b. Guiyang, China, Dec. 31, 1918; s. Shao-Long and De-Hui (Wen) H.; m. Zhenxiang Gan, Dec. 21, 1952; 1 child, Mingpei. B of Engring., Nat. Ctrl. U., Chongqing, China, 1942; MS of Sanitary Engring., U. Mich., 1949; PhD, U. Wis., 1951. Practice engr. Baotian Railway Constrn. Bur., Tianshui, China, 1942-43; tchg. asst. Chongqing U., 1943-44, Nat. Ctrl. U., China, 1945-47; design engr. Consoer, Townsend and Assocs., Chgo., 1954; assoc. prof. Tsinghua U., Beijing, 1955-60, prof., 1961-89, 90—; adv. group experts Beijing Mcpl. Govt., 1985-88, divsn. head, 1989-96. Author: Piping and Pumping Calculations Made Easy, 1973, Water Treatment, 1979, Modern Water and Wastewater Treatment, 1983 (Excellent Textbook award 1987), Contemporary theories of Water and Wastewater Treatment, 1991 (Excellent Textbook award 1995), Water Treatment: A Comprehensive Treatise, 1992 (Excellent Books of Sci. and Tech. award 1995); contbr. articles to profl. jours.; dep. chief editor Indsl. Water Treatment Jour., 1985-88. Mem. Chinese Soc. Chem. Engrs. (v.p. Inst. Indsl. Water Treatment 1981-88, v.p. Inst. Water and Wastewater Engring. 1985-90, pres. 1991-96, editl. bd. advisor jour. 1990—), Chinese Soc. Electronics (v.p. Clean Tech. Inst. 1982-85), Chinese Soc. Civil Engrs. (coun. mem. 1990-93, standing coun. 1994-98, hon. coun. mem. 1998—), Chinese Soc. Water and Wastewater engring. (pres. 1991-96, hon. pres. 1997—), Sigma Xi. Office: Tsinghua U Dept Environ, Sci and Engring, 100084 Beijing China

HSU, PI HUA, artist; b. Yun Lin, Taiwan, Apr. 16, 1957; d. Kuo Chih Hsu and Hsiu Jun Yang; m. Wen Bin Liu; 1 child, Wei Shoe. BA, Nat. Cheng Chi U., 1979. Libr. Nat. Cheng Chi U., Taipei, Taiwan, 1979-82; artist Pi Hua Hsu Art Studio, Taipei, 1981—. Author: Watercolors by Pi Hua Hsu, vol. 1, 1985, vol. 2, 1987, vol. 3, 1989, Notebook of Art and Poetry, vol. 1, 1991, vol. 2, 1993, Painting by Pi Hua Hsu, vol. 4, 1994. Recipient Excellent Novice award Art Mag., 1986, Spl. award Asian Art Exhbn., 1986, Art medal Chinese Assn. Arts and Lit. in Taiwan, 1993. Mem. Internat. Modern Artist Assn., Taipei Watercolor Assn., Traditional Chinese Flower Arrangement Found. Buddhist. Avocations: Chinese flower arranging, horticulture, swimming, music. Home and Office: PO Box 222 Mucha, 116 Taipei Taiwan

HSU, RUE RON, physics educator; b. Tainan, Taiwan, Dec. 28, 1958; s. Chin Hou and Jo Shin Hsu; m. Hsiu Yu Tseng, Feb. 19, 1984; 3 children. BS, Nat. Ctrl. U., Chung-Li, Taiwan, 1981, MS, 1984, PhD, 1987. Assoc. prof. dept. physics Nat. Cheng Kung U., Tainan, 1989-94, prof., 1994—. Contbr. articles to sci. jours., including Physics Letters, Classical and Quantum Gravity, Phys. Rev. Letters. 2d lt. Taipei Air Force, 1987-89. Mem. Astron. Soc. Republic of China (councillor 1999—), Phys. Soc. Republic of China, Astron. Soc. Pacific. Avocations: reading, classical music, painting, table tennis, badminton. Office: Nat Cheng Kung U, Dept Physics, Tainan 701, Taiwan

HSU, RUEY-FEN, otorhinolaryngological surgeon; b. Kaohsiung, Taiwan, Sept. 11, 1968; d. Shui-Li Hsu and Mei-Kuei Chen; m. Wu-Lang Yang, Dec. 3, 1997; 1 child, Chun-Yao Yang. MD, Kaohsiung Med. U., 1995. Lic. otolaryngologist. Intern Kaohsiung Med. U. Hosp., 1994-95; resident Chang Gung Meml. Hosp., Kaohsiung, 1995-98, chief resident, 1998-99, attending physician otolaryngology dept., 1999—. Inventor in field. Mem. AAAS, Taiwan Otolaryngol. Soc., N.Y. Acad. Sci. Office: Chang Gung Meml Hosp, 123 Ta-Pei Rd, 833 Niao Sung Hsiang Taiwan

HSU, SHU-EN, scientific research foundation administrator; b. Ho-pei, China, Aug. 29, 1929; s. H.G.K. and S.W. (Kuo) H.; m. Frances Chun Hwei Hsu, Jan. 15, 1959; children: Frank I.M., L.Y., Y.C. BS, Naval Coll. Tech., Tsao-ying, Taiwan, 1953; MS, Northwestern U., 1966; PhD, Stanford U., 1972. Engr. Naval Shipyard, Tsao-ying, 1953-63; researcher Chung Shan Inst. Sci. & Tech., Lungtan, Taiwan, 1967-78; prof. Nat. Taiwan U., Taipei, 1972-98; gen. mgr. China Engraving and Printing Works, Shin-dan, Taiwan, 1978-83; dir. Materials Rsch. and Devel. Ctr. Chung Shan Inst. Sci. and Tech., Lungtan, 1983-94; adj. prof. Nat. Taiwan U., Taipei, 1972-98; com. mem. Com. for Aviation and Space Industry Devel. of China, Taipei, 1989—; vis. prof. U. N.S.W., Sydney, Australia, 1992-98; cons. prof. Hong Kong U. Sci. & Tech., 1995; pres. HyTeC Co., Ltd., Taiwan, 1997—. Author: X-Ray Diffraction and Structure Analysis, 1993; co-editor: Advanced Composites and Structure, 1987; patentee in field; contbr. articles to sci. jours. Recipient Yun-Hwei medal Ministry Nat. Def., 1988, Hou Chin-Twai medal Hou's Culture Found., 1991, Dr. Sun Yet-Sen's medal for sci. creation, 1994. Fellow Asia Pacific Acad. Materials, Australian Acad. Technological Sci. and Engring.; mem. AAAS, Internat. Adv. Material Rsch. Soc., Soc. Mfg. Engrs., Soc. for Advancement of Materials and Proc., Chinese Soc. for Materials Sci. (past pres., Lu's Gold medal 1980), N.Y. Acad. Scis., Order Internat. Fellow. Home: 103 Lne 66 Hsing-Teh Rd, Win-Shan Taipei 11726, Taiwan

HSU, SING RONG, manufacturing executive, marketing professional; b. Maoli, Taiwan, Republic of China, Jan. 28, 1952; s. Koun Sen and Chun Mei (Lee) H.; m. Shau Yue Lin, Mar. 8, 1979; children: Chen-Whai, Yun-Guei, Raei-Hun. Grad., Taichung Comml. Coll. Sch., 1973, Tokyo Internat. U., 1980. Trading specialist Taichung Funai Electrics Co., 1973-75; supr. Kou-Hwa Ceramic Co., 1976-79; chief trading dept. Kun Nan Enterprise Co., Ltd., 1980-84, adminstrn. dept. mgr., 1984-85; dept. mgr. Center-Satellite

Coop. Assn., 1985-87; project leader Chinese-Japanese Tech. Coop., 1987-89; pres. Meek World-Wide Corp., 1989—; Japanese tour guide; Japanese/ Chinese translator; customs clearance specialist; bd. dirs. Champion Power Metallurgy Co., Ltd. Editor: Handbook of Sintered (P/M) Parts Design and Production, 1992, How to Launch Internation Marketing at Low Cost, 1993, Factory Managing of 5S, 1989; inventor traffic signal of special structure. Fax: 886-2-29133402. E-mail: sinei@usa.net. Home: 2F No 7 Ln 270 Chun-Hsin Rd, Sec 1 Hsin-Tien, Taipei Taiwan Office: Meek Worldwide Corp, 7F No 80 Hoping W Rd Sec 1, 100 Taipei Taiwan

HSU, SU-MING, pathologist, educator; b. Taiwan, Taiwan, Jan. 28, 1949; s. Tomhigh and Yu (Chen) H.; m. Pei-Ling; 1 child, Eugene. MD, Nat. Taiwan U., 1976. Diplomate Am. Bd. Anatomic Pathology. Resident Brown U., Providence, R.I., 1977-81; rsch. NIH, Bethesda, Md., 1981-84; adj. prof. U. Tex., 1984-90; prof. U. Ark., 1990-95, Nat. Taiwan Univ. Coll. Medicine, Taipei, 1995—. Office: Nat Taiwan Univ Hosp Path, #1 Jen Ai Rd 1st Sect, 100 Taipei Taiwan, Taiwan

HSU, TZU YAO, materials scientist, educator; b. Ningbo, Zhejiang, China, Mar. 21, 1921; s. Jue Qing and Qing Shan (Qiu) X. BS, Nat. Yunnan U., Kunming, China, 1942. Asst. rschr. Bur. Materials Rsch., Changqing, Nanjing, China, 1945-48; assoc. prof. Tangshan Jiao Tong U., Tangshan, China, 1949-53, Beijing U. Iron and Steel Tech., 1953-61; prof. materials sci. Shanghai Jiao Tong U., 1961—; hon. prof. Nanjing U. Sci. and Tech., 1996—, City U. Hong Kong, 1997—, Kunming U. Sci. and Tech., 1986—, Shandong Poly. U., 1984—, Yunnan U. Tech., 1984—; adj. prof. Shanghai U., 1981—. Adv. editor Internat. Materials Characterization, 1983—, ISIJ Internat., 1997—; author: Martersitic Transformation and Martensite, 1980, 81, 2d edit., 1999, Termodynamics of Materials, 1981, 2d edit., 1999, Bainitic Transformation and Bainite, 1991, Theory of Phase Transformation, 1988, 91, 99, Metallography of Low-Magenese Steels, 1979, Introduction to Materials Science, 1986, Principles of Metallography, 1964, Principles of Metallurgy, 1951; contbr. numerous articles to profl. jours. Recipient Nat. Natural Sci. prize of China, Nat. Commn. of Sci. and Tech., 1987, Progress of Sci. and tech. award State Commn. Edn., 1986, 87, 88, Nat. prize of progress in sci. and tech. Ministry of Sci. and Tech., 1999. Mem. Chinese Acad. Sci., Chinese Materials Rsch. Soc. (coun. 1991-95, hon. coun. mem. 1995—). Office: Shanghai Jiao Tong U, Hua Shan Rd, Shanghai 200030, China

HSU, WEN-MING, ophthalmologist; b. Tainan, Taiwan, July 10, 1948; s. Yung-Chiuan and Chuen-Tz (Chen) H.; m. Bi-Yu Huang, Apr. 3, 1975; children: Han-Pu (Henry), Chi-Hsin (Gregory), Shih-Ju (Jeff). MD, Tapei Med. Coll., 1973. Diplomate Nat. Health Dept., Taiwan. Resident dep. ophthalmology Vets. Gen. Hosp., Taipei, 1974-78, attending physician ophthalmology, 1978-83; chief, dept. of ophthalmology Vets. Gen. Hosp. Taichung, Taiwan, 1983-89; dir. oculoplastic section Vets. Gen. Hosp., Taipei, Taiwan, 1989-97; vice-dir. Yung-Kang Vets. Hosp., Tainan, Taiwan, 1997-98; chmn. Dept. Opthalmology Vets. Gen. Hosp., Taipei, Taiwan, 1998—; prof., chmn. dept. ophthalmology sch. medicine Nat. Yang-Ming U., Taiwan, 1999—; Fellow N.Y. Eye & Ear Infirmary, 1982, Pacific Med. Ctr., San Francisco, 1983, Moorfields Eye Hosp., London, 1989; assoc. prof. Nat. Yang-Ming U., Taipei, 1987—; clin. prof. Nat. Def. Med. Coll., 1996—. Author: Mini-Encyclopedia in Ophthalmology, 1993; editor Jour. Ophthal. Soc. of Republic of China, 1994—, Jour. Taipei Med. Assn., 1994-99. Fellow Internat. Coll. Surgeons; mem. Am. Acad. Aesthetic Restorative Surgery, Am. Acad. Ophthalmology, The Ophthal. Soc. Republic of China (v.p. 1993-96, 99—, dir. adv. bd. 1996-99). Avocations: golf, writing, stamp collecting. Office: Vets Gen Hosp Dept Ophthal, 201 Sect 2 Shih Pai Rd, Taipei Taiwan

HSU, YAU QUE, physician; b. Hong Kong, Feb. 28, 1953; s. Tak and Pui Chu (Yeung) H.; m. Brenda Kwok, June 22, 1986. BSc, U. Wis., 1975; AM, Harvard U., 1976; MBBS, Hong Kong U., 1981. Registrar U. Med. Unit Hong Kong U. Queen Mary Hosp., 1983-86; physician St. Teresa's Hosp., Hong Kong, 1986—; hon. clin. lectr. Hong Kong U., 1987—. Mem. Royal Coll. Physicians, Hong Kong Med. Assn., Phi Kappa Phi. Club: Harvard (Hong Kong). Office: Rm 802 Argyle Ctr Phase 1, 688 Nathan Rd, Hong Kong Hong Kong

HSU, YONG, research scientist; b. Jinan, China, Jan. 27, 1963; s. Chongan and Xilan (Fang) H. BS, Peking U., 1984, MA, 1987; PhD, U. Rochester, 1993. Asst. prof., assoc. scientist Mich. Molecular Inst., Midland, 1993-97; sr. rsch. sci. 3M Co., St. Paul, 1997—; cons. Dendritech, Inc., Midland, 1995—. Mem. AAAS, Am. Chem. Soc., Materials Rsch. Soc. Avocations: hiking, classical music, basketball. Office: 3M Center Bldg 201-2e08 Saint Paul MN 55144-1001

HU, BIN, mechanical engineering educator; b. Shucheng, China, Sept. 12, 1962; s. Jiongnan Hu and Xiying Wang; m. Yi Wu, Apr. 21, 1987; 1 child, Haoyue. B in Engring., Nanjing (China) U. Sci. Tech., 1983, M in Engring., 1986; PhD in Mech. Engring., U. Stuttgart, Germany, 1997. Tchg. asst. Nanjing U. Sci. and Tech., 1986-88, asst. prof. mech. engring., 1989-90; vis. scientist U. Stuttgart, Germany, 1991-97, rsch. fellow, 1998—. Contbr. articles to profl. jours. Mem. European Mechanics Soc., Chinese Soc. for Vibration Engring. Avocations: bridge, sightseeing. Home: Luxiyin 23 Apt 2-305, 210009 Nanjing China

HU, CHANG WEI, chemist, educator; b. Jun Lian, China, May 21, 1963; s. Zeyi Hu and Renshu Guo; m. Xiang Guang, Jan. 1, 1987; 1 child, Qi. BSc, Sichuan U., 1983, MSc, 1991, DSc, 1996. From asst. to prof. Sichuan U., Chengdu, China, 1983—, vice chair dept. chemistry, 1996—, dean faculty chemistry, 1998—. Mem. Chem. Soc. China (outstanding young chemist award 1992). E-mail: chwehu@mail.sc.cninfo.net. Office: Sichuan U Dept Chemistry, 29 Wangjiang Rd, 610064 Chengdu Sichuan, China

HU, CHENGLIE, mathematician, educator; b. Shanghai, China, Apr. 22, 1954; came to U.S., 1991; s. Li Yu and Wengiao Hu; m. Xianjing Xia, Jan. 21, 1982; 1 child, Bojun. BS, East China Normal U., 1977, MS, 1989; PhD, Wichita State U., 1995. Instr. E. China Normal U., Shanghai, China, 1980-91; tchg. fellow, rsch. asst. Wichita (Kans.) State U., 1991-95; asst. prof. Fort Hays (Kans.) State U., 1995—; reviwer Math. Revs. of Am., Math. Soc., 1996. Contbr. articles to profl. jours. Recipient Best paper award Math. Assn. Am. (Kans. sect.), 1995; grantee NSF, 1993-95. Mem. Sigma Xi, Kappa Mu Epsilon. Achievements include development of first software package on conformal mapping for doubly connected polygonal regions. Office: Ft Hays State U 600 Park St Hays KS 67601-4009

HU, CHUN PU, chemist, educator; b. Wuxi, Jiangsu, China, Mar. 12, 1939; s. Hong Zhao Hu and Li Xia Jiang; m. Mei Juan Li, Apr. 30, 1968; 1 child, Fei Fan Hu. BSc, East China U. Chem. Tech., Shanghai, 1961; MSc, Dalian (China) Inst. Tech., 1965. Tchg. asst. East China U. Sci. and Tech., Shanghai, 1965-78, lectr., 1978-83, assoc. prof., 1983-90, prof. chemistry, 1990—; vis. scientist U. Sheffield (Eng.), 1987-2000; dir. lab. spl. synthesis and processing of polymer materials East China U. Sci. and Tech., 1985—, pres. acad. com. materials, 1996—; supr. PhD students State Coun. China, 1993—; mem. acad. com., state key lab. synthetic fibers Donghua U., Shanghai, 1994—; mem. dept. structures and materials com. of sci. and tech. State Ednl. Dept. China, 1995—; mem. judgement group of material sci. and engring., com. of acad. degree, State Coun., China, 1997—; mem. found. jugdement group, dept. structures and materials Nat. Natural Sci. Found. China, 2000—. Author (book chpts.) Copolymerization, 1984, Advances in Polymer Blends and Alloys, vol. 4, 1993; patentee in field; mem. editorial coms. Polymer Bull., 1991—, Jour. Functional Polymers, 1992—, China Elastomers, 1992—, Jour. East China U. Sci. and Tech., 1996—, Acta Polymeric Sinica, 1999—, China Synthetic Rubber Industry, 1999—. Mem. Shanghai Assn. Sci. and Tech., Shanghai Assn. Cohering Tech. (pres. 1996—). Avocations: music, reading, bicycling, movies. E-mail: cphu@guomai.sh.cn. Fax: 86-21-64253539. Office: China U Sci Tech Inst Mat Sci Engring, 130 Meilong Rd East, Shanghai 200237, China

HU, DAN-NING, ophthalmologist; b. Shanghai, Dec. 25, 1936; came to U.S., 1989; s. Bing-Kui and Hua-Li (Liu) H.; m. Yuk-Shan Chu, May 6, 1973; 1 child, Ying Wu. MD, Shanghai First Med. Coll., 1955; postdoctoral fellow, Johns Hopkins U., 1981. Chmn. dept. ophthalmology Chiuchang Hosp., Shanghai, 1970-79; dir. Zhabei Eye Inst. and Hosp., Shanghai, 1979-89; chmn., prof. dept. med. genetics and dept. ophthalmology Tiedao Med. Coll., Shanghai, 1984-89; vice-dir. Nat. Ctr. of Genetic Medicine, Shanghai, 1988-89; dir. Tissue Culture Ctr. N.Y. Eye and Ear Infirmary, N.Y.C., 1989—; cons. Allergan, Inc., Irvine, Calif., 1993—; prof. dept. ophthalmology N.Y. Med. Coll., Valhalla, 1995—; cons. Pharmacia, Stockholm, 1993—, Kaoshing Med. U., Taiwan, 1999—; hon. prof. Shanghai First Hosp., China, 2000—. Author: Ophthalmic Genetics, 1988; assoc. editor: Pigment Cell Rsch., 1999—; inventor in field. Recipient Chinese Med. Rsch. award Chinese Health Ministry, 1980; grantee NIH, Bethesda, Md., 1986, IPE rsch. grantee Glaucoma Found., N.Y.C., 1994. Mem. Chinese Soc. Med. Genetics (exec. com. 1986—), Chinese Soc. Ophthalmic Genetics (chmn. 1979-89, award 1980), Internat. Fedn. Pigment Cell Soc. (chmn. ocular/extracutaneous expert group 1997—), Internat. Soc. Eye Rsch., Chinese Soc. Ophthalmology (com. 1979—), Soc. Ocular Pigment Cell Rsch. (chmn. 1997—). Office: NY Eye & Ear Infirmary 310 E 14th St New York NY 10003-4201

HU, DAVID CHUNG KUEN, interventional cardiologist, researcher; b. Hong Kong, Feb. 2, 1954; s. Shin Kan Hu and Ying Ching Niu; m. Janny Hu. BS, U. Minn., 1975; MD, Washington U., 1979. Diplomate Am. Bd. Internal Medicine, Am. Bd. Cardiology. Intern U. B.C., Vancouver, Can., 1979-80, resident, 1980-82, clin. instr., 1985-86, clin. asst. prof., 1986—; fellow Mayo Grad. Sch. Medicine, Rochester, Minn., 1982-85; interventional cardiologist Beth Israel Hosp./Harvard Med. Sch., Boston, 1998-99; cons. cardiologist Health Sci. Ctr. Hosp., Vancouver, 1985—; cardiology rep. B.C. Med. Assn., 1990-95. Author: (with John Burnett) Elevation of Atrial Natriuretic Factor in Heart Failure Science, 1985. Fellow Royal Coll. Physicians Can.; mem. Royal Coll. Surgeons Eng. Office: Rm 1512, 9 Queens Rd, Central Hong Kong

HU, FUNG-RONG, ophthalmologist, medical researcher, educator; b. Taichung, Taiwan, Sept. 1, 1956; s. Hui-Te and Chan-Chin (Chan) H.; m. Shan-Chwen Chang; children: Hao-Chun Chang, Hao-Yun Chang. MD, Nat. Taiwan U., Taipei, 1981. Intern Nat. Taiwan U. Hosp., Taipei, 1980-81, resident, 1981-85, attending staff, 1985—, lectr. ophthalmology, 1985-93; chief cornea sect. dept. ophthalmology Nat. Taiwan U. Hosp., 1996—; postdoctoral fellow Harvard Med. Sch., Boston, 1988-89; fellow in ophthalmology Mass. Eye and Ear Infirmary, Boston, 1988-89; assoc. prof. ophthalmology Nat. Taiwan U., Taipei, 1993-98; prof. Nat. Taiwan U., 1998—; cons. Lo-Ton (Taiwan) Po-Ai Hosp., 1985—, Cathay Gen. Hosp., Taipei, 1990—. Contbr. articles to profl. jours. Mem. Ophathlmol. Soc. of Republic of China (supr. 1994—, exec. gen. acad. com. 1991-93, exec. gen. fin. com. 1991-93), Formosan Med. Assn., Am. Acad. Ophthalmology. Avocations: music, playing piano, hiking, tennis, table tennis. Office: Nat Taiwan Univ Hosp, No 7 Chung-Shan South Rd, Taipei Taiwan

HU, HAIYAN, applied mechanics educator, consultant; b. Shanghai, Oct. 4, 1956; s. Luobai Wang and Mei Hu; m. Luna Wang, Aug. 2, 1982; 1 child, Lu Wang. BSc, Shandong U. Tech., Jinan, China, 1981, MSc, 1984; PhD, Nanjing U. Aeros.-Astronautics, China, 1988. Registered profl. mech. engr. Tchg. asst. Shandong U. Tech., 1984-85, prof., 1995—; rsch. fellow U. Stuttgart, Germany, 1992-94; lectr. applied mechanics Nanjing U. Aeros. and Astronautics, 1988-90, assoc. prof., 1990-92, prof., 1994—, dep. dir. Inst. Vibration Engring., 1990-92, dir., 1994-95, v.p., 1997—; cons. on vibration engrng. Assoc. editor Jour. Vibration Engring., 1992—; contbr. articles to sci. jours., including Jour. Sound and Vibration, Chaos, Solitons and Fractals, Chinese Jour. Aeros., Chinese Jour. Applied Mechanics. Named Outstanding Faculty Fellow, State Edn. Commn., Beijing, 1994, Outstanding Young Scientist, Nat. Sci. Found., Beijing, 1996; rsch. fellow Alexander von Humboldt Found., Bonn, Germany, 1991. Fellow Chinese Soc. for Vibration Engrng. (v.p.); mem. AIAA, Gesellschaft für Angewandte Mathematik und Mechanik. Avocations: photography, shooting. Office: Nanjing U Aeros and Astro, 29 Yudao St, Nanjing 210016, China

HU, HONG, mathematics educator, aerodynamics researcher; b. Hangzhou, Zhejiang, People's Republic China, Nov. 21, 1959; came to U.S., 1982; s. Zhiyu and Zhiruo (Xu) H.; m. Betty P. Tsang, July 25, 1985; children: Jenny T., Kevin J. BS, Zhejiang Inst. Tech., Hangzhou, 1982; M Engring., Old Dominion U., 1984, PhD, 1988. Prof. math. Hampton (Va.) U., 1988—; participant, presenter at nat. and internat. confs. Contbr. articles on computation fluid dynamics to jours., chpts. to books. Old Dominion U. fellow, 1986; grantee NASA, 1990—, U.S. Army, 1992-96. Mem. AIAA (sr.mem.), Am. Heliocopter Soc. Office: Hampton U Dept Math Hampton VA 23668

HU, JIANGUO, biochemist, researcher; b. Shanghai, Feb. 8, 1949; arrived in Japan, 1986; s. Jinfang Hu and Xinju Tang; m. Xiaoming Yang; 1 child, Qingyuan. BM, Chinese Traditional Med. U., Shanghai, 1982; PhD, Nagasaki (Japan) U., 1990. Pharmacy diplomate. Rschr. Inst. for Drug Control, Shanghai, 1982-86; guest rschr. Nagasaki U., 1986-90; chief rschr. BML Inc., Tokyo, 1991-2000; sr. mgr. overseas med. equipment Fuji Photo Optical Inc., Saitama, Japan, 2000—. Editor: Chinese Pharmacopia; contbr. articles to profl. jours. Mem. Japan Neurol. Soc., Japan Biochemistry Soc., N.Y. Acad. Scis. Office: Fuji Photo Optical Inc, 1-324 Uetake, Omiya, Saitama 330-8624, Japan

HU, JIANJUN, research scientist; b. Jilin, China, Nov. 17, 1964; parents Bang Hu and Guilan Chen; m. Conghui Yang, June, 1989; children: Xueyu, Esther Ping. BS, Peking U., Beijing, 1986; PhD, Chinese Acad. Scis., Beijing, 1991. Sr. engr. Capital Steel, Beijing, 1993-96; rsch. fellow Japanese Soc. for Promotion of Sci. Nagoya U., Japan, 1996-99; rsch. assoc. Northwestern U., Evanston, Ill., 1999—; vis. scientist Bremen U., Germany, 1991-93. Contbr. rsch. articles to profl. jours. Recipient 1st Class prize for natural sci. Chinese Acad. Scis., 1992. Mem. Microscop Soc. Am., Am. Inst. Physics, Japanese Soc. Electron Microscopy. Avocations: art, sports.

HU, JINLIAN, educator, researcher; b. Xishui, Hubei, China, Aug. 26, 1961; d. Yankun and Guifen (Pan) H.; m. Pingbiao Chen, Jan. 1, 1988; 1 child, Di. B of Engring., Wuhan Inst. Textile Sci. and Tech., China, 1982, PhD, 1994; M of Engring., China Textile U., Shanghai, 1986. Lectr. Chendu Textile Sch., China, 1982-83, Wuhan Inst. Textile Sci. and Tech., 1986-90; asst. prof. Hong Kong Poly U., 1994—. Fellow Textile Inst.; mem. Hong Kong Soc. Theoretical & Applied Mechanics. Avocations: reading, dancing, fashion. Office: Hong Kong Poly U, Hung Hom, Kowloon Hong Kong

HU, JIN-LIN, electrical engineering educator; b. Anqing, Anhui, China, July 8, 1966; s. Ming-Qi Hu and Hui-Qian Lu; m. Yan Ma, June 19, 1995; 1 child, Jun-Jie. BS, Northwestern Poly. U., Xian, China, 1989, MS, 1992; PhD, Xian Jiaotong U., 1998. Rschr. Northwestern Poly. U., 1992-94, asst. prof., 1994-98, assoc. prof., 1998-99; sr. rschr. City U. of Hong Kong, 1999—. Recipient Progress award of sci. tech. Ministry of Aerospace Industry, 1994, 96, 98. Mem. N.Y. Acad. Scis. Home: Northwestern Poly U, 710072 Xian Shaanxi China

HU, JINTAO, vice president of China; b. Jixi County, Anhui, China, Dec. 1942. Joined Chinese Communist Party, 1964, alt. mem. 12th cen. com., 1982; dir. constrn. com. Gansu Provincial Govt., 1982, mem. presidium, mem. standing com. 6th nat. com., 1983—; v.p. China Internat. Cultural Exch. Ctr., 1984—, People's Republic of China, 1998—; sec. com. Chinese Communist Party, Guizhou, 1985-88, mem. 13th ctrl. com., 1987-92, 14th ctrl. com., 1992—; pres. Ctrl. Party Sch., 1993—; permanent mem. Chinese Communist Party Politburo, 1992—, head ctrl. leading group for party bldg. work. Sec. Communist Youth League, 1982; chair Nat. Orgnl. Com. for Internat. Youth Year, 1984—; vice chair Ctrl. Orgnl. Com., 1993—. Mem. Soc. Young Pioneers Work (pres. 1984—). Office: Office of Pres, State Coun Sec Zhong Nan Hai, Beijing China*

HU, LI, art educator; b. Shanghai, China, Sept. 16, 1950; s. Renzhi Hu and Keren He; m. Ping Li, Feb. 22, 1988; children: Yichen Hu, Elina Hu. BFA, Shanghai U., 1986; MFA, U. S.D., 1993. Art designer Xiechang Sewing Machine Co., Shanghai, 1977-83; asst. prof. Shanghai U., 1986-89; assoc. prof. U. Wis., Oshkosh, 1993—. Solo shows include Morehead State U., Kent, 1999, U. Wis., Madison, 1999, Reno City Hall Gallery, 1999, Art Inst. and Gallery, Salisbury, Md., 1999, Art Ctr. in Orange, Va., 1999, Colo. State U., Ft. Collins, 1998, Coker Coll., Hartsville, S.C., 1998, Linfield State Coll., McMinnville, Oreg., 1998, McHenry County Coll., Crystal Lake, Ill., 1998, Chadron State Coll., Nebr., 1997, Kansas City Artists Coalition, Kansas City, Mo., 1997, Mont. State U., Billings, 1996, Corvallis Arts Ctr., Oreg., 1996, Minnetonka Ctr. for the Art, Wayzata, Minn., 1995, Bloominton Art Ctr., Minn., 1995, others; group shows include Leslie Powell Gallery, Lawton, Okla., 1997, Smithtown Twp. Arts Coun., St. James, N.Y., 1997, Korean Cultural Ctr., L.A.., 1996, Medici Art Ctr., Phila., 1996, San Francisco State U. Student Ctr. Art Gallery, Calif., 1995, Berkeley Art Ctr., Calif., 1995, Royal Garden Gallery, Copenhagen, 1987, Hunte Coll., N.Y., 1986, Kobe (Japan) Agr. Mus., 1986, Shanghai Art Mus., 1986, 87, 89, others; work collected at Sioux City Art Ctr., Iowa, U. S.D., Vermillion, Coal and Oil Corp., Ji Lu, Japan, Art Corp. of Japan-China, Kobe, Japan. Recipient Hon. Mention Okla.: Centerfold, Seventh, Leslie Powell Gallery, Lawton and the U. of Sci. and Art, Chickacha, 1997, Faculty Devel. Rsch. grant U. Wis., Oshkosh, 1996, 1995, Juror's award Berkeley Art Ctr. Assn., Calif., 1995, others. Home: 604 W 20th Ave Oshkosh WI 54902-6824

HU, MICHÈLE TAO-MING, neurologist; b. Oxford, London, Sept. 20, 1969; d. Yao-Su and Magdalene Hu; m. Simon Anthony Cudlip, 1995. Postgrad., U. London, MB BS, 1993. Rsch. fellow dept. neurology Kings Coll. Hosp., 1996-99; rsch. fellow dept. neurology MRC Cyclotron unit, Hammersmith Hosp., 1996-99, specialist registrar in neurology, 1996-99. Author: (with others) Handbook of Clinical Neurology, 1999; contbr. articles to profl. jours. Rsch. tng. fellowship Action Rsch., 1998—; travel grant Internat. Fedn. of Parkinson's Disease Founds., 1999. Mem. Royal Coll. of Physicians, Royal Soc. of Medicine, Am. Acad. of Neurology, Assn. of British Neurologists. Avocations: pottery, piano, Latin jive dancing. Office: MRC Cyclotron Unit, Hammersmith Hosp DuCane Rd, London W12 ONN, England

HU, PEI CHU, mathematician, educator; b. Qingzhou, Shandong, China, Aug. 26, 1961; s. Yao He and Guang Xiu (Li) H.; m. Jin Zheng, Jan. 25, 1987; 1 child, Zhong Yuan. BPhil, Shandong U., 1982, MPhil, 1985; PhD, Hong Kong U. Sci. and Tech., 1996. Tchg. asst. Shandong U., Jinan, 1985-88, lectr., 1988-96, assoc. prof., 1996-98, prof., 1998—; tchg. asst. Hong Kong U. Sci. and Tech., 1993-96. Author: (with Chung-Chun Yang) Value Distribution Theory and Its Applications to Meromorphic Mappings, 1996, Differentiable and Complex Dynamics of Several Variables, 1999; contbr. articles to profl. jours. Mem. Hong Kong Math. Soc., S.E. Asian Math. Soc., Am. Math. Soc. Avocations: reading novels, playing chess, travel, swimming, fishing. Office: Shandong U, Dept Math, 250100 Jinan Shandong, China

HU, SHUXIAN, neuroscientist, pediatric neurologist; b. Kunming, Yunnan, China; s. Fanxiang Hu and Quiqing Dan; m. Jie Min, Nov. 19, 1949; 1 child, Michael Min. MD, Beijing Med. U., 1982. Chief resident Beijing Med. U., 1984-85, attending physician, neurologist, 1986-88; fellow dept. neurosci. U. Minn., 1988-92; scientist Mpls. Med. Rsch. Found., Mpls., 1992—; asst. prof. medicine U. Minn. Med. Sch., Mpls., 1997—. Contbr. articles to profl. jours. Mem. AAAS, Internat. Immunocompromised Host Soc., Soc. for Neurosci., Upjohn Immunology and Infectious Disease (disting. rsch. scientist award). Avocation: sports. E-mail: haxxx031@maroam.tc.umn.edu. Office: Mpls med Rsch Found 914 S 8th St Minneapolis MN 55404-1204

HU, XIANDENG, engineering educator; b. Lianjiang, Gua, China, Mar. 17, 1957; s. Daohui and Xuexing (Huang) H.; m. Jinling Hu, May 18, 1960; children: Tianyi , Yixing. BS, South China U. Technology, Guangzhou, 1982; MS, Tianjin U., 1987; PhD, U. New Eng., 1998. Lectr. Tianjin U., China, 1982-90; scientist Qld. Dept. Primary Industries, Brisbane, 1993-94; lectr. James Cook U., Townsville, Australia, 1995-99; rsch. fellow U. Queensland, 1999—. Author: (computer software) Computer-Aided Design of Effluent Irrigation, 1998, Project Leaders: Integrated Turfgrass Management Systems for Golf Courses, 1998—; contbr. articles to profl. jours. Recipient award U. New Eng., Armidale, 1991, UNE Rsch. scholarship, 1992. Mem. Instn. of Engrs./Australia, Environ. Inst. of Australia, Inc., Australia Soc. of Soil Sci., Inc., Australian Water and Wastewater Assn. Avocations: table tennis, basketball, swimming. Office: U Queensland, Dept Civil Engring, Brisbane Queensland 4811, Australia

HU, XIAOMING, research scientist; b. Beijing, Oct. 18, 1963; came to U.S., 1998; m. Yan Wang, June 6, 1988; children: Colin, Sean. BSc, Peking U., Beijing, 1985; PhD, Aberdeen (U.K.) U., 1991. Rsch. fellow U. Warwick, Coventry, U.K., 1990-92, Inst. Physics, Beijing, 1993-96; vis. scholar Rsch. Ctr., Karlsruhe, Germany, 1996-98; asst. rsch. scientist U. Ariz., Tucson, 1998—. Contbr. articles to profl. jours. Mem. Am. Physics Soc. Achievements include research on phases of Ba adsorption on Si(100)-(2x1), nano-patterning and single electron tunneling using STM, generation and analysis of nano-scale AL islands by STM, hydrogen adsorption induced surface reconstructions on Si(113). E-mail: xhu@u.arizona.edu. Fax: 520-621-6778. Office: Optical Scis Ctr Univ Ariz Tucson AZ 85712

HU, XING, physics educator; b. Zhengzhou, Henan, China, Aug. 3, 1953; s. Yuanging Hu and Qiying Zhang; m. Yonghong Li; 1 child, Hu Hao. BS, Henan U., Kaifeng, China, 1982; MS, Zhengznou U., China, 1986; PhD, U. Kans., 1996. Asst. prof. Zhengzhou U., China, 1987-92, prof., 1997—. Contbr. articles to profl. jours. Recipient 1st rank award of sci. rsch. excellent articles of Henan Province, 1998. Mem. Chinese Physics Soc., Chinese Astronomy Soc. Office: Dept Physics, Zhengzhou Univ, 450052 Zhengzhou/Henan China

HU, YAO-SU, economist, educator, author; b. Tashkent, USSR, Aug. 7, 1946; s. Hung-Lick and Chi-Yung (Chung) H.; m. Magdalene Hübenthal, Dec. 17, 1968; children: Michele, Claire, Victor. BA with honors, Oxford U., 1968, MA, 1972, DPhil, 1973. Rsch. fellow Polit. and Econ. Planning, London, 1974-76; indsl. economist World Bank, Washington, 1976-78; sr. rsch. fellow Chatham House, London, 1978-80; sr. tutor Adminstrv. Staff Coll., Henley, U.K., 1980-83; sr. lectr., then reader in mgmt. studies Hong Kong U., 1983-88; gov. Shue Yan Coll., Hong Kong, 1984—; dir. internat. studies Henley Mgmt. Coll., Eng., 1988-90; Found. for Mgmt. Edn. chair internat. bus. U. Warwick, Eng., 1990-92; v.p. Hong Kong Shue Yan Coll., 1992—; vis. prof. Sci. Policy Rsch. Unit U. Sussex, 1992-93, hon. fellow, 1996—; mem. assoc. faculty Henley Mgmt. Coll., 1990—; vis. fellow Fed. Trust, London, 1996-98, sr. rsch. fellow, 1998—, prof. Coll. Europe (Natolin), 1998—. Author: Impact of U.S. Investment in Europe, 1973, National Attitudes and Financing of Industry, 1976, Europe Under Stress, 1981, Industrial Banking and Special Credit Institutions, 1984, (with Nicholas Jéquier) Banking and the Promotion of Technological Development, 1989, (with Sir Donald Maitland) Europe and Emerging Asia, 1998, The Asian Crisis and the European Union's Global Responsibilities, 2000; contbr. articles to profl. jours. Avocations: music, art, travel, Zen. Office: Hong Kong Shue Yan Coll, Braemar Hill Rd, Hong Kong China

HU, ZHI BIN, chemistry educator, researcher; b. Wuhan, Hubei, China, Mar. 26, 1913; s. Z. X. Hu and Y. D. Han; m. K. Y. Shu, Jan. 15, 1932 (dec. Feb. 1993). BS, Cen. China Coll., Wuhan, 1937; MS, U. Wis., 1949. Asst. Cen. China Coll., 1937-41, jr. lectr., 1941-43; lectr. South-Western Union U., 1943-45, Nankai U., China, 1945-46, South-Western Union U., 1946-47; asst. prof. Beijing Normal U., 1949—; cons. Nat. Surface Treatment Assn., China, 1988—. Contbr. articles to sci. jours. Recipient Capital prize, 1987; fellow Wis. Alumni Assn., 1948-49. Office: Beijing Normal U, Dept Chemistry, 100875 Beijing China

HU, ZHICHENG, research scientist; b. Jiangxi, China, May 1962; came to U.S., 1989; Bachelors degree, Zhejiang (China) U., 1982; masters degree, Tianjing (China) U., 1985; PhD, Tsukuba (Japan) U., 1989. Postdoctoral rsch. assoc. MIT, Cambridge, 1989-91; rsch. assoc. Engelhard Corp., Iselin, N.J., 1991—. Patentee in field; contbr. articles to profl. publs. Named N.J. Inventor of Yr., N.J. Inventor's Congress, Newark, 1997. Mem. IEEE, Am. Chem. Soc., Soc. Automotive Engrs., N.Y. Acad. Scis. E-mail: zhicheng.hu@engelhard.com. Office: Engelhard Corp 101 Wood Ave Edison NJ 08820-3504

HUA, JIESONG, microbiologist, researcher; b. Shanghai, Nov. 16, 1961; s. Danian and Jingping (Lu) H.; m. Jingwen Wang, Oct. 13, 1990; 1 child, Shuocheng. B Medicine, Shanghai Med. U., 1985; M Medicine, Shanghai 2d

Med. U., 1991; MS, Nat. U. of Singapore, 1998. Tchg. asst. Shanghai 2d Med. U., 1985-88, lectr., 1991-93; rsch. fellow Hosp. Pellegin, Bordeaux/Girondin, France, 1993-95; rsch. scholar Nat. U. of Singapore, 1995-97, rsch. asst., 1997-98, rsch. fellow, 1999—; mem. editl. bd. World Chinese Jour. of Digestion, Beijing, 1998—. Contbr. articles to profl. jours. Recipient French Fgn. Ministry fellowship, 1993-95, Nat. U. of Singapore scholarship, 1995-97. Avocations: swimming, jogging, reading newspaper. Home e-mail: huajiesong@yahoo.com. Office e-mail: michuajs@nus.edu.sg. Home: Goodman Rd 68, Singapore 345741, Singapore Office: Microbiol Nat U Singapore, Low Kent Bridge Rd, Singapore 117260, Singapore

HUA, JUEMING, science educator; b. Shanghai, Apr. 12, 1933; s. Disheng Hua and Xia Li; m. Shuyi Zhou; children: Hua-Schuller Hong, Hua Yue. BS, U. Tsinghua, Beijing, 1958; MS, Chinese Acad. Sci., Beijing, 1967. Asst. Gansu U. Industry, Lanzhou, China, 1958-64; prof. Inst. for History of Natural Sci., Chinese Acad. Sci., Beijing, 1986—, vice dir., 1988-93; dir. Inst. History of Sci. and Tech. U. Tsinghua, Beijing, 1993—; part-time prof. Chinese U. Sci. and Tech., Hefei, 1987—, Beijing U. Aeronautics and Astronautics, 1998—, U. Tongji, Shanghai, 1998—. Author: Collected Works in the History of Smelted-Casting in China, 1986, Metallurgy in Pre-Qin, 1993, Metallurgy in Ancient China, 1999; chief editor: Five Thousand Years of China's Science and Technology, 1997. Recipient 1st class prize sci. and tech. achievement Ministry of Culture, China, 1984, 1st class prize for excellent work Chinese Soc. for of Sci. and Tech., 1990, 2d class prize for excellent work Govt. Office for News and Pub., 1999. Mem. Soc. for History of Tech. (internat. scholar 1998-99), Internat. Com. for History of Tech., Chinese Soc. Traditional Tech. (chmn. 1995—). Home: Chinese Acad Sci, 18-5-310 Wei Zikeng Dorm, 100101 Chao Yang Beijing China Office: Inst History Natural Sci, 137 Chaonei St, 10010 Beijing China

HUA, SHIPING, political science educator; b. Hebei, China, Mar. 28, 1956; came to U.S., 1987; s. Jingwen and Suxia (He) H.; m. Jia Qin, Aug. 24, 1987; children: Xiaojia, James Hong. BA, Tianjin Fgn. Langs. Inst., China, 1982; MA, Chinese Acad. Social Sci., Beijing, 1986; PhD, U. Hawaii at Manoa, Honolulu, 1993. Degree assoc., vis. fellow East West Ctr., Honolulu, 1990-94; asst. prof. polit. sci. Eckerd Coll., St. Petersburg, Fla., 1996—. Editor, translator: Reporting and Writing the News, 1987; author: Scientism and Humanism: Two Cultures in Post-Mao China, 1995, Chinese Political Culture, 2000. Mem. Am. Polit. Sci. Assn., Assn. Asian Studies. E-mail: huasp@eckerd.edu. Office: 4200 54th Ave S Saint Petersburg FL 33711-4744

HUA, TONG-WEN, chemistry educator, researcher; b. Shanghai, China, Sept. 27, 1929; s. Bing-yuan and Yishan (Wu) H.; m. Yizhong Dong, May 7, 1955; children: Dong Mouqun, Dong Liqun. BS, Yanjing U., Beijing, 1951; MS, Peking U., Beijing, 1954. Teaching asst. chemistry dept. Yanjing U., Beijing, 1951-52; teaching asst. dept. chemistry Peking U., Beijing, 1954-56, lectr., 1956-60, assoc. prof., 1961-85, prof., 1986—; vis. scholar U. Conn., Storrs, 1982-83; dir. Div. Inorganic Chemistry Peking Univ., Beijing, 1956-85, Rsch. Ctr. Higher Chem. Edn., Beijing, 1986—. Author: (textbook) Principles of General Chemistry, 1989, 2d edit., 1993; translator: (textbook) Masterson's Chemical Principles, 1980, (reference book) Pimentel's Opportunities in Chemistry Today and Tomorrow, 1990, Ronald Breslow's Chemistry Today and Tomorrow-The Central, Useful and Creative Science, 1998; chief editor (jour.) Univ. Chemistry (Daxue Huaxue), 1986-96; contbr. articles to profl. jours. Recipient scholarship State Edn. Commn., 1989, 96, 97, Sci. and Tech. award State Petroleum Co., 1981. Mem. Internat. Union Pure and Applied Chemistry, Com. on Tchg. of Chemistry (nat. rep. 1983-95), Chinese Chem. Soc. (bd. dirs. 1986-90, standing com. 1991-94). Home: Peking U Zhong Guan Yuan 41-208, Beijing 100871, China Office: Peking U, Dept Chemistry, Beijing 100871, China

HUANG, AN-CHYAU, science educator; b. Taiwan, Apr. 9, 1962. PhD, U. Calif., Berkeley, 1994. Assoc. prof. Nat. Taiwan U. Sci. and Tech., Taipei, 1994—. Editor-in-chief Mechatronics Mag., 1999. Mem. IEEE. E-mail: achuang@mail.ntust.edu.tw. Fax: 886-2-2737-6460. Office: Nat Taiwan U Sci & Tech, 43 Keelung Rd Sect 4, Taipei 106, Taiwan, Republic of China

HUANG, BEN (HAIBIN), chemical engineer, researcher; b. Xian, Shanxi, China, Oct. 1, 1959; came to U.S., 1991; s. Yun Zhen and Wen Xian (Chen) H.; m. Meng Qiu Zheng, Aug. 19, 1995; 1 child, William Z. BS, Xian Inst. Metallurgy, China, 1981; MS in Polymer Chemistry, U. Sci. & Tech. of China, Hefei, China, 1988; MS in Chem. Engring., U. S. Fla., 1994, PhD in Chem. Engring., 1997. Process engr. Shanxi Chem Design Co., Xian, China, 1982-85; asst. prof. S. China U. Tech., Guang Zhou, China, 1988-91; rsch. chemist Film Techs Internat., St. Petersburg, Fla., 1997-98; R&D mgr. Film Techs Internat., St. Petersburg, 1998—. Contbg. co-author: Interfacial Aspects of Multicomponent Polymer Materials, 1997. Recipient Excellent Thesis award Anhui Acad. Soc., China, 1989. Mem. Am. Chem. Soc. Achievements include patent pending on trade secret; PASS mounting solution for safety window film installation; developed a three layered polymer matrix for fiber optical sensor; invented a technology to synthesize monodistributed, polymer encapsulated particles with the emulsion polymerization method. Avocations: hiking, travel, reading. Office: Film Techs Internat Inc 2544 Terminal Dr S Saint Petersburg FL 33712-1669

HUANG, CECILIA CHIUNG-I, classical violinist, pianist, educator; b. Nantou, Taiwan, Nov. 21, 1965; d. Yuh-feng Huang and Li-ching Wu; m. Allen Chiluen Wang, Sept. 20, 1996. BA, Nat. Taiwan Normal U., Taipei, 1989; MusM, Ind. U., 1991. 1st violinist Nat. Symphony Orch., Taipei, 1988-89, 91-96; lectr. violin Shih-chien U., Taipei, 1993-96; violinist Arioso Piano Trio, San Jose, Calif., 1997—, Oakland (Calif.) East Bay Symphony, 2000—; juror Keelung City Music Competition, 1996, Nat. U. Entrance Exam, Taiwan, 1995, Chinese Music Tchrs. Assn. No. Calif. Youth Music Comp., 2000. Violinist Chung-hwa Chamber Orch., Acad. Taiwan Strings, Taiwan Chamber Orch., Contemporary Chamber Orch. Taipei, New Art Chamber Orch.; founding mem. Arco String Quartet, 1992. Outstanding Music Student scholar Kawai, Inc., Taichung, Taiwan, 1981, Yamaha, Inc., Taipei, 1987; recipient 1st prize Taichung City Music Competition, 1984, 3d prize Nat. Taiwan Region Music Competition, 1984. Mem. Am. String Tchrs. Assn., Chamber Music Am., Chinese Music Tchrs. Assn. of No. Calif. (juror youth music competition, 2000). Roman Catholic. E-mail: ceciliah1121@yahoo.com.

HUANG, CHAO-CHING, pediatrician; b. Chai-Yi, Taiwan, Jan. 1, 1954; s. Kun-Tsan and Wan-Tsui (Lee) H.; m. Ling-Ling Pan, Nov. 27, 1982; children: Po-Hsiang, Po-Yin, Kevin. MD, Taipei Med. Coll., 1980. Resident Taipei Mackay Meml. Hosp., Taiwan, 1980-84, rsch. fellow in pediat. neurology, 1984-86, vis. staff in pediats., 1986-88; pediats. instr. Coll. Medicine Nat. Cheng Kung U., Tainan, Taiwan, 1988-91, assoc. prof. pediats. Coll. Medicine, 1991-98, prof. pediats. Coll. Medicine, 1998—; rsch. fellow in physiology and pediats. U. Pa., Phila., 1991-92. Mem. editl. bd. Taiwan Pediat. Assn., 1998; contbr. articles to profl. jours. including New Eng. Jour. Medicine and Radiology. Recipient Acad. Travel award Mead Johnson, 1991, Snow (Yukizirushi), 1993, 97. E-mail: huangped@mail.ncku.edu.tw. Office: Nat Cheng Kung U Hosp, 138 Sheng-Li Rd, Tainan 704, Taiwan

HUANG, CHAO-SHANG, physicist; b. Yushan, Jiangxi, China, Jan. 25, 1939; s. Zhang-Wen and Chang-E (Fang) H.; m. Xiu-Ping Xu, Sept. 5, 1973; 1 child, Wei. PhD, Academia Sinica, 1982. Asst. prof. Inst. Theoretical Physics, Academia Sinica, Beijing, China, 1982-86; assoc. prof. Academia Sinica, Beijing, China, 1986-91, prof., 1992—; head of first lab. Inst. of Theoretical Physics, Beijing, 1995-98. Editor: Procs. of the Internat. Symposium on Heavy Flavor and Electroweak Theory, 1996; contbr. articles to profl. jours. Mem. Chinese High Energy Physics Soc. Avocations: reading, swimming. Office: Inst Theoretical Physics, Acad Sinica PO Box 2735, Beijing 100080, China

HUANG, CHEIN-HO, chemistry educator; b. Taipei, Taiwan, Feb. 1, 1946; s. Zei-Shin and Zai-Un (Liu) H.; m. Li-ching Chen, Mar. 16, 1973; children: Yu-Chin, Yu-Hsuen, Yung-Han. MS, Tsing Hua U., 1971. Lectr. Tsing Hua U., Hsinchu, Taiwan, 1972-75; assoc. prof. Soochow U., Taipei, 1975-84, prof., 1985—; cons. Chung Shan Inst. Sci. and Tech., Lung-Tan, Taiwan, 1984—. Editor: Chinese Supplement of P&SF, 1993. Active social svc. Taipei Med. Coll. Hosp., 1994—. Lt. Taiwanese Army, 1971-72. Mem. Internat. Wire Assn., Am. Electroplaters and Surface Finishers Soc. (Kergan Wells Svc. award 1999). Avocations: piano, double base, philately, photography, hiking. Home: 4th Fl 64 Tung Huang Rd, Taipei 103, Taiwan Office: Soochow U Dept Chemistry, Shih-Lin, Taipei Taiwan

HUANG, CHENG-TEH JAMES, linguistics educator; b. Hualien, Taiwan, China, June 4, 1948; s. Ching-Fa Huang and Hsui-O Chen; m. Hsiao-Y Emily Huang, Nov. 30, 1977; children: Yiching Deborah, David J. BA, Nat. Taiwan Normal U., Taipei, China, 1972; MA, Nat. Taiwan Normal U., Taipei, Taiwan, 1974; PhD, MIT, 1982. Asst. prof. U. Hawaii, Honolulu, 1982-83, Nat. Tsing Hua U., Hsinchu, Taiwan, 1983-85; from asst. prof. to assoc. prof. Cornell U., Ithaca, N.Y., 1985-90; prof. U. Calif., Irvine, 1989—; vis. prof. Linguistic Inst., 1986, 91, 97, U. Paris, 1991; dir. Summer Inst. Chinese Linguistics, Santa Cruz, 1991, Cornell, 1997. Fulbright fellow, 1978-82, Guggenheim fellow, 1988-89, Sr. Scholar fellow Chiang Ching-Kuo Found., 1996-97, fellow Ctr. Advanced Study Behavioral Scis., 1997-98. Mem. Linguistic Soc. Am. (mem. program com. 1992-95, mem. com. linguistic insts. and fellowships 1997), Internat. Assn. Chinese Linguistics (pres. 2000). Home: 10 Owen Ct Irvine CA 92612-4041 Office: U Calif Irvine Dept Linguistics Irvine CA 92697-0001

HUANG, CHIH YAO, electronics engineer; b. Hsinchu, Taiwan, Republic of China, May 31, 1963; s. Ko Chih and Su Er (Chang) H.; m. Chien-Ting Hsu, Mar. 13, 1999. BS, Nat. Tsing-Hua U., Hsinchu, 1985; MS, Nat. Chiao-Tung U., Hsinchu, 1987, PhD, 1994. Postdoctoral fellow Nat. Nano Device Lab., Hsinchu, 1994-95; sr. R&D engr. Mosel/Vitelic Inc., Hsinchu, 1995-98; tech. asst. mgr. reliability tech. devel. dept. Winbond Electronics Corp., Hsinchu, 1998-99, sr. engr. logic device & reliability dept., 1999—; part-time lectr. Nat. Chiao-Tung U., Hsinchu, 1992-93; part-time assoc prof. Chung-Hua U., Hsinchu, 1997-98; abstract writer Sci. Info. Ctr., Nat. Sci. Coun, Taipei, 1993-97. Contbr. articles to profl. jours. including IEEE Transactions on Electron Devices and Solid-State Electronics. 2d lt. Chinese Air Force, 1987-89. Fellow Ministry of Edn., 1989-91, Nat. Sci. Coun., 1989-94, Indsl. Coop. Project, 1994-95. Mem. IEEE. Avocations: movies, swimming, tennis, photography, travel. Home: No 32 Ln 248 Sect 2, Ching-Kuo Rd, Hsinchu Taiwan 300

HUANG, CHUNG LIN, engineering educator; b. Taichung, Taiwan, China, Sept. 7, 1955; s. Jee-shee and Shu-jen H.; m. Shu-Ying Lai; 1 child, Neil. BS, Nat. Tsing-Hua U., Hsin-Chu, Taiwan, 1977; MS, Nat. Taiwan U., Taipei, 1979; PhD, U. Fla., 1987. Project engr. Unisys. Co., Calif., 1987-88; assoc. prof. dept. elec. engring. Nat. Tsing-Hua U., 1988-94, prof., 1994—. Office: Nat Tsing-Hua U, Dept Elec Engring, Hsin-Chu Taiwan

HUANG, CHUN-HSIUNG, dean, urology educator; b. Changhwa, Taiwan, Dec. 3, 1943; s. Ching-Hsiang and Su-Jung Huang; m. Shu-Li Huang-Chen; children: Shu-Pin, Shu-Chien, Shu-Hung. MD, Kaohsiung (Taiwan) Med. U., PhD. Resident Kaohsiung Med. Coll. Hosp., 1970-74; lectr. Kaohsiung Med. Coll., 1974-79, assoc. prof. urology, 1979-84, prof. urology, 1984—; dir. urology dept. Kaohsiung Med. Coll. Hosp., 1988—; dean, Sch. Medicine Kaohsiung Med. U., 1992—; med. sec. Kaohsiung Med. Coll. Hosp., 1989-90. Chief editor, Jour. Urol. Assn. of Republic of China. Lt., Army of Taiwan, 1969-70. Avocations: travel, golf. Office: Kaohsiung Med U Dept Urol, 100 Shih-Chuan 1st Rd, Kaohsiung 807, Taiwan

HUANG, CHUN-HUI, chemist, educator; b. Hebei, China, May 4, 1933; d. Jia-Pu Huang and Yu-Fen Zhao; m. Rong-Sen Zhang, Aug. 24, 1957; children: Kai, Jie. BS, Peking U., 1955. Asst., lectr., assoc. prof. chemistry dept. Peking U., Beijing, 1955-89, prof. Coll. Chemistry and Molecular Engring., 1989—; vis. scholar Iowa State U. Ames Lab., 1981-82, chemistry dept. Ariz. U., Tucson, 1982-83. Author: Coordination Chemistry of Rare Earths, 1997; co-author: Rare Earths, 1996; editor, author: Scandium and Rare Earths, 1992; contbr. more than 250 articles to profl. jours. Mem. Chemistry Soc. China, Rare Earth Soc. China. E-mail: hch@chemms.chem.pku.edu.cn. Office: Coll Chem/Molec Engring, Peking U, 100871 Beijing China

HUANG, CUN-BING, pathologist, educator, biomedical researcher; b. Guiyang, China, June 11, 1944; Swedish citizen, 1996.; m. Wei-Fang Xia; 2 children. Pathologist Tng. Cert., Guiyang Med. Coll., 1972; MSc, Nantong Med. Coll., 1982; MD, Nanjing Med. U., 1983. Technologist and head, part-time acupuncturist Sinan (China) Hosp., 1962-71, pathologist and head, part-time acupuncturist, 1973-78; pathologist, sr. lectr. Zunyi Med. Coll. and Tchg. Hosp., 1982-88, dir. and chief histochemistry lab., 1985-88; rsch. pathologist dept. pathonogy, nutritional rsch. Umeå (Sweden) Univ. Hosp., 1989-91, Karolinska Hosp./Karolinska Inst., Stockholm, 1991-92; vis. scientist UCLA, 1992; prof. dept. pathology Nantong Med. Coll., 1993-95; rsch. pathologist Ctr. Biotech. Karolinska Inst. at Novum, Huddinge Univ. Hosp., 1994-95; dir. Stockholm Anticancer Inst. HB, Stockholm; vis. prof. Cancer Rsch. Ctr. and Lab. for Molecular Pathology, Beijing Med. U., 1993, Dept. Ultrastructural Pathology, Jinling Hosp., Nanjing U. Med. Sch., 1993; vis. scientist dept. pathology U. Calif., Irvine, 1996, Johns Hopkins U., Balt., 1996, divsn. biology Calif. Inst. Tech., Pasadena, 1996; vis. prof. dept. pathology Beijing Med. U., 1997, Shanghai 2d Med. U., 1997, Inst. Genetics at Fudan U., Shanghai, 1997; vis. scientist cell biology and immunology divsn. Devel. Ctr. for Biotech., Inst. Molecular Biology, Academia Sinica, Nat. Health Rsch. Inst., Taipei, Taiwan, 1998, Nat. Taiwan Univ. Hosp., 1998, Cell Biology and Immunology divsn. Devel. Ctr. Biotech., taipei, 1998; spl. part-time rschr., advocate for rsch. responsibility Immunopathology Lab., Dept. Pathology and Oncology and Microbiology, Tumorbiology Ctr., Karolinska Inst. and Hosp., Stockholm, 1997-98; part-time prof. dept. pathology Nanjing Med. U., 1997—. Editor Sci.-Tech.-Soc., 1999—; contbr. numerous articles to profl. jours. Recipient Outstanding People of 20th century award, Internat. Biog. Ctr., 1999, Achievement Award of Sci. and tech., Guizhou Province, 1986, 85, Excellent Sci. Paper award Guizhou Province Assn. Sci. and Tech., 1986, 88. Mem. AAAS, N.Y. Acad. Sci., Swedish Cancer Soc., European Network on Young People and Tobacco, Chinese Med. Assn. Soc. of Pathology, Asia Pacific Assn. of Socs. of Pathologists, Chinese Anti-Cancer Assn., Chinese Assn. for Integration of traditional Chinese and Western Medicine. Office: Stockholm Anticancer Inst, Stockholm Sweden

HUANG, DA, university administrator, economics educator; b. Tianjin, China, Feb. 22, 1925; s. Shu-ren and Gao Huang; m. Shu-zhen Luo, June 28, 1952; children: Jian, Heng. Master's degree, No. China United Univ., 1947. Dep. dir. dept. fin. Renmin U., Beijing, 1954-66, dir. dept. fin., 1978-83, pres., 1991-94; v.p. People's Univ. of China, Beijing, 1983-91; mem., head econ. group acad. degree com. State Coun., China, 1988-91; mem. monetary policy com. People's Bank of China, 1997—; expert adv. com. on the humanities and social scis. studies State Edn. Commn., dir. 1997—. Author: Money and Its Circulation in the Chinese Economy, 1964, Socialist Fiscal and Financial Problems, 1981 (Excellent Textbook prize 1987), Introduction to Overall Balancing of Public Finance and Bank Credit, 1984 (Econ. Sci. prize 1986), Collection of Huang Da's Economic Papers, 1988, The Economics of Money and Banking, 1992, Macroeconomic Control and Money Supply, 1997; transl.: Gold in the Capitalist System Since World War II, 1965. Mem. Nat. People's Congress (mem. com. on fin. and economy 1993—), Chinese Soc. Fin. and Banking (chmn. 1995—), Chinese Soc. Pub. Fin. (vice chmn. 1983—), China Enterprise Confedn. (v.p. 1987—), Securities Assn. China (v.p. 1987—), chinese Assn. Internat. Understanding (mem. coun. 1982—), Chinese Com. on Econ. Edn. Exch. with the U.S. (chmn. 1985—). Avocations: calligraphy, running. Office: Renmin Univ, Office of Pres, Beijing 100872, China

HUANG, DADING, semiconductor materials administrator, researcher; b. Modong, Zhongqing, China, Feb. 3, 1941; s. Zhigang and Wengu (Shi) H.; m. Shihua Luo, Oct. 1, 1971; children: Rong, Yi. BS, U. Sci. and Tech., China, 1964. Rsch. asst. Inst. Semiconductors, Beijing, 1965-78, rsch. assoc., 1978-88, assoc. prof., 1988—, dep. head, 1987-91, head, 1995—; vis. fellow U. Salford, U.K., 1992-93. Contbr. articles to profl. jours. Recipient award Chinese Acad. Sci., 1985, 89. Avocation: Chinese gongfu. Home: No 402 Bldg 403 Science Pk, Datun Rd Chayang Dist, 100101 Beijing China Office: Inst Semiconductors, 35 Tsinghua E Rd Haidian Di, 100083 Beijing China

HUANG, FARONG, engineer, researcher, educator; b. Longyou, China, Oct. 11, 1962; s. Zhenhai and Yunqin (Zhang) H.; m. Jia Qi, Aug. 21, 1989; 1 child, Xu. B of Engring., East China U. Sci. and Tech., Shanghai, 1983, M of Engring., 1986, PhD, 1989. Lectr. East China U. Sci. and Tech., Shanghai, 1989-91, assoc. prof., 1991-93; Royal Soc. rsch. fellow U. St. Andrews, Scotland, 1994; assoc. prof. East China U. Sci. and Tech., Shanghai, 1995-97, prof., 1997—. Author in field. K.C. Wong fellow, 1994. Mem. Shanghai Soc. for Chemistry and Chem. Engring., Soc. Advancement of Material Process Engring. Avocations: sports, stamp collecting. Office: Sch Materials Sci/Engring, 130 Meilong Rd, Shanghai 200237, China

HUANG, HAN-PANG, electrical engineer, educator, researcher; b. Natou, Taiwan, China, Oct. 7, 1956; s. Te-Ching and Ching-Hsin (Liao) H.; m. Li-Chu Sheu, Mar. 25, 1990; children: Jong-Pyng, Quann-Ru. Diploma, Nat. Taipei Inst. Tech., 1977; MS, U. Mich., 1982, PhD, 1986. Cert. elec. engr. Assoc. prof. Nat. Taiwan U., Taipei, 1986-92, dir. Robotics Lab., 1987—, vice chair dept. mech. engr., 1992-93, prof., 1992—, assoc. dean Coll. Engring., 2000—; dir. IBM-Nat. Taiwan U. Edn. Ctr., Taipei, 1989—, Mfg. Automation Tech. Rsch. Ctr., Taipei, 1996-99; cons. Industry Devel. Bur. Ministry Econ. Affairs, Taipei, 1993-95, Inst. Info. Industry, Taipei, 1994-96; mem. adv. com. Nat. Sci. Coun., Taipei, 1998—, Ministry Edn., Taipei, 1998-99. Editor-in-chief Jour. Chinese Fuzzy Sys. Assn., 1997—, Internat. Jour. Fuzzy Sys., 1999—. Univ. Rsch. award Ford Motor Co., 1995. Mem. IEEE, Robotics and Automation Soc. of IEEE (chpt. chair 1995-97), Chinese Inst. Automation Engrs. Achievements include inventor of a Dextrous Hand, and micro hexapod robot. Avocations: reading, music, raquetball, table tennis. Office: Nat Taiwan U, Dept Mech Engring, Taipei 10660, Taiwan

HUANG, HESHENG, physicist, educator; b. He Xian, China, Nov. 22, 1942; s. Guorui Huang and Huixian Shi; m. Qin Xu, Feb. 8, 1971; 1 child, Chenyun. Grad., Tsinghua U., 1965. From asst. to prof. Tsinghua U., Beijing, 1965—. Office: Tsinghua U, Dept Physics, 100084 Beijing China

HUANG, HSIANG-HSI, industrial engineering educator; b. Keelung, Taiwan, Apr. 21, 1962; s. Hsiao-Lian and Rai-In (Cho) H.; m. Chun-Pin Hsu. BS in Indsl. Engring., Feng-Chia U., Taichung, Taiwan, 1985; MS in Indsl. Engring., U. Tex., Arlington, 1991, PhD, 1995. Indsl. engr. China Productivity Ctr., Taichung, 1984-85, Hong Kong Teak Wood Inc., Kaohsiung, Taiwan, 1988-90; NSF grad. rsch. asst. U. Tex., 1992-95, rsch. assoc. Automation and Robotics Rsch. Inst., 1995-96; assoc. prof. dept. indsl. mgmt. Nat. Pingtung (Taiwan) U. Sci. and Tech., 1996—; project reviewer Nat. Sci. Coun., Taipei, Taiwan, 1997—; paper reviewer Chinese Inst. Indsl. Engrs., 1997—; project co-leader, instr. Universal Furniture (Taiwan) Ltd., Pingtung, 1997—; mem. com. bd. curriculum planning and arrangement Nat. Pingtung U. Sci. and Tech., 1996-97, mem. com. bd. appeal for tchrs. affairs, 1996, mem. com. bd. sch. tchr. evaluation and hiring, 1997—. Contbr. chpt. to FMS: Recent Developments, 1995, Methods and Applications of Intelligent Control, 1997; also articles. Chmn. sr. high alumni assn. Feng-Chia U., Taichung, 1983, mem. com. bd. student coun., 1984; editor-in-chief Chinese Student Assn. at U. Tex., 1991-92. Sgt. Chinese Marine Corps, 1985-87. Nat. Sci. Coun. grantee, 1996, Best Rsch. award, 1996. Mem. Inst. Indsl. Engring., N.Y. Acad. Scis., Sigma Xi, Phi Beta Delta. Avocations: jogging, listening to music, reading novels. E-mail: hhuang@mail.npust.edu.tw. Fax: 886-8-7740321. Office: NPUST Dept Indsl Mgmt, 1 Hseuh-Fu Rd Nei-Pu Hsiang, Pingtung 91207, Taiwan ROC

HUANG, HSIEN-LU, electrical engineer; b. Hsiang-Hsiang, Hunan, China, Dec. 12, 1923; s. Shao-Ju and Ching (Yu) H.; m. Hui-Lien Peng Huang, Jan. 1, 1947; children: Su and Nan-Ching Chang, Kung and Janet Tu Huang, Chin and Samuel Lin, Hsin and Chris Lu, Sung-Ping and Emanuel Lin, Peter Sung-an and Nina Wang Huang. BSEE, Nat. Hunan U., 1944; MSEE, Va. Polytechnic Inst./State U., 1968, PhD in Elec. Engring., 1969. Cert. mgr. Rockwell Nat. Mgmt. Assn. Maj. Chinese Air Force, 1944-64; prodn. control chief, quality control officer, dep. squadron comdr. Chinese Air Force, Nanking and Taiwan, 1944-64; assoc. prof. in elec. engring. Taipei Inst. Technology, 1960-66; instr. in elec. engring. Va. Polytechnic Inst. and State U., Blacksburg, 1968-69; asst. prof. in elec. engring. W.Va. U., Morgantown, 1970-74; devel. design engr. Barber - Colman Co., Rockford, Ill., 1975-76, Bridgeport Machines Control Co., Horsham, Pa., 1977-79; sr. elec. engr. and reliability engr. specialist Ford Aerospace and Comms. Corp., Houston, 1979-85; lead reliability engr. Rockwell Space Opers. Co., Houston, 1986-96; mem. engring. staff United Space Alliance West, Houston, 1996—. Contbr. articles to profl. publs.; patentee candidate in field. Elder, advisor Phila. Chinese Bible Study Fellowship, Phila., 1977-79; elder, evangelist Clear Lake Chinese Ch., Houston, 1979—. Recipient Nat. Fidelity/Diligence medal Pres. of Rep. of China, Taipei, 1955, Group Achievement award Lyndon B. Johnson Space Ctr., Houston, 1983. Fellow AIAA (assoc.); mem. IEEE (life), Nat. Mgmt. Assn. (cert. mgr.). Avocations: Bible study, personal evangelism, Christian fellowship, church visitation, family spiritual retreat. Home: 470 Buoy Rd Webster TX 77598-2546 Office: United Space Alliance-West 600 Gemini St Houston TX 77058-2754

HUANG, HSIU-SHUANG, education educator; b. Chuang-Hua, Taiwan, Feb. 20, 1961; d. Chin-Yun and Yo-You (Chou) Huang; m. Shang-Liang Chen. MA, Cheng-chi U., Taipei, 1987; PhD, Liverpool (Eng.) U., 1993. Sr. svc. serviced Ministry of Edn., Taipei, 1986-89; assoc. prof. edn. Nat. Taipei Tchrs. Coll., 1993-94; assoc. prof. edn. Nat. Tainan (Taiwan) Tchrs. Coll., 1994-98, prof., 1998—, dir. secretariat, 1997—, dir. rsch. divsn., 1995-97, dir. secretariat, 1997-99. Author: The Principles of Instruction, 1997, The Three-Year Longitudinal Study of PhonologicalAwareness, Visual Skills and Chinese Reading, 1997 (Outstanding Rsch. award 1997); chief editor Jour. of Friends of Elem. Edn., 1995-97, Jour. of Classroom Mgmt., 1995-97. Recipient Outstanding Rsch. award Nat. Sci. Coun. Taipei, 1995, 96, 97, 99. Mem. APA. Avocation: reading. Office: Nat Tainan Tchrs Coll, No 33 Su-Lin St, 700 Tainan Taiwan

HUANG, HUAN-TSUNG, electrical engineer, educator; b. Chia-yi, Taiwan, Feb. 15, 1966; s. Yun-Chan Huang and Ming-Chuan Wu; m. Huei-Chun Wang. B in Engring., Nat. Cheng-Kung U., Tainan, Taiwan, 1988; MS, Nat. Chiao-Tung U., Hsinchun, Taiwan, 1990, PhD, 2000. Lectr. Ta-Hua Inst. Tech., Chung-Lin, Taiwan, 1992-2000; prin. engr. Taiwan Semiconductor Mfg. Co., 2000—. Contbr. articles to profl. jours. 2nd lt. Air Def. Missile Army, 1990-92, Hsinchu. Mem. IEEE (student). Avocations: reading, fishing. Home: 3F-2 No 1009 Ta-Hsueh Rd, Hsin-Chu 300, Taiwan

HUANG, HUNG-CHIA, microwave photonics researcher, educator; b. Beijing, Aug. 5, 1924; s. You-chang Huang and Kui-xu Li; m. Jin-ying Shen, Dec. 24, 1965; children: Huang Xiaojun, Huang Hai. BS in Elec. Engring., Nat. Assoc. Southwest U., China, 1944; DSc (hon.), Eurotech U., Hawaii, 1992; MS, U. Mich., 1949. Asst. Beijing U., 1946-47, Shanghai (China) Jiao Tong U., 1947-48; lectr. to prof. North Jiao Tong U., Beijing, 1950-64; rsch. prof., dir. Inst. Electronics, Academia Sinica, Beijing, 1956-64, Shanghai Inst. Optics and Fine Mechanics, 1964-79; prof. Shanghai U., 1979—, pres., 1979-87, hon. pres., 1987—; academician Academia Sinica, 1980—; mem. Electromagnetics Acad., MIT, 1989—; prin. scientist Nat. Ctr. Rsch. Lab on Milimeter Waves, Beijing, 1959-64; guest prof. U. Karlsruhe, Germany, 1984; vis. prof. Chinese U. Hong Kong, 1989, Cath. U. Leuven, Belgium, 1992; keynote spkr. Symposium 30 Yrs Microwaves, Dallas, 1982; chmn. PRC/Commn. B (Fields and Waves), Union Radio Sci. Internat., 1988—. Author: Microwave Approach to Highly Irregular Fiber Optics, 1998; contbr. articles to profl. jours. (award Instrument Soc. Am. 1994); patentee in field; mem. editl. bd. Microwave & Optical Tech. Letters, 1990—. Chmn. com. sci. and tech., Europe China Assn., Brussels, 1983-85. Major (interpreter), China-U.S.-U.K. Allied Force, 1944-45, Yunan-Burma Route War Area. Recipient Outstanding Contbn. Sci. award, Nat. Congress Sci., Beijing, 1979. Fellow Chinese Inst. Electronics. Avocations: photography, travel. E-mail: hjhuang@online.sh.cn. Fax: 86-21-59521407. Home and Office: Shanghai U, Shanghai 201800, China

HUANG, JIADONG, electronic engineer; b. Ningbo, China, June 1, 1944; s. Jinyou Huang and Yanli Guo; m. Zhiren Gong, Sept. 9, 1972; children: Ying. BS, Northwest Telecomms. Engring., Xian, China, 1966; MSc, Nanjing Comms. Engring. Inst., China, 1981. From asst. engr. to prof. Elec. Instrument Inst., Yangzhou, China, 1968—; vis. rschr. Cath. U. Louvain, Belgium, 1988-90; cons. Tai Go Comm., Inc., Changzhou, 1992—, Bao Hai Comm. Equipment, Inc., Suzhou, 1996—. Mem. IEEE (sr.). Roman

Catholic. Avocations: music, tourist, reading, swimming. Office: Elec Instrument Inst, 26 Nanhexia St, 225001 Yangzhou China

HUANG, JIAN PING, company executive; b. Changsha, Hunan, China, Sept. 26, 1960; came to U.S., 1988; s. Guo Guang Huang and Lai Zhen Peng; m. Jessica Poppele, Mar. 21, 1988 (div. Arp. 1991). BA in Linguistics, Sichuan Fgn. Studies U., Chongqing, China, 1982; MA in Lit., Xiamen (China) U., 1984; PhD in Econs., U. Internat. Bus. and Econs., Beijing, China, 1990. Dep. divsn. chief Ministry Fgn. Econ. Rels. and Trade, Beijing, 1985-87; gen.mgr. Kompass (China) Internat. Info. Svcs. Co. Ltd., Beijing, 1993-94; chmn. JP Internat. Inc., Alexandria, Va., 1990—; cons. Levi Strauss & Co., San Francisco, 1988-89, Coca Cola Co., Atlanta, 1989-90, U.S. EPA, Washington, 1990-92, Reed Info. Svcs., Greenstead, U.K., 1993—, Tadiran, Israel; chmn. China USA Bus. U., Best Com. Co. Ltd., Far East Agro-Tech. Co. Ltd., JP Swissino Co. Ltd., 1997—, Internat. Econ. & Social Devel. Rsch. Inst.; chmn., CEO JPI Group of Cos., www.jpi.com.cn. Author: China's Foreign Trade, 1987, China's Modernization, 1990. Councillor Fund for Bus. Edn., Beijing, 1991. Best scholar Sichuan Fgn. Studies U., Chongqing, China, 1981, Best Nat. Social Study Ministry Edn., Beijing, 1989. Mem. China Nat. Internat. Coop. Assn. (dir. 1985—), China Nat. Internat. Trade Assn. (dir. 1985—), China Nat. Aesthetics Assn. Home: 6121 Hyacinth Dr Alexandria VA 22310-1793 Office: JPI Group of Cos E Gate Plz, B Tower 5/F 29 Dongzhong St, Jiuxianqiao Lu Beijing 100027, China

HUANG, JINLIN, surgeon; b. Wuhan, Hubei, China, Aug. 1, 1951; s. Yunsheng Huang and Rongying Liu; m. Bingqin Sun, Aug. 1, 1980; 1 child, Jun. Student, Chinese Med. & Pharm. Shandong, Lalyang, China, 1974, 2nd Mil. Med. Coll. PLA, Shanghai, China, 1980, Gen. Shop. People's Lib. Army, Beijing, 1988, 4th Mil Med. Colll. PLA, Xian, China, 1995. Surgeon 401st Hosp. PLA Navy, Qingdao, China. Contbr. articles to profl. jours. Mem. Chinese Med. Assn., Chinese Antineoplastic Assn. Home: 2 Nantong Rd, 266071 Qingdao Shandong, China Office: 401st Hosp PLA Navy, 22 Minjiang Rd, 266071 Qingdao Shandong, China

HUANG, JOSEPH CHEN-HUAN, civil engineer; b. Nanking, China, Oct. 18, 1933; came to U.S., 1962, naturalized, 1972; MS in Structural Engring., Va. Poly. Inst. and State U., 1964, PhD 1988; m. Elizabeth C. Huang, Sept. 3, 1966; children: Edith, Eleanor, Evelyn, Edna. Registered profl. engr. N.Y., N.J., Pa., Del., Md., Va., W.Va., N.C., Fla., D.C. Project engr. Green Assos., Inc., Balt., 1964-68; pres. Gen. Engring. Consultants, Inc., Balt., 1968-76; chmn., chief exec. officer Highlights Corp., Towson, Md., 1976—; pres. HS Mgmt. and Svcs. Corp., 1992—. Mem. ASCE, Am. Concrete Inst., NSPE, Chinese Bus. Assn. Greater Washington (pres. 1993). Author: Prestressed Steel Structures, Strategies for Business; also tech. papers. Home: 3506 Templar Rd Randallstown MD 21133-2428 Office: 1248 E Joppa Rd Towson MD 21286-5805 also: 1045 Taylor Ave Baltimore MD 21286-8331 also: 825 N Hammonds Ferry Rd Ste B Linthicum Heights MD 21090-1355

HUANG, JUNLIAN, chemist, researcher; b. Shanghai, Oct. 8, 1946; s. Zhuxuan and Yueying (Zhang) H.; m. Youqian Hu; 1 child, Xiaoxing. MS, Shanghai Jiao Tong U., 1981; PhD, Fudan U., Shanghai, 1984. Asst. prof. U. Sci. and Tech. of China, Hefei, 1976-78; assoc. prof. Fudan U., Shanghai, 1988-92, prof. chemistry, 1993—, chmn. dept. macromolecular sci., 1993-96, dir. PhD students, 1994—; postdoctoral fellow U. Oslo, 1990; vice dir. Shanghai Ctr. for Advanced Materials, 1995—; vis. prof. Scandinavian Inst. for Dental Materials, Oslo, 1991-92. Contbr. articles to profl. jours.; patentee in field. Recipient 2d prize Electronic and Indsl. Ministry of China, 1990, 1st prize State Edn. Commn. China, 1995, 2d prize, 1996. Mem. AAAS, Chem. Soc. China. Avocations: table tennis, acrobatic fighting novel, basketball, football, volleyball. Home: No 45 Ln 650, Guo Shun Rd, Shanghai 200433, China Office: Fudan Univ Dept Macromolec, Han Dan Rd 220, Shanghai 200433, China

HUANG, KAI HUI, chemist, researcher; b. Xiamen, China, Nov. 10, 1932; s. Bi Xuan and Man Zhao (Jiang) H.; m. Su E. Zheng, Jan. 25, 1960; children: Jian Sheng, Jian Wei. BS, Xiamen (China) U., 1955, MD, 1958. Lectr. Xiamen U., 1961-77, assoc. prof., 1978-82, prof., 1984-93; dir. Chem. Inst. of New Star, Xiamen, 1993—; postdoctoral fellow Northwestern U., Evanston, Ill., 1982-83; vis. prof. U. Ill., Chgo., 1991-92; vis. rsch. prof. U. Calif., Berkeley, 1982, Cath. U. Louvain, Belgium, 1989-90. Author: Principles of Catalysis, 1983; editor Chinese Jour. Chem. Physics, 1987-97; contbr. articles to profl. jours. Recipient Chinese Nat. Nature Sci. Progress award China State Commn. Edn., Beijing, 1983, Advisor honor The Commn. of Chinese Inventors, Beijing, 1981. Fellow Chem. Fertilizer Soc. China (advisor 1981-90). Office: Xiamen U, PO Box 276, 361005 Xiamen Fujian, China

HUANG, KUN-YEN, physician, researcher, retired university dean; b. Hsinchu, Taiwan, Dec. 11, 1933; s. Hengchi and Tsamou (Yang) H.; m. Amy Hwei-mei Hsieh, Mar. 25, 1961; children: Susan, Amelia, Nellie. MD, Nat. Taiwan U., Taipei, 1959; PhD, George Washington U., 1967. Resident in surg. Nat. Tainan U. Hosp., Taipei, 1961-63; med. officer in rsch. Naval Med. Rsch. Inst., Bethesda, Md., 1963-68; asst. prof. microbiology George Washington U. Med. Sch., Washington, 1968-70, assoc. prof., 1970-76, prof., 1976-84; founding dean Cheng Kung U. Med. Coll., Tainan, Taiwan, 1982-95, dean emeritus, 1995—; co-dir. clin. rsch. Nat. Health Rsch. Inst., Taipei, 1999—; cons. Project Hope, Middlewood, Va., 1996-97. Author: (essays) Money Diplomacy, 1997, Tunnel Vision, 1998; weekly columnist China Daily. Recipient Golden Apple award Am. Assn. Med. Students, 1982. Fellow Infectious Diseases Soc. Am.; mem. Am. Soc. for Microbiology, Alpha Omega Alpha. Avocations: reading, writing, travel, history, golf. Home: 9D 230 Tun Hwa S Rd Sect II, Taipei Taiwan Office: Nat Health Rsch Inst, 128 Yen-Chiu-Yuan Rd Sect 2, Taipei Taiwan

HUANG, LIANG HSIUNG, microbiologist; b. I-Lan, Taiwan, July 16, 1939; came to the U.S., 1963; s. Kin Shi and A. Chaw (Huang) L.; m. Jane Huang, July 23, 1970; children: Grace, Amy. MS, U. Wis., 1965, PhD, 1971. Postdoctoral rsch. fellow Ohio State U., Columbus, 1972-73, U. Ga., Athens, 1973-75; rsch. scientist Pfizer Cen. Rsch., Groton, Conn., 1975-78, sr. rsch. scientist, 1978-83, sr. rsch. investigator, 1983-91, prin. rsch. investigator, 1991—; mem. adv. com. Am. Type Culture Collection, Rockville, Md., 1989-92. Contbr. articles to Internat. J. Systemic Bacteriology, Applied Microbiology, Arch. Biochem. Biophys., Mycotaxon, Jour. Indsl. Microbiology, Mycologia, Can. Jour. Botany, Am. Jour. Botany, Jour. Antibiotics; mem. editorial bd. Antimicrobial Agts. and Chemotherapy, 1977-82, Jour. Antibiotics, 1990—; editor: U.S. Fedn. for Culture Collections Newsletter, 1987-88. Active Conservation Com., East Lyme, Conn. Mem. U.S. Fedn. for Culture Collections (v.p. 1988-90, pres. 1990-92, exec. bd. mem., 1998—), Soc. for Indsl. Microbiology, Am. Soc. for Microbiology (selection com. J.R. Porter award 1989-91), Mycological Soc. Am., N.Y. Acad. Scis. Achievements include patents; action of gramicidin on mitochondria; discovery of new polycyclic ether antibiotics, of ansamycin antibiotics, of novel squalene synthase inhibitor, of novel quinolone compounds, of novel quinomycins, of novel macrolides, of novel erotomycins, of novel rapamycins, of novel topoisomerase II inhibitor, and of new development type of ascocarp centrum; description of new genus of actinomycetes and new species of Nocardia, Actinomadura, Nocardiopsis, Catenuloplanes, Aspergillus, Eleutherascus, Gliocephalotrichum, Neurospora, Triangularia, and Zopfiella. Home: 23 Sunrise Trail East Lyme CT 06333-1129 Office: Pfizer Inc Prizer Global R & D Eastern Point Rd Groton CT 06340-4947

HUANG, QIN, zoologist; b. Fuzhou, Fujian, China, July 8, 1958; s. Zhi and You-yu (Wu) H.; m. Qun Zhou, 1988; 1 child, Jun-li. BSc, Xiamen (China) U., 1982; PhD, U. Hong Kong, 1995. Asst. prof. Fujian Normal U., Fuzhou, China, 1982-92; postdoctoral fellow Swire Inst. Marine Sci., U. Hong Kong, 1996-99; dep. dir. Fuzhou Marine Biotech. R&D Ctr., 1999—; sr. cons. Fuzhou Agr. Com., 1999—; sr. scientist China Huaxia Bioengring. R&D Inst., 1999—. Contbr. articles to profl. jours. J.G. Phillips Meml. scholar, 1993-94; Hong Kong U. grantee, 1997; RGC rsch. grantee, 1999-2000; Sci. and Tech. Devel. Fund. grantee, 1999. Mem. AAAS, Fuzhou Biomed. Egnring. Assn. (coun. 1999—). E-mail: fzmbrd@pub3.fz.fj.cn. Office: Fuzhou Marine Biotech R&D, 105 Puxia Rd, Fuzhou, Fujian 350026, China

HUANG, RUNHUA, geography educator, researcher; b. Taishan, Guangdong, China, Sept. 11, 1938; Hongbang Huang and Yachang Ma; m. Qingyi Meng, Apr. 14, 1972; 1 child, Haiqian. BS, Sun Yat-Sen U., Guangzhou, China, 1959. Asst. Peking U., Beijing, 1959-78; lectr. Peking U., 1978-85, assoc. prof., 1985-91, prof., 1991—; vis. scholar Uppsala (Sweden) U., 1979-81; sr. vis. scholar Nottingham (Eng.) U., 1988. Author: Textbook of Soil Geography, 1991 (Excellent Geographic Publ. award Geog. Soc. China, 1994), Textbook of Environmental Science, 1997; editor: Jour. Natural Resources, 1986—, Environ. Sci., 1991—. Recipient Progress of Sci. and Tech. award State Commn. Edn., 1993, Nat. Environment Protection Agy. China, Ministry of Water Resources and Electric Power, 1980. Office: Peking U Dept Urban & Environ Scis, No 5 Yiheyuan Rd, 100871 Beijing China

HUANG, SHING-MOO, surgeon, researcher, consultant; b. Hualien, Taiwan, Apr. 19, 1954; s. Shih-Chin Huang and Dong-Hwa Chiu; m. Samantha Po-Liang Chao; children: Nana, Nancy, Tim. MB, Nat. Tawain U. Med. Coll., Taipei, China, 1979. Bd. of Medicine, special bd. of surgery, gastrointestinal surgery, digestive endoscopy, endoscopic surgery in China. Intern Nat. Taiwan U. Hosp., Taipei, 1978-79; surgical resident Vet. Gen. Hosp. Taipei, 1981-85, chief resident, 1985-86, attending surgeon, 1989-95; attending surgeon Nat. Taipei Nursing Coll. Hosp., 1986-89; supt. Der-Gee Hosp., Tao-Yuan, Taiwan, 1995—; clin. assoc. prof. Nat. Yang-Ming U., Taipei, 1989-94, Nat. Def. Med. Coll., Taipei, 1995; clin. assoc. prof. Nat. Yang-Ming U., 1989-94, lectr., 1995. Author: Inguinal Hernia: Advances or Controversies, 1993, Surgical Laparoscopy and Endoscopy, 1998. Active Rotary Internat., Tao-Yuan South RZ 3500, 1998— Lt. major Army Republic of China, 1979-81. Grantee Nat. Sci. Coun., Taipei, 1992, Vgh-Nthu Joint Rsch. Program, Taipei, 1994-95, Dept. Health, Exec. Yumu, Taipei, 1996. Fellow Internat. Collegium Chir. Digestive, Am. Coll. Surgeons; mem. Chinese Assoc. Endoscopic Surgery (Contribution award, 1999). Avocations: violin, choir, tennis, table tennis, mountain climbing. Home: 8 Ln 116 Tien-Shang St, Pa-Teh/Tao-Yuan 334, Taiwan Office: Der-Gee Hosp, 77 Sec 2 Jei-Shou Rd, Pa-Teh/Tao-Yuan 334, Taiwan

HUANG, SHOUHUA, electronics engineer; b. Hubei, China, Nov. 28, 1956; came to U.S., 1994; m. Dongmei; children: Davy, Andrew. BS, Nanjing U., 1980; ME, Wuhan Rsch. Inst. Posts and Telecomm., Wuhan, 1986; PhD, Beijing U. Posts and Telecomm., 1992. Engr. Ministry of Aeronautics and Space of China, 1980-83, Wuhan Rsch. Inst. of Posts and Telecomms., Wuhan, 1986-88; postdoctoral fellow Tsinghua U., Beijing, 1992-94; rsch. assoc. U. So. Calif., L.A., 1994-95; rsch. engr. E-Tek Dynamics, Inc., San Jose, 1995-97; sr. engr. Osicom Technologies, Inc., San Diego, 1997-99, Jet Propulsion Lab., Pasadena, Calif., 1999—. Patentee in field; translator: (books) Guide to Programs 1992/National Natural Science Foundation of China, Guide to Programs 1993, National Natural Science Foundation of China; contbr. articles to profl. jours. Mem. IEEE (sr.), Optical Soc. Am., Internat. Soc. for Optical Engring. Achievements include rsch. on 6-channel OC-48 (6x2.4 gb/s) 9,000 km WDM optical comm. system, 6x2.4 Gbit/s circulating loop with 100 km DSF (Dispersion Shifted Fiber), LD characterization systems, numerous others. Avocation: swimming.

HUANG, TAO, financial analyst; b. Qu-zhou, Zhejiang, China, Dec. 15, 1971; came to U.S., 1994; BS, Tsing Hua U., Beijing, 1994; MS, Columbia U., 1997, PhD, 1998. Tchg. asst. Columbia U., N.Y.C., 1995-98; quantitative analyst Citicorp, N.Y.C., 1998—; cons. All-China Market Rsch. Co., Beijing, 1992-94. Fellow Columbia U., 1995-98. Mem. Soc. Quantitative Analyst. Avocations: literature, music. Office: Citicorp 390 Greenwich St New York NY 10013-2375

HUANG, TE-HSIANG, astrologist, consultant, researcher; b. Tainan County, Taiwan, Jan. 20, 1952; s. San-Neng Huang and Chwen (Chen) Huang Chen; m. Hsiu-Chuan Kuo, Mar. 26, 1983; children: Ya-Lin, Liang-Yu. BS, FuJen Cath. U., Taipei County, Taiwan, 1975. Dir. East-White Rsch. Cr. Chinese Horoscope, Taichung City, Taiwan, 1981—; pres. East-White Astrology & Horoscope Cons. Co., Taichung City, 1990—; bd. chmn. Labor Union Astrology, Geomancy and Horoscope in Taichung, 1991. Author: East-White Chinese Lunar Calendar, East-White Chinese Nomenclature of a Person, 1987, Planning and Design of Human Life; contbr. articles to mags. and newspapers. With Taiwan Army, 1975-77. Recipient leading authority award Labor Union Astrology, Geomancy and Horoscope in Taichung, 1994; contbn. award Chinese Soc. Genesis Found., 1996. Mem. Chinese Soc. Astrology and Horoscope (authority award 1995), Rotary (Paul Harris fellow 1994). Avocations: golf, Chinese tea, singing, walking, music. Office: East-White Astrology, 299 Chung-Shan Rd, Taichung City 400, Taiwan

HUANG, TIAO-YUAN, engineering executive; b. Kaohsung, Taiwan, May 5, 1949; s. Ding-zong and Yeh-ying (cheng) H.; m. Cathy Nee, Feb. 24, 1981; 1 child, Quillan. BS, Nat. Cheng Kung U., 1971, MS, 1973; PhD, U. N.Mex., 1981. Mem. tech. staff Tex. Instruments Inc., Dallas, 1981-83; mem. rsch. staff Xerox Rsch. Ctr., Palo Alto, Calif., 1984-91; mgr. TD dept. Integrated Device Tech., Santa Clara, Calif., 1991-92, VLSI Tech. Inc., San Jose, 1992-94; prof. Nat. Chiao Tung U., Hsinchu, Taiwan, 1995—; v.p. rsch. and devel. Nat. Nana Device lab., Hsinchu, 1995—. Patentee in field; contbr. articles to profl. jours. Ensign Taiwanese Navy, 1973-75. IEEE fellow, 1995; recipient semiconductor award Internat. Tech. Achievement, 1988, award Found. for Outstanding Scholars, Taiwan, 1995. Mem. Internat. Conf. Solid State Devices and Materials (program com. 1996—), Internat. Electronic Devices and Materials Symposium (program com. 1998—). Avocations: jogging, travel, movies, mountain climbing, Chinese poetry. Home: 10509 Pineville Ave Cupertino CA 95014-4528 Office: Nat Nano Device Labs, 1001-1 Ta Hsueh Rd, Hsinchu 30050, Taiwan

HUANG, TING-CHIA, chemical engineering educator, researcher; b. Tainan, Taiwan, June 1, 1932; s. Tzuo and Nai (Yeh) H.; m. Juei-Chin Wan, Jan. 19, 1958; children: Ling-Yuang, Ling-Huei, Ping-Hsien, Chao-Cheng. BS, Nat. Cheng Kung U., Tainan, 1955; D Engring., U. Tokyo, 1979. Tchg. asst. dept. chem. engring. Nat. Cheng Kung U., 1956-60, instr., 1960-65, assoc. prof., 1965-68, prof., 1968—, chmn., dir. dept., 1981-87, v.p., 1995-97, acting pres., 1996-97; nat. chair prof. Ministry of Edn., 1997—; IAEA rsch. fellow Japan Atomic Energy Rsch. Inst., Tokai-mura, Ibaraki-Ken, 1962; rsch. assoc. U. Houston, 1969-70; tech. cons. ChiMeng Indsl. Co., Ltd., Hsin-Hua, Taiwan, 1979-99; cons. Ministry Edn., Taipei, Taiwan, 1988-94, Kang Hsiang Lan Pharmaceutice Co., Ltd., Yung-Kan Ind. Park, Tainan Syan, Taiwan, 1989—, Vedan Enterprise Corp., Shalu Taichung, Taiwan, 1999—. Author: Experimental Physical Chemistry, 1963, 20th edit., 1987, Chemical Engineering Thermodynamics, 1971, Physical Chemistry, 1978, 84, 5th edit., 1990, Experiments in Physical Chemistry, 1983, 3d edit., 1988; regional editor Waste Mgmt. jour.; contbr. over 180 articles to profl. jours. Recipient Engring. Sci. award Hsu's Found., 1975, Engring. Acad. award Ministry Edn., 1979, outstanding rsch. awards Ministry Edn., 1983, 84, Nat. Sci. Coun., 1986-94; named Outstanding Invited Rschr. Nat. Rsch. Coun., 1995-98. Mem. AIChE, Chinese Inst. Engrs. (best paper award 1975, 85, 96, 99, Outstanding Engring. Prof. award 1991), Chinese Inst. Chem. Engrs. (assoc. editor-in-chief jour. 1986—, Chin Kai-Ying award 1991, best paper award 1994, 95, 99, Chem. Engr. Inst. prize 1997), Chinese Chem. Soc., Soc. Chem. Engrs. Japan, Chinese Inst. Mining Engring. (best paper award 1989, 95), Phi Tau Phi. Avocations: reading, inventing, writing, music, table tennis. Address: 4th fl 23 Alley 17 Ln 133, Sec 2 Chong Hua E Rd, Tainan 70104, Taiwan Office: Nat Cheng Kung U, No 1 Ta'-Siue Rd, Tainan 70101, Taiwan

HUANG, TSUNG-JEN, orthopaedic surgeon, spine consultant; b. Taipei, Taiwan, Oct. 30, 1955; s. Yi-Po and Pao-Chu (Tsai) H.; m. Jin-Yann-Hung, Dec. 23, 1984; children: Hsin-Che, Hsin-Ju, Hsin-Yin. MD, China Med. Coll., Taichung, Taiwan, 1982; postgrad., Rush U., Chgo., 1993-94. Intern Nat. Taiwan U. Hosp., Taipei, 1981-82; resident in surgery Chang Gung Meml. Hosp., Taoyuan, Taiwan, 1984-86, resident in orthopaedics, 1986-88, chief resident, 1988-89, spine fellow, 1989-90, attending, 1990—, cons. spine surgeon, 1990—; assoc. prof. Chang Gung Meml. Hosp., 1997—, Chang Gung U., 1999—; pioneer surgeon, rschr. in video-assisted thoracic spinal surgery. Contbr. articles to profl. jours. Med. officer 1982-84. Grantee Nat. Sci. Coun., Taiwan, 1995-96, 98-99, 99-00, Chang Gung Meml. Hosp., 1996-97. Fellow Scoliosis Rsch. Soc. USA; mem. Pediatric Orthopaedic & Spinal Assn. Taiwan (bd. dirs. 1998—). Christian. Avocation: jogging. Office: Chang Gung Meml Hosp, No 5 Fu-Hsing St Kweishan, T'aoyuüan Taiwan

HUANG, WEI, engineer, researcher; b. Beijing, Apr. 6, 1966; s. Shuguo Huang and Donghui Wang; m. Wei Tan, Apr. 21, 1995. BS, Tsinghua U., Beijing, 1989, MS, 1992. Lectr. Beijing Poly. U., 1992-94; rschr. U. Hong Kong, 1994-97; sr. engr. Tsinghua Tongfang Control Co., Beijing, 1997—. Contbr. articles to sci. jours., including Fluid Engring., Energy and Bldgs., Procs. Engring. Thermophysics. Mem. AAAS, N.Y. Acad. Scis. Avocations: tennis, swimming, football, bridge.

HUANG, WEI-XIN, bank executive; b. Shanghai, Jan. 14, 1948; arrived in The Netherlands, 1987; s. Li-jun and Gui-nan (Shen) H.; m. Shi-rong Bao; 1 child, Xian-jia. MA, Shanghai U. Fin. & Econs., 1982, Internat. U. Japan, 1988; PhD, Erasmus U., Rotterdam, The Netherlands, 1992. Lectr. Shanghai U. Fin. and Econs., 1982-86; rsch. fellow Erasmus U., Rotterdam, 1986-87, 89-90; sr. mgr., Asia specialist Bank Mees Pierson, Rotterdam, 1990—; adj. prof. Maastricht Sch. Mgmt., Webster U., 1992—; cons. Deloitte Touche, Rotterdam, 1990—. Author: Economic Integration as a Development Device, 1991, The Stock Market, 1989; translator: Conference Interpretation, 1990; editor: Handbook on Correspondent Banking, 1995. Home: Kralingseplaslaan 80a, 3061 BA Rotterdam The Netherlands Office: Fortis Bank, Coolsingle 93, Rotterdam The Netherlands

HUANG, WENDING, forestry educator; b. Yixin, China, Sept. 12, 1951; s. Shunfa and Damei (Dong) H.; m. Qifen Xu; 1 child, Tianyu. MS, Nanjing Forestry U., China, 1981; DS, U. Helsinki, Finland, 1998. Asst. prof. Nanjing Forestry U., China, 1981-90, assoc. prof., 1991-92; sr. rschr. U. Helsinki, Finland, 1992-99, docent, 1999—. Author, editor: Agroforestry Management, 1991, Compound Agriculture in China, 1993. Office: U Helsinki Dept Forest Ecol, PO Box 28, FIN00014 Helsinki Finland

HUANG, WUNG HONG, physicist, educator; b. Touliuo, Taiwan, Feb. 10, 1953; p. Fu-Thon Huang and Kua-Thei Shaw; m. Li-Hua Lai, Sept. 17, 1956; 1 child, Huang; m. Kuo Wei. Undergrad., Chung-Kund U., Taiwan, 1975; PhD, Thsing-Hua U., Taiwan, 1985. Prof. Nat. Cheng-Kung U., Tainan, Taiwan. Avocation: bird watching. Home: Chung-Rong St, Tainan Taiwan Office: Physics Dept, Nat Cheng-Kung Univ, Tainan Taiwan

HUANG, XIANGQIAN, internist, consultant, medical educator, gastroenterologist; b. Gimo, China, July 3, 1923; s. Yunong Huang and Piyuan Zhou; m. Suyun Wang, Oct. 1, 1951; children: Guoqing, Yi, Jian. MD, Nanjing U., 1951. Resident dept. internal medicine Gen. Hosp.-Tianjin (China) Med. U., 1951-55, attending physician, 1955-78, assoc. prof., 1978-86, prof., 1986—; cons. Gastroenterology Unit, 3d Hosp., Tianjin Med. U., 1994—, Gastroenterology Unit, Nankai Hosp., China, 1980-84, Infectious Disease Hosp., Tianjin, 1978-84. Editor-in-chief: Therapeutics of Gastrointestinal Disease, 1996, Clinics of Internal Medicine and Its Development, 1993; mem. editl. bd. Chinese Jour. Digestion, 1980-99, World Chinese Jour. Gastroenterology, 1996—. Recipient 3d prize of sci. and tech. Tianjin Com. Sci. and Tech., 1994; grantee Tianjin Municipality, 1986. Mem. Royal Coll. Physicians and Surgeons Can., Tianjin Soc. Internal Medicine (chmn.), Chinese Med. Assn. Home: Box 235 22 Qixiangtai Rd, Tianjin 300070, China

HUANG, XIANG-YU, meteorologist; b. Beijing, China, Apr. 1, 1959; s. Litian and Juntiao (Yang) H.; m. Yueping Zhou, June 7, 1985; children: Jia, Kai. BSc, Peking U., 1982; PhD, Stockholm U., 1988. Asst. Stockholm U., 1984-88, lectr., 1988-92; sr. scientist Danish Meteorol. Inst., 1992—; guest prof. Beijing Meteorol. Coll., 1995-98. Contbr. articles to profl. jours. including Tellus, Monthly Weather Rev., Dynamics of Atmospheres and Oceans, Quar. Jour. of the Royal Meterol. Soc.. Mem. European Geophys. Soc. Avocations: table tennis, swimming. Home: Helgasvej 3, 2970 Hørsholm Denmark Office: Danish Meteorol Inst, Lyngbyvej 100, 2100 Copenhagen Denmark

HUANG, YAQI, biomedical and mechanical engineer, researcher; b. Changchun, China, Apr. 15, 1956; came to U.S., 1990; BS in Mechs., Beijing U., 1983, MS in Computational Fluid Dynamics, 1986; PhD in Biomed. and Mech. Engring., CUNY, 1996. Rsch. assoc. dept. mech. engring. MIT, Cambridge, Mass., 1996-99; fellow Harvard U. Med. Sch., Boston, 1999-2000; faculty Harvard U. Med. Sch., 2000—. Contbr. articles to profl. jours. (Best Paper award 1995, Melville medal ASME 1996). Recipient Harold Shames Biomed. Engring. award, 1996. Mem. ASME, Biomed. Engring. Soc., Sigma Xi. E-mail: yhuang@gcrc.bwh.harvard.edu. Office: Brigham & Women's Hosp 221 Longwood Ave # Rfb-486 Boston MA 02115-5804

HUANG, YEN TI, civil engineer; b. Taipei, Taiwan, Feb. 4, 1927; came to U.S., 1957; s. Tan Kun Huang and Mu Lin; m. Toshiko Naomi Saito Imano, July 4, 1958; 1 child, Philip Po-Wen. BSc, Nat. Taiwan U., Taipei, 1950; MASc, U. Toronto, Can., 1957; PhD, Columbia U., 1961. Registered profl. engr., Tex., N.Mex., Ont., Taiwan. Mem. rsch. staff Sperry Rand Rsch. Ctr., Sudbury, Mass., 1961-63; project geophysicist Atlantic Refining Co., Dallas, 1963-65; sr. geophysicist Geotech (subs. Teledyne Co.), Garland, Tex., 1965-68; mem. tech. staff Collins Radio Co., Richardson, Tex., 1968-70; CEO, pres. Y.T. Huang & Assocs., Dallas, 1970—, San Tai Internat. Corp., Dallas, 1973—; adj. prof. U. Tex., Arlington. Founder of numerical transform theorem used in digital transform; patentee gyroscopic apparatus, modular inflatable dome structures, modular space framed earthquake resistant structures, modular roof structures, and semi-submerged, movable, modular offshore platforms. Co-chair Tex. Asian Rep. Caucus, 1982, Spkr.'s Inner Circle, 2000. Econ. Coop. Am./Joint Commn. on Rural Reconstruction scholar Taiwan Dept. Edn., 1951-52; recipient Outstanding Alumnus, Nat. Taiwan U. Alumni Assn., 1999. Mem. ASCE (life; com. tower found. design stds. 1989-96), Internat. Soc. Offshore and Polar Engrs. (session chmn. 1991-94), N.Y. Acad. Scis., Tech. Club Dallas (v.p. 1993-95, pres.-elect 1996, pres. 1997), Rotary, Dallas Coun. on World Affairs. Unitarian. Avocations: photography, music, travel, history. Office: Y T Huang & Assocs Inc Windy Forest Pl 9405 Pinewood Dr Dallas TX 75243-6521

HUANG, YEN-CHIEH, researcher scientist, educator; b. Nantao, Taiwan, Oct. 1964. BSEE, Na. Sun Yat-Sen U., Kaohsiung, 1987; MSEE, Stanford U., 1991, PhD, 1995. Cons. scientist Stanford Synchrotron Radiation Lab., 1995; postdoctoral rsch. fellow Stanford U., 1995-97; asst. prof. Nat. Tsinghua U., Hsinchu, 1997—. Lt. Taiwan Army, 1987-89. Mem. IEEE, Optical Soc. Am., Soc. Photo-Optical Instrumentation Engrs. Office: Nat Tsinghua U, Dept Elec Engring, 30043 Hsinchu Taiwan

HUANG, YI-CHENG, mechanical engineer, educator; b. Taipei, Taiwan, Dec. 8, 1965; s. C.T. and K.F. H.; m. Jen-Ai Chao, July 18, 1992; 1 child, Yu-Jui. BSc, Nat. Ctrl. U., Chung-Li, Taiwan, 1988, MSc, 1990; MPhil, Columbia U., 1994, PhD, 1996. Cert. prof. cons. in environment waste water treatment. Rsch. asst. Nat. Ctrl. U., 1988-90; tchg. asst. Columbia U., N.Y.C., 1992-95, instr., 1995, course mgr., 1994-95; adj. assoc. prof. Dai-Yeh Inst. Tech., Taiwan, 1996-97; sr. mech. engr., front end project leader Philips Electronics, Hsin-Chu, Taiwan, 1996-97; assoc. prof. Nat. Chang Hua U. Edn., Taiwan, 1997—; adj. assoc. prof. Dai-Yeh U., 1997—; columnist Nat. Sci. Coun., Taipei, 1996-98; wastewater treatment cons. to several cos., 1992—; cons., mem. Innovation Incubator Ctr. Nat. Changhau U. Edn. Contbr. articles to profl. jours. 3d lt. Army of Taiwan, 1990-92. Recipient Rsch. award Nat. Sci. Coun., 1998. Mem. Automatic Tech., Sigma Xi. Home: 22-2 Chang Shun St, 50013 Chang Hua Taiwan Office: Nat Chang Hua U Edn Dept Indsl Edn, Paisha Village, Changhua 500, Taiwan

HUANG, YUNG-HUI, chemical engineer; b. Taipei, Taiwan, July 20, 1953; came to U.S., 1979; s. Lien-chih and Yu-Pei (Tsai) H.; m. I-Hung Huang, May 15, 1992; children: Caroline, Catherine. BS, Nat. Ctrl. U., Chung-Li, Taiwan, 1976; MS, U. S.C., 1982; PhD, U. Fla., 1986. Rsch. assoc. Auburn (Ala.) U., 1987-88, Mich. Molecular Inst., Midland, 1988-90; sys. engr. S3 Technologies, Columbia, Md., 1990-92; sr. process engr. Formosa Plastics Corp., Livingston, N.J., 1992-95; process devel. mgr. J.M. Huber Corp., Havre de Grace, Md., 1995—; vis. scholar Tech. U. Denmark, Lynby, 1984; organizer Polymer Symposium '95 Sci., Engring. and Tech., Houston, 1995. Contbr. articles to profl. jours. 2d lt. Chinese Army, 1976-78. Mem. AIChE, Soc. Plastics Engrs., Soc. for Advancement of Materials and Process

Engring., Sigma Xi. Achievements include 2 patents in field; avocations: basketball, tennis, music, literature, computer. Home: 963 Redfield Rd Apt I Bel Air MD 21014-4685 Office: J M Huber Corp 907 Revolution St Havre De Grace MD 21078-3723

HUANG, ZHIWEI, physicist, researcher, educator; b. Fuzhou, Fujian, China, Feb. 12, 1965; s. Muyan and Xuelian (Lin) H.; m. Wei Zheng, Mar. 15, 1993; 1 child, Yanxi. BSc with honors, Fujian Normal U., 1987, MSc, 1990; PhD, Nanyang Technol. U., Singapore, 1999. Rsch. assoc. Fujian Normal U., Fuzhou, 1990-93, lectr./dir., 1993-98, assoc. prof., dir., 1998—; rsch. scientist B.C. Cancer Rsch. Ctr., Vancouver, 1998; internat. cons. Internat. Ctr. for Sci. and High Tech., Trieste, Italy, 1999. Contbr. articles to profl. jours.; inventor in field. Recipient Outstanding Young Sci. Rschr. award Fujian Normal U., 1994, Award for excellent rsch. paper Sci. and Technol. Com. of Fujian, 1995, award for outstanding sci. and technol. achievements The Press of Chinese Sci. and Tech., Beijing, 1996. Mem. Fujian Physics Soc. of China, Fujian Optical Soc. of China. Avocations: swimming, travel, collecting stamps, photography. Office: Nanyang Technol U Div Phys, 469 Bukit Timah Rd, Singapore 259756, Republic of Singapore

HUB, LUDWIG A., business owner, consultant; b. Dubnany, Czech Republic, Apr. 24, 1937; arrived in Switzerland, 1968; s. Ludwig A. and Emily B. (Beinhofner) H.; m. Dagmar E. Smolka, Sept. 9, 1961 (div. Oct. 1978); children: Premysl, Eric. Diploma engring., Vscht, Prag, Czech Republic, 1961; PhD, ETH, Zurich, 1975. Rschr. Vusk, Kralupy, Czech Republic, 1961-68; rschr. Sandoz, Basel, Switzerland, 1968-72, group head, 1972-80, dept. head, 1980-95; dir. Safety Cons. Inst., Basel, Switzerland, 1995—; assoc. prof. VUT BRNO, Czech Republic, 2000; cons. Safety Cons. Inst., Basel, 1995—, dir., 1995—. Contbr. articles to profl. jours.; patentee in field. Avocations: sailing, music, sport. Office: Safety Cons Inst, Holeeholzweg 75, CH 4102 Binningen Switzerland

HUBÁČEK, MILAN, chemist, researcher; b. Pardubice, E. Bohemia, Czechoslovakia, June 18, 1957; s. Milan and Marta (Málková) H.; m. Kuniko Iinuma, Jan. 25, 1993; children: Johan, Manon. B in Nuclear Chemistry, Prague Tech. U., Czechoslovakia, 1981; D in Chemistry, Prague Inst. Chem. Tech., 1989. Researcher Iron and Steel Rsch. Inst., Karlstein, Czechoslovakia, 1981-89; asst. prof. Prague Inst. Chem. Tech., 1989-93; sr. researcher Nippon Steel Corp., Kawasaki, Japan, 1993-97; sr. rschr. Okayama Ceramics Ctr., Bizen, Japan, 1997—. Inventor novel crystallization and sintering methods in the hexagonal boron nitride (h-BN) system, others; contbr. articles to profl. jours.; patentee in field. Mem. Ceramic Soc. Japan, Am. Ceramic Soc. Avocations: music, travel, reading. Home: Nishikatakami 1196, Bizen Okayama 705, Japan Office: Okayama Ceramics Ctr, 1406-18 Nishikatakami, Bizen Okayama 705, Japan

HUBÁLEK, SLAVOMIL, psychologist; b. Prague, Czech Republic, June 13, 1947; s. Slavomil and Zdenka (Kautská) H.; m. Nataša Porgesová, June 16, 1978; children: Alžběta, Magdalena. Student, U. Chem. Engring., Prague, 1966-69; BA, Charles U., Prague, 1974, PhD, 1981. Clin. psychologist Mental Hosp., Czech Republic, 1974-82, Charles U., Prague, 1982-90; spokesman Ministry of Health, Prague, 1990-92; psychologist, mng. dir. Alea-Psychologie, Prague, 1992—; psychotherapist, Prague, 1974; ct. expert, Prague, 1982. Contbr. numerous articles to profl. jours. Cpl. Czechoslovak Army, 1974. Mem. Czech. Med. Soc., Czech Psychotherapeutical Soc. Roman Catholic. Avocation: reading. E-mail: alea@telecom.cz. Office: Alea-Psychologie, Michalská 12, 11000 Prague Czech Republic

HUBÁLEK, ZDENĚK, microbiologist, researcher; b. Brno, Moravia, Czech Republic, Aug. 22, 1942; s. Josef and Hedvika (Konecná) H.; m. Dagmar Necas; children: Sonja, Zora. BS, U. Brno, 1964, RNDr., 1970; PhD, Acad. Sci., Prague, 1972, DSc, 1987. Rsch. asst. Inst. Fodder Rsch., Brno, 1964-66; rsch. scientist Inst. Parasitology Czech Acad. Sci., Prague, 1966-83; sr. scientist Inst. Vertebrate Rsch. Czech Acad. Sci., Brno, 1984-86, sr. scientist Inst. Sys. Ecol. Biology, 1987-92, sr. scientist Inst. Landscape Ecology and Vertrebate Biology, 1993—, lab. head, 1984—; assoc. prof. microbiology Faculty of Sci., Masaryk U., Brno, 1999—. Author: (monograph) Fungi Associated with Free-Living Birds, 1974, (book) Cryopreservation of Microorganisms, 1996; contbr. over 200 articles to profl. jours. Recipient Purkynje medal Acad Scis. Biology, 1987. Mem. Czech Union of Ecologists, Czech Soc. Microbiology, Czech Soc. Zoology, N.Y. Acad. Scis. Achievements include research in ecology of arthropod-borne pathogenic bacteria and viruses. Avocations: ornithology, chamber music. Home: Lidická 26, CZ-69003 Břeclav Czech Republic Office: Czech Acad Scis Inst Ecology, Klášterní 2, CZ-69142 Valtice Czech Republic

HUBBARD, GREGORY SCOTT, physicist; b. Lexington, Ky., Dec. 27, 1948; s. Robert Nicholas and Nancy Clay (Brown) H.; m. Susan Artimissa Ruggeri, Aug. 1, 1982. BA, Vanderbilt U., 1970; postgrad., U. Calif., Berkeley, 1975-77. Lab. engr. physics dept. Vanderbilt U., Nashville, 1970-73; staff scientist Lawrence Berkeley Lab. Dept. Instrument Techs., Berkeley, Calif., 1974-80; dir. rsch. & devel. Canberra Industries, Inc., Detector Products Divsn., Novato, Calif., 1980-82; v.p., gen. mgr. Canberra Semiconductor, Novato, Calif., 1982-85; cons., owner Hubbard Cons. Svcs., 1978—; cons. SRI Internat., Nenlo Park, Calif., 1979-86, sr. rsch. physicist, 1986-87; divsn. staff scientist space exploration projects office Ames Rsch. Ctr., NASA, Moffett Field, Calif., 1987-90, chief space instrumentation and studies br., 1990-92; dep. chief space projects divsn., 1992-96, assoc. dir. space directorate, 1996-97, dep. dir. space directorate, 1997-99, assoc. ctr. dir., 1999—, Mars program dir. 2000—; mem. fed. Sr. Exec. Svc., 1997—; study mgr. Mars Pathfinder Mission, 1990-91, Ames project mgr., 1992-96; mission mgr. Lunar Prospector Mission, 1994-99; interim dir. NASA Astrobiology Inst., 1998-99, Mars program dir. NASA Hdqrs., 2000—; lectr. in field. Founders scholar Vanderbilt U., 1966; recipient Exceptional Achievement medal NASA, 1994, Outstanding Leadership medal, 1998, 99, Laurels for accomplishments in space Aviation Week, 1997, 98. Mem. AIAA (assoc. fellow), IEEE, Nuclear Sci. Soc., Am. Phys. Soc., Commonwealth Club Calif., Hon Order Ky. Cols.

HUBBARD, HOWARD JAMES, bishop; b. Troy, N.Y., Oct. 31, 1938; s. Howard James and Elizabeth D. (Burke) H. BA, St. Joseph's Sem., Yonkers, N.Y., 1960; STL, Gregorian U., Rome, 1964; DD (hon.), Siena Coll., 1977; LHD (hon.), Coll. St. Rose, 1977. Ordained priest Roman Catholic Ch., Rome, 1963; bishop of Albany Diocese of Albany, N.Y., 1977—; former parish priest St. Joseph's Ch., Schenectady, 1964; parish priest Cathedral Parish, Albany, 1964-65; asst. dir. Cath. Charities, Schenectady, 1966; chaplain Convent of the Sacred Heart, Kenwood, Albany, 1966; dir. Providence House, Albany, 1966; vicar gen. Diocese of Albany, 1976; dir. Cath. Interracial Coun.; coord. Urban Apostolate, from 1972; dir. Office of Pastoral Planning, Albany, 1974-76; diocesan consultor Diocese of Albany, 1976-77. Pres. Urban League. Office: Bishop of Albany Pastoral Ctr 40 N Main Ave Albany NY 12203-1481 Address: 125 Eagle St Albany NY 12202-1718

HUBBARD, STANLEY STUB, broadcast executive; b. St. Paul, May 28, 1933; s. Stanley Eugene and Didrikke A. (Stub) H.; m. Karen Elizabeth Holmen, June 13, 1959; children: Kathryn Elizabeth Hubbard Rominski, Stanley Eugene II, Virginia Anne Hubbard Morris, Robert Winston, Julia Didrikke Coyte. BA, U. Minn., 1955; hon. doctorate, Hamline U., 1995. With Hubbard Broadcasting, St. Paul, 1951—, pres., 1967—, chmn., CEO, 1983—; past chmn. U.S. Satellite Broadcasting Co., Inc., 1981-99; bd. dirs. Minn. Bus. Partnership; mem. broadcast adv. com. to comm. subcom. Ho. of reps., 1977-79; mem. FCC Adv. Com. on Advanced TV, 1988-95; mem. U.S. Nat. Inf. Infrastructure Adv. Coun., 1994-96. Contbr. articles to profl. jours. Chmn. St. Croix Valley Youth Ctr., 1968—; trustee Hubbard Found.; bd. dirs. U. Minn. Found., Mpls., Am. Friends of Jamaica, Assn. Maximum Svc. TV, U. St. Thomas, Minn. Bus. Partnership; past advisor Gov.'s Crime Commn., Ramsey County Ice Arena Com.; past bd. dirs. The Guthrie Theater, The Psychoanalytic Found. of Minn., Sci. Mus. of Minn.; past mem. Hazelden Adv. Com.; mem. Met. Airports Pub. Found. Adv. Bd. Recipient Mitchell Charnley award Northwest Broadcast News Assn., 1991, Internat. Humanitarian award Am. Friends of Jamaica, 1989, Arthur C. Clarke award Satellite Broadcasting and Comm. Assn., 1994, DreamMaker award Children's Cancer Rsch. Fund, 1994, Disting. Svc. award Nat. Assn. Broadcasters, 1995, Spurgeon award Boy Scouts Am., 1985, Avatar award Broadcast Cable and Fin. Mgmt., 1995, Human Rights award Am. Jewish Com., 1995, Cmty. Leadership award Mpls./St. Paul chpt. Alzheimer's Assn., 1995, Most Innovative Product award Minn. High Tech. Coun., 1995, Journalism Innovator award U. Nebr., 1996, Minn. Family Bus. award U. St. Thomas, 1996, Disting. Alumnus award Breck Sch., 1996, Minn. and Dakotas Entrepreneur of Yr. award, 1996, Heritage award U.S. Hockey Hall of Fame, 1996, U. Minn. M Club Hall of Fame Lifetime Achievement award, 1996, Broadcasters' Found. Golden Mike award, 1997, Acad. of Achievement's Golden Plate award, 1997; named to Broadcasting and Cable Hall of Fame, 1991, Soc. Satellite Profls. Internat. Space Hall of Fame, 1992, Acad. Achievement's Golden Plate award, 1997, Broadcast Pioneer award Minn. Broadcasters Assn., 1998; inductee St. Croix Valley Athletics Hall of Fame, 2000. Mem. NATAS (chmn. bd. trustees), Broadcast Pioneers, Internat. Radio and TV Soc. Avocations: sailing and boating, reading, photography. Office: Hubbard Broadcasting Inc 3415 University Ave W Saint Paul MN 55114-2099

HUBBARD, WALTER BRYAN, chemical engineer, consultant; b. Lawton, Okla., Oct. 14, 1954; s. Elise B. (Stakely) H.; m. Jana Sue Buchner; children: Kelli Krystin, Ashely Nicole. BS in Chemistry, North Tex. State U., 1983. Engring. technician Mostek Corp., Carollton, Tex., 1977-80; sr. engring. assoc. Texas Instruments, Dallas, 1980-83; photo/etch engr. VLSI, Inc., San Jose, Calif., 1983-84; etch/photo engr. Signetics Corp., Sunnyvale, Calif., 1984-85; dist. applications engring. mgr. Canon, USA, Irving, Tex., 1985-93; photolithography staff engr. VLSI, Inc., San Antonio, 1993—; R&D cons. engr. Piedra Drilling, Englewood, Colo., 1992—; cons. online entertainment Glitchmaster, Englewood, 1994—. Contbr. articles to profl. jours. Mem. Beta Sigma Phi. Achievements include patent and patent pending for semiconductor, photolithography technologies, innovations in lateral acoustical drilling detection and angular deflection; avocation: antiques. Office: VLSI Tech Inc 9651 Westover Hls San Antonio TX 78251-2701

HUBBARD, WILLIAM JAMES, library director; b. Grand Rapids, Mich., July 17, 1941; s. Willard Wright and Sara (Rast) H.; m. Barbara Ockun, Sept. 8, 1962; children: William, Thomas, James, Gregory. Engr., supr. Rochester (N.Y.) Telephone Corp., 1963-71; contract libr. Xerox Corp., Webster, N.Y., 1971-72; libr. circulation SUNY, Fredonia, 1973-75; libr. user svcs. Va. Poly. Inst. and State U., Blacksburg, 1975-80; dir. libr. svcs., dir.automation-networks, act. state libr. Va. State Libr., Richmond, 1980-88; univ. libr. Jacksonville (Ala.) State U., 1988—. Author: Stack Management, 1981; assoc. editor Ala. Librarian; contbr. articles to profl. jours. Mem. Am. Soc. Info. Sci., Ala. Libr. Assn., Nat. Assn. of Scholars. Office: State U Univ Libr Jacksonville AL 36265

HUBBELL, DAVID SMITH, surgeon, educator; b. Dallas, Aug. 29, 1922; s. Jay Broadus and Lucinda (Smith) H.; m. Barbara Baynard, July 3, 1947; children: Katherine, Lawrence, Daniel. AB, Duke U., 1943, MD, 1946. Diplomate Am. Bd. Surgery, Am. Bd. Thoracic Surgery. Pathologist U.S. Army Tripler Hosp., Honolulu, 1947-49; resident and Am. Cancer Soc. fellow in surgery Yale U. Hosp., New Haven, 1949-54; attending surgeon Bayfront and St. Anthony's Hosp., St. Petersburg, Fla., 1955-85; prof. depts. surgery and anatomy U. So. Fla., Tampa, 1985—, prof. emeritus, 2000—. Capt. M.C., U.S. Army, 1947-49. Recipient award for outstanding rsch. Moffitt Cancer Ctr., Tampa, 1994. Fellow Am. Cancer Soc. (life mem.); mem. ACS (pres. Fla. chpt. 1973-74), Fla. Assn. Thoracic Surgeons (pres. 1980-81), Pinellas County Med. Soc. (pres. 1969-70), Rotary. Republican. Presbyterian. Avocations: tennis, collecting and speaking on 1st editions by Mark Twain. Office: Moffitt Cancer Ctr 12902 Magnolia Dr Tampa FL 33612-9416

HUBEL, DAVID HUNTER, physiologist, educator; b. Windsor, Ont., Can., Feb. 27, 1926; s. Jesse Hervey and Elsie (Hunter) H.; m. Shirley Ruth Izzard, June 20, 1953; children: Carl Andrew, Eric David, Paul Matthew. BSc, McGill U., 1947, MD, 1951, DSc (hon.), 1978; AM (hon.), Harvard U., 1962; DSc (hon.), U. Man., 1983; DHL (hon.), Johns Hopkins U., 1990; DSci, U. Western Ont., 1993; DSc, Oxford U., 1994, Gustavus Adolphus Coll., 1994, Ohio State U., 1995; D honoris causa, U. Madrid, 1997, Univ. Miguel, 1998; JD honoris causa, Dalhousie U., 1998. Intern Montreal Gen. Hosp., 1951-52; asst. resident neurology Montreal Neurol. Inst., 1952-53, fellow clin. neurophysiology, 1953-54; asst. resident neurology Johns Hopkins Hosp., 1954-55; rsch. fellow Walter Reed Army Inst. Rsch., Washington, 1955-58; sr. fellow neurol. scis. group Johns Hopkins U., 1958-59; faculty Harvard U. Med. Sch., 1959—, George Packer Berry prof. physiology, chmn. dept., 1967-68, George Packer Berry prof. neurobiology, 1968-82, John Franklin Enders univ. prof., 1982—; George H. Bishop lectr. exptl. neurology Washington U., St. Louis, 1964; Jessup lectr. biol. scis. Columbia, 1970; James Arthur lectr. Am. Mus. Natural History, 1972; Ferrier lectr. Royal Soc. London, 1972; Harvey lectr. Rockefeller U., 1976; Weizmann meml. lectr. Weizmann Inst. Sci., Rehovot, Israel, 1979; George Eastman prof. Oxford, Eng., 1991-92; Eastman prof., Oxford, Eng., 1991-92; Fenn lectr. 30th internat. congress Internat. Union Psychol. Sci., Vancouver, B.C., Can., 1986; rschr. brain mechanisms in vision; bd. syndics Harvard U. Press, 1979-83; Brookhart lectr. Oreg. Health Scis., 1992, Murlin lectr. U. Rochester, 1992, Thurston lectr. Washington U., 1992; 1st ann. George A. Miller lectr. Cognitive Neurosci. Soc., 1995; keynote spkr. plenary session Am. Assn. for Lab. Animal Sci., Balt., 1995; Hoyt lectr. U. Calif. Sch. Medicine, San Francisco, 1995; Wilder Penfield lectr. Montreal Neurol. Inst. Speaker in field. Served with AUS, 1955-58. Recipient Trustees award Rsch. to Prevent Blindness, 1971, Lewis S. Rosentiel award for disting. work in basic med. rsch., 1972, Karl Lashley prize Am. Philos. Soc., 1977, Louisa Gross Horwitz prize Columbia U., 1978, Dickson prize in medicine U. Pitts., 1979, Ledile prize Harvard U., 1980, Nobel prize, 1981, Outstanding Sci. Leadership award Nat. Assn. for Biomed. Rsch., 1990, City of Medicine award, 1990, Glen A. Fry medal Coll. Optometry, Ohio State U., 1991, Charles F. Prentice medal Am. Acad. Optometry, 1993, Helen Keller prize Helen Keller Eye Rsch. Found., 1995; fellow Harvard Soc. Fellows, 1971—, Royal Soc. Medicine, 1991, First Ann. George A. Miller lectr. Cognitive Neurosci. Soc., Gerald award Soc. Neurosci., 1993, Hon. mem. Spanish Soc. Opth., 1997, Dr. Honoris Causa U. Madrid, 1997. Fellow AAAS, Am. Acad. Arts and Scis.; mem. NAS, Am. Physiol. Soc. (Bowditch lectr. 1966), Deutsche Akademie der Naturforscher Leopoldina, Soc. for Neurosci. (Grass lectr. 1976, Gerard award 1993), Assn. for Rsch. in Vision and Ophthalmology (Friedenwald award 1975), Johns Hopkins U. Soc. Scholars, Am. Philos. Soc. (Karl Spencer Lashley prize 1977), Royal Soc. London, Spanish Soc. Ophthalmology (hon.), Acadmica Europaea (fgn. mem.), Sigma Xi. Home: 98 Collins Rd Waban MA 02468-2235 Office: Harvard U Med Sch Dept Neurobiology 220 Longwood Ave Boston MA 02115-5701

HUBER, CLAYTON LLOYD, marketing professional, engineer, construction executive; b. Corpus Christi, Tex., May 4, 1955; s. James Lloyd and Lealla Jean (Snyder) H.; m. Verna Marlene May, Aug. 16, 1975; children: Konstanze Marlena, James Clayton, Katerina Nicole, Kassandra Kay. BS in Chem. Engring., W.Va. Inst. Tech., 1978. Registered profl. engr., W.Va.; cert. energy mgr. Project engr. Am. Cyanamid Co., Willow Island, W.Va., 1978-80; process engr. Mobay Chem. Corp., New Martinsville, W.Va., 1980-82; process design engr. Mobay Chem. Corp., Charleston, S.C., 1982-85; indsl. utilization specialist Hope Gas, Inc., Clarksburg, W.Va., 1985-88; mgr. mktg. tech. svc. Hope Gas, Inc., Parkersburg, W.Va., 1988-89; mgr. indsl. and tech. mktg. Hope Gas, Inc., Clarksburg, W.Va., 1989-95, mgr. residential, comml., tech. mktg., 1995-2000; gen. ptnr., mgr. Stillwood Development Group Ltd. Partnership, 1997—; v.p. TOP Gen. Bldg. Contractors, Inc., 1999—. Mem. W.Va. 4-H Club All Stars, Jacksons Mill, 1974—, Clarksburg Madrigal Singers; elder Ch. of Christ; steering com. W.Va. Clean State Program. Mem. NSPE, AIChE, Soc. Plastics Engrs., Assn. Energy Engrs., Am. Chem. Soc., Environ. Engrs. and Mgrs. Inst. of Assn. Energy Engrs. (charter), Nat. Coun. on Weights and Measures, W. Va. Natural Gas Vehicle Coalition (chair mktg. and devel. com.), W. Va. Environ. Inst., W. Va. Soc. Profl. Engrs. (pres. T. Moore Jackson chpt., state chmn. membership com., state bd. dirs.), Am. Assn. Cost Engrs. (bd. dirs.), Am. Inst. Archs. W.Va., Mid Ohio Valley Homebuilders Assn. Democrat. Avocations: racquetball, softball, fishing, hunting, golf. Office: TOP Gen Bldg Contractors Inc Stillwell Rd RR 1 Box 94A Davisville WV 26142-9774

HUBER, COLLEEN ADLENE, artist; b. Concordia, Kans., Mar. 30, 1927; d. Claude Irve and Freda (Trow) Baker; m. Wallace Charles Huber, Oct. 18, 1945 (dec.); children: Wallace Charles II (dec.), Shawn Dale, Devron Kelly (dec.), Candace Lynette, Melody Ann. Student, UCLA, 1974-78; BA cum laude, Calif. Poly. U., 1983. Co-owner, artist The Rocket (community newspaper), Garden Grove, Calif., 1955-58; quick sketch artist Walt Disney Prodn. Co., Burbank, Calif., 1958-59; v.p., art dir. Gray Pub. Co., Fullerton, Calif., 1968-76; tchr. North Orange County Sch. Dist., La Palma, Calif., 1974-76; art dir. Shoppers Guide, Upland, Calif., 1979-81; pub., owner Community Woman/Huber Ad Agy., Anaheim, Calif., 1976-79; artist Bargain Bulletin Pub., Fallbrook, Calif., 1979-82; graphic artist, designer Van Zyen Pub., Fallbrook, 1982-83; cons. sales East San Diego Mag./Baker Graphics, Rancho San Diego, Calif., 1978-88; owner, artist Coco Bien Objet d'Art, Laguna Beach, Calif., 1986-92; instr. Camp Fire Inc., 1990-92; instr. Coco Bien Objet d'Art, Temecula, Calif., 1992-93, Sun City, Calif., 1993—, Castle Rock, Wash., 1993—; dir. edn. Art Acad., Orange County, 1992-94; instr. Lake Elsinore Community Ctr., 1992—, San Jacinto C.C., 1997-98; 2nd v.p., membership chair, Fine Art Inst., San Bernadina Mus., San Bernardino, Calif., 1998-99, rec. sec., 2000—. Author: Gail, 1980 (1st Pl. award 1981, 2d Pl. award 1981); artist: Yearlings (2d Pl. award 1985), Penning (1st Pl. award 1987); exhibited at Temecula Art Coun. Wild Life Art Show, 1999. Participant Art-A-Fair, Laguna Beach Festival Show. Recipient certs. North Orange County ROP, 1976-77, 2d pl. San Bernardino Art Show, 1995, Hon. Mention Nat. Orange Show, 1996, City of Lake Elsinore, 1997, 1st pl. award FAI San Bernardino Mus., 1999. Fellow Zonta (2d v.p. 1990-91), Laguna Beach C. of C. (docent gallery night 1988); mem. Exec. Women, Calif. Press Women Assn. (chmn. jr. journalism contest Orange County chpt. 1985-86, pres. 1986-87; yearly chair Taste of Valley art show 1997), Wildlife Art Assn. Republican. Roman Catholic. Avocations: baseball fan, golf, swimming, dancing, theatre.

HUBER, DAVID LAWRENCE, physicist, educator; b. New Brunswick, N.J., July 31, 1937; s. Howard Frederick and Katherine Teresa (Smith) H.; m. Virginia Hullinger, Sept. 8, 1962; children: Laura Theresa, Johanna Jean, Amy Louise, William Hullinger. BA, Princeton U., 1959; MA, Harvard U., 1960, PhD, 1964. Instr. U. Wis., Madison, 1964-65, asst. prof., 1965-67, assoc. prof., 1967-69, prof., 1969—; dir. Synchrotron Radiation Ctr., 1985-97, Phys. Scis. Lab, Stoughton, Wis., 1992—; disting. vis. prof. U. Mo., Kansas City, 1988. A.P. Sloan fellow, 1965-67, Guggenheim fellow, 1972-73, Nat. Assn. State Univs. and Land Grant Colls. fellow Office of Sci. and Tech. Policy, 1990-91. Fellow Am. Phys. Soc.; mem. AAAS, Sigma Xi. Office: Univ Wis Phys Scis Lab 3725 Schneider Dr Stoughton WI 53589-3034 also: U Wis Dept Physics 1150 University Ave Madison WI 53706-1302

HUBER, JOHN CHARLES, fiberoptic executive; b. St. Louis, Feb. 13, 1940; s. George August Huber and Ethel Edith (Schall) Muehling; m. Sonia Ann Goldusky Huber, Aug. 25, 1962; children: Kris, Monica. BSEE, U. Mo.-Columbia, 1961, PhD, 1965; MBA, U. St. Thomas, St. Paul, Minn., 1982. Lic. profl. engr., Minn. Sr. rsch. specialist 3M/Central Rsch. Labs, St. Paul, Minn., 1965-76; mktg. mgr. 3M/Commercial Chem. Divsn., St. Paul, Minn., 1976-81; nat. sales and mktg. mgr. 3M/Interactive Sys. Divsn., St. Paul, Minn., 1981-85; mgr. of new product devel. 3M Co./Telecom Sys. Divsn., Austin, Tex., 1985-95; exec. v.p. Inst. for Invention and Innovation, Austin, Tex., 1995—; edtl. adv. bd. mem. Fiber Optic Product News, Morris Plains, N.J., 1991-95. Author one book and 26 other articles in refereed jours. inventive productivity, broadband communications, fiber optics, 1990—. Mem. Vestry St. Paul's Epis. Ch., Hidson, Wis., 1973-80; bd. dirs. St. Croix Valley Arts Guild, Hudson, Wis., 1974-78, Zachary Scott Theatre Ctr., Austin, Tex., 1986-90. Recipient Leadership award Austin Bus. Cmty. for the Arts, 1988, Honor award for Disting. Svc. in Engring., U. Mo.-Columbia, 1999. Mem. Soc. for Measurement and Control. Episcopalian. Avocations: history, antiques, photography, live theatre. E-mail address: jchuber@ccsi.com. Office: Inst for Invention and Innovation 500 E Anderson Ln Apt 238X Austin TX 78752-1207

HUBER, LYNN MANOS, artist, educator, administrator; b. St. Louis, Nov. 17, 1947; d. Robert Neal and Margie Ann (Fray) Manos; m. August Lafayette Huber III, Nov. 8, 1969 (div. Dec. 1993); 3 children. BFA, U. Kans., 1969; MA, U. Mo., 1978; ed., Kansas City (Mo.) Art Inst., 1973-75, 83-85. Instr. art Nelson-Atkins Mus. Art, Kansas City, 1969-82; artist Hallmark Cards, Kansas City, 1994-99; adj. instr. Kansas City Art Inst., 1988-90, 95-99, interim dir. continuing edn. and spl. programs, 1999-2000. Group exhbns. include U. Mo., Kansas City, 1995, Morgan Gallery, Kansas City, 1997, Nelson Art Gallery, 1998-99, Irving (Tex.) Arts Ctr., 1999; represented in collections at Mus. Nat. Belas Artes, Rio de Janeiro, Nelson-Atkins Mus. Art, Spencer Mus. Art, Lawrence, Kans. artist/instr. Young Audiences, 1992-98. Mem. Kansas City Artist Coalition, Friends of Art. E-mail: blhuber@worldinter.net.

HUBER, MICHAEL FREDERICK, journalist, educator; b. Oklahoma City, Okla., Dec. 4, 1952; s. James Arnold and Mary Frances (Kaho) H.; m. Cynthia Christine Morris, May 14, 1983; children: Eric William, Samuel James, Nicholas Andrew, Todd Michael. BA, Ind. U., Bloomington, 1974, MA, 1977. Reporter, editor The Chgo. Sun-Times, Chgo., 1977-79, The Courier-Journal, Louisville, Ky., 1979-82; night city editor The Miami Herald, 1982-86; exec. editor Review Publs., Miami, 1986-89; bus. writer The Miami Herald, 1989-91; asst. prof. Fla. Internat. U., Miami, 1992-; cons., Miami, 1991-; asst. dir. The Journalism Writing Project, Miami, 1992-; v.p. The Word Assn., Inc., Miami, 1995-. Co-author: (book) Words Into Flesh, 1994. Recipient award Ill. Press Editors, 1978, award Ill. Press Assn., 1978. Presbyterian. Home: 11100 Griffing Blvd Miami FL 33161-7250

HUBER, PAUL WILLIAM, biochemistry educator, researcher; b. Medford, Mass., July 23, 1951; s. William Francis and Catherine (Sheridan) H. BS, Boston Coll., 1973; PhD, Purdue U., 1978. NIH postdoctoral fellow U. Chgo., 1979-81, rsch. assoc., 1982-85; asst. prof. U. Notre Dame, Ind., 1985-92, assoc. prof., 1992—, assoc. chmn., 1993-97; vis. fellow Yale U., 1997. Contbr. articles to profl. jours. Mem. AAAS, Am. Soc. Biochemistry and Molecular Biology. Home: 1215 E Irvington Ave South Bend IN 46614-1417 Office: U Notre Dame Dept Chemistry/Biochemistry Notre Dame IN 46556

HUBER, ROBERT, biochemist, educator; b. Munich, Feb. 20, 1937; s. Sebastian and Helene (Kebinger) H.; m. Christa Huber, 1960; children: Ulrike, Martin, Robert, Julia. Diploma, Tech. Universität Munich, 1960, PhD, 1963, Habilitation, 1968; D (hon.), Louvain, Belgium, 1987, U. Ljubljana, Slovenia, 1989; D for Medicine and Surgery (hon.), U. 'Tor Vergata', Rome, 1991; D (hon.), Univ. Nova de Lisboa, Portugal, 2000. External prof. Tech. U. Munich, 1976; prof., dir. Max-Planck-Inst. for Biochemistry, Martinsried, Germany, 1972—. Editor Jour. Molecular Biology. Decorated grosse Verdienstkreuz mit Stern und Schulterband, Order for Merit for Sci. and Arts (Germany); recipient E.K. Frey medal Gesellschaft für Chirurgie, 1972, Otto Warburg medal Gesellschaft für Biologische Chemie, 1977, Emil van Behring medal U. Marburg, 1982, Keilin medal Biochem. Soc. London, Richard Kuhn medal Soc. German Chemists, 1987, E.K. Frey-E. Werle meml. medal, 1989, Kone award Assn. Clin. Biochemists, 1990, Sir Hans Krebs medal, 1992, Bayerischer Maximilianorden für Wissenschaft und Kunst, 1993, Linus Pauling medal, 1993, 94, Disting. Svc. award Miami Biotech. Winter Symposia, 1995, Max Tishler prize Harvard U., 1997, Max Bergmann medal U. Tübingen, 1997, co-recipient Nobel prize for chemistry, 1988. Fellow Royal Soc. London, Third World Acad. Scis., Am. Acad. Microbiology; mem. NAS (U.S.A.) (fgn. assoc.), European Molecular Biology Orgn. (coun. mem.), Japanese Biochem. Soc. (hon.), Deutsche Chemische Gesellschaft, Gesellschaft für Biologische Chemie, Am. Soc. Biol. Chemists (hon.), Swedish Soc. Biophysics (hon.), Bayerische Acad. der Wissenschaften, Deutsche Acad. der Naturforscher Leopoldina, Croatian Acad. Scis. and Art (corr.), Acad. Nazionale dei Lincei, European Molecular Biology Orgn. Office: Max Planck Inst Biochem, Am Klopferspitz 18A, Martinsried Munich 82152, Germany

HUBER, ROBERT LOUIS, art dealer; b. Rockford, Ill., Sept. 3, 1937; s. Edgar J. and Charlotte M. (Cichocki) H.; m. Marianne Jeanne Huber, Oct. 3, 1959; children: Michael Robert, Stephan Louis, Edward Francis. Univ. Wis., 1958, Mexico City Coll., Mexico City, Mex., 1960. Owner Huber Primitive Art, Dixon, Ill., 1972—; adv. in the formation of Pre-Columbian and Ethnographic collections, pvt. and museums, U.S., Europe, 1972—; lectr. Art Dept. Rockford Coll., 1986, Primitive Art Assn. Chgo., 1984, Notre Dame Primitive Art Assn., 1987, Nprstk Mus., Prague, Czech, 1996; educated his children at home, Mexico, 1968-76. Film maker: The Cuna,

1980, Nebaj, Cotzal, Chajul, 1987. Campaign assoc. Dem. Party, 1996—. Mem. Am. Assn. Dealers in Ancient Oriental and Primitve Art, Met. Mus. of Art, Precolumbian Art Rsch. Inst., Indpl. Ethnic Arts Coun. Avocations: world travel, wilderness hiking, built own home. E-mail: tellapple@aol.com. Home: 1012 Timber Trail Dr Dixon IL 61021-8934

HUBER, TONYA, education educator, writer; b. Lackawanna, N.Y., Feb. 28, 1958; d. H. Joseph and Elsie Garlick H. BS, Pa. State U., 1982, MEd, 1985, PhD, 1990. Assoc. prof. Coll. of Edn. Wichita (Ky.) State U., 1990—; internat. and overseas program faculty Coll. of N.J., Trenton, 1997—; cons. in field, workshop/conf. presenter in field, 1989—; rep. grad. coun. Wichita State U., 1998-2000. Author: (books) Teaching in the Diverse Classroom: Learner-Centered Activities That Work, 1993, Multicultural Planning to Maximize Learning: Creating Quality Learning Experiences, 2000; founder/editor: Jour. of Critical Inquiry Into Curriculum and Instrn., 1998—. Recipient Howard Soule Grad. fellow in Ednl. Leadership, Phi Delta Kappa, 1989. Mem. Nat. Assn. for Multicultural Edn. (pres. Kans. chpt. 1996-98, founding dir. 1994-96, chair Nat. Leadership Inst. 1996, recipient Svc. award 1990-98). Avocations: free weights, Western horseback riding, reading, theatre. E-mail: huber@twsu.edu. Office: Wichita State U Dept Curriculum/Instrn 1845 Fairmount St Wichita KS 67260-0001

HUBERMAN, JONATHAN SERGE, venture capitalist; b. Washington, July 8, 1965; s. Benjamin and Gisela Bialik Huberman; m. Susan Lynn Lutzker, May 1, 1993; 1 child, Mara. AB in Computer Sci., Princeton U., 1988; MBA, U. Pa., 1992. Mktg. mgr. future archs. Cray Rsch., Inc., Mpls., 1988-90; case leader Boston Consulting Group, Chgo., 1992-95; gen. ptnr. Idanta Ptnrs., San Diego, 1995—; bd. dirs. Boxer Cross, Menlo Park, Calif., Iomega Corp., Roy, Utah. Avocations: ice hockey, skiing. E-mail: jhuberman@idanta.com. Fax: 858-452-2013. Office: Idanta Ptnrs 4660 La Jolla Village Dr San Diego CA 92122-4601

HUBERT, JEAN-PAUL, ambassador; b. Grand-Mère, Que., Can., Dec. 16, 1941; s. Jean-Paul and Cécile (Laperrière) H.; m. Mireya Melgar, July 29, 1967 (div. Oct. 4, 1995); children: Jean-Philippe, Jean-Charles, Alexandra; m. Florence Fournier, Aug. 11, 1995. BCL, McGill U., 1966; M in Internat. Affairs, Columbia U., 1969; D in Polit. Sci., La Sorbonne, Paris, 1971; PhD in Internat. Affairs (hon.), Moncton (N.B.) U., 1996. Bar: Que., 1967. Dept. Fgn. Rels. and Internat. Trade Can. Diplomatic Svc., Ottawa, 1971-72; 2d sec., vice consul for Spain & Morocco Can. Diplomatic Svc., Madrid, 1972-74; legal affairs divsn. Can. Diplomatic Svc., Ottawa, 1974-76, pers. divsn., 1976-78; 1st sec. and consul Can. Diplomatic Svc., Havana, Cuba, 1978-81; dipol. polit. counselor, rep. Agy. for Cultural & Tech. Cooperation Can. Diplomatic Svc., Paris, 1991-95; econ. and treaty law divsn. Can. Diplomatic Svc., Ottawa, 1985-86, fed. coord. for La Francophonie, 1986-88; ambassador to Senegal, Mauritania, Guinea, Guinea-Bissau, Cape Verde Can. Diplomatic Svc., Senegal, 1988-90, high commr. to the Gambia, 1988-90, prime min. personal rep. La Francophonie, 1988-90, Dept. Fgn. Rels. and Internat. Trade Can. Embassy at Dakar, 1988-90; 1st ambassador, permanent rep. of Can. to OAS Can. Diplomatic Svc., Washington, 1990-93; sr. advisor Commonwealth La Francophonie/Hemispheric Affairs Can. Diplomatic Svc., Ottawa, 1993-94; personal rep. prime min. La Francophonie Can. Diplomatic Svc., Ottawa, Brussels, 1994-96; Dept. Fgn. Rels. and Internat. Trade ambassador to Belgium and Luxembourg, Brussels, 1994-98, Argentina and Paraguay, Buenos Aires, 1998—. Designated Order of la Pléiade Internat. Assn. of French-Speaking Parliamentarians, 1989. Avocation: genealogy. E-mail: jean-paul.hubert@dfait-maeci.gc.ca. Office: Canadian Embassy, Tagle 2828, Buenos Aires 1425, Argentina

HUBERT, JOHN F., metallurgical materials and processes engineer; b. Erie, Pa., Jan. 7, 1932; s. Felix Joseph and Helen Elizabeth (Plonski) H.; m. Joyce Mary Welch, Aug. 7, 1954; children: Karen, Kathleen, Kristen. B of Metall. Engring., Rensselaer Poly. Inst., 1954; MS in Metallurgy and Materials Sci., Lehigh U., 1966. Metall. engr. Bethlehem (Pa.) Steel Corp., 1954-68; metall. engr. and mgr. IBM Corp., Endicott, N.Y., 1968-76; materials scis. mgr. inkjet tech. Mead Corp., Dayton, Ohio, also Dallas, 1976-84; staff metall. materials and processes engr. space vehicles, satellites Martin Marietta Astronautics, Denver, 1984-92; gen. metall. and materials engr. locomotives MK Rail Co., Boise, Idaho, 1993-94; gen. metall. materials processes and fracture control engr. Lockheed Martin Corp., New Orleans, 1995—; engr. Space Shuttle Super Light Weight and X-33 Fuel Tanks, NASA, Michoud, La., 1995—. Author engring. evaluation documents, design guide; subject of feature article in Bus. Week, 1972. Vol. Heart Fund, Cancer Fund, Denver, 1990-93; swim coach Spl. Olympics, N.Y. State, 1970s; v.p. Broome County ARC, Binghamton, N.Y., 1976. Capt. USNR, 1955-77. Recipient Designer of Yr. award Tex. Turf Irrigation Assn., 1982, others. Mem. ASM Internat. (life), Am. Welding Soc., Soc. for Advanced Materials and Processes, Gardeners of Am. (nat. chmn. Yr. 2000 Conv.), Elks. Republican. Roman Catholic. Achievements include co-invention of synthesis of office atmospheres for accelerated corrosion testing of electrical circuit; first continuously regulated low temperature test cell. Avocations: landscape-irrigation-gardening, running, swimming, auto mechanics, flying. Home: 1225 Kingfisher Way Boise ID 83709-1239

HUBÍK, STANISLAV, philosopher, researcher; b. Hulín, Moravia, Czech Republic, Jan. 23, 1949; s. Miloš and Veronika (Ernestová) H.; m. Hana Olšanská, Aug. 8, 1970; children: Martin, Igor. MA in Sociology, Masaryk U., Brno, Czech Republic, 1973, MA in Philosophy, 1974, PhD in History of Philosophy, 1979. Asst. Inst. for Philosophy and Sociology, CSAV, Prague, 1974-77, Inst. for Rsch. of Social Consciousness, Brno, 1977-90; assoc. prof. Palacky U. Olomouc, 1990-95; assoc. prof. Ostrava U., 1995—, chief dept. social work, 1995-97; prof. Mendel U. Agr. and Forestry, Brno, 1997—. Author: Language and Metaphysics, 1983 (Award of Presidium of the Czech Acad. Scis. 1984), Postmodernism Through Linguistic Turn, 1994; co-author: Nature and Culture, 1990, Reason and Values, 1985. Recipient Award for Environment-Values-Ethics, Ministry of Environment, Czech Republic, 1992-94. Mem. Masaryk Sociol. Soc., Austrian Ludwig Wittgenstein Soc., European Soc. for Rsch. on the Edn. of Adults (mem. steering com. 1993). Mem. czech Husits Ch. Avocation: music. Home: Ant Slavika 9, 602 00 Brno Czech Republic Office: Ostrava Univ ZSF, 17 Listopadu 1790, 708 52 Ostrava Poruba Czech Republic

HÜBLER, ARVED CARL, university administrator; b. Bonn, Germany, July 25, 1960. D of Engring., Hochschule der Künste, Berlin, 1992; diploma in engring., Tech. U., Berlin, 1986. Cert. in media tech./sci. Tech. U. Bertelsmann AG, Gütersloh, Germany, 1994-97; inst. media tech. and sci. Contbr. numerous papers to profl. jours. Grantee Sternberg Stiftung, 1993. Office: Tech U Chemnitz, Inst Print & Media Tech, D-09107 Chemnitz Saxonia, Germany

HUBNER, WILLIAM FRANK, enterpreneur; b. L.A., July 25, 1934; s. Harvey William and Mable Eileen (Hall) H.; m. Carolyn Grace Coon, Oct. 10, 1952 (div. Aug. 1974); children: Karri, Bill Jr., Kim. Founder Allied Health Assn., 1963—, Paramount Fitness Corp., L.A., 1954-74; founding dir. Assn. Phys. Fitness Ctrs., Washington, 1975-93, chmn., 1980-81; chmn. bd. dirs., CEO Health Industries, Inc., 1984—; founder Nat. Credit Corp., 1961; co-founder Elite Aviation, Inc., Van Nuys, Calif., 1994—. Supporter Chuck Norris Kick Drugs Out of Am., Houston, 1992—; supporter various police depts. with fitness equipment Police Dept. Hist. Soc., L.A., 1990—. Mem. Vintage Club (Indian Wells, Calif.). Republican. Avocations: yachting, sports, reading.

HUCHANT, JEAN-LOUIS RAYMOND, financial executive; b. Paris, Sept. 12, 1950; s. Joseph Leon and Blanche Simone (Thievin) H.; m. Danielle Berangere Mabon, June 18, 1977; children: Pierre-Yves, Jean-Bernard, Alain-Xavier. B Econs., U. Lyon, France, 1973; MBA, U. Mich., 1975. Mgmt. cons. Bossard Cons., Paris, 1976-78, HB Conseil, Paris, 1978-79; CFO Extracorporeal (Johnson & Johnson) France, Neauphle, 1979-82; CFO Bayer SA, Puteaux, France, 1982-91, dir. fin., bd. dirs., 1991—; CEO, chmn. Distri, Puteaux, 1991—, mem. supervisory bd. Bayer Elastomeres, Lillebonne, France, 1991—, Bayer Diagnostics, Puteaux, 1990—, Bayer Pharma, Puteaux, 1990—; mem. supervisory bd. Borchers France, Castres, Bayer Classics, Puteaux, Haarmann et Reimer, St. Ouen l;Aumone, France, 1992—. French Fgn. Office scholar, 1973. Mem. Internat. Fiscal Assn., Inst.

Français des Avocat-Conseils Fiscaux, Assn. Directeurs Financiers, Assn. Français des Pr. Trésoriers. Avocations: history, tennis, skiing, literature. Home: 28 rue Le Sueur, 75116 Paris France Office: Bayer SA, 49/51 Quai de Dion Bouton, 92815 Puteaux France

HUCK, RICHARD FELIX, III, lawyer; b. St. Louis, Mar. 4, 1957; s. Richard Felix Jr. and Agnes Stewart (Kinsella) H.; m. Kathryn Ewing Otto, Apr. 7, 1984; children: Richard Dalton, Emily Stewart. BA, Washington & Lee U., 1979; JD, St. Louis U., 1982. Bar: Mo. 1982, U.S. Dist. Ct. (we. dist.) Mo. 1982, Ill. 1983, U.S. Dist. Ct. (ea. dist.) Mo. 1983, U.S. Ct. Appeals (8th cir.) 1983, U.S. Ct. Fed. Claims 1996. From assoc. to ptnr. Evans & Dixon, St. Louis, 1982-96; ptnr. Blumenfeld Kaplan & Sandweiss PC, St. Louis, 1996—. Mem. John Marshall Rep. Club., St. Louis, 1989. Mem. ABA, Bar Assn. Met. St. Louis, Forum on Constrn. Industry, Racquet Club, Noonday Club, St. Louis Country Club. Roman Catholic. Avocations: golf, squash. Home: 5 Glenmary Rd Saint Louis MO 63132-3608 Office: Blumenfeld Kaplan & Sandweiss PC 168 N Meramec Ave Ste 400 Saint Louis MO 63105-3758

HUCKABEE, HARLOW MAXWELL, lawyer, writer; b. Wichita Falls, Tex., Jan. 22, 1918; s. Edwin Cleveland and Gladys Idella (Bonney) H.; m. Gloria Charlotte Comstock, Jan. 10, 1942; children: Bonney M., David C., Stephen M. BA, Harvard U., 1948; JD, Georgetown U., 1951. Bar: U.S. Dist. Ct. D.C. 1952, U.S. Ct. Appeals (D.C. cir.) 1952. Cashier br. office Columbian Nat. Life Ins. Co., Boston, 1935-40; lawyer Fed. Housing Adminstrn., Washington, 1955-56; trial lawyer, criminal sect., tax divsn. U.S. Justice Dept., Washington, 1956-63; lawyer IRS, Washington, 1963-67; trial lawyer organized crime and racketeering sect. U.S. Justice Dept. Washington, 1967-68, trial lawyer criminal sect., tax divsn., 1968-80. Author: Lawyers, Psychiatrists and Criminal Law, 1980, Mental Disability Issues in the Criminal Justice System: What They Are, Who Evaluates Them, How and When, 2000; contbr. articles to profl. jours. and legal pubs. including Diminished Capacity Dilemma in the Federal System, 1991. Maj. U.S. Army, 1940-45, 48-55, ETO, Korea; lt. col. USAR, 1961. Methodist. Home: 5100 Fillmore Ave Apt 913 Alexandria VA 22311-5048

HUCKIN, WILLIAM PRICE, JR., prosecutor; b. Okmulgee, Okla., Aug. 20, 1920; s. William Price and Mary Louise H.; m. Freda Croom, Nov. 15, 1947; children: William Price III, David, Elizabeth, Barbara. BA, U. Okla., 1942, LLB, 1947. Bar: Okla. 1947; U.S. Dist. Ct. (no. dist.) 1953, U.S. Dist. Ct. (we. dist.) 1950, U.S. Ct. Appeals 1944. Asst. county atty. Tulsa, Okla., 1951-52, prosecutor, 1954-55, pvt. practice, 1956—; apttd. city prosecutor, Tulsa. Active First Presbyn. Ch., clk. of session, permanent jud. commn. 1st lt., pilot, U.S. Army Air Corps, 1943-45. Decorated EAME (Rome Arno and Air Offensive Europe) Theatre ribbon with 2 bronze stars, air medal, 1944, 2nd oak leaf cluster, 1944, unit citation, 1944. Mem. ATLA, Okla. Bar Assn., Tulsa County Bar Assn. (Disting. Svc. award 1986), Beta Theta Pi (pres. Gamma Phi chpt. 1947). Republican. Avocations: genealogy, chess. Home: 6706 S Florence Ave Tulsa OK 74136-4556 Office: 1206 Philtower Bldg 427 S Boston Ave Tulsa OK 74103-4141

HUCKINS, HAROLD AARON, chemical engineer; b. Cambridge, Mass., Nov. 28, 1924; s. Harold Aaron and Julia E. (Nugent) H.; m. Elizabeth L. Kearns, Nov. 15, 1952; children: Richard W., Robert M., Christopher N., Patricia A., Leslie K. BSChemE, Northeastern U., 1945; ASME, Lowell Inst., 1946; postgrad., Boston U., 1947-49, U. Pitts., 1950-52. Chem. process engr., asst. project mgr. Monsanto Chem. Co., Boston-Everett, Mass., 1945-49; sr. process engr., group leader Koppers Co. Chem. Div., Pitts., 1949-53; mgr. pilot plants, project mgr. Sci. Design Co., Inc., N.Y.C., 1953-66; v.p. tech. ops. Oxirane Chem. Co., Princeton, N.J., 1966-73; v.p. tech. assessment Halcon SD Group, N.Y.C., 1973-85; pres. Princeton Advanced Tech., Inc., 1985—; dir. Assn. Cons. Chemists and Chem. Engrs. div., N.Y.C., 1990-93, program chair, 1992-93; dir. Materials Tech., St. Louis, 1976-85. Co-author: The Chemical Plant, 1966; contbr. articles to profl. jours. Fellow AIChE (chair ctrl. Jersey sect. 1976-77, dir mgmt. divsn. 1981-82, dir. materials engring. and sci. divsn. 1992-93, chmn. tech. materials com. 1983-84, chmn. John Fritz medal commn. 1989, chmn. entrepreneurial com. 1994—, Chem. Engring. Practice award 1994); mem. Am. Soc. Materials, Am. Chem. Soc., Am. Ceramic Soc. Nat. Assn. Corrosion Engrs. (conf. chmn. 1984), Comml. Devel. Assn., Mensa Internat., Country Club of Hilton Head Island, Port Royal Racquet Club, Hilton Head Ski Club (bd. dirs.). Achievements include 10 U.S. patents for chemical process technology. Fax: 843-689-9212. E-mail: hhuckins@hargray.com. Office: Princeton Advanced Tech Inc 4 Bertram Pl Hilton Head Island SC 29928-3936

HUDA, MIRZA NAJMUL, development and management specialist; b. Dhaka, Bangladesh, Oct. 4, 1946; s. Mirza Nurul Huda and Umme Kulsum Siddiqua; m. Raihana Banu, Dec. 29, 1974 (dec. Feb. 1988); children: Sasha, Misha; m. Sayeeda Sultana, Nov. 18, 1988; 1 child, Sara. BSME, U. Engring. and Tech., Dhaka, 1968; MBA, U. Dhaka, 1970. Trainee Strabag Bau AG, Cologne, Germany, 1969-70; project mgr. Jurong Engring. Ltd., Singapore, 1972-81; tech. dir. Rahman Chems. Ltd., Dhaka, 1981-83; local cons. Planning Commn., Dhaka, 1983-85; dir. devel. Midas, Dhaka, 1985-91; program mgr. Can. Exec. Svc. Orgn., Bangladesh, 1988-91; local rep. Netherlands Mgmt. Coop. Program, Bangladesh, 1992-94; cons. Dhaka, 1991—; chmn. Saidpur Enterprises, 1994—; exec. com. mem. Prompt, NRT, IMCB; chairperson adv. com. NIPF. Fellow Instn. Engrs. Bangladesh; mem. ASME, IBA Alumni Assn., U. Dhaka (life). Avocation: traveling. Home: House 57 Rd 6A Dhanmondi, Dhaka 1209, Bangladesh Office: Champak Ltd, 57 Dhanmondi Rd 6A, Dhaka 1209, Bangladesh

HUDAK, JOSEPH DAVID, forensic engineer, educator, police investigator; b. Pottstown, Pa., Feb. 11, 1956; s. Joseph Andrew and Eleanore Barbara (Pierzchala) H.; children: Meredith Rebecca, Jonathan Michael, Wesley Robert; m. Joann Marie Kempf. BS in Civil Engring. with honors, Drexel U., 1979. Accredited accident reconstructionist Accreditation Commn. for Traffic Accident Reconstruction. Civil engr. IU Conversion Systems, Horsham, Pa., 1980-82, VFL Tech., Malvern, Pa., 1982-84; state trooper Pa. State Police, Harrisburg, 1984-2000; assoc. Robson-Lapina Inc. Forensic Engrs., Lancaster, Pa., 2000—; adj. faculty Tex. A&M U., 1995—; pres., forensic engring. cons. iE Forensic Cons., Inc., Newfoundland, Pa., 1997—; alternate rep. ACTAR bd. dirs., 1995-2000. Contbr. articles to profl. publs.; presenter in field of traffic homicide investigations. Mem. ASCE (assoc.), Soc. Automotive Engrs. (assoc.), Nat. Assn. Traffic Accident Reconstructionists and Investigators, Md. Assn. Traffic Accident Invesigators, Fraternal Order Police, Rotary, Tau Beta Pi, Chi Epsilon. Avocations: reading, sports, martial arts, stone masonry, weight training. Home: RR 1 Box 167C Newfoundland PA 18445-9772 Office: Robson-Lapina Inc Forensic Engrs 350 New Holland Ave Lancaster PA 17602-2301

HUDAK, ONDREJ, physicist, consultant; b. Michalovce, Czechoslovakia, Apr. 23, 1953; s. Ondrej and Magdalena (Kizivatova) H.; m. Tatiana Vargova, Apr. 22, 1978; children: Jana, Matej. Student, Charles U., Prague, Czechoslovakia, 1971-76; DSc, Charles U., Prague, Czech Republic, 1985; postgrad., Czechoslovakia. Diplomate in Theoretical Physics, Charles U. Scientist dept. phys. chemistry Šafarik's U., Košice, Czechoslovakia, 1977-79; grad student dept. dielectrics Inst. Physics, Prague, 1979-82, scientist, 1990-96; scientist solid state physics dept. Inst. Exptl. Physics, Košice, 1982-90; scientist dept. exptl. physics, faculty natural scis. Šafarik's U., 1996; lectr. in fins. M. Bell's U., Banska, Bystrica, Slovak Republic, 1997—; scientist faculty math. physics Comenius U., Bratislava, 1998; scientist Physics Materials and Tech., Slovak Technical U., Trnava, 1999—; sci. sec. Inst. Exptl. Physics, 1988-89; leading scientist Inst. Physics Czechoslovak Acad. Sci., Prague, 1990-96; cons., Slovak Republic, 1994—. Author: Technical Analysis and Our Capital Markets, 1994, O. Hudak, Technical Analysis, 1999; contbr. articles on material sci. and capital mkts. to profl. jours. Recipient Alexander Von Humboldt-Stiftung award, 1992. Mem. European Phys. Soc., Slovak Statis. and Demographical Soc., Slovak Phys. Soc., Slovak Geneal.-Heraldic Soc. Matica Slovenska. Avocations: travelling, swimming. E-mail: hudako@mail.pvt.sk. Home: Stierova 23/3, 04011 Kosice Slovak Republic Office: Faculty Finance, Tajovského 10, 97401 Banska Bystrica Slovak Republic

HUDAK, PAUL ALEXANDER, retired engineer; b. Youngstown, Ohio, Oct. 8, 1930; s. Paul and Elizabeth (Hoffman) H.; m. Ingrid Gertrud Matzke, June 6, 1964; children: Frank, David, Greta. BS in Math., Youngstown U.,

1958. Reliability/safety engr. N.Am. Aviation, L.A. and Downey, Calif., 1958-64, Douglas Aircraft, Long Beach, Calif., 1964-73, Chrysler Def., Sterling Heights, Mich., 1973-77, Boeing Airplane Co., Seattle and Everett, Wash., 1977-85, Mare Island Naval Shipyard, Vallejo, Calif., 1985-93; ret., 1993. Cpl. USMC, 1951-53. Mem. IEEE. Achievements include proposal for tech. ctr. to integrate edn. and work creation; proposal for devel. of world village of UN to meet social needs and promote world order. Home: 220 Bluebell Pl Vallejo CA 94591-8086

HUDDLESON, EDWIN EMMETT, III, lawyer; b. Oct. 20, 1945; s. Edwin Emmett and Mary (Taeusch) H.; m. Andra Nan Oakes, July 8, 1978; children: Michael, Jonathan. BS, Stanford U., 1967; JD, U. Chgo., 1970. Bar: Calif. 1970, D.C. 1977. Law clk. to Judge Charles M. Merrill U.S. Ct. Appeals (9th cir.), 1970-71; civil divsn. U.S. Dept. Justice, Washington, 1971-77. Author: Waiver of Miranda Rights, 1969, Confidentiality for Editorial Process, 1978, UCC Transaction Guide Leasing, 1989—, Appellate Advocacy, 1991, New Developments Leasing, 1993, Environmental Law Protections for Lenders, 1994; mem. U. Chgo. Law Rev., 1968-70, comment editor, 1969-70; contbr. articles on comml. law 1st Amendment, appellate advocacy to law jours. Fellow Am. Bar Found.; mem. ABA, FBA, Am. Law Inst., Charles Fahy Am. Inns of Ct. (master). Home: 1962 Upshur St NW Washington DC 20011-5354 Office: Driscoll & Draude 1230 31st St NW Washington DC 20007-3400

HUDEC, JAROSLAV, NATO official; b. Rozstáni, Czech Republic, Jan. 20, 1949; maried Jane Hudec; 3 children: Jaroslava, Zita, Sona. MEng., U. Transport, 1972; postgrad., Mil. Acad., Brno, 1983-86, Air War Coll., U.S., 1995-96. Commd. Czech Armed Forces, 1972, advanced through grades to maj. gen., air traffic contr. 6th fighter-bomber regiment, 1973-78, chief of staff, 20th fighter-bomber regiment, 1978-83, dep. chief of staff, 34th fighter-bomber divsn., 1986-89, with Air Force Hdqrs., 1989-91, with Air Force and Air Def. Hdqrs., 1991-92; gen. staff Mil. Acad., Brno, 1992-93; dep. chief of staff Air Force and Air Def. of Armed Forces Mil. Acad., 1993-95, gen. dir. Def. Planning Directorate of Min. of Def., 1996-99, mil. rep. of Czech Republic to NATO, 1999—. Office: NATO Hdqrs, Blvd Leopold III, 1110 Brussels Belgium*

HUDEC, LUBOMÍR JOSEF, educator; b. Opava, Czech Republic, June 21, 1935; s. Josef Václav and Anežka Marie (Provazníková) H.; m. Miroslava Kateřina Záková, Mar. 21, 1964; children: Hudec Tomáš, Hudcová Markéta. MSc, Czech Tech. U., 1958, PhD, 1966; DSc, Tech. U., 1981. Lectr. Czech Tech. U., Poděbrady, Czech Republic, 1958-61; sr. lectr. Czech Tech. U., Prague, 1962-70, reader, docent, 1974-80, prof., 1981-83; expert prof. Higher Inst. Electronics, Menouf, Egypt, 1971-73; prof. U. Chem. Tech., Prague, 1984—; mem. TESLA Vrsovice, Prague, 1990-93; mem. electric material processing IUVSTA, Corvallis, 1995, Fed. Coun. Material Electronics, Prague, 1987-92. Author: Electronic Devices, 1973, Synegetics and Stability Theory, 1982; co-author: Electronic Components, 1989, 92, Electronics Fundamentals, 1996; exec. editor Acta Polytechnica, 1977-84; contbr. articles to profl. jours.; inventor. Lt. A.A. Gunnery, radar specialist, 1959-60. Mem. Czech Engrs. Sci. Assn., Czech Engrs. Found. (bd. dirs.). Avocations: music and sports, volleyball. Home: Roosevelova 49/892, 160 00 Prague Czech Republic Office: Univ Chem Technology, Technicka 5, 166 28 Prague Czech Republic

HUDI, ISTVÁN, software engineer; b. Szeged, Hungary, July 7, 1963; s. Antal and Antalne (Magyary) H. MS in Physics, Physicist Diploma, Jozsef Attila U., Szeged, 1986, Medium Level State Lang. Exam English, 1993; postgrad., Gábor Dénes Informatical High Sch., Szeged, 1997—. Scientific assoc. dept. applied informatics Jozsef Attila U., Szeged, 1986-94; tchr. informatics Dugonics A. Piarist Grammar Sch., Szeged, 1993-94; programmer mathematican Biomondex Ltd., Szeged, 1994-95; sys. adminstr. Mav Regional Med. Ctr. Computers Dept., Szeged, 1996-98; software engr. Cygnus Ltd., Szeged, 1998—. Contbr. articles to profl. jours. Placed 3rd and 4th One Year Long Problem Solving Competition in Physics Eötvös Lorand Phys. Soc., 1981, 6th Phys. Competition in Memory of Ortvay R. Bolyai János, Eötvös Lorand, Phys. Soc., 1981, 2nd Mathemat. Competition in Memory of Gyula Szökefalvy-Nagy, 1981. Roman Catholic. Avocations: swimming, biking, computer programming in various languages, climbing hills.

HUDSON, CHARLES DAUGHERTY, insurance executive; b. La Grange, Ga., Mar. 17, 1927; s. J.D. and Janie (Hill) H.; m. Ida Cason Callaway, May 1, 1955; children: Jane Alice Hudson Craig, Ellen Pinson Hudson Harris, Charles Daugherty, Ida Hudson Russell. Student, Auburn U., 1945-48, LHD (hon.), 1992; LLD, La Grange Coll.; LHD (hon.), Mercer U., 1987. Ptnr. Hudson Hardware Co., La Grange, 1950-57; pres. Hammond-Hudson Ins. Agy., La Grange, 1957-58, owner, 1958-78; pres. Hammond, Hudson & Holder INc., 1978-94, chmn. bd., 1994—; bd. dirs. mem. exec. com. Citizens & So. Nat. Bank, La Grange, 1964-90; bd. dirs. Citizens & So. Ga. Corp., Citizens & So. Nat. Bank, Atlanta, C&S Investment Advisors, Inc., Atlanta, C&S Ga. Corp.; acting pres. La Grange Coll., 1979-80; v.p., bd. dirs. la Grange Industries, 1956—, Hudson Maddox Enterprises, 1965-95; ptnr. PCH Properties, 1981—; chmn. bd. dirs. First Annuity Corp., La Grange; bd. dirs., chmn. trust com. NationsBank of Ga. Recipient Pres.'s award Colonial Life Ins. Co., 1966, 69-70, 75-80, Disting. Alumni award Ga. Mil. Acad.-Woodward Acad., 1971, Disting. Svc. award Ga. Hosp. Assn., 1980, Respect La Law award Optimists Assn., 1977, Van Landingham Commitment to Edn. award, 1996, Pub. Svc. award Ga. Assn. AIA, 1977, Leading Producer award Aetna Life and Casualty, 1979; Paul Harris fellow, 1984. Mem. Am. Legion, Ga. Assn. Ind. Ins. Agts., Ga. Sck. Bd. Assn. (area dir.), SAR, Amicale de Group LaFayette (hon.). Chattahoochee Valley Art Assn., La Grange C. of C. (bd. dirs.), Newcomen Soc. N.Am., Ga. Hosp. Assn. (trustee 1980—), U. Ga. Gridiron Secret Soc., Highland Country Club (chmn. bd. 1999—), Lafayette Club, Commerce Club Atlanta, Aetna Life and Casualty Presidents, Masons, Shriners, Elks, Rotary (pres. 1964-65), Sigma Alpha Epsilon, Beta Gamma Sigma. Home: 407 Country Club Rd Lagrange GA 30240-2031 Office: Hammond Hudson & Holder Inc 206 W Haralson St Lagrange GA 30240-2722

HUDSON, CHRISTOPHER JOHN, publisher; b. Watford, Eng., June 8, 1948; s. Joseph Edward and Gladys Jenny Patricia (Madgwick); m. Lois Jeanne Lyons, June 16, 1979; children: Thomas, Ellen, Ronald, Timothy. BA with honors, Cambridge U., Eng., 1969, MA with honors, 1972. Promotion mgr. Prentice-Hall Internat., Eng., 1969-70; area mgr. Prentice-Hall Internat., Eng., France, 1970-71; mktg. mgr. Prentice-Hall Internat., Englewood Cliffs, N.J., 1971-74, dir. mktg., 1974-76, asst. v.p., 1976; group internat. dir. I.T.T. Pub., N.Y.C., 1976-77; pres. Focal Press, Inc., N.Y.C., 1977-82; v.p., pub. Aperture Found. Inc., N.Y.C., 1983-86; head publs. J. Paul Getty Trust, L.A., 1986—. Author: Guide to International Book Fairs, 1976; pub. Aperture, 1983-86, J. Paul Getty Mus. Jour., 1986—. Mem. adv. coun. Nat. Heritage Village, Kioni, Greece; mem. trade with eastern Europe com. Assn. Am. Pubs., N.Y., 1976-79, internat. fairs com., 1986-88. Mem. Internat. Assn. Mus. Publs. (Frankfurt, Fed. Republic Germany, chmn. 1992-95), U.S. Mus. Publ. Group (chmn. 1989—), Internat. Pubs. Assn., Hellenic Soc. (London), Oxford & Cambridge Club (London), Internat. Assn. Scholarly Pubs. (sec.-gen. 1994-97, chmn. internat. contracts com.). Avocation: rural preservation projects in England, Greece and California. Office: J Paul Getty Mus 1200 Getty Ctr Dr Ste 1000 Los Angeles CA 90049-1687

HUDSON, DARRIL, political scientist, educator; b. Trousdale, Okla., Dec. 18, 1931; s. Frank Wilks Hudson and Emma Lee (Jackson) Van Meter. BA, U. Calif., Berkeley, 1954; MSc in Internat. Rels., London Sch. Econs & Polit. Sci., 1960, PhD, 1965. Lectr. U. Md. Overseas Program, 1959-67; assoc. prof. Md. State Coll., Princess Anne, Md., 1967-68; prof. Calif. State U. Hayward, 1968-93, prof. emeritus, 1993—; vis. prof. Am. U., Paris, 1992-93; resident dir. German program Calif. State U., Heidelberg, Fed. Republic Germany, 1990-91; Fulbright prof. U. Heidelberg, 1981-82. Author: A Visitor's Guide to American Home Cooking, 1994, The World Council of Churches in International Affairs, 1978, The Ecumenical Movement in World Affairs, 1968. Vis. prof. Intelligence Svc., U.S. Army, 1955-58. Rsch. fellow Alexander von Humboldt Found., Bonn, Heidelberg, Fed. Republic Germany, 1966-67, 75, 89; recipient H.C. Richards prize Gray's Inn, London 1965. Mem. Mus. Soc. San Francisco. Democrat. Avocations:

cooking, writing, travelling. Home: 443 Fair Oaks St San Francisco CA 94110-3618

HUDSON, DAVID M., minister; b. Charleston, W.Va., Sept. 24, 1948; s. Charles R. and Margaret M. (Coleman) H.; m. Brenda J. Roach, Sept. 22, 1967; children: Nathaniel, Derek. Student, W.Va. State Coll., 1966, Apostolic Bible Inst., 1966-67, Tex. Bible Coll., 1968; DTh (hon.), Ind. Bible Coll., 1988. Ordained minister United Pentecostal Ch., 1973. Youth pres. United Pentecostal Ch., Indpls., 1980-85; sr. pastor Riverside Apostoic Ch., 1985—; exec. presbyter United Pentecostal Ch., St. Louis, 1994-96, harvestime radio commr., 1990—, gen. bd. presbyters, 1994-96; adj. prof. Ind. Bible Coll., Indpls., 1995—; bd. govs. Apostolic Coalition, Washington, 1987-91; mem. adv. bd. Passion-Fire Internat., 1998—; sec. treas. W.Va. dist. United Pentecostal Ch., Charleston, 1994—; internat. spkr. in field. Editor Apostolic Voice, 1987-89. Bd. dirs. Citizens Concerned for Cmty. Values, Morgantown, W.Va., 1990—; co-chmn. Israel prayer breakfast Religious Roundtable, Memphis, 1991. Named Nat. Pres. of Yr. United Pentecostal Ch., 1984, Internat. Pres. of Yr., 1985. Avocations: travel, reading, fitness. Home: PO Box 2069 Morgantown WV 26502-2069

HUDSON, DENNIS LEE, lawyer, retired government official, arbitrator, educator; b. St. Louis, Jan. 5, 1936; s. Lewis Jefferson and Helen Mabel (Buchanan) H.; children: Karen Marie, Karla Sue, Mary Ashley. BA, U. Ill., 1958; JD, John Marshall Law Sch., 1972. Bar: Ill. 1972, U.S. Dist. Ct. (so. and no. dists.) Ill. 1972. Ins. IRS, Chgo., 1962-72; spl. agt. GSA, Chgo., 1972-78, spl. agt.-in-charge, 1978-83, reginal insp. gen., 1983-87; supervisory spl. agt. Dept. Justice-GSA Task Force, Washington, 1978; arbitrator Circuit Ct. Cook County, Ill., 1989-94; prof. criminal justice Coll. of DuPage, Glen Ellyn, Ill., 1991—. Bd. govs. Theatre Western Springs, Ill., 1978-81, 91-92; deacon Grace Luth. Ch., LaGrange, Ill., 1977-81; lay eucharistic min. All Sts. Episcopal Ch., Western Springs, Ill., 1999—. With U.S. Army, 1959-61. John N. Jewett scholar, 1972. Mem. ABA, Ill. Bar Assn. Home: 109 51st Pl Western Springs IL 60558-2002 Office: Coll Dupage Bus & Svcs Div 22D St Lambert Rd Glen Ellyn IL 60137

HUDSON, DONALD J., retired stock exchange executive; b. Vancouver, B.C., Can., Sept. 26, 1930. BA in Econs. and Math., U. B.C., 1952; LLD (hon.), Simon Fraser U., 1993. With Shell Oil Co. of Can. Ltd., 1952-53; dir. sales devel. Can. Pacific Airlines, Vancouver, 1953-64; sr. v.p. Pacific div. T. Eaton Co., Ltd., Vancouver, 1964-81; pres. Vancouver Stock Exch., 1982-95; bd. dirs. Brit. Pacific Properties Ltd., Norwich Union Life Ins. (Can. bd.). Bd. dirs. Infowest Svcs., Inc., Internat. Fin. Ctr., Vancouver, Vancouver Bot. Garden Assn. Mem. Vancouver Lawn Tennis Club, Vancouver Club.

HUDSON, EDWARD VOYLE, linen supply company executive; b. Seymour, Mo., Apr. 3, 1915; s. Marion A. and Alma (Von Gonten) H.; m. Margaret Carolyn Greely, Dec. 24, 1939; children: Edward G., Carolyn K. Student, Bellingham Normal Coll., 1933-36, U. Wash., 1938. Asst. to mgr. Natural Hard Metal Co., Bellingham, 1935-37; ptnr. Met. Laundry Co., Tacoma, 1938-39; propr., mgr. Peerless Laundry & Linen Supply Co., Tacoma, 1939—; propr. Ind. Laundry & Everett Linden Supply Co., 1946-74, 99 Cleaners and Launderers Co., Tacoma, 1957-59; chmn. Tacoma Pub. Utilities, 1959-60; trustee United Mut. Savs. Bank; bd. dirs. Tacoma Better Bus. Bur., 1977—. Pres. Wash. Conf. on Unemployment Compensation, 1975-76; pres. Tacoma Boys' Club, 1970; v.p. Puget Sound USO, 1972-91; elder Emmanuel Presbyn. Ch., 1974—; past campaign mgr., pres. Tacoma-Pierce County United Good Neighbors. Recipient Disting. Citizen's cert. USAF Mil. Airlift Com., 1977; U.S. Dept. Def. medal for outstanding pub. svc., 1978. Mem. Tacoma Sales and Mktg. Execs. (pres. 1957-58), Pacific NW Laundry, Dry Clearning and Linen Supply Assn. (pres. 1959, treas. 1965-75), Internat. Fabricare Inst. (dir. dist. 7, treas. 1979, pres. 1982), Am. Security Coun. Bd., Tacoma C. of C. (pres. 1965), Air Force Assn. (pres. Tacoma chpt. 1976-77, v.p. Wash. state 1983-84, pres. 1985-86), Navy League, Puget Sound Indsl. Devel. Coun. (chmn. 1967), Tacoma-Ft. Lewis Olympia Army Assn. (past pres.), Elks Club (vice chmn. bd. trustees 1984, chmn. 1985-86), Shriners (potentate 1979), Masons, Scottish Rite, Tacoma Club, Tacoma Country and Golf Club, Jesters Club, Rotary (pres. Tacoma chpt. 1967-68), Tacoma Knife and Fork Club (pres. 1964). Republican. Home: 3901 N 37th St Tacoma WA 98407-5636 Office: Peerless Laundry & Linen Supply Co 2902 S 12th St Tacoma WA 98405-2598

HUDSON, ELIOT R., lawyer; b. Oakland, Calif., Apr. 22, 1950; s. Harter Glen and Alice Eliot Hudson; m. Susan K., Apr. 15, 1978 (div. 1998); 1 child, Christopher. BA in Econs., Polit. Sci., U. Calif., Davis, 1982; JD, U. Calif., San Francisco, 1985. Assoc. Dullicy, Casey, Schaeferh & Ceccotti, San Rafael, Calif., 1975-96, Kincaid, Gianunzio, Caudle & Hubert, Oakland, Calif., 1977-82; ptnr. McNamara, Houston, Dodge, McClura & Ney, Walnut Creek, Calif., 1996-97; atty. sr. litig. coun. law divsn. Aon Corp., San Francisco, 1997—. asst. cubmaster, cubmaster, asst. scoutmaster, cub com. chmn., troop com. chmn. Boy Scouts Am. Mt. Diablo Silverado Coun., 1987—; dir. Buckelew Ho., San Anselmo, Calif., 1975-77. Republican. Presbyterian. Home: 1 Owl Hill Ct Orinda CA 94563-3441 Office: Aon Law Divsn 1900 Spear St Tower One Market San Francisco CA 94105

HUDSON, GEOFFREY JOHN, retired nutritionist, researcher; b. Cambridge, Eng., Apr. 22, 1945; s. John Harold and Edith Hannah (Humm) H.; m. Christine Anne Huckle, Sept. 14, 1968; children: Nathan John Oliver, Robin Nicholas John. PhD, Coun. for Nat. Acad. Awards, 1992. Higher sci. officer Dunn Clin. Nutrition Ctr., Med. Rsch. Coun., Cambridge, 1974-99; freelance tech. editor, 1972—. Contbr. over 50 articles to sci. jours., including Jour. Sci. and Agr., Plant Foods for Man, Jour. Human Nutrition, Food Chemistry, Ecology, Food and Nutrition, Nutrition Reports Internat., Archives Disease in Childhood, Carbohydrate Rsch., Jour. Dairy Rsch., Vet. Record, Annals Nutrition and Metabolism, Growth Devel. and Aging, Nutrition Rsch., Cancer Epidemiology, Biomarkers and Prevention, Carcinogenesis, Analyst, Natural Toxins, European Jour. Gastroenterology and Hepatology, Brit. Jour. Nutrition, Internat. Congress Nutrition. Avocations: reading, writing, gardening, travel, table tennis.

HUDSON, IRENE LENA, mathematics educator; b. Littleborough, Eng., Mar. 13, 1953; arrived in Australia, 1958; d. Vladimir and Vera (Kuhalskyte) Romanov; m. Peter John Hudson (div.); 1 child, Sean Andrew. BS with honors, Adelaide U., South Australia, 1975; MS, Australian Nat. U., Canberra, 1978; Diploma in Maths. and Statistics, Cambridge U., Eng., 1979; PhD, LaTrobe U., Melbourne, Victoria, Australia, 1982. Statistical cons. divsn. animal behavior Med. Rsch. Coun. Cambridge U., 1977-79; tutor statistics sept. Monash U., Melbourne, Australia, 1982-83; head biostatistics unit Royal Children's Hosp., Melbourne, 1983-89; sr. cons. Statistical Cons. Ctr. U. Melbourne, 1989-93, rsch. fellow, sub program 1.2 leader Sch. Forestry, 1993-97; sr. lectr. dept. maths. and statistics Canterbury U., Christchurch, New Zealand, 1997—; head Rsch. Ctr. Health Techs. Canterbury U., Christchurch, 1998—, cons., mem. Soils Rsch. Ctr. Sch. Forestry, 1999; treas. Innovative Health Consortium Canterbury U. and Auckland (New Zealand) U., 1999; grants reviewer Nat. Health and Med. Rsch. Coun., 1987-97. Author: Sampling Plantation Eucalypts for Wood, 1997; co-author: Choloramphenicol Study, 1988-89. Grantee Nat. Health and Med. Rsch. Coun. Mem. Australian and New Zealand Statistical Assn., Australian Pulp and Paper Inst. (scientific and tech. assoc. 1994-99), Biometrics Soc., Women in Sci. Avocations: music, reading, writing, cinema, photography. Office: U Canterbury Dept Maths & Statistics, Pvt Bag 4800, Christchurch 1 Canterbury, New Zealand

HUDSON, LAURA LYN WHITAKER, research scientist, science administrator; b. Reno, May 24, 1960; d. Ernest Leo and Carol Suzanne (Kettering) Whitaker; m. Bradley Joe Hudson, Nov. 29, 1996; children from previous marriage: Jackie Kalinowski, Justin Stender, Jason Stender. AA, Scottsdale Community Coll., 1982; HPhD, London Inst. Applied Rsch., 1994. Habilitation technician Gompers's Rehab. Ctr. and Ariz. Tng. Program, Phoenix, 1979-82; sec., bookkeeper CEW Sound Recordings, Phoenix, 1979-82; sec. Electronic Test Ctr., Groton, Mass., 1984; exec. v.p., dir. sci. rsch., devel. and investment Children United to Save the Planet, Phoenix, 1991-94; exec. v.p. Arachne's Web, Phoenix, 1994—. Mem. Mentally Ill Kids In Distress, Phoenix, 1990, Lithium Alliance, Phoenix, 1992, Nat. Alliance for Mentally Ill, Phoenix, 1992, Smithsonian Inst., 1992. Named Internat. Woman of Yr., Internat. Biog. Ctr., England, 1991-92, Woman of Yr., Am. Biog. Inst., 1992; recipient Silver Shield of Honor, 1992. Mem. NAFE (assoc.), World Found. Successful Women (assoc.), Women's Inner Circle of Achievement, Lifetime Achievement Acad., Am. Biog. Inst. Rsch. Assn. (assoc. and advisor). Avocations: writing on uses and limitations of herbal medicines, animal dissection, North Am. Indian art and craft work. Home: PO Box 30931 Phoenix AZ 85046-0931

HUDSON, MARTIN FREDERIC, aviation medicine consultant; b. Boston, Eng., Nov. 10, 1941; s. Frederic Cecil Willis and Eleanor Dorothea (Loughton) H.; m. Susan Mary Garnett, July 4, 1964; children: Paul Martin, Philip John. MB BS, St. Bartholomew's Hosp., London, 1965. Med. specialist Royal Air Force, 1965-71; gen. practice Holmes Chapel, U.K., 1972-99; med. examiner Civil Aviation Authority, U.K., 1977—, FAA, 1997. Fellow Royal Coll. Physicians Edinburgh (Scotland). Avocations: music, golf, singing, travel, walking. E-Mail: martin-hudson@lineone.net. Home: 7 Swanwick Close Goostrey, Cheshire Holmes Chapel CW4 8NU, United Kingdom Office: Grasmere Med Svcs, 7 Swanwick Close, Goostrey Cheshire CW4 8XU, United Kingdom

HUDSON, MICHAEL JAMES, science educator; b. Weybridge, Surrey, England, Apr. 10, 1940; s. James Rowald and Gladys Ellen Emily (Johnson) H.; m. Cerris Eirwen Fishwick, Apr. 20, 1968; children: Giles Matthew, Clarie Racheol. BS in Chemistry with honors, U. Hull, 1962; PhD in Chemistry, U. Coll., London, 1966; cert. edn., Inst. Edn., London, 1966. Schoolmaster St. Paul's Sch., Barnes, England, 1966-71; lectr. U. Reading., England, 1971—; coord. Rschrs. Network of the European Union, 1997—; indep. advisor, England, 1998—; advisor cost program European Union, 1998—; advisor INTAS, Belgium, 1998—. Author: (textbook) Structure and Metals, 1973; contbr. articles to profl. jours. Recipient Studies on Ion Exchg. gold medal Japanese Sci. Soc., 1991. Mem. Royal Soc. Chemistry. Avocations: Dinghy sailing. E-mail: m.j.hudson@reading.ac.uk. Office: Reading U Chemistry Dept, PO Box 224 Whiteknights, Reading RG6 2AD, England

HUDSON, NOEL, artist; b. San Francisco, Dec. 27, 1943; d. Robert Denfeld and Isobel Franklin (Shaw) H.; m. Thomas Donald Reidy, Feb. 20, 1977. BA in Art, Scripps Coll., 1965; MA in Art, Claremont Grad. U., 1972. Instr. in art, ceramics Calif. H.S., Whittier, 1967-70; instr. in art Tachikawa Mid. Sch., Tachikawa AFB, Japan, 1970-73; instr. in painting and drawing Riverside (Calif.) City Coll., 1974; instr. in ceramics, off-loom fiber Redondo Beach (Calif.) H.S., 1974-80; instr. in painting, drawing, design N.Mex. Highlands U., Taos, 1981-83; instr. in drawing No. N.Mex. C.C., Taos, 1991-92; instr. in painting, color, theory U. N.Mex., Albuquerque, 1992-93; instr. in painting, drawing, design and art history Santa Fe C.C., N.Mex., 1993—; mem. various coll. coms. Santa Fe C.C.; coord. art tour Taos Art Assn., 1983-84; art cons. Taos Elem. Schs., 1983. One-woman shows include: Sumner & Dene Creations in Art, San Diego, 1998, Expressions in Fine Art Gallery, Santa Fe, 1997, Greg Flores Furniture Gallery, Taos, 1994, Southwest Passage Gallery, San Juan Capistrano, Calif., 1991, Montoya y Montoya Gallery, Denver, 1989, Wichita Art Mus., 1986, The Albuquerque Mus., 1995, 96, 97, 98, 99, 2000; collections include The Harwood Mus. Contemporary Collection, Taos, 1992, Santa Fe C.C., 1994. Democrat. Avocations: spiritual investigation, travel, hiking, reading. Home: 59 Balsa Rd Santa Fe NM 87505-8259 Office: Santa Fe CC 6401 Richards Ave Santa Fe NM 87505-4887

HUDSON, RAY, geography educator; b. Alnwick, Eng., Mar. 7, 1948; s. John and Jean (MacFarlane) H.; m. Geraldine Holder Jones, Aug. 2, 1975; children: Matthew, Anna. BA, Bristol (Eng.) U., 1969, PhD, 1974, DSc, 1996. Lectr. Durham (Eng.) U., 1972-84, sr. lectr., 1984-87, reader in geog., 1987-90, prof. geog., 1990—, dir. Ctr. for European Studies in Territorial Devel., 1990-99, dir. Nat. Online Manpower Info. Sys., 1987—, chair internat. ctr. regional regeneration & devel. studies, 1999—; Editor: Divided Europe: Society and Territory, 1999; author: Wrecking a Region, 1989. Author: Wrecking a Region, 1989, Digging Up Trouble: The Environment Protest and Opencast Coal Mining, 2000, Production, Places and Environment: Changing Perspectives in Economic Geography, 2000, Coalfields Regeneration: Dealing with the Consequences of Industrial Decline, 2000; editor: Divided Europe: Society and Territory, 1999; editor European Urban and Regional Studies, 1995—. Mem. Royal Geog. Soc. (v.p. 1999—, Edward Heath award 1989), Regional Studies Assn. Avocations: walking, reading, food and drink, travel. Office: U Durham, South Rd, Durham DH1 3LE, England

HUDSON, RICHARD L., retired educator, clergyman; b. Watertown, N.Y., Dec. 1, 1920; s. Milo Alfred and Marion (Davidson) H.; m. Beatrice Evalin Olson, Apr. 23, 1955; children: Margery Elise, Pamela Kristine. AB, Syracuse U., 1944, PhD, 1970; BD, Yale U., 1947, STM, 1950. Ordained to ministry United Meth. Ch., 1947;. Asst. minister Rome (N.Y.) Meth. Ch., 1946-48, Meth. Ch., Parish, N.Y., 1950-54; commentator Religion Makes News, Sta. WSYR, Syracuse, N.Y.; dir. pub. rels. Syracuse Area United Meth. Ch., 1954-56; minister Meth. Ch., Carthage, N.Y., 1956-58; Cokesbury fellow, grad. asst. Syracuse U., 1958-61; mem. faculty Wyoming Sem., Kingston, Pa., 1961-64; mem. faculty New Eng. Coll., Henniker, N.H., 1964-83, prof., 1971-83, prof. emeritus, 1983—, dean humanities, 1970-71; adj. prof. history Post Coll., Waterbury, Conn., 1985-91, Quinnipiac Coll., Hamden, Conn., 1987-97. Author: A Burden for Souls, 1950, A Student's Guide to the New Testament, 1963, The Challenge of Dissent, 1970; editor: The Only Henniker on Earth, 1980. Chmn. Henniker Hist. Soc., 1976-83; docent Canterbury Shaker Village, 1975-83, New Haven Colony Hist. Soc., 1984-93, bd. dirs. 1988-90. Mem. North Haven Mayflower Soc. (hon. mem.), Theta Chi Beta, Tau Theta Upsilon, Tabard. Home and Office: 44 Cloudland Rd North Haven CT 06473-4006

HUDSON, RICHARD MCLAIN, JR., journalist, researcher; b. L.A., June 18, 1925; s. Richard McLain Hudson and Helen Theodora Grant; m. Helen Aurora Lundstrom, Dec. 6, 1958; children: Lucinda, Anne. BS, U. Minn., 1946. Teaching asst. econs. U. So. Calif., L.A., 1946-47; editor Monrovia (Calif.) Daily News-Post, 1948-50, Pasadena (Calif.) Star-News, 1950-52, Stars & Stripes, Darmstadt, Germany, 1953-54, Picture News, N.Y.C., 1955-57; mng. editor Caracas (Venezuela) Daily Jour., 1958-60; founding editor War/Peace Report, N.Y.C., 1960-77, Global Report, N.Y.C., 1977—; exec. dir. Ctr. for War/Peace Studies, N.Y.C., 1960—; host weekly TV series Global Forum, Peace Through the UN, 1986-87; prin. arch. Binding Triad Sys. Global Decision-Making. Author: (with Ben Shahn) Kuboyama and the Saga of the Lucky Dragon, 1965. Mem. Dem. County Com., N.Y., 1980-92. Ensign, USN, 1944-46. Mem. UN Corrs. Assn., World Federalist Assn. (bd. dirs. 1980—). Avocations: fishing, photography, tennis, biking. E-mail: hudson@cwps.org. Home: 150 W 80th St New York NY 10024-6310 Office: Ctr for War/Peace Studies 180 W 80th St # 211 New York NY 10024-6301

HUDSON, STANTON HAROLD, JR., public relations executive, educator; b. Syracuse, N.Y., Jan. 28, 1951; s. Stanton Harold Sr. and Lucille (Shea) H. Cert. lang. and history, L'Univ. de Caen, France, 1970; BA in History/Polit. Sci., Canisius Coll., 1972; postgrad., SUNY Sch. of Law, Buffalo, 1974-76, Syracuse U., 1995-98. Legis. asst., asst. pub. rels. dir. Erie County Rep. Com., Buffalo, 1971-73; dir. pub. rels. and fin. Greater Niagara Frontier Coun. Boy Scouts Am., Buffalo, 1977-79; dir. pub. rels. Ellis Singer & Webb Advt., Buffalo, 1979-80; asst. v.p., mgr. mktg. communications M&T Bank, Buffalo, 1980-85; exec. dir. Shea's Ctr. for the Performing Arts, Buffalo, 1986; pres. Hudson Mktg. Communications, Buffalo, 1987-88; sr. dir. advt. and pub. rels. Blue Cross of Western N.Y., Inc., Buffalo, 1988-91; prin. Fredrickson & Hudson Assocs., Buffalo, 1991-92, Hudson & Assocs. Pub. Rels., Inc., Buffalo, 1992—; adj. prof. SUNY, Buffalo, 1987-93; asst. prof. Canisius Coll., 1993—, dir. grad. program Comm. & Orgnl. Devel., 1995—. Editor employee newsletter M&T Bank Observer, 1981, 82 (Project PICA Grand award United Way of Buffalo and Erie County); mng. editor employee newsletter Blue Cross Ink, 1991 (Excalibur award Pub. Rels. Soc. Am. 1990, 91, 94, 95, 97). Bd. mem. and mem. mktg. com. Am. Lung Assn., Western N.Y., Buffalo, 1983—; chmn. Erie/Niagara Tobacco Free Coalition, 1999—; bd. dirs. Am. Lung Assn., N.Y. State, Albany, 1987—, exec. com. 1992—, v.p., 1995, 96-97, pres., 1998—, chmn. ann. meeting com., 1994, chair N.Y. state coalition on smoking and health, 1995, Am. Lung Assn. Nat., 1995-96, vice chair mktg. and comms. com., 1999-2000, mktg. and comms. task force, 2000—, tobacco control steering com., task force on mktg., 1996-99, mem. revenue generation com., 1998-99, nat. customer svc. team mem., 1998-99, mem. nat. coun., 1999—, nat. bd., 2000—, mem. mgmt. oversight audit com., 1999—; chmn. pub. rels. and mktg. coms. Greater Buffalo chpt. ARC, 1989-92, bd. dirs., 1991-92; bd. dirs. ARC Blood Svcs., N.Y.-Pa. Region, 1993—; bd. dirs., exec. com. Greater Buffalo Opera Co., 1991-93; trustee, mem. mktg. com. Theodore Roosevelt Inaugural Nat. Hist. Site Found., 1994—, co-chair 2001 centennial celebration com.; bd. dirs. Buffalo Coun. on World Affairs, 1994-98, co-chair mktg. com., 1994-99; mem. Success By 6 awareness com. Buffalo and Erie County United Way, 1997—, mem. Leadership Coun., 1998—; mem. Erie County Cultural Resources Adv. Bd., Erie County, 1999—, exec. com. 2000—; bd. dirs. East Hill Found., 2000—. Recipient Francis V. Hanavan Meml. award for volunteer svc. Am. Lung Assn. We. N.Y., 1997, Gold Quill award Internat. Assn. of Bus. Communicators, 1984. Mem. Pub. Rels. Soc. Am. (accredited pub. rels. practitioner, counselors acad. educators sect., pres. Buffalo/Niagara chpt. 1990-91, treas. 1994-96, nat. assembly del. 1997—, treas. N.E. dist. 1992, chair-elect N.E. dist. 1993, chair 1994, nat. continuing edn. bd., 1993-95, nat. nominating com. 1995, nat. profl. advisor Pub. Rels. Student Soc. Am. 1996-2000, nat. women in pub. rels. com. 1996-98, nat. commn. pub. rels. edn. 1997-99, Practitioner of the Yr. Buffalo/Niagara chpt. 1993, Excalibur award 1993, 94, 95, 97, universal accreditation bd. 1998—, Nat. Paul M. Lund Pub. Svc. award 1997, Nat. Conf. for Cmty. and Justice Brotherhood/Sisterhood award 1999), Am. Mktg. Assn. (v.p. comms. Buffalo/Niagara chpt. 1991-92), Western N.Y. Comms. Steering Com. (chair 1991-92), Coordinated Care Mgmt. Corp. (mktg. com. 1994-98), Rotary (past dir.). Avocations: theater, jazz, reading, cross-country skiing, travel.

HUDSON, WILLIAM JEFFREY, JR., manufacturing company executive; b. Ill., May 20, 1934; s. William J. Sr. and Olga Georgevna (de Tarnowsky) H.; m. Margaret Royal, June 11, 1957; children: William J. III, Scott D., Robert C. BS in Elec. Engring., Cornell U., 1957, M. Cert. Elec. Engring., 1957; postgrad., Drexel U., 1959-61. With AMP Inc., Harrisburg, Pa., 1961—, market rschr., 1961-65, mgr. product planning Syscom, 1965, product mgr. Selective Signal, 1965-67, new product mgr. Capitron, 1967-73, new product mgr. Electron Devices Divsn., 1973-76, mgr. Devel. Engring. Circuit Components Divsn., 1976-77, mgr. Signal Components Divsn., 1977-81, group dir. connector and electronic products group, 1981-82, divisional v.p. connector and electronic products group, 1982-83; divisional v.p. Far East ops. AMP Inc., Tokyo, 1983-89, corp. v.p. Asia/Pacific, 1989-91; exec. v.p. internat. AMP Inc., Harrisburg, 1991-92, pres., CEO, 1993-98, vice chmn., 1998—, also bd. dirs.; bd. dirs. Goodyear Tire and Rubber Co., Keithley Instruments, Inc.; bd. dirs. carpenter Tech. Corp., Cornell U. Coun. Engring. Adv. Coun. Contbr. articles to profl. jours.; 12 patents in field. Bd. dirs. Pinnacle Health Found., 1994—; mem. bd. advisors Hershey Med. Ctr., 1994—; chmn. Pa. Export Trade Com., 1995-96; bd. dirs., exec. com. Team Pa., 1995—, work force investment bd. mem., chmn. employment stats. com., 1999—; mem. Pa. Human Resource Investment Coun., 1996—, chmn., 1996-99. Lt. (j.g.) USN, 1957-61. Mem. Nat. Elec. Mfrs. Assn. (exec. com., bd. govs. 1994-99), Nat. Assn. Mfrs. (exec. com., bd. dirs. 1993-98, vice chmn. 1997-98), Elec. Mfrs. Club (bd. dirs. 1993-98), Bus. Roundtable, U.S. Coun. Internat. Bus. (exec. com., chmn. Pa. Export Trade Coun., 1995-96, Team Pa. Human Resource Investment Coun., 1996-99, others). Office: AMP Inc 470 Friendship Rd Harrisburg PA 17111-1203

HUDSON, WILLIAM JOHN, chartered electrical engineering consultant; b. Carlisle, Cumbria, Eng., Feb. 21, 1964; s. Raymond Bracken and Mary Thoburn (Laidlow) H.; m. Michele Maria Ansell, Aug. 30, 1986; children: Victoria Elizabeth, Lavinia Alexandra. BSEE with honors, Staffordshire (Eng.) U., 1982-86, MS in Computing Sci., 1989; MBA, Nottingham Trent U., Eng., 1995; MPhil, Nottingham Trent U., 1997. Chartered elec. engr. Projects engr. TI Stainless Tubes, Ltd., Derbyshire, Eng., 1986-87; cons. Staffordshire, 1989—; engring. mgr. Sterling Tubes Ltd., Walsall, England, 1997-99; mng. dir. Sandvik Choksi Ltd., Village Rajpur, India, 1999—. Mem. Inst. Elec. Engrs.

HUE, JEAN BERNARD, physicist; b. Villedieu-Les-Poëles, France, Dec. 26, 1963; s. Bernard Martial and Andree Annette (Lecoulant) H. Lic. in electronics, U. Rennes, France, 1985, M Physics, 1987; diploma in engring., Materials, Physics, INPG, Grenoble, France, 1990; PhD, U. Grenoble, 1993. R&D physicist in laser damage field Laserdot, Nozay, France, 1990-93; R&D physicist CEA, Grenoble, 1993-96; NIF, LMJ physicist CEA, Livermore, Calif., 1996-98; R&D physicist laser damage field and optical thin films CEA, Grenoble, France, 1998—; involved in EUV photolithography. Contbr. articles to profl. jours. Roman Catholic. Avocations: tennis, bridge, stamps. Home: 49B rue de Aiguinards, 38240 Meylan France Office: CEA-G/LETI/DOPT/SCMDO, 17 Ave des Martyrs, 38054 Grenoble Cedex 09, France

HUEBNER, ULRICH, theologian; b. Neunkirchen, Germany, Apr. 16, 1952; s. Karl-Hermann and Linde (Pickel) H.; m. Renate Hinderling, June 30, 1978. DTheol, U. Heidelberg, 1991. Asst. U. Mainz, Germany, 1979-84; vicar Protestant Ch., Bad Kreuznach, Germany, 1984-86; asst. U. Heidelberg, Germany, 1986-94; prof. U. Kiel, Germany, 1994—; dir. Inst. Old Testament and Biblical Archaeology U. Kiel, 1995—; pres. Deutscher Palaestina-Verein, 1998—; co-dir. regional survey Petra, Jordan, 1997—. Author: Die Ammoniter, 1992, Spiele und Spielzeug im antiken Palaestina, 1992; contbr. articles to profl. jours. Mem. Am. Sch. Oriental Rsch., Br. Sch. Archaeology in Jerusalem. Avocation: music. Home: Jakob Steffan Str 12, D-55122 Mainz Germany Office: U Kiel Fac Theology, Leibniz str 4, D-24098 Kiel Germany

HUELSEN, ANTJE VON, media specialist, consultant; b. Hamburg, Germany, Mar. 28, 1966; d. Reinhard Franz-Daniel and Marga (Pedack) Meyns; 1 child, Henrike. Diploma in bus. adminstrn., U. Hamburg. Media planning asst. HMS CARAT, Hamburg, 1994-95, media planner, 1995-96; internat. media mgr. BBDO Media Team, Düsseldorf, Germany, 1996-97; media mgr. Media Direction, Düsseldorf, 1998—. Avocations: field hockey, tennis, skiing, family activities. Home: Roeschstrasse 13, 45470 Muelheim an der Ruhr Germany Office: Media Direction, Immermannstr 51, 40210 Düsseldorf Germany

HUENERGARDT, MYRNA LOUISE, college administrator, nurse practitioner; b. Medford, Oreg., Aug. 5, 1928; d. Henry and Matie Daisy (Vroman) H. BS, Columbia Union Coll., Takoma Park, Md., 1961; MA, Columbia U., 1963. RN, Calif.; cert. nurse practitioner. Charge nurse Glendale (Calif.) Adventist Hosp., 1954-57, 61-63; sch. nurse L.A. City Schs., 1957-60; instr. nursing Columbia Union Coll., Takoma Park, Md., 1964-68; dir. sch. nursing Branson Hosp. Sch. Nursing, Toronto, Ont., Can., 1968-71; chair paramed. dept. Southwestern C.C., Chula Vista, Calif., 1971-74; assoc. prof. nursing Loma Linda (Calif.) U., 1974-80; nurse rschr. U. So. Calif., L.A., 1981-83; nurse practitioner Community Health Projects, Covina, Calif., 1983-86; dir. student health svcs. Chaffey C.C., Rancho Cucamonga, Calif., 1986-94; med. edn. cons. Merck, Sharp & Dohme, West Point, Pa., 1991-96; nurse practitioner New Horizon Care Corp., Loma Linda, 1987-95; nurse cons., med. claims reviewer Aetna Ins., Loma Linda, 1994-97. Bd. dirs. ARC, Inland Empire, Calif., 1986-91; cons. Master Plan Com., Substance Abuse, San Bernardino County, Calif., 1990-95. Recipient Sameas award Outstanding Educators of Am., 1972, Disting. Leadership award Am. Biog. Inst., 1989; Fed. Govt. traineeship awards, 1961, 63, 64. Mem. Assn. of Calif. C.C. Adminstrs., Calif. Coalition of Nurse Practitioners, C.C. Health Svcs. Assn. of Calif. (pres. 1992-93), Sigma Theta Tau, Kappa Delta Pi. Republican. Avocations: travel, biking, gardening, concerts, singing. Home: 10636 Amapolas St Redlands CA 92373-8401

HUEPPI, ROLF, financial services executive; b. Uznach, St. Gall, Switzerland, Apr. 25, 1943; s. Lucas and Anna (Wespe) H.; children: Barbara, Claudia, Thomas, Marcus; m. Mary Margaret Young, Apr. 9, 1988. Cert., IMEDE, 1971, 76. Mgr. Zurich Ins. Co., Bombay, 1964-70; various mgmt. positions Zurich Ins. Co., 1970-84; pres., chief exec. officer Zurich Am. Ins. Co., Chgo., 1984-87; pres., chief operating officer Zurich Ins. Group, 1988-91, pres., chief exec. officer, 1991—, chmn., CEO, 1995—; chmn., CEO Zurich Fin. Svcs., 1998—; bd. dirs. numerous cos. Avocations: sailing, skiing, tennis.

HUET, PATRICK L., sports educator; b. Reims, France, July 6, 1946; s. Georges P. and Simone (Hubin) H.; m. Mary-Ellen Aron; 1 child, Veronique. PhD, U. Paris Sorbonne, 1971. Asst. producer French TV Sta. ORTF, Paris, 1964-68; asst. prof. U. Paris Sorbonne, 1968-73; prof. U. Paris, 1973—.

Author films about maths. and games. Mem. Soc. Math. de France, Soaring Club Cherence. Avocations: soaring and gliding, aircraft, flight instruction. Home: 60 Rue Baudricourt, 75013 Paris France Office: U Paris, 2 Place Jussieu, 75251 Paris France

HUETING, ROEFIE, environmental economomist, consultant, researcher; b. The Hague, The Netherlands, Dec. 16, 1929; s. Bernardus and Elisabeth (Steinvoorte) H.; m. Erna Jans Postuma, June 7, 1957; children: Tanja, Narda. Doctorandus, U. Amsterdam, The Netherlands, 1959; PhD, U. Groningen, The Netherlands, 1974. Pub. acct. Bureau, Hueting and Snethlage, The Hague, The Netherlands, 1959-62; labor mkt. rschr. Ministry Social Affairs, The Hague, 1962-65, Ministry Housing and Phys. Planning, The Hague, 1965-68; head dept. environ. stats. Statistics Netherlands, Voorburg, 1969-94, adviser, 1995—; cons., lectr. on environ. and econ. issues internationally, also nationwide to govts., industries and interested orgns.; pianist, leader Downtown Jazz Band, 1949—. Author: (books) What Is Nature Worth to Us?, 1970 (in Dutch), New Scarcity and Economic Growth, 1980, Methodology for the Calculation of Sustainable National Income, 1992; (ecological modelling), An Economic Scenario that Gives Top Priority to Saving the Environment, 1987. Decorated officer Orde van Oranje Nassau (The Netherlands); recipient Global 500 award UN, 1994. Avocations: music, lit. skating, running. Home: Roelofsstraat 6, 2596VN The Hague The Netherlands Office: Stats Netherlands, Prinses Beatrixlaan 428, 2273XZ Voorburg The Netherlands

HUETTER, BERND OTTO, neuropsychologist, researcher; b. Oberhausen, Rheinland, Germany, Feb. 15, 1960; s. Karl Otto and Dinelore (Birken) H.; m. Ursula Maria Lang, Nov. 13, 1993. Diploma in psychology, Ruhr U., Bochum, Germany, 1987; PhD, U. Freiburg, Germany, 1993. Rschr. dept. neurosurgery U. Freiburg, 1988-90, instr. dept. med. psychology, 1989-91; cons. neuropsychologist dept. neurosurgery U. Aachen, Germany, 1990—, sci. asst. dept. neurosurgery, 1994—, head neuropsychol. working group, 1995—. Author: Perception, Impact and Coping Processes with Invasive Procedures in Cardiology and Open Heart Surgery, 1984, Neuropsychological Sequelae of Subarachnoid Hermorrhage and its Treatment; contbr. articles to sci. jours., including Acta Neurochir, Neurosurgery, Jour. Clin. Exptl. Neuropsychology. Mem. German Soc. Med. Psychology, German Soc. Neuropsychology. Avocations: tennis, sports, gardening, arts. Office: U Aachen Neuro Clin, Pauwelstrasse 30, 52057 Aachen Germany

HUETTER, RALF, microbiologist; b. Basel, Switzerland, Sept. 15, 1931; s. Rita and Stehle, Aug. 23, 1956; children: Claudia, Ellen, Markus. Diploma in Agronomy, Swiss Fed. Inst. of Technology, Zurich, 1955, PhD, 1958, Privatdozent, 1964. Scientific collaborator Swiss Fed. Inst. of Technology, 1958-64, asst. prof., 1967-69, prof., 1969-88, v.p., 1988-96; postdoctoral fellow U. Calif. San Diego, La Jolla, 1965-66; cons. Ciba Corp., Basel, 1967-88. Contbr. articles to profl. jours. 1st lt. Inf., Swiss Army. Mem. Swiss Soc. Microbiology Switzerland (pres. 1995-98), Internat. Com. on Genetics of Indsl. Microorganisms (pres. 1986-94), Swiss Nat. Sci. Found. (pres.), Swiss Acad. Tech. Scis., Swiss Fed. Office for Intellectual Property (bd. dirs. 1995—), Technopark Zurich (bd. dirs. 1992-98), Hasler Found. Avocations: cross country skiing, jogging, mountain biking, swimming. Home: Rutistr 72, CH-8044 Gockhausen Switzerland

HUETTL, REINHARD F., ecologist; b. Regensburg, Germany, Jan. 1, 1957; s. Roman and Gertraud (Burkhard) H.; m. Beate R. Vogt, Apr. 28, 1989. MS, Albert Ludwigs U., 1983, PhD, 1986. Rsch. asst. Albert Ludwigs U., Freiburg, Germany, 1984-85; dept. head Kali & Salz AG/BASF, Kassel, Germany, 1986-90; asst. prof. U. Hawaii, Honolulu, 1990-91; inst. dir. Ctr. Agrl. Landscape and Land Use Rsch., Eberswalde, Germany, 1991-95; prof. Brandenburg Tech. U., Cottsus, Germany, 1993—, dir. Ctr. Post-mining Landscapes, 2000—; cons. World Resources Inst., Washington, 1987; working party chmn. Internat. Union Forest Rsch. Orgns., Vienna, Austria, 1987—; dir. Ctr. Excellence German Nat. Sci. Found., Cottbus, 1994—; vice-rector Brandenburg Tech. U., 1994-2000, German Sci. Coun., 2000—. Editor: Forest Decline in the Atlantic and Pacific Region, 1991, Nutrient Uptake and Cycling in Forest Ecosystems, 1994; co-editor: Management of Nutrition in Forests Under Stress, 1990; assoc. editor Water, Air and Soil Pollution, 1993-98. Mem. AAAS, Interntat. Soil Sci. Soc., Rotary, Berlin-Brandenburg Acad. of Scis. Roman Catholic. Avocations: jogging, skiing, beach walking, traveling, teaching. Office: Brandenburg Tech U, PO Box 101344, 03013 Cottbus Germany

HUETTNER, RICHARD ALFRED, lawyer; b. N.Y.C., Mar. 25, 1927; s. Alfred F. and Mary (Reilly) H.; children—Jennifer Mary, Barbara Bryan; m. 2d, Eunice Bizzell Dowd, Aug. 22, 1971. Marine Engrs. License, N.Y. State Maritime Acad., 1947; B.S., Yale U. Sch. Engring., 1949; J.D., U. Pa., 1952. Bar: D.C. 1952, N.Y. 1954, U.S. Ct. Mil. Appeals 1953, U.S. Ct. Claims 1961, U.S. Supreme Ct. 1969, U.S. Ct. Appeals (fed. cir.) 1982, also other fed. cts, registered to practice U.S. Patent and Trademark Office 1957, Canadian Patent Office 1968. Engr. Jones & Laughlin Steel Corp., 1954-55; assoc. atty. firm Kenyon & Kenyon, N.Y.C, 1955-61; mem. firm Kenyon & Kenyon, 1961-96, of counsel, 1996-98; specialist patent, trademark and copyright law. Trustee N.J. Shakespeare Festival, 1972-79, sec., 1977-79; trustee Overlook Hosp., Summit, N.J., 1978-84, 86-89, vice chmn. bd. trustees, 1980-82, chmn. bd. trustees, 1982-84; trustee Overlook Found., 1981-89, chmn. bd. trustees, 1986-89, emeritus trustee, 1991; trustee Colonial Symphony Orch., Madison, N.J., 1972-82, v.p. bd. trustees 1974-76. pres. 1976-79; chmn. bd. overseers N.J. Consortium for Performing Arts, 1972-74; mem. Yale U. Council, 1978-81; bd. dirs. Yale Communications Bd., 1978-80; chmn. bd. trustees Center for Addictive Illnesses, Morristown, N.J., 1979-82; rep. Assn. Yale Alumni, 1975-80, chmn. com. undergrad. admissions, 1976-78, bd. govs., 1976-80, chmn. bd. govs., 1978-80; chmn. Yale Alumni Schs. Com. N.Y., 1972-78; assoc. fellow Silliman Coll., Yale U., 1976—; bd. dirs., exec. com. Yale U. Alumni Fund, 1978-81; mem. Yale Class of 1949 Council, 1980—; bd. dirs. Overlook Health Systems, 1984—. Served from midshipman to lt. USNR, 1945-47, 52-54; cert. JAGC 1953; Res. ret. Recipient Yale medal, 1983, Disting. Svc. to Yale Class of 1949 award, 1989, Yale Sci. and Engring. Meritorious Svc. award, 1992. Fellow N.Y. Bar Found.; mem. ABA, N.Y. State Bar Assn., Assn. Bar City N.Y., N.Y. Patent Trademark Copyright Law Assn. (chmn. com. mtgs. 1961-64, chmn. com. econ. matters 1966-69, 72-74), AAAS, N.Y. Acad. Scis., N.Y. County Lawyers Assn., Am. Intellectual Property Law Assn., Internat. Patent and Trademark Assn., Am. Judicature Soc., Yale Sci. and Engring. Assn. (v.p. 1973-75, pres. 1975-78, exec. bd. 1972-79), Fed. Bar Coun. Clubs: Yale (N.Y.C.); Yale of Central N.J. (Summit) (trustee 1973-88, pres. 1975-77), Morris County Golf (Convent, N.J.); The Graduates (New Haven). Home: 150 Green Ave Madison NJ 07940-2513

HUFBAUER, GARY CLYDE, economist, lawyer, educator; b. San Diego, Apr. 3, 1939; s. Clarence Clyde and Arabelle Maxwell (McKee) H.; children: Randall Clyde Revelle (dec.), Ellen Arabelle Scripps, Romain Clyde; m. Valerie Parra, 1996. AB, Harvard U., 1960; PhD, King's Coll., Cambridge U., Eng., 1963; JD, Georgetown U., 1980. Bar: D.C. 1980, Md. 1980. Mem. faculty dept. econs. U. N.Mex., Albuquerque, 1963-74, prof., 1970-74; dir. internat. tax staff U.S. Dept. Treasury, Washington, 1974-77; dep. asst. Sec. Treasury, Internat. Trade and Investment Policy, 1977-80; mem. firm Rose, Schmidt, Chapman, Duff & Hasley, Washington, 1980-85; dep. dir. Internat. Law Inst., Georgetown Law Ctr., Washington, 1980-82; Wallenberg prof. fin. Georgetown U., Washington, 1985-92; dir. studies Coun. on Fgn. Rels., N.Y.C., 1997-98; sr. fellow Inst. Internat. Econs., Washington, 1982-85, 92-97, 98—; mem. Harvard Devel. Adv. Svc., Pakistan, 1967-69; vis. prof. Stockholm Sch. Econs., 1974, Cambridge U., 1973, Georgetown U., 1975. Author: Economic Sanctions Reconsidered, 1990, Western Hemisphere Economic Integration, 1995. Ford Found. fellow, 1966-67; Fulbright rsch. scholar, 1973. Mem. Am. Econ. Assn., Nat. Economists Club. Episcopalian. Office: Inst for Internat Econs 11 Dupont Cir NW Ste 600 Washington DC 20036-1224

HUFF, DENNIS LYLE, marketing professional; b. Chgo., Oct. 8, 1955; s. Barry Sanders Huff and Janada Jean (Patterson) Montgomery; 1 child, Alicia Jean; m. LouAnn Fae Gorder, Nov. 8, 1992. AS in Marine Tech., Coll. Oceaneering, 1984. Diver instr. Comml. Dive Ctr., Long Beach, Calif., 1984-87; owner Flight Shop, California City, 1987-90, Houston Export Co., 1990-92; exec. v.p. AMS, Inc., Oklahoma City, 1992-98; prin., owner Synergy Internat., Las Vegas, 1995—. With USMC, 1975-81. Avocations: skydiving, deep sea diving, camping, poetry, archaeology. Home: 1136 N Birch Cir Alpine UT 84004-1212 Office: Synergy Internat 8687 W Sahara Ave Ste 100 Las Vegas NV 89117-5868

HUFF, RICHARD G., recreational facility administrator; b. Homestead, Fla., Jan. 5, 1937; s. Richard Gates and Alice Theresa Huff; m. Gloria Virginia Huff, Feb. 13, 1983; children: Richard, Mark, Camilla. Grad. H.S., Homestead. Head golf profl. Redland Country Club, Homestead, 1957-61; tchg. profl. Desert Inn Country Club, Las Vegas, Nev., 1961-65; head golf profl. Winterwood Golf Club, Las Vegas, 1965-76; co-owner, mgr. Eagle Hills Golf Club, Eagle, Idaho, 1976-80; dir. golf Tropicana Hotel and Country Club, Las Vegas, 1980-90, Oakhurst Country Club, Clayton, Calif., 1990-95, Blackhawk Country Club, Danville, Calif., 1995-98; gen. mgr. Las Vegas Paiute Resort, 1998—. Mem. Profl. Golfers Assn. Am. (cert. class A, sec.-treas. Las Vegas chpt. 1970's, v.p. Las Vegas chpt. 1970's, sec.-treas. Rocky Mountain sect. 1974, Profl. of yr. Rocky Mountain sect. 1974, Tchr. of Yr. S.W. sect. 1989). Avocations: hunting, traveling, skiing. E-mail: teeup@lvpaiutegolf.com.

HUFF, RICKY WAYNE, sales executive; b. Willits, Calif., Sept. 30, 1953; s. Walter Richard and Janine Norma (Iles) H.; m. Donna Elizabeth Todd, Sept. 17, 1977; children: Brianne Ashley, Kendra Danielle. AA, Santa Rosa (Calif.) Jr. Coll., 1973; BA, Chico (Calif.) State U., 1975. Swim instr., lifeguard Chico YMCA, 1973; mall maintenance Chico Plz., 1973-74; warehouseman Stihl. Co., Chico, 1974-75; delivery driver Downey (Calif.) Unified Sch. Dist., 1975-76; regional mgmt. trainee Montgomery Ward, Norwalk, Calif., 1976-78; sr. sales rep. Fisher-Price Toys, East Aurora, N.Y., 1978-86; key account rep. Rubbermaid, Wooster, Ohio, 1986-87; dir. of sales Century Products Co., Macedonia, Ohio, 1987-96; owner, pres. RH Sales & Mktg., Downey, Calif., 1996—; nat. sales mgr. Relax-R Corp., St. Albans, Vt., 1998—. Author: (handbook) Contract Services, Retail Service Program, 1986, Independent Sales Force Sales Manual, 1989. Vol. YMCA, Downey, 1977—, campaigner, 1986, 93—, fin. com., 1995—, bd. mgrs., 1996—, mem. exec. com., 1998—, 2000 Teams chmn.; chief of Chonook tribe and wampon bearer YMCA Indian Princesses, Downey, 1992—, Nation Chief, 1997-99; bd. dirs. 1st Presbyn. Ch., Downey, 1987-89, Downey Family YMCA, 1996—; coach WNBA Sparks League Girls Basketball, YMCA, 1996—. Mem. Western Toy and Hobby Reps Assn., Downey DeMolay (adv. 1976-78), Willits DeMolay (master councilor 1970-71). Republican. Presbyterian. Avocations: basketball, biking, volleyball, running, remodeling houses. Home: 8432 Dacosta St Downey CA 90240-3934

HUFF, RUSSELL JOSEPH, public relations and publishing executive; b. Chgo., Feb. 24, 1936; s. Russell Winfield and Virgilist Marie (McMahon) H.; m. Beverly Diane Staschke, 1968; 1 child, Michelle Lynn. BA in Philosophy cum laude, U. Notre Dame, 1958; BS in Theology, Cath. U. Santiago (Chile), 1960; MA in Comm. Arts, U. Notre Dame, 1968. Ordained priest Roman Cath. Ch., 1962. Exec. editor Cath. Boy and Miss., Notre Dame, Ind., 1963-68; mng. editor Nation's Schs., McGraw Hill, Chgo., 1968-70; v.p. pub. affairs Homart Devel. Co., Chgo., 1971-76; dir. pub. rels. Sears, Roebuck Co. Internat. Ops., Chgo., 1976-82; dir. pub. affairs Sears Roebuck Found. Internat. Projects, Chgo., 1981-82; sr. v.p., sales and mktg. dir. Mineca Internat., Inc., Chgo., 1982-84; v.p., pub. rels. Lofino Poppa Devel. Corp., Sarasota, Fla., 1984-85; pres., co-owner R.J. Huff & Assocs., Inc., Sarasota, 1985—; real estate broker Sarasota, 1985—. Author: Come Build My Church, 1966, On Wings of Adventure, 1967, Wings of WWII, 1985, Companion to Wings of World War II, 1987, Winging It, Vols. I and II, 1992; editor, pub. (quar. jour.) Wings and Things of the World, 1987-93, Wings and Things of the World for Sale, 1993-95; cons., editl. contbr. Aviation Treasures, 1995—; sr. editor The Nobody's Fool Fin. Market Analyst Pub., 1996-98. Care min. leader Ch. Incarnation Parish Coun., mem. future planning and rev. com. Recipient Outstanding Mag. award Cath. Press Assn., 1965, 67; named for Best Cover, Nation's Schs., 1968; cert. Gemol. Inst. Am.; cert. jr. coll. tchr., Calif. Mem. Pub. Rels. Soc. Am. (accredited 1976—), Chicagoland Mil. Collectors Soc. (dir. quar. expositions 1981-82), Am. Soc. Mil. Insignia Collectors, Orders and Medals Soc. Am., Nat. Fgn. Trade Coun., Pub. Affairs Coun., Conf. Bd., Internat. Bus. Coun., Internat. Vis. Ctr. Chgo., Ptnrs. of the Ams. (cert. for advancement L.Am. rels. 1980), Sãa Paulo Ptnrs. (cert. for advancement Brazil-U.S. rels. 1979, dir. Ill.), Chgo. Assn. of Commerce and Industry, U.S.-Spanish C. of C. of Middle West (dir.), War Memorabilia Collectors Soc. (exec. dir.). Roman Catholic. Office: RJ Huff & Assocs Inc 4062 Kingston Ter Sarasota FL 34238-2632

HUFF, WILLIAM GREGG, economics; b. Lincoln, Nebr., Mar. 9, 1945; s. William N. and Mary C. (Albin) H.; m. Gillian C. Cronjé, Dec. 17, 1986; 1 child, William Hugh Anthony. BS with distinction, U. Pa., 1967; MSc, London Sch. Econ., 1968, PhD, 1986. Lectr. U. Lancaster, 1986-89, U. Durham, 1989-91; lectr. U. Glasgow, Scotland, 1991-94, sr. lectr., 1994—. Author: The Economic Growth of Singapore, 1994; contbr. articles to profl. jours. Mem. Royal Econ. Soc., Am. Econ. Assn., Econ. History Assn. Anglican. Office: Univ Glasgow Dept Econs, Adam Smith Bldg, G12 8RT Glasgow Scotland

HUFFMAN, DAVID GEORGE, electrical engineer; b. Fresno, Calif., Apr. 13, 1965; s. Fred Norman and Sharon (Richardson) H.; m. Johnnie Ann Valtierra, Sept. 21, 1991; children: Matthew Christopher Kenerly, Makenna Francisca-Elise. BSEE, Fresno State U., 1988. Field engr. Power Systems Testing Co., Fresno, Calif., 1988-93, dir. engring., 1993—, mgr., 1994—, gen. mgr., CEO, 1999—. Mem. Internat. Electronic and Electrical Engrs. Assn., Eta Kappa Nu. Avocations: golf, model building, reading, traveling, skydiving. Office: Power Systems Testing Co 4688 W Jennifer Ave Ste 108 Fresno CA 93722-6418

HUFFMAN, DEBRA ELLEN, research scientist; b. Teaneck, N.J., Jan. 3, 1960; d. William M. and Beaatrice Helen (Fabian) Friedman; m. William Lee Huffman, Nov. 13, 1994; 1 child, Jesse Lee. BS, Univ. S. Fla., 1988, M in public health, 1990, PhD, 1994. Rsch. scientist Univ. S. Fla., St. Petersburgh, 1994—; cons. Debra Huffman Cons. Inc., New Port Richey, Fla., 1997—; cons. Cartwright Olsen and Assocs. Author (book chpt.) The Continuing Threat of Waterborne Pathogens, 1999; contbr. articles to profl. jours. Recipient rsch. grants. Office: Univ South Fla 140 7th Ave S Saint Petersburg FL 33701-5001

HUFFMAN, DONNA LOU, interior designer; b. Uvalde, Tex., Sept. 25, 1948; d. Herbert Quarrells Jr. and Wanna Lou (Ray) Haile; children: Laura Anne, Christopher J. BS, U. Houston, 1969, MEd, 1973. Owner Rainbow Design LLC, Littleton, Colo., 1975—; owner Health By Design, www.designyourhealth.com; ind. bus. owner Rexall Showcase Internat.; spkr. in field. Designer Parade of Homes, 1989, Jr. Symphony Guild Showhome, 1996; designs featured in Colorado Homes and Lifestyles, Denver Post. Founder, pres. Priime Tiime Today, Littleton, Colo. Republican. Baptist. Avocations: water fitness, fly fishing, white water rafting. Office: Rainbow Design LLC PO Box 2829 Littleton CO 80161-2829

HUFFMAN, MICHAEL ALAN, zoologist, science film consultant, translator; b. Denver, Nov. 18, 1958; s. Robert Moris and Eleanor Ruth (Mentzer) H.; m. Fumie Naito, Apr. 8, 1993. BSc in Biology, Ft. Lewis Coll., Durango, Colo., 1983; MSc in Zoology, Kyoto (Japan) U., 1986, DSc in Zoology, 1989. Postdoctoral fellow Japan Soc. for Promotion Sci. Kyoto U., 1989-93, rsch. assoc. dept. zoology, 1994-96; rsch. staff Primate Rsch. Inst. Kyoto U., Inuyama, Japan, 1996-99, prof., 2000—; cons. Com. for Conservation and Care of Chimpanzees, 1986—; sci. advisor BBC, ANC Prodn., 1989—; dir. CHIMPP Group, Kyoto U., 1989—. Contbr. articles to profl. jours., chpts. to books. Named Frucht Meml. Lectr., U. Alta., 1997. Mem. Primate Soc. Japan (sec. pub. affairs 1995—, award for overseas rsch. 1993), Internat. Primate Soc., Soc. Française d'Ethnopharmacolagie. Avocations: kayaking, hiking, mountain climbing, painting. Home: 979 Glencoe St Denver CO 80220-4452 Office: Kyoto U, Primate Rsch Inst, Kanrin, Inuyama Aichi 484, Japan

HUFFMAN, PATRICIA NELL, entrepreneur; b. Springfield, Mo., Sept. 25, 1947; d. Rex Eugene and Helen Marie (Appleby) Riggs; m. Frank Dale Huffman, June 18, 1966; children: Chad, Heather, Tyler. Student, Joplin Jr. Coll., 1966. Saleswoman Sta. KTVJ-TV, Joplin, Mo., 1972-77; designer, mktg. ADI-Comml. Interiors, Tulsa, 1983-84; pres., designer Bittersweet, Inc., Joplin, 1984—; founder, pres. By Invitation Only, 1986—; co-owner, bd. dirs., sec. J-Town Billiards, Sports Bar and Grill, 1999—; cons. in field. Designer country gift items, 1978—. Vol. Mental Health Ctr., Joplin, 1965, Am. Heart Assn., Joplin, 1980, Family Self Help Ctr., Joplin, 1981—, United Way, Joplin, 1982; pres. Women's Support Group, Joplin, 1983-85, Family Violence Coun., 1996-97, bd. dirs., pres. bd.; bd. dirs. Children's Ctr., 1997—; co-founder S.A.F.E. Coalition, 1989-97. Recipient Women Helping Women award, 1998, House Resolution No. 785 for volunteerism with children and women State of Mo., 1994. Mem. Exch. Club (Book of Golden Deeds award for outstanding volunteerism with women and children 1996). Avocations: bridge, creative writing, billiards, painting, illustrating and writing children's books. Office: PO Box 2159 2502 S Main St Joplin MO 64803-2159

HUG, HUBERT PAUL, molecular biologist, researcher; b. Freiburg, Germany, Mar. 10, 1959; s. Paul Karl and Agnes (Müller) H. Student, U. Liverpool, Eng., 1984; diploma, U. Freiburg, 1985, PhD, 1988; postgrad., U. Zurich, Switzerland, 1985-88. Group leader U. Freiburg, 1988-92; postdoctoral fellow Osaka (Japan) Biosci. Inst., 1992-94; scientist U. Heidelberg, Germany, 1994-98, U. Ulm, 1996—; cons. Gödecke Ag, Freiburg, 1990-92. Author: The Neutra, 1994, (anthology) Furniture, 1994; patentee caspase kit. Mem. N.Y. Acad. Scis. Avocation: creative writing. Home: Kingskerswellweg 6, 89173 Lonsee Germany Office: Forschungslabore, Kinderklinik U Ulm 63, 89075 Ulm Germany

HUGE, HARRY, lawyer; b. Deshler, Nebr., Sept. 16, 1937; s. Arthur and Dorothy (Vor de Strasse) H.; m. Reba Kinne, July 2, 1960; 1 child, Theodore. AB, Nebr. Wesleyan U., 1959; JD, Georgetown U., 1963. Bar: Ill. 1963, D.C. 1965, S.C. 1985. Assoc. Chapman & Cutler, Chgo., 1963-65; from assoc. to ptnr. Arnold & Porter, Washington, 1965-76; sr. ptnr. Donovan, Leisure, Rogovin, Huge & Schiller, Washington, 1976-92, Shea and Gould Internat., Washington, 1992-94; ptnr. Powell Goldstein Frazer & Murphy, Washington, 1995—; chmn. Oncostasis, Inc., Charleston, S.C.; pres. Am. European Fund, Seattle, 1989—; chmn., trustee United Mine Workers Health and Retirement Funds, 1973-78; chmn. bd. dirs. Hollings Cancer Ctr. Med. U. S.C., Charleston. Contbr. articles to legal jours. Pres. Voter Edn. Project, Atlanta, 1974-78; mem. Pres.'s Gen. Adv. Com. Arms Control, 1977-81; trustee Nebr. Wesleyan U., 1978—; mem. task force local govt. Greater Washington Rsch. Ctr., 1981-82; spl. master Friends for All Children, Inc., U.S. Dist. Ct. D.C.; mem. Nat. Tobacco Settlement Arbitration Panel, Durham, N.C. With U.S. Army, 1960; officer USNG, 1960-65. Mem. ABA (co-chmn. legis. com. litigation sect. 1981), D.C. Bar Assn. (bd. profl. responsibility 1976-81), Inst. Human Virology (bd. dirs. U. Md. chpt.). Home: 25 E Battery St Charleston SC 29401-2740 Office: Powell Goldstein Frazer & Murphy 1001 Pennsylvania Ave NW Washington DC 20004-2505

HUGEL, RENE PAUL, engineering educator; b. Strasbourg, Alsace, France, Nov. 21, 1937; s. Modeste and Catherine (Kraemer) H.; m. Georgette Feuerstein, Oct. 11, 1935; children: Catherine, Veronique. BS, U. Strasbourg, 1955, D Physics, 1964; degree in engring., Ecole Nat. Sup. de Chimie, Strasbourg, 1960. Rsch. fellow CNRS, Strasbourg, 1960-66, MIT, Cambridge, 1966-67; prof. U. Reims, France, 1967—; dir. Ecole Sup. d'Ingenieurs en Emballage et Conditionnement, Reims, 1988-95; founder engring. sch. ESIEC, Reims, 1989. Lt. French Army, 1964-66. Office: ESIEC, F-51686 Reims France

HUGG, GERALDINE BERTHA NOVOTNY, retired gerontology specialist, journalist; b. N.Y.C., Oct. 15, 1913; d. Jerry Joseph and Bertha Ann (Strnad) Novotny; m. Alan Eddy Hugg, Mar. 10, 1982 (dec. Feb. 1997). BA in Journalism, U. Wis., 1949; MS in Pub. Rels., Boston U., 1953. lic. profl. gerontology U. Mich., Drake U. Departmental sec. U. Conn., Storrs, 1933-41, departmental asst., 1941-43; asst. editor, publs. editor divsn. comm. U. Conn., 1950-60; specialist Inst. Gerontology, U. Conn., 1960-67; dir. Windham Area Sr. Ctr., Willimantic, Conn., 1967; cons. and field rep. Conn. State Dept. Aging, Hartford, 1967-76; ret., 1976; advisor Conn. Coun. Sr. Citizens, 1960—; attended 9th Internat. Gerontol. Congress, Kiev, Russia, 1972. Contbg. editor Seniorage, 1976—; contbr. columns various newspapers. Vol. social action and edn. Conn. Soc. Gerontology, 1961-99, pres., 1981-83; participant Am. Exch. Corps, Caucuses, Russia, 1980, USSR People to People Program, China, 1994, South Africa, 1995, Russia and Estonia, 1996; active the Capitol Region Conf. Chs., 1996—; advcate for justice and peace Capitol Region Conf. of Chs., Hartford, Conn., 1997—; mem. Conn. Campaign to Abolish Nuclear Weapons, 1997; co-chmn. Conn. Coalition on Aging, Inc., Hartford, 1976-80; mem. United Srs. in Action, 1997—; mem. advocacy justice and peace Capitol Region Conf. Chs., Hartford, Conn., 1996— . Sgt. USMCR, 1943-45. Recipient David C. King award Conn. Soc. Gerontology, Hartford, 1985-98, award 100 Years of Women, U. Conn., Sterrs, 1993. Mem. Nat. Coun. on Aging (life), Nat. Coun. Sr. Citizens (life, mem. com. to establish 1st set of stds. for sr. ctrs.), Conn. Coun. Sr. Citizens, AAUW (past pres.), Czechoslovak Am. Club (pres. 1939-60), Zonta Internat. Club of West Hartford (bd. dirs. 1970—), Womens Internat. League Peace and Freedom, Ch. Women United (Conn. chpt. adv. bd. 1984), Czechoslovak Culture Group, United Srs. in Action (vol. activist), UN Assn. (Greater Hartford, Conn.). Democrat. Universalist. Avocations: swimming, oil painting, hiking. Home: 275 Steele Rd Apt 422 West Hartford CT 06117-2716

HUGGETT, RICHARD JOHN, geography educator, writer; b. Southgate, Middlesex, Eng., Oct. 29, 1948; s. Raymond Leonard and Jean Maude (Jeffrey) H.; m. Jane Elizabeth Firth, Aug. 1, 1970; children: James Alan, Sarah Anne, Edward John; m. Shelley Susan Dyer, Mar. 29, 1986; children: Daniel William, Zoë Jessica, Benjamin Richard. BSc in Geography first class, U. Coll. London, 1970, PhD in Geography, 1973. Geography master Haberdashers' Aske's Sch., Elstree, Eng., 1973-74; lectr. U. Manchester (Eng.), 1975-91, sr. lectr., 1991-2000, reader, 2000—. Author: Geoecology: An Evolutionary Approach, 1995, Environmental Change: The Evolving Ecosphere, 1997, Fundamentals of Biogeography, 1998. Mus. dir. Spotlight Singers; dir. amateur musicals. Anglican. Avocations: musical direction, amateur musicals. Office: U Manchester Sch Geography, Oxford Rd, Manchester M13 9PL, England

HUGGINS, CHARLES EDWARD, obstetrician, gynecologist, educator; b. Hartsville, S.C., Nov. 16, 1944; s. Charles Witherspoon Huggins and Frances Sue (Fountain) Evans; m. Mary Ellen Esto, May 29, 1966; children: Chadwick Edward, Laura Ruth, Mary Elizabeth. BS, Wofford Coll., 1965; MD, Med. U. S.C., 1969. Diplomate Am. Bd. Ob-Gyn. Intern Strong Meml. Hosp., Rochester, 1969-70; resident in ob-gyn. Med. U. S.C. Hosp., Charleston, 1970-74; chief of ob-gyn. Roper Hosp., Charleston; vice chmn. ob-gyn. dept. Bon Secours St. Francis Hosp., Charleston, 1999—; clin. assoc. prof. Med. U. S.C.; mem. exec. bd. Roper Hosp., Charleston,1992-95, perinatal adv. bd., Charleston, 1992-95. Leader Boy Scouts of Am., Mt. Pleasant, S.C., 1978-88; coach Hungry Neck Internat. Soccer, Mt. Pleasant, 1978-88. Lt. Cmdr. USN, 1974-76. Fellow ACOG, South Atlantic Assn. Ob-Gyn. (chair state com. 1995-98); mem. AMA, Am. Fertility Soc., NYAS, S.C. Med. Assn., Charleston County Med. Soc., Pi Kappa Phi (archon 1962—), Phi Rho Sigma. Presbyterian.

HUGGINS, CHARLOTTE SUSAN HARRISON, secondary school educator, author, travel specialist; b. Rockford, Ill., May 13, 1933; d. Lyle Lux and Alta May (Bowers) H.; m. Rollin Charles Huggins Jr., Apr. 26, 1952; children: Cynthia Charlotte Peters, Shirley Ann Cooper, John Charles. Student, Knox Coll., 1951-52; AB magna cum laude, Harvard U., 1958; MA, Northwestern U., 1960, postgrad., 1971-73; cert. in conversation French, Berlitz Lang. Sch. Asst. editor Hollister Publs., Inc., Wilmette, Ill., 1959-65; tchr. advanced placement English New Trier H.S., Winnetka, Ill., 1965—, master tchr., 1979, leader tchr., 1988; with Task Force Commn. on Grading, 1973-74; Sabbatical project 1 yr. world travel History-Lit. Prospectus; cons. Asian Studies New Trier, 1987-88; mem. New Trier Supts. Commn. on Censorship, 1991; critic tchr. Northwestern U.; cons. McDougall-Littel's Young Writer's Manual, 1985-88; asst. sponsor Echoes, 1981—, Trevia, 1982, 83; sponsor New Trier News, 1988—; pres. Harrison Farms, Inc., Lovington, Ill, 1976—; spkr. North Suburban Geneal. Soc., 1990; presenter Asian lit. Ill. Humanities Coun., 1992, Nat. Scholastic Press Assn., No. Ill. Sch. Press Assn., 1992, 93, 94; instr., travel expert New Trier Adult Edn. Keys to the World's Last Mysteries, 1986—. Author: A sequential Course in Composition Grades 9-12, 1979, A History of New Trier High School, 1982, Passage to Anaheim: An Historical Biography of Pioneer

Families, 1984, Cambodia: A Place in Time, 1987; (video tapes) The Glory That Was Greece, 1987, The World of Charles Dickens, 1987. Mem. women's bd. St. Leonard's House, Chgo., 1965-75; Ctrl. Sch. PTA Bd., Wilmette, 1960-64; mem. assocs. bd. Northwestern U. Settlement, Chgo., 1965-75, 98, pres. 1999—. Recipient DAR citizenship award, 1953, Phi Beta Kappa award, 1957, Am. Legion award, 1959; cert. of merit Graphic Arts Competition Printing Industries of Am., 1983, 1st place award Am. Scholastic Press Assn., 1990, cert. of merit Am. Newspaper Pubs. Assn., 1990. Mem. MLA, NEA, ASCD, Ill. Edn. Assn., New Trier Edn. Assn. (sec. 1992, pres.-elect 1994, pres. 1995-96), Nat. Coun. Tchrs. English, Ill. Assn. Tchrs. English, Women Comm., Inc., Northwestern U. Alumni Assn., Jr. Aux. U. Chgo. Cancer Rsch. Bd., Mary Crane League, Nat. Huguenot Soc., Ill. Huguenot Soc., Nat. Soc. DAR (historian 1999-2000, regent 2000—), Columbia Scholastic Press Assn. (del 1990, newspaper judge, medalist award), Ill. Journalism Edn. Assn. (awards chmn., bd. dirs. 1992—, sec. 1994-97), Quill and Scroll (George Gallup award 1990, bd. dirs. 1992-93), Nat. Scholastic Press Assn. (spring convention rep. 1991-92, 92-93, 93-94, 94-95, 95-96, newspaper judge, conv. del. 1991, All-Am. Newspaper award 1990-91, 91-92, Fall and Spring conv. presenter 1993-94, 94-95, 95-96, 96—), Art Inst. Chgo. (life), Chgo. Farmers, Terra Mus. Chgo. (charter), Lyric Opera (assoc.), Women's Club Wilmette, Mich. Shores Club, Univ. Club Chgo., Knox Coll. Alumni Assn., Radcliffe Coll. Alumnae Assn., Harvard U. Alumni Assn. (admissions candidate interviewer), Pi Beta Phi (North Shore Chgo. alumnae bd., publicity chair). Home: 700 Greenwood Ave Wilmette IL 60091-1748 Office: 385 Winnetka Ave Winnetka IL 60093-4238

HUGGINS, ELAINE JACQUELINE, nurse, retired army officer; b. San Jose, Calif., Mar. 26, 1954; d. William Burt and Edith Gwendolyn (Schindler) Moreland; m. Bruce Carlton Allanach, Oct. 8, 1976 (div. Oct. 1989); stepchildren: Dawn Louise, Christopher Bruce, Jeffrey Scott, Sean Michael; m. Michael Henry Huggins, Dec. 8, 1991; children: Phoebe Marie, Chloe Anne, Michael Henry Jr.; stepchildren: Abbey Rose, Jamin Michael. BSN, U. Md., 1976; MSN, Med. Coll. Ga., 1988; postgrad., Calif. Inst. Integral Studies. RN, Ga., Md., Calif. Commd. 2d lt. Nurse Corps U.S. Army, 1972, advanced through grades to maj., 1986; staff nurse gen. medicine-oncology Walter Reed Army Med. Ctr., Washington, 1976-78, team leader gen. medicine-oncology, 1978-79, head nurse med. splty. ward, 1979-80; asst. head nurse gynecol. oncology unit Tripler Army Med. Ctr., Honolulu, 1980-81, head nurse med. splty. clinic, 1981-83; staff nurse orthopedics Eisenhower Army Med. Ctr., Ft. Gordon, Ga., 1983-84, patient edn. coord., 1984-85, head nurse recovery rm., 1985-86; head nurse oncology/neurology unit Letterman Army Med. Ctr., Presidio of San Francisco, 1988-89, clin. nurse psychiat. unit, 1989-90, chief nursing adminstrn. E/N, 1990-92, ret., 1992; case mgr. Vis. Nurses Pomona, Claremont, Calif., 1993-94; nursing supr. Vis. Nurses Assn./Hospice of Pomona, San Bernadino, Calif., 1994-95, quality risk resource mgr., 1995-96; sabbatical to Australian outback with rsch. interests in cross-cultural health care and spirituality in health care, 1996-99; freelance writer, cons., 1999-2000; performance improvement mgr. Santa Barbara Vis. Nurses Assn., 2000—; mem. adj. faculty Sch. Nursing U. Phoenix-So. Calif. Campus, 1995-96; lectr. in field. Contbr. articles to nursing, mil., and med. publs. Mem. pub. edn. com. Am. Cancer Soc., Honolulu, 1982. Recipient Humanitarian Svc. medal, 1990. Mem. Am. Diabetes Assn., Am. Assn. Diabetic Educators, Grad. Student Nurses Assn. (sec. 1986-87), ANA, Mensa, Sigma Theta Tau. Avocations: reading, walking, beach combing. Home: 164 Auriga Ave Lompoc CA 93436-1216 Office: Santa Barbara Vis Nurses Assn 222 Canon Perdido Santa Barbara CA 93101-9637

HUGHES, ALAN MICHAEL, lexicographer, editor; b. Chelmsford, Essex, Eng., May 20, 1946; s. Fred and Joan (Dronfield) H.; m. Freda Joyce Thornton, July 20, 1990. BA, Queens Coll., Oxford, 1967, MA, 1968. Physicist Aluminium Labs., Ltd., Banbury, Oxon, 1967-68; editl. asst. Supplement to Oxford English Dictionary, Oxford, 1968-74; sr. editor Supplement to Oxford English Dictionary, 1974-85; sr. editor New Shorter Oxford English Dictionary, 1985-89, assoc. editor, 1989-91, gen. editor, 1991-93; chief sci. editor Oxford English Dictionary, 1993-99, assoc. editor, 1999—. Anglican. Avocations: local and topographical history, English countryside. Office: Oxford Univ Press, Great Clarendon St, Oxford OX2 6DP, England

HUGHES, ALFRED CLIFTON, bishop; b. Boston, Dec. 2, 1932; s. Alfred Clifton and Ellen Cecelia (Hennessey) H. A.B., St. John's Sem. Coll., 1954; S.T.L., Gregorian U., Rome, 1958, S.T.D., 1961. Ordained priest Roman Cath. Ch., 1957, ordained bishop, 1981. Asst. pastor St. Stephen's Parish, Framingham, Mass., 1958-59, Our Lady Help of Christians, Newton, Mass., 1961-62; lectr. St. John's Sem., Brighton, 1962-65, spiritual dir., 1965-81, rector, 1981-86; aux. bishop Archdiocese of Boston, 1981-93; regional bishop of Merrimack Region, 1986-90; vicar for adminstrn. Archdiocese of Boston, 1990-93; bishop of Baton Rouge, 1993—; chmn. com. on doctrine NCCB, 1991-94, com. on use of catechism, 1995—. Author: Preparing for Church Ministry, 1979, Spiritual Masters, 1999; contbr. articles to profl. jours. Mellon and Davis Founds. grantee, 1976. Mem. Catholic Theol. Soc. Am. Office: Cath Life Ctr PO Box 2028 1800 S Acadian Thruway Baton Rouge LA 70821-2028

HUGHES, ARTHUR HYDE, accountant, consultant; b. Lansing, Mich., May 15, 1952; s. Francis Aloysius and Alice Catherine (Hyde) H.; m. Ellen Marie Krempa, Feb. 13, 1982; children: Bradley Allan, Allison Marie. BS magna cum laude, Fla. State U., 1974; postgrad., U. Tex., Dallas, 1978. CPA, Tex. Treas. Excella Trading Corp., Ft. Worth, 1977-79; revenue analyst gas revenue acctg. ARCO, Dallas, 1975-82, sr. acct. oil revenue acctg., 1982-85, client rep. revenue projects group, 1985-87, supr. gas data svcs., 1987-88, supr. gas sys. redevel., 1988-89, prodn. acctg. cons., 1989-90, sr. revenue compliance auditor, 1990-96; internat. acct. ARCO Algeria, 1996; pvt. practice petroleum auditing, cons., 1996-97; mgr. exploration prodn. and fin. software Allegro Devel., Inc., 1997-98; prin. cons. Oracle Energy Co., 1998-2000; oil & gas subject matter expert Akili Sys. Group, 2000—; mem. Petroleum Data Exch. Steering Com., Denver, 1985-87, chmn. Gas Revenue Acctg., Data Exch. Com. (subs Petroleum Data Exch.) Dallas, 1986-87, spl. com. electronic data exch. of Coun. of Petroleum Acctg. Socs., Dallas, 1986—. Contbr. articles to profl. jours.; developer petroleum industry Gas Revenue Acctg. Data Exchange system with Gen. Elec., 1985. Alt. del. Tex. Rep. Conv., 1982; active Nat. Right to Life, Washington; active Citizen's Com. for Right To Keep and Bear Arms, Second Amendment Found. Mem. AICPA, Tex. Soc. CPAs, Petroleum Acctg. Soc., NRA (life), Tex. Rifle Assn., Ducks Unltd., Toastmasters, Gun Owner Am., Citizens Com. Right to Keep and Bear Arms, Second Amendment Found., Mensa, Intertel, Phi Eta Sigma, Phi Kappa Phi, Beta Gamma Sigma. Roman Catholic. Avocations: target shooting, reading, chess. Home and Office: 6405 Limerick Ln Garland TX 75044-3435

HUGHES, AUSTIN LELAND, biological sciences educator; b. Washington, Sept. 10, 1949; s. Edward Riley and Josephine (Nicholls) H.; m. Mary Ann Hughes, Apr. 23, 1980; children: Austin Leland, Helen W. AB, Georgetown U., 1969; MS, W.Va. U., 1980; PhD, Ind. U., 1984. Asst. prof. Pa. State U., University Park, 1990-96, assoc. prof., 1996-99; prof. biol. scis. U. S.C., Columbia, 2000—. Author: Evolution and Human Kinship, 1988, Adaptive Evolunion of General Genomes, 1999; mem. editl. bd. Immunogenetics, 1991—; contbr. more than 150 articles to sci. jours. Recipient Ryan Philosophy medal Georgetown U., 1969; NIH Rsch. Career Devel. awardee, 1992-97. Mem. Soc. for Study of Evolution, Soc. for Molecular Biology and Evolution. Roman Catholic. Office: Y SC 700 Sumter St Columbia SC 29208-0001

HUGHES, BARBARA BRADFORD, nurse, real estate manager; b. Bragg City, Mo., Jan. 21, 1941; d. Lawrence Hurl Bradford and Opal Jewel (Prater) Puttin; m. Robert Howard Hughes, Dec. 9, 1961; children: Kimberly Ann Hayden, Robert Howard II. ASN, St. Louis Community Coll., 1978; student, Webster U., 1980. RN, Mo. Med. surg. nurse Alexian Bros. Hosp., St. Louis, 1979-80; staff nurse Midwest Allergy Cons., St. Louis, 1980; nurse high altitude Aviation Nurse, Ltd., St. Louis, 1980-81; cardiac telemetry staff nurse Jefferson Meml. Hosp., Crystal City, Mo., 1992-94; vol. nurse Med. Ministry Internat., Plano, Tex., 1998—; owner, chmn. bd. Supreme Tool & Die Co., Fenton, Mo., 1998—; pvt. practice real estate mgmt., 1962—; mem. nursing adv. com. Jefferson Coll., Hillsboro, Mo., 1999. Vol. Luth. Hosp., St. Louis, 1967-70; mem. Mo. Bot. Garden, St. Louis, 1976—, Mo. Hist. Soc., 1993—, St. Louis Zoo Friends Assn., 1986-87, Nat. Trust for Hist. Preservation, 1990—; Channel 9-Ednl. TV, St. Louis; vol. blood drive ARC, St. Louis, 1980; vol. health tchr. Spartan Aluminum Products, Sparta, Ill., 1984; apptd. Jefferson Coll. Nursing Adv. Com., 1999—. U. Mo. scholar, 1959. Mem. AACN, Nat. Tool and Machining Assn., Wings of Hope (St. Louis), Mo. Pilots Assn., Women in Aviation Internat. (charter), U.S. Pilots Assn., Tyospaye Club, Aircraft Owners and Pilots Assn., Med. Ministries Internat. Republican. Avocations: flying, gardening, reading. Home and Office: 1536 Fenpark Dr Fenton MO 63026

HUGHES, BRIAN MICHAEL, psychologist, educator; b. Tuam, Ireland, Sept. 3, 1971; s. Thomas Jarlath and Mary Brigid (Leonard) H. BA with honors, Nat. U. Ireland, 1993, PhD, 1998. Llectr. in psychology Galway-Mayo Inst., 1995-98; lectr. in psychology Nat. U. Ireland, 1997-98; lectr. in psychology LSB Coll., Dublin, Ireland, 1998—, head psychology, 1999—, coord. skills program, 1994-98, access counselor, 1998; cons. Irish Soc. for Quality in Healthcare, Dublin, 1998—. Author papers in field. Mem. Irish Coun. for Civil Liberties, Dublin, 1999. Fellow Nat. U. Ireland, 1993-96. Mem. APA, Brit. Psychol. Soc., Psychol. Soc. Ireland. Avocations: philosophy, history of science, linguistics, television. Home: 16 Bel Air Dr, Tuam Ireland Office: LSB Coll, Balfe St, Dublin 1, Ireland

HUGHES, CRAIG MARTIN, management consultant; b. Melton Mowbray, Leicestershire, Eng., Oct. 6, 1966; s. Alun and Wray H.; m. Treasa Maria Kirby, 1999. BSc with hons., U. Warwick, Eng., 1988. Mgr. Andersen Consulting, Eng., 1988-96, N.Y.C., 1994; ptnr. M.A. Partnersocs., London, 1994—; dir. Smithfield Internet Svcs., Ltd., 2000—, Pin Striped Co., Ltd., 2000. Avocations: skiing, rollerblading, reading. Office: M A Partnership, 120 Old Broad St, London EC2, England

HUGHES, EDWARD T., retired bishop; b. Lansdowne, Pa., Nov. 13, 1920. Student, St. Charles Sem., U. Pa. Ordained priest Roman Catholic Ch. 1947. Ordained titular bishop Segia and aux. bishop Phila., 1976-86; 2d bishop Diocese of Metuchen, N.J., 1986-97; ret. Diocese of Metuchen, 1997.

HUGHES, GLYN, novelist, poet; b. Middlewich, Cheshire, Eng., May 25, 1935. Author: (novels) Where I Used to Play on the Green, 1981 (Guardian fiction prize 1982, David Higham award 1982), The Hawthorn Goddess, 1984, The Rape of the Rose, 1987, The Antique Collector, 1990, Roth, 1992, Bronte, 1996, Glynn Williams, 1998, Barry Burman. The Pilgrim's Progress, 1999, (non-fiction), Millstone Grit, 1975, Fair Prospects: Journeys in Greece, 1976, Andrzej Kuhn, 1994, (poetry) The Stanedge Bull, and Other Poems, 1966, Almost-Love Poems, 1968, Love on the Moor: Poems, 1965-68, 1968, Neighbours: Poems, 1965-69, 1969 (Welsh Arts Coun. Young Poet's prize 1969), Towards the Sun: Poems/Photographs, 1971, Rest the Poor Struggler: Poems, 1969-71, 1972, The Breast: A Poem, 1973, Alibis and Convictions, 1978, Best of Neighbours: New and Selected Poems, 1979, (plays) Alone on the Moors, 1975, One Man Alone, 1975, Mary Hepton's Heaven, 1984, (radio plays) The Yorkshire Women, 1978, Dreamers, 1979, Pursuit, 1999; editor: Selected Poems of Samuel Laycock, 1983; contbr. articles to periodicals including Times Lit. Supplement, Guardian, Malahat Rev., Kenyon Rev., New Statesmen, Poetry Wales, Mich. Quar. Rev., Critical Survey; given poetry readings on Arts coun. writers tours and at numerous Brit. and Am. univs. and colls. Arts Coun. scholar, 1970, 74. Office: Mor's House, 1 Mill Bank Rd, Sowerby Bridge Yorkshire HX6 3DY, England

HUGHES, GORDON F., research scientist, electrical engineer; b. L.A., Sept. 9, 1937; s. Thomas Whitsett and Elizabeth Hughes; m. Shirley Bordon, Nov. 4, 1982; children: Laura Marie, Eric Thomas. BS in Physics, Calif. Inst. Tech., 1959, MSEE, 1961, PhDEE, 1963. Aerospace scientist Autonetics, Anaheim, Calif., 1963-69; prin. scientist Xerox Palo Alto Rsch. Ctr., L.A., 1969-82; sr. dir. engring. Sengate Tech., Scotts Valley, Calif., 1982-97; sr. project scientist U. Calif., San Diego, 1997—; seagate and assoc. dir. Ctr. Magnetic Recording Rsch.; cons. Hughes Magnetics, San Diego, 1970—. Contbr. over 25 articles to profl. publs.; patentee in field. Mem. IEEE (sr.). Avocation: flying. Office: U Calif San Diego Ctr Magnetic Recording Rsch 9500 Gilman Dr La Jolla CA 92093-5004

HUGHES, JAMES DONALD, lawyer; b. Houston, June 5, 1951; s. D. E. and Ruby Christine (Wagstaff) H. BS, Stanford U., 1973; JD, U. Tex., 1976; LLM in Taxation, NYU, 1978. Bar: Tex. 1976, Ala. 1979, U.S. Dist. Ct. (so. dist.) Ala., 1979, U.S. Tax Ct. 1987, U.S. Dist. Ct. (no. dist.) Ala. 1999. Assoc. O.N. Baker Inc., Houston, 1977; ptnr. Armbrecht, Jackson, Demovy, Crowe, Holmes & Reeves, Mobile, Ala., 1978-99, Bradley, Arant, Rose & White, LLP, Birmingham, Ala., 1999—. Mem. ABA (taxation and real property probate and trust sects.), Small Bus. Coun. Am. (bd. legal advisers), Ala. State Bar (estate planning law specialist). Avocations: photography, stained glass, sports. Office: Bradley Arant Rose & White LLP 2001 Park Pl Ste 1400 Birmingham AL 35203-2736

HUGHES, JOHN HENRY, microbiology educator; b. Cleve., Jan. 7, 1942; s. James Wesley and Mary Ellen Hughes; m. Laura Josephine Greenlee, July 10, 1965; children: Paulo Jo Thomas, Jennifer Sue Carr, Darrell Allen, Eric David. BS, Ohio State U., 1964, PhD, 1972; MA, Bowling Green State U., 1967. Clin. microbiologist Children's Hosp., Columbus, Ohio, 1971-73; asst. prof. med. microbiology Ohio State U., Columbus, 1973-80, assoc. prof., 1980—; assoc. dir. Viral Diagnostic Lab., Children's Hosp., Columbus, 1981-94; bd. dirs. Am. Bd. Bioanalysis, St. Louis. Mem. editl. bd. Electronic Sci. Jour., 1995. Grantee NIH, Nat. Cancer Inst., NASA, 1974—. Achievements include inventor rotavirus diagnosis, rapid latex detection kit, latex immunoassay for rapid rotavirus detection, equipment for enhanced virus growth, enhanced production of poxvirus vectors by high speed rolling; patentee method for treatment and prevention of diseases caused by enveloped viruses including Herpes Simplex Virus Types 1 and 2 using 3, 4-dihydroxy-2H Benzopyran-2H-one. E-mail: hughes.7@osu.edu and hughesj@pediatrics.ohio-state.edu. Fax: 614-722-2716. Home: 4326 Oakview Dr Columbus OH 43204-1522 Office: Childrens Rsch Inst 308 Wexner 700 Childrens Dr Columbus OH 43205-2664

HUGHES, JOHN LLEWELLYN MOSTYN, telecommunications company executive; b. Bolton, Lancashire, Eng., July 20, 1951; s. Hugh Mostyn and Marion (Trohear) H.; m. Sue Lynn Lams, Dec. 27, 1980. BS, U. Hertfordshire, Eng., 1972. Tech. officer Brit. Govt., London, 1975-77; sales mgr. SEL Computers, Sutton, Eng., 1977-79, dir. European mktg., 1979-80; dir. bus. devel. SEL Computers divsn. Gould Inc., Ft. Lauderdale, Fla., 1980-83; dir. internat. sales Metheus Corp., Hillsboro, Oreg., 1983-84, v.p. sales, mktg. & svc., 1984-87; exec. v.p., COO Numerix Corp., Newton, Mass., 1987-88, pres., CEO, 1988-91; v.p., gen. mgr. Europe Convex Computer Corp., Dallas, 1991-95; dir. worldwide field integration Hewlett-Packard CXD, Dallas, 1995-97; chmn. IRTS Inc., N.Y.C., 1989-95; non-exec. dir. Micromuse plc, London, 1996, Riversoft Ltd., London, 1997; region pres. microelectronics group Lucent Techs. Europe, Middle East, Africa, Bracknell, Eng., 1997-99; pres. Worldwide GSM/UMTS Lucent Techs., Swindon, Eng., 1999-2000; non-exec. dir. Pixelfusion Group Plc., 2000. Area v.p. English Young Conservatives, Hertfordshire, 1974-78.

HUGHES, JULIAN CHRISTOPHER, psychiatrist; b. London, May 15, 1959; s. Peter John and Ann Catherine (Morrish) H.; m. Anne Marie Coulson, Aug. 10, 1985; children: Oliver James, Emma Catherine, Luke William Peter. BA in Philosophy, Politics, Econs., Oxford U., 1982, MA, 1986; Assoc., London Coll. Music, 1986; M.B.Ch.B. with distinction epidemiology, Bristol Med. Sch., 1988, MRCPsych, 1994; PhD, Warwick U., 2000. Registered physician, U.K. House physician/house surgeon Bristol Med. Sch., 1988-89; sr. house officer ob-gyn. Royal Air Force, 1989-90, gen. practice, 1990-92, trainee in psychiatry, 1992-95; sr. registrar in psychiatry Nat. Health Svc., Oxford, 1995-99; cons. in old age psychiatry Newcastle-upon-Tyne, 1999—; rsch. fellow Oxford Inst. for Ethics and Comm. in Health Care Practice, 1998—; hon. clin. lectr. U. Newcastle-upon-Tyne, 2000. Contbr. articles to profl. jours. Joint sec. Bristol Med. Group, 1986-87. Decorated Gulf War medal Min. of Def., 1991. Mem. royal Coll. Psychiatrists (mem. philosophy spl. interest group com. 1999—, Philip Davis prize in old age psychiatry 1995), Alzheimer's Disease Soc. Roman Catholic. Avocations: classical music (flute playing), architecture, running, swimming. Office: Gibside Unit/Newcastle Gen, Westgate Rd, Newcastle-upon-Tyne NE4 6BE, England

HUGHES, KAYLENE, historian, educator; b. Modesto, Calif., Aug. 4, 1952. BA, Miami-Dade (Fla.) Jr. Coll., 1972, Fla. Internat. U., 1976; MA, Fla. State U., 1977, PhD, 1985. Intern Fla. State Dept. Archives Records Mgmt., Tallahassee, 1977; Claims Control Supr. Sys. Devel. Corp., Tallahassee, 1978-81; editl. asst. Fla. Hotel and Motel Jour., Tallahassee, 1983-85; dir. edn., rsch. mgr. Fla. Hotel and Motel Assn., Tallahassee, 1985-87; historian U.S. Army Aviation & Missile Command, Redstone Arsenal, Ala., 1987—; grad. asst. Fla. State U., Tallahassee, 1976-77, tchg. asst., 1981-83; adj. instr. history John C. Calhoun C.C., Huntsville, Ala., 1990—. Author: Florida's Lodging Industry: The First 75 Years, 1987, The Missile's Red Glare, 1992, Redstone Army Airfield: A Tradition of Aviation Support, 1992, Redstone Arsenal's Role in Operation Desert Shield/Desert Storm, 1992; contbr. articles to jours. and newspapers. Grantee Fla. State U., 1983. Mem. Phi Alpha Theta (sec. 1982-85), Phi Theta Kappa. E-mail: kaylene.hughes@redstone.army.mil. Home: 342 Pawnee Trl SE Huntsville AL 35803-2280 Office: US Army Aviation and Missile Command Redstone Arsenal AL 35898

HUGHES, KENNETH, medical educator; b. Golborne, Lancashire, United Kingdom, Jan. 11, 1939; s. Thomas Henry and Esther (Green) H. BM, BCh, Oxford U., U.K., 1966, MD, 1989. Clin. medicine NHS, U.K., 1967-92; cons. WHO Smallpox Eradication Program, U.K., 1975-78; sr. lectr. dept. cmty. medicine Nat. U. Singapore, 1979-89, assoc. prof. dept. cmty. medicine, 1989-99, assoc. professorial fellow dept. cmty. medicine, 1999—; reviewer various internat. jours. Author: The Epidemiology of Cardiovascular Diseases in the Ethnic Groups of Singapore, 1993; contbr. various articles to profl. jours. Fellow FPHM, Royal Coll. Physicians, mem. Internat. Epidemiol. Assn., World Heart Fedn. section on epidemiology and prevention, Asian-Pacific Soc. Atherosclerosis and Vascular Diseases (mem. coun.). Avocations: golf, travel. Office: Nat U Singapore, Dept Faculty Medicine, Singapore 117597, Singapore

HUGHES, LEE EDWARD, ecologist; b. Ft. Robinson, Nebr., Feb. 19, 1943; s. Leland Stanford and Mildred Ricarda (Erickson) H.; m. Vickie Lynn Wiseth, May 28, 1971 (dec. Aug. 1996); children: Amber Lynn, Robert Leland. AS in Forestry, N.D. Sch. of Forestry, 1964; BS, Utah State U., 1966. Range conservationist Bur. of Land Mgmt., Battle Mountain, Nev., 1972-75, Glenwood Spring, Colo., 1975-77; range conservationist Bur. of Land Mgmt., St. George, Utah, 1977-90, ecologist, 1990—, facilities unit leader interagy. type 1 & 2 teams, 1990—. Contbr. articles to profl. jours. Trustee, bd. dirs. Dixie Care & Shares, St. George, 1988—; class leader Inst. Cont. Learning, 1990—. With USN, 1967-70, Vietnam. Mem. Soc. Range Mgmt. (future planning com. 1990-93, bd. dirs. 1994-96, membership com. 1997—, v.p. 1997-98, pres. 1999), Ariz. Riparian Coun., Ariz. Native Plant Soc. Democrat. Lutheran. Avocations: amateur astronomer, bicyclist, hiking, botany field trips. Home: 1828 Red Mountain Dr Santa Clara UT 84765-5266 Office: Bur Land Mgmt 345 E Riverside Dr Saint George UT 84790-6714

HUGHES, MAUREEN, casting director; b. Galway, Ireland, July 1, 1961; d. Sean and Margaret (Dunleavy) H. Exec. asst. Druid Theatre Co., Galway, 1984-94; casting dir. Abbey Theatre, Dublin, Ireland, 1992-94, Maureen Hughes Casting, Dublin, Ireland, 1994—. Avocations: music, reading, mountaineering, dancing, internet.

HUGHES, PATRICIA NEWMAN, academic administrator; b. Vicksburg, Miss., Apr. 16, 1964; d. Horace Wilbur Sr. and Florence (Hearn) Newman; m. Tommy Wade Hughes, Dec. 29, 1990; children: Newman Price, Dylan Wade; stepchildren: Amber Brooke, Kala Marie. BA, Miss. State U., 1986. Coord. prospect rsch. Office of Devel. Miss. State U., 1989-93, coord. prospect mgmt. Office of Devel., 1993-96, coord. prospect and donor rels. Office of Devel., 1997-98, asst. dir. devel., 1998—. Mem. Assn. Profl. Rschrs. for Advancement, Coun. Advancement and Support of Edn., Nat. Soc. Fundraising Execs. Democrat. Baptist. Avocations: reading, boating, camping. Office: Miss State U PO Drawer 6149 200 Walker Rd Mississippi State MS 39762

HUGHES, ROBERT NORMAN, psychologist, educator; b. Christchurch, New Zealand, Jan. 12, 1939; s. Arnot I. and Florence C. (Dumergue) H.; children: Cathryn Lisa, Emma Suzanne, Sarah Eve; m. Jennifer Irene Watson, May 11, 1996. BSc, U. New Zealand, 1961; MSc, U. Canterbury, 1963; PhD, Queen's U., 1967. Registered psychologist New Zealand. Lectr. U. Canterbury, Christchurch, 1964-65, Queen's U., Belfast, Ireland, 1965-67; from lectr. to sr. lectr., reader U. Canterbury, 1968—, head psychology dept., 1999—; mental health cons. WHO, Vietnam, 1995. Editor New Zealand Jour. Psychology, Internat. Jour. Comparative Psychology; contbr. articles to profl. jours. Fellow Am. Psychol. Soc., New Zealand Psychol. Soc., Psychol. Soc. Ireland. Avocations: genealogy, philately, musical appreciation. Home: Bells Rd, RD1 Christchurch New Zealand Office: U Canterbury, Dept Psychology PB 4800, Christchurch New Zealand

HUGHES, SARAH FARRELL, artist; b. Columbus, Ohio, July 28, 1969; d. George Gordon Hughes Sr. and Ann Farrell Hughes. BS in Photojournalism, Boston U., 1991; BFA, Calif. Coll. Arts and Crafts, Oakland, 1998; postgrad., Sch. for Internat. Tng., Kenya and Tanzania, 1989. Notary pub. Asst. film archivist and rschr. Anthropol. and Human Studies Film Archives, Smithsonian Mus., Washington, 1991-93; tchr. ESL and GED high sch. equivalency Lado Internat. Coll., Washington, 1992-95, exec. asst., 1992-95; exec. asst. Sierra Club, San Francisco, 1995-96; exhbn. asst., registrar, preparator Yerba Buena Ctr. for Arts, Mex. Mus., Jewish Mus., San Francisco, DeYoung Mus., New Langton Arts, San Francisco, 1998—; freelance artist San Francisco, 1990—; cons. to bd. dirs. for devel. of new artists' residence Villa Montalvo, Saratoga, Calif., 1999. Exhibited at So. Exposure, San Jose Conf. on Women Against Domestic Violence, 2000, Sculpture in Biennial Sculpture Competition, 1998, Interactive Performance with Sculptures, 1998. Tchr. Symposium on Teen Mothers Expectations, Oakland, 1997; photographer Eastern Market Historic Structure Report for Historic Preservations, Washington, 1992; photographer/builder Habitat for Humanity, Boston, 1989, 90. Villa Montalvo fellow, 1999; Women Artist scholar Montgomery County Women's Artist Collective, Rockville, Md., 1994. Democrat. Avocations: languages, travel, dance, swimming.

HUGHES, SHARON MARY, trade association executive; b. Chgo., July 28, 1952; d. George Ingersoll and Rose Myrtle (Reed) H. BA in Polit. Sci. and Comm. cum laude, Am. U., 1980, MS in Bus., Govt. Rels., 1985. Freelance photographer N.Y.C., 1972-76; advt. account exec. R.L. Newport and Co., N.Y.C., 1976-78; direct mail advt. mgr. John Wanamaker's, Phila., 1981-83; legis. intern U.S. Congressman James Florio, Washington, 1985; asst. dir. legis. affairs Nat. Food Processors Assn., Washington, 1985-87; mgr. govt. affairs Synthetic Organic Chem. Mfrs. Assn., Washington, 1987-89; exec. v.p. Nat. Coun. Agrl. Employers, Washington, 1989—. Mem., sodalist Holy Rosary Ch. Sodality, Washington, 1989— (sec. 1997-99). Mem. Women in Govt. Rels. (bd. dirs. 1996-98, co-chmn. environ. task force 1988-89, mem. agrl. task force 1989-90, co-chmn. congl. rels. com. 1992-93), Am. League Lobbyists, Am. Soc. Assn. Execs. (cert. assn. exec.), Greater Wash. Soc. Assn. Execs. Democrat. Roman Catholic. Avocations: photography, skiing, golf, history, travel. Fax: 202-728-0303. E-mail: hughesncae@aol.com. Home: 3506 Halcyon Dr Alexandria VA 22305-1330 Office: Nat Coun Agrl Employers 1112 16th St NW Ste 920 Washington DC 20036-4825

HUGHES, STELLA PLATT, sociology educator; b. Rapid City, S.D., Aug. 25, 1929; d. George Lee Platt and Josephine Ann Paulson; m. William Lewis Hughes, June 9, 1950; children: Elizabeth Holderman, James, Judith Cockrell, Michael. BS in Psychology, Okla. State U., 1973, MS in Corrections, 1976, PhD in Sociology, 1981. Undergraduate acad. counselor Okla. State U., Stillwater, 1981, lectr. dept. sociology, 1982, adj. asst. prof., 1982-88; assoc. prof. dept. liberal arts S.D. Sch. Mines and Tech., Rapid City, 1989-93, prof. dept. social scis., 1993-96, prof. emeritus, 1996—; cons. Okla. Hwy. Safety Office, 1985-88, HHS, 1992, 93, USDA, 1994; faculty assoc. Office Juvenile Sys. Oversight Okla. Commn. Children and Youth, 1986, U.S. Dept. Justice, 1986-87; project dir. Okla. Commn. Children and Youth/Dept. Mental Health, 1986; program evaluator S.D. Sch. Mines and Tech., 1992-93. Contbr. articles to profl. jours. Asst. leader, leader Girl Scouts Am., Stillwater, Okla., 1964-66; rep. to state bd. Okla. Assn. Children Learning Disabilities, Stillwater, 1971-72; bd. dirs. Cmty. Action Found.,

Stillwater, 1971-76, chmn. bd. dirs., 1974-76; bd. dirs. Sheltered Workshop Payne County, Stillwater, 1972-73; vol. counselor Payne County Vol. Program Misdemeanants, Inc., Stillwater, 1974-75; mem. steering com. Payne-Noble Family Planning, Stillwater, 1975-80; judge High Plains Sci. and Engring. Fair, 1990—, mem. sci. rev. com., 1991-94; mem. U.S. Senator Tom Dashle's Health Adv. Group, Rapid City, 1991—; bd. dirs. Black Hills Symphony Orch., Rapid City, 1996-99, v.p., 1997-99. Mem. AAAS, Norwegian-Am. Hist. Soc., Sons Norway, Nat. Geneal. Soc., Am. Sociol. Assn., Soc. Study Social Problems, Rsch. Soc. Alcoholism, Great Plains Sociol. Assn., Midwest Sociol. Soc., Southwestern Social Sci. Assn., New Eng. Hist. and Geneal. Soc., Alpha Kappa Delta. Avocations: genealogy, travel. Home: 6118 Greenleaf Ct Rapid City SD 57702-8845

HUGHES, STEPHEN ORMSBY, foreign correspondent; b. Crosby, Eng., Jan. 21, 1924; s. George and Juliet Winifred (Ormsby) H.; m. Raymonde Marie-Antoinette Million-Nietin Hughes, Sept. 3, 1951; children: Gregory Warwick, Kathleen Barbara. Student, St. Mary's Coll., Crosby, Eng. Pilot Royal Air Force, Eng., 1942-46; reporter Stroud (Eng.) Jour., 1946-48, Kent and Sussex Courier, Tunbridgewells, Eng., 1948-50; editor Sunday Ghibli, Tripoli, Libya, 1950-51; sub-editor Continental Daily Mail, Paris, 1951; corr. AP, Morocco, 1952-61; bur. chief Reuters, Rabat, Morocco, 1961-95; corr. BBC, Time-Life Inc., Morocco, 1995—. Author: Tight Lines and Dragonflies, 1972, Morocco Under King Hassan, 2000; co-author: Insight Guide to Morocco, 1989; translator (poetry) la Boite de Santale, 1974. Recipient Atlantic Star Royal Air Force, 1945; comdr., Wissam Alawite. Mem. Fgn. Press Assn. (pres.). Avocations: fly fishing, writing, drawing. Office: 17 Rue de Baghdad, 10000 Rabat Morocco

HUGHES, VESTER THOMAS, JR., lawyer; b. San Angelo, Tex., May 24, 1928; s. Vester Thomas and Mary Ellen (Tisdale) H. Student, Baylor U., 1945-46; B.A. with distinction, Rice U., 1949; LLB cum laude, Harvard U., 1952. Bar: Tex. 1955. Law clk. U.S. Supreme Ct., 1952; assoc. Robertson, Jackson, Payne, Lancaster & Walker, Dallas, 1955-58; ptnr. Jackson, Walker, Winstead, Cantwell & Miller, Dallas, 1958-76, Hughes, Luce, Hennessy, Smith & Castle, Dallas, 1976—, Hughes & Hill, Dallas, 1979-85, Hughes & Luce, Dallas, 1985—; bd. dirs. Exell Cattle Co., Amarillo, Tex., LX Cattle Co., Amarillo, Austin Industries, Dallas; adv. dir. First Nat. Bank Mertzon; tax counsel Communities Found. of Tex., Inc.; mem. adv. com. Tex. Supreme Ct., 1985-93. Contbr. articles on fed. taxation to profl. jours. Bd. dirs. Juvenile Diabetes Found. Inc., Dallas, 1982—; trustee Dallas Bapt. Coll., 1967-77; v.p., trustee, exec. com. Tex. Scottish Rite Hosp. for Children, 1967—; bd. overseers vis. com. Harvard Law Sch., 1969-75. 1st lt. JAGC U.S. Army, 1952-55. Mem. ABA (coun. sect. taxation 1969-73), Tex. Bar Assn., Dallas Bar Assn., Am. Law Inst. (coun. 1958—), Am. Coll. Tax Counsel, Southwestern Legal Found., Am. Coll. of Trust and Estate Counsel, Met. Club (Washington), Harvard Club (N.Y.C.), Masons, Order Ea. Star, Phi Beta Kappa, Sigma Xi. Democrat. Baptist. Avocations: traveling, community and church activities, reading. Office: Hughes & Luce 1717 Main St Ste 2800 Dallas TX 75201-4685

HUGHES, WILLIAM FRANKLIN, JR., ophthalmologist, emeritus educator; b. Indpls., Apr. 18, 1913; s. William F. and Alta (Rentschler) H.; m. Wanema Dickey, June 28, 1941 (dec. 1969); children: William Franklin III, Jacqueline Alter, Sarah Lee; m. Jane M. Stockdale, 1970. A.B., Amherst Coll., 1934; M.D., Johns Hopkins, 1938. Diplomate Am. Bd. Ophthalmology (mem. 1968-80). Intern, asst. resident and resident in ophthalmology Johns Hopkins, 1938-44, asst. prof. ophthalmology, 1944-46, research work, 1941-46; pvt. practice in ophthalmology Ind. U. Sch. of Medicine, 1946-47; prof. ophthalmology U. Ill., 1947—, head dept., 1947-58; ophthalmologist-in-chief Research and Ednl. Hosps. and Ill. Eye and Ear Infirmary, 1947-58; chmn. dept. ophthalmology Presbyn.-St. Luke's Hosp., Chgo., 1956-79; prof. ophthalmology Rush Med. Coll., 1971-81, prof. emeritus, 1981—; past mem. ophthalmology com. NRC. Author: Office Management of Ocular Diseases, 1953; mem. editorial bds. Archives of Ophthalmology, 1951-62, 81-84; editor Year Book Ophthalmology, 1959-81; contbr. articles on chem. burns of eyes, cataract extraction, beta irradiation, retinal detachment, corneal diseases and corneal transplantation. Mem. AMA, Assn. Research in Ophthalmology (trustee 1949-55), Am. Ophthal. Soc. (council 1971-76, pres. 1981), Chgo. Ophthal. Soc. (past pres.), Inst. of Med. Chgo., Billings Med. Club of Chgo. (pres. 1965), Sigma Xi, Alpha Kappa Kappa, Phi Kappa Psi. Home: 4 Court Of Mohawk Vly Lincolnshire IL 60069-3211

HUGHES, WILLIAM JOHN, former congressman, diplomat; b. Salem, N.J., Oct. 17, 1932; s. William W. and Pauline H.; m. Nancy L. Gibson; children: Nancy Lynne, Barbara Ann, Tama Beth, William John. AB, Rutgers U., 1955, JD, 1958, LLD (hon.), 1995; LHD (hon.), Mt. Vernon Coll., 1984; LLD (hon.), Richard Stockton State Coll., 1994, Glassboro State Coll., 1992; AA (hon.), Cumberland County Coll., 1994. Bar: N.J. 1959. Ptnr. Loveland, Hughes & Garrett, Ocean City, N.J., 1968-78; 1st asst. pros. atty. Cape May County, N.J., 1960-70; mem. 94th-103rd Congresses from 2d N.J. dist., Washington, D.C., 1974—; amb. to Panama U.S. Dept. State, 1995-98; Clifford P. Case prof. pub. affairs Rutgers U., 1997; disting. scholar ethics and pub. policy Richard Stockton Coll. N.J., Pomona, 1999—; prof. Rutgers U., 1999—; of counsel Riker, Danzig, Scherer, Hyland & Perretti, LLP, 2000—. Bd. govs. Shore Meml. Hosp., Sommers Point, N.J., 1972-76. Recipient Ann. Planning award Am. Planning Assn., 1979, Disting. Citizen award Atlantic Area coun. Boy Scouts Am., 1982, Legislator of Yr. award VFW, 1982, Pres.'s award Nat. Dist. Attys. Assn., 1982, Legis. Leadership award Nat. Assn. Chain Drug Stores, 1984, Humanitarian citiation Food Mktg. Chain Drug Stores and N.J. Food Council, 1984, Legis. award Nat. Assn. Police Orgns., 1984, Legis. Achievement award Fed. Law Enforcement Officers Assn., 1984, Man of Yr. award Girl Scouts Am., 1986, Legis. award N.J. Foster Parents Assn., 1986, Leo Fraser Super Achiever award Juvenile Diabetes Found., 1987, Arthur E. Armitage Sr. Disting. Alumni award Rutgers U., 1987, Disting. Info. Processing Pub. Service award Data Processing Mgmt. Assn., 1987, Rutgers U. medal, 1992, Distinction in Pub. Svc. award Am. Rivers, 1993, Congressional Advocacy award, 1994, Spirit of South Jersey award South Jersey Devel. Coun., 1994, Career Achievement award in pub. svc. N.J. Edn. Assn., 1995; named Congressman of Yr., Nat. Assn. Police Orgns., 1986, Hall of Disting. Alumni award Rutgers U., 1997, Jefferson medal award N.J. Intellectual Property Law Assn., 1995. Mem. ABA, N.J. Bar Assn., Ocean City Hist. Soc. (bd. dir. 1972-76), Ocean City C. of C. (bd. dir. 1960—), Exch. of Ocean City Club (pres. 1965-66, Nat. Big E. award 1965), Masons (master lodge, Worshipful Master 1969). Democrat. Epsicopalian. Home: 1019 Wesley Rd Ocean City NJ 08226-4754

HUGHEY, DAVID VAUGHN, business administration educator, dean; b. Henderson, Nev., Jan. 19, 1944; s. Vaughn V. and Janet R. (Taborsky) H. BA, Kent State U., 1967; postgrad., So. Ill. U., 1967-68; PhD, U. Pitts., 1977; BS, Internat. Coll., Newlands, Cayman Islands, 1987, M of Acctg., 1994, MS, 1995. Cert. instr. anthropology and biology Calif. C.C. Instr. bus. Stautzenberger Coll., Findlay, Ohio, 1988; acct., bookkeeper JEF Transport Co., Findlay, 1988-91; sr. lectr. biology U. Findlay, 1991; asst. prof. applied behavioral scis. Nat.-Louis U., Atlanta, 1991-92; prof. human resources, dean Internat. Coll., Newlands, 1992-95, prof. bus. adminstrn., dean, 1995—. Contbr. articles and revs. to profl. jours. and books. Contbr. Cayman Islands Nat. Mus., Georgetown, 1996—. With U.S. Army, 1969-71. Predoctoral fellow Andrew Mellon Found., 1974-76. Fellow Am. Anthropol. Assn.; mem. Caribbean Studies Assn. (life), Am. Acctg. Assn., N.Y. Acad. Scis., Pi Gamma Mu (hon.). Episcopalian. Avocations: poetry, photography, chess. Office: Internat Coll, Newlands Campus PO Box 136, Savannah Cayman Islands

HUGHEY, RICHARD KOHLMAN, author, lawyer; b. Chgo., July 6, 1934. BA cum laude, Santa Clara U., 1958, JD cum laude, 1963. Bar: Calif. 1964, U.S. Ct. Appeals (9th cir.) 1964, U.S. Supreme Ct. 1972. Atty. Pacific Gas & Elec. Co., San Francisco, 1963-69, Berry, Davis & McInerny, Oakland, Calif., 1969-71; ptnr. Caputo, Liccardo, Rossi & Kohlman, San Jose, 1971-75; lectr. law, dir. CLE Santa Clara (Calif.) U., 1975-80; mng. editor Bancroft-Whitney Co., San Francisco, 1980-91, Lawyers Coop. Pub. Co., Rochester, N.Y., 1992-94; history and lit. biography writer, 1995—; columnist Mountain Democrat, Placerville, Calif., 1997—. Bd. editors Calif. State Bar Jour., 1972-75; editor-in-chief Santa Clara Law Rev., 1961-63; author: Jeffers Country Revisited: Beauty Without Price, 1996, Computer Technology in Civil Litigation, 1990, Trial Lawyers Manual, 1978, Abalone Lite, 1997; co-author: Petroglyphs: Poetry and Fiction, 1994, Hey Lew: Homage to Lew Welch, 1997; editor: Am Jur Trials, 1980-90, Proof of Facts, 1982-90. Mem. citizen's adv. commn. U.S. Postal Svc., San Francisco, 1989-92; mem. adv. bd. Commn. on Future of the Cts., Jud. Coun. of Calif., 1992; dir. Cmty. Legal Svcs., San Jose, 1973-78. Recipient Merit award Calif. Psychol. Assn., 1985, Santa Clara County Bar Assn., 1973-75. Mem. ABA, Am. Acad. Forensic Scis., Assn. Trial Lawyers Am., Practicing Law Inst., Def. Rsch. Inst., Internat. Platform Assn., Writers and Books Club, Acad. Am. Poets, Modern Poetry Assn., San Jose Ctr. for Poetry and Lit. Avocations: creative writing, photography.

HUG-LEVY, SUZY, artist; b. Istanbul, Turkey, June 2, 1944; d. Sami and Fani (Hirsch) H.;m. Henri Levy, July 8, 1965; children: Eytan, Alida. BA, Robert Coll., Istanbul, Turkey, 1965. Internat. sculptor/performance artist. Instnl. exhibits Washington, Paris, Alexandria, Egypt, Sharjah, United Arab Emirates, Budapest, Hungary, others; works in worldwide collections. Trustee Istanbul Modern Art Mus. Found. Recipient Contemporary Art prize, 1993, Biennial award UAE, 1997, Best Sculptor award Turkish Arts Coun., 1999-2000. Mem. Internat. Assn. of Art, UNESCO, Turkish Plastic Arts Assn., SANART Assn. Avocations: contemporary art, classical music, modern dance, sailing. E-mail: suzy@atlas.net.tr. Fax: 90-212-251 5840. Home: 386/1 Ceudetpasa Cad, 80810 Istanbul Turkey Studio: 18 Bebek Dagi Gikmazi, 80810 Istanbul Turkey

HUGON, JACQUES, medical educator, neurologist; b. Saint-Maur, France, Dec. 19, 1950; s. Roger and Gilberte (Vercasson) H.; m. Francoise Barataud; 3 children. MD, U. Limoges, France, 1983; PhD in Cell Biology, U. Paris, 1987. Rsch. assoc. Albert Einstein Coll. Medicine, N.Y.C., 1984-86; prof. histology Faculty of Medicine, U. Limoges, 1989-2000; neurologist Limoges U. Hosp., 1987-2000; dir. Cell Neurobiology Lab. U. Limoges, 1990-2000, dir. Inst. Cellular and Molecular Biology, 1994-2000; chair prof., head dept. anatomy U. Hong Kong, 2000—, hon. clin. prof. dept. medicine and surgery, 2000—; cons. Oreg. Health Sci. U., 1994. Author sci. publs. Fax: 852 2817 0857. E-mail: jhugon@hkucc.hku.hk. Office: Fac Med Hist and Cell Biol, 2 rue du Dr Marcland, 87025 Limoges France

HUGOT-LE GOFF, ANNE J., science researcher; b. Asnieres, France, Feb. 7, 1939; d. Lucien Le Goff and Paulette Ponant; m. André Hugot; children: Emmanuelle, Yves David, Jullien. Grad., Ecole Superieure Elecricite, Paris, 1961; DS, U. Paris, 1966. Rsch. leader Ctr. Nat. Rsch. Sci., Paris; rschr. electrochem. lab. CNRS, Paris, 1961—. Mem. editl. bd. Thin Solid Films. Mem. Nat. Com. Mouvement des Citoyens. Mem. Internat. Soc. Electrochemistry, Electrochem. Soc. Roman Catholic. Home: 9 Ave de Colombes, 92600 Asnieres France Office: CNRS UPR 15, UPMC Tour 22, 75252 Paris Cedex 05, France

HUGUENIN, DENIS, research engineer; b. Macon, France, May 18, 1960; s. Jean-Pierre and Therese (Moreau) H. MS, U. Nancy, France, 1983; PhD in Physics, U. Grenoble, France, 1989. Rschr. C.E.N.G., Grenoble, 1984-85, 87-89, U. Tokyo, 1985-87; rsch. engr. Rhone Poulenc, Paris, 1989-97, Rhodia, Paris, 1998-99; energy dept. mgr. IMRA-Europe, Nice, France, 1999—. Contbr. papers to profl. publs.; patentee in field. Home: 1 place du Foulon, 06130 Plascassier France Office: IMRA-Europe, BP 213, 06904 Sophia Antipolis France

HUGUES, TOURVIEILLE DE LABROUHE, air transportation executive; b. La Rochefoucauld, Charente, France, Aug. 8, 1951; s. François and Marie Therese (Hymonnet) H.; m. Marie Laure Chabbert, Apr. 3, 1976; children: Stephane, Marion, Florent. Traffic mgr. Air Languedoc, Beziers, 1975-76; comml. dir. asst. Continentale Air Svc., Le Bourget, 1976-78; asst. mgr. Impression Technique et Publicitaire, Rueil Malmaison, 1978-79; comml. dir. Air Affaires Internat., Le Bourget, 1979-81, Euralair Internat., Le Bourget, 1981-99; sta. mgr. T.A.G. Aviation Co., France, Belgium, Luxembourg, 1999—. Decorated Chevalier de l'Ordre de l'Etoile de Bien et du Merite, Medaille d'Argent Grand Prix Humanitaire, Chevalier de la Croix de la Valeur Civique, Chevalier de l'Ordre Pro-Patria, Medal of Merit et Devouement Francais, Medal of Honor de l'Union Nat. des Anciens Combatants de l'Indochine et Territoire Afrique du Nord, Chevalier de l'Aide Aux Anciens Militaires. Mem. Assn. Representants Commerciaux des Compagnies Aériennes (v.p. 1981—), Assn. des Representants Interlines à Paris, St. James Paris, Skal Club, Habana Cigar Tourism Club, Aeroclub de France, Karate Club (v.p. Wezien chpt. 1989—). Avocations: tennis, karate, travel, reading, Asia. Fax: 33 1 41 69 17 18. Home: 18 Rue des Vignes, 95470 Saint Witz France Office: TAG Aviation, Le Terminal Bat 413, 93350 Le Bourget France

HUH, HOON, engineering educator; b. Seoul, Korea, Oct. 21, 1953; s. Naam and Kyungsoon (Park) H.; m. Sanghee Choy; children: Lynn, Hann, Vynn. BS, Seoul Nat. U., 1976, MS, 1978; PhD, U. Mich., 1986. Rsch. engr. Oriental Precision Co., Seoul, 1978-79; RA U. Mich., Ann Arbor, 1984-86, PD, 1986; from asst. to assoc. prof. Korea Advanced Inst. Sci. and Tech., Taejon, 1986-99, prof., 1999—; mem. steering bd. G-7 project Ministry of Sci. and Tech., Seoul, 1992-95; mem. planning and evaluating bd. Indsl. Tech. Evaluation and Planning/Ministry of Commerce, Industry and Energy, Seoul, 1994-99; mem. planning bd. Sci. and Tech. Policy Inst./Ministry of Sci. and Tech., Seoul, 1994. Guest editor: Internat. Jour. Vehicle Design, 1999-2000; editor: Metals and Materials, an Internat. Jour., 1997—, Internat. Jour. Automotive Tech., 2000—; contbr. articles to profl. jours. Rsch. engr. Army Hdqs., 1979-81. Recipient Korean Govt. Scholarship award Min. Edn., 1982, Korean-Am. Honor Scholarship award Korean Embassy in U.S., 1984. Mem. ASME, Asia-Pacific Conf. on Advances in Engring. Plasticity and Its Application (mem. internat. sci. com. 1994—), Asia Pacific Conf. on Materials Processing (mem. internat. sci. com. 1996—), Korean Soc. Tech. of Plasticity (editl. dir. 1991-99), Korean Soc. Mech. Engrs. (mem. editl. com., head Korea Advanced Inst. Sci. and Tech.), Soc. Engring. Sci., Korean Soc. Automotive Engrs. (editl. dir.), Korean Soc. for Composite Materials, Korean Soc. Theoretical and Applied Mechanics. Avocations: golfing, tennis, paintings, calligraphy. Office: Korea Adv Inst Sci and Tech, Dept Mech Eng Science Town, Taejon 305-701, Korea

HUH, HYUNG-TACK, oceanoprapher; b. San-Chung, Korea, Mar. 29, 1938; s. Hyun and Yung-Tae (Cho) H.; m. Yung-Hae Chun, Sept. 2, 1972; chilren: Seung, Wook, Gene. BS, Pukyung Nat. U., Pusan, Korea, 1960; MS, U. Wisc., 1969, PhD, 1975. Cert. fisheries biologist, Am. Fisheries Soc. Rschr. Nat. Fisheries R&D Inst., Pusan, Korea, 1960-61; rsch. scientist Nalco Environ. Scis., Inc., Evanston, Ill., 1970-72, Battelle Meml. Inst., Columbus, Ohio, 1976-77; principal scientist Korea Ocean R&D Inst., Seoul, 1978-81, dir., 1981-88, sr. rsch. fellow, 1989—; adv. Nat. Sci. Coun., Seoul, 1999—; vice-chmn. W. Pacific Oceanographic Commn., 1996—. Author: (books) The Oceans, The Last Frontier, 1981, Marine Biology, 1997. Recipient Wolhae Rsch. award, Wolhae Found., Seoul, 1990, Moran Jang award, Office Pres. Korea, 1990, Pacon Internat. award, Pacific Congress on Marine Sci. & Tech., 1998. Fellow Korean Acad. Sci., N.Y. Acad. Sci., Korean Soc. Futurology; mem. Korean Soc. Oceanography (pres.), N. Pacific Marine Sci. Orgn. (chmn.). Presbn. Home: 12-41 Bangbae-Dong Seochoku, 137-060 Seoul Korea Office: Korea Ocean R&D Inst, 1270 Sa-Dong Ansanshi, 425-600 Seoul Korea

HUH, SEUNG JAE, oncologist, educator; b. Seoul, Jan. 1, 1952; s. Joon and Hung Ok (Lee) H.; m. Ae Ja Park. MD, Seoul Nat. U., 1976; PhD, Chungang U., 1985. Intern Seoul Nat. U. Hosp., 1976-77, resident, 1977-81; assoc. prof. Soonchunghyang U., Seoul, 1985-94; prof., chmn. Samsung Med. Ctr., 1994-98. Contbr. articles to profl. jours. Capt. Army Hosp., 1981-84. Avocations: golf, tennis, jogging. E-mail: sjhuh@smc.samsung.co.kr. Office: Samsung Med Ctr, 50 Ilwon Dong Kangnam-ku, Seoul 130-710, Korea

HUHEEY, JAMES EDWARD, chemist, herpetologist and educator; b. Cin., Aug. 2, 1935; s. Edward O'Neill and Catherine (Smythe) H. BS, U. Cin., 1957; MS, U. Ill., 1959, PhD, 1961. Rsch. assoc. U. Mich., Ann Arbor, 1961; asst. prof. chemistry Worcester (Mass.) Poly. Inst., 1961-65; asst. prof. U. Md., College Park, 1965-68, assoc. prof., 1968-75, prof., 1975-98; prof. U. Tenn., Knoxville, 1998—; vis. prof. So. Ill. U., Carbondale, 1974-75, 89-90, UCLA, 1986, U. Tenn., Knoxville, 1998; pres., dir. Chem. Assocs. Md. Author: Inorganic Chemistry: Principles of Structure and Reactivity, 1972, 4th edit. 1993, (with Arthur Stupka) Amphibians and Reptiles of Great Smoky Mountains National Park, 1968, Diversity and Periodicity: An Inorganic Module, 1973, 78; contbr. articles to profl. jours. Recipient Young Chemists award D.C. chpt. Am. Inst. Chemists, 1971, Leo Schubert Teaching award, 1983; NSF grantee, 1965-67, 75-77, 78—; NSF fellow, 1959, duPont Teaching fellow, 1960; Sigma Xi grantee, 1963, Am. Philos. Soc. grantee, 1974. Fellow AAAS; mem. Am. Chem. Soc., Am. Soc. Ichthyologists and Herpetologists, Soc. Study Amphibians and Reptiles (dir.), Herpetologists League, Ecol. Soc. Am., Soc. Study Evolution. Home: Sourwood Mountain 215 Tucker Ln Lenoir City TN 37771-3405 Office: U Tenn Dept Chemistry Knoxville TN 27996

HUHN, DARLENE MARIE, county official, poet; b. Kearny, N.J., Feb. 13, 1967; d. Charles Joseph and Theresa Catherine (Foertsch) H. AAS, Essex County C.C., Newark, 1990. Sec. Hudson County Vo-Tech., North Bergen, N.J., 1983-84; law clk. Skoloff & Wolfe, Livingston, N.J., 1984-87; data entry clk. Robith, Lyndhurst, N.J., 1987-94; income maint. technician Hudson County Welfare, Jersey City, 1994—. Author: (poetry) Decisions, 1995, Have Faith, 1995 (Internat. Soc. Poetry Poet of Merit 1995, 96). Vice pres. Rosary Soc., East Newark, N.J., 1994-97; mem. pastoral coun. Deanery 14 Archdiocese of Newark, 1990-96. Recipient Golden Poet award World of Poetry, 1987-90, Achievement award Cath. Youth Orgn., 1991, Editor's Choice award Nat. Libr. Poetry, 1996; named Best Poet of 1988, Am. Poetry Assn., 1988, Famous Poet, Famous Poetry Soc., 1996, 98, Diamond Homer Trophy, 1998; inducted Internat. Poetry Hall of Fame, 1996. Mem. Phi Theta Kappa. Democrat. Wiccan. Avocations: poetry, science fiction book writing, classical music. Home: 330 N 2nd St East Newark NJ 07029-2721

HUHN, DIETRICH-JOACHIM, secondary school master; b. Dresden, Sachsen, Germany, Jan. 18, 1944; s. Joachim Albert and Elsbeth Anna (Just) H. Diploma in physics, U. Frankfurt, Germany, 1969, Dr. phil. nat., 1977; grad. mastership program, Studienseminar III, Frankfurt, 1979. Rschr., instr. U. Frankfurt and U. Hannover, Germany, 1969-77; lectr. Tech. Coll., Wiesbaden, Germany, 1981-84; master Humboldt Gymnasium, Bad Homburg, Germany, 1979-81, sr. master in physics and math., 1981—, head physics dept. Co-author: (manual) Handbuch der Experimentellen Physik, 1992; contbr. articles to profl. publs. Mem. Senckenbergische Naturforschende Gesellschaft. Avocations: horseback riding, yachting, tennis, classical music. Home: Königsteiner Strasse 114, 65812 Bad Soden Hessen, Germany

HUI, AI-MIN, surgeon, educator; b. Xingtang, Hebei, China, Nov. 24, 1962; s. Zhi-Zhong Hui and Jing-Min Wang; m. Lin Sun, Jan. 28, 1989; 1 child, Xiao-Yu. B Medicine, Hebei Med. U., Shijiazhuang, China, 1984; PhD, Shinshu U., Matsumoto, Japan, 1994. Asst. prof. Hebei Med. U., 1984-90; postdoctoral fellow Nat. Cancer Ctr., Tokyo, 1994-97; asst. prof. surgery U. Tokyo, 1997-2000, assoc. prof., 2000—. Author: Recent Advances in Gastroenterological Cardinogenesis, 1996, Molecular Genetics of Cancer, 2000; contbr. articles to profl. jours. Reciient Young Rschr. award Japan Soc. Gastroenterology Surg., 1993, Young Investigator award Internat. Conf. on Gastrointestinal Cancer, 1996; sci. rsch. grantee Japanese Govt., 1998-99. Mem. Assn. Chinese Scientists and Engrs. (councilor 1999—), Am. Assn. Cancer Rsch., N.Y. Acad. Scis., Internat. Gastro-Surg. Club. Avocations: reading, sports. Office: U Tokyo Dept Surgery, 7-3-1 Hongon Bunkyo-ku, Tokyo 113-0033, Japan

HUI, DESMOND CHEUK-KUEN, architecture educator; b. Hong Kong, Aug. 14, 1958; arrived in Can., 1981; s. Fong and Fung (Ng) H. BArch, Cornell U., 1982; MPhil, Cambridge U., 1986, PhD, 1997. Cert. Royal Archtl. Inst. of Can. Architect Barton Myers Assocs., Toronto, 1982-85; rsch. fellow St. Edmund's Coll. - U. Cambridge, U.K., 1989-90; lectr. U. Hong Kong, 1990-93, assoc. prof., 1993—; chmn. Hong Kong Soc. Chinese Trad. Dwellings, 1997—; vice-chmn. Hong Kong Inst. of Contemporary Culture, 1997—; guest scholar Canadian Ctr. for Architecture, Montreal, 1998. Mem. Antiquities Adv. Bd., Hong Kong, 1997—; mem. exec. com. Hong Kong Youth Hostel Assn., 1995—. Recipient scholarship Cornell U., 1977-82, Assn. of Commonwealth Univs., London, 1986-89. Mem. Ont. Assn. of Architects. Avocations: reading, sports, travel. Office: Dept Architecture, Univ Hong Kong/Pokfulam Rd, Hong Kong China

HUI, HO-WAH, pharmaceutical scientist; b. Hong Kong, June 20, 1957; came to U.S., 1976; s. Ching-Choi and Choy-Hing (Yong) H.; m. Julia Ying Chow, July 24, 1982; children: Jessica, Joanna. BS in Pharmacy with distinction, U. Wis., 1980, MS in Pharmaceutics, 1983, PhD in pharmaceutics, 1985. Registered pharmacist. Intern in pharmacy Madison (Wis.) Gen. Hosp., 1980-81; teaching asst. pharmacy U. Wis., Madison, 1981-83, research asst. pharmacy, 1983-85; rsch. pharmacist Abbott Labs., North Chicago, Ill., 1985-87; also bd. seminar com. Abbott Labs, North Chicago, Ill.; sr. rsch. scientist Abbott Labs., North Chicago, Ill., 1987-91, rsch. investigator, 1991-94, assoc. rsch. fellow vol. soc., 1994—; chmn. Exploratory Projects Discussion, Abbott Labs., 1988. Author: Oral Drug Products, 1987; contbr. articles to profl. jours. Counsellor, dir. Awana Youth Club, Vernon Hills, Ill., 1987—; pres. Madison Chinese Christian Fellowship, 1984, bd. dirs. exec. com., 1982-83; steering com. Chinese Christian Union. Ch., Chgo., 1986—, trustee, 1992—. Recipient Merck Sharp and Dohme scholarship U. Wis., 1984. Mem. Am. Pharm. Assn., Am. Assn. Pharm. Scientists (chmn. pharmaceutics and drug delivery publicity 1995, 96, chmn. drug delivery program 1990-91), Chicagoland Pharm. Discussion Group (chmn. membership com. 1993-96, program com. 1996—), Lake County Chinese Am. Assn. (pres. 1994-95, bd. dirs. 1995-98), Far East Broadcasting Co.-Chgo. (chmn. bd. dirs. 1997—). Avocations: swimming, table tennis, playing violin, singing. Office: Abbott Labs 14th And Sheridan Rd North Chicago IL 60064

HUI, PING, electrical engineering educator; b. Quzhou, Zhejiang, China, May 6, 1962; s. Zhongmo Hui and Hezheng Xie; m. Yuyin Lin, Jan. 6, 1993; children: An, Xin. BS, Changsha (China) Inst. Tech., 1982; MS, Zhejiang U., Hangzhou, 1984; PhD, Poly. U., Farmingdale, N.Y., 1991. Rsch. fellow Nanyang Tech. U., Singapore, 1991-94, lectr., 1994—, assoc. prof., 2000—. Contbr. articles to profl. jours. including Japanese Jour. Applied Physics, Jour. Applied Physics. Mem. IEEE (sr. mem.). Avocations: travel, swimming, reading. Home: Blk 905, Jurong West St 91 #04-155, Singapore 640905, Singapore Office: Nanyang Tech U, Elec Engring Sch, Singapore 639798, Singapore

HUIC, TOMISLAV, creative director; b. Zagreb, Croatia, Mar. 18, 1949; s. Stjepan Miho and Vera Jelena H.; m. Gordana Manojlovic, June 24, 1978; 1 child, Aleksandra. Diploma, High Acad. of Drama Arts, Zabreb; specialist in mktg. communication, Zagreb. Cameraman Zagreb, 1973-77; journalist Croatian Radio-TV, Zagreb, 1977-84; dir. of promotion The Lead and Aluminum products Factory, Zagreb-Kerestinec, 1984-88; mktg. dir. Polariod & Minolta, Zagreb, 1988-91; promotion & advt. counselor Croatian Min. of Tourism, Zagreb, 1991-93; creative dir. SRT Adv. Agy., Zagreb, 1993—. Creative dir. Vizual Identity of the Diary Industry in Split, 1995, Corp. Identity, 1995, TV commercial, 1996, Printed Ads, 1997. Recipient Honor for Realization of Croatian Advt. Festival Croatian Assn. Advts., 1994, Spl. Honor for Devel. of Croatina Advt. Festivald and Conv., 1996. Mem. Croatian Assn. Advt., Croatian Assn. Designers. Avocations: sailing, handcrafts. E-mail: srt@srt-advertising.com. Fax number: 00385 1 46 12 397. Home telephone: 003851 48 10 1923. Office telephone: 003851 46 12 630. Home: Djordjiceva 17, Zagreb HR 10000, Croatia Office: SRT, Kneza Mislava 11, Zagreb HR 10000, Croatia

HUIDOBRO, FERNANDO LÓPEZ, marketing professional; b. Barcelona, Spain, July 30, 1959; s. Guillermo López Cornejo and Consuelo Huidobro Ruiz. Higher Cert., Escuelas Pías San Antón, Barcelona, 1975; cert., STUCOM/BIT, Barcelona, 1983; qualification in analytic accountancy, INEM, Barcelona, 1990; qualification in databases, European Social Fund, Barcelona, 1991; qualification in mktg. and sales, Fomento del Trabajo Nacional, Barcelona, 1992; cert., Mediterranean Politicals Inst. Catalá de la Mediterránia d'Estudis i Cooperació, Barcelona, 1998. Acct. Chaflán 112 S.L., Barcelona, 1990; mktg. mgr. Barcelona Backstage/Barcelona Olympic Games, 1992; participant confs. in field. Mem. UNICEF, Spain, 1993-94, ANESVAD, Bilbao, 1999. Mem. Nat. Geographic Soc., Club Natació Montjuïc (Barcelona). Roman Catholic. Avocations: trekking, swimming, contemplation, cybernetics. Home: Mata 28 Prin 4, 08004 Barcelona Spain

HUIGNARD, JEAN PIERRE, research scientist; b. La Châtre L'Anglin, France, Aug. 28, 1944; s. Robert and Amédée (Delorme) H.; m. Ari Widjaja, Dec. 29, 1990; 1 child, Alexis. Engring. degree in optical scis., Ecole Superieure d'Optique, 1968; MS, U. Paris, Orsay, 1969; PhD, U. Orsay, 1974. Rsch. engr. Thomson-CSF Rsch. Lab., Orsay, 1969, head optics and signal processing lab., 1977-99, sr. scientist, 1999—, mem. Coll. Sci. Technique, 1990-99; editl. bd. sci. jours. in field.; gen. chair Conf. Lasers Electro-Optics, Europe, 1996; prof. in electro-optics U. Orsay, 1977; presenter, lectr. in field. Editor: Photorefractive Materials I and II; contbr. articles to profl. jours., chpts. to books.; patentee in info. storage, processing, holography, nonlinear optics, display. Recipient Laureate, French Optical Soc., 1976, French Acad. Scis., 1996, Nat. Merit award Ministery of Rsch. and Edn., 1995. Fellow Optical Soc. Am.; mem. IEEE (sr.), European Phys. Soc. (sec. quantum electronics optics). Avocations: scientific lectures, tennis. Home: 20 Rue Campo Formio, 75013 Paris France Office: Thomson-CSF/LCR, 91404 Orsay France

HUIJGENS, PETER C., internist, hematologist; b. Amsterdam, The Netherlands, Mar. 4, 1949; s. P. C. Huijgens and A. Peters; m. J. Brederoo, Jan. 3, 1974. MD, Free U., Amsterdam, 1973, PhD, 1986. Intern internal medicine U. Hosp. Vrije Universiteit, Amsterdam, 1973-78, staff internist dept. hematology, assoc. prof., 1987-97, prof., 1997—; staff mem., prof., dept. head dept. hematology Free U. Hosp., Amsterdam, 1978—. Contbr. articles to profl. jours. Mem. Dutch Soc. Hematology, Am. Soc. Hematology, European Hematology Assn. Avocation: hematology. Home: Amsterdamseweg 401, 1182 HC Amstelveen The Netherlands Office: Free Univ Hosp, de Boelelaan 1117, 1081 HV Amsterdam The Netherlands

HUISGEN, ROLF K.J., chemist; b. Gerolstein, Germany, June 13, 1920; m. Trudl Schneiderhan; children: Birge, Helga. Student, U. Bonn, 1939-40; PhD, U. Munich, 1943, Habil, 1947; Dr honoris causa, U. Complutense de Madrid, 1975, U. Freiburg, 1977, U. Erlangen, 1980, U. Wuerzburg, 1984, U. Regensburg, 1985, Technol. Inst., St. Petersburg, Russia, 1993. Assoc. prof. U. Tübingen, Germany, 1949-52; prof. organic chemistry U. Munich, 1952-88, prof. emeritus, 1988—; Carl Schurz prof. U. Wis., 1959; Baker lectr. Cornell U., 1963; Max Tishler lectr. Harvard U., 1963; vis. prof. U. Fla., Gainesville, 1968, U. Calif. Davis, 1972, 76, 79, U. Barcelona, 1978, Technion, Haifa, Israel, 1980, Hebrew U., Jerusalem, 1987, U. Milan, 1989, U. Pavia, 1993, U. Western Ont., 1996, others. Decorated Bavarian Order of Merit, Bavarian Maximilian Order Sci. and Art; recipient Liebig medal Gesellschaft Deutscher Chemiker, 1961, Lavoisier medal French Chem. Soc., 1965, P. Bruylants medal U. Louvain, 1968, Roger Adams award Am. Chem. Soc., 1975, Otto Hahn prize Gesellschaft Deutscher Chemiker, 1979, Internat. award Heterocyclic Chemistry, 1987, Adolfo Quilico medal Italian Chem. Soc., 1987, others. Mem. Bayer Akademie der Wissenschaften, Am. Acad. Arts and Scis., Deutsche Akademie der Naturforscher Leopoldina, Real Academia de Ciencias Exactas (Madrid), Nat. Acad. Scis. (Washington), Accademia Nazionale dei Lincei (Rome), Istituto Lombardo, Accademia di Scienze e Lettere (Milan), Polish Acad. Scis., French Chem. Soc. (hon.), Royal Soc. Chemistry London (hon.). Pharm. Soc. Japan (hon.), Polish Chem. Soc. (hon.), others. Office: U Munich/Dept Chemie, Butenandt Str 5-13, D-81377 Munich Germany

HUISMAN, INGMAR HARALD, food scientist, researcher, engineer; b. Goor, Overijssel, Holland, July 6, 1969; s. Reitze Cornelis and Olga Johanna (Kroonenberg) H. MSc in Chem. Engring. with honors, Twente U., Enschede, Holland, 1993, MSc in Applied Physics, 1993; PhD in Food Engring., Lund (Sweden) U., 1998. Postdoctoral rschr. Lund U., 1998, Valladolid (Spain) U., 1998-99; project mgr. TNO Food Rsch., Zeist, Holland, 1999—; tchr. Medborgaresholan, Lund, 1995-96; vis. rschr. Tech. U., Lappeenranta, Finland, 1996; Marie Curie rsch. fellow European Union, 1998. Composer, author, performing artist music CD Din Granne/Sunk, 1998; contbr. articles to profl. jours., chpt. to book. Recipient Nordic traveling grant NorFa, Finland, 1990. Mem. Marie Curie Fellows Assn. Avocations: music, theatre, languages. Office: TNO-Food Rsch, Postbus 360, 3700AT Zeist Utrecht, Holland

HUIZER, JOS, marketing professional, consultant; b. Edam, Netherlands, Mar. 24, 1957; m. Sandra de Moei, Apr. 6, 1997. Ing. in Elec. Electronic Engring. Tech Sch., 1985; RM/MBA, Cambridge (Eng.) U., 1995. Dir. Tratec Holding BV, Veenendaal, Netherlands; cons. mktg. Tratec Holding BV, Veenendaal. Office: Tratec Holding BV, De Smalle Zyde 10, NL-3900 Veenendaal LP, Netherlands

HUIZINGA, HARRY PIETER, economics educator; b. Haren, The Netherlands, May 3, 1963; s. Pieter Huizinga and Johanna Marie (De Jong) Schellenboom. AB magna cum laude, Princeton U., 1984; MA, Harvard U., 1988, PhD, 1988. Asst. prof. econs. Stanford U., Palo Alto, Calif., 1988-92; prof. internat. econs. Tilburg (The Netherlands) U., 1992—; economist World Bank, Washington, 1997; vis. scholar Internat. Monetary Fund, Washington, 1990, 93, 97; cons. fiscal affairs divsn. OECD, paris, 1994, 95. Contbr. articles to profl. jours. Avocation: hiking. Office: Tilburg U Dept Econs, PO Box 90153, 5000 LE Tilburg The Netherlands

HUKKINEN, JANNE ILMARI, environmental management educator; b. Helsinki, Finland, Oct. 6, 1957; s. Lars Johan and Maija Kaisa (Turja) H.; m. Tuula Anneli Lento, Mar. 28, 1985; children: Meri Amalia Lento, Tuomas Nikolai Lento, Hannes Konstantin Lento. MS, Helsinki U. Tech., 1984; PhD, U. Calif., Berkeley, 1990. Researcher Ministry of Environ., Finland, Helsinki, 1984-85; rsch. cons. Western Consortium Pub. Health, Berkeley, Calif., 1986; researcher Calif. Dept. Water Resources, Sacramento, 1987-88; environ. sci. and engring. fellow AAAS/U.S. EPA, Washington, 1990; postdoctoral rsch. fellow U. Calif., Berkeley, 1990-91; sr. researcher Tech. Rsch. Centre Finland, Espoo, 1991-93; assoc. prof. environ. mgmt. Maastricht (The Netherlands) Sch. Mgmt., 1993-96; prof. Arctic studies, dir. Arctic Ctr. U. Lapland, Rovaniemi, Finland, 1996-99; prof. environ. mgmt. Helsinki U. Tech., 1999—; rsch. cons. Imatran Voima Oy, Helsinki, 1992-93, Western Consortium Pub. Health, Berkeley, 1990-91; spl. rsch. cons. U.S. EPA, Washington, 1990. Contbr. articles to profl. jours. Recipient awards Acad. Fin., Berkeley, 1988, Finnish Cultural Fund, Berkeley, 1989, Harold D. Lasswel award, 1991; Fulbright YIT fellow, 1985. Mem. AAAS, Internat. Soc. Ecol. Econs., Finnish Waste Mgmt. Assn., Finnish Soc. Futures Studies. Office: Helsinki Univ Technology, PO Box 2300, 02015 Helsinki Finland

HUKUHARA, TOSIHIKO, biology educator; b. Niigata, Japan, Oct. 29, 1934; s. Takesi and Yayoi (Honma) H.; m. Kazuko Hirose, Nov. 10, 1961; children: Kazuhiko, Nobuhiko, Yayoi. Bachelor's degree, U. Tokyo, 1957, PhD, 1962. Asst. U. Tokyo, 1964-75; assoc. prof. Tokyo Noko U., 1975-88, prof., 1988-98; prof. Coll. Bioresource Sci., Nihon U., 1998—. Author: Insect Pathology, 1979, Atlas of Invertebrate Viruses, 1991; editor: Introduction to Sericultural Sciences, 1991. Recipient award Japanese Soc. Sericultural Scis., 1987. Mem. Japanese Soc. for Insect Pathology (pres. 1991-2000). Achievements include discovery of a virus enhancing factor and detection of polyhedra of a nuclear polyhedrosis virus in field soil. Avocations: movies, visiting foreign countries, Japanese chess. Fax: 0466-64-3627. E-mail: tosi@brs.nihon-u.ac.jp. Home: 4-26 3 chome Umezono, Kiyose Tokyo 204, Japan Office: Nihon U Coll Bioresources, 1866 Kameino, Fjjisawa 252-8510, Japan

HULBERT, SAMUEL FOSTER, college president; b. Adams Center, N.Y., Apr. 12, 1936; s. Foster David and Wilma May (Speakman) H.; m. Joy Elinor Husband, Sept. 3, 1960; children: Gregory, Samantha, Jeffrey. B.S. in Ceramic Engring., Alfred U., 1958, Ph.D., 1964. Registered profl. engr., La, S.C. Asst. varsity and freshman football coach Alfred U. (N.Y.), 1959-61; lab. instr. N.Y. State Coll. Ceramics, Alfred, 1958-59; instr. math and physics Alfred U., 1960-64; asst. prof. ceramic and metall. engring. Clemson U. (S.C.), 1964-68, head div. interdisciplinary studies, assoc. prof. materials and bioengring., 1968-71; assoc. dean engring research and interdisciplinary studies, prof. materials engring. and bioengring., dir. materials engring. and bioengring., 1970-73; prof. bioengring., dean Sch. Engring. Tulane U., New Orleans, 1973-76; pres.-designate spl. asst. to pres. Rose-Hulman Inst. Tech., Terre Haute, Ind., 1976, pres., 1976—; bd. dirs. Ind. Bus. Modernization & Tech. Corp., Integral Tech., Inc., Thomas & Skinner, Inc., Old Nat. Bank. Mem. editorial bd. Annals of Biomed. Engring., 1974, Jour. Biomed. Materials Rsch., 1970—; contbr. articles in field of biomaterials and artificial organ design to profl. jours. Mem. exec. com. Wabash Valley chpt. Boy Scouts Am.; mem. Ind. Humanities Coun., 1991—. Recipient medal Italian Soc. Orthopaedics, 1973, Delitala medal Instituto Ortopedico Rizzoli, 1973, Clemson award for outstanding contbns. to biomaterials, 1973, George Winters award European Soc. Biomaterials, 1982, Lifetime Achievement award Ind. Health Industry Forum, 1996; Ernst & Young Supporter of Indiana Entrepreneurship award, 1998. Fellow Am. Inst. for Med. and Biol. Engring., Am. Biomaterials Scis. and Engring., Internat. Acad. Ceramics; mem. Am. Soc. Artificial Internal Organs, Biomed. Engring. Soc., Soc. Biomaterials (dir. 1974—, pres. 1975-76), Am. Ceramic Soc., Nat. Inst. Ceramics Engrs., Am. Soc. Engring. Edn., Ind. Colls. and Univ. Assn., Ind. Colls. of Ind., Ind. Conf. Higher Edn., Assn. Ind. Tech. Univs. (sec., treas. 1977-78, pres. 1987-90), Presidents of Ind. Colls. and Univs., Vigo County Hist. Soc. (dir. 1979—, pres. 1995—), Keramos, Blue Key, Ind. Acad., Internat. Acad. Ceramics, Rotary, Sigma Xi. Republican. Office: Rose Hulman Inst Tech Office of Pres 5500 Wabash Ave Terre Haute IN 47803-3999

HULHOVEN, RÉGINALD MARCEL, internist, pharmacologist, educator; b. Brussels, Apr. 30, 1945; s. Leo Henri and Anne-Marie (Gaupin) H.; m. Myriam Cécile Rumbaut, Aug. 24, 1972; children: Catherine, Philippe, Astrid, Stephan. MD summa cum laude, Cath. U. Louvain, Belgium, 1970, specialist in internal medicine, 1975, PhD in Clin. Pharmacology, 1983. Rschr. FNRS, Belgium, 1978-80; asst. Cath. U. Louvain, 1980-86; clin. rsch. physician UCB, Braine-l'Alleud, Belgium, 1986-95; med. scientific advisor UCB, Braine-L'Alleud, Belgium, 1995-98, sr. med. advisor, 1999—; tchr., nursing sch., Brussels, 1970—; asst. tchr. clin. pharmacology Cath. U. Louvain, 1983-94, asst. tchr. clin. epidemiology, 1990-99, guest lectr. clin. epidemiology, 1999—; mem. State Jury for Nursing, Belgium, 1981-96; bot. advisor jour. De Tuinen van Eden/Les Jardins d'Eden, 1999—. Contbr. articles to scientific jours.; joint editor Louvain Med. Jour., 1978-87. Fellow Faculty Pharm. Medicine (U.K.); mem. AAAS, N.Y. Acad. Scis. Avocation: botany. Home: 5A Meerbeekse Steenweg, B-3020 Veltem-Beisem Belgium Office: UCB-Pharma Sector, Chemin du Foriest, B-1420 Braine-l'Alleud Belgium

HULL, GRAFTON HAZARD, JR., social work educator; b. Great Bend, Kans., Nov. 24, 1943; s. Grafton H. and Mary Kathryn (Hagerty) H.; m. Jannah Mather; children: Michael, Patrick, Robert Hurn, Jacob Hurn. BS, U. Wis., Madison, 1967; MSW, Fla. State U., 1969; EdD, U. S.D., 1979. Social worker Cen. State Hosp., Milledgeville, Ga., 1969; chief social work sect. Mental Hygiene Cons. Svc., Ft. Knox, Ky., 1969-71; social worker, then social work supr. Manitowoc County Dept. Social Svc., Manitowoc, Ky., 1971-74; asst. prof., chair dept. sociology Morningside Coll., Sioux City, Iowa, 1974-79; assoc. prof., chair dept. social welfare U. Wis., Whitewater, 1979-82, prof., chair dept., 1982-88; prof., chair dept. social work U. Wis., Eau Claire, 1988-93; dir. Sch. Social Work S.W. Mo. State U., Springfield, 1993-96; dir. divsn social work Ind. Univ. NW, Gary, 1996—; site visitor Coun. Social Work Edn., Washington, 1981—; cons. in field. Co-author: Understanding Generalist Practice, Building the Undergraduate Social Work Library, Case Studies in Generalist Practice, Generalist Practice with Organizations and Communities, The Macro Skills Workbook; cons. editor Jour. Social Work Edn., 1989-95, Aretê, 1993—; mem. editl. bd. Advances in Social Work; contbr. articles to profl. jours. Bd. dirs. Gary Neighborhood Svcs.; mem. Hoosier Boys Town Pub. Policy com.; chmn. Landmarks Commn., Whitewater, 1982-88; city councilman, mem. Planning and Architecture Rev. Commn., City of Whitewater, 1987-88. Capt. U.S. Army, 1969-71. Recipient Wis. Social Work Educator of Yr., 1991, City of Whitewater Hist. Preservation award, 1988, Outstanding Svc. award U. Wis.-Eau Claire, 1993, Outstanding Social Worker award Ind. House of Reps., 1999. Mem. NASW (chair west ctrl. Wis. br. 1989-91), Baccalaureate Program Dirs. Assn. (pres. 1991-93), Coun. Social Work Edn. (commn. on accreditation 1987-93, bd. dirs. 1993-96), Wis. Coun. Social Work Edn. (pres. 1984-91), Inst. Advancement Social Work Rsch. (sec.-treas. 1993-95), Mo. Consortium of Social Work Edn. Programs (pres. 1995-96), Ind. Assn. for Social Work Edn. (exec. com.). Democrat. Avocations: travel. Home: 2594 Walker Ln Salt Lake City UT 84117-7729 Office: Ind Univ NW Gary IN 46408

HULL, LEANNE VON NEUMEYER, public relations and communications executive, research consultant, writer; d. F. Louis and Greta Catherine (Clifford) von Neumeyer; children: Marc Lane, Kristin LeAnne, Michael Lane, Jamie Laird, Jeremy Leif, Breton Louis. Rschr., writer, owner Heritage Tree, Arcadia, Calif., 1970—; CEO von Neumeyer & Assocs., 1996—; project mgr., prodn. asst. One Light, KCM Prodns., 1999—; internat. bd. advisors, dir. protocol, mem. scholarship grant rev. com. Neeley Scholarship Found., 1988-89; dir. pub. comm. Ch. of Jesus Christ of Latter-day Saints, Foothill and Glendale regions, Calif., 1975-92, dir. cmty. rels., 1984-92, asst. dir. area coun., 1984; adminstrv. asst. Calif. Pub. Affairs Dept., L.A., 1990—; seminar coord. R.E.D.I., Inc., L.A., 1982-91, corp. rels. dir., 1984-91; design cons. H.M.J. Fine Jewelers Time & Eternity Collection, L.A., 1985-95; mem. nat. adv. coun. motion picture studio Brigham Young U., Provo, Utah, 1986-89; adminstrv. dir. Pasadena Geneal. Libr., Calif., 1977-82; writer, co-prodr. KBIG, Sideband Div. Radio, L.A., 1979-80; exec. asst. adminstr. Calif. Bicentennial Found. for the U.S. Constn., 1987; regional cons. Latter-Day, Sentinel Newspaper, L.A., 1985-89, exec. dir., 1988-89; mem. Brigham Young U. Marriott Sch. Bus. Mgmt. Soc., L.A., 1990—; mem. com. on child pornography legis. chmn. pub. info. portfolio com., 1988-91, L.A. County Comm. on Obscenity & Pornography, 1988-91; internet moderator 21stRenaissance.com, 1999. Author: Honored Heritage, 1975, Woman's Place of Honor, 1976, Prologue and Tapestry, 1976, Moments with the Prophets, 1977, Southern California: The Earthquake Threat, 1981, Quake!: Preparing Home, Family and Community, 1982, DreamQuest: Along the Trail, 1982, The Peregrine Papers, 1986, Bridget 'Biddy' Smith Mason: Her Legacy Among the Mormons, 1996, Etherea, 1999, Preparing Home and Family for Y2K, 1999, (novel and screenplay) The Dreamin' Jar, 2000; columnist Heritage Tree Foothill Intercity News, Knight-Ridder Pub., 1977-79; contbg. writer Women's Exponent Southern California edit., Sentinal: Journalism series, 1978-80; contbr. articles to profl. jours.; art exhibits include Wilshire Alma Exhibit, 1985, The Grand Artists Hall, 1986-88. Pres. Daus. Utah Pioneers-Los Angeles County, 1983-85; dir. protocol L.A. County Law Enforcement Conf., 1990; dir. recept. protocol State of Calif. Law Enforcement Conf. on Child Pornography, 1990; chmn. So. Calif. Task Force on Pornography, 1989-92; instr. earthquake preparedness and survival Arcadia chpt. ARC, L.A., 1983-85; mem. Cmty. Coordinating Coun., Arcadia, 1983-86; mem. exec. bd. Calif. Utah Women, L.A., 1977-79, 85-86, chmn. L.A. County Commn. Pub. Rels. Portfolio, 1988; exec. dir. Neeley Scholarship Found., 1989-91; coord. planning com. California '96: One Hundred Fifty Years LDS Sequicentennial, 1994—; display coord. L.A. Temple Hill Visitors Ctr., 1994-96; lineage rsch. dir. von Neumeyer-Burches & Assocs., 1992-96; specialist Y2K Task Force on Family Preparedness, 1998—. Recipient Best of Exhibit award Sculptor's West Workshop, 1982, cert. of recognition L.A. County, 1989, cert. appreciation L.A. County, 1990. Mem. Nat. Assn. Female Execs., Found. for Ancient Rsch. and Mormon Studies, Mormon Hist. Assn., Assn. Latter-Day Media Artists (assoc. editor Voice of ALMA 1978-83, exec. bd. 1977-81, chmn. spl. events 1985-90, internat. bd. govs. fellow 1981-83), Am. Film Inst., Deseret Bus. and Profl. Assn., Marriott Bus. Mgmt. Soc. (L.A. chpt.), Assn. L.D.S. Pub. Rels. Profls., Pub. Rels. Soc. Am. (L.A. chpt.), Nat. Mus. Women in the Arts (charter), Arcadia Tournament of Roses Assn., Arcadia C. of C. (chmn. industry commn. of women's divsn. 1983-85, mem. exec. bd. 1985-86). Avocations: sculpting, oil painting. Website: TheHeritageTree.com. Office: 1591 E Temple Way Los Angeles CA 90024-5801

HULL, LYNNE, environmental artist; 2 daughters. BA, U. Wyo., 1969; student advanced ceramics, U. Tex., Austin, 1976; studied with Ken Ferguson, 1975-77; studied with Richard DeVore, Ken Hendry, Colo. State U., 1980-82. adj. prof. art U. Wyo.; artist, cons. e-mail/internet project Getty ArtsEd Net and Ohio State U., 1996; artist in residence Yellowstone Nat. Park, 1992, Art Awareness, Lexington, Ky., 1993, Connemara Conservancy, Dallas, 1993, Missoula Mus. Arts, Mont., 1993, Jackson Hole Middle Sch., Wyo., 1995, Smoky Hills River Festival, 1995, Lakewood Park, Salina, Kan., 1995, U. Ill., Springfield, Lincoln Meml. Gardens, Ill. Audubon Soc., 1996, Toledo Bot. Garden, Ohio, 1996, Mt. Lake Workshop, 1999, Va. Tech. U., 1999; vis. artist Williams Coll., Williamstown, Mass., 1992, U. Colo., Colo. Springs, 1993, U. Colo, Pueblo, 1995, New Coll., Sarasota, Fla., 1999, Carnegie Mellon U., 1999;spkr., lectr. in field. Environ. siteworks Medicine Bow Nat. Forest, Wyo., 1989, raptor roosts, Wyo., Grizedale Forest Sculpture Park, Cumbria, Eng., 1991, Yellowstone Nat. Park, 1992, waterfowl sculptures Carsington Reservoir, Derbyshire, Eng., 1994, wetlands piece Salina, Kans., 1995, sites in Mex., many others; group shows include Bellevue Mus., Wash., 1987, Galleria Mesa, Ariz., 1988, Ucross Found. Gallery, Wyo., 1989, Emmanuel Gallery, Denver, 1989, Security Pacific Gallery, L.A., 1990, U. Arts., Phila., 1992, Tickon Internat. Symposium, Langeleand, Denmark, 1993, Soho 20 Gallery, N.Y.C., 1994, Adams State Coll., Alamosa, Colo., 1996, Ctr. for Art and Earth, N.Y.C., 1996, U. Oreg., 1997, Arvada Ctr. Arts, Colo., 1998, Durango Ctr. Arts, Colo., 1998, others; represented in permanent collections Arvada Ctr. for Arts, Colo., Nicolaysen Mus., Casper, Wyo., Wyo. State Mus., Cheyenne, Western Wyo. C.C.; works appear in (Lucy Lippard) On the Beaten Path, 1999, newspapers, mags.; subject numerous media articles. Fulbright fellow, 1993-94, fellow Wyo. Coun. Arts, 1979; grantee Nancy Gray Found. for Art in Environment, 1999, Wyo. Arts. Coun., 1991, 92, 93, Nat. Endowment Arts, 1990, U.S. Mex. Fund for Culture, 1997-98; residency Lila Wallace/Readers' Digest Found./Arts Internat., 1993-94, Grizedale Forest, Cumbria, Eng., 1991; numerous other grants and awards. Office: PO Box 1239 Fort Collins CO 80522-1239

HULL, RICHARD FRANKLIN, insurance brokerage executive; b. N.Y.C., Nov. 8, 1931; s. Washington and Emily G. (Stevenson) H.; children: Richard Franklin, David Townsend, Christopher Cornelius. Student, U. Va., 1953. Underwriter Crum & Forster Group, N.Y.C., 1953-56; pres. Hull & Co., Washington, 1956-62, Ft. Lauderdale, Fla., 1962—. Served with USMC, 1950-53. Mem. Am. Assn. Mng. Gen. Agts., Nat. Assn. Profl. Surplus Lines Assn., Ill. Surplus Lines Assn., Nat. Assn. Ins. Agts., Fla. Assn. Ins. Agts., Profl. Ins. Agts. Assn., Ind. Agts. Assn., Balboa Bay Club, Lauderdale Yacht Club, Lago Mar Country Club, Lloyd's Yacht Club, Rod and Reel Club, Ocean Reef Club, Lyford Cay Club, Cat Cay Club, Jockey Club, Royal Nassau Sailing Club, City of London Club. Home: 2401 Del Lago Dr Fort Lauderdale FL 33316-2301 Office: 2150 S Andrews Ave Fort Lauderdale FL 33316-3432

HÜLLEMANN, KLAUS-DIETHART, internist, psychotherapist, sports, social and rehabilitation physician; b. Eisenach, Germany, Apr. 5, 1938; s. Siegfried and Thekla H.; m. Brigitte Schube, May 16, 1975; children: Niko, Philipp, Mirko. Student, Frankfurt U., Fed. Republic Germany, 1958; MD, Heidelberg U., Fed. Republic Germany, 1964. Intern Psychiat. Hosp. Heidelberg, 1964-65; resident Gen. Hosp. Konstanz, 1966-67; with Ludolf-Krehl-Klinik, Heidelberg, 1968-75; dir. dept. medicine Höhenried (Fed. Republic Germany) Hosp., 1975-77; med. dir. St. Irmingard Hosp., European Pilot Hosp., WHO, Prien, Fed. Republic Germany, 1977—; prin. investigator German Cardiovascular Prevention Study, Bergen, 1979-91; prof. internal medicine, 1975, Munich U., 1978—; dir., prof. Dr.med. Klaus-D. Hüllman GmbH; coord., pres. German Network of Health Promoting Hosps., WHO, 1995—. Author, editor: Quo vadis-Medicine?, 1989, The Idea of Man in Medicine, Medicine in the Idea of Man, 1999, Fitness and Wellbeing, 1992; author: German Cardiovascular Preventive Study-GCP, 1998; contbr. over 250 articles to profl. jours. Mem. AAAS, N.Y. Acad. Scis., German Chinese Med. Assn., Internistenverband, Deutscher Sportärztebund. Avocations: cross-country skiing, hiking, piano, skiing. Office: Saint Irmingards Hosp, Osternacher Strasse 103, 83209 Prien am Chiemsee, Germany

HULSE, ROBERT DOUGLAS, high technology executive; b. Niagara Falls, N.Y., Aug. 16, 1943; s. Robert Edwin and Helen Louise (Kenny) H.; m. Nancy Louise Musser, Aug. 20, 1966 (div. 1986); children: Anne Warren, Robert Alexander; m. Karen Alice Karlberg, Dec. 31, 1987. AB, Princeton U., 1965; SMChemE, MIT, 1966, SM in Mgmt., 1968. Mgr. bus. analysis Halcon Internat. Inc., N.Y.C., 1968-73, dir. bus. planning, 1973-76; v.p., gen. mgr. Halcon Catalyst Industries, Little Ferry, N.J., 1976-82; v.p. planning & devel. Engelhard Industries, Iselin, N.J., 1982-84; pres., chief exec. officer i-STAT Corp., Princeton, N.J., 1984-86, Sunstone Inc., Dayton, N.J., 1986-87; vice chmn. Princeton Entrepreneurial Resources, 1988-90; pres., chief exec. officer SDTX Technologies, Inc., Princeton, 1989—; v.p. bus. devel. Enzon, Inc., Piscataway, N.J., 1991-94; exec. dir. The Sage Group, Bridgewater, N.J., 1995—, also bd. dirs.; COO, Hemispherx Biopharma, Inc., Phila., 1996-97; gen. ptnr. SAE Ventures, New Canaan, Conn., 1997—; cons. in field; dir. SDTX Technologies, Inc., Princeton, 1989—; pres., dir. Captiva Technologies, Princeton, 1989—; dir. Carnegie Venture Resources, Inc., Princeton, The Sage Group, Bridgewater. Dir. Gotham Light Opera Soc., N.Y.C., 1969-73; treas. Bloomingdale House of Music, N.Y.C., 1979-84. Named Univ. scholar Princeton U., 1961. Mem. The Licensing Execs. Soc., The Union League Club, Doubles, Sigma Xi, Phi Beta Kappa. Republican. Episcopalian. Avocations: chess, tennis. Home: 706 Sayre Dr Princeton NJ 08540-5835 Office: The Sage Group Inc 245 Rte 22 W Ste 304 Bridgewater NJ 08807-2560

HULSE, RUSSELL ALAN, physicist; b. N.Y.C., Nov. 28, 1950; s. Alan Earle and Betty Joan (Wedemeyer) H. BS, Cooper Union, 1970; MS, U. Mass., 1972, PhD, 1975. Rsch. assoc. Nat. Radio Astronomy Observatory, Charlottesville, Va., 1975-77; mem. tech. staff Princeton (N.J.) U. Plasma Physics Lab., 1977-80, staff rsch. physicist, 1980-84, rsch. physicist, 1984-92, prin. rsch. physicist, 1992—. Contbr. articles to profl. jours. Recipient Nobel prize in physics, 1993. Fellow Am. Phys. Soc., Inst. of Physics; mem. Am. Astron. Soc. Avocations: clay target shooting, bird watching, cross-country skiing, canoeing, hiking. Office: Princeton U Plasma Physics Lab James Forrestal Rsch Campus PO Box 451 Princeton NJ 08543-0451

HULSEBERG, PAUL DAVID, financial executive, educator; b. Elmhurst, Ill., Mar. 13, 1950; s. Arnold Henry and Viola (Kliewer) H.; m. Mary Kate Tessman, 1970 (div. 1977); children: Amy, Mandy; m. Gwen Ann Preston, May 17, 1980 (div. 1994); children: Christian, Nicole; m. Peggy Joyce Jones, 1997; children: Todd, Scott. BS in Mgmt., Oklahoma City, 1985; MBA in Info. Systems, Oklahoma City U., 1989. Cert. data processor. Database adminstr. Locke Supply Co., Oklahoma City, 1975-78; programming mgr. CMI, Inc., Oklahoma City, 1978-81; CFO NAPA Okla., Oklahoma City, 1981-98; fed. govt. employee Washington, 1999—; assoc. prof. info. systems, mgmt. and econs. Oklahoma City U., 1985-98; CEO Mirrorstone Mfg., mfrs. bd. game Tao, Oklahoma City, 1986—; regional exec. Okla. region Sports Car Clubs Am. Author boardgame Tao, 1986. Treas., trustee Edgemere Park Preservation, Inc., Oklahoma City, 1984-93. Mem. Alpha Chi, Beta Gamma. Methodist. Avocations: skiing, aikido, auto racing. Home: 5404 Brookland Rd Alexandria VA 22310-1805

HULSTAERT, FRANK, pharmaceutical company executive; b. Ghent, Belgium, July 4, 1960; s. Armand and Cecile (Poppe) H.; m. Martine Snoeck, Jan. 18, 1990; children: Eva, Lars. MD, State U. Ghent, 1985; MSc in Informatics, Free U. Brussels, 1992; postgrad., Limburgs U. Ctr., Diepenbeek, Belgium, 1993-94. Lic. physician, Belgium. Resident in internal medicine Univ. Hosp. Ghent, 1986-87; cons. in software Applied Artificial Intelligence N.V., Brussels, 1987-88; assoc. physician Becton Dickinson Immunocytometry Sys. Europe, Erembogem, Belgium, 1988-92; clin. rsch. physician Sandoz (Novartis), Brussels, 1992-97; head clin. R&D dept. Innogenetics, Ghent, 1997—. Contbr. articles to profl. jours.; inventor in field. Res. officer Med. Dept. NATO, 1985-86. Fellow Royal Coll. Physicians (U.K.), Faculty of Pharm. Medicine. Avocation: tennis. Office: Innogenetics NV, Industriepark 7 Box 4, B-9052 Ghent Belgium

HULT, GERT TOMAS MIKAEL, international business executive, educator; b. Uppsala, Sweden, June 11, 1967; came to U.S., 1987; s. Gert G. and L. Margareta (Söderkvist) H.; m. Laurie W., June 6, 1993. Mech. Engring. Degree, Fyrisskolan, Uppsala, Sweden, 1987; BSB, MBA, Murray State U., 1990, 91; PhD, U. Memphis, 1995. Cert. mech. engr. Founding mem. Inmark Consulting Group LLC, Memphis, 1994; asst. prof. internat. bus. U. Ark., Little Rock, 1994-96; dir. internat. bus. Fla. State U., Tallahassee, 1996-2000; cons. Fed. Express Corp., Memphis, 1993—. Editor: (book) Enhancing Knowledge Development in Marketing, 1997; contbr. articles to profl. jours. Mem. Acad. Internat. Bus., Am. Mktg. Assn. (program chair 1997, 98), Acad. of Mktg. Sci., Acad. of Mgmt., Decision Scis. Inst., So. Mktg. Assn. Lutheran. Avocations: golf, tennis, travel. Home: 1730 Highland Pl Tallahassee FL 32308-4752

HULT, SUSAN FREDA, history educator; b. Roslyn, N.Y., Jan. 29, 1956; d. Thomas Joseph and Rosemary (Arthur) Freda; m. Allan Richard Hult, Nov. 18, 1978 (div. 1982). BA in Polit. Sci., Fla. So. Coll., 1977; MA in History, Clemson U., 1985; postgrad., Rice U., 1985-89, U. Houston, 1989—. Read-a-Thon coord. Multiple Sclerosis Soc., Tampa, Fla., 1977-78; divsnl. sales mgr., asst. buyer Ivey's Fla., Winter Park, 1978-81; pers. dir. Tampa Hilton Hotel, 1981-82; grad. asst. Clemson (S.C.) U., 1984-85; prof. history Ctrl. Coll., Houston, 1986—, dept. chair history/philosophy/geography, 1995—; vis. asst. prof. history U. Alaska Southeast, Sitka, 1993-94; adj. instr. Sheldon Jackson Coll., Sitka, 1994; archivist Liberty Life Ins. Co., Greenville, S.C., 1985; pres. faculty assn. coun. Houston C.C. Sys., 1995-96, pres.-elect, 1994-95, sec., 1992-93, treas., 1991-92, chair, 1992-93, chair salary com., 1992-94, chair fundraising com., 1991-92, chair governance com., 1990-91; presenter in field. Editor CCHA Rev.; editl. asst. Papers of Jefferson Davis, Rice U., 1987-88, Jour. So. History, 1985-87; rev. editor C.C. Humanities Assn. Mem., docent Mus. Fine Arts Houston Guild; bd. dirs.. Houston Fedn. Profl. Women, 1999—; campaign worker various Dem. candidates, Houston, 1987— vol. Project Nicaragua, 1994, 95, 98, 99. NEH grantee, 1994-95, 98, 99-2000, Houston C.C. Sys. grantee, 1991-95, Fulbright-Hays grantee, 1994, 99, East-West Ctr. grantee, 1998; Illabelle Shanahan Morrisin fellow Alpha Chi Omega Found., 1985. Mem. Am. Assn. Women in C.C.s (Region VI dir.), Orgn. Am. Historians, Tex. C.C. Tchrs. Assn. (nat. bd. dirs. 1999—), Tex. Assn. Women C.C.s, Assn. Women Adminstrs., Houston Fedn. Profl. Women, C.C. Humanities Assn. (editor CCHA Rev.), Phi Alpha Theta, Omicron Delta Kappa, Kappa Delta Pi, Phi Theta Kappa (Tex. adv. bd. 1996-99, Horizon award 1996, seminar leader 1995-96, Robert Giles award 2000). Avocations: reading, singing, the arts, photography, tennis. Home: 4006 Julian St Houston TX 77009-5243 Office: Ctrl Coll/Houston CC Sys 1300 Holman St # 1229 Houston TX 77004-3834

HULTIN, SVEN OLOF, consulting company executive; b. Kittila, Finland, June 16, 1920; arrived in Switzerland, 1987; s. Erik Elias and Agnes Maria (Möller) H.; m. Agnes Cathrine Ekerodde, Dec. 29, 1946 (dec. Aug. 1987); children: Harriet Maria, Göran. MS, Abo (Finland) U., 1943, ScD, 1968. Registered profl. engr., Wash. Lectr. chem. engring. Abo U., 1948-51; project engr. Ekono Oy (architect engrs.), Helsinki, Finland, 1951-53, dept. head, 1953-59, v.p., 1960-63, pres., 1964-83; pres. ETY-Fin. Oy (holding co. of Ekono), Helsinki, 1984; ptnr. Nestor Ptnrs Oy (cons.), Espoo, Finland, 1985-96; chmn., CEO Ekono Inc., cons. engrs., Bellevue, Wash., 1973-84; vice-chmn. bd. Gruneko AG, cons. engrs., Basle, Switzerland, 1977-97; mem. bd. Oy Saab-Valmet AB, Helsinki, 1968-88; tech. dir. Voimayhdistys Ydin, Helsinki, 1956-65. Contbr. articles to profl. jours., chpts. to books. Mem. city coun., City of Uusikaupunki, Finland, 1948; mem. AEC, Govt. Finland, 1968-83; mem. bd. trustees of Abo U. Found., Finland, 1970-87. Lt. Finish mil., 1940-44. Named Comdr. of Finnish Lion Order Pres. of Finland, 1971; recipient Finnish Cross of Liberty, Supreme Comdr. Finnish Armed Forces, 1942, Cross of Finnish Sports in Gold, Minister Edn., Finland, 1983, Gold medal Acad. Tech. Scis., Finland, 1986, Silver medal Internat. Yacht Racing Union, 1990. Mem. Finnish Acad. Tech. Scis. (bd. dirs. 1967-70), Royal Swedish Acad. Engring. Scis. (fgn.), Soc. Finnish Engrs. (chmn. 1969-72), World Energy Coun. (exec. assembly chmn. 1980-86, hon. chmn. 1986—), Finnish Yachting Fedn. (chmn. 1969-77), Internat. Yacht Racing Union (chmn. measurement com. 1974-90), Offshore Racing Coun. (com. of honor 1986—), Rotary of Uusikaupunki (hon.). Lutheran. Avocations: yachting, aviation, swimming, slalom, golf. Home and office: Via Locarno 27, CH-6612 Ascona Switzerland

HULTMAN, ERIC HELMER, clinical chemist; b. Kristinehamn, Sweden, Oct. 10, 1925; s. Oskar Helmer and Hilda Maria (Eriksson) H.; m. Gunilla Barbro Holmgren; children: Per, Cajsa, Christin, Bjorn, Petra. B of Pharmacy, Royal Pharm. Inst., 1946; B of Medicine, Karolinska Inst., 1955, MD, 1956, PhD in Med. Sci., 1967; DSc (hon.), U. Waterloo, 1996. Physician Dep. Clin. Chem., Stockholm, 1956-70; head dept. clin. chem. Beckomberga Hosp., 1970-76; prof. clin. chem. Karolinska Inst., 1976-91; head dep. clin. chemistry Serafimer Hosp., Stockholm, 1976-79, Huddinge Univ. Hosp., 1980-91; prof. emeritus Karolinska Inst., 1992—; spl. prof. human metabolism Dept. of Physiology and Pharmacology U. Nottingham, 1995—; mem. rsch. group for neuromuscular disorders. Editor Scandinavian Jour. of Clin. and Lab. Investigation; contbr. 300 articles to profl. jours. Recipient Alvarenga Prize Swedish Med. Soc., 1966, McLaughlin award McMaster U., 1990. Mem. Swedish Soc. of Clin. Chemistry. Avocation: tennis. Home: St Eriksg 77, 11332 Stockholm Sweden Office: Huddinger Hosp, S-14186 Huddinge Sweden

HULTMAN, GUNNAR W., communications consultant; b. Gothenberg, Sweden, Oct. 19, 1951; s. Thure and Hjordis I. Hultman; m. Camilla Schrewelius, Aug. 25, 1975 (div. Jan. 1980); children: Erik, Henrik; m. Susanna M. Svartengren, June 4, 1988. LLB, U. Lund, 1978. Editor Affarsekonomi Mgmt., Stockholm, 1985-86; cons. Publicisterna, Stockholm, 1987-92; pres. Briggert, Hultman & Johard, Stockholm, 1993-94; sr. cons. Ruder Finn, Stockholm, 1994-95; pres. Hultman Pub. Rels. and Info., Lidingo, Sweden, 1995—; pub. NOS Newsletter on Brand Mgmt., Lidingo, 1996—. Dep. coun. mem. City Coun., Lidingo, 1998-99; bd. dirs., chmn. Lidingo SK Volleyball, 1996-98; bd. dirs. Stockholm 59 North-Soloists of the Royal Swedish Ballet, 1998—. Christian Democrat. Avocations: labrador retrievers, shooting. Fax: 0046 479 610 64. E-mail: gunnar.hultman@hpri.se. Office: HPRI, Starsholma, S-343 94 Almhult Sweden

HULTQUIST, PAUL FREDRICK, electrical engineer, educator; b. Holdrege, Nebr., Mar. 24, 1920; s. Fred Oscar and Lalan Ragnhild (Swanberg) H.; m. Juanita Marie Tokheim, Apr. 7, 1946; children: Fredrick James, Ann Marie. Student, Bethany Coll., Lindsborg, Kans., 1940-41, Hastings Coll., 1943-44; B.A. cum laude, U. Colo., 1945, Ph.D. (AEC predoctoral fellow) Physics, 1954. Instr. applied math. U. Colo., Boulder, 1945-48, 52-55; asst. prof. U. Colo., 1955-59, assoc. prof., 1959-63; prof., asst. dean engring. U. Colo., Colorado Springs, 1965-71; prof. elec. engring., assoc. dean U. Colo., Denver, 1971; prof. elec. and computer engring. U. Colo., 1971-88, prof. computer sci., 1982-88, prof. emeritus, 1988—; lectr. math. and computer sci. U. Nebr., Omaha, 1989-95; sr. scientist Tech. Support, Inc., Omaha, 1993—; assoc. dir. Univ. Computer Center U. Colo., 1973-76; assoc. rsch. scientist Lockheed Missiles and Space Co., Palo Alto, Calif., 1956-57; sr. staff scientist Ball Aerospace & Techs., Boulder, 1963-65; cons. in field. Author: Numerical Methods for Engineers and Computer Scientists, 1988; contbr. numerous articles, revs. to profl. publs. Trustee Bethphage Mission, Inc., Omaha, 1966-76, 78-84, 85-90, 91-96, chmn., 1980-84, 86-90, mem. human resources com., 1997—; trustee Bethphage Residential Ctrs., 1983-88, Bethphage Mission South, Austin, Tex., 1990-97; trustee Bethphage Mission East, Hartford, Conn., 1989-95, chmn., 1991-93; trustee Bethphage Mission Pacific, Portland, Oreg., 1995-97, chmn., 1995-97; chmn. bd. Advent Svcs., Inc., Omaha, 1998-99; mem. bd. parish edn. United Luth. Ch. Am., 1958-62, Luth. Ch. in Am., 1963-66, 68-72, mem. mgmt. com. divsn. parish svcs., 1972-78, 80-87, chmn., 1982-87; bd. dirs. Luth. Sch. Theology at Chgo., 1967-69, 72-78, chmn., 1975-78; bd. dirs. Pacific Luth. Theol. Sem., Berkeley, 1981-88; adv. mem. The Bethphage Found., 1992—; mem. steering com. Augustana Heritage Assn., 1998-2000. Mem. Assn. Computing Machinery, Soc. Indsl. and Applied Math., IEEE (sr.), Math. Assn. Am., Soc. Computer Simulation, Phi Beta Kappa, Sigma Xi, Tau Beta Pi. Democrat. Home: 6803 N 68th Plz Omaha NE 68152-2177

HULUGALLE, NILANTHA RUKMIN, soil scientist; b. Colombo, Sri Lanka, Jan. 6, 1956; s. Hiran and Shanti H.; m. Santhushti Ranasinha, Dec. 29, 1986; children: Kalinga, Ineshka. B in Agrl. Sci., La Trobe U., 1978, PhD, 1982. From jr. scientist to soil physicist Internat. Inst. Tropical Agriculture, Ibadan, Nigeria, 1983-91; soil scientist/rsch. officer NSW Agriculture, Narrabri, Australia, 1992-99, sr. rsch. scientist, 1999—. Maintenance com. St. Cyprion's Anglican Ch., Narrabri, 1997—. Mem. Internat. Soil Tillage Rsch. Orgn. (working groups 1994—). Avocations: reading, jogging, cricket, music, gardening. Home: 41 Gibbons St, 2390 Narrabri NSW, Australia Office: NSW Agriculture, Australian Cotton Rsch Inst, 2390 Narrabri NSW, Australia

HUMANN, L. PHILLIP, bank executive. Chmn. Trust Co. Bank subs. Trust Co. Ga., Atlanta, also bd. dirs., CEO, 1998-2000; chmn., pres. & CEO Sun Trust Banks, Inc., Atlanta, 2000—. Office: Suntrust Banks Inc 303 Peachtree St NE Atlanta GA 30308-3201*

HUMBERSTONE, GRAHAM DOUGLAS, journalist, television technician, computer programmer; b. Crayford, Kent, Eng., Feb. 1, 1952; came to Israel, 1976; s. Douglas Philip Ralph and Verda (Hardwick) H.; m. Ronit Chava Cohen-Tzedek, May 15, 1979; children: Daniel, David, Elazar, Benjamin, Joseph, Anna, Joshua, Yehuda, Sarah, Rachel. GCE in Math. and Physics, Rolls Royce Coll., Bristol, Eng., 1969-70. Cert. electronic journalist. Computer operator Lloyds Bank Plc., London, 1970-73; computer programmer Freshwater Ltd., London, 1973-74; computer operator De Bienkuff, Amsterdam, The Netherlands, 1974-75, S&A Geophysical, Swanley, Eng., 1975-76; 2d camera asst. Idan Studios, Jerusalem, 1976-77; 1st camera asst. CBS News, Jerusalem, 1977-78; 1st camera asst., soundman ABC News, Jerusalem, 1977-78; elec. news gathering covering Middle East affairs Worldwide TV News, Jerusalem, 1978-99; chief programmer, cofounder Namigra Ltd., Tel Aviv, 1999—; dir., programmer Chinese Astrology, Jerusalem, 1988-94; programmer Worldwide TV News, Jerusalem, 1988-91. Patentee dome irragation systems. Mem. Inst. Data Processing Mgmt. Assn., Soc. Motion Picture and TV Engrs. Avocations: cricket, travel, archeology, computer programming, short documentaries. Office: Namigra Ltd, 97 Ahad Ha'am St, Tel Aviv 64253, Israel

HUME, ALAN JAMES, accountant, management consultant; b. Auckland, New Zealand, Jan. 10, 1939; s. James Kinlay and Emily Blanche (Cahill) H.; m. Lynette Laura Goode; children: Patria Anne, Sheralyn Marie, Jarrod Charles. Chartered acct., U. New Zealand, 1960, B of Commerce, chartered sec., 1961, cost and mgmt. acct., 1963; M of Commerce, U. Auckland, 1966. Asst. acct. E.O. Faber Ltd., Auckland, 1956-58; asst. sec. Kauri Timber Co. Ltd., Auckland, 1959-61; chief acct. Fletcher Timber Co. Ltd., Auckland, 1962-63; sec. Fletcher Group Services Ltd., Auckland, 1964-71; corp. planning mgr. Fletcher Holdings Ltd., Auckland, 1972-79; gen. mgr. Fletcher Consulting Svcs. Ltd., Auckland, 1980-82; sr. mgmt. cons. PA Mgmt. Consultants Ltd., Auckland, 1983-89; mng. dir. Hume Mgmt. Consultants Ltd., Auckland, 1990—; current cost acctg. manual author U. Waikato, Hamilton, New Zealand, 1976-78; lectr. acctg. U. Auckland, 1959-66; dir. Designtec Mgmt. Ltd., Bangkok, 1991-98. Author: (book) New Zealand Housing Study, 1983, (manual and supplements) Current Cost Accounting, 1976-78; contbr. papers to profl. jours. Fellow New Zealand Soc. Accts. (chartered, examiner and moderator in acctg. 1959-79); mem. Inst. Chartered Secs. and Adminstrs., New Zealand Strategic Mgmt. Soc. (past nat. pres. and councilor). Avocations: tennis, table tennis, reading, writing, traveling. E-mail: hume management@xtra.co.nz. Office: Hume Mgmt Cons Ltd, 639 Glenfield Rd Glenfield, Auckland 1310, New Zealand

HUME, ELLEN HUNSBERGER, media analyst, journalist; b. Chevy Chase, Md., Apr. 24, 1947; d. Warren Seabury and Ruth (Pedersen) H.; m. John Shattuck, Feb. 14, 1991; 1 child, Susannah; stepchildren: Jessica, Rebecca, Peter. BA, Harvard U., 1968; PhD (hon.), Daniel Webster Coll., 1990. Reporter Somerville (Mass.) Jour., 1968-69; feature writer Santa Barbara (Calif.) News Press, 1969-70; pub. service dir., copy writer KTMS Radio, Santa Barbara, 1970-72; edn. reporter Ypsilanti (Mich.) Press, 1972-73; bus. reporter Detroit Free Press, 1973-75; met. reporter L.A. Times, 1975-77; congl. reporter L.A. Times, Washington, 1977-83; White House corr., polit. writer Wall St. Jour., Washington, 1983-88; exec. dir. Shorenstein Ctr. on Press and Politics Harvard U., Cambridge, Mass., 1988-93; moderator The Editors TV program, Montreal, Que., 1990-93; adj. lectr. Kennedy Sch. Govt., 1991-93, Medill Sch. Journalism, 1993-94; commentator Washington Week in Rev. PBS-TV, 1973-88, CNN, 1993-97; exec. dir. The Democracy Project, PBS, 1996-98. Kennedy Inst. Politics fellow Harvard U., 1981, Annenberg Washington Program fellow, 1993-95. Mem. Coun. of Fgn. Rels., Fund for Free Expression, Nat. Press Club. Methodist. Address: Am Embassy Prague Us Dept Ofstate Washington DC 20521-0001

HUME, JOHN, politician of Northern Ireland; b. Derry, No. Ireland, Jan. 18, 1937; s. Samuel and Anne (Doherty) H.; m. Patricia Hone, 1960; 5 children. Ed., St. Columb's Coll., Derry, St. Patrick's Coll., Maynooth, Nat. U. Ireland, PhD (hon.), U. Mass., 1985, Cath. U. Am., 1986, St. Joseph's U., 1986, Tusculum Coll., Tenn. Rsch. fellow Trinity Coll., LLD (hon.) Queens Coll., Belfast, 1995; assoc. fellow Ctr. for Internat. Affairs, Harvard; founding mem. Credit Union Irish League Credit Unions, pres., 1964-68; rep. Derry in No. Ireland Parliament, 1969-72, in No. Ireland Assembly, 1972-73; min. commerce, powersharing exec., 1974; rep. Derry in No. Ireland Conv., 1974-75; elected to European Parliament, 1979, No. Ireland Assembly, 1982; sponsor Irish Anti-Apartheid Movement; leader Social Dem. and Labour Party, 1979—; mem. Parliament for Foyle, No. Ireland, 1983—; mem. adv. com. protection of the Seas, 1989—. Recipient St. Thomas Moore award U. San Francisco, 1991, Nobel Peace Prize Norwegian Nobel Com., 1998. Office: 5 Bayview Ter, Derry BT48 7EE, Northern Ireland

HUME, ROBERT, pediatrician; b. Edinburgh, Scotland, Apr. 4, 1947; m. Shaena Finlayson Blair, Aug. 5, 1972. BSc, U. Edinburgh, 1969, MBChB, 1972, PhD, 1980. Fellow, lectr. pediat. U. Edinburgh, Scotland, 1975-92; lectr., reader U. Dundee, Scotland, 1993-97, prof., 1997—. Contbr. chpts. in books and articles to profl. jours. Recipient Margaret McLennan award, 1992. Fellow Royal Coll. Physicians Edinburgh, Royal Coll. Paediats. and Child Health. Office: Univ Dundee, Ninewells Hosp Med Sch, Dundee DD1 9SY, Scotland

HUMES, WILLEM J., investment manager; b. Bethesda, Md., Oct. 10, 1964; s. Samuel and Marijke (Oudegeest) H.; m. Elizabeth Vennema, Sept. 19, 1992; children: Willem J. Jr., Hendrik van der Haar. BA, Williams Coll., 1987. Analyst Mfrs. Hanover, N.Y.C., 1988-89; broker, v.p. Tullett & Tokyo/Eurobrokers, N.Y.C., 1989-90; v.p. Banco Santander, N.Y.C., 1990-91, Lehman Bros., N.Y.C., 1991-94; mng. dir. Weston Fin., N.Y.C., 1994-95; mng. ptnr. Van Eck Capital, N.Y.C., 1995—; bd. dirs., treas. South North Devel. Initiative; mem. Gibraltar-Am. Coun. Intern Dem. Senatorial Campaign Co., Washington, 1986. Mem. Brook Club. Home: 684 Carroll St Brooklyn NY 11215-2010 also: Northwest Hill Rd Pownal VT 05261 Office: Van Eck Global 99 Park Ave Rm 8R New York NY 10016-1507

HUMKE, RAMON LYLE, utility executive; b. Quincy, Ill., Nov. 19, 1932; s. E.G. and Florence K. (Koch) H.; m. Carolyn Jacobs Humke, Nov. 20, 1955; 1 child, Steven K. Ed., Quincy Coll., 1952-53, Springfield (Ill.) Coll., Ill., 1956-58, Carleton Coll., 1968; LLD, U. Indpls., 1988. Various mgmt. positions Ill. Bell Telephone Co., 1951-73; dir. forecasting and productivity AT&T, N.Y.C., 1974-75; v.p. pers. Ill. Bell Tel. Co., Chgo., 1978-82; v.p. corp. affairs Ameritech, Chgo., 1982-83; pres., CEO Ind. Bell Telephone Co. Inc., Indpls., 1983-89, Ameritech Svcs., Chgo., 1989-90; pres., COO Indpls. Power & Light Co., 1990—, also bd. dirs.; vice chmn. Ipalco Enterprises, Inc. Indpls., Indpls., 1991—; also bd. dirs. Ipalco Enterprises, Inc., Indpls.; chmn. bd. Meridian Ins. Group, Meridian Mut. Ins. Co.; bd. dirs. LDI Mgmt. Chmn. Infrastructure Commn., 1990, Indpls.; bd. dirs. Indpls. Downtown, Inc., 1992—; adv. bd. Crossroads of Am. chpt. Boy Scouts Am. With U.S. Army, 1953-56, ETO. Named Ky. Col., 1983, Ark. Traveler, 1985, Sagamore of the Wabash, 1987, 89; recipient medal of merit U.S. Treasury Dept., 1984, 85, Charles Whistler award, 1989, Benjamin Harrison medallion award, 1990, Americanism award, 1991, Good Scout award Boy Scouts Am., 1993, Hoosier Heritage award, 1993, Ind. Acad., 1996. Mem. Indpls. C. of C. (chmn. 1997-98, dir.), Columbia Club, Crooked Stick Golf Club, Indpls. Athletic Club, Meridian Hills Country Club, Skyline Club (bd. govs.), Twin Lakes Golf Club. Avocations: golf, wilderness hiking, U.S. history.

HUMLUM, OLE, geography educator, researcher, consultant; b. Esbjerg, Denmark, July 21, 1949; s. Arne and Ingeborg Humlum; m. Hanne Hvidtfeldt Christiansen, May 14, 1994. Sci. dir. Arctic Sta., Grenland, 1983-86; rsch. assoc. U. Copenhagen, 1976-83, assoc. prof. geography, 1986-99; prof. phys. geography UNIS, Svalbard, Norway, 1999—; vis. sr. lectr. U. St. Andrews, 1997-98, U. Torshavn, Faroe Islands, 1998; bd. dirs. Zefyr Software, Copenhagen. Contbr. articles to profl. jours. With arty. Danish Army, 1968-69. Mem. Royal Danish Geog. Soc. (coun., bd. dirs. 1989—). Avocation: mountain climbing, computer science. Office: UNIS, Univ Courses on Svalbard, N-9171 Lougyeasbyeu Norway

HUMMEL, HELMUT, physician; b. Schierling, Germany, Mar. 14, 1950; s. Josef and Margarete (Hng) H.; m. Jutta Hofmann, Apr. 7, 1974; children: Sonja, Quivin. Diploma, U. Regensburg, Germany, 1979, PhD, 1984. Scientific asst. U. Regensburg, Germany, 1980-84, acad. councillor, 1984; rschr. Siemens AG, Munich, Germany, 1984-86; asst. mgr. Siemens AG, Regensburg, Germany, 1986-88; prof. FH, Regensburg, Germany, 1988—; mng. dir. Mister, Regensburg, 1997—, Hummel & Wild, Regensburg, 1999—. Author: Physics for Engineers, 1997, Electricity and Magnetism, 1999. Avocations: music, camping. Office: FH Regensburg, Postfach 120327, 90325 Regensburg Germany Home: Hauptstv 6, 84069 Schierling Germany

HUMMEL, KONRAD, microbiologist; b. Metzingen, Reutlingen, Germany, Feb. 28, 1923; s. Alfred and Hedwig Lucie (Dorn) H.; m. Ute Hannelore Werner, Dec. 13, 1983. Diploma in Medicine, U. Freiburg, Germany, 1947; MD, U. Tuebingen, Germany, 1948. Asst. Inst. for Med. Microbiology/U. Freiburg, 1948-74; prof., dir. Inst. for Blood Group Serology/U. Freiburg, 1974-88; dir. Inst. for Blood Group Serology and Genetics, Freiburg, 1988—. Author: Tabellierte biostatistische Kenngroessen zur blutgruppenserologischen Vaterschaftsbegutachtung, 1992, Erblich-polymorphe Eigenschaften des Blutes zur Klaerung strittiger Blutsverwandtschaft und fraglicher Identitaet - hierzu benutzte biometrische Verfahren, 1997. Scholar Inst. Biology Physicochimique E. de Rothschild, Paris, 1961. Fellow Forensic Sci. Soc. India; mem. Internat. Soc. for Forensic Haemogenetics (hon.). Avocations: photography, numismatics, mineralogy. Home: Horbenerstr 34, D-79100 Freiburg Germany Office: Inst Blood Grp Serol/Genet, Sundgauallee 108, D-79110 Freiburg Germany

HUMPHREY, ALBERT S., business development executive; b. Kansas City, Mo., June 2, 1926; s. Albert Swartzendruver and Margaret Elizabeth (Benton) H.; m. Virginia Potter, Oct. 6, 1957 (div. Feb. 1970); children: Albert S. III, Virginia Potter, Jonathan Benton Cantwell, Heidi; m. Myrian Alice Octaaf de Baere, Oct. 20, 1983; children: Roosje Willems, Jonas Willems, Stephania Humphrey. BSc in Chem. Engring., U. Ill., 1946; MSc in Chem. Engring., MIT, 1948; MBA in Fin., Harvard U., 1955. Staff engr. East Coast Tech. Svc. Esso Standard Oil Co., Elizabeth, N.J., 1948-50; chief chem. and protective group Office of Chief Chem. Officer, U.S. Army Chem. Corp., Washington, 1952-54; asst. to pres. Penberthy Instrument Co., Seattle, 1955-56; chief product planning Boeing Airplane Co., Seattle, 1956-60; mgr. value analysis Small Aircraft Engine Divsn. G.E., Boston, 1960-61; mgr. rsch. and devel. planning P.R. Mallory & Co. Inc., Indpls., 1961-63; cons., presenter exec. seminars in bus. planning Stanford Rsch. Inst. and NASA Office Advance Rsch. & Tech., Menlo Park, Calif., 1965-70; chmn., CEO Bus. Planning & Devel. Inc., Kansas City, 1970—; mem. faculty Sch. Adult Edn. U. Wash., Seattle, 1955-58; vis. prof. Newcastle upon Tyne Poly. Sch. Bus. and Mgmt., Eng., 1982—; bd. dirs. Friborg Instruments, London, Hidden Valley Ltd., Birmingham, Eng., The Bank Consultancy Group, London, Randolph Crescent Mgmt. Co., London, Farkwood Films Ltd., Bedford, England, Newco Sewage Ltd., Wargrave, England; mem. exec. adv. bd. Nat. Bur. Cert. Cons., San Diego, dir. European ops.; bus. gov. John Kelly Tech. Colls., London. Contbr. articles to profl. jours. Lt. comdr. USN, 1944-46. Mem. British Inst. Dirs., British Inst. Mktg., Am. Inst. Chem. Engrs. (cert.), Harvard U. Alumni Assn., MIT Alumni Assn., U. Ill. Alumni Assn., Sigma Xi, Tau Beta Phi, Phi Delta Theta. Republican. Episcopalian. Avocations: assisting under-priviledged to start new bus. enterprises, skiing. Fax: 00 44 (0) 0207 266 0039. E-mail: humph@bpdev.demon.co.uk. Office: Bus Planning & Devel Co, The Lodge 1 Randolph Cresce, London W9 1DP, England

HUMPHREY, DIANA YOUNG, fund raiser, travel consultant; b. Balt., Feb. 7, 1938; d. Edwin Parson and Elizabeth Miller (Hoskins) Young; m. David Henry Carls, July 27, 1963 (div. Dec. 17, 1997); children: Peter Van Patten Carls, Elizabeth Roy Carls, Susan Montanye Carls; m. George Lee Humphrey, May 22, 1999. AB, Smith Coll., Northampton, Mass., 1960. Lic. real estate broker, Mass., 1978. Fgn. rights sales Little, Brown & Co., Inc., Boston, 1960-63; speech writer DNA Rsch., N.Y.C., 1963-64; vol. fund raiser John V. Lindsay, N.Y.C., 1964-65, Smith Coll., Northampton, Mass., 1970-75, 90-95, Smith Coll. Club, Concord, Mass., 1976-89, Jr. League of Boston, 1967—; bd. mem. devel. Ctr. House, Inc., Boston, 1981-94; fund raiser events Boston Symphony Orch., 1975—; fund raising, events Mass. Soc. for Prevention of Cruelty to Children, Boston, 1997—. Editor: Huntington Hartford Gallery Modern Art, N.Y.C., 1963. Speechwriter, Nelson A. Rockefeller Presdl. campaign, N.Y.C., 1963-64; active John V. Lindsay for Mayor, N.Y.C., 1964-65; mem., chmn. Wayland (Mass.) Planning Bd., 1976-81, Wayland Housing Partnership, 1987—; mem. Patriots' Trail coun. Girl Scouts U.S. Mem. Jr. League of Boston, Weston Golf Club. Episcopalian. Avocations: golf, travel, gardening, singing, politics. Home: 42 Cutting Cross Way Wayland MA 01778-3845

HUMPHREY, OWEN EVERETT, retired education administrator; b. Wautoma, Wis., Oct. 25, 1920; s. Marion A. and Flora A. (Helms) H.; m. Billye A. Cox, Apr. 6, 1946 (dec. Dec. 1974); children: Reba, Ivye. BS, U. Wis., Whitewater, 1947; MS, U. Ark., 1949; advanced cert., U. Ill., 1954. Life gen. supervisory cert. grades K-14. Elem. classroom tchr. Four Corners Sch., Plainfield, Wis., 1941-42; jr. high art and sci. tchr. Jefferson Sch., Sheboygan, Wis., 1947-48; elem. classroom tchr. and prin. Holcomb, Mo., 1949-50, Lincoln Sch., Mattoon, Ill., 1950-55; supervising prin. various elem. schs., Peotone, Ill., 1955-57; elem. tchr. Nameoki Sch., Granite City, Ill., 1957-59; elem. prin. Maryville Sch., Granite City, 1959-67; curriculum coord. Sch. Dist. #9, Granite City, 1967-79; adminstrv. asst. Regional Supt. of Schs., Madison County, Ill., 1979-81, 85-87; ret., 1987; leader parent study groups Ea. Ill. U., Mattoon, 1950-54; PTA field unit organizer Ill. Congress of Parents and Tchrs., Mattoon, 1952-54; coord. local dist. planning Sch. Dist. #9, Granite City, 1973-79; rep. Ill. State Curriculum Coun., Springfield, 1980-81. Co-author: The Greening of Gateway East, 1984; contbr. poetry to Nat. Libr. of Poetry anthologies; contbr. articles to profl. jours. Dir. chorus Area Coun. PTA, Mattoon, 1950-54, Granite City Area Coun. PTA, 1957-59; dir. Granite City Steel Mixed Chorus, 1958-60; actor Area Theatrical Soc., Collinsville, Ill., 1994. Sgt. U.S. Army Infantry, 1942-45, ETO. Recipient Area Coun. PTA award Granite City, Ill., 1979. Mem. NEA (life), ASCD (life), Ill. ASCD (life, bd. dirs.), Internat. Poets Soc. (life), Collinsville Area Theatrical Soc., Phi Delta Kappa (Gateway East chpt. sec., historian, v.p., pres., Svc. Key award 1984, George H. Reavis Assoc. award 1991). Avocation: composing music and lyrics. Home: 18 Wilson Park Dr Granite City IL 62040-3550

HUMPHREYS, DAVID ANDERSON, research engineer; b. Epsom, Surrey, Eng., Nov. 7, 1956; s. Archibald Anderson and Dorothy May (Diack) H.; m. Sharon Anita Stiles, May 7, 1983. BSc, Southampton (Eng.) U., 1978; PhD, London U., 1990. Chartered engr. Sci. officer laser and fibre optics measurement sect. Nat. Phys. Lab., Teddington, Eng., 1978-83, higher sci. officer laser and fibre optics measurement sect., 1983-86, sr. sci. officer laser and fibre optics measurement sect., 1986-91, grade 7 laser and fibre optics measurement sect., 1991—. Contbr. articles to profl. jours. Mem. IEEE (sr.), Inst. Elec. Engrs. UK (Ambrose Fleming Premium 1989). Avocation: music. Office: Nat Phys Lab, Queens Rd, Teddington TW11 OLW, England

HUMPHRIES, EDWARD FRANCIS, lawyer; b. S.I., N.Y., May 25, 1957; s. Robert Edward and Joan D. (Mauter) H.; m. Colleen Kennedy, July 21, 1990; 1 child, Stephen Edward. BBA, Bernard M. Baruch Coll., 1981; JD, Fordham U., 1984. Bar: N.J. 1984, U.S. Dist. Ct. N.J. 1984, N.Y. 1985, U.S. Dist. Ct. (ea. and so. dists.) N.Y. 1985, U.S. Dist. Ct. (we. dist.) N.Y. 1987, Pa. 1990, Hawaii 1990, U.S. Supreme Ct. 1990, U.S. Dist. Ct. Hawaii 1991. Assoc. Amabile & Erman, Bklyn., 1984-86, 87-92, ptnr., 1993—; assoc. Pegalis & Wachsman, Great Neck, N.Y., 1986-87. Trustee Soc. Hill East Condominium Assn., East Brunswick, N.J., 1987-90, pres., 1988-90; co-chmn. Homeowners Assn. Coun. East Brunswick, 1988-90; vice chmn. East Brunswick Planning Bd., 1989-90; pres. East Brunswick Rep. Club, 1989-91. Recipient Morton Wollman medal in Mgmt. Bernard Baruch Coll., 1981. Mem. N.Y. State Bar Assn., N.J. State Bar Assn., Hawaii Bar Assn., Beta Gamma Sigma, Sigma Iota Epsilon. Republican. Roman Catholic. Home: 451 Manor Rd Staten Island NY 10314-2963 Office: Amabile & Erman 1000 South Ave Staten Island NY 10314-3430

HUMPHRIES, JOAN ROPES, psychologist, educator; b. Bklyn., Oct. 17, 1928; d. Lawrence Gardner and Adele Lydia (Zimmermann) Ropes; m. Charles C. Humphries, Apr. 4, 1957; children: Peggy Ann, Charlene Adele. BA, U. Miami, 1950; MS, Fla. State U., 1955; PhD, La. State U., 1963. Registered lobbyist State of Fla. Part-time instr. psychology dept. U.

Miami, Coral Gables, Fla., 1964-66; prof. behavioral studies dept. Miami-Dade C.C., 1966—; Presenter, lectr. in field. Prodr., prin host (videos) Strategies in Global Modern Academia: Issues and Answers in Higher Education, 1993-94; prodr., host (video) Strategies in Global Modern Academia: Issues and Answers in Higher Education II, Strategies in Global Modern Academia, 1995, III, 1996-97, lect., Fostering, Enhancing and Improving Knowledge of American View of Constitutional Law from Psychological Perspective, given aboard cruise ship Costa Romantica; editl. staff, maj. author: The Application of Scientific Behaviorism to Humanistic Phenomena, 1975, rev. edit., 1979. Mem. Biofeedback Delegation to the People's Republic of China and Hong Kong, 1995, Citizen Amb. Program, Psychic Arts Delegation to Russia, 1997, Citizen Amb. Program, Am. Mus. Natural History, Pastorius Home Assn., Inc., Vizcayans (mus.), Aldren Kindred of Am., Inc., Nat. Trust Hist. Preservation, The Charles F. Menninger Soc., People to People (citizen amb.). Mem. AAUP (past v.p. and sec., pres. Miami-Dade C.C. chpt. 1986—, past v.p. Fla. conf., 1986-88, mem. exec. bd. Fla. conf. 1989-90, mem. nat.), AAUW (life, former v.p. Tamiami br. 1983-88, Appreciation award 1977), Biofeedback Soc. of Am. (pres. 1989—), Biofeedback Assn. Fla. (pres. 1990—), Internat. Platform Assn. (gov. 1979—, Silver Bowl award 1993), APA, Am. Psychol. Soc. (charter), Fla. Psychol. Assn., Mexico Beach C. of C. (bus. 1991-95), North Campus Speaker's Bur. (award for cmty. lecture series), Physicians for Social Responsibility, Internat. Soc. for Study Subtle Energies and Energy Medicine (charter), Inst. Evaluation, Diagnosis and Treatment (past v.p. 1975-87, pres. 1987—, former bd. dirs.), Dade-Monroe Psychol. Assn., Assn. Applied Psychophysiology and Biofeedback, Noetic Scis., Colonial Dames 17th Century, N.Y. Acad. Scis. (life), Regines in Miami, Soc. Mayflower Descs. (elder William Brewster colony), Hereditary Order of Descendants of Colonial Govs., Coral Gables Country Club (life), Historic Homeowners Coral Gables, Pilgrim John Howland Soc., Jockey Club (life), Phi Lambda (founder's plaque 1976, Appreciation award 1987), Phi Lambda Pi. Democrat. Achievements include research in biofeedback and human consciousness. Home: 1311 Alhambra Cir Coral Gables FL 33134-3521 Office: Miami Dade CC North Campus 11380 NW 27th Ave Miami FL 33167-3418

HUMS, JOSEPH ERICH, chemist, chemical engineer, consultant; b. Bamberg, Germany, Sept. 30, 1946; s. Georg and Annemarie (Firsching) H.; m. Eveline Goldmann, Mar. 2, 1979 (div. May 1985); m. Jutta Fischer, Dec. 28, 1993. Grad. in engring., Tech. U. Berlin, 1972; degree in chemistry, Free U. Berlin, 1978; PhD in Chemistry, U. Bayreuth, Germany, 1982. Mem. acad. coun. U. Bayreuth, 1982-85; developer Siemens AG, KWU, Erlangen, Germany, 1985-94, cons. engr. for tech. innovations, R & D support and patents, 1994-98; cons. engr. for tech. innovations, R & D support and patents Siemens AG, KWU, Redwitz, Germany, 1999—; asst. prof. Martin-Luther U., Halle-Wittenberg, Germany, 2000—; mem. internat. sci. com. post-conf. seminar on catalysis on eve of 21st Century, Boreskov Meml. Conf., Novosibirsk, 1997; mem. Internat. Scientific Bd. of 12th internat. Congress on Catalysis, Granada, Spain, 2000. Editor Europe and Asia Newsbrief sect. Applied Catalysis B: Environ. of Elsevier Sci. for Europe and Asia; contbr. articles to sci. jours.; patentee in fields catalysis, advanced materials, catalytic combustion, NOx abatement; exhibited in internat. group shows. Mem. German Assn. Fine Artists (former v.p. Bavaria). Avocation: fine arts. E-mail: erich.hums@red1.siemens.de. Office: Siemens AG KWU, KPW Bahnhofstrasse 43, D-96257 Redwitz Germany

HUND, BARBARA MAURER, English educator and speech broadcasting; b. Wilkes-Barre, Pa., Dec. 11, 1930; d. Robert Henry and Nerline Maude (Smith) Maurer; m. Henry John Hund, June 10, 1961; children: Kirsten, John. BA in English and Edn., Hofstra U., 1952; cert. in devel. western civilization, U. Edinburgh, Scotland, 1952; cert. in English, art, lit. and music, U. London, 1955; MA in Speech and Broadcasting, U. Wis., 1957; cert. in conversational Chinese, Yale U., 1966; EdD in Higher Edn., Coll. William and Mary, 1987. Cert. elem. and secondary tchr., N.Y., Wis., N.J., Md., Va. Elem. tchr., Baldwin, N.Y., Madison, Wis., Montclair, N.J., 1952-58; elem. tchr., Norfolk (Va.) Acad., 1972-76; tchr. TV, Washington County Sch. Sys., Hagerstown, Md., 1958-61; ednl. TV prodr. WMHT-TV Mohawk-Hudson Pub. Broadcasting, Schenectady, 1961-64; TV prodr. Chinese Broadcasting Co., Taipei, Taiwan, 1969-70; tchr. English, Taipei Am. Sch., 1969-70; prof. speech, English and broadcasting Tidewater C.C., Portsmouth, Va., 1976—, chmn. coll. internat. task force, 1995-96; chmn. distance edn. task force Tidewater C.C., Portsmouth, 1995-99; tchr. Beijing Broadcasting Inst., 1988-89, 1997; China coord. exch. agreement between Tidewater C.C. and Beijing Broadcasting Inst., 1989—; instr. Fulbright-Hays Study Seminar in Czech and Slovak Republics, summer 1993; instrnl. TV writer, prodr., broadcaster elem. math., sci. and enrichments lessons Washington County TV Project, 1958-61. Organizer, prodr., co-host comml. TV show Spotlight on Hampton Roads, Norfolk, 1986-87,. Edn. chmn. Luth. Ch., 1973-85, lay reader, lector, communion asst., 1985—; mem. cmty. adv. bd. WHRO Pub. Broadcasting, Hampton Roads, Va., 1980-84; leader leadership edn. and devel.. for 12 Luth. chs., Hampton Roads area, 1981-83; speaker on China experiences to local civic group and local TV stas., 1989-91; participant 1st Sino-Am. Conf. on Women's Issues, China and Ednl. Exch., Beijing, summer 1990, spring 1997. Named Outstanding Tidewater C.C. Faculty Showcase Mem., Va. C.C. Assn., 1994; scholar Hofstra U., 1948-52. Mem. AAUW, Am. Women in Radio and TV (charter, v.p., treas. Commonwealth chpt. 1962-99). Avocations: travel, reading, tennis, other sports. E-mail: bhund@mindspring.com.

HUNDEIKER, MAX EGON ERNST, physician, medical educator; b. Tempelburg, Pommern, Germany, June 28, 1937; s. Ernst H.W. and Elisabeth B.A. (Kortum) H.; m. Hanna Ratje, Aug. 7, 1964; children: Heike, Wibke, Ulf, Friederike. Degree in physics, U. Freiburg, 1959, MD, 1963, Habilitation, 1970. Asst. country hosps. Ratzeburg and Oldesloe, 1962-63; asst. in anatomy U. Freiburg, 1963-64, asst. dermatology Univ. Clinic, 1965-70, prof. dermatology, 1971-83; asst. Diakonissen-Krankenhaus, Kork, 1964-65; prof., chmn. dermatology Fachklinik Hornheide Münster, 1984—; sec. Vereinigung Operative Dermatologie, 1977-93; bd. dirs. Tumorzentrum Münsterland; sec. Arbeitsgemeinschaft/Krebsbekampfung, 1996—. Mem. editl. bd. Der Hautarzt, Internistische Praxis, 1984-96; editor: Zentralblatt Haut, 1984-96; contbr. more than 700 articles to profl. jours. Mem. German Dermatologic Soc., German Soc. Pathologists, Hungarian Dermatologic Soc. Office: Fachklinik Hornheide, Dorbaumstrasse 300, D-48157 Münster Germany

HUNDER, GENE GERALD, physician, educator; b. Lake City, Minn., Feb. 7, 1932; s. Tilman James and Melita Henrietta (Bremer) H.; m. Ingeborg Anne Hanson, May 6, 1990; children: Heidi, Jennifer, Gregory, Grant, Naomi, Stephanie. Student, St. Olaf Coll., 1950-52; BA, U. Minn. (Mpls.), 1954, MD, 1958, MS, 1963. Diplomate Am. Bd. Internal Medicine. Intern. Strong Meml. Hosp., Rochester, N.Y., 1958-59, resident, 1959-61; resident Mayo Clinic, Rochester, Minn., 1961-64; instr. internal medicine Mayo Grad. Sch., Rochester, Minn., 1966-67, asst. prof. internal medicine, 1968-73, assoc. prof., 1973-78, prof., 1978—, full mem. internal medicine, 1981—, cons. internal medicine and rheumatology; prof. internal medicine Mayo Clinic Mayo found., Rochester, Minn., 1978—; head sect. rheumatology Mayo Clinic, 1976-81; chmn. rheumatology rsch. com., 1976-81, 87, clin. investigator tng. program Mayo Grad. Sch., 1981-84, chmn. div. rheumatology 1987-96; Philip Showalter Hench lect. Ariz. Med . Soc., Phoenix, 1965; Charles W. Thomas lectr. Med. Coll. Va., Charlottesville, 1979; Carl Pearson lectr. Los Angeles County Med. Assn., 1983; Henry J. Lehrhoff lectr. Clarkson Hosp., Omaha, 1989, Nana Swartz lectr. Swedish Med. Soc., 1994, Gilbert Galens Meml. lectr. William Beaumont Hosp., Detroit, 1995. Co-author: Physical Examination of the Joints, 1978; editor: Rheumatology, 1978, Atlas of Rheumatology, 1998, Mayo Clinic on Arthritis, 1999; assoc. editor: Jour. Lab and Clin. Medicine, 1979-81; editor Jour. Current Opinion in Rheumatology, 1992-2000, Jour. Arthritis Care and Rsch., 2000—; mem. editl. bd. Jour. Rheumatology, 1982—, Jours. Musculoskeletal Medicine, 1983—, Ann. Intern. Med., 1998—. Mem. ho. dels. Arthritis Found., Atlanta, 1980-83, trustee, 1985; mem. exec. com. Minn. Arthritis Found., Mpls., 1984-90. Fellow ACP; Nu Sigma Nu scholar, 1995; Minn. Med. Found. acad. scholar, 1995. Mem. AMA, Am. Assn. Immunologists, Am. Fedn. Clin. Research, Am. Bd. Internal Medicine, AAAS. Cen. Clin. Research Club, Cen. Soc. Clin. Research (mem. program com.), Am. Soc. Clin. Rheumatology (pres.), Am. Coll. Rheumatology (mem. exec. com. 1976-77, v.p. cen. region 1987, pres. cen. region, 1989, bd. dirs. 1988-92, Master award 1997), Phi Beta Kappa, Alpha Omega Alpha. Republican. Lutheran. Home: RR 1 Box 132B Zumbro Falls MN 55991-9725 Office: Mayo Clinic 200 1st St SW Rochester MN 55905-0002

HUNG, HON CHEUNG GEORGE, engineering executive; b. Guangzhou, China, July 24, 1934; arrived in Can., 1991; s. Man Yu Hung and Sou Ling Kam. Diploma, Chinese U. Hong Kong, 1956. Mgr. Internat. Engring. Ltd., Hong Kong, 1957-79; pres. Sys. Engring. Ltd., Hong Kong, 1979—; mem. bd. trustees Chung Chi Coll., Chinese U. Hong Kong, 1973—, chmn. bd. trustees, 1993—; mem. coun. Chinese U. Hong Kong, 1993—. Recipient First prize Internat. Inventors Expn., 1991, Popular Sci. award, 1995, Best of What's New award, 1995. Mem. Heating, Refrigerating, Air Conditioning Engrs., Am. Mgmt. Assn., Assn. Energy Engrs., Rotary Club Hong Kong (pres. 1993-94). Achievements include invention of a new bicycle utilizing body weight called RISIGO (rise-sit-go) bicycle with patent in U.S. and 47 other countries and territories. Office: 16 1 F New Henry House, 10 Ice House St Ctrl, Hong Kong China

HUNG, JACKSON YAU-BONG, insurance company executive; b. Fukien, China, Aug. 4, 1949; s. Ang Johnny and Yu-Hsuan (Wu) Hung; m. Betsy Lai-Chu Ng, Nov. 4, 1978; children: Adrian, Desmond. Br. mgr. Sun Life of Can., Hong Kong, 1978-92; sr. unit mgr. Manulife (Internat.) Ltd., Hong Kong, 1993—; com. mem. 4th Asia Pacific Life Ins. Congress, Hong Kong, 1997. Fellow Life Underwriters Tng. Coun.; mem. Life Underwriters Assn. Hong Kong Ltd. (life), Hong Kong Achievers Toastmasters. Avocation: Chi-kung. Home: Flat C 17/F Block 5, Nan Fung Sun Chuen, Quarry Bay Hong Kong Office: Manulife (Internat) Ltd, 33 Hysan Ave 28/F, Causeway Bay Hong Kong

HUNG, MEI-JONG CHOW, social worker; b. Taipei, Taiwan, Republic China, Oct. 7, 1937; s. Wen-tung Yeh Chow; m. Chao-huang Hung, Mar. 24, 1964; children: Jennifer Ching-yi, John Ching-tsung. BS, Nat. Taiwan U., 1960; MSW, Simmons Coll. Sch. Social Work, 1963. Cert. social worker, hypnotherapist. Mental health counselor Taipei Pub. Health Teaching Demonstration, 1963-66; asst. prof. Taiwan U., 1964-66; social work supr. Johns Hopkins Hosp., Balt., 1969-71; pvt. practice social work Columbia, Md., 1972—. Vol. community recreational social work, 1988—; co-prodr. Opera Internat., Washington, 1999—. WHO fellow. Mem. NASW, Acad. Cert. Social Workers. Home and Office: 7255 Meadow Wood Way Clarksville MD 21029-1714 Address: PO Box 140 Fulton MD 20759-0140

HUNG, PAUL PORWEN, biotechnologist, educator, consultant; b. Taipei, Taiwan, Sept. 30, 1933; s. Yao-Hsun and Shiu-Chin (Wu) H.; m. Nancy Kay Clark, May 4, 1956; children: Pauline E., Eileen K., Clark D. BS in Arts and Sci., Millikin U., 1956; PhD in Biochemistry, Purdue U., 1960; DSc (hon.), Millikin U., 1997. Head molecular virology and biology Abbott Labs., North Chicago, 1960-81; gen. mgr. Bethesda Rsch. Lab., Gaithersburg, Md., 1981-82; asst. v.p. Wyeth Ayerst Labs., Radnor, Pa., 1982-95, disting. rsch. fellow, 1993-95; adj. prof. Northwestern U. Med. Sch., Chgo., 1975-86; chmn. bd. RDNA Corp., Bryn Mawr, Pa., 1995—; chmn. bd., pres. Global Briotech Inc., Taiwan; mem. Nat. Vaccine Adv. Com., Washington, 1990-95; cons. Am. Inst. Biol. Sci., Washington, 1992, UN Indsl. Devel. Orgn., Vienna, Austria, 1981. Author: (chpt.) Recombinant DNA, 1991, Hepatitis Vaccine, 1991; contbr. over 270 articles to profl. jours. Named Disting. Alumni of Yr. Purdue Univ., 1994. Mem. Am. Soc. Biochemistry and Molecular Biology, Am. Assn. Cancer Rsch., Internat. Assn. Biol. Standardization, Am. Inst. Chemists, Am. Soc. Microbiology, Am. Chem. Soc., AAAS, N.Y. Acad. Sci. Achievements include patents in field. Home: 506 Ramblewood Dr Bryn Mawr PA 19010-2041

HUNG, SHAN-LING, biology educator, researcher; b. Taipei, Taiwan, Republic of China, Dec. 6, 1962; came to U.S., 1985; d. Wei-Chang Hung and Mei-Tai Sze; m. Yen-Ting Chen, Mar. 10, 1991; children: Daniel, Jessica. BA, U. Tenn., Knoxville, 1987; PhD, U. Pa., 1992. Postdoctoral fellow U. Mich., Ann Arbor, 1992-94; assoc. prof. Nat. Yang-Ming U., Taipei, 1995—; committeeman radiation safety com. Nat. Yang-Ming U., 1995—, libr. com., 1999. Editl. bd. Jour. of Dental Sci., 1998-99. Recipient Nat. Rsch. Svc. award NIH, 1988-94, Grade A Rsch. award Nat. Sci. Coun., 1995; Career Devel. grantee Nat. Health Rsch. Inst., 1997-2000; Dr. Chji-Shuen Tsou rsch. grantee Med. Rsch. and Advancement Found., 1996-2000. Mem. The Chinese Soc. of Microbiology, Assn. of Dental Sci., The Taiwanese Assn. of Dental Rsch. Avocation: travel.

HUNG, TZU-CHEN, engineering educator; b. Peng-Hu, Taiwan, Oct. 20, 1957; s. King-Chung and Shar-Lan (Chen) H.; m. Gei-Mei Jeanne Shih, Dec. 12, 1987; children: H. Michelle, Y. Joshua. BS, Tsing-Hua U., Hsin-Chu, Taiwan, 1980, MS, 1982; MS, UCLA, 1987, PhD, 1989. Rsch. asst. UCLA, 1984-89; scientist Phys. Rsch., Inc., L.A., 1989; engr. Argonne (Ill.) Nat. Lab., 1990-92; dir. Global Energy Tech., Inc., Naperville, Ill., 1992-93; assoc. prof. I-Shou U. (former Kaohsiung Poly. Inst.), Taiwan, 1993—; rsch. assoc. Inst. Nuclear Energy Rsch., Tau-Yuan, Taiwan, 1983-84; cons. Global Energy Tech. Inc., Naperville, 1991-92, Tai-Power Co., Taipei, 1994—. Assoc. editor Jour. Cogeneration Report, 1997—; reviewer Nuclear Sci. Jour., 1995—, Internat. Jour. Numerical Methods in Fluids, 1995—; contbr. articles to profl. jours. Rsch. scholar UCLA, 1984; Small Bus. Innovative Rsch. grantee U.S. Dept. Energy, 1988, 89; recipient Nat. Sci. award, Taiwan, 1994, 97, 98, Paper award, Chinese Nuclear Soc., 1997. Mem. Chinese Soc. Engrs., Chinese Soc. Solar Energy, Chinese Soc. Cogeneration, Kaohsiung Met. Devel. Found. Avocations: music, sports. Home: 452 Jeou-Ru 2nd Rd, Kaohsiung Taiwan Office: I-Shou U, 1 Sect 1 Hsueh-Cheng Rd, Kaohsiung 84008, Taiwan

HUNG, YU-CHUN, anesthesiologist; b. Taipei, Taiwan, Oct. 27, 1962. Bachelor's degree, China Med. Coll., Taichung, Taiwan, 1989. Cert. in medicine. Resident of anesthesiology Makay Meml. Hosp., Taipei, 1989-93; attending in anesthesiology Taipei Med. Coll. Hosp., 1993-95; chief anesthesiology Ton Yen Gen. Hosp., Hsin Chu, Taiwan, 1995-97, cons. critical care medicine, 1997-99, sr. vis. of anesthesiology, 1999—. Mem. Soc. Anesthesiology of China (specialist 1993), Soc. Emergency and Critical Care Medicine (specialist 1994), Chinese Assn. for Study of Pain (specialist 1995). Avocation: photography.

HUNGATE, JAY W., artist, sculptor; b. Palo Alto, Calif., Jan. 11, 1965; s. Robert W. and JoAnne M. (Hinrichs) H.; m. Christine Theodoros, Sept. 7, 1996. BFA, Mass. Coll. Art, 1991. Artisan Robert Shure Co., Boston, 1988-90, Skylight Studios, Woburn, Mass., 1989-92; owner JWH Studio, Lowell, Mass., 1990—. Sculptures include Guardian of Hope & Dreams, 1990, Gossip Monger, 1995 (Best of Show award 1996). Mem. New Eng. Sculptors Assn. (v.p. 1998—, bd. dirs. 1997-98), New Eng. Sculptors Assn. Avocations: stone carving, gardening, bicycling, hiking, bonsai trees. Home: 48 Warwick St Lowell MA 01851-3722 Office: JWH Studio Statuary 99 Willie St Lowell MA 01854-4159

HUNGENBERG, THOMAS, radiologist; b. Cologne, Germany, July 23, 1955; s. Paul and Hedwig (Schiefer) H. MD, U. Cologne, 1982. Bd. cert. radiologist. Resident St. Katharinen Hosp., Frechen, Germany, 1981-83; resident Univ. Hosp., Cologne, 1983-88, Duesseldorf, Germany, 1989-90; dept. head Eduardus Hosp., Cologne, 1990—, hosp. head, 1995—; tchr. Teleradiologic Consulting Ctr., 1998—, Deutsche Gesellschaft für Ultraschall in der Medizin, Boeblingen, 1995—. Mem. Deutsche Roentgengesellschaft, Deutsche Gesellschaft für Ultraschall in der Medizin, Radiol. Soc. N.Am. Roman Catholic. Avocations: skiing, swimming. Office: Eduardus-Krankenhaus, Custodisstrasse 3-17, D-50679 Cologne Germany

HUNGERFORD, JOHN CHARLES, mechanical engineer; b. Detroit, Feb. 6, 1939; s. Joseph Vincent and Bertha Estelle (Warren) H.; m. Ruth Faye Wolkoff, Sept. 23, 1978; 1 child, Julia Michel. BSME, Ohio U., 1967, MS, 1968; PhD, Ohio State U., 1984. Cert. profl. ergonomist. Program analyst supr. Tenn. Dept. Mental Health, 1970-75; rsch. assoc. Ohio State U., 1975-79; assoc. prof. indsl. engring. U. Tenn., Knoxville, 1979—; cons. to nuclear industry; former cons. mental health programs; accident reconstructionist, forensics cons. Office of Edn. tng. grantee, 1973. Transp. Rsch. fellow; Office of Edn. tng. grantee 1973; recipient Grad. Rsch. award Ohio State U., 1978-79. Mem. Am. Soc. Engring. Edn., Human Factors and Ergonomics Soc., Am. Soc. Safety Engrs., Md. Assn. Traffic Accident Investigation, Nat. Assn. of Profl. Accident Reconstrn. Specialists, Ind. Indsl. Engrs. (regional v.p. 1993-95), Ergonomics Soc., Soc. Automotive Engrs., Alpha Pi Mu. Home: 7120 Stagecoach Trl Knoxville TN 37909-1113 Office: U Tenn Alumni Alumni Meml Bldg Rm 145 Knoxville TN 37996-0001

HUNG-LICK HU, HENRY, academic administrator; b. Shaoshing, China, Jan. 15, 1920; m. Chi-Yung Chung, Nov. 12, 1945; children: Y.S., F.C. LLB, Ctrl. U. Polit. Sci., Chungking, China, 1942; LLD, U. Paris, 1952. Atty. China, 1943-45; with Chinese Fgn. Svc., 1945-49; barrister Mid. Temple, London, 1954-55; atty. Hong Kong, 1955; pres. Shue Yan Coll. Author: Le Probleme Coreen, 1953, Nationality and Human Rights, 1956, Chinese Law and Custom in Hong Kong, 1956, Suez Canal Crisis, 1957. Avocations: reading, hiking, travel. Office: 602 Wah Cheong Bldg, 1 Glenealy Central, Hong Kong China

HUNING, ALOIS KONRAD, philosophy educator; b. Melle, Lower Saxony, Germany, Feb. 21, 1935; s. Johannes Mathias and Maria (Bartke) H.; m. Brunhilde Elisabeth Fedtke, Dec. 19, 1968; children, Mathias, Christian, Tobias. PhD, U. Louvain, Belgium, 1964. Lectr. OFM, Munster, 1965-68; mgr. Assn. German Engrs., Dusseldorf, 1969-73; prof. Acad. Pedagogies, Neuss, 1973-80, U. Dusseldorf, 1980-2000. Author numerous books. Pres. Christlich Demokratische Union Deutschlands, Wuelfrath, 1974-80, mem. bd. reps., 1975—; mayor Wuelfrath, 1989-95, dep. mayor, 1995—, mem. dist. parliament, 1994—. Roman Catholic. Avocations: arts, tennis. Home: Weissdornweg 12, D-42489 Wuelfrath Germany Office: Heinrich-Heine-Universitaet, Universitaetsstr 1, Düsseldorf D-40225, Germany

HUNJAN, TALJEET SINGH, hotel executive, consultant; b. Kisumu, Nyanza, Kenya, Apr. 18, 1965; s. Balbir Singh Hunjan and Surjit Kaur Padam; m. Wahida Ali Salim, Dec. 28, 1990; children: Nadia, Sadia, Abdulhasib. Diploma in Mgmt., British Tutorial Coll., Nairobi, 1986, diploma in Mktg. and Sales, 1987; MBA, Marlborough U., England, 1996, BA in Hotel Mgmt., PhD in Bus. Adminstrn., 1999. Gen. mgr. The Beat House, Nairobi, 1984-89, Reef Hotels, Mombasa, Kenya, 1989-90; mgr., acct. Dhaba Restaurant, Nairobi, 1991-92; resident mgr. Turtle Bay Beach Hotel, Malindi, Kenya, 1993-96; mgr., financial controller Gipsy Bar, Nairobi, 1996—; exec. H-M-C, Nairobi, 1997—; cons. Cook Internat. Ltd., Nairobi, 1997—, Sat Joiners Ltd., Nairobi, 1997—, Beauty & Beast Ltd., 1998, Raven Lounge Club, 1998, White Line Security, 1998, Vyombo Ctr., 1998, Gen. Merchants, 1999; dir. Hunjan Tours & Travel, Nairobi, 1996—, Hunjan Mgmt. Cons., Nairobi, 1997—, Four Sq. Enterprises, 1997, Four Sq. Co., 1998, Express Guarage, 1999. Vice chmn. Kanu Youth Patriots, Nairobi, 1992, coord., 1997. Recipient Adminstr. of Yr. trophy Wendy Entertainment Hilton Hotel, Nairobi, 1986. Fellow Chartered Inst. Bus. Adminstrn. (Ireland, certificate 1998), Marlborough (certificate 1996), Mensa (certificate 1997). Mem. Kanu Ch. Avocations: coin collecting, reading journals, corresponding, travel, food. Fax: 254(02)556440. E-mail: bil-lhunjan@hotmail.com. Home: PO Box 26628, Nairobi Kenya Office: Hunjan Management Cons, Keeckrock Rd PO Box 26628, Nairobi Kenya

HUNKIN, JOHN S., financial company executive. BA in Econ., U. Manitoba; MBA, York U. Various positions CIBC, 1969-80, gen. mgr., 1980-84, sr. v.p., 1984, exec. v.p. we. hemisphere, 1986, pres. investment and corp. banking ops., 1992, bd. dirs., 1993, chmn., CEO, 1999—; pres., CEO Wood Gundy Inc., 1992-99, dep. chmn., CEO, 1990-92; dir. Can. Psychiat. Rsch. Found.; chair adv. coun. Schulich Sch. Bus. York U.; bd. govs. York U.; bd. dirs. St. Michael's Hosp. Found. Bd. trustees Montreal Mus. Fine Arts Found. Office: Can Imperial Bank Commerce, Commerce Ct, Toronto, ON Canada M5L 1A2

HUNNECKE-ENFERT, EVELYN, German language and literature educator; b. Iserlohn, Germany, Aug. 14, 1955; arrived in France, 1985; d. Friedrich Wilhelm Hunnecke and Gerda Schmidt; m. Jean-Marie Enfert, Oct. 17, 1988; 1 child, Clara-Estelle Enfert. Staatsexamen, U. Tübingen, Germany, 1980, MA in German and French Studies, 1981; diploma of German studies, U. Aix-en-Provence, France, 1984, D d'Etat in German Lit., 1987. Sr. lectr. U. Toulouse, France, 1991-93; prof. U. Poitiers, France, 1993-94, U. Toulon, France, 1994—; mem. rsch. unit CERAM, U. Toulouse, 1992—, mem. rsch. unit BABEL, U. Toulon, 1996—. Author: Poésie et Poétique de Paul Celan; contbr. articles to profl. jours. Mem. German and French Assn. Germanists. Office: U Toulon Ave de, l'université BP 132, F-83957 La Garde France

HUNSAKER, RICHARD KENDALL, lawyer; b. L.A., June 2, 1960; s. Richard Allan and Patricia Kendall (Cook) H.; m. Laura Constance Haile, Oct. 8, 1988; children, Charles Nicholas, Laura Caroline. BA, U. Ill., 1982, MA, 1983; JD, Washington U., St. Louis, 1986. Bar: Ill. 1986, U.S. Dist. Ct. (cen. and no. dists.) Ill. 1987, U.S. Ct. Appeals (7th cir.) 1990, Wis. 1992. Speech coach Champaign (Ill.) Central High Sch., 1979-81; instr. speech communications, asst. debate coach U. Ill., Urbana, 1982-83; assoc. Heyl, Royster, Voelker & Allen, Springfield, Ill., 1986-87; assoc. Heyl, Royster, Voelker & Allen, Rockford, Ill., 1987-93, ptnr., 1994—. Author: Advanced Real Estate Law in Illinois - Environmental Liabilities, 1992, (with others) Advanced Real Estate Law in Illinois: Environmental Liability, 1992. Mem. ABA (tort and ins. practice, litigation and natural resources, energy and environ. law sects.), Ill. Bar Assn. (assoc., ins. law sect. 1990-92, civil practice and procedure, workers compensation, tort law and environ. control law sects.), Ill. Assn. Def. Trial Counsel, Winnebago County Bar Assn. (editl. bd. lawyer, legal-med., trial practice and continuing legal edn. coms.), Seventh Cir. Bar Assn., Def. Rsch. Inst. Methodist. Avocations: golf, biking, backpacking. E-mail: rhunsaker@hrva.com. Home: 1418 National Ave Rockford IL 61103-7144 Office: Heyl Royster Voelker & Allen 321 W State St Rockford IL 61101-1137

HUNSBERGER, ALICE CHANDLER, religion educator, human rights activist; b. Washington, June 25, 1952; d. George Shepherd and Ruth Margaret (Stillman) H.; m. Angelo Gelpi, Aug. 12, 1977 (div. Aug. 1994); 1 child, Adriane. BA cum laude, NYU, 1974; MA, Columbia U., 1977, MPhil, 1979, PhD, 1992. Rsch. asst. Middle East langs. Columbia U., N.Y.C., 1974-77; instr. Queens Coll./CUNY, N.Y.C., 1977, Aryamehr U. Tech., Isfahan, Iran, 1977-78, U. P.R., Rio Piedras, 1978; devel. assoc. Seamen's Ch. Inst., N.Y.C., 1984-88; assoc. dir. devel. Amnesty Internat., N.Y.C., 1988-99; adj. asst. prof. program in religion Hunter Coll./CUNY, N.Y.C., 1992-95; rsch. fellow Inst. Ismaili Studies, London, 1999—; lectr. in internat. human rights and Islamic philosophy; cons. various orgns., 1993—; seminar lectr. Cambridge (Eng.) U., 1994, Inst. for Ismaili Studies, London, 1997. Tech. editor Soc. for Islamic Philosophy and Sci., N.Y.C., 1980-91. Recipient 2d prize for Best Dissertation in Iranian Studies, Found. for Iranian Studies, 1992. mem. Middle East Studies Assn., Soc. for Iranian Studies (treas. 1992-94), Columbia U. Seminar in Iranian Studies (acting chair 1998-99), Am. Acad. Religion, Am. Philos. Soc. Democrat. Avocation: learning languages. Office: Inst Ismaili Studies 42-44 Grosvenor Gardens New York NY 10012

HUNSBERGER, ROGER MOORE, web developer, writer, lumber company executive; b. Washington, May 4, 1951; s. Emerson Franklin and Anne Chandler (Moore) H.; m. Linda Elizabeth Fleming, Aug. 16, 1969; children: Michelle Lynn Schahn, Eric John. Degree broadcast comms., RCA Insts., Inc., N.Y.C., 1972; student, Minn. Supreme Ct. Cont. Edn., St. Paul, 1986-89. Owner The Woodsmith, Mankato, Minn., 1975-79; terr. rep. Wadena (Minn.) Saw Mills, 1979-83; systems mgr. Indsl. Lumber & Plywood, Inc., Mpls., 1983-89; nat. sales mgr. Can. Forest Products, Ltd., Boise, Idaho, 1989-91; freelance writer St. Paul and Mpls., 1989—; owner A Writer on the Web, LLC, 1997—; creator, designer Xtravar.com, 2000—; cons., writer Orgn. Random Lengths Publs., Eugene, Oreg., 1992—; creator, presenter mgmt. seminars U. Minn., 1992. Author: Mark of the Coyote, 1990, Sojourn, 1994; contbr. articles to profl. jours. Mem. election com. Minn. House-Mark Piepho campaign, Mankato, 1977-82; chair fin. com. Holy Rosary Parish, Mankato, 1978-80. Mem. NRA, The Hunsberger Assn., The One Percent Club. Avocations: photography, hiking, woodworking, target shooting. Home: 3328 47th Ave S Minneapolis MN 55406-2345

HUN SEN, Prime Minister of Kampuchea; b. Kompang, Cham Province, People's Republic Kampuchea, 1952. Ed., Phnom Penh, People's Republic of Kampuchea; PhD in polit. sci., Nat. Inst. Politics, Hanoi, 1991. Joined Khmers Rouges, 1970, rising to comdt.; min. fgn. affairs Govt. Cambodia,

Phnom Penh, second prime min., 1993-98, prime min., 1998—; in Vietnam with pro-Vietnamese Kampucheans, 1978; returned to People's Republic Kampuchea after Vietnamese-backed takeover; minister for fgn. affairs People's Republic Kampuchea, 1979—, former prime minister; chmn. Council of Ministers, Republic of Kampuchea, 1985-89, State of Kampuchea, 1989-93. Office: Office of Coun Mins, Khemarin Palace, Phnom Penh Kampuchea

HUNSPERGER, ELIZABETH JANE, art and design consultant, educator; b. Phila., Aug. 30, 1938; d. Francis Charles and Elizabeth Julia Thorpe; m. Robert George Hunsperger, Sept. 13, 1958; 1 child, Lisa Marie. AA in Design, Santa Monica Coll., 1974; student, UCLA, 1975-76; BA in Art History, U. Del., 1978; postgrad., Rutgers U., 1978-81; MA in Edn., Del. State Coll., 1993. Designer Huntingdon Mills, Phila., 1960-63, Rothschild's, Ithaca, N.Y., 1963-65, Cornell U., Ithaca, 1965-67; freelance designer Malibu, Calif., 1967-76; art and design cons., lectr. Art & Sci. Assocs., Newark, Del., 1980—; art tchr. Cath. Diocese of Wilmington, 1988-95; art and spl. edn. tchr. Red Clay Consolidated Sch. Dist. A.I. duPont H.S., Greenville, Del., 1995-97, Shorehaven Sch., Chesapeake City, Md., 1997-99, A.I. duPont Inst., Wilmington, Del., 1999—; with Leech Sch., 1994; bd. dirs. Gallery 20, Newark, Del., 1982-86; cons. Arts and Sci. Assocs., Ednl. and Design Svcs., Newark, Del., 1995—. Exhbns. include Malibu Art Assn. Show, 1973, 74, Newark Art Show, 1987, 88. Founding mem. bd. dirs., v.p. Newark Housing Ministry, Inc., 1983-94, pres., 1989-91; mem. social concerns com. and drug and alcohol task force Del.; active Coun. Exceptional Children. Recipient Outstanding Svc. award YWCA, Santa Monica, Calif., 1972, award of recognition Missionhurst, 1982, Gov.'s Vol. of the Yr. award State of Del., 1990. Mem. Nat. Art Edn. Assn., Am. Craft Coun., Art Educators of Del. (bd. dirs., pres.), Debutante Assemlby Club (N.Y.C.). Episcopal. Home: 1014 New London Rd Newark DE 19711-2116

HUNSUCKER, ROBERT DUDLEY, physicist, electrical engineer, educator, researcher; b. Portland, Oreg., Mar. 15, 1930; s. Robert Deets and Johnnie Morris (Kuykendal) H.; m. Judith Mary Cotter, Apr. 28, 1956 (dec. Nov. 1980); children: Edith Louise, Jeanne Marie, Cynthia Lee; m. Phyllis Marie Hoover, July 25, 1981. BS in Physics, Oreg. State U., 1954, MS in Physics, 1958; PhDEE, U. Colo., 1969. Asst. prof. Geophysics Inst. U. Alaska, Fairbanks, 1958-64, assoc. prof. Geophysics Inst., 1971-78, prof. Geophysics Inst., 1978-87; physicist Nat. Bur. Standards, Boulder, Colo., 1964-67; sr. project leader ITS Office of Telecommunications Sci., Boulder, 1967-71; prof. emeritus physics and elec. engring., sr. cons. U. Alaska, Fairbanks, 1988—; radio propagation cons.; adj. prof. Pa. State U., Oreg. Inst. Technology. Author two tech. books; editor-in-chief Radio Sci., 1995-00; assoc. editor Radioscientist/URSI Bull.; contbr. over 100 articles to profl. jours. Served to lt. USNR, 1954-67. Fellow AAAS, IEEE (Alaska Engr. of Yr. Alaska sect. 1988, recipient outstanding achievement award IEEE region 6, 1988); mem. Am. Geophys. Union, U.S. Commission Internat. Union of Radio Sci., Sigma Xi, Sigma Pi Sigma, Eta Kappa Nu. Republican. Avocations: private pilot, fishing, amateur radio operation, writing. Office: Oreg Inst Technology Rm PV-282 EET Dept 3201 Campus Dr Klamath Falls OR 97601

HUNT, ALAN JOHN, English educator; b. Moscow, Idaho, Sept. 20, 1960; s. John P. and Marjorie (Lesher) H. BA in English, Wash. State U., 1984, MA in English, 1987, MA in Am. Studies, 1989. Instr. Wash. State U., Pullman, 1989-90, 93-94, Nishinomiya (Japan) Edn. Bd., 1990-92, Temple U. Japan, Osaka, 1992-93, Kansai U. of Fgn. Langs., Osaka, 1994-97; assoc. prof. Eichi U., Amagasaki, 1998—; active core curriculum project NEH, Wash. State U., 1987-90. Co-author: Intercultural Communication, 1996, Writing About the World, 1991, 2d edit., 1995; co-author Tchg. English in the Two-Yr. Coll., 1990; contbr. articles to profl. jours. Mem. TESOL, Japan Assn. Lang. Tchrs., Phi Kappa Phi, Phi Beta Kappa. Avocations: tennis, hiking, travel, reading, Japanese language.

HUNT, CHRISTOPHER JOHN, university librarian; b. Jan. 28, 1937; s. Richard John and Dorothy (Pendleton) H.; m. Kathleen Mary Wyatt, 1963. BA, U. Exeter; MLitt, U. Durham. Asst. libr. U. Newcastle upon Tyne, 1960-67; sub libr. U. Manchester, 1967-74; univ. libr. James Cook U. of North Queensland, 1974-81, La Trobe U., 1981-85; libr. Brit. Libr. Polit. and Econ. Sci., London Sch. Econs., 1985-91; dir., univ. libr. John Rylands U. Libr. of Manchester, 1991—; chmn. Internat. Com. Social Sci. Info. and Documentation, 1989—; acad. gov. London Sch. Econs., 1989-91. Author: The Leadminers of the Northern Pennines, 1970, The Book Trade in Northumberland and Durham to 1860, 1975; contbr. articles to profl. jours. Active Feofee Chetham's Hosp. and Libr., Manchester, 1993—; chmn. libr. panel Wellcome Trust, 1994—. Avocations: book collecting, scuba diving, wine. Office: U Manchester John Rylands Libr, Oxford Rd, Manchester M13 9PP, England*

HUNT, GARRY EDWARD, management consultant; b. London, May 23, 1942; s. Edward Bone and Amy Louisa (Butcher) H.; m. Wendy Thomas, Apr. 9, 1966; children: Sarah Jane, Susannah, Jonathan. BSc in Maths. with 1st class honors, U. London, 1964, PhD in Maths. Physics, 1966, DSc in Physics and Astronomy, 1981. Cert. mathematician. Sr. scientist Jet-propulsion Lab., Pasadena, Calif., 1970-72; prin. sci. officer Meteorlogical Office, Bracknell, Berks, Eng., 1972-77; dir. lab. planetary atmospheres U. Coll. London, London, 1977-82; dir. Ctr. Remote Sensing, head atmospheric physics Imperial Coll., London, 1982-86; bus. mgr. P.A. Cons. Group, London, 1986-88; CEO Logica Consultancy, Ltd., London, 1988-90; bus. devel. dir. ICL Plc., London, 1990-92; mng. ptnr. Elbury Enterprises, London, 1992—; vis. prof. U. Mo., St. Louis, 1984, U. Alexandria, Egypt, 1985, Eth Zurich, Switzerland, 1985, U. Md., Balt., 1986, City U. Bus. Sch., London, 1992—, City U. Bus. Sch., 1992-98, Kingston U. Bus. Sch., 1998—; non-exec. dir. Internat. Imaging Systems, 1974-86, Ctr. for Remote Sensing, Imperial Coll., 1982-86, Raynes Park Residents Holding Co., 1976—, Fleishman-Hillard, 1991-94, Workhouse, 1992-94, EDS, U.K., 1995-98, HW Group plc, 1998-2000, Smart ECommerce, 2000—, Access Internat., 2000—, Globebyte, 2000—, e Posit 2000—. Author 9 books and contbr. 300 articles to profl. jours. Pres. Raynes Park and London, 1992—; chmn. West Thames Br. Inst. of Dirs., Eng., 1994-97; Freeman City of London; Liveryman Worshipful Co. of Info. Techs. Recipient NASA awards, 1979, 82, 86, 89; named Internat. Scientist of Decade, ITN News, 1989. Fellow Royal Astron. Soc. (Gaskell medal 1983), Royal Meteorol. Soc., Royal Soc. Of Arts, British Interplanetary Soc., Inst. Dirs., Inst. Maths. and Its Applications; mem. Planetary Soc. (bd. advisor), British Computer Soc., Am. Geophys. Soc. Avocations: traveling, golfing. Fax: 44-20-8544-0158. E-mail: GarryEHunt@compuserve.com. Home and Office: Elbury House, 37 Blenheim Rd, London Raynes Park SW20 9BA, England

HUNT, GERALDINE BRIONY, veterinary surgeon, educator; b. Sydney, NSW, Australia, May 11, 1960; d. Peter and Susan Catherine Lebars (Williams) H. BVSc, U. Sydney, Australia, 1983; PhD, U. Sydney, 1989, Master Vet. Clin. Studies, 1991. Veterinarian Woden Animal Hosp., ACT, Australia, 1983-84; rsch. asst. Westmead Hosp., NSW, Australia, 1985-88; veterinarian Fairford Rd. Animal Hosp., Sydney, Australia, 1988; resident in small animal surgery U. Sydney, Sydney, 1989-91, lectr. in vet. anatomy, 1991-97, sr. lectr. in small animal surgery, 1997—; bd. examiners Australian Coll. Vet. Scientists, 1994-97, asst. chief examiner, 1997-99; adv. com. for the Registration of Vet. Specialists. Recipient Ian Clunies Ross Meml. award Australian Coll. Vet. Scientists, 1996. Fellow Australian Coll. Vet. Scientists. Avocations: horseback riding, swimming, walking, creative writing. Office: U Sydney, Dept Vet Clin Scis, Sydney 2006, Australia

HUNT, J. ROBIN, judge; b. Worcester, Mass., May 16, 1948; d. Malcolm H. and Betty Jean (Sprague) H.; m. Lawrence Robert Mills, June 1, 1970 (div. 1993); children: Christopher, Gregory; m. Arthur Michael Schmidt, Aug. 20, 1999. AB, Smith Coll., 1970; JD cum laude, Wayne State U., 1973. Law clk. Legal Aid & Defender, Detroit, 1971-72, Appellate Pub. Defender, Detroit, 1972-73, Wash. Atty. Gen., Olympia, 1972, U.S. Dist. Ct. (ea. dist.) Mich., Detroit, 1973-74; atty. Merdes, Schaible, Staley & DeLisio, Fairbanks, Alaska, 1974-75; from dep. to sr. dep. King County Prosecutor's Office, Seattle, 1976-83; mcpl. judge pro tem City of Winslow, Bainbridge Island, Wash., 1981-93, hearing examiner, 1985-96; judge State Washington Ct. Appeals, Tacoma, Wash., 1997—. Sch. bd. dir. Bainbridge Island, Wash., 1989-92. Mem. Congregational Ch. Avocations: music, sailing, cross-country skiing, hiking, performing arts. Home: State of Wash Ct Appeals Divsn Two 949 Market St Tacoma WA 98402

HUNT, JOHN J., historian, educator; b. Phila., Oct. 7, 1936; s. John J. and Ann M. H.; m. Rose Marie, Feb. 13, 1965; children: Michael, Stephen, Laura. BA, Villanova U., 1960, MA, 1960; PhD, Georgetown U., 1966. Prof. history St. Joseph Coll., West Hartford, Conn., 1965—. Mem. AAUP, Am. Hist. Assn., U. Faculty for Life. Roman Catholic. Avocation: astronomy, classical music, sports. Home: 12 Roaring Brook Rd Avon CT 06001-2323

HUNT, MAME, theater director, producer; b. Long Beach, Calif., Aug. 1, 1952; d. Edward W. and Joyce Eyber Hunt. BA, U. Calif., Santa Barbara, 1972; MFA, U. Calif., Davis, 1978. Literary mgr. L.A. Theatre Ctr., 1984-86, dir. new play devel., 1986-88; literary mgr. Berkeley (Calif.) Repertory Theatre, 1988-91; assoc. artistic dir. Magic Theatre, San Francisco, 1992, artistic dir., 1993-98; artistic dir. Bay Area Playwrights Festival, San Francisco, 1992-95; assoc. artistic dir. A Contemporary Theatre, Seattle, 1998-99; artistic assoc. Intiman Theatre, Seattle, 1999—; tchr. writing for performance Colo. Coll., Colorado Springs, 1995; cons. Rockefeller Found., N.Y.C., 1989-90. E-mail: mame@intiman.org. Office: Intiman Theatre PO Box 19760 Seattle WA 98109-6760

HUNT, MARTHA, sales executive, researcher; b. N.Y.C., May 17, 1924; d. Paul Andrew and Monika (Dobberstein) Pankau; children: Philip Brian Hunt, Susan Monica Hunt. Student, Syracuse U., 1943-47. Asst. controller Commonwealth Fund, N.Y.C., 1947-50; sales tech. Caldwell & Bloor, Mansfield, Ohio, 1958-64; sales promotion mgr. Vita Craft Corp., Shawnee, Kans., 1964-91, cons., 1964—; mem. Meeting Planners Internat., Kans. City, 1982—. Author and editor: cookbooks, 1965-91. Pres. LWV, Akron, Ohio, 1951-53; gov. Soroptimists, 1978-80, bd. dirs., Phila., 1978-80, coord. 1980-84, pres., Kansas City, 1973-74; bd. dirs. Kansas City chpt. Shepherd's Ctr., 1972—; nat. bd. dirs. Shepher's Ctrs. Am., 1990—; bd. dirs. Rose Brooks Ctr., 1979-86, v.p., 1984-85; bd. dirs., founder Safehome, Inc., 1979—, hon. chmn. as founder for Celebration of Safehome 1980-2000, 2000; pres. Metro Citizens Crusade Against Crime, Kansas City., 1983. Recipient Meritorious Svc. award, Kans. City Police Dept., 1975, Disting. Govs. award, Soroptimist Internat. Am., Phila., 1978-79, 79-80, Woman of Distinction award Santa Fe Trail Girl Scouts, 1993, Soroptimist Internat. Am., 1995, Milan Hulbert Humanitarian award Sales Profls. Internat., 1996, Mother of Our Movement award Kans. Coalition Against Sexual and Domestic Violence, 1999. Mem. Kappa Kappa Gamma (pres. 1948-49), Alumnae Assn. (N.Y.C.). Republican. Presbyterian. Avocations: traveling, volunteering.

HUNT, MARY REILLY, organization executive; b. N.Y.C., Apr. 17, 1921; d. Philip R. and Mary C. (Harten) Reilly; m. Robert R. Hunt, Apr. 10, 1943;; children: Marianne Schram, Philip R., Robert R., Elise Paul. Student, CCNY, 1939. Tax investigator Ind. Dept. Revenue, 1970-80; pres. Ind. Right to Life, 1973-77; treas. Nat. Right to Life Com., Washington, 1974, 77, 78, mem. exec. com., 1974, 76-81, vice chmn., 1976, exec. dir., 1978, dir. devel., 1979-94, v.p. devel., 1994-97, hon. bd. mem., 1983—; v.p. devel. Nat. Life Ctr., Woodbury, 1997—; pres. Mary Reilly Hunt & Assoc., Inc., South Bend, Ind., 1985—. Bd. dirs., v.p. YWCA, 1968-73, bd. dirs. Mental Health Assn. St. Joseph Co., 1972-78; candidate for state legis., 1988; mem. St. Joseph County Rep. Women precinct com., South Bend, 1964-79, alt. del. to Nat. Rep. Conv., 1976, 84, 88, 92; mem. South Bend Symphony Women's Assn. Recipient St. Patrick's medal St. Patrick's Coll. and Sem. (Ireland), 1996. Mem. NAFE, Women Bus. Owners, Am. Soc. Sovereign Mil. Order of Malta. Republican. Roman Catholic. Avocations: gardening, antique collecting. Office: Nat Life Ctr 1102 N Lafayette Blvd South Bend IN 46617-1136

HUNT, MAURICE ARTHUR, English educator, researcher; b. Lansing, Mich., Oct. 30, 1942; s. Elmore Clare and Irene Elizabeth H.; m. Pamela Helene Coyle, June 24, 1978; children: Alison, Jeffrey, Andrew, Thomas. BA, U. Mich., 1964; MA, U. Calif., Berkeley, 1966, PhD, 1970. Instr. English Coll. Marin, Kentfield, Calif., 1970-73; lectr. English Dominican Coll., San Rafael, Calif., 1974-75; vis. asst. prof. English Ariz. State U., Tempe, 1980-81; from asst. to assoc. prof. English Baylor U., Waco, Tex., 1981-93, prof. English, 1993—, chair dept. English, 1996—; mem. adv. bd. writing ctr. Tex. A&M U., College Station, Tex., 1985—; dir. Baylor Advanced Placement Inst., Waco, 1994-95, Baylor Freshman Composition Program, Waco, 1982-98; mem. exec. com. S. Ctrl. Renaissance Conf., College Station, 1988-90. Author: Shakespeare's Romance of the Word, 1990, Shakespeare's Labored Art, 1995; editor: Approaches to Teaching "The Tempest" and Other Late Romances, 1992, "The Winter's Tale": Critical Essays, 1995, Approaches to Teaching Shakespeare's "Romeo and Juliet", 2000; assoc. editor Papers on Lang. and Lit., 1996—, The Upstart Crow: A Shakespeare Jour., 1990—; mem. editl. bd. Shakespeare and the Classroom, 1993—; contbr. articles to profl. jours. Fundraiser United Way Bay Area, San Francisco, 1976-80; bd. dirs. Alameda County Tng. and Employment Bd., Oakland, Calif., 1977-78. Rsch. grantee Baylor U., 1986—. Mem. MLA, Fulbright Grants (mem. so. region, mem. nat. screening com.), Shakespeare Assn. Am., Greater Lansing Area Sports Hall of Fame, S. Ctrl. Renaissance Conf. (mem. exec. com. 1984—), Phi Beta Kappa. Democrat. Episcopalian. Avocations: jogging, sports. E-mail: Maurice Hunt@Baylor.edu. Home: 321 Oakwood Ln Hewitt TX 76643-3027 Office: Baylor U 500 Speight Ave Waco TX 76706-1458

HUNT, OLIVER RAYMOND, JR., thoracic and cardiovascular surgeon; b. Darlington, S.C., Apr. 23, 1923; s. Oliver Raymond Sr. and Annie Reid (Muldrow) H.; m. Eleanor Margaret Morgan, Dec. 16, 1944; children: David Morgan, Margaret Muldrow, Rebecca Elaine, Sarah Fredricka. AB, Berea Coll., 1947; MD, U. Louisville, 1951. Diplomate Am. Bd. Surgery, Am. Bd. Thoracic and Cardiac Surgery. Asst. in anatomy U. Louisville, 1950; intern Edward W. Sparrow Hosp., Lansing, Mich., 1951-52; fellow in surgery Mayo Found., Rochester, Minn., 1954-58, fellow in thoracic surgery, 1958-60; staff surgeon VA Hosp., Oteen, N.C., 1960-61; clin. assoc. SUNY, Buffalo, 1963-64, asst. prof. surgery, 1964-69, asst. dean, assoc. dean clin. affairs, 1965-67, 67-69; clin. asst., assoc. prof. surgery U. N.C., Chapel Hill, 1969-91; pvt. practice surgery Wilmington, N.C., 1969-91; CEO Regal Tomaoes Internat. Ltd., Nev., 1991—; v.p., bd. dirs. Jugoso Y Pulpas de San Gerado S.A., Costa Rica, 1989—; pres., CEO Mellinnium Environtl. Technologies Inc., 1995-98; v.p. med. staff Cape Fear Hosp., Wilmington, 1978, 79, pres., 1980-81, chief of staff, 1972, exec. com., 1978-82; cons. med. edn. Nat. U., Asuncion, Paraguay, 1965-67. Contbr. numerous articles to profl. jours.; inventor in field. Bd. dirs. New Hanover Bank, Wilmington, 1972-75, Planters Nat. Bank, Wilmington, 1976-87, Wilmington Devel. Corp., 1981-87, Wilmington Concert Assn., 1970-94; civil svc. commn. City of Wilmington, 1972-81. Lt. USNR, 1943-46. Named Rsch. scholar Dept. Chemistry U. Louisville, 1948-51; recipient Mosby prize for Scholarship, U. Louisville, 1948; named Hon. Prof., Nat. U. Asuncion, 1967. Mem. AMA, Am. Chem. Soc., N.C. Med. Soc., New Hanover Med. Soc., Soc. Thoracic Surgery, N.Y. Acad. Sci., N.C. Lung Soc., Alpha Omega Alpha, Phi Kappa Phi. Avocations: sailing, golf, scuba diving, fishing, painting, jewelry making.

HUNT, PETER ROGER, film director, writer, editor; b. London, Mar. 11, 1925; came to U.S., 1975; s. Arthur George and Elizabeth H.; widowed; 1 child, Nicholas Constantine. Student, London Sch. Music. Actor English Repertory Theater, London. Camera asst., asst. editor various documentaries; asst. editor various feature films. London Film Co.; scriptor various films Hill in Korea, Admirable Crichton, Next to No Time, Paradise Lagoon, Cry From the Streets, Greengage Summer (Am. title: Loss of Innocence), Ferry to Hong Kong, H.M.S. Defiant (Am. title: Damn the Defiant), Sink the Bismarck, Operation Snaffu; supervising editor, 2d unit dir.: Dr. No, Call Me Bwana, From Russia with Love, Goldfinger, Ibcress File, Thunderball, You Only Live Twice, Jigsaw Man, Desperate Hours; assoc. producer: Chitty Chitty Bang Bang; dir.: On Her Majesty's Secret Service, Gullivers Travels (film and animated), Gold, Shout at the Devil, Death Hunt, Wild Geese II, Assassination, Hyper Sapien, Marlowe, Shirley's World, Persuaders, (NBC-TV movie) Beasts in the Streets, (ABC-TV mini-series) Last Days of Pompeii, (CBS-TV spl.) Eyes of a Witness. Mem. Assn. Cinematic Technicians Great Britain, Broadcasting Entertainment Cinematograph Theatre Union, Dirs. Guild of Am., Motion Picture Acad. Arts, Acad. TV, Broadcasting, Entertainment, Cinematograph, Theatre Union. Office: Peter Hunt Films Inc PMB # 145 2337 Roscomare Rd # 2 Los Angeles CA 90077-1851

HUNT, ROBERT GARY, medical consultant, oral and maxillofacial surgeon; b. San Diego, July 10, 1945; s. Harvey E. and Pauline A. (Nazarovic) H.; m. Diane G. Hunt, Apr. 26, 1975; 1 child, Christine G. AA, Mesa Coll., San Diego, 1971; BS in Medicine, U. nebr., 1979, MD, 1979; DDS, U. So. Calif., 1976. Diplomate Am. Bd. Oral and Maxillofacial Surgery, Nat. Bd. Med. Examiners; lic. physician, Calif., Nebr.; lic. dentist, Calif., Nebr. Oral and maxillofacial surgeon in pvt. practice San Diego, 1981—. With USAF, 1965-70. Fellow Am. Assn. Oral and Maxillofacial Surgeons, Am. Coll. Oral and Maxillofacial Surgeons, Internat. Coll. Surgeons, Internat. Soc. Plastic, Aesthetic and Reconstructive Surgery, Am. Coll. Oral Implantology; mem. AMA, ADA, So. Calif. Acad. Oral Pathology, Mensa, Omicron Kappa Upsilon, Phi Kappa Phi, Alpha Tau Epsilon, Delta Sigma Delta, others. Home: 2240 Sunset Blvd San Diego CA 92103-1120

HUNT, ROBERT WILLIAM, theatrical producer, arts management consultant; b. Seattle, June 8, 1947; s. William Roland and Margaret Anderson (Crowe) H.; m. Marcie Loomis, Aug. 24, 1968 (div. Dec. 1975); 1 child, Megan; m. Susan Moyer, June 17, 1989 (div. Oct. 1997); children: Donovan, Jillian. BA, U. Wash., 1969. CPA, Wash. Data processing cons. Arthur Andersen & Co., Seattle, 1968-78; owner, cons. Robert W. Hunt & Assocs., Seattle, 1978—; exec. prodr. Village Theatre, Issaquah, Wash., 1979—; developer Francis J. Gaudette Theatre, Issaquah, Wash., 1994; cons. San Francisco Mus. Modern Art, 1981-90, Mus. of Flight, Seattle, 1983-90, Met. Mus. N.Y.C., 1984-85; contracted for acquired mgmt. Everett (Wash.) Performing Arts Ctr., 1998—. Creator arts computer software; prodr. (mus.) Eleanor, 1987, Heidi, 1989, Charlie and the Chocolate Factory, 1989, Book of James, 1990, Funny Pages, 1991, Jungle Queen Debutante, 1991, Glimmerglass, 1995, City Kid, 1995, Bootlegger, 1996, 4:00 AM Boogie Blues, 1998, Crossing Over, 1999, Making Tracks, 2000, Play It By Heart, 2000; creator, writer (pop group music and video) The Shrimps, 1984. Chmn. com. Seattle Arts Commn., 1975-78; treas. Arts Resource Svcs., Seattle, 1976-78; gen. mgr. Musicomedy Northwest, Seattle, 1977-79; bd. dirs. Theatre Puget Sound; treas., bd. dirs. Bellevue Fed. Little League, 1999—. Grantee Seattle Arts Commn., 1978-79, Wash. State Arts Commn., 1980—, King County Arts Commn., 1980—, Nat. Endowment for the Arts, 1992—. Mem. Wash. Soc. CPAs., Nat. Alliance for Musical Theatre (treas., bd. dirs.), Seattle Rotary. Office: Village Theatre 303 Front St N Issaquah WA 98027-2917

HUNT, ROBERT WILLIAM GAINER, colour consultant, educator; b. Sidcup, Kent, England, July 28, 1923; s. Frederick Richard William and Margorie St. Clare (Gainer) H.; m. Eileen Mary Redhead, July 26, 1947; children: Pamela, David, Philip, Margaret. BSc, Imperial Coll., Eng., 1943; PhD, London U., 1954, DSc, 1968. Experimental officer Ministry of Supply, Salisbury, Eng., 1943-46; asst. dir. rsch. Kodak Ltd., Harrow, Eng., 1946-82; colour cons. Salisbury, Eng., 1982—; vis. prof. color sci. U. Derby, Eng., 1993—. Author: The Reproduction of Colour, 5th edit., 1995, Measuring Colour, 3d edit., 1998. Recipient Judd-AIC medal Internat. Colour Assn., 1987, Gold Medal Inst. Printing, 1989. Fellow Royal Photographic Soc. (Progress medal 1984), Royal TV Soc., Royal Soc. Arts; hon. mem. Soc. Imaging Sci. and Tech. Mem. Evangelical Ch. Avocations: photography, travel, hill walking, christian preaching. Home and Office: Barrowpoint 18 Millennium, Close, Odstock Rd, Salisbury SP2 8TB, England

HUNT, RONALD FORREST, lawyer; b. Shelby, N.C., Apr. 18, 1943; s. Forrest Elmer and Bruna Magnolia (Brackett) H.; m. Judy Elaine Shultz, May 19, 1965; 1 child, Mary. A.B., U. N.C., 1966, J.D., 1968. Bar: N.C. 1968, D.C. 1973. Mem. staff SEC, Washington, 1968-69, legal asst. to chmn., 1970-71, sec. of commn., 1972-73; dep. gen. counsel, sec. Student Loan Mktg. Assn., Washington, 1973-78, sr. v.p., gen. counsel, sec., 1979-83, exec. v.p., gen. counsel, 1983-90; pvt. practice New Bern, N.C., 1991—; vice chmn. First Capital Corp., Southern Pines, N.C., 1984-90; bd. dirs. Student Loan Mktg. Assn., Washington, SLM Holding Corp., Reston, Va., e-Numerate Solutions, Inc., McLean, Va.; chmn. bd. dirs. Nat. Student Loan Clearinghouse, Reston, 1993-95, 97—. Mem. Montgomery County Commn. Landlord and Tenant Affairs, Md., 1976-81, chmn., 1979-81; bd. dirs. D.C. chpt. ARC, 1976-83; trustee Arena Stage, Washington, 1984-89, Washington Theatre Awards Soc., 1988-90. Republican. Presbyterian. Avocations: sailing; gardening.

HUNT, SWANEE G., public policy educator, former ambassador; b. Dallas, May 1, 1950; m. Charles Alexander Ansbacher; 3 children. BA, Tex. Christian U., 1972; MA, Ball State U., 1976; MA in Religion, Iliff Sch. of Theology, 1977, PhD, 1986; PhD (hon.), Webster U., 1994. Founder, chmn. Hunt Alternatives Fund, 1981—; co-founder, co-dir. Karis Community, 1980-83; min. pastoral care Capital Heights Presbyn. Ch., 1983; commr., vice chair Denver Community Mental Health Commn., 1983-87; with Gov. Policy Acad. on Families and Children at Risk, 1989-90; chair Colo. Coord. Coun. Housing and the Homeless, 1989-92; U.S. amb. to Austria, 1993-97; dir. women and pub. policy program Kennedy Sch. Govt.; commr. Rufugees United Nations High. Composer The Witness Cantata, 1985. Bd. dirs. Ctr. Reproductive Law and Policy, Charter Fund, Am. Mental Health Fund Nat. Adv. Bd., Colo. Children's Campaign, Denver Civic Ventures, Inc., The Missing Half, Pub. Edn. Coalition, U. Colo. Ctr. Health Ethics and Policy Rev. Bd., 1987-89, Women and Founds./Corp. Philanthropy; co-founder, trustee Women's Found. Colo.; trustee U. Denver; chair Mayor's Human Capital Agenda Coun., 1992-93; co-chair Denver Initiative Children and Families. Recipient Martin Luther King Humanitarian award U. Colo., 1992, NCCJ, 1992, Denver Urban Ministries, 1991, United Meth. Ch., 1989, Internat. Women's Forum, 1989, Sta. KUSA-TV, 1989, Caring Connection, 1989, Nat. Mental Health Assn., 1985, Mental Health Assn. Colo., 1984, 94, Mile High award United Way, 1993, Am. Heritage award Anti-Defamation League, 1995, Cordon Bleu du Saint Esprit Peace award, 1996, Humanitarian Lifetime Svc. award Denver Holocaust Awareness, 1997, Together for Peace award, 1997, 3 decorations Austrian Govt., 1997, Amb. award The Conflict Ctr., 1997, Inst. for Internat. Edn. award, 1998. Office: 168 Brattle St Cambridge MA 02138-3309 also: Kennedy Sch Govt 79 Jfk St Rm T110A Cambridge MA 02138-5801*

HUNT, T(HOMAS) W(EBB), retired religion educator; b. Mammoth Spring, Ark., Sept. 28, 1929; s. Thomas Hubert and Ethel Clara (Webb) H.; m. M. Laverne Hill, July 22, 1951; children: Melana Claire Hunt Monroe. MusB, Ouachita Bapt. U., 1950; MusM, N. Tex. State U., 1957, PhD, 1967. Faculty Southwestern Bapt. Theol. Sem., Ft. Worth, 1963-87; life cons. for prayer Bapt. Sunday Sch. Bd., Nashville, 1987-94, ret., 1994; lectr. in field; confs. on the five continents. Author: The Doctrine of Prayer, 1986, Music in Missions, 1986, The Disciple's Prayer Life, 1988, Church Ministry Prayer Manual, 1994, The Mind of Christ, 1995, In God's Presence, 1995; contbr. The Disciple's Study Bible, 1987. Home: 3915 Cypress Hill Dr Spring TX 77388-5798

HUNT, VALERIE VIRGINIA, electrophysiologist, educator; b. Larwill, Ind., July 22, 1916; d. Homer Henry Hunt and Iva Velzora Ames. BS in Biology, Fla. State Coll., 1936; MA in Physiol. Psychology, Columbia U., 1941, EdD in Sci. Edn., 1946; DD, Phoenix Inst., San Diego, 1984. Sci. tchr. Anniston (Ala.) H.S., 1936-38; asst. anatomy nursing dept. Columbia U., N.Y.C., 1939-40; chmn. health edn. Boston YWCA, 1942-43; instr. Columbia U. Tchrs. Coll. and Coll. Physicians and Surgeons, N.Y.C., 1943-46; asst. prof. U. Iowa, Iowa City, 1946-47; assoc. prof., dir. divsn. phys. therapy UCLA, 1947-64, prof. physiology, dir. electromyographic lab., 1964-80, prof. emeritus, 1980—; dir. BioEnergy Fields Lab. BioEnergy Fields Found., Malibu, Calif., 1980—; CEO Malibu Pub. Co., 1995—; cons. Nat. Bd. YWCA, 1943-46, Nat. Early Childhood Edn., 1948-50, UCLA Sch. Engring. Prosthetics Inst., 1949-51, Calif. Dept. Edn., 1950-60, Chrysler Motor Co. Space Divsn. Rsch., 1952, NASA Space Biology, 1958; field reader U.S. Dept. HEW, 1958-65; reviewer sci. textbooks McMillan Pub., Prentice-Hall, McGraw-Hill, W.B. Saunders & Co., 1959-67; cons. Fetzer Found. Energy Field Rsch., 1989, Heart Math Found., 1992. Author: Recreation for the Handicapped, 1955, Corrective Physical Education, 1967, Movement Education for Preschool, 1972, Guidelines for Movement Behavior: Curricula for Early Childhood Education, 1974, Infinite Mind: Science of the Human Vibrations of Consciousness, 1993, Mind Mastery Meditations, 1997, Naibhu, 1998; contbr. articles to profl. jours. Pres. United Cerebral Palsy, L.A., 1947-51; mem. adv. com. Harlan Shoemaker Clinic for Neurol. Disabilities, 1948-53; bd. dirs. Found. for Jr. Blind, 1949-52, Crippled Children Soc., 1953-58, YWCA, L.A., 1955-65; adv. com.,

Internat. Congress for Exceptional Children, 1964-72, Rory Found., L.A., 1998—; vestry bd. mem. St. Matthew Episcopal Ch., L.A., 1965-69. Rsch. grantee USPHS, 1957-61, Adelphi Found., 1960-63, Rolf Found., 1965-71; recipient Heritage award Calif. Dance Educator Assn., 1987, N.B. Rudman award Found. Exceptional Leadership, 1995; Dame Order of St. John of the Ams., 1996. Mem. NSF, N.Y. Acad. Scis., Pi Lambda Theta, Kappa Delta Pi. Avocations: travel, gardening, music, art, lecturing. E-mail: vhunt@bioenergyfields.org. Office: BioEnergy Fields Found PO Box 6653 Malibu CA 90264-6653

HUNTELAAR, MARK EDUARD, chemist, researcher; b. Alkmaar, The Netherlands, Aug. 11, 1964; s. Eduard Gerard Huntelaar and Clasina Catharina Bahnerth. M in chemistry, U. Amsterdam, 1990, PhD in thermodynamics, 1996. Chem. technician Netherlands Energy Rsch. Found. (name now Nuclear Rsch. & Consultancy Group), Petten, 1988-90, scientist, 1990—. Contbr. rsch. results to profl. jours. Mem. Royal Dutch Chemistry Soc. Avocations: biking, gardening, playing piano. Home e-mail: huntelaar@multiweb.nl. Office e-mail: huntelaar@nrg-nl.com. Home: W beckmanstraat 37, Alkmaar 1814 KR, The Netherlands Office: Nuclear Rsch & Consultancy Group, Westerduinweg 3, Petten 1755 LE, The Netherlands

HUNTER, DAVID JAMES, health policy and management educator, researcher, analyst; b. Irvine, Ayrshire, Scotland, Apr. 17, 1950; s. Thomas Drummond and Peggie Eileen (Scotcher) H.; m. Mairi Christine Hunter (div.); m. Jacqueline Floyd, Mar. 31, 1994; children: Eve Floyd, Miles Cameron. MA with honors, U. Edinburgh, Scotland, 1974, PhD, 1979. Hon. mem. faculty of pub. health medicine. Rsch. officer Outer Circle Policy Unit, London, 1977-80; health studies officer Royal Inst. Pub. Adminstrn., London, 1980-82; dir. Unit for Study of Elderly U. Aberdeen, Scotland, 1982-87; policy analyst King's Fund Inst., London, 1987-88; dir. Nuffield Inst. for Health, U. Leeds, Eng., 1989-97, prof. health policy and mgmt., 1989-99; prof. health policy and mgmt. U. Durham Bus. Sch., Eng., 1999—; trustee Dementia Svcs. Devel. Ctr., Stirling, Scotland, 1988-94; adviser WHO, Copenhagen, 1989—; non-exec. dir. Leeds (Eng.) Healthcare, 1990-96, 96-99; adviser House of Commons Social Svcs. Com., London, 1990-91; co-chair Assn. Pub. Health, 1998-2000; advisor health com. Ho. of Commons, 2000—. Contbr. articles to profl. jours.; editor Jour. Mgmt. in Medicine, 1997-99. Fellow Royal Coll. Physicians Edinburgh; mem. Faculty of Pub. Health Medicine (hon.), European Health Mgmt. Assn. (bd. dirs. 1990-95, 97-98, pres. 1995-97), U.K. Pub. Health Assn. (coun. mem. 1999—). Avocations: jazz music, swimming, reading, walking, cinema. Office: Durham U Bus Sch, 1 Mill Hill Ln, Durham DH1 3LB, England

HUNTER, DONALD FORREST, lawyer; b. Mpls., Jan. 30, 1934; s. Earl Harvey and Ruby Cecilia (Lagerson) H.; m. Marlys Ann Zilge; Jeffrey, Cheri, Kathryn. BA, U. Minn., 1961, JD, 1963. Bar: Minn. 1963, U.S. Dist. Ct. Minn. 1965, U.S. Ct. Appeals (8th cir.) 1965, Ill. 1977, U.S. Dist. Ct. (no. dist.) Ill. 1991, U.S. Supreme Ct. 1986. Assoc., then ptnr. Gislason, Dosland, Hunter & Malecki, New Ulm, Minn., 1963-76; exec. v.p., sec., gen. counsel Wirtz Prodn. Ltd. Ice Follies/Holiday on Ice, Chgo., 1976-79; ptnr. Gislason, Dosland, Hunter & Malecki, Mpls., 1979-99; of counsel Gislason & Hunter, 1999—; chmn. bd. dirs. Chgo. Milw. Corp., 1977-81; pres. Chgo. Milw. R.R., 1977-81; bd. dirs. First Security Bank, Chgo.; bd. dirs., officer First Security Bancorp, Inc., Chgo., 1993—; bd. dirs., sec. Wirtz Corp., Chgo. Blackhawk Hockey Team and related cos. Fellow Am. Coll. Trial Lawyers; mem. ABA, Am. Judicature Soc., Minn. Bar Assn. (bd. of govs. 1973-76), 5th Dist. Bar Assn. (pres. 1971-72), Hennepin County Bar Assn., Minn. Def. Lawyers Assn. (bd. dirs. 1976), Internat. Assn. Ins. Counsel, U.S. Supreme Ct. Hist. Assn. Office: Gislason & Hunter PO Box 5297 9900 Bren Rd E Ste 215E Hopkins MN 55343-9666

HUNTER, DOUGLAS LEE, media executive, former elevator company executive; b. Greeley, Colo., May 3, 1948; s. Delmer Eural and Helen Converse (Haines) H.; m. Janet Lee Snook, May 26, 1970; children: Darin Douglas, Joel Christopher, Eric Andrew, Jennifer Lee. BA, U. Sioux Falls, Enid, Okla., 1979; postgrad., N.Am. Bapt. Sem., Sioux Falls, S.D., 1977-79. Elevator constructor Carter Elevator Co., Inc., Sioux Falls, 1971-72, rep., 1972-74, contr., 1974-78, sec.-treas., 1978-82, v.p., 1982-87, pres., 1987-93; ptnr. Lifters Ltd., Sioux Falls, 1984-90, CEO, 1987-96; v.p. Fellowship or Cos. Christ, Internat., 1994-97; pres. Media Asia, 1997-99; Atlanta regional dir. Christians Leadership Concepts, 1999-2000; bd. dirs. Home Fed. Savs. Bank, HF Fin. Corp.; U.S. del. Forum Bus. in Vietnam, Ho Chi Minh City, 1993; guest lectr. Nat. Econs. U., Hanoi, Vietnam, 1995. Mem. gen. bd. Christian Ch., Indpls., 1984-88; mem. regional bd. Christian Ch. in the Upper Midwest, Des Moines, 1985-87; bd. dirs. Glory House, Sioux Falls, 1983-86; leader Bible Study Fellowship, Sioux Falls, 1981-92; vice chmn. Greater Sioux Empire Billy Graham Crusade, 1986-87; mem. internat. bd. dirs. Fellowship of Cos. for Christ Internat., 1993-95, v.p., 1994-97; pres. Media Asia, Inc., Atlanta, 1997-99; bd. dirs. Am. Mongolia Found., 1992-99; active S.D. Trade Del. to Mongolia, 1993-99; trustee N.Am. Bapt. Sem., 1989—; bd. dirs. Providence Christian Acad., 1998—, chmn., 1999—. Named Outstanding Young Religious Leader Sioux Falls Jaycees, 1974. Mem. S.D. Family Bus. Coun., Sen. Larry Pressler's Small Bus. Adv. Com., Nat. Assn. Elevator Contrs., Nat. Assn. Elevator Safety Authorities, Constrn. Specifications Inst., Christian Businessmen's Com. U.S., Sioux Falls C. of C. Republican. Avocations: golf, tennis, reading, music. Home: 695 Wyndham Place Cir Lawrenceville GA 30044-3629 Office: Christian Leadership Concepts Atlanta GA 30044

HUNTER, HOLLY, actress; b. Conyers, Ga., Mar. 20, 1958; d. Charles Edwin and Opal Marguerite (Catledge) H; m. Janusz Kaminski, May 20, 1995. BFA, Carnegie-Mellon U., 1980. Appeared in feature films Broadcast News, 1987 (Best Actress award N.Y. Film Critics Circle 1988, Best Actress award Berlin Film Festival 1988, Nat. Bd. Review award, Acad. award nominee best actress), Raising Arizona, 1987, Always, 1990, Miss Firecracker, 1989, Once Around, 1991, The Piano, 1993 (Best Actress award, Cannes Film Festival, 1993, Best Actress - Drama, Golden Globe, 1994, Acad. Award, Best Actress, 1993), The Firm, 1993 (Acad. award nominee, Best Supporting Actress, 1993), Home for the Holidays, 1995, Copycat, 1995, Crash, 1996, Hurly-burly, 1997, A Life Less Ordinary, 1997, Living Out Loud, 1998, Woman Wanted, 1999; TV prodns. Roe vs. Wade (Best Actress Emmy award 1989); Broadway stage prodns. Crimes of the Heart, The Wake of Jamey Foster; regional stage prodns. Buried Child, A Doll's House, Artichoke; other stage prodns. include A Lie of the Mind, L.A., Battery, N.Y.C., Miss Firecracker Contest, The Person I Once Was, N.Y.C.; cable TV prodns. Crazy in Love, 1992 (Ace award nominee), The Positively True Adventures of the Alleged Texas Cheerleader Murdering Mom, 1993 (Best Actress award Am. TV Awards, Emmy award - Outstanding Lead Actress in a Miniseries or Special, Cable Ace award, Best Actress in a Movie or Miniseries). Bd. dirs. Calif. Abortion Rights Action League.

HUNTER, JAMES GALBRAITH, JR., lawyer; b. Phila., Jan. 6, 1942; s. James Galbraith and Emma Margaret (Jehl) H.; m. Pamela Ann Trott, July 18, 1969 (div.); children: James Nicholas, Catherine Selene; m. Nancy Grace Scheurwater, June 21, 1992. B.S. in Engring. Sci., Case Inst. Tech., 1965; J.D., U. Chgo., 1967. Bar: Ill. 1967, U.S. Dist. Ct. (no. dist.) Ill. 1967, U.S. Ct. Appeals (7th cir.) 1967, U.S. Ct. Claims, 1976, U.S. Ct. Appeals (4th and 9th cirs.) 1978, U.S. Supreme Ct. 1979, U.S. Dist. Ct. (cen. dist.) Ill. 1980, Calif. 1980, U.S. Dist. Ct. (cen. and so. dists.) Calif. 1980, U.S. Ct. Appeals (5th cir.) 1982, U.S. Ct. Appeals (fed. cir.) 1982. Assoc. Kirkland & Ellis, Chgo., 1967-68, 70-73, ptnr., 1973-76; ptnr. Hedlund, Hunter & Lynch, Chgo., 1976-82, Los Angeles, 1979-82; ptnr. Latham & Watkins, Hedlund, Hunter & Lynch, Chgo. and Los Angeles, 1982—. Served to lt. JAGC, USN, 1968-70. Mem. ABA, State Bar Calif., Los Angeles County Bar Assn., Chgo. Bar Assn. Clubs: Metropolitan (Chgo.), Chgo. Athletic Assn., Los Angeles Athletic. Exec. editor U. Chgo. Law Rev., 1966-67. Office: Latham & Watkins Sears Tower Ste 5800 Chicago IL 60606-6306 also: 633 W 5th St Los Angeles CA 90071-2005

HUNTER, JOHN GRAHAM, investment management company executive; b. Edinburgh, Mar. 28, 1943; s. David and Catherine Valentina (Quillete) H.; m. Eileen Shannon, Nov. 1, 1969 (div. Mar. 1991); children: John, Sharryn. Assoc., Chartered Inst. of Mktg. Trainee Britannic Assurance, 1963-66, mgr., 1966-80; mktg. dir. Tyndall Holdings Plc, 1981-88, Refuge Overseas, Guernsey, 1988-92; chmn., CEO Apollo Investment Ltd., Guernsey, 1993—. Chmn. Action Rsch. for Multiple Sclerosis, Guernsey, 1986. Mem. United Club, Guernsey Sporting Club, Royal Channel Island Yacht Club. Avocations: literature, travel, golf. Home: Oakstone House, Rue de la Lande, Vale Guernsey GY3 5BQ, Channel Islands

HUNTER, JOHN HILTON, telecommunications company executive; b. Sydney, Australia, Nov. 6, 1948; s. Lewis Hilton and Marie (Andrew) H.; m. Constance Joanne Thew, Nov. 8, 1976; children: Edwina Robert, Joanne. BE, Univ. New South Wales, Syndey, 1970, MESc, 1972. Cadet engr. PMG Dept., Sydney, 1968-70; design engr. Telecom Australia, Sydney, 1970-74, construction & ops. engr., 1975-86, planning mgr., 1985-91; olympic bid mgr. Telstra, Sydney, 1991-93, gen. mgr. Sydney 2000 Olympics, 1993—; dir. Australiasian Teleconferencing Assn., 1994-95; chmn. Tech. Com. ATA, 1994-95; speaker in field. Contbr. articles to profl. jours. Recipient Trophy of Gratitude Barcelona Olympic Found., 1995. Fellow Inst. Radio Elec. Engring., Inst. Engrs. Australia; mem. Inst. of Elec. Engr. (sr.), Telecomm. Soc. Avocations: photography, bushwalking, family. Office: Telstra, 31/320 Pitt St, Sydney 2000, Australia

HUNTER, JOHN STEVENSON, sports sciences educator; b. Londonderry, Northern Ireland, July 25, 1940; s. John and Matilda (Stevenson) H.; m. Lesley Eileen Nuttall, July 20, 1984; children: Ximena, Angharad. Cert. in phys. edn., Stranmillis Coll., Belfast, No. Ireland, 1963; degree in phys. edn., Leeds (Eng.) U., 1973, MA, 1974. Phys. edn. tchr. Royal Sch., Armagh, 1963-64, head phys. edn., 1964-72; phys. edn. lectr. Borough Rd. Coll., West London, 1974-76; phys. edn. lectr. West London Inst., 1976-83, dean, head sch., 1983-95; dir. studies Brunel U., West London, 1995—; pres. 4th European Forum Sports Scis., London, 1995-97; sec. gen. U.K. Sports Recreation and Leisure, 1999—; adminstr. London Ctr. Sporting Excellence, 1986-93; chair Nat. Coaching Ctr., London, 1988-90. Contbr. articles to profl. publs. Trustee London Borough Houslow, West London,1 997—; mem. internat. adv. coun. Mason City (Iowa) Found., 1999—; mem. internat. faculty U.S. Sports Acad., Daphne, Ala., 1991-95; first team coach London Irish Rugby, 1975-78, Saracens Rugby, 1979-80, Richmond Rugby, 1981-83. Fellow U.K. Phys. Edn. Assn., 1997. Avocations: rugby, travel, music. Home: 30 Partridge Rd, Hampton Middlesex TW12 3SB, England Office: Brunel U, Borough Rd Isleworth, Middlesex TW7 5DU, England

HUNTER, JOHN THOMAS, biogeographer; b. Sydney, Australia, Dec. 21, 1967; s. John Anthony and Karmanina (Schwaski) H.; m. Vanessa Hewlett Pawlow, June 7, 1991; children: Briannon Phoebe, Calliden John. BSc, U. New Eng., 1992, PhD, 1999. Lectr. New Eng. Inst. Tech. & Further Edn., Armidale, Australia, 1991-97; mgr., prin. ecologist J. Hunter Pty Ltd., Armidale, 1997—; rsch. assoc. dept. natural resources U. New Eng., 2000—; Inverell-Yallaroi Native Vegetation Com., Inverell, Australia, 1999, Gwydir Unregulated River Catchment Com., Australia, 1999. Citizens Wildlife Corridors com., Armidale, 1997—. Mem. Royal Soc. Queensland, Am. Soc. Naturalists, Coast and Wetlands Soc., Field Naturalists Club Victoria. Avocations: antiquarian books, plant systematics. Home: 75 Kendall Rd, Invergowrie, Armidale NSW, Australia 2350

HUNTER, KERMIT, writer, former university dean; b. Hallsville, W.Va., Oct. 3, 1910; s. Otis John and Lillian Elizabeth Robinson (Farley) H. B.A., Ohio State U., 1931; M.A. in Theatre, U. N.C., 1949, Ph.D. in English Lit, 1956; D.Litt., Emory and Henry Coll., 1958; L.H.D., Okla. Christian Coll., 1971. Successively newspaper reporter C. of C. sec.; choir dir., organist, and piano study Juilliard Inst., 1931-40; bus. mgr. N.C. Symphony Orch., 1946; prof. drama Hollins Coll., Va., 1956-64; first dean Meadows Sch. Arts, So. Methodist U., Dallas, 1964-76; writer in residence So. Methodist U., 1976-78; sr. lectr. U. Tex., Arlington, 1978-93. Author, producer more than 40 hist. dramas, especially Unto These Hills, 1950, with total audience over 14 million. Served to lt. col. AUS, 1940-45. Decorated Legion of Merit. Home: 10412 Stone Canyon Rd #101N Dallas TX 75230-4834

HUNTER, LARRY LEE, electrical engineer; b. Versailles, Mo., Mar. 5, 1938; s. Donnan Kleber and Molly Opal (Roe) H.; m. Marcella Ann Avey, Feb. 1, 1959; children: Cynthia Lynn Hunter Hulen, Stuart Roe. BSEE, U. Mo., 1963; MBA, Fla. Inst. Tech., 1984. System test engr. McDonnell Aircraft Corp., St. Louis, 1963-65; design engr. Magnavox Co., Urbana, Ill., 1965-66, R&D engr., 1966-67; project engr. LTV Electrosystems, Garland, Tex., 1967-68, systems engr., 1968-70; program mgr. Dorsett Electronics, Tulsa, 1970-73; program mgr. Harris Corp., Melbourne, Fla., 1973-75, bus. area mgr., 1975-85; v.p. mktg., engring., program mgmt. Teledyne Lewisburg, Tenn., 1985-88; pres. L.H. Assocs., Columbia, Tenn., 1988-90; gen. mgr. Precision Cable div. AMP Inc., Greensboro, N.C., 1990-96, dir. global cable sys. bus. group, 1996-97; pres. L. Hunter Assocs., Inc., Tampa, Fla., 1997—. Inventor thermometer; contbr. articles to profl. jours. Mem. IEEE, Eta Kappa Nu. Republican. Methodist. Avocations: hunting, fishing, golf. Home: 16309 E Course Dr Tampa FL 33624-1127

HUNTER, LELAND CLAIR, JR., management consultant; b. Phila., Feb. 22, 1925; s. Leland Clair and Lillian Mae (Failor) H.; m. Elva Joy Charlton, July 5, 1946; children: Charlton Lee, Steven Kent, Brian Scott, Donna Joy. B.S., Villanova U., 1948; postgrad., Columbia U., 1944-45; M.B.A., Fla. Research Inst., 1971; grad., Advanced Mgmt. Program, Harvard U., 1973. Test engr. Gen. Electric Co., Phila., 1949-50; with Fla. Power & Light Co., 1950-88; v.p. indsl. relations Fla. Power & Light Co., Miami, 1966-72; v.p. transmission and distbn. Fla. Power & Light Co., 1972-73, group v.p., 1973-78, sr. v.p., 1978-88; pres. Leland Hunter Mgmt. Cons., Miami, 1988—; chmn. Hunter, Voehl and Lewis, 1995—; conf. co-chair Nat. Youth Crime Prevention Conf.; editor Charlton Pub. Co., 1998; mem. spl. labor com. Sec. of Labor U.S., 1975-76; mem. Labor and Mgmt. Polit. Action Com. for Utility Industry, 1977, Gov.'s Adv. Coun. Productivity, 1981—; pres. Leland Hunter Mgmt. Cons. Vice chmn. adv. com. Dade County (Fla.) Sch. Bd., 1966; bd. govs. Gold Coast AAU, 1967-68; bd. dirs. Crime Commn. of Greater Miami, 1974—; chmn. bd. Victoria Hosp., 1984-88; dir. Pro-Fish of Fla.; Fla. Lawyers Prepaid Legal Services Inc. Crime Commn. of Greater Miami, 1980—; bd. advisors Stetson U.; mem. bus. adv. com. Brookings Instn., Washington; exec. v.p. Atlantic Gamefish Found.; mem. Blue Ribbon Com. to Save Miami's Fin. Future, 1996; mem. County Mgrs. Com. to Stop Corruption in Dade County Politics. Served with USN, 1943-46. Recipient Key to City Toledo and Coral Gables Fla.). Mem. Am. Soc. Tng. Dirs. (pres. local chpt. 1955-56), Fla. Athletic Club (pres. 1962), Coral Gables Country Club, Univ. Miami Club. Home and Office: 7881 SW 180th St Miami FL 33157-6216

HUNTER, MOLLIE (MRS. MAUREEN M.H. MCILWRAITH), writer; b. Longniddry, East Lothian, Scotland, June 30, 1922; d. William George and Helen Eliza Smeaton (Waitt) McVeigh; m. Thomas McIlwraith, Dec. 23, 1940; children: Quentin Wright, Brian George. Ed., East Lothian, Scotland. Writer, 1953—; May Hill Arbuthnot lectr. U.S., 1975; lectr. Brit. Coun., Internat. Reading Assn. and edn. authorities for New Zealand and Australia, 1976; writer-in-residence Dalhousie U., Halifax, N.S., 1980, 81; organizer, tchr. writer's workshops; 29th Anne Carroll Moore Spring lectr., 1986; tchr. creative writing Aberlour Summer Sch. Gifted Children, 1987-88. Author: (plays) A Love-Song for My Lady, 1961, Stay for an Answer, 1962; (prose) Patrick Kentigern Keenan, 1963, Hi Johnny, 1964, The Spanish Letters, 1964, The Kelpie's Pearls, 1964, A Pistol in Greenyards, 1965, The Ghosts of Glencoe, 1966, Thomas and the Warlock, 1967 (Scottish Arts Coun. award), The Ferlie, 1968 (Child Study Assn. Am.'s Children's Book of Yr. citation 1968), The Bodach, 1970, The Lothian Run, 1970 (Book World's Children's Spring Book Festival honor citation 1970), The Thirteenth Member: A Story of Suspense, 1971 (Child Study Assn. Am.'s Children's Book of Yr. citation 1971), A Sound of Chariots, 1972 (Child Study Assn. Am.'s Children's Book of Yr. citation 1972, N.Y. Times Outstanding Book of Yr. citation 1972, Children's Book award Child Study Assn. Am. 1973, Phoenix award 1992), The Haunted Mountain: A Story of Suspense, 1972 (Child Study Assn. Am.'s Children's Book of Yr. citation 1972, N.Y. Times Outstanding Book of Yr. citation 1972, Scottish Arts Coun. award 1973), The Stronghold, 1974 (Child Study Assn. Am.'s Children's Book of Yr. citation 1974, Carnegie Medal for Children's Book Outstanding Merit Brit. Libr. Assn. 1974, Silver Pencil award 1975), A Stranger Came Ashore: A Story of Suspense, 1975 (Child Study Assn. Am.'s Children's Book of Yr. citation 1975, N.Y. Times Outstanding Book of Yr. citation 1972, Boston Globe Horn Book Honor Book 1976), Talent Is Not Enough: Mollie Hunter on Writing for Children, 1976 (Child Study Assn. Am.'s Children's Book of Yr. citation 1976), The Wicked One: A Story of Suspense, 1977 (Scottish Arts Coun. award book 1977), A Furl of Fairy Wind: Four Stories, 1977 (Child Study Assn. Am.'s Children's Book of Yr. citation 1977), The Third Eye, 1979, You Never Knew Her as I Did!, 1981, The Knight of the Golden Plain, 1983, The Dragonfly Years, 1983, The Three-Day Enchantment, 1985, I'll Go My Own Way, 1985, A Furl of Fairy Wind, 1986, Flora MacDonald and Bonnie Prince Charlie, 1987, The Mermaid Summer, 1988, The Pied Piper Syndrome, 1991, Gilly Martin the Fox, 1994, Day of the Unicorn, 1994, The King's Swift Rider, 1998. Performed vol. svcs. in serviceman's canteen during World War II. Mem. Soc. Authors (past chmn. Scotland chpt.). Scottish Nationalist. Episcopalian. Avocations: theatre, music, physical exercise, travel. Office: Rose Cottage, 7 Mary Ann Ct, Inverness 1V3 5BZ, Scotland

HUNTER, PATRICIA PHELPS, physician assistant; b. Nyack, N.Y., Oct. 11, 1952; d. Everett Edward and Evelyn Phelps; m. George Patton Hunter, June 26, 1982; children: Eric I., Kurt A. BA in Psychology & Spanish magna cum, Oneonta State U., 1974; BS in Physician Asst., Hahnemann Med. U., 1981; MS in Pub. Health, West Chester U., 1984. Rsch. asst. Oneonta (N.Y.) State U., 1973-74, Dartmouth Med. Sch., Hanover, N.H., 1974-76; paramedic San Francisco Ambulance, 1977-79; physician asst. Montgomery Hosp., Norristown, Pa., 1981—. Fellow Am. Acad. Physician Assts. (cert.); mem. Assn. for Retarded Citizens, Nat. Orgn. Rare Disorders, Nat. Orgn. Apraxia and Dyspraxia, Montgomery County Intermediate Unit Parents Group (recording sec. 1998—). Avocations: skiing, scuba diving. Home: 331 Collegeville Rd Collegeville PA 19426-3030 Office: Montgomery Hosp Clinic 15 W Wood St Norristown PA 19401-3300

HUNTER, PATRICIA RAE (TRICIA HUNTER), state official; b. Appleton, Minn., June 15, 1952; d. Harlan Ottowa and Clara Elizabeth (Tryhus) H.; m. Clark Waldon Crabbe, May 28, 1978 (div. July 1994); 1 child, Samantha Marcantonio. AS in Nursing, Good Samaritan Hosp., Phoenix, 1974; BS in Nursing, U. San Diego, San Diego, 1981; M Nursing, UCLA, 1985. RN; cert. oper. rm. nurse. Surg. svcs. educator Stanford Hosp., 1983-85; oper. rm. supr. Alexian Bros., San Jose, Calif., 1985-86; dir. surg. svcs. Cmty. Hosp. Chula Vista, Calif., 1986-89; mem. Calif. State Assembly, San Diego, 1989-92; spl. asst. Gov. Wilson Office Statewide Health Planning and Devel., Sacramento, Calif., 1993-94; sr. v.p., mng. dir. The Flannery Group, San Diego, 1997—; commr. Calif. Med. Assistance Commn., Sacramento, 1994-98, sr. v.p., mng. dir., 1998—; bd. mem. Premier Home & Health, Phoenix, 1994-95; cons. Summit Schs., Ontario, Calif., 1992-93, hosp., Monterey, Calif., 1984—; mem. adv. bd. Alheimers Assn., San Diego, 1990-92, Arthritis Found., 1990-92. Pres. Calif. Rep. League, 1995-97. Named Rockie Legislator of Yr., Calif. Psychol. Assn., 1990, Legislator of Yr. Calif. Nurse Practitioners Assn., 1992; recipient Alice Pauly award Nat. Women Polit. Caucus, San Diego, 1991. Mem. ANA (v.p. 1982-85), Assn. Oper. Rm. Nurses, NWPC, Bus. and Profl. Orgn., Rotary (bd. mem. 1993-94), San Diego Red Cross (bd. mem.), Sigma Theta Tau (leadership award 1991). Republican. Lutheran. Home: 3260 E Fox Run Way San Diego CA 92111-7723 Office: The Flannery Group 1121 L St Ste 501 Sacramento CA 95814-3943

HUNTER, ROBERT DOUGLAS, artist; b. Boston, Mar. 17, 1928; s. George Irvin and Hazel Francis (Costa) H.; m. Elizabeth Ives Valsam, Oct. 12, 1968; 3 children. Diploma, Vesper George Sch. Art, 1949. Instr. Vesper George Sch. Art, Boston, 1950-83, Worcester (Mass.) Mus. Fine Arts, 1965-75, Mt. Ida Jr. Coll., 1978. One man shows include Shore Studio Galleries, Boston, 1956, 61, Seattle Mus. Fine Arts, 1959, Tacoma Mus. Fine Art, 1959, Sacramento (Wash.) Mus. Fine Arts, 1959, Maryhill (Wash.) Mus. Fine Arts, 1959, Phila. Art Alliance, 1962, 67, 71, 74, Andover (Mass.) Gallery, 1970, Orleans (Mass.) Art Gallery, 1967, 68, Trees Pl. Gallery, Orleans, 1991, 96, 97, J. Todd Gallery, 1993, 95, 98, The Heritage Plantation Mus., Sandwich, Mass., 1997, The Zantman Gallery, Carmel, Calif., 1998, The Maryhill Mus. of Art, Goldendale, Wash., 1998; exhibited in group shows at Salmagundi Club, N.Y.C., Worcester (Mass.) Art Mus., others; represented in permanent collections at Maryhill Mus., Goldendale, Wash., Chrysler Mus., Norfolk, Va., others. Trustee Cape Mus. of Art, Dennis, Mass., 1991—. With USMCR, 1946-47. Recipient Richard Mitton Gold medal New Eng. Artist Exhbn., Boston, 1954-57, 59-61, 63-65, 67, 69-70, 74, Richard Mitton Silver medal, 1969, Pierson Meml. prize Ogunquit (Maine) Art Ctr., 1958, 63, Portrait prize, 1959, 66, 1st Painting award Acad. Artists, Springfield, Mass., 1961, Gold medal Am. Artists Profl. League, N.Y.C, 1962, Newington prize, 1966, 67, Bst Still LIfe award Grant Nat. exhbn., 1970, Popular prize Boston Arts Festival, 1962, John singleton Copley award Copley Soc., 1966, citation Gov. Mass., 1979, John Singleton Copley medallion, 1988, Best Still Life award North Shore Art Assn., 1981, award, 1993, Margarete Pearson Meml. award, 1996; named Copley Master, 1985. Master Am. Soc. Classical Realism; mem. Copley Soc. (bd. dirs. 1994-97), Provincetown Art Assn., Guld Boston Artists (past pres.). Address: 492 Lincoln Rd Walpole MA 02081-1209

HUNTER, ROSZELL DULANY, lawyer; b. Gastonia, N.C., Apr. 23, 1960; s. Roszell Dulany III and JoAnn (Selley) H. BA, Hampden-Sydney (Va.) Coll., 1982; JD, U. Va., 1986. Bar: Va. 1989, D.C. 1990. Asst. Senator John Warner, U.S. Senate, Washington, 1982-83; jud. clk. Judge Boyce Martin, U.S. Ct. Appeals, Louisville, 1986-87; assoc. Chief Justice Sir Anthony Mason, High Ct. Australia, Canberra, ACT, 1988; ptnr. Hunton & Williams, Richmond, Va. & Brussels, 1989—; chmn. bd. dirs. Ctr. for New Europe, Brussels, 1999—. Contbr. articles to newspapers and profl. jours. Office: Hunton & Williams, Ave Louise 326, B-1050 Brussels Belgium

HUNTER, WILLIAM JOHN, European commission director; b. London, Apr. 5, 1937; s. William George and Margaret (Beattie) H.; m. Estelle Edwards. MB, BS, U. London, 1961. Cert. occupl. health specialist. Casualty officer Westminster Hosp., London, 1962; house surgeon Gordon Hosp., London, 1962; house physician Brook Hosp., London, 1961; asst. pathologist Deptford Seaman's Hosp. Group, London, 1963-64; occupl. health physician Vauxhall Motors (GM Corp.), U.K., 1964-65, Gen. Foods Ltd., U.K., 1965-72; European dir. Gen. Foods Corp., U.K., 1972-74; prin. adminstr. European Commn., Brussels, 1974-82; head divsn.-occupl. health and hygiene European Commn., Luxembourg, 1982-87, dir. pub. health and safety at work directorate, 1987-99; dir. pub. health, 1999—; chmn. Com. Sr. Ofcls. Pub. Health, Brussels, 1987—, High Level Com. on Health, 1993—; jury mem. Europe et Medicine, 1993—. Decorated Officer Brother, Order of St. John of Jerusalem, 1996. Fellow Royal Coll. Physicians (internat. advisor), Faculty Medicine, Faculty Pub. Health Medicine (hon.); mem. Royal Coll. Surgeons. Avocations: swimming, scuba diving, photography, painting. Office: European Commn, Rue Alcide de Gasperi, L-2920 Luxembourg Luxembourg

HUNTER, WILLIAM SCHMIDT, engineering executive, environmental engineer; b. Bellwood, Pa., Mar. 24, 1931; s. William Franklin and Mary Mildred (Schmidt) H.; m. Barbara Ruth Crosland (dec. Mar. 1959); m. Sandra Lee Showalter, Aug. 26, 1961 (dec. Sept. 1991); m. Mary Elizabeth Tyson, Sept. 6, 1997; children: Felicia Fawn, Clarissa Cay, Patricia Schmidt. BSME, Lehigh U., 1953. Registered profl. engr., Pa. Project engr. W.Va. Pulp & Paper Co., Tyrone, Pa., 1953-56; plant engr. W.Va. Pulp & Paper Co., Williamsburg, Pa., 1956-61; project engr. St. Regis Paper Co., DeFeriet, N.Y., 1961-62; plant engr. Ga. Pacific Corp., Lyons Falls, N.Y., 1962-67; sr. project engr. Allied Paper Co., Kalamazoo, Mich., 1967-69, Hammermill Paper Co., Erie, Pa., 1969-80; chief engr. Stora Newton Falls, N.Y., 1980-81, v.p. engring., 1981-90, dir. environ. affairs, 1990-95; dir. environ. affairs Appleton Papers Inc., Newton Falls Mill, Newton Falls, 1995—. Bd. dirs. Am. Cancer Soc., Lewis County, N.Y., 1965, Clifton-Fine Econ. Devel. Corp., 1999-2000; vice chmn. Solid Waste Disposal Authority, St. Lawrence County, N.Y., 1992, 93, chmn., 1994, 95, 96, 97; com. chmn. Explorer Scouts, Boy Scouts Am., Williamsburg, Pa., 1959; councilman Williamsburg Borough Coun., 1961; pres., trustee Edinboro (Pa.) Presbyn. Ch., 1978-79; mem. mgmt. com. Devel. Authority North Country Solid Waste Mgmt., Lewis, Jefferson, St. Lawrence Counties, N.Y., 1994, 95, 96; mem. legis. adv. com. to state assembly woman, 1994-98; mem. Residents Com. to Protect the Adirondacks, 1996—; mem. The Adirondack Coun., 1997—. Mem. ASME, TAPPI, Altoona Engring. Soc. (bd. dirs. 1955-58), Adirondack Nature Conservancy, Sierra Club, The Nature Conservancy. Avocation: amateur radio. Home: 23 Colby Rd Star Lake NY 13690-3137 Office: Appleton Papers Inc Main St Newton Falls NY 13666

HUNTLEY, DONALD WAYNE, lawyer; b. Chgo., Sept. 22, 1942; s. Joseph Edward and Emily Rose (Beran) H.; m. Margaret Helen Kopacek, Aug. 27, 1966 (div. 1994); children: Richard A. II, Scott J., Mark B., C. Frederick M. BS, U. Ill., 1963, JD, 1966. Bar: D.C. 1967, Del. 1981, U.S. Supreme Ct. 1973. Patent counsel E. I. du Pont de Nemours & Co., Wilmington, Del., 1966-92, Remington Arms Co., 1985-89; founder present firm, 1993; asst. pub. defender State of Del., Wilmington, 1972-78; pntr. Huntley & Assocs., Wilmington. Bd. dirs. Del. Symphony Assn., 1972-86, 98—, pres., 1976-79, chmn. music com., 1979-86, trustee, 1988-98, chmn. past pres. coun., 1990—; bd. dirs. Kalmar Nyckel Commemorative Com., 1983-91, chmn. cultural com., 1983-86, mem. exec. com., 350th anniversary com., 1986-88; counsel Ctr. for Creative Arts, Yorklyn, Del., 1983-84. Mem. Rotary Club Wilmington, ABA, Del. Bar Assn., Phila. Intellectual Property Law Assn., Phi Delta Phi. Republican. Episcopalian. Home: 838 Summerset Dr Hockessin DE 19707-9338 Office: Huntley & Assocs PO Box 948 1105 N Market St Wilmington DE 19899-0948

HUNT OF WIRRAL, BARON DAVID JAMES FLETCHER, lawyer, former British government minister; b. May 21, 1942; married; 4 children. Ed., Liverpool (Eng.) Coll., U. Montpellier, France; degree in law, Bristol (Eng.) U. Opposition spokesman on shipping Ho. of Commons, 1977-79, Parliamentary pvt. sec. to sec. state for trade, and for def., 1979-81, asst. whip, 1981-83, lord commr. of Treasury (govt. whip), 1983-84, Parliamentary under sec. state for energy with responsibility for coal, 1984-87, dep. chief whip, 1987-89, min. state in dept. environ., 1989-90, mem. Privy Coun., 1990—, sec. state for Wales, 1990-93, sec. state for employment, cabinet min. responsible for women's issues, 1993-94, chancellor of the Duchy of Lancaster, 1994-95, cabinet min. pub. svc. and sci., 1994-95; sr. ptnr. Beachcroft Wansbroughs (ptnr. since 1968), 1999—; mem. Privy Coun., 1990—. Chmn. Brit. Youth Coun., 1971-74, Nat. Young Conservatives, 1972-73; former pres. Atlantic Assn. Young Polit. Leaders; former chmn. Brit. Atlantic Group Young Politicians; founder gov. European Youth Found., Strasbourg, France, 1978-79; vice chmn. Parliamentary Youth Lobby, 1978-79; vice chmn. in charge candidates Conservative Party, 1983-85; pres. Tory Reform Group, 1990-97; mem. parliament from Wirral, 1976-83, Wirral West, 1983-97; trustee Holocaust Ednl. Trust. Decorated mem. Order Brit. Empire. Mem. English Speaking Union (gov.). E-mail: lordhunt@bwlaw.co.uk. Fax: 020 7831 6630. Office: Beachcroft Wansbroughs, 100 Fetter Lane, London EC4A 1BN, England

HUNTOON, ROBERT BRIAN, chemist, food industry consultant; b. Braintree, Mass., Mar. 1, 1927; s. Benjamin Harrison and Helen Edna (Worden) H.; m. Joan Fairman Graham, Mar. 1, 1952; children: Brian Graham, Benjamin Robert, Elisabeth Ellen, Janet Lynne, Joelle. BS in Chemistry, Northeastern U., 1949, MS, 1961. Analytical chemist Mass. Dept. Public Health; microbiologist Met. Dist. Commn. Mass. Dept. Public Health, Boston, 1950-53; rsch. and devel. chemist Heveatex Corp., Melrose, Mass., 1953-56; with Gen. Foods Corp., 1956-70; acting quality control mgr. Gen. Foods Corp., Woburn, Mass., 1965-67; head group rsch. and devel. Gen. Foods Corp., Tarrytown, N.Y., 1967-70; dir. quality control U.S. Flavor div. Internat. Flavors & Fragrances, Teterboro, N.J., 1970-83, mgr. tech. svcs., 1983-87, mgr. product devel., 1987-89, cons., 1989-92; ind. cons. product devel., 1989—. Contbr. articles on flavor and food quality control to profl. and co. publs.; patentee gelatin compositions and mfg. processes. Served with USCG, 1945-46. Mem. Essential Oils Assn. (com. mem.), Flavor and Extracts Mfg. Assn. (com. mem.), Am. Chem. Soc., Inst. Food Technologists, Internat. Platform Assn., Indsl. Mgmt. Club (v.p. 1967) (Woburn), Croton Yacht Club, Saugus River Yacht Club (treas. 1967-68). Republican. Presbyterian. Office: 7 Scotland Hill Park Chestnut Ridge NY 10977-5908

HUNYADI, JANOS, dermatology educator; b. Szeged, Hungary, Aug. 22, 1943; s. Livia Labdy H.; m. Zsolt and Balazs Hunyadi. MD, U. Med. Sch., Szeged, 1967, cert. in dermatology, 1970, cert. in immunology, 1983, PhD, 1983. Cert. in allergology and clin. immunology U. Med. Sch., Debrecen, Hungary. Clin. asst. dept. dermatology U. Med. Sch., Szeged, Hungary, 1967-71, asst. dept. dermatology, 1971-77, asst. lectr. dept. dermatology, 1977-87, lectr., 1987-92, prof., head dept., 1992—. Contbr. articles to profl. jours. Mem. Rotary Club, Debrecen, Hungary, 1993. Recipient Dept. Dermatology fellowship U. Med. Sch., 1974-75, 85; named Postdoctorate Rsch. assoc. Nat. Naval Med. Ctr., Bethesda, 1979-80. Mem. German-Hungarian Dermatol. Soc., European Immuno-Dermatol. Soc., Hungarian Dermatol. Soc., Hungarian Allergological Clin. Immunological Soc., Hungarian Immunological Soc. Avocations: dermatology, immunology, allergology, tissue culture, experimental immunology. Office: U Debrecen Dept Dermatology, Nagyerdei krt 98, 4012 Debrecen Hungary

HUNYADY, GYÖRGY, social psychologist, educator; b. Budapest, Hungary, Aug. 13, 1942; s. Lajos Hunyady and Éva H. Balázs; m. Zsuzsanna Gárdonyi, Oct. 24, 1964; children: Orsolya, András. Diploma, Elte U., Budapest, 1965, Dr., 1967; Candidate of Scis., Hungarian Acad. Scis., Budapest, 1972, DSc, 1986. Head dept. psychology Kossuth Lajos U., Debrecen, Hungary, 1980-85; head dept. social and ednl. psychology, faculty humanities Eötvös Loránd U., Budapest, 1983—, dean faculty humanities, 1990-92, dir. Inst. Psychology faculty humanities, 1999—; head com. psychology Hungarian Acad. Scis., 1990—; pres. bd. Nat. Found. Pub. Edn., 1997-98; pres. 2d European Congress of Psychology, Budapest, 1991; mem. bd. TEMPUS-Hungary, 1990-95; chair nat. bd. Curriculum Devel. for Higher Edn. in Humanities and Social Scis., 1995-99. Author: Stereotypes During the Decline and Fall of Communism, 1998, Characterization of Social Categories in Psychological and Social Context, 1998; editor: (in Hungarian) Historical and Political Psychology, 1998, Group Perception, 1998. Recipient Deák Ferenc award Pro Renovanda Cultura Hungariae, 1997, Ránki György award Huntarian Acad. Scis., 1998. Mem. APA, Hungarian Psychol. Assn., Soc. for Social and Personal Psychology, European Assn. Empirical Psychology. Office: Eotvos Lorand U Inst Psych, Izabella u 46, 1064 Budapest Hungary

HUO, BONNIE KWAN, artist; b. Canton, China, Nov. 23, 1949; d. Hok Pui and Tai Wah (Wong) Kwan; m. Rex W.C. Huo, Feb. 10, 1972; 1 child, Alina. BA, U. Calif., Berkeley, 1971; postgrad. diploma in edn., U. Hong Kong, 1972. Sole proprietor Anything Aesthetic, Hong Kong, 1987—. One-woman exhibits include Kowloon Shangrila Hotel, Hong Kong, 1989, Shenzhen Art Mus., China, 1993, Letty's Gallery, Vancouver, 1994, Pristine Harmony Art Ctr., Taipei, 1995, Modest Art Gallery, Toronto, 1996, Traditional Chinese Cultural Soc., Montreal, 1996, Melbourne Chinese Mus. & Sydney Chinese Culture Ctr., 1998, World Jour. Gallery, San Francisco, 2000; represented in permanent collections Singapore Nat. Mus., Shenzhen Art Mus., Australia Chinese Mus., U. Indpls., Sotheby's Fine Modern Chinese Painting Auction. Recipient Cert. of Honor Suprs. of City and County of San Francisco and numberous art awards. Mem. Internat. Chinese Soc. Photography and Arts, Ling Nan Art Assn. Am., Fedn. Can. Artists, Fedn. Chinese Can. Artists in Vancouver, Hong Kong Artists Assn., White Cloud Hall, Hong Kong Lan Ting Soc. (com. mem.), Internat. Calligraphy Alliance (Hong Kong chpt.), Ling Nam Art Assn. (v.p.). Avocations: traveling, attending cultural events, golfing, reading, painting. Fax: (852) 2838-9362. E-mail: ufomail@netfront.net.

HUON, HUBERT JOHN, retired psychiatrist, neurologist; b. Douarnenez, France, June 6, 1936; s. Frank Allen and Mary Ann (Simon) H.; m. Mick Huon, Mar. 31, 1964; children: Nathalie, Renaud, John-Christopher, Valerie. BS, Coll. St. Francois Xavier, Vannes, France, 1953; MD, Faculty Medicine, Paris, 1971; Cert. in Psychiatry, Pediatrics, Faculty Medicine Paris, 1971-72; Cert. in Neurophysiology, Faculty Medicine, 1973. Intern, resident, asst. prof. biochemistry Hosps. of Paris, 1966-70; prof. asst. neurophysiology, psychiatry U. Paris, 1968-72; prof. asst. psychiatry Hosp. Brest, France, 1972-74; chief psychiat. service Ctr. Hosp. Specialise de St. Ave, Vannes, France, 1977-95, dir. sleep lab., 1980-99; dir. clin. teaching Hosp. Rennes, France, 1977-92; ret., 1999; cons. neurologist, Paris; expert ct. of justice, Rennes, 1973; clin. expert Ministry of Health, 1973; French del. World Council for Gifted and Talented Children, 1981-83; mgr. house constrn. firm. Author: The Children's Sleep, 1974; contbr. chpt. to book and med. research articles to profl. publs. Served as sgt. French armed forces, 1957-60, col. res. Mem. Sleep Research Soc., European Sleep Research Soc., French Soc. EEG and Neurophysiology, French Soc. Epidemiol. Psychology, Ordre Internat. des Anysetiers, Mensa. Roman Catholic. Achievements include research on intellegence and sleep. Avocations: tennis, astronomy, chess, sailing. Home: Kergoff, Douarnenez France

HUOT, NICOLAS, physicist; b. Troyes, France, Apr. 7, 1966. Diploma theoretical physics, U. Paris, 1989, PhD in Particle Physics, 1992. Nuclear physicist Framatome, France, 1993-95, Commissariat a l'Energie Atomique, France, 1995—. Mem. Am. Phys. Soc., European Phys. Soc.

HUOT, RACHEL IRENE, biomedical educator, research scientist, physician; b. Manchester, N.H., Oct. 16, 1950; d. Omer Joseph and Irene Alice (Girard) H. BA in Biology cum laude, Rivier Coll., 1972; MS in Biology, Cath. U. Am., 1976, PhD in Biology, 1980; MD, La. State U. Health Sci. Ctr., Shreveport, 2000. Sr. technician Microbiol. Assocs., Bethesda, Md., 1974-77; chemist Uniformed Svcs. Univ. of Health Scis., Bethesda, 1977-79; biologist Nat. Cancer Inst., Bethesda, 1979-82; postdoctoral fellow S.W. Found. for Biomed. Rsch., San Antonio, 1982-85, asst. scientist, 1985-87, staff scientist, 1987-88; instr. U. Tex. Health Sci. Ctr., San Antonio, 1988-89; asst. prof., dir. basic urologic rsch. La. State U., New Orleans, 1990-96; resident in internal medicine Med. Coll. Va. Hosps. Va. Commonwealth U., Richmond, 2000—; judge sr. div. Alamo Regional Sci. Fair, San Antonio, 1989-90. Contbr. articles to profl. jours. Vol. ARC, Christus Schumpert Hosp. (Vol. of Yr. award 1999), Shreveport; patient educator vol. Martin Luther King Clinic, Shreveport, La., 1996-2000. NSF grantee, 1972-74; recipient NIH Rsch. Svc. award, 1983-86, Searle Young Investigator award, 1994. Mem. AAAS, LWV, AAUW, AMA, Am. Soc. for Microbiology, Am. Soc. Internal Medicine, Am. Assn. Cancer Rsch., Am. Soc. Cell Biology, Med. Soc. Va., Fedn. Am. Scientists, Soc. for In Vitro Biology, N.Y. Acad. Scis., St. Vincent De Paul Soc., Sierra Club, Fedn. Am. Soc. Experiment Biology, Sigma Xi, Iota Sigma Pi, Delta Epsilon Sigma. Democrat. Roman Catholic. Avocations: drawing, painting, roadracing, reading, Volksmarching. Home: 2903 Oakland Ave Richmond VA 23228-5827

HUOVILA, TAPANI YRJÖ JARMO, communications educator; b. Jyväskylä mlk, Finland, Nov. 1, 1954; s. Aaro Johannes and Elli Margareta (Virkkunen) H.; m. Riitta Katriina Kinnunen, Aug. 9, 1980; children: Henna-Riikka, Antti. MA, U. Jyväskylä, 1982, PhD, 1987. Cert. tchr. history and social sci., journalist. Journalist Keskisuomalainen, Jyväskylä, 1984-87; lectr. U. Jyväskylä, 1987—, docent, 1996—, prof., 1996-98. Author: Layout as a Messsage, 1996, 2d edit., 2000. Bd. mem. Nat. Union Finnish Students, 1981-82, pres. cultural affairs, 1982. Mem. Finnish Assn. Mass Comm. Rsch. (bd. mem. 1992-95). Avocations: camping, astronomy. Office: U Jyväskylä, Matarankatu 6 PO Box 35, 40351 Jyväskylä Finland

HUPFER, ROBERT, engineering company executive; b. Krumbach, Bavaria, Germany, Aug. 2, 1968; s. Stefan and Edeltraud Hupfer; m. Nadine Hupfer. Diploma in EE, Tech. U., Munich, 1994. With BMW AG, Munich, 1994-95; project engr. Atlas Fahrzeugtechnik GMBH, Werdohl, Germany, 1995; project mgr. Atlas Fahrzeugtechnik GMBH, Werdohl, 1996-97, mgr. elec. devel., 1997-2000; mgr. elec. devel. Webast AG, Stockdorf, 2000—. Contbr. articles to profl. jours. Active German Mil., 1987-88. Mem. Verein Deutscher Ingenieure, Arbeitsgemeinschaft Simulation, Soc. Automotive Engrs. Avocations: sports, traveling. Home: Blumenweg 2A, 87727 Babenhausen Bavaria, Germany Office: Webasto Thermosys Internat, Kraillinger Strasse 5, 82131 Stockdorf Germany

HUPP, CAROL, elementary education educator, storyteller; b. Springfield, Ill., Mar. 1, 1951; d. Allen J. and Genieve R. Stieren; m. Larry D. Hupp, Apr. 26, 1969; children: Dean Allen, Clarrissa Ann, Joseph W., Anthony. AS, Lincolnland C.C., Springfield, 1988; BA, U. Ill., Springfield, 1989; MA, So. Ill. U., Edwardsville, 1999. Cert. tchr., Ill. Lead tchr. Step-by-Step Learning Ctr., Springfield, Ill., 1990-94; tchr. St. Mary's Sch., Taylorville, Ill., 1994-98; tchr. English Jeremia, Haiti, 1998-2000; tchr. St. Isidore's Sch., Farmersville, Ill., 2000—. Storyteller internat. festival, 1999. Vol. storyteller Ronald McDonald House, Springfield, 1996—. Tchr. in learning grantee Ill. Humanities Coun., 1998, tech. grantee Ill. Geography Alliance, 1998. Mem. Nat. Storytelling Assn. E-mail: hupp@ctllc.com. Home: 730 E Dean St Virden IL 62690-1514

HÜPPI, ROLF, financial company executive. With Zurich Fin. Svcs. Group, 1963—, group exec. bd., CEO Zurich orgn., dep. COO, 1987, COO, 1988, pres., CEO, 1991, also bd. dirs., 1993—, chmn. bd., 1995—. Office: Zurich Fin Svcs, Mythenquai 2, 8002 Zurich Switzerland*

HUPY, MICHAEL FREDERICK, lawyer; b. Milw., Oct. 11, 1946; s. Wilfred Joseph and Phyllis Marie (Heintz) H.; m. Suzanne Hupy. BA, Marquette U., 1968, JD, 1972. Bar: Wis. 1972, Ill. 1997, U.S. Dist. Ct. (we. and ea. dists.) Wis. 1972, U.S. Ct. Appeals (7th cir.) 1976, U.S. Supreme Ct. 1976. Ptnr. Hupy & Glasschroeder, Milw., 1972-76, Hausmann, McNally & Hupy S.C., Milw., 1976-89, Jacobson, O'Dess & Krings S.C., Milw., 1989-90, Jacobson & Hupy, S.C., Milw., 1990-76, Michael F. Hupy and Assocs., S.C., 1997—. Mem. ABA, Wis. Bar Assn., Milw. Bar Assn., Assn. Trial lawyers Am., Wis. Acad. Trial Lawyers. Office: 1110 W Wisconsin Ave # 1110 Milwaukee WI 53233-2314

HUQUE, AHMED SHAFIQUL, political science-public administration educator; b. Dhaka, Bangladesh, Aug. 1, 1952; s. Mohammad Manirul and Tabinda Akhtar (Khatun) H.; m. Khaleda Yasmin, Oct. 02, 1979; children: Shineen, Sakeen. BA with honors, U. Dhaka, 1974, MA, 1975; MA, U. Man., Winnipeg, Can., 1979; PhD, U. B.C., Vancouver, Can., 1984. Lectr. U. Chittagong, Bangladesh, 1976-78; teaching asst. U. Man., 1978-79, U. B.C., 1979-84; asst. prof. U. Chittagong, 1984-85, assoc. prof., 1985-88; assoc. prof. U. Dhaka, 1988-90; sr. lectr. City Poly. Hong Kong, 1990-92, prin. lectr., 1992-95; assoc. prof. City U. Hong Kong, 1995—; mem. publ. com. U. Chittagong, 1985-86. Author: Politics and Administration in Bangladesh, 1988, Paradoxes in Public Administration, 1990, Public Administration in the NICS, 1996, Social Policy in Hong Kong, 1997, The Civil Service in Hong Kong, 1998, Managing Public Services, 2000; editor-in-chief Pub. Adminstrn. and Policy; mem. editl. bd. several acad. jours.; contbr. articles to profl. jours. Moslem. Avocations: sports, music, reading. Office: City U Hong Kong/Social Adm, 83 Tat Chee Ave, Kowloon Hong Kong

HUR, JIN HO, high technology company executive; b. Taegu, Korea, Dec. 6, 1961; s. Jung Wook and Kyung Ja (Park) H.; m. Sue K. Kim, Apr. 20, 1988; 1 child, Sol. BS, Seoul (Korea) Nat. U., 1983; MS, Korea Advanced Inst. Sci., Seoul, 1985; PhD, KAIST, Seoul, 1990. Engrng. dir. Human Computer, Inc., Seoul, 1990-92; mktg. mgr. TriGem Computer, Inc., Seoul, 1992-94; pres., CEO Inet, Inc., Seoul, 1994-2000, Iworld Networking, Inc., Seoul, 2000—; acting chmn. Portsoft Group, Asia, 1990-91. Author: Report on Science Policy, 1993, also articles; mem. ISO/IEC JTC1/SC21/WG7, N.Y.C., 1987-90. Recipient Excellence award Ministry of Edn./Korea, Seoul, 1983. Mem. IEEE, Assn. for Computing Machinery, Asia Pacific Internet Assn. (chmn. 1997-98), Korea Internet Assn. (vice chmn. 1997-98), Networld and Interop (tech. adv. bd. 1995-97). Avocations: swimming, movies. Office: Iworld Networking Inc, 772 Yoksam-Dong, Kangnam-Ku Seoul 135-080, Republic of Korea

HUR, SUNMOO, research scientist; b. Kyoung Ki Do, Kwang Ju, Republic of Korea, Jan. 10, 1951; s. Myoung Hur and Ki Nam; m. Hoonja Park, Sept. 18, 1976; children: Jinsun, Seungbum. BS, Seoul Nat. U., Republic of Korea, 1973, MS, 1981; PhD, U. Fla., 1986. Rschr. Agy. Def. Devel., Seoul, 1976-80; sr. rschr. Agy. Def. Devel., Taejon, Republic of Korea, 1981-89; head tank & automotive propulsion sys. divsn. Agy. Def. Devel., Taejon, 1989-95, prin. rschr., 1990—, head. structural materials divsn., 1995-96. Contbr. articles to profl. jours. 1st lt. Korean Army, 1973-76. Recipient Encouraging award Min. Def., 1979, 93. Avocations: golf, climbing mountains. Fax: 82-42-823-3400. Office e-mail: sunmooh@sunam.kreonet.re.kr., home e-mail: HSM51@hanmail.net. Home: Expo 302-502, Jeonmin Dong, Yuseong Ku, 305-761 Taejon Republic of Korea Office: Agy Def Devel, Yuseong PO Box 35-5, 305-600 Taejon Republic of Korea

HUR, SU-RYONG, physician, anesthesiologist; b. Korea, Feb. 8, 1942; s. Hyung Keun and JaeKyung (Kim) H.; m. Myung Ja; children: Jennifer, Steven, Michelle. MD, Seoul Nat. U., 1966. Diplomate Am. Bd. Anesthesiology. Intern Union Hosp., Fall River, Mass., 1966-67; resident St. Vincent's Hosp, Worcester, Mass., 1967-68, Mass. Gen. Hosp., Boston, 1968-71; staff anesthesiologist St. Michael's Hosp., 1975—; asst. prof. anesthesiology Med. Coll. Wis., 1971-75, mem. clin. faculty anesthesiology, 1976—. Contbr. articles to profl. jours. Fellow Am. Coll. Anesthesiologists; mem. AMA, Internat. Anesthesia Rsch. Soc., Am. Soc. Anesthesiologists, Korean Am. Med. Assn., Wis. Soc. Anesthesiologists, State Med. Soc. of Wis., Med. Soc. of Milw. County, Milw. Soc. of Anesthesiologists. Home fax: 262-241-3415. Office fax: 414-527-5145. Office: St Michael Hosp Dept Anesthesiology 2400 W Villard Ave Milwaukee WI 53209-4999

HURD, BYRON THOMAS, newspaper executive, retired; b. Roseville, Mich., 1933; s. Clark Frank and Evelyn (Sybelden) H.; m. Barbara Jean Ekeroth; children: Thomas E., Roger A., J. Douglas, James B. BSBA in Advt. and Mktg., Wayne State U., 1954. Sales mgr. Detroit Free Press, 1954-55, Milne & Jones, Royal Oak, Mich., 1955-56, Detroit Times, 1956-59; account mgr. Milne Circulation Sales, Inc., Bloomfield Hills, Mich., 1959-65; agt. Bankers Life Co., Des Moines, Iowa, 1965-66; promotion mgr. Chgo. Today, Chgo. Tribune, 1966-74; owner, cons. Circulation Specialists, Homewood, Ill., 1974-77; exec. dir. circulation The Star Newspapers, Chicago Heights, Ill., 1977-95; ret., 1995; panelist, discussion leader, session master, com. mem. No. Ill. Newspapers Assn., DeKalb. Contbr. Publishers handbook, 1988. Elder, pres. governing bd. Flossmoor (Ill.) Community Ch., 1988. Mem. Cen. States Circulation Mgrs. Assn., Suburban Newspapers Am. (conf., sem. com. mem.), Audit Bur. Circulation (voting rep.), Circulation Mgmt. Ill., Rotary (dir. community svc. 1978-79, dir. internat. svc. 1979-80, sec. 1981-82, v.p. 1982-83, pres. 1983-84, dist. dir. pub. rels. 1984-86, dist. govs. aide 1986-87, dist. dir. vocat. svc. 1987-88, host Soviet Emerging Leaders 1988, Finnish 1989, dist. dir. group study exchange with India 1990, dist. conf. com. master ceremonies 1987-88, dist. conf. com. chmn. 1989-90), Flossmoor Country Club (sports and pastimes com. mem. 1988), Foxfire Golf and Country Club, Internat. Golfing Fellowship of Rotary (lifetime), U.S. Golfing Fellowship of Rotary (lifetime), Foxfire Country Club. Avocations: golf, skiing, racquetball, drawing, painting.

HURD, DOUGLAS RICHARD, British legislator; b. Marlborough, Wilts, Eng., Mar. 8, 1930; s. Anthony Richard and Stephanie (Corner) H.; m. Tatiana Elizabeth Michelle Eyre, Nov. 10, 1960 (div. 1982); children: Nicholas, Thomas, Alexander; m. Judy Smart, May 7, 1982; children: Philip, Jessica. King's scholar; Newcastle scholar, Eton, Trinity Coll., Cambridge U. With Her Majesty's Diplomatic Svc., Beijing; stationed at UN Her Majesty's Diplomatic Svc., Rome, 1952-56; dep. chair Nat. West Mkts., 1995-98; dir. Nat. West Group, 1995-99; chair Brit. Invisibles, 1997-2000, Prison Reform Trust, 1997—; dep. chmn. Coutts & Co., 1998—; chair Hawkpoink Ptnrs. Adv. Bd., 1998—; mem. staff rsch. dept. Conservative Party, 1966-68; pvt. sec. to leader of opposition, 1968-70; M.P. for Witney, Oxfordshire; polit. sec. to prime min., 1970-74, opposition spokesman on European affairs, 1976-79, min. of state Fgn. and Commonwealth Office, 1983-84, sec. of state No. Ireland, 1984-85, sec. of state for Home Affairs, 1985-89, sec. state fgn. and Commonwealth affairs, 1989-95; dep. chmn. Nat. West Markets, 1995-98. Author 3 hist. works, 9 polit. thrillers, created Life Peer, 1997. Decorated Companion of Honor, Privy Councillor, comdr. Order Brit. Empire. Mem. Beefsteak Club, Travellers Club. Conservative. Anglican. Avocation: writing. Office: House of Lords, Westminster, London SW1 OPW, England

HURD, GALE ANNE, film producer; b. L.A., Oct. 25, 1955; d. Frank E. and Lolita (Espiau) H. Degree in econs. and communications, Stanford U., 1977. Dir. mktg. and publicity, co-producer New World Pictures, L.A., 1977-82; pres., producer Pacific Western Prodns., L.A., 1982—. Producer: (films) The Terminator, 1984 (Grand Prix Avoiriaz Film Festival award), Aliens 1986 (nominated for 7 Acad. awards, recipient Best Sound Effects Editing award, Best Visual Effects award Acad. Picture Arts & Scis.), Alien Nation (Saturn award for best sci. fiction film), The Abyss, 1989 (nominated for 4 Acad. awards, Best Visual Effects award), The Waterdance, 1991 (2 IFP Spirit awards, 2 Sundance Film Festival awards), Cast a Deadly Spell, 1991 (Emmy award), Raising Cain, 1992, No Escape, 1994, Safe Passage (Beatrice Wood award for Creative Achievement), 1994, The Ghost and the Darkness, 1996, The Relic, 1996, Going West in America, 1996, Dante's Peak, 1997, Virus, 1997, Dead Man on Campus, 1997, Armageddon, 1998, Dick, 1998; exec. producer: (films) Switchback, 1997, Tremors, 1990, Downtown, 1990, Terminator 2, 1991 (winner 3 Acad. awards), Witch Hunt, 1994, Sugartime, 1995; creative cons. (TV program) Alien Nation, 1989-90. Juror Focus Student Film Awards, 1989, 90; chmn. Nicholl Fellowship Acad. Motion Picture Arts & Scis., 1989—; mem. Show Coalition, 1988—; mem. Hollywood (Calif.) Women's Polit. Com., 1987—; mem. U.S. Film Festival Juror; bd. dirs. IFP/West, Artists Rights Found.; trustee Am. Film Inst.; bd. dirs. L.A. Internat. Film Festival, Coral Reef Rsch. Found., Ams. for a Safe Future; mentor Peter Stark Motion Picture Producing Program, Sch. of Cinema-TV, U. of So. Calif., Women in Film Mentor Program. Recipient Spl. Merit award Nat. Assn. Theater Owners, 1986, Stanford-La Entrepreneur of Yr. award Bus. Sch. Alumni L.A., 1990, Fla. Film Festival award, 1994. Mem. AMPAS (prodr.'s br. exec. com. 1990—, festival grants com.), Am. Film Inst. (trustee 1989—), Americans for a Safe Future (bd. dirs. 1993—), Prodr.'s Guild Am. (bd. dirs.), Women in Film (bd. dirs. 1989-90), Inst. for Rsch. on Women and Gender (nat. adv. panel 1997—), Feminist Majority, Internat. Seakeepers Soc., Mulholland Tomorrow, The Trusteeship, Phi Beta Kappa. Avocations: scuba diving, Paso Fino horses. Office: Pacific Western Prodns 270 N Canon Dr Ste 1195 Beverly Hills CA 90210-5323

HURD, RICHARD NELSON, pharmaceutical company executive; b. Evanston, Ill., Feb. 25, 1926; s. Charles DeWitt and Mary Ormsby (Nelson) H.; m. Jocelyn Fillmore Martin, Dec. 22, 1950; children: Melanie Gray, Suzanne Dewitt. BS, U. Mich., 1946; PhD U. Minn., 1956. Chemist Gen. Electric Co., Schenectady, N.Y., 1948-49; R&D group leader Koppers Co., Pitts., $D, 1956-57; rsch. chemist Mallinckrodt Chem. Works, St. Louis, 1957-63, group leader, 1963-66; group leader Comml. Solvents Corp., Terre Haute, Ind., 1966-68, sect. head, 1968-71; mgr. sci. affairs G. D. Searle Internat. Co., Skokie, Ill., 1972-73, dir. mfg. and tech. affairs, 1973-77; rep. to internat. tech com. Pharm. Mfrs. Assn., Skokie, Ill., 1973-77; v.p. tech. affairs Elder Pharms., Bryan, Ohio, 1977-81; v.p. rsch. & devel. U.S. Proprietary Drugs & Toiletries div. Schering-Plough Corp., Memphis, 1981-83; v.p. sci affairs Moleculon, Inc., Cambridge, Mass., 1984-88; v.p. regulatory affairs Pharmaco-LSR, Inc., Austin, Tex., 1989-94; prin. Hurd & Assocs., Inc., Evanston, ILL., 1994—. Contbr. articles to profl. jours.; patentee in field. Mem. Ferguson-Florissant (Mo.) Sch. Bd., 1964-66; bd. dirs. United Fund of Wabash Valley (Ind.), 1969-71. With USN, 1943-46, 53-55. E.I. DuPont de Nemours & Co., Inc. fellow, 1956. Fellow AAAS; mem. Am. Acad. Dermatology (life), Am. Soc. Photobiology, Am. Chem. Soc., N.Y. Acad. Sci., Am. Pharm. Assn., Am. Assn. Pharm. Scientists, Food and Drug Law Inst., Drug Info. Assn., Sigma XI, Mich. Shores Club (Wilmette, Ill.). Presbyterian. Achievements include codevelopment of Ralgro and Oxsoralen; research in thioamides as a class of organic compounds; development of macrocyclic synthetic routes for natural products; development of psoralens for photochemotherapy of dermatologic disorders. E-mail: hurdreg@earthlink.net.

HURET, MARILYNN JOYCE, editor, puzzle constructor; b. N.Y.C., Dec. 5; d. Hyman and Clara (Weinberg) Moskowitz; m. Barry Saul Huret, Feb. 11, 1961; children: Abbey Beth, Eric Alan. BA in Math., Adelphi U., 1961. Tchr. math. Dist. 281, Robbinsdale, Minn., 1974-77; puzzle constructor Marvel Comics, N.Y.C., 1982-88, Great Puzzle Catalog, N.Y.C., 1982-83; editor, online sysop Crossword Am. LYRIQ Internat., 1995—; editor, Crossword America, puzzle mag. on-line LYRIQ Internat., Divsn. Enteractive, Inc., 1996-98; editor Crossroads Media Group, Inc., Newtown, Conn., 1998—; mem. Bucks County Courier Times Readers Adv. Group, 1995—; presenter in field; editor, developer, constructor Crossroads Media Group, Inc.; computer sci. tchr., coord. Politz Acad., Phila., 1999; mgr. editl. content, editor Crossroads Media Group, Inc. divsn. Katerra, Inc. puzzle constructor Soft Disk Electronic Pub., N.Y. Times, Bucks County Courier, Yardley News; writer biog. articles for crossword mag.; contbr. Crosswurd Mag., 1995—, Crosswords Diagramless Acrostics, Cryptograms For IDG Puzzle Series, Vols. I, II, III, IV, V, 101 Crossword Puzzles for Dummies, IDG Series; editor: Crossword Am. puzzle mag. on-line; crossword puzzle constructor N.Y. Times; writer, presenter More Bytes For the Buck (A Guide to Purchase of Computing Hardware & Components. Coop. weather observer Sta. WOR, N.Y.C., 1965-71; severe storm weather spotter NOAA,

1972-77, Mpls., 1977-79, Racine, Wis., 1980—, Phila., Mt. Holly, N.J.; commr. pub. safety City of Golden Valley, Minn., 1972-77; judge Delaware Valley Sci. Fairs, Phila., 1984—; adminstr. David Libr. of Am. Revolution, Washington Crossing, Pa., 1988-95.; dep. coord. emergency mgmt. Lower Makefield Twp., Pa., 1989—; bd. dirs. Delaware Valley Philharmonic Orch., mem. season planning com.; guild mem. Newtown (Pa.) Symphony; mem. MACA, 1997—. Recipient Svc. Appreciation award Golden Valley City Coun., 1977. Mem. LWV, AAUW (editor Makefield Area Connections 1993-96, Named Gift award 1994, Outstanding Woman of Yr. Makefield area 1995, organizer puzzle tournaments), Spl. Libr. Assn. (assoc.), Am. Cryptogram Assn., Am. Women in Computing, Nat. Puzzlers League, Bucks County Librs. Assn., Lower Bucks Computer Users Group, Adelphi U. Alumni Assn., Toastmasters, Spiffy's Gang. Home: 484 Kings Rd Yardley PA 19067-4652 Office: Crossroads Media Group Inc 3 Dinglebrook Ln Newtown CT 06470-1125

HURLBURT, HARLEY ERNEST, ocean modeling and prediction scientist; b. Bennington, Vt., Apr. 12, 1943; s. Paul Rhodes and Evelyn Arlene (Lockhart) H.; m. Cheryl Elaine Finch, Jan. 10, 1998. BS in Physics (scholar), Union Coll., Schenectady, 1965; MS, Fla. State U., 1971, PhD in Meteorology, 1974. NASA trainee Fla. State U., 1970-72; postdoctoral fellow advanced studies program Nat. Ctr. Atmospheric Rsch., Boulder, Colo., 1974-75; staff scientist JAYCOR, Alexandria, Va., 1975-77; oceanographer Naval Rsch. Lab. and related orgns., Stennis Space Center, Miss., 1977—, br. head, 1983-85; adj. faculty marine sci. U. So. Miss., Stennis Space Ctr., 1993—; adj. faculty meteorology Fla. State U., Tallahassee, 1995—; mem. nat. adv. panels NASA satellite surface stress working group, 1981-84, minerals mgmt. svc. interagy. adv. group, 1982-89, world ocean circulation experiment working group on numerical modeling, 1984-96, USN space oceanography working group, 1986-89; co-chmn. working group on global prediction sys., ocean prediction workshop, 1986; internat. working group on acoustic monitoring of world ocean Sci. com. Oceanic Rsch., 1991-98; internat. working group on modelling subarctic North Pacific circulation North Pacific Marine Sci. Orgn., 1994-95; mem. sci. steering team Global Ocean Data Assimilation Experiment, 1998—; project leader to develop the world's first eddy-resolving global ocean prediction model for the USN, 1987—. Contbr. numerous articles to profl. jours. V.p. Burgundy Citizens Assn., 1976-77. Weather officer USAF, 1965-69. Recipient Disting. Scientist medal 13th Internat. Colloquium, Liege, Belgium, 1981, Publ. award for best basic rsch. paper Naval Ocean R&D Activity, 1980, 90; grantee Office Naval Rsch., 1975-77, 84—, Dept. Energy, 1975-78, Tex. A&M U., 1976, Office of Naval Tech., 1987-93, Space Warfare Sys., 1989-94, Advanced Rsch. Projects Agy., 1993-95, Strategic Environ. Rsch. and Devel. Program, 1994-95, Def. Dept. High Performance Computing Challenge, 1997—, Nat. Ocean Partnership Program, 1997—; case study on Eddy-resolving Global Ocean Modeling and Prediction included in 2000 Computerworld Smithsonian Collection archived in Smithsonian's Nat. Mus. Am. History's permanent rsch. collection. Mem. Am. Meteorol. Soc., Am. Geophys. Union, Oceanography Soc., Phi Sigma Kappa, Sigma Xi (Kaminski Publ. award 1991), Sigma Tau, Chi Epsilon Pi. Methodist. Home: 507 Hermitage Ct Pearl River LA 70452-3903 Office: Naval Rsch Lab Code # 7304 Bay Saint Louis MS 39529

HURLBUT, ROBERT HAROLD, health care services executive; b. Rochester, N.Y., Mar. 9, 1935; s. Harold Leroy and Martha Irene (Fincher) H.; m. Barbara Cox, June 14, 1958; children: Robert W., Christine A. Hurlbut Bean. Student, Coll. Hotel Adminstrn., Cornell U., 1953-56. Adminstr., dir. Pillars Nursing Home, Rochester, 1956—, Elmcrest Nursing Home, Churchville, N.Y., 1960—, Elm Manor Nursing Home, Canandaigua, N.Y., 1960—, Penfield Nursing Home, Rochester, 1963—, Avon (N.Y.) Nursing Home, 1964—, Newark (N.Y.) Nursing Home, 1965—, Lakeshore Nursing Home, Rochester, 1972—; bd. dirs. HSBO, Blue Cross/Blue Shield Rochester, Living Ctrs. of Am., Excellus, Inc., Stong Meml. Hosp.; organizer, adminstrv. dir. hdqrs. Rohm Svcs. Corp., Rochester, 1964—; organizer, pres. hdqrs. Vari-Care Inc., Rochester, 1969-93; commr. N.Y. State Ins. Fund; mem. Cornell U. Hotel Sch. Adv. Coun. Mem. bd. trustees St. John Fisher Coll., 1983-98, trustee emeritus; bd. trustees Eastman Dental Ctr.; pres. Hurlbut Trust, 1994; mem. bd. govs. Strong Meml. Hosp., 1992-97. Fellow Am. Coll. Health Care Adminstrs.; mem. Greater Met. C. of C. (past chmn. bd. dirs.), Genesee Valley Club, Oak Hill Club, Cornell Club, Lambda Chi Alpha. Home: 200 Sheldon Rd Honeoye Falls NY 14472-9316 Office: Hurlbut Trust 740 East Ave Rochester NY 14607-2107

HURLE, DONALD THOMAS JAMES, physicist, researcher; b. Shepton Mallet, Eng., Mar. 31, 1935; s. Leslie Harry and Eleanor Ruth (Huntley) H.; m. Pamela Moreen Wilson, Aug. 1, 1961; children: Katherine Ruth, Clare Elizabeth. BSc in Physics, U. Southampton, Eng., 1956, PhD in Physics, 1960, DSc in Physics, 1972. Chartered physicist. Jr. rsch. fellow Royal Signals and Radar Establishment, Malvern, Eng., 1959-62, sr. sci. officer, 1962-65, prin. sci. officer, 1965-72; sr. prin. sci. officer Royal Signals and Radar Establishment, Malvern, 1972-85, dep. chief sci. officer, 1985-91; vis. indsl. prof. U. Bristol, Eng., 1987—; chmn. European Space Agy. Phys. Sci. Working Group, 1997—. Author: Crystal Pulling from the Melt, 1993; author, editor: (multi-vol.) Handbook of Crystal Growth, 1993-95; editor: Jour. Crystal Growth, 1980—; mem. hon. bd. Microgravity Quar., 1990—; contbr. articles to profl. jours.; patentee in field. Recipient Gustave Trasenster medal U. Liege, Belgium, 1986, Internat. Crystal Growth award Am. Assn. Crystal Growth, 1987. Fellow Inst. Physics, Brit. Assn. Crystal Growth (chmn. 1991-94, pres. 1997—). Achievements include pioneering work in discovering role of convection in crystal growth, dynamics and control of crystal pulling, thermodynamics of point defects in III-V compounds. Home: Scotscraig House Storridge, Malvern Worcs WR13 5EY, England

HURLEY, DEAN C., bank executive, lawyer; b. South Weymouth, Mass., Oct. 16, 1954; s. Dean C. and Neva (Richards) H.; m. Laura Ann Beck, Apr. 5, 1997; 1 child, Mackenzie Katherine. BS, Fairleigh Dickinson U., 1976, MBA, 1978; JD, N.Y. Law Sch., 1985. Bar: N.J. 1985, D.C. 1986. Asst. ops. mgr. Fieldcrest Mills, Inc., N.Y.C., 1976-77; spl. projects mgr. Citicorp Credit Svcs. Inc., N.Y.C., 1978-86; v.p., dir. fin. planning First Jersey Nat. Corp., Jersey City, 1986-88; v.p. asset strategies A/L. Mgmt. Dae Ichi Kangyo Bank div. The CIT Group, 1988-95; v.p. portfolio sales group Meenan, McDevitt & Co., Inc., 1996-98; v.p. DECC comml. mortgage acquisitions group Société Générale, N.Y.C., 1998—. Mem. Christian Ctr.; trustee, recording sec. Livingston Symphony Orch., 1993-97. Mem. Phi Delta Phi, Omicron Delta Epsilon. Republican. Avocation: piloting pvt. aircraft. Home: 23 Cider Mill Ln Port Murray NJ 07865-3202 Office: Société Générale 1221 Avenue Of The Americas New York NY 10020-1001

HURLEY, FRANCIS T., archbishop; b. San Francisco, Jan. 12, 1927. Ed., St. Patrick Sem., Menlo Park, Calif., Catholic U. Am. Ordained priest Roman Cath. Ch., 1951; with Nat. Cath. Welfare Conf., Washington, asst. sec., 1958-68; assoc. sec. Nat. Cath. Welfare Conf., now U.S. Cath. Conf., 1968-70; consecrated bishop, 1970; titular bishop Daimlaig and aux. bishop Diocese of Juneau, Alaska, 1970-71; bishop of Juneau, 1971-76, archbishop of Anchorage, 1976—. Office: Archdiocese Anchorage 225 Cordova St Anchorage AK 99501-2409

HURLEY, JEFFREY SCOTT, fabric company administrator; b. Pitts., Feb. 19, 1963; s. William Stephen and Mary Agnes (Wholey) H. BS in Chemistry, Gannon U., Erie, Pa., 1985; MS in Chemistry, Ga. Inst. Tech., Atlanta, 1990, PhD in Chemistry, 1992. Sr. rsch. chemist Hoechst Celanese Corp, Charlotte, N.C., 1992-95, bicomponent staple product devel. mgr., 1995-96, applications and devel. mgr. specialty staple products, 1996-97, mgr. bus. analysis and tech. assessment, 1997-98; mgr. absorbent products Buckeye Techs., Memphis, 1998—; cons., Atlanta, 1989-92; mem. adv. bd. Nonwovens Coop. Rsch. Ctr., 1997—; mem. tech. adv. bd. Assn. Nonwovens Fabvric Industry, 1997—. Author: Emerging Technologies in Hazardous Waste Management IV, 1994; contbr.: Phase Transfer Catalysis, 1994. Mem. Am. Chem. Soc. (organic, polymer material sci. and engring. and polymer divsn., Carolina Piedmont sect.). Achievements include development and support of a chemical mechanism modeling the generation of gaseous byproducts during the thermal decomposition of radioactive waste slurries stored at the Hanford (Wash.) Reservation, a new mechanism and kinetics concerning hydroxide promoted liquid-liquid phase transfer catalysis of simple organic reactions which contracts the current interfacial and extraction mechanisms; research and development of novel monomers and polymers from lab through production scale and investigation of novel polymerization techniques and polymerization process design and application. Office: Buckeye Techs PO Box 80407 Memphis TN 38108-0407

HURLEY, SUSAN LYNN, philosopher, educator; b. N.Y.C., Sept. 16, 1954; d. Roy Thomas and Esther (Sarchian) H. AB summa cum laude, Princeton U., 1976; B Philosophy with distinction, Oxford U., Eng., 1979, MA, 1981, PhD, 1983; JD cum laude, Harvard U., 1988. Jr. research fellow All Souls Coll., Oxford, Eng., 1981-84; Brockhues fellow, lectr. philosophy St. Edmund Hall Oxford U., 1985—; prof. polit. and ethical theory U. Warwick (Eng.), 1998—; vis. prof. law U. Calif. Berkeley, 1984; Meyer vis. prof. program law, philosopy, social theory NYU, 1987; vis. lectr. Harvard U. Law Sch., Cambridge, Mass., 1987; vis. fellow in Coun. of the Humanities, Princeton, N.J., 1988; fellow All Souls Coll., Oxford, England, 2000; sr. rsch. reader British Acad., 1990-92. Author: Natural Reasons: Personality and Polity, 1989, Consciousness in Action, 1998; co-editor: Foundations of Decision Theory, 1991, On Human Rights, 1993; contbr. articles on philosophy and law to profl. jours. Grad. scholar St. Catherine's Coll., Oxford, 1977-80; Nuffield Found. Social Sci. Rsch. fellow 1997-98. Mem. Anmesty Internat. Avocation: photography. Home and Office: U Warwick, PAIS, Coventry CV4 7AL, England

HURLIMANN, WERNER STEFAN, actuary; b. Balsthal, Switzerland, Feb. 23, 1953; s. Max Hans Hurlimann and Elise Hurlimann-Muller; m. Veronika Maria Zimmerli, Nov. 15, 1980; children: Isabelle, Corinne, Eliane. Diploma in math., ETH Zurich, Switzerland, 1977, DSc in Math., 1980. Asst. in math. ETH Zurich, 1977-81, postdoctoral fellow, 1983; postdoctoral fellow Yale U., New Haven, 1981-82, Max Planck Inst., Bonn, Germany, 1982-83; actuary Winterthur-Leben (Switzerland), 1984-88, 89—; vis. assoc. prof. actuarial sci. U. Toronto, Ont., Can., 1988-89. Contbr. articles to profl. publs. Recipient 1st prize Gunnar Benklander ASTIN Competition, 2000. Mem. AAAS, Am. Math. Soc., N.Y. Acad. Scis., Internat. Actuarial Assn. (sects. ASTIN, AFIR), French Math. Soc., Swiss Math. Soc., Swiss Assn. Actuaries, Assn. for Math., Econs. and Ops. Rsch., Soc. for Indsl. and Applied Math. Avocations: tennis, skiing, swimming, music, philately. Home: Schönholzweg 24, CH-8409 Winterthur Switzerland Office: Winterthur-Versicherungen, Paulstr 9 Value & Rish Mgmt, CH-8401 Winterthur Switzerland

HURLOCK, JAMES BICKFORD, lawyer; b. Chgo., Aug. 7, 1933; s. James Bickford and Elizabeth (Charls) H.; m. Margaret Lyn Holding, July 1, 1961; children: James Bickford III, Burton Charls, Matthew Hunter. AB, Princeton U., 1955; BA, Oxford U., 1957, MA, 1960; JD, Harvard U., 1959. Bar: N.Y. 1960, U.S. Supreme Ct. 1967. Assoc. White & Case, N.Y.C., 1959-66, ptnr., 1967—; dir. Orient Express Hotels, Ltd. Trustee N.Y. Presbyn. Hosp., Parker Sch. Fgn. and Comparative Law, Internat. Devel. Law Inst., Mystic Seaport Mus., Woods Hole Oceanog. Inst. Rhodes scholar, 1955. Mem. ABA, N.Y. State Bar Assn., Am. Law Inst., Am. Assn. Internat. Law. Republican. Episcopalian. Clubs: Links, River, N.Y. Yacht. Home: 46 Byram Dr Greenwich CT 06830-7008 Office: White & Case Bldg Ll 1155 Avenue Of The Americas New York NY 10036-2787

HURLOCK, JAMES BICKFORD, III, marketing executive; b. N.Y.C., May 3, 1962; s. James Bickford Jr. and Lynn (Holding) H.; m. Kathryn Buck, May 16, 1992; children: James Ross-Lewin, Warren Bickford. BA, Duke U., 1984; MBA, Columbia U., 1992. News reporter Pine Bluff (Ark.) Comml., 1984-85, Bus. Week Mag., Dallas, 1985-87, Cable News Network, N.Y.C., 1987-88; prodr. Blackwell Corp., Washington, 1988-90; mktg. exec. Home Box Office, N.Y.C., 1992-96; sales and mktg. Metro Goldwyn Mayer, Sydney, Australia, 1996-98, Paramount Pictures, Sydney, 1998—.

HURN, DAVID, photographer, lecturer; b. Redhill, Surrey, Eng., July 21, 1934; s. Stanley and Joan (Maynard) H.; m. Alita Naughton, 1964 (div. 1971); 1 child, Sian. Student, Royal Mil. Acad., Sandhurst, U.K., 1952-54. Asst. photographer Reflex Agy., London, 1955-57; free-lance photographer London, 1957-70, Tintern Gwent, Wales, 1971—; mem. Magnum Photos Coop. Agy., N.Y.C., Paris, London, 1967—; editorial adviser Album Photog. Mag., London, 1971; mem. Photography com. Art Coun. Great Britain, 1972-77; mem. art panel, 1975-77; head Sch. Documentary Photography, Gwent Coll. Higher Edn., 1973-90; com. mem. Coun. for Nat. Acad. Awards, 1978-87; Disting. vis. artist and adj. prof. Ariz. State U., Tempe, 1979-80; hon. fellow U. Wales, 1997. One-man shows include Biblioteque Nat., Paris, 1971, Photographers Gallery, London, 1974, Rencontres Internat. de Photographie, Arles, France, 1976, Northlight Gallery, Tempe, Ariz., 1978, U. N.Mex., Albuquerque, 1979, Imperial War Mus. Arts, 1987, Fifth Ave. Gallery, Scottsdale, Ariz., 1980; Sterling Coll. Art, Kans., 1980; Contrasts Gallery, London, 1982; Olympus Gallery, London, 1982; Malmö Mus. (Sweden), 1982; Palais des Congres, Lorient, France, 1982; Olympus Gallery, Tokyo, 1983; Palais des Beaux Arts, Charlerois, Belgium, 1983; Photogallery, Cardiff, 1984; Nat. Mus. Photography, Bradford, 1985; Axiom Gallery, Cheltenham, 1986, Stills Gallery, Edinburgh, 1986, Newport Mus., Wales, 1994, Nat. Mus. Wales, Cardiff, 2000; group shows include Personal Views 1850-1970, on tour U.K. and Europe, 1972, Images des Hommes, on tour Europe, 1978, Phoenix Art Mus., 1980, Photographers Gallery, London, 1983, Centre Nat. de La Photographie, Paris, 1985, Stills Gallery, Edinburgh, Photographic Art, Britian, 1945-89, Barbican, London, 1989, In Our Time, ICP, N.Y., 1989; represented in permanent collections Welsh Arts Coun., Cardiff; Contemporary Arts Soc. for Wales, Cardiff, Arts Coun. Great Britain, London; Brit. Coun., London; Bibliotheque Nationale, Paris; FNAC, Paris; Musé e du Chateau d'Eau, Tolouse, France; Internat. Ctr. Photography, N.Y.C.; George Eastman House, Rochester, N.Y.; Nat. Mus. Wales, Cardiff; Ctr. for Creative Photography, U. Ariz., Tucson; U. N.Mex. Art Mus., Albuquerque; San Francisco Mus. Modern Art; Calif. Mus. Photography, U. Calif.; Internat. Mus. Photography, George Eastman House, Rochester; Mus. Modern Art, N.Y.C., also pvt. collections; author: David Hurn: Photographs 1956-1976, 1979, On Being a Photographer, 1997, On Looking at Photographs, 2000, Land of My Father, 2000; contbr. articles to profl. publs. Recipient award for outstanding merit in living artist Welsh Arts Coun., 1971, award for social photography Kodak Social Photog. Bursary, 1971, Imperial War Mus. Arts award, 1987-88; U.K./U.S.A. Bicentennial fellow, 1979-80, Bradford fellow, 1993-94, Arts Coun. Wales Bursary, 1995.

HURN, F. ROGER, import/export company executive; b. June 9, 1938; s. Francis James and Joyce Elsa (Bennett) H.; m. Rosalind Jackson, 1980; 1 child. Degree, Marlborough Coll. Joined Smith Industries, 1958, export dir. motor accessory divsn., 1969, mng. dir. internat. ops., 1974, CEO,, 1981-96, chmn., 1991—, also bd. dirs.; chmn. Marconi plc; dep. chmn. Glaxo Wellcome plc; non-exec. dir. Ocean Transport & Trading, 1982-88, Pilkington, 1984-94, S.G. Warburg Group, 1987-95; liveryman Coachmakers and Coach Harness Makers' Co., 1979—. Gov. Henley Coll., 1986—. Decorated Knight, 1996. Mem. ICI. Office: Marconi Plc, One Bruton St, London W1X 8AQ, England*

HURNYAK, CHRISTINA KAISER, lawyer; b. Noblesville, Ind., Dec. 22, 1949; d. Albert Michael and Lois Angie (Gatton) Kaiser; m. Cyril Hurnyak, June 24, 1972. BA cum laude, Wittenberg U., 1972; JD, SUNY-Buffalo, 1979. Bar: N.Y. 1980, Pa. 1996, U.S. Dist. Ct. (we. dist.) Pa. 1998. Mem. support staff McKinsey & Co., Inc., mgmt. cons., Chgo., 1972-75; law clk. Justice Norman J. Wolf, N.Y. Supreme Ct., Buffalo, 1980-81; assoc. Dempsey & Dempsey, Buffalo, 1979-80, 81-90, Grossman, Levine & Civiletto, Niagara Falls, N.Y., 1990-95, The Tarasi Law Firm, Pitts., 1998—. Mem. ABA, ATLA, N.Y. State Bar Assn., Allegheny County Bar Assn., Pa. State Bar Assn., Pa. Trial Lawyers Assn. Democrat. Lutheran. Office: Tarasi Law Firm 510 3rd Ave Pittsburgh PA 15219-2107

HUROWITZ, VICTOR-AVIGDOR BENEDICT, Biblical and Ancient Near Eastern studies educator; b. Phila., Apr. 19, 1948; s. Bertram and Sadie (Shapiro) H.; m. Ann Fredda Roshwalb, Aug. 23, 1976; 1 child, Daniel Moshe. Student, Gratz Coll., Phila., 1965-69; BA, Temple U., 1969; MA, Hebrew U., Jerusalem, 1975, PhD, 1984. Instr. Hebrew Hebrew Union Coll., Jerusalem, Israel, 1977-79, instr. Assyriology, 1978-91; adj. lectr. Bible Ben Gurion U., Beer Sheba, Israel, 1978-86, lectr. Bible, 1986-91, sr. lectr. Bible, 1991-94, prof. Bible, 1994—. Author: I Have Built You An Exalted House, Temple Building in the Bible in Light of Mesopotamian and North West Semitic Writings, 1992, Inu Anum Sirum, 1994, Divine Service and Its Rewards, 1997; co-editor: Studies in Honor of Menahem Haran, 1996; contbr. articles to profl. jours. Recipient Most Significant Article in Bible award Bibl. Archaeology Soc., 1986, Most Significant Pub. in Bible, Hebrew U., 1990. Mem. Am. Oriental Soc., Assn. Jewish Studies. Jewish. Office: Ben Gurion Univ, Dept of Bible and ANE, Beer-Sheva Israel

HURST, CHARLES WILSON, lawyer; b. Salt Lake City, July 4, 1957; s. John Vann and Myra (Kasik) Piscane; m. Karen Buck, Jan. 5, 1985; children: Jeanette Q., Daniel C., Brian K., Matthew C., Robert W. Student, U. Chgo., 1975-77; BA cum laude, Wesleyan U., Conn., 1979; JD, Duke U., 1983. Bar: Pa. 1983, U.S. Dist. Ct. (ea. dist.) Pa. 1985, Calif. 1986, U.S. Dist. Ct. (cen. dist.) Calif. 1990. Assoc. Saul, Ewing, Remick & Saul, Phila., 1983-85; assoc. Wyman Bautzer Kuchel & Silbert, Orange County, Calif., 1985-89, ptnr., 1990; ptnr. Snell & Wilmer LLP, Orange County, 1990—. Dir. Pacific Art Found., 1994-2000; trustee Pegasus Sch., 1996—. Mem. ABA (comml. leasing com. of real property, probate and trust law sect.), Orange County Bar Assn. Office: Snell & Wilmer 1920 Main St Ste 1200 Irvine CA 92614-7230

HURST, LIONEL ALEXANDER, Antigua and Barbuda diplomat, lawyer; b. St. John's, Antigua and Barbuda, Dec. 4, 1950; s. Lionel Alexander and Agnes Hurst; m. Constance Beamon, Mar. 31, 1973 (div.); 1 child, Amira. BA, CUNY, 1980; MBA, L.I. U., 1982; JD, NYU, 1985. Amb. Antigua and Barbuda to U.S. and UN, Antigua and Barbuda Embassy, Washington. Office: Antigua and Barbuda Embassy 3216 New Mexico Ave NW Washington DC 20016-2745*

HURST, PATRICIA ANN, professional golfer; b. San Leandro, Calif., May 23, 1969. Student, San Jose U. Tchg. pro golfer La Quinta Country Club; golfer Players West mini-tour, winner 5 titles; winner USGA Jr., 1986, USGA Amateur, 1990; mem. U.S. World Amateur team; winner Oldsmobile Classic, 1997, Nabisco Dinah Shore, 1998, Electrolux USA, 2000. Office: care LPGA 100 International Golf Dr Daytona Beach FL 32124-1082

HURTADO, LARRRY WEIR, religious studies educator; b. Kansas City, Mo., Dec. 29, 1943; s. Weir Frank and Bonnie Jean (Burton) H.; m. Linda Ruth Bellah (div. 1975); 1 child, Tiffany; m. Shannon Lynne Hunter; children: Elisse, Jesse. BA, Ctrl. Bible Coll., Springfield, Mo., 1965; MA, Trinity Evang. Div. Sch., Deerfield, Ill., 1967; PhD, Case Western Res. U., 1973. Pastor North Shore Assembly of God, Skokie, Ill., 1971-75; asst. prof. N.T. Regent Coll., Vancouver, B.C., Can., 1975-78; prof. religion U. Man., Winnipeg, 1978-96; prof. N.T. lang., lit. and theology U. Edinburgh, Scotland, 1996—. Author: One God, One Lord: Early Christian Devotion and Ancient Jewish Momotheism, 1988, Text-Critical Methodology and the Pre-Caesarean Text, 1981, Mark: New International Bible, 1989, At the Origins of Christian Worship, 1999. Recipient Rh award for Outstanding Contbn. to rsch. in Humanities, U. Man., 1985; Soc. Scis. and Humanities Rsch. Coun. of Can. rsch. grantee, 1991-94, 95-97. Mem. Soc. for N.T. Studies, Soc. of Bibl. Lit. Office: Univ of Edinburgh New Coll, Mound Pl, Edinburgh EH1 2LX, Scotland

HURTIG, CHRISTIANE, political scientist, researcher, educator; b. Paris, Feb. 17, 1939; d. Alfred and Georgette (Moreau) Tirimagni; m. Serge Hurtig, July 8, 1965; 1 child, Marie-Odile. Lic. in Law, U. Paris, 1963; diploma, Inst. d'Etudes Politiques, Paris, 1964, PhD, 1985. Asst. Ministry of Agr., Paris, 1963-65; rschr. Immobiliere Constrn. Paris, 1966-67; rschr. Nat. Ctr. Sci. Rsch., Paris, 1973-79, sr. rschr., 1979—; prof. Inst. d'Etudes Politiques, 1991—. Author: From the SFIO to the New Socialist Party, 1970, Maharajahs and Politics in Contemporary India, 1988. E-mail: christiane.hurtig@ceri.sciences-po.org. Home: 86 Rue de la Federation, 75015 Paris France Office: Ctr d'Etudes/Recherches Int, FNSP, 56 rue Jacob, 75007 Paris France

HURTIG, SERGE, political scientist, educator, administrator; b. Bucharest, Romania, Apr. 16, 1927; s. Alexander and Anna (Stern) H.; m. Christiane Tirimagni, July 8, 1965; 1 dau., Marie-Odile. Student, Sch. Fgn. Svc., Georgetown U., 1946-48, Inst. Polit. Studies, U. Paris, 1948-50. Mem. Documentation Svcs. Fondation Nationale des Scis. Politiques, Paris, 1951, assoc. dir., 1957-69, tech. adviser, 1969-71, sec. gen., 1971-91, sci. dir., 1991-95, dir. studies and rsch. grad. program polit. sci.; lectr. Paris Inst. Polit. Studies, 1952—, prof., 1960-95. Editor Internat. Polit. Sci. Abstracts, 1963—; mem. bur. Internat. Com. for Social Scis. Info. and Documentation, 1989-95, chmn., 1993-95; contbr. articles on U.S., French and European politics to profl. jours. Bd. dirs. Fondation Franco-Américaine, 1976—, v.p., 1982—; bd. dirs. Fondation Nat. des Scis. Politiques, 1996—; exec. com. European Consortium for Polit. Rsch., 1970-76. Recipient Légion d'Honneur, Ordre Nat. du Mérite. Mem. Internat. Polit. Sci. Assn. (sec. gen. 1961-67, v.p. 1979-85), French Polit. Sci. Assn. (mem. coun. 1971-98), Am. Polit. Sci. Assn. Home: 86 rue de la Fédération, 75015 Paris France Office: 27 rue Saint-Guillaume, 75007 Paris France

HURWIC, JOZEF, physical chemist; b. Warsaw, Poland, May 23, 1911; arrived in France, 1969; s. Wolf and Zofia (Merecka) H.; m. Maria Janina Nowakowska, Apr. 7, 1952; children: Anna, Aleksander Wiktor. MS in Chem. Engring., Warsaw Inst. Tech., 1939, PhD, 1951. Prof. phys. chemistry Warsaw Inst. Tech., 1951-61, prof. physics, 1961-68, dean faculty chemistry, 1962-68; prof. phys. chemistry U. de Provence, Marseille, France, 1969-79. Author: Budowa materii, 1964, Tworcy nauki o promieniotworczosci, 1989, La Radioactivité, 1991, Kazimierz Fajans, 1991, Maria Sklodowska-Curie i promiemiotworczosc, 1993, Wspomnienia i refleksje, 1996; editor: Problemy jour., 1948-69; contbr. articles to sci. jours. Recipient Gold Cross Merit, Poland, 1953; named Comdr. of Polonia Restituta, 1966. Mem. Polish Chem. Soc. (hon. mem., pres. 1964-67), Polish Soc. Arts and Scis. Abroad, European Acad. Arts and Humanities (corr. mem.), Acad. Sci. Belles-Lettres d'Aix (corr. mem.). Achievements include dielectric and spectroscopic investigations on organic molecules structure. Home: 1 rue Désirée-Clary, 13003 Marseille France Office: 3 Pl Victor-Hugo, 13331 Marseille Cedex 03, France

HUSA, KAREL, composer, conductor, educator; b. Prague, Czechoslovakia, Aug. 7, 1921; came to U.S., 1954, naturalized, 1959; s. Karel and Bozena (Dongresova) H.; m. Simone Perault, Feb. 2, 1952; children: Catherine, Anne-Marie, Elizabeth, Caroline. M summa cum laude, Conservatory and Acad. Music, Prague, 1945, 47; grad., Conservatoire de Paris, France, 1948; license for conducting, Ecole Normale de Paris, 1947; MusD (hon.), Coe Coll., 1976, Cleve. Inst., 1985, Ithaca Coll., 1986, Baldwin-Wallace Conservatory, 1991, Hartwick Coll., 1997, New Eng. Conservatory, 1998; DHL (hon.), Coll. St. Vincent, 1996; ArtsD (hon.), Masaryk U., Czech Republic, 2000. Guest condr. Czechoslovak Radio, Prague, 1945-46; guest condr. orchs. in Hamburg, Brussels, Paris, Zurich, Suisse Romande, London, Manchester, Prague, Stockholm, Hong Kong; guest condr. orchs. in Singapore, Japan; guest condr. orchs. in Cin., Buffalo, N.Y.C., Boston, Rochester, N.Y., Balt., San Diego, Syracuse, N.Y.; faculty Cornell U., Ithaca, N.Y., 1954—; prof. music Cornell U. 1954—, dir. univ. symphony and chamber orchs., 1972-92, Kappa Alpha prof. music emeritus. Composer: Symphony, 1953, Fantasies for Orchestra, 1957, Divertimento for Brass, 1959, Poem for Viola and Orchestra, 1959, Elegy and Rondeau for Saxophone and Orchestra, 1961, Divertimento for String Orchestra, 1948, String Quartet No. 2, 1952, Portrait for String Orch., 1953, Mosaiques for Orchestra, 1961, Fresque for Orchestra, rev, 1964, Sonatina for Piano, 1943, Sonatina Violin and Piano, 1945, Sonata for Piano, 1949, Evocations of Slovakia for Clarinet, Viola and Cello, 1951, Eight Duets for Piano, 1955, Twelve Moravian Songs, 1956, Poem for Viola and Orchestra, 1962, Serenade for Woodwind Quintet and Orchestra, 1963, Concerto for Brass Quintet and Orch., 1965, Two Preludes; flute, clarinet, bassoon, 1966, Music for Percussion, 1966, Concerto for alto saxophone, concert band, 1967, String Quartet No. 3, 1968 (Pulitzer prize 1969), Music for Prague; for Band, 1968, for Orch., 1969, Apotheosis of this Earth for Winds, 1970, Concerto for Percussion and Winds, 1971, Two Sonnets from Michelangelo for Orch, 1971, Concerto for Trumpet and Wind Orch., 1973, Apotheosis of this Earth for Chorus and Orch, 1973, Sonata for Violin and Piano, 1972-73, The Steadfast Tin Soldier; for narrator and orch., 1974, Sonata for Piano, No. 2, 1975, Monodrama, ballet for orch, 1975, An American Te Deum; for mixed chorus, baritone solo, band and organ, 1976, for orch., 1978, Landscapes for Brass Quintet, 1977, Fanfare for Brass Ensemble, 1980, Pastoral for Strings,

1980, Three Moravian Songs, 1981, The Trojan Women, ballet for orch., 1981, Sonata a Tre, 1982, Concerto for Wind Ensemble, 1982 (Sudler award 1983), Cantata, 1983, Smetana Fanfare for Wind Ensemble, 1984, Variations for Violin, Viola, Cello and Piano, 1984, Symphonic Suite for Orch., 1984, Intrada for Brass Quintet, 1984, Concerto for Orchestra, 1986, Concerto for Organ and Orch., 1987, Frammenti for Organ solo, 1987, Concerto for Trumpet and Orch., 1987, Concerto for Violoncello and Orch., 1988 (Grawemeyer award 1993), String Quartet No. 4, 1990, Youth Overture, 1991, Cayuga Lake (Memories), 1992, Concerto for Violin and Orch., 1993, Five Poems for Wood-Wind Quintet, 1994, Les Couleurs Fauves, 1995, Midwest Celebration Fanfare, 1996, Celebration for Orchestra, 1997, Post-card from Home, 1997, others; commns. from, UNESCO, Koussevitsky Found., Nat. Endowment for Arts, Friends of Music at Cornell, Fine Arts Found. Chgo., Ithaca Coll., U. Ga., Chgo. Symphony Orchestra, Butler U., Washington Music Soc., Coe Coll., N.Y. Philharmonic, U. So. Calif., Kerze Found., also others.; editor: French Baroque Music: Reconstructions of Old French Baroque works by Lully and Delalande, 1961-68. Recipient prize Prague Acad. Arts, 1948, French Govt. award, 1946-47, L. Boulanger award, 1952, Pulitzer prize in music, 1969, Acad. Inst. Arts and Letters award, 1989, Grawemeyer award U. Louisville, 1993, Serge Koussevitzky Music Found. award, 1993, Czech Republic's medal of merit of 1st degree Pres. V. Havel, 1995, medal of Honor, City of Prague, 1998; Guggenheim fellow, 1964-65. Mem. Internat. Inst. Arts and Letters (life), Am. Acad. Arts and Letters, Belgian Royal Acad. Arts and Scis., Am. Music Ctr., Am. Acad. Arts and Letters, Internat. Soc. Contemporary Music, French Soc. Composers, Am. Fedn. Musicians, Kappa Gamma Psi (hon.), Kappa Kappa Psi (hon.), Delta Omicron (hon.), Phi Mu Alpha (hon.). Avocations: painting, sports. Home: 4535 S Atlantic Ave Apt 2106 Daytona Beach FL 32127-7047 Office: Cornell U Dept Music Ithaca NY 14853

HUSAIN, AJMAL, marketing consultant; b. Hyderabad, Sindh, Pakistan, May 9, 1971; s. Tajamal and Qamar Husain. BSc in Math. and Stats., U. Sindh-Jamishoro, Hyderabad, 1991, MBA, 1996. Sales and mktg. exec. Raazio Internat., Karachi, Pakistan, 1997-98, 2000—; bus. scis. faculty mem. Preston U., Hyderabad, 1999, Coll. Modern Scis., Hyderabad, 1999-2000; cons. Mktg. Decision Servers, Hyderabad, 1999—. Recipient Cert. of Appreciation, Marie Adelaide Leprosy Ctr., Pakistan, 1982, best cadet merit Nat. Cadet Corps, Pakistan, 1988. Mem. Mktg. Rsch. Soc. Pakistan, Pakistan Soc. Devel. Economists, Inst. Mktg. Mgmt. Pakistan (assoc.). Avocations: reading books, music, watching television, net surfing. E-mail: ajmal71@hotmail.com. Ajmal71@hyd.joaknet.com.ok. Home: B #10 Sindh U, Hyderabad 71000, Pakistan

HUSAIN, MOHAMMED HAMID, physician; b. Hyderabad, India, Oct. 10, 1940; arrived in United Kingdom, 1962; s. Mohammed Yousuf and Begum Asmat Unnisa (Jung) H.; m. Judith Margaret Houghton, June 27, 1969; children: Asif, Robina. B in medicine, B in surgery, Osmania, Hyderabad, 1962; MRCP, Royal Coll. Physicians, Glasgow, 1967; AOFM, Royal Coll. Physicians, London, 1980; MRCGP, Royal Coll. Gen. Practitioners, London, 1993; FRCP, Royal Coll. Physicians, Glasgow, 1982. House physician Glasgow Royal Infirmary, 1962-63, sr. house physician, 1963-64, dermatology registrar, 1964-66; medical registrar Rotherham, England, 1966-69, gen. medical practitioner, 1969—, occupational cons., 1974-2000; chmn. orgn. com. BMA, 1984-88, chmn. Trent regional coun., 1984-88; mem. Gen. Med. Svcs. Com., U.K., 1977-90; adviser and external assessor to Health Svc. Commr., England; mem. panel of apptd. persons, NHS Tribunals. Author: Practice Organization, 1981; contbr. articles to profl. jours. Pioneer and coordinator Multiple Sclerosis Rsch. Ctr. Appeal, 1990-92; founder and v.p. Rotherham Multiple Sclerosis Soc., 1992; organizer Help the Handicapped Campaign, Rotherham, 1975-77; vice chmn. Cmty. Rels. Coun., Rotherham, 1972-75; mem. Rotherhas Health Authority, 1982-90; mem. coun. British Medical Assn., 1980-88. Recipient OBE award Officer of the Most Excellent Order of the British Empire Her Majesty the Queen, 1995, Freeman of the City of London award, 1989; named Rotherham Citizen of Yr., 1992, Liveryman of the Soc. Apothecaries, 1993, Paul Harris fellow Rotary Internat., 1995, Freeman of the Met. Bourough of Rotherham, 1997. Mem. Medical Adv. Com., Home Office Tribunal for Misuse of Drugs, Rotherham Rotary Club (past pres.). Avocations: playing chess, watching cricket, listening to Schubert and reading political biographies, appreciation of classical art. Home: Barbot Hall Carr Hill, S61 4QL Rotherham England Office: Greasbrough Medical Cen, Munsbrough Rise, S614RB Rotherham England

HUSAIN, RAHAT, electrical engineer, researcher; b. North Lakhimpur, India, Jan. 22, 1959; s. Fasahat and Afsar (Bano) H.; m. Fareha Islam, Aug. 30, 1985; children: Aisha, Dawoud, Ishaaq. BSc in Engring., Aligarh Muslim U., India, 1980; MSc in Engring., King Fahd U. Petroleum & Minerals, Saudi Arabia, 1984. From rsch. asst. to engr. King Fahd U. Petroleum and Minerals, Dhahran, Saudi Arabia, 1981—; cons. in setting up an internal calibration facility for a specific bus., writing equipment calibration procedures, establishing quality assurance programs, conducting measurement surveys. Contbr. articles to profl. jours. Avocations: gardening, table tennis, reading. Home: New Kothi Near Kashana Nisar, Diggi Rd Civil Lines, 202002 Aligarh India Office: King Fahd U Petroleum & Minerals, KFUPM Box 527, 31261 Dhahran Saudi Arabia

HUSAIN, TANVEER, respiratory physiologist; b. Hardoi, India, Dec. 25, 1959; s.Tabshir Husain and Nayeema Begum H.; m. Shaheen Rizvi, Dec. 13, 1995; 1 child, Tanya. BS, U. Lucknow, 1982; MS, Inst. Ecology/Environ., New Delhi, 1996. Rsch. asst. Indsl. Toxicology Rsch. Ctr., Lucknow, 1984-91; respiratory physiologist Sanjay Gandhi Post Grad. Inst. Med. Scis., Lucknow, 1991—. Author: Environmental Issues, 1996; contbr. over 100 articles to profl. jours. Recipient Best Paper award Internat. Soc. Environ. Epidemiology Conf., Boston, 1998. Avocations: music, cricket, travel, pen friendship. E-mail: tanv99@yahoo.com. Office: Sanjay Gandhi Post Grad Inst Med Scis, Dept CVTS Rae Bareli Rd, Lucknow/Uttar Pradesh 226014, India

HUSAIN, TARIQ, plant pathologist, educator; b. Sitapur, India, Feb. 2, 1949; arrived in Pakistan, 1970; s. Akhlaq Husain and Zakira Khatoon; m. Farida Farooqi, Nov. 16, 1979; children: Nida Tariq Siddiqui, Shiza Tariq Siddiqui, Babar Tariq Siddiqui. BSc, U. Lucknow, India, 1968; MSc, U. Karachi, Pakistan, 1973. Rsch. asst. U. Karachi, 1974-76; lectr. edn. dept. Govt. Sindh, Pakistan, 1977-90; asst. prof. edn. dept. Govt. Sindh, 1991—. Contbr. articles to sci. jours. Avocations: keeping birds as pets, growing ornamental and rare plants, history. Home: H/12 Bhayani Heights, Abul Hasam Isphani Rd, Karachi Sindh, Pakistan Office: Adamjee Govt Sci Coll, Dept Botany, Karachi 74550 Sindh, Pakistan

HUSAR, ALEXANDRU MICIU, humanities educator, writer; b. Ilva Mare, Nasaud, Romania, Apr. 26, 1920; s. Coloman Andrew and Firoana (Miciu) H.; m. Margaret Costachi, Aug. 20, 1967. BA in Philosophy and Letters, U. Bucharest, Romania, 1945, PhD in Philosophy, 1973. Tchr. Romanian and philosophy George Cosbuc H.S., Năsăud, 1945-50; archives worker Cluj-Napoca (Romania) State Archives, 1950-51; prof. Babes Bolyai U., Cluj-Napoca, 1951-52, prof. history, 1952-59; prof. aesthetics and theory lit. U. Iasi, Romania, 1959-85; prof. emeritus Alexandru Ioan Cuza U., Iasi, 1996—; vis. prof. U. San Marcos, Lima, Peru, 1975-76; leader confs., Moscow, Leningrad Kiev, Stuttgart, Aachen, Cologne, 1964; pres. dept. history and theory of arts Iasi br. Romanian Acad., 1983; chair dept. world lit. Alexandru Ioan Cuza U., Iasi, 1970. Author: Beyond Ruins, 1959, The Return to Literature, 1970, Ars longa, Fundamentals of Arts, 1980, Metapoetics, Prolegomena, 1983, Sources of Arts, 1988, Irenikon, 1990, The European Idea, 1993, The Lessons of History, 1995, Anti-Gog, An Essay on the 20th Century,1997, O, tempora!, 1998, Miorita, Seatching through Memory, A Synthesis of Romanian Spirituality, 1999. Recipient Romanian Acad. award, 1985; DAAD Soc. scholar, Germany, 1970. Mem. Writers Union Romania (award 1995), Astra Soc. Romania (hon.), Soc. History and Philology (prs. Iasi br. 1964-70), Soc. Philology (pres. Iasi br. 1980-90), Internat. Gardening and Landscaping Acad. Rome. Home: et I, ap 6, Aleea Rozelor 9 Sc A, 6600 Iasi Romania

HUSAR, PETER, biomedical engineer, educator; b. Zilina, Slovakia, Sept. 18, 1956; s. Benadik and Stefania (Janikova) H.; children: Martin, Sylvia. Diploma in engring., Tech. U., Ilmenau, Germany, 1980, PhD, 1986. R&D engr. Electrotech. Rsch. Inst., Zilina, 1980-82; rschr. Rsch. Inst. for Computer Tech., Zilina, 1986-89; asst. prof. U. Slovakia, 1989-92; sr. rschr., R&D team leader Tech. U., Ilmenau, Germany, 1992—; scientist Siemens, 1987-88; R&D team leader U. Slovakia, 1989-92, Philips Comms. Industry, Nuernberg, 1989-90. Contbr. articles to profl. jours. including IEEE Trans. Biomed. Engring.; patentee in field. Recipient award European Union, 1992. Mem. IEEE (sr.), Internat. Soc. for Clin. Electrophysiology of Vision. Avocations: nature, skiing, reading, biking. Home: H Hertz-Str 60, PO Box 200130, D-98687 Ilmenau Germany Office: Tech U, G Kirchhoff-str 2, D-98684 Ilmenau Germany

HUSARIK, STEPHEN, music educator; b. Chgo., May 23, 1944; s. Stephen Husarik Sr. and Inez Medley. MusB with honors, U. Ill., 1970, MusM, 1972, postgrad., 1972-77; PhD, U. Iowa, 1983. Tchg. asst. U. Ill., Urbana, 1972-74; lectr. Sampson C.C., Clinton, N.C., 1976; tchg. asst. U. Iowa, Iowa City, 1977, 79; instr. Lewis U., Lockport, Ill., 1978, Trinity Coll., Palos Hills, Ill., 1980; instr. music and humanities Moraine Valley Coll., Palos Hills, Ill., 1984-89; head carillonneur Westark Coll., Ft. Smith, Ark., 1995—, instr. music and humanities, 1992—. Sr. editor Am. Keyboard Artists, 1987-92; co-author: A History of Westark Coll., 1999; editor Who's Who in the Humanities, 1990-92; contbr. numerous articles to Piano Quar., Am. Music, Clavier mag., Nat. Assn. Humanities Edn. Jour., Classical Mag.; rec. artist: (piano solos) Pictures at an Exhbn. by Mussorgsky, Scott Joplin and the Ragtime Classics. Field reader Council for Post-Secondary Edn., Washington, 1987. Recipient Nat. Edpress Assn. award, 1987, Master Tchr. award Whirlpool, 2000; grantee NEH, 1984, 89, 94, Ark. Humanities Coun., 1997. Mem. Am. Musicol. Soc., Am. Liszt Soc., Guild of Carillonneurs of N. Am., Coll. Music Soc., Nat. Assn. Humanities Edn. (newsletter editor 1993-94), Westark Coll. Faculty Senate (chair 1998), Westark Coll. Assn. (chair 1999). Office: Westark Coll Humanities Divsn Box 3649 Fort Smith AR 72913-3649

HUSBAND, WILLIAM SWIRE, computer industry executive; b. Hinsdale, Ill., Dec. 18, 1939; s. William Thompson and Arlene Martha (Frey) H.; m. Janet Goatley, Nov. 26, 1965; children: Scott, Andrea. BS, Iowa State U., 1962. Mktg. rep. IBM, San Francisco, 1966-70; dist. mktg. mgr. DPF, Des Plaines, Ill., 1971-78; v.p. Celtic Computer Investment Co., Palatine, Ill., 1978; pres. 20th Century Sys., Inc., Palatine, Ill., 1978-96; v.p. tech. AT&T Capital, Bloomfield Hills, Mich., 1996—, Newcourt Credit, 1998, CIT Group, 1999—; presenter symposium for U. Calif.-Berkeley Systems Technology Inst., Milan, 1987, 88, 89; speaker World Congress of Computing, Chgo., 1988. Author, pub.: Computer Acquisition and Disposition Planning, 7th edit., 1987; editor: COMPUTALK mag., 1987—, IBM Technology and Product Strategies in the 80's, 1986; contbg. editor: Computer Econs. mag., 1986—. Active Buehler YMCA, Palatine Boys' Baseball, 1978-85. Served to lt (j.g.) USN, 1962-66. Office: CIT Group 2285 Franklin Rd Fl 2 Bloomfield Hills MI 48302-0364

HUSBANDS, SIR CLIFFORD STRAUGHN, governor general of Barbados; b. Aug. 5, 1926; s. Adam Straughn and Ada Augusta (Griffith) H.; m. Ruby C.D. Parris, 1959; 3 children. Grad., Harrison Coll., Barbados; Middle Temple Inns of Ct., London. Bar: Middle Temple 1952. Pvt. practice Barbados, 1952-54, acting dep. registrar, 1954; legal asst. to atty. gen. Grenada, 1954-56, magistrate, 1956-57; magistrate Antigua, 1957-58; crown atty, magistrate and registrar Montserrat, 1958-60, acting crown atty, 1959; acting atty. gen. St. Kitts-Nevis-Anguilla, 1960; asst. to atty gen. Barbados, 1960-67, dir. pub. prosecutions, 1967-76; judge Supreme Court, Barbados, 1976-91; justice of appeal Barbados, 1991-96; gov. gen., 1996—; legal draughtsman, 1960-63; Queen's Counsel, Barbados, 1968. Avocations: music, swimming, photography, cricket. Office: Government House, Saint Michael Barbados

HUSEK, PETR IVAN, chemist, researcher; b. Brno, Moravia, Czechoslovakia, 1943; children: Miriam, Gabriela. MS, Inst. Chem. Tech., Prague, 1965; PhD, Charles U., Prague, 1979; DSc, U. Pardubice, Czech Republic, 1996. Rsch. chemist Inst. Endocrinology, Prague, 1966—. Contbr. chpt. to book, numerous articles to profl. jours. including Jour. Chromatography. Recipient award of Min. of Healthcare of the Czech Republic, 1995. Mem. Czech Chem. Soc. Roman Catholic. Avocations: politics, philosophy, theology, hiking. Office: Inst Endocrinology, Narodni Ave, 11694 Prague 1, Czech Republic

HUSEMANN, KURT, psychoanalyst; b. Herford, Germany, Apr. 24, 1947; s. Heinrich and Gertrud (Fleischer) H.; m. Evelyn Derenthal, June 7, 1996. Diploma in psychology, U. Cologne, Germany, 1972, D Natural Sci., 1975; grad. psychoanalyst and group analyst, German Acad. Psychoanalysis, Berlin, 1977. Clin. psychologist psychiat. day hosp., Cologne, 1972-75; pvt. practice, Duesseldorf, Germany, 1975—; lectr. psychosomatic medicine and psychoanalysis U. Herdecke, Germany, 1984-86; supr. mgrs., cons., coach various hosps., 1985—; supr. candidates, group tng. analyst Inst. for Group Analysis, Heidelberg, Germany. Contbr. articles on borderline patients group analysis, transcultural aspects of group analysis, psychotherapy with transsexual patients to nat. and internat. jours. Mem. Am. Group Psychotherapy Assn., Group Analytic Soc. (London), Internat. Assn. Group Psychotherapy, Internat. Coll. Psychosomatic Medicine, Cath. Acad. Circle Scientists Warsaw (hon.), German Work Group for Group Psychotherapy and Group Dynamics, German Assn. for Psychoanalysis, Psychotherapy, Psychosomatics and Deep Psychology, German Union Psychology, European Assn. for Transcultural Group Analysis (pres.), psychotherapeutic working grop for people who suffer from problems of the holocaust. E-mail: Hu.p-sy@t-online.de. Home and Office: Blücherstrasse 66, 40477 Düsseldorf Germany

HUSER, JOYCE MARIE, art educator; b. Wisconsin Rapids, Wis., Feb. 18, 1961; d. Charles augustine and Jane Elenor Huser; children: Peter, Colette, Joyce, Mark, David. BA, Cardinal Stritch Coll., 1988; grad. cert., U. Kans., 1996, MS, 1999. Cert. secondary edn., Wis. Tchr. Notre Dame H.S., Milw., 1989-90; mid. sch. tchr. Bruce Guadalupe Cmty. Sch., Milw., 1990-92; apprentice Smokey Vallery Pottery, Shawnee Mission, Kans., 1994-97; art instr. Lawrence (Kans.) Art Ctr., 1995-97; tech. trainer, rschr. U. Kans., Lawrence, 1997-99; elem. art tchr. Blue Valley Sch. Dist., Overland Park, Kans., 1996—. Exhibited in show at La Strada dell'Arte, 1998, 99. Sponsor Christian Found. for Children, Kansas City, Mo., 1993—. Grantee Kans. U. Alumni, 1995-97; recipient Tchr. Preparation cert. Pittsburg (Kans.) State U., 1997. Mem. Nat. Art Edn. Assn., U.S. Soc. for Edn. through Art, Nat. Assn. Multicultural Edn., Kans. Art Edn. Assn. (membership chair 1999—). Roman Catholic. Avocations: horseback riding, painting, ceramics, mountain biking, running. E-mail: johuser@hotmail.com. Office: Valley Park Elem Sch 12301 Lamar Ave Overland Park KS 66209-2702

HUSSAIN, AKMAL, economist, manufacturing executive, consultant; b. Lahore, Pakistan; s. Syed Alamdar H.; m. Rafia Hussain Sayed (dec. 1995); children: Syed Savail, Syed Jalal, Syed Abbas, Syed Amaan, Syed Akbar. BA in Econs., Philosophy, Punjab U., 1969; BA in Econs. with honors, U. Cambridge, 1972; PhD in Econs., Sussex U., Eng., 1980. Lectr., asst. prof. Punjab U., Lahore, Pakistan, 1973-76, 80-83; vis. prof. Pakistan Adminstrv. Staff Coll., Lahore, 1974—, Nat. Inst. Pub. Adminstrn., Lahore, 1974—, U. Calif., Riverside, 1983-84; cons. Internat. Labour Orgn./Asian Regional Team Employment Promo, Lahore, 1983-85, World Bank, 1993, 94; dir. Econ. Policy Research Unit, Lahore, 1983-85; chief exec. Sayyed Engrs. Ltd., Pakistan; country coord., assoc. project dir. Asian perspectives project UN U., South Asia, 1984-87; dir. Econ. Policy Rsch. Unit, Lahore, 1985—; cons. Swiss Devel. Corp.; mem. small farmers com. Nat. Commn. on Agr., Pakistan; mem. Prime Min.'s Consultative Com. on Econ. Policy, 1989-90; chmn. Prime Min.'s Task Force on Poverty Alleviation, 1997; mem. Econ. Adv. Bd.; sr. fellow Pakistan Inst. Devel. Econs., mem. econ. adv. bd. Author: Strategic Issues in Pakistan's Economic Policy, 1987, Poverty Alleviation in Pakistan, 1994; contbr. chpts. to books and articles to scholarly jours. Mem. Pakistan Human Rights Commn., Lahore, 1987. Mem. Soc. for Internat. Devel., Pakistan Soc. Devel. Economists, Pakistan Futuristics Inst., Soc. Advancement of Higher Edn. (founding). Club: Gymkhana (Lahore). Avocations: poetry, music, photography. Home: 11 Saint John's Park, Lahore Cantonment Pakistan Office: Sayyed Engrs Ltd, 1 Ahmed Block Garden Town, Lahore 3, Pakistan

HUSSAIN, ALTAF, financial controller; b. Karachi, Pakistan, May 18, 1964; s. Abdul Ghani and Khair-Un-Nissa; m. Ayesha A. Allarakha, Aug. 26, 1994; children: Amna, Hafsa. Degree, Inst. Cost and Mgmt. Accts., Karachi, 1988, Inst. Chartered Accts. of Pakistan, 1988. CPA, Colo. Audit trainee Zakaria Loya & Co., Karachi, 1984-88, audit mgr., 1988; auditor acct. Ernst & Young Internat., Riyadh, Saudi Arabia, 1988-90; asst. mgr. ABV Rock Group KB, Riyadh, 1991-95; fin. contr. Armetal Metal Industries Co. Ltd., Riyadh, 1995—; chmn. prof. devel. com. ABV Rock Group, Riyadh, 1993-94; sec. Pakistan Accts. Forum, Riyadh, 1994-95. Mem. AICPA, Inst. Chartered Accts. of Pakistan (assoc.), Inst. Cost and Mgmt. Accts. (assoc.), Karachi Gymkhana, Karachi Club. Office: Armetal Metal Industries Co, 9175 Riyadh Saudi Arabia

HUSSAIN, KAZI FAREEDUDDIN, engineering executive; b. Hyderabad, Deccan, India, Jan. 22, 1948; arrived in Saudi Arabia, 1991; came to U.S., 1966; s. Kazi Moinuddin and Niamath Begum (Khairat Ali) H.; m. Jeanne Marie Dodds, May 17, 1975; 1 child, Sarrah; m. Mahjabeen Muttee, Mar. 2, 1991. ASc, Donnelley Coll., Kansas City, Kans., 1970; BSBA, Ctrl. Mo. State U., Warrensburg, 1972, MS, 1974, EdS, 1975; ScD, Trinity U., 1994; Exec. PhD, Washington Internat. U., Bryn Mawr, Pa., 1999. Registered profl. engr.; cert. safety exec., hazard control mgr., environ. auditor, trainer; chartered cons.; qualified environ. profl. Asst. prof., chmn. Delgado Coll., New Orleans, 1975-76; supr. Monsanto, Nitro, W.Va., 1976-79; sr. regional engr. Mobil Oil, Paulsboro, N.J., 1979-80; mgr. program and project Mobil Oil, Beaumont, Tex., 1980-88; br. mgr. Tex. instruments, Sugarland, Tex., 1988-91; sr. advisor, project mgr. Saudi Arabian Mktg. and Refining Co., Jeddah, Saudi Arabia, 1991-93; exec. dir. Idea Network, Jeddah, Saudi Arabia, 1991-94; divsn. mgr. Saudi Binladin Group - O&M, Jeddah, Saudi Arabia, 1995—; founder, pres. SeviSystance, Internat., Internat. Bus. Network, TransArabia USA, Career & Coll. Counsel Internat.; prodr.-dir., pres. Trans World Comms.; bd. dirs. Real Food Products Pvt. Ltd., Burrgraff Co., HealthFirst Internat.; adj. prof. W.Va. State Coll., 1977-78, Marshall U., 1979, W.Va. Coll. Grad. Studies, 1976-78, Met. C.C., 1974-75; adj. prof., Greenwich Univ., St. Clements Univ., American Polytechnic Univ. bd. vis. scholars. Author: White Paper on Continuing Education and Professional Development in Western Saudi Arabia, 1994, Expatriate Recruiting and Management, Expatriate Policy and Procedures; editor: (newsletter) Nat. Safety Coun.'s Campus Safety, 1973-74; art editor: The Athenian; features editor: The Focus; writer, prodr., dir., actor several plays, radio, TV, video, and films; contbr. articles to profl. jours. Group leader Reagan-Bush Presdl. Campaign; precinct chmn. Jefferson County Rep. Party, 1982-88; bd. dirs. West End Family YMCA, 1986-88, S.E. Tex. chpt. Am. Diabetes Assn., 1986-87, Islamic Soc. Triplex, 1987-88; co-chair world trade coun. Beaumont C. of C., 1982-84, small bus. coun., 1985-86; bd. advisors Beaumont Mayor's Econ. Devel. Coun., 1987; co-chair issues com. Am. Bus. Jeddah. Fellow Royal Soc. Health, Inst. Diagnostic Engrs., Inst. Mgmt. Specialists, Instn. Mgmt.; mem. AIChE, Inst. Bus. Adminstrn. (chartered), Inst. Adminstrv. Mgmt. (chartered), Am. Inst. Plant Engrs., Am. Chem. Soc., Am. Soc. Safety Engrs., Am. Indsl. Hygiene Assn., Am. Businessmen Jeddah, Am. Indsl. Hygiene Assn. (mem. law com. 1978-81, mem. mgmt. com. 1984-87, mem. pub. affairs com. 1989-91), Islamic Soc. N.Am., Islamic Soc. Greater Houston, Arabian Soc. Human Resources Mgmt. (bd. dirs. western region). Republican. Islam. Avocations: swimming, music, traveling, reading, mass media and motion pictures. Home: PO Box 570897 Houston TX 77257-0897 Office: PO Box 122078, Jeddah 21332, Saudi Arabia

HUSSAIN, LIAQAT, pharmaceutical company manager; b. Peshawar, Pakistan, May 1; s. Hafiz Abdul Latif and Zeenat Un Nisa. FSc, Islamia Coll., Peshawar, 1993; BA, Peshawar U., 1997, MA in Econs. Territory mgr. Chiesi Pharm. (Italy), Pakistan, 1996—. Avocations: cricket, gardening, reading international magazines, touring. Home: H #1093 Mohallah Kotla, Rashid Khan I/S Gunj Gate, Peshawar City Pakistan

HUSSAIN, MANWAR, research chemist; b. Dhaka, Bangladesh, Aug. 28, 1960; s. Mohammed Jasim Uddin and Reza (Begum) H.; m. Taslima Akhtar Baby, June 19, 1987; 1 child, Nawara Manwar. BS, Jahangir Nagar U., Dhaka, 1985; MS, Jahangir Nagar U., 1987; PhD, Osaka U., Japan, 1996; postgrad., Mgmt. Inst. Bangladesh, 1992. Chemist Chem. Industry Bangladesh, Dhaka, 1987-92; rschr. Osaka U., 1992—; dir. Mazma Cera, Dhaka, 1996; advisor Hiroshi Internat., Osaka, 1998. Author rsch. papers. Recipient BCIC award BCIC Corp., Bangladesh, 1990, 1997. Avocations: travel, soccer, gardening. E-mail: manwar@sanken.osaka-u.ac.jp. Home: 1290 E Monipur, Mirpur 1216, Bangladesh Office: Osaka U, 8-1 Mihogaoka, Ibaraki 567 0047, Japan

HUSSAIN, MOHAMED ZAHIR, Maldivian government official. Min. pres. office Govt. Maldives, Malé, now min. of state for presdl. affairs, min. youth and sports. Office: Ghjaazee Bldg, Malé 20-05 Malé 20-05, Maldives*

HUSSAIN, MOHAMMAD GULAM, fish geneticist, research scientist; b. Mymensingh, Dhaka, Bangladesh, Feb. 1, 1954; s. Mohammad Jonab Ali and Ayesha Akhter Sundari Khatun; m. Habiba Akhter; children: Sazzad, Ali. BSc with honours, Bangladesh Agrl. U., Mymensingh, 1975, MSc, 1976; PhD, Stirling (Scotland) U., 1992. Sci. officer Dept. Fisheries, Mymensingh, 1978-81; fishery specialist UNDP, Al-Sin, Banias, Syria, 1981-83; aquaculture specialsit UNDP, Al-Ghab, Hama, Syria, 1983-86; prin. sci. officer Fisheries Rsch. Inst., Mymensingh, 1986-92, chief sci. officer, 1992—. Author: (with A.Chatterji, B. McAndrew and R. Johnstone) Theoretical and Applied Genetics, 1991, (with B. McAndrew, D. Penman and P. Sodsuk) Genetics and Evolution of Aquatic Organisms, 1994, (with A. Rahman, A. Bhadra and N. Begum) Aquaculture, 1995, Aquaculture International, 1998, (with D.J. Penman and B. McAndrews); contbr. articles to profl. jours. Freedom fighter Liberation Army, War of Liberation, Bangladesh, 1971. Recipient Lit. award for poems Bangla Acad., 1967, Man of Prodn. award Dept. Fisheries, Syrian Arab Republic, 1984. Mem. World Aquaculture Soc., Fisheries Soc. Brit. Isles, Asian Fisheries Soc., Network of Aquaculture Soc., Bangladesh Fisheries Soc., Bangladesh Zool. Soc., Bangladesh Environment Soc., Bangladesh Soc. Microbiologists. Muslim. Avocations: collecting world classical music, writing poems, world travel. Home: A-2 Quarter, BFRI Campus, 2201 Mymensingh Bangladesh Office: Bangladesh, Fisheries Rsch Inst, 2201 Mymensingh Bangladesh

HUSSAIN, MOINUDDIN SYED, geologist, reservoir engineer, consultant; b. Hyderabad, India, Dec. 28, 1931; s. Karimuddin Syed and Hafeeza Begum (Khan) H.; m. Aziza Moin Quadri, Aug. 20, 1942; children: Qutub, Ayesha, Arju. BS, Osmania U., Hyderabad, 1954; DIC, Imperial Coll., London, 1963; MS, London U., 1964. Registered profl. geologist, Calif. Asst. groundwater geologist Groundwater Devel. Orgn., Lahore, Pakistan, 1955-56; test geologist Std. Vacuum Oil Co. (ESSO), Karachi, Pakistan, 1956-62; superintending geologist Oil and Gas Devel. Corp., Karachi, Pakistan, 1962-69; mgr. exploration/projects Dawood Petroleum Ltd., Karachi, Pakistan, 1969-73; project geologist Hallenbeck McCoy and Assoc., Berkeley, Calif., 1973-75; sr. geologist Dow Chem. Co., USA, Houston, 1975-81; sr. internat. geologist Union Tex. Petroleum Corp., Houston, 1981-85; cons. Hycarbex, Inc., Houston, 1985-93; cons. in petroleum, energy, groundwater Katy, Tex., 1993—; mem. adv. bd. Hycarbex, Inc., Houston, 1985—; advisor Dawood Group of Industries, Karachi, 1969-73; del. to Pakistan, U.S. Dept. of Energy; mem. (with Dept. of Energy) Presdl. Mission to Pakistan, 1994-95. Founding mem. Internat. Explorationist Group, Houston, 1984. Mem. Am. Assn. Petroleum Geologists (cert. geologist, alt. del. 1984, Cert. of Recognition award 1987), Bangladesh Geol. Soc. (life), Pak-Am. Petroleum Soc. (founder 1983), Houston Geol. Soc. (Svc. award 1985). Republican. Muslim. Achievements include research on petroleum potential of Pakistan and Bangladesh resulting in several oil and gas discoveries; introduction of API stds. in these countries to replace Soviet technology; establishment of oil producing trend in San Marcos Arch area, Tex. thru Austic Chalk Formation; preparation of feasability studies for establishment of refineries, power plants, fertilizer plants, pig iron plants, LPG projects; design of oil and gas pipelines groundwater resource evaluation and development, basin evaluation, project development and implementation. Avocations: walking, hunting, fishing, reading. Office: Petroland Exploration Inc PO Box 218341 Houston TX 77218-8341

HUSSAIN, SYED MAHMOOD, eye surgeon; b. Madras, Tamilnadu, India, Aug. 27, 1939; s. Syed Ahmed Hussain and Ahmed Unisa Begum; m. Naseem Unisa Naseema; 6 children. MB, BChir, Madras (India) Med. Coll.,

1965, diploma in ophthalmology, 1978, M of Surgery in Ophthalmology, 1982, M.A.M.S., 1984, FMMC (hon.), 1983; D of Homeopathy, I.H.S., Calcutta, 1989; DSc (hon.), Internat. U., Colombo, Sri Lanka, 1990, PhD (hon.), 1995, D of Alternative Medicine, 1995. Chief med. officer G.O.H., Madras, 1973-76, G.E.S.I. Eye Care, Madras, 1976-79; D.M.O. S.O.S. Force, Kingdom of Saudi Arabia, 1979-84; prof. R.I.O. & G.O.H., 1984-90; cons. Rotary Club, Tanjore, India, 1975-90, Orphanage Soc., Bombay, 1970-85; rschr. in field; sec. gen. Soc. for Prevention of Blindness, WHO, 1976-90. Author: Simple Eye Treatment, 1979 (Best Author award), Health Eye, 1994 (Best Book award 1995). Chief Surgeon Govt. Eye Camps, Madras, 1987-89; dir. Health Resort Center, Tanjore, India, 1969-73; organizer Vol. Eye Soc. for Poor, 1978-95; convenor Irradication of Lepromatic Eye, 1990-96; ; vol. programs for prevention of blindness and trochoma, family planning and welfare programs; exec. coun. TN Med. Coun.; founder, pres. Universal Brotherhood of India. Fellow Royal Coll. Health (London), Odonto Osteokerato Prosthosis (Italy); mem. Heart Charitable Soc. (sec., Honors 1989), Healpage India (sec., Honors 1991), Human Right Soc. and Prevention of Cruelty to Destitute Women and Children (founder Madras chpt., pres.), Retinitis Pigmentosa Soc. (bd. dirs. 1985-90), C.S.I. Eye Soc. (bd. dirs. 1989-93), Glaucoma Prevention Soc. (pres. 1980-87), Univ. Acad. of Med. Soc., Pan Arab Coun. Ophthalmologists, World Eye Bank. Avocation: volunteer work. Home: Pursawalkam, 02 Grama St, Madras 600007, India Office: Dr Hussain Eye Care, 19 Mosque St Triplicane, Chennai 600005, India

HUSSAIN, TAJAMMUL, chemist; b. Lahore, Pakistan, Jan. 1, 1954; s. Aijaz Ali and Bilqis Ichamum; m. Sabiha Sultana, Oct. 20, 1980; children: Sal man Tajammul, Anslam Tajammul. BSc, U. Islamabad, 1970, MSc, 1974; MS, U. Manchester Inst. Sci. Tech., 1988, PhD, 1991. Rsch. asst. U. Islamabad, Pakistan, 1973-74; chemist ICI, Lahore, 1974-76, Ross Chems., Qazuin, Iran, 1976-79; chief sci. officer KRL, Pakistan, 1979—, also bd. dirs.; vis. faculty mem. u. islamabad, 1992—; tech. advisor Nat. Auth., Islamabad, 1997—; cons. PILA, Pakistan, 1996—, Chem-Serve, 1996—. Author: Chemistry for A Level, 1997; contbr. articles to sci. and profl. jours. Mem. Bd. Studies Quaid-e-Azam U., 1998—. Fellow Royal Soc. U.K., Chem. Soc. Pakistan (assoc.); mem. Am. Chem. Soc. Avocation: cricket. Home: #29/A St #28, F-10/1 Islamabad Pakistan Office: AQ Khan Rsch Labs KRL, PO Box 502, Rawalhindi Pakistan

HUSSEIN, ADEL MOKHTAR, nuclear engineer; b. Zawia, Libya, June 25, 1962; s. Abdulwahab Mokhtar Hussein and Radia Hassan Essuri; m. Entisar Amer Esh-Shain, Nov. 20, 1996; children: Ayat, Wajeeh. BSc in Nuclear Engring., Alfateh U., 1985. Asst. shift charge engr. Tripoli (Libya) West Power Sta., Gen. Elec. of Libya, 1986-89, efficiency engr., 1989-90; transformers and voltage breakers maintenance Tripoli (Libya) West Power Sta., Gen. Elec. of Libya, Zawia, 1990-91, Watt hour meters workshop, electromech. maintenance dept., 1991—; cons. Assn. of Indsl. Experts, Zawia, 1996; mem. Internat. Energy Found., Tripoli, 1997. Author: Basic Electrical Concepts, 1998, Guide to Electro-Mechanical Meters, 1998; contbr. articles to sci. and profl. jours. Mem. Engineers Union.

HUSSEIN, AHMED SOLIMAN, research scientist, nutritionist, educator; b. Cairo, June 27, 1947; s. Soliman El-Sayed Hussein and Amina Mohamed Attia; m. Mary Kay Rathke, Aug. 20, 1993; 1 child, Kareem Rabi. BS, Ain-Shams U., Cairo, 1970; MS, U. Calif., Davis, 1981; PhD, U. Ky., 1987. Rsch. assoc. U. Ky., Lexington, 1987-88; rsch. scientist U. Md. Ea. Shore, Princess Anne, 1988-90; asst. prof. United Arab Emirates U., Al-Ain, 1993-95, assoc. prof. dept. animal prodn., 1995—; vis. prof. U. Md. Ea. Shore, 1990-92, USDA/Agr. Rsch. Svc., Beltsville, Md., 1992-93; cons. United Arab Emirates poultry industry, 1993—; nutrition cons. Delmarva Poultry Industry, Nutrition and Feed Mfg. Com., Salisbury, Md., 1988-92. Contbr. articles to profl. jours. Vol. Peninsula Gen. Hosp., Salisbury, Md., 1992-93; coach Lexington Adult Soccer League, 1987. Rsch. grantee United Arab Emirates U., 1994, 95. Mem. Poultry Sci. Assn., Gamma Sigma Delta. Avocations: soccer, basketball, internat. travel, music. E-mail: ahussein@uaeu.ac.ae. Office: Dept Animal Prodn/Fac Agrl, Scis/PO Box 17555, Al-Ain/Abu Dhabi United Arab Emirates

HUSSEIN, LAILA ABBAS, nutritional scientist, researcher; b. Giza, Egypt, Jan. 2, 1938; d. Abbas Helmy Husstin and Souad Mohammed Salem. B Agr., Cairo U., 1958, MSc in Animal Nutrition, 1962; PhD in Agrl. Chemistry and Nutrition, U. Bonn, Bermany, 1967. Postgrad. fellow U. Calif., Davis, 1967-68; assoc. prof. U. Hamburg, Germany, 1975-77; rschr. Nat. Rsch. Ctr., Giza, 1978-79, 79—, head dept. nutrition sci., 1994-97; vis. prof. King Saud U., Riyadh, Saudi Arabia, 1993-94; nat. project leader FAO/TCP, Giza, 1997—; mng. training course use of stable isotopes Internat. Agy. Atomic Energy, 1999; rschr. in field; nat. project dir. Tech. Coop. Program Prodn. Nutrient Data Base for Local Egyptian Foods, 1997-99; prin. investigator food consumption patterns and average nutrient intakes project, 1994-99. Contbr. articles and papers to profl. jours. Recipient DAAD-Spende award, Germany, 1999; grantee Brit. Coun., 2000—. Mem. Steering Com. for Promotion, Nat. Nutrition Com., Acad. Sci. Rsch. and Tech. (mem. nutrition com. 1967—), Internat. Union Nutritional Scis. (mem. vitamin food description com.), Heliopolis Sporting Club. Avocation: charitable works. Home: Saleh Magdi 8, Cairo Egypt Office: Nat Rsch Ctr, El Tahrir, Giza 12311, Egypt

HUSSEIN, SADDAM, president of Republic of Iraq; b. Tikrit Dist., Iraq, Apr. 28, 1937; m. Sajida Khair-Allah; 2 sons, 3 daus. Student, College of Law, Egypt, 1961; law degree, U. Baghdad, 1971. Joined Arab Ba'ath (Renaissance) Socialist Party, 1956; participant attempt to overthrow Abdul-Karim Qasem, 1959; second in command Arab Ba'ath Socialist Party; mem. Regional Leadership, 1963; imprisoned, 1964-66, escaped 1966; re-elected mem. Nat. Command, Ba'ath Party, 1965; dep. sec. Regional Leadership, Arab Ba'ath Socialist Party, 1966; acting dep. chmn. Revolution Command Council, 1968-69, dep. chmn., 1969-79, chmn., 1979—; dep. sec. Ba'ath Regional Command, 1968-79, sec., 1979—; mem. Nat. Leadership, asst. sec.-gen., 1977-79; pres. Republic of Iraq, 1979—, prime min., 1994—; defacto chmn. Revolutionary Council, from 1968; dep. sec. Nat. Command, Ba'ath Party, from 1979. Author polit. and other treatises. Decorated 1st degree (civil) Rafidain, 1976. Address: Presdl Palce Karradat Mariam, Baghdad Iraq*

HUSSEIN, ZIAD A., electromagnetics scientist, researcher; b. Beirut; came to U.S., 1982, naturalized, 1998; s. Ali and Nawal Hussein; 1 child, Jennifer. BS, U. Mass., 1986; MS, Calif. State U., Northridge, 1991; postgrad., UCLA, 1994. Grad. rsch. asst. Calif. State U., 1987-89; mem. tech. staff Jet. Propulsion Lab., Calif. Inst. Tech., Pasadena, 1991—; session chmn. Progress in Electromagnetics Rsch. Symposium, Cambridge, Mass., 2000. Contbr. articles to sci. jours., including IEEE Geosci. and Remote Sension, IEEE Antennas Digest, IEEE Geosci. and Remote Sensing Digest, Progress in Electromagnetic Rsch. Recipient cert. of recognition NASA, 1997, 99. Mem. IEEE Geosci. and Remote Sensing Soc., IEEE Antennas and Propagation Soc. (session chmn., mem. tech. program com. 1995), IEEE Microwave Theory and Techniques Soc., Antennas Measurements Technique Assn. (orgn. com. 1994). Avocations: hiking, skiing. E-mail: ziad.a.hussein@jpl.nasa.gov. Home: 1401 N Los Robles Ave Apt 10 Pasadena CA 91104-5540 Office: Caltech/Jet Propulsion Lab 4800 Oak Grove Dr Pasadena CA 91109-8001

HÜSSEINOV, FARHAD VELIOĞLU, mathematician, economist, educator; b. Göychay, Azerbaijan, Mar. 29, 1948; s. Veli Kerimoğlu and Sekire Müslimgizi (Mirhadieva) H.; m. Emilia Baratgizi Karavelieva, 1979; children: Teymur, Tural. MSc, Azerbaijan State U., 1970; PhD, Moscow State U., 1976; DSc, Sobolev Inst. Math., Novosibirsk, 1990. Sr. rschr. Acad. Sci. Azerbaijan, Baku, 1975-80, 82-87, Moscow State U., 1980-82; prof., head Baku State U., 1987-92; vis. prof. Middle East Tech. U., Ankara, Turkey, 1992-94; vis. assoc. prof. Bilkent U., Ankara, 1994—; reviewer Am. Math. Revs., Ann Arbor, 1996—. Author: (with others) Mathematical Economics and Functional Analysis, 1974; contbr. articles to profl. jours. Mem. Econometric Soc. Home: Bilkent U Campus 4/2, 06533 Ankara Turkey Office: Bilkent U Econs Dept, 06533 Bilkent Turkey

HUSTED, WILLIAM ARMSTRONG, sales executive; b. London, Feb. 25, 1937; s. John Grinnell Wetmore and Helen Armstrong Husted. BS, Hobart Coll., 1959. Jr. analyst group actuarial divsn. Met. Life Ins. Co., N.Y.C., 1959-60, sr. analyst group actuarial divsn., 1961-63, sr. retention analyst group adminstrv. staff, 1964-70; distbr. Amway, Bedford, N.Y., 1976-98; ind. retail bus. owner Bedford, 1999—. Mem. Rep. Presdl. Legion of Merit, Washington, 1980—; mem. nat. adv. bd. Black America's Polit. Action Com., Hagerstown, Md., 1996—; nat. mem. Libr. of Congress, Washington, 1990—. Episcopalian. Avocations: collecting stamps, signed first edition books and fine antiques. Home and Office: 46 Greenwich Rd Bedford NY 10506-1509

HUSTER, ERNST-ULRICH, political scientist, educator; b. Welbsleben, Germany, Sept. 11, 1945; s. Ernst and Johanna (Bando) H.; m. Christa Maria Crecelius, July 9, 1971; children: Barbara, Stefan. Degree, Justus Liebig U., Giessen, Germany, 1970. Asst. J.L. Univ., Giessen, 1973-78, asst. prof., 1978-84; sci. employee Luth. Ch., Hannover, Germany, 1984-89; prof. polit. scis. Protestant U. of Applied Scis. Rheinland-Westfalen-Lippe, Bochum, Germany, 1989—; dean of dept. social work Protestant U. of Applied Scis., 1990-94, rector, 1995—. Author: Die Politik der SPD, 1945-50, 1978, Ethik des Staates, 1989, Armut in Europa, 1996, Reichtum in Deutschland, 1997. Mem. for Germany, European Commn.: Obs. on Nat. Policies to Combat Social Exclusion, 1992-94. Home: Steinstrasse 33, D 35415 Pohlheim Germany Office: Protestant U Applied Scis, Immanuel Kant Str 18-20, D 44803 Bochum Germany

HUSTON, DANIEL CLIFF, geophysicist; b. Anchorage, June 29, 1955; s. Arthur Cliff and Allie Mae (Ogdon) H.; m. Holly Hunter, Oct. 10, 1992; children: Lana Marie, Hayley Allison. BS in Geology and Geophysics, U. Hawaii, 1980, marine option program cert., 1980; MA in Geological Scis., U. Tex., 1987. Surveyor Trans Alaska Pipeline, 1975-78; geologist R&M Cons., Anchorage, 1980; geophysicist U.S. Minerals Mgmt. Svc., Anchorage, 1981-83; rsch. asst. Miss. Canyon Project, Austin, 1983-84; project SEER U. Tex. Inst. Geophysics, Austin, 1983-87; geophys. intern Sohio Petroleum Co., San Francisco, summer 1984; geophysicist leader advanced seismic methods group Unocal Sci. and Tech. Divsn., Brea, Calif., 1987-90; sr. geophysicist Unocal Oil and Gas Divsn., Houston, 1991-96; founder Hunter 3-D Inc., 1996—, Creekside Exploration, Inc., 1999—; pres. Creekside Exploration, Inc., 1999—; presenter in field. Contbr. articles to profl. jours. Fellow U. Tex. Indsl. Assocs., 1983. Mem. Am. assn. Petroleum Geologists, Soc. Exploration Geophysicists (presenter workshop 1984, ann. conv. 1986, regional conv. 1989). Methodist. Avocations: travel, scuba diving, skiing, weightlifting, reading history.

HUSTON, JANIS LYNNE, medical educator, consultant; b. Napoleon, Ohio, Sept. 14, 1952; d. Walter Ray and Betty Irene Huston. BS, Ohio State U., 1975; MEd, Bowling Green State U., 1983; PhD, U. Ky., 1997. Asst. dir. med. records Providence Hosp., Anchorage, Alaska, 1976-79; dir. med. record adminstrn. program Bowling Green (Ohio) State U., 1979-84; dir. med. records Crestview Hosp., Casper, Wyo., 1985-86; assoc. prof. Ea. Ky. U., Richmond, 1987-94; telemedicine rsch. assoc. U. Ky., Lexington, 1995-97; telemedicine cons. Histopathol. Lab., Wiesbaden, Germany, 1998-99, Reigate, England, 1999—; cons. Williams County Nursing Home, Bryan, Ohio, 1980-81, Henry County Hosp., Napoleon, Ohio, 1980-84, Midway (Ky.) Coll., 1990, Nat. City Bank, Lexington, 1990-91; vis. asst. prof. Ohio State U., Columbus, 1997-98. Contbr. articles to profl. jours. Mem. Am. Health Info. Mgmt. Assn. (registered health info. adminstr.), Royal Soc. Medicine (mem. telemedicine forum 1999). Avocations: sports, music, art.

HUSTON, JOHN, professional golfer; b. Mt. Vernon, Ill., June 1, 1961; m. Suzanne Huston; children: Jessica, Travis. Grad., Auburn U. Profl. golfer PGA, 1983—; winner Honda Classic, 1990, Walt Disney World/Oldsmobile Classic, 1992, Doral-Ryder Open, 1994, United Airlines Hawaii Open, 1998, Nat./Car Rental Classic/Disney, 1998. Medalist 1987 Qualifying Tournament; won Honda Classic, 1990, JC Penney Classic with Amy Benz, 1988, Walt Disney/Oldsmobile Classic, 1992, Doral-Ryder Open, 1994, Motorola Western Open, 1995, United Airlines Hawaiian Open, 1995, Buick Invitational Calif., 1995, Buick Challenge, 1995, Mercedes Championship, 1995. Office: PGA Am Box 109601 100 Avenue Of Champions Palm Beach Gardens FL 33410

HUSTON, JOHN CHARLES, law educator; b. Chgo., Mar. 21, 1927; s. Albert Allison and Lillian Helen (Sullivan) H.; m. Joan Frances Mooney, Aug. 1, 1954; children: Mark Allison, Philip John, Paul Francis James; m. Inger Margareta Westerman, May 4, 1979. AB, U. Wash., Seattle, 1950; JD, U. Wash., 1952; LLM, NYU, 1955. Bar: Wash. 1952, N.Y. 1964, U.S. Dist. Ct. (we. dist.) Wash. 1953, U.S. Ct. Appeals (9th cir.) 1953, U.S. Tax Ct. 1977, U.S. Supreme Ct. 1993. Assoc. Kahin, Carmody & Horswill, Seattle, 1952-53; teaching fellow NYU Law Sch., 1953-54; asst. co-dir. U. Ankara Legal Research Inst., Turkey, 1954-55; asst. prof. NYU, 1953-57; asst. prof. Syracuse U., N.Y., 1957-60, assoc. prof., 1960-65, prof., 1960-67; prof., assoc. dean U. Wash., Seattle, 1967-73, prof. law, 1973-96, prof. emeritus, 1996—; adj. prof. Asia-Pacific Law Inst., Bond Univ., Australia; of counsel Carney, Badley, Smith & Spellman, Seattle; vis. prof. U. Stockholm, 1986, U. Bergen, 1989, Bond U., Australia, 1991. Author: (with Redden) The Mining Law of Turkey, 1956, The Petroleum Law of Turkey, 1956, (with Muckleston and Cross) Community Property: General Considerations, 1971, (with Price and Treacy) 4th edit., 1994, (with Sullivan and others) Administration of Criminal Justice, 166, 2d edit., 1969, (with Miyatake and Way) Japanese International Taxation, 1983, supplements through 1997, (with Cross and Shields) Community Property Desk Book, 1989, supplement, 1997, (with Williams) Permanent Establishment, 1993. With USNR, 1945-46; capt. USAFR. Mem. ABA, Am. Coll. Trust and Estate Coun., Wash. State Bar Assn. (chmn. tax sect. 1984-85), King County bar Assn., Japanese Am. Soc. Legal Studies, Internat. Fiscal Assn. (past regional v.p., past mem. coun.). E-mail: huston@u.washington.edu Fax: 206-525-1758. Office: U Wash Sch Law 1100 NE Campus Pkwy Seattle WA 98105-6605

HUSTON, JOHN DENNIS, English educator; b. N.Y.C., Sept. 21, 1939; s. A. Arthur H. and Jacquelin (Buchenau) Hawkins; m. Priscilla Jane, June 13, 1964 (div. July 1985); children: Katherine, Penn; m. Lisa B. Bryan, Aug. 8, 1988; stepchildren: Rudy Bryan, Kirby Bryan. BA, Wesleyan U., 1961; MA, Yale U., 1964, PhD, 1966. Instr., English Yale U., New Haven, Conn., 1966-67, asst. prof., 1967-69; assoc. prof. Rice U., Houston, 1969-80, prof., English, 1980—; dir. freshman humanities Rice U., 1988-94, master Hanszen Coll., 1978-82, 92-98. Author: Shakespeare's Comedies of Play, 1981; co-editor: Classics of the Renaissance Theater, 1969. Named CASE Prof. of Yr., 1989-90, Disting. Alumnus Wesleyan U., 1991; recipient Wilbur Cross medal Yale Grad. Sch., 1992. Mem. Coll. English Assn. (bd. dirs. 1989-92), Phi Beta Kappa. Democrat. Avocations: running, racquetball, squash, skiing, fishing. Home: 4115 Mcduffie St Houston TX 77098-3419 Office: Rice U Dept English PO Box 1892 Houston TX 77251-1892

HUSTON, MARGO, journalist; b. Waukesha, Wis., Feb. 12, 1943; d. James and Cecile (Timlin) Bremner; student U. Wis., 1961-63; AB in Journalism, Marquette U., 1965; m. James Huston, Dec. 9, 1967 (div.); 1 son, Sean Patrick. Editorial asst. Marquette U., Milw., 1965-66; feature editor, reporter Waukesha Freeman, 1966-67; feature reporter Milw. Jour., 1967-70; reporter Spectrum, women's and food sections, 1972-79, edit!. writer, 1979-84, polit. reporter, 1984—, asst. picture editor, 1985-91, copy editor, 1992-95; reporter Milw. Jour. Sentinel (merger Milw. Jour. and The Sentinel), 1995—; instr. mass comm. U. Wis., Milw. Recipient Penney-Mo. award for consumer abortion series, 1977, Pulitzer Prize for investigation into plight of elderly, 1977, Clarion award, 1977, Knight of Golden Quill award, Milw. Press Club, 1977, Wis. AP writing award, 1977, special award Milw. Soc. Profl. Journalists, 1977, Penney-Mo. Paul Myhre award for excellence, 1978; By-Line award Marquette U. Coll. of Journalism, 1980; Wis. UPI best editorial award, 1982; Wis. Women's Network award for journalist achievement for women's issues, 1983, Dick Goldensohn Fund award, 1991, 1st place award for investigative reporting Inland Press Assn., 1997, 98, 2d award Enterprise interpretive reporting Wis. Newspaper Assn., 1998; Wis. Arts Bd. Literary Arts grantee, 1992. Mem. Milw. Press Club. Office: Milwaukee Journal Sentinel 333 W State St Milwaukee WI 53203-1309

HUTCHENS, EUGENE GARLINGTON, college administrator; b. Birmingham, Ala., Nov. 26, 1929; s. Wallace Luther and Reydonia (Corry) H.; m. Betty Frances Goode, Aug. 26, 1951; children: Dale Eugene, Wayne Goode, Dennis Wade. BA, Samford U., 1952; ThM, New Orleans Bapt. Theol. Sem., 1970; MS in Econs., U. Mo.-Columbia, 1972. Ordained to ministry, 1952. Min. North Brewton (Ala.) Bapt. Ch., 1952-56, 1st Bapt. Ch., Ashland, Ala., 1956-63, Highlands Bapt. Ch., Huntsville, Ala., 1963-67; tchr. pub. schs. Huntsville, 1967-71; instr. econs. N.W. Ala. State Jr. Coll., 1972-77, acting pres., 1981, dir. Tuscumbia campus, 1977-89; adminstrv. asst. Shoals C.C., 1989-93, asst. to dean, 1993-95; pastor emeritus Weeden Heights Bapt. Ch., Florence, 1995; owner radio stas., WKNI AM, Lexington, Ala., WFIX, Rogersville, Ala., 1991-96, mem. Ala. Bapt. State Exec. Bd., 1961-63; v.p. Ala. Bapt. State Pastors Conf., 1966, Ala. Bapt. Historical Commission, 1992—. NSF grantee, 1971-72. Mem. NEA, Ala. Edn. Assn., Ala. Jr. and C.C. Assn. (exec. com. 1981-84). Home: 801 E 2nd St Tuscumbia AL 35674-2206

HUTCHENS, PAT MERCER, art educator; b. Winnfield, La.. BA in Art, tchg. cert., Wheaton Coll., 1959; MFA in Art Theory and Practice, Northwestern U., 1980; MS, Nat. Louis U., 1990; postgrad., Betzelel Art Sch., Jerusalem, Corcoran Sch. Art, Chgo. Art Inst., Northwestern State U., No. Va. Coll., Pasadena City Coll., Wheaton Grad. Sch. Tchr. painting and drawing Wheaton Coll., 1965-66, 70-72; tchg. asst. art theory and practice Northwestern U., Evanston, Ill., 1978-80; tchr. printmaking and drawing George Mason U., Fairfax, Va., 1980-81; tchr. painting Lord Fairfax Coll., Middletown, Va., 1999—; tchr. portrait painting, painting Corcoran Coll. Art and Design, Washington; tchr. design No. Va. Coll.; pvt. art tchr., 1980—; founder, dir. Washington Art Works, 1980—. Solo and group shows include Nineveh Gallery, Tel Aviv, Gallery 41, Rananna, Israel, Assn. Painters and Sculptors Gallery, Tel Aviv, Nat. Etchings Exhbn., Tel Aviv, New Orleans Studio 8 Gallery, N.Y.C. and So. Pines, N.C., Ill. Bell Art Exhbn., North Shore (Chgo.) Art League, U. Calif., San Bernardino Fine Arts Gallery, Pasadena City Coll. Exhbn., Wheaton Coll., Northwestern U., Fairfax Coun. on Arts, Greater Washington Collection Fine Art, Washington Ballet Art Exhbn., The Gallery, Leesburg, Va., Greater Reston (Va.) Art Ctr., D.C. Union Sta., 1999, Nat. Press Bldg., Washington, 1999, others; collections include Standard Oil, Edward M. Kennedy, Irwin Edlovitch, others; work featured in books, art jours. Israel, U.S. Mem. Nat. Scholastic Honor Soc. E-mail: yaelpat@aol.com. Home: 705 Forest Park Rd Great Falls VA 22066-2908

HUTCHEON, ANDREW WILLIAM, physician, consultant, research; b. Aberdeen, Grampian, Scotland, May 21, 1943; s. George and Elsie Sophia (Murison) H.; m. Christine Gray Cusiter, July 28, 1945; children: Louise Gray, Andrew Barry, Wendy Lyn. MBCLB, Aberdeen U., 1968; MRCP, Glasgow-Royal Coll., Glasgow, Strath Clyde, 1971; MD, Aberdeen U., 1977; FRCP, Glasgow & Edinburgh U., 1980. House officer Nat. Health Svc. Aberdeen (Scotland) Hosps., 1968-69; sr. house officer Nat. Health Svc. Glasgow (Scotland) Hosps., 1969-71; registrar Nat. Health Svc. Glasgow Hosps., 1973-75; sr. registrar Nat. Health Svc. Glasgow (Scotland), London, 1975-78; cons. physician Nat. Health Svc. Aberdeen (Scotland) Hosps., 1978—; cons. physician, Nat. Health Svc., Aberdeen, cons. med. oncologist; sr. lectr. in med. Aberdeen U. Recipient FRCP, Royal Coll., Glasgow, 1983, Royal Coll., Edinburgh, 1989. Mem. British Assn. for Cancer Research, European Assn. for Med. Oncology, Scottish Soc. of Physicians (sec. 1987-89), Scottish Soc. for Experimental Med. (sec. 1983-87). Avocations: skiing, curling, golf, mus. Office: Dept of Clin Oncology, Aberdeen Royal Infirmary, Grampian, Scotland, Aberdeen AB2 2YS, Great Britain

HUTCHERSON, CHRISTOPHER ALFRED, marketing, recruiting and educational fundraising executive; b. Memphis, June 13, 1950; s. Alfred Wayne Hutcherson and Loretta (Morris) Kindsfather; m. Glenda Ann Champ, May 22, 1971 (dec. 1995); m. Barbara A. Haralson, Sept. 27, 1998. BS, U. Houston, 1972, MA in Adminstrn., 1977, postgrad., 1977-79. Cert. tchr. and adminstr., Tex. Pvt. music instr. Spring Br. and Pasadena Ind. Sch. Dists., Tex., 1968-75; jr. high and high sch. band dir. Deer Park (Tex.) Ind. Schs., 1972-80; recruiter M. David Lowe Personnel, Houston, 1981; sales dir. Instl. Financing Svcs., Benicia, Calif., 1982-85; sales mgr. Instl. Financing Svcs., Benicia, 1985-87; nat. tng. dir. Champion Products and Svcs., San Diego, 1987-88, west coast and midwest sales mgr., 1988-89; pres. Camelot, Inc., Auburn, Calif., 1989-91; pres., CEO Camelot Telephone Assistance Program, Inc., Folsom, Calif., 1991-92; nat. dir. sales and mktg. edn. and devel. Nat. Scrip Ctr., Inc., Santa Rosa, Calif., 1992-95; exec. v.p. Scrip Plus Inc., Fresno, Calif., 1995-96; chmn., pres., CEO Children's Heros, Inc., Auburn, 1996—; fund raising cons. non-profit orgns., 1982—; speaker in field; creator kitchen table mktg. sys., 1992. Judge Tex. jr. high and high sch. bands, 1974-81, regional band chmn., 1973-77; choir dir. St. Hyacinth Ch., Deer Park, 1979-81; vice chmn. Ch. Coun. St. Hyacinth Ch., 1980; founder Tex. Region XIX Jr. High Band Competition, 1973 (Spl. Achievement award 1979); 1st chair clarinet Tex. All-State Band, 1968; founder, pres. Glenda Hutcherson Heros Found., 1996—; creator Heroes Reward Card Program, 1996—; founder, pres. Childrens Heros Fund; pres. Sunshine Valley Homeowners Assn., 1999-2000. Mem. Kappa Kappa Psi (v.p. Outstanding Mem. award 1970). Republican. Roman Catholic. Avocations: golf, reading, movies. Home: 14105 Lodestar Dr Grass Valley CA 95949-8362

HUTCHESON, J(AMES) STERLING, lawyer; b. Nanking, China, Oct. 17, 1919; s. Allen Carrington and Strausie (McCaslin) H.; m. Marilyn Brown, Dec. 26, 1944; children—James Sterling, Holly Hutcheson Jasperson, Joanne Hutcheson Denton, Scott Brown, Allen McCaslin. B.A., Princeton U., 1941; LL.B., Stanford U., 1949. Bar: Calif. 1949, U.S. Dist. Ct. (no. dist.) Calif. 1949, U.S. Ct. Apls. (9th cir.) 1949, U.S. Dist. Ct. (so. dist.) Calif. 1950, U.S. Ct. Mil. Appeals 1955, Clk. jud. com. Calif. State Assembly, 1949; assoc., then ptnr. Gray, Cary, Ames & Frye, San Diego, 1950-93; ptnr. emeritus Gray, Cary Ware & Freidenrich, 1994—. Mem. San Diego City Traffic Commn.; bd. dirs. San Diego County Hosp. and Health Facility Planning Commn.; trustee Francis Parker Sch., San Diego, 1956-59, pres. bd., 1957-58; trustee La Jolla (Calif.) Country Day Sch., 1956-59. Served to comdr. USNR, 1941-45. Mem. Internat. Assn. Def. Counsel (state editor 1958, 61-63, 66-67, chmn. legal malpractice subcom. 1962, exec. com. 1976-79), State Bar Calif. (lectr. continuing edn. bar 1960, 63, mem. disciplinary bd. 1973-77, referee rev. bd. 1979-83, client security fund 1977-78), San Diego County Barristers, San Diego County Bar Assn. (sec. 1963-64, v.p. 1964-65, chmn. med. legal ccm. 1961-62), Am. Bd. Trial Advs., Assn. So. Calif. Def. Counsel (dir. 1974-76), Southwestern Legal Found. (lectr. 1963), Am. Coll. Trial Lawyers, Def. Research Inst. (regional v.p. Pacific 1971-74), Navy League, Phi Alpha Delta. Republican. Presbyterian. Club: Princeton of San Diego (pres. 1955-71). Home: 7784 Hillside Dr La Jolla CA 92037-3944 Office: Gray Cary Ware & Freidenrich 401 B St Ste 1700 San Diego CA 92101-4297

HUTCHESON, JERRY DEE, manufacturing company executive; b. Hammon, Okla., Oct. 31, 1932; s. Radford Andrew and Ethel Mae (Boulware) H.; B.S. in Physics, Eastern N. Mex. U., 1959; postgrad. Temple U., 1961-62, U. N.Mex., 1964-65; m. Lynda Lou Weber, Mar. 6, 1953; children—Gerald Dan, Lisa Marie, Vicki Lynn. Research engr. RCA, 1959-62; sect. head Motorola, 1962-63; research physicist Dikewood Corp., 1963-66; sr. mem. tech. staff Signetics Corp., 1966-69; engring. mgr. Litton Systems, Sunnyvale, Calif., 1969-70; engring. mgr. Fairchild Semiconductor, Mountain View, Calif., 1971; equipment engr., group mgr. Teledyne Semiconductor, Mountain View, 1971-74; dir. engring. DCA Reliability Labs., Sunnyvale, 1974-75; founder, prin. Tech. Ventures, San Jose, Calif., 1975—; chief exec. officer VLSI Research, Inc., 1981—. Democratic precinct committeeman, Albuquerque, 1964-66. Served with USAF, 1951-55. Registered profl. engr., Calif. Mem. Nat. Soc. Profl. Engrs., Profl. Engrs. Pvt. Practice, Calif. Soc. Profl. Engrs., Semiconductor Equipment and Materials Inst., Soc. Photo-Optical Instrumentation Engrs., Am. Soc. Test Engrs., Presbyterian. Club: Masons. Contbr. articles to profl. jours. Home: 5950 Vista Loop San Jose CA 95124-6562 Office: VSLI Rsch 1754 Technology Dr Ste 117 San Jose CA 95110-1320

HUTCHINGS, ANDREW J., copywriter; b. Woolwich, England, Feb. 26, 1962; s. Peter and Elizabeth (Webster) H.; m. Anna-Louise Kenny, July 17, 1993. B in Commerce, U. Melbourne, 1981. Acct. CRA Ltd., Melbourne, 1981-83; investment analyst Citicorp Scrimgeour Vickers Australia Ltd., Melbourne, 1983-86, Jardine Fleming Australia Ltd., Sydney, 1986-88; investment dir. GT Mgmt. Australia Ltd., Sydney, 1988-94; global funds coord. GT Global Asset Mgmt. PLC, London, 1994-98; chmn. Universal Copywriters Ltd., Woollahra, Australia, 1998—. Mem. Assn. Investment Mgmt. Sales Execs. Office: Universal Copywriters Ltd, 2 Boderton Mews Duncton, Petworth West Sussex UK

HUTCHINS, BRIAN R., attorney general; b. Oklahoma City, Aug. 18, 1954; s. Richard D. and M. (Elaine) H.; m. Aug. 4, 1984 (div. May 1995); children: Courtney, Meredith. BA in Polit. Sci., Calif. State U., Fullerton, 1976; JD cum laude, Calif. Western Sch. Law, San Diego, 1979. Bar: Calif. 1979, Nev. 1981, U.S. District Court, U.S. Ct. Appeals (9th cir.), U.S. Supreme Ct. Law clk. to Assoc. Justice Noel E. Manoukian Nev. Supreme Ct., Carson City, 1979-80; dep. atty. gen. State Nev., Carson City, 1980-86, chief dep. atty. gen. criminal justice divsn., 1987-89, chief dep. atty. gen. transp. and pub. safety divsn., 1990—; spl. prosecutor Carson City Grand Jury, 1982; lectr., presenter of various courses, seminars, confs. Contbr. to profl. jours. Mem. Staff Parish Com., Carson City, 1985-86, 96-98; treas., sec., v.p., pres. Boys & Girls Club West Nev. Carson City, 1996-2000; chmn., youth coun. First United Meth. Ch., Carson City, 1998-99; layleader, 1987-88; mem. various bds., commns., 1980—; supt. Sunday Sch., 1988-90; tchr., leader Sunday Sch., 1987-94; leader Christcare Small group trng., 1995—; asst. coach, umpire Carson City Little League, 1980-85; instr. Carson City Youth Ski program, 1980-82; youth soccer coach AYSO Carson City, 1998-99; asst. scoutmaster, Boy Scouts Am., 1980-82. Mem. Fifth Ave. Townhouse Assn. (bd. dirs. 1980-94). Avocations: running, softball, volleyball, skiing, mountain biking. Fax: 702-888-7309. Home: 1696 Rankin Dr Carson City NV 89701-6857 Office: Office Atty Gen 1263 S Stewart St Carson City NV 89712-0001

HUTCHINS, EDITH ELIZABETH, accountant; b. Prince Frederick, Md., July 14, 1966; d. Aaron Ray and Alma Marie (Phillips) H.; 1 child, Jonathan Alexander Sawyer. BS in Acctg. summa cum laude, Hampton (Va.) U., 1988; postgrad., Am. U., 1997—. CPA, Md. Staff acct. Deloitte & Touche, Morristown, N.J., 1988-89; account exec. KEZB Radio, El Paso, Tex., 1990; cost acct. Helen of Troy, El Paso, 1990; payroll adminstr. Calvert County Pub. Schs., Prince Frederick, Md., 1992—; fin. cons., Prince Frederick, 1993—; tax preparer, Lexington Pk., Md., 1993—; writer, prodr. radio commls., 1990. Vol. NAACP, Calvert County, 1996. Mem. AICPA, Md. Assn. CPAs, Alpha Kappa Alpha. Democrat. Avocations: missionary work, acting, promotional modeling, tennis, travel. Home: 650 Gunsmoke Cir Lusby MD 20657-5156

HUTCHINSON, ALAN, computer scientist, educator; b. York, Eng., July 30, 1948; s. George William and Christine Anne (Rymer) H.; m. Catherine Mary Finney, July 5, 1996; children: Timothy, Rebecca. BA, St. John's Coll., Cambridge U., 1969; MSc, Warwick U., 1970, MPhil, 1975. Programmer Oriel Ltd., Oxford, 1976, Regional Health Authority, Oxford, 1977-81; higher sci. officer Nat. Engring. Lab., East Kilbride, 1981-83; lectr. U. Manchester (Eng.) Inst. Sci. and Tech., 1983-85, King's Coll., London, 1986—. Author: Algorithmic Learning, 1994; editor: Machine and Human Learning, 1989. Mem. London Math Soc., European Assn. for Theoretical Computer Sci., Assn. for Computational Linguistics. Avocations: bell ringing, cycling, mountain walking, badminton. Office: Kings Coll, Dept Computer Sci, London WC2R 2LS, England

HUTCHINSON, GEORGE BAIN, English and American studies educator; b. Evanston, Ill., Nov. 21, 1953; s. James Moore and Iris Louise (Bain) H.; m. Portia Babbette Spencer, Aug. 28, 1982; children: Spencer Paul, Geoffrey Bain. AB, Brown U., 1975; MA, Indiana U., 1980, PhD, 1983. Well digger U.S. Peace Corps, Burkina Faso, W. Africa, 1975-77; grad. fellow Indiana U. Am. Studies Program, Bloomington, 1977-78; assoc. instr. Indiana U. Dept. English, Bloomington, 1978-82; asst. prof. English U. Tenn., Knoxville, 1982-88, assoc. prof. English, 1988-96, prof., 1996-2000; chair literary studies Ind. U., Bloomington, 2000—; chmn. Am. Studies Program U. Tenn., Knoxville, 1987—. Author: The Ecstatic Whitman, 1986, The Harlem Renaissance in Black and White, 1996; contbr. articles to profl. jours. Recipient Alcoa Found. scholarship, Aluminum Co. Am., 1971-75, Am. Studies fellowship, Ind. U., Bloomington, 1977-78, NEH summer stipend, 1988, NEH fellowship, 1989-90. Mem. Modern Lang. Assn., South Atlantic Modern Lang. Assn., Am. Studies Assn., Walt Whitman Assn., Knoxville Rowing Assn. (pres. 1985-98). Avocations: sculling, hiking, writing. Office: U Tenn Dept English Knoxville TN 37996-0430

HUTCHINSON, JERRY JAMES, medical products executive; b. Bromsgrove, England, Nov. 29, 1955; s. James Haliday and Joyce Hudson (Bird) H.; m. Gillian Elizabeth Dye, Sept. 4, 1982; children: David, Emma, Claire. BSc with honors, U. Leeds, Eng., 1977, PhD, 1981. Rsch. fellow U. Birmingham, Eng., 1980-83; scientist E R Squibb, Moreton, Eng., 1983-85; sect. head and higher positions Convatec Ltd., Deeside, Eng., 1985-96, dir., 1997—. Co-editor: Wound and Skin Physiology, 1995; contbr. articles to profl. publs., chpts. to books in field. Mem. Soc. Gen. Microbiology, Wound Healing Soc., European Wound Mgmt. Assn. Avocations: classic motorcycle restoration, white water kayaking, swimming, fitness. Office: Convatec Ltd, 1st Ave Deeside Indsl Pk, Deeside CH5 2NU, England

HUTCHINSON, JOSEPH CANDLER, retired foreign language educator; b. Hazelhurst, Ga., Jan. 10, 1920; s. George Washington and Lillie Arizona (Rowan) H.; m. June Cruce O'Shields, Aug. 12, 1950 (div. 1980); children: Junie O'Shields, Joseph Candler. BA, Emory U., 1940, MA, 1941; PhD, U. N.C., 1950; postgrad., U. Paris, 1951,53. Tchr. Tech. High Sch., Atlanta, 1941-42; instr. French, German, Italian Emory U., Atlanta, 1946-47; instr. U. N.C., Chapel Hill, 1947-50, asst. prof., 1954, assoc. prof., 1954-57; asst. prof. Sweet Briar (Va.) Coll., 1950-51, 53-54; assoc. prof. Tulane U., New Orleans, 1957-59; fgn. lang. splst. U.S. Office Edn., Washington, 1959-64; acad. adv. hqrs. Def. Lang. Inst., Washington, 1964-74; acad. adv. hqrs. Def. Lang. Inst., Monterey, Calif., 1974-77, dir. tng. devel. Fgn. Lang. Ctr., 1977-82; asst. acad. dean Def. Lang. Inst., Monterey, 1982-85, dean of policy, 1985-88; vis. prof. U. Va., Charlottesville, 1966, Arlington, 1970, Georgetown U., 1968, Am. U., 1971; cons. Coun. Chief State Sch. Officers, 1960, U. Del., 1966, U. Colo., 1968, U. Ill., 1968; U.S. del. Bur. Internat. Lang. Coordination NATO, 1964-79, 81-82, 86-87. Author: Using the Language Laboratory Effectively: School Executive's Guide, 1964, The Language Laboratory: Equipment and Utilization in Trends in Language Teaching, 1966, others; editor: Dialogue on Language Instruction, 1986-88; contbr. articles to profl. jours. Served with U.S. Army spl. agent counter intelligence corps, 1942-46, 51-53. Decorated Bronze Star, 5 Battle Stars-Europe, battlefield commn. Mem. Am. Coun. Edn. (task force on internat. edn. 1973), NEA (sec. dept. fgn. langs. 1961-64), AARP/VOTE (17th congl. dist. team), Higher Edn. Assn., Monterey Peninsula, Am. Coun. Tchg. Fgn. Lang., MLA, Am. Mgmt. Assn., Am. Soc. Tng. and Devel., Nat. Assn. Ret. Fed. Employees (v.p. Monterey chpt. 1990, pres. 1991-92), Monterey Choral Soc., Camerata Singers, Washington Linguistics Club (v.p. 1970-72). Episcopalian. Home: PO Box Ab Pacific Grove CA 93950-0525

HUTCHINSON, LESLIE JULIAN, preventive medicine physician; b. Cin., June 22, 1957; s. Joseph Edward and Evelyn (Moss) H.; m. Stephanie Ellyn Leffingwell, Dec. 22, 1989. BS, Xavier U., 1978; MD, U. Cin. Coll. of Medicine, 1984; MPH, The Johns Hopkins U., 1990. Diplomate Am. Bd. Preventive Medicine Specialist in Occupl. Medicine; MD, Calif., Ga., Ohio; registered hazardous substances profl. Chemist EPA, Cin., 1982; Ctrs. for Disease Control vis. program staff fellowship Nat. Inst. for Occupl. Safety and Health, Cin., 1984; resident in internal medicine Wright State U., Dayton, Ohio, 1984-85; med. officer Agy. for Toxic Substances and Disease Registry, Atlanta, 1986-92; occupl. medicine resident Emory U., Atlanta, 1992-93; adj. assoc. prof. environ. and occupl. health Emory U. Sch. Pub. Health, Atlanta, 1990—; pres. HLM Consultants, Atlanta, 1993—; on-site peer reviewer Tex. Air Control Bd., Galveston, 1987-88; mem. Emory U. Acad. Adv. Coun. on Occupl. and Environ. Health, Atlanta, 1989—; instr. environ. risk mgr. certification U. Southwest Tex., San Marcos, 1996—. Contbr. articles to profl. jours. instr. med. coll. admission text preparation program for minority students Atlanta U., 1987-90. Recipient Performance Mgmt. and Recognition System award Dept. Health and Human Svcs., 1989, Spl. Act or Svc. award Dept. of Health and Human Svcs., 1992, Xavier U. Achievement and Nat. Merit scholarships, Xavier Biology prize. Mem. Nat. Environ. Health Assn., Am. Coll. Occupl. and Environ. Medicine, Delta Omega, Alpha Omega Alpha, Sigma Pi Sigma. Avocations: photography, Oriental philosophy. E-mail: hlm@mindspring.com. Office: HLM Consultants 214 Wynfield Way Auburn GA 30011-2849

HUTCHINSON, PARK WILLIAM, JR., theatre educator; b. Lancaster, Pa., Apr. 14, 1935; s. Park William and Thelma Mae (Beam) H.; m. Patsy Ann Flory, Aug. 15, 1955 (div. May 1981); 1 child, Suzanne Flory Hutchinson; m. Jeri Ann McElroy, Sept. 18, 1982. BA, Franklin Marshall Coll., 1957; BD, Princeton Theol. Sem., 1960; MA, Columbia U., 1962; PhD, Northwestern U., 1968. Instr. Tougaloo (Miss.) Coll., 1962-64, asst. prof., 1964-65, dir. speech & theater, 1962-65; asst. prof. theatre R.I. Coll., Providence, 1968-71, assoc. prof., 1971-74, prof., 1974—, chair dept. theater and dance, 1996-98, chair dept. music theater and dance, 1998—; dir. dance & drama Mathewson St. United Meth. Ch., Providence, 1969-75; dir. R.I. Gov.'s Sch. for Youth in the Arts, Providence, 1970-72; art. dir. NewGate Theatre, Providence, 1991-92. Dir. over 100 plays and readings, 1957—. Mem. exec. bd. R.I. Festival Theatre, Providence, 1971, Coll. of Fellows, New Eng. Theatre Conf., Boston, 1987—; theatre coord. R.I. Arts in Edn. Project, Providence, 1970-72. Danforth Found. fellow, 1965-66, 67-68; grantee R.I. Com. for Humanities, 1975—, R.I. Coun. Arts, 1978—. Mem. Assn. Theatre in Higher Edn., Phi Beta Kappa. Avocations: hist. portrayals: Jefferson, Thoreau, Wilde, Poe, Darrow, etc. Home: 7 Wadsworth Ave Smithfield RI 02917-4109 Office: RI Coll 600 Mount Pleasant Ave Providence RI 02908-1924

HUTCHINSON, PHILIP, education educator; b. Bishop Auckland, Durham, U.K., July 26, 1938; s. George and Edna (Routh) H.; m. Joyce Harrison, Sept. 7, 1960; children: Barbara Helen, John Paul. BS in Physics with hons., U. Durham, 1959; PhD, U. Newcastle-upon-Tyne, 1963; D (hon.), U. Lund (Sweden), 1999. Chartered physicist, chartered engr. Rsch. scientist theoretical physics divsn. AERE Harwell, Didcot, Eng., 1962-69; rsch. scientist Didcot, Eng., 1970-75; head of thermodynamics and fluid mechs. group AERE Harwell, Didcot, Eng., 1975-80; head of engring. physics br. AEFE Harwell, Didcot, Eng., 1980-85, head of engring. scis. divsn., 1985-87; head of sch. of mech. engring., prof. statis. fluid mechs. Sch. of Mech. Engring./Cranfield Univ., Cranfield, Eng., 1987—; vis. fellow U. Houston, 1969-70; chmn. Internat. Energy Agy., exec. com. on fundamental rsch. in combustion, Paris, 1977-81; vis. prof. Imperial Coll., London, 1980-85, U. Leeds, 1985—; mem. Watt Com. on Energy, London, 1980s; dir. Cranfield Flow Tech. Cons. Ltd., 1987-99, Norseca Ltd., Belgium; chmn., mng. dir. Engring. Tech. and Cons., Ltd., Wantage, Eng., 1987—; prin. Royal Mil. Coll. Sci., 1996—; dep. vice chancellor Cranford U., 1996—, pro vice chancellor, 1996-99. Contbr. articles to profl. jours. and publs. Chmn. govs. King Alfreds Sch., Wantage, Eng., 1984. Fellow Royal Acad. Engring.; mem. European Rsch. Community on Flow Turbulence and Combustion (chmn. 1994—), Inst. of Physics, Royal Instn. Avocations: music, reading, gadgets. Office: Cranfield Univ, Sch of Mech Engring, Beds MK43 OAL Cranfield England

HUTCHISON, JAMES ARTHUR, JR., architectural and engineering company executive; b. Gainesville, Mo., Oct. 25, 1917; s. James Arthur and Dora Ethel (James) H.; m. Imogene Cox, Dec. 5, 1946; children: Judith Lynn, Janet Gayle, James Arthur III. BS in Mech. Engring., Okla. State U., 1940; BS in Aero. Engring., Spartan Sch. Aeronautics, 1942; BS in Acctg., Okla. Sch. Accountancy, 1963. Registered profl. engr. Del., N.J., Md., V.I. Asst. chief engr. Spartan Aircraft Co., Tulsa, Okla., 1943-51; owner H&H Engring. & Constrn. Co., Tulsa, 1951-68; sr. liaison engr. ILC Industries Inc. Appollo Astronaut Program, Dover, Del., 1968-72; v.p. Diamond State Engring., Inc., Dover, 1972-78; founder, chmn. bd. dirs. The JAED Corp., Smyrna, Del., 1978—. Chmn. bd. trustees, chmn. bldg. com. 1st Bapt. Ch., Dover, 1979-90, 97-2000. Mem. Am. Inst. Steel Constrn., Am. Concrete Inst., Ctrl. Del. Pilots Assn. (pres. 1977-78). Republican. Avocation: aircraft flight instruction. Office: The JAED Corp 6 Village Sq Smyrna DE 19977-1852

HUTCHISON, JANE CAMPBELL, art history educator, researcher; b. Washington (D.C.), July 20, 1932; d. James Paul and Leone Bailey (Warrick) H. BA fine arts, Western Maryland Coll., 1954; MA art history, Oberlin Coll., 1958; PhD art history, U. Wis., 1964. Tech. illustrator/ Dept. Model Basin U.S. Navy, Washington (D.C.), 1954-56; rsch libr. Toledo Mus. of Art, 1957-59; teaching asst. U. Wis., Madison, 1959-60,61-63; vis. asst. prof. Temple U., Phila., summer 1968; from instr. to assoc. prof. U. Wis., Madison, 1964—, prof., 1975—, dept. chmn., 1977-80, 92-93; cons. NEH, Washington (D.C.), 1972-77, Inst. Internat. Edn., N.Y.C., 1977, 82, 89, Nat. Gallery of Art, Washington, 1982-83, Rijksmuseum, Amsterdam, 1984, 98, Cin. Art Mus., 1990—; expert witness U.S. Dist. Ct. (so. dist.) N.Y., 2000. Author: Master of the Housebook, 1972, Early German Artists, vol. 8, 1980, vol. 9, 1981, vol. 9 part 2, 1991, vol. 8 part 6, 1996, Albrecht Dürer: A Biography, 1990 (German edit., 1994), Albrecht Dürer: A Guide to Research, 2000. Pres. Madison chpt. AAUP, 1979-81, Midwest Art History Soc., 1983-85; sec.-treas. Historians of Netherlandish Art, 1995-99; pres. St. Andrew's Soc. Madison, 1995—. Grad. fellow Oberlin Coll., 1955-57, fellow U. Wis., 1959-60, 61-63, Fulbright fellow Rijksuniversiteit Utrecht, Netherlands, 1960-61, rsch. grantee NEH, Germany, 1982, German Acad. Exch. Svc., Germany, summer 1989; Grant in aid Am. Coun. Learned Soc., Amsterdam, 1984; recipient Alumni award Western Md. Coll. Trustees, 1987. Mem. AAUP (pres. Madison chpt. 1979-81), Internat. Coun. Mus., Am. Assn. Mus., Medieval Acad. Am., Coll. Art Assn., Univ. Club U. Wis. (bd. dirs. 1976-80, pres. 1980), Wis. Assn. Scholars (v.p. Madison chpt. 1990—), Midwest Art History Soc. (pres. 1983-85), Historians of Netherlandish Art (sec.-treas. 1995-99), Print Coun. Am. E-mail: jchutchi@facstaff.wisc.edu. Home: 2261 Regent St Madison WI 53705-5321 Office: U Wis Dept Art History 800 University Ave Madison WI 53706-1414

HUTCHISON, KEITH ROBERT, history and philosophy of science educator; b. Strathfield, Australia, Sept. 20, 1944; s. Ronald Edward and Rita (Parkes) H.; m. Mary Katharine Farrow Macdonald, Sept. 20, 1969; children: Benjamin, Oliver. BSc, Australian Nat. U., 1967; MSc, Monash U., 1968; diploma in history/philosophy of sci., Oxford U., 1969, D.Phil., 1977. Lectr. Riverina Coll. Advanced Edn., Wagga Wagga, Australia, 1973-75, Swinburne Coll., Melbourne, 1977; lectr. U. Melbourne, 1978-79, rsch. fellow, lectr., 1980—. Mem. Australasian Assn. for History Philosophy and Social Studies of Sci., History of Sci., History of Sci. Soc., Nat. Com. History and Philosophy of Sci. Office: U Melbourne, Dept History and Phil Sci, Parkville VIC 3052, Australia

HUTCHISON, RICHARD LYNN, technical writer; b. Ft. Worth, Nov. 1, 1953; s. Prentiss Lynd and Frances Josephine (Hammack) H.; m. Christine Louise Cooley, Aug. 5, 1978; children: Matthew Ryan, Michelle Renee, Mary Rebecca, Marcus Richard. BA in History, U. Tex., Arlington, 1977, MA in History, 1982; AA in Mgmt. Devel., Tarrant County Jr. Coll., Ft. Worth, 1993. Cert. elem. tchr., Tex. Tchr./coach Arlington Ind. Sch. Dist., 1978-82; tech. writer Global Group, Inc., Ft. Worth, 1983-84; tchr. White Settlement Ind. Sch. Dist., Ft. Worth, 1984-85; tech. writer, data adminstr., manpower/material estimator Bell Helicopter/Textron, Inc., Ft. Worth, 1985—; instr. (part-time) U.S. History Tarrant County Jr. Coll., 1983-89, 1990—; adj. instr. World History Southwestern Coll., Phoenix, 1990. Bd. mgrs. N.E. Br. YMCA, Ft. Worth, 1991-94, 1997— (chmn. 1995-96); mem. sch. com. Glenview Christian Sch., Ft. Worth, 1993—. Vol. of Yr. Ft. Worth YMCA, 1994. Mem. Orgn. Am. Historians, Optimists (v. p. baseball N.E. Optimist Club 1997-98, pres. 1999, club pres. 2000). Republican. Baptist. Avocations: Sunday Sch. tchr., golf, coaching baseball. E-mail: rhutchison@bellhelicopter.textron.com. Home: 5521 Maurie Dr Fort Worth TX 76148-3823 Office: Bell Helicopter Textron Inc PO Box 482 Fort Worth TX 76101-0482

HUTCHISON, ROBERT EDWARD, hematopathologist; b. Springfield, Mo., Feb. 8, 1951; s. James Camden and Janice Marie Hutchison; m. Debra Lee Hutchison, Dec. 21, 1978; children: Camden, Raymond, Samuel. BA, U. Mo., 1973, MD, 1977. Diplomate Am. Bd. Pathology. Physician Mid Mo. Mental Health Ctr., Columbia, 1977-79; resident in pathology U. Mo., Columbia, 1980-84; hematology fellow SUNY Upstate Med. U., Syracuse, 1984-86, hemapathologist, 1989—; blood bank dir. St. Jude Children's Research Hosp., Memphis, 1986-89. Co-author: Clinical Diagnosis by Laboratory Methods, 2000, Pediatric Neoplasia, 1997. Mem. Am. Soc. Hematology, Soc. Hematopathology, Cancer & Leukemia Group, Pediatric Oncology Group (pathology chair 1988-00). Democrat. Roman Catholic. Avocations: photography, music, triathlon. Office: SUNY Upstate Med U 750 E Adams St Syracuse NY 13210-2306

HUTH, WILLIAM EDWARD, lawyer; b. South Bend, Ind., July 26, 1931; s. Edward Andrew and Margaret Mary (Emonds) H.; m. Mary Pamela Hall, Aug. 11, 1962; children: Katharine Louise, Stephen Edward (dec.), Alan Edward. BS, U. Dayton, 1952; JD, Yale, 1957. Bar: N.Y. 1958, U.S. Dist. Ct. (so. dist.) N.Y. 1959, Mich. 1962, U.S. Dist. Ct. (ea. dist.) Mich. 1962, U.S. Supreme Ct. 1969, Pa. 1975, Conn. 1978. Assoc. Kelley, Drye, Newhall & Maginnes, N.Y.C., 1958-61; group counsel Chrysler Corp., Detroit, 1962-72; ptnr. Ziegler, Dykhouse, Wise & Huth, Detroit, 1973-74; assoc. gen. counsel Westinghouse Electric Corp., Pitts., 1974-76; asst. sec., asst. gen. counsel Combustion Engring., Inc., Stamford, Conn., 1976-90; ptnr. Huth, Grinnell & Flaherty, Stamford, 1991—; adj. prof. law Wayne State U., Detroit, 1969-74, adj. prof. law Pace U. Sch. of Law, 1999—. Contbr. articles to profl. publs. 1st lt. AUS, 1952-54. Mem. ABA (antitrust sect., internat. law sect., bus. law sect., intellectual property sect.), Am. Soc. Internat. Law, Am. Arbitration Assn. (Blue Ribbon Panel Arbitrators & Mediators, mem. copr. coun. com.), Inter-Am. Bar Assn., Inter-Pacific Bar Assn., Internat. Bar Assn., Conn. Bar Assn. (chmn. corp. coun. sec. 1991-94), Assn. of Bar of City of N.Y., Westchester-Fairfield Corp. Counsel Assn. (pres. 1987, bd. dirs. 1984-88), U.S. C. of C. (mem. antitrust adv. coun.), Yale Club N.Y.C., N.Y. Yacht Club, The Army and Navy Club (Washington), Indian Harbor Yacht Club (Greenwich), Order of Coif. Roman Catholic. Home: 39 Balmaha Ct Fairfield CT 06432-1173 Office: Huth Grinnell & Flaherty 1055 Washington Blvd Stamford CT 06901-2216

HUTHLOFF, CHRISTA ROSE, library and information science educator; b. Aichelberg, Germany, Oct. 4, 1946. Grad., Libr. Sch., Hamburg, Germany, 1969. Head interlibr. loan Lower Saxonian State Libr., Hannover, Germany, 1969-76; lectr. Libr. Sch., Hannover, 1976-80; lectr. libr. & info. sci. Fach Hoch Sch, Hannover, 1980—. Author: GRIPS Fuer BRZN und DBI, 1991; co-author: Online - Bibiliographieren in allgemeinbibliographiochen, 1985; editor: Informationsvermittling, 1988; contbr. articles to profl. jours. Mem. Verein der Diplom Bibliothekare an Wissenschaft Lichen Bibliotheken, Deutsche Gesellschaft für Informationswissenschaft und Informationspraxis. Office: Fach Hoch Sch Info und Komm, Ricklinger Stadtweg 120, 30459 Hannover Germany

HUTLEY, TREVOR JOHN, research scientist; b. Gillingham, Eng., May 29, 1955; s. John Charles and Isabel Norah (Osborne) H.; m. Julie Carman, Sept. 18, 1976; children: Kelly Ann, Katie Elizabeth. BTech with 1st class honours, Brunel U., 1977; MBA summa cum laude, Bus. Sch. Lausanne, Switzerland, 1991; PhD, Cranfield Inst. Tech., 1985. Group leader dept. materials applications Dunlop, Birmingham, Eng., 1977-82; packaging group exec. British Plastics Fedn., London, 1976; rsch. officer Polymer Composites Group, Cranfield Inst. of Tech., 1982-85; rsch. scientist DuPont (U.K.) Ltd., Eng., 1985-89; sr. rsch. scientist DuPont de Nemours Internat., Geneva, 1989-96; regional tech. mgr. Asia-Pacific, DuPont China Ltd., Kowloon, Hong Kong, 1997-98; rsch. assoc. DuPont Internat. SA, Geneva, 1998-2000; polymer cons. Arrabon Technologies, Onex/GE, Switzerland, 2000—; market devel. cons. DuPont de Nemours Internat., Geneva, 1992-93, mem. regional bus. team, 1994-96; lectr. polymer group Cranfield Inst. of Tech., U.K., 1983-85. Contbr. articles to profl. jours. Treas. Crossroads Cmty. Ch., Geneva, 1990-92, elder, house-group leader; mem. Corp. Com. Polymer Experts, 1994-96. Recipient Corp. Environ. Excellence award, 1991. Mem. Inst. Materials, Soc. Mfg. Engrs. (sr.), Soc. Plastics Engrs. (sr.), Royal Soc. Chemistry (chartered chemist). E-mail: trevorhutley@consultant.com. Home and Office: chemin de Belle-Cour 60, CH-1213 Onex/GE Switzerland

HUTNIK, NIMMI, psychologist; b. Hong Kong, Apr. 3, 1954; d. Urumese Lonappen and Clare (Paul) Parambi; m. Michael Ivan Hutnik, Aug. 8, 1980; children: Anna, Tanya. BA with honors, Lady Shri Ram Coll., Delhi, India, 1974; MA, Arts Faculty, Delhi, 1976; PhD, Dept. Exptl. Psychology, Oxford, U.K., 1985. Cert. Transactional Analyst. Reader Lady Shri Ray Coll., New Delhi, 1977-98; sr. lectr. U. Surrey, Roehampton, U.K., 2000—; cons. Gallup - MBA, India, 1996-97, Varkey Ednl. Svcs., India, 1997, Sahayata, India, 1990—; exec. bd. dirs. Indian Assn. Family Therapy. Author: Ethnic Minority Identity: A Social Psychological Perspective, 1991. Chmn. Sahara House, New Delhi, 1986-88; rschr. at Mental Health Found., London 1999-2000; con. Spastic Soc. of India, New Delhi; founding mem. Aashiana: A Therapeutic Cmty., New Delhi, 1978-82. Recipient Fulbright Am. Sr. Rsch. fellowship L.A., 1997, Commonwealth Acad. Staff scholarship, Oxford, 1982-85, Pres.'s Gold medal, New Delhi, 1976. Mem. Tarshi (exec. bd. 1997), TASI (exec. bd. 1993-95), IAFT (exec. bd. 1995-97). Avocations: painting and drawing.

HUTSON, JEFFREY WOODWARD, lawyer; b. New London, Conn., July 19, 1941; s. John Jenkins and Kathryn Barbara (Himberg) H.; m. Susan Office, Nov. 25, 1967; children: Elizabeth Kathryn, Anne Louise. AB, U. Mich., 1963, LLB, 1966. Bar: Ohio 1966, Hawaii 1970. Assoc. Lane, Alton & Horst, Columbus, Ohio, 1966-74, ptnr., 1974—. Trustee, vice-chair 6 Pence Sch., 1983-88; mem. com. creeds and professionalism Ohio Supreme Ct., 1989-90; chair, bd. dirs. N.W. Counseling Svcs., 1990-92, regional v.p. Def. Rsch. Inst., 1991-93. Lt comdr. USNR, 1967-71. Fellow Am. Coll. Trial Lawyers, Am. Bar Found., Ohio State Bar Found., Columbus Bar Found.; mem. Ohio Bar Assn. (past chair litigation sect.), Ohio Assn. Civil Tiral Attys. (past pres.), Columbus Bar Assn., Internat. Assn. Def. Counsel, Faculty Def. Coun. Trial Acad., Scioto Country Club, Athletic Club. Avocations: cycling, reading, music. Office: Lane Alton & Horst 175 S 3rd St Ste 700 Columbus OH 43215-5100

HU TSU TAU, RICHARD, Singapore government official; b. Singapore, Oct. 30, 1926; m. Irene Tan Dee Leng; 2 children. BSc in Chemistry, U. Calif., Berkeley, 1952; diploma in chem. engring., U. Birmingham, Eng., 1954, PhD in Chem. Engring., 1957. Lectr. chem. engring. U. Manchester, Eng., 1958-60; with Shell Oil Co., Singapore and Malaysia, 1960-70; dir. mktg., gen. mgr. Shell Oil Co., 1970-73; with Shell Internat. Petroleum Co., The Hague, The Netherlands, 1973-74; chief exec. Shell Cos., Malaysia, 1974-77; chmn., chief exec. Shell Cos., Singapore, 1977-82; chmn. Shell Cos., 1982-83; mng. dir. Monetary Authority Singapore, 1983-84, Govt. of Singapore Investment Corp. Pte. Ltd., 1983-84; elected mem. Parliament, 1984; min. trade and industry, 1985; chmn. Monetary Authority Singapoer also Bd. Commrs. Currency, Singapore, 1985—; min. fin., 1985—, min. health, 1985-87, min. nat. devel., 1992-94. Avocations: golf, swimming. *

HUTT, PETER BARTON, lawyer; b. Buffalo, Nov. 16, 1934; s. Lester Ralph and Louise Rich (Fraser) H.; children: Katherine Zurn, Peter Barton, Sarah Henderson, Everett Fraser. BA magma cum laude, Yale U., 1956; LLB, Harvard U., 1959; LLM, NYU, 1960. Bar: N.Y. 1959, D.C. 1961, U.S. Supreme Ct. 1967. Assoc. Covington & Burling, Washington, 1960-68, ptnr., 1968-71, 75—; chief counsel FDA, Washington, 1971-75; bd. dirs. Cogetix, Inc., Salt Lake City, Circe Biomed., Inc., Lexington, Mass., Emisphere Tech., Inc., Hawthorne, N.Y., PhaseForward, Inc., Waltham; mem. adv. com. to dir. NIH, 1976-81; mem. com. on rsch. tng. NAS, 1976-80; bd. dirs. Calif. Health Care Inst., San Diego, 1996—; counsel to Alcoholic Beverage Med. Rsch. Found., 1984-85, chmn. bd. dirs., 1986-92; mem. Nat. Com. to Review Current Procedure for Approval of New Drugs for Cancer and AIDS, Nat. Cancer Inst., 1988-90; mem. nat. bd. Scripps Clinic and Rsch. Found., La Jolla, 1977-85, 90-95; mem. internat. bd. Scripps Instns. of Med. and Sci., 1995—, Ctr. for Study Drug Devel., Tufts U. Ctr., 1976-99, Calif. Healthcare Inst., San Diego, 1996—, Ctr. for Advanced Studies, U. Va., 1982—, Inst. for Health Policy Analysis, 1982—, Am. Pharm. Inst., Washington, 1988-92; mem. Com. on Food Laws and Regulations, Inst. Food Tech.; mem. adv. com. Progress and Freedom Found., 1994-97; mem. adv. bd. Frazier Healthcare Investments, Seattle, 1993—, Sprout Group, N.Y. and Menlo Park, 1993—, Polaris Venture Ptnrs., Waltham, Mass., 1995—, Vanguard Medica Ltd., Guildford, Eng., 1993-99; mem. various panels U.S. Congl. Office Tech. Assessment; lectr. on food and drug law Harvard U., 1994—, Stanford U., 1998; mem. adv. bd. Columbia U. Sch. Pub. Health, 1997—. Author: (with Patricia Wald) Dealing with Drug Abuse, 1972, (with Richard Merrill) Food and Drug Law, 1991, (with Bruce Kuhlik) Understanding Export Law, 1998; editor-in-chief U.S. Food Labeling Law, 1991—; contbg. editor: Legal Times of Washington, 1978-86; mem. editorial bd. various jours.; editor: Food and Drug Law: An Electronic Book of Student Papers. Bd. dirs. Sidwell Friends Sch., Washington, 1976-84; bd. dirs. Legal Action Ctr., N.Y.C., 1976—, vice-chmn., 1984-98; bd. dirs. Found. for Biomed. Rsch., 1976—, vice chmn., 1989— ; trustee Washington Lawyers Com. for Civil Rights & Urban Affairs, 1976—; bd. dirs. Soc. Risk Analysis, 1985-88, 89-92, counsel, 1992—; mem. vis. com. Harvard Sch. Pub. Health, 1980-86. Recipient award of merit FDA, 1972, 75, Disting. Svc. award HEW, 1974, Underwood-Prescott award MIT, 1977. Fellow

Soc. Risk Analysis; mem. ABA (former chmn. life scis. com., sect. on sci. and tech.), Inst. Medicine of NAS (mem. Devel. of Drugs and Vaccines Against AIDS roundtable 1988-94, bd. on health care svcs. 1998—). Episcopalian. Club: Metropolitan (Washington). Home: 402 Prince St Alexandria VA 22314-3114 Office: Covington & Burling 1201 Pennsylvania Ave NW Washington DC 20004-2401

HUTTELOVA, RENATA, embryologist; b. Lanskroun, Czech Republic, Feb. 5, 1970; d. Emil and Margita (Dolnakova) Grocholova; m. Martin Huttel, Sept. 13, 1996. MSc, Charles U., 1993, PhD, 1998. Embryologist Inst. Care Mother and Child, Prague, Czech Republic, 1993-95, Pronatal Pvt. IVF Ctr., Prague, 1996—. Mem. Scientists Reproductive Medicine, European Soc. Human Reproduction and Embryology. Office: Pronatal Pvt IVF Ctr, Na Dlouhe Mezi 4, 147 00 Prague 4, Czech Republic

HUTTER, BERND, molecular biologist, researcher; b. Chingen, Germany, Feb. 10, 1969; arrived in Singapore, 1997; s. Guenter and Magda (Bosch) H.; m. Grit Richter, July 14, 1994; children: Philip, Denise. MSc, U. Bayreuth, Germany, 1994; PhD, U. Braunschweig, Germany, 1996. Rsch. fellow Inst. Molecular & Cell Biology, Singapore, Singapore, 1997—. Contbr. articles to profl. jours.; patentee in field. Mem. Am. Soc. Microbiology.

HUTTIN, CHRISTINE CLAUDE, economist; b. Nancy, France, Mar. 25, 1957; d. Roger and Micheline (Martin) H. MBA, Essec, France, 1980; diploma, Coll. Europe, 1981; PhD, Ecole Haute Etudes Scis Social, Paris, 1986. Tech. advisor French Treasury, Paris, 1986-87; economist Credit Nat., Paris, 1987-88; tech. advisor European Commn., Brussels, Belgium, 1990-91; vis. prof. Hong Kong U. Sci. & Technology, 1991-92; assoc. prof. U. Paris, 1988—; cons. WHO, Bulgaria, Albania, Copenhagen, 1998-99, European Commn., 1992-94, World Bank, Indonesia, 2000. Author: Economics of Pharmaceuticals, 1989; editor, author: The Prescription Drug Market: International Perspective and Challenges for the Future, 1992. Fulbright scholar, Berkeley, Calif., 1990; Takemi fellow Harvard Sch. Pub. Health, 1995. Mem. Acad. Mgmt., N.Y. Acad. Scis., Coll. Econs. de Sante. Avocations: hiking, music, skiing. Home: BP14, 92420 Vaucresson France

HUTTO, DANIEL DOUGLAS, philosopher, educator; b. Yonkers, N.Y., Nov. 12, 1965; s. William Erving and Margaret Scott (MacKenzie) H.; m. Sharifah Farakial Farah Alyahya, July 21, 1989; children: Alexander, Justin. BA in English Lit., Marist Coll., 1987; MPhil in Logic and Metaphysics, U. St. Andrews (Scotland), 1990; DPhil, U. York (Eng.), 1994. Tchr. 4th grade Fielday Sch., N.Y., 1988-89; tutor philosophy U. York (Eng.), 1990-93, asst. lectr., 1992-93; lectr. U. Hertfordshire (Eng.), 1993-95, study abroad coord., scheme officer cognitive sci., 1994-99, rsch. leader, sr. lectr., 1995-99, reader in philosophy of psychology, 1999; vis. lectr. U. Sunderland, Eng., 1991-92; dir. Ctr. Meaning and Metaphys. Studies, Hertfordshire, Eng., 1996-99, head of philosophy, 1999—. Author: The Presence of Mind, 1999, Beyond Physicalism, 2000; co-author: Space Infantry, 1982; co-editor: Current Issues in Idealism, 1996. Mem. Am. Philosoph. Assn., Soc. Philosophy and Psychology, European Soc. Analytic Philosophy. Office: U Herts Watford Campus, Dept Philosophy, WD2 8AT Watford Herts, England

HUTTON, ANGUS FINLAY, cattle breeder, consultant; b. Mysore, Karnataka, India, Apr. 8, 1928; arrived in Australia, 1962.; s. Henry William and Dorothy Lillian (Franklin) H.; m. Muriel Gem Robertson, Aug. 18, 1953; children: William McNab, Christine Margaret. Degree, Lawrence Meml. Royal Mil. Coll, 1944; diploma in agr., Kenya, 1956. Asst. mgr. Tea Estates India Ltd., 1945-52; sr. asst. mgr. Uganda Tea Estates Ltd., 1952-54; mgr. Ea. Produce Tea Estates Ltd., Kenya, 1954-62; scientific officer in charge Dept. Agr. Tea Rsch. Sta. and Factory, Papua New Guinea, 1962-78; proprietary farmer Small Crops/Cattle/Forestry Property, Queensland, Australia, 1978—; product/pasture inspector quaranting Inspection Svc. Dept. Primary Industry, Queensland, 1994—; cons. in field; nat. coord. Insvc. Farming and Trading Agy., Papua New Guinea, 1974-78. Author book chpts., articles, proposals in field. Mem. Wildlife Mgmt. Bd. India, 1948-52; hon. ranger Uganda and Kenya Nat. Park, 1954-63; v.p. Waria Local Govt. Coun., Papua New Guinea, 1969-78; hon. protector Nat. Parks and Wildlife Svc., Queensland, 1978—; s.p. constable Kenya Police Res., 1954-62. Cpl., trooper Indian Army Cavalry, 1944-47. Recipient Efficiency Decoration, Def. medal, Freedom of the Forest award Govt. of India, 1952, Independence medal Papua New Guinea, 1971. Fellow Zool. Soc. London (life), Royal Entomol. Soc. London; mem. Returned Serviceman's League of Australia (Gold medal, cert. 1971). Mem. Australian City Country Alliance Party. Presbyterian. Avocations: climbing, bush walking, horseback riding, fishing, photography.

HUTTON, DEBORAH SPENCE, academic administrator; b. Winnipeg, Man., Can., Mar. 10, 1952; d. Frances Spence and Bette Margaret (Brown) H. BSc (hons.), Queen's U., 1975, BEd, 1977; MSEd, Northern Ill. U., 1981; EdS, Ind. U., 1998. Tchr. social studies Bishop's Coll. Sch., Lennoxville, Canada, 1977-80; from project asst. tchr. edn. project to co-instr. Ind. U., Bloomington, 1983-94, coord. outreach & spl. projects Ctr. Study Global Change, 1996—; Co-author: African Social Studies Program 1, 1991, African Social Studies Program 2, 1991; contbr. articles to profl. jours., chpts. to books. cons. Russian Global Schs. Initiative, 1994-95; cons. com. Ctr. Canadian Studies Franklin (Ind.) Coll., 1993-94. Co-chair bldg. expansion steering com. Unitarian-Universalist Ch., Bloomington, 1995-98; pres. Georgetown Village Condominium Assn., Bloomington, 1991-94; mem. City Commn. on Status of Women, Bloomington, 1983-84. Mem. Nat. Coun. Social Studies, Ind. Coun. Social Studies, Global Edn. Network, Pi Lambda Theta. Avocations: gardening, bird watching, canoeing, reading. Office: Ind U Ctr Study Global Change 201 N Indiana Ave Bloomington IN 47408-4001

HUTTON, WINFIELD TRAVIS, management consultant, educator; b. L.A., Aug. 17, 1935; s. Travis Calhoun and Frances (Gardemann) H. BS in Mgmt. summa cum laude, Ohio State U., 1956, MBA, 1957, PhD, 1959. Consumer economist Fed. Res. Bank Atlanta, 1959-62; prof. econs. Hunter Coll., CUNY, 1962-68; prof. European divsn. U. Md., 1968-79, 93-99; prof. Troy State U.-Europe, Germany, 1979-93; cons. on mgmt., mktg. and econs. in Europe, 1968—. Author: (mgmt. computer simulations) City France, 1994, Simanage, 1998; author computer programs for rsch. stats.; contbr. articles to profl. jours. Lay reader St. Alban's Episcopal Ch., Kaiserslauten, Germany, 1981-88. Mem. AAUP, Am. Mktg. Assn. (manuscript reviewer 1983-94), Am. Econ. Assn., Beta Gamma Sigma. Avocations: opera, folk dancing, walking, cycling, travel. Address: 15138 Stone Ln N Apt B106 Shoreline WA 98133-6259 also: Goethestr 66, 19053 Schwerin Germany

HUTTUNEN, JUSSI KALERVO, health institute administrator; b. Helsinki, Finland, Aug. 27, 1941; s. Reino Tapio and Maire Tuulikki (Ahonen) H.; m. Raili Annikki, June 4, 1963; children: Kati, Outi. MD, Dr. Med. Sci., U. Helsinki, 1966. Specialist cert. in internal medicine. Rschr. U. Helsinki, 1963-68; rsch. fellow U. Calif., San Diego, 1968-70; resident Univ. Hosp. of Helsinki, 1970-74; assoc. prof. U. Kuopio, Finland, 1975-78; dir.-gen. Nat. Pub. Health Inst., Helsinki, 1978—. Recipient Jacob Paulsen prize Nordic Insulin Found., Copenhagen, 1981. Mem. Finnish Diabetes Rsch. Found. (pres. 1985-91), Finnish Heart Assn. (v.p. 1990-93, pres. 1998—), Finnish Cancer Assn. (pres. 1992-95), Finnish Soc. Physicians (pres. 1996-99). Home: Mäntytie 21 A 5, 00270 Helsinki Finland Office: Nat Pub Health Inst, Mannerheimintie 166, FIN00300 Helsinki Finland

HUUNAN-SEPPÄLÄ, ANTTI JOHANNES, insurance company executive; b. Tampere, Finland, June 24, 1945; m. Irja Suojärvi, June 8, 1968; children: Karoliina, Henriikka. MD, U. Helsinki, 1972, special competence in ins. medicine, 1994. Lectr. dept. pub. health U. Helsinki, 1972-74; med. expert Social Ins. Instn., Helsinki, 1973, head social medicine office, 1974-78, dep. dir. med. affairs, 1979-84, dir. med. affairs, 1984—; docent U. Tampere, 2000. Co-author: Inability to Work: The Role and Possibilities of Research, 1979, Aging and Care of the Elderly, 1981, Nutrition Research, 1983, Vakuutuslääketiede, 1999. Pres. Rheuma Found., Finland, 1985—, Prosthetic Found., Finland, 1988—, Rehab. Found., Finland, 1991—, Punkaharju Rehab. Hosp. Found., Finland, 1993—. Decorated Knight First Class of Order of White Rose of Finland Pres. of Finland, 1989. Mem. Royal Soc. of Health, Rehab. Internat. (pres. Finnish com. 1993—), Internat. Rehab. Med. Assn. (councillor 1986-90), Internat. Social Security Assn. (reporter 1989), Finnish Ins. Med. Assn. (pres. 1982-85). Avocations: music, literature, golf. E-mail: antti.huunan-seppala@kela.memonet.fi. Office: Social Ins Instn, PO Box 450, FIN-00101 Helsinki Finland

HUVOS, ANDREW, internist, cardiologist, educator; b. Budapest, Hungary, Apr. 23, 1930; came to U.S., 1950; s. Julian Gyula and Magdolna (Matyas) H.; m. Monique Chatriot, June 8, 1959; children: Christine, Anne, Philip. Student, Free U. Brussels, 1948-50, Harvard U., 1951; MD, Boston U., 1955. Diplomate Am. Bd. Internal Medicine, Am. Bd. Cardiovascular Disease. Resident in medicine Yale-New Haven Med. Ctr., 1955-59; fellow in cardiology Mass. Gen. Hosp., Boston, 1961-63; physician-in-charge cardiac catheterization lab. Univ. Hosp., Boston, 1963-70; chief cardiology Faulkner Hosp., Boston, 1970-74, chief medicine, 1974-95; lectr. medicine Harvard Med. Sch., Boston, 1974-86; lectr. medicine and physiology Boston U. Sch. Medicine, 1976—; prof. medicine Tufts U. Sch. Medicine, Boston, 1985-97, prof. emeritus, 1997—; dir. Tufts Assoc. Health Plan, 1979-81. Contbr. articles to med. jours., chpts. to books. Chmn. bd. trustees Ecole Bilingue, Inc., Arlington, Mass., 1970-74; trustee Boston Med. Libr., 1981-85. Capt. M.C., U.S. Army, 1959-61. Recipient Excellence in Teaching award Boston U. Sch. Medicine, 1974; USPHS grantee, 1977-83. Fellow ACP, Am. Coll. Cardiology, Am. Coll. Chest Physicians (pres. New Eng. States chpt. 1981-83); mem. Am. Heart Assn. (fellow couns. clin. cardiology and circulation), Dorchester Med. Club, Roxbury Clin. Record Club, Alpha Omega Alpha. Presbyterian. Avocations: opera, classical music. Office: Faulkner Hosp Boston MA 02130

HUXLEY, SIR ANDREW (FIELDING), physiologist, educator; b. London, Nov. 22, 1917; s. Leonard and Rosalind (Bruce) H.; m. Jocelyn Richenda Gammell Pease, July 5, 1947; children: Janet Rachel, Stewart Leonard, Camilla Rosalind, Eleanor Bruce, Henrietta Catherine, Clare Marjory Pease. BA, Cambridge (Eng.) U., 1938, MA, 1941, ScD (hon.), 1978; MD (hon.), U. Saar, 1964, Marseille U., 1979, Humboldt U., Berlin, 1985, Ulm U., 1993, Charles U., Prague, 1998; DSc (hon.), U. Sheffield, Eng., 1964, U. Leicester, Eng., 1967, London U., 1973, U. St. Andrews, Scotland, 1974, U. Aston, Birmingham, Eng., 1977, U. Western Australia, 1982, Oxford U., 1983, U. Pa., 1984, Harvard U., 1984, U. Keele, 1985, East Anglia U., 1985, U. Md., 1987, Brunel U., 1988, U. Hyderabad, 1991, Glasgow U., 1993, Witwatersrand U., 1998; LLD (hon.), U. Birmingham, 1979, Dundee U., 1984; Dr (hon.), York U., 1981, Toyama Med. and Pharm. U., 1995; DHL (hon.), NYU, 1982. Mem. rsch. staff Anti-Aircraft Command, 1940-42, Admiralty, 1942-45; fellow Trinity Coll., Cambridge, 1941-60, 90—, hon. fellow, 1967-90, master, 1984-90, dir. studies, 1952-60; demonstrator Cambridge U., 1946-50, asst. dir. rsch., 1951-59, reader exptl. biophysics, 1959-60; Jodrell prof. physiology U. Coll. London, 1960-69, Royal Soc. rsch. prof., 1969-83, hon. fellow, 1980; emeritus prof. physiology U. London, 1983—; Herter lectr. Johns Hopkins U., 1959; Jesup lectr. Columbia U., 1964; Forbes lectr., 1966; Croonian lectr. Royal Soc., 1967, Florey lectr., 1982, Blackett Meml. lectr., 1984; Fullerian prof. Royal Inst., London, 1967-73; Hans Hecht lectr., Chgo., 1975; Sherrington lectr. Liverpool U., 1976-77; Centenary Colloquium lectr. Berlin Inst. Physiology, 1977; Cecil H. and Ida Green vis. prof. U. B.C., 1980; 6th ann. Darwin Lecture, 1982, Romanes Lecture, Oxford U., 1983; Tarner lectrs. Trinity Coll., Cambridge, 1988; Maulana Abul Kalam Azad Meml. Lecture, New Delhi, 1991; C.G. Bernhard lecture, Stockholm, 1993; Davson lecture Am. Physiol. Soc., 1998; Wartenweiler lecture Internat. Soc. of Biomechanics, Calgary, 1999. Author: Reflections on Muscle, 1980; editor Jour. Physiology, 1950-57, chmn. bd. Publs. on analysis of nerve conduction (with Hodgkin), physiology of striated muscle, devel. of interference microscope and ultramicrotome. Trustee Brit. Mus. (Natural History), 1981-90, Sci. Mus., 1984-88. Created knight bachelor, 1974; decorated Order of Merit, 1983, Grand Cordon of Sacred Treasure (Japan), 1995; recipient (with A.L. Hodgkin and J.C. Eccles) Nobel prize for physiology or medicine, 1963, Swammerdam medal Soc. for Advancement of Natural Scis., Medicine and Surgery, Amsterdam, 1997; Imperial Coll. Sci., Tech. and Medicine hon. fellow, 1980; Queen Mary and Westfield Coll. fellow, 1987. Fellow Royal Soc. (Copley medal 1973, council 1960-62, 77-79, 80-85, pres. 1980-85), Royal Acad. Engring. (hon.), Inst. Biology (hon.), Royal Soc. Can. (hon.), Royal Soc. Edinburgh (hon.), Royal Coll. Physicians (hon.), Acad. Med. Sci. (hon.), Indian Nat. Sci. Acad. (fgn.); mem. Physiol. Soc. (hon., rev. lectr. on muscular contraction 1973), Internat. Union Physiol. Scis. (pres. 1986-93), Brit. Biophys. Soc., Royal Acad. Scis., Letters and Fine Arts Belgium (assoc.), Muscular Dystrophy Campaign (chmn. med. research com. 1974-81, v.p., 1981—), Royal Instn. Gt. Britain (hon.), Anat. Soc. Gt. Britain and Ireland (hon.), Am. Philos. Soc., Brit. Assn. Advancement Sci. (pres. 1976-77), NAS (U.S.) (fgn. assoc.), Royal Acad. Medicine Belgium (assoc.), Dutch Soc. Scis. (fgn.), Am. Soc. Zoologists (hon.), Royal Irish Acad. (hon.), Japan Acad. (hon.), Nature Conservancy (coun. 1985-88). Home and Office: Manor Field, 1 Vicarage Dr Grantchester, Cambridge CB3 9NG, England

HUXLEY, CAROLE CORCORAN, state education commissioner; b. Evanston, Ill., Jan. 1, 1938; d. Harold Francis and Angela Mary (Dawson) Corcoran; m. Michael Remsen Huxley, Mar. 27, 1971; children: Samuel Dawson, Ian Matthew Remsen. BA, Mount Holyoke Coll., 1960; MA in Tchg., Harvard U., 1961. Tchr. Woodbury (Conn.) H.S., 1961-62; area supr. to divisional dir. Am. Field Svcs., N.Y.C., 1962-71; program officer Nat. Endowment for the Humanities, Washington, 1971-79, dep. dir. state programs, 1979-80, dir. spl. programs, 1980-82; dep. commr. cultural edn. N.Y. Dept. Edn., Albany, 1982—. Trustee Mount Holyoke Coll., 1982-98, Albany Med. Coll., Albany Med. Ctr., 1983-88, Commn. on Preservation and Access, 1988-98, Rsch. Librs. Group, 1998—; del. White House Conf. on Librs., 1990-91. Mem. N.Y. Coun. Humanities (bd. dirs. 1984-90, v.p.). Roman Catholic.

HUXLEY, MARY ATSUKO, artist; b. Stockton, Calif., Mar. 5, 1930; d. Henry K. and Kiku H. (Kisanuki) Taniguchi; m. Harold Daniels Huxley, 1957. Student, Armstrong Coll., Berkeley, Calif., 1950, San Francisco Art Inst., 1968; pvt. studies with, Thomas C. Leighton, 1970-75. art show judge regional art clubs, corps., pvt. orgns., and county fairs, 1972-99. Solo shows include Artists' Coop., San Francisco, 1973, 75, 76, The Univ. Club Invitational, San Francisco, 1976, I. Magnin, San Mateo, 1976, Palo Alto Med. Found., 1992, Galerie Genese, San Mateo, 1993; exhibited in juried group shows at Catharine Lorillard Wolf Art Club, N.Y.C., 1979, Knickerbocker Artists of Am., N.Y.C., 1979, Salmagundi Club Ann., N.Y.C., 1981, Butler Inst. Am. Art, Youngstown, Ohio, 1982, Am. Artists Profl. League, N.Y.C., 1982, 83, 86, 87, 88, Oil Painters of Am. Ann. Nat. Juried Shows, Gallery at Long Grove, Ill., 1993, 94, Taos, N.Mex., 1997, Oil Painters of Am. Ann. Pacific Coast Regional Juried Show, Jones & Terwilliger Gallery, Carmel, Calif., 1997, San Francisco Ann. Art Festival, 1970-74, Renaissance Gallery, Santa Rosa, Calif., 1973, Paramount Theater, Oakland, Calif., 1974, Met. Club Invitational, San Francisco, Marin Soc. Artists Ann., Ross, Calif., 1976, 79, Soc. Western Artists Ann., San Francisco, 1976, 78, 80, Peninsula Art Assn. Ann., Belmont, Calif., 1980, Fresno (Calif.) Fashion Fair Ann., 1981, 84, De Saisset Gallery, U. Santa Clara, Calif., 1979, Lodi (Calif.) Ann. Grape and Art Festival, 1970, 71, 72, 73, 74, 75, 76, 77, 78, 79, 81, San Mateo County Ann. Floral Fiesta, 1975, 76, 77, 78, 79, 81, Charles & Emma Frye Mus. Gallery, Seattle, 1975, Redwood City Women's Club Ann. Flower Show, 1978, Fremont Art Assn. Anns., 1987, 88, 89, John Muir Med. Ctr. invitational, 1999-2000, 3 Com-Synopsis Invitational Traveling Exhibit, 2000—; numerous others; represented in numerous pvt. and corp. collections in U.S., Europe and Asia. Recipient Marjorie Walter Spl. award San Mateo County Exhbn., 1975, Gold medallion and 1st award San Mateo County Fair Fine Arts Exhbn., 1976, Best of Show award Cultural Arts of Palo Alto and Palo Alto Art Club, 1979, Best of Show and 1st award U. Art Ctr. and Palo Alto Art Club Ann., 1981, Spl. Merit award Oakland Art Assn., John Muir Med. Ctr. Ann., 1989, 1st award Burlingame Art Soc. Anns., 1976, 77, 1st award Redwood City Women's Club Ann. Flower Show, 1978, 1st award Soc. Western Artists Palo Alto Med. Ctr. Ann., 1983, 1st award Soc. Western Artists John Muir Med. Ctr. Ann., 1986, 1st award Fremont Art Assn. Ann., 1989, numerous others. Fellow Am. Artists Profl. League; mem. Soc. Western Artists (signature, trustee 1986-97, bd. dirs. 1972-75, 98, chmn. juried exhbns. 1972-81), Am. Soc. Classical Realism, Oil Painters Am. (signature), Allied Artists Am., Marin Soc. Artists (signature). Studio: PO Box 5467 San Mateo CA 94402-0467

HUYBRECHTS, GUY HENRI, food products executive; b. Antwerp, Belgium, May 12, 1956; s. Luc and Helena (Bosch) H.; m. Corine Taymans, Dec. 13, 1986; 1 child, Frederic. Degree in Comml. Engr., Solvay ULB, Brussels, 1980. Supr. fin. adminstr. Procter & Gamble Benelux, Brussels, 1980-83; prof. accountancy, mktg. and mgmt. EPHEC, Brussels, 1983; asst. fin. dir. Petrofina, Antwerp, Belgium, 1983-88; dir. fin. and adminstrn. Petrofina, Gabon, 1988-89; div. mgr. N.V. Vamo Mills, Ghent, Belgium, 1989-93; gen. mgr. profl. products N.V. Vamix, Ghent, 1993-95; mng. dir. N.V. Alpro, Wevelgem, Belgium, 1995—; mem. group exec. com. Vandemoortele Group, Izegem, Belgium, 1995—; dir. gen. Sojinal S.A., France, 1996—; v.p. Sojaxa, Paris, 1997—; mem. exec. mktg. mgmt. programme Stanford U., Bus. Grad. Sch., 1997; mem. advanced mgmt. programme Insead Fontainebleau, France, 1998. Mem. Solvay Union Engrs., Ridder In De Kroonorde. Office: NV Alpro, Vlamingstraat 28, 8560 Wevelgem Belgium

HUYPENS, JOZEF MARIA ALFONS, communication consultant; b. Geel, Antwerp, Belgium, Mar. 7, 1948; s. Robert Huypens and Maria Vangeel; m. Bertje Sterckx, July 28, 1969 (dec. Apr. 1999); children: Sven, Inge. Lic. Social Scis., Cath. U. Leuven, 1971, Doctor Comml. Scis., 1980. Journalist Gazet Van Antwerpen, Belgium, 1971-85, dep. editor-in-chief, 1985-91, editor-in-chief, 1991-96; prof. U. Antwerp, Belgium, 1992—, U. Leuven, Belgium, 1998—; gen. mgr. Communicado Int., Belgium, 1996—. Author: De Plaatselyke Nieuwsfabriek, 1980; co-author: Public Relations Non-Profit Organization, 1983; editor: Media en Politiek, 1999; contbr. articles to profl. publs. Senator Jaycees Internat., 1982—; pres. Vrienden Van Ter Wende, 1988—. Mem. Orde Van den Prince. Avocations: squash, music. Home: 's Hertogenlaan 58, 3000 Leuven Belgium Office: Communicado Int, 'S Hertogenlaan 58, 3000 Leuven Belgium

HUYSMAN, JAMES DAVID, healthcare executive, consultant; b. N.Y.C., Jan. 27, 1955; s. Michel and Arlene Muriel (Weiss) H.; m. Betsy Catherine Bergner, May 29, 1988. BA in Cmty. Psychology with high honors, U. Fla., 1977; M in Clin. Social Work, Barry U., Miami Shores, Fla., 1987. Diplomate NASW; lic. clin. social worker; cert. addictions profl.; registered lic. real estate broker. Dir. vocat. program Fellowship House, South Miami, Fla., 1984-86; therapist Ctrs. for Psychol. Growth, Miami, Fla., 1986-88; v.p. outreach The Bradford Group, Birmingham, Ala., 1988-92; dir. aftercare The Geraldo Rivera Show, N.Y.C., 1991—; v.p. devel. CareNet Psychol. Mgmt., Nashville, 1993-96; chmn., CEO Ptnrs. in Health Mgmt., Ft. Lauderdale, Fla., 1996—; dir. Aftercare Leeza Show, 1996—; cons. to Rev. Jesse Jackson, Rainbow Coalition, Washington, 1990-91, largest pub./pvt. treatment grant, Washington, 1989-90, Howell Heflin D.C. Treatment Grant, Bradford Group, Washington, 1989-90, Bennett/Klehr Drug Policy Office, Washington, 1989-90, Geraldo Rivera, Montel Williams, Les Brown, Leeza, other talk shows; founder, dir. 1st Healthcare Network and Aftercare Program for Talk TV; creator nat. talk show; CEO At the End of the Day Prodns. Contbr. over 300 articles to nat. newspapers; appeared on over 70 nat. syndicated talk shows. Bus. devel. OrNoA Healthcorp. Tenet Health Sys. Recipient Friends Day Founder recognition Cmty. Mental Health Agys., Miami, 1986. Mem. ACLU, Nat. Wildlife Fedn., Nature Conservancy, World Wildlife Fund, Habitat for Humanity, Fla. Alcohol and Drug Abuse Assn. Democrat. Jewish. Avocations: motorcycling, travel, Miami ballet, theater, collecting animation and memorabilia. Office: Ptnrs in Health Mgmt Ste 309 1100 Lee Watner Blvd Fort Lauderdale FL 33315 also: Ptnrs in Health Mgmt 3050 Biscayne Blvd Ste 908 Miami FL 33137-4143

HUZL, FRANTISEK, occupational health physician, educator; b. Roznov under Radhost, Czech Republic, Sept. 22, 1926; s. Frantisek and Frantiska (Dockalova) H.; m. Anna Slamova, Aug. 25, 1951 (dec. Oct. 22, 1984); children: Helena, Vladimir; m. Eva Hrda, Nov. 22, 1990. MD, Charles U., Prague, Czech Republic, 1951, Candidate of Med. Sci., 1959, DSc, 1985. Specialist in occupl. diseases and indsl. medicine; specialist of 1st grade in internal medicine. Dr. 1st internal clinic Faculty Hosp., Prague, 1951-52; dr. clinic occupl. diseases Faculty Hosp. and Charles U., Prague, 1952-55; asst. specialist internal clinic Faculty Hosp. and Charles U., Pilsen and Prague, 1955-59; dep. chief dept. occupl. diseases and toxicology Faculty Hosp., Pilsen, 1957-59, chief dept. occupl. diseases and toxicology, 1959-86; chief clinic occupl. health and indsl. medicine Faculty Hosp. and Charles U., Pilsen and Prague, 1987-92; prof. faculty medicine Charles U., Prague, 1987—; dep. chief dept. occupl. health, head outpatient divsn. Mcpl. Hygienic Sta., Pilsen, 1992-98; ext. prof. faculty pedagogy West Bohemia U. Pilsen, 1994-96. Editor: Vibration Disease/Vibration Induced White Fingers, 1959, Delta Aminolevulinic Acid in Urine and Activity Dehydratase d-ALA in Blood in the Course of Influence of Lead and Cadmium, 1969, 75, Results of Prevention of Vibration Diseases in Metallurgy Industries in Heavy Engineering Industries and in Forestry, 1985, Association of Coal Workers Pneumoconiosis or Silikosis with Rheumatoid Arthritis, 1993; contbr. 290 articles to profl. jours. and procs. 1st lt. Mil. Health Svc., 1951. Recipient Hon. Appreciation award Czech Agr. Acad., 1981. Mem. J.E. Purkyně Med. Soc. of Czech Republic, Occupl. Health Soc. of Czech Republic (hon., Hon. medal 1983), J.E. Purkyně Soc. Internal Medicine, J.E. Purkyně Soc. Pathophysiology of Respiration, J.E. Purkyně Soc. Occupl. Health Medicine (hon.). Avocations: gardening, reading. Home: B Smetana St # 1, 30135 Pilsen Czech Republic Office: Mcpl Hygenic Sta Dept Occpl, Tylova St # 20, 30125 Pilsen Czech Republic

HVIDT, CHRISTIAN, NATO official; b. July 15, 1942; m. Jane Hvidt; 2 children; 3 children from previous marriage. Commd. lt. Danish Armed Forces, 1962, advanced through grades to gen., 1996, with flying svc., 1962-69, test pilot, tehn dep. squadron comdr. F-35 Draken, 1969-74, br. chief Tactical Air Command, 1975-79, squadron comdr., 1979-83, staff officer, br. chief plans and policy divsn., 1983-87; comdg. officer Danish Armed Forces, Air Sta. Karup, 1987-88; chief of staff Tactical Air Command Danish Armed Forces, 1989-90, with plans and policy, ops., budget and finance, 1990-94; perm. Danish mil. rep. to NATO Hdqrs. Mil. com. Brussels, 1994-96; chief of staff HQ Chodden, 1996, chief of def., Danish Armed Forces, 1996—. Decorated Nat. Order of Merit of French Republic, Disting. Flying Cross, Danish Air Force Badge of Honor, Comdr. of Order of Dannebrog. Office: NATO Hdqrs, Blvd Leopold III, 1110 Brussels Belgium also: Hdqrs Chief of Def Denmark, PO Box 202, 2950 Vedback Denmark*

HWANG, CHANG-CHOU, engineering educator; b. Chang-Hwa, Taiwan, July 28, 1950; s. Chun-Ba and Chang-Yuan (Chang) H.; m. May-Hui Lin, Nov. 12, 1975; 1 child, An-Pu. B in Engring., Nat. Taipei (Taiwan) Inst., 1972; M in Engring., Rensselaer Poly. Inst., 1981; PhD, Nat. Tsing Hua U., Hsin-Chu, Taiwan, 1989. Registered profl. engr., Taiwan. Engr. Taiwan Sanyo Electric Co., Taipei, 1974-75, Nat. Chung-Shan Inst. Sci. and Tech., Tao-Yuan, Taiwan, 1976-92; lectr. Chiensien Coll., Tao-Yuan, 1983-87; vis. rsch. scholar Rensselaer Poly. Inst., Troy, N.Y., 1987-88; assoc. prof. engring. Feng Chia U., Taichung, Taiwan, 1992-97, prof., 1997—, sec. Coll. Computer Sci. and Elec. Engring., 1999-2000; dir. dept. elec. engring. Feng Chia U., Taichung, 2000—. Mem. IEEE, Chinese Inst. Elec. Engring., Chinese Assn. for Magnetic Tech. Avocations: mountain climbing, stamp collecting, painting. Home: 41 Nine Dragon St, Pei-Twen, Taichung 406, Taiwan Office: Feng Chia U, Sea-Twen, 100 Wenhwa Rd, Taichung 407, Taiwan

HWANG, CHANG-SING, physicist; b. Taipei, Taiwan, Taiwan, Republic of China, May 10, 1952; s. Lan-gi and Zen-Twou (Wang) H.; married, May 10, 1977; children: Li-Ming, Li-Tzong, Li-Ping. BS, Chung-Cheng Inst. Tech., Tau-Yen, Taiwan, Republic of China, 1974; MS, Nat. Tsing Hua U., Hsinchu, Taiwan, Republic of China, 1978; PhD, U. N.Mex., 1985. Asst. scientist Chung Shen Inst. Sci. and Tech., Lung-Tan, Taiwan, Republic of China, 1978-85; assoc. scientist Chung Shen Inst. Sci. and Tech., Lung-Tan, Republic of China, 1985-89, Inst. Nuclear Energy Rsch., Lung-Tan, 1989—; assoc. prof. Nat. Tsing Hua U., Hsinchu, 1988—. Inventor in field. Mem. Am. Physics Soc. Home and Office: Inst Nuclear Energy Rsch, PO Box 3-4, Lungtan 32500, Taiwan

HWANG, CHI-HUNG, mechanical engineering researcher; b. Tainan, Taiwan, Aug. 2, 1967; s. Deng-Lin and Xiu-Rong (Chen) H.; m. Ling-Sun Kong, July 7, 1999. MSc, Tsing Hua U., Hsinchu, Taiwan, 1993, Dr, 1996. Lectr. Ming-Hsin Poly., Taiwan, 1994-95; assoc. rschr. PIDC, Taiwan, 1996—, mech. group leader, 1999—. Patentee in field of optics. 2d lt., arty. Taiwan Army, 1996. Mem. SPIE, Soc. for Extpl. Mechanics, Chinese Soc. Mech. Engrs. Office: Precision Instrument Devel, R&D rd VI, Hsin Chu Taiwan

HWANG, DAVID HENRY, playwright, screenwriter; b. L.A., Aug. 11, 1957; s. Henry Yuan and Dorothy Yu (Huang) H.; m. Kathryn A. Layng, Dec. 17, 1993; 1 child, Noah. BA in English, Stanford U., 1979; postgrad., Yale Drama Sch., 1980-81. Playwright: FOB, 1980 (Obie award 1981), The Dance and the Railroad, 1981 (CINE Golden Eagle award 1982), Family Devotions, 1981, Sound and Beauty, 1983, The Sound of a Voice, 1984, As the Crow Flies, 1986, Rich Relations, 1986, M. Butterfly, 1988 (Tony award for best play 1988, Outer Critics Circle award for best Broadway play 1988, Pulitzer prize for drama nomination 1988), (musicals) 1000 Airplanes on the Roof, 1988, Bondage, 1992, Face Value, 1993, Trying to Find Chinatown, 1996, Golden Child, 1996-98 (Obie award 1997, Tony nomination Best Play 1998), The Silver River, 1997, (adaptation) Peer Gynt, 1998; librettist: The Voyage, 1992; screenwriter: (films) M. Butterfly, 1993, Golden Gate, 1994, (television) Forbidden Nights, 1990. Mem. Pres.'s Com. Arts and Humanities, 1994—. Fellow Rockefeller Found., 1983, Guggenheim Found., 1984, Nat. Endowment Arts, 1987; recipient Drama-Logue award 1980, 86, 98, John Gassner award, 1988. Mem. Dramatists Guild (bd. dirs. 1988—). Democrat. Office: Writers & Artists Agy care William Craver 19 W 44th St Ste 1000 New York NY 10036-6095 also: CAA 9830 Wilshire Blvd Beverly Hills CA 90212-1804

HWANG, HYUNSANG, science educator; b. Daegu, Korea, Apr. 7, 1966; parents Wontak Hwang and Munsun Lee; m. Jungmin Kim, Dec. 25, 1994; children: Woochan, Jaewon. PhD, U. Tex., 1992; BS, Seoul Nat. U., 1988. Prin. rschr. LG Semicon, Seoul, 1992-97; assoc. prof. Kwangju (Korea) Inst. Sci. & Tech., 1997—. Patentee in field. Fax: 062-970-2304. E-mail: hwanghs@kjist.ac.kr. Office: Kwangju Inst Sci & Tech, 1 Oryong Puk-gu, Kwangju 500-712, Korea

HWANG, KAO PIN, physician, educator, consultant, researcher; b. Taichung, Taiwan, Republic of China, June 27, 1952; s. San Liang and Chao (Chiu) H.; m. Ying Lu, Dec. 29, 1977; 3 children. B degree, Kaohsiung Med. Coll., 1977, M degree, 1982, PhD, 1988. Attending physician in pediats. Kaohsiung Med. Univ. Hosp., Taiwan, 1981—, asst. prof. pediats., 1982-88, sec. Hosp. Infection Control Com., 1984-98, chief Rsch. Ctr. for Tropical Medicine, 1991-93, chief gen. pediats., 1992-93, assoc. prof., 1988—, chmn. Hosp. Infection Control Com., 1998—. Exec. editor Acta Paediatrica Sinica, 1993; dep. editor-in-chief Nosocomial Infection Control Jour., 1996; standing editor Chinese Jour. Pest Control, 1997; pub. Nosocomial Infection Control Jour., 1999—. Commr. adv. com. nosocomial infection control Dept. Health, Taipei, 1990—, commr. com. for qualification of tchg. hosp., 1992—, commr. cons. com. of vaccination, 1993—, commr. adv. com. enteroviral infection, 1998—, chmn. adv. com. Dengue Hemorrhagic Fever, 1999—. Recipient Mead Johnson Pediat. Rsch. award Pediat. Assn. Republic of China, 1979, Ann. Nestle award of Pediat. Rsch., 1986, 88. Mem. Nosocomial Infection Control Soc. (pres. 1996—), Infectious Diseases Soc. (dir. 1996—), Chinese Soc. Parasitology (supr. 1991-97, dir. 1998—), Am. Soc. Tropical Medicine and Hygiene, Am. Soc. for Microbiology, Assn. for Profls. in Infection Control and Epidemiology. Avocations: golf, tennis, music, travel, reading. Home: No 243 Chien-Hsin Rd, 807 Kaohsiung Taiwan Office: Kaohsiung Med Coll, No 100 Shih-Chuan 1st Rd, 807 Kaohsiung Taiwan

HWANG, KEUM TAEK, food science educator; b. Chonju, Korea, Mar. 26, 1958; s. Ho Jum and Gil Sun (Kim) H.; m. Chonpun Choe Hwang, Sept. 15, 1984; children: David Jiwon, Peter Byungwuke. BS, Seoul Nat. U., Korea, 1979; MS, Cornell U., Ithaca, N.Y., 1988, PhD, 1991. Food technologist Baik Wha Brewery, Kunsan, Korea, 1981-84; sea grant scholar N.Y.S. U., Ithaca, 1986-90; grad. rsch. asst. Cornell U., Ithaca, N.Y., 1991; rsch. chemist USDA-ERRC, Phila., 1991-93; prof. Mokpo (Korea) Nat. U., 1993-96, Chonbuk (Korea) Nat. U., 1996—; adv. Korea Food and Drug Adminstrn., Kwangju, Korea. Contbr. scientific papers in field. Recipient N.Y. Sea Grant Inst. Scholar award, 1986-90, Albert Flegenheimer Meml. Grad. Fund award Cornell U., Ithaca, N.Y., 1991. Mem. Inst. of Food Technologists, Am. Oil Chemists' Soc., Korean Soc. Food Sci. and Technology, The Korean Soc. of Food Sci. and Nutrition. Avocations: gardening, skiing, travel. E-mail address: Kthwang@moak.chonbuk.ac.kr. Fax: 652-270-3854. Office: Dept Food Sci & Nutrition, Chonbuk National Univ, Chonju 561-756, Korea

HWANG, KI-YOUNG, mechanical engineer, researcher; b. Yangyang, Rep. of Korea, Sept. 7, 1957; s. Hoo-Bong Hwang and Bok-Deok Son; m. Soo-San Lee, Apr. 5, 1986; children: Byung-Won, Byung-Jo. BSME, Ulsan Inst. Tech., Rep. of Korea, 1980; MSME, Yonsei U., Seoul, Rep. of Korea, 1986, PhD in Mech. Engring., 1994. Cert. in 1st class heat-control engring. Rschr. Grad. Sch. Yonsei U., 1990-94; rschr. Agy. Def. Devel., Taejon, Rep. of Korea, 1979-87, sr. rschr., 1988—. Contbr. rsch. articles to sci. publs. Mem. Korean Soc. Mech. Engrs., Korean Soc. Propulsion Engrs., Korean Soc. Automotive Engrs., Korean Soc. Aero. and Space Scis., Korean Soc. Air-conditioning and Refrigerating Engrs. Roman Catholic. Avocations: hiking, tennis, sightseeing. E-mail: kiyhwang@hananet.net. Home: 115-406 Noori Apt, Wallpyung-dong Seo-ku, Taejon 302 283, Republic of Korea Office: Agy Def Devel, PO Box 35-5 Yuseong, Taejon 305 600, Republic of Korea

HWANG, SEONG SIK, materials scientist, researcher; b. Taejon, Korea, June 15, 1963; s. Su Won Hwang and Jeong Ok Lee; m. Soon Kee Min; children: Seok Joon, Seok In, Seok Chan. BS, Yonsei U., Seoul, Korea, 1986, MS, 1988, PhD, 1997. Sr. rschr. Korea Atomic Energy Rsch. Inst., Taejon, 1989—. Contbr. articles to profl. jours. Mem. Corrosion Sci. Soc. Korea. E-mail: sshwang@nanum.kaeri.re.kr. Office: Korea Atomic Energy Rsch, PO Box Yusong 105, Taejon 305-600, Korea

HWANG, SUNG-HO, mechanical engineer; b. Chong-Ju, Chungbuk, Korea, Aug. 18, 1965; s. Eui-Gon Hwang and Choon-Bum Kim; m. Soo-Young Jung, May 25, 1992; children: In-June, In-Chan. BS, Seoul (Korea) Nat. U., 1988, MS, 1990, PhD, 1997. Sr. rschr. Korea Inst. Indsl. Tech., ChonAn, 1992—; cons. Hydro-Electronic Devel. Mfg., Buchon, Korea, 1997—. Contbr. articles to profl jours. Mem. SAE, KSAE, KSME, KSPE, ICASE. Avocations: ping-pong, ba-duk. Home: 101-1006 Il-Sung Apt, SsangYong-Dong, 330-090 ChonAn Chung Nam Korea Office: Korea Inst Indsl Tech, 35-3 HongChonRi IbJang Myun, 330-820 ChonAn ChungNam Korea

HWANG, TAE-WOOK, engineering researcher; b. Seoul, Korea, Oct. 9, 1964; came to U.S., 19963; s. Il Soo and Hyung Ok (Lee) H.; m. Myung Woo Hwang Bang, July 25, 1992; children: Ha Hyun, Hannah. BS, Korea U., Seoul, 1987; MS, Korea Adv. Inst. Sci./Tech., Seoul, 1989; PhD, U. Mass., 1997. Rsch. asst. Koreal Advanced Inst. of Sci. and Tech., Seoul, 1987-89; sr. rsch. engr. Samsung Advanced Inst. of Tech., Yong In, Korea, 1989-93; rsch. asst. U. Mass., Amherst, 1994-97; rschr. Nat. Inst. Stds. and Tech., Gaithersburg, Md., 1997—. Author: Ceramic Translations, 1999; contbr. articles to profl. jours. Home: 547 Coachman Dr Apt 2 Troy MI 48083-1514 Office: Nat Inst Stds and Tech Mfg Engring Lab Gaithersburg MD 20899-0001

HWANG, TZONELIH, computer scientist, educator; b. Tainan, Taiwan, Mar. 16, 1958; s. Fong-Yung and Kwei-Inn (Lin) H.; m. Ginger Lee, Dec. 25, 1989; children: Kwang-Lin, Kwang-Chin. BSc, Nat. Cheng Kung U., Taiwan, 1980; MSc, U. S.W. La., 1986, PhD, 1988. Rsch. asst. U. S.W. La., Lafayette, 1985-88, computer scientist, 1988; assoc. prof. computer sci. Nat. Cheng Kung U., 1989-93, prof., 1993—; cons. Indsl. Tech. Rsch. Inst., Hsinchu, Taiwan, 1992-93; adminstr. Info. Security Soc. Republic of China, Taiwan, 1994—; program chair Internat. Conf. on Cryptology and Info. Security, Internat. Computer Symposium, 1996, 98. Editor Jour. Edn. and Info. Edn., 1990—; patentee in field. 2d lt. Republic of China Marine Corps, 1980-82. Rsch. grantee Nat. Sci. Coun. Republic of China, 1989-94, recipient Excellent Rsch. award, 1994. Mem. IEEE, Internat. Assn. Ctyptographic Rsch. Avocations: tennis, swimming, golf, badminton, hiking. Home: 35-99 Ann Si Li Jar Li Jen, Tainan Shein Taiwan Office: Inst Info Engring, Nat Cheng Kung U, Tainan Taiwan

HWANG, TZU-YANG, minister; b. Kaohsiung, Taiwan, Republic of China, Sept. 21, 1953; came to U.S., 1985; d. Chi-Chou and Iu-Chih (Tsai) Huang; m. Wei-Chih Shih Hwang, Sept. 6, 1980. MDiv, Tainan Theol. Sem., 1980; ThM, Princeton (N.J.) Theol. Sem., 1986; PhD, Chinese for Christ Theol. Sem., Rosemead, Calif., 1990. Ordained to ministry Presbyn. Ch. Chairperson, min. Presbytery's Zrhlin Dists. Ch., Champhua, Taiwan, 1981-83; min., lectr., sr. editor Tainan Theol. Sem., 1983-85; founder, min. The Youth Fellowship of Kingston Presbyn. Ch., Princeton, 1985-86; head of religion edn., lectr. Good Shepherd Formosan Presbyn. Ch., Monterey Park, Calif., 1987-88; head of religion edn., lectr. Chinese for Christ Theol. Sem., 1987-88, dir. theology and philosophy, dean students, sr. editor, 1990-94; founder., pres., prof., CEO Am. Chi Chou Theo-Philosophical Inst., 1995—; Vis. Scholar, Harvard U. Div. Sch., Duke U. Div. Sch., 1991-92; sr. pastor, pres. Light Christ Ch.; chmn., pres., incorporator, bd. dirs., Light Christ Found., 1994—. Contbr. numerous articles to profl. jours. With Chinese Def., 1972-74. mem. Am. Acad. Religion, Soc. Biblical Literature, ABIRA (internat. and continental gov., internat. Order of Ambassadors), Internat. Biog. Ctr. (dir. gen. honors list), Assn. IBC (advisor of Dir. of Gen.), Internat. Order of Merit (bd. mem.), Leading Intellectuals of World (founding charter mem., noble mem. and world laureate), others. Home and Office: 11768 E Roseglen St El Monte CA 91732-1446 Office: Am Chi Chou Theo Phil Inst PO Box 6143 11804 Hemlock St El Monte CA 91732-1413

HWANG, WENG-SING, materials engineer; b. Kang-Shan, Taiwan, Jan. 2, 1955; s. Dann-Hai and Jin-Jy (Liu) H.; m. Chiou-Jung Lee, Sept. 27, 1986; children: Pao-Yao, Po-Chung. BS, Nat. Cheng Kung U., 1976; MS, U. Pitts., 1981, PhD, 1985. Engr. China Steel Corp., Kaohsiung, Taiwan, 1978-79; rschr. Battelle Columbus (Ohio) Lab., 1985; dep. dir. metals processing rsch. lab. Nat. Cheng Kung U., Tainan, Taiwan, 1988-90; prof. dept. materials sci. and engring. Nat. Cheng Kung U., Tainan, 1990—, assoc. dean engring., 1999—; vis. rschr. Tohoku U., Sendai, Japan, 1990-91. Contbr. articles to profl. jours. Lt. Taiwan Army, 1976-78. Recipient Outstanding Rsch. award Nat. Sci. Coun., 1992, 94. Mem. Chinese Foundrymen's Assn. (bd. dirs., sec. gen. 1994-96, Paper award 1989, 91, 96, 98, 99), Chinese Forging Assn. (supr. 1992—). Avocations: movies, classical music, swimming, hiking. Home: 10 Alley 24 Ln 243, Chung-Hwa East Rd Sect 2, Tainan Taiwan Office: Nat Cheng Kung Univ, Dept Materials Sci & Engring, Tainan 701, Taiwan

HWANG, WOEI-YANN PAUCHY, physics educator; b. Miao-Li, Taiwan, Republic of China, Aug. 25, 1948; s. A.S. and T.-M. (Chang) H.; m. Jane Su-Chen, June 4, 1977; children: Justin Han-Che, Irving Hua-Hsuan. BS in Physics, Taiwan U., Taipei, Taiwan, 1971; PhD in Physics, U. Pa., 1977. Rsch. assoc. U. Wash., Seattle, 1978-81; asst. prof. Ind. U., Bloomington, 1981-83, assoc. prof., assoc. scientist, 1983-86; vis. assoc. prof. Carnegie-Mellon U., Pitts., 1986-88; prof. Taiwan U., Taipei, 1987—, chmn. dept. physics, 1997—; adj. prof. Carnegie-Mellon U., Pitts., 1988—; collaborator Los Alamos (N.Mex.) Nat. Lab., 1986—. Co-author: (textbook) Relativistic Quantum Mechanics and Quantum Fields, 1991; editor Chinese Jour. of Physics, 1988—; co-editor of 8 books; series editor Trends in Particle and Nuclear Physics, 1993—. Recipient Humboldt award, 1990-91, Outstanding Rsch. award Nat. Sci. Coun., 1989-91, 91-93, 95-97, named Outstanding Rsch. Investigator, 1998—, Nat. Chair Prof. Ministry of Edn., 1998—. Mem. Am. Phys. Soc., Internat. Astron. Union, Phys. Soc. Republic of China, Sigma Xi.

HWU, HAI-GWO, psychiatry educator; b. Tainan, Taiwan, Feb. 20, 1947; s. Chuang and Te (Hsieh) H.; m. Suher Liaw; two children. MD, Nat. Taiwan U., 1972. Bd. cert. psychiatrist, Taiwan. Lectr. Nat. Taiwan U., Taipei, 1983-86, assoc. prof., 1986-92, prof., 1992—; chmn. dept. mental health Taipei City Psychiat. Ctr., 1980-83; supt. Provincial Taoyuan Hosp., 1989-92; dir. sect. cmty. dept. psychiatry Nat. Taiwan U. Hosp., 1996—, dir. adult psychiatry dept., 1996-98. Author: Manual of Psychiatric Diagnosis, 1991, Modern Psychiatric Therapy, 1995, Schizophrenia-Descriptive Psychopathology, 1999; author/editor: Biological Psychiatry, 1995; chief editor Taiwanese Jour. Psychiatry, 2000—. Lt. Taiwanese Army, 1972-73. Fellow Pacific Rim Coll. Psychiatrists; mem. Chinese Soc. Psychiatry (Taiwan), World Psychiat. Assn. (mem. sect. epidemiology and community psychiatry 1990-99), Chinese Mental Health Assn. (bd. dirs. Taipei chpt. 1980—, pres. 1997-99), Formosan Med. Assn., Chinese Soc. Molecular and Cell Biology (Taiwan), Chinese Soc. Genetics (Taiwan), Internat. Soc. Psychiat. Genetics, Asian-Oceanian Soc. Biol. Psychiatry, Internat. Neuropsychiat. Assn., World Fedn. Mental Health. Office: Nat Taiwan Univ Hosp, No 7 Chung-Shan South Rd, 100 Taipei Taiwan

HYATT, DAN RICHARD, judge; b. Seattle, Nov. 23, 1949; m. Robin L. Hinkle, Dec. 20, 1973 (div. 1988); m. Kathleen Lyons; children: Casey, Dorianne. BA in English, U. Oreg., 1975; JD, Lewis & Clark Coll., Eugene, Oreg., 1978. Bar: Oreg. 1978, U.S. Dist. Ct. Oreg. 1978, U.S. Ct. Mil. Appeals 1984, U.S. Ct. Appeals (9th cir.) 1985, U.S. Ct. Fed. Claims 1986, U.S. Supreme Ct. 1993. Ptnr. Hyatt, Jackson & Vause, Portland, Oreg., 1978-82; sr. def. counsel USN, Guam, 1983-84; spl. asst. U.S. atty. Dept. Justice, Seattle, 1984-85; pvt. practice, Portland, 1985-97; lawyer's chair MOMS, Frederick, Md., 1991-97; nat. counsel Am. Fighter Aces Assn., Mesa, Ariz., 1994-97, Nat. Spiritualist Assn., Lilydale, N.Y., 1990-94. Elder Westminster Presbyn. Ch., Portland, 1986-89. Comdr. USNR, 1984—. Mem. Oreg. State Bar Assn. (counsel to bar-ethics 1993-97, chair mil. and vets. sect. 1995-97, bd. govs. (ex-officio 1995—), Judge Advocates Assn., Am. Legion, Am. Fighter Aces Mus. Found. (counsel 1994-97), False Memory Syndrome Found. Avocations: forensic psychology, carpentry. Office: 601 SW 2nd Ave Fl 17 Portland OR 97204-3154

HYATT, JAMES ARMSTRONG, university administrator; b. Chilliwack, B.C., Can., May 28, 1949; s. Delbert Harold and Agnes (Barr) H.; m. Sandra Allard, May 23, 1981; children: Kathryn Barr, John Allard. BA, U. Wash., 1972, MBA, 1976. Mgmt. analyst Dept. Social and Health Svcs., Olympia, Wash., 1976-77; planning analyst U. Wash., Seattle, 1977-79; dir. fin. mgmt. ctr. Nat. Assn. Coll. and Univ. Bus. Officers, Washington, 1979-86, exec. v.p., 1986-87; asst. vice chancellor U. Md., College Park, 1987-91; assoc. chancellor U. Calif., Berkeley, 1991-98, vice chancellor, 1998—; bd. dirs., mem. exec. com. Nat. Ctr. for Higher Edn. Mgmt. Sys., Bolder, Colo., 1984-86; cons. U. Mass., Amherst, 1982, Am. U., Washington, 1988-89, U. Md. Sys., College Park, 1994; primary rep. Coun. on Govtl. Rels., 1994—; mem. nat. higher edn. adv. panel Nat. Ctr. on Ednl. Stats., 1983-86; mem. nat. planning com. project to develop Integrated Post-Secondary Edn. Data Sys., U.S. Dept. Edn., 1983-86; mem. nat. task force econs. of rsch. librs. project Coun. on Libr. Resources, 1983-86. Author: Reallocation: Strategies for Effective Resource Management, 1984, University Libraries in Transition, 1986, Financial Management of Colleges and Universities, 1986, Presentation and Analysis of Financial Management Information, 1989. Avocations: writing, sketching, bicycling. Office: U Calif 200 California Hall Berkeley CA 94720-1502

HYDE, CATHERINE RYAN, writer, short story writer; b. Buffalo, N.Y., Apr. 17, 1955. instr. writer's conf. Cuesta Coll., San Luis Obispo, Calif.; adminstrv. asst. Santa Barbara (Calif.) Writer's Conf. Author: (novels) Funerals for Horses, 1997, Pay It Forward, 2000, (short story collection) Earthquake Weather, 1998. Recipient Raymond Carver Short Story contest Humboldt State U., 1994, 96, Tobias Wolff award for fiction The Bellingham Rev., 1997; cited in Best American Short Stories, 1999. E-mail: info@book-logic.com. Office: The Hardy Agy 3020 Bridgeway Ste 204 Sausalito CA 94965-2839

HYDE, KEVIN DAVID, mycology educator; b. Cheltenham, Eng., May 3, 1955; arrived in Australia, 1989; s. John Stanley and Majorie Phylis (Gibbons) H.; m. Virlie Arimas, June 16, 1996; children: Kale, Tamsin. BSc, U. Cardiff, Wales, 1979; MSc, U. Portsmouth, Eng., 1980; PhD, U. Portsmouth, 1985. Prin. plant pathologist Dept. Prim. Industries, Govt. of Queensland, Australia, 1989-92; assoc. prof. Hong Kong U., 1992—. Editor: Biodiversity of Tropical Microfungi, 1997; contbr. articles to profl. jours. Office: Ctr Rsch Fungal Diversity, U Hong Kong, Hong Kong Hong Kong

HYDE, MICHAEL ARTHUR, chemical company executive; b. Kingston, Ont., Apr. 17, 1942; s. Arthur Edwin and Isabell Mary (Moran) H.; m. Monica Jill Hill, Sept. 9, 1964 (div. 1972); children: David Michael, Andrew Tyler; m. Yoko Igaya, May 19, 1981; children: Keri Kazumi, Amanda Izumi. BS in Engring., Queen's U., Kingston, Ont., 1965. Registered profl. engr., Ont. Tech. mgr. constrn. divsn. rsch. Dow Chem. Can., Sarnia, Ont., 1971-76; dist. sales mgr. constrn. divsn. Toronto, 1980-83, nat. sales mgr. constrn. divsn., 1984-85; mgr. new ventures and diversification, 1986-88, dir. environ. affairs plastics dept., 1989—, dir. Ont. govt. affairs, 1994—; dir. rsch. Dow Chem. Japan, Gotemba, Japan, 1976-80; v.p., sec. Mod-Lok Wall Sys. Ltd., Vancouver, B.C., Can., 1986-88; mem. Fire Test Bd., Ottawa, Ont., 1974-76. Patentee in field. Mem. Ont. Indsl. Roofing Assn. (bd. dirs. 1981-84), Assn. Profl. Engrs., Constrn. Specs. Can. Conservative (dir., sec. treas., policy com., mem. exec. com.), Recycling coun. Ont. (chmn. pub. affairs com., mem product stewardship com., mgmt. com.), Environ. and Plastics Inst. Can. (recycling and degradability sub-coms., Canplast award 1991), Corps. Supporting Recycling (corp. mem.), Collecte Selectif Quebec (corp. mem.), Can. Polystyrene Recycling Assn. (chmn. 1989-91), Can. Plastics Industry Assn. (nat. environ. health and safety com.), Vinyl Coun. Can. (steering exec. and crisis response coms.), Plastic Film Mfrs. (recycling com.), Bus. Rsch. Netwwork, Can. Chems. Prodrs. Assn. (Ont. regional exec. com.), Ont. Region Bus. Econ. and Govt. Com. (chmn.), Thursday Group, Global Climate Change Liaison Group. Avocations: swimming, boating, water skiing, cross-country skking. Home: 61 Greengrove Crescent, Don Mills, ON Canada M3A 1H8 Office: Dow Chem Can Inc, PO Box 363, Don Mills, ON Canada M3C 2S7

HYDE, THOMAS HORACE, mechanical engineering educator; b. South Shields, Eng., Oct. 14, 1949; s. Thomas and Florence May (Baker) H.; m. Marguerite Eileen Tarrant, Sept. 24, 1949; children: Thomas Robert, Christopher James. BSc, U. Aston, Birmingham, Eng., 1972, MSc, 1973; PhD, U. Nottingham, Eng., 1976, DSc, 1994. Student apprentice BSA, Birmingham, 1968-71; rsch. asst. U. Nottingham, 1976-78, lectr., 1978-87, reader, 1987-89, prof. mech. engring., 1989—, head Sch. of Mech., Materials, Mfg. Engring. and Mgmt., 1998—; rschr., 1976—; dir. Rolls Royce U. Tech. Ctr. in gas turbine transmission sys., 1997—. Contbr. over 170 articles to sci. and tech. jours. Rsch. grantee in field. Fellow Inst. Mech. Engring., Inst. Materials. Avocations: guitar, sports, reading. Office: U Nottingham Dept Mech Engr, University Park, Nottingham NG7 2RD, England

HYDÉN, DAG, otorhinolaryngologist; b. Stockholm, May 16, 1945; s. Holger Viktor and Ingrid Elsa (Bergström) H.; m. Else Mattsson, Apr. 19, 1974 (div. Aug. 1986); children: Åsa, Lisa; m. Gunilla Margaretha Kjellgren, July 20, 1987; 1 child, Johan. MD, U. Uppsala, Sweden, 1973, PhD, 1983. Cert. in otorhinolaryngology Swedish Med. Bd., 1979. Intern in medicine and surgery Härnösand, Sweden, 1973-75; rsch. resident Lab. Otoneurlogy and Physiology U. Toronto, Can., 1980-81; resident Ear, Nose and Throat Clin., Univ. Hosp., Linköping, Sweden, 1975-79, staff., 1981-86, asst. head., 1987-92, head, 1993—. Author: The Man Behind the Syndrome, 1989, The Women and the Men Behind the Syndrome, 1996; contbr. articles to profl. jours. Gunnar Nyström scholar U. Uppsala, 1972, otoneurological studies scholar Workers Found., U. Toronto, 1980. Mem. Swedish Otorhinolaryngological Soc., Swedish Vestibular Soc., Swedish Ear Surgery Soc., Neuroequilobriometric Soc., Barany Soc. Avocations: art, literature, old home restoration. Home: Ingenjörsgatan 7, S 58737 Linköping Ostrglnd, Sweden Office: ENT Clin, Univ Hospital, S 58185 Linköping Ostrglnd, Sweden

HYDER, RUMY TABREZ, physician; b. Dhaka, Bangladesh, June 1, 1960; s. Mohammad Salehuddin and Bela (Kasem) H.; m. Shamim Ara Lipi, June 15, 1999. HSC, Notre Dame Coll., Dhaka, Bangladesh, 1978; MBBS, Dhaka Med. Coll., 1985. Asst. surgeon Dhaka Med. Coll. Hosp., 1985-86; med. officer Rajdhani Clin., Dhaka, 1986, Upazilla Health Complex, Jhenaidah, 1986-88, Shaheed Suhrawardy Hosp., Dhaka, 1988-89; gen. physician Ministry Health & Med. Edn. Iran, Bandar-Abbas, 1990-94; hon. med. officer Dhaka Shishu Hosp., 1995-96; resident emergency physician Al-Jafar Hosp., Saudi Arabia, 1997-2000. Educator blood donor awareness, Sandhani, 1985. Avocations: reading, jogging, music, table-tennis, sightseeing. Home: 222/ka Malibagh Flat-5, 1217 Dhaka Bangladesh Office: Al-Jafar Hosp, 31982 Al-Hassa Saudi Arabia

HYDERABADI-(ALIKHAN), AKBAR, retired architect, poet; b. Hyderabad, A. P., India, Jan. 20, 1925; arrived in Eng., 1955; s. Ahmed and Shaher Bano (Khan) Alikhan; m. Carmelina Shireen Mauro; children: Rehana Siraj-Allan, Najaf Alikhan. Diploma in architecture. Author: (poems) Khat-E-Rahguzar, 1971, Numoo Ki Aag, 1981, Awazon Ka Shaher, 1988 (Alami Urdu award 1988), Zarron Sé Sitaron Tuk, 1993 (Best Poetry Book of Yr. 1993). Home: 30 Tuffley Rd, Bristol BS10 5EG, England

HYLAND, ANTHONY DAVID CHARLES, architecture educator; b. Surrey, Eng., Aug. 8, 1935; s. Cyril Henry Vincent and Joan Wilhelmina (Rendall) H.; m. Vivien Denzille Risdon, July 30, 1966; children: Daniel, Francis. BA in Architecture, U. London, 1959; MA in Conservation Studies, U. York, Eng., 1979. Pvt. practice architecture, Accra, Ghana, 1961-67, Durham, Eng., 1980-82; lectr. architecture U. Kumasi, Ghana, 1967-75, assoc. prof., 1975-78; dep. dir. Ctr. for Archtl. R & D Overseas, U. Newcastle upon Tyne, Eng., 1982-93; head dept. architecture, assoc. prof. European U. Lefke, Northern Cyprus, 1996-98; cons. archtl. conservation and heritage mgmt.; prof., chmn. dept. architecture Nat. U. of Sci. and Tech., Bulawayo, Zimbabwe, 1998—; cons. UNESCO, The Gambia, 1982, 95, Ghana, 1995-96, UN Devel. Program, Ghana, 1989-92, USAID, Ghana, 1992-97. Co-author: Elmina: A Conservation Study, 1982, Rives Coloniales: Architectures de St. Louis à Douala, 1993; editor The Arab House, 1984; prin. works include Leech Hall, St. John's Coll., Durham, 1987. Chmn. bd. govs. Ridge Sch., Kumasi, Ghana, 1971-78. Fellow Ghana Inst. Archs.; mem. Royal Inst. Brit. Archs. (assoc.), Internat. Coun. on Monuments and Sites. Anglican. Avocations: choral singing, poetry, painting and drawing, walking.

HYLANDER, WALTER RAYMOND, JR., retired civil engineer; b. Memphis, July 22, 1924; s. Walter Raymond and Mary Howard (Douglass) H.; m. Marjorie Jean Gunter, Mar. 8, 1951; children: Walter Raymond, Joyce Elizabeth. BS, U.S. Mil. Acad., 1945; MS in Civil Engring., MIT, 1950. Registered profl. engr., N.Y., Miss. Commd. 2d lt., U.S. Army, 1945, advanced through grades to col., 1969, ret., 1973; tng. dir. Bechtel Power Corp., Grand Gulf, Miss., 1974-76; tng. and edn. mgr. Saudi-Arabian Bechtel Co., Jubail, 1976-77; tng. dir. St. Regis Paper Co., Montecello, Miss., 1978-79; chief civil engr. Bechtel Power Corp., Grand Gulf, 1979-86; chmn. Panel of Experts on Mine Warfare, NATO, London, 1962-65; sr. advisor on engr. tng., Vietnam, 1967-68; mem. U.S. Army Com. on Mil. History, West Point, N.Y., 1972-73; mem. U.S. ACDA, Washington, 1968-69. Contbr. articles to profl. jours. Fellow ASCE; mem. Soc. Am. Mil. Engrs., Nat. Assn. Model Railroaders, La. Miss. Christmas Tree Assn., Phi Kappa Phi. Methodist. Avocations: growing Christmas trees, model railroading, Civil War history. Home: Rosswood Plantation Lorman MS 39096

HYLLSETH, BJØRN, veterinary virology educator; b. Skoger, Vestfold, Norway, May 30, 1927; s. Kolbjørn and Andrine (Bakke) H.; m. Randi Tellefsen, May 9, 1958; children: Sonja, Arne, Rolf, Elisabeth. B Vet. Sci., Sydney (Australia) U., 1957; postgrad., Norwegian Coll. Vet. Medicine, Oslo, 1964; PhD, Royal Vet. Coll., Stockholm, 1973. Active vet. medicine Franklin Vet. Club, New Zealand, 1958-63; lab. veterinarian Nat. Vet. Inst., Stockholm, 1965-73; assoc. prof. Norwegian Coll. Vet. Medicine, 1973-85, prof., 1985-95; hon. assoc. prof. Royal Vet. Coll., Stockholm, 1973—; rschr. dept. vet. microbiology Wash. State U., Pullman, 1982-83; spl. adviser microbiology KLEAN Inc., 1995—. Author: Virus Infections in Ruminants; papers, abstracts and revs. to sci. jour. Mem. European Soc. for Vet. Virology (Norwegian coordinating mem.), Norwegian Vet. Soc., Norwegian Soc. for Microbiology, Norwegian Soc. for Virology. Mem. Conservative Party. Lutheran. Achievements include research on equine arteritis virus infection; UVC irradiation and air filtration to control microbial contamination in various medical facilities and food industry; System KLEAN patented in 65 countries. Home: Leanglia 48, N-1387 Asker Norway Office: Klean ASA, PO Box 62, N-1351 Rud Norway

HYMAN, ANDREW THEODORE, patent lawyer, physicist; b. Boston, Mar. 3, 1962; s. Lester Samuel Hyman and Helen Reeder Sidman. BS, U. Mass., 1987; JD, Lewis and Clark Coll., 1994. Bar: Conn. 1996, D.C. 1998, U.S. Patent Office 2000; Environ. law cert. Sci. data editor MIT Lincoln Lab., Lexington, Mass., 1989-90; mgr. Hostelling Internat., Knoxville, Md., 1995-2000; telecom. advisor Appalachian Trail Conf., Harpers Ferry, W.Va., 1997-2000; atty. Ware, Fressola, VanderSluys & Adolphson, Monroe, Conn., 2000—. Contbr. articles to Am. Math. Monthly, Am. Jour. Physics, European Jour. Physics, Nuovo Cimento, Denver Jour. Internat. Law; referee Am. Jour. Physics, 1999—. Decorated Army Achievement medal U.S.

Army, Wiesbaden, Germany, 1984. Avocations: hiking, swimming. E-mail: mail@andrewhyman.com. Office: PO Box 224 755 Main St Monroe CT 06468-2830 Office: 755 Main St PO Box 224 Monroe CT 06468-0224

HYMAN, BRUCE MALCOLM, ophthalmologist; b. N.Y.C., May 22, 1943; s. Malcolm A. and Sylvia S. H.; AB, Columbia U., 1964; MD, NYU, 1968. Intern in surgery Albert Einstein Coll. Medicine/Bronx Mcpl. Hosp., 1968-69; resident in ophthalmology Manhattan Eye, Ear and Throat Hosp., N.Y.C., 1971-74; pvt. practice medicine specializing in ophthalmology, N.Y.C., 1974—; tchr. attending surgeon Manhattan Eye, Ear and Throat Hosp., 1974—; med. cons. U.S. Seaplane Pilots Assn., 1975—, Health Ins. Plan Greater N.Y., 1977—; ophthalmologist to Hotel Trades Coun., Hotel Assn. N.Y.C., 1974—; attending ophthalmologist Roosevelt Hosp., N.Y.C., 1979—, dir. adult outpatient ophthalmology, 1980—; police surgeon N.Y.C., 1977—, dep. chief police surgeon, 1978—; attending ophthalmologist Doctors Hosp., 1979—, Le Roy Hosp., 1979—, St. Luke's Hosp., 1980—; outpatient ophthalmologist N.Y. Hosp., 1975-77; clin. ophthalmologist Columbia Coll. Physicians and Surgeons, 1981—. Served with USPHS, 1969-71. Diplomate Am. Bd. Ophthalmology. Fellow ACS; mem. N.Y. State, N.Y. County med. socs., Am. Acad. Ophthalmology and Otolaryngology. Contbr. articles to profl. jours. Office: 133 E 64th St New York NY 10021-7045

HYMAN, EDWARD SIDNEY, physician, consultant; b. New Orleans, Jan. 22, 1925; s. David and Mary (Newstadt) H.; m. Jean Simons, Sept. 29, 1956; children: Judith, Sydney, Edward David, Anne. BS, La. State U., 1944; MD, Johns Hopkins U., 1946. Diplomate: Am. Bd. Internal Medicine, Intern Barnes Hosp., Washington U., St. Louis, 1946-47; fellow in medicine Stanford U., San Francisco, 1949-51, asst. resident in medicine, 1950-51, Peter Bent Brigham Hosp., Boston, 1951-53; teaching fellow in medicine Harvard U., Boston, 1952-53; practice medicine specializing in internal medicine, New Orleans, 1953—; dir. kidney unit Charity Hosp., New Orleans, 1953-55; investigator Touro Research Inst., New Orleans, 1959; dir. Hyman Corp.; mem. staff Sara Mayo Hosp., 1954-79, chief of staff, 1968-70, trustee, 1970-78; mem. staff Touro Infirmary, New Orleans, St. Charles Hosp.; panelist Pres.'s Commn. on Health Needs of Nation, 1952; cons. water quality New Orleans Sewerage and Water Bd., 1978; mem. research adv. com. Cancer Assn. New Orleans, 1976-81, La. Bd. Regents, 1983. Contbr. articles to profl. jours. NIH grantee, 1960-81; Am. Heart Assn. grantee, 1962-65. Fellow ACP; mem. Am. Fedn. Clin. Rsch., Am. Soc. Artificial Internal Organs, Am. Physiol. Soc. Biophys. Soc. (chmn. local arrangements 1971, 77, 81, 87), Am. Soc. Microbiology, AAAS, Pvt. Drs. Am. (co-founder 1968, v.p. 1968-84, Dist. Svc. award 1981), Orleans Parish Med. Soc. (gov. 1972-80), La. State Med. Soc. (ho. of dels. 1970-81), Surfaces in Biomaterial Found. Jewish. Subspecialties: Internal medicine; Biophysics. Current work: Clincial internal medicine, biochemistry, biophysics, nephrology, artificial organs, water quality, government in medicine, cause of death in renal failure, significance of bacteria in urine. Isolated aldosterone, 1949; patentee sheet plastic oxygenator (artificial heart), oil detection device; inventor telephone transmission of electrocardiogram, early data transmission; inventor hydrogen platinum detection of heart shunts, Method for detection of bacteria in urine, Systemic Coccal Disease (SCD), Desert Storm Syndrome (following the Persian Gulf War) as a bacterial disease (SCD), grantee treatment of Gulf War Syndrome as a form of SCD, Silicone Implant Disease as a bacterial disease, as a manifestation of Systemic Coccal Disease. Office: 3525 Prytania St Ste 220 New Orleans LA 70115-3586

HYMAN, LEONARD STEPHEN, finanical consultant, economist, author; b. N.Y.C., June 5, 1940; s. Milton and Elsie (Reiter) H.; m. Judith N. Siegel, July 4, 1965; children: Andrew S., Robert C. BA, N.Y. U., 1961; MA, Cornell U., 1965. Fin. analyst Chase Manhattan Bank, N.Y.C., 1965-72; ptnr. H.C. Wainwright & Co., N.Y.C., 1972-77; v.p. Wainwright Securities, N.Y.C., 1977-78; v.p., head utility rsch. group Merrill Lynch Capital Markets, N.Y.C., 1978-94, first v.p., 1987-94; pres. Pvt. Sector Advisors, Inc., Sleepy Hollow, N.Y., 1994—; mng. dir. Fulcrum Internat., Ltd., 1995-96; sr. industry advisor Salomon Smith Barney, Inc. 1997—; mem. bd. advisors Electric Power Rsch. Inst., 1993-99, Enertech Capital, 1999—, Excelergy, 2000—; mem. lunar energy enterprise case study task force NASA, 1988-89. Author: America's Electric Utilities, 1983; co-author: The New Telecommunications Industry, 1987, The Water Business, 1998, A Blueprint for Transmission, 1999; contbr. Electric Power Strategic Issues, 1983, The Future of Electrical Energy, 1986, Deregulation and Diversification of Utilities, 1988, The Electric Industry in Transition, 1994, The Virtual Utility, 1997, Power Systems Restructuring, 1998, Pricing in Competitive Electricity Markets, 2000; editor: The Privatization of Public Utilities, 1995; contbr. article to profl. jours.; mem. editl. bd. Forum for Applied Research and Public Policy, 1993—, Cogeneration and Competitive Power Jour., 1999—. Mem. Pa. Task Force on Electric Utility Efficiency, Harrisburg, 1982-83; mem. adv. com. U.S. Congress-Office Tech. Assessment, Washington, 1983, 86-87, 87-88, 92-93; mem. North Am. Elec. Reliability Coun. Elec. Reliability Panel, 1997. Mem. AAAS, Soc. Utility Regulatory Fin. Analysts (bd. dirs. 1998—), N.Y. Soc. Security Security Analysts, Fin. Analysts Fedn., Inst. Chartered Fin. Analysts, U.S. Energy Assn., Phi Beta Kappa. Democrat. Jewish. Avocations: skating, travel, music, canoeing. Home and Office: Private Sector Advisors Inc 34 Fremont Rd Sleepy Hollow NY 10591-1118

HYMAN, MISTY DAWN, Olympic athlete; b. Mesa, Ariz., Mar. 23, 1979. Recipient Gold medal 200-meter butterfly Sydney Olympics, 2000, Bronze medal 200-meter butterfly, Gold medal 4 x 400-meter medley relay (team) World Championships, 1998; winner 3 individual NCAA titles, 1998, mem. 2 championship relay teams NCAA, 1998; named NCAA Swimmer of Yr., 1998. Office: USA Swimming 1 Olympic Plz Colorado Springs CO 80909-5746*

HYMAN, ROGER DAVID, lawyer; b. Oak Ridge, Tenn., Apr. 23, 1957; s. Marshall Leonard and Vera Lorraine (McKinney) H.; m. Elsa Laurencio; 1 child, Cristina Alicia. BA, Vanderbilt U., 1979; JD, U. Tenn., 1984. Clk. Oak Ridge Nat. Lab., 1977-78, 81; air personality, news reporter Stas. WKDA, WKDF, Nashville, 1979; program dir. Sta. WBIR-FM, Knoxville, Tenn., 1979-80; assoc. atty. Hindman & Holt, Attys., Knoxville, Tenn., 1984-85; asst. atty. gen. State of Tenn., Knoxville, 1986-95; with Law Offices of Roger D. Hyman Powell, Tenn., 1995-97; ptnr. Hyman & Carter, Attys., Powell, Tenn., 1997—. Bd. dirs. Knoxville Christian Sch., 1991-93. Democrat. Mem. Ch. of Christ. Home: 2713 Windemere Ln Powell TN 37849-3782 Office: Hyman & Carter PO Box 1304 Powell TN 37849-1304

HYMAN, SIGMUND M., benefits consultant; b. Balt., Aug. 4, 1921; m. Mary Bloom, Nov. 28, 1947; children: Carol A. Hyman Williams, Nancy L. BS in Econs., Franklin and Marshall Coll., 1947. CLU. Chmn. S.M. Hyman Co., Balt., 1956-77, S.M. Hyman Co. Ltd., London, 1971-77, Bus. Data Services, Balt., 1963-77; gen. agt. New Eng. Life Ins. Co., Boston, 1960-79; v.p. William M. Mercer, Inc., Balt., 1977-80; benefits cons. Balt., 1980—; assoc. Coun. Profit-Sharing Industries, 1960-82, Am. Pension and Profit-Sharing Inst. Purdue U., 1961-82, Balt. Mayor's Pension Study Com., 1966-90, Mayor's Bus. Adv. Coun., 1977-86; mem. Gov.'s Commn. on Competitive Forces Facing Md.'s Horse Racing Industry, 1994—. Mem. exec. com. Greater Balt. Com., 1960-80; vice chmn. Md. Acad. Scis., 1970-90; bd. dirs. Balt. Mus. Art, 1973-79, Goodwill Industries Balt., 1981—; trustee emeritus Franklin and Marshall Coll., Lancaster, Pa., 1973—; chmn. internat. affairs com. Johns Hopkins U., Balt., 1979-80. 1st lt. AUS, 1941-46, ETO, 1951-53, Korea. Decorated Purple Heart; named Disting. Citizen of Balt., 1976, Outstanding Alumnus, Franklin and Marshall Coll., 1981. Mem. Balt. C. of C. (v.p. 1970-78), Balt. Center Club, Suburban Balt. Country Club. Avocations: ham radio, golf, art collecting. Office: PO Box 248 Stevenson MD 21153-0248

HYMAS, JUNE HOPPER, librarian; b. Schenectady, N.Y., Sept. 14, 1935; d. Jack Hicks and Olga (Butler) Hopper; m. Scott Simpson Hymas, June 21, 1955; children: Kimberli Susan Shomin, Scott Bradford, Robert Kipp, Alison Michele. BA, Brigham Young U., 1961; MLS, Case Western Res. U., 1964. Contbr. poems to mags. Recipient 2d place award Montalvo Poetry Competition, 1989, 3d place, 1985. Mem. Calif. Libr. Assn. (pres. Calif. poetry bibliographers sect. 1990-91, multicultural svcs. com. 1979-96), Yuki Teikei Haiku Soc. (pres. 1991-93), Calif. Native Plant Soc., Nature Conservancy of Calif., Santa Clara Valley Audubon Soc. Democrat. Avocations: poetry, photography, choral singing, watercolor painting, study. E-mail: hymas@aol.com.

HYNDMAN, ROBIN JOHN, statistician, educator; b. Dandenong, Victoria, Australia, May 2, 1967; s. Ian Thomas and Judith Marie (Richards) H.; m. Leanne Kim Saxon, Dec. 9, 1989; children: Naomi, Timothy, David, Abigail. BSc with honors, U. Melbourne, Victoria, 1988, PhD, 1992. Statis. cons. U. Melbourne, 1985-92; lectr. U. Melbourne, Parkville, Victoria, 1993-94; lectr. stats. Monash U., Clayton, Victoria, 1995-96, sr. lectr., 1997—, dir. statis. cons. svc., 1996-98, dir. cons., 1999—; dir. Key Ctr. for Statis. Sci., Melbourne, 1996-97. Author: Forecasting: Methods and Applications, 3d edit., 1998. Mem. Am. Statis. Assn., Statis. Soc. Australia (sec. 1993-95). Christadelphian. Office: Monash U Dept Econometrics, and Bus Stats Wellington Rd, Clayton VIC 3800, Australia

HYODO, HARUO, radiologist, educator; b. Honai-chyo, Nishiuwa-gun, Ehime, Japan, Mar. 3, 1928. B of Medicine, Tokushuma U., 1959, MD, 1966. Chief clinic of radiology Nat. Kochi Hosp., 1963-65; chief divsn. of radiology Ehime Prefectural Ctrl. Hosp., 1970-77; prof. dept. radiology Dokkyo U. Sch. Medicine, Mibu, Tochigi, Japan, 1977-90; dir. emeritus Ikeda Meml. Hosp., Sukagawa, Fukushima, Japan, 1990—; asst. dir. Fukuda Meml. Hosp., Mooka, Tochigi, 1993—; guest prof. Dokkyo U. Sch. Medicine, 1994—, Tenjin (China) 2d Med. Coll., 1986—. Patentee in field. With Japanese Navy, 1944-45. Mem. German Radiol. Soc., Japanese Radiol. Soc. (cert. radiologist), Japanese Soc. Med. Imaging Tech. (pres. ann. gen. mtg. 1989-90), Japan Biliary Assn. (pres. ann. congress 1987-88), Japanese Med. Imaging Tech. Assn. (councilor 1980-95). Avocations: photography, motoring, bowling, fishing. Home: 1-9-3 Saiwai-chou, Mib-machi, Shimotsuga-gun Tochigi 321-0203, Japan Office: Fukuda Meml Hosp, 3-10 Namikichou, Mooka Tochigi 321-43, Japan

HYSLOP, DAVID JOHNSON, arts administrator; b. Schenectady, June 27, 1942; s. Moses McDickens Hyslop; m. Sally Fefercorn, Aug. 12, 1995; 1 child, Alexander. BS in Music Edn., Ithaca Coll., 1965. Elem. sch. vocal music supr. Elmira Heights, N.Y., 1965-66; mgr. Elmira Symphony Choral Soc., 1966; asst. mng. dir. Minn. Orch., Mpls., 1969-72; gen. mgr. Oreg. Symphony Orch., Portland, 1972-78; exec. dir. St. Louis Symphony Soc., 1978-89, pres., 1989-91; pres. Minn. Orch., 1991—. Bd. dirs. Am. Symphony Orch. League, 1988-96, chmn., 1994, mem. exec. and nominating coms., 1990-93; bd. dirs. Minn. Citizens for Arts, Mpls. Downtown Coun., 1992-97, Mpls. Visitors and Conf. Bur., 1996-98; mem., co-chmn. arts edn. task forMo. Arts Coun., 1989-90; mem. rec. panel Nat Endowment for Arts, 1986-88, mem. challenge grant panel, 1987-88, mem. music overview panel, 1987-88, mem. music creation and presentation panel, 1999; chmn. music and performing arts com. Regional Commerce and Growth Assn., St. Louis, 1987-89. Martha Baird Rockefeller grantee, 1966. Mem. Am. Symphony Orch. League (chmn. major mgrs. and policy com. 1985-87, orch. mgmt. fellowship program 1979-88, orch. assessment program 1988), Regional Orch. Mgrs. Assn. (founder), Minn. Orchestral Assn., Mpls. Club, Arena Club. Avocations: basketball, travel, reading, study of German. Home: 2019 Irving Ave S Minneapolis MN 55405-2521 Office: Minn Orch 1111 Nicollet Ave Minneapolis MN 55403-2406

HYSONG, NICK, olympic athlete; b. Winslow, Ariz., Dec. 9, 1971; s. Cranston Hysong. Degree in mktg., Ariz. State U., 1994. Pole vaulter U.S. Track and Field Team; winner Gold Medal Sydney, 2000. Placed 2nd U.S. Nat. Championships, 1999, 2nd meet, Rome, 2000. Office: USA Track and Field Team RCA Dome Ste 140 Indianapolis IN 46225*

HYTNER, BENET ALAN, barrister; b. Dec. 29, 1927; s. Maurice and Sarah H.; m. Joyce Myers, 1954 (div. 1980); 4 children. Grad., Cambridge; MA, Nat. Svc.; RASC, 1949-51. Called to bar, 1952, created Queen's counsel, 1970; elected bencher Mid. Temple, 1977, sr. bencher, 1997. Mem. Gen. Coun. of Bar, 1969-73, 86-88; recorder Crown Court, 1972-97; mem. Senate of Inns of Ct. and Bar, 1977-81, 84-86; judge of appeal Isle of Man, 1980-97; leader No. Cir. Bar, 1980-84. Office: 22 Old Bldgs Lincoln's Inn, London WC2A 3UJ, England

HYUN, EUNSOOK, education educator; b. Seoul, Republic of Korea, Sept. 18, 1962; came to the U.S., 1987; d. Jisung Hyun and Soongil Lee; m. Yaesock Roh, July 4, 1987 (div. Mar. 1995); 1 child, Yevin A. BEd in Early Childhood Edn., Duksung Women's U., Seoul, 1985, MEd in Early Childhood Edn., 1987; PhD in Curriculum and Instrn., Pa. State U., 1995. Cert. early childhood edn. tchr. Republic of Korea. Grad. rsch. asst. Duksung Woman's U., Seoul, 1985-87; kindergarten tchr. Child Devel. Lab. Sch., Seoul, 1985-87; instr. dept. early childhood edn. SangJi U., Won Ju, Korea, 1987; presch. and kindergarten tchr. Child Devel. Lab. Grambling (La.) State U., 1989-90; presch. tchr. Child Devel. Ctr., University Park, Pa., 1992-93; grad. tchg. asst. Pa. State U., University Park, 1992-95; asst. prof. Clarion U. Pa., 1995-97; asst. prof. Fla. Gulf Coast U., Ft. Myers, 1997-99, assoc. prof., 1999—; presenter in field. Author: Making Sense of Developementally and Culturally Appropriate Practice in Early Childhood Education, 1998; contbr. articles to profl. jours. Prof. Redlands Christian Migrant Assn., Immokalee, Fla., 1997—. Grantee in field. Mem. ASCD, Am. Ednl. Rsch. Assn. (session chair, proposal reviewer, nat. bd. mem.), Nat. Assn. for the Edn. Young Children (ad hoc com. for developmentally appropriate curriculum and assessment 1997-2000), Nat. Assn. Early Childhood Tchr. Educators, Assn. Tchr. Educators. Avocations: reading, collecting stamps, kayaking. E-mail: ehyun@fgcu.edu. Office: Fla Gulf Coast Univ 10501 Fgcu Blvd S Fort Myers FL 33965-0001

HYUN, MYUNG-KWAN, investment company executive; b. Sept. 2, 1941; married; 2 sons. BA in Law, Seoul Nat. U., 1963; MA in Econs., Keio U., 1974. CEO Samsung Corp., Seoul, Korea; vice chmn., CEO Samsung. Office: Samsung Corp, 310 Taepyung-ro 2-ga Chung-gu, CPO Box 1144 Seoul 100-102, South Korea*

HYUN-MIN, KIM, material scientist; educator; b. Seoul, Korea, Dec. 20, 1965; arrived in Japan, 1993; s. Kim Kap-Jin and Choi Seung-Ho; m. Ahn Hyun-Jung, June 10, 1995; 1 child, Da-Young Kim. BSc, Yonsei U., Korea, 1989, MSc, 1991; PhD, Kyoto (Japan) U., 1997; D Engring. in Material Chemistry. Rsch. scientist Korea Inst. Sci. and Tech., 1992-93; rsch. assoc. Kyoto U., 1997-99, asst. prof., 1999—. Contbr. articles to profl. jours. 2d lt. Army of Republic of Korea, 1991-92. Rsch. fellow Japan Soc. for Promotion of Sci., 1997-99. Mem. Am. Chem. Soc., Chem. Soc. Japan, Japanese Soc. Biomaterials (young investigator award 1998). Home: Sakyo-ku Takano Higashi-Hiraki 20, Kastrom Raknhoku 316, Kyoto 606-8107, Japan Office: Kyoto U Grad Sch Engring, Yoshida Sakyo-ku, Kyoto 606-8501, Japan

HYYPPA, KALEVI, electrical engineering educator; b. Helsinki, Jan. 5, 1941; arrived in Sweden, 1942; s. Esa and Vappu (Salminen) H.; m. Gunhild Wiss, July 19, 1964; 1 child, Maria. MSEE, Royal Inst. Tech., Stockholm, 1967; PhD, Lulea U. Tech., Sweden, 1993. Rsch. engr. Royal Inst. Tech., Stockholm, 1967-75; sr. rsch. engr. Lulea U. Tech., Sweden, 1975-94, sr. lectr., 1994—. Inventor in field. Mem. IEEE, Svenska Elektroingenjörers Riksförbund. Avocations: cross-country skiing, windsurfing. Home: Slipvagen 13A, SE-97341 Luleå Sweden Office: Lulea U Tech, SE-97187 Lulea Sweden

IACOBUCCI, FRANK, lawyer, educator, jurist; b. Vancouver, B.C., Can., June 29, 1937; s. Gabriel and Rosina (Pirillo) I.; m. Nancy Elizabeth Eastham, Oct. 31, 1964; children—Andrew Eastham, Edward Michael, Catherine Elizabeth. B of Commerce, U. B.C., Vancouver, 1959, LLB, 1962; LLM, Cambridge U., Eng., 1964, Diploma in Internat. Law, 1966; LLD (hon.), U. B.C., 1989, U. Toronto, 1989, U. Ottawa, 1995, U. Victoria, 1996, Law Soc. Upper Can., 2000. Bar: Ont. 1970, Queen's Counsel, 1986. Assoc. Dewey Ballantine et al, N.Y.C., 1964-67; assoc. prof. law U. Toronto, 1967-71, prof. law, 1971-85, assoc. dean faculty of law, 1973-75, v.p. internal affairs, 1975-78, dean faculty of law, 1979-83, v.p., provost, 1983-85; vis. fellow Wolfson Coll., Cambridge, Eng., 1978; dep. min. of justice and dep. atty. gen. Govt. of Can., Ottawa, Ont., 1985-88; chief justice Fed. Ct. of Can., Ottawa, 1988-90; justice Supreme Ct. Can., Ottawa, 1991—; mem. Permanent Ct. of Arbitration, 1997—; former cons. Ont., Alta., Can. govts.; mem. Ont. Securities Commn., Toronto, 1982-85; dir. Cambridge Can. Trust, 1984-91; mem. Can. Jud. Coun., 1988-91, exec. com., edn. com.; gov. Can. Jud. Centre, 1989-91; gov. Nat. Jud. Inst., 1992—; mem. adv. coun. Internat. Centre Criminal Law Reform and Criminal Justice Policy, 1991-93, dir. 1993—. Co-author: Canadian Business Corporations, 1977, Cases and Materials on Partnerships and Canadian Business Corporations, 1983; co-editor: Materials on Canadian Income Tax, 6th edit., 1985; contbr. chpts. to books, articles to profl. jours. Mem. Islington Residents and Ratepayers Assn., 1971-85; dir. Multicultural History Soc., Ont., 1976-88; v.p. Nat. Congress Italian Cans., 1980-83, dir. Toronto dist., 1979-83; v.p. Can. Inst. Advanced legal Studies, 1981-85, bd. govs., 1981-85, 91-98; mem. adv. com. Faculty of Law, McGill U., 1996—; dir. U. Toronto Found., 1997—; mem. adv. bd. Inst. Can. Studies, U. Ottawa, 1998—. Newton Rowell fellow Can. Inst. Internat. Affairs, 1962, McKenzie-King traveling fellow U. B.C., 1963; recipient Law Soc. medal Law Soc. Upper Can., 1987, Ordine al merito Nat. Congress Italian Canadians, Toronto Dist., 1989, 125th Anniversary of Confedn. Can. medal, 1992, Lion d'Or award, Ordre des Fils d'Italie au Canada (Montreal), 1995, Cosentino dell'Anno award, Fedn. of Clubs Cosentini of Ont., 1995, Man of the Yr. award Can. Italian Bus. and Profl. Assn. Toronto, 1985, Italo-Can. of the Yr. award Confratellanza Italo-Canadese, Vancouver, 1985, Commendatore dell'Ordine Al Merito della Repubblica Italiana, 1993, Man of Yr. award Brotherhood Interfaith Soc., Vancouver, Can., 1999; named hon. citizen Mangone, Italy, 1996; hon. fellow St. John's Coll., Cambridge U. Fellow Am. Coll. Trial Lawyers (hon.); mem. Can. Bar Assn., Le Club de Golf Rivermead (Aylmer, Quebec), Sigma Tau Chi, Phi Gamma Delta (Disting. Fiji award 1987). Avocations: tennis, golf, other sports. Office: Supreme Ct Can, Wellington St, Ottawa, ON Canada K1A 0J1

IACOVIDES, ALKIS, automotive company executive; b. Famagusta, Cyprus, Sept. 16, 1951; s. Iacovos Vasiliou and Magda (Skeparnidou) I.; m. Nina Ppollou, Jan. 7, 1979; 3 children. Degree, Filton, Bristol, England, 1972, Bristol Polytech., 1975; Diploma in Mgmt. Sci., Bristol U., 1976. Dir. Fairway Motor Inc., Nicosia, Cyprus, 1977—; mng. dir. A.I. Motokinisi, Nicosia, Cyprus, 1992—; chmn. Reliable Motor Cars, Nicosia, 1989—, Harley Davidson Ctr., Nilosia, 1992—, J.J.A. Motosport Ctr., Nicosia, 1997—, Onasia Holdings, Nicosia, 1997—. Consul Gen. of Republic of Korea to Cyprus, 1997. With Cyprus Army, 1969-70. Office: Fairways Motors, PO Box 25674, Nicosia Cyprus

IAFRATE, GERALD CARL, motion picture company executive, lawyer; b. Denver, Aug. 17, 1951; s. Vincenzo and Anita M. (Iacobelli) I.; m. Linda S. Hartzell, June 26, 1980 (div. Jan. 1983); 1 child, Mario J.; m. Jennine Saltzman, Dec. 10, 1992 (dec. May 1994). BS in Anthropology, NYU, 1971; DC, Cleve. Chiropractic Coll., Kansas City, Mo., 1975; JD, U. San Francisco, 1988. Bar: Calif., 1988, N.Y., 1988; diplomate Nat. Bd. Chiropractic Examiners, 1975; lic. chiropractor Mo., 1975. Pvt. practice, ptnr. Midwest Chiropractic Clinics, Inc., Cameron, Mo., 1976-83; legal affairs commnr. USPHS, Washington, 1989-94; dep. insp. gen., Atlantic Maritime Adminstrn., Washington and London, 1991-92; admiralty law counsel U.S. Naval Inst., Annapolis, Md., 1992-98; pres. Ilex-Ryder Entertainment, Inc., L.A., 1995-98; of counsel for admiralty and maritime affairs Mass. Heavy Industries, Inc., Quincy, Mass., 1998—; CFO Roustabout Films, L.A., 1999—. Contbr. treatise Columbia Internat. Law Rev., 1988. Mem. Emissary Assembly World Jewish Congress, N.Y.C., 1991—. Rear admiral USPHS, 1989-94. Diplomate Command Staff Coll., Ft. Leavenworth, Kans., 1990. Mem. ABA, Res. Officers Assn., Am. Legion (Honor award 1996), Brit. Royal Anthropol. Soc. Republican. Jewish. Office: Ilex-Ryder Entertainment 1901 Avenue Of The Stars Los Angeles CA 90067-6001 also: Ilex-Ryder Prodns Kaufman Astoria Studios 34-12 36th St Astoria NY 11106

IAKOVOS (DEMETRIOS A. COUCOUZIS), retired archbishop; b. Imvros, Turkey, July 29, 1911; s. Athanasios and Maria Coucouzis. Grad., Theol. Sch. of Halki, Ecumenical Patriarchate, 1934; STM, Harvard, 1945; DD, Boston U., 1960, Bates Coll., 1970, Dubuque U., 1973, Assumption Coll., 1980; LHD, Franklin and Marshall Coll., 1961, Southeastern Mass. Tech. Inst., 1967, Am. Internat. Coll., 1972, Cath. U., 1974, Loyola Marymount U., 1979, Queen's Coll., 1982; LLD, Brown U., 1964, Seton Hall U., 1968, Coll. Holy Cross, 1966, Fordham U., 1966, Notre Dame U., 1979, N.Y. Law Sch., 1982, St. John's U., 1982; HHD, Suffolk U., 1967, Stonehill Coll., 1980; DST, Berkeley Div. Sch., 1962, Gen. Theol. Sem., 1967, Thessalonica U., 1975; DLitt, PMC Colls., 1971; others. Ordained deacon Greek Orthodox Ch., 1934; archdeacon Greek Orthodox Ch., Met. Derkon, 1934-39; prof. Archdiocese Theol. Sch., Pomfret, Conn., 1939; ordained priest, 1940; parish priest Hartford, Conn., 1940-41; preacher Holy Trinity Cathedral, N.Y.C., 1941-42; parish priest St. Louis, 1942; dean Cathedral of Annunciation, Boston, 1942-54; dean Holy Cross Orthodox Theol. Sch., Brookline, Mass., 1954, now pres.; bishop of Holy Cross Orthodox Theol. Sch., Melita, Malta, 1954-56; rep. Ecumenical Patriarchate, World Council Chs., Geneva, 1955-59; then co-pres. coun. Ecumenical Patriarchate, World Council Chs., 1959-68; elevated to Metropolitan, 1956; archbishop, N. and S. Am., Holy Synod of Ecumenical Patriarchate, 1959-96; ret., 1996; chmn. Standing Conf. Canonical Bishops in the Americas; mem. adv. bd., v.p. Religion in American Life. Author works in Greek, French, English, German. Pres. St. Basil's Acad., Garrison, N.Y.; chmn. trustees Hellenic Coll., Brookline; trustee Anatolia Coll., Salonika, Greece. Recipient Man of Yr. award B'nai B'rith, 1962; recipient Nat. award NCCJ, 1962, Clergyman of the Yr. award Religious Heritage Am., 1970, Presdl. Citation as Disting. Am. in Voluntary Service, 1970, Man of Conscience award Appeal of Conscience Found., 1971, Presdl. Medal of Freedom, 1980, Interreligious award Religion in Am. Life, 1980, Clergyman of Yr. award N.Y.C. Council Churches, 1981, others. Mem. Am. Bible Soc. (bd. mgrs.). Address: 31 Park Dr S Rye NY 10580-1826*

IALONGO, PAOLO, surgeon, researcher; b. Bari, Puglia, Italy, Oct. 30, 1966; s. Carlo Piero and Maria (Zanoletti) I. MD, U. Bari, 1991. Asst. dept. hepatic transplantation/hepato-pancreato-biliary Hosp. Paul Brousse, Paris, 1994-95; asst. dept. kidney/hepatic transplantation/digestive surgery U. Rennes, France, 1995-96; asst. dept. hepatic transplantation/digestive surgery U. Nice, France, 1996; surgeon, rschr. U. Bari, 1996—. Contbr. articles to profl. jours. Recipient Prof. Marinaccio Found. award, 1991. Mem. A. De Blasi Soc. of Surgery, N.Y. Acad. Scis. Roman Catholic. Avocations: tennis, skiing. Home: Piazza Eroi del Mare 13, 70121 Bari Puglia, Italy Office: U Bari Dept Hep Transp/DigS, Policlinin Piazza G Cesare, 70124 Bari Italy

IAMANDI, PETRU, English educator, translator; b. Galati, Romania, Feb. 20, 1951; s. Gheorghe and Maria (Neacsu) I. BA, U. Iasi, Galati, 1974; M.A., High Sch. 8, Galati, 1990. Tchr. Ali Cuza H.S., Galati, 1974-77, High Sch. 8, 1977-90; instr. English and English and Am. lit. Vasile Alecsandri Coll., Galati, 1990-99; lectr.eng. dept. Lower Danube Univ., Galati, 1999—; coord. Blue Danube River Project, Galati, 1991-99. Author: English-Romanian Dictionary, 2000; co-author: English Textbook for the 10th Grade, 2000; translator: (into English) Contemporary Political Doctrines (Anton Carpinschi), 1991, Requiem for the Second Millenium (V. Ghica), 1997, House of the Sky (Victor Sterom), 1999, (into Romanian) Murder at the Manor (Margaret Broadhurst-Clegg), 1991, Murders at Tynewydd (Broadhurst-Clegg), 1992, July's People (Nadine Gordimer), 1993, Sundipper (Paul B. Thompson), 1994, (with Dan Starcu and Doru Tatar) Knights of the Galactic Empire, 1995, Warlock Games (Richard Lee Byers), 1995, Times without Number (John Brunner), 1996, States and Markets (Susan Strange), 1997, (with Mihaela Ghiță) Nietzsche's Children (Raymond Humphreys), 1998, The Red Ghost (Joel Chace), 1999, Democracy and its Critics (Robert A. Dahl), 2000; editor: (books in English) Borderlines (Phil Carradice), 1997, Carmilla (J.S. Le Fanu), 1997, Living Words (Raymond Humphreys), 1998, (with Humphreys) The Time Traveller, 1998, River Empathy, 1999; contbr. prose and poetry and theatre transls. to over 100 profl. publs., including The Third Half, Illuminations, Xenos, Cambrensis, Borderlines, Beyond the Boundaries, Target, Fortress. Cons. Astralis Found., Galati, 1997. Mem. Costache Negri Writers Assn. Avocations: soccer, tennis, theatre. Home: Bloc 0 Apt 32 Sc 2, Micro 17, 6200 Galati Romani Office: Lower Danube Univ, Str Domneasca No 47, 6200 Galati Romania

IANCU, ION, computer science and mathematics educator; b. Sopot, Romania, June 6, 1954; s. Dumitru and Lucica (Stuparu) I.; m. Maria Vascu,

June 16, 1986 (dec. Dec. 1989); children: Vlad, Mihnea Marian; m. Silvia Popescu, Jan. 20, 1990. D in Math., Bucharest U., 1997. Rschr. U. Craiova, Romania, 1978-89, asst. prof., 1989-92, lectr., 1992-98, reader, 1998—. Author: The Theory of Compilers Writing, 1997, Compilers Writing and Semantics Programming Languages-Practical Guide, 1998; contbr. articles to profl. jours. Avocations: sports, historical and geographical literature. Fax: 40-51-413728. E-mail: i iancu@central.ucv.ro. Home: Th Aman Bl 731116, 1100 Craiova Romania Office: U Craiova, 13 A i Cuza, 1100 Craiova Romania

IANCU, OVIDIU CORNELIU, education educator; b. Ianca, Braila, Romania, Oct. 14, 1940; s. Dumitru and Maria (Calinescu) I.; m. Monica Nechifor, July 14, 1967; 1 child, Raluca-Ioana. Grad. Degree in Electronics, Politech. Inst., Bucharest, 1962; Grad. Degree in Physics, U. Bucharest, 1969; Philos. Degree, Politech. Inst., Bucharest, 1972. Asst. prof. Politech. Inst., 1962-76, prof., 1976—; cons. Metro, Bucharest, 1979-96, Nat. Inst. Microtechnology, Bucharest, 1996—. Author: (books) Electronic Materials and Devices, 1972, Dielectric and Magneting Devices, 1979; contbr. articles to profl. jours. Recipient Nicolae Teclu award Romanian Acad., Bucharest, 1976. Mem. IEEE, SPIE. Office: Univ Politechnica Bucharest, Bd Iuliu Maniu 1-3 NR, 77202 Bucharest Romania

IANÍ, ETTORE, sociologist; b. Argusto, Catanzaro, Italy, Nov. 12, 1948. M in Sociology, U. Rome, 1974. Dir. Inst. for Rsch. of Sea, Rome, 1986-93; vice-chmn. Lega/Pesca, Rome, 1987-92, chmn., 1992—; dir. Lega/Pesca News, Rome, 1995—; chmn. bd. Consortium Uniprom, Rome, 1995—; mem. fin. com.R&D, Rome, 1990—; mem. ctrl. com. for fisheries, Rome, 1995—; mem. E.V. Fisheries Com., Brussels, 1990—; vice-chmn. CO.Ge.C.A. Fisheries, Brussels, 1997—; mem. Legacoop Nat. Com., Rome, 1994—. Author: (book) Il Mercantilismo, 1981, Il mercato Internazionale, 1981, Lira Nuova E Azienya Italia, 1986. Mayor City of Argusto, Italy, 1975-77; chmn. bd. dirs. Consortium Mediterraneo, Rome, 1991-93; vice commr. Port Authority Gioia Tauro, Italy, 1998—. Office: Lega Pesca, Via Nazionale N 243, 00184 Rome Italy

IANKOV, IVAN, oil company executive; b. Koinare, Pleven, Bulgaria, Aug. 15, 1949; s. Ianko Iankov and Rosa Georgieva (Vatseva) Stankov; m. Roumiana Tomova Ivancheva, Dec. 25, 1949; 1 child, Vladimir Ivanov. CE, High Inst. Civil Engrs., Sofia, Bulgaria, 1975; degree in Economy, Acad. Fgn. Trade, Moscow, 1982. Cert. in internat. econ. relationships, civil engring. Capt. Bulgarian Army, 1968-70; engr. Bldg. Inst. Investigation Rsch., Sofia, Bulgaria, 1975-79; trade rep. Technoexport, Tripoli, Libya, 1983-86, Bioinvest, Benghazi, Libya, 1986-89; economist Agroengineering Ltd., Sofia, 1990-91; trader Quorum JV, Moscow, 1991-94; dir. Petroquorum Ltd., Moscow, 1994—. Co-author: Building- Light Steel Structure, 1977. Avocation: philately. Fax #: (095) 937-67-94. E-mail: virex.glasnet.ru. Office: Petroquorum Ltd, 27 Malaija Nikitskaij St, 121069 Moscow Russia

IANNELLO, SILVIA, internal medicine researcher, medical educator; b. Catania, Italy, May 9, 1948; d. Natale and Rosa (Tricomi) I.; m. Francesco Belfiore, July 31, 1974; children: Eleonora, Rosanna. MD, U. Catania, 1973, specialist in hematology, 1978, specialist in diabetology, 1982. Resident in internal medicine U. Catania, 1973-77, Ministry Edn. fellow, 1977-80, clin. investigator internal medicine, 1982—; vis. rsch. assoc., U. So. Calif., L.A., 1982. Author: Advances in World Diabetes Research; contbr. numerous articles to internat. profl. jours. Mem. Am. Diabetes Assn., Internat. Diabetes Fedn., European Assn. Study of Diabetes, European Assn. Study of Obesity. Avocation: painting. Home: Via XX Settembre N 19, I-95027 San Gregorio Catania, Italy Office: Garibaldi Hosp Internal Med, U Catania, I-95123 Catania Italy

IANNICELLI, JOSEPH, chemical company executive, consultant; b. N.Y.C., Aug. 5, 1929; s. Peter and Catherine (Gugliotti) I.; m. Betty Peterson, June 28, 1978; children: Mark, Rex, Gina. SB, MIT, 1951, PhD, 1955. Rsch. chemist Textile Fibers, E.I. DuPont, Wilmington, Del., 1955-60; tech. dir. Clay Div. J.M. Huber, Macon, Ga., 1960-70; founder, chief exec. officer Aquafine Corp., Brunswick, Ga., 1970—, Aero-Instant Corp., Brunswick, Ga., 1988—; co-founder IMPEX Corp., Brunswick, Ga., 1988—; cons. Consol. Goldfields Australia, Sydney, 1976-78, Rio Tinto, Madrid, 1980-82, Hoganes, Malmo, Sweden, 1984. Author: Evaluation and Comparison of Crossfield and Solenoid Field Magnetic Filters, 1981; co-author: A Survey-Benneficiation of Industrial Minerals, 1980; contbr. over 30 articles to profl. jours. Pres. Ga. Tidewater Conservation Assn., Brunswick, 1991-92; bd. dirs. Jekyll Island (Ga.) Citizens Assn., 1992-96, pres., 1993-95; govt. appointment as mem. Jekyll Island (Ga.) Citizens Resource Coun., 1995-97; foreman Glynn County Grand Jury, Brunswick, 1989-; chmn. Glynn Union of Taxpayers, 1996—; mem. Glynn County Bd. Edn., 1998—. Recipient Rsch. grant NSF, 1980, 84, Elec. Power Rsch. Inst., 1980, Resolution of Commendation, Ga. Ho. of Reps., 1995. Fellow Am. Inst. Chemists; mem. Tech. Assn. of Pulp and Paper Industry (chmn. pigments com. 1971-72). Achievements include over 100 patents including paramagnetic separator and process, silane modified organo clays, mercaptan scrubber; performed first high temperature superconducting magnetic separation of minerals as part of a team consisting of Aquafine, DuPont and Sumitomo, 1996. Home: 28 Saint Andrews Dr Jekyll Island GA 31527-0901 Office: Aquafine Corp 3963 Darien Hwy Brunswick GA 31525-2423

IANNONE, EUGENIO, communications engineer, researcher; b. Rome, Dec. 28, 1960; s. Augusto and Clelia (Quaranta) I.; m. Flavia Giannoli, May 3, 1986; children: Emanuele, Maria Grazia, Gabriele. B in Engring., U. Rome La Sapienza, 1984. Rschr. U. Bordoni Found., Rome, 1986-97; project mgr. for rsch. projects Pirelli Cavi e Sistemi, Milan, 1997-99; with Cisco Photonics, 2000—. Author: Coherent Optical Communications Systems, 1995, Nonlinear Optical Communications Networks, 1998; contbr. articles to profl. jours.; reviewer IEEE Jour. Light Tech. 1992-96, Photonics Tech. Letters (1992-97), Jour. Selected Areas (1995); reviewer Optics Letters., 1997; patentee in field. Catechist, Roman Cath. Ch., Rome. Soldier, Italian Army, 1985, Rome. Mem. IEEE. Roman Catholic. Avocations: role-playing games, chess, reading, music. E-mail: liannone@cisco.com. Home: Viale Brianza 22, I-20127 Milan Italy Office: Cisco Photonics, Viale Sarca 222, I-20126 Milan Italy

IANNUZZI, JOHN NICHOLAS, lawyer, author, educator; b. N.Y.C., May 31, 1935; s. Nicholas Peter and Grace Margaret (Russo) I.; m. Carmen Marina Barrios, Aug. 1979; children: Dana Alejandra, Christina Maria, Nicholas Peter II, Alessandro Luke; children from previous marriage: Andrea Marguerite, Maria Teresa. BS, Fordham U., 1956; JD, N.Y. Law Sch., 1962. Bar: N.Y., U.S. Dist. Ct. (so. and ea. dists.) N.Y. 1964, U.S. Dist. Ct. (no. and we. dists.) N.Y. 1965, U.S. Ct. Appeals (2d cir.) 1965, U.S. Supreme Ct. 1971, U.S. Dist. Ct. Conn. 1978, U.S. Tax Ct. 1978, U.S. Ct. Appeals (5th and 11th cirs.) 1982, U.S. Ct. Appeals (4th cir.) 1988, Wyo. 1994. Assoc. Law Offices of H.H. Lipsig, N.Y.C., 1962, Law Offices of Aaron J. Broder, N.Y.C., 1963; ptnr. Iannuzzi & Iannuzzi, N.Y.C., 1963—; adj. prof. trial advocacy Fordham U. Law Sch. Author: (fiction) What's Happening, 1963, Part 35, 1970, Sicilian Defense, 1974, Courthouse, 1977, J.T., 1984, (non-fiction) Cross-Examination: The Mosaic Art, 1984, Trial Strategy and Psychology, 1992, Handbook of Cross-Examination, 1999, Handbook of Trial Strategy, 2000. Mem. ABA, N.Y. County Bar Assn., N.Y. Criminal Bar Assn., Columbian Lawyers Assn., Lipizzan Internat. Fedn. (v.p.). Roman Catholic. Home: 118 Via Settembre, 9 Rome Italy Office: Iannuzzi & Iannuzzi 233 Broadway New York NY 10279-0001 also: 775 Park Ave Huntington NY 11743-3976 also: Front St Millbrook NY 12545 also: 345 Franklin St San Francisco CA 94102-4427 also: Advokatunburo Schumacher, Bunishoferstrasse 51, 8706 Zurich Switzerland also: 1592 Pine Ave W, Montreal, PQ Canada also: 120 Adelaide St W, Toronto, ON Canada H3B 3G3

IANZINI, FIORENZA, radiobiologist, educator; b. Rome, Mar. 13, 1957; d. Marcello and Maria (Stecconi) I.; m. Michael Austin Mackey, Mar. 15, 1996; 1 child, Matilda. MSc, Liceo Scientifico Morgagni, Rome, 1976; PhD, U. Rome, 1980. Rsch. fellow NIH, Rome, 1981-83; vis. scientist endocrinology & metabolism Charles U., Prague, Czechoslovakia, 1983; postdoctoral rsch. U. Wis., Madison, 1984-86; fellow NIH, Rome, 1986-88, rsch. scientist biophysics dept., 1988-96; asst. prof. radiology Washington U. Med. Sch., St. Louis, 1996—; vis. scientist Ctrl. Rsch. Inst. Chemistry Hungarian Acad. Scis., Budapest, 1986; med. rsch. coun. radiobiology unit Boyer Ctr. Molecular Medicine, Didcot, England, 1989; med. rsch. coun. dept. therapeutic radiology Yale U. Sch. Medicine, New Haven, 1993. Avocations: reading, music, skiing, outdoors. E-mail: ianzini@radonc.wustl.edu. Office: Washington U 4511 Forest Park Ave Saint Louis MO 63108-2138

IAQUINTA, LEONARD PHILLIP, university official; b. Kenosha, Wis., Aug. 1, 1944; s. Anthony Sam and Mary Natalie (Gallo) I. BJ, Northwestern U., 1966; M in Journalism, Columbia U., 1967. Dir., cons. World Studies Data Bank Acad. for Ednl. Devel., N.Y.C., 1969-76; dir. field svcs. for alumni rels. Northwestern U., Evanston, Ill., 1977-81; dir. nat. alumni program Columbia U., N.Y.C., 1981-82; devel. officer, alumni dir. CUNY, 1982-86; dir. devel. and alumni affairs Ind.-Purdue Univs., Ft. Wayne, 1986-95, Northeastern Ill. U., Chgo., 1995—; spkr. various profl. confs. Assoc. editor: Notes on Negotiating, 1974; contbr. articles to profl. jours.; author various devel. manuals. Exec. dir. Kenosha United Way, 1976-77. Recipient 4 nat. alumni programming and fundraising awards Council for Advancement and Support of Edn., 1981, 84, 88, 98, 15 Who Care award Vol. Connection of Switchboard of Ft. Wayne, 1990. Mem. Nat. Soc. Fund Raising Execs., Coun. for Advancement and Support of Edn., Chgo. Planned Giving Coun., Rotary, Sigma Delta Chi. Mem. Congregational Ch. Avocations: gardening, reading, travel. Home: 6033 N Sheridan Rd Apt 31-g Chicago IL 60660-3048 Office: Northeastern Ill U Dir Devel and Alumni Rels 5500 N Saint Louis Ave Chicago IL 60625-4679

IAQUINTO, JOSEPH FRANCIS, electrical engineer; b. Phila., Nov. 9, 1946; s. Francis Edward Iaquinto and Maria Carmina (Mancini) Feldman; m. Jo-Carol Maniscalco, Nov. 21, 1977; children: Joseph Michael, Jonathan Franklin. BSEE, Drexel U., 1969; MSEE, Stanford U., 1971. Registered professional engineer, Pa., Va. Teaching asst. Stanford (Calif.) U., 1969-71; sr. project engr. GM Corp., 1971-75; regional system engring. mgr. Memorex Corp., King of Prussia, Pa., 1975-77; sr. prin. engr. Computer Sci. Corp., Falls Church, Va., 1977-80; dir. devel. Tesdata Systems Corp., Tyson's Corner, Va., 1980-82; staff engr. HRB-Singer Co., Lantham, Md., 1982-84; sr. staff engr. Lockheed Electronics Co., Vienna, Va., 1984-86; mem. tech. staff MRJ div. Perkin Elmer, Oakton, Va., 1986-89; system engr. Ford Motor Co., Dearborn, Mich., 1989-93; engring. mgr. A.C. Nielsen, Dunedin, Fla., 1993-94; mgr. sys. engring. E'On Corp., Reston, Va., 1994-95; mem. tech. staff TASC, Reston, Va., 1995—. Author: Memorex 1380 Internal and Lesson Plan, 1977, Simulation of Microwave Propagation in the Atmosphere, 1987; co-author: (with H. Brandt) Control Engineering Application to Automobiles, 1973; author: (with others) Secure Internetwork Data Communications, 1979, Mission Planning System Specification, 1985; contbr. articles to tech. publs. Instr. ARC, Mich. and Pa., 1971-77; treas. Macomb County Young Reps., Sterling Heights, Mich., 1975; councilman Longacre PTA, Farmington, Mich., 1990-92. Recipient acad. scholarship Phila. Sch. System. Mem. IEEE, Nat. Soc.Profl. Engrs., Inst. Soc. Am. Roman Catholic. Achievements include development of first microprocessor based direct digital engine fuel control algorithm at GM, of first microcomputer based direct digital wheel lock control algorithm at GM; co-invention of a classified secure network inter network communications protocol; co-conversion of classical signal processing algorithms to massively parallel computer algorithms; modification of system engineering technology to suit automotive electronics applications; invented methodology to use FMEAs and reliability engineering processes to create robust Network Management & Control system for wireless/wireline data communications network.

IATROPOULOS, MICHAEL JOHN, health research executive, pathology educator; b. Athens, Greece, Nov. 8, 1938; came to U.S. 1966; s. John Michael and Marina (Yancoglu) I.; m. Barbara Jeanne McNeil, Aug. 27, 1966; children: John Michael, Mary Ellen. AB, Athens Coll., Greece, 1958; MD, U. Tuebingen, Ger., 1964; Dr.Med.Sc., U. Tuebingen, 1965. Research assoc./resident Div. Biomed. Sci., Brown U., Providence, 1966-67; resident dept. internal medicine U. Cologne, Ger., 1967-68; instr. pathology div. biomed. sci. Brown U., 1968-70; resident dept. pathology U. Mo., Columbia, 1970-71; spl. fellow toxicology CEPT Albany (N.Y.) Med. Coll., 1972-74; asst. prof. ICES Albany Med. Coll., Alamogordo, N.Mex., 1974-77; assoc. prof., dep. dir. ICES Albany Med. Coll., 1977-78; dept. head MRD Am. Cyanamid Co., Pearl River, N.Y., 1978-89; head regulatory pathology and histopathology Am. Health Found., Valhalla, N.Y., 1989-99; pres. Labpath Mgmt., Inc., Suffern, N.Y., 1989-99; prof. pathology N.Y. Med. Coll., N.Y., 1989—. Author: New Anticancer Drugs, 1983, Gastrointestinal Toxicology, 1986, Carcinogenicity, 1988, Toxicokinetics and New Drug Development, 1989, Toxicokinetics, 1993; assoc. editor Jour. Toxicologic Pathology, 1999—. Fellow Acad. Toxicol. Scis.; mem. Soc. Toxicology, Soc. Toxicologic Pathologists (councillor 1981-86), Internat. Fedn. Soc. Toxicologic Pathologists (sec.-gen. 1989-95), Japanese Soc. Toxicologic Pathology (hon. mem.), Internat. Acad. Toxicologic Pathology (bd. dirs. 2000—). Home: 6 Bruce Ct Suffern NY 10901-3310 Office: NY Med Coll Dept Pathology Grasslands Rd Valhalla NY 10595

IATROPOULOS, THEODORE, technical consultant; b. Athens, Feb. 6, 1927; s. Nikolaos and Antigoni (Zouzouki) I.; m. Georgina Praka, July 20, 1968; children: Antigoni/Vassoula, Nikolaos, Marina. BS in Marine Engring., Royal Hellenic Naval Acad., Piraeus, Greece, 1948, MS in Marine Engring., 1949; MS in Mech. Engring., Columbia U., 1958. Registered cons. marine surveyor; European engr./registered. Asst. supr. Nat. Shipping and Trading, N.Y.C., 1956-57; project engr. Aircraft Porous Media, N.Y.C., 1958-59; marine port engr. Marinus Inc., N.Y.C., 1959-60, marine supt., 1960-63; tech. mgr. Atlantic Maritime Enterprises, N.Y.C., 1963-71; mng. dir. Vanta Marine Co. S.A., Athens, 1971—. Lt. comdr. Greek Navy, 1948-56. Fellow Inst. Marine Engrs.; mem. ASME, Am. Soc. Naval Architects and Marine Engrs. Home: Filothei, Kapodistriou 3, Filothei, Filothei Athens 152-37, Greece Office: Vanta Marine Co SA, Eth Antistaseos 63B, Halandri, Filothei Athens 152-37, Greece

IBAÑEZ, LUIS ALFONSO, insurance executive; b. Cochabamba, Cercado, Bolivia, May 4, 1951; s. Alberto and Nora Ibanñez; m. Maria Ximena Quintanilla; children: Ximena, Viviana, Alfonso. BA, U. Catholica Boliviana, La Paz, 1976; MBA, INCAE, Managua, Nicaragua, 1979. Regional mgr. Vascal Bottling Co., 1979-84; CIA. mng. asst. Cia Boliviana de Seguros, 1984-97; CEO Cia La Vitalicia Seguros Vida, 1998-2000; prof. bus. adminstrn. Cath. U., 1986-2000. Mem. Bolivian Ins. Assn. (pres. 1984-2000). Roman Catholic. Avocations: mountain biking, camping, reading. Home: Calle Coyote D-7, Valle de aranjuez Box 6512, La Paz Bolivia Office: La Vitalicia Seguros & Reaseguros, de Vida SA Av 6 De Agosto #2170, Edif Hoy Mezz La Paz Box 8424, Bolivia

IBARRA, BALDEMAR, astrophysicist, educator; b. Veracruz, Mexico, Apr. 9, 1969; s. F. Gilberto Ibarra and Margarita Escamilla; m. Lidia Garrido, July 1, 1995; children: Adalid, Gilberto. BS in Electronics, Autonomous U. of Puebla, Mex., 1996; MS in Optics, Nat. Inst. Astrophysics, Optics and Electronics, Mex., 1996, PhD in Optics, 1999; postdoctoral, U. Dayton, 2000. Rschr. Nat. Inst. of Astrophysics, Optics and Electronics, Puebla, 1999—. Contbr. articles to profl. jours. Roman Catholic. Avocations: soccer, classical and Mex. music, Science literature, children. Office: Nat Inst Astrophys Optics, Calle Luis Enrique Erro #1, Puebla 72000, Mexico

IBARRA, SILVIA, marketing professional; b. Matamoros, Tamaulipas, Mex., Aug. 30, 1974; arrived in U.S., 1995; d. Horacio Wale and Silvia Ibarra. BS in Internat. Mktg., Mktg. U. Monterrey, Mex., 1997. Product mgr. Torrey, Monterrey, 1997-98; with internat. dept. Tex. State Bank, Brownsville, 2000—. Roman Catholic. Home: Apt 103 C 24 Calle Retama Brownsville TX 78520-7356

IBATULLIN, ILDUS IBATULLOVICH, academic administrator; b. Kayuki Village, Russia, Mar. 22, 1946; s. Ibatulla Bictimirovich Bictimirov and Khanifa (Khasanovna) Bictimirova; m. Flera Zhaferovna Bilukova, Aug. 20, 1974; children: Ibatullin Shamil Ildusovich, Ibatullin Marat Ildusovich. Diploma, Kazan (Russia) State Vet. Inst., 1970; D in Agr. Sci., Ukrainian State Agrl. U., Kiev, 1993. Asst. Kazan State Vet. Inst., 1970-71; sr. scientist Agronomy Rsch. sta., Kiev, Ukraine, 1975-79, head lab. chem. adds animal nutrition, 1980-85, dep. dir., 1985-86; assoc. prof. Ukranian Agrl. Acad., Kiev, 1986-90; dep. vice-rector sci. and rsch. Ukranian State Agrl. U., Kiev, 1990-95; vice rector sci. and rsch. Nat. Agrl. U. Ukraine, Kiev, 1996—; chmn. specialized sci. coun. Nat. Agrl. U., Kiev, 1996-99, mem. specialized sci. coun., 1999; chmn. expert coun. Prin. Sci. Com., Kiev, 1999. Name Disting. Scientist Ukraine, 1998. Mem. Ukrainian Acad. Higher Edn. Scis., Ukrainian Acad. Agrarian Scis. (corr.). Office: Nat agrl U Ukraine, Gerojiv Oborony str. 15, 03041 Kiev Ukraine

IBBS, SIR (JOHN) ROBIN, retired bank executive; b. Birmingham, Eng., Apr. 21, 1926; s. T.L. and Marjorie (Bell) I.; m. Iris Barbara Hall, 1952; 1 child. Student, Upper Can. Coll., Toronto, U. Toronto, Trinity Coll., Cambridge, Eng.; MA, Cambridge U., 1950; DSc (hon.), Bradford U., 1986; LLD (hon), Bath U., 1993. Bar: Lincolns Inn 1952, hon. bencher 1999. With CA Parsons & Co. Ltd., 1949-51, ICI, 1952-88; exec. dir. Imperial Metal Industries Ltd., 1972-74, non exec. dir., 1974-76; gen. mgr. planning ICI, 1974-76, exec. dir., 1976-80, 82-88; dir. ICI Ams. Inc., 1976-80, ICI Australia Ltd., 1982-87; dir. Lloyds Bank Plc, 1985-97, dep. chmn., 1988-93, chmn., 1993-97; chmn. Lloyds Mcht. Bank Holdings Ltd., 1989-92, Lloyds TSB Group, 1995-97; head cen. policy rev. staff Cabinet Office, 1980-82; mem. coun. Chem. Industries Assn., 1976-80, 82-87, v.p., 1983-87, hon. mem., 1987; mem. Top Salaries Rev. Body, 1983-88; advisor to Prime Min. on efficiency and effectiveness in govt., 1983-88; mem. Sierra Leone arms investigation, 1998; chmn. coun. U. Coll. London, 1989-95; trustee, dep. chmn. Isaac Newton Trust, 1988-99. Leader Rev. Ho. Commons Svcs., 1990. Lt. Royal Navy, 1947-49. Office: care Lloyds Bank PLC, 71 Lombard St, London EC3P 3BS, England

IBN ALFRED, SHAREEF, marketing professional; b. Phila., Jan. 1, 1968; s. Alfred and Sandra Mae Goodwin; m. Khadeejah Bint Robert; m. Malkia Abd-Al Kareen, Dec. 3, 1998; children: Imani, Suffeeyah, Mu'ad. BA, Morehouse Coll., 1995; MBA, Lancaster (Eng.) U., 1995; cert. in Islamic Studies, Madinah U., 1998, Oslamic Soc. N.Am., 1996. Cert. network marketer U. Ill. Chgo. CEO, founder Shareef Afred & Assocs., Atlanta, 1998—, Shareef Alfred Found., Atlanta, 1998—, Health and Wealth, Inc., Atlanta, 1998—; pres., founder Muslim Network Marketers, Atlanta. Field organizer Qunan Wa Sunnah Soc., Detroit, 1995—; anti-racism officer Nat. Union of Students, 1993-94; fundraiser Am. Fellowship, Lancaster, 1994-95, Am. liaison Madinah U., 1998—. Mem. Nat. Honor Soc., Morehouse Coll., 1994-95. Mem. Toastmasters Internat. Muslim. Avocations: akido martial art, bicycle riding, walking, learning Arabic, travel.E-mail: shareef@chek.com. Office: Shareef Alfred & Assocs 134 Chappell Rd SW Atlanta GA 30314-2529

IBRAGIMOV, VAGIF RZA OGLY, mathematics educator, researcher; b. Nachechivan, Azerbaijan, May 9, 1947; s. Rza Ibragim Ismailov and Siddiga Alekper Ismailov; m. Kifayat Aliyeva, May 9, 1971; children: Naila, Ilkhama, Abbas. B, State U. Baku, Azerbaijan, 1969, postgrad., 1964-69, Candidate of Scis. (hon.), 1981. Rsch. student State U. Baku, 1972-75, tchr., 1975-81, head tchr., 1981, docent dept. computational math., 1985—; researcher univs. in Bulgaria, Czechoslovakia, 1980. With USSR army, 1970-72. Islamic. Home: Narimanov St 51/53, 370006 Baku Azerbaijan Office: State U Baku Z Khalilov 23, Dept Math, 310602 Baku Azerbaijan

IBRAHIM, ABDULHAMID S., psychology educator, dean; b. Cairo, June 4, 1949; s. Ibrahim Abdulwahab; m. Azza Ahmed Sharaf, Aug. 19, 1979; children: Tarek, Sarah, Hatem. BA in Psychology, Ainshams U., Cairo, 1971, M of Psychology, 1978, PhD in Psychology, 1983. Journalist Al-Ahram Newspaper, Cairo, 1976-78; rschr. Ednl.-Rsch. Ctr., Riyadh, Saudi Arabia, 1978-83; assoc. prof. Coll. Edn., Riyadh, Saudi Arabia, 1983-91; head ednl. tech. dept. Coll. Specific Edn., Portsaid, Egypt, 1993-94, dep. dean, 1994-96, dean, 1996—; cons. IBN-Khaldoun Ctr. for Devel. Rschs., Cairo, 1991-95, High Coun. Accident Prevention, Riyadh, 1987; dir. Program for Developing Random Housing Areas in Egypt, Cairo, 1994—. Author: Woman in Egyptian Public Life, 1995; translator: (into Arabic) The Social Psychology of Prejudice, 1997; translator: (into Arabic) (ref. book) Experimental Social Psychology, 1994; co-author (booklet) Ethical Principles for Egyptian Psychologists, 1995; dep. chief editor Psychol. Studies, 1993—; mem. editl. bd. Future of Arab Edn., 1994—. Mem. Egyptian Transparency Orgn., Cairo, 1997, Orgn. for Supporting Egyptian-Women Voters, Cairo, 1997, Egyptian Psychol. Studies Assn., 1983. Capt. Egyptian Army, 1971-76. Mem. APA, Egyptian Psychol. Assn. (treas. 1992—). Avocations: travelling, reading, computer programming, public service, writing newspaper articles. Home: 11 Salman El Farsy, Nozha-Heliopolis, Cairo Egypt Office: Coll Edn, Suez Egypt

IBRAHIM, AHMAD ZAINI, oil industry executive; b. Alor Setar, Malaysia, June 4, 1966; s. Sultan Mohamad Saudh Ibrahim and Rusikoh Abdul Rahman. BS, Sultan Abdul Hamid Coll., Alor Setar, 1983. Clk. Rank Venture SMI, Jitra, Malaysia, 1995; asst. libr. IPDA U., Jitra, Malaysia, 1996—. Mediator polit. parties, Kuala Lumpur, 1986. Recipient Tun Paduka Nila award Agong, Istana Negara, 1985. Parti Islam Semalaysia. Avocations: travel, education. Office: Inst Perguruan Darulaman, Bandar Darulaman, 06000 Jitra Malaysia

IBRAHIM, AHMED, urological surgeon, educator; b. Dongola, Sudan, Sept. 15, 1945; s. Ibrahim Ahmed Ibrahim and Amna Ziyada Mohamed; m. Zeinab Hassan Satti, Sept. 21, 1972; children: Husam, Muhannad, Mazin, Akram, Tamer, Dalia. MB BCh, Cairo U., 1966. House officer Cairo U. Hosps., 1966-67; med. officer Khartoum (Sudan) Hosp., 1967-69; sr. med. officer Darfur Province, Sudan, 1969-70; surg. registrar Ministry of Health Hosps., Sudan, 1970-72, Newcastle Upon Tyne, Eng., 1972-75; lectr. in surgery U. Khartoum, 1975-78, assoc. prof. urology, 1978-86; assoc. prof. urology King Saud U., Abha, Saudi Arabia, 1986-93, chmn. dept. surgery, 1991-94, prof. urology, 1993—. Contbr. more than 69 articles to profl. jours. Fellow Royal Coll. Surgeons Edinburgh, Internat. Coll. Surgeons, Am. Coll. Surgeons; mem. Brit. Assn. Urol. Surgeons. Avocations: reading, table tennis, photography. Home: PO Box 1544, Abha Saudi Arabia Office: Coll Medicineand Med Scis, King Kahlid U PO Box 641, Abha Saudi Arabia

IBRAHIM, FOUAD SAYED, mathematician, researcher; b. Samalout, Egypt, July 27, 1953; s. Sayed Ibrahim Zedan and Sageda Husaen Esmaiel; m. Mervat Ibrahim Abdel-Hamid, Jan. 15, 1981; children: Ahmed, Mahmoud, Mohamed. BSc, Assiut U., 1976, MSc, 1980, PhD, 1987. Cert. in math. Demonstrator math. dept., faculty sci. Assiut U., 1976-80, asst. lectr. math. dept., faculty sci., 1980-87, lectr. dept. math., faculty sci., 1987—; head math. dept. Faculty Tchrs., Elmadena, Elmnora, Saudi Arabia, 1995-96. Contbr. papers to profl. jours. Soldier, 1976-77. Mem. Math. Soc. Egypt. Avocations: reading, sports, traveling. Fax: 202 088 342708. E-mail: fibrahim@aun.eun.eg. Office: Assiut U Math Dept, Elgamaa, Assiut 71516, Egypt

IBRAHIM, HISHAM RADWAN, biochemist educator; b. Cairo, Egypt, Apr. 1, 1957; s. Radwan I. BSc, Cairo U. Faculty Agriculture, Egypt, 1979; MSc, Yamaguchi (Japan) U., 1990; PhD, Tottori (Japan) U., 1993. Rschr. Misr Dairy Inc., Cairo, Egypt, 1981, Schweppes Inc., Cairo, Egypt, 1982-87; rsch. fellow Faculty of Agriculture Yamaguchi (Japan) U., 1987-88; rsch. group leader Taiyo Kagaku Inc., Mie, Japan, 1993-95; asst. prof. Faculty of Agriculture Kagoshima (Japan) U., 1995—; guest scientist Ctr. for Antimicrobial Rsch., Calif. Polytech. U., 2000—. Author: CRC Press, Inc., 1997, 2000; patentee in field; contbr. articles to profl. jours. Mem. AAAS, N.Y. Acad. Sci., Japan Soc. for Biosci., Biotech. and Agrochemistry. Avocations: swimming, tennis, camping, aviation (sky sports). Home: 28-1-509 Kamoike 2-chome, Kagoshima 890-0063, Japan Office: Kagoshima Univ Faculty of Agriculture, Kagoshima U Fac of Agrl, 21-24 Korimoto 1-chome, Kagoshima 890-0065, Japan

IBRAHIM, KIMBALL YUSUF, aerospace engineer; b. Washington, Mar. 14, 1952; s. Walid Yusuf and Barbara (Lawlor) I.; m. Sharon Elaine Brown, Aug. 3, 1979; children: Barbara Elaine, Christina Marie. BS, George Mason U., 1978; MS, U. Houston, 1982. Intern in biology NASA-Hdqr. Office of Space Sci., Washington, 1978-79; scientist GE, Houston, 1979-82, ops. supr., 1982-89; sr. engr. McDonnell Douglas, Houston, 1989; lead aerospace engr. mission integration br. E042 NASA-Marshall Space Flight Ctr., Huntsville, Ala., 1989-96, project mgr. Payload Projects Office JA21, 1996—, chief electro-optics br. EB53, Astrionics Lab., 1996-99, dep. chief Avionics systems group, Avionics dept., 2000—; dep. mission mgr. STS78 Life and Microgravity Spacelab Mission, 1996. Contbr. articles to profl. jours. With USAF, 1972-76. Mem. AIAA, N.Y. Acad. Sci., Aerospace Med. Assn., Tri Beta, Alpha Chi. Achievements include research on payload crew utilization

for spacelab missions, lead payload flight controller on Atlas-1 Shuttle Mission and dep. mission mgr. STS78 Life and Microgravity Spacelab Mission, 1996. Office: NASA Marshall Space Flight Ctr Avionics Systems Group ED15 Huntsville AL 35803

IBRAHIM, M. MEDHAT SOLIMAN, chemical company executive; b. Alexandria, Egypt, Apr. 16, 1956; s. Soliman Osman Ibrahim and Safeeya Mohamed Maassarani; m. Amera Yossef Marray; children: Sherien, Rewan. Diploma, BSC, Alexandria, 1979. Safety inspector Safety Sector, Alexandria, 1984-88, fire officer, 1988-94, fire sect. head, 1994-96, safety sect. head, 1996-97, safety dep., 1997—. Mem. Hydrocarbon Processing, Nat. Safety Coun. Office: Egyptian Petrochem Co, KM 36 Alex Rd, Alexandria Egypt

IBRAIMO, ISMAEL MAHOMEDE, financial executive; b. Ibo, Mozambique, July 18, 1953; s. Mahomede Aide Ibraimo and Maria Telma Eduardo Frias Costa; m. Maria de Fatima Binace, Sept. 6, 1956; children: Quissange, Samantha Damuela, Isaac de Sousa. Degree in acctg. and mgmt., Inst. Comml., Maputo, 1980. Local sr. estate adminstr. Estate Tete, Mozambique, 1973-74, Ministry of Interior, Maputo, 1975-76; fin. and adminstrv. dir. Imigration Dept. Nat. I Svcs., Maputo, 1976-80, N.I.S., 1980-82; area dir. Socimo, Lda, Maputo, 1982-89; group mng. dir. Sage, Lda, Maputo, 1989—; sr. cons. trade and fin. Interfranca, Maputo, 1989-91. Developer varous bank products. 1st v.p. Ibo Island Friendship Orgn., Pemba, 1991—. Sgt. Colonial Portuguese Army, 1974-75. Recipient honor diploma Aemo-Nat. Writers, 1993. Mem. Am. Mgmt. Assn., Chamber of Trade of Maputo, Aeprimo (pres. fiscal coun. 1994). Avocations: soccer, music, swimming, volleyball, basketball. Home: Av D Afonso Henriques 204, PO Box 2429, Maputo Mozambique Office: Sage Lda Investimentos, Rua da Resistencia 1746 10, POB 4047 Maputo Mozambique

IBRAIMOVA, ELMIRA, diplomat. Permanent rep. of the Kyrgyz Republic to the UN. Office: Permanent Mission Kyrgyzstan Republic 866 U N Plz Rm 477 New York NY 10017-1822

IBSEN, HANS, internist, educator; b. Oct. 23, 1942. MD, U. Copenhagen, 1970, D Med. Sci., 1980. Vis. asst. prof. internal medicine U. Mich., 1981-82; chief of medicine, dept. internal medicine Holbaek Hosp., 1986-90; chief of medicine, dept. internal medicine and cardiology Glostrup (Denmark) Hosp., U. Copenhagen, 1990—; assoc. prof. internal medicine, U. Copenhagen, 1990—; mem. editl. bd. Jour. Clin. Hypertension, Jour. Hypertension, Blood Pressure. Contbr. articles to internat. profl. jours., chpts. to books. Mem. Danish Soc. Hypertension (v.p. 1983-86, pres. 1986-88, Rsch. award), Internat. Soc. Hypertension (coun. mem. 1986-94, sec. 1988-92), World Hypertension League (exec. bd. 1991-94).

IBSSA, SEIFU, accountant; b. Addis Abeba, Shoa, Ethiopia, Nov. 19, 1958; came to U.S., 1982; s. Ibssa Ido and Gudetu Ilala; m. Mulu Berhane, May 1, 1963; children: Girum S., Aklil S., Nobell S., Simon s. AA in Acctg., Comml. Coll., Addis Ababa, 1980; ASBA, Santa Monica Coll., Calif., 1986; BS in Internat. Bus., San Jose State U., 1992. Supr. acctg. GenPharm Internat., Mountain View, Calif., 1990-94; sr. acct. NEC Electronics, Roseville, Calif., 1994-99; fin. sys. splst. McClatchy Corp., Sacramento, Calif., 1999—. Bd. chmn. Ethiopian Cmty. Ctr., Sacramento, 1997-98. Mem. Inst. Mgmt. Accts. Avocations: photography, playing accordian. Office: 2001 P St Sacramento CA 95814-5232

IBY, PAUL, Roman Catholic bishop; b. Raiding, Burgenland, Austria, Jan. 23, 1935; s. Stefan and Elisabeth (Zolles) I. Degree in Theology, Vienna U., Austria, 1959; Dr. Jur. Can, Gregoriana U., Rome, 1967. Ordained priest Roman Cath. Ch., 1959. Asst. priest Cathedral of Eisenstadt, Austria, 1959-61, episcopal master of ceremonies, 1961-63, episcopal sec., 1967-74; mgr. of charity Diocese of Eisenstadt, 1969-77, mgr. of religious tchg., 1973-85, dir. of episcopal sec., 1974-92, chancellor, 1977-84, vicar gen., 1984-92, designed bishop, 1992, ordained bishop, 1993—. Office: Bischofshof, St Rochus-Strasse 21, A-7000 Eisenstadt Burgenland, Austria

ICATLO, FAUSTINO CERENO, JR., research scientist; b. Vinzons, Camarines, The Philippines, Feb. 14, 1957; s. Faustino Quinito Sr. and Asuncion (Cereno) I.; m. Rosalina Sahagun Perez, Jan. 4, 1986; children: Josemari Angelo, Louis Carlo. DVM, U. of the Philippines, Quezon City, 1981. Head dept. animal rsch. Rsch. Inst. for Tropical Medicine, Metro Manila, 1985-88, sci. rsch. specialist, 1982-88; rsch. scientist R&D Divsn. Ghen Corp., Gifu City, Japan, 1988-95, sr. rsch. scientist Immunology Rsch. Inst., 1996—. Contbr. articles to profl. jours. including Jour. Biol. Chemistry; inventor immunotherapeutic drug for helicobacter pylori, anti-helicobacter pylori chemotherapeutic drug. Recipient scholarship Nat. Sci. and Tech. Authority, 1985, scholarships U. of the Philippines, 1980. Mem. Philippine Assn. Lab. Animal Sci. (pres., founder 1988). Roman Catholic. Avocations: fishing with my children, guitar, karaoke, basketball, table tennis. Home: 101 Residence May, 22-1 Oritate, Gifu City 501-1132, Japan Office: Immun Rsch Inst/Ghen Corp, 839-1 Sano, Gifu 501-1101, Japan

ICHIHARA, YOSHIAKI, industry executive; b. Osaka, Japan, Nov. 7, 1937; m. Machiko Koizumi Ichihara, Apr. 5, 1944; children: Hiroaki, Naoki. B in Engring., U. Tokyo, 1960. Engr. TEPCO, Tokyo, 1960-81; deputy gen. mgr. R&D TEPCO, 1981-87, head branch office, 1987-91, gen. mgr. R&D planning, 1991-95, dir. R&D, 1995-97, fellow, 1997—; dir. Japan Inst. Elec. Engring., Tokyo, 1990-92; deputy chmn. Japan Soc. vor Computational Engring. and Sci., 1995-97; vis. rschr. Inst. of Indsl. Sci. U. Tokyo, 1997-98; vis. prof. Ctr. for Internat. and Indsl. Collaboration Rsch. U. Tokyo, 1997—; advisor rsch. Inst. Indsl. Sci. U., Tokyo, 1999—. Inventor: Optical fiber mounted ground wire for tranmission lines, 1986. Mem. IEEE (sr.), Japan Inst. Elec. Engring. Avocations: painting, cultural and technology history. Home: 3-22-6 Kotsubo, Zushi 249-0008, Japan Office: Tokyo Elec Power Co, 1-1-3 Uchisaiwaicho, Tokyo 100, Japan

ICHIKAWA, ATSUNOBU, Japanese government official; b. Kobe-shi, Hyogo Pre., Japan, Aug. 3, 1930; s. Tozo and Umeko (Anbiru) I.; m. Toshiko Hosoda; children: Ikuta Ichikawa Yoko, Hiroyuki. BS, Tokyo Inst. Tech., 1953, MS, 1955, PhD, 1958. Rsch. assoc. Princeton (N.J.) U., 1959-60; assoc. prof. engrng. Tokyo Inst. Tech., 1961-70, prof., 1970-71; dir. gen. Nat. Inst. Environ. Studies, Tsukuba, Japan, 1991-94; commr. Nat. Pers. Authority, Tokyo, 1994—; dir. R & D divsn. Nat. Ctr. for Sci. Info., 1986-88; mem. Sci. Coun. Japan, Tokyo, 1988-94, Sci. Coun. (Monbusho), Tokyo, 1990-94. Author: Making a Breakthrough in Research and Deelopment, 1996, also 5 other books; editor: Automatic Control Handbook; contbr. over 150 articles to profl. jours. Mem. Engring. Acad. Japan. Home: 1-8-8 Ogawa Machida, Tokyo 194-0003, Japan Office: Nat Pers Authority, 1-1-1 Kasumigaseki Chiyoda, Tokyo 100-8913, Japan

ICHIKAWA, TADAYUKI, language institute executive; b. Hiroshima, Japan, Mar. 1, 1944; s. Saibo and Tamiko Ichikawa; m. Mitsuko Nakamura, Oct. 10, 1968; 1 child, Seita. B in Econs., Yokohama (Japan) Nat. U., 1966. Br. mgr. Yamaha Piano and Organ Sales Co., Ltd., Otaru, Japan, 1967-69, Sapporo, Japan, 1969-70; market researcher Hamamatsu, Japan, 1971-73; pres., CEO, EC Lang. Inst., Sapporo, 1973—, EC Internat., Sapporo, 1980—; ofcl. fgn. langs. supplied Winter Olympic Games, Nagano, Japan, 1998. Editor, pub. directory, investment guide and bus. guide for Hokkaido, Japan. Advisor Hokkaido Bd. Edn., 1996—. Named hon. interpreter 1st Winter Asian Games Com., Sapporo, 1986. Mem. System Analyst Soc., Rotary. Avocation: tennis. Home: 5-10 Miyanomori 3-12, Chou-ku Sapporo Hokkaido 064-0953, Japan Office: EC Internat, Pres Bldg Minami-1 Nishi-5, Chuo-ku Sapporo Hokkaido 060-0061, Japan

ICHIKAWA, YOSHIO, wood trade company executive; b. Feb. 12, 1914; s. Keisaburo and Eyi I.; m. Shizuko Satch, May 26, 1946; children: Yoshiro, Shigeo. Law degree, U. Tokyo, 1938. Mem. staff Ministry of Fin., 1938-48, chief investigator rsch. dept., 1957-54; chief acct. Tobata Chem. Co., Ltd., Tokyo, 1954-74; mng. dir. Kinugasa Co., Ltd., Tokyo, 1964—; mng. dir. Daiwa Shoji Co., Tokyo. Mem. Tokyo C. of C. and Industry. Jehovah's Witnesses. Avocation: travel. Home: 1-1-2-913 Oyada, Adachi-ku, Tokyo 120, Japan Office: 219 Koskudoro Bldg, 10 Ginzanishi-8 chuo-ku, PO Box 207 Kyobashi, Tokyo 104-8603, Japan

ICHIMURA, TAKAHISA, history educator, philosophy educator; b. Himeji, Japan, Feb. 16, 1933; s. Masahiro and Ikue (Ando) I.; m. Yasuko Nonaka, Nov. 16, 1960; children: Kouichi, Kanako. BA, Waseda U., 1956, MA, 1958, DLitt, 1986. Assoc. prof. Kitasato U., Kanagawa, Japan, 1965-71; assoc. prof. Waseda U., Tokyo, 1971-72, prof., 1973—. Author: The Founding Process of the 6-3-3 Plan in America, 1987, Emerson and His Era, 1994. Mem. Japanese Soc. Philosophy of Edn., Japanese Soc. Hist. Studies of Edn., John Dewey Soc. Japan. Home: 3-22-8 Kajiwara, Kamakura Kanagawa 247-0063, Japan Office: Waseda U, 1-6-1 Nishiwaseda, Shinjuku-ku Tokyo 169-8050, Japan

ICHINO, MANABU, engineering educator, college dean; b. Abashiri, Hokkaido, Japan, Feb. 20, 1944; s. Kyozo and Yaeko (Morikuni) I.; m. Hiroe Miki, Oct. 4, 1968; children: Makoto, Hiromi. B Engring., Tokyo Denki U., 1967, M Engring., 1970, D Engring., 1974. Asst. Tokyo Denki U., 1967-74, lectr., 1974-76, asst. prof., 1976-84, prof. engring., 1984—, dept. chmn., 1989-93, dean, 1993-97, chmn. grad. sch., 1997-98, trustee, 1993-97, 98—. Contbr. articles to profl. jours. Mem. IEEE, Pattern Recognition Soc., Classification Soc. Am. Office: Tokyo Denki U, Ishizaka, 350-03 Hatoyama Saitama, Japan

ICHINO, YOKO, ballet dancer; b. Los Angeles, Cali.. Studied with Mia Slavenska, L.A. Mem. Joffrey II, N.Y.C., Joffrey Ballet, N.Y.C., Stuttgart Ballet, Fed. Republic Germany; tchr. ballet, 1976; soloist Am. Ballet Theatre, 1977-81; guest appearances, 1981-82; prin. Nat. Ballet Can., Toronto, Ont., 1982-90; various guest appearances including World Ballet Festival, Tokyo, 1979, 85, Tokyo Ballet, 1980, with Alexander Godunov and Stars, summer, 1982, Sydney Ballet, Australia, N.Z. Ballet, summer 1984, Ballet de Marseille, 1985-87, Deutsche Opera Ballet Berlin, 1985-90, Munich Opera Ballet, 1987-90, Australian Ballet, 1987, 89, Staatsoper Berlin, 1989, 90, Komische Opera, Berlin, 1991-93, David Nixon's Dance Theater, Berlin, 1990, 91, Birmingham Royal Ballet, 1990-93, Deutsche Opera Ballet, Berlin, 1994-95; tchr. Australian Ballet, 1989, Birmingham Royal Ballet, 1991, 93, Nat. Ballet of Can., 1993, Cullberg Ballet, Sweden, 1994, Nat. Ballet Sch., 1994, 95, Ballet de Monte-Carlo, 1994, Geneva Ballet, 1995-98, Nederlands Dance Theater, 1995, Rambert Dance, 1995, Royal Winnipeg Ballet, 1999; tchr. numerous ballet workshops; dir. profl. program Ballet Met, 1995—. First Am. women recipient medal Third Internat. Ballet Competition, Moscow, 1977.

ICHINOHASAMA, RYO, hematopathologist, educator; b. Kashimadai, Miyagi, Japan, May 10, 1957; s. Jinya and Hisa (Ito) I.; m. Rie Yamamoto, Oct. 31, 1987; children: Leo, Guy, Serah. MD, Hirosaki U., 1982; PhD, Tokyo Med. and Dental U., 1986. Staff Nat. Cancer Ctr. Rsch. Inst., Tokyo, 1986-87, Nat. Hosp. Sendai, Japan, 1987-89; rsch. asst. Tohoku U. Hosp., Sendai, 1989-96; assoc. prof. Tohoku U. Sch. Dentistry, Sendai, 1996—; vis. scientist Beth Israel Hosp. and Harvard Med. Sch., Boston, 1995-96. Home: 2-10 Fukuzawa-machi Aoba-ku, Sendai Miyagi 980 0002, Japan Office: Tohoku U Sch Dentistry, 4-1 Seiryo-machi Aoba-ku, Sendai Miyagi 980-8575, Japan

ICHINOSE, YUKITO, surgeon; b. Nagasaki, Japan, May 31, 1953; s. Kashio and Sachiko (Ushio) I.; m. Noriko Matsui, May 5, 1979. MD, Nagasaki U., 1978, D in Med. Sci., 1988; hon. prof., Liaoning Tumor Hosp., Shenyang, China, 1997. Vis. scientist MD Anderson Hosp., Houston, 1986-87; head dept. chest surgery Nat. Kyushu Cancer Ctr., Fukuoka, Japan, 1993; clin. prof. Kyushu U., Fukuoka, 1999—; lectr. Kyushu U., Fukuoka, Japan, 1993-98. Contbr. articles to profl. jours. Recipient Shinoi and Kawai award Japan Lung Cancer Soc., Chiba, 1993; grantee Ministry of Health and Welfare Japan, 1993—. Fellow Am. Coll. Chest Physicians; mem. Am. Assn. Cancer Rsch., Internat. Assn. Study of Lung Cancer. Avocation: swimming. Office: Nat Kyushu Cancer Ctr, 3-1-1 Notame Minami-ku, Fukuoka 811-1395, Japan

ICKIS, JOHN CATHER, business administration educator; b. Cleve., May 7, 1943; arrived in Costa Rica; s. Lynn Sherman and Elizabeth (Cather) I.; m. Norma Emes, Apr. 1, 1978; children: Laura, Elizabeth, Catherine Ann. B of Internat. Studies, Miami U., Oxford, Ohio, 1966; B of Fgn. Trade, Thunderbird Grad. Inst., Glendale, Ariz., 1967; MBA, Harvard U., 1971, DBA, 1978. Assoc. rsch. Harvard U., Boston, 1985; rsch. assoc. INCAE, Montefresco, Nicaragua, 1971-73; program dir. INCAE, Montefresco, Costa Rica, 1975-79, acad. dir., 1980-84, 86; dean INCAE, Alajuela, Costa Rica, 1986-89, Montefreso, 1992-94; prof. bus. adminstrn. INCAE, Alajuela, 1994—; pres. J.E. Austin Assocs., Inc., Cambridge, Mass., 1989-92. Co-editor: Beyond Bureaucracy, 1987; mem. editl. adv. bd. Jour. Health Mgmt.; contbr. articles to profl. jours. Vol. Peace Corps, Veraguas, Panama, 1967-69; vol. Earthquake Relief, Managua, Nicaragua, 1973. Recipient Hon. Citizenship, Soweto, South Africa, 1991, award for doctoral studies Ford Found., Mexico City, 1973. Mem. ASTD (strategic leadership forum), Internat. Agribus. Mgmt. Assn. Avocations: sailing, golf. Home: Calle Miraflores # 09, Residencial Dona Claudia, Ciudad Cariari Heredia, Costa Rica Office: INCAE, Apdo 960-4050, Alajuela Costa Rica

IDAHOSA, PATRICIA OKIEMUTE, librarian; b. Warri, Nigaria, Mar. 21, 1966; d. Egavon Mathias and Ayowie (Igbasogie) I. B Libr. and Info. Sci., U. Maiduguri, Nigeria, 1987; diploma in mgmt., Lagos (Nigeria) Bus. Sch., 1995. Libr. Internat. Inst. Tropical Agr., Nigeria, 1987-89, Lagos Bus. Sch., 1994—; rsch. officer Crusader Ins., Nigeria, 1989-90; libr./documentatio officer African Regional Ctr. for Engring. Design and Mfg., Nigeria, 1990-94; cons. Nigeria LIbr. Assn., 1995, African Devel. Cons. Group. Mem. Lagos Bus. Sch. Alumni Assn. (fin. sec. 1995—), Nigerian Libr. Assn. (treas. 1993-94), Nigarian Inst. Mgmt., Spl. Libr. Assn. (bus. and fin. sec. 1997). Avocations: reading, travel, walking, bird watching. E-mail: patidahosa@hotmail.com. Office: 11 Ademola St off Awolowo, Ikoyi PO Box 53988 Falomo, Lagos Nigeria

IDÄNPÄÄN-HEIKKILÄ, JUHANA ELJAS, health organization administrator, pharmacologist; b. Pihtipudas, Finland, July 1, 1937; s. Martti and Vieno (Leppänen) I.-H.; m. Ulla Marja Möttölä, Mar. 11, 1977; children: Ilona, Juhana, Klaus. MD, Helsinki (Finland) U., 1966, PhD in Med. Scis., 1968, docent in pharmacology, 1971; prof. pharmacology, Kuopio (Finland) U., 1977. Vis. prof. medicine U. Tex., Houston, 1968-69; asst. prof. medicine U. Oulu, Finland, 1969-71; chief med. officer Nat. Bd. Health of Finland, 1972-90; vis. scientist U.S. FDA, Rockville, Md., 1982-83; sr. advisor UN Fund for Drug Abuse, Vienna, Austria, 1988-89; dep. dir., divsn. drug mgmt. and policites WHO, Geneva, Switzerland, 1990-95, dir., divsn. drug mgmt. and policies, 1995-99; prof. Inst. Biomedicine U. Helsinki, Finland, 1999—; mem. UN Commn. on Narcotic Drugs, 1984-87, vice chmn., 1986, chmn., 1987; rep. of Finland to the Pompidou Group, Coun. of Europe, 1987-90; sr. adviser to coun. Internat. Orgns. Med. Scis., Geneva, 1999—. Contbr. over 100 articles to scientific publs. 1st Med. Lt., Finnish Def. Power, 1987—. Decorated Order of the White Rose, Finland, 1987. Avocation: classical music. Home: Kanavamäki 22A, 00840 Helsinki Finland Office: Univ Helsinki, 00840 Helsinki Finland

IDDAMALGODA, ARUNASIRI, veterinary surgeon, livestock consultant; b. Colombo, Sri Lanka, Sept. 29, 1963; s. Martin and Karunawathie (Kiriella) I.; m. Nayana Manoj de Silva Kalinga, May 26, 1993; 1 child, Banuka Amila. B Vet. Sci., U. Agrl. Scis., Bangalore, India, 1990; MSc, Gifu (Japan) U., 1996, PhD, 1999. Cert. vet. surgeon. Vet. surgeon Mahaweli Devel. Project, Colombo, 1990-92; vet. rsch. officer Vet. Rsch. Inst., Peradeniya, Sri Lanka, 1993; postgrad. rschr. Gifu U., 1996—; vet. cons. Mahaweli Authority, Sri Lanka, 1990-92. Contbr. articles to profl. jours. Mem. Japanese Vet. Med. Assn., World Poultry Sci. Assn., Japanese Poultry Sci. Assn., Vet. Coun. Sri Lanka. Avocations: singing, sports. Home: 701 Haitsu Soden, Soden Odori 2-14, Gifu 502-0902, Japan Office: Gifu U Faculty Agr, 1-1 Yanagido, Gifu-shi 501-1112, Japan

IDE, HISATO, landscape architect; b. Tokyo, Sept. 9, 1936; s. Gentaro and Yukiko (Kato) I.; m. Masako Otsuka, Sept. 26, 1938; 1 child, Nogiku. B Agr., U. Tokyo, 1961, M Agr., 1963, PhD Agr., 1970. Asst. prof. U. Tokyo, 1963-73, assoc. prof., 1973-84, prof., 1984-97, prof. emeritus, 1997—; vis. rschr. Nat. Inst. of Vegetation Sci., Germany, 1968-69; mem. Sci. Coun. of Japan, 1994-97; pres. Japan Inst. of Landscape Architecture, 1993-95, v.p. City Planning Inst. of Japan, 1995-99. Author: Ecology for the Conservation of Open Spaces, 1980, Land Use Planning Based on Natural Sites, 1985, Landscape Architecture, 1986, Landscape Ecology, 1993. Recipient Ishikawa award City Planning Inst. of Japan, 1965, JILA prize Japan Inst. of Landscape Architecture, Tokyo, 1972, Hon. for Internat. Advancement, Internat. Turfgrass Soc., 1989. Mem. Japan Soc. of Revegetation Tech. (v.p. 1991-93), Rural Planning Assn. (pres. 1992-94). Avocations: gardening, perspective sports. Home: Honcho 31-4-412, Saitama Prefecture, Wako 351-0114, Japan

IDEI, NOBUYUKI, electronics executive; b. Nov. 21, 1937; m. Teruyo Idei; 1 child, Mari. Grad., Waseda U., 1960. Joined Sony, 1960; head corp. comm. and brand image Sony of France; mng. dir. Sony Corp., 1989-95, pres., 1995-99, corp. chmn., CEO, 2000—. Avocations: golf, movies, music. Office: Sony Corp, 6-7-35 Kitashinagawa, Shinagawa-ku Tokyo 141-0001, Japan*

IDING, ALLAN EARL, lawyer; b. Milw., Apr. 29, 1939; s. Earl Herman and Erna Adeline (Albrecht) I.; m. Anne Louise Chaconas, July 9, 1961; children: Kent Earl, Krista Anne Templeman, Bradford A., Andrea Beth Brozynski. BS, Marquette U., 1961, LLB, 1963; DHL (hon.), Nashotah (Wis.) House, 1990. Bar: Wis. 1963, U.S. Dist. Ct. (ea. dist.) Wis. 1963, U.S. Ct. Appeals (7th cir.) 1963. Law clk. U.S. Ct. Appeals (7th cir.), Chgo., 1963-64; assoc. Whyte Hirschboeck Dudek, S.C., Milw., 1964-71, mem., 1971—; bd. dirs. Elicar Corp. Trustee Nashotah House, 1976—; pres., bd. dirs. Wis. DeMolay Found., Milw., 1985—, Wis. Health and Ednl. Facilities Authority, 1978-85, Todd Wehr Found., Inc., Wis. Masonic Home, Inc.; mem. Wauwatosa (Wis.) Police and Fire Commn., 1978-83. Mem. Blue Mound Golf and Country Club (bd. dirs.), Milw. Athletic Club, Masons (grand master Wis. 1981-82). Republican. Episcopalian. Avocation: golf. Home: 9212 Wilson Blvd Milwaukee WI 53226-1729 Office: Whyte & Hirschboeck Dudek SC Ste 2100 111 W Wisconsin Ave Milwaukee WI 53203-2501

IDLA, KATRIN, chemist, educator; b. Suure-Jaani, Estonia, Apr. 29, 1966; d. Ants and Tiina (Aasa) I.; 1 child: Katariina. MSc in Chemistry cum laude, Tartu U., 1989; MSc in Chem. Engring., Tallinn Tech. U., 2000. Jr. scientist U. Tartu, 1988-89; jr. scientist Tallinn (Estonia) Tech. U., 1989-91, project scientist, 1993—, asst. lectr., 1992—; vis. scientist Helsinki U. Tech., 1994-96, 98-99, cons., 1997-98; cons., vis. scientist Linköping (Sweden) U., 1996, 97, 99, 2000; coord. tech. mgmt. program Concordia Internat. U., Estonia, 1999-2000. Editor Sci. and Tech. News in Estonian State TV, 1999—; contbr. articles to profl. jours.; patentee in field. Grantee Johnson Found., Sweden, 1996, Estonian Sci. Found., 1993—, CIMO, Helsinki, 1993-94, Acad. Finland, 1995-97, Royal Swedish Acad. Scis., 1999-2000. Mem. Internat. Soc. Electrochemistry. Avocations: music, hiking, movies. Office: Tallinn Tech U, Ehitajate TEE5, 19086 Tallinn Estonia

IDLE, ERIC, actor, screenwriter, producer, songwriter; b. South Shields, Eng., Mar. 29, 1943. Pres. The Cambridge Footlights, 1964-65. TV shows include The Frost Report, Monty Python's Flying Circus, 1969-74, Rutland Weekend TV, 1975, Suddenly Susan, 1999-2000; films include And Now For Something Completely Different, 1971, Monty Python and the Holy Grail, 1975, The Rutles, 1978, Monty Python's Life of Brian, 1979, Monty Python Live at the Hollywood Bowl, 1982, Monty Python's The Meaning of Life, 1983, Yellowbeard, 1983, National Lampoon's European Vacation, 1985, Transformers: The Movie, 1986, The Adventures of Baron Munchausen, 1988, Nuns on the Run, 1990, Too Much Sun, 1991, Mom and Dad Save the World, 1993, Splitting Heirs, 1993, Casper, 1995, The Wind in the Willows, 1996, Burn Hollywood Burn, 1998, Dudley Do-Right, 1999, South Park: Bigger, Longer and Uncut (voice), 1999. Office: Grant & Tani Inc 9100 Wilshire Blvd Ste 1000 Beverly Hills CA 90212-3415 also: William Morris 151 S El Camino Dr Beverly Hills CA 90212-2704

IDLE, JEFFREY ROBERT, pharmacology educator, consultant; b. Kendal, Eng., Sept. 17, 1950; s. Robert William and Margaret Joyce (Golightly) I.; 1 child, Nadia Karim. BSc, Hatfield Poly., 1972, BSc with honors, 1973; PhD, St. Mary's Hosp. Med. Sch., London, 1976. Chartered chemist, biologist. Technician Geigy Ltd., Manchester, Eng., 1971; rsch. chemist Wander Ltd., 1972; lectr. biochemistry St. Mary's Hosp. Med. Sch., 1976, lectr. biochem. pharmacology, 1976-83, Wellcome Trust sr. lectr., 1983-85; reader pharmacogenetics U. London, 1985-88; prof. U. Newcastle, Eng., 1988-95, head Sch. clin. Med. Scis., 1992-95, chmn. dept. pharm. scis., 1993-95; prof. medicine and molecular biology Norwegian U. Sci. and Tech., Trondheim, 1996—; hon. prof. clin. pharmacology U. Extremadura, Badajoz, Spain, 1999—; exec. dir. Nivy Blacksmith Music, Děpoltovice, Czech Republic, 1999—; chief exec. Genotype Ltd., U.K., 1992-95. Founding editor, editor-in-chief Pharmacogenetics, 1990-98; contbr. over 350 articles to profl. jours., chpts. to books. Recipient numerous rsch. grants, 1983—. Fellow Royal Soc. Chemistry, Inst. Biology. Avocations: music, languages, history, culture, film. Home: Zlatá 34, 36005 Karlovy Vary Czech Republic Office: Nivy Blacksmith Music, Nivy 4, 36225 Děpoltovice KV, Czech Republic

IDO, YOSHIMITSU, communication company executive; b. Tokyo, Oct. 19, 1941; s. Yoshio and Teiko (Sasa) Ido; m. Kazuko Nishino, Apr. 30, 1970; children: Yoko, Reiko. BE, Tokyo U., 1965. Engr. Nippon Kokan, Tokyo, 1965-70, asst. mgr., 1970-78, gen. mgr. corp. planning, 1983-86; mng. tech. mgmt. Engring. Assn. of Japan, Tokyo, 1978-80; program dir. Convex Computer, Richardson, Tex., 1991-96; mng. dir. CIO KVH Telecomm., Tokyo, 1999—; cons. Electronics Co., Tokyo, 1988-91, Med. Co., Tokyo, 1989-90. Translator: Industrial Project Management, 1984, Basic Electronics for Scientist, 1986; mng. editor Handbook of Control and Measurement, 1984; editor Personal Computer Musium, 1991-92. Mem. IEEE, Inst. of Physics, Inst. of Physics Japan. Avocations: dancing Tango, tea celemony, collection old personal computers. Home: 6-5-19 Kaminagaya Konanku, Yokohama 233-0012, Japan Office: KVH Telecom Shim Aoyama Bld, 1-1-1 Minami Aoyama, Tokyo 107-0062, Japan

IDOL, JAMES DANIEL, JR., chemist, educator, inventor, consultant; b. Harrisonville, Mo., Aug. 7, 1928; s. James Daniel and Gladys Rosita (Lile) I.; m. Marilyn Thorn Randall, 1977. A.B., William Jewell Coll., 1949; M.S., Purdue U., 1952, Ph.D., 1955, D.Sc. (hon.), 1980. With Standard Oil Co., Ohio, 1955-77; rsch. supr. Standard Oil Co., 1965-68, rsch. mgr., 1968-77; mgr. venture rsch. Ashland Chem. Co., Columbus, Ohio, 1977-79; v.p., dir. corp. R & D Ashland Chem. Co., 1979-88; Disting. prof. materials sci. and ceramics Sch. Engring. Rutgers U., New Brunswick, N.J., 1988—, dir. Ctr. for Packaging Sci. and Engring., 1988—, dep. dir. Ctr. for Plastics Recycle Rsch., 1988-95; mem. adv. bd. NSF Presdl. Young Investigators Awards; cons. in field; lectr. chem. engring. dept. Northwestern U., 1978, Stanford U., 1982, 83, U. Calif., Berkeley, 1986, Yale U., 1988; lectr. Lawrence Berkeley Lab., 1985, 86; mem. adv. bd. Petroleum Rsch. Fund, 1974-76; v.p., program coord. 1st N.Am. Chem. Congress, 1975; program coord. 1st Pacific Rim Chem. Cong., 1979; indsl. rep. Coun. for Chem. Rsch., 1983—, mem. governing bd., 1985—; mem. panel on frontiers in fossil fuel energy rsch. NRC, 1986, mem. com. on tracking toxic wastes, 1989-93, panel on polymers in the environ. Internat. Union of Pure and Applied Chemistry, 1996; mem. adv. bds. U. Tex., Tex. A&M, Ohio State U., Purdue U., Okla. State U., Ariz. State U., U. Mass., Inc., Case Western Reserve U., 1965-75; mem. com. on energy conservation in processing of indsl. materials; mem. adv. bd. Nat. Inst. Sci. and Tech., 1997—; mem. com. polymers recycling Internat. Union Pure and Applied Chem., 1993—; mem. U.S. Coun. Chem. Rsch., 1981-89, gov. bd. 1985-88. Contbr. articles to profl. jours., handbooks and encys., chpts. to books; mem. editl. adv. bd. Indsl. & Engring. Chemistry Jour., 1976-84, Chem. and Engring. News, 1977-81, Am. Chem. Soc. Symposium Ser., 1978-84, Advances in Chemistry Ser., 1979-84, Chem. Week Mag., 1980-82, Science, 1986-91, Jour. Applied Polymer Sci., 1988—; inventor ammoxidation process for manufacture acrylonitrile (over 80 plants in 30 countries-this ammoxidation process was designated as Nat. Hist. Chem. Landmark 1997 by Am. Chem. Soc.); patentee in several fields. Active Cleve. Welfare Fedn. Recipient Modern Pioneer award NAM, 1965, Disting. Alumnus citation William Jewell Coll., 1971. Fellow AAAS, Am. Inst. Chemists (life; bd. dirs. 1981—, vice chmn. 1986, chmn. 1987, Chem. Pioneer award 1968, Mems. and Fellows lectr. 1980); mem. Nat. Acad. Engring., Soc. Plastics Industry, Soc. Mfg. Engrs.-Composite Group, Am. Chem. Soc. (indsl. and engring. chemistry divsn., chmn. 1971, chem. innovator designation Chem. and Engring. News mag. 1971, Joseph P. Stewart Disting. Svc. award 1975, Creative Invention award 1975), Am. Mgmt. Assn. (R&D coun. 1985-88, Coun. award for Disting.

Svc. pkg. coun. 1989-97, mfg. and tech. coun. 1997—), Dirs. of Indsl. Rsch., Am. Inst. Chem. Engrs., Licensing Execs. Soc., Soc. Plastics engrs., Indsl. Rsch. Inst. (rep., chmn. bd. editors 1983-86), Plastics Pioneers Assn., Soc. Chem. Industry (Perkin medal 1979), Ind. Acad. Sci., Catalysis Soc. (Ciapetti award/lectureship 1988), Cleve. Athletic Club, Cosmos Club (Washington), Worthington Hills Country Club, Masons, Shriners, Sigma Xi, Alpha Chi Sigma, Theta Chi Delta, Kappa Mu Epsilon, Alpha Phi Omega, Phi Gamma Delta. Mem. Christian Ch. (Disciples of Christ).

IDOWU, ISIAKA ADIO, socio-economics consultant, agriculturist; b. Ijale-Papa, Nigeria, Feb. 13, 1949; s. Sulaimon Alabi and Sidikat Agbeke (Faleti) I.; m. Taiwo Aderonke Kalejaiye, Dec. 1, 1992; 4 children. BSc in Internat. Agrl. Econ. with honors, U. Kassel, Witzhausen, Germany, 1980; MSc in Agrl. Devel., Tech. U. Berlin, 1983, DSc in Internat. Agrl. Devel., 1988. Profl. cert. in Agr. and Ambiance, Fachoberschwe, Witzenhausen, Germany, 1978; Ccert. in agr. IAR&T, U. Ife Sch. Agr., Akure, Nigeria, 1972. Agrl. ext. sta. officer Lagos (Nigeria) State Ministry Agr. & Coop., 1970-73; rsch. fellow Internat. Inst. Tropical Agr., Ibadan, Nigeria, 1985-86; country case rschr. Internat. Inst. Tropical Agr./Internat. Svc. Nat. Agrl.Rsch., Nigeria, The Netherlands, 1988-89; lectr., coord. dept. agr. ext. U. Agr., Abeokuta, Nigeria, 1989-98, acting dir. agrl. media resources & ext. (AMREC), 1998—; cons. socio-economist Internat. Inst. Tropical Agr./IDRC, Ibadan, 1995-98, devel. cons. Farmer's Union of Nigeria, Abeokuta, 1996—, dir. AMOCI/NGO, Abeokuta, 1996—. Author: Links Between Agricultural Research and Extension oin Nigeria, 1988. Activist World Hunger Project, Germany/Nigeria, 1986-87; sec. Ijale Cmty. Devel. Assn., 1990—; mem., nat. zonal coord. Nat. Children's Agrl. Project, 1998—. Post-doctorate fellow Fed. Ministry Econ. Cooperation, Bonn, Germany, 1993; recipient Ford Found./Nest Rsch. Competition award, 1993. Fellow Inst. Farmers of Nigeria (hon., patron, Merit award 1990); mem. Agr. Soc. Nigeria, Agr. Ext. Soc. Nigeria, Nigeria Rural Sociology Assn. Pentecostal Christian. Avocations: photography, gardening, travel, singing. Office: U Agr Abeokuta, Agrl Media Res Ctr AMREC, POB 2240 Abeokuta Ogun, Nigeria

IDREES, MUHAMMAD, engineering designer, consultant; b. Faisalabad, Punjab, Pakistan, Feb. 1, 1971; s. Atta Muhammad and Kalsoom (Akhtar) Malik; m. Nayyar Chughtai, Nov. 3, 1995; 1 child, Ol-Laaiba Nawaal. FSc, Govt. Coll., Fiasalabad, Pakistan, 1987; BSME, UET, Lahore, Pakistan, 1993; diploma in Workshop Tech., Germany, 1994. Registered profl. engr., Pakistan. Engrng. quality assurance PEL, Lahore, 1993-94; engr. ISO-9000 project EMCO, Lahore, 1994; exec., mgr. tech. PEDFACS, Faisalabad, 1994—, HPI, Faisalabad, 1994—; tech. cons. PEDFACS, 1994—, HPI, 1997—; incharge Tech. Cons. Svcs., Faisalabad, 1996—; dir. Spl. Machines Divsn., Faisalabad, 1997—, GM-Almaalik Internat. Group. Inventor hydraulic integrated systems, handicap motorbike, fabric A-frame/batcher free sys. with handling and storing and other spl. handling pieces of equipment. Gen. sec. Green Home, Faisalabad, 1997. Recipient Innovative Tech. award PIQC, Lahore, 1997, Recognition award M.D. GTM, Karachi, Pakistan, 1997, Recognition award EPB Pakistan, 1997. Mem. AEP, PEC (life), Lions Club Internat., Amnesty Internat. Avocations: innovative ideas with research and development, gardening, humanitarian, badminton, family get togethers. Home: 562 Sarfraz Colony St No 7, 38090 Faisalabad Pakistan

IDRISA, AUDU LAWAN, obstetrician, gynecologist, educator; b. Ngoshe, Borno, Nigeria, June 26, 1959; s. Lawan and Zainabu Attawa Idrisa; m. Halima Audu Abubakar, Aug. 23, 1982; children: Jamila, Zainab, Muhammad Nur, Al-Amin, Idris. MB, BS, U. Maiduguri, Nigeria, 1983. Intern tchg. hosp. U. Maiduguri, 1983-84, med. rsch. fellow, 1986-91, lectr. I in ob-gyn., 1991—, sr. lectr. ob-gyn., 1994-97, assoc. prof., head dept. ob-gyn., 1993—, cons. ob-gyn. tchg. hosp., 1991—, coord. family planning tchg. hosp., 1993—, assoc. prof. ob-gyn., 1997—, chmn. health svcs. com., 1999—; registrar ob-gyn. U. Coll. Hosp., Ibadan, Nigeria, 1986-89, sr. registar ob-gyn., 1989-91; hall master Kashin Ibrahim Hall, U. Maiduguri, 1995—; chmn., dir. reproductive health Fed. Ministry Health, N.E. Zone, Nigeria, 1996—. Contbr. articles to profl. jours. Mem. tech. com. UN Fund for Population Activities, Borno, 1996. Fellow Internat. Coll. Surgeons, West African Coll. Surgeons; mem. Nigerian Med. Assn., Med./Dental Cons. Assn. Nigeria, Soc. Gynaecology Obstetrics Nigeria. Achievements include organization of undergraduate and postgraduate curriculum in obstetrics and gynecology at Univ. Maiduguri; coordination of family planning activities in North Eastern Nigeria (Sub Sahara Africa); coordination of reproductive health in North Eastern Nigeria (Federal Health Zone D). Office: U Maiduguri Dept Ob-Gyn, PO Box 1069, Maiduguri Borno, Nigeria

IEKO, TOHRU, military officer, researcher; b. Zushi, Kanagawa, Japan, Apr. 25, 1964; s. Makoto and Aiko Ieko; m. Chikako Iida, Feb. 10, 1990; children: Takashi, Kimika. B of Engring., Nat. Def. Acad., Yokosuka, Kanagawa, 1988, M of Engring., 1993; D of Engring., Shinsyuu U., Nagano, Japan, 1999. Cert. in engring. Platoon leader Japan Ground-Def. Force, Asaka, Saitama, Japan, 1989-91; rsch. fellow dept. aerospace engring. Nat. Def. Acad., Yokosuka, Kanagawa, 1993-97; rsch. fellow 1st Rsch. Ctr. Tech. R & D Inst. Japan, Meguro, Tokyo, 1998—. Contbr. tech. papers to profl. jours. Maj. Japan Ground Self-Def. Force. Mem. AIAA, IEEE, Japan Soc. for Aero. and Space, Scis. Sensing Instrument Control Engring. Fax: 81 3 3713 6077. E-mail: ieko@msn.com. Home: 1753-20 Oyamacho, Machida Tokyo 194-0212, Japan Office: Tech R & D Inst Japan, 2-2-1 Nakameguro, Meguro Tokyo 153-0061, Japan

IEMMA, UMBERTO, engineering educator; b. Rome, Aug. 10, 1962; s. Ottavio and Enza (Sampo) I. Maturita scientifica, A Righi, Rome, 1981; engrng. degree, U. Rome, 1990, PhD in Aerospace Engring., 1994. Postdoctoral fellow U. Rome, 1994-96, asst. prof., 1996—; resp. Graphic Simulation Lab., Italy, 1999—. Avocations: music, photography, cinema. Address: Dept Mech Engring U Rome, Via Vasca Navale 79, 00146 Rome Italy

IERARDI, ERIC JOSEPH, school system administrator; b. Bklyn., May 11, 1950; s. Joseph and Angelina (Vitale) I. BA, St. Francis Coll., 1973; MEd, Fordham U., 1987. Asst. dir. James A. Kelly Local Hist. Studies Inst., 1973; St. Francis Coll. tchr. St. Bartholomew's Sch., 1974-78; tchr. Our Lady of Grace Sch., Bklyn., 1978-86; tchr. St. Mary Star of Sea Sch., 1986-87, asst. on edn. to Bklyn. borough pres., 1979; dist. rep., mgr. Congressman Stephen J. Solarz, 1981-82; prin. St. Francis Xavier Sch., Vicksburg, Miss., 1987-89, St. Francis Paola Sch., Bklyn., 1989-91, St. Pius V, Jamaica, Queens, N.Y., 1991-96; adminstr. David A. Boody Intermediate Sch. 228, Bklyn.; instr. prof. Hinds C.C., Miss.; U.S. delegate Gruppo Savoia, 2000. Author: Gravesend: The Home of Coney Island, 1975, Gravesend: Brooklyn, Coney Island & Sheepshead Bay, 1996, Brooklyn in the 1920s, 1998; contbg. editor Bklyn. Mag., 1978-79. Past mem. Cmty. Planning Bd. 11, Bklyn.; past pres. Gravesend Dem. Club; commr. deeds City N.Y.; apptd. U.S. del. GRUPPO SAVOIA. Named Hon. Mayor, Gravesend, Eng., 1977; recipient Calabrian of Yr. award Brutium Cultural Club, 1979; knighted, named to Order of Merit of Savoy, His Royal Highness Prince Victor Emmanuel IV of Savoy, 1999. Mem. Assn. Tchrs. Social Studies, Columbia Tchrs. Assn., Gravesend Hist. Soc. (pres.), Circolo Culturale Club, Univ. S. Fla. Club, Order Sons of Italy. Democrat. Roman Catholic. Home: PO Box 5 Upper Black Eddy PA 18972-0005 Office: IS 228 228 Avenue S Brooklyn NY 11223-2746

IEREMIA, MIRCEA CONSTANTIN, engineering educator; b. Ploiesti, Romania, June 25, 1939; s. Ioan and Valeria Lelia (Georgescu) I.; m. Georgeta Ecaterina Marinescu, July 16, 1964 (dec. Dec. 1986); children: Ieremia Diana Anca, Ieremia Andrei Ion. PhD, Civil Engring. U., Bucharest, Romania, 1971. Prof. Civil Engring. U., Bucharest, Romania, 1963—; engr. Constrn. Enterprise, Bucharest, Romania, 1961-63, Indsl. Project Inst., Bucharest, Romania, 1963-72, Bldg. Project Inst., Bucharest, Romania, 1986-88, Tech. Computer Applications, Brussels, Belgium, 1992-95; dir. Design Mgmt. Rsch. Bldgs. Co., Bucharest, 1992—; chmn. Internat. confs. on Finite Elements, Romania, 1991-93; cons. in field. Author: Theoretical and Applied Mechanics, 1975, Theory and Calculus of Orthotropic Plates, 1983 (Romanian Acad. award 1983), Theory of Elasticity and Plates in Constructions Design, 1986, Strength of Materials, 1987, Elasticity, Plasticity, Nonlinearity, 1998, European/World Conference on Earthquake Engineering, 1990—; chief editor Computing Jour. Mem. U. Alliance from Romania, Bucharest, 1990. Capt. Artillery Res. Mem. Internat. Assn. Bridge and Structural Engring., Earthquake Engring. Rsch. Inst., Assn. Francaise Genie Parasismique, Soc. Computer Aided Engring. Bucharest (pres.), N.Y. Acad. Scis. Avocations: symphony music, software creation, swimming, travel, political books. E-mail: mieremia@hidro.utcb.ro. Home: 2-4 Fainari Str, Bl 51 Sc C Ap 100, 72161 Bucharest Romania Office: Tech U Civil Engring, 122-124 Lacul Tei Blvd, 72302 Bucharest Romania

IERMOLI, ROBERTO HECTOR, physician, educator; b. Mendoza, Argentina, Nov. 14, 1950; s. José Jorge and Blanca Angela (Gordillo) I.; Karen Elisabeth Mikkelsen, Dec. 19, 1980; children: Nicolás Gabriel, Cecilia Inés, Lucía Florencia, Laura Valeria. MD with honors, U. Nacional Cuyo, Mendoza, Argentina, 1974; postgrad., Washington U., St. Louis, 1981-86. Intern U. Nacional Cuyo, 1975-76; resident U. Buenos Aires, 1977-80, head of residence, 1980-81, specialist in internal medicine, 1982, asst. prof., 1987; head of residence Policlin. Bancarios, Buenos Aires, 1981-82, instr. of residence, 1982-84; chief svcs. Clin. Modelo Morón, Buenos Aires, 1985-90, vice dir. residence, 1985—; area chief physician Hosp. Clínicas U. Buenos Aires, Buenos Aires, 1987—, prof. internal medicine, 1995—; cons. Editorial Med. Panamericana, Buenos Aires, 1979-86, med. dir., 1986—; jr. tchr. Hospital Clínicas, 1981-84, sr. tchr., 1984-87, asst. prof., 1987-95, prof. medicine, 1995; cons. Orgn. Panamericana de Salud, Buenos Aires, 1987—; dir. residence Hosp. Español, Buenos Aires, 1991-93. Author: El Especialista en Medicina Interna, 1992, Farmacología, 1993. Mem. AAAS, Am. Soc. Hypertension, N.Y. Acad. Scis. Roman Catholic. Avocations: outdoor activities, camping. Home: Soler 6076 4 C, 1425 Buenos Aires Argentina Office: Med Office, Thames 2237 PB A, 1425 Buenos Aires Argentina

IERY, MICHAELA RAE, public relations specialist; b. Madrid, Dec. 15, 1971; d. David Douglas and Gillian Mary I.; m. Joseph Anthony Allred (div. Nov. 1995). BA in Journalism, Kent State U., 1993; postgrad., U. Phoenix. Journalist The News Jour., Mansfield, Ohio, 1993-95; comm. rels. dir. Richland Newhope Ctr., Mansfield, 1995-98; pub. info. officer Ohio Dept. Mental Retardation & Devel. Disabilities, Columbus, 1998—; mem. Ohio Pub. Images com., 1999; former co-chair comms. com. Richland County Vision Com., Mansfield. Author article series "The Berger Sons," 1995 (award AP 1995). Vol. Spl. Olympics, Mansfield, 1997-98, Cat Welfare Assn., Columbus, 1999. Avocations: website design, creative writing, knitting. Office: Ohio Dept MR/DD 1810 Sullivant Ave Columbus OH 43222-1055

IESAN, DORIN, mathematics educator; b. Radauti, Suceava, Romania, Apr. 8; s. Ioan and Despina Meletia (Curelaru) I.; m. Elena Plesea, July 20, 1964; 1 child, Ciprian-Sextil. M in Math., U. Al. I. Cuza, Iasi, Romania, 1963, PhD, 1968. Asst. prof. U. Al. I. Cuza, Iasi, 1963-68, lectr., 1968-75, assoc. prof., 1975-81, prof. math., 1981—. Author: Theory of Thermoelasticity, 1979, Saint-Venant's Problem, 1987, Prestressed Bodies, 1989, Thermoelastic Deformations, 1996. Recipient prize Ministry of Edn., 1967, Simion Stoilow award Acad. of Romania, 1974; fellow Nat. Rsch. Coun. of Italy, Rome, 1972. Mem. Am. Math. Soc., Gesellschaft fur Angewandte Math. und Mechanik. Home: str Macazului 11C Apt 1, 6600 Iasi Romania Office: U Al I Cuza Faculty Math, Bd Copou Nr 11, 6600 Iasi Romania

IFANTIS, EVANGELOS K., mathematics educator; b. Palamas, Karditsa, Greece, Nov. 1, 1934; s. Konstantinos A. and Hariclia E. (Buri) I.; m. Eleni Simos Malamateniou, Oct. 8, 1970; children: Hariclia, Konstantina. Ptychion, U. Athens, Greece, 1959, PhD, 1969. Cert. mathematician. Rschr. Nuclear Rsch. Centre, Democritos, Athens, 1964-74; prof. dept. math. U. Patras, Greece, 1974—. Author: Measure Theory, 1990, Operator Theory, 1992. Officer Mil. Air Forces, 1960-62. Christian Orthodox. Office: U Patras, Dept Math, Patras Greece

IFENNE, DENNIS ISAAC, medical educator; b. Igwu-Orokam, Benue, Nigeria, Sept. 15, 1956; s. Ifenne Ochani Abaikwe and Onyukwo Helen Onoja; m. Beatrice Ada Ameh, Oct. 1, 1994; 1 child, Deborah Fatu. MBBS, Ahmadu Bello U., Zaria, Nigeria, 1980. Pre-registration housemanship Murtala Mohammed Splst. Hosp., Kano, Nigeria, 1980-81; med. officer Nat. Youth Svc. Corps., Akure, Nigeria, 1981-82; sr. house officer Ahmadu Bello U. Tchg. Hosp., Zaria, Nigeria, 1982-83; mem. hosp. mgmt. com., 1985-90, 96-98; registrar Ahmadu Bello U. Tchg. Hosp., Zaria, 1983-89, sr. registrar, 1989-91; lectr., cons. Ahmadu Bello U. and Ahmadu Bello U. Tchg. Hosp., Zaria, 1992-97, sr. lectr., cons., 1997—; mem. Nat. Tech. Com. Maternal and Child Heath, 1992—; team leader, project dir. Prevention Maternal Mortality, 1992-96; external examiner ob-gyn. three med. schs. in Nigeria, 1997—; mem. visitation team for accreditation of tng. instns. West African Coll. Surgeons in Ob-Gyn., 1997—. Mem. Campaign Against Unwanted Pregnancy, Nigeria, 1986—, Post Abortion Network Nigeria, 1997—. Fellow West African Postgrad. Med. Coll., Internat. Coll. Surgeons; mem. Nigeria Med. Assn. (chmn. nat. com. on family health and population activities 1993—, mem. nat. exec. coun. 1992—), Soc. Ob-Gyn. Nigeria (mem. scientific rsch. com. 1996—), Nigerian Cancer Soc. Roman Catholic. Avocations: travel, reading, table tennis, dancing, swimming. Office: Ahmadu Bello Tchg Hosp, PMB 1026, Zaria Kaduna, Nigeria

IFFY, LESLIE, medical educator; b. Budapest, Hungary, May 17, 1925; came to U.S., 1969; s. Zoltan and Rozsa (Lantos) I.; m. Maureen B. Deeney. MD, U. Budapest, Hungary, 1949; MD (hon.), Semmelweis U., Budapest, 1993. Diplomate Am. Bd. Ob-Gyn. Resident, fellow Országos Testnevelési és Sportegészségügyi Intézet Hosp. Ministry of Health, Budapest, 1951-56; fellow U. Wash., Seattle, 1964; asst. prof. Temple U., Phila., 1969-70; assoc. prof. U. Ill., Chgo., 1971-72, Jefferson Med. Coll., Phila., 1972-73; prof. U. Medicine and Dentistry of N.J., Newark, 1974—; dir. obstetrics U. Hosp., Newark, 1974—. Contbr. over 170 articles to profl. jours. and chpts. to books; editor: Perinatology Case Studies, 1978, 85, Obstetrics and Perinatology, 1981 (in English and Spanish), Operative Perinatology, 1984 (in English, Spanish and Japanese), Operative Obstetrics, 2d edit., 1992. Recipient Dr. Robert Jardine Rsch. prize U. Glasgow, 1963, Ford Found. rsch. fellowship, Seattle, 1964, hon. fellowship Hungarian Obstet. Soc., 1986. Fellow Royal Coll. Surgeons (Can.); mem. Cen. Assn. Ob-Gyn. (life), Chgo. Gynecol. Soc., Am. Coll. Legal Medicine (bd. dirs. 1989-95), Royal Coll. Physicians (Edinburgh, Scotland, licentiate), Royal Faculty Physicians and Surgeons (Glasgow, Scotland, licentiate), Romanian Soc. Obstetricians and Gynecololists (hon.). Avocations: music, chess, literature. Home: 5 Robin Hood Rd Summit NJ 07901-3718 Office: NJ Med Sch UMDNJ 150 Bergen St Newark NJ 07103-2406

IFRIM, MIRCEA GHEORGHE, anatomist, general physician, scientist, educator; b. Calata, Cluj, Romania, May 4, 1943; s. Gheorghe Vasile and Veturia Horatiu (Crucin); m. Feng Chen, June 27, 1997. MB, Med. U., Bucharest, Romania, 1963; MD, Med. U., Cluj, Romania, 1971; postgrad. studies Edn. Mgmt., U. Oradea, Romania, 1989, D Honoris Causa, 1998. Diplomate, Med. Examiners, Romania. Asst. prof. Med. U., Cluj., Romania, 1967-70; lectr. Med. U., Cluj., 1970-78; vis. prof. Med. U., Bucharest, Romania, 1978-90; prof. Med. U., Bucharest, 1991—; dean, founder of faculty Med. Faculty, Oradea, Romania, 1991—; dir. Med. Rsch. Inst., Oradea, 1991—; chmn. Br. Acad. Scis., Oradea, 1996—; vice rector V. Goldis U., Arad, Romania, 1997—; bd. dirs. Internat. Orgn. for Assessment of Quality in Higher Edn., 1991—; gen. sec., chair UNESCO, Bucharest, Romania, 1994-97; v.p. Internat. Conf. for Edn., Geneva, Switzerland, 1996—. Author: Physical Education and Sports Anatomy and Biomechanics, 1980, Malformative Risk in Human Reproduction, 1983, Human Body Anatomy Atlas, 3 vols., 1985 (Victor Babes award), Anthropology, 1987, Connective Tissue Morphology and Pathology, 1988 and 11 other monographs; contbr. over 108 articles to profl. jours. and 111 essays included in the summary books of different specialty nat. and internat. congresses. First counselor, Ministry of Edn., Romania, 1990-92; counselor for edn. Romanian Govt., 1992-93; gen. sec. UNESCO-CNR, 1994-97. Decorated with Sci. Merit award, Romanian Govt., Bucharest, 1989; recipient award Romanian Acad. Scis., Bucharest, 1988, Diploma with hons. for sportive anthropology research, Internat. Orgn. of Sports Medicine, 1989, Hon. Diploma for Human Rights Defense Europ Coun. ECOFOR. Mem. Internat. Soc. German Lang. Speaking Anatomists (Lübeck, Germany, hon.), Internat. Fedn. Anthropology and Genetics in Sports (v.p. Warsaw 1986), Nat. Soc. Normal and Pathological Morphology (v.p. Bucharest, 1994), Nat. Union of Scientists (v.p. Bucharest), Acad. Scis. and Culture (Sao-Paulo, Brazil, hon. comdr. 1996). Avocations: Far East lit., Buddhism, parapsychology, occultism, flowers. Home: 20 Radu Robescu, OPHR-39 Bucharest 2, Romania Office: U Oradea Med Faculty Dean, # 10 1 Decembrie St, 3400 Oradea Bihor, Romania

IFTAR, ALTUG, electrical engineering educator, researcher; b. Istanbul, Turkey, June 28, 1960; s. Ismail and Beyhan (Bulbul) I.; m. Gonul Selver Kircaali, Dec. 23, 1988; 1 child, Dora. BS, Bogazici U., Istanbul, 1982; MS, Ohio State U., 1984, PhD, 1988. Tchg. asst. Bogazici U., 1980-82; tchg. and rsch. assoc. Ohio State U., Columbus, 1983-88; rsch. assoc. U. Toronto, 1988-92; assoc. prof. elec. engrng. Anadolu U., Eskisehir, Turkey, 1992-97, prof., 1997—, chair dept. elec. engring., 1993—; Contbr. chpts. to books, articles to Automatica, IEEE Trans. on Automatic Control, Internat. Jour. Control. Engring. scis. field editor Anadolu U. Jour. Sci. and Tech., 1999—. Recipient Young Investigator award Sci. and Tech. Rsch. Coun. Turkey, 1993. Mem. IEEE (bd. govs. Turkey sect. 1996-99, chair Control Sys. Soc. chpt. 1999—). E-mail: aiftar@anadolu.edu.tr. Office: Anadolu U, Dept Elec Engring, 26470 Eskisehir Turkey

IFTODE, LIVIU, computer science educator; b. Sibiu, Romania, Apr. 13, 1959; s. Vasile and Lucretia Iftode; m. Cristina Iftode. BS, Poly. Inst., Bucharest, Romania, 1984; MA, Princeton U., 1993, PhD, 1998. Asst. prof. Rutgers U., Piscataway, N.J., 1997. Office: Rutgers U Dept Computer Sci Piscataway NJ 08854

IFVARSSON, CARL-ANDERS, Swedish government official; b. Stockholm, Sweden, Nov. 7, 1939; s. Folke and Ebba (Bergman) I.; m. Katarina Adolfsson (div. 1988); children: Caroline, Carl. LLM, Stockholm U., 1966. Sec. Liberal Group in Swedish Parliament, 1964-67; asst. to commr. of pers. City of Stockholm, 1967-70; city commr. City of Lidingö, Sweden, 1971-78; undersec. of state Ministry Health and Social Affairs, Sweden, 1978-82, 91-94; dep. dir. gen. Nat. Bd. Health and Welfare, Sweden, 1982-91; dir. gen. Swedish Patent and Registration Office, 1995—; chmn. Swedish Coun. on Social Rsch., 1978-79, Commn. on Family Economy, 1979-83, Commn. on Social Legislation, 1991-95; rep. for Sweden, Adminstrv. Coun. of European Patent Office; mem. adminstrv. bd. Office for Harmonisation in the Internal Market, European Union, 1995—, chmn., 2000; head Swedish del. Governing Bodies of World Internat. Property Orgn., 1995—. City councilor City of Lidingö, 1967-82; chmn. exec. com. Liberal Party, Stockholm, 1976-82. Avocations: literature, modern art, golf, sailing. Home: Talltunet 8, S-18148 Lidingö Stockholm Sweden Office: Swedish Patent/Regis Office, Valhallavagen 136, S-10242 Stockholm Sweden

IGAMBERDIEV, ABIR UBAEVICH, plant physiologist; b. Alma-Ata, Kazakhstan, July 4, 1959; s. Ubai Igamberdiev and Marina Fedorovna Dashkova; m. Natalia Vyacheslavovna Bykova, Sept. 11, 1992; 1 child, Timur. BSc in Biology, Voronezh (USSR) U., 1979, MS in Biology, 1981, Candidate Scis. in Biology, 1985; DSc in Biology, Russian Acad. Scis., Moscow, 1992. Asst. prof. Voronezh U., 1981-92, assoc. prof., 1992-93, head dept. plant physiology and biochemistry, 1993—; vis. rsch. prof. dept. botany U. Wyo., Laramie, 1997-98; vis. rsch. prof. dept. plant physiology U. Umea, Sweden, 1998—. Contbr. articles to profl. jours. Recipient stipent Pres. Russian Fedn., Russian Acad. Scis., Moscow, 1995, 97; named Soros prof. Internat. Sci. Found., N.Y., 1995, 96, 98; grantee Volkswagen Found., Germany, 1995, Russian Fund for Basic Rsch., Moscow, 1995-98. Mem. Russian Soc. Plant Physiologists (corr., mem. presidium). Avocations: philosophy, classical music, art. E-mail: abir.igamberdiev@plantphys.umu.se. Fax: 46 90 786 66 76. Home: Stipendiegrand 4B-205, S-901 87 Umea Sweden Office: Dept Plant Physiology, Univ Umea, S-901 87 Umeå Sweden

IGARASHI, KAZUEI, biochemist; b. Shirone, Niigata, Japan, July 7, 1941; s. Kyushirou and Fuyo (Ichikawa) I.; m. Kiyoko Kadota, May 29, 1969; children: Kazutsugu, Keiko. B in Pharm. Scis., Chiba U., 1963, M in Pharm. Scis., 1965; D in Pharm. Sci., U. Tokyo, 1970. Rsch. assoc. Chiba U., 1970-74, asst. prof., 1975-79, assoc. prof., 1980-83, prof., 1984—, dean, 1999—; cons. Environtl. Conservation, Kisarazu, Japan, 1996—. Editl. bd. Internat. Jou. of Biochemistry and Cell Biology, 1997—, Yakugaku Zasshi, 1997—; author: Physiological Functions of Polyamines (in Japanese), 1993. Mem. Am. Soc. for Biochemistry and Molecular Biology, The Japanese Biochem. Soc., Pharm. Soc. of Japan (Abbott prize 1979), Japanese Cancer Assn. Avocations: reading, traveling. Home: 3-3-2 Higashichiba, Chuou-ku, Chiba 260-0041, Japan Office: Pharm Scis Chiba Univ, 1-33 Yayoi-cho Inage-ku, Chiba 263-8522, Japan

IGARASHI, MASARU, art museum curator, consultant; b. Tokyo, May 6, 1961; parents Shigeru and Chiyoko (Tada) I.; m. Kyoko Maruyama. BA, Seijo U., 1984; PhD, CUNY, 1996. Curator Sezon Mus. Art, Tokyo, 1984-91; lectr. Met. Mus. Art, 1995-97; dir. Itochu Gallery, Tokyo, 1996-98; chief curator Aoki Internat. Collection, Tokyo, 1997—, Yasuda Kasai Mus. Art, Tokyo, 1999—. Grantee Asian Cultural Coun., U.S., 1991, KAO Cultural Found., 1991, Smithsonian rsch. grantee, 1992. Home: 1-19-6 Kameido #608 Koto-ku, Tokyo 136-0071, Japan Office: Yasuda Kasai Mus Art, 1-26-1 Nishi-Shinjuku, Shinjuku-ku Tokyo 160-8338, Japan

IGARASHI, TAKASHI, chemist; b. Aizubange, Fukushima, Japan, Dec. 20, 1950; s. Susumu and Toshiko (Narita) I.; m. Shizue Ono, Oct. 1, 1974; children: Riki, Yuki. BS, Waseda U., Japan, 1974, PhD, 1982. Fellow Advanced Rsch. Inst. for Sci. and Engring. Waseda U., Japan, 1982; rsch. fellow The Inst. of Phys. and Chem. Rsch., Japan, 1983-84; rschr. Mitsui Toatsu Chems. Inc., Japan, 1984-96; asst. mgr. The Assn. for the Progress of New Chemistry, Japan, 1996-98; gen. mgr. for tech. Japan Chem. Innovation Inst., Japan, 1998—. Mem. Am. Chem. Soc.

IGARASHI, YASUO (DAVID), language educator; b. Tokyo, Dec. 27, 1933; s. Yumatsu and Yoshino (Takagi) I.; m. Masano (Martha) Hoshikawa, May 14, 1963; children: Tatsuyuki, Eiji. BA, Tokyo U. Edn., 1956, MA, 1959; postgrad., U. Tex., 1972-73, U. Mich., 1973. Lectr. Iwate (Japan) U., 1960-64; from lectr. to assoc. prof. Chuo U., Tokyo, 1964-68; assoc. prof. Seijo U., Tokyo, 1968-76, prof. English, 1976—, chair dept. English, 1993-95, chair internat. exch. com., 1995-96, 99—; chmn. com. 12th World Congress Applied Linguistics, Sci. Coun. Japan, 1998-2000; spl. mem. Nat. Accreditation Com. for Univs. Min. Edn., Japan, 1999—; vis. scholar linguistics London U., 1981-91, Leeds (Eng.) U., 1991-92; vis. scholar U. B.C., Can., 1996; vis. rschr. Monash U., Australia, 1996-97. Author: Phonological Contrasts Between English and Japanese, 1999, For the Better English Pronunciation, 2000; co-author: The Science of Language, 1994, The Modern Dictionary of Linguistics, 1988; co-editor The Teaching of English in Japan, 1978 (JACET prize 1979). Exch. rsch. grantee Japan Found. for Promotion of Sci., 1972. Mem. Japan Assn. Coll. Tchrs. English (bd. dirs. 1982—). Home: 2572 Onoji, Machida Tokyo 195-0064, Japan Office: Seijo U, 6-1-20 Seijo, Seijo Tokyo 157, Japan

IGBINEWEKA, ANDREW OSABUOHIEN, public administration, political science educator; b. Benin City, Edo State, Nigeria, Nov. 30, 1947; came to U.S., 1973, naturalized; s. Igbineweka Moses Iditua and Victoria Ilekhue (Idahor) Igbineweka; m. Pauline Omono Airen, June 24, 1980; children: Ofumwegbe, Oyemwen, Osagie, Osasu, Osaruyi. BA, U. Mary Hardin-Baylor, 1976; MA, U. North Tex., 1979, PhD, 1982. Libr. Immaculate Conception Coll., Benin City, 1968-69; clerical officer High Ct. of Justice Jud. Dept., Benin City, 1969-73; tchg. asst. U. North Tex., Denton, 1976-79; lectr. II, asst. prof. U. Benin, Benin City, 1983-85, lectr. I, 1985-89, sr. lectr., 1989-92, head dept., 1990-91; Disting. vis. prof. U. Calgary, Alta., Can., 1992; vis. prof. Indiana U. Pa., 1992-94; ind. rsch. cons. Pitts., 1994—; mem., cons. U. Benin Consulting Svcs., 1984-92; therapist Suzanne and Assocs. and Western Bell, Pitts., 1997—; casemanager Shuman Juvenile Detention Ctr., Pitts., 1998—; therapeutic staff support, therapist Sharp Visions Inc., Pitts., 1999—, therapeutic staff support and mobile therapist, Pressly Ridge Schs, Pitts., 1999—. Contbr. chpts. to books and articles to profl. jours. Chmn. Getty's Dormitory, U. Mary Hardin-Baylor, Belton, Tex., 1974-75, v.p. Internat. Club, 1974-75, chmn. Bapt. Students Union Internat., 1974-76, pres., founder chess club, 1975-76; chmn. constn. revision com. Nigerian Students Assn., U. North Tex., 1977, pres., 1981-82; senate mem. U. Benin, 1990-91; chmn. Aduwa Club constn. revision com., Benin City, 1992; vol. Lay Reader's Assn., St. Albert's Cath. Ch., U. Benin, 1984-92, Parish Laity Coun., 1984-92, Group Svcs. to Aged Patients of Beacon Manor, Inc., spring 1994; active St. Paul Cathedral, 1999—. Recipient Internat. Student Scholarship award Southwestern U., Georgetown, Tex.,

1973-74, U. Mary Hardin-Baylor, Belton, 1974-76, 75-76, Hon. Scholarship award, 1975-76; grantee U. Benin, Benin City, 1984-85, 87-88, Indiana U. Pa., 1992-93, 93-94. Mem. ASPA, Am. Polit. Sci. Assn., Policy Studies Orgn., Internat. Polit. Sci. Assn. (rsch. com.), Nigerian Inst. Mgmt. Cons. (pub. rels. officer 1986-97), U.S. Chess Fedn. (U. Pitts. chess club chpt.), Pitts. Chess Club, Pi Sigma Alpha, Phi Alpha Theta. Avocations: chess, billiards, soccer coaching, religious activities, cruising the Internet.

IGIMI, SHIZUNOBU, microbiologist; b. Iida, Japan, June 25, 1957; s. Mikio and Noriko (Yazawa) I.; m. Yachiyo Nagatoro, Jan. 1988; children: Shinji, Saki, Yayoi. BS, Tokyo U., 1984, MS, 1986, PhD, 1989. Rschr. Nat. Inst. Infectious Diseases, Tokyo, 1989-96, sr. rschr., 1996—. Office: Nat Inst Infectious Disease, 1-23-1 Toyama Shinjuku-ku, 162-8640 Tokyo Japan

IGLAUER, EDITH, writer, reporter; b. Cleve., Mar. 10, 1917; arrived in Can., 1976; d. Jay and Bertha G. (Good) I.; m. John Heywood Daly, Mar. 1, 1976 (dec. Feb. 1978); m. Philip Hamburger, Dec. 24, 1942; children: Jay Philip Hamburger, Richard Shaw Hamburger. BA, Wellesley Coll., 1938; MS, Columbia U., 1939. Freelance writer, 1939—. Author: The New People, The Eskimo's Journey Into Our Time, 1966 (Outdoor Sci. Club award), Denison's Ice Road, 1975, 3d edit., 1992, Inuit Journey, 1979, revised edit., 2000, Seven Stones: A Portrait of Arthur Erickson, Architect, 1981, Fishing with John, 1988 (Shortlisted Gov. Gens. award), The Strangers Next Door, 1991; contbr. articles to newspapers and popular mags. Active Harbour Commn., Pender Harbour, B.C., 1993-95; bd. dirs. Grips, Sechelt Peninsula, 1996-98, Francis Point Marine Park Soc., 1998—. Geneva scholar Sch. Internat. Studies, 1937; recipient Woodrow Wilson Prize in modern politics Wellesley Coll., 1938, Cleve. Creative Achievement in Lit., Womens City Club, 1983, Short-Listed, Gov. Gen's award for Non-Fiction, Can., 1988. Mem. Authors Guild, Writers Union Can., Cosmopolitan Club, N.Y., Cleve. Play House Club. Democrat. Avocations: swimming, travel, cooking, grandchildren. Fax: 604-883-9322. E-mail: edaly@uniserve.com. Home: PO Box 116, Garden Bay, BC Canada Office: The New Yorker Mag 4 Times Sq New York NY 10036-6561

IGLEHART, PATRICIA ANN, strategy and market planning executive; b. Waco, Tex., Jan. 2, 1944; d. Stephen Austin and Susie Odell (White) I.; m. Lance Dunn Shaw, June 11, 1965 (div. Dec. 1970). Student, Tex. A&M U., 1962-65; BS, N.Mex. State U., 1966; M in Natural Scis., Ariz. State U., 1971; MS in Applied Math. & Statistics, SUNY, Stony Brook, 1975; MS in Math., NYU, 1978; PhD in Math., Stevens Inst. Tech., 1996. Math. tchr. Gadsden H.S., Anthony, N.Mex., 1966-67, Glendale (Ariz.) Union H.S. Dist., 1968-69; math. dept. chmn. Phoenix H.S. Dist., 1969-73; sys. engr. IBM U.S. Eastern Area, Springfield, N.J., 1977-79, Piscataway, N.J., 1979-84; product adminstr. IBM ISG U.S., White Plains, N.Y., 1984-86; sys. engring. mgr. IBM NA Eastern Area, Harrison, N.Y., 1986-89; sr. program mgr. market rsch. studies and IT opportunity analysis IBM NA S&D Market Analyses, White Plains, N.Y., 1989-98; e-bus. market intelligence Internet divsn. IBM Somers, N.Y., 1998-99; IBM/Lotus knowledge mgmt. project office IBM Software Group, Somers, N.Y., 1999-2000; mem. IBM NA Sr. Fin. Mgmt. Group, 1998; CEO, owner Dry-Glo Mktg., Carmel, N.Y., 1987-90. Bd. dirs. Carmel Civic Assn.; bd. mgrs. Woodland Trail; mem. Mission Ch. Assembly of God, Holmes, N.Y. Mem. Am. Math. Soc., Math. Assn. Am., Phi Kappa Phi. Democrat. Avocation: playing piano. Home: S-75 Woodland Tr Carmel NY 10512

IGLESIAS, ENRIQUE V., bank executive, former government minister; b. Asturias, Spain, July 26, 1930; s. Isabel Garcia de Iglesias. D in Econs. and Adminstrn., U. de Montevideo, 1953. Mng. dir. Union de Bancos del Uruguay, 1954-62; tech. dir. Nat. Office of Planning, Uruguay, 1962-66; pres. Cen. Bank, Uruguay, 1966-68; minister fgn. affairs Uruguay, 1985-88; pres. Inter-Am. Devel. Bank, Washington, 1988—; exec. sec., 1972, UN asst. sec. gen., under sec. gen.; rep. Inter-Am. Com. on the Alliance for Progress, 1972-85; sec. gen. UN conf on New and Renewable Sources of Enrgy, Nairobi, Kenya, 1981; chmn. UN Inter-Agy. Group on the Devel. of Renewable Sources of Energy; sec. gen, spl. advisor to UN Dir. Gen. for Devel. and Internat. Econ. Coop., 1982; chmn. Gen. Agreement on Tariffs and Trade, 1986; prof. Univ. Rep., chmn. econ. devel., dir. Inst. Econs., 1952-67; mem. Bd. Latin Am. Social Scis. Coun.; bd. trustees Inst. for Iber-Am. Coop., Spain. Contbr. articles to profl. jours. Recipient Prince of Asturias award, 1982. Office: IDB 1300 New York Ave NW Washington DC 20577-0001*

IGLESIAS, FRANCISCO JAVIER, biology educator; b. Santiago de Compostela, Galicia, Spain, Aug. 11, 1966; s. Jose Manuel Iglesias and Maria Mercedes Pineiro; m. Adelina Casal; children: Africa, Xavier. B Biology, Faculty of Biology, Santiago, 1989, D Biology, 1995. Assoc. prof. U. Santiago, 1997—. Author: (book) Sndil Forming Techniques, 1997; inventor in field. Grantee Galician Govt., Santiago, 1993-95, U. Santiago, 1996. Mem. Galician Assn. Snail Farmers.

IGLSEDER, HEINRICH RUDOLF, space engineer, researcher; b. Salzburg, Austria, May 15, 1957; arrived in Germany, 1977; s. Heinrich and Berta (Wiltschko) I.; m. Christina Scholle, Oct. 20, 1989; children: Christian-Andreas, Lisa-Maria. Engr. diploma, Tech. U., Munich, 1983, D of Engring., 1986; D of Tech., Tech. U., Vienna, 1987. Cert. space technology engr. Sci. asst. Ctr. Space Tech. and Microgravity Zarm, Bremen, Germany, 1987-90; project mgr., head space tech. div. Zarm, Bremen, 1990-92, head predevel. divsn. space tech. and advanced projects, 1992-95; project scientist Chair for Astronautics and Space, Munich, 1987—; cons. Space Tech. and Micro Systems, Sittensen, Germany, 1993-95; assoc. prof. Inst. Space and Astronautical Sci., Sagamihara, Kanagawa, Japan, 1995-96, head predevel. divsn. Vorwerk Elektrowerke, Wuppertal, Germany, 1996-98; dir. of product devel. and engring. Wilkhahn, 1999—. Contbr. articles to profl. jours. Roman Catholic. Home: IM Fasanenkamp 10, D-31552 Rodenberg Germany

IGNARRO, LOUIS J., pharmacology educator; b. Bklyn., May 31, 1941. BA in Pharmacy, Columbia U., 1962; PhD in Pharmacology, U. Minn., 1966. Prof. dept. molecular and med. pharmacology UCLA Sch. Medicine. Contbr. articles to profl. jours. Postdoctoral fellow NIH, 1966-68; recipient Rsch. Career Devel. award USPHS, 1975-80, Nobel prize in Medicine, 1998. Mem. NAS, Alpha Omega Alpha (hon.). Achievements include research in the biochemical, physiological, and pathophysioilogical roles of nitric oxide and cyclic GMP in mammalian cell function; the transcriptional, translational and catalytic regulation of constitutive and inducible nitric oxide synthases; the role of other biochemical pathways in the regulation of biosynthesis and metabolism of nitric oxide; the biochemical and chemical mechanisms by which nitric oxide elicits cytotoxic effects on invading target cells and microorganisms; the role of nitric oxide as a neurotransmitter in non-adrenergic non-cholinergic neurons innervating various issues. Office: UCLA Sch Medicine Dept Molecular & Med Pharmacology 23-315 Chs 10833 Leconte Ave Los Angeles CA 90095-0001*

IGNAT, ADORIAN NICOLAE, information and telecommunications professional; b. Timisoara, Romania, Jan. 12, 1959; came to U.S., 1990; s. Gheorghe and Maria (Sima) I.; m. Ana Mihes, Aug. 21, 1982; 1 child, Andrei Dumitru. BSME, Poly. Inst., Timisoara, 1984, MS of Thermal Engines, 1985; MS in Telecom. and Info. Mgmt., Poly. U., 1999. Cert. netware engr. Chief mech. engr. Comtim, Timisoara, 1985-88, work safety and sys. integrating dir., 1988-90; night auditor, sys. adminstr. The Broadway Am., N.Y.C., 1990-91; maintenance/info. sys. supr. The Peninsula, N.Y.C., 1991-92; asst. dir. engring., MIS coord. Hyatt Hotels and Resorts, Hyatt Regency, Greenwich, 1992-94; asst. regional MIS dir. Hyatt Hotels and Resorts, Grand Hyatt N.Y., N.Y.C., 1994-97; sr. MIS cons. Jacoby Med. Ctr. N.Y.C. Health and Hosps. Corp., 1997-98; dir. telecomms., info. sys. integration North Bronx Healthcare Network, 1998-99, dir. info. tech., 1999—; MIS cons. Telecom. Info. Mgmt. Integrated Solutions, N.Y.C., 1996—. Lt. Romanian Army, 1978-80. Mem. ASME, Network and Sys. Profls. Assn. Avocations: swimming, skiing, scuba diving, biking. Home: 3217 Tierney Pl Bronx NY 10465-4023 Office: NYC Health and Hosp Corp North Bronx Healthcare NW 1400 Pelham Pkwy S # Bn4 Bronx NY 10461-1138

IGNATOV, ALEXANDER, plant pathologist, researcher; b. Butovo, Moscow, Russia, Jan. 20, 1965; s. Nikolas Ignatov and Evdokia Kostenetskaia. MSc, diploma in agronomy, Moscow Agrl. Acad., 1987; PhD, Russian Inst. Vegetable Breeding, Moscow, 1993. Asst. technician Russian Inst. Phytopathology, Moscow, 1987-89; sr. rschr. Russian Inst. Vegetable Breeding, Moscow, 1993-98, Ctr. Bioengring., Moscow, 1998—; vis. rschr. Hort. Rsch. Internat., Wellsbourne, U.K., 1994-95; post-doctoral fellow Nat. Rsch. Inst. Vegetable, Ornamental Plants and Tea, Ano, Japan, 1997-98; dep. chmn. com. on bacterial plant diseases Russian Acad. Agrl. Scis., Moscow, 1998—. Contbr. articles to profl. jours. Recipient stipend Pres. for Young Scientists from Russian Fedn., Russian Acad. Scis., Moscow, 1993; scholar Brit. Coun., U.K., 1994; fellow Japanese Sci. and Tech. Agy., 1996. Mem. Russian Soc. Plant Pathologists. E-mail: ignatov@biengi.ac.ru. Fax: 7 095 135 05 71. Office: Ctr Bioengring, Pr 60-letiya Oktyabrya 7/1, 117312 Moscow Russia

IGNATOV, OLEG VLADIMIROVICH, microbiologist; b. Saratov, Russia, Jan. 16, 1962; s. Vladimir Vladimirovich and Valentina Aleksandrovna (Golovashkina) I. PhD, All-Union Anti-Blaque Sci. Rsch. Inst., 1992. Jr. scientist Saratov Trawmatology Inst., 1985-89; scientist Saratov Br. of VNII Genetica, 1989-93; sr. scientist Inst. of Biochem. Physiol. Plants Russian Acad. Scis., 1993—. E-mail: oignatov@ibppm.saratov.su. Home: Socolvaja str 44/62-102, 410030 Saratov Russia Office: Russian Acad Scis, Entuziastov av 13, 410015 Saratov Russia

IGNATOVICH, VLADIMIR KAZIMIROVICH, physicist, researcher; b. Moscow, Aug. 17, 1937; s. Kazimir Frantsevich Ignatovich and Mariya Ivanovna Veskova; m. Galina Mikhailovna Golyakevich, 1960 (div. 1976); 1 child, Aleksandr; m. Svetlana Nikolaevna Kosheleva, May 7, 1976; children: Philipp, Igor. Diploma, Moscow U., 1962; degree in physics, JINR, Dubna, Russia, 1976. Jr. scientist, researcher JINR LTP, Dubna, 1965-68, engr., 1968-74, scientist, 1974-80; sr. scientist FLNP JINR, Dubna, 1980—. Author: The Physics of Ultra Cold Neurtrons, 1990; contbr. articles to profl. jours. Mem. Jt. Inst. for Nuclear Rsch. Avocations: music, poetry, politics, teaching. Office: JINR FLNP, 141980 Dubna Moscow, Russia

IGNOZZI, BRYAN K., management consultant; b. Pitts., Feb. 3, 1971; s. Gus Kenneth and Edith Jan (Andring) I. BS, Allegheny Coll., 1993; MBA, Rollins Coll., 1997. Real estate assoc. J&K Realty, Lower Burrell, Pa., 1991-94; cons. PNC Bank Corp., Pitts., 1994-96; prof. So. Coll., Orlando, 1998—; mgmt. cons. Dreifus Assocs. Ltd., Orlando, 1997-99; sr. cons. KPMG, LLP, Charlotte, N.C., 1998—. Vol. Habitat for Humanity. Mem. Nat. Assn. Campus Card Users, Smart Card Industry Assn., Am. Mktg. Assn. Roman Catholic. Home: 3283 Leechburg Rd Lower Burrell PA 15068-2846 Office: KPMG LLP 2800 Two First Union Ctr Charlotte NC 28282

IGUCHI, HARUO, history educator; b. Manila, The Philippines, Mar. 29, 1964; s. Takeo and Katsuko Iguchi; m. Yoko Okabe. BA in Bus. Econs., Brown U., 1986; MA in History, U. Chgo., 1990, PhD in History, 1995. Asst. prof. Doshisha U., Kyoto, Japan, 1996-99, assoc. prof., 1999—. Contbr. articles to profl. jours. The Edwin O. Reischauer Inst./Harvard U. Postdoctoral fellow, 1995-96; Mellon Found. grantee, 1994-95; U. Chgo. scholar, 1991-94. Mem. Internat. House of Japan, Am. Hist. Assn., Orgn. for Am. Historians, Brown Alumni Club of Japan. Office: Doshisha U Ctr Am Studies, Kamigyo-ku, Kyoto 602-8580, Japan

IGUCHI, KAZUMOTO, theoretical physicist, researcher; b. Kofu, Yamanashi, Japan, Oct. 13, 1957; s. Minoru and Michiko (Tanzawa) I.; m. Kazuko Kondo, Aug. 3, 1991; children: Isaac, George. Grad., Sci. U. Tokyo, 1980; M in Engring., Osaka U., Toyonaka, Japan, 1982; PhD in Physics, U. Utah, Salt Lake City, 1990. Researcher Sumitomo Cement Co. Ltd., Funabashi, Chiba, Japan, 1985, Fujitsu Ltd., Ota-ku, Tokyo, Japan, 1991-93, Inst. Phys. and Chem. Rsch., Wako-shi, Saitama, Japan, 1993-96. Mem. Japan New Party, 1992-93, Heisei Ishin No Kai, 1992-93. Mem. Am. Phys. Soc., The Phys. Soc. Japan, The Planetary Soc.

IGUCHI, YASUO, computer scientist, educator, researcher; b. Fukuoka, Japan, Mar. 6, 1930; s. Sadao Okasaka and Kunie Iguchi; m. Ikuko Nomoto, Mar. 14, 1956; children: Fumio, Tomoko. BS, Tokyo U. Edn., 1953, MS, 1964, DS, 1977. Tchr. Pub. Jr. H.S., Tokyo, 1953-61; asst. Tsukuba (Japan) U., 1978-82, lectr., 1983-86; asst. prof. U. East Asia, Shimonoseki, Japan, 1987, prof., 1988-93; prof. computer sci. Takamatsu (Japan) Jr. Coll., 1994-95, 2000—, Takamatsu U., 1996-2000; dir. libr. Takamatsu Jr. Coll., 1995; dean of students, Takamatsu U., 1996-97, dir. univ. ext. ctr., 1998-2000; internat. refereeing com., Scientific Coun., Krasnoyarsk, Russia, 1992-93. Contbr. articles to profl. jours. Mem. AAAS, N.Y. Acad. Scis., Charles Darwin Assn., Phys. Soc. Japan. Buddhist. Avocations: classical music, reading, gardening. Office: Takamatsu U, 960 Kasuga-cho, Takamatsu 761-0194, Japan

IGWE, SAMUEL AGINA, pharmacologist, lecturer, researcher; b. Port Harcourt, Nigeria, Mar. 18, 1953; s. Isaiah Okike and Esther Ekodu (Princess Okafor) I.; m. Julie Ijeoma Okorie, Nov. 2, 1990; children: Chibuzor, Chimamaka, Chikezie. BSc in Pharmacology, U. Ibadan, Nigeria, 1980; MSc in Pharmacy and Therapeutics, U. Nigeria, Nsukka, 1983; PhD in Biochem. Pharmacology, Nnamdi Azikiwe U., Awka, 1995. Cert. in in vivo/in vitro testing technique for P Falicaparu sensitivity WHO, 1985, cert. in computer proficiency, 1994. With Nat. Youth Svc. Gen. Hosp., Macurdi, Nigeria, 1981-82; rsch. asst. Tchg. Hosp., Enugu, Nigeria, 1983-88; lectr. Imo State U., Okigwe, Nigeria, 1988-94; lectr. Abia State U., Uturu, Nigeria, 1994—, head ocular pharmacology Sch. Optometry, 1988—, head dept. pharmacology, 1994—, dir. malaria control, 1996—; mem. Univ. Senate Abia State U., 1994; external examiner U. Nigeria, U. Port Harcourt, Nnamdi Azikiwe U. Editor: Perspectives in Visual Sciences, 1996; editor Jour. Health/Visual Scis., 1998; contbr. articles to profl. jours. Sec. Ndiuche Youth Movement, Arondizuogu, Nigeria, 1985—; mem. coll. bd. medicine Coll. Medicine Abia State U., 1993—. Mem. African Soc. for Pharmacologists, West African Soc. Pharmacology, N.Y. Acad. Sci. Anglican. Avocations: tennis, badminton, walking, photography. E-mail: jovel@infoweb.abs.net. Office: Abia State U, Coll Medicine and Hlth Scis, PMB 2000 Uturu Nigeria

IHAMUOTILA, KRISTIINA, textile artist; b. Helsinki, Feb. 7, 1939; d. Jussi and Paula Malmivuo; m. Risto Ihamuotila, 1960; children: Jari, Mika, Laura. Student, Pohjanheimo Textile Sch. Freelance textile artist. Textile work included in 50 collections. Recipient Order Comdr. Isabel La Catolica, 1989, Order Comdr. Avec Couronne, Adolphe de Nassau, 1993. Mem. Indsl. Designers' Union. Avocations: jazz dance, farming. Home: Histantie 1A, 02820 Espoo Finland

IHARA, MASATAKA, pharmacy educator; b. Ito City, Japan, Apr. 5, 1942; s. Michihiro and Myrako (suzuki) I.; m. Reiho Kobayashi, Jan. 15, 1967; children: Tomoko, Masayuki, Yumiko. B, Tohoku U., Sendai, Japan, 1965, M, 1967, PhD, 1970. Asst. prof. Tohoku U., Sendai, Japan, 1971-81, assoc. prof., 1981-97, prof., 1997—; vis. assoc. prof. Kyoto U., Japan, 1994. Recipient Miyata award, Nagoya, Japan, 1992; postdoctoral fellow Cambridge U., England, 1971-74. Mem. Pharm. Soc., Am. Chem. Soc., Royal Soc. Chemistry. Avocations: reading, driving, skiing. Home: 3-34-17 Midorigaoka, Sendai 982-0021, Japan Office: Tohoku U, Grad Sch Pharm Scis, Sendai 980-8578, Japan

IHDE, AARON JOHN, history of science educator emeritus; b. Neenah, Wis., Dec. 31, 1909; s. John Lewis and Ella (Haase) I.; m. Olive Jane Tipler, June 14, 1933 (dec. Mar. 28, 1988); children: Gretchen (Mrs. Hendrick Serrie), John. BS, U. Wis., 1931, MS, 1939, PhD, 1941. Chemist Blue Valley Creamery Co., Chgo., 1931-38; instr. chemistry Butler U., Indpls., 1941-42; mem. faculty U. Wis.-Madison, 1942—, prof. chemistry, integrated liberal studies and history of sci., 1958-80, emeritus prof., 1980—, chmn. dept. integrated liberal studies, 1963-70; Carnegie intern in gen. edn. Harvard, 1951-52; Mem. Wis. Food Standards Adv. Com., 1955-68, chmn., 1964-65. Author: The Physical Universe, 1963, Development of Modern Chemistry, 1964, 2d edit., 1984, Selected Readings in the History of Chemistry, 1965, (with others) Joseph Priestley, Scientist, Theologian, and Metaphysician, 1980, Chemistry: As Viewed from Bascom's Hill, 1990. Recipient Dexter award history of chemistry divsn. Am. Chem. Soc., 1968, U. Wis. Chancellors award for disting. teaching, 1978. Mem. AAAS, History of Sci. Soc., Am. Chem. Soc. (Dexter award history of chemistry div. 1968), Soc. History of Tech., Wis. Acad. Scis., Arts and Letters (pres. 1963-64), Sigma Xi, Phi Lambda Upsilon. Unitarian. Home: 636 Mecca Dr Sarasota FL 34234-2713

IHM, SON-KI, chemical engineering educator, researcher; b. Seoul, Aug. 13, 1946; s. Geun-Hyuk and Hee-Won (Chang) I.; m. Haeng-Ja Koo, Dec. 20, 1975; children: Peter Sung-Hoh, Jung-Hyun, Sung-Hwan. BS, Seoul Nat. U., 1969; MS, SUNY, Buffalo, 1975, PhD, 1977, postgrad., 1978. Asst. prof. chem. engring. Korea Advanced Inst. Sci. and Tech., Seoul, 1978-81, assoc. prof., 1981-87, prof., 1987-92; prof. Korea Advanced Inst. Sci. and Tech., Taejon, 1992—, chmn. chem. engring., 1990-91, dir. applied sci. rsch., dean applied engring., 1995-97; vis. prof. Av Humboldt Found., Braunschweig, Germany, 1983-84, Kyoto (Japan) U., 1981; cons. Korean Ministry Labor, 1987-97, Korean Ministry Trade and Industry, 1988-90, Korean Ministry Environ., 1993-97. Editor Korean Jour. Chem. Engring., 1986-88; contbr. articles to sci. jours., including Jour. Chem. Engring. Japan, Jour. Catalysts, Applied Catalaysis, Macromolecules. Decorated Nat. medal (Republic of Korea). Mem. Korean Acad. Sci. and Tech., Nat. Acad. Engring. Korea, Korean Inst. Chem. Engrs. (life, chmn. internat. cooperation 1998, award for best paper of yr. 1986, chmn. catalysis divsn. 2000). Avocations: golf, tennis, Go, walking. Office: Korea Adv Inst Sci and Tech, 373-1 Kusung-dong Yusung-gu, Taejon 305-701, Republic of Korea

IHNKEN, KAI ARNDT, surgeon, researcher; b. Hannover, Germany, Sept. 17, 1962; came to U.S., 1991; s. Gert and Barbara Ihnken; m. Victoria Lynn Ihnken, Sept. 17, 1994; children: Linda, Sarah. MD, Justus Liebig U., Giessen, Germany, 1989. Intern in thoracic and cardiovascular surgery Johann Wolfgang Goethe U., Frankfurt, Germany, 1989-90, resident in surgery, 1990-91; prof. surgery UCLA Sch. Medicine, 1991-93; resident in thoracic and cardiovascular surgery Johann Wolfgang Goethe U., 1994-95; resident in cardiovascular surgery Albert Ludwigs U., Freiburg, Germany, 1995-96; resident in surgery Stanford (Calif.) U. Hosp., 1997—. Contbr. articles to profl. jours. Recipient Young Investigators award Am. Coll. Angiology, 1993, Am. Coll. Angiology, 1995, Ernst Derra prize German Assn. Thoracic and Cardiovascular Surgery, 1997. Mem. Am. Heart Assn. (Young Investigators award 1992), European Soc. Cardiovascular Surgery (Dos Santos award 1994), European Assn. Cardiothoracic Surgery, German Assn. Cardiothoracic and Vascular Surgery, German Heart Assn., German Assn. Cardiology. Home: 35 Creek View Cir Larkspur CA 94939-1488 Office: Stanford Univ Hosp Rm H3680 Dept Surgery 300 Pasteur Dr Stanford CA 94305

II, JACK MORITO, aerospace engineer; b. Tokyo, Mar. 20, 1926; came to U.S., 1954, naturalized, 1966; s. Iwao and Kiku Ii.; children: Keiko, Yoshiko, Mutsuya. BS, Tohoku U., 1949; MS, U. Wash., 1956, PhD in Aero. and Astronautics, 1964; M in Aero. Engring., Cornell U., 1959; PhD in Engring., U. Tokyo, 1980. Reporter Asahi Newspaper Press, Tokyo, 1951-54; aircraft designer Fuji Heavy Industries Ltd. Co., Tokyo, 1956-58; mem. staff structures rsch. Boeing Co., Seattle, 1962—. Contbr. numerous articles on aerodyns. to sci. jours. Mem. AIAA, Japan Shumy and Culture Soc. (pres. 1976-96), Sigma Xi. Congregationalist. Office: The Boeing Co MS 67-HC Seattle WA 98124

IIDA, ITSUO, precious metal catalyst company executive; b. Tanashi, Tokyo, Japan, July 4, 1947; s. Sajiro and Yasuko (Suzuki) I.; m. Kayoko Nagato; children: Naoto, Mikako, Chiyoko. BS, U. Tokyo, 1971, MS, 1973, PhD in Chemistry, 1978. Rsch. chemist Sagami Chem. Rsch. Ctr., Sagamihara, Kanagawa, Japan, 1973-79, Nippon Engelhard, Ichikawa, Chiba, Japan, 1979-97; prodn. mgr. N.E. Chemcat, Numazu, Shizuoka, Japan, 1997-99; dir., gen. mgr. N.E. Chemcat, Ichikawa, 1999—. Editor: Chemistry and Application of Precious Metals, 1984, Story of Catalysis, 1997. Recipient meritorious award Catalyst Mfrs. Assn. Japan, 1999. Avocation: shogi (Japanese chess). Office: NE Chemcat, 3-19-3 Nakakokubun, Chiba Ichikawa 272-0835, Japan

IIDA, KEIJI, cardiologist, educator; b. Tokyo, Sept. 11, 1952; s. Yoshio and Motoko (Takeyasu) I.; m. Yuko Kawatani; children: Rihito, Sunato, Korehito. MD, Nippon Med. Sch., 1978; PhD, U. Tsukuba, 1984. Asst. prof. U. Tsukuba, Japan, 1984—; rsch. fellow Harvard Med. Sch., Boston, 1989-91. Contbr. articles to profl. jours. Mem. Japanese Circulation Soc. Avocation: tennis. Home: 1-39-10 Daita, Setagaya Tokyo 155, Japan Office: Univ Tsukuba Inst Clin Med, 1-1-1 Tennodai, Tsukuba Ibaraki 305, Japan

IIDA, NORIHIKO, psychiatrist, educator; b. Ogaki, Japan, Feb. 24, 1947; s. Koichi and Tsuya (Ohta) I.; m. Hatsuko Kuriyama, June 10, 1974; children: Tomoko, Masahiko, Nobuko. MD, Osaka (Japan) Med. Coll., 1971. Instr. psychiatry Osaka Med. Coll., 1972-76, 78-81; rschr. Tokyo Met. Neurosci. Inst., 1976-78; v.p. Shin-Abuyma Hosp., Osaka, 1981-86; dir. Med. Ctr. Kansai U., Osaka, 1986—, prof., 1991—. Contbr. articles to profl. jours. Pres. com. health promotion planning Taito City, Tokyo, 1995—. Recipient Kusuda prize, Japan Jour. Multiphasic Health Testing and Svc., 1997. Mem. AAAS, World Fedn. Mental Health, World Psychiatry Assn., N.Y. Acad. Sci., Japanese Assn. of Univ. Health Adminstrn. (supr.), Japanese Assn. of Univ. Mental Health (councilor), Japan Assn. of Sch. Mental Health (councilor, editor), Japanese Soc. of Psychosomatic Medicine (councilor). Avocations: piano, playing flute, skiing, billiards. E-mail: iidan@ipcku.kansai-u.ac.jp. Office: Kansai Univ, Yamate Cho 3 3 35, 5648680 Suita Japan

IIDA, SHUICHI, physicist, educator; b. Kobe, Hyogo-Ken, Japan, Jan. 30, 1926; s. Shunzoh and Sono (Ueda) I.; m. Kyoko Matsuoka, Apr. 29, 1955; children: Mariko Takahara, Junko Kose. BS in Physics, U. Tokyo, 1947, PhD in Physics, 1958. Asst. prof. physics U. Tokyo, 1952-58, assoc. prof., 1958-68, prof., 1968-86, prof. emeritus, 1986; prof. Teikyo U., Sagamiko, Kanagawa, Japan, 1988-89, Utsunomiya, 1989-96; vis. prof. AT&T Bell Labs., Murray Hill., N.J., 1961-63. Contbr. articles to profl. jours. Mem. Am. Physics Soc., Magnetics Soc. IEEE, Japan Soc. Powder and Powder Metallurgy, N.Y. Acad. Sci., Charles Darwin Assocs., Magnetics Soc. Japan, Japan Inst. Metals, Physics Soc. Japan. Achievements include patents for ferrites; founder of unifying frame for physics; introduction of essential q-number theory in biophysics; solution of EPR problem; solution of wave-particle dualism; proposal of frontier notion principle; proposal of filamentary current loops for c-number structure of lepton and hadron particles; proposal of parasiton state pion in nuclei, existence of contra-particle for neutrinos and pions, Iida diagram for parity violation problems, completely electromagnetic origin of particle masses; completely electromagnetic origin of weak and strong interactions, proposal of chipped photon mechanism for redshifts and denial of big bang cosmology, finding a new thermal principle called transient energy principle, and rigorous proof for perfect diamagnetism of perfect conductors. Home and Office: 4-23-11 Funabashi, Setagaya-ku Tokyo 156-0055, Japan

IIDA, TOHKO, virologist, educator; b. Takaoka, Japan, Dec. 13, 1970; d. Syuji and Noriko (Sano) I. M in Agr., PhD, Kyoto (Japan) U., 1995. Lectr. Kyoto Prefectural U. Medicine, 1995—. Office: Dept Microbiology, Kyoto U Medicine Kamikyo-ku, Kyoto 602 8566, Japan

IIJIMA, MASAAKI, psychiatrist, educator; b. Izumo, Shimane, Japan, Aug. 11, 1960; p. Teietsu and Hiroko (Kouda) I. MD, PhD, Shimane Med. U., Izumo, 1992. Instr. dept. psychiatry Shimane Med. U., Izumo, 1990-93, asst. prof. dept. psychiatry, 1993-95, 96—; vis. clinician Mayo Clinic, Rochester, Minn., 1995-96. Avocation: music. E-mail: iijima@shimane-med.ac.jp. Fax: 81-853-20-2260. Office: Shimane Med Univ, Enya-cho 89-1, Izumo 693-8501, Japan

IIMURA, OSAMU, cardiologist, nephrologist, endocrinologist; b. Ochiai town, Karafuto, Japan, Jan. 28, 1931; s. Haciro and Sotoe (Watanabe) I.; m. Kyoko Kudo, Feb. 2, 1964; 2 children. BSc, Hokkaido U., Sapporo, Japan, 1953; MD, Sapporo Med. U., 1958, PhD, 1963. Asst. prof. Sapporo Med. U., 1963-65, 68-80, lectr., 1965-68, prof. of medicine, 1980-96; pres. Sapporo Med. Univ. Hosp., 1992-96; chief med. cons. Hokkaido JR Sapporo Hosp., 1996—. Editor-in-chief: Hypertension research - Clinical and Experimental, 1996-99; editor Jour. Hypertens, 1990-92, Clin. and Exptl. Pharmaco and Physiol, 1986—, Clin. autonom Rsch., 1990-96. Recipient Hokkaido Med.

Assn. award, 1981, Hokkaido Gov. award, 1981, Hokkaido Sci. and Tech. award, 1994. Fellow Am. Heart Assn.; mem. Japan Circulation Soc. (dir. 1983-94), Japan Soc. Hypertension (dir. 1981-96), Japan Soc. Preventive Cardiology (pres. 1992-99), Japan Soc. Gerontology (dir. 1988—), European Soc. Cardiology, Internat. Soc. Hypertension. Avocations: classical music, travel, reading. Office: Hokkaido Rwy Co Sapporo Hos, N-3 E-1 Chuo-ku, Sapporo 060-0033, Japan

IINO, HIROSHI, engineering educator; b. Kanazawa, Ishikawa, Japan, Dec. 15, 1933; s. Sutekiti and Hatsu (Orito) I.; m. Kuniko Mori, Feb. 17, 1942; children: Tamura Shoko, Hiroya. BS, Tokyo U., 1956, MS, 1958; ScD, MIT, 1967. Cert. engr. Plant mgr. Nippon EVR Co., Tokyo, 1973-79; rep. dir. Teijin-Memorex Co. Ltd., Tokyo, 1978-87; dir. Teijin Ltd., Tokyo, 1989-95, gen. mgr. rec. media divsn., 1991-95; prof. Kanazawa (Japan) Inst. Tech., 1996—. Author: (book) Becoming and Being Engineers, 1998; contbr. articles to profl. jours. Examiner New Industry Devel. Found., Ishikawa Prefecture, Kanazawa, 1998—. Mem. IEEE, ASEE, MIT Assn. of Japan (coord. 1967—.). Office: Kanazawa Inst Tech, 7-1 Ohgzgaoka Nonoichi, Ishikawa 921-8501, Japan

IIYOSHI, ATSUO, academic administrator; b. Tokyo, Sept. 17, 1936; s. Seiichi and Taeko (Mori) I.; m. Masako Saito, Nov. 11, 1965; children: Hiroko, Kyoko. B of Engring., Keio U., Japan, 1960, PhD, 1965. Prof. plasma physics lab. Kyoto U., 1971-89, dir. plasma physics lab., 1988-89; dir.-gen. Nat. Inst. Fusion Sci., Toki, Gifu, Japan, 1989—; head dept. fusion sci. Sch. Math. and Phys. Sci. Grad. U. for Advanced Studies, 1992—; prof. emeritus Kyoto U., 1996—; pres. Chibu U., KAsugai, Japan, 1999—; prof. emeritus The Grad U. Advanced Studies, 1999—, Nat. Inst. Fusion Sci., 1999—. Author: Introduction to Controlled Thermonuclear Reaction, 1975. Recipient Tech. Progress award Atomic Energy Soc. Japan, 1982. Mem. Japan Soc. Plasma Sci. and Nuclear Fusion Rsch. (pres.). Home: 802 4-19-1 Hakusan-cho, 507 Tajimi Gifu, Japan Office: Chubu U, 1200 Matsumoto-cho, Kasugai-city 187-8501, Japan

IIZUKA, HISAKAZU, electronics company laboratory administrator; b. Kashiwazaki, Japan, Feb. 9, 1941; s. Kazuo and Kikuyo (Miida) I.; m. Yoshie Ashida, Apr. 28, 1965; 2 children. BSc, Tohoku U., Sendai, Japan, 1963, MSc, 1965, D of Engring., 1968. Sr. mgr. VLSI rsch. dept. Toshiba Co., Kawasaki, Japan, 1984-88, sr. mgr. technol. adminstrn. dept., 1988-89, sr. mgr. metals and ceramics lab., 1989-93; technology exec. liquid crystal device dept. Toshiba Co., Himeji, Japan, 1993-95; gen. mgr. Display Device Engring. Lab., Yokohama, Japan, 1995—. Author: Silicon Integrated Circuits, Applied Solid State Science Part A, 1981, Semiconductor Technologies, 1986; patentee semicondr. memory device. Mem. Japanese Inst. Elec. Engrs. (mem. tech. expert com. 1979-85, 86-89), Inst. Electronics and Comm. Engrs. (tech. expert com. 1986-89), Japan Soc. Applied Physics (bd. dirs. 1988-90), Assn. for Human Orgn. (mem. mng. com. 1994—). Home: 19-2-A401, Higashiterao Kitadai, Tsurumi-ku Yokohama 230, Japan Office: Toshiba Corp, 8 Shinsugita-cho, Isogo-ku Yokohama 235, Japan

IJÄS, TEUVO TAPIO, federal agency administrator; b. Halikko, Finland, Aug. 4, 1941; s. August and Eeva Ester (Kohonen) I.; m. Mirja Orvokki Kuittinen, Apr. 23, 1944; 1 child, Susanna Tuulikki. M in Social Sci., U. Helsinki, Finland, 1966, M in Law, 1975. Officer Min. of Def., Helsinki, Finland, 1966-72; inspector Min. of Def., Helsinki, 1973-75; legal officer UN Forces, Nicosia, 1972-73; chief of bur. Nat. Housing Bd., Helsinki, 1975-77, dep. dir. gen., 1979-93; sec. gen. Housing Coun., Helsinki, 1977-79; dir. gen. Min. of Environ., Helsinki, 1979-93, Housing Fund of Finland, Helsinki, 1993—; v.p. Suomi-Finland Housing and Planning, Helsinki, 1992-94, pres., 1995—; mem. bur. Internat. Fedn. Housing and Planning, 1994—; chair Finnish Housing Fair Co-operation, 1994—. Decorated Order of Knighthood of White Cross, 1980; recipient UN medal, Helsinki Gold medal, 2000. Mem. Finnish Housing Assn. (chmn. 1993—). Avocations: tennis, golfing, gardening, hunting, writing. Office: Housing Fund of Finland, Asemapaallikonkatu 14, 00520 Helsinki Finland

IJI, PAUL ADE, animal scientist, researcher; b. Opeim-Owo, Benue, Nigeria, Jan. 5, 1962; s. Iji Ijogo and Priscilla Onwu (Igbala) Ijogo; m. Dorcas Ugwo Ominyi, Oct. 28, 1998; 1 child, Moses. BSc, U. Maiduguri, Nigeria, 1986; MSc, U. Aberdeen, Scotland, 1990; PhD, U. Adelaide, Australia, 1998. Lectr. Ahmadu Bello U., Zaria, Nigeria, 1987-98; rschr. U. Natal, PM'Burg, S. Africa, 1999—. Contbr. articles to profl. jours. Oda Shared scholar, 1989-90; Australian Devel. Coop. scholar AusAID, 1994-98. Assoc. Physiol. Soc.; mem. Brit. Soc. Animal Sci., World's Poultry Sci. Assn. Avocations: reading, swimming, travelling. Office: U Natal, Dept Animal Sci, Private Bag X01, Scottsville 3209, South Africa

IJSSELMUIDEN, CAREL, public health physician, epidemiologist; b. Winterthur, Zürich, Switzerland, Apr. 11, 1954; arrived in South Africa, 1980; s. Aloysius Johannes I. and Maria Leonie Kohschulte Brokhaus; m. Joëlle-Laure Neustetel, Jan. 23, 1980; children: Samuel Tsunduka, Misha Tsakani, Aline Lindiwe. MD, Erasmus U., Rotterdam, The Netherlands, 1980; DTM&H, Med. U. South Africa, Pretoria, 1983; MPH, Johns Hopkins U., 1990. Med. splst. Med. officer St. Clara Academic Hosp., Rotterdam, The Netherlands, 1980; sr. med. officer Elim Hosp., N.P. Province, South Africa, 1980-84; lectr. dept. cmty. health U. Witwatersrand, Johannesburg, South Africa, 1985-88; dep. med. officer of health Johnannesburg Health Dept., 1988-90; sr. lectr. dept. cmty. health Med. U. So. Africa, Medunsa, 1990-95; prof., chair dept. cmty. health Faculty of Medicine U. Pretoria, South Africa, 1995—, dir. Sch. Health Sys. and Pub. Health, 1999—; study dir. Nat. Vamin A Study, Southfrica, 1994-96. Tech. editor: South. Africa Jour. Epidemiology and Infection, 1988—; rev. nat. and nternat. jours.; contbr. articles to profl. jours. Mem. nat. Essential Nat. Health Rsch. Commn. Fellow Faculty Cmty. Health Coll. Medicine; mem. Internat. Epidemiol. Assn., Epidemiol. Soc. So. Africa (sec. 1986-90), Hastings Ctr. Bioethics. Avocations: gliding, photography. E-mail: Carel@medic.up.ac.za. Office: U Pretoria Faculty Medicine, Dept Cmty Health PO Box 667, 0001 Pretoria Gauteng, South Africa

IKÄVALKO, JOHANNA EIRA, biologist, researcher; b. Helsinki, Finland, June 7, 1965; d. Johannes and Sirkka-Liisa (Venovirta) I. MS, U. Helsinki, 1991, Lic. Phil., 1994, PhD, 1997; docent, 2000. Hydrobiologist; protist taxonomist. Stipendiate Walter and Andrée de Nottbeck Found., Finland, 1990-91, 93-96; asst. hydrobiology U. Helsinki, 1991-2000; stipendiate Acad. Finland, 1996-97; rschr. U. Calif. Inst. Marine Scis., Santa Cruz, 1998, Acad. Finland, 1999; lectr. Open U., Helsinki, 1991-96, 99-2000, Adult Learning Ctr., Lahti, Finland, 1992-96, 98—, U. Helsinki. Co-author: Freshwater Ecology, 1991, 3rd edit., 1993; editor: 2nd Workshop Baltic Sea Protists, 1992; illustrator: (scientific report) Biodiversity in the Arctic, 1997. Grantee Walter and Andrée de Nottbeck Found., 1990-91, 93-96, Finnish Ministry Trade and Industry, 1995-96, Acad. Finland, 1995-96, U. Kiel, Germany, 1996-97. Mem. Internat. Phycological Soc., Phycological Soc. Am., Systematics Assn. Eng. Lutheran. Avocations: sports, arts, nature. E-mail: johanna ikavalko@hotmail.com. Home: Huopalahdentie 15 A 3, Fin00350 Helsinki Finland Office: U Helskini Divsn Hydrobiol, PO Box 7, FIN00014 Helsinki Finland

IKAWA, HIROYUKI, ceramic science and engineering educator; b. Hiroshima, Japan, Aug. 9, 1941; s. Toyoichi and Masuno Ikawa; m. Fusako Maruo, Mar. 25, 1972; children: Takahiro, Kouta. Bachelors, Tokyo Inst. Tech., 1966, MS in Engring., 1968, D of Engring., 1971. Rsch. asst. Tokyo Inst. Tech., 1971-85, assoc. prof., 1985-93; prof. ceramic engring. Kanagawa Inst. Tech., Atsugi, Japan, 1993—; vis. scientist Pa. State U., State College, 1989-90. Author: Dictionary of Fine Ceramics, 1987, Handbook of Ceramic Engineering, 1989, Proton Conductors, 1992, Ceramic Data Book, 1993. Mem. Am. Ceramic Soc., Ceramic Soc. Japan (Scholarship award 1992), Chem. Soc. Japan. Home: Koma 2-21-236, Ooiso-machi 255-0001, Japan Office: Kanagawa Inst Tech, Shimo-ogino 1030, Atsugi 243-0292, Japan

IKEDA, HIROAKI, retired engineering educator; b. Iwata, Shizuoka, Japan, Mar. 21, 1935; s. Ken-Ichi and Kane (Mutoh) I.; m. Kimiko Mayeda, Nov. 3, 1960; children: Yuki Nagai, Motoko. BS, Shizuoka U., Hamamatsu, Japan, 1957; PhD, U. Tokyo, 1975. Engr. Japan Broadcasting Corp., Tokyo, 1957-73, sr. scientist, 1973-78, sr. engring. staff mem., 1978-82, 83-87, mgr., 1982-83; prof. Shizuoka U., Hamamatsu, 1987-98; tech. mem. Venture Enterprise Ctr., Tokyo, 1984-95; vis. scientist Shizuoka Prefecture, 1989-91, 93-94; scientist Nagoya Indsl. Sci. Labs., Nagoya, Japan, 1993-2000; project leader Telecom. Advancement Orgn. Japan, 1996-99. Contbr. articles to profl. jours. Recipient Invention and Rsch. award Met. of Tokyo, 1982, OHM award Elec. Sci. and Tech. Found., Tokyo, 1988; rsch. award Takayanagi Found., Hamamatsu, 1991. Mem. IEEE (sr.), Inst. Electronics, Info. and Comm. Engrs. (tech. paper reviewer 1974-81), Inst. Elec. Engrs. Japan, IEEE Industry Applications Soc. (mfg. sys. devel. and applications dept.). Home: 2157-26 Naruse, Machida Tokyo 194-0044, Japan

IKEDA, HIROSHI, educational measurement educator; b. Kurashiki-city, Japan, Apr. 19, 1932; s. Riichiro and Toyoko (Tanaka) I.; m. Fusako Matsumoto, Apr. 20, 1959; children: Yoko, Eiko. BA, U. Tokyo, 1956, MA, 1958; PhD, U. Ill., 1965. Assoc. prof. St. Paul's U., Tokyo, 1965-73, prof., 1973-79, 82-98; prof. Tokyo Inst. Tech., 1979-82; guest prof. Nat. Ctr. of Univ. Entrance Exam., Tokyo, 1978-90, U. of Air, Chiba, Japan, 1992-98; Fulbright sr. rschr. U. Pitts., 1985-86; bd. dirs. Soc. for Testing English Proficiency, Tokyo. Author: (book) Research Methods for Behavioral Sciences, 1971, The Science of Testing, 1992, Modern Test Theory, 1994; editor and author: Handbook of Statistical Methods, 1989. Recipient Disting. Contbn. award The Behavior Metric Soc. of Japan, 1992. Mem. Am. Ednl. Rsch. Assn., Nat. Coun. on Measurement in Edn., Japanese Assn. Ednl. Psychology. Avocation: computer programming. Home and Office: 4-23-10 Jindaiji-Motomachi, Chofu-shi 182-0017, Japan

IKEDA, KAZUYOSI, physicist, poet; b. Fukuoka, Japan, July 15, 1928; s. Yosikatu and Misao (Misumi) I.; m. Mieko Akiyama, Nov. 20, 1956; children: Hiroko Ikeda Yamaguti, Yosihumi. 1st degree Rigakusi, Kyushu U., Fukuoka, Japan, 1951, DSc, 1957; D Environ. Sci. (hon.), Internat. Earth Environment U., 1993; DLitt (hon.), London Inst. Applied Rsch., 1995; diploma of honor, Inst. Affaires Internat., 1995. Asst. dept. physics Kyushu U. Faculty Sci., Fukuoka, 1956-60, assoc. prof. dept. physics, 1960-65; assoc. prof. dept. applied physics Osaka (Japan) U. Faculty Engring., 1965-68, prof. theoretical physics dept. applied physics, 1968-89, prof. theoretical and math. physics dept. math. scis., 1989-92, prof. emeritus, 1992—; pres. Internat. Earth Environment U., Japan, 1995—, prof. theoretical physics, 1992—; bd. advisory coun. Ansted U., 1999—. Author: Statistical Thermodynamics, 1975, Mechanics Without Use of Mathematical Formulae--From a Moving Stone to Halley's Comet, 1980, Invitation to Mechanics--From the Fundamentals of Calculus to the Motion of a Comet, with Appendix on a comet in ancient times, 1985, (collection of poems) Bansyoo Hyakusi, 1986, Basic Mechanics, 1987, Basic Thermodynamics--From Entropy to Osmotic Pressure, 1991, The World of God, Creation and Poetry, 1991, Poems on the Hearts of Creation, 1993, Mountains, 1995, North South East and West, 1996, Graphical Theory of Relativity, 1998, Hearts of Myriad Things in the Universe, 1998, Kazuyosi's Poetry on the Animate and the Inanimate, 1998, Poems on Love and Peace, 1998, Songs of the Soul, 1999, Hearts of Innumerous Things in Heaven and Earth, 2000; editor Modern Poetry, 1996—; contbr. more than 100 articles to profl. jours.; author serialized poems, essays on poetry. Hon. founder, Japan rep. Olympoetry Movement, 1992—. Recipient Yukawa Commemorative Scholarship award Yukawa Found., 1954, World Biographical Hall of Fame award Hist. Preservations Am., 1990, prize Catania e il suo Vulcano, Accademia Ferdinandea Sci. Lettere Arti, 1994, Albert Einstein Acad. Cert. award for outstanding achievement Albert Einstein Internat. Acad. Found., 1998, Internat. Artistic-Literary prize of Primavera Catanase, Accademia Ferdinandea, Sci. Lettere Arte, 1997, Pandit prize Indian Coun. Natural Medicine Rsch., 1999; named Knight of Yr., Internat. Writers and Artists Assn., 1995, Knight Templar Order, Lofsensic Ursinius Order, Holy Grail Order, Universal Knights Order, San Ciriaco Order, 1995, Order of Pegasus Highest Degree, Olympoetry Movement Fund, 1996, Pandit prize, Indian Coun. of Natural Medicine and Rsch., 1999, Cultural Doctorate in Poetical Lit., World U. Roundtable, 1999, Best World Poet of Yr. award Poets Internat., 1999, Poet of Millennium award Internat. Poets Acad., 2000. Fellow United Writers' Assn. (life), World Lit. Acad. (life), Internat. Poets Acad. (life, Internat. Eminent Poet award 1993); mem. N.Y. Acad. Scis., Am. Biog. Inst. Rsch. Assn. (dep. gov. 1989—, continental gov. 1998—), World Inst. Achievement (life), Lifetime Achievement Acad. (life, Golden Acad. award 1991), Phys. Soc. Japan (com. mem. 1970—, chmn. Osaka br. 1976-77, 83-84, editor jour. 1976-78), Internat. Biog. Assn. (life patron 1990—), Internat. Biog. Ctr. (dep. dir. gen. 1989—), World Acad. Arts and Culture (life), World Congress of Poets (life), Confedn. Chivalry (mem. grand coun. 1991—, Chevalier Grand Cross 1991), Accademia Ferdinandea Scienze Lettere Arti (academician of honor 1994—), Order Internat. Fellowship (charter 1994—), World Parnassians Guild Internat. (hon. dir. 1995—), Acad. M.I.D.I. (senator 1995—), Coun. of States for Protection of Life (senator 1995—, minister plenipotentiary for Asian States 1999—), Academia Argentina (academician 1995—), Internat. Parliament for Safety and Peace (Medalla al Merito 1995, senator 1999—, minister plenipotentiary for Japan 1999—), Modern Poets Soc. (bd. dir. 1996—), Accademia Internazionale Trinacria Lettere-Arte-Scienze (academician of merit 1997—), Leading Intellectuals of the World (founding charter mem. 1998—), Internat. Govs. Club, London Diplomatic Acad. (founder). Home: Nisi-7-7-11 Aomadani, Minoo-si Osaka 562-0023, Japan Office: Osaka U Fac Engring Dept Math Scis, 2-1 Yamadaoka, Suita-si Osaka 565-0871, Japan

IKEDA, SHUJI, semiconductor engineer; b. Koganei, Tokyo, Japan, Mar. 27, 1956; s. Shinichi and Chizuko (Iwasaki) I.; m. Hiroko Oinuma, Dec. 12, 1981; children: Yuki, Ayano, Sho. BS, Tokyo Inst. Tech., 1978; MSEE, Princeton U., 1987. Engr. Hitachi Ltd., Tokyo, 1986-91, sr. engr., 1991—. Author (video) Semiconductor Manufacturing Process, 1982. Head coach elem. sch. soccer team, Tokyo, 1994—. Mem. IEEE (Internat. Electron Devices Meeting subcom. 1993-94, Asian arrangement chmn. 1995—, mem. exec. com. 1998—). Avocations: soccer, football, camping. Home: 3-30-8 Nukuikita, Tokyo Koganeishi 184, Japan Office: Hitachi Ltd, 6-16-3 Shiumachi, Ome, Tokyo 198-8512, Japan

IKEDA, TADASU, diabetologist; b. Yonago, Japan, Mar. 15, 1947; s. Takamasa and Miyako (Tahara) I.; m. Mitsuko Nadao, Mar. 25, 1973; children: Rinko, Teiko, Ruiko, Mizuha. D of Med. Sci., Tottori U., 1980. Resident Tottori U. Hosp., Yonago, Japan, 1971-73, mem. med. staff, 1973-77; rsch. asst. 1st Dept. Internal Medicine Faculty Medicine, Yonago, Japan, 1977-83, assoc. prof., 1983-90; prof. dept. nursing Tottori U. Coll. Med. Care Tech., Yonago, Japan, 1990—; prof. faculty medicine Tottori U., Yonago, Japan, 1999—; chief dept. nursing Tottori U. Coll. Med. Care Tech., 1992-96. Rsch. fellow Vanderbilt U. Sch. Medicine Dept. Molecular Physiology, Nashville, 1995-96; recipient Shimoda Mitsuzo award, 1986. Fellow Japan Diabetic Soc.; mem. Am. Diabetes Assn. Avocations: mountain climbing, catching butterflies. Office: Faculty Medicine Tottori U, 133-2 Nishi-machi, Yonago 683-0826, Japan

IKEDIFE, DOZIE ONYEANUSI, obstetrician-gynecologist, researcher; b. Nnewi, Nigeria, Aug. 24, 1932; s. Dunu-Ifeneti Ikedife Dunu-Ugochukwu and Ejeagha (Nzewi) Ikedife; m. Christie Onyebuchi Anazodo; children: Dozie Jr., Kenechukwu, Okeoma, Chiazor, Somadina, Onyedika, Ziesaluchukwu (Zikora). BSc, U. London, 1958; MBChB, U. Glasgow, Scotland, 1959; diploma in obstet., Royal Coll. Ob-Gyn., 1960; D in Pub. Adminstrn., World U., Tucson, 1983. Sr. ho. officer, registrar in ob-gyn. Stobhill Hosp., Glasgow, 1960-63; med. officer spl. grade Ministry of Health, Lagos, Nigeria, 1964-66, Eastern Region, Enugu, Nigeria, 1966-67; founder, specialist-in-charge City Hosp., Aba, Nigeria, 1967-70, Specialist Med. Ctr. and Ikedife Hosp., Nnewi, Nigeria, 1970—; reader in ob-gyn. Nnamdi Azikiwe U. Coll. Health Scis., Nnewi, Nigeria, 1995—; examiner in ob-gyn. U. Nigeria, Nsukka, 1981, Nnamdi Azikiwe U., Awka, 1994, Nigerian Nat. Postgrad. Med. Coll., 1978-84, West African Postgrad. Med. Coll., 1994—. Contbr. articles to profl. jours. and conf. procs. 1st chmn. Cmty. Coun., Nnewi, 1972-75; hon. commr. for econ. devel. East Ctrl. State of Nigeria, 1975; 1st hon. commr. fin. and econ. devel., Anambra State, 1976; 1st spl. asst. to 1st exec. pres., Fed. Rep. Nigeria, 1979-83; mem. Nnewi Royal Cabinet, 1972; co-founder, 1st chmn. Confidence Newspapers Ltd., Nnewi, 1995; established Dozie Ikedife Ann. Medal and Prize for Best Graduating Med. Dr., Nnamdi Azikiwe U., Awka, 1995, and Dr. Dozie Ikedife Ann. Prize for Best Student in Cmty. Health, U. Nigeria, Nsukka, 1988. Awarded 1st Chieftancy title (Ikuku Ebu Nkpu) by 14 towns in Nnewi North, Nnewi South, Ekwusigo local govt. areas, Anambra State, 1980; awarded Hon. Chieftancy title (Ikenga Nnewi) by the Igwe, his Royal Cabinet, and the people of Nnewi, 1981; awarded Hon. Chieftaincy title of Odezuligbo Umueje, 1997. Fellow Med. Coll. Ob-Gyn. (Nigeria), West African Coll. Surgeons, Royal Coll. Ob-Gyn., Internat. Coll. Surgeons (pres. Nigeria nat. sect. 1987-95, fedn. sec. 1991-94, mem. exec. coun. 1991-94, world v.p. 1994-96), Learners Soc. Nigeria (founder); mem. Nigerian Med. Assn. (1st Nnewi zonal chmn. 1972-76), Soc. Ob-Gyn. of Nigeria (exec. mem. 1976-84), Internat. Soc. Cardio-Thoracic Surgeons (hon.), Rotary Club Internat. (dist. officer dist. 9140), Rotary Club of Nnewi (charter pres. 1984-86, One Star Paul Harris Fellow, Vocat. Svcs award 1997), Peoples Club of Nigeria, Anaedo Social Club of Nigeria. Avocations: horseback riding, growing Iroko trees, chess, classical music. Home: No. 23 Ikedife St, PO Box 32, Otolo Nnewi, Nigeria Office: Ikedife Hosp Spl Med Ctr, 33 Igwe Orizu Rd PO Box 32, Nnewi Nigeria

IKEGAMI, HIDETSUGU, physicist, educator; b. Tottori, Japan, Feb. 1, 1930; s. Eiji and Shigeno (Inoue) I.; m. Noriko Matsuzono, Nov. 3, 1956; children: Sayaka, Masako, Hatsuyo. BS, Kyoto U., 1952, DSc, 1959; PhD (hon.), Uppsala U., 1990. Rsch. assoc. Kyoto U., Japan, 1952-56; asst. prof. Tokyo U., 1956-64, Brookhaven Nat. Lab., N.Y.C., 1962-64; assoc. prof. Tokyo Inst. Technology, 1964-72; prof. Osaka U., Japan, 1972-93, dir. RCNP, 1985-93, prof. emeritus, 1993—; guest prof. Uppsala U., Sweden, 1993—. Avocation: studying J. Haydn. Home: Hibarigaoka 2-12-50, 665-0805 Takarazuka Japan

IKEGAWA, MASATO, engineering researcher; b. Yokohama, Japan, Jan. 12, 1951; s. Masamichi and Ayako (Kosuge) I.; m. Reiko Yajima, Apr. 7, 1979; 1 child, Taisuke. BS, Tokyo U., 1974, MS, 1976, PhD, 1990. Rschr. Mech. Engring. Rsch. Lab., Hitachi Ltd., Tsuchiura, Japan, 1976-86, sr. rschr., 1987—; vis. rschr. U. Calif., Berkeley, 1983-84. Author: Genshi Bunshi no Nagare, 1996, Computational Mechanics (VI), 1999; contbr. articles to profl. jours.; inventor, patentee in field. Mem. ASME, Electrochem. Soc., Japan Soc. of Mech. Engrs. Achievements include development of first scroll compressor for air conditioning; development of Monte-Carlo deposition-profile computer program for semiconductor manufacturing; development of rarefied gas flow simulation for etching and CVD reactors; development of magneto-microwave plasma simulation. Avocation: tennis. Office: Mech Engring Rsch Lab, Hitachi Ltd 502 Kandatsu, Tsuchiura, Ibaraki 300-0013, Japan

IKEHIRA, HIROO, radiologist, researcher; b. Kyoto, Japan, Feb. 28, 1955; s. Hiroshi and Reiko (Negoro) I.; m. Junko Harasawa; 1 child, Hiroaki. MD, Kobe (Japan) U., 1980; PhD, Chiba (Japan) U., 1987. Lic. specialist diagnostic radiology and radiotherapy, supr. radiation protection, specialist nuclear medicine and magnetic resonance in medicine and biomed. physics. Intern Chiba U. Hosp., Chiba-shi, Japan, 1980; resident Aberdeen (Scotland) Royal Infirmary, 1982; asst. prof. Yamanashi U. Sch. Medicine, Kofu, Japan, 1981-83; rschr. Nat. Inst. Radiol. Scis., Chiba, Japan, 1983-88, sr. rschr., 1989-92; sr. lectr. Chiba U. Sch. Medicine, 1992-98, assoc. prof., 1998-99; head informative molecular rsch. Nat. Inst. Radiol. Scis., Chiba, 1999—; exch. scientist Lawrence Berkeley (Calif.) Lab., 1987-88; guest lectr. Tohoku U., Sendai, Japan, 1990-99, Showa U., Tokyo, 1995-99; guest scientist Nat. Inst. Radiol. Scis., Chiba, 1992-99. Editor Japanese Jour. Magnetic Resonance in Medicine, 1990-98. Mem. Japan Soc. Magnetic Resonance in Medicine (bd. dirs. 1996-2000). Avocation: haiku (poem, Japanese short poem). Home: 3-38-10 Izumidai, Ichihara-shi 299-0114, Japan Office: Nat Inst Radiol Scis, 4-9-1 Anagawa, Inage-ku Chiba-shi 263-8555, Japan

IKEKAWA, NOBUO, academic administrator; b. Iiyama, Nagano, Japan, Oct. 12, 1926; s. Kumaji and Tsune (Takahashi) I.; m. Sanae Numata. BS in Pharm. Sci., U. Tokyo, 1951, PhD, 1959; postgrad., Kyushyu U., Japan, 1955. Rsch. assoc. Inst. Applied Microbiology U. Tokyo, 1955-61; vis. scientist NIH, LC, NIAMD, 1958-60; sr. chemist Inst. Phys. and Chem. Rsch., Japan, 1961-69; prof. dept. chemistry Tokyo Inst. Tech., 1969-87; prof. Coll. Sci. and Engring. Iwaki Meisei U., 1987-95; pres. Niigata (Japan) Coll. Pharmacy, 1995—; vis. assoc. prof. Inst. for Lipid Rsch., Baylor Coll. Medicine, 1966; bd. dirs. Rsch. Found. for Pharm. Scis., Japan, 1997—; chmn. bd. dirs. Niigata Inst. Sci. and Tech., 1996—; rschr. on biological active sterols, 1951-95. Author: Studies on Biologically Active Steroi. Recipient Sato Meml. award, 1979, M.S. Tswett Chromatography medal, 1982, Shimadzu award, 1992, Rsch. Contbn. award Japan Biomed. Mass Spectrometry Soc., 1996. Mem. Japan Assn. Pharm. Coll. (bd. dirs. 1997—), Pharm. Soc. Japan (bd. dirs. 1984-94, award 1981, Mem. of Merit award 1998). Buddhist. Avocation: golf. Office: Niigata Coll Pharmacy, Kamishinei-chou 5-13-2, Niigata 950-2081, Japan

IKENBERRY, STANLEY OLIVER, education educator, former university president; b. Lamar, Colo., Mar. 3, 1935; s. Oliver Samuel and Margaret (Moulton) I.; m. Judith Ellen Life, Aug. 24, 1958; children: David Lawrence, Steven Oliver, John Paul. BA, Shepherd Coll., 1956; MA, Mich. State U., 1957, PhD, 1960, LHD (hon.); LLD (hon.), Millikin U.; LHD (hon.), Ill. Coll., Rush U., W.Va. U., Towson State U., Bridgewater (Va.) Coll., Bradley U., Shepherd Coll., Roosevelt U., Mich. State U. Instr. office Mich. State U., 1958-60, instr. instl. rsch. office, 1960-62; asst. to provost for instl. rsch., asst. prof. edn. W.Va. U., 1962-65, dean coll. human resources and edn., assoc. prof. edn., 1965-69; prof., assoc. dir. ctr. study higher edn. Pa. State U., 1969-71, sr. v.p., 1971-79; pres. U. Ill., Urbana, 1979-95, pres. emeritus, Regent prof., 1995—; pres. Am. Coun. on Edn., Washington, 1997—; bd. dirs. Pfizer, Inc., N.Y.C., UtiliCorp United Inc., Kansas City, Mus. Natural History; bd. overseers Tchrs. Ins. and Annuity Assn./Coll. Retirement Equities Fund. Contbr. articles to profl. jours. Past chmn. Carnegie Found. for Advancement Tchg.; bd. dirs. Nat. Mus. Natural History. Named hon. alumnus Pa. State U. Mem. Am. Coun. Edn. (past chmn., pres. 1996—), Assn. Am. Univs. (past chmn.), Comml. Club Chgo., Mid-Am. Club, Tavern Club (Chgo.), Cosmos Club (Washington). Office: Am Coun on Edn One Dupont Cir Washington DC 20007

IKEO, KYOICHI, marketing researcher, educator; b. Zushi-shi, Kanagawa, Japan, Sept. 29, 1950; s. Kiyoshi and Hiroko (Watase) I.; m. Atsuko Sato, Feb. 2, 1981; children: Sayaka, Erika. BA, Keio U., Tokyo, 1973, MA, 1975, PhD, 1991. Asst. prof. Kwansei Gakuin U., Nishinomiya, Japan, 1979-83; assoc. prof. Kwansei Gakuin U., Nishinomiya, 1983-88; assoc. prof. Keio U., Tokyo, 1988-94, prof., 1994—. Author (book) Consumer Behavior and Marketing Strategy, 1991 (Disting. Rsch. award Japanese Soc. Mktg. and Distbn. 1993), Innovation of Japanese Marketing, 1999; co-author (books) New Frontier in Consumer Behavior Analysis, 1984, Theory of Commerce, 1989, Basic Knowledge in Management for Reading the Nikkei, 1991. Recipient Disting. Rsch. Paper award Japan Soc. Advertising, 1984. Mem. Japan Assn. for Consumer Rsch. (pres. 1998-99), Japan Soc. Mktg. and Distbn. Avocations: skiing, tennis, snorkeling. Home: 5-13-22 Seijo, Setagaya Tokyo 157-0066, Japan Office: KEIO U Grad Sch Bus Admin, 2-1-1 Hyoshi-honcho, Kohokuku Yokohama 223-8523, Japan

IKEYAMA, MASAMI, scientific researcher; b. Japan, Sept. 23, 1959. MS, Nagoya U., Japan, 1984, DS, 1989. Rschr. Govt. Indsl. Rsch. Inst., Nagoya, 1988-93, sr. rschr., 1993—. Contbr. articles to profl. jours. Mem. Japan Soc. Applied Physics, Japan Soc. Powder and Powder Metallurgy, The Meteorol. Soc. Japan. Avocations: audio, photography. Office: Nat Indsl Rsch Inst Nagoya, 1-1 Hirate-cho Kita-ku, Nagoya 462-8510, Japan

IKLÉ, FRED CHARLES, former federal agency administrator, policy advisor, defense expert; b. Fex, Switzerland, Aug. 21, 1924; s. Fritz A. and Hedwig M. (Huber) I.; m. Doris Eisemann, Dec. 23, 1959; children—Judith, Miriam. M.A. in Social Sci, U. Chgo., 1948, Ph.D. in Sociology, 1950. Research assoc. Columbia Bur. Applied Social Research, 1950-54; mem. social sci. dept. Rand Corp., 1955-61; head social sci. dept. Rand Corp., Santa Monica, Calif., 1968-73; research assoc. Ctr. for Internat. Affairs Harvard U., 1962-63; prof. polit. sci. Mass. Inst. Tech., 1964-67; dir. U.S. ACDA, Washington, 1973-77; chmn. Conservation Mgmt. Corp., 1978-81, 88—; under-sec. for policy Dept. Def., Washington, 1981-88; Disting. scholar Ctr. for Internat. and Strategic Studies, 1988—; bd. dirs. Zurich-Financial Svcs., Nat. Endowment for Democracy; chmn. Telos Corp., 1995—; mem. adv. bd. dirs. RAND Drug Policy Ctr.; mem. Nat. Com. on Terrorism, 1999-00. Author: The Social Impact of Bomb Destruction, 1958, How Nations Negotiate, 1964, Every War Must End, 1971. Mem. Internat. Inst. Strategic Studies, Am. Coun. Fgn. Rels., Met. Club. Republican. Home: 7010 Glenbrook Rd Bethesda MD 20814-1223 Office: Ctr Strategic & Internat Studies 1800 K St NW Washington DC 20006-2202

IKOSSI-ANASTASIOU, KIKI, electrical and computer engineer; b. Nicosia, Cyprus, Dec. 23, 1954; came to U.S., 1978; d. George J. and Margarita K. (Vavlitis) Ikossi; m. Chris Anastasiou, Aug. 27, 1977; children: Georgia-Charithea, Michael-George. BSEE, Nat. Tech. U., Athens, Greece, 1977; MS, U. Cin., 1982, PhD, 1986. Rsch./tchg. asst. U. Cin., 1980-86; sr. rsch. scientist Universal Energy Sys., Dayton, Ohio, 1986-90; asst. prof. elec. and computer engring. La. State U., Baton Rouge, 1990-96, assoc. prof., 1996-99; mem. staff Naval Rsch. Lab., Washington, 1999—; Naval Rsch. Lab., 1998—, reviewer NSF, Washington, 1993—; summer faculty rsch. fellow Navy-Am. Soc. Engring. Edn., Naval Rsch. Lab., Washington, 1991, sr. summer faculty rsch. fellow, 1992-98. Contbr. articles to profl. publs. Recipient 7 awards for contbns. Am. Soc. Engring. Edn./Navy, 1991-98, DON Contbn. award, 1999, Alan Berman Outstanding Rsch. Publs. Awd., US Navy, 1998; U. Cin. coun. rsch. fellow, 1982, 83, 79-85; rsch. grantee NSF, USN, La. Quality Support Edn., 1991—. Mem. IEEE (co-chairperson MTT's Internat. Microwave Symposium 1996-99, mem. tech. program com. for internat. microwave symposium, reviewer 1995—), AAAS, AAIP, AAUW, Soc. Women Engrs., Assn. Women in Sci., Am. Soc. Engring. Edn., Washington Acad. Sci., N.Y. Acad. Sci., Electrochem. Soc. Metall. Achievements include refinement of method of moments for deep level transient spectroscopy studies in semiconductors; one of the first scientists to incorporate antimonides in III-V compound microelectronic devices; patent pending on monolithic tandem solar cells with antimonides; patentee indium phosphide microelectronic device processing. Avocation: animal rights. Home: 6275 Gentle Ln Alexandria VA 22310-2260 Office: care NRL Code 6856 4555 Overlook Ave SW Washington DC 20375-0001

IKPEBA, VICTOR, soccer player; b. Dec. 6, 1973. Forward Monaco (France) Football Club. Address: Assn Sportive Monaco Football Profl, 7 Avenue des Castelans, 98014 Manaco France*

IKULAYO, PHILOMENA BOLAJI, physical education educator; b. Ikoro-Ekiti, W. Region, Nigeria, June 2, 1948; d. Simeon Olanipekun and Reginah Dada (Babatunde) Falade; m. Alfred Olaiya Ikulayo, Dec. 28, 1964; 5 children. BEd, Sussex Sch. Edn., Eng., 1975; MEd, Manchester U., Eng., 1978; PhD, U. Lagos, Nigeria, 1985. Tchr. Igede, Nigeria, 1967, Dick Shepperd Comprehensive Sch., London, 1975-77, Dunraven Grammer Sch., London, 1978; asst. lectr. U. Ife, Ile-Ife, Nigeria, 1978-79; from lectr. II to prof. U. Lagos, 1979—; mem. caretecar com. Nat. Sports Commn., 1984-85, 85-89; hall mistress U. Lagos, 1997-99. Author: Physical Education Fundamental, 1982, Understanding Sports Psychology, 1990, sports Psychology Digest, 1991, Family Life and Sex Education, 1999. Treas. Nigerian Assn. Phys. Health Edn., Recreation, Sports & Dance, 1993-99. Fellow Phys. Edn. Assn. U.K., Sports Psychology Assn. Nigeria (founder, first nat. pres.); mem. Internat. Soc. Sport Psychology (v.p. 1993-97), Internat. Coun. Health, Phys. Edn. Recreation, Sports & Dance (sec. gen. 1991-99), Africa Zone, Nigeria Assn. Profl. Educator (mem. exec. com.), Internat. Soc. Sports Psychology (chmn. 1997—), Women Sports Internat., Internat. Assn. Physical Edn. (African rep.). Roman Catholic. Office: U Lagos, Dept Phys & Health Edn D24, Lagos Nigeria

IKURA, YOSHIHIRO, pathologist, educator; b. Ibaraki City, Osaka, Japan, Jan. 31, 1965; s. Tadao and Setsuko (Minato) I.; m. Kiyoko Hashimoto, June 1, 1991; 1 child, Shogo. MD, Osaka City U., 1989, D in Medicine, 1996. Surg. resident Kobe (Japan) City Gen. Hosp., 1989-91; staff pathologist Osaka City U. Med. Sch., 1991-99, asst. prof., 1999—. Contbr. articles to profl. jours. Recipient Osaka Mayor's award, 1998; grantee Ministry Edn., Sci. and Culture, 1996, 99. Mem. Internat. Acad. Pathology, Japanese Soc. Pathology, Japanese Soc. Gastroenterology, Am. Assn. Study of Liver Diseases. Avocations: motorcycling, travel, swimming. Home: 4-1-32-402 Kusugaokacho, Nada-ku Kobe 657-0024, Japan Office: Osaka City U Med Sch Path, 1-4-3 Asahimachi, Abeno-ku Osaka 545-8585, Japan

IKUTA, MUNEHIRO, medical educator; b. Kamakura, Japan, Mar. 10, 1948. Cert. occupational therapy, Sch. of Rehab., Kiyose, Japan, 1971; BS, Kanazawa (Japan) Econ. Coll., 1985; MD, Kanazawa U., 1990. Occupational therapist Yokohama (Japan) U. Hosp., 1972-79; asst. prof. Kanazawa U., 1979-92, prof., 1992—. Author: Kansetsu Kado Shogai, 1990; contbr. articles to profl. jours. Com. mem. Ishikawa Prefecture, Japan, 1996—; social welfare com. mem. Kanazawa City, Japan, 1997—. Mem. Japanese Assn. Occupational Therapist (dir.). Office: Kanazawa U Sch Health Scis, Fac Med Kodatsuno 5 chome, Kanazawa 920-0942, Japan

IKUTA, NOBUAKI, electrical engineering educator; b. Kochi City, Japan, Oct. 22, 1929; s. Ekitaro and Reiko (Hirobe) I.; m. Chieko Sakaki, May 22, 1961; children: Noriko, Naoko. Grad., Tokushima Tech. Coll., 1951; PhD in Engring., Tokyo U., 1972. Tchr. Tokushima Tech. H.S., 1953-63; asst. faculty engring. Tokushima U., 1964-65, lectr. Tech. Coll., 1965-67, asst. prof., 1968-72, prof. elec. engring., 1973-87, prof. faculty engring., 1987-94; prof. Rsch. Inst. Chiba Inst. Tech., 1995—. Contbr. articles to profl. jours. Recipient Prize for outstanding progress Inst. Electrostatics of Japan, 1982. Mem. Inst. Elec. Engrs. Japan (head Shikoku br. 1990, mem. technol. com. on discharge 1986-90, Prize for Outstanding Paper, 1972), Phys. Soc. Japan, Japan Soc. Applied Physics. Avocations: classical music, wood and metal working. Home: 939-1 Ishii, Ishii Tokushima 779-3233, Japan Office: Rsch Inst Chiba Inst Tech, 2-17-1 Tsudanuma, Narashino Chiba 275, Japan

ILARI, VIRGILIO, history educator; b. Rome, Nov. 2, 1948; s. Ottorino and Matilde (Sista) I.; m. Marisa Meddi, Apr. 2, 1973. LLD, U. rome, 1970. Asst. in Roman law U. Siena, Italy, 1972-73, U. Rome, 1973-79; assoc. prof. Roman law U. Macerata, Italy, 1979-90; assoc. prof. mil. history Cath. U., Milan, 1990—; rsch. dir. Mil. Ctr. Strategic Studies, Rome, 1989-93; cons. Italian Parliament, Rome, 1997. Author: Gli Italici Nelle Strutture Militari Romane, 1974, Le Forze Armate Tra Politica e Potere, 1979, Guerra e Diritto Nel Mondo Antico, 1980, L'Interpretazione Storica del Diritto di Guerra Romano, 1981, Storia del Servizio Militare in Italia, 5 vols., 1989-91, Storia Militare Della Prima Repubblica, 1943-93, 1994, Il Generale Col Monocolo, 1907-73, 1995, Inventarsi Una Patria, 1996; co-author: (with F. Botti) Il Pensiero Militare Italiano 1919-1949, 1985, (with Antonio Sema) Marte in Orbace, 1989, (with C. Paoletti and G. Boeri) Tra I Borboni e Gli Asburgo, 1701-33, 1996, La Corona Di Lombardia 1733-63, 1997, (with P. Crociani and C. Paoletti) La Guerra delle Alpi 1792-96, 2000; contbr. articles to Internat. Mil. and Def. Ency., 1991. Served with Italian Army, 1971-72. Fellow Interuniv. Seminar on Armed Forces and Soc. Home: Via Bosco Degli Arvali 32/c/6, 00148 Rome Italy Office: Cath U, 1 Largo A Gemelli, 20123 Milan Italy

ILAVSKY, MICHAL, physicist, researcher, educator; b. Liptovsky Peter, Slovakia, Nov. 21, 1940; s. Michal and Zuzana (Halkova) I.; m. Marie Mazurkova, Nov. 25, 1962; children: Jan, Michaela. MSc, Tech. U., Prague, 1962; PhD, Faculty of Math. Physics, Prague, 1966; DSc, Charles U., Prague, 1987. Sr. rsch. fellow Czechoslovak Acad. Scis., Prague, 1966—, chief scientist, 1987—; chief scientist Faculty of Math. and Physics Charles U., Prague, 1994—, prof., 1997—; rsch. fellow Inst. Organometallic Compounds, Acad. Scis., Moscow, 1964-65; sr. rsch. fellow in chemistry Syracuse (N.Y.) U., 1969-70; vis. prof. U. Ulm, 1991, Delft (The Netherlands) U. of Tech., 1992-93; lectr. at internat. and domestic confs. in the field of structure and properties of polymers, especially polymer networks. Mem. editl. bd. Polymer Gels and Net, 1993; contbr. more than 170 articles to profl. jours. including Macromolecules, Polymer, Polymer Bull., Jour. Polymer Sci., among others; patentee in field. Recipient prize Czechoslovac Acad. Scis., 1971, 81. Mem. Internat. Network Group, Czech Group of Rheology, Czech Soc. for Sci. and Tech. Avocations: tennis, chess, skiing. Home: Soukenicka 29, 11000 Prague 1, Czech Republic Office: Charles U Faculty Math and, Physics V Holesovickach 2, 1800 Prague 8, Czech Republic

ILES, ROGER DEAN, financial educator; b. Detroit, June 11, 1950; s. Virgil Llewellyn and Mary Elizabeth (Lynn) I.; m. Gail Ann Swatzell, Jan. 10, 1971; 1 child, Gwendolyn Christine. AA, Regents Coll., 1990; BS magna cum laude, Crichton Coll., 1992; MBA, U. Memphis, 1997. Enlisted USN, 1969, advanced through grades to chief electronics technician, 1969-89; ret., 1989; switchman Mich. Bell Telephone Co., Dearborn, 1968-69; acct., cashier, alumni advisor Crichton Coll., Memphis, 1989-99; adj. faculty Crichton Coll., Memphis, 1998—, U. Memphis, 1998—; chmn., mgr. Shade Tree Engring., Inc., Munford, Tenn., 1992—. Mem. Gideons Internat. (zone leader, pres. Tipton County South Camp). Republican. Baptist. Avocations: auto racing, target shooting. Fax: 901 837-0499. E-mail: wuzzo@bigriver.net. Home: 59 Jennifer Cv Brighton TN 38011-6056 Office: 2359 Beaver Rd Brighton TN 38011-6215

ILICETO, SABINO, cardiologist, researcher; b. Bari, Italy, May 11, 1953; s. Nicola and Emilia Ferrara Iliceto; m. Mariella Boccuzzi, 1982; 1 child, Silvia. MD, U. Medicine, Bari, Italy, 1977; cardiology specialist, Inst. of Cardiology, Bari, Italy, 1980. Fellow Inst. of Cardiology, Bari, 1977-80, asst. cardiologist, 1980-83, chief echo lab., 1983-84; prof. cardiology Inst. of Cardiology, Cagliari, Italy, 1994—; prof., chief of cardiology Dept. Cardiovascular Scis., Cagliari, 1997—; prof. cardiovascular semiology Sch. of Cardiology, Bari, 1987-94; dir. Sch. of Cardiology, Cagliari, 1999. Author: Ecocardiografia Clinica, 1989, Ultrasound in Coronary Artery Disease, 1991, Cardiac Ultrasound, 1993; contbr. over 500 articles to profl. publs. Rsch. fellowship Rotary Internat., 1979,. Fellow Am. Coll. Cardiology; mem. European Soc. of Cardiology, Italian Soc. of Cardiology. Avocations: golf, skiing, jogging. Fax: 39-070-62747. E-mail: iliccard@pacs.unica.it. Home: Via Beatillo 43, 70121 Bari Italy

ILIES, BEATRICE GEORGETA, English language educator; b. Seini, Romania, Nov. 25, 1952; d. Nicolae Radu and Gizela (Patovan) I. BA, Tchr. Tng. Coll., Baia Mare, Romania, 1976, U. Bucharest, Romania, 1980; postgrad., U. Lancaster, Eng., 1997—. Tchr. English Fine Arts H.S., Baia Mare, 1976-77; tchr. English lang. Sch. No. 17, Baia Mare, 1977-92, Lucaciu H.S., Baia Mare, 1992-98; sr. lectr. North U., Baia Mare, 1993—. Contbr. articles to profl. jours. Mem. European Soc. Study English, Romanian Soc. Anglo-Am. Studies. Avocations: painting, target shooting, religion, crafts. E-mail: gbilies@mail.alphanet.ro. Home: 6/43 Caragiale, 4800 Baia Mare Romania Office: North U, 76 Victoriei, 4800 Baia Mare Romania

ILIESCU, MIHAI, military officer; b. Mihaileni, Romania, Nov. 8, 1942; s. Dumitru and Elena Iliescu; m. Maria Popescu, May 31, 1973; 1 child, Cristina-Mihaela. Student, Superior Mil. Sch., Brasov, Romania, 1960-64; D Mil. Sci., Mil. Acad., Bucharest, Romania, 1976. Served to gen. Air Force and Air Def. Staff; tech. officer Anti-aircraft Missiles Unit, 1964-72; comdr. Anti-aircraft Arty. Battery, 1972-74, chief of staff, 1976-77; ops. officer territory Anti-aircraft Def. Command, 1977-79; gen. staff officer Air Force Anti-aircraft Def. Dept., 1979-85; chief of staff Anti-aircraft Missiles Brigade, 1985-89, bridage comdr., 1989-91; comdr. Territory Anti-aircraft Def. Command, 1991-93; 1st dep. Air Force and Air Def. Staff, 1993—. Coord.: History of Romanian Artillery and Missiles, Vol. 2, 1996-97; contbr. articles to profl. jours. Home: 1 Radu Voda St, Bucharest Romania Office: Air Force and Air Def Hdqrs, SOS Bucuresti-Plqiesti, Bucharest Romania

ILIOPOULOU, EVGHENIA, plastic surgeon; b. Tirgoviste, Romania, Sept. 20, 1952; d. Athanasios and Vasiliki (Vafiadou) I. Sr. house officer, gen. surgeon U. Alex-Polis, 1982-84; registrar plastic surgeon Kat. Hosp., Athens, 1984-87; registrar NTL clinic Gen. Hosp., Athens, registrar urology clinic; specialist in plastic surgery, 1988; jr. cons. dept. plastic surgery K.A.T. Gen. Hosp., Athens, 1989-97, sr. cons. dept. plastic surgery, 1997—. Author: Burn—What Next, 1997; contbr. articles to profl. jours. Mem. Am. Burn Assn., Med. Burn Assn., Internat. Soc. Burn Injuries, European Burn Assn., IPRAS. Avocation: writing articles for newspapers. Home: 3is Sept 119, Athens 11251, Greece

ILKER GELI EN, MEHMET, pharmaceutical company executive; b. Mar. 11, 1953. BS, Izmir Coll.; MD, Hacettepe U., Ankara, Turkey; postgrad. in anesthesiology, Wuppertal, Germany. Asst. in anesthesiology Wuppertal, Germany, 1978-84; med. dir. CIBA-Geigy, Turkey, 1985-90, Hoechst, Turkey, 1990-91; asst. med. dir. Pfizer, Turkey, 1991-92, product scientist, 1992-94; med. dir. Bristol-Myers Squibb, Turkey, 1995—; participant numerous nat. and internat. med. confs. Contbr. articles to sci. and profl. jours. Mem. Turkish Med. Assn., Turkish Hypertension and Atherosclerosis Assn., Turkish Infectious Diseases Assn., Turkish Clin. Pharmacology Assn., Drug Info. Assn., Bornova Anadolu Lisesi Edn. Found. (steering com.), Turkish pharmaceutical Mfrs. Assn. (audit com.), Turkish Pharmaceutical Technologists Assn., Turkish Pharmacology Assn. Avocations: reading, travel, history, med. anthropology, old photos of Turkish cities Istanbul, Ankara and Izmir. Office: Sayhan Sitesi F, Blok # 8, 80840 Istanbul Turkey

ILKIN, BAKI, diplomat. Turkish amb. to Copenhagen; spl. advisor to fgn. min. Govt. of Turkey; Turkish amb. to The Hague; Turkish amb. to USA Washington, 1998—. Fax: 202-659-0744. Office: Embassy of the Republic of Turkey 2525 Massachusetts Ave NW Washington DC 20008-2826

ILLANES, ALEJANDRO MORA, physician, educator, researcher; b. Concepcion, Chile, May 10, 1928; s. Alejandro Benavides Illanes and Emelina Delord Mora; m. Javiera Araya, July 17, 1954 (dec. Jan. 1982); children: Alejandra, Javier; m. Eliana Giglio, July 8, 1983. B Math., U. Chile, Santiago, 1947, B Biology, 1948, lic. in medicine, 1955, MD, 1956; postgrad., Tulane U., 1961. Instr. Pharmacology Inst. U. Chile, 1956-61, asst. prof. Pharmacology Inst., 1961-68, prof., head exptl. medicine dept., 1969-73; subrogating prof. Bern (Switzerland) U. Physiol. Inst., 1974-75; vis. prof. pharmacology dept. Man. CHF, Winnipeg, Can., 1975-76; prof. pharmacology, chief physiol. scis. dept. Orient U., Bolivar, Venezuela, 1976-96; fellow in pharmacology Harvard U. Sch. Medicine, 1962-63; mem. health com. Consejo Nacional de Investigacion, Santiago, 1970-73; founder, mem. Orient Ctr. Toxicology, Bolivar, 1978-81; med. rsch. cons. Ministry of Health, Govt. of Chile, 1970-73; pres., coord. med. scis. sect. Nat. Scis. Congress, 1972. Author, editor: Scorpion Venom Pharmacology, 1982; contbr. articles to profl. jours. Pres. Chilean Nat. Formulary Com., 1971-73; organizer, sec. Guayana sect. Venezuela Assn. for Advancement of Scis., Bolivar, 1984-90; organizer, editor bull. Sci., Tech. and Edn. of Guayana, Bolivar, 1984-90. Recipient Honor award Venezuelan Assn. for Advancement of Sci., 1994, U. Venezuela, 1996, Meritory Prof. award and diploma Nat. Univ. Sys., 1995, Meritory Rsch. award P.E.I.-UDO, Venezuela, 2000. Mem. Chilean Coll. Physicians, Internat. Soc. Heart Rsch., N.Y. Acad. Scis. Roman Catholic. Avocations: classic cars, writing, photography, collecting pens and watches.

ILLERIS, SVEN, geography educator; b. Copenhagen, June 8, 1936; s. Tage Philipson and Bodil Illeris; m. Gerd Jönsson, June 4, 1963; children: Jacob, Lotte, Naja. MSc in Geography, U. Copenhagen, 1962, DSc in Geography, 1988. Prin. Ministry of the Environment, Copenhagen, 1962-79; dir. rsch. Local Govts.' Rsch., Copenhagen, 1979-89; prof. Roskilde (Denmark) U., 1989—; chmn. Com. on Village Shops, Copenhagen, 1978-80; expert European Commn., Brussels, 1984-86, mem. monitoring and evaluation com. on European City Cooperation Sys./Ouverture, 1995-99; chmn. com. on regional policy Nordic Inst. Regional Rsch., Helsinki, Finland, 1986-89; councillor Réseau Svcs. et Espace, 1994—. Author: Services and Regions in Europe, 1989, Essays on Regional Development in Europe, 1994, The Service Economy: A Geographical Approach, 1996; editor Byplan, 1967-83. Home: Saettedammen 10, DK-3400 Hillerød Denmark

ILLÉS, LÁSZLÓ, literary historian, educator; b. Szijártóháza, Zala, Hungary, Aug. 12, 1928; s. Vendel and Mária (Soós) I.; m. Ilona Strauss, Sept. 10, 1954; children: Erika, Judit. Diploma of tchg. lang. and lit., Eotvos Lorand U., Budapest, Hungary, 1955; PhD, Hungarian Acad. Scis., Budapest, 1967. Iron turner Csepel Works Machine Factory, Budapest, 1951-58; dir. gen. Petőfi Lit. Mus., Budapest, 1970-75; rschr. Inst. Lit. Studies, Hungarian Acad. Scis., 1958-69, section head, 1976-93; asst. prof. habil. Miskolc (Hungary) U., 1994—. Author: Józanság és Szenvedély, 1966, A Megörzött Utópia, 1988; editor: Nagyvilág, 1961-93; co-editor: Hungarian Studies on György Lukács, 1993, Üzenet Thermophülébõl, 1999. Mem. Hungarian Writer's Assn., Hungarian P.E.N., Schiller-Gesellschaft, Internat. Comparative Lit. Assn. Avocations: swimming, walking, gardening.

ILLÉS-ALMÁR, ERZSÉBET ROZÁLIA, astronomer, researcher; b. Szekszárd, Tolna, Hungary, Nov. 15, 1936; d. Gyorgy and Gyorgyné (Márkvárt) Illés; m. Iván Almár, Aug. 3, 1959; children: Edit, Ákos. Diploma, L. Eötvös U., Budapest, Hungary, 1959; PhD, Hungarian Acad. Scis., Budapest, 1994. Asst. Konkoly Obs., Budapest, 1959-62, scientist, 1962-94, sr. scientist, 1994—. Mem. Internat. Astron. Union, Com. on Space Rsch. Office: Konkoly Obs, PO Box 67, H-1525 Budapest Hungary

ILLGEN-WILCKE, BRUNHILDE, biologist; b. Zagreb, Yugoslavia, Apr. 14, 1950; d. Werner and Nada (Sušić) I.; m. Wilko Wilcke, Mar. 26, 1990. Dipl.Biol., Univ., Tubingen, Germany, 1975, Dr. rer.nat., 1983; MD, Univ., Zagreb, 1985, D in Med. Sci., 1986. Clin. rschr. Merz & Co., Frankfurt, Germany, 1986; head microbiology, lab. animal breeding Ciba, Stein, Switzerland, 1986-96, head lab. animal breeding, 1995-96; head microbiology, lab animal svcs. Novartis, Basle, Switzerland, 1997-2000; head microbiol. svcs. MicroBioS, Münchenstein, Switzerland, 2000—. Mem. German Assn. Lab. Animal Sci., Am. Assn. Lab. Animal Sci., Swiss Assn. Lab. Animal Sci., Com. Hygiene, Swiss Assn. Tropical Medicine and Parasitology. Office: MicroBios GmbH, 4142 Münchenstein Switzerland

ILLI, ESKO ANTERO, military career officer; b. Mäntsälä, Uusimaa, Finland, Oct. 18, 1945; s. Toivo Johannes and Taimi Regina (Anttila) I.; m. Pirkko Marketta Laurila, Oct. 13, 1973; children: Markku Antero, Risto Johannes. Naval officer, Finnish Naval Acad., Helsinki, 1968; gen. staff officer, Finnish War Coll., Helsinki, 1977; M in Polit. Sci., Helsinki U., 1981; grad., U.S. Naval War Coll., 1991. Commdg. officer Minelayer Pohjanmaa, Helsinki, 1984-86; cos Helsinki Naval Base, Upinniemi, Finland, 1986-87; comdr. Missile Squadron, Turku, Finland, 1987-90; dir. Nat. Def. Courses, Helsinki, 1991-94; pres. Nat. Def. Coll., Helsinki, 1994-96; cinc Finnish Navy, Helsinki, 1997—; mil. mem. Supreme Ct., Helsinki, 1996—; bd. dirs. Def. Forces Found., Helsinki, 1997—. Vice admiral Finnish Navy, 1964—. Recipient UN medal UN Truce Supervision Orgn., Jerusalem, 1975; named Comdr. 1st Class, Order of the Lion of Finland, 1995, Royal Swedish Order of the North Star, 1996. Office: Finnish Naval HQ, Pohjoiskaari 36, 00201 Helsinki Finland

ILLMAN, SÖREN ARNOLD, mathematician, educator; b. Helsinki, Finland, May 12, 1943; s. Arne and Hebe Dorotea (Nordström) I.; m. Kerstin Gunhild Anna Johansson, Aug. 25, 1968; children: Erik Jerker, Johanna Kristel. MS, U. Helsinki, 1966; PhD, Princeton U., 1972. Asst. U. Helsinki, 1965-66, prof., 1975—; rsch. asst. Acad. of Finland, 1971-72, jr. rsch. fellow, 1972-75; mem. Inst. for Advanced Study, Princeton, N.J., 1974-75; vis. rsch. fellow Inst. des Hautes Études Scientifiques, Bures-sur-Yvette, France, 1977, Math. Inst. Oxford U., Eng., 1978, Forschungs Inst. für Matematik, ETH, Zürich, Switzerland, 1982, 85, Dept. Math. Yale U., New Haven, 1996; vis. scholar U. Mich., Ann Arbor, 1983; vis. prof. Dept. Math., Purdue U., West Lafayette, Ind., 1983; vis. prof. Rsch. Inst. Math. Scis., Kyoto (Japan) U., 1986-87; vis. prof. Max-Planck-Inst. für Math., Bonn, Fed. Republic of Germany, 1989, 92; vis. prof. Dept. Math., Princeton (N.J.) U., 1991-92; sr. mem. Math. Scis. Rsch. Inst., Berkeley, Calif., 1992; vis. prof. Forschungs Institut für Mathematik, ETH, Zürich, 1993, Math. Inst. U. Oxford, Eng., 1995, 96; organizer, co-chmn. Group Actions on Manifolds, Mathematisches Forschungsinstitut Oberwolfach, Germany, 1998; co-organizer Symposium on Transformation Groups, Toyohasi City, Japan, 1999; lectr. in field. Contbr. articles to math. jours. Recipient Grand award Oscar Öflund Found., 1993, Magnus Ehrnrooth Found. award, 1997; decorated Knight 1st class Order of White Rose of Finland, 1994; Fulbright grantee, 1967-68, Acad. of Finland grantee, 1982, 86, 91-92, 95-96, 99-2000. Mem. Finnish Soc. Scis. and Letters (chmn. math.-phys. sect. 1988-91), Finnish Math. Soc. (sec. 1966, vice chmn. 1991—), Am. Math. Soc., Finnish Acad. Sci. and Letters. Avocations: music, travel, movies. Home: Johannesbrinken 1B 46-47, 00120 Helsinki 1, Finland Office: U Helsinki Dept Math, PO Box 4 Yliopistonkatu 5, FIN-00014 Helsinki Finland

ILLMANN, MARGARET LOUISE, ballet dancer; b. Adelaide, Australia, Dec. 9, 1965; arrived in Canada, 1989; d. Kevin Murray and Jennifer Coralie (Manser) I. Student, Annesley Coll., Adelaide, 1982, Australian Ballet Sch., Melbourne, 1983-84. Soloist Australian Ballet Co., Melbourne, 1985-89; corps de ballet Nat. Ballet of Canada, Toronto, 1989-90, prin. dancer, 1991-96; prin. Stuttgart Ballet, 1996-98; freelance artist, 1998-99; guest prin. dancer Deutsche Opera, Berlin, Germany, 1999—; guest dancer Leningrad Fundraiser at Kirov, 1991, Rome Opera Ballet, 1992, 96, 97, 98, Hamburg Ballet, 1993, 95, 96, Eng. Nat., 1994, 99, N.Y.C. Ballet, 1994, 95, Dresden Staatsoper, 1995, 98, UNICEF Gala Rome, 1995, Teatro San Carlo Naples, 1996, 98, 99, La Scala Spain Tour, 1998, La Scala Milan, 1999, Munich Bayerische Opera Ballet, 1998, 99. Prin. ballet roles include Eurydice Glen Tetley's Orpheus, 1988, Macmillan's Gloria, 1989, Bayadere, 1989, Snow Queen/Sugar Plum in Nutcracker, 1990, Kitri in Don Quixote, 1990, Olga in Onegin, 1991, Titania in Ashton's Midsummer Nights Dream, 1998, Spoerlis, 1999, Juliet in Cranko, Neumeier, Amodio and Vamos' Romeo & Juliet, Aurora in Sleeping Beauty, 1991, Odette/Odile in Swan Lake, 1991, Giselle in Giselle, 1992, Red Couple in Kylian's Forgotten Land, 1992, Who Cares?, 1994, Swanhilda in Coppelia, 1994, The 4 Seasons, 1995, Tchaikovsky P.D.D. '95, Afternoon of a Faun, 1998, Cinderella in Ben Stevenson's 1995, Cannito's 1997, Catherine et Clefves in Prejlokajs Le Parc, 2000, (Broadway) The Red Shoes, 1993 (The Astaire award 1993, The World Theater award 1993, Drama Desk nomination); appeared in 2 Bravo Spls., Can. TV Series 'Zoya' Daniel Steele; Children's Film Rossini's Ghost. Recipient Louise Pommery Ballet grant, Paris Opera Sch., 1987, South Australian Young Achiever Arts award South Australia, 1990, Creations by William Forsythe, Lar Lubovitch, Glen Tetley, John Neumeier Luciano Cannito, Ricardo Nunez and Mauro Bigonzetti, Berliner Zeitung Critics award, 2000. Avocations: reading, travelling, further education. Fax: 347 87 274. Office: c/o Deutsche Oper Ballet, Richard-Wagner-Str 10, D-10585 Berlin Germany

ILLMENSEE, KARL OSKAR, geneticist, clinician; b. Lindau, Bodensee, Germany, July 29, 1939; Naturalized Austrian citizen.; s. Karl Illmensee and Erika Haag. PhD, U. Munich, Germany, 1971. Prof. U. Geneva, 1977-87, U. Salzburg, Austria, 1988-94, U. Innsbruck, Austria, 1994—; co-dir. Vitategbiotech. GmbH, 1999—; mem. sci. bd. Internat. Soc. Devel. Biology, Basel, Switzerland, 1981, Ludwig Inst., Brussels, 1981-83, Hofmann-LaRoche Inst., Basel, 1982-83, Yamaha Conf., Kyoto, Japan, 1984; session chmn. Human devel. Internat. Conf., Wien, Austria, 1986; co-organizer Cologne Internat. Conf., 1983; organizer internat. workshop, Arolla, Switzerland, 1981. Co-editor: Genetic Manipulation, 1984; mem. editl. bd. MGG Jour. 1980—; patentee for 1st mammalian cloning, 1981. Recipient Otto Mangold award, Freiburg, Germany, 1981, Marcel Benoist award, Bern, Switzerland, 1982, Johannes Pfaffenstiel medal, Kiel, Germany, 1982, Ioannes Paulus II medal, Rome, Vatican, 1982. Mem. European Molecular Biology Orgn., European Soc. for Human Reprodn., Med. Soc. WHO (hon.). Avocations: skiing, wind surfing, tennis, painting. Office: Innsbruck U, Frauenklinik Anichstr, A-6020 Innsbruck Austria

ILLNEROVA, HELENA, physiologist, science administrator; b. Prague, Czechoslovakia, Dec. 28, 1937; d. Karel and Libuse (Baxova) Lagus; m. Michal Illner, Oct. 4, 1963; children: Jakub, Srbova Libuse. RNDr, Charles U., Prague, 1967; PhD, Czechoslovak Acad. Sci., Prague, 1966, DSc, 1990. Rsch. assoc. Inst. Physiology/Czechoslovak Acad. Sci., 1966-86, head dept., 1986-93, vice dir., 1990-93; head dept. physiology, v.p. Acad. Sci. Czech Republic, Prague, 1993-99. Author: Circadian Rhythms in the Mammalian Pineal Gland, 1986; contbr. chpt. to book, articles to profl. jours. Leader, Children Tourist Club, Prague, 1975-85. Recipient award of Otakar Jandera, Czechoslovak Union for Phys. Edn. and Sports. Mem. Soc. Rsch. Biol. Rhythms (adv. bd. 1990), European Pineal Soc. (coun. 1990-99), Czech. Soc. Neurosci. (coun. 1994—), Learned Soc. of the Czech Republic. Avocations: grandmothering, literature, tourism, skiing. Home: Bronzova 2021, 155 00 Prague Czech Republic Office: Inst Physiology/Acad Sci, Videnska 1083, 142 20 Prague Czech Republic

ILLUM, LISBETH, pharmaceutical scientist, educator; b. Aalborg, Denmark, Mar. 30, 1947; d. Hans Erik and Grethe Elisabeth (Due Pedersen) I.; m. Gunnar Karup, Oct. 1967 (div. 1977); 1 child, Morten; m. Stanley Stewart Davis, Nov. 24, 1984; 1 child, Daniel. MPharm, Royal Danish Sch. Pharmacy, 1972, PhD, 1978, DSc, 1987. Lectr. Royal Danish Sch. Pharmacy, 1972-75, sr. lectr., 1978-90; spl. prof. Nottingham (Eng.) U., 1990—; mng. dir. Danbiosyst U.K. Ltd., 1990-99; chief scientific advisor West Pharm. Svcs., Nottingham, Eng., 1999—. Editor: Microspheres and Drug Therapy, 1984, Polymers in Controlled Drug Delivery, 1987, Delivery Systems for Peptide Drugs, 1987, Pharmaceutical Applications of Cell and Tissue Culture to Drug Transport; contbr. over 270 articles to profl.jours.; mem. sci. bd. numerous pharm. jours.; patentee in field. Recipient The Amersham award, 1987, Marie Longgaard's award Copenhagen U., 1988, Brite/Euram awards European Union, 1989, 91, 96. Fellow Am. Assn. Pharm. Scientists; mem. Controlled Release Soc. Avocations: tennis, skiing,

water sports, films, concerts. Office: West Pharm Svcs, Nottingham Sci and Tech Pk, Nottingham NG7 2TN, England

ILOGU, NOEL OBIAJULU, physician; b. Ibadan, Oyo, Nigeria, Dec. 15, 1961; came to U.S., 1994; s. Edmund Christopher and Elizabeth Chineze (Obiago) I.; m. Sandra Nneka Ike, July 15, 1995; children: Chudi, Chisom. MD, U. Benin, Nigeria, 1985. Diplomate Am. Bd. Internal Medicine. Sr. house officer NHS Hosps., U.K., 1988-92; career registrar Burnley (Eng.) Gen. Hosp., 1992-94; resident St. Peter's Med. Ctr., New Brunswick, N.J., 1994-97; pvt. practice, Somerset, N.J., 1997—; cons. on tobacco issues in Africa, Lagos, Nigeria, 1997—. Contbr. articles to profl. jours. Mem. AMA, ACP, APHA, Am. Soc. Addiction Medicine, Royal Coll. Physicians (Edinburgh), NAACP. Avocations: squash, swimming, golf, listening to jazz. Home: 35 Stratford Dr Somerset NJ 08873-4825 Office: 680 Easton Ave Ste 3 Somerset NJ 08873-1865

ILOZUMBA, KRIS CHINYERE, ceramics company executive; b. Port Harcourt, Nigeria, July 16, 1961; s. Gebriel Irunna and Patrician Ngboye (Okoli) I.; m. Celestina Adaku Onwuazombe, Sept. 8, 1990; children: Lilian, Chineze, Chisom. Diploma bus. mgmt., Trans-World Tutorial Coll., Jersey, Britain, 1981. Gen. mgr. I. Franco Comml. Stores, Ebute Metta, Lagos, Nigeria, 1980-83; exec. dir. Krisilo Motors & Co., Ebute Metta, 1984—; chmn., CEO Krisilo Internat., Ltd., 1995—; chmn. CEO Krisilo Ceramics Industries Ltd., Ebute Metta, 1993—; cons. Daxion Enterprises Ltd., Festac Town, Lagos, 1993—. Dep. sec. Obeledu Progressive Union, Lagos, 1990-94. Avocations: soccer, lawn tennis, table tennis, badminton & handball. Home: 35 Ishaga Rd Surulere, Lagos Nigeria Office: Krisilo Motors & Co, 117 Herbert Macaulay St, Ebute Metta Lagos Lagos, Nigeria

ILSON, BERNARD, public relations executive; b. N.Y.C.; s. Abraham and Goldie Itzkowitz; m. Carol Ruth Geller; children: David, James. BA, Bklyn. Coll.; MA, Columbia U.; PhD, NYU, 1998. Writer NBC TV, N.Y.C., 1955-57; acct. exec. David Alber Assocs., N.Y.C., 1957-58; v.p. Rogers, Cowan and Brenner, N.Y.C., 1958-63; pres. Bernie Ilson, Inc., N.Y.C., 1963—; founder Hall of Fame of Am. Humor; past/present clients include The Ed Sullivan Show, The Beatles at Shea Stadium, All in the Family, The Monkeys, The Patridge Family, Grammy Awards, Entertainer of Yr. Awards, Motown Records, Tony Bennett, Liberty Mut. Ins. Co., Control Data Corp., Am. Soc. for Hypertension, Missoula Children's Theater, Grand Ole Opry, Hee Haw, The Negotiation Inst., Liberty Mut. Legends of Golf, NBC TV Network, Simon and Schuster, The City of Mobile Tricentennial. Watercolor artist: Bklyn. Mus. Biennial Watercolor Show, 1954; one-man shows: Keulik Gallery, N.Y.C., Nemisis Galley, N.Y.C.; pub., founder Ilson's Inside Information, 1991—. Mem. Writers Guild Am., Acad. TV Arts and Scis., Country Music Assn., Mobile C. of C., Kappa Delta Pi. Club: Explorers. Avocations: painting, fishing. Office: 65 W 55th St New York NY 10019-4913

ILVES, TOOMAS HENDRIK, diplomat; b. Stockholm, Dec. 26, 1953; came to U.S., 1993; s. Endel and Irene Ilves; m. Merry Bullock, Dec. 31, 1980; children: Luukas Kristjan, Juulia. BA, Columbia U., 1976; MA, U. Pa., 1978. Rsch. asst. Dept. Psychology Columbia U., N.Y.C., 1974-76, 79; English tchr., asst. to the dir. Ctr. Open edn., Englewood, N.J., 1979-81; arts adminstr., dir. Vancouver (Can.) Lit. Ctr., Washington, 1981-82; lectr. Estonian Lit. Linguistics Simon Fraser U., Vancouver, 1983-84; analyst Radio Free Europe, Munich, 1984-88, dir. Estonian Svc., 1988-93; amb. Estonia, Washington, 1993—; apptd. Min. Fgn. Affairs, Estonia, 1996—. Editor, pub. Porp!, 1988; translator numerous collections of Estonian poetry; contbr. more than 80 articles to profl. publs. Mem. Estonian P.E.N. Lutheran. Office: Min Fgn Affairs, Rävala 9, EE0100 Tallinn Estonia*

ILVESMAKI, MIKA JUHANI, research scientist, consultant; b. Helsinki, Finland, Jan. 31, 1969; s. Pekka Jussi Ilvesmaki and Eva Orvokki Kristiina Mikkolanniemi. MSc, Helsinki U. Tech., Espoo, Finland, 1996. Sr. rsch. scientist Helsinki U. Tech., Espoo, 1996—; cons. Teleware Oy, Helsinki. Sgt. Finnish Army, 1989-90. Nokia scholar Nokia Found., 1999. Mem. IEEE (student, Student Travel grantee 1998), Finnish Karate Fedn. (Dan). Avocation: Japanese martial arts. Office: Helsinki U Tech, Otakaari 5 A, 02015 Espoo Finland

ILYINA, VERA, Olympic athlete; b. Moscow, Feb. 20, 1974; came to U.S., 1996; Student, U. Tex. Winner Silver medal springboard European Championships, 1991, 93, 97; winner springboard Goodwill Games St. Petersburg, 1994; winner Silver medal springboard World Championships, 1994, winner Gold medal European Championships, 1995; winner Gold medal springboard Sydney, 2000. Named NCAA Nat. Women's Diver of Yr., 1997. Office: All-Russia Athletic Fedn, Luzhnetskaya Nab 8, Moscow 119871, Russia*

ILYUSHIN, BORIS BORISOVICH, physicist, researcher; b. Pavlodar, Kazakhstan, Dec. 9, 1963; arrived in Russia, 1982; s. Boris Andreevich and Balentina Nikolaevna (Lyulyukina) I.; m. Elena Maratovna Shastova, Aug. 6, 1984 (div. Apr. 1990); m. Olga Leonidovna Shestakova, Dec. 14, 1995; 1 child, Boris. PhD, Inst. Theoretical & Applied Mechanics, Russia, 1994. Plant worker Pavlodar, 1980-82; rsch. scientist Inst. Theoretical and Applied Mechanics, Russian Acad. Scis., Novosibirsk, Russia, 1989—. Contbr. articles to profl. jours. Sgt. USSR Air Force, 1985-87. Fax: 7-3832-343480. E-mail: ilyush@itp.nsc.ru. Office: Inst Thermophysics, 1 Acad Lavrentyev Ave, 630090 Novosibirsk Russia

ILYUSHIN, YAROSLAW ALEXANDROVICH, physicist, researcher, consultant; b. Moscow, Russia, Aug. 26, 1970; s. Alexander Sergeevich and Vera Alexandrovna (Volzhenskaya) I.; m. Anna Sergeevna Vinogradova. MSc, Moscow State U., 1993, PhD, 1996. Rsch. assoc. Moscow State U., 1996-98, asst. prof., 1998—; cons. Method Co., Russia, 1998-00. Contbr. articles to profl. jours. including Crystallography Reports, Acoustical Physics, and Doklady Acad. Scis. Avocation: ham radio. Office: Moscow State U, Phys Fac, 119899 Moscow Russia

IM, KAYE SOON, humanities educator; b. Seoul, Korea, Sept. 13, 1944; d. Bong Jae and Soon (Rye) I.; m. Paek Je Cho, Dec. 21, 1968; children: Sang Joon, Nam Joon, Dong Joon. BA, Ewha Womans U., Seoul, 1967, MA, 1967; MA, U. Ill., 1975, PhD, 1981. Assoc. prof. Acad. Korean Studies, Seoul, 1981-84, dir. rsch. materials dept., 1982-84; chmn. history dept. Hanyang U., Seoul, 1987-89, 95-97, prof., 1984—; vis. prof. Beijing U., 1991-92; dir. Asia Pacific Inst., Seoul, 1997—. Author: The Light of Love: Everyday Life of Underprivileged Blind People, 1987, The Rise and Decline of the Eight Garrisons in the Qing Period, 1993, Korean's One-sided Love of China, 1994, The China's Magic Stone, Hong Kong, 1997. Arbitrator the Family Ct., Seoul, 1995—; advisor Citizen's Alliance for Consumer Protection of Korea, 1996—. Mem. Korean History Assn., Korean Soc. 18th Century Studies (bd. govs. 1997—), Soc. Asian History Studies. Avocations: swimming, oriental painting. Office: Hanvang U History Dept, 17 Haengdangdong Sengdongku, Seoul 133-070, Korea

IMADA, MASANORI, information processing educator; b. Tokyo, Aug. 23, 1935; s. Kinsuke and Mitsu (Ogura) I.; m. Miyoko Nishimura, Nov. 5, 1962; children: Masahiro, Yuki, Joe. B in Electro-Comm. Engring., U. Electro-Comm., Tokyo, 1960. From mgr. quality assurance to mgr. new products IBM Japan, Yasu, 1972-76; sr. advisory product mgr. IBM Japan, Tokyo, 1977-82, from mgr. product evaluation to mgr. sys. devel., 1982-91; info. processing educator Tokyo Tech. Coll., 1991—. Mem. IEEE, N.Y. Acad. Scis., Info. Processing Soc. Avocations: sculpting, painting with oils. Home: 4-6 Mejirodai, 3 Chome, Hachioji, Tokyo 1930833, Japan Office: Tokyo Tech Coll, 1-15-5 Higashi Kunitachi, Tokyo 186 0002, Japan

IMADE, GODWIN EREMWAN, medical researcher; b. Usen, Nigeria, Oct. 1; s. Imade Philip and Mure Agatha (Uwadiae) Obairogboi; m. Esther Tayo Olawuyi; children: Andrew, Victor, Philip. Diploma in med. lab. sci., Carmarthen Tech., Wales, 1979; diploma in bacteriology, Inst. Med. Lab. Tech., Lagos, Nigeria, 1982, diploma in chem. pathology, 1988; MSc in Endocrinology, U. Jos, Nigeria, 1992; grad. diploma in reproductive sci., Monash U., Melbourne, Australia, 1996. Jr. med. lab. sci. officer trainee Singleton HOsp., Swansea, Wales, 1978-79; med. lab. scientist trainee Univ. Coll. Hosp., Ibadan, Nigeria, 1981-82; med. lab. scientist Bapt. Hosp., Ogbomoso, Nigeria, 1982-83; med. lab. scientist U. Jos, 1985-91, rsch. fellow, 1991—; rsch. trainee Monash U., Melbourne, 1995-97. Mid. Manpower Tng. grantee Nigerian Govt./Brit. Coun., 1977-79, Radioimmunoassay/Non Isotopic Tng. Tech. grantee WHO, Nairobi, Kenya, 1987, rsch. tng. grantee, Australia, 1995-97. Fellow Inst. Med. Lab. Tech. Nigeria; mem. Nigerian Venereal Disease Assn., Am. Fertility Soc. Baptist. Avocations: swimming, soccer, table tennis.E-mail: imadeg@unijos.edu.ng. Office: U Jos Faculty Med Scis, Dept Ob-gyn, PMB 2084 Jos Plateau State, Nigeria

IMADO, FUMIAKI, mechanical, systems engineering educator; b. Komagome, Tokyo, Mar. 1, 1945; s. Bunzo Ishiwara and Yoshi Imado; m. Mikiko Wakabayashi, Oct. 11, 1976; children: Eisuke, Tomoko, Kenji. BS, U. Tokyo, 1968, PhD, 1975. Registered profl. engr. Engr. Ctrl. Rsch. Lab. Mitsubishi Electric Co., Amagasaki, Hyogo, 1973-77, sr. engr., 1977-84, chief engr., 1984-94, chief engr., mgr., 1991-94; prof. dept. mech. systems engring. Shinsu U., Nagano, Japan, 1994—; guest lectr. Chun Shan Inst. Sci. and Tech., Lung-Tan, Taiwan, 1990-93, 97, Ryukoku U., Otsu, Japan, 1991-94, Nagano Indsl. Engring. U., 1994—; rschr. Nat. Aerospace Lab., Mitaka, Tokyo, 1993—. Contbr. articles to Jour. GN & C, Jour. Aircraft, Computers Math. with Appl. Mem. AIAA (sr.), Japan Soc. Aeronautics and Astronautics (bd. dirs. 1990-92, jour. editor 1983—, chief flight dynamics dept. 1995—), Japan Soc. Biomechanism, Soc. for Instrument and Control Engrs. Achievements include patent for artficial satellite, missile guidance and control field; rsch. in finding optimal fighter maneuvers against PNG missiles; design of missile guidance systems; development of softwares in the fields, satellites, bombs. Home: 5-14-1-101 Wakasato, Nagano 380-0922, Japan

IMADO, KEIJI, tribologist, researcher; b. Usa-shi, Oita, Japan, Dec. 9, 1953; parents Takaji and Harue Imado; m. Harumi Imado, Mar. 14, 1982. Doctor, Kyushu U., Fukuoka, Japan, 1996. Cert. engr. Engr. Mazda Motor Co., Hiroshima, Japan, 1974-76; lectr. Oita U., 1977—. Contbr. articles to sci. jours.; inventor in field. Mem. Japan Soc. Mech. Engrs., Japanese Soc. Tribologists, Japan Soc. Precision Engring., Japan Soc. Clin. Biomechanics. Avocations: diving, trekking. Fax: +81-97-554-7507. E-mail: imado@cc.oita-u.ac.jp. Office: Oita U, 700 Dannoharu, Oita Oita-shi 870-1192, Japan

IMAI, TAKASHI, steel manufacturing executive; b. Kamakura, Japan, 1929. Student, U. Tokyo, 1952. Joined Fuji Iron and Steel, 1952, various positions, 1952-63, mgr. raw materials, 1963-70; dep. gen. mgr. fuel and ferrous metals Nippon Steel (formed by merger of Fuji Iron and Steel and Yawata Steel), Tokyo, 1970-73, gen. mgr. iron ore, 1973-83, mng. dir., 1983-89, exec. v.p., 1989-92, pres., 1992—; chmn., rep. dir. Tokyo. Avocation: go. Office: Nippon Steel Corp, 6-3 Ohtemachi 2-chome, Chiyoda-ku Tokyo 100-8071, Japan*

IMAIZUMI, NOBU THEODORE, educator; b. Nishinomiya, Japan, Dec. 21, 1941; s. Isamu and Asa (Nagai) I.; m. Carol Marie Jones, Dec. 28, 1969; children: Ryan Yukio, Rebecca Sayuri. BA, Kwansei Gakuin U., Nishinomiya, Japan, 1965; MTh, So. Meth. U., 1969. Pastor Christ United Meth. Ch., Santa Maria, Calif., 1969-72; instr. Allan Hancock Coll., Santa Maria, Calif., 1969-72; pastor Visalia (Calif.) United Meth. Ch., 1972-74; instr. Coll. Sequdias, Visalia, 1972-73; pastor Pine United Meth. Ch., San Francisco, 1974-78; prof. Kwansei Gakuin U., Nishinomiya, Japan, 1995—. Recipient Mental Health award State of Calif., Visalia, 1973. Democrat. Methodist. Avocations: tennis, travel. Home: 44-38 Nishi 2-chome, Hyogo 661-0034, Japan Office: Kwansei Gakuin U, 2-1 Gakuen Sanda, Hyogo 669-1337, Japan

IMAKITA, ATSUKO, English language educator; b. Sapporo, Hokkaido, Japan, June 23, 1972; parents Isamu and Kumiko Imakita. B of Commerce, Otaru U. Commerce, 1994. Cert. in edn. Tchr. h.s. Hokkaido Ednl. Bd. Japan, Sapporo, 1994—; English tchr. Chitose Hokuyo H.S., 1994-99, Setana Comml. H.S., Setana/Hokkaido, 1999—. Transl. Chitose (Japan) Vol. Translator Orgn., 1998-99. Fulbright grantee, 1998. Avocations: traveling, reading. Fax: 81 1378 7 3243. E-mail: atz99@hotmail.com/. Office: Setana Comml H S, 651 Honcho, Setana Hokkaido 049-4805, Japan

IMAM, AHMAD FAHMY, lawyer; b. Cairo, June 1, 1937; came to Belgium, 1968; s. Fahmy Imam and Saida (Mohamed) Ismail; m. Sabine Imam-Puddig, Dec. 16, 1972; children: Marc Karim, Patrick Amir. Lic. in Law, Cairo U., 1957, higher diploma in polit. economy, 1959, higher diploma in Pub. Law, 1961; Lic. in Econ., U. Brussels, 1969; PhD in Internat. Tax Laws, 1974. Prof. comml. law High Inst. Commerce, Mansoura, Egypt, 1961-65; judge State Coun. Cairo, 1965-68; lectr. tax law Faculty Law, Mansoura, Egypt, 1974-75; banker European Arab Bank, Brussels, 1975-85; expert UN Devel. Programme, IMF, Washington, 1986—, UNOID, Vienna, 1986—; pres., lawyer Arab African Bur. Legal Cons., Brussels, 1987—; fellow, arbitrator Chartered Inst. Arbitrators, London, 1991; arbitrator Am. Arbitration Asns., N.Y.C., 1987, Euro-Arab System of Arbitration, Paris, 1985. Author: Financial Markets in Arab Countries, 1981, Arab Financial Aid Through Arab Financial Markets, 1984, La Charte des Investissement De Les Pays en Voie de Developpement, 1998. Mem. Assn. Euro-Arab, Jurist, Assn. Law and Econs. Egypt. Socialist. Moslem. Avocations: table tennis, swimming, chess. Office: Arab African Bur Legal Cons, Armendylaan 34, 1933 Brussels Belgium

IMAM, M. ASHRAF, materials scientist, educator; b. Patna, Bihar, India, Sept. 7, 1945; came to U.S. 1970; s. Naimuddin Ahmad and Zakia (Begum) Ahmad; m. Shamim Akhtar, June 22, 1979; children: Nabil S., Rahil U., Mariam S. BS, Ranchi U., India, 1966; MS, Carnegie-Mellon U., 1972; DSc, George Washington U., 1976. Rsch. assoc. George Washington U., Washington, 1976-78, rsch. scientist, 1978-81, adj. prof., 1981 ; guest scientist Nat. Inst. Standard, Gaithersburg, Md., 1974 ; sr. rsch. scientist Geo-Centers Inc., Newton, Mass., 1981-84; metallurgist Naval Rsch. Lab., Washington, 1984 . Contbr. articles to profl. jours.; editor: Structure and Deformation of Boundaries, 1986, Advances in Low-Carbon High Strength Ferrous Alloys, 1993, Advanced Materials and Processing, 1998. MRL fellow Carnegie Mellon U., 1971-72, CSIR fellow, 1966-68, others. Fellow Am. Soc. of Metals Internat.; mem. ASM, The Minerals, Metals, Materials Soc. (titanium com. 1980—, phys. metallurgy com. 1980 , mech. metallurgy com. 1980—), Sigma Xi. Achievements include 8 patents. Home: 1159 Mill Garden Ct Great Falls VA 22066-1845 Office: Naval Rsch Lab Code 6320 4555 Overlook Ave SW Washington DC 20375-0001

IMAM, MUHAMMAD HASAN, engineer educator; b. Gaya, Bihar, India, July 12, 1946; s. Muhammad Alley and Hasbunnisa Imam; m. Surriya Jabeen Jilani, Dec. 11, 1976; children: Muhammad Ahmad, Fatimah, Muhammad Arshad, Muhammad Muddassir, Muzzammil. B in Engring., U. Karachi, Pakistan, 1968; MS, U. So. Calif., 1973, PhD, 1977. Registered profl. engr., Ont., Can. Rsch. assoc. U. So. Calif., L.A., 1977-79; staff rsch. engr. Gen. Motors Rsch. Labs., Warren, Mich., 1979-83; prof. N.E.D. U. Engring. and Tech., Karachi, 1983-84, Umm Al-Quar U., Makkah, Saudi Arabia, 1984—; cons. Engring. Optimization Software, Deltona, Fla., 1995-97; presenter in field. Contbr. articles to company newsletters and profl. jours. Mem. Pakistan Engring. Coun. (life mem.), Internat. Soc. Structural and Multi-disciplinary Optimization. Avocations: computer programming, genetic algorithms, design optimization. Home: PO Box 885, Makkah Saudi Arabia

IMAMOĞLU, EMINE OLCAY, social psychologist, educator; b. Izmir, Aegean, Turkey, Dec. 1, 1944; d. Ömer and Mazlume Cahide (Uğur) Kaya; m. Vacit Imamoğlu, Sept. 6, 1968; children: Cağri, Selen. BS, Middle East Tech. U., Ankara, Turkey, 1968; MA, U. Iowa, 1969; PhD, U. Strathclyde, Glasgow, 1974. Instr. Hacettepe U., Ankara, 1969-72, asst. prof., 1975-79, assoc. prof., 1979-81; assoc. prof. Middle East Tech. U., Ankara, 1981-88, prof. dept. psychology, 1988—, prof. gender and women's studies, 1994—, chmn. dept. psychology, 1982-84, 88-97; vis. acad. scholar UCLA, 1984-85; vis. rschr. Environ. Psychol. Unit, Lund, Sweden, 1988. Author: Related to Kindness, 1979, People's Homes and Environments, 1996; contbr. articles to profl. jours.; corr. editor Internat. Soc. for Study of Behavioral Devel. Jour., 1978-83, Newsletter, 1982-94; acad. advisor Turkish Jour. Psychology, 3P-Jour. Psychiatry, Psychology and Psychopharmacology. Asst. chair Nursery Sch. Exec. Bd., Hacettepe U., 1978-81; organizing mem. 2d Nat. Family Conv., Ankara, 1994; spkr. Turkish Radio and TV, Ankara. Am. Field Svc. scholarship, 1961-62, Fulbright scholar, 1968-69, 84-85; NATO Sci. Commn. grantee, 1978, 79. Mem. Turkish Assn. Psychologists, Turkish Intelligence Found. (one of originating mems.), Turkish Assn. Social Scis. Avocations: collecting Roman and historical pottery and glass from Anatolia, Ottoman silver jewelry, copper, Turkish rugs and kilims. Home: 105 Sokak No 2, Binsesin Sitesi, 06531 Umitkoy Turkey Office: Middle East Tech Univ, Dept Psychology, 06531 Ankara Turkey

IMAMURA, MASASHI, chemist, educator, researcher; b. Nanao, Ishikawa, Japan, Feb. 8, 1924; s. Shigeyuki and Misao (Sugie) I.; m. Mieko Noda, Dec. 19, 1947; 1 child, Machiko. BS, Osaka (Japan) U., 1946; DSc, Tohoku U., Sendai, Japan, 1958. Asst. prof. Osaka City U., 1949-58, assoc. prof., 1958-60; prin. scientist Inst. Phys. and Chem. Rsch., Wako, Saitama, Japan, 1960-84; prof. Tokyo U. Info. Scis., Chiba, Japan, 1988-94; prof. emeritus Inst. Phys. and Chem. Rsch., Wako, 1984—; rsch. assoc. Boston U., 1960-62; vis. prof. Inst. Atomic Energy, Sao Paulo, Brazil, 1973; com. mem. Sci. Coun. Japan, Tokyo, 1981-91; councilor Internat. Assn. Radiation Rsch., Amsterdam, The Netherlands, 1980-84. Author 7 books; editor 3 books; contbr. 150 sci. papers to profl. jours. Mem. Am. Chem. Soc., Chem. Soc. Japan, Japanese Soc. Radiation Chemistry (v.p. 1973-75, pres. 1981-83), Japanese Assn. Radiation Rsch. Avocations: photography, music, languages. Fax: 81-48-476-1711. Home: 11-15 Honcho-3, Shiki Saitama 353-0004, Japan

IMAMURA, NOBUTAKA, physician, educator, researcher; b. Hiroshima, Japan, Apr. 13, 1943; s. Tamotsu and Kiyono (Kimura) I.; m. Hiroko Harada; children: Yoshitaka, Sohkichi, Shigehiro. MD, Hiroshima U., 1968, PhD, 1973. Asst. prof. Rsch. Inst. Nuclear Medicine and Biology, Hiroshima, 1984—; guest prof. R.E. Kavetsky Inst. Exptl. Oncology, Nat. Acad. Scis. of Ukraine, 1997—, Hematology Dept., Kiev Hosp., Ukraine, 1998—. Author 20 books; contbr. over 200 articles to profl. publs. including Brit. Jour. Hematology, European Jour. Hematology, The Lancet, New Engl. Jour. Med., Blood, Japan Soc. Ins.; assoc. editor Exptl. Oncology, 2000—. Rep. non govtl. orgn. humanitarian support for Chernobyl victims, 1996—. Recipient Hiroshima Peace grant 1997, 98, 99, 20th Century Achievement award, Outstanding Achievement award Internat. Biog. Ctr., Cambridge, Eng.; named 1000 Leaders of World Influence Am. Biog. Inst. Mem. Japanese Assn. Cancer Rsch., Japanese Assn. Internal Medicine, Counsellors of Japanese Assn. Hematology, Japanese Assn. Clin. Hematology, Internat. Counsellors of Model Devel. Sys. Achievements include research in aggressive NK cell leukemia. High incidence of Neutropenia among Atomic bomb survivors. Avocations: music, tennis. Home: 14-24 Nishi-asahimachi, Minamiku Hiroshima 734-0002, Japan

IMAMURA, SADAO, hospital administrator, retired educator; b. Kyoto, Japan, Feb. 5, 1935; s. Shiro and Yuki (Tsuda) I.; m. Kimi Tanaka, May 14, 1966; children: Sadahiro, Takehiro. MD, Kyoto U., 1968. Lectr. Kyoto U., 1960-70, asst. prof., 1972-78, assoc. prof., 1978-80, prof., 1980-97, prof. emeritus, 1997—; head dermatology sect. Kori Hosp., Neyagawa, Japan, 1970-71; dir. Matsue City (Japan) Hosp., 1997—. Recipient culture award Kyoto Newspaper Co., 1997. Mem. Rotary. Home: 58-1 Uo-machi, Shimane Matsue City 690-0062, Japan Office: Matsue City Hosp, 101 Nadamachi, Shimane Matsue City 690-8509, Japan

IMAMURA, SHOHEI, film director; b. Tokyo, Japan, Sept. 15, 1926. Dir., instr. Broadcasting and Movie Tech. Sch., Yohohama, Japan; former asst. dir. Yasujiro Ozu. Dir. 15 films including: Pigs and Battleships, 1961, Insect Woman, 1963, Vengeance is Mine, 1979, Eijanaika, 1981, The Ballad of Narayama, 1983, Zegen, 1988, Black Rain, 1990, Unagi, 1997, Kanzo Sensei, 1998; also made documentaries for TV. Winner Japanese Acad. award for best film (Ballad of Narayama), 1983, Cannes Film Festival's Golden Palm award, 1983. Address: care Tori Co Ltd, 3-2-17 Ginza, Chuo-ku Tokyo 104, Japan*

IMAMURA, TAIRA, chemistry educator; b. Tokyo, Jan. 27, 1944; m. Kazuko Suzuki. BA, Yamagata U., Japan, 1967; MS, Hokkaido U., Sapporo, Japan, 1969, DS, 1972. Postdoctoral rsch. fellow Hokkaido U., 1972-73, 77, assoc. prof., 1992—; postdoctoral rsch. fellow U. Iowa, 1972-73; vis. rsch. fellow Miami U., 1973; postdoctoral rsch. fellow U. Ill., 1974-76. E-mail: timamura@sci.hokudai.ac.jp. Office: Divsn Chem Grad Sch Sci, Hokkaido Univ, Sapporo 060-0810, Japan

IMAMURA, TOHRU, physicist; b. Nagoya, Aichi, Japan, Sept. 29, 1945; s. Ryokichi and Sumi (Shibayama) I.; m. Seiko Kimizuka, Oct. 25, 1970; children: Yuko, Shioko. BSc, U. Tokyo, 1969. Rsch. officer NRLM, Tokyo, 1969-79, sr. rsch. officer, 1979—; office of internat. rels. NRLM, Tsukuba, 1985—. Author: Theoretical and Applied Mechanics, 1973; contbr. articles to profl. jours. Chmn. Parents and Tchrs. Assn., 1985-87. Mem. Acoustical Soc. Am., Acoustical Soc. of Japan, Soc. Franco-Japonaise Tech. Indstr. Achievements include research on the theory of ultrasonic field. Home: 5-508-2 Matsushiro, Tsukuba 305-0035, Japan Office: Nat Rsch Lab of Metrology, 1-1-4 Umezono, Tsukuba 305-8563, Japan

IMAMURA, TORU, molecular cell biologist; b. Kagoshima, Japan, Feb. 25, 1956; s. Hiroshi and Eiko (Ishikawa) I.; m. Reeko Urabe, Mar. 15, 1986; children: Mayumi, Ryota. BS, Tokyo U., 1979, MS, 1981, PhD, 1984. Researcher Fermentation Rsch. Inst., Tsukuba, 1984-88; vis. scientist ARC, Rockville, Md., 1988-90, 92-93; biotech. cons. Ministry Internat. Trade and Industry, Chiyoda and Tokyo, 1991-92; sr. scientist Nat. Inst. Biosci. and Human Tech., Tsukuba, 1993—, group leader, 1997—, lab. head, 1998—; chmn. radiation safety com. Fermentation Rsch. Inst., 1987-88, chmn. pollution prevention com., 1990-91; contact person Japan-U.S. aggreement in sci. and tech. Mechanism of Growth Signaling, 1992—, adj. prof. Sci U Tokyo, 1995—. Contbr. articles to profl. jours. Recipient Tsukuba Encouragement prize, 1996, Dir.-Gen. award Agy. Indsl. Sci. and Tech., 1999. Mem. AAAS, N.Y. Acad. Scis., Am. Soc. for Cell Biology, Am. Soc. for Biochemistry and Molecular Biology, Japan Biochem. Soc., Japan Cell Biology Soc., Japanese Soc. Molecular Biology, Japanese Soc. Carbohydrate Rsch. (councilor). Avocations: art, tennis, reading, travel, music. Home: 2-20-12-1301, Senju-Azuma, Adachi 120-0025, Japan Office: Nat Inst Biosci & Human Tech, 1-1 Higashi, Tsukuba 305-8566, Japan

IMAN (IMAN ABUDULMAJID), model; b. Somalia, July 25, 1955; m. Spencer Haywood (div. 1987); 1 child, Zulekha; m. David Bowie, Apr. 24, 1992. Student, U. Nairobi, Kenya. Joined Wilhelmina Model Inc., 1975; introduced to U.S. Iman's Kikois. Appearences include (films) The Human Factor, 1979, Out of Africa, 1985, Star Trek VI, 1986, No Way Out, 1987, Surrender, 1987, House Party II, 1991, Exit to Eden, 1994, The Deli, 1997, Omikron: The Nomad Soul, 1999, (TV) Heart of Darness, 1994; (TV series) Miami Vice, The Cosby Show, In the Heat of the Night.

IMANAKA, KUNIYASU, psychologist; b. Tokyo, Dec. 20, 1950; s. Sukeyoshi and Haruko Imanaka; m. Yasuko Kataoka, Feb. 10, 1978; 1 child, Kaoru. B in Engring., Saitama U., Urawa, Japan, 1973; M in Phys. Edn., Tokyo U. Edn., 1975; PhD, U. Queensland, Brisbane, Australia, 1991. Lectr. Nagasaki (Japan) U., 1979-83, assoc. prof., 1983-91, prof., 1991-95; prof. Tokyo Met. U., 1995—. Contbr. articles to profl. jours. Sci. rsch. grantee Ministry of Edn., Sci., Sport and Culture of Japan, 1993—. Mem. Japanese Psychol. Assn., Japan Soc. Exercise and Sports Physiology, Japanese Soc. Sport Psychology. Office: Tokyo Met U Dept Kinesiolog, 1-1 Minami-Ohsawa, Hachioji 192-0397, Japan

IMANI, NIKITAH OKEMBE-RA, anthropologist, sociologist; b. Atlanta, July 29, 1967; s. Eulas C. and Eloise Strong; 1 child, Kamau Okembe-Ra Imani. BSFS in Internat. Politics, Georgetown U., edu9; MA in Polit. Sci., MA in Sociology, U. Fla., 1991, 92, PhD in Sociology, 1995. Asst. prof. sociology James Madison U., Harrisonburg, Va., 1995—; co-pastor Imani Temple Ch., Atlanta, 1999—; pastor Reap a Life Ministries, Harrisonburg, 1995—; adj. assoc. prof. Blue Ridge C.C., 2000—. Co-author: (book) The Agony of Education, 1996. E-mail: imanino@jmu.edu. Office: James Madison Univ Msc 7501 Harrisonburg VA 22807-0001

IMATAKE, MIDORI, industrial design company executive; b. Osaka, Japan, Feb. 13, 1937; d. Shichiro and Sachiko (Matsuura) I. B.Indsl. Design, Pratt Inst., N.Y.C., 1962. 1st class cert. architect, Japan. Pres. Imatake & Assocs., Inc., Nishinomiya, Japan, 1972—, Osaka Indsl. Design

Inst., 1987—; prof. Otemae Coll.; chmn. planning com. Hort. Landscape Inst. f Hyogo Prefecture, 1991—; mem. promotion com. Pan-Pacific Design Exch. Program, 1992—; committeeman Urban Landscape Deliberative Coun. of Osaka Prefecture, 1998—. Author: The Effective Basic design Method, 1964; editor: Woman Designers of America, 1975; designer City Planning with Greens project (Citizen's Culture award Nishinomiya City 1998). Recipient award for work for refreshing the town Hyogo Prefecture, 1994. Mem. DAS Designers Assn. (trustee 1987—), Internat. Soroptimist of Ashiya. Home: 3-28 Hagoromocho, Nishinomiya 662-0051, Japan

IMBARDELLI, AMEDEO PATRICK, marketing professional; b. Melbourne, Victoria, Australia, June 5, 1960; s. Aristed Mario and Andalusia (DiBari) I.; m. Judith Anne Adams (div. May, 1988); children: Lisa Michelle, Ashley Steven. BBA in Hotel Adminstrn., Cornell U., 1980, MBA, 1985; student, Saigon Open U., Vietnam, 1991. Gen. mgr. Hilton Hotels, Brisbane, Australia, 1987-89; area gen. mgr. SPHC Group, Vietnam, 1989-92; area gen. mgr. Melbourne, 1992-94, India, 1994-96; regional dir. New Zealand, 1996-97; gen. dir. mgmt. St. Leonards, Australia, 1997—; dep. COO So. Pacific Hotel Corp. Group, 1999—. Bd. dirs. Lincoln U., New Zealand, 1996-97, Canterbury Tourism, New Zealand, 1996-97 (chmn.), Melbourne Tourism, 1992-94, Vietnam Fgn. Investment, 1989-92; com. mem. Young Liberals, Melbourne, 1975-79. Recipient Appreciation award Melbourne Variety Club, 1993; identified Young Exec. Bull. Mag., Australia, 1983. Fellow Australian Inst. Mgmt., Inst. Mktg. (com.), Global Hotel Assn., Variety Club Australia (bd. dirs. 1998—). Roman Catholic. Avocations: skiing, theatre, scuba diving, Formula One racing. Office: SPHC Group, 504 Pacific Hwy, Saint Leonards NSW 2065, Australia

IMBERT, JEAN-CLAUDE, orthopedic physician and surgeon; b. Toulon, Var, France, Oct. 21, 1935; s. Pierre and Marie-Berthe (Drapier) I.; m. Daniele Dussert, Aug. 9, 1962; children: Anne, Pierre. MD, U. Lyon, 1966. Cert. orthopedic surgeon. Intern state hosps. Lyon, 1962-66, resident state hosps., 1967-69; dept. head Orthopedic Clinic, St.-Etienne, France, 1970—; cons. French Football Fedn., Paris, 1975—, St.-Etienne Football Team, 1972—. Author: Current Concepts in Knee Traumatology and Surgery, Encyclopedie Medico-Chirurgicale, 1984-87, 92-2000; mem. editl. bd.: Knee Surgery Sport Traumatology Arthroscopy, 1993—; mem. sci. com.: Maitrise Orthopedique, 1993—. Lt. Armed Med. Svc., Algeria, 1960-62. Mem. European Fedn. for Orthopedic and Sport Traumatology (pres. 1993-95), Internat. Soc. for Orthopedic and Trauma Surgery, French Soc. Trauma in Sports (sec.), French Arthroscopic Soc. (v.p.). Roman Catholic. Avocations: scuba diving, cooking, trekking, classical music. Office: Clinique de la Digonniere, 60 rue Robespierre, 42100 Saint-Étienne France

IMBODEN, JOHN BASKERVILLE, psychiatry educator; b. Morrilton, Ark., Sept. 17, 1925. MD, Johns Hopkins U., Balt., 1950. Diplomate Am. Bd. Neurology and Psychiatry; lic. physician, Md. Intern Cin. Gen. Hosp., 1950-51; resident Johns Hopkin's Hosp., 1951-52, 54-56; pvt. practice psychiatry Balt., 1963—; chief dept. psychiatry Sinai Hosp. of Balt., 1969-90; assoc. prof. psychiatry Johns Hopkins U., Balt., 1963—. Co-author: Practical Psychiatry in Medicine; contbr. articles to profl. jours, chpts. to books. With U.S. Army, 1952-54. Fellow Am. Psychiat. Assn.; mem. Am. Psychoanalytic Assn. Office: 600 Wyndhurst Ave Baltimore MD 21210-2489

IMEL, JOHN MICHAEL, lawyer; b. Cushing, Okla., Aug. 4, 1932; s. Arthur Blaine and Hazel Monnet (Kelly) I.; m. Patricia Ann Carney, July 31, 1954; children: Blythe Michele, Kathryn Ann, Dixie Lynn, Sally Louise. BS, U. Okla., 1954, JD, 1959. Bar: Okla. 1959, U.S. Dist. Ct. (no. dist.) Okla. 1961, U.S. Ct. Appeals (10th cir.) 1961, U.S. Supreme Ct. 1962, U.S. Dist. Ct. (we. dist.) Okla. 1967, U.S. Dist. Ct. (ea. dist.) Okla. 1971. Asst. atty. County of Tulsa, 1959-60; mcpl. judge City of Tulsa, 1960-61; U.S. atty. U.S. Dept. Justice, Tulsa, 1961-67; ptnr. Moyers, Martin, Santee Imel & Tetrick, Tulsa, 1967—. Regent U. Okla., Norman, 1981-88, chmn., 1987-88; trustee Children's Med. Ctr., Tulsa, 1979-84. Capt. USNR, 1954-56. Fellow Am. Bar Found., Am. Coll. Trial Lawyers (state chmn. 1987-88); mem. Am. Inns of Ct. (program chmn. 1989-90, Exemplary Leadership award 1996), So. Hills Country Club (bd. govs. 1993-99), Tulsa Club (pres. 1990), Rotary (pres. 1968-69). Democrat. Methodist. Avocations: golf, swimming, tennis, reading. Home: 3920 E 58th Pl Tulsa OK 74135-7823 Office: Moyers Martin Santee Imel & Tetrick 320 S Boston Ave Ste 920 Tulsa OK 74103-3722

IMHOF, HERWIG, radiologist; b. Pressburg, Slovakia, Feb. 9, 1943; arrived in Austria, 1945; s. Ernst and Margarethe (Schiefer) I.; m. Ilse Rummelhardt, Aug. 24, 1968; children: Klaus, Andrea. MD, U. Vienna, Austria, 1968. Cert. Austrian Bd. Physicians. Asst. physician I. Med. Klinik/U. Vienna AKH, 1968-71; asst. physician radiology I. Med. Klinik/U. Vienna Allgem Krankenhaus, 1972-75; asst. physician II Surgic Clinic/Allgem Krankenhaus-Radiology, 1971-72; asst. prof. radiology U. Chgo., 1975-76; dozent Zentr Inst. Radiology U. Vienna - Allgem Krankenhaus, 1976-87, leiter, prof. MR Inst., 1987-99, leiter, prof. osteology, 1991—; spkr. med. faculty Kuriensprecher, 1992-99, mem. senate, 1998—. Office: U Klinik f Radiodiagnostik AKH Vienna, Waehringerguertel 18-20, A-1090 Vienna Austria

IMHOF, MARGARETE LYDIA, psychology educator; b. Erbach, Odenwald, Germany, July 22, 1958; d. Albin Robert and Sigrid Johanna (Troll) I.; m. Jobst Noelle, July 22, 1998. Diploma in psychology, Würzburg U., 1983, MA in English, 1984; PhD in Psychology, Bamberg U., 1995. Lectr. Luther Coll., Decorah, Iowa, 1987-88, U. Ill., Chgo., 1989; asst. prof. Bamberg U., Germany, 1990-95, Frankfurt U., Germany, 1995. Author: Motor Activity and Concentration in Listening Situations, 1995. Mem. Internat. Listening Assn. (Ralph G. Nichols award 1998), Internat. Sch. Psychology Assn., Deutsche Gesellschaft fuer Psychologie. Office: Johann Wolfgang Goethe U, Senckenberganlage 15, 60054 Frankfurt Germany

IMHOF, RENE, pharmaceutical company executive, researcher; b. Baden, Switzerland, Sept. 28, 1945; m. Elisabeth Kappeler, July 29, 1972; children: Sabina, Dino. Diploma in chemistry, Swiss Fed. Inst. Tech., Zürich, 1969, DSc in Tech., 1972. Cert. Roche Lectr. in Medicinal Chemistry, 1980. Dept. dep. head CNS F. Hoffmann-La Roche, Basel, Switzerland, 1985-90, scientific lab head, 1976-82, group head CNS, 1982-85, dept. head logistics rsch., 1990-94, head nonclin. devel. Basel, 1994-96, global head nonclin. devel., 1996-98, head of rsch., 1998—, also bd. dirs. dir.; asst. dir. Roche Basel, 1988-94, dep. dir., 1994—; lectr. scientific meetings, 1972—. Contbr. articles to profl. scientific publs.; patentee in field of utilities in prevention and treatment of human diseases. Chmn. 2 polit. campaigns against 2 constnl. initiatives to restrict/abolish animal experimentation for scientific purposes, 1991-93. Mem. Internat. Union Pure and Applied Chemistry. Office: F Hoffmann-La Roche Ltd, Bldg 69 Room 311, CH-4070 Basel Switzerland

IMIELINSKI, BRUNON LESŁAW, neurosurgeon, researcher; b. Brzesc, Polesie, Poland, Apr. 16, 1928; s. Jan Casimir and Janina Maria (Łapińska) I.; m. Halina Izabela Lipińska, Jund 19, 1953; 1 child, Tomasz. MD, Med. U. Gdańsk, Poland, 1953, PhD, 1965. Intern 3rd univ. dept. surgery Med. Sch. Gdansk, 1953-54, resident dept. neurosurgery, 1954-60; asst. prof. dept. neurosurgery Med. U. Gdańsk, 1953-65, assoc. prof., 1967-73, prof., 1974-75, 77—; sr. house officer Regional Neurosurg. Ctr., Liverpool, U.K., 1966; rsch. asst. U. Edinburgh, U.K., 1966-67; dir. Inst. Neurosci. Med. U. Gdańsk, 1976-79, chmn. dept. neurosurgery, 1985-98, lectr. ethics in medicine, 1999—; chmn. dept. neurosurgery Garyounis U., Benghazi, Libya, 1979-81; sr. del. Polish Soc. Neurosurgery to World Fedn. Neurosurg. Socs., 1997. Editor: Surgery of Pituitary Gland and Its Area, 1977, Skull Base Surgery and Minimal Invasive Surgical Techniques, 1998; inventor in field. Mem. Mcpl. Coun. Health Svc., City of Gdańsk, 1971-74; sec Com. of Devel. of Med. Care, Gdańsk, 1981-90; mem. med. sect. Nat. Coun. High Edn., Warsaw, 1996-99. Capt. M.C., Polish mil., 1955. Mem. Romanian Soc. Neurosci. (hon.), Polish Soc. Neurosurgeons (hon., mem. bd. 1985—), European Assn. Neurosurg. Socs. (mem. stds. and adminstrv. coun. 1983-87. Avocations: tourism, skiing, classical music, swimming. Home: Olejarna 8/1, 80-843 Gdańsk Poland Office: Med U Gdańsk, ul Debinki 7, 80-211 Gdańsk Poland

IMMING, MARIE ELIZABETH, public relations professional; b. St. Louis, Dec. 4, 1966; d. William Charles and Margaret H. (Parker) I. BA in Communication, Avila Coll., 1989, BA in Psychology, 1989. Camera operator Avila Coll./sta. KSHB-TV, Kansas City, Kans., 1986-88; promotion intern KMBC-TV, Kansas City, Kans., 1988-89; pub. rels. staff mem. J.I. Case, Kansas City, Kans., 1990—. Editor Avila Examiner, 1989. Com. mem., Alcohol Awareness Week, Kansas City, 1988. Mem. Kansas City Media Profls. Home: 5311 Hallet St Shawnee KS 66216-5147

IMPARATO, EDWARD THOMAS, writer; b. Flushing, N.Y., Jan. 6, 1917; s. Charles and Romilda (Delli Bovi) I.; m. Jean Catherine De Garmo, Aug. 1, 1947. BS, U. Tampa, 1963. V.p. Merrill Lynch, Clearwater, Fla., 1963-74; fin. cons. J.C.I., Inc., Belleair, Fla., 1974-92; free-lance author Belleair, Fla., 1992—; CEO, chmn. (INSAT) Internat. Systems, Clearwater, 1987-92. Author: How to Manage Your Money, 1964, Into Darkness, 1994, MacArthur-Melbourne to Tokyo, 1996, Rescue from Shangri-La, 1997, History of the 374th Troop Carrier, 1997, General Douglas MacArthur Speeches and Reports 1908-1964, 2000, The Wisdom and Vision of Douglas MacArthur-General USA, 2000, Gen. MacArthur "Acclaimed", 2000. Col. USAF, 1938-61. Decorated Legion of Merit, D.F.C., Air medal with oak leaf cluster, Am. Def. Svc. medal; recipient WWII Victory medal, 1945, Natl. Def. Svc. medal, 1945, Am. Campaign award, 1945, Medal for Humane Action, 1945; named to Sr. Hall of Fame for vol. svc., 1998; honored as Father of Morton F. Plant Hosp. Found., 1978. Mem. Order Daedalians, Retired Officers Assn. Independent. Home and office: 155 Bayview Dr Belleair FL 33756-1403

IMPELLIZZERI, ANNE ELMENDORF, insurance company executive, non-profit executive; b. Chgo., Jan. 26, 1933; d. Armin and Laura (Gundlach) Elmendorf; m. Julius Simon Impellizzeri, Oct. 12, 1961 (dec.); children: Laura, Theodore (dec.). BA, Smith Coll., 1955; MA, Yale U., 1957. CLU; ChFC. Tchr. Amity Regional H.S., Woodbridge, Conn., 1957-58; adminstrv. and editl. asst. East Europe Inst., N.Y.C., 1958-59; health educator Met. Life Ins. Co., N.Y.C., 1959-62, 71-76, adminstrv. asst. pub. affairs, 1976-78, asst. v.p. corp. social responsibility, 1978-80, v.p., 1980-85, v.p. group ins., 1985-88; v.p. N.Y.C. Partnership, 1988-90; pres., CEO Blanton-Peale Inst., N.Y.C., 1990-98; exec. dir. Russel Wright's Manitoga, Garrison, N.Y., 1998—; bd. dirs. Nuveen Mcpl. Funds, 1994—, Support Ctr. for Nonprofit Mgmt., 1995—, Bard Music Festival, 1990—; bd. dirs. Scenic Hudson, 1997—, treas., 1999—; trustee Smith Coll., 1991-96; mem. Bus. Urban Issues Coun. of the Conf. Bd., 1981-85, chair, 1983-85. Trustee Lakeland Bd. Edn., Westchester County, N.Y., 1967-71, pres., 1970-71; bd. dirs. Nat. Safety Coun., 1974-80; pres. Am. Assn. Gifted Children, 1975-85, chair, 1985-90. Named to Acad. of Women Achievers, YWCA N.Y., 1978; Fulbright grantee, 1955-56. Mem. Assn. Yale Alumni (bd. govs. 1985-88), Phi Beta Kappa. Office: Manitoga PO Box 249 Garrison NY 10524-0249

IMPERATO, JOSEPH JOHN, lawyer, composer; b. Jersey City, N.J., Mar. 14, 1956; s. Joseph Francis Imperato and Edith Roslyn (Dubin) Schwimmer. Student, Oberlin Coll., 1974-76; BA, Fla. State U., 1978, JD, 1981. Bar: Fla. 1983. Trial atty., tng. instr. Office of Pub. Defender, Miami, Fla., 1982—; lectr., mock trial coach Dade County sec. schs. and univs., Miami, 1993—. Composer musical scores Fox TV Network, 1992-94; composer comml. jingles, 1975— (Addy award 1976), original songs, 1974— (Billboard Mag. Songwriting award 1995); composer, producer original childrens' musicals, 1997—. Mem. ASCAP, Audio Enging. Soc. Office: Office of Pub Defender 1320 NW 14th St Miami FL 33125-1609

IMPERATO, PASCAL JAMES, physician, health administrator, author, editor, medical educator; b. N.Y.C., Jan. 13, 1937; s. James Anthony and Madalynne Marguerite (Insante) I.; m. Eleanor Anne Maiella, June 4, 1977; children: Alison Madalynne, Gavin Humbert, Austin Clement. BS, St. John's U., 1958, DSc (hon.), 1977; MD, SUNY, Downstate Med. Ctr., 1962; M in Pub. Health and Tropical Medicine, Tulane U., 1966, DSc (hon.), 1996. Diplomate Am. Bd. Preventive Medicine, Nat. Bd. Med. Examiners. Fgn. fellow Assn. Am. Med. Colls., Kenya, Tanzania, Uganda, 1961; intern dept. internal medicine L.I. Coll. Hosp., 1962-63, resident dept. medicine, 1963-65; fgn. rsch. fellow Tulane Univ.-U. del Valle, Cali, Colombia, 1965; N.Y. Acad. Medicine/Glorney Raisebeck fellow Tulane U., New Orleans, 1965-66; med. epidemiologist smallpox eradication-measles control program Ctrs. Disease Control/USPHS, Mali, 1966-72; dir. Bur. Infectious Disease Control, N.Y.C. Dept. Health, 1972-74, prin. epidemiologist, dir. immunization program, 1972-74, 1st dep. commr., 1974-77, dir. pub. health residency tng. program, 1974-77; chmn. N.Y.C. Swine Influenza Immunization Task Force, 1976-77; commr. health N.Y.C., 1977-78; chmn. N.Y.C. Bd. Health, 1977-78; chmn. bd. N.Y.C. Health and Hosps. Corp., 1977-78; chmn. exec. com. N.Y.C. Health Systems Agy., 1977-78; acting health services adminstr. N.Y.C., 1977-78; clin. instr. dept. medicine Cornell U. Med. Coll., N.Y.C., 1972-74, asst. clin. prof., 1974-78, asst. clin. prof. dept. pub. health, 1974-77, assoc. clin. prof., 1977-78, adj. prof., 1979-2000; clin. assoc. prof. dept. preventive medicine, cmty. health SUNY Health Sci. Ctr. at Bklyn., 1974-77, lectr., 1977-78, prof. and chmn., 1978-94; disting. svc. prof. and chmn., 1994—; mem. staff N.Y. Hosp. 1972-78, L.I. Coll. Hosp., 1973—, State U. Hosp., 1978—, Kings County Hosp., 1978—; lectr. dept. cmty. medicine Mt. Sinai Sch. Medicine, CUNY, 1974-90; lectr. dept. health adminstrn. Sch. Pub. Health, Columbia U., 1982-89; cons. N.Y. State Dept. Edn., 1982-87, NAS, 1985, dept. cmty. health svcs. and ambulatory care Brookdale Hosp. Med. Ctr., 1987-96; med. cons. Africa Bur., U.S. AID, 1974; cons. program for appropriate tech. in health U.S. AID, 1985-89; med. dir. R&D and Epidemiology Island Peer Rev. Orgn., 1991—. Author: Doctor in The Land of the Lion, 1964, (with Osa Johnson) Last Adventure, 1966, Bwana Doctor, 1967, The Treatment and Control of Infectious Diseases in Man, 1974, The Cultural Heritage of Africa, 1974, A Wind in Africa: A Story of Modern Medicine in Mali, 1975, What To Do About the Flu, 1976, African Folk Medicine, 1977, Historical Dictionary of Mali, 1977, 3rd edit., 1996, Dogon Cliff Dwellers: The Art of Mali's Mountain People, 1978, Medical Detective, 1979, (with Eleanor Imperato) Mali: A Handbook of Historical Statistics, 1982, The Administration of a Public Health Agency: A Case Study of the New York City Department of Health, 1983, Buffoons, Queens and Wooden Horsemen, 1983, (with Greg Mitchell) Acceptable Risks, 1985, (with Robert I. Goler) Early American Medicine, 1987, Arthur Donaldson Smith and the Exploration of Lake Rudolf, 1987, Mali: A Search for Direction, 1989, (with Eleanor Imperato) They Married Adventure: The Wandering Lives of Martin and Osa Johnson, 1992, Quest for the Jade Sea: Colonial Competition Around an East African Lake, 1998; editor: Acquired Immunodeficiency Syndrome: Current Issues and Scientific Studies, 1989; Historical and Contemporary Aspects of Infectious Disease Control, 1996, (with Ronald E. Coons and J. Winthrop Aldrich) Over Land and Sea: Memoir of an Austrian Rear Admiral's Life in Europe and Africa, 1857-1909 (Ludwig Ritter von Höhnel), 2000; contbr. articles to profl. jours.; cons. editor N.Y. State Jour. Medicine, 1983, dep. editor, 1983-86, editor, 1986-93; editor Jour. Cmty. Health, 1985—; mem. editl. bd. Explorers Jour., 1979-88, Am. Jour. Chinese Medicine, 1985—, The Pharos, 1995—; mem. med. adv. bd. Med. Herald, 1992—; chairperson publs. com. Annals of Epidemiology, 1996-99. Bd. dirs. Pub. Health Rsch. Inst., 1977-78, Cmty. Coun. Greater N.Y., 1977-78, Med. Health and Rsch. Assn., 1977-78, Greater N.Y. Hosp. Assn., 1977-78, N.Y. Heart Assn., 1983-84, Primary Care Devel. Corp., 1995—; bd. trustees Milton Helpern Libr. Legal Medicine, 1977-89, hon. trustee, 1989—; hon. trustee Martin and Osa Johnson Safari Mus., 1964—; mem. adv. bd. Physicians for Social Responsibility, 1983—; mem. N.Y. State Bd. Medicine, 1985-95, vice chmn., 1990-93, chmn., 1993-95; mem. bd. zoning and appeals Village of Plandome Heights, N.Y., 1986-90, trustee, 1990-92; mem. sci. adv. bd. Explorers Club, 1988-93; chmn. N.Y.C. Met. Area Task Force on Syphilis, 1990-91; mem. bd. regents L.I. Coll. Hosp., 1992—; mem. N.Y.C. Mayor-Elect Giuliani's Health Care Adv. Group, 1993; mem. N.Y. State Coun. on Grad. Med. Edn., 1994-98; co-chmn. adv. commn. on pub. health N.Y.C. Coun., 1994—; mem. N.Y. State Bd. for Profl. Med. Conduct, 1994—; mem. Fulbright Selection Com., Africa, 1999—. Lt. comdr. USPHS, 1966-69. Recipient Meritorious Honor award and medal Dept. State, 1971, US AID Meritorious Honor award and medal, 1970, Outstanding Alumnus award Tulane U., 1978, Delta Omega Nat. Merit award, 1978, Frank Babbot award SUNY, 1980, Disting. Alumni Achievement award, and medal SUNY, 1987, Spl. Service award for smallpox eradication USPHS, 1987, Pub. Health Achievement award N.Y.C. Dept. Health, 1999, Nat. Acads. Practice Interdisciplinary Creativity award, 2000; Fulbright scholar, North Yemen, 1985. Master ACP, Fellow: Royal Soc. Tropical Medicine and Hygiene, Royal African Soc., Am. Coll. Epidemiology, Am. Coll. Preventive Medicine; mem. Am. Soc. Tropical Medicine and Hygiene, N.Y. Soc. Tropical Medicine (v.p. 1976-77, pres. 1989-90), East African Wildlife Soc., African Studies Assn., Author's Guild, Explorers Club, Delta Omega, Alpha Omega Alpha. Roman Catholic. Office: Box 43 450 Clarkson Ave Brooklyn NY 11203-2056

IMRE, GYÖRGY, ophthalmologist; b. Budapest, Hungary, Aug. 17, 1927; s. Kálmán and Kálmánné (Reményik Sarolta) I.; m. Györgyné Balogh Edit, Oct. 16, 1955 (dec. July 1958); 1 child, Miklós; m. Györgyné Kiss Ilona, Sept. 24, 1959; 1 child, László. MD, Semmelweis Med. U., Budapest, 1951; DMS, 1968. Clinician 2nd dept. ophthalmology Semmelweis Med. U., 1951-56, asst., 1956-77, 1st asst., 1977-80, asst. prof., 1980-83, prof., 1983-96, dir. 2d dept. ophthalmology. Contbr. more than 130 articles to sci. publs., chpts. to books. Mem. Hungarian Ophthal. Soc. (mem. governing body 1961—, sec. gen. 1968-71, Hirschler award 1995, Imre-Blaskovics award 1998), Internat. Ocular Inflammation Soc. (founding, mem. internat. coun. 1992—). Avocations: bird watching, rowing. Home: Süveg U. 14/a, H-1112 Budapest Hungary Office: Semmelweis Med Univ 2nd Dep, Ophthalmol, Mária u 39, H-1085 Budapest Hungary

IMRE, LÁSZLÓ, literature educator; b. Csorna, Hungary, Nov. 17, 1944; s. Sándor Imre and Julia Happich; m. Theodóra Mezey. Grad., U. Kossuth, Debrecen, Hungary, 1968. Cert. tchr. lang. and lit., Hungary. Asst. U. Kossuth, 1969-73, 1st asst., 1973-84, asst. prof., 1984-98, prof., 1998—, dean faculty of arts, 1989-92, head dept., 1989—, vice rector, 1998—; guest prof. U. Helsinki, Finland, 1992-96;. Author: Rákos Sándor, 1973, Brjusoff and the Russian Symbolic Novel, 1973, The Hungarian Novel in Verse, 1990, The Mood of Existence of Literary Genres, 1996. Recipient Toldy Rerenc Dij award Magyar Irodalomtörténeti Társaság, 1992. Home: Hadházi u 44 A, 4028 Debrecen Hungary Office: Debreceni Egyetem, Egyetem tér 1, 4010 Debrecen Hungary

IMRE, LÁSZLÓ, energy engineering educator, designer, researcher; b. Apátfalva, Hungary, Aug. 4, 1929; s. József and Margit (Szabados) I.; m. Emoke Nádas, 1954; children: Emoke, Györgyi. Diploma engr. in mech. enging., Tech. U. Budapest, Hungary, PhD, 1965; DSc, Hungarian Acad. Sci., Budapest, 1985. Lectr. dept. energy Tech. U. Budapest, 1951-57, asst. prof., 1957-65, assoc. prof., 1965-87, prof., 1987—, dep. dir. Inst. Thermal Energy and Sys. Enging., 1978-92; prof. dept. energy Tech. U. Budapest, Budapest, 1992-99; prof. emeritus Tech. U. Budapest, 1999—. Author, editor: Handbook of Drying, 1974, Thermal Performance of Electric Machines and Devices, 1982; author: Heat Transfer in Composite Devices, 1983; contbg. author: Handbook of Industrial Drying, 1987, 95, Industrial Drying of Foods, 1997. Chmn. Hungarian Solar Energy Soc., Budapest, 1983. Recipient gold medal of inventors Hungarian Patent Office, 1971, acad. prize Hungarian Acad. Sci., 1984. Mem. IEEE, Internat. Solar Energy Soc. (bd. dirs. 1993). Avocations: fishing, traveling, sailing, painting. Office: Tech U Budapest Dept Energy, Müegyetem rkp 3, H-1111 Budapest Hungary

IMRE, MEHMET FEHMI, writer; b. Ankara, Turkey, Feb. 13, 1957; s. Fethi Cemal and Edibe (Ünlü) I. BA, Faculty of Lang. History Geog., Ankara, 1979. Editor Yanki Weekly News mag., Ankara, 1979-82; freelance writer Ankara, 1983—. Author: Onehundredandseventysix Years, 1992, Stories of Silence (in english also), 1994, Heaven and Hell, 1995, Peace, 1997, How to Be Champion in Football, 1998, I God, 1999. Avocations: astronomy, physics, geology, anthropology. Home: 119/4, Küçükesat Caddesi, 06660 Ankara Turkey

IMWINKELRIED, EDWARD JOHN, law educator; b. San Francisco, Sept. 19, 1946; s. John Joseph and Enes Rose (Gianelli) I.; m. Cynthia Marie Clark, Dec. 30, 1978; children: Marie Elise, Kenneth West. BA, U. San Francisco, 1967, JD, 1969. Bar: Calif., Mo., U.S. Supreme Ct. Consumer atty. San Francisco Neighborhood Legal Svcs., 1969-70; capt. U.S. Army, 1970-74; prof. law U. San Diego, 1974-79, Washington U., St. Louis, 1979-85, U. Calif., Davis, 1985—; disting. faculty Nat. Coll. Dist. Attys., Columbia, S.C., 1978—; mem. legal issues working group DNA Commn., Washington, 1998—. Author: Evidentiary Foundations, 1998; contbr. articles to profl. jours. V.p. St. James Coun., Davis. Mem. Am. Acad. Forensic Sci., ABA (criminal justice sect.), Nat. Assn. Criminal Def. Lawyers. Democrat. Roman Catholic. Avocation: jogging. Home: 2204 Shenandoah Pl Davis CA 95616-6603

INABA, KOSAKU, heavy manufacturing executive; b. Jan. 16, 1924; m. Hiroko Inaba. Student, Tokyo Inst. Tech., 1946. With Ishikajima Shibaura Turbine, 1946; with Ishikawajima-Harima Heavy Industries Co., Tokyo, 1972—, chmn., CEO, 1995—; chmn. Japanese Aero Engines Corp.; bd. dirs. Toshiba Corp., Tokyo. Mem. Japan Chamber Commerce and Industry (chmn.). Avocation: golf. Office: Ishikawajima-Harima Heavy Inds, 2-2-1 Otemachi, Chiyoda-ku Tokyo 100-8182, Japan also: Nippon Shoko Kaigisho, 3-2-2 Marunouchi, Chiyoda-ku Tokyo Japan*

INABA, MOTOKICHI, writer, management educator, organizational scientist; b. Yokohama, Japan, July 12, 1935; s. Tatsuzo and Chiyo (Kato) I.; m. Haruko Hiraga, Nov. 24, 1967; children: Yushi, Yohei, Eiki. B in Econs., U. Tokyo, 1963, M in Econs., 1965. Lectr. Yokohama Nat. U., 1968-69, assoc. prof., 1969-81, prof., 1981-98, trustee, 1989-96, dean faculty bus. adminstrn., 1991-93, dean grad. sch. internat. devel. studies, 1994-96; prof. Seijo U.; prof. emeritus Yokohama Nat. U., 1998—; vis. scholar Sloan Sch. Mgmt., MIT, Cambridge, Mass., 1972-73, 86-87. Author: (in Japanese) Business Organization, 1971, A Theory of Business Behavior, 1982, Foundations of Modern Management, 1991, Corporate Dynamics, 2000; co-author: Analysis of the Firm Behavior, 1985, Administration-Interdisciplinary Approaches, 1986, Current Perspectives of Management Thought, 1986; editor: Contemporary Management Theories, 1994. Mem. Acad. Assn. for Orgnl. Sci. (dir.), Japan Acad. Internat. Bus. Studies (dir.), Soc. Hist. Mgmt. Theories (dir.), Internat. House of Japan, Acad. Mgmt. (U.S.), The Sci. Coun. Japan. Buddhist. Avocations: tennis, hiking, coins. Home: 13-9 Minamikaruizawa, Nishi-ku, Yokohama 220-0002, Japan Office: Seijo U Faculty Econs, 6-1-20 Setagaya-ku, Tokyo 157-8511, Japan

INABA, TOSHIO, veterinary medicine educator; b. Amagasaki, Hyogo, Japan, Jan. 9, 1952; s. Nobuyoshi and Sueko (Imada) I.; m. Mikiko Kawabe, May 2, 1982; children: Tetsushi, Natsuki. DVM, Osaka (Japan) Prefecture U., 1974, MSc, 1976, PhD, 1982. Rsch. fellow Washington U., St. Louis, 1978-80; rsch. assoc. Osaka Prefecture U., Sakai, 1980-91, asst. prof., 1992-95, assoc. prof., 1996—. Author: Endocrinological Examinations in Obstetrics and Gynecology, 1978, Reproduction in the Dog and Cat, 1989, Clinical Signs and Diagnosis in Small Animal Practice, 1993, Textbook of Theriogenology, 1995, Seventh Lake Shirakaba Conference, 1996, Veterinary Dictionary, 1989, Dictionary of Dairy Terminology, 1993; contbr. numerous articles to profl. jours. Recipient Acad. award Japanese Soc. Farm Animal Vet. Medicine, 1992, acad. award Osaka Vet. Med. Assn., 1999. Mem. Japanese Soc. Vet. Sci. (councilor), Japanese Soc. Animal Reproduction (Acad. award 1989), N.Y. Acad. Scis. Avocations: cycling. Fax: 81 722 549918. E-mail: inaba@vet.osakafu-u.ac.jp. Home: 1-5-2 Tachibanacho, Toyonaka, Osaka 560-0025, Japan Office: Osaka Prefecture U, Dept Animal Reprodn, Sakai Osaka 599-8531, Japan

INABA, YOSHIYUKI, patent and trademark lawyer; b. Osaka, Japan, Mar. 8, 1950; s. Yoshisada and Kaori (Yokokoji) I.; m. Kayoko Takamatsu, June 10, 1984; children: Kanako, Daisuke. BS, Sophia U., Tokyo, 1973; postgrad., Patent Acad., 1980. Bar: Japan; lic. patent atty. Assoc. Unuma & Assocs., Tokyo, 1974-78, 80-85; assoc., trainee Koda & Andriola, L.A., 1978-80; trainee Stevens, Davis et al, Washington, 1980; prin. Inaba & Assocs., Tokyo, 1985-90; ptnr. TMI Assocs., Tokyo, 1990—; spkr. Am. Intellectual Property Law Assn., 1983; lectr. Santa Clara U. Sch. Law Summer Program, Tokyo, 1998—. Mem. Internat. Assn. for the Proetction of Indsl. Property, , Internat. Trademark Assn. (spkr.), Asian Patent Atty. Assn. Office: TMI Assocs, 5-1 Toranomon 3-chome #803, Minato-ku Tokyo 105-0001, Japan

INABA, YUTAKA, medical educator, epidemiologist; b. Tokyo, Aug. 10, 1942. MD, U. Tokyo, 1968, D of Health Sci., 1973, D of Med. Sci., 1983. Med. diplomate. Lectr. U. Tokyo, 1973-79; assoc. prof. Juntendo U., Tokyo, 1979-88, prof., 1988—; rsch. assoc. U. Hawaii, Honolulu, 1975-76. Editor-in-chief Japanese Jour. Biometerology, Juntendo Med. Jour.; editor The

Japanese Jour. Epidemiology. Home: 4-6-12 Kotesashi-cho, Tokorozawa City 359-1141, Japan 359 Office: Jutendo U Sch Medicine, 2-1-1 Hongo, Bunkyo-ku, Tokyo 113-8421, Japan

INADA, YUJI, biochemistry and biotechnology educator, researcher; b. Kobe, Hyogo, Japan, Aug. 22, 1927; s. Tokuzo and Sachi Inada; m. Mitsue Hirota, Nov. 22, 1955; children: Sakiko, Motoko. Bachelor's degree, Kyoto (Japan) U., 1952; DSc, Tokyo U., 1961. Instr. Kyoto U., 1952-57; lectr. Kyoto Women's U., 1957-59; asst. researcher Tokugawa Inst. Biol. Rsch., Tokyo, 1959-61; from asst. prof. to assoc. prof. Tokyo Inst. Tech., 1961-82, prof., 1982-88; prof. Toin U. Yokohama, Japan, 1988—; prof. Symposium of Bio-Hybrid, Japan, 1986—; vis. prof. Ji Lin U., Liao Ning U., Chaina Med. U. Author: Chemical Modification of Proteins, I, II, III, 1987-90, Mysteries of Life, 1992, Bioconjugate Drugs, 1993, Neoglycoconjugate, 1995. Mem. Chem. Soc. Japan, Japanese Cancer Assn., Japanese Assn. for Drug Delivery System, Japanese Biochem. Soc. (mem. coun.), Internat. Soc. Thrombosis and Haemostasis, N.Y. Acad. Scis. Avocations: reading, classical music. Home: 1-808 Shimomaruko, 2-24-10, Oota-ku Tokyo 146-0092, Japan Office: Toin U Yokohama Human Sci Tech Ctr, 1614 Kuroganecho Aoba-ku, Yokohama 225-8502, Japan

INAGAKI, KOSAKU, information scientist, physicist, philosopher; b. Osaka, Japan, Mar. 30, 1949; s. Junzaburo (Kanazawa) and Teruko I.; m. Haruyo Takagi, March 18, 1978; children: Hiroyuki, Hitomi. BEE, Kyoto U., 1972, MEE, 1974, PhD in Info. Sci., 1977. Rsch. assoc. Kyoto U., Japan, 1977-82, assoc. prof., 1982—. Author: (books) The Doomsday of Computer Society, 1990, New Human Beings in Information Age, 1991, Coming Turning Point of Information Society, 1992, Information and Strategy, 1994, Unhappy Network Games, 1995, Gigabit Society, 1996, Basics of Computer Science, 1996, Information Media in the 20th Century, vol. 2, 1996, Complex, All Too Complex, 1996, Basics of Computers, 1997, Philosophy of Network Civilizations, 1997, Complex Systems, Complex Invariants, 1997, Game Theory in Everyday Life, 1998, Complex Systems and Beyond, 1999; contbr. articles to profl. jours. Recipient Pattern Recognition Soc. paper award, 1986. Mem. Japan Info. Culture Soc. (dir. 1997—), Inst. Electronics, Info. and Comm. Engrs., Info. Processing Soc. E-mail: inagaki@kuis.kyoto-u.ac.jp. Home: 52-7 Shimogamo Tadekura, Sakyo Kyoto 606-0806, Japan Office: Grad Sch Info Kyoto U, Yoshida-Honmachi, Sakyo Kyoto 606-8501, Japan

INAO, SHIGENORI, orthopaedic surgeon, researcher, educator; b. Asahikawa, Hokkaido, Japan, July 31, 1957; s. Shigeru and Kyoko (Iriyama) I.; m. Yuka Nagano, June 12, 1994; children: Takaaki, Kazuka. MD, Asahikawa Med. Coll., 1982, D of Med. Sci., 1986. Rsch. assoc. dept. biochemistry U. Ill., Urbana, 1986-89; med. staff Asahikawa Red Cross Hosp., 1990-91, Shindo Orthopaedic Hosp., Asahikawa, 1991-92; asst. dept. orthopaedic surgery Asahikawa Med. Coll., 1989-90, instr. dept. orthopaedic surgery, 1992—. Author: Prevention of Congenital Dislocation of the Hip in Infants: Experience and Results in Japan, 1993; contbr. articles to profl. jours. Grantee for sci. rsch. Ministry of Edn. of Japan, 1993, 94, 95-96; Am. Orthopaedic Assn. travelling fellow, 1999. Mem. Japanese Orthopaedic Assn., Japanese Soc. of Hip Joint, Japanese Soc. Cartilage Metabolism. Avocations: golf, jogging. Office: Asahikawa Med Coll/Orth Sur, Midorigaoka-higashi 2-1 1-1, Asahikawa, Hokkaido 078-8510, Japan

INAYAT-HUSSAIN, SALMAAN HUSSAIN, biochemical toxicologist; b. Kuala Terengganu, Malaysia, Sept. 5, 1968; s. Amir Muhammad and Rais Fatima (Abdul Razak) I.-H.; m. Michelle Nunis, Oct. 28, 1992; 1 child, Danial Imran. BSc with honors, U. Kebangsaan Malaysia, Kuala Lumpur, 1991; PhD, U. Leicester, Eng., 1997. Hosp. svc. rep. Pfizer Corp., Kuala Lumpur, 1991-92; tutor U. Kebangsaan Malaysia, 1992-97, asst. prof., 1997—; vis. rsch. assoc. Sch. Pharmacy, U. Colo. Health Scis. Ctr., Denver, 1999-2000; environ. impact assessment cons. for Union Carbide Corp., Consultancy Bur., U. Kebangsaan Malaysia; sec. Nat. Health Scis. Symposium, Kuala Lumpur, 1998; vis. scientist German Cancer Rsch. Ctr., Heidelberg, 1998. Contbr. articles to profl. jours. Young Scientists travel fellow IUBMB/FEBS, 2000, fellow Dan Charitable Fund for Rsch. in Biol. Scis., 2000; Wellcome rsch. travel grantee, 1999; Nat. U. Malaysia grantee, 1993-97. Mem. Mountain West Soc. Toxicology, Malaysian Soc. Physiology and Pharmacology, Malaysian Health Soc., Brit. Toxicology Soc. Islamic. Avocations: badminton, swimming, reading. E-mail: salmaan@medic.ukm.my. Office: Univ Kebangsaan Malaysia, Jalan Raja Muda Abdul Aziz, Kuala Lumpur 50300, Malaysia

INBAL, ELIAHU, conductor; b. Feb. 16, 1936; s. Jehuda Joseph and Leah (Museri) I.; m. Helga Fritzsche, July 29, 1968; 3 children. Student, Ednl. Acad. Music, Jerusalem, 1952-56, Conservatoire nat. Superieur, Paris, 1961-63. Chief condr. Radio Symphony Orch., Frankfurt, Germany, 1974-90, Teatro La Fenice, Venice, 1984-87; hon. condr. RSO Frankfurt, 1995—, Nat. Symphony Orch. RAI, Turin, 1996—; chief condr. Berlin Symphony Orch., 2001—; Guest condr. with numerous orchs., including Milan, Rome, Berlin, Munich, Hamburg, Stockholm, Copenhagen, Vienna, Budapest, Amsterdam, London, Paris, Tel Aviv, N.Y.C., Chgo., Toronto, and Tokyo, Phila. Condr. numerous recs. Office: Hessischer Rundfunk, D-60222 Frankfurt Germany also: care Kaylor Mgmt Inc 130 W 57th St Apt 8G New York NY 10019-3311

INBAR, MICHAEL, social psychology educator, consultant; b. Paris, Oct. 10, 1931; arrived in Israel, 1958.; BA, Hebrew U., Jerusalem, 1964; PhD, Johns Hopkins U., 1966. Asst. prof. U. Mich., Ann Arbor, 1966-67; vis. scholar Russell-Sage Found., N.Y.C., 1975-76; prof. sociology and psychology U. Haifa, Israel, 1976-77; lectr. through sr. lectr. Hebrew U., 1968-75, prof. sociology, 1977-81, Mandel prof. cognitive social psychology and edn., 1981—, dean Faculty Social Scis., 1984-88; vis. scholar Grad. Ctr., CUNY, 1982-83; vis. fellow Princeton (N.J.) U., 1988-89; sr. cons. Mandel Inst., Jerusalem, 1989—. Author: The Vulnerable Age Phenomenon, 1976; co-author: Ethnic Integration in Israel, 1976; founder, editor Simulation and Games, 1970-71; author simulation game The Community Response Game, 1966. Mem. Israeli Sociol. Assn., Am. Sociol. Assn., Am. Psychol. Soc. Avocation: chess. Office: Hebrew U, Dept Sociology, Jerusalem Israel

INCHINGOLO, GIUSEPPE MARTINO, anthropologist; b. Genoa, Italy, July 11, 1952; s. Antonio and Maria (Barbiani) I.; m. Tamara Maria Mendelevich, Dec. 11, 1980. Diploma in chemistry, Tech. Inst. of Chem. Industry, Genoa, 1975; degree in biology, U. Genoa, 1981. Cons. rschr. Italian Nat. Rsch. Ctrs. on Aging, Genoa, 1975—; cons. rschr. Inst. Anthropology U. Genoa, 1976-86, cons. rschr. Mus. Ethnomedicine, 1984-86. Contbr. articles to sci. jours. Mem. AAAS, Italian Soc. Anthropology and Ethnology, Italian Soc. Medicine and Geriat., N.Y. Acad. Scis. Avocations: blues and rock music, game theory. Fax: 1 651 319 6465. E-mail: inkpi@yahoo.com. Home: Via S Bernardo 17/12A, I-16123 Genoa Italy Office: PO Box 575, I-16100 Genoa Italy

INCZE, FERENC JÓZSEF, anesthesiologist; b. Budapest, Hungary, Dec. 28, 1928; s. Ferenc Béla and Flora Emma (Glückseel) I.; m. Maria Ágnes Ferencz, Sept. 12, 1959 (div. Sept. 1977); children: Ferenc Miklós, László Tamás, Katalin Judit. MD, Med. U. Budapest, 1953; PhD, Hungarian Acad. Scis., Budapest, 1977. Cert. pathology, surgery, anesthesiology, intensive care. Intern Med. U. Budapest, 1952-53, resident in pathology, 1954-55, resident in surgery, 1955-60, asst. prof. surgery, 1960-65; specialist in surgery Polyclinic 20th Dist. Budapest, 1965-70; head anesthesist Met. István/Stephan Hosp., Budapest, 1970-79; resident Med. Coll. Wis., Milw., 1971-73; head dept. anesthesiology and intensive care St. Roche Hosp., Budapest, 1979-95, cons. dept. anesthesiology and intensive care, 1996—; chief med. officer in anesthesiology and intensive care Pest County, 1979—; redactor Orvosi Hetilap/Med. Weekly, 1994—. Co-author: Surgery of Rectal Cancer, 1969, Respiratory Diseases, 1995; contbr. numerous articles to profl. jours. Active Trade Union Physicians and Health Care Workers, 1953-89. Med. Coll. Wis. fellow, 1981; recipient Ministry of Health award, Budapest, 1978, 86, Semmelweis prize Pest County, 1996, Scientific and Ednl. Work medal Hungarian Chamber of Physicians, 1996, Markusovszky Lajos prize Springer Med. Pub., 1999. Fellow Am. Coll. Anesthesiologists; mem. Hungarian Soc. Surgeons, Hungarian Soc. Anesthesiology and Intensive Care, Hungarian Acad. Scis., Hungarian Chamber of Physicians (Semmelweis prize of Pest County 1996). Avocations: numismatics, photography, home video, swimming, rowing. Home: Dohány Utca 30/b, H-1077 Budapest Hungary Office: St Roche Hosp, Gyulai Pál Utca 2, H-1085 Budapest Hungary

INCZE, KÁLMÁN, science administrator; b. Budapest, Hungary, Aug. 13, 1936; s. János and Maria (Tóth) I.; m. Anikó Rybár, Dec. 10, 1960; children: András, Zoltán, Kálmán. Diploma, Agrl. U., Gödöllö, Hungary, 1959; D of Natural Sci., Eötvös L. U., Budapest, 1965; PhD in Microbiology, Acad. Scis., Budapest, 1975. Rschr. Hungarian Meat Rsch. Inst., Budapest, 1959-69, sr. rschr., 1969-78, dept. head, 1978-85, rsch. dir., 1985-90, dir., 1990—; assoc. prof. U. Horticulture and Food Industry, Budapest, 1991—; cons. Iowa State U., Ames, 1989. Co-author: (books) Handbook of Meat Industry, 1973, Microbiology of Canning, Meat and Refrigeration Industry, 1980; co-editor: (book) Microbial Associations and Interactions in Food, 1984; editor-in-chief: (periodical) A HUS/Meat/, 1990—. Recipient Sigmond Elek medal Hungarian Sci. Assn. for Food Industry, 1992, Lörincz Ferenc medal Meat Rsch. Inst., 1995, Small Cross, Republic of Hungary, 1999. Mem. Sci. Assn. for Meat Industry (bd. dirs. 1995—), Sci. Assn. for Food Microbiology (bd. dirs. 1985—), Acad. Scis. (mem. com. for food sci. 1991—). Avocations: traveling, music, do it yourself activities, languages. Office: Hungarian Meat Rsch Inst, Gubacsi ut 6/b, 1097 Budapest Hungary

INCZÉDY, JANOS JOSEPH, retired chemical engineering educator; b. Budapest, Hungary, June 26, 1923; s. Janos Inczédy-Meissner and Anna Freysinger; m. Sara Ruzsicska, Mar. 1949; children: Janos, Sara, Susan, George. Diploma in chem. engring., Tech. U., Budapest, 1946, D in Technology, 1959; DSc, Hungarian Acad. Sci., Budapest, 1966. Cert. chem. engring. Engr. Leather Factory, Vác, 1945-49; dep. tech. dir. Pannonia Leatherf, Budapest, 1949-51; asst. Tech. U., Budapest, 1951-70; prof. Veszprem (Hungary) U., 1970-93, prof. emeritus, 1993—. Author: Analytical Application of Ion Exchanges, 1966, Analytical Application of Complex Equilibria, 1976, Continuous and Automatic Analysis, 1984. Mem. Internat. Union Pure and Applied Chemistry (divsn. V., com. V1 1969-95), Hungarian Chem. Soc. (pres. 1981-89, hon. pres. 1989—), Hungarian Acad. Sci. (divsn. chemistry). Avocation: music. Home: Budafoki ut 45, H-1111 Budapest Hungary Office: Univ Vesprem, Eqyetem u 10, H-8200 Veszprem Hungary

INDAHL, TROND MARINUS, museum curator; b. Sarpsborg, Norway, Oct. 10, 1953; s. Odd and Bjørg (Kolstad) I. Magister in History of Art, U. Oslo, Norway, 1980. Curator Nordlandsmuseet, Bodø, Norway, 1980-81, Trondheim (Norway) Mus. Applied Art, 1981-83; cons. for protection of architecture Sør-Trøndelag County Adminstrn., Trondheim, 1983-87; curator, head dept. The West Norway Mus. Applied Art, Bergen, 1987—; leading museologist at restoration project for Damsgård Country Mansion, Bergen, 1987-93. Home: Krohnengsmuget 9, N-5003 Bergen Norway Office: Western Norway Mus Applied Art, Nordahl Brunsgate 9, N-5014 Bergen Norway

INDARGO, EVELYN, music educator, concert pianist; b. Surabaya, Java, Indonesia, Nov. 1, 1975; d. Heru and Aida (Lisawati) Indargo. BMus, Staatliche Hochschule Musik, Freiburg, Germany, 1996; MMus, U. So. Calif., L.A., 1998. Cert. Yamaha tchr. Accompanist U. So. Calif., L.A., 1997-98; music instr. Yamaha Music Sch., Cerritos, Calif., 1998—; music dir. Indonesian Cath. Ch., L.A., 1996-98; concert pianist radio recording, TV appearances at TVRI, Surabaya, Indonesia, 1996. Mem. Music Tchrs. Assn. Calif., Pi Kappa Lambda.

INDERJIT, econogist, researcher; b. Delhi, India, Dec. 24, 1963; s. Nirmaljit Singh and Amerjit (Kaur) Ahluwalia. BSc, HansRaj Coll., Delhi, 1984; MSc, Panjab U., Chandigarh, India, 1986; PhD, Delhi U., 1993. Jr. rsch. fellow dept. botany U. Delhi, 1987-89, sr. rsch. fellow dept. botany, 1989-93, rsch. scientist, 1993-94; postdoctoral fellow Lakehead U., Thunder Bay, Can., 1995-97; STA fellow PERC, Sapporo, Japan, 1997-98; asst. prof. KVL U., Copenhagen, 1998-99; assoc. prof. Panjab U., Chandigarh, India, 2000—; vis. scientist Hokkaido Tokai U., Sapporo, 1995, Va. Tech., Blacksburg, 1997; vis. prof. Second Napoli (Italy) U., 1996. Sr. editor: Allelopathy Organisms, Processes and Applications, 1995, Principles and Practices in Plant Ecology: Allelochemical Interactions, 1999; contbr. articles to Plant and Soil, Jour. Chem. Ecology, Bot. Rev., Am. Jour. Botany, others. Mem. Ecol. Soc. Am., Bot. Soc. Am., Weed Sci. Soc. Am., Internat. Soc. Chem. Ecology, Internat. Weed Sci. Soc. Home: 3923 Tri Nagar, St No 18, Delhi 110035, India Office: Botany Dept, Panjab Univ, Chandigarh 160014, India

INDIRA, C.J., electrochemical research scientist; b. Adoor, India, Dec. 7, 1945; ss. Sri P.P. Padmanabha Pillai and Smt. N. Janaki Amma; m. K.V. Prasad, Jan. 24, 1971; children: Lakshmi, Jyothi. BSc, Kerala (India) U., 1966, MSc, 1969. Jr. scientific asst. CECRI Karaikudi, Tamil Nadu, India, 1972-77, sr. scientific asst., 1977-82, scientist A, 1982-83; scientist B CECRI Cochin Unit, Kerala, 1983-88, scientist C, 1988-93, scientist E, 1993—. Patentee in field; contbr. articles to profl. jours. Fellow Soc. Advancement Electrochem. Sci. and Tech. India (life fellow); mem. Swadeshi Sci. Movement India. Avocations: reading, music, dance, library activities. Home: Anupama near CUSAT Guest Ho, Kochi, 682 022 Kerala India Office: CECRI Cochin Unit, KD Plot, PO S Kalamassery, 683 109 Kochi Kerala, India

INDIRKAS, TAYFUN ABDULHALIK, holding company executive; b. Adana, Turkey, Mar. 23, 1945; s. Celalettin and Mehpare Z. (Onan) I.; m. Zühre Taskin, Mar. 4, 1972; 1 child, Ugur S. BS in Econs., Middle East Tech. U., Ankara, Turkey, 1971; MBA, U. Tex., 1977. Fin. mgr. Tümosan, Ankara, 1977-80, Eczacibasi O.A.S., Istanbul, Turkey, 1980-83; mng. dir. Eczacibasi Dash, Istanbul, 1983-86; v.p. Eczacibasi Holding, Istanbul, 1986—. Exec. bd. mem. Istanbul Found. for Culture and Art, 1990—. Mem. Fedn. European des Fabricants de Ceramics Sanitáires (bd. mem. 1988—), Galatasaray Soccer Club. Avocations: classical music, history. Office: Eczacibasi Holding AS, Büyükdere Cad 193, 80640 Istanbul Turkey

INDJIC, DRAGO, investment company executive; b. Belgrade, Serbia, Yugoslavia, June 23, 1965; s. Trivo and Snezana (Djuric) I.; m. Tamara Ast, Aug. 4, 1995; 1 child, Ana. Diploma in engring., U. Belgrade, 1990; PhD, Imperial Coll., London, 1993. Rsch. assoc. Mihailo Pupin Inst., Belgrade, 1983-90; sr. quantitative analyst Econostat, Wargrave, U.K., 1993-97; risk analyst Kuwait Investment Office, London, 1998-99; rsch. cons. 1st Quadrant Ltd., London, 1999-2000; head rsch. Fauchier Ptnrs. Ltd., London, 2000—; expert cons. European Comm., Brussels, 1997—; vis. prof. European Ctr. for Peace and Devel., Belgrade, 1997—; vis. rschr. London Bus. Sch., 1998—. Contbr. articles to profl. jours. Advisor Petnica Sci. Ctr., Valjevo, Yugoslavia, 1984—. Mem. IEEE, Inst. Elec. Engrs. Office: 2 Cavendish Sq, London W1G OPA, England

INDRAYAN, ABHAYA, statistician; b. Meerut, India, Nov. 11, 1945; s. Mahesh Prakash and Shakuntala (Devi) Prabhakar; m. Asha Rastogi, Oct. 15, 1972; children: Rahul, Swati. BSc, Meerut Coll., 1963, MSc, 1965; MS, Ohio State U., 1976, PhD, 1977. Lectr. Med. Coll., Allahabad, India, 1969-74; reader U. Coll. Med. Scis., Delhi, India, 1977-87; prof., dir. divsn. biostatistics, med. informatics U. Coll. Med. Scis., Delhi, 1987—; tchg. assoc. Ohio State U., Columbus, 1974-77, vis. faculty, 1983-84; project adviser Indian Coun. Med. Rsch., New Delhi, 1983-96; advisor WHO, Delhi, 1994, 96, Geneva, 1995, Hacettepe U., Ankara, 1997, Bangkok, 1998; project dir. Indian Coun. Social Sci. Rsch., New Delhi, 1995-97; cons. Danish Assistance to Blindness Control, New Delhi, 1995; project dir. UNAIDS India Database, New Delhi, 2000. Author: Solution Manual for Introduction to Statistical Methods, 1986, Medical Biostatistics, 2000; editor: Health Issues in Delhi, 1995, HIV/AIDS Research in India, 1997; contbr. articles to profl. jours. Grantee WHO, 1995. Fellow Indian Soc. Med. Statistics (convener curr. com. 1986-88, bd. dirs. 1994-97, Best Paper award 1995), Computer Soc. India (convener spl. interest group med. informatics 1994—), Nat. Acad. Med. Scis.; mem. Internat. Biometric Soc. (mem. internat. tech. com. 1995-98), Internat. Epidemiol. Assn., Internat. Statis. Inst. Avocations: computers, plants, foliage. Office: U Coll Med Scis, Dilshad Garden, Delhi 110 095, India

INDROVA, MARIE, immunologist; b. Ceske Budějovice, Czech Republic, Sept. 9, 1949; d. Jaromir and Marie (Masakova) Sefcikova; m. Miroslav Indra, Sept. 9, 1972; children: Marie, Madgalena. PhD, Inst. Molecular Acad. Sci., Prague, Czech Republic, 1980. Jr. rsch. worker Inst. Molecular Genetics, Czech Acad. Sci., Prague, 1980-94, rsch. worker, 1994—. Acad. Sci. Czech Republic grantee, 1995-97, 2000—, Grant Agy. of Czech Republic grantee, 1998-2000. Office: Inst Molecular Genetics, Flemingovo n 2, 16637 Prague Czech Republic

INDURAIN LARRAYA, MIGUEL, retired professional racing cyclist; b. Villava, Navarre, Spain, July 16, 1964. Profl. racing cyclist, 1986-97, ret. Amateur Cycling Champion of Navarre and Spain, 1983; Spanish Cycling Champion, 1993; 1st pl. Vuelta a Murcia and Tour del Porvenir, 1986, Vuelta a los Valles Mineros, 1987, Volta a Catalunya, 1988, 91, 92, Paris-Nice Cycling Classic, 1988, 89, 90, Critérium Internat., Avignon, France, 1988, San Sebástian Cycling Classic, 1990, Tour de France, 1991, 92, 93, Giro d'Italia, 1993; Bronze medalist World Long-Distance Cycling Championship, 1992, Gold medal Individual Time Trial Atlanta Olympics, 1996; recipient Principe de Asturias prize for Sports; decorated Grand Cross Order of Sports Merit, 1993; named to Legion of Honor, France, 1993. Address: Fed Espanola de Ciclismo, Ferraz 16, E-28008 Madrid Spain Address: Villava, Pamplona Spain*

INDYK, MARTIN S., diplomat; b. London, July 1, 1951. BE, Sydney U.; PhD in Internat. Rel., Australian Natl. U. Spec. asst. to the pres. & sr. dir. for Near East & So. Asian affairs Natl. Sec. Council; deputy dir. current intelligence for the Mid-East Australia, 1978; exec. dir Washington Inst. for Near East Policy, 1985; U.S. amb. to Israel U.S. Dept. of State, 1995—; asst. sec. Near Ea. affairs, 1997—; sr. mem. Sec. Christopher's Mid-East peace team; White House Rep. U.S.-Israel Sci. & Tech. Commission; adj. prof. Johns Hopkins Sch. Adv. Internat. Studies. Office: US Dept State Am Emb Tel Aviv, Israel Washington DC 20521-9700

INEICHEN, GUSTAV, linguistics educator; b. Luzern, Switzerland, June 6, 1929; s. Jules and Anna (Schmid) I.; m. Gertrud Luthin, Aug 10, 1955 (div. 1982); children: Wolfram, Markus. Lic.Phil., U. Fribourg, 1953, Dr.Phil., 1957; PhD, U. Zurich, 1963. Rsch. fellow Fondazione Cini, Venice, Italy, 1957-63; asst. prof. U. Zurich, 1963-65; prof. linguistics U. Gottingen, Germany, 1965-70, 75—; dir. Swiss Inst., Rome, 1970-75; vis. prof. U. Nanjing, China, 1985, U. Perugia, Italy, 1986, 88, Pusan, South-Corea, 1996. Author: El libro agregà de Serapion, 2 vols., 1962, 66, Arabisch-orientalische Sprachkontakte in der Romamia, 1997, Typologie und Sprachvergleich im Romanischen, 1999. Lt. Swiss Army, 1952-65. Mem. Corrispontente Acad. Padova, N.Y. Acad. Scis. Office: Romance Inst, Humoldtallee 19, 37073 Gottingen Germany

INFELD, ERYK, theoretical physicist; b. Toronto, Ont., Can., Jan. 8, 1940; Polish and Can. citizen; s. Leopold and Mary Helen (Schlauch) I.; 1 child, Ewa Joanna. BA, Cambridge (Eng.) U., 1962, MA, 1968; MA, Warsaw (Poland) U., 1964, PhD, 1966; DSc, Soltan Inst., Warsaw, 1972. Culham assoc. Culham (Eng.) Labs., 1964-65; assoc. Soltan Inst., Warsaw, Poland, 1963-64, adj. prof., 1965-73, assoc. prof., 1973-90, full prof., 1990—; prin. rsch. fellow Warwick (Eng.) U., 1978; vis. prof. U. Montreal (Can.), 1990-91; rsch. fellow U. Coll. London, 1992-93, Royal Soc. visitor, Warwick, Eng., 1998; vice chmn. Plasma Sect., Polish Acad. Sci., Warsaw, 1982-88, 93-96. Co-author: (with Rowlands) Nonlinear Waves, Solitons and Chaos, 1990 (Macmillan-Newbridge Book of the Month 1990, Doubleday Book Club 2000), 2nd edit., 2000; author: The Price of the Prize, 2000; co-editor: Nonlinear Dynamics Chaotic and Complex Systems, 1997; editor: Leopold Infeld, 1978; assoc. editor: Jour. Plasma Physics, 1988—, Jour. Tech. Physics, 1993—; contbr. numerous articles to profl. jours. Decorated Gold Cross Polish govt., 1989; recipient Polish Acad. Scis. award, 1990. Mem. Oxford and Cambridge Soc. Montreal, Am. Phys. Soc., Am. Math. Soc., Internat. Soc. for the Interaction between Math. and Mech., Polish Phys. Soc. (exec. com. 1983-86), Polish Electromagnetic Soc. (pres. 1990-91), Soc. for Sci., Polish Acad. Scis. (physics com.). Avocation: horseback riding, writing novels. Home: Boya 2 no 8, 00621 Warsaw Poland Office: Soltan Inst, Hoza 69, 00681 Warsaw Poland

INFIELD, PAUL LOUIS, barrister; b. London, July 1, 1957; s. Gordon Mark and Roda Molca (Lincoln) I.; m. Catharine Grace Evans, Feb. 6, 1987; children: Samuel Francis, Margery Joan. LLB, Sheffield U., 1979. Bar: Eng., Wales. Barrister London, 1980—. Contbr. The Prisons Handbook, 1997-98; co-author: The Law of Harassment and Stalking: Butterworths, 2000. Chmn., bd. visitors HM Prison, Wandsworth, London, 1996-98. Jewish. Avocations: penal affairs, cycling, children, scuba diving. Office: 5 Paper Buildings Temple, London EC4Y 7HB, England

INGBER, ARIEH, dermatology educator; b. Vasharoshnomyen, Hungary, Dec. 25, 1947; s. Abraham and Zehava (Perelstein) I.; m. Tova Levy, Feb. 2, 1975; children: Moria, Shira, Esthy, Renana, Abraham, Israel, Noam. MD, Tel-Aviv U., 1973; Specialist for Dermatology, Beilinsom Med. Ctr., Petach-Tikua, Israel, 1984. Resident dept. dermatology Beilinsom Med. Ctr., Petach-Tikua, 1979-84, sr. dermatologist, 1984-93, dep. head, 1993-95; chmn. dept. dermatology Hadassah Hosp., Jerusalem, 1995—; chmn. Israeli Contact Dermatitis soc., 1993—; sr. dermatologist dept. dermatology, Beilinson Med. Ctr., 1984; lectr. in dermatology and venereology, Sackler Sch. of Medicine, Tel Aviv U., 1985; participant Christian Albrechts Hosp., U. Kiel, 1985; lectr. dept. dermatology Baylor Coll. of Medicine, Tex. Med. Ctr., Houston, 1988; intern. Assaf-Harofe Med. Ctr., Zerifin, Israel, 1974; gen. physician villages near Ashkelon, Israel, 1976-77; others. Author numerous publs. in field. Recipient awards Katzenellenbogen Rsch. Found., Sackler Sch. of Medicine, Tel Aviv U., 1981, 1992, Israel Cancer Rsch. Fund award, 1986, Vol.'s award Am. Acad. of Dermatology, 1993, award Am. Contact Dermatitis Soc. Ann. Mtg., Washington, 1993.

INGEL, LEV KHANAANOVICH, geophysicist, researcher; b. Nizhny Tagil, USSR, May 15, 1946; s. Khanaan Isaacovich and Fruma Solomonovna (Al'perovich) I.; m. Faina Isaacovna Shtern,June 25, 1975 (div. Sept. 1982); 1 child, Ann; m. Irina Edwardovna Sklobovskaya, Jan. 5, 1990. Grad., Gorky (USSR) State U., 1968; PhD, Inst. Exptl. Meteorology, Obninsk, USSR, 1979; D in Physics and Math., Hydrometeo Ctr. Russia, Moscow, 1998. Engr. Inst. Salute, Gorky, 1969-73; engr. Inst. Exptl. Meteorology, Obninsk, USSR, 1973-75, scientist, 1975-83; sr. scientist Inst. Exptl. Meteorology, Obninsk, USSR/Russia, 1983—, dir. postgrad. study, 1985-95. Contbr. articles to profl. jours. Pres. Kaluga Region Br. Dem. Russia Movement, 1992-97; sec. Obninsk Regional Human Rights Soc., 1995—. Grantee Internat. Sci. Found., 1993, Russian Found. Fundamental Rsch., 1997, 98. Mem. Fed. Party Dem. Russia. Avocations: modern history, running, football, walking in Russian forests. Home: Mira St 4 flat 45, 249038 Obninsk Russia Office: Inst Exptl Meteorology, Prosp Lenina 82, 249030 Obninsk Russia

INGELMAN-SUNDBERG, AXEL, obstetrics and gynecology educator; b. Uppsala, Sweden, Dec. 22, 1910. MD, Uppsala (Sweden) U., 1938; asst. prof. ob-gyn., Karolinska Inst., 1947-58, royal prof., 1958-77. Asst. in gen. chemistry Uppsala U., 1929, asst. in histology, 1930-31, asst. in pathology, 1937; sr. surgeon dept. ob-gyn. Sabbatsberg U., Stockholm, 1949-79; cons. Sophiahemmet Hosp., 1983-88; surg. dept. Ersta Hosp., 1977—; prof. emeritus ob-gyn. Karolinska Inst., Stockholm, 1978—; cons. Swedish Nat. Bd. Health, 1960-79, Swedish Def. Forces, 1969-79; hon. prof. U. Montevideo, 1962; pres. 5th World Congress on Fertility and Sterility, 1966; prof. (hon.) Faculty of Medicine U. Buenos Aires, 1998. Author: Rectal Injuries Following Radium Treatment of Cancer of the Cervix Uteri, 1947, The Childbearing Years, 1951; co-author: A Child Is Born, 1965-82; chief editor: Acta Obstet., Gyn. Scandinav., 1970-77; asst. editor: Internat. Jour. Gynecol. Obst., Internat. Jour. Fertility; contbr. numerous sci. papers to profl. jours. Recipient Hwasser prize, 1943. Mem. Swedish Soc. Ob-Gyn. (pres. 1961-69), Scandinavian Assn. of Ob-Gyn. (pres. 1966-68), Scandinavian Assn. for Study of Fertility (pres. 1961, 74), Internat. Fertility Assn. (pres. 1968-74), Internat. Fedn. Fertility Socs. (treas. 1968-80), Fedn. Internat. Gyn.-Ob. (v.p. 1973-76, pres. sci. com. 1976-79, medal 1994), Internat. Urogynecol. Assn. (pres. 1976-81, pres. 15th ann. meeting 1990), , others. Avocation: salmon fishing.

INGEMANSSON, RICHARD STIG BERNT, cardiothoracic surgeon; b. Lund, Sweden, Sept. 8, 1963; s. Stig Gerhard and Sol-Britt Barbro (Anderson) I. MD, U. Lund, Sweden, 1990; PhD, 1995. At doctor Dept. Surgery Medicine, Fagersta, Sweden, 1990-92; MD Dept. Cardiothoracic Surgery,

Lund, Sweden, 1992-95; PhD, 1995, st-doctor, aud. doctor, 1999. Author: Progress in Applied Microcirculation, 1996; contbr. articles to profl. jours. Capt. Reserve, 1984-97, Sweden. Mem. Svenska lakarsallskapet, Svensk thorax.kir. forening, The Swedish Hunting Assn. Avocations: hunting, fishing, sailing, golf. Home: Allahelgona kyrkogata 6A, 22362 Lund Sweden Office: Dept Catdiothoracic Surgery, University Hospital of Lund, S-22185 Lund Sweden

INGENKAMP, HEINZ GERD, philologist, educator; b. Krefeld, Germany, Nov. 22, 1938; m. Barbara Brigitta Kutsche, Aug. 4, 1964; children: Konstantin, David, Julian. PhD, Bonn (Germany) U., 1966. Extraordinary prof. Bonn U., 1971-79, univ. prof., 1980—. Author: Plutarchs Schriften über die Heilung der Seele, 1971, Schillers Werke, Nationalausgabe, Band 15 I, 1993, Friedrich Schiller, Werke und Briefe, Band 9, 1995; co-editor Schopenhauer-Jahrbuch, 1984—, Beitrage zur Philosophie Schopenhauers, 1998—; editor: Die Antike und ihr Weiterleben, 1997—. Mem. Schopenhauer-Gesellschaft (pres. 1992-00). Home: Am Helpert 5, D-53177 Bonn Germany Office: U Bonn Philologisches Seminar, Am Hof 1 e, D-53113 Bonn Germany

INGERMAN, PETER ZILAHY, infosystems consultant; b. N.Y.C., Dec. 9, 1934; s. Charles Stryker and Ernestine (Leigh) I.; m. Carol Mary Pasquale, Dec. 19, 1970 (div. May 1980); m. Colleen Frances McGaffey, Sept. 13, 1996. AB, U. Pa., 1958, MSEE, 1963; PhD, Greenwich U., 1991. CLU; cert. data processor, computer programmer, sys. profl., emergency med. technician. Rsch. investigator U. Pa., Phila., 1958-63; tech. dir. programming rsch. Westinghouse, Balt., 1963-65; mgr. RCA, Cherry Hill, N.J., 1965-72; sr. staff cons. Equitable Life Assurance Soc. of U.S., N.Y.C., 1972-77; ind. computer cons. Willingboro, N.J., 1977—; adj. prof. computer sci. Pratt Inst. Tech., 1968-73; mem. working groups Internat. Fedn. Info. Processing, 1962—; rep. Conf. Data Systems Langs., 1967-71, Am. Nat. Standards Inst., 1960-69; bd. dirs. Phila. Health Plan, Inc., 1975-77, Crossroads Runaway Program, Inc., 1981-82, Willingboro Emergency Squad, 1986-89, Compliance, Inc., 1989—, Providence House, 1991-94, vice chair, 1991-94. Author: A Syntax-Oriented Translator, 1966, Russian transl., 1969; contbr. articles to profl. jours.; patentee electronic circuits. Fellow Brit. Computer Soc.; mem. IEEE (life sr.), AAAS, Assn. Computing Machinery, Data Processing Mgmt. Assn., Am. Cryptogram Assn., Brit. Engring. Coun. (chartered info. sys. practioner, chartered info. sys. engr., chartered engr.), Independent Computer Cons. Assn. (treas. 1999—), Am. Guild Organists (co-dean S.W. Jersey chpt. 1997-98, dean 1998-99, treas. 1999—), N.J. Acad. Scis., Mensa, Triple Nine Soc., Assn. Former Intelligence Officers, Sigma Xi (life), Upsilon Pi Epsilon. Office: 40 Needlepoint Ln Willingboro NJ 08046-1928

INGERSOLL, GAIL LAURA, nursing administrator, nursing educator, nursing researcher; b. Utica, N.Y., Apr. 25, 1949; d. Robert James and Elnora Catherine (Bracken) I. AAS in Nursing, Alfred State Coll., 1971; BSN, Alfred U., 1980; MSN, U. Rochester (N.Y.), 1983, EdD in Adminstr., 1986. RN, N.Y., Ind., Tenn. Asst. clinician surg. ICU U. Rochester Med. Ctr., 1974-77, surg. ICU staff nurse, 1971-74, 77-79, clinician I surg. outpatient dept., 1979-82, assoc. dir. office clin. practice evaluation, 1988-89, dir. rsch. clin. nursing practices, 1988-89; clin. nurse specialist/instr. critical care U. Rochester Sch. Nursing, 1985-86, clin. nurse specialist/instr. trauma/spinal cord injury, 1985-86, asst. prof., 1986-92, interim chmn. div. health restoration, 1988-89; chmn. div. health restoration U. Rochester (N.Y.) Sch. Nursing, 1989-91; assoc. prof., chmn. dept. nursing adminstrn. and tchr. edn. Ind. U. Sch. Nursing, Indpls., 1992-96, prof., 1995-96; asst. dir. nursing for adminstrn. Ind. U. Hosps., Indpls., 1992-96; prof. Ind. U. Sch. Nursing, Indpls., 1995-96; assoc. dean for rsch., Chenault prof. nursing Vanderbilt U., 1996-99; vis. prof. U. Rochester, 1999—; lectr. and cons. in field; manuscript reviewer Critical Care Nurse, 1986-89, Image, The Jour. Nursing Scholarship, 1989-98, Nursing Outlook, 1992—. Robert Wood Johnson Clin. Nurse scholar, U. Pa., postdoctoral fellow, 1988. Fellow Am. Acad. Nurses; mem. ANA, Nat. League for Nursing, Sigma Theta Tau (Leadershpi award Delta Sigma chpt.), Kappa Delta Pi, Sigma Xi. Office: Box 619-7 601 Elmwood Ave Rochester NY 14642-0001

INGERSOLL, RICHARD KING, lawyer; b. Algoma, Wis., Aug. 13, 1944; s. Robert Clive and Bernice Eleanore (Koehn) I.; m. Caroline Soi-Keu Yee, Aug. 31, 1968; children: Kristin Paula Juk-Yee, Karin Eleanor Juk-Ling. BBA, U. Mich., 1966; JD, U. Calif.-Berkeley, Berkeley, 1969. Bar: Ill. 1969, Hawaii 1973. Asst. prof. U. Ill.-Champaign, Champaign, 1969-70; assoc. Sidley & Austin, Chgo., 1970-73; ptnr. Rush, Moore, Craven, Kim & Stricklin, Honolulu, 1973-88, Gelber, Gelber, Ingersoll Klevansky & Faris, Honolulu, 1989—; speaker tax law seminars. Author various law materials. Mem. ABA (taxation, bus. and internat. law coms.), Waialae Country Club (sec.). Home: 944 Waiholo St Honolulu HI 96821-1226

INGERSOLL, TED MERIAM, adversiting executive; b. Cleve., Oct. 3, 1939; s. Edumund Meriam and Helen (Storer) I.; m. Jean M. McCutcheon, June 30, 1962; children: Karen Marie, Kristen James, Kimberley Sue. BFA, Kent State U., 1962. V.p., acct. exec. The Marschalk Co., Cleve., 1969-73; v.p., mgmt. supr. Tracy-Locke Advt., Denver and Dallas, 1973-81; exec. v.p. First Columbia Fin. Corp., Denver, 1981-84; dir. Mason Best Co., Dallas, 1984-87; pres. Richards/Ingersoll, Dallas, 1987-90; exec. v.p. Valentine Radford Advt., Dallas and Kansas City, Mo., 1991—; bd. dirs., adv. bd. Bryan's House, Dallas, 1987—; bd. dirs. Communities in Schs., Dallas, 1994—. Capt. USAF, 1962-68. Republican. Presbyterian. Avocations: snowskiing, golfing, music. E-mail: ted.ingersoll@valrad.com. Home: 3525 Turtle Creek Blvd Apt 5B Dallas TX 75219-5515 Office: Valentine Radford Inc PO Box 13407 Kansas City MO 64199-3407

INGHAM, KENNETH DALE, communication educator; b. Pottstown, Pa., May 2, 1963; s. Kenneth Leroy Ingham and Ruth Elizabeth Overholtzer. BS, Kutztown (Pa.) U., 1988, MS summa cum laude, 1991. News dir. WPAZ Radio, Pottstown, Pa., 1988-91; prof. comm. Alvernia Coll., Reading, Pa., 1993—; videographer, prodn. asst. Broadcast Images, Allentown, Pa., 1988; prodr. cable TV commls., 1991, tech. advisor corp. tng. video, 1992. Dir., writer, prodr. Seduction of Innocence, 1991. Avocations: photography, autograph collecting, fishing, movies, musical theatre.E-mail: dale@newmail.net.

INGLE, PANDHARINATH ONKAR, agricultural educator; b. Shemba Bk, India, Oct. 19, 1948; s. Onkar Ninaji and Kasabai Onkar (Rakhonde) I.; m. Sarala Pandharinath Dandge, FEb. 11, 1974; 2 children. BS in Agr., Coll. Agr., Nagpur, India, 1968, MS in Agr., 1970; PhD in Ext. Edn., Dr Panjabrao Deshmukh Agrl. U., Akola, India, 1981; LLB, Nagpur (India) U., 1984. Cert. agrl. educator, rschr., ext. expert. Sr. rsch. asst. Dr. Panjabrao Deshmukh Agrl. U., Akola, 1971-76; asst. prof. Dr. Panjabrao Deshmukh Agrl. U., Sindewahi, India, 1977-80; supt. Agrl. Sch., Warud (Pusad), India, 1980-81; asst. prof. Postgrad. Inst. PDKV, Akola, 1981-90, assoc. prof. agr., 1990—, rector, 1987—; mem. acad. coun. Dr. Panjabrao Deshmukh Agrl. U., Akola, 1997—, mem. faculty agr., 1996—, mem. bd. studies, 1997—. Author: Congruity and Innovation in Indian Agriculture, 1987, Scientific Report Writing, 1999; contbr. articles to profl. jours. Mem. Internat. Soc. Ext. Edn. (life), Indian Soc. Ext. Edn. (life), Maharashtra Soc. Ext. Edn. (life, Best Rsch. Paper award 1985, 89, Best Use of AV Aids in Paper Presentation 1990). Avocations: reading, writing, farming, playing badminton. Home: B/19 Krishinagar PDKV, Akola 444 104, India Office: Dept Ext Edn, PDKV Krishinagar, Akola 444 104, India

INGLE, RONALD FERGUSON, family physician; b. Jinan, Shandong, China, May 8, 1927; arrived in South Africa, 1958; s. Laurence Mansfield and Agnes Sinclair (Ferguson) I.; m. Pauline Cornwell Marshall, Feb. 13, 1960. BA, Cambridge (Eng.) U., 1948, MB, BChir, 1952, MA, 1953. Med. supt. All Saints Mission Hosp., Transkei, South Africa, 1958-76; chief med. officer in primary care Dept. Health, Transkei, 1977-80, dep. sec. (profl.), 1980-82; Tb officer Dept. Health and Welfare, Eastern Cape, South Africa, 1982-85; sr. lectr. Med. U. So. Africa, Medunsa, South Africa, 1985—; mem., vice chmn. Cons. Com. for South African Med. Missions, 1970-76; mem. coun. South African Nat. Coun. for Health Edn., 1977-82; mem. com. Transkei and Ciskei Rsch. Soc., 1978-84; mem. health edn. com. South African Nat. Tb Assn., 1985-94. Contbr. articles to sci. publs. Chmn. Beacon Bay br. Progressive Fed. Party, 1983-84. Flight lt. Royal Air Force, 1953-57. Mem. South African Med. Assn., Brit. Med. Assn., Royal Air Force Club London, Mensa. Avocations: medical informatics, research methodology, bird watching, travel, literature. Home: 678 Punctata St, Gauteng Pretoria North 0182, South Africa Office: Med Univ So Africa, Dept Family Medicine, Medunsa 0204, South Africa

INGLE, STEPHEN JAMES, political science educator; b. Ripon, Yorkshire, Eng., Nov. 6, 1940; s. James and Violet Grace (Stephenson) I.; married Aug. 5, 1964; children: Jonathan James-Stuart, Benedict John Stephen, Cassie Louise. BA with honors, U. Sheffield, Eng., 1962, MA in Econs., 1965; PhD, Victoria U., Wellington, New Zealand, 1967. Lectr. politics U. Hull, Eng., 1967-79, sr. lectr. politics, 1980-91, head of dept., 1985-90; prof., head of dept. U. Stirling, Scotland, 1991—; vis. rsch. fellow Victoria U., Wellington, 1993. Author: Socialist Thought in Imaginative Literature, 1979, Parliament and Health Politics, 1981, The British Party System, 1987, 3d edit., 2000, George Orwell: A Political Life, 1993. Active East Yorkshire Health Authority, 1985-90, various sch. bds. of govs., 1985-90. Mem. Polit. Studies Assn. (sec. 1987-88). Avocations: fell walking, music, theater. Home: The Ridings, Perth Rd, Dunblane FK15 OHA, Scotland Office: U Stirling, Dept Politics, Stirling FK9 4LA, Scotland

INGLE, SUD RANGANATH, management consultant; b. Pune, India, Oct. 6, 1942; Came to U.S., 1965; s. Ranganath V. and Sita R. I.; m. Neelima Kulkarni Ingle, June 21, 1970; children: Geeta, Vinita. B in Engring., Coll. Engring., Pune, 1964; MS in Indsl. Engring., Purdue U., 1966; MBA, U. Wis., Oshkosh, 1972. Quality control engr. Giddings and Lewis, Fond du Lac, Wis., 1966-70; quality control engr. Mercury Marine, Fond du Lac, 1970-77, gen. mgr., 1977-82; pres. Quality Circles Services, Fond du Lac, 1982—; cons., trainer in field; assoc. prof. bus. Marian Coll. Fond du Lac, Wis., 1987—, initiator of Quality Productivity Mgmt. degree program, 1988, co-initiator MS program in Quality Values and Leadership, 1991. Author: Quality Circles Master Guide, 1982, Quality Circles in Service Industries, 1983, In Search of Perfection, 1985, (video programs and workbooks) Implementing ISO 9000 Standards Series, Organizational Quality Improvement, Implementing Quality Circles. Mem. Fond du Lac Art Council, 1970; local rep. Fox Valley India Soc., Appleton, Wis. 1979. Mem. Internat. Assn. Quality Control (founding), Am. Soc. Quality Control. Home: 318 Pheasant Ct Fond Du Lac WI 54935-5425 Office: PO Box 812 Fond Du Lac WI 54936-0812

INGLEHART, RONALD FRANKLIN, political science educator; b. Milw., Sept. 5, 1934; s. Gerald Almon and Helen Clara (Krippene) I.; m. Babette Feinberg, Aug. 16, 1963 (div. Sept. 1968); children: Elizabeth Lynn, Rachel Jennifer; m. Marita Rohr Rosch, May 5, 1986; children: Ronald Charles, Marita Helen. BA, Northwestern U., 1956; MA, U. Chgo., 1962, PhD, 1967. Asst. prof. U. Mich., Ann Arbor, 1967-71, assoc. prof., 1971-76, prof. polit. sci., 1977—, program dir. Inst. for Social Rsch., 1984—; vis. prof. U. Mannheim, Germany, U. Geneva, U. Kyoto, Japan, U. Kobe, Japan, Free U., Berlin, Leiden U., U. Rome, U. Belo Horizonte; mem. adv. coun. Berlin Sci. Ctr., 1992—, Ctr. for Polit. Studies, Ann Arbor, 1995—. Author: The Silent Revolution, 1977, Culture Shift, 1990, Modernization and Postmodernization, 1997, Human Values and Beliefs, 1998; mem. editl. bd. seven scholarly jours. Co-founder Euro-Barometer Surveys, Brussels, 1974—; pres. World Values Surveys Hdqrs., Ann Arbor, 1988—, Global Environ. Survey, 1996—. Mem. Internat. Soc. for Polit. Psychology, Internat. Polit. Sci. Assn., Am. Polit. Sci. Assn., Midwest Polit. Sci. Assn. Avocation: writing childrens stories. Home: 2626 Geddes Ave Ann Arbor MI 48104-2715 Office: Inst for Social Rsch 326 Thompson St Ann Arbor MI 48104-2225

INGLES, ERNIE BOYCE, academic administrator, chief librarian; b. Calgary, Alta., Can., Dec. 30, 1948; s. Robert Howard and Muriel E. (Boyce) I.; m. Claire E. Chapman, Aug. 28, 1971; 1 child, Erin. BA, U. Calgary, 1970, MA, 1973; MLS, U. B.C., Can., 1974. Head dept. rare books U. Calgary, 1974-78; exec. dir. Can. Inst. of Hist. Microre Prodns., Ottawa, Ont., Can., 1978-84; univ. librarian U. Regina, Sask., Can., 1984-90; dir. libraries U. Alberta, 1990-95, assoc. v.p. learning sys., 1995—. Compiler: Canada: The Printed Record, 1981, Canada: World Bibliographical Series, 1990, Bibliography of Canadian Bibliography, 1994. Exec. dir., founder Northern Exposure to Leadership Inst., 1993—; trustee Ottawa Pub. Libr. Bd., 1982-84. Recipient Ruth Cameron medal, U. B.C., 1974, Marie Tremaine medal for bibliography, 1996; named Outstanding Acad. Librarian, Can. Assn. of Coll. and Univ. Librs., 1994, Innovator of Year, Can. Info. Tech., 1996. Mem. Can. Libr. Assn. (pres. 1990-91), Bibliog. Soc. of Can. (pres. 1989-91), Hist. Soc. Alta. (exec. dir. 1977-78). Avocation: riding. Address: 1-3J University Hall, Edmonton, AB Canada T6G 2J9

INGOLFSSON, THORSTEINN, diplomat. Permanent rep. to NATO Govt. of Iceland, Brussels, 1994-98; permanent rep. to UN Govt. of Iceland, N.Y.C., 1998—. Office: Permanent Mission Iceland to UN 800 3rd Ave Fl 36 New York NY 10022-7604

INGRAHAM, HUBERT ALEXANDER, Bahamian government official; b. Pine Ridge, Bahamas, Aug. 4, 1947; m. Delores Miller; 5 children. Bar: Bahamas, 1972. Sr. ptnr. Law Firm of Christie, Ingraham & Co.; prime min. The Bahamas, 1992—; mem. Her Majesty's most hon. Privy Coun., 1993—; chmn. The Bahamas Mortgage Corp. Elected to nat. gen. coun. Progressive Liberal Party, 1975, re-elected 1982, elected nat. chmn., 1976, mem. House of Assembly, 1977, expelled 1986, elected ind. mem. 1987; joined Official Opposition, 1990, apptd. parliamentary leader, leader Free National Movement, 1990. Mem. Nassau Jaycees (officer), Bahamas Jaycees (officer). Office: Office the Prime Min, West Bay St POB N-7147, Nassau Bahamas*

INGRAHAM, JOHN WRIGHT, banker; b. Evanston, Ill., Nov. 10, 1930; s. Harold Gillette and Mildred (Wright) I.; m. Barbara Gaye Barker, Nov. 8, 1967; children—Kimberly, Elizabeth, Scott. A.B., Harvard U., 1952, M.B.A., 1957; postgrad., NYU Grad. Sch. Bus., 1963-68. Jr. lending positions Citicorp, N.Y.C., 1957-66, sr. lending positions, 1966-70, head instl. recovery mgmt., 1970-78, dep. chmn., credit policy com., 1979-92, sr. v.p. oversight N.Am lending, 1979-84, sr. v.p., mem. credit policy com. for Latin Am. and investment banks, 1985-88, sr. v.p., mem. credit policy for global pvt. bank, 1989-92; sr. v.p., line risk mgr. for global pvt. bank Dynamo M Fund, Nassau, Bahamas, 1993-99; sr. v.p., line risk mgr. Citigroup Global Asset Mgmt. and Pvt. Banking, N.Y.C., 2000—; bd. dirs. Dynamo M Fund, Nassau, Bahamas; past bd. dirs. Ark. Best Corp., Ft. Smith, Sprague Techs., Inc. Greenwich, Conn.; chmn. audit com. Presto Industries, Houston, 1986-88; vice chmn. bd. Penn Cen. Corp., Cin., 1978-84, chmn. fin. com., 1982-91, past bd. dirs.; rep. banking industry before coms. and hearings U.S. Ho. Reps., U.S. Senate, 1976-78; mem. N.Y. Crime Stoppers, N.Y.C. Police Found., 1993—. Trustee Noble and Greenough Sch., Dedham, Mass., 1987-94; mem. bus. adv. coun. to dean Grad. Sch. Bus., U. Ark, Fayetteville, 1985-95; mem. com. for Asia rsch. HArvard U. John King Fairbanks Ctr., Cambridge, Mass., 1993—. Lt. USN, 1952-55, Korea. Mem. Fin. Acctg. Standards Bd. (task force 1974-81), Robert Morris Assocs. (bd. dirs. 1972-75, Disting. Svc. award 1978), Union Club, Piping Rock (Locust Valley, L.I.), Gulfstream Bath and Tennis Club (Fla.), Ocean Club (Fla.), Harvard Club Boston, St. Andrews Soc. State of N.Y. Republican. Christian Scientist. E-mail: john.ingraham@citicorp.com. Home: 950 Park Ave New York NY 10028-0320 Office: Citicorp 399 Park Ave New York NY 10022-4614 also: 6880 N Ocean Blvd Boynton Beach FL 33435-3348

INGRAM, JAMES BROWN, retired educator; b. Cullen, Scotland, June 2, 1930; s. John Forsyth and Charlotte Baxter (Brown) I.; m. Elizabeth Ann Macbeth, Aug. 4, 1958; children: Alan Macbeth, Cameron John, Gillian Margaret. MA, Aberdeen (Scotland) U., 1950, BD, 1953; MEd, Edinburgh (Scotland) U., 1955; MSc, Strathclyde (Scotland) U., 1983. Asst. tchr. Jordanhill Coll. Sch., Glasgow, Scotland, 1955-61; head dept. divinity, asst. vice prin. Tchrs. Coll., Bulawayo, Rhodesia, 1962-65; lectr. in edn. U. Coll. Rhodesia, Salisbury, 1965-70, City of Leeds (Eng.) and Carnegie Coll. Edn., 1970-72; prin. lectr. curriculum studies Margaret McMillan Coll. Edn., Bradford, Eng., 1972-77; BEd course dir. Bradford (Eng.) and Ilkley C.C., 1977-80, prin. lectr. fin. and investment, 1980-90; retired, 1990; rschr., writer UNESCO, Paris, Hamburg, 1977-79. Author: Curriculum Integration and Lifelong Education, 1979; contbr. articles to profl. jours. Mem. Killin Heritage Soc., Killin Golf Club. Presbyterian. Avocations: golf, gardening, music, mathematics, economics.

INGRAM, JAMES CARLTON, economist, educator; b. Roanoke, Ala., Jan. 11, 1922; s. John Henry and Isabelle (Shanks) I.; m. Alice Jane Graham, May 1, 1948; children: Deborah, Susan, Melissa. B.S., U. Ala., 1942; A.M., Stanford, 1947; Ph.D. (Social Sci. Research Council fellow), Cornell U., 1952. Research analyst Indsl. Indemnity Ins. Co., San Francisco, 1947-48; successively asst. prof., assoc. prof., prof. econs. U. N.C., Chapel Hill, 1952—; dean U. N.C. (Grad. Sch.), 1966-69; vis. mem. London Sch. Econs., 1963-64; vis. prof. Thammasat U., Bangkok, Thailand, 1969-71; guest scholar Brookings Instn., 1976; disting. vis. prof. Johns Hopkins U. Bologna Ctr., 1984; vis. prof. Hopkins-Nanjing China Ctr., 1988. Author: Economic Change in Thailand Since 1850, rev. edit, 1971, Regional Payments Mechanisms, 1962, International Economic Problems, 1966, 3d edit., 1978, International Economics, 1983, 3d edit., 1993; Mng. editor: So. Econ. Jour, 1961-65. Served with AUS, 1942-46. Ford Found. fellow, 1963-64. Mem. Am. Econ. Assn., So. Econ. Assn. (mem. exec. com., pres. 1972-73). Home: 1012 Highland Woods Rd Chapel Hill NC 27514-4410

INKSTER, JULI, professional golfer; b. Santa Cruz, Calif., June 24, 1960; m. Brian Inkster, July, 1980. Student, San Jose State U. Professional golfer LPGA, 1983—; winner Nabisco/Dinah Shore Invitational, 1984, 89, DuMaurier Classic, 1984, Lady Keystone Open, 1985, 86, McDonald's Classic, 1986, Atlantic City Classic, 1986, 88, Crestar Classic, 1988, 89, Safeco Classic, 1988, Bay State Classic, 1991, JAL Big Apple, 1992, U.S. Women's Open, 1999, Longs Drugs Challenge, 1999, Welch's/Circle K Championships, 1999; mem. U.S. Solheim Cup teams, 1992, 98. Victories include Samsung World Championship of Women's Golf, 1997, 98, McDonald's LPGA Championship, 1999, Longs Drug Challenge, 2000. Office: care LPGA 100 International Golf Dr Daytona Beach FL 32124-1082

INLOW, RUSH OSBORNE, chemist; b. Seattle, July 10, 1944; s. Edgar Burke and Marigale (Osborne) I.; m. Glora Elisa Duran, June 7, 1980. BS, U. Wash., 1966; PhD, Vanderbilt U., 1975. Chemist, sect. chief U.S. Dept. Energy, New Brunswick Lab., Argonne, Ill., 1975-78; chief nuclear safeguards br. Cruise missile sys., 1983-84, program mgr. Navy strategic sys., 1984-85, dir. weapon programs divsn., 1985-88, dir. prodn. ops. divsn., 1988-90, asst. mgr. safeguards and security, 1990-94, asst. mgr. nat. def. programs, 1994-96, dep. mgr., 1996-2000; mem. tech. staff Sandia Nat. Labs., 2000—; apptd. Fed. Sr. Exec. Svc., 1985. Served with USN, 1966-71. Tenn. Eastman fellow, 1974-75; recipient Pres. Meritorious Exec. awrd The White House, Pres. Clinton, 1994. Mem. Am. Chem. Soc., Sigma Xi. Republican. Episcopalian.

INMAN, CULLEN LANGDON, telecommunications scientist; b. N.Y.C., June 24, 1933; s. Claude Colbert Sr. and Myra Eugenia (Langdon) I.; m. Patricia Anne McDonough, Dec. 23, 1965; children: Cathleen Elaine, Elisabeth Myra. AB in Math., Univ. Calif., 1956; PhD in Physics, N.Y.U., 1965. NAS/NRC rsch. assoc. Goddard Inst. Space Studies, N.Y.C., 1965-66; group leader systems and analysis, tech. staff info. divsn. Am. Inst. Physics, N.Y.C., 1967-72; cons., 1972-74; programmer analyst, mem. tech. staff N.Y. Telephone/Bell Labs., 1974-89. Contbr. articles to profl. jours. Mem. Am. Physical Soc., Am. Math. Soc., Assn. Computing Machinery. Achievements include research for first calculation of binding energy of a neutron star, calculation of weak induced magnetic moment of the muon's neutrino.

INMAN, EDWARD OLIVER, museum director; b. Oslo, Norway, Aug. 12, 1948; s. John and Peggy Florence (Beard) I.; m. Elizabeth Douglas, Mar. 4, 1971 (div. 1982); children: James, Louise; m. Sherida Lesley Sturton, June 27, 1984; 1 child, Isabel; stepchildren: Rachel, Harriet. MA, Gonville & Caius Coll., 1969, Sch. Slavonic Studies, London, 1970. Rsch. asst., directing staff Imperial War Mus., London, 1972-78; keeper Imperial War Mus. Duxford, Cambridge, 1978-82; dir. Imperial War Mus., Cambridge, 1982—; gov. 2d Air Divsn. Meml. Libr., Norwich, U.K., 1994—; dir. Cultural Heritage Nat. Tng. Orgn. (formerly Mus. Tng. Inst.), Bradford, U.K., 1998—. Decorated Order Brit. Empire. Fellow Royal Aero. Soc. Office: Imperial War Museum, Duxford Airfield, Cambridge CB2 4QR, United Kingdom

INMAN, JAMES RUSSELL, claims consultant; b. Tucson, May 24, 1936; s. Claude Colbert and Myra Eugenia (Langdon) I.; m. Charleen M. Bowman, Feb. 22, 1964 (div. 1977); m. Margaret Williams Kendrick, Apr. 26, 1996. Student, Pomona Coll., Claremont, Calif., 1954-60. Supr. res. dept. Honnold Libr. Claremont Coll., 1959-60; supr. casualty claims CNA Ins., L.A., 1961-70; asst. mgr., asbestos specialist, head entertainment claims Firemen's Fund, L.A., Beverly Hills, 1970-83; pres. Wilnor Corp., L.A., 1982—; claims auditor dirs. and officers claims Harbor/Continental Ins., L.A., 1984-86; claims mgr. Advent Mgmt., L.A., 1987, Completion Bond Co., Century City, Calif., 1988; asst. to pres., claims specialist Am. Multiline Corp., L.A., 1988-92; sr. claims specialist Reliance Ins. Co., Glendale, Calif., 1992-94; expert witness in field. Mem. First Century Families: Calif.; mem. com. Baldwin Hills Dam Disaster, 1968-72; pres. Alcohol Info. Ctr., L.A., 1983-85. Mem. L.A. Athletic Club, Wilshire Country Club. Avocations: Classic cars, American and English silver. Home: 623 S Arden Blvd Los Angeles CA 90005-3814

INNES, BRIAN, writer, designer; b. Croydon, Surrey, Eng., May 4, 1928; s. Stanley George and Laura Florence (Thornton) I.; m. Felicity McNair Wilson (div. 1965); m. Eunice Mary Lynch, Apr. 2, 1971 (div. 1984); children: Simon, Andrew, Jamey. BSc, U. London, 1949; student, King's Coll., London, London Coll. Printing, Ctrl. Sch. Art & Crafts, Chelsea Coll. Art. Rsch. biochemist Kemball, Bishop & Co., London, 1949-53; asst. editor Chem. Age, London, 1953-55; assoc. editor The Brit. Printer, London, 1955-60; art dir. Paul Hamlyn Group, London, 1960-62; dir. Temperance Seven Ltd., London, 1961—, Animated Graphic and Publicity, London, 1964-65; prin. Brian Innes Agy., London, 1965-67, Immediate Books, London, 1966-70, FOT Libr., London, 1966—; script editor Zeta Mag., London, 1967; art dir. BPC/Purnell Pub., London, 1967-70; creative dir., dep. chmn. Orbis Pub., London, 1970-86; dir. Macdonald Pub., London, 1986-87; editl. dir. Mirror Pub., London, 1987-88; cons. Brown Pkg., London, 1990-95. Author: The Book of Pirates, 1966, The Book of Spies, 1967, The Book of Revolutions, 1967, Die Seeraüberei, 1969, The Book of Outlaws, 1969, Flight, 1969, The Lore of the Railways, 1970, Horoscopes, 1977, The Tarot, 1978, The Red Baron Lives, 1982, The Book of the Havana Cigar, 1983, Red Red Baron, 1983, (with Francis King) Fate and Fortune, 1989, Crooks and Conmen, 1992, Catalogue of Ghost Sightings, 1996, History of Torture, 1998, Death and the Afterlife, 1999, The Book of Dreams, 2000, Bodies of Evidence, 2000, (as Neil Powell) Alchemy, the Ancient Science, 1979, The Book of Change, 1980, (with Stuart Holroyd) Mysteries of Magic, 1976, Geheimisvolle Wissenschaften, 1978, Geheimzinnige Wetenschappen, 1978 and others; contbr. Encyclopedia Britannica, Cordon Bleu Cookery Course, History of the English Speaking Peoples, World War II, American Destiny, On Four Wheels, The Sea, Greenfingers, Wings, Take Off, the Elite, The Story of Scotland, Discover Scotland, Real Life Crimes, Marshall-Cavendish Encyclopedia of Life Sciences; contbr., co-editor: Man Myth & Magic, 1995; contbr. numerous photographs; appeared in plays A Doll's House, 1935, A Christmas Carol, 1935, Pickwick, 1936, Quality Street, 1937, The Bed Sitting-Room, 1963, The Royal Commission Revue, 1964, Oom-Pah-Pah, 1964; appeared in films, including The Guinea Pig, 1948, It's Trad Dad, 1962, Take Me Over, 1962, Toto di Notte, 1962, The Wrong Box, 1965; numerous recordings, radio and TV appearances. Royal variety command performance, London, 1961. Fellow Royal Soc. Arts, Chartered Soc. Designers; mem. Inst. Printing, Arts Club, Brit. Actors' Equity (life), Soc. Authors, Crime Writers' Assn., Soc. Nautical Rsch., Cruising Assn. Avocation: music. Home: Les Forges de Montgaillard, 11330 Montgaillard France

INNES, CATHERINE LYNETTE, English studies educator; b. Mudgee, NSW, Australia, Jan. 26, 1940; arrived in England, 1975; d. Ian Charles and Myriam Sarah (Mirza) I.; m. Martin Paul Scofield, Dec. 31, 1975; children: Robin Mary, Rachel Joy. BA, U. Sydney, Australia, 1960; MA, U. Oreg., 1965; PhD, Cornell U., 1973. Tchg. fellow U. Sydney, 1961-63; instr. Ctrl. Wash. State Coll., 1966-67, Tuskegee Inst., Ala., 1968-70; asst. prof. U. Mass., Amherst, 1973-75; lectr. U. Kent, Canterbury, 1978-92, prof., 1992—, equal opportunities officer, 1990-93. Assoc. editor WASAFIRI, 1990-99; author: The Devil's Own Mirror, 1990, Chinua Achebe, 1990, Woman and Nation in Irish Literature, 1993; editor: African Short Stories, 1985. Labor organizer La Huelga, Calif., 1966. Mem. Brit. Assn. for Australian Studies

(v.p. 1988-90), Assn. for Tchg. Caribbean and African Lit. (pres. 1978-79). Avocations: music, theatre, travel. Office: U Kent, Sch English, Canterbury Kent CT2 7NX, England

INNES, JOHN, accounting educator; b. Edinburgh, Scotland, July 11, 1950; s. Joseph and Marjory I.; m. Tina Graham, March 25, 1982. BCom, U. Edinburgh, 1972, PhD, 1985. Auditor KPMG, Edinburgh, 1972-75; internat. auditor Uniroyal, Oxford, 1975-78; lectr., sr. lectr. U. Edinburgh, 1978-91; prof. U. Dundee, Scotland, 1991—; lead tchg. assessor Funding Coun., Scotland, 1995-96; vis. prof. U. Nantes, France, 1997-99. Co-author: Contemporary Cost Management, 1995; editor, contbr.: Handbook of Mgmt. Acctg., 1998; contbr. articles to profl. jours. Office: U Dundee, Dept Acctg Bus Fin, Dundee DD1 4HN, Scotland Address: U Dundee Acctg Bus Fin Dept, Perth Rd, Dundee DD1 4HN, Scotland

INNES-BROWN, GEORGETTE MEYER, real estate broker, insurance broker; b. Wilmington, Del., Mar. 20, 1918; d. George and Flora Sue (Saunders) Meyer; m. Andrew T. Innes, Jr., Nov. 26, 1947 (dec.); m. Roy Glen Brown, Jr., Mar. 6, 1991. Grad. Real Estate Law, theory, Conveyancing and Practice, Phila. Bd. Realtors Sch., 1945; grad. Fire, Marine, Casualty Ins., North Phila. Realty Bd. Sch., 1946; cert. appraiser, Villanova Coll., 1974. Lic. realtor, Pa., ins. broker and appraiser, Phila. Ins. broker, realtor Phila., 1945—, ins. broker, 1946—, also appraiser; residential and single family home builder, Bucks County, Pa., Princeton, N.J., 1955-61. Mem., spkr. Juniata Pk. Civic Assn., Phila., 1984. Recipient Knights Legion award Italian-Am. Press, 1971. Mem. Nat. Assn. Realtors (sec.-treas. and v.p. chpt. 1975-80), Am. Bus. Women's Assn. (chpt. v.p. 1971, Businesswoman of Yr. 1971), Phila. Women's Realty Assn. (pres. bd. govs. 1949-85, pres. 1949-51, Woman of Yr. 1972-73), Phila. Bd. Realtors (v.p. residential divsn. 1975), North Phila. Realty Bd. (v.p. 1975, 76, pres. 1977, Gustav A. Wick award 1979), Del. Coun. Realty Bds. (sec. 1974), Real Estate Multiple Listing Burs. (treas. 1972-76), Sigma Lambda Soc. (chpt. pres. 1948). Avocations: golf, dancing, gardening, cooking, embroidery. Home: 1162 Walnut Ter Boca Raton FL 33486-5565

INNIS, PAULINE, writer, publishing company executive; b. Devon, England; came to U.S., 1954; m. Walter Deane Innis, Aug. 1, 1959. Attended, U. Manchester, U. London. Author: Hurricane Fighters, 1962, Ernestine or the Pig in the Potting Shed, 1963 (paperback 1992), The Wild Swans Fly, 1964, The Ice Bird, 1965, Wind of the Pampas, 1967, Fire from the Fountains, 1968, Astronumerology, 1971, Gold in the Blue Ridge, 1973, 2d edit., 1980, My Trails (transl. from French), 1975, Prayer and Power in the Capital, 1982, The Secret Gardens of Watergate, 1987, Attention: A Quick Guide to Armed Services, 1988, Desert Storm Dairy, 1991, The Nursing Home Companion, 1993, Bridge Across the Seas, 1995, The Gospel of Joseph, 1998, I've Smashed the Devil's Window, 1999; co-author: Protocol, 1977. Bd. dirs. Washington Goodwill Industries Guild, 1962-66; membership chmn. Welcome to Washington Club, 1961-64; co-chmn. Internat. Workshop Capital Spkr.'s Club, 1961-64; pres. Children's Book Guild, 1967-68; dir. Ednl. Commn., bd. dirs. Internat. Conf. Women Writers and Journalists, Nat. Arboretum, 1992—; criminal justice com. D.C. Commn. on Status of Women; founder vol. program D.C. Women's Detention Ctr.; chmn. women's com. Washington Opera, 1977-79; mem. Liaison Com. Med. Edn., 1979-85; nat. trustee Med. Coll. Pa., 1980—; mem. Edn. Commn. for Fgn. Med. Grads., 1986—. Named Hoosier Woman of Yr., 1966. Mem. Soc. Women Geographers, Authors League, Smithsonian Assocs. (women's bd.), English-Speaking Union, Spanish-Portuguese Group D.C. (pres. 1965-66), Br. Inst. U.S., Am. Newspaper Women's Club (pres. 1971-73), Internat. Soc. Poets (disting.), Sulgrave Club, Internat. Clubs (co-chair 1997), Venerable Order St. John Jerusalem, Internat. Neighbors Club. Home: 2700 Virginia Ave NW Washington DC 20037-1908

INNOCENTI, ANTONIO CARDINAL, retired archbishop; b. Poppi, Fiesole, Tuscany, Aug. 23, 1915. Ordained Roman Cath. Ch., 1938. Consecrated bishop Titular See Aeclanum, 1968; archbishop of Eclano; then archbishop Apostolic Nuncio Spain; proclaimed cardinal, 1985, retired; prefect Congregation for the Clergy; pres. pontifical commn. Ecclesia Dei, 1991. Home and Office: Piazza della Citta Leonina 9, 00193 Rome Italy*

INOGUCHI, TAKASHI, political scientist, educator; b. Nigata, Japan, Jan. 17, 1944; s. Kokichi and Mitsuko I.; m. Kuniko Yokota, Aug. 8, 1976. BA, U. Tokyo, 1966, MA, 1968; PhD, MIT, 1974. Assoc. prof. polit. sci. Sophia U., Tokyo, 1974-77; assoc. prof. polit. sci. U. Tokyo, 1977-88, prof., 1988—; sr. vice rector The United Nations U., 1995-97; Japan Found. vis. prof. Grad. Inst. Internat. Studies, Geneva, 1977-78, Australian Nat. U., 1986; disting. vis. prof. Nat. U. Singapore, 1999. Author: Peking, Pyongyang, Moscow, 1961-66: A Quantitative Analysis of International Relations, 1970, A Comparative Study of Diplomatic Style, China, Britain, Japan, 1978, International Political Economy, 1982, Contemporary Japanese Political Economy, 1983, Introduction to Social Sciences, 1985, The Political Economy of International Relations, 1985, Beyond Free Ride: Japan's New Role in the Changing World, 1987, States and Societies, 1988, Negoatiation, Alliance and War, 1990, Contemporary International Politics and Japan, 1991, Japan: The Governing of an Economic Superpower, 1993, Japan's Foreign Policy in an Era of Global Change, 1993, Contemporary Japanese Diplomacy, 1993, System Change and International Politics, 1994, The Task of a Political Scientist, 1996, Global Change: A Japanese Essay, 2000; co-author: Japanese Electoral Behavior, 1986, Electoral Behavior in the 1983 Japanese Elections, 1986, Tribal Legislators: Japan's Liberal-Democratic Parliamentarians in Action, 1987, Deciphering the World, 1990, Assessing the Gulf War, 1991; editor: Leviathan: Japanese Jour. Polit. Sci., 1987—, Jour. Japanese Studies, 1989—; editor Internat. Orgn., 1986-91, World Politics, 1990-93, Japanese Jour. Polit. Sci., 1999—, Internat. Rels. Asia-Pacific, 2000—; co-editor The Polit. Econ. of Japan, vol. 2, The Changing Internat. Context, 1988, The Total Vision of Aging Societies, 1991, Politics in Pacific Asia Since WWII, 1993, U.S.-Japan Rels. and Internat. Institutions After the Cold War, 1995, North-East Asian Regional Security: The Role of Internat. Institutions, 1996, Japanese Politics Today: Beyond Karaoke Democracy?, 1997, The Vitality of Japan, 1997, The Changing Nature of Democracy, 1998, Internat. Security Mgmt. and The United Nations, 1999, Cities and the Enrironment, 1999, Democracy, Governance, and Economic Performance: East and Southeast Asia, 2000, American Democracy Promotion, 2000, Japanese Foreign Policy Today: Beyond Karaoke Diplomacy?, 2000; editor Contemporary Polit. Sci. Series, 1988—, E. Asian States and Societies Series, 1992-93, Frontiers of Knowledge Series, 1999—; assoc. editor other jours. Grantee Ministry Edn., 1978, 79-81, 81-83, 85-88, 87-90, 88-90, 93-95 98-99, 99—; Fulbright vis. scholar Ctr. Internat. Affiars HArvard U., 1983-84, U. Delhi, 1989, U. Aarhus, 1990, Sch. Advanced Internat. Studies Johns Hopkins U., 1990, Gadjah Mada U., Jogjakarta, Indonesia, 1990, Peking U., Beijing, China, 1993, Inst. Internat. Studies U. Calif., Berkeley, 1993; affiliate scholar UN U., Tokyo, 1990-94. Mem. Japanese Polit. Sci. Assn., Am. Polit. Sci. Assn., Internat. Polit. Sci. Assn., Japanese Assn. Internat. Relations (v.p. 1998—), Internat. Studies Assn., Econ. Coun. People's Living, Acad. Coun. Japanese Govt. Office: 7-3-1 Hongo, Bunkyoku Tokyo 113-0033, Japan

INOKUCHI, HIROO, education administrator, escientist; b. Hiroshima, Danbara, Japan, Feb. 3, 1927; s. Toyohachiro and Yoshiko (Mikami) I.; m. Yasuko Ishibshi, Feb. 3, 1961; children: Wataru, Makoto, Satoko. BSc, U. Tokyo, 1948, MSc, 1950, DSc, 1956; PhD, Nottingham U., 1957, DSc, 1987. Rsch. assoc. U. Tokyo, 1950-59, assoc. prof., 1959-67, prof., 1967-75; prof. Inst. for Molecular Sci., 1975-87, dir. gen., 1987-93, rsch. advisor, 1995—; pres. Okazaki Nat. Rsch. Inst., 1993-95; vice dir. Internat. Inst. Advanced Studies, 1996—; chief scientist Space Utilization Rsch. Program, NASDA, 1996—. Contbr. articles to profl. jours. Recipient Japan Acad. award, 1965, Prize of Fujiwara Found., 1989, Person of Cultural Merit, 1994. Mem. Engring. Acad. Japan, Japan Acad., Chinese Acad. Sci. Home: 4-18-9 Mejiro Toshima, Tokyo 171-0031, Japan Office: Inst Molecular Sci, 38 Myodaiji, Okazaki 444-8585, Japan

INOUE, AKIRA, law educator; b. Japan, 1938. LLB, Hitotsubashi U., Tokyo, 1962, LLM, 1967. Cert. full prof. grad. sch. of law, coun. for establishment of univs., Minister of Edn., Japan. Asst. prof. Seijo U. Faculty Law, Tokyo, 1977-79, prof., 1980—, prof. Grad. Sch. Law, 1987—; vis. scholar Inst. Comparative Law, U. Jean Moulin (Lyon III), Lyon, France, 1976-77, 89, Inst. Comparative Law Paris, U. Law, Econs. and Social Scis. (Paris 2), 1989. Co-author: (with others) (books) Important Problems of Modern Commercial Law, 1983, Grand Dictionary on Law of Corporations, 1984, Present Problems of Commercial Law, 1985, Powers and Liablilites of Directors, 1994. Mem. Japan Assn. Private Law, Assn. Econ. Jurisprudence, Japanese Maritime Law Assn., The Air Law Inst. of Japan. Office: Seijo U Faculty of Law, 6-1-20 Seijo Setagaya-ku, Tokyo 157, Japan

INOUE, HIDENORI, law educator; b. Kyoto, Japan, Dec. 20, 1950; s. Tsuyoshi and Toshiko Inoue. B of Politics, Waseda U., Tokyo, 1975, LLM, 1977. Instr. Mesei U., Tokyo, 1984-89, assoc. prof., 1989-95, prof., 1995—; committeeman Japan Energy Law Inst., Tokyo, 1984-95, Inst. Developing Economies, Tokyo, 1992-96, Clean Japan Ctr., Tokyo, 1992, Nuc. Material Control Ctr., 1997-98; rapporteur Internat. Bar Assn., London; bd. dirs. Japan Ctr. for Human Environ. Problems, Japanese Assn. Environ. Law and Policy, Japanese Assn. Land and Environment. Mem. Internat. Bar Assn., Am. Soc. Internat. Law, Japanese Assn. Internat. Law, Japanese Assn. World Law, Japanese Assn. Traffic Law, Japanese Assn. Water Resources and Environment, Soc. Environ. Sci. Japan. Home: # 206 14-18 Kamisoshigaya, 5 chome Setagaya-ku, 157-0065 Tokyo Japan Office: Meisei U, 1-1 Hodokubo 2 chome, 191-8506 Hino Tokyo, Japan

INOUE, HISAYUKI, chemist; b. Onomichi, Hiroshima, Japan, Sept. 3, 1951; s. Tsuyoshi and Hidee (Yoshikawa) I.; m. Kaori Inoue; children: Eri, Yuki, Takuya. BS in Chemistry, Nagoya Inst. Tech., 1974; MS in Chemistry, Kyoto U., 1976, PhD in Chemistry, 1980. Rschr. Meteorol. Rsch. Inst., Tsukuba, Japan, 1980-86, sr. rschr., 1986-91; sr. rschr. Meteorol. Rsch. Inst., Tsukuba, 1991-97, head, 1997—; postdoctoral fellow Groningen U., The Netherlands, 1991. Author rsch. in field. Mem. Japan Chem. Soc., Japan. Meteorol. Soc. (Horiuchi Shorei Kikin medal 1990), Am. Geophys. Union. Avocations: skiing, swimming, baseball reading, visiting old temples. Office: Meteorol Rsch Inst, 305 0052 Tsukuba Ibaraki Japan

INOUE, KAZUHIRO, physiatrist, researcher; b. Miyazaki, Japan, Sept. 3, 1959; s. Kazushige and Tomiko (Watanabe) I. MD, U. Occup. and Environ. Health, Japan, 1985; PhD, U. Occup. and Environ. Health, 1991. Mem. med. staff dept. rehab. medicine U. Occupational and Environ. Health, Kitakyushu, Japan, 1985-91, instr., 1991-92; chief dept. rehab. medicine Hamamatsu (Japan) Rosai Hosp., 1992-95; instr. dept. rehab. medicine U. Occupational and Environ. Health, Kitakyushu, Japan, 1995-96; chief dept. rehab. medicine Junwakai Meml. Hosp., 1996—. Contbr. articles to profl. jours. Mem. AAAS, N.Y. Acad. Scis., Japanese Assn. Rehab. Medicine, Internat. Soc. Autonomic Neuroscis., Japan Soc. Neurovegetative Rsch., Japan Soc. Med. Electronics and Biol. Engring. Fax: 81-985-47-8558. E-mail: kazinoue@orange.ocn.ne.jp. Office: Junwakai Meml Hosp Rehab Md, 1119 Komatsu, Miyazaki 880-2112, Japan

INOUE, NAOHISA, physicist, educator; b. Ichikawa, Chiba, Japan, Aug. 21, 1944; s. Yoshio and Tama Inoue; m. Shiomi Hashimoto; children: Mino, Hisami. BS, Tokyo U., 1969, MS, 1971, PhD in Physics, 1973. Rschr. NTT Labs, Tokyo, 1973-83; supr. NTT Labs, Atsugi, Japan, 1983-95; prof. physics Osaka Prefecture U., 1995—. Co-author: Handbook of Nanophase Materials, 1997, Defects and Properties of Semiconductors, 1987; contbr. articles to profl. jours. Avocations: travel, tennis, ancient history, cacti. Home: 5-12-16 Hanakoganei, Kodaira Tokyo 187-0002, Japan Office: Osaka Prefecture Univ, 1-2 Gakuencho, Sakai Osaka 599-8570, Japan

INOUE, SHUN, sociologist; b. Sendai, Miyagi, Japan, Sept. 8, 1938; s. Noboru and Tadako (Ishihara) I.; m. Mayako Shigematsu, Mar. 14, 1967. BA, Kyoto U., 1963, MA, 1965. Asst. lectr. Kyoto U., 1967-70; lectr. Kobe U. Commerce, 1970-72; assoc. prof. Osaka Nat. U., Japan, 1972-80, prof., 1980-96; prof. Kyoto U., 1996—. Author: The Loss of Meaning in Death, 1973, A Sociology of Play and Games, 1977, Play and Culture, 1981, A Social Psychology of Lies and Lying, 1982, A Choice of Nightmares, 1992; co-author: Introduction to Sociology, 1993; editor: A Sociology of Contemporary Culture, 1998, Contemporary Sociology Series, 26 vols., 1995-97, Studies in the Sociology of Sport, 1999. Mem. Japan Sociol. Assn., Japan Soc. Sport Sociology, Kansai Sociol. Assn. Home: 3-23-13 Nagaoka, Nagaokakyo-shi, Kyoto 617-0823, Japan Office: Kyoto U Dept Sociology, Yoshida-Honmachi, Sakyo-ku, Kyoto 606-8501, Japan

INOUE, TAKASHI, food products executive; b. Tokyo, Japan, Aug. 12, 1935; s. Seishiro and Chiyo (Sekimizu) I.; m. Akiko Hirasawa, Feb. 7, 1965; children: Haruko, Naoko, Ken, Makoto. Student, Tokyo U., 1959, D of Agriculture, 1977. Head research group Kirin Brewing Co., Takasaki, 1972-84, gen. mgr. brewing sci. lab., 1984-87, gen. mgr. cen. lab. key tech., 1987-89; exec. mng. cons., 1989—; part-time lectr. Tokyo U. of Agr. and Tech., 1984—. Mem. Inst. Food Technologists, Master Brewers Assn. Am. (corr. chmn. 1985—), Am. Soc. Brewing Chem. Home: 1-20-13 Takaidonishi, Suginamiku Tokyo 168, Japan Office: Beer div Kirin Brew Co, 6-26-1 Jingumae, Shibuyaku Tokyo 150, Japan

INOUE, TAKAYUKI, vascular surgeon; b. Osaka, Japan, Sept. 21, 1929; s. Kenichi and Hisa (Takashima) I.; m. Yachiko Torii, Oct. 17, 1964; children: Tadashi, Kyoko. BS, Osaka City U., 1950, MD, 1954, PhD, 1961. Med. diplomate Japanese Ministry of Health and Welfare, 1955. Resident in surgery Osaka City U. Hosp., 1955-57; resident in anesthesia The Jewish Hosp. of Bklyn., 1957-59; rsch. fellow in surgery Columbia U.-Presbyn. Med. Ctr., N.Y.C., 1959-61; instr. surgery Osaka City U. Med. Sch., 1962-64; fellow in surgery U. Colo. Med. Ctr., Denver, 1964-66; surgeon in chief Osaka Mcpl. Shirokita City Hosp., 1967-71; asst. prof. surgery Kawasaki Med. Coll., Okayama, Japan, 1971-76; prof. surgery Kawasaki Med. Coll., Okayama, 1976-81; surg. dir. Soryukai-Inoue Hosp., Osaka, 1981-86; dir. North Osaka Clinic, 1986-91; hon. dir. Iseikai Hosp., Osaka, 1992—. Contbr. articles to profl. jours. Mem. North Osaka Cultural Saloon, 1994—. Mem. Japanese Soc. Surgery, Internat. Soc. Surgery, Internat. Cardiovascular Soc., Internat. Soc. for Artificial Organs. Avocations: reading, painting, photography, travel. Home: 4-12-25-601 Hanjo, Minoh City Osaka 562-0044, Japan Office: Iseikai Hosp, 6-2-25 Sugawara, Higashi 533-0022, Japan

INOUE, TAKESHI, psychiatrist; b. Kumamoto, Japan, Sept. 3. 1932; s. Tatsuichi and Shigeye (Matsushita) I.; M.D., Kumamoto U., 1957, Ph.D., 1962; m. Michiko Takeshita, Oct. 8, 1961; children: Hiroko, Takao. Lectr. dept. biochemistry Kumamoto U. Med. Sch., 1957-61; lectr. U. Calif. Med. Sch., San Francisco, 1961-73, postdoctoral fellow, 1968; postdoctoral fellow dept. biochemistry Temple U. Med. Sch., Phila., 1968-70; asst. prof. dept. neuropsychiatry Kumamoto U. Med. Sch. (Japan), 1971-83; dir. Minamata Hosp., 1983-85, dir., 1985-93; dir. Kohsei Hosp., 1993—. Mem. AAAS, Japanese Neurochem. Soc., N.Y. Acad. Scis., Sigma Xi. Home: 16-15 2 Chome Musashigaoka, Kumamoto 862, Japan Office: 1125-2 Shimoharadamachi, Hitoyoshi 868, Japan

INOUE, YOSHIHARU, biochemistry educator; b. Kitakyushu, Fukuoka, Japan, Sept. 21, 1961; s. Masato and Tamae (Yasunari) I.; m. Keiko Katsura, June 18, 1989; children: Fumiyoshi, Hiroyoshi. BS, Kyoto (Japan) U., 1985, MSc, 1987, PhD, 1991. Asst. prof. Rsch. Inst. for Food Sci., Kyoto U., 1988-95, assoc. prof., 1995—; mem. editl. bd. Process Biochemistry, Elsevier, 1998—, Applied Microbiol. Biotech., 2000—. Author: Genome Microbiology, 1999; contbr. articles to sci. jours., including Jour. Biol. Chemistry. Recipient young scientist award Japan Soc. for Biosci. Biotech. and Agrochemistry, 1999. Mem. Yeast Soc. (com. 1998—), Soc. for Biosci. and Engring. (com. for fortification of Society 1995—). Office: Kyoto U, Rsch Inst for Food Sci, Uji Kyoto 611-0011, Japan

INOUE, YOSHISUKE, business administration educator; b. Nagasaki, Japan, Apr. 21, 1932; s. Arata and Masa I.; m. Motoko; children: Mari, Mika, Yumi. BME, Waseda U., 1956; MS (Fulbright scholar), Case Inst. Tech., 1960. Control engr. Yawata Iron & Steel Co. Ltd., Yawata, Japan, 1956-70, asst. mgr. office of pres., 1965-67, mgr. info. systems dept., 1968-76; dept. gen. mgr. info systems dept. Nippon Steel, Tokyo, 1976-80, gen. mgr. system devel. office, 1980-86; assoc. prof. bus. adminstrn. St. Andrew's U., Osaka, Japan, 1987-91; prof. bus. adminstrn. St. Andrew's U., Osaka, Japan, 1991—; dean bus. adminstr. St. Andrew's U., Osaka, 1996-98. Mem. Japan Soc. Mech. Engring., Sigma Xi. Anglican. Home: 1250-204 Oyamada-cho, Kawachinagano-City, Osaka 586-0094, Japan Office: St Andrews U Dept Bus Admin, 1-1 Manabino Izumi-city, Osaka 594-1152, Japan

INOUYE, TAMON, mathematician; b. Tokyo, Oct. 9, 1936; s. Kaoru and Mitsuko (Shibuya) I.; m. Kazuko Hatoyama, Oct. 6, 1967; children: Shin, Ayako. BS, U. Tokyo, 1959, MS, 1961, ScD, 1966. Rschr. Toshiba R & D Ctr., Kawasaki, Japan, 1961-71, sr. rschr., 1971-78; prof. U. Tsukuba, Japan, 1984-2000, prof. emeritus, 2000—, dean grad. sch., sci. & engring. dept., 1997-99; dir. Inst. Applied Physics U. Tsukuba, 1999-2000; vis. scientist MIT, 1966-67. Rsch. fellow Toshiba Rsch. & Devel. Ctr., 1978-84. Mem. Japanese Soc. Magnetic Resonance Medicine (sec. gen. 1991, bd. trustees 1986-90, 94-98, 2000—), Japan Assn. Med. Imaging and Tech. (sec. gen. 1996, bd. trustees 1990—). Achievements include development of first diagnostic magnetic resonance imager in Japan. Home: 3-16-14 Nishi-Shinagawa, Shinagawa-ku Tokyo 141-0033, Japan Office: Inst Applied Math, 2-8-8-401 Amakubo, Tsukuba 305-0005, Japan

INSALATA, S. JOHN, arbitrator; b. Chgo., Nov. 2, 1933; s. Sabato Chistopher and Marie Olivia (Gomes) I.; m. Bernadine Borst, 1968 (div. 1969). JD, Loyola U., Chgo., 1957, M in Social and Indsl. Rels., 1965; cert., Hague Acad., World Court, Holland, 1962. Bar: Ill. 1958, U.S. Dist. Ct. Ill. 1958, U.S. Ct. Appeals 1958, U.S. Supreme Ct. 1960. Clk. Taylor, MIller, Bush, Magnor, Chgo., 1957-58; legis. counsel N.A.M.A. Trade Assn., Chgo., 1958-65; gen. counsel Ill. Bar Assn., Springfield, 1966; asst. prof. adminstrv. law and legis. DePaul U., Chgo., 1967-70; pvt. practice Chgo. Contbr. articles to profl. jours. Named Atty. of Yr., DePaul U., Chgo., 1964. Mem. Scottish Rite Masons, Medinah Shriners, Pi Kappa Delta. Avocations: writing, speaking, photography, philetaly, travel. Home and Office: 426 W Briar Pl Apt 1C Chicago IL 60657-4701

INSANALLY, SAMUEL RUDOLPH, diplomat; b. Guyana, Jan. 23, 1936. Grad., U. London, U. Paris. Tchr. modern langs. Kingston Coll., Jamaica, Queen's Coll., Guyana, U. Guyana, 1959-66; counsellor Guyanese Embassy, Washington, 1966-69; charge d'affaires Guyanese Embassy, Venezuela, 1970; amb. Guyanese Embassy, 1972-78, amb. to Belgium (accredited to Sweden, Norway and Austria), 1978-81, amb. to Colombia, 1982-86; dep. permanent rep. of Guyana UN, N.Y.C., 1970-72, permanent rep., 1987—; head polit. divsn. I Ministry Fgn. Affairs, 1982-86; high comdr. to Barbados, Trinidad and Tobago and Ea. Caribbean Govt. of Guyana, 1982-86; bd. govs. Inst. Internat. Rels., Trinidad and Tobago, 1982-86; pres. 48th session, UN General Assembly, 1993—. Office: Permanent Mission of Guyana UN 866 U N Plz Rm 555 New York NY 10017-1822*

INSARDI, NINA ELIZABETH, benefits administrator; b. Port Chester, N.Y., Dec. 8, 1960; d. Albert Charles and Dorothy Elizabeth (Adis) I. BA in English magna cum laude, U. Richmond, 1982. Cert. employee benefits specialist. From exec. sec. to assoc. dir. benefits comm. CBS Inc., N.Y.C., 1984-97; dir. health benefits CBS (divsn. Viacom, Inc.), N.Y.C., 1998—. Tutor Literacy Vols. of Am., Westchester, N.Y., 1989-94; fundraising vol. U. Richmond, N.Y. Alumni Chpt., 1993-97; election dist. leader Rye (N.Y.) Dem. Com., 1992—. Mem. Phi Beta Kappa. Democrat. Presbyterian. Avocations: travel, reading, camping. E-mail: neinsardi@cbs.com. Office: Viacom Inc 1515 Broadway New York NY 10036-8901

INSULZA, JOSÉ MIGUEL, Chilean government official; b. 1943; m. Georgina Nuñez V.; 3 children. Student, St. George' Coll., U. Chile, Facultad Latinoamericana de Ciencias Sociales, U. Mich. Prof. polit. theory U. Chile, 1973; prof. polit. scis. Pontifícia U. Católica de Chile, 1973; pol. adviser Ministry Fgn. Rels., Santiago, Chile, 1973, head multilateral econ. affairs dept., 1990-94, under-sec. fgn. affairs, 1994, min., 1994—; dir. Diplomatic Acad., 1973; rschr., then dir. Instituto de Estudios de Estados Unidos, Centro de Investigación y Docencia Económicas, Mex., 1981-88; prof. U. Autónoma de Mex., 1990-94; dep. chair Internat. Cooperation Agy., 1990-94; min. sec. of the pres. Govt. of Chile, Santiago, min. of interior; bd. dirs. Instituto de Fomento de Desarrollo Científico y Tecnológico; mem. Consejo Chileno de Relaciones Internacionales, Consejo de Redacción, Nexos Mag., Mex., Corporación de Desarrollo Tecnológico Empresarial. Office: Ministry Fgn Rels, Palacio de la Moneda, Santiago Chile*

INTISAROW, MIKHAIL MIKHAILOVICH, microbiology educator; b. Moscow, July 13, 1936; s. Mikhail Avakovich Intisarow and Marija Ivanovna (Skrilova) Schepkina; m. Tamara Sergeevna Karpikova, Feb. 25, 1962 (div. 1964); 1 child, Sergej; m. Tatiana Troitskaja, Jan. 31, 1970; 1 child, Mikhail. MS, Acad. Vet. Sci., Moscow, 1960; postgrad., Acad. Vet. Sci., Kusminki, Russia, 1969. Veterinarian Rjasan, Russia, 1960-61; sr. technician Russian Acad. Scis., Moscow, 1962-65; lectr. Acad. Vet. Sci., Moscow, 1972-79; rschr. SRLEBM Acad. Med. Scis., Jurlowo, 1980-86, mem. Sci. Coun., 1987—; reader Acad. Vet. Medicine, Moscow, 1986-89, prof., 1989—. Author: Theoretical and Practical Problems of Gnotobiology, 1986, Depths of the Matter, 1993, Theologynizing, 1996. Mem. N.Y. Acad. Scis. Christian Orthodox. Avocations: classical music, painting. Home: Ul Tashkentskaja 34-3-31, 109472 Moscow Russia Office: Acad Vet Medicine, Ul Skrjabina 23, 109472 Moscow Russia

INTRILIGATOR, DEVRIE SHAPIRO, physicist; b. N.Y.C.; d. Carl and Lillian Shapiro; m. Michael Intriligator; children: Kenneth, James, William, Robert. BS in Physics, MIT, 1962, MS, 1964; PhD in Planetary and Space Physics, UCLA, 1967. NRC-NASA rsch. assoc. NASA, Ames, Calif., 1967-69; rsch. fellow in physics Calif. Inst. Tech., Pasadena, 1969-72, vis. assoc., 1972-73; asst. prof. U. So. Calif., 1972-80; mem. Space Scis. Ctr., 1978-83; sr. rsch. physicist Carmel Rsch. Ctr., Santa Monica, Calif., 1979—; dir. Space Plasma Lab., 1980—; cons. NASA, NOAA, Jet Propulsion Lab.; chmn. NAS-NRC com. on solar-terrestrial rsch., 1983-86, exec. com. bd. atmospheric sci. and climate, 1983-86, geophysics study com., 1983-86; U.S. nat. rep. Sci. Com. on Solar-Terrestrial Physics, 1983-86; mem. adv. com. NSF Divsn. Atmospheric Sci. Co-editor: Exploration of the Outer Solar System, 1976; contbr. articles to profl. jours. Recipient 3 Achievement awards NASA, Calif. Resolution of Commendation, 1982. Mem. AAAS, Am. Phys. Soc., Am. Geophys. Union, Cosmos Club. Achievements include being a participant Pioneer 10/11 missions to outer planets; Pioneer Venus Orbiter, Pioneers 6, 7, 8 and 9 heliocentric missions. Home: 140 Foxtail Dr Santa Monica CA 90402-2048 Office: Carmel Rsch Ctr PO Box 1732 Santa Monica CA 90406-1732

INTRILIGATOR, MARC STEVEN, lawyer; b. Oceanside, N.Y., July 14, 1952; s. Alan and Sally (Jacobs) I.; m. Roxann Kathleen Hoff, Aug. 28, 1977; children: Seth Adam, Joshua Ross, Daniel Benjamin. BA, SUNY, Binghamton, 1974; JD, Boston U., 1977. Bar: N.Y. 1978. Assoc. Dreyer and Traub, N.Y.C., 1977-83, assoc. ptnr., 1984-85, sr. ptnr., 1985-96; of counsel Fischbein Badillo Wagner Harding, N.Y.C., 1996—. Projects editor: Boston U. law rev., 1976-77. Past pres. Croton Jewish Ctr. Mem. ABA, Assn. of Bar of City of N.Y., Highlands Country Club (pres., trustee), Tau Epsilon Phi. Office: Fischbein Badillo Wagner Harding 909 3rd Ave New York NY 10022-4731

INYANG, HILARY INYANG, geo-environmental engineer, researcher; b. Uyo, Nigeria, Nov. 8, 1959; came to U.S., 1982; s. Inyang Amos and Abigail (Affiong) I.; children: Imikan Hilary, Abigail. BS in Geology with honors, U. Calabar, Nigeria, 1981; BS, N.D. State U., 1985, MS, 1986; PhD, Iowa State U., 1989. Soil technician Midwest Soil Testing Lab., Fargo, N.D., 1984; program asst. FHWA Tech. Transfer Ctr., Fargo, N.D., 1985-86; rsch. asst. Spangler Geotechnical Lab., Ames, Iowa, 1986-88; resident researcher Wis. Dept. of Transp., Madison, summer 1989; vis. asst. prof. Purdue U., West Lafayette, Ind., summer 1990; asst. prof. U. Wis., Platteville, 1988-93; sr. geoenvironmental engr. U.S. EPA, Washington, 1991-93; pres. Geoenvironmental Design and Rsch., Fairfax, Va., 1991-95; prof., dir. Ctr. Environ. Engring., Sci. and Tech. U. Mass., Lowell, 1995—; chmn. environ. engring. com., sci. adv. bd. EPA, Washington, nat. adv. couns. mem., 1998—. Mem. editorial bd. Internat. Jour. Surface Mining and Reclamation, Rotterdam, The Netherlands, 1991—, Rsch. Conservation and Recycling, Amsterdam, The Netherlands, 1992—, Jour. Environ. Systems, N.Y.C., 1992—, Internat. Jour. Pub. Works, Washington, 1991—, Internat. Jour. Environ. Issues, Rotterdam, 1992—, CRC Reviews Environ. Control, Fla., 1992—; contbr. articles to profl. jours. Team mem. Dubuque (Iowa) Tennis Club, 1989-91; chmn. engring. minority com. U. Wis., Platteville, 1990-91; affiliate mem. United Meth. Ch., Falls Church, Va., 1992—. Recipient

scholarship U.S. Dept. or Energy, 1986-88, scholarship Fed. Govt. of Nigeria, 1983-85, Geology award Shell-British Petroleum Co., 1978. Fellow AAAS (EPA Environ. Sci. and Engring.), Geol. Soc. London; mem. ASCE (co-editor publ. 1992, Essay 1st prize 1984), ASTM, Transp. Rsch. Bd., Geol. Soc. Am., World Rock Boring Assn., Internat. Soc. Rock Mech., Internat. Assn. Engring. Geol. Achievements include development of techniques for protection of foundation systems in contaminated land, new device for impact strength measurements on rocks, contribution to advances in theoretical analysis for contaminant barriers, leaching processes and waste containment system reliability analyses. Home: PO Box 648 N Chelmsford MA 01863-0648 Office: U Massachusetts CEEST Rm 114 One University Ave Lowell MA 01854

IOANNIDES, CHARIS ODYSSEAS, plastic and reconstructive surgeon; b. Athens, Attika, Greece, Jan. 1, 1955; s. Alexandros and Irene (Bakoyanni) I.; m. Albertina Johanna Tyssen, July 19, 1992; 1 child, Alexandros. DMD, Dental U. Athens, Greece, 1977; MSc, Med. U. Athens, 1978, MD, 1989; PhD, Med. U. Nymegen, The Netherlands, 1987. Diplomate European Bd. Maxillofacial/Plastic Surgery. Asst. U. Hosp., Nymegen, The Netherlands, 1979-83, asst. prof., 1985-87; staff surgeon Athens (Greece) Naval Hosp., 1984-85; asst. prof. U. Hosp., Leuven, Belgium, 1989-92; hon. clin. asst. U. Coll. Hosp., London, 1992-95, cons., 1996—. Mem. editl. bd. Jour. Cranio-Maxillofacial Surgery, Germany, 1989—; contbr. chpts. to books. 2nd lt. Greek Navy, 1984-85. Recipient Leibinger prize European Soc. Cranio/Maxillofacial Surgery, Athens, 1988. Avocations: 19th century paintings, golf. Office: U Coll Hosp Dept Plastic Surgery, Mortimer St, London W1N 8AA, England

IOANNIDIS, DIMITRIS NIKOLAOS, economist, marketing consultant; b. Thessaloniki, Greece, Oct. 26, 1963; s. Nikolaos Dimitris and Athina Roxani Ioannidis; m. Katerina Agni, May 5, 1990; children: Athina, Irini. Dipl., Aristotle U., 1987, econ., 1991. Mgr. sales Tziata M., Thessaloniki, 1987; rschr. MRB Hellas, Thessaloniki, 1988-90; mgr. area Delta S.A., Thessaloniki, 1992; mgr. mktg. Apostolou S.A., Thessaloniki, 1993-94, Mevgal S.A., Thessaloniki, 1994-95; asst. prof. Technol. Ednl. Inst., Thessaloniki, 1995—; rschr. Pantion U., Athens, Greece, 1994—; mktg. cons. Hellenic Catering, Athens, 1996—; bus. cons. several enterprise and orgns. Greece. Author: Biotechnology and Agroindustrial Complex in Greece, 2000; contbr. articles to profl. jours. With Greek Army, 1992. Mem. Mktg. Inst. Greece, Greek Execs. Inst., Econ. Chamber Greece, Hellenic Assn., for Internat. Devel. Avocations: photography, mountain climbing. Home and Office: 13 Ethn Antistasis St, 56625 Thessaloniki Greece

IOANNOU, PANAGIOTIS, chemistry educator; b. Mytilene, Lesvos, Greece, Aug. 29, 1945; s. Vasili and Maria (Tsagaraki) I.; m. Grammatiki Voutsinos, Apr. 19, 1982; children: Maria, Vasili. BS in Chemistry, U. Athens, 1969; MS in Molecular Enzymology, U. Warwick, Coventry, Eng., 1972, PhD in Molecular Scis., 1976. Postdoctoral rsch. assoc. U. Warwick, 1976, SUNY, Stony Brook, 1976-77; from lectr. to asst. prof. to assoc. prof. U. Patras, Greece, 1978-91; prof. U. Patras, 1991—. Contbr. rsch. articles to profl. jours. Rsch. grantee Onassis Found., 1980, Greek Nat. Rsch. Inst., 1982, Greek Govt., 1989, 92. Mem. Am. Chem. Soc., Assn. Greek Chemists. Greek Orthodox. Avocations: hunting, farming. Office: U Patras, Dept Chemistry, Patras Greece

IOANNOU, PANAYIOTIS A., gene therapist, researcher; b. Kalogrea, Kyrenia, Cyprus, Jan. 26, 1951; arrived in Australia, 1997; s. Andreas Ioannou and Maria A. Hatzicharitou; m. Athina Photiou, Aug. 17, 1980; children: Ioanna, Andreas, Evagoras. BSc with honors, Univ. Coll., London, 1972, PhD in Biochemistry, 1976. MRC postdoctoral rsch. fellow St. Mary's Hosp. Med. Sch., London, 1976-78; rsch. fellow Univ. Coll. Hosp., London, 1978-79; officer Thalassaemia Ctr., Nicosia, Cyprus, 1980-95; dir. dept. molecular genetics Cyprus Inst. Neurology and Genetics, Nicosia, 1990-96; prin. rsch. fellow gene therapy group The Murdoch Inst., Melbourne, Australia, 1997; sr. scientist, group leader gene therapy group The Murdoch Inst., Melbourne, 1998—; hon. sr. scientist The Cyprus Inst. Neurology and Genetics, 1997—. Contbr. articles to profl. jours.; patentee in field. Founding mem. Friends of the U. of Cyprus, 1988. Fellow WHO, Oxford (Eng.) U., 1987-88, Cagliari U., Sardinia, Italy, 1988, rsch. fellow Duke U., 1989, UNESCO fellow Human Genome Project, Lawrence Livermore (Calif.) Nat. Lab., 1992, rsch. fellow Roswell Park Cancer Inst., Buffalo, 1993, rsch. fellow Lineberger Comprehensive Cancer Rsch. Ctr., U. N.C., Chapel Hill, 1995; grantee Am. Muscular Dystrophy Assn., 1992-95, Cyprus Anti-Anemia Assn., EEC, 1993-96, Nat. Multiple Sclerosis Soc., 1994, Internat. Atomic Energy Agy., UN High Commn. for Refugees in Cyprus, Assn. Française contre les Myopathies. Mem. European Group on Human Gene Therapy (founding), Australian Gene Therapy Soc. (founding, organizer), Human Genome Orgn., Cyprus Thalassemia Assn., Thalassemia Internat. Fedn., U.K. Thalassemia Soc. (hon.), Cyprus Acad. Scis., Am. Soc. Human Genetics, Am. Soc. Gene Therapy, N.Y. Acad. Scis. Office: The Murdoch Inst, Flemington Rd Parkville, Melbourne VIC 3052, Australia

IODICE, EMILIO FRANCIS, science administrator; b. N.Y.C., Apr. 13, 1946. BS, Fordham U., 1968; MBA, Bernard Baruch U., 1971; DBA internat. bus., applied econs., George Washington U., 1986. Corp. planning staff Continental Group, N.Y.C., 1971-73; economist, office dir. U.S. Dept. Commerce, Washington, 1973-78; chief economist Customs Svc., U.S. Dept. Treasury, Washington, 1978-82; comml. counselor U.S. and Fgn. Comml. Svc. U.S. Embassy, Brasilia, Brazil, 1982-85, Mexico City, 1985-87; comml. counselor U.S. Embassy, Rome, 1985-87; minister comml. affairs U.S. Embassy, Rome, 1987-92, Madrid, 1992-96, Paris, 1996-98; exec. v.p. Lucent Techs., Cedex, France, 1998—; prof. George Mason U., 1980-82, N.V.C. Coll., Annadale, Va., 1975-82, Boston U., Rome, 1989—, Am. U., Rome, 1989—. Contbr. articles to profl. jours. Dir. bd. regents Marymount Internat., Rome, 1989-91. Recipient Superior Performance award U.S. Dept. Commerce, 1985, Meritorious award, 1984, Silver medal, 1983; Gold medal award for heroism, 1985; Plaque, Va. Coal Assn., 1985. Mem. Am. Econ. Assn., Beta Gamma Sigma. Roman Catholic. Avocations: writer, historian.

IOFFE, MARAT EVSEEVICH, researcher; b. Moscow, USSR, Feb. 17, 1931; s. Evsey Lasarevich Diment and Minna Leibovna Ioffe; m. Valentina Nikolaevna Mats, Mar. 8, 1963 (div. 1965); m. Natalia Konstantinovna Tomashevskaia, Dec. 12, 1969; 1 child, Inna. MD, Med. Inst., Moscow, 1955; PhD, Inst. Higher Nervous Activity, Moscow, 1963, DSc, 1976. Traumatologist local hosp. Stalinogorsk, USSR, 1955-57, Kuntsevo, USSR, 1957-58; jr. rschr. Inst. Higher Nervous Activity and Neurophysiology, Moscow, 1961-72, sr. rschr., 1972-86, head of unit, 1986-88, head of lab., 1988—; head of lab. of motor learning Inst. Higher Nervous Activity and Neurophysiology, Moscow, 1988—. Author: (books) Corticospinal Mechanisms of Instrumental Motor Reactions, 1975, Mechanisms of Motor Learning, 1991, (book chpts.) Stance and Motion: Facts and Concepts, 1988, Motor Control, Today and Tomorrow, 1999, Complex Brain Function: Conceptual Advances in Russian Neurosciences, 2000, Progress in Motor Control II, 2000; contbr. numerous articles to profl. jours. Mem. Internat. Brain Rsch. Orgn., N.Y. Acad. Scis. Home: 2 Vargi Str Apt 174, 117133 Moscow Russia Office: Inst Higher Nervous Activity, Butlerov Str 5a, 117865 Moscow Russia

ION, DUMITRU BARBU, physicist, researcher; b. Podul Pitarului, Bucharest, Romania, July 25, 1937; s. Barbu Alexandru and Maria Ion (Filip) I.; m. Reveica Constantin Mihai, Dec. 2, 1965; children: Alexandru Cristian, Mihai Laurian. Diploma in tchg., Pedagogical Sch., Bucharest, 1955; diploma in physics, Bucharest U., 1962, D in Physics, 1971. Tchr. various elem. schs., Bucharest, 1955-56; sr. rschr. Joint Inst. Nuc. Rsch., Dubna, Soviet Union, 1971-76; physicist Inst. Atomic Physics, Bucharest, 1962-69, sr. rschr. 3, 1979-90, sr. rschr. 1, prof., 1990—; guest rschr. G.S.I. Darmstadt, Germany, 1987, Tubingen (Germany) U., 1989-90, INFN-FRASCATI, Italy, 1994-95; guest prof. Ludwig Maximilians U. Munchen, Germany, 1990-96. Contbr. articles to profl. jours including Nuc. Physics (award of Romanian Acad., 1981), Astroparticle Physics, Elem. Particles and High Energy Physics, others. Mem. European Physical Soc. (hon.), Romanian Physical Soc., NY Acad. Scis. (hon.). Romanian Orthodox. Avocations: chess, tourism, painting, fishing. Home: BL 61 AP 180 SC E, Str Cernisoara Nr 29-39, Bucharest Romania Office: Inst Atomic Physics, Magurele PO Box MG-6, Bucharest Romania

IONESCU, EUGEN CONSTANT, neurosurgeon, consultant; b. Iasi, Romania, July 3, 1963; s. Ramiro Ioan and Juliette Elena Ionescu; m. Carmen Simona Dumbrava, Apr. 27, 1991; children: Stejarel Valerian, Ruxandra Cecilia. MD, U. Medicine, Iasi, 1988, postgrad., 1996—. Diplomate Romanian Head & Neck Surgery Bd. Resident in gen. medicine Departmental Hosp., Miercurea Ciuc, Romania, 1988-90; resident in gen. medicine Univ. Hosp., Iasi, 1990-91, resident in otorhinolaryngology, 1991-94; surgeon, neuro-otologist Neurosurgical Hosp., Iasi, 1994—, resident in neurosurgery, 1996—; resident in neurosurgery Neurosurgical Hosp., Lyon, France, 1999—; asst. prof. U. Claude Bernard, Lyon, 1994-95; cons. Soros Found., Iasi, 1998. V.p. Liberal Nat. Party, 1998—. Sgt. Romanian Army, 1981-82. Mem. Romanian Soc. Neurosurgery, Romanian Soc. Otorhinolaryngology. Romanian Orthodox. Avocations: soccer, tennis, internet, politics. Fax: 40-3217-30-20. Office: Neurosurgical Hosp, str.Ateneului nr.2, 6600 Iasi Romania

IONESCU, GEORGE, psychiatrist, educator; b. Buciumeni, Romania, June 24, 1933; s. Isaia and Rada (Predescu) I.; m. Aurelia Stoian, May 9, 1978; children: Andrei, Sorin. MD, U. Medicine and Pharmacy, Bucharest, Romania, 1959; PhD in Medicine, U. Bucharest, 1970, PhD in Psychology, 1987. Med. diplomate, cert. psychologist. Intern U. Medicine and Pharmacy, Bucharest, 1959-61, jr. lectr., 1965-66, lectr., 1966-71, sr. lectr., 1971-72, reader, 1972-91, prof., 1991—; physician in pvt. practice, 1959-65; specialist in psychiatry, 1965-71; psychiatrist in pvt. practice, 1971—; chief dept. psychiatry Al. Obregia Hosp., Bucharest, 1980—, Univ. Medicine and Pharmacy, Bucharest, 1997—. Author: Introduction to Medical Psychology, 1973, The Psychosomatic, 1975, Psychopathology, 1979, clinical Psychology, 1985, Textbook of Medical Psychology and Psychotherapy, 1995, 99, Personality Disorders, 1997, Clinical Psychiatry, 2000, others; editor Romanian Rev. of Psychiatry and Med. Psychology, 1993—. Romanian Acad. grantee, 1986. Mem. Romanian Acad. Med. Scis., Romanian Psychiat. Assn. (pres.), Internat. Psychiat. Assn., South-Eastern Psychiat. Soc. (dirs. com.). Orthodox Christian. Home: Calea Plevnei Nr1 ScB ap 22, Bucuresti sector 5, 70628 Bucharest Romania Office: Alexandru Obregia Hosp, I Clin Dept Soseaua, 10 Bucharest 4, Romania

IONESCU TULCEA, CASSIUS, research mathematician, educator; b. Bucharest, Rumania, Oct. 14, 1923; naturalized, 1967; s. Ioan and Ana (Caselli) Ionescu Tulcea. M.S., U. Bucarest, 1946; Ph.D., Yale, 1959. Mem. faculty U. Bucarest, 1946-57, assoc. prof., 1952-57; research assoc. Yale U., 1957-59, vis. lectr., 1959-61; assoc. prof. U. Pa., 1961-64; prof. U. Ill., Urbana, 1964-66; prof. Northwestern U., Evanston, Ill., 1966-90, prof. emeritus, 1990—. Author: Hilbert Spaces (in Rumanian), 1956, A Book on Casino Craps, 1980, A Book on Casino Blackjack, 1982; co-author: Probability Calculus (in Rumanian), 1956, Calculus, 1968, An Introduction to Calculus, 1969, Honors Calculus, 1970, Topics in the Theory of Liftings, 1969, Sets, 1971, Topology, 1971, A Book on Casino Gambling, 1976; contbr. articles to profl. jours. Recipient Asachi prize Rumanian Acad., 1957. Office: Northwestern U 2033 Sheridan Rd Evanston IL 60208-0830

IONITA, MARIA ILEANA, chemical engineer, researcher; b. Bucharest, Romania, Nov. 14, 1956; d. Stancu and Elena (Alexe) Lica; m. Veniamin Niculae Ionita; 1 child, Claudiu Stefan. Degree in chem. engring., Poly. Inst. Bucharest, 1980, M, 1988; PhD, Romanian Acad. Sci., 1997. Chem. engr. Equipment for Measurements and Control Enterprise, Bucharest, 1980-85; chem. engr. Ctrl. Inst. Chemistry, Bucharest, 1985-90, sci. rschr., 1988—; chem. engr. S.C. Zecasin S.A., Bucharest, 1990—; tchg. asst. Faculty of Indsl. Chemistry, Poly. Inst. Bucharest, 1987-94; chair photoelectrochemistry symposium 49th Ann. Meeting Internat. Soc. Electrochemistry, Kitakyushu, Japan, 1998. Patentee in field. Avocations: crosswords, music, photography, table tennis, drawing. Home: 14 Ghe Manu St Sector 1, 78112 Bucharest Romania Office: S C Zecasin S A, 202 Spl Independentei, sect 6, 77208 Bucharest Romania

IOPPOLO, FRANK S., JR., lawyer; b. Rockville Centre, N.Y., Nov. 13, 1966; s. Frank S. and Carmella L. (Marrone) I. BA, Wake Forest U., 1988; JD, Fordham U., 1991. Bar: Fla. 1991, U.S. Dist. Ct. (mid. dist.) Fla. 1991, D.C. 1992, N.Y. 1992, U.S. Dist. Ct. (so. dist.) Fla. 1992, U.S. Supreme Ct. 1995. Assoc. Baker & Hostetler, Orlando, Fla., 1991-96, Greenberg Traurig, Orlando, 1996—. Bd. regents Leadership Fla., 1995-96, 97-98; chmn. bd. Orlando Marine Insts., Inc., 1995-97; bd. dirs. Assoc. Marine Insts., Inc., 1995-97; pres., chmn. bd. Bay Point of Bay Hill Property Owners Assn., Inc., Orlando, 1994-96; bd. dirs. Communities in Schs., Orange County, Fla., 1997-99. Mem. ABA, Fla. Bar Assn., Orange County Bar Assn., N.Y. State Bar Assn., D.C. Bar Assn., Wake Forest U. Alumni Assn. Ctrl. Fla. (pres. 1995-98). Avocations: sailing, snow and water skiing, reading, fishing, target shooting. Office: Greenberg Traurig 111 N Orange Ave Fl 20 Orlando FL 32801-2316

IORDACHE, MIHAI, engineering educator; b. Lunca-Corbului, Arges, Romania, Nov. 19, 1944; s. Gheorghe and Constantina (Pantoiu) I.; m. Diana Ileana Bordelanu, July 26, 1969; children: Razvan-Gabriel, Georgiana-Mona. MSc, Poly. U., Bucharest, Romania, 1967, PhD, 1977. Cert. elec. engr. Asst. prof. Poly. U., Bucharest, 1967-78, lectr., 1978-90, assoc. prof., 1990-93, prof. engring., 1993—. Author 20 books including Computer-Aided Numeric Analysis of Nonlinear Large-Scale Electric Circuits, 1995, Electrical Engineering Problems, Algorithms and Implementation, 1995, Modern Theory of Electrical Circuits: Fundamentals, Applications, Algorithms and Computer Programs, vol. I, 1998, vol. II, 2000; contbr. articles to profl. jours. Mem. IEEE, Romanian Assn. of Medling and Simulation in Engring., Romanian Assn. of Elec. Machines Rschrs. Avocations: tennis, reading, music, theater. Home: Tirgul Neamt 18, 77486 Bucharest Romania Office: Poly U Bucharest, Splaiul Independentei 313, 77206 Bucharest Romania

IORDANOW, PAUL STANISLAS, marketing professional; b. Nice, France, Sept. 9, 1946; s. Serge and Marguerite Marie (Mizgier de Turzina) I.; m. Beatrice Euphemie de Wazieres, June 29, 1973. Grad., Ecole Superieure Scis., Paris, 1971. Head mktg. dept. Citroen, Paris, 1972-82; transport dept. mgr. Brule Ville Assocs., Versailles, France, 1982-90; advt. dept. dir. Brule Ville Assocs., Viroflay, France, 1990-92; chmn. Maxicom, Versailles, 1992—. Contbr. articles to profl. jours. Mem. Am. Mktg. Assn., Esomar, Assn. Anciens Eleves de L'Essec. Roman Catholic. Avocations: golf, skiing, finance. Home: 3 Rue de Castellane, 75008 Paris France Office: Maxicom SA, 16 Rue Champ Lagarde, 78000 Versailles France

IORDANSKII, ALEXEY LEONIDOVICH, polymer chemist; b. Moscow, Dec. 22, 1945; s. Leonid Alexandrovich and Nina Il'inichna (Nekrasova) I.; m. Larisa Igorevna Ivanova, Aug. 24, 1944; 1 child, Dmitrii Alexeevich. BD, Moscow State U., 1968; PhD, Semenov's Inst. Chem. Physics, Moscow, 1975, DSc in Chemistry, 1990. Jr. rsch. worker Inst. Chem. Physics, Moscow, 1968-80, sr. rsch. worker, 1980-90, leader rsch. worker, 1990-95, head lab., 1995—, assoc. prof., 1996—; lectr All-Union Soc. "Knowledge", Moscow, 1975—; lectr., cons. State Inst. of Requalification of Adminstrn., Moscow, 1976-90. Author: Is Diffusion friend or Enemy?, 1976, Diffusion of Electrolytes in Polymers, 1988, Interaction of Polymers with Corrosive and Bioactive Media, 1994, Transport Phenomena in Polymer Systems, 1978. Mem. Mendeleev's Soc., Moscow, 1970—. Recipient Gold Medal award All-Union exhbn. Advancements Advancement in Med. Polymers, Moscow, 1987, 850 Yr.'s Anniversary of Moscow medal, 1997, U.S. Civilian R&D Found. awardee, 1997—. Mem. Internat. Controlled Release Soc. Avocations: canoe travel, fishing. E-mail: iozdan@chph.zas.zu. Office: Semenovs Inst Chem Physics, 4 Kosyginstr, 117334 Moscow Russia

IOSEBASHVILI, ALEXANDER, research scientist, educator; b. Tbilisi, Georgia, Russia, Jan. 26, 1965; came to U.S., 1978; s. Otar and Rachael (Krikhel) I. DSc, NYU, 1991. Rsch. sci. Exxon Chem. Co., N.Y.C.; hon. prof. sci. NYU, 1993. Organizer internat. collaboration for unity of scis. and their orgns. for helping humanity; mem. Am. Mus. Natural History, Nat. Geog. Soc., N.Y. Pub. Libr., Am. Liver Found. Recipient Cert. Excellence and Honor achievements sci. Mem. AAAS, N.Y. Acad. Sci., Am. Psychol. Soc., Mus. Nat. History, Acad. Polit. Scis., Astron. Soc. of Pacific, Drs. of World, People's Med. Soc., Smithsonian Inst. Jewish. Achievements include elaborism and research of an important postulated scientific information scientific material in different spheres; analysis and discovering scientific problems of a crime; explanation adn postulation mathematically, physico-philosophically and cosmologically of the questions regarding the interpretation of connection and nucleus; elaboration of the issues of classification of transformation of conception ONE into conception TWO. Home: 99 05 63rd Dr Apt 9 V Rego Park NY 11374

IOSIFOVA, EKATERINA KONSTANTINOVNA, paleontologist; b. Moscow, Feb. 13, 1963; d. Konstantin V. and Julia I. PhD, Geol. Inst. Russian Acad. Sci., 2000. From probationer to scientist Geol. Inst., Russia, 1987—. Home: Akad Anokhina 6-3-484, 117602 Moscow Russia

IOSLOVICH, ILYA, mathematician; b. Moscow, Russia, Aug. 23, 1937; s. Veniamin Ioslovich and Natalia Polyakova; m. Alexandra Bryandinskaya, Febr. 5, 1959 (div. Dec. 1967); 1 child, Andrey; m. Lilia Sapozhnikova, Nov. 4, 1973; 1 child, Alexei. MSc, Moscow State U., 1960; PhD, Moscow Inst. Physics & Tech. Sr. rsch. engr. Inst. Equipment Design, Moscow, 1960-65; rsch. fellow Inst. Econs. State Planning Com., Moscow, 1966-68; sr. rsch. fellow Inst. Control Systems, Moscow, 1968-72; head lab. Inst. Network Scheduling, Moscow, 1972-76; head dept. Rsch. Inst. Control & Automation Systems, Soviet Coop., Moscow, 1976-91; rschr. Faculty Agrl. Engring., 1991-98, assoc. rsch. prof., 1999—. contbr. numerous articles to profl. jours. Recipient Silver Achievement medal Com. All-Union Exhbn. for Indsl. Achievements, 1976, 83. Home: St. Hazait 17/21, 36751 Nesher Israel Office: Faculty Agrie Engrn, 32000 Haifa Israel

IP, FRANCIS, hotel executive; b. Hong Kong, Sept. 3, 1947; s. Kam-Hung and Au-Yeung Fu (Ying) I.; m. Beatrice Wu, Apr. 17, 1970; 1 child, Andrea; m. Sheila Shih, May 24, 1995. BA in Hotel Adminstrn., Pacific Western U., 1983; cert. hotel adminstr., Profl. Bus. and Tech. Mgmt. Inst., 1989; cert. bus. mgmt. and adminstrn., Brit. Inst. Mgmt. Specialists, 1992; cert. profl. mgr., Can. Inst. Mgmt. Reservation and ticketing supr. Pan Am. World Airways, 1969-79; sr. tng. officer Cathay Pacific Airways, 1980-82; front office mgr. Hyatt Regency Hotel, Hong Kong, 1983-86; dep. gen. mgr. Taipei Fortuna Hotel, 1987-93; resident dir. Riviera Hotel Taipei, 1993—. Fellow Profl. Bus. and Tech. Mgmt. Inst. (life, founder 1983—), Brit. Inst. Mfg. (life), Brit. Inst. Mgmt. Specialists (life); mem. N.Y. Acad. Scis., Com. of Rep. China Outstanding Corp. Leaders (Golden Pyramid award 1998). Avocations: reading, gardening. Office: The Riviera Hotel Taipei, 646 Linsen North Rd, Taipei Taiwan Republic of China

IP, HORACE HO-SHING, computer science educator; b. Hong Kong, Jan. 9, 1957; s. Edward Ming-Cheung Ip and Nancy Wai-Ling Ng; m. Annie Wai-Lan Ng; 1 child, Francesca. BSc in Applied Physics with honors, U. London, 1980, PhD in Image Processing, 1983. Postdoctoral rsch. assoc. Univ. Coll. London Imaging Processing Group, 1983-84; rsch. fellow, Rsch. Computing Unit Imperial Cancer Rsch. Funds Lab., London, 1984-87; project mgr., sr. engr. Cambridge (Eng.) Consultants, 1987-89; sr. lectr. City Univ. Hong Kong, Dept. Computer Sci., 1989-91, prin. lectr. to Univ. Sr. Lectr., 1991-96, prof., head dept. computer sci., 1997—; chmn. tech. panel on multimedia and comm., Hong Kong Indsl. Tech. Ctr. Corp., 1998—; mem. adv. peers group Open Learning Inst., 1994—; chair, program com. mem. various internat. confs.; official advisor 9th Internat. Computer Expo and Conf., Hong Kong; co-editor: Lecture Notes in Computer Science 1024: Image Analysis Applications and Computer Graphics, 1995, Lecture Notes in Computer Science 1464: Multimedia Information Analysis and Retrieval, 1998; contbr. chpts. to books. Assoc. editor, editl. bd. (internat. jour.) Pattern Recognition, 1995—; editor Jour. Computer-Aided Design and Computer Graphics; spl. issue editor Real-Time Imaging Jour.; chair editl. adv. bd. The IT Mag., 1994—; editor-in-chief Hong Kong Computer Jour., 1993-94; contbr. articles to profl. jours.; reviewer various jours., conf. procs., rsch. grants. Fellow Hong Kong Instn. Engrs.; mem. IEEE (chair computer chpt. 1996-97), Engring. Coun., Inst. Physics U.K., Inst. Elec. and Electronics Engrs., Hong Kong Computer Soc. (dir. edn. and tng. 1994-95, editor newsletter 1994-95), Hong Kong Soc. Multimedia and Image Computing (founding pres. 1992-95), Internat. Assn. Pattern Recognition (mem. governing bd. 1992—, founding co-chair tech. com. multimedia and image comm. 1994—). Avocations: Chinese calligraphy and painting. Office: City Univ Hong Kong, Tat Chee Ave, Kowloon Hong Kong China

IP, NANCY YUK-YU, life sciences educator; b. Hong Kong, July 30, 1955; d. Chung Yin Yip and Siu Ling Lee; m. Kai Yang Chu, Aug. 12, 1984; children: Derek, Cathryn. BS, Simmons Coll., Boston, 1977; PhD, Harvard U., 1983. Postdoctoral fellow Harvard Med. Sch., 1983-84, Sloan-Kettering Inst., 1984-85; head lab. med. genetics Lifecodes Corp., 1987-89; sr. staff scientist Regeneron Pharms., 1989-93; project dir. Shanghai (China) Rsch. Ctr. of Life Scis. Chinese Acad., 1995—; assoc. prof. life scis. Hong Kong U. Sci. and Tech., 1993-97, prof. life. scis., 1998—, assoc. dean of sci., 1998—; sci. cons. Regeneron Pharms., 1993-96; dir. Biotech. Rsch. Inst., Hong Kong, 1996—. Patentee in field. Rsch. Infrastructure grantee, 1995—. Mem. Soc. for Neurosci., N.Y. Acad. Scis., Chinese Soc. of Neuroscis. (founding mem.). Office: Dept Biology, Hong Kong U Sci & Tech, Clear Water Bay Hong Kong China

IP, SAI YIN, physician; b. Hong Kong, Sept. 27, 1962; s, Y.N. and M. (Wong) I.; m. Yu Wai Ho, Aug. 25, 1989; 1 child, Honora. MB, ChB, Chinese U. Hong Kong, 1987. Diplomate Am. Bd. Internal Medicine. Resident in medicine Faulkner Hosp., Boston, 1990-93; physician in pvt. practice, Hong Kong, 1994—. Fellow Mass. Med. Soc., The Royal Australian Coll. Gen. Practitioners, Hong Kong Coll. Family Physicians; mem. ACP. E-mail: ip963226@netvigator.com. Office: Clinic 1 M Floor, Belvedere Garden Phase One, Tsuen Wan Hong Kong

IP, W. KIN, dermatologist; b. Hong Kong, Aug. 24, 1957; s. Shing-Fu and Shiu-Bing (Mok) I.; m. Wai-Ling Ng, Dec. 27, 1983; children: Hugh Ian, Nora Ann. MB, BChir, U. Hong Kong, 1982. Pathology registrar Princess Margaret Hosp., Hong Kong, 1984-85; med. registrar Palmerston North & Waikato Hosp., New Zealand, 1985-86; sr. dermatology registrar Christchurch Pub. Hosp., New Zealand, 1986-88; cons. dermatology Evangel and Precious Blood Hosp., Hong Kong, 1991-96; dermatologist TW Adventist Hosp., Hong Kong, 1991—; cons. dermatology Hong Kong Ctrl. Hosp., 1996-97, St. Paul's Hosp., Hong Kong, 1995—, Bapt. Hosp., Hong Kong, 1998-99. Fellow Royal Coll. Physicians (London and Edinburgh), Am. Acad. Dermatology; mem. Brit. Assn. Dermatology, European Acad. Dermatology. Avocations: swimming, wine tasting, antique watches, tennis. Office: 1811 Argyle Ctr I, 688 Nathan Rd, Kowloon Hong Kong China

IP, WINNIE S. C., music educator; b. Hong Kong, May 20, 1960; came to U.S., 1975; d. Yun Chi and Pui Fong Yue Yip. MusB, Hartford U., 1984; MusM, Cath. U., 1986; cert. in adminstrn. and mgmt., Harvard U.; diploma with merit in advanced chamber music, Assoc. Bd. Royal Schs. of Music, Eng., 1993. Music dir., founder The Ip Piano Sch., Boston, 1992—; rep. Assoc. Bd. of Royal Schs. of Music, Boston, 1990—. Mem. New Eng. Piano Tchr. Assn. (bd. dirs. 1998—). Roman Catholic. Office: The Ip Piano Sch 72 Kneeland St Ste 501 Boston MA 02111-1928

IPATOV, SERGEI IVANOVICH, mathematician; b. Moscow, Nov. 10, 1952; s. Ivan Iosiphovich and Alexandra Ivanovna (Ropakova) I.; m. Artjuhova Valentina, June 14, 1986. MS, Moscow U., 1975; PhD, Inst. Applied Math., Moscow, 1982; DSc, Inst. Applied Math., 1997. Probationer, investigator Inst. Applied Maths. Russian Acad. Scis., Moscow, 1975-77, jr. scientist, 1977-87, scientist, 1987-90, sr. scientist, 1990-97, lead scientist, 1997—; lectr. Moscow U., 1998. Author: Migration of Celestial Bodies in the Solar System, 2000; contbr. articles to profl. jours. Grantee NSF, 1992, Russian Found. Basic Rsch., 1993-98, Russian Fed. Program Astronomy, 1997—, European So. Obs., 1995, 98, Deutsche Acad. Austauschdienst, 1996, Internat. Sci. Found., 1995, Internat. Astron Union, 1998, 2000, Belgian Office for Scientific, Technical and Cultural Affairs, 1998; named Outstanding People of the 20th Century medal, 1998, Outstanding Scientist of the 20th Century, 1998. Fellow Internat. Biograph. Assn.; mem. European Astron. Soc., Euro-Asian Astron. Soc., Com. Space Rsch., Russian Acad. Natural Scis. (corr.), Russian Acad. Scis & Arts. Avocations: gardening, walking. Home: Apt 252, Micklukho Macklaya St 55, 117279 Moscow Russia Office: Keldysh Inst Applied Math, Miusskaya Sq 4, 125047 Moscow Russia

IPEKCI, AHMET, holding company executive; b. Istanbul, Turkey, Jan. 8, 1944; s. Nevzat and Fatma (Demirbag) I.; m. Tolgay Tümer, Apr. 22, 1944. Economist, Sisli Coll., Istanbul, 1968; Doctorate, Istanbul U., 1973. CPA. From asst. to asst. prof. to assoc. prof. Istanbul Tech. U., 1969-82; v.p. Tekfen Constrn., Istanbul, 1983-94; gen. coord. Tekfen Holding, Istanbul, 1994—; bd. dirs. Tekfen Bank, Istanbul, Hallesche Mittel Deutsche Bau Ag., Halle, Germany; chmn. Tekfen Fgn. Trade, Tekfen Securities Co. Author: Introduction to Business Administration, 1980. Home: Salcikir Sokak # 66, 80880 Istanbul Turkey Office: Tekfen Holding, Tekfen Sitesi, 80600 Istanbul Turkey

IPLIKCIOGLU, AHMET CELAL, neurosurgeon, educator, researcher; b. Ankra, Turkey, Jan. 10, 1957; s. Abdullah Suat and Nimet Iplikcioglu; m. Nurten Okutan, May 20, 1995; 1 child, Suat Baris. MD, Hacettepe U., Ankara, 1981, Neurosurgeon, 1987. Neurosurgeon Corum (Turkey) State Hosp., 1988-89; chief resident Ankara Hosp., 1989-92, vice chief, 1992-93; pvt. practice, Istanbul, Turkey, 1996—; chief SSKk Tepecik Tchg. Hosp., Izmir, Turkey, 1993-96, SSK Okmeydani Tchg. Hosp., Istanbul, 1996—. lt. Turkish Marine Forces, 1987-88. Mem. Turkish Neurosurg. Soc. Fax: 902122478696. E-mail: acelal@doctor.com. Home: Oyak Sitesi 33/A:13 Ayazaga, Istanbul Turkey Office: Valikonagy Cad 127/7, Nisantasi, Istanbul Turkey

IPOUSTEGUY, JEAN, sculptor, designer, engraver, painter; b. Dun-sur-Meuse, France, 1920. Studies with Robert Lesbounit, 1938. One-man shows in sculpture in Europe and U.S. include galerie Claude-Bernard, 1961-83, Fondation Nationale des Arts graphiques et Plastiques, Paris, 1979, Kunsthalle, Berlin, 1980, Galerie D.M. Sarver, Paris; Guggenheim Mus., N.Y.C., 1983, Chelsea Harbor, London, 1999; group shows include Venice Biennale, 1964, Weiner Festwochen, Vienna, 1981, Seven Dials Gallery, London, 1982; executed monumental sculptures for cities including Berlin, Lyons, Grenoble, Washington (French Embassy), Melbourne, Australia, water-colour Galerie Sarver, Paris, 1988, sculpture The Land Scapes, 1989, Charcoal, 1989, Gerhard Marcks Haus, Bremen, Germany, 1997, galerie The Art Alliance, N.Y., 1997. Decorated chevalier French Legion of Honor, 1984; recipient prize Bright Found., Venice, Biennale, 1964, Heitland Found., 1989; retrospective a la Kunsthalle de Berlin, 1992, Mort de l'Eveque Neuman, Eveque de Phila., Dun sur Meuse, 1995, Ambassade de France, Washington, 1997. Home: 35 rue Chevreul, 94600 Choisy le Roi France

IPPEN, ERICH PETER, electrical engineering educator; b. Fountain Hill, Pa., Mar. 29, 1940; s. Arthur Thomas and Elisabeth Anne (Wagenplatz) I.; m. Dorothea Ellen Swansen, Sept. 24, 1966; children: Erich Peter, Jason Timothy. S.B., MIT, 1962; M.S., U. Calif.-Berkeley, 1965, Ph.D., 1968. Mem. tech. staff Bell Labs., Holmdel, N.J., 1968-80; vis. prof. MIT, Cambridge, 1977-78, prof. elec. engring., 1980—, Elihu Thomson prof. elec. engring., 1987—, prof. physics, 1996—; cons. Bell Labs., 1981—, Allied Corp., Mt. Bethel, N.J., 1982-90. Contbr. articles to profl. jours.; patentee in field. Recipient Edward Longstreth medal Franklin Inst., 1982, Harold E. Edgerton award Soc. Photo-Optical Instrumentation Engrs., 1989, John Scott award City of Phila., 1991. Fellow Am. Acad. Arts and Scis., Optical Soc. Am. (R.W. Wood prize 1981), IEEE (Morris E. Leeds award 1983, Wuantum Elecs. award 1997), Am. Phys. Soc. (Arthur L. Schawlow prize 1997); mem. NAS, NAE, Sigma Xi. Home: 156 School St Belmont MA 02478-3516 Office: MIT 77 Massachusetts Ave Cambridge MA 02139-4307*

IPPOMMATSU, MASAMICHI, gas company engineer, executive; b. Osaka, Japan, Dec. 20, 1954; s. Yasuo and Hiroko (Suzisi) I.; m. Yukari Uematsu, Mar. 21, 1986 (div. 1994); 1 child. BSc, Tokyo U., 1977, MSc, 1979, DSc in Phys. Chemistry, 1988. Rschr. Osaka (Japan) Gas Co., Ltd., 1979-86, sr. scientist, 1986-93, chief engr. (mgr.), 1993-2000, head mgr., 2000—. Contbr. articles to profl. jours. Recipient Disting. Svc. award Japan Gas Assn., 1989, 91, 92, 93, 98. Mem. Electrochem. Soc. Japan, Ceramic Soc. Japan, Gas Turbine Soc. Japan. Home: 8-31 Ohata, Hyogo Nishinomiya 662-0836, Japan Office: Osaka Gas Co Ltd, 5-11-61 Torishima, Osaka Konoha ku 554-0051, Japan

IQBAL, JAMSHAID, physician, microbiologist, consultant; b. Rawalpindi, Punjab, Pakistan, Nov. 6, 1953; s. Mohammad Rafique and Hafizan Baigum; m. Robina Nazeer; children: Umer, Saad. MD, QMC, Pakistan, 1978; MSc, U. Birmingham, England, 1985; PhD, U. Stockholm, 1994. Cons. WHO, 1986-90; head immunology NIH, Pakistan, 1985-90; WHO fellow U. Stockholm, 1990-94; EU fellow Inst. Pasteur, Paris, 1994-95; asst. prof. Faculty Medicine Kuwait U., 1995—; cons. microbiologist Al Kabeer Hosp., Kuwait, 1995—; cons. immunologist NIH, Pakistan, 1985-90. Mem. Am. Soc. Tropical Medicine and Hygiene, N.Y. Acad. Scis., Brit. Soc. Immunology, Coll. Physicians and Surgeons (Pakistan). Avocations: hiking, sightseeing. Offfice: Faculty Medicine, Kuwait U, 24923 Safat 13110, Kuwait

IQBAL, MUHAMMAD, botanist, educator, dean; b. Khatauli, Uttar Pradesh, India, Sept. 30, 1952; m. Ameer Jahan; children: Rabea, Abida, Bushra. BSc with honors, Aligarh (India) Muslim U., 1972, MSc in Botany, 1974, MPhil in Botany, 1975, PhD in Botany, 1979. Lectr. botany Govt. P.G. Coll., Uttar Kashi, India, 1981-82; lectr. botany Aligarh Muslim U., Aligarh, India, 1982-87, reader in botany, 1987-90; prof. botany Hamdard U., New Delhi, 1990—, dean of sci., convener, 1990-92, 94-96; convener Nat. Symposia on Citrus, 1991, Emerging Technologies in Environ. Conservation, 1994, Reclamation of Wasteland by Cultivation of Medicinal Plants, 1994, Consequences of Environ. Degradation, 1997, Environmental Protection Through Plants, 1998, Attitude of Public and Profls. towards Environ. Pollution, 1999; mem. sci. adv. com. CCRUM, Ministry of Health and Family Welfare, New Delhi, 1994—; co-opted mem. bd. studies Ctr. for Bioscis., Jamia Millia Islamia, New Delhi, 1993-99; mem. acad. coun. Aligarh Muslim U., 1996-98; mem. sci. adv. subcom. for cultivation of medicinal plants Ministry of Health and Family Welfare, Govt. India, 1994-96; mem. acad. com. environ. studies Inst. Objective Studies, New Delhi, 1996—; mem. com. infrastructure develop. misc. projects, Ministry of Environ. and Forests, New Delhi, 1998-2000; mem. res. degree com. Barkatullah U. Bhopal, 1999—; mem. bd. rsch. studies Kashmir U. Srinagar, 1997-2000; mem. adv. com. Hamdard Study Circle, New Delhi, 2000—; PhD thesis examiner of 12 univs.; included in panels of experts drawn by Dept. Sci. and Tech., Govt. India, 1991—, Homi Bhabha Fellowship Coun., Bombay, 1991—, Tamil Nadu Pub. Svc. Commn., Madras, 1992—, Rajasthan Pub. Svc. Commn., Ajmer, 1993—, Ctrl. Coun. for Rsch. in Unani Medicine, 1994—, Nat. Bot. Rsch. Inst., Lucknow, 1991—, Dept. Environ., Govt. of India, 1998—, Dept. Edn., Govt. of India, 1998—. Editor: The Vascular Cambium, 1990, Growth Patterns in Vascular Plants, 1994, The Cambial Derivatives, 1995, Plant Response to Air Pollution, 1996, Environmental Hazards: Plants and People, 2000; editl. bd. mem. Rsch. Jour. of Plant and Environment, Indian Jour. Applied and Pure Biology, Environmental and Chemical Research, Jour. Environ. Biology; contbr. over 130 articles to profl. jours., 15 chpts. to books. Recipient H.L Chakravarty award Indian Sci. Congress Assn., 1986, Al-Biruni award Muslim Assn. Advancement Sci. and TWAS, 1988, Cert. of Merit, Ministry of external Affairs, Govt. of Iran, 1995, World Environ. Cong. award, 1997. Fellow Linnean Soc. of London, Indian Botanical Soc., Nat. Environ. Sci. Acad., Acad. Environ. Biology, United Writers' Assn.; mem. Indian Soc. Citriculture (v.p. 1996), Internat. Soc. Plant Morphologists (life), Indian Soc. Tree Scientists (life), Assn. for Indian Bot. Contractor (life), Indian Sci. Congress Assn. (life), Soc. of Environ. Scientists (life), Muslim Assn. for Advancement of Sci. (life), Indian Bot. Soc. (life), Nat. Acad. Scis. (life), All India Muslim Ednl. Conf. (life), Indian Assn. for Environ. Mgmt. (life), Internat. Soc. Environ. Botanists (life), Nat. Environ. Sci. Acad. (life), Nat. Inst. Ecology India (life), Acad. Environ. Biology (life), Nat. Acad. Plant Sci. India (life), Nat. Info. Welfare Trust (life), United Writers' Assn. (life), Coun. for Promotion of Sci. (founder mem.), Internat. Assn. Wood Anatomists. Achievements include research in structural and developmental botany, environmental botany, medicoethnobotany. Office: Hamdard U Faculty of Sci, Dept Botany, New Delhi 110062, India

IQBAL, MUHAMMAD, mathematics educator, researcher; b. Jallandhar, Panjab, India, Apr. 5, 1941; arrived in Pakistan, 1947; s. Nawab Ali and Bibi Bir; m. Zohra Begum; children: Tasneem, Adnan, Salman, Imran, Fozia. MA, Panjab U., Lahore, Pakistan, 1963; MSc, Dundee (Scotland) U., 1973; PhD, U. Wales, Cardiff, 1989. Lectr. Gordon Coll., Pindi, Pakistan, 1963; lectr. Panjab U., 1963-71, asst. prof., 1971-86, assoc. prof., 1986-91; assoc. prof. math. King Fahd U. Petroleum and Minerals, Dhahran, Saudi Arabia, 1991—. Author: Introduction to Numerical Analysis, 1991, Introduction to BASIC Language, 1989, FORTRAN 66 and 77, 1989, Fundamentals of Complex Analysis, 1992; contbr. articles to internat. sci. jours. Mem. Pakistan Math. Soc., Panjab Math. Soc. (life), London Math. Soc. Avocations: reading, research. Office: King Fahd U Petroleum and, Minerals Dept Math Sci, Dhahran 31261, Saudi Arabia

IRAM, YAACOV, education educator; b. Siedlce, Poland, Sept. 29, 1939; arrived in Israel, 1948; s. Shmuel and Malka (Barneboim) Shtutman; m. Edi Sapir, 1961; children: Yaron, Galya, Asaf. BA, Hebrew U., Jerusalem, 1963; MA, Dropsie U., 1971, PhD, 1972; postgrad., U. Pa., 1973. Postdoctoral U. Pa., Phila., 1973; lectr. Technion-Israel Inst. Tech., Haifa, 1973-74, 81-82; prof. Bar Ilan U., Ramat Gan, Israel, 1974—; Head Burg Chair in Edn. for Human Values, Tolerance and Peace, 1995—. Author: Theories and Practice in Jewish Education, 1977, The Educational System in Israel, 1998, Development of Teaching in Israel, 1999; contbr. articles to profl. jours. Fulbright scholar in residence USIA, 1988; Finland-Israel Scholars Exch. grant, 1994, The German Academic Exch. grant, 1995. Mem. World Assn. Ednl. Rsch. (pres. 1993-97, v.p. 1999), Am. Assn. Ednl. Rsch., Comparative and Internat. Edn. Soc., Israel Hist. Edn. Soc. (pres.). Office: Bar Ilan U, Sch Edn, 52900 Ramat Gan Israel

IRANDOUST, SAID, chemical reaction engineering educator, scientist; b. Tabriz, Azerbaijan, Iran, Sept. 23, 1960; arrived in Sweden, 1979; s. Amir-Agha Irandoust and Rofia Shirvanli; m. Airi Aulikki Hirvonen, Apr. 9, 1988; children: Aila, Sanna. MSc, Chalmers U. Tech., Goteborg, Sweden, 1984, PhD, 1989. Cert. engring. Rsch. asst. Chalmers U. Tech., Goteborg, 1990-94, assoc. prof., 1994-97, prof., 1998—, v.p., 1999—; rschr. pedagogical devel. Chalmers U. Tech., Goteborg, 1994—. Contbr. chpts. to books. Recipient Pedagogical prize Student Fedn., 1987, 96, Chalmers U. Tech., 1994. Avocations: music, sports, oriental carpets. Office: Dept Chem Reaction Engring, Chalmers Univ Tech, SE-412 96 Göteborg Sweden

IRANI, RAY R., oil, gas and chemical company executive; b. Beirut, Lebanon, Jan. 15, 1935; came to U.S., 1953, naturalized, 1956; s. Rida and Naz I.; children: Glenn R., Lillian M., Martin R. BS in Chemistry, Am. U. Beirut, 1953; PhD in Phys. Chemistry, U. So. Calif., 1957. Rsch. scientist, then sr. rsch. scientist Monsanto Co., 1957-67; assoc. dir. new products, then dir. research Diamond Shamrock Corp., 1967-73; with Olin Corp., 1973-83, pres. chems. group, 1978-80; corp. pres., dir. Olin Corp., Stamford, Conn., 1980-83, COO, 1981-83; chmn. Occidental Petroleum Corp. subs. Occidental Chem. Corp., Dallas, 1983-94; CEO Occidental Petroleum Corp., subs. Occidental Chem. Corp., Dallas, 1983-91; chmn. Can. Occidental Petroleum Corp. Ltd., Calgary, 1987-99; exec. v.p. Occidental Petroleum Corp., L.A., 1983-84, pres., COO, 1984-91, pres., 1991-96, chmn., CEO, 1991—, also bd. dirs.; bd. dirs. Am. Petroleum Inst., Oxy Oil and Gas USA Inc., Occidental Oil and Gas Corp., Occidental Petroleum Investment Corp., Cedars Bank, Kaufman and Broad Home Corp., Jonsson Cancer Ctr. Found./UCLA. Author: Particle Size; also author papers in field; numerous patents in field. Vice chmn. Am. U. Beirut; trustee U. So. Calif., St. John's Hosp. and Health Ctr. Found., Natural History Mus. Los Angeles County; bd. govs. Los Angeles Town Hall, Los Angeles World Affairs Coun. Mem. Nat. Petroleum Coun., Am. Inst. Chemists, Am. Chem. Soc., Sci. Rsch. Soc. Am., Indsl. Rsch. Inst., The Conf. Bd., The CEO Roundtable, Nat. Assn. Mfrs. (bd. dirs.), Am. Petroleum Inst. (bd. dirs.), U.S.-Russia Bus. Coun. Office: 10889 Wilshire Blvd Los Angeles CA 90024-4201

IRARRAZAVAL, ISMAEL MENDEZ, engineering executive; b. Santiago, Chile, Aug. 2, 1952; s. Ismael Rozas and Gabriela Amunategui (Mendez) I.; m. Carolina Garcia de la Huerta Lagos, May 17, 1980; children: Maria Jose, Ismael, Pablo, Miguel Luis, Diego, Carolina. BS, St. Georges Coll., Santiago, 1969; Degree in Indsl. Mechanics, U. Santa Maria, Valparaiso, Chile, 1974; postgrad., U. santiago, 1976. Mgr. Comercial Ind. Pacific, Santiago, 1974-78; tech. asst. Saavedra Benard, Santiago, 1978-80; dir. Plastigen S.A., Santiago, 1980-86; dir. mgr. IIM Ingenieria Industries, Santiago, 1986—. Recipient ACTIM scholarship Agence pour la Coop. Techniques Industrielle et Economique (ACTIM), Paris, 1986. Mem. Assn. Chilean French Engrs. and Technicians (v.p. 1996), Soc. Plastics Engrs. (sr.). Roman Catholic. Home: Av Charles Hamilton 120, Santiago Chile Office: IIM Ingenieria Ind SA, Gral Jofre 42, Santiago Chile

IRAZUSTABARRENA, MIGUEL ANGEL, marketing professional; b. Buenos Aires, Dec. 25, 1938; s. Miguel Ignacio and Maria (Iarza) I.; m. Sara Maria Fernandez, Nov. 13, 1965 (div. Sept. 1992); children: Miguel Javier, Maria Fernanda. CPA, MBA, U. Buenos Aires, Argentina, 1970; prof. internat. trading, Getulio Vargas U., Rio de Janeiro, Brazil, 1974. Exec. pres. Apeco Do Brazil, San Pablo, Brazil, 1971-72; internat. mktg. dir. Apeco Internat., Chgo., 1972-73, Alpha Crux, Buenos Aires, 1973-75, F. V. Argentina S.A., Buenos Aires, 1977—; dir. Docol-FV, Joinville, Brazil, 1979—; pres., dir. Fravi Do Brasil, San Pablo, 1983—. Home and Office: 1602 Florida, Av San Martin 2719 1o C, Buenos Aires Buenos Aires, Argentina

IREDALE, PETER, health authority chairman; b. Brownhills, England, Mar. 15, 1932; s. Harry and Annie (Kirby) I.; m. Judith Margaret Marshall, April 11, 1957; children: John Peter, Susan Caroline, Helen Jane, Alison Sarah. BSc, U. Bristol, Eng., 1952, PhD, 1955; DSc (hon.), Oxford (Eng.) Brookes U., 1993. From rsch. physicist to dir. United Kingdom Energy Authority, Harwell, Oxfordshire, Eng., 1955-87; dir. Harwell (Eng.) lab. United Kingdom Energy Authority, 1987-90; dir. Harwell, Culham (Eng.) sites Oxfordshire, 1990-92; chmn. Oxfordshire Health Authority, Oxford, Eng., 1992—; chmn. U.K. Wave Energy Dept. Energy, 1979-84. Contbr. articles to profl. jours. Fellow Inst. Physics, Inst. Elec. Engrs. Avocations: family, reading, architecture, music, woodworking. Home: 25 Kirk Close, OX2 8JL Oxford England Office: Oxfordshire Health Authorit, Richards Bldg Old Rd Headin, OX2 8JL Oxford England

IRELAND, KEVIN (MARK), poet; b. Auckland, New Zealand, July 18, 1933. LittD (hon.), Massey U. Writer-in-residence Canterbury (New Zealand) U., 1986; Sargeson fellow Auckland, 1987; lit. fellow Auckland U., 1988. Writings include: (poems) Face to Face, 1963, Educating the Body, 1967, A Letter from Amsterdam, 1973, Orchids Hummingbirds & Other Poems, 1974, A Grammar of Dreams, 1975, Literary Cartoons, 1977, The Dangers of Art: Poems 1975-80, 1981, Practice Night in the Drill Hall, 1985, The Year of the Comet, 1986, Selected Poems, 1987, Tiberius at the Beehive, 1990, Skinning a Fish, 1994, Anzac Day: Selected Poems, 1997, Sleeping with the Angels, Stories, 1994, (novels) Blowing My Top, 1996, The Man Who Never Lived, 1997, The Craymore Affair, 2000, (memoir) Under the Bridge and Over the Moon, 1999. Recipient Nat. Book award for Poetry, Mont. award; decorated Order Brit. Empire; recipient Commemoration medal, 1990. Mem. PEN (nat. pres. New Zealand 1990-92). Office: 8 Domain St, Devonport New Zealand

IRGENS, KAYA MOWINCKEL, retired library director; b. Bergen, Norway, Aug. 15, 1937; d. Hakon and Althild (Heiberg) Mosby; m. Jacob Irgens, July 2, 1960; children: Elisabeth, Benedicte. Grad., Libr. Sch., Oslo, 1960; MA in English, Lang. and Literature, U. Bergen, 1989. Dept. libr. Bergen Pub. Libr., 1960-64, 72-81; documentalist Veritas, Bergen, 1985-87; libr. Bergen Tech. Coll., 1981-85; sect. mgr. Novsk Hydro, Bergen, 1987-94; libr. dir. Bergen Coll., 1994-99, ret., 1999. Columnist Bergens Tidende Newspaper; contbr. articles to profl. jours. Leader Bergens Tidende Found., 1986—; active Women Liberation Movement, 1972—. Mem. Norwegian Libr. Organ. Avocations: music, literature, arts & crafts. Home: Ovre kalfarlien 41, 5018 Bergen Norway

IRI, MASAO, mathematical engineering educator; b. Jan. 7, 1933; s. Jin-ichi and Yasumi (Kuga) I.; m. Yumi Mizoo, March 19, 1960; children: Chika, Masato, Yuka. B in Engring., U. Tokyo, 1955, M in Engring., 1957, D in Engring., 1960. Rsch. asst. Kyushu U., Fukuoka, Japan, 1960, asst. prof., 1960-62; from assoc. prof. to prof. U. Tokyo, 1962-93, prof. emeritus, 1993—; prof. Chuo U., Tokyo, 1993—; dir. Inst. Sci. and Engring., Chuo U., Tokyo, 1996—. Author: Network Flow, Transportation and Scheduling, 1969, also 27 books in Japanese, 10 books transl. into Japanese; editor-in-chief Jour. Ops. Rsch. Soc. Japan, 1980-82, Japan Jour. Indls. & Applied Math, 1997—; Asian regional editor Jour. Circuits, Sys. and Computers, 1990-95, Optimization Methods and Software, 1992-97; adv. editor Networks, 1975-99, European Jour. Operational Rsch., 1985-99, Zeitschrift fur Ops. Rsch., 1991-94, Math. Methods of Ops. Rsch., 1995—; assoc. editor Math. Programming, 1976-88, Math. Programming Series A, 1989-98, Internat. Jour. Computational Geometry and Applications, 1990—, Investigacion Operativa, 1992-97; mem. editl. bd. Discrete Applied Math., 1979—, European Jour. Combinatorics, 1981-95, numerous others. Recipient Matsunaga prize Matsunaga Found., 1965, New Tech. prize Inst. Chem. Engrs. Japan, 1968, Toray Sci. and Tech. prize Toray Found., 1993, Purple Ribbon medal Prime Minister Japan, 1995. Fellow IEEE (sr. mem. 1984-89); mem. Ops. Rsch. Soc. Japan (v.p. 1984-85, pres. 1992-94), Math. Programming Soc., Japanese Soc. Quality Control, Life Support Tech. Soc. (v.p. 1985-87), Math. Soc. Japan, Linguistic Soc. Japan, Inst. Electronics Info. and Comm. Engrs. Japan (Paper prize 1969, 76, Achievement prize 1989, editor-in-chief Transactions on Fundamental Electronics Comm. and Computer Scis. 1993-94), Info Processing Soc. Japan (Paper prize 1981, 88, 90), Soc. Instruments and Control Engrs. Japan, Japan Soc. Indsl. Applied Math. (v.p. 1992-93, pres. 1996-97), Engring. Acad. Japan, N.Y. Acad. Sci., Geog. Info. Sys. Assn. (pres. 1994-96), Internat. Fedn. Operational Rsch. Socs. (v.p. 1983-85), Assn. Asian-Pacific Operational Rsch. Socs. (pres. 1992-94), Sigma Xi. Fax: 81-3-3817-1681. Home: 4-11-1-402 Higashi-Komagata, Sumida-ku Tokyo 130-0005, Japan Office: Chuo U Dept Info Sys Engr, 1-13-27 Kasuga Bunkyo-ku, Tokyo 112-8551, Japan

IRIE, PHILIP SHINAZO, physician, scientist; b. Osaka, Japan, Aug. 25, 1920; came to U.S., 1957; s. Rokuro and Taneko (Watanabe) I.; m. Masako Hinoue, May 29, 1969; children: Hanna Yoko, Robert Eiichi. BS, Daishi Coll., Kanazawa, Japan, 1942; MD, Osaka Imperial U., 1945; ScD, Osaka City U., 1961. Rsch. fellow Mt. Sinai Hosp., Chgo., 1957-58, Hahnemann Med. Coll., Phila., 1958-60, Sloan-Kettering Cancer Inst., N.Y.C., 1960-61; rsch. fellow N.Y. Med. Coll., N.Y.C., 1969-70, mem. faculty, 1971—; rsch. fellow Mt. Sinai Med. Sch., NYU, N.Y.C., 1967-69, mem. faculty, 1972—. Contbr. articles to profl. jours. Recipient Physician Recognition award AMA, 1969, Ministry award Dept. Health and Pub. Welfare, Japan, 1992, Disting. Svc. award Yomiuri Newspaper, 1992. Mem. N.Y. State Med. Soc., N.Y. County Med. Soc., Mt. Sinai Med. Sch. Alumni Coun. Achievements include exploration of diuretic to control hypertension prolonging human life; diuretic and antihypertensive activity of luminous substance 3-aminophthalhydrazide; anticancer activity of some Latices and Luciferin. Office: 11035 71st Ave Forest Hills New York NY 11375-4560

IRIE, SEIJI, hematologist, educator; b. Okayama, Japan, Feb. 28, 1955; m. Hiroko Irie, Nov. 3, 1984; 1 child, Saeko. PhD, Okayama U., 1983. Intern, resident Okayama (Japan) U. Med. Sch., 1979-81; instr. in medicine Inst. for Thermal Spring Rsch. Okayama U., Misasa, Tottori, Japan, 1983-84; instr. Inst. for Environment and Diseases Okayama U., Misasa, Tottori, Japan, 1986-88; instr. dept. hematology-oncology U. Miss. Med. Ctr., Jackson, 1984-86; rsch. fellow dept. hematology-oncology Inst. Med. Sci. U. Tokyo, 1988-94; instr. in medicine Juntendo U., Tokyo, 1994-97; dir. divsn. of hematology Kanto Rosai Hosp., Kawasaki, 1997—. Contbr. articles to profl. jours. Recipient Beecham award So. Soc. for Clin. Investigation, 1986. Mem. Internat. Soc. for Exptl. Hematology, AAAS, Japanese Cancer Assn., Japan Soc. Clin. Hematology, Japanese Soc. Hematology, Japanese Soc. Internal Medicine. Home: Somechi 2-10-1-409 Chofu, Tokyo 182-0023, Japan Office: Kanto Rosai Hosp Div Hemat, Kizuki-Sumiyoshi-cho 2035, Nakahara-ku Kawasaki 211-0021, Japan

IRITANI, TOSHIO, psychology educator; b. Tokyo, Setagayaku, Japan, July 30, 1932; s. Tomosada and Fumi (Shimzu) I.; m. Yukie Umeda, Mar. 28, 1974. BEd, Tokyo U. Edn., 1955, MA, 1957; postgrad. studies (non-degree), Harvard U., 1958-61; PhD, Clark U., Worcester, 1962. Rsch. assoc. MIT, Boston, 1960-61; vis. rschr. U. Geneva, Switzerland, 1961-62; rsch. assoc. and vis. lectr. U. Hawaii, Honolulu, 1966; instr. Tokai U., 1963-68, assoc. prof., 1968-73, prof., 1973-98, prof. emeritus, 1998—; rschr. and vis. prof. Polish Acad. Sci., U. Warsaw, 1976-77; vis. scholar Hoover Instn., Stanford U., 1982; vis. prof. St. Anthony's Coll. Oxford (Eng.) U., 1993-94; mem. peace study com. Internat. Union of Psychol. Sci., Brussels, 1989—; prof. Chofu Women's Coll., 1998-2000. Author: The Value of Children-A Cross-National Study, Vol. 6, 1979, Group Psychology of the Japanese in Wartime, Japanese edit. 1986, Chinese edit., 1989, English edit., 1991, New Social Psychology, Rev. 5th edit., 1991, Power: A Study of Social and Psychological Analysis, Japanese edit. 1993, Korean edit., 1996;. Bd. dirs. Population Problems Rsch. Coun., Mainichi Newspapers, Tokyo, 1970. Recipient Disting. award Mainichi Nespapers, 1942, Tokyo, Wundt medal German Psychol. Soc., Leipzig, Germany, 1980. Mem. Assn. Applied Psychology (exec. com., divsn. polit. psychology, U.S.), Group for Psychol. Study of Peace Tokyo (chmn. 1986—), Internat. Coun. Psychologists, Washington (bd. dirs. 1993-96, Planck Disting. Svc. award 1997)., Internat. Mozart Soc., Salzburg, Austria. Avocations: pianist (classical), collector potteries, ceramics, drawing, writing, travel. Home: 3-21 4-Chome Daita, Setagaya Tokyo 155-0033, Japan

IRIZARRY, FRANCISCO A., comnputer information systems official, lawyer; b. San Juan, P.R., Feb. 7, 1962; s. Francisco Irizarry Cancel and Gloria Gonzalez; m. Kathleen Gladys Ryan, May 23, 1987; 1 child, Kevin. BA cum laude, U. Dayton, 1984, JD, 1987. Bar: Ohio 1988. Assoc. Rieser & Marx, Dayton, Ohio, 1988-90; mgr. content devel. and ops. NEXIS, Lexis-Nexis, Dayton, 1988-99, mgr. computer info. sys. products, 1999—. Trustee CityFolk, Dayton. Mem. Phi Alpha Delta, Pi Sigma Alpha. Roman Catholic. Fax: 937-865-1668. E-mail: francisco.irizarry@lexis-nexis.com. Home: 5524 Hearthside Ct # Dt Dayton OH 45424-5231 Office: Lexis-Nexis 9443 Springboro Pike Miamisburg OH 45342-4425

IRMAY, SHRAGGA, engineering educator, lexicographer; b. Lodz, Poland, July 1, 1912; arrived in Israel, 1924; s. Dawid and Sara Nena (Danziger) Szeps; m. Rinna Irena Zaks, Sept. 9, 1950; children: Ron, Amnon. Civil Engr., Liége (Belgium) U., 1935, Colonial Engr., 1935; MSc (hon.), Technion-Israel Inst. Tech., Haifa, 1958. Asst. dept. chemistry Med. Sch. Liége U., 1934-35; asst. Technion-Israel Inst. Tech., Haifa, 1938-41, prof., 1958-80, prof. emeritus, 1980—; tchr. Nautical H.S., Technion's Tech. H.S., Haifa, 1939-41; founder, head Hydrotech. Soil Mechanics Lab., Technion, Haifa, 1949-52; head Divsn. Hydraulic Engring., Haifa, 1954-56; acting v.p. for rsch. Technion, Haifa, 1960-62; dean Technion Grad. Sch., acad. coord. for rsch., Haifa, 1966-68; chmn. Senate Com. on Improvement of Engring. Edn., 1961-62, Technion Com. for Photography and Tchg. Aids, 1963-64, Technion Interdisciplinary Bioengring. Com., 1966, other coms.; cons. Inst. Français de Pétrole, 1964; founder sect. on applied math. Sanit Engring. Lab Faculty Agr. Author: (book) Collected Papers, 1981; editor, co-author: (book) Physical Principles of Water Percolation and Seepage, UNESCO, 1968; editor: Technion Sci. Publs., 1942-43; co-author 50 multilingual dictionaries; contbr. over 200 articles to profl. jours.; Israel Minerals patent, 1953-55. Sec. Assn. Students of Palestine, Liége, 1931-32; edn. officer, cofounder ARP., Hagana, Haifa, 1939; mem. Govt. Agrl. Coun., Israel, 1955-58, Govt. Coun. of Engrs. and Archs., Israel, 1961-79; chmn. Adv. Bd. Ashdod Harbor Devel., Israel, 1957-58; mem. Acad. Coun. Beer Sheva U., 1962-66. Overseas fellow Churchill Coll., 1977; recipient medals Liege U. and Ghent U., 1964, hon. cert. Assn. Engrs. and Architects in Israel, 1993, Israel Inst. Standards, 1998. Mem. European and Mediterranean Com. Water Planning (hon., medal), Am. Geophys. Union (hon.), Water Resources Mgmt. and Kidmah (mem. editl. bd.), Technion Faculty Assn. (chmn. 1951), Acad. Hebrew Lang., Acad. Royale des Scis. d'Outre-Mer (hon. corr.),. Home: 12/7 Klebanoff St, 32804 Haifa Israel Office: Technion-Israel Inst Tech, Borowitz Bldg, 32000 Haifa Israel

IRMICI, MANLIO, journalist; b. Bianchi, Italy, May 22, 1939; s. Elia and Concetta (Nista de la Rouerie) I.; m. Francis Barone; 1 child, Elia. Degree in medicine, U. Paris, 1960; degree in literature, U. Bari (Italy), 1980. Author: Rorschach Technique, 1975, The Friend, 1986, The Run in the Dark, 1986; author of poems. Recipient Golden medal s. Valentino, Terni, Italy, 1979, Rd. Gabrieli, Rome, 1979. Roman Catholic. Avocations: naturalist, entomologist, poet.

IROH, JUDE ONWUEGBU, chemistry educator; b. Umulogho Obowo, Nigeria, Sept. 2, 1958; came to the U.S., 1986; s. Konkwo and Rita (Akuichi) I.; children: Bright Jude Obinna, Jude Onwuegbu Jr. BS in Applied Chemistry, U. Jos Jos, Nigeria, 1980; MS in Polymer Sci. and Tech., U. Manchester, 1984; PhD in Materials Sci., U. Conn., 1990. Grad. asst. Fed. U. Tech., Owerri, Nigeria, 1981-84, asst. lectr., 1985-86, lectr. II, 1986-90;

grad. asst. U. Conn., Storrs, 1986-90; postdoctoral fellow Temple U., Phila., 1990-91; asst. prof. chemistry U. Cin., 1991-97, assoc. prof., 1997—; student cons. engr. UTRC, Hartford, Conn., 1989; cons. G-Cat Co., Hartford, 1990-95. Advocate, mentor U. Cin., 1992-95, faculty advisor, 1993-95. Mem. Am. Chem. Soc., SAMPE, AIChE (assoc.), Adhesion Soc. (award com. 1993—). Achievements include patent for electrochemical method and product; co-inventor electrochemical technique for insi.tu impregnation of graphite fiber-polyimide composites. Home: 11957 Blackhawk Cir Cincinnati OH 45240-1405 Office: U Cin 408B Rhodes Hall Ml12 Cincinnati OH 45221-0001

IRONS, JEREMY JOHN, actor; b. Cowes, Eng., Sept. 19, 1948; s. Paul Dugan and Barbara Anne (Sharpe) I.; m. Sinead Moira Cusack, Mar. 28, 1978; children: Samuel James, Maximilian Paul. Actor: (stage appearances) including John the Baptist in Godspell, 1973, Mick in The Caretaker, 1974, Petruchio in The Taming of the Shrew, 1975, Harry Thunder in Wild Oats, Royal Shakespeare Co., 1976-77, 86, James Jameson in Rear Column, 1978, The Real Thing, 1984 (Tony award 1984); title role in Richard II, Leontes in Winter's Tale, The Rover, Royal Shakespeare Theater, Stratford-Upon-Avon, Eng., 1986-87; (films) Nijinsky, 1979, The French Lieutenant's Woman, 1981, Betrayal, 1982, Moonlighting, 1982, The Wild Duck, 1983, Swann in Love, 1983, The Mission, 1985, Chorus of Disapproval, 1988, Australia, 1988, Dead Ringers, 1988 (named Best Actor N.Y. Film Critics' Circle, 1988), Danny, the Champion of the World, 1989, Reversal of Fortune, 1990 (Acad. award for best actor, 1991, Golden Globe for best actor), Kafka, 1991, Waterland, 1992, Damage, 1992, M. Butterfly, 1993, The House of the Spirits, 1994, The Lion King, 1994 (voice), Die Hard with a Vengeance, 1995, Stealing Beauty, 1996, Lolita, 1997, The Chinese Box, 1997, Man in the Iron Mask, 1998; (TV appearances) Alex Hepburn in The Captain's Doll, 1982, Charles Ryder in Brideshead Revisited, 1980-81, Tales from Hollywood, 1992, Longitudre, 1999. Decorated officer Legion d'Honneur (France). Address: Hutton Mgmt, 4 Old Manor Close, Askett Bucks HP27 9NA, England

IRONS, WILLIAM GEORGE, anthropology educator; b. Garrett, Ind., Dec. 25, 1933; s. George Randall and Eva Aileen (Veazey) I.; m. Marjorie Sue Rogasner, Nov. 4, 1972; children—Julia Rogasner, Marybeth Rogasner. BA, U. Mich., 1960, MA, 1963, PhD, 1969; postgrad., London Sch. Econs., 1964-65. With Army C.E., 1956-58; asst. prof. social relations Johns Hopkins U., 1969-74; asst. prof. anthropology Pa. State U., 1974-78; assoc. prof. anthropology Northwestern U., Evanston, Ill., 1978-83, prof., 1983—; cons. Nat. Geog. Soc., NSF, AAAS, Social Sci. Research Council, Time-Life Books, U. Wash. Press, Random House, Worth Pubs., Rutgers U. Press, U. Tex. Press, Pelenum Press, Oxford U. Press, Cornell U. Press. Author: Perspectives on Nomadism, 1972, The Yomut Turkmen, 1975, Evolutionary Biology and Human Social Behavior, 1979, Adaptation and Human Behavior, 2000; mem. bd. editors Ethology and Sociobiology. Mem. coun. Human Behavior and Evolution Soc., pres. elect, 1999. With AUS, 1954-56. Recipient Lifetime Achievement award Commn. on Nomadic Peoples, Internat. Union Anthropol. and Ethnological Scis.; grantee NSF, 1973, 76, 83, 85, 86, Ford Found., 1974, Harry Frank Guggenheim Found., 1976. Fellow AAAS, Am. Anthrop. Assn.; mem. Assocs. in Current Anthropology, Human Behavior and Evolution Soc. (pres.-elect), Internat. Soc. Human Ethology, Internat. Soc. for Behavioral Ecology, Ctr. for Advanced Studies in Religion and Sci., Inst. for Religion in an Age of Sci., Phi Kappa Phi. Achievements include research on Turkmen of Iran, human behavioral ecology, evolutionary ethics. Home: 2604 Payne St Evanston IL 60201-2133 Office: Northwestern U Dept Anthropology 1810 Hinman Ave Evanston IL 60208-0809

IRONS, WILLIAM LEE, lawyer; b. Birmingham, Ala., June 9, 1941; s. George Vernon and Velma (Wright) I. BA, U.Va., 1963; JD, Samford U., 1966. Bar: Ala. 1966, U.S. Dist Ct. (no. dist.) Ala. 1966, U.S. Ct. Appeals (5th cir.) 1966. Dir. mil. justice Maxwell AFB, Ala., 1963-69; law clk. Speir, Robertson & Jackson, Birmingham, 1964-66; asst. judge adv. Whiteman AFB, Mo., 1966-67, Gunter AFB, 1967-68; ptnr. Speir, Robertson, Jackson & Irons, 1970-71, Speir & Irons, 1971-72, William L. Irons & Assocs., 1972—; U.S. trustee, 1964-86; instr. sr. officers Judge Adv. Gen.'s Sch. Air War coll., Air Univ., Maxwell AFB. Candidate Ala. Ho. Reps. 1966. Deacon, Sunday sch. supt. Mountain Brook Bapt. Ch. Served to capt. USAF Strategic Air Command. Decorated Commendation medal and citation USAF, Cong. medal of honor; named Outstanding Jr. Officer Vietnam War, USAF, 1969; DuPont Regional scholar U.Va. Mem. ABA, Birmingham Bar Assn., Assn. Trial Lawyers Am., Nat. Assn. Cert. Judge Advs., Fed. Bar Assn., Nat. Res. Officer Assn., Newcomen Soc., St. Andrews Soc., SAR (pres. Ala. chpt., writer numerous cover stories on Am. Revolution era, Taylor award 1990, U.S. Senate Commendation for Authorship of Colonial Navy 1992, senate commendation state of N.Y. for Chronicles of the Am. Revolutionary War 1995), Descendants of Washington's Army at Valley Forge (capt. of the guard, com. admiral state of Md. 1995), Nat. Lawyers Club, Birmingham Exec. Club (pres. 1978-79), Sigma Delta Kappa. Democrat. Baptist. Home: 3855 Cove Dr Birmingham AL 35213-3801 Office: 1227 City Federal Building Birmingham AL 35203-3714

IRSHAD, MOHAMMAD, biochemistry educator; b. Muzaffar Nagar, India, June 4, 1954; s. Abdul and Bashiran Hamid; m. Khalida Begum; 2 children. MSc, DAV, 1975; PhD, Meerut U., 1980. Rsch. assoc. All India Inst. Med. Scis., New Delhi, 1981-83, rsch. officer, 1983-90, asst. prof., 1990-95, assoc. prof., 1995-99, prof., 1999—; mem. various coms. AIIMS, New Delhi, 1991—. Contbr. articles to profl. jours. Recipient Nat. Oration award ICMR, 1990. Fellow Internat. Med. Sci. Acad.; mem. Nat. Acad. Med. Scis., Soc. of Biochemistry, Soc. of Immunologists, N.Y. Acad. Sci., Nat. Acad. of Sci. Avocations: music, cricket, new scientific activities. Home: E-18 Ansari Nagar, New Delhi 110029, India Office: All India Inst Med Scis, Ansari Nagar, New Delhi 110029, India

IRUDAYARAJ, JOSEPH, agricultural engineering educator; b. Coimbatore, Tamil Nadu, India, Nov. 8; came to U.S., 1983; BS, Coll. Agrl. Engring., Coimbatore, 1983; MS, U. Hawaii, 1986, 87; PhD, Purdue U., 1990. Asst. prof. U. Sask., Saskatoon, 1991-94, Utah State U., Logan, 1995-98, Pa. State U., University Park, 1998—. Author, editor: Modeling of Food Systems, 2000; contbr. articles to profl. jours. Grantee USDA, Dairy Mgmt. Inc., Dept. Energy. Mem. Am. Soc. Engring. in Agr., Food and Biol. (rsch. spectroscopy, biosensors, novel food processing). Avocations: traithlons, soccer, tennis. Home: 373 Glengarry Ln State College PA 16801-7091 Office: Pa State U 227 Agrl Engring Bldg University Park PA 16802

IRURRE PEREZ, JOSE, chemistry educator, researcher; b. Barcelona, Spain, Oct. 23, 1940; s. Prudencio Irurre Esteve and Maria C. Pérez López. Degree in chem. engring., Inst. Quimic de Sarria, Barcelona, 1964; Lic. in Sci., U. Barcelona, 1982; PhD in Chem. Engring., Inst. Quimic de Sarria, 1969. Prof. auxiliar Inst. Quimic de Sarria, Barcelona, 1964-67, adj. prof., 1967-73, prof. agregado, 1973-77, prof. catedratico, 1977—; chief sect. Estereoquimica Inst. Quimic de Sarrià, U. Ramón Llull, 1967—, dir. dept. organic chemistry, 1992-98. Mem. Real Sociedad Espanola de Quimica, Asociacion Antiguos Alumnos. Office: Via Augusta 390, 08017 Barcelona Spain

IRVINE, BARON OF LAIRG ALEXANDER ANDREW MACKAY, Lord Chancellor of England and Wales; b. June 23, 1940; s. Alexander and Margaret Christina I.; m. Alison Mary McNair, 1974; 2 children. BA with honors, LLB with honors, Christ's Coll., Cambridge, Eng.; MA, LLB, Glasgow (Scotland) U. Univ. lectr. LSE, 1965-69; called to Inner Temple, 1967; with Queen's Counsel, 1978; head 11 King's Bench Walk Chambers, 1981-87; with Bencher of the Inner Temple, 1985, Recorder, 1985-88; dep. high ct. judge, 1987-97; hon. Bencher of the Inn of Ct. of No. Ireland, 1998; shadow spokesman on legal affairs/home affairs Labour Party, 1987-92; shadow lord chancellor, 1992-97; lord chancellor Govt. of U.K., 1992—; privy councillor, 1997; joint pres. House of Lords, Brit. Am. Parliamentary Group, Commwealth Parliamentary Assn., Intr-Parliamentary Union; vice-patron World Fedn. of Mental Health. Scholar Christ's Coll. Mem. Garrick Club. Avocations: cinema, theatre, collecting paintings, travel. Office: House of Lords, Westminister, London SW1A 0AA, England SW1A 0PW*

IRVINE, EDMUND, race car driver; b. Newtownards, No. Ireland, Nov. 10, 1965. Profl. race car driver Formula 1 Rogues, 1983—. 2-time champion Formula Ford, 1983-87, winner Jordan F3000, 3d in overall series, Hockinheim, 1990. Fax: 39-536-949-436. Office: Ferrari SpA, Via Ascari 55-57, I-41053 Maranello Italy*

IRVINE, IAN ALEXANDER NOBLE, media company executive, director; b. Derby, U.K., July 2, 1936; m. Noelle Elizabeth Morgan. BSc in Econ., London Sch. Econ., 1957. Articled clk. Amsdon, Cossart & Wells, London, 1957-61; chartered acct. Touche Ross & Co., London, 1961-65, ptnr., 1965-82; mng. dir. Fleet Holdings PLC, London, 1982-85; chief exec. Octopus Pub. Group PLC, London, 1986-90; dir. Reed Internat. P.L.C., London, 1987-97, dep. chief exec., 1990-92, dep. chmn., 1993-94, chmn., 1994-97; exec. dir. Reed Elsevier plc, London, 1994-96, chmn., 1994-96; dir., chmn. Video Networks Ltd., 1997—; chmn. So. Star Circle Plc, 1997-99; apptd. by Sec. State for Trade and Industry as inspector to investigate Roadships Ltd., 1973; apptd. asst. to inspector to investigate Court Line Ltd., 1974; apptd. by Sec. State for Industry as mem. Indsl. Devel. Adv. Bd., 1974-85; dir. Reuters Holdings PLC, 1984-86, TV-AM PLC, 1983-90, chmn., 1988-90, Brit. Satellite Broadcasting Ltd., 1990-91, Capital Radio plc, 1982-90, 91—, chmn., 1992-96, MEPC plc, 1992-93; chmn. Brit. Sky Broadcasting Ltd., 1990-91; dir., chmn. Southern Star Circle Plc, 1997-99; dir. Piedmont Internat. SA, 1997, Saatchi & Saatchi Plc, 1998-2000. V.p. Marine Conservation Soc., U.K., chmn., 1992-93, 97—. Fellow Inst. Chartered Accts. (Eng., Wales), Royal Geographic Soc., Royal Soc. Arts; mem. Honourable Artillery Co., Brit. Inst. Mgmt. (companion), Newspapers Pub. Assn. Ltd. (coun. 1982-85), Garrick Club, Brit. Sub-Aqua Club (chmn. 1983-86). Avocations: scuba diving, fly fishing, photography, travel. Office: MIAssociates, 14 Treguntor Rd, London SW10 9LR, England

IRVINE, PHYLLIS ELEANOR, nursing educator, administrator; b. Germantown, Ohio, July 14, 1940; m. Richard James Irvine, Feb. 15, 1964; children: Mark, Rick. BSN, Ohio State U., 1962, MSN, 1979, PhD, 1981; MS, Miami U., Oxford, Ohio, 1966. Staff nurse VA Ctr., Dayton, Ohio, 1962-66; mem. nursing faculty Miami Valley Hosp. Sch. Nursing, Dayton, 1968-78; teaching asst., lectr. Ohio State U., Columbus, 1979-82; assoc. prof. Ohio U., Athens, 1982-83; prof., dir. N.E. La. U., Monroe, 1984-88; prof., dir. sch. nursing Ball State U., Muncie, Ind., 1988—. Reviewer Health Edn. Jour., Reston, Va., 1987; contbr. articles to profl. jours. Mem. Mayor's Commn. on Needs of Women, La., 1984-88; 1st v.p., bd. dirs. United Way of Ouachita, La., 1986-88. Mem. ANA, Ind. Nurses Assn., Ind. Coun. Deans and Dirs. of Nursing Edn. (pres. 1992-98), Internat. Coun. Women's Health Issues (bd. dirs. 1986-92, 98-2000), Assn. for the Advancement Health Edn., Sigma Theta Tau. Office: Ball State U Cn418 Nursing Muncie IN 47306-0001

IRVINE, REED JOHN, media critic, corporation executive; b. Salt Lake City, Sept. 29, 1922; s. William John and Edna (May) I.; m. Kay Araki, Aug. 14, 1948; 1 son, Donald. A.B., U. Utah, 1942; postgrad., U. Colo., 1943-44, U. Wash., 1949; M.Litt., Oxford U., Eng., 1951. With Gen. Hdqrs. of Allied Occupation of Japan, Tokyo, 1946-48; economist bd. govs. Fed. Res. System, Washington, 1951-63, adviser internat. fin., 1963-77; chmn. bd. Accuracy in Media, Inc., Washington, 1971—; editor AIM Report; syndicated columnist, radio commentator; chmn. Accuracy in Academia, 1985—. Author: Media Mischief and Misdeeds, 1984; co-author: (with Cliff Kincaid) Profiles of Deception, 1990, (with Joseph C. Goulden and Cliff Kincaid) The News Manipulators, 1993. Dir. Council Def. of Freedom, Washington, 1970—. Served with USNR, 1942-43, USMC, 1943-46, PTO; to capt. USMCR, 1944-46. Recipient George Washington medal Freedom Found., 1980, Ethics in Journalism award World Media Assn., 1987. Mem. Phi Beta Kappa. Mem. LDS Ch. Office: Accuracy in Media Inc 4455 Connecticut Ave NW # 330 Washington DC 20008-2328

IRVINE, ROSE LORETTA ABERNETHY, retired communications educator, consultant; b. Kingston, N.Y., Nov. 14, 1924; d. William Francis and Julia A.; m. Robert Tate Irvine Jr., Dec. 18, 1965 (dec. June 1968). BA, Coll. St. Rose, 1945; MA, Columbia U., 1946; PhD, Northwestern U., 1964. Tchr. English, Kingston H.S., 1946-47; tchr. English and speech Croton-Harmon H.S., Croton-on-Hudson, N.Y., 1947-49; instr. speech SUNY, New Paltz, 1949-53; asst. prof. SUNY, New Platz, 1953-57, assoc. prof., 1957-64, prof. speech communication, 1964-85, prof. emeritus, 1985—; guest prof. Yon Sei U., Seoul, 1970; U.S. del. U.S. Bi-Nat. Conf., Manila, 1976; adv. bd. Rondout Nat. Bank Norstar (now Fleet Bank), 1973-85; U. Chancellor's adv. bd. SUNY Senate, Albany, 1974-80; guest prof. Celtic lore Princess Grace Libr., Monaco, 1987; mem. faculty sr. rsch. partnership program SUNY, Albany, 1999—cons., rschr., writer, 1985—; presenter in field. Contbr. articles to Speech Teacher, Educational Forum, Readers Theatre, others. Mem. Nat. Jr. League, Kingston, 1958-90; dir. Puppet Theater for Srs., N.Y., 1982-83; bd. trustees Friends of the Senate House State Hist. Site, Kingston, 1996-99, pres. 1999; bd. Ulster County adv. coun. to Office for Aging, 1998—, v.p., 2000—; mem. allocations com. United Way Ulster County, 1998—. Honor Tuition scholar Coll. St. Rose, Albany, N.Y., 1941; named Outstanding Educator of Am., 1971. Mem. AAUW (liaison SUNY New Paltz 1966-85), Speech Comm. Assn. (mem. legis assembly 1967-68, emeritus), N.Y. State Speech Assn. (emeritus), Zeta Phi Eta, Delta Kappa Gamma, Kappa Delta Pi, Pi Lambda Theta. Roman Catholic. Avocations: historic preservation, golf, swimming, travel, local history. Home: 105 Lounsbury Pl Kingston NY 12401-5231 Office: SUNY Communications Dept New Paltz NY 12561

IRVINE, WILLIAM BURRISS, management consultant; b. Wheeling, W.Va., July 20, 1925; s. Russell Drake and Elizabeth (Carney) I.; m. Allen Claywell; children: William, Mary, Edward. BA in Econs., Cornell U., 1949. V.p. Basil L. Smith Sys., Phila., 1949-66; pres. Pa. Graphic Arts, Inc., Phila., 1966-78, Classified Devel. Corp., Bryn Mawr, Pa., 1978—; pres. Victor O'Neil Studios divsn. Herff Jones, Inc., N.Y.C., 1972-75; trustee Cornell Delta Phi Ednl. Found., N.Y., 19855; bd. dirs. Main Ling Sch. Night, 19985. Author: Treasury of College Humor, 1947. Mem. St. Elmo Club of Phila., St. Elmo Club of N.Y., Lake White Club, Delta Phi (sec. 1960-62). Republican. Roman Catholic.

IRVING, DAVID OWEN, biotechnology company executive; b. Sydney, NSW, Australia, Feb. 16, 1954; s. Geoff and Ellen Jane (McLaughlan) I.; m. Anne-Marie Clarke, Jan. 7, 1977; children: James, Edward, Harry. BSc, James Cook U., Townsville, Australia, 1974, BSc with honors, 1975; MSc, Australian Nat. U., Canberra, 1977, PhD, 1984. Tech. officer Australian Nat. U., 1977-80; fellow, assoc. Rockefeller U., N.Y.C., 1983-86; fellow CSIRO, Sydney, Australia, 1986-87; sr. rsch. scientist Biotech Australia, Sydney, 1987-90, mgr. molecular biology rsch. dept., 1990-97, head R&D divsn., 1997—; hon. assoc. MacQuarie U. Sch. Biol. Scis., Sydney, 1998; dir. Biotech Australia, Sydney; mem. sci. adv. bd. Pi2Ltd. Patentee in field; contbr. articles to profl. jours. Australian Wool Corp. postgrad. scholar, 1980; CSIRO postdoctoral fellow, 1983; recipient new investigator rsch. award NIH, 1984. Mem. Australian Soc. for Biochemistry and Molecular Biology, Australian Biotech. Assn. Avocations: home renovation, jogging, aerobics and weight training, children's sports, reading. Office: Biotech Australia Pty Ltd, 28 Barcoo St Roseville, Sydney 2069 NSW, Australia

IRVING, JAN ELIZABETH, publisher; b. Upper Ferntree Gully, Victoria, Australia, July 13, 1962; d. David Vaughan Howy and Barbara Lina (Wilhelm) I. BSc with honors, Monash U., Melbourne, Australia, 1985, diploma in edn., 1986; diploma comml. art and graphic design, Stotts, 1988. Rsch. asst. in pharmacology Monash U., 1983; census collector Australian Govt., 1986; personal asst. to Mrs. LMP Buchanan Melbourne, 1987-91; editor, pub. Erinrac Enterprises, Melbourne, 1991—; dir. Sixty Sixth Rave P/L, Melbourne, 1984-92. Author: The Cashmere Book, 1986, Dog Games, 1995; editor, author: Clumber Spaniel: Australasian Handbook, 1986, Clumber spaniels, 1998; editor internat. mag. Clumber Spaniel Corr., 1987—; editor Australian mag. Canine Collectables Courier. Mem. Mcpl. Fire Prevention Com., Pakenham Shire, 1987-93, mem. Mcpl. Waste Mgmt. Com., Pakenham Shire, 1993. Fellow Canine Mus. Found.; mem. Clumber Spaniel Clubs (Sweden, U.K. and Australia), Rarer Gundog Spaniel Club. Anglican. Avocation: dog exhibitions. Office: Erinrac Enterprises, Erinrac Upper Beaconsfield, 3808 Victoria Australia

IRVING, JEFFREY ALAN, management consultant, educator, lawyer; b. N.Y.C., May 20, 1947; s. Herbert and Florence (Rapoport) I.; m. Maureen Pickett, July 20, 1988; children: Tara, Michael. BSBA cum laude, U. Denver, 1969; JD, U. Okla., 1973; MBA with honors, Harvard U., 1980. Bar: N.Y. 1974, U.S. Dist. Ct. (ea. and so. dists.) N.Y. 1975, U.S. Ct. Appeals (2d cir.) 1975, U.S. Supreme Ct. 1978. Legal intern Legal Aid Soc., Norman, Okla., 1972-73; assoc. Pincus, Hutner, Seeman & Hasen, N.Y.C., 1973-74; exec. v.p., gen. counsel Global Sysco divsn. Sysco Corp., Garden City, N.Y., 1974-91; pres. food svcs. divsn. Seabrook Bros. and Sons. Inc., 1991-92; founder, mng. dir. cons. firm, Great Neck N.Y.; mem. faculty Hofstra U. Coll. Bus. Administrn. Editor Human Rights Rsch. Jour., 1972-73; contbr. articles to Inc. mag., Food Svc. Distbr. mag. Bd. dirs. L.I. chpt. March of Dimes, 1975-91. Mem. Bar N.Y., Nassau County Bar Assn. (ethics com. 1974-80), Freight Users Assn. N.Y. (pres. 1978, bd. dirs. 1975-92). Republican. Avocations: tennis, sailing. Office: Irving Consulting Group 11 Middle Neck Rd Ste 307 Great Neck NY 11021-2301

IRWIN, GAIL PATRICIA, university official, consultant; b. Christchurch, New Zealand, Apr. 9, 1947; d. Clarence Francis and Joan Patricia (Farrier) Wilkins; m. William John Irwin, Jan. 29, 1968; children: Christopher Andrew Angus, Angela Leucine Quintana. MSc (hon.), Victoria U. Wellington, New Zealand, 1968, LLB, 1994; PhD, Waikato U., Hamilton, New Zealand, 1971. Rsch. scientist Wallaceville Animal Rsch. Ctr., Upper Hutt, 1966-71; lectr. chemistry and biochemistry Wellington Poly., 1971-80, sr. lectr., 1980-90, head liaison and edn. svcs., 1990-93, head Sch. Bus. and Info. Sys., 1993-97, acad. dir., 1998-99; with Massey U. Wellington Campus, 1999—; bd. mem. Toxic Substances Bd., 1983—, New Zealand YwK Consultative Com., 1999-2000,. Author: Development of Intellectual Property Policies, 1993, 94, The Germination of Seeds, 1971; contbr. articles to profl. jours. Justice of Peace Appt. by Govt., New Zealand, 1992—. Recipient Innovative Teaching Grants, 1981, 83, Postdoc Study award, 1973, Postgrad. scholarship, 1968, Dept. Edn., Chemistry prize New Zealand Inst. Chemistry, Wellington, 1965. Fellow New Zealand Inst. Mgmt.; mem. Wellington Regional C. of C. (dir. 1993—); Wellington C. of C. (councillor 1993-96), Wellington Law Soc., New Zealand Assn. Scientists. Avocations: philately, oil and water color painting, batik, computers. Fax: 64-4-8012790. E-mail: gpirwin@massey.ac.nz. Office: Massey U Wellington Campus, Private Box 756, Wellington New Zealand

IRWIN, JOHN ALAN GIBSON, plant pathologist, educator; b. Brisbane, Queensland, Australia, July 16, 1950; s. John Thomas George and Ethel (Gibson) I.; m. Hilary Paget, Jan. 16, 1950; children: Genevieve, Vivienne. B in Agrl. Sci., U. Queensland, Brisbane, 1972, M in Agrl. Sci., 1975; PhD, U. Wis., 1980; D in Agrl. Sci., U. Queensland, 1992. Cert. Practicing Agriculturalist, Australian Inst. Agrl. Sci. Plant pathologist Queensland State Govt., Brisbane, 1972-77; Australian Meat Rsch. Com. overseas rsch. fellow U. Wis., Madison, 1977-80; plant pathologist Queensland State Govt., 1980-82; lectr. botany U. Queensland, 1982-84, sr. lectr. botany, 1984-86, reader in botany, 1987-92, prof. botany, 1992—; dir. Coop. Rsch. Ctr. Tropical Plant Pathology, U. Queensland, 1992-98, CEO, 1999—; mem. Austrlian Oilseeds Rsch. Coun., 1989-91; mem. crop improvement com. Australian Grains R & D Corp., 1991-93. Mem. editl. adv. bd. Australian Jour. Exptl. Agr., 1986-88, chmn., 1989-90; mem. editl. adv. bd. Australian Jour. Agrl. Rsch., 1992-98, chmn., 1998—; contbr. over 150 refereed publs. in internat. jours. on plant pathology; co-breeder disease-resistent alfalfa. Recipient Urrbrae medal Urrbrae Found., South Australia, 1993. Fellow Am. Phytopath. Soc., Australian Inst. Agrl. Sci. (Australian medal Agrl. Sci. 1992), Australasian Plant Pathology Soc. (Daniel McAlpine meml. lectr. 1997); mem. Genetics Soc. Am. Avocation: gardening. Office: U Qld Coop Rsch Ctr Plant P, Lev 5 John Hines Bldg, Brisbane QLD 4072, Australia

IRWIN, LESLIE ROBSON, orthopedist; b. Consett, England, May 9, 1962; s. Robson and Olga Madge (Padgett) I.; m. Catherine Pope, Apr. 25, 1987. BA, Oxford U., England, 1983, BM, BChir, 1986, MA, 1988. Cons. orthopaedic & hand surgeon Sunderland (Eng.) Royal Hosp., 1999—. Contbr. articles to profl. jours. Fellow Royal Coll. Surgeons; mem. British Orthop. Assn., British Soc. for Surgery of the Hand, British Elbow and Shoulder Soc. Office: Sunderland Royal Hosp, Kayll Rd, Sunderland SR4 7TP, England

IRWIN, LINDA BELMORE, marketing consultant; b. Portland, Oreg., Apr. 29, 1950; d. Calvin C. and Dorothy B. (Belmore) Harper; m. Michael Hugh Irwin, June 24, 1989. Student, Portland State U., 1968-72. With Hyatt Regency, New Orleans, 1975-78; catering Hyatt Regency-Capitol Hill, Washington, 1978-80; dir. catering Hyatt, Anaheim, Calif., 1978-80; mgr. Dockside Yacht Sales, Annapolis, Md., 1981-85; dir. sales and mktg. Loew's Hotel, 1985-86; dir. mktg. Annapolis Marriot, 1986-88; ind. mktg. cons. Washington, Dallas, Cin., 1988—. Amb. State of Md., Annapolis, 1986-88; mktg. chair Tourism Coun. Annapolis and Anne Arundel County; curricula advisor Anne Arundel C.C.; mem. fund raising com. Ch. Circle Beautification Trust. Mem. Nat. Banquet mgrs. Guild (founder L.A. chpt.), Nat. Assn. Female Execs. (area dir. 1985—), Annapolis C. of C. (ambassador 1985-88), Greater Washington Soc. of Assn. Execs., Anne Arundel Trade Coun., Md. Tourism Coun. (adv. bd.), Internat. Platform Assn. Republican. Episcopalian. Avocations: calligraphy, sailing, traveling, literature, ballet.

IRWIN, PATRICK NOEL, insurance company executive; b. London, Dec. 15, 1939; arrived in South Africa, 1947; s. Henry Joseph and Kathleen Sarah (Evans) I.; m. Lone Butty, Apr. 25, 1968; children: Pia Nicola, Michaela Britt. With Guardian Royal Exch. Assurance, London, other locations, 1966-78; gen. mgr. Irano British Ins., Tehran, Iran, 1978-80, Nat. Ins., Manama, Bahrain, 1980-83; mng. dir. Antah Sedgwick Chartered Ins., Kuala Lumpur, Malaysia, 1983-86, Saudi Ins. Broking Assocs., Jeddah, Saudi Arabia, 1987-90, Bahrain Ins. Co., Manama, 1991—; gen. mgr. Bahrain Nat. Holding Co. and Bahrain Nat. Ins. Co., 1999—. Sec. Bahrain British Bus. Forum, Manama, 1995. Fellow Inst. Mgmt.; mem. Bahrain Ins. Assn. (treas. 1995, 98). Roman Catholic. Avocations: golf, travel. Office: Bahrain Ins Co, PO Box 843, Manama Bahrain

IRWIN, PETER JOHN, orthopaedic surgeon; b. East St. Louis, Ill., July 7, 1934; s. Peter and Anne (Sokalski) Iwasyszyn; m. Kathryn Swanson, June 15, 1960; children: Kathryn Linda, Mary Elizabeth, Amy Marie, Kenneth John, James Patrick. BS in Biology, St. Louis U., 1955, MD, 1959. Diplomate Am. Bd. Orthopaedic Surgery, Am. Bd. Forensic Medicine. Intern Creighton Meml. St. Joseph Hosp., Omaha, 1959-60; resident in orthopaedic surgery U. Ark. Med. Ctr., Little Rock, 1961-65, tchg. staff, 1965-97; pvt. practice Fort Smith, Ark., 1965-97; mem. staff Sparks Regional Med. Ctr., 1965-97, St. Edward Mercy Med. Ctr., 1965-97, retired, 1997; mem. staff St. Edward Mercy Med. Ctr., 1965-97—; mem. staff Sparks Regional Med. Ctr., 1965-97, chief of staff, 1979, bd. dirs., 1980-87; ret. 1998. Lt. comdr. M.C., USN, 1966-68. Fellow ACS, Am. Acad. Orthopaedic Surgeons (councillor 1983-89); mem. AMA, So. Med. Assn., Sebastian County Med. Soc. (pres. 1997), Ark. Orthopaedic Assn. (pres. 1976-77), Mid-Am. Orthopaedic Assn. (founding mem., pres. 1993-94), Clin. Orthopaedic Soc., Inc., Mid-Ctrl. States Orthopaedic Soc. (pres. 1979-80), So. Orthopaedic Assn., Am. Orthopaedic Soc. for Sports Medicine, Am. Soc. Sports Medicine, Ark. Hand Club.

IRWIN, RICHARD DENNIS, electrical engineering educator; b. Albany, Ga., Mar. 27, 1958; s. Vernon Hugh and Martha Lucille (Carson) I.; m. Charlotte Anita Yancey, Mar. 8, 1981; children: Katherine Virginia, Thomas Ralph, Elizabeth Martha. BSEE, Miss. State U., Starkville, 1980; MS, Miss. State U., 1983; PhD, Miss. State U., Starkville, 1986. Registered profl. engr., Ohio. Instr. Miss. State U., 1983-86; assoc. sr. staff engr. Control Dynamics Co., Huntsville, Ala., 1986-87; asst. prof. Ohio U., Athens, 1987-90, assoc. prof., 1990-96, prof., 1996—, chair Sch. EECS, 1997—, Grad. chair, 1993-97; pres. Austral Engring. and Software, Inc.; cons. Control Dynamics Co., Huntsville, 1988, Systran, Dayton, Ohio, 1991, Wright State U., Dayton, 1990-92, Nichols Rsch., Huntsville, 1992; mem. steering com. Southeastern Symposium on Sys. Theory, 1988—, gen. chmn., 1994. Contbr. articles to Jour. Guidance, Control, Dynamics, Jour., Astron. Sci., Jour. Materials Engring. and Performance, Jour. Optimal Control and Applications, others. Recipient Outstanding Achievement award Ohio Soc. Profl. Engrs., 1989, Russ Rsch. award, 1993; NASA faculty fellow, 1988, 89, 90; grantee NASA, 1988-95, Dept. Edn., 1999—. Mem. IEEE (sr.), AIAA, Am. Astron. Soc., Am. Soc. Engring. Edn., I.F.A.C. (aerospace tech. com. 2000—), Sigma Xi, Phi Kappa Phi, Tau Beta Pi, Eta Kappa Nu. Democrat. Achievements include development of frequency domain system identificaiton techniques for flexible systems; demonstration of control system design using experi-

mental data models, first Internet accessible flexible structures control lab. Office: Ohio U Stocker 333 Athens OH 45701

IRWIN, ROBERT HUGH CRAWFORD, manufacturing company executive; b. Chadds Ford, Pa., Mar. 26, 1928; s. Andrew Polluck and Helen Baker (Chalfant) I.; m. Elizabeth Symonds; children: Lauren, Lisa. BSME, U. Del., 1951. Various engring. positions Chrysler Corp., Detroit, 1951-60; exec. mfg. positions Chrysler Australia Ltd., Adelaide, 1960-67, Chrysler St. Louis Truck Plant, 1967-68; dir. mfg. Chrysler U.K., London, 1968-77; dir. internat. mfg. Chrysler Corp., Detroit, 1977-80; v.p. ops. Batesville (Ind.) Casket Co., 1980-84, pres., 1984-89; vice chmn., CEO LeRoy Industries, 1991-94; bd. dirs. Exide Corp., Leroy Industries, Die Moulding Co. Avocations: golf, swimming, boating, farming. Home: 831 Newhall Rd Unionville PA 19375

IRWIN, WILLIAM EDWARD, III, health physicist; b. Balt., Dec. 26, 1956; s. William Edward Jr. and Janice Lelea (English) I.; children: Kathryn, Irwin. BA, Coll. William and Mary, 1980; MBA, N.H. Coll., 1992; MS, U. Mass., 1994, candidate for DSc, 1995—. Diplomate Am. Acad. Health Physics; cert. health physicist Am. Acad. Health Physics. Health physics cons. various locations in Ariz., Ala., S.C., N.C., Va., 1984-85; lead instr. chemistry Ariz. Pub. Svc., Wintersberg, 1985-90; sr. instr. health physics N. Atlantic Energy Svcs., Seabrook, N.H., 1990-92; health physicst MIT, Cambridge, 1992—; occupl./environ. health cons. Praecis Pharm., Inc., Cambridge, 1994—, Cubist Pharms., Inc., Cambridge, 1994—, Arcturus Pharms., Woburn, Mass., 1994—, Duracell, Inc., Needham, Mass., 1994—, W.R. Grace, Co., 1994—, Sontra Med., Cambridge, 1996—, Bell Atlantic Mobile, 1995—, Visidyne, Inc., 1996—, Implant Scis., 1998—, AT&T Wireless Svcs., 1996—, Sprint PCS, 1997—, Omnipoint Comms., 1997—, Lasertron, Inc., 1997—, Suntory Phram. Rsch. Labs., 2000—. Recipient Vigil Honor, Order of the Arrow, Eagle Scout, Boy Scouts Am., Newport News, 1972; Am. Acad. Nuc. Tng. fellow Inst. Nuc. Power Ops., 1992. Mem. AAAS, Am. Nuclear Soc., Health Physics Soc., Am. Indsl. Hygiene Assn., Am. Conf. Govtl. Indsl. Hygienists. Avocations: mountain climbing, rock climbing, skiing. Office: 77 Massachusetts Ave Cambridge MA 02139-4301

ISAAC NASH, EVA MAE, educator; b. Natchitoches Parish, La., July 24, 1936; d. Earfus Will Nash and Dollie Mae (Edward) Johnson; m. Will Isaac Jr., July 1, 1961 (dec. May 1970). BA, San Francisco State U., 1974, MS in Edn., 1979, MS in Counseling, 1979; PhD, Walden U., 1985; diploma (hon.), St. Labre Indian Sch., 1990. Nurse's aide Protestant Episcopal Home, San Francisco, 1957-61; desk clk. Fort Ord (Calif.) Post Exchange, 1961-63; practical nurse Monterey (Calif.) Hosp., 1963-64; tchr. San Francisco Unified Schs., 1974; counselor, instr. City Coll. San Francisco, 1978-79; tchr. Oakland (Calif.) Unified Sch. Dist., 1974—; pres. sch. adv. coun., Oakland, 1977-78, faculty adv. coun., 1992-93; advt. writer City Coll., San Francisco, 1978; instr. vocat. skill tng., Garfield Sch., Oakland, 1980-81; pub. speaker various ednl. insts. and chs., Oakland, San Francisco, 1982—; lectr. San Jose State U., 1993; creator Language Arts-Step By Step program E. Morris Cox Elem. Sch., Oakland, 1995, 96; author, presenter material in field. Author video tape Hunger: An Assassin in the Classroom, 1993-94. Recipient Community Svc. award Black Caucus of Calif. Assn. Counseling and Devel., 1988, Cert. of Recognition, 1990; named Citizen of the Day, Sta. KABL, 1988. Mem. ASCD, Internat. Reading Assn., Nat. Assn. Female Execs., Am. Personnel and Guidance Assn., Calif. Personnel and Guidance Assn., Internat. Platform Assn. (Hall Fame 1989, Profl. Speaking cert. 1993), Phi Delta Kappa. Democrat. Avocations: travel, hiking, tennis, music, dancing. Office: Oakland Unified Sch Dist 1025 2nd Ave Oakland CA 94606-2296

ISAACS, HAROLD, history educator; b. Newark, Dec. 19, 1936; s. Albert Lewis and Bertha (Wohl) I.; m. Doris Carol Mack, Apr. 25, 1974. BS in History, U. Ala., University, 1958, MA in History, 1960, PhD in History, 1968. Grad. tchg. fellow in history U. Ala., University, 1959-62; instr. in history Memphis State U., 1962-65; asst. prof. history Ga. Southwestern State U., Americus, 1965-70, assoc. prof. history, 1970-79, prof. history, 1979—; bd. dirs. Ga. Consortium, Inc., World Communities Theater. Author: Jimmy Carter's Peanut Brigade, 1977; founder, editor Jour. of Third World Studies, 1984—. Advisor Young Dems., Ga. Southwestern State U., 1965-80; founder, coord. Third World in Perspective Program Seminar Series, 1981—; coord. Black Leaders Lecture Series, 1981. Recipient Tchr. of Yr. award Alpha Phi Alpha, 1982, Outstanding Svc. award Americus Early Bird Civitan Club, 1983, Outstanding Historian and Humanitarian award SABU, 1994, Presdl. Citation for Disting. Svc., 1995, Outstanding Svc. to African Am. and Third World Studies SABU 1996-97, 1997. Mem. Assn. Third World Studies, Inc. (founder, pres., exec. dir., 1983-91, treas. 1983-97, Presdl. award 1992), Latin Am. Studies Assn., World History Orgn., Am. Hist. Assn. Democrat. Jewish. Home: 180 Lakeshore Dr Americus GA 31709-8233 Office: Ga Southwestern State U Dept History and Polit Sci 800 Wheatley St Americus GA 31709-4376

ISAACS, RICHARD B., investigative and protective services professional; b. Evanston, Ill., Nov. 12, 1942; s. Harry Columbus and Natalie I.; m. Catherine Anne Nicodemo, Oct. 25, 1980 (div. 1994). BA, NYU, 1964; MA, Columbia U., 1975. Cert. CPP. V.p. Blackstone & West, Inc., Phila., 1967-69; indsl. photographer N.Y.C., 1970-76; programmer STSC, Inc., N.Y.C., 1976-81; pres. Blackstone & West, Inc., N.Y.C., 1981-89; prin., sr. v.p. The Lubrinco Group, Inc., N.Y.C., 1989-2000; dir. ASR Instrs. Coun., Arlington, Tex., 1983-2000. Author: (book) The Seven Steps to Personal Safety, 1993, rev. 1998; editor: The Bus. Security e-Jour., 1998-2000; others. Vol. Peace Corps, Colombia, 1964-66. Mem. Am. Soc. Law Enforcement Trainers (mem. security com. 1999-2000), Tactical Response Assn., Soc. Competitive Intelligence Profls., Internat. Assn. Counterterroism and Security Profls. Avocations: poetry, translating, flying, 50-meter free pistol, Aikido. Office: The Lubrinco Group Inc 215 Park Ave S Ste 711 New York NY 10003-1603

ISAAK, GEORGE RICHARD, physicist, researcher; b. Pilica, Poland, Mar. 7, 1933; s. Alexander Julian and Berta (Fischer) I.; m. Ümit Hasnedaroglu, Aug. 29, 1964; children: Katherine Gudrun, Erica Helen. BSc, U. Melbourne, 1955, MSc, 1958; PhD, U. Birmingham, Eng., 1965. Rsch. physicist Imperial Chem. Industries (Australia and New Zealand), Melbourne, 1958-60; rsch. assoc. U. Birmingham, 1961-64, lectr. in physics, 1964-69, sr. lectr., 1969-82; rsch. assoc. U. Minn., Mpls., 1974; Gauss prof. Georg August U., Göttingen, Germany, 1980-81; reader U. Birmingham, 1982-84, prof. physics, 1984—; adj. prof. physics U. Minn., 1996—. Contbr. articles to profl. jours.; patentee resonance spectrometers. Recipient Max Born medal Inst. Physics and German Phys. Soc., 1985, Hughes medal Royal Soc. (London), 1993. Fellow Inst. of Physics, Royal Astron. Soc. (Herschel medal 1995). Avocation: swimming. Office: U Birmingham, Edgbaston, Birmingham B15 2TT, England

ISAAZ, KARL, cardiologist; b. Argenteuil, France, Feb. 5, 1955; s. Raymond and Hélène (Masarovic) I.; m. Nicole Larose, June 2, 1979; children: Alexandre, Sandra, Marion. MD, U. Nancy, France, 1985. Intern I. Hosp., Nancy, France, 1979-82, U. Nancy, 1982-85; chef de clinique U. Nancy Divsn. Cardiology, 1985-89, cardiologist, 1989-94; prof. medicine, chief divsn. cardiology U. Saint-Etienne, France, 1994—. Reviewer Am. Jour. Cardiology, Jour. of Am. Coll. Cardiology. Fogarty Internat. Rsch. fellow NIH, Washington, 1988, Rsch. fellow Cardiovascular Rsch. Inst. U. Calif., San Francisco, 1988-89; recipient Rsch. award commemorating the 50th anniversary of French Soc. Cardiology, 1987. Fellow Am. Coll. Cardiology, European Soc. Cardiology; mem. AAAS, Am. Soc. Echocardiocragphy, European Soc. Biomechanics. Avocations: Spanish guitar, fly fishing. Home: 4 Place Jean Plotton, 42000 Saint-Etienne France Office: Svc de Cardiologie-Hosp Nord, Chu de Saint-Etienne, 42055 Saint Priest en Jarez France

ISAF, FRED THOMAS, lawyer; b. Jacksonville, N.C., Nov. 18, 1950; s. Thomas Fred and Rowanda (Maloof) I.; m. June J. Jeffcoat, Aug. 18, 1973; children: Julie, Thomas, Christa. BA, Duke U., 1972; JD, Emory U., 1975, LLM in Taxation, 1978. Bar: Ga. 1975. Ptnr. Peterson, Young, Self & Asselin, Atlanta, 1980-86; shareholder Roberts and Isaf, PC, Atlanta, 1986-94, Roberts, Isaf & Summers, PC, Atlanta, 1994-99; ptnr. McGuire Woods Battle & Boothe, Atlanta, 1999—. Contbr. article to profl. jour. Dir. Pinecrest Acad., 1995—. Mem. State Bar Ga., Cherokee Town and Country Club (dir. 1994-96, 99, sec. 1993, v.p. 1997, pres. 1998), Order of the Coif, Order of Barristers. Office: McGuire Woods Battle & Boothe Ste 2200 285 Peachtree Center Ave NE Atlanta GA 30303-1261

ISAKAEV, EMIN KHASAEVICH, physicist; b. Ahmedkent, Russia, Aug. 12, 1940; s. Isakay and Eva (Kadieva) Khasaev; m. Natalie Emilievna Levit, May 8, 1965 (div. May 1980); 1 child, Vladimir; m. Valentina Petrovna Golubeva; 1 child, Michael. Physicist, Dagestan U., Makhachkala, Russia, 1962; D-r, Moscow U., 1967. Tchr. secondary sch., Madjalis, 1962-63; postgrad. Moscow U., 1963-66; tchr. Dagestan U., Makhachkala, Russia, 1966-68; rschr. Associated Inst. High Temperatures/Russian Acad. Scis., Moscow, 1968—. Office: Inst for High Temperatures, Izhorskaya 13/19, 127412 Moscow Russia

ISAKOV, SERGEY LEONIDOVICH, physicist; b. Vereshchagino, Russia, Mar. 12, 1961; s. Leonid and Nina (Bashenyova) I.; m. Natalia Gavrichenkova, Sept. 14, 1991; two children. BSc, Phys. Tech. Inst. Moscow, 1985, PhD, 1989. Scientific worker Kurchatov Atomic Energy Inst., Moscow, 1983-92; svc. mgr. Sch. Svc., Moscow, 1993-95; cash flow rschr. Bank Optimum, Moscow, 1995-96; dep. chief Albus, Moscow, 1996—. Home: Stroitelny pr 4A-52, 143400 Krasnogorsk Russia

ISARD, PHILLIP ISAAC, medical nutritionist, consultant; b. L.A., May 18, 1949; s. Henry and Claris (Kaufman) I.; m. Pennel Donoher, May 20, 1977 (div. June 1990). BS in Biochemistry, Temple U., 1971; D Holistic Health, Am. Holistic Coll. Nutrition, Birmingham, Ala., 1992; DSc, Clayton Coll., Birmingham, 1994. Cert. med. nutritionist, N.Y. Rsch. asst. dept. exptl. surgery Hahnemann Hosp., Phila., 1967-72, rsch. assoc. dept. surg. rsch., 1968-72; chief small animal surgery Biokinetics Rsch. Lab., Temple U., Phila., 1969-74; rsch. assoc. dept. pharm. rsch. Med. Coll. Pa., Phila., 1974-81; medico-legal rschr. Med-Leg Rsch. Assocs., Huntingdon Valley, Pa., 1981-95; med. nutritionist Northumberland Valley Nutrition, Bethayres, Pa., 1992—; cons. Med. Nutritional Cons. NED, Huntington Valley, 1994—; tchr. various cmty. colls., Phila., 1990—; nutrition cons. free clinic Nutrition Ptnrs., Bethayres, Pa., 1991—. Contbr. articles to profl. jours. Vol. Pennypack Watershed Assn., Willow Grove, Pa., 1970—; tchr. emergency com. Pa. Amateur Radio Club, Huntingdon Valley, 1990—. Rsch. grantee NSF, NIH, Def. Advanced Rsch. Projects Agy., 1967-74. Unitarian-Universalist. Achievements include research on muscle hypertrophy more efficient than cytologic hyperplasia in augmenting muscle physiologic parameters concerned with work requiring maxmal O2 uptake and utilization; avocations: aviation, equitation, amateru radio, astronomy, electronics, computers, reading, volleyball. Home and Office: Med Nutricon NED 567 Hoyt Rd Huntingdon Valley PA 19006-8101

ISARESCU, ANDREEA, olympic athlete; b. Onesti, Romania, July 3, 1984. Mem. gymnastics team Romania, 1997—; winner jr. title European Championship, 1998, winner silver in all-around, 1998, winner silver in vault, 1998; winner gold team all-around Olympics, Sydney, Australia, 2000. Office: Romanian Gymnastics Ctr Romanian Studies, Ofcl Postal I Casuta Postala 108, 6600 Iasi Romania*

ISĂRESCU, MUGUR, banker; b. Drăgăsani, Valcea, Romania, Aug. 1, 1949; married; children: Costin, Lacramioara. Grad., Acad. Econ. Studies, 1971; PhD in Econs., 1989. Chmn. Romanian Nat. Bank Socialist Republic Romania; prime minister Romania, 1999—. Office: Nat Bank Romania, Str Lipscani 25B, 70421 Bucharest Romania*

ISAYEV, AVRAAM ISAYEVICH, polymer engineer, educator; b. Privolnoe, Azerbaijan, Russia, Oct. 17, 1942; s. Isai S. and Basia (Rabayeva) I.; m. Lubov M. Dadasheva, July 26, 1969; 1 child, Daniela. MSChemE, Azerbaijan Inst. Oil & Chem., Baku, 1964; PhD in Polymer Engring., USSR Acad. Scis., Moscow, 1970; MS in Applied Maths., Inst. Electronic Machine Bldg., Moscow, 1975. Rsch. assoc. State Rsch. Inst. Nitrogen Industries, Severodonetsk, Russia, 1965-66; predoctoral Inst. of Petrochem. Synthesis Russia Acad. Sci., Moscow, 1967-69, rsch. assoc., 1970-76; sr. rsch. fellow Israel Inst. Tech., Haifa, 1977-78; sr. rsch. assoc. Cornell U., Ithaca, N.Y., 1979-83; assoc. prof. Inst. Polymer Engring., U. Akron, Ohio, 1983-87, prof., dir. mold tech., 1987—; guest prof. U. Aachen, Germany, 1986, U. Linz, Austria, 1993, Kyoto Inst. Technology, Japan, 1996, Inst. Polymer Rsch., Dresden, Germany, 1997, U. Sao Carlos, Brazil, 1997; expert on plastics processing technologies, Malaysia, 1995. Editor: Injection Compression Molding Fund, 1987, Modelling of Polymer Processing, 1991, Liquid Crystalline Polymer Systems Technological Advances, 1996; mem. editorial bd. Advances in Polymer Tech., 1989-90, Jour. Elastomers and Plastics, 1992—, Progress in Polymer Processing Series, 1993—, Jour. Applied Polymer Sci., 1995—, Jour. Polymer Engring., 1997—; contbr. articles to Internat. Ency. of Composites, Ency. of Polymer Sci. and Engring., others. Expert witness U.S. Ho. of Reps., Washington, 1988; expert U.S. Army Rsch. Office, 1991; mem. rev. panel NSF, Washington, 1991, 94, 2000. NASA fellow, 1985; recipient Laureate of Young Scientists USSR Acad. Scis., 1970, Cert. of Appreciation, U. Akron Bd. Trustees, 1988, 93, Outstanding Rschr. award U. Akron Alumni Assn., 1996, Silver medal The Inst. Materials, London, 1997, Vinogradov prize G. V. Vinogradov Soc. Rheology, Moscow, 2000, Omnova Solutions Signature Univ. award, Akron, 2000; named Disting. Corp. Inventor, Am. Soc. Patent Holders, 1995. Mem. Am. Chem. Soc. (Melvin Mooney Disting. Tech. award rubber divsn. 1999), N.Y. Acad. Scis., Soc. Plastics Engrs. (Cert. of Recognition 1994), Polymer Processing Soc. (treas. 1989-91), Soc. Rheology. Jewish. Achievements include (20) patents for Self-Reinforced Composites, Devulcanization of Rubbers and Decrosslinking of Crosslinked Plastics; fundamental research in polymer and composite processing. Office: U Akron Inst Polymer Engring 260 S Forge St Akron OH 44325-0001

ISAZA, DIANA MARIA, medical technologist, researcher; b. Medellin, Antioquia, Colombia, May 2, 1964; d. Hector Isaza and Leonor Guzman; m. Fernando Peñaranda, Apr. 28, 1990. Med. Technologist, Colegio Mayor Antioquia, Medellin, Colombia, 1985; advanced tng., UN U., 1991; MS, U. Antioquia, Medellin, Colombia, 1995; advanced tng., The Brit. Coun., 1996. Rschr. Corp. para Investigaciones Biologicas, Medellin, Colombia, 1985-92; researcher Inst. Colombiano Medicina Tropical, Medellin, 1992—; instr. Inst. de Ciencias de la Salud, Medellin, 1997—. Contbr. articles to profl. jours. Avocation: cross stitch. Home: Calle 14 A No 43 D 56 (406), Medellin Antioquia Colombia Office: Inst Colombiano MedicinaTropical, Apartado Aereo 52162, Medellin Antioquia Colombia

ISBELL, HAROLD M(AX), writer, investor; b. Maquoketa, Iowa, Sept. 20, 1936; s. H. Max and Marcella E. Isbell; m. Mary Carolyn Cosgriff, June 15, 1963; children: Walter Harold, Susan Elizabeth, David Harold, Alice Kathleen. BA cum laude, Loras Coll., 1959; MA, U. Notre Dame, 1962; grad., U. Mich., 1982. Instr. U. Notre Dame, South Bend, Ind., 1963-64; asst. prof. San Francisco Coll. for Women, 1964-69; assoc. prof. St. Mary's Coll., 1969-72; with Continental Bank & Trust Co., Salt Lake City, 1972-83, v.p., 1977-83, comml. credit officer, 1978-83, also bd. dirs. Editor, translator: The Last Poets of Imperial Rome, 1971, Ovid: Heroides, 1990; contbr. to publs. in field of classical Latin lit. and contemporary Am. lit. Trustee Judge Meml. Cath. H.S., Salt Lake City, 1977-84; mem. Utah Coun. for Handicapped and Developmentally Disabled Persons, 1980-81; bd. dirs. Ballet West, 1983-90, emeritus, 1990—, Story Line Press, 1994-99, Smuin Ballets, San Francisco, 1994-99; founder Cath. Found. Utah, pres., 1984-86, trustee, 1984-89. Mem. AAAS, MLA, Medieval Acad. Am., Alta Club. Democrat. Roman Catholic.

ISBERG, ANNIKA MARIA, oral and maxillofacial radiologist, researcher, educator; b. Stockholm, Jan. 5, 1943; d. Gunnar Axel and Mildred Maria (Brodin) I.; m. Torsten Hans Holm, 1967 (div. 1981); children: Anders Holm, Maria Holm; m. Gunnar Adolf Fredrik Siegel, Oct. 3, 1992. DDS, Karolinska Inst., Stockholm, 1968, PhD, 1980. Cert. specialist of Oral and Maxillofacial Radiology; diplomate Swedish Med. Rsch. Coun. Asst. prof. Karolinska Inst., Stockholm, 1968-74, assoc. prof., 1974-92; prof. Umeå (Sweden) U., 1993—; pres. The C.O. Henrikson's Found., Sweden, 1991-95. Contbr. numerous articles to sci. publs. Grantee Swedish Med. Rsch. Coun., 1982—; recipient Calvin Case Rsch. award, 1995. Mem. Swedish Soc. Dentomaxillofacial Radiology (bd. dirs. 1982-95, pres. 1988-95). Avocations: archeology, classical music, literature, theater, hiking, traveling. Office: Umeå U, Dept Oral-Maxillofac Radiol, S-901 87 Umeå Sweden

ISBISTER, DENNIS JOHN, physicist, educator; b. Sydney, N.S.W., Australia, July 4, 1947; s. Herbert Gale and Gwendolyn (Keegan) I.; m. Gail Audrey Lawther, Aug. 4, 1973; children: Sam, Kate. PhD, U. N.S.W., 1977. Rsch. fellow RMC U. N.S.W., Canberra, 1974-89, lectr., 1989-93, sr. lectr., 1993-99, assoc. prof., 1999—; vis. prof. chemistry McGill U., Can., 1993, Colo. Sch. Mines, 1998, 99, 2000; vis. fellow Rsch. Sch. of Chemistry, 1999—.

ISBISTER, JENEFIR DIANE WILKINSON, microbiologist, researcher, educator, consultant; b. Rahway, N.J., June 4, 1936; d. Edwin Guy and Alvira Marie (Andrews) Wilkinson; m. James David Isbister, July 23, 1960; children: Wendy Jill Isbister Kalavritinos, Kirstin Ann Isbister Hammond. BS, Newberry (S.C.) Coll., 1957; MS in Med. Tech., Jefferson Med. Sch., Phila., 1958; PhD in Microbiology, U. Md., 1977. Med. technologist Princeton (N.J.) Hosp., 1958-60; instr. med. tech. sch. George Washington U., Washington, 1960-62, rsch. asst., 1976-77; rsch. microbiologist Environ. Biospherics, Inc., Rockville, 1978-80; group leader environ. microbiology dept. Atlantic Rsch. Corp., Alexandria, Va., 1980-89; pvt. practice cons. microbiologist Potomac, Md., 1989—; sr. tech. advisor ARCTECH, Inc., Chantilly, Va., 1989-92; adj. prof. George Mason U., 1988-92, rsch. prof., 1992—; cons. Orkand Corp., Silver Spring, Md., 1979-80, U.S. DOE, Pitts., 1988-89. Contbr. to book, articles to profl. jours. Sci. fair judge Montgomery and Fairfax County Schs., Md. and Va., 1975—; bd. dirs. Bedford (Pa.) Springs Music Festival, 1984-89. Va.-Carolina Chem. Corp. scholar, 1953; recipient Congl. High Tech. award Congl. Caucus for Sci. and Tech., 1985. Mem. ASTM (vice chair 1983-92, 99—), Am. Soc. for Microbiology, Am. Soc. for Clin. Pathologists, Cosmos Club, Phi Kappa Phi, Phi Sigma, Chi Beta Phi. Episcopalian. Avocations: reading, music, tennis, restoring old houses and furniture. Home: 9521 Accord Dr Rockville MD 20854-4302 Office: George Mason U SRIF Dept Fairfax VA 22303

ISBISTER, JOHN WILLIAM, economist, educator; b. Toronto, Can., Aug. 21, 1942; came to U.S., 1964; s. Claude Malcolm adn Frances Ruth I.; m. Elizabeth Ruth, June 20, 1965 (div. 1978); children: Victoria, David, Peter; m. Roswell Linda Spafford, June 26, 1987; 1 child, Will. BA, Queen's U., 1964; PhD, Princeton U., 1969. From asst. prof. to prof. econs. U. Calif., Santa Cruz, 1968-78, prof. econs., 1978—; provost Merrill Coll. U. Calif., Santa Cruz, 1984-99. Author: Promises Not Kept, 1991, 4th edit. 1998, Thin Cats, 1994, The Immigration Debate, 1996. Pres., bd. dirs. Santa Cruz Cmty. Credit Union, 1979-99. Democrat. Mem. Unitarian Ch. Avocations: skiing, swimming, bicycling. E-mail: isbister@cats.ucsc.edu. Office: Economics Dept Social Scis I Univ Calif Santa Cruz CA 95064

ISCOE, CRAIG STEVEN, lawyer; b. Austin, Tex., May 10, 1953; s. Ira and Louise N. (Kosches) I.; m. Rosemary Anne Hart, Apr. 16, 1983; children: David Hart, Mark Samuel. BA, U. Tex., 1974; JD, Stanford U., 1978; LLM, Georgetown U., 1979. Bar: D.C. 1978, U.S. Dist. Ct. D.C. 1978, U.S. Dist. Ct. Tenn., 1992, U.S. Supreme Ct. 1982, Tenn. 1992. Grad. fellow/staff atty. Inst. for Pub. Representation, Washington, 1978-79; asst. to dir. FTC, Washington, 1980-82; assoc. Arent, Fox, Washington, 1982-85; vis. prof. Georgetown U., Washington, 1986; asst. U.S. atty. U.S. Atty. for D.C., 1986-91, 92-97; asst. prof. Vanderbilt U., Nashville, 1991-92; assoc. dep. atty. gen., 1997—; adj. prof. Georgetown U. Law Sch., 1990, 92—; instr. Nat. Inst. Trial Advocacy, Washington, 1993-95, N.Mex., 1995. Contbr. articles to profl. jours., chpts. to books. Bd. dirs. Wash. Coun. Lawyers, 1989-91, 93-95, cons. Am. Bar Assn. Ctrl. & East European Law Initiative, (CEELI). Recipient Spl. Achievement award Dept. Justice, 1994, 95. Democrat. Jewish. Avocations: running, woodworking. Office: Office of Dep Atty Gen US Dept Justice 950 Pennsylvania Ave NW Washington DC 20530-0001

ISDALE, CHARLES EDWIN, chemical engineer; b. DeQuincy, La., Mar. 10, 1942; s. Vester Edwin and Katherine Gwendolyn (Wincey) I.; m. Lucille Brown, Aug. 26, 1962; children: Charles Edwin Jr., Jennifer Denise Hunt, Amberly Lauren. BSChemE, La. State U., 1965; MBA, So. Ill. U., 1978. Registered profl. engr., Ill., La. Chem. engr. Firestone Synthetic Rubber, Lake Charles, La., 1965-69, A.E. Staley Mfg. Co., Decatur, Ill., 1969-72; dir. engring. and maintenance VIOBIN Corp., Monticello, Ill., 1972-80; pres. Control Enterprises, Inc., Savoy, Ill., 1980-95; Control Enterprises, Inc., College Station, Tex., 1995-97; sr. lectr. dept. chem. engring. Tex. A&M U., College Station, 1998—; cons. Nabisco Brands, East Hanover, N.J., 1984—, Clorox, Jackson, Miss., 1987—, Alpharma, Chicago Heights, Ill., 1987—, Chinook Group, Sombra, Ont., Can., 1987—. Active Brazos Valley Cmty. Ch., Bryan, Tex. Mem. AIChE (sect. chmn. 1972-73), Instrument Soc. of Am. (Man of Yr. 1986). Achievements include design of a configurable multivariate control method, a method for removal of solvent to low ppm levels from enzymes, design of a batch wheat germ oil extraction plant, design of an animal gland extraction plant; patents on processing beef lung for production of heparin. Home: 715 Canterbury Dr College Station TX 77845-7903 Office: PO Box 10297 College Station TX 77842-0297

ISE, NORIO, chemistry educator; b. Kyoto, Japan, Oct. 19, 1928; s. Jiro and Kinu (Haruta) I.; m. Nobuko Otsuki, Nov. 25, 1963; children: Tadashi, Kiyoshi, Naoko. BS, Kyoto U., Japan, 1954, MS, 1956, PhD, 1959. Assoc. prof. Kyoto U., Japan, 1962-70, prof., 1970-92; guest prof. Johannes-Gutenberg U., Mainz, Germany, 1981; Turner Alfrey vis. prof. Mich. Molecular Inst., Midland, Mich., 1984; mem. macromolecular divsn. Internat. Union Pure and Applied Chemistry, Oxford, Eng., 1981-87, titular mem., 1989-93, 98—; coun. mem. Internat. Assn. Colloid & Interface Scientists, Wageningen, Holland, 1990-94. Co-author: Introduction to Polymer Chemistry, 1970, 2d edit. 1995; editor, author: An Introduction to Speciality Polymer, 1983; translator: Wasan, Japanese Mathematics, 1993. Recipient The Chem. Soc. of Japan award, 1986, Japan Acad. award, 1999. Avocation: music. Home: 23 Nakanosaka, Kamigamo Kita-ku, Kyoto 603, Japan

ISELY, HENRY PHILIP, association executive, integrative engineer, writer, educator; b. Montezuma, Kans., Oct. 16, 1915; s. James Walter and Jessie M. (Owen) I; m. Margaret Ann Sheesley, June 12, 1948; children: Zephyr, LaRock, Lark, Rodin, Kemper, Heather Capri. Student, South Oreg. Jr. Coll., Ashland, 1934-35, Antioch Coll., 1935-37. Organizer Action for World Fedn., 1946-50, N.Am. Coun. for People's World Conv., 1954-58; Organizer World Com. for World Constl. Conv., 1958, sec. gen., 1959-66; sec. gen. World Constn. and Parliment Assn., Lakewood, Colo., 1966—; organizer worldwide prep. confs. World Constn. and Parliment Assn., 1963, 66, 67, 1st session People's World Parliament and World Constl. Conv., Switzerland, 1968; editor assn. jour. Across Frontiers, 1959—; co-organizer Emergency Coun. World Trustees, 1971; co-organizer World Constituent Assembly, Innsbruck, Austria, 1977, Columbo, Sri Lanka, 1978-79, Troia, Portugal, 1991; organizer Provisional World Parliament 1st session, Brighton, Eng., 1982, 2nd Session, New Delhi, India, 1985, 3d Session, Miami Beach, Fla., 1987; mem. parliament, 1982—; sec. Working Commn. to Draft World Constn., 1971-77, pres. World Svc. Trust, 1972-78, ptnr. Builder Found., Vitamin Cottages, 1955—, (chmn. bd. dirs., 1985—), pres. Earth Rescue Corps., 1984-90, sec.-treas. Grad. Sch. World Problems, 1984— (prof. world problems, 1990—), cabinet mem. Provisional World Govt., 1987—, pres. World Govt. Funding Corp., 1986—, Emergency Earth Rescue Adminstrn., 1995—, co-organizer Global Ratification and Elections Network, 1991— (sec. 1992—), prin. organizer 4th session Provisional World Parliament, Barcelona, 1996, organizer first More Oxygen for the World conf., San Antonio, 1998; prof. world problems Grad. Sch. World Problems, now organizing 5th session of Provisional World Parliament Ougadougou Correction Ctr., Sirte, Libya, 2000. Author: The People Must Write the Peace, 1950, A Call to All Peoples and All National Governments of the Earth, 1961, Outline for the Debate and Drafting of a World Constitution, 1967, Strategy for Reclaiming Earth for Humanity, 1969, Call to a World Constituent Assembly, 1974, Proposal for Immediate Action by an Emergency Council of World Trustees, 1971, Call to A Provisional World Parliament, 1981, People Who Want Peace Must Take Charge of World Affairs, 1982, Plan for Emergency Earth Rescue Administration, 1985, Plan for Earth Finance Credit Corporation, 1987, Climate Crisis, 1989, Technological Breakthroughs for A Global Energy Network, 1991, Bill of Particulars: Why the U.N. Must Be Replaced, 1994, Manifesto for the Inauguration of World Government, 1994, Call to the Fourth Session of the Provisional World Parliament, 1995, Fifth Session, 1997, Critique of the Report of the Commission on Global Governance, 1995, Using Credit Cards and Electronic Accounting to Initiate New Global Finance System, 1996, Double

Jeopardy and the Phytoplankton Project, 1997, The Fallacy of Treating Labor as a Commodity, 1998, The Immediate Economic Benefits of World Government, 2000; co-author, editor: A Constitution for the Federation of Earth, 1974, rev. edit., 1991, also author several other world legis. measures adopted at Provisional World Parliament, 1968-96; co-author: Plan for Collaboration in World Constituent Assembly, 1991, Creator treatment for screen drama History Hangs by a Thread, 1993; designer: prefab modular panel sys. constrn., master plan Guacamaya project, Costa Rica. Candidate for U.S. Congress, 1958. Recipient hon. rsch. doctorate in edn., 1989, Honor award Internat Assn. Educators for World Peace, 1975, Ghandi medal, 1977, Honor award Internat Soc. Universalism, 1993. Mem. ACLU, Am. Acad. Polit. Sci., Fellowship of Reconciliation, World Union, World Federalist Assn., World Future Soc., Earth Island Inst., Populatin Reference Bur., Earth Action, People's Congress, Life Ext. Found., Interfaith Alliance, Internat. Assn. for Hydrogen Energy, Friends of Earth, Wilderness Soc., Solar Energy Soc., Sierra Club, Amnesty Internat., World Resources Inst., Human Rights Watch, Nat. Nutritional Foods Assn., Environ. Def. Fund, Greenpeace, Ctr. for Study of Democratic Instns., War Resistors League, Audubon Soc., Worldwatch Inst., Internat. Assn. Constl. Law, Earth Regeneration Soc., Zero Population Growth, Caner Control Soc., Mt. Vernon Country Club. Socialist. Fax: 303-237-7685. E-mail: wcpaliament@uswest.net. Home: Lookout Mountain 241 Zephyr Ave Golden CO 80401-9589 Office: 8800 W 14th Ave Lakewood CO 80215-4817

ISER, WOLFGANG, English and comparative literature educator, writer; b. Marienberg, Germany, July 22, 1926; s. Paul and Else (Steinbach) I.; m. Lore Reichert, May 24, 1952. Student, U. Leipzig, Germany, 1946, U. Tuebingen, Germany, 1946-47; PhD, U. Heidelberg, Germany, 1950. Instr. in English U. Heidelberg, Germany, 1951-52, asst. prof., 1955-57, assoc. prof. English, 1957-60; asst. lectr. in German U. Glasgow, Scotland, 1952-55; prof. English and comparative lit. U. Wuerzburg, Germany, 1960-63, U. Cologne, Germany, 1963-67, U. Constance, Germany, 1967-91, U. Calif., Irvine, 1978—. Writings include: (lit. criticism) Die Weltanschauung Henry Fieldings, 1952, Walter Pater: Die Autonomie des Aesthetischen, 1960, English transl., 1987, Die Appelstruktur der Texte, 1970, English transl., 1972, Spensers Arkadien: Fiktion und Geschichte, 1970, Der Implizite Leser, 1974, English transl., 1974, The Act of Reading: A Theory of Aesthetic Response, 1979, Sterne: Tristram Shandy, 1988, Prospecting: From Reader Response to Literary Anthropology, 1989, Staging Politics: The Lasting Impact of Shakespeare's Historical Plays, 1993, The Fictive and the Imaginary: Charting Literary Anthropology, 1993, The Range of Interpretation, 2000; editor: Dargestellte Geschichte in der europaeischen Literatur des 19 Jhdts., 1970, Theorien der Kunst, 1982, Languages of the Unsayable: The Play of Negativity in Literature and Literary Theory, 1989, Translatability of Cultures-Figurations of the Space Between, 1996. Office: U Calif Irvine Dept English Irvine CA 92697-0001

ISEUX, JEAN-CHRISTOPHE, international relations specialist; b. Lyon, Rhône, France, Nov. 11, 1967; s. Jean Victor Iseux and Colette Ponsot. BSc, Strasbourg (France) U., 1988, MSc, 1989; diploma in engring., Geophysics Inst., Strasbourg, 1990; MSc in Mgmt., U. Oxford, Eng., 1991. With Nat. Atomic Commn., Paris, 1991-92; attaché French Embassy, Bonn, Germany, 1992-94; analyst Credit Lyonais Capital Market, London, 1994-95; v.p. Oxford Analytica Ltd., 1995-97; rsch. prof. EOS-Japan Found., 1997—; dir. China studies Regulatory Policy Rsch. Ctr., Hertford Coll., U. Oxford, 1998—; spkr. UN Conf. on Disarmament, 1996, World Trade Orgn. Ministerial Conf., 1996; spl. adv. People's Rep. China, 1998—; vis. prof. People's U. China, 1998—; MBA prof. Qinghua U. China, 1999-2000; chmn. adv. bd. East-India Co., 1998—. Patentee nuc. sci. and petroleum engring. fields. Govt. observer UN Conf. on Disarmament, Geneva, 1996-2000; govt. del. World Trade Orgn., Geneva, 1996-97. Fellow Royal Geog. Soc.; mem. Inst. Internat. Strategic Studies, Lansdowne Club, Soc. Petroleum Engrs. Avocation: fox hunting (master of foxhound). E-mail: iseux@hotmail.com. Home: Venaille, 71120 Charolles France

ISHAQ, MOUSA HANNA, materials engineer; b. Aboud, Jordan, Dec. 30, 1951; came to U.S., 1977; s. Hanna Yacoub and Salma Azar Ishaq; m. Kristin M. Peterson, Jan. 14, 1978; 1 child, John P. BS in Engring., Am. U., Cairo, 1977. Jr. engr. IBM, Essex Junction, Vt., 1978, assoc. engr., 1978-82, sr. assoc. engr., scientist, 1982-85, staff engr., scientist, 1985-87, adv. engr., scientist devel., 1987-97, sr. engr., scientist devel., 1997—; tech. transfer rev. bd. IBM, 1998—. Inventor in field. Pres. Burlington-Bethlehem-Arad Sister City Project, Burlington, Vt., 1995—, task force, 1991; adv. bd. U.S./Arab Children's Artwork Exch., Burlington, 1991-94; mem. Vermonters for Peace in the Middle East, Vergennes, Vt., 1985—, Resettlement Coordinating Cambodian Refugees, Burlington, 1983-85. Democrat. Lutheran. Avocations: travel, gardening, reading, swimming, fishing. Home: PO Box 341 Essex Junction VT 05453-0341 Office: IBM 1000 River St Essex Junction VT 05452-4299

ISHAY, JACOB SCHECTMANN, biologist; b. Podul Iloaiei, Romania, Jan. 13, 1931; arrived in Israel, 1947; s. Israel and Debora (Schapira) Schechtmann; m. Ada Brizel, children: Isac, Michal. BSc, Tel-Aviv Univ., Tel-Aviv, Israel, 1959, postgrad. studies, 1959-60, MSc, 1960; PhD, The Hebrew Univ., 1967. Asst. Sackler Sch. Medicine, Tel-Aviv, 1966-67; instr. Tel-Aviv Univ., 1967-69, lectr., 1969-74, sr. lectr., 1974-81, assoc. prof., 1981-87, prof., 1987—; chairperson Assn. Sr. Staff, Tel-Aviv, 1987-91; 1st Israeli Space experiment with NASA, 1992. Contbr. more than 200 articles to profl. jours. on social insect behavior. Honorary Texan, 1996. Jewish. Achievements include research on hornet and wasp toxins and semiconductive properties of their silk and cuticle. Avocations: bee-keeping, literature. Home: Bd Emanuel 15, Tel Aviv Israel Office: Sackler Medical Sch, Levanon St, 69978 Tel Aviv Israel

ISHCHENKO, MICHAIL ALEXEEVICH, chemistry educator; b. Leningrad, Jan. 30, 1947; s. Alexei Yakovlevich and Ludmila Alexandrovna (Tsvetkova) I.; m. Raisa Ignatievna Ponomareva, Jan. 22, 1982; children: Ishchenko Ekatherina, Ishchenko Olga. Engr. Chemist, State Inst. Technology, Leningrad, 1971, Cand. Chem. Scis., 1975, D Chem Scis, 1989, Prof, 1997. Jr. scientist State Inst. of Tech., Leningrad, 1971-72, 75-77, lectr., 1977-83, sr. lectr., 1983-91, asst. prof., 1991-94; prof. State Inst. of Tech., St. Petersburg, Russia, 1994—, head of chem. dept., 1995—. Contbr. articles to profl. jours.; inventor in field. Avocations: vegetable and fruit growing, hunting, fishing, water tourism. Home: Marshal Zhukov prospect 47, Apt 9, 198330 Saint Petersburg Russia Office: State Inst Technology, Moskovsky prospect 26, 198013 Saint Petersburg Russia

ISHIBASHI, AKIRA, physicist, laboratory administrator, educator; b. Saga-city, Saga, Japan, July 17, 1958; s. Fusao Fukutomi and Masako Ishibashi; m. Chieko Soejima, Sept. 1, 1993; 1 child, Yutaro. BSc, U. Tokyo, 1981, MSc, 1983, PhD, 1990. Cert. in physics, optoelec. device engring. Rsch. asst. Lawrence Berkeley Nat. Lab., Berkeley, Calif., 1982-83; physicist Sony Corp. Rsch. Ctr., Yokohama, Japan, 1982-90; vis. faculty dept. physics U. Ill., Urbana-Champaign, 1990-91; project leader BLD project Sony Corp., Yokohama, 1992-97, mgr., physicist Frontier Sci. Lab., 1998—; vis. prof. Tohoku U., Sendai, Japan, 1998—; group leader H-10 Kakenhi-Basic Rsch., Yamaguchi, Japan, 1998—. Co-author: (book) Blue-Emitting Optical Devices, 1997; co-editor: (book) Physics and Simulation of Optoelectric Devices VI, 1998; patentee in field. Vice-chmn. Terasuhausu Town Com., Sasanocdai, 1996. Mem. IEEE (sr.), SPIE, Phys. Soc. Japan, Japan Soc. Applied Physics. Avocations: cycling, guitar. Office: Sony Corp Rsch Ctr, 134 Goudo Hodogaya, 240-0005 Yokohama Japan

ISHIBASHI, EIICHI, engineering researcher and educator; b. Fukuoka, Japan, Mar. 7, 1929; s. Hajime and Miyako (Inoue) I.; m. Shizuko Ushijima, Mar. 1957; 1 child, Masahiro. B of Engring., Kyushu U., Fukuoka, 1952, DEng, 1968. Engr. Hitachi (Japan) Co., 1952-62; sr. rschr. Hitachi Rsch. Lab., 1962-69; rsch. mgr. Power Reactor and Nuclear Fuel Devel. Corp., Oarai, Japan, 1969-76; prof. Oita (Japan) U., 1976-92, designated prof., 1991-92; prof. Nippon Bunri U., Oita, 1992-2000; adviser Kyushu Elec. Co., Fukuoka, 1979-80; dir. Solar Energy Rsch. Lab., Oita U., 1981-83, mem. coun., 1987-89; chmn. Rsch. Commn. on The Energy Problem, Ecol. Fedn., Kyushu-Yamaguchi, 1994-99. Contbr. articles to profl. jours. Recipient Tech. Devel. award Atomic Energy Soc. Japan, 1977. Mem. Japan Soc. Mech. Engrs. (prize 1969). Avocations: fishing, classical music. Home: 1-1-35 Miyazaki-dai, Oita 870-1137, Japan

ISHIBASHI, HIROMI, medical educator, researcher; b. Nagasaki, Japan, Oct. 4, 1946. MD, Kyushu U., Fukuoka, Japan, 1971, PhD, 1980. Med. diplomate internal medicine. Resident Kyushu U. Hosp., Fukuoka, Japan, 1971-73, sr. resident, 1974-76; biochemistry rsch. fellow U. Tex. Health Sci. Ctr., Dallas, 1976-78; rsch. assoc. internal medicine Kyushu U. Faculty of Medicine, Fukuoka, Japan, 1979-91, asst. prof. internal medicine, 1991-95, assoc. prof. internal medicine, 1995—; gen. sec. 95th gen. meeting Japanese Soc. Internal Medicine, Fukuoka, Japan, 1998. Contbr. articles to profl. jours. Grantee Ministry of Health and Welfare of Japan, 1995, 96, 97, 98, 99, 2000. Fellow ACP, Am. Coll. Gastroentrology, Japanese Soc. Internal Medicine, Japanese Soc. Gastroentrology, Japan Soc. Hepatology, Japanese Soc. Ultrasonics in Medicine; mem. Internat. Assn. for Study of the Liver, Asian-Pacific Assn. for Study of the Liver. Avocations: computers, books, classical music, cinema. Home: 1-21-5 Momochi Sawara-ku, Fukuoka 814-0006, Japan Office: Kyushu Univ Fac Med 1st Dept Int Med, 3-1-1 Maidashi Higashi-ku, Fukuoka 812-8582, Japan

ISHIDA, HAJIME, pharmacologist, educator, researcher; b. Osaka, Japan, May 29, 1936; s. Koshi and Setsuko (Itoi) I.; m. Reiko Yata, April 11, 1969; children: Masami, Tomomi. D in Dentistry, Osaka U., 1964, PhD, 1968. Rsch. asst. Dept. Pharmacology Osaka U. Dental Sch., 1968-77, lectr., 1977; prof. Dept. Pharmacology Tokushima U. Dental Sch., 1977—. Author: Medical Dictionary, 1987; author, editor: Dental Pharmacology, 1997; contbr. articles to profl. jours. Trustee Iwadare Ednl. Assn. Dental Grad. Students, Osaka, 1977, dir. 1990. Mem. AAAS, N.Y. Acad. Sci., Japanese Pharmacol. Soc. (councillor 1972—), Japanese Assn. Oral Biology (councillor 1977—), Japanese Assn. Oral Biology (supt. 1999—), Japanese Salivary Gland Soc. (councillor 1979—). Home: 1-16-56 Higashikori 1 chome, Hirakata 573-0075, Japan Office: Dept Pharm Tokushima U, 3-18-15 Kuramoto-cho, Tokushima 770-8504, Japan

ISHIDA, MASAHARU, political history educator; b. Fukuoka, Japan, Oct. 6, 1947; s. Norio and Chiyoko Ishida. B of Engring., Kyushu U., Fukuoka, 1971, LLB, 1973, LLM, 1979, PhD, 1992. Staff mem. Asahi Shimbun, Tokyo, 1973-77; assoc. prof. Kyushu U., Fukuoka, 1984-91, prof., 1991—. Author: (book) Formation of Cold-War-State, 1993; co-author: (books) Origins of Vietnam War, 1984, 1968: Prelude to Change, 1995; contbr. articles to profl. jours. Mem. Japan Assn. Internat. Rels., Japanese Polit. Sci. Assn. Home: 2-33-15 Wakamiya Higashi-ku, Fukuoka City 813-0036, Japan Office: Kyushu U Grad Sch of Law, 6-19-1 Hakazaki Higashi-ku, Fukuoka 812-8581, Japan

ISHIDA, MASARU, chemical engineer, educator; b. Yokohama, Kanagawa, Japan, Mar. 11, 1942; s. Takio and Shizue (Nagano) I.; m. Toshie Horiguchi, May 27, 1969; children: Hiroshi, Kazumi. B in Engring., Tokyo Inst. Tech., 1964, M in Engring., 1966, D of Engring., 1969. Rsch. assoc., assoc. prof. Tokyo Inst. Tech., 1969-84, prof., 1984—, dir. chem. resources lab., 2000—. Author: Thermodynamics - Its Perfect Comprehension and Applications, 1995; patentee in field. Mem. ASME (Edward F. Obert award 1999), AIChE, Japan Inst. Energy (Excellent Rsch. award 1996), Chem. Engr. Soc. Japan (Excellent Paper award 1974, Excellent Rsch. award 1996). Home: 2600-125 Kozukue Kouhoku-ku, Kanagawa Yokohama 222-0036, Japan Office: Tokyo Inst Tech Chem Res Lab, 4259 Nagatsuta Midori-ku, Kanagawa Yokohama 226-8503, Japan

ISHIGOHKA, TAKESHI, engineering educator; b. Tokyo, Mar. 10, 1944; s. Tadashi and Nobuko (Yoshizawa) I.; m. Terue Hamanaka, Nov. 28, 1971; children: Satoru, Megumi. B of Engring., Seikei U., Tokyo, 1966, M of Engring., 1968, D of Engring., 1974. Asst. Seikei U., 1971-77, lectr., 1977-78, assoc. prof., 1978-89, prof., 1989—. Recipient Matsunaga Meml. prize Elec. Power Rsch. Inst. Japan, 1978. Mem. Japanese Inst. Elec. Engring., Japanese Cryogenic Engr.'s Assn. Buddhist. Avocations: tennis, playing flute, writing poetry, painting, reading. Home: 2-4-13 Akatsuki-cho, Tokyo Hachioji-shi 192-0043, Japan Office: Seikei Univ, 3-3-1 Kichijoji-Kita, Tokyo Musashino 180-8633, Japan

ISHIGURO, RYOJI, mechanical engineer; b. Sapporo, Hokkaido, Japan, May 28, 1930; s. Naoyuki and Setsuko (Kimura) I.; m. Kuniko Kimura, Jan. 10, 1960; 1 child, Suguru. B in Engring., Hokkaido U., 1953, M in Engring., 1955, DEng, 1968. Lectr. mech. engring. Hokkaido U., Sapporo, 1957-58, assoc. prof., 1958-70, prof. nuclear engring., 1970-94; rsch. fellow U. Del., Newark, 1962-63, Japan Atomic Energy Rsch. Inst., Tokai, 1969-70; cons. Hokkaido Electric Power Co., Inc., Sapporo, 1994—. Editor-in-chief: Jour. of the Atomic Energy Soc. of Japan, and Nuclear Sci. and Technology, 1977-78; contbg. author: Introduction to Nuclear Engineering, 1977, Material of Heat Transfer, 4th edit., 1986; author: Heat Transport Theory, 1993. Trustee Hokkaido U., 1989-91. Hill Found. fellow U. Minn., Mpls., 1961-62. Mem. Atomic Energy Soc. of Japan (bd. dirs. 1976-78), Japan Soc. Mech. Engrs. (councilor 1989-90, prize for acad. excellence 1988, prize for thermal engring. 1995), The Heat Transfer Soc. of Japan (pres. 1990-91). Avocations: skiing, fishing. Home: 4-1 Yamate 7, Kitahiroshima Hokkaido 061-1148, Japan Office: Hokkaido Electric Power Co-The Wonder Lab, 1-chome Naebo-cho Higashiku, Sapporo 065-0043, Japan

ISHIHARA, KANICHIRO, publishing company executive; b. Miyakonojo, Miyazaki, Japan; s. Yasusaburo and Kesayo (Yamashita) I.; m. Sumiko Ishihara, Apr. 1, 1948 (died 1999); children: Mitsuko, Reiko. Engr. Kawasaki Aircraft Co., Japan, 1938-40; pres. Ishihara Kogyo Co., Japan, 1959—, Myoken Ishihara Hotel, Japan, 1988—, Ishihara Pub. Co., Japan, 1990—; chmn. Miyakonajo J/H Assn., Japan, 1990—. Author: (books) Decade Diary Book, 1969, Learning from T. Saigo, 1989; inventor in field. Recipient citation Police Office, 1955, citation Min. Welfare Dept., 1994. Mem. Hotel Assn. (dir. 1951—), Buddhist Assn. (br. rep. 1967—), Lion's Club (chmn. 1967—). Avocations: scientific laboratory research, traveling.

ISHIHARA, KOUSAI, English language educator; b. Mitama, Yamanashi, Japan, Apr. 20, 1943; s. Koudou and Yuri (Nagai) I.; m. Etsuko Shirai, Mar. 13, 1969; 1 child, Chitose. Lectr. Iwamizawa (Japan) Komazawa Jr. Coll., 1968-71; lectr. Komazawa U., Tokyo, 1971-75, assoc. prof., 1975-82, prof., 1982—; dir. Shakespeare Inst., Tokyo, 1987. Author: Rural England, 1987, Northrop Frye on Shakespeare, 1991, Shakespeare and the Super Natural, 1991, Historical Stories of London, 1994, A Literary Journey Through England, Part I, 1995, A Literary Journey Through England, Part II, 1996, Stories of London Pub, 1997, London: A Mysterious City, 1999. Mem. Hitsuji-kai, Tokyo, 1993—. Zen Buddhist. Home: 2-17-14 Edakita Aoba-ku, Yokohama Kanagawa 225-0015, Japan Office: 1-23-1 Komazawa Setagaya-ku, Tokyo 154, Japan

ISHIHARA, KUNI, crop scientist; b. Zushi, Kanagawa, Japan, May 27, 1933; s. Uichi and Miyoko (Inoue) I.; m. Kayoko Hashimoto; children: Takeshi, Itaru. B Agr., U. Tokyo, 1957, M Agr., 1959, D Agr., 1962. Assoc. rschr. U. Tokyo, 1962-66; assoc. prof. Tokyo U. Agr. and Tech., 1966-80, prof., 1980-97, dean United Grad. Sch., 1992-96, mem. coun., 1988-96; prof. Utsunomiya U., 1997-99, Tokyo U. Agr., 1999—. Author, editor: Science of Rice Plant: Physiology, 1995; contbr. articles to profl. jours. Recipient Crop Sci. award Japanese Soc. Crop Sci., 1981, Agronomy award Japanese Soc. Agronomy, 1994, Yomiuri Agronomy award Yomiuro Newspaper Co., 1994. Avocation: tennis. E-mail: ishihara@nodai.ac.jp. Home: Daita 4-16-6 Setagya-ku, Tokyo 155 033, Japan Office: Tokyo U Agr Internat Devel, 1-1-1 Sakuragoaka, Satagaya, Tokyo 156 8502, Japan

ISHII, AKIHIKO, chemist, educator; b. Shinjuku, Tokyo, Japan, May 20, 1959; s. Shoichi and Minayo (Omiya) I.; m. Naoko Kumon, Mar. 12, 1989; children: Tomoaki, Minoru. BSc, Saitama (Japan) U., 1982; PhD, U. Tokyo, 1987. Asst. prof. Saitama U., 1987-94, assoc. prof., 1994—; vis. prof. U. Caen, France, 1997. Mem. Chem. Soc. Japan, Soc. Synthetic Organic Chemistry Japan (progress award chemistry of dithiiranes 1996), Internat. Coun. Main Group Chemistry Inc. Office: Saitama U Faculty Sci, Shimo-okubo 255, Urawa 338-8570, Japan

ISHII, MASAMI, hospital director, neurosurgeon; b. Iwaki, Fukushima, Japan, Jan. 8, 1951; s. Tadashi and Michiko (Hisa) I.; m. Atsuko Yanagi, Mar. 12, 1978; children: Akira, Masashi. MD, Hirosaki U., 1979, Nat. Inst. Neurosurgery, Budapest, Hungary, 1979, Saitama (Japan) Med. Coll., 1981. Diplomate Japan Neurosurg. Soc. Asst. dept. neurosurgery Hirosaki U., 1980-82; head doctor dept. neurosurgery Iwaki (Japan) Kyoritu Hosp., 1982-85; dir. Ishii Hosp. Neurosurgery and Ophthalmology, Iwaki, 1985—; v.p. Iwaki-city Med. Assn. Contbr. articles to profl. jours.; inventor in field. Mem. AAAS, Japan Neurosurg. Soc. (bd. dirs.), Japanese Assn. Rehab. Medicine, Iwaki-City Med. Assn. (exec.). Avocations: piano, painting, photography, audio. Office: Ishii Hosp Neurosurgery and Ophthalmology, 3-1 Tsukamae Rinjo Onahama, Iwaki 971-8122, Japan

ISHII, SAKAE, physicist, researcher; b. Osaka, Japan, Sept. 21, 1940; s. Hikoichi Taki and Kunie Ishii. BEE, Osaka U., 1964, MEE, 1966, PhD, 1971. Rschr. Osaka U., 1966—. Contbr. articles to profl. jours. Mem. AAAS, N.Y. Acad. Scis., Nat. Geog. Soc., Nature Conservation Soc. of Osaka, Planetary Soc. Home: 4-9-9 Kofudai, Toyono Toyono Osaka 563-0104, Japan Office: Osaka U Grad Sch Engring, Dept Electronics Yamada-Oka, Suita 5650871, Japan

ISHII, TORU, physician; b. Ueda, Nagano, Japan, Oct. 2, 1918; s. Kosaku and Nobu Ishii; M.D., Niigata U., 1943; m. Nagako Mitani, Oct. 23, 1948; children—Chiaki, Junji. Tutor biochemistry Niigata U., 1946—; dir. clin. labs. First Nat. Hosp., Tokyo, 1962—; mem. faculty Showa U. Med. Sch., 1964—, prof. clin. biochemistry and clin. pathology, 1971—, also univ. trustee; prof. emeritus, dir. Sch. of Showa Med. Tech. and Dental Hygiene, from 1984; cons. Tokyo hosps. Served as officer M.C., Japanese Navy, 1945. Mem. Japanese Soc. Clin. Pathology (insp.), Japanese Soc. Diabetes (councilor). Editor med. jours. Home: 1-16-16-311 Toyama, Shinjuku-ku, Tokyo 162-0052, Japan Office: 1-5-8 Hatanodai Shinagawa-ku, Tokyo 142, Japan

ISHII, YOSHINORI, environmental science educator; b. Tokyo, Mar. 14, 1933; s. Kichijiro and Kei Ishii; m. Hiroko Hisamune, Nov. 24, 1963; children: Yutaka, Makoto, Akira. BS, U. Tokyo, 1955, ED, 1977. Exploration geophysicist Teikoku Oil Co., Tokyo, 1955; rsch. geophysicist Japan Petroleum Exploration Co., Tokyo, 1955-67, sr. geophysicist, 1970-71; sr. geophysicist Japan Nat. Oil Corp., Tokyo, 1967-70; assoc. prof. geophysics U. Tokyo, 1971-78, prof. geophysics, 1978-93, prof. emeritus, 1993—; dep. dir. gen. Nat. Inst. Environ. Studies, Ibaraki, Japan, 1994-96, dir. gen., 1996-98; pres. Inst. Environ. Tech. Promotion in Asia, 1998—; prof. Toyama U. Internat. Studies, 2000—; mem. Sci. Coun. of Japan, Tokyo, 1988-91. Author: Introduction to Remote Sensing, 1981, Geophysical Engineering, 1988, Energy and Global Environmental Problems, 1995; co-author several books; contbr. numerous articles to profl. jours. Mem. Engring. Acad. Japan, Soc. Exploration Geophysicists of Japan (pres. 1984-85, 1988-89, Best Paper award, Tokyo, 1976), Remote Sensing Soc. Japan, (v.p. 1981-88, pres. 1990-92), Japanese Assn. for Petroleum Tech. (v.p. 1982-86), Soc. Environ. Sci. Japan, Japan Soc. of Water Environment. Avocations: golf, computer. Home: 8-2-14 Hisagi, Zushi, Kanagawa 249-0001, Japan Office: 1-5-17 Kagawa Bldg 4F, Chuo City Yaesu, Tokyo 103-0028, Japan

ISHIKAWA, AKIRA, global management educator; b. Odawara, Kanagawa, Japan, Apr. 20, 1934; s. Ryoji and Hisako Ishikawa; m. Minako Shirai, June 22, 1958; 1 child, Makoto. MA in Bus. Adminstrn., U. Wash., 1970; PhD, U. Tex., 1972; postgrad., MIT, 1973; Cultural Doctorate (hon.), Univ. of the World, La Jolla, Calif., 1985; PhD (hon.), Internat. Inst. Advanced Study, 1999. Cert. pub. statistician, Japan. Cons. SAFECO Corp., Seattle, 1969-70; instr., rsch. assoc. U. Tex., Austin, 1970-72; asst. prof. NYU, N.Y.C., 1972-76; assoc. prof. Rutgers U., Newark, 1976-83, prof., 1984-87; prof., dir. Internat. Exch. Ctr. Aoyama Gakuin U., Tokyo, 1988-90, chair internat. bus. Grad. Sch. Internat. Politics, Econs. and Bus., 1997—; sr. rsch. fellow U. Tex., Austin, 1989—; cons. Taisho Pharm. Co., Tokyo, 1991-92. Chair. Doc. program Grad. Sch. of Internat. Politics Economics and Bus., Internat. Bus. Area, Ayoyama Gakuin U., 1997—. Author: Corporate Planning and Control Model Systems, 1975, Strategic Budgeting, 1985, Future Computer and Information Systems, 1986, Strategic Budget Control, 1993; author, editor: Global Information Network, 1992, Ambiguity and Fuzziness, 1993, Fuzzy Research Strategy, 1991, Information Strategy for Global Firms, 1994, The Global Information Network: English Edition, 1995, Analysis and Evaluation of Fuzzy Systems, 1995, Modern International Accounting, 1996, Revolution of Electronic Meeting Systems, 1997, Why Is Seven-Eleven Japan So Mighty?, 1998, World No. 1 Companies in Japan, 1999, Kyoto Model, 1999, Cybernetic Renaissance, 1999, Ecological Accounting and Information Systems, 2000; editor-in-chief Assn. Info. Edn. in Colls. and Univs. in Japan, 1993-2000. Mem. U.S. Security Coun. Found., Washington, 1993; mem. com. East Asian Econ. Cooperation, Tokyo, 1993; mem. com. Advanced Inst. German-Japanese Studies, Ulm, Germany, also Tokyo, 1993. Recipient Outstanding Scholarly Contbn. award Sys. Rsch. Found., 1995, Book of Yr. award Internat. Inst. for Advanced Studies in Sys. Rsch. and Cybernetics, 1994; Telecomm. Adv. Found. grantee, Tokyo, 1991, 92, 93, Lab. for Internat. Fuzzy Engring. Rsch. grantee, Yokohama, 1990. Mem. Japan Soc. for Fuzzy Theory (trustee, mem. adv. bd. 1991—), Japan Info.-Culture Soc. (bd. dirs. 1997—), Soc. Mgmt. Analysis (bd. dirs.), Assn. Info. Edn. in Colls. and Univs. (chair promotion com. 1992-2000), Human Systems Mgmt. (editorial bd. 1991—), Group Decision and Negotiation (assoc. editor 1992—), Japan Soc. Mgmt. Acctg. (bd. dirs. 1992-98), Sigma Iota Epsilon, Beta Alpha Psi. Avocations: swimming, golf, jogging, table tennis, Igo. Home: 5-11-22-401 Minami-aoyama, Minato-ku Tokyo 107, Japan Office: Aoyma Gakuin U, 4-4-25 Shibuya-Shibuya-ku, Tokyo 150, Japan

ISHIKAWA, HIROSHI, medical educator; b. Tokyo, Nov. 11, 1941; s. Hachitaro and Hisa Ishikawa; m. Yoshiko Takahashi, Mar. 23, 1968; children: Mayumi, Takaki. MD, Jikei Univ., 1968, Physician's diploma, D Med. Sci., 1972. Lectr. diplomate Showa Univ. Sch. Medicine, Tokyo, 1972-74; assoc. prof. Tohhoku Univ. Sch. Medicine, Sendai, Japan, 1974-80; postdoctoral fellowship UTHSCSA, San Antonio, 1976-78; assoc. prof. Jikei Univ. Sch. Medicine, 1980-85, prof., chmn., 1985—; mem. edn. com. Jikei U. Sch. Medicine, 1981-91, med. examiner, 1973—. Author: Modern Appliat. Cultured Cells, 1985, Modern pathology, 1994, Histology, 1989, Anatomy, 1990. Recipient award Japanese Endocrinol. Soc., 1984, Japanese Soc. Mammalian Ova Rsch., 1999. Mem. N.Y. Acad. Sci. Home: 3-5 1 Banchou Chiyoda-ku, Tokyo 102, Japan Office: The Jikei U Sch Medicine, 3-25-8 Nishi Shinbashi, Tokyo 105-8461, Japan

ISHIKAWA, IKUO, metallurgist, researcher; b. Oe, Yamagata, Japan, June 16, 1949; s. Hiromatu and Mitue (Maki) I.; m. Yoshiko Hirabayashi, Oct. 18, 1974; children : Chisako, Atushi. BS, Tokyo U., 1972, M of Engring., 1974. Rschr. Tohoku Nat. Indsl. Rsch. Inst., Sendai, Japan, 1974-88, sr. rschr., 1988—. Contbr. articles to sci. jours. Avocations: calligraphy, social dancing. Home: 1-1-45-817 Itsutsubashi, Aoba-ku 17 Itsutsubashi, Sendai Miyagi 980-0022, Japan Office: Tohoku Nat Indsl Rsch Inst, 4-2-1 Nigatake, 983-8551 Sendai Miyagi, Japan

ISHIKAWA, ISAO, periodontologist, educator; b. Osaka, Japan, Dec. 6, 1940; s. Yoshioki and Kikue (Komatsu) I.; m. Dominique Agnes Dotte, Sept. 24, 1970; children: Nicole-Ayako, Satoshi-Olivier, Sabine-Kazuko. DDS, Tokyo Med. and Dental U., 1965, PhD, 1971. Rsch. fellow U. Geneva, 1968-70, charge de recherche, 1974-76; lectr. Tokyo Med. and Dental U., 1973-79, assoc. prof. periodontology, 1980-84, prof., 1984—. Chief editor: Periodontology, 1996; mem. editorial bd. Jour. Periodontology, 1990—. Mem. Asian Pacific Soc. Periodontology (sec. gen. 1993—), Internat. Soc. Laser in Dentistry (treas. 1990—). Home: Tsudanuma 1-13-24, 275 Narashino Japan Office: Tokyo Med and Dental U, Yushima 1-5-45, 113 Bunkyo-ku Tokyo Japan

ISHIKAWA, KOSUKE, management consultant; b. Hokkaido, Japan, Oct. 10, 1959; s. Haruki and Keiko (Inoue) I. BA in Mgmt., Gakushuin U., 1984; MBA, Wake Forest U., 1996. With Isuzu Motors, Tokyo, 1984-87, ABB, Tokyo, 1988-93; asst. mgr. Coors Japan, Tokyo, 1996-97; cons. JMA Mgmt. Ctr., Tokyo, 1997—; sec. of com. Asea Brown Boveri, Tokyo, 1991-92, comm. mem., 1991-92. Mem. Am. C. of C. (HRM com.), Can. C. of C. in Japan, Tokyo Can. Club. Home: 4-42-17-204 Yoyogi, Shibuya-ku, Tokyo 151-0053, Japan Office: JMA Mgmt Ctr Inc, 301038 Shiba Koen, Minata-ku 105-8520, Japan

ISHIKAWA, MOTOO, electrical engineer, educator; b. Kyoto, Japan, Jan. 12, 1949; s. Ryodo and Hiroko (Tsubouchi) I.; m. Machiko Ishikawa, Nov. 23, 1976; 1 child, Hiroki. PhD, Kyoto U., 1978. Instr. Kyoto U., 1976-82, assoc. prof., 1983-97; prof. U. Tsukuba, 1998—; vis. scholar U. Tenn. Space

Inst., Tullahoma, 1980-81. Contbr. articles to Jour. Energy, Jour. Propulsion and Power, Jour. Nuclear Sic. and Tech., Energy Conversion and Mgmt., Fusion Engring. and Design. Achievements include devel. of numerical analyses of magnetohydrodynamics electrical power generation and direct energy conversion in fusion reactors. Home: Gokasho Sanbanwari 18-1, Uji Kyoto 611-0011, Japan Office: Mechanics and Systems, U Tsukuba Inst Engring, Tsukuba 305-8753, Japan

ISHIKAWA, NOBUTAKA, civil engineer, educator; b. Harbin, China, Nov. 9, 1937; arrived in Japan, 1946; s. Keiichi and Sadako Ishikawa; m. Keiko Kubota; children: Norito, Takako, Katsuaki. B in Engring., Nat. Def. Acad., 1960; M in Engring., Kyushu U., 1965, D of Engring., 1969. Asst. prof., assoc. prof. Dept. Civil Engring. Nat. Def. Acad., Yokosuka, Japan, 1969-79; prof. Nat. Def. Acad., Yokosuka, 1979—; mem. Internat. Sci. Adv. Com., Structure under Shock and Impact, 1994, Shock and Impact Load of Structure, 1996, Earthquake Resistant Engring. Structures, 1996. Author: Introduction of Plastic Analysis, 1988; editor: Impact Behavior and Design of Structure, 1993; editl. adv. bd. mem. Internat. Jour. Engring Optimization, 1990-94. Exec. Assn. Mil. Christian Fellowship Japan, Tokyo, 1987—. Mem. ASCE, Can. Soc. Civil Engrs., Japanese Soc. Civil Engrs. (subcom. chmn. Impact Problems Structural Engring 1989-94). Avocation: tennis. Office: Nat Def Acad Dept Civ Engr, 1-10-20 Hashirimizu, Yokosuka 239, Japan

ISHIKAWA, TAKEO, educator; b. Sakado, Japan, Jan. 1, 1956; m. Etsuko Ishikawa, Mar. 24, 1961; children: Takuya, Tomoya. B of Engring., Saitama U., Urawa, Japan, 1978; M of Engring., Tokyo Inst. Tech., 1980, D of Engring., 1983. Rsch. assoc. Gunma U., Kiryu, Japan, 1983-91, assoc. prof., 1991—; part-time lectr. Joubu U., Gunma, Japan, 1994—. Translator: IEEE Standard Dictionary of Electrical and Electronics Terms, 1989; contbr. articles to profl. jours. Mem. IEEE (reviewer 1996—, treas. VTS Japan chpt. 2000—), IEE Japan (reviewer 1997—, mem. tech. com. 1995—, sec. Gunma sect. 1996-2000, chair Gunma sect. 2000—), Japan Soc. Simulation Tech. Office: Gunma U Elec Engring, 1-5-1 Tenjin-cho, Kiryu, Gunma 376-8515, Japan

ISHIKAWA, TETSUYA, information science educator; b. Tokyo, May 27, 1943; m. Sachiko Ishikawa. MA, Keio U., Tokyo, 1972; D, Waseda U., Tokyo, 1992. Prof. U. Libr. and Info. Sci., Tsukba, Japan. Fax: 81-298-59-1093. E-mail: ishikawa@ulis.ac.jp. Office: Univ Libr/Info Sci, 1-2 Kasuga, Tsukuba 305-8550, Japan

ISHIKAWA, TOSHIHISA, biochemist, educator; b. Kawanoe, Ehime, Japan, Sept. 4, 1954; came to U.S., 1991; s. Kazuo and Tsuyako (Shinohara) I.; m. Naoko Fukasawa, Mar. 6, 1982. BS in Chemistry, Hokkaido U., Sapporo, Japan, 1977, MS in Biochemistry, 1979, PhD in Biochemistry, 1982. Acad. rsch. fellow Min. Edn. Sci. and Culture, Japan, 1982; postdoctoral fellow U. Düsseldorf, Germany, 1982-87; asst. biochemist Osaka (Japan) U. Med. Sch., 1987-89; project leader German Cancer Rsch. Ctr., Heidelberg, 1989-91; asst. prof. U. Tex. M.D. Anderson Cancer Ctr., Houston, 1991-95; sect. chief Cen. Rsch. Pfizer Pharms. Inc., Aichi, Japan, 1995-97, mgr., 1997-99; dir. Pfizer Healthcare Acad., 1999-2000; prof. grad. sch. biosci. and biotech. Tokyo Inst. Tech., Yokohama, Japan, 2000—; gen. sec. internat. conf. Osaka, 1988; chmn. meeting Soc. Free Radical Rsch. Kyoto, Japan, 1988; session chmn. Gordon Rsch. Conf. on Drug Metabolism, Plymouth, N.H., 1995; vis. prof. U. Nancy, France, 1990; participant numerous confs.; presenter numerous seminars. Regular reviewer Biochemical Pharmacology, London, 1986-87; edit. advisor Biochemical Jour., London, 1989—; contbr. articles, abstracts to profl. jours. Recipient Rsch. award Internat. Life Scis. Inst., 1993; scholar Deutscher Acad. Austauschdienst, 1982-83; grantee Minn. Edn., Sci. and Culture Japan, 1987-89, Deutsche Krebsforschungsstiftung, 1989-91, Deutsche Forschungsgemeinschaft, 1990-91, Internat. Life Sci. Inst. Rsch. Found., 1993-95, NIH/Nat. Cancer Inst., 1994—. Mem. Am. Assn. Cancer Rsch., European Soc. Biochem. Pharmacology, German Biochem. Soc., Japanese Biochem. Soc., Brit. Biochem. Soc., N.Y. Acad. Scis. Home: 4-17-30 Kirigaoka, Midorikui, Yokahama 226-0016, Japan

ISHIKAWA-FULLMER, JANET SATOMI, psychologist, educator; b. Hilo, Hawaii, Oct. 17, 1925; d. Shinichi and Onao (Kurisu) Saito; m. Calvin Y. Ishikawa, Aug. 15, 1950; 1 child, James A.; m. Daniel W. Fullmer, June 11, 1980. B of Edn., U. Hawaii, 1950, MEd, 1967; MEd, U. Hawaii, 1969, PhD, 1976. Diplomate Am. Acad. Pain Mgmt. Prof. Honolulu Bus. Coll., 1953-59; prof., counselor Kapiolani Community Coll., Honolulu, 1959-73; prof., dir. counseling Honolulu Community Coll., 1973-74, dean of students, 1974-77; psychologist, pres., treas. Human Resources Devel. Ctr., Inc., Honolulu, 1977—; cons. United Specialties Co., Tokyo, 1979, Grambling (La.) State U., 1980, 81, Filipino Immigrants in Kalihi, Honolulu, 1979-84, Legis. Ref. Bur., Honolulu, 1984-85, Honolulu Police Dept., 1985; co-founder Waianae (Hawaii) Child and Family Ctr., 1979-92. Co-author: Family Therapy Dictionary, 1991, Manabu: The Diagnosis and Treatment of a Japanese Boy with a Visual Anomaly, 1991; contbr. articles to profl. jours. Commr. Bd. Psychology, Honolulu, 1979-85; co-founder Kilohana United Meth. Ch. and Family Ctr., 1993—. Mem. APA, ACA, Hawaii Psychol. Assn., Pi Lambda Theta (sec. 1967-68, v.p. 1968-69, pres. 1969-70, 96-98), Delta Kappa Gamma (sec., v.p. scholarship 1975, Outstanding Educator award 1975, Thomas Jefferson award 1993, Francis E. Clark award 1993). Avocations: jogging, tennis, dancing. Home: 154 Maono Pl Honolulu HI 96821-2529 Office: Human Resources Devel Ctr 1750 Kalakaua Ave Apt 809 Honolulu HI 96826-3725

ISHIMARU, KANJI, plant biochemist; b. Matsuyama, Ehime, Japan, Sept. 19, 1959; s. Motoaki and Fuyue (Miyoshi) I.; m. Keiko Tamai, Nov. 12, 1989; 1 child, Hiromasa. MS, Kyushu U., 1987. Rschr. Kyushu U., Fukuoka, Japan, 1987-88, Japan Health Sci. Found., Tokyo, 1988-90; assoc. prof. Saga (Japan) U., 1990—. Author: Biotechnology in Agriculture and Forestry, 1996, Recent Research Development in Phytochemistry, 1997; editor Japanese Soc. of Food Chemistry, 1996—; contbr. articles to profl. jours. Mem. Saga Frontier 21, 1996—. Rsch. support grant San Ei Gen Found., 1995—, Japan Health Sci. Found., 1995—, Sci. and Tech. Agy., 1995—. Avocations: writer, gardening, photography. Home: Mikashima, Mikazuki 845-0025, Japan Office: Saga U, Honjo, Saga 840-8502, Japan

ISHIMARU, MASAHIKO JOHN, psychiatrist researcher; b. Fukuoka, Japan, Mar. 20, 1957; s. Akihiko and Setsuko (Nishihara) I.; m. Kazuko Elizabeth Hashimoto, May 4, 1990; children: Takahiko, Yoshihiko. Mitsuhiko. LLB, Tokyo U., 1979; MD, Tokyo Med. and Dental U., 1986, PhD, 1994. Med. diplomate. Intern dept. psychiatry Tokyo Med. and Dental U., 1986-87; clin. staff Tsurumidai Hosp., Beppu, Japan, 1987-88, Haryugaoka Hosp., Koriyama, Japan, 1988-91; resident dept. psychiatry Tokyo Med. and Dental U., 1991-92, faculty staff Med. Rsch. Inst., 1992-2000; assoc. prof. Med. Rsch. Inst., Tokyo, 1999-2000, Obirin U., Tokyo, 2000—; vis. rschr. Dept. Psychiatry, Washington U., St. Louis, 1994-97. Recipient Shimazaki-Shimazono-Takahashi Meml. prize Tokyo Med. & Dental U., 1996. Christian Ch. of Japan. Avocations: writing novels and essays, playing violin, swimming. Home: 2-8-1-501 Ookayama, Meguro-ku Tokyo 152-0033, Japan Office: Obirin U, 3758 Tokiwa-machi, Tokyo 194-0294, Japan

ISHIMARU, TADASHI, otolaryngologist; b. Kanazawa, Japan, Mar. 2, 1961; s. Mikio and Takako Ishimaru. MD, Kansai Med. U., Moriguchi, Japan, 1987, PhD, 1992. Resident Kanazawa U., 1987-88; ear nose and throat surgeon Fukui (Japan) Prefectural Hosp., 1992-93; chief ear nose and throat dept. Ushitsu (Japan) Gen. Hosp., 1993-94; co-chief ear nose and throat dept. Ishikawa Prefectural Ctrl. Hosp., Kanazawa, Japan, 1994-95; mem. ear nose and throat ednl. instr. Kanazawa U., 1995—. Contbr. articles to profl. jours. Office: Otorhinolaryngol Dept, Kanazawa U 13-1 Takaramachi, Kanazawa 920-0934, Japan

ISHIMARU, TAKANORI, dentist, educator; b. Tokuyama, Yamaguchi, Japan, Mar. 3, 1952; s. Kyouri and Eiko Ishimaru; m. Yukiko Okuda; children: Naoko, Yoshifumi, Reiko. DDS, Kyushu Dental Coll., Kitakyushu, Fukuoka, Japan, 1980. Dental diplomate, Japan. Instr. dept. dental anesthesiology Kyushu Dental Coll., Kitakyushu, 1980-85; dental staff Ohtemachi Hosp., Kitakyushu, 1986-89; instr. dept. oral and maxillofacial surgery Yamaguchi U. Sch. Medicine, Ube, Japan, 1989—. Contbr. articles to profl. jours. Mem. Internat. Assn. Oral and Maxillofacial Surgery. E-mail: tishimar@po.cc.yamaguchi-u.ac.jp. Fax: 836-22-2298. Home: 2-10-202 Kitakotoshiba, 1 Choume, Ube Yamaguchi 755-0036, Japan Office: Yamaguchi U Sch Medicine, 1-1-1 Minamikogushi, Ube Yamaguchi 755-8505, Japan

ISHIMORI, KOICHIRO, researcher, educator; b. Kyoto, Japan, May 12, 1961; s. Katsumi and Fumiko (Ochiai) I.; m. Rie Koshiba, June 2, 1991. B of Engring., Kyoto U., 1984, M of Engring., 1986, PhD, 1989. Cert. in biochemistry, bioinorganic chemistry, biophys. chemistry. Rsch. assoc. Kyoto U., 1989-95; assoc. prof. Kyoto U., 1995—. Contbr. articles to profl. jours. Postdoctoral fellow U. Wis., Madison, 1993-94. Mem. Am. Chem. Soc., Am. Soc. Biochemistry and Molecular Biology. Home: 208 1-8-23 Tennou Ibaraki, 567-0876 Osaka Osaka, Japan Office: Kyoto U Dept Molec Engring Grad Sch Engring, Kyoto U Dept Molec Engring, Yoshida Honmachi Sakyoku, 606-8501 Kyoto Japan

ISHIMOTO, COE, electronics company executive; b. Tokyo, July 10, 1950; s. Shaw and Mitsuko (Shibata) I.; m. Tokiko Sato, Apr. 19, 1980; children: Akiko, Kota, Satoko. BS, MIT, 1972, PhD, 1979; MA, Harvard U., 1975. Gen. mgr. Frontier Sci. Labs., Sony Corp., Yokohama. Mem. IEEE, Soc. for Info. Display.

ISHIMOTO, YASUO, law educator; b. Tanabe, Japan, Dec. 5, 1924. LLB, U. Tokyo, 1948, LLD, 1961. Asst. law faculty U. Tokyo, 1948-52; asst. prof. law Osaka (Japan) City U., 1953-60, prof. law, 1960-81; prof. law Jochi U., Tokyo, 1981-95, Kanagawa U., Yokohama, Japan, 1998—. Author: Historical Considerations on the International Law of Neutrality, 1958, Treaties and the People, 1960, Structural Changes in the International Law, 1998. Mem. Internat. Law Assn. (Japan br. sec.-gen. 1991—), Japanese Assn. Internat. Law (pres. 1982-85). Home: 945-11 Kashima, Hachioji 192-0353, Japan

ISHIURA, YOSHIHISA, internist, allergist, researcher; b. Kurobe, Japan, Feb. 26, 1964; s. Kaji and Takayo (Kaneda) I.; m. Naoko Uchiyama, Sept. 15, 1993; children: Yoshiaki, Akie. MD, Tottori (Japan) U., 1983; PhD, Kanazawa (Japan) U., 1993. Postdoctoral fellow Toyama (Japan) Med. and Pharm. U., 1989-91; physician Kurobe City Hosp., 1991-92; postdoctoral fellow, rschr. Kanazawa U., 1993—; respirologist, Kurobe City Hosp., 1991—, allergist and respirologist, Kanazawa U., 1993—. Author: Common 350 Drugs in Japan, 1996, Current Therapy for Respiratory Disease, 1997. Fellow Japanese soc. Internal Medicine, Japanese Soc. Chest Disease, Japan Soc. Bronchology. Avocations: skiing, photography. Fax: 81-76-234-4252. Home: 102 2-3 Sugihiramachi, Nishinokusa, Wajima City Ishikawa 928-0011, Japan Office: Wajima Mcpl Hosp, Ha 1-1 Yamagishi-machi, Wajima City Ishikawa 928-8585, Japan

ISHIWARA, HIROSHI, electronics engineer; b. Yamaguchi, Japan, Nov. 6, 1945; s. Sei-icihiro and Nobuko Ishiwara; m. Kayoko Hoshi, Apr. 7, 1974; 2 children. BEng, Tokyo Inst. Tech., 1968, MEng, 1970, DEng, 1973. Rsch. assoc. Tokyo Inst. Tech., 1973-76, assoc. prof., 1976-89, prof., 1989—. Author: Semiconductor Devices, 1990; editor: Heteroepitaxy on Silicon: Fundamentals, Structure, Devices. Recipient Japan IBM Sci. prize Japan IBM Sci. Prize Com., 1990, Inoue Sci. prize, 1994, Ichimura Tech. prize, 1994. Mem. IEEE (sr.), Material Rsch. Soc., Japanese Soc. Applied Physics. Achievements include research of heteroepitaxy of conductive and insulating thin films on semiconductor substrates and research on ferroelectric memory. Home: 4-22-6 Denenchofu Otaku, Tokyo 145-0071, Japan Office: Tokyo Inst Tech, 4259 Nagatsuda Midoriku, Yokohama 226-8503, Japan

ISHIWATARI, HIROMASA, biomedical electronics educator, researcher; b. Kawasaki, Japan, Jan. 9, 1935; s. Shokichi and Mitsu (Uyama) I.; m. Junko Hamada, Apr. 24, 1967; children: Hironobu, Hirotoshi. BSEE, U. Electro-Comms., Tokyo, 1958, PhD, 1995; MS in Biomed. Engring., U. Pa., 1964; PhD, U. Electro-Comms., 1995. Gen. mgr. Sanei Instrument Co., Tokyo, 1970-73; from project leader to gen. mgr. Matsushita Electronics, Osaka, Japan, 1973-95; prof. Suzuka U. Med. Sci., Japan, 1995—; chmn. Suzuka U. Med. Sci., 1996-97, dean, 1997—. Author: Basics of Laser Engineering, 1995, Guidebook of Laser Safety, 1989; contbr. articles to profl. jours. Mem. Inst. Elec. Info. and Comm. Engrs., Soc. Instrument Control Engrs., Soc. Med. Elec. and Biomed. Engring. Avocations: handmaking violins, woodcraft, hiking. Home: 57-1-510 Higashi-chisato, Kawage, Agegun 510-0303, Japan Office: Suzuka U Med Sci, 1001-1 Kishioka, Suzuka 510-0293, Japan

ISHIZAKA, KAZUYOSHI, electronics company executive; b. Mar. 12, 1921. Degree, Tokyo U., 1942. Pres., chmn. bd. dirs. Kenwood Corp., Tokyo, former chmn. bd. dirs., co. adviser. Office: Kenwood Corp, 14-6 Dogenzaka 1-chome Shibuya-ku, Tokyo 150-8501, Japan*

ISHIZAKA, SHIGEAKI, immunologist, researcher; b. Nakanojo, Gunma, Japan, Aug. 4, 1945; s. Rinzaburo and Katsu (Tomita) I.; m. Yoshiko Takahashi, 1985; 1 child, Yasuki. MD, Nara Med. U., Kashihara, Japan, 1971; PhD, Osaka (Japan) City U., 1978. Clin. rschr. Osaka City U., 1978-81; guest investigator Karolinska Inst., Stockholm, 1981-83; asst. prof. Nara Med. U., Kashihara, 1983-84, lectr., 1984-93, assoc. prof., 1993-95, prof., 1995—. Mem. editl. bd. Internat. Jour. Immunopathological Pharmacology, 1993—; patentee in field of parotin peptide. Recipient Soc. Osaka award Osaka City, 1978, Found. Osaka Clin. Immunology award Osaka Clin. Immunology, 1983, Health Sci. award Health Sci. Found., Tokyo, 1995, Superior award Japan Soc. Salivary, 1996. Mem. Japan Soc. Clin. Parasitology (councilor 1994—), Japan Soc. Parasitology (councilor 1995—), Japan Soc. Salivary (councilor 1985—), N.Y. Acad. Scis. Avocations: art, archery. Office: Nara Med U Dept Parasitol, 840 Shijo-Cho, 634-8521 Kashihara Nara, Japan

ISHIZAKI, TATSUSHI, physician, parasitologist; b. Tochigi, Japan, Mar. 8, 1915; s. Takaji and Satoko I.; M.D., Tokyo (Japan) U., 1939, Ph.D., 1951; diploma pub. health, Singapore U., 1959; m. Yuriko Sase, Nov. 5, 1946; children: Terumi, Michiharu. With U. Tokyo Sch. Medicine, 1939, sr. asst. dept. phys. therapy and medicine, 1946-55; chief 2d divsn. dept. parasitology Nat. Inst. Health, Japan, 1953-67, chief dept., 1967-74; mem. emeritus, 1980—; lectr. clin. allergy U. Tokyo Sch. Medicine, 1956-71; prof. clin. immunology Dokkyo U. Sch. Medicine, 1973-82, prof. emeritus, 1982—, chmn. clin. profs., 1978-80; panelist Japan-U.S.A. Coop. Study Parasitology, 1965-74. Hon. fellow Am. Coll. Allergists; mem. Japanese Soc. Allergy (exec. com., pres., hon. fellow 1981—), Korean Soc. Allergy (hon.), Japanese Soc. Tropical Medicine (hon. fellow, exec. com.), Japan-German Assn. Protozoan Diseases (pres.), Rsch., publs. on skin tests for various antigens; standardization of criteria of positive skin test basic phenomena of skin reaction especially mast cell degranulation mechanism analysis of onset of asthma attacks especially related to air pollution, weather; analysis of mechanisms of occupational allergy, others. Home: 8-15 Torimachi Mibumachi, Tochigi Japan

ISHIZUKA, TOSHIAKI, immunologist, cardiologist, vascular cell biologist; b. Musashino, Tokyo, Japan, Dec. 17, 1963; s. Toshio and Reiko (Yamataka) I.; m. Yuko Ito, Oct. 26, 1997; 1 son. MSc, Nat. Def. Med. Coll., Tokorozawa, Saitama, Japan, 1988; MD, Keio U., Tokyo, 1998. Med. diplomate cardiology, immunology. Resident Nat. Def. Med. Coll. Hosp., Tokorozawa, Japan, 1988-90; rsch. fellow Nat. Def. Med. Coll., Tokorozawa, Japan, 1990-97, rsch. fellow divsn. biomedical engring., 1997-98; dir. Japan Grand Self-Def. Force Kasumigaura Med. Ctr., 1998-2000, The Med. Office of the Def. Agy., Tokyo, 2000—. Co-author: Current Medical Technology Reviews, 1991, Ministry of Health and Welfare Report, 1992-93, Arteriosclerosis - For New Clinical Therapy, 1995. Major Japanese Grand Self-Def. Force (JGSDF), 1988—. Grantee Japanese Ministry of Health and Welfare, 1991-93; recipient Nat. Def. Med. awards, 1999. Fellow Japanese Soc. Internal Med., Japan Rheumatism Assn.; mem. Japanese Vascular Biology Orgn. Avocations: tennis, driving, sightseeing. Office: Med Office Japan Def Agy, 5-1, Ichigayahonmuracho, Tsuchiura Shinjuku, Tokyo 162-0845, Japan

ISHMAEL, MOHAMMED ALI ODEEN, Guyana diplomat; b. Britannia, Guyana, Jan. 29, 1948; s. Hamid and Zowrah (Khan) I.; m. Evangeline Majid, Mar. 30, 1975; children: Safraz Waseem, Nadeeza. BA in Geography, U. Guyana, Georgetown, 1974, diploma in edn., 1976; PhD in Edn., Pacific Western U., L.A., 1989. Elem. sch. tchr. Ministry Edn., Guyana, 1964-70, secondary sch. tchr., 1970-83, dep. headmaster, 1983-85; tchr. Ctrl. Edn. Authority, Bahamas, 1985-93; amb. to U.S., Guyana Embassy, Washington, 1993—; permanent rep. to OAS, Washington, 1993—, vice chmn. environ. com., 1993-94, v.p. permanent coun., 1993, pres. permanent coun., 1994, vice-chmn. com. on sustainable devel., 1996-97; chief negotiator for Guyana at Summit of the Ams., 1994, 98, Hemisphere Summit on Sustainable Development, 1997. Author: Problems of the Transition of Education in the Third World, 1990, Towards Education Reform in Guyana, 1993, Amerindian Legends of Guyana, 1995, The Trail of Diplomacy, 1999; contbr. articles to various publs. Recipient Gandhi Centenary Gold Medal, 1974, Nat. award Cacique Crown of Honor, 1997. Mem. Nat. Geographical Soc., Acad. Polit. Sci. Mem. People's Progressive Party. Muslim. Avocations: reading, writing, coin collecting. Office: Embassy of Guyana 2490 Tracy Pl NW Washington DC 20008-1633

ISHMAEV, SERGEY NIKOLAYEVICH, physicist, researcher; b. St. Petersburg, Russia, Nov. 4, 1938; s. Nikolay Rodyonovich and Faina Sergeyevna (Smirnova) I.; m. Nina Stepanovna Tereshchenko, Apr. 30, 1961; 1 child, Tatyana. Degree in physics, Physics & Engring. Inst., Moscow, 1962; PhD in Neutron and Solid State Physics, Kurchatov Inst., Moscow, 1993. Sr. rschr. Kurchatov Inst., 1962—; referee ISTI, Moscow, 1991-94. Contbr. articles to profl. jours. Office: I V Kurchatov Inst, 1 Kurchatov Square, 123 182 Moscow Russia

ISIK, NEJAT, neurosurgeon; b. Ankara, Turkey, Jan. 1, 1956; s. Mehmet and Betül (Yakin) I.; m. Nihal Çetinerler, Mar. 5, 1983; children: Mehmet Can, Yamaç Alican. MD, Hacettepe U., Ankara, 1980, specialization in neurosurgery, 1986; PhD in Microsurgery, Makmara U., Istanbul, Turkey, 1998. Asst. physician dept. neurosurgery Hacettepe U. Med. Sch., 1980-86; neurosurgeon Zonguldak (Turkey) State Hosp. Neurosurgery Clin., 1987-90; neurosurgeon SSK Göztepe Hosp. Neurosurgery Clin., Istanbul, 1990—, asst. chief, 1993—. Lt. Turkish land forces, 1986-87. Mem. Turkish Med. Assn., Turkish Neurosurg. Soc., European Neurosurg. Soc. Avocation: photography. Home: Serap Caddesi, 2 Serap Sokak 4/16, Maltepe Istanbul 81530, Turkey

ISIRIMAH, NNAEMAKA OGU, agricultural studies educator; b. Kafanchan, Nigeria, Jan. 18, 1937; s. Thomas Ogu and Mary Osiago (Woko) I.; m. Eunice Uchenna Okoroafor; children: Chijioke, Okechuku, Nnamdi, Mary Durcas, Cioma. BSc with honors, Tuskegee Inst., 1967; MSc, U. Wis., 1969, PhD, 1972. Cert. tchr. Tchr. Yolun Tary Anglican Agy., Dwerri, 1957-60; sr. pivotal tutor Anglican Grammar Sch., Onichauboma, 1962-63; project assoc. Water Rsch. Ctr./U. Wis., Madison, 1972-73; prin. lectr. Coll. Sci. & Tech., Port Harcourt, Nigeria, 1973-80; prof. soil and environ. biochemistry Rivers State U. Sci. and Tech., Port Harcourt, Nigeria, 1980—; Nigerian lang. culture tchr. USAID Peace Corps. Divsn., Washington, summers 1964-66; chmn. Rivers State com. Operation Feed the Nation, 1976-80; cons. in field. Contbr. articles to profl. jours. Chmn. Cmty. Devel. Com., Obrikom, Onelga, 1989-96; gov. bd. Cocoa Rsch. Inst. Nigeria, 1980-83; active Nigerian Coun. for Mgmt. Devel., Lagos, 1981-83; rep., bd. trustees Christ Ch., 1999—; chmn. spl. duty com. Full Gospel Businessmen Fellowship Internat., 1998-99. Fulbright fellow La. State U., 1984; recipient Merit cert. Niger Delta North Diocese, Port Harcourt, 1999; U. Wis. scholar, 1970. Mem. Soil Sci. Soc. Nigeria (editl. bd. 1999—). Anglican. Avocations: music, reading, walking, gardening, singing. Home: PO Box 8, 5 Umuenyike Rd, Omoku Onelga Nigeria Office: State U Sci & Tech Crop Soi, PO Box 5080, Port Harcourt Nigeria

ISKANDER, GEORGE MINA, chemistry educator, researcher; b. Omdurman, Sudan, Oct. 28, 1942; s. Mina Iskander Butros and Lola Ibrahim George; m. Daisy Ramzi Shihata, Nov. 22, 1969; children: Mary George, Yousif George. Degree, Comboni Coll., Khartoum, Sudan, 1951, degree with honors, 1956. Rsch. fellow U. Liverpool, London, 1974, Royal Holloway and Bedford Coll., London, 1984-85; demonstrator dept. chemistry U. Khartoum, 1970, lectr., 1974, assoc. prof., 1978-82, prof., 1982—; cons. in chemistry U. New South Wales, Sydney, 1994—, Sch. Biol. Scis., 1997—. Author: Problems in Organic Chemistry, 1987. Fellow Royal Chem. Soc.; mem. Swiss Chem. Soc. Mem. Labor Party. Avocations: playing chess, backgammon, pre-1970 football. Home: 97 Southee Circuit Oakhurst, Sydney NSW 2761, Australia Office: U New South Wales, Sydney NSW 2052, Australia

ISKRA, MARIA, chemist, researcher; b. Międzychód, Poland, Aug. 16, 1950; d. Jan and Leokadia (Jandy) Krawiecka; m. Antoni Augustyn Iskra, Nov. 20, 1971; children: Magdalena, Karolina. MS, Adam Mickiewicz U., Poznań, Poland, 1973; PhD, Karol Marcinkowski U. Med. Scis., Poznan, Poland, 1983. Cert. in chemistry. Asst. Karol Marcinkowski U. Med. Scis., Poznań, 1975-83, adjunct, 1983—. Contbr. papers to profl. jours. Mem. Internat. Atherosclerosis Soc., Polish Atherosclerosis Soc. Avocations: historical books, music, painting, gardening, photography. Office: K M U Med Scis, 6 Grunwaldzka St, 60-780 Poznań Poland

ISLAM, BADR UL, lawyer; b. Hariawala, Gujrat, Pakistan, Sept. 21, 1953; s. Inaam Ullah and Qamar Inaam (Chatha) Khan; m. Farzana Badr Hayat, Oct. 30, 1987; children: Zao Fishan, Zafar, Navak, Nabil, Hamzah. BA in Econs. and Polit. Sci., U. Punjab, Lahore, Pakistan, 1983; LLB, Karachi (Pakistan) U., 1986. Ptnr. Abbasi Law Assocs., Karachi, Pakistan, 1987-88, Badr Islam & Co., Gujrat, Pakistan, 1989—; Chmn. anti-corruption com. bar, 1995, bar accountability com. 1997, dist. crimes control com., 1995, dist. narcotic control com., 1995, peace com., 1995. Sec. gen. Gujrat br. Pakistan People's Party, 1990-94. Mem. Nat. Soc. Minorities' Rights (pres. 1998), Punjab Bar Coun., Dist. Bar Assn. (v.p. 1995, exec. com. 1997-98, Medal for outstanding svcs. in field of human rights 1997), Human Rights Soc. Pakistan (pres. 1991-96), Lawyers for Human Rights (pres. 1996—), Lawyers' Club (adminstr. 1998). Home: By-Pass Hariawala, 50700 Gujrat Punjab, Pakistan Office: Badr Islam & Co, District Courts, 50700 Gujrat Punjab, Pakistan

ISLAM, MOHAMMED SHAHIDUL, horticulturist, food scientist, researcher; b. Jessore, Bangladesh, July 31, 1964; s. A.K.M. Shamsul and B. Shaira Haque; m. Sharmin Khan, Aug. 14, 1990; children: Intisar, Ishrar. Higher secondary, Govt. M.M. Coll., Jessore, 1981; BSc in Agr. with honors, Bangladesh Agrl. U., Mymensingh, Bangladesh, 1988, MS in Horticulture, 1990; PhD in Postharvest Horticulture, Ehime U., Matsuyama, Japan, 1996. Cert. agriculturist. Rsch. asst. Bangladesh Agrl. U., Mymensingh, 1988-90; sci. officer Bangladesh Agrl. Rsch. Inst., Giazipur, 1990—; fgn. rschr. Kagawa U., Takamatsu, Japan, 1996-97, vis. scientist, 1996; Japan Soc. for the Promotion of Sci. postdoctoral rsch. fellow Chiba U., Matsudo City, 1998—. Contbr. articles to profl. jours. Mem. AAAS, Am. Soc. Horticultural Sci., Bangladesh Bot. Soc., Plant Breeding and Genetics Soc. Bangladesh, Bangladesh Horticultural Sci. Soc. (life), Crop Sci. Soc. Bangladesh, Agriculturist Soc. Bangladesh, Agrl. Scientist Soc. Bangladesh. Avocations: table tennis, football, cricket, music, travel. Office: Chiba U Dept Veg Sci, 648 Matsudo, Chiba 271-8510, Japan

ISLAM, MUHAMMAD NURUL, securities trader; b. Chittagong, Bangladesh, Sept. 13, 1943; s. Osman and Amena (Khatun) Sowdagar; m. Shamsun Nahar; Nov. 24, 1968; 1 child, Zia. BA, U. Dhaka, Bangladesh, 1963. Ptnr. Gani & Sons, Chittagong, Bangladesh, 1968—; dir. Cooperator's Enterprise, Chittagong, 1966—; mng. dir. Solex Ltd., Chittagong, 1981—; pres. Solex Rsch., Chittagong, 1994—, Solex Corp., Chittagong, 1997—; CEO Solex Securities Ltd., Chittagong, 1995—. Pub. (books) Japaner Shahitya O Shahityik, 1999, Lenin Ghumube Ebar, 1999. Founder/Pres. Nippon Acad., 1985, Chattagram AOTS Alumni Soc., 1987; founder Chattagram JICA Alumni Soc., 1989; founder/v.p. OISCA-Chittagong, 1993; hon. counsull Japan, 1990—. Mem. Bangla Acad., Chittagong Stock Exhange, World Future Soc., Rotary Internat. Avocations: photography, reading, social work, pub. speaking. Office: Solex Securities Ltd., Osman Ct 70 Agrabad, 4100 Chittagong Bangladesh

ISLAM, RAFIQUL, chemical engineer, educator; b. Magura, Bangladesh, Mar. 31, 1956; s. Shamsuddin Ahmed. MSc in Petro-Chem. Engring. & Tech. with honors, Jhenidah Cadet Coll., 1980; PhD in Chem. Engring., Azerbaijan Inst. Petroleum & Chemistry, 1985. Process engr. Eastern Refinery Ltd., 1981, Bangladesh Petroleum Corp., 1982-86; scientist Ctrl.

Rsch. Lab. Baku Oil Refinery, 1982-85; process design engr. Bangladesh Che. Industries Corp., 1986-87; prof. U. Dhaka, Bangladesh, 1987—; European Commn. postdoctoral rsch. fellow, scientist German Petroleum Inst. Rsch., 1992-93; UNESCO sr. scholar fellow, vis. prof. E. China U. Sci. & Tech., Shanghai, 1998-99; founder mem.-sec. Environment Study Ctr. Bangladesh; participant numerous internat. seminars and confs. Contbr. approximately 40 articles to profl. jours. Recipient Marie Curie Bursary award European Commn., 1992, Great Wall award UNESCO, 1992; 2-time winner Moscow Olympics, 1984, 85. Fellow Inst. Engrs. Bangladesh; mem. Bangladesh Chem. Soc. (life), Bangladesh Assn. Advancement Sci., Asiatic Soc. Bangladesh. Moslem. Home: Flat 214, Anowar Pasha Bhaban, Dhaka 1000, Bangladesh Office: U Dhaka, Dept Applied Chemistry, Dhaka 1000, Bangladesh

ISLAM, SK NAZRUL, pharmacist; b. Dhaka, Bangladesh, Oct. 1, 1955; s. Sk abdul and Begum (Sanawara) Mannan; m. Monira Ahsan, Sept. 4, 1985; children: Sheikh Khaled Saifulla Sadi, Sheikh Faisal Ashadulla Mahdi, Sheikh Fuad Abdulla Hadi. B.Pharm.(hons.), U. dhaka, 1980, M.Pharm., 1982; PhD, U. Strathclyde, U.K., 1994. Registered pharmacist, Bangladesh. Rsch. asst. dept. pharmacy U. Dhaka, 1982-83; mfg. pharmacist Amico Labs., Ltd., Dhaka, 1984-85, Squibb of bangladesh Ltd., Dhaka, 1985-86; lectr. Inst. Nutrition and Food Sci. U. Dhaka, 1986-94, asst. prof., 1994-98, assoc. prof., 1998—; vis. rschr. Strathclyde U., Glasgow, 1990; house tutor Ziaur Rahman Hall, Dhaka U., 1988-89, Salimullah Hall, 1996—. Contbr. articles to profl. jours. Bd. govs., Inst. Nutrition and Food Sci., U. Dhaka, 1994-95. UN Univ. fellow, 1998; David Livingstone grantee Strathclyde U., 1990-94, univ. postgrad. scholar, 1991-94. Mem. Bangladesh Pharm. Soc., Nutrition Soc. of Bangladesh, Bangladesh Assn. for Advancement of Sci. Avocations: travel news, music, community activities, world events. E-Mail: snlslam@bangla.net. Home: Dhaka Univ, Salimullah Hall, Dhaka 1000, Bangladesh Office: Inst Nutrition and Food Sci, Dhaka Univ, Dhaka 1000, Bangladesh

ISLAS YEPEZ, OSCAR ALBERTO, healthcare company executive, educator; b. Mexico City, Mex., Dec. 2, 1966; s. Alfonso and Luz Maria (Yépez) I. B of Acctg., U. Panamericana, Mexico City, Mex., 1988. CPA, Mexico. Auditor Arthur Andersen & Co., Mexico City, Mex., 1986-87; fin. analyst Smithkline & French, Mexico City, Mex., 1989-90; fin. planning mgr. Smithkline Beecham, Mexico City, Mex., 1991-92, controller pharms., 1993-95; finance dir. Smithkline Beecham, Rio de Janeiro, 1996; controller Mex. Smithkline Beecham, Mexico City, 1996-99, dir. spl. projects, 1997-99; controller Glaxo Wellcome, Mexico City, 1999—; prof. U. Panamericana, Mexico City, 1989—. Contbr. articles to profl. jours. Recipient México's Best Student award El Diario de México Jour., 1989; U. Panamericana scholar, 1984. Mem. U. Panamericana Acctg. Sch. Acad. Bd. (pres. alumni bd. 1989-93). Roman Catholic. Avocations: collecting comics, reading, chess, swimming. Home: Cerro San Andres #240, 04200 Mexico City Mexico Office: Glaxo Wellcome, Calz México-Xochimilco 4900, 14370 Mexico City Mexico

ISMAEL, NABIL FATHY, civil engineer, educator, consultant, researcher; b. Sherbin, Egypt, Mar. 21, 1946; arrived in Kuwait, 1978; s. Mohammed Fathy and Galila Ibrahim (Gabr) I.; m. Seham Mohammed Darweesh Mostafa, Aug. 20, 1979; children: Hussam, Hisham, Dalya. BSc with honors in Engring., Cairo U., 1966; MSc in Engring., Duke U., 1970, PhD in Engring., 1974. Registered profl. engr., Egypt. Tchg. instr. Cairo U., 1966-68; rsch. asst. Duke U., Durham, N.C., 1969-72; civil engr. II Port Authority of N.Y. and N.J., 1972-74; sr. engr. Ont. Hydro, Toronto, 1974-78; asst. prof. Kuwait U., 1978-81, assoc. prof., 1981-93, prof., 1993—; cons. Ministry Pub. Works, Kuwait, 1980-90, Ministry of Justice, 1991-00, Office Consultation and Career Devel., Kuwait U., 1986-00. Contbr. articles to profl. jours. including Jour. Geotech. and Geoenviron. Engring., ASCE, Can. Geotech. Jour., Transp. Rsch. Record, Soil and Found., IEEE, among others. Recipient Best Student award Ministry Edn., Egypt, 1958-61; rsch. assistantship Duke U., 1969-72; rsch. grantee Kuwait U., 1988-00, Kuwait Found. for Advancement Sci., 1979-84. Mem. ASCE, Soc. Engrs. (Egypt). Avocations: tennis, ping pong, volleyball, reading. Office: Kuwait U Dept Civil Engring, PO Box 5969, Safat Kuwait 13060, Kuwait

ISMAGILOVA, ROZA NURGALIEVNA, anthropologist, researcher; b. Tomsk, Russia, Mar. 29, 1928; d. Nurgali Sadreevitch Ismagilov and Zoya Umarovna Abdrashitova; div. 1962. Degree, U. Tashkent, USSR, 1950; D of History, Inst. Ethnography, Moscow, 1955, Docteur d'Etat, 1971; cert. prof., Inst. African Studies, Moscow, 1991. Rschr. Inst. of Ethnography, 1950-60; rschr. Inst. for African Studies, 1960-65, sr. rschr., 1965-79, dir. dept. ethno-cultural studies, 1979-98; dir. Ctr. for Editing Ency. "Africa", 1999—. Contbr. over 200 articles to profl. publs.; author 4 books. V.p. Soviet Assn. Friendship with African Peoples, 1960-92, Assn. for Bus. and Cultural Cooperation with African Countries, 1992-95. Honored Scientist, Russian Fedn., 1989, Order Friendship of Peoples, 1984. Mem. Internat. Sociol. Assn. (bd. dirs. rsch. com. 05,1984—), Assn. for Study Ethnicity and Nationalism. Avocations: classical musics, foreign languages, gardening, yoga. E-mail: rismagil@inafr.msk.su. Home: 9 Gubkina Apt 69, 117312 Moscow Russia Office: Inst African Studies, 30/1 Spiridonovka, 103001 Moscow Russia

ISMAIL, AMAT, Chinese government official; b. Qira County, Hotan, People's Republic of China, 1935. Dep. sec. CYL, Qira County, 1955-56, CPC, Qira County, 1956-58; dep. dir. dept. polit. work in culture and edn. Xinjiang, 1974-85; vice-chmn. Regional Rebolutionary Com., Xinjiang, 1974-79; polit. commisar Xinjiang Mil. Region, 1976-82; 1st dep. dir. Xinjiang Party Sch., 1977-79; chmn. Xinjiang Regional People's Govt., 1979; vice-chmn. CPC CC, 1988, Nationalities Com. under 7th CPC CC, 1988; minister State Nationalities Affairs Commn., 1986—; state councillor, 1993—. Office: care State Coun Secretariat, Zhong Nan Hai, Beijing People's Republic of China*

ISMAIL, ESSAM ABDUL RAHIM, pediatrician, consultant; b. Alexandria, Egypt, Nov. 16, 1951; m. Nahla Mohamad Abdou, Aug. 9, 1979; children: Fadi, Sherif, Rami. Cert. edn., Al Tabary, Cairo, 1970; MBChB, Sch. Medicine, Alexandria, 1976; diploma, Ireland, 1984; MRCP, U.K., 1989. Rotator Alex Univ., Alexandria, 1976-77; gen. practitioner Buhaira Polyclinic, Damanhour, Egypt, 1977-78; house officer Thawra Hosp., Baghdad, 1978, resident, 1979; family medicine doctor Polyclinic, Kuwait, 1980-87; cons. Farwaniya Hosp., Kuwait, 1987—, pediatrician, 1997; tutor Kuwait Univ. Medical Sch., 1993—, Univ. Dublin Ireland, 1992-94; lectr. Kuwait Inst. of Applied Scis., 1992-94. Contbr. numerous articles to profl. jours. Mem. Egyptian Medical Assn., Kuwait Medical Assn., Royal Coll. Physicians (U.K.). Avocations: table tennis, swimming, fishing, soccer. Home: PO Box 936, Hamad A Mubarak St, 22010 Kuwait Kuwait Office: Farwaniya Hosp, Kuwait Kuwait

ISMAIL, GAMAL ALI FOUAD, mathematics educator; b. Zagazig, El Sharkia, Egypt, Oct. 29, 1950; d. Ali Fouad Ismail Sabry and Souad Ahmed Mahmoud; m. Hussein Abdel Wahab Abdel Gawad, Feb. 21, 1974; children: Ayman, Ihab, Assmaa. BSc, Ain Shams U., Cairo, 1972, MSc, 1976, PhD, 1985. Demonstrator Women's Coll., Cairo, 1972-76, from asst. lectr. to lectr., 1976-95, assoc. prof., 1995—; mgr. computer unit Women's Coll., Cairo, 1995—. Mem. Egyptian Math. Soc. Avocations: reading, listening to music, tennis, traveling. Home: 82 A Abdel Aziz Fahmy St, Cairo Egypt

ISMAIL, KAMAL ABDEL RADI, mechanical engineering educator, consultant; b. Suez, Egypt, June 29, 1940; arrived in Brazil, 1973; s. Abel Elradi and Halima Ismail; divorced; children: Darryl Mark, Jason Andrew. BSME, U. Cairo, 1963; MSc, Assiut (Egypt) U., 1967; PhD, Southampton (Eng.) U., 1972. Demonstrator Assiut U., 1963-66; vis. prof. U. Mosul, Iraq, 1972-73; sr. lectr. mech. engring. State U. Campinas, Brazil, 1973-74, adj. prof., 1974-80, prof., 1980—; cons. Nt. Rsch. Ctr., Sorocaba, Brazil. Author: Experimental Transport Phenomena, 1980, Basic Engineering Instrumentation, 1998, Bancos de gelo, fundamentos e modelagem, 1998. Recipient rsch. award State U. of Campainas, 1997, Brasilian Nat. Rsch., 1998. Achievements include research in heat pipes, energy storage, heat transfer and fluid mechanics. Avocations: sports, swimming. E-mail: kamal@fem.unicamp.br. Office: State U Campinas Univ City, Br Geraldo, CP 6122, 13083970 Campinas SP, Brazil

ISMAIL, MICHAEL MOHAMMED, financial consultant; b. Hong Kong, Feb. 26, 1964; arrived in U.K., 1990; s. Danny I. and Gladys (Kan) I.; m. Shammee Catherine Ismail, Dec. 5, 1993. B Engring. with honors, Hong Kong Polytechnic U., 1988; postgrad. in pub. adminstrn., Oxford U., U.K. Tng. engr. Hong Kong Telephone, 1986-87; adminstrv. officer Hong Kong Govt., 1988-93; br. mgr. Zagle Star, 1993—. Mem. Hong Kong Instn. of Engrs. (chmn. young mem.'s com. 1993-95), Instn. Elec. Engrs., IEEE, Million Dollar Round Table, Gen. Agts. and Mgrs. Assn. (Career Devel. award). Avocations: motoring, music, swimming, cycling, computing. Office: GPO Box 10821, Hong Kong Hong Kong

ISMAIL, SAAD MOHAMED, agricultural studies educator; b. Fayied, Ismailia, Egypt, Aug. 25, 1952; s. Mohamed Ismail and Marium Hassan Rabeih; m. Sahar Salah El-Din Ali, Sept. 15, 1986; children: Allaa, Sarah. BSc, Zagazig (Egypt) U., Moshtohor, 1976, MSc, 1981; PhD, Mich. State U., 1989. Demonstrator Zagazig U., 1977-81; asst. lectr. Suez Canal U., Ismailia, Egypt, 1982-89, asst. prof., 1989-93, assoc. prof., 1993-98, prof., 1998—; postgrad. rsch. asst. U. Calif., Davis, 1987-89; rsch. asst. prof. U. Waterloo, Can., 1991-93; prin. investigator project Ministry Agr., Cairo, 1996-99, pesticides in medicinal plants project, 1996-97; rschr. in field. Contbr. articles to profl. jours., chpt. to book. Officer Egyptian Army, 1976-77. Rsch. grantee Ministry Agr., Egypt, 1996-97, 98-99, Fgn. Rels. Coord. Unit-U.S. AID, 1998-99. Fellow Am. Chem. Soc. (reviewer 1995-99). Avocations: swimming, running, reading, helping people. Office: Suez Canal U Faculty Agr, Dept Plant Protection, Ismailia 41522, Egypt

ISMAIL, SADEQ AL-HAJ JAFAR, educational studies educator; b. Kuwait, Oct. 12, 1944; s. Jafar Ali and Seddiqah Redha (Mohsen) I.; m. Fawziyah Abdul Baqi Al-Jamali; children: Abdul Aziz, Aliya, Lamiya. BA, U. Baghdad, 1968; MA, U. Calif., Berkeley, 1974, MA in Near Eastern Studies, 1974, PhD in Edn., 1974; diploma, Harvard U., 1976. Chmn. dept. edn. Kuwait U., 1976-79, dean Coll. Arts and Edn., 1979-80; exec. dir. Sultan Qaboos U., Muscat, 1981-89; edn1. advisor Islamic U., Beyroth, Lebanon, 1997-98; pres. London U. Sci. and Humanities, 1999—; ednl. advisor Ministry of Edn., Muscat, Oman, 1986-89, United Arab Emirates U., Al-Ain, 1990-91, Qatar U., 1991-92; cons. Coll. Edn. Arabian Gulf U., Bahrain, 1977-78, Islamic U., Beyroth; chmn. Estab. Cmty. Colls., Muscat, 1984, Sultan Quaboos U., Muscat, Sultantate of Oman, 1981-89. Recipient award Tchr.'s Assn., 1977, U. Tanessee, 1983, Tchr.'s and Psychol. Assn., Damascus U., 1997, 98. Mem. Future Soc., Philosophy of Edn., Profs. Assn., Critical Thinking Soc. Avocations: swimming, jogging, bicycle riding, camel riding, caring for animals. Fax: (00965) 484-6749. Address: PO Box 117, Safat Kuwait City 13012, Kuwait Office: Kuwait U Coll Edn, PO Box 1117, Safat 13012, Kuwait

ISMAIL, SUZAN ROUSHDY, medical geneticist; b. London, Apr. 24, 1938; d. Roushdy and Dawlat (El Sayed) I.; m. Nabil Abbas El Kharadly; children: Sherine, Rasha, Roushdy. MBBCh, Ain Shams U., 1960; PhD, Univ. Coll. London, 1966. House officer Ain Shams U. Hosp., Cairo, Egypt, 1961-62; sr. house officer Royal Infirmary, Edinburgh, Scotland, 1962-63; rsch. asst. Univ. Coll. London, 1964-66; from lectr. to prof. Med. Rsch. Inst. Alexandria U., Egypt, 1967—; dept. head. Med. Rsch. Inst., 1972—; cons. Min. Health, Egypt, 1990—, others. Author: Human Genetics, 1990; contbr. articles to profl. jours. Bd. dirs. Illiteracy Eradication Program, Alexandria, 1995. Mem. Genetic Counseling Soc. (chmn. 1986—), Leprosy Care Soc., Old Age Care Soc. Avocations: swimming, music, tennis, traveling. Home: 19 El Pharaana St Bab Shark, Alexandria Egypt Office: Med Rsch Inst, 165 El Horreya Ave, Alexandria Egypt

ISMAIL, WAN AZIZCH WAN, government party leader; b. Malaya, Dec. 3, 1952; m. Anwar Ibrahim; six children.; Grad., Royal Coll. of Surgeons, Dublin. Pres. Nat. Justice Party, Malaysia. Avocations: baking cakes, fishing. Office: Nat Justice Pty No 1018 201, Block A Pusa/Dagagan Phileo, Selanger Darul Ehsan Malaysia*

ISMAIL-ZADEH, ALI TOFIK, geophysicist, researcher; b. Baku, Azerbaijan, Sept. 28, 1961; s. Tofik Ali and Sima Dziavad (Bagiroff) Ismail-Z.; m. Sofia MIkhailovna Salman, June 20, 1992. MSc, Baku U., 1983; PhD, USSR Acad. Scis., Moscow, 1989; DSc, Russian Acad. Scis., Moscow, 1997. Math. diplomate; geophys. diplomate. Sr. rsch. fellow Internat. Inst. Earthquake Predicition Russian Acad. Scis., Moscow, 1994—, rschr., 1990-94; jr. rschr. Inst. Geology, Azerbaijanian Acad. Scis., Baku, 1983-88; vis. rschr. U. Trieste, Italy, 1995, Royal Inst. Tech., Stockholm, 1996, U. Uppsala, Sweden, 1997-98, U. Cambridge, Eng., 2000; chief dept. projects Internat. Inst. Earthquake Prediction Theory and Math. Geophysics, Moscow, 1993—; vis. scholar Swedish Royal Soc., 2000. Contbr. articles to profl. jours. Recipient award Internat. Sci. Found., 1993, Russian Federation's pres., 1999; grant Swedish Royal Acad. Scis., Stockholm, 1997; named Young Rschr. Acad. Europeae, London, 1995; A Von Humboldt rsch. fellow, 2000; Internat. Sci. & Tech. Ctr. grantee, 1999-2002. Mem. Geophys. Union (life), Eurosci. (founder, bd. mem.), European Geophys. Soc. Avocations: music, theater, swimming. E-mail: aismail@mitp.ru. Office: Internat Inst Earthquake, Warshavskoye Sh 79-2, 113556 Moscow Russia

ISMIEL, MOTHAFAR ABDUL-GHAFOOR, marketing professional; b. Qadisiya, Iraq, May 22, 1958; s. Abdul-Ghafoor Ismiel Al-Bakri and Badria Abdul-Majeed Al-Hashimi; m. Wafa Abdul-Karim Al-Youzbeki, Apr. 1, 1984; children: Muhammed, Mays, Yusr, Rand. BSc in Pharmacy, Coll. Pharmacy, Baghdad, Iraq, 1981. Rsch. pharmacist Sci. Rsch. Coun., Baghdad, 1982-92; office mgr. Julphar Pharma Industries, Ras Al-Khaima, United Arab Emirates, 1993-97; area mgr. Pharmadule, Nacka, Sweden, 1997—; market rschr. Julphar Pharma Industries, Ras Al-Khaima, United Arab Emirates. Contbr. articles to profl. jours., including Cancer Letters, Jour. EthnoPharmacology, Neurosci. Capt. Med. Svc., Iraqi Army, 1982. Avocations: music, sports. Home: Nakheel Ras Al-Khaima, Abu Dhabi United Arab Emirates Office: Julphar Pharma Industries, PO Box 997, Ras Al-Khaima United Arab Emirates

ISNARD, PASCAL GEORGES MICHEL, pharmaceutical executive, researcher; b. Tours, France, Feb. 27, 1957; s. Hubert Isnard and Suzanne Mercier; m. Yvette Morin, Sept. 18, 1996; children: Florence, Christophe. Diploma in engring., Inst. Chimie et Phys. Indsl., Lyon, France, 1979; PhD, U. Lyon, 1984. Rschr. Rhone-Poulenc, Lyon, 1985-93, head waste treatment lab., 1993-96, head ecotoxicology lab., 1996-98, sci. adviser environ. affairs, 1998—; mem. sci. com. Pnetox, Paris, 1994—, Rhone Méditerranée-Corse Water Agy., Lyon, 1999—. Author: Chemical Exposure Predictions, 1992; contbr. articles to profl. jours. Mem. Setac, Secotox. Avocation: mountaineering. Home: Grande Rue, 01600 Miserieux France Office: Aventis Pharma, 9 quai Jules Guesde, 94400 Vitry sur Seine France

ISOBE, SYUZO, astronomer, educator; b. Osaka, Japan, July 16, 1942; s. Matsujiro and Toyoko Isobe; m. Nagako Miyauchi, Aug. 21, 1946; 1 child, Kotoha. BD, U. Tokyo, 1965, MD, 1967, PhD, 1971. Asst. U. Tokyo, 1968-88; asst. prof. astronomy Nat. Astronomy Observatory, Tokyo, Japan, 1988—. Author Diffuse Nebulae, 1982, Observatories in the World, 1983, Toward the Edge of the Universe, 1988, Mechanism of Our Universe, 1993. Pres. Japan Spaceguard Assn., Tokyo, 1999—. Mem. Astron. Soc. Japan. Avocations: baseball, skiing. Home: 2 48 14 Hagoromo, Tachikawa Tokyo 190, Japan Office: Nat Astron Observatory, 2 21 1 Osawa, Mitaka Tokyo 181, Japan

ISOGAI, YUKIHIDE, physician, hematologist, diabetologist, educator, clinical hemorheology researcher; b. Tokyo, July 30, 1929; s. Masaaki and Tokuyo Isogai; m. Hisa Furuta, Nov. 3, 1955; children: Masahiro, Kumiko, Junko. MD, Jikei U., Tokyo, 1954, PhD, 1960. Intern The 2nd Tokyo (Japan) Nat. Hosp., 1955; rsch. resident in hematology and hemorheology Jikei U. Sch. Medicine, Tokyo, 1960-67, lectr. in medicine, 1967-76, assoc. prof., 1976-83, prof. medicine, 1983-95; physician Clinic for Hematology and Diabetology, Jikei U. Hosp., Tokyo, 1955-95; coun. mem. Kyoritsu Coll. of Pharmacy, 1993—; guest prof. Jikei U. Sch. Medicine, 1995—, vis. prof. Kyoritsu Coll. of Pharmacy, 1995-2000; cons. Kinugasa Gen. Hosp., Yokosuka, 1995—, Shimizu Corp., Health Mgmt., Tokyo, 1995—; rsch. advisor Mitsubishi Chem. Corp., Tokyo, 1995-97. Editor: Clinical Hemorheology, 1981—; hon. editor: Biorheology (Japan), 1987—. Med. Rsch. grantee Sankyo Found. Life Sci., Tokyo, 1984-85, Chiyoda Mutual Life Found., Tokyo, 1993. Mem. Internat. Soc. Biorheology (chmn. 1992, pres. 1992-95, past pres. 1995-99), World Soc. Biomechanics (coun. mem. 1990-98), European Soc. Microcirculation, Japanese Soc. Internal Medicine (coun. mem. 1984-95), Japanese Soc. Hematology (mem. of merits), Japanese Soc. Angiology (mem. of merits), Japanese Soc. Thrombosis and Hemostasis (coun. mem. 1991-95), Japanese Soc. Biorheology (coun. mem.), Japanese Soc. Microcirculation (coun. mem.), Japanese Soc. Diabetes (mem. of merits), Portugal Soc. Hemorheology (hon.), N.Y. Acad. Sci. Avocations: photography, swimming, golf, travel. Home: 19-12 Kugahara 1 Chome, Ohta-Ku Tokyo 146-0085, Japan Office: Liaison Office Internat Soc Biotheology in Japan, 19-12 Kugahara 1 chome Ohta-ku, Tokyo 146-0085, Japan

ISOLANI, PAULO CELSO, chemistry educator, researcher; b. São Paulo, Brazil, Oct. 9, 1947; s. Vitorio and Serafina (Rupolo) I.; m. Maria da Graça Boggi, Dec. 21, 1985. BSc in Chemistry, U. São Paulo, 1970, PhD in Phys. Chemistry, 1974, Habilitation, 1987. Tchng. aux. U. São Paulo, 1973-74, asst. prof., 1974-87, assoc. prof., 1987—; nat. rep. phys. chemistry IUPAC, Geneva, 1994-96. Assoc. editor Anais da ABQ Jour., 1994—. Mem. Associação Brasileira de Quimica (dir. internat. affairs 1994-2001), Acad. Sci. State São Paulo. Avocations: mechanical shop work, electronics. Office: U São Paulo Inst Quimica, Caixa Postal 26077, 05513970 São Paulo Brazil

ISON, MIRTA SUSANA, psychologist, researcher; b. Mendoza, Argentina, May 9, 1964; d. Osvaldo Manuel Ison and Nélida Noemí Ison Zintilini. Lic. in psychology, U. Aconcagua, Mendoza, 1988; M, Phd, U. Nat. San Luis, Argentina, 1995. Rschr. Consejo Nat. de Investigaciones Centifices, Tecnicas, Argentina, 1990-96, 97—; tchr. U. Nat. San Luis, 1997—; tchr. U. del Aconcagua, 1989—. Contbr. articles to jours. in field. Mem. APA, Assn. Argentina Ciencios del Comportamiento. Avocations: music, cinema, volleyball. Office: INCIHUSA/CRICYT, Ave Adrion Ruiz Leal, 5500 Mendoza Argentina

ISOPESCU-CIOBANU, LAURA, internist, pneumologist; b. Jassy (Iasi), Romania, May 5, 1966; d. Dimitrie A. and Silvia (Sarghie) Isopescu; m. Adrian P. Ciobanu, Oct. 15, 1988. MD, U. Grigore T. Popa, Iasi, Romania, 1990; PhD, U. Medicine and Pharmacy "Grigore T. Popa", 1999. Asst. prof. U. Popa Gr.T., Iasi, Romania, 1994-2000; internist Rehab. Hosp., Iasi, 1995-2000; med. cons. Coca-Cola Co., Iasi, 1995-99; cons. gen. ultrasonography, Iasi, 2000. Avocations: opera, classical music, dancing, poetry, Oriental culture. Home: Anastasie Panu Nr 52 H2/7/3, 6600 Iasi Romania Office: Rehab Hosp, P.Halipa Nr 14, Iasi 6600, Romania

ISOUN, TURNER TIMIMIPRE, animal pathologist, veterinarian, consultant; b. Odi, Yenagoa, Nigeria, Sept. 2, 1938; s. Mark Ebidi and Dali Fekiseimo (Amgbapu) I.; m. Miriam Jean Forbes, Sept. 13, 1964; children: Diseye T., Ebitari Ellen, Tariye Louise. BSc, Mich. State U., 1963, DVM, 1965, PhD, 1970; DSc, Rivers State U. Sci. & Tech., Port Hascourt, Nigeria, 1991. Lic. veterinarian. Prof. veterinarian pathology U. Ibadan, Nigeria, 1968-79; spl. advisor on sci., tech. Rivers State Govt., Nigeria, 1979-80; vice chancellor Rivers State U. Sci. & Tech., Port Harcourt, Nigeria, 1980-84; editor African Acad. Scis., Nairobi, Kenya, 1989-96; chmn., trustee, dir. Niger Delta Wetlands Ctr., Port Harcourt, Nigeria; vis. scientist MIT, Cambridge, 1976, Bernard Nocht Inst. of Tropical Medicine, Hamburg, Germany, 1979; cons. Rivers State Govt., Port Harcourt, Nigeria, 1980-83, The World Bank, Nigeria, 1994, Fed. Environ. Protection Agy., Nigeria, 1996-97; advisor Bayelsa State Govt., Nigeria, 1996—. Author: Evolutions of Science & Technology in Nigeria, 1987; editor: Mobilization of African Scientific Talent for Development, 1988; editor (jour.) Discovery and Innovation: Quar. Editls., 1989-95; contbr. numerous articles, procs. to profl. jours.; reviewer in field. Gubernatorial candidate Rivers State, Nigeria, 1985; advisor So. Minorities Movement, Nigeria, 1993-97, Nigerian Nat. Congress, 1993—; mem. Corps of Mediators, Nigeria, 1997—. Recipient disting. faculty award and citation U. Ibadan, Nigeria, 1983. Fellow African Acad. Scis. (treas. 1996-98); mem. Internat. Union of Concerned Survivors, Nat. Corps of Mediators (Nigerian chpt.). Home: Plot 100 GRA, 16 Elelenwo and Amaji Sts, Port Harcourt Nigeria Office: PO Box 7390, Port Harcourt Nigeria

ISOYAMA, SHOGEN, medical researcher; b. Ibaraki Prefecture, Japan, July 16, 1947; s. Shoichi and Eiko (Kashimura) I.; m. Yoko Nakamura, Oct. 10, 1985; children: Kai, Sho, Sei. BS, Tohoku U., Sendai, Japan, 1968, MD, 1972, PhD, 1980. Med. intern Tohoku U. Hosp., 1972-73, resident in medicine, 1973-74; rsch. fellow Harvard U. Med. Sch. and Beth Israel Hosp., Boston, 1984-87; asst. prof. internal medicine Tohoku U. Sch. Medicine, 1979-90, assoc. prof., 1990—; prof. medicine Tohoku Bunka Gakuen U., Sendai, Japan; vis. prof. China Med. Sch., Sjenyan, China, 1991. Author: Diastolic Relaxation of the Heart, 1994, Recent Advances in Aging Science, 1994. Recipient Cardiovasc. Rsch. awards Am. Heart Assn., Boston, 1985, 86; grantee Ministry of Edn., Sci. and Culture, Tokyo, 1988-94. Buddhist. Avocations: fishing, playing baseball. Fax: 81-22-233-6299. Home: 2-24 Akaishidai 4-chome, Tomiya-machi Kurokawa-gun, Miyagi 981-3332, Japan Office: Tohuka Bunka Gakuen U, 45-16 Kunimi 6-chome, Aoba-ku Sendai 981-8550, Japan

ISPANY, MARTON, mathematician, educator; b. Miskolc, Hungary, July 23, 1966; s. Marton and Maria (Lantos) I. MSc, Kossuth Lajos U., Debrecen, Hungary, 1989, PhD, 1997. Rsch. asst. Computer Ctr. of Kossuth Lajos U., Debrecen, 1989-91; lectr. Inst. Math. and Informatics, KLTE, Debrecen, 1991-96, asst. prof., 1996—. Farkas grantee BJMT, Hungary, 1999. Avocations: basketball, reading, music, skiing. E-mail: ispany@math.klte.hu. Office: Inst Math and Info, Kossuth Lajos/Egyetem ter 1, Debrecen Hungary 4010

ISQUITH, FRED TAYLOR, lawyer; b. N.Y.C., June 6, 1947; s. Stanley and Rita (Hoskwith) I.; m. Susan Nora Goldberg, May 23, 1976; children: Fred, Rebecca. BA, CUNY, 1968; JD, Columbia U., 1971. Bar: N.Y. 1972, D.C. 1976, U.S. Dist. Ct. (so. and ea. dists.) N.Y. 1975, U.S. Dist. Ct. (no. dist.) N.Y. 1988, U.S. Dist. Ct. (we. dist.) Mich. 1992, U.S. Dist. Ct. Ariz. 1994, U.S. Dist. Ct. (ctrl. dist.) Ill. 1996, U.S. Ct. Appeals (2d cir.) 1975, U.S. Ct. Appeals (8th cir.) 1985, U.S. Ct. Appeals (3d cir.) 1986, U.S. Ct. Appeals (4th cir.) 1990, U.S. Supreme Ct. 1983, U.S. Dist. Ct. Colo. 1999, U.S. Dist. Ct. Nebr. 2000, U.S. Ct. Appeals (1st cir.) 2000. Assoc. Fulbright & Jaworski, N.Y.C., 1971-75, Kaye Scholer et al, N.Y.C., 1975-80; ptnr. Wolf Haldenstein Adler Freeman & Herz, N.Y.C., 1980—; zd. trustees St. Chad's Coll. Found.; bd. dirs. 103 East 84th St. Corp., N.Y.C., Sheinkopf Comm., Ltd.; lectr. Am. Conf. Inst., N.Y. State Bar Assn.; mediator Supreme Ct. State N.Y. County N.Y. Comml. Divsn.; arbitrator Am. Arbitration Assn.; lectr. in field. Author: An Introduction to Securities Arbitration, 1994, Real Estate Exit Strategies, 1994, Fundamental Strategies in Securities Litigation, 2000, Federal Civil Practice, 2000; editor, weekly columnist The Class Act. Mem. ABA (mem. internet com. anti-trust law sect.), N.Y. State Bar Assn. (coms. on securities and legis., arbitrator securities industry disputes sect.), N.Y. County Lawyers Assn. (chmn. bus. torts), D.C. Bar Assn., Assn. of Bar of City of N.Y. (Fed. Cts. com.), Bklyn. Bar Assn. (civil practice law and rules com., legis. com. and fed. cts. com.), Columbia Club. Office: Wolf Haldenstein Adler Freeman & Herz 270 Madison Ave New York NY 10016-0601

ISRAEL, EDMOND SYLVAIN, banker; b. Luxembourg, May 5, 1924; s. Gustave and Erna (Lande) I.; m. Renée Israel Rudowski, March 17, 1999. Dr. Honoris Causa, U. Fribourg, Sacred Heart U. With Banque Internat. à Luxembourg, 1946-88, dir. gen., dir. gen., hon. gen. dir., 1989-96; chmn. bd. dirs. Cedel, 1970-90, hon. chmn., 1990; vice-chmn. Asia-Europe Found., 1998, chmn. bd. govs., 1999; hon. chmn. Luxembourg Stock Exch., 1996, hon. chmn. bd. dirs. BNP Luxembourg and Soc. Européenne de Banque. Contbr. banking articles to profl. pubs. and spoken at confs. Decorated comdr. Ordre Couronne de Chene, officer Order Civil Mil. Adolphe Nassau, comdr. Ordre Nat. du Mérite, comdr. Order of Brit. Empire, comdr. Ordre de Léopold, comdr. Ordre Nat. Mérite Rep. Française, Grosses Verdienstkreuz des Verdienstordens der Budesrepublik Deutschland. Mem. Brit. C. of C. Luxembourg (hon. chmn.). Lodge: Lions. Avocations: theoretical physics, philosophy, music. Office: Clearstream Internat, 3-5 Place Winston Churchill, L 2964 Luxembourg Luxembourg

ISRAEL, LUCIEN ISIDORE, oncologist, educator; b. Apr. 14, 1926; s. Jacques and Alice Allegra Israel; m. Germaine Bach, Jan. 31, 1949; children: Daniele, Dominique, Guillaume. MD, U. Paris, 1956. Chief clinic U. Paris

Med. Sch., 1957-62, mem. faculty, 1963—, prof. medicine, 1973-95, emeritus prof. oncology, 1995—; chief oncology svc. Univ. Hosp. Lariboisere, 1971-76, Univ. Hosp. Avicenne, 1976-95; ret.; mem. French-Am. Cancer Agreement Com., 1976-92; dir. Inst. d'Oncologie Cellulaire et Moleculaire Humaine, U. Paris, 1986-95; mem. Conseil Nat. de l'Enseignement Supèrieur de la Recherche, 1994-96. 1st lt. French Army, 1951-52. Recipient Jean Dagnan Bouveret prize French Acad. Scis., 1974; grantee U.S. Nat. Cancer Inst., 1976-78. Mem. Inst. France, Internat. Assn. Study Lung Cancer, European Orgn. Study Treatment Cancer, French Soc. Respiratory Diseases, Am. Assn. Cancer Rsch., Am. Soc. Clin. Oncology, Acad. Nat. Scis. Morales et Politiques. Home: 36 Mont Thabor, 75001 Paris France

ISRAEL, MICHEL ALBERT, computer science educator; b. Paris, Sept. 9, 1947; s. Simantov and Sarah (Chaul) I.; m. Nicole Blot, Mar. 22, 1972; 1 child, Yael. PhD, Marie Curie U., Paris, 1987. Prof. CNAM-IIE, Paris, 1973-91, Evry (France) U., 1991—; dean Evry (France) U. Coll. Fundamentals and Applied Scis., 1998; chmn. computer sci. lab. Evry U. Coll. Fundamentals and Applied Scis., 1998; chmn. dept. math. and computer sci., Evry U., 1991-97. Mem. IEEE-Computer Sci. (sr., chair design automation tech. com. 1994—, sec., bd. govs. 1997, treas. 1998-99, v.p. tech. activities 2000, Outstanding award 1990). Office: Evry U, Cours Monseigneur Romero, 91025 Evry France

ISRAELI, RAPHAEL, Asian studies educator; b. Fes, Morocco, Sept. 15, 1935; s. David and Ruhama (Amazig) I.; m. Margalit Fyrbjork; children: Shlomit, Avi, David. BA, Hebrew U., Israel, 1963; MA, U. Calif., Berkeley, 1970, PhD, 1974. Commd. Israel Def. Forces, 1953, advanced through grades to maj., 1964; ret., 1974; prof. Hebrew U., Jerusalem, Israel, 1974—; vis. prof. Pitts. U., 1981, York U., Toronto, 1983-84; vis. scholar Harvard U., Boston, 1984-85, Australian nat. U., Canberra, 1996, Naruto U., Japan, 1997, Ghent (Belgium) U., 1997. Author, editor books; contbr. 80 articles to profl. jours. Fellow Truman Inst. (sr.). Jewish. Home: Bialik 4, Jerusalem Israel Office: Hebrew U Truman Inst, Mt Scopus, Jerusalem 91505, Israel

ISRAELIT, MARK, general relativity and cosmology physics educator; b. Klaipeda-Memel, Lithuania, Feb. 29, 1928; arrived in Israel, 1971; s. Shlomo and Esther (Szereszewsky) I.; m. Mila Modilevsky, Apr. 29, 1956; children: Diana, Shlomo. MSc in Physics, Latvian State U., Riga, 1952; DSc in Physics, Technion, Haifa, Israel, 1975. Lectr., sr. lectr. Moscow Polygraphic Inst.-Latvian Br., Riga, 1961-71; lectr. dept. physics Technion, Haifa, 1971-75; lectr. dept. physics and math. U. Haifa, 1976-81, sr. lectr. dept. physics and math., 1981-96, emeritus, 1997—; vis. prof. dept. physics U. Konstanz, Germany, 1985-86, 92-93, 96; vis. prof. Inst. Theoretical Physics, U. Goettingen, Germany, 1986; vis. prof. physics and astronomy U. Victoria, B.C., Can., 1993; lectr. in field. Referee Math. Revs., 1983-88, The Basic Rsch. Found., 1989—, Gen. Relativity and Gravitation, 1989—, Founds. of Physics, 1990—, The Astrophys. Jour., 1990—, Astrophysics and Space Sci., 1992—; author: (monograph) The Weyl-Dirac Theory and our Universe, 1999; contbr. over 60 articles to profl. jours. Office: Dept Physics, U Haifa Oranim, 36006 Tivon Israel

ISRAIL, MICHAELA ANCA, physician; b. Bucharest, Romania; d. Mihail Dumitru and Adriana Maria (Palade) I. MD, Sch. Medicine, Bucharest, Romania, 1964; D in Med. Scis., Sch. Medicine, 1976. Teaching asst. Sch. Medicine, Dept. Microbiology, Bucharest, Romania, 1964-78; microbiologist Cantacuzino Inst., Bucharest, Romania, 1978-80, sr. microbiologist, 1980—, head cholera dept., 1996—. Contbr. articles to profl. jours. Humboldt Found. fellow, Bonn, 1973-74, 78, 91-92. Mem. Humboldt Club. Avocations: classical music, arts, history, philosophy. Office: Inst Cantacuzino, Bd Splaiul Independente 103, 70100 Bucharest Romania

ISSHIKI, MASAYUKI, sociologist; b. Suzuka, Japan, Oct. 21, 1950; s. Mikio Isshiki and Michiko Isshiki-Fujii; m. Miwa Terada, Dec. 28, 1988. BA in Sociology, Sussex Coll., 1980, D in Sociology, 1986. V.p. Sanas Corp., Yokkaichi, Japan, 1980-83; rsch. scientist Triad PCL, Hong Kong, 1986-91; ptnr. Triad Cons., Suzuka, Japan, 1991-93; prof. Suzuka Internat. U., 1994—. Author: Economic Development in Southeast Asia, 1991, Development of Bamboo, 1992, U.S. Watch, 1995—. Avocations: skiing, farming. Home and Office: Rm C-101, 15-11-C-101 Minami-Ejima, Suzuka Mie 510-0235, Japan

ISSING, OTMAR, banking executive, economist; b. Wuerzburg, Germany, Mar. 27, 1936; s. Hans and Josefine (Käfer) I.; m. Sieglinde Böhm; children: Peter, Frank. Diploma, U. Wuerzburg, 1960, Dr. rer. pol., 1961, habilitation, 1965. Lectr. U. Wuerzburg, 1965-67; prof. U. Erlangen-Nuremberg, Fed. Republic Germany, 1967-73, U. Wuerzburg, 1973-90; mem. directorate Fed. Republic Germany, Deutsche Bundesbank, 1990-98; mem. exec. bd. European Ctrl. Bank, 1998—; coun. econ. experts, Fed. Republic Germany, 1988-90. Author: Introduction to Monetary Theory, 11th edit., 1998, Introduction to Monetary Policy, 6th edit., 1996; co-editor: Wist Jour., 1972-90. Mem. Am. Econ. Assn., Verein fur Socialpolitik, List Gesellschaft, Acad. Scis. and Lit. Roman Catholic.

ISTOCK, VERNE GEORGE, banker; b. Sept. 20, 1940. BA in Econs., U. Mich., 1962, MBA in Fin., 1963. Credit analyst trainee NBD Bancorp, Inc., Detroit, 1963-71, group head, 1971-77, head U.S. divsn., 1977-82, sr. v.p., 1979-82, exec. v.p., 1982-85, vice chmn., dir., 1985-93, chmn., CEO, 1994-95, also bd. dirs.; chmn. NBD Bank; pres., CEO First Chgo. NBD Corp., Chgo., 1995-98, chmn., 1996-98; chmn. bd. Bank One Corp., Chgo., 1998-2000, pres., 2000—; bd. dirs. Kelly Svcs. Inc.; former dir. Internat. Monetary Conf., Masco Corp., Detroit Renaissance, Fed. Res. Bd. Chgo. Dir. Chgo. Coun. on Fgn. Rels. Mem. U. Mich. Alumni Assn. (past pres., lifetime dir.), Bankers Roundtable (past dir.), Econ. Club Chgo., Mich. Bus. Roundtable, Comml. Club of Chgo., Econ. Club Detroit (bd. dirs.), Ill. Bus. Roundtable (bd. dirs.). Office: Bank One Corp 1 Bank One Plz Chicago IL 60670-0001

ISUPOV, VLADISLAV ALEKSANDROVICH, physicist, researcher; b. Nolinsk, USSR, July 20, 1927; s. Aleksandr Ivanovich and Anna Dmitrievna (Kuznetsova) I.; m. Evgeniya Nikolaevna Nikitina, Dec. 17, 1957; children: Marina Vladislavovna, Nataliya Vladislavovna. Engr., Poly. Inst., St. Petersburg, Russia, 1952; M of Phys.-Math. Scis., Russian Acad. Scis., St. Petersburg, 1960, D of Phys.-Math. Scis., 1970, cert. prof., 1993. Jr. scientist Inst. Semiconductors-Russian Acad. Scis., St. Petersburg, 1957-66, sr. scientist, 1966-70; sr. scientist A.F. Ioffe Phys-Tech. Inst.-Russian Acad. Scis., St. Petersburg, 1971-85; leading scientist A.F. Ioffe Phys.-Tech. Inst.-Russian Acad. Scis., St. Petersburg, 1985—. Co-author: Ferroelectrics and Antiferroelectrics, 1971, Ferroelectrics and Related Materials, 1983, Physics of Ferroelectric Phemomena, 1985; contbr. over 280 articles to profl. jours.; inventor in field. Recipient State prize in chemistry USSR Com., Moscow, 1975. Avocation: gardening. Home: ul Bela Kun 23-161, 192236 Saint Petersburg Russia Office: AF Ioffe Phys Tech Inst RAS, Polytekhnicheskaya 26, 194021 Saint Petersburg Russia

ITAKETO, UMANA THOMPSON, systems and control engineer; b. Edem Aya, Ikot Abasi Akwa Ibom State, Nigeria, Oct. 30, 1969; s. Thompson Itaketo Umana and Dina Thompson Itaketo; m. Ima Umana Essiet, Dec. 26, 1995. Diploma with distinction, Petroleum Tng. Inst., Warri, Nigeria, 1979; B Engring. with honors, U. Tech., Enugu, Nigeria, 1985; M Engring., U. Nigeria, Nsukka, Nigeria, 1989; PhD, Fed. U. Tech., Owerri, Nigeria, 1999. Indsl. attachee Nigerian Agip Oil Co., Pt. Harcourt, Nigeria, 1978, Mobil Oil Co., Eket, Nigeria, 1983; univ. lectr. U. Nigeria, Nsukka, 1986-89; instrumentation engr. Mobil Oil Co., Eket, 1987—; instrumentation engr., cons. and rsch. engr., Eket, 1991—. Author: The Design and Implementation of Interface Level Controller, 1985, Investigation into Various Controller Types/Tuning Methods for Improved Systems Response, 1988, State-Space/Matrix System Approaches in the Analysis and Control of Time Delays in Control Loops, 1995 (Coren Regd. 1992), The Development of Optimal Control Strategy for the Control of Non-Linear Systems Under Dynamic States, 1998, The Development of Performance Criterion for Optimal Control Studies on Non-Linear Systems, 1998, The Method of Isoclines In Determining the Stability of Non-Linear Systems Under Dynamic States, 1999, Application of Lyapunov's Second Method in the Stability Analysis of Oil/Gas Separation Process, 1998, Application of Isocline Plots of Non-Linear Systems for Aircraft Stability Under Dynamic States, 1999, The Stability of Non-Linear Systems Under Dynamic States, 1999, The Control of 2nd Order Non-linear Systems by a Proportional-plus-Integral-plus Derivative (PID) Controller, 1999, The Design and Installation of a Dissipation Array System for Lightning Prevention, 1999; contbr. articles to profl. jours. Active Nat. Youth Svc. Corp., 1985-86. Acad. scholar Cross River State Govt., 1980, Mobil Producing Nigeria, 1980, Fed. Govt. Nigeria, 1986, award Nigerian U. Engring. Students Assn., 2000. Mem. IEEE, Instrument Soc. Am., Internat. Fedn. Automatic Control, Nigerian Soc. Engrs., Coun. Registered Engrs. Nigeria (registered profl. engr.). Methodist. Avocations: football, playing chess, high jump athlete, artist, sprinter. Office: Mobil Prod Nigeria Qua Iboe Terminal 3225 Gallows Rd Fairfax VA 22037-0002

ITAMI, YOSHIHIKO, communications executive; b. Tokyo, Nov. 26, 1925; s. Shintaro and Nami (Ariga) I.; m. Reiko maeda Itami, Jan. 29, 1950; children: Janie, Marie. BA, Keio U., Tokyo, 1950. With Mitsui & Co., Ltd., 1950—; bd. Mitsui & Co. Ltd., Tokyo, 1981-85; exec. v.p. Japan Comms. Satellite Co., 1985-91, chmn., 1991-93; pres., CEO Japan Bus. TV, Inc., Tokyo, 1993-97; outside bd. mem. Mall of TV, Inc., Tokyo, 2000—. Home: 4-4-14 Minami Azabu, Minato-ku, Tokyo 106-0047, Japan

ITHAKISSIOS, DIONYSSIS S., pharmaceutical educator; b. Zante, Greece, 1941; m. Xanthi Papaeliou; children: Fotini, Eliana, Constantina. BSc in Pharmacy, U. Athens, Greece, 1965, PhD in Medicinal Chemistry, 1969; PhD in Bionucleonics, Purdue U., 1973. Fellow Greek Atomic Energy Commn., Athens, 1967-69, Purdue Rsch. Found., Lafayette, Ind., 1971-73; sr. radiochemist Nuclear Med. Lab., Minn. Mining and Mfg. Co., 1973-78; fellow French Atomic Energy Comm., 1980-81; radiopharmacist isotope dept., 1968-71; head radioimmunochem. lab., 1981-82; dir. Radioisotopes and Radiodiagnostic Products Inst., 1989-95; prof. pharm. tech. and radiopharmacy U. Patras (Greece) Sch. Pharmacy, 1983—; dir. Radioisotopes and Radiodiagnostic Products Inst.; bd. mem. Nat. Ctr. Sci. Rsch. Demokritos, 1989-95; chmn. bd., dir. Nat. Ctr. for Sci. Rsch. Demokritos, Athens, 1996—. Author 2 textbooks; contbr. over 160 articles and abstracts to internat. sci. jours. Fellow French Atomic Energy Comm., 1980-81; recipient Disting. Alumnus Awd., Purdue Univ. Ind. Sch. Health Scis., 1999. Mem. AAAS, Soc. Nuclear Medicine, European Nuclear Medicine Soc., Am. Assn. for Clin. Chemistry, Clin. Ligand Assay Soc., European Ligand Assay Soc., Internat. Pharm. Fedn., N.Y. Acad. Scis., Sigma Xi (hon.), Rho Chi, Phi Lambda Upsilon. Achievements include basic and applied research for development of new diagnostic and therapeutic radio medication, new diagnostic technologies and methods for substance measurements in biological samples; evaluation of the importance, relationship and diagnostic value of biological indices in diseases; dosage form design (polymers, nonparticles, microspheres and liposones? for delivery or targeting of drugs; radiopharmaceuticals for several applications; pharmakinetics. Office: U Patras, Pharm Tech Lab, 26110 Patras Greece

ITINA, TATIANA EUGENIEVNA, physicist, researcher; b. Ivanova, Russia, Apr. 23, 1971; arrived in France, 1996.; d Evgeny Alexandrovich and Tamara Semenovna (Barass) Govorykha; m. Sergvei Pavlovich Itin, Aug. 07, 1993 (div. Aug. 1997). MS, Inst. of Phyics and Tech., Moscow, 1994; PhD, ESM2 Marseille U., France, 1999. Rsch. asst. Rus. Acad. Scis., Moscow, 1992-93; rschr. Radon, Moscow, 1993; rsch. asst. TSNiimash, Korlev, Russia, 1993-98. Contbr. articles profl. jours. Grantee French Minstry Foreign Affairs, 1996-99. Mem. N.Y. Acad. Sci. Avocations: reading, table tennis, swimming. Office: irphe-lp3, 163 Ave de Luminy Case 918, 13288 Marseille France

ITKES, ALEXANDER VENIAMINE, biology educator, researcher; b. Kiev, USSR, July 22, 1952; s. Veniamine Mikhail and Klaudia Nikolai (Vorobyova) I.; m. Vera Leonidovna Tunitskaya, Aug. 22, 1980; 1 child, Alexander. Grad. in biology, Moscow State U., 1978; PhD, Inst. Molecular Biology, Moscow, 1981, DSc in Biology, 1990. Rschr. Inst. Molecular Biology, 1981-91, prin. rschr., 1991-97; prof. biology Moscow State U., 1993—; head dept. biology and genetics Med. Sch. People's Friendship U., Moscow, 1997—. Home: Volgin St 31 Bldg 3 Apt 205, 117437 Moscow Russia Office: Med Sch RPFU, Miklukho-Maklay St 8, 117198 Moscow Russia

ITO, KOICHI, engineering educator, antenna researcher; b. Nagoya, Aichi, Japan, June 4, 1950; s. Shigeharu and Sakae (Kano) I.; m. Setsu Tomita, Jan. 21, 1974; children: Hiroshi, Eiji. BS, Chiba (Japan) U., 1974, MS, 1976; D Engring., Tokyo Inst. Tech., 1985. Rsch. assoc. Tokyo Inst. Tech., 1976-79; rsch. assoc. Chiba U., 1979-89, assoc. prof. elec. engring., 1989-97, prof., 1997—; vis. prof. U. Rennes, France, 1989, 94, 98. Author: Handbook of Microstrip Antennas, 1989; contbr. articles to profl. publs.; patentee in field. Mem. AAAS, IEEE, Inst. Electroics, Info. and Comm. Engrs. (chmn. bio-electromagnetic phantoms tech. group), Inst. TV Engrs. Japan (chmn. radio and optical tech. group), Japanese Soc. Hyperthermic Oncology. Avocations: driving, travel. Home: Hanamigawa-ku, 2-19-401 Asahigaoka, Chiba 262-0017, Japan Office: Chiba U Dept Elec Engring, 1-33 Yayoi Inage, Chiba 263-8522, Japan

ITO, MASAO, physiologist; b. Nagoya, Aichi, Japan, Dec. 4, 1928; s. Rikuo and Chiyo (Inagaki) I.; m. Midori Watanabe, May 29, 1931; children: Minami, Yukari. MD, U. Tokyo Med. Sch., 1953, DMS, 1959. Asst. prof. med. faculty Kumamoto (Japan) U., 1954-57; asst. prof. med. faculty U. Tokyo, 1958-62, assoc. prof. med. faculty, 1963-70, prof. med. faculty, 1970-86, dean med. faculty, 1986-88; dir. gen. Frontier Rsch. Sys. Inst. Phys. and Chem. Rsch., Wako, Japan, 1991—; dir. RIKEN Brain Sci. Inst., Wako, Japan, 1997—; emeritus prof. U. Tokyo, 1989—. Co-author: (book) The Cerebellum as a Neuronal Machine, 1967; author: The Cerebellum and Neural Control, 1984-2000; editor-in-chief Neuroscience Rsch. Decorated chevalier Legion d'Honneur (France), Order of Culture (Japan); recipient Fujiwara Found. prize, 1981, Imperial prize Japan Acad., 1986, Neural Plasticity prize IPSEN Found., 1993, Person of Cultural Merit award Japanese Govt., 1996, Japan prize The Sci. and Tech. Found. of Japan, 1996. Mem. Royal Swedish Acad. Scis., Royal Soc. London, Russian Acad. Scis., French Acad. Scis., Armenian Acad. Scis., Japan Acad., French Acad. Scis., Internat. Brain Rsch. Orgn. (pres. 1980-86), Internat. Union Physiol. Scis. (pres. 1993-97), Sci. Coun. Japan (pres. 1994-97). Avocations: travel, book reading. Office: Brain Sci Inst, RIKEN Wako, Saitama 351-0198, Japan

ITO, MITSUO, science administrator, molecular spectroscopist; b. Kitakyushu, Fukuoka, Japan, Mar. 24, 1929; s. Nobuo and Shizuko (Matsui) I.; m. Tamiko Iwata, Nov. 10, 1958. BS, Kyushu U., Fukuoka, Japan, 1951, PhD, 1960. Rsch. assoc. Kyushu U., Fukuoka, 1951-64; assoc. prof. Tokyo U., 1965-69; prof. Tohoku U., Sendai, Japan, 1970-92; dir. gen. Inst. Molecular Sci., Okazaki, Japan, 1993-99; pres. Okazaki (Japan) Nat. Rsch. Inst., 1999—. Decorated Purple ribbon with medal of honour, Japan, 1997; recipient awards Chem. Soc. Japan, Tokyo. 1988, Spectroscopic Soc. Japan, Tokyo, 1989. Avocations: oil painting, sketching. Office: Okazaki Nat Rsch Inst, Myodaiji, Okazaki Aichi 444-8585, Japan

ITO, NOBORU, electric power industry executive; b. Qindao, Santon, China, Dec. 17, 1921; s. Eisho and Raiko (Watanabe) I.; m. Sachiko Tsuchiya (dec. Nov. 1978); children: Junko, Kyoko. B degree, Tohoku U., Sendai, 1946, D degree, 1973. Engr. Toyo Comm. Co., Kawasaki, 1946-50, Oi Electric Co., Tokyo, 1950-57; chief rschr. Oi Electric Co., Yokohama, 1964-69, dir., 1970-83, cons., 1984-91; pres. Leo-B Corp., Yokohama, 1992—; scientist Tokyo U., 1960-63, 89-91; lectr. Yamagata U., 1982-83; scientist U. So. Calif., L.A., 1985-86. Recipient invention prize Japan Inst. Invention, 1982, dir. prize Sci. and Tech. Agy. of Japan, 1982, yellow ribbon prize Japan Govt., 1984. Mem. IEEE (sr.), N.Y. Acad. Scis., Japan Phys. Soc., Japan Merits Club. Avocations: learning foreign languages, car trips. Office: Leo-B Corp, R1012 6-13-53 Kikuna, Kohokuku Yokohama 222, Japan

ITO, SADAMOTO, American literature educator; b. Kobe, Japan, Nov. 8, 1935; s. Mamoru and Shizue (Hirano) I.; m. Hiroko Yoshida, Nov. 11, 1969; children: Satoko, Takayuki, Kaori, Tetsuya. BA, Kyoto (Japan) U., 1960, MA, 1964. Asst. U. Osaka (Japan) Prefecture, 1964-67, asst. prof., 1968-72, assoc. prof., 1973-84; prof. Nara (Japan) Women's U., 1985-99, Baika Women's Coll., Ibaraki, Japan, 1999—; vis. fellow Princeton U., 1978-79. Co-author: (books) A New Development in American Literature: Novelists, 1983, An Introduction to American Literature, 1987, A History of American Literature, 1989, The River in American Literature, 1992. Mem. The Am. Lit. Soc. Japan (bd. reps. 1995—, editor Studies in Am. Lit. 1987-94), The Kansai Am. Lit. Soc. (editor Kansai Am. Literature 1985-87, exec. mgr. 1989-91, councilor 1989—, v.p. 1995-97, pres. 1997—), The English Literary Soc. of Japan (councilor 1993-96), The Japanese Assn. for Am. Studies. Avocations: music, tennis, theatre, travel. Home: 6-4-5 Suzurandai, Nishimachi, Kita Ku, Kobe 651-1114, Japan Office: Baika Womens Coll, 2-19-5 Shukunosho, Ibaraki 567-8578, Japan

ITO, TETSUO, electrician, researcher; b. Hitachi, Ibaraki, Japan, Feb. 12, 1951; s. Chuichiro and Akiko Ito; m. Kumiko Miyata, Nov. 15, 1980; 1 child, Tomokazu. BS, Ibaraki U., Hitachi, 1973, MS, 1975. Rschr. Hitachi, Ltd., 1975-92, sr. rschr., 1993—. Contbr. articles to profl. jours. Avocations: tennis, driving, piano playing. Office: Hitachi Ltd Ctrl Rsch Lab, 7-1-1 Ohmica-cho, Hitachi 319-12, Japan

ITO, TOMOHIRO, mechanical engineer; b. Yamaguchi, Japan, Oct. 31, 1951; s. Takafumi and Yaeko I.; m. Akiko Harada, May 5, 1980. M in Engring., Osaka U., 1977; D in Engring., Tokyo Met. U., 1995. Sr. rschr. Mitsubishi Heavy Industry, Takasago, Japan, 1986-92; asst. chief rschr. Mitsubishi Heavy Industry, Takasago, 1993—. Contbr. articles to profl. jours. Mem. Japan Soc. Mech. Engrs. Office: Mitsubishi Heavy Industry, 2 1 1 Shinhama Araicho, Takasago 676-8686, Japan

ITO, UMEO, neurosurgeon; b. Nagano City, Japan, Jan. 9, 1934; s. Fukuei and Naoko Ito; m. Umeno Horiko, Sept. 19, 1967; 1 child, Seiro. Diploma in gen. culture, Tokyo U., 1954; MD, Tokyo Med. and Dental U., 1960, PhD, 1965. Asst. Tokyo Med. and Dental U., 1965-72, asst. prof., 1972-76, assoc. prof., 1976—; dir., neurosurgeon in chief Musashino Red Cross Hosp., Tokyo, 1980—; vis. fellow NIH, Bethesda, Md., 1972-74; asst. U. Mainz (Germany), 1974; invited prof. U. Bern, Switzerland, 1985; cons. Tokyo Rsch. Inst. Psychiatry, 1987-92, Jichi Med. Sch., Tochigi, Japan, 1989—, Tokyo Met. Inst. for Neurosci., 1997—. Editor: Maturation Phenomenon in Cerebral Ischemia, 1992, Brain Edema IX, 1994, Brain Edema X, 1997, Maturation Phenomenon in Cerebral Ischemia II, 1997, Maturation Phenomenon in Cerebral Ischemia III, 1999; contbr. articles to profl. jours.; patentee in field. Recipient Masuda award Japan Red Cross Soc., 1990, Internat. Honored Citizenship award City of New Orleans, 1999, award for 1st description of maturation phenomenon in cerebral ischemia and leadership in neurosci. Neurosci. Ctr. of Excellence, La. State U., 1999; scholar Esso-Std. Oil Co., Tokyo, 1964. Fellow Am. Heart Assn. (stroke coun.); mem. World Fedn. of Neurosurgeons, Japan Soc. of Neurosurgery, Am. Assn. Neurol. Surgeons, N.Y. Acad. Sci. Avocations: playing cello for string quartet, painting, playing tennis, walking, skiing. Home: 4-22-24 Zenpukuji, Suginami-ku, Tokyo 1670041, Japan Office: Neurosurg Musashino Red Cross Hosp, 1-26-1 Kyonan-cho, Musashino-shi Tokyo 180, Japan

ITO, YOICHIRO, pathologist; b. Dec. 22, 1928; came to U.S., 1968, naturalized, 1978; s. Taichi and Ai (Kubota) I.; m. Ryoko Tanioka, Dec. 23, 1963; children: Koichi, Shin. MD, Osaka City U., 1958. Rotating intern U.S. Yokosuka (Japan) Naval Hosp., 1958-59; resident in pathology Cleve. Met. Gen. Hosp., 1959-61, Michael Reese Hosp., Chgo., 1961-63; instr. physiology Osaka City U. Med. Sch., 1963-68; vis. scientist Nat. Heart, Lung and Blood Inst., NIH, Bethesda, Md., 1968-78, med. officer, 1978—. Recipient 1st pl. award ann. sci. rsch. presentation at Cleve. Met. Gen. Hosp., 1960, Tech. Excellence award for devel. blood cell separator, 1979; Fulbright exch. scholar, 1959-63; WHO rsch. travel fund grantee Nat. Inst. Med. Rsch., London, 1968. Mem. N.Y. Acad. Scis., Kenshinkai. Achievements include research on innovation in separation sci., including continuous development of countercurrent chromatography, cell separation methods; initiated and developed countercurrent chromatography; patentee coil planet centrifuge, rotating-seal-free flow-through centrifuge, pH-zone-refining countercurrent chromatography, centrifugal precipitation chromatography. Office: NIH 9000 Rockville Pike Bethesda MD 20892-0003

ITO ACOSTA, JAVIER YUTAKA, financial consultant; b. Juarez, Mex., Dec. 3, 1919; s. Jose Kaname Ito and Enriqueta Acosta; m. Luz Maria Varela, Sept. 4, 1943; children: Silvia, Graciela, Luz Oralia, Javier, Rosalina, Eduardo. Diploma in acctg., Escuela Tech. Comml., Juarez, 1935, El Paso Tech. Sch., 1938; BA, Palmore Bus. Coll., 1942; CPA, Escuela Bancaria y Commerce, Mexico City, 1948. Gen. acct. Juarez Gas Co. S.A., 1950-92, gen. mgr., 1993-97; fin. cons. Grupo Imperial Corp. S.A., Juarez, 1998—; cons., auditor Toko, S.A. (Japan), Juarez, 1973-75; acctg. cons. Gas Natural de Juarez, 1998—; fin. cons. Ito, Gamez, Lievano & Correa, Juarez, 1974-80. Mayor pro-tem, city treas. City of Juarez, 1969-71; chmn. Juarez C. of C., 1968-69; founder, mem. Intercity Group, Juarez, 1978-99. Mem. Fedn. Accts. Norte Centro (Chihuahua rep.), Assn. Mex. Japonesa (Chihuahua rep.), Asociados del Svc. Gas Natural (bd. dirs. 1999). Roman Catholic. Avocations: golf, travel.

ITOH, GEN, medical educator; b. Ichinomiya shi, Japan, Jan. 19, 1939; s. Kyubei and Kiyoko (Ishiguro) I.; m. Yoshiko Koike, Nov. 21, 1966; children: Wataru, Takashi. MD, Nagoya (Japan) U., 1963, PhD, 1968. Asst. sch. medicine Nagoya U., 1968-75; assoc. prof. Aichi Med. U., Nagakute-Aichi, Japan, 1975-79; prof. Aichi Med. U., Nagakute-Aichi, 1979—; mem. Adv. Bd. BAsic and Applied Myology. Co-author: Kijun Byorigaku. Mem. Am. Soc. Investigative Pathology, N.Y. Acad. Sci. Avocations: tennis, golf, paintings, classical music. Home: 1646 Kushitsukuri Hagiwara, Ichinomiya shi 491-0376, Japan Office: Aichi Med U, 21 karimata Nagakute cho, Aichi gun 480 11, Japan

ITOH, HIROYASU NICOLAS, computer, communications and optical scientist; b. Ishinomaki-City, Miyagi, Japan, Mar. 17, 1954; s. Yoshimitsu and Yukiko (Arai) I.; m. Takako Theresa Tanaka, Oct. 22, 1988; 1 child, Hiroki. BSEE, Sophia U., Tokyo, 1976; MS in Indsl. Engring., U. Ariz., Tucson, 1978, PhD in Systems Engring., 1982. Sr. rschr. Racal-Milgo Inc., Miami, Fla., 1982-84; system design engr. Rockwell Internat., Newport Beach, Calif., 1984-85; engr. Comms. divsn. Fujitsu Ltd., Kawasaki, Japan, 1985-88; rschr. Optical Signal Processing Lab., Fujitsu Labs., Kawasaki, Japan, 1988-92; rschr., coord. internat. rels. and advanced rsch. R & D Planning and Coord. Office, Fujitsu Labs., Kawasaki, 1994-98; rschr. Fujitsu Rsch. Inst., Makuhari, Japan, 1992-94; sr. coord., adminstr. sub-tarabyte optical memory project Optoelectronic Industry and Tech. Devel. Assn., 1998-99; with patent promotion divsn. Fujitsu Labs., Ltd., 1999—. Author: Photonic Switching II, 1990; author, editor: Corporate Analysis Measures and Models, 1994; editor: Electronic Money, 1997; contbr. articles and tech. reports to profl. jours.; patentee in field. Mem. IEEE (sr.), Sophia Sci. and Tech. Assn. (com. mem. 2000—), Inst. Electronics, Info. and Comm. Engrs. of Japan, Japanese Ops. Rsch. Soc. (editl. bd. 1993-97), N.Y. Acad. Scis. (Charles Darwin assoc.), Info. Processing Soc. of Japan (steering com. distributed processing systems study group 1996-98), Sophia U. Alumni Assn. (rep.), Rotary Internat. Fellows Tokyo (steering com. 1999—). Roman Catholic. Avocations: walking, tennis, swimming, piping, jazz music. Office: Fujitsu Labs Ltd Patent, Prom Divsn 10-1 Wakamiya, Morinosato Atsugi City Kanagawa, Japan

ITOH, ISAO, humanities educator; b. Kakamigahara-shi, Gifu-ken, Japan, Sept. 19, 1949; s. Kunihiko and Tsutako (Yamada) I.; m. Nobuko Nishiwaki; two children. MA, Meijigakuin U., Tokyo, 1974. Tchr. Kokugakuin Sr. H.S., Tokyo, 1974-90; asst. prof. Nagoyajiyugakuin Jr. Coll., Nagoya, Japan, 1990-95; prof. Tokyo Seitoku Coll., 1995-2000, Aichi U., Toyohashi, Japan, 2000—; part-time lectr. Waseda U., Tokyo, 1995—. Author: The Collected Poems: The Moonlight Reflected in the Stream, 1981, Pater-His Quest for Beauty, 1986, The Collected Poems: The Sound of Oneness, 1991; collaborator: The World of Walter Pater, 1995, Nishiwaki Junzaburo the Paterean, 1999. Dir. The Mcpl. Judo League of Urawa, Urawa-shi, Japan, 1995. Mem. Pater Soc. Japan (dir. 1990—), Wilde Soc. Japan (dir. 1995—), English Literary Soc. Japan, Modern Poetry Soc. Japan, Japan Writer's Assn. Buddhist. Avocation: judo (fourth degree black belt). Home: 336-0031 Saitama-ken, Urawa-shi, Shikatebukuro 4-11-15, Japan Office: 441-8522 Aichi-ken, Toyohashi-shi, Machihata-machi 1-1 Japan

ITOH, KAZUYOSHI, educator; b. Himeji, Hyogo, Japan, Nov. 21, 1948; s. Satoru and Takako (Oguni) Kodama; m. Kae Itoh, Dec. 17, 1972; children: Daigo, Machiko. B. of Engring., Osaka (Japan) U., 1971, M. of Engring., 1975; D. of Engring., Hokkaido U., Sapporo, Japan, 1984. Engring. and math. diplomate. Rschr. Nippon Kokan K.K., Kawasaki, Japan, 1971-72, Matsushita Electric Indsl. Co. Ltd., Kadoma, Japan, 1975-78; rsch. assoc.

Hokkaido U., Sapporo, 1978-86; rsch. assoc. Osaka U., 1986-88, assoc. prof., 1988-95, prof. dept. applied physics, 1995—. Co-author: Progress in Optics XXXV, 1996, Ultrafast and Ultra Parallel Optoelectronics, 1995; contbr. articles to profl. jours. Fellow Optical Soc. Am., SPIE; mem. Japan Soc. Applied Physics, Optical Soc. Am., Internat. Soc. Optical Engring. Home: Hanayashiki 1-27-16, Kawamishi 666-0035, Japan Office: Osaka U Grad Sch Engring, Yamada-oka 2-1, Suita Osaka 565, Japan

ITOH, NOBUYA, biochemist, educator; b. Suzuka, Mie, Japan, Sept. 8, 1955; s. Tomihiro Iwata and Yoshie Itoh; m. Noriko Yamagiwa, June 1988; children: Maiko, Hiroya. B of Engring., Kyoto (Japan) U., 1978, M of Engring., 1980, D of Agr., 1988. Rschr. Amano Pharm. Co. Ltd., Aichi, Japan, 1980-89; lectr. Fukui (Japan) U., 1989-91, assoc. prof., 1991-97; prof. Toyama (Japan) Prefectural U., 1997—. Recipient Incentive award Japanese Soc. Biosci. Biotech. Agrochemistry, 1995. Office: Toyama Prefectural U, Kurokawa 5180, Kosugi Toyama 939-0398, Japan

ITOH, SHINJI, physiologist, researcher; b. Ise-City, Mie-ken, Japan, Feb. 16, 1912; s. Motoichi and Kuni (Hayashi) Ito; m. Eiko Ito, June 9, 1937; children: Yukiko, Toru, Hiroko, Yutaka. MD, Nagoya (Japan) U., 1935, PhD, 1941. Asst. Nagoya U., 1937-41, assoc., 1941-47, assoc. prof., 1947-57; prof. Hokkaido U., Sapporo, Japan, 1957-75, prof. emeritus, 1975—; rsch. advisor Shionogi Rsch. Inst., Osaka, Japan, 1975-93; guest lectr. Yamagata (Japan) U., 1985-99; guest prof. Guelph (Can.) U., 1976. Editor: Essential Problems in Climatic Physiology, 1960, Integrative Mechanism of Neuroendocrine System, 1968, Advances in Climatic Physiology, 1972, Physiology of Cold-Adapted Man, 1974, Circumpolar Health, 1976; patentee on memory enhancer, 1985, new peptide (improves brain functions), 1985. Recipient Sunrising medal Japanese Govt., 1985, Sci. and tech. prize Hokkaido Govt., 1968, Hokkaido Med. Assn. prize, 1971. Mem. AAAS, Japan Physiol. Soc. (special), Japan Endocrinology Soc. (hon.), Japan Neuroendocrinology Soc. (hon.), Internat. Soc. Neuroendocrinology (hon.), Japan Biometeorol. Soc. (hon.), Internat. Soc. Biometeorology, Neurosci. Soc. Home: 2-6-31 Nishikoori, Otsu 520 0027, Japan

ITOH, SHOKO, American literature educator; b. Kobe, Hyogo, Japan, Mar. 30, 1944; d. Shigetaka and Fusako (Sakuma) Narashiba; m. Takaaki Itoh, Dec. 28, 1969; children: Rei, Rena. BA, Hiroshima (Japan) U., 1966, MA, 1968, PhD, 1997. Lectr. Notre Dame Jr. Coll., Hiroshima City, 1968-75, assoc. prof., 1975-83; assoc. prof. Hiroshima U., 1983-89, prof. Am. lit., 1989—; part-time prof. Okayama U., 1993, Yasuda Grad. Sch., Hiroshima, 1994—. Author: The Road to Arnheim: The World of Edgar Allen Poe, 1986, Reading Nature of American Literature, 1996, American Authors and Europe, 1997, Sauntering to the Inner Wilderness: Nature Writing and American Society, 1998, American Jeremiads: Puritanism in American Literary History, 1999; transl. New Historicism, 1995, Faith in a Seed, 1995; contbr. articles to profl. jours. Fulbright sr. rschs., 1986-87. Mem. MLA, Poe Soc., Am. Lit. Soc. of Japan (rep. com. 1991—, editor 1997—), Japan Nathaniel Hawthorne Soc. (dir. 1991-93), Chu-Shikoku Am. Lit. Soc. (dir. 1991—), Japan Henry Thoreau Soc. (v.p. 1996-98, pres. 2000—), Assn. for Study of Lit. and Environment of Japan (mng. dir. 1994—, editor 1997—), U.S. Assn. Studies in Lit. and Environment (editl. bd. 1997—). Office: Hiroshima Univ, 1-7-1 Kagamiyama, Higashihiroshima 739-0046, Japan

ITOH, SONOE, medical technologist, cytologist; b. Kurume, Fukuoka, Japan, Feb. 8, 1958; d. Terumi and Kumoi (Yamaguchi) Nakamura; m. Tsutomu Itoh, Apr. 4, 1982; 2 children. Grad., Oita (Japan) Med. Profl. Sch., 1979. Med. technologist in pathology St. Mary's Hosp., Kurume-shi, Japan, 1979—. Mem. Japan Acad. Cytology, Internat. Acad. Cytology. Home: 347-3 Miyanozin-machi, Goroumaru, 839-0802 Kurume-shi Fukuoka Japan Office: St Mary's Hosp Dept Path, 422 Tsubukuhon-machi, 830-8543 Kurume-shi Fukuoka Japan

ITOH, SUMIKO, theoretical scientist; b. Chiba-city, Japan. MSc, Tokyo Inst. of Tech., 1982, PhD, 1987. Invited lectr. Yokohama Nat. U., Japan, 1988-93, Inst. of Molecular Sci., Okazaki, Japan, 1990; assoc. prof. The Nishi-Tokyo U., Japan, 1990-93; vis. scholar Oxford U., 1993-94; vis. scientist Cavendish Lab., Cambridge, Eng., 1994-96; vis. scientist dept. applied math. and theoretical physics Cambridge U., Eng., 1994-96; assoc. prof. grad. sch. energy sci. Kyoto U., Japan, 1996—. Contbr. articles to profl. jours. including Zeitschrift fur Naturforschung, Bull. of Chem. Soc. Japan. Mem. European Phys. Soc., Am. Phys. Soc., Math. Soc. Japan, Phys. Soc. Japan, Electrochem. Soc., Am. Math. Soc. Avocation: arts. Office: Kyoto U Grad Sch Energy Sci, Gokashou, Uji Kyoto 611-0011, Japan

ITOH, TADASHI, trading company executive; b. Japan, Jan. 6, 1922; m. Fumiko Itoh. Grad., Tokyo U., 1949. Chmn. Sumitomo Corp., Tokyo, Internat. Civil and Comml. Law Ctr. Japan; hon. advisor Sumitomo Corp. Home: Kami Shakujii Heim 2-808, 4-1, Shakujii-dai Nerima-ku Tokyo 177, Japan Office: Sumitomo Corp, 2-2 Hitotsubashi 1-chome, Chiyoda-ku Tokyo 100, Japan*

ITOH, TAKAO, physical chemist, lepidopterist, educator; b. Tokyo, Feb. 21, 1951; m. Yoshie Honda, Dec. 1, 1985. BA, Hokkaido U., Sapporo, Japan, 1974, MS, 1976, ScD, 1980. Rsch. assoc. U. Calif., Riverside; founder, rep. Rsch. Group on Insects, Hokkaido, U., 1970-73. Author: Studies of High Temperature Sueprcondutors, vol. 5, 1990; contbr. over 70 articles to profl. jours. NIH vis. fellow, 1985-86. Mem. Am. Chem. Soc., Chem. Soc. Japan, Japan Photochem. Assn., Lepidopterists Soc. Office: Miyazaki Med Coll, Kiyotake-cho, Miyazaki Gunma, Japan 8891692

ITOH, TOSHIAKI, university educator, researcher; b. Hashima, Japan, Sept. 26, 1959; s. Isamu Itoh and Masako Katayama; m. Kumiko Daibo, Mar. 28, 1995. BS, Tokai U., 1982; MS, Tokyo U., 1984, PhD, 1987. Cert. applied mathematics. Rsch. fellow Japan Soc. for Promotion of Sci. for Japanese Jr. Scientists, Hiroshima, Japan, 1987-88; asst. prof. bus. adminstrn. Kobe (Japan) U., 1988-94; assoc. prof. integrated arts and scis. Tokushima (Japan) U., 1995—. Contbr. articles to profl. jours. Mem. Phys. Soc. Japan, Info. Processing Soc. Japan, Soc. for Indsl. Applied Math., Japan Soc. for Indsl. and Applied Math., Am. Math. Soc. Avocations: painting, electric music, radio control models. Office: Tokushima U Fac Integ A&S, 1-1 Minamijosanjima-cho, Tokushima 770-8502, Japan

ITOH, WILLIAM H., former ambassador; b. Tokyo, Japan, May 30, 1943; m. Melinda White; children: Charlotte, Caroline. BA in Social Science, MA in History, Anthropology, U. N.Mex., 1971. Sec. tchr. Albuquerque Pub. Schs., 1967-68; asst. prof. history Calif. State U., Humboldt, 1972-73; U.S. Dept. State staff asst. and exec. officer Bur. Congressional Rels., 1975-76, congressional rels. office, 1980-83; country officer for Japan Bur. East Asian and Pacific Affairs, 1978-80, spl. asst., 1983-84; spl. asst. Office of Under Sec. for Pol. Affairs, 1984-86; consular and pol. officer U.S. Embassy, London, 1976-78; U.S. consul gen. Western Australia, Perth, 1986-90; dep. exec. sec. and acting exec. sec. Dept. State, 1991-93; exec. sec. Nat. Security Council White House, Washington, 1993-95; amb. to Kingdom of Thailand U.S. Dept. of State, 1995-98; vis. prof. Kenan-Flager Bus. Sch., U. N.C., Chapel Hill. Logistics officer USAF, 1967-69. Address: 2782 N Wakefield St Arlington VA 22207-4152

ITOI, EIJI, medical educator, orthopedist; b. Morioka, Iwate, Japan, Jan. 14, 1956; s. Yuichi and Teiko (Nakamura) I.; m. Mika Iino, Apr. 19, 1986; children: Sakae Shori. MD, Tohoku U., 1980, PhD, 1989. Jr. resident Nat. Mito (Japan) Hosp., 1980-82, sr. resident, 1982-83; asst. Tohoku U. Hosp., Sendai, Japan, 1983-87; instr. Tohoku U. Hosp., Sendai, 1987-93; asst. prof. Akita (Japan) U. Hosp., 1994—; vis. scientist Mayo Clinic, Rochester, Minn., 1997-98. Contbr. articles to profl. jours. Recipient Neer award Am. Shoulder Elbow Surgeons, 1992, grant award Japan Orthop. and Traumatology Found., Tokyo, 1995, Sci. Exhibit award Radiol. Soc. N.Am., 1996; rsch. fellow Mayo Clinic, Rochester, Minn., 1990-91, sr. rsch. fellow, 1991-93, travelling fellow Japan Shoulder Soc./European Soc. Surgery Shoulder & Elbow, 1994, Am. Orthop. Assn., 1997. Mem. Internat. Soc. Orthop. and Traumatology, Asian Shoulder Assn., Am. Shoulder Elbow Surgeons. Avocation: music. Home: 1-18 Kitamachi Tegatayama, Akita 010-0842, Japan Office: Akita U Sch Medicine, Hondo 1-1-1, Akita 010-8543, Japan

ITSKOVSKY, MATVEY AVRAAM, physicist, researcher; b. Kiev, Ukraine, Oct. 16, 1937; came to Israel, 1991; s. Avraam Isaac and Bronia Avraam (Rivkind) I.; m. Ira Aaron Kinsburg, Aug. 9, 1963 (div. Dec. 1984); children: Anna, Inessa. MSc, Voronezh State Univ., Russia, 1966; PhD, Donetsk State Univ., 1973. Sr. researcher Inst. of Physics, Kiev, 1965-91; prof. asst. Technion IIT, Haifa, Israel, 1992—; vis. prof. asst. Max-Planck Inst., Grenoble, France, 1994-95; cons. Polytech. Inst., Kiev, 1967-72; lectr. The All Union Scientifically Popular Soc., Ukraine, 1982-91. Contbr. articles to profl. jours. With Soviet Army, 1957-60. Recipient rsch. grants Min. of Immigrant Absorption, Israel, 1992-94, Minerva Found., Germany, 1993-95, Arc-en-Ciel program, France, 1995, Gil'adi Found., Israel, 1996—, Israel Sci. Found. Israel Acad. Scis. and Humanities, 1999-01. Mem. Israel Physical Soc. Avocations: reading, swimming, tourism. Office: Technion Israel Inst Tech, Chem Dept, 32000 Haifa Israel

ITURRIAGAGOITIA, JUAN RAMON, lawyer; b. Barcelona, Spain, Jan. 29, 1953; arrived in Belgium, 1987; s. Juan Ramon Iturriagagoitia y del Solar and Maria Blanca Bassas Carbó; m. Hendrika de Geest, Aug. 21, 1956; children: Xavier, Arthur. B degree, German Sch. San Alberto Magno, Barcelona, 1972; lic. in law, U. Barcelona, 1983; LLM, Georgetown U., 1985. Bar: Brussels (list B), Madrid. Assoc. Law Office Antonio Roca Puig, Barcelona, 1975-77, Law Office J.M. Planas Bassas, Gerona, Spain, 1978-79; ptnr. Gabinete Juridico, Barcelona, 1979-84; counsel Secretariat of the Internat. C. of C. Ct. of Arbitration, Paris, 1985-87; assoc. JYB Cremades & Assocs., Brussels, 1988-90, resident ptnr., 1991-94; charge de cours U. Rene Descartes, Paris, 1987-90; invited prof. U. Antwerp, Belgium, 1988-89. Author: Transposition of EC Directives in Spanish Commercial Law, 1993, Synopsis des Relations Juridiques de L'Entrepreneur Etranger en Espagne, 1993; co-author: Handbook in Provisional Remedies in International Commercial Arbitration, 1992. Mem. Internat. C. of C. (commn. on law and practices relating to competition 1989—, commn. on fin. svcs. 1991—), Ordre Francais des Avocats du Barreau de Bruxelles (commn. des membres des barreaux etrangers etablis a Brussels 1992—). Office: Rue Le Correge 93, 1000 Brussels Belgium

ITZIKOWITZ, ANGELA JANE, law educator, consultant; b. Benoni, South Africa, Mar. 17, 1958; d. Harry Findlay and Omnia (Nock) Roberts; m. Gary Itzikowitz, Oct. 10, 1984; children: Raffy, Gina. BA, U. Stellenbosch, South Africa, 1979, LLB, 1982. Advocate of High Ct. of South Africa. Lectr. Witwatersrand Law Sch., Johannesburg, South AFrica, 1984-90, sr. lectr., 1990-95, assoc. prof., 1995-98; cons. Chuene, Kunene, Motsatsi Inc., Johannesburg, 1998—; dir. LLM in Banking and Stock Exch. Law, RAU, Johannesburg, 1997—; participating flelow London Inst. Internat. Banking Fin.and Devel. Law; professorial fellow Asian Inst. Internat. Fin. Law, Hong Kong, 1997—. Co-author, editor: Cases and Mateirals on Bills of Exchange, 1998. Mem. Lawyers for Human Rights, Johannesburg, 1990-96; mem. South African Law Commn. on Money Laundering, Johannesburg, 1996; mem. Transparency Internat., 1995—. Mem. Assn. Banking Lawyers So. Africa (founder). Avocations: squash, walking, horseback riding. Home: 17A 8th Ave, Parktown North, 2193 Johannesburg South Africa Office: Faculty of Law/Wits U, PO Box 2050, 2000 Johannesburg South Africa

IUE, SATOSHI, electronics executive. CEO, chmn. bd. Sanyo Electric, Osaka, Japan, chmn. bd. Office: Sanyo Electric, 2-5-5 Keihan-Hondori, Moriguchi City Osaka 570-8677, Japan*

IUGA, ALEXANDRU IULIU, engineering educator; b. Dobra, Romania, Aug. 15, 1942; s. Ioan and Terezia (Finteusan) I.; m. Silvia Gabriela Pop, Aug. 21, 1974; 1 child, Anca-Ioana. MSEE, Mining Inst., 1966; MSPh, U. Babes-Bolyai, 1973; PhD, Poly. Inst. Iasi, 1984. Engr. Electricity Co., Hunedoara, Romania, 1966-67; asst. prof. Polytech. Inst., Cluj, Romania, 1974-90; assoc. prof. Tech. U., Cluj, 1990-92, prof., 1992—, doctorate supr., 1991—; expert Nat. Edn. Ministry, Romania, 1997—. Co-author: Handbook of Electrical Measurements, 1974; contbr. articles to profl. jours.; patentee in field. Mem. IEEE (sr.), Electrostatics Soc. of Am. Avocations: music, trips, athletics. Home: Str Mehedinti 2 ap 25, RO-3400 Cluj-Napoca Romania Office: Tech Univ of Cluj-Napoca, 15 C Daicoviciu St, RO-3400 Cluj-Napoca Romania

IVANČEVIĆ, DARKO, nuclear medicine educator; b. Zagreb, Croatia, June 14, 1929; s. Drago and Josipa (Kodrić) I.; m. Elizabeta Stemberger, May 21, 1958; children: Klara Purgar, Iva Kanajet. MD, U. Zagreb, 1956, MSc in Phrmacy, 1966, PhD, 1970. Cert. nuclear medicine bd., Croatia (examiner 1978—). With Rebro Hosp., Zagreb, 1960—, chief divsn., 1975-91, chmn. dept., 1991-94; fellow Atomic Energy Commn. Inst. F. Joliot, Orsay, France, 1966-67; asst. internal medicine clinic U. Zagreb Med. Faculty, 1960-80, asst. prof. nuclear medicine, 1980-83, assoc. prof., 1983-87, prof., 1987-96, prof. emeritus, 1996—; sci. asst. Vanderbilt U., Nashville, 1973; mem. European Bd. Nuclear Medicine, 1995—. Editor: Clinical Nuclear Medicine, 1999; contbr. articles to med. jours. Mem. Croatian Soc. Nuclear Medicine (pres. 1992-96, v.p. 1996—), Croatian Med. Assn., Yugoslavia Assn. Nuclear Medicine (sec. 1970-74, diploma for spl. merit 1975). Avocation: photography. Home: Vinogradska 20 a, 10 000 Zagreb Croatia Office: Rebro Hosp Dept Nuclear Med, Kišpatićeva 12, 10 000 Zagreb Croatia

IVANČEVIĆ, VELIMIR, physician; b. Zagreb, Croatia, Aug. 18, 1958; s. Željko and Vesna (Vrkljan) I.; m. Birgit Stüwe, May 22, 1987; 1 child, Janko. MD, U. Zagreb, 1986, PhD, 1993. Diplomate German Bd. Nuclear Physicians. Intern Univ. Hosp., Zagreb, 1985-86, resident, 1987-90; rschr. U. Zagreb, 1989-90; resident Bethesda Hosp., Duisburg, Germany, 1990-91, Univ. Hosp., Göttingen, Germany, 1991-94; head physician Univ. Hosp. Charité, Berlin, 1994—. Contbr. chpts. to books and articles to profl. jours. IAEA grantee, Moscow, St. Petersburg and Kiev, 1987; Familie Gerhard Wuth-Stiftung rsch. grantee, Phila., 1996. Mem. N.Y. Acad. Scis., European Assn. Nuclear Medicine, German Assn. Nuclear Medicine. E-mail: velimir.ivancevic@charite.de. Office: Univ Hosp Charite Clinic, Schumannstr 20-21, 10098 Berlin Germany

IVANCHENKO, LIANA ANATOLYIVNA, physicist, researcher; b. Moscow, Jan. 15, 1941; d. Anatoliy Ivanovich and Ludmila Izraylevna (Trachtengold) Andryushchenko; m. Leonid Vasylyovich Ivanchenko, Dec. 25, 1965; children: Vasyl, Myckaylo. Grad., State Univ. Odessa, Ukraine, 1963; degree, Nat. Acad. Sci. Ukraine, Kiev, Ukraine, 1972, D, 1993. Aspirant Phys. Inst. Acad. Scis. of USSR, Moscow, 1963-66; engr. Inst. for Problems of Materials Sci. Nat. Acad. of Sci. Ukraine, Kiev, 1967-72, jr. scientist, 1972-76, sr. scientist, 1976-94; leading scientist Kiev, 1994—. Patentee in field; contbr. articles to profl. jours. Home: 1-B Dobrokhotova app 27, 03142 Kiev Ukraine Office: Nat Acad Sci Ukraine, 3 Krzhyzhanovsky, 03142 Kiev Ukraine

IVANI, GIORGIO, anesthesiologist, educator, consultant; b. Genoa, Italy, Apr. 15, 1954; s. Giovanni Battista and Luciana Ivani; m. Marina Scaglia, Dec. 22, 1990; children: Simone, Alessia. Sci. Lic., U. Genoa, 1979. Specialist in pediats., anesthesia, intensive care, and pain therapy. Cons., head pediatric anesthesia and postoperating pain control in gen. surgery Gaslini Children's Hosp., Genoa, 1996-98; assoc. prof. pediatric anesthesia and intensive care U. Genoa, 1996-98; chmn. dept. anesthesia and intensive care unit Regina Margherita Childen's Hosp., Turin, 1998—; prof. pediat. anesthesia and intensive care U. Turin, 1998—; Italian del. Fedn. of European Assns. of Pediat. Anesthesia, 1997-2004; adj. prof. anesthesia and ICU in pediats., U. Genoa; invited spkr. and participant numerous workshops and congresses in field of pediat. anesthesia. Contbr. chpts. to books, articles to profl. jours.; editor: Anestesia Loco-Regionale Pediatrica, 1996, Pain Treatment in Children, 2000; mem. editl. bd. Jour. Local and Regional Anesthesia and Pain Therapy, Regional Anesthesia, Pediat. Anesthesia; guest editor Regional Anesthesia and Pain Medicine. Mem. Italian Soc. Pediat. Anesthesia (pres. 1997-99), European Soc. Regional Anesthesia, Am. Soc. Regional Anesthesia, Assn. Pediat. Anesthesia of Gt. Britain and Ireland, French Assn. Pediat. Anesthesia. Fax: 39 011 6614612. E-mail: gioivani@ipsnet.it. Office: Regina Margherita Children's Hosp, Piazza Polonia 94, 10126 Turin Italy

IVANIER, PAUL, steel products manufacturing company executive; b. Cernauti, Romania, Oct. 12, 1932; s. Isin and Fancia Ivanier; m. Lily Neilinger, June 13, 1954; children: Shirley Retter, Janet Neuman, Philip. McGill U., 1957; PhD (hon.), Ben-Gurion U. Chartered acct. With Ivaco Inc. (formerly Sivaco Wire and Nail Co.), Montreal, v.p. ops., exec. v.p., 1969-76, pres., chief exec. officer, dir., 1976—; bd. dirs. Ivacan Inc., Docap (1985) Corp., Bakermet Inc. Grand patron Montreal Mus. Fine Arts; mem. bd. govs. U. Montreal, Concordia U., Royal Victoria Hosp. Corp.; internat. bd. govs. Ben-Gurion U.; bd. dirs. Weizmann Inst. Scis., Med. Rsch. Found. Jewish Gen. Hosp. Mem. Can. Steel Producers Assn. (bd. dirs. past vice chmn.), Can. Steel Trade and Employment Congress (bd. dirs., founder), Order of Can., Club des Entrepreneurs/Conseil du Patronat du Quebec (Laureate 1989), Elmridge Golf and Country Club, Mt. Royal Club. Office: Ivaco Inc, 770 rue Sherbrooke St W, Montreal, PQ Canada H3A 1G1

IVANISHKO, YURI ALEXANDROVICH, research ophthalmologist; b. Rostov-on-Don, Russia, Feb. 13, 1954; s. Alexander Ivanovich Ivanishko and Pana Markovna Zhelesnjak; m. Natalia Mikhilovna Semjonkina; children: Maria, Ekaterina. MB in Surgery, Rostov State Med. U., 1976, MB in Ophthalmology, 1978, MD; PhD, Scientific Rsch. Inst. Eye, Moscow, 1983, DSc, 1994. Academician Russian Laser Acad. Sci., cert. in laser ophthalmomicrosurgery. Chief dr. North Caucasion Ophthal. Ctr., Rostov State Med. U., 1982; cons. med. Regional Med. Svcs. Ministry Internal Affairs, Rostov, 1982, Rostov Regional First-Aid Hosp., 1985; with Rostov Bur. Med. Jurisprudence Exams., 1990; chief dr., med. dir. Ophthalmology Ctr. InterYUNA, Rostov, 1992. Contbr. over 60 articles to profl. jours. on laser microsurgery with patology of retina; author new principles and methods of lasermicrosurgery of forea area of retina. Recipient Inventor of USSR badge, USSR State Com. on Innovation and Invention, 1984; recipient Silver medal Peoples Econ. Achievement exhbn., 1988. Avocations: children, literature, sports, hunting. E-mail: Ivanishko@interyuna.ru. Fax: 7 8632 659086. Office: Ophth Ctr InterYUNA, B Sadovaja str 115, 344021 Rostov-on-Don Russia

IVANITSKY, ALEXEY MICHAILOVICH, physiologist; b. Moscow, June 2, 1928; s. Michail Feodorovich and Natalia Iosifovna (Appak) I.; m. Luidmila Petrovna Osipova, Nov. 28, 1953; children: George, Irina. MD, 1st Moscow Med. Inst., 1952; D of Med. Scis., Inst. Higher Nervous Activity, Moscow, 1965. Jr. scientist Inst. Higher Nervous Activity, Moscow, 1956-61; head electrophysiological lab. Serbsky State ctr. Social & Forensic Psychiatry, Moscow, 1961-90; head lab. human higher nervous acivity Inst. Higher Nervous Activity & Neurphysiology, Moscow, 1987—; vice chmn. Nat. Com. Russian Physiologists, Moscow, 1990-99; coord. expert coun. sect. social problems medicine & human ecology Russian Humanitarian Found., Moscow, 1996—. Author: Brain Mechanisms of Signal Evaluation, 1976, (with V.B. Strelets & I.A. Korsakov) Informational Brain Processing and Mental Activity, 1984. Recipient I. P. Pavlov Gold medal Russian Acad. Scis., 1996; Honored Scientist Russian Federation, 1999. Mem. Russian Physiological Soc. (v.p. 1990-93), Internat. Acad. of Astronautics (corr. mem. 1998). Office: Inst High Nervous Activity, 5a Butlerov str, 117865 Moscow Russia

IVANITZ, JOHN MICHAEL, operations supervisor; b. Regina, Sask., Can., Nov. 4, 1939; arrived in Libya, 1990; s. John and Lena (Morse) I.; m. Nualchant Katlingham, Mar. 25, 1980; 1 child, Joanne Michele. BSc in Geol. Engring., Mich. Tech. U., 1964. Geophysicist Pan Am. Oil (Amoco), Calgary, Alta., Can., 1964-68; party chief, resident mgr. Western Geophys., Houston, 1968-85; ops. supr. North African Geophys. Exploration Co., Tripoli, Libya, 1990—. Avocations: golfing, stamp collecting. Home: PO Box 38, 40000 Khon Kaen Thailand Office: PO Box 1141, Tripoli Splaj

IVANKOVICH, ANTHONY D., anesthesiologist, educator; b. Debeljaca, Yugoslavia, Mar. 25, 1939; came to U.S., 1965; m. Olga Ivankovich. MD, U. Zagreb, Croatia, 1963. Lic. physician, Ill.; diplomate Am. Bd. Anesthesiology. Resident in internal medicine County Hosp. Nunberg, Fed. Republic Germany, 1963-65; rotating intern Edgewater Hosp., Chgo., 1966; resident in anesthesiology U. of Chgo. Hosps., 1967-68; asst. prof. anesthesiology Stritch Sch. Medicine Loyola U., Maywood, Ill., 1970-71; instr. anesthesiology Pritzker Sch. Medicine U. Chgo., 1969, assoc. prof. anesthesiology, 1972-74; faculy Sch. Medicine Cook County Postgrad., Chgo., 1975—; prof. anesthesiology Rush Med. Coll. Rush-Presbyn. St. Luke's Med. Ctr., Chgo., 1980—, dir. Rush Pain Ctr., chmn. anesthesiology, 1980—; attending anesthesiology Stritch Sch. Medicine, Loyola U., Chgo., 1970-71, lectr., anesthesiology, 1971-81; cons. anesthesiology Suburban TB Sanatorium, Hinsdale, Ill., 1970-71, Shriner's Hosp. for Crippled Children, Chgo., 1977-82; attending anesthesiology Michael Reese Med. Ctr., Chgo., 1971-74; chief oper. rm. svcs. 801st Gen. Hosp., USAR, Lincolnwood, Ill., 1971-73, chief surgery, 1973-74, assoc. chief profl. svcs., 1974-76; dir. anesthesia rsch. Michael Reese Med. Ctr., Chgo., 1971-74; chmn. anesthesiology Ill. Masonic Med. Ctr., Chgo., 1974-80, Rush-Presbyn.-St. Luke's Med. Ctr., Chgo., 1980—, chmn. coun. surg. chmn. divsn. surg. scis. and svcs., 1992-94, dir. Surg. Hosp., assoc. v.p., 1993—, dir. Women & Children's Hosp., assoc. v.p., 1994—; assoc. examiner Am. Bd. Anesthesiology, 1978; presenter in field. Author: (books) Nitroprusside and Other Short-Acting Hypotensive Agents, 1978, (book chpts. with others) Perspective in High Frequency Ventilation, 1983, Current Controversies in Thoracic Surgery, 1986, Anesthesia and ENT Surgery, 1987, Liposomes as Drug Carriers, 1987, Effective Hemostasis in Cardiac Surgery, 1988, Adjuncts to Cancer Therapy, 1989, Advances in Anesthesia, 1990, Cardiothoracic and Vascular Anesthesia Update, 1991, Cardiothoracic and Vascular Anesthesia Update, 1991, Clinical Anesthesia, 1992, Clinical Anesthesia Updates, 1992, Liposomes in Drug Delivery, 1992; contbr. articles and abstracts to profl. jours. Fellow Am. Coll. Anesthesiologists; mem. AMA, Internat. Assn. for Study of Pain, Internat. Anesthesia Rsch. Soc., Am. Soc. Anesthesiologists, Am. Heart Assn., Am. Coll. Chest Physicians, Am. Pain Soc., Pan Am. Med. Assn., Soc. for Intravenous Anesthesia, Ill. Med. Soc., Ill. Soc. Anesthesiologists, Soc. Neurosurg. Anesthesia and Neurologic Supporting Care, Midwest Pain Soc., Chgo. Med. Soc., Chgo. Soc. Anesthesiologists, Inst. of Medicine of Chgo., Chgo. Heart Assn., Circanes Soc., Sigma Xi. Office: Rush-Presbyn-St Luke's Med Ctr Dept Anesthesiology 1653 W Congress Pkwy Chicago IL 60612-3833

IVANOV, DMITRY EVGENYEVICH, physiologist, researcher; b. Saratov, Russia, Jan. 13, 1963; s. Evgeny Gavrilovich Kusarashvili and Nina Nicolaevna Ivanova. MS, U. Saratov, 1985; postgrad., Inst. Gen. Genetics, Moscow, 1987-90; PhD in Physiology, Russian Acad. Scis., Moscow, 1991. Trainee Inst. Biophysics, Pushchino, Russsia, 1985-87; asst. prof. U. Saratov, 1990-92; scientist Inst. Traumatology and Orthopedics, Saratov, 1992-95, sr. scientist, 1995—. Contbr. articles to sci. jours., including Russian Jour. Devel. Biology, Biology Bull. of USSR Acad. Scis., Progress in Physiol. Scis., Path. Physiology and Exptl. Therapy. Mem. N.Y. Acad. Scis. Fax: (845) 2-263-965. Home: K-97(4-97), Kosmonavtov St Dom-4, Saratov 410002, Russia Office: Inst Traumatology-Orthoped, Ul Chernischevskogo 148, 410002 Saratov Russia

IVANOV, IGOR SERGEYEVICH, federal official; b. Moscow, Sept. 23, 1945; married; 1 child. Student, Moscow Pedagogical Inst. Fgn. Langs. Jr. rschr. Inst. World Econs. and Internat. Rels., USSR Acad. Scis., 1969-73; second then first sec., counsellor, counsellor-envoy USSR Embassy, Spain, 1973-83; expert first European dept. Ministry Fgn. Affairs, 1983-84, counsellor of min., 1984-85, asst. min., 1985-86, dep. chief then chief dept., 1987-92, chief gen. sec., mem. bd., 1989-91, Russian amb. to Spain, 1991—, 1st dep. minister fgn. affairs, 1994—. Office: Ministry Fgn Affairs, Pr Mira 49A, Moscow 120110, Russia*

IVANOV, IOLIAN MARINOV, investment manager, consultant; b. Sofia, Bulgaria, Nov. 4, 1959; s. Marin Tzonkov and Iordanka Dishkova (Ionovska) I. BSc, Tech. Sch. Mech. and Elec., Gabrovo, Bulgaria, 1978; MSc, Tech. U., Sofia, 1985; PhD, Bulgarian Acad. Scis., Sofia, 1992; cert., U. Ctrl. Lancashire, Preston, Eng., 1993, Georgetown U., 1998. Mktg. mgr. Bulgarian Austrian Joint Venture, Sofia, 1990-92; pres. IOLI Co., Sofia, 1991—; sci. assoc. Inst. Robotic Systems Bulgarian Acad. Scis., Sofia, 1992-94; project mgr. Inst. Control and System Rsch. Acad. Scis., Sofia, 1994-95; head dept. Privatization Agy. Bulgaria, 1994-95; dir. Eurocapital Joint Stock Co., Sofia, 1995—; exec. dir., mem. bd. Eurocapital JSCo, Sofia, 1997-98; mgr. Eastern Europe Euro Fidelity, U.S. and Bulgaria, 1999—; sci. rschr. Bulgarian Acad. Scis., 1990. Author: Optimization of a Robotic Arc Welding System, 1991. Recipient awards Ministry of Edn. and Scis., Sofia, 1984-85, 87-90, Know-How Fund Tng. award, U.K., 1993; Overseas Tech. scholar, Japan, 1994; fellow USAID, 1996, Pew Charity Trust, 1998. Mem.

Am. Welding Soc., Union Scientists Bulgaria, Am. C. of C. in Bulgaria, Am. Fin. Assn., Assn. Energy Engrs. Avocations: skiing, tennis, windsurfing, theatre, travel. E-mail: ivanovi@gusun.georgetown.edu. Home: 179 Kniaz Boris I St, 1202 Sofia Bulgaria Office: Euro Fidelity, PO Box 5, 1303 Sofia Bulgaria

IVANOV, IVAN TANEV, physicist, educator; b. Samuilovo, Bulgaria, Oct. 9, 1951; s. Tanyo Ivanov and Gospodina Dobreva (Gavazova) Tanev; m. Tanka Ganeva Marcheva, Oct. 30, 1983 (div. Oct. 1987); 1 child, Tanyo Ivanov Tanev. Univ. degree, Sofia (Bulgaria) State U., 1974; PhD, Stara Zagora Med. Inst., 1995. Controling physicist Nuclear Electrostation, Kozluduy, Bulgaria, 1974-76; physicist Chem. Plant, Stara Zagora, Bulgaria, 1976-84; asst. prof. Med. Inst., Stara Zagora, 1984-98, assoc. prof., head dept., 1998—. Contbr. articles to profl. jours.; patentee in field. Mem. Union Bulgarian Scientists. Bulgarian Orthodox. Avocations: travel, folk music. Home: Flat 26, Armejska Str 16 E, 6000 Stara Zagora Bulgaria Office: Thracian Univ, Stara Zagora Med Inst, 6000 Stara Zagora Bulgaria

IVANOV, KYRILL PAVLOVICH, physiologist; b. Leningrad, Russia, Jan. 3, 1927; s. Pavel Vasilievich and Anna Leontevna (Grigorieva) I.; m. Natalia Vladimirovna Chezhina, Oct. 25, 1968. D of Med. Sci., I.P. Pavlov Inst. Physiolology, Leningrad, Russia, 1965. Jr. rschr. I.P. Pavlov Inst. Physiology, Leningrad, Russia, 1956-62, sr. rschr., 1962-65; head dept. thermoregulation, bioenergetics I.P. Pavlov Inst. Physiology, St. Petersburg, Russia, 1965—, vice dir., 1966-77, dir., 1977-81. Author: Biological Computing Centre, 1975, Energy Demands an dOxygen Supply of Brain, 1979, The Principles of Energetics in Organism vol. 1, 1990, vol. 2, 1993. Deputy Mcpl. Coun. Vsevologhsk, 1978-82. Mem. IBRO, Russian Physiological Soc., Russian Acad. Sci. (scientific coun. 1992—). Avocations: music, sports, history. Office: IP Pavlov Inst Physiology, nab Makarova 6, 199034 Saint Petersburg Russia

IVANOV, LYUBOMIR LALOV, mathematician, foundation executive; b. Sofia, Bulgaria, Oct. 7, 1952; s. Lalo Ivanov Krastev and Mita Tsvetkova Dunchovska; m. Penka Borislavova Dobreva, June 25, 1982; children: Borislava, Nusha. MSc in Math., Sofia U., 1977, PhD in Math., 1981. Rsch. assoc. Inst. Math., Sofia, 1981-88; vis. rsch. fellow Oslo U., Norway, 1985; sr. rsch. assoc. Inst. Math., Sofia, 1988—; MP, chmn. parliamentary group Parliament, Sofia, 1990-91; parliamentary sec. Fgn. Min., Sofia, 1991; chmn. sect. logic Inst. Math., Sofia, 1990—; mem. Communal Place-naming Commn., Sofia, 1991; sec. Antarctic Place-names Commn., Bulgaria, 1994—; topographic surveyor Bulgarian base Antarctica, 1994-95, 95-96; mem. working group interministerial com. NATO Integration, 1997—. Author: (book) Algebraic Recursion Theory, 1986, (topographic maps) various, 1996; participant: (drafting and adoption) Constitution of the Republic of Bulgaria, 1991. Found. mem., v.p. Wilderness Fund, 1989—; coord. coun. Union Democratic Forces, 1990-91; pres. Manfred Wörner Found., 1994—; mem. exec. bd. Civil Soc. Devel. Found., 1997—; coord. Marshall Meml. Fellowship for Bulgaria, 1997—; coun. mem. Atlantic Treaty Assn., 1996—. Sgt. Artillery Reconnaissance, 1970-72. Recipient Nikola Obreshkov prize Acad. Scis. & Sofia U., 1987. Mem. Union Bulgarian Mathematicians, Atlantic Club of Bulgaria (v.p. 1999—), Friends Aleko Konstantinov Club. Mem. Bulgarian Greens Party. Avocations: mountain hiking, skiing, swimming, map collecting. E-mail: antar@math.bas.bg. Home: 2 Biser St, 1000 Sofia Bulgaria Office: Manfred Wörner Found, 29 Slavyanska St, 1000 Sofia Bulgaria

IVANOV, MIKHAIL SAMUILOVICH, aerodynamic researcher; b. Moscow, Apr. 19, 1945; s. Samuil Mikhailovich Katz and Nina Petrovna Ivanova; m. Lyudmila Alexeevna Egorova, Aug. 12, 1964; 1 child, Yanina. MSc, Moscow State U., 1968; PhD, Russian Acad. Scis., Novosibirsk, Russia, 1979, DSc, 1993. Jr. rsch. scientist Inst. Theoretical and Applied Mechs. Siberian Br. Russian Acad. Scis., Novosibirsk, 1968-73, rsch. scientist, 1973-78, sr. rsch. scientist, 1978-83, leading rsch. scientist, 1983-88, head computational aerodynamics lab., 1988—; vis. prof. Brownschweig Tech. U., 1991, Deutsche Forschungsanstalt für Luft und Raumfahrt e.V., 1992, 95, Aachen Tech. U., 1994; vis. scientist USAF, 1995, 98. Contbr. articles to profl. jours. Mem. AIAA, N.Y. Acad. Scis. Office: Inst Theor and Applied Mech, 4/1 Institutskaya Str, 630090 Novosibirsk Russia

IVANOV, SLAVTSCHO KUNEV (SLAVI IVANOV), petrochemistry educator, researcher; b. Novi Pazar, Bulgaria, Feb. 10, 1935; s. Kuni Slavov and Raina Ilieva (Dimanova) I.; m. Jordanka Petrova, Mar. 12, 1961; children: Kuni, Peter. Grad., Moscow Petroleum Inst., 1958; PhD, Inst. Organic Chemistry, Sofia, Bulgaria, 1966, DSc, 1982. Tech. rsch. worker Bulgarian Acad. Scis., Sofia, 1958, rsch. worker, 1960-69, rsch. asst., 1969-84, prof. petrochemistry, 1984-97; pres. SciBulCom Ltd., Sofia, 1994—; prof. petrochemistry U. Konstantin Preslavski, Shumen, Bulgaria, 1977-84, U. Plovdiv, Bulgaria, 1969-84, U. Asen Zlatarov, Burgas, 1984—. Editor-in-chief Oxidation Comm., 1989—, Jour. Balkan Tribological Assn., 1994—; author: Houben-Weyl Methoden der organischen Chemie Band E 13/teil2, 1988, Reaction Mechanism of Inhibitors-Peroxide Decomposers, 1988; contbr. chpt. to book, over 100 articles to profl. chem. jours. Mem. Assn. Bulgarian Experts in Eco-Technology (pres. 1996), Bulgarian Chem. Soc. (v.p. 1993—), Balkan Tribological Assn., Internat. Assn. Stability and Handling of Liquid Fuels. Avocations: travel, working in country house. E-mail: scibulcom@globalcons.com. Home: 7 Nezabravka Str, 1113 Sofia Bulgaria Office: SciBulCom Ltd, PO Box 249, 1113 Sofia Bulgaria

IVANOV, VADIM TIKHONOVICH, biochemist; b. Pheodosia, Russia, Sept. 18, 1937; s. Tikhon Timofeevich and Lidia Ivanovna (Pavlova) I.; m. Raisa Aleksandrovna Osadchia, Feb. 24, 1962; children: Elena, Piotr. Grad., Lomonosov State U., 1960. Postgrad. Shemyakin and Ovchinnikov, Moscow, 1960-63; jr. rschr. Inst. of BioOrganic Chemistry, Russia, 1963-65, sr. rschr., 1965-71, head of lab., 1971—; dep. dir. Acad. Scis., Moscow, 1972-88, dir., 1988—; academician, sec.; prof., bioorganic chair Biol. Dept., Lomonosov State U., 1976—; dir. Shemyakin-Ovchinnikov Inst. Bio-organic Chemistry; bd. dirs. Protein Rsch., Natick, Internat. Jour. of Peptide and Protein Rsch., Copenhagen. Editor-in-chief Bioorganicheskaya Kimiya, Moscow, 1988—; contbr. numerous articles to profl. jours. Recipient Lenin prize Govt. USSR, 1975, State prize, 1985. Mem. Russian Acad. of Scis., Russian Acad. of Agrl. Scis., European Peptide Soc., N.Y. Acad. Scis. Office: Shemyakin-Ovchinnilov Inst, ul Miklukho-Maklaya 16/10, 117871 Moscow Russia also: Russian Acad Scis, 117901 Leninsky Pr 14, Moscow Russia*

IVANOV, VICTOR BORISOVICH, plant physiologist, educator; b. Moscow, May 22, 1937; s. Boris Ivanovich and Olga Victorovna (Okolskaya) I.; m. Svetlana Nikolaevna Dmitrieva, Aug. 6, 1963; 1 child, Oleg Victorovich. Magistr, Moscow State U., 1959; PhD, Inst. Plant Physiology, Moscow, 1964, DSc, 1972. Cert. plant physiologist. Jr. scientist Inst. Elemetoorganic Chemistry, Moscow, 1959-65; head dept. biochem. rsch. Inst. Gen. Chemistry, Russian Acad. Sci., Moscow, 1965-98; head dept. root physiology Inst. Plant Physiology, Russian Acad. Scis., Moscow, 1998—; prof. Moscow Pedagogical U., 1975-99. Author: (in Russian) Cellular Basis of Plant Growth, 1974, Physiology of Crop Plants, 1967, Active Dyes in Biology, 1981, Cell Proliferation in Plant, 1987; (in English) Reactive Dyes in Biology, 1986; contbr. articles to profl. jours.; patentee in field. Avocation: phylately. Office: Inst Plant Physiology, Botanicheskaya Str 35, 127276 Moscow Russia

IVANOV, VLADIMIR PETROVITCH, medical educator; b. Issyilkul, Omsk, Russia, Sept. 1, 1944; s. Peter Kirilovitch Gutovsky and Ekaterina Afanasievna Ivanova; m. Yelena Leonidovna Baulina, July 2, 1966; children: Yelena, Marina. Candidate of medicine, Med. Inst., Karaganda, USSR, 1974; MD, Med.-Genetic Sci. Ctr., Moscow. Tchr. Med. Inst., Karaganda, 1969-72, sr. tchr., 1974-76, dean faculty, 1974-87, lectr., then asst. prof., 1976-87, pro-rector, 1979-84; head dept. Med. Univ., Kursk, Russia, 1987—; prof. Med. Inst., Kursk, Russia, 1989—, Pedagogical Inst., Kursk, 1993—. Contbr. articles to med. jours. Sec. YCL, Karaganda, 1965-73; mem. CPSU Com., Karaganda, 1969-91. Recipient Diploma, Presidium of Supreme Soviet of Kazakhstan, 1969, Jubilee Hon. badge YCL, 1968, Hon. badge, 1971. Mem. Russian Acad. Med. Scis. (corr.), Acad. Ecology and Security of Activity, Internat. Acad. Nature and Soc., Regional Soc. Med. Geneticists (chmn. 1993—), Inter-Regional Soc. Med. Geneticists. Avocation: reading. Home: K Marks, 72/12-17, 305021 Kursk Russia Office: Med State Univ, K Marks, 3, 305000 Kursk Russia

IVANOVA, GINKA GEORGIEVA, chemical engineer; b. Varbovka, Bulgaria, Jan. 10, 1938; s. Georgi and Nedka (Hadjieva) Kalbukovi. PhD, Moscow Inst. Chem. Technology, 1975. From rsch. asst. to rsch. assoc. Bulgarian Acad. Scis., Sofia, 1976-93. Avocation: occult science. Home: Dist Druzhba 2, Apt 38 EntB Bl 224, 1582 Sofia Bulgaria

IVANOVA, OLGA MICHAELOVNA, cardiologist, researcher. MD, 2d Med. Inst., St. Petersburg, 1978; M in Internal Medicine, 1st Med. Inst., St. Petersburg, 1984, PhD in Cardiology, 1990. Physician Rsch. and Treatment Ctr., St. Petersburg, Russia, 1990—. Contbr. articles to profl. jours. Mem. Russian Med. Assn. E-mail: Olga@simolg.spb.su. Office: Rsch and Treatment Ctr, 56 Enthusiasts Ave Apt 111, Saint Petersburg 195030, Russia

IVANOVA, PAVLINA KRASTEVA, geophysical engineer; b. Beli Izvor, Vratca, Bulgaria, July 14, 1935; d. Kristio Dimitrov and Ivanka Stoyanova Ivanova; m. Dinko Dimitrov Grozev, May 20, 1960 (div. 1981); children: Svetlana Gospodinova Grozeva, Maria Gospodinova Grozeva. Engr., Geol.-Geophys. Inst., Moscow, 1959; mathematician, Sofia (Bulgaria) U., 1965; PhD, Bulgarian Acad. Scis., 1977, DSc in Physics, 1996. Contbr. articles to profl. jours. including Geomagnetism and Aeronomy, Planetary Space Sci. Recipient Badge of Honor, Bulgarian Acad. Scis., 1985. Mem. N.Y. Acad. Scis. Achievements include research in geomagnetic phenomena and interplanetary magnetic field (IMF); in inverse geophysical problems. Home: Tcarigradsko Shose Str, Iztok Bl 11 VH 2, 1113 Sofia Bulgaria Office: Geophys Inst Bulgarian Acad Sci, Akad G Bonchev Str Bl 3, 1113 Sofia Bulgaria

IVANOVA, TANIA NENOVA, electrical engineer; b. Sofia, Bulgaria, Sept. 9, 1946; d. Neno Slavchev and Ekaterina Vassileva (Peeva) Stoyanov; m. Mintcho Ivanov, Mar. 23, 1969; children: Katia, Nelly. Elec. Engr., Tech. U. Sofia, 1969; PhD in Physics, Ctrl. Lab. for Space Rsch., Sofia, 1981. Engr. Sci. Group on Space Physics, Sofia, 1969-73; rsch. fellow Ctrl. Lab. for Space Rsch., Sofia, 1973-81; sr. rsch. scientist Space Rsch. Inst., Sofia, 1984—, head space biotech. dept., 1987—, head space engring. divsn., 1990-95, sci. sec., 1996; expert cons. Bulgarian Aerospace Agy., Sofia, 1995-97; rep. Bulgarian Sci. Tech. Subcom., Com. on Peaceful Uses of Outer Space, Vienna, Austria, 1995-96; mem. internat. sci. coun. Biol. Life Support Sys., Russia, 1995—. Contbr. articles to profl. jours.; patentee in field. Recipient Medal for Work, golden, Govt. Bulgaria, 1980, Medal for Sci. "Kiril and Methodi" 1st degree, 1984, East-West Euro Intellect, silver, 1995. Achievements include: scientific and engineering experience with experimental methods, systems, and scientific equipment in the field of Space Plasma Physics (1969-83) and Space Biotechnology; creation of the first SVET Spae Greenhouse for plant growth onboard MIR Space Station (1990—). Avocations: classical music, viola playing, gymnastics, skiing, tourism. Office: Space Rsch Inst, 6 Moskovska Str PO Box 799, 1000 Sofia Bulgaria

IVANOVIC, DANIZA MARINCOVICH, biologist, educator; b. Iquique, Chile, June 30, 1947; d. Rodolfo Carrasco Ivanovic and Maria Tolosa Marincovich. BS, Pontifical Cath. U. Chile, Santiago, 1970; MS in Food and Nutrition Planning, U. Chile, Santiago, 1981. Assoc. prof. U. Chile Inta, Santiago, 1976—. Author: (chpt.) Food and Nutrition Policies and Programs in Chile: A Successful Experience, 1993; editor: Rendimiento escolar y estado nutricional, 1988; contbr. articles to profl. jours. De. Ramon Corbalan Melgarejo, Med. Soc. Santiago, 1991. Mem. Chilean Nutrition Soc. Roman Catholic. Avocations: piano. Office: U Chile Inta, Jose Pedro Alessandri 5540, PO Box 138 11, Santiago Chile

IVANSIC, IVAN, mathematician; b. Gradiste, Croatia, July 9, 1931; s. Stjepan and Mara (Lukic) I.; m. Zlatka Tartaro, Sept. 13, 1958 (dec. Jan. 1996); 1 child, Dubravko. B of Engring., El. Eng. Sch., Zagreb, Croatia, 1956; MS, Sch. Nat. Sci., Zagreb, 1968; PhD, U. Zagreb, 1970. Asst. U. Zagreb, 1957-61, lectr., 1961-71, from asst. prof. to assoc. prof., 1971-82, prof., 1982—; vis. assoc. prof. U. N.C., Greensboro, 1978-79, Okla. U., Norman, summers 1998, 99. Editor-in-chief: (math. jour.) Glasnik Matematicki, 1973-90; contbr. rsch. articles to profl. jours. Lt. former Yugoslav Army, 1965-80. Recipient Rudjer Boskovic award Croatian Govt., 1980. Mem. Am. Math. Soc., Croatian Math. Soc. (pres. 1980-83). Home: Gregorciceva 6, 10000 Zagreb Croatia Office: Fac Elec Eng & Computing, Unska 3, 10000 Zagreb Croatia

IVÁNYI, ATTILA SZILÁRD, operations research specialist, educator; b. Budapest, Hungary, Nov. 13, 1942; s. Kázmér István and Jolán (Csepreghy) I.; m. Margit Balogh, May 31, 1969; children: Dalma, Kinga, Krisztina. Diploma in Mech. Engring., Poly. U., Miskolc, Hungary, 1966; MBA, Budapest U. Econ. Scis., 1974, postgrad. diploma, 1978; PhD, Hungarian Acad. of Sci., 1979, DSc in Econs., 1986. R&D leader Láng Machine Factory, Budapest, 1966-74; asst. prof. Econs. BUES Hungary, 1974-80, assoc. prof. Econs, 1980-88, prof. Econs, 1988—, vice chmn. dept. Indsl. Mgmt., 1985-92, chmn. Innovation Mgmt. Group dept. Applied Econs., 1992—; dir. Economum consulting firm, Budapest, 1985—; prof. Newport U., Calif., 1997—. Improving the Marketability of Products Through Value Analysis, 1980, Value Analysis in Organizing Production, 1984, Product Strategy, Production Policy and Technical Development, 1985, (with Ilona Hoffer) Innovation Management, 1993, Innovation Methodology, 1996. Recipient award Ministry of Edn., 1983. Mem. Acac. of Sci. (indsl. econs. com. 1991), Value Analysis Soc. of Hungary (scientific pres. 1990). Avocations: swimming, table tennis. E-mail: econovum@mail.elender.hu. Home: Mandula u 31, 1O25 Budapest Hungary Office: Budapest U Econ Scis, Fovam ter 8 sz, 1O93 Budapest Hungary

IVÁNYI, JÁNOS, endocrinologist; b. Bekéssámson, Hungary, Dec. 12, 1924; s. János and Erzsébet (Csete) I.; m. Ella Toth; children: János, Béla, Tibor. MD, U. Szeged, Hungary, 1949; PhD, Hungarian Acad. Scis., 1993. Med. Diplomate. Asst. physician Dept. Medicine Univ. Sch., Szeged, Hungary, 1949-55; head physician Dept. Medicine City Hosp., Jászberény, Hungary, 1955-60, County Hosp., Çyula, Hungary, 1960-95; ret., 1995; chief internist, diabetologist County Békés, 1968-95. Author: (book) Theory and Practice of Intensive Care, 1977; contbr. chpt. to book. Lt. Army of People, Hungary, 1951-52, Budapest. Recipient Ministry of Health award Helsinki, Finland, 1964. Mem. European Diabetes Assn. Lutheran. Home: Árpád St 20, H-5700 Gyula Hungary

IVATURI, RAO, nutritionist, educator, consultant; b. Madras, India, Jan. 20, 1960; came to U.S., 1981; s. Subba Rao and Raja Rajeswari (Chaganti) I.; m. Indira Venkateshwararao Pingali, Nov. 25, 1988. BS in Agr., Andhra Pradesh Agrl. U., Hyderabad, India, 1981; MS in Food and Nutrition, Kans. State U., 1983; PhD in Nutrition, U. Nebr., 1986. Cert. nutrition specialist. Nutrition coord. U. Nebr. Health Ctr., Lincoln, 1985-86; assoc. prof. nutrition Ind. State U., Terre Haute, 1986—; nutrition cons. West Cen. Ind. Econ. Devel. Dist., Terre Haute, 1988—; teaching and rsch. activities related to hunger; seminar leader, weight mgmt. clinic Ind. State U. Adult Fitness Program. Contbr. articles to profl. jours. Coord. World Food Day Teleconf., Ind. State U., 1986, 88, 92-94. Recipient Caleb Mills Disting. Tchg. award Ind. U. Mem. Am. Inst. Nutrition, Fedn. Am. Socs. for Exptl. Biologies. Office: Family/Consumer Svcs Dept Ind State U Terre Haute IN 47809-0001

IVENS, MARY SUE, microbiologist, mycologist; b. Maryville, Tenn., Aug. 23, 1929; d. McPherson Joseph and Sarah Lillie (Hensley) I.; B.S., E. Tenn. State U., 1949; M.S. (NIH research trainee), Tulane U. Sch. Medicine, 1963; Ph.D., La. State U. Sch. Medicine, 1966; postgrad. Oak Ridge Inst. Nuclear Studies, Emory U. Sch. Medicine. Dir. microbiol. and mycol. labs. Lewis-Gale Hosp., Roanoke, Va., 1953-56; rsch. mycologist Ctrs. Disease Control, Atlanta, 1957-60; rsch. assoc. La. State U. Sch. Med., 1963-66, instr. medicine, 1966-72, instr. Microbiology, 1966-72, clin. prof., 1972—; dir. mycology lab, La. State U. Sch. Med., 1963-72; lectr. Sch. Dentistry, La. State U. Med. Ctr., 1968-70; assoc. prof. natural scis. Dillard U., New Orleans, 1972—; assoc. Marine Biol. Lab., Woods Hole, Mass., 1978— ; cons. in field. Commr. WHO conf. on ctr. for Mycotic sera 1969; chmn. Gold Medal Award Com. Sigma Xi, 1978; mem. La. assn. def. counsel expert witness bank, 1985—; bd. dirs. La. coun. Girl Scouts U.S., Community Relationships Greater New Orleans, Zoning Bd. River Ridge (La.); mem. exec. bd. River Ridge Civic Assn., 1982—, sec., 1982-84; chmn. pers. bd. Riverside Bapt. Ch., River Ridge; dir. Outreach First Baptist Ch., New Orleans, 1989—. Recipient Rosicrucian Humanitarian award, 1981; Macy fellow, MBL, Woods Hole, 1978-79; grantee NSF, NIH; diplomate Am. Bd. Microbiology. Mem. Internat. Soc. Human and Animal Mycology, Med. Mycological Soc. Am., Am. Soc. Microbiology (nat. com. on membership 1983-87), AAAS, Nat. Inst. Sci., Sigma Xi. Author articles in field. Home: 408 Berclair Ave New Orleans LA 70123-1504 Office: Dillard U Div Natural Sci New Orleans LA 70122

IVERSEN, BENJAMIN RUPERT LARS, investment banker; b. Cambridge, Eng., May 10, 1969; s. Leslie Lars and Susan Diana (Kibble) I.; m. Barbara Steffen, July 25, 1997. MA, Cambridge U., 1991. Exec. Cazenove Co., London, 1991-95, Credit Lyonnais Securities, London, 1995-96; dir. Credit Lyonnais Securities, Hong Kong, 1996-99, Merrill Lynch, Singapore, 2000—; dir. Panos Therapeutics, Oxford, 1995—. Mem. Securities Inst., Macau Golf Club. Avocations: portfolio investment, reading, golf, skiing. Office: Merrill Lynch 29F Millenia, Tower, 1 Temasek Ave, Singapore 039 192, Republic of Singapore

IVERUS, LENNART JAN GUSTAF, artist; b. Skara, Sweden, Feb. 8, 1930; s. Gustaf Herbert and Sonja Maria (Lundgren) I.; m. Ann-Charlotte Taube; children: Martina, Charlotta. BA, U. Stockholm, 1955; postgrad., Royal Acad. Fine Arts, Stockholm, 1961-65, Royal Coll. Arts, London, 1963-64. Tchr. U. Coll. of Arts, Crafts and Design, Stockholm, 1975-95. Bd. dirs. The Graphic Soc., Stockholm, 1965-67, 92-94, Swedish Artists Assn., 1977-80. Home: Maltesholmsvägen 180, 165-62 Hässelby Sweden

IVES, MARGARET CHRISTYNE, foreign language educator; b. Grimsby, England, Dec. 22, 1938; d. George and Marjorie Winifred (Pettifer) I. BA, London U., 1960, MA, 1964; PhD, Lancaster U., 1979. Lectr. U. Cambridge, England, 1964-69, Lancaster U., England, 1974-97; external examiner Strathclyde U., Scotland, 1985-89, Bristol U., England, 1988-92, Leicester U., England, 1988-92, Leeds U., England, 1996-99, East Anglia U., Eng., 1996-2000. Author: The Analogue of Harmony, 1970, Enlightenment and National Revival, 1979, The Mystic Veil, 1998, Women of the Passion, 1998. Lay reader Ch. of England, Lancaster, 1989—. German studies fellow Girton Coll., Cambridge, 1962-70, Brith Coun. Exch. fellow, Budapest, 1972-73. Mem. Ch. of England. Avocation: walking. Office: Lancaster U., Lonsdale Coll, Lancaster LA1 4YN, England

IVESTER, MELVIN DOUGLAS, retired beverage company executive; b. New Holland, Ga., Mar. 26, 1947; s. Howard Edward and Ada Mae (Pass) I.; m. Victoria Kay Grindle, Mar. 20, 1969. BBA cum laude, U. Ga., 1969. Acct. Ernst & Ernst, Atlanta, 1969-75; mgr. Ernst & Whinney, Atlanta, 1975-79; asst. contr., dir. corp. auditing The Coca-Cola Co., Atlanta, 1979-81, v.p., contr., 1981-83, sr. v.p. fin., 1983-84, sr. v.p., CFO, 1985-89; pres. European Cmty. Group, 1980-90, Coca-Cola USA, 1990-91; pres. Coca-Cola N.Am. Group, 1991-93, prin. oper. officer, 1993-94, pres., COO, 1994-97, also bd. dirs., chmn., CEO, 1997-2000, ret., 2000; bd. dirs. Georgia Pacific Corp., Sun Trust, Inc., trustee Morehouse Coll.; former trustee, dir. U. Ga. Found. Home: 411 Peachtree Battle Ave NW Atlanta GA 30305-4032

IVEZIĆ, MARIJA NEDJELJKA, entomologist, nematologist, educator; b. Vrpolje, Sinj, Croatia, Aug. 10, 1947; d. Ivan and Luca (Žuljević) Šušnjara; m. Miroslav Ivezić; children: Tihana, Vladimir. Agronomist, U. Osijek, 1970, MSc, 1976, PhD, 1980. Asst. rschr., asst. Faculty Agr., Osijek, Croatia, 1971-80; docent, assoc. prof. Faculty Agr., Osijek, 1981-90, prof., 1991—; cons. U. J.J. Strossmayer, Osijek, 1997-2000; mem. Nat. Coun. Higher Edn., Zagreb, Croatia, 1994-2000, coun. sci., Zagreb, 2000—. Contbr. articles to profl. jours. Recipient Cert. of Appreciation USDA, 1986, Pres. award Republic Croatia, 1995-97, award for Sci., 1999. Mem. European Soc. Nematologists (v.p. 1990-94), Croatian Soc. Entomologists, Croatian Soc. Agronomists. Roman Catholic. Avocations: table tennis, walking, swimming. Office: Univ JJ Strossmayer, Trg sv Trojstva 3, 31 000 Osijek Croatia

IVLIYEV, ANDREI DMITRIYEVICH, physics educator; b. Vladivostok, Russia, Jan. 11, 1948; s. Dmitri Ivanovich Ivliyev and Elga Genrikhovna Stromberg; m. Eugeniya Vladimirovna Grunina, June 13, 1974; children: Larisa, Aleksandra. Degree in radioengring., Ural Polytech. Inst., Ekaterinburg, 1972; degree in physics, Ural State U., Ekaterinburg, 1978. Sci. worker Ural Polytech. Inst., Ekaterinburg, 1972-80; asst. lectr. Ural State Acad. Mining and Geology, Ekaterinburg, 1980-82, assoc. prof., 1982-92, prof., 1992—. Author: Physics, 1993; co-author: Hall Effect in Transition Metals at High Temperatures, 1985, Thermal Diffusivity...Metals...Near Phase Transition, 1982; patentee in field. Mem. N.Y. Acad. Scis. Avocations: theater, music, basketball, skiing, swimming. Home: 17 Apt 25 Manevrovaya Str, Ekaterinburg 620050, Russia Office: Ural State Acad Mining/Geol, 30 Kuibysheva str, 620144 Ekaterinburg Russia

IVONIN, VLADIMIR MICHAYLOVITCH, ecologist, agricultural engineer; b. Glazov, Russia, Dec. 13, 1938; s. Michail Yakovlevitch and Myzha Pavlovna (Malginova) I.; m. Olga Vasilyevna Kaverina, May 29, 1968 (div. Sept. 1973); 1 child, Inna Vladimirovna; m. Ludmila Grigorevna Sorokina, Feb. 18, 1977. Forestry engr., Land Reclamation Inst., Novocherkassk, Russia, 1968; PhD, Donskoy Agrl. Inst., Persianovka, Russia, 1972; DSc, All-Union Scientific Inst., Volgograd, Russia, 1985; prof., WAK, Moscow, 1987. Sr. scientific collaborator Donskoy Agrl. Inst., 1969-75; sr. scientific collaborator All-Union Scientific and Rsch. Inst. Forestry, Pushkino, Russia, 1975-76, Volgograd, Russia, 1976-79; head lab. soil conservation All-Union Scientific and Rsch. Inst. Forestry, Barnaul, Russia, 1979-85; head chair ecology Land Reclamation Acad., Novocherkassk, 1985—. Author: Forest Recultivation of Slopes Damaged by Gullies, 1983, Recultivation of Gullies, 1992, The Ecological Foundations of Land Reclamation, 1995, Forest and Agricultural Reclamation of Gully Lands, 1998. Sgt., Army Arty., 1962-64, Rostov-on-Don. Recipient scientific investigation prize Russian Ministry Agr., Moscow, 1996, North Caucasus Railroad Bd., Rostov-on-Don, 1996, Nat. Park, Sochi, 1997. Mem. Russian Acad. Agrl. Edn. Avocations: poetry, literature, fishing. Home: 25-a Komsomolskay str Apt 9, 246029 Novocherkassk Russia Office: Land Reclamation Acad, 111 Pushkinsky Str, 346409 Novocherkassk Russia

IVRY, DAVID, diplomat; b. Gedera, Israel, 1934; m. Ifra Ivry; three children. BS in Aero. Engring., Technion U., 1977. Chief rep. U.S.-Israel Strategic Dialogue, 1986-88; dir.-gen. Ministry Def., 1986-96; prin. asst. Min. Def. for Strategic Affairs, 1996-99; nat. security advisor, head Nat. Security Coun., 1999-2000; Israel's amb. to U.S. Washington, 2000—; head Inter-Ministerial Steering Com. on Arms Control, 1986-96; lead Israel's del. Multilateral Working Group on Arms Control and Regional Security, 1986-96. Bd. dirs. El-Al, 1978-82, Israel Aircraft Industries, 1982-92; bd. govs. Technion U., Haifa, 1987—. Maj. gen., comdr. Israel Air Force, 1977-82. Decorated Legion of Merit, USAF; recipient Disting. Svc. Order award Govt. Singapore, Amitai Distinction award for ethical adminstrn. and conduct State of Israel. Fax: 202-364-5423. E-mail: ask@israelemb.org. Office: Embassy of Israel 3514 International Dr NW Washington DC 20008-3099

IVSHINA, IRENA BORISOVNA, microbiologist; b. Perm, USSR, June 12, 1950; d. Boris A. Milashin and Valentina I. Milashina; m. Nikolai S. Ivshin; children: Yelena N., Nikolai N. Bsc with 1st class honors, Perm State U., 1972; PhD, Russian Acad. Sci., 1982. Rschr. Inst. Natural Sci., Perm, 1972-75; rschr. Inst. Ecology and Genetics Microorganism, Perm, 1975-85, sr. rschr., 1985-87, head alkanotrophic microoganism lab., 1988—; chief regional specialised collection alkanotrophic microorganisms. Recipient medal Order, Russia, 1999. Mem. World Fedn. Culture Collection (mem. exec. bd.), N.Y. Acad. Scis. Achievements include Russian patent. Home: Plekhanov str h 22 fl 33, 614068 Perm Russia Office: Inst Ecology & Genetics Microrg, 13 Golev Str, 614081 Perm Russia

IVY, BENJAMIN FRANKLIN, III, financial and real estate investment advisor; b. Bremerton, Wash., May 18, 1936; s. Edward Byron Ivy and Ada Josephine (Anderson) Steele; m. Karen Yvonne Thompson, July 14, 1961 (div. June 1979); children: Britt Annemarie Ivy, Zenah Blair; m. Emily Cecile

Rawlins, Apr. 18, 1982 (div. June 1992); m. Catherine Elaine Bracken, May 23, 2000. BME, Cornell U., 1959; MBA, Stanford U., 1961. CFP. Purchasing agent U. Calif., Berkeley, 1960-62; contract adminstr. Lockheed Missiles and Space div., Sunnyvale, Calif., 1962-64; asst. to pres. Tridea subsidiary McDonnell Douglas, Pasadena, Calif., 1964-68; v.p. Mitchum, Jones & Templeton, Inc., Palo Alto, Calif., 1968-74, Paine Webber, Palo Alto, 1974; pres. Morgan Investment Svcs., Inc., Palo Alto, 1974-84; v.p. Morgan, Olmstead, Kennedy & Gardner, Inc., 1974-84; pres., chmn. Ivy Fin. Enterprises, Inc., Palo Alto, 1984—; pres. Ivy Fin. Svcs., Palo Alto; v.p. and registered prin. Assoc. Group, Inc., L.A., 1984—, dir., 1994-98, Cert. Fin. Planner, 1989—. Founder, former dir. Found. to Eliminate the Nat. Debt, Palo Alto, 1992. Mem. Internat. Assn. Fin. Planners (charter, bd. dirs. 1972-73), Pacific Exch. (assoc.), Cornell U. Alumni Assn., Stanford Alumni Assn. (life), Stanford Bus. Sch. Alumni Assn. (life), Sharon Heights Golf and Country Club, Masons, Elks, Kappa Sigma. Avocations: golf, tennis, poetry, opera, international travel. Office: Ivy Fin Enterprises Inc 525 University Ave Fl 6 Palo Alto CA 94301-1903

IVY, MICHELLE DENEEN, actress, playwright, executive assistant; b. Chgo., Dec. 12, 1973; d. Jonathan Melvin and Jessie Rein Ivy. Student, Robert Morris Coll., Chgo., 2000—. Asst. choreographer, camp counselor CAST Summer Youth Theater Camp, Oak Park, Ill., summer 1993; mem. security staff No. Ill. U., DeKalb, 1994-96; actress, prodr., dir., writer Chgo., 1996—; owner Satin Comforts, Bolingbrook, Ill., 1996-99; office mgr., tech. asst. DePaul U., Chgo., 1998-99; exec. asst. Info. Resources, Inc., Chgo., 1999, Arthur Andersen, Chgo., 2000—; counselor, motivator Ivy Prodns., Chgo.; motivational spkr. EbonyEnergy.com., Chgo., 2000, 3d Unitarian Scholarship Com., Chgo. Author: (poetry) Original Creations from the Mind of Michelle, 1999; scriptwriter: Shante's Reality Check, 1999; founder, choreographer, dancer Rhythm Nation Dance Troupe, 1995-96. Scholar 3d Unitarian, Chgo., 1992, Gammon United Meth., Chgo., 1992. Mem. NAFE. Avocations: writing poetry, plays, songs, acting, dancing, public and motivational speaking. Home: 3628 W Polk St Fl 1 Chicago IL 60624-4049

IWAHASHI, MAKIO, chemistry educator, chemist; b. Ohmuta, Fukuoka, Japan, Feb. 22, 1946; s. Masatoshi and Tsuneyo (Tawara) I.; m. Tomoko Okabe, Mar. 21, 1971; children: Takuya, Mie. BS, Tokyo U. Sci., 1968; MSc, Tokyo Met. U., 1970, PhD, 1975. Rsch. instr. Tokyo Met. U., 1970-84; postdoctoral fellow Clarkson U., Potsdam, N.Y., 1979-81; asst. prof. Kitasato U., Sagamihara, Kanagawa, Japan, 1984-92, assoc. prof., 1993-94, prof. chemistry, 1994—, dean of libr. of sch. sci., 1994-98. Author: Thermodynamics of Molecules, 1996. Mem. Am. Chem. Soc., Japan Chem. Soc. (chief of planning sect. divsn. colloid and interface sci. 1998-2000, regular organizer Kanto br. 1998—), Spectroscopy Soc. Japan, Japan Oil Chemists' Soc. (dir. 1998-99), Surface Sci. Soc. Japan, Japan Liquid Crystal Soc. (dir. 2000—), Soc. Applied Spectroscopy. Home: 1444-4 Isobe, Kanagawa Sagamihara 228-0827, Japan Office: Kitasato U Sch Sci, 1-15-1 Kitasato, Kanagawa Sagamihara 228-8555, Japan

IWAHASHI, MASAHIRO, engineering educator; b. Tachikawa, Tokyo, Japan, Feb. 24, 1965; s. Kazuhiro and Toshiko Iwahashi; m. Rie Iwahashi. B.Engring., Tokyo Met. U., 1988, M.Engring., 1990, Dr.Engring., 1996. Rschr. Nippon Steel Co. Ltd., Tokyo, 1990-93; rsch. asst. Nagaoka U. of Tech., Niigata, 1993-98, assoc. prof. dept. elec. engring., 1998—; JICA expert Thammasart U., Bangkok, 1998-99. Contbr. articles to profl. jours. Mem. IEEE, Inst. of Electronics, Infor. and Comm. Engrs. Avocations: violin, windsurfing, telemark skiing. Office: Nagaoka Univ of Tech, 1603-1 Kamitomioka, Nagaoka Niigata 940-2188, Japan

IWAHORI, SHUICHI, fruit science educator; b. Yokohama, Kanagawa, Japan, Aug. 9, 1938; s. Shozaburo and Ryuko I.; m. Takako Igarashi, Apr. 13, 1963; 1 child, Seiko Nakajima. B in Agrl. Sci., U. Tokyo, 1961, M in Agrl. Sci., 1963, PhD, 1966. Post doctoral fellow U. Calif., Davis,, 1966-67, Riverside, 1967-69; asst. prof. agrl. sci. U. Tokyo, 1969-71; assoc. prof. Kagoshima (Japan) U., 1971-82, prof., 1982-91; prof. U. Tsukuba, Japan, 1991—; chmn. Inst. Agrl. Forestry U. Tsukuba, 1994-98, dean doctoral program in agrl. sci., 1999—. Fulbright Travel grantee, 1966. Mem. Japanese Soc. Hort. Sci. (coun. 1990-96, v.p. 1993-96, 96-99, pres.), Internat. Soc. Hort. Sci. (mem. editl. bd. 1969—, coun. 1993—), Soc. for Chem. Regulation of Plants (coun. 1990-2000, mem. editl. bd. 1996-2000), Tropical Agr. Rsch. Assn. Japan (editor-in-chief 1995—, coun. 1995—). Avocation: playing Go. Office: U Tsukuba, Inst Agr and Forestry, Tsukuba 305-8572, Japan

IWAI, KAZURO, physician and research consultant; b. Tokyo, Mar. 8, 1927; s. Shosaburo and Yoshi (Okanoya) I.; m. Yoshiko Kimura, Oct. 23, 1955; children: Akiko Asakura, Yukiko Tabata, Setsuko Iwai. Diploma, Kyoto U. Med. Sch., Japan, 1949; MD (hon.), Kyoto U., 1959. Chief pathology sect. Rsch. Inst. Tuberculosis, Kiyose, Tokyo, 1959-76, head dept. rsch., 1977-79, vice dir., 1980-83, dir., 1984-87, cons., 1987—; mem. rsch. com. intractable disease Ministry Health and Welfare, Japan, 1970-95; chmn. rsch. com. diesel exhause health effect Environ. Agy., Japan, 1986-98. Chief editor (computer program): Respiro-Navi, 1998; contbr. articles to profl. jours. Mem. Japanese Soc. Tuberculosis (dir. 1978—), Japanese Soc. Sarcoidosis (hon.), Japan Antituberculosis Assn. (dir. 1985—). Avocation: sailing by cruiser. Home: 2-4-16 hibarigaoka-kita, Hoya-shi, Tokyo 202-0002, Japan Office: Japan Antituberculosis Assn, 3-1-24 Matsuyama Kiyose-shi, Tokyo 204-0022, Japan

IWAI, ZENTA, engineering educator; b. Tokyo, Apr. 4, 1941; s. Fumio and Makie (Sindo) I.; m. Michiko Nunoi, July 7, 1968; children: Ken, Yoshi. BSc, Kyoto U., 1964, MSc, 1966, Dr.Engring., 1970. Rsch. assoc. Kyoto U., 1964-70; assoc. prof. Kumamoto (Japan) U., 1970-80, prof., 1980—. Author: Observer, 1988, Mechanical Engineering Dictionary, 1997, Control Engineering, 1999, Lecture and Exercise of Vibration Engineering, 2000. Bd. dirs. Kumamoto U., 1999—, dean Faculty of Engring, 2000—. Mem. Soc. Instrument and Control Engrs. (bd. dirs. 1997-99, Best Paper award 1970, pres. Kyushu Br 2000), Japan Soc. Mech. Engrs. (mem. coun. 1990, 97, Contbn. award as reviewer 1997), Inst. of Sys., Control and Info. Engrs. (mem. coun. 1983—), Kyushu Assn. Engring. Edn. (Best Contbn. award 2000). Avocations: fishing, gardening. Office: Kumamoto Univ, Dept Mech Engring, Kumamoto 860-8555, Japan

IWAKAWA, SEIGO, pharmaceutical scientist; b. Fuchu, Hiroshima, Japan, Aug. 30, 1952; s. Sei-ichi and Kiyoko (Yoshioka) I.; m. Nobuko Okuda, Apr. 29, 1984; children: Shinya, Yumi. BS in Pharmacy, Hiroshima U., 1975, MS in Pharmacy, 1977; PhD in Pharmacy, Kyoto (Japan) U., 1986. Pharmacist Kyoto U. Hosp., 1983-84; instr. Kyoto U., 1984-89; lectr. Kobe (Japan) U., 1989-93, vice dir. dept. pharmacy, 1990-93; assoc. prof. Kobe Pharm. U., 1993-98, prof., 1998—; lectr. Kobe Gakuin U., 1990-93. Mem. AAAS, Japanese Soc. for Study of Xenobiotics, Pharm. Soc. Japan. N.Y. Acad. Scis. Home: Ibukidaihigashi 2-1-1-305, Nishi-ku, Kobe 651-2242, Japan Office: Kobe Pharm U, Motoyamakita 4-19-1, Higashinada-ku Kobe 658-8558, Japan

IWAMA, HIROSHI, anesthesiologist; b. Kamaishi, Iwate, Japan, Nov. 28, 1960; s. Teruo and Kimiko (Sasaki) I.; m. Naomi Suzuki, Oct., 1991; children: Yuki, Tomomi. B in Medicine, Oita (Japan) Med. U., 1986; MD, Fukushima (Japan) Med. Coll., 1994. Cert. emergency medicine physician, specialist in anesthesiology, specialist in intensive care medicine; pain clinic cert. Rschr. in forensic medicine Oita (Japan) Med. U., 1986-87; resident in emergency medicine Nippon Med. Sch., Tokyo, 1987-89; staff anesthesiologist Ctrl. Aizu Gen. Hosp., Aizuwakamatsu, Japan, 1989-92; dir. anestheisology and emergency medicine Ctrl. Aizu Gen. Hosp., Aizuwakamatsu, 1994—; staff anesthesiologist Fukushima (Japan) Med. Coll., 1992-94. Contbr. articles to profl. jours. including Jour. Anesthesia, Anesthesiology,, Can. Jour. of Anaesthesia, Jour. of Trauma, Acta Anaesthesiologica Scandinavica, Anaesthesia, Surgery Today, Brit. Jour. Anaesthesia, Jour. Clin. Anesthesia, Regional Anesthesia and Pain Medicine, Jour. Emergency Medicine, others. Mem. Japanese Assn. Acute Medicine, Japan Soc. Anesthesiology, Japan Soc. Pain Clinicians, Japanese Soc. Intensive Care Medicine, Japan Surg. Soc. Avocation: scuba diving. Home: Lions Mansion 1301, 3-1-8 Chuo Fukushima, Aizu-Wakamatsu 965-0037, Japan Office: Ctrl Aizu Gen Hosp, 1-1 Tsuruga-machi Fukushima, Aizu-Wakamatsu 965-0011, Japan

IWAMOTO, MASAKAZU, chemistry educator; b. Shimabara, Nagasaki, Japan, Oct. 26, 1948; s. Masatomo and Hiroko M.; m. Tomoko Kaetsu, Apr. 22, 1978; children: Fumiko, Michiharu, Nobuko, Shouko. B in Engring., Kyushu U., 1971, M in Engring., 1973, DEng, 1976. Asst. prof. Nagasaki U., 1976-81, assoc. prof., 1981-87; prof. chemistry Miyazaki U., 1987-90, Hokkaido U., 1990-00, Tokyo Inst. Tech., 2000—; dir. catalysis rsch. ctr. Hokkaido U., 1997-00. Recipient Chem. Soc. Japan awards, 1982, 94, 2000, Catalysis Soc. Japan awards, 1986, 97, Found. for New Tech. award, 1990, Inst. Mech. Engring. award, 1993, Hokkaido PTA Assoc. award, 1999. Avocations: skiing, tennis, golf. Home: Kamihirama, 1254-2108 Nakahara-ku, Kawasaki 211-0013, Japan Office: Tokyo Inst Tech Chem Rsch, Nagatsuta 4259 Midori-ku, Yokohama 226-8503, Japan

IWAMOTO, SOUICHI, engineering educator, scientific researcher; b. Kobe, Hyogo, Japan, Sept. 21, 1943; s. Koudo and Haruko Iwamoto; m. Kayoko Iwamoto, July 1970; children: Chitaru, Akeshi. Student, U. Tokyo, 1967, postgrad., 1969, PhD, 1974. Rschr. Chief, Tokyo, 1974-79; prof. Toyo U., Saitama, Japan, 1979—. Contbr. papers to profl. jours. Mem. IEEE, AAS, AMS, APS. Republican. Buddhist. Avocations: violin, Go, golf. Home: 1384-86 Suneori, 350-2213 Tsurugashima Saitama, Japan

IWAMOTO, YOSHIHISA, biochemistry and microbiology educator; b. Shizuoka, Japan, Mar. 6, 1943; s. Kenkichi and Jun Iwamoto; m. Kikuko Matsuzono, Mar. 27, 1968; children: Kumiko, Takayoshi, Yukiko. B, Shizuoka Coll. Pharmacy, Japan, 1965, M, 1967, PhD, 1979. Rsch. assoc. Shizuoka Coll. Pharmacy, 1968-84, asst. prof., 1984-87; asst. prof. U. Shizuoka Sch. Pharamcy, 1987-91, assoc. prof., 1991-97, prof. Sch. Nursing, 1997—; postdoctoral fellow U. Ala., Birmingham, 1979-80, U. South Ala., Mobile, 1980-81; vis. scientist Cancer Rsch. Lab., U. Auckland, New Zealand, 1991. Inventor Mutation Rsch., 1985, 92, Photochem. Photobiology, 1985, 88, Photodermatology, 1991, Chem. Pharm. Bull., 1992, 93, Biol. Pharm. Bull, 1994, 95, Microbiol. Immunol., 1996. Avocations: soft tennis, reading, travel, tennis. Home: 34-24 Nakada Honcho, Shizuoka 422, Japan Office: U Shizuoka, 52-1 Yada, Shizuoka 422, Japan

IWAŃCZAK, WOJCIECH JÓZEF, historian; b. Wrocław, Poland, Jan. 19, 1948; s. Edward and Sabina (Staniszewska) I.; m. Irena Dubiel, June 8, 1985; children: Paweł, Przemysław. MA in History, Warsaw U., 1970; D in Humanities, Polish Acad. Scis., 1981. Editor Tygodnik Kulturalny, Warsaw, 1973-76; rschr. Inst. of History, Polish Acad. Scis., Warsaw, 1976-80; lectr. Pedagogical U., Kielce, Poland, 1982-92; head of medieval dept. Pedagogical U., Kielce, 1990—, prof., 1992—; fellowship Czechoslovak Acad. Scis., Prague, Czech Republic, 1979, Istituto Luigi Sturzo, Rome, 1985-87; Geisteswissenschaftliches Zentrum Geschichte und Kultur Ostmitteleuropas e.V., Leipzig, Germany, 1997; v.p. Polish-Czech sect. of the com. of historical scis. Polish Acad. Scis., Warsaw, 1994—; pres. Polish-Czech sect. of the com. of hist. scis. Polish Acad. Scis., Warsaw, 2000—; pres. Hist. Soc. in Warsaw, 1999—; invited lectr. various univs. Author: On the Trail of Knightly Adventure, 1985, Men of the Sword, Men of Prayer, Men of Work, 1989, Teaching in the Old Times, 1997; contbr. over 110 articles to profl. jours. Mem. Medieval Acad. Am., Medieval Inst. of Leeds, Assn. of Scientific Authors. Avocations: skiing, tennis, sailing, languages. Office: Pedagogical U Inst History, Żeromskiego 5, 25-369 Kielce Poland

IWARSON, STEN AXEL, infectious diseases physician educator; b. Svenljunga, Sweden, Apr. 28, 1940; s. Stig L. and Elsa C. (Lind) I.; m. Birgitta R. Rennerfelt, Nov. 14, 1964; children: Matts, Pelle, Charlotte, Susanne. MD, U. Göteborg, Sweden, 1967, PhD, 1973. Head dept. infectious diseases Sahlgrenska U. Hosp., Göteborg, 1980—; vis. scientist Office Biologies, FDA, Bethesda, Md., 1983-84; prof. Infectious Diseases, Göteborg U.; med. advisor Nat. Bd. Health, Sweden, 1980—; med. expert Med. Products Agy., Sweden, 1990—. Author, editor: (textbooks) Infectious Diseases; contbr. articles to profl. jours. Fellow Infectious Diseases Soc. Am., Royal Coll. Physicians Edinburgh, Royal coll. Physicians London (hon.). Avocation: collecting Swedish glass art. Home: Mimersvagen 47, S-43364 Partille Sweden Office: Sahlgrenska U Hosp Ostra, Dept Infectious Diseases, S-41685 Göteborg Sweden

IWASAKI, HIDESUKE, biochemistry educator; b. Kure, Hiroshima, Japan, Jan. 3, 1930; s. Saisuke and Yone (Kawato) I.; m. Ikuko Kosumi, May 17, 1959; children: Toshisuke I., Kuniko Yoshida. PhD, Kyoto (Japan) U., 1961. Pharm. diplomate. Researcher Takeda Chem. Industries Ltd., Osaka, Japan, 1954-63; vis. scientist NIH, 1963-64; lab. chief Takeda Chem. Industries Ltd., Osaka, 1964-84, liaision officer, 1984-90; lectr. Mukogawa Women U., Nishinomiya, Japan, 1976-2000; rep. for Japan to toxicology test group Orgn. Econ. Cooperation and Devel., Luxenbourg, 1979; vice chmn. safety com. Japan Soc. Pharm. Mfrs., Tokyo, 1976-86; R&D Com. MITI Japanese Govt., Tokyo, 1985-86. Editor: Standard Operating Procedures in Toxicology, 1981; discoverer new antibiotic; author inventions Jour. Antibiotics, 1955-76. Dir. Soc. Welfare Annuitants, Itami City, Japan, 1992—. Mem. Am. Soc. Microbiology, Japan Pharm. Soc. Avocations: bonsai, classic music. Home: 5-5-8 Minamino, Itami Hyogo 664-0865, Japan

IWASAWA, ISOO (FRANCIS), accountant, management consultant; b. Yokohama, Kanagawa, Japan, Jan. 9, 1936; d. Matasaku (Joseph) Ninomiya and Haruno (Ann) I.; m. Kinuko (Kay) Sato, March 15, 1963; children: Isoaki, Lia, Chiharu, Leo. BSc, St. Martin's Coll., Olympia, Wash., 1960; postgrad., U. Wash., 1960-61, Georgetown U., 1961. CPA, Wash. Prin. Ernst & Whiney, Hong Kong, 1984-86; ptnr. Arthur Young, Hong Kong, 1986-89; mng. dir. Asahi Iwasawa & Assocs. Mgmt. Cons. Ltd., Hong Kong, 1989—. Avocations: gardening, sailing, golfing. Office: China Resources Bldg FL 43, No 26 Harbour Rd Rm 4303, Wanchai Hong Kong Address: AIA Mgt Cons Ltd Cindic Tow, 128 Gloucester Rd Rm E &F8F, Hong Kong Hong Kong

IWATA, FUMIHIRO, internist; b. Nagoya, Aichi, Japan, May 25, 1960; s. Sumio and Kimiko (Itoh) I.; m. Noriko Hasegawa, Oct. 10, 1990; 3 children. MD, Nagoya (Japan) City U., 1985, PhD, 1995. Physician dept. internal medicine Midori Mcpl. Hosp., Nagoya, 1986-90; rschr. dept. internal medicine Sch. Medicine Nagoya City U., 1990-92; rsch. fellow Sepulveda (Calif.) VA Med. Ctr., UCLA, 1992-94; physician, rschr. dept. internal medicine Nagoya Kouseiin Hosp., 1995-96; chief endoscopy ctr. dept. internal medicine Kosai (Japan) Gen. Hosp., 1996-98; physician dept. internal medicine NTT West Tokai Hosp., Nagoya, 1998—. Contbr. articles to profl. jours. Mem. Japanese Soc. Internal Medicine, Japanese Soc. Gastroenterology, Japan Gastroenterol. Endoscopy Soc. Home: 3-18-11 Chiyoda Naka-ku, Nagoya Aichi 460-0012, Japan Office: NTT West Tokai Hosp, 2-17-5 Matsubara Naka-ku, Nagoya Aichi 460-0017, Japan

IWATA, FUMIO, marine zoologist; b. Yokohama, Kanagawa, Japan, Mar. 6, 1925; s. Hikosaburo and Hisa (Yoneyama) I.; m. Mutsuko Kawashima, Jan. 6, 1951; children: Mineo, Tomomi. DSc, Hokkaido U., Sapporo, 1959; PhD (hon.), Marquis Giuseppe Scicluna IUF, 1988; DSc (hon.), Albert Einstein I.A.F., 1993. Asst. Hokkaido U., 1950-59, asst. prof., 1959-74, prof., 1974-88, prof. emeritus, 1988—; prof. Kushiro Pub. U. of Econs., Kushiro, Japan, 1988-95. Recipient Sabin Commemorative medallion AEIAF, 1995. Home: Momijidai Nishi 5-9-13, Atsubetsuj-ku Sapporo 004-0013, Japan

IWATA, YOSHIKAZU, neurosurgeon; b. Osaka, Japan, May 20, 1936; s. Yoshiharu and Shigeyo (Masui) I.; m. Hisako Shizukuishi, Sept. 16, 1940; children: Kazuko, Hideo, Sumiko. MD, Osaka U., 1962, PhD, 1967. Cert. Ednl. Coun. for Fgn. Med. Grads. House officer Nat. Osaka Hosp., 1967-74; resident Cerebral Stereotaxic Inst., Phila., 1970-72; intern St. Luke's and Children's Med. Ctr., Phila., 1971-72; staff Osaka U. Hosp., 1975-82; neurosurgeon-in-chief Minoh City Hosp., Osaka, 1982-94, dir., 2000—; judge Med. Ins. Payment, Osaka, 1988—. Contbr. articles to profl. jours. Mem. N.Y. Acad. Scis., Japan Neurosurg. Soc. Avocation: world travel. Office: Minoh City Hosp Neurosurg, 5-7-1 Kayano, Osaka Minoh 562-8562, Japan

IWATSUBO, EIJI, urologist; b. Nagasaki, Japan, Nov. 27, 1941; s. Torao and Aya I.; m. Izue Nono, Apr. 29, 1970; children: Shiori, Hiroko, Yasuyo, Takahiro. MD, Kyushu U., 1967, PhD, 1982. Intern U.S. Naval Hosp., Yokosuka, Japan, 1967-68; resident in urology Kyushu U. Hosp., Fukuoka, Japan, 1968-70, Beppu Nat. Hosp., Oita, Japan, 1970-72; asst. prof. Kyushu U. Sch. Medicine, 1972-78; lectr. Harvard Sch. Medicine, Boston, 1978-79; chief urology Spinal Injuries Ctr. Labor Welfare Corp., Iizuka, Japan, 1979—; clin. prof. Kyushu U. Sch. Medicine, 1976—; vis. prof. Miyazaki Med. Coll., Japan, 1977—, Saga Med. Coll., Japan, 1980—, Kurukme U. Sch. Medicine, Japan, 1984—, Coll. Occupl. and Environ. Health, Japan, 1998—; mem. WHO Expert Adv. Panel on Accident Prevention, 1997—. Author: Atlas of Urological Surgery, 1983, Illustrated Urology, 1991, Q&A for Sexuality of Paraplegia, 1994, Guidebook for Sexuality and Childbirth of the Paralyzed, 1996. Mem. Fukuoka Urol. Soc. (bd. dirs. 1987—), Japan Incontinence Soc. (hon. cons. 1992—), Internat. Med. Soc. Paraplegia (nat. del. 1999—), Internat. Incontinence Soc. Avocation: Japanese martial arts. Office: Labor Welfare Corp, Spinal Injuries Ctr, 820-8508 Iizuka Fukuoka, Japan

IWAYAMA, TAJIRO, university president, educator; b. Kyoto, Japan, Jan. 10, 1933; s. Hikoichi and Toku (Fukui) I.; B.A., Doshisha U., 1955, M.A., 1958; M.F.A., State U. Iowa, 1962 Legum Dr., Carleton Coll., 1997; m. Ikuyo Takami, Mar. 16, 1960. Research asst. Doshisha U., Kyoto, 1958-63, instr. Am. lit., 1963-65, asst. prof., 1965-70, prof., 1970—, dean acad. affairs, 1979-80, 89-90, dir. Ctr. Am. Studies, 1983-86, dean Faculty of Letters, 1986-88, now pres.; dir. Kyoto Am. Studies Summer Seminar, 1981-86 . Fulbright grad. fellow, 1960-62, Am. Council Learned Socs. fellow, 1972-73. Mem. Japanese Assn. Am. Lit. (exec. sec.), MLA, English Lit. Assn. Japan, Japanese Assn. Am. Studies. Author: English Composition Manual, 1978; Saul Bellow, 1982, Invitation to American Literature, 1987, The Gilded Age and American Literature, 1987; editor: East-West Review, 1964-67. Home: 46 Hitsujisaru-cho, Katsura, Nishikyo-ku Kyoto 615-8084, Japan Office: Doshisha U, Karasuma Imadegawa, Kyoto Kamigyo-ku 602-8580, Japan*

IWUH, PASCHAL CHINAENYE, petroleum and chemical engineer, researcher; b. Ekwereazu, Nigeria, Aug. 20, 1971; s. Patrick Enyeribe and Pauline Nwaurasi (Aririguzo) I. BS in petroleum engring., U. Ibadan, Nigeria, 1995; postgrad., Tech. U. Budapest, Hungary, 1997-99; MS in chem. engring., 1999. Engr. Mobile Producing (NIG) Ultd., Lagos, Nigeria, 1996-97. Exch. scholar Ga. Inst. Tech., Atlanta, 1998. Mem. AIChE, Soc. Petroleum Engrs., Am. Chem. Soc., Nigeria Soc. Engrs. Avocations: chess, Scrabble, soccer, table tennis, swimming. Home: 611 Hawthorne Square Oakdale PA 15071 Address: Bayer Corporation 100 Bayer Rd Pittsburgh PA 15205

IYAKUTTI, KOMBIAH THEVAR, physics educator; b. South Vijayanarayanam, India, Apr. 15, 1949; s. S. Kombiah Thevar and Smt. Arumugathammal; m. Valli Iyakutti, June 8, 1978; children: Lakshmi, Kobi Sundar. BSc, Madurai U., 1970; MSc, U. Madras, 1972, PhD, 1978. Jr. rsch. fellow U. Madras, India, 1972-74, rsch. asst., 1974-78, lectr., 1978-84; postdoctoral fellow Uppsala U., Sweden, 1981-82; reader Madurai (India) Kamaraj U., 1984-87, prof., 1987—; hon. dep. dir. Sci. Edn. Ctr., Madurai, 1986-88; head dept. Madurai Kamaraj U., 1993—, head, coord. Sch. of Physics, 1995-97, sr. prof. 1998—, mem. syndicate 2000-03. Contbr. articles to profl. jours. Jr. rsch. fellowship Coun. of Scientific and Indsl. Rsch., 1972, internat. seminar fellow SIDA, 1981-82; vis. scientist grant ICTP, 1989. Fellow Tamil nadu Acad. of Scis.; mem. Indian Sci. Congress, The Victoria Edward Hall. Office: Madurai Kamaraj U, Sch Physics, Palkalainagar, Madurai 625 021, India

IYE, MASANORI, astronomy educator; b. Sapporo, Hokkaido, Japan, Aug. 13, 1949; s. Masaharu and Tomoko Iye; m. Etsuko Katori, July 1, 1979; children: Kenya, Tetsuya. BS, U. Tokyo, 1972, MS, 1974, DSc, 1977. Rsch. fellow Japan Soc. for Promotion of Sci., Tokyo, 1977; tenure rsch. assoc. faculty sci. U. Tokyo, 1977-81, tenure rsch. assoc. Tokyo Astron. Obs., 1981-86, assoc. prof. Tokyo Astron. Obs., 1986-88; assoc. prof. Nat. Astron. Obs., Tokyo, 1988-93, prof., 1993-99, dir. large telescope divsn., 1994-96, dir. optical and infrared astronomy divsn., 1999—; exec. sec. nat. com. for astronomy Japan Coun. for Sci., Tokyo, 1995-98; 8.2m Subaru Telescope Project scientist Nat. Astron. Obs., Tokyo, 1994-00. Editor: (with T. Nishimura) Science and Engineering Frontiers for 8-10m Telescopes, 1995; patentee in field; contbr. articles to profl. jours. Brit. Coun. scholar, 1982; fellow European So. Obs., 1983; numerous rsch. grants Ministry of Edn., Sci. and Culture, 1984-99, Japan Soc. for Promotion of Sci., 1999-00. Mem. Astron. Soc. Japan (v.p. 1999-00), Japan Coun. for Sci. (chairperson com. for internat. collaboration in astronomy 1999-01), Soc. for Photo-Optical Instrumentation Engrs. (symposium chair 1999-00). Avocations: tennis, guitar, igo. Fax: 81 422 34 3527. E-mail: iye@optik.mtk.nao.ac.jp. Office: Nat Astron Obs, Osawa 2-21-1, Mitaka Tokyo 181-8588, Japan

IYENGAR, NARAYANA RANGACHAR, administrator, researcher; b. Tumkur, India, June 2, 1943; s. Rangachar S. and Padmasini R. I.; m. Vaijayanthi N., Oct. 14, 1977; 3 children. BCE, U. Mysore, India, 1962; MS in Engring., Indian Inst. Sci., Bangalore, 1966, PhD, 1969. Lectr. Indian Inst. Sci., Bangalore, 1969-74, asst. prof., 1974-81, assoc. prof., 1981-86, prof., 1986-94; dir. CBRI (CSIR), Rookee, India, 1994—; vis. asst. prof. Purdue U., West Lafayette, Ind., 1970-71; rsch. assoc. Columbia U., N.Y.C., 1971; nat. rep. IUTAM, 1989-92; spkr. in field; dist. Schmidt vis. prof. Fla. Atlantic U., 1995. Editor: Nonlinear Stočhastic Dynamics, 1995. Von Humboldt fellow, 1978-80, 92, 97; vis. scholar Bklyn. Polytech., N.Y.C., 1971; recipient M. Visvesvaraya award for sr. scientists Govt. of Karnataka, 1995. Fellow Indian Acad. Scis., Indian Acad. Engring., Indian Nat. Acad. Scis.; mem. Internat. Assn. St. Safety and Reliability (hon.). Hindu. Avocations: tennis, classical music, sanskrit. Home: A 11 Shanti Nagar, Roorkee 247667, India Office: Ctrl Bldg Rsch Inst, Roorkee 247667, India

IYENGAR, RAJANI GIRIDHAR, pharmaceutical chemistry educator, researcher; b. Chennai, Tamil Nadu, India, Mar. 3, 1953; d. Rathangapani and Mohana Pani Sampathkumar; m. Giridhar Sesha Iyengar, July 1, 1979; 1 child, Satish Giridhar. BPharm, Madras (India) U., 1973; MPharm, Birla Inst. Tech. and Scis., Pilani, Rajasthan, India, 1975; PhD in Pharmacy, Makaraja Sayajirao U., Baroda, India, 1987. Tchg. asst. pharmacy dept. Maharaja Sayajirao U., Baroda, 1975-76, lectr. pharm. chemistry, 1976-84, reader pharm. chemistry, 1984—, rsch. coord. rsch. projects, 1981-91; chief coord. All India Coun. Tech. Ednl. R&D Project, 1999—. Contbr. articles to profl. jours. Recipient Gold medal Indian Drugs Mfg. Assn., Bombay, 1973. Achievements include inventor in field. Avocations: internet surfing, reading, music. Home: 105 Anand Bhavan, Opp Polo Grounds, Baroda Gujarat 390 001, India Office: Pharmacy Dept, MS Univ Baroda, Baroda Gujarat 390 001, India

IYER, RAM, manufacturing engineer; b. Bombay, India, Mar. 15, 1970; came to U.S., 1993; M in Indsl. Engring., Tex. Tech. U., 1993. Mfg. engr. U.S. Industries, Dallas, 1994-97, Compaq Computer Corp., Houston, 1997—. Mem. Inst. Indsl. Engrs. Office: Compaq Computer Corp 20555 SH249 Houston TX 77070

IYER, RAMASWAMY HARIHARA, nuclear chemist, radiochemist; b. Thuravoor, Kerala, India, Aug. 27, 1936; s. Vanchiswaran Ramaswamy and Bhageerathi Iyer; m. Jayalakshmi Harihara Mahadevan, Nov. 2, 1966; children: Jyothi, Hema, Mahalakshmi. BSc, Maharaja's Coll., Ernakulam, India, 1956, MSc, 1958; PhD, Purdue U., 1966. Cert. in nuclear chemistry. Sci. officer Bhabha Atomic Rsch. Ctr., Mumbai, India, 1959-91; head radiochemistry divsn. Bhabha Atomic Rsch. Ctr., Mumbai, 1991-96, emeritus scientist CSIR, 1996—; postdoctoral fellow Purdue U., West Lafayette, Ind., 1966-68; vis. scientist San Diego State U., 1974-75; expert in nuclear chemistry Atomic Energy Commn., Damascus, Syria, 1991; Internat. Atomic Energy Agy. expert in nuclear chemistry Rangoon U., Myanmar, 1992, Ministry of Energy and Mineral Resources, Amman, Jordan, 1994. Mem. editl. bd.: Radiation Measurements, 1995. Named Emeritus Scientist Coun. Sci. and Indsl. Rsch., New Delhi, 1996—. Mem. Nuclear Track Soc. India (pres. 1995-98, patron 1998—). Hindu. Avocations: social work, religion and philosophy, music. Home: Anushree, C-6/20/2:3 Sector 6 CBD, Belapur Navi Mumbai 400614, India Office: Bhabha Atomic Rsch Ctr, Waste Mgmt Projects Divsn, Mumbai 400085, India

IYER, VISWANATH, advertising company executive; b. Bombay, Nov. 29, 1949; s. Mahadevan Iyer and Subbalakshmi Mahadevan; m. Anandi Rangan, Apr. 23, 1976; children: Dorshan, Anirudh. BS, Bombay U., 1970. Acct. exec. L.P.E. Aiyers Advt., Bombay, 1973-76; from acct. exec. to mng. dir. Creative Unit Pvt. Ltd., Bombay, 1976—; mng. dir. Video Magic Ltd., Bombay, 1995—; bd. dirs. Media Audience, Bombay, 1987—; chmn. Brahma

On-Line, Bombay, 1999—. Avocations: cricket, swimming, reading. Office: Creative Unit Pvt Ltd, 43 Mahatma Ghandi Rd, 400 023 Mumbai India

IYNEDJIAN, PATRICK BERNARD, biomedical researcher; b. Lausanne, Switzerland, Mar. 3, 1943; s. Aram and Georgette (Abrezol) I.; m. Dietlinde C. Mayer, May 16, 1971; children: Nicolas Pierre, Marc Alexander. BA, Gymnase Classique Cantonal, 1962; MD, U. Lausanne Sch. Medicine, 1968. Postdoctoral fellow dept. pharmacology U. Lausanne, 1969-73; postdoctoral fellow Fels Rsch. Inst., Temple U. Sch. Medicine, Phila., 1973-75, rsch. assoc. dept. biochemistry, 1975-77; lab. head dept. pharmacology U. Lausanne, 1977-83, lectr. divsn. endocrinology-metabolism, 1994—; invited scientist Inserm U145, Nice, France, 1983; lab. head divsn. clin. biochemistry U. Geneva Sch. of Medicine, 1984—. Contbr. articles to profl. jours. including Am. Jour. Physiol., Jour. Biol. Chemistry, Proc. Nat. Acad. Sci., Jour. Clin. Invest. Mem. Swiss Soc. Pharmacology, Biochem. Soc. Achievements include cloning of mammalian glucokinase gene. Office: Div Clin Biochem U Geneva, 1 Rue Michel-Servet, 1211 Geneva Switzerland

IYODA, MITSUHIKO, economics educator; b. Aichi, Japan, Oct. 1, 1943; m. Masako Chojahara, Jan. 7, 1975; 1 child, Muneyoshi. BA in Econs., Wakayama Nat. U., Japan, 1966; MA in Econs., Osaka City U., Japan, 1969; DPhil in Econs., Buckingham U., Eng., 1995. Assoc. prof. Momoyama Gakuin U., Osaka, Japan, 1972-82, prof., 1982—; vis. fellow Lancaster U., Eng., 1982-83; dir. Rsch. Inst. Momoyama Gakuin U., Osaka, 1985-89, dean faculty econs., 1990-92; vis. rsch. prof. U. Buckingham, Eng., 1993-94; dir. Internat. Centre, 1998-2000. Author: Profits, Wages, and Productivity in the Business Cycle: A Kaldorian Analysis, 1997. Mem. Japanese Econ. Assn., Internat. Assn. for Rsch. in Income and Wealth, Japan Soc. Econ. Policy, Royal Econ. Soc. (Eng.), Japan Assn. for Evolutionary Econs. Avocations: tennis, music. Home: 3-6-14 Momoyama-dai, Sakai-shi, Osaka 590-0141, Japan Office: Momoyama Gakuin U, 1-1 Manabino, Izumi-shi, Osaka 594-1198, Japan

IZAKOVIČOVA HOLLA, LYDIE, physician, educator; b. Valtice, Czech Republic, Nov. 7, 1971; d. Pavel and Alena (Šotnarová) H.; m. Vincent Izakovič, May 15, 1999. MD, Med. Faculty MU, Brno, Czech Republic, 1996, PhD, 1999. Rschr. Med. Faculty Masaryk U., Brno, 1996-97, asst. lectr., 1997-99, sr. lectr., 1999—; pvt. practice Brno, 1996—; resident Vera Maskova's Stomatol. Clinic, 1996—. Contbr. articles to profl. jours. Mem. Czech Allergology and Immunology Soc., Czech Dental Chamber, Czech Med. Chamber. Avocation: statistics. Office: Inst Pathol Physiology, Med Fac Masaryk U Kom nam 2, 662 43 Brno Czech Republic

IZARD, JACQUES YVES, histology educator, biologist; b. Saint-Girons, France, Jan. 2, 1933; s. Paul and Lina (De Napoli) I. MD, U. Toulouse, 1960. Asst. Med. Sch. U. Toulouse, 1960-66; prof. Med. Sch. U. Caen, 1966-98, pres., 1971-75; head of lab. Caen Hosp., 1966-98; ret., 1998. Avocation: history. Home: 19 rue Poliveau, 75005 Paris France

IZETBEGOVIC, ALIJA, government official; b. Bos Šamac, Bosnia-Herzegovina, Aug. 8, 1925; s. Mustafa and Hiba (Dzabija) I.; m. Halida Repovac, May 26, 1949; children: Lejla, Sabina, Bakir. BS in Law, U. Sarajevo, Bosnia-Herzegovina, 1956. Bar: Boznia-Herzegovina, 1960. Dir. Niskogradnja, Sarajevo, 1950-56; legal advisor PUT, Sarajevo, 1956-64, I.P.S.A., Sarajevo, 1964-81, Sarajevo, 1981-83; chmn. presidency Nat. Govt. Bosnia and Herzegovina, 1990-98; pres. Govt. of Bosnia, 1998—; legal advisor Sarajevo U., 1970-81. Author: Islamic Declaration, 1970, Problems of Islamic Awakening, 1977, Islam Between East and West, 1986. Chmn. Party of Dem. Action, Sarajevo, 1989. Recipient King Faisal Internat. prize for serving Islam, The Selection Com., Riyadh, Saudi Arabia, 1993. Moslem. Office: Party Democratic Action Office Pres, Musala Omlandinska bb, 71000 Sarajevo Bosnia-Herzegovina

IZHEVSKY, SERGEI SERGEJEVITCH, entomologist, ecologist; b. Moscow, Dec. 7, 1938; s. Sergei Alexandrovitch and Tatjana Nikolajevna (Furina) I.; m. Tatjana Ivanovna Ivankina, Feb. 18, 1964; 1 child, Maria. PhD, Moscow Forestry Inst., 1961, D (hon.), 1967; DSc (hon.), Plant Protection Inst., St. Petersburg, Russia, 1988. Rsch. scientist Nature Protection Lab., Moscow, 1961-63, Moscow Forestry Inst., 1963-67, The Main Bot. Garden, Moscow, 1967-70, Inst. Evolutional Animal Morphology, Moscow, 1970-73; head Russia Lab. Biol. Control, Moscow, 1973-76; head dept. entomology Inst. for Plant Quarantine, Moscow, 1976—; lectr. Moscow State U., 1978-81; sec. gen. East Palaearctic sect. Internat. Orgn. Biol. Control, Moscow, 1990-92. Author: Introduction and Application of Entomophages, 1990; co-author: (with R.S. Ushatinskaya) Colorado Potato Beetle, 1984, (with V. Guliy) Biological Plant Protection Glossary, 1986; co-author, co-editor: (with A. Akhatov) Pests of Protected Crops, 1999; mem. editl. bd. Russian Entomol. Jour., 1999—. Avocation: journalism. Home: 1 Rizhsky per 3-66, 129278 Moscow Russia Office: Russian Inst Plant Quarantine, Pogranitchnaya 32, 140150 Bykovo Russia

IZMAILOV, VLADIMIR VASILIEVICH, physics educator; b. Zheleznovodsk, Russia, July 10, 1949; s. Vasily Andreevich and Ludmila Alexandrovna (Retunskaya) I.; m. Natalia Borisovna Kopylova, Feb. 25, 1983. Degree in mech. engring., Tver U. Tech., Russia, 1971; DS, Moscow Rsch. Inst. Railway, 1996. Rsch. scientist Tver U. Tech., Russia, 1971-78, sr. lectr., 1978-80, asst. prof., 1980-97, prof., 1997—. Author: Handbook on Electrical Apparatus, 1988; contbr. articles to profl. jours. Mem. Russian Phys. Soc. Home: Konopliannikova St 11-36, 170041 Tver Russia Office: Tver State U Tech, 22 A Nikitin emb, 170026 Tver Russia

IZQUIERDO, JOSE MANUEL, physicist; b. Valencia, Spain, Jan. 24, 1963; s. Jose and Isabel (Rodriguez) I.; m. Alicia Alvarez, June 28, 1997. Grad. in physics, U. Valencia, 1986, PhD, 1991. Postdoctoral fellow Cambridge U., UK, 1993-95; postdoctoral fellow U. Valencia, 1996, assoc. prof., 1997—. Author: Lie Groups, Lie Algebras, Cohomology and Some Physical Applications, 1995; contbr. articles to profl. jours. Mem. Spanish Royal Soc. Physics, Marie Curie Fellowship Assn. Office: U Valladolid Fac Scis, Prado de la Magdalena S/N, 47011 Valladolid Spain

IZQUIERDO, LUIS SALVADOR, literature educator; b. Barcelona, Feb. 27, 1936; s. Antonio and Trinidad (Salvador) I.; m. Anna Llopart Ramon, July 4, 1961; children: Antoni, Miguel, Pol. Degree, U. Barcelona, 1964, PhD cum laude, 1980. Vis. asst. prof. U. Cin., 1964-66; prof. Escuela de Periodismo, Barcelona, 1966-69; prof. encargado de curso U. Barcelona, 1969-80, prof. adjunto contratado, 1980-82, prof. titular, 1982-89, catedratico de literatura espanola, 1990—; vis. prof. Howard U., Washington, 1965, NYU, 1984, Ctr. for European Studies, Harvard U., 1995; v.p. Inst. d'Humanitats, Barcelona, 1987—; literary advisor Plaza & Janes, Barcelona, 1989-91; mem. jury-literat City Hall, Barcelona, 1988—; literary advisor Barrarl, Barcelona, 1977-85. Author: Kafka, 1981, Antologia de J. Moreno Villa, 1982, Supervivencias, 1970, El Ausente, 1979, Calendario del nomada, 1983, Senales de Nieve, 1995, Sesion Continua, 1998; contbr. critical introductions to various books. Recipient Jury Cervantes prize 1999. Avocations: walking, travel, museums, history of painting. Office: U Barcelona, 585 Gran Via Corts Catalanes, 08007 Barcelona Spain

IZRAILEV, YURIY LVOVICH, metrologist; b. Gorodnya, Ukraine, Oct. 1, 1939; s. Lev Abramovich and Yulia Gershevna (Reznikova) I.; m. Elena Georgievna Khotyleva, Oct. 30, 1960 (dec. Oct. 1997); 1 child, Tatyana Yurievna. Degree energetics engring., Moscow Inst. Transport Engring, 1961; PhD, Russian Acad. Sci., 1997. Supt. Trust Sibenergomontazh of Energetics, Ministry of USSR, Novosibirsk, Russia, 1961-65; chief engr. Trust Mosenergoremont of Energetics, Ministry of USSR, Moscow, 1965-69; major engr. All-Russian Thermal Engring. Inst., Moscow, 1969-77, leading rschr., 1977—; pres. scientific industry co. Survivability of Power Plants, Moscow, 1994-96; major technologist metrologist Russian Joint Stock Co., Moscow, 1996—; co-chmn. Inter-Indsl. Coordinating Coun., Moscow, 1986—. Author: Fundamentals of the Theory of Turbine Survivability, Recommendations and Expertise, Vols. I, II, 1992, (with others) Thermal Stress and Strength Analysis of Turbine Rotors and Casings, 1988; contbr. articles to profl. publs.; patentee in field. Recipient Min. Coun. award Creation Scientific Fundamentals of Failure Mechanics, 1983. Mem. Russian Acad. of Humanity Rsch., N.Y. Acad. of Sci. Home: Krzhizhanovskaya St 34-91, 117218 Moscow Russia Office: All Russian Thermal Engring, 14/23 Avtojavodskaya St, 109 280 Moscow Russia

IZRAYLEVICH, SERGEY, ecological entomologist, researcher; b. Krivoy Rog, Ukraine, Oct. 4, 1966; arrived in Israel, 1990; s. Vladimir and Olga (Grossman) I.; m. Natalia Belkova, Mar. 30, 1990; children: Iris, Victoria. BSc, Pedagogical Inst., Krivoy Rog, 1990; PhD in Biology with honors, Hebrew U. Jerusalem, Rehovot, Israel, 1996. Rsch. asst. Hebrew U. Jerusalem, 1990-91, lectr., 1991-95, investigator, 1991-95; lectr. Tel-Hay Coll., Kiriat-Shmone, Israel, 1994-95; mng. dir. Hortan Ltd., Paris, 1995—; invited spkr. Symposium European Assn. Acarolgists, Amsterdam, The Netherlands, 1996. Contbr. articles to profl. jours. Recipient 1st prize for Outstanding Original Presentation IX Internat. Congress Acarology, Ohio, 1994, Max Shlomiok's Honor award Senate of Hebrew U., 1996; recipient rsch. grant for theoretical ecology Inter-Univ. Fund, Tel-Aviv, 1995, Mifal Ha Pais's prize, 1997. Mem. Ecol. Soc. Am., Entomol. Soc. Am., European Assn. Acarologists. Avocations: snooker, tennis. Office: Hortan Ltd, 4 Place des Saisons, 92036 Paris La Défense 1 cedex, France

IZSÁK, JÁNOS KORNÉL, biologist, applied mathematician, educator; b. Zalaegerszeg, Zala, Hungary, Jan. 11, 1944; s. Gyula Endre and Jolanda (Morandini) I.; m. Emma Ernhardt, Jan. 18, 1975; children: József, Ferenc, Rudolf. MS in Biology and Chemistry, Eötvös U., 1967, MS in Applied Math., 1974; PhD, Hungarian Acad. Sci., 1984. Lectr. Eötvös U., Budapest, Hungary, 1967-76; statistician Health Dept. of County Coun., Zalaegerszeg, 1976-78; assoc. prof. dept. math. Coll. Financy and Accountancy, Zalaegerszeg, 1978-84; prof., head dept. biology Berzsenyi Coll., Szombathely, Hungary, 1984-90; prof., head dept. zoology Berzsenyi Coll., Szombathely, 1990—; mem. supraindividual com. Hungarian Sci. Rsch. Fund, Budapest, 1995-98; mem. biometrical and biomath. com. Hungarian Acad. Sci., Budapest, 1993—, mem. ecol. com., 1997—. Editor: (in Hungarian) Introduction to Biomathematics, 1981; contbr. articles to profl. jours. Mem. Internat. Biometric Soc., Hungarian Biometrical Soc., Hungarian Gerontol. Soc. Home: Fö tér 19 2 14, H-9700 Szombathely Hungary Office: Berzsenyi Coll, Karolyi Gaspar ter 4 #170, H-9701 Szombathely Hungary

IZSAK, SAMUEL, medical educator; b. Tirgu Mures, Transilvania, Romania, Dec. 20, 1915; s. Izsak and Rachel I.; m. Sarah Ungar, Sept. 6, 1945; children: George, Andrew. MD, U. Cluj, Romania, 1948. Asst. U. Cluj, 1948-52, asst. prof., 1952-77, prof., 1977-81, retired prof., 1981—; chief of medicine history discipline, U. Cluj, 1964-81; founder and organizer The Collection Mus. of Pharmacy History of Cluj, 1954-63. Author: (books) The pharmacy along the centuries, 1979, Studies of medicine history, 1962, Aspects from the past of Romanian medicine, 1954, Dr. Iulius Baras - a great popularizer of the natural sciences, 1956, Romanian-Hungarian Medical Relations, 1956, The life and work of Stefan Stinca 1865-1897, 1956, Hippocratic Disputes Medical Srudies and Conferences, 1971-72; With Dr. Gh. Bratescu, 1999; On the Ways of the Past, Writings on Medical Culture, 1999, numerous others; co-author: History of Universal Medicine, 1970, History of Romanian Medicine, 1972; contbg. author books in field; contbr. articles to profl. jours. Recipient State award Govt. of Romania, 1957, Scientific award Class II, Ministry of Edn., Romania, 1962. Mem. Romanian Soc. Med. History, Internat. Acad. Pharmacy History, Internat. Soc. of Medicine History, Italian Acad. of Pharmacy History, Hungarian Assn. of Medicine History. Avocation: history of scis. Home: Str Napoca nr.27, 3400 Cluj Romania

IZUCHUKWU, JOHN IFEANYICHUKWU, industrial and mechanical engineer; b. Uke, Nigeria, May 6, 1955; came to U.S., 1976; s. Michael Chike and Cecilia Obiageli (Ikeakor) I.; m. Michele Anthea Palmer, July 22, 1989; children: Michael, John, Joseph. BS in Indsl. Enring., U. Portland, Oreg., 1980, MS in Mech. Engring., 1984; PhD in Indsl. Engring., Northeastern U., 1994. Base mgr. OEM Mfg., Digital Equipment Corp., Portland, Oreg., 1980-85; computer-aided software engring. mgr. Digital Equipment Corp., Marlboro, Mass., 1985-87, mgr. mech. design automation, 1987; mgr. concurrent engring. and application ctr. for tech. Digital Equipment Corp., Rochester, N.Y., 1989-91; group mgr. aerospace product strategy Digital Equipment Corp., Marlboro, 1991-93, worldwide strategy mgr., integrated product devel., 1993-95; team leader, R & D Ethicon Endo-Surgery, Inc., Cin., 1995—; sr. dir. global rsch., devel. and engring. Mallinckrodt, Inc., St. Charles, Mo., 1998—; adj. prof. decision scis. Babson Coll., Wellesley, Mass., 1994-95. Contbr. articles to engring. jours., including Jour. Mfg. Sci. and Engring.; patentee in field. Mem. ASME, Inst. Indsl. Engring. (sr. mem.). Home: 18002 Pine Canyon Ct Wildwood MO 63005-4938 Office: Mallinckrodt Inc 3 Missouri Research Park Dr Saint Charles MO 63304-5685

IZUMI, OSAMU, materials scientist, educator, researcher; b. Sendai, Japan, Mar. 26, 1926; s. Koichiro and Aiko (Suzuki) I.; m. Keiko Oka; 2 children. B in Engring., Tohoku U., Sendai, 1950, D in Engring., 1962. From asst. to prof. emeritus Tohuku U., Sendai, 1950-89, prof. emeritus, 1989—; dir. The Metals Mus., Sendai, 1998—; vice chmn. Internat. Conf. Titanium, Kyoto, 1978-81; chmn. Internat. Symposium Compounds, Sendai, 1987-91. Editor Material Rsch. Soc., 1985-86. Mem. Japn Inst. Metals (hon., Award of Thesis 1980, 82, Honda Meml. Lectr. 1989, Tanigawa-Harris prize 1986, Gold medal 1993. Home: 4 10 13 Mukaiyama Taihaku, Sendai 982-0841, Japan

IZURIETA MORA BOWEN, RAUL O., lawyer, journalist; b. Quito, Ecuador, June 8, 1945; s. Ricardo J. Izurieta and Blanca C. Mora Bowen. M of Laws, Tulane U., 1968; JD, Ctrl. U., Quito, 1969; diploma, Inst. Higher Studies, Ecuador, 1977. Sr. ptnr. Izurieta Mora Bowen Law Firm, Quito, 1969—; pres. various bus. dirs. Editor: El Universo Newspaper, 1990—, Comments on Current Issues, 1989—, Comments on Legal Issues; pres. editl. com. Channel 33TV, 1996—. Recipient Nat. Medal Republic Ecuador, 1991, 96, Nat. Justice award Govt. Spain, 1983. Mem. ABA (liaison), Spanish Bar Assn. (hon.), Peru Bar Assn. (hon.), former pres. of Quito Bar Assn. (past pres.), Ecuadorian Bar Assn., Interam. Bar Assn., Ecuadorian Assn. Radio & TV, Jr. Chamber (life), Club Lawyers (pres. 1981-84), Club La Union-Quito. Roman Catholic. Avocations: playing guitar, swimming. E-mail: Izurieta@uio.Telconet.net. Home: 2020 Diguja, Quito Ecuador Office: Izurieta Mora Bowen, Amazonas N35-89, Quito Ecuador

IZUS, GONZALO GREGORIO, physicist; b. Mar del Plata, Argentina, June 14, 1963; s. Osvaldo Gregorio and Maria Elena (Castellano) I. D of Physics, Nat. U. Mar del Plata, Argentina, 1996. Rschr. Nat. U. Mar Del Plata, Argentina, 1996—; rschr. Mediterranean Inst. for Advanced Studies, 1998-2000; cons. in field. Contbr. articles to profl. jours. With Argentine Mil., 1983-85. Nat. U. Mar del Plata fellow, 1991-93, CONICET fellow, 1993-95, 95-97. Mem. Health Found. (cons.). Avocations: fishing, camping. Office: Nat U Mar del Plata, Funes 3350, 7600 Mar del Plata Argentina

IZUYAMA, TAKEO, physicist, educator; b. Tokyo, Nov. 30, 1931; s. Sadashichi and Toshiko I.; m. Atsuko; children: Marie, Toshio. BS, U. Tokyo, 1954, MS, 1956, DSc, 1959. Rsch. assoc. Kyoto (Japan) U., 1959-61; lectr. Nagoya (Japan) U., 1962-64; assoc. prof. U. Tokyo, 1964-78, prof., 1978-92, prof. emeritus, 1992—; prin. The Kaisei Academy, Tokyo, 1992—; vis. prof. Northeastern U., Boston, 1969-70, The Toho U., Funabashi, Chiba, Japan, 1992—; guest physicist Centre d'Etudes Nucleaires de Saclay, Gif-sur Yvette, France, 1970-71; lectr. dept. physics Saitama (Japan) U., 1977—, Yokohama (Japan) City U., 1987—; chmn. environtl. study Inst. Ednl. Study Japan, Hachiouji, Tokyo, 1999—; chmn. bd. edn. Arakawa-Tokyo, 1999—. Chmn. editorial bd. Jour. of Phys. Soc. of Japan, 1983-85; contbr. articles to profl. jours. Mem. Bd. Edn., Arakawa-Tokyo, 1996—. Mem. Phys. Soc. Japan, Am. Phys. Soc., Internat. House Japan, Masion Franco-Japonaise, Internat. Assn. Math. Physics. Home: 4-2-19 Sendagi Bunkyo-ku, Tokyo 113-0022, Japan Office: The Kaisei Acad, 4-2-4 Nishi-Nippori, Arakawa-ku, Tokyo 116-0013, Japan

IZZAT, MOHAMMAD BASHAR, cardiothoracic surgeon, educator; b. Damascus, Syria, Oct. 1, 1964; s. Ahmad Walid and Hanna (Atassi) I. MD, Damascus U., Syria, 1987; MCh, U. Bristol, Eng., 1996. Cert. Intercollegiate Bd. Cardiothoracic Surgery. Resident in internal medicine U. Hosp., Damascus, Syria, 1987-88, resident in emergency surgery, 1988-89; sr. house officer in gen. surgery Walsgrave Hosp., Coventry, Eng., 1989; sr. house officer in urology Addenbrooke Hosp., Cambridge, Eng., 1989-90; sr. house officer in orthop. Brook Gen. Hosp., London, 1990; sr. house officer in gen. surgery Clatterbridge Hosp., Liverpool, Eng., 1990-91; jr. registrar in gen. surgery Southport (Eng.) Dist. Gen. Hosp., 1991-92; sr. house officer in cardiac surgery The Cardiothoracic Ctr., Liverpool, 1992; jr. registrar in cardiothoracic surgery No. Gen. Hosp., Sheffield, Eng., 1992-93; registrar in cardiothoracic surgery Bristol Royal Infirmary and Frenchay Hosp., Eng., 1993-95, sr. registrar in cardiothoracic surgery, 1995-96; assoc. prof., cons. surgeon, head sect. cardiac surgery Prince of Wales Hosp., Hong Kong, 1996-98; cons. cardiothoracic surgeon Damascus U. Cardiovascular Surg. Ctr., 1998—; dir. cardiac surgery svs. Shami Hosp., Syria, 1998—; vis. assoc. prof. Caribbean heart care U. The West Indies, Trinidad, 1996, The Am. Univ. of Beirut, Lebanon, 1997; dir. Hong Kong Homograft Bank. Author: Minimally Invasive Cardiothoracic Surgery, 1999, Echocardiography in Adult Cardiac Surgery, 1999; contbr. articles to profl. jours. Rsch. grantee U. Bristol, Eng., 1995, Brit. Heart Found., U.K., 1993, Rsch. Coun., Hong Kong, 1997. Fellow Am. Coll. Chest Physicians, Internat. Coll. Surgeons, European Soc. Thoracic Surgery, Royal Coll. Surgeons Ireland, Royal Coll. Surgeons England, Royal Coll. Surgeons Edinburgh, Coll. Surgeons Hong Kong, Am. Coll. Cardiologists, Soc. Thoracic Surgeons, Mediterranean Assn. for Cardiology and Cardiac Surgery. Avocations: airbrush painting, photography.

IZZUDDIN, BASSAM AFIF, computing in civil engineering, educator; b. Broummana, Lebanon, Sept. 11, 1965; arrived in England, 1986; s. Afif Khalil and Souheila (Qontar) I.; m. Hala Aboul Hosn, July 30, 1994; children: Hanadi, Sari. B of Civil Engring., Am. U. Beirut, 1986; MS in Steel Structures, Imperial Coll., 1987, PhD in Nonlinear Analysis, 1991. Structural analyst Steel Constrn. Inst., Ascot, England, 1987-90; lectr. engring. computing Imperial Coll., London, 1990-99, reader in computational structural mechanics, 1999—; cons. in field. Contbr. articles to profl. jours. Mem. ASCE, Instn. Structural Engrs. (U.K.). Avocations: playing the lute, squash, chess. Office: Dept Civil/Environ Engring, Imperial Coll Rd, London SW7 2BU, England

JAAFAR, MOHAMED ALI, accountant, financial consultant; b. Kota Bharu, Kelantan, Malaysia, June 8, 1924; s. Mohamed Bin Jaafar and Fatimah (Saadiah) Mohamed Ali; m. Siti Fatimah, 1944; m. Sabariah, 1956; children: Rosharumi, Rosmawar, Sabri, Rosnilam, Darma, Atma, Rosdelima, Roslinda. PhD, U. Ga., 1981. Tutor Islah Sch., Kota Bharu, 1949-51; mgr. Coop. Soc., Kelantan, 1951-53; officer IRS, Malaysia, 1954-72; acct. State Econ. Devel. Corp., Terengganu, Malaysia, 1973-80. Mem. Australian Soc. Accts., CPA Assn. Home: Wisma Harumi Kelulut, Marang, 21600 Terengganu Malaysia Office: Mohamed Ali & Co, 11-W 2D Fl Jalan Kota Lama, 20300 Kuala Terengganu Malaysia

JAASKELAINEN, ANTTI JUHANI, forensic scientist; b. Viipuri, Karjala, Finland, May 8, 1939; s. Toivo Sippo Juho and Kerttu Katri Kylllikki (Pesola) J.; m. Hanna Hillervo Mietakangas, June 6, 1960; children: Satu, Leena, Minna-Kaisa, Sanna, Miika. MD, U. Turku, Finland, 1968. Lic. forensic pathologist, Finland. Pathologist U. Turku, 1964-65, asst. medicine dept. sci., 1965-69, asst. prof. dept. pub. health, 1970-71, sr. lectr. forensic sci., 1970—; forensic scientist State of Finland, 1970—; lectr. U. Tampere, Finland, 1972-91; examiner traffic accidents Finish Accident Prevention Orgn., 1971—; examiner, lectr. Mass Catastrophy Investigation in Finland, 1976—; mem. coun. safety Province of Turku, 1975. Contbr. articles to profl. jours. Sec. Finnish Assn. for Sci., 1972-79; chief medicine local health sta. State Employees in Turku, 1982—; chmn. working safety commn. Provincial Govt., Turku, 1980—. Lt. Finland mil., 1973. Paul Harris fellow, 1988. Mem. Rotary Internat. (past pres.), Finish Lion (comdr. 1984). Conservative. Lutheran. Avocations: astronomy, mathematics, classical music, tennis. Home: Loukkaankatu 3 A, 20300 Turku Finland

JABBOUR, NABIL MILAD, ophthalmologist; b. Beirut, Nov. 11, 1955; came to U.S., 1979; s. Milad S. and Rose J. (Hatem) J.; m. Nina R. Khalifé, Aug. 19, 1979; children: Noel, Jad. BSc, Am. U. Beirut, 1976, MD, 1980. Lic. physician W.Va., N.Y., Kans., Mass. Intern in internal medicine Am. U. Beirut, 1979-80, resident dept. ophthalmology, 1980-83; fellow Retina Assocs./Mass. Eye & Ear Infirmary Eye Rsch. Inst. Harvard Med. Sch., Boston, 1983-85; chief fellow Retina Assocs./Mass. Eye & Ear Infirmary Eye Rsch. Inst. Harvard Med. Sch., 1984-85; asst. prof. ophthalmology W.Va. U., Morgantown, 1985-89, assoc. prof. ophthalmology, 1989-91; founder, owner Mid-Atlantic Retina Consultations, Morgantown, 1991—; dir. retina and vitreous svc. W.Va. U., Morgantown, 1987-91, chmn. med. student edn. com., 1989-91, mem. biomed. rsch. support com., 1988-91; pres. ForSight Found., 1991—; chmn. med. records com. W.Va. U. Hosp., 1990-91, mem. patient care rev. com., 1990-91; educator, lectr., presenter in field. Contbr. numerous articles to profl. jours.; creator videotape Jabbour-Nutter Diathermy System Transconjunctival and Transscleral Diathermy; inventor in field. Pres. Parents' Assn. Alliance Christian Sch., 1988-89, bd. dirs., 1989—, pres. bd. dirs., 1991-93; pres. Homeowners' Assn. Willow Wick, 1989-90; chmn. W.Va. Diabetes Eye Coun., 1990-9; mem. W.Va. Diabetes Control Coun., 1990—; pres., trustee Trinity H.S., Morgantown, 1995—; v.p., trustee H.O.M.E., Houston, 1994—. Fellow ACS; mem. AMA, Am. Acad. Ophthalmology, W.Va. State Med. Assn., W.Va. Acad. Ophthalmology, Schepens Internat. Soc. (founding), Vitreous Soc., Sigma Xi. Achievements include development of Iris Speculum for open sky vitrectomy, vitreoretinal dissection set, high viscosity contact lens for vitreous surgery, transscleral diathermy electrode, diathermy return path, illuminated dissection spatula for vitrectomy, suction tip with soft guard, irrigation/aspiration manual set, illuminated wide angle contact lens for vitrectomy, right-angled infusion cannula. Office: Mid-Atlantic Retina Consultations Inc 3120 Collins Ferry Rd Morgantown WV 26505-3305

JABBOUR, WAFAA NAJIB, biologist, consultant; b. Kfarhata, Koura, Lebanon, Apr. 10, 1959; s. Najib and Leila (Sakr) J. Med. Biologist, Angers (France) U., 1990, Dr. Pharmacy, 1992. Rschr. cellular biology Univ. Hosp., Angers, France, 1987-95; med. biologist Dr. Jabbour Lab., Mansourieh, Lebanon, 1996—; cons. INSERM UZ98, Angers, 1991-94; cons. cellular biology Univ. Hosp., Angers, 1995—. Co-author: Senile Dementias: Early Detection, 1987; contbr. articles to profl. jours. Mem. N.Y. Acad. Scis., Internat. Brain Rsch. Orgn., French Soc. Neurosci. Avocations: music, gastronomy, Pétanque. Home: Main St Mokhayber Bldg, PO Box 1410, Beit Mery Mein, Lebanon Office: Dr Jabbour Lab, Main St, Mansourieh Mein, Lebanon

JABER, LUTFI ABDULFATAH, pediatrician, genetics researcher, educator; b. Taibe, Israel, Sept. 23, 1945; s. Abdulfatah Abdul Kader and Soad Asad Jaber; m. Chozaima Hosni Jbara; children: Sohale, Manal, Soha, Samir, Amir. MD, Tel Aviv U., 1974; postgrad., Tulane U., 1992-93. Intern Golda Med. Ctr., Petah Tiqva, Israel, 1971-72; resident in internal medicine Beilinson Med. Ctr., Petah Tiqva, 1974-79, sr. pediatrician, 1979-81, sr. pediatrician, hematologist, 1987-92; cons. Mother and Child Health Ctrs. Ministry of Health, Taibe, 1981-87; Hubert Humphrey fellow Tulane U., New Orleans, 1992-93; dir. The Bridge to Peace Pediat. Ctr., Taibe, 1993—; sr. lectr. pediat. Sackler Sch. Medicine, Tel Aviv U. Contbr. articles to profl. jours. Mem. Israel Med. Assn., Israel Assn. Clin. Pediat., Israel Soc. Ambulatory Pediat. Home: Box 27, 40400 Taibe Israel Office: The Bridge Peace Pediat Ctr, 40400 Taibe Israel

JABER FILHO, JORGE ANTÔNIO, psychiatrist; b. Vacaria, Brazil, Mar. 15, 1952; s. Jorge Antonio and Etelvina Netto (Carvalho Netto) J.; children GabrielGlat, Lucia Glat. MD, State U. Rio de Janeiro, 1979; MBA. Med. diplomate specializing in psychoanalysis. Pvt. practice Rio de Janeiro, 1983; dir. Jorge Jaber Clinic, 1990; prof., coord. postgrad. course for psychotherapy WFMH, 1980-87; cons. Comty. Svc. Barra do Tiouca, Rio de Janeiro, 1993. Lt. Brazilian Army, 1978-79. Mem. World Fedn. Mental Health, Am. Psychiat. Assn., Brazilian Assn. Alcoholism, N.Y. Acad. Scis. Avocations: judo, soccer, jogging, reading. Office: Rua Gal Venancio Flores, 305 Sl 602 Leblon, Rio de Janeiro 22441090, Brazil

JABŁOŃSKA-CEGLAREK, ROMUALDA BOGUSŁAWA, agricultural educator; b. Józefów, Silesia, Poland, Jan. 6, 1939; d. Szczepan and Maria (Dzieło) J.; children: Dariusz, Bernadeta. MSc, Agr. U., Szczecin, Poland, 1961, PhD, 1970; prof. asst., Agr. U., Warsaw, 1979; assoc. prof., U. Podlasie, Siedlce, Poland, 1986, prof., 1991. Head Vegetable Crops Catedry,

Siedlce, 1978—; dean agr. dept. U. Podlasie, Siedlce, 1980-81, 83-97, v.p., 1984-87. Author: Basic of Vegetable Crops, 1984 (Ministry of Edn. award 1985), Horticulture, 1986 (Ministry of Edn. award 1987). Active Polish Hort. Sci. Soc., Warsaw, 1980; mem. hort. com. Polish Acad. Sci., Warsaw, 1993. Recipient award for rsch. work Ministry Edn., Warsaw, 1980, award for tchg. students Ministry Edn., Warsaw, 1983. Roman Catholic. Avocations: literature, music, theatre. Office: U Podlasie, B Prusa 14, 08-110 Siedlce Poland

JABLONSKA-GIERDALSKA, BEATA JOANNA, scientific researcher; b. Warsaw, June 29, 1965; d. Stanislaw Andrzej and Danuta Zofia (Szczepanek) J.; m. Marcin Pawel Gierdalski, Sept. 23, 1995; 1 child, Mateusz. MSc in Pharmacy, Med. Acad., Warsaw, 1991; PhD in Neurobiology, The Nencki Inst. Exptl. Biol., Warsaw, 1997. Sci. rschr. The Nencki Inst. of Exptl. Biology, 1991-99; postdoctoral fellow Uniformed Svcs. U. of the Health Sci., Bethesda, Md., 1999—. Contbr. articles to profl. jours. Recipient Award for Disting. Young Grad. Student, Found. for Polish Sci., 1996, Award for disting. Young Scientist, French Acad. Sci. and Rhone Poulenc, 1996, Award Dept. Life Scis., Polish Acad. Sci., 1994, 95, Award for Outstanding PhD Thesis, 1998, Award Dept. of Life Scis., 1999; fellow European Neurosci. Assn., 1993, 94, 95, UNESCO, 1994, 95, European Sci. Found., 1994, Fedn. of European Biochem. Soc., 1996, Inst. de France and Rhone Poulenc, 1996, Henry M. Jackson Found. for Advancement of Mil. Medicine, 1999. Mem. Polish Neurosci. Soc., European Brain and Behavior Soc., Internat. Brain Rsch. Orgn.

JACCHIERI, SAUL GDANSKI, chemist; b. SÃo Paulo, Brazil, Dec. 3, 1952; s. Carlos and Mary (Gdanski) J. BSc in Chemistry, U. Fed. Sao Carlos, 1977; M in Chemistry, U. São Paulo, 1982; D in Physics, Centro Brasileiro Pesquisas Fisicas, Rio de Janeiro, 1983. Adj. prof. U. Fed. Pernambuco, Recife, 1983-84, U. Fed. Minas Gerais, Belo Horizonte, Minas Gerais, 1985-94; vis. scientist U. Fla., Gainesville, 1991-92; vis. rschr. Inst. Butantan, São Paulo, 1995—; cons. Rsch. Support Found. São Paulo State, 1997; adv. bd. U. Fed. Minas Gerais, Belo Horizonte-Minas Gerais, 1994. Contbr. articles to profl. jours. Grantee Rsch. Support Found. São Paulo State, 1998, Frederick Biomed. Supercomputer Ctr., 1992. Mem. AAAS, Protein Soc., Am. Chem. Soc. Achievements include development of computer programs peptide21, SEQspace, matrix algorithm with variables ranges of interaction. Home: Rua General Waldomiro, de Lima 289, 04344070 São Paulo Brasil Office: AC Camargo Cancer Hosp, Rua Prof A Prudente 211, 01509090 São Paulo SP01246-902, Brazil

JACHNA, JOSEPH DAVID, photographer, educator; b. Chgo., Sept. 12, 1935; m. Virginia Kemper, 1962; children: Timothy, Heidi, Jody. BS in Art Edn., Inst. Design, Ill. Inst. Tech., 1958, MS in Photography, 1961. Part-time photographic asst. Derwin Studio Darkroom, Chgo., 1953-54; photo-technician Eastman Kodak Labs., Chgo., 1954; photographer's asst. DeSort Studio, Chgo., 1956-58; free-lance photographer Chgo., 1961—; instr. photography Inst. Design, Ill. Inst. Tech., Chgo., from 1961; instr. photography U. Ill., Chgo., from 1969, now prof. One-man shows include Art Inst. Chgo., 1961, St. Mary's Coll., Notre Dame, Ind., 1963, U. Ill., Chgo., 1965, 77, Lightfall Gallery Art Ctr., Evanston, Ill., 1970, U. Wis., Milw., 1970, Ctr. for Photog. Studies, Louisville, 1974, Nikon Photog. Salon, Tokyo, 1974, Afterimage Gallery, Dallas, 1975, Visual Studies Workshop Gallery, Rochester, N.Y., 1979, Chgo. Ctr. for Contemporary Photography, 1980, Focus Gallery, San Francisco, 1981, Photogenesis, Albuquerque, 1983, Andover (Mass.) Gallery, 1984, Chgo. State U., 1985, Tweed Mus. Art, Duluth, Minn., 1986, Gallery 954, Chgo., 1993, State of Ill. Galleries, Chgo., Lockport and Springfield, 1994, Fermilab, Batavia, Ill., 1995, Stephen Daiter Gallery, Chgo., 2000; exhibited in group shows at Art Inst. Chgo, 1963, 83, MIT, Cambridge, 1968, Walker Art Ctr., Mpls., 1973, 89, Renaissance Soc. Gallery U. Chgo., 1975, Mus. Contemporary Art, Chgo., 1977, 96—, Mus. Art RISD, Providence, 1978, Carpenter Ctr. Visual Arts, Harvard U., Cambridge, 1981, Nexus, Atlanta, 1983, Nat. Mus. Art., Washington, 1984, San Francisco Mus. Modern Art, 1985, Internat. Ctr. Photography, Tucson, 1992, Gallery 312, Chgo., 1996, Stockholm Subway, Sweden, 1999; represented in permanent collections, Mus. Modern Art, N.Y.C., Internat. Mus. Photography, George Eastman House, Rochester, N.Y., MIT, San Francisco Mus. Modern Art, Mpls. Inst. Arts, Art Inst. Chgo., Ctr. Photog. Studies, Louisville, Ctr. for Creative Photography, U. Ariz., Tucson. Ferguson Found. grantee, 1973; Nat. Endowment for Arts grantee, 1976; Ill. Arts Council, 1979; Guggenheim fellow, 1980. Office: U Ill Sch Art and Design 106 Jefferson Hall M/C036 929 W Harrison St Chicago IL 60607-7038

JACHOWICZ, RYSZARD SLAWOMIR, electronics educator, researcher; b. Wilno, Lithuania, Mar. 13, 1945; came to Poland, 1945; 010s. Piotr and Weronika (Zydowicz) J.; m. Maria Szklennik, Sept. 12, 1970; 1 child, Malgorzata. BS, MS, Warsaw U. Tech., Poland, 1969, PhD, 1973, DSc, 1981. Asst. Aviation Inst. Warsaw, 1969; sr. instr. dept. electronics Warsaw U. Tech., 1969-74, asst. prof. dept. electronics, 1974-81, prof. dept. electronics, 1991—, prof. nominated by State, 1996—; guest scientist Nat. Bur. Stds., Washington, 1977-78; rsch. specialist dept. electronic engring. and computer sci. MIT, Cambridge, 1978-79, assoc. prof. dept. electronics, 1981-91; vis. prof. Tech. U. Vienna, Austria, 1994; head sensors rsch. group dept. electronics Warsaw U. Tech., 1975—, vice dean dept. electronics, 1984-87; leader Polish-USA Rsch. Project, Warsaw and Washington, 1979-82, Warsaw and Bethlehem, Pa., 1994-98. Contbr. articles to profl. jours.; patentee in field. Chmn. 3d conf. on Opto- and Electronic Sensors, 1994, Internat. Conf. Eurosensors XI, 1997; mem. sci. coun. Electronic Indsl. Inst., Warsaw, 1992—, chmn., 1999—; mem. steering com. EuroSensors, Ann. Conf., 1994—. Served to cpl. Poland Army, 1965, 68. Recipient III Grade award Ministry of Sci. and Tech., Poland, 1980, 7 Sci. Achievement awards Pres. Warsaw. Mem. IEEE (sr., vice chmn. Poland sect. 1992—, chmn., 1997—), Polish Elec. Soc. (sr.), Polish Acad. Sci. (com. metrology sect. chmn. 1994—, Sci. Achievement award 1976), Polish Soc. Sensors Tech. (organizing com. co-chmn. 1991-92). Roman Catholic. Avocations: skiing, yachting. Home: ul Oginskiego 28 m 16, 03-357 Warsaw Poland Office: Warsaw Univ Tech, ul Nowowiejska 15/19, 00-665 Warsaw Poland

JACHYMSKI, JACEK ROBERT, mathematics educator, researcher; b. Łódź, Poland, June 28, 1959; s. Stefan and Jadwiga (Okrasa) J.; m. Zofia Krystyna Jacewicz, Dec. 20, 1986; children: Krzysztof, Ignacy, Zofia. MSc, Tech. U. Łódź, 1981, PhD, 1987. Rsch. asst. Tech. U. Łódź, 1981-87, asst. prof. math., 1987-2000, assoc. prof. math., 2000—; vis. prof. math. U. Natal, Durban, South Africa, 1996. Contbr. articles to profl. jours. Mem. Am. Math. Soc., N.Y. Acad. Scis., Polish Alpine Assn. (instr. alpinism 1993—), Japan Assn. Math. Sci. Avocations: climbing, mountain cycling, classical music, skiing. Office: Tech U Lodz Inst Math, Zwirki 36, 90-924 Lodz Poland

JACINTO, RAMON PEREYRA, broadcast executive, musician; b. Pasay City, Manila, The Philippines, June 3, 1945; s. Fernando Pantangco and Bernardina Reyes (Pereyra) J.; m. Marilou Tuason Arroyo, Oct. 24, 1964; children: Beatriz, Nadine, Luccia, Nicole; m. Frannie Osorio Aguinaldo, Nov. 16, 1990; children: Natalia, Ramon. Degree in econs., Ateneo de Manila, The Philippines, 1966. Pres. Rajah Broadcasting Network, 1963-72; v.p. Jacinto Steel, 1965-72; exec. v.p. Iligan Integrated Steel, 1968-72; vice chmn. F. Jacinto USA, N.Y.C., 1969-86; chmn. Rajah Broadcasting Network, 1986—, RJ Holdings, Inc., 1986—; pres. cons. Pres. Pamos for Com. on Flagship Programs and Projects, 1985-90. Composer, lyricist Baguio, Here We Come, 1962 (gold record 1962), Don't Let Go, 1977. Co-chmn. fin. Lakas Polit. Party, 1993-98. Recipient Presdl. citation Pres. of the Philippines, 1998. Mem. World Pres.'s Orgn., Rotary (Makati S.W. chpt.). Roman Catholic. Avocations: music, golf, running.

JACINTO, SYLVIA S., dermatologist; b. Manila, Nov. 5, 1939; d. Carmelo Pongco and Concepcion (Sayoc) Jacinto; children: Marie Therese, Gary, Maria Jasmin, Jennifer, Marietta. MD, U. Philippines, 1962; grad., Sheffield Sch. Interior Design, 1990. Adj. resident Dept. Internal Medicine Philippine Gen. Hosp., Manila, 1962-63, asst. resident, 1963-64, instr., 1967-72; resident NYU-Bellevue Med. Ctr. Dept. Dermatology, N.Y.C., 1964-67; dir. Philippine Dermatol. Soc., Manila, 1970-74, 79-84, pres., 1975-76, 77-78; founder, treas. J&J Med. Clinics, Inc., Makati, 1976—, Gary's Corp., Manila, 1989; clin. prof., chmn. dept. dermatology Skin and Cancer Found., Inc., 1984—; chmn. dept. dermatology Asian Hosp., 2000—; cons. dermatologist Med. Ctr. Manila, 1967-87, U.S. Embassy, 1968—, Cardinal Santos Med. Ctr., Mandaluyong, 1975-92, 96—, St. Martin de Porres Charity Hosp., San Juan, 1980-92, Ctrl. Bank Philippines, 1972—, U.S. Peace Corps., 1968-86, Can. Embassy, 1986—. Contbg. author: Diseases of the Skin, Textbook of Pediatrics and Child Health, 1976, 82, 90, 95; editor, founder Philippine Jour. of Dermatology and Dermatologic Surgery, 1979-95; mem. editl. bd. Jour. Philippine Dermatol. Soc., 1993-98; one-woman painting exhbns. at Ayala Mus., Makati, 1993, Gallery Y, Mandaluyong, 1995. Pres. White Plains Ladies' Assn., Quezon City, 1976-77, White Plains Assn., Inc., 1995, 96; mem Manila chpt. Zonta Internat., 1976-84, Manila Mahikari Okiyomesho Ctr., 1984-88; bd. trustees Christian Parenting for Peace and Justice Found., Inc., 1995-97; founding pres. Hospice Philippines Found. Inc., 1997—. Recipient Enrile Award of Distinction Philippine Bd. Med. Examiners, 1962. Fellow Am. Acad. Dermatology; mem. Internat. Soc. Dermatol. Surgery (adv. bd. Philippines 1978—), Am. Acad. Cosmetic Surgery, Am. Contact Dermatitis Soc., Pacific Dermatol. Assn., Internat. Soc. Dermatology, Am. Soc. Dermatol. Surgery, Am. Coll. Phelbology, Soc. Investigative Dermatology, Nail Disorders, Venous Forum of the Philippines (charter mem.), Am. Soc. for Hair Restorative Surgery, Am. Holistic Med. Assn., Skin and Cancer Found. Inc. (pres., co-founder, exec. dir. 1984—), Dermatology Found. (Century mem. 1988-92, 93—), Am. Coll. Cryosurgery (corr. mem. 1978—), Internat. Soc. Pediatric Dermatology, Skin Cancer Found. (mem. adv. bd. Philippines 1995—), Internat. Sheng Zhen Soc., U. Philippines Med. Alumni Soc. (life), Nat. Rsch. Coun. of Philippines, Philippine Med. Assn. (life), Philippine Soc. Cryosurgery, White Plains Country Club, Valley Golf Club (Cainta), Palicpican Sports and Country (Ternate). Avocations: Qigong, playing piano, interior design, sculpture (terracotta, ceramic, paper mache), flamenco dancing. Office: Skin Clinic, 1311 Batangas St, Makati City 1200, The Philippines

JACK, DAVID EMMANUEL, governor general; b. Victoria Village, St. Vincent and the Grenadines, July 16, 1918; s. John and Margaret (Lewis) J.; m. Esther Veronica Mc Kay, Apr. 24, 1946; children: Wilson (dec.), Joel, Theresa, Gloria. Tchr's cert., 1941; external course, La Salle Ext. U., Chgo., 1943-46; diploma in higher accountancy, 1947. Primary sch. tchr., 1934-43; oil refinery operator Curacao, N.A., 1943-45; asst. acct. Corea & Co. Ltd., St. Vincent, 1945-48; cost acct. Govt. Cotton Ginnery, 1948-50; acct. Arrowroot Assn., 1950-69, gen. mgr., 1950-69; sec., chief acct. Hazells Ltd., 1980-81; mgr. St. Vincent Automotive Co-op Gas Sta., 1983-84; min. Housing, Labour and Community Devel., 1984-86; min. of health Dept. of Health, 1987-89; chmn., bd. dirs. Nat. Comml. Bank of St. Vincent & The Grenadines, 1989; acting gov. gen. Kingstown Govt., St. Vincent & The Grenadines, 1989—, gov. gen.; elected to St. Vincent & The Grenadines House of Assembly, 1984-89. Past pres. St. Vincent Meth. Local Preachers' Assn.; past chief ranger Ancient Order of Foresters. Recipient Cert. of Merit Meth. Ch. of the Caribbean and the Ams. Avocations: carpentry, classical music. Home: New Montrose, PO Box 381, Kingstown Saint Vincent and the Grenadines Office: Office of Governor General, Kingstown Saint Vincent and the Grenadines*

JACK, DIXIE LYNN, software consultant, social worker; b. Orlando, Fla., Apr. 7, 1943; d. Alex and Dorothy Ellen (Dixon) J. BA, U. Wash., 1965; AA, Highline C.C., Des Moines, 1971. Tchr. Archdioces, Burien, Wash., 1968-70, Tukwila (Wash.) Sch. Dist., 1970-75; fin. svcs. technician Dept. Welfare, Seattle, 1982-84; social worker, supr. Dept. Children and Family Svcs., Everett, Wash., 1984-94; user support/tng. mgr. Lockheed Martin, Hartford, Conn., 1995-97; computer based tng. mgr. Am. Mgmt. Sys., Manchester, Conn., 1997; implementation, bus. process cons. Ctr. for Support of Families, Chevy Chase, Md., 1998; cons. Juvenile Justice, Supreme Ct., Seattle, 1988-95. Mem. Assn. Univ. Women, Hartford Club. Home: 13116 E 41st Dr Yuma AZ 85367-6146

JACK, IAN GRANT, editor, writer; b. Farnworth, Lancashire, Eng., Feb. 7, 1945; s. Henry Archibald and Isabella Ramsay (Gillespie) J.; m. Aparna Bagchi, Mar. 6, 1979 (div. 1992); m. Rosalind Sharpe, Feb. 28, 1998; children: Isabella, Alexander. Grad. H.S., Fife, Scotland, 1962. Journalist East Kilbride News, Scotland, 1965-66, Scottish Daily Express, Glasgow, 1966-70, The Sunday Times, London, 1970-86, The Observer, London, 1986-88; editor The Ind. on Sunday, London, 1991-95, Granta, London, 1995—. Author: Before The Oil Ran Out, 1987. Named Journalist of Yr., 1986, Reporter of Yr., 1989, Nat. Newspaper Editor of Yr., 1993. Mem. India Internat. Ctr. Avocations: reading (particularly history), steam navigation, travel. Office: Granta, 2/3 Hanover Yard Noel Rd, London N1 8BE, England

JACKAMAN, MICHAEL CLIFFORD JOHN, retired food products executive; b. Nov. 7, 1935; s. Clifford Thomas and Lily Margaret J.; m. Valerie Jane Pankhurst, 1960; 2 children. MA with honors, Jesus Coll., U. Cambridge. Dep. mng. dir. Harveys of Bristol, 1976-78; mktg. dir. Allied Breweries, 1978-83; dir. Allied Domecq plc, 1978-96, chmn., 1991-96; dir. Kleinwort Benson Group plc, 1994-98; chmn. Hiram Walker Allied Vintners, 1983-91, John Harvey & Son Ltd., 1983-93. Mem. coun. adminstrn. Chateau Latour, 1983-91; bd. dirs. Fintex of London Ltd., 1986-92, Rank Orgn., 1992-97; gov. Bristol Polytech, 1989-91; appeal chmn. Royal Hosp. for Sick Children, Bristol. Decorated comdr. Bontemps du Médoc et des Graves (France). Mem. Keepers of Quaich (grand master 1996-97, Scotland). Avocations: walking, tennis, potting. Office: The Grand Appeal, 24 Upper Maudlin St, Bristol BS2 8DJ, England

JACKEL, SIMON SAMUEL, food products company executive; b. N.Y.C., Nov. 11, 1917; s. Victor and Sadie (Unger) J.; m. Betty Carlson, Jan. 22, 1954; children: Phyliss Marcia (dec.), Glenn Edward. BS, CCNY, 1938; postgrad., U. Ill., 1941-42; AM, Columbia U., 1947, PhD, 1950. Head fermentation divsn. Fleischmann Lab., Stamford, Conn., 1944-59; v.p. R & D Vico Products Co., Chgo., 1959-61; lab. dir. Quality Bakers of Am. Coop. Inc., Greenwich, Conn., 1961-74; v.p. rsch. dir. Sunbeam Baked Foods, Greenwich, 1974-84; dir. R & D, operating com. Bakers R&D Svcs., Greenwich, 1969-84; pres. Plymouth Tech. Svcs., Tarpon Springs, Fla., 1951—; internat. cons., 1984—; sci. adv. com. Am. Inst. Baking, 1970-91, sanitation edn. adv. com., 1978-81. Tech. editor Bakery Prodn. and Mktg. Mag., 1968-85; contbr. articles to profl. jours.; patentee in field. Dir. hearing aid audiology Jewish Home and Hosp. for Aged, N.Y.C., 1951-76; mem. industry adv. com. N.D. State U., 1977-85; chmn. investment com., bd. dirs. Found. Unitarian Universalists of Clearwater, 1994—; treas., bd. dirs. Unitarian Universalists of Clearwater, 1997-98. Recipient USAAF Exceptional Civilian Svc. award 1943, Wisdom Hall of Fame award, 1978, Rsch. grant USPHS, 1947-50. Fellow AAAS, Am. Inst. Chemists, Am. Assn. Cereal Chemists (chmn. milling and baking divsn. 1973-74, Charles N. Frey award 1981, bakery columnist Cereal Foods World 1984-95, hon. fellow 1993); mem. Am. Chem. Soc. (50 yr. Membership award 1995), Am. Soc. Bakery Engrs. (chmn. tech. info. svc. com. 1979-95), Am. Bakers Assn. (nutrition com. 1971-77, chmn. tech. liason com. to U.S. Dept. Agr. 1975-87, food tech. regulatory affairs com. 1977-91; alt. gov. 1978-87, assoc. gov. 1988-95), Ind. Bakers Assn. (cons. food safety com. 1977-80, labeling com. 1978-84, tech. affairs com. 1978-84, co-chmn. labeling and good mfg. practices com. 1984-94), Inst. Food Technologists (50 yr. Membership award 2000), N.Y. Acad. Sci., N.Y.C. Chemists Club, Sigma Xi, Phi Lambda Upsilon. Home and Office: 684 Hidden Lake Dr Tarpon Springs FL 34689-2600

JACKLIN, ANTHONY, professional golfer; b. Scunthorpe, Eng., July 7, 1944; s. Arthur David Jacklin; m. Vivien Jacklin, 1966 (dec. Apr. 1888); 3 children; m. Astrid May Waagen, Dec. 1988; 1 son; 2 stepchildren. Profl. golfer, 1962-85, 88—; dir. golf Sam Roque Club, Cadiz, Spain, 1962—; owner, mgr. Tony Jacklin Golfscape, golf course design, Lewisburg, W.Va., 1991—; winner Lincolnshire Open Championship, 1961, Brit. Assn. Pro Championship, 1965, Pringle Tournament, 1967, Dunlop Masters, 1967, 73, Greater Jacksonville Open, 1968, 72, Greater Greensboro Open, 1968, 72, Brit. Open Championship, 1969 (first Brit. player to win since 1951), U.S. Open Championship, 1970 (first Brit. player to win since 1920), Benson & Hedges, 1971, Brit. Profl. Golfers Assn., 1972, 82, Bogota Open, 1973, 74, Italian Open, 1973, Scandinavian Open, 1975, Kerrygold Internat., 1976, English Nat. P.G.A. Championship, 1977, German Open, 1979, Venezuelan Open, 1979, Jersey Open, 1981, P.G.A. Championship, 1982, First of Am. Classic, 1994, Franklin Quest Championship, 1995; first player since 1900 to hold U.S. and Brit. Open titles simultaneously; player Ryder Cup, 1967-80, team capt., 1983, 85, 87, 89. Author: Golf With Tony Jacklin, 1969, The Price of Success, 1979, (with Peter Dobereiner) Jacklin's Golfing Secrets, 1983, Tony Jacklin: The First Forty Years, 1985. Decorated Order Brit. Empire, comdr. Brit. Empire; winner Franklin Quest Championship, 1995. Mem. Brit. Profl. Golfers' Assn. (hon. life pres.), European Tour (hon. life), PGA Tour, Sr. PGA Tour, PGA of Am.

JACKSON, ALAN, neuroradiologist; b. Oldham, England, Feb. 24, 1957; s. John and Jean J.; m. Susan Caroline Beards, June 6, 1986. BSc, U. Manchester, 1978, PhD, 1981, MBChB, 1984. Sr. house officer Univ. Hosp., Manchester, 1985-87; sr. house officer in oncology Christie Hosp./Holt Radium Inst., Manchester, 1987, registrar in med. oncology, 1987; registrar in diagnostic radiology NW Regional Tng. Rotation, Manchester, 1990-91; sr. registrar in neuroradiology Manchester Royal Infirmary, 1991-93; sr. lectr. neuroradiology, prof. U. Manchester, 1993—. Mem. Radiol. Soc. N.Am., Internat. Soc. Magnetic Resonance in Medicine, Br. Inst. Radiology, Royal Coll. Radiologists. Office: U Manchester Dept Diag Rad, Oxford Rd, Manchester M13 9PT, England

JACKSON, ANDREW PRESTON, library director; b. Bklyn., Jan. 28, 1947; s. Walter Luther Sr. and Bessie (Lindsey) J. BS, CUNY, 1990, MLS, 1996; pub. librs. profl. cert., SUNY. Asst. supr. pers. processing unit Human Resources Adminstrn. Agy. Child Devel. Pers. Dept., N.Y.C., 1968-70, coord. pers. svcs., 1970-76; customer rels. mgr., contracts mgr. Robinson Chevrolet, Novato, Calif., 1976-79; office mgr. Sesame Press, Inc., N.Y.C., 1979-80; exec. dir. Langston Hughes Cmty. Libr. and Cultural Ctr., Corona, N.Y., 1980—; lectr. Black history, N.Y.C., 1986—; cons. evaluating black heritage collections. Contbr. articles to profl. jours. Bd. mem. Cmty. Adv. Bd. Elmhurst (N.Y.) Hosp. Ctr., 1983-97, Queens Pub. TV, Flushing, N.Y., 1989—, York Coll. Alumni, Inc., Jamaica, N.Y., 1990-93, 96—; vice-chair cmty. adv. bd. Otis Bantum Correctional Ctr. N.Y.C. Dept. Corrections, Rikers Island, N.Y., 1990-95; convener Churchman's Fellowship Corona Congl. Ch., 1987-89; chmn. Gen. Social Svcs. Adv. Coun., Cmty. Planning Bd., Area 3 and 5, 1984-87; treas. No. Blvd. Mcht.'s Assn. Corona, 1985—; mem. York Coll. Cmty. adv. Coun., 1997—; mem. N.Y. State Freedom Trails Commn., Queens Underground R.R. com. Staff sgt. USAF, 1964-68, Vietnam. Decorated Bronze Star; named Man of Yr., Nat. Assn. Negro Bus. & Profl. Women's Club, Inc., 1991, Ombudsman award, 1982, East Elmhurst Alumni Inc. Hall of Fame, 1998; recipient Cmty. Svc. award East Elmhurst Track Club, 1986, Tabernacle Cmty. C.M.E. Ch., Nat. Assn. Univ. Women (north shore br.), Cmty. award East Elmhurst-Corona Civic Assn., 1989, Outstanding Leadership in Queens award Queens Fedn. of Churches, 1988, Cert. of Appreciation Kiwanis, 1991, Cmty. Svc. award Minority Mgmt. Assn., N.Y.C., 1992, Cert. of Recognition August Martin H.S., 1992, Gov.'s award African-Americans of Distinction, N.Y. State Gov., 1994, Disting. Grad. award Nat. Assn. Equal Opportunity in Higher Edn., 1994, Cert. of Honor, Queens Borough Pres., 1994, Giving It Back, award W.C. Bryant H.S., 1995, Youth Devel. award 115th Police Precinct Coun., 1994; Disting. Alumni award York Coll. Alumni Assn., Inc., 1996, Fufilling The Dream award CBS-TV, 1996, Scroll of Honor, 4W Circle of Arts and Enterprise, 1996, Cmty. Svc. award Nat. Coun. Negro Women, 1997, Cmty. Svc. award Elmcor Alumni Assn., 1998, Comty. Svc. award Concerned African-Am. of Flushing, 1998, Lamplighter award Queens Borough Pub. Libr., 1999. Mem. NAACP, ALA, ALA Black Libr. Caucus (exec. bd. 1999—, Libr. Advocacy award 1999, Libr. Outreach award 1999), Pub. Librs. Assn., Libr. Adminstrn. and Mgmt. Assn., N.Y. Black Librs. Caucus, N.Y. Libr. Assn. Avocations: speaking with youth, reading. Home: 25-14 97th St East Elmhurst NY 11369-1923 Office: Queens Borough Pub Libr Langston Hughes Comm Libr 100-01 Northern Blvd Corona NY 11368-1038

JACKSON, BERNARD STUART, legal and religious studies educator; b. Liverpool, Eng., Nov. 16, 1944; m. Rosalyn Young, 1967; children: Iain Charles, Judith Deborah. LLB with honors, U. Liverpool, 1965; DPhil, Oxford U., 1969; LLD, U. Edinburgh, Scotland, 1987; DHL honoris causa, Hebrew Union Coll., Cin., 1998. Lectr. dept. civil law U. Edinburgh, 1969-76; prin. lectr. divsn. law Preston Poly., 1976-77; head dept. law Liverpool Poly., 1977-85, prof. law, 1980-85; prof. law U. Kent, Canterbury, 1985-89; Queen Victoria prof. law U. Liverpool, 1989-97; Alliance prof. modern Jewish studies U. Manchester, 1997—; mem. Conseil d'administration Assn. Européenne pour la philosophie du droit, 1996—; sr. assoc. fellow Oxford Ctr. for Postgrad. Hebrew Studies, 1984-96; emeritus prof. U. Liverpool, 1997—; vis. asst. prof. U. Ga. Sch. Law, 1968-69; Brit. Coun. lectr. Acad. Interchange with europe Scheme, U. Rotterdam, U. Amsterdam, 1975; Littman fellow Oxford Ctr. for Postgrad. Hebrew Studies, Hilary term, 1977; faculty lectr. theology Univ. Coll. North Wales, 1980; Catriona Gibson lectr. Faculty of Law, Queen's U., Kingston, Ont., 1980; Lady Davis vis. prof. dept. bible Hebrew U., Jerusalem, 1981; Spkr.'s lectr. in bibl. studies U. Oxford, 1983-86; prof. invité U. Paris X, Nanterre, 1987-88; prof. U. Bologna, 1988; Caroline and Joseph Gruss vis. prof. in Talmudic legal studies Harvard Law Sch., 1992; Gastprof. Rechstheorie Katholieke U., Brussels, 1992—; assoc. prof. U. Paris I, Pantheon-Sorbonne, 1994; mem. mgmt. com. Nat. Ctr. for Cued Speech, 1985-89. Author: Theft in Early Jewish Law, 1972, Essays in Jewish and Comparative Legal History, 1975, Semiotics and Legal theory, 1985, Law, Fact and Narrative Coherence, 1988, Making Sense in Law, Linguistic, Psychological and Semiotic Perspectives, 1995, Making Sense in Jurisprudence, 1996, Studies in the Semiotics of Biblical Law, 2000; editor: Studies in Jewish Legal History in Honour of david Daube, 1974, Modern Research in Jewish Law, 1980, Jewish Law in Legal History and the Modern World, 1980, The Jerusalem Conf. Vol., 1986, The Halakhic Thought of R. Isaac Herzog, 1991, The Jerusalem 1990 Conference Vol., 1992, Legal Visions of the New europe, 1993, Legal Semiotics and the Sociology of Law, 1994, An Introduction to the History and Sources of Jewish Law, 1996; joint editor Section II: Compendia Rerum Judaicarum ad Novum Testamentum, 1973-78; editor The Jewish Law Annual, 1978-97; editor-in-chief The Liverpool Law Rev., 1979-85; editl. bd. Internat. Jour. Semiotics of Law, 1984—, Internat. Jour. of the Legal Profession, Semiotic Crossroads, Zeitschrift für altorientalische und biblische Rechtsgeschichte; mem. internat. adv. bd. Legal Ethics, 1997—; editl. adv. bd. Archivos Latinoamericanos de Metodologia y Filosofia del Derecho, Venezuela, Ctr. for Semiotic Rsch. in Law, Govt. and Econs., Pa. State U.; contbr. numerous articles to profl. jours. Mem. mgmt. com. U.K. Law Tech. Ctr., 1989-92; chmn. BILETA Inquiry into Computer Provision in U.K. Law Schs., 1989-91; mem. no. cir. com. on computer support for litigation, 1991—; mem. Lord Chancellor's Area Criminal Justice Adv. Com., 1992—. Mem. Jewish Law Assn. (hon. pres. 1984-88, chmn. pubs. com. 1984-88, exec. com. 1978-92), Brit. Assn. Jewish Studies (hon. pres. 1993), Oxford Ctr. for Hebrew and Jewish Studies (sr. assoc. 1997—, corr. fellow 1996-97), Internat. Assn. for Semiotics of Law (sec.-gen., treas. 1987-93), Soc. for Computers and Law (com. mem. Liverpool br. 1993-96). E-mail: bernard.jackson@man.ac.uk. Fax: 44-151-729-0371. Home: 173 Mather Ave, Liverpool L18 6JZ, England Office: U Manchester Ctr Jewish Stu, Oxford Rd, Manchester M13 9PL, England

JACKSON, BETTY EILEEN, music and elementary school educator; b. Denver, Oct. 9, 1925; d. James Bowen and Fannie (Shelton) J. MusB, U. Colo., 1948, MusM, 1949, MusB in Edn., 1963; postgrad., Ind. U., 1952-55, Hochschule fur Musik, Munich, 1955-56. Cert. educator Colo., Calif. Tchr., accompanist, tchr. H.L. Davis Vocal Studios, Denver, 1949-52; tchg. assoc. U. Colo., Boulder, 1961-63, vis. lectr., summers 1963-69; tchr. Fontana (Calif.) Unified Sch. Dist., 1963-92; pvt. studio, 1966—; lectr. in music Calif. State U., San Bernardino, 1967-76; performer, accompanist, music dir. numerous musical cos. including performer, music dir. Fontana Mummers, 1980—, Riverside Cmty. Players, Calif., 1984—; performer Rialto Cmty. Theatre, Calif., 1983—; head visual and performing arts com. Cypress Elem. Sch., 1988-92. Performances include numerous operas, musical comedies and oratorios, Cen. City Opera, Denver Grand Opera, Univ. Colo., Ind. Univ. Opera Theater (leading mezzo), 3 tours of Fed. Rep. Germany, 1956-58; oratorio soloist in Ind., Ky., Colo., and Calif., West End Opera (lead roles), Riverside Opera (lead roles). Judge Inland Theatre League, Riverside, 1983-92; mem. San Bernardino Cultural Task Force, 1981-83; bd. dirs. Riverside-San Bernardino Counties Met. Auditions, 1988—; mem. adv. bd. Riverside Concert Opera, 1990-95. Fulbright grantee, Munich, 1955-56; named outstanding performer Inland Theatre League, 1982-84; recipient Outstanding Reading Tchr. award, 1990, Tchr. of Yr. nominations, 1990, 91, hon. svc. award, 1992. Mem. AAUW (bd. dirs., cultural chair 1983-86), NEA, Nat. Assn. Tchrs. Singing (exec. bd. 1985-89), Internat. Reading Assn., Music Educators Nat. Conf., Calif. Tchrs. Assn., Calif. Elem. Educators Assn.,

Fontana Tchrs. Assn., Music Tchrs. Assn., Arrowhead Reading Coun., San Bernardino Vly. Concert Assn. (bd. dirs. 1977-83), Internat. Platform Assn., Nat. Assn. Preservation and Perpetuation of Storytelling, Order Eastern Star, Kappa Kappa Iota (v.p. 1982-83), Sigma Alpha Iota (life), Chi Omega. Avocations: community theater and opera, travel, collecting Hummels and plates. Home: PO Box 885 Rialto CA 92377-0885

JACKSON, BETTY L. DEASON, real estate developer; b. Wichita, Kans., Mar. 31, 1927; d. Orville John and Ida Mabel (Wolfe) Deason; m. James L. Jackson, July 2, 1966 (dec. Feb. 1983); children: Rebecca Lou, Jennifer Mae. AA, SW Baptist U., Bolivar, Mo., 1946; BA, Cen. Mo. State U., 1963; MA, U. Mo., 1964. Lic. realtor, Kans. Salesperson Sears, Kansas City, Mo., 1943-44; bookkeeping clk. Hallmark Cards, Kansas City, Mo., 1945-46; civil service Camp Pendleton, Oceanside, Calif., 1947; sec. Ford Motor Co., Kansas City, Mo., Jim Taylor Olds Co., Independence, Mo., 1952-54; tchr. Consol. Sch. Dist. #2, Mo., 1954-55; tchr. adminstr. Consol. Sch. Dist. #2, Raytown, Mo., 1963-78; owner mgr. B.J.'s Florist Car Wash Laundramat, Stockton, Mo., 1979-82; owner, ptnr. J and S Realty, Stockton, Mo., 1983—; officer J-S Corp., Stockton, 1986-94. Mem. Nat. Assn. Realtors, Mo. C. of C., AARP, Greater Ozark Bd. Realtors. Democrat. Baptist. Avocations: play organ, piano, church clubs. Home: 1316 Lakeview Cir Stockton MO 65785-9394 Office: Coldwell Banker J-S Realty PO Box 159 Stockton MO 65785-0159

JACKSON, CEPHUS, educational administrator, consultant; b. Whatley, Ala., Feb. 5, 1946; s. Cephus and Darnell Jackson; m. Lynda Loving; 1 child, Kia Jannell; m. Mary Dawn Jackson, June 29, 1994. BS, Jackson (Miss.) State Coll., 1968; MS, Va. Poly. Inst. and State U., 1994; PhD, U. So. Miss., 1998. Football player L.A. Rams, 1968; tchr. Richmond (Va.) City Schs., 1969-82, lead tchr., 1988-94; pharm. salesman Upjohn Co., Kalamazoo, 1982-88; asst. prin. Picayune (Miss.) Schs., 1994-96; prin. Gulfport (Miss.) Sch. Dist., 1996—; cons. Bogalusa (La.) City Schs., 1996, Hancock County Sch., Kiln, Miss., 1996, Marion County Schs., Columbia, Miss., 1997, New Iberia (La.) Schs., 1999. Pres. Ctrl. Ward Polit. Action Com., Richmond, 1981-86; mem. Federated Arts Coun., Richmond, 1982-84, Leadership Gulf Caost, Gulfport, 1988—. Mem. Miss. Assn. Elem. Sch. Adminstrs. (pres.-elect), Phi Delta Kappa. Avocations: golf, walking. E-mail: gport.cjackson@mdek12.state.ms.us. Office: Bayou View Elem Sch 4898 Washington Ave Gulfport MS 39507-4499

JACKSON, CHARLES WAYNE, food products executive, former telecommunications industry executive; b. Louisville, June 3, 1930; s. Wayne O. and Geneva Drake J.; m. Sallie I. Lambert, June 21, 1952 (div. Feb. 1980); m. Elizabeth J. Soptic, June 1, 1979; children: Thomas, Carol E., Charles N. BEE, Ga. Inst. Tech., 1952. Student engr. AT&T, Cin., 1954-55; dist. plant engr. AT&T, Jacksonville, Fla., 1955-56; comml. rep to acctg. asst. AT&T, Atlanta, 1956-59; transmission systems engr. to plant design engr. AT&T, Kansas City, 1963-66; project mgr. to dir. major project Western Elec. Co., N.Y.C., 1966-69; engr. dir. TWX coord. to bus. relations dir. AT&T, N.Y.C., 1969-75; dir. pvt. lines rates Long Lines Co., Somerset, N.J., 1975; dir. pvt. lines rates to dir. planning Long Lines Co., Bedminster, N.J., 1975-81; dir. data prog. svcs. to dir. svc. devel. mktg. dept. AT&T, Bedminster, 1981-87; cons. pvt. practice Brandenburg, Ky., 1987-90; v.p. H&R Block Franchise, 1990-92; owner Squire Taber Apple Orchard, 1992—; v.p. Echo Enterprises, Inc., 1991—. 1st. lt. U.S. Army, 1952-54. Mem. Ky. State Horticulture Soc. (v.p., dir.), Elks. Methodist. Avocations: photography, horticulture. Home and Office: 1194 Adkins Rd Rineyville KY 40162-9722

JACKSON, DARNELL, agency director; b. Saginaw, Mich., Feb. 2, 1955; s. Roosevelt and Annie Lois (Pratt) J.; m. Yvonne Kay Givens, July 29, 1978; children: Brandon Darnell, Elliott Stephen. BA, Wayne State U., 1977, JD, 1981; AA, Kalamazoo C.C., 1993. Office mgr., shift supr. Wayne State U., Detroit, 1979-81; mng. ptnr. Allan & Jackson, P.C., Saginaw, 1983-85; asst. city atty. Saginaw City Atty.'s Office, 1985-86; asst. prosecuting atty. Saginaw County Prosecutor's, Saginaw, 1986-89; assoc. Braun, Kendrick, Finkbeiner et al, Saginaw, 1989-90; instr. Paralegal Inst. Delta Coll., University Center, Mich., 1986; instr. Northeastern Basic Police Acad. Delta Coll., University Center, 1991-96; dep. chief asst. prosecuting atty. Saginaw County Prosecutor's Office, 1990-93; adminstrv. dep. chief of police Saginaw Police Dept., 1993-96; dir. Office of Drug Control Policy State of Mich., Lansing, 1996—; mem. Drug Edn. Adv. Com., Lansing, Mich., 1996—, DARE Policy Adv. Bd., Lansing, 1996—, Mich. Dispute Resolution, Saginaw, 1989-92, Sen. Cisky Adv. Com., Saginaw, 1992-94; co-chair Partnership for Drug Free Mich., 1997—; speaker in field. Bd. dirs. United Way of Saginaw County, 1996, Westchester Village/Essex Manor, 1994-96, Saginaw County Child Abuse and Neglect Coun., 1994-96, Mr. Rogers Say No to Drugs Program, 1991-95; mem. Saginaw Valley Sate U. Multicultural Adv. Com., 1991-96; adv. bd. Saginaw St. Mary's Hosp., 1991-94, State Sen. Jon Cisky Minority Affairs Adv. Com., 1992-94. Recipient award for Profl. Excellence, FBI/Saginaw County Gang Crime Task Force, 1995, Frederick Douglass award for Community Svc., Mich. State Legis., 1991, award for Effort in War on Drugs, Saginaw Police Dept. Spl. Ops. Unit, 1989, Spl. Tribute for Community Svc., Mich. State Legis., 1985, Comm. Svc. awards Wayne State Univ. Free Legal Aid Clin, 1980-81. Mem. Mich. Bar Assn., Saginaw County Bar Assn., Fraternal Order of Police, Internat. Assn. of Chiefs of Police, Mich. Assn. of Chiefs of Police, Nat. Orgn. of Black Law Enforcement Execs. Office: Office Drug Control Policy Lewis Cass Bldg 320 S Walnut St Lansing MI 48933-2014

JACKSON, DEBORAH CHERYL, mathematician; b. Melbourne, Victoria, Australia, Feb. 2, 1955; d. Frederick Arthur and Beryl Victoria (Potter) Trueman; m. Clive Warwick Jackson, Jan. 6, 1990. BA (Double Honours), Monash U., Clayton, Victoria, 1978, PhD, 1981, A.Mus. A. (A.M.E.B), 1986. Tutor Monash U., 1981-83, sr. tutor, 1984-85; lectr. Swinburne Univ. Tech., Hawthorn, Australia, 1986-98; reviewer Math. Revs., Ann Arbor, Mich., 1983—. Contbr. articles to profl. lit. Australian Commonwealth Univ. scholar Monash U., 1973, Commonwealth postgrad. research awardee, 1979-81. Chair Victorian Algebra Group, 1996—. Mem. Australian Math. Soc., Am. Math. Soc., Inst. Math. Stats., Australian Stat. Soc., Australasian Assn. Engrng. Edn. Mem. Anglican Ch.

JACKSON, ELIJAH, JR., communication executive. AA in Gen. Studies and Broadcasting, Ricks Coll., Rexburg, Idaho, 1982; AA in Theatre, Brigham Young U., Hawaii, 1984, AA in Speech Comm., 1984; BA in Comm., U. Hawaii, Manoa, 1987; postgrad., U. Southwestern La., Lafayette, Polk C.C., Winter Haven, Fla.; LLM in Taxation, U. Hawaii, Manoa, 1988; D of Juridicial Sci. in Taxation, Washington Sch. Law, Sandy, Utah, 1999; DSc in Taxation, Washington Inst. Grad. Studies. Tng. Prog. by Federal Mogul Corp., 1998; entrepreneurship tng., Hawaii C. of C., Honolulu, 1987; Bus. Etiquette and Protocol, U. of Hawaii Manoa, 1986; Fin. Mgmt. for Closely held Bus., Bank of Hawaii, 1985; Eng. Tech., Tampa Tech. Inst., 1981. Editor Oceanic Cablevision, Am. TV Corp., Time Warner Inc., Honolulu TV Com. Corp.; pvt. practice radio and TV project budget mgr., prodr., dir, videographer; legal rschr., legis. aide Com. on Consumer Protection and Commerce State of Hawaii Legislature; CEO Jackson Program, 10 years, Jackson Pacific Joint Venture, 10 years, Jackson Instructional TV Sys., 10 years; trustee, fiduciary, promoter JBS Inc. Parent Corp., Hawaii, Fla.; CEO, pres., promoter Jackson Family Limited Partnership, Ltd., 13 years, Jackson Family Limited Trust, 13 years, JBS Inc. Parent Corp., 13 years, Elijah Jackson, Jr., Inc., 13 years; CEO, pres., chmn., promoter Delesia Renee Jackson Inc., 13 years; legal rschr., legislative aide State of Hawaii, 13th Legislature Com. on Consumer Protection and Commerce, Hawaii, 1 year; intern field prod., videographer, ABC affiliate, KITV channel 4, 1 year; graphic design, photography, cons. video system design Sony and CMX videos, 2 years; with Washington Inst. Grad. Studies Grad. Tax Program, Sandy, Utah; trustee, pres. Jackson Internatl. Mgmt. Limited, Nassau, Bahamas; assoc. mgr. trainee DIscount Auto Parts, Inc.; sales assoc. Anderson News Co., Lakeland, Fla. , Tampa, Fla., Knoxville, Tenn; legal rschr., real estate rschr., paralegal JBS Mgmt. and Properties, JBS Land and Water Entertainment and Sports; pres., CEO, trustee, financer, ptnr., tax matter person, nominee, residual interest holder, promoter Jackson Family Limited Partnership, Ltd., Jackson Family Limited Trust, JBS Inc. Parent Corp., Jackson Broadcasting Sys., Inc., JBC Inc. Lead Corp. of Fla. Divsn., JacksonBoroadcasting Co., Inc., Elijah Jackson, Inc., Jr., Inc., Jackson Enterprises, Inc., Jackson Commodity Credit Corp., Cashland Inc., Jackson Internat. Telecom. Corp., Jackson, Inc., Jackson Internat. Fin. Corp., others; chmn. bd. Elias, Elisha and Elisabeth Jackson Inc., JBS Mgmt. Corp., Jackson Entertainment Svcs., Inc., EJJ Productions Inc. Radio/TV project budget mgr., prod., dir., videographer; editor for Oceanic Cablevision a/k/a Amer. TV Corp. a/k/a Time Warner Inc. d/b/a Honolulu TV Comm. Corp. Recipient cert. of appreciation VFW, 1998, 99. Mem. ABA, Amer. Payroll Assn. Fax: 863-686-4659. Address: PO Box 92895 Lakeland FL 33804-2895 Office: Wash Inst Grad Studies 2268 Newcastle Dr Sandy UT 84093-1743

JACKSON, FELICITY ANNE, performing arts organization administrator; b. Hitchin, Hertfordshire, Eng., Apr. 16, 1949; d. Brian John and Jacqueline Anne (Barnes) J. BA with honors, Cambridge U., Eng., 1970; B Philosophy, Exeter U., Eng., 1972. Planning coord. Glyndebourne Festival, Sussex, Eng., 1979-82; head artistic planning Nat. Opera, Brussels, 1982-84; casting mgr. Glyndebourne Festival, Sussex, Eng., 1988-90; casting cons. Leipzig Opera, Germany, 1990-92, Netherlands Opera, Amsterdam, Holland, 1990-92; artistic adminstr. Can. Opera Co., Toronto, Can., 1992-94; dir. artistic adminstrn. Glimmerglass Opera, N.Y., 1994-97; gen. mgr. European Union Opera, London, 1997-98; casting cons. Fla. Grand Opera, 2000—; mem. adv. bd. Rosa Ponselle Found., Balt., 1992—; artistic cons. Chgo. Opera Theater, 2000—. Avocations: canoeing, travel.

JACKSON, JANE W., interior designer; b. Asheville, N.C., Aug. 5, 1944; d. James and Willie Mae (Stoner) Harris; m. Bruce G. Jackson; children: Yvette, Scott. Student, Boston U., 1964; BA, Leslie Coll., 1967; postgrad., Artisan Sch. Interior Design, 1980-82. Tchr. Montessori, Brookline, Mass., 1969-72; interior designer, owner Nettle Creek Shop, Honolulu, 1980-88; owner Wellesley Interiors, Honolulu, 1988—. Active Mayor's Com. for Small Bus., Honolulu, 1984. Mem. Honolulu Club. Democrat. Office: Wellesley Interiors PO Box 1622 Kaneohe HI 96744-1622

JACKSON, JEROME ALAN, biological scientist, educator, researcher; b. Ft. Benning, Ga., Feb. 4, 1943; s. Wayne Clark and Phyllis Mae (Monroe) J.; m. Nancy Ann Niemann, Aug. 7, 1965 (div. Mar. 1983); children: Jerome Alan, Paul Clark, Ann Christine, Peter Michael; m. Bette Jean Schardien, Mar. 12, 1984; children: Steven Brent, Matthew Clifford. BS, Iowa State U., 1965; PhD, U. Kans., 1970. Instr. biology West H.S., Bakersfield, Calif., 1965-66; asst. prof. dept. zoology Miss. State U., Mississippi State, 1970-74, assoc. prof., 1974-79, curator of birds, 1970—, curator of mammals, 1987—, prof. dept. biol. scis., 1979—; pres. Eco-Inventory Studies, Inc., Mississippi State, 1988—; co-host Ms. Outdoors, WCBI TV, Columbus, Miss., 1988—; scientist, expdn. to Cuba, Nat. Geographic Soc., 1988; short term tech. advisor in Indonesia, Acad. for Edn. Devel./U.S. Agy. Internat. Devel., 1994. Author/editor 12 books about birds or nature, including Vulture Biology and Management, 1993; contbr. over 200 articles to profl. jours. and over 100 articles to popular mags. Trustee N.Am. Loon Fund, 1986-89. Recipient Excellence in Sci. Teaching award Miss. Sci. Tchrs. Assn., 1992, Outstanding Cmty. Environ. award Southwire Co., 1993, Outstanding Contbn. to Sci. in Miss. award Miss. Acad. Scis., 1990; named Man of Yr., Inland Bird Banding Assn., 1976. Fellow AAAS, Am. Ornithologists Union, Explorers Club; mem. Wilson Ornithol. Soc. (pres. 1983-85, editor Wilson Bull. 1974-78), Assn. Field Ornithologists (editor jour., v.p. 1997—), Miss. Ornithol. Soc. (editor Miss. Kite 1976—, pres. 1971-72). Methodist. Avocations: flying, diving, photography. Office: Miss State U Dept Biol Scis Box GY Mississippi State MS 39762 Address: Jackson & Whitaker Center 10501 Fgcu Blvd S Fort Myers FL 33965-0001

JACKSON, JESSE LOUIS, civic and political leader, clergyman; b. Greenville, S.C., Oct. 8, 1941; s. Charles Henry and Helen Jackson; m. Jacqueline Lavinia Brown, 1964; children: Santita, Jesse Louis, Jonathan Luther, Yusef DuBois, Jacqueline Lavinia. Student, U. Ill., 1959-60; B.A. in Sociology and Economics, N.C. A&T State U., 1964; postgrad., Chgo. Theol. Sem., D.D. (hon.); hon. degrees, N.C. A&T State U., Pepperdine U., Oberlin U., Oral Roberts U., U. R.I., Howard U., Georgetown U. Ordained to ministry Baptist Ch., 1968; founder (with others) Operation Breadbasket joint project So. Christian Leadership Conf., Chgo., 1966; nat. dir. Operation Breadbasket joint project So. Christian Leadership Conf., 1967-71; founder, exec. dir. Operation PUSH (People United to Serve Humanity), Chgo., 1971—; candidate for Democratic nomination for Pres. U.S., 1983-84, 87-88; nat. pres. Nat. Rainbow Coalition Inc., Chgo.; founder PUSH-Excel and PUSH for Econ. Justice; lectr. for high schs., colls., prof. audiences in Am., Europe. Interviewer TV program Both Sides with Jesse Jackson. Active Black Coalition for United Community Action, 1969. Recipient Presdl. award Nat. Med. Assn., 1969; Humanitarian Father of Year award Nat. Father's Day Com., 1971; Third Most Admired Man in Am. Gallup Poll, 1985; named one of six new leaders on the rise U.S. News World Report. Address: Rainbow PUSH Coalition 930 E 50th St Chicago IL 60615-2702

JACKSON, JOHN HERMAS, financial company executive; b. Cambridge, Jamaica, July 28, 1948; s. Frederick E. and Lucille Frederica (Burgess) J.; m. Celia Patricia Stewart, July 31, 1952; children: Suzanne (dec.), Steven, Jo-Anne. Sr. acct. KPMG Peat Marwick, Montego Bay, Jamaica, 1969-76; bus. mgr. Sevens Ltd., May Pen, Jamaica, 1976-78; fin. mgr., internal auditor Nat. Sugar Co. Ltd., Kingston, Jamaica, 1978-83; ptnr. Jackson Burnett Parkinson Jackson, Kingston, Jamaica, 1983—; CEO, dir. Capital Market Svc. Ltd., Kingston, Jamaica, 1985—; chmn., CEO Bridgeton Mgmt. Svc. Ltd., Kingston, Jamaica, 1975—; chmn. Point Village Resorts, Ltd., 1996; dir. Eagle Unit Trust Mgmt. Co., Ltd., Kingston, 1987-2000. Mem. Inst. Chartered Accts. Jamaica (mem. sub-com.), Jaycees (pres. 1976), Jamaica Club, Liguanea Club. Baptist. Avocations: tennis, table tennis, monopoly, scrabble, dominoes. Home: 26 Norbrook Acres Dr, Kingston 8, Jamaica Office: Bridgeton Mgmt Svcs Ltd, 12 Merrick Ave, Kingston 10, Jamaica

JACKSON, KATHERINE CHURCH, former elementary school educator, reading educator; b. Phila., Apr. 26, 1925; d. John Edward and Katherine Darlington (Short) C.; m. James Kermit Jackson, Dec. 20, 1953; children: James Kermit, Quentin Winfield, Karen A. Jackson White. BS in Edn., Cheyney (Pa.) State Tchrs. Coll., 1946; MEd, Temple U., 1951; DEdin Adminstrn., Nova U., 1981. Cert. elem. sch. tchr., supr., prin., Pa. Elem. tchr. Pub. Schs., Oxford, N. Glenside, Pa., 1946-54; collaborator lang. arts, t.v. tchr. Pub. Schs., Phila., 1956-67, asst. dir., tng. specialist office of sch. vols., 1967-70, dist. supr., dir. reading, 1970-77, elem. prin., 1971-82; asst. prof. Lincoln U., Pa., 1986-87, reading and writing specialist, 1986—. Prodr., photographer: (slide presentation) Parents Help With Reading, 1965; writer, prodr. (t.v. series, script) Reading Inservice for Teachers, 1965; creator, prodr., photographer (slide presentation) PL-142 Works for the Handicapped, 1980. Pres. bd. YWCA, West Chester, Pa., 1984-89; bd. dirs. Cmty. Ctr., West Chester, 1984-91. Recipient Profl. award Bus. and Profl. Women, 1966, Cmty. and Club Svc. award Keystone Federated Women's Club, 1989, Spirit of YWCA, YWCA of Greater West Chester, 1990. Mem. AAUW, Fanny J. Coppin Federated Women's Club (chpt. pres. 1984—), Bus. Profl. Women (pres. Phila. chpt. 1965-69). Democrat. Episcopalian. Avocations: reading, singing, opera. Home: 1210 Cheyney Rd West Chester PA 19382-8502 Office: Lincoln U ACT 101 Time Program Lincoln University PA 19352

JACKSON, L. DUANE, agriculturist; b. Frederick, Okla., Feb. 15, 1942; s. Dale L. and E. Lucille J. BS, Okla. State U., 1964; MS, Wash. State U., 1967; PhD, Tex. A&M U., 1970. Cert. prof. agronomist and soil scientist. Lab. asst. Okla. State U., Stillwater, 1962-64; rsch. and teaching asst., rsch. assoc. Tex. A&M U., College Station, 1966-69; asst. prof. agr. Ohio State U., Columbus, 1970-72; agrl. cons. Ohio Crop Prodn., Columbus, 1972-74; cons. agronomist, entomologist, agrl. engr., soil scientist Field Crop Svc., Sterling, Colo., 1976—; pres. Ind. Agrl. Cons. Colo., 1991. Okla. State U. Sch. Agr. scholar, 1962. Mem. Am. Soc. Agronomy, Gideons. Office: Field Crop Svc PO Box 1055 Sterling CO 80751-1055

JACKSON, LARRY C., publishing executive; b. Austin, Tex., Apr. 14, 1944; s. Laurence C. and Mary Ruth (McAngus) J.; m. Susan Blackburn, Dec. 15, 1966; children: Laurence III, Deborah Jackson McClure, Edward. BA in Journalism, U. Tex., 1968. City editor Arlington (Tex.) Daily News, 1967-69; City editor Laredo (Tex.) Times, 1969-71; mng. editor Henderson (Tex.) Daily News, 1971-72; gen. mgr. Austin Citizen, 1972-73; publ. Round Rock (Tex.) Leader, 1973-84, Pecos (Tex.) Enterprise, 1984-87, Corona (Calif.)-Norco Independent, 1987-91; editor, gen. mgr. Wharton (Tex.) Journal-Spectator, 1991—; v.p. River Pubs., Inc., 1994—. Charter pres. YMCA, Round Rock, Tex., 1981; mem. City Charter Commn., Round Rock, 1977; chmn. U.S. Bicentennial Commn., Round Rock, 1975-76; bd. dirs. Tex. Newspaper Found., 1994—; mem. City Beautification Commn., Wharton, Tex., 1999—; life mem. Disciples of Christ Hist. Soc.; bd. dirs. Wharton County His. Mus., 2000—. Paul Harris fellow Rotary Internat. Found., 1995; named Citizen of Yr. Round Rock C. of C., 1984. Mem. Tex. Press Assn. (pres. 1998-99), S. Tex. Press Assn. (pres. 1996), Rotary Club (pres. Wharton 1994-95), Wharton (Tex.) C. of C. (v.p. 2000). Republican. Mem. Ch. of Christ. Avocations: tchg. Bible class, playing Oboe, travelling by train. Home: 1203 N Fulton St Wharton TX 77488-3129 Office: Wharton Journal-Spectator 115 W Burleson St Wharton TX 77488-5003

JACKSON, MARIAN NELL, counselor; b. Ville Platte, La., May 10, 1974; d. Marion Jackson and Mary Ann Doucet. BA, U. La., 1996; MEd, So. U., Baton Rouge, 1999. Tchr. St. Landry Parish Sch. Bd., Opelousas, La., 1996-99; counselor U. La., Lafayette, 1999—. Advisor 4-H Club, Opelousas, 1996-99. Mem. Mid-S. Ednl. Rsch. Assn., Delta Sigma Theta (sch. Am. chair 1993—), Kappa Delta Pi, Golden Key Honor Soc. Avocations: internet, research. Fax: 337-482-6833. Home: 248 Belle Ridge Rd Opelousas LA 70570-0840 Office: U La Lafayette Upward Bound II Program PO Box 43452 Lafayette LA 70504-0001

JACKSON, MICHAEL, talk show host; b. London, Apr. 16, 1934; came to US, 1958.; s. Harry and Terry E. J.; m. Alana Ladd, Oct. 16, 1965; children: Alan Ladd, Alisa Sue, Devon Michael. High sch. diploma, King Edward VII, Johannesburg, South Africa, 1951; LLD (hon.), We. State U. Announcer, prodr. S.A.B.C., Johannesburg, 1952-56, B.B.C., London, 1956-58; talkshow host, disc jockey WHYN Radio and TV, Springfield, Mass., 1958-60; disc jockey KYA Radio, San Francisco, 1960-61; talkshow host KEWB Radio, Oakland and San Francisco, 1961-62, KHJ Radio/TV, L.A., 1962-63, KNX Radio, L.A., 1963-64, KCET (PBS) TV, L.A., 1963-65, KABC TV, L.A., 1965-67, KABC Radio, L.A., 1966-98, KRLA Radio, L.A., 1998—. Recipient Golden Plate award Acad. Achievement, 1961, Emmy awards (7), Golden Mike awards (4), star on Hollywood Walk fo Fame; named Radio Talkshow Host of Yr. Nat. Assn. Radio Talkshow Hosts, 1997-98; decorated Legion of Merit, 1986, Most Excellent Order Brit. Empire, 1988. Avocations: photography, horseback riding, skiing, gardening, cooking. Office: KRLA Radio (CBS) Los Angeles CA 90086

JACKSON, MICHAEL HERBERT, environmental health educator; b. Hornchurch, Essex, Eng., July 17, 1940; s. Herbert and Emily Alice (Bennett) J.; m. Diana Evelyn Evans, Mar. 16, 1966; children: Karen Elizabeth, Wendy Kathryn. BA, Open U., 1975; PhD, Strathclyde (U.K.) U., 1986. Environ. health officer local govt., 1957-77; lectr. U. Strathclyde, 1977-86, sr. lectr., 1986-92, reader, 1992-94, prof. environ. health, 1994—; cons. to various govt. and indsl. orgns., U.K., 1980—. Author: Environmental Health Reference Book, 1989; editor Internat. Jour. Environ. Health Rsch., 1990—. Rsch. grantee Chest, Heart and Stroke Assn., 1983, Overseas Devel. Agy., 1989, Health and Safety Exec., 1990, Ministry of Agr., 1991, 92, Water Rsch. Coun., 1990, 91, 92, 93, Sci. and Engring. Rsch. Coun., 1993, various indsl. orgns., 1984, 85, 89, Nat. Health Svc., 1996, Brit. Coun., 1998, 99, Scottish Higher Edn. Funding Coun., 1998. Fellow Royal Coll. Pathology, Royal Soc. Health, Royal Soc. Arts, Inst. Biology, Chartered Inst. Environ. Health, Royal Environ. Health Inst. Avocations: gardening, reading, do-it-yourself projects, wine tasting. Office: U Strathclyde Environ Health Divsn, John Anderson Bldg, Glasgow G4 0NG, Scotland

JACKSON, MICHAEL PEART, university administrator; b. Oldham, Lancashire, Eng., Jan. 7, 1947; s. Herbert and Norma (Peart) J.; m. Sylvia Woodferth; children: Karen, Callum. BA, U. Hull, Eng., 1968, MA, 1971. Lectr. U. Stirling, Scotland, 1970-78, sr. lectr., 1978-85, prof., 185-90, sr. dep. prin., 1990—. Author: Decentralisation of Collective Bargaining, 1993, Policy Marking in Trade Unions, 1989, An Introduction to Industrial Relations, 1990, Labour relations on the Docks, 1993. Justice of the Peace, 1990—. Mem. Inst. of Pers. and Devel. Office: Univ of Stirling, Dept Mgmt and Orgn, Stirling FK9 4LA, Scotland

JACKSON, NONA ARMOUR, writer, illustrator; b. Denison, Tex., Sept. 22, 1939; d. Thomas Jefferson and Novella Mae (Binion) A.; m. R.L. Jackson, Jr., Apr. 16, 1966. Supr., illustrator Diaper Jeans, Inc., Denison, 1959-62; clothing pattern maker, designer Srader's Sportswear, Denison, 1963-65; receptionist Glad Tidings Ch., Sherman, Tex., 1981-84; pastor elderly ministry Glad Tidings Ch., Sherman, 1984-87; author Pottsboro, Tex., 1987—; spkr. in field. Author, illustrator, photographer: The Cotton Mill! Can Anything Good Come from There? Vol. I-IX, 1995, Industries 1973-1981, Vol. I, 1995, Churches 1906-1991, vol. II 1995, Schools 1890-1964, vol. III, 1995, Golden Rule Independent School Extra-Curricular Activities, vol. IV, 1995, Cotton Mill Community, vol. V, 1995, The People: A Biography in Three Volumes, Vols. VI-VIII, 1995, Associates, Vol. IX, Index, Vols. VI-IX, 1995; author, illustrator: Pioneers of North West Grayson County, Texas Mid to Late 19th Century and Early 20th Century: Delaware Bend, Red Branch/Prairie Valley, Rock Creek with Some Dexter, Texas Data, 1996, Pioneers of Central Grayson County, Texas Mid to Late 19th Century and Early 20th Century: Cherrymound and Ambrose, 1996, Pioneers of Central Grayson County, Texas Mid to Late 19th Century and Early 20th Century: Cedar Community, 1996, Pioneers of South East Grayson County, Texas Mid to Late, 19th Century and Early 20th Century: Pilot Grove, 1996, Series 1 (4000 B.C.-A.D. 1607) The Overseas Connection, Big Oaks from Little Trees Grow, vols. I-III, 2000, Series 2 (A.D. 1607-A.D. 1837) Immigrant & Colonial Ancestors, vols. IV-VIII, 2000, Series 3 (A.D. 1937-A.D. 1987) A Grayson County, Texas Epic-One Hundred and Fifty Years, vols. IX-XV, 2000, Series 4 (A.D. 1855-A.D. 1991), Twentieth Century-Big Oaks-Precious Memories, vols. XVI-XVII, 2000, Series 5-10 The Collective Works of Nona Jackson vols. XVIII-XXXIX, 2000, Series 11, Jesus or Die!, Father, Son & Holy Ghost, Obedience, and Walking With God, vols. XL-XLII, 2000; contbr. articles and photographs to publs. Sec., treas., young people's supt. Sunnyside Bapt. Ch., Denison, 1963-65; Sunday sch. tchr. Glad Tidings Ch., Sherman, 1978-83; tour guide, hostess Grayson County Frontier Village, Inc., Denison, 1978-97; active Adopt a Nursing Home, Tex. Dept. Human Resources, 1999—. Mem. Grayson County Humane Soc., Nat. Audubon Soc., Nat. Trust Hist. Preservation, Libr. Congress Assoc. (charter). Republican. Assembly of God. Avocations: guitar, art, nature, theology, genealogy. Home: Unit 1 109 Houston Ave Pottsboro TX 75076-3031

JACKSON, PATRICK JOHN, public relations counsel, editor, author, public speaker; b. Grand Rapids, Mich., Sept. 5, 1932; s. Ira William and Edythe Jane (Minnema) J.; children: Richard, Kevin, Pamela, Roberta, Jennie, Alexandra, Jeremy; m. Stacey E. Smith, 1995. Student, Kenyon Coll., 1950-53; M.Ed., Antioch U., 1979. Dir. sports publicity Kenyon Coll., 1951-52; reporter Grand Rapids Press, 1953-54; advt. dir. Beckley (W.Va.) newspapers Corp., 1954-55; v.p. Jackson, King & Griffith, Waynesboro, Va., 1956-59; account exec. Ruder & Finn, N.Y.C., 1958; sr. counsel, co-founder Jackson, Jackson & Wagner, Exeter, N.H., 1959—; editor PR Reporter, 1976—, Who's Who in Pub. Relations, 1976—, Channels, 1982—; adj. prof. public relations Boston U. Sch. Public Communication, 1973-82; vis. prof. Universidad de Segrado Corazon, 1990, Hearst scholar Northern Iowa U., 1995. Editor: N.H. Conservation Directory, 1970-80; ed. Improving Productivity, 1983, co-author: Public Relations Practices: Managerial Case Studies and Problems, 1990, 5th edition, 1994, Actionable, Practical Research for Public Relations Purposes, 1994, A Probing Look at Employee Relations Today, 1998. Chmn. Strafford-Rockingham Regional Coun., 1977-78; chmn. Southeastern N.H. Regional Planning Commn., 1976-77; mem. Gov.'s Com. on N.H. Future, 1978-79; co-founder, legis. agt. Environ. Coalition, 1972-83; mem. Gov.'s Com. on Forest Resources, 1981-82; founder, lobbyist Statewide Program of Action to Conserve our Environment, 1968-93, dir., 1993—; founder, dir. N.H. Environ. Found., 1975—; dir. Granite State Pub. Radio; mng. trustee Richmond Realty Trust, 1973—; trustee Antioch U. 1981-88, First Amendment Congress, 1980-98; chmn. N.H. Agr. Task Force; founder N.Am. Pub. Rels. Coun., 1980—; founder, chmn. Epping Planning Bd., 1967-72; pres. Seacoast Region Assn., 1978-82; bd. dirs. N.H. Social Welfare Coun., 1982-85, Youth Communication, Inc., 1985-93; mem. bd. vis. Def. Info. Sch., 1984-98, chmn., 1989-98; trustee Internat. Bus. Communicators Found., 1991-95, PRSA Found., 1994-98; chmn. pub. rels. adv. bd. Ferris State U., 1988—; trustee Soc. for the Protection of N.H. Forests, 1994—; mem. adv. bd. Ball State U., Rowan U.,

Grand Valley State U., Antioch New England Grad. Sch. Recipient Communicator of Yr. award Glassboro State U., 1980, Arthur W. Page award U. Tex., 1984, Vern C. Shrantz award Ball State U., 1982, Gold Anvil award, 1986, Learning & Liberty award, 1987, first winner Pathfinder award Kent State U., 1993; first inductee to Pub. Rels. Hall of Fame Rowan Univ. N.J., 1996. Fellow Pub. Rels. Soc. Am. (pres. New Eng. chpt. 1974-75, nat. dir. 1976-77, nat. sec. 1978, nat. pres.-elect 1979, pres. 1980, Lincoln award for pub. svc. 1978); mem. Am. Assn. Pub. Opinion Rsch., Nat. Sch. Pub. Rels. Assn. (Pres. award 1993), Orgn. Devel. Network, Canadian Pub. Rels. Soc., Arthur W. Page Soc., Internat. Assn. Bus. Communicators (mem. commn. on pub. rels. measurement and evaluation 1999—), Portsmouth Athanaeum, Delta Kappa Epsilon. Quaker. E-mail: pjackson@jjwpr.com. Home: 51 Central Rd Rye NH 03870-2523 Office: Jackson Jackson Wagner 14 Front St Exeter NH 03833-2795

JACKSON, PETER ANTHONY, psychology educator; b. London, Mar. 25, 1938; arrived in New Zealand, 1971; s. Robert A. and Georgina L. (Bailey) J.; m. Sylvia E. Perry, Apr. 1959 (div. 1980); children: Leigh, Gail; m. Christine W. Skulander, Mar. 1980 (div. 1990); children: Joanne, Miles; m. Kathleen G. Livingston, July 1992. BA in Psychology, Massey U., New Zealand, 1989, MA in Psychology, 1992, PhD in Psychology, 1998. Tchr. engrng. Open Poly. New Zealand, 1975-91, tchr. psychology, 1991-93, head psychology, 1993—. Mem. New Zealand Psychol. Soc., New Zealand Royal Soc. Avocations: running, motorcycle touring, swimming.

JACKSON, PHILIP DOUGLAS, professional basketball coach; b. Deer Lodge, Mont., Sept. 17, 1945; m. June; 5 children. Grad., North Dakota, 1967. Basketball player N.Y. Knicks, 1967-78; basketball player N.J. Nets, 1978-80, asst. coach, 1980-82; head coach Albany Patroons (Cen. Basketball Assn.), 1982-87; asst. coach Chicago Bulls, 1987-89, head coach, 1989-98; head coach Los Angeles Lakers, Los Angeles, 1999-. Mem. NBA Championship Team, 1970, 73; coach NBA championship team, 1991, 92, 93,96; named Coach of Yr., NBA, 1996. Office: Los Angeles Lakers PO Box 10 3900 W Manchester Blvd Inglewood CA 90306

JACKSON, RAYMOND SIDNEY, JR., lawyer; b. Bklyn., Sept. 17, 1938; s. Raymond Sidney and Mary Frost (McInerney) Van Vranken. BA, William Coll., 1960; JD, Harvard U., 1966. Bar: N.Y. 1967, U.S. Dist. Ct. (so. and ea. dists.) N.Y. 1969, U.S. Ct. Appeals (2d cir.) 1969. Assoc. Thacher, Proffitt & Wood, N.Y.C., 1966-76, ptnr., 1976-94, of counsel, 1994—. Mem. South St. Seaport Mus., N.Y.C., 1974—, Gramercy Neighborhood Assocs., N.Y.C., 1974—, Nat. Assn. Coll. and Univ. Attys., 1972. Mem. ABA (vice chmn. admiralty and maritime law com. sect. of tort and ins. practice 1990-92), N.Y. State Bar Assn. (admiralty and maritime com. internat. law and practice sect. 1989-94), Assn. Bar City N.Y. (admiralty com. 1984-85, 88-91), Maritime Law Assn. U.S. (com. on practice and procedure 1976-91). E-mail: rsjacksonj@aol.com. Office: Thacher Proffitt & Wood 2 World Trade Ctr New York NY 10048-0005

JACKSON, REGINALD SHERMAN, JR., lawyer; b. Oct. 8, 1946; s. Reginald Sherman and Frances (Holland) J.; m. Joanne Marie Warren, Aug. 31, 1968; children: Reginald Sherman III, Michael W., Adam H. BA, Ohio State U., 1968, JD, 1971. Bar: Ohio 1971, U.S. Supreme Ct. 1976; cert. civil trial advocate Nat. Bd. Trial Advocacy. Mem. Fuller, Henry, Hodge Snyder, Toledo, 1971-76; asst. U.S. atty. no. dist. Ohio U.S. Dept. Justice, 1976-78; ptnr. Connelly, Jackson & Collier, Toledo, 1978—; adj. prof. trial practice U. Toledo Coll. Law, 1976-89. Fellow Am. Bar Found., Ohio State Bar Found. (trustee 1998—), Toledo Bar Found. (pres. 1993-98); mem. ABA (ho. of dels. 1996-99, litigation sect.), Am. Bd. Trial Advocates, Ohio Bar Assn. (pres. 2000-01), Toledo Bar Assn. (pres. 1989-90), Toledo Country Club (trustee 1981-93, pres. 1991-93), Rotary (trustee 1994-96, 1st v.p.). Home: 2907 River Rd Maumee OH 43537-3740 Office: Connelly Jackson & Collier 405 Madison Ave Ste 1600 Toledo OH 43604-1226

JACKSON, ROBBI JO, non-hazardous agricultural products company executive, lawyer; b. Nampa, Idaho, Apr. 12, 1959; d. William R. Jackson and Marilyn K. Samp Jackson Nunez. BS in Fin., U. Colo., Boulder and Denver, 1981; JD, U. Denver, 1987, LLM in Taxation, 1990. Bar: Colo. Asst. office mgr. Jerome Karsh & Co., Denver, 1982; office mgr. Almirall & Assocs., Englewood, Colo., 1983-84; assoc. Moye, Giles, O'Keefe, Vermeire & Gorrell, Denver, 1989-90, Holme Roberts & Owen, Denver, 1990-92; in-house gen. counsel Cmty. Corrections Svcs., Denver, 1992-96; CEO Enviro Cons. Svc., LLC, Evergreen and Lakewood, Colo., 1996—. Mem. staff Adminstrv. Law Rev., Denver, 1985, editor, 1985, mng. editor, 1986-87; co-author course of study materials; presenter in field. Mem. fin. com. Mile-High chpt. ARC, Denver, 1990-92; food delivery person Vols. of Am., Meals-on-Wheels, Denver, 1990-92. Recipient scholarships. Mem. ABA, Colo. Bar Assn. (ethics com.). Republican. Avocations: running marathons and other races, biking, hiking, swimming, piano and organ playing.

JACKSON, ROBERT HOWARD, food company executive, scientist; b. Pitts., Jan. 3, 1932; s. Robert and Anna J.; m. Betty Jean Jackson, June 15, 1957; 1 child, Jay Michael. BS, Penn. State Univ., 1953, MS, 1955; PhD, Mich. State Univ., 1959. Asst. prof. Univ. Mass., Amherst, 1955-57; group leader R.J. Reynolds Industries, Winston-Salem, N.C., 1961-64; tech. dir. Lehigh Valley Dairies, Allentown, Pa., 1964-68; v.p. ops. Marriott Corp., Washington, 1968-79; pres.,COO Marshall Foods, Inc., Marshall, Minn., 1979-82; pres., CEO Nutrisearch Co., Cin., 1982-85; CEO Bioproducts Internat., Inc., Sarasota, Fla., 1985—; bd. dirs. Marshall Foods, Inc., 1979-82, Imperial Biotechnology, Ltd., London, 1985-91; adv. bd. Einstein Medical, Inc., LaJolla, Calif., 1995-96; bd. dirs. J Group, Inc., Chgo., 1992—; dir. bus. devel. Quest Internat. (Unilever), Sydney, Australia, 1991-94. Contbr. articles to profl. jours. With U.S. Army, 1959-61. Mem. Inst. of Food Tech., Soc. Sigma Xi, Food Industry Assocs., Am. Men of Sci. Republican. Episcopalian. Avocations: physical fitness, golf, fishing, bass violinist. E-mail: jubilance@worldnet.att.net.

JACKSON, ROBERT KEITH, manufacturing company executive; b. South Bend, Ind., Apr. 20, 1943; s. Orval Russell and Dorothy Alice (Gailey) J.; m. Cheryl Dee Bronkhorst, Nov. 6, 1965; children: Jennifer Lynn, Stephen Robert. BS, Western Mich. U., 1966; MBA, Vanderbilt U., 1987. Vocat. tchr. Warren (Mich.) Consol. Schs., 1967-68; mfg. engr. Eaton Corp., Kalamazoo, 1968-77, gen. supt., 1977; gen. supt. Eaton Corp., Kings Mountain, N.C., 1977-80; plant mgr. Eaton Ltd., Manchester, Eng., 1980-84, Eaton Corp., Shelbyville, Tenn., 1984-91; mgr. mfg. and quality assurance Truck Components Ops. Eaton Corp., Kalamazoo, 1991-93; plant mgr. Eaton Corp., Humboldt, Tenn., 1993-96; ops. specialist Eaton Corp., China, 1996-97; gen. mgr. Eaton Truck and Bus. Components (Shanghai) Co., Ltd., 1997—; mem. adv. coun. indsl. studies Mid. Tenn. State U., Murfreesboro, 1985-91, Sch. Bus., 1990-91; mem. machine tool tech. adv. com. Jackson (Tenn.) State C.C., 1994-96; mem. devel. com. U. Tenn. at Martin, mem. mech. engring. adv. bd., 1995-96. Trustee Eaton Pub. Policy Assn., Cleve., 1985-89. Mem. Tenn. Assn. Bus. (bd. dirs. 1989-91), Rotary, Elks, KC. Republican. Roman Catholic. Home: 640 Dogwood Dr Monteagle TN 37356-2010 Office: Wai Gao Qiao Free Trd Zone, 388 Ai Du Rd, Pu Dong Shanghai 200131, China

JACKSON, ROBERT WILSON, biologist; b. Kirkcaldy, Fife, Scotland, Oct. 8, 1970; s. Robert Stevenson Jackson and Denise Margaret (O'Neill) Burton; m. Dawn Louise Arnold, July 6, 1996. BSc in Applied Biol. Scis. with honors, U. of the West of Eng., Bristol, 1994, PhD, 1997. Rsch. assoc. U. of the West of England, Bristol, 1998—. Contbr. articles to profl. jours. Mem. Soc. of Gen. Microbiology, British Soc. of Plant Pathology. Mem. Ch. of England. Avocations: walking, travelling, history, wildlife. Office: U of the West of Eng, Coldharbour Ln, Frenchay BS16 1QY, England

JACKSON, RYNO MARSHALL, forensic psychologist, consultant; b. Reading, Pa., Oct. 12, 1934; s. Jesse and Helen Adelia (Taylor) J.; m. Jacqueline Estelle Coleman, Aug. 10, 1963; children: Michael, David, Tracy. BA in English Edn., Glassboro State U., 1961; MA, Newark State U., 1972; PsyD, Rutgers U., 1985. Cert. sch. psychologist, N.J.; diplomate Am. Coll. Forensic Examiners, Am. Coll. Psychol. Treating Addictions. English tchr. Scotch Plains-Fanwood, N.J., 1961-70; sch. psychologist Plainfield (N.J.) Bd. Edn., 1970-89; forensic psychologist Forensic Psychology, Flemington, N.J., 1989—; cons. Union County Juvenile and Domestic Rels. Ct., Elizabeth, N.J., 1972-82, Middlesex County Coll., Woodbridge, N.J., 1988-92, Greenbrook Acad., Boundbrook, N.J., 1990—; adj. prof. Newark State Coll., Union, N.J., 1992-96. Juvenile conf. com. advisor, Plainfield, 1986-87; search and rescue pilot CAP, Linden, N.J., 1975-85; coach Little League Baseball, Plainfield, 1972-78, Pee Wee Football, 1975-78. Mem. APA, N.J. Psychol. Assn., N.J. Assn. Black Psychologists, Internat. Soc. Police Surgeons, Am. Mensa, Am. Coll. Forensic Psychology. Home: 1208 Salem Rd Plainfield NJ 07060-3323 Office: Assocs in Forensic Psychology 260 Rt 202-31 N Flemington NJ 08822

JACKSON, SAMUEL L., actor; b. Washington, Dec. 21, 1948; m. LaTanya Richardson; 1 child, Zoe. Performances include: (TV series) Movin' On, 1972, Ghostwriter, 1992; (TV movies) The Trial of the Moke, 1978, Uncle Tom's Cabin, 1987, Common Ground, 1990, Dead and Alive: The Race for Gus Farace, 1991, Simple Justice, 1993, Assault at West Point, 1994, Against the Wall, 1994; (films) Together for Days, 1972, Ragtime, 1981, Eddie Murphy Raw, 1987, Coming to America, 1988, School Daze, 1988, (voice-over) Mystery Train, 1989, Do The Right Thing, 1989, Sea of Love, 1989, A Shock to the System, 1990, Def by Temptation, 1990, Betsy's Wedding, 1990, Mo' Better Blues, 1990, The Exorcist III, 1990, Goodfellas, 1990, Return of Superfly, 1990, Jungle Fever, 1991 (Best Actor award Cannes International Film Festival), Strictly Business, 1991, Juice, 1992, White Sands, 1992, Patriot Games, 1992, Johnny Suede, 1992, Jumpin' at the Boneyard, 1992, Fathers and Sons, 1992, National Lampoon's Loaded Weapon 1, 1993, Amos & Andrew, 1993, Menace II Society, 1993, Jurassic Park, 1993, True Romance, 1993, Hail Caesar, 1994, Fresh, 1994, Hail Caesar, 1994, The New Age, 1994, Pulp Fiction, 1994, Losing Isiah, 1995, Kiss of Death, 1995, Fluke, 1995, Die Hard With a Vengeance, 1995, The Great White Hype, 1996, Trees Lounge, 1996, The Search for One Eye Jimmy, 1996, A Time to Kill, 1996, The Long Kiss Goodnight, 1996, 187, 1997, Jackie Brown, 1997, Hard Eight, 1997, Eve's Bayou, 1997, Sphere, 1998, Out of Sight, 1998, The Negotiator, 1998, Rules of Engagement, 1999, Mefisto in Onyx, 1999, Star Wars Episode I: The Phantom Menace, 1999, Deep Blue Sea, 1999, Shaft, 2000, others.

JACKSON, STANLEY EDWARD, retired special education educator; b. Washington, Sept. 3, 1918; s. Eugene Edward and Inez Christine (Booth) J. BS, Miner Tchrs. Coll., Washington, 1939; MA, Columbia U., 1947, Profl. Diploma, 1948, EdD, 1958; postgrad., Johns Hopkins U., Peabody Inst. Elem. tchr. D.C. Pub. Schs., 1940-58, elem. sch. prin., 1958-66, dir. spl. edn., 1966-72; gov.-at-large Coun. for Exceptional Children, Reston, Va., 1971-72, asst. exec. dir., membership, 1972-82; lectr. Cath. U., Washington, 1965-66, asst. prof. edn., 1967; instr. D.C. Tchrs. Coll., 1971-72; initiator Tchr. Aide Program Spl. Edn. Classes D.C. Pub. Schs., 1968; founder Juvenile Decency Corps Uplift House, 1964; co-planner Mamie D. Lee Sch. Mentally Retarded, 1968. Author: School Organization for the Mentally Retarded, 1973, Educational Strategies and Services for Exceptional Children, 1976. Pres. Area K Bd. Commrs. Youth Coun., Washington, 1959-65; founder UPLIFT Cmty. House, Washington, 1963, pres. Chpt. 49, 1962-64, 1st pres. Fedn. 524, 1965-66; bd. dirs. Found. for Exceptional Children, 1978. With U.S. Army, 1941-45, WWII. Decorated four Battles Stars; recipient Yes I Care award Found. for Exceptional Children, 1992, Stanley E. Jackson scholarship established in his honor Found. for Exceptional Children, 1980; Plaque for Outstanding Cmty. Svc., Commrs. Coun., Washington, 1963, Outstanding Ret. Tchr. award Jr. Citizens Corps, 1979; Stanley E. Jackson spl. edn. award established in his honor Bd. Edn. D.C. Pub. Schs., 1973, Stanley E. Jackson Scholarships established Peabody Prep., Johns Hopkins U., 1989. Mem. NEA, AAUP, NAACP, D.C. Congress Parents and Tchrs. (life), Coun. Exceptional Children, Dept. Elem. Sch. Prins., AMVETS, Urban League, Johns Hopkins Assoc. Program, Kappa Delta Pi, Phi Delta Kappa. Avocations: music, numismatics, writing, philanthropy. Home: Apt 703 One E University Pky Baltimore MD 21218

JACKSON, STEPHEN ERIC, police official; b. Seymour, Ind., July 9, 1946; s. Ralph Marshall Jackson and Dolly Katherine (Britt) Tudor; m. Cheryl Jane Hallman, June 23, 1967 (div. 1985); children: Kirstina Leigh, Brandi Annette; m. Margaret Ann Skelton, Oct. 17, 1986 (div. 1989); m. Candy Sandler Clinard, Sept. 30, 1995. BA in Sociology, N. Tex. State U., 1976; grad., Tex. Law Enforcement Inst., 1991; MPA, U. North Tex., 1993. Lic. mediator, 1996. Police officer, sgt. Denton (Tex.) Police Dept., 1970-81; customer svc. mgr. Amerace Corp., Denton, 1981-83; dir. police and traffic svcs. U. North Tex., Denton, 1983-98; ptnr. Pathways Ednl. Corp., Irving, Tex., 1998—; pres. Pathways Life Mgmt. Seminars, 1999—; adj. faculty applied econs. U. North Tex., 2000—; public speaker, life mgmt. coord, v.p. Denton County Chiefs of Police, 1986-94. Contbr. articles to profl. jours. Precinct chmn. Denton County Rep. Party, 1982-85; mem. Pub. Transp. Task Force, Denton, 1989; chmn. steering com. Leadership Denton, 1990-95, 95-97, Leadership Denton Alumni Assn., 1991—; mem. parking com. Main St. Denton, Inter-Assn. Task Force on Alcohol and Other Substance Abuse Issues, 1995-97, local assoc. Nat. Coalition Bldg. Inst., 1990—; del./panelist White House Conf. on Hate Crimes, 1997. Mem. Internat. Assn. Campus Law Enforcement Adminstrs. (v.p. 1995-96, pres. elect 1996-97, pres. 1997-98), Tex.-N.Mex. Assn. Coll. and Univ. Police Depts. (Pres.'s award 1985, treas. 1993-96, Adminstr. of Yr. 1993), Internat. Assn. Chiefs of Police. Avocations: rugby, golf, tennis. Office: Pathways Ednl Corp 4201 Wingren Dr Ste 210 Irving TX 75062-2763

JACKSON, SUSAN, secondary education educator; b. N.Y.C., Jan. 13, 1945; d. Peter Van Rennsalaer Weeks and Eugenia Mortlock Flatow; children: Lori Moussapour, Michael Madoff, Nigel, Marissa. BA, Cornell U., 1965; MA, Montclair State U., 1979. Tchr. Aurora County Secondary Sch., N.Y., 1965-66, Thornton Donovan Sch., New Rochelle, N.Y., 1968-69, Beacon (N.Y.) H.S., 1970-72, Int. Sch. 162, N.Y.C., 1972-76, Hackensack (N.J.) H.S., 1976-90, Hackensack Mid. Sch., 1990—; co-advisor Nat. Jr. Honor Soc., Hackensack, 1992—; instructional leader Hackensack Mid. Sch., 1998—. Del. Hackensack Edn. Assn., 1992-95; chairperson bd. dirs. Ctr. Modern Dance Edn., Hackensack, 1985-93. Avocations: poetry, travel. Home: 365 Lookout Ave Hackensack NJ 07601-2804 Office: Hackensack Mid Sch 360 Union St Hackensack NJ 07601-4394

JACKSON, THIRSTON HENRY, JR., retired adult education educator; b. Camden, N.J., Mar. 28, 1913; s. Thirston Henry and Elizabeth Loraine (Keck) J.; m. Grace Roberta Ballard, Sept. 26, 1934 (dec. Dec. 1993); 1 child, Diane Jackson Bove. BSEE, Duke U., 1934; MA in Edn., Calif. Luth. U., 1984. Registered profl. engr., Calif.; registered tchr., Calif. Physicist Hughes Aircraft, Hawthorne, Calif., 1932-40; radio engr. Northrop Aviation, Hawthorne, 1940-50; electronic engr. N.Am. Aviation, Inglewood, Calif., 1950-60; sr. design engr. N.Am. Aviation, Downey, Calif., 1960-72; asst. chief engr. Marquardt Aircraft, Van Nuys, Calif., 1972-79; exec. v.p. 21st Century Tech., L.A., 1979-82; tchr. electronics Simi Adult Sch., Simi Valley, Calif., 1982-90; ret., 1990. Patentee automatic navigation device; developer missile navigation heat seeker. Scoutmaster Boy Scouts Am., N.J., 1929-32, N.C., 1932-33, L.A., 1933-54. Mem. Nat. Eagle Scout Assn. (sr.). Avocation: model railroading. Home: 6694 Tremont Cir Simi Valley CA 93063-3945

JACKSON, THOMAS GENE, lawyer; b. N.Y.C., Mar. 9, 1949; s. Alan Clark and Clare Seena (Werther) J.; m. Beatrice Lafrance Korab, June 11, 1972; children: Sarah Ann, Alan Edward. AB magna cum laude in English, Dartmouth Coll., 1971; JD, U. Va., 1974. Bar: N.Y. 1975, U.S. Dist. Ct. (so. and ea. dists.) N.Y. 1975, U.S. Ct. Appeals (2d cir.) 1975, U.S. Ct. Appeals (5th cir.) 1978, U.S. Supreme Ct. 1978, U.S. Ct. Appeals (D.C. cir.) 1986. Editor The Rsch. Group, Charlottesville, Va., 1973-74; assoc. Phillips Nizer Benjamin Krim & Ballon LLP, N.Y.C., 1974-82, ptnr., 1982—; fed. bar coun. com. 2d Cir. Cts., 1997—, chmn. subcom. on tech. in the cts., 1997—. Mem. Village of Irvington Cable TV Adv. Com., N.Y., 1979-91, 95—, chmn. franchise renewal com., 1991-95; sec. Village of Irvington Environ. Conservation Bd., 1983-87, chmn., 1987—; mem. Dartmouth Coll. Alumni Coun., 1986-89. Mem. ABA (sect. antitrust law, Clayton Act com., premerger notification subcom. 1982—), Fed. Bar Coun. (com. 2d cir. cts. 1997—, chmn. subcom. tech. in cts. 1997—), Am. Arbitration Assn. (panel of arbitrators, comml. tribunal 1986—), Assn. of Bar of City of N.Y. (antitrust and trade regulation com. 1988-92, mergers acquisitions and joint ventures subcom. 1991-92), Dartmouth Coll. Club Officers Assn. (exec. com. 1988-91), Dartmouth Coll. Class Secs. Assn. (v.p. 1984-85, pres. 1985-86), Dartmouth Club Westchester (sec. 1984-87, 90—, pres. 1987-90). Home: 32 Hamilton Rd Irvington NY 10533-2311 Office: Phillips Nizer Benjamin Krim & Ballon LLP 666 5th Ave New York NY 10103-0001

JACKSON, WYNELLE REDDING, children's services educational administrator, tax preparer; b. Atlanta, Sept. 3, 1947; d. Edwin Turner and Eva Josephine (Davis) Redding; m. Ronald Van Watson, Aug. 10, 1974 (div. Aug. 1978); m. Toney Jackson, Sept. 16, 1995. BA in Elem. Edn., CUNY, 1968; MEd in Supervision and Adminstrn., U. N.H., 1982. Lic. notary pub., N.Y. Tchr. Pub. Sch. 129 N.Y.C. Bd. Edn., Bklyn., 1969-74, coord. career edn. dist. 16, 1974-75, tchr. Pub. Sch. 243, 1975-80; tchr. Pub. Sch. 85 N.Y.C. Bd. Edn., Queens, 1980-82; dir. ednl. svcs. The Salvation Army Social Svcs. for Children, N.Y.C., 1982—. Treas. Black Am. Heritage Found., Jamaica, N.Y., 1982—; mem. Wayanda Civic Assn., Queens Village, N.Y., 1994—. Recipient Josephine H. Pettie Humanitarian award Black Am. Heritage Found., 1993. Mem. ASCD, Nat. Notary Assn., N.Y. State Assn. Supervision and Curriculum Devel., Phi Delta Kappa, The Nat. Sorority of Phi Delta Kappa, Inc. (fin. sec. Beta Omicron chpt. 1980-81, treas., 1983-87, fin. sec. eastern region 1991-95). Episcopalian. Avocation: bowling. Home: 99-10 211th St Queens Village NY 11429 Office: The Salvation Army Social Svcs for Children 132 W 14th St New York NY 10011-7389

JACOB, FRANÇOIS, biologist; b. Nancy, France, June 17, 1920; s. Simon and Therese (Franck) J.; m. Lysiane Bloch, Nov. 27, 1947 (dec. 1984); children: Pierre, Laurent, Odile, Henri; m. Geneviève Barrier, 1999. M.D., Faculty of Medicine, Paris, 1947; D.Sc., Faculty of Scis., Paris, 1954; D.Sc. (hon.), U. Chgo., 1965; Dr honoris causa, various univs. Asst. Pasteur Inst., 1950-56, head dept. cellular genetics, 1960-92, pres., 1982-88; prof. cellular genetics Coll. of France, 1964-92; prof. emeritus Coll. of France and Inst. Pasteur, 1992—. Author: The Logic of Life, 1970; The Possible and the Actual, 1981, The Statue Within, 1987, Of Flies, Mice and Men, 1997. Recipient Charles Leopold Mayer prize, 1962; Nobel prize in physiology and medicine (with A. Lwoff and J. Monod), 1965. Mem. Académie des Sciences (Paris), Académie française Paris; fgn. mem. Royal Danish Acad. Scis. and Letters, Am. Acad. Arts and Scis., Nat. Acad. Scis. (U.S.), Am. Philos. Soc., Royal Soc. (London), Académie Royale de Médecine de Belgique, Acad. Scis. Hungary, Royal Acad. Scis. Madrid. Achievements include rsch. on genetics bacterial cells and viruses; contbr. to mechanisms of info. transfer (messenger RNA) and genetic basis of regulatory circuits, early stages of the mouse embryo. Office: Pasteur Inst, 25 Rue du Dr Roux, 75724 Paris Cedex 15, France

JACOB, JOHN EDWARD, corporate executive, communications executive; b. Trout, La., Dec. 16, 1934; s. Emory and Claudia (Sadler) J.; m. Barbara Singleton, Mar. 28, 1959; 1 child, Sheryl Renee. BA, Howard U., 1957, MSW, 1963; LHD (hon.), Old Dominion U., 1983, Fisk U., 1984; LLD (hon.), LaFayette Coll., 1985, Tuskegee U., 1986, Cen. State U., 1986, Fla. Internat. U., 1988, Dominican Coll., 1988, Howard U., 1990, Am. U., 1993; LHD (hon.), Morris Brown U., 1991, So. Ill. U., Boston Coll., Boston Coll., 1992. Caseworker, then child welfare casework supr. Balt. Dept. Public Welfare, 1960-65; mem. staff Washington Urban League, 1965-70, acting exec. dir., 1968-70; dir. community orgn.-tng. Eastern region Nat. Urban League, 1970; exec. dir. San Diego Urban League, 1970-75; pres. Washington Urban League, 1975-79; exec. v.p. Nat. Urban League, N.Y.C., 1979-81, former pres., chief exec. officer; corp. exec., exec. v.p., chief comms. officer Anheuser-Busch Cos., 1994—; field work instr. Howard U. Sch. Social Work, 1963-65, lectr., 1967-69, chmn. bd.; cons., lectr. in field; bd. dirs. Local Initiative Support Corp., Bennett Coll., Nat. Westminster Banco, Anheuser Busch Cos., Nat. Park Found., Bennett Coll., N.Y. Tel. Co., Continental Corp., Coca-Cola Enteprises Inc., LTV Corp. Author weekly column To Be Equal, 1982. Vice chmn. bd. trustees Howard U., 1971-78, chmn. 1988-91, chmn. emeritus 1991—; mem. jud. nominating commn. U.S. Dist. Ct. and U.S. Cir. Ct., Washington, 1978; bd. overseers U. Calif., San Diego, 1974-75; bd. dirs. NCCJ, 1983-88, Eisenhower Found., 1984-86, Ind. Sector, 1984-89, Jr. Achievement, 1985-91; chmn. Citizens' Commn. on AIDS for N.Y.C. and No. N.J., 1985. With AUS, 1957-58. Recipient Whitney M. Young Meml. award Washington Urban League, 1979, United Way Am. profl. leadership award, Public Service award United Black Fund Washington, 1979, Achievement award Eastern province Kappa Alpha Psi, 1976, Outstanding Community Service award Howard U. Sch. Social Work Alumni Assn., 1979, Spl. Citation Atlanta Club, Howard U. Alumni Assn., 1980, Hudson L. Lavell Social Action award, Phi Beta Sigma, 1982, Exemplary Servcie award, Alumni Club L.I. Howard U., 1983, Achievement award, Zeta Phi Beta, 1984, Blackbook's Bus. & Profl. award, Dollars and Sense mag., 1985, Nat. Kappaman Achievement award Durham Alumni Chpt., Kappa Alpha Psi, 1984, Bayard Rustin Humanitarian award, 1989, Lifetime Achievement award St. Louis chpt. NAACP, 1991, Equal Justice award Nat. Bar Assn., 1991. Democrat. Episcopalian. Office: Anheuser-Busch Cos One Busch Pl Saint Louis MO 63131-1139

JACOB, PIERRE, philosophy educator; b. Neuilly-sur-Seine, France, Jan. 1, 1949; s. François and Lise (Bloch) J.; m. Marie-Noëlle de Rohozinska, May 10, 1985; children: Claire, Sarah, Raphaël. Agregation de Philosophie, Ecole Normale Supérieure, St. Cloud, France, 1972; PhD in History of Sci., Harvard U., 1978. Tchr. philosophy Lycee du Perreux, France, 1978-79; head rsch. CR2 C.N.R.S., Aix-en-Provence, France, 1980-84, head rsch. CR1, 1984-87; head rsch. CR1 C.N.R.S., Paris, 1987-94, dir. rsch. DR2, 1994—. Author: L'Empirisme Logique, 1980, De Vienne A Cambridge, 1980; editor: L'Age de la Science, 1988-92, What Minds Can Do, 1997. Harkness Found. fellow, 1973-75, Thyssen Stiftung fellow, 1979-80. Mem. European Soc. for Analytic Philosophy, European Soc. for Philosophy and Psychology. Home: 75 Boulevard Saint Michel, 75005 Paris France Office: CREA Ecole Polytechnique, Inst Cognitive Scis, 67 blvd Rinel, 69675 Lyon France

JACOB, TEUKU, bioanthropologist, educator; b. Peureulak, Aceh, Indonesia, Dec. 6, 1929; s. Teukoe and Tjoet (Kariman) Soeleiman; m. Nuraini Umar, Dec. 17, 1972; 1 child, Tjut Nila Nurilani. MD, Gadjah Mada U., Yogyakarta, Indonesia, 1956; MS, Howard U., 1960; PhD, U. Utrecht, The Netherlands, 1967; DSc (hon.), Internat. Open U., Colombo, Sri Lanka, 1992. Asst. bioanthropology Gadjah Mada U., Yogyakarta, 1954-57, lectr., 1962-65, assoc. prof. bioanthropology, 1965-71, prof. bioanthropoloy, 1971-00, prof. emeritus, 2000—, head lab. bioanthropology, 1968—, vice dean faculty of medicine, 1973-75, dean, 1975-79, rector, 1981-86; instr. anatomy Howard U., Washington, 1959-61; vis. prof. human paléontology San Diego State U., 1968; invited prof. Inst de Paléontologie Humaine, Paris, 1991, 99; fgn. prof. Coll. de France, Paris, 1992, 99; chmn. Indonesian Soc. of Medical Polemology, 1985, advisor Indonesian Tchrs. Found., Yogyakarta, 1994—, Ctr. for the Study of Nat. Identity, Yogyakarta, 1995—. chmn. bd. trustees, Ctr. for Security and Peace Studies, 1996—. Editor: Community Medicine, 1972; author: Man, Science and Technology, 1988, Polemology: The Science of War and Peace, 1992, The Future, 1991 (Indonesian Best Book Found. award 1994), Toward a Humane Technology, 1996. Mem. People's Consultative Assembly, Republic of Indonesia, Jakarta, 1982-87. Recipient Medal for Sci. Rsch., Ministry of Edn., Jakarta, 1982, Sci. Prize for Rsch., Indonesian Med. Assn., 1984, Gold medal Indian Bd. Alternative Medicines, Calcutta, 1993, Sultan Hamengkubuwono award 1997. Mem. AAAS, N.Y. Acad. Sci., Internat. Assn. for Study Human Paleontology (exec. com.), Centro Int. di Studi e Ricerche sul Popolamento Preistorico e Protoistorico del Piemonte Sudorientale (hon.), Indonesian Soc. of Bio and Paleoanthropology (chmn.) Gadjah Mada Alumni Assn. (vice chmn. 1977-85), Indonesian Acad. of Scis., Indonesian Anthropol. Assn., Longgupo Inst. of Paleoanthropology (China acad. adviser). Islam (Sunni). Avocations: reading, essay writing, travel, photography, music. Home: Sekip M 4, Yogyakarta 55281, Indonesia Office: Lab of Bio and Paleoanthrop, Sekip Medika Rd, Yogyakarta 55281, Indonesia

JACOBOWITZ, HAROLD SAUL, lawyer; b. N.Y.C., Aug. 26, 1950; s. William and Miriam (Spector) J.; m. Estrella B. Rivera, Oct. 26, 1972. BA, CUNY, 1972; JD, Rutgers U., 1977. Bar: N.Y. 1977, U.S. Dist. Ct. (so. dist.) N.Y. 1978, U.S. Dist. Ct. (ea. dist.) N.Y. 1978. Assoc. Goldman & Heffernan, N.Y.C., 1977-78, Zola & Zola, N.Y.C., 1978-79, Goldberg & Lysaght, N.Y.C., 1979-82; atty. of record Am. Internat. Group (Jacobowitz, Spessard, Garfinkel & Lesman), N.Y.C., 1982-88, regional mng. atty., 1988-89, chief counsel, 1989-90, v.p., 1990—, chief tech. officer property/casualty

claims, 1998—; arbitration panel U.S. Dist. Ct. (ea. dist.) N.Y. Mem. ABA, N.Y. State Bar Assn., Assn. Bar City N.Y., N.Y. County Lawyers Assn., Assn. Trial Lawyers N.Y.C. (bd. dirs.). Office: Am Internat Group 70 Pine St New York NY 10270-0002

JACOBS, ALICIA MELVINA, account executive; b. Newark, June 24, 1955; d. Alvin and Melvina (McKinney) J. BA, Oberlin Coll., 1977. Caseworker Essex County Welfare Bd., Newark, 1977-78; sr. audit analyst N.J. Blue Cross, Newark, 1978-80; fin. analyst N.Y. State Office of the Spl. Cont., N.Y.C., 1980-81; account exec. Fortune Temporary Personnel, N.Y.C., 1981-84; sales mgr. Wall St. Temporary, N.Y.C., 1984-85; account exec. Prentice Hall, N.Y.C., 1985-90; account exec. Rsch. Inst. Am., Newark, 1990-91, Westfield, 1992-93, Century City, Calif., 1993-96; regional acct. mgr. Interactive Search, Calif., 1997-98; regional acct. mgr. Giga Info. Group, Calif., 1998-99, v.p., dir. bus. devel., 1999—. Fund-raising chmn. The Africa Project, N.Y.C., 1989-91; sec. We Are Family, Newark, 1989—; mentor, tutor Welcome Bapt. Ch., Newark, 1991—; vol. Scott-Krueger Cultural Ctr., Newark, 1991—; vol. mentor Jr. Achievement, Sisters Having Our Say, SOS Group, Faithful Central Employment Vol., The Restaurant Club, Women Who Cook 1994; chairperson Oberlin Coll. AA Cluster Reunion, Ohio, 1997. Recipient Heroine award Montclair (N.J.) High Sch., 1990, Participant award Madison Ave. Sch., Newark. Mem. NAACP, N.J. Law Librs. Assn., Coalition of 100 Black Women. Avocations: teaching children, aerobics, reading. Home: 6922 Knowlton Pl Apt 305 Los Angeles CA 90045-2099

JACOBS, DIANA PIETROCARLI, botanical illustrator; b. Glen Cove, N.Y., Aug. 22, 1950; d. Frank and Elizabeth (Ranaldo) Pietrocarli; m. David Jacobs, Feb. 12, 1977; children: Aaron Michael, Molly Sarah. BA, U. Pitts., 1971. Cert. bot. and zool. illustrator Los Angeles County Mus. Comml.; artist agt. Mary Louise Flock Assn., N.Y.C., 1971-74; freelance illustrator, painter Los Angeles, 1976—; bot. illustrator Huntington Bot. Gardens, San Marino, Calif., 1981—; instr. Otis Parsons Sch. Design, 1985-86; v.p. Roundelay Prodns., 1977—. Illustrator: Celebrating the Wild Mushroom, 1986; solo shows include Nat. Mus. History L.A., 1989, Biota Gallery, 1992, Gene Sinser Gallery, 1993, McHenry Coll., 1995, U. Wis., 1995, Santa Barbara Arts Commn., 1996, The Casements, Fla., 1996, McCaffery Gallery, Calif., 1997, Laredo Ctr. for Arts, 1997, Maturango Mus., 1997, Cathedral Heritage Soc., 1997, Artists, Residents of Chgo., 1998, Sierra Arts Found., 1999, Pacific Grove Art Ctr., 1999. Bd. dirs. Los Angeles County Mus. Natural Hist. Alliance. Recipient Silver award Art of Calif. Discovery, 1st place award Thousand Oaks Art Assn., Gold award Art of Calif. Discovery, award of merit Redding Mus. Art and History, Purchase award Minot State U., Exhibit award Santa Cruz Art League.

JACOBS, ELEANOR ALICE, retired clinical psychologist, educator; b. Royal Oak, Mich., Dec. 25, 1923; d. Roy Dana and Alice Ann (Keaton) J. B.A., U. Buffalo, 1949, M.A., 1952, Ph.D., 1955. Clin. psychologist VA Hosp., Buffalo, 1954-83; EEO counelor VA Hosp., 1962-79, chief psychology service, 1979-83; clin. prof. SUNY, Buffalo, 1950-83; speaker on psychology to community orgns. and clubs, 1952—; Mem. adult devel. and aging com. NICHD, HEW, 1971-75. Researcher for publs. on hyperbaric medicine, hyperoxygenation effect on cognitive functions in aged. Recipient Outstanding Superior Performance award Buffalo VA Hosp., 1958, Spl. Recognition award SUNY, Buffalo, Spl. Recognition award SUNY, 1971; W.L. McKnight award Miami Heart Inst., 1972; Adminstrs. commendation VA, 1974; Dirs. commendation VA Med. Center, Buffalo, 1978; Disting. Alumni award SUNY, Buffalo, 1983; named Woman of Yr. Bus. and Profl. Women's Clubs, Buffalo, 1973. Mem. Am. Psychol. Assn., Eastern Psychol. Assn., N.Y. State Psychol. Assn., Am. Group Psychotherapy Assn., Am. Soc. Group Psychotherapy and Psychodrama, Psychol. Assn. Western N.Y. (Disting. Achievement award 1976), Group Psychotherapy Assn. Western N.Y., Undersea Med. Soc., Sigma Xi. Home: PO Box 432, Ridgeway, ON Canada L0S 1N0

JACOBS, EUGENE GARDNER, JR., psychiatrist, psychoanalyst, educator; b. Providence, Jan. 3, 1926; s. E. Gardner and Edna Jacobs; m. Alice L. Smith, Apr. 12, 1951 (div. 1980); children: Susan, Nancy, John, Peter. AB, Yale U., 1948; MD, U. Pa., 1952. Diplomate Am. Bd. Psychiatry and Neurology. Intern Pa. Hosp., Phila., 1952-53; resident Neurol. Inst. N.Y., N.Y.C., 1953-54; rsch. fellow Columbia U., N.Y.C., 1954-55; resident N.Y. State Psychiat. Inst., Columbia Presbyn. Hosp., N.Y.C., 1955-58; pvt. practice Phila., 1958—; cons. psychiatrist Pa. Hosp., 1997—; staff psychiatrist Inst. of Pa. Hosp., Phila., 1958-62, sr. attending psychiatrist, 1974-97; chief psychiatrist Student Health Svc., Temple U., Phila., 1973-77; chief dept. psychiatry Phila. Naval Hosp., 1981-85; clin. asst. prof. U. Pa., 1970-81, 97—; clin. assoc. prof. MCP Hahnemann U., Phila., 1981-98, adj. clin. assoc. prof., 1998—. Capt. USNR, ret. Fellow Am. Psychiat. Assn. (life); mem. Phila. Assn. for Psychoanalysis, Am. Psychoanalytic Assn., Phila. Psychiat. Soc. Fax: 215-842-0571. Home and Office: 5400 Wissahickon Ave Philadelphia PA 19144-5223

JACOBS, FRANCIS GEOFFREY, lawyer, educator; b. June 8, 1939; s. Cecil Sigismund and Louise (Fischhof) J.; m. Ruth Freeman, 1964; 1 child; m. Susan Felicity Gordon, 1975; 4 children. MA, DPhil, U. Oxford. Bar: Middle Temple, 1964, Queen's Counsel, 1984, Bencher, 1990. Lectr. jurisprudence U. Glasgow, 1963-65; lectr. law LSE, 1965-69; secretariat European Commn. Human Rights and Legal Directorate Coun. Europe, Strasbourg, France, 1969-72; legal sec. Ct. Justice European Communities, Luxembourg, 1972-74, advocate gen., 1988—; prof. European law U. London, 1974-88; dir. Ctr. European Law King's Coll., London, 1981-88, vis. prof., 1989—; UK del. conf. supreme adminstrv. cts. EEC, 1984-88; part-time practice, 1974-88; mem. Adminstrn. Tribunal, Internat. Inst. for Unification Pvt. Law, Rome; Cooley lectr. U. Mich., 1983, Bishop lectr., 1989; gov. Brit. Inst. Human Rights, 1985—. Author: Criminal Responsibility, 1971, The European Convetion on Human Rights, 1975; author: (with others) References to the European Court, 1975, The Court of Justice of the European Communities, 1977, The European Union Treaty, 1986; editor: European Law and the Individual, 1975; editor: (with others) The European Community and GATT, 1986, The Effect of Treaties in Domestic Law, 1987, Liber Amicorum Pierre Pescatore, 1987; editor Yearbook of European Law, 1981-88; mem. editl. bd. Yearbook of European Law, Cahiers de Droit Européen, Common Market Law Review, European Law Review, Jour. Environ. Law, King's Coll. Law Jour., Rivista di Diritto Europeo; gen. editor Oxford European Community Law series, 1986—. Comdr. Ordre de Mérite. Mem. U.K. Assn. European Law (hon. sec. 1974-81, v.p. 1981—). Avocations: books, music, nature, travel. Office: Ct Justice European Communities, Palais de la Cour de Justice, L-2925 Luxembourg Luxembourg*

JACOBS, FRANCK MORGEN, physicist; b. St. John's, Antigua, Jan. 13, 1950; s. Theophilos Jeremiah and Iris Louisa (Peters) J.; m. Arlene Sheryl Henry, July 27, 1991; 1 child, Mario Dmitri. BSc in Physics, U. W.I., 1985; postgrad., Loyola Bus. Sch., 1986, U. Sussex, 1988; diploma in Engring., U. Reading, 1996. Asst. meteorologist Govt. Antigua, 1970-71, sr. statis. asst., 1975-81, statistician, 1985-86, dir. statistics, 1987—; rschr., cons. Cmty. Health Aide Program Evaluation, Antigua, 1978-79; census officer Govt. Antigua, 1991—; lectr. U. W.I., 1993—. Fellow Royal Statis. Soc.; mem. AAAS, Am. Phys. Soc., Interam. Statis. Inst., Antigua Artists Soc., Am. Assn. Physics Tchrs., Masons, Am. Math. Soc. Islamic. Avocations: chess, martial arts, drawing and painting, scientific research. Office: Ministry Finance Stats Divsn, Redcliffe St, Saint John's W I Antigua and Barbuda

JACOBS, GEORG ANDREAS, oncologist; b. Saarbruecken, Germany, June 1, 1963; s. Hermann H. and Christel M. (Klein) J.; m. Nicole C. Risse; children: Helena, Nicolas. MD, U. Saarland, Germany, 1988, PhD, 1991. Physician U. Saarland, Germany, 1988-95; attending physician Cath. Hosp., Saarbruecken, Germany, 1996-97; oncologist Clinics for Oncology, Saarbruecken, Germany, 1997—; cons. in field. Mem. European Soc. Medicine, Internat. Soc. Oncology. Office: Praxis Fuer Heamatologie, 78 AM Ludwigsberg, 66113 Saarsbruecken Germany

JACOBS, HARA KAY, lawyer; b. Phila., Dec. 22, 1969; d. Ellis R. Jacobs and Sandy K. Sacks; m. Clifford I. Ward, Oct. 10, 1998. BA, U. Mich., 1991; JD, Duke U., 1994. Bar: Pa. 1994, U.S. Dist. Ct. (ea. dist.) Pa. 1995, N.J. 1995, U.S. Dist. Ct. N.J. 1995, U.S. Dist. Ct. (ea. and so. dists.) N.Y. 1997, N.Y. 1998. Assoc. Ballard Spahr Andrews & Ingersoll, Phila., 1994-97, Hall Dickler, N.Y.C., 1997-98, Pryor Cashman Sherman & Flynn, N.Y.C., 1998—. Mem. ABA (intellectual property sect.), Internat. Trademark Assn. (project editl. bd.), N.Y. Bar Assn., Phi Beta Kappa. Avocations: basketball, skiing, running. Office: Pryor Cashman Sherman & Flynn 410 Park Ave Fl 10 New York NY 10022-4407

JACOBS, HAROLD ROBERT, mechanical engineering educator, practitioner; b. Portland, Oreg., Nov. 19, 1936; s. Harold Henry and Catherine Mae (Gill) J.; m. Georgeen Kirkpatrick, Aug. 26, 1961; children: Sara Catherine, Harold Robert, Kenneth Patrick. BS cum laude, U. Portland, 1958; MS in Mech. Engring., Wash. State U., 1961; PhD in Mech. Engring., Ohio State U., 1965. Registered profl engr., Utah, Wash. Engr. GE, San Jose, Calif., Hanford, Wash., 1958-59, 60; instr. dept. mech. engring. Wash. State U., Pullman, 1959-61; rsch. engr. aerospace divsn. Boeing Co., Seattle, 1961-62, 63; insr. mech engring. Ohio State U., Columbus, 1963-64; mem. tech. staff Aerospace Corp., San Bernadino, Calif., 1964-67; prof. dept. mech. engring. U. Utah, Salt Lake City, 1967-69, from asst. prof. to assoc prof., 1969-74, chmn. fluid mechanics divsn. Coll. Engring., 1974-79, prof. mech. engring., 1974-84, chmn. applied mechanics divsn., 1977-84, chmn. dept. civil engring., 1978-79, assoc. dean rsch., 1981-84; prof. mech engring., head dept. Pa. State U., University Park, 1984-94, prof. emeritus, 1994—; dean Coll. Engring., prof. mech. engring. Colo. State U., Ft. Collins, 1994-99; chief engr. CEEMS, Bothell, Wash., 1999—; mem. summer faculty Sandia Nat. Labs., Livermore, Calif., 1981; vis. prof. U. Strathclyde, Glasgow, Scotland, 1976-77; vis. prof. Imperial Coll., U. London, summer 1992; cons. numerous corps. Mem. internat. adv. bd. Russian Jour. Engring. Thermophysics, 1991—; contbr. numerous articles to profl. jours.; patentee in field; reviewer numerous jours. Ohio State U. fellow, 1962-63. Assoc. fellow AIAA (assoc. adv. coun. Utah sect. 1971-77, treas. 1972-73, chmn. 1974-75, Engr. of Yr. award 1973, numerous coms.); fellow ASME (chmn. gen. papers, coordinating com. heat transfer divsn., chmn. com. on heat transfer in mfg. and material processing 1991-94, mem. numerous coms., tech. editor Jour Heat Transfer 1986-92); mem. ASEE, Am. Inst. Chem. Engrs. (dir. thermal systems divsn. 1994-96, dir. 1994-96, vice chair 1999—), Sigma Xi (Ohio State Outstanding Engring. Alumnus 1991). Office: CEEMS 13816 26th Ave SE Bothell WA 98012-4606

JACOBS, IVOR MARK, administrator; b. Nottingham, England, Aug. 11, 1960; s. Phillip J. and Ann Mellors; m. Donna Michelle Watters, July 11, 1992; childre: Dannielle, Roxi. Degree in biochem, Peoples Coll., Nottingham, 1978. Mng. dir. Heatshield Ltd., Nottingham, England, 1983-89, Coldseal Ltd., Nottingham, England, 1990—, Trade Frame Ltd., Nottingham, England, 1991—, Esquire Estates, Nottingham, England, 1995—; chmn. Air Attack Ltd., Nottingham, England, 1994—; chief exec. Roxdan-Devel., Nottingham, England, 1996—; cons. in field. Avocations: motor sports, show jumping, helocopters, travel. Office: Coldsead Ltd, Queens Rd Beeston, Nottingham NG9 1FD, England

JACOBS, JACK BERNARD, judge; b. July 23, 1942; s. Louis K. and Phoebe J.; m. Marion Antiles, Apr. 2, 1967; 1 child, Andrew Seth. AB, U. Chgo., 1964; LLB, Harvard U., 1967. Bar: Del. 1968, U.S. Dist. Ct. Del. 1968, U.S. Ct. Appeals (3d cir.) 1968, U.S. Supreme Ct. 1975. Law clk. Del. Chancery and Superior Cts., 1967-68; assoc. Young, Conaway, Stargatt & Taylor, Wilmington, Del., 1968-71; ptnr. Young, Conaway, Stargatt & Taylor, Wilmington, 1971-85; vice chancellor Ct. of Chancery State of Del., 1985—; adj. prof. Widener U. Sch. Law, 1986—; chmn. Bar-Bench-Media Conf. Del., 1992-93; mem. various faculty continuing legal edn. programs. Contbr. articles to profl. jours. Vice chmn. Nat. Jewish Cmty. Rels. Adv. Coun., 1985-89; bd. dirs. Jewish Fedn. Del., 1981-87, Del. Symphony Assn., 1991-95, Del. Cmty. Found., 1994—, chair grants com., 1998-2000; pres. Milton & Hattie Kutz Home, 1990-92. Mem. ABA (litigation sect., bus. law sect., mem. com. corp. laws), Am. Law Inst., Am. Judicature Soc. (bd. dirs. 1999—), Del. Bar Assn., Harvard Law Sch. Del. (pres. 1986-87), Phi Beta Kappa. Democrat. Jewish. Home: 28 Beethoven Dr Wilmington DE 19807-1923 Office: Ct of Chancery 1000 N King St Wilmington DE 19801-3303

JACOBS, JEFFREY LEE, lawyer, education network company executive; b. Boston, Jan. 20, 1951; s. Philip and Millicent T. (Katz) J.; m. Deborah R. Rath, June 7, 1981; children: Alison, Hannah. BA, U. Pa., 1973; MPA, U. So. Calif., 1979; JD, Pace U., 1985. Bar: Conn. 1985, N.Y. 1988. Asst. to comptroller gen. U.S. Gen. Acctg. Office, Washington, 1976-80; sr. rsch. assoc. Nat. Acad. Pub. Adminstrn., Washington, 1980-83; dir. of seminars Prentice Hall, Clifton, N.J., 1985-87; pres. Profl. Edn. Network, Inc., Westport, Conn., 1987—; lectr. Ga. Tax Inst., Ohio Fed. Tax Inst.; adj. prof. Quinnipiac Coll., U. New Haven; cons. KeepSmart.com. Co-author: GAO: Government Accountability, 1979; producer, writer TV series The CPA Report, 1988-91; producer, writer radio series Legal Practice Alert, 1990—. Trustee Westport Pub. Libr. Mem. ABA (taxation sect.), Acad. Legal Studies in Bus. Home: 16 Janson Dr Westport CT 06880-2568 Office: KeepSmart.com 12 Skyline Dr Hawthorne NY 10532-2133

JACOBS, JIM, actor, playwright, composer, lyricist; b. Chgo., Oct. 7, 1942; m. Diane Rita Gomez, June 5, 1965 (div. 1974); 1 child, Kristine; m. Denise Nettleton, Apr. 29, 1978. Student, Chgo. City Coll., 1962-63. Appeared in over 50 cmty. and profl. theatre prodns. including Until the Monkey Comes, 1966, Take Me Along, 1967, Flora, The Red Menace, 1968, Entertaining Mr. Sloane, 1969, The Serpent, 1969, Don't Drink the Water, 1970, Jimmy Shine, 1970, all Chgo., No Place to Be Somebody, nat. touring co., 1971, on Broadway, 1971, The Magnolia Club, Chgo., 1975, The Local Stigmatic, Chgo., 1976; dir. The Ruffian on the Stair, Chgo., 1975; actor: (films) Medium Cool, 1969, Love in a Taxi, 1976, (TV series) Open All Night, 1982; author, lyricist, composer: (with Warren Casey) Grease, Broadway, 1972-80, (Tony award nomination 1972, Grammy award nomination 1972), London-West End, 1973, 77, motion picture, 1979, (revival) Grease, London, 1993— (Olivier award nomination), (revival) Broadway, 1994-98 (Tony award nomination), Grease On Ice (Am. Ice Show Tour), 1998—; author: (with Warren Casey) Island of Lost Coeds, 1979; (with Jim Weston) Bats in the Belfry, 1982; (with Jim Weston) Remember the Night, 1988. Recipient Humanitarian of Yr. award Young Adult Inst., N.Y.C., 1992. Mem. Dramatists Guild, Authors League Am., ASCAP, Actors Equity Assn., Screen Actors Guild., AFTRA. Office: care Ronald Taft PC 18 W 55th St New York NY 10019-5315

JACOBS, JOHN PATRICK, lawyer; b. Chgo., Oct. 27, 1945; s. Anthony N. and Bessie (Montgomery) J.; m. Linda I. Grams, Oct. 6, 1973; 1 child, Christine Margaret. BA cum laude, U. Detroit, 1967, JD magna cum laude, 1970. Bar: Mich. 1970, U.S. Dist. Ct. Mich. (ea. dist.) 1970, U.S. Ct. Appeals (6th cir.) 1974, U.S. Ct. Appeals (D.C. cir.) 1988, U.S. Supreme Ct. 1978. Law clk. to chief judge Mich. Ct. Appeals, Detroit, 1970-71; assoc., then ptnr. Plunkett & Cooney P.C., Detroit, 1972-92, also bd. dirs.; founding ptnr., prin. mem. O'Leary, O'Leary, Jacobs, Mattson, Perry & Mason P.C., Southfield, Mich., 1992-99; prin., owner John P. Jacobs, P.C., 1999—; investigator Atty. Grievance Com., Detroit, 1975-84; mem. hearing panel Atty. Discipline Bd., Detroit, 1984-87, 94—; adj. prof. law Sch. Law, U. Detroit, 1983-84, faculty advisor, 1984-89, Pres.'s Cabinet, 1982—; elected rep. State Bar Rep. Assembly, Lansing, Mich., 1980-82, 91-92, 93-96; fellow Mich. State Bar Found., 1990-98; spl. appellate counsel State Bar Mich., 1998—; treas., mem. steering com. Mich. Bench-Bar Appellate Conf. Com., 1994—; apptd. mem. Mich. Supreme Ct. Com. on Appellate Fees, 1990; spl. mediator appellate negotiation program Mich. Ct. Appeals, 1995—; mem. exec. com. Mich. Appellate Bench-Bar Conf. Found., 1996—. mem. profl. ethics com. State Bar Mich., 1998, mem. multi-disciplinary practice com., 1999. Bd. dirs. Boysville of Mich., Clinton, 1988-95, 99—, chmn. pub. policy com., 1993-95, pub. policy liaison, 1999—; apptd. mem. State Bar Mich. Blue Ribbon Com. Improving Def. Counsel-Insurer Rels., 1998-99, spl. amicus curiae counsel to Mich. Supreme Ct., 1999. Recipient Robert E. Dice Med. Malpractice Def. Atty. award Mich. Physicians, 1986; Reginald Heber Smith fellow, 1971-72. Fellow Am. Acad. Appellate Lawyers, Mich. Std. Jury Instn. (subcom. employment law 1984-87); mem. ABA (litigation sect., appellate subcom., torts and ins. practice), Internat. Assn. Def. Counsel (v.p., amicus curiae com., med. and legal malpractice coms., product liability com.), Fedn. Ins. and Corp. Counsel, Mich. Def. Trial Counsel (chmn. amicus curiae com. 1986-88, chmn. future planning com., bd. dirs. 1989—, treas. 1993-94, sec. 1994-95, v.p. 1995-96, program chair 1990, 94, 95, pres., 1996-97), Def. Rsch. Inst. (state rep. 1997-98, Outstanding Performance Citation 1997, appellate com. steering com. 1997—), Cath. Lawyers Soc. (bd. dirs. 1988-98, emeritus dir. 1998—; pres. 1994-95). Democrat. Roman Catholic. Avocations: collecting antique law books, film. Office: 1 Towne Sq Ste 1400 Southfield MI 48076-3705

JACOBS, KAREN LOUISE, medical technologist; b. Kingston, N.Y., May 7, 1943; d. William Charles and Vera Elizabeth (Kelly) J. BS in Applied Tech., Empire State Coll., 1976; MS in Pub. Svc. Adminstrn., Russell Sage Coll., 1982. Sr. lab. tech., hosp. lab. supr. City of Kingston Labs., 1962-68; sr. rsch. asst. Dudley Obs., Albany, N.Y., 1972-75; lab. adminstr. Albany Med. Coll., 1976-99; tchr. environ. edn. Five Rivers Environ. Edn. Ctr., Delmar, N.Y., 1999—; faculty, 1982-97; guest lectr. Sage Coll.; coord. complex labs. JCAHO regulations, 1997; infection control com. and subcoms. on AIDS mgmt. and human immunodeficiency virus universal precautions Albany Med. Ctr. Infection Control, 1987-97, accreditation regulatory oversight com.; pvt. piano tchr. Albany Acad. for Boys, 1999. Bd. dirs. chpt. Leukemia Soc. Am., 1983-87; judge sci. and tech. summer issue on excellence in Am. U.S. News and World Report; vol. asst. naturalist Five Rivers Environ. Ctr. Mem. Clin. Lab. Mgmt. Assn. (del. citizen amb. program to China 1989), Am. Soc. Clin. Pathologists, Sierra Club, Earthwatch, Nat. Speleological Soc., Hudsonia (bd. dirs. 1995). Home: 50 Meadowbrook Dr Apt 149 Slingerlands NY 12159-2146

JACOBS, LOUIS JACOBUS, education educator, psychologist, consultant; b. Springs, Gauteng, South Africa, June 21, 1946; s. Cornelius Johannes and Christina Louisa (Oosthuizen) J.; m. Johanna Hendrina Engelbrecht, Dec. 13, 1969; children: Riaan, Renier. MA, Univ. South Africa, South Africa, 1969, DLitt in Philosophy, 1974, MEd, 1972, DEd, 1975. Cert. higher edn. tchr. Sr. tchr. Tchrs. Diploma, South Africa, 1968-73; sr. rschr. Human Sci. Rsch. Coun., South Africa, 1974-75, Univ. South Africa, South Africa, 1975-79; sr. lectr. Univ. South Africa, 1980-84, assoc. prof., 1985-86, prof., 1987-97; prof., head dept. ednl. guidance and counseling U. Pretoria, 1997—; with Child Welfare, South Africa, 1985-90, psychologist, 1991-96; psychologist Tng. Interns, South Africa, 1983-97. Author: Family Therapy, 1991, Interpretations of Childrens Drawings, 1992, Dynamics of the Self-Concept, 1993, Projection in Pedodiagnosis, 2d edit., 1996. Recipient grant U. South Africa, 1974, 75. Mem. Edn. Assn. S. Africa, Psychology Inst. S. Africa. Mem. Dutch Reformed Ch. Avocation: photography. Home: PO Box 37 Wingate Park, Pretoria 0153, South Africa Office: U Pretoria, Dept Guidance/Counselling, Pretoria 0002, South Africa

JACOBS, PAUL FRANCIS, physicist; b. N.Y.C., Dec. 21, 1938; s. Bertram Lawrence and Margaret Veronica J.; m. Starla Kay Reed, Aug. 16, 1980 (div. Oct. 1997). BS, Union Coll., Schenectady, N.Y., 1960; MS, Princeton U., 1963, PhD, 1966. Prin. physicist Xerox Electro-Optical Sys., Pasadena, 1966-84; chief scientist Xerox Spl. Info. Sys., Pasadena, 1984-89; dir. R&D 3D Sys., Inc., Valencia, Calif., 1989-97; v.p. tech. Express Tool Inc., Warwick, R.I., 1997—; adj. prof. mech. engring. Clemson U., 1995—; adj. prof. engring. Worcester Poly. Inst., 1997—. Prin. author/tech. editor: Rapid Prototyping and Manufacturing: Fundamentals of Stereolithography, 1992, Stereolithography and Other RP&M Technologies, 1996; patentee in field. Achievements include research on the development of production rapid tooling inserts utilizing high thermal conductivity materials in conjunction with conformal cooling channels to achieve significantly enhanced thermal management, reduced cycle time, improved productivity, decreased residual injection molding stress and reduced part distortion; developer of basic equations of stereolithography; advanced theory of "random noise shrinkage" associated with phase change processes. E-mail: pjacobs@expresstool.com. Home: 20 Jacalyn Dr Saunderstown RI 02874-2029 Office: Express Tool Inc PO Box 484 Westfield MA 01086-0484

JACOBS, PETER, retired haematology educator, haematologist; b. Pretoria, Transvaal, South Africa; s. Conrad Cornelius and Marie (Viljoen) J.; m. Margaret Ann Botbyl, Jan. 21, 1961; children: Séan Keiran, Wayne Clinton. MB, BCh, U. Witwatersrand, Johannesburg, South Africa, 1959, MD, 1966, PhD, 1974. Registrar (internship) Johannesburg Gen. Hosp., South Africa, 1960-62; clin. tutorial registrar Johannesburg Gen. Hosp., 1963-67; sr. rsch. bursar U. Witwatersrand, Johannesburg, 1961-66; cons. and therapeutics trial physician Univ Witwatersrand, Johannesburg, 1970-72; sr. rsch. fellow haematology U. Wash., Seattle, 1967-69; found. prof. haematology U. Cape Town, South Africa, 1972-94, prof. emeritus, 1994—; hon. cons. Groote Schuur Hosp., Cape Town, 1995—, Tygerberg Hosp., Cape Town, 1995—, WHO, 1996; hon. prof. haematology Stellenbosch U. and Tygerberg Acad. Hosp. Co-author: (books) (with A. Bird), Basic Haematology, 1983, (with L. Wood), General and Oncologic Haematology for Nursing and the Paramedical Professionals, 1995; also monograph and articles. Grantee: Med. Rsch. Coun., Capetown, 1986-88. Fellow ACP, Royal Coll. Physicians (Edinburgh), Royal Coll. Pathologists (Eng.), Coll. Physicians (South Africa). Home: Toison D'Or, 4 Van Reenen Hof Newlands, W Cape Cape Town 7700, South Africa Office: Constantiaberg Medi-Clinic, Dept Haemat, Burnham Rd, Plumstead Cape 7800, South Africa

JACOBS, RENÉ GASTON, editor, retired educator; b. Fumel, France, Oct. 4, 1920; s. Robert and Alice (Delbrel) J.; m. Marie Mary Jacobs, Sept. 14, 1949; 1 child, Alice. Grad., Ecole Normale, Cahors, France, 1940. Instr. St-PROJET (Lot), St. Bonnet de Gignac, France, 1940-50, Inst. dans. la Seine, Bondy, France, 1950-76; editor UNIR, pres. Union Interlinguistic France, Les Pavillons, France, 1962—. Translator: Les cinq sous de Lavarède, 1995. Home: 75 Allée Danièle Casanova, 93 320 Les Pavillons France

JACOBS, RICHARD ALAN, management consultant; b. Portland, Maine, Aug. 16, 1934; s. Harry Gordon and Bernice (Levine) J.; m. Nancy Dean, Feb. 8, 1958; children: Karen, Alison. BS, MIT, 1956; MBA, Roosevelt U., Chgo., 1979. Mgr. engring. Mobil Chem., Macedon, N.Y., 1956-60; plant mgr. Champion Internat., Ft. Wayne, Ind., 1960-63; v.p. Quester Corp., Toledo, 1963-66; sr. v.p A. T. Kearney, Inc., Chgo., 1966-96; mgmt. cons. Supply, N.C., 1996—. Author: Production Control, 1970, Systems Management, 1978. Trustee Village of Northbrook, Ill., 1980-84; trustee MIT, Cambridge, Mass., 1993—, dir. alumni bd., 1980—, chmn. alumni fund, 1987-89. 1st lt. U.S. Army, 1957-58. Mem. Soc. Plastics Engrs. (pres., bd. dirs. 1976-77), MIT Alumni Assn. (pres. 1992), MIT of Chgo. Club (bd. dirs. 1977—). Home and Office: PO Box 879 Supply NC 28462-0879

JACOBS, TED SETH, artist, educator; b. Newark, June 11, 1927; s. Maurice and Jessie (Jacobson) J.; m. Dorris Hodgson (div.); m. Janet Adams (div.); m. Gundula Wien, (div.); children: Jodiah, Caleb, Carey Wren, Amadeus; m. Maura McDonnell. Student, Art Students League, 1943-46. Former instr. life painting and drawing Art Students League, N.Y.C.; former instr. N.Y. Acad. Life Drawing and Painting, N.Y.C.; founder, instr. Ecole Albert DeFois, Anjou, France. One man shows include Adelson Gallery, Boston, Wickersham Gallery, N.Y.C., Beaudine Fine Arts, N.Y.C., Coe Kerr, N.Y.C., Drawing Shop, N.Y.C., Galerie Vollombreuse Biarritz, Galerie Mouffe, Paris, St. Vincent's Coll., Latrobe, Pa., Dance and Music Drawings, Castle of Martigné-Briand, 1995, An Am. View of France paintings Chapel St. Catherine, Fontevraud, 1995, oil portraits Castle of Martigné-Briand, 1995; exhibited in group shows Alan Stone Gallery, Kennedy Galleries, Chapel St. Jean, Saumur, Greensburg Mus., Walker Art Ctr., Randolph-Macon Coll., Chrysler Mus.; numerous portrait and mural commns.; author: Drawing with an Open Mind, Light for the Artist; creator Restructured Realism. Founding mem. First Lamaist Budhist Inst., Washington, N.J., 1959. Recipient medals Salon de Vittel, City of Montaigu, Tourist Offices of Anjou. Mem. Internat. Aikido Fedn., Carnatic Music Soc. E-mail: tedart77@aol.com. Home: Mes Illusions, 49310 Les Cerqueux sous Passavant France

JACOBS, THEODORE JOSEPH, psychiatrist, educator; b. July 3, 1931. AB, Yale U., 1953; MD, U. Chgo., 1957. Clin. prof. psychiatry Albert Einstein Coll. Medicine, Bronx, N.Y., 1985—; tng. and supervising analyst N.Y. Psychoanalytic Inst., N.Y.C., 1985—, NYU Psychoanalytic Inst., N.Y.C., 1985—. Author: The Use of the Self: Countertransference and Communication in the Analytic Situation, 1991; co-editor: On Beginning an Analysis, 1991. Mem. Assn. for Child Psychoanalyis (pres. 1996-98). Address: 46 Walworth Ave Scarsdale NY 10583-1430 also: 170 E 77th St New York NY 10021-1912

JACOBS, TIMOTHY ANDREW, epidemiologist, international health consultant, medical missionary; b. St. Petersburg, Fla., Nov. 5, 1944; s. W. Andrew and Virginia (Ott) J.; m. Carolyn Martin, Nov. 4, 1972; 1 child, Jenny Thuy Ha. BSN, U. Fla., 1970; MS, PNP, U. Utah, 1976; PhD, Internat. Inst. Advanced Studies, 1979; C.T.M., Liverpool (Eng.) Sch. Tropical Medicine, 1982; cert. hosp. epidemiology, U. Iowa, 1985; MPH, Yale U., 1991; cert. in internat. (Spanish) living, Sch. Internat. Tng., Brattleboro, Vt., 1984. Nat. design and media cons. Nat. Assn. Pediatric Nurse Assocs. and Practitioners, Cherry Hill, N.J., 1977-83; asst. prof., co-coord. community health nursing U. N.D., Grand Forks, 1980; vol. epidemiologist, pub. health specialist Vinh Children's Hosp., Vinh City, Vietnam, 1989; pediatric staff nurse I U. Fla. Pediatric Svc., Shands Teaching Hosp., Gainesville, 1970; instr. pediatric nursing U. Utah Coll. Nursing, Salt Lake City, 1976-77; pvt. cons. Internat. Cmty. Health and Epidemiology, New Haven, 1990-94; med. supr., health svcs. mgr. Brown & Root Logcap Med. Clinic, Port-au-Prince, Haiti, 1994-95; med. tech. proposal cons. UN, Rwanda, Angola, 1995; specialist Home Health Care, Tampa, Fla., 1996—; vol. pub. health scientist, cons. Hanoi (Vietnam) Sch. Pub. Health; cons. epidemiologist Vinh and Huong Son, Vietnam, 1993; internat. edn. cons. U. Am., New Orleans, 1994; cons. infectious disease epidemiology, consulate of Nicaragua, Miami, Health for Health Svcs. Hurricane Mitch, 1998; cons. Christian Haitian Outreach Clinics and Orphanages, Jeremie and Mariani, Haiti, 1998—. Contbg. editor Episource, 1991, 97, Resources in Epidemiology; contbr. articles to profl. jours.; contbr. to poetry jours.; anthologies Daybreak on the Land, 1997, Audiotape Sounds of Poetry, 1997, Archive of the Vietnam Conflict, Personal Papers Collection, 1999. Donor, contbr. Asian Family and Comty. Empowerment Ctr., St. Petersburg, Fla. Capt. Nurse Corps, U.S. Army, 1968-73, Vietnam. Recipient Cert. of Achievement in HIV-AIDS Edn., AIDS Project, New Haven, Conn., 1994, Editor's Choice award for outstanding achievement in poetry Nat. Libr. Poetry, 1997. Fellow Royal Soc. Tropical Medicine and Hygiene (London), Am. Biog. Inst. (advisor, rsch. adv. bd.); mem. AMA, VFW, Am. Legion, Vietnam Vets. Am., Nat. Assn. Pediatric Nurse Assocs. and Practitioners (com. dir. graphics & logos mil. chpt., former chmn. nat. art and exhibits subcom., former mem. pub. rels. com., Cert. Recognition 1983), Am. Pub. Health Assn. (epidemiology sect., internat. healthsect., mem. caucus pub. health and faith cmty.), Internat. Assn. Med. Assistance to Travellers, Fla. Pub. Health Assn., Nat. Adolescent Health Promotion Network, Assn. Mil. Surgeons U.S., Ret. Army Nurse Corps Assn., Liverpool Tropical Sch. Assn. (Eng.), Assn. Yale Alumni in Pub. Health, Consortium for Internat. Nursing Edn., Rsch. & Practice, U.S.-Vietnam Friendship Assn., Doctorate Assn. N.Y. Educators, Fleet Marine Force Corpsman Assn. (former Conn. rep., charter mem.), U.S. Navy Corpsmen United Assn., Am. Assn. Navy Hosp. Corpsmen, U.S. Army (Vietnam) 24th Evacuation Hosp. Assn. (com. asv. reunion 1993), Vets. Vietnam Restoration Project, U.S. Com. Scientific Cooperation with Vietnam, N.Y. Acad. of Sci., Walter Reed Army Med. Ctr. Soc. (charter), Spl. Ops. Med. Assn., Sigma Xi, Sigma Theta Tau (charter mem. Gamma Rho chpt.), Phi Kappa Phi. Home: 11333 Calgary Cir Tampa FL 33624-4804

JACOBS, WENDELL EARLY, JR., lawyer; b. Detroit, Nov. 15, 1945; s. Wendell E. and Mildred P. (Horton) J.; m. Elaine M. Lott (div.); children: Wendell Early III, Damon R. BFA, Denison U., 1969; JD, Wayne State U., 1972. Bar: Mich. 1972, U.S. Dist. Ct. (ea. dist.) Mich. 1973, Fla. 1974. Asst. prosecutor Jackson County, Mich., 1973-76; ptnr. Jacobs & Engle, Jackson, 1977—. Mem. Mich. Coun. on Crime and Delinquency. Mem. Nat. Assn. Criminal Def. Lawyers, Criminal Def. Attys. Mich., Jackson County Bar Assn., Eagles Club, Grotto Club, Elks. Avocations: paddleball, motorcycling. Home: 9281 Greenwood Rd Grass Lake MI 49240-9590 Office: Jacobs & Engle 1104 W Michigan Ave Jackson MI 49202-4123

JACOBS, WENDY, editor. BA, U. Conn., 1974; postgrad., Norwich U., 1974, Ind. U., 1975, U. Toronto, 1979. Mem. editl. dept. Plenum Pub., N.Y.C., 1974-77; editor Macmillan Pub., Toronto, Ont., Can., 1978-79; cons., writer, editor Bus., Govt. Pub., Toronto, 1980-91, Bus., Acad. Pub., New Orleans, 1991—. Office: 3508 Robert St New Orleans LA 70125-4808

JACOBS, WILFRIED DESIRE SERAPHIN, banker; b. Zemst, Belgium, Apr. 19, 1954; s. Frans and Juliana (Mertens) J.; m. Viviane Jacobs, May 29, 1981; children: Steven, Peter. BA in Applied Econs., Cath. U. Leuven, Belgium, 1977, MBA, 1979. Territorial mgr. Burroughs, Gent, Belgium, 1980-81; br. mgr. Bank Brussels Lambert, Antwerp, Belgium, 1981-86; corr. banking officer Bank Brussels Lambert, Brussels, 1986-89; corp. mgr. Lloyds Bank, Brussels, 1989-91; regional mgr. Soc. Gen., Antwerp, 1991-96; regional mgr. Flanders Banca Monte Paschi Belgio, Antwerp, 1996—; gen. mgr. Woodcreek Buba, 1999—; judge Ct. of Comml. Law, Antwerp, 1998—; gen. mgr. Woodcreek BVBA, 1999—. Maj. Belgian Air Force, 1981—. Mem. Commn. for Def. and Security Issues of Interallied Confedn. of Res. Officers (spokesman), French-Belgian C. of C. (bd. dirs. 1993-98), Jr. C. of C. (treas., v.p. 1986-94). Roman Catholic. Avocations: photography, travel, philately. E-mail: jacobs@online.be. Home: Mercatorlaan 10, 3191 Boortmeerbeek Belgium Office: Banca Monte Paschi Belgio, Grote Markt 27, 2000 Antwerp Belgium

JACOBSEN, GRETE KRAG, pathologist; b. Copenhagen, Sept. 27, 1943; d. Per Krag J. and Marie Louise (Gorrisson) Hanssen; m. Joachim Knop, Apr. 27, 1987; children: Nikolaj, Filip. MD, U. Copenhagen, 1977, Dr.med., 1985. Lic. pathologist. Jr. registrar Mcpl. Hosp., Dept. Pathology, Copenhagen, 1971-73, Mcpl. Hosp., Dept. Dermatology, Copenhagen, 1974-75; registrar dept. pathology Gentofte Hosp., 1975-76; sr. registrar Herlev Hosp., Dept. Pathology, Copenhagen, 1976-80; asst. prof. pathology Herlev Hosp., Copenhagen, 1980-82; sr. registrar dept. pathology Hvidovre Hosp., Copenhagen, 1982-85; cons., chief pathologist Gentofte Hosp., Copenhagen, 1985—; lectr. in field. Author: Atlas of Germ Cell Tumours, 1989; contbr. articles to profl. jours.; exhibited art in shows, 1976—. Grantee in field, 1976—. Fellow Med. Soc. Copenhagen (v.p., pres. 1997-99); mem. Danish Soc. Pathology (chmn. 1989-92), others. Home: Bispebjerg Parkallé 11, 2400 NV Copenhagen Denmark Office: Kas Gentofte Dept Pathology, Niels Andersensvej, 2900 Hellerup Denmark

JACOBSEN, JOHANNES, electronics company executive; b. Nykøbing Mors, Denmark, Aug. 25, 1940; s. Hans O. and Margrethe (Dohn) J.; m. Emma Hoffmann Graversen, July 11, 1964 (dec. Aug. 1991); m. Margit Vils Pedersen Graversen, Aug. 1, 1992. MSEE, Tech. U. Denmark, Copenhagen, 1965, PhDEE, 1968. Asst. prof. Tech. U. Denmark, 1968-69; sr. engr. European Space Agy., Nordwijk, The Netherlands, 1974-77; head R & D, ITT, Horsens, Denmark, 1977-79; engr. TERMA Elektronik AS, Aarhus, Denmark, 1969-74, v.p. tech., 1979-83, pres., CEO, 1983—; vice chmn. Micro Matic Holding A/S, Odense, Denmark, 1994; bd. dirs., mem. exec. com. Confedn. Danish Industries, Copenhagen, 1992-98; bd. dirs. Danish Employrs' Confedn., Copenhagen, 1989-98. Contbr. articles to sci. jours., including Electronics Letters, Can. Jour. Physics, IEEE Trans. on Antennas and Propagation. Mem. IEEE (sr., Spl. Recognition award 1970), Assn. Danish Engrs. Decorated Order of Chivalry (Denmark). Home: Søsvinget 38, DK-8250 Egå Denmark Office: TERMA Elektronik AS, Hovmarken 4, DK-8520 Lystrup Denmark

JACOBSEN, KLAUS, orthopaedic surgeon, consultant, researcher; b. Frederiksberg, Copenhagen, Denmark, Mar. 23, 1939; s. Christian and Signe Henriette Margrethe (Skjold) J.; m. Kirsten Klinge Sørensen, Oct. 14, 1961; children: Jørgen Henrik Klinge, Jacob Klinge, Mår Klinge. MD, U. Copenhagen, 1965, PhD in Surgery, 1981. Diplomate in gen practice, orthopaedic surgery. Sr. registrar Orthopaedic Hosp., Copenhagen, 1979-80; sr. registrar neurosurgery dept. Glostrup Hosp., Copenhagen, 1980-81; sr. registrar in orthopedic surgery Rigshosp., Copenhagen, 1981-83, Frederiksberg Hosp., 1984; asst. cons. in orthopaedics Gentofte Hosp., Denmark, 1984-85; sr. cons., head dept. orthopaedics Frederiksberg Hosp., 1985-97; chief of arctic Inuit Hosp in Qaanaag, Thule, Greenland, 1997—; lectr. Copenhagen U., 1984-85, Danish Orthopaedic Soc., 1973-87. Author: Klaus Jacobsen: Stress Radiography of the Human Knee, 1981, (with others) Danish Textbooks of Surgery; contbr. articles to profl. jours. Grantee Danish Med. Rsch. Coun., 1972-74, Danish Coun. for Sports Rsch., 1974, Found. for the Handicapped, 1974, Poul Guildahl Found., 1981. Mem. Danish Orthopaedic Soc. (exec. com. 1986-90, chmn. 1988-90), Danish Surg. Soc., Scandinavian Orthopaedic Soc., European Soc. Knee Surgery and Arthroscopy. Avocations: drawing, wood carving, sailing, skiing, husky dogs. Home: Chefdistriktslaegen, Qaanaaq Hosp, 3971 Greenland Denmark

JACOBSEN, PETER ERLING, professional golfer; b. Portland, Oreg., Mar. 4, 1954; m. Jan; children: Amy Kristen, Mickey. Grad., U. Oreg. Profl. golfer PGA, 1976—. Won Western Australian Open, 1979, Buick-Gooodwrench Open, 1980, Johnnie Walker Cup, Spain, 1981, 82, Colonial Nat. Invitation, Sammy Davis, Jr.-Greater Hartford Open, 1984, Oreg. Open, 1976, Calif. Open, 1986, (with Curtis Strange) Fred Meyer Challenge, 1986, Bob Hope Chyrsler Classic, 1990, Pebble Beach Nat. Pro-Am, Buick Invitational, 1995. Office: care PGA Box 109601 100 Ave of Champions Palm Beach Gardens FL 33410 also: care Cedar Bay Prodns 5119 NE 42d St Seattle WA 98105

JACOBSEN, SHIRLEY MARIE, business owner, songwriter, artist; b. Sioux City, Iowa, Aug. 1, 1944; d. Elmer and Edith Nancy (Lyght) Rich; m. George Allen Archer, Mar. 28, 1965 (div. Feb. 1973); children: David Allen Archer, John Travis Archer; m. Gerald Lee Jacobsen, June 1, 1974; children: Mark Allen Jacobsen, Steven Lee Jacobsen. BCA cum laude, S.W. Assemblies of God U., 1993. Office mgr. Lindsay Soft Water, Fremont, Nebr., 1964; info. asst. Northwestern Bell Telephone Co., Omaha, Nebr., 1964-68; contract acctg. asst. Peter Kiewit Sons Co., Omaha, 1968-69; asst. pricer Ready Mixed Concrete Co., Omaha, 1971-73; head accounts receivable dept. Lyman Richey Sand and Gravel, Omaha, 1973-74; br. office adminstr. DialAm. Mktg., Omaha, 1984-85; pres. asst. Lyric Co., Omaha, 1985-86; vol. libr. Henderson County Library, Chandler, Tex., 1992-97; mgr. real estate Pvt. Partnership, Nebr. and Tex., 1974—. Author: Cancer Review, 1983, Successful Telemarketing Business, 1986, A Second Start in Life, 1995, Feelings of the Heart, 1998; songwriter Perfect Peace, He'll Take You Back, 1996, Some Water to Drink, From Thorns to Gems, 1997. S.W. Assemblies God U. divsn. scholar, 1993; named to Internat. Poetry Hall of Fame, 1998. Mem. Am. Assn. Bible Colls., World Jewish Congress, So. Gospel Music Assn., Broadcast Music, Inc., Women in the Arts, Christian Country Music Assn., Internat. Country Music Assn., Internat. Order of Fellowship, Internat. Biog. Ctr. (Cambridge, Eng., founder mem.), London Diplomatic Acad., Clinton Presdl. Libr., Delta Epsilon Chi (hon.). Avocations: reading/research, writing, art, music, travel. E-mail: jaylee@up2me.com. Office: 3511 N 55th St Omaha NE 68104-3519

JACOBSEN, SØREN LANGE, financial consultant; b. Virum, Denmark, Nov. 28, 1951; parents Robert and Ruth (Lange) J. PhD in Econs., Copenhagen U., 1983. Acct. Revisor Centret, Copenhagen, 1975-78; salesman Borsen Newspaper, Copenhagen, 1979-81; cons. Albertslund Mcpl., Copenhagen, 1981-87; fin. contr. Nilpeter, A/S., Copenhagen, 1987-89; cons. NOAH, Copenhagen, 1989—; mgr. Theatre Banden, Odense, 1990-93, Kolding Highsch., 1993-94; cons., rschr. and lectr. on transp. and culture, Aarhus, 1994—; bd. dirs. Scan Link No Way, Coun. of Transport, Denmark, JuneMovement, Denmark; cons. Ministry of Environment and Energy, Copenhagen, 1996—. Avocations: stamps, sailing.

JACOBSEN, THEODORE H. (TED H. JACOBSEN), labor union official, educator; b. N.Y.C., July 27, 1933. BS, Fordham U., 1955; postgrad., Hunter Coll., 1957-80, NYU, 1957-80, Columbia U., 1957-80. Cert. high sch. English tchr., N.Y.C. Tchr. English N.Y.C. Bd. Edn. (on leave), 1957-86; editor Labor News and Trade Union Handbook N.Y.C. Ctrl. Labor Coun., AFL-CIO, N.Y.C., 1986—; mem. exec. bd. Jewish Labor Com., N.Y.C., 1977—. Workers Def. League, N.Y.C., 1986—, Am. Labor ORT, N.Y.C., 1986—; regional v.p. Union Label and Svc. Trades Dept., N.Y., 1980-96; mem. adv. bd. Harry Van Arsdale Jr. Coll. Labor Studies, Empire State Coll., N.Y.C., 1986—; mem. adv. coun. for occupation edn. N.Y.C. Bd. Edn., 1986—, vice-chmn., 1989—; bd. dirs. Nat. Ethnic Coalition Orgns., Inc.; mem. bd. govs. The Forum; sec. N.Y.C. Ctrl. Labor Coun. AFL-CIO. Mem. Cmty. Bd. 8, N.Y.C., 1987-93, N.Y.C. Sch.to-Work Regional Coun. Regional Planning Assn.; mem. exec. bd. Workman's Circle Home-Geriatric Ctr., 1986-89, treas., 1989—; sec. Robert F. Wagner Labor Archives, NYU, 1986—; bd. dirs. Cath. Interracial Coun., 1987—, United Way N.Y., 1988-95, Coun. on Environ., N.Y.C., 1988-95, Italian Acad. Found., Nat. Ethnic Coalition Orgns., Inc., Italic Studies Inst.; trustee Italian Hosp. Soc., ARC in Greater N.Y., 1989—; mem. bd. advisors Transition Ctr., N.Y.C. Bd. Edn., 1991, Svc. Area Planning Group, 1991; mem. exec. bd. Friends A. Philip Randolph Campus H.S. at City Coll., 1990—; mem. Naval War Coll. Found., 1989—; mem. N.Y. State coastal mgmt. adv. com. N.Y. Harbor Maritime Industry, 1988—; charter mem. Battle of Normandy Found., 1988—; chmn. N.Y. Trade Union Coun. for Histadrut, 1992—; mem. Asian Pacific Am. Labor Alliance; life mem. Workmen's Circle Arbeter Ring; patron N.Y.C. Met. Opera; trustee Italian Hosp. Soc., ARC in Greater N.Y., 1989—. Decorated knight Order of Merit (Italy), knight officer Order of Sts. Maurice and Lazarus, comdr. Order of Merit of Savoy; recipient Cope awards N.Y. State United Tchrs., 1975, 78, Best Newsletter award, 1974, 75, 79, 80, 81, spl. award educators chpt. Jewish labor Com., 1986, Roberto Clemente award Nat. Assn. for Puerto Rican Civil Rights, 1988, 75th Anniversary Cert. of Appreciaition, U.S. Dept. Labor, 1988, Hurricane Hugo Disaster Relief citation ARC, 1991, 80th Anniversary Exemplar award NAACP, N.Y. br. 1991, Good Scout award Greater N.Y. Couns. Boy Scouts Am., 1992, Spl. Recognition award Hispanic Labor Com., 1992, George Meany award, Leadership Svc. Recognition award United Way of N.Y.C., 1992, Consumer Merit award N.Y. Consumer Assembly, 1992, Torch of Hope award Pride of Judea, 1993, Congl. Ellis Island Medal Honor, 1993, N.Y.C. Coun. Citation, 1993, Coalition of Labor Union Women award, 1994, John LaFarge award for interrracial justice Cath. Interracial Coun. N.Y., 1995, N.Y.C. NOVA Ancora Job Tng. Program Award of Appreciation, N.Y.C. Dept. Probation, 1995, Disting. Svc. award Internat. Brotherhood Elec. Workers, Local 3, J Divsn., 1996, Robert Briscoe award Emerald Isle Immigration Ctr., 1996, George Meany award Gtr. N.Y. Couns. Boy Scouts Am., 1999; named Man of Yr., Jewish Heritage Com. and Educators chpt., 1980, Educator of Yr., Assn. Tchrs. of N.Y., 1986; proclamation from Queens borough pres. declaring June 23, 1993 Theodore 'Ted' Jacobsen Day. Mem. AFTRA (bd. govs. 1996—), NATAS (bd. govs. N.Y. chpt.), NAACP (golden life heritage), United Fedn. Tchrs. (editor newsletter, chpt. chmn. 1974-86, mem. P.M. staff 1973—, Eli Trachtenberg award 1966, 74, 77, 81, Albert Lee Smallheiser citation 1976), Order Sons of Italy in Am., Jewish Tchrs. Assn., Cath. Tchrs. Assn., Internat. Labor Comm. Assn., Coalition Labor Union Women, Black Trade Unionists Leadership Com., Jewish Heritage Com., Irish-Am. Studies Com., Irish-Am. Heritage Mus. (charter), Loyal League Yiddish Sons Erin (hon.), U.S. Naval Inst., Internat. Platform Assn., B'nai B'rith (lodge 2201, trustee 1989-96, bd. dirs. Adelstein Family Project HOPE Found. Housing for Elderly 1992—), The Actor's Fund (life), U.S. Holocaust Meml. Mus. (charter), Lower East Side Tenement (hon. commr. 1992—), U.S. Naval Inst., Amigos del Teatro Teresa Carreno (patron Caracas, Venezuela), The Discovery Ctr. (Ft. Lauderdale, Fla.), TV and Radio Working Press Assn., The Asia Soc., Met. Mus. Art, Elks, Nat. Italian-Am. Found. Avocations: theater, opera, travel. E-mail: thjnycusa@aol.com. Office: NYC Cen Labor Coun AFL-CIO 386 Park Ave S New York NY 10016-8804

JACOBSON, ALBERT HERMAN, JR., industrial and systems engineer, educator; b. St. Paul, Minn., Oct. 27, 1917; s. Albert Herman and Gertrude Jacobson; m. Elaine Swanson, June 1960; children: Keith, Paul. BS Indsl. Engring./Adminstrn. cum laude, Yale U., 1939; SM Bus. and Engring. Mgmt., MIT, 1952; MS in Applied Physics, U. Rochester, 1954; PhD in Indsl. and Mgmt. Engring., Stanford U., 1976. Registered profl. engr., Calif. Pers. asst. Yale U., New Haven, Conn., 1939-40; indsl. engr. in electronics Radio Corp. of Am., Camden, N.J., 1940-43; prodn. officer USN BuORD, 1943-44; RINSMAT USN Colonial Radio Corp. (Sylvania), Buffalo, 1944-45; INSORD USN Eastman Kodak Co., Rochester, N.Y., 1945-46; chief engr., dir. quality control Naval Ordnance Office, Rochester, N.Y., 1946-57; staff engr. Space Satellite Program Eastman Kodak Co., Rochester, 1957-59; assoc. dean Coll. Engring. and Architecture Pa. State U., University Park, Pa., 1959-61; v.p., gen. mgr. to pres. Knapic Electro-Physics Inc., Palo Alto, Calif., 1961-62; prof. of indsl. and systems engring. Coll. of Engring. San Jose State U., 1962—, co-founder, coord. Cybernetic Systems grad. program, 1968-88; cons. in field, Lockheed, Motorola, Santa Fe R.R., 20th Century Fox, Alcan-Aluminium Corp., Banner Container, Sci. Mgmt. Corp., No. Telecom, Siliconix, others. Author: Military and Civilian Personnel in Naval Administration, 1952, Railroad Consolidations and Transportation Policy, 1975; editor: Design and Engineering of Production Systems, 1984; contbr. articles to profl. jours. Mem., chmn. Pers. Commn. City of Mountain View, Calif., 1968-78; troop chmn., scoutmaster, mem. Stanford Area Coun. Boy Scouts of Am., Palo Alto, 1970-83; chmn. Campus Luth. Coun. San Jose State U., 1981-86; mem. Santa Clara Valley Luth. Parish Coun., 1991—; pres. N.Y. State Young Adults Coun. YMCA, 1954-55. Lt. comdr. USNR. Recipient commendation USN, 1946; Alfred P. Sloan fellow Program Exec. Devel. MIT, 1951-52, NSF fellow, Stanford U., 1965-66; recipient Scouters Key and Award of Merit Stanford Coun. Boy Scouts Am., 1976. Mem. Am. Soc. Engring. Edn., Inst. Indsl. Engrs., Am. Prodn. and Inventory Control Soc. (bd. dirs. 1975—), Masons, Sigma Xi, Tau Beta Pi. Lutheran. Avocations: orchestra and choir, swimming, tennis, skiing, photography. Home: 1864 Limetree Ln Mountain View CA 94040-4019 Office: San Jose State U Coll Engring 1 Washington Sq San Jose CA 95192-0001

JACOBSON, CLAIRE E., music therapist; b. N.Y.C., Sept. 28, 1929; d. Philip and Sophie Winkler; children: Sandra, Jerry; m. Marvin Roth, Mar. 6, 1994. BA in Psychology, Fla. Internat. U., 1976, postgrad., 1993—; diploma, Nat. Guild Piano Tchrs., 1948. Music dir. Jewish Cmty. Ctr., Miami, Fla., 1979—; music therapist Dade County Schs., Miami, 1980—. Performer, therapist for the elderly, Miami Beach, Fla., 1979—; bd. dirs. Caravel Homeowners Assn., Miami, 1980—. Mem. Hadassah, Sierra Club, B'nai B'rith, Golden Key, Psi Chi, Phi Kappa Phi. Jewish. Avocations: piano, singing, writing. Home: 6741 SW 91st Ave Miami FL 33173-2423

JACOBSON, DAN, writer; b. Johannesburg, South Africa, Mar. 7, 1929; s. Hyman Michael and Liebe (Melamed) J.; m. Margaret Pye, Feb. 13, 1954; children: Simon Orde, Matthew, Jessica. B.A., U. Witwatersrand, Johannesburg, 1949, DLitt (hon.), 1997. Journalist and tchr., 1950-54, profl. writer, 1954—; fellow in creative writing Stanford U., 1956-57; vis. prof. English lit. Syracuse U., 1965-66; lectr. Univ. Coll., London, 1975-79; reader in English U. London, 1980-87; prof. of English U. London, 1988-94, emeritus, 1994; vis. fellow SUNY Buffalo, 1971, Humanities Rsch. Centre Australian Nat. U., 1981; vice chmn. lit. panel Arts Coun. Gt. Britain, 1972-74. Author: The Trap, 1955, A Dance in the Sun, 1956, Price of Diamonds, 1957, The Zulu and the Zeide, 1959, Evidence of Love, 1960, No Further West, 1961, The Beginners, 1966, Through The Wilderness, 1968, The Rape of Tamar, 1970, Inklings, 1973, The Wonder-Worker, 1974, The Confessions of Josef Baisz, 1978, The Story of the Stories, 1982, Time and Time Again: Autobiographies, 1985, Her Story, 1987, Adult Pleasures, 1988, Hidden in the Heart, 1991, The God-Fearer, 1992, The Electronic Elephant, 1994, Heshel's Kingdom, 1998; translator A Mouthful of Glass, 2000. Recipient John Llewelyn Rhys award Nat. Book League, 1958, W. Somerset Maugham award Soc. Authors, 1964, H.H. Wingate award Jewish Chronicle, 1978, J.R. Ackerley award for autobiography P.E.N. Club of Gt. Britain, 1986, MAry Elinore Smith Poetry prize; Soc. Authors travelling fellow, 1986. Address: care Am Heath & Co, 79 St Martins Ln, London WC2N 4AA, England

JACOBSON, EDWIN JAMES, medical educator; b. Chgo., June 27, 1947; s. Edwin Julius and Rose Josephine (Jirinec) J.; m. Martha Shanks; 1 child, Emily. BA, U. So. Calif., 1969; MD, UCLA, 1976. Diplomate Nat. Bd. Med. Examiners, Am. Bd. Internal Medicine; lic. physician, Calif. Intern in medicine UCLA Hosp., 1976-77, resident in medicine, 1977-79, fellow in nephrology, 1979-81, chief resident in medicine, 1979-81; asst. clin. prof. of medicine UCLA, 1981-88, assoc. clin. prof. medicine, 1988-94, clin. prof. medicine, 1994—; adj. asst. prof. medicine, UCLA, 1980-81; mem. med. sch. admissions com. UCLA, 1981—, med. staff credentials com., 1984—, med.staff exec. com., 1990-94, med. staff/hosp. adminstrn. liaison com. 1991-94, hosp./med. sch. faculty rels. com., 1991—, nat. kidney found., 1991—, med. adv. bd., 1991—; prin. investigator A/M Group Grant, UCLA Med. Ctr., 1993, Peter Langer Meml. Fund Award, 1993; lectr. in field. Author: Medical Diagnosis: An Algorithmic Approach, 1989, rev. edit., 2000; co-author: (with P. Healy) Il Processo Decisionale nella Diagnosi Medica, 1992; manuscript rev. bd.: Bone Marrow Transplantation, 1988—, Jour. Am. Geriatrics Soc., 1989—; editor for symposia in field; contbr. articles to profl. jours.; editor book chpts. Recipient Upjohn Achievement award, 1977. Mem. ACP, Alpha Omega Alpha. Office: UCLA 100 Ucla Medical Plz Ste 690 Los Angeles CA 90024-6992

JACOBSON, HAROLD GORDON, radiologist, educator; b. Cin., Oct. 12, 1912; s. Samuel and Regina (Dittman) J.; m. Ruth Enenstein, Aug. 10, 1941; children: Richard, Arthur. B.S., U. Cin., 1934, M.B., 1936, M.D., 1937. Diplomate Am. Bd. Radiology (trustee 1971-82, chmn. written exams com. in diagnostic radiology 1973-81, co-chmn., mem. 1981—, treas. 1976-78, v.p. 1978-80, pres. 1980-82, mem. residency rev. com. 1976-82, vice-chmn. 1979-80, chmn. 1980-82, exec. com. 1976—). Intern Los Angeles County Gen. Hosp., 1936-38; fellow in pathology Longview Hosp., Cin., 1938; resident Mt. Sinai Hosp., N.Y.C., 1939-41, Associated Hosps. U. Tex., 1941-42; asst. in radiology U. Tex., 1941-42; assoc. radiologist New Haven (Conn.) Hosp.; also instr. Yale U., 1952; asst. chief, asso. radiologist VA Hosp., Bronx, N.Y., 1946-50; chief radiology service VA Hosp., 1950-53, cons., 1958—; asst. clin. prof. N.Y. U., 1952-53, clin. prof., 1953-59, prof. clin. radiology, 1959-64; prof. radiology Albert Einstein Coll. Medicine, 1964-71; prof., chmn. Albert Einstein Coll. Medicine of Montefiore Hosp. and Med. Center, N.Y.C., 1972-85; prof. radiology Albert Einstein Coll. Medicine of Montefiore Hosp. and Med. Center, 1985-86, prof. emeritus, chmn., Disting. Univ. Prof. radiology, 1986—; dir. dept. roentgenology Hosp. for Spl. Surgery, N.Y.C., 1953-55; radiologist-in-chief Montefiore Hosp. and Med. Center, N.Y.C., 1955—; sr. cons. in radiology Nat. Bd. Med. Examiners, 1975—, mem. bd., 1979-83; vis. prof. radiology Inst. Orthopaedics, U. London, 1975—; vis. prof., lectr., UCLA Med. Ctr., 1986, 88, various socs., med. schs., univs. in Israel, Brazil, Finland, Cuba, Eastern Europe; vis. prof., lectr., med. ctrs. Republic of China and guest Chinese Radiol. Soc., 1986; named lectures include Felson Lecture, Carman Lecture, Baylin Lecture, Beeler Lecture, Freedman Lecture, Pfahler Lecture, Chamberlain Lecture, Evans Lecture, Sampson Lecture, Wolf Meml. Lecture, Caffey Lecture, Grubbe Lecture, Myron Melamed Lecture; Double Day lectr. U. Tex., 1992, Spl. lectr. N.Y. Roentgen Soc., 1992; head del. of radiologists to Republic of China, 1984. Author: (with Clarence Schein, William Z. Stern) The Common Bile Duct, 1967, Neuroradiology Workshop, Vol. III, 1968, (with Ronald O. Murray) Radiology of Skeletal Disorders: Exercises in Diagnosis, 1971, 2nd edit. 1977, 3rd edit. 1989; co-author: Bone Disease Syllabus, 1972, 2d series, 1976, 3d series, 1980, 4th series 1989, Index for Roentgen Diagnosis, 3d edit. 1975; co-editor in chief Jour. Internat. Skeletal Soc., 1976—; co-chief editor Skeletal Radiology, 1975; mem. editorial bd. Excerpta Medica, 1974—, Jour. AMA, 1979—, others. Served as maj. M.C. AUS, 1942-46. Recipient Gold medal Assn. Univ. Radiologists, 1982, Gold medal Phi Lambda Kappa, 1983, Spl. Excellence award (in lieu of Hon. Doctorate) U. Cin., 1987, Spl. award N.Y. Roentgen Soc., 1993, Alumni Staff Assn. Montefiore Med. Ctr., 1993; spl. named lecture in his honor Roentgen Soc., 1992. Fellow Am. Coll. Radiology (councilor 1960—, bd. chancellors, chmn. com. on radiol. coding 1967—, mem. commn. on credentials 1968—, chmn. commn. on affairs Am. Inst. Radiology 1971—, co-chmn. com. on diagnostic coding index and thesaurus 1973—, Gold medal 1978, selected for video taping as living legend in radiology), Royal Coll. Radiologists (London) (hon.); mem. Am. Roentgen Ray Soc. (Cert. Appreciation 1983, Gold medal 1989), N.Y. Roentgen Soc. (pres. 1959-60, historian 1967—, spl. lecture 1992), AMA, N.Y. State Med. Soc., N.Y. Med. Soc., Soc. of Chairmen Acad. Radiology Depts. (mem. exec. council 1972—, pres. 1973-74), Radiol. Soc. N.Am. (pres. 1966-67, mem. bd. censors 1968—, Diamond Jubilee lectr. 1989, Gold medal 1972), Royal Soc. Medicine (hon.), Internat. Skeletal Soc. (co-founder, pres. 1974-75, chmn., mem. exec. com. 1976—), Chinese Radiol. Soc. (hon.), Cuban Radiol. Soc. (hon.), Alpha Omega Alpha (Rigler lectr. 1964, 70, Crookshank lectr. London 1974, Holmes lectr. Boston 1974, Doubleday lectr. Houston 1991). Home: 3240 Henry Hudson Pky Bronx NY 10463-3212 Office: Montefiore Med Ctr Dept Radiology 111 E 210th St Bronx NY 10467-2401

JACOBSON, JEFFREY E., lawyer, consultant; b. N.Y.C., Aug. 19, 1956; s. Murray and Adele (Ebert) J.; m. Linda Moel, Aug. 11, 1984; children: Justin Myles, Sari Amanda. BA, Fordham U., 1976; JD, N.Y. Law Sch., 1980. Bar: N.Y. 1982, D.C. 1982, U.S. Tax Ct. 1982, U.S. Ct. Internat. Trade 1982, U.S. Dist. Ct. (so. and ea. dists.) N.Y. 1982, U.S. Ct. Appeals (2nd cir.) 1988, U.S. Supreme Ct. 1988. Assoc. SESAC, Inc., N.Y.C., 1980-82; sole practice N.Y.C., 1982-85; sr. ptnr. Jacobson & Colfin, P.C., N.Y.C. and L.I., 1985-90; mng. mem. Jacobson & Colfin, P.C., N.Y.C. and Washington, 1991—; v.p., sec. Fifth Ave. Media, Ltd., N.Y.C., 1995—; assoc. prof. Five Towns Coll., N.Y., 1999—; asst. mgr. Embassy Theatre, N.Y.C., 1975, Victoria Theatre, N.Y.C., 1975; asst. Theatre Confections, Inc., N.Y.C.,

1975; mgr. Criterion Theatre, N.Y.C., 1976; mgr., sec. Squirrels Prodns. Ltd., N.Y.C., 1976-88; pres. Aldous Demian Prodns., Ltd., N.Y.C., 1980-82; counsel Box Office Media, N.Y.C., 1982-88, Eggink, N.Y.C., 1982-89, Performance Records, 1988-97, J&J Mus. Enterprises, Ltd., 1982-95,, Anamaze Records, 1982-95, Cynthia Entertainment Group, Ltd., 1989-91, Roir Records, 1992—, Super Bubble Music Corp., 1992-99, Sergei Artemiev Benefit, 1993, New Riders of the Purple Sage, 1985—, Mick Taylor Music, 1985—, Best Film and Video Corp., 1988-91, Marty Balin, 1988—, Andrew Tosh, 1990—; spkr. CMJ Music Marathon & Musicfest, 1995, Phila. Music Confs., 1993, 94, 95, 96, 97. Mem. editl. bd. Mealey's Intellectual Property Litigation Law Report, 1992-93; contbr. articles to profl. jours.; music and internat. promotion mgmt., 1984-85; columnist IMPS Jour., 1990-95, Replication News, 1998—. Mem. Rep. candidate assembly; v.p. Pelham Pkwy., 1983-88; speaker Songwriter's Guild, N.Y.C., 1983-88, NARAS, 1991; entertainment arbitrator Am. Arbitration Assn., N.Y.C., 1984-95; guest speaker Ctr. for Media Arts, N.Y.C., 1985, Fordham U., N.Y.C., 1986, N.Y. Law Sch., 1987, Detroit Sch. Law, 1991, 93; counsel Pelham Pkwy. Block Assn., Inc., 1991; panelist Mid-Am. Music Conf., Detroit, 1993, Black Radio Exclusive, Econs. of Music, 1993; league lawyer Hewlett-Woodmere Little League, 1994-2000. Recipient Eagle Scout Silver Palm award Boy Scouts Am., 1972, Cert. of Merit Bronx House, Nathan Burkan award ASCAP, 1980, Plaque of Appreciation, Am. Arbitration Assn., 1985; named Most Admired Men and Women of Yr., 1993, Two Thousand Notable Am. Men, 1993, Man of Yr., 1996. Mem. ABA (chmn. subcom. on satellites, chmn. subcom. on copyright compliance, chmn. subcom. on copyright renewal, mem. patent trademark, copyright law sect., forum com. on entertainment and sports law sects., mem. spl. com. on corp. practice 1992-97, mem. spl. com. on atty. opinions 1994—, mem. spl. com. on internet 1997—), forum com. on comm. law, young lawyer's divsn., vice chmn. 1992-94, patent, trademark, intellectual property sect. exec. com., 1992-93, media law com., young lawyers divsn., founder Urban Intellectual Property Law seminars 1993-95, dir., 1993-95, mem. com. on atty./client opinions, mem. spl. com. Internet usage), Assn. of Bar of City of N.Y. (entertainment law com. 1992-95, trademark law com. 1997-2000), Copyright Soc. USA (com. on Bicentennial of copyright, mem. editl. bd. Jour. of Copyright Soc. 1991-93, 97—), Nat. Acad. Rec. Arts and Scis. (edn. com., columnist N.Y. chpt. newsletter 1997-2000), Rock and Roll Hall of Fame and Museum, Internat. Assn. Entertainment Lawyers, B'nai B'rith (v.p. 1988-91), Order of the Arrow Brotherhood, Sephardic Jewish Brotherhood Am., Audubon Soc. Inc., Phi Delta Phi. Jewish. Avocations: music, photography, swimming, stereo equipment, traveling. Office: Jacobson & Colfin PC 19 W 21st St Rm 603A New York NY 10010-6805

JACOBSON, MICHAEL DAVID, journalist; b. Aylesbury, Eng., Mar. 26, 1923; s. Maurice and Suzannah Constance (Davies) J.; m. Nita Mary Maynard Moyce, Sept. 4, 1952 (div. Feb. 1976); 1 child, Sallyann Maynard; m. Gela Jane Peters, Mar. 19, 1976 (div. Oct. 1996). Student, Bishop's Stortford Coll., Herts, U.K., 1936-39. Fgn. corr. and night fgn. news editor Daily Mail, London, 1951-62; various freelance editor positions, 1962-84; sr. sub-editor The Sunday Times, London, 1965-85, The Observer, London, 1985-90; editor Dordogne Telegraph, France, 1990-93; editor, pub. rels. cons. Anglers' Conservation Assn., Grantham, Eng., 1989—; dir. T.A. Cutbill and Ptnrs., London, 1975-81; British pub. rels. cons. Chevron Oil (U.K.) Ltd., London, 1969-84; pub. rels. cons. The Angling Found., 1975-79, 88-93. Author: Pros and Cons, 16th edit. 1977, 17th edit. 87; translator North Africa, 1954, Traveller's Guide to France, 1988; contbr. numerous articles to profl. jours. Magistrate Brent Petty Sessions Area, Middlesex, Eng., 1983-93; chmn. Brent South Liberal Dem. Constituency Party, Middlesex, Eng., 1984-85. With Royal Navy, 1942-46. Fellow Brit. Assn. Communicators in Bus.; mem. Inst. Pub. Rels., Confédération Européenne de Relations Publiques. Office: BPI, 24250 La Roque Gageac France

JACOBSON, RICHARD LEE, lawyer, educator; b. Los Angeles, Nov. 2, 1942; s. Joseph and Betty (Koenig) J.; children: David, Peter, Michael. S.B., U. Chgo., 1964; J.D., U. So. Calif., 1970. Bar: Calif. 1971, U.S. Ct. Appeals (9th cir.) 1971, D.C. 1980, U.S. Ct. Appeals (4th cir.) 1980, U.S. Ct. Appeals (D.C. cir.) 1980, U.S. Supreme Ct. 1980, U.S. Ct. Appeals (6th cir.) 1983. Law clk. U.S. Ct. Appeals (9th cir.), 1970-71; law clk. to Assoc. Justice William O. Douglas U.S. Supreme Ct., Washington, 1971-72; assoc. Irell & Manella, Los Angeles, 1973-76; mem. trial unit SEC, Washington, 1977-78, spl. counsel to chmn., 1978-79; ptnr. Mayer, Brown & Platt, Washington, 1980-85; spl. counsel Heller, Ehrman, White & McAuliffe, Palo Alto, 1986-88; of counsel Fulbright & Jaworski, Washington, 1988-89, ptnr., 1990—; adj. prof. law Georgetown U. Law Ctr., Washington, 1979-86; mem. bd. advisors, sec. Reform Act Litig. Reporter, 1998—. Exec. editor So. Calif. Law Rev., 1969-70; contbr. articles to profl. jours. Bd. dirs. Washington Lawyers Com. for Civil Rights and Urban Affairs, 1983—. Mem. ABA (chmn. subcom. uniformity of local discovery rules 1983-85, chmn. subcom. securities class actions 1995—, fed. regulation securities com., securities litigation com.), Am. Law Inst., Washington Coun. Lawyers (bd. dirs. 1982-86, 88-99, pres. 1985-86), D.C. Bar Assn. (nominations com. 1984-85, steering com. computer law divsn. 1985-86), Assn. SEC Alumni (pres. 1995-97, dir. 1998—), Order of Coif. Office: Fulbright & Jaworski LLP 801 Pennsylvania Ave NW Washington DC 20004-2615

JACOBSON, RICHARD PHILIP, lawyer; b. Livingston, N.J., May 15, 1962; s. Allen Sander and Carol Jacobson; m. Susan B. J., July 22, 1989; children: Rachel Amanda, William Rutter. BA, U. Conn., 1984; JD, Georgetown U., 1987. Bar: N.J. 1987, N.Y. 1996, D.C. 1996, U.S. Ct. Appeals (2d cir.), U.S. Ct. Appeals (3d Cir.). Lawyer Wilentz, Goldman & Spitzer, Woodbridge, N.J., 1987-92, Dunn, Pashman, Hackensack, N.J., 1992-95, Colucci & Umans, N.Y.C., 1995—. Office: Colucci & Umans 101 E 52d St New York NY 10022

JACOBSSON, RICHARD AKE, experimental particle physicist; b. Stockholm, Sweden, Mar. 4, 1969; s. Borje Ake and Rose-Marie Ingrid (Hammarstrom) J. BSc in Physics, U. Stockholm, 1991, PhD in Physics, 1996. Scientific assoc. CERN, Geneva, 1991-97; postdoctoral rschr. Stockholm U., 1996-97; particle physics rsch. fellow CERN, Geneva, 1997-2000, staff physicist, 2000—. Particle Physics Rsch. fellow CERN, Geneva, 1997-2000. Mem. Sea Environment Assn. (pres. 1997—). Avocations: marine environmental studies, diving, nature photography, trekking. Home: Rue De Champ Novaz, 01630 Challex France Office: European Orgn Nuclear Rsch, Meyrin, CH 1211 Geneva 23, Switzerland

JACOBUS, CHARLES JOSEPH, lawyer, title company executive, author; b. Ponca City, Okla., Aug. 21, 1947; s. David William and Louise Graham (Johnson) J.; m. Heather Jeanne Jones, June 6, 1970; children: Mary Helen, Charles J. Jr. BS, U. Houston, 1970, JD, 1973. Bar: Tex. 1973; cert. specialist residential and commerical real estate law Tex. Bd. Legal Specialization. Pvt. practice Houston, 1973-75; staff counsel Tenneco Realty, Inc., Houston, 1975-78; gen. counsel Tenneco Realty, Inc., Deerfield, Ill., 1979-83; chief legal counsel Speedy Muffler King, Deerfield, 1978-79; v.p. Commerce Title Co., Houston, 1983-85; sr. v.p. Charter Title Co., Houston, 1986—; ptnr. Jacobus & Melamed PC, Houston; 1998 Jenkens & Gilchrist, Houston, 1998-99; pvt. practice Bellaire, Tex., 1999—; adv. dir. Heritage Bank, Houston; adj. faculty Tex. A&M U., 1986-90; adj. prof. U. Houston Law Ctr., Houston C.C., Champions Sch. Real Estate; instr. advanced real estate law State Bar Tex., course dir., 1990, Tex. Land Title Assn. Sch. Author: Real Estate Law, 2d edit., 1996, Texas Real Estate, 8th edit., 1998; co-author: Mastering Real Estate Titles and Title Insurance in Texas, 1996, Georgia Real Estate, 1995, Ohio Real Estate, 2d edit., 1990, Calif. Real Estate, 1989, Keeping Current with Texas Real Estate, updated annually, Real Estate Principles, 8th edit., 1999, Real Estate, An Introduction to the Profession, 8th edit., 1999, Texas Title Insurance, updated annually, Texas Real Estate Brokerage and the Law of Agency, 2000; co-author: Real Estate Brokerage Law and Practice; editor: Building Blocks of a Commercial Transaction, 1992, Building Blocks of a Residential Real Estate Transaction, 1994, Texas Real Estate Law Deskbook, 1995; editor-in-chief Tex. Forms Manual. Chmn. Planning and Zoning Commn., Bellaire, Tex., 1976-77; bd. dirs. Tax Increment Fin. Dist., Bellaire, 1984-91; chmn. task force on edn. Tex. Real Estate Commn.; chmn. profl. adv. com. dept. urban and regional planning Tex. A&M U., 1988-89; 1st asst. scoutmaster Boy Scout World Jamboree, Holland, 1995, scoutmaster, Chile, 1999; scoutmaster Nat. Boy Scout Jamboree, 1997; mayor City of Bellaire, 1998-2000; sec.-treas. Harris County Mayors and Coun. Assn. 1999. Recipient Peggy Hayes Tchg. Excellence award TLTA, 1993. Mem. ABA (acquisitions editor books and pubs. com., chmn. brokers and brokerage com. 1986-93), Internat. Wine Food Soc. (host Houston chpt. 1993-94), Am. Coll. Real Estate Lawyers, Nat. Assn. Corp. Real Estate Execs. (chpt. v.p.), Am. Land Devel. Assn. (bd. dirs.), Tex. Land Title Assn. (chmn. forms manual com., TREC earnest money contract task force), Houston Real Estate Lawyers Coun., Real Estate Educator's Assn. (pres. 1987-88, Real Estate Educator of Yr. 1986, 2000), Houston Bar Assn. (chmn. real estate sect. 1987-88), Bellaire/S.W. Houston C. of C. (Outstanding Real Estate Educator in Tex. 1986, Outstanding Businessman of Yr. 1990), chmn. Tex. Real Estate Commns. Edn. Task Force, 1999—), U. Tex. Mortgage Lending Inst. (faculty), U. Houston Law Alumni Assn. (bd. dirs.), Universal Order Knights of Vine (master barrister Houston chpt.), Les Amis Escoffier, Amici della Vite. Republican. Roman Catholic. Home: 5223 Pine St Bellaire TX 77401-4820 Office: 6800 West Loop S Ste 460 Bellaire TX 77401-4525

JACOBY, COLEMAN, scriptwriter; b. Pitts.; s. Harry and Etla (Bernstein) J.; m. Gaby Monet, June 17, 1955; children: Catherine, Antoinette. Grad. high sch., Pitts. Ind. TV scriptwriter, 1950—. Original writer Jackie Gleason Show, creator The Poor Soul, Reggie Van Gleason, Joe the Bartender characters; scriptwriter: (TV series) The Phil Silvers Show (Sgt. Bilko), The Garry Moore Show, Kraft Music Hall, numerous HBO spls., (teleplays) The Wonderful Worls of Burlesque (Emmy award nomination), The Bachelor (Sylvania award). Recipient 4 Emmy awards Nat. Acad. TV Arts and Scis., Christopher award, Sylvania award. Mem. Writers Guild Am. East (life). Democrat. Club: Friars (N.Y.C.). Home and Office: 350 E 84th St New York NY 10028-4405

JACOBY, NEIL HERMAN, JR., astronautic engineer, consultant; b. Chgo., Oct. 20, 1940; s. Neil Herman and Clair (Gruhn) J. BA in Astronomy, UCLA, 1965, MS in Engring., 1969. Sci. guide Griffith Obs., L.A., summer 1962; comuter program cons. UCLA Western Data Processing Ctr., 1966-67; tchg. asst. in astrodynamics UCLA Sch. Engring. and Applied Sci., summer 1968; staff scientist Computer Scis. Corp., L.A., 1972-76; sys. analyst Sys. Devel. corp., Santa Monica, Calif., 1977-81; cons. in astrodynamics, astronautics L.A., 1981—; ind. property mgr., L.A., 1979—. Contbr. articles to sci. and profl. jours. Bd. dirs. Westwood Homeowners Assn., L.A., 1981—. Mem. AIAA, AAAS, Am. Astronautical Soc. (sr.), N.Y. Acad. Sci., Internat. Biog. Assn. (Cert. of Merit), Planetary Soc., Alpha Gamma Sigma. Achievements include development of a time series for rapid missile trajectory determination, and an orbit determination method using 5 observations. Also, a novel method of non-co-planer orbital transfer for a geocentric satellite. Determined that three observations of right ascension and declination of a comet are substantially better than five observations in accurately determining an orbit of a comet because of the very high eccentricity of the comet's orbit, determined that three observations are better than five in determining highly eccentric orbits of comets. Avocations: astrodynamics/astronautics, surfing, jogging, swimming. Home and Office: 1434 Midvale Ave Los Angeles CA 90024-5406

JACOMB, SIR MARTIN, banker; b. Chiddingfold, Eng., Nov. 11, 1929; s. Hilary W. and Felise Jacomb; m. Evelyn Heathcoat Amory, 1960; children: Emma, Matthew, Thomas. Student, Eton Coll., Eng.; MA in Law, Oxford U., 1953, hon. doctorate, 1997; hon. doctorate, U. Humberside, 1993, U. Buckingham, 1997. Pvt. practice law, 1955-68; with Kleinwort Benson Ltd., 1968-85, vice chmn., 1976-85; dep. chmn. Barclays Bank PLC, 1985-93; chmn. Barclays de Zoete Wedd Ltd., 1986-91, Postel Investment Mgmt. Ltd., 1991-95; dep. chmn. Comml. Union Assurance Co., 1988-93, Bank of Eng., 1986-95, The Daily Telegraph, 1986-95; chmn. Brit. Coun., 1992-98, Prudential plc, 1995-2000, Delta plc, 1993-2000; dir. Marks and Spencer plc, 1991-2000, Rio Tinto plc, 1988-2000, Canary Wharf Grp plc, 1999-2000, Minorplanet Sys. plc, 2000—. Dir. The Royal Opera House, Covent Garden, 1987-92; mem. fin. com. Oxford U. Press, 1971-95; trustee Nat. Heritage Meml. Fund, 1982-97, World Monuments Fund, 1999—; chancellor U. Buckingham, 1998—. Created knight, 1985; hon. fellow Worcester Coll., Oxford, 1994. Mem. Inner Temple (hon. master of the bench 1987). Avocations: theater, family bridge, tennis. Office: Delta plc, 1 Kingsway, London WC2B 6XF, England

JACOMET, THIERRY, lawyer; b. Paris, Oct. 27, 1944; s. André Jacomet and Hélène Cathala; m. Irene des Graviers, Jan. 13, 1968; children: Amélie, Edouard, Ombline, Quentin. Degree in Law, U. Paris, 1966, degree in English, 1968; M Comparative Law, Columbia U., 1967. Bar: Paris 1970. Assoc. Gide Loyrette Nouel, Paris, 1970-78; ptnr. Gide Loyrette Novel, Paris, 1978—; lectr. Inst. Bus. Law, Aix en Provence, France, 1984—. Author: Les Relations Financières avec l'Etranger, 1982, 5th edit., 1990. Vice chmn. Scouts Unitaires de France, 1984-96. Office: Gide Loyrette Nouel, 26 Cours Albert 1er, Paris France

JACQMAIN, MONIQUE HERMANCE JULIENNE, Italian language educator; b. Antwerp, Belgium, Jan. 3, 1934; d. Gaston Jacqmain and Marguerite Van Honsté. BA in Romance Philology, Ghent State U., Belgium, 1954; MA in Romance Philology, Ghent State U., 1956; PhD, Brussels Free U., 1968. Tchr. French Rijksnormaalschool, Tongeren, Belgium, 1957-59, Atheneum, Deurne, Belgium, 1959-64; tchr. Italian Atheneum, Deurne, 1962-66; prof. Italian Antwerp State U., 1964-99, sect. head, 1990-99, ret., 1999; cons. in field. Author: Il Linguaggio della Pubblicità, 1973, Profili Italiani, 1985, Is je Italiaans Perfect? E' perfetto il tuo neerlandese?, 1995; translator: Il mio amico assassino, 1974, Il Fuoco fatuo, 1975, Gioacchino di Babilonia, 1977, De idyllische Nederlanden, 1987, Atila, 1993; contbr. articles to profl. jours. Avocations: music, theater, creative writing. Home: Jan Moorkensstraat 17 bus 4, 2600 Antwerp Belgium

JACQMIN, ROBERT P., nuclear engineer. PhD, MIT, 1991. Engr. Argonne (Ill.) Nat. Lab., 1991-95, CEA Cadarache, Saint-Paul-Lez-Durance, France, 1995—. Office: CEA Cadarache SPRC/LEPH, Bat 230, 13108 Saint-Paul-Lez-Durance France

JACQUEMYN, YVES, obstetrician/gynecologist; b. Merksem, Antwerp, Belgium, July 25, 1962; s. Roger-Felix Jacquemyn and Liliane Peeters; m. Machteld Leontina Claes, May 16, 1986; children: Nathalie, Mathieu. Humaniora Latina, Antwerp Jesuit Coll., 1980; Med. Candidate, RUCA Antwerp U., 1983; MD, UIA Antwerp U., 1987. Specialist in ob/gyn. Rsch. asst. dept. physiology RUCA U., Antwerp, 1983-87; clin. asst. U. Hosp., Antwerp, 1987-90, sr. asst., 1991-92, resident, 1992-93; clin. asst. Maria Mediatrix Hosp., Deurne, 1990-91; resident Antwerp Middelheim, 1993-98; tchr., head dept. obstet. Antwerp U., 1998—, tchr. in obstetrics, 1998—; cons. St. Elisabeth Hosp., Antwerp, 1993-98, FOB Med. Ctr., Antwerp, 1993-98. Contbr. articles to profl. jours. Elected mem. Univ. Dept. Coun., Antwerp, 1986. Lt. Med. Svc. Germany mil., 1992-93. Mem. Internat. Perinat. Soc., Psychosomatic Working Group, Fedn. Internat. Gynecologists, European Soc. Human Reprodn., Brit. Med. Ultrasound Soc., World Fedn. Ultrasound Medicine, Internat. Soc. Ultrasound Ob-Gyn., Brit. Perinatal Soc. Avocation: pianist. Home: Strijdersstraat 24, Antwerp Edegem 2650, Belgium Office: U Hosp Antwerp, Wilrijkstraat 10, Edegem 2650, Belgium

JACQUESSON, ALAIN L., librarian; b. Geneva, Switzerland, Nov. 3, 1946; s. Guy and Elisabeth (Giddey) J.; m. Marie-Jose Chanez, Feb. 8, 1975; children: Severine, Mathieu. Responsable Ecole de bibliothecaires, Geneva, 1978-81; project chief U. Geneva, 1981-88; dir. Bibliothèques Municipales, Geneva, 1988-93, Bibliothèque Publique et Universitaire, Geneva, 1993—. Mem. ALA, Assn. of Swiss Libr., Assn. French Librs., Am. Soc. Info. Sci. E-mail: alain.jacquesson@bpu.ville-ge.ch. Fax: 4122 418-28-01. Office: Bibliotheque Publique Univ, Parc des Bastions, 1211 Geneva 4, Switzerland

JACYNA-ONYSZKIEWICZ, ZBIGNIEW MARIA, physicist, educator; b. Cracow, Poland, Aug. 10, 1944; s. Józef and Aleksandra (Ciszak) Jacyna-O.; m. Irena Helena Pycz, July 26, 1969; 1 child, Tymoteusz. MSc, A. Mickiewicz U., Poznań, Poland, 1967, PhD, 1975, DSc, 1981; prof., Pres. Poland, 1992; DSc (hon.), Kaliningrad (Russia) State U., 1995. From rsch. asst. to assoc. prof. physics A. Mickiewicz U., 1967-95, prof. physics, 1995—; dept. fellow U. Fla., Gainesville, 1985-86, fellow Joint Inst. Nuc. Rsch., Dubna, Russia, 1990; vice dir. Inst. Physics, Poznan, 1987-93, head divsn. magnetic theory, 1991—, vice dean Faculty of Physics, 1993-99. Author: Unified Treatment of Quantum and Statistical Mechanics, 1983, Fundamental Problems and Achievements of Modern Physics, 1991, Principles of Quantum Thermodynamics, 1996, Genesis Principles of Quantum Cosmology, 1999, Metakosmology, 1999; contbr. chpt. to book, articles to more than 100 sci. publs. Mem. Solidarity Trade Union, Gdánsk, Poland, 1980—. Recipient awards Polish Min. Edn., 1980, 83, 88; recipient Gold Cross of Merit, 1988, Nat. medal edn., 1995. Mem. European Soc. Study Sci. and Theology, Polish Phys. Soc., Pax Romana. Roman Catholic. Avocations: swimming, space flights, theology. E-mail: zbigonys@main.amu.edu.pl. Home: ul Z Lisowskiego 12/2, 61-606 Poznan Poland Office: A Mickiewicz U Fac Physics, ul Umultowska 85, 61-614 Poznan Poland

JADHAV, JAYAWANT DADAJI, agro-meteorology educator; b. Ambason, India, Oct. 15, 1964; s. Dadaji Kadaji and Leelabai Dadaji (Kor) J.; m. Jayawant Dadaji Jadhav, May 24, 1992; 1 child. BSc in Agr., MPKV, Rahuri, India, 1988, MSc in Agr., 1991, PhD, 2000. Agrl. officer Mahatma Phyle Krishi Vidyapeeth, Solapur, India, 1991—; fellow SCIR, New Delhi, 1997-99. Inventor in field. Rsch. fellow ICAR, New Delhi, 1989-90. Mem. N.Y. Acad. Scis., Indian Jour. Dryland Agr. Avocations: drama. Home and Office: Krishna Bhavan, Near DAV Coll, Solapur 413002, India

JADHAV, SURESH SAKHARAM, pharmaceuticals company executive; b. Amravati, India, Jan. 21, 1950; s. Sakharam and Indumati (Deshmukh) J.; m. Supriya Marunrakkal, Apr. 22, 1951; children: Swapnil, Sachin. B in Pharm., Nagpur U., 1970, M in Pharm., 1972; PhD, Haffkine Inst., Bombay, India, 1978. Sr. sci. officer Haffkine Inst., 1977-79; from mgr. to exec. dir. Serum Inst. India Ltd., Pune, 1979—; cons. EXIM Bank, India, Consultancy Devel. Ctr., Govt. India; expert panel tech. info. forecasting & assessment coun. Govt. India; mem. rev. com. on animal husbandry WHO. Mem. W.H.O. rev. com. on Animal Husbandry; vol. Indian Red Cross Soc. Mem. India Pharmacol. Soc., Internat. Soc. Toxicology, AAAS, Internat. Assn. Biol. Standardization, Indian Acad. Vaccinology & Immunobiology, Indian Virol. Soc., N.Y. Acad. Scis. Avocations: hiking, sightseeing, reading, photography. Home: 16 Sadhana Society, 222/1 Hadapsar, Pune 411 028, India Office: Serum Inst India Ltd, 212/2 Hadapsar, Pune 411 028, India

JADIN, EMILE JOSEPH, finance company executive, consultant; b. Quenast, Belgium, Mar. 26, 1943; s. Leon Alphonse Jadin and Nelly Clara Tresinie; m. Christiane Zulma Goossens, July 30, 1966; children: Benoit, François, Anne. Grad., Inst. St. Marie Arlon, Belgium, 1961; lic. in comml. scis., Hautes Etudes Comml. St. Louis, Brussels, 1968. CPA, Belgium. Sect. chief. Banque de la Société Générale de Belgique, Brussels, 1961-68; sr. auditor Arthur Andersen, Brussels, 1968-72; internal auditor PRB, Brussels, 1972-77, chief acct., 1977-83; fin. dir. PRB-Gechem, Brussels, 1984-90; CFO Gechem-Recticel, Brussels, 1991-98; ind. chartered acct., 1998—. Roman Catholic. Avocations: football, bicycling, swimming, crosswords. Home: Chemin du Croly 99, 1430 Quenast Belgium Office: chemin du Croly 58, 1430 Quenast Belgium

JAECKEL, CHRISTOPHER CAROL, memorabilia company executive, antiquarian; b. N.Y.C., Jan. 2, 1941; s. Theodore Ridgway and Yolanda (Benjamin) J.; m. Elizabeth McGreevy Billmire, July 5, 1969; 1 stepchild, Garrett O'Neil Billmire III. BA in English, Princeton U., 1964. Producer, dir. WBAL-TV, Balt., 1966-68, TV news reporter, anchor, 1968-71; pres. Walter R. Benjamin Autographs, Hunter, N.Y., 1971—. Contbr. author: Autographs and Manuscripts, 1978; editor mag./catalog The Collector, 1990. Chmn. Town of Hunter Planning Bd., Tannersville, N.Y., 1978; mem., vice chmn. Bd. Assessment Rev., Hunter, 1980-96; chmn. Rep. Com., Hunter, 1980-82; pres. Hunter Fire Co., 1980-82. Mem. Mountaintop Hist. Soc. (pres. 1978-80), Lions (v.p. Rip Van Winkle club 1980-82). Roman Catholic. Avocations: travel, reading, writing, photography. Office: Walter Benjamin Autographs 664 Scribner Holw Hunter NY 12442

JAEGER, ADOLF OTTO, psychology educator, researcher, consultant; b. Usseln, Waldeck, Germany, June 25, 1920; s. Karl and Adelheid (Winckler) J.; m. Inge Deutsch, July 17, 1947 (dec. Apr. 1987); children: Renate, Sabine, Katrin. Diploma in psychology, U. Goettingen, Germany, 1954, D Natural Scis., 1958; Venia Legendi, U. Giessen, Germany, 1965. Asst. U. Goettingen, 1954-55; chmn. psychology German Soc. for Personalwesen, Frankfurt am Main, 1955-68; chmn. dept. orgnl. psychology U. Giessen, 1963-68; ordinary prof. psychology Free U. Berlin, 1968-87, emeritus, 1987—, founder Inst. Psychology, 1970; cons. Bundesministerien, Bundeslaender, Grossbetriebe, 1955-70; mem., chmn. Testkurtorium des BDP, 1958-64. Author: Dimensions of Intelligence, 1967, 3d edit., 1973, Personnel Selection, 1970, Berlin Intelligence Structure Model, 1982, Validity of Intelligence Tests, 1986, (with H.M. Süss and A. Beauducel) Berlin Intelligence Structur Test, 1997; editor, co-editor Diagnostica, 1967-95; contbr. articles to sci. jours. Lt. German Army, 1941. Mem. APA (affiliate), German Soc. for Psychology (hon.), Berufsverband Deutscher Psychologen, Gesellschaft für Arbeitswissenschaft. Evangelical. Avocation: photography. Home: Erlenweg 72 Apt 262, 14532 Kleinmachnow Germany Office: Free U Berlin Inst Psych, Habelschwerdter Allee 45, 14195 Berlin Germany

JAEGER, ARNO, operations research educator; b. Berlin, July 10, 1922; s. Gustav and Amalie (Beau) J.; m. Charlotte Streichan, Oct. 29, 1998. Diploma in math., U. Goettingen, 1948, D in Natural Scis., 1949. Brit. coun. fellow Manchester (Eng.) U., 1949-50; lectr. U. Coll. Ibadan, Nigeria, 1950-52; rsch. assoc. U. Ill., Urbana, 1952-53; assoc. prof. U. Cin., 1953-59, prof., 1959-68, Charles Phelps Taft prof., 1968-70, dir. grad. studies, 1961-70; prof. Ruhr U., Bochum, Germany, 1970—, dir. Inst. Mgmt. Sci. and Ops. Rsch., 1971—; vis. prof. U. Wuerzburg, 1956, Free U., Berlin, 1957, U. Goettingen, 1957, Miami U., Oxford, Ohio, 1958, U. Munich, 1958, 62, U. Mannheim, 1965, U. Karlsruhe, 1966-68, Tongji U., Shanghai, 1982, Fachhochschule Bingen, 1991-92, U. Potsdam, 1992-93. Author: Introduction to Analytic Geometry and Linear Algebra, 1967, Mathematik und Leben—Eine seltene Gleichung, 1997; co-author: Lineare Wirtschaftsalgebra, 1969, Lineare Algebra und Lineare Programmierung, 1987; editor Econometrics and Ops. Rsch., 1965—; translator: Lineare Programmierung und Erweiterungen, 1966. Home: Nussbaumweg 25, D-44799 Bochum Germany Office: Ruhr U, Universitaetsstr 150, D-44780 Bochum Germany

JAEGER, DAVID LEONARD, chemical engineer; b. Muskegon, Mich., Feb. 12, 1954; s. Leonard Fredrick and Ada Maxine (Abendroth) J. BS in Chemistry, Mich. Technol. U., 1977, BSChemE, 1982. Environ. chemist Muskegon County WWTP, 1978-80; plant chemist Eastshore Chem. Co., Muskegon, 1980-81; chemist, chem. engr. Aquatic Sys., Inc., Ludington, Mich., 1982-85; rsch. chemist Widger Chemist-BASF, Warren, Mich., 1985-90; chem. engr. Super Environ., Inc., Brighton, Mich., 1990-91; sr. chem. engr. Engring.-Sci., Inc., Birmingham, Mich., 1991-93; sr. remediation engr. Swanson Environ., Inc., Farmington Hills, Mich., 1993-95; sr. assoc. Wolke & Assoc., Shelby Twp., Mich., 1995-98; sr. ops. engr. CRA Svcs., Romulus, Mich., 1998—; mem. pub. rels. com. Mich. Environ. Cons./Contractor's Assn., Lansing, 1993-94; branch chief Environ. Operations-Marine Safety and Environ. Protection Dept., USCG (Aux.), 1996-97. Co-author monographs in field. Unit commr. Clinton Valley coun. Boy Scouts Am., Mich., 1990-92; vol., divsn. staff officer USCG Aux., 1989-95. Recipient Group Action citation USCG, 1992, Operational Svc. award USCG, 1994, Meritorious Team Commendation with bronze star USCG, 1995, award of adminstrv. merit USCG, 2000. Mem. Mich. Assn. Environ. Profls., Water Environ. Fedn., Engring. Soc. Detroit, Elks. Presbyterian. Achievements include design and construction of more than a dozen small, medium, and large scale groundwater clean-up operations; design of industrial wastewater treatment operations; startup and operations of a 0.5 MGD wastewater treatment plant. Office: CRA Svcs Ste 160 11100 Metro Airport Center Dr Romulus MI 48174-1467

JAEGER, MARC M., judge; b. Luxembourg, Oct. 4, 1954. M, U. Strasbourg, France, 1979. Advocat Barreau Luxembourg, 1981-83, attache de justice, 1983-84; judge Tribunal D'Arrondissement, Luxembourg, 1984-86; magistrat detache Referendaire Cabinet de L'Avocat Gen., 1986-88, Referendaire Cabinet du Judge, 1988-96; judge Tribunal Premiere Instance, 1996—. Office: Ct 1st Instance European Cntys, Blvd Konrad Adenauer Kirchberg, Luxembourg L-2925, Luxembourg*

JAEGER, PHILIPPE, physician, educator; b. Fribourg, Switzerland, Sept. 10, 1949; s. Louis and Jacqueline (Bunge) J.; m. Nicole Baechtold, Oct. 2, 1982; 1 child, Hélène. B of Arts and Scis., Coll. St. Michel, Fribourg, 1968; MD, U. Lausanne, Switzerland, 1975. Diplomate Swiss Bd. Internal

Medicine. Rsch. fellow in renal physiology Yale U., New Haven, 1976-77, resident in nephrology, 1982-83; rsch. fellow in hypertension U. Lausanne, 1975-76, resident in internal medicine, 1978-80, chief resident, 1980-82, adj. physician dept. medicine, 1983-88; physician-in-chief U. Berne, Switzerland, 1988—; instr. medicine Univ. Hosp., Lausanne, 1984, asst. prof. nephrology, 1985; prof. medicine, dir. Policlinic of Medicine, Univ. Hosp., Berne, 1988; hon. pres. Internat. Congress on Renal Stone Analysis, Bordeaux, France, 1993. Editor: Métabolisme Electrolytique et Minéral, 1994; editor Praxis, 1990-00; contbr. numerous articles and abstracts to New Eng. Jour. Medicine, Kidney Internat., Jour. Bone and Mineral Rsch., Jour. Clin. Investigation, Am. Jour. Physiology, The Lancet, others. Served to capt. Swiss Med. Soc. Recipient prize Swiss Soc. Urology, 1985. Fellow ACP (hon.); mem. European Assn. Internal Medicine (pres.-elect 1994-96), European Fedn. Internal Medicine (pres. 1998—), Swiss Soc. Internal Medicine (pres. 1995-98), French Soc. Nephrology (v.p. 1995-97, pres. 1997-99), Swiss Soc. Nephrology (coun. mem. 1991-99), Swiss Assn. Against Osteoporosis (coun. mem. 1989—). Roman Catholic. Avocations: history, tennis, bicycling, piano. Office: Univ Hosp, 3010 Bern BE, Switzerland

JAEGGI, MARTIN NIKLAUS RICHARD, river engineer; b. Solothurn, Switzerland, May 18, 1947; s. Peter and Margrit (Reinert) J.; m. Alica Elisabeth Kis, Aug. 24, 1975; children: Dominique, Pascal, Adrian. Diploma in rural engring., Swiss Fed. Inst. Technology, 1970, PhD, 1983. Rsch. asst. Lab. Hydraulic ETH, Zurich, 1971-75, head river sect., 1975-89, head river divsn., 1989-94; cons. Ebmatingen, Zurich, Switzerland, 1994—; with Lincoln Coll., Canterbury, New Zealand, 1978-79; part-time lectr. Swiss Fed. Inst. Tech., Zurich, 1983-92, part-time reader, 1992—. Contbr. articles to profl. jours. Mem. Swiss Assn. Engrs. and Architects, Kiwanis (pres. Zuercher Oberland club 1994). Roman Catholic. Avocation: sports. Office: Zuerichstrasse 108, 8123 Ebmatingen Switzerland

JAEGLE, ANDRE, retired engineer; b. Uccle, Belgium, Mar. 11, 1930; s. Jean Charles-Edouard J. and Andree Helene Rossel; m. Madeleine Mary Hassan, July 26, 1952; children: Mireille, François, Agnes. Grad., Ecole Poly., Paris, 1952. Nat. sec. UGICT-CGT Engrs. Union, Paris, 1968-81; with employment dept. Office of Prime Min., Paris, 1981-82; dep. mgr. Cabinet of Transp. Min., Paris, 1982-84; mgr. Geographic Inst., Paris, 1955-68, from chief engr. to sr. engr., 1984-94; ret.; pres. French Nat. Commn. for Automation in Cartography, 1965-75. Chief editor Options mag., 1978-80. Pres. World Fedn. Sci. Workers, Montreuil, France, 1996—. Fax: 03033-1-48188003. E-mail: fmts@wanadoo.fr. Office: FMTS, Case 404, 93514 Montreuil Cedex, France

JAENEN, CORNELIUS JOHN, history educator, consultant; b. Cannington Manor, Can., Feb. 21, 1927; m. Ina May Turner Jaenen. MA, U. Manitoba, Winnipeg, Can., 1950; BEd, U. Manitoba, Can., 1958; PhD, U. Ottawa, Can., 1963; LLD, U. Winnipeg, Can., 1981. Diplome de fin d'etudes, Bordeaux, France. Housemaster Ravenscourt Sch., Winnipeg, Can., 1949-52; instr. Imperial Ethiopian Govt., Addis Ababa, 1952-55; tchr. City if Winnipeg Schs., 1955-58; asst. prof. Meml. U., St. John's, Can., 1958-59; asst. full prof. United Coll., Winnipeg, Can., 1959-67; prof. U. Ottawa, Can., 1967-92, emeritus prof., 1992—; founding pres. Canadian Ethnic Studies Assn., 1971-73; pres. French Colonial Hist. Soc., 1986-88, Canadian Hist. Assn., 1988-89; chmn. Ethnic Histories Panel, Sec. of State, Can., 1971-86. Author: Friend and Foe, 1976 (Sainte-Marie prize, 1974), The Role of the Church in New France, 1976, The French Regime in the Upper Country of Canada, 1996' author, editor: Les Franco-Ontariens, 1993 (Legault prize, 1993); contbr. chpts. to books and essays to jours. Mem. Manitoba Adv. Com. on Bilingualism, Winnipeg, 1963-65, Canadian Consultative Com. on Multiculturalism, Ottawa, 1973-76, Ontario Coun. on Grad. Studies, Toronto, 1973076; cons. Canadian Mus. Civilization, Ottawa, 1991-97. Recipient Ronsard medal Govt. France, 1947, Gold medal in Edn., U. Manitoba, 1958. Fellow Royal Soc. Can. (sec. 1999—, J.B. Tyrrell medal 1994). Home: 9 Elma St, Gloucester, ON Canada K1T 3W8 Office: Dept History, University of Ottawa, Ottawa, Canada K1N 6N5

JAENSSON, BERNT OLOF, materials engineer; b. Nybro, Sweden, Oct. 4, 1940; s. Olof and Estrid J.; m. Barbro Osterberg, Aug. 18, 1962; 1 child, Jenny. MSc, Chalmers U. Technology, 1965, PhD, 1972; DSc, Linkoping U., 1989. R&D engr. Soderfors Bruk, Sweden, 1965-68, Saab-Scania AB, Linkoping, Sweden, 1972-95, CSM Materialteknik, Linkoping, 1995—. Mem. Swedish Soc. Materials Technology. Home: Sune Gjutares grand 5, S-59631 Skanninge Sweden Office: CSM Materialteknik AB, Box 13200, S-58013 Linköping Sweden

JAFAR, MUHAMMAD MAMUN, distribution company executive; b. Kumasi, Ashanti, Ghana, June 15, 1965; s. Jafar Issah and Maimuna Musah; m. Umurutu Muhammad, July 5, 1994. BA with honors, U. Lagos, Nigeria, 1974; MBA, U. Pa., 1984; MA, U. London, Eng., 1988; Internat. Bus. Rsch. Cert., U. Sussex, Eng., 1990. Dir. T.T.L., Tema, Ghana, 1970-74; gen. mgr. F.E., Kumasi, Ghana, 1974-77; pres. U.A.C., Kumasi, 1977-90; chmn., founder El Mamun Enterprise, Kumasi, Ashanti, 1990—, Internat. Gen. Bus. Rsch., 1988—; cons. I. of I. Biz. Freetown, Sierra Leone, 1980-88. Author: (books) Echo ofIslam, 1978, Macay Image, 1982. Constituency organizer Nat. Dem. Congress Polit. Party of Ghana, 1992-96. Recipient B.O.I.R. C. of C., Eng., 1979. Mem. Meridian Club. Islam. Avocations: reading, travel, athletics. Office: El-Mamun Enterprise, PO Box AO 182, Kumasi Ashanti, Ghana, West Africa

JAFFÉ, ERNST RICHARD, medical educator and administrator; b. Chgo., Jan. 4, 1925; s. Richard Hermann and Berta (Kohn) J.; m. Anne Jane Sylvestre, Aug. 5, 1950; children: Stephanie Anne Green, Richard Sheridan Jaffé. BS, U. Chgo., 1945, MD, 1948, MS in Pathology, 1948; DHL (hon.), Yeshiva U., 1987. Diplomate Am. Bd. Internal Medicine, Hematology, Nat. Bd. Med. Examiners; lic. physician, N.Y. Intern Med. Presbyn. Hosp., N.Y.C., 1948-50, resident, 1953-55; postdoctoral fellow Albert Einstein Coll. of Medicine, Bronx, N.Y., 1955-57, instr., asst. prof., 1957-62, assoc. prof., 1962-69, prof. medicine, 1969-84, acting dean, 1972-74, 83-84, sr. assoc. dean, 1974-83, 84-91, disting. univ. prof. medicine, 1984-92, disting. univ. prof. medicine emeritus, 1992—; mem. hematology study sect. Nat. Inst. Health, Bethesda, Md., 1972-82, Hirschl Sci. Adv. Com. I.T. Hirschl Trust, N.Y.C., 1974-92, N.Y. Community Trust Blood Disease Panel, N.Y.C., 1978-97; dir. Belfer Inst. for Advanced Biomed. Studies, 1978-92. Co-editor Seminars in Hematology, 1968-2000, co-editor emeritus, 2000—; editor-in-chief Blood, 1975-77; contbr. articles to profl. jours. Nat. bd. govs. ARC, Washington, 1984-90, chmn. blood svcs. com., 1988-90; bd. dirs. Nat. Marrow Donor Program, 1987-2000; bd. dirs. Henry M. and Lillian Stratton Found., 1985-96, pres., 1989-96; trustee Bergen Cmty. Regional Blood Ctr., 1997-2000 . With U.S. Army, 1944-46; capt. USAF, 1951-53. Named Career Scientist, Health Rsch. Coun.; recipient Charles R. Drew award ARC, 1990. Fellow Internat. Soc. Hematology (counselor 1980-88, v.p. 1984-88, historian 1990—); mem. Am. Soc. Hematology (pres. 1983, historian 1993—), Assn. Am. Physicians, Am. Fedn. Clin. Rsch., Am. Soc. Clin. Investigation, Am. Physiol. Soc., Assn. Am. Med. Colls. (emeritus), Coun. Acad. Socs. (adminstrv. bd. 1985-90, chmn. 1989), N.Y. Soc. Study Blood (pres. 1978-80), Soc. for Exptl. Biology and Medicine (pres. 1993-95, past pres. 1995-97), U. Chgo. Alumni Assn. (Profl. Achievement citation 1992), U. Chgo. Med. Alumni Assn. (Disting. Svc. award 1981), Phi Beta Kappa, Sigma Xi, Alpha Omega Alpha. Lutheran. Avocations: philately, photography, reading. Office: Albert Einstein Coll Medicine 1300 Morris Park Ave Bronx NY 10461-1926

JAFFE, EVAN, rabbi; b. Balt., Jan. 3, 1953; s. Marvin and Carolyn J.; m. Phyllis Lerner, June 6, 1982; children: Jordana Tatiana, Atara. BA, Columbia U., 1982; MA, Jewish Theol. Sem. Am., N.Y.C., 1987. Ordained rabbi, 1987. Rabbi Flemington (N.J.) Jewish Cmty. Ctr., 1987—; chaplain Hunterdon Devel. Ctr., Clinton, N.J., 1990—, Greenbrook (N.J.) Regional Ctr., 1992—, Edna Mahon Correctional Ctr., Clinton, 1998—, Hagedorn Geriatric Ctr., Glen Gardner, N.J., 1990-96; pres. Women's Crisis Svcs., Flemington, 1994-95; bd. dirs. Jewish Family Svcs., Somerville, N.J., 1996—. Author: Illustrated Dictionary of Ballet, 1980. Avocations: jogging, playing recorder, skiing. Home: 51 Coppermine Vlg Flemington NJ 08822-1570

JAFFE, FREDRICK F., surgeon; b. N.Y.C., June 3, 1942; s. David A. and Mildred C. (Leibner) J.; m. Mary E. Mark, June 14, 1964 (div. Dec. 1994); children: David, Harry; m. Deborah L. Moody, Nov. 5, 1995. BS, Tufts U., 1964, MD, 1968. Diplomate Am. Bd. Orthopedic Surgery. Surg. intern N.Y. Hosp., N.Y.C., 1968-69, surg. fellow, 1969-70; orthopedic resident Hosp. for Joint Diseases, N.Y.C., 1970-73, fellow, 1973-74, attending orthopedic surgeon, 1974—, chief adult reconstructive surgeon, 1991-94; attending orthopedic surgeon Beth Israel Med. Ctr., N.Y.C., 1994—, chief adult reconstructive surgery Singer Divsn., 1994-96, sect. chief hip svc. Singer Divsn., 1997—; dir. Insall, Scott, Kelley Inst. for Orthopaedics and Sports Medicine, N.Y.C., 1994—. Fellow Am. Acad. Orthopedic Surgery, ACS, Am. Assn. Hip and Knee Surgeons, N.Y. Acad. Medicine; mem. Orthopaedic Rsch. Soc., Ea. Orthopedic Assn., N.Y. State Orthopedic Assn. Avocations: sailing, skiing, scuba diving, tennis, photography. E-mail: kneehipmde@aol.com. Fax: 212-759-5332. Office: 401 E 55th St New York NY 10022-4103

JAFFE, JAY M., company executive, management consultant; b. Chgo., Nov. 23, 1943; s. Jules S. and Reva Goodman Jaffe; 1 child, Sara. Reporter, bus. editor Augusta (Ga.) Chronicle, 1967-69; pub. rels. dir. U. Hosp., Augusta, 1969-70; editor, pub. Columbia News, Martinez, Ga., 1970-72; news dir. WRDW-TV, Augusta, 1972-75; asst. staff dir., house ethics com. U.S. Ho. Reps., Washington, 1975-79; pres., CEO Jaffe Assocs., Washington, 1979—. Dir., com. chair Greater Washington Bd. Trade, 1979-90; dir. Nat. Press Club Bldg., Washington, 1992-98. Cpl. U.S. Army, 1964-67. Avocations: skiing, fishing. E-mail: jaffej@get-serious.com. Fax: 301-881-6993. Home: 10932 Wickshire Way Rockville MD 20852-3221

JAFFE, JEFF HUGH, retired food products executive; b. Washington, Dec. 25, 1920; s. Henry A. Jaffe and Mildred (Loewenberg) Auslander; m. Natalie Rubin, Dec. 31, 1945; children: Bonita Jaffe Berens, Holly Anne. BS in Archtl. Engring., Va. Poly. Inst. and State U., 1943. Chmn. bd. dirs., pres. The Chunky Corp. (now Ward Candy, Inc.), 1950-69; pres., CEO candy, chocolate and biscuit group Ward Foods Inc., 1969-71, pres., COO, 1971-72; also bd. dirs. Ward Foods, Inc., 1972-74; chmn. bd. dirs., pres. Schutter Candy Co., 1958-67, Klotz Confection Co., 1960-67; pres., CEO The Schrafft Candy Co., 1974-78; v.p. consumer products group Gulf and Western Industries, 1974-78; pres., CEO Bernan Foods, Inc., 1980-85, ret., 1985; bd. dirs. Community Nat. Bank of S.I., N.Y., Ward Foods, Inc., Ward Candy Co., Oxford Energy Co.; guest lectr. Harvard Bus. Sch., 1970-84. Bd. dirs. Young Pres.'s Orgn., Woodmere Acad., Village Hewlett Bay Park (past chmn. and pres.). Mem. Assn. Mfrs. of Confectionery and Chocolate (past chmn.), Candy Execs. Club, Property Owners Assn. (Sailfish Point, Fla., chmn. transition com., chmn. emeritus, CEO). Home: 6500 SE Harbor Cir Stuart FL 34996-1952

JAFFE, KATHARINE WEISMAN, retired librarian; b. Cambridge, Mass., Apr. 27, 1927; d. Maurice and Esther (Feinberg) W.; m. Myron I. Jaffe, Dec. 18, 1949; children: Stephen Philip, Jane Elizabeth J. Martin, Samuel Morris. AB in Am. Civilization, Colby Coll., 1948; MS in Libr. Sci., Simmons Coll., 1952. Asst. children's libr. Boston Pub. Libr., 1948-51; libr. Mishkan Tefila Synagogue, Newton, Mass., 1955-58, Temple Emmanuel, Newton, 1958-59; reserve libr. Brandeis U., Waltham, Mass., 1960-62; reference libr., archives libr. Boston Coll., 1963-75; vol. libr. and archives libr. Berkshire Hist. Soc., Pittsfield, Mass., 1994-96; chairperson Friends of Libr., New Marlborough, Mass., 1978-94. Libr. rep. to design referenc and Atrium New Libr. Boston Coll., 1973-75; founding chair bookstore Brandeis Women's Com., Noami Lodge, 1950-75; book group leader, organizer, 1955-75; edn. chair South and Ctrl. Berkshire chpt. LWV, 1994-96, 97—, pres. 1996-97, mem. governing bd.; docent Edith Wharton Home, Mount Lenox, 1988-92. Democrat. Jewish. Avocations: reading mysteries and U.S. and international politics, travel. Home: PO Box 113 144 Brewer Hill Mill River MA 01244

JAFFE, SUSAN, ballerina; b. Washington. Student, Md. Sch. Ballet; student, Sch. Am. Ballet, Am. Ballet Theatre Sch. With Am. Ballet Theatre II, 1978-80; with Am. Ballet Theatre, 1980—, soloist, 1981-83, prin., 1983—. Repertoire includes: Le Corsaire, Apollo, La Bayadere, Bouree Fantastique, Carmen, Cinderella, Concerto, Duets, Giselle, The Guards of Amager, Push Comes to Shove, Symphonie Concertante, Ballet Imperial, Coppelia, Etudes, Giselle, Jardin auxLilas, Romeo and Juliet, The Sleeping Beauty, Other Dances, Theme and Variations, Swan Lake, La Sylphide, Undertow, Voluntaries, Dim Lustre, Manon, Gala Performance, Don Quioxte, Cruel World, Sextet, The Snow Maiden, Fall River Legend, Grande Pas Classic, Stepping Stones, Anastasia, others; created role Lynne Taylor-Corbett's Great Galloping Gottschalk, Bruch Violin Concerto No. 1, Serious Pleasures; appeared Spoleto in An Evening of Jerome Robbins Ballets, 1982, Known by Heart (Twyla Tharp); appeared with Kirov Ballet, 1988; guest appearances with The Royal Swedish Ballet, The Royal Danish Ballet, The English Nat. Ballet, La Scala Ballet, Milan, 1997, 98, The Royal Ballet, 1998, Stuttgart Ballet, 1998, The Munich Opera Ballet, The Vienna State Opera Ballet. Recipient N.Y. Woman-Lancome Paris Woman of Yr. award, 1989. Office: Am Ballet Theatre 890 Broadway 3d Fl New York NY 10003-1211

JAFFE, WILLIAM J(ULIAN), industrial engineer, educator; b. Passaic, N.J., Mar. 22, 1910; S. Elias and Ida (Rosensohn) J. BS in Math and Physics, NYU, 1930; MA in Math., Columbia U., 1931, MS in Indsl. Engring., 1941; ScD in Engring., NYU, 1953. Registered profl. engr., Calif. Cons. engring. math. pvt. practice, 1931-41, 45—; naval architect U.S. Navy Phila. Naval Yard, 1941-45; from instr. to disting. prof. N.J. Inst. Tech., Newark Coll. Engring., 1946-75, disting. prof. emeritus, 1975—; mem. bd. standards rev. Am. Nat. Standards Inst., N.Y.C., 1981-89; adj. prof. NYU Grad. Coll. Engring., 1953-54; mem. Clark bd. internat. mgmt. Com. de l'Orgn. Scientifique, 1957-60, chmn. Clark bd., 1960; vis. prof. Sangyo Nohritsu Diagaku, Sanno Inst. Mgmt., Tokyo, 1960. Author: L.P. Alford: Evolution of Modern Industrial Management, (with Lillian M. Gilbreth) Management's Past: A Guide to Its Future; editor: Industrial Engineering Terminology; contbr. numerous articles to profl. jours. Fellow AAAS (coun.), ASME (bd. standardization, codes and standards ednl. commn., Dedicated Svc. award, Centennial award), Inst. Indsl. Engrs., N.Y. Acad. Medicine (chmn. biomed. engring. sect.), Soc. for Advancement of Mgmt.; mem. Am. Math. Soc. (hon., life). Home: 1175 York Ave Apt 9E New York NY 10021-7173

JAFFRÉ, ERIC, financier; b. Paris, France, Apr. 2, 1956; s. Denis and Marcelle (Clavel) J. Degree in Finance, Arts et Metiers, Paris, 1996. Financier Etabtinement Public pom l'Amenagement de la Defense, Paris la de Fense, 1988—. Roman Cath. Avocation: books. Home: Tour Eve 1911 Place du Sud, 92800 Puteaux France

JAFFRIN, MICHEL YVES, biomedical engineer, educator, consultant; b. Nice, France, June 11, 1938; s. Louis Rene and Mireille (Nataf) J.; m. Nicole Monique Lespinasse, Aug. 1, 1960; children: Stefan, Manuel. Degree in aero. engring., Ecole Nationale Superieure d Aeronautique, Paris, 1960; PhD in Engring., Brown U., 1964; PhD, U. Paris VI, 1976. Rsch. engr. Alcatel Alstom, Marcoussis, 1966-67; prof. MIT, Cambridge, 1967-73; maitre de confs. Ecole Polytechnique, Paris, 1984-96; prof. U. Compiegne, 1973—; sci. coun. Nat. Ctr. for Sci. Rsch., Paris, 1989-91; hon. vis. prof. U. NSW, Sydney, 1984; sr. mem. Inst. Universitaire de France, 1997—. Editor: Biological Flows, 1996, Biomechanics of Fluids and Tissues, Masson, 1998, Cardiovascular and Pulmonary Dynamics, 1977; mem. editl. bd. Jour. Med. Engring. and Physics, Jour. Biomed. Engring., Jour. Biomechanics, others; contbr. over200 articles to profl. jours.; patentee in field. Lt. French Air Force, 1965-66. Mem. European Soc. Artificial Organs (gov. 1992—), Soc. Biomechanics (pres. 1995-97), Internat. Soc. Artificial Organs. Avocations: skiing, photography. E-mail: michel.jaffrin@utc.fr. Office: U Compiegne Dept Biological, Engring BP 20529, 60205 Compiegne France

JAFREE, MOHAMMED JAWAID IQBAL See GEOFFREY, IQBAL

JAGA, KUSHIK, medical researcher; b. Johannesburg, South Africa, Feb. 20, 1960; came to the U.S., 1994; p. Vallabh and Jesmine Jaga. MB, BChir, Mangalore U., Manipal, India, 1988; postgrad. diploma occupl. health, U. Witwatersrand, Johannesburg, 1993; MPH, N.Y. Med. Coll., 1998. Med. diplomate. Sr. med. officer Nat. Ctr. for Occupl. Health, Johannesburg, 1990-94; rsch. asst. dept. infectious diseases Westchester Med. Ctr., Valhalla, N.Y., 1996; rschr. dept. trauma Westchester Med. Ctr., Valhalla, 1998—; adminstrv. asst. Admissions's Office N.Y. Med. Coll., Valhalla, 1997; cons. Nat. Ctr. for Occupl. Health, Johannesburg, 1990-94. Contbr. articles to profl. jours. Mem. Am. Pub. Health Orgn., South African Med. and Dental Coun., Karnataka State Med. Coun. India. Hindu. Avocations: music, arts, cooking, swimming, reading. E-mail: kushik jaga@nymc.edu. Home: 31 S Stone Ave # 2 Elmsford NY 10523-3611 Office: Westchester Med Ctr Dept Trauma 100 Grasslands Rd Valhalla NY 10595-1612

JAGABANDHU, MALATI, radiologist; b. Poona, India, Oct. 14, 1942; d. Kasturi and Devaki Pangan; m. Nandyala Jagabandhu (dec.); 1 child, Sridaar. B Medicine and Surgery, U. New Delhi, 1965, AB in Radiology, 1975. Pvt. practice radiology Madras, India, 1976—; cons. radiologist, Madras; chief Vijaya Hosp., Madras, 1976—. Avocations: reading, music, meditation. Home: 56/6 Luz Church Rd, Chennai Mylapore 60004, India

JAGACINSKI, CAROLYN MARY, psychology educator; b. Orange, N.J., Apr. 12, 1949; d. Theodore Edward and Eleanor Constance (Thys) Jagacinski; m. Richard Justus Schweickert, Dec. 27, 1980; children: Patrick, Kenneth. AB with honors in psychology, Bucknell U., 1971; MA in Psychology, U. Mich., 1975, PhD in Psychology and Edn., 1978. Rsch. assoc. U. Mich., Ann Arbor, 1978-79; rsch. assoc. Purdue U., West Lafayette, Ind., 1979-80, vis. asst. prof., 1980-83, rsch. psychologist, 1983-86, vis. lectr., 1986-88, asst. dean, 1988-89, asst. prof. psychology, 1988-94, assoc. prof., 1994—. Contbr. articles to profl. jours. U. Mich. predoctoral fellow, 1977-78, dissertation grantee, 1977-78; Exxon Edn. Found. grantee, 1983-84. Mem. APA, Midwestern Psychol. Assn., Soc. for Judgment and Decision Making, Am. Ednl. Rsch. Assn., Psychonomic Soc., Sigma Xi, Psi Chi. Avocations: tennis, reading. Office: Purdue Univ Dept Psychol Scis West Lafayette IN 47907

JAGAN, DEREK CHUNILALL, barrister; b. Port Mourant, Berbice, Guyana, May 25, 1930; s. Jagan and Bachaoni Jagan; m. Roshenara Gajraj, Oct. 20, 1962; children: Renita Savita Sullivan, Brian Arvind. Degree of Utter Bar, Hon. Soc. of Mid. Temple, London, 1956. Lic. barrister. Mem. gen. coun. People's Progressive Party PPP, Guyana, 1958-73, mem. nat. assembly, 1961-73, mem. exec. coun., 1965-73; dep. spkr. Nat. Assembly, Guyana, 1971-73, mem. Police Svc. Commn., 1987-92, spkr., 1992—; v.p. Amazonian Parliament, S.Am., 1993—; mem. adv. com. Nat. Ins. Scheme, Guyana, 1975-78; exec. mem. Legal Practitioners, Guyana, 1971-80; mem. rules com. Supreme Ct., Guyana, 1982-92; conf. participant Commonwealth Parliamentary Assn., Jamaica, 1964, Trinidad and Tobago, 1969, 1999, Malyasia, 1996, Mauritus, 1997, New Zealand, 1998; participant conf. on strenghtening of civil soc. Inter Am. Devel. Bank, Washington, 1994. Contbr. articles to profl. jours. Named Commn. of Oaths, Guyana, 1970, Justice of Peace, 1970, Sr. Counsel, 1991, Notary Pub., 1993, Cacique Crown of Honour, 1996, Order of Roraima, 2000. Mem. Guyana Bar Assn., Everest Cricket club, Georgetown Cricket Club, GeorgetownClub. Mem. People's Progressive Party. Avocation: cricket. Home: 356 East St, Georgetown Guyana Office: Lot 1 Croal St, Georgetown Guyana

JAGAN, JANET, retired president of Republic of Guyana; b. Chgo., Oct. 20, 1920; d. Charles and Kathryn Roberts; m. Cheddi Jagan, Aug. 5, 1943; children: Cheddi Jr., Nadira. Student, U. Detroit, 1938-39, Wayne U., Detroit, 1939-40, Mich. State Coll., 1940-42, Cook County Sch. Nursing, Chgo., 1942-43. Editor Thunder, 1950-57; dep. speaker House Assembly, 1953, min. labour, health & housing, 1957-61, min. home affairs, 1963-64; editor Mirror Newspaper, 1973-97; prime min., first v.p., elected pres. Republic of Guyana, 1997-99. Author: History of the People's Progressive Party, 1963, The Struggle of the People's Progressive Party for Guyana's Independence, 1966, Army Intervention in 1973 Elections in Guyana, 1973, 2d edit., 1974, An Examination of National Service, 1974, also 5 books of children's stories. M.P., 1953, 57-61, 63-64, 76-97; mem. Election Com., 1967-68; mem. Georgetown City Coun., 1950; chmn. Commn. on the Rights of the Child, 1993-97. Named One of Outstanding Women of Yr., U. Guyana, 1989; recipient Order of Liberator Simon Bolivar, Venezuela, Order of Excellence, Republic of Guyana, Gold medal for Peace, Democracy and Women's Rights, UNESCO, 1997. Mem. Union Guyanese Journalists (pres.), Women's Progresive Orgn. (pres. 1970—), People Progressive Party (gen. sec. 1950-70, internat. sec. 1970-84, exec. sec. 1984-91, exec. com.). Avocation: writing children's stories. Home: 65 Pln Bel Air, Georgetown Demerara, Guyana

JAGANNATH, PALEPU, oncologic surgeon; b. Visakhaptnam, India, Jan. 13, 1956; s. Haranath and Savithri Palepu; m. Gouri, Nov. 18, 1983; children: Sowmya, Meghana. MB, BChir, S.V. U., Kurnool, India, 1978; MS, Madras U., 1992. From jr. resident to surgeon Tata Meml. Hosp., Bombay, India, 1982—; cons. in field. Fellow ACS, Internat. Coll. Surgeons, Internat. Med. Sci. Acad.; mem. Nat. Acad. Med. Scis., Assn. Surgeons India, Assn. Gastroenterology, Indian Soc. Oncology, Indian Soc. Study of Liver, Internat. Hepatobiliary Assn. Avocations: swimming, table tennis, gymnastics, art, reading. Home: Flat 22 Alka Plot G-615, 15th Rd Santacruz (W), Bombay 400 054, India Office: Tata Meml Hosp Dept Surgery, Tata Meml Hosp Surg Oncolog, E borges Marg Parel, 400 012 Bombay India

JAGANNATHAN, SESHADRI, chemist; b. Madras, Tamil Nadu, India, July 27, 1960; came to U.S., 1981; s. Srinivasan and Champa (Desikachari) J. BS, Bangalore U., India, 1981; MS, Clarkson U., 1985, PhD, 1987. Postdoctoral fellow U. Conn., Storrs, 1986-87, U. Calif., Riverside, 1987-88; rsch. assoc. U. Pitts., 1988-92; sr. rsch. scientist Eastman Kodak Co., Rochester, N.Y., 1992-98, rsch. assoc., 1998—; mem. phys. chemistry delegation to People's Rep. of China, Citizen Amb. Program People-to-People, Spokane, Wash., 1996. Patentee in field. Rsch. grantee NSF, U. Calif., Riverside, 1988. Mem. Am. Chem. Soc., Gamma Sigma Epsilon, Sigma Xi. Avocation: yoga. Office: Rsch Labs/Eastman Kodak Co 1999 Lake Ave Rochester NY 14650-0001

JÄGER, JÜRGEN, research engineer; b. Laufenburg, Baden, Germany, Dec. 31, 1955; s. Klaus and Hildegard (Lapat) J. Diploma in engring., U. Karlsruhe, Germany, 1979; PhD, U. Delft, The Netherlands, 1992. Asst. U. Karlsruhe, 1980-85; engr. Industriewerke Karlsruhe Augsburg, Karlsruhe, 1986-90; ind. rschr. Germany, 1990-98; rsch. engr. Ingenieurbüro für Awendungen im Maschinenbau, Erlangen, Germany, 1998—. Contbr. over 25 articles to profl. publs., including Jour. Applied Mechanics, Engring. Fracture Mechanics, others. Home: Blattwiesenstr 7, 76227 Karlsruhe Germany Office: IBAMA, Goerdelerstr 8, 91058 Erlangen Germany

JÄGER, LUDWIG, philology educator; b. Homburg/Saar, Germany, Oct. 24, 1943; s. Karl and Anna-Maria (Schappo) J.; m. Cornelia Epping, Dec. 6, 1986. MA, U. Heidelberg (Germany), 1969; PhD, U. Düsseldorf (Germany), 1975, Habilitation, 1978. Rsch. asst. U. Düsseldorf, 1975-79, asst. prof., 1979-82; vis. prof. Rheinisch Westfälische Tech. Hochschule, Aachen, Germany, 1979, 80-82; prof. humanities, PhD Rheinisch Westfälische Tech. Hochschule, Aachen, 1982—, head German dept., 1982-84, dean Faculty Humanities, 1985-87; co-dir. spl. rsch. br. Sonderforschungsbereich/Forschungskolleg 427, Cologne, Germany, 1999. Author: On the Historical Semantics of German Emotional Words, 1988, German Studies in the Media Society, 1994, Changeover: The Case of Schneider/Schwerte and the Discretion of the Field of German Studies, 1998. Head Deutscher Germanistenverband Frankfurt am Main, 1991-94. Mem. Cercle Ferdinand de Saussure, Inst. Deutsche Sprache. Office: Lehrstuhl Deutsche Philol, Germanistisches Inst RWTH, 52062 Aachen Germany

JÄGER, MANFRED WALTER, paleontologist; b. Eimbeckhausen, Germany, May 3, 1954; m. Elke Langstein, Nov. 9, 1989. Grad., Tech. U. Hannover, Germany, 1979, D of Natural Scis., 1983. Sci. collaborator Bodensee-Naturmuseum, Konstanz, Germany, 1982-87; mus. custodian Fossilienmuseum im Werkforum, Dotternhausen, Germany, 1988—. Contbr. articles to profl. jours. Mem. Paleontology Soc. (mem. adv. bd. 1987-89), Natural History Soc., Deutscher Museumsbund. Office: Fossilienmuseum Werkforum, Rohrbach Zement, D-72359 Dotternhausen Germany

JÄGER-ZÜRN, IRMGARD FLORA, botanist, researcher; b. Tetschen, Czechoslovakia, May 29, 1936; d. Rudolf and Irmtraut Flora (Reiniger) Jäger; m. Herbert Erich Dieter Zürn, Apr. 19, 1963; children: Jörg Tilmann, Veit Rüdiger. PhD, U. Vienna, Austria, 1962. Lectr., sci. asst. U. Heidelberg, Germany, 1962-67; ind. rscher. Madras, India, 1967-71, König-

stein, Germany, 1986—. Contbr. numerous articles to profl. publs. Mem. governing body Regional Protestant Ch., Synode, 1990—. Avocations: home, freehand drawing. Address: Hainerbergweg 61, D-61462 Königstein Germany

JAGGERNAUTH, RABINDRA, management consultant; b. San Fernando, West Indies, June 26, 1955; s. Satnarayan and Samadai (Arjoon) J.; m. Jacinta Therese Chin Aleong, Aug. 17, 1985; children: Justin, Ryan. B of Math., U. Waterloo, Ontario, Can., 1979; MSc, U. Aston, Birmingham, Eng., 1982. Dir. trade info. ctr. Export Devel. Corp., Port of Spain, Trinidad, 1985-89; dir. Ernst & Young Cons. Ltd., Port of Spain, Trinidad, 1990-95; ptnr. Ernst & Young, Port of Spain, Trinidad, 1995—; mgr. KPMG Peat Marwick, Port of Spain, 1987-90; dir. JCA Optical Lted., Diego Martin, Trinidad, 1990—. Bd. dirs. Rotary, 1993. Recipient Gold medal Duke of Edinburgh Award Scheme, Trinidad and Tobago, 1973, Queens Scout award Scout Assn. Trinidad and Tobago, 1973. Mem. British Computer Soc., Info. Tech. Profl. Soc. (pres.), Info. Systems Audit and Control Assn, Inst. of Cert. Mgmt. Cons. Avocations: cricket, camping, hiking. Office: Ernst & Young, PO Box 158 53-55 Abercromby St, Port of Spain Trinidad and Tobago

JAGIRDAR, MOHD IQBAL YASZNKHAN, foreign language educator; b. Dgadag, Karnatak, India, Mar. 8, 1944; s. Yasinkhan Walikhan and Hajra Yasinkhan Jagirdar; m. Qamartaj Abdul Majid Mulla, Dec. 29, 1969; three children. BA, Karnatak (India) U., 1969, MA in Hindi, 1971, MA in Urdu, 1973, diploma English-Hindi translation, 1979. Lectr. J.G. Commerce Coll., Hubli, India, 1971-72, A.U.C.J. Coll., Hubli, 1972-77; prof. Poona Coll., Maharashtrar, 1977—. Mem. All India Translator's Bd., Poona U. Tchrs. Assn. Avocations: reading English Hindi Urdu literature, traveling, friendship. Home: Flat 1 Godavari Society, Near Sadhna Bank, Ghorpadigaon Pune 411001, India Office: Hindi Dept Poona Coll, Camp Area, Pune 411001, India

JAGLAND, THORBJØRN, member of parliament; b. Drammen, Norway, Nov. 5, 1950; m. Hanne Grotjord, 1975; 2 children. Exec. sec. Norwegian Labour League Youth, 1977-81; project and planning officer Norwegian Labour Party, 1981-86, acting gen. sec., 1986, gen. sec., 1987, chair, 1992—, mem. Parliament, chmn. Parliamentary Caucus, 1993-96, 97—; prime min. Govt. Norway, 1996-97; v.p. The Socialist Internat., 1999—; chmn. standing com. on fgn. affairs Govt. Norway, 2000, min. fgn. affairs, 2000—; chmn. Middle-East com. Socialist Internat., 2000—. Author: Min europeiske drøm, 1990, Ny solidaritet, 1993, Brev, 1995; co-author: For det blir for sent, 1982; contbr. articles to newspapers and profl. jours. Office: Ministry Fgn Affairs, PO Box 8114 Dep, 0032 Oslo 1, Norway

JAGSCH, ALBERT, biologist, researcher; b. Linz, Austria, May 17, 1947; s. Leopold and Franziska (Eibl) J.; m. Waltraud Maria Elisabeth Albert, July 21, 1972; 1 child, Viktor. PhD, Karl Franzens U., Graz, Austria, 1972. Cert. biologist. Asst. Fed. Inst. Fisheries, Scharfling, Austria, 1972-87, dir., 1987—; lectr. U. Salzburg, 1979—. Editor: Jour. Oesterreichs Fischerei, 1984—. Mem. Austrian Fisheries Assn. (mgr. 1975-87), Austrian Soc. Environ. Protection (mem. exec. com. 1976—), Am. Fisheries Soc. Home and Office: Fed Inst Water Ecology, Fisheries, Biology & Lake Rsch, Scharfling 18, A-5310 Mondsee Austria

JAGTAP, KRISHNA KONDIRAM, economics educator; b. Yeola, Nashik, India, July 26, 1964; s. Kondiram Sudam and Jankabai Kondiram Jagtap; m. Shindu Sambjl Bansode, May 5, 1991; 1 child, Kum Kirti Krishna. MA, S.S.G.M. Coll., Kopargaon, India, 1997. Lectr. K.S.S. Instn. Sataru, 1988-89. Social worker, reporter R.P.I., Maharashtra, 1985. Mem. Deambedkur Edn. Soc. (dir. 1985). Home: Hudcco Colony, 191/151 Ybola, Yeola India Office: Arts & Com Coll, Mokhada Dist Therue, Mokhadu Konken, India

JAGTIANI, RAM ALIMCHAND, investment counselor; b. Hyderabad, Sind, India, Dec. 11, 1936; arrived in Hong Kong, 1948; s. Alim P. and Sawitri A. (Savitri) J.; m. Roma R. Jagtiani, Aug. 1, 1963; children: Ranjeev R., Neesha R. Student, St. Joseph's Coll., Hong Kong, 1955, Pitman Exam Inst., Hong Kong, 1956. Mng. dir. Alimsons & Co., Ltd., Hong Kong, 1956-87; ptnr. United Stock Brokers, Hong Kong, 1970; agt. Transamerica Occidental Life, Hong Kong, 1960-79, gen. agt., 1980—; mng. dir. Ram A. Jagtiani, Ltd., Hong Kong, 1982—. Mem. Million Dollar Round Table (life), Nat. Assn. Life Underwriters, Life Underwriters Assn. of Hong Kong, Royal Hong Kong Golf Club, Hong Kong Country Club, Royal Hong Kong Jockey Club, Indian Club, Nav Bharat Club, Kowloon Cricket Club, Rotary, Shriners. Avocations: tennis, squash, snooker, coin collecting. Home: C2 12/F Fairland Gdns, 7 Homantin Hill Rd, Kowloon Hong Kong Office: Transamerica Occidental, 6 Hennessy Rd 6/F1 Sincere Ins Bldg, 1001 Wanchai Hong Kong

JAHAN, FERDOUSE, research scientist; b. Rajshahi, Bangladesh, Nov. 17, 1957; arrived in Australia, 1996; d. Fazlul Haque and Aysha Begum; m. Mohammed Hedayetul Islam, July 15, 1983; three children. BSc with honors, Rajshahi U., Bangladesh, 1979, MSc, 1982; PhD, Brunel U., London, 1988. Scientist Atomic Energy Commn., Bangladesh, 1983; lectr. Rajshahi U., Bangladesh, 1983-86, asst. prof., 1987-91, assoc. prof., 1991-95; rsch. fellow U. Tech., Sydney, Australia, 1996-97; scientist Commonwealth Sci. & Indsl. Rsch. Orgn., Sydney, 1998—. Contbr. articles to profl. jours. Recipient Gold medal Pres. Bangladesh, 1975; Commonwealth scholar Assn. Commonwealth Univs., U.K., 1983. Mem. Australian Inst. Physics, Inst. Physics U.K., Phys. Soc. Bangladesh. Avocations: reading books and journals, listening to music, playing indoor games, dress making. Office: CSIRO Divsn Telecom, Bradfield Rd West Lindfield, Sydney NSW 2070, Australia

JAHANGIR, ARSHAD, cardiologist; b. Karachi, Sind, Pakistan, Nov. 12, 1960; s. G. Ashraf and Sabra Bilquis J.; m. Huma A. Khan, Nov. 9, 1991; children: Ahad A., Imaan A. MBBS, U. Karachi, 1986. Diplomat Am. Bd. Internal Medicine, Cardiology and Cardiac. Cardiologist, cardiac electrophysiologist Mayo Clinic, Rochester, Minn., 1997—. Contbr. articles to profl. jours. Avocations: photography, art and music, travel. E-mail: jahangir.arshad@mayo.edu. Office: Mayo Clinic 200 1st St SW Rochester MN 55905-0001

JAHIEL, RENE INO, physician; b. Boulogne, Seine, France, Mar. 29, 1928; s. Richard and Cecile (Lwovsky) J.; m. Deborah Berg, May 8, 1955; children: Abigail, Richard, Beth. BA, NYU, 1946; MD, SUNY (Downstate Med. Coll.), Bklyn., 1950; PhD, Columbia U., 1957. Intern Montefiore Hosp., N.Y.C., 1950-51; resident Mt. Sinai Hosp., N.Y.C., 1952, fellow in virology, 1952-55; exptl. immunologist Nat. Jewish Hosp., Denver, 1957-59; asst. attending pathologist, exptl. pathology Mt. Sinai Hosp., 1959-61; asst. prof. pub. health cornell U. Med. Coll., Ithaca, N.Y., 1961-66; rsch. assoc. prof. preventive medicine NYU, N.Y.C., 1967-70, rsch. prof., 1970-76, rsch. prof. medicine, Sch. Medicine, 1976-88; cons. health svcs. rsch., policy and planning, 1989—; adj. prof. health svcs., rsch. and policy New Sch. for Social Rsch., 1991-96; dean faculty of sci. and pub. health, Ecole Libre des Hautes Etudes of N.Y., 1991-94, v.p. scis., 1994—; vis. prof. dept. cmty. medicine and healthcare, U. Conn. Health Ctr., 1995—; pres. Internat. Health Policy Rsch. Corp., N.Y.C., 1995—; med. dir. Southbury (Conn.) Tng. Sch., 1993-95; med. cons. State of Conn. Dept. Mental Retardation, 1996-97; tchr. met. leadership program, U. Coll., NYU, 1969-73; physician Assn. for Help for Retarded Children, 1982-88, Young Adult Inst., 1984-89, Assn. for Children with Retarded Mental Devel., 1988-93; cons. Nat. Ctr. for Health Svcs. Rsch., 1983-85; bd. dirs. N.Y. Scientists Com. Pub. Info., 1974-79, Physicians Forum, 1975-84. Author sci. rsch. articles on tissue culture, virology, interferon, preventive medicine, health policy, health svcs. rsch., homelessness, sociology of knowledge: editor: Homelessness: A Prevention-Oriented Approach, 1992. Mem. interferon adv. com. Am. Cancer Soc., 1984-93; mem. nat. bd. Com. for Nat. Health Svc., 1976-79, coalition, 1980-85. Lt. USNR, 1955-57. Grantee USPHS, 1966-79. Mem. APHA (chmn. com. health svcs. rsch. 1980-87, governing coun. 1983-85, 99—, chmn. homelessness study group 1984-90, chmn. policy com. caucus on disablement 1989-92, founding chmn. caucus on homelessness 1990-91, Med. Care sect. award 1985, chmn. membership com. spl. interest group on disability 1993-97, chair 1998-99), Internat. Health Econs. Assn., Internat. Assn. Health Policy (bd. dirs. 1998—), Physicians for Social Responsibility, Internat. Soc. Sys. Sci. Health Care, Assn. Health Svcs. Rsch. (Spl. Recognition award 1986), World Assn. for Psychosocial Rehab. (chmn. com. on mental handicaps 1992-94). Home: 24 Park Pl Apt 17K Hartford CT 06106-5027

JAHKOLA, KAARLO ANTERO, retired engineering educator; b. Korpilahti, Finland, Feb. 5, 1931; s. Kalle Ilmari and Ida Lydia (Kytönen) J.; m. Oili Orvokki Gustafsson, Apr. 18, 1954; children: Outi Helena, Juha Kaarlo. MSc in Engring., Tech. U. Helsinki, Finland, 1956; D in Engring. (hon.), Tech. U. Tallinn, Estonia, 1993. Planning engr. Imatran Voima, Helsinki, 1957-62; asst. dept. head Imatran Voima, 1963-74; prof. Tech. U. Helsinki, 1974-94. 2d lt. Finnish armed forces, 1956. Mem. Finnish Assn. Profs., Finnish Soc. Tech., Finnish Assn. Elec. Engrs., Finnish Acad. Technology, Estonian Acad. Scis., N.Y. Acad. Scis. Avocation: sailing.

JAHN, DIETER, biochemist, educator; b. Jesberg, Germany, Aug. 1, 1959; s. Werner and Anneliese (Wolf) J.; m. Martina Johanna Will, June 16, 1988; children: Christopher, Robert. Diploma, U. Marburg, 1984, Dr.rer.nat., 1987. Postdoctoral fellow U. Marburg, 1987-88, asst. prof., 1992-96; postdoctoral fellow Yale U., New Haven, 1988-92; prof. U. Freiburg, 1996-2000, U. Braunschweig, Germany, 2000—; cons. in field. Contbr. articles to profl. jours. Home: In Den Schoenen Morgen 14, 38300 Wolfenbuettel Germany Office: Inst Microbiology, Spiel Mannstr 7, 38106 Braunschweig Germany

JAHN, EGBERT KURT, social scientist, educator; b. Berlin, Germany, May 26, 1941; m. Brigitte Sigrid Amelung. PhD, Sch. Philosophy, Marburg, Germany, 1969. Asst. prof. U. Marburg, Germany, 1969-70; rschr. Peace Rsch. Inst., Frankfurt, Germany, 1970-76, rsch. dir., 1974-90; prof. U. Frankfurt, 1975-93, U. Mannheim, 1993—; guest prof. U. Copenhagen, Denmark, 1986-87, U. Calif., Irvine, 1988; dean Sch. Social Scis. U. Frankfurt, 1977-78, U. Mannheim, 1995-96; acting dir. Peace Rsch. Inst., Frankfurt, 1975-76, 81-82, chmn. 1977-79. Author: Die Deutschen in der Slowakei, 1971, Buerokratischer Sozialismus-Chancen der Demokratisierung?, 1982; editor: Soviet Foreign Policy, 1978, Elements of World Instability, 1981, European Security: Problems of Research on Non-Military Aspects, 1987, Issledorania problem mira vperiod i posle konflikta Vostok-Zapad, 1997, (seires) Studien zu Konflikt und Kooperation in Osten, 1994—. Mem. German Assn. Polit. Sci., German Peace Rsch. Assn., Internat. Peace Rsch. Assn. Office: U Mannheim, A5, 68131 Mannheim Germany

JAHN, JENS-EBERHARD P.W., sociologist, linguist, educator; b. Berlin, Germany, June 1, 1967; s. Paul Eberhard and Ingrid Irmgard Elsbeth (Beckmann) J.; m. Jutta Pistor, Feb. 20, 1998. MA, Freie U., Berlin, Germany, 1995. Asst. tchr. ITC Peano, Florence, Italy, 1989-90; asst. prof. pvt. schs., Berlin, Germany, 1990-95, U. Mannheim, Germany, 1998; customer svc. Santa Cruz Biotech., Inc., Heidelberg, Germany, 1998-99; asst. prof. U. Heidelberg, Germany, 1996—, pvt. and pub. schs., Heidelberg, Germany, 1998—; dons., organizer ICE, Dresden, Germany, 1999; translator, cons. Interdisciplinary Project Narcism, Berlin, Germany, 1988-90; interpreter City of Neuruppin, Germany, 1994. Translator: (poems) Narziss and Narzissmus, 1992; playwrite: Die Friesen, 1994; author: H. Boell: Glaubensgemeinschaft und Kirchl Institution, 1999; contbr. articles to profl. jours. Treas. IKUS, Berlin, Germany, 1993-99. Grantee DFG, Heidelberg, Germany, 1995-98. Mem. IKUS, Soc. for Engangered Langs., AG Ital. Geschichte. Roman Catholic. Avocations: canoeing, ethnology, cooking, gardening, literature. Home phone: 49 6224 929782. Home: Welfenallee 9/12, D-69181 Leimen Germany Office: IKUS, Koenigstr 15A, D-13589 Berlin Germany

JAHN, RENATE ELISABETH, surgeon; b. Luebeck, Germany, July 10, 1946; d. Willy Georg and Elisabeth Maria (Lange) Steltner; m. Wilfried Andreas Jahn, July 17, 1946; 1 child, Kjell. Diploma in nursing, St. Georg Hosp., Leipzig, Germany, 1966; MD, Karl-Marx-U., Leipzig, 1972. Specialist edn. Leipzig, 1972-74, specialist edn. surgery, 1974-78, specialist in surgery, 1978-81; specialist in surgery Bad Oldesloe, Germany, 1981-83, BE Klinik, Hamburg, Germany, 1983-89; specialist in accident surgery U. Hamburg, 1990—, lectr. in surgery, 1991—, head working accident surgery laser rsch., 1990—; lectr. in field, 1991—; mem. sci. com. Jour. Laser in Medicine and Surgery, 1990. Contbr. numerous articles to profl. jours.; author videos, posters in field. Mem. German Soc. Laser Medicine, Am. Soc. Lasers in Medicine and Surgery, Optical Soc. Am. Avocation: painting. Fax: (0) 4188/81 82. Office: U Hosp/Accident Surgery, Martinistr 52, D-20146 Hamburg Germany

JAHNKE, JUERGEN, psychologist, educator; b. Helmstedt, Germany, Oct. 26, 1939; s. Harald and Gertrud (Bandholt) J.; m. Heide Palmgren, Sept. 4, 1965; children: Jasper, Julie. Dr.rer.nat., U. Goettingen, Germany, 1971. Counseling psychologist U. Goettingen, 1966-71; lectr. psychology U. Edn., Freiburg, Germany, 1971-75, prof. psychology, 1975—, prorector, 1990-94. Author: Interpersonale Warnehmung, 1975, Sozialpsychologie der Schule, 1982; co-author: Zwischen Apathie und Protest, 1974; editor: Aufklaerung—Projekt der Vernunft, 1998, Psychologiegeschichte— Beziehungen zu Philosophie und Grenzgebieten, 1998. Mem. European Soc. for History of Human Scis., Internat. Soc. 18th Century Studies, Lichtenberg Soc., New Bach Soc. Lutheran. Avocations: history of psychology, literature 18th Century. Home: Weberdobel 11, D-79256 Buchenbach Germany Office: Paedagogische Hochschule, Kunzenweg 21, D-79117 Freiburg Germany

JAHODAR, LUDEK, pharmacognosist; b. Budyne upon Ohre, Czech Republic, Dec. 17, 1948; s. Alois and Marie (Boukalova) J.; m. Blazena Pospisilova, July 21, 1972; children: Ludek, Helena. BS, U. Komensky, 1972, DPharm, 1973; PhD in Pharmacy, Charles U., 1981. Jr. lectr. pharmacy U. Bratislava, Slovak Republic, 1972-74; sr. lectr. pharmacy U. Prague, Czech Republic, 1975-88, assoc. prof. pharmacy, 1988-94; prof. pharmacy Charles U., Prague, 1995—. Mem. Pharm. Soc. Avocations: painting, nature photography, tourism, tennis. Office: Charles U Faculty Pharmacy, Heyrovsky, 50005 Hradec Kralové Czech Republic

JAI, LEE HUN, government executive; b. Apr. 17, 1944; married; 2 children. Grad., Seoul Nat. U.; M of Econs., Boston U. Chmn. Fin. Supervisory Commn., Korea. Office: Min Fin & Economy, 1 Chungangdong, Kwachon Korea*

JAIKUN, SUWIT, university official; b. Nong Kae, Thailand, Nov. 26, 1942; s. Jalern and Cha-Loy (Phong-Are-Morn) J.; m. Noul-Jan Glangchai; children: Srivieng, Chet-Tha, Anu-Shah. Degree in safety, health and environ. en, Sukothai U., Bangkok, 1997. Asst. to mng. dir. Thai Phardex, Pattaya, Thailand, 1991-97; mng. dir. Pure Water & Ice Cube Mfg., T Non Soong, Thailand, 1997—. Mem. Dem. Party. Bhuddist. Home: 859 Udorn-Konkan Rd Km 16, Ban Non Soong T Non Soong, MU-2 J Udonthani 41330, Thailand Office: Pure Water and Ice Cube Mfg, Km 16 Udon-Konkan Rd Ban Non Soong, T Non Soong J Udonthani 41330, Thailand

JAIMOUKHA, IMAD MAHMOUD, electrical and electronic engineering educator; b. Amman, Jordan, Sept. 22, 1960; arrived in U.K., 1978; s. Mahmoud Abdel Rahman and Zahra Yusuf (Shekeh) J. BSc, U. Southampton, Eng., 1983; MSc, Imperial Coll., London, 1986, PhD, 1990. Rsch. asst. Imperial Coll., London, 1990-94, lectr., 1994—. Contbr. articles to profl. jours. With Jordanian Armed Forces, 1983-85. Recipient scholarship Arab-Brit. C. of C., London, 1986, studentship Com. Vice-Chancellors and Principles of the Univs. of U.K., 1987. Mem. Inst. Engring. Jordan. Muslim. Avocations: reading, playing piano, walking. Office: Imperial Coll, Exhibition Rd, London SW7 2BT, England

JAIN, ANIL K., chemicals executive; b. Bundi, Rajasthan, India, Jan. 11, 1963; s. Kailashchandra N. and Premlata K. Jain; m. Anita A. Anita, Jan. 28, 1988; children: Pranay, Prachi. B in Commerce, Dalamia Coll., Mumbai, India, 1983. Owner Gangwal Chems. Ltd., Mumbai, 1988; ptnr. S. A. Chems., Mumbai, 1991—. Fellow Inst. Chartered Accts. India. Office: SA Chems, 220, Udyog Bhawan Goregadn, Mumbai 400063, India

JAIN, B. M., international political studies educator; b. Chohatan, India, Sept. 2, 1946; s. Multan Mal and Agri Devi Jain; m. Manju Jain. MA, U. Jodhpur, India, 1967, PhD, 1983. Fellow Univ. Grants Commn., Jaipur, India, 1977-81; prof. polit. sci. U. Rajasthan, Jaipur, 1988—; fellow Indian Coun. Social Sci. Rsch., Jaipur, 1987-88; vis. scholar Kyungnam U., Seoul, 1997, Henry L. Stimson Ctr., Washington, 1998; invited lectr. internat. univs., 1988—. Author: India and the United States, 1987, Nuclear Politics in South Asia, 1994, Nuclearization in South Asia, 1999; editor-in-chief Indian Jour. Asian Affairs, 1988—. Grantee Charles Wallace Trust India, London, 1997. Mem. Internat. Peace Rsch. Assn., Internat. Polit. Sci. Assn., Assn. Third World Studies, Global Peace and Devel. Rsch. Inst. (hon. bd. dirs. 1997—). Avocations: tennis, astrology, poetry, music. Home: 4/87 Jawahar Nagar, Jaipur 302004, India Office: U Rajasthan South Asia, Studies Ctr, Jaipur 302004, India

JAIN, BIRENDRA, geophysicist; b. Gaya, Bihar, India, Nov. 15, 1947; came to U.S., 1971; s. S.C. and M.D. Jain; m. Lata R. Jain, Feb. 17, 1976; children: Sarika, Smita, Monica. BS, Indian Sch. Mines, 1970; MS, U. Calif., Berkeley, 1973, D Engring., 1978. Geophysicist Oil India Ltd., 1970-71; rsch. asst. U. Calif., Berkeley, 1973-78; staff geophysicist Phoenix Corp., McLean, Va., 1978-81, Mobil Oil Corp., Dallas, 1981-92; chief goephysicist O.N.G.C., New Delhi, 1992-96, dep. gen. mgr., 1997—. Mem. Soc. Exploration Geophysicists, Am. Geophys. Union. Home: A-136 Sector 27, Noida UP, India Office: Directorate Gen Hydrocarbon, 18-20 K G Rd, 110001 New Delhi India

JAIN, DIL SUKH, engineering executive; b. Mandalgarh, Rajasthan, India, Dec. 13, 1953; s. Chand Mal and Ratan Devi (Patni) J.; m. Chanda Badjatya, Jan. 19, 1976; 1 child. B Engring. with honors, BITS, Pilani, India, 1975, M Engring. in Electronics, 1977. Sr. sci. asst. CEERI, Pilani, 1977-79; head imaging divsn. Nat. Remote Sensing Agy., Hyderabad, India, 1979—, ops. dir. IRS-1B, 1991—, dep. project dir. IRS-P5 project, 1996—, project dir. ASDF project, 1997—. Patentee in field; designer electronic instrumentation. Named Outstanding Young Person, Secunderabad Jr. Chamber, 1991, A.P. Jr. Chamber, 1991, Outstanding Young Indian, Indian Jr. Chamber, 1991. Mem. IEEE, Indian Soc. Remote Sensing (life). Avocations: writing articles, lecturing, reading technical journals, indoor games, sightseeing. Home: 48/B S R Nagar, Hyderabad 500038, India Office: Nat Remote Sensing Agy, Balanagar, Hyderabad 500037, India

JAIN, GHISA LAL, dean, agronomy educator; b. Udaipur, Rajasthan, India, July 2, 1937; s. Bhanwar Lal and Sunder Bai (Jodhawat) Sagrawat; m. Suman Bhandari, Feb. 8, 1964; children: Sanjay Sagrawat, Shipra Chelawat. BSc in Agr., Rajasthan Coll. Agr., Udaipur, 1960, MSc in Agronomy, 1962; PhD, Ctrl. Arid Zone Rsch. Inst., Jodhpur, India, 1966. Demonstrator RCA, Udaipur, 1962-63; asst. prof. Udaipur U., 1966-70; assoc. prof. Sukhadia U., Udaipur, 1970-82; prof., univ. head Rajasthan Agrl. U., Udaipur, 1983-91, assoc. dir. rsch., 1992-93; dean postgrad. studies Rajasthan Agrl. U., Bikaner, India, 1994-97, dean Coll. Agr., 1997; sec. Indian Soc. Arid Zone Rsch., Jodhpur, 1964-66; mem. study team on maize Nat. Commn. on Agr., Delhi, India, 1972-73; mem. Ad Hoc Group for Advance Funding, Jaipur, India, 1994-96; vis. scientist prodn. agronomy CIMMYT, Mexico City, 1979; cons. Indian Coun. Agr. Rsch., Fertiliser Assn. of India, Indian Farmers Fertiliser Co-Operative Ltd., Krishak Bharti Co-Operative Ltd., others; cons. Uduipur Nat./internat. cons. Editor: Agr. Sect. Lok Vigyan, 1966-70; chief editor Prabudha Krishak, 1987-89; mem. editl. bd. Agr. Sci. Digest, 1989—, Indian Jour. Agr. Rsch., 1994-97; referee various rsch. jours., 1973—; contbr. articles to profl. jours. Bd. dirs. Mahaveer Interant., Udaipur, 1990, Mahaveer Internat., Bikaner, 1996-97. Recipient Shri Govind Hari Singhania award, 1969; jr. rsch. fellow Coun. Sci. and Indsl. Rsch., 1963-64, U. Grants Commn., 1964-66, postdoctoral fellow Govt. Netherlands, Wageningen, 1968-69, sr. postdoctoral fellow Alexander Von Humboldt Found., Germany, 1974-76, fellow Internat. Res. in Sci. and Tech., U.K., 1986-87; merit scholar Govt. of Rajasthan, 1961, Sahu Jain Trust, 1962-63, Govindram Sexaria Charity Trust, 1959-61. Fellow Indian Soc. Agronomy (life, councillar 1981-83, 87, 88). Avocations: travel, listening to music, writing, reading. Home: 2-A Ambamata Scheme, Udaipur 313 004, India

JAIN, L. C., engineering executive. Dir., founder Knowledge-Based Intelligent Engring. Systems Ctr. Univ. South Australia, Mawson Lakes, South Australia; presenter numerous confs. Founding editor-in-chief Internat. Jour. of Knowledge-Based Intelligent Engring. Systems; assoc. editor IEEE Transactions on Indsl. Electronics; editor-in-chief Internat. Book Series on Computational Intelligence. Mem. Electronics Assn. of South Australia (v.p. 1997). Fax: 618-8302-3384. E-mail: l.jain@unisa.edu.au. Office: KES U South Australia, Mawson Lakes 5095, South Australia

JAIN, NARENDRA PRAKASH, publisher; b. Lahore, Punjab, India, Jan. 16, 1939; s. Shantilal and Lajwanti Jain; m. Anuradha Shimla, Oct. 7, 1964; children: Vasudha, Anurag, Priya, Tushar, Tanvi. BA with honors, St. Stephen Coll., Delhi, India, 1961; diploma in bus. mgmt., Delhi Sch. Econs., 1963. Mng. dir. Motilal Banarsidass Publs., Delhi, 1984—; vice-chmn. Bhogilal Leharchand Inst. Indology, Delhi, 1987—; sec. Vishwakalyan Atma Jain Found., Delhi, 1992. Named Best Bookseller Fedn. of Indian Publs., 1997. Mem. India Internat. Ctr. Avocations: classical music, poetry, dance, drama, spiritual literature. Home: 41 UA, Bungalow Rd Jawahar Nagar, Delhi 110007, India

JAIN, PANKAJ KUMAR, publisher; b. Gurgaon Haryana, India, Apr. 14, 1954; s. Satya Prakash and Bimla Devi J.; m. Renu Jain, Dec. 6, 1981; two children. BA, DSD Coll., Gurgaon, India, 1974. Dir. Indian Documentation Svc., 1975—. Treas. Blessings (Ctr. for Mentally and Neurologically Disabled Children), 1995—. Office: Indian Documentation Svc, 887/5 Patel Nagar PB # 13, 122001 Gurgaon/Haryana India

JAIN, PREM CHAND, mechanical engineer; b. New Delhi, India, Jan. 26, 1936; s. Kishori Lal and Kapoori Devi Jain; m. Renu Jain, Oct. 3, 1965; 1 child, Payal. BME, Banaras Hindu U., 1957; MSME, U. Minn., 1960, PhD of Mech. Engring., 1967. Trainee engr. ICI Australia, Melbourne, 1956-57; sr. rsch. engr. Carrier Corp. RDC, Syracuse, N.Y., 1967-69; vis. prof. Indian Inst. Tech., Kanpur, 1970-71; sr. engr. Stein Doshi Bhalla, New Delhi, India, 1971-79; chmn., mng. dir., pres. Spectral, New Delhi, 1980—; vis. prof. Sch. Architecture, New Delhi, 1973—; bd. dirs. IEE India, Hyderabad, 1983; cons. engr. with 40 yrs. experience in design of HVAC, electrical, pub. health, fire suppression, BMS, security, data and voice transmissions systems for bldgs., India and worldwide. Bd. dirs. Triveni Kala Sengam, New Delhi and RLJ Trust, Delhi. Fellow Am. Soc. Heating Refrigerating & Air Conditioning Engrs (founding pres. India chpt. 1991), Inst. Refrigeration London, Instn. Engrs. India, Instn. Energy Engrs. India, Indian Soc. Lighting Engrs.; mem. ASME (U.S.), Internat. Solar Energy Soc. (Germany), Nat. Fire Prevention Assn., Illum Engrs. Soc. N.Am., Cons. Engr. Assn. (India), Indian Soc. Heating, Refigeration & Air Conditioning Engrs. (pres. emeritus 1993—). Avocations: reading, classical music, fashion design, indoor games. Fax: 91-11-647-0947. E-mail: sscin@giasd101.vsnl.net.in. Home: S 126 Greater Kailash II, New Delhi 110048, India Office: Spectral Svcs Cons, E6 Masjid Moth, Greater Kailash III New Delhi 110048, India

JAIN, PUSHPENDRA KUMAR, physics educator, researcher; b. Saharanpur, India, Sept. 7, 1946; s. Prakash Chand and Kamal Jain; m. Priti Jain, Feb. 24, 1978; children: Gauri, Shilpi, Shitesh. BSc, Agra (India) U., 1965; MSc, Meerut (India) U., 1967; PhD, U. Conn., 1975; cert. in Russian, U. Delhi, India, 1977; cert. in French, Alliance Francaise, Gaborone, Botswana; Chartered Physicist, Inst. Physics, U.K., 1989. Rsch. asst. Indian Inst. Tech., Delhi, 1968-70; grad. asst. U. Conn., Storrs, 1970-75; scientist Nat. Phys. Lab., Delhi, 1975-78; lectr. Birla Inst. Tech. and Sci., Pilani, India, 1978-83; lectr. I U. Zambia, Lusaka, 1983-86; lectr. physics U. Botswana, Gaborone, 1987-90, sr. lectr., 1990-99, assoc. prof., 1999—; founder mem. Botswana nat. com. World Energy Coun., 1994—, interim chmn., 2000—. Editor: Physics in the Service of Africa, 1991; contbr. articles on new and renewable energy, physics and materials sci. to scholarly jours., chpt. to book. Grantee, fellow UNESCO, Brit. Coun., Commonwealth Sci. Coun., 1985, 91, 92, 94, 98, 2000. Mem. Inst. Physics (U.K.), Indian Physics Assn. (life), South African Inst. Physics, Internat. Vegetarian Union (regional sec. Africa region 1997—), Vegetarian Soc. Botswana (founder, chmn. 1995—), Energy Soc. Botswana (founder, chmn. 1990-98), Phi Beta Kappa, Phi Kappa Phi, Sigma Pi Sigma. Jainist. Avocations: numismatics, travel and tourism, reading, videos on nature, wildlife. Home: Plot 4807 Ext 11, Jn

of, Nyrere Dr-Okavango Close, Gaborone Botswana Office: U Botswana Dept Physics, P/Bag 0022, Gaborone Botswana

JAIN, RANJAN, executive; b. Hazaribagh, India, Apr. 12, 1966; s. Uttam Chand and Mani J.; m. Charu, Feb. 18, 1995; 1 child. BS, Luckrow Christian Degree Coll., India, 1986. Asst. personnel officer Debur India Ltd., Delhi, 1989-91, Stencil Apparel Biards, Delhi, 1991-93; mgr. EIH Ltd., Bangalore, India, 1994-97, Amid Mills Ltd., Ahmedabad, India, 1997-98; head Amtrex hitachi Appliances, Ahmedabad, India, 1998—. Mem. APRD Network (mem. exec. com. 1998—). Office: Amtrex Hitachi Appliances, 901 Abhijit Bldg, Ahuedabad 380006, India

JAIN, RATAN LAL, business executive, consultant engineer; b. Alwar, Rajasthan, India, Jan. 10, 1933; s. Hazari Lal and Tarawati (Jain) J. BSc, Kanpur (India) U., 1951; Grad. in Marine Engring., Marine Coll. Calcutta, 1955. Cert. engr. with 1st class cert. of competency, India. Jr. engr. Clan Line Steamers Ltd., London, 1955-58; 2d engr. MacAndrews Ltd., Liverpool, Eng., 1958-59; 3d and 2d engr. India Steamship Ltd., Calcutta, 1961-64, chief engr., 1964-66; chief engr. P&O Group, London, 1969-71; tech. mgr. Cosmos Steels Ltd., Calcutta, 1968-69; draftsman, mech. engr. Liverpool Regional Hosp. Bd., 1958-61; surveyor Lloyds Register, London, 1966-68; rep. in India, New Sulzer Diesel Ltd., Winterthur, Switzerland, 1972-94; cons. engr. Ratan L. Jain & Co., Bombay, 1994—. Author: Training and Assessment Record Books as Per the Requirements of International Maritime Organisation, London for Marine Engineers, 1999. Chmn. Internat. Maritime Conf., Bombay, 1986, 90, 94, Inst. Marine Engrs. (India). Recipient Vikas Ratna award Indian Internat. Friendship Soc., 2000. Fellow Inst. Marine Engrs. India (pres. 1991-93, 95-97), Inst. Marine Engrs. London (chartered engr.), Instn. of Engrs. India (prs. 1991-93, 95-97), Instn. Mech. Engrs. London. Avocations: dancing (Silver medals in Latin and Ballroom dance), German and Japanese languages, western light and classical music, Indian light and classical music. Home: 703A Bafna Apts, Mogul Lane, Mahim, Mumbai 400016, India

JAIN, SUBIN, internist, consultant; b. New Delhi, July 13, 1967; s. Surinder Kumar and Bina Devi Jain; m. Nandita Telang, Apr. 18, 1993; 1 child, Ananya. MB, BS, Maulana Azad Med. Coll., New Delhi, 1991. Diplomate Am. Bd. Internal Mdicine, Am. Bd. Pulmonary Medicine. Intern L.I. Jewish Med. Ctr., N.Y.C., 1992-93; resident in internal medicine U. Conn., Farmington, 1993-95, chief resident, 1995-96; fellow in pulmonary medicine Baylor Coll. Medicine, Houston, 1996-99; assoc. cons. Singapore Gen. Hosp., 1999—. Contbr. articles to med. jours., including Am. Juor. Respiratory and Critical Care Medicine, Critical Care Clinics: Environ. Emergencies, Critical Care Clinics: Mech. Ventilation, Chest. Mem. Am. Coll. Chest Physicians (Young Investigator award 1999), Am. Thoracic Soc., Singapore Thoracic Soc. Fax: 65-227-1736. E-mail: subinjain@usa.net. Office: Singapore Gen Hosp, Outram Park, Singapore Singapore

JAIN, SUDHANSHU KUMAR, ethnobotanist, taxonomist; b. Amroha, Uttar Pradesh, India, June 30, 1926; s. Prakash Chandra and Shri Devi (Gupta) J.; m. Satya Kumari Mittal, May 5, 1948; children: Sunil, Arun, Yogesh. BS, U. Allahabad (India), 1943, MS, 1946; PhD, U. Poona (India), 1965. Asst. prof. Meerut (India) U., 1947-49; sr. scientific asst. Coun. Sci. and Indsl. Rsch., New Delhi, 1951-56; botanist Botan. Survey India, Calcutta, 1956-71, dy., jt. dir., 1971-78, dir., 1978-84; emeritus scientist dept. sci. tech., environ. forests Coun. Sci. and Indsl. Rsch., Lucknow, India, 1984-94; dir. Inst. Ethnobiology, Lucknow, India, 1995—; cons. Uttar Pradesh (India) Dept. Environment, Lucknow, 1986, Coun. of Sci. and Indsl. Rsch./Dept. Sci. and Tech., Lucknow, 1986—; prin. investigator United Nations Devel. Program, Lucknow, 1994-95, Coun. Sci. and Indsl. Rsch./Wenner-Gren Found., U.S.A., 1996-98. Author 25 books on ethnobiology, flora, rare plants, including Dictionary of Indian Folk Medicine and Ethnobotany, Medicinal Plants, 1991, Tribal Medicine, 1998, Dictionary of Ethnoveterinary Plants of India, 1999; editor: 8 books on medicinal plants, rare plants, including Contributions to Indian Ethnobotany, Threatened Plants of India, Flora India, Ethnobiology in Human Welfare, 1968-96; chief editor: Fascicles of Flora of India, 1978-84, Jour. Ethnobotany, 1989-95, 99—; mem. editl. bd. numerous profl. jours. Pres. Kaul Sci. Found., 1992-96. Fellow Soc. Ethnobotanist (pres. 1980-88, 91-95, Harshberger medal 1992), Indian Botan. Soc. (Maheshwari medal 1982, pres. 1987), Nat. Acad. Sci. (Gold medal 1960, pres. biology 1987), Indian Nat. Sci. Acad. (S.B. Saxena medal 1996), Soc. for Econ. Botany (Disting. Econ. Botanist 1999), Assn. Plant Taxon (pres. 1998—). Follower of Jain religion. Avocations: photographer, writing popular science, nature study, archival materials. Fax: 205836. Home: A-26 Mall Ave Colony, Lucknow 226001, India Office: Inst Ethnobiology, Nat Botan Rsch Inst, Lucknow 226001, India

JAIN, SUDHIR KUMAR, civil engineering educator; b. Lalitpur, U.P., India, July 4, 1959; s. Narendra Kumar and Magan Mala J.; m. Abhilasha Jain, June 6, 1985; children: Saumya, Nikhil. BE in Civil Engring., U. Roorkee, India, 1979; MS in Civil Engring., Calif. Inst. Tech., 1980, PhD in Civil Engring., 1983. Lectr. Indian Inst. Tech., Kanpur, India, 1984-85, from asst. prof. to prof., 1985—; vis. scholar, vis. prof. U. Mich., 1994; team leader post-earthquake reconaissance for 5 earthquakes, India, 1988, 91, 93, 97, 99. Contbr. over 80 rsch. articles to profl. jours. Robert A. Millikan fellow, 1982-83, Indo-US Sci. and Tech. fellow, 1994; Nat. Merit scholar, 1973-79; grantee nat. agencies. Mem. Am. Concrete Inst., Indian Soc. Earthquake Tech., Indian Concrete Inst., Indian Bldg. Congress, Indian. Instn. Bridge Engrs., New Zealand Soc. Earthquake Engring., Earthquake Engring. Rsch. Inst. (U.S.), Internat. Assn. for Earthquake Engring. (bd. dirs. 2000—). Office: Indian Inst Tech, Dept Civil Engring Prof, Kanpur 208 016, India

JAIN, SURESH CHAND, electrical engineering and physics educator and researcher; b. Saharanpur, India, Dec. 5, 1926; s. R.C. and S. Jain; m. Sudha Govila, July 23, 1950; chidren: Amitabh, Rita Atkinson, Rajeev. BSc, U. Allahabad, India, 1947, MSc, 1949; PhD, U. Delhi, India, 1955. Rsch. trainee Nat. Phys. Lab., New Delhi, India, 1949-55; rsch. fellow Leeds (Eng.) U., 1955-59; head solid state divsn. Nat. Phys. Lab., New Delhi, 1959-64; prof., dean sci. faculty Indian Inst. Tech., New Delhi, 1964-69; dir. solid state lab. Ministry of Def., Delhi, 1969-84; prof., sr. rsch. fellow Oxford (Eng.) U., 1987-88, 90-93, Cath. U. Leuven, Belgium, 1993—. Author: Ge-Si Strained Layers, 1994, Compound Semiconductor Strained Layer Devices, 2000; ; editor: New Metallic Crystals, 1970, III-V Strained Layer Devices; contbr. over 300 articles to profl. jours. Recipient SSBB award Govt. of India, 1965. Fellow Inst. of Physics (Londno), Indian Nat. Acad., Inst. Elec. and Telecomm. Engrs. India; mem. IEEE (sr.). Jain religion. Avocations: writing popular science, history of science, music. Office: IMEC, Kapeldreef 75, 3001 Leuven Belgium

JAIN, VIJAY PRAKASH, international marketing executive; b. Meerut, Uttar Pradesh, India, Aug. 13, 1944; arrived in Denmark, 1972; s. Sumat Prasad and Pushpa Devi (Lata) J.; m. Karen Nielsen, July, 18, 1970; children: Camilla, Anja. Diploma, Sch. World Trade, Vienna, Austria, 1968; MBA, U. Western Ont., London, Can., 1971. Researcher York U., Toronto, Can., 1971-72; lectr. Sch. Commerce, Naestved, Denmark, 1972-76; dir. Lemvig-Fog & Jain Pvt. Ltd., Copenhagen, 1974-79; mng. dir. Silkotex Aps, Silkeborg, Denmark, 1981-91; pres. Inst. for Tng. in Intercultural Mgmt., Denmark, 1995—; prof. Sch. Internat. Mktg. and Export, Herning, Denmark, 1980—. Author: Eksport, 1982. Bd. dirs. Internat. Student Ctr. Mem. Soc. for Intercultural Relations. Avocation: tennis. Home and Office: TDT Internat ApS, Vestergade 72, 8600 Silkeborg Denmark

JAIN, YATISH, environmental educator; b. Sagar, India, Sept. 25, 1970; s. Suresh and Maya J. BSc, Rani Durgavati U., 1989, MSc, 1991, B in Edn., 1995, PhD, 1997, LLB, 2000. Environmentalist Orbit Biotech Innovation Pvt. Ltd., Jabalpur, India, 1990-92; project coord. Nat. Environ. Engring. Rsch. Inst. India, Nagpur, 1992-94; environmental scientist Econ Pollution Control Pvt. Ltd., Bombay, India, 1994-95; rschr. Govt. Sci. Jabalpur, 1995—; Cons. Mahakoushal Pipe Industries, Jabalpur, 1995—. Author: Environmental Laws (in Hindi), 2000; editor: Paryavaran Deepika, 1995; contbr. articles to profl. jours. Pres. Jain Youth Cultural Soc., 1994-96. Mem. Prakriti Mitra Environ. Soc. (bd. dirs. 1990—), Assn. Environ. Educationists (bd. dirs.), Indian Assn. Environ. Mgmt., Rotary, Lions. Avocations: traveling, politics. Home: Kendriya Vidyalaya Campus, GCF 482 011, Jabalpur India Office: Govt Sci Coll, Dept Environ Sci, 482 001 Jabalpur India

JAIRAM, KHELANAND VISHVAYKANAND, lawyer; b. Queenstown, Essequibo, Guyana, Nov. 29, 1946; came to U.S., 1988; s. Kaiser and Narainee Jairam; m. Joyce B. Gafur, Dec. 2, 1967; children: Shashi, Nishall, Ashwini. Barrister at Law, Inns Ct. Sch., London, 1974; LLB with honors, U. London, 1988; LLM, U. N.Y., N.Y.C., 1990. Bar: Eng. 1974, Wales 1974, Guyana 1974, N.Y. 1991, U.S. Dist. Ct. (so. and ea. dists.) 1991, Trinidad and Tobago, 1997. Pvt. practice Georgetown, Guyana, 1974-88; tax counsel N.Y.C. Dept. Fin., 1991-94; pvt. practice Law Office K.V. Jairam, N.Y.C., 1994—; mem. parliament, Govt. of Guyana, 1980-85. Mem. ABA, Am. Trial Lawyers Assn., N.Y. State Bar Assn., Queens County Bar Assn. Democrat. Hindu. Avocations: tennis, cricket. Home: 230 Main St East Rockaway NY 11518-1715 Office: 18915 Jamaica Ave Hollis NY 11423-2513

JAISWAL, DINESH KUMAR, pharmaceutical scientist, educator; b. Howrah, India, Mar. 5, 1947; came to U.S., 1983; s. Jagadish Prasad and Phool Kumari Jaiswal; m. Manju Jaiswal, Feb. 10, 1971; children: Rahul, Kunal. BS in Pharmacy, Banaras Hindu U., Varanasi, India, 1970, MS in Pharmacy, 1972, PhD in Pharmacy, 1978. Assoc. prof. Banaras Hindu U., 1973-75, 78-83; chemist Phoenix Lab., Hicksville, N.Y., 1983-84; sr. chemist Superpharm, Islip, N.Y., 1984-86; mgr. Quad Pharm., Indpls., 1986-90; sr. devel. pharmacist GAF Chem. Co., Wayne, Ind., 1990-93; prin. scientist Mova Pharm., Caguas, P.R., 1993-96, Forest Labs., Inwood, N.Y., 1996—. Contbr. articles to profl. jours., including Jour. Pharm. Scis., PHarm. Rsch., USA, Pharmatech/Manchester. Jr. rsch. fellow UGC, New Delhi, India, 1975, sr. rsch. fellow, 1976, rsch. assoc., 1977. Mem. Am. Assn. Pharm. Scientists, Parenteral Drug Assn. and Controlled Release Soc. Achievements include patent for pharmaceutical tablet with PVP having enhanced drug dissolution rate. Avocations: sports, music, tourism. Home: 6 Sunflower Ct Holtsville NY 11742-2520 Office: 300 Prospect St Inwood NY 11096-2035

JAISWAL, RAVINDRA SINGH, psychogeriatrician; b. Allahabad, U. Pradesh, India, Dec. 11, 1951; arrived in Eng., 1977; s. Misri Lal and Kamla (Kumari) J.; m. Sunita Jayaswal, Feb. 18, 1981; children: Shivani, Vishal. MB BS, M.L.N. Med. Coll., Allahabad, India, 1975; DPM, Royal Coll. Physicians, and Surgeons, London, 1980. House officer in psychiatry Durham Area Health Authority, Darlington, Eng., 1977-78; registrar in psychiatry Durham Area Health Authority, Sedgefield, Eng., 1978-79; house officer/registrar in psychiatry St. Bartholomew's Hosp., London, 1979-82; registrar in psychiatry Bromley (Eng.) Health Authority, 1983-86; clin. asst. Bedford Hosp., Bedford, Eng., 1987-93; assoc. specialist Bedford & Shires Nat. Health Svc. Trust, Bedford, 1993—; cons. Bedford & Shires Nat. Health Svc. Trust, Bedford, 1987—. Fellow Royal Soc. Health; mem. Internat. Psychogeriatric Assn., Brit. Med. Assn.(regional rep.), Royal Coll. Psychiatrists (affiliate). Avocations: swimming, kite flying, stamp collecting, cricket. Office: Bedford Hosp Wellerwing SW, Kempston Rd, Bedfordshire Bedford MK42 9DJ, England

JAISWAL-DALE, AMEETA, dean, financial consultant; b. Hyderabad, India; came to U.S., 1983; m. John P. Dale. MA in Econs., Osmania U., Hyderabad, 1976; MS in Econometrics, U. Rennes, France, 1983, PhD in Applied Econs., 1983. Asst. prof. dept. econs. Ea. Ill. U., Charleston, 1984-88; asst. prof. Coll. St. Catherine, St. Paul, 1988-90; assoc. prof. dept. fin. U. St. Thomas, St. Paul, 1990-99; asst. dean Grad. Sch. Bus. U. St. Thomas, Mpls., 1999—; cons. Customized Svcs., St. Paul, 1989—; corp. trainer fin. mgmt. Individual Customized Svcs., St. Paul, 1990—; vis. prof. U. Caen, France, 1991—; treas. World Trade Week, St. Paul, 1996—; invited prof. Palacky U., Olonviouc, Czech Republic, 1997; pres. Pulsai Techs., St. Paul, 1997—. Contbr. articles to profl. jours. Vol. Minn. Internat. Ctr., 1990—, India Assn. Minn., 1990—, Ho. Hope & Hindu Temple, St. Paul, 1997—, Met. Airports Commn., 1998—. Internal grantee U. St. Thomas, Coll. St. Catherine, 1988-98. Mem. Fin. Mgm. Assn., European Fin. Mgmt. Assn., Com. Women Economists, Assn. Enterprises and Firms. Avocations: cooking, wine, travel, gardening, performing arts. Office: U Saint Thomas MPL 331 1000 La Salle Ave Minneapolis MN 55403

JAK, MICHIEL J. G., chemist, researcher; b. Gouda, The Netherlands, Sept. 21, 1969; s. Joop G. and Irene V. (van den Berg) J.; m. Annelieke E. Hooiring, June 20, 1994. MSc in Materials Sci. Engring., Delft U. Tech., The Netherlands, 1994, PhD in Chem. Tech., 1999. Postdoctoral rschr. in inorganic chemistry Delft U. Tech., 1998—. Contbr. articles to sci. jours. Travel grantee European Sci. Found., Shell, Netherlands Orgn. Sci. Rsch. Mem. Electrochem. Soc. (spkr. internat. conf. 1996, 98). Achievements include patent for ceramic li-ion batteries. Avocation: tennis. Office: Delft Tech U Inorganic Chem, Julianalaan 136, 2628 BL Delft The Netherlands

JAKAB, IRENE, psychiatrist; b. Oradea, Rumania; came to U.S., 1961, naturalized, 1966; d. Odon and Rosa A. (Riedl) J. MD, Ferencz József U., Kolozsvar, Hungary, 1944; lic. in psychology, pedagogy, philosophy cum laude, Hungarian U., Cluj, Rumania, 1947; PhD summa cum laude, Pazmany Peter U., Budapest, 1948; Dr honoris causa, U. Besançon, France, 1982, U. Pécs, Hungary, 1999. Diplomate Am. Bd. Psychiatry, Am. Bd. Pediatric Neuropsychology. Rotating intern Ferencz József U., 1943-44; resident in psychiatry Univ. Hosp., Kolozsvar, 1944-47, resident in neurology, 1947-50; resident internal medicine Univ. Hosp. for Internal Medicine, Pécs, Hungary, 1950-51; chief physician Univ. Hosp. for Neurology and Psychiatry, Pécs, 1951-59; staff neuropathol. rsch. lab. Neurol. Univ. Clinic, Zurich, 1959-61; sect. chief Kans. Neurol. Inst., Topeka, 1961-63; dir. rsch. and edn., 1966; resident psychiatry Topeka State Hosp., 1963-66; asst. psychiatrist McLean Hosp., Belmont, Mass., 1966-67; assoc. psychiatrist McLean Hosp., 1967-74; prof. psychiatry U. Pitts. Med. Sch., 1974-89, prof. emerita, 1989—, co-dir. med. student edn. in psychiatry, 1981-89; dir. John Merck Program, 1974-81; mem. faculty dept. psychiatry Med. Sch., Pecs, 1951-59; asst. Univ. Hosp. Neurology, Zurich, 1959-61; assoc. psychiatry Harvard U., Boston, 1966-69, asst. prof. psychiatry, 1969-74, program dir. grad course mental retardation, 1970-87; lectr. psychiatry, 1974—. Author: Dessins et Peintures des Aliénés, 1956, Zeichnungen und Gemälde der Geisteskranken, 1956, Pictorial Expression in Psychiatry, 1998; editor: Psychiatry and Art, 1968, Art Interpretation and Art Therapy, 1969, Conscious and Unconscious Expressive Art, 1971, Transcultural Aspects of Psychiatric Art, 1975; co-editor: Dynamische Psychiatrie, 1974; mem. editl. bd. Confinia Psychiatrica, 1975-99; contbr. articles to profl. jours. Recipient 1st prize Benjamin Rush Gold medal award for sci. exhibit, 1980, Bronze Chris plaque Columbus Film Festival, 1980, Leadership award Am. Assn. on Mental Deficiency, 1980; Menninger Sch. Psychiatry fellow, Topeka, 1963-66. Mem. AMA, Am. Psychol. Assn., Am. Psychiat. Assn., Société Medico Psychologique de Paris, Internat. Rorschach Soc., N.Y. Acad. Scis., Internat. Soc. Psychopathology of Expression (v.p. 1959—), Am. Soc. Psychopathology of Expression (chmn. 1965—, Ernst Kris Gold Medal award 1988), Royal Soc. of Medicine (overseas fellow), Internat. Soc. Child Psychiatry and Allied Professions, Internat. Assn. Knowledge Engrs. (v.p. for medicine 1988-95), Deutschsprachige Gesellschaft für Psychopathologie des Ausdruckes (hon. Prinzhorn prize 1967), Hungarian Psychiat. Assn. (hon. 1992), World Psychiat. Assn. (co-chmn. sect. on mass and media and mental health, co-chmn. sect. on psychopathology of expression). Home and Office: 74 Lawton St Brookline MA 02446-5801

JAKACKI, DIANE KATHERINE, web production and marketing executive; b. Englewood, N.J., July 27, 1964; d. Bernard and Barbara (Logie) J. BA, Lafayette Coll., 1986. From asst. to mktg. mgr. to website exec. prodr. Home Box Office, N.Y.C., 1987—. Author: (plays) Beowulf: A 20th Century Evening in a 10th Century Mead Hall, 1992, Blocked, 1994, Rubbing Brass, 1996. Youth group leader Congl. Ch., New Canaan, Conn., 1994-96. Avocations: theatre, computers, British history, golf, cycling. Office: HBO 1100 Ave of Americas New York NY 10036

JAKAS, MARIO M., science educator; b. Corrientes, Argentina, Sept. 5, 1952; s. Vicente R. Jakas and Celia Iglesia; m. Rosa Albisu, Jan. 19, 1974; children: Vicente, Santiago, Veronica, Anthony. MSc, Inst. Balseiro, Argentina, 1975, PhD, 1983. Cert. physicist. Staff scientist Atomic Energy Comm., Argentina, 1977-85, Investigacion Aplicada, Argentina, 1985-89; prof. U. de La Laguna, Spain, 1991—; adj. prof. USN, Monterey, Calif., 1983-85; vis. prof. U. Autónoma, Madrid, 1989-90. Author: (book) Atomic Ion Collisions in Solids and at Surfaces, 1997. Fellow Inst. Physics (U.K.); mem. Sigma Chi (Monterey chpt.). Office: U de La Laguna, Astrofisica Sanchez 5/N, 38201 La Laguna Spain

JAKEE, KEITH ERIC, economics researcher, educator; b. Detroit, Mar. 4, 1962; arrived in Australia, 1997; s. G. and Leota Mae (Goosby) J.; m. Sheilagh M. Riordan, May 9, 1992. BA magna cum laude, No. Mich. U., 1984; MA in Applied Econs., U. Mich., 1989; MA, George Mason U., 1991, PhD, 1996. Ind. cons. Medora Cons., Arlington, Va., 1989-92; lectr. econs. U. Coll. Cork, Ireland, 1993-95; rsch. scholar City U. Stockholm, 1995-96; lectr. econs. Monash U., Melbourne, Australia, 1997—; lectr. in field, Stockholm, Oslo; expert testimony U.S. Ho. Reps., Washington, 1990; presenter numerous confs., Ireland, The Netherlands, Germany, Austria, Canada, Australia, Sweden, U.S., 1992—. Author: (monograph) Economics of Swedish Norms, 1996; contbr. articles and rsch. reports to profl. jours. Active Big Brothers, Marquette, Mich., 1984-85. Fulbright scholar Uppsala (Sweden) U., 1992-93, Mich. Competitive scholar State of Mich., 1980-84; faculty rsch. grantee U. Coll. Cork and Monash U., Australian Rsch. Coun. grantee. Mem. Am. Econ. Assn., Am. Polit. Sci. Assn. Avocations: music performance, traveling. Office: Monash U, Dept Econs, 3800 Clayton Victoria, Australia

JÄKEL, THOMAS ERICH, parasitologist, researcher; b. Siegen, Germany, Dec. 16, 1960; s. Erich and Karin (Bertelmann) J. Diploma in Biology, U. Hohenheim, Germany, 1988, PhD in Natural Scis., 1994. Tech employee, rschr. U. Hohenheim, 1986-88, rsch. scientist, 1989-93; project coord., rschr., mgr., cons. German Tech. Coop., Eschborn, Germany, 1993—. Contbr. articles to profl. jours. Grantee German Tech. Coop., 1987, PhD grantee, 1989. Mem. AAAS, German Soc. Parasitologists, German Soc. Herpetologists. Office: U Hohenheim Div Parasitol, Emil Wolff Str 34, 70599 Stuttgart Germany

JAKÓBISIAK, MAREK WŁODZIMIERZ, immunologist, researcher; b. Warsaw, Poland, Aug. 18, 1944; s. Stanisław and Eugenia (Szczap) J.; m. Elżbieta Błaszczyk, Sept. 28, 1971; children: Marta, Katarzyna. MD, Sch. Medicine, Warsaw, 1968, Docent, 1982; PhD, Inst. Exptl. Medicine, Warsaw, 1972. Rsch. asst. Sch. Medicine, Warsaw, 1972-82, assoc. prof., 1982-90, prof. immunology, 1990—, head dept., 1993; mem. com. immunology Polish Acad. Sci., 1996. Co-author, editor: Immunology, 1996; contbr. articles to profl. jours. Mem. Polish Soc. Immunology. Office: Sch Medicine Dept Immunol, Chałubińskiego 5, 02-004 Warsaw Poland

JAKOBOVITS, ÁKOS ANTAL, obstetrician, gynecologist, consultant; b. Szeged, Csongrad, Hungary, Feb. 27, 1957; s. Antal Ferenc and Rozália Veronika (Molnár) J.; m. Ilona Tösèr, Oct. 8, 1994 (div.). MD summa cum laude, Univ. Sch. Medicine Szeged, 1982; specialist in Ob-Gyn., Postgrad. Med. Sch. Budapest, 1987. Asst. Békéscsaba (Hungary) Hosp., 1982-84; asst. Cegléd (Hungary) Hosp., 1984-87, cons., 1987—; guest physician dept. ob-gyn U. Hosp., Zurich, 1997. Contbr. articles to profl. jours. including Am. Jour. Obstetrics and Gynecology, Early Human Devel., Acta Anatom., Basel, Acta Ob-Gyn. Scandinavica, Jour. Pediatrics, European Jour. Ob-Gyn., Reproductive Biology, Fertil. Steril, J. Ultrasound Med. Fellow Alexander von Humboldt Found. Aachen, 1991-92. Home: Vasas szent Peter u 7, H-6723 Szeged Hungary Office: Toldy Ferenc Hosp, Törteli ut 1-3, H-2701 Cegled, County Pest Hungary

JAKOBSEN, JOHANNES, neurology educator, neurologist; b. Aarhus, Denmark, Feb. 4, 1945; s. J.B. and C. (Nielsen) J.; m. Lena B. Dalgaard, July 18, 1967 (div. 1972); 1 child, Jon Dalgaard; m. Kirsten Vinther-Jensen, Feb. 14, 1979; children: Eske, Tua. MD, Aarhus U., 1972, PhD, 1979. Tng. position neurology Aarhus U. Hosp., 1972-74; rsch. fellow Aarhus U., 1974-81, Mayo Clnic, Rochester, Minn., 1979-80; tng. position neurology U. Hosp. Copenhagen, 1981-91; rsch. fellow Washington U., St. Louis, 1989-90; cons. Aarhus U. Hosp., 1991—; prof. neurology U. Aarhus, 1992—; chmn. neurology Aarhus U. Hosp., 1996—; chmn. coun. consultants Aarhus U. Hosp., 1994-2000. Co-editor Acta Neurologica Scandinavia, 1998—. Chmn. Danish Neurol. Soc., 1997,; bd. mem. European Study Group for Diabetic Neuropathy, 1997—. Recipient Gold medal U. Copenhagen Med. Sch., 1969; recipient award Soc. for Poliomyelitis, Copenhagen, 1981, Carl Holst-Knudsens award Aarhus U., 1984, Henry og Karla Hansens award Copenhagen U., 1986. Home: Emil Aarestrupsvej 5, DK-08000 Århus Denmark Office: Aarhus Univ Hosp, Nørrebrogade 44, DK-8000 Århus Denmark

JAKOBSEN, KAARE, superintendent, school system administrator; b. Öksnes, Norway, May 24, 1916; s. Jens Nikolai and Regine Othilie Jakobsen. Grad., Tchrs. Tng. Coll., 1944, Coll. Music, 1955, Postgrad. Coll., 1953-58. Tchr. secondary modern sch. Gildeskål, Norway, 1944-45; headmaster boarding sch. Öksnes, Norway, 1945-53; tchr. primary sch. Trondheim, 1953-60; tchr. second modern sch. Malm, Norway, 1960-65; supt. schs. Gamvik, Norway, 1965-70, Dönna, Norway, 1970-74; lectr. in field; auditor to bank, Öksnes, 1934-36, bank mgr., 1945-53. Author: The Play of Vibrations I, 1995, II, 1996; contbr. articles to profl. jours. Organist, parish clk., Öksnes, 1945-53; organist, Gamvik, 1965-70. Mem. AAAS, Rosicrucian Order AMORC, N.Y. Acad. Scis. Lutheran. Avocations: philosophy, languages, writings, travel, astronomy, physics. Home: Linbastavägen 5, S510 21 Satila Sweden

JAKOBSEN, TOVE HYGUM, journalist; b. Roruig, Denmark, Apr. 6, 1945; d. Rasmus Marinus and Gunhilde (Larsen) Carstensen; m. Preben Hygum Jakobsen, July 17, 1965 (dec. Mar. 1995); children: Mette, Kamilla. Student, Danish Sch. Journalism, Arhus, Denmark, 1964. Trainee, staff journalist Sjællands Tidende, Slagelse, Denmark, 1962-69; v.p. Danish Union Journalists, Copenhagen, 1980-84, pres., 1984-90; staff journalist Danish Radio Corp., Copenhagen, 1969—; bd. dirs. Internat. Fedn. Reproduction Rights, chair authors rights expert group, 1988—; mem. Govtl. Expert Com. Media Liability, Copenhagen, 1986-90. Co-author: The Copyright is Yours, 1988, Authors Rights in the Modern Mass Media, 1997. Mem. Danish Copyright Collecting Soc. (pres. 1994-97). Home: Midtermolen 2, DK 2100 Copenhagen Ø, Denmark Office: Danish Radio Broadcasting Corp, Rosenoerns Alle 22, Copenhagen Denmark

JAKOBSON, BJÖRN ANDERS, research and development engineer; b. Tidaholm, Sweden, Nov. 22, 1943; s. Karl-Gustav Samuel and Gerda Maria Elisabet (Andersson) J.; m. Britt Elfström, May 25, 1968; children: Jenny, Jesper. Grad. in engring., Tech. Inst., Stockholm, 1967. Automotive electrician Osterman AB, Stockholm, 1964-66; foreman Electro Diesel, Kiruna, Sweden, 1967-74; devel. engr. Peltor AB, Värmano, Sweden, 1974—. Office: Aearo Peltor, Box 2341, 331 02 Värnamo Sweden

JAKOPČIĆ, KRESIMIR, retired chemistry educator; b. Zagreb, Croatia, Nov. 30, 1930; s. Miroslav and Marija (Srdarević) J.; m. Olga Franić, Oct. 24, 1959; 1 child, Sanja. Degree in Chem. Engring., U. Zagreb, 1956, DSc, 1963. Asst. Inst. Rugjer Bošković, Zagreb, 1957-63, sr. asst., 1963-67, head lab., 1962-68; postdoctoral rsch. asst. chem. dept. U. Manchester, Eng., 1966-67; lectr. Faculty Tech., Zagreb, 1967-73, assoc. prof., 1973-78, prof., 1978-91, head dept., 1973-87, dean, 1977-79; prof. Faculty Chem. Engring. and Tech., Zagreb, 1991-97; ret., 1997. Contbr. numerous articles on chemistry of heterocyclic compounds and organic photochemistry to profl. jours. Mem. Internat. Soc. Heterocyclic Chemistry, European Photochemistry Assn., Croatian Chem. Soc. (hon.), N.Y. Acad. Scis. Roman Catholic. Avocations: photography, Alpine skiing. E-mail: kjapkop@pierre.fkit.hr. Home: Nazorova 66, HR-10000 Zagreb Croatia Office: Faculty Chem Engring & Tech, Marulićev Trg 20, HR-10000 Zagreb Croatia

JAKSA, MARK BRIAN, civil engineering educator, researcher; b. Adelaide, Australia, Feb. 10, 1961; s. Stan and Maria Nivis (Clappis) J.; m. Marie Helen White, Jan. 21, 1989; children: Matthew, Christopher. BEng with honors, U. Adelaide, 1984, PhD, 1996. Geotech. engr. Coffey & Ptnrs. Pty Ltd., Adelaide, 1984-85; civil engr. B.C. Tonkin & Assocs., Adelaide, 1985-87; tutor U. Adelaide, 1988-91, lectr., 1992-98, sr. lectr., 1998—; sr. engr. G.J. Perry & Assocs. Pty Ltd., Adelaide, 1988-95; chmn. 7th Australia New Zealand Conf. on Geomechanics Organizing Com., Adelaide, 1993-96. Editor: Geomechanics in a Changing World, 1996; contbr. articles to profl. jours. Recipient James Hardie pipeline award James Hardie Industries,

Australia, 1983; grantee Australian Rsch. Coun., 1993-95. Mem. Instn. Engrs. Australia (cert.), Australian Geomechanics Soc. (hon. sec. 1994-96, chmn. 1997—, joint award with New Zealand Geotech. Soc. 1996). Roman Catholic. Home: 12 Paul St Hectorville, Adelaide SA 5073, Australia Office: U Adelaide, Dept Civil & Enviro Engring, Adelaide SA 5005, Australia

JAKUBASSA-AMUNDSEN, DORIS HEIDEMARIE, physicist, mathematician; b. Munich, Oct. 17, 1947; d. Ernst and Liselott (Strauss) Jakubassa; m. Per Amund Amundsen, June 6, 1980; 1 child, Ragnhild. Diploma, Tech. U. Munich, 1972, PhD in Natural Scis., 1975; privatdozent, U. Frankfurt, Germany, 1989; dipl. mathematics, U. Munich, 2000. Rsch. assoc. Tech. U. Munich, 1975-78, univs., Norway and Denmark, 1978-80, Tech. U. Munich, 1980-86, U. Munich, 1987-91, U. Frankfurt, U. Munich, 1992—. Avocations: swimming, music, sewing. Office: U Munich Physics Sect, Am Coulombwall 1, 85748 Garching Germany

JAKUBETZ, HANSJOERG, chemist; b. Herrenberg, Germany, Mar. 4, 1965; s. Franz and Ilse J. Grad., Eberhard-Karls U., 1993, DSc, 1997. Asst. lectr. Eberhard-Karls U., Tuebingen, Germany, 1997-98; from group leader analytical svcs. to gen. mgr. CarboGen Labs., Marly, 1999—. Author: The Impact of Stereochemistry on Drug Development and Use, 1997; contbr. articles to profl. jours. Mem. Am. Chem. Soc., GDCH, Nat. Geographic Soc. Office: CarboGen Labs Marly AG, Rte de L'Ancienne Papeterie, Marly Fribourg 1723, Switzerland

JAKUBOWSKY, FRANK RAYMOND, religious writer; b. Belfield, N.D., Oct. 11, 1931; s. William and Catherine (O'bach) J. Student, U. N.D., 1950-52. Chemist Sherwin-Williams Paint Co., Emeryville, Calif., 1958-85; pres. Bold Books, Oakland, Calif., 1978—; editor Spiritfest, Berkeley, Calif., 1997—. Author: Creation, 1978, Jesus Was a Leo, 1979, The Psychological Patterns of Jesus Christ, 1982, The Creative Theory of the Universe, 1983, Caldecott, 1985, Frank on a Farm, 1988, Lake Merritt, 1988, Thank God, I Am Alive, 1989, Whitman Revisited, 1989, Spiritual Symbols for the Astrology of the Soul, 1990, This New World; Birth: Sept. 8, 1958, 1990, Perceptive Types, 1993, Father Figure Frank's Stories, 1996, Inspiration Stories, 1998, Universal Mind, 1998, Big Bang Goes Puff, 1999. Pfc. U.S. Army, 1952-54. Mem. Urantia Fellowship, Inst. Noetic Scis., Nat. Coun. Geocosmic Rsch. Roman Catholic. Avocations: writing songs for children on fraimba. Home: 1565 Madison St Apt 308 Oakland CA 94612-4511

JALAJ, JAY KUMAR, retired academic administrator; b. Lalitpur, Uttar Prad, India, Oct. 2, 1934; s. Dhanna Lal and Kesar (Bai) Jain; m. Preeti Jain, May 15, 1959; children: Shraddha Ghate, Smita Humbad. BA, Allahabad (India) U., 1955, MA, 1957; PhD, Vikram U., Ujjain, India, 1977. Asst. prof. Allahabad U., 1961-62, Govt. of Madhya Pradesh Colls., various cities, 1959-72; prof. Govt. of Madhya Pradesh Colls., Ratlam, 1972-83, degree prin., 1983-84, postgrad. prin., 1984-94, ret., 1994—; mem. program adv. com. All India Radio, Indore, 1994—; working chmn. Ctrl. Sch., Ratlam, 1984-94. Author: Suraj Si Aasthha, 1958, Dhvani aur Dhavanigram Shastra, 1962 (M.P. Govt. Kamtaprasad Guru award 1967), Aitihasik Bhasha Vijanan Siddhant Aur Vyavhar, 1972, Sankrit Aur Hindi Natak Rachana Eavam Rangakarm, 1985 (M.P. Govt. Bhoj award 1987); co-author: Tum Kahan Se Aaye, 1964. Recipient Sahitya Saraswat award Hindi Sahitya Sammelan, Prayag, India, 1998. Mem. Kalaveethika (chmn. 1990—), Surabhi, Rotary (hon.). Avocations: reading, creative writing. Home: 30 Indira Nagar, Ratlam 457 001, India

JALENAK, JAMES BAILEY, lawyer; b. New Orleans, Sept. 5, 1939; s. Leo R. and Reha (Lichterman) J.; m. Natalie Block, Dec. 27, 1965; children: Margaret Amie Jalenak Wexler, Catherine Ann Jalenak Levit. BA in Politics & Econs. magna cum laude, Yale U., 1961, JD, 1964. Assoc. Paul, Weiss, Rifkind, Wharton & Garrison, N.Y.C., 1964-65; ptnr. Hanover, Walsh, Jalenak & Blair, Memphis, 1965—; lectr. in law U. Memphis, 1971-76. Sec., gen. counsel Memphis Zool. Soc., also past bd. dirs.; v.p. S.W. coun. Union Am. Hebrew Congregations; chmn. legal com. Henry S. Jacobs Camp; pres. Temple Israel, Memphis, 1992-94; past pres. Memphis Pub. Edn. Fund, Memphis Yale Club; past bd. dirs. Jewish Children's Regional Svc., New Orleans, Memphis Jewish Cmty. Ctr.; past officer, bd. dirs. Plough Towers, Jewish Family Svc.; past chmn. ctrl. area adv. com., supt.'s adv. com., commn. on excellence Memphis City Schs.; v.p. Memphis Jewish Fedn. Recipient Golden Rule award Vol. Ctr. of Memphis, 1994, Cmty. Svc. award Memphis Urban League, Humanitarian of Yr. award NCCJ, 2000. Fellow Tenn. Bar Found.; mem. Memphis Bar Assn. (bd. dirs.), Memphis Rotary (pres. 1998-99), Order of Coif, Phi Delta Phi. Jewish. Avocation: photography. Home: 5260 Sycamore Grove Ln Memphis TN 38120-2242 Office: Hanover Walsh Jalenak Blair 22 N Front St Memphis TN 38103-2162

JALILI, NADER, mechanical engineer, educator; b. Tehran, Iran, Oct. 26, 1970; came to U.S., 1995; s. Ahmad and Delnaz (Doulat Abadi) J.; m. Jaleh Esmailzadeh, Dec. 5, 1993; children: Paneed Fatemeh, Jalili. BSc with 1st class honors, Sharif U. tech., Tehran, 1992, MSc with 1st class honors, 1995; PhD, U. Conn., 1998. Design cons. Iranian truck Mfg., Tehran, 1992-93; tchg. asst. Sharif U. Tech., Tehran, 1993-95; design engr. Iranian Crane Mfg., Tehran, 1993-95; lectr. Azad U. Karaj, Iran, 1994-95; rsch. asst. U. Conn., Storrs, 1995-98; asst. prof. dept. mech. engring. No. Ill. U., DeKalb, 1999—; computer cons. Sharif U. Tech., 1993-94, U. Conn., 1997-98; design cons. Indsl. Mixers Mfg. Co., Esfehan, Iran, 1994-95. Contbr. articles to profl.. jours. U. Conn. scholar fellow, 1995-98. Mem. ASME (assoc.), AIAA (assoc.), IEEE (assoc.). Moslem. Avocations: volleyball, running, soccer. Home: 854 Issaqueena Trl Apt 705 Central SC 29630-9368 Office: Northern Illinois Univ 590 Garden Rd Dekalb IL 60115-2378

JALILIAN-MARIAN, JAMAL, physicist; b. Iran, May 4, 1963. BA, U. Ill., Chgo., 1990; PhD, U. Minn., 1997. Rsch. assoc. Lawrence Berkeley Lab., Calif., 1997—. Office: LBNL 1 Cyclotron Rd Berkeley CA 94720-0001

JALISI, QAZI M.H., medical educator; b. Budaun, U.P., India, Feb. 5, 1937; s. Zahur-ul Hasnain and Zainab Khatoon (Qadri) Qazi; m. Humaira Qadri Jalisi, Aug. 23, 1964; children: Hasan, Farah, Farrukh, Scharukh. MBBS, Liaquat Med. Coll., 1959; DLO, Royal Coll. Surgeons Physician, 1963, FRCS, 1964; FICS (hon.), Internat. Coll. Surgeons, 1967; FCPS (hon.), Coll. Physicians Surgeons, Pakistan, 1987; FCBS (hon.), Bangladesh Coll. Surgeons, 1993. Cert. O.R.L. Head Neck surgeon specialist. Prof. Nishtar Med. Coll., Multan, Pakistan, 1969-70, Liquat Med. Coll., Jamshoro, Pakistan, 1970-71, Jinnah Post-grad. Med. Ctr., Karachi, Pakistan, 1979-86; prof. Dow Med. Coll., Karachi, 1971-79, 1986-97; prin. Sindh Med. Coll., Karachi, 1986-87, dean faculty med. Karachi U., 1992-94, dean faculty ORL, Coll. Physicians Surgeons Pakistan, Karachi, 1992—. Author: Short Book of ENT Diseases 1st-9th Eds, Fundamentals of O.R.L., 1969, Current Problems in O.R.L., 1991; contbr. articles to prof. jours. Bd. govs. Pakistan Med Rsch. Coun., 1992-94; counsillor Pakistan Med. Coun., 1992-94, life councillor, regional sec. Internat. Fed. Otoloryngology Soc., 1993—. Reciepent gold award 8th Asia-Oceania Congress, 1995, gold award Pakistan E.N.T. Soc., 1997, gold award Internat. Fed. Otholaryngology Socs., 1997. Fellow Internat. Coll. Surgeons, Royal Soc. Med., Pakistan Coll. Physicians Surgeons. Avocations: reading, writing, traveling. Office: JJ Hosp, Al-Haroon Bld Garden Rd, Karachi Pakistan

JALLIN, FRANCOIS, judge. Pres. Tribunal Supérieur d'Appel, St. Pierre and Miquelon. Office: Tribunal Superieur d'Appel, BP 4215, Saint Pierre 97500, Saint Pierre and Miquelon*

JALURIA, YOGESH, mechanical engineering educator; b. Nabha, Punjab, India, Sept. 8, 1949; came to U.S., 1970; s. Jagdishwar and Maya (Verma) J.; m. Anuradha Malhotra, Sept. 9, 1975; children: Pratik, Aseem, Ankur. BS, Indian Inst. Tech., Delhi, 1970; MS, Cornell U., 1972, PhD, 1974. Mem. tech. staff Bell Labs., Princeton, N.J., 1974-76; asst. prof. Indian Inst. Tech., Kanpur, 1976-80; asst. prof. Rutgers U., New Brunswick, N.J., 1980-82, assoc. prof., 1982-85, prof. of mech. engring., 1985-91, prof. II, disting. prof., 1991—; cons. David Sarnoff Lab., SRI, Princeton, 1989-90, Steel Authority, Ranchi, India, 1977-80, others; mem. NSF grants rev. panel, other panels, 1996-98; NSF vis. scientist Indian Inst. Tech., 1988-89; lectr. in field; participant workshop on natural convection NSF, Colo., 1982, Indo-Australian Solar Energy Workshop, New Delhi, 1978, others; assoc. tech. editor J. Heat Transfer, 1993-99; mng. editor Computational Mechanics, 1994—, co-editor, 2000—; spkr. in field. Author: Natural Convection Heat and Mass Transfer, 1980; co-author: (book) Computational Heat Transfer, 1986, Buoyancy Induced Flows, 1988, (with others) Computer Methods for Engineering, 1988, Design and Optimization of Thermal Systems, 1998, (book chpts.) Natural Convection, 1985, Handbook of Single-Phase Convective Heat Transfer, 1987, Energy Storage Systems, 1989, Handbook of Fire Protection, 1995, numerous others; contbr. more than 300 articles and papers to profl. jours. and confs. including Rev. Sci. Instrum., Jour. Heat Transfer, Jour. Thermophysics Heat Transfer, Numerical Heat Transfer, Jour. Fluid Mech., Jour. Numerical Meth. Engring.; mem. numerous editorial bds. including mem. editorial adv. bd. Numerical Heat Transfer, 1987—; mem. editorial bd. Internat. Jour. Numerical Meth. Heat and Flow, 1990—; reviewer including Applied Mechanics Rev., Jour. Fluid Mechanics, Jour. Heat Transfer, Jour. Solar Energy Engring.; referee numerous articles. NATO Disting. lectr., 1984, 88; recipient cert. of recognition Dept. of Commerce, 1982, Disting. Alumnus award IIT, 1994. Fellow ASME (chmn. nat. heat transfer conf., coord. com. 1991-92, exec. com. heat transfer divsn. 1998—, Heat Transfer Mem. award 1995, Worcester Reed Warner medal 1999, Freeman scholar 2000), Am. Phys. Soc., Combustion Inst., India Assn. of East Brunswick (pres. 1985, 91, 94-96), Cornell India Assn. (v.p. 1972-73). Democrat. Hindu. Achievements include patents for Methods and apparatus for heating articles, for Methods and apparatus for avoiding undesirable deposits in crystal growing operations; copyrighted computer software in materials processing and electronics cooling; research in thermal processing of materials, fires, computational heat transfer, natural convection, cooling of electronic equipment and environmental flows, flows rising above finite heated bodies, interaction of buoyant flows with surfaces, buoyant jet flows, mixed convection in enclosures, heat removal from heated elements on a vertical surface, thermal stratification and heat rejection problems, solar energy storage in salt-gradient solar ponds, numerical and experimental simulation of thermal processes in manufacturing systems, computer aided design of thermal systems, knowledge based design methodology, and enclosure fire growth processes. Office: Rutgers U Mech Engring Dept New Brunswick NJ 08903

JAMAL, MOEZ AHAMED, banker; b. Mombasa, Kenya, June 15, 1955; s. Ahamed and Shamsultan (Kalyan); m. Nadia Eboo, June 23, 1979; children: Nijhad, Shazia. BA in Econs. with honors, Manchester U., 1976; MBA, NYU, 1979. 1st v.p. Lloyds Bank, N.Y., 1979-85; v.p. Credit Suisse, London, 1985-93; treas. Credit Suisse, N.Y.C., 1993-96; mng. dir., golbal head money markets/funding Credit Suisse First Boston, N.Y.C., 1997—. Mem. R.A.C. Club, Overseas Bankers Club, City Swiss Club. Moslem. Home: 33 High Farms Rd Glen Head NY 11545-2222

JAMALIPOUR, ABBAS, electrical engineer, educator; b. Isfahan, Iran, May 31, 1963; arrived in Australia, 1998; m. Zohreh Heidari, Mar. 21, 1988; children: Soroush, Sepehr. BSEE with honors, Isfahan U. Tech., 1988; MSEE with honors, Sharif U. Tech., Iran, 1990; PhD in Elec. Engring., Nagoya (Japan) U., 1996. Lectr. Sharif U. Tech., 1991-92, rsch. engr., 1990-92; tchg. asst. Nagoya U., 1994-96, asst. prof., 1996-98; sr. lectr. U. Sydney, 1998—; cons. Iran Telecom. Rsch. Ctr., Tehran, 1989-91. Author: Low Earth Orbital Satellites for Personal Communication Networks, 1998; contbr. articles to profl. jours. Recipient Young Scientist award Internat. Union of Radio Sci., 1996, Inoue Rsch. award for young scientists, 1996, award Telecomms. Advancement Found. Japan, 1997. Mem. IEEE (sr., student grantee 1994), Internat. Union Radio Sci., Inst. Electronics, Info. and Comm. Engrs. (Japan), Symposium of Info. Theory and Its Applications, Australian Assn. for Engring. Edn. Avocations: driving, reading, books. E-mail: a.jamalipour@ieee.org. Office: U Sydney, Sch Elec & Info Engring, Sydney 2006, Australia

JAMAR, STEVEN DWIGHT, law educator; b. Ishpeming, Mich., May 11, 1953; s. Dwight W. and Lorraine (Persgard) J.; m. Shelley June Von Hagen-Jamar, May 19, 1979; children: Alexander S., Eric D. BA, Carleton Coll., 1975; JD cum laude, Hamline U., 1979; LLM with distinction, Georgetown U., 1994. Bar: Minn. 1979, D.C. 1993, U.S. Supreme Ct. 1985. Jud. clk. Minn. Supreme Ct., St. Paul, 1979-80; assoc. Meagher & Geer, Mpls., 1980-86; clin. instr. William Mitchell Coll. of Law, St. Paul, 1987-89; pvt. practice Mpls., 1987-89; vis. asst. prof. law U. Balt., 1989-90; asst. prof. law Sch. Law Howard U., Washington, 1991-94, assoc. prof. law, 1994-96, prof. law, 1996—, dir. legal rsch. and writing program, 1990—; cons. on environ. legal info. sys. project NASA, 1998—. Co-author: Essential Lawyering Skills: Interviewing, Counseling, Negotiation, and Persuasive Fact Analysis, 1999; contbr. articles to profl. jours. Bd. dirs. Legal Advice Clinics, Hennepin County, Mpls., 1980-89, mem. exec. com., 1986-89, sec.-treas., 1988-89; coach Soccer Assn. Columbia, 1991-96. Mem. Legal Writing Inst. (bd. dirs. 1992-2000, exec com., 1994-98, pres., 1997-98), ABA, ACLU, Am. Soc. Internat. Law, Amnesty Internat., Computer Law Assn., Assn. Legal Writing Dirs. (bd. dirs., exec. com. 1996-97), Sierra Club, Howard County Go Club. Avocations: canoe camping, soccer, go. Office: Howard U Sch Law 2900 Van Ness St NW Washington DC 20008-1106

JAMARD, MICHEL HUBERT, corporate communications specialist; b. Paris, Jan. 16, 1948; s. Michel Louis and Jacqueline (Blain) J.; m. Noelle Laurence Girard, Nov. 6, 1975; 1 child, David. Degree in Journalism, Ecole Superieure Journalisme, Paris, 1971. Reporter Argus des Collectivites, Paris, 1975-77, L'Agence Nouvelle, Paris, 1977-78; chief reporter L'Agence Economique et Financiere, Paris, 1978-83; press officer Alcatel CIT, Paris, 1983-87; pub. rels. mgr. Alcatel, Brussels, 1987-88; dep. dir. comms. Alcatel Alsthom, Paris, 1988-90; dir. comms. Alcatel Cable, Clichy, France, 1991-96; dir. corp. comm. Alcatel Alsthom, Paris, 1995; dir. comms. OTV Group-Générale des Eaux (Vivendi), 1997-2000; v.p. corp. comm. COGEMA Group, 2000—. Editor mag. Profile, 1987, Cable, 1990. Reicpinet Corp. Advt. Grand Prix Strategies, Paris, 1989, 90, 95. Avocations: reading, tennis. Home: 6 Ave de Cluny, Saint Maur 94100, France Office: l'Aquarène, 1 place Montgolfier, 94417 Saint-Maurice France

JAMEEL, FATHULLA, government official; b. Malé, Maldives, Sept. 5, 1942; s. Mohamed and Shareefa Jameel; m. Fathimath, Oct. 30, 1989. B.A. in philosophy and islamic studies, Al-Azhar U., Cairo, 1967; diploma in edn., Ein-Shams U., Cairo, 1968; spec. diploma in edn., Ein Shams U., Cairo, 1969; fgn. svc. training, Minstry of Foreign Affairs, Canberra, Australia, 1974. Tchr. Majeediyya Sch., 1969-73; undersec., Ministry of External Affairs Republic of Maldives, Malé, 1973-76, dep. head, Ministry of External Affairs, 1976-77, acting undersec., dept. fgn. aid, 1974; acting undersec., Ministry of Transport Republic of Maldives, 1975; perm. rep. Maldives to the U.N., 1977-78; min. fgn. affairs Republic of Maldives, Malé, 1978—; gov. Maldives Internatl. Monetary Fund, Asian Devel. Bank, 1979-83, The World Bank,, 1979—; gov. maldivesto Islamic Devel. Bank, 1980—; acting min. planning and devel. Republic of Maldives, Malé, 1982-83, min. state for planning and devel., 1990-91; chmn., Maldives Fisheries Coop., 1990-91, Nat. Youth Coun., 1979-81; mem. Fisheries Adv. Bd., 1979—, Nat. Planning Coun., 1981—, Tourism Adv. Bd., 1981—, Nat. Edn. Coun., 1989—; mem. bd. dirs. Maldives Monetary Authority, 1981—; chmn. DHIRAAGU, Natl. Telecommunication Co., 1988—, mem., Parliament, 1989—; mem. Supreme Coun. Islamic Affairs, 1997—. Office: Ministry Fgn Affairs, Baduthakufaanu Magu, Male 20-05, Maldives

JAMES, ANNETTE L., financial planner; b. Mount Clare, W.Va., Apr. 23, 1937; d. William E. and Eva Elizabeth (Thompson) Cunningham; m. Ronald G. James, Dec. 26, 1959; children: Janet E., R. Eric. BS, Alderson-Broaddus Coll., 1959; MSN, U. Rochester, 1961. CFP; cert. practice of Kinlein. Asst. prof. Alderson-Broaddus Coll., Philippi, W.Va., 1968-75, W.Va. U., Morgantown, 1976-80; ptnr. James, Williams & Assocs., 1980-98; pvt. practice kinleiner, 1999—; v.p., trustee Alderson-Broaddus Coll. Co-author: The Joy of Listening, 1993. Mem. Ptnrs. in Edn. Harrison County Pub. Schs., Shinnston, W.Va.; trustee Alderson-Broaddus Coll. Recipient Apollo award Alderson-Broaddus Coll., 1993, Disting. Alumni award, Alderson Broaddus Coll., 1995. Mem. WVBC Ministers Wives Assn. (pres. 1997-98), Woman's Club (Shinnston). Baptist. Home: 7108 Adelphi Rd Hyattsville MD 20782-1001 Office: Practice of Kinlein Metro 3 Bldg Ste 637B Hyattsville MD 20782

JAMES, BARBARA FRANCES, school nurse, special education educator; b. Elizabeth, N.J., June 29, 1941; d. Edward Joseph and Frances Veronica (Szypula) Turkiewicz; 1 child, John Wayne James. Certificate in group tchg., Kean Coll., 1981; diploma, Elizabeth Gen. Sch. Nursing, 1962; BS magna cum laude, Jersey City State Coll., 1994. Cert. tchr. health edn., cert. sch. nurse, cert. infant specialist, cert. family svc. provider trainer, N.J.; RN, N.J. Oper. room nurse Alexian Bros. Hosp., Elizabeth, 1962-63; obstetrical nurse Rahway (N.J.) Hosp., 1964-65; pvt. duty nurse Alexian Bros., St. Elizabeth and Elizabeth Gen. Hosps., 1964-65; office nurse Stephan S. Halabis, MD, Linden, N.J., 1965-71; tchr. developmentally disabled Assn. for Retarded Citizens, Winfield, N.J., 1971-76; early intervention tchr., home trainer The Arc of Union County/Kohler Child Devel. Ctr., Winfield, 1976—; sch. nurse Kohler Child Dev. Ctr., Winfield, N.J., 1976—; guest lectr. developmental disabilities Kean Coll., Middlesex County Coll., Rutgers U., Jersey City State Coll., Fla. Atlantic U., Union Coll., 1980-92; mem. pres. com. on mental retardation U.S. Dept. Health and Human Svcs., N.J. State Nurses Assn., Elizabeth Pub. Schs. One-woman shows include Elizabeth Gen. Med. Ctr., Woodbridge, N.J., 1984; exhibited in group shows at N.J. State Mus., Trenton, 1959, Elizabeth Gen. Med. Ctr., 1960-62, Found. Arts and Scis., Long Beach Island, 1981, Kean Coll., Union, N.J., 1981, Woodbridge (N.J.) Mall, 1981; author, illustrator (booklet) Recognizing Childhood Illness, 1973. Mem. legis. com. Union County Protection Coun., Elizabeth, 1975; mem. supervisory com. Winfield Fed. Credit Union, 1977; active Dem. com. Twp. of Winfield, 1978, mem. drug alliance coun., 1990; active local, county and state health fairs. Recipient Health Fair Pub. Svc. award State of N.J., Rutgers U., 1986; Garwood (N.J.) Women's Club scholar, 1959; named Teacher of the Year ARC of Union County, 1981. Mem. Coun. for Exceptional Children, League for Ednl. Advancement of Nurses. Avocation: fine arts painting. Home: 66B Wavecrest Ave Winfield Park NJ 07036-6633 Office: The Arc of Union County Kohler Child Devel Ctr 39 1/2 Wavecrest Ave Winfield Park NJ 07036-6630

JAMES, BRUCE RICHARD, investor; b. Cleve., Oct. 19, 1942; s. George R. and Dorothy B. (Watson) J.; m. Jo Ann Osborn, Feb. 5, 1966 (div. Feb. 1982); children: Michael, Jeffrey, Stephen; m. Nora Ellen Thomas, May 11, 1985. BS, Rochester (N.Y.) Inst. Tech., 1964. V.p. Keller-Crescent Co., Evansville, Ind., 1964-70; v.p. Cardinal Co., San Francisco, 1970-73; pres., CEO Uniplan Corp., San Francisco, 1973-83, Electrographic Corp., San Francisco, 1983-93; chmn., CEO Barclays Law Pubs., San Francisco, 1986-94; pres., CEO Nev. New-Tech, Inc., Incline Village, Nev., 1993—; mem. dean's adv. coun. U. Nev. Las Vegas Boyd Sch. of Law, 1999—; bd. dirs. BIPAC, Washington; chmn. bd. dirs. Polish-Am. Print Co., Warsaw, 1990-93; pres. Printing Industries of Calif., 1989-91; mem. dean's adv. bd. U. Nev.-Las Vegas Boyd Sch. of Law. Candidate U.S. Senate, 1997-98; vice chmn. bd. trustees Rochester Inst. Tech., 1993—; chair bd. trustees Sierra Nev. Coll., Incline Village, 1997—; mem. Bd. of Equalization, Reno, 1995-97; trustee U. Nev. Desert Rsch. Inst., 1999—; dir. Nev. Test Site Devel. Corp., 1999—, Western Folklife Ctr., Elko, Nev., 1999—; bd. dirs. Cmty. Found. Western Nev., 1999—; fin. chmn. Nev. Rep. Party, 2000—. Commencement spkr. Rochester Inst. Tech., 1998, Alumnus of Yr., 1997; recipient Silver Beaver award Boys Scouts Am., 1992. Mem. NMA, Printing Industries of Am. (chair congl. roundtable), Las Vegas C. of C., Nat. Fedn. Independent Businesses, World Trade Club of San Francisco, Internat. Wine & Food Soc., Confrerie de la Chaine des Rotisseurs, Alexis de Tocqueville Soc. (Nev. state chmn. 1999—), Genesee Valley Club (Rochester, N.Y.). Republican. Episcopalian. Office: Nev New Tech Inc PO Box 9167 Incline Village NV 89452-9167

JAMES, DARRELL SCOTT, biology educator, consultant; b. Nampa, Idaho, May 30, 1963; s. William Darrel and Lucille Ann James; m. Alina Fujie, Dec. 27, 1986; 1 child, Travis Hirorni. BS in Biology, Pacific U., 1986; MS in Marine Sci., Oreg. State U., 1990. Cert. tchr., Calif. Biology cons. Coll. Bd., San Jose, Calif., 1990—; biology instr. Modesto (Calif.) Jr. Coll., 1991—; marine biology instr. Chapman U., Modesto, 1996—; sci. curriculum coord. Modesto City Schs., 1997—; biology instr. Beyer H.S., Modesto, 1985—. Named Calif. Tchr. of Yr. Calif. League H.S., 1997. Republican. Home: 2628 Maestro Way Modesto CA 95355-9672 Office: Fred C Beyer HS 1717 Sylvan Ave Modesto CA 95355-1312

JAMES, DAVID GERAINT, physician; b. Treherbert, Wales, Jan. 2, 1922; s. David James and Sarah (Davies) J.; m. Sheila Patricia Sherlock, Dec. 15, 1951; children: Amanda Melys, Auriole Zara. BS, U. Cambridge, Eng., 1941; MB BS, U. London, 1945; postgrad., Columbia U., N.Y.C., 1950-51; LLD (hon.), U. Wales, 1985. Rsch. fellow Columbia U., N.Y.C., 1950-51; pvt. practice London, 1959—; dean Royal Northern Hosp., London, 1968-87; prof. medicine U. London, 1987—; prof. medicine, Royal Free Hosp. Sch. Medicine, U. Miami, Fla., U. Santo Domingo; consulting physician, Royal Navy. Author: Sarcoidosis and Other Granulomatous Disorders, 1994; mem. editorial bd., Postgrad. Med. Jour., Hosp. Doctor, Brit. Jour. Clin. Practice; editor-in-chief: Internat. Jour. Sarcoidosis; contbr. numerous sci. papers to profl. publs. Knight, Order of Christopher Columbus, Dominican Republic; recipient gold medal, Barraquer Inst. Ophthalmology, Barcelona, Spain. Fellow ACP (hon.), Royal Coll. Ophthalmology; mem. World Assn. Sarcoidosis and Other Granulomatous Disorders (pres.), Harvey Soc. London (past. pres.), Med. Soc. London (past pres., trustee), Osler Soc. London (past pres.), Am. Osler Soc., World Congress of History of Medicine (organizing sec. 1972), Hunterian Soc. Eng. (councillor), Royal Cymmrodorian Soc. (v.p.), Royal Coll. Physicians, Nat. Acad. Medicine France. Office: 149 Harley St, London W1N 1HG, England

JAMES, DAVID LEE, lawyer, international advisor, author; b. Chgo., Aug. 23, 1933; s. Roy L. and Ethel (Wells) J.; m. Sheila Feagley, May 26, 1962; children: Pamela, James, Winifred, Paul, Brian, Adam. A.B., Harvard U., 1955; J.D., U. Chgo., 1960; grad. exec. program, Stanford U., 1979. Bar: N.Y. 1961, N.J. 1967, Hawaii 1976, Ill. 1987. With various law firms N.Y.C., 1960-67; counsel and asst. gen. counsel, asst. sec. Texasgulf Inc., 1967-75; gen. counsel, sec. Dillingham Corp., Honolulu, 1975-77, v.p., gen. counsel, sec., 1977-84; v.p. legal affairs, sec. Dillingham Corp., San Francisco, 1984-85; asst. gen. counsel, asst. sec. Crown Zellerbach Corp., San Francisco, 1985-86; sr. ptnr., sr. corp. atty. Arnstein & Lehr, Chgo., 1987-90, of counsel, 1990-96; chmn. bus. programs East-West Ctr., Honolulu, 1990-92; chief of party and sr. law devel. advisor USAID and Govt. of Indonesia, Jakarta, Indonesia, 1992-93; pres. Bus. Strategies Internat., San Francisco, Calif., 1993—; hon. consul of Malaysia, Hawaii, 1977-84; adv. bd. Internat. and Comparative Law Ctr., Southwestern Legal Found., Dallas, 1976-91; adv. com. Law of Sea Inst., Honolulu, 1977-84; lectr. in law Stanford U. Sch. Law, 1996-98. Author: Doing Business in Asia, 1993, The Executive Guide to Asia-Pacific Communications, 1995; contbg. editor Upside mag.; contbr. various articles on bus. and legal subjects. Bd. dirs. Chgo. Chamber Orch., 1988-90, pres. 1989-90, Jr. Achievement Hawaii, 1976-84, Hawaii Opera Theatre, 1981-84, Friends of East-West Ctr., 1982-84; mem. Morristown (N.J.) Bd. Edn., 1967-68. Served to lt. (j.g.) USNR, 1955-57. Mem. Outrigger Canoe Club (Honolulu), World Trade Club (San Francisco), Harvard Club (N.Y.C.). E-mail: djames@bsicorp.net. Office: Bus Strategies Internat 425 Market St Ste 2200 San Francisco CA 94105-2434

JAMES, DAVID LINDON, academic administrator; b. Detroit, Sept. 1, 1955; s. Lindon Donald and Sharon Rose (Kyle) J.; m. Debra Marie Ketterer, Dec. 30, 1977; children: Collin, Nathan, Leah. BA, Western Mich. U., 1977; MA, Central Mich. U., 1979; EdD, Wayne State U., 1998. Adj. instr. St. Clair Community Coll., Port Huron, Mich., 1979-80; coordinator program promotion Siena Heights Coll., Adrian, Mich., 1980-82, dir. admissions, 1982-86; dir. admissions U. Mich., Flint, 1986-96; dean acad. and student svcs. Oakland C.C., Waterford, Mich., 1996—. Author (books of poems) A Heart Out Of This World, 1984, Do Not Give Dogs What Is Holy, 1994. Recipient Creative Writers award Mich. Council for the Arts, 1983. Office: Oakland CC 7350 Cooley Lake Rd Waterford MI 48327-3864

JAMES, GARY DOUGLAS, biological anthropologist, educator, researcher; b. Norwich, Conn., Dec. 6, 1954; s. Godfrey Merchant and Joan (McIlwaine) J.; m. Kathleen Louise Wilson, July 28, 1979. BA, Wake Forest U., 1976; MA, Pa. State U., 1980, PhD, 1984. Part-time instr. Pa. State U., University Park, 1982-84; postdoctoral assoc. Cornell U. Med. Coll., N.Y.C., 1984-86; asst. prof. physiology and biophysics Med. Coll. Cornell U., N.Y.C., 1986-91, asst. prof. physiology in medicine, 1986-91, assoc. rsch. prof. of physiology in medicine, 1991-98, assoc. rsch. prof. of

physiology and biophysics, 1991-98; rsch. prof. Decker Sch. Nursing SUNY, Binghamton, 1998—, dir. Inst. for Primary and Preventative Health Care, adj. prof. dept. anthropology, 1999—, adj. prof. dept. psychology, 2000—. Contbr. chpt. to book, articles to profl. jours. Recipient New Investigator Rsch. award NIH, 1986, Internat. Man of the Yr. award Internat. Biog. Ctr., 1993; NIH postdoctoral trainee, 1984. Fellow Human Biol. Assn. (sec.-treas. 1992-96, exec. com. 1996—), Soc. Behavioral Medicine; mem. AAAS, Am. Assn. Phys. Anthropologists, Internat. Platform Assn., Soc. for Study Social Biology, Am. Soc. Hypertension, Soc. for Epidemiol. Rsch., Am. Dermatoglyphics Assn. (exec. com. 1996-98, sec. 1998-99), The Harvey Soc. Lutheran. Office: Decker Sch of Nursing Binghamton Univ SUNY Box 6000 Binghamton NY 13902-6000

JAMES, GORDON, III, lawyer; b. Montclair, N.J., Feb. 24, 1947; s. Ernest Gordon Jr. and Betty (Wackerman) J.; m. Adelia Louise Medlin (div. Sept. 1989); children: Deidre Leigh, Diana Catherine, Gordon Daniel; m. Gwen Aline Campanile, Jan. 5, 1991 (div. June 1993). BS, U. Tenn., 1969; JD, Vanderbilt U., 1972. Bar: Fla. 1972, U.S. Dist. Ct. (so. dist.) Fla. 1972, D.C. 1973, U.S. Ct. Appeals (11th cir.) 1980, U.S. Dist. Ct. (mid. dist.) Fla. 1985, U.S. Dist. Ct. (no. dist.) Fla. 1986, U.S. Supreme Ct. 1988. Assoc. Bradford, Williams, Kimbrell, et al, Miami, Fla., 1972-76; ptnr. Druck, Grimmett, Norman, Weaver, Scherer, Ft. Lauderdale, Fla., 1976-77, Druck, Grimmett, Scherer, James, Ft. Lauderdale, 1977-78, Grimmett, Scherer, James, Ft. Lauderdale, 1978-79, Conrad, Scherer, James & Jenne, Ft. Lauderdale, 1979-95, Heinrich Gordon Hargrove Weihe & James, Ft. Lauderdale, 1995—. Eucharistic lay minister, All Saints Episcopal Ch., 1991—. Capt. USAR, 1969-77. Mem. ABA, Fla. Bar Assn. (vice chmn. civil rule of procedure com. 1990-91), Nat. Assn. R.R. Counsel, Am. Acad. Hosp. Attys., Am. Bd. Trial Advs. (cert., Ft. Lauderdale chpt. pres. 1998), Def. Rsch. Inst., Fla. Def. Lawyers (pres. 1991-92). Republican. Avocations: fishing, snow skiing, scuba diving, physical and aerobics exercise. Office: Heinrich Gordon Hargrove Weihe & James 500 E Broward Blvd Fort Lauderdale FL 33394-3000

JAMES, GRAHAM RICHARD, bishop; b. Torrington, Devon, Eng., Jan. 19, 1951; s. Lionel Dennis and Florence May James; m. Julie Anne Freemantle, Jan. 21, 1978; children: Rebecca Alice, Dominic Richard. BA, U. Lancaster, 1972; diploma in theology, U. Oxford, Eng., 1974; cert. in theology with distinction, Oxford Theol. Coll., 1975. Ordained as deacon, Ch. of Eng., 1975, priest, 1976, bishop, 1993. Curate Christ Ch., Peterborough, 1975-78; team vicar Christ the King, Welwyn Garden City, 1979-83; sr. selection sec. Ch. of Eng., 1983-87; chaplain Archbishop of Canterbury, 1987-93; bishop St. Germans, Truro, Cornwall, 1993-99; bishop of Norwich Eng., 1999—; vice-moderator Ch. Commn. for Inter-Faith Rels., 1993—. Contbr.: (book) Say One for Me, 1991; editor: New Soundings, 1997. Dir. Cornwall Alcohol and Drugs Agy., 1994—; pres. St. Petroc's Soc., U.K., 1993—. Mem. Athanaeum Club (London), Norfolk Club (Norwich). Avocations: theatre, cricket, collecting secondhand books. Fax: 01603 761613. E-mail: bishop@bishopofnorwich.org. Home and Office: Bishop's House, Norwich NR3 1SB, England

JAMES, GREGORY CYRIL, linguist; b. Redruth, Cornwall, Eng., Dec. 26, 1947; m. Zelinda Kit-Ying; children: Kendrick Hak-Kun, Llywelyn Wai-Loong. MA, U. Edinburgh, Scotland, 1970, MSc, 1979; M Phil., U. Reading, Eng., 1978; PhD, U. Exeter, Eng., 1989. Lectr. Regional Inst. English, Bangalore, India, 1970-72; tutor English Padworth Coll., Reading, Eng., 1972-74; head apprentice lang. tng. Mil. Tech. HighSch., Masjed-e Soleiman, Iran, 1974-78; lectr. U. Exeter, Eng., 1979-89, sr. lectr., 1989-90; vice prin. Inst. Lang. in Edn., Hong Kong, 1983-85; dir. Lang. Ctr. U. Sci. and Tech., Hong Kong, 1990—, prof., 1998—. Author: Tamil Lexicography, 1991; co-author: English in Computer Science, 1994, Colloquial Cantonese, 1994, English in Business Studies, 1996, Dictionary of Lexicography, 1998, History of Tamil Dictionaries, 2000. Recipient Faculty Enrichment award Govt. Can., Toronto, 1988; fellow G.K. Delmas Found., N.Y.C., Venice, 1986, Indian Coun. Hist. Rsch., Delhi, 1990, Internat. Inst. Tamil Studies, Madras, 1980, Dictionary Rsch. Ctr., U. Exeter, Eng., 1995; Assoc. in Linguistics Macquarie U., Australia, 1995. Fellow Inst. Linguists. Office: Hong Kong U Sci and Tech, Lang Ctr, Clear Water Bay, Kowloon Hong Kong

JAMES, KEITH, immunology educator; b. Frizington, Cumbria, Eng., Mar. 15, 1938; s. George Stanley and Alice (Dixon) J.; m. Valerie Spencer Jubb, Sept. 30, 1967; children: Mark, Stephen Gordon, Daniel. BSc, Birmingham (Eng.) U., 1959, PhD, 1962; DSc, U. Edinburgh, Scotland, 1970. Rsch. fellow Birmingham U., 1962-64; rsch. assoc. U. Calif., San Francisco, 1964-65; sr. lectr. immunology U. Edinburgh, 1965-77, reader, 1977-91, prof., 1991—. Co-author: Introducing Immunology, 1986, 2d edit., 1993; mem. editl. bds. 5 jours.; contbr. over 250 articles to sci. jours. Fellow Royal Soc. Edinburgh, Royal Coll. Pathologists, Inst. Biology; mem. Brit. Soc. for Immunology (treas. 1974-79, ednl. sec. 1980-85, trustee 1988-95), Internat. Union Immunological Socs. (sec. gen. 1992-98). Avocation: walking. Office: U Edinburgh Lister Labs, Royal Infirm, Lauriston Pl, Edinburgh EH3 9YW, Scotland

JAMES, LOUIS GABRIEL, writer, English literature educator; b. Shrewsbury, Eng., May 2, 1933; s. Henry Gerard and Grace Mary (Dunham) J.; m. Louise Annabel McConnell, May 29, 1994; children: Nicola, Michele, Hilary, Adrian. MA with honors, Oxford (Eng.) U., 1955, PhD, 1960. Staff tutor U. Hull, Eng., 1958-63; lectr. U. W.I., Kingston, Jamaica, 1963-66, U. Kent, Canterbury, Eng., 1966-80; prof. English and Commonwealth Lit. U. Singapore, 1986-87, U. Kent, 1987—. Author: Fiction for the Working Man, 1830-1850, 1963, Print and the People, 1976, Jean Rhys, 1978, Islands In Between, 1968, Caribbean Literature in English, 1998. Office: U Kent, Rutherford College, Canterbury CT2 7NX, England

JAMES, MILTON GARNET, economist; b. Guyana, Jan. 27, 1937; came to U.S., 1969, naturalized, 1976; s. Reginald Nathaniel and Caroline Elizabeth J.; m. Joyce Fernandes, July 31, 1960; children: Milton Garnet, Michael, Mark. BS, U. London, 1964; MBA, St. John's U., N.Y., 1972; PhD, U. London, 1973. Instr. econs. Baruch Coll. CUNY, 1972-74; asst. prof. mktg. Ramapo Coll., N.J., 1974-77; cons. econs. N.Y.C., 1978—. Chmn. Guyanese Cmty. Coun., U.S., 1976—. Recipient Pub. Svc. award Guyanese Cmty. Coun., 1982. Mem. Am. Econs. Assn., Caribbean Studies Assn., Masons. Episcopalians. Achievements include research in economic development, econometric forecasting, monetary and fiscal policies. Home: 649 E 23rd St Brooklyn NY 11210-1127

JAMES, NIGEL TERENCE, statistics consultant, former educator; b. Dec. 16, 1940. MA, MD, BChir, Cambridge (Eng.) U., 1967; MSc, Oxford (Eng.) U., 1970; MSc in Applied Stats., Coun. Nat. Acad. Awards, 1988. Sr. lectr. biomed. sci. Med. and Pure Scis. Faculties, U. Sheffield, Eng., 1967-97; dir. SigmaMetrics Statis. Cons. Svcs., Sheffield, 1997—. Author books; contbr. over 200 articles to med. and sci. jours. Mem. United Oxford and Cambridge U. Club (London). Avocation: music. Home: Park Holme, Sheffield S10 3EL, England Office: SigmaMetrics, PO Box 1462, Sheffield S10 3XP, England

JAMES, PATRICK FREDERICK, biology educator; b. Wellington, New Zealand, Oct. 14, 1928; arrived in Wales, 1929; s. Edward Frederick and Esther Minnie (Holswick) J.; m. Anne Christine Brettell-Stokes, Sept. 2, 1957; children: John Edward, Michael Fraser, Catherine Rebbeccah, Sarah Brettell. BSc, London U., 1956, MSc, 1969. Chartered biologist; cert. further edn. adminstrn. Part time lectr. Westham Tech. Coll., London, 1955-57, Isleworth Poly., London, 1956-57; tchr. Port Antonio Secondary Sch., Jamaica, 1957-60, Cranhorne Chase Sch., Wardour Castle Wilts, Eng., 1960-66; lectr. Salisbury (Eng.) Tech. Coll., 1966-93. Contbr. articles to profl. jours. Observer Royal Observer Corps, Salisbury, 1960-88; chmn. Liberal Club, Tisbury Nu Salisbury, Eng., 1960-80; ch. warden Swallowcliffe, Nu Tisbury, 1966-96. Signalman Royal Signals, 1948-50. Fellow Linnear Soc. (Bonhole Bequest award 1994); mem. Inst. Human Biology, Eugenics Soc. (Marie Stopes award 1976), Inst. Biology. Anglican. Avocations: visiting relatives, archery, swimming, reading. Home: Homewood Swallowcliffe, Salisbury SP3 5PW, England

JAMES, P(HYLLIS) D(OROTHY) (BARONESS JAMES OF HOLLAND PARK OF SOUTHWOLD IN COUNTY OF SUFFOLK), author; b. Oxford, Eng., Aug. 3, 1920; d. Sidney Victor and Dorothy May Amelia (Hone) J.; m. Connor Bantry White, 1941 (dec. 1964); children: Clare Bantry, Jane Bantry. Student Brit. schs.; LittD (hons.), U. Buckingham (Eng.), 1992, U. Hertfordshire (Eng.), 1994, U. Glasgow (Scotland), 1995, Durham U., 1998, Portsmouth U., 1999; DLitt, U. London, 1993; D. U. Essex, Eng., 1996. Adminstr. Nat. Health Service, 1949-68; apptd. prin. Civil Svc. Home Office, 1968; prin. Police Dept., 1968-72, Criminal Policy Dept., 1972-79. Author: Cover Her Face, 1962, A Mind to Murder, 1963, Unnatural Causes, 1967, Shroud for a Nightingale, 1971; (with T.A. Critchley) The Maul and the Pear Tree, 1971; An Unsuitable Job for a Woman, 1972, The Black Tower, 1975, Death of an Expert Witness, 1977, Innocent Blood, 1980, The Skull Beneath the Skin, 1982, (play) A Private Treason, 1985, A Taste for Death, 1986, Devices and Desires, 1989, The Children of Men, 1992, Original Sin, 1994, A Certain Justice, 1997, Time to be in Earnest, 1999. Gov. BBC, 1988-93; bd. dirs. Brit. Coun., 1988-93; bd. dirs., chair lit. adv. panel Arts Coun. Gt. Britain, 1988-92. Decorated Order Brit. Empire, 1983; created life peer (Baroness) of U.K., 1991; Assoc. fellow Downing Coll., Cambridge, 1986; hon. fellow St. Hilda's Coll., Oxford, 1996, Girton Coll., Cambridge, 2000; recipient Grandmaster award Mystery Writers of Am., 1999. Fellow Royal Soc. Lit., Royal Soc. Arts; mem. Soc. of Authors (chmn. 1984-86, pres. 1997—), Detection Club. Office: Greene & Heaton Ltd, 37 Goldhawk Rd, London W12 8QQ, England

JAMES, STEPHEN DAVID, water industry executive; b. Southport, Lancashire, England, Mar. 5, 1964; s. Michael and Elizabeth (Rimmer) J.; m. Valerie Jane Pearce, Oct. 4, 1993; children: Luke, Orrin, Darcy. BSc in Chem. Sci. with honors, U. Leeds, England, 1986. Scheduler Brit. Pipeline Agy., Hemel Hempstead, England, 1988-89, movements technologist, 1989-91, movements mgr., 1991-94; ops. mgr. Brit. Pipeline Agy., England, 1994-95, sr. cons., 1995-96, sr. cons. health, safety, environ., total quality mgr., 1996-97; devel. mgr. Anglian Water, Cambridgeshire, Eng., 1997-98; set up Anglianwaterdirect.com, 1999, comml. devel. mgr., 2000—; group chief inspector Brit. Pipeline Agy., 1995-96. Sub lt. Royal Navy, 1986-88. Avocations: sailing, mountaineering, hockey. Home: 31 Mill Rd, Buckden Cambs PE18 9SS, England Office: Anglian Water Plc, Ambury Rd Huntingdon, Cambridge PE18 6NZ, England

JAMES, STUART, librarian; b. Borehamwood, U.K., Mar. 17, 1944; s. George Alexander and Margaret Betty (Munn) J.; m. Gillian Margaret Buckman, Mar. 3, 1943; children: Josephine, Matthew. BA, Birmingham U., 1965. Sr. libr. asst. Leeds (Eng.) City Librs., 1965-69; libr. Northampton (Eng.) Devel. Corp., 1970-71; info. specialist Irvine (Scotland) Devel. Corp., Ayrshire, 1971-78; dep. libr. Paisley (Scotland) U., 1978-89, libr., 1989—; chmn. Ayrshire Libs. Forum, 1998—. Author: Using Literature (Analytical Chemistry by Open Learning), 1987; editor Libr. Rev., 1986—, Reference Revs., 1990—. Fellow Libr. Assn., Royal Soc. Arts; mem. Inst. Info. Scientists, Scottish Libr. Assn. (v.p. 1999-2000). Avocations: history of aviation, collecting books. Home: 13 Ronaldsay Ct Dreghorn, Irvine Ayrshire KA11 4JJ, Scotland Office: Univ Paisley, Univ Library, Paisley PA1 1BE, Scotland

JAMES, THOMAS NAUM, cardiologist, educator; b. Amory, Miss., Oct. 24, 1925; s. Naum and Kata J.; m. Gleaves Elizabeth Tynes, June 22, 1948; children: Thomas Mark, Terrence Fenner, Peter Naum. BS, Tulane U., 1946, MD, 1949. Diplomate Am. Bd. Internal Medicine (mem. bd. govs. 1982-88), Bd. Cardiovasc. Diseases (bd. dirs. 1972-78). Intern Henry Ford Hosp., Detroit, 1949-50, resident in internal medicine and cardiology, 1950-53, staff, 1959-68; instr. medicine Tulane U., New Orleans, 1955-58, asst. prof., 1959; prof. medicine U. Ala. Med. Ctr., Birmingham, 1968-87, prof. pathology, 1968-73, assoc. prof. physiology and biophysics, 1969-73, dir. Cardiovasc. Rsch. and Tng. Ctr., 1970-77, chmn. dept. medicine, dir. divsn. cardiovasc. disease, 1973-81, Mary Gertrude Waters prof. cardiology, 1976-87, Disting. prof., 1981-87; prof. medicine, prof. pathology U. Tex. Med. Br., Galveston, 1987—, pres., 1987-97, dir. WHO Cardiovasc. Ctr., 1988-98, Thomas N. and Gleaves T. James disting. chair cardiol. scis., 1997—; U. Tex. Med. Br., Galveston, 1997—; physician-in-chief U. Ala. Hosps., 1973-81; mem. adv. coun. Nat. Heart Lung and Blood Inst., 1975-79; pres. 10th World Congress Cardiology, 1986; mem. cardiology del. invited by Chinese Med. Assn. to China, 1978; Campbell orator Queens U., Belfast, No. Ireland, 1982; Mikamo lectr. Japan Circulation Soc., 1982; Sir Thomas Lewis lectr. Brit. Cardiac Soc., 1983; Einthoven lectr. U. Leiden, The Netherlands, 1993, Bailey K. Ashford lectr. U. P.R., 1995; hon. lectr. U. Padua, 1998. Author: Anatomy of the Coronary Arteries, 1961, The Etiology of Myocardial Infarction, 1963; Mem. editl. bd. Circulation, 1966-83, Am. Jour. Cardiology, 1968-82, Am. Heart Jour, 1976-79; contbr. articles to profl. jours. Capt. M.C. U.S. Army, 1953-55. Recipient 50-year Lifetime Achievement award Tulane Med. Alumni Assn., 1999. Fellow ACP (gov. Ala. 1975-79, master 1983); mem. AMA, Am. Clin. and Climatological Assn. (v.p. 1992-93, councillor 1992-93), Assn. Am. Physicians, Am. Soc. Clin. Investigation, Assn. Univ. Cardiologists (pres. 1978-79), Am. Heart Assn. (pres. 1979-80, Herrick award Coun. on Clin. Cardiology 1999), Am. Coll. Cardiology (v.p. 1970-71, trustee 1970-71, 76-81, First Disting. Scientist award 1982, chmn. publs. com. 1994-97), Am. Soc. Pharmacology and Exptl. Therapeutics, Soc. Exptl. Biology of Medicine, Am. Coll. Chest Physicians, Ctrl. Soc. Clin. Rsch., Internat. Soc. and Fedn. Cardiology (pres. 1983-84), WHO (expert adv. panel on cardiovascular diseases 1988-97), So. Soc. Clin. Investigation, Am. Fedn. Clin. Rsch., Ala. Acad. Honor. Philos. Soc. Tex., Phi Beta Kappa, Sigma Xi, Omicron Delta Kappa, Alpha Omega Alpha, Alpha Tau Omega, Phi Chi. Presbyterian. Clubs: Cosmos, Mountain Brook, Galveston Artillery. Office: U Tex Med Br 301 University Blvd Galveston TX 77555-5302

JAMES, TRACEY FAYE, screenwriter; b. Wilmington, Ohio, Feb. 4, 1963; d. James Whitney and Lydia Wanell (Wethington) J. Student, Art Instrn. Schs., 1980, Arlington Career Ctr., 1985. Freelance screenwriter San Antonio, 1981—; sports photographer No. Va. Sun, Arlington, Va., 1988. Author (screenplays): Nights of Terror, 1987, Dark Lords, 1991, Diamond Run, 1996, At the Hands of Mercy, 1997, A Lesson in Murder, 1999. Recipient award for patriotic svc. U.S. Treasury, 1981. Republican. Episcopalian. Avocations: writing, drawing, bowling, movies, music.

JAMES, WILFRED MARTIN, telecommunications executive, engineer; b. Singapore, Sept. 26, 1964; came to U.S., 1987; s. Daniel and Agatha J.; m. Suzanne Mercedes James, Aug. 6, 1995; children: Cameron, Nicole, James. BSEE, Oreg. State U., 1990; cert. in data comm., U. Wash., 1993. Mgr. US West Comm., Seattle, 1990-91, traffic engr., network planner, 1991-93, project mgr., 1993-94; sr. cons. Andersen Consulting, Seattle, 1994-96; mgr. network implementation Toll Free Cellular, Seattle, 1996-97, dir. carrier relations, 1997; dir. carrier rels., dir. network Global Mobility Sys., Bellevue, Wash., 1998, dir. product mgmt., 1998—; dir. product mgmt. @Mobile.com, 1999—; cons. Wilfred M. James Cons., 1999—; chmn. exhibits and seminars NORTHCON 96 Conf., Seattle, 1996. Inventor and patentee in field. Sponsor Children Internat., 1990—. Waldo Cumming scholar Oreg. State U., Corvallis, 1989. Mem. IEEE, World United Soccer Club (player, mgr., coach, founder), Telecomm. Industry Assn. (tech. com., wireless industry stds. com.). Avocations: soccer, driving, music, web page design. Home and Office: 2635 232d Pl SE Issaquah WA 98029

JAMES, WILLIAM HALL, former state official, educator; b. North Providence, R.I., July 20, 1910; s. John William and May (Hall) J.; m. Virginia Stowell, June 24, 1950, 1 child, Hillery Stowell. Student, U. Lausanne, 1928-29; BPhil, Brown U., 1933; MA, Yale U., 1946, PhD, 1953; LLD, U. New Haven, 1976. Tchr. New Canaan (Conn.) Bd. Edn., 1933-36; teaching prin. Easton (Conn.) Bd. Edn., 1936-42, 46-47, supervising prin., 1947-53, supt. schs., 1953-58; supt. schs. Branford (Conn.) Bd. Edn., 1958-66; staff Commn. Higher Edn., Hartford, Conn., 1966-77; dir. accreditation and scholarships Commn. Higher Edn., Hartford, 1966-77; ret., 1977; cons. Greater New Haven State Tech. Coll., 1977-78, Conn. Commn. Higher Edn., 1980-81; adj. prof. history So. Conn. State Coll., New Haven, 1947-49, adj. prof. econs. and labor-mgmt. rels., 1981-92, adj. prof. labor-mgmt. rels.; adj. prof. internat. rels., Eurasian affairs and history Western Conn. State Coll., Danbury, 1949-58; adj. prof. ednl. adminstrn. U. Bridgeport, Conn., 1958; adj. prof. econs. and indsl. rels. U. New Haven, West Haven, Conn., 1979-90, adj. prof. indls. rels.; adj. prof. labor-mgmt. rels., mgmt. Teikyo Post U., Waterbury, Conn., 1988-93; lectr. in field. Author: The Monetarists and the Current Crisis, 1975. Mem. North Branford (Conn.) Commn. Econ. Devel., 1980-95, chmn., 1981-95; mem. PTA. Maj. USAAF, 1942-46. Recipient Disting. Friend of Greater New Haven State Tech. Coll. award, 1984. Mem. SAR, NEA, Conn. Edn. Assn., Conn. Assn. Pub. Sch. Supts., Conn. Assn. Advancement Sch. Adminstrn., Am. Assn. Sch. Adminstrs., Yale Post-Doctoral Seminar Group (pres. 1968-69), Conn. State Employees Assn., Conn. Coun. Higher Edn. (treas. 1971-77), Am. Assn. Higher Edn., Royal Can. Geog. Soc., Numerical Control Soc., Rotary, Schoolmasters Rotary U.S. (sec.-treas. 1965-69), Am. Legion (post comdr. Easton 1948-49), China-Burma-India Vets. Assn., Exchange Club. Home: 373 Reeds Gap Rd Northford CT 06472-1106

JAMES BAILEY, JULIE CHRISTINA, actor, humanities educator, filmwriter; b. London, July 16, 1935; arrived in Australia, 1938; d. Willem John Heyting and Florence Gertrude James; m. Peter Goodwin Bailey, Oct. 7, 1964 (dec. Jan. 1980); children: Pippa, Robin. Cert., Royal Acad. Dramatic Art, 1953; BSc in Econs., U. London, 1973. Prodr. ind. TV cos., London, 1958-67; head rsch. Australian Film, TV and Radio Sch., 1975-84; mem. Australian Broadcasting Tribunal, 1984-89; prof. Griffith U., Brisbane, Australia, 1990-95, adj. prof., 1995—; mem. Australian com. UNESCO, 1980-84. Writer numerous TV programs and films. Home: 13 Battersea St, Abbotsford, Sydney 2046, Australia

JAMESON, PAULA ANN, lawyer; b. New Orleans, Feb. 19, 1945; d. Paul Henry and Virginia Lee (Powell) Bailey; children: Paul Andrew, Peter Carver. BA, La. State U., 1966; JD, U. Tex., 1969. 010BAr: TEx. 1969, D.C. 1970, Va. 1973, N.Y. 1978, U.S. Dist. Ct. D.C. 1970, U.S. Dist. Ct. (ea. dist.) Va. 1976, U.S. Ct. Appeals (D.C. cir.) 1972, U.S. Ct. Appeals (4th cir.) 1976, U.S Ct. Appeals (5th cir.) 1978, U.S. Ct. Appeals (2d cir.) 1985, U.S. Supreme Ct. 1973. Asst. corp. counsel D.C. Corp. Counsel's Office, 1970-73; sr. asst. county atty. Fairfax County Atty.'s Office, Fairfax, Va., 1973-77; atty. Dow Jones & Co., Inc., N.Y.C., 1977-79, house counsel, 1979-81, asst. to chmn. bd., 1981-83, house counsel, dir. legal dept., 1983-86; sr. v.p., gen. counsel, corp. sec. PBS, Alexandria, Va., 1986-98; ptnr. Arter & Hadden, Washington, 1998-2000; v.p., chief adminstrv. officer, gen. counsel Gibson Guitar Corp., Nashville, 2000—; mem. FCC WRC-2000 Industry Adv. Com. Mem. ABA, Fed. Comms. Bar Assn., D.C. Bar Assn., Computer Law Assn., Copyright Soc. U.S.A. (past trustee). Democrat. Roman Catholic. Office: Gibson Guitar Corp 309 Plus Park Blvd Nashville TN 37217-1005

JAMIL, TARIQ, computer engineer, educator; b. Pakistan, Nov. 9, 1965; arrived in Australia, 1997; p. Mohammad and Raib-al-Manoon Jamil. BSEE, NWFP U. Engring. and Tech., Pakistan, 1989; MS in Computer Engring., Fla. Inst. Tech., 1992, PhD in Computer Engring., 1996. Registered profl. engr., Pakistan; chartered engr., U.K. Grad. tchg. asst. Fla. Inst. Tech., Melbourne, 1994-96; asst. prof. Ghulam Ishaq Khan Inst. Engring. Scis. and Tech., Topi, Pakistan, 1997; lectr. U. NSW, Sydney, Australia, 1997-98, U. Tasmania, Launceston, Australia, 1999-2000; asst. prof. Sultan Qaboos U., Muscat, Oman, 2000—. Nat. Talent scholar, 1981-89, Quaid-e-Azam scholar Fla. Inst. Tech., 1990-94. Mem. IEEE (student activities com. 1995-97, student editor Potentials mag. 1995-97), IEEE Computer Soc. (award for acad. excellence 1996), Instn. Elec. Engrs. U.K. Islamic. Avocations: coin collecting, stamp collecting, reading autobiographies, reading computer magazines. E-mail: t.jamil@ieee.org. Fax: 968-513416. Address: Elec & Electronics Engring, PO Box 33, Al-Khodh 123, Sultante of Oman Office: U Tasmania, Sch Computing, Launceston TAS 7250, Australia

JAMINDAR, RASESH CHATURBHAI, historian; b. Mehmadabad, Gujarat, Bharat, July 19, 1934; s. Chaturbhai Chhaganbhai and Manibahen Chaturbhai (Bhatt) J.; m. Meena Rasesh CBhatt, May 11, 1958; children: Nilay, Sonal, Malay. BA with honors, Gujarat U., Ahmadabad, Bharat, 1958, MA, 1961, PhD, 1967. Lectr. Gujarat Vidyapith, Ahmadabad, 1963-66, sr. lectr., head, 1966-82, PhD supr., 1971-97, reader, head, 1982-85, prof., head, 1985-94, coord. univ. grants commn. program, 1991-94, ret., 1997; dir. independent study project fgn. students Gujarat Vidyapith, Ahmadabad, 1965-82, mem. acad. coun., 1966-94; mem. archival coun. Gujarat State, 1993—; faculty mem. record mgmt. programs, 1986—; adv. com. Gujarat Stae Archaeology Dept., 1998—; faculty mem. IAS tng. courses Sardar Patel Seva Samaj, and Sardar Patel Inst. Pub. Adminstrn., Ahmedabad, 1997—. Author: Bibliography of the History of Gujarat, Vol. 2, 1961, Vol. 8, 1985, Indological Studies in the Gujarat Vidyapith, 1972, History and Culture of Gujarat During Western Kshatrapas, 1975, Itihas Samshodhan, 1976, Central Asia, 1977, History of India from Guptas to the Advent of Europeans, 1980, revised edit., 2000, History: Concept and Researches, 1988, Cultural Heritage of Gujarat, 1989, History of Freedom Movement in Gujarat, 1990, Economic Life in Early India, 1991, Concept of History Writing, 1992, Concept of Archives, 1992, Pre-Gupta Coinage of India, 1994, (with R.N. Mehta) History of the Early World, 1995, revised edit., 2000; co-editor: (rsch. jour.) Vidyapith, 1977-94, mem. editl. bd., 1995-2000; co-editor: Concept of Indology, 1973, Twentieth Century India in Historical Perspectives, 1977, Epigraphical Resources in Gujarat, 1981, New Perspectives in History, 1987; contbr. articles to profl. jours. Recipient Gold medal Gujarat History Congress, 1981; rsch. fellow Univ. Grants Commn., New Delhi, 1961-62, 62-63, sr. fellow Indian Coun. Hist. Rsch., New Delhi, 1996-97; grantee Univ. Grants Commn., New Delhi, 1964, 84-85, 85-86, Indian Coun. Hist. Rsch., New Delhi, 1975. Mem. Gujarat History Congress (exec. mem. 1962-86, treas. 1962-66, v.p. 1972-76, pres. 1990-92, mem. adv. com. 1992-97), Indian History and Culture Soc. (mem. steering com. 1980-83, vice-chmn. 1992-96, pres. 1997), Epigraphical Soc. India (mem. exec. com. 1980-82), Place-Names Soc. India (mem. exec. com. 1980-86). Avocations: research, writing, coin and stamp collecting, traveling. Home: B-10 Vasu Apts Naranpura, Ahmadabad Gujarat 380013, Bharat Office: Gujarat Vidyapith, Ashram Rd Near Gandhi Bridg, Ahmadabad Gujarat 380014, Bharat

JAMMEH, YAHYA ABDULAZIZ JEMUS JUNKUNG, Gambian government official; b. May 25, 1965. D Civil Laws, St. Mary's U., Halifax, Can., 1999. Head Mil. Police, 1991; enlisted Gambia Nat. Gendarmerie, 1984, advanced through grades to col., 1996, spl. intervention unticomdr. in chief of armed forces, 1984-86, spl. guards unit mobile gendarmerie, 1986-87, officer commdg. mobile gendarmerie, 1991, officer commdg. mil. police unit, 1991, officer commdg. mil. police yundum barracks Gambia Nat. Army, 1991-94, ret., 1996; head of state, chmn. armed forces provisional ruling coun. Republic of Gambia, 1994-97, pres., head of state, comdr. in chief of armed forces, 1997—. Named Hon. Citizen of Ga., 1993, Hon. Lt. Col. ADC, Ala. State Mil., 1994, Grand Comdr. Order AL-FATAH, highest Libyan Insignia, 1995, Order of Brilliant Jade with Grand CORDON of ROC, highest Chinese Insignia, 1996, Hon. Admiral, Ala. State Navy, 1998, Grand Order of Bravery by Lybian Leader, 1998; recipient Pan-African humanitarian award Pan-African Found. and World Coun., 1997, Islamic Worldwide Grand Prix, Cheikhna Cheikh Saad Bouh Found., Dakar, 1998, 2000. Office: Office Pres, State House, Banjul The Gambia

JAMROGIEWICZ, DEBRA LYNN, educational consultant; b. Indpls., Jan. 18, 1953; d. Marion Alfred and Phyllis Ann (Sperback) Fieber; m. Andrew Mark Jamrogiewicz, Mar. 8, 1975; children: Andrew, Peter. BA, Purdue U., 1974. Tchr. All Saints Sch., Ft. Worth, 1975-76; program dir. YMCA, Ft. Worth, 1976-77; office mgr. Canton Corps., Mpls., 1977-79; sch. bd. dirs., chair Wayzata (Minn.) Pub. Schs., 1992-98; bd. dirs. N.E. Safe Kids Coalition, Mpls., 1992-96; dir. edn. Ch. of St. Anne, Medina, Minn., 1990-95; pres. Leadership Strategies for Success, Inc., Mpls., 1998—; cons. Hazard, Young, Attea and Assocs., Chgo., 1996—. Bd. dirs. Assn. of Met. Sch. Dists, Mpls., 1995-97; mem. Twin West Women's Network, Mpls., 1996-97; pres. PTA, Wayzata, 1990-91. Mem. Nat. Sch. Bds. Assn., Minn. Sch. Bd. Assn., Twin West-Wayzata-N.W. C. of C. Roman Catholic. Avocations: volunteerism, golf, reading.

JAN, CHWU-CHING HWANG, environmental chemistry consultant; b. Taipei, Taiwan, July 10, 1956; d. Chau-Ching and Hsiu-Mei (Lin) Huang; m. Deng-Yang Jan; 1 child, Avery. BS, Nat. Cheng-Kung U., 1978; MBA, U. Chgo., 1995; PhD, Ohio State U., 1986. Rsch. asst. Nat. Sci. Found., Taipei, Taiwan, 1978-79; lab. mgr. Nat. Tsing Hua U., Hsinchu, Taiwan, 1979-81; sr. rsch. chemist UOP, Des Plaines, Ill., 1986-92; cons. Iris DC Inc., Elk Grove Village, Ill., 2000, pres., 1993-2000; ptnr. Russian Investment Solutions, L.P., Chgo., 1998-2000; advisor technology CASDAY Co., Ltd., Hsinchu, Taiwan, 1993-2000. Contbr. articles to profl. jours. including Jour. Electro.-analytical Chem., Interfacial Electrochem., Analytical Chemistry. Mem. Am. Chem. Soc. (internat. student grant 1985), U. Chgo. Alumni Club, U. Chgo. Women's Bus. Group. Achievements include patents for

hydrotreating processes for organic and halogenerated organic feedsocks containing undesirable olefinic and/or halogen components and/or organic materials, process for decomposing peroxide impurities in a tertiary butyl alcohol feedstock. Avocations: playing piano, singing. Office: Iris DC Inc 1644 Von Braun Trl Elk Grove Village IL 60007-3100

JAN, JIRI, electronics engineer, educator; b. Brno, Czech Republic, June 2, 1941; s. Jaroslav and Vanda (Kramarova) J.; m. Drahomira Svandova, Nov. 20, 1970; children: Vit, Jitka. MSEE, Tech. U., Brno, 1963, PhD, 1969. From asst. to assoc. prof. Tech. U., Brno, 1963-91, full prof., 1991—, vice dean faculty electronic engring. and computer sci., 1990-94; head dept. biomed. engring., 1990—. Author: Digital Signal Filtering, Analysis and Restoration, 1997, 2000; contbg. author Computer Analysis of Images and Patterns, 1995; editor: Analysis of Biomedical Signals and Images, 1996, 98, 2000; contbr. numerous articles to profl. jours. and conf. procs.; patentee in field. European Commn. grantee, 1992-93, 95-99. Mem. IEEE (assoc. editor Transactions on Biomed. Engring. 1996—), EURASIP (Central European liaison 1994—), Czech Soc. Biomed. Engring. (nat. com.), Engring Acad. of Czech Republic (founding mem. 1994—). Avocations: classical music, pipe organ building, nature. E-mail: jan@dbme.fee.vutbr.cz. Home: Zizkova 68, CZ 61600 Brno Czech Republic Office: Tech U Dept Biomed Engring, Purkynova 118, CZ-61200 Brno Czech Republic

JAN, SARDAR AHMED SHAH, real estate agent; b. Peshawar, Pakistan, Oct. 19, 1939; s. Sardar Ahmed and Badrun-Nissa Ahmed Jan; m. Nazparwar Ahmed Sharif, Mar. 9, 1967; children: Ayesha Ahmed, Saira Ahmed, Mohammed Faisal. BA in English Lit. with honors, U. Peshawar, 1962, MA in English Lit., 1963; ednl. planning and mgmt. course, Allama Iqbal Open U., Islamabad, Pakistan, 1978. Tutor English P.A.F. Acad., Risalpur, Pakistan, 1965-71; head English dept. Libyan Air Force, Okba-Bin-Nafa, Tripoli, Libya, 1972-74; directing staff English Jr. Command & Staff Sch., P.A.F., Karachi, Pakistan, 1974-76; directing staff individual studies scheme P.A.F. Base, Badaber, Peshawar, 1976-82; comdr. officer Sch. Edn. & Mgmt. P.A.F. Base, Kohat, Pakistan, 1982-84; real estate agt. Peshawar, 1984—. Pres. mess com. P.A.F. Base, Kohat, 1983-84. Wing comdr., 1965-84. Mem. Peshawar Officers Club. Sunni Muslim. Avocations: public speaking, golf, shotgun shooting. Home: #3 Khalid Rd, Peshawar 25000, Pakistan

JANA, ATANU HRISHIKESH, dairy technology educator, researcher; b. Manipal, India, Apr. 10, 1962; s. Hrishikesh Sripati and Shova (Karmakar) J.; m. Madhumita Atanu Sen Gupta, May 9, 1985; 1 child, Piyali. BS in Dairy Tech., S.M.C. Coll. Dairy Sci., Anand, India, 1984, MS in Dairy Tech., 1989, PhD in Dairy Sci., 1999. Cert. dairy technologist. Rsch. asst. S.M.C. Coll. Dairy Sci., Anand, India, 1984-89, asst. prof., 1989—; tchr. Dairy Plant course Anand, India, 1990, 96; external examiner Rajasthan Agr. U., Bikaner, India, Rejendra Agrl. U., Pusa, India, Dairy Sci. Coll., Raipur, India. Contbr. articles to profl. jours. Mem. Bengal Cultural Assn., Ahmedabad, India, 1980—, Durga Puja Com., Anand, India, 1983—, Boho Club, Nat. Dairy Devel. Bd., Anand, India, 1986—. Recipient ICAR Jr. fellowship Indian Coun. Agrl. Rsch., New Delhi, India, 1985. Mem. (life) Indian Dairy Assn. New Delhi, Assn. Food Scientists & Technologists (Mysore) India. Avocations: swimming, mnemonics, rifle shooting, writing articles. Home: 25 Krishna Pk, Borsad Rd, Anand 388 001, India Office: SMC College Dairy Science, Anand Campus, Anand 388 110, India

JANA, MANAS KUMAR, agriculturist, educator; b. Midnapur, India, July 19, 1932; s. Bipin Bihari and Sushila Bala (Maity) J; m. Ahuti Mandal, June 4, 1963; children: Tumpa, Sumana. BSc in Agr., Banaras Hindu U., Varanasi, India, 1951, MSc in Agr., 1953; M Tech., Indian Inst. Tech., Kharagpur, 1960, PhD, 1962. Cert. agrl. scientist, geneticist. Rsch. asst. Govt. West Bengal, India, 1953-54; rsch. asst., assoc. lectr. Indian Inst. Tech., Kharagpur, 1954-66, lectr., 1967-72, asst. prof., 1973-81, prof., 1981-93, prof. emeritus, 1993—, head agrl. and food engring. dept., 1989-91, chmn. horticulture unit, 1988-91; organizing chmn. Joint Entrance Exam., Indian Inst. Tech., Kharagpur, 1985-86, vice chmn., 1982, 83, tchr. Nat. Svc. Scheme, 1970-78; vis. scientist Colo. State U., Ft. Collins, 1983, U. Calif., Davis, 1979, 83, U. Sask. Saskatoon, Can., 1978-79, U. Liege and U. Brussels, Belgium, 1965-66, Inst. Kulturpflanzenforschung, Gatersleben, Germany, 1966; visitor insts. in U.S., Can., Eng., France, Japan, Sweden, Denmark, Chechoslovakia, Italy, Thailand and Germany. Editor The Harvester; editl. bd. Exptl. Genetics. contbr. articles to profl. jours. Advisor Ushagram Trust, West Bengal, 1996—. Recipient Rsch. Assoc. award Internat. Devel. Rsch. Ctr., Ottawa, Can., 1978, UNESCO fellowship/Belgian Govt. scholarship, 1965, Ford Found. fellowship Colo. State U., Ft. Collins, 1983, U. Calif., Davis, 1979, 83. Fellow Indian Cryogenic Coun., West Bengal Acad. Sci. and Tech., Indian Soc. Genetics and Plant Breeding; mem. Soc. Cryobiology, Indian Sci. Congress Assn., Soc. Genetics and Breeders; life mem. Indian Red Cross Soc. Home: B10/199, Kalyani 741 235, India Office: Indian Inst Tech, West Bengal 721 302, India

JANARDANAN, CHATHOTH, chemist, educator; b. Cannanore, India, May 15, 1960; p. K.M. Kunhikannan and Chathoth Thala; m. Girija Pilavullathil, Apr. 28, 1995; 1 child, Harshin. BSc, Nirma Lagiri Coll., India, 1981; MSc, Calicut U., Cannanore, 1983, PhD, 1989. Scientist Calicut U., 1985-89; lectr. in chemistry Nirmalagiri Coll., 1989-90; lectr. Sree Narayana Coll., Cannanore, 1990—. Contbr. articles to profl. jours. Fellow Indian Chem. Soc., Indian Acad. Scis., Indian Coun. Chemistry. Avocations: reading, playing. Home: Chathoth House, PO Nirmalagiri, 670701 Cannanore India Office: Sree Narayana PG Coll, PO Thottada 7, Cannanore 670 007, India

JANÁS, FRANTIŠEK, publisher, economist; b. Nová Lhota, Hodonín, Czech Republic, Sept. 15, 1946; s. Tomáš and Anna (Szentesi) J.; m. Jana Malárová, Apr.2, 1966; children: Robert, Lucie. Grad., Acad. Bus., Brno, Czech Republic, 1982. Worker Svit, Zlín, Czech Republic, 1963-66; worker Bldg. Co., Brno, 1966-71, clk., 1971-89, chief divsn. employment, 1990-91; holder, pub. Edice 33, Brno, 1979—; holder Gallery Art Fine Guns, Brno, 1991-94. Editor some 40 books, including: The Raven, 1979, 81, The Sonets, 1979, The Flowers of Evil, 1980, Vltava, 1980, The Twelve Texts, 1981, The Flight of Swallows, 1981, Don Quijote, 1981, The Story of Mr. Valdemar, 1982, 84, 90, The Six, 1983, The Sacrifice Approbation, 1984, Ota Janeček and Vincenc Kramár, 1984, The Night Divertimento, 1984, The Dreams, 1985, The Fragments of Poe's Poems, 1985, The Dead Shepherd, 1988, The New Twelve Lyrical Texts, 1987, The Outskirts-The Hommage to Camil Lhoták, 1987, The Enamel Stars-The Hommage to Bohumil Hrabal, 1988, The Graphic, 1988, Eyes Eyes, 1991, Rhymes to Be Traded for Bread, 1993, From Kafka's Diaries, 1994, 96, The Blue Mist Poems, 1998, others. Fellow Trade Union, Brno, 1983-90. Fellow Club of Friends of Fine Arts; mem. Assn. Czech Bibliophiles, Assn. Hollar. Roman Catholic. Avocations: tourism, collecting fine arts. Office: Edice 33, Herčíkova 4, 612 00 Brno Czech Republic

JANČA, JOSEF ALOIS, chemist, educator; b. Kroměříž, Moravia, Czech Republic, Nov. 16, 1944; s. Josef and Helena (Hrabálková) J.; m. Eva Kotrbová, Nov. 10, 1973; children: Eva, Josef. PhD in Macromolecular Chemistry, Acad. Scis., Prague, Czech Republic, 1975; DSc, U. Chem. Tech., Prague, 1984. Head lab. Inst. Macromolecular Chemistry Acad. Scis., Prague, 1975-80; dir. Inst. Analytical Chemistry, Brno, Czech Republic, 1980-90; vis. assoc. prof. U. Utah, Salt Lake City, 1978-79, Ecole Supérieure de Physique el de Chimie Industrielles, Paris, 1991-93, U. P. et M. Curie, Paris, 1993; prof. chemistry U. de La Rochelle, France, 1993—; rsch. scientist Ecole Supérieure Chimie Mulhouse, France, 1969-70; co-chmn. Symposium on Chromatography of Polymers and Polymers in Chromatography, Prague, Czech Republic, 1978; chmn. Internat. Symposium on Polymer Analysis and Characterization, Brno, Czech Republic, 1990; mem. gov. bd. ISPAC Ltd., U.S., 1988—. Author: Steric Exclusion Liquid Chromatography of Polymers, 1984, Field-Flow Fractionation: Analysis of Macromolecules and Particles, 1988, Field-Flow Fractionation, 1992; mem. editl. bd. Internat. Jour. Polymer Analysis and Characterization, 1979—, Jour. Lig. Chromatography, 1979—, Mikrochimica Acta, 1987—; contbr. chpts. to books, over 120 articles to profl. jours.; patentee in field. Mem. Czechoslovak Chem. Soc. (v.p. chromatography sect. 1981-95), Czech Chem. Soc., Groupe Français d'Etudes et d'Applications des Polymères, Internat. Union Pure and Applied Chemistry. Avocations: classical music, photography, tennis, skiing, mountain biking. Office: U de La Rochelle, Ave Marillac, 17042 La Rochelle France

JANCSO, GABOR, neuroscientist; b. Szeged, Hungary, Aug. 8, 1948; s. Miklos and Aranka (Gabor) J.; m. Marta Ruth Katona, Sept. 11, 1972; children: Daniella, Judit. MD, U. Szeged Med. Sch., 1972; PhD, Hungarian Acad. Scis., 1983, DSc, 1994. Asst. prof. anatomy Univ. Med. Sch., Szeged, Hungary, 1972-81, assoc. prof. physiology, 1981-95; prof. physiology Albert Szent-Györgyi Med. Sch., Szeged, Hungary, 1995—. rsch. fellow Med. U. Wurzburg, Germany, 1977-78, U. Graz., Austria, 1980, Univ. Coll., London, 1981, U. Bristol, U.K., 1986-88, Max-Planck-Institut, Bad Nauheim, Germany, 1990. Mem. Internat. Brain Rsch. Orgn., European Neurosci. Assn., Hungarian Physiol. Soc. (jubilee award 1980). Home: Petofi S sgt 25, 6722 Szeged Hungary Office: U Szeged Dept Physiol, Dom ter 10, 6720 Szeged Hungary

JANCUK, KATHLEEN FRANCES, educational administrator; b. Balt., Apr. 1, 1950; d. Joseph Frank and Dorothy Jane (Lowry) J. BA in Elem. Edn., Notre Dame Coll., Balt., 1974; MEd in Reading, Towson State U., 1985; MEd in Adminstrn., Loyola Coll., Balt., 1992. Cert. tchr., reading specialist, adminstr. and supr., Md. Substitute tchr. St. Wenceslaus, Balt., 1970-72; tchr. 5th grade St. Boniface, Phila., 1972-77; tchr. 5th grade Cath. C.C., Balt., 1977-82, reading specialist K-5, 1982-88; reading specialist K-8 St. Mary's Elem. Sch., Annapolis, Md., 1988-91; prin. St. Clare Sch., Balt., 1991-97, St. John Neumann Sch., Cumberland, Md., 1997—. Non-voting mem. St. Clare Sch. Bd., Balt., 1991-97, St. John Neumann Sch. Bd., 1997—; mem. Sch. Sisters of Notre Dame, 1991—; mem. area pastoral coun., 1993-97. Recipient Recognition of Svc. award Archdiocese of Balt., 1993. Mem. ASCD, Elem. Sch. Prins. Assn. (exec. bd. dirs. 1994-97), Nat. Cath. Ednl. Assn., Internat. Reading Assn., Mid. States Assn. Sch. Evaluation Teams. Democrat. Roman Catholic. Avocations: collecting clowns, puppetry, swimming, singing, playing guitar and piano. Office: St John Neumann Sch 151 Fayette St Cumberland MD 21502-2998

JANCZAK, ANDREW ANTHONY, executive; b. Buenos Aires, Feb. 20, 1950; came to U.S., 1955; s. Zygmunt and Gertrude (Sierocki) J.; m. Helen Mary Gimber, Jan. 27, 1973; children: Andrew S., Jeanette M. BS in Aerospace Engring., Polytech. Inst. Bklyn., 1972, MS in Mgmt., 1976. Mktg. dir. Telsonic/Trescott, Inc., L.I. City, N.Y., 1973-76; pres. Belzona, Inc., Uniondale, N.Y., 1976-83; pres., owner Molecular Systems, Inc., Edgewood, N.Y., 1983-90; pres. Enecon Corp., Bethpage, N.Y., 1990—. Patentee in field. Avocations: golf, boating. Office: Enecon Corp 700 Hicksville Rd Ste 110 Bethpage NY 11714-3469

JANDAGHI ALAEE, MAJID, civil engineer; b. Semnan, Iran, June 17, 1960; s. Yaghobali Jandaghi Alaee and Fatemeh Sharifi; m. Nayareh Bardideh, Mar. 23, 1985; children: Morteza, M. Amin. BSc in Civil Engring., Amir Kabir U. Tech., Tehran, Iran, 1985, MSc in Hydraulic Structures, 1985; PhD, U. Western Australia, Perth, 1984. Project engr. Ports and Shipping Orgn., Tehran, 1986-88, head design office, 1988-90, dir. gen. design and supervision, 1990-91, head coastal engring. dept., 1998—. Avocations: sports, computers. Home: No 18 Chamn e Sharghi, Tehran Iran Office: Ports and Shipping Orgn, No 751 Enghelab Ave, Tehran 15994, Iran

JANDELEIT, JÜRGEN, physicist, researcher; b. Aachen, Germany, Jan. 16, 1967; s. Otto and Luise (Recker) J. Diploma in Physics, RWTH, Aachen, 1993, PhD, 1997. Asst. Lehrstuhl für Lasertechnik, Aachen, 1994-97; head diode laser group Fraunhofer-Inst. for Laser Tech., Aachen, 1997—. Roman Catholic. Avocations: photography, music. Office: Fraunhofer-Inst Laser Tech, Steinbachstr 15, D-52074 Aachen Germany

JANDERA, PAVEL, chemistry educator, researcher; b. Hradec Králové, Czechoslovakia, Apr. 1, 1944; s. Jiri and Zdenka (Jelinková) J.; m. Marie Hojná, June 28, 1974; 1 child, Jana. MS in Engring., U. Chem. Tech., Pardubice, Czechoslovakia, 1967, PhD, 1977; DSc, U. Chem. Tech., Prague, Czech Republic, 1989. Asst. prof. U. Chem. Tech., Pardubice, 1970-90, assoc. prof., 1990, 91-92; rsch. prof. U. Tenn., Knoxville, 1990-91; prof. analytical chemistry U. Pardubice, 1992—; nat. rep. Commn. on Separation Methods, Internat. Union Pure and Applied Chemistry, 1996—. author: (in Czech) Liquid Chromatography with Programmed Composition of the Mobile Phase, 1984, Introduction to HPLC, SNTL Prague, 1984, (in English) Gradient Elution in Liquid Column Chromatography, 1985; mem. editl. bd. Jour. Chromatography, 1989-98; contbr. articles to profl. jours. Mem. Czech Chem. Soc. (mem. com. analytical chem. sect. 1991—, mem. com. chromatography sect. 1987—). Avocations: literature, hiking, history. Office: Pardubice Univ, Faculty Chem Tech, 532 10 Pardubice Czech Republic

JANDOVA, ANNA MILADA, oncologist, researcher; b. Prague, Czechoslovakia, July 26, 1931; d. Adalbert and Anna (Teskova) Gubo; m. Jiří Janda, May 26, 1962; children: Iva Pravdova, Dana Tesarova, Vera Masopustova. MD, Charles U., Prague, 1963. Oncology rschr. 2d Gynecol. Clinic, Prague, 1965-95, Charles U. Physiology Inst., Prague, 1995-97, Inst. Radio Engring. and Electricity, Prague, 1998—; cons. Charles U. Physiology Inst., 1990—. Patentee in field. Mem. Czech Med. Soc. Roman Catholic. Avocations: nature, travel. Office: Inst Radio Eng & Elec CAS, Chaberska 57, 182 51 Prague 8 Czech Republic

JANDRELL, IAN ROBERT, electrical engineer, educator; b. East London, Ea. Cape, South Africa, June 8, 1963; s. Theodore Walter and Dorothy Hazel (Marillier) J.; m. Heidi Müller, Jan. 25, 1986. BSc in Engring., U. Witwatersrand, Johannesburg, South Africa, 1985, grad. diploma in Engring., 1987, PhD in Engring., 1990. Registered profl. engr., Engring. Coun. South Africa. Lectr. U. Witwatersrand, Johannesburg, 1990-94, sr. lectr., 1995-97, joint programme leader, lightning/EMC rsch. programme, 1996—, assoc. prof., 1998—; cons., Sandton, South Africa; temp. lectr. U. Witwatersrand, Johannesburg, 1989-90; dir. Crown Publs., Bedfordview, South Africa, 1994—, Expo for Young Scientists, Pretoria, South Africa, 1995—, divsn. continuing engring. ed., U. Witwatersrand, 1997—. Editor Electricity & Control, 1990— (winner Specialist Press Assn. 1990, 91, 92, 93, Spa PICA Engring. Tech., 1994); contbr. over 65 articles to profl. publs. Recipient Y rating Found. Rsch. Devel., South Africa, 1995, C rating, 1998. Sr. mem. South African Inst. Elec. Engrs. (coun. mem. 1993-97, chairperson edn. trng. com. 1994-96, Engr. of Yr. 1994); mem. Engring. Assn. South Africa (v.p. 1997—), South Africa rep. study com. 15 1997-99, Electric Power Coordination Com. (tech. sec. 1991-95, exec. bd.), Nat. Stds. Body, Engring. 06, Mfg. and Tech.,1998. Lutheran. Avocations: railroad modelling, fly fishing. Office: U Witwatersrand, 1 Jan Smuts Ave, Johannesburg Gauteng, South Africa

JANDT, KLAUS DIETER, dental materials and biomaterials science scholar, researcher, educator; b. Hamburg, Germany, Aug. 15, 1961; s. Herbert Emil Friedrich and Hedwig (Dorroch) J.; m. Karin Sutmöller, July 7, 1990. Diploma in physics magna cum laude, Hamburg (Germany) U., 1989; D of Natural Scis. magna cum laude, Tech. U. Hamburg Harburg, Hamburg, 1993. Product developing engr. Philips Comp., Hamburg, 1989; rsch. scientist Tech. U. Hamburg Harburg, 1989-93; rsch. assoc. U. Bristol, Eng., 1993; rsch. fellow Cornell U., Ithaca, N.Y., 1994-96; sr. lectr. (assoc. prof.) U. Bristol, Eng., 1996—; chmn. Alexander von Humboldt Chpt., Bristol, 1997—. Author: (book) Polymer-Metal-Epitaxy in Computer Simulation and Experiment, 1993; patentee blue LEDs for polymerization oral biomaterials. Feodor-Lynen fellow Alexander von Humboldt Assn., 1994. Mem.Am. Assn. for Advancement of Sci (AAAS), Internat. Assn. for Dental Rsch (IADR), Deutsche Physikalische Gesellschaft (DPG), Soc. for Biomaterials. Avocations: tennis, beekeeping, music, cooking. Office: U Bristol Oral & Dental Sci, Lower Maudlin St, BS1 2LY Bristol England

JANE, BEVERLEY LOIS, science and technology educator; b. Melbourne, Victoria, Australia, July 20, 1946; d. William Thomas and May Victoria (Brown) J.; m. Warren John Leeds Walsh, May 11, 1968 (div. 1990); children: Melinda Jane, Martine Nicole. EdB, LaTrobe U., Melbourne, 1988; EdM, LaTrobe U., 1991; PhD, Monash U., Melbourne, 1996. Cert. secondary education educator, 1966. Biology, sci. and math. tchr. Victorian secondary schs., 1967-68; sci. tchr. RAAF Sch., Penang, Malaysia, 1969-71; biology tchr. Eltham Coll., Melbourne, 1978-88; sr. rsch. asst. Monash U., 1988; early childhood lectr. U. Melbourne, 1989; sr. lectr. in primary sci. and tech. Deakin U., Melbourne, 1990—. Co-author (with Fleer): Technology for Children-Developing Your Own Approach, 1999; contbr. book chpt., articles to profl. jours.; author: (video recordings) Children Linking Science with Technology, 1994, Coolart: A Wetlands Experience, 1995, Quality Materials Technology: Family and Food, 1999. Mem. Tech. Edn. Assn. of Victoria (v.p. 1997), Sci. Tchrs. Assn. of Victoria, Australasian Sci. Edn. Rsch. Assn. Anglican. Avocations: gardening, theology, travel, markets, wave skiing. Office: Deakin U, 221 Burwood Hwy, Burwood 3125, Australia

JANES, JOSEPH ANTHONY, JR., optometrist; b. El Paso, Tex., Nov. 1, 1951; s. Joseph Anthony and Mildred Caroline (Dechant) J.; m. Janet Elaine Johnson, Jan. 10, 1976; children: Kelly Marie, Michael Harrison, Stephen Christopher. BS in Optometry, U. Houston, 1974, OD, 1976. Optometrist Farah Mfg., El Paso, Tex., 1976-77, Bellaire (Tex.) Eye Assocs., 1977-80; lectr. U. Houston Coll. Optometry, 1978-80, asst. prof., 1980-84; pres., optometrist Bellaire Contact Lens. Assoc., Houston, 1982—; adj. asst. prof. U. Houston Coll. Optometry, 1984-90; adj. assoc. prof. U. Houston, 1991—; v.p., sec. Laser Eye Ctr L.L.C., 1996—; adv. bd. Vistakon Inc., Jacksonville, Fla., 1986; bd. dirs. Laser Eye Inst. Houston, 1996—. Contbr. articles to profl. jours. Fellow Am. Acad. Optometry, Nat. Acad. Eye Surgery; mem. Am. Optometric Assn., Tex. Optometric Assn., Harris County Optometric Assn. (exec. coun. 1997—, v.p. 1998, pres. 1999), Optometric Found., Am. Soc. for Laser Medicine and Surgery, Sigma Nu Frat. (treas. alumni assn. 1981). Avocations: golf. Office: Bellaire Contact Lens Assoc 5420 Dashwood Dr Ste 207 Houston TX 77081-5332

JANES, ROBERT ROY, museum executive, archaeologist, museum consultant; b. Rochester, Minn., Apr. 23, 1948; m. Priscilla Bickel; children: Erica Helen, Peter Bickel. Student, Lawrence U., 1966-68, BA in Anthropology cum laude, 1970; student, U. of the Ams., Mexico City, 1968, U. Calif., Berkeley, 1968-69; PhD in Archaeology, U. Calgary, Alta., Can., 1976. Postdoctoral fellow Arctic Inst. N.Am., U. Calgary, 1981-82; founding dir. Prince of Wales No. Heritage Centre, Yellowknife, N.W.T., 1976-86, project dir. Dealy Island Archaeol. and Conservation Project, 1977-82; founding exec. dir. Sci. Inst. of N.W.T.; sci. advisor Govt. of N.W.T., Yellowknife, 1986-89; exec. dir., pres., CEO Glenbow Mus. Art Gallery Libr. and Archives, Calgary, 1989-2000; fellow Glenbow-Alta. Inst., 2000—; mus./heritage cons., 2000—; adj. prof. archaeology U. Calgary, 1990—. Author: Preserving Diversity-Ethnoarthcaeological Perspectives on Culture Change in the Western Canadian Subarctic, 1991, Museums and the Paradox of Change, 1995, 2d edit., 1997; author: (with others) The Arctic Institute of North America Technical Paper No. 28, 1983; author manuscripts, monographs; contbr. articles o profl. jours. mem. First Nations/CMA Task Force on Mus. and First Peoples, 1989-92; bd. dirs. Yoho Burgess Shale Found.; mem. nat. adv. bd. Ctr. for Cultural Mgmt., U. Waterloo. Recipient Nat. Parks Centennial award Environ. Can., 1985, Can. Studies Writing award Assn. Can. Studies, 1989, Disting. Alumni award Alumni Assn. of U. Calgary, 1989, L.R. Briggs Disting. Achievement award Lawrence U., 1991; Can. Coun. doctoral fellow, 1973-76; rsch. grantee Govt. of Can., 1974, Social Scis. and Humanities Rsch. Coun. Can., 1988-89. Fellow Arctic Inst. N.Am. (bd. dirs. 1983-90, vice chmn. bd. 1985-89, hon. rsch. assoc. 1983-84, chmn. priorities and planning com. 1983-84, exec. com. 1984-86, assoc. editor Arctic jour. 1987-97), Am. Anthrop. Assn. (fgn. fellow); mem. Can. Archaeol. Assn. (v.p. 1980-82, pres. 1984-86, co-chmn. fed. heritage policy com. 1986-88), Current Anthropology (assoc.), Can. Mus. Assn. (hon. life mem., cert accreditation 1982, Outstanding award in Mus. Mgmt., Outstanding Achievement award for publ. 1996), Internat. Coun. Mus., Can. Art Mus. Dirs. Orgn. (mem.-at-large bd. dirs.), Can. Mus. Assn. (bd. dirs., v.p. 1999), Alta. Mus. Assn. (moderator seminars 1990, Merit award 1992, Merit award for Museums and the Paradox of Change 1996), Assn. Cultural Execs. (bd. dirs. 1999-2000, ACE award for Can. Cultural Mgmt. 1998), Sigma Xi. Home: Box 32 Site 32, RR 12, Calgary, AB Canada T3E 6W3

JANES, WILLIAM SARGENT, real estate corporation executive; b. Cambridge, Mass., Mar. 24, 1953; s. G. Sargent and Ann (Brown) J.; m. Alice Maxine Rowley, June 19, 1982; children: Pack Sargent, Maxine Cotton. BA, Bowdoin Coll., 1976. Sr. sales cons. Coldwell Banker, Washington, 1976-84; ptnr. Lincoln Property Co., Washington, 1984-89; pres. Rock Creek Ptnrs., Inc., Washington, 1990—; prin. RMB Realty, Washington, 1990—; bd. dirs. Brazos Fund L.P., Brazos Advisors, Carr Real Estate Svcs., Pragon Group, Inc., CapStar Hotel Co. Mem. young pres. orgn. and devel. com. Washington Nat. Cathedral; bd. dirs. Paragon Group Inc.; mem. adv. bd. Brazos Asset Mgmt., Carr Real Estate Svcs., Cap Star, EquiStar, Brazos Advisors. Mem. Urban Land Inst., Soc. Indsl. Realtors, Nat. Assn. Indsl. and Office Pks. Home: PO Box 1204 Middleburg VA 20118-1204 Office: RMB Realty Inc 1133 Connecticut Ave NW Washington DC 20036-4305

JANG, AN SOO, medical educator; b. Kwangju, Korea, Oct. 6, 1964; p. Yun Jang and Yeon Sun Park J.; m. Eun Mee Park, Feb. 10, 1989; children: Jun Hak, Hwan Hee, Don Ho. Premed., Chonnam U., Kwangju, 1983-84; med. sch., Chonnam U., 1985-89, grad. sch., 1993-95. Intern Chonnam U. Hosp., Kwangju, 1989-90; resident Chonnam U. Hosp., 1993-97, fellow in allergy, 1997-98; asst. prof. Seonam U. Coll. Medicine, Kwangju, 1998—. Contbr. articles to profl. jours. Mem. Korean Soc. Allergology, Korean Acad. Tuberculosis & Respiratory Medicine, Korean Soc. for Immunology, Korean Med. Assn. Avocation: tennis. E-mail: jas877@chollian.net. Office: Seonam U Hosp, Seoug Marukdong 120-1, Kwangju 502-157, Korea

JANG, DO-HYUN, engineering educator; b. Chunan, Chungnam, Korea, Aug. 24, 1956; s. Duck-Jin Jang and Jung-Ja Bae; m. Young-Sun Jee, Oct. 9, 1983; children: Sung-Jun, Sung-kun. BS, Hanyang U., Seoul, Republic of Korea, 1980; MS, Seoul Nat. U., 1982, PhD, 1989. From asst. prof. to assoc. prof. Hoseo U., Chunan, 1986-96, prof., 1997—; vis. scholar Tex. A&M U., College Station, 1993-94. 2d lt. Korean Army, 1982-83. Mem. IEEE, Korean Inst. Elec. Engrs. (backbencher 1996, Sci. award 1989), Korean Inst. Power Electronics (editor 1998-2000). Avocations: hearing music, climbing, travel. Fax: (82)-418-532-4246. Home: Songpa-Ku Moonjung-Dong, Family Apt 301-404, 138-200 Seoul Korea Office: Hoseo U Dept Elec Engring, Baebang-myung Sechul-ri 29-1, 336-795 Asan-si Chungnam, Korea

JANG, GUN-EIK, educator; b. Yeosu, Korea, May 8, 1956; s. Jong-Pil and Bong-Ju (Park) J.; m. Hwa-Young Gwak, Jan. 10, 1961; 1 child, Ji-Hee. BS, Han Tang U., Seoul, 1982; MS, U. Utah, 1987; PhD, Mich. State U., 1992. Rschr. Kum Kang Co., Seoul, 1983-85, Korea Advanced Inst. Sci. Tech., Taejon, 1993-94, Korea Atomic Energy Rsch. Inst., Taejon, 1994-95; asst. prof. Chungbuk Nat. U., Cheongju, Korea, 1995—. Author: Japanese Journal of Applied Physics, 1994, Superconductor Science and Technolog, 1994, Thin Solid Film, 1999. Office: Chungbuk NAt U, Gesin-dong San 48, Chongju 360-763, Korea

JANG, HYUN MYUNG, materials engineering and science educator; b. Chilgok, Republic of Korea, Jan. 21, 1953; s. Tae-Hee and Kwang-Hwan (Choi) J.; m. Kyung-Hee Lee, June 21, 1978; 1 child, Albert Young-Woo. BSc in Chemistry with honors, U. Seoul (Republic of Korea) Nat., 1976; MSc in Chemistry, Washington U., St. Louis, 1980; PhD in Materials Sci., U. Calif., Berkeley, 1985. Rsch. assoc. Lawrence Berkeley Nat. Lab., Berkeley, 1981-85; rsch. fellow MIT, Cambridge, 1986-87; asst. prof. Pohang (Republic of Korea) U. Sci. and Tech., 1987-90, assoc. prof., 1991-95, prof., 1996—, head dept. materials sci. and engring., 1998—; chmn. sci. program com. 3rd Internat. Meeting of Pacific Rim Ceramic Socs., 1996—; mem. internat. adv. com. World Ceramics Congress, Faenza, Italy, 1996—. Author: (with others) Chemical Processing of Ceramics, 1994; contbr. or co-contbr. more than 80 articles to internat. sci. jours., 1986—. Recipient Best Rsch. award Rsch. Inst. Indsl. Sci. and Tech., Pohang, 1989, Best Civilian award Lions Clubs Internat., 1997; named one of Top 33 Scientists in Ceramics-related Basic Sci., World Ceramics Congress, 1996. Mem. Am. Ceramic Soc., Materials Rsch. Soc. Internat. (tech. dir. 1996—), Nat. Acad. Engring. of Korea. Buddhist. Avocations: mountain climbing, hiking, singing. Office: Pohang U Sci and Tech, Dept Materials Sci and Engr, Pohang 790-784, Republic of Korea

JANG, IK-KYUNG, cardiologist; b. Seoul, Korea, July 13, 1954; came to U.S., 1987; s. Bong-Taek and Ki-Ho (Pyun) J.; m. Youn-Chul Moon; children: Monica, Peter. MD, Kyung-Hee U., 1980; PhD, Leuven U., 1987.

Fellow, clin. asst. Mass. Gen. Hosp., Boston, 1987-94, med. asst., 1994-97, asst. physician, 1997—. Author: Textbook of Interventional Cardiology, 1994; contbr. articles to profl. jours. Fellow Am. Coll. Cardiology, European Soc. Cardiology; mem. Mass. Med. Soc., Paul Dudley White Soc. Roman Catholic. Avocation: tennis. Office: Mass Gen Hosp 55 Fruit St Boston MA 02114-2696

JANG, JAE-YEON, medical educator; b. Seoul, Republic of Korea, Aug. 17, 1957; s. Dong-Ik Jang and Busoon Jo; m. Soo-Nam Jo, Apr. 22, 1989; children: Min-Seok, Seo-Won. BS, Seoul (Korea) Nat. U., 1981, MS, 1983, PhD, 1988. Rschr. Inst. for Environ. Rsch., Yonsei U., Seoul, 1984-88; sr. rsch. Inst. for Occupl. Health, Seoul, 1989-92, Inst. for Occupl. Health Sci., Lausanne (Switzerland) U., 1993-94; prof. Ajou U., Suwon, Republic of Korea, 1994—; exec. com. Environment and Pollution Rsch. Group, Seoul, 1989—, Ctr. for Worker's Health, Seoul, 1991—; com. for toxicity test of chems. Ministry of Labour, Seoul, 1992; mem. Com. for Quality Assurance of Environ. Analysis, Inchon, Republic of Korea, 1992—; rsch. com., editl. com. mem. Korean Fedn. for Environ. Movement, Seoul, 1993—; mem. Com. for Quality Assurance of Occupl. Disease Diagnosis, Inchon, 1994—; bd. dirs. Environ. and Pollution Rsch. Corp., Seoul. Author: Problems and Solutions of Pollution, 1991; contbr. articles to profl. jours. 2d lt. Korean Army, 1983. Mem. Internat. Soc. Exposure Analysis, Internat. Occupl. Hygiene Assn., Am. Conf. Govtl. Indsl. Hygienists, Korean Indsl. Hygienists Assn., Korean Worker's Health and Safety Rsch. Assn., Korean Soc. Environ. Toxicol. (bd. dirs., editl. com. 1996—). Avocations: hiking, swimming, Go. Office: Ajou U Occupl-Environ Med, 5 Wonchon Paldal, Suwon 442-749, Republic of Korea

JANGID, RADHEY SHYAM, engineering educator; s. Gokul and Girija (Devi) Chand; m. Vandna Jangid, May 5, 1994; 1 child, Bulbul. BE, U. Jodhpur, 1989; MTech, Indian Inst. Tech., New Delhi, 1991, PhD, 1993. Rsch. assoc. Indian Inst. Tech., Delhi, 1993-94; lectr. Bits Pilani, India, 1994, Indian Inst. Tech. Bombay, Mombai, India, 1994—. Author: Strucutural Analysis, 1997. Avocations: playing cards, tracking, watching crickets. Home: 4 Vihar House IIT Campus, Powai 400076, India Office: Dept Civil Engring, Indian Inst Tech, Powai Mumbai 400076, India

JANIAK, MAREK KRZYSZTOF, pathophysiologist; b. Warsaw, Aug. 14, 1950; s. Zdzislaw and Marianna (Pacholska) J.; m. Maria Teresa Walach, Nov. 12, 1977. MD, Mil. U. Sch. Medicine, Lodz, Poland, 1974; PhD, Mil. Inst. Hygiene & Edipemiol, Warsaw, 1978. Rsch. asst. Mil. Inst. Hygiene & Epidemiology, Warsaw, 1975-78, sr. rsch. assoc., 1978-87, asst. prof., 1988-89; asst. prof. dept. pathophysiology Inst. Rheumatology, Warsaw, 1989-93; asst. prof., head dept. Mil. Inst. Hygiene & Epidemiology, 1995-98, assoc. prof., dept. head, 1998—; vis. scientist U. Alberta, Edmonton, Can., 1992-94; cons. in field. Author: AIDS - The Disease History, 1987. Mem. Soc. Neutrality of the State with Respect to the Outlook on Life, Warsaw, 1990—. Lt. col. Polish Mil., 1968-89, 99—. Mem. Am. Assn. Cancer Rsch., Polish Soc. Immunology, European Assn. Cancer Rsch. Avocations: literature, music, theater, film, sailing, skiing. Home: Bora-Komorowskiego 52-36, 03-982 Warsaw Poland Office: Mil Inst Hygiene/Epidemiolo, Kozielska 4, 01-163 Warsaw Poland

JANICE, BARBARA, illustrator; b. Bklyn., Jan. 25, 1949; d. Irving and Blanche (Lass) Rothman; 1 child, Stacey-Alissa Mirsky. BS in Biology, L.I. U., 1971; studied with, Frank Netter, MD. Staff illustrator Courier-Life Pubs., Bklyn., 1975-78, The Village Voice, N.Y.C., 1978-80; art dir., dept. anatomy SUNY Health Sci. Ctr., Bklyn., 1989-91; freelance illustrator Walt Disney Prodns., N.Y.C., 1990-95, Orlando, Fla., 1990-95; art dir. EuroDisney, Paris, 1990-95; illustrator EuroDisney, Orlando, N.Y.C., 1991-94; art dir. for Donald Duck character EuroDisney, Ft. Lauderdale, Fla., 1994—; sr. sys. specialist for L.Am., Microsoft Corp., 1995-99; cons. Parkland, Fla., 1999—; dir. Barbara Janice Graphics, N.Y.C. and Fla., 1980—, Barbara Janice Cons., Inc., 1999—; guest spkr. Pratt Sch. Art and Design, Bklyn., 1991; art dir. for character Donald Duck, EuroDisney, Paris, 1992—. Illustrator: Current Operative Urology, 6th edit., 1989, A Historical Profile of the Children's Medical Center, 1990, 2d rev. edit., 1992, The Human Body on File, 1992; represented in permanent collections SUNY Health Sci. Ctr., Bklyn., EuroDisney, Paris, Tokyo Disneyland. Vol. artist Coalition for the Homeless, N.Y.C., 1985, 91, AIDS Coalition, Ft. Lauderdale, N.Y.C., 1992—. Recipient 1st place N.Y. Art Critics award, 1984, 2d place award, 1992, Outstanding Artists & Designers of 20th Century award Oxford U., Cambridge, England, 1999. Mem. Assn. Med. Illustrators, Soc. Illustrators (1st place 34th ann. exhbn. 1991, 2d place 33d ann. exhbn. 1990, 1st place 40th ann. exhbn. 1997), Graphic Artists Guild (profl. rep.), Am. Biog. Inst. (bd. advisors), Internat. Biog. Ctr. (bd. govs.). Home: 5537 NW 124th Ave Parkland FL 33076-3430

JANIGA, MARY ANN, art educator, artist; b. Lackawanna, N.Y., June 14, 1950; d. Jacob and Julia (Zatlukal) Mazurchuk; m. William B. Janiga, Nov. 23, 1972; children: Nicholas, Matthew. BS, State U. Coll., Buffalo, 1972, MS, 1974, cert. advanced study, 1995. Cert. in sch. adminstrn. and supervision. Tchr. art Buffalo Pub. Schs., 1972—; art facilitator Olmsted Sch., Buffalo, 1985—; supervising tchr. State Univ. Coll., Buffalo; liaison Albright-Knox Art Gallery, 1994—; art presenter fed. pre-kindergarten program, 1998. Exhibited in group shows at Cheektowaga (N.Y.) Art Guild, 1979, Erie County Parks Art Festival, 1979, Lockport Art Festival, 1980, Allentown Art Exhibit, Kennan Ctr. Recipient various awards for art; grantee Buffalo Tchr. Ctr., 1986-90, Olmstead Home Sch. Assn., 1991-97, Allentown Village Soc., 1994. Mem. NEA, PAT (life), Olmsted Home Sch. Assn., SUNY-Buffalo Alumni Assn., Buffalo Tchrs. Fedn., Buffalo Fine Arts Acad., Buffalo Soc. Natural Scis., Zool. Soc. of Buffalo, Lancaster H.S. Home Sch. Assn. (rec. sec. 1998-99, co-pres. 1999-01). Avocations: reading, concerts, theater, art exhibits. Office: Olmsted Sch 911 Abbott Rd Buffalo NY 14220-2423

JANIK, ANDRZEJ, law educator; b. Warsaw, Poland, Sept. 26, 1951; s. Jozef and Pelagia Janina (Bonarska) J.; m. Malgorzata Derkacz, Aug. 5, 1978; 1 child, Piotr. LLM, Warsaw U., 1973, PhD of Law, 1979. Asst., lectr., asst. prof. Warsaw Sch. Econs., 1974-92, prof., 1995—; counsel Bank Handlowy Warsaw, 1985-95; ptnr. Haarmann, Hemmelrath & Ptnr., Warsaw, 1996—. Author: Product Liability-A Comparative Study, 1988, (monograph) Produkthaftung International, 1988, Panstwo i Prawo, 1984, Internationales Steuerrecht, 1997. Mem. Polish Bar Assn., Legal Advisors Assn. Roman Catholic. Avocations: classical music, opera, jogging. Home: Czterech Wiatrów 16, 02-800 Warsaw Poland Office: Warsaw Sch Econs, Al Niepodleglosci 162, 02-554 Warsaw Poland

JANIK-CZACHOR, MARIA ZOFIA, physicochemist; b. Warsaw, Poland; d. Waclaw Eugeniusz and Maria Irena (Tarnawa-Malczewska) Janik; m. Andrzej Cezary Czachor, June 14, 1962; 1 child, Maria Paulina. MS in Chemistry, Tech. U. Warsaw, 1963; PhD in Phys. Chemistry, Polish Acad. Sci., Warsaw, 1968, Habilitation, 1982. Asst. Tech. U. Warsaw, 1963-64; adj. Polish Acad. Sci., Warsaw, 1968-84, sr. ind. rsch. fellow, 1984, rsch. group leader, 1982-93, chair dept., 1993-96; vis. rsch. fellow Northwestern U., Evanston, Ill., 1980, 82; cons. Corrosion Rsch. Ctr., U. Minn., Mpls., 1983; vis. prof. Tohoku U., Sendai, Japan, 1989, U. Geneva, 1996. Nat. Poly. Inst. Toulouse, France, 2000; mem., co-organizer internat. adv. bds. and organizing coms. symposia and confs, 1985—; initiated and co-organized a series of cyclic internat. interdisciplinary Symposia Warsaw, 1993, Sendai, 1998; cons. in field; nat. standardization com. ISO Fedn., 1999—. Co-editor Passivity and its Breakdown ECS Pennington vol. 97-26, 1998; contbr. sci. articles to profl. jours. Alexander von Humboldt fellow, 1974, 86, Japanese Soc. Prom. Sci. fellow, 1989, Conv. Intercantonale Pour L'Enseignement du 3e Cycle en Chimie fellow, 1996; recipient Civil award Polish Cross of Merit. Mem. Internat. Electrochem. Soc., Polish Chem. Soc., Polish-Japan Soc. Roman Catholic. Avocations: history of art, architecture, classical music, theater. Office: Polish Acad Sci Inst Phys Chemistry, Kasprzaka 44/52, 01-224 Warsaw Poland

JANIN, ANNE, pathology educator; b. Paris, Dec. 31, 1951; d. Robert and Solange Mercier; m. Jean François Janin, June 28, 1975; children: Marianne, Cécile, Camille, Mathilde, Axelle. MD, Paris Med. U., 1977, Pathologist, 1978, Immunologist, 1981, Dermatologist, 1986. Resident U. Hosp., Paris, 1975-78; asst. U. Hosp., Clermont Ferrand, France, 1979-86; assoc. prof. U. Hosp., Lille, France, 1986-95; head dept. pathology Hosp. Saint Louis, Paris, 1995—; coord. French Orgn. of Pathological Tissue Banks, 1999—; mem. editl. bd. Amales de Pathologie, Paris, 1986-88; cons. for molecular biology, U. Hosp., Lille, France, 1990-96. Contbr. over a hundred articles to profl. jours including Am. Jour. Pathology, Blood, Lancet, Immunology, Human Pathology, Jour. of Exptl. Medicine, Gastroenterology, Brit. Jour. Dermatology, Archives of Dermatology; also chpts. to books including Stress Proteins in Medicine, 1995, Sjögren's Syndrome: State of the Art, 1994. Grantee: Am. Acad. Allergy and Clin. Immunology, 1985, Univ. Rsch., 1986, 89, 93, Ligue Contre le Cancer, 1995, Assn. pour La Recherche sur Le Cancer, 1998. Mem. European Soc. Pathology. Office: Hosp Saint Louis Dept Path, 1 Ave C Vellefaux, 75745 Paris Cedex 10, France

JANKE, JOHN ERIC, secondary educator; b. Longview, Wash., Mar. 30, 1960; s. John Charles and Rose Kathryn (Albertson) J. AA, Lower Columbia Coll., 1982; BA in History, Ctrl. Wash. U., 1984, MEd, 1999; BA in Edn., Western Wash. U., 1986. Cert. tchr., Wash. Jr. sch. high tchr. Bd. Edn., Kelso, Wash., 1986-94; jr. high tchr. Bd. Edn., Longview, 1986-94, Spannaway, Wash., 1994-2000. Named Alumni of Yr. Ctrl. Wash. U., 1997. Mem. NEA, Wash. Edn. Assn., Bethel Edn. Assn. Avocations: golfing, stamp collecting, pool. E-mail: johnjanke@yahoo.com. Home: 2843 Magnolia St Longview WA 98632-3544

JANKE, KENNETH, investment consultant; b. Ft. William, Ont., Can., May 13, 1934; s. Adolf Earthman and Julianna (Dika) J.; m. Sally Mildred Roach, June 29, 1957; children: Kenneth Stuart, Laura Lynn, Julie Ann. Student, Mich. State U., 1952-56. Asst. mgr. Household Fin. Co., Detroit, 1958-60; gen. mgr. Nat. Assn. Investors, Royal Oak, Mich., 1960-76, pres., CEO, 1976—; bd. dir. Investment Edn. Inst., Royal Oak, pres. 1995—; bd. dirs. World Fedn. Investors, Brussels, pres., 1995—. Author: Ask Mr. Naic, 1982, Golf Is A Funny Game (But It Wasn't Meant To Be), 1992, Starting and Running a Profitable Investment Club, 1996; co-author: Wit and Wisdom of Golf, 1997; columnist mag. Better Investing. Chmn. Mich. Golf Hall of Fame, Lake Orion; pres. Am. Cancer Soc.-Oakland Country, Southfield, Mich., 1974-75; pres., bd. dirs. NAIC Growth Fund, Royal Oak; bd. dirs. AFLAC, Inc., Columbus, Ga.; bd. advisors Mich. PGA, West Bloomfield. With U.S. Army, 1956-58, ETO. Recipient Disting. Svc. award Investment Edn. Inst., 1972, Founder award Am. Cancer Soc., 1970. Fellow Fin. Analysts Soc. Detroit (pres. 1984—), Fin. Analysts Fedn.; mem. Nat. Investor Rels. Inst. (pres. Detroit 1985—), Western Golf Assn. (bd. dirs., pres.), Indianwood Golf and Country Club (Lake Orion), Renaissance Club (Detroit), NFL Alumni (Lauderdale, Fla.), Scalawag's Country club (Mt. Clemens, Mich.), Masons. Republican. Episcopalian. Avocations: golf, golf collecting. Home: 4305 W Maple Rd Bloomfield Hills MI 48301-2901 Office: Nat Assn Investors Corp 711 W 13 Mile Rd Madison Heights MI 48071-1806

JANKLOW, MORTON LLOYD, lawyer, literary agent; b. N.Y.C., May 30, 1930; s. Maurice and Lillian (Levantin) J.; m. Linda Mervyn LeRoy, Nov. 27, 1960; children: Angela LeRoy, Lucas Warner. AB, Syracuse U., 1950; JD, Columbia U., 1953. Bar: N.Y. 1953, D.C. 1961, U.S. Dist. Ct. (so. and ea. dists.) N.Y., U.S. Ct. Appeals (2nd cir.), U.S. Supreme Ct. Chmn., CEO Morton L. Janklow Assocs., Inc., 1977-89; ptnr. Janklow & Ashley, LLP, N.Y.C., 1989—; sr. ptnr. Janklow & Nesbit Assocs., 1989—; trustee Managed Accts. Svcs., PaineWebber PACE funds, 1996—; chmn. Janklow & Nesbit (U.K.); bd. dirs. Revlon, Inc., 1997-2000, Orbis Comm., Inc., N.Y.C., 1986-89, Revlon, Inc.; bd. dirs., mem. finance com. McCaffrey & McCall, Inc., N.Y.C., 1962-87; chmn. exec. com. Harvey Group, Inc., N.Y.C., 1968-71, Cable Funding Corp., N.Y.C., 1971-73; mem. exec. com. Sloan Commn. Cable Comm., 1970-71, Andrew Wellington Cordier fellow Columbia U. Sch. Internat. Affairs; vis. lectr. Radcliffe Coll., Columbia U. Law Sch., NYU; bus. and fin. adv. bd. NYU Press and NYU Sch. Arts, 1977—; donor, founder Morton L. Janklow Professorship of Lit. and Artistic Property, Columbia U. Sch. Law; life mem., Harlan Fiske Stone fellow of Columbia U. Law Sch.; founder Morton L. Janklow Program for Advocacy in the Arts, Columbia U. Law Sch.; mem. dean's coun. Columbia U. Law Sch., 1992—. Bd. dirs., exec. com., devel. chmn. City Center Music and Drama, 1971-75; bd. dirs. Film Soc., Lincoln Ctr., 1972-75, Am. Cinematheque, 1971-75; bd. govs. Jewish Mus., 1969-75; dir., chmn. Janklow Found.; trustee Mr. and Mrs. Harry M. Warner Found., 1965—, Sidney Sheldon Found.; mem. Council of Friends, Whitney Mus. Am. Art, 1973-82, also mem. com. on paintings and sculptures; ad hoc com. on pub. and merchandising activities Met. Mus. Art; bd. advisors Princeton U. Art. Mus., 1984-89; mem. adv. bd. Guggenheim Mus., 1980-86; adv. council Sch. Arts, NYU; mem. Ind. Com. on Arts Policy; bd. advisors Columbia U. Jour. Art and the Law; assn. of fellows Pierpoint Morgan Libr., N.Y.C.. Served with AUS, 1953-55. Decorated chevalier l'Ordre des Arts et des Lettres de la Republique Française. Mem. ABA, N.Y. Bar Assn., Assn. of Bar of City of N.Y. (membership com. 1967—), N.Y. County Lawyers Assn., Fed. Comms. Bar Assn., Am. Judicature Soc., Coun. on Fgn. Rels., Com. on the Rsch. Librs., N.Y. Pub. Libr. Office: 445 Park Ave New York NY 10022-2606

JANKOVIC, JOSEPH, neurologist, educator, scientist; b. Teplice, Czechoslovakia, Mar. 1, 1948; came to U.S., 1965; m. Cathy Sue Inselberg, May 26, 1973; children: Jason, Daniel, Zachary. MD, U. Ariz., 1973. Diplomate Am. Bd. Neurology. Med. intern Baylor Coll. Medicine, Houston, 1973-74, asst. prof. neurology, 1977-84, assoc. prof., 1984-88, prof., 1988—; resident in neurology Columbia U., N.Y.C., 1974-76, chief resident in neurology, 1976-77; dir. Parkinson's Disease Ctr. and Movement Disorder Clinic, Houston, 1977—; sr. attending physician Meth. Hosp., Houston, 1988—. Author over 500 articles and book chpts. in field; editor/co-editor 16 med. books; mem. editorial bd. jours. Movement Disorders, Clin. Neuropharmacology, Neurology Jour., Jour. Neurology Psychiatry. Chmn. sci. adv. bd. Blepharospasm Rsch. Found.; mem. adv. bd. Dystonia Med. Rsch. Found., Internat. Tremor Found., Tourette's Syndrome Med. Adv. Bd. Grantee disease rsch. founds., pharmaceutical cos., NIH. Fellow Am. Acad. Neurology; mem. AMA, Am. Neurol. Assn., Soc. for Neurosci., Movement Disorders Soc. (pres.-elect 1991-94, pres. 1994-96). Avocations: tennis, family activities, music. Office: Baylor Coll Medicine 6550 Fannin St Ste 1801 Houston TX 77030-2744

JANKOVIC, NIKOLA, internist, nephrology consultant; b. Zagreb, Croatia, May 12, 1953; s. Mojmir and Neva (Sket) J.; m. Vera Katalinic, Apr. 16, 19778; children: Mateja, Andrej. Student, Med. Faculty Zagreb, 1978, postgrad. clin. pharmacology, 1980, M of Med. Sci., 1990. Bd. cert. in internal medicine, specialty in nephrology. Internist Sveti Duh Hosp., Zagreb. Contbr. numerous articles to med. jours. and chpts. to books. Lt. Croatian Army Res. Mem. Croatian Med. Soc., Internat. Soc. Peritoneal Dialysis, Internat. Soc. Nephrology, Internat. Soc. Artificial Organs, N.Y. Acad. Scis., Tennis Club (bd. dirs.). Roman Catholic. Avocation: tennis. Office: Sveti Duh Hosp, Sveti Duh 64, 10000 Zagreb Croatia

JANKOVIĆ, SLOBODAN, aerodynamics educator, researcher; b. Brussels, Aug. 10, 1932; s. Dušan and Ljubica (Apostolović) J.; m Ksenija, July 3, 1960 (div. 1975); 1 child, Jelena; m. Zorica, Sept 18, 1975 (div. 1982);1 child, Ana; m. Melinda Djelmiš, Dec. 30, 1982. BS in Civil Engring., Ecole d' Application, Brussels, 1959; M in Aerospace, U. Beograd, Yugoslavia, 1964, PhD in Aerospace, 1967. Ballistics researcher Military Tech. Inst., Beograd, Yugoslavia, 1960-67; aerodynamic researcher Military Tech. Inst., Beograd, 1979-84; asst. prof. Hight Military Tech. Sch., Zagreb, Yugoslavia, 1967-73; prof. Hight Military Tech. Sch., Zagreb, 1984-91; asst. prof. U. Beograd., 1973-79; aerodynamic researcher Maritime & Defense Inst., Zagreb, 1991-94; prof. U. Zagreb, 1994—; cons. United Metal Industry, Sarajevo, 1975-91; adv. bd. Metorol. Inst., Zagreb, 1985-92. Author: (military edition) Exterior Ballistics, 1977, Missile's Aerodynamics, 1979, Flight Mechanics of Missiles, 1998. Col. Yugoslavian army tech. br., 1960-73. Recipient Sci. award, Ministr of Defense, Beograd, 1966, 1971. Mem. AIAA, Croation Soc. Mechanics. Roman Catholic. Home: Av Vukovar 240, Zagreb Croatia

JANKOVIĆ, STIPAN, radiologist, neuroradiologist; b. Strizirep, Croatia, Nov. 5, 1948; s. Ivan and Nevenka (Rančič) J.; m. Gorana Bais, Nov. 27, 1973; children: Ivana, Hrvoje. MD, Med. Sch., 1972, MS, 1979, PhD, 1982. Resident in radiology Clin. Hosp., Split, Croatia, 1974-77; asst. in radiology Med. Sch., Split, 1978-85, assoc. prof., 1985-88, prof., 1988—; vice-head radiology Clin. Hosp., Split, Croatia, 1982-95, head radiology, 1995—. Editor (with others) Harison's Principles of Internal Medicine, 1995; editor, author Selective Chapters in Urgent Medicine, 1998; contbr. articles to profl. jours. Maj. Croatian Army Res., 1991-96. Grantee Spomenica Domovinske Zahvalnosti, Red Hrvatskog Trolista, Spomenica Domovinskog rata, Medalja Oluja. Mem. European Soc. of Neuroradiology, European Soc. Radiology, Croatian Soc. of Radiology, Oncology and Rheumatology, N.Y. Acad. Scis. Roman Catholic. Avocations: hiking, bowling, foreign literature. Home: Starčevićeva 24A, 21000 Split Croatia Office: Clin Hosp Split, Spinciceva 1, 21000 Split Croatia

JANKOWSKI, ROBERT, civil engineering educator; b. Gdynia, Gdańsk, Poland, Dec. 26, 1968; s. Tadeusz and Kazimiera Wladyslawa (Reszka) J.; m. Monika Izabela Chamera, July 3, 1993. BSc, U. Sheffield, Eng., 1992; postgrad., U. Roskilde, Denmark, 1993; MSc, Tech. U. Gdansk, 1993; PhD, U. Tokyo, 1997. Rsch. assoc. Tech. U. Gdansk, 1992-94, asst. prof. civil engring., 1997—. Contbr. articles to profl. jours. Recipient scholarships Govt. European Cmty., 1991-92, Govt. Japan, 1994-97, Found. for Polish Sci.; award for best MSc thesis Govt. Poland, Warsaw, 1994. Mem. Japan Soc. Civil Engrs. Roman Catholic. Avocations: cycling, tennis, computers. Home: ul Rylkego 4, 80-307 Gdańsk Poland Office: Tech U Gdańsk, Ul Narutowicza 11/12, 80-952 Gdańsk Poland

JANKOWSKI, STANISŁAW JAN, microbiologist; b. Lwów, Poland, Aug. 4, 1938; s. Wiktor Jan Jankowski and Janina Zopoth; div.; 1 child. MS, U. Wrocław, Poland, 1963; PhD, Polish Acad. Sci., 1971; Habilitation, Med. U., 1991. Asst. Med. U., Wrocław, 1963-70, asst. prof., 1970-96, head dept. biology, 1996—. Contbr. articles to profl. jours. Mem. Polish Microbiology Soc., Polish Genetic Soc., Polish Immunol. Soc. Roman Catholic. Avocations: traveling, Napoleon Bonaparte. E-mail: jank@biolog.am.wroc.pl. Home: Pl Grunwaldzki 4/37, 50 384 Wrocław Poland Office: Dept Biology Med Univ, Mikulicza Radeckiego St 9, 50 367 Wrocław Poland

JANKOWSKI, TADEUSZ, mathematician, educator; b. Kolo, Poznan, Poland, Apr. 8, 1940; s. Stefan and Janina (Banasiak) J.; m. Kazimiera Reszka, Dec. 31, 1961; children: Jacek, Robert. MSc, U. Poznan, 1963; PhD, U. Gdansk, Poland, 1971; DSc, Tech. U. Warsaw, Poland, 1995. Asst. Computer Ctr. Tech. U. Gdansk, 1963-71, asst. prof. dept. math., 1971-84; mem. faculty engring. sci. U. Benghazi, 1984-89; asst. prof. dept. math. Tech. U. Gdansk, 1989-96, assoc. prof., head differential equations dept., 1996—, prof., 1998—. Author 3 textbooks; contbr. numerous rsch. articles to profl. jours. Mem. Internat. Fedn. Nonlinear Analysts, Polish Math. Soc. Roman Catholic. Office: Tech U Gdansk, 11/12 Narutowicz St, 80-952 Gdansk Poland

JANKUHN, STEFFEN, physicist, researcher; b. Erfurt, Thuringia, Germany, Mar. 14, 1967; s. Helmut and Anita (Postel) J. Diploma, U. Leipzig, Germany, 1995. Rsch. scientist U. Leipzig, 1995-2000, Inst. f. Oberflachenmod e.V., Leipzig, 2000—. Contbr. articles to profl. jours. Scholar Free State Saxony, 1999-2000. Mem. German Phys. Soc. Office: Inst Oberflachenmod, Permoserstr 15, 04303 Leipzig Saxony, Germany

JANN, JOEFON, computer scientist; b. Hong Kong, China; came to U.S., 1967; m. Pratap Pattnaik. B in Math., Wellesley Coll., 1970; M in Math., CUNY, 1972; M in Computer Sci., Columbia U., 1977. Adj. lectr. math. Lehman Coll., Bronx, N.Y.; tech. staff Network Analsysis Corporation, Glen Clove, N.Y.; APL programmer ISTG Hdqs. IBM, Harrison, N.Y.; sys. programmer ISTG Hdqs. IBM; adv. sys. engr. N.Y. Banking Branch Office IBM, N.Y.C., tech. staff Math. Analysis & Computation Ctr.; computer scientist T.J. Watson Rsch. Ctr. IBM, Yorktown Heights, N.Y., 1989—; tech. mem. IBM Deep Blue Chess Team, 1996-97. Mem. Inst. Elec. and Electronics Engs. Inventor Home Node Migration for Distributed Shared Memory Sys., 1999. Avocations: playing piano, classical music, photography. Fax: 914-945-4425. E-mail: joefon@us.ibm.com. Office: IBM TJ Watson Rsch Ctr PO Box 218 Yorktown Heights NY 10598-0218

JANN, PETER, international justice; b. 1935. D of Law, U. Vienna. Judge, then magistrate; referent Ministry of Justice, Austrian Parliament; mem. Constitutional Ct., Vienna; judge Ct. of Justices of European Cmtys., Luxembourg, 1995—. Office: Ct Justice European Cmtys, Palais de Cour de justice, Kirchberg L-2925, Luxembourg*

JANNATPOUR, SEYED ALI, software engineer, educator; b. Tehran, Iran, Mar. 2, 1975; s. Hashem Jannatpour and Zahra Saemi Ford. BS in Computer-Software Engring., Azad U. of Tehran, 1995; MS in Computer Engring. in Artificial Intelligence, Amir Kabir U. of Tech., Tehran, 1998—; postgrad., Shahid Beheshti U. of Tech. Software engr. Tarfand Rayaneh Co., Tehran, 1995, IRNET Co., Tehran, 1995-96, Bamdad Computer Co., Tehran, 1996-97; cons. dept. mgr. ERAware Technologies, Tehran, 1997-99; part-time instr. computer engring. dept. Shahid Sattari Air U., Tehran, 1999—; part-time software engr. PATSA Co., Tehran, 1999—; univ. instr. Shahid Beheshti U. of Tech., 2000—. Programmer, designer Windows Persian Programming Tools 1.1, 1995. 1st lt. Tehran Army, 1999-2000. Recipient Appreciation award 10th Internat. Music Festival, 1995. Avocation: playing piano. Fax: 98-21-874-7761. E-mail: ali@jannatpour.com. Home: PO Box 13955-331, Tehran Iran Office: PATSA Co No 20, 19h St Bokharest Ave, Tehran Iran

JANNERSTEN, PER E., publisher, writer; b. Gothenburg, Sweden, Oct. 17, 1948; s. Eric R. and Anna M. (Kaellberg) J.; m. Britt M. Carlbom, Feb. 16, 1972; children: Anna, Carl. BA, U. Stockholm, 1971, MA, 1971. CEO EJT Printing House, Avesta, Sweden, 1972-83; Jannersten Forlag, Avesta, Sweden, 1983—; exec. Internat. Bridge Press Assn., 9 Miles City, Mont., 1984—. Author: Bridge in One Night, 1986; co-author: The Tournament Director, 1990, Movements—A Fair Approach, 1994; contbr. (newspaper) Svenska Dagbladet, Stockholm, 1982—; contbg. editor Swedish Acad. Dictionary, 1982—. Office: Jannersten Forlag AB, Bjorkstigen 8, SE 77427 Avesta Sweden

JANNO, JAAN, mathematician; b. Kuressaare, Estonia, Feb. 18, 1961; s. Jüri and Juta Janno; m. Signe Avent, May 29, 1987; children: Liis, Marten. Dipl.Math., U. Tartu, Estonia, 1984; PhD, Inst. Math. and Mechanics, Russia, 1988. Jr. rsch. worker Inst. Cybernetics, Estonian Acad. Scis., Tallinn, Estonia, 1987-88, sr. rsch. worker, 1988-97; sr. rsch. worker Inst. Cybernetics, Tallinn Tech. U., 1997—. Contbr. articles to profl. jours. Mem. Estonian Math. Soc. (Award of A. Humal 1992). Avocations: classical music, health sport. Home: Liiva 4-44, 72712 Paide Estonia Office: Inst Cybernetics, Akadeemia tee 21, 12618 Tallinn Estonia

JANNUZI, EUGENE FREDRIC, retired manufacturing executive; b. Beaver Falls, Pa., Nov. 9, 1915; s. Raphael and Teresa Anita (Silvester) J.; m. Margaret Anna Moltrup, Feb. 10, 1945. BS, Geneva Coll., Beaver Falls, 1936; MEd, U. Pitts., 1941. Sci. tchr. Beaver Falls Sch. Dist., 1936-42; reporter Pitts. Post-Gazette, 1946-51; asst. dir. pub. rels. & advtg. Jones & Laughlin Steel Corp., Pitts., 1951-66; chmn., pres. Moltrup Steel Products Co., Beaver Falls, 1966-89; ret., 1989. Author: (novel) Bright Star, 1997. Mem. Beaver County Planning Commn., 1966-89; past trustee Geneva Coll.; past dir. Am. Iron & Steel Inst.; elder 1st Presbyn. Ch., Beaver Falls. Lt. USN, 1942-46 ETO. Recipient Others award Salvation Army, Beaver Falls, 1993. Mem. Pitts. Press Club, Beaver Valley Country Club, Rotary (pres. Beaver Falls club 1972-73), Am. Legion (life). Republican. Avocations: tennis, golf, writing, speaking. Home: 308 7th St Patterson Hts Beaver Falls PA 15010-3234

JANO, PATRICE JOSE, optical engineer; b. Epernay, Champagne, France, Apr. 15, 1946; s. Roger J. and Renee P. (Guennelon) J.; m. Veronique Mh Super, July 12, 1975; children: Melusine, Enguerrand, Perceval. M Physics, U. Reims, France, 1970; Optics Engr., Ecole Sup. Optique, Orsay, France, 1972. Lic. engr. Head high energy laser divsn. Dir. des Rschrs. et Etudes Techniques, Paris, 1972-77; project mgr. mil. applications of lasers LDM, Marcoussis, France, 1982-86; head indsl. lasers activities Cilas, 1986-88; head Extended Air Def. Act Thomson-CSF, Bagneux, France, 1988-95; head large lasers systems Thomson-CSF, Guyancourt, France, 1995—. Founder Opto. Mem. Old Fellow of Superieure Optique Sch. (pres. 1996). Achievements include patents on laser missile guidance, laser technology, laser alignment, others. Home: 20 Rue de Melun, 77240 Seine Port France Office: Thomson-CSF Optronique, Rue Guynemer BP 55, 78283 Guyancourt France

JÁNOS, SZÖLLÖSI, obstetrician; b. Mezotur, Hungary, Nov. 11, 1939; s. Szöollösi and Takács (Róza) J.; m. Irén Kovács, Aug. 22, 1975; children: Dalma, Agnes. MD, U. Szeged, Hungary, 1964. Dir. outpatient dept. andrology Szeged, 1972—; asst. prof. dept. ob.-gyn. U. Med. Sch., Szeged, 1991—; mgr. WHO Andrological Rsch. Team U. Med. Sch., Szeged, 1980—. Editor: Magyar Andrologia; contbr. articles to profl. jours. Mem. European Soc. Human Reproduction. Home: Traktor u 26, H-6726 Szeged Hungary Office: Albert Szent Gyorgyi Med Sc, Semmelweis ul, 6725 Szeged Hungary

JANOSKI, HENRY VALENTINE, banker, former investment counselor, realtor; b. Nanticoke, Pa., Feb. 14, 1933; s. Bruce and Marie (Rozmarek) J.; m. Rita Rosemary Ruane, Sept. 27, 1980; children: Maria, Elizabeth. BA magna cum laude, Yale U., 1955; MBA, U. Pa., 1960. Sr. credit analyst Nat Bank Detroit, 1960-63; asst. cashier First Nat. Bank, Wilkes-Barre, Pa., 1963-65; sr. v.p. Northeastern Bank, Scranton, Pa., 1965-80; investment counselor, fin. planner Clarks Summit, Pa., 1980-92; realtor assoc. Clarks Summit, 1992; chief trust investment officer Penn Security Bank and Trust Co., Scranton, 1992—; instr. fin. Marywood Coll., Scranton, 1983. Bd. dirs. Cmty. Med. Ctr., Scranton, 1974-97, asst. treas., 1976-91; bd. dirs. Emergency Med. Svcs. Northeastern Pa., Pittston, 1976—, pres., 1985-87; bd. dirs. Polish Am. Congress No. Pa. divsn., Scranton, 1972—, v.p., 1972-89, pres., 1989—; bd. dirs. Ethics Inst. N.E. Pa., Dallas, 1991-96; bd. dirs., treas. Keystone chpt. Am. Heart Assn., Scranton, 1968-74; chmn. Campaign for Yale U., Northeastern Pa., 1976-78; incorporating dir. Lackawanna County U.S. Comstn. Bicentennial Commn., 1987-88; treas. Grove St. Home Sch. Assn., Clarks Summit, 1987-90; lectr. Christ the King Ch., Dunmore, 1982-87, Our Lady of the Snows Ch., Clarks Summit, 1987—, Ch. of St. Benedict, Newton Twp., 1991—; allocations vol. United Way, 1988-91. 1st lt. AUS, 1955-57. Recipient Assn. U.S. Army award, 1954, Disting. Mil. Student award, 1955, Am. Legion award, 1947, 51, Cert. Leadership Lackawanna, 1989. Mem. Am. Bankers Assn., Pa. Bankers Assn., Am. Inst. Banking, No. Anthracite Bankers Assn., Fin. Analysts Phila., Fin. Analysts Fedn., Inst. Chartered Fin. Analysts (chartered fin. analyst), Assn. for Investment Mgmt. and Rsch., Estate Planning Coun. Northeastern Pa., Nat. Assn. Realtors, Pa. Assn. Realtors, Greater Scranton Bd. Realtors, Experiment in Internat. Living (France), Le Cercle Francais (treas. 1994—), Ecologia/Ekologiya, Wyo. Hist. and Geol. Soc., Greater Scranton C. of C., Esperanto League for N.Am., Universala Esperanto Asocio, Friends of Poland of Lackawanna County, Polish Nat. Alliance, Polish Falcons Am., Polish Am. Hist. Assn., Kosciuszko Found., Assn. Yale Alumni (rep. 1988-91), Aircraft Owners and Pilots Assn., Schultzville Airport Pilots Assn., Westmoreland Club (Wilkes-Barre), Scranton Club, Yale Club of Northeastern Pa. (sec. 1985-88, alumni sch. com. interview applicants), U. Pa. Club (Lackawanna County), Leadership Lackawanna Alumni Assn., Phi Beta Kappa. Republican. Roman Catholic. Avocations: skiing, flying, travel, languages. Home: 107 Carteret Dr Clarks Summit PA 18411-1009 Office: Penn Security Bank & Trust Co 150 N Washington Ave Scranton PA 18503-1843

JANOUSEK, IVO PETR, museum director; b. Ostrava, Czechoslovakia, July 8, 1938; s. Jan and Blanka (Hummel) J.; m. Jarmila Hrubant, 1965 (div. 1977); 1 child, Jan. Diploma Engring., Tech. U., Prague, Czechoslovakia, 1963, PhD, 1987; BA, Charles U., Prague, 1989. Rschr. Rsch. Inst. Automation, Ostrava, Czechoslovakia, 1964-68; asst. prof. Tech. U., Ostrava, 1968-77; prof. Conservatory, Ostrava, 1968-72; rschr. CKD Semiconductors, Prague, 1977-87, sci. worker, 1987-90; dir. Nat. Tech. Mus., Prague, 1990—; lectr. U. for Chemistry, Pardubice, Czechoslovakia, 1968-73, Charles U., Prague, 1993—. Author: Acoustics for Musicians, 1977, Technical Diagnostics, 1988 (award 1988), Computers and Art, 1989, 3 other books, 9 univ. textbooks; critic, journalist for art various mags., 1970; patentee in field. Leader underground activities, mgr. art exhbns., pub. samizdats, Ostrava, 1970-89. Recipient diplomas Ministry Edn., 1972, 74, Silver award Union Technicians, 1987, award for lit. Czech Found. Technicians, 1989, Gold award ICTP, 1997; fellow Internat. Com. for History of Tech. Nat. Com., 1992, Engring. Collaborative for Sci., Industry and Tech. Exhbns. Mem. Centreeurropean Union Tech. Museums (pres. 1993), Com. Internat. Mus Sci. of Tech./Internat. Coun. Museums (mem. exec. 1992), European Coll. Sci. Industry & Tech. (exec. com. 1996), Assn. Machine Engring. (senator), Engring. Acad., European Acad. Sci. & Art. Avocations: classical and jazz music, visual arts design and architecture. Fax: 33371801. E-mail: info@ntm.cz. Home: U Havlickovych sadu 1, Prague 2, Czech Republic Office: Nat Tech Mus, Kostelni 42, 170 78 Prague 7, Czech Republic

JANOVER, ROBERT H., lawyer; b. N.Y.C., Aug. 17, 1930; s. Cyrus J. and Lillian D. (Horwitz) J.; m. Mary Elizabeth McMahon, Oct. 23, 1966; 1 child, Laura Lockwood. BA, Princeton U., 1952; postgrad., U. Vienna, 1956; JD, Harvard U., 1957. Bar: N.Y. 1957, U.S. Supreme Ct. 1961, D.C. 1966, Mich. 1973. Practice law N.Y.C., 1957-65; cons. Office of Edn., HEW, Washington, 1965; legis. atty. Office of Gen. Counsel, HEW, Washington, 1965-66; asst. gen. atty. Mgmt. Assistance Inc., N.Y.C., 1966-71; atty. Ford Motor Credit Co., Dearborn, Mich., 1971-74; mem. firm Freud, Markus, Slavin, Toohey & Galgan, Troy, Mich., 1974-79; pvt. practice Detroit, 1979-82, Bloomfield Hills, Mich., 1982—. Contbr. articles to profl. jours. Bd. dirs. Oakland Citizens League, 1976-96, v.p., 1976-79, pres., 1979-96; bd. dirs. Civic Searchlight, Inc., 1976-96. 1st lt., arty. U.S. Army, 1952-54, Korea. Mem. ABA, Mich. State Bar, N.Y. State Bar, Detroit Met. Bar Assn., Bar Assn. D.C., Assn. Bar of City of N.Y., Am. Inns Ct. (master of the bench 1996-99), Princeton Club of Mich. (pres. 1991-92), Princeton Club of N.Y., Nassau Club (Princeton, N.J.), Harvard Club (N.Y.C.). Home: 685 Ardmoor Dr Bloomfield Hills MI 48301-2415 Office: 100 W Long Lake Rd Ste 200 Bloomfield Hills MI 48304-2774

JANOWIAK, FRANCISZEK, plant physiologist, researcher; b. Lipnica Wielka, Orawa, Poland, Sept. 20, 1956; s. Karol and Joanna (Jasiorka) J.; m. Bozena Mazur, June 4, 1985; 1 child, Joanna. MS, Agrl. U., Cracow, Poland, 1982, PhD, 1992. Cert. engr. Rsch. asst. Inst. Plant Physiology, Polish Acad. Scis., Cracow, 1982-86, sr. rsch. asst., 1986-92, adiunkt, 1992—; doctoral fellow U. Hamburg, Germany, 1989-91. Rsch. grantee State Com. Sci. Rsch., Warsaw, 1993, 98, European Union, Brussels, 1994. Office: Inst Plant Physiology, Polish Acad Scis Podluzna 3, 30239 Cracow Poland

JANOWITZ, WARREN ROBERT, physician, lawyer; b. N.Y.C., Nov. 6, 1947; s. Norman and Pearl (Saltzman) J.; m. Ellen Rose Kirschner, June 15, 1969 (dec. 1982); m. Elizabeth Ann Rafey, Mar. 20, 1983; children: Michelle, Scott, Allison. BS in Nuclear Engring., NYU, 1968, MD, 1972; JD, U. Miami, Fla., 1986. Bar: Fla. 1987. Intern U. Miami Affiliated Hosps., 1972-73; resident in internal medicine and nuclear medicine U. Miami Affiliated Hosps., Mt. Sinai Med. Ctr., 1973-76; asst. prof. radiology U. Miami, 1978-92; pvt. practice Shea & Gould, Miami, 1987-94; dir. vascular lab. divsn. nuclear medicine and ultrasound Mt. Sinai Med. Ctr., Miami Beach, Fla., 1978-96; assoc. dir. nuclear medicine Bapt. Hosp. Miami/Miami Cardiac & Vaxcular Inst., 1996—; gen. ptnr. Diagnostics Miami Beach (Fla.) Ltd., 1986-90; of counsel Shea & Gould, Miami; adv. bd. radiation protection State of Fla. Dept. Health. Contbr. chpts. to book, articles to profl. jours. Served to lt. comdr. USNR, 1976-78. Named Rep. New Inductees to Fla. Bar Supreme Ct. Fla., 1987. Fellow Am. Coll. Cardiology; mem. ABA, Fla. Med. Assn. (specialty council 1981-87). Jewish. Office: Miami Cardiac and Vascular Inst 8900 N Kendall Dr Miami FL 33176-2118

JANS, DAVID ANDREW, biochemist, research scientist; b. Melbourne, Victoria, Australia, Oct. 19, 1958; s. Vacys Zigmundas and Jessie Hume (Clement) J.; m. Patricia Rossi, June 26, 1987; children: Marianna Sophia, Angela Barbara. BSc with honors, U. Melbourne, Australia, 1981; PhD, Australian Nat. U., Canberra, 1985. Rsch. scientist Friedrich Miescher Inst., Basel, Switzerland, 1984-87; vis. scientist Max Planck Inst. for Biophysics, Frankfurt, Germany, 1987-91; rsch. fellow Westfälische Wilhelms Univ., Münster, Germany, 1991-92; vis. prof. Rsch. Ctr. for Molecular Diagnostics, Moscow, 1993; fellow Level C John Curtin Sch. Med. Rsch., Canberra, Australia, 1993—, fellow Level D, 1997—; grant reviewer Australian Rsch. Coun., 1995—, Wellcome Found., 1996—; article reviewer EMBO Jour./Jour. Cell Biology/Proc. Nat. Acad. Sci., 1995—. Author: The Mobile Receptor Hypothesis: The Role of Membrane Receptor Lateral Movement in Signal Transduction, 1997; contbr. articles to profl. jours. Named Eminent Scientist of Yr., Internat. Rsch. Progress Coun., 1999; fellow UICC-Internat. Union Against Cancer, 1996; grantee Australian Rsch. Coun., 1994, Clive and Vera Ramaciotti Found., 1994-96, Nat. Health and Med. Rsch. Coun., 2000, Wellcome Trust, 2000. Mem. Am. Soc. for Cell Biology, Royal Microscopy Soc., Australian Soc. for Exptl. Pathology. Avocations: music, literature, art, history, sculpture. Home: 35 Jamieson Crescent, Kambah ACT 2902, Australia Office: John Curtin Sch Med Rsch, PO Box 334, Canberra ACT 2601, Australia

JANS, ROBERT MACIEJ, environmental company executive, consultant; b. Poznań, Poland, Mar. 24, 1963; s. Władysław and Felicja (Bekas) J.; m. Iwona Bozena Śnieg, June 27, 1985; children: Igor, Milosz, Arnika. MSc, Tech. U., Poznań, 1986. Asst. of sci., lectr. of sci. Tech. U., Poznań, 1985-89; designer Miriaba Ltd., Poznań, 1988-90; mktg. mgr. Ekolog, Pita, Poland, 1989-91; dir. Ekolog's Div., Poznań, 1992-93; pres., CEO Ekolog Systems Ltd., Poznań, 1994—; lectr., rschr. Tech. U., Poznań. Contbr. articles to profl. jours. Mem. Water Environment Fedn., Internat. Assn. Water Quality, Wielkopolska C. of C. (coun. 1995—). Avocation: kung fu, rock music, movies. Office: Ekolog Systems, Ziębicka 35, 60-164 Poznan Poland

JANSEN, DENNIS WILLIAM, economics educator, consultant; b. St. Louis, Oct. 23, 1956; s. Elmer H.V. and Rosemary F. (Sievers) J.; m. Debra J. Hennessey, June 24, 1978; children: Megan, Amy, Mary. AB in Econs. and Math., St. Louis U., 1978; PhD in Econs., U. N.C., 1983. Instr. N.C. State U., Raleigh, 1982-83; vis. scholar Fed. Res. Bank St. Louis, 1988-89; asst. prof. econs. Tex. A&M U., College Station, 1983-88, assoc. prof., 1989-93, prof., 1994—, head dept., 1996—; tchg. fellow U. N.C., Chapel Hill, 1989-94; mem. vis. faculty Cath. U. Louvain, Belgium, 1990, 92, Erasmus U., Rotterdam, the Netherlands, 1990, Ind. U., 1991. Author: Intermediate Macroeconomics, 1994; Money, Banking and Financial Markets, 1995; contbr. articles to profl. jours. Mrs. Victor Humphrey fellow U. N.C., 1978, Earhart Found., Japan, 1988; rsch. fellow PERC, 1992—. Mem. Am. Econ. Assn., Royal Econ. Assn., We. Econ. Assn., So. Econ. Assn. Roman Catholic. Avocations: reading, soccer, coaching little league. Home: 1704 Emerald Pky College Station TX 77845-5543 Office: Tex A&M U Dept Econs College Station TX 77843-4228

JANSEN, DONALD WILLIAM, lawyer, legislative administrator; b. Luverne, Minn., Aug. 21, 1948; s. William John and Florence Catherine (Tisdell) J.; m. Jacqueline Skeens, Sept. 30, 1978; children: Christopher Donald, Morgan Whitney, Madison Maarten. BA in Polit. Sci., Ariz. State U., 1970; JD, Gonzaga U., 1975. Bar: Ariz. 1975, U.S. Dist. Ct. Ariz. 1977, U.S. Supreme Ct. 1987, U.S. Ct. Appeals (9th cir.) 1998. Asst. rules atty., counsel to ethics com. Ariz. Ho. of Reps., Phoenix, 1976-83, counsel to majority leader, 1983-87, gen. counsel, 1987; dir. Ariz. Legis. Coun., Phoenix, 1987-92; policy advisor and counsel Ariz. Ho. of Reps., Phoenix, 1992-98, gen. counsel, 1998—. Contbr. to Ariz. State Law Jour., 1988. 1st lt. U.S. Army, 1970-72. Mem. State Bar Ariz., Nat. Conf. State Legislatures, Western Legis. Conf. Roman Catholic. Home: 4389 E Olney Dr Phoenix AZ 85044-1018 Office: Ariz House of Reps 1700 W Washington St Phoenix AZ 85007-2812

JANSEN, EPPO, retired international government official; b. Bucarest, Romania, Oct. 6, 1935; s. Hubertus Johannes and Jansje (Sluis) J.; m. Terttu Liisa Heikurainen, July 1964; children: Aino, Arvi. Head Information Office European Parliament in the Netherlands, The Hague; ret., 2000. Home: Delistraat 36, 2585 XB The Hague The Netherlands Office: European Parliament, Korte Vijverberg 6, 2513 AB The Hague The Netherlands

JANSEN, ERIK CHRISTIAN, physician, anesthesiologist; b. Copenhagen, Nov. 10, 1943; s. Knud Frede and Else Maria (Andersen) J.; m. Birgit RÜgge, May 9, 1974; children: Tejs, Neel, Grit. MD, U. Copenhagen, 1972, PhD, 1988. Anesthesiology specialist. Resident Glostrup (Denmark) Hosp., 1972-73, Gentofte (Denmark) Hosp., 1973-75, 78-80; sr. resident Bispebjerg Hosp., Copenhagen, 1980-82; sr. resident Herlev (Denmark) Hosp., 1975-78, 82-86, acting chief, 1984-85; sr. resident Univ. Hosp., Copenhagen, 1986-89, chief anesthesia, 1989—, dir. hyperbaric medicine, 1994—; acting dir. Biomechanics Lab., Hellerup, 1972-94; vice chmn. Outer Copenhagen Hosps., 1974-76; cons. Greenland Telecom, Copenhagen, 1982-93, Greenland Health, 1992—; lectr. U. Copenhagen, 1980-86; chief specialist tng. in anesthesiology, 1988-92; examiner European Acad. Anesthesiology, 1993—; mem. European COST-scientific group in hyperbaric medicine; mem. diving com. Danish Navy, 1995—. Editor: Spelling Without Language, 1991; contbr. articles to profl. jours. Mem. 5th Pearyland Expdn., Greenland, 1968, Anglo-Danish Ingolffjeld Expdn., Greenland, 1973, Broenlund Meml. Expdn., Greenland, 1984. Recipient Study award Hafnia Ins. Ltd., 1972, 74, Lykfelt's Found., 1978, Danish Med. Found., 1972, 76, 88, Guidal award Danish Orthopedic Soc., 1978, 88. Mem. Danish Soc. Anesthesiology (Study award 1988), Nordic Assn. Anesthesiologists. Avocations: arctic explorations, sailing, archaeology, music. Office: Rigohosp Copenhagen U Hosp, AN 4132 Blegdamsvej 9, DK-2100 Copenhagen Denmark

JANSEN, JOHAN FRANZ, chemist; b. Emmen, The Netherlands, July 5, 1963; s. Joop and Truida Moorman) J.; m. Coby van der Veen, June 20, 1990; children: Folkert, Robert, Nils, Ivar. DS, State U. Groningen, 1991. Rsch. chemist D.S.M., Geleen, The Netherlands, 1995—. Author of 1 book; patentee in field. Mem. KNCV, ACS. Avocations: badminton, reading. Home: Maristraat 11, 6165AP Geleen The Netherlands Office: DSM Rsch, PO Box 18, 6160MD Geleen The Netherlands

JANSEN, LAMBERTUS, state agency administrator, retired judge; b. Salt Lake City, Oct. 27, 1934; s. Lambertus Christianus and Cobi Maria (van Ekelenburg) J.; m. Rosemary Van Dyke, Aug. 22, 1958 (div. 1969); children: Jackie Lyn, David Scott; m. LaNita Joyce Lindley, Sept. 10, 1982. AA, Westminster Coll., Salt Lake City, 1954, BS, 1959; JD, U. Utah, 1968. Bar: Utah 1968, N.Y. 1983. Tchr. English Jordan Sch. Dist., Sandy, Utah, 1959-61; fraud investigator Utah Job Svc., Salt Lake City, 1962-65; instr. U. Utah, Salt Lake City, 1965-68; lawyer Jansen Law Office, Salt Lake City, 1968-83, Hyatt Legal Svcs., Syracuse, N.Y., 1983-87, Shanley Law Office, Oswego, N.Y., 1987-92; city ct. judge Oswego, 1992-2000; ret.; hearing officer Utah Dept. Health, Salt Lake City, 2000—. Dir. Utah Housing Devel. Agy., Salt Lake City, 1969-71; mem. steering com. Oswego County Anti-Drug Program, 1996-97; mem. Oswego County Drug Ct. Program, 1996-97. Mem. Am. Judges Assn., N.Y. State City Ct. Judges Assn., Am. Trial Lawyers Assn., Utah State Bar, Utah Bar Assn., Salt Lake County Bar. Roman Catholic. Avocations: skiing, hiking, golf, camping. Home: 1382 E 850 N Tooele UT 84074-9026

JANSEN, OLAV, physician, neuroradiologist; b. Hamburg, Germany, Mar. 26, 1961; s. Max and Helga (Schlueter) J.; m. Sabine Langeloh, Aug. 5, 1988; children: Peer, Liu, Finn. PhD. Med. diplomate. Resident in radiology U. Lubeck, Germany, 1986-92, fellow in neuroradiology, 1992-93; mem. staff dept. neuroradiology U. Heidelberg (Germany) Med. Sch., 1993-97, lead attending staff, 1997—. Contbr. over 50 articles to med. jours. Mem. German Soc. Neuroradiology (Kurt-Decker award 1996). Evangelist. Avocations: sailing, jogging, skiing. Office: U Heidelberg Dept Neurorad, IM Neuenheimerfeld 400, 69120 Heidelberg Germany

JANSKY, LADISLAV, physiologist; b. Hradec Kralove, Czech Republic, Aug. 1, 1931; s. Ladislav and Jana (Jandova) J.; m. Jarmila Richterova, Oct. 3, 1933; children: Petr, Jarmila. MS, Charles U., Prague, Czech Republic, 1954, PhD, 1958, DS, 1990. Asst. Charles U., Prague, Czech Republic, 1954-58; asst. prof. Charles U., Prague, 5, 1958-68; rsch. officer Nat. Rsch. Coun., Ottawa, Can., 1965-66; prof. Charles U., 1968—; chmn. Postgrad. Sch. Medicine, Prague, 1992—. Author: Adaptational Physiology, 1979, Physiology of Animals and Man, 1981; editor: Nonshivering Thermogenesis, 1971, Regulation of Depressed Metabolism and Thermogenesis, 1976. Mem. Czech Physiol. Soc. (hon.). Home: Jipouská 1158, 142 00 Prague 4, Czech Republic Office: Charles U Faculty Sci, Viničná 7, 128 00 Prague 2, Czech Republic

JANSON, BARBARA JEAN, publisher; b. Mason City, Iowa, Mar. 7, 1942; d. Harley Arnold and Helen Victoria (Henrickson) J.; m. W. John Shallenberger, Feb. 24, 1963 (div. Sept. 1980); children: Mona, Ann; m. John Batty Henderson, Sept. 8, 1984 (div. 1990); m. Arthur R. Hilsinger, Aug. 31, 1997. BS in Math., Iowa State U., 1965; MS in Math., Trinity Coll., 1970; MBA, U. R.I., 1982. Cert. math. tchr., Iowa, N.Y., Conn. Math. tchr. Pub. High Schs., Avon, Farmington, Bloomfield, Conn., 1966-68, Ulster Acad., Kingston, N.Y., 1971-73; math. instr. Ulster County Community Coll., Kingston, 1973; math. editor Houghton Mifflin Co., Boston, 1974-77; math. instr. Bristol County Community Coll., Fall River, Mass., 1977-78; asst. dir. editorial Am. Math. Soc., Providence, 1978-81, dir. of publ., 1982-85; founder, pres. Janson Publs., Inc. (purchased by Tribune Edn. Group), Providence and Dedham, Mass., 1985-96; pres. Janson Assocs., Dedham, 1996-98; pub. cons. Everyday Learning/Tribune Edn. Group, 1996-98; pres. Janson Assocs., Dedham, 1996—; mem. expert panel materials devel. ref. NSF, 1996-99; rep. sci. publ. com. Am. Heart Assn., 1986-90; mem. R.I. State Adv. Commn. on Librs.; mem. R.I. Legis. Commn. for Math. and Sci. Edn., 1991; mem. adv. com. R.I. State Systemic Initiative in Math. and Sci., 1993-94. Editor: Scholarly Publishing: Managing Today, Planning for Tomorrow, 1986. Bd. dirs. Planned Parenthood of R.I., Providence, 1986-87, First Parish Unitarian Ch., Beverly, Mass., 1975-76; mem. steering com. Am. Math. Project, Berkeley, Calif., 1986-92; mem. oversight com. Resources Math. Reform Ednl. Devel. Ctr., Newton, Mass.; adv. mem. R.I. State Coun. on Librs. Recipient Mortar Bd. award Iowa State U., 1965. Mem. AAAS, LWV, Soc. for Scholarly Publishing (bd. dirs. 1986-90, chair ann. meeting 1985), N.Y. Acad. Sci., Am. Math. Soc., Math. Assn. Am., Nat. Coun. Tchrs. Math., Assn. Am. Publishers (jours. com. 1982-85), Nat. Assn. Women Bus. Owners. Unitarian. Home and Office: 8 Jackson Pond Rd Dedham MA 02026-5524

JANSON, TORE, linguist; b. Stockholm, Feb. 12, 1936; s. Tage and Signe (Sundberg) J.; children from previous marriage: Harald, Eskil; m. Christina Westman, Sept. 3, 1976. MA, Stockholm U., 1958, PhD, 1964. Asst. prof. UCLA, 1964-66; docent Stockholm U., Stockholm, 1966-82; rschr. Humanistisk-samhälls-vetenskapliga forsknings-rådet, Stockholm, 1983-85; prof. Latin Göteborg (Sweden) U., 1986-97, dean humanities, 1993-97, prof. African langs., 1998—; Swedish rep. European Sci. Found., Strasbourg, France, 1986-90. Author: Latin Prose Prefaces, 1964, Prose Rhythm in Medieval Latin, 1975, (with J. Tsonope) Birth of a National Language: The History of Setswana, 1991, (with L.G. Andersson) Languages in Botswana: Language Ecology in Southern Africa, 1997; contbr. 50 articles to profl. jours. Mem. Linguistic Soc. Am., The Botswana Soc. Home: Dr Lindhs gata 3, S 41325 Göteborg Sweden Office: Göteborg U, S 40530 Göteborg Sweden

JANSSEN, HERMAN, marketing and sales executive; b. Lier, Belgium, Mar. 5, 1956; s. Lodewijk and Simone (Hendrickx) J.; m. Marie-Louise De Groof, Sept. 16, 1982; children: Bart, Leen. Degree in indsl. engring., Indsl. H.S. Antwerpen Mechelen, 1979. Sales mgr. Benelux Mitsui & Co., Belgium, 1981-87; sales mgr. Benelux ECC Internat., Belgium, 1987-90, sales & mktg. mgr. Europe-Africa-Mid. East, 1991—. Sgt. Belgian med. forces, 1979-80. Avocations: football, tennis, film. Home: Waversesteenweg 58, 2500 Lier Belgium

JANSSEN, JAMES ROBERT, consulting software engineer; b. Frederick, Md., June 14, 1959; s. Robert James and Kathryn Doris (Randolph) J.; m. Deborah June Dellwo, Mar. 15, 1986 (div. Sept. 20, 1988). BSEE, Stanford U., 1981, MSEE, 1982. Simulation technician Varian Assocs., Palo Alto, Calif., 1981; hardware design engr. Fairchild Test Systems, San Jose, Calif., 1982-86, Factron Test Systems, Latham, N.Y., 1986-87; software, sys. designer Schlumberger Technologies Labs., Palo Alto, 1988; software engr. Photon Dynamics, Inc., San Jose, 1989-90, ADAC Labs., Milpitas, Calif., 1990-92; software, system designer ADAC Labs., Aalborg, Denmark, 1992, Milpitas, 1992-94; consulting software engr. self-employed, Sunnyvale, Calif., 1994-96; mem. tech. staff Netscape Comms. Corp., Mountain View, Calif., 1996-99, Am. Online Inc., Mountain View, 1999—; pres., founder Digital Studio Systems, Inc., Sunnyvale, 1990-93. Patentee multiple timing signal generator. Civic vol. City of Sunnyvale, 1993. Mem. Tau Beta Pi. Avocations: motocross racing, guitar playing, auto race driving, auto race spectating. Home and Office: 2028 Lockhart Gulch Rd Scotts Valley CA 95066-2923

JANSSEN, MICHAEL ALLEN, astronomer; b. Boise, Idaho, Sept. 30, 1937; s. Winfred Stuart and Glenys (Bassett) J.; m. Elizabeth Goodspeed Fredrick (div. Sept. 1974); children: Aaron Michael, Elizabeth Goodspeed; 1 stepson, Daniel Benbenisty; m. Saundra Zena Sutton, June 4, 1979. BA, U. Calif., Berkeley, 1963, PhD, 1972. Physicist Lawrence Radiation Lab., Livermore, Calif., 1963-67; rsch. asst. U. Calif., Berkeley, 1971-72; resident rsch. assoc. NRC, Jet Propulsion Lab., Pasadena, Calif., 1972-74; sr. scientist NRC, Jet Propulsion Lab., Pasadena, 1974-76, mem. tech. staff, 1976-96, group supr., 1989-91, sect. mgr., 1991-93, lead scientist, astrophysics, 1994-97, sr. mem. tech. staff, 1996—, asst. mgr. divsn. earth and space scis., 1997—. Editor: Atmospheric Remote Sensing by Microwave Radiometry, 1993; contbr. more than 50 articles to profl. jours. Recipient Exceptional Sci. Achievement medal, NASA, 1992. Mem. Am. Astron. Soc., Internat. Union Radio Sci., Internat. Astron. Union, Am. Geophys. Union. Achievements include participation in discovery of cosmic background anisotropy. Avocation: golf. Office: Jet Propulsion Lab Mail Stop 169-506 4800 Oak Grove Dr Pasadena CA 91109-8001

JANSSEN, PAUL-EMMANUEL, bank executive; b. Brussels, Feb. 22, 1931; s. Charles-Emmanuel and Marianne (Boël) J.; m. Nadine van der Straten Waillet, July, 1961 (div. July 1978); children: Valérie de Spoelberch, Emmanuel Janssen; m. Cecilia Löfgren, July, 1980. LLD, U. Libre de Brussels, 1954; postgrad., Harvard U., 1957. With Société Belge de Banque; with Générale de Banque, mng. dir., 1965—, chmn. exec. com., 1989-92, chmn. bd. dirs., 1992—; chmn. Belgian Banking Assn., 1976-79; mem. Trilateral Commn.; exec. com. Fedn. des Entreprises de Belgique; bd. dirs. mfg. cos.; chmn. soc. Immobilire du Brabant; chmn. bd. dirs. Soc. Atlas Copco Airpower; bd. dirs. Atlas Copco AB, Sweden; dir. Union Financiere Boël, Brussels. Avocations: forestry, riding, music lover. Office: Gen de Banque SA, 3 Montagne Du Parc, B-1000 Brussels Belgium*

JANSSEN-ARTS, THEODORA J. F., civic worker; b. Antwerp, Belgium, Aug. 22, 1936; d. Joseph Arts and Maria Dekkers; m. Paul A.J. Janssen, July 1, 1957; children: Garziëlla, Herwig, Yasmine, Pablo, Maroussia. Grad. secondary sch., Antwerp. Hon. pres. Friends of Opera Monnaie, Brussels; pres. Montgomery Club; adminstr. Compagnie Benelux Paribas, Mus. of Dynasty, Brussels, Mus. Art, Antwerp, also other mus. Avocations: taking care of private museum, pre-Columbian arts. Fax: 32 14 41 96 28. Home: Antwerpse Stw 20, 2350 Vosselaar Belgium

JANSSENS, DANNY DENIS, transportation company executive; b. Turnhout, Belgium, Mar. 24, 1959; s. Georges and Francine J.; m. Marina Louisa Mattys, Aug. 28, 1981; 1 child, Gavin. B, Horito, Turnhout, Belgium, 1980. Software cons. Compex Data Systems, The Netherlands, 1980-82; project leader Data Process, Antwerp, Belgium, 1982-87; internat. project leader Banksys, Brussels, 1987-92; mgr. systems devel. Fedex, Brussels, 1992-96, mng. dir., 1996-98, v.p. info. tech., 1998—. Avocations: tennis, skiing, gardening, reading. Office: Fedex Europe Mid-East Afric, Pl St Gudule 14, B1000 Brussels Belgium

JANSSENS, JESSICA ROLANDE JULIENNE, publisher, literary agent; b. Deurne, Antwerpen, Belgium, July 8, 1962; d. Jan and Mireille (Truyens) J. Grad., STLBW, Antwerpen, 1980-83, degree in pub. libr. mgmt., 1981; degree, Acad. Music, Antwerpen, 1981. Cert. librarian. Head librarian Pub. Libr., Gravenwezel, Belgium, 1981-83; asst. mgr. Toneelfonds J. Janssens, Antwerp, 1983-86, managing dir., 1986—. Avocations: astrology, cycling. E-mail: jessica.janssens@toneelfonds.be. Office: Toneelfonds J Janssens BVBA, Te Boelaerlei 107, B-2140 Antwerp Belgium

JANSSENS, MARCEL, literature educator; b. Grembergen, Belgium, Feb. 28, 1932; s. Eduard Pauwel and Maria Eugénie (DeWilde) J.; m. Catherine Aerts; children: Elisabeth, Eduard, Margaretha, Antoon. D of Philosophy and Letters, Cath. U. Leuven, Belgium, 1951; D (hon.), U. Potchefstroom, South Africa, 1996, U. Wroclaw, Poland, 1997, U. Lublin, Poland, 1997. Prof. faculty arts Cath. U. Leuven, 1968-97, prof. emeritus, 1997—; mem. Koninrelyke Akademie voor Nederlands Taalk en Letteriunde, Ghent, Belgium. Author: De Maat Van Drie, 1985 (Triannal award 1985). Home: Boetsenberg 15, 3053 Haasrode Belgium

JANSSON, AKE ROLAND, engineer; b. Sjalevad, Sweden, Feb. 26, 1923; s. Sven Teodor and Selma Martina (Norman) J.; m. Erna Euphrasia de Simpelaere, Aug. 27, 1949; 1 child, Yvonne. Engr., Tech. U. Harnosand, Sweden, 1943. Rsch. engr. Klippan Finepaper, Sweden, 1945-57, Royal Tech. Inst., Stockholm, 1958-60; mill mgr. Cellulose Products, Johannesburg, South Africa, 1960-62, Skåpafors Tissue Mill, Sweden, 1962-66, Mabelpap Paper Mill, Stembert, Belgium, 1966-87; cons. Swemac, Brussels, 1987-91. Mem. Tech. Assn. Pulp and Paper Mfg., Swedish Paper Engrs. Assn. Achievements include patents in waste paper treatment. Home: Chadriat, F-24120 Terrasson France

JANTANAVIVAT, CHUN, parasitologist, medical scientist and researcher; b. Supanburi, Thailand, Feb. 22, 1949; s. Daeng Phong and Hong Ti (Ang) Han; m. Kanchana Saisawang; children: Krit, Sutthisa. BSc in Biology, Ramkamheng U., Bangkok, 1983; MSc in Tropical Medicine, Mahidol U., Bangkok, 1987. Med. lab. asst. Women's Hosp., Dept. Med. Svc., Ministry of Pub. Health, Bangkok, 1970-78; med. asst. scientist, dept. protozoology Faculty of Tropical Medicine, Mahidol U., 1978-87, med. scientist, 1988-94, rschr., scientist, 1990—, affirmanter, 1992-93; co-preceptor med. com. Children's Hosp., Bangkok, 1990-94; lectr. med. com. Paholpolpyuhasena Gen. Hosp., Kanchanaburi, Thailand, 1991-93; active rschr. Inst. for Thai Traditional Medicine Investigation and Rsch., Chaengmai, Thailand, 1990—; advisor sci. and tech. sect. Wat Noi Nopakul Secondary Sch., Bangkok, 1990. Mem. editl. bd. Telecomm. Mag., 1994-99; local correlator The Min. Mag., 1998—; contbr. articles to profl. jours.; presenter on daily TV program Thai Sky TV, 1993. Mem. Congress for Social-Welfare and Pub. Svc. Corp. Thailand, Bangkok, 1991. Mem. AAAS, N.Y. Acad. Sci., Tropical Medicine Assn. Thailand, Teparuk Radio Amateur Club (membership chair 1994-96). Avocations: amateur radio, social work. Home: 2/2 Judsarn Suthorn 11, Nongborn, Bangkok 10260, Thailand Office: Faculty Tropical Medicine, 420/6 Rajvithi Rd, Bangkok 10400, Thailand

JANTEA, CHRISTIAN L., orthopaedic and hand surgeon, educator; b. Bucuresti, Romania, May 11, 1956; Immigrated to Germany, 1969; Dr. med., 1984, Priv. doz., 1993. Cons. for orthopaedic, arthritis, tumor, hand and upper limb surgery Orthopaedic Dept., Heinrich-Heine U., Dusseldorf, Germany, 1987—. Mem. German Soc. Orthopaedics and Traumatology, German Soc. Hand Surgery, Am. Orthopaedic Rsch. Soc., European Soc. Biomechanics, European Rheumatoid Arthritis Surg. Soc., European Soc. Surgery of the Shoulder and Elbow. Office: Orthopaedic Dept, Heinrich-Heine U Dusseldorf, Moorenstr 5 D-40275 Düsseldorf Germany

JANTSCH, WOLFGANG JOHANNES, physics educator; b. Vienna, Austria, Aug. 21, 1946; s. Hans and Marlene D. (Ratzersdorfer) J.; m. Katharina Maria Maly, June 27, 1973; children: Stephanie, Andreas, Nikolaus, Matthias. PhD, U. Vienna, 1971. Postdoctoral fellow Lakehead U., Thunder Bay, Ont., Can., 1971-72; asst. prof. Inst. fü Exptl. Physik U. Linz (Austria), 1971-79; scientist Max-Planck Inst. f. Festkorper forschung, Stuttgart, Fed. Republic Germany, 1980-81; lectr. Inst. fü Exptl. Physik U. Linz, 1982-90, prof., 1990—; chmn. 17th Internat. Conf. on Defects in Semiconductors, 1993. Contbr. articles and revs. to profl. jours.; patentee in field. Recipient Förderungspreis, Theodor-Koerner Stiftung, Vienna, 1975, Landeskulturpreis fuer Wissenschaft, Govt. of Upper Austria, 1988. Mem. Austrian Phys. Soc. (sec. 1991-93, Fritz-Kohlrausch Preis 1986). Home: Asangerweg 10a, A 4040 Linz Austria Office: Johannes Kepler U, Altenbergerstr 69, A 4040 Linz Austria

JÄNTTI, AHTI JOHANNES, German language educator; b. Helsinki, Finland, May 8, 1942; s. Martti Johannes and Elvi Johanna (Mikkonen) J.; m. Aino Mirjami HäKKinen, April 19, 1969; 1 child, Katri. MA, U. Helsinki, Finland, 1970, Licentiate of Philosophy, 1976; Doctor of Philosophy, 1978. Scientific asst. U. Bonn, Germany, 1970-72; lectr. U. Jyväskylä, Finland, 1972-76; assoc. prof. U. Turku, Finland, 1976-79; jr. rschr. Acad. Finland, Helsinki, 1979-80; assoc. prof. U. Tampere, Finland, 1980-86; sr. rschr. Acad. Finland, 1984; prof. U. Jyväskylä, 1986—, dir., German dept., 1986-92; dir. Finnish Inst., Berlin, Germany, 1992-99. Author: Zum Passiv und Reflexiv, 1978; editor: Festschrift Lauri Seppänen, 1984, Probleme der Modalität, 1989, Schicksalsschwere Zeiten, Marschall Mannerheim und die Deutsch-Finnischen Beziehungen 1939-1945, 1997, Finnisch-Deutsche Kulturbeziehungen seit dem Mittelalter, 1998, Sibelius und Deutschland, 2000. Recipient 1st Class Knight of the Finnish White Rose Govt. of Finland, 1992. Mem. Finnish-German Soc. Jyräskylä (pres. 1988-92), Assn. Finnish-German Socs. (pres.). Avocations: music, literature, internat. activities. Home: Kenttäkatu 22, 40720 Jyväskylä Finland Office: U Jyväskylä, German Dept Seminaarink 15, 40100 Jyväskylä Finland

JANTZEN, J(OHN) MARC, retired education educator; b. Hillsboro, Kans., July 30, 1908; s. John D. and Louise (Janzen) J.; m. Ruth Patton, June 9, 1935; children: John Marc, Myron Patton, Karen Louise. A.B., Bethel Coll., Newton, Kans., 1934; A.M., U. Kans., 1937, Ph.D., 1940. Elementary sch. tchr. Marion County, Kans., 1927-30, Hillsboro, Kan., 1930-31; high sch. tchr., 1934-36; instr. sch. edn. U. Kans., 1936-40; asst. prof. Sch. Edn., U. of Pacific, Stockton, Calif., 1940-42; assoc. prof. Sch. Edn., U. of Pacific, 1942-44, prof., 1944-78, prof. emeritus, 1978—, also dean sch. edn., 1944-74, emeritus, 1974—, dir. summer sessions, 1940-72; condr. overseas seminars; mem., chmn. commn. equal opportunities in edn. Calif. Dept. Edn., 1959-69; mem., chmn. Commn. Tchr. Edn. Calif. Tchrs. Assn., 1956-62; mem. Nat. Coun. for Accreditation Tchr. Edn., 1969-72. Bd. dirs. Ednl. Travel Inst., 1965-89. Recipient hon. svd. award Calif. Congress Parents and Tchrs., 1982, McCaffrey disting. Svc. award in recognition of leadership in higher edn., cmty. relationships and internat. svc. San Joaquin Delta Coll., 1996. Mem. NEA, Am. Edn. Rsch. Assn., Calif. Edn. Rsch. Assn. (past pres. 1954-55), Calif. Coun. for Edn. Tchrs., Calif. Assn. of Colls. for Tchr. Edn. (sec., treas. 1975-85), Rotary (Outstanding Rotarian of Yr. award North Stockton 1990, Paul Harris fellow 1980), Stockton Coun. PTA Found., Phi Delta Kappa. Methodist. Home: 117 W Euclid Ave Stockton CA 95204-3122

JANULAITIS, EUGENIJUS ARVYDAS, molecular geneticist; b. Panevezys, Lithuania; s. Andrius and Eleonora Juodyte) J.; m. Kazimiera Jotautaite, Nov. 6, 1968; children: Julija, Monika. PhD, St. Petersburg U., 1972; DSc, Inst. Protein, Moscow, 1985. Rsch. assoc. Kaunas Med. U., Lithuania, 1967-69, Inst. Botany, Vilnius, Lithuania, 1972-75; from dept. head to sr. scientist Inst. Biotechnology, Vilnius, 1975—. Author: Restriction Enzymes and Their Application, 1989. Mem. Royal Swedish Acad. Engring. Scis., Academia Europaea. Roman Catholic. Avocations: basketball, sports. E-mail: janulait@fermentas.lt. Office: Inst Biotechnology, Graiciuno 8, Vilnius Lithuania LT-2028

JANUSCHOWSKI, RAINER, internist, endoscopist, gastroenterologist; b. Hannover, Germany, July 24, 1950; s. Walter and Margarete (Sajonz) J.; m. Sun-Young An, Oct. 10, 1980; children: Tim, Kai. Med. diploma, U. Essen, 1977, dr.'s degree, 1981; diploma internal specialist, 1984, diploma gastroenterology/endoscopy, 1985. Asst. dr. internal dept. Preetz, 1979-80; asst. dr. radiology Celle, 1980-89, asst. dr. internal, 1981-87; asst. dr. gastroenterology Wilhelmshaven, 1983-86; asst. med. dir. internal dept. Herford, 1986-88, vice med. dir., 1988—; mem. mng. bd. Federation of Employed Specialists, 1997—. Recipient Award of the North German Cmty. of Gastroeneterology, 1995. Roman Catholic. Avocations: tennis, sailing, jogging, piano, guitar. Home: Sauerbruchstr 77, 32049 Herford Germany

JANUSHEVSKIS, ALEXANDER, mechanical engineer, research administrator; b. Sigulda, Latvia, Sept. 23, 1951; s. Vladimirs and Veneranda (Novokshanova) J.; m. Liene Spangere, Feb. 2, 1980; children: Janis, Jekabs, Ieva, Anna. M in Engring., Poly. Inst. Riga, Latvia, 1974, PhD, 1989; DSc, Riga Tech. U., 1992. Rsch. assoc. Riga Poly. Inst., 1974-81, rsch. fellow, 1981-85, sr. rschr., 1985-91, head rsch. lab., 1991—; cons. Mechanobr Rsch. Inst., St. Petersburg, Russia, 1987-90, Volga Automobile Works, Togliatti, Russia, 1991-92; vis. assoc. prof. U. Wales, Swansea, 1997; mem. Latvian Nat. Mechanics Com., 1995—. Author: Automation of Dynamic Calculations for Designing of Multibody Systems, (in Russian) 1990; contbr. articles to profl. jours.; patentee in field of vibro impact pressing of materials. Mem. N.Y. Acad. Scis. Roman Catholic. Avocations: computers, cars, books, nature, music. Office: Riga Tech U, 6 Ezermalas St, LV-1006 Riga Latvia

JANUSZKIEWICZ, ANNA, anesthesiologist; b. Lowicz, Poland, May 15, 1958; arrived in Sweden, 1991; d. Wladystaw and Walentyna (Balachowicz) J. MD, Lodz Acad. Medicine, Poland, 1983. Anesthesiologist Inst. Pediats. Med. Acad. Lodz, 1985-88; anesthesiologist dept. pediat. and ICU Polish Mother's Health Ctr., Lodz, 1988-90; asst. anesthesiologist dept. ICU Huddings Univ. Hosp., Sweden, 1990-91, sr. registrar dept. anesthesia & ICU, 1991—. Mem. Swedish Med. Assn. Avocations: books, music, golf. Home: Fatburs Kvarng 5 3tr, 11864 Stockholm Sweden Office: Huddinge Univ Hosp, 141 86 Huddinge Sweden

JANZEN, JAN, physician, pathologist; b. Schwerin, Germany, Nov. 14, 1964; s. Walter and Gisela (Ziegenhagen) J.; m. Katrin Rothenberger, Dec. 1, 1997. Dipl-med, Humboldt U.-Charité, Berlin, 1989, med. diploma, 1991; MD, Humboldt U., Berlin, 1992. Spl. cert. in surg.-based pathology. Physician various hosps., Switzerland, 1991-94, 95-96; physician Paris, 1994-95, Germany, 1997-2000. Contbr. articles to jours. in Switzerland, France, Germany, Netherlands, Denmark, Eng. and U.S. Recipient nat. and internat. medals in sports. Office: Inst Pathology, Röntgenstrasse 2, D-88048 Friedrichshafen Germany

JANZEN, LEE, professional golfer; b. Austin, Minn., Aug. 28, 1964. Mem. Ryder Cup Team, 1993. Winner No. Telecom Open, 1992, Phoenix Open, 1993, U.S. Open, 1993, 98; Buick Classic, 1994; The Players Championship, 1995; Kemper Open, 1995; Sprint International, 1995. Office: Sports Link 545 Delaney Ave Ste 4 Orlando FL 32801-3866

JANZEN, NORINE MADELYN QUINLAN, medical technologist; b. Fond du Lac, Wis., Feb. 9, 1943; d. Joseph Wesley and Norma Edith (Gustin) Quinlan; m. Douglas Mac Arthur Janzen, July 18, 1970; 1 son, Justin James. BS, Marian Coll., 1965; med. technologist, St. Agnes Sch. Med. Tech., Fond du Lac, 1966; MA, Ctrl. Mich. U., 1980. Med. technologist Mayfair Med. Lab., Wauwatosa, Wis., 1966-69; supr. med. technologist Dr.'s Mason, Chamberlain, Franke, Klink & Kamper, Milw., 1969-76, Hartford-Parkview Clinic, Ltd., 1976-94; patient svc. ctrs. supr. Med. Sci. Labs., Wauwatosa, Wis., 1994-97, Poole Med. Tech. Med. Sci. Labs, 1997-98; clin. mgr. Planned Parenthood Wis., 1997-99; coord. health in bus. Hartford Parkview Clin., 1990-91, drug program coord., 1991-94; outreach coord. Cmty. Meml. Hosp., Menomonee Falls, Wis., 2000—; co-chair joint mtg. Clin. Lab. Mgrs. Assn. and Wis. Assn. for Clin. Lab. Scientists, 1993-94. Substitute poll worker Fond du Lac Dem. Com., 1964-65; mem. Dem. Nat. com., 1973—; coord. Warhawk Band Booster Uniform Project, 1997-99; post card ministry coord. Methodist Ch.; cmty. league youth vol., recognition coord. Mem. AAUW (rec. sec. 1996-98, pub. policy chair 1998—, pres.-elect 2000—), Cmty. League, LWV, Am. Soc. for Clin. Lab. Scientist (people to people clin. lab. scientist del. to People's Republic of China 1989, Mem. of Yr. award 1997), Nat. Soc. Clin. Lab. Scientists (awards com. chair 1984-87, 88-91, nominations com. 1989-92), Wis. Assn. Clin. Lab. Scientists (exec. sec. 1991—, chmn. awards com. 1976-77, 84-85, 86-87, treas. 1977-81, pres.-elect 1981-82, pres. 1982-83, dir. 1977-84, 85-87, mem. of yr. award 1982, 95, numerous svc. awards, chair ann. meeting 1987-88), Clin. Lab. Mgmt. Assn. (co-chair joint meeting 1993-94), Milw. Soc. Clin. Lab. Scientists (pres. 1971-72, bd. dirs. 1972-73, exec. sec. 1999—), Comms. of Wis. (originator, chmn. 1977-79), Southeastern Suprs. Group (co-chmn. 1976-77), Warhawk Band Boosters (trysting place tent party fundraiser 1997-2000, uniform fundraiser chair 1996-98), Alpha Delta Theta (nat. dist. chmn. 1967-69, nat. alumnae dir. 1969-71), Alpha Mu Tau. Methodist. E-mail: nmjanzen@aol.com. Home: N98W17298 Dotty Way Germantown WI 53022-4618 Office: Cmty Meml Hosp W180 N 8085 Town Hall Rd Menomonee Falls WI 53051

JANZEN, RUDOLF WILHELM CHRISTIAN, neurologist; b. Hamburg, Germany, Sept. 20, 1940; s. Rudolf and Helene (Carstensen) J.; m. Irmgard Jessen, Sept. 19, 1969; children: Ulrike, Wiebke, Annette. MD, U. Hamburg, Germany, 1967, privat dozent, 1977, prof., 1983. Cert. clin. neurologist Landesarztekammer Hamburg. Asst. Neurophysiologie, Munster, Germany, 1969-71; asst. Neurologie, Hamburg, 1971-78, sr., 1978-85; head dept. Neurologie, Frankfurt, 1985; dir. Hosp., Frankfurt, 1986-88. Author: Pain Analysis, 1989, Neurocritical Care, 1994, Intensive Care Medicine, 1994, Neurologic Intensive Care Medicine, 1999. Mem. European Soc. Neurology, N.Y. Acad. Scis., Euroacademia Multidisciplinaria Neurotraumatologica, German Interndisciplinary Assn. Critical Care Medicine, German Assn. Clin. Neurophysiology, German Assn. Neurologists, Rotary. Avocations: music, painting. Office: Nordwest Klinik Neurology, Steinbacher Hohl 2-26, 60488 Frankfurt Germany

JAO, SHU-WEN, colon and rectal surgeon; b. Pin-Tong, Taiwan, Jan. 19, 1952; s. Yean-Shion and Shiou-Huey (Chen) J.; m. Shu-Mei Wu Jao, Jan. 22, 1978; children: Kai-Yuan, Ya-Fang. MD, Nat. Def. Med. Ctr., Taipei, Taiwan, 1977. Medical diplomate. Resident in surgery Tri-Service Gen. Hosp., Taipei, Taiwan, 1977-81; chief resident in surgery TSGH, Taipei, Taiwan, 1981-82; attending surgeon of colon and rectal surgery, 1982-97; vis. clinician Mayo Clinic, Rochester, Minn., 1983-84; chief of colon and rectal surgery TSGH, Taipei, Taiwan, 1997—; prof. surgery Nat. Def. Med. Ctr., Taipei, Taiwan, 1990—; directorship Soc. Colon and Rectal Surgeons, R.O.C., Taipei, Taiwan, 1992—; editor Chinese Med. Jour. Taipei, Taiwan, 1993—, Med. Digest, Taipei, Taiwan, 1989-93; chief Med. Libr. Tri-Service Gen. Hosp., Taipei, Taiwan, 1993-97. Inventor: UK Patent, 1995, U.S. patent, 1997; contbr. articles to profl. jours. Col. Tri-Service Gen. Hosp., 1977-97, Taipei. Recipient Rsch. award nat. Sci. Coun. R.O.C., Taipei, Taiwan, 1983, 85, 93. Mem. Am. Soc. Colon and Rectal Surgeons, Internat. Soc. Univ. Colon and Rectal Surgeons, Internat. Coll. Surgeons. Avocations: golf, volleyball. Home: No 32 Sect 3 Ting-Chow Rd, Taipei Taiwan Office: Tri-service General Hospital, No 8 Sect 3 Ting-Chow Rd, Taipei Taiwan

JAOUEN, HERVE JEAN, electrical engineer; b. Mont de Marsan, Landes, France, Feb. 24, 1956; s. Jean Lucien and Anne (Madec) J.; m. Nathalie Garcia, Sept. 7, 1964; children: Edouard, Geoffrey. Elec. engr., ENSERG, 1979; DEA, INPG, 1979, PhD, 1984. Assoc. prof. CNRS, France, 1981-89; TCAD engr. Ctrl. R&D ST, France, 1989-94, TCAD mgr., 1994—. Patentee in field. With French Army, 1980-81. Mem. IEEE, MRS. Avocations: computer science, skiing, horses, travel, walking. Office: ST Microelectronics, 850 Rue Jean Monnet, 38926 Crolles France

JAPARIDZE, TEDO ZURAB, diplomat; b. Tbilisi, Georgia, Sept. 28, 1946; came to the U.S., 1994; s. Zurab Japaridze and Helen (Korsaveli) Korsaveli-Fedotova; m. Tamar Chikvaidze, Mar. 25, 1981; 1 child, Nika. Faculty of langs. and European lit., Tbilisi (Georgia) State U., 1972; PhD, USA and Can. Studies Inst., Moscow, 1979. Sr. rschr. USA and Can. Studies Inst., Moscow, 1974-89; vice chmn. for UNESCO affairs Ministry of Fgn. Affairs, Tbilisi, 1989-90, dep. fgn. min., 1990-91, first dep. fgn. min., 1991-92; nat. security adviser to head of state Office of the Head of State, Tbilisi, 1992-94; amb. to the U.S. Embassy of Republic of Georgia, 1994—. Co-author: Political System of the U.S. History and Contemporary Situation, 1989. Christian Orthodox. Avocations: sports, music. Home: 4701 Willard Ave Chevy Chase MD 20815-4643 Office: Embassy of Republic of Georgia Ste 300 1615 New Hampshire Ave NW Washington DC 20009-2520*

JAPP, NYLA F., infection control services administrator; b. Sterling, Colo., Jan. 8, 1948; d. Leonard W. and Eleanor M. (Barnts) J. Diploma, Pikes Peak Inst. Med. Tech., 1970; Assoc. in Nursing, Garden City Community Coll., 1980; diploma, Pikes Peak Inst. Med. Tech., 1970; BS in Human Resources Mgmt., Friends U., 1992; MS in Health Adminstrn., Kennedy Western U., 1997, Kennedy-Western U., 1997. RN, Kans. With surg. unit St. Catherine Hosp., Garden City, Kans.; sanitarian Finney County Commrs., Garden City; mgr. sterile processing St. Catherine Hosp., Garden City, Kans., mgr. infection control, dir. infection control svcs.; nurse mgr. U. Kans. Hosp., Kansas City, Kans.; area sites dir. STEROUT Inc., Miami Lakes, Fla.; area dir. BW Med. Group, Inc., Sterout, Inc.; regional infection control nurse Providence Med. Ctr., Kansas City. Mem. Am. Soc. Hosp. Ctrl. Svc. Pers. (pres. elect, regional bd. dirs., chmn. recognition com., chmn. membership com., mem. tech. cert. com., APIC liaison, AORN liaison, JCAHO liaison, AAMI liaison, regulatory adv. com., Educator of Yr., Tom Samuels rsch. award), Great Plains Soc. Hosp. Ctrl. Svc. Pers. (chmn. program com., mem. newsletter com., chmn. nominating com., rsch. com., pres., bd. dirs.), Nat. Inst. for Cert. Healthcare Sterile Processing and Distbn. Pers. (bd. dirs.), Internat. Assn. Hosp. Ctrl. Svc. Mgmt., Assn. Practitioners in Infection Control. Home: 10325 Earnshaw St Overland Park KS 66215-2233

JAQUES, JOSEPH M, trauma consultant; b. Michigan City, Ind., July 30, 1967; s. Vernon Guy and June Violet J.; m. Kelly A. Jaques, Nov. 23, 1991; children: Kaylen E., Peyton E., Jillian E. BBA, Ind. State U., 1989. Sales cons. Jaymar Ruby, Inc., Michigan City, Ind., 1989-91, Bristol-Meyers Squibb, Princeton, N.J., 1991-93, SmithKline Beecham, Phila., 1993-97; trauma cons. Synthes, USA, Paoli, Pa., 1997—. pres. Michiana Med. Assn., 1993-94. Republican. Home: 13851 Lexington Cir N Granger IN 46530-4972

JAQUETTE, JANE STALLMAN, foreign studies educator; b. Chgo., Nov. 10, 1942; d. Roy Andrews and Mary Frances Agnes (Nielsen) Stallmann; m. David Leaf Jaquette, June 13, 1964 (div. 1981); children: Christopher David, Sarah Jane; m. Abraham F. Lowenthal, Jan. 20, 1991. BA, Swarthmore Coll., 1964; PhD, Cornell U., 1971. Asst. prof. politics Occidental Coll., L.A., 1969-72, assoc. prof. politics, 1972-81, prof. politics, 1981—; policy analyst U.S. Agy. for Internat. Devel., Washington, 1979-81; bd. dirs. Acad. and Profl. Programs for Ams., Cambridge, Mass., U.S. Com. UN Fund for Women. Editor, contbr.: Women in Politics, 1974, The Women's Movement in Latin America, 1989, 2d edit., 1994; co-editor: Women and Democracy: Latin America and Central and Eastern Europe, 1998. Mem. Pacific Coun. on Internat. Policy, Coun. of Fgn. Rels., L.Am. Studies Assn. (pres. 1995-97), Assn. for Women in Devel. (pres. 1990-92), Am. Polit. Sci. Assn. Office: Occidental Coll 1600 Campus Rd Los Angeles CA 90041-3314

JAQUITH, GEORGE OAKES, ophthalmologist; b. Caldwell, Idaho, July 29, 1916; s. Gail Belmont and Myrtle (Burch) J., m. Pearl Elizabeth Taylor, Nov. 30, 1939; children: Patricia Ann Jaquith Mueller, George, Michele Eugenie Jaquith Smith. BA, Coll. Idaho, 1938; MB, Northwestern U., 1942, MD, 1943. Intern Wesley Meml. Hosp., Chgo., 1942-43; resident opthalmology U.S. Naval Hosp., San Diego, 1946-48; pvt. practice medicine, specializing in opthalmology Brawley, Calif., 1948—; pres. Pioneers Meml. Hosp. staff, Brawley, 1953, dir. exec. com. Calif. Med. Eye Coun., 1960—, v.p. Calif. Med. Eye Found., 1976—. Sponsor Anza coun. Boy Scouts Am., 1966—, Gold card holder Rep. Assocs., Imperial County, Calif., 1967-68, PTO. Served with USMC, USN, 1943-47. Mem. Imperial County (pres. 1961), Calif. Med. Assn. (del. 1961—), Nat., So. Calif. (dir. 1966—, chmn. med. adv. com. 1968-69), Soc. Prevention Blindness, Calif. Assn. Opthalmology (treas. 1976—), San Diego, L.A. Opthal. Socs., L.A. Rsch. Study Club, Nathan Smith Daivs Soc., Coll. Idaho Assocs., Am. Legion, VFW, Res. Officers Assn., Basenji Assn., Nat. Geneal. Soc., Cuyamaca Club (San Diego), Elks, Phi Beta Phi, Lambda Chi Alpha (Hall of Fame). Presbyterian (elder). Office: PO Box 511 Brawley CA 92227-0511

JARALLAH, JAMAL SALEH, family physician, educator; b. Al-Ula, Madinah, Saudi Arabia, Apr. 5, 1958; s. Jarallah Saleh and Jameelah Mohammed (Shwaikan) J.; m. Nahiba Fahad Al-Shalhoub; 6 children. MBBS, King Saud U., Riyadh, Saudi Arabia, 1983, MSc, 1986. Med. diplomate. Intern King Khalid U. Hosp., Riyadh, 1983, family medicine program, 1984-86; resident Dept. of Family Medicine, U. Liverpool, 1986-87; demonstrator King Saud U., 1984-86, lectr., 1986-88, asst. prof. dept. cmty. medicine, 1988-92, assoc. prof., 1992-98, prof., 1998—. Mem. Royal Coll. Gen. Practitioners, World Orgn. of Nat. Colls. and Acads. of Family Medicine (mem. coun. 1994—), Saudi Soc. of Family and Cmty. Medicine (mem. coun. 1990—). Muslim. Avocations: football, swimming, poetry. Office: Kind Saud U, Dept Family & Cmty Medicine, PO Box 2925, Riyadh 11462, Saudi Arabia

JARAMILLO, RICARDO MEJIA, mechanical engineer; b. Manizales, Caldas, Colombia, Nov. 11, 1948; s. Ricardo and Blanca Jaramillo; m. Amparo Jaramillo, Dec. 15, 1972; children: Daniel, Ana Maria, Juan David. BSME, Univ. P. Bolivariana, Medellin, Colombia, 1971; MSME, U. Mich., 1975. Cert. vibration specialist. Asst. prof. Univ. P. Bolivariana, Medellin, 1971-73, dean mech. engring. dept., 1975-76; cons. Medellin, 1977—. Contbr. articles to profl. jours. Mem. Vibration Inst. Chgo., N.Y. Acad. Sci. Avocations: photography, astronomy, biology, wood work.

JARBATH, HEBERT MICHEL, civil engineer, consultant; b. Jacmel, Haiti, Nov. 19, 1936; s. Dalloze Robert and Clelie Elizabeth (Pierre) J.; m. Marie-Alice Margareth Degraff, Aug. 28, 1976; children: Didier, Olivier. Civil Engr., U. Haiti, 1959; postgrad., Carnegie Tech., Pitts., 1959-61. Project engr. Marndr, Port-au-Prince, Haiti, 1961-63; chief engring. office, cons. Onatra, Kinshasa, Zaire, 1963-87; exec., dir., cons. Pochep, Port-au-Prince, 1987-91; oper. dir., cons. Camep, Port-au-Prince, 1991-94; gen. mgr., cons. Cogec-Sa, Port-au-Prince, 1994-99. Recipient Silver medal Govt. Kinshasa, Zaire, 1983, Gold medal, 1984. Fellow ASCE; mem. Can. Soc. Civil Engrs., Can. Soc. Engring. Mgmt. Roman Catholic. Achievements include patent in field. Home: Bourdon, No 3 Impasse Charlevoix, Port-au-Prince Haiti Office: Cogec SA No 74 Ruelle Waag, PO Box 16021, Petition-Ville Haiti

JÄRBE, TORBJÖRN ULF CHRISTIAN, psychologist, educator; b. Kristianstad, Sweden, May 6, 1946; came to the U.S., 1991; s. Bengt O. and Kajela E. (Lochner) J.; m. Esta R. Kroon (div.); children: John, Shamalee; m. Diane A. Mathis, Dec. 28, 1991 (dec.). BA in Psychology, U. Uppsala, 1969, MS, 1972, PhD, 1977. Project leader dept. psychology U. Uppsala, Sweden, 1972-91; vis. scientist ctr. for addiction rsch. U. Medicine and Dentistry N.J., 1991; vis. assoc. prof. divsn. addiction rsch. and treatment Hahnemann U., Phila., 1991-92, rsch. assoc. prof., 1992—; postdoctoral fellow in pharmacology U. N.C., 1977-78. Referee numerous scientific jours.; contbr. articles to profl. jours. Björnström-Stephenson fellow Am.-Sweden Found., 1977-78. Mem. European Neurosci. Assn., Internat. Brain Rsch. Orgn., Swedish Soc. for Alcohol and Drug Rsch., Soc. for Stimulus Properties of Drugs (pres. 1990), European Behavioral Pharmacology Soc., Internat. Cannabis Rsch. Soc., Internat. Behavioral Neurosci. Soc., Coll. on Problems in Drug Dependence, Am. Psychol. Assn. Home: 141 E Valleybrook Rd Cherry Hill NJ 08034-3824 Office: Temple U Coll Liberal Arts 265 67 Weiss Hall Psych Dep 1701 N 13th St Philadelphia PA 19122-6011

JÁRDÁNHÁZY, TAMÁS, neurologist; b. Kiskunmajsa, Hungary, Oct. 11, 1946; s. Jozsef Tivadar and Terezia Judit (Mayer) J.; m. Klara Domonkos, Sept. 11, 1971; 1 child, Anett. MD, Szote U., 1971, dr. habil. med., 1994; PhD, MTA-TMB, 1985. Resident Szote Neurol./Psychiat., Szeged, Hungary, 1971-75, registrar, 1975-84, asst. prof., 1984-90, assoc. prof., 1990-97, prof., 1997—; rsch. fellow AZU-KNF, Utrecht, Holland, 1982-83. Recipient Apathy Istvan medal Szote U., 1971, Medal for Univ. Studies Ministry of Edn., 1971. Mem. MIEOT, Hungarian Soc. Clin. Neurophysiology, World Fedn. Neurology. Avocations: cycling, travel, electronic and computer techniques. Office: Szote Dept Neurol/Psychiat, Semmelweis u 6, H-6725 Szeged Hungary

JARDAS, IVAN, biologist; b. Vrbovsko, Croatia, May 4, 1942; s. Vjekoslav and Stanka (Hriberski) J.; m. Nada Brajdic, May 22, 1971; 1 child, Ivana. MS, U. Zagreb, Croatia, 1970, PhD, 1977. Scientific Inst. Oceanography & Fisheries, Split, Croatia, 1968-70, scientific officer, 1970-77, sr. scientific officer, 1977-80, prin. scientific officer, 1980—; prof. dept. marine & maritime affairs U. Split, 1993—. Author: Fauna and Flora of the Adriatic: Jabuka Pit, 1989, The Adriatic Ichthyofauna, 1996, Fishes and Cephalopoda of the Adriatic Sea, 1997. Mem. Soc. Europaea Ichthyologorum, Croatian Biol. Soc. Avocations: philately, photography, painting, mountain climbing. Office: Inst Oceanography, I Mestrovica 63, 21000 Split Croatia

JARDILLIER, JEAN-CLAUDE, biochemistry and pharmacy educator; b. Amiens, France, Mar. 19, 1939; s. Marcel and Raymonde (Hubert) J.; m. Huguette Derbesse, July 4, 1962; children: Helene, Philippe, Claire. Pharmacy Degree, U. Lille, 1963; PhD, Faculty of Pharmacy, Paris, 1968. Asst. U. Amiens, France, 1966-69; maitre asst., 1969-72; prof. U. Reims, France, 1972-74; head dept., 1974—; dean Faculty Pharmacy, 1981-87; clin. biochemist Hosp. and Anticancer Inst., Paris, Reims, 1966-96 ; expert analyst Ministery of Health, Paris, 1973—; v.p. U. Reims, 1994—; research dir. Ministery of Edn., Paris, 1980-86; cons. pharm. cos., France, 1981-86; head panel French Clin. Biochemistry Soc., Paris and Europe,

1982—. Co-author: Clinical Biochemsitry, Vol. 1, 1977, Vol. 2, 1980, Vol. 3, 1988; co-editor: Symposium on Marihuana, 1979; contbr. arciles to profl. jours. Recipient Thesis award Louis Dorch U. Paris, 1970. Mem. Biol. Chemistry French Soc., European Assn. Cancer Rsch., N.Y. Acad. Scis., Am. Assn. Clin. Chemistry (Outstanding Speaker award 1997), Am. Assn. Cancer Rsch., Internat. Union Pure and Applied Chemistry (nat. rep. 1978-85), Nat. Acad. Pharmacy, French Soc. Clin. Biology (v.p. 1993-96, pres. 1996-99, past pres. 1999—). Republican. Roman Catholic. Office: Faculty of Pharmacy, 51 rue Cognacq Jay, 51100 Reims France

JARDIM, LUIS EDUARDO, electronics industry executive; b. Lisbon, Portugal, July 29, 1960; s. Guilherme Ivens Ferraz and Maria do Rosário (Corrêa de Barros) J.; m. Maria João Freire Themudo, Sept. 29, 1990; children: Mariana, Guilherme Afonso, Maria João. Diploma in electrical engrng., inst. Superior Technico, Lisbon, 1986. Asst. Inst. Sup. Technico, 1985-86; devel. mgr. Timex Corp., Lisbon, 1986-87; devel. engr. Philips, Tilburg, The Netherlands, 1987-88; project leader Philips, Ovar, Portugal, 1988-91, devel. mgr., 1991-95, unit mgr., 1995-98; dir. Siemens Transformer Factory, Sabugo, Portugal. Mem. Ordem dos Engenheiros, Planetary Soc., Nat. Geographic Soc. Roman Catholic. Avocations: tennis, farming, reading. Office: Philips Portuguesa Siemens SA, Apartado 1 Pero Pinneiro, 2715 Sabugo Portugal

JÄREMO, PETTER, hematologist, researcher; b. Copenhagen, Sept. 10, 1953; arrived in Sweden, 1959; s. Svend Aage Jacobsen and Shna Järemo; m. Pirjo Irmeli Harakka, May 28, 1993; children: Helena, Mikael. Degree, Erlangen (Germany) U., 1980. Physician Örebro (Sweden) Regionsjukhus, 1981-93; rsch. assoc. Rikshospitalet, Oslo, 1992, Thomas Jefferson U., Phila., 1994; physician Vrinnevisjukhuset, Norrköping, Sweden, 1995-99, Univ. Hosp., Linköping, Sweden, 1999—. Contbr. articles to profl. jours.; inventor in field. Home: Morängatan 2, S-60386 Norrköping Sweden Office: Univ Hosp, Dept Cardiology, S-58185 Linköping Sweden

JARGIELLO, PRZEMYSLAW, investment company executive; b. Gdansk, Poland, Jan. 28, 1964. M in Philosophy, Acad. Cath. Theology, 1995; diploma in capital investment, Postgrad. Banking Sch., 1996. Dir. mktg. and sales dept. Skarbiec Investment Fund Co., Warsaw, 1997-2000; mem. mgmt. bd. Pohjola Life Ins. Co., Warsaw, 2000—. Mem. Assn. Investment Fund. Cos. Office: Pohjola Life Ins Co, Wauelska Str 15B, 02-034 Warsaw Poland

JÀRMAI, KÀROLY, engineering educator; b. Miskolc, Hungary, Jan. 23, 1955; s. Jarmai and Jarmaine (Molnàr) J.; m. Anikó Diòszegi, Jan. 28, 1978; children: Tamas, Peter. Diploma in engring., U. Miskolc, 1978, D of Univ., 1979, Habilitation, 1995; European engr., FEANI, Paris, 1991; D of Tech. Sci., Hungarian Acad. of Sci., Budapest, 1996. Rsch. worker U. Miskolc, 1978-90, assoc. prof. engring., 1991-96, prof., 1996—. Author: Analysis and Optimum Design of Metal Structures, 1997; vice-editor GÈP, 1992—; co-editor conf. procs., VII Internat. Symposium on Tubular Structures, 1996. Cpl. Border Guard, Nyirbator, 1980. Mem. Sci. Soc. Mech. Engrs. (pres. 1993—, Pattantyus award 1994), Internat. Inst. of Welding (del. XIII commn. 1996—), Internat. Assn. Structural and Multidisc Optim). Avocations: travel, music.

JARMAN, THERESA KAY, fire chief; b. Indpls., June 3, 1956; d. John Bowers Jarman and Ramona Catherine Hilgenburg. BS, San Diego State U., 1978; AS, Miramar Coll., 1986; MPA, San Diego State U., 1997. Cert. state fire officer; cert. hazardous materials specialist. Fire recruit San Diego Fire Dept., 1983-84, fire fighter, 1984-90, fire engr., 1990-94, fire capt., 1994-98; fire bn. chief San Diego Fire and Life, 1998-99; dep. chief San Diego Fire and Life Safety Svcs., 1999—; plans officer Urban Search & Rescue, San Diego, 1996-98; dir. comms. San Diego Fire and Life Safety Svcs. and San Diego Med. Svcs. Enterprise, 1998-99. U.S./Mex. Innovative Tech. Assistance grantee U.S. EPA, 1993-95, local emergency planning com. grantee Calif. EPA, 1993-95. Mem. Internat. Assn. Fire Fighters, Internat. Assn. Fire Chiefs, Nat. Fire Info. Coun., Women in the Fire Svc. Avocations: hiking, kayaking, golfing. Office: San Diego Fire and Life Safety Svcs Ste 604 1010 2nd Ave San Diego CA 92101-4912

JARMUSCH, JIM, director, actor; b. Akron, Ohio. Actor: (films) American Autobahn, 1984, Straight to Hell, 1987, Running Out of Luck, 1987, Helsinki Napoli All Night Long, 1987, Leningrad Cowboys Go to America, 1989, The Golden Boat, 1990, In The Soup, 1992, Iron Horsemen, 1994, Tigrero: A Film That Was Never Made, 1994, Blue in the Face, 1995, Typewriter, the Rifle & the Movie Camera, 1996, Cannes Man, 1996, Sling Blade, 1996, Divine Trash, 1998, (TV series) Fishing With John, 1991, American Cinema, 1994; writer, dir., editor, prodr., composer: Permanent Vacation, 1982 (Joseph von Sternberg prize Mannheim, Internat. Critics prize Figueira da Foz, Portugal 1981); dir., writer, editor: Stranger Than Paradise, 1984 (Camera D'Or Cannes Film Festival 1984, Best Picture of Yr. Nat. Soc. Film Critics 1984); dir., writer: Down By Law, 1986 (Best Film award Locarno, Best Fgn. Film Norway, Denmark and Israel), Mystery Train, 1989 (Highest Artistic Achievement prize Cannes Film Festival), Dead Man, 1995 (World Premiere Cannes Film Festival 1995, Felix award Best Non-European Film 1996, Best Cinematography award N.Y. Critics Cir. 1996); dir., writer, prodr.: Ghost Dog: The Way of the Samurai, 1999; dir.: Coffee and Cigarettes I, 1993 (Golden Palm Cannes Film Festival 1993); exec. prodr.: When Pigs Fly, 1993; dir., cinematographer: Year of the Horse, 1997; cinematographer: You Are Not I, 1981; dir., writer, prodr.: Night on Earth, 1991 (Grand award Best Feature Film Houston Internat. Film Festival 1992, Ind. Spirit award Best Cinematography 1993); dir.: Coffee and Cigarettes, 1986, Coffee and Cigarettes II, 1986. *

JARNAGAN, HARRY WILLIAM, JR., project control manager; b. Cedar Rapids, Iowa, Nov. 7, 1953; s. Harry William and Virginia Lillian (Grusy) J.; m. Anne Therese Tompkins, June 7, 1975; children: Douglas William, Michael Patrick, Marianne Virginia. BS, U.S. Mil. Acad., 1975; M of Engring., Tex. A&M, 1984. Registered profl. engr., Tex. Project mgr. Dunbar & Dickson, Inc., Clute, Tex., 1980-83, 84-85; grad. teaching asst. Tex. A&M U., College Station, 1983-84; cost. engr. Bechtel Power Corp., Houston, 1985-87; project control engr. Tenn. Valley Authority, 1987-88, Fluor-Daniel, Inc., Rochester, N.Y., 1988-90, MK-Ferguson Co., Oak Ridge, Tenn., 1990-95; mgr. Avlis project controls U.S. Enrichment Corp., Livermore, Calif., 1995-97; western region project controls mgr. Internat. Tech. Corp., Pleasanton, Calif., 1997-98; program controls mgr. Hatch Mott McDonald, San Jose, Calif., 1998—. Capt. U.S. Army, 1975-80. Mem. Am. Assn. Cost Engrs. (cert., v.p. fin.), Tau Beta Pi. Lutheran. Avocations: running, weight lifting, sky diving. Home: 875 Henderson Way Tracy CA 95376-8944 Office: Hatch Mott McDonald 6140 Stoneridge Mall Rd Ste 250 Pleasanton CA 94588-3232

JARNAGIN, WILLIAM ROBERT, surgeon, surgical oncologist; b. Somerville, Mass., July 21, 1960; s. Robert Lee and Frances Mary Jarnagin; m. Laura Q. Quintiliani, Mar. 17, 1984; 1 child, Emma. BA, Dartmouth Coll., 1982; MA, Brandeis U., 1984; MD, Rush Med. Coll., 1988. Diplomate Am. Bd. Surgery, Nat. Bd. Med. Examiners. Intern, resident U. Calif., San Francisco, 1988-96; clin. fellow Meml. Sloan-Kettering Cancer Ctr., N.Y.C., 1996-97, asst. attending surgeon, 1997—; rsch. fellow U. Calif., San Francisco, 1990-93; instr. Cornell Med. Coll., N.Y.C., 1997—. Lt. comdr. USNR Med. Corps, 1995—. Recipient Individual Nat. Rsch. Svc. award NIH, 1993, Sr. Fellowship award Am. Gastroenterol. Assn., 1993. Mem. ACS (oncology group), Soc. Surg. Oncology, Soc. for Surgery of Alimentary Tract, Am. Assn. for Study Liver Diseases, Alpha Omega Alpha. Roman Catholic. E-mail: jarnagiw@mskcc.org. Office: Meml Sloan-Kettering Cancer Ctr Dept Surgery 1275 York Ave New York NY 10021-6094

JARNI, ROBERT, soccer player; b. Eakovec, Croatia, Oct. 26, 1968. Midfielder FC Hajduk, 1986-91, FC Bari, 1991-93; previously with Bari, Torino and Juventus, Italy, 1991-95; midfielder Real Betis (Spain) Football Club, 1995-98, Real Madrid, 1998—. Office: Real Madrid, Concha Espina 1, 28036 Madrid Spain*

JAROLÍM, LADISLAV, urologist, researcher; b. Novy Bor, Czech Republic, Mar. 31, 1949; s. Ladislav and Jiřina (Polanecká) J.; m. Ružena Golková, Aug. 1, 1985; children: Lucie, Kateřina, Jakub. MD, Charles U., Prague, Czech Republic, 1973, PhD, 1985; 1st degree in surgery, Postgrad. Med. Sch., Prague, Czech Republic, 1976, 2d degree in urology, 1983. Intern dept. surgery Charles U., Prague, 1973-74, intern dept. urology, 1977-79, vis. asst. prof., 1980-86, assoc. prof., 1987—; intern dept. surgery State Sanatorium, Prague, 1975-76; head divsn. urology dept. surgery Prague, Czech Republic, 1985-89; dir. dept. urology Charles U., 1989-90. Contbr. articles to profl. jours.; editor: Advances in Urology, 1996; editor Endoscopy Jour., Prague, 2000. Grantee Healthcare Ministry, Czech Republic, 1997. Mem. European Assn. Urology, Internat. Urol. Assn. (nat. del. of Czech Republic 1985—), Czech Prostate Health Coun. (chmn. 1993). E-mail: ladislav.jarolim@lf1.cuni.cz. Office: Dept Urology Charles U, Ke Karlovu 6, 128 08 Prague Czech Republic

JAROLMEN, JOSEPHINE TUZEO, social worker, psychotherapist, educator; b. N.Y.C., May 2, 1945; d. Fortunato and Mary Caponetto Tuzeo; m. Howard Jarolmen, Dec. 15, 1980; chlidren: Michele Catanzaro, Richard Catanzaro. BA, William Paterson U., 1970; MSW, Fordham U., 1984; PhD, Rutgers U., 1996. Social worker Pascack Valley H.S., Hillsdale, N.J., 1974-99; pvt. practice psychotherapist Ridgewood, N.J., 1983—; prof. Ramapo Coll., Mahwah, N.J., 1984—. Home: 352 Corona Pl Ridgewood NJ 07450-2802

JAROSZ, SLAWOMIR, chemist, educator; b. Warsaw, Poland, May 16, 1952; s. Ryszard and Zofia (Stawikowska) J.; m. Malgorzata Pruss, June 8, 1974; 1 chld, Magdalena. MSc, U. Warsaw, Poland, 1974; PhD, Inst. Organic Chemistry, Warsaw, 1979, DSc, 1990. Rschr. Inst. Organic Chemistry, 1975-78, 1978-83, sr. rschr., 1983-95, asst. prof., 1995-99, prof., 1999—. Co-editor Polish Jour. of Chemistry, 1997—; contbr. articles to profl. jours. Mem. Polish Chem. Soc. (pres. Warsaw br. 1995—, co-editor jour. Orbital 1991-97). Avocations: walking, books, cosmology. Office: Polish Acad Sci, Kasprzaka 44, 01-224 Warsaw Poland

JAROSZEWSKI, VERDA M., English educator; b. Peru, Ill., Oct. 22, 1957; d. Joseph and Verda Mankowski; m. David Louis Jarosewski, May 31, 1980; children: Abraham, Theresa. BA, Marquette U., 1979, MA, 1981, PhD, 1997. Instr. U. Wis., Platteville, 1981-83, Marquette U., Milw., 1983-85; lectr., instr. U.N.C., Charlotte, 1998—. Mem. Adj. Assn. for Faculty (chair 1999—). Roman Catholic. E-mail: verdabet@freewwweb.com. Office: UNC Charlotte Univeristy Ave Charlotte NC 28223

JARRELL, GLENN, city planner, farmer; b. Beckley, W.Va., June 8, 1958; s. Roy and Anna Mae Jarrell; m. Brooklyn Mae Jarrell. BA, W.Va. U., 1988, MA, 1991. Clk. Jarrell's Gen. Store, Arnett, W.Va., 1978-83; night clk. Rick's Supermarket, Glen Daniel, W.Va., 1983-87; rsch. asst. Regional Rsch. Inst., Morgantown, W.Va., 1987-88; supr. Summer Youth Program, Beckley, W.Va., 1988; rsch. asst. W.Va. U., Morgantown, 1989, tchg. asst., 1988-90; planner W.Va. Solid Waste Mgmt. Bd., Charleston, 1991—. Mem. FFA, W.Va. Geog. Club. Avocations: reading, traveling, computers, sports, farming. Home: PO Box 306 Fairdale WV 25839-0306

JARRETT, THOMAS WILLIAM, urological surgeon; b. N.Y., June 5, 1961; s. William John and Margaret Elizabeth J.; m. Martha Ann Burke, May 29, 1997; 1 child, John Burke. BA in anthropology, Duke Univ., 1983; MD, Emory Univ., 1987. Surgery resident Emory Univ., Atlanta, 1987-89; urology resident N.Y. Hosp., N.Y.C., 1989-93; fellowship Long Island Jewish Hosp., New Hyde Park, N.Y., 1993-94; asst. prof. urology George Washington Univ., Washington, 1994-97, Johns Hopkins Univ., Balt., 1997—; audio, video rep. Am. Urological Assn., 1999—; cons. manuscript review Urology, Balt., 1998—, Jour. Urology, 1998—. Recipient rsch. grant Nat. Kidney Found., 1999, Johns Hopkins Univ., 1997, 98, 99. Mem. Endurological Soc., AMA, Mid Atlantic Am. Urology Assn. Avocations: tennis, skiing, running. E-mail: twjcjhmi.edu. Office: Johns Hopkins Medical Inst 4940 Eastern Ave Baltimore MD 21224-2735

JÄRV, JAAK, chemistry educator; b. Tartu, Estonia, Nov. 5, 1948; s. Lembit and Rufina (Platov) J.; m. Kiira Ellman, Sept. 8, 1973 (div. May 1997); children: Laur, Kadri; m. Heli Väärtnou, May 7, 1999. Grad. with honors, Tartu U., 1972, PhD, 1976; PhD (hon.), Kuopio U., Finland, 1991; DSc in Chemistry, Moscow U., 1990; D of Med. Scis. (hon.), Uppsala U., Sweden, 1996. Cert. docent in organic chemistry, 1983, prof. organic chemistry, 1991. Rsch. fellow Tartu U., 1972-73, 76-77, assoc. prof., 1977-83, dep. prorector, 1983-91, prof., 1991—, dean faculty physics and chemistry, 1999—; panel mem. Estonian Sci. Found., 1993—; mem. Tartu U. Coun., 1992-95, 99—. Mem. editl. bd. Bioorganic Chemistry Acad. Press, 1985—; contbr. more than 150 sci. articles to profl. jours., 12 book chpts. Mem. panel Baltic Assn. Com. Culture and Sci., Tallinn, Estonia, 1996-98; mem. publ. com. Fedn. European Biochem. Socs., 1998—. Rsch. grantee Estonian Sci. Found., 1994, Internat. Sci. Found., N.Y., 1994-98, INCO grantee European Union DG XII, Brussels, 1997—. Mem. Estonian Biochem. Soc., European Peptide Soc., Am. Chem. Soc., European Neurochem. Soc., Biochem. Soc. U.K., Sr.'s Assembly, Rotary Internat., Estonian Acad. Sci. Avocation: water sports. Office: Tartu, 2 Jakobi St, EE51014 Tartu Estonia

JARVIK, LISSY F., psychiatrist; b. The Hague, Netherlands; m. Murray E. Jarvik, Dec. 19, 1954; children: Laurence A., Jeffrey G. AB cum laude, Hunter Coll., N.Y.C.; MA, Columbia U., PhD; MD, Western Res. U. Diplomate Am. Bd. Pediat. From rsch. asst. to psychiatrist II N.Y. State Psychiat. Inst., N.Y.C.; rotating intern Mt. Sinai Hosp., N.Y.C.; resident in pediatrics Babies Hosp., Columbia Presbyn. Med. Ctr., Vanderbilt Clinic, N.Y.C.; resident in psychiatry N.Y. State Psychiat. Inst., N.Y.C., 1965-68; asst. attending, then attending psychiatrist Vanderbilt Clinic, 1962-72; from rsch. assoc. to assoc. prof. Columbia U. Coll. Phys. and Surg., 1956-72; chief psychogenetic unit West Los Angeles VA Med. Ctr., 1970-82, chief psychogeriatric unit, 1982-87; prof. psychiatry UCLA Med. Sch., 1982-94, prof. emeritus, 1994—; M.S. McLeod vis. prof. U. Adelaide, Australia, 1981; vis. prof. Australian Postgrad. Med. Found., 1981; Disting. Physician Dept. VA, 1987-93, emeritus, 1993—; dir. GetSmart program, 1991—, dir. Upbeat Program, 1993—; cons. in field, mem. numerous task forces. Mem. editl. bd. profl. jours.; founding co-editor Alzheimer Disease and Associated Disorders--An Internat. Jour.; contbr. over 300 articles to profl. jours. Recipient R. Thornton Wilson award, 1967, Woman in Sci. award UCLA, 1981, Group Research award Assn. for Specialists in Group Work, 1984, Research award Alzheimer Disease and Related Disorders Assn., L.A. chpt., 1985, Jack Weinberg Memorial award Am. Psychiatric Assn., 1986, Robert W. Kleemeier award Gerontol. Soc. of Am., 1986, Edward B. Allen award Am. Geriatrics Soc., 1986, Disting. Scientific Achievement award Calif. State Psychol. Assn., 1987, Irving S. Wright award Am. Fedn. for Aging Rsch., 1988, William C. Menninger Meml. award ACP, 1993, Svc. to Psychogeriat. award Internat. Psychogeriat. Assn., 1995, C. Charles Burlingame award The Inst. Living, 1998; named Woman of Achievement, Women's Equality Day, 1980, Woman of Yr., AAUW, Santa Monica, 1985; named to Hunter Coll. Alumni Assn. Hall of Fame, 1991; Foundation fellow Ctr. for Advanced Study in Behavioral Scis., 1988-89. Fellow AAAS, Gerontol. Soc. Am. (Joseph T. Freeman award 1996), Am. Geriatric Soc., Internat. Soc. Twin Studies, Am. Acad. Pediatrics, Am. Psychol. Assn. (div. pres.); mem. Am. Med. Womens Assn., Am. Soc. Human Genetics, Am. Psychopath Assn., Am. Aging Assn., Am. Soc. on Aging, Behavior Genetics Assn., Internat. Assn. Gerontology, Am. Psychiat. Assn. (Disting. Psychiatrist Lectr. 1996), Am. Assn. for Geriat. Psychiatry (past pres., Founders award 1990-91, Sr. Investigator award, 1993), Internat. Psychogeriat. Assn., N.Y. Acad. Scis., West Coast Coll. Biol. Psychiatry, World Psychiat. Assn., Sigma Xi. Office: 760 Westwood Plz Los Angeles CA 90095-8353 also: VA Med Ctr 11301 Wilshire Blvd # 11L Los Angeles CA 90073-1003

JÄRVINEN, PEKKA TAPANI, occupational physician; b. Helsinki, Finland, Mar. 9, 1954; s. Lauri Johannes and Irja Kaarina (Jokiranta) J.; m. Riitta Helena Jyrä, Sept. 6, 1980; children: Lasse, Heikki, Anna. MD, U. Turku, Finland, 1979. Pvt. practice Finland, 1979-85; occupl. physician Ahlsthom Corp., Eura, Finland, 1986-87, Turku Regional Inst. Occupl. Health, 1988, Rauma, Finland, 1989, Rauma Ltd., Pori, Finland, 1990-99, Valmet Corp., Jyväskylä, Finland, 1999—. Office: Valmet Corp, PO Box 587, 40101 Jyväskylä Finland

JARVINEN, VESA MATTI, clinical physiologist; b. Espoo, Finland, Apr. 27, 1954; s. Pauli Olavi and Tuulikki (Autio) J.; m. Irmeli Anna Irene Creutz, Nov. 3, 1979; children: Vappu, Ilari. BSc, Turengin Yhteiskoulu, Turenki, Finland, 1974; MD, Helsinki U., 1980. Gen. practitioner Nurmijarvi County, Finland, 1981-86; jr. house officer Laakso Hosp., Helsinki, 1986-89, Helsinki Univ. Ctrl. Hosp., 1989-91; specialist in clin. physiology Kiljava Hosp., Finland, 1991, med. supt., 1991—; cons. Medi-Metro OY, Helsinki, 1991—; rschr. Dept. of Radiology, Helsinki U. Ctrl. Hosp., 1991—. Mem. Finnish Soc. Clin. Physiology (Heikki Wendelin award 1995, bd. mem. 1998—), Finnish Cardiac Soc. Avocations: photography, sailing, traveling, sports, gardening. Office: Kiljava Hosp, FIN05250 Kiljava Finland

JARVIS, DARRYL STUART LESLIE, social sciences educator, consultant; b. Nottingham, Midlands, Eng., Sept. 23, 1963; s. John Staurt and Jean Jarvis. Student, Flinders U., Adelaide, Australia, 1981-85, MA, 1990; PhD, U. B.C., Vancouver, Can., 1995. Rsch. assoc. Inst. Internat. Rels. U. B.C., Vancouver, 1995-96, sessional prof., 1996; lectr. internat. rels. faculty econs. and bus. U. Sydney, NSW, Australia, 1997—; polit. risk cons. Strategic Assessment Internat., Ctr. for Pub. and Internat. Affairs, U. Sydney, 1999—. Mem. Internat. Studies Assn., Am. Polit. Sci. Assn. Anglican. Avocations: mountain hiking, skiing, sailing. E-mail: djarvis@presto.net.au and darrylj@bullwinkle.econ.usyd.edu.au. Fax: 02 9351-3624. Home: Unit 79, 304-308 Pitt St, Sydney NSW 2000, Australia Office: Dept Govt & Internat Rels, Univ Sydney, Sydney NSW 2006, Australia

JARVIS, DONALD BERTRAM, judge; b. Newark, N.J., Dec. 14, 1928; s. Benjamin and Esther (Golden) J.; m. Rosalind C. Chodorcove, June 13, 1954; children: Nancie, Brian, Joanne. BA, Rutgers U., 1949; JD, Stanford U., 1952. Bar: Calif. 1953. Law clk. to justice John W. Shenk Calif. Supreme Ct., 1953-54; assoc. Erskine, Erskine & Tulley, 1955, Aaron N. Cohen, 1955-56; law clk. Dist. Ct. Appeal, 1956; assoc. Carl Hoppe, 1956-57; adminstrv. law judge Calif. Pub. Utilities Commn., San Francisco, 1957-91, U.S. Dept. of Labor, San Francisco, 1992—; mem. exec. com. Nat. Conf. Adminstrv. Law Judges, 1986-88, sec. 1988-89, vice-chair, 1990-91, chair-elect, 1991-92, chair 1992-93; pres. Calif. Adminstrv. Law Judges Coun., 1978-84; mem. faculty Nat. Jud. Coll., U. Nev., 1977, 78, 80; mem. U.S. Bd. of Alien Labor Cert. Appeals, 1995—. Chmn. pack Boy Scouts Am., 1967-69, chmn. troop 1972; class chmn. Stanford Law Sch. Fund, 1959, mem. nat. com., 1963-65; dir. Forest Hill Assn., 1970-71; patron San Francisco Opera. Served to col. USAF Res., 1949-79. Decorated Legion of Merit. Mem. ABA (mem. ho. of dels. 1993-99, vice chair jud. divsn. 1997-98, chair elect 1998-99, chair 1999-2000), State Bar Calif., Bar Assn. San Francisco, Calif. Conf. Pub. Utility Counsel (pres. 1980-81), Air Force Assn., Res. Officers Assn., Ret. Officers Assn., San Francisco Gem and Mineral Soc., Stanford Alumni Assn., Rutgers Alumni Assn., Phi Beta Kappa (pres. No. Calif. 1973-74), Tau Kappa Alpha, Pi Alpha Theta, Phi Alpha Delta. Home: 530 Dewey Blvd San Francisco CA 94116-1427 Office: 50 Fremont St San Francisco CA 94105-2230

JARVIS, JOHN ARNOLD KUYS, lawyer; b. Kroonstad, South Africa, Dec. 11, 1942; s. Arnold Kuys and Valmee (Rodda) J.; m. Ann Elizabeth Lowry, Sept. 11, 1971; children: Matthew, Penelope. B Comm., U. Stellebosch, South Africa, 1963; LLB, U. Potchefstroom, South Africa, 1965; MA, Cambridge (Eng.) U., 1968. Artilled clk. Williams Gaisford & Steyn, Potchefstroom, 1965-66; profl. asst. Webber Wentzel Hofmeyer Turnull & Co., Johannesburg, South Africa, 1968-70; ptnr. Webber Wentzel Bowens, Johannesburg, 1970—; dir. Kongskilde SA (Pty) Ltd., Johannesburg, 1996—. Contbr. articles to profl. jours. Mem. Rand Club, Country Club Johannesburg, Tuxffontein Race Club. Avocations: fly fishing, music, walking. Home: 103 Central Ave, Sandton 2109, South Africa Office: Webber Wentzel Bowens, 60 Main St PO Box 61771, Marshalltown 2107, South Africa

JASANI, BHARAT, pathology educator, histopathology consultant; b. Nairobi, Kenya, Jan. 20, 1947; s. Keshavlal Bhimji and Prabhavati (Chandarana) J.; m. Annand Prakash Myrrpurey, July 7, 1973; children: Karishma, Maya. BSc with honours in Biochemistry, U. Glasgow, Scotland, 1969; PhD in Exptl. Pathology, U. Birmingham, Eng., 1973, MB, ChB, 1976. House officer in medicine East Birmingham (Eng.) Hosp., 1976, house officer in surgery, 1977, sr. house officer in pediatrics, 1977; sr. house officer, lectr. in pathology U. Wales Coll. Medicine, Cardiff, 1977-79, registrar in pathology, lectr., 1980-82, sr. registrar, sr. lectr., 1982-89, cons., sr. lectr., 1989—, dir. immunocytochemistry and molecular pathology unit, 1993—; dep. dir. rsch. oncology unit Velindre Hosp. NHS Trust, 2000, mem. med. students selection panel, 1999; assessor U.K. Nat. Quality Assurance Scheme, London, 1992—; mem. bd. biomed. methods course, Cardiff, 1987—. Prin. author: Immunocytochemistry in Diagnostic Histopathology, 1993; also more than 200 articles. Mem. Welsh Distinction Awards Com., 1999. Grantee Amersham Internat., 1983, Welsh Scheme for R & D, 1984, 94; recipient Nat. Distinction award in Pathology, 1998. Fellow Royal Coll. Pathologists (Becton Dickinson travel fellow 1982); mem. Am. Assn. Cancer Rsch., Assn. Clin. Pathologists (rep. working group on quality assurance 1990—, immunology com. 1999), Path. Soc. Gt. Britain, N.Y. Acad. Scis. Achievements include patent for DNP-Hapten sandwich staining procedure, diaminobenzidine silver enhancement technique; discovered metallothionein as a prognostic marker in human cancer, light chain restricted plasma cells in autoimmune disease; principle British researcher of SV40 Association with human cancer. Office: U Wales Coll Medicine, Heath Park, Cardiff CF4 4XN, Wales

JASEN, J(UNE) E., artist, designer, enamelist; b. N.Y.C., 1952. BFA, U. Cin., 1973; MA in Arts and Edn., NYU, 1976. Artist j.e. jasen studio, N.Y.C., 1979—. One-woman exhbns. include Mobilia Gallery, Cambridge, Mass., 1982, Langman Gallery, Willow Grove, Pa., 1983, Elements Gallery, Greenwich, Conn.,1984, New Morning Gallery, Ashville, N.C., 1984, Art Forms, Red Bank, N.J., 1987, Judith Wolov Gallery, Boston, 1992, Gallery of Wearable Art, N.Y.C., Del Mano Gallery, L.A., Window or Main Street Gallery, others; exhibited in group shows at Marrietta Coll. Craft Nats., Marietta, Ohio, 1980, Mamaroneck Artist Guild Exhbn., N.Y., 1981, Western Colo. Ctr. for Arts, Grand Junction, 1981, Gallery 500, Phila., 1982, Pindar Gallery, N.Y.C., 1982, Joy Horwich Gallery, Chgo., 1982, Mill Gallery, Guilford, Conn., 1983, Detroit Gallery of Contemporary Crafts, 1983, Carol Hooberman Gallery, Birmingham, Mich., 1983, Vitti Gallery, Upper Montclair, N.J., 1984, Eve France Gallery, Houston, 1984, Rocking Horse Gallery, Fort Worth, Tex., 1985, Reese Palley Gallery, Atlantic City, 1985, Mind's Eye Gallery, Scottsdale, Ariz., 1986, Hudson River Gallery, Ossining, N.Y., 1986, Affinity Gallery, Louisville, 1987, Jacqueline Gallery, Carmel, Calif., 1988, Joan Michelin Gallery, N.Y.C., 1988, Tennyson Gallery, Provincetown, Mass., 1989, Dee Erlien Gallery, Milwaukee, 1990, Judith Wolov Gallery, Boston, 1992, Brookfield Gallery, Conn., 1993, Greater Jewish Cmty. Ctr. Wash., D.C., 1993, New Visions Gallery, Marshfield, Wis., 1994, Margo Jacobsen Gallery, Portland, Oreg., 1995, SOHO Gallery, Pensacola, Fla., 1996, Schenectady Mus., N.Y., 1996, The Sight Gallery, San Francisco, 1997, Hoy Inst. Fine Arts, New Castle, Pa., 1997, Walter Anderson Mus. Art, Ocean Springs, Miss., 1997, Birger Sandzen Meml. Gallery, McPherson, Kans., 1998, womanMADE Gallery, Chgo., 1998, St. Vincent Hosp. & Woman's Health Ctr. & Toucan Gallery, Billings, Mont., 1999, Silvermine Guild Arts Ctr., New Canaan, Conn., 1999, Randon Modern Gallery, Tacoma, Wash., 2000, Target Gallery, Alexandria, Va., 2000, Baker's Art Found., Liberal, Kans., 2000, others; represented in permanent collections Judith Fliegal, N.Y.C., Goodies Inc., Knoxville, Tenn., HMO/U.S. Health Care, Blue Bell, Pa., UPS, N.Y.C., Am. Crafts Coun. slide library collection; lectr. in field. Named one of Outstanding Women in Am., 1982; Wash. Square Outdoor Art Exhbn. 3 time award winner, 1980-81,; recipient Enamels Into a New Decade award Enamel Guild West, 1981, cert. outstanding achievement Women in Design Internat., 1983, . Mem. Am. Craft Coun., Nat. Enamelist Guild, Enamelist Guild South, Enamel Guild West, N.W. Enamelist Guild, Midwest Enamelist Guild, Ariz. Enamelist Guild, Enamelist Guild North/East (bd. mem., founder steering group), Enamel Soc. (charter mem.), Brit. Enamelist Soc., Empire State Crafts Alliance, Design Internat., Safety in the Arts. E-mail: jejasen@aol.com. Home and Office: j e jasen studio 36 E 10th St New York NY 10003-6219

JASINSKI, LESZEK JERZY, economist, educator; b. Lebork, Pomerania, Poland, Feb. 9, 1952; s. Władysław and Krystyna (Starnawska) J.; m. Elżbieta Markisz, June 28, 1975; children: Adam, Tomasz, Michał, Anna. MA, Ctrl. Sch. Planning & Stats., Warsaw, Poland, 1974, D in Econs.,

1977; D in Econs. habilitation, Acad. Econs., Cracow, Poland, 1988. Chair Inst. Econometrics Ctrl. Sch. Planning and Stats., Warsaw, 1974-80; asst. Inst. for Market Rsch., Warsaw, 1980-89; asst. prof. Fgn. Trade Rsch. Inst., 1989-96; prof. Inst. Econs., Polish Acad. Scis., 1996—; advisor to min. European Integration, 1992—. Author: Analysis of Integration, Reform of the European Union, Polish Exchange Rate Policy in 1990-1998, Poland's Foreign Economic Relations Under Communism; co-author: Polish Tranformation From Perspective of European Integration; contbr. articles to profl. jours. Roman Catholic. Home: Zamiany 14 m 21, 02-786 Warszawa Poland Office: Polish Acad Scis Inst Econs, Marszalkowska 77/79, 00-683 Warszawa Poland

JASINSKI, PIOTR, electronic engineer, researcher; b. Gdansk, Poland, June 21, 1968; s. Roman and Maria Jasinski; m. Marzenna Domanska, Sept. 26, 1992. MSc in Engring., Tech. U. Gdansk, 1992. Asst. Tech. U. Gdansk, 1992—; bursar City U. London, 1993, Christian Albert U., Kiel, Germany, 1996. Roman Catholic. Avocations: basketball, computers. E-mail: pijas@pg.gda.pl. Fax: 48 58 3471757. Office: Tech Univ Gdansk, ul Narutowicza 11/12, 80-952 Gdansk Poland

JASINSKI-CALDWELL, MARY L., company executive; b. Chester, Pa., May 8, 1959; d. A. Robert and Helen M. Jasinski; m. William A. Caldwell, Aug. 4, 1990; children: Helaina M., Anna L. Student, Loyola Coll., Balt., 1980, Loyola Coll., Balt., 1980; AS, Goldey Beacom Coll., Wilmington, Del., 1982, BS, 1983. Registered orthotic fitter; cert. sr. pharmacy technician. Gen. mgr. pension plan City Pharmacy of Elkton (Md.), Inc., 1975-96, treas., 1987-96, jr. ptnr., 1994, v.p., 1996—; founder, pres. City Home Health Care, Inc., Elkton, 1997—; disc jockey, promoter Garfield's Restaurant, Elkton; editl. writer local newspapers; pro-life columnist KC newsletter. Creator ednl. program PARTICIP.A.A.T.E. For Life. Bd. dirs. Cecil County chpt. ARC, 1996—, fin. devel. chmn., 2000—; bd. dirs. Mission Am., Inc.; bd. dirs. Md. Right to Life, 1993-94, co-chair Cecil County chpt.; adv. Cecil County Pregnancy Ctr., Cecil County Bd. Edn. Textbook Adoption Policy Com., 1995; pro-life educator City Pharmacy of Elkton, Inc. Speaker of March For Life of Md., 1997-98, Md. Pub. TV, 1997. Alpha Chi scholar, Lindback scholar; recipient J.W. Miller award, Outstanding Achievement in Excellence award K.C., 1994, Ralph and Eleanor Hicks Outstanding Vol. svc. award ARC, Cecil County, Md., 1999-2000; named Family of Yr., 1995; named to Honor Roll of Best 250 Independents in U.S., Drug Topics, 1992. Mem. NAFE, NRA, Am. Mgmt. Assn., Nat. Fedn. Ind. Bus., Bd. Orthotic Cert., Am. Assn. Pharm. Technicians, Nat. Right to Life Com., Am. Life League, Internat. Platform Assn., Pro-Life Md., Christian Coalition, Cath. Alliance, Cecil County C. of C., Stop Internat., Human Life Internat., Concerned Women for Am., Pharmacists for Life, Goldey Beacom Coll. Alumni Assn., Movement for a Better Am., Cath. League, Liberty Alliance, Susan B. Anthony List, Alpha Chi. Republican. Roman Catholic. Avocations: home improvement, gardening, social concerns, pro-life education, reading. Office: City Pharmacy Inc 723 N Bridge St Elkton MD 21921-5398

JASKIERNIA, JERZY, Polish government official; b. Kudowa Zdroj, Poland, Mar. 21, 1950; s. Zofia and Mieczyslaw Jaskiernia; m. Alicja Slowinska, 1980; 2 children. Master of Law, Jagiellonian U., Poland, 1972, Doctor of Legal Scis., 1977; D habil. in Legal Scis., Polish Acad. Scis. Inst. Law, 1994. Asst. law and adminstrn. faculty Jagellonian U., Crakow, 1972-75, sr. asst., 1975-77, adj. faculty, 1977-81; chair Polish Socialist Youth Union Gen. Bd., 1981-84; dep. Sejm, 1985-89, 91—, chair legis. com., 1993-95, 96-97; counsellor Embassy of Poland, Washington, 1988-90; prof. adminstrn. and mgmt. faculty Kielce (Poland) Pedagogical Coll., 1995—; dep. chmn. European Integration Com., 1997—; advisor to min. Ministry of Fgn. Affairs, 1987-88; chair Polish-Brit. Parliamentary Group, 1993—; active Nat. Assn. Constnl. Com., 1992-95, Parliamentary Assembly Coun. of Europe, 1994—, chmn. subcom. on human rights of com. on legal affairs and human rights, 1998—, min. justice-atty. gen., 1995-96; dep. chmn. Joint Parliamentary Com. of the Republic of Poland and European Union, 1997—. Author: Pozycja stanow w systemie federalnym USA, 1979, Dylematy mlodych, 1984, Dialog nasza szansa, 1985; co-author: System polityczny PRL w procesie przemian, 1988, Problemy pluralizmu, porozumienia narodowego i consensusu w systemie politycznym PRL, 1989, Stany Zjednoczone a wspolczesne procesy i koncepcje integracji europejskiej, 1992, Zasada rownosci w prawie wyborczym USA, 1992, Wizja parlamentu w nowej Konstytucji Rzeczypospolitej Polskiej, 1994, Zasady demokratycznego państwa prawnego w sejmowym postepowaniu ustawodawczym, 1999, Zgromadzenie Parlamentarne Rady Europy, 2000. Mem. Main Bd. Socialist Youth Union, 1973-76; mem. Polish Socialist Youth Union, 1976-85; mem. Main Arbitration Bd., 1976-80, chair, 1980-81; active PZPR, 1970-90, dep. mem. ctrl. com., 1982-86, vice chair youth com., 1981-86, mem. inter-party problems com., 1986-88; active Nat. Coun. Patriotic Movement for Nat. Rebirth, 1983-89, sec.-gen., 1984-87; mem. sci. bd. Rsch. Inst. Youth Problems, Warsaw, 1984-89; active Social Dem. of Republic of Poland, 1990-91; mem. ctrl. exec., 1991-92, head parliament and self-govt. affairs dept., 1990-91, mem. presidium of nat. com., 1993-97; dep. chmn. Dem. Left Alliance (SLD) Parliamentary Caucus, 1996—; mem. nat. com., chmn. Com. on Internat. Cooperation, 1997-99; active Dem. Left Alliance, 1999—, mem. Nat. Exec. Bd., 2000—. Office: Wiejska 6 pok C-D 109, 00 902 Warsaw Poland

JASKOLL, TINA FELICE, geneticist; b. New York, Jan. 24, 1950; d. Saul and Edith (Alva) J. BA, Yeshiva U., New York, 1971; PhD, CUNY, 1978. Fellow craniofacial biology U. So. Calif. Sch. Dentistry, Los Angeles, 1977-80; rsch. asst. prof. U. So. Calif. Sch. Dentistry, 1980-86, rsch. assoc. prof., 1986-87; assoc. prof. Yeshiva U., New York, 1987-88; rsch. assoc. prof. U. So. Calif. Sch. Dentistry, Los Angeles, 1988-91; asst. prof./co-dir. lab. devel. genetics U. So. Calif., Los Angeles, 1988-91, 1995-99; prof./co-dir. U. So. Calif., 1999—; grant reviewer NIH, NSF, Washington, 1988, 96, 98. Jour. reviewer: Anatomical Record, Acta Anatomica, Developmental Biology, Teratology, 1998—; editl. bd.: (jour.) Jour. Craniofacial Genetics and Developmental Biology, 1997—; contbr. over 50 articles to profl. jours. Judge Calif. State Fair, L.A., 1991, 93-2000, L.A. Ednl. Partnership Outreach Pub. Sch. Tchrs., 1985; mem. orgn. com. 10th Congress Internat. Soc. Devel. Genetics, 1985. Recipient Dr. Samuel Belkin award profl. achievement, Yeshiva U., 1994; fellowship, NIH, L.A., 1977-80; grantee NIH, 1988-2001. Mem. AAAS, Am. Soc. Cell Biology, Endocrine Soc., Soc. Developmental Biology. Avocations: antiquing, crafting. Fax: 213-740-7560. E-mail: tjaskoll@hsc.usc.edu. Office: USC Sch Dentistry Lab Devel Genetics 925 W 34th St # 4264 Los Angeles CA 90089-0058

JASKULA, MARIAN JÓZEF, chemist; b. Cracow, Poland, Aug. 26, 1948; s. Aleksander and Zofia (Banczak) J.; m. Teresa Regina Chwistek, June 17, 1973; children: Anna, Maria, Jerzy. MSc, Jagiellonian U., Kraków, Poland, 1971, PhD in Phys. Chemistry, 1979, Dr. habil. in Electrometallurgy, 1992. Asst. Faculty of Chemistry Jagiellonian U., Kraków, Poland, 1971-79, adj. asst. prof., 1979—; head Electrochemical Group, 1993—; privat dozent Rheinisch-Westfalische Technische Hoschschule, Aachen, Germany, 1992-99; aussenplanmassiger prof. Rheinisch-Westfalische Technische Hochschule Aachen, Germany, 1999—. Co-author: Physical Chemistry Exercises, 1989; contbr. over 80 papers to sci. publs.; patentee in field; co-author of two student books. Pres. UJ-Tchrs. Trade Union, Kraków, 1976-80, 80-81. Grantee Austrian Govt., 1982-83, Denmark Govt., 1984, 92-93, 1999-2000; Humboldt fellow, 1987-90; recipient Polish Ministry for Sci. award, 1979, 85, Friedrich-Wilhelm Preis award, Aachen, 1992, Gold Cross of Merit, 1995, Silver medal Tech. U. Kosice, Slovakia, 1995. Mem. Polish Chem. Soc., Polish Chemistry Engrs. Soc. Roman Catholic. Avocations: travel, sport. E-mail: jaskula@chemia.uj.edu.pl. Home: Obopólna 3/39, 30-039 Cracow Poland Office: Jagiellonian U, 3 Ingardena Str, 30-060 Cracow Poland

JASON, J. JULIE, money manager, author, lawyer; b. Owensboro, Ky., May 14, 1949; d. Richard and Grazina Pauliukonis; m. Marius J. Jason, Dec. 19, 1970; children: Ilona, Leila. BA, Baldwin-Wallace Coll., 1971; JD, Cleve. State U., 1974; LLM, Columbia U., 1975. Bar: Ohio 1974, N.Y. 1976, U.S. Dist Ct. (so. dist.) N.Y. 1976, U.S. Ct. Appeals (2d cir.) 1976, U.S. Supreme Ct. 1978. Pvt. practice N.Y.C., 1974-78; asst. gen. counsel Paine Webber, N.Y.C., 1978-83; pres. P.W. Trust and Paine Webber Futures Mgmt. Co., N.Y.C., 1983-88; sr. fin. svcs. atty. Donovan, Leisure, Newton & Irvine, N.Y.C., 1988-89; co-founder, mng. dir. Jackson, Grant & Co., Stamford, Conn., 1989—; arbitrator NYSE; mediator U.S. Bankruptcy Ct., 1997. Author: You and Your 401(K), 1996, The 401(K) Plan Handbook, 1997; weekly columnist "401-OK" Times Mirror Publ., 1998—. Mem. ABA, AAUW (chair scholarship com. 1992-93), Nat. Assn. Securities Dealers (cert. arbitrator, cert. mediator), Am. Soc. Journalists & Authors, Investment Co. Inst. (sec. regulation com. 1978-83), The Corp. Bar, Columbia U. Alumni Club of Fairfield County (pres. 1993-94, chair pres.'s coun. 1994-96). Office: Jackson Grant & Co 1177 High Ridge Rd Stamford CT 06905-1203

JASPERT, W. PINCUS, editor; b. Frankfurt, Germany, Mar. 21, 1926; s. Willem Otto and Isolde (Anger) J.; m. Hella Mandl, Feb. 20, 1940 (div. 1965); children: Elisabeth (dec.), Beatrice; m. Julia Merrell Boreham, Feb. 17, 1970 (div. 1997); children: Anna, Willem John, Augustus James Ulysses; m. Barri Clark Limpus, Apr. 3, 1998. Trainee mgr., asst. prodn. mgr. F. Bruckmann Pub., Munich, 1948-49; asst. pub. F. Bergmann-Springer Verlag, Heidelberg; asst. prodn. mgr. Butterworth-Springer Sci. Publs., London, 1950; asst. editor Amstutz & Herdeg Pubs., Zurich, 1951; editor Blandford, London, 1952-56; mktg. exec. Jarrold & Sons, Norwich, England, 1956-57; assoc. cons. Edward McSweeney Assocs., N.Y.C., 1957-66; tech. advisor Sunday Times, London, 1965, Fin. Times, London, 1968-96; cons. editor World-Wide Printer, various cities, 1970-96. Author, editor: Encyclopedia of Type Faces, 11th edit., 1993, State of the Art Reports Comprint, 1982-2001. Fellow Inst. of Printing; mem. Internat. Soc. Optical Engring., Tech. Assn. Graphic Arts, Rsch. and Engring. Coun. Graphic Arts. Address: 6859 Willoughby Ave Apt 2 Los Angeles CA 90038-2437

JASSO, GUILLERMINA, sociologist, educator; b. Laredo, Tex., July 22, 1942; d. José Jasso-Rodríguez and Guillermina de los Santos-Lozano. BA, Our Lady of the Lake Coll., 1962; MA, U. Notre Dame, 1970; PhD, Johns Hopkins U., 1974. Asst. prof. Barnard Coll. and Columbia U., N.Y.C., 1974-77; spl. asst. to commr. U.S. Immigration and Naturalization Svc., Washington, 1977-79; dir. rsch. U.S. Select Commn. on Immigration and Refugee Policy, Washington, 1979-80; asst. prof. U. Mich., Ann Arbor, 1980-82; assoc. prof. U. Minn., Mpls., 1982-86, prof., 1986-87; prof., dir. theory workshop U. Iowa, Iowa City, 1987-91; prof. NYU, N.Y.C., 1991—, dir. methods workshop, 1991-97; mem. study sect. on social sci. and population NIH, 1991-95; mem. U.S. Com. for Internat. Inst. for Applied Sys. Analysis, 1993—; mem. various programs NSF, 1987-96, 98-99; mem. panel on demographic and econ. impacts of immigration NAS, 1995-97; mem. population rsch. subcom. Nat. Inst. Child Health and Human Devel., NIH, 1998—; vis. prof. Zentrum Umfragen, Methoden, und Analysen, Mannheim, Germany, 1995, U. Leipzig, Germany, 1996; mem. core rsch. team bination study on migration between Mex. and U.S., U.S. Commn. on Immigration Reform, 1995-97; mem. editl. bd. Social Justice Rsch., 1985—, Jour. Math. Sociology, 1985—, Rationality and Society, 1999—, European Sociological Review, 2000-04; dep. editor Am. Sociol. Rev., 1996-99; disting. alumni lectr. U. Notre Dame, 1987; univ. pub. lectr. Our Lady of Lake U., 1989. Author: The New Chosen People, 1990; contbr. articles to profl. jours. Grantee Russell Sage Found., 1983-85, Rockefeller Found., 1985-86, NSF, 1994-97, NIH, 1995-99; fellow Ctr. for Advanced Study in Behavioral Scis., Stanford, Calif., 1999-2000. Fellow Johns Hopkins Soc. Scholars; mem. Am. Sociol. Assn. (chair internat. migration sect. 1996-99, chair theory sect. 1996-99), Sociol. Rsch. Assn. E-mail: gjl@is3.nyu.edu. Office: NYU Dept Sociology 269 Mercer St 4th Fl New York NY 10003-6633

JASTHI, SIVA RAMA KRISHNA, software professional, consultant; b. Guntur, India, June 8, 1965; s. Pullaiah and Drakshayani (Modukuri) J.; m. Bhaskarani Chennupati, Aug. 31, 1994; 1 child, Tapan. B Tech., Jawahrlal Nehru Tech. U., Anantapur, India, 1987; M Tech., P.S.G. Coll. Tech., Coimbatore, India, 1990; PhD, Indian Inst. Tech., New Delhi, 1994; CMII grad., Ariz. State U., 1999. Rsch. scholar Indian Inst. Tech., Delhi, 1990-93, sr. sci. officer, 1993-95; sr. software engr. Computervision India, Pune, 1995-96, Computervision Corp., Bedford, Mass., 1996-98; prin. software engr. Metaphase Tech. Inc., Arden Hills, Minn., 1998—; cons. Bharat Heavy Elecs. Ltd., Bhopal, India, 1993-95. Reviewer Computer and Indsl. Engring. jour.; contbr. articles to profl. jours. Mem. Indian Instn. Indsl. Engrs. (life), Instn. Engrs. India (life, Best Rsch. Paper award 1994), Indian Soc. Tech. Edn. (life). Avocations: net surfing, writing for kids, indoor games. Office: Structural Dynamics Rsch Corp Metaphase Tech Divsn 4233 Lexington Ave N Ste 3290 Saint Paul MN 55126-6160

JASWON, MAURICE ARTHUR, mathematics educator; b. Dublin, Ireland, June 19, 1922; s. Tobias and Fanny (Cohen) J.; m. Rachel Miller, Aug. 26, 1948; children: Mervyn, Jeremy. BSC, Trinity Coll., Dublin, 1944, MA, 1951; PhD, Birmingham (Eng.) U., 1949. Rsch. fellow Birmingham U., 1947-49; lectr. Imperial Coll., London, 1949-57; reader London U., 1957-67; vis. prof. Brown U., Providence, 1963-64, U. Ky., Lexington, 1965-66, Inst. Tech., Delhi, 1973; prof., dept. head City U., London, 1967-87, vis. prof., 1987—. Author: (with G.T. Symm) (monograph) Integral Equation Methods in Potential Theory and Elastostatics, 1977. Fellow Inst. Maths. and Applications of London; mem. AAAS. Office: City U, St John St, London EC1, England

JASZBERENYI, CSABA JOSEPH, chemist, researcher; b. Budafok, Hungary, Aug. 19, 1948; s. József and Erzsebet (Sotter) J.; m. Erzsebet Vekony; children: Mark, Aron, Sara. Ph.D., Lajos Kossuth U., Debrecen, Hungary, 1975, C.Sc., 1985; D.Sc., Hungarian Acad. Scis, Budapest, 1994; Ph.D., Dr. Habil., Tech. U. Budapest, 1995. Asst. prof. Lajos Kossuth U., Debrecen, 1974-76, assoc. prof., 1976-81, rsch. fellow, 1981-84, sr. rsch. fellow, 1984-94; vis. prof. Tex. A&M U., 1988-94, sr. scientist, 1991-94; sr. scientist Tech. U., Budapest, 1994—, Széchenyi prof., 1997—; pres. Comporganics Co., Budapest, 1994—; pres. Barton Found. Contbr. book chpts.; U. textbooks. Achievements include patents in medicinal chemistry, agrochemicals, among others. Office: Tech U Budapest, Müegyetem Rkp 3, H-1111 Budapest Hungary

JATEGAONKAR, RAVINDRA VINAYAK, aeronautical engineer; b. Bhiwandi, India, Sept. 3, 1950; s. Vinayak and Vimal J.; m. Padma Jahagirdar, June 26, 1977; two children. BSc, Calicut U., 1972, MSc, 1975; PhD, Indian Inst. Sci., Bangalore, 1986. Scientist NAL Bangalore, India, 1975-86; from guest scientist to sr. scientist DLR Inst. Flight Mechs., Braunschweig, Germany, 1981—. Mem. AIAA (sr., mem. tech. com. Atomspheric Flight Mechanics). Home: Aurikelweg 23, 38108 Braunschweig Germany

JATIYA, SATYANARAYAN, government official; b. 1945. Elected to Madhya Pradesh Legis. Assembly, India, 1977, Lok Sabha, India, 1980; min. Ministry Labor, New Delhi, India, 1998—. Office: Ministry Labor, Shram Shakhti Bhawan, Rafi Marq New Delhi 110 001, India*

JAUBERT, JEAN MARIE, marine biology educator; b. Oran, Algiers, June 14, 1941; s. Amédée P. and Marie (Fabre La Maurelle) J.; m. Josette P. Brillouet, Apr. 6, 1964; 1 child. MSc, U. Marseille, France, 1966, PhD in Biol. Oceanography, 1971; DSc, U. Nice, France, 1987. From asst. prof. to assoc. prof. U. Nice, 1967-86, prof. marine biology, 1987—; dir. European Oceanographic Inst., Monaco, 1990—; sci. officer Ministry of Fgn. Affairs, Paris, 1982-87; mem. nat. com. Nat. Coun. for Sci. Rsch., 1996-98. Contbr. articles to profl. jours.; patentee in field. purification of water. Decorated Palmes Academiques, 19885 recipient medal Soc. Oceanography, 1995. Mem. AAAS, Acad. Interdisciplinary Scis. Paris, N.Y. Acad. Scis. Avocations: scuba diving and photography, plane gliding, aquarium. Office: European Oceanographic Inst, Sci Ctr Monaco, MC 9800-Ville Monaco Monaco

JAUMANN, HERBERT, literary educator; b. Noerdlingen, Bavaria, Germany, July 27, 1945; s. Gregor and Rosa (Doerflinger) J. PhD, U. Munich, 1974; Dr. habilitation, U. Bielefeld, Germany, 1988. Rsch. asst. U. Tuebingen, Germany, 1975-79; asst. prof. German lit. U. Bielefeld, 1980-89; full prof. German lit. U. Toronto, Can., 1990-94; prof. German lit. U. Greifswald, Germany, 1994—; vis. prof. U. Kiel, Germany, 1989, U. Padova, Italy, 2000. Author: Deutsche Barockliteratur, 1975, Critica, 1995; co-author: Wieland: Author, Work, Reception, 1994; editor: Der Goldne Spiegel, 1979, L'An 2440, 1982, 89; editor, co-author: Rousseau in Germany, 1995, Kaspar Schoppe (1576-1649): Philologe im Dienste der Gegenreformation, 1998; contbr. articles and book revs. to profl. jours. Mem. MLA, Internat. Soc. of the Classical Tradition, Renaissance Soc. Am. Home: Herderstr 5, D-12163 Berlin Germany Office: Univ Greifswald, D-17487 Greifswald Germany

JAUNAUX, YVES, physician; b. Reims, Champagne, France, July 23, 1944; s. Robert and Jeanne (Hoyet) J.; m. Thérèse Blonde, June 12, 1974; children: Anne, Laure. MD, U. Reims, 1971. Physician various hosps., Reims, 1962-70, Exercice Libéral, La Ferté Gaucher, 1970—; Co-dir. L'Essentiel de L'Actualité Politique et Parlementaire (newspaper), 1986-97; v.p. Club Avenir et Liberté, 1983-87, sec. gen., 1987-97, pres., 1997—. Named Chevalier de l'Ordre du Mérite, 1987. Rassemblement pour la République. Roman Catholic. Avocations: tennis, skiing, sailing, piano. Office: Avenir et Liberté, 18 rue Molière, 75002 Paris France also: 26 rue des Promenades, 77320 La Ferté Gaucher France

JAUSLIN, JEAN-FRÉDÉRIC, library director; b. Neuchâtel, Switzerland, July 31, 1954; s. Emile and Yvonne (Guyot) J.; m. Carol Berthoud, Sept. 15, 1984; children: Jérôme, Pascal, Raphaël. Lic., Univ. Neuchâtel, 1978; PhD, Tech. U., Zurich, 1984. Sci. advisor Winterthur (Switzerland) Ins., 1984-85; head computer sci. dept. Neuchâteloise Ins., 1985-90; dir. Swiss Nat. Libr., Bern, 1990—. Mem. Lions (pres. 1993-94). Office: Swiss Nat Libr, Hallwylstr 15, 3003 Bern Switzerland*

JAVANAYOTHIN, PHLAVUT, electric power industry executive; b. Bangiok, Jan. 1, 1941; s. Suraphol and Wichitra Javanayothin; m. Kannakorn Kumpanatsaenyakorn, Jan. 16 , 1967; 1 child, Kongkamol. B in Engring., Chulalongkorn U., Bangkok, 1962; MSEE, Ill. Inst. Tech., 1970. Engr. Provincial Electricity Authority, Bangkok, 1963-65; asst. regional engr. Provincial Electricity Authority, Lopburi, Thailand, 1965-67; chief sect. Provincial Electricity Authority, Bangkok, 1967-73, engr. level 3, 1973-78, asst. mgr., 1978-87, dir. dept., 1987-94, inspector, 1994-96, asst. gov., 1996-97, dep. gov., 1997—; cons. engr. The Govt., Chiang Rai, Thailand, 1990; com. mem. Chulalongkorn U., Bangkok, 1998, Narasuan U., Phitsanulok, Thailand, 1998; cons. The Indsl. of Thailand, Bangkok, 1998. Cons. The Reps. Parliament, Bangkok, 1997, Internal Security Ops. Command, Bangkok, 1998; com. mem. Office of the Prime Min., Bangkok, 1999. Mem. Engring. Assn. Thailand, Inst. Elec. and Electronics Engrs. Thailand (chmn.), Thai Mech. and Elec. Contractor Assn. (hon.). Office: Provincial Electricity Auth, 200 Ngam Wong Wan Rd, Bangkok 10900, Thailand

JAVERI, SULTANALI MAHOMEDALI, fire protection consultant; b. London, Dec. 26, 1953; s. Mahomedali Cassamali and Fatma (Munjee) J.; m. Christine Leontine Fauche, may 21, 1983; children: Sebastien Sultanali, Florian Georges Sultanali. BS with honors, City U., London, 1975. Chartered mech. engr. Trainee Ministry of Def., U.K., 1975-79; fire prevention engr. Factory Mut. Ins., U.K., 1979-83; boiler and machinery cons. Factory Mut. Ins., Paris, 1983-88; mgr. property loss control Axa Grand Risques, Paris, 1988-95; chief engr. Axa Global Risks, Paris, 1995-98; mgr., sr. account engr. Protection Internat., Paris, 1998-99; exec. dir. Guthel Maroe, Esbly, France, 1999—; cons. tech. coms. Nat. Fire Protection Assn., Boston, 1994—, cons. internat. adv. com., 1997—; cons. Assemblee Pleniere des Socs. D'Assurance Dammages; cons. to the fire coun. Underwriters Lab., Chgo., 1998—; cons. to fire rsch. adv. coun. Nat. Fire Protection Rsch. Found., Boston, 1998—. Contbr. articles to profl. jours. Mem. Nat. Fire Protection Assn., Royal Overseas League, Instn. of Mech. Engrs. Avocations: woodworking, model and tool making, horseback riding. Office: Guthel Maroe ZAC de la Pierre, Tourneville Isles Le Villenoy, 77440 Esbly France

JAVIERRE ORTAS, ANTONIO MARIA CARDINAL, archbishop, writer, educator; b. Sietamo, Huesca, Spain, Feb. 21, 1921. Grad. theology studies, U. Salamanca, U. Louvain, Belgium, U. Pontificia Gregoriana, Rome. Ordained priest Roman Cath. Ch., 1949, joined Order of Salesian Monks, 1951; consecreated archbishop titular Meta, 1976; created cardinal 1988. Prof. theology Ateneo Pontificio Salesiano, Rome, 1959-71, dean faculty theology, 1971, vice chancellor, 1976; with Prefect Congregation for Divine Worship and Discipline of Sacraments, Vatican City; elevated to cardinal Roman Cath. Ch., 1998—; mem. Congregation for Doctrine of Faith, Congregation of Bishops, Congregation of Clergy, Congregation for Cath. Edn., S.T. Signature Apastolicae, and Pontifical Cons. for Promoting Christian Unity, Pontifical Cons. for the Laity; cons. De Legum Textibus. Author: Sucesión apostólica en la I Clem, 1958, Sucesión apostólica en Mt., 1958, El tema literario de la sucesión, 1963, Diálogo ecuménico, 1966, Promoción, conciliar fel diálogo ecuménico, 1966, Il padre tuo che è nel segreto, 1974, Christo Parola e parola di Christo, 1975, La Unión de las Iglesias, 1977, La Educación Universitaria Católica, 1988. Office: Via Rusticucci 13, 00193 Rome Italy*

JAVIER-ZEPEDA, CARLOS ALBERTO, pathologist, laboratory director; b. Comayaguela, Honduras, Mar. 29, 1945; s. Carlos A. Javier-Santos and Andrea (Zepeda) de Javier; m. Jennie E. Medina, June 2, 1947; children: Juan Carlos, Alida, Leonardo. MD, U. Honduras, Tegucigalpa, 1969. Diplomate Am. Bd. Anatomic and Clin. Pathology, Med. Microbiology. Prof. dept. pathology Sch. Medicine U. Honduras, Tegucigalpa, 1975-88; dir. Clin. Microbiology Lab. Hosp. Escuela, Tegucigalpa, Honduras, 1976—, Labs. Medicos, Tegucigalpa, Honduras, 1976—. Editor Medicina Clinica, Tegucigalpa, Honduras. Mem. Am. Soc. Clin. Pathologists (fgn. mem.), Coll. Am. Pathologists (affiliate), Am. Soc. Microbiology. Roman Catholic. Avocations: photography, walking.

JAVITT, JONATHAN C., physician, health policy analyst, writer; b. N.Y.C., Nov. 7, 1956; s. Norman B. and Suzanne (Markovits) J.; m. Marcia C. Fishman, June 29, 1986; children: Zachary, Matthew, Gabrielle. AB with honors, Princeton U., 1978; MD, Cornell U., 1982; MPH, Harvard U., 1984. Diplomate Am. Bd. Ophthalmology. Intern Lenox Hill Hosp., N.Y.C., N.Y., 1982-83; resident Wills Eye Hosp., Phila., 1984-87; fellow Johns Hopkins Hosp., Balt., 1988-89; instr. Johns Hopkins U., 1987-90, asst. prof., 1990-99; prof. Johns Hopkins U., Balt., 1999—; asst. prof. Georgetown U., Washington, 1990-93, assoc. prof., 1993-96; prof. Sch. Medicine, prof. sch. Pub. Policy Georgetown U., Washington, Md., 1996—; founder, chmn. Certitude, Inc., Mpls., 1994—; sr. v.p., nat. med. dir. United Health Care/Applied Health Care Informatics, Mpls., 1997-98; chmn. Health Directions LLC, Bethesda, 1998—; founder, pres., vice chmn. EMEDX, Inc., 1999—; bd. dirs. Brookdale Inst. Social Policy, Am. Joint Distribution Com.; expert cons. Health Care Fin. Adminstrn., Balt., 1987—; spl. employee The White House Health Reform Task Force, Washington, 1992; cons. Nat. Eye Inst./NIH, 1990—, Nat. Inst. Diabetes Digestive and Kidney Disease/NIH, 1991—, Agy. for Health Care Policy Rsch., 1994—, The World Bank, Washington, 1993—, Swedish Coun. on Tech. Improvement, 1997, Japanese Min. of Health, 1993, Australia Min. of Health, 1994—. Sect. editor Archives of Ophthalmology, 1993—, Ophthalmology Times, 1993—; author more than 200 books, chpts., articles; patentee in field. Com. chair Nat. Health Policy Coun., Washington, 1992—; cmty. speaker on health care The White House, 1992—. Recipient Cert. of Appreciation, USAF, 1991, Physician Scientist award Nat. Eye Inst., 1988; U.S. Presdl. Letter of Appreciation, 1993; Kellogg Found. fellow, 1983; guest of honor Japanese Glaucoma Soc., 1996, New England Ophthalmologic Soc., 1997. Fellow Am. Acad. Ophthalmology (Honor award 1990), Am. Glaucoma Soc.; mem. AMA, AOPA, NBAA, Assn. for Rsch. in Vision and Ophthalmology, Assn. for Health Svc. Rsch., Am. Glaucoma Soc., Kehilath Jeshurun, Royal Ocean Racing Club, Princeton Club, Harvard Club, Cosmos Club. Republican. Jewish. Avocations: sailing, aviation. Office: Health Directions LLC 3 Bethesda Metro Ctr Ste 100 Bethesda MD 20814-6310

JÁVOR, TIBOR, internist, pharmacologist, gastroenterologist, educator; b. Debrecen, Hungary, Apr. 10, 1926; s. Jenő Jakobovics and Hermina Rosenfeld; m. Kornelia Terner, Jan. 18, 1979; 1 child, István. MD, U. Med. Sch., Debrecen, 1951. Asst. prof. U. Med. Sch., Debrecen, 1951-58; assoc. prof. U. Med. Sch., Szeged, Hungary, 1958-68; prof., head dept. Pècs (Hungary) U. Med. Sch., 1968-93; med. advisor Kèri Pharma, Budapest, 1997—. Author 12 textbooks of internal medicine; mem. editl. bd. Clin. Pharmacology Rsch.; contbr. over 200 articles to profl. jours. Mem. Hungarian Gastroent. Soc. (pres. 1978-88), Drug Registration Com. E-mail: h13775jar@ella.hu. Home and Office: Lónyay Str 19, 1093 H Budapest Hungary

JAVORKA, KAMIL, physiologist, educator; b. Teplicka n Vah, Zilina, Slovakia, July 5, 1944; s. Adolf and Anna (Singliarova) J.; m. Jana Benovska, Oct. 8, 1945; children: Kamil, Michal. MD, Comenius U., Bratislava, Slovakia, 1968, PhD, 1975, Habilitation, 1981, DSc, 1991. Asst. dept.

physiology faculty medicine Comenius U., Martin, Slovakia, 1968-81, assoc. prof. faculty medicine, 1981-91, prof. faculty medicine, 1991—; head dept. physiology Comenius U., 1986—, vice dean Jessenius Med. Faculty, 1996—; sci.-sec. European Respiratory Soc. Work Group Reg. Breathing, Paris, 1995—; assoc. mem. com. clin. physiology Internat. Union of Physiol. Scis., 1995—. Author: Circulation in Fetuses (in Slovak), 1992 (Slovak Lit. Found. prize 1993), Clinical Pediatric Physiology (in Slovak), 1996, (textbook) Practical Course in Physiology, 1993. Recipient Laufberger's medal Czechoslovakia Physiology Soc., 1991, Silver medal Comenius U., 1993, Silver medal Slovak Med. Soc., 1994. Mem. Slovak Soc. Physiology Pathology Breathing (pres. 1993—), Slovak Physiology Soc. (v.p. 1993—), N.Y. Acad. Scis. Home: Moyzesova N 19, 036 01 Martin Slovakia Office: Comenius Univ Jessenius Med, Mala Hora 4 Dept Physiology, 037 54 Martin Slovakia

JAVORSKA, MAGDA, psychologist; b. Ostrava, Czech Republic, Oct. 10, 1950; d. Karel and Stepanka (Stiborova) Filip; m. Magda Filipova Javorska, Feb. 10, 1973; children: Eva, Zora. Degree in Psychology, U. Palackeho, Czech Republic, 1979, PhD, 1987. Trade asst. C-C Co., Czech Republic, 1971-73; mgr. House of Technic, Ostrava, Czech Republic, 1973-76; rsch. worker Rsch. Inst., Ostrava, Czech Republic, 1979-87; psychologist City Hosp. Ostrava, Czech Republic, 1987—. Office: MNOF, Janovskeho 8, 72880 Ostrava Czech Republic

JAW, TWEI-SHIUN, pediatric radiologist, educator; b. Nan-Tou, Taiwan, Republic of China, Dec. 12, 1952; s. Kun-Chan and Chin-Chih (Lai) J.; m. Meng-Chuan Chiang, Jan. 7, 1972; Yen-Chun, Min-Wu, Min-Fang. MB, Kaohsiung (Taiwan) Med. Coll., 1978, M in Med. Sci., 1984. Resident Kaohsiung Med. Coll. Hosp., 1978-82, lectr., 1984-91; assoc. prof. Kaohsiung Med. Coll., 1991-99; prof. radiology and pediats. Kaohsiung Med. U., 1999—; vis. staff Kaohsiung Med. U. Hosp.; fellow in pediat. radiology U. Tsukuba, Ibaraki, Japan, 1985; fellow in pediat. radiology Internat. Cath. Hosp., Tokyo, 1986. Co-author: Teaching Files of Computed Tomography, 1978; contbr. more than 30 articles to profl. jours. Mem. Radiol. Soc. Rep. China, Soc. Ultrasound Medicine (supr. 1994-96, 98—), Radiol. Soc. N.Am. (corr.), Taiwan Pediat. Assn., Formosan Med. Assn. Avocations: travel, bridge, swimming. E-mail: jaw4241@ms23.hinet.net. Office: Kaohsiung Med U Hosp, 100 Shih-Chuan 1st Rd, Kaohsiung, Taiwan 807, Republic of China

JAWAD, ABDUL JALIL, anthropology educator, researcher; b. Musaiyab, Babil, Iraq, Jan. 15, 1926; s. Jawad Hammoud Kambar and Hashmiyah Fadhidl; m. Johanna Jabaay, Jan. 15, 1964; children: Jamil, Samir, Ferida, Besim, Karim. License, Higher Tchrs. Coll., Iraq, 1947; MA, U. Chgo., 1957, PhD, 1962. Tchr. secondary sch. Iraq, 1947-53; supr. Directoral of Antiquies, Iraq, 1962-63; conservator Mus. of Ethnology, Holland, 1964-68, analyst, rschr., 1976-77; lectr. U. Eastern Ill., 1968-69, assoc. prof., 1969-71; asst. prof. Coll. of Art, U. Baghdad, Iraq, 1971-75; social rschr. Royal Tropical Inst., Holland, 1977-84; ret. Author: The Advent of the Era of Township in Northern Mesopotamia, 1965.

JAWAD, SAID TAYEB (SAID TAYEB DJAWAD), political commentator, writer; b. Kandahr, Afghanistan, Feb. 27, 1958; came to U.S., 1986; s. Mir Hussain and zakia Shah; m. Shamim Rahman, Nov. 16, 1986. Student, Kabul (Afghanistan) U., 1976-80, Wilhelms U., Muenster, Germany, 1984-86, Long Island U., 1986. Paralegal Lehnardt & Bauman, N.Y.C., 1988-89, Steefel, Levitt & Weiss, San Francisco, 1989—; polit. commentator various newspapers, radio and TV stas. including BBC. Editor weekly newspaper OMAID, 1992-95; pub. Substratum of Human Rights Violations in Afghanistan, Modern Dictatorship, The United States and the Afghan Resistance, Soviets Expansionto the South, Fundamentalism in Central Asia; contbr. articles to BBC World Reports (London) and to profl. jours. throughout world. Bd. dirs. Afghanistan Cultural Soc., San Francisco, 1990-92; mem. Internat. Soc. for Human Rights, Frankfort, Germany, 1983-86; mem. nat. adv. bd. Info. Am., Atlanta, 1991-94; active Amnesty Internat., N.Y.C., 1987—. Mem. World Affairs Coun. Home: One St Francis Pl # 3506 San Francisco CA 94107

JAWAHEER, GIRISH, pediatric surgeon, researcher; b. Phoenix, Mauritius, Aug. 6, 1963; s. Sanjaye and Somlata (Ramdaursingh) J.; m. Catherine Louise Conway, Oct. 22, 1993. MB, ChB, U. Manchester, Eng., 1988. Sr. house officer in pediatric surgery Royal Liverpool (Eng.) Children's Hosp., 1991, registrar, 1992; sr. house officer in gen. surgery Countess of Chester (Eng.) Hosp., 1991-92; rsch. fellow Fazakerley Hosp., Liverpool, 1992-95; specialist registrar in pediatric surgery Royal Hosp. for Sick Children, Edinburgh, Scotland, 1995-97, Royal Victoria Infirmary, Newcastle-Upon-Tyne, Eng., 1997-99; fellow in pediatric hepatobiliary surgery/liver transplant Children's Meml. Hosp., Chgo., 1999—. Contbr. articles to med. jours., including Archives of Disease in Childhood, Early Human Devel., Archives Disease in Childhood, European Jour. Pediatric Surgery, Am. Jour. Ob-Gyn. Recipient 1st prize for best presentation Liverpool Pediatric Club, 1995, 1st prize for best poster Brit. Assn. Parenteral and Enteral Nutrition, 1995. Fellow Royal Coll. Surgeons (Eng.); mem. Brit. Assn. Pediatric Surgeons (assoc., presenter Rotterdam 1994, Sheffield, Eng. 1995, Jersey, 1996, Istanbul, Turkey 1997), Scottish Soc. Pediatric Surgeons. Avocations: swimming, gardening, music, travel. Office: Childrens Meml Hosp 2300 N Childrens Plz Chicago IL 60614-3394

JAWAN, JAYUM ANAK, political science educator; b. Malaysia, Oct. 12, 1958. BA in Polit. Economy, U. N.C., 1980; MA in Polit. Sci. Internat. Rels., Appalachian State U., 1982; PhD in Politics and Devel. S.E. Asia, U. Hull, Eng., 1992. Grad. tchg. asst. polit. sci. Appalachian State U., Boone, N.C., 1981; lectr. social scis. Faculty Ednl. Studies U. Pertanian Malaysia, 1982—, sr. lectr. social sciences, 1990—; assoc. prof. social devel. studies Faculty Human Ecology U. Putra Malaysia, 1994—; part-time lectr. in social scis. U. Malaysia Sarawak, 1995-96; cons. Malaysian Strategic Rsch. Ctr., 1996, cons. various private colls. offering Malaysian Politics and Govt. course, 1998, cons., Natl. Bd. of Accreditation, Ministry of Edn. on the Malaysian Studies Curriculum, 1998, Ministry Edn., 1998; participant, attendee seminars, symposia, and confs. Mem. editl. bd. Malaysian Jour. Social Rsch., 1992, Jour. Dinamika, 1995; contbr. chpts. to books; contbr. articles to profl. jours. Grantee Brit. Coun., 1995; recipient scholarships Trinity United Meth. Ch. (U.S.), 1977-79, Lee Found., 1977-80, Fed. Govt. Malaysia, 1980-81, Sir Frederick Galleghan Meml. award Australia-Singapore-Malaysia Assn., U. Sydney, 1986. Fellow Borneo Rsch. Coun.; mem. Malaysia Social Scis. Assn. (v.p. 1996-97), Inst. Consultancy, Malaysian Assn. for Am. Studies. Office: U Putra Malaysia, Dept Social Devel Studies, 43400 Serdang, Selangor Malaysia

JAWIEŃ, JACEK, physician researcher; b. Cracow, Poland, Nov. 28, 1965; s. Eugeniusz and Halina (Pławny) J. MD with honors, Jagiellonian U., Cracow, 1990, PhD with honors, 1994. Asst. Dept. Allergy and Clin. Immunology, Cracow, 1990-97, Dept. Pharmacology, Cracow, 1997—. Contbr. articles to profl. jours. Mem. European Soc. Clin. Investigation (councillor coun. 1998-2001), N.Y. Acad. Scis. Avocations: history. Home: Kolberga 14/7, 31-160 Cracow Poland Office: Dept Pharmacology, Grzegórzecka 16, 31-531 Cracow Poland

JAWORSKA, TAMARA, painter, tapestry maker; b. Archangel, Russia; arrived in Can., 1969; d. Antonio Jankowski; m. Tadeusz Jaworski, 1957; children: Eva, Pyotr. BFA with honors, State Acad. Fine Arts, Lodz, Poland, 1950, MFA in Art Weaving, 1952; M of Painting honoris causa, Accademia Italia, 1982. From asst. prof. to sr. asst. prof., lectr. Stae Acad. Fine Arts, Poland, 1952-58. Exhibited in solo shws at Leo Kamen Gallery, Toronto, Art Galleries of London and Windsor, Ont., Glendon Art Gallery, Toronto, Art Gallery of Hamilton, also exhibits in France, West Germany, Belgium, Switzerland, luxembourg; group exhbns. include Warsaw and Lodz art galleries, Pushkin Mus., European Art Gallery, Moscow, Richard Demarco Gallery, Edinburgh, Fine Art Mus., Plymouth, Eng., Merton Gallery, Toronto, Hermitage Leningrad Mus., USSR, Nat. Art Gallery, Tehran, Mus. Modern Art, Mexico City, Art Gallery of Ont., RCA-Art 2000, Toronto and Stratford, 2000; exhibited tapestires at New Coll., Galerie Inard, Ctr. Nat. de la Tapisserie d'Abusson, Paris, later in Madrid, Barcelona, Valencia, San Sebastian, Paris, Munich, Zurich, others; works in permanent collections of Pushkin Nat. Mus., European Art Gallery, Moskau, Russia, Nat. Mus., Warsaw, Nat. Mus. of Textile Arts, Lodz, Poland, Nat. Mus. of Home Army, King City, Krakow, Poland, Galashields Art Inst., Scotland, Bank of Montreal, Toronto, Bell Can., Ottawa, Molson Canadian, Toronto, Mutual Ins. of Can., Toronto and many corp. and pvt. collections in Europe, Am., Mid. East; subject of articles in art books and mags. Decorated Order of Can.; recipient Interior Design and Architecture award Triennale de Milano, 1957, award for excellence Montreal, 1973, Golden Centaur award Academia Italia, 1982, Gold medal and 1st prize Internat. Juried Art competition, N.Y.c., 1985, Commemorative medal Can. Fedn., 1993. Fellow Royal Coll. Art; mem. Royal Acad. Arts, Accademia Italia delle Arti e del Lavoro (academician). E-mail: tamtad@ica.net. Home: 49 Don River Blvd, Toronto, ON Canada M2N2M8

JAY, CHRISTOPHER EDWARD, stockbroker; b. Walla Walla, Wash., May 2, 1949; s. Orville Elmo and Juanita Hope (Beckius) J.; m. Mardra Marguerite Jones, July 25, 1981; children: Pohaku Kepano, Hope Lauren, Christopher James. BS, Lewis and Clark Coll., 1972; MA, U. Nev., 1975. 1st v.p. Merrill Lynch & Co., Anchorage, 1975—. Dist. chair Rep. Cen. Com., Anchorage, 1980-81; bd. trustees Lewis and Clark Coll., Portland, Oreg., 1988—; bd. dirs. Anchorage Mus. History and Art Found., 1988-90, KSKA Pub. Radio, Anchorage, 1991-93, Alaska Pub. Broadcasting Inc., Anchorage, Providence Hosp. Found., Anchorage; bd. dirs., treas. Anchorage Symphony Orch.; active 1st Presbyn. Ch., Anchorage. Named one of nation's top brokers Registered Rep. mag., 1995, 1998 Broker Hall of Fame, Rsch. Mag., 1998; recipient Disting. Alumni award Lewis and Clark Coll., 1996. Mem. Rotary (pres. Anchorage chpt. 1989-90, Paul Harris fellow 1989, co-chmn. dist. conv. 1997, elected del. to nat. Rep. conv. 2000). Republican. Presbyterian. Avocations: reading, walking, travel, civic activities. Home: 11060 Hideaway Lake Dr Anchorage AK 99516-1183 Office: Merrill Lynch & Co 3601 C St Fl 14 Anchorage AK 99503-5925

JAYABALAN, NARAYANASAMY, botanist, researcher; b. Mahadevimangalam, Tamil Nadu, India, Jan. 19, 1954; s. Suruttaipillai Narayanasamy and Narayanasamy Kuppu Ammal; m. Jayabalan Menaka, May 27, 1981; children: Nirmal Jayabalan, Yamini Jayabalan. BSc in Botany, Govt. Arts Coll., Tiruvannamalai, India, 1975; MSc in Botany, Presidency Coll., Madras, India, 1977; PhD in Botany, Bharathidasan U., Trichy, India, 1988. Tech. asst. Bharathidasan U., Tiruchy, India, 1982-89, lectr. plant sci., 1989-96, reader plant sci., 1996—; consulting botanist Bharathidasan U., Tiruchy, India, 1985—, treas. faculty forum, 1997. Contbr. articles to profl. jours., newsletters. Mem. Indian Botanical Soc. (life), Indian Soc. for Genetics and Plant Breeding, Swamy Botanical Club (life), N.Y. Acad. Scis. Avocations: watching TV, reading, gardening. Home: HC 672 Anna Nagar, Tamil Nadu, Tiruchirapalli 620 026, India Office: Bharathidasan Univ, Palkaliperur Tamil Nadu, Tiruchirapalli 620 024, India

JAYAKUMAR, SHUNMUGAM, Singapore government official; b. Singapore, Aug. 12, 1939; m. Lalitha Rajahram, 1969; 3 children. Student, U. Singapore, Yale U. Permanent rep. of Singapore to U.N., 1971-74, high commr. to Can., 1971-74; dean, prof. Law Faculty, U. Singapore, 1974-80; m.p. Govt. of Singapore, 1980—, min. state for law and home affairs, 1981-83, min. labour, 1983-85, min. home affairs, 1985-94, min. law, 1988—, min. fgn. affairs, 1994—. Contbr. articles to profl. jours. Office: Ministry of Fgn Affairs, 250 North Bridge Rd # 07-00, Raffles City Tower Singapore Singapore 179101

JAYAPRAKASHA, GUDDADARANGAVVANA HALLYKRISHNAREDDY, chemistry educator; b. Chitradurga, Hindu, India, July 20, 1961; d. K. Krishna and M.R. Puttamma Reddy; m. S.V. Savitha Jayaprakasha, June 27, 1993; 2 children. BSc, Mysore (India) U., 1983, MSc, 1985. Quality control chemist Belur Alginates (P) Ltd., Mysore, 1986-87; plant supr. Kap-Chem. Ltd., Mysore, 1988. Flavours & Essences (P) Ltd., Mysore, 1988-90; jr. sci. asst. Ctrl. Food Technol. Rsch. Inst., Mysore, 1990-95, sr. sci. asst., 1995—. Inventor in field; contbr. articles to profl. jours. Mem. Assn. Food Scientists and Technologists India (life). Home: C-40 Cftri Staff Quarters, Mysore 570 013, India Office: Ctrl Food Technol Rsch Inst, Mysore 570 013, India

JAYARAMAIAH, KARAGADA MUNISWAMAPPA, academic administrator; b. Venkatagiri kote, Karnataka, India, July 25, 1937; s. Karagada Hosur Narayanamma Muniswamappa; m. Subbareddy Thejovathi, May 9, 1965; children: J. Shiva Prasad, J. Mamatha, J. Prashanth. BSc, Coll. Agriculture, Bangalore, India, 1960; MS, Inst. Agriculture, Knoxville, Tenn., 1972; PhD, Indian Agrl. Rsch. Inst., New Delhi, India, 1981. Agrl. ext. officer Dept. Agrl., India, 1960-66; instr. U. Agrl. Scis., Dharwad, India, 1966-72; training officer U. Agril. Scis., Bangalore, India, 1972-75; ext. leader, 1975-80; prof. agrl. ext. U. Agrl. Scis., Bangalore, India, 1981-93, regional coord., 1993-96, registrar, 1996-97, retired, 1997—. Editor Mysore Jour. Agrl. Scis., 1983-86, Current Research, 1983-86; editor: Agricultural Education & Rural Development, 1986, Rural Development: Selected Strategies & Case Studies, 1985, Afforestation & Wastelands Development, 1994; contbr. articles to profl. publs. Indian Agrl. Rsch. Inst. scholar, New Delhi, 1977-80; fellow U.S. Agy. Internat. Dev., Washington, 1970-72. Mem. Internat. Fed. Women in Agriculture, Indian Soc. Ext. Edn. (v.p. 1996-99), Internat. Coun., Internat. Union of Forestry Rsch. Orgns. Austria, Lions Club (appreciation award, 1991, pres. Bangalore Hebbal chpt. 1990-91, dist. chmn. agriculture and tree planting com. 1991-92). ISKCON. Avocations: social svc., reading. Home: 103 B 3rd Main 6th Cross, Ganganagar Bangalore 560 032, India

JAYATILAKA, DYLAN, chemist; b. Kuala Lumpur, Malaysia, Apr. 4, 1966; s. Basil D. and Grace M. (Samuel) J.; children: Brynne Michelle, Tamlyn Kelsey. BSc with honors, U. Western Australia, Perth, 1987; PhD, Cambridge (Eng.) U., 1992. Nat. rsch. coun. rsch. assoc. NASA Ames Rsch. Ctr., 1992-93; rsch. fellow U. Western Australia, Perth, 1972-93, Australian rsch. coun. rsch. fellow, 1993-95, Queen Elizabeth II rsch. fellow, 1995—. Office: U Western Australia, Dept Chemistry, 6907 Perth Australia

JAYAWARDENA, A.S., banker. Gov. Cen. Bank Sri Lanka, 1995—. Office: Cen Bank Sri Lanka POB 590, No 30 Janadhipathi Mawatha, Colombo 00100, Sri Lanka

JAYNE, JOHN EBEN, mathematician, educator; b. Davenport, Iowa, May 29, 1943; s. John E. and Helen (Loose) J. AB, U. Calif., Berkeley, 1965; PhD, Columbia U., 1971; DSc, U. London, 1986; DSc (honoris causa), U. Sofia, 1996, U. Shoumen, 1998. Prof. math. U. London, 1972—; vis. prof. various univs. Austria, Czech Republic, France, Italy, Poland, Russia, Spain, U.S. Contbr. over 1000 pages to profl. math. rsch. jours. Grantee govts. of 5 countries, NATO, European Cmty. Mem. Am. Math. Soc., London Math. Soc. Home: 47 Fitzroy St, 4 Fitzroy House, London W1P 5HR, England Office: Univ Coll London-Dept Math, Gower St, London WC1E 6BT, England

JAYSON, MALCOLM IV, rheumatology educator; b. London; m. Judi Tauber; children: Gordon, Robert. MB, BChir, U. London; MD, U. Bristol; MSc, U. Manchester. Cons., sr. lectr. U. Bristol and Royal Nat. Hosp. for Rheumatic Diseases, Bath, Eng., 1967-77; prof. rheumatology U. Manchester, 1977-99, emeritus prof. rhematology, 1997—; past pres. Arachnoiditis Trust, Rheumatology sect. Royal Soc. Medicine. Author: Back Pain: The Facts, Rheumatism and Arthritis, Understanding Back Pain. Fellow Royal Coll. Physicians London; mem. Brit. Soc. for Rheumatology (hon. Heberden libr.), Internat. Soc. for Study of the Lumbar Spine (pres.), European Spine Soc., Australian Spine Soc. (hon.), Soc. Chiropodists and Podiatrists (hon., pres.). Avocations: antiques, clocks, sundials, game fishing. Home: The Gate House, 8 Lancaster Rd Didsbury, Manchester M20 2TY, England Office: Rheumatic Diseases Ctr, Hope Hosp, Salford M6 8HD, England

JAYSON, RICHARD ANDREW, accountant; b. London, June 16, 1968; s. Bernard Ronald and Carole Linda (Aarons) J.; m. Belinda Nicole Brahams, June 2, 1996. B of Elec. Engrng. with honors, Leeds U., England, 1990. Mgr. Price Waterhouse, England, 1991-97; sr. mgr. Price Waterhouse Coopers, Israel, 1997-99, England, 1999—; advisor Israeli High Tech. Industry, 1997—. Mem. IEEE, ICEAW. Office: Pricewaterhouse Coopers, 10 Bricket Rd, Saint Albans AL1 3JX, England

JAZDZEWSKI, KRZYSZTOF HENRYK, zoologist, hydrobiologist, educator; b. Warsaw, Poland, Nov. 27, 1938; s. Konrad and Stefania (Jasnorzewska) J.; m. Teresa Zofia Pawłowska, June 22, 1963; children: Krzysztof Leszek, Anna Maria. MSc in Zoology, U. Łódź, Poland, 1960, MSc in Biochemistry, 1963, DSc in Biol. Scis., 1967. Tech. asst. Inst. Zoology Polish Acad. Sci., Łodź, 1960-62; asst. dept. gen. zoology U. Łódź, 1962-68, adj., 1968-76, assoc. prof., 1976-89, prof. dept. invertebrate zoology and hydrobiology, 1989—; dir. Inst. Environ. Biology, U. Łódź, 1981-83, head lab. polar biology and oceanbiology, 1983—, head dept. invertebrate zoology and hydrobiology, 1983-90, vice rector, 1990-96; mem. presidium com. zoology Polish Acad. Sci., 1990—, presidium (v.p.) com. on polar rsch., 1996—, com. marine rsch., 1999—. Author: Malacostraca-Catalogus faunae Poloniae Vol. 13, 1995 (prize Ministry of Edn. 1996); editor-in-chief Folia limnologica Acta U. Łódź, 1983-89, Polish Polar Rsch., 1985—. Decorated Knight's Cross of Polonia Restituta Order, Pres. of Poland, 1993. Mem. Royal Inst. Natural Sci. of Belgium (rsch. assoc.), Crustacean Soc., Biol. Soc. of Wash. Roman Catholic. Avocations: skiing, scuba diving, canoeing. Home: Apt 260, Łagiewnicka st 102/116, 91-456 Łódź Poland Office: U Łódź, Banacha St 12/16, 90-237 Łódź Poland

JE, IMSHUN, hydrogeologist; b. Toronto, Ont., Can., Dec. 27, 1971; s. Jin Wan and Fumiko Tsuchida Je. BSc with honors, U. Toronto, 1995, MSc in Geology, 1997. Rsch. asst. U. Toronto, 1994-95, tchg. asst., 1995-97; geologist Ghana Mining, Toronto, 1997; hydrogeologist Azimuth Environ., Barrie, Ont., 1997-98; project hydrogeologist Handex of Ill., Naperville, 1998—. Contbr. chpt. to book in field. Fellow U. Toronto, 1995, 96; undergrad. summer rsch. fellow Nat. Sci. and Engring. Rsch. Coun. Can., 1994; J.P. and C.P Dickson geology scholar, 1994. Mem. Internat. Assn. Hydrogeologists, Assn. Geoscientists of Ont. Avocations: spiritual learning, hiking, skiing, painting. Fax: (630) 527-8174. E-mail: ije@handexmail.com. Home: 1811 4 Lakes Ave Apt 3K Lisle IL 60532-2908 Office: Handex of Ill 1701 Quincy Ave Ste 31 Naperville IL 60540-6683

JEAN, (BENOIT GUILLAUME MARIE ROBERT LOUIS ANTOINE ADOLPHE MARC D'AVIANO), Grand Duke of Luxembourg; b. Berg Castle, Luxembourg, Jan. 5, 1921; s. Felix, Prince of Bourbon-Parma and Prince of Luxembourg and Charlotte, Grand-Duchess of Luxembourg; m. Princess Josephine-Charlotte of Belgium, Apr. 9, 1953; children: Marie Astrid, Henri (hereditary grand duke), Jean, Margaretha, Guillaume. Ed., Luxembourg and Ampleforth Coll., Eng., Laval (Que., Can.) U., 1940-42; Dr. Hon., Miami U., Oxford, Ohio, 1979, Strasbourg U., 1957. Mem. Luxembourg Council of State, 1951-61; lt.-rep. of Grand Duchess, 1961-64, grand duke of Luxembourg, 1964—, chief scout of Luxembourg, 1945—; col. regiment Irish Guards, 1984—; mem. Internat. Olympic Com., 1946—. Served as capt. Irish Guards, Brit. Army, 1942-45; col. Luxembourg Army, 1945, gen., 1964. Decorated Croix de Guerre (Luxembourg, France, Belgium and The Netherlands); Silver Star (U.S.). Home: Chateau de Berg, Colmar-Berg L-2013, Luxembourg Office: Grand Ducal Palace, L-2013, Luxembourg Luxembourg

JÉAN, ROSARIE PAMELLA, elementary education educator; b. Kingston, Jamaica, Apr. 18, 1958; d. Roal George Mitchell and Barbara Theresa Escoffery; m. Francis Jean, Sept. 17, 1988; children: Aymar Christian, Mikhail D'Amore. BA in Psychology, UCLA, 1982; cert. in facility mgmt., NYU, 1998; M in Secondary Edn., Mercy Coll. Sales mgr. Macy's East Inc., N.Y.C., 1985-87, MIS coord., 1988-90, ops. mgr., 1991-99, com. person, parade ofcl., 1993-99, asst. buyer, 1997-98; instr. Eleanor Roosevelt Middle Sch., N.Y.C., 1999—. Coach Closter Jr. Football League, 1999—, dir. Closter cheerleaders, 1999—. Avocations: reading, developing programs for children. E-mail: dvinedestiny@aol.com. Home: 91 Chestnut Ave Closter NJ 07624-3101

JEANGUILLAUME, CHRISTIAN, physician, physicist; b. Paris, Jan. 29, 1951; s. Rene and Marie-Therese (Eude) J.; m. Liliane Doulanjon, Oct. 27, 1984; children: Arnaud, Marine. MD, U. Paris XII, Creteil, 1979; CES nuclear medicine, U. Paris V, 1982; PhD in Physics, U. Paris XI, Orsay, 1989. Maitre de conf. praticien hospitalier faculte de medecine Creteil. Rschr. CNRS Lab. de Physique des Solides LA002, Faculte des Scis., Orsay, 1979—; asst. des Hopitaux asst. des univ. Assistance Publique Hosp. Henri Mondor Faculte de Medecine, Creteil, 1980-85, maitre de conf. des Univ. Praticien Hosp., 1986. Contbr. articles to profl. jours.; inventor in field. Mem. IEEE (assoc.), Soc. Francaise de Medecine Nucleaire, European Assn. Nuclear Medicine. Office: Lab de Physique des Solides, Faculte des Scis 91405 Orsay France

JEANNE, PIERRE PAUL, retired chief financial officer; b. Montigny, France, May 29, 1932; s. Louis and Anne-Marie (Malherbe) J.; 1 child, Katherine. Grad. econs., Conservatoire National des Arts et Metiers, Paris, 1985. Asst. chief acct. Selection Du Reader's Digest, Paris, 1960-68, controller, 1968-83, chief fin. officer, 1983-92. Served with French Army, 1952-56. Avocation: scuba diving. Office: Reader's Digest France, 5-7 Ave Louis Pasteur, 92220 Bagneux France

JEBANESAN, SUBRAMANIAM SEBANESAN, bishop; b. Manipay, Sri-Lanka, Mar. 28, 1940; s. Narayanapillai and Kanagammah (Vinasithamby) Subramanian; m. Seeta Vimalalakshmi Rajakulendran Jebanesan; children: Hyacinth Nirmalene Christene Gitanjely. BA, U. Ceylon, Peradeniya, Sri-Lanka, 1962; BDiv, U. Serampore, India, 1979; MA, U. Sri-Lanka, Peradeniya, 1981; PhD, U. Jaffna, Sri-Lanka, 1987. Tchr. English lang. St. Anthony's Coll., Kandy, Sri-Lanka, 1962-69; tchr. English and history Jaffna Coll., Vaddukaddai, Sri-Lanka, 1969-75, vice prin., 1986-88, prin., 1988-93; bishop Jaffna Diocese, Ch. South India, Sri-Lanka, 1993—. Author: Contribution Made to Tamil by the American Missionaries, 1985, The Higher Educational Enterprize of the American Missionaries who Served in Sri-Lanka, 1990. Coun. mem., selection com. for mgmt. studies faculty Jaffna U., 1990—; patron Sri-Lanka Red Cross Com., Valigamam West, 1991-93. Office: Ch South India, 39 Fussels Ln, Colombo 06, Sri Lanka

JEBSI, KHAILEDDINE, economist, educator; b. Sousse, Tunisia, Sept. 17, 1968; m. Béchir Jebsi and Farjia Kalthouni; m. Chahnez Jaafoura, Aug. 10, 1998. Degree in Econs., Faculty de Droit et Dose Econ., Montepellier, 1990, lic., 1991, maîtrise, 1992, DEA, 1993; PhD, Faculty de Droit et Dose Econ., 1995, 96. Asst. prof. CNAM, Millau, France, 1994-96, ISG, Tunis, Tunisia, 1997, Faculté Sch. Econs., Sousse, Tunisia, 1997-98; master asst. prof. Faculté Sch. Econs., Sousse, 1998—; rschr. LAMETA, Montpellier, 1993—.

JECH, ČESTMÍR, physical chemist, researcher; b. Bezdědice, Czech Republic, Nov. 22, 1925; s. Alois and Jana (Kaulerova) J.; m. Naděžda Zelenkova, Nov. 2, 1950; children: Libor, Tomas. D Natural Scis., U. Charles, Praha, Czech Republic, 1950, DS, 1991. Rschr. Inst. Phys. Chemistry, Acad. Sci., Praha, 1953—; lectr. in nuclear chemistry U. Charles, 1957-70. Author: Radioactive Aerosols, 1955, Interaction of Energetic Ions in Solids, 1974; co-author: Nuclear Methods in Chemical Research, 1989; contbr. articles to profl. jours. Hon. mem. environ. orgn. Children of the Earth, Praha, 1990. Recipient State prize Pres. of Czech Republic, 1954, J. Heyrovsky medal Czechoslovakian Acad. Sci., 1985. Mem. Czech Chem. Soc., Union Czech Math. and Physics (hon. medal 1996). Avocations: arts, wood carving. Office: Inst Phys Chemistry, Dolejškova 3, 182 23 Praha 8, Czech Republic

JECHOVA-VOISINE, HANA, humanities educator; b. Humpolec, Czechoslovakia, Apr. 19, 1927; naturalized French citizen, 1978; d. Bohumil and Božena (Bartáková) Sánerová; m. Vladimir Jech, July 10, 1948 (div. June 1975); m. Jacques Renè Voisine, Dec. 21, 1984. PhD, Charles U., Prag, Czechoslovakia, 1951; Candidata Scientiarum, Acad. Scis., Prag, Czechoslovakia, 1962; Dr. habilitation, U. Warsaw, Poland, 1965; Dr. d'Etat, U Paris III, 1972. Editl. staff Pedagogical Pub. Inst., Prag, 1951-55; reader Polish lit. U. Olomouc, Czechoslovakia, 1955-69; reader comparative lit. U. Paris III, 1969-71, vis. prof., 1978-82; vis. prof. Czech lang. and lit. U. Paris, 1982-86, prof., 1986-95; ret., 1995; mem. mng. com. Writers' Assn., Prag, 1953-69; vis. prof. comparative lit. U. François Rabelais, Tours, France, 1971-73, 76-78. Contbr. articles to profl. jours. Decorated chevalier Legion of Honor (France). Home: 57 rue Jean le Galleu, 94200 Ivry Sur Seine France

JEDINAKOVA-KRIZOVA, VĚRA, chemist, educator; b. Prague, Czech Republic, Apr. 21, 1940; d. Jan Slanec and Ruzena (Brabcová) Slancová; m. Petr Jedinák, Nov. 11, 1962 (div. 1979); 1 child, Petr; m. Rudolf Kříž, Nov. 28, 1991. MSc, Inst. Chem. Tech., Prague, 1962, PhD, 1966; DSc in Nuclear Chemistry Engring., Tech. U., Prague, 1987. Expert for environ. impact assessment of Czech Republic, 1994—. Asst. prof. Inst. Chem. Tech., Prague, 1966-69, sr. rsch. scientist, 1969-84, leading rsch. scientist, 1984-86, prof. nuclear chemistry, 1987—; chairperson Commn. for PhD Program, Prague, 1986-93; mem. Commn. for DSc Program, Czech Republic and Slovakia, 1999—; vis. investigator Inst. Stable Isotope, Dresden, Germany, 1967-70, Royal Tech. U., Stockholm, 1975; adviser Ministry of Environment, Prague, 1996-99. Co-authors: Recent Developments in Separation Science, 1986, (textbooks) Extraction Separation of Radionuclides, 1986, Gama Spectrometry in Laboratory Praxis, 1992, 93, 97; contbr. over 160 articles to profl. jours. Grantee Agy. of Czech Republic, 1997—. Mem. Czech Chem. Soc. (chmn. nuclear chemistry sect. 1991-96, vice-chmn. 1996—). Home: Pretlucka 1/2154, 100 00 Prague 10, Czech Republic Office: Inst Chem Tech, Technická 5, 166 28 Prague 6, Czech Republic

JEDLICKA, MIROSLAV, electronic engineer, researcher; b. Simonovice, Czech Republic, Sept. 30, 1929; s. Josef Antonin and Anna (Urbanova) J.; m. Olga Marie Souckova Jedlickova, Oct. 1, 1957; children: Ivan, Petr. MS, Czech Tech. U., Prague, 1952; PhD, 1961. Tutor Elec. Faculty of Czech Tech. U., Prague, 1952-53; researcher Vacuum Electronics Rsch. Inst., Prague, 1953-67, chief of research, 1967-88; scientific sec. TESLA Vacuum Engring., Prague, 1988-90; dir., 1991-92; pres. Czech and Slovak Soc. for Photonics, Prague, 1992—; lectr., examiner Elec. Faculty Czech Tech. U., Prague, 1957-87; cons. Czechoslovk Office for Standards and Measurement, 1961-89. Author: Photoelectricity, 1975; co-author of six books on photoelectronic image devices and camera tubes, 1963-85; author, co-author of more than 250 articles and papers to profl. jours. Mem. Czech Olympic Com., Prague, 1993-96; pres. Ski Assn. of Czech Republic, 1968-70, 90-94. Mem. Internat. Measurement Confedn. (sec.), Czech and Slovak Soc. for Photonics. Achievements include finding of technology of effective Te-Cs-Rb-Na-K-Sb and Sb-Rb-Cs photocathodes for photomultipliers and image devices, finding of technology of sprayed CdSe layers and amorphous Si layers for television camera tubes, determination of conditions for photomultiplier stability. Home: Jemenska 581, 16000 Prague Czech Republic

JEDRYSEK, MARIUSZ ORION, geoscience educator; b. Gklibczyce, Poland, Apr. 28, 1962; s. Zdzislaw and Jozefa (Stefaniszyn) J.; m. Albina Anna Wroblewska Jedrysek, Aug. 11, 1984; 1 child, Tymoteusz. MS, U. Wroclaw, Poland, 1985, PhD, 1989. Postdoc. fellow Mitsubishi Kasei Inst. for Life Scis., Japan, 1990-91; head of lab. U. Wroclaw, Poland, 1994—, head of dept., 1998—, prof., 1999—; organizer, 1990-92, chmn., 1992-94, Internat. Isotope Soc. Editor: Coursebook on Isotope Geology, 1990, Isotope Workshop Extended Abstracts, 1994; author: Geochemica et Cosmochimica Acta, vol. 59, 1995, Chemical Geology, vol. 159, 1999. stipend fellow Found. for Polish Sci., Warsaw, 1993; Min. of Nat. Edn. award, Warsaw, 1999. Mem. Internat. Isotope Soc., European Soc. Isotope Rsch., Geochem. Soc. Japan, Am. Geophys. Union, Geochem. Soc. Avocations: scuba diving at night, football, singing. Office phone: 48-77-3288924. Office: Dept Applied Geology, University of Wroclaw, 50-205 Wroclaw Poland

JEDRZEJEWSKA, BARBARA KINGA, epidemiologist, researcher; b. Białystok, Poland, July 13, 1951; d. Dymitr and Janina (Popławska) Wasilewski; m. Dariusz Wincenty Jedrzejewski, Feb. 26, 1977; 1 child, Michal. MSc in Pharmacy, Med. U. Lublin (Poland), 1975, PhD in Natural Scis., 1984. Asst., sr. asst. Agrl. Acad. Dept. Biochemistry, Lublin, 1975-81; with dept. epidemiology Med. U. Lublin, 1984—. Co-author: Epidemiologia-Skrypt Dla Studentów, 1985, Epidemiologia-Podrecznik Dla Lekarzy i studentów, 1995, Sanalogia, 1998, 2nd edit., 1999. Mem. Polish Biochem. Soc., Polish Epidemiol. and Infectious Disease Soc., Polish Soc. of the History of Medicine, Polish Gerontol. Soc. Roman Catholic. Avocations: poesy, skiing, walking, collecting. Home: 9 Zywiecka, 20-870 Lublin Poland Office: Dept Epidemiology Med U, 85 Lubartowska, 20-123 Lublin Poland

JĘDRZEJEWSKI, JERZY WITOLD, mechanical engineering educator, consultant; b. Radom, Poland, July 8, 1932; s. Wacław and Leokadia (Rybka) J.; m. Katarzyna Stanisława Bocho, July 18, 1970; children: Bartosz, Magdalena. MSc, Tech. U. Wroclaw, Poland, 1956, PhD, 1965. Instr. mech. engring. Tech. U. Wroclaw, 1954-65, asst. prof., 1965-70, assoc. prof., 1970-86, prof., 1986—, mgr. sci.-tech. divsn., 1969-73, head machine tool design divsn., 1970—, v.p., 1973-75, interuniv. design lab. head, 1999—; vis. prof. Tech. U. Baghdad, Iraq, 1989-90, Naggaoka (Japan) U. Tech., 1995; adviser Polish Ministry Industry and Commerce, Warsaw, 1994-96, Ministry of Economy, 1997—; gov. Cadsol Design AB, 1998—; nominator of the Japan Prize, 1996—;. Editor, co-author: Thermal Behavior Intelligent Diagnostics and Supervision of Machining Systems, 1996; editor Machine Engring. Jour., 1996—. Decorated Cross of Merit, Cross of Order (Poland); recipient award European Cmty., 1995; named Man of the Yr. ABB, 1997. Mem. Internat. Instn. for Prodn. Engring. Rsch., Engrs. Acad. Poland, Polish Soc. Mech. Engrs. (gold honor badge 1977, Mierzejewski Disting. award 1996), N.Y. Acad. Scis. Avocations: skiing, swimming, sailing, music, painting. Home: ul Kamienna 4 m 64, 53-308 Wrocław Poland Office: Wroclaw U of Tech, Wybrzeze Wyspianskiego 27, 50-370 Wroclaw Poland

JEE, INNHO, computer and information educator; b. Ansung, Korea, Nov. 11, 1958; s. Kunjong Jee and Eunun Kim; m. Aeja Yoo; 1 child, Frank Wonseok. BS, Seoul Nat. U., 1980, MS, 1983; PhD, Poly. U., N.Y.C., 1995. Sr. rschr. Agy. for Def. Devel., Daejon, Korea, 1982-88; rsch. asst. Poly. U., N.Y.C., 1991-95; asst. prof. Hongik U., Seoul, 1995—; mem. adv. com. Chungnam Provincial Office, Daejon, 1997—, Hongik U., Seoul, 1997—. Contbr. articles to profl. jours. Recipient award Min. of Nat. Def., 1986, Award of Republic of Korea's Pres., Ministry of Govt. Adminstrn., 1987. Mem. IEEE, Inst. Elec. Engrs., Inst. Elec. Engrs. Korea, Korean Inst. Comm. Scis., Acoustical Soc. Korea, Koean Inst. Elec. Engrs. Avocation: golf. Home: 102-1405 Banpo Hansin Twr A, Seochogu 137-030 Seoul Korea Office: Hongik U Div Info & Comm, Sinan-ri Chochi-won, 339-701 Chochiwon Chungman, Korea

JEET, SURJIT SINGH, historian, research scholar; b. Jallandhar, Panjab, India, June 1, 1946; arrived in Eng., 1976; m. Avtar Kaur Saggu; four children. BA with honors, Punjab U., Chandigarh, India, 1968, MA in History, 1971; MA in Religious Edn., Punjab U., Patiala, India, 1973. Rsch. scholar U. Chandigarh; dir. Inst. Namdhari Sikh Studies, London, 1993; head libr. H.H. Satguru Jagjit Singh Lab., London, 1996. Author: Maharaja Duleep Singh and Government, The Namdhari Documents; editor: The Namdhari Sikhs. Social worker Cmty. Work Counseling. Named Man of Yr., Vishaw Namdhari Ednl. Soc., India, 1995. Mem. Exec. Club, World Congress of Faiths, Inst. of Peace and Global Understanding and Mediation Svs., Inst. Hist. Rsch. Studies (sch. gov.). Avocations: collecting antiques, books, mpas, relics about Sikh history and religion. Home: 36 Margery Park Rd, Forest Gate, London E7 9JY, England

JEFFERS, IAN LLOYD, newspaper executive; b. Brisbane, Australia, July 1, 1943; s. Lloyd and Jean (Carr) J.; m. June Mavis Jarvis, May 1, 1965; children: Lisa, Bruce. Acct. Gold Coast Bull., 1965-78, gen. mgr., 1978-91, mng. dir., 1992—; dir. Gold Coast Pubs., 1987—. Chmn. Gold Coast Tropicarnival Festival, 1988—. Mem. Pacific Area Newspaper Assn. (pres. 1991-93), Internat. Newspaper Mktg. Assn. (pres. Pacific divsn. 1990-92, internat. bd. dirs. Dallas 1993-96). Avocations: fishing, golf.

JEFFERSON, JOSEPH MURRAY, banker; b. Heilwood, Pa., July 9, 1919; s. Ernest Maloy and Edith (Morris) J.; m. Mary Margaret Kerr, May 27, 1943 (dec. Mar. 1991); children: James Murray, Sharon Lee; m. Mary Jo Greenly, Dec. 11, 1999; 1 stepchild, Traci Romedy. BS, Waynesburg (Pa.) Coll., 1943; postgrad., Ind. U., 1949-51, Dartmouth Coll., 1963-64. Laborer Buckeye Coal Co., Nemacolin, Pa., 1936-41; sec. First Fed. S&L Assn., Waynesburg, Pa., 1945-52; exec. v.p., CEO Provident Fed. S&L Assn., Pitts., 1953-61; v.p. First Fed. S&L Assn. of Pitts., 1961-68; pres., CEO Washington (Pa.) Fed. Savs. Bank, 1968-86, dir. emeritus, 1995—; dir., vice chmn. Fed. Home Loan Bank of Pitts., 1986-91. Bd. dirs. Pa. Indsl. Devel. Agy., Harrisburg, 1963-64, Pa. Econ. League, Harrisburg, 1985-95, YMCA, Washington, 1968-85. With U.S. Army Aircorps, 1941-42, lt. USN, 1943-46. Named to Pa. Cmty. Bankers Hall of Fame, 1992. Mem. U.S. S&L League (dir. exec. com. 1968-71), Pa. S&L League (pres. 1963-64), Masons (32 deg.), Lions (Melvin Jones fellow). Avocations: golf, public speaking. Home: 151 Hallock St Pittsburgh PA 15211-1367

JEFFERY, CHRISTINE ELIZABETH, academic researcher; b. Weston-s-Mare, UK, May 17, 1966; d. David and Patricia (Montgomery) Rye; m. Paul Alan Jeffery, Apr. 25, 1992; children: Emily, Kerenza. B in German & Librarianship, U. Wales, 1988. Sr. researcher Morgan Stanley Internat., London, 1988-92; from rsch. officer to hasst. dir. projects and rsch. Oxford Univ. Devel. Office, UK, 1992—. Avocation: parenting, needlecrafts. Office: Oxford U Devel Office, Oxenford House Magdalen St, OX13AB Oxford England

JEFFORDS, EDWARD ALAN, former assistant state attorney general; b. Nov. 28, 1945; s. Roy Ezra and Sylvia Belle (Dickinson) J. AA, Victor Valley Coll., 1967; student, U. Wis. Mgmt. Inst., 1977; BS, USNY-Albany, 1983; JD, Baylor U. Sch. Law, 1985; postgrad, Harvard U., 1991; DHL (hon.), Harington Coll., 1976. Bar: Tex. 1985, U.S. Dist. Ct. (we. dist.) Tex. 1985, U.S. Ct. Appeals (5th cir.) 1985, U.S. Dist. Ct. (so. dist.) Tex. 1986, U.S. Dist. Ct. (no. dist.) Tex. 1988, U.S. Supreme Ct. 1989; bd. cert. civil trial law, personal injury law, Tex. bd. legal specialization, 1990; cert. civil trial adv., Nat. Bd. Trial Advocacy, 1995. Editor Auburn (Wash.) Globe-News, 1967-70; fine arts editor Tacoma News-Tribune, 1970-75; exec. dir. Ozark Inst., Eureka Springs, 1976-82; asst. atty. gen. State of Tex., Austin, 1985-92; exec. dir. Pan Am. Ednl. Found., 1989—; adj. prof. Nat. U. of Costa Rica, 1989-90; trustee Regents Coll. Alumni Assn., USNY, 1990-99; advocate Nat. Coll. Advocacy. Exec. editor Baylor Law Rev., 1984-85. With USAF, 1963-67. Mem. ABA, Travis County Bar Assn., Tex. Trial Lawyers Assn., Assn. Trial Lawyers Am., Am. Judicature Assn., Tex. Group Legal Ethics, Trial Lawyers for Pub. Justice, Order of Barrister, State Bar Coll., State Pro Bono Coll., Univ. Club, Million Dollar Adv. Forum, Delta Theta Phi. Office: PO Box 2521 Austin TX 78768-2521

JEFFREDO, JOHN VICTOR, aerospace engineer, manufacturing company executive, inventor; b. Los Angeles, Nov. 5, 1927; s. John Edward and Pauline Matilda (Whitten) J., m. Elma Jean Nesmith (div. 1958); children: Joyce Jean Jeffredo Ryder, Michael John; m. Doris Louise Hinz, (div. 1980); children: John Victor, Louise Victoria Jeffredo-Warden; m. Gerda Adelheid Pillich, 1980. Grad. in aeronautical engring., Cal-Aero Tech. Inst., 1948; AA machine design, Pasadena City Coll., 1951; grad. in electronics, The Ordnance Sch. U.S. Army, 1951; postgrad, U. So. Calif., 1955-58, Palomar Coll., 1977-96; MBA, La Jolla U., 1980, PhD in human rels., 1984. Design engr. Douglas Aircraft Co., Long Beach and Santa Monica, Calif., 1955-58; devel. engr. Honeywell Ordnance Corp., Duarte, Calif., 1958-62; cons. Honeywell Devel. Labs, Seattle, 1962-65; supr. mech. engring. dept. aerospace divsn. Control Data Corp., Pasadena, Calif., 1965-68; project engr. Cubic Corp., San Diego, 1968-70; supr. mech. engring. dept. Babcock Electronics Co., Costa Mesa, Calif., 1970-72; owner, operator Jeffredo Gunsight Co., Fallbrook, Calif., 1971-81; chief engr. Western Designs, Inc., Fallbrook, Calif., 1972-81, exec. dir., 1981-88, CEO, 1988-96, owner, operator, 1981-87; owner, operator Western Design Concepts, Inc., 1987-94; exec. dir. JXJ, Inc., San Marcos, Calif., 1981-88, CEO, 1988—; mgr. Jeffredo Gunsight divsn., 1981-94, chief engr. JXJ, Inc., 1987-92 (merger JXJ, Inc. and Western Design Concepts, Fallbrook, Calif.), prin. 1992—, owner, mgr., Energy Assocs., San Diego, 1982-86, pres. Jeffredo Internat., 1984-88, founder, CEO John-Victor Internat., San Marcos, Calif., Frankfurt, Fed. Rep. Germany, 1988-99, The Jeffredo Solution, Fallbrook, 1996—, engring. cons. Action Instruments Co., Inc., Gen. Dynamics, Alcyon Corp., Systems Exploration, Inc. (all San Diego), Hughes Aircraft Co., El Segundo, Allied-Bendix, San Marcos, bd. dirs.Indian World Corp., JXJ, Inc., John-Victor Internat.; chmn., bd. dirs., pres. Maritime Shoshone, Inc., 2000—; owner, operator The Badger Creek Studio, Fallbrook, 1997—. Author: Gabrieleño, New Perspective on the Island Gabrielino, The Ocean People, Wildcatting; contbr. articles to trade jours. and mags.; guest editl. writer Town Hall, San Diego Union; narrator: (film) The Sacred Desert, 1994; spkr. in field; patentee agrl. frost control, vehicle off-road drive system, recoil absorbing system for firearms, telescope sight mounting system for firearms, breech mech. sporting firearm, elec. switch activating system, 37 others, others pending. Mem. San Diego County Border Tsk Force on Undocumented Aliens, 1979-80, 81-82, mgr., rep. Island Gabrieleno Group, NAGPRA repatriation project, 1995—, historian Maritime Shoshone, 1995—, spokesman Island Shoshone, 1995—, chmn. Native Californian Coalition, 1982—, bd. dirs. Nat. Geographic Soc., 1968. With U.S. Army, 1951-53. Recipient Superior Svc. Commendation award U.S. Naval Ordnance Test Station, Pasadena, 1959. Mem. AIAA (sr.), NRA (life), Soc. Automotive Engrs., San Diego Zool. Soc., Sierra Club (life), The Wilderness Soc., Catalina Island Conservancy, The Nature Conservancy, Clan Stewart Soc. Am., Ducks Unlimited, Pechanga Band of Luiseno Indians (life), Cova, Catalina Island Mus. Soc., The Planetary Soc., Soc. for Calif. Archaeology, Skeptics Soc., North County Scots. Avocations: chess, music, archaeology, conservation, sculpture. Home: PO Box 387 Bonsall CA 92003-0387

JEFFREE, ROSS ANTHONY, research scientist; b. Sydney, Australia, Feb. 2, 1951; s. Benjamin John and Yvonne Joyce (Barlow) J.; m. Wendy Patricia Jennings, Mar. 1, 1980; children: Christopher Ryan, Paris Yvonne. BS with honors, U. Sydney, Australia, 1974; PhD, U. New Eng., Armidale, Australia, 1985. Exptl. officer I Australian Atomic Energy Commn., Sydney, 1974-78, exptl. officer II, 1978-83, exptl. officer III, 1983-87; sr. rsch. scientist Australian Nuclear Sci. Tech. Orgn., Sydney, 1987-92, prin. rsch. scientist, 1992-94; nuclear counselor Australian High Commn., London, 1994-98; EIS mgr. replacement rsch. reactor project Australian Nuclear Sci. and Tech. Orgn., Sydney, 1998—, group mgr. environ. biology, 1998-99, leader radioecology affinity group, 1999—; tutor Sch. Biol. Scis., U. Sydney, 1973; lectr. U. Tech., Sydney, 1985-87; advisor sch. adv. com. Sch. Biomed. and Life Scis., Univ. Technology Sydney, 1993-94; nat. rep. coodinated rsch. programs marine and freshwater radioecology IAEA, 1986—, rsch. assoc. IAEA Marine Environment Lab., dept. cellular physiology U. Rouen, France; nat. del. Orgn. Econ. Coop. and Devel. - Nuc. Energy Agy. Contbr. articles to profl. jours. Sec. Ramsgate Life Saving Club, Sydney, 1993-94. Fellow Australian Inst. Biology, Eco-Ethics Internat. Union; mem. Australasian Soc. for Ecotoxicology (state rep. 1994), Soc. Limnology, Internat. Union Radioecology, South Pacific Environ. Radioactn. Assn., Australian Nuc. Sci. and Tech. Orgn. (Dir. award for Prodn. 1993). Achievements include mechanistic and predictive model of metal accumulation in freshwater bivalves and turtles; biogeochemical model of radionuclide concentrating mechanism in oligotrophic marine environments; use of osteoderms to monitor lead contamination in estuarine crocodiles. Home: 45 Casuarina Rd, 2234 Alfords Point NSW, Australia Office: Austral Nuclr Sci/Tech Org, PMB 1, Menai 2234, Australia

JEFFREY, FRANCIS, software developer, forecaster; b. Calif., 1950. BA in Computational Neurophysiology, U. Calif., Berkeley, 1972. Research assoc. U. Calif., San Diego, 1972-73; cons. Sci. Applications, Inc., La Jolla, Calif., 1973-75; entrepreneur Big Sur, Calif., 1973-77; cons. Alive Systems Info. Scis., San Francisco, 1978-87; founder, pres., chief exec. officer Alive Systems, Inc. and Elfnet, Inc., Malibu, Calif., 1987—; cons. Inst. for Advanced Computation, Sunnyvale, Calif., 1973-75, Human-Dolphin Found., 1980-82, 87-89, Esalen Inst., 1982-83; co-founder (with Sir. A.C. Clarke, R.W. Benshert, A.F. Alles) Arthur C. Clarke Comms., Singapore, Calif., 2000—. Author: (with others) Handbook of States of Consciousness, 1986, John Lilly So Far, 1990, (with others) Voices from The Edge, 1995, Patent Cooperation Treaty International Publication WO 97/24663, 1997, Japanese edit., 1998, European Cmty. edit., 1999; originator Malibu civic dolphin protection resolution, 1992, whales as living cultural resources resolution, 1994; designer com. co-piloting; creator symposium Radical Connectionsim and the Visualization of Network Programs, 1999—; patentee in field. Co-founder New Forum, Monterey, Calif., 1984, Gt. Whales Found., San Francisco, 1986, chmn., CEO, Malibu (Calif.) Dolphin Recovery Ctr., 1996—; co-founder Big Sur chpt. L5 Nat. Space Soc.; creator Annual Malibu (Calif.) Symposium on Radical Connectionism and the Visualization of Network Programs, 1999—; mem. multi-author panel discussion series Techno 2000, Beyond 2000. Mem. AAAS, IEEE, Assn. for Computing Machinery, Am. Soc. for Cybernetics (founding, control sys. group), Amnesty Internat. (leadership group), Cousteau Soc. (life mem.), Raoul Wallenberg Inst. Ethics (adv. bd.). Achievements include invention of communication co-pilots, conscious networks system, "Adverteasing" (trademark) for the suspended resolution of hypertext links. E-mail: francis@elfi.com. Home and Office: PO Box 6844 Malibu CA 90264-6844

JEFFREYS, ELYSTAN GEOFFREY, geological engineer, petroleum consultant and appraiser; b. Apr. 26, 1926; s. Geoffrey and Georgene Frances Theodora (Littell) J.; m. Pat Rumage, May 1, 1946 (div.); children: Jeri Lynn, David Powell; m. Peggi Villar, Feb. 28, 1975. Geol. Engr., Colo. Sch. Mines, 1951, grad. in Econ. Evaluation and Investment Decision Methods, 1972, 91. Registered prof. engr., Miss., land surveyor, Miss., geologist, Tenn.; profl. geologist, Ala.; sr. appraiser of oil and gas properties. Ptnr. G. Jeffreys & Son, 1951-53, Jeffreys & Launius, 1953-55; pvt. practice petroleum exploration, 1954-77; exploration mgr. Arrowhead Exploration Co., Bovile and Brewton, Ala., 1977-83; cons. petroleum geologist, 1964—; pres., chmn. bd. CE) Major Oil Co., Jackson, Miss., 1961-84, v.p., 1984-98; v.p. The Jeffreys Co., Inc., Mobile, 1976-96, pres., CEO, 1996—; mgr. Koala Energy Co., LLC, 1994-2000; asst. mgr. Kee Energy Co., LLC, 1996-2000. Vestryman Trinity Episcopal Ch., Mobile, 1989-92, 94-96, sr. warden, 1991-92; bd. trustees The Appraisal Found., 1993-94. With 3d U.S. Army, 1944-46, ETO. Mem. Miss. Geol. Soc., Ala. Geol. Soc., New Orleans Geol. Soc. Am. Assn. Petroleum Geologists, Am. Soc. Appraisers (accredited sr. appraiser in tech. valuation of oil and gas, chief examiner, internat. bd. examiners for oil and gas 1993-99), Gulf Coast Assn. Geol. Socs. (treas. 1960, Cert. of Svc. 1971), Soc. Petroleum Evaluation Engrs., Miss. Assn. Petroleum Landmen, Assn. Petroleum Landmen of Ala., Masons (32 degree), Shriners, Pi Kappa Alpha. Address: 115 Fairway Dr Daphne AL 36526-7401

JEFFREYS-JONES, RHODRI, history educator; b. Carmarthen, Wales, July 28, 1942; s. Thomas Ieuan and Nancy (Watkins) Jeffreys-J.; m. Janetta Carolina Minkiewicz, Aug. 15, 1970 (div. 1992); children: Gwenda, Rowena; m. Mary Fenton, Mar. 21, 1992. BA, U. Coll. Wales, Aberystwyth, 1963; postgrad., U. Mich., 1965-65, Harvard U., 1965-66; PhD, U. Cambridge, 1969. Tutor Harvard U., Cambridge, Mass., 1965-66, fellow, 1971-72; tutor Fitzwiliam Coll. of Cambridge (Eng.) U., 1966-67; lectr., reader U. Edinburgh, Scotland, 1967-97, prof. Am. history, 1997—; vis. prof. U. Toronto, Ont., Can., 1993. Author: American Espionage, 1977, Violence and Reform in American History, 1978, The CIA and American Democracy, 1987, Changing Differences: Women and the Shaping of American Foreign Policy, 1917-1994, 1995, Peace Now! American Society and the Ending of the Vietnam War, 1999; co-editor: North American Spies: New Revisionist Perspectives, 1992, The Growth of Federal Power in American History, 1983, Eternal Vigilance? 50 Years of the CIA, 1997, American- British-Canadian Intelligence Relations 1939-2000, 2000; editor: Eagle Against Empire: American Opposition to European Imperialism, 1914-1982, 1983. Fellow Can. Govt., Toronto, 1993. Mem. Orgn. Am. Historians, Soc. Historians of Am. Fgn. Rels., British Assn. for Am. Studies, Scottish Assn. for the Study of Am. (chair). Avocations: snooker, vegetable gardening, opera. Office: U Edinburgh Dept History, WRB 50 George Sq, Edinburgh EH8 9JY, Scotland

JEFFREY-SMITH, LILLI ANN, biofeedback specialist, educator, administrator; b. Bedford, Ind., 1944; d. Charles Constantine and Adelai (Malon) Jeffrey-Smith. Grad. Ind. Bus. Coll., 1963; B.S., Ind. U., 1973; grad. Psychosomatic Medicine Clinic, Berkeley, Calif. (accredited by Albert Einstein Coll. Medicine); PhD in Behavioral Sci., Kennedy-Western U., 1988. Diplomate Am. Bd. Disability Analysts (sr.); cert. biofeedback specialist. Project assoc., stress mgmt. clinician City of Indpls., 1973-79; cons. Airport Med. Clinic, Indpls., 1981; outreach coord. Abbot-Northwestern Hosp., Mpls., 1981; dir. biofeedback dept. Sister Kenney Inst., Mpls., 1979-81, Noran Neurol. Clinic, Mpls., 1981-83; instr., dir. Biofeedback Tng. and Treatment Ctr., Edina, Minn., 1979—; pres. Biofeedback Rsch. and Devel. Co. Ltd., Edina, 1983—; cons. to biofeedback depts. St. Joseph Hosp., Mankato, Minn., 1984—, Lakeview Clinic, Waconia, Minn., 1983, Psychiat. Clinic of Mankato, 1983—, Fairview Ridges Hosp., Burnsville, Minn., 1987—. Author, narrator health and wellness tape series. Mem. Republican Presdl. Task Force, 1984—, NSC, 1985; co-chmn. Mayor's Handicapped Task Force, Indpls., 1975; founder, pres. Miss Wheel Chair of Ind., Inc. Named Hon. Lt. Gov., State of Ind., 1978; given Key to the City of Indpls., 1973, Flag of the City of Indpls., 1975. Mem. ABDA, NAFE, AAUW, AAAS, Am. Inst. Stress, N.Y. Acad. Sci., Edina C. of C., Minn. Women's Network, Biofeedback Soc. Am., Biofeedback Soc. Minn., Am. Assn. Control Tension, Am. Assn. Behaviorial Therapists, Am. Assn. Biofeedback Clinicians, Nat. Assn. Women Bus. Owners, Soc. Open Focus and Tng. Rsch., Am. Assoc. of U. Woman, Nat. Assoc. of Female Execs., Assn. Trainers in Clin. Hypnosis, Internat. Stress and Tension Control Assn., Minn. Assn. Rehab. Providers, Nat. Assn. Exec. Women, Internat. Platform Assn. Avocations: music, stamp collecting, shooting, poetry. Office: Biofeedback Tng & Treatment Ctr 7300 France Ave S Ste 200 Minneapolis MN 55435-4542

JEGEDE, KAYODE JOHN, educational administrator; b. Akure, Nigeria, Sept. 20, 1939; s. Gabriel and Janet J.; m. Margaret Jolayem Longe, July 24, 1965; four children. LLB, Holborn Coll. Law, 1964; LLM, Univ. Coll. London, 1967. State counsel Fed. Min. Justice, Lagos, Nigeria, 1969; asst. registrar U. Lagos, 1969-77, dep. registrar, 1977-80; sec. Coun. Legal Edn., Lagos, 1980-93; from acting dir. to dir. gen. Nigerian Law Sch., Lagos, 1993—; lectr. profl. ethics Nigerian Law Sch., 1989—; sr. adv. Nigeria, 2000—. Mem. Nigerian Bar Assn., Internat. Bar Assn., Commonwealth Bar Assn., Nigerian Body of Benchers. Avocations: gardening, reading, music, traveling, playing games.

JEHENSON, PHILIPPE MARIE GEORGES, physician, physicist, researcher; b. Namur, Belgium, Nov. 7, 1955; arrived in France, 1982; s. Pierre S.M. Jehenson and Elisabeth Piron; m. Sylvie M.A. Peroueme, June 24, 1995. MD, U. Pavia, Italy, 1978; BSc in Physics, Imperial Coll. Sci. & Tech., London, 1982; nuclear medicine specialization, U. Paris, 1986, PhD, 1992, habilitation for professorship, 1992. Postdoctoral staff radiation protection European Union/French Atomic Energy Authority, Paris, 1982-83; rsch. asst. in nuclear magnetic resonance French Atomic Energy Authority, Paris, 1984, rschr. nuclear magnetic resonance, 1985—, head nuclear magnetic resonance spectroscopy in medicine, 1986-94, head nuclear magnetic resonance and metabolic pathology, 1994-97; sci. expert, med. rsch. European Commn., Brussels, 1997—; lectr. U. Paris, 1988—; sci. expert, cons. European Union, Brussels, 1995-97, French Ministry Health, Paris, 1995—; med. rsch. expert European Commn.; reviewer various jours. Contbr. articles to profl. jours. Scholar Imperial Coll. Sci. and Tech., London, 1980, 81, 82; grantee Wellcome Trust, London, 1981; European Commn. Post-Doctoral grantee European Union, Brussels, 1983; Frederic Joliot grantee French Atomic Energy Authority, Paris, 1984. Mem. Internat. Soc. for Magnetic Resonance in Medicine, European Soc. for Magnetic Resonance in Medicine and Biology, French Soc. Nuclear Medicine, French Magnetic Resonance Group (v.p. and meeting organizer 1993-97). Avocations: skiing, tennis, ballroom dancing. Home: 9 Bis Rue Gazan, 75014 Paris France Office: CEA Sv Hosp Frederic Joliot, 4 Pl du General Leclerc, F-91406 Orsay France also: European Commn/Dir Gen Rsch, Rue de la Loi 200, B-1049 Brussels Belgium

JEHLIČKOVÁ GUCKLEROVÁ, MARIE ANNA, writer, economist, publishing executive; b. Opava, Silesia, Czech Republic, July 18, 1941; d. Otto de Grande and Hedvika (Kawanová) von Guckler; m. Milan Jehlička, Oct. 31, 1963; children: Zdeněk, Daniel. BS in Econs., Univ. of Econs. Grads., Prague, Czech Republic, 1964. Economist State Record Pub. Ho., Prague, 1964-78, chief editor, 1978-90; cons. Apon (cultural firm), N.Y.C., 1968-71; writer, Czech Ministry of Culture, 1966, Czech Press Agy., 1967-69; editor Czechoslovak Fgn. Broadcasting, Prague, 1968-71. Author: (phonograph records) Fairy-Tales, 1975, 76, 77, 79, The Water Castle, 1980, (audiotapes) Fairy-Tales, 1980, 94, 95, Fairy-Tales from Castles, Seas and Woods, 1992; (books) The Celtic Crown, The Celts-the Ancestors of the Europeans, An American. Democrat. Roman Catholic. Avocation: research on roots of European nations, including Celts. Home: Kloboučnická 7, 140 00 Prague Czech Republic Office: Mariadan, Kloboučnická 7/1627, 140 00 Prague Czech Republic

JEKUNEN, ANTTI PEKKA, health facility administrator, oncologist; b. Oulu, Finland, Feb. 22, 1960; s. Lauri E. and Helli (Syväniemi) J.; m. Maarit Helena Murtomäki, Aug. 22, 1981; children: Noora, Jaakko, Veera. MD, U. Oulu, 1986, PhD, 1988; cert. med. oncology and radiotherapy, U. Helsinki,

1996. Pvt. practice Oulu, Oulainen, Kokkola, Vaasa, Finland, 1987-88; acting physician Vaasa Cen. Hosp., 1988; fellow U. Calif., San Diego, 1990-92; sr. registrar Oncology Clinic, Helsinki, Finland, 1993-95; sr. lectr. oncology Helsinki U., 1995-99; sr. cons. oncology Helsinki U. Ctrl. Hosp., 1996; med. dir. Rhône-Poulenc Rorer, Helsinki, Finland, 1997—; sr. lectr. applied oncology Turku, Finland, 1999—; st. lectr. clin. drug. rschr. Helsinki, 1999—; med. dir. Aventis Pharma, Helsinki, 2000—. Contbr. articles to profl. jours. 2d lt. Finish mil., 1989. Grantee Acad. Cancer Rsch., San Diego, 1991, Finnish Cancer Found., 1992, 94-95. Mem. Am. Assn. Cancer Rsch. (Travel award 1992), Am. Soc. Clin. Oncology, N.Y. Acad. Scis. Home: Täysikuu 3 B 44, 02210 Espoo Finland Office: Aventis Pharma, Maistraatinportti 4A, 00241 Helsinki Finland

JELASKA, DAMIR TIHOMIR, mechanical engineering educator; b. Split, Dalmatia, Croatia, Mar. 25, 1947; s. Tihomir Maksimilijan and Marija Nikola (Pentić) J.; m. Maja Petar Katić, Dec. 30, 1971; children: Goran, Igor. BSc, U. Zagreb, Croatia, 1971, MSc, 1980; PhD, U. Rijeka, Croatia, 1982. Asst. Naval Acad., Split, 1973-78, lectr., 1978-84; rschr. Shipyard, Split, 1984-87; prof. Faculty of Electro-technics, Mech. Engring. and Naval Arch., Split, 1987—, chief machine elements chatedra, 1988—, chief mech. engring. dept., 1994-96; cons. Former Yugoslav Navy, Split, 1980-84, Jugoplastika, Split, 1988-91; adviser Inst. Shipbuilding Industry, Split, 1985-88, Ad-Plastik, Solin, Croatia, 1991-97. Contbr. articles to profl. jours.; patentee in field. Mem. Union Yugoslav Comunists, Split, 1976-88. Maj. Yugoslav Navy, 1973-84. Decorated medal with silver swords for mil. merit Marshall Tito, 1977, Golden medal for mil. merit Marshall Tito, 1979, Medal of Work, Presidency of Sfry, 1987. Fellow Croatian Mech. Design Soc.; mem. Internat. Fedn. for Theory of Machines and Mechanisms-Croatia, N.Y. Acad. Scis. Avocations: fishing, humanitarian activities, chess, walking. Office: Faculty Mech Engring Naval Architecture, R Boskovića B B, 21000 Split Dalmatia, Croatia

JELAVIC-KOJIC, FRANKA MARIA-LOUISE, radiologist, researcher; b. Zagreb, Croatia, Oct. 21, 1963; d. Frane and Vesna (Božic) J.; m. Branimir Kojic, Mar. 19, 1988; children: Ivana Petra, Frane Tomislav, Marko Juraj. MD, U. Zagreb, 1987, postgrad., 1987-88, 89-90, 92-93; postgrad., Interuniversity Sch. Med. Ultrasound, Dubrovnik, 1989-90, Interuniversity Sch. Med. Ultrasound, Zagreb, 1993. Cert. radiologist Croatian Ministry Health. Med. dr. Clinic for Infectious Diseases, Zagreb, Croatia, 1989; resident radiology Sv. Duh. Gen. Hosp., Zagreb, Croatia, 1990-95, radiologist, 1995—; co-investigator internat. project, Antwerp, Belgium, 1994-97; presenter, lectr. in field. Contbr. articles to profl. jours. Recipient Cert. of Attendance Am. Austrian Found., 1994. Mem. Croatian Med. Assn., Croatian Soc. Radiology (bd. dirs. 1993-98), European Assn. Radiology, Croatian Jr. Radiologists Forum (chmn. 1993-95, 95-97, sr. adv. bd. 1998—), Eurpean Assn. Radiology, Jr. Radiologists (nat. rep. 1993-98), Internat. Postgrad. Orgn. Knowlege Transfer and Tchg. Excellent Students Croatia (I-POKRATES-CROATIA) (founder). Roman Catholic. Avocations: travel, communications, family walks by the seashore, reading, movies. Home: Strossmayerov trg 7, 10 000 Zagreb Croatia Office: Gen Hosp Sv Duh Dept Radiology, Sv Duh 64, 10 000 Zagreb Croatia

JELIN, SHELDON C., judge; b. Nanticoke, Pa.. BS, Temple U., 1954, JD, 1957. Bar: Pa. Pvt. practice Phila., 1957-88; judge Ct. of Common Pleas of Phila., 1st Jud. Dist., 1988—; mem. ethics com. Pa. Conf. State Trial Judges, 1991—; mem. Pa. Coun. on Aging, 1992-95. Former mem., bd. dirs. Mid City Lodge, B'nai Brith, Phila.; bd. trustees Youth Devel. Ctr., Bensalem, Pa., 1993-97. With USAR, 1958-64. Mem. Phila. Bar Assn., Lawyers Club Phila., Masons. Office: Phila Ct of Common Pleas 360 City Hall Philadelphia PA 19107-3201

JELINCH, FRANK ANTHONY, lawyer; b. San Jose, Calif., July 22, 1943; s. Frank Anthony and Minnie Leona J.; m. Roberta Katherine Magi, Dec. 27, 1975; 1 child, Michelle. BA cum laude, San Jose Sate U., 1965; JD, U. Calif., Berkeley, 1968. Bar: Calif. 1969, U.S. Dist. Ct. (no. dist.) Calif. 1969, U.S. Supreme Ct. 1972. Ptnr. Jelinch & Rendler, Cupertino, Calif., 1980—; instr. Lincoln U. Sch. Law, San Jose, 1980; founder Cupertino Nat. Bank. Chmn. San Francisco Shakespeare Festival, 1997-98, Terra Found., San Jose, 1980—; commr. Los Gatos Parks Commn., 1980-88, Cupertino Parks & Recreation, 1996—, Cupertino Fine Arts Commn., 1990-94; chair Am. Heart Assn. Cardiac Fundraising Drive, 1996; pres. Los Gatos Friends of the Arts; . Capt. U.S. Army, 1969-73, Command Judge Advocate, 1st Signal Brigade, USARV, 1971, legal officer Op. Homecoming (Vietnam returning POW's) 1973. Recipient Bronze Star, Oak Leaf Cluster, Army Commendation Medal (1st Oak Leaf Cluster), Vietnam. Mem. ABA (EEOC com.), Sunnyvale-Cupertino Bar Assn. (pres. 1990), Cupertino C. of C. (pres. 1998-99, del. trade delegation to Taiwan 2000), Santa Clara County Bar Assn. (gov. 1990), Calif. State Bar Assn., Santa Clara County Trial Lawyers Assn., U.S. Supreme Ct. Hist. Soc., Phi Alpha Theta, Pi Sigma Alpha. Office: Jelinch & Rendler 20863 Stevens Creek Blvd Cupertino CA 95014-2125

JELINEK, FRANTISEK, radio engineering and electronics researcher; b. Boskovice, Czechoslovakia, June 23, 1933; s. Frantisek and Stepanka (Nezvalova) J.; m. Alena Chmelarova, Sept. 14, 1956; 1 child, Jana (div. Dec. 1979). MS, Czech Tech U, Prague, 1956; PhD, Acad. Scis., Prague, 1965. Cert. elec. engr. Engr. Inst. Radio Engring. and Electronics, Prague, 1956-59, rschr., 1965-80, sr. rschr., 1980—, dept. head, 1992-98, dep. dir., 1990-98, supr., 1970—; external lectr. Czech Tech. U., Prague, 1984-90; com. mem. Trade Union Orgn., Inst. Radio Engring. and Electronics, 1968-70. Co-author: Gunn Diodes and Avalanche Diodes, 1974, Fourth Conference on Nonlinear Oscillations, 1968. Recipient medal Czechoslovak Govt., 1959. Mem. Czech Elec. Soc. Mem. Evangelical Ch. Czech Brethren. Avocations: photography,l tourist travel, skiing, gardening. Home: Werichova 954, 15200 Prague 5, Czech Republic Office: Inst Radio Engring & Elec, Acad Scis Chaberska 57, 182 51 Prague 8, Czech Republic

JELÍNEK, MILAN, linguist; b. Brno, Czech Republic, June 22, 1923; s. Emil and Božena (Konečná) J.; m. Marie Tvaružková, Dec. 30, 1948 (div. Feb. 1966); children: Zdeněk, Ivan; m. Jana Poláková, Feb. 26, 1966; children: Milan, Petr, Ota. CandSc., Masaryk U., Brno, 1958, PhD, 1949. Tchr. secondary sch., Holešov, Czech Republic, 1948-49; rsch. worker Acad. Scis., Brno, 1950-58, 71-83; lectr., sr. lectr., prof. Faculty of Arts Masaryk U., 1958-71; prof. Masaryk U., Brno, 1990-93, rector, 1990-92; external prof. U. Silesia, 1993—; vis. prof. Arndt U., Greifswald, Germany, 1961-62, Sorbonne, Paris, 1965-66; mem. Sci. Coun., 1993—. Author: On Language and Style of Newspapers, 1957, Nouns of Action, 1967, Stylistic Aspects of Grammatical System, 1974, Stylistics, 1995, Argumentation and Art of Communication, also numerous articles. Decorated comdr. Palmes Académiques (France); recipient medal for Loyalty 1939-1945, medal of 50th Anniversary of Establishment of ČSR, 1958, Gold medal Masaryk U., 1993. Mem. Assn. of Linguists, Masaryk Soc. Brno, Linguistic Circle of Prague. Social Democrat. Avocation: stylistics. Home: Zborovská 39, 616 00 Brno Czech Republic Office: Masaryk U Filozofická Fakulta, A Nováka 1, 660 88 Brno Czech Republic

JELINOVIĆ, ZVONIMIR STANKO, economics educator; b. Travnik, Bosnia and Herzegovina, Feb. 19, 1916; s. Stanko Petar and Ana Petar (Jazvo) J.; m. Dragica Petar Tepšić, Apr. 3, 1949. Grad., U. Zagreb Sch. Law, Croatia, 1949; PhD, U. Zagreb Sch. Econs., Croatia, 1953, postdoctoral, 1958. Diplomate Rlwy Traffic, 1942. Officer, high command Yugoslav Army Engring. Corps., 1938-41, Ministry of Def., Zagreb, 1941-45; chief Dept. Traffic of Zagreb City Coun., 1945-50; rsch. asst. in econs. U. Zagreb, 1950-58, asst. prof. econs., 1958-63, assoc. prof. econs., 1963-69, prof. econs., 1969-85; fellow Rsch. Inst. Transport Traffic and Maritime, Zagreb, 1969-70, Fed. Inst. Rsch., Belgrade, Yugoslavia, 1950-58; mem. Fed. Commn. Codification, Belgrade, 1951-58; advisor City Coun. for Housing and Communal Works, Zagreb, 1950-67. Author: 18 books including Economics of Transportation, 1972, Maritime Economics, 1975, Economics of Air Transport Traffic, 1976, Struggle for Adriatic Railway, 1957; contbr. articles to profl. jours. Mem. Croatian Coun. Traffic Safety, 1975—; court expert for traffic accidents, Govt. Croatia, 1955-65. 2d lt., 1941-45, Independent State of Croatia, Zagreb. Recipient Gold medal Yugoslav Acad. Sci. and Arts, 1969, Life Works award Parliament of Croatia, 1986, UN scholarship Yale U., 1961-62. Fellow Am. Inst. Traffic, Inst. Policy Studies Balt.; mem. Croatian Assn. Traffic Engrs. (pres. 1975—). Roman Catholic. Avocations: motoring, mountaineering, swimming. Home: Vrbanićeva 37, 10000 Zagreb Croatia

JELLOWS, TRACY PATRICK, software engineer; b. Quincy, Mass., Oct. 15, 1951; d. Henry David and Dorothy Margret (Joyce) J. BS in Physics, Bridgewater (Mass.) State Coll., 1981; postgrad., U. Mass., Boston, 1982. Software engr. Lotus Devel. Corp., Cambridge, Mass., 1984-85, sr. software engr., 1985-89; prin. engr. 1-2-3 Graphics Lotus Devel. Corp., 1989-90; prin. engr. Edsun Labs., Waltham, Mass., 1990-91; prin. engr., cons. Saturn Software, Brockton, Mass., 1991-96; prin. engr. Thomson Fin. Svcs., Boston, 1996-98; cons. engr. Saturn Software, Brockton, Mass., 1998—. Mem. IEEE, Assn. Computing Machinery, Aircraft Owners and Pilots Assn., Mensa. Democrat. Roman Catholic. Avocations: music, computer software and hardware, boating, general aviation. Home: 9 Toby Rd Brockton MA 02302-1947

JELVED, MARIANNE, government executive; b. Charlottenlund, Denmark, Sept. 5, 1943. MEd in Danish Lang. and Lit., 1979. Tchr. Denmark, 1967-89, Royal Danish Sch. Ednl. Studies, 1979-87; chmn. Social Liberal MPs, Denmark, 1988; min. for econ. affairs Denmark, 1993—; min. for nordic cooperation Govt. of Denmark, Copenhagen, 1994—, leader SLP Parliamentary Group, 1988, min. econ. affairs, 1993—. Co-author: BRUD-Radikale vaerdier i en forandret tid, 1994; author, editor Danish textbooks. Elected mem. Social Liberal Party Det Radikale Venstre, Gundsø, 1982-89; dep. mayor, Gundsø, 1982-85. Office: Ministry Econ Affairs, Ved Stranden 8, 1061 Copenhagen K, Denmark*

JEMELJANOVS, ALEKSANDRS, research center administrator, educator; b. Riga, Latvia, Feb. 5, 1938; s. Vladimirs and Herta (Truze) J.; m. Maija Leinerte, Nov. 6, 1959; children: Egils, Valdemars, Sandra, Aija. Grad., Latvia Agr. U., Riga, 1961; postgrad., Latvian Rsch. Inst., 1969; Dr.Med.Vet., Vitebsk Acad. Vet. Medicine, Belarus, 1971; Dr.habil.agr., Russia Sci. Rsch. Inst., St. Petersburg, Russia, 1991. Tchr. Bebrene Vet. Tech. Sch., Latvia, 1961-62; mgr. Bebrene Vet. Dist., 1962-63; dir. Daugavpils State Artificial Insemination Sta., Latvia, 1963-66; rschr. Latvian Rsch. Inst. Animal Husbandry and Vet. Sci., Sigulda, 1969-82, dir., 1985—; dep. minister Min. of Agr., Riga, 1982-85; prof. Faculty Vet. Medicine, Latvia U. Agr. Contbr. articles to profl. jours.; patentee in field. Mem. Couns. of Promotion of Vet. Medicine and Animal Breeding, 1992, Coun. of Faculty of Vet. Medicine, Jelgava, 1992, Coun. of Emeritus Scientists, Riga, 1996; mem. adv. coun. State Vet. Svcs., Riga, 1997. Recipient Hon. Diploma, Presidium of Supreme Coun. of Latva, 1983, prize Coun. of Ministers of USSR, 1985; named Excellent Agriculturist, Min. Agr., Latvia, 1988. Mem. N.Y. Acad. Scis., Latvian Acad. Scis., Acad. Agr. and Forestry Sci. (v.p. 1992—), Scandinavian Agr. Scientists Assn. (mem. Baltic br. 1991—), World Poultry Sci. Assn. (Latvia br.), Intelligentsia Assn., Scientists Assn., Hunters Soc. Avocations: hunting, touring, gardening. Office: Rsch Ctr Sigra Latvia U Agr, 1 Instituta St, LV-2150 Sigulda Latvia

JENG, DONG-SHENG, engineering educator; b. Taidong, Taiwan, Dec. 5, 1964; arrived in Australia, 1997; s. Kang-Sheng Jeng and Kung Ning Wang; m. Kin Wa Kwok, Feb. 28, 1997; 1 child, Cathryn. B Engring., Nat. Chung-Hsing U., Taiwan, 1987, M Engring., 1989; PhD, U. WA, Australia, 1997. Rsch. assoc. Nat. Chung-Hsing U., Taiwan, 1991-92, 98-99; postdoctoral rschr. Univ. WA, Australia, 1997-99; lectr. Griffith U., Australia, 1999—. Recipient Excellent Article award Inst. Chinese Engrs., Taiwan, 1993. Mem. Am. Soc. Civil Engring. Office: Griffith Univ Sch Engring, PMB 50 Gold Coast Mail Ctr, Queensland 9726, Australia

JENG, MU-DER, electrical engineering educator; b. Taipei, Taiwan, China, June 25, 1961; s. Shan-Chin and Feng-Chu (Yu); J.; m. Na-Na Kao, May 13, 1988; children: Catherine, Christopher. BS, Nat. Cheng-Kung U., Taiwan, 1983, MS, 1985; PhD, Rensselaer Poly. Inst., 1992. Rsch. asst. Nat. Cheng-Kung U., 1983-85; 2d lt. officer Bur. Intelligence, Taipei, 1985-87; assoc. engr. Inst. for Info. Industry, Taipei, 1987-88; tchg. asst., rsch. asst. Rensselaer Poly. Inst., Troy, N.Y., 1988-92; assoc. prof. Nat. Taiwan Ocean U., Keelung, Taiwan, China, 1992-98, prof., 1998—; vis. scientist INRIA, France, 1999, 2000. Author: Petri Nets in Manufacturing, 1993; contbr. numerous papers to jours. and conf. procs. Recipient rsch. awards Nat. Sci. Coun. Taiwan, 1994, 95, 96, 97, 98, 99. Mem. IEEE (sr. mem., F.V. Taylor award 1993), Phi Tau Phi. Avocations: tennis, music, movies. Office: Nat Taiwan Ocean U Dept Elec Engring, 2 Pei-Ning Rd, 202 Keelung Taiwan

JENG, WOEI-LIH, oceanography educator; b. Lung-chi, Fu-chien, China, Apr. 3, 1945; s. Chia-Miao Jeng and Su-Hua Chen. BS, Nat. Taiwan Normal U., Taipei, 1967; MS, Nat. Taiwan U., Taipei, 1971; PhD, U. Tex., 1976. Instr. Nat. Taiwan U., Taipei, 1976-77, assoc. prof., 1977-82, prof., 1982—. Contbr. articles to profl. jours. Office: Nat Taiwan U Inst Oceanography, PO Box 23-13, Taipei 106, Taiwan

JENG, YANN-CHYN, quality engineer; b. Shin-Chu, China, May 9, 1948; parents Wei-Sheng Jeng and Jung-Mei Ro; m. Yueh-Lien Lo, Sept. 23, 1977; children: White-Chi, White-Yu. MS, Cheng-Kung U., 1975, U. Fla., 1980; PhD, Tsing-Hwa U., 1991. Group leader CSIST, Taiwan, China, 1975-91; dept. head I-Shou U., Taiwan, China, 1993-96, dean student affairs, 1996-99; cons. Philip Co., Taiwan, 1991-99, TACO Co., Taiwan, 1981-90. Buddhist. Avocation: badminton. Office: 1 Sec 1 Ta-Hsu Hsiang, Kaoshing County Taiwan, China 84008

JENGER, JEAN ANTOINE, civil servant; b. Nice, France, Nov. 26, 1930; s. Camille and Jeanne Adrienne (Wagner) J.; divorced 1982; children: Michel, Daniele. Student, Nat. Sch. Administrn., 1962-64. Head office teaching Art and Architecture Min. Culture, Paris, 1965-66, head office modern architecture, 1966-69, asst. dir. architecture, 1972-78; asst. dir. Caisse Nat. Monuments Historiques, Paris, 1970-71; dir. Pub. Establishment Orsay Mus., Paris, 1978-87; dir. French documentation, 1987-95; pres. Le Corbusier Found., 1982-92; bd. dirs. Corbusier Found.; commd. for the restoration of the castle of Chamarande, France. Author: Orsay de la Gare au Musée, 1986, Souvenirs de la Gare d'Orsay, 1987, Orsay Metamorphosis of a Monument, 1987, Souvenirs de la Tour Eiffel, 1989, Le Corbusier un Autre Regard, 1992, Le Corbusier l'Architecture pour émouvoir, 1993. Named Commander Nat. Order Merit, Officer Legion Honor, Officer Arts and Letters, Officer Palmes Academiques. Mem. Paris Acad. Architecture (assoc.). Avocations: photography, piano. Home: 7 Ave Verdier, 92120 Montrouge France

JENISCH, UWE KARLHEINZ, lawyer, German ministry official; b. Lötzen, E. Prussia, Germany, Apr. 9, 1941; s. Hans B. and Waldtraut (Kuhnert) J.; m. Barbara M. Coler, Dec. 1, 1967; children: Katrin, Jenny. 1st law degree, U. Kiel, Germany, 1966, DJ, 1970; 2d law degree, Superior Ct. Hamburg, Germany, 1970. Counsellor Fed. Ministry for Rsch., Bonn, Germany, 1970-72; sci. attachée German Embassy, Brussels, 1971; counsellor Ministry for Econs., Kiel, 1973—; German del. Law of the Sea Conf., N.Y.C., 1975-82; adj. instr. Law of the Sea, U. Kiel, Germany, 1977-81; mem. European Marine Sci. and Tech. Com., Brussels, 1992-96; bd. dirs., tchr. Inst. for Law of the Sea, Rostock, U., 1993—; vis. rschr. Harvard Law Sch., 1968. Author: 7 monographs and bibliographies including The Legality of Peacetime Naval Activities on the High Seas, 1970, Analysis of Informal Composite Negotiating Text, UN Session 3, 1977, The Law of the Sea (A Bibliography), 1988; Bibliographie des Deutschen Schrifttums zum Internationalen Seerecht, 1982-96; contbr. over 80 articles to profl. jours; extensive lecturing in sci. and industry, adult education, TV. Initiation German candidate for seat on Internat. Tribunal of Law of the Sea, Hamburg. Capt. German Navy Res., 1995. Mem. Am. Soc. Internat. Law, Law of the Sea Inst. Lutheran. Avocations: sailing, skiing. Office: Ministry Econs PO Box 1192, Land Schleswig-Holstein, 24105 Kiel Germany

JENKIN, JAMES THOMAS, videotape editor; b. Monclair, N.J., Apr. 28, 1964; s. David Alan and Dolores Ann (Hyland) J. Student, Raritan Valley Coll., Somerville, N.J., 1987-88; cert. advanced non-linear editing, Avid Sch. Forman Rising Sun Coatings, Flemington, N.J., 1985-89; with dept. videotape playback Picsonic Prodns., N.Y.C., 1989-91, videotape editor, 1991—; sr. editor program Headliners and Legends MSNBC, 1999—; pres. Thought Bubble Media. Contbr. articles to mags. Recipient various Telly awards, 1991, 92, 95, Communicator award, 1997, Videographer award, 1998. Mem. Internat. TV Soc. Avocations: music composition, softball, tennis, movie research. Office: Picsonic Prodns 25 W 45th St New York NY 10036-4902

JENKINS, BERNARD LOUIS, parking lot company executive, consultant; b. Paris, Mar. 10, 1931; s. Henry John J.; m. Sophia Vardoulaki. Ecole Ctrl. Paris, 1955. Diplomed engr. Exec. Larco Metallurgical & Mining AS, 1970-85; chief exec. Larco Metallurgical & Mining AS, Greece, 1986-89; cons. Usinor-Sollac, Greece, 1990-93; mng. dir. SETEX-HELLAS, 1994—; freelance cons., Athens, 1993—. Lt. French Air Force, 1956-57, Algeria. Decorated Valeur Mil., French Army, 1957, Ordre Nat. du Merite French Fgn. Affairs, 1975. Mem. Assn. Démocratique des FranÇais de l'etranger. Home: Aspasias 3, 156-69 Papagos Greece Office: Setex-Hellas AS, Chalandri Greece

JENKINS, BERNARD STEPHEN, cardiologist, consultant; b. Croydon, London, Eng., Dec. 21, 1939; s. Bernard Pizzy and Jane (Webb) J.; m. Elizabeth Ann Winder, Nov. 3, 1995. MA, Cambridge U., 1961, MB, 1964, BChir, 1966. Chmn. med. com. St. Thomas Hosp., London, 1981-84, chief exec., 1987-91, cons. cardiology, 1971—; dist. gen. mgr. West Lambeth Health Authority, 1984-87; cons. cardiologist Guy's and St. Thomas trust, London, Cromwell Hosp. Contbr. articles to profl. jours. Fellow Royal Coll. Physicians (London), Royal Inst. of Arts; mem. British Cardiac Soc. Avocations: piano playing. Home: 13 Richborne Terr, London SW8 1AS, England Office: Cardiology Dept, St Thomas Hosp, London SE1 7EH, England

JENKINS, EARNESTINE L., art history educator; b. Mar. 16, 1956. PhD in African History, Mich. State U., 1997. Asst. prof. art history U. Memphis, Tenn., 1999—.

JENKINS, EVERETT WILBUR, JR., lawyer, author, historian; b. Oklahoma City, Nov. 28, 1953; s. Everett Wilbur and Lillie Bell (Ingram) J.; m. Monica Lynn Endsley, June 3, 1978; children: Ryan, Camille, Jennifer, Cristina. BA, Amherst Coll., 1975; JD, U. Calif., Berkeley, 1978. Bar: Calif. 1979. Dep. county counsel Contra Costa County, Martinez, Calif., 1980-81; dep. city atty. City of Richmond, Calif., 1981-84; asst. city atty. City of Richmond, 1984—; bd. atty. West County Agy., Richmond, 1981-90; authority atty. Solid Waste Mgmt. Authority West Contra Costa, Richmond, 1985-87, 88-91; legal rep. tech. adv. com. Contra Costa County Solid Waste Commn., Martinez, Calif., 1986-87; pub. mem., 1987-88; adv. atty. West Contra Costa Transp. Adv. Com., San Pablo, 1994—; bd. atty. Richmond Housing Authority, 1992-99. Author: Pan-African Chronology, 1996, II, 1998, The Muslim Diaspora, 1999, vol. 2, 2000. Rep. Contra Costa County Hazardous Materials Commn., Martinez, 1987-88; bd. dirs. YMCA of the East Bay, Oakland, 1996—; bd. dirs. West Contra Costa YMCA, Richmond, 1987—, chair program com., 1991-92, vice chair bd. dirs. 1992-96, chair bd. dirs., 1996-98, chair cmty. gifts campaign, 1992-94 (named Rita Davis Vol. of the Yr., 1993); umpire Little League Baseball, 1997—, ASA Softball, 1997—. Mem. State Bar Calif. (exec. bd. pub. law sect. exec. com. 1987-91, editor Pub. Law News 1988-91, liaison to bd. govs. 1991-92), Charles Houston Bar Assn., Continuing Edn. Bar (joint adv. com. 1993-96). Independent. Office: City Atty's Office 2600 Barrett Ave # 330 Richmond CA 94804-1654

JENKINS, J. CRAIG, sociology educator; b. Bryan, Tex.. BA, U. Tex., 1970; MA, SUNY, Stony Brook, 1974; PhD, SUNY, 1975. From asst. to assoc. prof. sociology U. Mo., Columbia, 1976-86; prof. sociology Ohio State U., Columbus, 1986—. Author: The Politics of Insurgency, 1985; editor: The Politics of Social Protest, 1995. Mem. adv. bd. Nat. Com. for Responsive Philanthropy, Washington, 1997—. Fellow Inst. for Policy Studies Yale U., 1980, 83. Mem. Am. Sociol. Assn., Internat. Studies Assn. Office: Ohio State U Dept Sociology 310 Bricker Hall 190 N Oval Columbus OH 43210

JENKINS, JAMES WILLIAM, osteopath, medical consultant; b. Columbus, Ohio, May 15, 1953; s. William Harvey and Irene Barbara (Kacsor) J.; m. Deborah Susan Dorrance, June 16, 1987. BA in Biology, Calif. State U., Fullerton, 1976; DO, Coll. Osteopathic Med. Pacific, 1984; diploma in emergency medicine, Ohio State U., 1988. Cert. correctional health profl.; cert. ambulatory medicine. Intern Warren (Ohio) Gen. Hosp., 1984-85; resident in emergency medicine Meml. Osteopathic Hosp., York, Pa., 1985-87; rsch. fellow, clin. instr. Coll. Medicine, Ohio State U., Columbus, 1987-88; clin. emergency physician, med. edn. coord. emergency dept. Dr.'s Hosp., Columbus, 1988-89; med. dir. emergency dept. Greenfield (Ohio) Area Med. Ctr., 1989-93, clin. emergency/trauma physician, 1991-93; med. dir. Chillocothe (Ohio) Correctional Inst., 1993-96; clin. physician, healthcare cons. Ross Correctional Inst., Chillicothe, 1996—; emergency med. svc. med. advisor Franklin Twp. Fire Dept., Columbus, 1988-89; clin. asst. prof. Coll. Osteo. Medicine Pacific, Pomona, Calif., 1989. Contbr. articles to profl. publs., chpt. to book. Mem. CPR com. ARC, Santa Ana, Calif., 1978-81; instr. trainer Am. Heart Assn., Santa Ana, 1972-80; instr., course coord. basic trauma life support Am. Coll. Emergency Physicians, Columbus, 1988—. Rsch. grantee Emergency Medicine Found., 1988, Kellogg Found., 1979-80; recipient rsch. fellow award Emergency Medicine Residents Ohio, 1988, Armstrong Lit. award, 1980. Mem. Am. Assn. Physician Specialists, Am. Acad. of Ambulatory Care, Beta Beta Beta. Avocations: collecting books, martial arts.

JENKINS, KEITH PELLOW, religious organization executive; b. Kingsbridge, U.K., Dec. 28, 1941; m. Frances Murphy; 2 children. MA, U. Oxford, U.K., 1963. Pvt. practice law, 1971-81; exec. sec. cmty. and race rels. unit Brit. Coun. Chs., 1981-86, asst. sec. gen., 1986-90; sec.-gen. European Ecumenical Commn. for Ch. and Soc., Brussels, 1990—. Avocations: theology, politics, economics. Office: Ecumenical Centre, Rue Joseph II 174, B-1040 Brussels Belgium*

JENKINS, MARGARET ANNE, biochemist; b. Warragul, Victoria, Australia, Apr. 20, 1944; d. Anthony Allard and Grace Evelyn (Petschack) Pettit; m. Ian McPherson Jenkins, Jan. 28, 1966; children: Anita, David. BS, Monash U., 1964; Diploma of Fin. Planning, Deakin U., 1991. Biochemist Queen Victoria Hosp., Melbourne, 1965; sole technologist West Gippsland Hosp., Warragul, 1965-68; relieving technologist West Gippsland Hosp., 1968-72, sole biochemist, 1972-76; biochemist Preston & Northcote Cmty. Hosp., Preston, Australia, 1976-83, Austin & Repatriation Med. Ctr., Heidelberg, Australia, 1983—. Mem. Australian Assn. Clin. Biochemists (br. edn. rep. 1987-91, mem. com. Victorian br. 1985-87, traveling scholarship 1991, Nancy Dale scholarship 1993, Roche Poster award 1999), Australian Electrophoresis Soc. (com. mem. 1996-98). Avocations: piano, reading, gardening. Office: Austin & Repatriation Med, Ctr Studley Rd, Heidelberg 3084, Australia

JENKINS, RACHEL, psychiatrist; b. Manchester, U.K., Apr. 17, 1949; d. Peter Osborne and Beryl (Braddock) McDougall; m. David Keith Jenkins (div. 1999); children: Ruth, Ben. BA with honors, Cambridge (Eng.) U., 1971, BA, B in Surgery, MA, 1974, MD, 1984. Registrar Mandsley Hosp., London, 1975-78; rsch. fellow Inst. of Psychiatry, London, 1978-79, lectr., 1980-82, sr. lectr., 1983-85, dir. WHO Collaborating Ctr., 1997—; sr. lectr. St. Bartholomew's Hosp., London, 1985-87; prin. med. officer Dept. of Health, London, 1988-96. Trustee Mental Health Found., London, 1997—. Fellow Royal Coll. of Psychiatrists, Royal Coll. of Pub. Health and Hygiene, Faculty of Occupl. Health Medicine (hon. 1998), Am. Psychiat. Assn. (disting. 1999). Avocation: ecology. Office: WHO Collaborating Ctr, De Crespigny Pk, London SE5 8AF, England

JENKINS, RICHARD ERIK, patent lawyer; b. Newport News, Va., Jan. 12, 1946; s. Willard Erette and Ina Beatrice (Porter) J.; m. Susan Rankin Thurston, Aug. 24, 1968 (div. Nov. 1991); 1 child, Anna. BS, N.C. State U., 1968, M in Stats. and Econs., 1971; JD, U. N.C., 1975. Engr. Celanese Corp., Charlotte, N.C., 1971-72; assoc. atty. Stevens, Davis, Miller & Mosher, Washington, D.C., 1975-76, Bell, Seltzer, Park & Gibson, Charlotte, N.C., 1976-78; ptnr. Adams &Jenkins, Charlotte, 1978-80; asst. patent counsel Burlington Industries, Inc., Greensboro, N.C., 1980-84; sr. ptnr. Jenkins & Wilson, Durham, N.C., 1984—; adj. assoc. prof. Duke U., Durham, 1989—, N.C. State U., Raleigh, N.C., 1992—. Trustee N.C. Ctrl. U., Durham, 1992-95; bd. govs. Univ. Club, Durham, 1994-98; bd. dirs. Coun. Entrepreneurial Devel., 1988-90. Mem. AMA, N.C. Bar Assn., Ro-

tary, Hope Valley Country Club, Univ. Club, Carolina Club. Republican. Presbyn. Avocations: golf, yard, reading, sports cars. Office: Jenkins & Wilson PA 3100 Tower Blvd Ste 1400 Durham NC 27707-2563

JENKINS, ROBERT ROWE, lawyer; b. Norwalk, Ohio, Aug. 8, 1933; s. Robert Leslie and Millie Leona (Rowe) J.; m. Francis Jean Cline, June 12, 1955 (div. July 1972); children: Diane Elaine, Katherine Eileen; m. Jean Dingus, July 9, 1972. Student, Lebanon Valley Coll., 1951-55; BS in Chemistry, Eastern Coll. (now U. Balt.), 1967; JD, U. Balt., 1975. Bar: Md. 1976, U.S. Dist. Ct. Md. 1976, U.S. Ct. Appeals (4th cir.) 1979, U.S. Supreme Ct. 1979. Atty. Social Security Adminstrn., Balt., 1975-76; trial atty. Nelson R. Kandel, Balt., 1976-77; sole practice Balt., 1977-81; ptnr. Jenkins Block & Mering, Balt., 1981—; faculty continuing profl. edn. of lawyers Md. Inst., Balt., 1986—. Ruling elder Faith Christian Fellowship Presbyterian Ch. Am., Balt., 1982—. Served with U.S. Coast Guard, 1955-59. Mem. ABA, Md. Bar Assn., Balt. City Bar Assn., Assn. Trial Lawyers Am., Md. Trial Lawyers Assn., Christian Legal Soc., Nat. Orgn. Social Security Claimant's Rep. (exec. com.). Republican. Avocations: fishing, boating. Home: 1003 Travers St Cambridge MD 21613-1543 Office: Jenkins Block and Assocs 711 W 40th St Ste 235 Baltimore MD 21211-2186 also: 1011 E Main St Ste 212 Richmond VA 23219-3537 also: 516 Poplar St Cambridge MD 21613-1834 also: 33 W Franklin St Ste 102 Hagerstown MD 21740-4826

JENKINS, ROY HARRIS (LORD JENKINS OF HILLHEAD), writer, politician; b. Nov. 11, 1920; s. Arthur and Hattie J.; m. Jennifer Morris, 1945; 3 children. Ed., Oxford (Eng.) U.; numerous hon. degrees. Mem. staff Indsl. and Comml. Fin. Corp., 1946-48; Labour Party mem. Ho. of Lords, 1948-77, Social Dem. mem., 1982-87, leader Liberal Dems., 1988-98; pres. Royal Soc. Lit., 1988—; chmn. Fabian Soc., 1957-58; mem. coun. Britain in Europe; dep. chmn. Common Market campaign, 1961-63; dir. fin. ops. John Lewis Partnership Ltd., 1963-64; min. aviation, 1964-65; sec., 1965-67; chancellor of exchequer, 1967-70; dep. leader Labour party, 1970-72; home sec., 1974-77; pres. Commn. European Cmtys., 1977-81; privy Councillor, 1964; a founder, first leader Social Dem. Party, 1981. Author: Mr. Attlee: An Interim Biography, 1948, New Fabian Essays, 1952, Pursuit of Progress, 1953, Mr. Balfour's Poodle, 1954, Sir Charles Dilke: A Victorian Tragedy, 1958, The Labour Case, 1959, Asquith, 1964, Essays and Speeches, 1967, Afternoon on the Potomac, 1972, What Matters Now, 1972, Nine Men of Power, 1974, Partnership of Principle, 1985, Truman, 1986, Baldwin, 1987, Twentieth Century Portraits, 1988, European Diary, 1989, (autogiobraphy) A Life at the Centre, 1991, Portraits and Miniatures, 1993, Gladstone, 1995, The Chancellors, 1998. With Royal Arty., 1942-46. Decorated Order of Merit (Luxembourg and Italy), grand cross Order of Charles III (Spain), Comandeur Légion d'Honneur (France), mem. Brit. Order of Merit; recipient Charlemagne prize, 1972, Robert Schuman prize, 1972, Prix Bentinck, 1978. Fellow British Acad.; mem. Am. Acad. Arts and Scis. (hon. fgn.). Office: House of Lords, SW 1 London England

JENKINS, SPEIGHT, opera company executive, writer; b. Dallas, Jan. 31, 1937; s. Speight and Sara (Baird) J.; m. Linda Ann Sands, Sept. 6, 1966; children: Linda Leonie, Speight. B.A., U. Tex.-Austin, 1957; LL.B., Columbia U., 1961; DMus (hon.), U. Puget Sound, 1992; HHD, Seattle U., 1992. News and reports editor Opera News, N.Y.C., 1967-73; music critic N.Y. Post, N.Y.C., 1973-81; TV host Live from the Met, Met. Opera, N.Y.C., 1981-83; gen. dir. Seattle Opera, 1983—; classical music editor Record World, N.Y.C., 1973-81; contbg. editor Ovation Mag., N.Y.C., 1980—, Opera Quar., Los Angeles, 1982—. Served to capt. U.S. Army, 1961-66. Recipient Emmy award for Met. Opera telecast La Boheme TV Acad. Arts and Scis., 1982. Mem. Phi Beta Kappa Assocs. Presbyterian. Home: 903 Harvard Ave E Seattle WA 98102-4561 Office: Seattle Opera PO Box 9248 Seattle WA 98109-0248

JENKINS, WILLIAM E., business executive; b. L.A., Sept. 30, 1949; m. Catherine D. Jenkins; children: Laura J. Gann, Richard M. Jenkins. BS, No. Ariz. U., 1974; MS, U. Ariz., 1976. Cert. safety profl. Safety engr. Am. Smelting & Refining Co., Tucson, 1976-78; loss prevention engr. Mobil Oil S.E. Inc., New Orleans, 1978-80; supr. environ. health and safety engring. Mobil Exploration Norway Inc., Stavanger, 1980-82; supr. engring. P.T. Arun NGL Co., Lhok Seumawe, Indonesia, 1982-83; supr. loss prevention engring. Mobil Saudi Arabia, Jeddah, 1983-85; mgr. internat. environ., health & safety engring. Mobil Exploration & Production Divsn., Dallas, 1985-88; mgr. environ., health & safety divsn. Mobil North Sea Ltd., Aberdeen, Scotland, 1988-94; mgr. environ., health & safety sys. & strategic planning Mobil Exploration & Prodn. Inc., Dallas, 1995; mgr. global environ., health & safety risk mgmt. Mobil Oil Corp., Dallas, 1995-96; mgr. environ., health & safety ctr. for risk mgmt. Mobil Oil Corp., Fairfax, Va., 1996-97; v.p. Mobil Oil Shipping and Transp., Fairfax, 1997-99; pres. Exxonmobil Internat. Marine Transp., London, 1999—; dir. Internat. Tanker Owners Pollution Fedn. Ltd., London, 2009—, Cristal Ltd., Bahamas, 2000—. Contbr. articles to profl. jours. Mem. Am. Soc. Safety Engrs., U.K. Inst. Occupational Safety & Health, Soc. Petroleum Engrs. Achievements include development of first comprehensive environ. health and safety management system in oil and gas industry, first competency-based professional development system for loss prevention engineers in oil and gas industry.

JENKINS, WILLIAM MCLAREN, engineering educator, civil engineer, researcher; b. Newstevenston, Scotland, June 28, 1927; s. Archibald McLaren and Janet (Hamilton) J.; m. Carol Eveline Nutten, Mar. 31, 1956; children: Douglas Alan, Alison Kathleen Whittaker. BS in Civil Engring., Glasgow (Scotland) U., 1953, PhD in Civil Engring., 1958; D of Tech., Coun. Nat. Acad. Awards, Gray's Inn Road, London, 1992. Apprentice civil engr. Appleby-Frodingham Steel Co., Scunthorpe, Eng., 1943-49; civil engr. in tng. Civil Engring. Contractors-Local Authorities, Eng., 1951-53; lectr. civil engring. King's Coll.-U. London, 1955-63; reader civil engring. U. Bradford, Eng., 1964-68; head dept. civil and structural engring. and bldg. Teesside Poly., Middlesbrough, Eng., 1968-81; assoc. dean, prof., dir. studies civil engring. U. Hertfordshire, Hatfield, Eng., 1981-87, prof. emeritus, 1987—; part-time tchr., rschr. dept. civil engring. Leeds (Eng.) U., 1988—; rsch. dept. computer sci. U. York, Eng., 1997—; vis. prof. civil engring. U. East London, 1997—; advisor to rsch. couns.; cons. in field; external examiner various univs. Author: Matrix and Digital Computer Methods in Structural Analysis, 1969 (also in Japanese, 1975), Structural Mechanics and Analysis, 1982 (also in Spanish, 1985), Structural Analysis Using Computers, 1990; co-author: Basic Computing for Civil Engineers, 1983, Moment-transmitting Bolted Endplate Conditions, Structural Stability and Strength, 1990; contbr. over 25 articles to profl. jours. Sci. Rsch. Coun. grantee, 1964-68, British Steel Corp., 1975-80, 82-88, U.K. agencies for collaborative rsch. with Hong Kong, 1983-85. Fellow Instn. Civil Engrs. (examiner Part II exam. 1960-70), Instn. Structural Engrs. Mem. United Reformed Ch. Avocations: classical music, playing violin, water color and pastel painting. Office: U Leeds, Dept Civil Engring, Leeds LS2 9JT, England

JENNER, WILLIAM ALEXANDER, meteorologist, educator; b. Indianola, Iowa, Nov. 10, 1915; s. Edwin Alexander and Elizabeth May (Brown) J.; m. Jean Norden, Sept. 1, 1946; children: Carol Beth, Paul Williams, Susan Lynn. BA, Ctrl. Meth. Coll., Mo., 1938; cert. meteorology, U. Chgo., 1943; MEd, U. Mo., 1947; postgrad., Am. U., 1951-58. Instr. U. Mo., 1946-47; rsch. meteorologist U.S. Weather Bur., Chgo., 1947-49; staff Hdqrs. Air Weather Svc., Andrews AFB, Md., 1949-58, Scott AFB, Ill., 1958-84; dir. tng. Hdqrs. Air Weather Svc., Scott AFB, 1960-84. Mem. O'Fallon (Ill.) Twp. H.S. Bd. Edn., 1962-99, sec., 1964-71, pres., 1971-83, 85-87, 93-99, v.p., 1990-93; mem. gov. bd. Belleville Area Spl. Svcs. Coop., 1996-99; pres. St. Clair County Regional Vocat. Sys. Bd., 1986-89, active, 1986-99; vice chmn. southwestern divsn. Ill. Assn. Sch. Bds., 1987-89, chmn., 1989-95, dir., 1994-99; comdr. 507th Fighter Group Assn. Inc., 1987-89; mem. O'Fallon Planning Commn., 1973-84, sec., 1979-81, sub-divsn. chmn., 1978-84; alderman City of O'Fallon, 1984-93. With AUS, 1942-46. Recipient Disting. Svc. award O'Fallon PTA, 1968, Exceptional Civilian Svc. award Dept. Air Force, 1984, Disting. Svc. award City of O'Fallon, 1985, Merit cert. St. Clair County, 1987, 99, Cmty. Svc. award O'Fallon Toastmasters Club, 1991, Master Bd. Mem. award Ill. Assn. Sch. Bds., 1991, award of excellence O'Fallon C. of C., 1991, Spl. Recognition award Ill. State Bd. of Edn., 1995, Lifetime Disting. Svc. award, 1998, Disting. Alumni award Ctrl. Meth. Coll., 1999, Those Who Excel award of excellence, 1999; Jenmer award established by Air Weather Svc., 1984. Fellow Am. Meteorol. Soc.; mem. AAAS, APA, Am. Psychol. Soc., Wilson Ornithol. Soc., Am. Philatelic Soc., Am. Philatelic Congress, Nat. Soc. Study Edn., Nat. Audubon Soc., Nat. Arbor Day Found., Tree City USA, Nat. Parks and Conservation Assn., Nat. Wildlife Fedn., Nat. Resources Def. Coun., Nature Conservancy, Vt. Inst. Natural Sci., Leadership St. Louis, Focus St. Louis, The World Wildlife Fund, N.Y. Acad. Scis., VFW, Am. Legion, The Wilderness Soc., The Wildlife Conservation Soc., Rails to Trails Conservancy, Masons, Shriners, Sierra, Phi Delta Kappa, Psi Chi. Home: 307 Alma St O'Fallon IL 62269-2449

JENNINGS, BARRY RANDALL, physicist, educator, director, cleric; b. Purley, Surrey, Eng., Mar. 3, 1939; s. Albert James and Ethel Victoria (Randall) J.; m. Margaret Penelope Wall, Sept. 1, 1964; children: Carolyn Sarah, Samantha Jane. BSc, Southampton U., 1961, PhD, 1964, DSc, 1976. Chartered physicist, chemist; ordained min. Ch. of Eng. Rsch. fellow Strasbourg (France) U., 1964-65; lectr. physics London U., 1966-71; prof., physics dept. head Brunel (Eng.) U., 1971-84; prof. optics U. Reading, Eng., 1984-89; worldwide rsch. dir. English China Clays plc, 1990-97; rsch. physics prof. U. Reading, 1997—; chmn. Plymouth (Eng.) U. Consultancy Co., 1997—; vis. prof. La Pampa (Argentina) U., 1979, San Luis (Argentina) U., 1979, U. Reading, 1990-93; vis. prof. chemistry Bristol (U.K.) U., 1992-98; vis. prof. elec. engring. South Bank U. of U.K., 1994—; asst. curate St. Germans with Hessenford and Tideford, 1998-2000, Truro Diocese Cornwall; asst. curate Callikngton with South Mill, 2000—. Co-author: (with V.J. Morris) Atoms in Contact,; editor: Electro Optics of Macromolecules and Colloids, 1979; co-editor: (with S.P. Stoylov) Colloid and Molecular Electro-optics, 1992; edit. bd. mem. Jour. Physics; Applied Physics, 1987-90, Polymer, 1980-99, Internat. Jour. Biol. Molecules, 1981-84, Semiconductor Sci. and Tech., 1987-88; patentee in field; contbr. 230 articles to profl. jours. Pres. Cornish Fedn. Male Voice Choirs, Cornwall, U.K., 1991—. Recipient Freeman award City of London, 1997, Kerr Medal for Molecular Electro-Optics Soc., 1994, Polymer prize Soc. Chem. Industry, 1969. Mem. Assn. Internat. Cancer Rsch. (com. 1984-90), Brit. Biophys. Soc. (pres. 1982), Brit. Polymer Physics Group (chmn. 1977-85), Mineral Industry Rsch. Assn. (v.p. 1990-97). Avocations: long case clocks, antiquarian books, swimming, music, science and faith. Home: Pitt Meadow, St Dominic, Cornwall PL12 6SX, England Office: U Reading Dept Physics, White Knights, Reading RG6 6AF, England

JENNINGS, JOHN MARK, historian, writer; b. Phila., Nov. 26, 1962; s. Thomas Raymond and Elizabeth Ann Jennings; m. Kayoko Jennings, Jan. 6, 1989; children: Thomas Katsumi, James Katsuya. BA, Pa. State U., 1985; MA, U. Hawaii at Manoa, 1988, PhD, 1995. Journalist, film reviewer Suburban Pub., Inc., Wayne, Pa., 1985-86; vis. rschr. Sophia U., Tokyo, 1991-95; vis. asst. prof. Old Dominion U., Norfolk, Va., 1995-96, adj. asst. prof., 1996; adj. asst. prof. Norfolk State U., 1996-97; asst. prof. history U.S. Air Force Acad., Colorado Springs, 1997-99, assoc. prof., 2000—. Author: The Opium Empire, 1997; contbr. articles to profl. jours. Recipient David H. Zook award Dept. History, U.S. Air Force Acad., 1999. Mem. Assn. for Asian Studies, Soc. for Historians of Am. Fgn. Relations, Rocky Mountain World History Assn. Avocations: classical music, fishing, Sherlock Holmes. Office: US Air Force Acad Dept of History 2354 Fairchild Dr U S A F Academy CO 80840-6299

JENNINGS, NICHOLAS ROBERT, education educator, researcher; b. London, Dec. 15, 1966; s. R.G. and V.A. (Macey) J.; m. J.M. Smith Jennings, Aug. 1994; children: Anna Elizabeth, Matthew James. BS, U. Exeter, U.K., 1988; PhD, U. London, 1992. Rschr. Queen Mary and Westfield Coll., London, 1988-89, lectr., 1989-95, reader, 1995-98, prof., 1998-99; prof. electronics and computer sci. U. Southampton, Eng., 1999—; cons. Mitsubishi Electric, London, 1995—, IBM, Raleigh, 1996; chief sci. officer Lost Wax Media. Author: Cooperation in Industrial Milti-Agent System, 1995; editor: Intelligent Agents, 1996, Foundations of Multi-Agent System, 1996, Agent Technology: Markets and Implementations, 1998. Mem. IEEE, Am. Assn. Artificial Intelligence, Inst. Electrical Engrs. Avocations: football, cricket, golf. Office: U Southampton, Electronics/Computer Sci, Southampton SO17 1BJ, United Kingdom

JENNINGS, PETER CHARLES, television anchorman; b. Toronto, Ont., Can., July 29, 1938; s. Charles and Elizabeth (Osborne) J.; children: Elizabeth, Christopher. Student, Trinity Coll. Sch., Port Hope, Ont., Carleton U., Ottawa, Ont.; LLD, Rider (N.J.) Coll. Began career with Sta. CFJR, Ont.; formerly with CBC, Montreal, Que., CJOH-TV, Ottawa; former parliamentary corr., network anchorman Canadian TV, Ottawa; network anchorman, nat. corr. ABC News, N.Y.C., from 1964; London anchorman World News Tonight, until 1983, anchorman, sr. editor, 1983—; also involved with prodn. numerous network documentaries.; anchorman Peter Jennings Reporting, 1990—; moderator news spls. for children; anchorman Capital to Capital; anchor TV series The AIDS Quarterly, PBS. Recipient 9 Emmy awards for news reporting, Alfred I. DuPont-Columbia U. award. Mem. Internat. Radio and TV Soc., Overseas Press Club (awards). Office: ABC Press Relations 47 W 66th St Fl 2 New York NY 10023-6201

JENNINGS, SIR ROBERT YEWDALL, judge; b. Bradford, West Riding of Yorkshire, Eng., Oct. 19, 1913; s. Arthur Jennings and Edith Schofield Brotherton; m. Christine Dorothy Bennett, Aug. 4, 1955; children: Richard David Yewdall J., Philippa Mary J., Joanna Felicity. MA, LLB, Cambridge U., Eng., 1936, LLD (hon.), 1993; Choate fellowship, Harvard U., 1936-37; LLD (hon.), Saarland U., Germany, 1981, Hull U., Eng., 1987, Rome U., Italy, 1990, Cambridge U., 1993, Oxford U., 1996. Queen's Counsel. Whewell prof. internat. law Cambridge U., 1955-81; judge Internat. Ct. of Justice, Hague, Netherlands, 1981-95, pres., 1991-94; mem. Permanent Ct. Arbitration, 1981; appointing authority Iran-U.S. Claims Tribunal, 1999—. Author: The Acquisition of Territory, 1963, General Course on International Law, 1967, Collected Works, 2 vols., 1998; editor: Brit. Yearbook of Internat. Law, 1959-83. Maj. British Army, 1940-46. Hon. Bencher, Lincoln's Inn, 1970; knighted, 1981; hon. fellow Jesus Coll., Cambridge, 1981, Downing Coll., 1981, London Sch. Econs. & Polit. Sci., 1994. Hon. mem. Am. Soc. Internat. Law (Manley Hudson medal 1993); mem. Institut de Droit Internat. (pres. 1981). Avocations: reading, music, walking, watching cricket.

JENNINGS, WIRT HOLMAN, JR., retired marketing executive; b. Newberry, S.C., Oct. 5, 1927; s. Wirt Holman and Dorothy Elizebeth (Suber) J.; m. Carrie Lucille Braswell, Oct. 26, 1947; children: Michael Earl, Martha Jane, Dorothy Elizebeth. BS in Math. and Chemistry, Newberry Coll., 1949; grad., Lynhurst U., 1958. Area rep. to mgr. T.A. Edison, Inc., West Orange, N.C., 1949-52; sales trainee Esso Std. Oil, N.J., Columbia, S.C., 1952-55; sales rep. Esso Std. Oil, N.J., Bennettsville, S.C., 1955-56; sales supr., asst. dist. mgr. Esso, Humble, Enco, Columbia, 1956-64; dist. mgr. Esso, Humble, Enco, Birmingham, Ala., 1964-67; project coord. Esso, Humble, Enco, Memphis, 1967-68; nat. project coord. Exxon Co. USA, Houston, 1968-75; innovative project coord. Exxon Co. USA, Charlotte, N.C., 1975-80, Memphis, 1980-83, Houston, 1983-85; pres. Mktg. Expeditors, Inc., Houston, 1985-93; councilman Newberry County Coun., 1997—. Co-founder, pres. Cayce/West Columbia (S.C.) Jaycees, 1956; pres. Ala. Petredeum Coun., Birmingham, 1966; v.p. AARP, Newberry, 1997—; chmn. Rep. Party, Newberry, 1997—; mem. founding bd. dirs. Nat. Ins. Automotive Svc. Excellence, Washington, 1972-74; bd. trustees Newberry Coll., 2000—; bd. dirs. Houston Water and Sewer, 1971-75. With USN, 1945-46. Mem. Newberry Coll. Home Guard (chair 1997—), Columbia Exxon Annuitant Club (ex-officio, pres. 1998—). Avocations: fishing, hunting, golfing. Home: 51 Jennings Pt Prosperity SC 29127-8842

JENNINGS-HARRISON, DIAN THERESA, physician; b. Pointe-A-Pierre, Trinidad and Tobago, June 30, 1962; d. Ronald and Carole E. (Chinapoo) Jennings; m. Leslie Samuel DeWitt Harrison, Sept. 15, 1990; 1 child, Matthew. BS, U. W.I., Mona, Jamaica, 1985; MBBS, U. W.I., Cave Hill, Barbados, 1992. Med. registration Trinidad and Tobago, Jamaica, Gen. Med. Coun., U.K. Sr. lab. technician Caribbean Indsl. Rsch. Inst., 1986; med. intern Ministry of Health of Trinidad and Tobago, San Fernando, 1992-93, house officer, 1993-95; primary health care physician Jamaica, 1995—. Mem., guitarist Cath. Soc., U. W.I., 1981-85. Mem. Trinidad and Tobago Med. Assn., Jamaica Med. Assn., N.Y. Acad. Scis., Friends of Blood Bank, Guild of Grads. U. W.I., Caribbean Coll. Family Physicians. Roman Catholic. Avocations: stamp collecting, chess, movies, theater, guitar. Home: 3 Waddell St, Vistabella San Fernando Trinidad WI Office: Gen Hosp San Fernando, Paradise Pastures, San Fernando Trinidad and Tobago

JENNISON, BRIAN LESTER, environmental specialist; b. Chelsea, Mass., June 13, 1950; s. Lewis L. and Myra S. (Piper) J. BA, U. N.H., 1972; PhD, U. Calif., Berkeley, 1977; cert. hazardous materials mgr., U. Calif., Davis, 1986. Teaching, rsch. asst. U. Calif., Berkeley, 1972-77; staff rsch. assoc. Dept. of Molecular Biology, Berkeley, 1978-80; instr. dept. biology Calif. State U., Hayward, 1977; sr. biologist San Francisco Bay Marine Rsch. Ctr., Emeryville, Calif., 1980-81; inspector I Bay Area Air Quality Mgmt.Dist., San Francisco, 1981-83, inspector II, 1983-88; enforcement program specialist Bay Area Air Quality Mgmt. Dist., San Francisco, 1988-92; dir. air quality mgmt. div. Washoe County Dist. Health Dept., Reno, Nev., 1992-00; dir. Lane Regional Air Pollution Authority, Eugene and Springfield, Oreg., 2000—; cons. U.S. Army Corps of Engrs., L.A., 1980, San Francisco, 1981; instr. U. Calif., Berkeley ext., 1990-93, Assoc. Bay Area Govs., 1990-92; adj. prof. U. Nev., Reno, 1994-2000. Contbr. articles to profl. jours. Postdoctoral fellow, Harbor Br. Found., 1977-78. Mem. AAAS, Air and Waste Mgmt. Assn. (chmn. Ea. Sierra chpt. 1994-96, chmn.-elect Nev. sect. 1999), Navy League of U.S. (life), Springfield, Oreg., Rotary Club, Phi Beta Kappa. Avocations: railroad history, photography. Office: LRAPA 1010 Main St Springfield OR 97477-4879

JENNY, CHRISTIAN JAKOB, former insurance executive, educator; b. Aarau, Switzerland, Nov. 24, 1937; s. Hanns Erich and Helene (Mahler) J.; m. Turid Mariendal, Dec. 26, 1964; 1 child, Pierre Christian. MEE, Stanford U., 1964; PhD, Swiss Fed. Inst. Tech., Zurich, 1981. Sys. engr. Data Processing Divsn. IBM, San Francisco, 1963-65, adv. sys. engr., 1965-67; adv. sys. engr. IBM, Caracas, Venezuela, 1967; mem. rsch. staff Sci. Ctr. IBM, Palo Alto, Calif., 1968-70; mem. rsch. staff Rsch. Lab. IBM, Rüschlikon, Switzerland, 1970-82; data processing coord. Zurich Ins. Co., 1982-85, mgr. info. tech., 1985-87, chief info. officer, sr. v.p. info. tech., 1987-95; dir. Found. for Info. Mgmt. U. St. Gallen, 1995-99; mem. selection bd. Swiss Nat. Found., Berne, 1991-93, 95-99; info. mgmt. lectr. Swiss Sch. for Mgmt. Edn., Brunnen, 1993-95, U. St. Gallen, 1997—, lectr., chief recruiting officer and info. exec. for postgrad. program Master in Bus. Engring., U. Gallen. Contbr. articles to profl. jours.; inventor multiprocessor for line switching. 1st lt. Swiss Arty. Mem. Swiss Informatics Soc. (sec. 1979-83), Assn. Computing Machinery (chmn. Swiss chpt. 1972-74). Home: Seestrasse 149, CH-8800 Thalwil Switzerland Office: U St Gallen IWI HSG, Muller-Friedberg Strasse 8, CH-9000 St Gallen Switzerland

JENNY, FREDERIC YVES, economist, educator; b. Geneva, Switzerland, Sept. 29, 1943; s. Frederic Marc and Madeleine (Permezel) J.; m. Sarah Harrison Beers, Feb. 4, 1984. Student, Ecole Superieure des Scis. Econ. et Comml., Paris, 1966; PhD in Econs., Harvard U., 1975; Doctorat d'Etat, U. Paris, 1977; Dr. Honoris Causa, U. Wuhan, China, 1983. Prof. econs. ESSEC, Cergy-Pontoise, France, 1972—; rapporteur Commission de la Concurrence, Paris, 1980-85, rapporteur gen., 1985-86; rapporteur gen. Conseil de la Concurrence, Paris, 1987-93, vice-chmn., 1993—; mem. conseil des études Inst. Nat. de la Statistique et des Etudes Economiques, Paris, 1982-86; mem. Conseil Scientifique de l'Evaluation, Paris, 1990-96; chmn. competition law and policy com. Orgn. Econ. Cooperation and Devel., 1994—; chmn. com. in internat. trade and competition World Trade Orgn., 1997—. Co-author: Concentration et politique des Structures industrielles, 1975, L'Entreprise et les politiques de concurrence, 1976, Initiation a la theorie micio-economique, 1983. Decorated Officier Ordre Nat. du Mérite, 1999, Chevalier Ordre Nat. de la Légion d'Honneur, 1993. . Avocations: photography, sailing. Office: Conseil de la Concurrence, 11 rue de l'Echelle, Paris 75001, France

JENS, ELIZABETH LEE SHAFER (MRS. ARTHUR M. JENS, JR.), civic worker; b. Monroe, Mich., Jan. 25, 1915; d. Frank Lee and Mary (Bogard) Shafer; m. Arthur M. Jens, Jr., Aug. 14, 1937; children: Timothy V., Christopher E., Jeffrey A. Student, Kalamazoo Coll., 1932-34, U. Wis., 1935, Northwestern U., 1934-36; BS, Northwestern U., 1936; postgrad., Wheaton Coll., 1965; Lic. Practical Nurse, Triton Coll., 1968-69. Gray lady Hines (Ill.) Hosp., 1948-49, 51-53; vol. Elgin (Ill.) State Hosp., 1958-72; writer Newsletter Vol. Planning Coun., 1960-62. Writer column Mental Health and You for Press Publs., 1969-90, Life Newspapers, 1982-93, Pioneer Newspapers, 1984, Herald Newspapers, 1986-94; author: The Jewelled Flower: The True Account of a Courageous Young Man's Life and Death By His Own Hand, 1987. Mem. Family Svc. Assn. DuPage County; vol. coord., organizer, chmn. bd. dirs., treas. of the Thursday Evening Club, social club for recovering mental patients DuPage County, 1966—; vol. FISH orgn., 1973-84; bd. dirs. DuPage County mental Health Soc., 1962-68, sec., 1963-64, 65-68, chmn. forgotten patient com., 1963-68, chmn. new projects, 1965-68; co-chmn. Glen Ellyn unit Ctrl. DuPage Hosp. Assn. Women's Aux., 1959-60; bd. dirs. chmn. com. on pesticides, Ill. Audubon Soc., 1963-73; mem. Ill. Pesticide Control Com., 1963-73, Citizens Com. Dutch Elm Disease, Glen Ellyn, 1960; bd. dirs. Natural Resources Coun. Ill., 1961-67, sec., 1961-64; bd. dirs. DuPage Art league, 1958-68, chmn. bd., 1961-63, Paint-out chairperson, 1968-84, 91—, chmn. new bldg. com., 1968-75, Best in Show award 1991; bd. dirs. mem. planning com., publicity chmn. DuPage Fine Arts Assn., 1965-67; bd. dirs. Friends Libr. Glen Ellyn, 1967-68; mem. adv. bd. Rachel Carson Trust for Living Environment 1971-74; bd. dirs. Mental Health Assn. of DuPage, 1973—, sec., 1973-75, pres., 1980-81, chmn. cmty. liaison, 1981-89, chmn. action group, 1976—; mem. DuPage Subarea adv. coun. Suburban Cook County-DuPage County Health Sys. Agy., 1977-83; bd. dirs. DuPage County Comprehensive Health Planning Agy., 1976, DuPage County Bd. of Health, 1987-95; mem. DuPage County Behavioral and Mental Health Adv. Bd., 1977—; mem. com. on midlife and older women Ill. Commn. on Status of Women, 1978-85; bd. dirs., publicity chmn. DuPage County Coun. Vol. Coords., 1977-78; bd. dirs., membership chmn. Homemakers Equal Rights Assn. in DuPage County, 1979-84; publicity chmn., v.p. Homemakers Coalition for Equal Rights, 1984-97; mem. ERA Ill. Bd., 1987-92, v.p., 1994-97; mem. DuPage County Health Planning Coun., 1984-94, chairperson task force on residencies for mentally ill, 1990-93; mem. Community Care Coalition of DuPage County, 1988-93, NAACP; mem. pub. rels. com. Bethlehem Ctr. Food Bank of DuPage County, 1987-89; tour guide Stacy's Tavern-Glen Ellyn Hist. Mus., 1986-96; chmn. Grass Roots Com. to Pass Ill. Marital Property Act, 1982-97; mem. adv. bd. Older Adult Inst. Coll. DuPage, 1989—; del. for Mental Health Assn. DuPage to DuPage County Consortium, 1989-97, DuPage Consortium, Prevention and Intergenerational Task Force, 1991-97; vol. Hospice of DuPage, 1990—; bd. dirs. Willowbrook Wildlife Found., 1992-96, v.p., 1992-94; bd. dirs. DuPage area Older Women's League, chairperson publicity, 1992-96 (recipient Wonderful Older Woman ann. award 1990); with Clown Min. Fox Valley Unity Ch., 1991-95; vol. Ill. Dept. Mental Health, DuPage County. Recipient Pathfinders award, ERA Ill., 1965; hon. mention in Nat. Sonnet contest, 1967; Vol. of Yr. Ill Mental Health Assn., 1975; Svc. award Ill. Rehab. Assn., 1980; named DuPage County Outstanding Woman Leader in Arts and Culture W. Suburban YWCA, 1984, Friend of the Mentally Ill, Alliance for the Mentally Ill of DuPage County Ann. award, 1988, Adade Wheeler award Coll. of DuPage, 1994, Mental Health Person of Yr., Mental Health Assn. of Ill., 1995, Pub.. Svc. award Ill. State Med. Soc., 1996; vol. DuPage County Health Dept. Mental Health Svcs., 1999—. Mem. Mental Health Assn. DuPage, Wilderness Soc., Humane Soc. U.S., Nat. Trust for Hist. Preservation, DuPage County Hist. Soc. (life) Glen Ellyn Hist. Soc. (life), Nat. Audubon Soc., Nat. Writers Club (monthly meeting chmn. Midwest chpt. 1973-74, 4th award Ann. Mag. Contest 1978), DuPage Art League (hon. life, Best of Show award 1991), Defenders of Wildlife, Theosophical Soc. Am. (Quest Study Group 1992—), Nature Conservancy Ill. (hon.), Chgo. Art Inst. (life), Ill. Assn. Mental Health (dir. (1966-68), Amnesty Internat., Pi Beta Phi. Home: 22 W 210 Stanton Rd Glen Ellyn IL 60137-7111

JENSEN, ARTHUR SEIGFRIED, consulting engineering physicist; b. Trenton, N.J., Dec. 24, 1917; s. Emil Anthony and Emma Anna (Lund) J.; m. Lillian Elizabeth Reed, Aug. 9, 1941; children: Deane Ellsworth, Alan Forrest, Nancy Lorraine. BS, U. Pa., 1938, MS, 1939, PhD, 1941; diploma in advanced engring., Westinghouse Sch. Applied Sci., 1972, diploma in computer sci., 1977. Registered profl. engr., Md. Research physicist U.S. Naval Research Labs., Washington, 1941; research physicist RCA Labs., Princeton, N.J., 1945-57; mgr. spl. electron devices Westinghouse Electronic Tube Div., Balt., 1957-65; sr. adv. physicist Electronics Systems Ctr., Balt., 1965-91; cons. physicist Westinghouse Electronic Systems Ctr., Balt., 1991-

94; co-owner, chief engr. Jensen Cons. Engring., 1994—; mem. Md. State Bd. Registration Profl. Engrs., 1979-86, vice chmn., 1983-86; cons. Nat. Acad. Sci., 1970. Contbr. articles to profl. jours.; 25 patents. Mem. Endowed Sons of Norway Found., Nancy Lorraine Jensen Meml. Scholarship Fund. Served to capt. USN, 1941-46, USNR, 1946-77, ret., 1977—. Hector Tyndale fellow, 1939, George Lieb Harrison fellow, 1940; recipient outstanding svc. award Engrs. Coun. Md., 1986, Gov.'s citation, 1986, Westinghouse spl. patent award, 1972; endowed Sons of Norway Found., Nancy Lorraine Jensen Meml. Scholarship Fund. Fellow IEEE (life), Washington Acad. Scis.; mem. AAAS, AIAA, Res. Officers Assn., Ret. Officers Assn., Naval Res. Assn., Am. Phys. Soc., Am. Assn. Physics Tchrs., Soc. Photo-Optical Instrumentation Engrs., Optical Soc. Am., N.Y. Acad. Scis., Md. Acad. Scis. (chmn. awards com.), Nat. Coun. Engring. Examiners (chmn. internat. rels. com.), Infrared Info. Symposium, Am. Legion, Fleet Res. Assn., Sons of Norway, Nat. Eagle Scout Assn., Vigil Honor Order of Arrow, Sigma Xi, Pi Mu Epsilon, Kappa Phi Kappa. Club: U.S. Naval Acad. Officers and Faculty. Achievements include patents in field. Home and Office: Chapel Gate 1104 Oak Crest Village 8820 Walther Blvd Parkville MD 21234-9025

JENSEN, BEVERLY ANN, communications specialist; b. Worthington, Minn., July 18, 1948; d. Waldo Alfred and Georgiann Mary (Ulrich) J.; m. Abdolhosain Katirayi, Mar. 23, 1975 (div. Feb. 1989); children: Leila, Angela, Laura. BJour, U. Mo., 1970, MA, 1977; PhD in Comm., U. Wash., 1987. Gen. reporter Loveland (Colo.) Reporter-Herald, 1970-71; staff writer Stephens Coll., Columbia, Mo., 1972-74; news dir. Stephens Coll., Columbia, 1974-76; teaching asst. Sch. Journalism, U. Mo., Columbia, 1976-77; predoctoral teaching assoc. dept. communication U. Wash., Seattle, 1978-80; instr. journalism Mich. State U., East Lansing, 1982-83; comms. cons. Communication Mgmt. Rsch., Seattle, 1978-93; founder, dir. New Thought Childcare Ctr., Seattle, 1988-90; asst. prof. Am. U., Cairo, 1993-97, internat. devel. comm. cons., 1993-98; sr. mgr. Price Waterhouse Coopers, Washington, 1998—. Contbr. articls to profl. jours. Mass media advisor Beijing Workers' Union, 1996. Mem. Soc. for Internat. Devel., World Assn. Pub. Opinion Rsch. Democrat. Mem. Religious Sci. Ch. Avocations: cooking, photography, collecting Oriental rugs. E-mail: jabeverly@get.net.

JENSEN, CRAIG LOUIS, pediatrician, medical educator; b. Provo, Utah, Sept. 8, 1956; s. Louis Wells and Patrea (Egbert) J. BA, U. Utah, 1979, MD, 1983. Diplomate Nat. Bd. Med. Examiner; cert. Am. Bd. Pediatrics (pediatrics and pediatric gastroenterology), cert. Am. Bd. Nutrition (clin. nutrition). Rsch. asst. prof. Baylor Coll. Medicine, Houston, 1989-91, asst. prof., 1991—; attending physician Tex. Children's Hosp., Houston, 1989—. Contbr. articles to profl. jours. Fellow Am. Acad. Pediatrics; mem. N.Am. Soc. for Pediatric Gastroenterology and Nutrition, Houston Gastroenterologic Soc. Home: 3023 Teague Rd Houston TX 77080-2515 Office: Tex Childrens Hosp 6621 Fannin St # Mc3-3391 Houston TX 77030-2303

JENSEN, ELWOOD VERNON, biochemist; b. Fargo, N.D., Jan. 13, 1920; s. Eli A. and Vera (Morris) J.; m. Mary Welmoth Collette, June 17, 1941 (dec. Nov. 1982); children: Karen Collette, Thomas Eli; m. Hiltrud Herborg, Dec. 21, 1983. AB, Wittenberg U., 1940, DSc (hon.), 1963; PhD, U. Chgo., 1944; DSc (hon.), Acadia U., 1976, Med. Coll. Ohio, 1991; MD (hon.), U. Hamburg, 1994. Mem. faculty U. Chgo., 1947-90, assoc. prof. biochemistry Ben May Inst. Cancer Rsch., 1954-60, prof., 1960-63, Am. Cancer Soc. research prof. physiology, 1963-69, dir. Ben May Inst., 1969-82, dir. Biomed. Ctr. Population Research, 1972-75, prof. physiology, 1969-73, 77-84, prof. biophysics, 1973-84, prof. biochemistry, 1980-90, Charles B. Huggins disting. svc. prof., 1981-90, emeritus prof., 1990—; research dir. Ludwig Inst. for Cancer Research, 1983-87; scholar-in-residence Fogarty Internat. Ctr. NIH, 1988, Cornell U. Med. Coll., 1990-91; prof. Inst. for Hormone and Fertility Rsch. U. Hamburg, Fed. Republic Germany, 1992-97; Nobel vis. prof. Karolinska Inst., Huddinge, Sweden, 1998, STINT vis. scientist, 1998-99, prof. emeritus, 1999—; vis. prof. Max-Planck-Inst. für Biochemie, Munich, Germany, 1958; mem. chemotherapy rev. bd. Nat. Cancer Inst., 1960-62, bd. sci. counselors, 1969-72; mem. Nat. Adv. Coun. Child Health and Human Devel., 1976-80; mem. adv. com. biochemistry and chem. carcinogenesis Am. Cancer Soc., 1968-72, coun. for rsch. and clin. investigation, 1974-77; mem. assembly life scis. NRC, 1975-78; mem. com. on sci., engring. and public policy Nat. Acad. Scis., 1981-82; mem. rsch. adv. bd. Clin. Rsch. Inst. of Montreal, 1987-96, Klinik für Tumor Biologie, Freiburg, 1993—, Strang Cancer Prevention Ctr., 1994—; cons. Rockefeller U. Hosp., 1990-92. Mem. editl. adv. bd. Perspectives in Biology and Medicine, 1966—, Archives of Biochemistry and Biophysics, 1979-84; mem. editl. bd. Biochemistry, 1969-72, Life Scis., 1973-78, Breast Cancer Rsch. and Treatment, 1980—, Endocrine-Related Cancer, 1994—, Jour. Biol. Markers, 1998—; assoc. editor: Jour. Steroid Biochemistry, 1974-94; contbr. articles to profl. jours. Recipient D.R. Edwards medal, 1970, La Madonnina prize, 1973, Pap award, 1975, prix Roussel, 1976, Nat. award Am. Cancer Soc., 1976, Gregory Pincus Mem. award, 1978, Gairdner Found. award, 1979, Lucy Wortham James award, 1980, Charles F. Kettering prize, 1980, Golden Plate award, 1980, Nat. Acad. Clin. Biochemistry award, 1981, Scientist of Yr. award Achievement Rewards for Coll. Scientists Found., 1981, Pharmacia award, 1982, Hubert H. Humphrey award, 1983, Rolf Luft medal, 1983, Renzo Grattarola medal, 1984, Fred C. Koch award, 1984, Axel Munthe award, 1985, Humboldt Sr. Rsch. prize, 1992, Joseph Bolivar DeLee award Chgo. Lying-In Hosp., 1995; Guggenheim fellow, 1946-47. Mem. NAS (council 1981-84), AAAS (Amory prize 1977), Am. Soc. Biochemistry and Molecular Biology, Am. Chem. Soc., Am. Assn. Cancer Rsch. (G.H.A. Clowes award 1975), Endocrine Soc. (pres. 1980-81), Am. Gyn/Ob Soc. (hon.), St. Paul Surg. Soc. (hon.), EORTC Receptor and Biomarker Group (hon.). Address: Karolinska Inst Dept Med, Nutrition Novum, S-141 86 Huddinge Sweden

JENSEN, FINN VERNER, computer science researcher; b. Tønder, Denmark, June 13, 1945; s. Karl Verner and Sigrid Flensted (Hvid) J.; m. Kirsten Bangsø Nielsen, Aug. 19, 1967; children: Marianne Bangsø, Olav Bangsø. Cand. Scientist, Århus (Denmark) U., 1970; D in Math., Warsaw (Poland) U., 1974. Secondary sch. tchg. cert. Rsch. asst. Århus U., 1970-72, rsch. fellow, 1972-74; assoc. prof. Aalborg (Denmark) U., 1974-86, reader, 1989-98, prof., 1998—; project mgr. Judex Internat., Aalborg, 1986-89; prin. rschr. Oper. & Decision through Inference Networks, Aalborg, 1990-96, Aalborg U.-Hewlett Packard Lab., Aalborg, 1998—; gen. mgr. Hugin Support Ltd., Aalborg, 1996—. Author: An Introduction to Bayesian Networks, 1996; designer (computer sys.) Hugin, 1989. Editor Brønderslev Avis, 1975-79; chmn. Brønderslev Amatør Scene, 1990-94; regional chmn. Dansk Amatøteater Samvirke, North Jutland, 1995-98, bd. mem., 1997-98. Mem. IEEE, Am. Assn. Artificial Intelligence. Avocations: drama, team handball, golf. Home: Olufsgade 26, 9700 Brønderslev Denmark Office: Aalborg Univ, Fredrik Bajersvej 7E, 9220 Ålborg Denmark

JENSEN, HANNE, rheumatologist, consultant; b. Copenhagen, May 30, 1946; d. G. Stefansen; m. Henning S. Jensen, Mar. 8, 1970; children: Olof, Torben. Diploma in Philosophy, U. Copenhagen, 1966, Cand.Med. & Surg., 1974, Specialist in Internal Medicine, 1984, D Med. Sci., 1992. Houseman/registrar North Canterbury Hosp. Bd., Christchurch, New Zealand, 1974-77; houseman/registrar Univ. Hosps. of Copenhagen, 1977-83, specialist registrar in internal medicine/rheumatology, 1983-93; cons. U. Hosp., Copenhagen, 1993—; postgrad tutor KAS Gentofte, Copenhagen, 1984-87; clin. lectr. U. Copenhagen, 1986-93. Contbr. articles to profl. jours. Danish Rheumatism Assn. grantee, 1988-89; specialist recognition in rheumatology, 1991. Mem. Danish Internal Medicine Orgn., Danish Rheumatol. Soc., Danish Soc. for Med. Rheumatology (sec. 1986-95), Danish Assn. for Sr. Physicians (bd. 1998—), Young Drs. Assn. State Univ. Hosp. (chmn. 1992-93), Drs. Assn. Office: Kas Gentofte, Univ Hosp PO Box 263, DK-2900 Hellerup Denmark

JENSEN, HANS FRANDSEN, historian, educator; b. Lejrskov, Denmark, Apr. 19, 1937; s. Johannes and Anna (Frandsen) J.; m. Inge-Marie Skovsböl, Dec. 21, 1963; children: Anders, Karen, Kristian. Tchr.'s cert., Gedved Tng. Coll., Denmark, 1961. Tchr. Virklund Sch., Denmark, 1962-68, Sortebakkeskolen, Nöragcr, Denmark, 1968-97; tchr. Sydhimmerlands Mus., Hobro, Denmark, 1981—, mgr. nature sch., Boldrup, Denmark, 1992—. Author: Life in the Country A Hundred Years Ago, 1974, We Work with History, 1986, vol. 2, 1989; editor: People Tell, 1978—. Home: Bredgade 50, 9610 Nöráger Denmark Office: Sydhimmerlands Mus, Vestergade 23, 9500 Hobro Denmark

JENSEN, HENRIK, economics educator; b. Aarhus, Denmark, May 24, 1961; m. Inge Laustsen, May 28, 1988; children: Mikkel, William. Cand.Econ., U. Aarhus, 1989, PhD, 1995. Economist Econ. Coun., Copenhagen, Denmark, 1992-94; assoc. prof. econs. U. Copenhagen, 1995—. Contbr. articles to profl. jours. Recipient 60 Yr. Jubilee prize Faculty Social Scis., 1996. Office: Inst Econs, Studiestaede 6, DK-1455 Copenhagen Denmark

JENSEN, JOHN ROBERT, lawyer; b. Rapid City, S.D., Aug. 9, 1946; s. Edwin Robert and Roxina Althier (Hollinger) J.; m. Susan McClelland, Aug. 27, 1977; children: Margaret Marie, Jennifer Jo, Edwin Robert II, James Peder. BA, Calif. State U., Northridge, 1971; JD, Baylor U., 1976. Bar: Tex. 1977, U.S. Dist. Ct. (no. dist.) Tex. 1977, U.S. Ct. Appeals (5th cir.) 1982. Asst. ins. dir. Groesbeck Fin., L.A., 1971-73; v.p. Capital Cons., Dallas, 1973-74; assoc. McConnell & Assocs., Arlington, Tex., 1977; sole practice Arlington, Tex., 1984—. Author: Checklist for Texas Lawyers, 1979, 2d edit., 1981. Served with U.S. Army, 1966-68, Vietnam. Decorated Army Commedation medal. Mem. Arlington Bar Assn., Baylor Order Barristers, Tex. Bd. Legal Specialization (cert. personal injury trial law), Nat. Bd. Trial Adv. (cert. civil trial adv.), Delta Theta Phi (treas. Baylor chpt. 1976). Lutheran. Office: Jensen & Jensen 6025 Interstate 20 W Arlington TX 76017-1077

JENSEN, KARSTEN HØGH, engineering educator, researcher; b. Nykoebing Sj., Denmark, Mar. 7, 1952; s. Henning and Astrid (Olsen) J.; m. Lisbet Juul, July 17, 1992; 1 child, Sarah. MSc in Civil Engring., Tech. U. Denmark, 1977, PhD, 1983. Hydrologist Danish Hydraulic Inst., Horsholm, 1977-88; rsch. asst. Tech. U. Denmark, 1979-83, postdoct. researcher, 1983-88, assoc. prof., 1988-90, docent, 1990-99, prof., 1999—; vis. scientist MIT, 1987; permanent cons. Carl Bro Group Cons. Engrs., Denmark, 1988-91; vis. prof. U. Colo., Boulder, 1992-93; chief engr. Water Quality Inst., Denmark, 1994-99. Fulbright scholar Fulbright Commn., 1992-93. Mem. Internat. Assn. Hydrol. Scis. (pres. internat. com. atmosphere, soil, vegetation rels. 1997). Home: Gadevangen 49, DK-2800 Lyngby Denmark Office: Tech U Denmark, ISVA Bldg 115, DK-2800 Lyngby Denmark

JENSEN, KARSTEN ULRIK, management educator; b. Gilleleje, Sealand, Denmark, Nov. 24, 1947; s. Svend Erik and Kirsten (Magnussen) J.; m. Lone Johansen, June 6, 1992. Cert. vocat. tchr. Planner Internat. Svc. Sys. Univ., Copenhagen, Denmark, 1969-73, br. mgr., 1973-75, cons., 1975-77, planning mgr., 1977-78, tng. cons., 1978-91, mgr. total quality mgmt. tng. Quality Inst., 1991-96; chief cons. The Danish Assn. of Mgrs. and Execs., 1996; ptnr., owner K&K Bus. Excellence i/S, 1997—; cons., tchr. Denmarks Forvaltnings-Hojskole, 1984—; assessor to European Quality Award, European Found. for Quality Mgmt., Brussels, 1994, 95, 96. Producer, author: (training videos) Methods, 1991. With inf. Denmark Marine Corps., 1968-69. Mem. European Found. Quality Mgmt., Danish Assn. Bus. Excellence, Catalyst. Avocations: golf, classical music. Home: Dyndetvej 24, DK-4140 Borup Denmark

JENSEN, KLAUS BRUHN, media and communications educator, researcher; b. Aarhus, Denmark, Oct. 20, 1956; s. Helge and Ritta (Rasmussen) J.; m. Grethe Krogh Skylv, Oct. 15, 1994 (dec. Feb. 1998); m. Ghita Juul Nielsen, July 29, 2000. MA, U. Aarhus, 1982, Dr.Phil., 1986. Rsch. fellow U. Aarhus, 1983-85; asst. prof. U. Copenhagen, 1986-90, assoc. prof., 1990—; cons. Sage Publs., Edward Arnold Publs., European Commn. Human Rights, The Netherlands, 1989, Danish Media Commn., Denmark, 1994-95, UNESCO, Paris, 1991-95; mem. global expert panel future media program London Bus. Sch. and Markle Found.; adj. prof. U. Oslo, 1996—. Author, contbr.: Communication Yearbook, 1991; editor: Danish Media History, 3 vols., 1996-97, News of the World, 1998; co-editor: A Handbook of Qualitative Methodologies for Mass Communication Research, 1991 (Spanish version 1993, Chinese version 1996, Portugese version 2000); author: The Social Semiotics of Mass Communication, 1995 (Spanish version 1997, Italian version 1999); mem. editl. bd. Jour. Broadcasting and Electronic Media, Journalism: Theory, Practice and Criticism, Comm., Social Semiotics, European Jour. Comm. Fellow Fulbright Commn., 1981, Am. Coun. Learned Socs., 1988-89. Mem. Internat. Assn. Mass Comm. Rsch., Internat. Comm. Assn. Avocations: traveling, music, jogging.

JENSEN, OLE, energy researcher; b. Hjorring, Jutland, Denmark, Aug. 21, 1932; s. Ole Pedersen and Agnes (Olesen) J.; m. Gerda Christensen, July 4, 1959 (dec. Feb. 1974); children: Jesper, Birgitte, Mette Lise, Hans; m. Inger Brygger, July 4, 1987. MSME, Tech. U. Copenhagen, 1958. R & D engr. Sabroe Refrigeration, Aarhus, Denmark, 1960-63; asst. prof. Tech. U., Copenhagen, 1963-70, assoc. prof., 1970-77; with Danish Bldg. Rsch. Inst., Hoersholm, 1977—; mgr. R & D Energy Rsch. Program, Copenhagen, 1977—; mem. energy R & D coun. Danish Ministry Energy, Copenhagen, 1977—, mem. solar R & D Coun., 1988—; mem. exec. com. for energy conservation Internat. Energy Agy., 1980—, mem. solar exec. com., 1988—; mem. steering group Air Infiltration and Ventilation Ctr., 1986—. Editor Kulde (Refrigeration), 1962-68; contbr. articles to profl. jours. Lt. Danish Army, 1960-61. Recipient award Nordic Innovations, 1983. Mem. Danish Assn. Civil Engrs., Danish Heating and Ventilation Engrs., Internat. Bldg. Coun. Achievements include research on energy conservation in buildings, termodynamics of compressors, solar energy in buildings, energy research and development programs and strategies. Home and Office: Bernhard Bangs Alle 11, DK2000 Frederiksberg Denmark

JENSEN, PAUL EDWARD TYSON, business educator, consultant; b. New Orleans, Apr. 27, 1926; s. Paul Christian and Nena Laura (Robertson) J.; m. Jule Valerie Geisenhofer, Jan. 10, 1953; children: Christian, Elena, Constance. BS in Physics, Tulane U., 1947, BBA, 1949; MBA, Golden Gate U., 1976. Asst. mgr. Cuban Atlantic Sugar Co., Lugareño, Cuba, 1952-55; sr. engring. specialist GTE, Mountain View, Calif., 1955-82; sr. staff engr. TRW, Inc., Sunnyvale, Calif., 1982-92; dean Sch. of Bus., Northwestern Poly. U., Fremont, Calif., 1988—, also bd. trustees; cons. geog. info. sys. TRW, Inc., Sunnyvale, 1993-94. Capt. USMCR, 1945-61, WWII, Korea. Fellow Soc. Tech. Comm. (assoc.); mem. IEEE (life, sr. mem.), Am. Phys. Soc., Soc. Computer Simulation, World Future Soc., Assn. Old Crows. Presbyterian. Avocations: amateur radio, jogging, photography, travel. Home: 8033 Regency Dr Pleasanton CA 94588-3131 Office: Northwestern Poly U 117 Fourier Ave Fremont CA 94539-7482

JENSEN, PETER KJESTRUP AXEL, clinical geneticist, consultant; b. Vandel, Denmark, Jan. 28, 1951; s. Anders Kjestrup and Margrethe Axel (Nielsen) J.; m. Karin Elin Nissen, Mar. 12, 1982; children: Lena, Lars. MD, U. Aarhus, Denmark, 1978. Med. staff Univ. Hosp. Aarhus, 1978-79; rschr. U. Aarhus Inst. Human Genetics, 1979-95; med. staff U. Aarhus Dept. Clin. Genetics, 1979-95; head dept. clin. genetics Univ. Hosp. Aarhus, 1995—; cons. in clin. genetics, Jylland, Denmark, 1982—. Author: Human Origins and Evolution, 1996, Chromosomal Disorders in Man, 1998. Mem. European Soc. Dermatologic Rsch., Danish Soc. Med. Genetics, Danish Cytogenetics Register. Avocations: amateur geology, study of human origins. Home: Egevej 16, 8680 Ry Denmark Office: Univ Hosp Aarhus, Dept Clinical Genetics, 8000C Århus Denmark

JENSEN, ROBERT GORDON, nutritionist, consultant; b. Carthage, Mo., Jan. 2, 1926; s. Wiggo England and Thelma Nancy (Judd) J.; m. Helene Catherine Wickstrom, Dec. 20, 1947; children: Gordon, Jeffrey. BS, U. Mo., 1950, MS, 1951, PhD, 1954. Instr. U. Mo., Columbia, 1954-55, asst. prof., 1955-56; asst. prof. U. Conn., Storrs, 1956-61, assoc. prof., 1961-66, prof., 1966-91, prof. emeritus, 1991—. Author, editor: Handbook of Milk Composition, 1995; contbr. more than 130 articles to profl. jours. With USN, 1944-46, ETM. Fellow Am. Dairy Sci. Assn., 2000. Fellow Internat. Soc. Rsch. Human Milk Lactation (founding mem., 1st recipient Macy-Gyorsy award 1995); mem. Am. Oil Chem. Soc. (Supelco-Nicholas Pelick award 1998), Am. Soc. Nutrition Sci. Home: 186 Chaffeeville Rd Storrs Mansfield CT 06268-2637

JENSEN, ROBERT GRANVILLE, geography educator, university dean; b. Seattle, June 16, 1935; s. John Granville and Eva Phyllis (Watson) J.; m. Nansie Jean Gilfillan, June 8, 1957; children: Carolyn, Maryann, Paul. BS, Oreg. State U., 1957; MA, U. Wash., Seattle, 1962, PhD, 1964. Acting asst. prof. Portland (Oreg.) State U., summer 1963; from asst. prof. to assoc. prof. geography Syracuse (N.Y.) U., 1964-78, prof., 1979—, chmn. dept., 1973-90, interim dean Grad. Sch., 1989-90, dean Grad. Sch., 1990-94, interim dean Coll. Arts and Scis., 1993-94, dean Coll. Arts and Scis., 1994—, dir. Soviet and East European Studies, 1968-75; del. Soviet-Am. Seminar on Cities, Moscow, 1975. Contbr., editor: (with Shabad and Wright) Soviet Natural Resources in the World Economy, 1983 (Geog. Soc. Chgo. award 1984, named one of outstanding acad. books, Choice 1984-85); assoc. editor Soviet Geography, 1983-87; co-editor Soviet Economy, 1984-88; contbr. articles to profl. jours. Mem. Commr.'s Doctoral Coun. N.Y. State Dept. Edn., 1989-92. Served to 1st lt. USMC, 1957-60. Fgn. Area fellow to USSR Am. Council Learned Socs., 1965-66; Fulbright-Hays faculty research fellow to USSR, 1970-71; Sr. Exchange scholar Internat. Research and Exchanges Bd., 1970-71; NSF grantee, 1977-80. Mem. Am. Assn. for Advancement Slavic Studies, Am. Geog. Soc., Assn. Am. Geographers (chmn. splty. group 1980-81, 83-84, honors award for contbns. to Soviet and East European scholarship 1993). Democrat. Avocations: alpine skiing, tennis. Home: 61120 Riverbluff Trl Bend OR 97702-1991 Office: Syracuse U Office of Dean Arts & Scis 300 Hall Of Langs Syracuse NY 13244-0001

JENSEN, SØREN KROGH, research scientist; b. Herning, Denmark, Dec. 2, 1959; s. Alfred Krogh and Kirsten Feldborg (Nielsen) J.; m. Ulla Holm Jakobsen, July 29, 1989; children: Anne, Niels, Kristian. MSc in Agronomy, Royal Vet. and Agrl. U., Copenhagen, 1987, PhD, 1991. Tchr. Royal Vet. and Agrl. U., Copenhagen, 1987; rsch. chemist Novo Nordisk, Bagsvard, Denmark, 1988-90; rschr. Danish Inst. Agrl. Sci., Tjele, Denmark, 1991-94, sr. rschr., 1995—; external examiner Royal Vet. and Agrl. U., Copenhagen, 1996—. Contbr. articles to profl. jours. Mem. Groupe Consultatif Internat. Recherche sur le Colza. Avocations: breeding sportshorses, riding, hunting. Home: Vibaekvej 33, DK-8800 Viborg Denmark Office: Danish Inst Agrl Sci, Rsch Ctr Foulum, DK-8830 Tjele Denmark

JENSEN, TOM RISDAHL, diplomat; b. Hjoerring, Denmark, Sept. 28, 1947; s. Lavst and Eva Maria (Larsen) J. MA, Aarhus U., Denmark, 1975; MS in Polit. Sci., Aarhus U., 1981. Head sect. Ministry Fgn. Affairs and Fgn. Posts, Copenhagen, Denmark, 1977-81, 84-88; head of dept., 1992-97, undersect., ambassador, 1997—; first sec. permanent representation Danish Embassy, Brussels, 1981-84; econ. counselor Danish Embassy, Bonn, Germany, 1988-92. Home: Martensens Alle 4A 1 Fl, DK-1828 Copenhagen V, Denmark Office: Ministry Fgn Affairs, DK-1448 Copenhagen K, Denmark

JENSEN, W. LYNNE, family nurse practitioner; b. Salt Lake City, July 23, 1957; d. Percy Leondo and Wilma Beth (Oswald) Neal; children: Michael Wayne, Laura Ann. ADN, Weber State U., 1985; BSN, Tex. A&M U., 1995, MSN, 1998. RN, Tex.; cert. family nurse practitioner; cert. ACLS, CPR, NALS instr., PALS instr., trauma nurse care course provider. Staff nurse McKay-Dee Hosp., Ogden, Utah, 1984-85; med.-surg. staff nurse Tooele Valley (Utah) Regional Med. Ctr., 1985-86, ICU staff nurse, 1986-90, edn. coord., 1989-90; DON Tooele Valley Home Health, 1990-91; ICU staff nurse Fountain Valley (Calif.) Regional Med. Ctr., 1991-92; house supr., ICU staff nurse Bee County Regional Med. Ctr., Beeville, Tex., 1991-92; instr. LVN program Bee County Coll., 1992-93; edn. mgr., performance improvement coord. Bee County Regional Med. Ctr., Beeville, Tex., 1993-97; dir. nursing, post surg. unit Spohn Bee County Hosp., Beeville, 1997-98; family nurse practitioner Roel & Assocs., Beeville, 1998-99, Bear River Med. Arts, PA, Garland, Utah, 1999—; coord. seminars and workshops for cmty. and health profls. Leader, Ch. of Jesus Christ of Latter Day Saints, 1990—; mem. medi-tech computer task force, 1997; mem. Bee County Health Edn. Cmty. Task Force; bd. dirs. Area Health Edn. Com., Coastal Bend, 1997—; mem. adv. bds. Bee County Rural Initiatives, facilitator support and edn. groups, CQ Com.; adv. bd. Robert Wood Johnson Found. nursing workforce 2000; spkr. at various civic and cmty. events; facilitator for support groups Am. Cancer Soc. Mem. ANA, AACN (mem. bd. dirs. 1994, rural health outreach rep. 1994), Coastal Bend Health Care Assn. (v.p. Corpus Christi area 1993-94), Tex. A & M, Corpus Chriti Nursing Alumni Assn., Sigma Theta Tau. Avocations: music, reading, family. Home: 51 E 200 S # 3 500 S Hillside Dr Apt 503 Beeville TX 78102-5353 Office: Bear River Med Arts PA 104 S Jefferson St Garland UT 84312

JENTSCH, WERNER RUDOLF, animal nutritionist; b. Dresden, Germany, May 7, 1929; s. Rudolf Ernst and Marianne Gertrud (Kirsten) J.; m. Jutta Martha Elsbeth Kramer, Mar. 20, 1956; children: Friedrich Rudolf Holger, Bruno-Otto Thorsten. Dr. agr., U. Rostock, Germany, 1960; Dr.sc.agr., Agr. Acad. Berlin, Germany, 1971; Dr.agr.habil., U. Rostock, 1991. Leader calorimetry group Oskar-Kellner-Inst., Rostock, Germany, 1958-75, leader respiration group, 1960-94; leader animal feeding group Agr. Exhbn. Leipzig, Germany, 1971-85, Agr. Scientific Assn., Rostock, 1974-89; mem. rsch. Coop. Animal Nutrition Agr. Acad., Berlin, 1971-90, Coop. Beef Cattle Acad., Berlin, 1971-90; cons. in field. Co-author: Tierernahrung und Allgemeine Futterungslehre, 1968, Energetische Futterbewertung, 1971, Rostocker Futterbewertungssytem, 1971, 7th edit., 1989, Ackerfutter, 1976, 2d edit., 1990; contbr. articles to profl. jours. Avocations: ornithological observations, travel. Home: Etkar-Andre-Str 44, 18069 Rostock Germany Office: Inst Biology Farm Animals FB Nutritional Physiology, J-v-Liebig Weg 2, 18059 Rostock Germany

JENTZ, GAYLORD ADAIR, law educator; b. Beloit, Wis., Aug. 7, 1931; s. Merlyn Adair and Delva (Mullen) J.; m. JoAnn Mary Hornung, Aug. 6, 1955; children: Katherine Ann, Gary Adair, Loretta Ann, Rory Adair. BA, U. Wis., 1953, JD, 1957, MBA, 1958. Bar: Wis. 1957. Pvt. practice law Madison, 1957-58; from instr. to assoc. prof. bus. law U. Okla., 1958-65; vis. instr. to vis. prof. U. Wis. Law Sch., summers 1957-65; asso. prof. to prof. U. Tex., Austin, 1965-68, prof., 1968-98, prof. emeritus, 1998—, Herbert D. Kelleher prof. bus. law, 1982-98, chmn. gen. bus. dept., 1968-74, 80-86. Author: (with others) Business Law Text and Cases, 1968, Business Law Text, 1978, Texas Uniform Commercial Code, 1967, rev. edit., 1975, West's Business Law: Alternate Edition, 7th edit., 1999, Legal Environment of Business, 1989, Texas Family Law, 7th edit., 1992, West's Business Law: Text and Cases, 7th edit., 1998, Fundamentals of Business Law, 5th edit., 2000, Business Law Today, 5th edit., 2000, Business Law Today-Comprehensive Edition, 5th Edit., 2000, Business Law Today-The Essentials, 5th edit., 2000, Business Law Today-Alternate Essentials Edition, 4th edit., 1997; dep. editor Social Sci. Quar., 1966-82, editl. bd., 1982-94; editor-in-chief Am. Bus. Law Jour., 1969-74, adv. editor, 1974—. Served with AUS, 1953-55. Recipient Outstanding Tchr. award U. Tex. Coll. Bus., 1967, Jack G. Taylor Tchg. Excellence award, 1971, 89, Joe D. Beasley Grad. Tchg. Excellence award, 1978, CBA Found. Adv. Coun. award, 1979, Grad. Bus. Coun. Outstanding Grad. Bus. Prof. award, 1980, James C. Scorboro Meml. award for outstanding leadership in banking edn. Colo. Grad. Sch. Banking, 1983, Utmost Outstanding Prof. award, 1989, CBA award for excellence in edn., 1994, Banking Leadership award Western States Sch. Banking, 1995, U. Tex. Civitatis award, 1997; inducted to CBA Hall of Fame, 1999. Mem. Southwestern Fedn. Adminstrv. Disciples (v.p. 1979-80, pres. 1980-81), Am. Arbitration Assn. (nat. panel 1966-96), Acad. Legal Studies in Bus. (pres. 1971-72, exec. com. 1989-94, Faculty award of excellence 1981), So. Bus. Law Assn. (pres. 1967), Tex. Assn. Coll. Tchrs. (pres. Austin chpt. 1967-68, exec. com. 1979-80, state pres. 1971-72), Wis. Bar Assn., Omicron Delta Kappa, Phi Kappa Phi (pres. 1983-84). Home: 4106 N Hills Dr Austin TX 78731-2826 Office: U Tex CBA 5.202 MSIS Dept Austin TX 78712

JENYON, MALCOLM KEELING, geologist, consultant; b. Manchester, Eng., Sept. 16, 1930; s. Cecil Alfred and Elsie (Parker) J.; m. Ann Whitworth, Aug. 21, 1957; children: Amanda, Elizabeth, Joanne. BS, U. Manchester, 1953, MS, 1985, DS, 1989. Geologist/geophysicist Seismograph Svc. Ltd., Tulsa, 1953-88; cons. North Yorkshire, U.K., 1988—. Author: Salt Tectonics, 1986, Oil and Gas Traps, 1990; co-author: (with A.A. Fitch) Seismic Reflection Interpretation, 1985; co-editor: Seismic Atlas of Structural and Stratigraphic Features, 1988; contbr. articles to profl. jours. With Royal Navy, 1946-48. Fellow Birkbeck Coll. U. London, 1990-91. Fellow Geol. Soc. (chartered); mem. Petroleum Exploration Soc. Gt. Britain, Mensa. Avocations: music, skeet shooting, languages. E-mail: mjenyon@compuserve.com. Home and Office: Kirkbank House, Bellerby Leyburn, North Yorkshire DL8 5QP, United Kingdom

JEON, BEOM S., medical educator. MD, Seoul Nat. U., Republic of Korea, 1982, PhD, 1993. Resident Seoul Nat. U. Hosp., 1983-87, U. Minn., Mpls., 1987-91; fellow Columbia U., N.Y.C., 1991-93; faculty Seoul Nat. U.

Hosp., 1993—. Merritt fellow Columbia U., 1997-98. Office: Seoul Nat U Hosp, Dept Neurology, Seoul 110-744, Republic of Korea

JEON, CHANG-JIN, neuroscientist; b. Taegu, Korea, June 29, 1959; m. Moon-Sook Kim, Feb. 14, 1987; children: Min-Jee, Tae-Heon. BS, Kyungpook Nat. U., 1983, MS, 1985; PhD, U. Tenn., 1991. Rsch. fellow Harvard Med. Sch., Boston, 1992-94; from asst. prof. to assoc. prof. Kyungpook Nat. U., Taegu, Korea, 1994—; vis. prof. Harvard Med. Sch., Boston, 1999-2000. Mem. Soc. Neurosci., Korean Assn. Creation Rsch. Office: Kyungpook Nat U Biology, 1370 Sankyuk-dong, Taegu Korea 702-701

JEON, HAE MYUNG, surgeon, educator; b. Seoul, Korea, Apr. 12, 1955; s. Young Soon Jeon and Jeong Hee Kim; m. Hye Sook Rhee, May 23, 1987; 1 child, Seung Hee. Degree in medicine, Cath. U., Seoul, 1979, MS, 1989, MD, 1992. Diplomate Bd. Gen. Surgery. Intern Cath. U./St. Mary's Hosp., Seoul, 1982-83, 1983-87; instr. Cath. U./St. Mary's Hosp., Uijongbu, Korea, 1987-92, asst. prof., 1992-96, assoc. prof., 1996-99; asst. prof. Cath. U./St. Mary's Hosp., Seoul, 1999—; fellow U. Tex./M.D. Anderson Cancer Ctr., Houston, 1993-95. Contbr. articles to profl. jours. Capt. Korean armed. forces, 1979-82. Mem. Korea Med. Assn., Am. Colorectal Surgeons, Korean Surg. Assn., Rotary. Democrat. Roman Catholic. Avocations: golf, tennis, hiking. Home: Kangnam-Ku Apt 21-303, Apgujeoung-Dong Misung, Seoul 135-120, Korea Office: St Mary's Hosp Dept Surgery, Youido-dong Youngdeungpo 62, Seoul 150-010, Korea

JEON, SANG-WOON, writer, science historian; b. Won San, Korea, Nov. 21, 1928; s. Kyung-hwa and Ui-suk (Ham) J.; m. Os Park, May 9, 1957; children: He-Kyung, He-rim, Tae-il. BS, Seoul Nat. U., 1956, Diploma, 1966; LittD, Kyoto U., 1977; DSc, William Penn U., 1986. Prof. Sungshin U., Seoul, 1966-85, pres., 1985-89; Tasan prof. Yonsei U., Seoul, 1996-97; vis. prof. Kyoto U., 1981, 85, 90, 91, Needham R. Inst., Cambridge, U.K., 1991, 92; sr. advisor Min. of Sci. and Tech., Seoul, 1981-85; chmn. Org. Com. 8th ICHSEA, Seoul, 1995-96; advisor Korea Broadcasting System, 1985-87, Seoul Met. Mus., 1995—. Author: (books) Science and Technology in Korea, 1966, 76, 78, 98, Korean Scientific Cultural Properties, 1987, New Understanding for Traditional Korean Science, 1998. Named Most Outstanding Author, The Hanguk Ilbo, Seoul, 1966; recipient prize for sci. and tech. Korean Govt., Seoul, 1973, Oesol-sang prize Oesol-hoe Soc., Seoul, 1979. Mem. Cultural Property Cmty., 1981-2001, Nat. History Compilation Com./Korea, 1987-94, Korean Acad. of Sci. and Tech., Korean History of Sci. Soc. (pres. 1982-84). E-mail: jeontaeil@hanmail.net.

JEONG, BYUNG YONG, educator; b. Seoul, Korea, Mar. 21, 1962; s. Han Jo Jeong and Hyung Soon Hur; m. Myung Han Kim, June 27, 1992; 2 children: Ji Hyun, Ju Hyun. BS, Korea U., 1984; MS, Korea Advcd. Inst. Sci./Tech., 1986; PhD, KAIST, 1995. Assoc. prof. Hansung U., Seoul, Korea, 1990—, chmn. indsl. engring., 1992-93, chmn. indsl. safety engring., 1993-96; dean grad. sch. of safety and health mgmt. Hansung U., Seoul, 1999—. Contbr. articles to profl. jours. Mem. Human Factors & Ergonomics Soc. Avocations: tennis. E-Mail: byjeong@hansung.ac.kr. Office: Hansung U, 389 Samsun-Dong Sungbuk-Gu, Seoul 136-792, Republic of Korea

JEONG, HONG, education educator; b. Seoul, S. Korea, May 16, 1953; s. Young-Jin Jeong and Il-Jae Cho; m. Myong-Ja Bae; children: Sang-Won, Jeong. BS, Seoul Nat. U., 1977; MS, KAIST, Seoul, 1979; SM in EECS, MIT, 1984, EE in EECS, 1986, PhD in EECS, 1988. Reg. profl. elec. engr. Lectr. Kyungpook Nat. U., Taegu, Korea, 1979-82; asst. prof. Postech, Pohang, Korea, 1988-94, assoc. prof., 1994—; cons. Bell labs, Murray Hill, N.J., 1986-87; adminstr. Brain Rsch. Ctr., Pohang, 1998-99; exec. sec. Soc. AI, Neuro and Fuzzy Sys., Seoul, 1991-95; vice-chmn. Soc. Neurocomputing, Seoul, 1994-96; mem. com. Internat. Conf. Neural Info. Processing, 2000. Author: (books) Advances in machine Vision, 1989, Introduction to Neural Computer, 1992, Biologically Motivated Computer Vision, 2000; contbr. numerous articles to profl. jours.; 13 patents in field, Korea. Judge Korean Inst. Sci. and Tech. Evaluation and Planning, Seoul, 1995—, Kyunpook Sci. Exhbn., Pohang, 1995—, Engring. Rsch. Ctr., Korea Sci. and Engring. Found., 2000. Recipient Iron Tech. award Pohang Iron and Steel Co., Pohang, 1996; overseas dispatch prof. Korea Rsch. Found., Seoul, 1996, overseas study Ministry of Edn., Seoul, 1982. Mem. Sigma Xi. Avocations: photography, hiking, skiing, jogging, half marathons. Office: Postech EE Dept, 790-784 Pohang South Korea

JEONG, JAE-JUN, nuclear engineer, researcher; b. Youngcheon, Kyungbook, South Korea, Jan. 16, 1962; s. Tae-Yong and Sang-Soo (Kwon) J.; m. Hye-Sook Kwon, Jan. 7, 1989; children: Hyun-Jae, Hyun-Su. BS, Seoul Nat. U., 1984; MS, Korea Advanced Inst. Sci. and Tech., 1986, PhD, 1990. Rsch. asst. Korea Advanced Inst. Sci. and Tech., Seoul, 1986-89; sr. rschr. Korea Atomic Energy Rsch. Inst., Taejon, 1990—; vis. scientist Commn. a l'Energie Atomique, Grenoble, France, 1994-95. Contbr. articles to profl. jours. including Nuclear Engring. and Design, Nuclear Tech., Annals of Nuclear Energy, Jour. Nuclear Sci. and Tech., Jour. Korean Nuc. Soc. Recipient scholarship Combustion Engring. Korea, 1987. Mem. Korean Nuclear Soc. (Best Paper award 2000). Avocations: tennis, golf, go. Office: Korea Atomic Energy Rsch, Dukjin 150, Yusung Taejon 305-600, South Korea

JEONG, JAE-TACK, science educator; b. Kwangju, South Korea, Nov. 23, 1957. BS, Seoul Nat. U., Korea, 1980; MS, Korea Advanced Inst Sci. &Tech, Seoul, 1982, PhD, 1986. Prof. Kumoh Nat. U. of Tech., Kumi, Kyongbuk, Korea, 1986-95, Chonnam Nat. U., Kwangju, Korea, 1995—. E-mail: jtjeong@chonnam.ac.kr. Office: Chonnam Nat U Mech Engring, 300 Yongbong dong, Kwangju 500-757, Korea

JEONG, JI HWAN, mechanical engineering educator; b. Jeonjoo, Jeonbook, Republic of Korea, June 27, 1965; s. Shik Geun Jeong and Keum Nam Lee; m. Hyun Jung Kim, Jan. 21, 1994; 1 child, Kyung Ho. BA, Seoul Nat. U., 1988; degree in nuclear engring., Korea Advanced Inst. Sci. and Tech., Taejon, 1990, PhD, 1995; postgrad., Oxford (Eng.) U., 1995-96. Sr. rschr. Korea Advanced Inst. Sci. and Tech., 1995; sr. rschr. Korea Atomic Energy Rsch. Inst., Taejon, 1996-99, cons., 1999—; lectr. mech. engring. Chonan (Republic of Korea) Coll. Fgn. Studies, 1999—. Contbr. articles to sci. jours., including Nuclear Engring. and Design, Internat. Jour. Multiphase Flow, Heat and Mass Transfer. Brit. Chevening scholar Fgn. and Commonwealth Office, 1995; Kosef postdoctoral fellow Korea Sci. and Engring. Found., 1995. Mem. Korean Nuclear Soc., Korean Soc. Mech. Engrs., Am. Chem. Soc. Avocations: swimming, hiking, go, travel. Home: Doorae Apt 107-904, Sinbang-Dong, Chonan Choongnam 330-260, Republic of Korea Office: Chonan Coll Fgn Studies, Anseo-Dong, Choongnam, Chonan 330-750, Republic of Korea

JEONG, JONGKOO, chemical company executive; b. Seoul, Sept. 16, 1948; s. Rakmo Jeong and Oaknyo Lee; m. Sungja Hong, Dec. 28, 1978; children: Jisoo, Jiwon. BS, Seoul Nat. U., 1972; MS, U. Akron, 1983, PhD, 1985. mem. judging com. Nat. Tech. Devel. Fund. Rsch. scientist Hyosung Ltd., Anyang, 1975-91; v.p. Dongbu Hannong Chem. Co., Seoul, 1992—. Author: (book) Environmental Map of Ulsan City, 1994. Dir. Citizens' Environ. Rsch. Coun., Ulsan, 1994—. 1st lt. Korean Navy, 1972-75. Mem. Am. Chem. Soc., Korean Polymer Soc. (adv. bd. 1997—). Avocations: playing classical guitar music, writing scientific essays. Fax: 82 2 565 8532. E-mail: jkjeong@dongbuchem.com. Office: Dongbu Hannong Chem Co, 838 Yokesamdong, Seoul Korea

JEONG, LAK SHIN, chemist, educator; b. Seoul, Korea, Jan. 5, 1961; s. Sun Young and Young Sook (Kwon) J.; m. Heaok Kim, June 10, 1988; children: Heain, Hyung Woo. BS, Seoul Nat. U., 1984, MS, 1986; PhD, U. Ga., 1992. Rsch. assoc. Seoul Nat. U., 1985-86, 87-88; rschr. Nat. Cancer Inst./NIH, Bethesda, Md., 1993-95; asst. prof. pharmacy Ewha woman's U., Seoul, 1995-97, assoc. prof., 1997—, dir. Gen. Instrument Lab., 1997—; cons. FDA (Korea), Soul, 1998-99. Assoc. editor Pharm. Soc. Korea jour., 1996-98; contbr. articles to profl. jours.; patentee in field. Lt. Korean Army, 1986-87. Recipient Outstanding Rsch. award Ewha Woman's U., 1998. Mem. Am. Chem. Soc., Pharm. Soc. Korea, Sigma Xi, Rho Chi. Avocations: basketball, skiing, travel, jogging, meditation. Office: Ewha Womans Univ Coll Pharm, 11-1 Daehyun-dong, Seodaemoon-ku Seoul 120-750, South Korea

JEONG, MYUNG HO, cardiologist, educator; b. Nam Won, Chon Buk, Korea, Oct. 25, 1958; s. Jeong JaeWan and Lee Jung Suk; m. Jeong Jin Suk Dec. 11, 1983; children: Chan Yong, Chan Uk. MD, Chonnam Nat. U., Kwang Ju, Korea, 1983, PhD, 1989. Fellow in cardiology Chonnam Nat. U., Kwang Ju, Korea, 1989, instr., 1992-94, asst. prof., 1994-98, assoc. prof., 1998—; fellow in cardiology Mayo Clinic, Rochester, Minn., 1994-95; dir. health screening ctr., foreigner's clin., catheterization lab. Chonnam Nat. U. Hosp., 1998—. Contbr. articles to profl. jours. Capt., med. officer Korean Army, Korea, 1989-92. Recipient Rsch. award, Korean Soc. Circulation, 1996, Rsch. award Korean Soc. Internal Medicine, 1998; grantee Korean Ministry of Health and Welfare, 1998-2001. Fellow Soc. Cardiac Angiography, Am. Coll. Cardiology; mem. AHA. Home: 172 Bong Sun Bong, Nanku Kwang-Ju 503-062, Korea Office: Chonnam Nat U Hosp, 8 Hak Dong, Dong-ku Kwang-Ju 501-757, Korea

JEONG, YONG HWAN, materials scientist, researcher; b. Koesan, Chungbuk, Korea, Oct. 8, 1956; s. Dong Ok and Sun Jun (Cho) J.; m. Mi Suk Choi, Mar. 5, 1983; children: Da Min, Da Hoon. MS, Yonsei U., Seoul, Korea, 1985, PhD, 1991. Rschr. Korea Atomic Energy Rsch Inst., Taejon, 1985-88, sr. rschr., 1988-91, prin. rschr., project mgr., 1994—; rsch. engr. Siemens/KWU, Erlangen, Germany, 1992-93. Contbr. articles to profl. jours. including Jour. Nuclear Materials; patentee in field. With Korean Army, 1978-80. Fellow IAEA, 1992. Mem. Korean Inst. Metal and Materials, Korea Nuclear Soc., Materials Rsch. Soc. Korea. Avocation: mountain climbing. Home: Aeundong Hanbit, Apt 103-502, Yusong, Taejon 305-333, Korea Office: Korea Atomic Energy Rsch, PO Box 105, Yusong, Taejon 305-600, Korea

JEPPSON, LAWRENCE SMITH, publisher fine arts, consultant; b. Logan, Utah, June 5, 1926; s. Robert Baird and Elsie (Smith) J.; m. Frances Bennett, Nov. 5, 1952; children: Marian J. Stoddard, Carolyn J. Richards, Morgan B., Alison J. Hyde, Anne J. Bradham, Bryan B. Cert. civil engring., Oregon State U., 1946; BS, U. Utah, 1948; MS, Boston U., 1952. Missionary, mag. editor Church of Jesus Christ of Latter-day Saints, France, Belgium, Paris,, Geneva,, Switzerland, 1948-51; pub. rels. dir. Washington, 1952-56; pres., owner Lawrence Jeppson Pub. Rels. Svc., Industries Agy., Advt., Washington, 1951-80; pres. Jeppson Galleries and Lawrence Jeppson Assocs. Fine Arts, Bethesda, Md., 1958—; editor, publ. contemporary art Bethesda, Md., 1964-68; co-founder and art mgr. Collectors' Investment Fund, Washington, L.A., 1970-80; pres., owner Art Circuit Svcs., Bethesda, 1965—; pres., chmn. Mathieu Matégot Found. for Contemporary Tapestry, Washington, Bethesda, 1989—; owner, publ. AcroEditions & Legacy Press, Bethesda, 1978—; lectr. in field. Author: Murals of Wool, 1960, The Fabulous Frauds...Great Art Forgeries, 1970, The Neo-Iconography of Tsing-fang Chen, 1978, Un Coup d'Oeil Honnête Sur Les Mormons, 1951, The Spirit of Liberty, 1986, The Art of Dr. T.F. Chen: Neo-Iconography, 1990, Ecstasies in Wool, 1998; editor, publ. Contemporary Art Reports; TV and radio appearances; contbr. articles to profl. jours. Bd. visitors U. Md. Pub. Rels. Dept., 1957, Citizen Adv. bd. Montgomery Co. Dept. Recreation, 1980; ofcl. U.S. del. ARCO, Madrid, 1987. Recipient fellowship rsch. Cultural Ministry, France, 1970. Republican. LDS. Avocations: writing, traveling. Office: Lawrence Jeppson Assoc 9004 Honeybee Ln Bethesda MD 20817-6927

JEPSON, ANTHONY MICHAEL, solicitor; b. Stockport, Cheshire, Eng., Oct. 8, 1937; s. Alfred and Beatrice May (Barker) J.; m. Susan Mary Glover, Sept. 21, 1967; children: Alistair, Caroline. LLB, Leeds U., 1957. Solicitor, ptnr. Foysters, Manchester, Eng., 1961-72; corp. finance mgr. Singer & Friedlander Ltd., Manchester, 1972-75; ptnr. Colombotti & Ptnrs., London, 1975-80, Jepson Goff, London, 1980-96, Gordon Dadds/Jepson Goff, London, 1996—; dir. Coventry City Football Club Ltd., 1991—; mem. Legal Working Party FA Premier League, 1997—. Author: What To Do With the Family Company; co-author: Tax Planning for Wills. Mem. Chartered Inst. Taxation, Soc. Trust and Estate Practitioners. Avocations: shooting, golf, wine, gardening. Home: Field Cottage St Leonards, Near Tring HP23 6NS, England Office: 80 Brook St Mayfair, London W1Y 2DD, England

JEPSON, HANS GODFREY, investment company executive; b. Spencer, W.Va., July 24, 1936; s. Hans G. and Juanita Imogene (Shears) J.; m. Barbara Gayle Keller, Dec. 3, 1966. A.B. magna cum laude, Princeton U., 1958. Exec. editor Arnold Bernhard & Co., N.Y.C., 1961-68; v.p., research dir. Dominick & Dominick, Inc.,, N.Y.C., 1968-70; dir., sr. v.p., research dir. Alliance Capital Mgmt. Corp., N.Y.C., 1970-76; exec. v.p., chief investment officer U.S. Trust Co. N.Y., N.Y.C., 1976-80; pres. Valquest Assocs., Inc., N.Y.C., 1980—, Lafayette Enterprises, Inc., N.Y.C., 1983—, The Stanton Corp., Del., 1994—; dir. United News & Media, Inc., Del. Bd. dirs. J. Aron Charitable Found. 2d lt. U.S. Army, 1958-59, capt. USAR, 1959-66. Mem. Assn. for Investment Mgmt. and Rsch., N.Y. Soc. Security Analysts, Dial, Elm and Cannon Club (Princeton, N.J.), Princeton Club (N.Y.C.), Econ. Club (N.Y.C.), La Boule New Yorkaise (N.Y.C.), Fedn. Petanque USA, Inc. Home: 11 5th Ave New York NY 10003-4342 Office: Lafayette Enterprises Inc 126 E 56th St Fl 23 New York NY 10022-3639

JERATH, NEELIMA KHOSLA, ecologist, reseacher; b. Sindri, India, June 20, 1956; d. Ved Prakash and Krishna (Bhalla) K.; m. Vinod Kumar, July 26, 1979; children: Kinshuk, Kanay. BS, Gorakhpur U., India, 1975; MS, Gorakhpur U., 1977, PhD, 1981; PG Diploma in Environ. and Ecology, Inst. Ecoloyg and Environ., New Delhi, 1990; Diploma in Mgmt., Indira Gandhi Open U., New Delhi, 1996. Lectr. Govt. Coll. for Girls, Chandigarh, 1981-88; sr. scientific officer Punjab State Coun. Sci. and Tech., Chandigarh, 1988-95, principal scientific officer, 1995—; rschr. Gorakhpur Pub. U., 1977-81. Editor: (book) Changing Scenario of our Environment, 1992, Punjab Enviroment Status Report, 1995, Some Facets of Biodiversity, 1996, Infusing Environment Issues in Technical Education, 1998; Co-author: (book) Ramsar Sites of India, 1994. Recipient Punjab State award for environ. work, Govt. Punjab, 1999, Environ., Edn. and Awareness award, Pub. Sahitya Kala Manch, 1996, Gold Medal for 1st in MS women candidates, 1982. Fellow Inst. of Environ. Engrs.; mem. Internat. Soc. Environmental Botanists, Indian Soc. Tree Scientist, Prof. Women's Adv. Bd., Am. Biographical Inst. (bd. dirs.). Avocations: reading, quizzing, embroidery, cooking. Home Phone: 91-0172-771969. Office Phone: 91-0172-702602/720224. Office: Punjab State Coun Sci, SCO 2935-36 Sector 22-C, 160022 Chandigarh India

JERI, ARTURO R., endocrinologist, gynecologist, researcher; b. Huancayo, Peru, Nov. 23, 1955; s. raul Niceforo and Juana (Jaimes) J.; m. Susan Powell, Oct. 30, 1999; children: Ingrid, Jürgen. B.Medicine, San Marcos U., Lima, 1984, MD, 1985. Med. diplomate. Intensive care physician San Juan Hosp., Ica, Peru, 1986-87; postgrad. in ob-gyn. Cayetani Heridic U., Lima, 1987-90, chief resident ob-gyn., 1989; phyestrogens rschr. Inst. Gynecology and Reprodn., Lima, 1995—, chief menopause unit, 1998-99; med. dir. Las Palmeras Health Ctr., 1992-97, chief of ob-gyn. dept., 1992—. Contbr. articles to profl. jours. Active mem. Peruvian Red Cross, Lima, 1982, Amarant Menopause Found., Australia; custodian N.S.W. State Libr., 1997. Mem. Peruvian Menopause Soc. (founder), Australasian Menopause Soc., Internat. Menopause Soc., N.Y. Acad. Scis., Osteoporosis Soc., Masons. Roman Catholic. Avocations: Australian culture, Australian philatelic. Home: Hinchinbrook, 2 Goose Close, Sydney 2168 NSW, Australia Office: Inst Gynecol/Reprodn, Av Monterrico 1045, Lima 33, Peru

JERMIASON, JOHN LYNN, elementary school educator, farmer, rancher; b. Rochester, Minn., Jan. 9, 1958; s. Orlyn and Evelyn S. Jermiason; m. Ann M. Gebhardt, July 30, 1990. BA in Music, Psychology, St. Olaf Coll., 1981; AS in Agr., N.D. State U., 1982; BS in Edn., Minot State U., 1990. Sales rep. Century 21 Real Estate, Minot, N.D., 1989; ind. farmer, rancher Minot, 1982—; substitute elem. tchr. Minot Pub. Schs., 1993—. Prin. violist Minot Symphony Orch., 1983—, bd. dirs., 1996—; mem. ch. coun. Augustana Luth. Ch., Minot, 1989-91; mem. No. Lights String Quartet. Mem. Elks, Phi Mu Alpha, Kappa Delta Pi. Avocations: church choir. Home: PO Box 452 Minot ND 58702-0452

JERMYN, WILLIAM ALEXANDER, agricultural scientist; b. Blenheim, New Zealand, Aug. 18, 1947; s. Alan John and Ellen Jermyn; m. Jane Lancaster. B in Agrl. Sci., U. Canterbury, New Zealand, 1970, M in Agrl. Sci. with honors, 1973; PhD, U. Sask., Can., 1976. Plant breeder New Zealand Inst. Crop and Food Rsch., Christchurch, 1972—. Contbr. more than 35 articles to profl. jours. Fellow Agronomy Soc. New Zealand; mem. New Zealand Inst. Agrl. Sci., New Zealand Inst. Food Sci. and Tech., Piedmontese Soc. New Zealand (coun. 1995—). Office: Crop & Food Rsch, Pvt Bag 4704, Christchurch New Zealand

JERN, NILS STEFAN, psychologist; b. Stockholm, Sweden, Feb. 23, 1945; s. Nils and Kity (Edenholm) J.; m. Marianne Fontaine, July 1968; children: Sara, Johan, Patrik. BA, Lund U., 1967, MA, 1968, PhD, 1971. From asst. tchr. to lectr. Lund U., Sweden, 1967-73; from clin. psychologist to head psychol. svcs. Aengelholm Gen. Hosp., Sweden, 1973-96; sr. lectr. dept. edn./ Linkoping U., Sweden, 1996-98; sr. lectr. dept. psychology Lund U., 1998—; clin. inst. Lund U. Hosp., 1981; bd. mem. EPPA EC, 1999—; cons. in field. Co-author, co-editor: Group Relations, 1984, The Hard to Catch Organization, 1996. Fellow Swedish Psychol. Assn.; mem. APA (fgn.). Home: Fridhemsgatan 10, SE-6253 Angelholm Sweden

JERNIGAN, ALVIN, JR., retired automobile sales executive; b. Marshall, Tex., Sept. 4, 1933; s. Alvin Jernigan Sr. and Katherine Whitfield; m. Dorothy Jernigan, June 15, 1981 (div. May 1990); children: Darnell J., Delbert W., Dori Ann. Student, Bay City Jr. Coll., 1953-54; AA in bus. and mktg., Delta Coll., 1979. Food svc. supr. VA Hosp., Downey, Ill., 1959-62; TWA comms. West Side VA, Downey, 1962-64; with prodn. dept. Gen. Motors, Flint, Mich., 1964-65; with sales dept. Garber Pontiac Cadillac, Saginaw, Mich., 1966-80; ins. agent Allstate Ins. Co., Saginaw, 1980-85; auto sales exec. Labadie Old Cadillac GMC, Bay City, Mich., 1986-99; ret., 1999. Sch. bd. mem. Buena Vista Sch. Dist., 1988—, pres. 1996-98; mem. Buena Vista Recreation Com., Saginaw, 1985—, IOC Adv. Bd. Fundraising Group, Saginaw, 1991-93, Buena Vista Cmty. Coun., 1988-91; vol. United Negro Coll. Fund, Saginaw, 1991-93. Mem. Cadillac Cres Club (with distinction), Frontiers Club (pres. 1982-83, Man of Yr. 1980), Saginaw Bay Fish Masters (v.p. 1993-94), Optimist Club. Democrat. Baptist. Avocations: fishing, golf. Home: 3010 Welland Dr Saginaw MI 48601-6914

JERNUDD, BJÖRN HOLGER, educator; b. Stockholm, Sweden, May 7, 1942; s. Hadar Evert and Ingrid Maria (Andersson) J.; m. Birgitta Maria (Börjesson), Sept. 8, 1962, (div. July 1974); children: Tor, Asa, Disa, Ulf; m. Sharon Jean Mann, Aug. 12, 1985; children: Sigrid, Ingrid. Uppsala U., Umea, Sweden, 1963, Stockholm Sch. Econs., 1966. Lectr. Monash U., Melbourne, Australia, 1966-69; sr. lectr. Monash U., 1970-74; project specialist The Ford Found., Cairo, Egypt, 1974-76; rsch. asssoc. East West Ctr., Honolulu, 1976-87; sr. fellow Nat. U. Singapore, 1987-91; reader H Baptist U., Hong Kong, 1992-94; chair prof. H Baptist U., 1994—; faculty mem. Advanced Inst. Delhi India, 1987, rsch. fellow Inst. African Asian Studies, 1973-73, rsch. assoc. Stanford U., 1971-72. Author: Lectures on Language Problems; editor/author: The Politics of Language Purism, Can Language be Planned?; editor: The New Language Planning Newsletter. Chmn. adv. bd. Lingnan U., editorial com. Swedish Chamber Commerce, ct. and coun. mem. Hong Kong Baptist U. Mem. Linguistic Soc. Am., Sudan Studies Assn., Ladies Recreation Club. Avocations: running, reading.

JEROME, DOMINIQUE YVES, research executive; b. La Tronche, France, June 1, 1943; s. Etienne and Yvonne Jerome; m. Marie-Christine Langlois, May 27, 1978; children: Sylvain, Aurélie. Ingénieur Chimiste, Lycée Janson de Sailly, Paris; PhD in Chemistry, U. Oreg., 1970; Doctorat Sciences Physiques, U. Paris, 1972. Rsch. asst. U. Oreg., Eugene, 1967-70; rsch. assoc. U. Paris, 1970-75; sci. advisor Ministry of Rsch., Paris, 1975-81; dir. R&D Quartz et Silice, Paris, 1982-84; mgr. chemistry and materials dept. Agence Nationale de Valorisation de la Recherche, 1984-95; mgr. rsch. divsn. Regional Coun. of Ile-de-France, Paris, 1995—. Contbr. articles to profl. jours. Fulbright fellow U. Oreg., 1970. Mem. Meteoritical Soc., Soc. Francaise de Mineralogie et Cristallographie, Sigma Xi. Home: 18 Rue du Pavillon, 92100 Boulogne France Office: Regional Coun Ile-de-France, 35 Blvd des Invalides, 75007 Paris France

JERRAM, JAMES, rail transportation executive; b. Aug. 7, 1939; s. Lionel and Kathleen (Cochrane) J.; m. Ruth Middleton, 1965; 4 children. MA Selwin Coll., Cambridge. With Arthur Andersen & Co., 1963-71, Standard Telephones & Cables, 1971-87; bd. mem. fin. British Railways Bd., London, 1991, vice chmn., CFO. Office: British Railways Bd, Euston House 24 Evershot St, London NW1 1 DZ, England also: Whittles House, 14 Pentonville Rd, London W1 9HF, England*

JERSILD, PER CHRISTIAN, writer, physician; b. Katrineholm, Sweden, Mar. 14, 1935; s. Christian and Svea (Bengtsson) J.; m. Ulla Flyxe, Oct. 22, 1960; children: Jonas, Mattias. MD, Karolinska Inst., Sweden, 1962; PhD (hon.), Royal Inst. Tech., Sweden, 1999; MD (hon.), U. Uppsala, Sweden, 2000. Author 30 books, including, The Animal Doctor, 1975, Children's Island, 1986, After the Flood, 1986, House of Babel, 1987, A Living Soul, 1988. Mem. Royal Acad. Sci. Sweden. Home: Rosendalsvagen 20, 194 63 Upplands Vasby Sweden

JERVIS, DAVID THOMPSON, political science educator, academic administrator; b. Bryn Mawr, Pa., Mar. 16, 1954; s. Walter T. and Mary Charlotte (Abernethy) J. BA, Eastern Coll., St. Davids, Pa., 1976; MA, Villanova U., 1978; PhD, Temple U., 1985. Asst. prof. Washburn U., Topeka, 1985-92, assoc. prof. polit. sci., 1992-96, prof., 1996-2000, asst. dir. Washburn Internat. Ctr., 1991-1999; dir. Office of Internat. Edn. SUNY, Oneonta, N.Y., 2000—; vis. prof. U. Orebro, Sweden, 1995, U. Witwatersrand, South Africa, 1995. Contbr. articles to profl. jours. Bd. dirs. Internat. Ctr. Topeka, 1988-1999. Fulbright scholar U. Zagreb, 1997-98. Mem. Internat. Studies Assn., Pi Sigma Alpha, Phi Alpha Theta, Phi Kappa Phi, Phi Beta Delta. Avocations: reading, sports, travel. Office: SUNY-Oneonta Office of Internat Edn SUNY Oneonta Oneonta NY 13820

JERVIS, SIMON SWYNFEN, historic buildings director; b. Yoxford, Suffolk, Eng., Jan. 9, 1943; s. John Swynfen Jervis and Diana Elizabeth (Marriott) Parker; m. Fionnuala MacMahon, Apr. 19, 1969; children: Thalia Swynfen Jervis, John Swynfen Jervis. BA in Classics, History of Art, U. Cambridge, 1964. Student asst./asst. keeper of art Leicester (Eng.) Mus. Art Gallery, 1964-66; asst. keeper dept. furniture Victoria & Albert Mus., London, 1966-75; dep. keeper Victoria & Albert Mus., 1975-89, acting keeper, 1989, curator, 1989-90; dir., Marlay curator Fitzwilliam Mus., Cambridge, Eng., 1990-95; dir. historic bldgs. Nat. Trust, London, 1995—; chmn. Nat. Trust Arts Panel, London, 1987-95; editor Furniture History, London, 1987-92; trustee Royal Collection Trust, 1993—; dir. Burlington Mag., 1993—, trustee, 1997—; pres. Soc. Antiquaries of London, 1995—. Author: Victorian Furniture, 1968, Printed Furniture Designs Before 1650, 1974, High Victorian Design, 1983, Penguin Dictionary of Design and Designers, 1984. Trustee Sir John Soanes Mus., 1999—. Mem. Furniture Soc. (chmn. 1998—). Office: The National Trust, 36 Queen Anne's Gate, London SWIH 9AS, England

JESIEN, LESZEK ANTONI, political scientist; b. Warsaw, Poland, June 13, 1962; s. Piotr and Marianna (Zarzycka) J.; m. Katarzyna Anna Krol, Jan. 7, 1994; 1 child, Karolina Anna. MA, Warsaw U., 1987, PhD, 1995. TV prodr. Teleart Ltd., Warsaw, 1987-89; fgn. reporter Obserwator TV News, Warsaw, 1990-91; fgn. editor Obserwator Codzienny Daily, Warsaw, 1991-92; fgn. affairs specialist Govt. Press Office, Warsaw, 1992-93; western European editor Gazeta Wyborcza Daily, Warsaw, 1993-95; expert European Integration Office, Warsaw, 1995-96; rsch. fellow Coll. of Europe, Natolin, Warsaw, 1997-98; advisor prime min. and chief negotiator Poland Accession to European Union, Warsaw, 1998—; sr. assoc. mem. St. Antony's Coll., Oxford, 1993-94. Author: After Amsterdam, Before Enlargement. A Political Landscape of the European Union, 1998, Europe in the Mirror of Euroscepticism, 1999, The Choice or Inertia. The Amsterdam Treaty and Theories of European Integration, 2000; contbr. articles to profl. jours. Brit. Chevening scholar U.K. Fgn. and Commonwealth Office, 1993; Nat. Forum Found. vis. fellow, 1993; recipient award Western European Union Inst. for Strategic Studies, 1997. Avocations: film, classical music. Home: Sardynska 5/21, 02-761 Warsaw Poland

JESKY, T. J., pharmaceutical products executive; b. Chgo., Feb. 15, 1947; s. Henry J. and Joan F. (Lalko) J. Student, Universidad de las Ams., Mex., 1964-65; BA Mktg. and Retailing, Bradley U., 1969. Field rep. Morton Norwich, Chgo., 1973-76, major account rep., 1976-79; Chgo. dist. mgr. Norwich Eaton Pharms., N.Y., 1979-80; N.Y.C. dist mgr. Norwich Eaton (A Procter & Gamble Co.), N.Y., 1980-83; mgr. Midwest and P.R. divsn. Norwich Eaton, Oak Brook, Ill., 1983-90; mgr. P.R. divsn. nat. accounts, mgr. nat. hosp. divsn. Procter & Gamble Pharms., Norwich, N.Y., 1990-93; mgr. Can. divsn. Procter & Gamble Pharms., Cin., 1994-95; pres., CEO Studebaker's, Inc., Scottsdale, Ariz., 1995-97, Ionosphere, Inc., Scottsdale, 1997-98, Barrington Labs., Inc., Las Vegas, 1998—. Contbr. articles to profl. jours. Mem. Pharm. Mfr. Assn., Am. Mgmt. Assn., Nat. Pharm. Coun. Home: PO Box 8744 Scottsdale AZ 85252-8744

JESSE, HORST, minister; b. Wagendruessel, Slovacia, Apr. 17, 1941; arrived in Germany, 1945; s. Ladislaus and Luise (Kueffer) J.; m. Christine Katharina Theile, Sept. 20, 1968; children: Friederike Luise, Johannes Daniel, Wulf Martin, Nikolaus, Arnold. Master degree, Fern U., Hagen, Germany, 1990; PhD, Ludwig Maximilians U., Munich, 1994. Ordained to ministry Evang. Luth. Ch., 1970. Vicar Evan. Luth. Ch., Hoechstadt, Germany, 1968-71; parish min. Evan. Luth. Ch., Nuernberg, Germany, 1971-74, Augsburg, Germany, 1974-88, Munich, 1988—; assoc. mem. Iona Cmty., Great Britain. Author: Das Augsburger Bekenntins in drei Jahrhunderten, 1980, Die Lyrik Bertolt Brechts, 1994, Brecht in Berlin, 1994, Leben und Wirken des Philipp Melanchthan, 1998, Die retrospektive Widerspiegelung der Identitatsentwicklung Jugendlicher, 2000, others; contbr. articles to profl. jours. Mem. Internat. Brecht Soc., Brechtkreis Augsburg (founder), Goethe Gesellschaft Weimar, Verband der Historiker Deutschlands. Home: Berlstrasse 6A, 81375 Munich Germany

JESSEE, ROY MARK, lawyer; b. Kingsport, Tenn., Feb. 8, 1966; s. Roy Claude and Myrtle Delight (Robinette) J.; m. Cortney Wynn Williams, June 30, 1990. BA, King Coll., 1988; JD, U. Va., 1991. Bar: Va. 1991, U.S. Dist. Ct. (we. dist.) Va. 1992. Law clk. Ct. of Appeals of Va., Bristol, 1991-92; assoc. atty. Mullins, Thomason & Harris, Norton, Va., 1992-94; shareholder, prin., atty. Mullins, Thomason, Harris & Jessee, Norton, Va., 1995-98; shareholder, prin. Mullins, Harris & Jessee, Norton, Va., 1998—. Contbr. articles to legal jours. Chmn. Scott County Dem. Party, 1993-95, 95-97. Named one of Outstanding Young Men in Am., 1989. Mem. ABA, Wise County Bar Assn. (pres.-elect 1998, pres. 1999), Am. Judicature Soc., Va. Assn. Def. Attys. Democrat. Baptist. Avocations: running, weight lifting, reading, writing poetry. Home: PO Box 353 112 B Elm St Gate City VA 24251 Office: Mullins Harris & Jessee PO Box 1200 30 Seventh St Norton VA 24273

JESSEN, EIKE, computer science educator; b. Göttingen, Germany, Aug. 28, 1933; s. Jens and Käthe (Scheffer) J.; m. Inge Nagler, Sept. 25, 1965; children: Anna, Julia. Diploma in engring., Tech. U. Berlin, 1960, DEng, 1964. Asst. Tech. U. Berlin, 1960-64; mgr. large scale computer devel. AEG-Telefunken, Konstanz, Germany, 1964-72; prof. computer sci. U. Hamburg, Germany, 1972-77, 78-83, U. Bundeswehr, Munich, 1977-78; prof. computer sci. Tech. U. Munich, 1983—, v.p., 1994-96; advisor Fed. Ministry Rsch. and Tech., Bonn, Germany, 1972-82, Nat. Rsch. Found., Bonn, 1986—; pres. German Nat. Rsch. Network, 1988-90, 97—. Author: Rechnerarchitektur, 1975, (with R. Valk) Rechensysteme, 1986. Decorated Bundesverdienstkreuz, Munich, 1994. Mem. Soc. for Informatics (ofcl.), Assn. German Electrotech., Assn. for Computing Machinery. Home: Lange Strasse 28, 82327 Tutzing Bavaria, Germany Office: Tech U Munich, Inst for Informatics, 80290 Munich Germany

JESSERAMSING, CHITMANSING, ambassador; b. Mahebourg, Mauritius, Aug. 25, 1933; s. Jeewoonarain and Banitha (Bindah) J.; m. Usha Seereeram; children: Devendra (dec.), Janita, Anjali. B.A. with honors, Delhi U., 1957, M.A. with honors, 1959; Diploma in Diplomatic Studies, Canberra U., 1966, Queen's Coll., Oxford U., 1967; M.A., Georgetown U., 1974. Prin. Islamic Cultural Coll., Mauritius, 1961-62; edn. officer English Dept. Royal Coll., Curepipe, 1962-66; diplomatic officer Prime Minister's Office Govt. of Mauritius, 1967-68; 1st sec. Mauritius Embassy, Washington, 1968-79, min.-counsellor, charge d'affaires, 1979-81, ambassador to U.S., also accredited to Can., Brazil, Argentina, Cuba, Trinidad and Tobago, Jamaica, Barbados, Mex., 1982-93, 96—, fgn. policy advisor to leader of opposition, 1993-95. Mem. Royal Coll. Philos. Soc. (founder, pres. 1962-66), Univ. Club (Washington). Club: International (Washington). Avocations: reading; philosophy discussions. Home: 8926 Harvest Square Ct Potomac MD 20854-4475 Office: Embassy Mauritius 4301 Connecticut Ave NW Ste 441 Washington DC 20008-2304

JESSOP, PHILIP GREGORY, chemistry educator; b. Ottawa, Ontario, Can., June 26, 1963; came to U.S., 1996; s. Alan M. and Patricia A. J.; m. Lorena Dawn Crook, Aug. 16, 1986: children: David, Michael. BSc, U. Waterloo, Can., 1986; PhD, U. Brit. Columbia, Vancouver, Can., 1991. Rsch. asst. Shell Can., Oakville, Ontario, Can., 1986 summer; postdoctoral fellow U. Toronto, Can., 1991-92; rschr. Rsch. Devel. Corp. Japan, Nagoya, Japan, 1993-96; asst. prof. U. Calif., Davis, 1996—. Editor Chemical Synthesis Using Supercritical Fluids, 1999; contbr. articles to profl. jours. Mem. Chem. Inst. Can., Am. Chem. Soc. Achievements include three Japanese patents in field and European patent pending. Office: U Calif Dept Chemistry 1 Shields Ave Davis CA 95616-5200

JESSUP, JAN AMIS, arts volunteer, writer; b. Chgo., Aug. 10, 1927; d. Herman Harvey and Anita (Lincoln) Sinako; m. Everett Orme Amis, Dec. 20, 1970 (dec. Nov. 1981); m. Joe Lee Jessup, Apr. 16, 1989. BA, U. Minn., 1948; postgrad., Rutgers U., 1969-70. bd. dirs., exec. com. Broward Ctr. for Performing Arts Pacers, Fort Lauderdale, Fla., 1985-88, pres., 1987-88; speaker U. Internat. Bus., Beijing, 1985. Active not-for-profit orgns. including Girl Scouts U.S., Boy Scouts Am., Presbyn. Ch.; beautification com. Lighthouse Point, Fla., 1978-89, sec., 1988-91; rep. to Fla. Art Orgns., 1987-88; bd. dirs. Archways, Ft. Lauderdale, 1987-91, Fla. Grand Opera, 1993—; trustee Miami City Ballet, 1991-94; adv. bd. Guild of the Palm Beaches, 1994-95; bd. govs. Fla. Philharm. Orch., 1981—, v.p. representing all affiliates, 1985-87, 92, 94-96, exec. com., 1989-93, v.p. individual giving, 1991-92, bd. dirs., 1994—, chmn. affiliate com., 1994-95, v.p. vols., 1995-96, chmns. adv. coun., 1996-98; bd. trustees The Harid Conservatory, Boca Raton, 1997—; mem. Blue Ribbon steering com. The Harid Conservatory Sch. Music at Lynn U., 1999—, Concert Assn. Fla., Inc., 1995-98; mem. Palm Beach Cultural Coun., 1993—; advisor Friends of Philharm., 1996-97; founding pres. The Harid Guild of The Harid Conservatory, 1997-99, bd. dirs., 1997—; mem. Nat. Youth Orch. Festival 2000 Com. Mem. Nat. Soc. Arts and Letters, Am. Symphony Orch. League (vice chmn. 1989-90, sec. vol. coun. 1986-87, v.p. 1987-88, pres. 1989-90, advisor 1990-91, assoc. Resource Devel. Inst. 1996—, bd. dirs. 1998—, liaison and com. mem. Nat. Youth Orch. Festival 2000 Com.), The Opus Soc. (bd. dirs., m. exec. com. 1981-95, chmn. 1981-85, pres. 1989-93), Ft. Lauderdale Philharm. Soc. (bd. dirs. 1986—), Opera Soc. (sec. 1986-87, v.p. pub. rels. 1987-88, bd. dirs. 1986—), Royal Palm Dinner Theatre (bd. dirs. 1998-2000), Gold Coast Jazz Soc. (bd. dirs. 1992-98, v.p. 1994-98), Royal Dames of Cancer Rsch. (bd. trustees 1995-97), Boca Raton Resort and Club , Royal Palm Yacht and Country Club, Royal Palm Yacht and Country Club Women's Club, Sea Grape Garden Club (past pres.), Ocean Reef Club. Republican. Avocations: music listening, boating, fishing, writing, bridge playing. Home: 133 Coconut Palm Rd Boca Raton FL 33432-7975

JESSUP, JOE LEE, business educator, management consultant; b. Cordele, Ga., June 23, 1913; s. Horace Andrew and Elizabeth (Wilson) J.; m. Janet Amis, Apr. 16, 1989. BS, U. Ala., 1936; MBA, Harvard U., 1941; LLD (hon.), Chung-Ang U., Seoul, Korea, 1964. Sales rep. Proctor & Gamble, 1937-40; liaison officer bur. pub. rels. U.S. War Dept., 1941; spl. asst. and exec. asst. Far Ea. div. and office exports Bd. Econ. Warfare, 1942-43; exec. officer to chief of staff Svcs. of Supply-Europian Theatre, 1943-44; exec. officer, office deptl. adminstrn. Dept. State, 1946; exec. sec. adminstr.'s adv. coun. War Assets Adminstrn., 1946-48; v.p. sales Airken, Capitol & Service Co., 1948-52; assoc. prof. bus. adminstrn. George Washington U., 1952, prof., 1952-77, prof. emeritus, 1977—, asst. dean Sch. Govt., 1951-60; pres. Jessup and Co., Ft. Lauderdale, Fla., 1957—; bd. dirs. Giant Food, Inc., Washington (audit comm. 1974-75), 1971-75, Am. Equity Investors, Inc., 1986-87, Hunter Assn. Labs, Fairfax, Va., 1964-69 (exec. comm. 1966-69, exec. v.p. 1967, gen. mgr. 1969), coordinator Air Force Resources Mgmt. program, 1951-57; del. in edn. 10th Internat. Mgmt. Conf., Sao Paulo, Brazil, 1954, 11th Conf., Paris, 1957, 12th Conf., Sydney and Melbourne, Australia, 1960, 13th Conf., Rotterdam, Netherlands, 1966, 14th Conf., Tokyo, 1969, 15th Conf., Munich, Germany, 1972; mem. Md. Econ. Devel. Adv. Commn., 1973-75. Mem. Civil Svc. Commn., Arlington County, Va., 1952-54; mem. nat. adv. coun. Ctr. for Study of Presidency, 1974-99; mem. bd. overseers Lynn U., Boca Raton, 1991—; mem. adv. bd. Youth Automotive Tng. Ctr., Hollywood, Fla., 1993—; mem. Atlanta regional panel for selection of White House fellow, 1990-95, mem. Miami regional panel, 1994-95; trustee Tng. Within Industry Found., Summit, N.J., 1954-58, Philharm Orch., Fla., 1986-91; mem. Chaine des Rotisseurs, 1987-92. Decorated Bronze Star; recipient cert. of appreciation Sec. of Air Force, 1957. Mem. Harvard Club (N.Y.C.), Univ. Club (Washington), Royal Palm Yacht and Country Club. Home: 133 Coconut Palm Rd Boca Raton FL 33432-7975

JESTCZEMSKI, FRANK, physicist, researcher; b. Essen, Germany, Mar. 4, 1964; s. Heinrich and Elfriede (Henke) J.; m. Anette Lehnheuser, Apr. 1, 1999. Diplom-Physiker, Ruhr-U., Bochum, Germany, 1990; Dr. Rer. Nat., Justus Liebig U., Giessen, Germany, 1995. Scientific co-worker Inst. Biochemistry and Endocrinology Justus-Liebig U., Giessen, Germany, 1990-95; scientific cons. Medisyst GMBH, Linden, Germany, 1996; analyst Input GMBH, Langgöns, Germany, 1996-98; sr. analyst, cons. Meta Group GmbH, Bad Homburg, Germany, 1998—; sr. cons. META Group Deutschland GmbH. Contbr. articles to profl. jours. Mem. Deutsche Physikalische Gesellschaft, Gesellschaft Deutscher Naturforscher Und Ärzte, Gesellschaft für Deutsche Sprache, N.Y. Acad. Scis. Avocations: tango. Office: META Group Deutschland GmbH, Saalburgstr 1572, D-61350 Bad Homburg Germany

JESZENSZKY, GEZA, historian, politician; b. Budapest, Hungary, 1941; married; 2 children. BA in English and History, 1966, PhD, 1980. Secondary tchr., 1966-68; rschr. Nat. Szechenyi Libr.; libr., since 1973; tchr. Dept. Internat. Rels. U. Econs., since 1976; M.P. Parliament of Hungary, Budapest, 1994-98; dean Faculty of Social Scis. U. Econs., 1989; min. Ministry Fgn. Affairs, Budapest, 1990-94; amb. extraordinary & plenipotentiary to U.S. Rep. Hungary, 1998—; lectr. Santa Barbara U., Calif., 1986, U. Mich., Ann Arbor, 1996. Author numerous books, studies and sci. publs. Founder Hungarian Dem. Forum. Fulbright scholar, 1984-86. Mem. Hungarian Profl. and Sci. Assn. Avocations: reading, skiing. Office: 3910 Shoemaker St NW Washington DC 20008

JETER, KATHERINE LESLIE BRASH, lawyer; b. Gulfport, Miss., July 24, 1921; d. Ralph Edward and Rosa Meta (Jacobs) Brash; m. Robert McLean Jeter, Jr., May 11, 1946. BA, Newcomb Coll. of Tulane U., 1943; JD, Tulane U., 1945. Bar: La. 1945, U.S. Dist. Ct. (we. dist.) La. 1948, U.S. Tax Ct. 1965, U.S. Supreme Ct. 1971, U.S. Dist. Ct. (ea. dist.) La. 1975, U.S. Ct. Appeals (5th cir.) 1981, U.S. Dist. Ct. (mid. dist.) La. 1982. Assoc. Montgomery, Fenner & Brown, New Orleans, 1945-46, Tucker, Martin, Holder, Jeter & Jackson, Shreveport, 1947-79; ptnr. Tucker, Jeter, Jackson and Hickman and predecessors, Shreveport, 1980—; judge pro tem 1st Jud. Dist. Ct., Caddo Parish, La., 1982-83; mem. adv. com. to joint legis. subcom. on mgmt. of the community; pres. YWCA of Shreveport, 1963; hon. consul of France; Shreveport, 1982-91; pres. Little Theatre of Shreveport, 1966-67; pres. Shreveport Art Guild, 1974-75; mem. task force crim justice La. Priorities for the Future, 1978; pres. LWV of Shreveport, 1950-51. Recipient Disting. Grad. award Tulane U., 1983. Mem. Am. Law Inst., La. State Law Inst. (mem. coun. 1980—, adv. com. La. Civil Code 1973-77, temp. ad hoc. com. 1976-77, sr. officer 1993—), Am. Law Inst., Pub. Affairs Rsch. Coun. (bd. trustees 1976-81, 91—, exec. com. 1981-84, area exec. committeeman Shreveport area 1982), ABA, La. Bar Assn., Shreveport Bar Assn. (pres. 1986), Nat. Assn. Women Lawyers, Shreveport Assn. for Women Attys., C. of C. Shreveport (bd. dirs. 1975-77), Order of Coif, Phi Beta Kappa. Author: (with Fredricka Doll Gute) Historical Profile, Shreveport 1850, 1982; author: A Man and His Boat, The Civil War Career and Correspondence of Lieutenant Jonathan H. Carter, 1996; contbr. articles on law to profl. jours. Home: 3959 Maryland Ave Shreveport LA 71106-1021 Office: 401 Edwards St Ste 905 Shreveport LA 71101-5509

JETER, WAYBURN STEWART, retired microbiology educator, microbiologist; b. Cooper, Tex., Feb. 16, 1926; s. Joseph Plato and Beulah (Stewart) J.; m. Margaret Ann McDonald, May 30, 1947; children—Randall Mark, Monette Ann, Marcus Kent. B.S., U. Okla., 1948, M.S., 1949; Ph.D., U. Wis., 1950. Diplomate: Am. Bd. Microbiology. Mem. faculty U. Iowa, 1950-63, assoc. prof., 1958-63; prof. microbiology U. Ariz., Tucson, 1963-89, prof. microbiology emeritus, 1989—, prof. pharmacology and toxicology, 1983-91, prof. pharmacology and toxicology emeritus, 1991—, head dept. microbiology and med. tech., 1967-83, dir. lab. cellular immunology, 1976-91; dir. med. tech. program U. Ariz., 1976-79; vis. prof. immunology and med. microbiology U. Fla., 1980; pres. Scientific Rels. Svcs., Inc., 1988—. Contbr. articles profl. jours. Served with USNR, 1943-46. Fellow AAAS; mem. Am. Acad. Microbiology, Am. Assn. Immunologists, Ariz. Acad. Sci., Am. Soc. Microbiology (mem. council 1975-77), Soc. Exptl. Biology and Medicine, Sigma Xi. Democrat. Presbyterian. Home: 5140 N Via Sempreverde Tucson AZ 85750-5966

JETHMALANI, RAM, government official; b. Pakistan, Sept. 14, 1923; married; 4 children. Elected to Lok Sabha, 1977; mem. Rajya Sabha, 1988—; min. Ministry Law & Justuce, 1996, Ministry Urban Devel., 1998—. Office: Ministry Urban Devel, Dr Rajendra Prasad Rd, New Delhi 110 001, India*

JETLEY, SURRINDER KUMAR, career officer; b. Mandi Bahauddin, Pakistan, May 16, 1940; s. Kharaiti Lal and Raj Kumari (Jhingan) J.; m. Kiran Suri, Sept. 30, 1968; children: Komal, Radhika, Sameer. MS in Defense Studies, Madras U., 1984, Allahabad U., 1987; MBA, Symbiosis Inst. Bus. Adminstrn, Pune, India, 1998. Commd. 2d lt. Army of India, 1960, advanced through grades to capt., 1967, advanced through grades to maj., 1972, advanced through grades to lt. col., 1978, advanced through grades to col., 1985, advanced through grades to brig. gen., 1988, advanced through grades to maj. gen., 1990, advanced through grades to lt. gen., 1993, dep. chief of staff, 1999—. Recipient Disting. Svc. award, 1987, 98, Sena medal for gallantry during ops., 1972. Home: #6 Rajaji Marg, 110 011 New Delhi India Office: Army Hdqts, DHQ PO, 110 011 New Delhi India

JETTMAROVÁ, ZUZANA, linguist; b. Prague, Bohemia, Czech Republic, Oct. 18, 1952; d. Josef Stehno and Marie Bestakova. Diploma in Translation, Interpretaion, Charles U., Prague, Czech Republic, 1976, PhD Slavonic Studies, 1979; MSc Applied Linguistics, Edinburgh U., Scotland, 1990. Free lance translator, interpreter Prague, Czech Republic, 1976-81; tchr. Charles U., Prague, 1981; dir. Lang. Ctr., Prague, 1985-91; also dir. Inst. Translation Studies, Prague, 1991—; internat. programs mgr. Faculty of Arts, Prague, 1991-95; SOCRATES coord. Faculty of Arts, Prague, 1997—; vice chmn. Czech Com. for Translation-Interpreting Prague, Czech Republic, 1997—; v.p. European Soc. Translation Studies, 1998—. Author: Encyclopedia entry, Übersetzung, translation, traduction; co-editor (series) Folia Translatologica vols. 2 and 3, 1993-94; co-author: (bibliography) Czech and Slovak translation studies, 1995; co-editor EST 1995 Procs. Intercultural Communication, 1997. Mem. Internat. Fedn. Translators (com. for qualifications and tng. 1997—), European Soc. Translation Studies (v.p. 1998—), N.Y. Acad. Scis., European Lang. Coun. (com. for translation and interpreting 1998—). E-mail: jettmar@ff.cuni.cz. Office: Inst Translation Studies, Hybernská 3, 110 00 Prague Czech Republic

JEW, HENRY, pharmacist; b. Hong Kong, June 10, 1950. BS in Pharmacy, U. Ga., 1974. Preceptor to externship program So. Sch. of Pharmacy, U. Ga., 1974-78; researcher Brompton's Mixture, 1977-78; pharmacist VA Med Ctr, Decatur, Ga., VNS Inc., Atlanta.

JEWELER, ROBIN, lawyer; b. Washington, Sept. 11, 1951; d. David Baer and Jeanne Carolyn (Weiss) J.; m. Laurence Donald Wiseman, May 29, 1978; children: Justin Jeweler, David Baer. BA with honors, U. Md., 1973; JD, George Washington U., 1976. Bar: Md., Washington. Jud. clk. Supreme Ct. Appeals, Charleston, W.Va., 1977-78; atty. Matthew Bender, Inc., N.Y.C., 1978-79; legis. atty. Congrl. Rsch. Svc., Libr. Congress, Washington, 1980—. Contbr. articles to profl. jours. Bd. dirs. Jewish Hist. Soc., Washington, 1996-2000, sec., 1999, asst. treas., 2000; pres. Bells Mill PTA, 1993. Mem. Internat. Women's Insolvency and Restructuring Confedn., Fed. Bar Assn., Am. Bankruptcy Inst. Fax: 202-707-8595. E-mail: rjeweler@crs.loc.gov. Home: 10621 Democracy Ln Potomac MD 20854-4016 Office: Libr Congress 101 Independence Ave SE Washington DC 20540-0002

JEWISON, NORMAN FREDERICK, film producer, director; b. Toronto, Ont., Can., July 21, 1926; s. Percy Joseph and Irene (Weaver) J.; m. Margaret Ann Dixon, July 11, 1953; children: Kevin Jefferie, Michael Philip, Jennifer Ann. Student, Malvern Collegiate Inst., Toronto, 1940-44; BA, Victoria Coll., U. Toronto, 1944; LLD (hon.), U. Western Ont., 1974, U. Trent, 1985, Ryerson Inst., 1986. With CBC, 1952-58, CBS, 1958-61, Universal Studios, 1961-64; freelance film dir., producer, exec. producer, 1965—; presenter student film award CNE, 1980-81; dir. Harry Belafonte, Jackie Gleason, Andy Williams, Judy Garland, Danny Kaye TV shows; produced 1981 Acad. Awards; pres. of jury Avoriaz Film Festival, France, 1981. Dir.: (TV films) 40 Pounds of Trouble, The Thrill of it All, 1963, Send Me No Flowers, 1964, (feature films) Art of Love, The Cincinnati Kid, 1965, In the Heat of the Night, The Thomas Crown Affair, 1967, Gaily, Gaily, 1968; producer, dir.: (films) The Russians are Coming, 1966, Fiddler on the Roof, 1970, Jesus Christ Superstar, 1972, F.I.S.T., 1977, And Justice For All, 1979, Best Friends, 1982, Only You, 1994; producer: (films) The Landlord, 1969, Billy Two Hats, 1972, Rollerball, 1974; exec. producer: (films) Dogs of War, 1980, Iceman, 1983, The January Man, 1988; exec. producer, dir.: (films) A Soldiers Story, 1984, Agnes of God, 1985, Moonstruck, 1988, In Country, 1989; co-producer, dir. (film) Other People's Money, 1991. Served with Royal Can. Navy, 1945-46. Decorated companion Order of Can., 1982; named Dir. of Yr., Nat. Assn. Theatre Owners, 1982, Best Dir. Berlin Film Festival, 1988; recipient Can. Liberty award, 1958, Irving G. Thalberg Meml. award, 1999, Emmy award, 1960, Emmy award nominations, 1961-62, TV Dirs. award, 1961, Golden Globe award, 1966, Acad. award nominations, 1966-67, 72, 74, 84, 88; honored by Calif. ACLU, 1984. Mem. Can. Ctr. for Advanced Film Studies (founder, co-chmn. 1986), Dirs. Guild Am. (goals and purposes com. 1982, award nominations 1966, 67, Outstanding Directorial Achievement award nomination 1984). Avocations: skiing, yachting, tennis. Office: Yorktown Prodns Inc Bldg 2465 3000 Olympic Blvd Santa Monica CA 90404-5073

JEX, IGOR, physicist, researcher; b. Bratislava, Slovakia, Oct. 16, 1962; s. Ja'n and Anna (Kulískova') J.; m. Soňa Kocíbova'; children: Michal, Martin. Diploma in Engring., Czech Tech. U., Prague, 1987, habilitation, 1997, DSc, 2000; PhD, Inst. Physics, Bratislava, 1991. Rschr. Inst. for Solid State Physics, Tokyo, 1992, Max-Planck Soc., Berlin, 1993, U. Helsinki, Finland, 1994, Max-Planck Soc., 1995; asst. Czech Tech. U., 1996—. Avocation: philosophy. Office: Czech Tech U Dept Physics, Brehova 7 FNSPE, 11519 Prague Czech Republic

JEYAKUMAR, RAMANUJAM, physicist; b. Kovilpatti, India, Sept. 24, 1966; s. Venkataswamy Ramanujam and Ramanujam Sivagamy; m. Jeyakumar Ramaprabha, June 16, 1999. BSc in Physics, Madurai Kamaraj U., 1986, MSc in Physics, 1988; PhD in Physics, Nat. Phys. Lab., New Delhi, 1998. Tchr. G Venkataswamy Naidu Coll., Kovil Patti, India, 1989-90; rsch. fellow Ctrl. Electrochem. Rsch. Inst., Karaikudi, India, 1991-93; sr. rsch. fellow Nat. Phys. Lab., New Delhi, 1994-98; rsch. assoc. Met. Phys. Lab., New Delhi, 1998-2000, Indira Gandhi Ctr. for Atomic Rsch., Kalpakkam, India, 2000; post doctoral fellow U. Waterloo, Canada, 2000—. Avocations: book reading, TV watching, playing chess, basketball. E-mail: jkrnaidu@yahoo.com, rjayakum@ece.uwaterloo.ca. Office: U Waterloo, Dept Elec Computer Engring, Waterloo, ON Canada N2L 3G1

JEYASEELAN, SITHAMPARAPILLAI, instrumentation/control systems engineer; b. Mulay, Sri Lanka, Sept. 26, 1953; arrived in Australia, 1981; s. Ramaswamy and Kantha (Muthusamy) S.; m. Chandragowry Cumarevelu, Aug. 19, 1985; children: Ahilan and Jeevan. BSc, Univ. Westminster, London, 1980. Field instrument engr. Geo Systems Ltd., Perth, Australia, 1981-85; asst. field seismologist Seismograph Svcs. Ltd., Adelaide, Australia, 1985-86; rsch. & devel. engr. Tracker Communications Ltd., Adelaide, Australia, 1986-87; elec. engr. Tulsa Pty Ltd., Adelaide, Australia, 1987-88; sr. engr. BHP Steel, Whyalla, Australia, 1988-96; sr. instrument & control engr. Water Corp., Perth, 1996—. Mem. The Inst. of Elec. Engrs., The Inst. of Mesurement & Control, The Inst. of Engrs., Inst. of Instrumentation and Control. Avocations: current affairs, reading, playing squash and badminton. Home: 34 Central Ave, Ardross 6153, Australia Office: Water Corp, 629 Newcastle St, 6007 Leederville 6007, Australia

JEYASOTHY, SELVADURAI, hotelier, actor; b. Kuala Lumpur, Malaysia, Nov. 24, 1950; s. Selvadurai Muthu and Potkody Nagalingam; m. Mugunthadevy Murugesu Jeyasothy, May 27, 1984; children: Athithan, Abeegithan. Grad., Hindu Coll., Colombo, Sri Lanka, 1969. Asst. Coop. Weawing Mill, Chankanai, Jaffna, Sri Lanka; hotel employee Riyadh, Saudi Arabia, 1981—. Actor, dir., comedian. Pres. Chempithoddam, Araly, 1972; Maru Malarchy Dramatic Soc., 1974; dep. pres. Sana Samagu Seva Sangam, 1978; organizer Social Work Com., Arly, 1979; mem. Coop. Soc., Araly, 1979-80. Recipient Best Actor award Village Com., Araly, Arank Olir Asan award Dramatic Soc. Araly, People Entertainer awrad Music Soc. Mem. Staff Welfare Soc. (v.p.). Hindu. Avocations: collecting foreign currency, listening to music, debate, acting, social work. Home: Apt c7, 93 2/5 Peterson Ln, Colombo 6, Sri Lanka

JEZEK, KAREL, computer science educator; b. Stankov, Czech Republic, June 17, 1942; s. Karel Jezek and Anna (Holubova) Jezkova; m. Marie Blazkova, Aug. 20, 1971; children: Karel, Petr. MSc, Tech. U., Pilsen, Czech Republic, 1964; PhD, Tech. U., Prague, Czech Republic, 1981. Registered profl. engr. Lectr. Tech. U., Pilsen, 1965-68, asst. prof., 1968-88, assoc. prof., 1988-90; mem. parliament Fed. Assembly of Czechoslovakia, 1990-92; head computer sci. dept. West Bohemia U., Pilsen, 1993—. Author: Special Programming Languages, 1986; co-author: Informatics, 1990, Data Protection, 1992, Parallel Architecture and Programs, 1999, Compiler Construction, 1999. Dep. Civic Forum, Prague, 1990. Mem. IEEE Computer Sci. Soc., Assn. Computing Machinery. Avocations: classical music, skiing, turistic. Home: K Svetle 10, 32318 Pilsen Czech Republic Office: West Bohemia U Dept Computer Sci, Univerzitni 22, 30614 Pilsen Czech Republic

JEZEK, PETR, biochemist, biophysicist, researcher; b. Prague, Czechoslovakia, Apr. 22, 1957; s. Frantisek and Jindriska (Bardounova) J.; m. Zuzana Strouhalova, Aug. 12, 1978; children: Jan, Petra. Diploma in Physics, Charles U., Prague, 1981, DrRerNat, 1982; PhD in Animal Physiology, Acad Sci., Inst. Physiology, 1987. Postdoctoral fellow dept. pharmacology Med. Coll. Ohio, Toledo, 1988-90; rschr., dept. head Inst. of Physiology, Prague, 1991—. Mem. editorial bd. Internat. Jour. Biochemistry and Cell Biology, 1996—; contbr. articles to Jour. Biol. Chemistry. Vice mayor Cakovice quarter Prague,1994—; local chmn. Civic Dem. Party, Prague, 1991—. Fogarty Internat. grantee, 1992-94; U.S.-Czech Sci. Technol. Program grantee, 1995-99; Deutsche Forschungsgemeinschaft grantee, 1996-99, others. Mem. N.Y. Acad. Scis., Czech Biochem. Soc. Achievements include hypothesis of affinity and effector parts of binding site, revealing new substrotes of uncoupling protein and bringing evidence for fatty acid cycling mechanism, by which all mitochondria are partially uncoupled; confirming discovery of uncoupling protein in plants. E-mail: jezek@biomed.cas.cz. Office: Institute of Physiology, Dept 375 Videnska 1083, CZ 14220 Prague Czech Republic

JEZERNIK, KAREL, electrical engineer, educator; b. Dokležovje, Slovenia, Apr. 11, 1942; s. Karel and Marija (Vindiš) J.; m. Zinka Savnik, Apr. 25, 1970; 2 children. B in Engring., U. Ljubljana, Slovenia, 1968; M in Engring., U. Ljubljana, 1974, PhD, 1976. Engr. ISKRA, Ljubljana, 1968-70; from asst. to prof. U. Maribor, Slovenia, 1970-74; lectr; rschr. Tech. U., Braunschweig, Germany, 1974-75; dean faculty electrotech. engring. U. maribor, 1977-81, dir. electrotech. rsch. inst., 1981-85, vice rector, 1985-87. Author: Springer Verlag, 1994; contbr. articles to profl. jours. Mem. IEEE, Nat. Rsch. Found. Tech. Slovenia (pres. 1982—). Office: U Maribor, Smetanova 17, 2000 Maribor Slovenia

JEZIOROWSKI, JÜRGEN, retired theologian, journalist; b. Würzburg, Bavaria, Germany, Sept. 18, 1936; m. Inge Mäusbacher, Oct. 9, 1962; children: Thomas, Marja, Jörg. Student, U. Erlangen, Germany, U. Berlin, U. Basel, Switzerland. Pastor Bavaria, 1962-67; student pastor Stuttgart, Germany, 1967-69; oberkirchenratin Hannover, Germany, 1970-98; ret., 1999. Author books, TV films, articles. Evangelical Lutheran.

JEZOWSKI, JACEK MARIA, chemical engineering educator; b. Krakow, Poland, Feb. 28, 1950; s. Zygmunt and Maria Krzysztofa (Wartanowicz) J.; m. Alina Jadwiga Bysiek, Feb. 21, 1948; children: Anna, Maciej, Barbara. MS, Tech. U., Poland, 1972, PhD, 1976, DSc. Lectr. to sr. lectr. Tech. U., Wroclaw, 1976-93; prof., vice head Rzeszow U. of Tech., Poland, 1993—; head of dept. Univ. Wroclaw, 1980-81, U. Rzeszow, 1995-97. Author: (book) Designing Heat Recovery Subsystems at Certain Data, 1995, Designing Heat Recovery Subsystems at Uncertain Data, 1995; editl. bd. Hungarian Jour. of Indsl. Chemistry, 1990-96. Roman Catholic. Avocations: reading history books, tennis, basketball. Office: Rezeszow Univ Tech, Al Powstancow Warszawy 6, 35959 Rzeszow Poland

JHABVALA, RUTH PRAWER, writer; b. Cologne, Germany, May 7, 1927; lived in India, 1951-75; came to U.S., 1975; d. Marcus and Eleonora (Cohn) Prawer; m. Cyrus S. H. Jhabvala, 1951; 3 children. MA, London U., 1951, DLitt (hon.), 1986, LHD (hon.), 1995, D Arts (hon.), 1996. Author: (novels) To Whom She Will, 1955, The Nature of Passion, 1956, Esmond in India, 1957, The Householder, 1960, Get Ready for Battle, 1962, A Backward Place, 1965, A New Dominion, 1972, Heat and Dust, 1975 (Booker award for fiction Nat. Book League 1975), In Search of Love and Beauty, 1983, Three Continents, 1987, Poet and Dancer, 1993, Shards of Memory, 1995; (short story collections) Like Birds, Like Fishes and Other Stories, 1964, A Stronger Climate: Nine Stories, 1968, An Experience of India, 1971, How I Became a Holy Mother and Other Stories, 1976, Out of India: Selected Stories, 1986, East Into Upper East, 1998; (film scripts) The Householder, 1963 (with James Ivory), Shakespeare Wallah, 1965 (with Ivory), The Guru, 1968, Bombay Talkie, 1970, Autobiography of a Princess, 1975, Roseland, 1977, Hullabaloo over Georgie and Bonnie's Pictures, 1978, The Europeans, 1979, Jane Austen in Manhattan, 1980, Quartet, 1981, Heat and Dust, 1983, The Bostonians, 1984, A Room With a View, 1986 (Writers Guild of Am. award for best adapted screeplay 1986, Acad. award for best adapted screenplay 1986), (with John Schlesinger) Madame Sousatzka, 1988, Mr. and Mrs. Bridge, 1990, Howards End, 1992 (Acad. award for best adapted screenplay 1992), Remains of the Day, 1993 (Acad. award nomination for best adapted screenplay 1993), Jefferson in Paris, 1995, Surviving Picasso, 1996, (with James Ivory) A Soldier's Daughter Never Cries, 1998, The Golden Bowl, 2000. Decorated comdr. Brit. Empire; Guggenheim fellow, 1976; Neil Gunn. Internat. fellow, 1979; MacArthur Found. fellow, 1984-89. Home: 400 E 52d St New York NY 10022-6404

JI, CHAOZHU, United Nations official, diplomat; b. China, July 30, 1929; s. Chi Kungchuan; m. Wang Xiangtong, 1957; 2 children. Attended, Harvard U., Tsinghua U., Peking, China. Stenographer, typist Panmunjom, Korea for Chinese People's Vols., 1952-54; counsellor Liaison Office of China, Washington, 1973-75; dep. dir. dept. for internal orgs. and confs. Min. Fgn. Affairs, 1975-79, dep. dir. Am. and Oceanic affairs, 1979-82; minister-counsellor Chinese Embassy, Washington, 1982-85; amb. to Fiji, Kiribati and Vanuatu, 1985-87, U.K., 1987-91; under-sec. for tech. cooperation for devel. UN, 1991-92, under sec.-gen. dept. econ. devel., 1992-93, under sec.-gen. dept. for devel. support and mgmt. svcs., 1993-96; vice-chmn. All-China Fedn. Returned Overseas Chinese, 1997—; sr. cons. China Inst. Internat. Strategic Studies, 1996—; English interpreter Chmn. Mao, Premier Chou En-lai and other Chinese leaders, 1955-73. Avocations: swimming, archaeology, history. Home: The Pinnacle 11201 Queens Blvd Apt 18 D Forest Hills NY 11375 Office: 1 Beixinqiao Santiao, Beijing 100007, China

JI, HANBING, property development merchant, information technology merchant and developer, neural network specialist, researcher; b. Shanghai, China, June 26, 1965; arrived in Hong Kong, 1993; s. Ruirong Ji and Jiashan Li; m. Chogau Cheung, Dec. 19, 1995. B in Engring., Shanghai Jiao Tong U., 1986, MS in Engring., 1989, PhD, 1992; PhD, Chinese U. Hong Kong, 1997. Rsch. asst. Shanghai Jiao Tong U., 1986-92, Hong Kong U. Sci. and Tech., 1993, Chinese U. Hong Kong, 1993-96; computer/comm. network specialist Cathay Pacific Airways, Ltd., 1996-97; mng. dir. Carifull Devel., Ltd./Fung Yuen Property, Ltd./Fung Yuen Land Devel./Infosys.com, Ltd., Hong Kong, 1997—. Inventor in field; contbr. articles to profl. jours. and conf. procs.; reviewer IEEE Trans. on Neural Networks, 1996—, Internat. Journ. Neural Systems, 1997, IEEEFUZZ '92, 1991, Internat. Jour. of Neural Systems, 1997. Named Outstanding Grad. Student, Shanghai Jiao Tong U., 1988, 91. Mem. IEEE, Internat. Neural Network Soc. Avocations: soccer, basketball, swimming.

JI, MINGGANG, mechanical engineering educator; b. Shanghai, Jan. 15, 1935; s. Linggi Ji and Tsuitsui Du; m. Huili Shen, Aug. 8, 1959; children: Shanmei, Shanhong. BS, Northwestern Poly. U., Xi-an, China, 1957. Asst. Northwestern Poly. U., 1957-63, instr., 1964-81, assoc. prof., 1981-86, prof., 1986—; mem. specialty com. Nat. Edn. Com., 1990-95. Editor: Principles of Finite Element Method in Fluids, 1985; contbr. articles to profl. publs. Recipient 2d Class Sci. and Tech. award Nat. Edn. Com., China, 1986, Theoretical Rsch. award Ministry of Aviation, 1982, 3d Class Nat. Invention award, 1988. Fellow Chinese Soc. Aeronautics and Astronautics (mem. com. 1990—); mem. Chinese Soc. Mech. Engring., Chinese Soc. Engring. Thermophysics. Avocation: classical music. Office: Northwestern Poly U, Dept Mech Engring, Xian Shaanxi 710072, China

JI, YU, research scientist, electrical engineer; b. Chuangchun, Jilin, China, Sept. 7, 1962; came to U.S., 1997; s. Guangqian Ji and Jialing Xie; m. Youyang Jin, Oct. 18, 1987; children: Megan Nantian, Nancy Tianhe. BSc, Heilongjiang U., 1984; MS, Shizuoka U., 1987, PhD, 1990. Rsch. asst. Harbin (China) Inst. Tech., 1984-85; rsch. engr. Graphica Computer Corp., Tokyo, 1990-91; rsch. assoc. U. Western Sydney, Australia, 1991-92; postdoctoral fellow Comm. Rsch. Lab., Tokyo, 1993-95; rsch. scientist ATR Adaptive Comm. Rsch. Labs., Kyoto, Japan, 1995-97; rsch. assoc. Calif. Inst. Tech. Jet Propulsion Lab., Pasadena, Calif., 1997-2000; product mgr. Santec USA, Hackensack, N.J., 2000—; cons. Sofcom, Ltd., Tokyo, 1993-96. Inventor in field. Mem. IEEE, Inst. Electronics Info. and Comm. Engrs. Japan, Inst. Electronics, Info. and Comms. Engrs. Avocations: swimming, table tennis, travel, reading. Home: 202 Center St Milford NJ 07646-3432 Office: Santec USA Jet Propulsion Lab 433 Hackensack Ave Hackensack NJ 07601-8001

JI, YUSHENG, computer engineering educator; b. Nanjing, Jiangsu, China, Oct. 1960; s. Bingxian Ji and Guisheng Chu; m. Linghua Meng, Mar. 1988; 1 child, Jing Jing. B of Engring., U. Tokyo, 1984, M of Engring., 1986, D of Engring., 1989. Rsch. assoc. Nat. Ctr. for Sci. Info. Sys., Tokyo, 1990-95, assoc. prof., 1995—; vis. asst. prof./scientist U. Wis., Madison, 1992-93; vis. rschr. U. Calif., Santa Cruz, 1997-98. Co-translator: (book) Design and Implementation of 4.3 BSD UNIX Operating System, 1991; contbr. papers and articles to profl. jours. Mem. IEEE, Inst. Electronics, Info. and Comm. Engrs., Info. Processing Soc. Japan.

JIA, CHUNWANG, Chinese government official; b. Beijing, 1938. Lectr. physics CYL Com./Qinghua U., 1964-77; mem. CCP, 1962—; mem. standing com. CYL, 1978-82, sec. Beijing br., elected mem. standing com., 1982-84; dep. sec. Beijing CP, 1984-85; minister of state security, elected mem. CPC CC, 1985-99, min. of pub. security, 1999—. Office: East Dist, 14 Dong Chang An Jie, Beijing 100741, People's Republic of China*

JIA, WEI JIA, computer science educator, researcher; b. Pan Xian, Guizhou, China, Nov. 10, 1957; s. Dao Xing Jia and Zhu Ying Fu; m. Mei Xie, Jan. 8, 1986; 1 child, Si (Sally). BS in Computer Sci., Ctr. South U. Tech., Changsha, China, 1982, MS in Computer Sci., 1984; MS in Applied Sci., Faculty Poly. Mons (Belgium), 1992, PhD in Computer Sci., 1993. Asst. lectr. dept. computer sci. City U. Tech., Changsha, China, 1984; lectr. dept. computer sci. City U. Tech., Changsha, 1988-91; guest researcher dept. computer sci., vis. scholar U. Ottawa (Can.), Ont., 1987-88; with Gesellschaft fur Math. und Datenverarbeitung (GMD), St. Augustin, 1993-95; asst. prof. dept. computer sci. City U. Hong Kong, 1995—; prin. investigator rsch. projects supported by Strategic Rsch. Grants City U. Hong Kong and RGC Rsch. Grants, Hong Kong; mem. program com. Internat. Conf. on Parallel and Distributed Sys., 1998, 99, Annual Symposiums on High Performance Computing Sys., 1998; mem. organizing com. Internat. Confs. 1997 Internat. Joint Computer Sci. Conf. and Asia Software Engring. Conf.; session chmn. Internat. Computer Sci. Conf., 11th Annual Internat. Symposium on High Performance Computing Sys., 1997, 7th internat. workshop Hong Kong Computer Soc.; mem. program com. 4th Real-time Computing Sys. and Applications, 2000; program co-chair 4th IEEE Internat. Conf. on Algorithm and Arch. on Parallel Processing; spkr., presenter in field. Author: Object-Oriented Programming-Smalltalk, 1990; contbr. numerous articles to profl. jours., chpts. to books. Rsch. grantee City U. Hong Kong, 1995, 96, 97, 98, 99, 2000, RGC Rsch. Grants, 1996, 97, 98, 2000. Office: Dept Computer Sci City U, 83 Tat Che Ave, Hong Kong Hong Kong

JIA, XINGDONG, electrical engineering educator, researcher; b. Taiyuan, China, Aug. 29, 1963; s. Yunxiu Jia and Naiqin Sun; m. Lei Yang, May 28, 1988; 1 child, Chaoxiang. B, Xi'an (China) Jiaotong U., 1983, MS, 1986; PhD, City U. Hong Kong, 1998. Lectr. Xi'an Jiatong U., 1986-92; rsch. scholar City U. Hong Kong, 1992—. Contbr. articles to profl. jours. Mem. IEEE, China Inst. Electronics, China Inst. Elec. Techniques. Avocations: bridge, swimming, music. Office: City U Hong Kong, Sch Creative Media, Hong Kong China

JIA, YUMIN, engineer; b. Beijing, July 4, 1958; s. Yuxian Yuan; m. Fanning Lind, Aug. 18, 1992; 1 child, Jason. M, Nat. U. Singapore. Engr. Philips, Beijing, 1982-90; rschr. U. Tenn., Knoxville, 1991-93; engr. Nat. U. Singapore, 1994—. Contbr. articles to profl. jours. Mem. Microscopy Soc. Am. Office: Nat U Singapore, Singapore 119260, Singapore

JIANG, CHENGYONG, immunologist; b. Yanjin, Henan, China, Aug. 22, 1963; s. Songhong and Xiouying (Shen) J. MD, First Med. U., Guangzhou, 1983. Physician Nanjing Hosp., China, 1983-86; postgrad. Chinese Acad. Med. Sci., Beijing, 1986-89; asst. prof. Inst. Basic Med. Sci., Beijing, 1989-92; vis. rschr. U. VI of Paris, France, 1993; Postdoctoral fellow U. Tex. H.S.C., San Antonio, 1994-95; postdoctoral fellow UCLA-Harbor Med. Ctr., 1996; microbiologist/immunologist Tex. Ctr. Infectious Disease, San Antonio, 1997-2000; Contbr. articles to profl. jours. Avocations: travel, photography, movies. Fax: 210-531-4550. E-mail: chengyong.jiang@tdh.state.tx.us. Office: Tex Ctr Infectious Dis 2303 SE Military Dr San Antonio TX 78223-3542

JIANG, CHONGJUN, chemical engineer; b. Laiyang, Shandong, China, Mar. 6, 1957; came to Australia, 1988; s. Dunxiang Jiang and Yuying Zhou; m. Liyan Ma, Nov. 16, 1983; children: Wei Jiang, Sarah Jiang, Emma Jiang. BS in Chem. Engring. with honors, East China Petroleum Inst., China, 1982; PhD in Chem. Engring., U. New South Wales, Australia, 1992. Tchr. Wandi H.S., Lai Yang, China, 1974-77; process engr. Rsch. Inst. Petroleum Processing, Beijing, China, 1982-85; prin. engr. Rsch. Inst. Petroleum Processing, 1986-88; rsch. assoc. Sch. Chem. Engring. U. New South Wales, Australia, 1989-92; post-doctoral rsch. fellow U. New South Wales, 1992-95; project mgr. James Hardie Tech. Unit, Sydney, Australia, 1995—; gen. exec. J&M Chem. Egnring. Tech. Cons., Sydney, Australia, 1996—; visiting sci. Japan Petroleum Coop. Ctr., Tokyo, 1985—. Mem. Assn. Chinese Scis. and Engrs. in Australia (v.p., 1992-97), N.Y. Acad. Scis. Achievements include a patent for the production of hydrogen from methanol at room temperature. Avocations: fishing, drama, opera, photography. E-mail: jiang.chongjun@jameshardie.com.au. Home: 49 Waverly St Belmore, Sydney NSW 2192, Australia Office: James Hardie Tech Unit, 1 Grand Ave Camellia, Sydney NSW 2142, Australia

JIANG, DE-SHENG, physicist, educator; b. Shanghai, Sept. 21, 1940; s. Yi-Ling Jiang and Zhong-Xiu Zhou; m. Guan-Li Wu, May 1, 1968; children: Shan, Ming. Student, Nanjing U., China, 1963, Chinese Acad. Scis., Beijing, 1967. Rsch. asst., rsch. assoc., assoc. prof., prof. Inst. Semicondrs., Chinese Acad. Scis., Beijing, 1967—; vis. scientist Max-Planck-Inst. for Solid State Rsch., Stuttgart, Germany, 1979-81, 86, 89, 93, Laboratoire de Physique des Solides, Toulouse, France, 1992, Paul-Drude-Inst. for Solid State Electronics, Berlin, 1996; mem. acad. com. Nat. Lab. for Supelattices and Microstructures, Beijing, 1991-95, 95—; project head Nat. Found. Natural Scis., 1988-91, 92-95, 96-98. Contbr. rsch. articles to profl. publs. Mem. Electronics Soc. China (sr. mem.), Physics Soc. China. Avocations: music, philately. Office: Inst Semicondrs Chinese Acad Scis, PO Box 912, 100083 Beijing China

JIANG, HE, biomedical scientist, entrepreneur; b. Chengdu, Sichuan, China, Feb. 13, 1958; came to U.S., 1994; s. Xintian Jiang and Youbai Shan; m. Kang Rao, Aug. 1, 1983; children: Kelen T., Lan T. MD, Luzhou (China) Med. Coll., 1982; MSc, 3d Mil. Med. U., Chongqing, China, 1985; PhD, U. Man., 1994. Lic. MD, Chinese Ministry Health and Ednl. Com. Asst. prof. 3d Med. U., Chongqing, China, 1985-87; vis. prof. faculty medicine U. Man., Winnipeg, 1987-88, rsch. scientist dept. physiology, 1988-90; guest rschr. NIH, Bethesda, Md., 1994—; chmn. Kela Global Exchange, Ltd., 1998. Rsch. in molecular motor, asthma, diagnostics; contbr. articles to profl. jours., chpts. to books. Recipient 3d Natural Scis. Rsch. award China State Nature and Sci. Com., Chongqing, 1987, Vis. Scholarship award China State Edn. Com., Can., 1987-88, Studentship award Man. Health Rsch. Coun., Can., 1988, 89, Man. Lung Assn., Can., 1988, Major Student Rsch. award, 1990, 94, St. Boniface Gen. Hosp. Rsch. Found., 1988, Man. Med. Svc. Found. award, 1989, Sigma Xi Student Rsch. award U. Man., 1991. Fellow Med. Rsch. Coun. Can. (Postdoctoral fellowship 1990-94, 94-97); mem. Nat. Soc. Med. Scientists (Top Ten Young Med. Scientists in U.S. award), Biophys. Soc., Am. Physiol. Soc., Can. Ctrs. Excellence Respiratory (affiliate), Chinese Pathophysiol. Soc., N.Y. Acad. Scis. Avocations: volleyball, photography, trade, multimedia and animation design, music and singing. Office: Lab Molecular Cardiology NIH 8N202 10 9000 Rockville Pik Bethesda MD 20892

JIANG, JIA-QIAN, environmental engineer, chemist; s. Qi-Yu and Xiu-E (Zhang) J; m. Yi-Ping Zhu; children: Ann, Allen. BSc, Shanghai Inst. Tech., 1982; PhD, Imperial Coll./U. London, 1995. Chartered engr., U.K., chartered chemist, U.K. Rsch. engr. Shanghai Inst. Tech., 1982-86; chief engr., head Lab. of Water and Waste Water, Shanghai Inst. Tech., 1986-90; acad. visitor Imperial Coll., London, 1991-92, rschr., 1992-95, rsch. fellow, 1995-99; lectr. U. Surrey Ctr Environ Health Engring, Eng., 1999—; forum mem. Environ. Office of Imperial Coll., 1997—. Contbr. articles to profl. jours.; patentee in field. Recipient Unwin prize Imperial Coll., London, 1997, Excellent Paper prize Shanghai Water Assn., 1984. Mem. Royal Soc. Chemistry, Chartered Inst. Water and Environ. Mgmt., Internat. Assn. Water Quality. Avocation: reading historical books. Office: U Surrey Ctr Environ Health, Dept Civil Engring, Guildford Surrey GU2 5XH, England

JIANG, JING PING, education educator; b. Ningbo, Zhejiang, China, Dec. 1, 1935; s. Xian Cheng and Xiang Ying (He) J.; m. Li Li Dai, May 12, 1967; 1 child, Pin Shan. MS, Mich. State U., 1958. Lectr. Zhejiang U., Hangshou, 1958-78, assoc. prof., 1978-85, prof., 1985—; vis. scholar U. Wis., Madison, 1979-81, Reading (Eng.) U., 1988-89. Contbr. articles to profl. jours. Sino-British Friendship scholar, 1989. Mem. IEEE (sr. mem., chmn. Shanghai subsect. 1995-97). Avocations: photography, fishing. Home and Office: Zhejiang U, Yu Gu Rd # 20, Hangzhou 310027, China

JIANG, LEI, mechanical engineer, researcher, consultant; b. Xi'an, Shaanxi, People's Republic of China, Mar. 24, 1963; arrived in Can., 1986; s. Yan-Zhi Jiang and De-Xin Zheng; m. Juan Zhou, Aug. 18, 1986; children: Patricia Min, Christopher Liang. BSc, Xi'an Jiaotong U., 1985; PhD, U. N.B., Fredericton, Can., 1989. Rsch. asst., tchg. asst. U. N.B., 1986-89; rsch. assoc. U. Victoria, Can., 1989-90; sr. rsch. engr. Martec Ltd., Halifax, Can., 1990—; vis. scientist U. Victoria, 1992, 93, 95. Reviewer tech. jours. including Jour. Sound and Vibration, 1992, 97, Internat. Jour. Numerical Methods in Engring., 1993; contbr. articles to profl. jours. including Jour. Sound and Vibration, Internat. Jour. for Numerical Methods in Engring., ASME Jour. Applied Mechanics. 1st class scholar Xi'an Jiaotong U., 1983. Mem. ASME, Can. Soc. Mech. Engring., U.S. Assn. Computational Mechanics. Avocations: Chinese calligraphy, travel, table tennis, music. Home: 44 Plateau Crescent, Halifax, NS Canada B3M 2V8 Office: Martec Ltd, 1888 Brunswick St Ste 400, Halifax, NS Canada B3J 3J8

JIANG, QINGTANG, educator; b. Wen Cheng, China, Sept. 21, 1965; s. Shousong and Songzhu (Hu) J.; m. Hong Chen; 1 child, Boyang. BS, Hangzhou U., China, 1986, MS, 1989; PhD, Peking U., Beijing, 1992. Asst. prof. Peking U., Beijing, 1992-94, assoc. prof., 1994—. Contbr. articles to profl. jours. Postdoctoral fellow Nat. U. Singapore, 1995-97, rsch. fellow, 1997—. Office: Nat U Singapore Dept Math, 10 Kent Ridge Crescent, Singapore 119260, Singapore

JIANG, SHI YANG, astronomer; b. Huaying, China, Feb. 10, 1936; s. Chang Song Jiang and Rui Qing Tang; m. Gui Hua Peng, Feb. 5, 1968; children: Ruo-Ju Jiang, Luo-Hua Jiang. BS, U. Nanjing, China, 1958. Asst. Beijing Astron. Observatory, 1958-63, assoc., 1963-78, assoc. prof. astronomy, 1978-86, prof. astronomy, 1986—; prof. astronomy Shanxi Astron. Observatory, Xian, China, 1987—; head stellar physics dept. Beijing Astron. Observatory, 1983-89; vis. astronomer U. Durham, Eng., 1983. Inventor of spectrograph design. Recipient Nat. Sci. award Chinese Acad. Scis., Beijing, 1996. Mem. Internat. Astron. Union (mem. orgn. com. Commn. no. 27 1994—), Astron. Soc. China (bd. dirs. 1989-94, Zhang Yu-Zhe award 1996). Office: Beijing Astronomical Observ, Datun Rd 20A, Beijing 100012, China

JIANG, SHUN-YUAN, medical educator; b. Tau-Yuan, Taiwan, July 20, 1959; d. Ren-Kong Jiang and Mei-Chi Chang; m. Rong-Yaun Shyu, June 3, 1984; 2 children. BS, Nat. Taiwan Normal U., 1982; MS, Nat. Def. Med. Ctr., Taipei, Taiwan, 1984; PhD, U. Wis., 1992. Asst. rschr. Nat. Def. Med. Ctr., Taipei, 1984-87, 92-93, assoc. prof., 1993-99, prof., 1999—. Mem. Am. Cancer Soc., Cellular and Molecular Biology Soc. of Republic of China, Oncology Soc. of Republic of China. Office: Rm 8315 No 161 Sec 6, Ming-Cheung East Rd, Taipei 114, Taiwan

JIANG, SONGSHENG, physics educator; b. Guongfeng, Jiangxi, China, Oct. 18, 1935; s. Meifang Jiang and Yun-yue Zhou; m. Wenyu Qian, Jan. 1969; children: Haiyin, Haiming. Grad., Peking U., Beijing, 1957. Rsch. asst. Lab. Neutron Physics, Joint Inst. for Nuclear Rsch., Dybna, USSR, 1959-60; rsch. asst. Lab. Neutron Physics, Inst. Atomic Energy, Academia Sinica, Bijing, 1961-64, rsch. scientist, 1965-80; rsch. scientist dept. nuclear technique China Inst. Atomic Energy, Bijing, 1981-91, prof. dept. nuclear physics, 1992—; vis. scientist Nuclear Structure Rsch. Lab., U. Rochester, N.Y., 1986-88. Contbr. articles to sci. jours., including Nuclear Instruments and Methods, Chinese Physics Letters. Recipient award China Com. Sci. and Tech., 1995. Avocations: fishing, classical music, watching television, walking. Home: 205 Yuanxinxiru, Xinzhen, Fangshan 102413, China Office: China Inst Atomic Energy, PO Box 275(49), Beijing 102413, China

JIANG, TIANZI, computer scientist, mathematician, educator; b. Yongzhou, Hunan, China, Apr. 17, 1962; s. Meixi Jiang and Xiaomei Yang; m. Shuhong Luan, Aug. 29, 1995; 1 child, Yining Jiang. BSc, Lanzhou (China) U., 1984; MSc, Hangzhou (China) U., 1992, PhD, 1994. Asst. prof. Suzhou (China) U., 1989; assoc. prof. Nat. Lab. Pattern Recognition, The Inst. Automation, Beijing, 1996-99, head computational vision workgroup, 1994-97, prof. Nat. Pattern Recognition, 1999—; vis. scientist Max-Planck Inst. Cognitive Neurosci., Leipzig, Germany, 1999—. Contbr. articles to profl. jours., including Internat. Jour. Computer Math. Recipient Natural Sci. award Chinese Acad. Sci., 1996; youth rsch. grantee Nat. Natural Sci. Found. China, Beijing, 1998; rsch. fellow Nat. Lab. Pattern Recognition, Inst. Automation, Beijing, 1994, vice-chancellor's postdoctoral rsch. fellow U. New South Wales, Sydney, Australia, 1997-99, Max-Planck fellow Max-Planck Soc., Leipzig, 1999. Mem. IEEE, Computer Soc. of IEEE, N.Y. Acad. Scis. Avocations: travel, reading, fishing, movies. Fax: +49-341-9940221. E-mail: jiang@cns.mpg.edu. Office: MP Inst Cognitive Neurosci, Stephanstr 1, 04103 Leipzig Germany

JIANG, WOEI-JIA, biochemist, consultant; b. Kaohsiung City, Taiwan, Jan. 10, 1963; s. K.S. and S.F. (Hong) J.; m. L.K. Chou, 1990; 1 child, Amy. BSc, Nat. Cheng Kung U., Tainan, Taiwan, 1986, MSc, 1988; PhD in Medicine, Monash U., Melbourne, Australia, 1998. Asst. rsch. scientist Devel. Ctr. Biotech., Taipei, Taiwan, 1990-93; demonstrator Monash U., Melbourne, Australia, 1994-98, rsch. fellow, 1998—; cons. Unison Herbal Pharms. Ltd., Melbourne, 1998—; R&D mgr. Unison Tech. Australia Ltd., Melbourne, 1999—. Patentee in field. With Taiwan Army, 1988-90. Recipient grad. scholarship Monash U., 1994-97. Mem. Australian Biotech. Assn., Australian Soc. Biochemistry and Molecular Biology, Australian Diabetes Soc., Drug Info. Assn., Taiwanese Bus. Assn. Melbourne (vice chmn.). Fax: 61-3-9905-4699, 61-3-9738-1889. E-mail: woeijaijiang@hotmail.com. Home: 3/19 Gardiner Rd, Clayton 3168 Vic, Australia Office: Monash U Dept Biochem, Wellington Rd, Clayton 3168 Vic, Australia also: UHP/UTA, 12/11 Havelock Rd, Bayswater VIC 3153, Australia

JIANG, ZEMIN, Chinese government official; b. Yangzhou City, Jiangsu, People's Republic of China, Aug. 17, 1926. Grad. in elec. engring., Jiastong U., Shanghai, People's Republic of China, 1947. Dir. power subplant Changchun No. 1 Motor Vehicle Plant, from 1956; dir. Shanghai Elec. Equipment Sci. Rsch. Inst., Wuhan Heat Power Machinery Rsch. Inst., until 1970; dep. dir., then dir. Fgn. Affairs Bur., 1st Ministry Machine Bldg. Industry, 1971-79; vice min. Adminstrv. Commn. for Import and Export Affairs, 1980-82, State Fgn. Investment Commn., 1981-82; vice min. electronics industry, 1982-83, min. electronics industry, dep. head leading group, 1983-85; mayor City of Shanghai, 1985-88; chmn. Ctrl. Mil. Commn., 1990—; pres. China, 1993—; mem. Chinese Communist Party, 1946—, mem. Politburo of Cen. Com., 1987—, mem. standing com. of Politburo of Cen. Com., 1989—, gen. sec., 1989—; dep. sec. Shanghai Municipality Communist Party, 1985. Office: Office of the Pres care State Coun Secretariat, Zhong Nan Hai, Beijing China*

JIANG, ZHAO-HUI, mechanical engineering educator, scientist; b. Qiqihar, China, May 3, 1957; s. Yugui Jiang and Suzhen Wang; m. Kwok-Yee Fung, Feb. 26, 1991; 1 child, Henry Hong-Ru. BS, Harbin (China) Inst. Tech., 1982; M Engring., Chiba (Japan) U., 1985; PhD, Tohoku U., Sendai, Japan, 1988. Sr. rschr. China Devel. Inst., Shenzhen, 1989-90; lectr. Hiroshima (Japan)-Denki Inst. Teh., 1990-93; sr. rsch. scientist U. Toronto, Ont., Can., 1994-96; assoc. prof. Hiroshima Inst. Tech., 1997—, dir. robotics and automation lab., 1997—; dept. dir. China Devel. Inst., 1989-90. Contbr. articles to profl. jours. Recipient Young Investigator award Robotics Soc. Japan, 1988, Best paper award Robotics Soc. Japan, 1990. Fax: 0829 23-3267. Office: Hiroshima Inst Tech, 2-1-1 Miyake Saeki-ku, Hiroshima 731-5193, Japan

JIANG, ZHI-CHENG, physical chemist, educator; b. Lanzhou, Gansu, China, Apr. 21, 1943; s. Shen and Yu-Feng (Li) J.; m. Cun-Ying Gao, Sept. 19, 1942; children: Xi-Heng, Xi-Xiang. Grad., Lanzhou (China) U., 1967. Tchr. H.S. Lanzhou, 1968-78; rsch. asst. Lanzhou Inst. Chem. Physics, Chinese Acad. Scis., 1978-81, rsch. assoc., 1981-86, assoc. prof., 1987-95, prof., 1996—, divsn. dir., 1986-98; vis. scholar Pa. State U., State College, 1987-88, 94-95, vis. scientist adv., TDK-SAE Magnetics, Ltd., 1999—. Contbr. articles to profl. jours. Fellow Chinese Chem. Soc., Chinese Soc. Physics. Avocations: classical music, ice skating, swimming. Office: Lanzhou Inst Chem Physics, Chinese Acad Scis, 730000 Lanzhou Gansu, China

JIANGPING, TU, metallurgist, educator; b. Nanchang, Jiangxi, China, Nov. 25, 1963; s. Tu Puzheng and Xiao Guilian; m. Zhu Liping, Jan. 23, 1990; 1 child, Xiyue. BS, Shanghai Jiaotang U., 1985; MS, Zhejiang U., Hangzhou, China, 1990, PhD, 1994. Engr. China Shipbuilding Indsl. Corp., Jiujiang, 1985-88; lectr. Zhejiang U., 1994-96, assoc. prof., 1996-97, prof., 2000—, asst. dir. dept. material sci. engring., 1995-97; rschr. Hiroshima (Japan) U., 1998-99. Author: Advanced Composites, 1995; contbr. articles to profl. jours. Fellow Japan Soc. for Promotion Sci.; mem. MRS, Mech. Soc. China, N.Y. Acad. Scis. Avocations: bridge, sports, music. Office: Hiroshima U Dept Chem Engr, Kagamiyama 1-4-1, Higashi Hiroshima 739-8527, Japan

JIAXUAN, TANG, government agency official; b. Jiangsu, China, Jan. 1938; married; 1 son. Grad., Fudan U., Shanghai, 1958; postgrad. diploma, Beijing U., 1962. Intern Japanese Lang. sect. Radio Broadcastng Bur., China, 1962-64; mem. staff interpretation and translation team Fgn. Ministry, 1964-70; coun. mem. Sino-Japanese Friendship Assn., Chinese Pe-

ople Assn. Friendship Fgn. Countries, 1970-78; 2d sec., 1st sec. Embassy of People's Republic of China, Japan, 1978-83; min.-counsellor, then min. Embassy of the People's Republic of China, Japan, 1988-91; dep. dir.-gen. Dept. Asian Affairs Ministry Fgn. Affairs, Beijing, 1983-88, asst. fgn. min., 1991-93, dep. fgn. min., 1993-98, fgn. min., 1998—. Office: Ministry Fgn Affairs, No 2 Chaoyangmen Nan Dajie, Beijing China

JIBIN, LIU, federal official. Min. of def. China. Office: 25 Huang Si Da Jie De Sheng, Men Wai East Dist, Beijing 100011, China*

JIE-QING, WU, engineering educator, consultant; b. Shanghai, Sept. 20, 1926. B of Engring., Zhejiang U., China, 1949. Engring. diplomate. Asst. Shangtong U., China, 1949-50; asst. Zhejiang U., 1950-53, lectr., 1953-81, prof., 1981—; supr. postgrad. students Zhejiang U., 1981—, dir. metal performance ctr., 1980-84. Inventor in field. Mem. Am. Soc. Metal. Avocations: riding motorcycle, volleyball. Office: Zhejiang U Dept Mechanics, Zhe-Da Rd, 310027 Hangzhou Zhejiang, China

JIHA, JACQUES, economist; b. Port-au-Prince, Haiti, Apr. 4, 1958; came to U.S., 1979; s. Jacob Jiha and Mercilie Jerome; m. Marie Chantale Fulcher, Dec. 15, 1984; children: Christine Amanda, Kimberly. BA, Fordham U., 1985; MA, New Sch. Social Rsch., 1988, PhD, 1991. Prin. economist N.Y. State Assembly, Ways & Means Com., Albany, 1988-91; exec. dir. N.Y. State Legis. Tax Study Commn., Albany, 1992-94; chief economist office of the comptroller City of N.Y., 1994-97, deputy comptroller, 1997—. Contbr. articles to profl. jours. Mem. Am. Econ. Assn. Democrat. Avocations: reading, sports, beer making, cooking. Office: City of NY Office of Comptroller 1 Centre St Rm 510 New York NY 10007-1602

JILEK, JAMES PARKER, state agency official; b. Cleve., June 2, 1945; s. Edward Eugene and Jeanette Claire Jilek; m. Karen Susak Jilek, July 23, 1949; children: Krista Marie, James Matthew, Jeffrey Parker. BS in Edn., Bowling Green (Ohio) State U., 1967; MS in Pers. Counseling, Wright State U., 1973; PhD in Guidance and Counseling, Ohio State U., 1975. Cert. h.s. tchr., sch. counselor, edn. adminstr., specialist pupil pers., ednl. adminstr. specialist ednl. rsch, ednl. adminstr. specialist supr. Tchr. h.s. Leipsic (Ohio) Schs., 1967-69; tchr. jr. h.s. Jefferson Towns (Ohio) Schs., 1969-73; social worker Westside Youth Svcs., Dayton, Ohio, 1973-74; coord. counseling Urbana (Ohio) Coll., 1974-76; fina. aid counselor Ohio State U., Columbus, 1976-78; pers. mgr. R.G. Barry Co., Canal Winchester, Ohio, 1978-80; ednl. cons. Ohio Dept. Edn., Columbus, 1980-89, chief effective schs., 1989-94, asst. dir. continuous improvement, 1994—. Editor: Continuous Improve Planning Reference Guide, 1998. Presenter Marriage Encounter, Columbus, 1980-84; leader Boy Scouts Am., Gahanna, Ohio, 1990-93. Mem. Ohio Edn. Assn., Phi Delta Kappa. Roman Catholic. Home: 553 Theori Ave Gahanna OH 43230-2222 Office: Ohio Dept Edn 65 S Front St Rm 1009 Columbus OH 43215-4183

JILEK, JAROSLAV, economist; b. Olomouc, Czech Republic, Feb. 8, 1931; s. Vaclav and Bozena (Hovorkova) J.; m. Bibiana Csaszarová, Mar. 10, 1962; children: Martin, Milan. Degree in econs., Econ. U. Bratislava, 1954, PhD, 1963. Asst. prof. Econ. Univ., Bratislava, Slovakia, 1954-60; from asst. prof. to prof. U. Econs., Praha, Czech Republic, 1960—; vice dir. Isnt. Statistics, Praha, 1968-70; v.p. Federal Statistical Office, Praha, 1990-92; editor Statistika, 1991—. Mem. Czech Econ. Soc., Czech Statis. Soc. (v.p. 1991-94). Home: Sokolovska 179/1996, 190 00 Praha Czech Republic Office: Univ Econs, Nam W Churchilla 4, 130 67 Praha Czech Republic

JILEK, JOSEF H., polymer chemist; b. Vienna, Austria, Mar. 16, 1950; s. Josef R. and Ingeborg (Guss) J. Diploma in chem. tech., Ryerson Poly. Inst., Toronto, Ont., Can., 1972, B Tech, 1975; PhD, N.D. State U., 1979. Resin chemist Inmont Can., Toronto, 1972-75; sr. chemist Dow Chem. Co., Horgen, Switzerland, 1979-83, Rheinmuenster, Fed. Republic Germany, 1984-85; market devel. mgr. Dow Pipe Systems, Vienna, 1985-86; group leader Isovolta, Vienna, 1986-90; market devel. mgr. Rohm and Haas, Vienna, 1991—. Author: Powder Coatings, 1991; editor-in-chief Tech. Mktg. Corp., Norwalk, Conn., 1980-83; contbr. articles to profl. jours.; patentee in field. Western Pub. Co. scholar, 1976-78. Mem. Fedn. Socs. for Coatings Tech., Am. Chem. Soc., Brit. Oil and Color Chemists' Assn., N.Y. Acad. Scis. Home: Mariengasse 27, A-1170 Vienna Austria Office: Rohm and Haas, Diefenbachgasse 35-41, A-1150 Vienna Austria

JÍLEK, MILOŠ, mathematician, researcher; b. Řeporyje, Czech Republic, June 2, 1931; s. Adolf and Marie (Bartáková) J.; m. Jiřina Hamplová, Dec. 13, 1958. MSc, Charles U., Prague, Czech Republic, 1954, PhD, 1964. Asst. Rsch. Inst. Food Industry, Prague, 1954-62; rsch. fellow Inst. Microbiology Czechoslovak Acad. Sci., Prague, 1962-92; cons. Inst. Biophysics Czechoslovak Acad. Sci., Brno, 1984-90. Author: Statistical Tolerance Limits (in Czech), 1988 (Czech Lit. Fund award 1989, Czech Tech. Soc. award 1989); co-author: (with D. Přikrylová and J. Waniewski) Mathematical Modeling of the Immune Response, 1992. Recipient award Czechoslovak Acad. Scis., 1980, 88, J.E. Purkyně medal, 1988. Mem. Bernoulli Soc. Probabilities and Stats., Soc. Czech Mathematicians and Physicists, Czech Statis. Soc. Avocations: literature, history, heraldry.

JILER, LINDA CERISE, retired fire and aviation program technician, fire emergency dispatcher, consultant, researcher, writer; b. Santa Monica, Calif., Dec. 30, 1956; d. Milton John "Jack" Jiler and Peggy Jean Williams. AA, Lassen Coll., 1979, Cert. Forestry Technician, 1980. Cert. Calif. Dept. Forestry and Fire Protection Fire Acad., 1990. Fire clk./firefighter-wildland Lassen Coll. Contract Crew, Susanville, Calif., 1976-77; forestry technician (fire) U.S. Forest Svc. Lassen Nat. Forest/Eagle Lake Ranger Dist./Bogard Ranger Sta., Susanville, Calif., 1977-80; dist. personnel technician U.S. Dept. Interior-Bur. Land Mgmt., Susanville Dist., Calif., 1981-86; pub. contact rep. U.S. Dept. Interior Bur. Land Mgmt. Susanville Dist., Susanville, Calif., 1986; wildland firefighter/dispatcher Lassen Coll. Contract Fire Crew, Susanville, Calif., 1986-87; fire, aviation program asst., lightning detection specialist U.S. Dept. Interior Bur. Land Mgmt., Calif. State Office, Sacramento, 1988-93; 9-1-1 interagy. fire dispatcher Calif. Dept. Forestry and Fire Protection, Camino, 1988-93; 9-1-1 interagency emergency commd. ctr. operator Calif. Dept. Forestry and Fire Protection, Camino Interagency Emergency Command Ctr., 1988-93; cons. info. svcs. Sacramento, 1993—; speaker in field; pub. info. officer USDA-FS, U.S. Dept. Interior-Bur. Land Mgmt., CDF, 1983-93. Author: How to Get A Job with the Federal Government, 1983, rev. edit., 1985, 86, Injury and Claim Processing Manual, 1985, Demobilization Training Guide, 1985, Train-the Trainer Wildland Fire Timekeeping Procedures, 1985, (manual) California State Office SOP for Intelligence Gathering, 1987-88; co-author: (manual) California Interagency Mobilization Guide, 1988, Bur. of Land Management's State Policy for Handling of Burn Victims, 1988. Recipient Cert. of Appreciation, Lassen County Bd. Suprs., 1986, 87, Cert. of Appreciation and Cert. of Recognition for Outstanding Performance, U.S. Forest Svc. Pacific S.W. Region, 1987, Nat. Wildland Coord. Group award for Outstanding Performance, U.S. Forest Svc. Pacific N.W. Region and Wallow Whitman Nat. Forest, 1986, Superior Achievement and Profl. Contbns. award U.S. Dept. Agriculture Forest Svc. and U.S. Dept. Interior Bur. Land Mgmt., 1990; cert. Appreciation Eldorado Bd. Suprs. U.S. Forest Svc., 1992, Recognition award Oakland Athletics Baseball Club, 1987, Recognition award San Diego Padres Baseball Club, 1988. Mem. ACLU, Calif. State Employees Assn. (classification rep. 1989-93), Calif. Profl. Firefighters, Chronic Fatigue Immune Dysfunction Syndrome Support Groups, Nat. Wildlife Fedn., Nat. Trust for Hist. Preservation, Nat. Conf. Incident Command System Fin. Officers, Nat. Australian Shepherd Club Am., Sigma Kappa (alumni past pres.), Sierra Club. Democrat. Avocations: Australian shepherds, calligraphy, sociology studies, child support issues, commercial radio (voice overs).

JILES, DAVID COLLINGWOOD, physicist, materials science educator; b. London, Sept. 28, 1953; s. Kenneth Gordon and Vera Ellen (Johnson) J.; m. Helen Elizabeth Graham, Oct. 29, 1979; children: Sarah Jane, Elizabeth Anne, Andrew John, Richard David. BSc, Exeter (Eng.) U., 1975; MSc, Birmingham (Eng.) U., 1976, DSc, 1990; PhD, Hull (Eng.) U., 1979. Registered profl. engr.; chartered engr. Postdoctoral fellow Victoria U., Wellington, New Zealand, 1979-81; rsch. assoc. Queens U., Kingston, Ont., Can., 1981-84; rsch. fellow Iowa State U., Ames, 1984-86, assoc. physicist, 1986-88, physicist, 1988-90, assoc. prof., 1988-90, sr. physicist, 1990—, prof., 1991—; chmn. Conf. on Properties and Applications of Magnetic Materials, Chgo., 1985—; pres. Magnetics Tech. Inc., Ames, 1989—; cons. engr. State of Iowa, Des Moines, 1996; sci. adv. Brit. Admiralty, 1991-92, NATO, 1992-98, U.S. Nuc. Regulatory Commn., 1996-97; vis. prof. U. Hull, Eng., 1991, 94, U. Saarland, Germany, 1992, 97, Tech. U. Vienna, 2000; vis. scientist Czech Acad. Scis., 1999. Author: Introduction to Magnetism and Magnetic Materials, 1991, 2d edit., 1998, Introduction to Electronic Properties of Materials, 1994; editor: IEEE Transactions on Magnetics, 1992—, Nondestructive Testing and Evaluation, 1988—; contbr. more than 290 articles to profl. jours. Recipient Fed. Lab. Consortium award U.S. Dept. Energy, 1994, Magnetics Soc. Disting. Lectr. award, 1997. Fellow IEEE, Inst. Elec. Engrs. U.K., Inst. Physics, Am. Phys. Soc. (chair topical group on magnetism and it's applications, 1997—), Magnetics Soc. (adminstrv. com. 1995—), Inst. Math. and its Applications. Achievements include 12 patents; developer of various models relating to non-linear effects and theory of ferromagnetic hysteresis. Avocations: classical music, chess, squash, soccer, jogging. Office: Ames Lab Iowa State U Ames IA 50011-0001

JIMÉNEZ, BLANCA, waste water treatment specialist, researcher; b. Mexico City, Nov. 17, 1958; d. Armando and Ines (Cisneros) J.; m. Héctor Garduño; children: Andrea, Diana. Grad. in environ. engring., U. Autonoma Met., Mexico City, 1980; diploma d'Etudes Approfondies, Nat. Inst. Applied Scis., Toulouse, France, 1982, PhD, 1985. Assoc. rschr. Engring. Inst. Nat. Autonomous U. Mex., Mexico City, 1985-88; coord. environ. engring. Ingring. Inst. Nat. Autonomous U. Mex., Mexico City, 1989-91; coord. profl. devel. Mex. Inst. Water Tech., Mexico City, 1991-93; coord. grad. studies Sch. Engring., Nat. Autonomous U. Mex., 1992-93; sr. rschr. Engring. Inst., Nat. Autonomous U. Mex., 1989—, dep. dir., 1997—. Contbr. articles to profl. jours.; patentee in field. Grantee Internat. Found. Sci., Stockholm, 1987-92, Technol. Devel. for ecology award CIBA, Mexico City, 1993, Emilio Rosenblueth award Nat. Acad. Engring., Mexico City, 1994, Young Academicians award Nat. Autonomous U. Mex., 1996, fellowship Trojan Co., Can., 1997, Technol. Rsch. award Mex. Acad. Sci., 1997. Mem. Nat. Acad. Engring., Mex. Assn. Environ. Engrs. (v.p. 1996—). E-mail: bjc@pumas.iingen.unam.mx. Office: Ambiental Inst Ingenieria, Circuito Escolar S/N, 04510 Ciudad Universitaria Mexico

JIMENEZ, JOSEPHINE SANTOS, portfolio manager; b. Lucena, Quezon, Philippines, June 6, 1954; came to U.S., 1972; d. Jose Hirang and Virginia Villapando (Santos) J. BS, NYU, 1979; MS, MIT, 1981. Securities analyst Mass. Mut. Life Ins. Co., Springfield, 1982-83; investment officer One Fed. Asset Mgmt., Boston, 1984-87; sr. analyst, portfolio mgr. Emerging Markets Investors Corp., Washington, 1988-91; mng. dir., portfolio mgr. Montgomery Asset Mgmt., San Francisco, 1991—; founding ptnr. Montgomery Emerging Markets Fund. Mem. Inst. Chartered Fin. Analysts. Office: Montgomery Asset Mgmt 101 California St San Francisco CA 94111-5802

JIMÉNEZ, RAMIRO, biotechnologist, educator, translator; b. Havana, Cuba, May 31, 1941; s. Ramiro and Leonor Jiménez; m. Lidia Jiménez, July 31, 1966; 1 child, Carlos. BSc in Chem. Engring., U. Havana, 1966, postgrad. Rsch. fellow Inst. Cubano de Investigaciones de los Derivados de la Caña de Azucar, Havana, 1964-67; grad. instr. Superior Poly. Sch., Havana, 1967-68; rsch. fellow Inst. Investigaciones para la Industria Alimenticia, Havana, 1968—; cons. Commn. for Single-Cell Protein, Havana, 1981—; postgrad. faculty IIIA, Havana, 1984—, UNI, Managua, Nicaragua, 1994; rsch. work on fermentation tech., fermentation products used in food industry, flavor enhancers. Author: Biotecnologia, Conceptos Fundamentales y métodos, 1994; contbr. articles to profl. jours. UNESCO grantee, UN Univ. grantee. Mem. Assn. for Food Sci. and Tech. Avocations: cinematography, classical music, philosophy, history. Home: Plaza 10600, 45 #1109 entre Ave 26 y Ulloa, Havana Cuba Office: IIIA, Carr Guatao Km 3-1/2 Lisa, 19200 Havana Cuba

JIMENEZ, VALENKA, bank executive; b. Santo Domingo, Dominican Republic; came to U.S., 1978; d. Leonidas Jimenez and Gertrudis Castillo. BS, Bentley Coll., 19996; postgrad., Georgetown U. Banker Bank of Am., Austin, 1997-98, Citibank, FSB, Washington, 1998-99, KPMG LLP, Washington, 2000—. Vol. Rep. Party, 1997—. Mem. NAFE, D.C. C. of C., Women of Washington, Iberro C. of C. Republican. Roman Catholic. Home: PO Box 1529 Washington DC 20013-1529

JIMENEZ-ACOSTA, FRANCISCO JAVIER, dermatologist; b. Las Palmas, Spain, May 16, 1960; s. Francisco Jimenez and Margarita Acosta; m. Inmaculada Artero; 1 child, Carla Jimenez. MD, U. Navarra, Pamplona, Spain, 1983; PhD, U. Madrid, 1988. Resident in dermatology U. Madrid, 1987; fellow in dermatopathology U. Miami, Fla., 1988-89; dermatologist Hosp. Insular, Las Palmas, 1989-92; fellow in dermatol. surgery Duke U., Durham, N.C., 1992-94; fellow in hair restoration surgery Stough Clin., Hot Springs, Ark., 1995; dermatologist Clin. La Zarzuela, Madrid, 1996-98; dir. Skin Laser Ctr., Clin. San Roque, Las Palmas, 1998—. Internat. editor Dermatologic Surgery, 1996-99; contbr. over 50 articles to med. jours., also 4 chpts. to books. Grantee Govt. of Canary Islands, FISS. Avocation: sports. Office: Derm and Laser Ctr, Reyes Catolicos 20, 35001 Las Palmas CIslands, Spain

JIMÉNEZ-BELTRAN, DOMINGO, executive; b. Zaragoza, Spain, Apr. 2, 1944; s. Mariano and Maria Gloria (Beltran) J.; married; one child. Indsl. engr. Polytech U., Madrid, 1967; environ. engring. cons., 1968-82; exec. advisor Min. Pub., Works & Planning, 1983-85; deputy dir. gen. Internat. EU Rels., 1985-86; head divsn. health, phys. safety & quality Consumers Policy Svc., European Commn., 1987-91; dir.-gen. environ. policy Ministry Pub. Works, Transport and Environment, Spain, 1991-94; exec. dir. European Environ. Agy., Copenhagen, Denmark, 1994—. Contbr. articles to profl. jours. Office: EEA, 6 Kongens Nytorv, DK-1050 Copenhagen Denmark*

JIMENEZ LORA, FELIX ANTONIO, tourist company executive; b. La Vega, Dominican Republic, Jan. 17, 1950; s. Felix A. and Iluminada M. (De Lora) Jimenez; m. Denisse Ortiz, Oct. 14, 1978 (div. 1980); m. Elina Katsman, June 23, 1987; children: Rachel Eliana, David Gabriel. Architect degree, Universidad Nacional Pedro Henriquez Ureña, Santo Domingo, Dominican Republic, 1972; tourism planner, Interam. Inst. Tourism, Mexico City, 1975; tourism mktg., George Washington U., 1991. Cert. architect. Design chief Alpaca Contrns., Santo Domingo, 1970-73; architect Baquero, Lora & Assocs., Santo Domingo, 1974-76; gen. dir. Turinter, S.A., Santo Domingo, 1976-81; gen. mgr. Co. Operacion Hotelera, Samana, Dominican Republic, 1981-87; pres. Turinter S.A., Santo Domingo, 1987—; pres. Tour Operators Nat. Assn., Santo Domingo, 1987-89, 97-99; gen. sec. Am. Fedn. Youth Travel Orgn., Mexico City, 1986-92; vice chmn. Am. Sightseeing Internat., 1998-2000, chmn., 2000—. Bd. dirs. Found. for East Region Devel., San Pedro de Macoris, 1986. Mem. Club 20-30 (Santo Domingo), Lions Club (Samana). Rotary Club Santo Domingo. Roman Catholic. Avocations: playing piano, reading, sailing. E-mail: turintersdg@codetel.net.do. Home: 39 Anacaona Ave, Santo Domingo Dominican Republic Office: Turinter SA, Leopoldo Navarro #4, Santo Domingo Dominican Republic

JIMENEZ-MONTANO, MIGUEL ANGEL, biophysicist; b. Mexico City, Mex., Sept. 21, 1941; s. Miguel Angel and Graciela Aubert (Montano) J.; m. Maria Enriqueta Castellanos-Gallegos, Mar. 3, 1965; children: Sybelle, Elmar. MS, U. Wis., 1967; DS, U. Copernicus, Torun, Poland, 1976. Tchr. physics U. Veracruz, Xalapa, Mex., 1965-67, prof., 1970-71, rschr., 1976-90; prof. U. Am., Puebla, Mex., 1991—; co-dir. rsch. U. Am., 1984—. Coauthor: (chpt.) Theoretical Biology, 1989; co-editor La Ciencia y Hombre mag., 1988—; contbr. articles to profl. jours. Vis. Fulbright fellow U. Calif., San Francisco, 1982-83; recipient Scientific Rsch. award U. Veracruz, Mex., 1989, rsch. award Fundacion Miguel Aleman, Mex., 1990. Mem. Mexican Phys. Soc., Mexican Math. Soc., Soc. Math. Biology, N.Y. Acad. Scis., Gamma Sigma. Avocations: graphic arts, mountain climbing, yoga. Office: U Am, Santa Catarina Martir AP47, Cholula Puebla 72820, Mexico

JIMENEZ-VARONA, JOSE, research engineer; b. Seville, Spain, Apr. 15, 1963; s. Jose Paulino Jimenez-Moreno and Carmen Varona-Alvarez; m. Carmen Barrera-Pavon, Aug. 3, 1996; children: Daniel, Jose. BS, Martinez-Montañes, Seville, 1981; M Engring. Aeronautics, U. Madrid, 1988. Rsch. engr. Nat. Rsch. Ctr. Aeronautics, Madrid, 1990—. Contbr. articles to profl. jours.; patentee Fortran code for wing design. With Spanish Navy, 1989-90. Roman Catholic. Avocations: reading, history, soccer, flute. Office: INTA, Carretera Ajalvir Km 4'5, 28850 Torrejon de Ardoz Spain

JIMENO, RITA LINDA VENTURA, lawyer; b. Manila, Sept. 12, 1952; d. Antonio Pambid and Leonor Sacro (Sabas) Ventura; m. Nicanor Barcelon Jimeno, Jan. 15, 1977; children: Laarni Julia, Karen Olivia, Nikki Sarah, Fidel Paolo. AB in Broadcast Comm., U. of the Philippines, Quezon City, 1973, LLB, 1985. Bar: Philippines, 1986. Chief cmty. rels. and info. office Nat. Housing Authority, Quezon City, 1975-78; journalism instr. De La Salle U., Manila, 1978-80; mng. dir., exec. prodr. Beta Promotions, Manila, 1980-85; assoc. Barcelona Perlas Joven & Academia Law Offices, Makati, The Philippines, 1986-89; ptnr. Barcelona Barcelona Jimeno Magdamit & Garlitos Law Offices, Makati, 1989-92; mng. ptnr. Jimeno & Assocs. Law Offices, Makati, 1992-95, Jimeno Jalandoni & Cope Law Offices, Makati, 1995—; dir., corp. sec. BBK, inc., Makati, 1991—, Total Solutions Software, inc., Makati, 1993—, Crawford & Co. Philippines, Inc., Makati, 1995—, Oppax Group Holding, Inc., Makati, 1997—, Tourist Ctr., Makati, 1998—, Filipino Travel Ctr. Corp., Manila., 1998—; corp. sec. Little Giant Steel Pipe Inc., Makati, 1997—, Goodyear Steel Pipe Inc., Quezon City, 1997—, Milwaukee Industries Corp., Makati, 1997—; dir., pres. Saklolo Abogado Prodns., Inc., Makati, 1999—; bd. dirs. HB&A Rsch. Internat., Inc., Makati; legal cons. Las Pinas Doctor's Hosp., Inc., 1987—, TV Asahi, Manila, 1991—, Muntinlupa (Philippines) Polymedic Inc., 1992—, Yakult Phillippines, Inc., Manila, 1992—, Selecta Feeds Inc., Quezon City, 1992—, Cover and Pages Corp., Manila., 1992—, Arcecon Dairy Products, Quezon City, 1993—, Family Care Hosp., Inc., Laguna, The Philippines, 1993—, Filmundo Export Corp., Pasig, 1994—, Eastmont Advt. Inc., Pasig, 1995—, Tourist Ctr., Inc., Makati, others. Program host Saklolo Abogado Radio Program, Pasig City, The Philippines, 1995-99, Todo-todong Saklolo, Pasig City, 1999—, Saklolo Abogado TV Show, Quezon City, 1999—; regular columnist People's Jour., Manila, 1998—. Dir. United Way Philippines, Quezon City, 1998-2000. Recipient Bronze medalist Cmty. Chest Found., Caloocan City, The Philippines, 1968, Plaque of Commendation for Outstanding Svc., Nat. Housing Authority, 1997; coll. scholar U. Philippines, 1970-73. Mem. Philippine Bar Assn. (2nd v.p., dir., treas. 1997-98, 98-99, Presdl. award of merit 1990, Spl. Appreciation award 1998), Integrated Bar of the Philippines, Women Trial Lawyers Orgn. of the Philippines (dir. 1998—), U. Philippines Womens Lawyers Cir., Fedn. Internat. De las Abogadas. Roman Catholic. Avocations: dancing, swimming, singing, literary writing, reading. Office: Jimeno Jalandoni & Cope Law, 189 Salcedo St, Makati 1229, Philippines

JIN, BO, government agency executive, engineering educator; b. Yinchuan, Ningxia, China, Mar. 16, 1958; s. Sheng Gui Jin and Mei Hua Tian; m. Xiu Quan Yan, Feb. 14, 1988; 1 child, Haoyi. BChemE, Ningxia U., 1982; MSc in Environ. Sci. and Tech., 1 Internat. Inst. Hydraulic and, Delft, The Netherlands, 1993; PhD in Environ. and Biotech. Engring., U. New Eng., NSW, Australia, 1998. Lectr. applied chemistry Taole Tech. Sch., Ningxia, 1982-86; environ. engr., asst. rsch. fellow Ningxia Inst. for Water Conservancy, Yinchuan, 1986-90, vice dir. rsch. ctr., project mgr., 1990-94; exec. rsch. project engr. Weston Bioproducts, Brisbane, Australia, 1995-98; sr. rsch. scientist Weston Bioproducts, Melbourne, Australia, 1998-99; gen. exec. engr., prof. Ninxia Environ. Protection Agy., Yinchuan, 1999—. Contbr. articles to profl. jours. Fellow Netherlands Govt., 1992; recipient Australia Overseas Postgrad. Rsch. award Ministry of Employment and Edn., Queensland, 1996. Mem. Internat. Soc. Biochemistry and Biotech., Australia Water and Wastewater Assn. Avocations: music, sports, travel. Office: Griffith Univ, Sch Environ Engring, 4111 Queensland Australia

JIN, HYUNG JONG, biological sciences educator; b. Seoul, Rep. of Korea, Feb. 3, 1959; s. Bong-Sang Jin and Jung-Joo Kim; m. Ae-Kyung Park, May 4, 1991; children: Oh-Kyun, Min-kyun, Sung-Hee. BS, Seoul Nat. U., 1982, MS, 1987, PhD, 1991. Lic. pharmacist Korean Ministry Health and Social Affairs. Asst. prodn. mgr. Yuhan Corp., Kunpo, Rep. of Korea, 1983-85; rsch. assoc. U. Wis., Madison, 1991-94; rschr. Coll. of Medicine, N.E. Ohio U., Rootstown, 1994-96; asst. prof. U. Suwon, Rep. of Korea, 1996—. Author: Antibiotics and Development of Antibiotic Resistance Factor Inhibitor, 1997; contbr. articles to sci. jours. including Molecular Cells, Jour. of Bacteriology, others. Deacon. Sgt. Korean Army, 1982-83. Grantee Pacific Chem. Co., Yongin, 1996-99, Korean Ministry of Edn., Seoul, 1997, 98, Korean Rsch. Found., Seoul, 1997, 98, 99, Korean Sci. and Engring. Found., Seoul, 1998, 2000—. Mem. Biochem. Soc. Korea, Microbiol. Soc. of Korea (councillor 1998—, mem. editl. bd. 1997—), Korean Soc. Molecular Biology (life), Pharml. Soc. of Korea. Presbyterian. Avocations: jogging, mountain climbing, tennis, reading. Fax: 82-31-220-2290. E-mail: hjjin@mail.suwon.ac.kr. Office: U Suwon Wawoo-Ri San 2-2, Bongdamyeub Whasung-goon, Kunggi Do 445-743, Republic of Korea

JIN, JIAN-XUN, metallurgical and electrical engineer, researcher; b. Beijing, Aug. 12, 1962; arrived in Australia, 1989; s. Huaizhe Jin and Jing Lin; m. Hai-Yan Zhang, May 27, 1988; children: Fan, Helen. B Engring., Beijing U. Sci. and Tech., 1985; MSc, U. NSW, Sydney, Australia, 1995; PhD, U. Wollongong, Australia, 1997. Assoc. editor Metall. Industry Press, Metall. Industry Ministry China, Beijing, 1985-89; rsch. asst. U. NSW, 1991-92; rsch. fellow Wollongong U., 1997-99, chief investigator ARC large rsch. project, 2000—. Assoc. editor Sci. and Tech. Bus. Computer; contbr. articles to sci. jours., including Jour. Elec. and Electronics Engring., IEEE Trans. on Applied Superconductivity, Physica C, Philos. Mag. B., Engring. World. Avocations: radiotechnics, electronic and electrical instrument amateur, photogrphy, computers, sports. E-mail: jianxun jin@uow.edu.au. Home: PO Box 364, Rockdale NSW 2216, Australia Office: Wollongong U Inst for, Superconducting-Elec Mat, Wollongong NSW 2522, Australia

JIN, NYUM, federal official. Min. of fin. Kyonggi, South Korea. Office: 1 Chungang-dong, Wachon, Kyonggi Province South Korea*

JIN, SHAOHONG, pharmacist; b. Shanghai, China, Oct. 6, 1946; s. Pinfang J. and Xiunzheng Qian; m. Jianjun Wei. B, Beijing Med. U., 1970; postgrad., Chinese Acad. Med. Scis., Beijing, 1980. Pharmacist Xian Mcpl. Inst. Drug Control, China, 1972-78; pharmacist Nat. Inst. Control Pharm. & Biol. Products, Beijing, 1982-84, chief divsn. antibiotics, 1984-89; prof. chief divsn. antibiotics Nat. Inst. Control Pharm. & Biol. Products, 1992-97. Editor: Chinese Pharmacopoeia, 1995. Vis. scholar Health Protection Br. Drug Rsch. Lab., Ottawa, Can., 1980-82, vis. scholar Inst. Superiore Sanita, Rome, 1989-92. Mem. Chinese Pharm. Com., Chinese Pharm. Soc., Am. Soc. Microbiology. Office: Nat Inst Control Pharm, Tiantan Xili No 2, Beijing 100050, China

JIN, TAE EUN, mechanical engineer; b. Seoul, Republic of Korea, Sept. 7, 1957; s. Ik Sang and Hong Ja (Sim) Jin; m. Jeong Min Woo, May 18, 1985; children: Yoo Jeong, Seung Eun, Min Gyu. Bachelor's, Yonsei U., Seoul, 1981, MS, 1985, PhD, 1994. Rschr. Korea Power Engring. Co., Seoul, 1985-87, sr. rschr., 1988-91, supr. rschr., 1992-93, project mgr., 1994—, dir., 1998—; cons. Korea Inst. Nuclear Safety, Seoul, 1996; mem. ISO Tech. Com., Seoul, 1998—. Contbr. articles to profl. jours. Sgt. Korean Army, 1981-83. Mem. Korean Soc. Mech. Engrs. (rev. com. mem. 1995—), Internat. Assn. Structural Mechanics in Reactor Tech. 15 (sci. com. 1998—), Korean Nuclear Soc. Avocations: golf, skiing. Office: Korea Power Engring Co, 360-9 Mabuk-ri Kusong-myon, 449-713 Yongin-si Republic of Korea

JIN, XUECHENG, engineering researcher; b. Harbin, People's Republic China, May 28, 1966; came to U.S., 1995; s. Shixia Jin and Yicheng Liang; m. Shujie Zhao, Jan. 15, 1992; 1 child, Joy Oiu, Jin. B in Engring., Tsinghua U., Beijing, China, 1990; MSc, Stanford (Calif.) U., 1997, student, 1998—. Rsch. scholar Nat. U. of Singapore, 1992-93; assoc. rsch. fellow Gintic Inst. of Mfg., Singapore, 1993-95; rschr. Stanford U., 1995—; sr. tutor Nat. U. Singapore, 1995—. Contbr. articles to profl. publs.; inventor micromachined ultrasonic transducer fabrication. Recipient RWB Stephens prize Ultrasonic Internat., 1997, region 3.6.9. winner IEEE Engring. Medicine and Biology Soc., 1998, region 10 winner, 1994, Engring. Acoustics award Acoustic Soc. of Am., 1997. Mem. IEEE. Avocation: tennis. Home: 71 Escondido Vlg Apt B Stanford CA 94305-7193 Office: Edwards L Einzton Lab Stanford U Stanford CA 94305

JIN, YONG, chemical engineering educator; b. Beijing, July 30, 1935; s. Rong Jin and Xiu-Ying Wang; m. Yuan-Yi Qiu, Oct. 2, 1960 (dec. 1973); children: Ning, Jie; m. Hua Hu, Jan. 18, 1977; 1 child, Jin-Ming. BS, Ural Poly. Inst., Svirdelovsk, USSR, 1959; postgrad., Tienjing (China) U., 1960. Asst. lectr. Sci. and Tech. U., Beijing, 1960-73; assoc. prof. Tsinghua U., 1973-85, prof., 1985—; concurrent prof. grad. sch. U. Mineralogy China, Beijing, 1992; concurrent prof. Fu-Shun (China) Petrochem. Inst., 1993—, Guangxi U., Nanning, China, 1995—; cons. dv. bd. Chem. Engrng. & Tech., VCH, Weinheim, Germany, 1992; cons. People's Govt. Beijing, 1986—; vice dir. Chem. Engring. Inst., Tsinghua U., 1992—, dir. Fluidization Lab., 1979—. Co-author: Circulating Fluidized Bed, 1996; editor procs. in field.; contbr. articles to profl. publs.; patentee concurrent downflow chem. reactor. Outstanding Contbg. Specialist, State Coun. People's Republic China, 1987; mem. specialist groups Nat. Degree Granting Com. China, 1990. Recipient Nat. Innovation award II, Nat. Sci. and Tech. Com. China, 1987, Nat. Tech. Devel. award II, Nat. Sci. and Tech. Com. China, 1995, Fundamental Rsch. award Nat. Edn. Com. China, 1987, 92, 95, Outstanding Tchr. award Nat. Edn. Com. China, 1995, awrd Nat. Labour Union China, 1998. Mem. Chinese Soc. Particnology (standing dir. 1995), Chinese Acad. Engring. Office: Tsinghua U, Dept Chem Engring, Beijing 100084, China

JIN, ZHE, food science educator; b. Wang Qing, People's Republic of China, Nov. 11, 1963; s. Bo Shun and Jin Yu (Wu) J.; m. Su Jing Cui, Aug. 8, 1988; children: Xiao Chen. BSc, N.E. Normal U., 1985; MSc, Jilin Agrl. U., Chang Chun, China, 1993; PhD, Iwate U., 1998. Lectr. Jilin Agrl. U., 1986-94; vice dir. physics lab. Jilin U., 1991-94; vis. scholar Iwate (Japan) U., 1994-95, vis. rschr., 1998—. Co-author: Experiment of Physical Technology, 1992; contbr. articles to profl. jours. Mem. Assn. of Med. Biophysics of China, Japanese Soc. for Food Sci. and Tech., Japan Soc. for Biosci., Biotech. and Agrochemistry. Avocations: gymnastics, soccer, volleyball, music. Home: 2-19-13-305 Kuriyagawa, Morioka City 020-0124, Japan

JINADU, YUSUF, management consultant; b. Lagos, Nigeria, May 16, 1967; s. Anbaliu and Falilatu (Akinwunmi) J.; m. Omolara Oni, Jan. 21, 1997; 1 child, Remilekun. Diploma, Inst. Adminstrv. Mgmt. of Nigeria, 1989, Inst. Commerce of Nigeria, 1991, Rafadek Inst. Mgmt. and Tech., Nigeria, 1994. Mktg. officer Prentice (Nigeria) Ltd., 1990-93, mktg. mgr., 1994-98, adminstrv. mgr., 1999—. Moslem. Avocations: reading, travel, people, table tennis, research. Home: 8 Adegoroye St, Lagos Nigeria Office: Prentice Nigeria Ltd, 9 Demurin St PO Box 5581, Surulere Lagos Nigeria

JINBU, YOSHINORI, dentist; b. Ooishida, Japan, May 30, 1955; s. Tsunetaro and Teruyo (Taira) J.; m. Chieko Hagiwara, Mar. 24, 1984; 1 child, Genta. DDS, Kanagawa Dental Coll., 1980; PhD, Tokyo Med. and Dental U., 1984. Asst. prof. Tokyo Med. and Dental U., 1984-85; asst. prof. Kanagawa Dental Coll., Yokosuka, 1985-86, lectr., 1990-93; asst. prof. Jichi Med. Sch., Tochigi, Japan, 1986-90, lectr., 1993—; rschr. Calif. State U., Fresno, 1989-90. Contbr. articles to profl. jours. Named Best Rschrs. of Yr., Kanagawa Odontol. Soc., 1985, 90. Mem. Internat. Assn. Dental Rsch., Japanese Biochem. Soc., Japanese Soc. Stomatology. Avocations: traveling, driving. Home: 3-20-17 Nishigaoka Izumiku, Yokohama Japan Office: Jichi Med Sch 3311-1 Yakushiji, Minamikawachi, Kawachi gun 32904, Japan

JINDAL, NARESH, veterinarian; b. Hisar, Haryana, India, Oct. 15, 1967; s. Tejbhan and Satya Devi (Goyal) J.; m. Anita Agarwal, July 16, 1994; children: Mohit, Keshav. B in Vet. Sci. and Animal Husbandry, Chaudhary Charan Singh Haryana Agr. U., Hisar, 1989, MVSc in Vet. Pub. Health & Epidemiology, 1991, PhD in Vet. Pub. Health & Epidemiology, 1999. Tng. assoc., jr. scientist Chaudhary Charan Singh Haryana Agr. U., Hisar, 1993, asst. disease investigation officer, 1993-96, asst. disease investigation officer dept. vet. pub. health, 1996-99; asst. disease investigation officer, dept. vet. epidemiology and preventive medicine, 1999—. Author: Aflatoxicosis in Animals and Man, 1997. Mem. World Poultry Sci. Assn. (grantee 1998-99), Indian Vet. Assn., Mountaineering Club (adviser). Avocation: reading. Home: H.No. 157, Friends Colony, Hisar 125 001, India Office: CCS Haryana Agr U, Dept Vet Epid and Prev Medicine, Hisar 125 004, India

JINDAL, SANGITA, publisher; b. Calcutta, Aug. 30, 1962; d. Kailash Kumar Kanuria and Urmila Modi Kanuria; m. Sajjan Jindal; children: Tarine, Tanui, Parth. BA, St. Xavier's U., Ahmedabad, India, 1980. Pub. Art News Mag. of India, 1997—. Chmn. Jindal Edn. Trust, Mumbai, 1985—, Jindal Art Found., Bombay, 1982—; hon. dir. Jindal Arts Creative Interaction Ctr., 1992—; festival dir. Artfest 2000, Mumbai, 2000. Avocations: badminton, swimming, cultural activities. Home: 32 Waskeshwar Rd, Mumbai India Office: Nat Ctr Performing Arts, Mumbai India

JINDRA, JIŘÍ, electrochemist; b. Prague, Czech Republic, June 7, 1938; s. Jindřich and Marie (Otradovská) J.; m. Jaroslava Štulová, Feb. 22, 1969; children: Jiří, Jaroslav, Jan. MSc, Charles U., Prague, 1961; D of Natural Scis., Charles U., 1966; PhD, Czech Acad. Scis., Prague, 1965. Scientist J. Heyrovsky Inst. Phys. Chem. Electrochemistry, Prague, 1965-93; mgr. Inst. Contemporary History, Prague, 1993—; vis. scientist U. Bonn, Germany, 1970-71, Tech. U., Darmstadt, Germany, 1990-91, 95, 97; abstractor Chem. Abstracts Svc./Am. Chem. Soc., Columbus, Ohio, 1963-90; head dept. J. Heyrovsky Inst., 1990-93. Contbr. articles to profl. jours.; patentee in field. Recipient prize Czech and Bulgarian Acads. of Scis., 1984, Czech and East German Acads. of Scis., 1986. Mem. Czech Chem. Soc. Home: Brodského 6/1665, 149 00 Prague 4, Czech Republic Office: Inst Contemporary History, Vlašská 9, 118 40 Prague 1, Czech Republic

JINGLES, JULIAN See REYNOLDS, RAYMOND JULIAN ARTHUR

JINNO, KENJI, physician, researcher; b. Niihama, Ehime, Japan, Aug. 29, 1946; s. Miyoshi and Kazuko (Kunita) J.; m. Michiko Kurokawa, Oct. 10, 1973; children: Tomonori, Maki, Akiko. BD, Okayama (Japan) U. Med. Sch., 1971; MD, PhD, Okayama (Japan) Med. Sch., 1975. Med. diplomate Ministry of Health and Welfare, Japan. Physician Nat. Iwakuni (Japan) Hosp., 1976-79; dir. internal medicine Shikoku Cancer Ctr. Hosp., Matsuyama, 1979-92, dir. clin. rsch. and internal medicine, 1992-99, head dir. clin. div., head dir. int. med., 1999—; mem. organizing com. 4th Internat. Symposium on Treatment of Liver Cancer, Tokyo, 1995. Author: Hepatocellular Carcinoma (in Japanese), 1991. Grantee Ministry of Health and Welfare, Japan, Tokyo, 1994, 95, 96, 97. Mem. Med. Assn. Ehime Prefecture (mem. com. 1992—), Med. Assn. Matsuyama City (mem. com. 1992—), Japanese Soc. Internal Medicine (councilor 1995—), Japanese Soc. Hepatology (councilor 1989—), Japanese Soc. Gastroenterology (councilor 1988—), Liver Cancer Study Grp. of Japan (organizer, 1998—). Buddhist, Shingon. Avocations: oil painting, reading. E-mail: kjinno@bochan.shikoku-cc.go.jp. Office: Shikoku Cancer Ctr Hosp, 13 Horinouchi, Matsuyama 790-0007, Japan

JINNOUCHI, SEISHI, radiologist, educator; b. Ohkuchi, Kagoshima, Japan, Jan. 3, 1957; s. Mareo and Tsuya (Tajima) J.; m. Kazuko Arimitsu, Nov. 23, 1982; children: Yuko, Yoriko, Hiroshi. MD, Miyazaki Med. Coll., 1981. Resident Miyazaki Med. Coll. Hosp., 1981-82, asst. prof., 1982-91, lectr., 1991-94, 95-96, assoc. prof., 1997—; rsch. fellow Royal Marsden Hosp., Sutton, Eng., 1994-95, Frankfurt (Germany) U. Hosp., 1995. Co-author: Clinical PET in Oncology, 1993. Mem. Soc. Nuclear Medicine, European Assn. Nuclear Medicine, Japan Radiol. Soc. Avocations: personal computers, golf. Home: 3-26-9 Tsunehisa, Miyazaki 880-0913, Japan Office: Miyazaki Med Coll Dept Radiology, 5200 Kihara, Kiyotake-cho Miyazaki 889-1692, Japan

JINRIGHT, NOAH FRANKLIN, vocational school educator, security executive; b. Banks, Ala., Dec. 5, 1936; s. William Carroll and Ila Marie (Garrett) J.; m. Sarah Ann (Graham) Nickolson, Nov. 21, 1959 (div. Sept. 1974); children: Charlene M., Lisa A., Michael D.; m. Frances Lenora Gaskins, June 11, 1978; children: Diana Carol, Jonathan Franklin. Cert. archtl. and mech. drafting, Columbus (Ga.) Tech., 1971, cert. plate and pipe welder, 1984, CNC, 1983. Lic. ins. agent, Ga; cert. security officer. Operator scale Bibb Textiles, Columbus, 1954-56; operator press and share Columbus Iron Works, 1957-58; ins. agt. Interstate Life, Columbus, 1958-61; winder starter/generator Joe Hooten, Inc., Columbus, 1960; fireman City of Columbus, 1960-66; advt. rep. Jinright Enterprises, Columbus, 1966; ins. agt. Security Life of Ga., Columbus, 1966; operator share and press Pascoe Steel, Columbus, 1966-67; machinist Goldens' Foundry and Machine Works, Columbus, 1967; carpenter, roofer Muscogee County Sch. Dist., Columbus, 1968-72; pattern maker Pekor Iron Works, Columbus, 1972-78; instr. metals tech. Spencer H.S., Columbus, 1978-91, Carver H.S., Columbus, 1991-94; security officer Sizemore Security Internat, 1994-95, 97-99; instr. metals tech. Kendrick H.S., Columbus, 1994-99; ret., 1999; security officer Sizemore Security Internat., 1999—; past mfg. rep. printing and advtg. specialties; cons. Voc. Tng. and Rsch. Inst., Seoul, Korea, 1989-90; instr., ptnr. with M/Davis; fire protection supr. 9311th AFRESRSQD Col., Ga., (T Sgt.). Contbr. articles to local newspapers. Sponsor Spencer H.S. AWS Club, 1979-81; exec. trainer Precision Metalforming Assn., 1996-99; past trustee Epworth United Meth. Ch., ch. usher; mem. Columbus Confederate Drill Team. Tech. sgt. USAFR, 1963-65. Recipient Recruiting cert. USAF, 1991-92, Best Drilled Soldier award D-Co., 3-Times Nat. Guard; named top marksman in Co.D. 560th Armn. Engr. Bn. (48th divsn.), Bn. Champion, 1962, 3d Best in State Ga., 1962, NCO instr. in Bn. Mem. NEA, Internat. Soc. Welding Educators (1st symposium program adv. bd. mem.), Am. Foundry Soc., Am. Welding Soc. (adv. bd.), Vocat. Indsl. Clubs Am. (advisor, cert. of appreciation region VIII 1996), Trade and Indsl. Educators Ga. (mem. West Ga. Sch. to work-evaluation team 1994-99), Muscogee Edn. Assn., Ga. Assn. Educators, Ga. Vocat. Assn., Am. Vocat. Assn., Precision Metalforming Assn., Am. Foundrymen's Soc., Ga. Teacher's Union, So. Assn. Colls. and Schs., Ga. Assn. Educators,. Methodist. Avocations: fishing, hunting, camping, model building, photography. Home: PO Box 63 Columbus GA 31902-0063 Office: 2040 Lee Rd 427 Phenix City AL 36867

JIPA, ALEXANDRU, physics educator; b. Vărbilău, Prahova, Romania, Sept. 25, 1957; s. Ion and Emilia (Teleanu) J.; m. Silvia Somesan, Nov. 24, 1984; 1 child, Andra. BSc in Physics, U. Bucharest, Romania, 1981, MSc in Physics, 1982, PhD in Physics, 1990. Physicist Inst. Nuc. Power Reactors, Pitesti, Romania, 1982-84; rschr. Inst. Elec. Engring., Bucharest, 1984-88; asst. prof. physics U. Bucharest, 1988-91, lectr., 1991-97, assoc. prof., 1997—; vice head exptl. physics group Inst. Nuc. Power Reactors, Pitesti, 1983-84; vice head atomic and nuc. physics dept. Faculty Physics, U. Bucharest, 1996—; mem. profl. coun. Faculty of Physics, U. Bucharest, 2000; head exptl. physics group Inst. Elec. Engring., Bucharest, 1986-88; mem. EPS and fellow organizing com. ICHEP, Glasgow, Scotland, 1994, Warsaw, Poland, 1996; Internat. Nuclear Physics conf., Paris, France, 1998, Physics of Strangeness Program, U. Wash., Seattle, 1998, 11th EPS General Conf., London, Eng., 1999; cons. in field, 1991—. Co-author: Nuclear Physics Problems, 1996, Elements of Relativistic Nuclear Physics, 1999, Elements of Relativistic Nuclear Physics, 2000; contbr. articles to profl. publs. 2nd lt. Romanian Army, 1981. Mem. Romanian Phys. Soc. (sec. 1990-94, bd. dirs. 1994-96, sec. nuclear physics divsn. 1997—), European Phys. Soc., N.Y. Acad. Scis. Avocations: lecturing, history, theatre. Home: Sector III, Marius Emanoil Buteica Nr 8, R-74366 Bucharest Romania Office: Univ Bucharest Fac Physics, Atomistilor Nr 1, R-76900 Bucharest Romania

JIRANEK, VLADIMIR, microbiologist, educator; b. Prague, Czech Republic, Jan. 5, 1966; arrived in Australia, 1969; s. Zdenek Josef and Anna (Widemannova) J.; m. Danielle Louise Cornell, Nov. 28, 1987; children: Milan Cornell, Grace Anne. BSc with honors, U. Adelaide, Australia, 1987; PhD, U. Adelaide, 1993. Rsch. asst. Enterovax Pty. Ltd., Adelaide, 1987; rschr. Australian Wine Rsch. Inst., Adelaide, 1988-92; postdoctoral fellow Carnegie Mellon U., Pitts., 1992-95; lectr. microbial physiology/fermentation tech. U. Auckland, New Zealand, 1995-97; lectr. in oenology U. Adelaide, 1997—; cons. wine industry, Australia, 1988-92, 97—; cons. biotechnology industry, USA, 1992-95, New Zealand, 1995-97; mem. sci. adv. panel Cerechen Corp., 1998—; spkr. in field. Contbr. chpt. in book and articles to profl. jours. Mem. AAAS, Australian Soc. for Biochemistry and Molecular Biology, Am. Soc. for Oenology and Viticulture, Soc. for Indsl. Microbiology. E-mail: vladimir.jiranek@adelaide.edu.au. Office: Adelaide U, PMB 1, Glen Osmond SA 5064, Australia

JIRAVA, EMIL, maxillofacial surgeon; b. Prague, Czechoslovakia, Apr. 26, 1930; s. Emil and Berta (Skachova) J.; m. Libuse Chylkova, June 14, 1933; children: Konecna Ivana, Jirava David. MUDR, Med. Faculty, Prague, 1953; Assn. Prof., Med. Faculty, Olomouc, 1968, Prof., 1981; DSc, Charles U., Prague, 1979. Med. diplomate. Doctor Med. Faculty, Olomouc, 1953-54, asst. lectr., 1954-68, assn. prof., 1968-81, prof., 1981—; vice-dean Med. Faculty, U. Palacky, Olomouc, 1989-94; vis. lectr. Oreg. Health Scis. U. Chef editor: Jour. of Czech Dentistry Prague, 1987—; author publs. in field. Recipient nat. award Czech Republic, 1983. Mem. N.Y. Acad. Scis., Assn. of Maxillofac. Surgery (pres. 1984-89), Czech Dental Assn. (hon.), Czech Med. Assn. (hon.), Pierre Fauchard Acad. Avocations: poetry, tourism, cooking. Home: Erenburga 42, 77900 Olomouc Czech Republic Office: Clin of Maxillofacial Surg, 1.P.Pavlova 6, 77520 Olomouc Czech Republic

JIRICEK, ONDREJ, physics educator; b. Praha, Czechoslovakia, July 9, 1964; s. Frantisek and Vaclava (Paulova) J.; m. Eva Kubistova, Oct. 31, 1987; children: Vaclav, Marie. MSc, Czech Tech. U., Prague, 1986, PhD, 1993. Rsch. student CETIM, Senlis, France, 1990-91; grad. asst. Czech Tech. U., 1987-90, asst. prof. physics, 1990-98, assoc. prof. physics, 1998—; sec.-gen. Czech. Acoustical Soc., Prague, 1992—. Contbr. articles to profl. jours.; dancer Dance Theater Bu-Fo, Prague, 1992, Dance Theater Chorea Bohemica, Prague, 1980-92. Recipient Active Control of Aerodynamic Noise award, 1993, award for Exptl. Equipment for Measurment of Sound Energy Transfer, 1993. Mem. Assn. Czech and Slovak Mathematicians and Physicists, Czech Acoustical Soc., Acoustical Soc. Am. Avocations: dancing, playing violin, guitar, skiing. Office: Czech Tech Univ, Technicka 2, 166 27 Prague 6, Czech Republic

JIŘICKA, ZDENĚK, pathologist; b. Horice v Podkrkonosi, Czech Republic, May 19, 1922; s. Josef and Vlasta (Chlemestová) J.; m. Eva Suzanne Procházková, Oct. 27, (1949 dec. 1995); children: Vojtěch, Dana. MD, Charles U., 1949; PhD, Acad. Scis. Czech Republic, 1964. Physician City Hosp., Prague, 1949-54; lectr. in pathology faculty of medicine Charles U., Praha, Bohemia, 1954-58; exptl. pathologist Acad. Scis. Czech Republic, Praha, 1959—; vis. scientist Tulane U., New Orleans, 1966-67. Contbr. articles to profl. jours. Fellow Czech Pathol. Soc. Avocations: classical music, classical literature, photography. Home: Severni II 25, CZ-14100 Praha Czech Republic Office: Inst Pharmacology AVČR, Videnska 1083, CZ-14220 Praha Czech Republic

JIRKA, JIŘÍ, nephrologist, researcher; b. Kroměříž, Czech Republic, Mar. 5, 1927; s. Josef and Pavla (Skládalová) J.; m. Hana Černá, Sept. 28, 1957; children: Tomáš, Jan. MD, Charles U., Prague, 1951; PhD, Acad. Scis., Prague, 1958; DSc, Charles U., 1989. Ho. officer City Hosp., Most, Czechoslovakia, 1951-53; trainee in rsch. Inst. Cardiovasc. Rsch., Prague, 1953-58, sr. investigator, 1958-70; head clin. dept., 3d Med. Rsch. Unit Inst. Clin. and Exptl. Medicine (IKEM), Prague, 1971-89, dir. Clinic of Nephrology, 1990-91, cons. Clinic of Nephrology, 1992—; cons. Min. Pub. Health, Havana, Cuba, 1964-65, Intertransplant, Prague, 1974-90. Co-author: Rejection Nephropathy, 1979 (Czechoslovak Min. Health prize 1979), Renal Allograft Biopsy, 1997; contbr. 212 articles to profl. jours., 231 abstracts of oral presentations. Fulbright fellow, 1987. Mem. Czech Soc. Nephrology (hon. com. mem. 1997), European Renal Assn. Avocations: trout fishing, hunting. Home: Újezd 15/415, 150 00 Prague 5 Czech Republic Office: IKEM, Vídeňská 1958/9, 140 21 Prague 4 Czech Republic

JIRSA, MILAN, biochemist; b. Prague, Czechoslovakia, Mar. 21, 1923; s. Frantisek and Eleonora (Falterova) J.; m. Vera Buchalova, Nov. 16, 1949; children: Milan, Zuzana Vancikova. Diploma Engring., Sch. Indl. Chemistry, Prague, 1944; MD, Charles U., Prague, 1949, PhD, 1957, DSc, 1968. Registrar faculty medicine Charles U., Prague, 1949-54; rsch. worker rsch. unit for hepatol. Charles U., 1954-65, chief rsch. worker for hepatol., 1968-90, rsch. worker, 1991—; rsch. fellow Royal Free Hosp., London, 1966-67; mem. adv. bd. med. faculty, Charles U., 1990-95. Rschr./inventor in field. Recipient State prize, 1986, Gold plaque J.E. Purkynje's, Czechoslovak Acad. Scis., 1988; grantee in field. Mem. Czech Soc. for Photobiology and Photodynamic Therapy (pres. 1995—). Home: Tocita 17, 140 00 Praha 4 Czech Republic Office: 1st Dept Medicine, 1st Fac Med/U nemocnice 2, 128 08 Praha 2 Czech Republic

JIRSÁK, OLDŘICH, educator; b. Hradec Králové, Czech Republic, July 22, 1947; s. Oldrich and Marie (Netiková) J.; m. Jitka Hrbácová, Aug. 11, 1972; children: Lucie, Samuel. Dr., rerum naturalium, U. PJS, 1975; PhD, Slovac Acad. Sci., 1980. Rsch. asst. U. Olomouc, Czechoslovakia, 1970-71; rschr. Chemlon, Humenne, Czechoslovakia, 1972-79; sr. rsch. officer U. Liberec, Czechoslovakia, 1979-90; asst. prof. U. Liberec, 1990—, head dept. nonwovens, 1991—. Contbr. articles to profl. jours.; patentee in field. Mem. N.Y. Acad. of Sci. Office: Tech Univ of Liberec, Halkova 6, 46117 Liberec Czech Republic

JIRUM, XU, science educator; b. Huaiyin, Jiangsu, China, Mar. 18, 1955; s. Xu Bilun and Zhou Xinglan; m. Hu Fang, July 24, 1984; 1 child. BS, South-Ctrl. Industry U., Changsha, China, 1981; MS, Northeatern U., Shenyang, China, 1986, PhD, 1989. Asst. Northeastern U., 1982-88, lectr., 1988-92, asst. prof., 1993-97; postdoctoral vis. scholar Imperial Coll. Sci., Tech. and Medicine, London, 1992-93; asst. prof. Dalian (China) U., 1997-98, prof., 1998—. Author: Theory of the Flow Field in Hydrocyclones, 1998; contbr. articles to profl. jours. Mem. N.Y. Acad. Scis. Avocations: literature, swimming, football. Office: Dalian U, Dept Chem Engring, 116622 Dalian Liaoning, China

JITPIMOLMARD, SUTHIPUN, medical educator; b. Khon Kaen, Thailand, June 20, 1958; s. Kobkait and Rayup Jitpimolmard; m. Buskorn Chairungsri, July 23, 1986; children: Jukrapope, Disya. MD, Khon Kaen U., 1981, BS, 1979; diploma in clin. neurology, U. London, 1988. Diplomate Thai Bd. Neurology. From lectr. to asst. prof. to assoc. prof. Khon Kaen U., 1988-99, prof., 1999—; cons. neurologist Srinagarind Hosp., Khon Kaen, 1988—; dep. dir. R&D Inst., Khon Kaen U., 1999—. Author: (book) Ambulatory Medicine, 1992; author, editor: (books) Symptomatology in General Medicine, 1996, Hemifacial Spasm and Other Movement Disorders of the Face, 1998; editor: (jour.) Bull. of Neurol. Soc. Thailand, 1996—. Rsch. fellow Royal Free Hosp. Sch. Medicine, U.K., 1986-87, Brit. Coun. fellow Inst. Neurology, U. London, 1987-88. Mem. Am. Acad. Neurology, Queen Square Assn. (U.K.), Assn. Brit. Neurologists (U.K.). Avocations: stamp collecting, swimming, reading books. Office: Khon Kaen U Divsn Neurology, 123 Friendship Hwy, Khon Kaen 40002, Thailand

JIUYONG, SHI, judge; b. Zhejiang, China, Sept. 10, 1926. BA in Govt. and Pub. Law, St. John's U., Shanghai, 1948; MA in Internat. Law, Columbia U., 1951, postgrad., 1951-54. Asst. rsch. fellow Internat. Law Inst. Internat. Rels., Beijing, 1956-58; sr. lectr., assoc. prof. Internat. Law Fgn. Affairs Coll., Beijing, 1958-64; rsch. fellow Internat. Law Inst. Internat. Law, Beijing, 1964-73, 73-80; tchr. Internat. Econ. Law Dept. Law Peking U., 1980-85; prof. Internat. Law Fgn. Affairs Coll., Beijing, 1984-93; prof. Law Fgn. Econ. Law Tng. Ctr. Min. Justice People's Republic China, Beijing, 1987-88; judge Internat. Ct. of Justice, The Hague, The Netherlands, 1994—, v.p., 2000—; adviser Chinese Soc. Internat. Law, Beijing, Chinese del. 35th session Gen. Assembly UN, China's Alt. Rep. Sixth Com. to 35th session, Chinese del. to 36th, 37, 38th sessions UN Gen. Assembly and China's del. Sixth Com. at same sessions, 1981-83; legal adviser Ministry Fgn. Affairs People's Republic China, 1980-93, Office Chinese Sr. Rep. Sino-Brit. Joint Liaison Group on Hong Kong plenary sessions, 1985-93, Chinese Ctr. Legal Consultancy, Beijing, 1989-93, Chinese del. 1980 Ann. Meeting Bd. Govs. Internat. Monetary Fund and Internat. Bank Reconstruction and Devel., del. Ministry Fin. People's Republic China Internat Bank Reconstruction and Devel., Chinese del. talks between Govt. China and Asian Devel. Bank, 1986, Chinese side Working Group Sino-Brit. Negotiations regarding Hong Kong, 1984, Chinese del. Disarmament Conf., 1991-92; del. Chinese del. to sessions Asian-African Legal Consultative Com., 1981, 85, 93, Chinese del. legal consultations between Ministry Fgn. Affairs of People's Republic China and Dept. State U.S. Am., 1983, 1984, Chinese del. negotiations between Govt. People's Republic China and Govt. U.S. Am. on Mut. Promotion and Protection of Investment Agreement, 1983, 1984; expert sr. legal experts meeting rev. Montevideo program, UN Environ. Program, Geneva, 1991, Nairobi, 1991; lectr. internat. fin. instns. Nat. Bureau Oceanography, People's Republic China, 1986, protection of private fgn. investment Hague Acad. Internat. Law Regional Program, Beijing, 1987, Grad. Inst. Internat. Studies, Geneva, 1988, autonomy in Internat. Law Sem. UN Office, Geneva, 1988, certain issues relating to legal status of Hong Kong Spl. Adminstrv. Region, internat. trade regulation, 1985-86, others; chmn. panel discussions new internat. econ. order Beijing Conf. Law of the World World Peace through Law, 1990; participant symposium internat. law arms control and disarmament, Geneva, 1991, Seminar Draft Code Crimes and internat. criminal jurisdiction, symposium on tchg., dissemination and rsch. internat. law in devel. countries, Beijing, 1992. Mem. Am. Soc. Internat. Law, Internat. Law Commn. (rep. to 45th session UN gen. Assembly 1990, 30th meeting of Asian-African Legal Consultative Conf. 1991, mem. 1987-93, rapporteur, 1988, chmn. 1990, lectr. 1991), Inst. Hong Kong Law Chinese Law Soc., Standing Com., Beijing Com., Eighth Ann. Com., Chinese People's Polit. Consultative Conf., Fgn. Econ. and Trade Arbitration Commn., China Coun. Promotion Internat. Trade, Steering Com. Office: Internat Ct of Justice, Peace Palace, 2517 KJ The Hague The Netherlands*

JIWKOW, WASIL, violin maker; b. Jakimovo, Bulgaria, Dec. 12, 1926; s. George and Todora J. Master Diploma for stringed instrument making with Master Manachil Crastew, Sofia, Bulgaria, 1951. Internat. exhbns.; Concours Internat. de Quatuor a Cordes, Liege, Belgium, 1957, 60, 63, 69, 72, Societa Filarmonica Ascolana, Mostra Internazionale di Luteria, Viola Moderna, Ascoli, Italy, 1959, Concours Internat. for Stringed Instruments, Poznan, Poland, 1967, The Violin Soc. of Am. Internat. Bicentennial Exhbn. and Competition, Phila., 1976; exhibited 24 original instruments (violins, violas, celloes) at Arts Acad., Interlochen, Mich., 1975. Recipient numerous certs. and first prizes, including: 2d prize for violin, Poznan,, 1972, 1st prize for best making and style Quartet Competition, Liege, Belgium; Diploma for Mordern Viola, 1959, diploma for best making and tone, Phila., 1976, diploma for workmanship, viola, La Jolla, Calif., 1978. Office: Artistic Atelier Violin Making, Mueller-Strasse 26, 80469 Munich Germany

JIYA, JONATHAN YISA, national government official, preventive medicine; b. Kuciworo, Niger, Nigeria, May 30, 1950; s. Ndabayisa Samuel and Nnaala Eunice (Tswanya) J.; m. Elizabeth Halima Umaru, Apr. 7, 1977; 4 children. MB, BS, Ahmadu Bello U., Zaria, Nigeria, 1976; MPH, Boston U., 1983; MNI, Nat. Inst., Kuru, Jos, Nigeria, 1986. Registered mem. Nigerian Med. Coun. House officer Ahmadu Bello U. Tchg. Hosp., Kaduna, Nigeria, 1976-77, sr. house officer, 1978; with nat. svc. St. Gerard's Hosp., Kaduna, Nigeria, 1977-78; med. officer Lafiya Clinic, Kaduna, Nigeria, 1981; sr. med. officer Gen. Hosp., Minna, Nigeria, 1981-83, prin. med. officer, 1983-84; dir. health svcs. State Health Svcs. Bd. State of Niger, Nigeria, 1984-90; dir. disease control State of Niger Ministry of Health, Nigeria, 1990-94; dep. dir. disease control, nat. coord. health Fed. Ministry of Health, Maitama, Abuja, Nigeria, 1994—. Chief editor nat. newsletter, Onchocerciasis Control in Nigeria, 1997; contbr. Nigeria Onchocericiasis Rev., 1998. Recipient scholarship State Govt. Niger, Ahmadu Bello U., Zaria, 1969, 76, scholarship Fed. Govt. Nigeria, Boston U., 1982. Mem. Nigerian Med. Assn., Am. Pub. Health Assn., Nigerian Inst. Mgmt., Golf Club Minna, Nigeria (pres. 1987-90), Polo Club, Minna (pres. 1989-90), UN Club (chmn. Minna 1990—). Avocations: golf, gaming, reading. Office: Fed Ministry Health, Shehu Shagari Way, Maitama Abuja, Nigeria

JIZBA, JOSEF VACLAV, chemist, researcher; b. Prague, Czechoslovakia, June 5, 1952; s. Josef and Marie (Belingerová) J. Grad. engr., Inst. Chem. Tech., Prague, 1975; PhD, Czechoslovak Acad. Sci., Prague, 1983. Stage rschr. U. Tubingen, Germany, 1982; rsch. worker Inst. Microbiology, Prague, 1983-94; rsch. worker mgr. Lab. Bioactive Compounds, Prague, 1994—. Contbr. articles to profl. jours.; patentee in field. Grantee UNESCO and local instns., 1982—. Roman Catholic. Avocations: gardening, yoga. Office: Lab Bioactive Compounds, Ježovická 99, 190 16 Prague Czech Republic

JO, MASATOSHI, chemist; b. Shirahama, Japan, Aug. 31, 1958; s. Hiromu and Akiye (Nakagawa) J. BS, Kyoto U., Japan, 1981, MS, 1983, DS, 1987. Rschr. Electrotech. Lab., Tsukuba, Japan, 1987-90, sr. rschr., 1990—; officer indsl. sci. and tech. frontier program AIST, MITI, 1996-97. Contbr. articles to profl. jours. Mem. Japan Soc. Applied Physics, Surface Analysis Soc. Japan (editl. com., mem. inspector, auditor), N.Y. Acad. Scis. Achievements include development of a new method for analyzing inelastic background of X-ray photoelectron spectroscopy by solving Tougaard's formula. Office: Electrotech Lab, Umezono 1-1-4, Tsukuba 305-8568, Japan

JO, SOOK JIN, artist; b. Kwangu, Korea, Oct. 20, 1960; came to U.S., 1988; d. Seok Hyung Cho and Won Jung Lee. BS, In Ha U., Incheon, Korea, 1982; MFA, Hong Ik U., Seoul, Korea, 1989, Pratt Inst., 1991. Gallery artist O.K. Harris Works of Art, N.Y.C., 1990—; dir. Sook Jin Jo Atelier, N.Y.C., 1991—; reporter Art & Info, Broadcasting Comm. Coll., Incheon, 1984-85; appeared in Art Today, N.Y., KBS, Seoul, WMBC-TV,, N.Y.; lectr. in field. Exhibited in 13 one-woman shows and 50 group exhbns., including Exit Art, N.Y., Il Min Mus., Seoul, Bobbit Visual Arts Ctr., Albion, Mo., Montclair State Coll., Upper Montclair, N.J., Korean Cultural Ctrs. N.Y. and L.A., Nat. Mus. Modern Art, Seoul, Fine Arts Ctr., Seoul, Kyoto (Japan) City Art Ctr.; represented in over 30 pvt. collections, including Housatonic Mus. Art, Conn., Erie Mus. Art, Pa.; art published in numerous newspapers, mags. and books, including Art in Am., N.Y. Times, Flash Art, Rev. Mag., Art Asia Pacific, Metro Times, Mich., Korea Times, Ctrl. New, Saegae Times, Art in Pocket, Japan; documentary film of her wood constrn. and pub. art installation Color of Life by WMBC, N.Y.; contbr. over 50 articles to mags. and newspapers. Fellow Korea Arts Found. Am., 1993, Pollock-Krasner Found., 1996, Socrates Sculpture Park, 1999. Avocations: swimming, yoga, cats. Home: 266 W 25th St Apt 5R New York NY 10001-7308

JO, UN-BOCK, anatomist, educator; b. Hungnam, Korea, Nov. 3, 1941; s. Jong-Ho Jo and Gi-Nam Ju; m. Soo-Ja Kim, May 18, 1968; children: Gi-Jin Jo, Gi-Wook Jo. BS, Pusan Nat. U., Korea, 1965, MS, 1969, PhD, 1975. Instr. Coll. of Medicine/Pusan Nat. U., 1969-74, asst. prof., 1974-78, assoc. prof., 1978-79, 1979-84; prof. Coll. of Edn./Pusan Nat. U., 1984—; vis. prof. Saint-mariana Med. Sch., Japan, 1979; assoc. dean Pusan Nat. Grad. Sch., 1982-83, chmn. dept. biology edn., 1985-91, dir. Sci. Edn. Ctr., 1991-92. Editor: (books) Environmental Biology, 1995, Comparative Anatomy of Vertebrate, 1997; editl. staff: Korean Jour. of Electron microscopy, 1995—. Pres. Pusan Christian Faculty Assn., 1976-77, Pusan-South Presbytery, Men's Missionary Assn., 1987-88; elder Sojung Presbyn. Ch., 1982—; chief Wheat Grain mission, Milyang, Korea, 1988. 2d lt. land forces Korean mil., 1965-67. Recipient award of merit minister of Edn., Seoul, 1991, Meritorious Svc. award Pusan City Tchr.'s Assn., 1998. Mem. Korean Assn. Anatomy (bd. dirs. 1996—), Korean Assn. Environ. Edn. (bd. dirs. 1996—). Presbyterian. Avocations: oil painting, photography. E-mail: ubjo@hyowon.cc.pusan.ac.kr. Office: Pusan Nat Univ/Biology Edn, 30 Jangjeondong Kumjeong Gu, Pusan 609-735, Republic of Korea

JO, WON HO, engineeing educator; b. Kimhae, Korea, Nov. 5, 1950; s. Kyu Deok and Tong E. (Park) J.; m. Young Hee Jung; children: Jay Hyun, Hyun Hwa. BS, Seoul Nat. U., 1973, MS, 1975; MS, Polytech. Inst. of N.Y., 1977, PhD, 1979. Asst. prof. Seoul Nat. U., 1980-84, assoc. prof., 1984-90, prof., 1990—; vis. scholar U. Tex., 1987-88, U. Mass., 1996-97. Contbr. more than 130 articles to profl. jours. Recipient Best Paper award Korean Fedn. of Sci. and Tech. Socs., 1992. Mem. Polymer Soc. of Korea (bd. dirs. 1996—), Korean Soc. of Rheology (bd. dirs.). Avocations: classical music, go. Office: Dept Fiber/Polymer Sci, Seoul Nat U, Seoul 151-742, Republic of Korea

JOA, EUGEN ERNST, educational association administrator; b. Adelsberg, Germany, June 1, 1937; arrived in Italy, 1964; s. Franz and Elisabeth (Michler) J.; m. Christine Franziska Schneider, Aug. 21, 1974; 1 child, Kathrin. With Uhlmann-Eyraud, Geneva, Switzerland, 1961-64; dir. CLM, Trento, Italy, 1966-92; mng. dir. Centro di Lingue Moderne, The Bell Ednl. Trust, Trento, 1992—. Roman Catholic. Avocations: tennis, cross-country skiing, skiing, reading. Home: Via Lungadige 81, I-38100 Trento Italy Office: CLM-Bell, Via Pozzo 30, 38100 Trento Italy

JOANNIDIS, MICHAEL, internist, researcher; b. Brixen, Italy, Oct. 31, 1960; arrived in Austria, 1961; s. Michael and Lydia J. MD, U. Innsbruck, Austria, 1986. Postdoctoral rschr. Inst. Physiology, Innsbruck, 1986-89; fellow in nephrology Beth Israel Hosp.-Harvard Med. Sch., Boston, 1992-94; resident Univ. Hosp., Innsbruck, 1989-92, staff mem. dept. medicine, 1995—, head med. emergency room, 1995—, attending med. ICU,, 1995—; assoc. prof. U. Innsbruck, 1998. Contbr. articles to profl. jours. Grantee Austrian Sci. Found., 1992-94. Mem. Austrian Physicians Assn. (cert.), Austrian Soc. Nephrology (bd. dirs. 1994—), Am. Soc. Nephrology, European Soc. Intensive Care Medicine. Avocations: skiing, windsurfing, tennis. Office: U Internal Medicine, Anichstrasse 35, A 6020 Innsbruck Tyrol, Austria

JOAQUIM, RICHARD RALPH, hotel executive; b. Cambridge, Mass., July 28, 1936; s. Manuel and Mary (Marrano) J.; m. Nancy Phyllis Reis, Oct. 22, 1960; 1 child, Vanessa Reis. BFA, Boston U., 1955, MusB, 1959. Social dir., coord. summer resort Wolfeboro, N.H., 1957-59; concert soloist N.H. Symphony Orch., Vt. Choral Soc., Choral Arts Soc.,, 1957-60; coord. performance functions, mgr. theatre Boston U., 1959-60, asst. program dir., 1963-64, dir. univ. programs, 1964-70; gen. mgr. Harrison House of Glen Cove; dir. Conf. Svc. Corp., Glen Cove, N.Y., 1970-74, sr. v.p. dir. design and devel.; v.p. Aritec, also mng. dir. Sheraton Internat. Conf. Ctr., 1975-76; pres. Internat. Conf. Resorts, Inc., 1977, Western Conf. Resorts; concert solist U.S. Army Field Band, Washington, 1960-62; creative arts cons., editorial cons., concert mgr. Commr. recreation Watertown, Mass., 1967—; mem. Spl. Study Com., Watertown, 1967—, Glen Cove Mayor's Urban Renewal Com., Nat. Com. for Performing Arts Ctr. at Boston U., Jacob K. Javits Fellows Program Fellowship Bd.; bd. dirs. Nat. Entertainment Conf.; trustee Boston U., 1983—, Hotel and Food Adminstrn. Program Adv. Bd., Boston U., 1986—, Ariz. Opera Co. With AUS, 1960-62. Recipient Disting. Alumni award Boston U., 1991. Past mem. Assn. Coll. and Univ. Concert Mgrs., Am. Symphonic League, Am. Fedn. Film Socs., Assn. Am. Artists, Am. Pers. and Guidance Assn.; mem. LaChaine des Rotisseurs, Knights of the Vine, Order of St. John, Nat. Alumni Coun. Boston U., The Lotos (N.Y.) Club. Office: 5600 N Saguaro Rd Paradise Vly AZ 85253-5235

JOAQUIN, DOMINGO CASTELO, finance educator, management consultant; b. Manila, Nov. 20, 1954; s. Eleuterio Baltazar and Encarnacion Castelo Joaquin. PhD in Regional Sci., U. Pa., Phila., 1986; MSc in Stats. and Probability, Mich. State U., 1994, PhD in Fin., 1997. Project coord. Devel. Acad. of the Philippines, 1975-78; asst. prof. econs. St. Olaf Coll., Northfield, Minn., 1986-89; asst. prof. econs. and bus. adminstrn. Hope Coll., Holland, Mich., 1989-91; asst. prof. fin. Ill. State U., Normal, 1998—; cons. Econ. and Corp. Fin. Modeling Assocs., Portland, Oreg., 1999—. Contbr. articles to profl. jours. Mem. Fin. Mgmt. Assn. E-mail: dcjoaqu@ilstu.edu. Home: 1507 Tearose Ln Bloomington IL 61704-8268 Office: Dept Fin Ins & Law Ill State Univ Normal IL 61790-0001

JOB, CHARLES KAMALAM, pathologist, educator; b. Nigercoil, India, Nov. 2, 1923; s. Joseph Charles and Ponnammal (Jacob) Kamalam; m. Jennie Thankal Gunamony, May 14, 1954; children: Anand, Sudharshini and Subhashini. MBBS, Madras U., 1953, MD, 1959. Dir. Schieffelin Leprosy Rsch. and Tng. Ctr., Karigiri, India, 1959-68; head pathology dept., prof. Christian Med. Coll. and Hosp., Vellore, India, 1966-75; med. supt., prof. pathology Christian Med. Coll. and Hosp., Vellore, 1975-78; prin., prof. pathology Christian Med. Coll., Vellore, 1978-81; chief pathology rsch. dept. Nat. Hansen's Disease Ctr., Carville, La., 1981-91; cons. pathologist St. Thomas Hosp. and Leprosy Ctr., Tamil Nadu, India, 1991—; emeritus scientist Schieffelin Leprosy Rsch. and Tng. Ctr., Karigiri, 1991—, cons., 1962-81; clin. prof. pathology Tulane U., New Orleans, 1982-91; pres. The Leprosy Mission Internat., London, 1999. Pres. Leprosy Mission Internat., London, 1999. Recipient K.D. Sahu Gold medal Hind Kusht Nivaran Sangh, 1971, Damien-Dutton award, 1993. Fellow Indian Acad. Med. Scis., Royal Coll. Pathologists, Indian Coll. Pathologists (coun. chmn.); mem. Indian Assn. Leprologists (v.p. 1968-71, pres. 1972-73), Indian Assn. Pathologists, Internat. Acad. Pathologists, Internat. Assn. Leprologists (v.p. 1984-88, hon. v.p. 1988—), Christian Med. and Dental Soc., N.Y. Acad. Med. Scis. Office: St Thomas Hosp-Leprosy Ctr, Chettupattu, TSR Tamil Nadu 606 801, India

JOB, RAYMOND FRANKLIN SOAMES, psychologist; b. Dubbo, Australia, July 13, 1954; s. Raymond Wallace and Nancy Colleen (Cook) J.; m. Mai Peedo, Oct. 4, 1986; children: Shannon, Lara, Lawson. BA with honors, U. Sydney, 1977, PhD, 1986. Tutor U. Sydney, 1977-80, lectr., sr. lectr. then assoc. prof., 1986—; sr. behavioral scientist Roads and Traffic Authority, Sydney, 1980-82; sr. behavioural scientist Nat. Acoustic Labs., Sydney, 1982-85; dir. Fleming Job & Assocs., 1988-93, Soames Job & Assocs., 1995—; cons. Roads and Traffic Authority of N.S.W., 1989—. Author: (with D. Kenny) Australia's Adolescents: A Health Psychology Perspective, 1995; contbr. numerous articles to profl. jours. Recipient Tasman Lovell Meml. medallion U. Sydney, 1986; large grants scheme Australian Rsch. Coun., 1992, 93, 94, 95, 96, 97, 98, Australian Rsch. Coun. Infrastructure grant, 1997, Fed. Office of Road Safety grants, 1993-94, 96-97, 99-2000; Commonwealth scholar 1971-72, 73, 1977-80. Mem. Australian Psychol. Soc., Australian Coll. of Road Safety (assoc. fellow, v.p. 1998—), Internat. Commn. Biol. Effects of Noise (sec. 1998—). Avocations: scuba diving, surfing. Office: Dept Psychology U Sydney, Broadway, Sydney 2006, Australia

JOBS, STEVEN PAUL, computer corporation executive; b. Feb. 24, 1955; adopted s. Paul J. and Clara J. (Jobs); m. Laurene Powell, Mar. 18, 1991. Student, Reed Coll. With Hewlett-Packard, Palo Alto, Calif.; designer video games Atari Inc., 1974; co-founder Apple Computer Inc., Cupertino, Calif., chmn. bd., 1975-85, former dir.; pres. NeXT, Inc., Redwood City, Calif., 1985-96; chief exec. officer NeXT, Inc. (bought by Apple, 1996), Redwood City; interim CEO Apple Computer, Cupertino, Calif., 1997—, now CEO, chmn.; chmn., chief exec. officer Pixar Animation Studios, 1986-. Co-designer: (with Stephan Wozniak) Apple I Computer, 1976. Recipient Nat. Medal Tech. presented by Pres. Ronald Reagan, Entrepreneur of the Decade award, Inc. Mag., Jefferson award for Pub. Svc. Office: Pixar Animation Studios 1001 W Cutting Blvd Richmond CA 94804-2028

JOCHNER, MICHELE MELINA, lawyer; b. Naperville, Ill., May 19, 1966. BA summa cum laude, Mundelein Coll., Chgo., 1987; JD with honors, DePaul U., 1990, LLM in Taxation Law, 1992. Bar: Ill. 1990, U.S. Dist. Ct. (no. dist.) Ill. 1990, U.S. Ct. Appeals (7th cir.) 1996, U.S. Supreme Ct. 1996. Law clk. U.S. Securities & Exch. Commn., Chgo., 1989; legal rsch. asst. to prof. Marlene Nicholson DePaul U. Sch. Law, Chgo., 1989-91; legal rsch. asst. to assoc. dean Vincent Vitullo DePaul U. Sch. Law, 1989-91; law clk. extern U.S. Dist. Ct. (no. dist.) Ill., Chgo., 1989-90; judicial law clk. Cir. Ct. of Cook County, Chgo., 1991-92; staff atty. Cir. Ct. of Cook County, 1992-93, sr. staff atty., 1993-95, acting supr. legal rsch. divsn., 1995-96; staff atty. permanency project child protection divsn. Cir. Ct. Cook County, Chgo., 1996-97; jud. law clk. to Hon. Mary Ann G. McMorrow Ill. Supreme Ct., Chgo., 1997—; mem. subcom. money transfers and adminstrv. regulations Ill. Supreme Ct., 1995-96; adj. prof. law John Marshall Law Sch., Chgo., 1994—, judge Herzog moot ct.competition, 1997—; adj. prof. law DePaul U. Coll. Law, 1998—; spkr. in field. Contbr. articles to profl. jours. Recipient Harold A. Shertz award Film, Air & Package Carriers Conf., Alexandria, Va., 1990. Mem. ABA, Ill. Bar Assn. (Lincoln award 2d pl. 1994, 97, 2000, 1st pl. 1996, 99, mem. gen. practice sect. coun., chair continuing legal edn. subcom., mem. standing com. legal edn., admission and competence, mem. tradition of excellence award subcom., elected assembly mem. 2000), Fed. Bar Assn., Chgo. Bar Assn., U.S. Supreme Ct. Hist. Soc., Order of Coif, Kappa Gamma Pi, Phi Sigma Tau. Avocations: writing fiction, non-fiction.

JOCIC', DANKO RADOSAV, mathematician; b. Foča, Yugoslavia, June 10, 1960; s. Radosav Milutin and Vinka Miloš (Stanojevic') J.; m. Svjetlana Mitar Elez; children: Andrej, Aleksej. Mathematician, U. Belgrade, 1983, M of Math. Sci., 1986, PhD, 1991. Asst. U. Kragujevac, Yugoslavia, 1984-85; rschr. Inst. for Applied Math. and Electronics, Belgrade, 1987-94; asst. U. Belgrade, 1994-96, asst. prof., 1996—; vis. scholar Ind. U., Bloomington, 1991. Author: Measure Theory, Functional Analysis, Operator Theory, Belgrade, 1999; contbr. articles to profl. jours. Grantee Nat. Scientific Fund, 1991. E-mail: jocic@matf.bg.ac.yu. Office: Blaža Jovanovic'a 22/1, 11160 Belgrade Yugoslavia Also: U Belgrade Fac Math, Studentski trg 16 POB 550, 11000 Belgrade Yugoslavia

JOEBSTL, HANS ANTON, forest economist, educator, scientist; b. Limberg/Wolfsberg, Austria, June 13, 1944; s. Johann and Josefine (Eberhard) J.; m. Elfriede Stampf, Feb. 14, 1977; 1 child. Degree in engring., U. Bodenkultur, Vienna, 1968, DSc, 1973. From asst. to prof., 1968—; prof. bus. mgmt. forestry and timber industries U. Bodenkultur, Vienna, 1979—; cons. in field, 1977—; sr. lectr. U. Trento, Italy, 1990—. Author: A Model of the Permanent Forest Enterprise, 1973, Sustainable Enterprise Planning in Forestry, 1978, Managerial Economics in Forestry, 1995, Accounting in Forestry and Forest Product Industry, 1996, Rotation Period of Norway Spruce under Changed Market Conditions, 1997, Cost and Performance Accounting, 2000; contbr. articles to profl. jours. Mem. Internat. Union Forestry Rsch. Orgn. (coord. rsch. group 1987—, Disting. Svc. award 2000), Internat. Acctg. Assn. Office: U Bodenkultur, Gregor Mendel-Strasse 33, A 1180 Vienna Austria

JOENSEN, JÓAN PAULI, ethnology and history educator, academic administrator; b. Sorvagur, Faeroe Islands, Apr. 30, 1945; s. Peter Ole and Irene (Haraldsen) J.; m. Louisa Lamhauge, Jan. 8, 1977; children: Birita, Durita. BA, U. Lund, Sweden, 1971, MA, 1973, PhD, 1975; DPhil, U. Aarhus, Denmark, 1987. Rschr. U. Lund, 1973-75, The Danish Humanistic Rsch. Consul, 1976-77; curator Nat. Mus., Faeroe Islands, 1977-89; external lectr. U. Faeroes, Torshavn, Faeroe Islands, 1980-89, prof. ethnology and history, 1989—, rector, pres., 1990-98; prof. ethnology, head of sect. U. Bergen, Norway, 1998—; mem. bd. Nordic Soc., The Faroe Islands, Torshavn, 1976-82, Faroese Soc. Sci., 1977-93, The Sci. Found. of Faroe Sav. Bank, Torshavn, 1987-97; chmn. Faroese Rsch. Coun., 1996-98. Author books and articles on Faroese history and culture, 1975-93. Mem. Royal Gustavus Adolphus Acad., Folklore Fellows (assoc.), Societas Scientiarum Faeroensis. Office: Inst Kulturstudie Kunsthistorie, Sydnespl 13, 5007 Burpen Faeroe Islands also: Univ Faroes, JC Svabosgoeta 7, FO-100 Torshavn Faeroe Islands*

JOERGENSEN, STEEN BO, financial services executive; b. Copenhagen, Dec. 7, 1957; s. Bent E. and Ulla M. (Christensen) J.; m. Pia Maria Skogstad Johnson, June 15, 1985; children: Mads G., Anders G., Amalie M. MSc in Econs., U. Copenhagen/London Sch Econs, 1981. V.p. Unibank, Denmark, 1981-92; CFO Finanssektorens Pensionskasse, Denmark, 1992; mng. dir., CEO Finanssektorens Pensionskasse, Denmark, 1993—; bd. dirs. Coun. Pension Funds, Denmark, Britannia Invest, Denmark, Britannia Invest Holland B.V., Ejendomsselskabet Accumulus, Denmark, Ejendomsinteressentskabet Vestervang III, 1998—; bd. advisors Hambros Advanced Technology Trust, England, 1994—, Danish Venture Fin., Denmark, Laan & Spar Bank, Denmark, Spar Nord Bank, Denmark, Amtssparekassen Fyn, Denmark, Cross Atlantic Ptnrs., USA/Denmark, 1998—. Avocations: tennis, jogging, downhill skiing. Office: Finanssektorens Pensionkasse, Amaliegade 27, DK-1256 Copenhagen K, Denmark

JOERGER, JAY HERMAN, psychologist, entrepreneur; b. Freeport, N.Y., Sept. 23, 1957; s. Herman Alexander and Ellen Rose (Becker) J.; m. Diana Botero, Mar. 27, 1993; children: Nicholas Alexander, Richard Andrew. BS, Union U., 1980; MA, Colgate U., 1981; EdD, Columbia U., 1987. Diplomate Am. Bd. Profl. Disability Cons., Wellness Profl., Substance Abuse Psychology, Clin. Psychology, Psychology Assessment, Evaluation and Testing, Child Custody Evaluation; lic. psychologist, N.Y.; bd. cert. forensic examiner; bd. cert. in forensic medicine; registered hypnotherapist. Drug abuse counselor Drug Abuse Coun., Norwich, N.Y., 1980-81; vocat. rehab. counselor Community Workshop, Glens Falls, N.Y., 1981-83; assoc. psychologist N.Y. State, Wingdale, N.Y., 1986-96; pres. Mentors Resource and Devel. Corp., 1991—; mem. group practice Ctr. Stress Reduction, 1993-97, Carmel Psychol. Assocs., 1993-94; admission and hosp. privileges Four Winds Hosp., Katonah, N.Y., 1995—; cons., Somers, N.Y., 1988—; adj. asst. prof. Iona Coll., 1993-95; adj. prof. Lehman Coll., 1994-97; founding coord. Alcoholism and Drug Abuse Counselor Tng. Program Lehman Coll., 1996; bd. dirs. Rapid Rabbit, Inc.; forensic psychol. cons. and expert witness. Author: A Participant Manual for Mentally Ill Chemical Abusers, 1989, Living Successfully: A Self-Study Guide, 1993; co-author: The Physical, Psychological and Social Effects of Chemical Abuse - A Clinician's Workbook, 1994, 2d edit., 1995, Substance Abuse: Evaluation and Treatment Training Program, 1995; (book, audio tape) Living Successfully: Relax and Enhance Your Life, 1996. Amateur radio operator, mil. affiliate radio operator Westchester Emergency Comm. Assn., Westchester County, 1983—; bd. dirs. Hudson Valley Fedn., Clintondale, N.Y., 1987-88. Recipient Excellence in Psychology award Med. Staff Orgn., Harlem Valley Psychologists, 1990. Mem. Am. Coll. Forensic Examiners (life), Am. Bd. Profl. Disability Cons., N.Y. State Psychol. Assn. (sec.-treas. addiction divsn. 1993-95, liaison managed care task force 1994-95), Westchester County Psychol. Assn. (pres. indsl. orgn. divsn. 1992-95). Avocations: amateur radio, motorcycling, cooperatives, martial arts. Office: 1 Edgewater Dr Middletown NY 10940-2106 also: Rt 202 and Lovell St Lincolndale NY 10540

JOERGES, CHRISTIAN HARALD, lawyer, educator; b. Weissenfels, Germany, Sept. 27, 1943; s. Harald and Maria (Heyden) J.; m. Annette Rothenberg, Mar. 20, 1972; children: Johanna, Charlotte. Student in law, Frankfurt (Fed. Republic of Germany) U., 1962-66, JD, 1971; student, Inst. for Internat. and Fgn. Trade Law, Washington, D.C., 1966-67, Netherlands Inst. for Advanced Study, 1985-86. Fellow Inst. Internat. and Fgn. Trade Law, Washington, 1966-67; asst. Law Sch., Frankfurt U., 1972-73, docent, 1973-74; prof. law U. Bremen, Fed. Republic of Germany, 1974-98, co-dir. Ctr. for European Legal Policy, 1982-87; prof. European U. Inst., Florence, Italy, 1998—; part-time prof. European U. Inst., Florence, Italy, 1987. Author, editor books and articles in law jours. Author, editor books and articles in law jours. Recipient Walter Koib Gedaechtrius prize U. Frankfurt, 1971. Office: European U Inst Law Dept, Via Boccaccio 121, D-50123 Florence Italy

JOERGES, JASDAN BERNWARD, science journalist, curator; b. Saarbruecken, Germany, July 26, 1965; s. Bernward Josef and Zahra Ellaheh (Sokhansandj) J. Diploma, Free Univ., Berlin, 1992, PhD summa cum laude, 1996. Rsch. asst. Free Univ., Berlin, 1996-98; sci. journalist Berlin, 1998; curator Berliner Festspiele GMBH, Berlin, 1998-2000, Deutsches Hygiene Mus., Dresden, 2000—; vis. scientist Salk Inst., San Diego, 1993-94. Author, programmer (computer game) Kinetik, 1987; artist (computer art, video installation) Calightoscope, 1988-89 (ARS Electronica award 1989); contbr. articles to profl. jours.

JOFFE, BARBARA LYNNE, computer management professional, computer artist; b. Bklyn., Apr. 12, 1951; d. Lester L. and Julia (Schuelke) J.; m. James K. Whitney, Aug. 25, 1990; 1 child, Nichole. BA, U. Oreg., 1975; MFA, U. Mont., 1982. Cert. project mgr. IBM; cert. project mgmt. profl. Project Mgmt. Inst. Applications engr., software developer So. Pacific Transp., San Francisco, 1986-93; computer fine artist Barbara Joffe Assocs., San Francisco, Englewood, Colo., 1988—; instr. computer graphics Ohlone Coll., Fremont, Calif., 1990-91; adv. programmer, project mgr.-client/server Integrated Sys. Solutions Corp./IBM Global Svcs. So. Pacific/Union Pacific Railroads, Denver, 1994-97; applications sys. mgr. IBM Global Svcs./CoBank, Greenwood Village, Colo., 1997-99; exec. project manager IBM/GM Web Hosting, 2000—. Artwork included in exhibits at Calif. Crafts XIII, Crocker Art Mus., Sacramento, 1983, Rara Avis Gallery, Sacramento, 1984, Redding (Calif.) Mus. and Art Ctr., 1985, Euphrat Gallery, Cupertino, Calif., 1988, Computer Mus., Boston, 1989, Siggraph Traveling Art Shown, Europe and Australia, 1990, 91, 4th and 7th Nat. Computer Art Invitational, Cheney, Wash., 1991, 94, Visual Arts Mus., N.Y.C., 1994, 96, IBM Golden Circle, 1996. Recipient IBM Project Mgmt. Excellence award, 1998. Mem. Assn. Computing Machinery, Project Mgmt. Inst. (cert.). Avocations: art, gardening, hiking.

JOFFE, BARRY ISAAC, physician; b. Johannesburg, South Africa, Oct. 24, 1939; s. Eli and Celia (Brand) J.; m. Rebecca Ede Berkowitz, Nov. 11, 1964; chidlren: Harry, Daniel, Gideon, Aviva. MB, BCh, Witwaterstrand U., 1962, DSc, 1975. Med. intern Baragwanath Hosp., Johannesburg, 1963-64; postgrad. fellow Nat. Inst. of Neurology, London, 1965; med. resident Coronation Hosp., Johannesburg, 1966-67, 69-70; rsch. assoc. Endocrin Rsch. Unit, Cape Town, 1968-69; cons. physician Non-European Hosp., Johannesburg, 1970-80; assoc. prof. medicine Witwatersrand U., Johannesburg, 1981-88, prof. metabolic medicine, 1989—; prin. physician Hillbrow Hosp., Johannesburg, 1981-93, prof. medicine, 1994-97; clin. head, prof. medicine Johannesburg Hosp., 1998—; mem. faculty bd. Faculty of Medicine, Witwatersrand U., Johannesburg, 1981—, mem. of senate, 1989—, mem. postgrad. com., 1989-93; vice chmn. Med. adv. com. Hillbrow Hosp., Johannesburg, 1990, 91, 94-96. Contbr. articles to profl. jours. Rsch. grant Witwatersrand U., 1994-99, Med. Rsch. Coun., 1994-97. Fellow Royal Coll. Physicians; mem. Soc. for Endocrinology Metabolism, Diabetes of So. Africa (sec. 1975-82), The Endocrine Soc. Achievements include development of an experimental model for hyperosmolar diabetic coma; elucidation of the pathogenesis of diabetes in the African communities of So. Africa. Office: Witwatersrand U Med Sch Dept Med, 7 York Rd Parktown, Johannesburg 2193, South Africa

JOFFE, DAVID JONATHON, lawyer; b. Manhatten, N.Y., Mar. 8, 1962; s. Seymour Joffe and Saretta Hoyt (Hill) Prescott; m. Hillary Ray Joffe, June 25, 1994; children: Alexander Seymour, Zachary Nathan. BA, Fla. State U., 1984; JD, U. Miami, Coral Gables, Fla., 1988. Bar: Fla. 1989, U.S. Dist. Ct. (so. dist.) Fla. 1989, U.S. Dist. Ct. (mid. dist.) Fla. 1989, U.S. Ct. Appeals (11th cir.) 1989. Legal intern Dade County Pub. Defenders, Miami, 1988-89; assoc. Randy S. Maultasch, Esquire, Miami, 1989-90; owner, ptnr. Ticket Attys., P.A., Coconut Grove, Fla., 1992—; pvt. practice Coconut Grove, 1990—; mem. C.J.A. Panel Atty. for So. Dist. of Fla. Dir., chmn. com. Dade County Young Dems., Miami, 1990. Mem. ABA, ATLA, Nat. Assn. Criminal Def. Lawyers, Assn. Fla. Trial Lawyers, Fla. Assn. Criminal Def. Attys. Democrat. Jewish. Avocations: working out (exercise), reading, pistol and skeet shooting. Office: 2900 Bridgeport Ave Ste 401 Coconut Grove FL 33133-3606

JOFFE, JOSEF, editor, columnist; b. Lodz, Poland, Mar. 15, 1944; m. Christine Brinck; children: Jessica, Janina. BA, Swarthmore Coll., 1965; MA, Johns Hopkins U., 1967; PhD, Harvard U., 1975. Sr. editor Die Zeit, Hamburg, Germany, 1976-82; fellow Woodrow Wilson Ctr. for Scholars, Washington, 1982-83; sr. fellow Carnegie Endowment, Washington, 1983-84; editl. page editor Süddeutsche Zeitung, Munich, 1985-2000; vis. prof. govt. Harvard U., Cambridge, Mass., 1990-91; vis. lectr. Princeton U., 1998, Payne Disting. Lectr., 1999-2000; lectr. Internat. U. of Bremen, European Coll. of Liberal Art, Berlin; assoc. Olin Inst., 1990—; mem. adv. bd. Nixon Inst. for Peace and Freedom, Washington; trustee Atlantik-Brücke, Bonn, Germany, Fed. Security Acad., Bonn, Leo Baeck Inst., N.Y.; mem. internat. adv. bd. Hollinger Corp., Trilateral Commn., 1987; bd. dirs Am. Acad., Berlin. Author: The Limited Partnership: The U.S., Europe, and the Burdens of Alliance, The Great Powers and the Future International Politics; mem. editl. bd. The Nat. Interest, Prospect; contbg. editor Time mag.; co-editor: Die Zeit, Hamburg, 2000—; contbr. articles to profl. jours. Pres. Harvard Club Munich. Recipient Fed. Order of Merit, Germany, 1996, various journalism prizes in Germany. Mem. Internat. Inst. for Strategic Studies, Am. Coun. on Germany. Home: S Auffahrtsallee 25, 80639 Munich Germany Office: Die Zeit, 20079 Hamburg Germany

JOFFE, ROBERT DAVID, lawyer; b. N.Y.C., May 26, 1943; s. Joseph and Bertha (Pashkovsky) J.; children by prior marriage: Katherine, David; m. Virginia Ryan, June 20, 1981; stepchildren: Elizabeth DeHaas, Ryan DeHaas. A.B., Harvard U., 1964, J.D., 1967. Bar: N.Y. 1970, U.S. Dist. Ct. (so. and ea. dists.) N.Y. 1971, U.S. Ct. Appeals (2d cir.) 1972, U.S. Supreme Ct. 1973. Maxwell Sch. Africa Pub. Svc. fellow (funded by Ford Found.) Republic of Malawi, 1967-69, state counsel, 1968-69; assoc. Cravath, Swaine & Moore, N.Y.C., 1969-75, ptnr., 1975—, dep. presiding ptnr., 1997-98, presiding ptnr., 1999—; apptd. to bd. dirs. by Pres. Clinton, Romanian Am. Enterprise Fund, 1994—. Bd. dirs. Lawyers Com. for Human Rights, The Jericho Project, 1985-97, Fiduciary Trust Co. Internat.; chair Harvard Law Sch. Nat. Fund, 1995-97, Dean's Adv. Bd., 1997—. Mem. ABA, N.Y. Bar Assn., Assn. of the Bar of the City of N.Y. (chmn. trade regulation com. 1980-83, exec. com. 1995-99), Coun. on Fgn. Rels., Human Rights Watch/Africa (adv. com.), Harvard Club. Home: 300 W End Ave Apt 13A New York NY 10023-8156 Office: Cravath Swaine & Moore 825 8th Ave Fl 46 New York NY 10019-7416

JOH, YASUSHI, science administrator, chemist; b. Naruo, Hyogo, Japan, Mar. 19, 1933; s. Kenzo and Kotoko Joh; m. Mariko Omi, Oct. 10, 1979. MS in Chemistry, Osaka (Japan) U., 1958, DSc in Organic Chemistry, 1963, PhD in Polymer Sci., 1963. Supr. Mitsubishi Rayon Co., Hiroshima, Japan, 1959-70; rsch. assoc. U. Mich., Ann Arbor, 1970-73; sr. rsch. scientist Nippon Zeon Co., Kawasaki, Japan, 1974-85; assoc. dir. med. tech. and mktg. dept. corp. rsch. and devel. Ube Industries Ltd., Tokyo, 1985-95; med.

cons. IMEC Corp., 1995—; dir. Fuji Mentenir Co., 1995—; CEO, chmn. Percussionaire Japan; cons. internat. med. cons.; bd. dirs. Fuji Mentenir Co. Mem. Am. Assn. for Respiratory Care, Am. Soc. Artificial Internal Organs, Internat. Soc. Artificial Organs, European Soc. Artificial Organs, Japanese Soc. Artificial Organs, Japanese Soc. Biomaterials. Achievements include 172 patents for Synthetic Polymer and Fibers (acrylic fibers); 278 patents for Artificial Organs (kidneys, hearts, biomaterials and related things); commercialized artificial kidney (dialyzer), artificial heart (ventricular assist device) as the first governmentally approved device, and artificial blood vessels (vascular grafts) in Japan. Home: #401 998-1 Futo-o-cho, Kohoku-ku, Yokohama 222-0031, Japan Office: IMEC # 401, 998-1 Futo-o-cho Kohoku-ku, Yokohama 222-0031, Japan Office: c/o Fuji Mentenir Co, 5-2 Kanda-mitoshiro-cho, Chiyoda-ku Tokyo 101-0053, Japan

JOH, YONG-GOE, food science educator; b. Haman-gun, Republic of Korea, Aug. 13, 1939; s. Soong-ku Joh and Tow-im Lee; m. In-Ja Lee, Dec. 15, 1970; children: Jeung-hoon, Hea-lin, Yong-lin, Jeung-hyen. BSc, Pusan Nat. U. Fisheries, Korea, 1965, MSc, 1968; PhD, Tohoku U., Sendai, Japan, 1976. Asst. prof. Kunsan (Korea) Nat. Jr. Coll. Fisheries, 1968-72, 76-77, Cheju (Korea) Nat. U., 1977-80; prof. Dong-A U., Pusan, 1980—. Contbr. articles to profl. jours. Cpl. Korean Army, 1961-63. Recipient Devotion to Ednl. Devel. award Assn. Pusan Edn. Fedn., 1999. Mem. Korean Oil Chemists' Soc. (editor 1982-95, v.p. 1995-99), Japan Oil Chemists' Soc., Am. Oil Chemists' Soc. Roman Catholic. Avocations: scuba diving, carpentering. Home: 27/5 573/33-bunji, Daeyeon 3-dong Nam-gu, Pusan 608-023, Republic of Korea Office: Univ Dong-A, 840 Hadan 2-dong Saha-gu, Pusan 604-714, Republic of Korea

JOHANET, OLIVIER, finance executive, educator; b. Paris, Jan. 20, 1954; s. Christian J. and Brigitte M. (Courtinat) J.; m. Dominique M. Gourlez de Lamotte, Sept. 16, 1977; children: Cecile, Capucine, Christian, Paul. Diploma, Inst. Politics, Paris, 1975, U. Paris II, 1977, Ctr. Perfectionnement aux Affaires, Paris, 1986. Insp. Soc. Generale, Paris, 1977-82; head credit dept. Banque Vernes, Paris, 1982-85, dep. mgr. fin. dept., 1985-88; head mktg. and sales dept. Fimagest, Paris, 1988-92; CEO Focale Fin., Paris, 1992; head investors team Credit Agricole, Paris, 1992—; bd. dirs. Credit Agricole Asset Mgmt., K.K., Tokyo; tchr., bd. tchrs. Centre de Perfectionnement Aux Affairs, 1988—; head internat. sales, bd. dirs. Indocam-Credit Agricole Group, Morocco. Avocations: wood modelling, pastry, plomb soldiers painting. Home: 86 Rue Gallieni, 92100 Boulogne-Billencourt France Office: Credit Agricole, 90 Bd Pasteur, 75015 Paris France

JOHANNES, HELGI (HELGI JONSSON), writer; b. Reykjavik, Iceland, Sept. 5, 1926; s. Jon and Jonina (Johannesdottir) Matthiasson; m. Margret Guttormsdottir, Dec. 31, 1969; children: Jon Gauti, Guttormur Helgi. Grad., Sch. Commerce, Reykjavik, 1949; student, Luxembourg, 1991-93. Sailor, 1949-52; sec. Icelandic Parliament, 1952-62; archivist Reykjaviks City Archive, 1971-73; freelance writer, 1973—; lang. tchr., Bergen, Norway, 1987-91. Books include: Any Weather Whatever, 1957, Looked upon the Frozen Snow, 1958, The Painter's House, 1961, The White Sails, 1962, Black Ceremony, 1965, The Carousel, 1969, Phantoms Assemble to a Conference, 1971, Sailor in Peace and at War, 1976, Gifts You are Offered, 1976, A Boy from the East Coast, 1977, 2d vol., 1978, Aiming for the Sky, 1979, The Composer, 1980, Head of Police Force during the British and American Occupation of Iceland in the Second World War, 1981, Valur Gislason and the Theater, 1981, 211 Comic Tales, 1982, Heard and Seen, 1983, The Story of Communications in Iceland, 1986, Otto, the Initiator, 1997, Far and Wide, A Collection of Essays and Other Pieces, 1999; (radio play) An Island in the Ocean, 1975; translator: The Unknown Soldier (v. Linna), 1971, Our Honor and Power (Nordahl Grieg), 1977, The Legend of the Holy Drinker (J. Roth), 2000; columnist Morgunbladid Daily, 1975—; contbr. short stories to anthologies including World Prize Stories, 1956. Recipient 1st prize short story Eimreidin Mag., 1955, award Icelandic Nat. Broadcasting Sta., 1971; grantee Icelandic Govt., 1956—, Icelandic Cultural Ministry, 1972. Mem. Icelandic Writers Found. (mem. adversary com. 1975, lit. prize 1976, 80, 88, 96).

JOHANNES, ILLE, chemist; b. Tallinn, Estonia, Aug. 12, 1939; d. Karl and Leena (Kivik) Juul; m. Edgar Johannes, Mar. 31, 1973; children: Eero, Tarmo. BSc, Tech. U., Tallinn, 1963; PhD in Chem. Engring., Mendeleyev Inst. Chem. Tech., Moscow, 1973. Jr. rschr. Inst. Chemistry, Tallinn, 1963-74, sr. rschr., 1974—. Contbr. articles to profl. jours.; patentee in field. Estonian Sci. Found. grantee, 1995, 96, 97, 98, 99, 2000. Mem. Estonian Chem. Soc., N.Y. Acad. Scis. Avocations: family, home. Home: Liivaluite 3-5, 11214 Tallinn Estonia Office: Inst Chemistry, 15 Akadeemia Rd, 21618 Tallinn Estonia

JOHANNESSEN, ERLING AARSAND, development engineer; b. Bergen, Norway, May 4, 1967; s. Haakon and Martha (Aarsans) J.; m. Vivi Greve, Oct. 18, 1997; 1 child, Haakon Greve. MSEE, Norwegian Inst. Tech., Trondheim, 1993; PhD, Norwegian U. Sci. and Tech., Trondheim, 1997. Rsch. asst. Norwegian Inst. Tech., Trondheim, 1993-94, rsch. fellow, 1994-97; project mgr. Kvaerner ASA, Oslo, Norway, 1997-99; sr. project engr. Ulstein Bergen AS, Bergen, Norway, 1999—. Mem. IEEE (sec., chmn. student br. Trondheim 1995-97). Home: Barliveien 6, Fyllingsdalen N-5142, Norway Office: Ulstein Bergen AS, PO Box 924, Bergen N-5808, Norway

JOHANNESSEN, JAN VINCENTS, pathology educator; b. Kristiansand, May 25, 1941. MD, U. Bergen; PhD, U. Oslo. Pres., CEO The Norwegian Radium Hosp. and Inst. for Cancer Rsch., Oslo, 1983—; clin. prof. pathology Columbia U. Coll. Physicians and Surgeons, N.Y., 1979—; rep. Norwegian Press Coun., 1989—; founder, dir. Montebello Ctr. i Mesnali, 1991—; spkr., presenter in field. Editor-in-chief: Electron Microscopy in Human Medicine, Ultrastructural Pathology, 1980—, Cancer Mag.; columnist various Norwegian newspapers and mags.; contbr. numerous articles to profl. jours.; song writer, jewelry designer. Recipient Nyco prize, Purkyne medal, Semmelweis medal, Karl Evang's prize for outstanding contbns. to health info., Primus Motor prize of manpower Norwegian Inst. Pers. Adminstrn., Norwegian prize for productivity Internat. Soc. Productivity Scis., Polytechnic Soc. Norway, Lighthouse prize Salvation Army, Gold medal of honour City of Porto, Portugal; named hon. prof. Internat. Med. Soc. Bulgaria; comdr. Royal Swedish North Star Order, Royal Dutch Oranje Nassau Order, Royal Belgian Order of the Crown, Presdl. German Order of Merit; knight Premier Cross of Royal Norwegian Order of St. Olav. Mem. Internat. Union Against Cancer (coun. mem.), European Soc. Pathology (pres., chmn. coun.), European Soc. Pathology (hon.), Hungarian Soc. Pathology (hon.), Portuguese Soc. Pathology (hon.), Cell Path Soc. (hon.), Polish Acad. Scis. (hon.), Norwegian Acad. Tech. Scis., Norwegian Cancer Soc., Polytechnic Soc. Norway (pres.), Nordic Cancer Union (Rsch. prize), Oncology Forum, Found. for Pub. Promotion of Sci. Info. (chmn.). Fax: 47 22 52 30 09. Office: Norwegian Radium Hosp, Montebello, N-0310 Oslo Norway

JOHANNESSEN, JON-ARILD, systems thinking and cybernetics executive; b. Mehamn, Norway, Dec. 8, 1949; s. Johannes and Magdalene (Danielsen) J.; m. Siri Hopland, July 21, 1990. MSc, Oslo U., 1979, Stockholm U., 1988; PhD, Stockholm U., 1990. Prof. Bodö Grad. Sch. Bus., 1988—; cons. Ruder Rsch. Found., 1995—; prof. organizational behavior Norwegian Sch. Mgmt., 1999—. Author 7 books; also over 40 articles. Address: Evenvollen 46, 2653 Gausdal Norway

JOHANNESSON, INGOLFUR ASGEIR, education educator; b. Akureyri, Iceland, Apr. 1, 1954; s. Johannes Kristjansson and Benediktsdottir Gerdur. BA, U. Iceland, 1979, postgrad., 1983; PhD, U. Wis., 1991. Elem. sch. tchr. Breidholt (Iceland) Mid. Sch., 1980-81; secondary sch. tchr. Jr. Coll. East, Reykjavik, 1982-86; divsn. chief Traffic Coun., Iceland, 1992-95; asst. prof. U. Akureyri, Iceland, 1995-97, assoc. prof., 1997—. Author: Menntakerfi i motun, 1983, Heimabyggdin, 1985, Reykjavik: Landshoettir, 1988, Reykjavik: Atvinna, 1988, Reykjavik: Lifshaettir, 1991; co-author: (chpts.) Natturusyn, 1994, Foucaults Challenge, 1998, Education Governance and Social Integration and Exclusion, 1999; contbr. articles to profl. jours. Office: U Akureyri, 602 Akureyri Iceland

JOHANNESSON, KERSTIN INGRID, marine biologist, educator; b. Molndal, Sweden, Dec. 16, 1955; d. Gunnar and Ingrid (Svensson) Janson; m.Bo Johannesson, Nov. 20, 1987; children: Klara, John. BA in Biology with honors, Goteburg U., Sweden, 1979, PhD, 1986. Asst. lectr. Goteburg U., 1982-83, assoc. prof., 1991-92, prof. marine ecology, head dept., 1997-2000; asst. prof. Swedish Natural Sci. Rsch. Coun., 1986-91, assoc. prof., 1992-96; dir. Tjärnö Marine Biol. Lab., Sweden, 1999—. Editor: Progress in Littorinid and Muricid Biology, 1990; contbr. articles to profl. jours. Rsch. grantee Goteburg U., 1980-82, 83-86. Mem. Soc. Study of Evolution. Avocation: sailing. Office: Tjarno Marine Biol Lab, S-452 96 Stromstad Sweden

JOHANNSEN, CARL GUSTAV, library information scientist, educator; b. Haderslev, Denmark, Apr. 2, 1951; s. Carl Gustav and Esther (Eyser) J.; m. Ulla Traerup, Dec. 1, 1978 (div. Jan. 1995); children: Rikke, Anders. PhD, The arhus Sch. Bus., Denmark, 1996; MA in History and Danish Lit., U. Aarhus, 1997. Lectr. U. Aarhus, 1974-78; assoc. prof. Royal Sch. Librarianship, Aalborg, Denmark, 1978-92; prof. Royal Sch. Librarianship, Copenhagen, 1992—; assoc. prof. The Aarhus Sch. Bus., 1997—; referee Info. Processing and Mgmt., 1992—, Jour. of Info. Sci., 1993—. Author: Quality Management in the Library and Information Services Sector; contbr. articles to profl. jours. Mem. Internat. Fedn. Libr. Assns. (mem. hon. com. 1997), Danish Rsch. Libr. Assn., Danish Assn. Info. and Documentation (pres. 1993-94). Avocations: history, opera, gastronomy, ornithology, fishing. Office: Royal Sch Librarianship, 6 Birketiwget, 2300 Copenhagen Denmark

JOHANNSEN, MONIKA, food chemist, researcher; b. Hamburg, Germany, May 24, 1966; d. Peter and Irmtraut (Kroeber) J. Diploma in Food chemistry, U. Hamburg, 1990; PhD, Tech. U. Hamburg-Harburg, 1995. Cert. in food chemistry. Scientist Tech. U. Hamburg-Harburg, 1992-95, 98—, F. Hoffmann-La Roche Ltd., Basle, Switzerland, 1996-98. Contbr. articles to profl. jours. Avocations: travel, dancing, reading. Home: Rotdornstieg 65, D-25469 Halstenbek Germany Office: Tech U Hamburg-Harburg, Eissendorfer Strasse 38, D-21073 Hamburg Germany

JOHANNSEN DE BLOCK, ANNE CHRISTINE, real estate agent; b. Mexico City, Feb. 27, 1925; d. Ludwig and Minna (Trube) J.; m. Rudolph Block III, June 26, 1965 (dec. Apr. 22, 1993). Grad., Niebuell H.S., Germany. Sec. to asst. mgr. Pierre Marques Hotel, Acapulco, Mex., 1956-64; mgr. Real Estate Office PRODASA, 1965—. Mem. Navy League, Smithsonian. Avocation: reading. Home: Apartado Postal 549, 39300 Acapulco Mexico

JOHANNSSON, KJARTAN, politician; b. Reykjavik, Iceland, Dec. 19, 1939; s. Johann and Astrid Dahl Thorsteinsson; m. Irma Karlsdottir, 1964; 1 child. Student, Reykjavik Coll., Tech. U. Stockholm, U. Stockholm, Ill. Inst. Tech. Consulting engr. Reykjavik, 1966-78; tchr. Faculty Engring. & Sci., prof. Faculty Econs. & Bus. Adminstrn. U. Iceland, 1966-78, 80-89; chair Orgn. Support Elderly, Hafnarfjordur, Fisheries Bd. Mcpl. Trawler Co., Hafnarfjordur, 1970-74; mem. Mcpl. Coun., Hafnarfjordur, 1974-78; mem. party coun., exec. coun. Social Dem. Party, 1972-89, vice-chair, 1974-80, chair, 1980-84; mem. Icelandic Parliament, 1978-89, spkr. of lower house, 1988-90; min. fisheries Govt. Iceland, 1978-80, min. commerce, 1979-80; permanent rep. UN, Geneva, 1989-94; sec.-gen. European Free Trade Assn., Geneva, 1994—. Office: European Free Trade Assn, 9-11 rue de Varembé, 1211 Geneva 20, Switzerland Office: 74 Rue de Treves, 1040 Brussels Belgium*

JOHANSEN, HANS CHRISTIAN, economic historian, educator; b. Aarhus, Denmark, June 27, 1935; s. Vilhelm and Clara (Andersen) J.; m. Kirstine Madsen; children: Jens, Hanne. MA in Econ., U. Aarhus, 1963, PhD, 1968. Sr. lectr. U. Aarhus, Denmark, 1964-70; prof. U. Odense, Denmark, 1970—. Author books and articles on internat. econ. and social history. Mem. Danish Royal Acad. Sci., Norwegian Acad. Sci., Academia Europaea, Finnish Acad. Sci. Home: Anne Maries Alles 4a, DK-5250 Odense SV, Denmark Office: U Odense, Campusvej, DK-5230 Odense M, Denmark

JOHANSEN, LARS EMIL, Greenland government official. Former prime min. Govt. of Greenland, Nuuk, now v.p. Mem. Siumut. Office: Royal Greenland A/S, Aalisartut aggutaat 47, DK-3900 Nuuk Greenland

JOHANSEN, ROBERTO MIGUEL, entomologist, researcher; b. Chihuahua, Mexico, Sept. 19, 1944; s. Arthur Michael Johansen and Maria Consuelo Naime. B in Biology, U. Nat. Autonoma Mexico, 1972, MSc, 1974, DSc, 1977. Lectr. comparative histology U. Veracruzana, Jalapa Veracruz, Mexico, 1969-71; assoc. rschr. Inst. Biología, U. Nat. Autonoma Mexico, 1975-83, sr. rschr., 1984-99, head dept. zoology, 1985-87, head editl. unit, 1987-91; lectr. in insect morphology U. Nat. Autonoma Mexico, 1982-84; entomology cons. Consejo Nacional Consultivo Fitosanitario Mexico, 1996-99; lectr. Colegio Postgraduados Montecillo, Texcoco, Mex., 1998-99. Contbr. over 100 articles to profl. jours. Named Nat. rschr. Sistema Nacional de Investigadores, Mexico, 1983. Fellow Soc. Mexicana de Entomología (pres. 1999—), Entomol. Soc. Am. (bd. cert.), Academia Mexicana de Ciencias, Real Soc. Española Historia Natural. Avocations: music, photography. Fax: 550-01-64. Office: Inst Biol UNAM Dept Zool, AP 70-153, 04510 Mexico City Mexico

JOHANSEN, SHARON FRANCES, tourism company executive; b. Paeoroa, Thames, New Zealand, Aug. 14, 1946; d. Anthony Sperry and Molly Kerswell (Bond) Leonard; divorced; children: Damian Russell, Karsha. Sch. cert., Hauraki Plains Coll., New Zealand, 1964. Cert. Kiwi host and superhost; std. first aid cert. Order of St. John. Bank clk. ANZ Bank Ltd., New Zealand, 1964-70, agy. mgr., 1970-76; co-founder, co. dir. Coromandel Holiday Resort Ltd., New Zealand, 1976-94; owner, co. dir. Johansen Guiding Adventures Ltd., 1994—; co-founder, co. dir. Wincorp-Corp. Team Learning, 1996—; mem. exec. bd. Tourism Coromandel. Author: Fodors Travel Guide, 1996-97. Named Waikato Bus. Person of Yr., Waikato Bus. Assn., 1992; recipient Inaugural Eco-Tourism award for high achievement in conservation and pub. edn., 1990, New Zealand Trade and Devel. Commendation award for valuable contbn. to tourism, 1991. Mem. Pacific Asian Travel Assn., New Zealand Tourism Fedn., New Zealand Tourism Industry Assn., Pauanui Recreation and Sports Club, Zonta. Avocation: traveling internationally, nature, music, movies, reading. E-mail: adventures@coronandel.net.nz. Home: Settlement Rd, 2850 Pauanui Beach New Zealand Office: Johansen Guiding Adventures, 430 Settlement Rd Box 76, Pauanui Beach 2850, New Zealand

JOHANSEN, TOR FREDRIK, finance company executive; b. Barum, Norway, May 10, 1946; s. Nicolai B. and Anne-Marie (Larsen) J.; m. Ida Helliesen, Aug. 29, 1970; children: Helle, Håkon. MBA, Norwegian Sch. Bus. Adminstrn., Bergen, 1970. Rsch. asst. Norwegian Sch. Bus. Adminstrn., 1970-73; fin. sec./cons. Norsk Hydro, Oslo, 1973-77; various positions Eksportfinans, Oslo, 1977-80, head fin., 1980-87, exec. v.p., 1987-91, pres., CEO, 1991—; chmn. Kommunekreditt Norge As, 1999—; mem. econ. policy coun., Assn. Norwegian Banks, Oslo, 1994—; chmn. Norwegian Registry of Securities, Oslo, 1993-99; mem. Norwegian Export Coun., 1992-96; dep. bd. mem. Nordic Environment Fin. Corp., 1990-96. Avocations: cross-country skiing, windsurfing, mountain hiking. Office: Eksportfinans ASA, Dronning Maudsugt 15, 0119 Oslo Norway

JOHANSEN, TRULS ERIK BJERKLUND, urologist, surgeon; b. Larvik, Vestfold, Norway, Feb. 9, 1951; s. Konrad August and Gerd Bye (Karlsen) J.; m. Inger Corneliuseen, July 23, 1976; children Marie Cathrine, Astrid Helene, Ingrid Kristine, Liv Inger. MD, U. Oslo, 1976, PhD, 1988. Chief surgeon Sandefjord (Norway) Hosp., 1984-85; chief urologist Akershus Ctrl. Hosp., Oslo, 1986-88; chief urologist and chief gen. surgeon Telemark Ctrl. Hosp., Porsgrunn, Norway, 1988—; head Norwegian Inst. Urology, TromsÖ, Norway, 1991—; prof. urology U. TromsÖ, 1995—; founder, head author nat. Integrated Svcs. Digital Network network for rsch., edn. and quality assurance in a med. specialty. Inventor: The urethraring for catherization of ruptured male urethra; contbr. articles to profl. jours. Lt. Norwegian Air Force, 1982-83. Recipient CR Bard Urology award Norwegian Urolog. Assn., Oslo, 1986; Best Paper prize Scandinavian Assn. Urology, Finland, 1991, Qualty prize Norwegian Med. Assn., Oslo, 1996; several other awards. Mem. Norwegian Surg. Assn. (bd. dirs. 1993-99, v.p. 2000—), Scandinavian Assn. Andrology (dep. bd. mem. 1991—, Alexander Malthes award of honor 1990), European Assn. of Urology (award 1992, 97).

JOHANSON, GREGORY JOHN, psychotherapy trainer, minister; b. Portland, Ore., Jan. 29, 1947; s. Knut Harry and Liv Angel (Einarsen) J.; m. Cherith Hope Hansen, May 20, 1967; 1 child, Leif Nathan. BA in Psychology and Philosophy, Willamette U., 1969; MDiv Pastoral Care, Emory U., 1972; postgrad., Pacific U. Grad. Sch., 1979-82; MPhil, Drew Grad. Sch., 1994, PhD, 1997. Lic. profl. counselor N.J. Pastor United Meth. Chs., Oreg. and N.J., 1969—; pvt. practice as pastoral psychotherapist Oreg. and N.J., 1979—; dir. counseling svcs., chaplain Plz. Santa Maria Hosp., Baja, Calif., 1980-81; lectr. in psychology Western State Chiropractic Coll., Portland, Oreg., 1981-82; lectr. Nat. Coll. Naturopathic Medicine, Portland, 1981-82, Mt. Hood Cmty. Coll., 1981-82; contract therapist Luth. Family Svcs., Klamath Falls, Oreg., 1982-87; psychotherapy trainer, founding trainer Hakomi Inst., Boulder, Colo., 1982—, also bd. dirs.; clin. assoc. prof. marriage and family therapy Ctrl. Conn. State U., New Britain, Conn., 1998—; editor Hakomi Forum, Hakomi Inst., Boulder, 1982—; faculty tutor PhD students Union Grad. Sch., Yellow Springs, Ohio, 1989—; book rev. editor pastoral care sect. Pulpit Digest, San Francisco, 1986-91; guest lectr. Western Oreg. State Coll. Psychology Hons. Program, Monmouth, Oreg., 1980, Drew U. DMin Program, Madison, N.J., summer 1996, Columbia Coll. Master's Program, Chgo., 1993, Australian Sch. of Applied Psychology, Sydney, Australia, 1996. Author: Grace Unfolding, 1991, Sanfte Stärke: Heilung im Geiste des Tao te King, 1993, Revelacion de la Gracia: Psicoterapia en el Espiritu de el Tao-te King, 1994; editor: Feed My Sheep, 1984, Pastoral Care Issues In the Pulpit, 1984; co-editor The Jour. of Self-Leadership; mem. editl. bd. The Jour. of Pastoral Care, 2000—; contbr. numerous articles to books and periodicals. Ordained elder United Meth. Ch., 1974. Lelia S. Bortzmeyer scholar Willamette U., 1966, Dean's award scholar Emory U., 1970, Shirley Sugerman scholar Drew Grad. Sch., 1987; postdoctoral fellowship Princeton U., 1999—. Mem. Assn. for Clin. Pastoral Edn., Clin. Theology Assn. (profl., Eng.), Am. Assn. of Pastoral Counselors, Soc. for Pastoral Theology, Internat. Pastoral Care Network for Social Responsibility, Assn. for Transpersonal Psychology, Am. Acad. Religion, U.S. Assn. for Body Psychotherapy, Forge Inst. for Spirituality and Social Change, Integral Inst. of Spirituality. Republican. United Methodist. Avocations: stained glass work, sailing, wood construction, cabinet making, sports. Home and Office: PO Box 625 Branchville NJ 07826-0625

JOHANSSON, ALF GUNNAR, civil engineer, educator; b. Lidköping, Sweden, Sept. 13, 1939; s. Karl Henning and Sigrid Emelia (Carlsson) J.; m. Britt Lisbeth Mattiasson, 1967 (div. 1991); children: Mikael, Mattias. MSc, Chalmers U. Tech., Göteborg, Sweden, 1965. Surveying engr. Nils P. Lundh AB, Västerås, Sweden, 1966-67; hwy. engr. Swedish Nat. Rd. Adminstrn., Göteborg, 1967-74; supt. engr. Hwy. Dept., Mölndal, Sweden, 1974-80; rsch. and devel. dir. Göteborgs Förorter, Göteborg, 1980-84; lectr. Polhemsgymnasiet, Göteborg, 1981-92; head of dept. Chalmers U. Tech., 1989-98; cons. AJ-Konsult, Partille, Sweden, 1984-95. Author: Light Public Works Engineering, 1984, The Engineer in the Process of Public Works Engineering, 1989, Road Quality Definition and Monitoring in Maintenance Procurement, 1997, Internal Clients, Contractors and Inspection: Six Swedish Municipalities, 1999. Capt. Swedish Army, 1961-94. Mem. Internat. Shooting Union (judge 1992—). Home: Enetångsvägen 2, S-43376 Partille Sweden Office: Applied Bldg Civil Engring, Chalmers U Tech Box 8873, S-40272 Göteborg Sweden

JOHANSSON, ALLAN ÅKE, chemistry educator; b. Helsinki, Dec. 19, 1941; s. Ulrica Christina Zilliacus, Feb. 25, 1967; children: Karatina, Sofie. DiplEng, Helsinki U. Tech., 1966, TeknLic, 1969, DrTech, 1973. Lectr. Helsinki U. Tech., 1967-69; scholar Cambridge (Eng.) U., 1969-70; asst. prof. Åbo (Finland) Akademi, 1970-73; sr. cons. Linotek Cons. Engring., Helsinki, 1973-78; group leader Battelle Geneva Rsch. Ctr., 1978-83; rsch. prof. VTT Chem. Tech., Finland, 1983—; dir. VTT Non-Waste Rsch., Helsinki, 1986-96; vis. prof. Lund (Sweden) U., 1996—; mem. sci. com. European Environ. Agy., Copenhagen, 1996—. Author: Technology Beyond Our Means?, 1996, Clean Technology, 1992; editor: Technology and the Environment: Facing the Future, 1989; contbr. more than 100 articles to profl.jours.; holder more than 20 patents. Decorated knight 1st class Order of Finnish Lion. Mem. Finnish Acad. Tech. Scis., Swedish Acad. Tech. Scis. in Finland. Avocations: sailing, karate, olive cultivation, oil painting. Office: VTT Chem Tech, Biologinkuja 7, 02044 VTT Finland

JOHANSSON, GUNN N.M., psychology educator; b. Stockholm, Sweden, July 11, 1941; d. August and Louisa (Boj) J.; m. Kjell I. Johansson, Oct. 2, 1965 (dec. Dec. 1994). MA, Stockholm U., 1964, degree in philosophy, 1970, PhD in Psychology, 1973. Rsch. asst. Stockholm U., 1965-73, project coord., 1973-79, rsch. assoc., 1978-84; rsch. sec. Bank of Sweden Tercentenary Found., Stockholm, 1975-78; rsch. fellow Swedish Coun. for Rsch. in the Humanities and Social Scis., Stockholm, 1985-89; prof. work psychology Stockholm U., 1989—; prof. work psychology Swedish Office Labour Market Policy Evaluation, Uppsala, also bd. dirs.; bd. dirs. Natur & Kultur Publ. Co., Stockholm; chair ethics com. Swedish Coun. for Rsch. in the Humanities and Social Scis., Stockholm, 1990-95. Editor: (with B. Gardell) Working Life: A Social Science Contribution to Work Reform, 1981, (with J.V. Johnson) The Psychosocial Work Environment, Work Organization, Democratization, and Health, 1991. Mem. Royal Swedish Acad. Engring., Royal Swedish Acad. Letters, History and Antiquities. Office: Stockholm U, Dept Psychology, S-10691 Stockholm Sweden

JOHANSSON, LEIF VALDEMAR, automotive company executive, mechanical engineer; b. Gothenburg, Sweden, Aug. 30, 1951; s. Lennart and Inger Johansson; m. Eva Birgitta Fjellman; children: Andreas, Emelie, Marcus, Charlotte, Louise. M Sci. and Engring., Chalmers U. Tech., Gothenburg, 1977. R & D mgr. Centro Morgardshammar, Sweden, 1977; pres. Husqvarna Motorcyklar, Sweden, 1979, Facit, Atvidaberg, Sweden, 1982; major appliances divsn. mgr. Electrolux Group, Stockholm, 1983, exec. v.p., 1988, pres., 1991, CEO, 1994; pres., CEO AB Volvo, Gothenburg, Sweden, 1997—; bd. dirs. Fedn. Swedish Industries. Mem. Royal Swedish Acad. Engring. Scis. Office: AB Volvo, SE-405 08, Göteborg Sweden

JOHANSSON, LENNART VALDEMAR, Swedish industrialist; b. Gothenburg, Oct. 3, 1921; s. Waldemar and Alma (Nordh) J.; m. Inger Hedberg, 1944; 3 children. AB, SKF, 1943; DTech (hon.), Chalmers U., 1979, Sarajevo U., 1983. Mng. of mfg., 1961, gen. mgr., 1966, dep. mng. dir., 1969, pres., group CEO, 1971-95, chair, 1985-92, hon. chair, 1992—. Recipient King of Sweden's medal, Finnish Order of the Lion John Ericsson medal, 1986. Avocations: sailing, swimming. Home: AB SKF, SE-41550 Göteborg Sweden*

JOHANSSON, ROLF NILS, physician, educator; b. Osby, Sweden, Aug. 17, 1953; s. Arvid Ingemar and Birgit Elisabet Johansson; m. Boel Margareta Ahnberg, 1987; children: Helena, Hillevi, Vibeke. MSc, Lund (Sweden) Inst. Tech., 1977, PhD, 1983; BMed, Lund U., 1980, MD, 1986. Tchhg. asst. automata theory Lund Inst. Tech., 1976-80; tchg. asst. control theory Lund U., 1979-83, tchg. asst. math. stats., 1979-80; rsch. assoc. CNRS Laboratoire d'Automatique, Grenoble, France, 1985-86; docent Uppsala (Sweden) U., 1985; asst. prof. Lund Inst. Tech., 1983-85, assoc. prof., 1986—, prof. control sci., 1999—; coord. dir. program in robotics Lund Inst. Tech., 1993—. Author: System Modeling and Identification, 1993. Recipient Innovation Cup award, 1988, Ebeling prize Swedish Soc. Medicine, 1995. Avocations: private aviation, forestry, language study. Office: Lund Inst Tech, Dept Automatic Control, S22100 Lund Sweden

JOHARI, MUHAMMAD FERHAD BIN, lawyer, educator; b. Singapore, Mar. 26, 1967; s. Johari Bin Kassim and Sharifah Rukiah Binte Syed-Sagaff. B of Law, Staffordshire (Eng.) U., 1992; postgrad. diploma in Singapore law, Nat. U., Singapore, 1997. Bar: Supreme Ct. of the Republic of Singapore, 1988. Atty. Edwin Chan & Co., Singapore, 1998—. Corporal Singapore Armed Forces, 1986-88. Named Hon. col. The Confederate Air Force, 1999. Mem. Singapore Judo Fedn. (asst. sec. gen. 1996—), Singapore Judo Club (sec.-gen.). Avocations: Judo, bodybuilding, writing, poetry, English literature, philosophy. Office: 111 N Bridge Rd, #14-01 Peninsula Plz, Singapore 179098, Singapore

JOHN, SIR DAVID GLYNDWR, industrial gases company executive; b. July 20, 1938; s. William Glyndwr and Marjorie (Gaze) J.; m. Gillian Edwards, 1964; 2 children. BA, Christ's Coll., 1962; MA, Cambridge U., Eng., 1966; MBA, Columbia U., N.Y.C., 1966; grad. Internat. Sr. Mgmt. Program, Harvard U., 1984. With United Steel Co., 1962-64, Rio Tinto Zinc Corp., 1966-73, Redland plc, 1973-81, Inchcape, 1981-95; chmn. BOC Group, 1996—, Premier Oil, Plc., 1998—; devel. dir. then CEO Gray Mackenzie & Co., Middle East, 1981-87; CEO Inchcape Bhd, Singapore, 1987-90, chmn. 1990-95, Inchcape Middle East, 1991-94, Inchcape Toyota, 1994-95; non-exec. dir. St. Paul Co., 1996—, Balfour Beatty TLC, 2000—. with Brit. Army, 1957-59. Avocations: sailing, gardening, reading. Office: BOC Group PLC, Chertsey Rd Windlesham, Surrey GU20 6HJ, England

JOHN, ELTON HERCULES (REGINALD KENNETH DWIGHT), musician; b. Pinner, Middlesex, Eng., Mar. 25, 1947; s. Stanley and Sheila Eileen (Farebrother) Dwight. Student, Royal Acad. Music, London, 1959-64. Singer, songwriter, musician; began playing piano, 1951; joined group Bluesology, 1965; appeared in movie Tommy, 1975; toured America 10 times 1970-76; composer, performer: Empty Sky, 1969, Elton John, 1970, Tumbleweed Connection, 1971, 11.17.70, 1971, Friends, 1971, Madman Across The Water, 1971, Honky Chateau, 1972, Don't Shoot Me I'm Only The Piano Player, 1973, Goodbye Yellow Brick Road, 1973, Caribou, 1974, Greatest Hits, 1974, Empty Sky, 1975, Captain Fantastic and the Brown Dirt Cowboy, 1975, Rock of the Westies, 1975, Here and There, 1976, Blue Moves, 1976, Greatest Hits Vol. II, 1977, A Single Man, 1978, Victim of Love, 1979, 21 at 33, 1980, Jump Up, 1982, Too Low For Zero, 1983, The Fox, 1983, Breaking Hearts, 1984, Ice on Fire, 1985, Leather Jackets, 1986, Your Songs, 1986, Live in Australia, 1987, Reg Strikes Back, 1988, Sleeping with the Past, 1989, The Thom Bell Sessions, 1989, To Be Continued, 1990, The One, 1992, Duets, 1993, Made in England, 1995, The Big Picture, 1997, Elton John & Tim Rice's AIDA (toured with Billy Joel), 1998-99, The Road to El Dorado, 2000; composer, performer singles: Lady Samantha, 1969, From Denver to L.A., 1970, Take Me to the Pilot/Your Song, 1970, Border Song, 1970, Friends, 1971, Levon, 1971, Tiny Dancer, 1972, Rocket Man, 1972, Honky Cat, 1972, Crocodile Rock, 1972, Daniel, 1973, Saturday Night's Alright for Fightin', 1973, Goodbye Yellow Brick Road, 1973, Step into Xmas, 1973, Bennie and the Jets, 1974, Don't Let the Sun Go Down on Me, 1974, The Bitch Is Back, 1974, Lucy in the Sky with Diamonds, 1974, Philadelphia Freedom, 1975, Someone Saved My Life Tonight, 1975, Island Girl, 1975, I Feel like a Bullet (In the Gun of Robert Ford), 1976, Don't Go Breaking My Heart, 1976, Sorry Seems to Be the Hardest Word, 1976, Bite Your Lip (Get Up and Dance), 1977, Ego, 1978, Song for Guy, 1979, Mama Can't Buy You Love, 1979, Victim of Love, 1979, Part-Time Love, 1979, Johnny B Goode, 1979, Little Jeannie, Song for Guy, 1978, Are You Ready for Love, 1979, Little Jeannie/Conquer the Sun, 1980, Don't Ya Wanna Play This Game No More?, 1980, Chloe, 1981, Empty Garden (Hey Hey Johnny), 1982, Blue Eyes, 1982, I'm Still Standing, 1983, Kiss the Bride, 1983, I Guess That's Why They Call It the Blues, 1983, Sad Songs (Say So Much), 1984, Who Wears These Shoes, 1984, Wrap Her Up, 1986, Nikita, 1986, Heartache All Over the World, 1986, Candle in the Wind, 1987, I Don't Wanna Go on with You Like That, 1988, Town of Plenty, 1988, Candle in the Wind (live), 1988, A Word in Spanish, 1988, Healing Hands, 1989, Sacrifice, 1990, You Gotta Love Someone, 1991, Easier to Walk Away, 1991, Don't Let the Sun Go Down on Me, 1991, The One, 1992, Believe, 1995, Made in England, 1995; composer music (film) The Lion King, 1994 (Best Original Song Acad. award for "Can You Feel the Love Tonight?"); albums include Love Songs, 1996. Chmn. Watford Football Club, 1976-90, pres. Watford Football Club, 1990—; established Elton John Aids Found., 1993. Recipient Gold Discs for all albums composed; played to over 2 million people across 4 continents, 1984, 86; first popular Western singer to perform in USSR, 1979; Best British Male Artist Brits award, 1991; Grammy award, 1981, Grammy Legend award, 2000; inducted into Rock & Roll Hall of Fame, 1994. Address: Twentyfirst Artists Ltd, 1 Blythe Rd, London W14 OH9, England Mailing: Ste 370 8900 Wilshire Blvd Beverly Hills CA 90211*

JOHN, GEORGE, psychiatrist, consultant; b. Mavelikara, Kerala, India, Aug. 14, 1947; arrived in Eng., 1974; s. Philipose and Saramma (George) J.; m. Anna Varkey, May 21, 1973; children: Kieran George, Philip George. MB, BS, Kasturba Med. Coll., Mangalore, India, 1973. Registrar Nottingham (Eng.) Rotational Tng., 1974-77; sr. registrar St. Thomas Hosp., London, 1977-80; cons. psychiatrist Thames Gateway NHS Trust, Dartford, Eng., 1980—; med. dir. Godden Green Clinic, Sevenoaks, Eng., 1989—; hon. rsch. fellow Inst. Psychiatry de Crispingy Park, London; clin. tutor Hayes Grove Priory Hosp., Bromley, Eng., 1983-87. Author: Pharmakokinetics of Phenothiazines, 1984. Recipient Freedom of City of London award Lord Mayor's Office, Guildhall, London, 1997; named yeoman Worshipful Soc. Apothecaries, London, 1998. Fellow Linnean Soc.; mem. Royal Coll. Psychiatrists, Athenaeum Pall Mall, London Golf Club (premier mem.). Mem. Indian-Syrian Orthodox Ch. Avocations: golf, poetry, Shakespeare. E-mail: docgjohn@aol.com. Home: Mangalam St George's Rd, Bickley Kent BR1 2LD, England Office: Godden Green Clinic, Kent Sevenoaks BR1 2LD, England

JOHN, GERALD WARREN, hospital pharmacist, educator; b. Salem, Ohio, Feb. 16, 1947; s. Harold Elba and Ruth Springer (Pike) J.; m. Jean Ann Marie Orris, Nov. 5, 1977; children: Patrick Warren, Jeanette Lynn. BS in Pharmacy, Ohio No. U., 1970; MS, U. Md., 1974. Registered pharmacist, Ohio, S.C. Staff pharmacist North Columbiana County Cmty. Hosp., Salem, 1970-72; asst. resident in hosp. pharmacy U. Md. Hosp., Balt., 1972-73, sr. resident, 1973-74, chmn. patient care pharmacies, 1974-76; dir. pharmacy Ohio Valley Hosp., Steubenville, 1976-97; exec. dir. Tri-State Health Svcs., Inc., 1997—; mem. adv. bd. Contemporary Pharmacy Practice, 1977-83; preceptor profl. externship program Ohio No. U. Sch. Pharmacy, 1977—; adj. clin. instr. practical experience program Duquesne U. Sch. Pharmacy, 1976—; adj. clin. instr. Ohio State U. Sch. Pharmacy, 1988-99; dir. of pharmacy Trinity Med. Ctr., Steubenville, 1997—. Columnist Weirton Daily Times, 1990-94. Trustee, v.p. Valley Hospice Inc., 1985-98, 2000—. Named Hosp. Pharmacist of Yr., Md. Soc. Hosp. Pharmacists, 1976, Outstanding Young Man of Am., U.S. Jaycees, 1977. Fellow Am. Soc. Con. Pharmacists; mem. Am. Soc. Hosp. Pharmacists, Ohio Soc. Hosp. Pharmacists, Jefferson County Acad. Pharmacy, Southeastern Ohio Soc. Hosp. Pharmacists (pres. 1985-87), Rho Chi, Phi Eta Sigma. Methodist.

JOHN, GERHARD ROBERT DUTT, oil company executive; b. London, Aug. 5, 1946; s. Paresh and Johanna Gertrud (John) Dutt. BSc Econs./Internat. Rels. with honors, Univ. Coll., London, 1970; MA in Internat. Rels. with distinction, U. So. Calif., 1980; postgrad., King's Coll., London, 1982-83; MSc in Econs. and Indsl. Rels., London Sch. of Econ., 1985; diploma, Inst. Pers. Mgmt., 1985, membership diploma, 1986. Acctg. asst. Texaco Ltd., London, 1970-71, mktg. asst., 1971-74, personnel asst., 1974-78; cons. DSA, London, 1979-84; recruitment coord. Jawaby Oil, London, 1986-92, head personnel & recruitment, 1992—. Contbr. articles to profl. jours. and newspapers. Mem. Chartered Inst. Pers. Devel., Royal Overseas League. Avocations: mountain walking, photography. Home: 81 Grange Gardens, London N14 6QW, England also: Haus Theodul, 3921 Randa Switzerland Office: Jawaby Oil Svc, 15-17 Lodge Rd, London NW8 7JA, England

JOHN, GREGORY DAVID, management consultant; b. Newcastle, Australia, Aug. 23, 1943; s. Owen Henry and Joan Fyfe (Walkley) J.; m. Lynne Williams, Apr. 8, 1967; children: Carolyn, Andrew. Student, Harvard U., 1988. Asst. indsl. and pers. officer State Dockyard, Newcastle, Australia, 1961-66; with Assn. Profl. Engrs. Australia, 1966-75, sr. indsl. officer, 1975-76, dir. indsl. rels., 1977-81; gen. mgr. ops. Victorian Chamber of Mfrs., 1981-82; corp. gen. mgr. indsl. rels. Wormald Internat. (Australia) Pty. Ltd., 1982-84; assoc. dir. planning Australian Chamber of Mfrs., 1984-85, dir., 1985-87, dep. nat. chief exec., dir. NSW divsn., 1987-89; dir. indsl. rels. Victorian Employers' Fedn., 1989-91; dir. ops. Victorian Employers' C. of C. and Industry, 1991-92, dir. strategy and corp. relationships, 1995-97; dep. sec. employee rels. and employment Dept. Bus. and Employment of Victoria, 1992-94; gen. mgr. indsl. rels. Crown Casino Ltd., 1994-95; mng. dir. The Chessmen Group, Melbourne, Australia, 1997—; mgmt. rep. bus. and industry adv. com. Orgn. Econ. Cooperation and Devel., Paris, 1990; Australian del. Internat. Labour Orgn., Geneva, Switzerland, 1992. Contbr. articles to profl. jours. Chmn. Kingswood Coll., Melbourne, 1989-92. Mem. The Athenaeum Club, Pacific Inst. of Australia Inc., Rotary. Avocations: reading, international affairs, gardening, opera, music. Office: The Chessmen Group, 55 Collins St Level 43, Melbourne 3000, Australia

JOHN, NANCY R., librarian, writer; b. Bklyn., Feb. 1, 1948; d. Rex K. and Gwendolyn K. J.; m. Edward J. Valauskas, May 3, 1980. AB, Stanford U., 1969; MLS, UCLA, 1973. Cataloger Nat. Gallery Art, Washington, 1974-77; catalog libr. U. Ill. Chgo. Cir., 1978-79, asst. univ. libr., 1980—; internet advisor U.S. Mission to Internat. Orgns., Geneva, Switzerland, 1995-96; cons. U. Arts, Phila., 1991-93. Co-author: Internet Troubleshooter, 1994; co-editor: Internet Initiative, 1995; editor: (by K.G. Saur) Libri, 1995—. Recipient Esther J. Piercy award ALA, 1982. Mem. ALA, Internat. Fedn. Libr. Assn. and Instns. (profl. bd. 1989-93, 2d v.p. 1997-99, 1st v.p. 1999-2001), Assn. for Libr. Collections and Tech. Svcs. (pres. 1989-90). Avocation: golf, needlework. Fax: 312/413-0424. E-mail: nrj@uic.edu. Home: 5050 S Lake Shr Apt 3214 Chicago IL 60615-6601 Office: UIC Univ Libr PO Box 8198 Chicago IL 60680-8198

JOHN, RICHARD, chemistry educator; b. Wollongong, NSW, Australia, Dec. 29, 1965; s. David Llewellen and Kathleen (Cooney) J.; m. Melinda Jane Spencer, Nov. 3, 1990; 1 child, David. BSc with honors, U. Wollongong, 1988, PhD in Chemistry, 1993. Sr. lectr. Keble Coll. Oxford (Eng.) U., 1992-94, Royal Soc. rsch. fellow, 1992-94, rsch. scholar U. Coll., 1992-95; rsch. fellow U. Wollongong, 1995-96; sr. lectr. chemistry Griffith U., Gold Coast, 1996—; bd. dirs. Centre for Chem. and Biol. Analysis, Gold Coast. Contbr. more than 30 articles to profl. jours. Fellow Royal Soc., 1992-94, Australian Rsch. Coun., 1995-96; recipient rsch. scholar award U. Coll., Oxford, 1992-95; grantee Royal Soc., Australian Rsch. Coun., numerous Australian indsl. cos. Mem. Royal Australian Chem. Inst. (treas. 1997—). Office: Griffith U, Parklands Dr Southport, Gold Coast QLD 4210, Australia

JOHN, SARAH, physicist; b. Trivandrum, India, Feb. 18, 1953; came to U.S., 1981; d. Walliaveetil John and Sarah (Thomas) J. BSc, Univ. Coll., Trivandrum, India, 1971, MSc, 1973; MS, Coll. William and Mary, 1984, PhD, 1986. Tchg. asst. Coll. William and Mary, Williamsburg, Va., 1981-86; staff scientist Sci. & Tech. Corp., Hampton, Va., 1988-91, Vigyan, Inc., Hampton, Va., 1991-92; vis. asst. prof. U. Mo., Columbia, 1994-97. Contbr. articles to profl. jours. Nat. Sci. Talent Search awardee, India, 1968. Mem. Am. Phys. Soc. Achievements include development of a novel computational technique for quantum dynamics as a stochastic process and formulating a geometric model for nuclear absorption from microscopic theory.

JOHNNERFELT, BENGT ÅKE, electrical engineer, administrator; b. Bjursad, Dalarna, Sweden, Apr. 13, 1951; s. Ingvar Rolf and Anna-Great (Lang) J. MS in Elec. Engring. Test engr. ASEA AB, Ludvika, Sweden, 1976-78, devel. engr., 1978-84; design mgr. ABB Switchgear, Ludvika, 1984-98; BU SA R&D mgr. ABB Baths, Ludvika, 1998—; Author in field. Mem. IEEE/SPDC (Standards medallion 1999), IECTK37 (sec. 1991). Avocations: golf, bridge, growing orchids, tropical discus fish. Home: Rasfallsgatan 18, 77141 Ludvika Sweden

JOHN PAUL, HIS HOLINESS POPE, II (KAROL JOZEF WOJTYLA), bishop of Rome; b. Wadowice, Poland, May 18, 1920; s. Karol and Emilia (Kaczorowska) W. Student, Jagiellonian U., Krakow, 1937-39, ThD, 1949; studied in underground sem., Krakow, 1942-46; D. ethics, Pontifical Angelicum U., Rome, 1948; Dr. (hon.), J. Guttenberg U., Mainz, Fed. Republic Germany, 1977. Ordained priest Roman Cath. Ch., 1946; pastor St. Florian's Parish, Krakow, 1948; student chaplain Jagiellonian U., 1949; prof. moral theology Krakow, 1953; prof. ethics, then chmn. dept. philosophy Cath. U. of Lublin, 1954-58, dir. ethics inst., 1956-58; aux. bishop of Krakow, 1958, archbishop of Krakow, 1964-78; great chancellor Pontifical Theol. Faculty, Krakow; created cardinal by Pope Paul VI, 1967; elected Pope, Oct. 16, 1978, installed, Oct. 22, 1978. Author of: books, poetry, plays, including The Goldsmith's Shop; Play Easter Vigil and Other Poems, 1979, Love and Responsibility, 1960, The Acting Person, 1969, Foundations of Renewal, 1972, Sign of Contradiction, 1976; encyclicals: The Redeemer of Man, 1979, On Human Work, 1981, The Apostles of the Slavs, 1985, The Lord, the Giver of Life, 1986, Redemptoris Mater, 1987, Sollicitudo Rei Socialis, 1987, Dives in Misericordia, 1989, Crossing the Threshold of Hope, 1994; contbr. articles on philosophy, ethics and theology to various jours. Mem. Polish Acad. Scis. Address: Palazzo Apostolico, Vatican City 00120, Vatican City

JOHN PETER, GIBBONS, linguistics educator, linguist; b. Hatfield, Eng., Jan. 21, 1946; arrived in Australia, 1983; s. Harry John and Ada Alice (Moretti) G. BA with hons., U. Exeter (Eng.), 1968; MA, U. Lancaster (Eng.), 1974; PhD, U. Reading (Eng.), 1983. Cert. edn., U. London, 1969. Tchr. Briam Inst., Madrid, 1966-67, Jamhuri H.S., Nairobi, Kenya, 1969-71, Haringey Lang. Resource Ctr., London, 1972-73; lectr. U. Hong Kong, 1975-83; lectr., sr. lectr. U. Sydney, 1983—; cons. in English lang. Internat. Devel. Program, Canberra, Australia, 1986-93; chair expert English panel Coun. on Overseas Profl. Qualifications, Canberra, 1986-87, regional adv. com. Nat. Accreditation Authority for Translators and Interpreters, Sydney, 1991-93. Author: Code-Mixing and Code Choice: A Hong Kong Case Study, 1991; editor: Language and the Law, 1994; co-editor: Learning, Keeping and Using Language, 1991; contbr. articles to profl. jours. Mem. Applied Linguistics Assn. Australia, Brit. Assn. Applied Linguistics, Internat. Assn. Forensic Linguists. Anglican. Avocations: blues music, bush walking, theatre. Office: U Sydney, Dept Linguistics, Sydney 2006, Australia

JOHNS, ALLAN THOMAS, electrical engineering educator; b. Exeter, Devon, Eng., Apr. 14, 1942; s. William George and Ivy Maud (Camble) J.; m. Marion Franklin; children: Louisa Anne, Victoria Helen. BSc with 1st class honors, U. Bath, Eng., 1966, PhD, 1971, DSc, 1982. Chartered engr. Asst. dist. engr. S.W. Elec. Bd., Bristol, Eng., 1966-69; rsch. fellow U. Bath, 1969-70, lectr., 1970-77, reader, 1977-85, prof. elec. engring., 1991—, dir. overseas devel., 1998—; prof. City U., London, 1985-91; non-exec. dir. EEM Consultancy Svcs. Ltd., Hong Kong; chmn., non-exec. dir. Intalec Ltd.; cons. Gen. Elec. Co., Stafford, Eng., Govt. Abu Dhabi, United Arab Emeritus, Ctrl. Electricity Generating Bd. and Nat. Grid Co., London, KEPCO Korea. Editor books Instn. Elec. Engrs.; editor Power Engring. Jour., 1986-99. Chmn. Sci. and Engring. Coun., Elec. Power Industries Com., Swindon, 1991—, Electricity Rsch. Co-Funding Scheme Com., Swindon, 1990—; vice-chmn. Greendown Sch., Swindon, 1991—. Rsch. grantee Sci. and Engring. Rsch. Coun., Eng., 1984—. Fellow Instn. Elec. Engrs., Royal Soc. Arts; mem. Swindon N Bowling Club (pres. 1989-98). Avocations: ice dancing, walking, singing, piano, bowling.

JOHNS, BEVERLEY ANNE HOLDEN, special education administrator; b. New Albany, Ind., Nov. 6, 1946; d. James Edward and Martha Edna (Scharf) Holden; m. Lonnie J. Johns, July 28, 1973. BS, Catherine Spalding Coll., 1968; MS, So. Ill. U., 1970; postgrad., Western Ill. U., 1973-74, 79-80, Western Ill. U., 82, U. Ill., 1984-85. Cert. adminstr., tchr. Ill. Demonstration tchr. So. Ill. U., Carbondale, 1970-72; instr. MacMurray Coll., Jacksonville, Ill., 1977-79, 90-93; intern Ill. State Bd. Edn., Springfield, 1981; program supr. Four Rivers Spl. Edn. Dist., Jacksonville, 1972—; chair Ill. Spl. Edn., 1982-85; conf. coord. Ill. Alliance, Champaign, 1982-94; lectr., cons. in field. Author: Report on Behavior Analysis in Education, 1972; (with V. Carr) Techniques for Managing Verbally and Physically Aggressive Students, 1995; (with V. Carr, and C. Hoots) Reduction of School Violence: Alternatives to Suspension, 1997; (with J. Keenan) Techniques for Managing a Safe School, 1997; editor: Position Papers of Ill. Council for Exceptional Children, 1981; contbr. articles to profl. jours. Bd. dirs. Jacksonville Area Assn. Retarded Citizens, v.p., 1993-94, sec. 1996-99; govt. rels. chair Internat. Coun. Exceptional Children, 1984-87; fed. liason Ill. Adminstrs. Spl. Edn., 1985-86. So. Ill. U. fellow, 1968; resolution honoring Beverly H. Johns Internat. Coun. for Exceptional Children Conv., 1982; recipient Recognition cert. Ill. Atty. Gen., 1985, Outstanding Leadership award Internat. Coun. Exceptional Children, 2000; named Jacksonville Woman of Yr., Bus. and Profl. Women, 1988, Unsung Hero Jacksonville Jour.-courier, 1993. Mem. ASCD, Assn. Retarded Citizens (com. 19825), Ill. Coun. for Children with Behavioral Disorders (founder, past pres., pres. Ill. divsn. for learning disabilities 1991-92, Presdl. award 1985), Ill. Alliance for Exceptional Children (v.p. 1982-94), Learning Disabilities Assn. (bd. dirs., pres. 2000—), Ill. Coun. Exceptional Children (past pres., chair govt. rels. com. 1982-95, 97-98, governing bd. 1984-95, Presdl. award 1983, Lifetime Achievement award 1989, First Lady 1993), Internat. Coun. for Children with Behavioral Disorders (pres. 1997), West Cen. Assn. for Citizens with Learning Disabilities (founder, com. chair 19975), Internat. Pioneer Press (editor CEC pioneer divsn., pres. internat. pioneers divsn.), Internat. Divsn. Learning Disabilities (exec. bd.), Delta Kappa Gamma (chpt. pres. 1988-90, state exec. bd. 19915), Phi Delta Kappa. Roman Catholic. Avocation: world travel. Home: PO Box 340 Jacksonville IL 62651-0340 Office: Four Rivers Spl Edn Dist 936 W Michigan Ave Jacksonville IL 62650-3113

JOHNS, DAVID PETER, hospital administrator, medical researcher; b. Iserlohn, Germany, Jan. 17, 1952; arrived in Australia, 1978; s. Peter Frederick and Christina Lilian (Reynolds) J.; m. Maureen Florence Snyman, Sept. 5, 1976; children: Daniel Peter, Andrew David; m. Marion Joy Little, June 1, 1993; children: Jarney, Lauren. Degree with Distinction in Applied Biology and Nutrition, Southbank Polytech., London, 1975; PhD, Monash U., Clayton, Australia, 1998. Cert. respiratory function scientist. Asst. sci. officer dept. nutrition Lab. of Govt. Chemist, London, 1969-74; med. physics technician lung function unit Brompton Heart & Chest Hosp., London, 1974-78; scientist-in-charge Austin Hosp., Melbourne, Australia, 1978-89; sr. scientist Alfred Hosp., Melbourne, 1989-93, head scientist physiol. svcs. dept. respiratory medicine, 1993—; dir. Lungcare Pty Ltd., Melbourne; cons. Stds. Australia, Melbourne, 1992-94; hon. sr. lectr. depts. physiology and medicine Monash U., Melbourne, 1993—; grant assessor Nat. Health and Med. Rsch. Coun., 1990-91, Australian Rsch. Coun., 1994-95, Nat. Health and Med. Rsch. Coun., 1999—; lectr. cmty. hosps., confs., orgns., univs. and symposiums. Author book; contbr. articles to profl. jours, chpts. to books. Recipient Trunoff award Royal Australian Engrs., Australian Army, 1981, sci. and tech. travel scholarship Whole Time Med. Specialists, Alfred Hosp., 1994. Mem. Australian and New Zealand Soc. Respiratory Sci. (found. editor 1982-89, bd. mem. 1980-89, 92-94, chmn. minimum stds. 1988-92, best rsch. presentation 1990), Inst. Biology, Thoracic Soc. Australia and New Zealand, Med. Scientist Assn. Victoria. Avocations: astronomy, reading, wind surfing. Home: 4 Hearthside Ct, Ringwood VIC 3134, Australia Office: Alfred Hosp Dept Resp Med, Commercial Rd, Prahran VIC 3181, Australia

JOHNS, MARGARET BUSH, neuroendocrinologist, researcher, educator; b. Boston, July 31, 1928; d. Ernest William Bush and Ellinor (Brennan) Gazik; m. D. Craig Johns, Jan. 15, 1953 (div. 1982); children: Katherine Adrian, Sara Elizabeth; m. H. Peter Stern, May 30, 1985. Student, George Washington U., 1945-47, NYU, 1951-53; BA, Hunter Coll., N.Y.C., 1971; PhD, Rutgers U., 1979. Postdoctoral NIH rsch. fellow Mt. Sinai Med. Sch., N.Y.C., 1978-81; instr. dept. biol. scis. Hunter Coll., N.Y.C., 1982-83; rsch. scientist NYU, N.Y.C., 1985; ind. rschr. in neuroendocrinology Mountainville, N.Y., 1985—; cons. Lederle Labs., 1984; reviewer NIH, NSF, 1982—. Contbr. articles to Nature, Endocrinology, Annals of N.Y. Acad. Sci. Vol. tutor non-English-speaking children N.Y. Pub. Sch. Sys., N.Y.C., 1964; vol. landscape coord. Neighbors United for Justice in Housing, Newburgh, N.Y., 1988—, vol. edn. cons. Harlem Valley Secure Ctr., Wingdale, N.Y., 1998—. Fellow The Endocrine Soc. Democrat. Achievements include the first to discover a function of the vomeronasal organ in mammalian physiology; first to discover specific and saturable in vitro uptake of serotonin in gonadotrophs in the anterior pituitary of rats and humans. Avocations: pastel painting, gardening, travel. Home: 192 6th Ave New York NY 10013-1228 Office: PO Box 330 Mountainville NY 10953-0330

JOHNS, MURRAY WILLIAM, sleep physician, consultant, researcher; b. Geelong, Victoria, Australia, Feb. 11, 1937; s. William Norman and Monica Thelma (Walsh) J.; m. Penelope Sue Roberts, Aug. 24, 1967; children: Diana Frances, Fleur Elizabeth. BSc, Melbourne U., 1958; MB BS, Monash U., Melbourne, 1966, PhD, 1973. Geologist Geol. Survey of Victoria, 1958-60; jr. resident med. officer Alfred Hosp., Melbourne, 1967-68, sr. resident med. officer, 1968-69, rsch. fellow in surgery, 1969-72; postdoctoral rsch. fellow UCLA, 1973; mem. sci. staff Environ. Physiology Unit Med. Rsch. Coun., London, 1974-76; pvt. practice Melbourne, 1977-87, cons., rschr. in sleep medicine, 1988—; dir. Epworth Sleep Ctr. Epworth Hosp., Melbourne, 1988—; mem. external adv. com. Sch. Biophys. Scis. and Elec. Engring. Swinburne U. Tech., Melbourne, 1995—; dir. Sleep Diagnostics Australia Pty. Ltd., Melbourne, 1996—; mem. adv. com. Grad. Sch. Integrative Med., Swinburne U. Tech., Melbourne, 1998—; adj. prof. Sch. Biophys. Scis. and Elec. Engring., Swinburne U. Tech., Melbourne, 1998—. Contbr. more than 60 articles to profl. jours. including Sleep, Brit. Med. Jour., Med. Jour. Australia, Archives of Internal Medicine, Jour. Applied Physiology, Chest, Electroencephalography and Clin. Neurophysiology, Ergonomics, among others. Recipient rsch. scholarship Nat. Health and Med. Rsch. Coun. Australia, 1969-71; rsch. fellow Edward Wilson Meml. Rsch. Found., Alfred Hosp., Melbourne, 1972-73. Mem. Australasian Sleep Assn., Am. Acad. Sleep Medicine, Royal Soc. Victoria. Avocations: maritime history of Australia, tennis, bookbinding. Home: 76 Hotham St, East Melbourne VIC 3002, Australia Office: Epworth Sleep Ctr, 187 Hoddle St, Richmond VIC 3121, Australia

JOHNS, TIMOTHY ROBERT, judge; b. Aberdeen, S.D., July 17, 1948; s. Frank Edward Johns and Helen Theresa Mock; m. LeAnn L. Thoresen, Nov. 25, 1978; children: Nicholas, Justin. BA, No. State U., 1970; JD, U. S.D., 1974. Dep. states atty. Butte County, S.D., 1974-75; atty. City of Nisland, S.D., 1974-75; pvt. practice Belle Fourche, S.D., 1974-75; magistrate State of S.D., Deadwood, 1975-89, cir. ct. judge, 1989—; mem. S.D. Jud. Qualifications Commn., 1997—. Mem., pres. Deadwood-Lead (S.D.) Jaycees, 1978-85; bd. dirs. Adv. Coun. Black Hills coun. Boy Scouts Am., Northern Hills Adjustment Tng. Ctr., Spearfish, S.D., Northern Hills YMCA of Lead, State Bd. S.D. Spl. Olympics. Recipient Keyman award Deadwood-Lead Jaycees, 1982-83; named Outstanding Young Man of Am. Mem. S.D. Judges Assn. (pres. 1995-96), KC, Kiwanis. Roman Catholic. Avocations: reading, hunting, fishing, boating. Home: 110 S Main St Lead SD 57754-1541 Office: 8th Jud Cir Ct PO Box 626 78 Sherman St Deadwood SD 57732-1341

JOHNS, VARNER JAY, JR., medical educator; b. Denver, Jan. 27, 1921; s. Varner Jay and Ruby Charlene (Morrison) J.; m. Dorothy Mae Hippach, Dec. 7, 1944; children—Marcia Johns Hinshaw, Donna Johns Bennett, Varner Jay III. B.S., La Sierra Coll., 1944; M.D., Coll. Med. Evangelists, 1945. Diplomate: Nat. Bd. Med. Examiners, Am. Bd. Internal Medicine, Am. Bd. Cardiovascular Disease. Intern White Meml. Hosp., Los Angeles, 1944-45; resident White Meml. Hosp., 1945-47; resident pathology Loma Linda (Calif.) U., 1947-48; head physician Los Angeles County Hosp., 1951; assoc. dean Sch. Medicine Loma Linda U., 1951-54, chmn. dept. medicine, 1956-69, 80-86, prof. medicine, 1957-86, prof. emeritus, 1986—; assoc. dean continuing edn. Sch. Medicine Loma Linda U. (Sch. Medicine), 1975-86; chief med. service White Meml. Hosp., Los Angeles, 1956-62, 78-80, hon. visitng physician, 1986—; chief med. service Loma Linda U. Hosp., 1964-69, 80-86, hon. visitng physician, 1986—; co-physician in chief Los Angeles County Hosp., 1958-64; cons. Office Surgeon Gen., Dept. Army, 1956-67; vis. colleague Inst. Cardiology, London, 1962-63; hon. vis. physician Nat. Heart Hosp., London, 1962-63; cons. Jerry L. Pettis Meml. VA Hosp., Loma Linda, 1978-86; bd. dirs. Am. Sound and Video Corp., 1986-91. Editorial bd.: Calif. Medicine, 1964-74; contbr. articles to profl. jours. Pres. bd. govs. Alumni Fedn. Loma Linda U., 1970-71; trustee Loma Linda U., 1952-54, Loma Linda Med. Ctr., 1984-86; bd. dirs. Audio/Digest Found., 1975-86, pres. 1986-91. Served to maj. M.C. AUS, 1954-56. Fellow A.C.P. (gov. So. Calif. region II 1972-76), Am. Coll. Cardiology; mem. Los Angeles Acad. Medicine (governing bd. 1965-68, 74-79, treas. 1977-78, v.p. 1978-79, pres. 1979-80), San Bernardino County Heart Assn. (dir. 1966-72), Am. Heart Assn. (fellow council clin. cardiology), Western Assn. Physicians, Royal Soc. Medicine, AMA (del. 1987-91), Calif. Med. Assn. (del. 1974-91), Los Angeles Soc. Internal Medicine (pres. 1961-62), Inland Soc. Internal Medicine (pres. 1988-89), Alpha Omega Alpha, San Bernardino County Med. Soc. (v.p. 1972-73, pres. 1974-75), Redlands Country Club (Calif. bd. dirs. 1995-98). Home: 11565 Hillcrest Ct Loma Linda CA 92354-3553

JOHNS, WARREN LEROI, lawyer; b. Nevada, Iowa, June 9, 1929; s. Varner Jay and Ruby Charlene (Morrison) J.; m. Elaine C. Magnuson, July 24, 1955 (div. June 1983); children: Richard Warren, Lynn Cherie Johns-Pence; m. Ruth Page Scott, Sept. 29, 1985. BA, La Sierra U., 1950; MA, Andrews U., 1951; JD, U. So. Calif., 1958. Bar: Calif. 1959, U.S. Dist. Ct.

(cen. dist.) Calif. 1959,U.S. Supreme Ct. 1963, Md. 1976, D.C. 1976, U.S. Dist. Ct. Md. 1976, U.S. Dist. Ct. D.C. 1976, U.S. Tax Ct. 1976, U.S. Ct. Appeals (4th cir.) 1976, U.S. Ct. Appeals (10th cir.) 1977, U.S. Ct. Customs and Patent Appeals 1979. Gen. counsel So. Calif. Conf. Seventh-day Adventists, Glendale, 1959-63, Pacific Union Conf. Seventh-day Adventists, Glendale and Sacramento, 1964-69; pvt. practice Sacramento, 1969-75; gen. counsel Gen. Conf. Seventh-day Adventists, Washington, 1975-92, trustee; pvt. practice Brookeville, Md., 1992-98; mem. adv. bd. Ctr. for Ch./State Studies, De Paul U. Coll. Chgo., 1987-93, spl. counsel to gen. conf., 1992-95; spl. counsel Adventist HealthCare Corp., Columbia Union HealthCare Corp., 1992-97. Author: Dateline Sunday USA, 1967, Ride to Glory, 1999; founding editor JD, 1978-92. Chmn. bd. dirs., pres. Sacramento Area Econ. Opportunity Coun., 1974. Recipient Frank Yost award Ch. State Coun., Glendale, Alumnus of Achievement award Andrews U., 1981, Alumnus of Yr. award La Sierra U., 1994. Mem. AAAS, ABA (vice-chmn. com. on torts, non-profit, charitable and religious orgns., sect. of tort and ins. practice 1990-91). Democrat. Avocations: sports, photography, book collecting. Office: 21320 Georgia Ave Brookeville MD 20833-1132

JOHNSEN, ANDERS HOLTEN, scientist, biochemist; b. Copenhagen, Denmark, July 3, 1950; s. Bent and Agnethe (Holten) J.; m. Susanne Ammendrup; children: Ina, Maja. MS, U. Copenhagen, 1978, PhD in Biochemistry, 1982, DSc, 1998. Rsch. fellow U. Copenhagen, Denmark, 1978-81; clin. chemist County Hosp., Naestved, Denmark, 1981-84, Finsen Institute, Copenhagen, 1984-86; scientist, biochemist Rigshospitalet, Copenhagen, 1986-92, sr. scientist, 1992-98, chief biochemist, 1998—. Contbr. over 90 articles to sci. jours. Mem. bd. dirs. & chmn. various youth instns., 1994—. Mem. N.Y. Acad. Scis., Assn. Biomolecular Resource Facilities, Danish Biological Soc., Danish Biochemical Soc. Office: Dept Clin Biochemistry-Rigshospitalet KB3011, Blegdamsvej 9, DK-2100 Copenhagen Denmark

JOHNSEN, ARVE, lawyer; b. Borre, Norway, Feb. 18, 1934; s. Arthur Johannes and Svanhild (Ekeberg) J.; m. Tove Elisabeth Nilssen, Sept. 17, 1960; children: Marianne Elisabeth, Ninia Margrethe, Eva Marie. BA in Bus. Adminstrn., Norges Handelshoyskole, Norway, 1957; MA in Econs., U. Kans., 1960; Law Degree, U. Oslo, 1960. Cert. atty. MNA. Sec. Norsk Hydro, Oslo, Norway, 1961-64, sales mgr., 1965-71; asst. judge State, Oslo, Norway, 1964-65; pres. Statoil, Stavanger, Norway, 1972-88; pvt. practice law Oslo, Norway, 1990—; chmn. Inst. for Energy, Norway, 1992, Hitec, Norway, 1994, The Oslo Philharm. Orch., Norway, 1997, Navis, Norway, 1997, NORFUND, Norway, 1997, A. Ugland & Sons, Norway, 1998. Dep. min. Bratteli Govt., Norway, 1971-72. 2nd lt. Norwegian Army, 1957-58. Recipient Disting. Svc. award Offshore No. Seas Found., Stavanger, 1990; named Oilman of the Yr., Stavanger Petroleum Explorer, 1988. Mem. Norwegia Assn. of Attys. (cert. attys.). Social Democrat. Fax: 47-22 55 70 04. Office: Drammensveien 78, 0271 Oslo Norway

JOHNSEN, SIGBJØRN, governor; b. Lillehammer, Oct. 1, 1950; m. Helle Laier; 3 children. Student, Norwegian Sch. Mgmt. Bank cashier, dir. studies, acct.; dep. rep. Nat. Assembly Hedmark, 1973-76, permanent mem., 1976-77, elected rep., 1977-97, mem. various coms., 1976-97; min. fin. Norway, 1990-96; gov. County Hedmark; vice chmn. Norwegian Labour League Youth, 1975-77; dep. chmn. Equal Status Coun., 1976-83; del. Coun. Europe's Parliamentary Assembly, 1985-89; mem. bd. Nat. Bank, 1999—. Office: Staten Hus, N-2306 Hamar Norway

JOHNSON, ADDIE COLLINS, secondary education educator, former dietitian; b. Evansville, Ind., Feb. 28; d. Stewart and Willa (Shamell) Collins; m. John Q. Johnson, Sept. 6, 1958 (dec. Aug. 1991); 1 child, Parker. BS, Howard U., 1956; MEd, Framingham State Coll., Mass., 1967. Registered dietitian, Mass. Dietitian Boston Lying-In Hosp., 1957-61; dietitian Diet Heart Study, Harvard U. Sch. Pub. Health, Boston, 1962-63; tchr. Foxboro (Mass.) Pub. Sch., 1967—; dietitian Sch. Medicine Boston U., 1975-77, Westinghouse Health Systems, Boston; faculty Dept. Nursing Boston State Coll., 1979-82; nutrition cons. Head Start program Westinghouse Sch., Boston, 1979-82; instr. dept. nursing U. Mass., 1981—, Bridgewater (Mass.) State Coll., 1982-97; mem. state adv. coun. Dept. Edn Bur. Nutrition Edn., 1981-83; participant NSF Project Seed, 1992; chmn. edn. com., bd. dirs. Consumer Credit Counseling Svcs. of Mass., Inc., 1996-99. Bd. dirs. Norfolk-Bristol County Home Health Assn., Walpole, Mass., 1975-78; presenter Nat. Social Studies Assn., Boston, 1984-85; instr./trainer health svcs. edn. ARC, 1987-90. Mem. AAUW, NAACP (life), Am. Dietetic Assn., Am. Home Econs. Assn., Ea. Mass. Home Econs. Assn. (bd. dirs. 1978), Mass. Tchrs. Assn. (higher edn. com. 1984-87), Soc. Nutrition Edn., Mass. State Dept. Edn. (adv. bd. 1995—), Consumer Credit Counseling Svc. (bd. chair edn. com. 1998-99), Delta Kappa Gamma (journalist Iota chpt. 1986-88, membership com. 1988-92, v.p. 1994, pres. Iota chpt. 1996-98), Delta Sigma Theta. Avocations: travelling, bicycling. Home: 92 Morse St Sharon MA 02067-2719 Office: Foxboro Pub Schs Mechanic St Foxboro MA 02035-2028

JOHNSON, ADRIAN, religious organization executive; b. Bucuresti, Ilfov, Romania, Aug. 6, 1935; arrived in Norway, 1982; s. Ioan and Alexandrina Adina (Dragusin) Turlea; m. Gabriela Somai, Oct. 9, 1976 (div. 1995); children: Johnson, Beatrice, Christina. B. Mktg. in Econy, A.J. Theol. Sem., 1955; MBA, Granton Inst., 1986. Mng. dir., owner Oslo, Norway, 1983—; pres. The Gospel's Message, Oslo, Norway, 1986—. Contbr. articles to profl. pubs. Mem. N.Y. Acad. Scis. Avocations: violin, skiing, bicycling. Home and office: Brochmannsgt 4, 0470 Oslo Norway

JOHNSON, ALAN ARTHUR, physicist, educator, consultant; b. Beckenham, Eng., Aug. 18, 1930; came to U.S., 1962; s. Frederick W. and Dorothy (Tew) S.; m. Elizabeth Ann Banks, June 22, 1958 (div. Dec. 1981); children: Stephen Graham, Michael Andrew, David Nicholas, Brian Philip, Susan Christine; m. Barbara Davidson Pinkerton, Mar. 11, 1990. B.Sc. with spl. honours in Physics, Reading (Eng.) U., 1952; M.A. in Physics, U. Toronto, 1954; Ph. D. in Metal Physics, U. London, Eng.; diplomate, Imperial Coll., London, 1960. Sci. officer Royal Naval Sci. Service, Eng., 1954-56; lectr. metallurgy Imperial Coll. Sci. and Tech., U. London, 1960-62; dir. rsch. Materials Rsch. Corp., Orangeburg, N.Y., 1963-65; prof. phys. metallurgy Bklyn. Poly. Inst., 1965-71, head dept. phys. and engring., metallurgy, 1967-71; prof. materials sci., chmn. dept. Wash. State U., 1971-75; dean Grad. Sch. U. Louisville, 1975-76, prof. materials sci., 1975—; cons. to govt. and industry, 1960—; pres. Metals Rsch., Inc., 1988—. Editor: Water Pollution in the Greater New York Area, 1971; editor in chief Internat. Jour. Ocean Engring., 1968-75; assoc. editor, 1975-88, editor emeritus, 1988—; contbr. over 115 articles to profl. jours. and conf. procs. Recipient Kentuckiana Metroversity award for innovative tchg., 1995, Disting. Citizen of Louisville, 1996, Cmty. Svc. award U. Louisville, 1998. Fellow AAAS, Inst. Materials, Inst. Physics, Am. Soc. for Metals (nat. nominating com. 1980-81, chmn. Louisville chpt. 1981-82, 89-90, 96-97, chmn. metals engring. inst. com. 1982-83); mem. Coun. Engring. Instns. (chartered engr.), Sigma Xi, Tau Beta Pi, Phi Kappa Phi. Office: U Louisville Ernst Hl Rm 311 Louisville KY 40292-0001

JOHNSON, ALBERT WESLEY, consultant on governance; b. Insinger, Sask., Can., Oct. 18, 1923; s. Thomas William and Louise Lillian (Croft) J.; m. Ruth Elinor Hardy, June 27, 1946; children: Andrew, Frances, Jane, Geoffrey. BA, U. Sask., 1942; MA, U. Toronto, Ont., Can., 1945; MPA (Littauer fellow), Harvard U., 1950, PhD (Littauer fellow), 1963; LLD (hon.), U. Regina, 1977, U. Sask., 1978, Mt. Allison U., 1982, Queen's U., 1992, Carleton U., 1999. Dep. provincial treas. Govt. of Sask., Regina, 1952-64; asst. dep. minister fin. Govt. of Can., Ottawa, Ont., 1964-68; econ. adviser to prime minister on constn. Govt. of Can., 1968-70, sec. treasury bd., 1970-73, dep. minister nat. welfare, 1973-75; pres. CBC, Ottawa, 1975-82; Skelton-Clark fellow Queens U., 1982-83; prof. polit. sci. U. Toronto, 1983-89, prof. emeritus, 1989—; sr. fellow Can. Centre for Mgmt. Devel., Ottawa, 1989-91; cons. on governance Internat. Monetary Fund, Indonesia, 1988, 91, S. Africa, 1992-99; chmn. task force on univ. programs, Sask., 1992-93; sr. fellow Massey Coll., 1999—. Contbr. articles to profl. pubs.; editorial bd.: Can. Public Policy, 1974-75. Bd. dirs. Nat. Film Bd., 1970-82, U. Sask. Hosp., 1957-64; mem. Nat. Arts Centre, 1975-82; bd. govs. U. Sask., Saskatoon, 1952-63. Recipient Gold medal Profl. Inst. of Pub. Svc. of Can., 1975; decorated Companion of the Order of Can., 1997. Mem. Ottawa Polit. Economy Assn. (pres. 1969-70), Inst. Public Adminstrn. Can. (pres. 1962-63, Vanier medal 1976, nat. council 1951-69), Can. Polit. Sci. Assn. (exec. council 1963-64). Mem. United Ch. of Can.

JOHNSON, ALBERTA CLARK, psychology educator; b. Chattanooga, Apr. 19, 1942; d. William Ross and Helen W. Clark; m. John Burlin Johnson, Mar. 12, 1965; children: Sonya K., Roxanne Johnson Dingman. BA, U. N.C., Greensboro, 1964; MS, U. Ariz., 1979, PhD, 1988. Cert. family life educator, Nat. Coun. Family Rels. Membership dir. Tucson Area Coun. Camp Fire, 1981-83; asst. dir. Ext. Winter Sch., Tucson, 1984-87; human devel. specialist U. Ariz. Coop. Ext. Svc., Tucson, 1983-87; assoc. faculty Pima C.C., Tucson, 1987-88; family life specialist U. Ariz. Coop. Ext. Svc., 1989-92, U. Ark. Coop. Ext. Svc., Little Rock, 1989-92; cons. Little Rock, 1992-93; asst. prof. psychology and edn. Floyd Coll., Rome, Ga., 1993-97, assoc. prof. psychology, 1997—. Contbr. articles to profl. jours. Sec., governing state bd. dirs. Parents Anonymous of Ariz., Phoenix, 1983-84; mem. Gov.'s Coun. on Children, Youth and Families, Phoenix, 1983-84; pres. bd. dirs. Pima County chpt. Parents Anonymous, Tucson, 1985-86; v.p. Women's Info. Network, Inc., Rome, 1997; bd. dirs. Ga. Breast Cancer Coalition, 2000—. Named Woman of Excellence, 1998, Women in Mgmt. and Greater Rome C. of C. Mem. AAUP, Nat. Coun. on Family Rels., Nat. Assn. for Edn. of Young Children, Coun. Tchrs. of Undergrad. Psychology, Ga. Assn. for Young Children, Psi Beta, Kappa Omicron Nu, Pi Lambda Theta. Avocations: photography, hiking, camping, reading. Office: Floyd Coll PO Box 1864 3175 Highway 27 N Rome GA 30162-1864

JOHNSON, ALEX CLAUDIUS, English language educator; b. Freetown, Sierra Leone, Aug. 14, 1943; came to U.S., 1991; s. Eunice Angela (Thorpe) J.; m. Daphne Marvel Taylor; children: Marvin, Joyemi. BA in English Lang. and Lit. with honors, U. Durham, Eng., 1968; MA in English and Am. Lit., U. Kent, Canterbury, Eng., 1971; MPhil in Linguistics, U. Leeds, Eng., 1974; PhD in English, U. Ibadan, Nigeria, 1982. Tchr. various h.s., Freetown, Sierra Leone, 1968-69, 71-72; sr. lectr., lectr. English dept. Fourah Bay Coll., Sierra Leone, 1974-88, sr. lectr., acting head classics/philosophy dept., 1987-88, assoc. prof., head English dept., 1988-91; prof. English lang. and Creole studies U. Bayreuth, Germany, 1982-84; vis. prof. S.C. State U., Orangeburg, 1991-92, prof., 1992; acting vice prin. Fourah Bay Coll., summer 1989, 90, dean faculty of arts, 1989-91; cons. UNESCO, 1985-89; external assessor U. Cape Coast, Ghana, 1988. Contbr. articles to internat. profl. jours., papers to internat. confs. and symposia. Chief examiner West Africa Examinations Coun., Accra, Ghana, 1978-91, Inst. Edn., U. Sierra Leone, 1980-91; chair Nat. Primary Curriculum Revision Com., 1981. Mem. SAMLA, South Ea. Renaissance Conf., Coll. Lang. Assn., African Lit. Assn., West African Linguistic Soc. (sec., organizer 13th West African Langs. Congress, Freetown, 1978), West African MLA (exec. com. 1981-82). Episcopalian. Home: 767 Windmill Way Orangeburg SC 29118-2838

JOHNSON, ANNE HALE, educational association administrator; b. Rochester, N.Y., Oct. 12, 1923; d. Ezra Andrews and Josephine (Booth) Hale; m. Arthur William Johnson, July 20, 1957; children: Joy Sanborn, Randall, Christiane Brooks (dec.). BA, Smith Coll., 1945; MA, Columbia U., 1952; MDiv, Union Theol. Sem., N.Y.C., 1956. Exec. dir. Rochester Assn. for the UN, 1946-49; asst. to dir. World Fedn. UN Assns./Internat. Student Movement for UN, Paris, 1950-51; exec. dir. Citizens for Ike, Rochester, 1951-52; midwest field rep. U.S. Com. for UNICEF, Chgo., 1953; dir. Christian edn. Swarthmore (Pa.) Presbyn. Ch., 1956-57; tchr. and coord. adult edn. issues Georgetown Presbyn. Ch., Washington, 1957-72, 85—; tchr. Old and New Testament courses Madeira Sch., McLean, Va., 1961-62; spkr. in fields of fgn. policy, religious activities, women's issues. Contbr. articles to newspapers. Mem. bd. Union Theol. Sem., 1990—, chair, 1996—; mem. bd. Madeira Sch., 1993-97, Faith and Politics Inst., Washington, 1992—, Presbyn. Women, Washington, 1992-96; v.p. bd. The Living Pulpit, Bronx, N.Y., 1991—; sec.-treas. Safe Travel Am., Potomac, Md., 1987—; founding bd. mem. Rep. Coalition for Choice, Washington, 1989—; mem. Montgomery County Rep. Ctr. Com., 1994—; mem. steering com. Covenant Network of Presbyns., 1998. Republican. Presbyterian. Home: 10600 Red Barn Ln Potomac MD 20854-1953

JOHNSON, ANTONIA AXSON, corporate executive; b. Sept. 6, 1943; d. Axel Axson and Antonia Johnson; m. P. Göran Ennerfelt; children: Alexandra Mörner, Caroline Mörner, Axel Mörner, Sophie Mörner. Student, Radcliffe Coll., 1963-64; MA in Psychology and Econs., U. Stockholm, 1971. With Nordstjernan AB, 1971-79; with Axel Johnson AB, Stockholm, 1979—, chmn., 1982—; chmn. bd. Axel Johnson Inc., Stamford, Conn., Hemkopskedjan AB, Sweden, City Mission of Stockholm; chmn. World Childhood Found.; bd. dirs. Axel Johnson Internat., Sweden, Nordstjernan AB; chmn. The Axel and Margaret Axson Johnson's Found., NCC Nordic Constrn. Co., Stockholm Environ. Inst.; mem. IVA-Royal Swedish Acad. of Engring. Scis., Xerox Corp. Named Profl. Woman of Yr., 1987, Fin. Woman of Yr., 1988; named # 1 of Am.'s Top 25 Women Bus. Owners, Nat. Found. for Women Bus. Owners and Working Woman, 1992, named # 4 of Am.'s Top 50 Women Bus. Owners, 1993. Office: Axel Johnson AB, Villagatan 6 PO Box 26008, S-100 41 Stockholm Sweden also: Axel Johnson Inc 300 Atlantic St Ste 701 Stamford CT 06901-3522

JOHNSON, ARLENE LYTLE, government agency official; b. Pitts., Jan. 20, 1937; d. Willis and Minnie Lee (Blackman) Neal; children: Robin Gerome Lytle, Cheryl Rose Lytle Campbell. Student, various profl. courses. Clk.-typist Pa. Dept. Revenue, Harrisburg, 1955; office sec. Akron (Ohio) Jewish Ctr., 1956-57; clk.-stenographer Pa. Employment Service, Pitts., 1960-61, Dept. Treasury, Washington, 1961; sec.-stenographer Dept. HEW, Washington, 1961-70; exec. sec. to dir. Bur. Cmty. Health Svcs., Health Svcs. Adminstrn., Dept. HEW, Rockville, Md., 1970-81; staff asst. to dep. asst. sec. for children and families Dept. HHS, 1981-93, staff asst. to asst. sec. for children and families, 1993—. Recipient Spl. Recognition award USPHS, 1991, Superior Svc. award Health Svcs. and Mental Health Adminstrn., 1973, Sustained Superior Svc. award HHS, 1984-90, 2000, Spl. Recognition award Human Devel. Svcs. Adminstrn. for Children and Families, 1989, 91. Jehovah's Witness. Home: 15609 Everglade Ln Apt 103 Bowie MD 20716-3270 Office: Rm 600 370 Lenfant Promenade SW Washington DC 20447-0001

JOHNSON, ARTIS, educational administrator, clergyman; b. Thomasville, Ga., Oct. 3, 1948; s. Moses and Lillie Ruth (Ross) J.; m. Myrtle Elizabeth Woodruff, Sept. 16, 1969; children: Latoya, Mike, Jamal, Isaac, Solomon, Artis II, Simon, Kelvin, Stephanie, Chad, Alvin. AA, Birdwood Jr. Bapt. Coll., 1968; BS, Albany State Coll., 1970; MEd, Valdosta State Coll., 1971, MS, 1971; D Ministry, Bethany Theol. Sem., Dothan, Ala., 1992; PhD, Bethany Theol. Sem., 1993, DBS, 1006. 4th grade tchr. Harper Elem. Sch., Thomasville, Ga., 1971-76, Scott Elem. Sch., Thomasville, 1976-81; tchr., asst. headmaster Vashti Methodist Sch., Thomasville, 1981-82; from tchr. to dean students Howard Mid. Sch., Monticello, Fla., 1982-93; prin. Jefferson County Adult Sch., Monticello, 1993—; pastor Bethany Congl. Ch., Thomasville, 1971-81, Evergreen Congl. Ch., Beachton, Ga., 1974—. Author: (children's book) Oliver Wants a Pony, 1978. Mem. NAACP (life), Am. Soc. Notaries, Ga. Notaries, Ga.-S.C. Assn. Congl. Mins., Monticello Ministerial Assn., Fla. Assn. Sch. Adminstrs., Literacy Vols. Am., Kiwanis (youth advisor 1994—, Kiwanian of Yr. award 1996), Masons. Democrat. Avocations: fishing, hunting, bicycling, swimming. Home: 3888 Ga Highway 33 Boston GA 31626-4000 Office: Jefferson County Adult Sch 760 E Washington St Monticello FL 32344-2549

JOHNSON, BADRI NAHVI, sociology educator, real estate business owner; b. Tehran, Iran, Dec. 1, 1934; came to U.S., 1957; d. Ali Akbar and Monir Khazraii Nahvi; m. Floyd Milton Johnson, July 2, 1960; children: Rebecca, Nancy, Robert. BS, U. Minn., 1967, MA, 1969; postgrad., 1994—. Stenographer Curtis 1000, Inc., St. Paul, 1958-62; lab. instr. U. Minn., Mpls., 1966-69, teaching asst., 1969-72; chief exec. officer Real Estate Investment and Mgmt. Enterprise, St. Paul, 1969—; prof. sociology Anoka-Ramsey C.C., Coon Rapids, Minn., 1973—; pub. speaker, bd. dirs., sponsor pub. radio KFAI, Mpls., 1989-93; established an endowed scholarship for women Anoka Ramsey C.C., 1991. Radio talk show host KCW, Brookline Parks, Minn., 1993. Organizer Iranian earthquake disaster relief, 1990; bd. dirs. dist. 7 Cmty. Coun., 1996-98. Recipient Earthquake Relief Orgn. citation Iranian Royal Household, 1968. Mem. NEA, Nat. Soc. Scis. Assn., Women's Leadership Forum, Minn. Edn. Assn., Sociologists of Minn., U. Minn. Alumni Assn., Minn. Club, St. Petersburg Yacht Club. Avocations: world travel, classical and historical novels, exotic food, gardening. Home: 1726 Iowa Ave E Saint Paul MN 55106-1334 Office: Anoka-Ramsey Community Coll 11200 Mississippi Blvd NW Minneapolis MN 55433-3470 also: U Minnesota Soc Dept Minneapolis MN 55455

JOHNSON, BARBARA ANN, health services educator; b. Rochester, N.Y., July 3, 1953; d. Ray Clifford and Helen Frances (Lindgren) J.; m. William A. Perison, Feb. 28, 1986 (dec. 1998); 1 child, Alyssa Ann. BSEd, Worcester State COll., 1975; MA, U. Mass., 1977; PhD, U. Fla., 1982. Lic. speech-lang. pathologist, Tex., La., N.Y., Calif. Speech therapist Killingly Pub. Schs., Danielson, Conn., 1975-76; grad. tchg. asst. dept. comm. disorders U. Mass., Amherst, 1976-77; level II trainee VA Med. Ctr., Gainesville, Fla., 1977-78; grad. tchg. asst. Eng. Lang. Inst. U. Fla., Gainesville, 1978-79, grad. tchg. asst. speech dept., 1980-81; pvt. practice speech-lang. pathologist North Ctrl. Fla., 1980-81; asst. prof. speech sci., pathology and audiology dept. St. Cloud (Minn.) State U., 1983-84; dir. speech-lang. pathologist South County Speech-Hearing-Learning Ctr., Gilroy, Calif., 1984-85; vis. asst. prof. speech dept. Nat. Inst. for Deaf Rochester (N.Y.) Inst. Tech., 1985-90; asst. prof. speech dept. La. Tech. U., Ruston, 1990-92; assoc. prof., chair/dir. dept. comm. disorders U. Tex.-Pan Am., Edinburg, 1992-96, interim dean, assoc. prof. Coll. Health Scis. & Human Svcs., 1996-98, prof., chair dept. comm. disorders, 1998-99; prof., chair dept. speech pathology and audiology Ithaca (N.Y.) Coll., Edinburg, 2000—; presenter, mentor in field. Author: Language Disorders in Children: An Introductory Clinical Perspective, 1996; contbr. articles to profl. pubs. Grantee Crippled Children's Soc. Santa Clara County, 1985, U.S. Dept. Edn., 1993, 94, U. Tex.-Pan Am., 1994, Pro-Tec Equipment, 1995, Health Career Opportunity Program, 19965. Mem. Am. Speech-Lang.-Hearing Assn. (cert. clin. competence, Svc. Recognition award 1993, mem. profl. svcs. bd. 1991-93, multi-site com. 1991-93), Tex. Speech-Lang.-Hearing Assn., Coll. Health Deans, Tex. Soc. Allied Health Professions, Coun. Grad. Programs in Comm. Scis. and Disorders, Coun. Suprs. in Speech-Lang. Pathology and Audiology (pres. 1997), Kappa Delta Pi.

JOHNSON, BARBARA JEAN, retired judge, lawyer; b. Detroit, Apr. 9, 1932; d. Clifford Clarence and Orma Cecile (Boring) Barnhouse; m. Ronald Mayo Johnson, June 24, 1965; 1 child, Belinda Etezad. BS, U. So. Calif., 1953, JD, 1970. Bar: Calif. 1971. Ptnr. Angela, Burford, Johnson & Tookay, Pasadena, Calif., 1970-77; judge L.A. Mcpl. Ct., 1977-81, L.A. Superior Ct., 1981-97; ret., 1997; lectr. U. So. Calif. Law Sch. profl. program; adj. prof. Southwestern U. Law Sch. Recipient Ernestine Stahlhut award, 1981. Mem. Calif. Judges Assn., 1977-98, Nat. Assn. Women Judges, 1980-98, Calif. Women Lawyers Assn. (pres. 1976-77), Women Lawyers Assn. L.A. (pres. 1975-76), World Jurist Assn. Home: 1000 Prospect Blvd Pasadena CA 91103-2810

JOHNSON, BETTY LOU, secondary education educator; b. Stockwell, Ind., Apr. 4, 1927; d. Paul Stanley Jones and Ethel Leona (Royer) J.; m. Kenneth Odell Johnson, Aug. 5, 1950; children: Cynthia Jo (Mrs. James P. Greaton), Gregory Alan. BS in Home Econs., Purdue U., 1948; postgrad., Northwood Inst. Culinary Arts, 1981, 83. Cert. home economist. Tchr. LaCrosse (Ind.) Jr.-Sr. High Sch., 1948-49, Wendell L. Willkie High Sch., Elwood, Ind., 1949-51, Thomas Carr Howe High Sch., Indpls., 1951-57; substitute tchr. Gt. Oaks Joint Vocat. Sch. Dist., Cin. Mem. AAUW, Am. Home Econs. Assn. (life), Ohio Home Econs. Assn. (life), John Purdue Club, Purdue Pres.'s Coun., Purdue U. Alumni Assn. (life), Gamma Sigma Delta. Home: Indian Hill Village 8360 Arapaho Ln Cincinnati OH 45243-2718

JOHNSON, BRIAN KEITH, electrical engineering educator; b. Madison, Wis., Mar. 11, 1965; s. Alton Cornelius and Virginia Rae (Kroener) J.; m. Elizabeth M. Williams, Jan. 3, 1998; 1 child, Erica Pearl. BS, U. Wis., 1987, MS, 1989, PhD, 1992. Registered profl. engr., Wis., Idaho. Teaching asst. U. Wis., Madison, 1988, rsch. asst., 1988-92; engr. Lawrence Livermore Nat. Labs., Livermore, Calif., 1989; asst. prof. U. Idaho, Moscow, 1992-97, assoc. prof., 1997—; instr. Coll. Engring. Tchg. Asst. Tng., U. Wis., Madison, 1988, Engring. profl. devel., 1992-98; co-advisor Iron Cross Leadership Soc., Madison, 1988-92, U. Idaho IEEE Student Chpt., 1995—; dir. Western Virtual Engring., 1996-99. Lodge chief Order of the Arrow, Boy Scouts Am., 1982-84, dir. Brownsea Double 2Course, Madison, 1987, advisor, 1990-92. Recipient Vigil Hon. Membership, Order of the Arrow, Boy Scouts Am., 1988, Leadership award, Exploring Boy Scouts Am., 1986, Outstanding Young Faculty award U. Idaho Coll. Engring., 1985. Mem. IEEE (co-chair working group on utility applications of superconductors 1999—), NSPE, Am. Soc. Engring. Edn., Wilderness Soc., CIGRE, USNC. Lutheran. Avocations: cross country ski racing, bicycling, backpacking. Office: U Idaho Dept Elec Engring Moscow ID 83844-0001

JOHNSON, CAMMARIE, behavior analyst; b. Detroit, June 15, 1960; d. Charles Warren and Norine Carroll (Goode) J.; m. Charles Jonathan Burlile, July 24, 1993; 1 child, Kathryn Johnson Burlile. BA in Psychology, Pitzer Coll., Claremont, Calif., 1982; BA in English, Pitzer Coll., 1982; MA in Psychology, Northeastern U., 1992. Lic. mental health counselor, Mass. Psychologist I W.E. Fernald State Sch., Waltham, Mass., 1984-88; clin. ednl. specialist New Eng. Ctr. for Children, Southborough, Mass., 1988-92; dir. edn. New Eng. Ctr. for Children, Southborough, 1992-95; program dir. New Eng. Ctr. for Autism, Southborough, 1995—; assoc. psychologist E.K. Shriver Ctr., Waltham, 1993—; faculty MS program in applied behavior analysis Northeastern U., Boston, 1994—; curriculum com. chairperson, New Eng. Ctr. for Children, 1992—; presenter (original rsch.) local and nat. confs. Contbr. articles to profl. jours. Mem. human rights com. New Eng. Ctr. for Children, 1989-96. Recipient fellowships Northeastern U., 1986, 87, 88. Mem. Assn. for Behavior Analysis, Berkshire Assn. for Behavior Analysis and Therapy. Avocations: travel, creative writing, hiking, quilting, bird watching. Home: 17 Cedar St Dedham MA 02026-3221 Office: The New Eng Ctr for Children 33 Turnpike Rd Southborough MA 01772-2108

JOHNSON, CARL FREDERICK, marriage and family therapist; b. July 18, 1947. BA in Psychology, Northwestern U., 1969; MA in Clin. Psychology, Ga. State U., 1975. Lic. marriage and family therapist, Ga. Grad. tchg. asst. Ga. State U., Atlanta, 1972-73; family therapist Bridge Family Ctr., Atlanta, 1973-80; pvt. practice The Family Workshop, Atlanta, 1979—; adj. instr. Dekalb C.C., Clarkston, Ga., 1981-82; appointee Ga. Composite Bd. Profl. Counselors, Social Workers and Marriage and Family Therapists, 1985-93; exec. dir. Ga. Assn. Marriage and Family Therapy, Atlanta, 1997—. Contbr. articles to profl. jours. Fellow Am. Assn. for Marriage and Family Therapy (Divnsl. Contbn. award 1993); mem. Ga. Assn. for Marriage and Family Therapy (Outstanding Ctbn. award 1983, 85, 93, Lifetime Achievement/Disting. Svc. award 1996, chair legis. affairs com. 1980-85, 93-95), Assn. Marital and Family Therapy Regulatory Bds. (founder, pres. 1987-91, coord. devel. nat. licensing exam in marital and family therapy 1989-92). Home: 751 N Parkwood Rd Decatur GA 30030-5023 Office: Family Workshop Ste 410 2957 Clairmont Rd NE Atlanta GA 30329-1647

JOHNSON, CAROLYN A., retired computer specialist; b. Macon, Ga., Oct. 5, 1941; d. Clair Warren and Leone (Powell) J. BA, U. Utah, 1964; MSA, George Washington U., 1973. Part-time sec. Navy Fed. Credit Union, Washington, 1960-64; sec. U. Minn., Mpls., 1964-67; computer specialist Dept. of Army, Washington, 1968-98; ret. E-mail: caj202@gateway.net.

JOHNSON, CARRIE, singer, folklorist; b. St. Augustine, Fla., Feb. 20, 1935; d. Norman James and Robbie Louise (Frazier) J.; widowed 1989; children: Mylinda Watts, W. Norman Barbes, Charles Barbes, Levi Barbes, Carrie D. McCrary, June Lester. Student, Edward Waters Coll., 1953-55, Fla. Meml. Coll., 1955. Tchr. Pub. Schs., Miami, 1966-83; newspaper columnist St. Augustine Record, 1996; singer, folklorist, performer, 1976—. Performer (one-woman show) Harriet Tubman, 1997—; singer (cassette) The Voice of Lincolnville, 1995. Trustee Ft. Mose Hist. Soc., St. Augustine, 1999—, St. Johns Housting Partnership, St. Augustine, 1996—; chaplain Lincolnville Crime Watch, St. Augustine, 1997—. Recipient Good Samaritan award Catholic Charities Bur., St. Augustine, 1998; named among 25 leaders of the present St. Augustine Record, 1999. Mem. Emil Maestre Music Assn., Marjorie Kinnan Rawlings Soc. Mem. African Meth. Episcopal Ch. Avocation: bicycle riding. Home: 30 Desoto Pl Apt 202 Saint Augustine FL 32084-4364

JOHNSON, CHARLES FOREMAN, architect, architectural photographer, planning architecture and system engineering consultant; b. Plainfield, N.J., May 28, 1929; s. Charles E. and E. Lucile Johnson; m. Beverly Jean Hinnendale, Feb. 19, 1961; children: Kevin, David. Student, Union Jr. Coll., 1947-48; BArch, U. So. Calif., 1958; postgrad., UCLA, 1959-60. Draftsman Wigton-Abbott, P.C., Plainfield, 1945-52; arch., cons. graphic, interior and engring. systems designer, 1953—; designer, draftsman H.W. Underhill, Arch., L.A., 1953-55; tchg. asst. U. So. Calif., L.A., 1954-55; designer with Carrington H. Lewis, Arch., Palos Verdes, Calif., 1955-56; grad. arch. Ramo-Wooldridge Corp., L.A., 1956-58; tech. dir. Atlas Weapon Sys. Space Tech. Labs., L.A., 1958-60; advanced planner and systems engr. Minuteman Weapon Sys. TRW, L.A., 1960-64; divsn. staff ops. dir. TRW, 1964-68; cons. N.Mex. Regional Med. Program and N.Mex. State Dept. Hosps., 1968-70; prin. Charles F. Johnson, arch., L.A., 1953-68, Santa Fe, N.Mex., 1968-88, Carefree, Ariz., 1988-97, Carpenteria, Calif., 1998—; freelance archtl. photographer, Santa Fe, 1971—; tchr. archtl. apprentice program, 1974—; program writer, workshop leader, keynote spkr. Mich. Archtl. Design Competition, 1993; keynote spkr. Mex. Inst. Tech. y de Estudios Superiores, 1993; lectr., spkr., judge III Bienal Arch. and Urbanism Costa Rica, 1996. Major archtl. works include: residential bldgs. in Calif., 1955-66; Bashein Bldg. at Los Lunas (N.Mex.) Hosp. and Tng. Sch., 1969, various residential bldgs., Santa Fe, 1973—, Kurtz Home, Dillon, Colo., 1981, Whispering Boulders Home, Carefree, 1981, Hedrick House, Santa Fe, 1983, Kole House, Green Valley, Ariz., 1984, Casa Largo, Santa Fe (used for film The Man Who Fell to Earth), 1974, Rubel House, Santa Fe, 1986, Smith House, Carefree, 1987, Klopfer House, Santa Fe, 1988, Janssen House, Carefree, 1988, Art Start Gallery, 1988, Dr. Okun's House, 1990, Luterback House, Carefree, 1992, Phillips House, Carefree, 1992, Balagura House, Santa Fe, 1993, additions to homes, 1993, 94, Carpmteria, 1998—; subject mag. articles, projects in books, shown on TV; contbr. articles on facility planning and mgmt. to profl. publs.; contbr. archtl. photographs to mags. in U.S., Eng., France, Japan and Italy; contbr. articles on facility mgmt., planning info. systems, etc. to profl. jours. Pres. Santa Fe Coalition for the Arts, 1977; set designer Santa Fe Fiesta Melodrama, 1969, 71, 74, 77, 78, 81, Ariz. Audiophilo Soc., 1997; designer Jay Miller & Friends Fiesta float, 1970-88 (winner 20 awards). Recognized for work in organic architecture and siting bldgs. to fit the land; named among top 100 Archs., Archtl. Digest mag., 1991. Mem. Desert Mountain Golf Club, Ariz. Audiophile Soc. (bd. dirs.), Delta Sigma Phi. Avocations: music, photography, collecting architecture books, Frank Lloyd Wright works. Home: 3271 Beach Club Rd Carpinteria CA 93013-1112

JOHNSON, CHARLES OWEN, retired lawyer; b. Monroe, La., Aug. 18, 1926; s. Clifford U. and Laura (Owen) J. BA, Tulane U., 1946, JD, 1969; LLB, Harvard U., 1948; LLM, Columbia U., 1955. Bar: La. 1949. Sole practice Monroe, 1949-50; mem. law editl. staff West Pub. Co., St. Paul, 1953; atty. Office of Chief Counsel, IRS, Washington, 1955-79, chief Ct. Appeals br. Tax Ct. divsn., 1968-79. Author: The Genealogy of Several Allied Families, 1961. Served with AUS, 1950-52. Mem. FBA, La. Bar Assn., Nat. Lawyers Club, Nat. Gavel Soc. (past treas., past pres.), Soc. Colonial Wars (past dep. gov. D.C. soc., lt. gov., gov.), SAR, S.R. (past pres. D.C. Soc.), Soc. of 1812 (past pres. D.C. soc.), S.C.V., Soc. Colonial New Eng. (past gov. gen. nat. soc.), Nat. Soc. Desc. Early Quakers (past nat. presiding clk.), Sons Union Vets., St. Andrew's Soc. Washington, Royal Soc. St. George, Sons and Daus. of Pilgrims (past treas., 2nd dep. gov. gen.), Huguenot Soc. S.C., Huguenot Soc. La. (past pres.), Soc. Descs. Jersey Settlers, La. Colonials, Sons. and Daus. of Province and Republic of West Fla. 1763-1810 (past gov.), Jamestowne Soc., Soc. Descs. Old Plymouth Colony, Order Ams. of Armorial Ancestry (past pres.), Soc. Descs. Colonial Clergy (past chancellor gen.), Hereditary Order Descs. Colonial Govs. (past gov. gen.), First Families of Ga. (past chancellor gen.), Order Founders and Patriots of Am. (past gov. D.C. and La. Soc.), Order First Families Miss. 1699-1817 (gov. gen. 1967-69), Mil. Order Stars and Bars (past judge adv. gen.), Soc. Cin., Hereditary Order First Families of Mass. (registrar gen.), Va. Geneal. Soc., Miss. Hist. Soc., Va. Hist. Soc., Order First Families of R.I. and Providence Plantations 1636-1647 (past gov. gen.), Order of Descs. of Colonial Physicians and Chirurgiens (past pres. gen.), Sons and Daus. of Colonial and Antebellum Bench and Bar 1565-1861 (past pres. gen.), Nat. Soc. Sons and Daus. of Antebellum Planters 1607-1861 (pres. gen.), Order of Scions of Colonial Cavaliers (gov.), Army and Navy Club Washington, City Tavern Club. Home: Apt 809S 2111 Jefferson Davis Hwy Arlington VA 22202-3121

JOHNSON, CHARLES ROBERT, lawyer; b. Dallas, July 30, 1934; s. Calvin Thor and Lula Martha Pool Johnson; m. Agnes McGuire, Jan. 1957; children: Erin, Hunter, Thor. BBA, Tex. A&M U., 1955; LLB, So. Meth. U., 1961. Bar: Tex. 1961. Assoc., ptnr. Locke Purnell, Dallas, 1961-68; ptnr. Stalcup Johnson, Dallas, 1968-77, Johnson Smith Kourney, Dallas, 1977-78, Coke & Coke, Dallas, 1978-81, Pettit & Martin, Dallas, 1981-88, Shank Irwin, Dallas, 1988-91, Johnson & Steinberg, Dallas, 1991-94, Johnson Jordan Nipper & Monk, Dallas, 1994—; assoc. editor Southwestern Law Jour., 1960-61; guest instr. fed. income taxation and estate planning So. Meth. U. Sch. Law, 1964-65; vis. prof. fed. income taxation, corp. taxation and bus. assns. I and II So. Meth. U. Sch. Law, 1976-77. Chmn. Joni and Friends Ministries, Dallas; 1st lt. aircraft artillery U.S. Army, 1957-58. Fellow Am. Coll. Trust & Estate Coun., Nat. Assoc. Estate Planning Coun.; mem. Dallas Bar Assn., Am. Bar Assn., State Bar Tex., Estate Planning Coun. N. Tex. (former pres., bd. dirs.), Order of Woolsack, Barristers, Delta Theta Phi. Avocations: reading, walking, gardening. E-mail: cjohnson@jjnmlaw.com. Office: Johnson Jordan Nipper & Monk PC 13355 Noel Rd Ste 1880 Dallas TX 75240-6829

JOHNSON, CLARENCE TRAYLOR, JR., state judge; b. Trenton, Fla., Aug. 16, 1929; s. Clarence Traylor and Jessie Grande (Wilson) J.; m. Shirley Ann Traxler, Aug. 30, 1957; children: James Waring, Robert Dale, Douglas Earl, Jan Elizabeth. BSBA, U. Fla., 1955, JD, 1958. Ptnr. Cone, Wagner, Nugent, Johnson, McKeown & Dell, West Palm Beach, Fla., 1958-71; sr. cir. ct. judge 18th Jud. Cir. of Fla., Brevard and Seminole Counties, 1971-92; chmn. Fla. Conf. of Cir. Judges, 1990-91; mem. Fla. Bench Bar Commn., State of Fla., 1990-92; faculty Fla. Jud. Coll., 1988-90; mem. Fla. Fed.-State Jud. Coun., 1989-91, Jud. Coun. Fla., 1989-91. Pres. Jr. C. of C., Cocoa, Fla., 1963-64; chmn. bd. Cen. Brevard YMCA, Cocoa, 1965-66; pres. YMCA, Brevard County, 1968-71, Rotary, Cocoa, 1965-66; charter pres. Vassar B. Carlton Am. Inn of Ct., 1992-93. With USAF, 1950-54. Recipient Disting. Svc. award Cocoa Jaycees, 1965, Jud. Achievement award Acad. Fla. Trial Lawyers, 1987. Mem. ABA, Brevard County Bar Assn. (pres. 1969-70), The Fla. Bar (bd. govs. 1970-71). Lutheran. Avocation: fishing. Home: 600 Heron Dr Merritt Island FL 32952-4022

JOHNSON, CLARION ELLIS, physician; b. Bklyn., Dec. 31, 1950; s. Clarion and Eddye Pride Scott J.; m. Heather Lee Mitchell, June 26, 1976; children: Clarion Ellis III, Sarah Elizabeth. BA, Sarah Lawrence Coll., 1972; MD, Yale U., 1976. Diplomate Am. Bd. Internal Medicine in cardiovasc. diseases, Nat. Med. Bd. Examiners, Am. Bd. Preventive Medicine. Intern Downstate Med. Ctr., Bklyn.; resident Harlem Hosp. Ctr., N.Y.C.; dir. CCU/ICU, staff cardiologist, dir. Echocardiography Lab. Kimbrough Army Cmty. Hosp., Ft. Meade, Md., 1981-83; staff rschr. dept. microwave rsch. Walter Reed Army Inst. Rsch., Washington, 1984-86, staff cardiologist, 1984-86; dir. critical care support lab., asst. prof. dept. medicine Howard U. Sch. Medicine, Washington, 1986-87; sr. med. officer, rschr. Evaluation Rsch. Corp. Internat., Fairfax, Va., 1987-88; assoc. clin. dir. Mobil Corp., Fairfax, 1988-93, clin. dir., 1993-94, sr. clinic dir., 1994-98, acting dir. med. clinics, co-lead med. leadership team, 1998, gen. mgr., med. dir. Global Med. Svcs., 1998—; asst. prof. dept. medicine Uniformed Svcs. U. Health Scis., F. Edward Hebert Med. Sch., Bethesda, Md., 1982—; attending physician Fairfax (Va.) Hosp., 1990—; adv. bd. Ctr. for Sci. and Tech. in the Media, Washington, 1991-94; vol. Washington Free Clinic, 1995—; bd. dirs. Mobil Found. Contbr. articles to profl. jours. Pres. bd. dirs. City Lights Sch. Maj. U.S. Army, 1979-86. Walter Reed Army Med. Ctr. fellow, 1979-81, 83-84. Mem. ACP (assoc.), Va. Occupl. Med. Soc. (bd. mem. 1995, conf. com. 1996), Bio-Electro Magnetic Soc., Yale Club N.Y.C. Democrat. Roman Catholic. Avocations: marathon running, martial arts. Home: 5504 Dorset Ave Chevy Chase MD 20815-6626 Office: Mobil Oil Co Med Dept Rm FP0511 3225 Gallows Rd Fairfax VA 22037-0002

JOHNSON, CLARK EUGENE, JR., electronics and computer company executive, magnetics physicist; b. Mpls., Aug. 3, 1930; s. Clark Eugene and Betty (Wiggenhorn) J.; m. Nancy De Man, Apr. 21, 1951 (div. 1965); children: Wendy, Taylor, Brett, Clark Eugene III, Timothy, Carrie; m. Irma Shirley Rubin, Dec. 25, 1965 (div. 1984); m. Nora Gail Hill, Dec. 1993. BS in Physics, U. Minn., 1950, MSEE, 1961. V.p. Vibrac Corp., Chelmsford, Mass., 1968-72; pres. Micro Communications, Waltham, Mass., 1972-77; dir. rsch. Buckeye Internat., Columbus, Ohio, 1977-81; pres. Vertimag Systems Corp., Mpls., 1981-83, chmn., chief tech. officer, 1983-85, cons., 1985-86, IEEE congl. sci. and engring. fellow, 1988; ind. cons. in magnetic rec., 1959—; cons. on high-resolution sys. Advanced Rsch. Projects Agy. Dept. Def.; bd. dirs. High Iron Travel, Mpls.; founder, bd. dirs. Pres. Rastech Corp., Mpls., 1986-95; founder, pres. CARD Sys. Testing Lab., Inc., Mpls., 1989-95; mem. tech. adv. bd. Optex Comms., Rockville, Md.; co-founder, co-dir. rsch. program on comms. policy MIT, 1989-97; pres. Pandora Techs., Inc., Mpls., 1995—; pres., co-founder USA-Nat. Host, Inc., 1995-99; exec. v.p. Transaction Media, Inc., 1997—; pres. Caritas Techs., Corp., Mpls., 2000—. Contbr. numerous articles on magnetic rec. to profl. publs.; patentee in field. Founder, bd. dirs. Com. for Preservation Recs., Balt., 1982-85; dir., mem. exec. com. Minn. High Tech. Coun., Mpls., 1984-86. Fellow IEEE (magnetics soc., v.p. 1980-82, pres. 1982-84); mem. Am. Assn. Pvt. R.R. (bd. dirs. 1988-98), High Definition TV (co-founder ad hoc com.). Democrat. Home: 3315 Saint Paul Ave Minneapolis MN 55416-4317

JOHNSON, CLIFTON HERMAN, historian, archivist, former research center director; b. Griffin, Ga., Sept. 13, 1921; s. John and Pearl (Parrish) J.; student U. Conn., 1943-44; BA, U. N.C., 1948, PhD, 1959; MA U. Chgo., 1949; postgrad. U. Wis., 1951; m. Rosemary Brunst, Aug. 2, 1960; children: Charles, Robert, Virginia. Tutor, LeMoyne Coll., Memphis, 1950-53, asst. prof., 1953-56, prof., 1960-61, 63-66; asst. prof. East Carolina Coll., 1958-59; asst. libr. and archivist Fisk U., 1961-63; exec. dir. Amistad Rsch. Ctr., New Orleans, 1966-92, emeritus, 1992. Bd. dirs. La. World Expn., 1980-82, Lillie Carroll Jackson Mus., 1978-89, Countee Cullen Found., 1981-87, Friends of Archives La., 1978-90, La. Folklife Commn., 1982-85, Ctr. for Black Music Rsch., 1986—, New Orleans Urban League, 1994—; exec. bd. dirs. All Congregations Together, 1997—; cons. DreamWorks Prodns., 1997. With AUS, 1940-45. Recipient NEH fellow, 1994. Mem. So. Hist. Assn., Soc. Am. Archivists, Assn. for Study Negro Life and History, Orgn. Am. Historians, Nat. Assn. Human Rights Workers. Author: (with Carroll Barber) The American Negro: A Selected and Annotated Bibliography for High Schools and Junior Colleges, 1968, A Legacy of La Amistad: Some Twentieth Century Black Leaders, 1989, Abolitionism in the Antislavery Movement, 1997; editor: God Struck Me Dead: Religious Conversions and Experiences and Autobiographies of Ex-Slaves, 1969.

JOHNSON, CONSTANCE ANN TRILLICH, minister, internet service provider, small business owner, librarian, lawyer, writer, researcher, lecturer; b. Chgo., Apr. 16, 1949; d. Lee and Ruth (Goodhue) Trillich; m. Robert Dale Neal, Dec. 25, 1972 (div. 1988); 1 child, Adam Danforth; m. Lewis W. Johnson Jr., Feb. 14, 1990. BA in French, U. Tenn., 1971, cert. Sorbonne, 1970; MLn, Emory U., 1979; JD, Mercer Law Sch., 1982; PhD magna cum laude Internat. Sem., 1995. Bar: Ga. 1982. Reservationist AAA, Tampa, Fla., 1971-72; libr. tech. asst. I, Mercer U., Macon, Ga., 1973-74, libr. tech. asst. II, 1974-78; teaching asst. Mercer Law Sch., Macon, 1981; asst. prof. Mercer Med. Sch., Macon, 1980-82; pvt. practice, Macon, 1982-86; min. Ch. Tzaddi, 1986-89; writer/researcher ADC Project, 1988-89; min. Alliance of Divine Love, 1988—; co-owner Cmtys. OnLine, Winter Park, Fla., 1990—, Christians on the Net, 1995—; of counsel Read Found., Evansville, Ind., 1989; mgr. Lifestream Assocs., 1989; freelance editor Page Design Co., 1989; assoc. AA Computer Care, Winter Park, Fla., 1989; founder House of the Lord, 1989—; rsch. asst. Ctr. Constl. Studies, Macon, 1983; instr. bus. Wesleyan Coll., Macon, 1982; web designer Christians On The Net, 1995—; curator Angel Art Gallery, 1995—; webmaster World Wide Super Net, 1996—, internet editor, Discovery Newspaper, Orlando Fla., 1998—; Mem. Unitarian Universalist Soc., 1997—. Author: (book) Treasures From Heaven, 1995; editor (periodical) Ray of Sunshine, 1989; assoc. prof., libr. Internat. Sem., Plymouth Fla., 1991. Bd. dirs. Unity Ch., Middle, Ga., 1987, Sec., 1987. Bd. dirs. Macon Council World Affairs, 1981-82, Light of Creative Awareness, Northville, Mich., 1989; mem. Friends Emory Libraries, Atlanta, 1980-87; mem. Friends Eckerd Coll. Library, St. Petersburg, Fla., 1980-87. Mem. ABA, Am. Soc. Law and Medicine, Am. Judicature Soc., DAR (Kaskaskia chpt.), Mercer U. Women's Club (treas. 1974, pres. 1986, bd. dirs. 1987), Am. Assn. U. Women, Friends of the Libr., Mid. Ga. Gem and Mineral Soc., Macon Mus. Arts and Scis., La Leche League (sec. 1985), Phi Alpha Delta. Republican. Office: Communities OnLine 1416 Pelican Bay Trl Winter Park FL 32792-6131

JOHNSON, CRANE, writer, lawyer; b. Bayard, Nebr., June 30, 1921; s. Carl Arthur and Pearl (Haskins) J. MA, U. So. Calif., 1948; postgrad., Stanford U., 1949; PhD, Case We. Res. U., 1960; LLB, N.Y. Law Sch., 1960; LLM, NYU, 1968. Bar: N.Y., 1962. Vol. legal aid lawyer. Author: Past Sixty, 1953, Thirty-Five One Act Plays, 1967, Presque Isle Village, 1995, Three Jacumba Tales, 1998, Ten Stories, 1999, Twelve Jacumba Tales, 1999. U.S. rep. at ednl. confs. in London and Vienna. Served with AUS, WWII. Mem. N.Y. Bar Assn. Address: PO Box 158 Jacumba CA 91934-0158

JOHNSON, DANIEL LEON, aeronautical engineer; b. Manistee, Mich., Jan. 24, 1936; s. Malcolm Storer and Viola Johanna (Hinkle) J.; m. Dorothy Gwynn Chandler, Sept. 22, 1963; children: Romer D., Olin M., Daniela D., Wenona B., Conrad C., Garrett H. BS, U.S. Mil. Acad., West Point, N.Y., 1958; MS in Aero. Engring., U. Mich., 1960, MS in Instrumentation Engring., 1960; PhD in Aero. Engring., U. Colo., 1971. Comd. 2d lt. USAF, 1958, advanced through grades to col., 1978; engr. Material Command, Beale AFB, Calif., 1960-62; engr., chief missle test Logistics Command, Hill AFB, Utah, 1963-67; engr., liason Logsitics Command, Vietnam, 1967-68; engr. Aerospace Med. Rsch. Lab., Wright-Patterson AFB, Ohio, 1971-78, chief tech. svcs. divsn., 1978-84; chief scientist Larson-Davis Labs., Provo, Utah, 1984-89; dir. biophysics ops. EG&G MSI, Kirtland AFB, N.Mex., 1989-97; pres. Interactive Acoustics Inc., 1998—; mem. phys. agts. TLV com. Am. Conf. Govtl. Indsl. Hygienists, 1992—; mem. com. on hearing, bioacoustics and biomechanics steering com. NRC, 1990-93. Contbr. over 90 articles to profl. jours., chpts. to books. Decorated Bronze Star, Legion of Merit; recipient Harry G. Armstrong award Aerospace Med. Rsch. Lab., 1977. Fellow Acoustical Soc. Am. (chmn. noise com. 1992-94, vice chmn. com. on stds. 1993-97, dir. com. on stds. 1997—, chmn. ANSI S1 and S12 coms. 1984-96); mem. Soc. Automotive Engrs., Nat. Hearing Conservation Assn., Inst. Noise Control Engring., Am. Indsl. Hygiene Assn. Achievements include development of the analysis that is used by the current International Standard that relates noise exposure to noise induced hearing loss; development (with others) of the measurement metric for environmental noise; determination of the safety limits of low frequency sound; determination in part of the safety limits of some types of impulsive sounds. Office: Brüel Bertrand & Johnson Acoustics Inc 4719 Mile High Dr Provo UT 84604-6305

JOHNSON, DAVID BLACKWELL, safety engineer; b. Annapolis, Md., June 16, 1954; s. Charles McCoy and Jane (Ingling) J.; m. Jacalyn Benjamin, Aug. 7, 1976; children: Sarah Ingling, Jeffrey Blackwell, Kevin Berington. BA, Drew U., 1976; postgrad., NYU, 1976-78. Cert. safety profl. Am. Bd. Cert. Safety Profls. Rsch. assoc. NYU Med. Ctr., 1978-79; safety engr., indsl. hygienist Burroughs Corp., Plainfield, N.J., 1979-80; mgr. safety and indsl. hygiene Unisys Corp., Plainfield, 1980-81; corp. supr. hazardous materials Revlon, Inc., Edison, N.J., 1981-82; mgr. safety and health Revlon, Inc., 1982-84; mgr. indsl. hygiene and safety Celanese Engring. Resins, Inc., Chatham, N.J., 1984-87; corp. dir. environ., health and safety affairs Hoechst Celanese Corp., Somerville, N.J., 1987-96; v.p. environ., health and safety affairs Givaudan-Roure Corp., Clifton, N.J., 1996-99; sr. v.p. ops. N.Am. Givaudan-Roure Corp., Mt. Olive, N.J., 1999—; bd. dirs., Celanese Emergency Brigade Tng. Ctr., Rock Hill, S.C., 1987—. Adviser safety com. City of Summit, N.J., 1985; pres. Summit Regional Bd. Health. Mem. Am. Indsl. Hygiene Assn. (treas. N.J. sect. 1984-85), Am. Soc. Safety Engrs., Nat. Safety Mgmt. Assn., Am. Pub. Health Assn., Kiwanis. Episcopalian. Avocations: baseball, fishing, golf. Home: 25 Waldron Ave Summit NJ 07901-2805 Office: Givaudan-Roure Corp 300 Waterloo Valley Rd Mount Olive NJ 07004-3560

JOHNSON, DAVID GALE, economist, educator; b. Vinton, Iowa, July 10, 1916; s. Albert D. and Myra Jane (Reed) J.; m. Helen Wallace, Aug. 10, 1938; children: David Wallace, Kay Ann. BS, Iowa State Coll., 1938, PhD, 1945; MS, U. Wis., 1939; student, U. Chgo., 1939-41; LHD (hon.), Iowa State U., 1995. Research assoc. Iowa State Coll., 1941-42, asst. prof. econs., 1942-44; with dept. econs. U. Chgo., 1944—, rsch. assoc. to assoc. prof., 1944-54, prof., 1954—, now emeritus prof., assoc. dean div. social scis., 1957-60, dean, 1960-70, chmn. dept. econs., 1971-75, 80-84, acting dir. library, 1971-72, dir. Office Econ. Analysis, 1975-80, v.p., dean of faculties, 1975, provost, 1976-80; acting dir. William Benton Fellowship in Broadcast Journalism, 1991-92; dir. Ctr. East Asian Studies, 1994-98; economist OPA, 1942, Dept. State, 1946, Dept. Army, 1948; mem. food adv. com. Office of Tech. Assessment, U.S. Congress, 1974-76; cons. TVA and Rand Corp., AID, 1962-68; pres. Nat. Opinion Rsch. Ctr., 1962-75, 79-85; agrl. adviser Office of Pres.'s Spl. Rep. for Trade Negotiations, 1963-64; mem. Pres.'s Nat. Adv. Commn. on Food and Fiber, 1965-67; adv. bd. Policy Planning Coun. State Dept., 1967-69, Nat. Commn. on Population Growth and the Am. Future, 1970-72; mem. steering com. Pres.'s Food and Nutrition Study, NAS, 1975-77; chmn. bd. dirs. Univ. Savs. and Loan Assn., 1986-88, chmn. exec. com., 1988-92; mem. com. Econ. Edn. and Rsch. in China, 1984-94; co-chmn. working group on population growth and econ. devel. NAS, 1984-86, chmn. delegation to Bulgaria, 1991; team leader World Bank Food Sector Reform Mission to USSR and Republics, 1991-92; cons. European Bank for Reconstrn. and Devel., 1993; mem. internat. adv. com. China Ctr. for Econ. Rsch. Peking U., 1995—; hon. prof. Beijing U., 1999. Author: Forward Prices for Agriculture, 1947, Agriculture and Trade: A Study of Inconsistent Policies, 1950, (with Robert Gustafson) Grain Yields and the American Food Supply, 1962, The Struggle Against World Hunger, 1967, World Agriculture in Disarray, 1973, 2d edit., 1991, World Food Problems and Prospects, 1975, (with Karen Brooks) Prospects for Soviet Agriculture in the 1980's, 1983, The People's Republic of China: 1978-90, 1990, Long-Term Agricultural Policies for Central Europe, 1996; editor Economic Development and Cultural Change, 1986—. Bd. dirs. Wm. Benton Found., 1980-92; pres. S.E. Chgo. Commn., 1980—. Recipient Loyola-Mellon Social Sci. award Loyola U. Chgo., 1992. Fellow Am. Acad. Arts and Scis., Am. Agrl. Econs. Assn.; mem. NAS, Social Sci. Rsch. Coun. (dir. 1953-56), Am. Econ. Assn. (pres.-elect 1998, pres. 1999), Am. Farm Econ. Assn. (pres. 1964-65), Phi Kappa Phi, Alpha Zeta. Home: 1700 E 56th St Apt 1307 Chicago IL 60637-1934 Office: U Chgo Dept Econs 1126 E 59th St Chicago IL 60637-1580

JOHNSON, DAVID K., oceangrapher, transportation executive; b. Monrovia, Dazabah, Liberia, Oct. 29, 1961; s. David K. Sr. and Sonnie Duwor; m. Emmoa C. Robinson, Feb. 22, 1988 (div. Nov. 1992); m. Tenneh K. Johnson, Oct. 1, 1999; children: Karmassah, Sonie, Korpoh. BA in Marine Affairs, U. R.I., 1993; postgrad., SUNY, Bronx, 1999—. Cert. ship chartering Assn. Ship Brokers and Agents. Export docs. clk. Logistics Svcs., Inc., Carteret, N.J., 1994-95; docs. supr. Target Shipping, Cranford, N.J., 1995-97; pres. Liberia Lonestar Shipping, Co., N.Y.C., 1997—. Mem. Fed. Lofa Assn. (interim pres. 1999-00), Liberian Cmty. Assn. N.Y. (counil mem. 1995-97. Baptist. Avocations: Reading, sports, recreation, music. E-mail: liberia.lonestarship@netgenie.com. Office: Liberia Lonestar Shipping Co 2645 8th Ave Apt 5F New York NY 10030-1521

JOHNSON, DAVID PAUL, orthopedic surgeon; b. Manchester, Eng., June 7, 1958; m. Ingrid Frederika Pattje, Aug. 24, 1986; children: Teejay, Justin. MB, BChir, Manchester U., 1980, MD, 1990. Registrar trainee Nuffield Orthop. Ctr., Oxford, Eng., 1984-86; rsch. fellow dept. orthop. U. Bristol, Eng., 1986-87; lectr. in orthop. surgery U. Bristol, 1987-91; fellow in knee surgery Austin Hosp., U. Monash, Melbourne, Australia, 1990, Sydney, Australia, 1990-91; cons. orthop. surgeon Bristol, 1991—; mem. anterior creciate ligament study group North Sydney Inst. Sports Medicine, Sydney, 1994. Author: Infection and Failed Wound Healing Following Knee Arthroplasty, 1990, Patellar Tendants, 1997, 99; contbr. articles to profl. jours. Fellow Royal Coll. Surgeons (London)(higher surg. tng. 1990), Royal Coll. Surgeons (orthop.)(Edinburgh), mem. European Soc. Sports Medicine and Knee Surgery (traveling fellow 1994, faculty 1995—, Theo Von Rens prize 1992), Am. Orthop. Soc. Sports Medicine, Brit. Orthop. Assn. (Muckerjee prize 1989, Robert Jones prize, Gold medal 1990). Avocations: skiing, golf, sailing. Fax: (44) 1179706633. E-mail: sportsmed@orthopaedics.co.uk. Office: Chesterfield Hosp, 3 Clifton Hill, Bristol BS8 1BT, England

JOHNSON, DAVID WESTLEY, organic chemist; b. Adelaide, Australia, July 6, 1951; s. Jeffrey William and June Lucretia (Smith) J.; m. Katherine Lynn Lewis, Dec. 13, 1981; children: Sarah Elizabeth, Frances Gaenor. BS, U. Adelaide, 1971, BS with honors, 1972, PhD, 1975. Postdoctoral rsch. asst. U. Cambridge, U.K., 1976; sr. rsch. officer The Queen Elizabeth Hosp., Woodville, Australia, 1977-85; prin. hosp. scientist Women's and Children's Hosp., 1986—. Nat. Health & Med. Rsch. Coun. grantee, 1986, 89. Mem. Royal Australian Chem. Inst., Am. Soc. for Mass Spectrometry. Mem. Seventh Day Adventist Ch. Avocations: constructional electronics, microcomputing, reading, philately. Office: Womens-Childrens Hosp Dept Chem, Path 72 King William, 5006 North Adelaide 5006, Australia

JOHNSON, DAVID WOLCOTT, psychologist, educator; b. Muncie, Ind., Feb. 7, 1940; s. Roger Winfield and Frances Elizabeth (Pierce) J.; m. Linda Mulholland, July 7, 1973; children: James, David, Catherine, Margaret, Jeremiah. BS, Ball State U., 1962; MA, Columbia U., 1964, EdD, 1966. Asst. prof. ednl. psychology U. Minn., Mpls., 1966-69, assoc. prof., 1969-73, prof., 1973—, Emma Birkmaier prof. in ednl. leadership, 1994—; orgnl. cons., psychotherapist. Author: Social Psychology of Education, 1970, (with Goodwin Watson) Social Psychology: Issues and Insights, 1972, Reaching Out, 1972, 6th edit., 1997, 7th edit., 2000, Contemporary Social Psychology, 1973, (with F. Johnson) Joining Together, 1975, 6th edit., 1997, 7th edit., 2000, (with D. Tjosvold) Porductive Conflict Management, 1983, Circles of Learning, 1984, 4th edit., 1993, (with R. Johnson) Learning Together and Alone, 1975, 5th edit., 1998, Human Relations and Your Career, 1978, 3d Edit., 1991, Educational Psychology, 1979, (with R. Johnson, E. Holubec) Cooperative Learning, 1984, 7th edit., 1998, (with R. Johnson) Structuring Cooperative Learning, 1987, (with R. Johnson) Creative Conflict, 1987, (with R. Johnson) Leading the Cooperative School, 1989, 2d edit., 1994, (with R. Johnson) Cooperation and Competition: Theory and Research, 1989, (with R. Johnson) Teaching Students to be Peacemakers, 1991, 3d edit., 1995, also video, 1991; (with R. Johnson, K. Smith) Active Learning: Cooperative Learning in the College Classroom, 1991, 2nd edit., 1998, (with R. Johnson) Learning Mathematics and Cooperative Learning, 1991, (with R. Johnson) Creative Controversy, 1992, 3d edit., 1995, (with R. Johnson, E. Holubec) Advanced Cooperative Learning, 1988, 3d edit., 1998, Cooperative Learning: Increasing College Faculty Instructional Productivity, 1991, Academic Controversy, 1997, (with R. Johnson, H. Holubec) Cooperation in the Classroom, 1984, 7th edit., 1998, (with R. Johnson) Positive Interdependence, 1992, (video) 1992, (with R. Johnson and E. Holubel) The Nuts and Bolts of Cooperative Learning, 1994, (with R. Johnson) Meaningful and Manageable Assessment Through Cooperative Learning, 1996, (with R. Johnson) Learning to Lead Teams, 1997, Human Relations: Valuing Diversity, 1999; editor Am. Ednl. Rsch. Jour., 1981-83; contbr. over 350 articles to profl. jours. Bd. dirs. Walk-In Counseling Ctr., 1971-74. Recipient Gordon Allport award Soc. for Psychol. Study of Social Issues, 1981, Helen Plante award Am. Soc. Engring. Edn., 1984, Outstanding Rsch. award Am. Pers. and Guidance Assn., 1972, Nat. Coun.l for the Social Studies Rsch. award, 1986, Outstanding Rsch. award Am. Assn. Counseling and Devel., 1988, award for Outstanding Contbn. Am. Edn. Minn. Assn. for Supervision and Curriculum Devel., 1990, Outstanding Alumni of Yr. award Ball State U., 1990, Rsch. and Practice award S.W. Ohio Planning Coun. for Insvc. Edn., 1990, Excellence in Tchg. award Dept. Def. Schs., Panama, 1994, Emma Birkmaier Prof. in Ednl. Leadership Coll. Edn. U. Minn., 1994-97. Fellow Am. Psychol. Assn.; mem. Am. Sociol. Assn., Am. Ednl. Rsch. Assn. (award for Outstanding Contbn. to Coop. Learning 1996), Am. Mgmt. Assn., Am. Assn. for Counseling and Devel., Nat. Rsch. Coun. Home: 7208 Cornelia Dr Minneapolis MN 55435-4160 Office: U Minn 330 Burton Hall Minneapolis MN 55455

JOHNSON, DEWEY E(DWARD), JR., dentist; b. Charleston, S.C., Mar. 19, 1935; s. Dewey Edward and Mabel (Momeier) J. AB in Geology, U. N.C., 1957, DDS, 1961. Pvt. practice dentistry, Charleston, 1964-92; assoc. to Stanley H. Karesh, DDS Charleston, 1970-77, tech. market rschr., designer, 1970-90; indsl. designer, various orgns., 1965, 75, 77, 88, 91, 92. Served to lt. USNR, 1961-63. Mem. ADA, Royal Soc. Health, Charleston C. of C. (cruise ship com. 1969), Charleston Dental Soc., Hibernian Soc.,

Charleston Mus., Internat. Platform Assn., Charleston Libr. Soc., S.C. Hist. Soc., Gibbes Art Gallery, Preservation Soc. of Charleston, Navy League U.S., Optimist Club, Phi Kappa Sigma, Sigma Gamma Epsilon, Psi Omega. Achievements include various scientific and engineering designs; patentee in dental matrix device. Home: 112 Folly Road Blvd Charleston SC 29407-7509

JOHNSON, DIAN L. LAWLER, voice educator, technician; b. Birmingham, Ala., Oct. 29, 1951; d. William Lister Lawler Jr. and Ann Elizabeth Dismukes; m. James Goree Johnson III, July 8, 1989. Student, U. Montevallo, 1970-72; MusB in Vocal Performance, Converse Coll., 1974; MusM in Vocal Performance, U. Ill., 1976. Cert. McClosky vocal technician. Instr. voice Jacksonville (Ala.) State U., 1976-85; instr. U. Ala., Tuscaloosa, 1986-88; instr. voice and theory Carver Creative and Performing Arts Ctr., Montgomery, Ala., 1988-89; instr. voice Dunwoody (Ga.) Sch. Arts, 1989-98; pvt. studio instr. Roswell, Ga., 1989—; instr. Truett-McConnell Coll., Cleve., Ga., 1993-95, Shorter Coll., Rome, Ga., 1997—. Editor, cons.: Functional Lessons in Singing, 3d edit., 1985; operatic performance Brevard Music Ctr. Opera, 1971-73, 83, So. Regional Opera, 1972-83, Am. Inst. for Musical Studies, Graz, Austria, 1974, Goldovsky Opera Workshop, 1981. Mem. Nat. Assn. Tchrs. Singing (membership chmn. Ga. 1976-00), Music Tchrs. Nat. Assn., Atlanta Music Club (chmn. young performers concerts 1994-98), Alpharetta jr. Woman's Club, Mu Phi Epsilon, Pi Kappa Lambda. Avocations: walking, yoga, Alabama football, coaching pageant contestants, reading mystery books. Home: 1180 Lea Dr Roswell GA 30076-4626

JOHNSON, DIANA LEE, insurance specialist; b. Cin., Oct. 7, 1952; d. Earl Richard and Rosemary (Fey) Peterson; m. William W. Johnson, Apr. 7, 1978; children: Anthony Joseph, Scott Alan, Brandi Marie, Gregory James. BA in Math., Miami U., Oxford, Ohio, 1975. Rate analyst Ohio Casualty Group, Hamilton, 1976-89, tech. analyst, 1989-98, programmer, 1998-2000, software engr., 2000—. Recipient Intro to Ins. cert. Ins. Inst. Am., 1991, Intro to Claims cert. Ins. Inst. Am., 1992, Supervisory Mgmt. cert. Ins. Inst. Am., 1994. Mem. Ins. Data Mgmt. Assn. (test grader 1993—, designation 1993). Home: 335 Belle Ave Hamilton OH 45015-1104 Office: Ohio Casualty Group Ins Cos 9450 Seward Rd Fairfield OH 45014

JOHNSON, DON EDWIN, lawyer; b. Decatur, Ill., Jan. 29, 1939; s. B. Edwin and Mary Louise (Pitzer) J.; m. Suzanne Curtis, Aug. 23, 1959; children: Jennifer, Marc Wade. BA cum laude, Millikin U., 1959; LLB, U. Ill., 1961, JD, 1968. Bar: Ill. 1961, U.S. Dist. Ct. (so. dist.) Ill. 1961, U.S. Tax Ct. 1986. Law clk. Ill. Supreme Ct., Springfield, 1961-63; assoc. Hohlt, House & DeMoss, Pinckneyville, Ill., 1961-66; ptnr. Johnson Seibert & Bigham, Pinckneyville, 1966—; state's atty. Perry County, Ill., Pinckneyville, 1968-72; bd. dirs. 1st Nat. Bank, Pinckneyville, First Perry Bancorp, Pinckneyville. Contbr. articles to profl. jours. City atty. DuQuoin, Ill., 1965-68, Pinckneyville, 1983—; bd. dirs. Rend Lake Coll. Found., Ina, Ill., 1981-90; bd. visitors U. Ill. Coll. Law, 1984-88. Fellow Am. Coll. Trust and Estate Counsel, Am. Bar Found., Ill. Bar Found. (chmn. 1986-87); mem. Ill. State Bar Assn. (chmn. fed. tax sect. 1983-84, chmn. mineral law sect. 1984-86, 94-95, 96-97), Energy and Mineral Law Found. (trustee 1985—), Nat. Acad. Elder Law Attys., Pinckneyville C. of C. (pres. 1968), So. Ill. Golf Assn. (pres. 1997—), USGA (sectional affairs com. 1994—), Rotary (pres. 1966, 76), Elks, Scottish Rite, Shriners, Chaine des Rotisseurs, Red Hawk Country Club, Crab Orchard Golf Club, Kelly Greens Golf and Country Club, Delta Sigma Phi. Republican. Presbyterian. Avocations: golf, travel, stamp and coin collecting. Fax: 618-357-3314. E-mail: JSBAttorneys@Midamer.net. Home: 605 W South St Pinckneyville IL 62274-1236 Office: Johnson Seibert & Bigham One N Main St Pinckneyville IL 62274

JOHNSON, DONALD HARRY, JR., government official, educator; b. Chgo., May 30, 1950; s. Donald Harry and Dorothy Wright (Millard) J.; m. Kathryn Elizabeth Wiersum, June 24, 1972 (div. Aug. 1987); children: Eric Donald, Christine Melin. BA Elem. Edn. and History, Carthage Coll., Kenosha, Wis., 1972; postgrad., Harvard U., 1977, 2000; MA Higher Edn. Adminstrn., U. Mich., 1979, MA Polit. Sci., 1980, PhD, 1982; MA, Inst. (Fair Housing) John Marshall Law Sch., 1998, 99, John F. Kennedy Sch. Govt., 2000. Cert. tchr. K-8, social scis., Ill., Wis., Colo., V.I. Equal opportunity specialist/civil rights analyst U.S. Dept. HUD, Chgo., 1988—; elem. edn. tchr. All Sts. and V.I. Pub. Schs., St. Thomas, 1972-75; commr. V.I. Athletic Assn., 1973-75; higher edn. adminstr. Carthage, Suomi Coll., Springfield (Ill.) Coll., U. Mich., 1975-83; dir. admissions Suomi Coll., 1977-78; adminstr. Disabled Student Newsletter, U. Mich., 1978-79; adminstrv. asst. Office of Minority Svcs., U. Mich., 1978-79, admissions officer U. Mich., 1979-81; dean coll. Springfield Coll., 1981-83; exec. coun. Ctrl. Ill. Fgn. Lang. Coll. Consortium, 1981-83, chmn. internat. studies group, 1981-83; cons. polit. candidates, Ann Arbor, Washington, Chgo., 1979—; polit. sci. prof. U. Mich., Lincolnland Coll., U. Ill.-Springfield, Coll. DuPage, Triton Coll., Elmhurst Coll., Aurora (Ill.) U., 1980-90; rsch. affiliate Caribbean Rsch. Inst., U. V.I., 1980-82; rsch. cons. Afro-Am. Thematic Project, U. Ill.-Springfield, 1983-85; chmn. HUD Disabled Employee Adv. Com., Chgo., 1988—, labor/mgmt. exec. com., 1996-98; cons. colls. and univs.; lectr. in field. Contbg. author: Theory and Practice of 3rd World Solidarity, 1998; guest commentator NBC Today, 1982, Nat. Pub. Radio, 1984; author, ERIC, Nat. Inst. Edn., Boulder, Colo., 1982; editor: Disabled Student Newsletters, U. Mich., 1978-79. Disting. guest Embassy of Finland, Washington, 1995; candidate local sch. coun., Chgo., 1994; ednl. guest speaker Com. of Ill. State Bd. Edn., Chgo., 1994; mem. com. ACCESS LIVING, Chgo., 1991—, ednl. com. Chamber of Commerce, Springfield, 1982; disability trainer to pub. and pvt. sector individuals, 1978—. Named Disting. Young Alumnus award Carthage Coll., Kenosha, Wis., 1982; Rackham grantee U. Mich., 1980-82, others.; recipient HUD Superior Accomplishment award 1999. Mem. Am. Fedn. Govt. Employees (election chmn. 1991, exec. coun. 1997-99), Phi Alpha Theta. Lutheran. Avocations: freelance writing, bicycling, scuba diving. Home: 2206 W Morse Ave Chicago IL 60645-4820 Office: US Dept HUD 77 W Jackson Blvd Ste 2101 Chicago IL 60604-3511

JOHNSON, DONALD LELAND, sales executive; b. Ithaca, N.Y., Jan. 4, 1929; s. Howard W and Jeanette Younkin (Bergiel) J.; m. Marilyn Fitzgerald, Sept. 3, 1929; 1 child, Judy. Grad. high sch., Las Vegas, Nev., 1946. Expediter U.S. Atomic Energy Commn., Nev., 1956-58; gen. mgr. Ideal Plumbing Supply, Las Vegas, 1958-75, TFI Bldg. Materials, Las Vegas, 1978-81; owner, mgr. D.L. Johnson Sales Co., Las Vegas, 1981-97. Chmn. bd. Order of Rainbow for Girls, 1969. With U.S. Navy, 1946-51, PTO. Mem. Mason (past master), Shrine, Jesters Club. Democrat. Baptist. Avocations: big game hunting, auto racing, snowmobiling, world traveling. Home: 2494 Green Mountain Ct Las Vegas NV 89135-1537

JOHNSON, DONALD RAYMOND, lawyer; b. N.Y.C., June 26, 1960; s. Donald Francis and Jacqueline E. (Barnett) J. BA, Liberty U., 1982, MA, 1984; JD, Washington and Lee U., 1989; postgrad., Va. Polytech. Inst., Yale U., U. Va. Bar: Va. 1989, D.C. 1991, N.Y. 1995, U.S. Dist. Ct. (no., so., and ea. dists.) N.Y., U.S. Dist. Ct. (ea. and we. dists.) Va., U.S. Ct. Appeals (fed. cir.), U.S. Supreme Ct. Pvt. practice Charlottesville, Va., 1989-96; dir., pres. Internat. Brokerage & Investment Co., Charlottesville, 1991-99; dir., v.p. Internat. Investment Svcs., Inc., Charlottesville, 1991-2000; pvt. practice N.Y.C., 1995—. Bd. dirs. Excellence in Edn., Charlottesville, 1990-92, Heritage Soc., Charlottesville, 1990-92, World of Life Internat., 2000—; U.S. del. German-Am. Multiplicitorian Seminars; founder Mission, Inc., 2000—. Named one of Outstanding Young Men of Am., Alumnus of the Yr.; recipient numerous awards and honors for ednl., civic, and social activities. Mem. ABA, ATLA. Republican. Baptist. Avocations: running, sailing, tennis. E-fax: (603) 687-1173. E-mail: drjohnson@attglobal.net. Home: 126 Atlantic Ave Massapequa Park NY 11762-2328 Office: 90 Schermerhorn St Brooklyn NY 11201-5028

JOHNSON, DOUGLAS WELLS, lawyer; b. May 31, 1949; s. Robert Douglas and Mildred Irene (Fehr) J.; m. Kathryn Ann Hoberg, Oct. 18, 1980. BA, U. Denver, 1971, JD, 1974. Bar: Colo. 1974, U.S. Dist. Ct. Colo. 1974, U.S. Ct. Appeals (10th cir.) 1974, U.S. Supreme Ct. 1977, Ill. 1980, U.S. Dist. Ct. (no. dist.) Ill. 1980, U.S. Ct. Appeals (7th cir.) 1981, D.C. 1981, U.S. Ct. Internat. Trade 1981, U.S. Dist. Ct. (ea. dist.) Mich. 1983, U.S. Ct. Appeals (6th cir.) 1984, U.S. Ct. Appeals (fed. cir.) 1984, U.S. Dist. Ct. (no. dist.) Ind. 1986, U.S. Ct. Appeals (4th and 8th cirs.) 1986. Ptnr. Mellman, Mellman & Thorn, Denver, 1974-80; sr. atty. Amoco Corp., Chgo., 1980-91; mgr. real estate Amoco Oil Co., Chgo., 1991-94; sr. atty. Amoco Corp., Chgo., 1994-98; chief legal counsel BP Amoco Pipeline Co., 1998—. U. Denver Alumni scholar, 1967-71. Mem. ABA, Ill. Bar Assn., D.C. Bar Assn., Chgo. Bar Assn., Kappa Delta Pi. Office: BP Amoco Corp 200 E Randolph St Ste 1907B Chicago IL 60601-6436

JOHNSON, EDNA SCOTT, English language educator, volunteer; b. Sioux Falls, S.D., Aug. 15, 1913; d. George Emil and Emma Erika (Pearson) Nelson; m. Preston William Scott, May 29, 1939 (dec. Apr. 1969); children: William Scott (dec. 1969), Gregory N. Scott; m. Merritt W. Johnson, Jan. 1, 1973 (dec. May 1978). BA, U. S.D., 1936. Cert. secondary tchr. English instr. Beresford (S.D.) High Sch., 1936-39; pres. Hecla (S.D.) Sch. Bd., 1950-63, Assn. Sch. Bds., S.D., 1954-60, state pres. nat. exec. com.; del. to White House Conf. on Edn., 1955; cons. Am. Social Hygiene Soc., 1956; exec. com. Gov.'s Lay Conf. Edn., S.D., 1962; mem. Landmarks Commn., 1975-84. Author: School Board Members Handbook, 1957, Brown County History, 1981, Bethlehem Lutheran Church History, 1984, (booklet) Railroads of Brown County, 1984; editor Brown County LWV Bull., 1991-92. Den mother Cub Scouts, 1951-61; leader Brown County Sch. Dist. Reorganization Bd., S.D., 1953-57; mem. devel. com. U. S.D., 1958-66; pres. Brown County Libr. Bd., 1958-77, S.D. PTA, 1960-62, state pres. nat. bd.; pres. Brown County Hist. Soc., 1986-88, Community Concerts Bd., Aberdeen, 1981-85; gen. chmn. Diamond Jubilee, Hecla, 1960-61, Declaration of Independence Celebration, Brown County, 1976, Brown County State Centennial Celebration, S.D., 1988-90; bd. dirs. Aberdeen United Way, 1983-84; sheriff Dakota Midlands Western Corral, pres. 1989-91; bd. pres. Dakotah Prairie Mus., 1954—; mem. Bethlehem Luth. Ch. Choir. Recipient Outstanding Svc. award U. S.D., 1956, Outstanding Sch. Bd. Mem. award S.D. Sch. Bd. Assn., Sch. Bell award S.D. Sch. Bd. Assn., 1984; named First Lady of Aberdeen, 1984. Mem. AAUW (pres.), NEA, S.D. Edn. Assn., P.E.O., O.E.S., Aberdeen Area Arts Coun., Fedn. Women's Clubs, N.S.U. Faculty Wives, Aberdeen Area Geneal. Soc., LVW (pres. 1996-98), Sons of Norway, MC3 Club, Time Club, Chi Omega, Delta Kappa Gamma. Avocations: research and writing, reading, history, walking. Address: PO Box 1566 Aberdeen SD 57402-1566

JOHNSON, ELEANOR MAE, education educator; b. St. Paul, Mar. 22, 1925; d. Emil H. and Leona W. (Warner) Busse; m. Edward Charles Johnson, May 13, 1950; 1 child, Mary Jo Johnson Tuckwell. BS, U. Wis., Stout, 1946, MS, 1959, edn. specialist, 1981. Cert. home economist, tchr., Wis. Instr. home econs. various pub. schs., Wis., 1946-48, 56-64; home economist U. Wis. Extension, various locations, 1948-51, 52-56; tchr. educator U. Wis.-Stout, Menomonie, 1965-87; ret., 1987; summer session guest prof. U. Man., Winnipeg, Can., 1970, 71, S.D. State U., Brookings, 1978; dir. Native Am. curriculum for home econs. Fed. Vocat. Project, U. Wis.-Stout, 1978-80; cons. vocat. evaluation team U. Wis.-Stout, 1982-90; presenter at profl. confs.; team mem. interdisciplinary consumer edn. teaching materials Joint Coun. Econ. Edn., 1980-82. Editor teaching materials for Native Ams., 1978-80. Sr. statesman Wis. Coalition on Aging, 1990-2000; adv., vol. Office of Aging, 1992-2000. Mem. Am. Home Econs. Assn. (del. nat. and internat. confs., Inner City fellow 1970), Am. Vocat. Assn., Wis. Edn. Assn., U. Wis.-Stout Alumni, Assn. Tchr. Educators, Am. Assn. Ret. Persons. Avocations: national and international travel, collecting historical canning jars, stamps, antique dolls, genealogy. Home: 623 Elm Ave Barron WI 54812-1712

JOHNSON, ELIZABETH MISNER, communications executive; b. Lewiston, Idaho, May 16, 1939; d. Gervase Arthur and Blenda N. (Westerlund) Misner; m. Dohn Robert Johnson, Oct. 13, 1962; children: Dohn Robert Jr., Kevin Arthur. BS in Acctg., U. Idaho, 1961. CPA, Calif., Wash. Audit staff Randall, Emery, Campbell & Parker (now Coopers & Lybrand), Spokane, Wash., 1961-62; audit staff, sr. Price Waterhouse, L.A., 1962-65; CPA L.A., 1966-73; CFO KLP, Inc. dba Call-America, Mesa, Ariz., 1995-98; treas., pres., hon. life mem. Arts Coun. Calif. State U., Northridge, 1975—; internat. dir. alumnae devel. Alpha Gamma Delta (recipient unusually outstanding svc. award, 1993), U.S. and Can., 1988-98, com. mem. 2004 Internat. Com. (restructure internat. orgn.), 1994—; chmn. bd. trustees Alpha Gamma Delta Found., 1998—. Pres. Soroptimist Internat., Coeur d'Alene, Idaho, 1991-92, regional nominating com., 1993-94. Mem. Ariz. Soc. of CPAs. Home: 14839 S 47th Way Phoenix AZ 85044-6881

JOHNSON, EUGENE CLARE, data processing company executive; b. Whitehall, Wis., Nov. 19, 1940; s. Paul Reuben and Clara Theresa (Severson) J.; m. Livia Ann Baynes, Sept. 23, 1967; children: Andrew Paul, Anthony Alexander. Student, Madison Coll., 1959, Pasadena Coll., 1961, Purdue U., 1962, Harvard U., 1974. Vol. Peace Corps, Chile, 1962-64; acct. Am. Ins. Underwriters, N.Y.C., 1964-66; advanceman to Pres. Richard M. Nixon N.Y.C., 1966-68; asst. treas. Bristol-Myers Co., N.Y.C., 1968-69; spl. asst. to Gov. Nelson Rockefeller N.Y.C., 1969-77; mgr. advanced systems div. U.S. Postal Service, Washington, 1971-80; with govt. relations dept. ITT, Washington, 1980-85; exec. v.p., chief operating officer TCom Systems, Inc., Washington, 1985-88; v.p. market devel. Diversified Data and Communications Inc., Washington, 1988-90; pres., chief exec. officer Bus. Mail Express, Inc., Washington, 1990-95, Mail 2000, Washington, 1995—; founder Electronic Funds Transfer Assocs., Washington, 1977. Patentee performance analyzer. Sr. adviser Reagan Presdl. Transition Team, 1980; presdl. appointee U.S. Archtl. and Transp. Barriers Compliance Bd., 1988-90; adv. bd. Peace Corps., 1990-92. Club: Kenwood Golf and Country (Bethesda, Md.) (chmn. bd. dirs. 1987). Avocations: tennis, golf, jogging. Home: 5525 Chamberlin Ave Chevy Chase MD 20815-6643 Office: Mail 2000 Inc 5420 Butler Rd Bethesda MD 20816-1500

JOHNSON, EVELYN BRYAN, airport terminal executive; b. Corbin, Ky., Nov. 4, 1909; d. Edward William and Myme Estelle (Fox) Stone; m. Wyatt J. Bryan, Mar. 21, 1931 (dec. 1963); m. Morgan N. Johnson, Feb. 25, 1965 (dec. Mar. 1977). Grad., Tenn Wesleyan Jr. Coll., 1929; student, U. Tenn., 1930-32. With Morristown (Tenn.) Flying Svc., Inc., 1947-97, chief flight instr., 1949-97, sec.-treas., 1949-62, pres., 1962-82; mgr. Moore Murrell Airport, 1962—; gov.'s appointee Tenn. Aero. Commn., 1983-86, vice-chmn., 1987-89, chmn., 1989, 94-96, 96—. Recipient Carnegie Hero medal, 1958, Svc. to Mankind award Morristown Sertoma Club, 1981, Kitty Hawk award, FAA, 1991, Friends of Aviation award Tenn. Aviation Assn., 1992, Stewart G. Potter Aviation Edn. award Aviation Distbrs. and Mfrs. Assn., 1992, Elder Statesman of Aviation award Nat. Aeronautics Assn., 1993; named Flight Instr. of Yr., Nashville Dist. 1973, 79, So. region 1979, Nat., 1979 (all FAA), Outstanding Alumnus Tenn. Wesleyan Coll., 1981, Inductee Women in Aviation Pioneers Hall of Fame, 1994, Hamblen Women Hall of Fame, 1997, Flight Instr. Hall of Fame, EAA Air Venture Mus., Oshkosh, 1997; holder of record most flying time for women pilots, 1995, Guiness Book of Records 1995-96, 97, 98, 99. Mem. CAP, Morristown Area C. of C., Nat. Assn. Flight Instrs. (bd. dirs., treas 1987-88, award 1992), Ninety-Nines, Whirly Girls (plaque 1992), Aircraft Owners and Pilots Assn., Silver Wings (bd. dirs. 1987—, Woman of Yr. 1981, Carl Fromhagen award 1992, Ninety Nines award of merit 1994). Republican. Baptist. Home: 775 Commanche Dr Jefferson City TN 37760-5125 Office: PO Box 1013 Morristown TN 37816-1013

JOHNSON, EVERETT CLARK, banker; b. Colfax, Wash., Apr. 14, 1955; s. Donald McGregor and Doris Jean (Woolverton) J.; m. Lorraine Jean Colvin, Sept. 22, 1978. Student, Eastern Wash. U., 1973-77, BA in Bus. Adminstrn., 1999. Br. rep. Capital Fin., Columbus, Ohio, 1978; clk. Floyd's Thrift, Potlatch, Idaho, 1980-81; v.p. State Nat. Bank, Garfield, Wash., 1981-97; enumerator U.S. Census Bur., 2000—; ptnr. DEJ Investments, L.L.C, Garfield, Wash., 1997—, sec., treas. SMROK, Inc., Garfield, Wash., 1981—; clk.-cashier WalMart, 2000—. Home: 507 W Adams St Garfield WA 99130

JOHNSON, FRANK, retired state official, educator; b. Ogden, Utah, Mar. 12, 1928; s. Clarence Budd and Arline (Parry) J.; m. Maralyn Brewer, Aug. 15, 1950; children: Scott, Arline, Laurie, Kelly, Edward. BS, U. Utah, 1955; MS, U. Ill., 1958, PhD, 1960. Instr. U. N.D., Grand Forks, 1955-56; teaching asst. U. Ill., Urbana, 1956-59; rsch. asst. prof. U. Del., Newark, 1959-60; prof. U. Utah, Salt Lake City, 1960-93, assoc. dean, 1970-77; dir. divsn. pub. utilities State of Utah, Salt Lake City, 1989-95; cons. Gen. Foods, Sears, Magnavox, Albertsons, Zion Bank, Nat. Food Brokers Assn., others; part-owner Old Post Office Bldg., Ogden, Utah, Seventeenth St. Storage; bd. dirs. Enterprise Mentors Internat. Legis. Utah House of Reps., Salt Lake City, 1982-88; mem. Humanitarian Svc. Mission, eastern Europe, 1998-99. Republican. Avocations: mountains, boating, travel, reading, public service. Home: 2373 Dayspring Ln Salt Lake City UT 84124-1887

JOHNSON, GREGORY CARL, pilot, astronaut, career officer; b. Seattle, July 30, 1954; s. Raleigh Osmond and May Ann (Linneman) J.; m. Christine Rochelle Scott, Aug. 10, 1974; children: Scott Gregory, Kent Christopher. BS in Aeronautics and Astronautics, U. Wash., 1977; exptl. test pilot, USAF Test Pilot Sch., 1984. Cert. airline transport pilot. Head maintenance dept. USN, Oak Harbor, Wash., 1989-90; project pilot NASA Johnson Space Ctr., Houston, 1990-94, chief maintenance and engring., 1994-98, astronaut candidate pilot tng., 1998-99, astronaut support pilot, 1999—; commdg. officer Naval Sta. Rota Spain USNR, New Orleans, 1993-95; commdg. officer Naval Air Sta. New Orleans USNR, 1995-97; commdg. officer naval rsch. lab. USNR, Houston, 1998—; primary test pilot multiple projects, 84, 86, 87, 92. Capt. USNR, 1977—. Mem. AIAA, Soc. Exptl. Test Pilots, Naval Reserve Assn. Avocations: car repair, running.

JOHNSON, H. THOMAS, business educator; b. Chgo.; m. Elaine B. Johnson, July 17, 1971; 1 child, Thomas C. AB, Harvard U., 1960; MBA, Rutgers U., Newark, 1961; PhD, Wis. U., 1969. Auditor Arthur Andersen & Co., Boston, 1961-64; prof. econs. U. Western Ont., London, Can., 1968-78; prof. bus. Wash., 1978-88; Retzlaff chair bus. Portland (Oreg.) State U., 1988—. Author: Relevance Lost, 1987, Relevance Regained, 1992, Profit Beyond Measure, 2000. Office: Portland State U Sch Bus Portland OR 97035

JOHNSON, HARDWICK SMITH, JR., school psychologist; b. Millen, Ga., Aug. 13, 1958; s. Hardwick Smith Sr. and Louise (Joiner) J. BA, Atlanta Christian Coll., 1981; MEd, Ga. So. Coll., 1984; EdS, Ga. State U., 1988; DSc (hon.), Holy Trinity Coll. Cert. spl. edn. tchr., Ga.; cert. sch. psychologist. Ga. Spl. edn. resource tchr. Claxton (Ga.) High Sch., 1983-86; sch. psychologist, 1986—; genealogist, 1980—; supervising tchr. Author: The History of the Johnson Family and Johnson Church, 1976, The Aaron Family, 1986, Some Descendants of James and Rachel Oglesby, 1785-1991, 1991. Organizing club pres. Young Reps. Coweta County. Named Tchr. of the Yr., Coun. for Exceptional Children, Claxton, 1985, Hon. Order Ky. Col., 1986, hon. admiral Tex. Navy Gov. of Tex., 1987, lt. col. a.d.c. Gov. of Ga., 1987, citizen State of Okla., citizen of L.A., col. Gov. La., lt. col. Gov. Ala., hon. mem. Coweta Tribal Town of the Creek Indian Nation (now Okla.); recipient Liberty medal with oak lead cluster SAR, Meritorious Svc. award SAR, Silver Good Citizenship medal SAR, medal of honor NSDAR, medal of honor NSDAC, Minuteman medal NSSAR, 1994. Fellow Am. Coll. Genealogists; mem. SAR (v.p. chpt. 1985-86, pres. Statesboro chpt. 1986-87, state sec. 1987—, Meritorious Service medal Ga. soc. 1987, state pres., v.p. gen. South Atlantic dist. 1991-92), Sons of Confederate Vets., Nat. Soc. Sons of Am. Colonists (nat. v.p. 1986—, gov. Ga. soc. 1987—, gov. gen. 1989-91, Mil. Order of the Stars and Bars), Council for Exceptional Children (pres.-elect, v.p. 1985-86), Ga. Assn. Educators (sch. rep. 1985—, pres.-elect 1986-87), NEA (sch. rep.), Ga. Assn. Sch. Psychologists, Continental Soc. Sons Indian Wars (founding gov. gen., nat. pres.), The Nat. Gavel Soc., Jamestowne Soc., Gen. Soc. Colonial Wars, Colonial Order Acorn, First Families Ga. (founding sec./treas. gen., gov. gen. 1993—), Nat. Huguenot Soc., Gen. Soc. War 1812 (former v.p. gen.), Sons Revolution in State of Ga., Hereditary Order Descendants Colonial Govs. (gov. gen. 1999—), Nat. Soc. Descendants Early Quakers, Nat. Soc. Ams. of Royal Descents (recorder), Order Indian Wars of U.S., Order Ams. Armorial Ancestry, Hereditary Order Descendants Loyalists and Patriots Am. Revolution (dep. gov. gen.), Order Colonial Lords of Manors in Am., Baronial Order of Magna Charta, Order of The Three Crusades,(1096-1192), Order of The Crown of Charlemagne in the United States of Am., The Colonial Soc. Pa., Descendants Washington's Army at Valley Forge (organizing cmdr. Ga. brigade), Aztec Club of 1847-Mil. Soc. of the Mex. War (former v.p.), Baronial Order of Magna Charta, St. George's Soc. (Jacksonville, Fla.), Nat. Soc. Sons and Daughters of Pilgrims (gov. gen. 1993-95), Sons and Daughters of the Colonial, Antebellum Bench and Bar, Order of Scions of Colonial Cavaliers, The Old Guard (Atlanta), Sons and Daughters of Antebellum Planters, DeMolay (master councilor 1977-78), Am. Priory Most Venerable Order of Hosp. of St. John of Jerusalem (assoc. officer brother), Soc. for the Preservation of Early Am. Art, City Tavern Club, Kappa Delta Pi (historian 1983—), Phi Delta Kappa. Republican. Avocations: heraldry, travel, writing, reading. Home: 15 Watson Dr Newnan GA 30263-2935

JOHNSON, HOWARD WESLEY, former university president, business executive; b. Chgo., July 2, 1922; s. Albert H. and Laura (Hansen) J.; m. Elizabeth J. Weed, Feb. 18, 1950; children: Stephen Andrew, Laura Ann, Bruce Howard. B.A., Central Coll., Chgo., 1943; MA, U. Chgo., 1947; cert., Glasgow (Scotland) U., 1946; LLD (hon.), Harvard U., U. Miami, 1966, U. Mass., 1969, Oklahoma City U., 1970, U. Cin., 1973, Babson Coll., 1978; ScD (hon.), Lowell Tech. Inst., Tufts U., Bryant Coll., 1967; LHD (hon.), Northea. U., 1966, Roosevelt U., 1969; LittD (hon.), Clarkson Coll. Tech., 1973. From asst. to assoc. prof., dir. mgmt. rsch. U. Chgo., 1948-51, 53-55; asst. to v.p. pers. adminstrn. Gen. Mills, Inc., 1952-53; assoc. prof., dir. exec. programs, assoc. dean Sloan Sch. Mgmt., MIT, 1955-59, prof., dean, 1959-66; pres. MIT, 1966-71; chmn. corp., 1971-83, hon. chmn. corp., 1983-90, life mem. corp., 1983-97, life mem. emeritus, 1997—; exec. v.p. Federated Dept. Stores, 1966; chmn. Fed. Res. Bank Boston, 1968-69; trustee Putnam Funds, 1961-71; mem. Pres.'s Adv. Com. on Labor-Mgmt. Policy, 1966-68; chmn. Environ. Studies Bd. NAS-NAE, 1973-75; mem. sci. adv. com. Mass. Gen. Hosp., 1968-70; mem. Nat. Manpower Adv. Com., 1967-69, Nat. Commn. on Productivity, 1970-72; trustee Com. Econ. Devel., 1968-71, Wellesley Coll., 1968-86, trustee emeritus 1986—; trustee Radcliffe Coll., 1973-79; hon. trustee Aspen Inst. for Humanistic Studies, Inst. Deaf Analyses, 1971-79; mem. corp. Woods Hole (Mass) Oceanog. Instn. Author: Holding the Center: Memoirs of a Life in Higher Education, 1999. Trustee WGBH Ednl. Found., 1966-71, Henry Francis du Pont Winterthur Mus., 1984-87, Dibner Inst., 1992-97; mem. corp. Mus. Sci., Boston; overseer Boston Symphony Orch, 1968-72; mem.-at-large Boy Scouts Am.; pres. Boston Mus. Fine Arts, 1975-80, trustee 1971-72, chmn. bd. overseers, 1980-83, chmn. exec. com., 1983-87, hon. life trustee 1992—; trustee Alfred P. Sloan Found., 1982-95, chmn. bd. 1988-95; bd. dirs. Nat. Arts Stablzn. Found., 1983-87, Museo de Arte de Ponce, 1983-87. With AUS, 1943-46. Recipient Alumni medal U. Chgo., 1970. Fellow AAAS, Am. Acad. Arts and Scis.; mem. Coun. Fgn. Rels., Am. Philos. Soc., Century Assn. (N.Y.C.), Comml. Club (Boston), Tavern Club (Boston), St. Botolph Club (Boston), Phi Gamma Delta. Office: MIT 77 Massachusetts Ave Cambridge MA 02139-4307

JOHNSON, IAN MARTIN, information and library science educator,; b. Sheffield, Yorkshire, Eng., Mar. 17, 1945; s. Herbert William and Dorothy (Clements) J.; m. Gillian Atkinson, Sept. 16, 1967 (div. 1978); m. Patricia Jane (Jean) Trevena, Apr. 14, 1979. BA, Leeds (Eng.) Poly., 1975. Chartered libr. Various positions City Librs., Sheffield, 1962-74; seconded as profl. asst. to libr. advisers Dept. Edn. and Sci., London, 1970-72; sr. tng. officer Rotherham (Eng.) Borough Coun., 1974-78; dir. liaison and tng. svcs. Coll. Librarianship Wales, Aberystwyth, Wales, 1978-89; head Sch. Info. and Media, Robert Gordon U., Aberdeen, Scotland, 1989—; mem. adv. com. for bibliog. svcs. Brit. Libr., 1993-97; participant profl. confs. Mem. editl. bd. Edn. for Info., 1992—, Jour. Librarianship and Info. Sci., 1992-97; co-editor: Libri, 2000—; contbr. over 50 articles to profl. jours., chpts. to books. Fellow Libr. Assn. (coun. 1996—); mem. Inst. Mgmt., Inst. Info. Scientists, Internat. Fedn. Libr. Assns. (chmn. profl. bd. 1993-95), Brit. Assn. for Info. and Libr. Edn. and Rsch. (chmn. heads of schs. and depts. com. 1997—), European Assn. Libr. and Info. Edn. and Rsch. (chmn. exec. bd. 1999—). Home: 3 Beechwood Gardens, Westhill AB32 6YE, Scotland Office: Robert Gordon U Sch Info, and Media, Garthdee Rd, Aberdeen AB10 7QE, Scotland

JOHNSON, J. SUSAN, psychologist; b. Ramey AFB, P.R., Mar. 24, 1948; d. Wesley Roger and Marie Dolores (Stecher) J. BA in Psychology, San Diego State U., 1970, Ma in Psychology, 1974. Nat. exec. lab. coord. Navy Nat. Elec. Lab., San Diego, 1970-72; assoc. dir. clin. decisions Navy Health Rsch. Ctr., San Diego, 1972-78; exec. dir. The Edwards Assocs., San Diego, 1978—; clin. intern in clin. psychology TRI Community Svcs. Outpatient Clinic, San Diego, 1978-80; exec. dir., v.p. Strategic Vision, San Diego,

1983—; cons. in field; co-founder Ctr. for Value Centered Life, 1999; key spkr., program coord. for nat. presidencies, prime mins., Fortune 100 CEO's, 1978—; pvt. practice on theoretical devel. of value centered psychology, 1972—. Contbr. articles to profl. publs. Avocations: skiing, boating, scuba diving, landscaping.

JOHNSON, JAMES A., financial organization executive; b. Benson, Minn., Dec. 24, 1943; s. Alfred I. and Adeline (Rasmussen) J.; m. Katherine Marshall, Feb. 15, 1969 (div. 1973); m. Maxine Isaacs, Jan. 12, 1985; 1 child, Alfred Isaacs. BA, U. Minn., 1965; MA, Princeton U., 1968. Spl. asst. to Sen. Walter Mondale U.S. Senate, Washington, 1972; dir. pub. affairs Dayton Hudson Corp., Mpls., 1973-76; exec. asst. to v.p. Walter Mondale The White House, Washington, 1977-81; pres. Pub. Strategies, Washington, 1981-85; mng. dir. Lehman Bros., N.Y.C., 1985-89; vice-chmn. Fannie Mae, Washington, 1990-91, chmn., 1991-98, chmn. exec. com. bd. dirs., 1999; chmn., CEO Johnson Capital Ptnrs., Washington, 2000—; bd. dirs. Target Corp., Goldman Sachs Inc., Cummins Engine, Temple-Inland. Chmn. John F. Kennedy Ctr. for Performing Arts; chmn. bd. trustees The Brookings Instn.; bd. dirs. The Enterprise Found., Kaufman & Broad Home Corp., Nat. Alliance to End Homelessness, Nat. Housing Endowment, United Healthcare Corp., Nat. Assn. on Fetal Alcohol Syndrome. Democrat. Avocations: tennis, golf, travel. Office: Johnson Capital Ptnrs 600 New Hampshire Ave NW Washington DC 20037-2414

JOHNSON, JAMES HARDING, advertising executive; b. Perry, Iowa, Sept. 26, 1940; s. Richard Harding and Dorothy Margarite (Nelson) J.; m. Kathy Novak, Dec. 27, 1980; children: Ann Katherine, Alexander Simon, Elizabeth Ashely; children by previous marriage: Jennifer Lynn, James Harding. BA, U. Wash., 1963; PHD, U. Minn., 1972. Lic. psychologist, Utah, Va., Ill. Asst. prof. psychology U. Utah, Salt Lake City, 1975-77, dir. divsn. psychology Med. Sch., 1976-77; assoc. prof., vice chmn. dept. psychiatry Ea. Va. Med. Sch., Norfolk, 1977-79; chmn. Va. Consortium for Profl. Psychology, Norfolk, 1978-79; prof., dir. clin. psychology Ill. Inst. Tech., Chgo., 1979-83; pres. Human Edge Software, Inc., San Mateo, Calif., 1983-87, Text Generations Techs., San Mateo, 1987-89, Johnson Direct Advt., Palo Alto, Calif., 1988-89; CEO Connected Brands, 1989—. Author: Mental Health in the 21st Century, 1979, Technology in Mental Health Care Delivery Systems, 1980, How to Buy Almost Any Drug Legally Without a Prescription, 1990; co-author: Mind Prober, 1985; mem. editl. bd. Computers in Psychiatry and Psychology, Computers in Human Service, Behavior Rsch. Methods and Instrumentation, 1977, Computers in Psychiatry and Psychology, Computers and Behavioral Sci.; contbr. articles to profl. jours. Recipient Rush bronze medal Am. Psychiat. Assn., 1975. Mem. APA. Office: Connected Brands 400 Seaport Ct Ste 100 Redwood City CA 94063-2799

JOHNSON, JAMES NORTH, surgeon, educator; b. Blackburn, Lancashire, Eng., Nov. 13, 1946; s. Edwin and Elizabeth Marjorie (North) J.; m. Gillian Christine Markham, Oct. 28, 1972; children: Katharine Sarah Markham, Charles Henry North. MB ChB, Liverpool (Eng.) U., 1970, MD, 1980. Sr. registrar in vascular surgery Royal Liverpool Hosp., 1983-84, acting cons. surgeon, 1984; sr. registrar vascular surgery Broadgreen Hosp., Liverpool, 1984-85; assoc. postgrad. dean U. Liverpool, 1990-93; cons. vascular surgeon Halton Gen. Hosp., Cheshire, 1985—, dir. surgery, 1993-97; hon. clin. lectr. U. Liverpool, 1987—. Contbr. papers to profl. jours. Fellow Royal Coll. Surgeons Eng. (accredited in gen. surgery, chmn. joint consultants' com. 1998—); mem. Brit. Med. Assn. (mem. coun. 1992—, chmn. cen. cons. and specialists com. 1994-98), Athenaeum Club. Avocation: traveling. Home: Talgarth 66 View Rd, Rainhill Prescot L35 OLS, England Office: Brit Med Assn, BMA House Tavistock Sq, London WC1H 9JP, England

JOHNSON, JANE PENELOPE, freelance writer; b. Danville, Ky., July 1, 1940; d. Buford Lee Carr and Emma Irene (Coldiron) Sebastian; m. William Evan Johnson, July 15, 1958; children: William Evan Jr., Robert Anthony. Grad., Famous Writer's Sch. Fiction, Westport, Conn., 1967; grad. writer's div., Newspaper Inst. Am., N.Y.C., 1969; LittD (hon.), The London Inst. Applied Rsch., 1997. Freelance writer Lexington, Ky., 1969—. Contbr. poetry to Worldwide Poetry Anthologies, Sparrowgrass Poetry Forum, Internat. Libr. of Poetry; author song lyrics: Everlasting Freedom, Answered Prayer, Glory Bound; recs. include America, 1997-98, The Light of the World, 1998-99; included in Hilltop Gospel Songbook; contbr. poetry to books and mags and articles to profl. publs. Patron Menninger. Ennobled by Prince John, The Duke of Avram, Tasmania, Australia; semifinalist Internat. Libr. Poetry, N.Am. Poetry Open; finalist Poetry Open Poetry Guild N.Y., Poetry Competition Iliad Press, Amherst Soc. Competition for Emily Dickinson award; recipient 28 Editor's Choice awards for poetry Nat. Libr. of Poetry, 1994, Editor's Choice award Internat. Libr. Poetry, 2000, Coat of Arms, Coll. of Heraldry; inductee Internat. Poetry Hall of Fame, 1996; named World Laureate. Fellow The World Lit. Acad. Eng.; mem. NAFE, Smithsonian Assocs., Peale Ctr. for Christian Living, Sweet Adelines, Internat. Soc. Poets (life, advisor), Internat. Platform Assn., Charles Menninger Soc. (life), Internat. Order of Merit, Nat. Writer's Club, Poetry Guild N.Y., Internat. Libr. of Poetry. Democrat. Avocations: swimming, skating, dancing, piano. Office: PO Box 8013 Gardenside Br Lexington KY 40504

JOHNSON, JOHN ANDREW, construction executive; b. Grand Rapids, Mich., Apr. 10, 1942; s. Arnold L. and Ione A. (Christenson) J.; m. Peggy J. Ruckman, June 12, 1971 (dec. Apr. 1996); children: Perry T., John C-G. (dec.); m. Luisa Moncada Ruiz, June 30, 1997; 1 child, Andrew L. Assoc. in Engring., Mich. State U., E. Lansing, 1964; diploma, U.S.A. Signal Sch., Ft. Monmouth, 1966, Detroit Diesel Allison, Indpls., 1972. Tech. writer Massey-Ferguson, Inc., Indpls., 1965-66, 1969-70; svc. rep. Massey-Ferguson, Inc., Akron, Ohio, 1970-73; regional svc. mgr. Massey-Ferguson, Inc., Detroit, 1973-78; regional sales mgr. Massey-Ferguson, Inc., Columbus, Ohio, 1978-84; pres. Johnson and Assocs., Ind., 1984-86; svc. mgr. Hanomag Baumaschinen GmbH, Hannover, Fed. Republic Germany, 1986-90, Samsung Constrn. Equipment, Seoul, Republic of Korea, 1990-98; dir. Internat. Cons., Pierceton, Ind., 1998-99, Volvo Constrn. Equip. N.Am. Inc., Asheville, N.C., 1999—. With U.S. Army, 1966-69. Mem. Soc. Automotive Engrs., Profl. Photographers Assn., Pierceton C. of C., Am. Legion. Republican. Lutheran. Avocations: golf, fishing, hunting, photography. Home: 1052 Columbine Rd Asheville NC 28803-2398 Office: Volvo Construction Equip N Amer 1 Volvo Dr Asheville NC 28803-3447

JOHNSON, JOHN HENRY, film director, producer, photographer, educator; b. Pueblo, Colo., Oct. 31, 1951; s. William Admiral "Buddy" and Matilda Marie (Trabucco) J.; m. Nadine Sue Milosavich, Aug. 24, 1974; children: Rebecca Sue, Thomas William. Student, U. So. Colo., 1970-73; Assoc. in Fine Arts, Rochester Inst. Tech., 1973, BFA summa cum laude, 1975; MFA, Cranbook Acad. Art, 1977. Photographer Colo. Hwy. Dept., Eisenhower Tunnel, 1971; cinematographer, prodn. asst., writer various prodn. cos., Colo., 1979-80; prodn. asst. Metro-Goldwyn-Mayer, Canon City, Colo., 1983; studio cameraman, flr. dir. Sta. KOAA-TV, Pueblo, 1970, 97—; dir., cinematographer, editor Humanities div. film series, U. So. Colo., Pueblo, 1971-72; photographer Pueblo Chieftain & Star Journal, 1975; pres., founder Tamarack Prodns., Inc., Pueblo, 1982—; grad. teaching asst. Cranbrook Acad. Art, Bloomfield Hills, Mich., 1977; instr. photography Arapahoe Community Coll., Littleton, Colo., 1978, Community Coll. Denver, 1979; instr. filmmaking, photography and design Colo. Inst. Art, Denver, 1978-79, U. So. Colo., 1980-81; instr. filmmaking Learning Tree U., Chatsworth, Calif., 1992; instr. photography, filmmaking, art and humanities Pueblo C.C., 1994—. Dir., cinematographer, co-writer, co-editor (documentary film) Damon Runyon's Pueblo, 1981 (Golden Eagle award Council on Internat. Nontheatrical Events 1983); dir., writer, producer, cinematographer, editor: (documentary film) Zebulon Pike & The Blue Mountain, 1984 (Golden Eagle award Council on Internat. Nontheatrical Events 1985, Commendation cert. Am. Assn. for State and Local History 1986); dir., writer, producer, cinematographer, editor (feature film) Blue Lights, 1988 (invited feature at the Internat. Sci. Fiction and Fantasy Film Festival, Rome, 1990); photographer represented in books including Visual Concepts for Photographers, 1980 (Chinese edit. 1998), Photographic Materials & Processes, 1986 (also Italian edit. 1993), View Camera Technique, 5th edit., 1986, 6th edit., 1993, 7th edit., 1998, Orlin Helgoe-Shaman of the Prairie, 1986, Southwest Fine Arts Biennial Catalogue, 1976; contbg. editor: Focal Encyclopedia of Photography, 3d edit., 1993. Grantee Thatcher Found., 1973-77, Profl. Photographers Am., 1974, Cranbrook/Ford Found., 1977, NEH, 1979, Colo. Endowment for the Humanities, 1979, U. So. Colo., 1979. Avocations: skiing, music, genealogy, movies.

JOHNSON, JOSEPH STEVE, communications educator, broadcaster; b. Butte, Mont., Dec. 28, 1937; s. Steve C. and Goldeen (Petersen) J.; m. Sylvia Ann Fuller, Aug. 7, 1959; children: Tamara, Steven, Jacqui, Jeffrey. BA, U. Utah, 1961; PhD, Mich. State U., 1970. Asst. prof. U. Utah, Salt Lake City, 1964-65, dir. grad. program, 1972-75, dept. chair, 1992-98; dir. programming KSL, Salt Lake City, 1965-67; prof. comms. San Diego State U., 1967—; vis. scholar People's Rep. of China, 1985-86. Author: Modern Radio Station Practices, 1972, 2nd edit., 1977 (Broadcast Preceptors 1973); author: (with others) International World of Eclectronic Media, 1996; narrator, spokesman film and tv documentaries. mem. Internat. Comms. Coun., Broadcast Edn. Assn., Sierra Club. Mem. LDS Ch. Avocations: outdoor sports, travel. Home: 92 Kawela Plantation Kaunakakai HI 96748 also: PO Box 609 La Mesa CA 91944-0609 Office: San Diego State U Sch Comm 5402 College Ave San Diego CA 92115-2435

JOHNSON, KATHARYN PRICE (MRS. EDWARD F. JOHNSON), civic worker; b. Smyrna, Del., Mar. 24, 1897; d. Lewis M. and Jennie Cairl (Smithers) Price; grad. Centenary Coll., 1915, LHD (hon.), 1997; student Goucher Coll., 1915-18; m. Edward F. Johnson, Nov. 16, 1920; children: Edward A., Jane Cairl Johnson Kent. With Liberty Loan Com. for Md. and Liberty Loan Assn. of Balt., 1918-20; dir. Scarsdale Woman's Club, 1933-36; dir. White Plains Thrift Shop, 1930-43, pres., 1936-43; mem. exec. com. Scarsdale Community Fund, 1934-38; active Scarsdale council Girl Scouts, 1937-53, commr., 1939-41, now hon. mem. Scarsdale-Hartsdale council, 1953-69; mem. region 2 com. Girl Scouts U.S.A., 1942-56, mem. nat. bd., exec. com., 1947-55, chmn. orgn. and mgmt. dept., 1952-55, mem. nat. field com., 1943-55, mem. equipment service com. 1956-69, mem. internat. com., 1956-60, mem. meml. gifts com., 1974-81; mem. Bd. Edn., Scarsdale, N.Y., 1943-46; disaster chmn. Scarsdale chpt. ARC, 1942-45; mem. Commn. Human Rights, 1958-69, Commn. Status of Women, 1957-69; rep. World Assn. Girl Guides and Girl Scouts to UN, 1957-71, mem. NGO com. on UNICEF, 1965-72, sec., 1968-70; participant World Confs., World Assn. Girl Guides and Girl Scouts, Greece, 1960, Denmark, 1963, Japan, 1966, Finland, 1969, Can., 1972, Eng., 1975, Iran, 1978, World Conf., U.S., 1984. Recipient Juliette Low World Friendship medal Girl Scouts USA, 1984. Mem. Nat. Coun. Women U.S., Scarsdale Hist. Soc., Olave-Baden-Powell Soc. (founder), Pi Beta Phi. Republican. Presbyterian. Clubs: Scarsdale Woman's (life), Scarsdale Golf, Nat. Women's Republican; Shenorock Shore. Home: 165 Brewster Rd Scarsdale NY 10583-2021

JOHNSON, KEITH LIDDELL, chemical company executive; b. Darlington, England, July 22, 1939; came to U.S., 1948, naturalized, 1958; s. Arthur Henry and Beatrice (Liddell) J.; m. Margaret Elaine Meston, Aug. 29, 1959; children: Leslie Margaret, Kevin Liddell, Gregory Norman, Kathleen Elaine; 1 ward, Ann Louise Warwick. BA, U. Mich., 1960. Chem. technician Ajem Labs., Livonia, Mich., 1956-60; rsch. chemist labs. Swift & Co., Chgo., 1960-63, project mgr., 1963-67; group leader R&D ctr. Swift & Co., Oak Brook, Ill., 1967-71; adminstrv. asst. to exec. v.p. Swift & Co., Chgo., 1971-72, quality assurance dir., 1974-78, group mgr. plant quality assurance, 1978-82; quality assurance mgr. refinery divsn. Swift Edible Oil Co. subs. Swift & Co., Chgo., 1972-73, corp. quality assurance mgr., 1973-74; tech. dir. Norman Fox & Co., L.A., 1982-83, br. mgr., 1983-88, gen. mgr., 1988—, exec. v.p., dir., 1989—, pres., 1993—; bd. dirs. Lexard Corp., L.A., v.p. 1990—; mem. Chgo. Manpower Area Planning Com., 1971; mem. industry adv. bd. South Coast Air Quality Mgmt. Dist., Calif., 1982-84. Contbr. articles to profl. jours. V.p., dir. St. Martha's Sr. Care Ctr., West Covina, Calif., 1993—, chmn. bd., 1995—, vestry St. Martha's Episcopal Ch., sr. warden 1991-96, 98—; bd. dirs. St. Martha's Epsicopal Sch., 1999—. Mem. Chgo. Chemists Club, Chem. Art Forum Chgo. (v.p. 1980, pres. 1981), Am. Chem. Soc., Soc. Cosmetic Chemists (membership chmn. Bay area chpt. 1985, chmn. 1987-88), Am. Oil Chemists Soc., Jr. Assn. Commerce and Industry (dir. 1968, v.p. 1969, exec. v.p. 1970, pres. 1971), Chem. Mktg. Assn. So. Calif., U.S. Jr. C. of C. (dir. 1972), Ill. Jr. C. of C. (v.p. 1972). Episcopalian. Achievements include 17 U.S. and 25 fgn. patents. Home: 342 Amberwood Dr Walnut CA 91789-2473 Office: PO Box 58727 Los Angeles CA 90058-0727

JOHNSON, KELLY ANNE, music educator; b. San Pedro, Calif.; d. Mark A. and Gay E. Smith; m. Todd A. Johnson, Aug. 8, 1992. B in Music Edn., Ctrl. Mo. State U., 1993; MusM in Clarinet Performance, Ariz. State U., 1995, Mus D in Clarinet Performance, 1999. Instr. Mesa (Ariz.) C.C., 1995-97, Scottsdale (Ariz.) C.C., 1995-97, U. Ctrl. Ark., Conway, 1997-98, Ctrl. Bapt. Coll., Conway, 1998-99, Ark. Tech. U., Russellville, 1999—. Prin. clarinetist Ark. Symphony Orch., Little Rock, 1997—; albums include Clarinet Unlimited, 1999. Mem. Nat. Assn. Coll. Wind and Percussion Instrs., Internat. Clarinet Assn. (performer 1998, 99), Coll. Music Soc., Sigma Alpha Iota, Pi Kappa Lambda. Avocations: traveling, movies, reading. Office: Ark Tech U Witherspoon 208 Russellville AR 72801

JOHNSON, KENNETH LEROY, airport executive; b. Vero Beach, Fla., Oct. 30, 1965; s. Franklin Roosevelt and Helen (Perry) J. BSc, Tenn. State U., 1987. Equipment svc. employee Northwest Airlines, Orlando, Fla., 1989-91; asst. dir. ops. Hillsborough County Aviation Authority, Tampa, Fla., 1991—. Democrat. Baptist. Avocations: golf, working out. E-mail: jstone32@gte.net. Home: #2214 10231 Woodford Bridge St # 2214 Tampa FL 33626-1819

JOHNSON, KENNETH OWEN, retired audiologist; b. St. Paul, Jan. 26, 1920; s. Ernest Wilbert and Anna Mae (Little) J.; m. Dorothy Schlesselman, Sept. 5, 1949 (dec. Aug. 1995). BA, Macalester Coll., St. Paul, 1946; MA, U. Minn., 1948; PhD, Stanford, 1952. Chief, audiology and speech correction program VA, Washington, 1954-56; cons. acoustical audiology, dir. San Francisco Hearing and Speech Ctr., 1956-57; asst. clin. prof. dept. surgery Stanford Med. Sch., 1957; exec. sec. Am. Speech and Hearing Assn., 1957-80; dir. Deafness, Speech and Hearing Publs., 1959-78; sec.-treas., past pres.; chmn. Coalition Ind. Health Professions, 1970-71; cons. for speech, hearing and lang. to Head Start program, 1968-72; mem. research fellowship bd. U.S. Vocational Rehab. Adminstrn., 1964-71. Bd. dirs. Com. Handicapped, People to People Program; trustee Am. Speech and Hearing Found. Kenneth O. Johnson Edn. Ctr. named in his honor, Rockville, Md., 1983; recipient Disting. Citizen award Macalester Coll., 1946. Fellow Am. Speech and Hearing Assn. (cert. speech pathology and audiology, editor jour.); mem. AAAS, Am. Psychol. Assn., Speech Assn. Am., Internat. Assn. Logopedics and Phoniatrics (v.p. 1977-80), So. Calif. Golf Assn. (bd. dirs. 1988-92, vice chmn. rules and competition com. 1988-92, course rating com. and rules and competition com. 1988-97, v.p. Rancho Bernardo Golf Club 1994). Home: 15591 Walton Heath Row San Diego CA 92128-4477

JOHNSON, KRAIG NELSON, lawyer, mediator; b. Landstuhl, Germany, July 8, 1959; came to U.S., 1966; s. Howard Arthur and Joy Anne (Nelson) J.; m. AmberJade F. Leca, Nov. 13, 1993. BA with honors, Eckerd Coll., 1981; M in Internat. Mgmt., Am. Grad. Sch. Internat. Mgmt., Glendale, Ariz., 1982; JD, Baylor U., 1992. Bar: Fla. 1993; cert. mediator and arbitrator Supreme Ct. of Fla. Mktg. mgr. Jack Eckerd Corp., Clearwater, Fla., 1982-85; mktg. systems mgr. NCS, Inc., Houston, 1985-87; dir. ops. Petro, Inc., El Paso, 1987-90; atty. and shareholder Zimmerman, Shuffield, Kiser & Sutcliffe, P.A., Orlando, Fla., 1992—. Editor: Florida Workers' Compensation Practice, 1994; contbr. articles to profl. jours. Mem. internat. trade and investment adv. bd. Econ. Devel. Commn. of Mid-Fla., Orlando, 1997—; mem. Task Force on Title IX, Baylor U. Bd. of Regents, Waco, 1992-93; bd. dirs. Asian-Am. C. of C., Orlando, 1994-95. Fellow Soc. of Antiquaries of Scotland; mem. Am. Immigration Lawyers Assn., St. Andrew's Soc. of Ctrl. Fla. (bd. dirs., v.p. 1996-98, pres. 1998—), Fla. Bar Assn. (sect. on internat. law and litig.), Order of Barristers. Avocations: sailing, flying, shooting sports, Mandarin Chinese and German languages. Home: 509 N Hampton Ave Orlando FL 32803-5516 Office: Zimmerman Shuffield Kiser & Sutcliffe PA 315 E Robinson St Ste 600 Orlando FL 32801-4308

JOHNSON, LAURENCE F., college executive; b. Corpus Christi, Tex., Dec. 17, 1950; s. Howard E. and B. Louise (Franklin) J.; m. Maria Guadalupe Cisneros-Solis, Dec. 15, 1979; children: Alexis Elizabeth, Laurence Alejandro. BA, U. Tex., 1975, PhD, 1993; MBA, S.W. Tex. State U., San Marcos, 1988. Divsn. chair Austin C.C., 1983-93; assoc. dir. League for Innovation in the C.C., Mission Viejo, Calif., 1994-96; exec. v.p. Terra C.C., Fremont, Ohio, 1996—; mem. adv. bd. Invest Learning, Inc., San Diego, 1994-96; postdoctoral trainee Inst. for Ednl. Mgmt., Harvard U., 1998. Author: Embracing the Tiger, 1997; contbr. articles to profl. jours.; editor: Leadership Abstracts, 1994-96, Learning Without Limits, 1996, Common Ground, 1996; gen. editor C.C. Jour. Rsch. and Practice, Denton, Tex., 1994-97. Mem. Tri-County Mental Health Bd., Fremont, Ohio. Recipient Sloan Rsch. award Am. Assn. C.C.s, Washington, 1996, Goodman Malamuth award Am. Assn. Univ. Adminstrs., Washington, 1994, Internat. Tchg. Excellence award Nat. Inst. for Staff and Orgnl. Devel., 1991; named to Exec. Leadership Inst., League for Innovation, Costa Mesa, Calif., 1995. Mem. Nat. Coun. Instrnl. Adminstrs., Continuous Quality Improvement Network (instl. rep.), Nat. Learning Infrastructure Initiative (instl. rep.), Phi Kappa Phi, Kappa Delta Pi. Avocations: music, scuba, skiing, reading. Office: Terra C C 2830 Napoleon Rd Fremont OH 43420-9814

JOHNSON, LAYMON, JR., management analyst; b. Jackson, Miss., Sept. 1, 1948; s. Laymon and Bertha (Yarbrough) J.; m. Charlene J. Johnson, Nov. 13, 1982. B in Tech., U. Dayton, 1970; MS in Sys. Mgmt., U. So. Calif., 1978. Mem. tech. staff Rockwell Internat., Canoga Park, Calif., 1975-77; sr. dynamics engr. Gen. Dynamics, Pomona, Calif., 1978-83; fin. sys. specialist Northrop Corp., Pico Rivera, Calif., 1983-90; utility budget analyst dept. water and power City of L.A., 1991-97; mgmt. analyst L.A. Police Dept., 1997—. Lt. comdr. USNR, 1970-92. Mem. Internat. Assn. Law Enforcement Intelligence Analysts, Inc., Am. Philatelic Soc., Libr. Congress Assocs., So. Calif. Crime Analysts Assn., L.A. County Mus. Art, Music Ctr. L.A., L.A. World Affairs Coun., Inst. Safety and Sys. Mgmt. Triumvirate, Trojan Club, Tau Alpha Pi. Democrat. Roman Catholic.

JOHNSON, LEONARD GUSTAVE, research mathematician, consultant; b. Neguanee, Mich., Mar. 12, 1918; s. Werner Leonard and Sophia (Larsson) J.; m. Taimi Marie Lappi, July 5, 1944; 1 child, Virginia. BA, No. Mich. U., 1940; MA, U. Mich., 1941. Math. tchr. Channing (Mich.) H.S., 1941-42; rsch. mathematician Gen. Motors Corp., Detroit, 1945-74; seminar leader Detroit Rsch. Inst., Grosse Pointe Farm, Mich., 1958-98. Author: The Statistical Treatment of Fatigue Experiments, 1964, Theory and Technique of Variation Research, 1964; editor Statis. Bull. Detroit Rsch. Inst., 1961-98. State Coll. scholar U. Mich., 1940-41. Fellow Am. Soc. Quality (cert. reliability engr.); mem. Soc. Automotive Engrs., Indsl. Math. Soc. (treas. 1950-51, pres. 1994-97, Gold award 1991), Kappa Delta Pi, Phi Beta Kappa. Avocations: writing poetry, computer software development. Home and Office: 31811 Bretz Dr Warren MI 48093-1670

JOHNSON, LESTER LARUE, JR., artist, educator; b. Detroit, Sept. 28, 1937. BFA, U. Mich., MFA. Prof. Ctr. for Creative Studies, Detroit. Exhibited in group shows at Whitney Mus. Art, Nat. Acad. Design, N.Y.C., Kalamazoo (Mich.) Inst. Arts, Saginaw (Mich.) Art Mus., Detroit Inst. Arts, U. Mich. Mus. of Art, Ann Arbor; represented in permanent collections Osaka U. Arts, Japan, Detroit Inst. Arts, Flint Inst. Arts, Grand Rapids Mus. Art; prin. works include Bishop Internat. Airport, Flint. Recipient John S. Newberry Purchase prize, 54th Exhibit Mich. Artists, Detroit Inst. Arts, 1964, recognition award African-Am. Music Festival; grantee Andrerw W. Mellon Found. Office: Ctr for Creative Studies Coll Art and Design 201 E Kirby St Detroit MI 48202-4048

JOHNSON, LETHA E.(VELYN), archivist; b. Concordia, Kans., Mar. 18, 1974; d. (stepfather) Eugene and Lillian Joyce Vogan. B in U.S. History, Washburn U., 1997; postgrad., Emporia State U., 1999—. Minority student intern Kansas City Area Archivists, 1994; move/laborer Kans. State Hist. Soc., Topeka, 1995, libr. page, 1995-96, office asst. II, 1996-99, archivist I Gov.'s trainee, 1999—. Docent Treasures of the Tzars, Topeka, 1995. Mem. Soc. Am. Archivist (Minority Student award 1996), Kansas City Area Archivists (minority student intern 1994, membership com. 1996, 97, mem. minority student com. 1997—, sec. 1999—), Phi Alpha Theta (sec. Alpha Beta Beta chpt. 1995-96, pres. 1996-97). Avocations: reading, listening to music, waterskiing, boating. Office: Kans State Hist Soc 6425 SW 6th Ave Topeka KS 66615-1099

JOHNSON, MARK PAUL, obstetrics and gynecology educator, geneticist; b. Fargo, N.D., Sept. 28, 1953; s. Milton Leslie Johnson and Jean Nora (Edhlund) McNeil; m. Christine Marie Jerpbak, May 5, 1984; children: Jennifer, Erik, Rolf. BA in Biology magna cum laude, Concordia Coll., Moorhead, Minn., 1976; MS in Med. Genetics, U. Minn., 1980, MD, 1984. Diplomate Am. Bd. Ob-Gyn., Am. Bd. Med. Genetics. Grad. rsch. fellow dept. lab. medicine and pathology U. Minn. Med. Ctr., Mpls., 1979-80; resident in ob-gyn. U. Mich. Med. Ctr., Ann Arbor, 1984-88; fellow in med. genetics, clin. instr. ob-gyn. Wayne State U. Sch. Medicine, Detroit, 1988-90, clin. instr. dept. molecular biology and genetics, 1988-90, asst. prof. ob-gyn., molecular medicine-genetics, pathology, 1990-96, assoc. prof. ob-gyn., molecular medicine-genetics, pathology, 1997-98, assoc. dir. div. reproductive genetics, 1990-98, assoc. dir. Ctr. for Fetal Diagnosis and Therapy, 1990-98, assoc. dir. grad. program in genetic counseling, 1996-98; assoc. prof. ob-gyn. and surgery U. Pa., Phila., 1998—; dir. obstetrics svcs., divsn. fetal surgery Children's Hosp., Phila., 1998—; vis. asst. prof. ob-gyn. Med. Coll. Ohio, Toledo, 1991-93; numerous presentations, condr. workshops in field. Editor: (with others) Maternal Genetic Disease, 1995, Invasive Outpatient Procedures in Reproductive Medicine, 1996; mem. editl. bd. Fetal Diagnosis and Therapy, 1991—; contbr. numerous articles, abstracts and revs. to med. jours., chpts. to books. Recipient Bronze Beeper award Galens Med. Soc., 1987, 1st place award for outstanding rsch. paper Wayne State U.-Hutzel Hosp., 1990, Faculty Achievement award Alpha Omega Alpha, 1998; grantee March of Dimes Birth Defects Found., 1991, Nat. Inst. Child Health and Human Devel., 1994-97. Fellow ACOG (1st place award for outstanding rsch. paper 1990), Am. Coll. Med. Genetics (founding); mem. AMA, Am. Soc. Human Genetics, Internat. Fetal Medicine and Surgery Soc. (pres. 1997), Soc. Maternal-Fetal Medicine, Ctrl. Assn. Obstetricians and Gynecologists, Mich. Med. Soc. (med. ethics com. 1995), Wayne County Med. Soc. (med. ethics com. 1993-98), Sigma Xi, Alpha Omega Alpha. Avocations: sailing, fly fishing, classic cars. Office: Pediatric Gen and Thoracic Surgery Childrens Hosp of Phila 34th and Civic Ctr Blvd Philadelphia PA 19104

JOHNSON, MARLENE M., nonprofit executive; b. Braham, Minn., Jan. 11, 1946; d. Beauford and Helen (Nelson) J.; m. Peter Frankel. BA, Macalester Coll., 1968. Founder, pres. Split Infinitive, Inc., St. Paul, 1970-82; pres., bd. dirs. Face to Face Health and Counseling Clinic, 1977-78; with Working Opportunities for Women, 1977-82; lt. gov. State of Minn., St. Paul, 1983-91; sr. fellow Family Support Project, Ctr. for Policy Alternative, 1991-93; assoc. adminstr. for adminstrn. GSA, Washington, 1994-95; v.p. for people and strategy Rowe Furniture Corp., McLean, Va., 1995-97; CEO NAFSE: Assn. Internat. Educators, 1998—; founder, past chmn. Nat. Leadership Conf. Women Execs. in State Govt.; mem. exec. com., midwestern chair Nat. Conf. Lt. Govs.; bd. dirs. AFS-USA, Inc., 1992-98, Nat. Capitol Region coun. Girl Scouts U.S., 1997—; mem. adv. bd. Ctr. for Children in Poverty, Columbia U.; mem. commn. on internat. edn. Am. Coun. for Edn., 1999—. Chmn. Minn. Women's Polit. Caucus, 1973-76, Dem.-Farmer-Labor Small Bus. Task Force, 1978, Child Care Task Force, 1987; dir. membership sect. Nat. Women's Polit. Caucus, 1975-77; vice chmn. Minn. Del. to White House Conf. on Small Bus., 1980; co-founder Minn. Women's Campaign Fund, 1982; bd. dirs. Nat. Child Care Action Campaign; chair Children's 2000 Commn., 1990; candidate for Mayor St. Paul, 1993. Recipient Outstanding Achievement award St. Paul YWCA, 1980, Disting. Svc. award St. Paul Jaycees, 1980, Disting. Citizen citation Macalester Coll., 1982, Disting. Contbns. to Families award Minn. Coun. on Family Rels., 1986, Minn. Sportfishing Congress award, 1986, Royal Order of Polar Star Govt. Sweden, 1988, Children's Champion award Def. Fund, 1989, Jane Preston award Minn. State Coun. on Vocat. Tech. Edn., 1989, Legis. Leadership award Am. Fedn. Tchrs., 1991; named One of Ten Outstanding Young Minnesotans, Minn. Jaycees, 1980; Swedish Bicentennial Commn. grantee, 1987. Mem. Nat. Assn. Women Bus. Owners (past pres.).

JOHNSON, MARTIN CLIFTON, physician; b. Santa Fe, Nov. 16, 1933; s. Henry J. and Dorothy (Clifton) J.; m. Priscilla Bollam, June 13, 1959; children: Martin Clifton II, Kurt B., Kirsten L. Ustach, Katharine E. AB,

Stanford U., 1955, MD, 1959. Diplomate Am. Bd. Neurol. Surgery, Am. Bd. Pediat. Neurosurgery, Am. Bd. Forensic Examiners, Am. Bd. Forensic Medicine. Intern in surgery Palo Alto (Calif.) Stanford U. Hosp., 1959-60; fellow in neurosurgery Mayo Found., Rochester, Minn., 1960-61; asst. resident gen. surgery Presbyn. Med. Ctr., San Francisco, 1963-64; asst. resident, sr. resident, chief resident in neurosurgery U. Cin., 1964-68; pvt. practice neurosurgery/pediat. neurosurgery Portland, Oreg., 1968-99. Col. M.C. USAR ret.; lt. comdr. M.C. USNR, 1961-63. Fellow ACS, Am. Acad. Pediats.; mem. AMA, Portland Met. Med. Soc., Oreg. Med. Soc., Congress Neurol. Surgeons, Am. Assn. Neurol. Surgeons, Soc. Critical Care Medicine, N.W. Pediatric Soc., Oreg. Neurosurg. Soc., Internat. Soc. for Pediatric Neurol. Surgery, Am. Assn. Pediatric Neurosurgery, Portland Acad. Pediatrics, Multnomah Athletic Club, Columbia Edgewater Country Club, Columbia Aviation Club. Office: Pacific Northwest Neurol Assocs PC 31870 SW Country View Ln Wilsonville OR 97070-7476

JOHNSON, MARY KATHERINE (KATIE JOHNSON), elementary education educator; b. Prescott, Wis., June 12, 1945; d. Walter Frank and Mary Jane (Larson) Johnson; m. William F. Hilton, June 23, 1968 (div. 1985); children: Bradley Eric, Karin Louise. BA, Mich. State U., 1967, MA, 1970; postgrad., U. Calif., Berkeley, 1970—. Cert. elem. tchr., Calif. Tchr. East Lansing (Mich.) Pub. Schs., 1967-68, Hall's Crossroads Sch., Aberdeen, Md., 1968-69, Oakland (Calif.) Pub. Schs., 1970-82; tchr., cons. Bay Area Writing Project, Berkeley, 1978—, Bay Area Math. Project, Berkeley, 1994—, Bay Area Calif. Arts Project, Berkeley, 1997—; cons. Child Devel. Project, San Ramon, Calif., 1985; tchr. Berkeley Unified Sch. Dist., 1986—; coord. pub. programs, math. edn. program Lawrence Hall of Sci., U. Calif., Berkeley, 1996-98; mem. MATHTEQ U. Calif., Berkeley, 1987-90; mem. com. of credentials Commn. for Tchr. Preparation and Licensing, Sacramento, 1974-76; spkr. Asilomar Math. Conf., 1991—, mem. program com., 1995-2000; spkr. Wine Country Math. Conf., 1992, Calif. chpt. Assn. for Persons with Severe Handicaps Conf., 1992, 94, 97, 98, 2000, bd. dirs., 1997—; spkr. Assn. for Persons with Severe Handicaps Internat. Conf., 1993, Supported Life Conf., 1992; rep. No. Regional Spl. Edn. Local Plan Area Com., Region III Full Inclusion Task Force for State of Calif., 1994-98; participant Calif. Rsch. Inst., 1992; mem. adv. task force on tchr. preparation in mainstreaming Calif. Commn. on Tchr. Credentialling, 1996; adv. bd. Profl. Internship Program., U. Calif., Berkeley. Contbg. author: Portfolio Assessment in Mathematics, 1990, Teacher Handbook on Homework, C.M.C. Communicator, 1993. Coord. children's coun. Epworth Meth. Ch., Berkeley, 1985-88, 96-98, Youth Coun., 1993-95; cert. lay spkr. Bay View dist. Calif.-Nev. United Meth. Ch., Berkeley, 1989—, bd. trustees, 1994-96, 98—; pres. bd. trustees Maya's Music Therapy Fund, 1994—; mem. adv. bd. Calif. Urban Partnership Program, 1999—. Named Math. Tchr. of Yr. Alameda/Contra Costa Counties Math. Educators, 1996; Berkeley Pub. Edn. Found. grantee, 1988, 89, 90, 92, 94, 95, 98, In Dulce Jullibo Inc. grantee, 1989, 90, 92, 94, 95, 99, BAMP grantee, 1995, Calif. Math. Coun. grantee, 1995; fellow Bay Area Math. Project, 1994, Oakland-Bay Area Writing Project, 1977, Bay Area Writing Project, 1978, 98, Bay Area Calif. Arts Project, 1997. mem. Nat. Coun. Tchrs. English, Nat. Coun. Tchrs. Math., Calif. English Coun., Calif. Math. Coun., P.E.O.; bd. dirs. CA Chpt. Assn. Persons with Severe Handicaps, 1997—, Alameda-Contra Costa County Math. Educators (pres. 2000—). Democrat. Avocations: singing, jogging, swimming, gourmet cooking, sewing. Home: 1016 Keeler Ave Berkeley CA 94708-1404 Office: Oxford Sch 1130 Oxford St Berkeley CA 94707-2624

JOHNSON, MARYANNA MORSE, business owner; b. Oxford, Miss., Dec. 21, 1936; d. Hugh McDonald and Anna Sullivan (Virden) Morse; children: Julianna, Hunter, Cynthia, Capp. Student, Miss. U. for Women, 1957; BSN cum laude, Tex. Woman's U., 1986. RN, Tex. Owner MM Johnson Network India, Boulder, Colo., 1968—, MJM Assocs., Boulder; health promotion cons., 1986—. Recipient Lane Zunker Excellence award, 1999. Mem. Sigma Theta Tau. Home: 3102 Bell Dr Boulder CO 80301-2277

JOHNSON, MARYL RAE, cardiologist; b. Fort Dodge, Iowa, Apr. 15, 1951; d. Marvin George and Beryl Evelyn (White) J. BS, Iowa State U., 1973; MD, U. Iowa, 1977. Diplomate Am. Bd. Internal Medicine, Am. Bd. Cardiovasc. Diseases. Intern U. Iowa Hosps., Iowa City, 1977-78, resident, 1978-81, fellow, 1979-82; assoc. in cardiology U. Iowa Hosps. and Clins., Iowa City, 1982-86, asst. prof. medicine cardiovasc. divsn., 1986-88; asst. prof. medicine Med. Ctr. Loyola U., 1988-92, assoc. prof., 1992-94; assoc. prof. Rush. U., 1994-97, Northwestern U. Med. Sch., 1998—; med. dir. cardiac transplantation U. Iowa Hosp., 1986-88, assoc. med. dir. cardiac transplantation Loyola U., 1988-94; assoc. med. dir. Rush Heart Failure and Cardiac Transplant Program, 1994-97; dir. Heart Failure Cardiac Transplant Program, Northwestern U. Med. Sch., 1998—. Assoc. editor Jour. Heart and Lung Transplantation, 1995-99; mem. editl. bd. Jour. Heart and Lung Transplantation, 2000—. Mem. Nat. Heart Lung and Blood Adv. Coun., Bethesda, Md., 1979-83; mem. biomed. rsch. tech. rev. com. NIH, 1990-93, chairperson, 1992-93, chair biomed. rsch. tech. spl. emphasis panel, 1999—. Barry Freeman scholar, 1974; recipient Jane Leinfelder Meml. award U. Iowa Coll. Medicine, 1977, Clin. Investigator award NIH, 1981, New Investigator Rsch. award, NIH, 1981, 86. Mem. AMA, AAAS, ACP, Internat. Soc. Heart and Lung Transplantaiton, Am. Heart Assn., Am. Coll. Cardiology (bd. councillors Ill. chpt.), Am. Soc. Transplantation, Cen. Soc. for Clin. Rsch., Ill. Med. Soc., Chgo. Med. Soc., Order of Rose, Alpha Lambda Delta, Phi Kappa Phi, Iota Sigma Pi, Alpha Omega Alpha. Office: Northwestern U Med Sch 250 E Superior St Ste 520 Chicago IL 60611-2958

JOHNSON, MATILEE HOWARD, retired headmistress; b. Palmetto, Ga., Dec. 9, 1934; d. Amplus Dilworth and Mattie (King) Howard; m. Andrew Emerson Johnson III, Dec. 27, 1977. BS, U. Ga., 1957; MA in Adminstrn., Ga. State U., 1970; postgrad., Colgate U., 1960, 63, Emory U., 1966-67, Oxford (Eng.) U., 1980. Cert. ednl. adminstrn., Ga. Tchr. Everglades Sch. for Girls, Miami, 1957-61, The Hamlin Sch., San Francisco, 1960-61; tchr., dean of students Westminster Girls' Sch., Atlanta, 1961-66, dean of students, 1966-72, head mistress, 1972-77, ret., 1977; substitute tchr., Dana Hall, Wellesley, Mass., 1990; ednl. cons. Pingry and Kent Place Schs., Elizabeth, N.J., 1972; conf. chmn. Midsouth Assn. Ind. Schs., Atlanta, 1973; conv. com. Nat. Assn. Prins. Schs. for Girls. Adv. bd., convocation chmn., March of Dimes, Atlanta, 1974; mem. Cmty. Coun. Montgomery, 1997-98. mem. spl. acquisition com. Montgomery Mus. Fine Arts, 1997-99; bd. dirs. Landmarks Found., Montgomery, 1996-99, Montgomery Chorale, 1994-98; mem. women's com. Carnegie Mus., Pitts., 1983-98. Methodist. Avocations: creating jewelry, swimming, skiing, decorating, flower arranging. E-mail: aejmhj@bellsouth.net. Home: 2302 Allendale Pl Montgomery AL 36111-1635

JOHNSON, MATTHEW HILL, structural engineer; b. Boston, May 21, 1970; s. Gerard Griffin and Jean (Hill) J. BSCE, Ohio U., 1994, MSCE, 1996. Civil engr. Bryant Assocs., Boston, 1997; structural engr. David M. Berg Assocs. Inc., Needham, Mass., 1997—. Mem. ASCE (assoc.), Am. Inst. Steel Constrn., Boston Soc. Civil Engrs. (assoc.). Avocations: surfing, skiing, mountain biking, running. Home: 26 Worcester Sq Apt 4 Boston MA 02118-2944 Office: David M Berg Assocs Inc 570 Hillside Ave Needham MA 02494-1225

JOHNSON, MATTIEDNA, nurse, retired diaconal minister; b. Amite County, Miss., Apr. 7, 1918; d. Isaac and Minnie (Ramsey) J.; m. Robert William Kelley, Oct. 19, 1943 (div. May 1980); children: Bobby Lou, Robert William Jr., Patricia Elaine, Frances Minette. RN, Terrell Meml. Hosp.; postgrad., Homer G. Phillips Hosp.; MA, Ashland Theol. Sem. RN, Tenn., Mont., Minn.; diaconal min. United Meth. Ch. Head nurse Jane Terrell Hosp., Memphis; staff nurse Homer G. Phillips Hosp., St. Louis; lab. tech. U.S. Army U. Minn., Mpls.; pvt. duty nurse Mpls. Dist. Minn. State, Mpls.; medical missionary Gbarnga (Liberia) Meth. Mission; pvt. duty night nurse Mo., Tenn., Ohio. Author: Tots Goes to Gbarnga, 1994, Johnson's Instructors Guide, 1949, Johnson's Manual-Church Nursing, 1994. Created ch. nursing Am. Red Cross, 1949—, vol. instr. Mem. ANA, Nat. Black Nurses Assn. (sec. 1970—). Achievements include crystallization of penicillin mold for gun shot wounds; tests of staphlococcus germs and terrible mice mold against streptococcus hymolyticus germ of scarlet fever; developed R13 Mold penicillin crystals for the injectable IV-Intra Muscular. Home: 13606 Abell Ave Cleveland OH 44120-3954

JOHNSON, MICHAEL, track and field Olympic athlete; b. Dallas, Sept. 13, 1967. Student, Baylor U., 90. Recipient Gold medal 200 meters Goodwill Games, 1990, 94, 4 x 100 relay Barcelona Olympics, 1992, 200 meters and 400 meters Summer Olympics, Atlanta, 1996, Jesse Owens award, 1994; winner 200 meters World Athletic Championships, 1991, 400 meters, 1993; U.S. Nat. champion 200 meters, 1990-92, 95; named Athlete of Yr. USA Track & Field, 1993-94; world record holder indoor 400 meters, 200 meters at 1996 Olympics; gold medal for 400 meters World Championship, 1997., gold medalist, 400m & 4 x 400m, Sydney Olympic Games, 2000. Office: USA Track & Field PO Box 120 Indianapolis IN 46206-0120

JOHNSON, MICHAEL RAYMOND WALTER, geologist, retired; b. Nottingham, Eng., Apr. 12, 1930; s. Walter and Florence (Thomason) J.; m. Mary Rita Lyden (div. 1987); children: Patrick, Frances; m. Anne McNab Brown, Sept. 22, 1988. BS, U. Nottingham, 1953; PhD, Imperial Coll., 1955. Geologist Brit. Geol. Survey, 1955-57; lectr. U. Edinburgh, Scotland, 1957-68; reader U. Edinburgh, 1968-97; ret., 1997. Contbr. articles to profl. jours. Fellow Royal Soc. Edinburgh, Geol. Soc. London, Geol. Soc. Edinburgh. Avocations: music, walking. Office: Univ Edinburgh Dept Geology, W Mains Rd, Edinburgh EH9 3JW, Scotland

JOHNSON, MICHAEL ROSS, corporate communications executive, writer; b. Delphi, Ind., Nov. 23, 1938; s. Myron and Eileen (Rahilly) J.; m. Jacqueline Zimbardo, Apr. 15, 1966; children: Stephanie, Raphaelle, Delphine. BA, San Jose U., 1960; cert., Columbia U., 1967. Corr. AP, Moscow, 1967-71; bur. chief McGraw Hill World News, Paris, 1971-76; dir. McGraw Hill World News, N.Y.C., 1976-82; editor-in-chief Internat. Mgmt., London, 1982-90; editl. dir. C.E.P. Comm., Paris, 1990-92; media dir. Burson Marsteller, London, 1992-97; global media dir. ICO Global Comms., London, 1997-00, dir. corp. comm., 2000—. Author: Business Buzzwords, 1986, Guide to European Business Cultures, 1988, French Resistance, 1996, Workaholism: Getting a Life in the Killing Fields of Work, 2000. Dir. World Piano Competition, London, 1997—. Seaman first class USCG, 1961-62. Avocations: piano, writing, drawing, painting.

JOHNSON, MICHAEL WARREN, international relations specialist; b. Mpls., Oct. 2, 1948; s. Warren Redy and Lorraine Agnes (Capistran) J.; BS, U.S. Mil. Acad., 1970; MA in Internat. Relations, U. So. Calif., 1973; PhD in Polit. Sci., MIT, 1985; postgrad., Harvard U., 1987; m. Jeanine Ann Tyldesley, Feb. 6, 1971 (div. 1991); children: Benjamin T., Joseph A., Katherine E.; m. Deborah V. Matthews, July 26, 1991; children: Maximilian N., Scott M. Commd. 2d lt. U.S. Army, 1970, advanced through grades to capt., 1974, resigned, 1975; sr. middle east analyst U.S. Army Mil. Intelligence, 1975; stockbroker Merrill Lynch, Pierce, Fenner & Smith, Inc., Boston, 1975-81; v.p. Thomson McKinnon Securities Inc., Boston, 1981-82; 1st v.p. Jefferies & Co., Boston, 1982-84; sr. v.p. Moseley, Hallgarten, Estabrook & Weeden, Inc., Boston, 1984-88; internat. rels. cons. Geopolitical Strategist, Inc., 1984—. Fgn. policy adviser to Congl. candidate, 1980. Mem. Assn. of Grads. U.S. Mil. Acad.

JOHNSON, MORGAN BURTON, artist, writer; b. Santa Monica, Calif., Nov. 25, 1952; s. Arnold and Roma (Burton) J. BA in Psychology, U. Calif., San Diego, 1974; Cert. Fgn. Studies, Lycee du Universite, Dijon, France, 1968. Mgr. Coronet Stores, Las Vegas, Nev., 1975; mgr., chef Diver's Cove Restaurant, Long Beach, Calif., 1977-80; prodn. control asst. Century Plastics, Compton, Calif., 1980; prodn. supr. Analytichem Internat., Harbor City, Calif., 1980-81; sr. planner Sci. Mfg./Am. Hosp., Emeryville, Calif., 1982-85; materials mgr. Applied Biosys. (Perkin-Elmer), Foster City, Calif., 1985-90; owner, pres. Two Bears Restoration, 1990—. Exhibited in group shows at Medford (Oreg.) Ctr., 1993, Mills House Art Gallery, Garden Grove, Calif., 1979, San Bernardino Mus. Art, 1980-81, Calif. Poly. State U., San Luis Obispo, 1985, West Coast Biennial, Pacific Grove Art Ctr., 1985, Cunningham Meml. Art Show, Bakersfield, Calif., 1985, The Rogue Gallery, Medford, 1984, 85, 90, 91, C. Erickson Gallery, Half Moon Bay, Calif., 1986-90, Britt Music Festival, Jacksonville, Oreg., 1994; solo shows include Daleo Farms, Sams Valley, Oreg., 1995, Cache Salon, Walnut Creek, 1996, First Congl. Ch., Long Beach, 1996; included in pvt. collections; author: Trees of Other Colors, 1994, Condemned to a Life of Painting Pretty Pictures, 1994, Circle of the White Buffalo, 1996, Memories of Aunt Aura, 2000; published in Nat. Libr. Poetry Anthology, 1997, 98, 99, 2000; creator website, 2000. Mem. So. Oreg. Arts Coun., Medford, 1990—, San Francisco Artist's Coop, 1980-83; fin. sec. Long Beach Art Assn., 1978-79; hanging com. mem. San Diego Art Inst., 1974-76. Recipient 1st prize Recreation and Parks Dept., L.A., 1965, 66, Long Beach Art Assn., 1977, 3d pl. award Downey Mus. Art, 1977, 78, So. Oreg. Lambda Excellence award for art, 1998. Avocations: hiking, gardening. Home and Office: 2130 Capital Ave Medford OR 97504-6944

JOHNSON, NAOMI BOWERS, nurse; b. Ft. Benning, Ga., Aug. 17, 1954; d. Bob and Henrietta Violet (Hoomalu) Bowers; m. James William Johnson, Dec. 7, 1973 (div.); children: Amelia, Melissa, Charity, James-William. ADN, Troy State U., Montgomery, Ala., 1974. Office supr., lab. supr., nursing coord. physician's office, Selma, Ala.; patients care coord. West. Ala. Home Health Agy., Selma; discharge planning/social svcs., SOBRA and clin. case mgmt. coord. Vaughan Regional Med. Ctr. Hosp., Selma; DON Dunn Nursing Home, Selma, Capitol Hill Health Care Ctr.; dir. mktg. and admissions Mariner Post Acute Health Care Network, Montgomery, Ala.

JOHNSON, NEAL FREDERICK, psychological scientist, educator; b. Willmar, Minn., May 1, 1934; s. Malcolm Ruben and Helen Laura Johnson; m. Kathleen A. Crimmins, Sept. 9, 1960; children: Neal, Margaret, Elizabeth, Michael. BA, U. Minn., 1956, PhD, 1961. Prof. psychology Ohio State U., Columbus, 1961—; vis. prof. U. Calif., Berkeley, 1965, 74, 75, 77, 78, 83. Contbr. articles to profl. jours.; assoc. editor Jour. Memory and Lang., 1984-88; consulting editor Jour. Verbal Learning and Verbal Behavior, 1965-84, Memory & Cognition, 1972-82, Jour. Exptl. Psychology: Human Perception and Performance, 1978-82, Jour. Exptl. Psychology: Learning, Memory and Cognition, 1982-89, Jour. Memory and Lang., 1988-94, Gen. Psychology Rev., 1996—. Mem. com. Troop 312 Boy Scouts Am., Columbus, 1974-81. Rsch. scholar Tozer Found., Stillwater, Minn., 1959; grantee U.S. Office Edn., NIH, NSF. Fellow APA (pres. Soc. Gen. Psychology 1995, pres. divsn. exptl. psychology 1996), AAAS (governing coun. 1998-2000); mem. Psychonomic Soc. (pres. 1997), Coun. Sci. Soc. Presidents, Midwestern Psychol. Assn. (pres. 1987). Presbyterian. Avocations: downhill skiing, fencing. Home: 5478 Rockwood Rd Columbus OH 43229-4324 Office: Dept Psychology Ohio State U Columbus OH 43210

JOHNSON, OLIN CHESTER, education educator; b. Phila., Sept. 19, 1941; s. Benjamin F. and Eva M. Johnson; m. Vernetta Dudley, Nov. 22, 1964; children: Quanda, Olin Jr. BS, Cheyney State Coll., 1965; MEd, Temple U., 1969; MS, U. Pa., 1972. Cert. elem. edn., social studies, elem. prin., secondary prin., supt., Pa. Tchr. Phila. Sch. Dist., 1965-68, supr., 1968-72, dir., coord. urban career ednl. ctr., 1973-75, prin., 1976—; prin. William Bryant Sch., 1977-80, Charles R. Drew Sch., 1981—; mem. secondary sch. com. U. Pa., Phila.; adj. asst. prof. Drexel U., Phila., 1989—, mem. ednl. adv. com. Chmn. Cmty. Concern 13, Inc., 1970—, B.F. Johnson Scholarship Fund, 1971—; vice-chmn. Phila. M.H. Multi-Purpose Learning Ctr., 1975-85; bd. dirs. Open Door Bapt. Ch. Recipient award Nat. Tchr. Corp., 1970, Four Chaplains Cmty. Svc. award, 1971, 73, Phila. Prin. Merit award Phila. Sch. Dist. #1, 1978, OIC commendation, 1973, Pa. Dept. Edn. Planning and Testing citation, 1987, Prin. Outstanding Leadership C.R. Drew award, 1987; Ford Found. fellow U. Pa., 1971-74. Mem. Am. Assn. Sch. Adminstrs., Pa. Congress Sch. Adminstrs., Phi Delta Kappa, Kappa Alpha Psi.

JOHNSON, ORA J., clergyman; b. Aug. 31, 1932; s. Ora F. and Thelma Pauline (Julian) J.; m. Wanda Mae Lockamy, Aug. 11, 1952; children: David Russell, Kent Alan, Vicki Jeanne. BS, Oakland City U., 1971, MS, DD, 1996. Ordained to ministry Bapt. Ch., 1966;. Sales rep., staff sales mgr. Western & So. Ins. Co., Evansville, Ind., 1956-70; pastor Corydon (Ky.) Gen. Bapt. Ch., 1965-68, Wadesville (Ind.) Gen. Bapt. Ch., 1968-70, North Haven Gen. Bapt. Ch., Evansville, 1970-75; nat. dir. evangelism and ch. growth Gen. Bapt. Hdqs., Poplar Bluff, Mo., 1976-82; pastor 1st Gen. Bapt. Ch., Malden, Mo., 1982-88, Howell Gen. Bapt. Ch., Evansville, 1988-90; asst. v.p. for denomination rels. Oakland City U., 1990-93, exec. v.p., 1995—; pres. O.J. Johnson Property Mgmt. Co.; pastor 1st Gen. Bapt. Ch., Owensboro, Ky., 1993-95; moderator Gen. Assn. of Gen. Bapts. Nat. Conv., 1991; producer, dir. weekly TV program Moments of Worship, 1973-74; pres. Greater Evansville Sunday Sch. Assn., 1975; pres. Gen. Bapt. Home Mission Bd., 1972-73, Gen. Bd. Gen. Bapts., 1972-76; pres. Evansville Clergy Assn., 1975-76. Named Outstanding Theologian of 1971, Gen. Bapt. Brotherhood; recipient Good Shepherd award Boy Scouts Am., 1980. Mem. Christian Resource Assn., Evangelization Forum, Nat. Assn. Evangelicals, Malden Ministerial Alliance (pres. 1983), Malden C. of C. (pres. 1985-86), Malden Optimist, Kiwanis (bd. dirs. Evansville club 1975, Poplar Bluff club 1981-83, Oakland City club 1997-99), Evansville C. of C. Home: 110 N Lucretia St Oakland City IN 47660-1038 Office: Oakland City U 143 N Lucretia St Oakland City IN 47660-1037

JOHNSON, PETER FORBES, transportation executive, business owner; b. Salem, Mass., May 7, 1934; s. William Bennett and Sarah Loraine (Nee) J.; m. Mikell Kraus, Oct. 11, 1958; children: Krista, Todd, Karyn, Jennifer. BS, U.S. Mcht. Marine Acad., 1957. Deck officer Texaco, Port Arthur, Tex., 1958-63; from deck officer to master Reynolds Metals Co., Corpus Christi, Tex., 1963-65, port capt., 1965-68, operating mgr., 1968-71; internat. marine mgr. Gulf Miss. Marine Corp., New Orleans, 1971-72; cons. Peter F. Johnson & Assocs., New Orleans, 1972-73; exec. v.p. Pyramid Marine, Inc., New Orleans, 1973-76; pres., chief exec. officer, owner, chmn. bd. Pacific-Gulf Marine, Inc., New Orleans, 1976—; trustee Am. Maritime Officers, Dania, Fla. Lt. (j.g.) USNR, 1959-63. Mem. Coun. Am. Master Mariners, Soc. Naval Architects and Marine Engrs., Propeller Club U.S. (Maritime Man of Yr. 1986), U.S. Navy League, Southern Yacht Club, English Turn Country Club. Republican. Roman Catholic. Avocations: fly fishing, golf, hunting, sailing. Home: 3 Lakeway Ct New Orleans LA 70131-3322 Office: Pacific Gulf Marine Inc PO Box 6479 New Orleans LA 70174-6479

JOHNSON, PHILIP LESLIE, lawyer; b. Beloit, Wis., Jan. 24, 1939; s. James Philip and Christabel (Williams) J.; m. Kathleen Rose Westover, May 12, 1979; children: Celeste Marie, Nicole Michelle. AB, Princeton U., 1961; JD, U. South Calif., 1973. Bar: Calif. 1973, U.S. Ct. Appeals (9th cir.) 1975, U.S. Ct. of Military Appeals, 1978, U.S. Supreme Ct. 1980. Pilot U.S. Marine Corps., 1961-70; assoc. Law Office Wm. G. Tucker, L.A., 1973-78; ptnr. Engstrom, Lipscomb & Lack, L.A., 1978-92; judge pro tem Calif. State Bar Ct., 1990-95; ptnr. Lillick & Charles, Long Beach, Calif., 1993-99, Woolley, Russell & Johnson, Long Beach, 1999—; chmn. aerospace law com. Def. Rsch. Inst. Contbr. articles to profl. jours. Pres., bd. dirs. U. So. Calif. Legion Lex, 1992-93; chmn. com. to nom. alumni trustees Princeton U., 1996-97, mem. exec. com. of alumni coun., 1996-97; chmn. Marine Corps Scholarship Found. L.A. Ball, 1997-99. Mem. ABA, (aviation & space law com., torts & ins. practice section), Princeton Club (So. Calif., bd. dirs.). Avocations: flying, snow skiing, jazz. Home: 5340 Valley View Rd Rancho Palos Verdes CA 90275-5089 Office: Woolley Russell & Johnson 444 W Ocean Blvd Ste 1700 Long Beach CA 90802-4525

JOHNSON, PHILIP WAYNE, judge; b. Greenwood, Ark., Oct. 24, 1944; s. John Luther and Flora (Joyce) J.; m. Carla Jean Newsom, Nov. 6, 1970; children: Betsy, Carl, Jeff, Laura, Philip. B.A., Tex. Tech. U., 1965, J.D., 1975. Bar: Tex. 1975, U.S. Dist. Ct. (no. and we. dists.) Tex. 1976, U.S. Ct. Appeals (5th cir.) 1984, U.S. Supreme Ct. 1984; cert. in civil trial and personal injury trial law, Tex. Bd. Legal Specialization. Assoc. Crenshaw Dupree & Milam, Lubbock, Tex., 1975-80; ptnr. Crenshaw Dupree & Milam, 1980-98; justice Tex. State Ct. of Appeals (7th dist), Amarillo, 1999—. Bd. dirs., pres. Lubbock County Legal Aid Soc., Tex., 1977-79; bd. dirs., chmn. Trinity Christian Schs., Lubbock, 1978-83, 85-89; bd. dirs., pres. S.W. Lighthouse for Blind, Lubbock, 1978-85. Served to capt. USAF, 1965-72. Decorated Silver Star, D.F.C.; Cross of Gallantry (Vietnam). Fellow Am. Bar Found., Tex. Bar Found. (life); mem. ABA, Tex. Bar Assn., Amarillo Bar Assn., Lubbock County Bar Assn. (pres. 1984-85), Phi Delta Phi. Home: 7818 Covington Pkwy Amarillo TX 79121-1940 Office: Seventh Ct of Appeals 501 S Fillmore St Rm 2A Amarillo TX 79101-2449

JOHNSON, RALPH RAYMOND, ambassador, federal agency administrator; b. Portland, Oreg., Mar. 31, 1943; s. Ralph Wilson and Margaret Mary (Munly) J.; m. Ann Frances Huetter, Aug. 19, 1967; children: David, Timothy. BA in Polit. Sci., Seattle U., 1963; MA in Internat. Rels., Columbia U., 1965. Mgmt. trainee Seattle First Nat. Bank, 1968-69; vice-consul U.S. Embassy, Georgetown, Guyana, 1969-71; econ. officer U.S. Embassy, Warsaw, Poland, 1973-76, La Paz, Bolivia, 1977-79; asst. chief indsl. and strategic materials U.S. Dept. State, Washington, 1979-81, chief trade agreements div., 1981-83, office dir. European regional polit./econ. affairs, 1985-86, dep. asst. sec. state, 1986-91, prin. dep. asst. sec. state, 1991-93, coord., aid to Eastern Europe with rank of amb., 1993-95; U.S. amb. to Slovak Republic, 1995-99; dep. trade rep. bilateral affairs Japan-Europe U.S. Trade Rep.'s Office, Washington, 1983-85; prin. dep. High Rep. Sarajevo, Bosnia, 1999—. Sgt. U.S. Army, 1965-68. Mem. Am. Fgn. Svc. Assn., Seattle U. Alumni Assn. (Disting. Pub. Svc. award 1994). Roman Catholic. Avocations: photography, building furniture, running, scuba diving.

JOHNSON, RALPH THEODORE, JR., physicist; b. Salina, Kans., Apr. 29, 1935; s. Ralph Theodore and Mary Alice (Wallerius) J.; m. Ruth Elaine Rohrer, Jan. 25, 1958; children: Barbara A., Thomas T., Gregory E., Janet E. MS in Physics, Kans. State U., 1959, PhD, 1964. Staff mem. GE, Cin., 1957-58; rsch. and teaching asst. Kans. State U., 1958-63; from rsch. scientist to mgr. Sandia Nat. Lab., Albuquerque, 1965-97; mem. N.Mex. Govs. Energy Task Force, 1974; mem. assessment panel Nat. Rsch. Panel, 1978-90; mem. Am. Nat. Std. Writing Com., 1990-97. Contbr. articles to profl. jours. Pres., bd. dirs. Marriage Enrichment Nonprofit Corp. 1st lt. USAF, 1963-65. Achievements include patent for neutron radiation detector; memory phenomenon in amorphous semiconductors; ionic conduction in solid electrolytes; radiation effects in semiconductors and electronics; metrology program development; marriage program development. Home: 6601 Arroyo Del Oso Ave NE Albuquerque NM 87109-2733

JOHNSON, RICHARD DARRELL, consulting firm executive, management consultant; b. Columbus, Ohio, Aug. 1, 1935; s. Darrell Dean and Gretchen Price (Motz) J.; m. Ann Elizabeth Sektnan, Apr. 9, 1960; children: Julie Ann, Jennifer Lynn, Douglas Richard. B of Indsl. Engring., Ohio State U., 1958, MBA, 1962. Registered profl. engr., Ohio; CPA, Ohio, Ill.; cert. in computer processing Inst. for Cert. of Computer Profls. Consulting staff Arthur Andersen & Co., Cleve., 1962-65, consulting mgr., 1965-70, consulting mng. ptnr., 1971-75; cons. retail industry head Arthur Andersen & Co., 1969-75, chmn. adv. coun., 1976-78; country mng. ptnr. Arthur Andersen & Co., Tehran, Iran, 1975-77; mng. ptnr. profl. edn. Arthur Andersen & Co., Chgo., 1977-79, mng. ptnr. edn. consulting, 1979-86; mng. ptnr. change mgmt. Andersen Consulting, Chgo., 1986-91, ret. ptnr., 1991; pres. VIA Internat. Ltd., Chgo., 1992-99; chmn. VIA Internat. LLC, Chgo., 1998-99; pres. RDJ Ltd. Mgmt. Conss., 1999—. Treas. Lake Forest (Ill.) Symphony Assn., 1979-81, v.p., 1981-83, exec. v.p., 1983-89, adv. bd., 1989—; gen. coord. Chgo. campaign Am. Cancer Soc., 1983; mem. Ill. Dist. 67 Bd. Edn., Lake Forest, 1984-90, sec., 1984-85, v.p., 1988-90, chmn. edn. com., 1987-90, chmn. strategic planning com. 1989-90; dir. United Way Lake Forest, Lake Bluff, Ill., 1981—, treas., 1984-86, pres., 1986-88; trustee Ravinia Festival Assn., Highland Park, Ill., 1988-95, 96—, vice chmn. 1998—, devel. com., chmn. 1998—, long range planning com. 1996—, fin. com., ann. fund com., 1979—; life mem. Ohio State U. Pres. Club, 1971—, adv. com., 1991-2000, vice chmn., 1995-96, chmn., 1996-98; mem. Chgo. adv. bd. Coll. Engring., Ohio State U., 1988-91, alumni adv. coun., 1996-99, Alumni Assn. bd. dirs., 1999—, Coll. of Bus. Adv. Coun., 1976-83, 1st v.p., 1978-79, Ruth Weimer Mount Leadership Initiatives Fund, 1997—. 1st lt. USAF, 1958-61. Recipient Internat. Disting. Svc. award Assn. Sys. Mgmt., 1976, Alumni Citizenship award Ohio State U., 1998, Gerlach award, 1998. Mem. Chgo. Coun. on Fgn. Rels., Execs. Club Chgo., Pelican Isle Yacht Club (Naples, Fla.), Sloane Gardens Club (London) (treas. 1993-94), Vail (Colo.) Racquet Club. Avocations: skiing, boating, classical music, tennis, international travel. Home: 351 Sussex Ln Lake Forest IL 60045-2057 Office: RDJ Ltd 351 Sussex Lane Lake Forest IL 60045-2057

JOHNSON, RICHARD FRED, lawyer; b. Chgo., July 12, 1944; s. Sylvester Hiram and Naomi Ruth (Jackson) J.; m. Sheila Conley, June 26, 1970; children: Brendon, Bridget, Timothy, Laura. BS, Miami U., Oxford, Ohio,

1966; JD cum laude, Northwestern U., 1969. Bar: Ill. 1969, U.S. Dist. Ct. (no. dist.) Ill. 1969, U.S. Ct. Appeals (7th cir.) 1977, U.S. Supreme Ct. 1978, U.S. Ct. Appeals (2d cir.) 1980, U.S. Ct. Appeals (9th cir.) 1991, U.S. Ct. Appeals (5th cir.) 1993. Law clk. U.S. Dist. Ct. (no. dist.) Ill., Chgo., 1969-70; assoc. firm Lord, Bissell & Brook, Chgo., 1970-77, ptnr., 1977—; lectr. legal edn. Contbr. articles to profl. jours. Recipient Am. Jurisprudence award, 1968. Mem. Chgo. Bar Assn., Union League. Home: 521 W Roscoe St Chicago IL 60657-3518 Office: Lord Bissell & Brook 115 S La Salle St Ste 3200 Chicago IL 60603-3902

JOHNSON, RICHARD TENNEY, lawyer; b. Evanston, Ill., Mar. 24, 1930; s. Ernest Levin and Margaret Abbott (Higgins) J.; m. Marilyn Bliss Meuth, May 1, 1954; children: Ross Tenney, Lenore, Jocelyn. AB with high honors, U. Rochester, 1951; postgrad., Trinity Coll., Dublin, Ireland, 1954-55; LLB, Harvard, 1958. Bar: D.C. 1959. Trainee Office Sec. Def., 1957-59; atty. Office Gen. Counsel. Dept. Def., 1959-63; dep. gen. counsel Dept. Army, 1963-67, Dept. Transp., 1967-70; gen. counsel CAB, 1970-73, mem., 1976-77; gen. counsel NASA, 1973-75, ERDA, 1975-76; chmn. organizational integration Dept. Energy Activation, Exec. Office of Pres., 1977; ptnr. firm Sullivan & Beauregard, 1978-81; gen. counsel Dept. Energy, 1981-83; ptnr. Zuckert, Scoutt, Rasenberger & Johnson, 1983-87; prin. Law Offices of R. Tenney Johnson, Esq., Washington, 1987—; gen. counsel Assn. of Univs. for Rsch. in Astronomy, 1987—. Lt. USNR, 1951-54. Mem. ABA, Fed. Bar Assn., Cosmos Club, Phi Beta Kappa, Theta Delta Chi. Office: 2121 K St NW Ste 800 Washington DC 20037-1829

JOHNSON, RICHARD WALTER, entrepreneur; b. Mpls., Oct. 2, 1928; s. Walter Benjamin and Evelyn (Peterson) J.; m. Marlys Jean Tiller, Feb. 21, 1988; children: Richard Walter, William Charles, Nancy Ann, Thomas Gregory, Michael Richard. B.B.A. with distinction, U. Minn., 1949. C.P.A., Nebr., Ill. With Arthur Andersen & Co. (C.P.A.'s), 1949-74; mng. partner Arthur Andersen & Co. (C.P.A.'s), Omaha, 1960-74; chmn. bd., chief exec. officer Western Securities Co. of Del., Omaha, 1975—; pres., CEO Modern Equipment Co., Omaha, 1975—. Bd. dirs., exec. com. Jr. Achievement Omaha, 1962—, pres., 1966-67; gen. campaign chmn. Heart of the Midlands United Way, 1972, chmn. pacemaker sect. fund raising campaign, 1964, chmn. corporate standards com., 1966, assoc. gen. chmn., 1968, treas., mem. exec. com., 1969; bd. dirs. Fontenelle Forest Nature Ctr. Assn. Mid-Am. council Boy Scouts of Am., Omaha Symphony Assn., Omaha Big Bros. Assn., Omaha Playhouse Assn.; Trustee Creighton U. Pres.'s Council. Recipient One of Outstanding Young Men in Am. award, 1965, Gifford award Fontenelle Forest Assn., 1997. Mem. AICPA, Nebr. Soc. CPAs, Newcomen Soc. N.Am., Omaha C. of C. (chmn. membership rels. com. 1962—, bd. dirs. 1965-76, mem. exec. com., v.p. 1968-72), Omaha Club, Omaha Country Club, Garden of the Gods Club (Colorado Springs), Masons, Shriners, Rotary Internat., Beta Gamma Sigma, Beta Alpha Psi. Home: 1323 N 98th Ct Omaha NE 68114-2112 Office: 2000 Cuming St Omaha NE 68102-4324

JOHNSON, ROBERT ALLAN, psychologist; b. Clun, Shropshire, Eng., Feb. 24, 1951; s. John Thomas and Rosalind Elizabeth (Ingram) J.; m. Bruna Zizmond, Nov. 24, 1979; 1 child, Brendan Giancarlo. BA, Macquarie, NSW, Australia, 1983; M in Clin. Psychology, Macquarie U., NSW, Australia, 2000; MLitt, U. New England, Australia, 1986; MSc, U. NSW, 1990; PhD, U. Sydney, NSW, 1995, B in Applied Sci., 1996. Radiol. technologist orgns. in pvt. and pub. sector, Eng. and Australia, 1975-98; rsch. scholar U. Sydney, 1991-94; rsch. fellow U. NSW, 1995-96; rschr. U. NSW and U. Sydney, 1991-96; psychologist pub. sector, Australia, 1997—; pvt. practice Sydney, 1991—. Mem. APA, AAAS, Am. Psychol. Soc., Australian Psychol. Soc., Am. Inst. Radiology, Soc. Radiology, Internat. Assn. for Study of Pain. E-mail: johnson1@bigpond.net.au. Office: 15 Mount St, NSW Clovelly 2031, Australia

JOHNSON, ROBERT ARNOLD, physician, cardiologist, poet; b. Caldwell, Idaho, May 31, 1942; s. Robert Lyle and Ellen Lora (Salisbury) J.; m. Judith Suzanne Gibson, Sept. 7, 1962 (div. Apr. 1989); children: Heidi Johnson Judge, Heather Johnson Warner, Erin Johnson Shaw; m. Susan Eileen Pickett, Apr. 29, 1989. BS in Zoology, Wash. State U., 1964; MD, U. Wash., 1969. Intern, then resident in medicine Beth Israel Hosp., Boston, 1969-73; fellow in cardiology Mass. Gen. Hosp., Boston, 1971-74; from instr. to asst. prof. medicine/cardiology Mass. Gen. Hosp./Harvard Med. Sch., Boston, 1974-83; cardiologist Walla Walla (Wash.) Clinic, 1983-97; med. dir. cardiac svcs. St. Mary Med. Ctr., Walla Walla, 1997—. Author, co-editor: The Practice of Cardiology, 1980, 2d edit., 1988; author book-length epic poem; contbr. articles to profl. jours. Bd. dirs., chair fundraising Walla Walla Symphony Soc., 1994-97. Mem. Am. Heart Assn. (fellow coun. on clin. cardiology), Acad. Am. Poets, Nat. Assn. Advancement of Sci., Phi Beta Kappa, Alpha Omega Alpha. Democrat. Avocations: music (audience, criticism), travel (Italy), cooking, wine tasting. Home: 362 S 3rd Ave Walla Walla WA 99362-2847 Office: St Mary Physician Group 401 W Poplar St Walla Walla WA 99362-2846

JOHNSON, ROBERT BRUCE, historic preservationist; b. Salina, Kans., Dec. 14, 1941; s. Robert Alexander and Virginia Belle (Keen) J.; m. Dora Koundakjian, May 14, 1966 (div. May 1986); children: Martin, Alicia; m. Genevieve Whittemore, Oct. 18, 1986; 1 child, James Trevor Johnson. BA, Wheaton Coll., 1964; JD, Cath. U. Sch. of Law, Washington, 1976. Orgnl. sales leader The Southwestern Co., Nashville, 1963-65; asst. housing mgr. Nat. Capitol Housing Authority Housing Urban Devel., Washington, 1966-67; project dir. Archdiocese of Washington Office of Edn., Washington, 1967-70; dep. dir. Dept. Labor Youth Svcs., Washington, 1970-75; pres. Intown Properties Inc., Washington, 1977-81, Mt. Vernon Realty Inc., Washington, 1981-86, Premier Realty Svcs. Inc., Washington, 1986-90; sr. v.p. AmeriFund Inc., Washington, 1990-95; devel. dir. Patrick Henry Inst., Lynchburg, Va., 1995-98; cons. Nat. Trust for Hist. Preservation, Washington, 1982-83, New Covenant Schs., Lynchburg, Va.; ptnr. Towne Ctr. Assocs., Staunton, Va., 1979-92, Capitol Link Devel. Assocs., Washington, 1986-89, Coolidge House Assocs., Washington, 1987-94. Contbr. articles to profl. jours. Treas., co-founder New City Montessori Sch., Washington, 1969-73; mem. Cmty. Advisors on Equal Employment, Washington, 1967-70; patron Nat. Children's Choir, 1979-89, treas., initiator Bottle Bill Initiative Campaign, Washington, 1985-86. Recipient Silver Palm Eagle Scout Boy Scouts Am., 1957. Mem. Nat. Trust for Hist. Preservation, Hist. Staunton Found. (ann. preservation award 1982, 83), Victorian Soc. Am., Lynchburg Acad. Music Theatre. Home: Villa Mozart 517 Washington St Lynchburg VA 24504

JOHNSON, ROBERT DOHENY, portfolio manager; b. Aruba, The Netherlands, Antilles, Jan. 3, 1946; s. Robert Archie and Helen Joan (Doheny) J.; m. Monika Cristina Schenkel, Aug. 21, 1981; 1 child, Christopher Michael. BS in Econs., U. Pa., 1968. Registered rep. White, Weld & Co., N.Y.C., 1970-74; Caracas rep. Bank Julius Baer, Zurich, 1974-88; ptnr. Johnson & Stuber Asset Mgrs., Zurich, 1989—. Mem. Union Club (life), N.Y., Cum Laude Soc., Caracas Country Club, Club Baur au Lac, The Brook, N.Y. Home: Harzerstrasse 23, 8704 Herrliberg Switzerland Office: Johnson & Stuber Asset Mgrs, Olgastrasse 4, 8024 Zurich Switzerland

JOHNSON, ROBERT EUGENE, physiologist; b. Conrad, Mont., Apr. 8, 1911; s. Arthur D. and Florence May (Disbrow) J.; m. Margaret Hunter, Jan. 11, 1935; children: Thomas Arthur, Charles William, Katherine Helen (dec.). B.S. in Chemistry, U. Wash., 1931; B.A. in Physiology (Rhodes scholar), U. Oxford, Eng., 1934, D.Phil. in Biochemistry, 1935; M.D., Harvard U., 1941. Research asst. advancing to asst. prof. indsl. physiology Harvard Fatigue Lab., 1935-46; expert cons. QMC 3, AUS, 1941-46; dir. U.S. Army Med. Nutrition Lab., Chgo., 1946-49; prof. physiology U. Ill. at Urbana, 1949-73, head dept., 1949-60, dir. univ. honors program, 1959-67, acting dean Grad. Coll., 1952-53; prof. biology Knox Coll., Galesburg, Ill., 1973-79; coordinator Knox Coll.-Rush U. Med. Program, 1973-79; sci. cons. Presbyn.-St. Luke's Hosp., Chgo., 1973-83; pres. Horn of the Moon Enterprises, Montpelier, Vt., 1980—; vis. prof. physiology U. Vt., 1983—. Co-author: Metabolic Methods, 1951, Physiological Measurements of Metabolic Functions in Man, 1963; author: Sir John Richardson, 1976; also articles in profl. jours. NSF Sr. Postdoctoral Research fellow, 1957-58; Guggenheim Meml. Found. fellow, 1964-65. Mem. Am. Soc. Clin. Investigation, Am. Physiol. Soc., Nutrition Today, History of Sci. Soc., Phi Beta Kappa, Sigma Xi. Home and Office: 5 East Terr South Burlington VT 05403-6145

JOHNSON, ROBERT LEE, JR., physician, educator, researcher; b. Dallas, Apr. 28, 1926; s. Robert L. and Doris (Miller) J.; m. Aileen Johnson, 1952; children: Stephen Lee, Robert Edward. BS, So. Meth. U., 1947; MD, Northwestern U., 1951. Intern Cook County Hosp., Chgo., 1951-52; resident in internal medicine Parkland Meml. Hosp., Phila., 1952-55; fellow nat. foun. infantile paralysis and clin. instr. U. Tex. Southwestern Med. Ctr., Dallas, 1955-56; fellow dept. physiol. and pharmacology Grad. Sch. Medicine U. Pa., Phila., 1956-57; asst. prof. U. Tex. Southwestern Med. Ctr., Dallas, 1959-65, assoc. prof., 1965-69, prof. medicine, 1969—; vis. staff Parkland Meml. Hosp., Dallas, 1957—, Zale Lipshy U. Hosp., Dallas, 1989—; cons. chest diseases VA Hosp., Dallas, 1966—; dir. chest medicine clinic Parkland Meml. Hosp., 1983—; mem. parent rev. com. Nat. Heart, Lung, and Blood Inst. for Spl. Ctrs. of Rsch. proposals, 1983-85; mem. Nat. Heart, Lung, and Blood Rsch. Rev. Com., 1985-89; mem. respiratory and applied physiology study sect. NIH, 1991-94. Mem. editl. bd. Jour. Clin. Investigation, 1972-77, Jour. Applied Physiology, 1980-82, 96-2000, Circulation, 1996—; guest referee editor Jour. Applied Physiology, Am. Jour. Physiology, Chest, Circulation, Circulation Rsch., Am. Rev. Respiratory Disease, Am. Jour. Med. Sci., Jour. Clin. Investigation, Early Human Devel., Kidney Internat.; contbr. articles to profl. jours. With Naval ROTC, 1945-46; with USNR, 1944-46; maj. USAR, 1962. Mem. Am. Heart Assn. (cardiopulmonary coun. exec. com. mem. 1990-92, nominating com. cardiopulmonary coun. 1989-93, chmn. 1990-92), Am. Thoracic Soc. (planning com. mem. 1987-90, com. proficiency standards 1985-94, Scientific Accomplishment award 1996, recipient Scientific Accomplishment award 1996), Am. Coll. Chest Physicians, Am. Fedn. Clin. Rsch., Am. Physiol. Soc., Am. Soc. Clin. Investigation, Assn. Am. Physicians, Cen. Soc. Clin. Rsch., So. Soc. Clin. Rsch., Soc. Sigma Xi. Fax: 214-648-8027. E-mail: robert.johnson@email.swmed.edu. Office: UT Southwestern Med Ctr 5323 Harry Hines Blvd Stop 7200 Dallas TX 75390-7200

JOHNSON, ROBERT LOUIS, cable television company executive; b. Hickory, Miss., Apr. 8, 1946; m. Sheila Crump, Jan. 19, 1969. BA in History, U. Ill., 1968; M in Pub. Affairs, Princeton U., 1972. Press. sec. Hon. Walter E. Fauntroy, Congl. del. from Washington, 1973-76; v.p. govt. rels. Nat. Cable TV Assn., 1976-79; founder, pres. Black Entertainment TV, Washington, 1979—, Dist. Cablevision, Inc., 1980—; chmn., pres., CEO BET Holdings, Inc. (formerly Black Entertainment TV), Washington, 1993—. Recipient Image award NAACP, 1982, Bus. of Yr. award D.C. C. of C., 1985, Exec. Leadership Coun. award Turner Broadcasting, 1993, 20/20 Vision award Cablevision Mag., 1995, Hall of Fame award Broadcasting and Cable Mag., 1997, Good Guys award Nat. Women's Polit. Caucus, 1998, Disting. Alumni award Princeton U., 1998. Office: BET Holdings Inc 1900 W Pl NE Washington DC 20018-1211

JOHNSON, RODNEY MARCUM, lawyer; b. Dayton, Ohio, Feb. 6, 1947; s. Marvin Clarence and Frances (Marcum) J.; m. Martha Elizabeth Mapp, Sept. 3, 1967 (div. 1974); m. Madolyn Gorman, May 5, 1979; children: Kristine Janeen, Jarrod Marcum, Jason Oliver. AS in Bus. Mgmt., Sinclair C.C., 1968; BS in Bus. Econs., Wright State U., 1975; JD, Cleve. State U., 1978. Bar: Ohio 1979, U.S. Dist. Ct. (so. dist.) Ohio 1980, U.S. Tax Ct. 1980, U.S. Ct. Mil. Appeals 1983, U.S. Supreme Ct. 1983, Fla. 1985, U.S. Dist. Ct. (no. dist.) Fla. 1986. Methods engr. Delco Moraine Divsn. GMC, Dayton, 1965-71; sys. analyst D.W. Mikesell, Inc., Dayton, 1971-74; prin. Johnson Tool Co., Savannah, Ga., 1974-75; pvt. practice Dayton, 1979-81; dist. chief legal counsel Fla. Dept. Health, Pensacola, 1986—. Lt. comdr. JAGC, USN, 1981-86. Mem. Escambia-Santa Rosa Bar Assn. Avocations: boating, fishing, scuba diving. Office: Fla Dept Health 1295 W Fairfield Dr Pensacola FL 32501-1107

JOHNSON, RUFUS NORMAN, JR., electrical engineer; b. Pleasant Hill, N.C., Aug. 11, 1958; s. Rufus Norman J. and Catherine Fay Butler. Diploma, Halifax C.C., 1977, AA in Bus. Adminstrn., 1986. Cert. Nachi Robotics Sys. Elec. engr. Cummins Engine Co., Whitakers, N.C., 1988—. Author: The Legend of the Landkeepers, 1999. Former fire chief Gaston (N.C.) Vol. Fire Dept. Mem. N.C. Fossil Club. Avocation: amateur paleontologist. Home: 937 Gray St Roanoke Rapids NC 27870-2358

JOHNSON, RUFUS WINFIELD, lawyer; b. Montgomery County, Md., May 1, 1911; s. Charles L. and Margaret (Smith) J.; m. Rosena L. Allen, June 21, 1939 (div. May 1971); m. Vaunda Louise Griffith, May 29, 1971; step-children: Yvonne, Jackie, Karen, Rodney, Michelle. AB, Howard U., 1934, postgrad., 1934-36, LLB, 1939. Bar: Calif., Ark., Supreme Ct. Ark., Supreme Ct. Calif., D.C. Dist. Ct., U.S. Ct. Appeals, D.C., U.S. Supreme Ct., Supreme Ct. of South Korea; cert. counsel Judge Advocate Gen. Sch., Washington. Pvt. practice D.C., Calif., Ark., 1945—; originator Lawyer's Pro Bono Svc. Ret. lt. col. USAR. Recipient Combat Infantry badge, U.S. Army, 1944, Purple Heart, 1944, Bronze Star, 1944, Spl. Citation Bravery, 1944. Mem. VFW (life), Am. Judicature Soc., Am. Acad. Polit. and Social Sci., Mil. Order Purple Heart, Internat. Soc. Poets, Am. Kempo Karate Assn., Sr. Citizens Coalition, Ret. Officers Assn., Am. Legion, Masons, Am. Karate Assn. (5th degree Shorin-Ryu Black Belt), Lions. Baptist. Home: PO Box 776 Mason TX 76856-0776

JOHNSON, RUTH FLOYD, educator, consultant; b. Plateau, Ala., Apr. 19, 1935; d. Nathan Daniel and Ora Anna (Ellis) Floyd; children: Anthony, Walter, Camille, Quinitta, Annette. Student, Tuskegee Inst., 1951-53; BS in History, Bowie (Md.) State U., 1970; MEd in Counseling, U. Md., 1977; PhD in Human Svcs. Adminstrn., Univ. for Humanistic Studies, San Diego, 1982. Cert. tchr., counselor. Radio personality Sta. WMOZ, 1953-56; owner, dir. Azalea Sch. Dance, 1954-56; numerous posts for fed. govt., 1957-69; tchr., adminstr. Pub. Schs. of Prince George's County, Md., 1970-78; tchr.-counselor Dunbar S.T.A.Y. Sch., Washington, 1974-75; instr. child and youth study divsn. U. Md., 1977-78; CEO Diametron Corp., 1979-81; tchr. L.A. Unified Sch. Dist., 1980-82, Pasadena (Calif.) Unified Sch. Dist., 1982-83, Rialto (Calif.) Unified Sch. Dist., 1984—; profl. devel. coord. Calif. State Polytech. U., 1995—. Author: Remediating Mass Poverty: Development of a Model Program, 1982, Pep Squad handbook, 1991, (with others: Government/Contemporary Issues: A Curriculum Guide, 1976. Active PTAs; mem. organizing com. Peppermill Village Civic Assn., 1966; vol. Boy Scouts Am., 1968-72, Sr. Citizens of Prince George's County, 1974-76; bd. dirs.Mill Point Improvement Assn., 1975-78, Combined Communities in Action, 1976-78; mem. Prince George's County Hosp. Commn., 1978; mem. Altadena Town Coun., 1983; founder Rialto Freedom and Cultural Soc., 1988; mem. Calif. 36th Dist. Bicentennial Adv. Com., 1989; mem. exec. com. Rialto Police/Community Rels. Team, 1993. Recipient Outstanding Svc. to Children and Yourh award Md. Congress PTA, 1969, Services to Boy Scouts Am. award, 1969, Svcs. to Sr. Citizens award, 1975, Community Svc. award Rialto Freedom and Cultural Soc., 1993, others. Mem. NEA, NAACP, Nat. Assn. Univ. Women, Nat. Coun. Negro Women, Zeta Phi Beta, Gamma Phi Delta. Avocations: world travel, theatre, tennis, spectator sports, outdoor activities. Home: PO Box 1946 Rialto CA 92377-1946

JOHNSON, SAMMYE LARUE, communications educator; b. Dallas, Oct. 8, 1946. BS in Journalism with distinction, Northwestern U., 1968; MS in Journalism with highest distinction, 1969. Asst. editor Where Mag., Chgo., 1969; feature writer Chicago Today newspaper, Chgo., 1969-71, editor Sunday mag., 1971-73; editor San Antonio Mag., 1976-79; comms. dir. VIA Met. Transit Sys., San Antonio, Fed. Rep. Germany, 1979; asst. prof. journalism William Allen White Sch. Journalism U. Kans., Lawrence, 1979-80; asst. prof. journalism Trinity U., San Antonio, 1980-85, assoc. prof. comm., 1980-91, prof. comm., 1991—, Carlos Augustus de Lozano chair journalism, 1998—; cons. pub. rels. Community Guidance Ctr., San Antonio, 1985-88, Funding Info. Ctr., San Antonio, 1983—, Bexar County Women's Ctr., San Antonio, 1984—. Author: The Magazine from Cover to Cover, 1999, Magazine Publishing, 2000; contbr. articles to profl. jours., consumer and trade mags., newspapers. Named Today's Woman of Achievement San Antonio Light Newspaper, 1981, Pub. Rels. Educator of Yr. Tex. Pub. Rels. Assn., 1984-85. Mem. Women in Comms. (dir. 1978-80, pres. chpt. 1983-84, Proliner award 1981, 82, 83, 86, 87, 88, 90, 93, 96, 97, Comms. Headliner of Yr. 1984), Internat. Assn. Bus. Communicators (bd. dirs. 1979, Gold Quill award 1979, named Communicator of Yr. 1981, numerous other awards 1976-96), Assn. for Edn. in Journalism and Mass Comms. (sec., vice chair, chair mag. divs. 1985-89, Mag. Educator of Yr. 1997), Kappa Tau Alpha. Home: 7523 Bridgewater Dr San Antonio TX 78209-3113 Office: Trinity U Dept Communication 715 Stadium Dr San Antonio TX 78212-7200

JOHNSON, SAMUEL CURTIS, wax company executive; b. Racine, Wis., Mar. 2, 1928; s. Herbert Fisk and Gertrude (Brauner) J.; m. Imogene Powers, May 8, 1954; children: Samuel Curtis III, Helen Johnson-Leipold, Herbert Fisk III, Winifred Johnson Marquart. BA, Cornell U., 1950; MBA, Harvard U., 1952; LLD (hon.), Carthage Coll., 1974, Northland Coll., 1974, Ripon Coll., 1980, Carroll Coll., 1981, U. Surrey, 1985, Marquette U., 1986, Nijenrode U., 1992. With S.C. Johnson & Son, Inc., Racine, 1954—, internat. v.p., 1962-63, exec. v.p., 1963-66, pres., 1966-67, chmn., pres., chief exec. officer, 1967-72, chmn., chief exec. officer, 1972-88, chmn., 1988—; bd. dirs. Deere & Co., Moline, Ill., H.J. Heinz Co., Phila., Mobil Corp., N.Y.C.; chmn. bd. dirs. Johnson Worldwide Assocs., Inc., Johnson Internat. Inc. Trustee Am. Mus. Natural History, N.Y.C.; trustee emeritus The Mayo Found., Cornell U., presdl. councillor; chm Johnson's Wax Fund, Inc., Johnson Found., Inc.; founding chmn. emeritus Prairie Sch., Racine; chmn. adv. coun. Cornell U. Grad. Sch. Mgmt.; regent emeritus Smithsonian Instn.; hon. mem. Bus. Coun.; mem. nat. bd. govs. The Nature Conservancy. Mem. Chi Psi. Clubs: Cornell (N.Y.C., Milw.); Univ. (Milw.); Racine Country. Home: 4815 Lighthouse Dr Racine WI 53402-2666 Office: S C Johnson Wax 1525 Howe St Racine WI 53403-2236

JOHNSON, SANDRA ANN, elementary education educator, counselor; b. Houston, Apr. 27, 1958; d. Johnnie and Area (Bradford) J. AA, Houston C.C., 1991; BBA, Tex. So. U., 1994; MA, Prairie View A&M U., 1998; PhD, Tex. So. U., 2000; PhD in Psychology, Berne U. Lic. profl. counselor. Tchr. computers Houston Sch. Dist., 1981—; instr. North Harris Coll., Houston, 1996—, Houston C.C. Vol. Herman Hosp., Houston, 1987-88, Houston Recovery Ctr.; counselor Vision of Hope Women, Houston, 1996-97, Cmty. Devel. Corp.; contact person Houston Mayor's Camp, 1997; pres. H.; bd. dirs. Vision of Hope. Named Disting. Role Model of Houston, North Main Ch. of God in Christ, 1998. Mem. Chi Sigma Iota. Democrat. Baptist. Avocations: tennis, golf, jogging, reading, racquetball. Office: Mary Bethune Acad 1500 S Victory Dr Houston TX 77088-7102

JOHNSON, SHARON MARGUERITE, social worker, clinical hypnotherapist; b. San Diego, July 23, 1962; d. James Hugh and Efstathia (Bliziotis) J.; m. Sandy L. Scott, July 6, 1995; children: Devon, Rocky, Madonna, Sadie, Audre, Maya, Yoko. AAS, So. Maine Tech. Coll., South Portland, 1983; BA in Social Work, U. Maine, Orono, 1992, MSW, 1993. Lic. clin. social worker, mental health rehab. technician IV, transformational breath facilitator. Head cook Meals for Maine, Inc., Bangor, 1985-88; instr. ARC, Bangor, 1987-92; counselor assoc. substance abuse Wellspring, Inc., Bangor, 1987-93; counselor aide Onward Program U. Maine, Orono, 1989-92; intensive case mgr. Cmty. Health and Counseling Svc., Bangor, 1993-95, mental health therapist, 1993-97; consultation liaison clinician Acadia Hosp., Bangor, 1997-99, team leader, crisis cons., 1999—; pvt. practice psychotherapy, 1997—; adj. social work faculty U. Maine, Orono, 1995; adj. mem. human svc. faculty U. Coll., Bangor, 1997—; field interviewer Rsch. Triangle Inst., 1997. Mem. edn. com. Peace and Justice Ctr. Eastern Maine, Bangor, 1993-96, mem. steering com., 1995-96; mem. admissions com. U. Maine Sch. Social Work, Orono, 1994-95; asst. to vol. coord. Maine Won't Discriminate, Bangor, 1995. Mem. NASW (Maine chpt. chair clin. com. 1995-96, BASW student rep. 1991-92, pres.-elect 1994-95, BASW Ray Dow Meml. award 1992, named MSW Outstanding Student 1993), Am. Assn. Profl. Hypnotherapists (cert.), No. New Eng. Soc. Clin. Hypnotherapists, Phi Beta Kappa, Phi Kappa Phi. Democrat. Avocations: metaphysics, pet therapy, guitar. Home: PO Box 147 Winterport ME 04496-0147 Office: The Acadia Hosp Stillwater Ave Bangor ME 04401

JOHNSON, SHIRLEY Z., lawyer; b. Burlington, Iowa, Mar. 6, 1940; d. Arthur Frank and Helen Martha (Nelson) Zaiss; m. Charles Rumph, Jan. 19, 1979. BA summa cum laude, U. Iowa, 1962; JD with honors, U. Mich., 1965. Bar: Calif. 1966, D.C. 1976, U.S. Supreme Ct. 1979. Trial atty. antitrust divsn. U.S. Dept. Justice, San Francisco, 1965-72; counsel antitrust subcom. U.S. Senate Jud. Com., Washington, 1973-75; ptnr. Baker & Hostetler, Washington, 1976-85; pvt. practice Washington, 1985-98; ptnr., chair antitrust and trade regulations dept. Greenberg Traurig, Washington, 1998—; adv. bd. BNA Antitrust & Trade Regulations Reporter, 2000—; mediator U.S. Dist. Ct., Washington, 1990—. Contbr. articles to profl. jours. Trustee The Textile Mus., Washington, 1991—, v.p. bd. trustees, 1994—. Mem. ABA, Women's Bar Assn. (bd. dirs. 1989-91), Am. Law Inst., Order of Coif, Phi Beta Kappa. Democrat. Avocation: collecting Asian art. Office: Greenburg Traurig 800 Connecticut Ave NW Washington DC 20006-2709

JOHNSON, SONDRA LEA, accountant; b. Kansas City, Mo., May 11, 1952; d. Albert John Oscar and Dorothy Mae (Hudgens) J. AA, Longview Coll., 1972; BSBA cum laude in Acctg., Cen. Mo. State U., 1974, MBA, 1980. CPA, Mo. Acct. Farmland Industries, Kansas City, 1974-76; acct., auditor Ernst & Whinney, Kansas City, 1976-79, Laventhol & Horwath, Kansas City, 1980-81; corp. acct., mgr. Butler Mfg. Co., Kansas City, 1981-84; audit supr. Grant Thornton Internat., Kansas City, 1984-89; sr. fin. analyst Hoechst Marion Roussel, Kansas City, 1989-95; with fin. reporting dept. UtiliCorp United, Inc., Kansas City, 1996-99; sr. fin. analyst ERC/GE, Overland Park, Kans., 1999—; specialized instr. nat. continuing edn. tng. program, Grant Thornton Internat., various locations U.S.A.; acctg. instr. Cen. Mo. State U., Warrensburg, 1979-80, Rockhurst Coll., Kansas City, 1981-82, Avila Coll., Kansas City, 1989-90. Mem. AICPAs, Inst. Mgmt. Accts., Mo. Soc. CPAs, Women's C. of C. of Kansas City, Phi Kappa Phi. Democrat. Lutheran. Avocations: travel, collecting ltd. edition figurines, spectator sports, music. Office: ERC GE 5200 Metcalf Ave Overland Park KS 66202-1296

JOHNSON, STEPHEN WALTER, veterinarian; b. Columbus, Ohio, Apr. 21, 1960; s. Walter Eugene and Annemarie J.; m. Lynette Sue Johnson, Jan. 25, 1986. BS, Colo. State U., 1982, DVM, 1986. Hosp. owner and dir. Allard Animal Hosp., Loveland, Colo., 1986—. State rep. Dist. 49 Colo. Gen. Assembly, Denver, 1997—; chmn. Larimer County Colo. Planning Commn., Ft. Collins, 1987-96; pres. United Way of Loveland/Berthoval, 1994-95; bd. dirs. Loveland C. of C., 1991-94. Republican. Baptist. Avocations: stamp collecting, hockey, current events.

JOHNSON, STEWART WILLARD, civil engineer; b. Mitchell, S.D., Aug. 17, 1933; s. James Elmer Johnson and Grace Mahala (Erwin) Johnson Parsons; m. Mary Anis Giddings, June 24, 1956; children: Janelle Chiemi, Gregory Stewart, Eric Willard. BSCE, S.D. State U., 1956; BA in Bus. Adminstrn. and Polit. Sci., U. Md., 1960; MSCE, PhD, U. Ill., 1964. Registered profl. engr., Ohio. Commd. 2d lt. USAF, 1956, advanced through grades to lt. col.; prof. mechs. and civil engring. Air Force Inst. Tech. USAF, Dayton, Ohio, 1964-75; dir. civil engring. USAF, Seoul, Republic of Korea, 1976-77; chief civil engring. research div. USAF, Kirtland AFB, N.Mex., 1977-80; ret. USAF, 1980; prin. engr. BDM Corp., Albuquerque, 1980-94, Johnson and Assocs., Albuquerque, 1994—; cons. in site surveys, found. design, constrn. of grund stas. for satellite comm. sys., 1992-96; cons. space sci. and lunar basing NASA, U. N.Mex., N.Mex. State U. and Los Alamos Nat. Lab., 1987-92; adj. prof. civil engring. U. N.Mex., 1987-92; prin. investigator devel. concepts for lunar astron. obs. U. N.Mex., N.Mex. State U., NASA, 1987-94; tech. chmn. Space '88, Space '90, Space '94, Space '96, Space '98, Space 2000, Internat. Confs., Albuquerque; vis. lectr. Internat. Space U., Japan, 1992, Huntsville, Ala., 1993, Barcelona, Spain, 1994, Stockholm, 1995; mem. panel on siting lunar base European Space Agy., 1994; gen. chair Space 96 and RCEII Conf., Albuquerque, 1996; gen. chmn. Space Conf., Albuquerque, 1998, 2000, Robotics Conf., Albuquerque, 1998, 2000. Editor Engineering, Construction, and Operations in Space, I, 1988, II, 90, V, 96, Space 2000 Procs.; contbr. articles to profl. jours. Pres. ch. coun. Ch. of Good Shepherd United Ch. of Christ, Albuquerque, 1983-85, chmn. bd. deacons, 1991-93, moderator, 1996-97; S.W. Conf. (United Ch. Christ) del. to Gen. Synod XIX, St. Louis, 1993, Gen. Synod XX, Oakland, Calif., 1995, Gen. Synod XXI, Columbus, Ohio, 1997; trustee Lunar Geotech. Inst., 1990—; mem. adv. bd. Lab. for Extraterrestrial Structures Rsch., Rutgers U., 1990—. Fellow Nat. Acad. Scis. NRC, 1970-71; recipient World Bar Assn. Space Humanitarian award, 1996. Fellow ASCE (chmn. exec. com. aerospace divsn. 1979, tech. activities com. 1984, chmn. com space engring. and constrn. 1987—, mem. nat. space policy com. 1988—,

chmn. 1990—, Outstanding News Corr. award 1981, Aerospace Scis. and Tech. Applications award 1985, 90, Edmund Friedman Profl. Recognition award 1989); mem. AIAA (space logistics com., Engr. of Yr. region IV 1990), Soc. Am. Mil. Engrs., Am. Geophys. Union, Soc. Am. Milit. Engrs., Sigma Xi, Pi Sigma Alpha. Republican. Mem. United Ch. of Christ. Avocations: photography, swimming, walking, gardening, hiking.

JOHNSON, THANGIRALA SUDHAKAR, biotechnologist, researcher; b. Vijayawada, Andhra Pradesh, India, Oct. 13, 1965; s. John and Manikyam T.; m. Pushpanjali, Apr. 25, 1995. BS, Loyola Coll., Vijayawada, India, 1985; MS, Kakatiya U., Warangal, India, 1988; PhD, Ctrl. Food Technol. Rsch. Inst, Mysore, India, 1994. Plant biotechnology researcher. Researcher Ctrl. Food Technol. Rsch. Inst., Mysore, India, 1988-94; sr. scientist Dabur Rsch. Found., New Delhi, India, 1994—. Author: Recent Advances in Biotechnology Applications of Plant Tissue Culture, 1997, Role of Biotechnology in Medical and Aromatic Plants, 1997; contbr. articles to profl. jours. Recipient Best Oral Presentation Assn. Microbiologists of India, 1990, Shared Laljee Godhoo Smarak award for Excellence in R & D Assn. Food Scientists and Technologists, 1996, Young Scientist award, 1997, Indian Sci. Congress award, 2000. Mem. Internat. Assn. Plant Tissue Culture, Asia-Pacific Assn. Micropropagators, Soc. Biol. Chemists (Best Rsch. Poster Presentation 1991, 92, 93, 94, 95). Avocations: reading, listening to music, cricket, playing drums, photography. Office: Dabur Rsch Found, 8/3 Asaf Ali Rd, 110 002 New Delhi India

JOHNSON, THEA JEAN, internet and intranet security service provider; b. Conshohocken, Pa.; d. Andrew Edward and Mary Rachel (Hillyard) Lewis; m. Lewis Edward Johnson, Apr. 30, 1966; 1 child, Vanessa Rachel. BS in Indsl. Mgmt., Temple U., 1968; Diploma in Computer Systems Engring., IBM Edn. Ctr., N.Y.C., 1968; AMA Cert., Villanova U., 1976. Internet/Intranet security svc. provider RGI, Falls Church, Va., 1981-84; pres. NESS, Reston, Va., 1984—. Facilitator/co-author: (book) Lifelong Learning, 1992 (plaque 1992), others. Bd. dirs. Reston Community Assn., 1988-89; mem. Fairfax County Commn., 1989-92; nat. del. Dem. Nat. Conv., San Francisco, 1984; chair Fairfax County Coun. Arts, 1993; fgn. rels. commr. Internat. Children's Festival, Wolf Trap; deacon Martin Luther King Ch.; co-chairperson Va. del. White House Conf. on Small Bus., 1995; mem. White House Conf. on Small Bus. Summit, 1996; founder IBM Acad Tng. Program for Phila. h.s. children at risk. Recipient Svc. award U.S. Dept. Health and Human Svcs., Washington, 1992, citation Outstanding Vol. Reagan/Bush, Washington, 1985, Outstanding Contbn. to White House Conf. on Small Bus. Pres. William J. Clinton, others. Mem. Network Entrepreneurial Women (charter mem.), LWV (exec. bd. Reston chpt. 1989-91), Va. Assn. Female Execs. (adv. bd. 1989-93), Alpha Kappa Alpha. Democrat. Baptist. Avocations: intergenerational community programs, gourmet cooking, tennis, puzzles, decorating. Office: NESS Inc 2022 Swans Neck Way Ste 2B Reston VA 20191-4035

JOHNSON, THOMAS DALE, management consultant; b. DeKalb, Ill., Aug. 9, 1942; s. Orville J. and Dorace G. (Gonterman) J.; m. Patricia T. Riley, Sept. 6, 1969; children: Christopher, Todd, Shawn, John Scott. BS in Chem. Engring., Purdue U., 1965, MS in Indsl. Adminstrn., 1966. Cons. Price Waterhouse & Co., Washington, 1969-71; adminstrv. mgr. Nat. Coun. Equal Bus. Opportunity, Washington, 1971-73; owner Riley & Johnson, Washington, 1971—; v.p. Washington Mgmt. Group, 1978-83, Wayne Mid-Atlantic, 1980-90; v.p. fed. regulatory products Info. Handling Svcs., 1983-87; pres. Bus. Rsch. Svcs., Inc., 1991—; v.p. mktg., sales and sys. gen. mgr. Asia United Press Internat., 1996-97; pub. Bradford's Directory Mktg. Rsch. Agys., 1999—; founder, CIO, dir. Biosupplies.com, 1999—. Contbr. articles to profl. jours. Pub. mkt. rsch. directories, govt. advisories; treas. St. Columba's Ch., 1980-82; bd. dirs. Neighborhood Planning Coun., 1986-93; treas. Nat. Dir. Pub. Assn., 1993—; co-founder Capital Content Network, Online Pubs. Assn., 1999—. Served with Chem. Corps, U.S. Army, 1967-68. Mem. Nat. Directory Publ. Assn. (treas.). Episcopalian. Office: 4201 Connecticut Ave NW Washington DC 20008-1158

JOHNSON, TRACEY LOUISE, mathematics educator; b. Balt., Aug. 8, 1967; d. Bernard Milton and Mary Allen Johnson. BS, Hampton N.S.U., 1991; MS, U. Ga., 1998, postgrad., 1998—. Data analyst Bullock Electoral Cons., Atlanta, 1994-95; asst. V.p. Acad. Affairs, Athens, Ga., 1994-95; ednl. program specialist Upward Bound Trio-Program, Athens, 1994-96; math faculty Athens Area C.C., 1996—, U. Ga., Athens, 1998—; co-advisor Obtaining Student Excellence, Athens, 1996—; reviewer pilot calculator program Ohio State U., Athens, 1996; acad. cons. McGraw Hill, Chgo., 1998—; cons. Clarke County Sch. Bd., Athens, 1999—; presenter in field. Co-editor: Business Math, 1999; contbr. articles to profl. jours. instr. Upward Bound, U. Ga., 1995, 96; judge of elections Bd. Election Suprs., Balt., 1998. Recipient Outstanding Svc. award Grad. Profl. Scholars, Svc. award Athens '96 Olympic Com., 1996. Mem. Nat. Coun. Tchrs. Math., North Ga. Assn. Developmental Educators (polit. liaison 1999—), Classic Ga. Links, Inc. (founder, v.p. 1999—), United Meth. Women (v.p. 1997—). Avocations: interior decorating, ballroom dancing, wine tasting, yoga, travel. E-mail: tjohnson@coe.uga.edu. Office: Univ Ga 301 Milledge Hall Athens GA 30602

JOHNSON, W. THOMAS, JR., media executive; b. 1941. BJ, U. Ga., 1963; MBA, Harvard U., 1965. With Tex. Broadcasting Corp., Dallas, 1965-75; exec. v.p. Tex. Broadcasting Corp., 1965; pub. Dallas-Herald Times, 1975; with L.A. Times, 1975—, pres., 1977, pub., 1980, sr. v.p., 1986, vice chmn., chmn. bd. dirs.; pres., bd. dirs., chmn., CEO Cable News Network, 1990—; chmn. bd. dirs. Times Mirror Newspaper mgmt com.; v.p. Turner Broadcasting Sys., Atlanta. Dep. press sec., spl. asst. Pres. Lyndon B. Johnson, 1969. White House fellow, 1965; named Pub. of Yr., Adweek Mag., 1984, Cable Exec. of Yr., Adweek Mag., 1991; Recipient Horatio Alger Distinguished Am. award, 1987. Mem. Stanford Profl. Journalism Fellowship Program (chmn.), Lyndon B. Johnson Found. (chmn.), Mayo Found. (bd trustees), Knight Found. (bd. trustees). Office: Cable News Network 1CNN Ctr NW PO Box 105366 Atlanta GA 30348-5366

JOHNSON, WALLACE, retired army officer; b. Oklahoma City, Aug. 8, 1939; s. Carroll Wallace and Pauletta (Bibbs) J.; m. Lela Mae Johnson, Dec. 25, 1959; children: Wallace, Steven, Valerie Lynne, Sharon Denise. BS, U. Okla., 1961; MBA, Ala. A&M U., 1973. Commd. 2d lt. U.S. Army, 1961, advanced through grades to lt. col., 1978; lt. inf. platoon leader, exec officer 1/58th Inf. (Mech), Ft. Benning, Ga., 1962-64; detachment comdr. Co. A-29 C 10th spl. forces Bad Tolz, West Germany, 1964-66, detachment comdr. A333, 5th spl. forces group, Republic Vietnam, 1966-67; br. chief instr. USAMMCS Redstone Arsenal, Ala., 1969-71; security plans, ops. officer 23d support group, Republic Korea, 1971-72; chief orgn. br. USAMMCS, Redstone Arsenal, 1973-75; exec. officer 101st Ordnance Bn., Heilbronn, W. Ger., 1976-78; surety insp. Office of Insp. Gen., Heidelberg, W. Ger., 1978-79; sr. logistics instr. Command and Gen. Staff Coll., Ft. Leavenworth, Kans., 1979-84; chief materiel and logistics systems div. Army Ordnance Missile and Munition Ctr. and Sch., 1984-85; sr. program analyst CAS, Inc., 1985-86; mgr. logistics integration Acustar, Inc. Mil.-Pub. Electronic Systems, 1986-88, mgr. bus. devel. dept., automatic test equipment (ATE)/test program sets (TPS) and electroluminescent display products Chrysler Corp., 1986-91; dir. mktg. Automation Rsch. Systems Ltd., 1991-93, program mgr., 1993-94 GMU, 1994—; dir., mentor-protege program; instr. U.S. Army service shcs.; sr. parachutist, jump master. Decorated Combat Inf. Badge, Bronze Star. Mem. Assn. U.S. Army, Am. Def. Preparedness Assn., Internat. Platform Assn., Soc. Logistics Engrs., Unmanned Vehicle Assn., Spl. Forces Assn., Nat. Def. Industry Assn. Republican. Baptist. Club: Jaywalkers of Ft. Leavenworth (v.p. 1980-81), Kiwanis, Nat. Space Club (vice chmn.). Lodge: Sertoma (Leavenworth chpt. pres. 1981-84). Home: 9513 Retriever Rd Burke VA 22015-4515 Office: George Mason U Fairfax VA 22030-3409

JOHNSON, WALTER FRANK, JR., lawyer; b. Georgiana, Ala., Apr. 14, 1945; s. Walter F. and Marjorie Ellen (Carnathan) J.; m. Emily Waldrep, Nov. 23, 1969; children—Brian W., Stacey E. BS in Bus. Adminstrn., Auburn U., 1968; JD, Samford U., 1973. Bar: Ala. 1973, Ga. 1974. Assoc. Hatcher, Meyerson, Oxford and Irvin, Atlanta, 1973-74, Thompson and Redmond, Columbus, Ga., 1974-78; sole practice, Columbus, Ga., 1978—; asst. pub. defender, Columbus, 1978; acct. Union Camp Corp., 1968-70. Mem. ABA, Ala. State Bar, State Bar of Ga., Columbus Lawyers Club. Methodist. Home: 3235 Flint Dr Columbus GA 31907-2029 Office: PO Box 6507 3006 University Ave Columbus GA 31907-2106

JOHNSON, WILLIAM BRUCE, retail executive; b. Nassau, The Bahamas, Aug. 24, 1940; s. William Kenneth Johnson and Wilhelmine Violet (Hussey) Eyres; m. Calliope Klonaris, Apr. 27, 1969 (div. Oct. 1979); m. Janet Loren McKay, Feb. 25, 1984; 1 child; Bruce William John. Grad., Lindsay Collegiate Inst., 1958. Clerk, bookkeeper Bahamian Paint Supply, Nassau, 1958-60, acting mgr., 1960-66; gen. mgr. Bahamian Paint Supply Ltd., Nassau, 1966-70, pres., minority shareholder, 1970-81, pres., majority shareholder, 1981—; pres. La Boheme Ltd., Friar Ltd. Methodist. Avocations: swimming, billiards. Home: 98 Yorkshire St, Nassau The Bahamas Office: Bahamian Paint Supply Ltd, PO Box N-1321, Nassau Bahamas

JOHNSON, WILLIAM POTTER, newspaper publisher; b. Peoria, Ill., May 4, 1935; s. William Zweigle and Helen Marr (Potter) J.; m. Pauline Ruth Rowe, May 18, 1968; children: Darragh Elizabeth, William Potter. AB, U. Mich., 19957. Gen. mgr. Bureau County Rep., Inc., Princeton, Ill., 1961-72; pres. Johnson Newspapers, Inc., Sebastopol, Calif., 1972-75, Evergreen, Colo., 1974-86; pres. Canyon Commons Investment, Evergreen, 1974—, Johnson Media, Inc., Granby, Colo., 1987—. Author: How the Michigan Betas Built a $1,000,000 Chapter House in the '80s. Alt. del. Rep. Nat. Conv., 1968. Lt. USNR, 1958-61. Mem. Colo. Press Assn., Nat. Newspaper Assn., Maple Bluff Country Club, Madison Club, Bishops Bay Country Club, Beta Theta Pi. Home: 5302 Lighthouse Bay Dr Madison WI 53704-1114 Office: PO Box 409 Granby CO 80446-0409

JOHNSON-BROWN, HAZEL WINFRED, nurse, retired army officer; b. West Chester, Pa., Oct. 10, 1927; d. Clarence Lemont and Garnett (Henley) J. RN diploma, Harlem Hosp., N.Y.C., 1950; BSN, Villanova U., 1959; MSN, Tchr.'s Coll., Columbia U., 1963; PhD in Ednl. Adminstrn., Cath. U. Am., 1978. 1st lt. U.S. Army Nurse Corps, 1955, advanced through grades to brig. gen., 1979; mem. staff U.S. Army Med. R&D Command, Washington, 1967-73; dir. Walter Reed Army Inst. Nursing, Washington, 1976-78; asst. for nursing Office of Surgeon Med. Command, Korea, 1979-83; chief Army Nurse Corps Office of Surgeon Gen. Dept. of the Army, Washington, 1983-86; dir. govtl. affairs office Am. Nurses Assn., 1986-96; prof. Coll. Nursing and Health Sci. George Mason U., 1989-96; dir. Ctr. for Health Policy George Mason U., 1996—; cons. Nursing Edn. Health Policy, Health Adminstrn. Decorated Disting. Svc. medal, Legion of merit, Meritorious Svc. medal, Army Commendation medal; recipient Evangeline G. Bovard Army Nurse of Yr. award Letterman Army Med. Ctr., San Francisco, 1964, Dr. Anita Newcomb McGee award DAR, Washington, 1971. Mem. Assn. Balck Nursing Faculty, Black Women United for Action, Assn. U.S. Army, Nat. Assn. Military Family, Am. Nurses Assn., Nat. League Nursing, Sigma Theta Tau.

JOHNSON-LAIRD, PHILIP NICHOLAS, psychologist; b. Rothwell, Eng., Oct. 12, 1936; s. Frederick Ryberg and Dorothy (Blackett) J.-L.; m. Maureen Mary Sullivan, Aug. 1, 1959; children: Ben, Dorothy. BA with honors, Univ. Coll., London, 1964; PhD, Univ. Coll., 1967; Doctorate (hon.), U. Gothenburg, Sweden, 1983, Padua (Italy) U., 1997, Trinity Coll., Dublin, Ireland, 2000. Asst. lectr., then lectr. psychology Univ. Coll., London, 1966-73; vis. mem. Inst. for Advanced Study, Princeton, N.J., 1971-72; reader, prof., chair exptl. psychology Sussex U., Brighton, Eng., 1973-82; spl. appointment, asst. dir. Med. Rsch. Coun. Applied Psychology Unit, Cambridge, Eng., 1982-89; prof., Stuart prof. psychology Princeton U., 1989—; vis. prof. cognitive sci. Stanford (Calif.) U., 1980, vis. prof. psychology, 1985; vis. prof. Trieste (Italy) U., 1990, Univ. Coll., 1992, NYU, 1996. Author: Mental Models, 1983, The Computer and the Mind, 1988, (with Ruth Byrne) Deduction, 1991, 7 others; contbr. over 200 articles to profl. jours. Mem. Campaign for Disarmament, London, 1959-82. Recipient Medaglia D'Onore, U. Florence, Italy, 1989. Fellow Brit. Acad., Royal Soc. U.K.; mem. Am. Psychol. Soc., Brit. Psychol. Soc. (Spearman medal 1974, Pres.' award 1985), Soc. Exptl. Psychologists. Avocations: modern jazz piano, arguing. E-mail: phil@princeton.edu. Office: Princeton U Dept Psychology Princeton NJ 08544-0001

JOHNSON-LEWIS, ANGELA DAWN, therapist; b. Des Moines, Feb. 8, 1971; d. Dennis Keith and Norma June (Snider) Johnson; m. Philip Duane Lewis, Nov. 25, 1995. BA, U. Iowa, 1993, MA, 1996. Cert. alcohol and drug counselor, Iowa Bd. Substance Abuse. Substance abuse counselor Area Substance Abuse Coun., Cedar Rapids, Iowa, 1994-98; therapist Prairie Health Ptnrs., Inc., Iowa City, 1998—. Mem. Am. Psychol. Assn., Am. Counseling Assn. Avocations: reading, hiking, canoeing. Office: Prairie Health Ptnrs Inc PO Box 755 Independence IA 50644-0755

JOHNSON VELAZCO, NANCY RUTH, marketing professional; b. Phila., Feb. 4, 1948; d. Samuel Blaine and Ruth Dorothy (Carpenter) Johnson; m. Julio Horacio Velazco, Dec. 6, 1982 (div. Oct. 1984); 1 child, Cristine. BA in Spanish, Ursinus Coll., Collegeville, Pa., 1970; MA in Spanish, Villlanova U., 1974; MBA, The Wharton Sch. U. Pa., 1978. Secondary tchr. Spanish, William Penn Sch. Dist., Lansdowne, Pa., 1970-76; indsl. rsch. analyst indsl. rsch. unit Wharton Sch., U. Pa., Phila., 1976-78; sales rep. pharms. Eli Lilly & Co., Providence, 1978-79; market rsch. analyst Eli Lilly & Co., Indpls., 1979-80; mktg. mgr. Eli Lilly & Co., Buenos Aires, 1980-82; Intron product mgr., bus. devel. mgr. Schering Plough Corp., Miami, Fla., 1983-84, regional mktg. dir. for L.Am., 1984-89; dir. respiratory, dermatology and antifungals Schering Plough Corp., Kenilworth, N.J., 1989-90, sr. mktg. dir. global mktg., 1991—. Author: The Political, Economic and Labor Climates in Mexico, 1977, The Political, Economic and Labor Climates in Peru, 1978. Chmn. party events Children's Specialized Hosp., Mountainside, N.J., 1994—. Mem. Nat. Soc. DAR (treas. Westfield chpt. 1995—). Republican. Home: 727 Glen Ave Westfield NJ 07090-4326 Office: Schering-Plough Corp 2000 Galloping Hill Rd Kenilworth NJ 07033-1328

JOHNSTON, BERNARD FOX, foundation executive, writer; b. Taft, Calif., Nov. 19, 1934; s. Bernard Lowe and Georgia Victoria (Fox) J.; m. Audrey Rhoades, June 9, 1956 (div. Sept. 1963); 1 child, Sheldon Bernard. BA in Creative Arts, San Francisco State U., 1957, MA in World Lit., 1958. Lectr. philosophy Coll. of Marin, Kentfield, Calif., 1957-58; lectr. humanities San Francisco State U., 1957-58, 67-68; instr. English Contra Costa Coll., San Pablo, Calif., 1958-63; Knowles Found. philosophy fellow, 1962; fellow Syracuse (N.Y.) U., 1964-66; freelance writer Piedmont, Calif., 1968-77; pres. Cinema Repertory, Inc., Point Richmond, Calif., 1978-89; pres., exec. dir. Athena Found., Tiburon, Calif., 1990—, Incline Village, Nev., 1990—; exec. prodr. (TV series) The Heroes of Time, (TV documentary) The Shudder of Awe; CEO The Athena Found., Inc., 1997, Mahler Festival, U. Colo., Boulder, 1998. Author: (screenplay) Point Exeter, 1979, Ascent Allowed, 1988 (award); author, editor: Issues in Education: An Anthology of Controversy, 1964, The Literature of Learning, 1971; festival pianist Lake Tahoe Internat. Film Festival, 1998; resident pianist Tahoe-Chrysler Corp., 1998; pianist (CD) Time Remembered; musical dir., featured pianist Lake Tahoe Summer Music Series, 2000. Arts grantee Silicon Valley Community Found., 1998. Mem. Dirs. Guild Am., Writers Guild Am., Coun. for Basic Edn., Wilson Ctr. Assocs., Assn. Lit. Scholars and Critics, Smithsonian Instn., Donner Land Trust, Nat. Assn. Scholars, Calif. Assn. Scholars, San Francisco State Alumni Assn., Commonwealth Club of Calif. Avocations: classical and jazz piano, backpacking, softball. Office: 845 Southwood Blvd Ste 50 Incline Village NV 89451-9463

JOHNSTON, DAVID WILLIAM, city manager; b. Warsaw, Ind., Nov. 30, 1959; s. Maynard Baker Johnston and Katherine Mary Povich; m. Caroline Jo Babinec, Feb. 11, 1995. BA in Am. Studies, U. Notre Dame, 1982; MPA, Ind. U., Indpls., 1986. Adj. faculty mem. Sch. Pub. and Environ. Affairs Ind. U., 1988-91; dir. transp. planning office State of Ind., Indpls., 1986-89, dir. traffic safety, 1989-92; dir. stewardship Cath. Diocese of Gary, Merrillville, Ind., 1992-94; adminstrv. dir. Ind. Health Ctrs., Indpls., 1994-97; village adminstr. Village of Coal City, Ill., 1997—. Bd. dirs. Ind. Pub. Health Assn., Indpls., 1996-97, Alzheimer's Assn., Kankakee, Ill., 1998—, Cmty. Action of Greater Indpls., 1995-97; mem. com. Transit Adv. Coun., City of Indpls., 1996-97. Recipient Sagamore of the Wabash award, Gov. of Ind., 1988, 92, Pub. Safety award Hoosier Safety Coun., 1991, Cert. of Svc. award Ind. State Police, 1992. Mem. Am. Planning Assn., Am. Econ. Devel. Coun., Internat. City/County Mgmt. Assn., Grundy County C. of C. (bd. dirs. 1999—). Roman Catholic. Avocations: map reading, walking, hiking, reading historical non-fiction. E-mail: johnsmanor@uti.com. Home: 1421 Shawnee Rd Indianapolis IN 46260-4078

JOHNSTON, DONALD JAMES, civic organization official; b. Ottawa, Ont., Can., June 26, 1936; s. Wilbur Austin and Florence Jean Moffat Tucker J.; m. Heather Bell Maclaren, Dec. 11, 1965; children: Kristina, Allison, Rachel, Sara. BA, BCL, McGill U., Montreal, Que., Can., 1958. Created Queen's counsel. Assoc. Stikeman & Elliott, 1961; founder Johnston, Heenan & Blaikie; lectr. fiscal law McGill U. Faculty Law, 1964-77; mem. Can. Ho. of Commons, Ottawa, 1978-88; pres. Treasury Bd. Can., 1989-82; min. of state for sci. and tech. Econ. and Regional Devel., 1982; min. Justice Atty. Gen. of Can., 1984; pres. Liberal Party Can., 1990-94; sec.-gen. Orgn. Coop. and Devel., Paris, 1996—. Contbr. articles to profl. jours.; editor, author three books on public policy. Mem. Cercle du Bois de Boulogne, Tir aux Pigeons, Mt. Royal Club, Montreal Indoor Tennis Club. Avocations: writing, tennis, piano. Home: 92 Ave Henri-Martin, 75116 Paris France Office: OECD, 2 rue Anshé Pascal, 75775 Paris Cedex 16, France

JOHNSTON, ELLIOTT FRANK, retired supreme court judge; b. Adelaide, Australia, Feb. 26, 1918; s. William Stewart and Elsie Vivian (Elliott) J.; m. Elizabeth Teesdale-Smith, Apr. 17, 1942; 1 child, Ian. LLB, Adelaide (Australia) U., 1940; LLD (hon.), Plinders U. S. Australia, Adelaide, Australia, 1996. Solicitor Adelaide, Australia, 1941; army AIF, Australia, 1941-45; solicitor, barrister Adelaide, Australia, 1946-51; organiser Communist Party, Australia, 1951-57; solicitor, barrister Adelaide, Australia, 1957-70, QC barrister, 1970-83; judge Supreme Ct., South Australia, 1983-88; royal commr. Laverton Royal Comm., West Australia, 1974-75, Aboriginal Deaths in Custody Royal Comm., 1988-91; assoc. prof. law Plinders U., Australia, 1992-95; ret., 1995. Co-editor: Left Debate for Political Change, Australian Options. Mem. state com., nat. orgn. Communist Party of Australia, 1941-83; pres., mem. Labour Lawyers, 1979-83; pres. Aboriginal Legal Rights, South Australia, 1969-76. Lt. Australian Army, 1941-45. Recipient AO award Gov.-Gen., Australia, 1994. Avocations: bridge, croquet, reading. Home: 398 Gilles St, Adelaide 5000, Australia

JOHNSTON, J. BROOKE, JR., lawyer; b. N.Y.C., Mar. 2, 1940; s. J. Brooke Johnston and Margaret Adelia Simpson; m. Judith Noble, June 22, 1963 (div. Dec. 1972); 1 child, Tracy Leigh; m. Marjorie Harris, May 22, 1976; stepchildren: Jeffrey Wooden, Wendy W. Barze. BA, Williams Coll., 1962; JD, Fordham U., 1967. Bar: N.Y. 1967, Ala. 1975. Mgmt. trainee Equitable Life, N.Y.C., 1962-67; assoc. Breed, Abbott & Morgan, N.Y.C., 1967-75; ptnr. Berkowitz, Lefkovitz & Patrick, Birmingham, Ala., 1975-78, Haskell Slaughter Young & Johnston, Birmingham, 1979-96, Baker, Johnston & Wilson LLP, Birmingham, 1998—; sr. v.p., gen. counsel MedPartners, Inc., Birmingham, 1996-98; bd. dirs. United Leisure Corp., L.A., Grand Havana Enterprises, Inc., L.A. Mem. ABA, N.Y. State Bar Assn., Ala. State Bar Assn., Birmingham Bar Assn. Republican. Episcopalian. Avocations: reading, golf, travel. E-mail: jbj@bakerjohnston.com. Home: 3704 Montrose Rd Birmingham AL 35213 Office: Baker Johnston & Wilson LLP Ste 322 1 Independence Plz Birmingham AL 35209-2634

JOHNSTON, JOHN THOMAS, engineering executive; b. St. Louis, Jan. 24, 1930; s. Herbert Johnston and Mabel (Farris) Seeley; m. Shirley Wiladean Trulove, Nov. 25, 1950; children: John David, Thomas Daniel. Cert. in mech. tech., Washington U., St. Louis, 1960, BS in Physics, 1963; MBA, Lindenwood Coll., 1978. Structural engr. McDonnell Aircraft, St. Louis, 1955-66, 67-70, project engr., 1970-83, integrator-engr., 1983-87; chief engr. Lear Jet, Wichita, Kans., 1966-67; mgr. aero tech. E-Systems, Greenville, Tex., 1987-92, mem. tech. staff, 1992-93; pvt. practice cons. Greenville, Tex., 1993—; pres. Tech. Engring. Cons., Greenville, Tex., 1995—; designated engring. rep. FAA, Kansas City, Mo., 1967-75; chief exec. officer Midwest Travel Inst., St. Peters, Mo., 1985-90. Contbr. articles to profl. publs.; patentee in field. Fundraiser Lindenwood Coll., St. Charles, Mo., 1987; organizer Jr. Achievement, St. Charles, 1975; juvenile officer Jud. Dist. 11, St. Charles, 1970's. Sgt. U.S. Army, 1950-53. Mem. AIAA. Home and Office: 3 Thornhill Dr Greenville TX 75401-9404

JOHNSTON, MARGARET ELIZABETH, agricultural science educator, researcher; b. Merthyr Tydfil, Wales, Nov. 15, 1949; d. Gordon Reiniecke and Judith Mary (Elliott) McKay; m. Kerry Lawrence Johnston; children: David Lawrence, Cameron Robert, Katherine Sarah. B in Agrl. Scis. with honors, Univ. Queensland, Brisbane, Australia, 1972; M in Agrl. Scis., Univ. Queensland, 1979, PhD, 1994; U. So. Queensland, Toowoomba, Australia, 1991. Registered tchr. Bd. Tchr. Registration; PAg cert. Australian Inst. of Agrl. Sci. and Tech. Sr. horticulturist Dept. Prim Ind., Brisbane, 1972-82; joint owner pvt. farm Dalby, 1982-84; cons., part time tchr. TAFE, Dalby, Queensland, 1984-88; adj. lectr. U. Queensland, Gatton, 1988; lectr. U. Queensland, 1989-96, sr. lectr., 1996—. Author: Plant Breeder Rights, 1999. Grantee Parkdale Nursery, 1998; Affirmative Action scholar, 1993; Churchill Fellowship, 1996; recipient gold medal Best New Plant Floralies Internat. de Nantes, 1999. Mem. Royal Australian Inst. Parks and Recreation, Australian Flora Found., Nat. Tertiary Edn. Union (pres. Gatton Sule br. 1996-98, v.p. 1995-96, 98-99), Australian Inst. Agrl. Sci. (sec. Queensland br. 1977-78), Australian Soc. Hort. Sci. Avocation: walking. Office: U Queensland, QLD Gatton 4345, Australia

JOHNSTON, MARILYN FRANCES-MEYERS, physician, medical educator; b. Buffalo, Mar. 30, 1937. BS, Dameon Coll., 1966; PhD, St. Louis U., 1970, MD, 1975. Diplomate Am. Bd. Pathology, Diplomate Nat. Bd. Med. Examiners. Fellow in immunology Washington U., St. Louis, 1970-72; resident in pathology Washington U. Hosp., St. Louis, 1975-77, St. John's Mercy Med. Ctr., St. Louis, 1977-79; research fellow hematology St. Louis U. Sch. Medicine, 1979-80; instr. biochemistry St. Louis U., 1972-75, asst. prof. pathology, 1980-87, assoc. prof., 1987-92, prof., 1992-99, prof. emeritus, 1999—, dir. transfusion svcs., 1980-99; staf pathologist Christian Hosp. Barnes Jewish Christian Hosps., St. Louis, 1999—; med. dir. Mo./Ill. Regional Red Cross, 1983-88; area chmn. for inspection and accreditation Am. Assn. Blood Banks, Arlington, Va., 1984; med. dir. transfusion svc. Christian Hosps., Barnes-Jewish-Christian Hosp. Sys., St. Louis, 1999—. Author: Transfusion Therapy, 1985. Recipient Transfusion Medicine Acad. award Nat. Heart, Blood and Lung Inst., 1984; Goldberger fellow AMA, 1979. Mem. Am. Assn. Blood Banks, Am. Assn. Immunologists, Internat. Soc. Blood Transfusion, Am. Soc. Clin. Pathologists, Sigma Xi. Office: Christian Hosp NE 16560 Chesterfield Airport Rd Chesterfield MO 63017-1412

JOHNSTON, NEIL CHUNN, lawyer; b. Mobile, Ala., Feb. 23, 1953; s. Vivian Gaines and Sara Niel (Chunn) J.; m. Ashley Monroe Hocklander, Dec. 20, 1980; children: Katie, Neil Jr. BA, Southwestern at Memphis (name changed to Rhodes Coll.), 1975; JD, U. Ala., 1978. Atty. Hand, Arendall L.L.C., Mobile, Ala., 1978—; Com. mem. Ala. Law Inst. Com., Tuscaloosa, Ala., 1990; mem. Gov.'s Wetland Mitigation Task Force, 1994. Contbr. articles to profl. jours. Pres. Project CATE Found, Inc., Mobile, 1987—; trustee Nature Conservancy, Ala., 1990-96; mem. Wetland Mitigation Banking Task Force, 1994-96; bd. dirs. Am. Jr. Miss Program. Recipient Ala. Gov.'s award-Water Conservationist, Ala. Wildlife Fedn., 1987, EPA Region IV Wetlands Recognition award, 2000. Mem. ABA, Ala. State Bar Assn. (chmn. environ. law sect. 1984-91, corp. banking, bus. law sect. 1993, Mobile Bar Assn., Ala. Forestry Assn., Ala. Law Inst. (mem. com. 1990), Rotary (pres. Mobile 1996-97). Office: Hand Arendall LLC 3000 FNB Bldg Royal St Mobile AL 36602

JOHNSTON, ROSEMARY ROSS, educator, researcher; b. Sydney, N.S.W., Australia, Feb. 16; d. Royston Frederick Darling and Dorothy Patricia Cowley; m. Malcolm Charles Ferguson, Dec. 17, 1966; children: Emily-Jane Melinda, Annabel Rosemary, Malcolm Ross, Sarah Elizabeth, Robert Charles. BA, Sydney U.; MA, Macquarie U., N.S.W., 1993, PhD, 1995, Diploma in Edn. Cert. tchr., N.S.W. Secondary tchr. N.S.W. Dept. Edn.; writer, prodr. Ednl. TV; primary, secondary tchr. Sydney Japanese Sch.; sr. lectr. U. Tech. Sydney, 1995—, dir. Ctr. for Rsch. and Edn. in the Arts, 1997—; bd. mem. Montgomery Inst.; rsch. prof. Abo Akademi Univ., Finland, 2000. Co-author: Reading, Writing and Children's Literature, 2000; contbr. articles to profl. jours. Bd. mem., bd. edn. Uniting Ch.; chmn. commn. for sch. edn., 1996—. Mem. Internat. Fedn. Langs. and Modern Lit. (assoc sec. gen. 1996—), Internat. Rsch. Soc. for Children's Lit. (sec. 1997—), Australian Coll. Edn., Australian Assn. for Rsch. in Edn., Children's Lit. Assn. Avocations: reading, writing, gardening, walking. Home: 8

Suncrest Ave, NSW Newport 2106, Australia Office: U Tech Sydney, Eton Rd, NSW Lindfield 2070, Australia

JOHNSTON, SEAN FRANCOIS, physicist, historian of science; b. Edmonton, Alta., Can., Oct. 30, 1956; arrived in Eng., 1988; s. Harold Henry and Frances Henriette (Coulombe) J.; m. Elisabeth McNair Lewis, June 7, 1986. BSc, Simon Fraser U., Vancouver, B.C., Can., 1978, MSc, 1980; PhD, U. Leeds, Eng., 1994. Chartered physicist, U.K. Image analyst Can. Ctr. for Remote Sensing, Ottawa, Ont., Can., 1980-81; group leader systems engring. Bomem Inc, Quebec City, Que, Can., 1981-87; chief engr. analytical div. Lloyd Instruments PLC, Southampton, Eng., 1988-89; instrument mgr. Laser Monitoring Systems, Ltd., Hull, Eng., 1989-92; rsch. fellow U. Leeds, Eng., 1992-96, U. York, Eng., 1996-99; lectr. sci. studies Crichton Coll., U. Glasgow, Dumfries, Scotland, 1999—. Author: Fourier Transform Infrared: A Constantly Evolving Technology, 1991; translator: Optical Fibers, 1986. Mem. Inst. Physics, Optical Soc. Am., Brit. Assn. History of Sci. Office: Crichton Coll, Crichton U Campus, Dumfries DG1 4ZL, Scotland

JOHNSTON, WILLIAM J., JR., neurosurgeon; b. Sept. 11, 1945. BS, U. Southwestern La., 1969; MD, La. State U., 1973. Neurol. surgeon Neurosurg. Assocs., Metairie, La., 1979—; chief of staff E. Jefferson Gen. Hosp., Metairie, 1992. Office: 4228 Houma Blvd Ste 220 Metairie LA 70006-3006

JOHNSTONE, ALEXANDER HENRY, retired chemistry educator; b. Edinburgh, Scotland, Oct. 17, 1930; s. William and Jean Henry Johnstone; m. Martha Young Cuthbertson, Aug. 21, 1954; children: David Alexander, Alan John. BSc 1st class, U. Edinburgh, 1953; postgrad. cert. in edn., Moray House Coll., Edinburgh, 1954; PhD, U. Glasgow, Scotland, 1972. Chemistry tchr. George Watson's Coll., Scotland, 1956-62; head of chemistry Stirling H.S., Scotland, 1963-72; lectr. in chemistry U. Glasgow, Scotland, 1972-73, asst. prof. in chemistry, 1973-80, assoc. prof. in chemistry, 1980-89, prof. in chemistry, 1989-92, prof. sci. edn., 1992—; found. dir. of learning svc. U. Glasgow, 1992-95, found. dir. ctr. for sci. and edn., 1980-98; Verhagen chair Limburg U. Centre, 1993; lectr. Fedn. of European Chem. Socs., 1998. Author: Chemistry Takes Shape, vols. 1 - 5, 1964-96, A Worksheet Introduction to Chemical Spectroscopy, 1969, Test Your Chemistry, 1970, Chemistry Check-Up, 1974, Energy, Chaos and Chemical Change, 1977, Words in Chemistry, 1978, Understanding Non-Technical Words in Science, 1980, Chemistry About Us, 1980, Words That Matter in Science, 1985, Meaning Beyong Readability, 1988, Practical Problem Solving in Chemistry, 1989, Starter Projects for Sixth Year Studies Chemistry, 1993, More Starter Projects for Sixth Year Studies Chemistry, 1995, Evaluation in Innovations, 1998; contbr. numerous articles to profl. publs. Lt. British Army, 1954-56. Recipient Mellor medal Royal Australian Chem. Inst., 1987, Illuminati medal Italian Chem. Soc., 1991, Brasted medal Am. Chem. Soc., 1997. Fellow Royal Soc. of Chemistry (pres. edn. divsn. 1978-80, v.p. 1978-80, Nyholm medal 1979). Mem. United Free Ch. of Scotland. Avocations: hill walking, archaeology, lay preaching. Home: 7 Shirra's Brae Rd, Stirling FK7 OAY, Scotland Office: Ctr for Sci Edn, U Glasgow, Glasgow G12 8QQ, Scotland

JOHNSTONE, C. BRUCE, investment company executive; b. N.Y.C., Nov. 7, 1940; s. R. Adam and Muriel S. (Smith) J.; m. Helen Louise Lott, Aug. 27, 1963; children: Brent Paul, Reed Evan. AB cum laude, Harvard U., 1962, MBA, 1966. CFA. V.p. portfolio mgr. Fidelity Equity Income Fund, Boston, 1972-90; portfolio group leader income and growth funds Fidelity Mgmt. & Rsch. Co., Boston, 1981-90, sr. v.p., 1984-89, bd. dirs., 1989-90, exec. v.p. chmn. investment com., 1990; sr. v.p. Fidelity Mgmt. Trust Co., Boston, 1982-90, also bd. dirs.; mng. dir. Fidelity Investments, Boston, 1983—; founding mem., dir. Needham Edn. Found. class chair Harvard U. Bus. Sch., 1966—, class sec., 1986—; mem. com. on univ. resources Harvard U., 1987—. Lt. USNR, 1962-68. Mem. Chartered Fin. Analysts, Boston Security Analysts Soc., Wellesley Country Club, Harvard Varsity Club, Harvard Club Boston. Home: 827 Charles River St Needham MA 02492-1007 Office: Fidelity Investments 82 Devonshire St Boston MA 02109-3605

JOHNSTONE, GREGG MARTIN, communications executive; b. San Diego, Apr. 6, 1947; s. Ralph E. and Maxine Ann O'Dell J.; m. Jane Marie Sammon, Jan. 20, 1973; children: Erik Michael, Katie Marie, Kevin Matthew. BS in Physics, Va. Polytechnic Inst., 1970. Application engr. Video Engring. Co., Washington, 1970-73; field svc. engr. Internat. Video Co., Sunnyvale, Calif., 1973-77; pres. Nat. Video Svcs., Inc., Newtown, Ct., 1977—, Intermed Video Technologies Inc., Newtown, Conn., 1991—; ptnr. Tech. Investments, Inc., 1991—, J & J Investments. Patentee in field. Mem. Soc. Motion Picture and TV Engrs., IEEE, Internat. TV Assn., Am. Radio Relay League. Avocation: amateur radio operator (N1GFH). Office: Nat Video Svcs Inc 18 Commerce Rd Newtown CT 06470-1607

JOHNSTONE, MEGAN-JANE, nursing educator; b. Dannevirke, New Zealand, Nov. 27, 1955; arrived in Australia, 1984; d. John and Laurel (Walkley) J. BA, Waikato U., Hamilton, New Zealand, 1985; MA, Monash U., Melbourne, Australia, 1985; PhD, LaTrobe U., Melbourne, Australia, 1993. Cert. gen. nursing and obstetrics. RN Wakato Hosp., Hamilton, 1977-78, 80-84; sister-in-charge Arobiginal Health Program, Cunnamulla, Australia, 1978; lectr. Phillip Inst. of Tech., Melbourne, 1987-93; assoc. prof. RMIT U., Melbourne, 1994-97, prof., 1997—; cons., vis. expert Ministry of Health, Singapore, 1996; cons. in ethics and human rights Royal Coll. of Nursing Australia, Internat. Coun. of Nurses, Geneva, Switzerland, 1998—, Austin and Repariation Med. Ctr., Melbourne, 1996—. Author: Nursing and the Injustices of the Law, 1994, Bioethics: A Nursing Perspective, 3rd edit., 1999; editor: The Politics of Euthanasia; a Nursing Response, 1996; contbr. articles to profl. publs. Co-founder, exec. mem. Transcultural Health Care Coun., Melbourne, 1984-94; mem. Victorian Found. for Survivors of Torture, Melbourne, 1990—, Australians Against Child Abuse, Melbourne, 1999—. Annie M. Sage Nursing Meml. scholarship Royal Coll. of Nursing Australia, 1990; recipient Inaugural Mona Menziew Postdoctoral Rsch. award Nurses Bd. of Victoria, 1998. Fellow Royal Coll. of Nursing, NSW Coll. of Nursing; mem. Australian Nursing Fedn., Internat. Assn. of Bioethics. Avocations: horse riding (trails), visual arts, classical music, reading, movies. Home: PO Box 328, Melbourne VIC 3078, Australia Office: RMIT Univ, Plenty Rd, Melbourne VIC 3083, Australia

JOIREMAN, JEFFREY ALAN, psychology educator; b. Spokane, Wash.; s. James Edward and Gloria Ann Joireman; m. Esther Tonny Worley. BA in Psychology, Ea. Wash. U., 1987; MA in Social Psychology, U. Del., 1992, PhD in Social Psychology, 1996. Asst. prof. psychology Seattle Pacific U., 1996—; statis. cons. Army Rsch. Labs., Aberdeen, Md., 1994. Contbr. articles to profl. jours. Fulbright fellow, 1994-95, grad. fellow U. Del., 1995-96. Mem. Am. Psychol. Soc., Western Psychol. Assn., Soc. for Personality and Social Psychology. Avocations: hiking, cycling, photography. E-mail: joireman@spu.edu. Office: Seattle Pacific U 3307 3d Ave W Seattle WA 98119

JOKINEN, OLLI TAPIO, research mathematician; b. Helsinki, Finland, July 27, 1966; s. Tapani Veikko Juhani and Salme Johanna (Raitala) J. MS in Engring., Helsinki U. Tech., 1991, lic. in tech., 1993, DSc in Tech., 2000. Rschr., Inst. Math. Helsinki U. Tech., 1990-92, rsch. scientist, Inst. Photogrammetry and Remote Sensing, 1993—. 2d lt., Signal Corps, 1985-86, Riihimäki, Finland. Heikki and Hilma Honkanen Found. scholar, 1993, Found. Tech. in Finland scholar, 1993. Lutheran. Avocations: trumpet, piano, singing. Office: Helsinki U Tech, PO Box 1200, FIN02015 Hut Finland

JOKIO, PEKKA JOHANNES, orthopedist; b. Porvoo, Kerkkoo, Finland, Aug. 22, 1929; s. Juho Henrik and Eine Eufrosyne (Hautala) J.; m. Helvi Maria Pyykonen, Jan. 24, 1955 (div. Nov. 1981); children: Marja-Leena, Kirsti, Paivi, Jaana; m. Sirpa Ansa Markkula, Aug. 4, 1984. MD, U. Helsinki, Turku, 1957; specialization in orthopedics, Invalid Found., Helsinki, 1982. Med. officer Dist. Hosp., Ivalo, 1958-63; asst. surgeon Maria Hosp., Helsinki, 1963-65; gen. surgeon Regional Hosp., Iisalmi, 1969-79; asst. surgeon U. Hosp., Helsinki, 1979-81; asst. orthopedist Invalid Found., Helsinki, 1981-85; orthopedist Mil. Hosp., Helsinki, 1985-94; physician Pvt. Hosp. Mehilainen, Helsinki, 1994—. Med. 1st lt. Helsinki Mil., 1989-94. Mem. Lions Internat. Coalition Party. Evang.-Lutheran. Avocations: aviation, golf, tennis, literature, history. Office: Pvt Hosp Mehilainen, Runeberginkatu 47 A, SF-00260 Helsinki Finland

JOKL, MILOSLAV VLADIMIR, mechanical engineer; b. Prague, Feb. 9, 1933; s. Bronislav and Ludmila (Mullerova) J.; m. Jana Marie Spetova, Feb. 14, 1964; children: Miloslav, Daniel. MSc, Tech. U., Prague, 1956, PhD, 1963, DSc, 1975; postgrad. in Eng. Lang., Brown U., 1986. With Tech. U. Prague, 1956-76, mem. faculty bldg. sci., 1977—; lab. head Inst. Hygiene and Epidemiology, Tech. U. Prague, Prague, 1956-76; cons. Min. of Health, Prague, 1966-69, Inst. Rationalization, Prague, 1968-89, Inst. Aviation Medicine, Prague, 1958-83, Tech. Univ. Denmark, 1984, Kans. State U., 1986-87. Author: (books) Microenvironment, 1989 (Oustanding Book award Czech Biomed. Soc. 1990), Theory and Optimization of Indoor Environment, 1986 (Outstanding Textbook award Rector of Tech. U., 1988); inventor: Stereothermometer, 1977 (Czech State award 1978), Space Ship Microclimate Evaluation, 1966 (Scientiae Rerum Montanorum Pribram award 1967). Vol. Charity of Czech Evangelic Ch., Prague, 1990-93; elder Czech Evangelic Ch., Prague, 1996—. Recipient Tech. U. of Kosice medal U. Kosice, 1993, J.E. Purkyne medal Czech Med. Soc., Prague, 1983, Czech State award, Prague, 1979, recipient Tech. U. Prague Gold Medal U. Prague, 1998. Fellow Indoor Air Int. (scientific sec. 1992-95), Internat. Soc. Built Environ. (mem. coun. 1996—), Soc. Environ. Engring. (mem. coun. 1990—). Avocations: swimming, tennis. Office: Technical Univ Prague, 7 Thakurova, CZ 16629 Prague Czech Republic

JOKL, VLADIMÍR, analytical chemistry educator, researcher; b. Hustopeče, Moravia, Czech Republic, Jan. 18, 1926; s. Francis and Adèla Zakovská; m. Miloslava Skalniková; children: Helena, Olga. BS in Pharmacy, Masaryk U., Brno, Czechoslovakia, 1949, MS, 1952; PhD, U. Comen, Bratislava, Slovakia, 1961; DS, Tech. U., Prague, Czech Republic, 1974. Asst. lectr. Faculty of Pharmacy Masaryk U, Brno, Czechoslovakia, 1950-59; sr. lectr. Faculty of Pharmacy, Bratislava, Czechoslovakia, 1960-63; asst. prof. Faculty of Pharmacy, Bratislava, 1964-77; prof. Faculty Pharmacy, Charles U., Hradec Králové, Czech Republic, 1978-91; ret., 1991—; dept. head Charles U. Faculty of Pharmacy, Hradec Králové, 1970-89, vice dean, 1970-85. Author: (book) Textbook of Analytical Chemistry, 1989; contbr. over 70 articles to sci. jours. including Jour. of Chromatography and many others. Mem. Czech Chem. Soc. Office: Charles U Faculty Pharmacy, Heyrovského 1203, Hradec Králové Czech Republic

JOLIOT, PIERRE ADRIEN, biologist; b. Paris, Mar. 12, 1932; s. Jean Frédéric and Iréne (curie) J.; m. Anne Gricouroff, Jan. 7, 1961; children: Marc, Alain. Lic. Biology Sci., U. Paris, 1956, PhD, 1960. Rschr. CNRS, Paris, 1954-81, dir. rsch., 1974; prof. Coll. France, Paris, 1981—; chef svc. Inst. Biology Physico-chimique, Paris, 1975, adminstr., 1994, dir. 1997; dir. dept. biology Ecole Normale Superieure, Paris, 1987-92; pres. Comets CNRS, 1998. Scientific advisor Prime Minister, Paris, 1985-86; mem. com. nat. evaluation rsch. CNER, Paris, 1989-92. Recipient Charles F. Kettering award Excellence in Photosynthesis, 1970. Mem. NAS, Acad. Scis., Acad. European Socs., Acad. Europea. Avocations: tennis, sailing, skiing. Home: 16 rue de la Glacière, 75013 Paris France Office: Inst Biology Physico-chim, 13 rue Pierre Marie Curie, 75005 Paris France

JOLLES, GEORGES EDGAR RENÉ, scientist; b. Vienna, Austria, Apr. 10, 1929; s. Henri and Marguerite (Weinber) J.; m. Bernadette Bergeret, July 4, 1959; children: Charles, Francois, Brigitte. Lic. es Scis., Ecole Superieure de Chimie, Lyons, France, 1950; PhD, U. Paris, 1953; postgrad. U. Louvain, 1953-54, U. Wis., 1954-55. Research assoc. Rhone-Poulenc Group, Paris, 1956-70, dir. pharm. research, 1970-76, research dir. health div., 1976-82, sci. dir., 1982—; mem. French Nat. Research Council, 1970-80. Author: Histochimie Normale et Pathologique, 1969, Drug Design, Fact or Fantasy?, 1984, Immunostimulants, Now and Tomorrow, 1987, In Vitro Methods in Toxicology, 1992, neurodegenerative diseases, 1994; contbr. articles to profl. jours.; patentee in field. Recipient Galien award Medecine Mondiale, 1973; laurcate of the French Acad. of Scis., 1993; named Knight of French Nat. Order Merit. Mem. Am. Chem. Soc., Internat. Soc. Chemotherapy, Soc. Chimique de France, Societe de Chimie Biologique, N.Y. Acad. Scis. Roman Catholic. Home: 1 Allée des Pins, 92330 Sceaux France Office: 20 Ave Raymond Aron, 92165 Antony France

JOLLEY, R. GARDNER, lawyer; b. Salt Lake City, May 12, 1944; s. Reuben G. and Varno J.; m. Sharon Lea Thomas, Aug. 21, 1965; children—Christopher Gardner and Jennifer Lea. B.S. in Econs., U. Utah, 1966; J.D., U. Calif.-Berkeley, 1969. Bar: Calif. 1970, Nev. 1970, U.S. Dist. Ct. Nev. 1970. Law clk. to presiding justice Nev. Supreme Ct., 1969-70; assoc. Wiener, Goldwater and Galatz, Las Vegas, 1970-73; ptnr. Jolley, Urga, Wirth & Woodbury, Las Vegas, Nev., 1974—; lectr. new law clks. for Nev. judges, 1973-74; instr. Clark County Community Coll., 1975-77; instr. Nev. Continuing Legal Edn., 1983. Bd. dirs. Catholic Community Services, 1973-80; bd. govs. Easter Seal Soc., 1977-78. Mem. Nev. State Bar Assn. (bd. govs. 1976-86, pres. 1985-86), ABA (Nev. rep. to Ho. Dels. 1986-88), Assn. Trial Lawyers Am., Nev. Trial Lawyers Assn.

JOLLY, DANIEL EHS, dental educator; b. St. Louis, Aug. 25, 1952; s. Melvin Joseph and Betty Ehs (Koehler) J.; m. Paula Kay Haas, 1972 (div.); 1 child, Farrell; m. Karen Lynn Small, 1998; stepchildren: Ryan, Ariel. BA in Biology and Chemistry, U. Mo., Kansas City, 1974, DDS, 1977. Resident in hosp. dentistry VA Med. Ctr., Leavenworth, Kans., 1977-78; pvt. practice Newcastle, Wyo., 1978-79; asst. prof. U. Mo., Kansas City, 1979-87; chief restorative dentistry Truman Med. Ctr., Kansas City, 1979-87; dir. dental oncology Trinity Luth. Hosp., 1982-87; assoc. prof., dir. gen. practice residency program Ohio State U., Columbus, 1987—; prof., dir. gen. practice residency program, 1993—; dir. Honduras Clinic Project, 1992—; bd. dirs. Rinehart Found., U. Mo. Dental Sch., Kansas City, 1985-87; cons. Lee's Summit (Mo.) Care Ctr., 1984-87, Longview Nursing Ctr., Grandview, Mo., 1986-87; sec. Combined Hosp. Dental Staff, Columbus, 1989-90, v.p., 1990-91, pres., 1991-92. Author: (manual) Hospital Dental Hygiene, 1984, Hospital Dentistry, 1985, OSU Manual of Hospital Dentistry, 1989—, (booklet) Nursing Home Dentistry, 1986, Dental Oncology, 1986. Mem. regional coun. Easter Seal Soc., Kansas City, 1985-87, mem. profl. adv. coun. Nat. Easter Seal Soc., 1986-92; sec. bd. dirs. Easter Seal Rehab. Ctr., Columbus, 1990-93; pres. Health Profls. Serving Humanity. With U.S. Naval Sea Cadet Corps, 1998-99. Recipient Alumni Achievement award in dentistry U. Mo., Kansas City, 1995, Ohio Dental Assn. Humanitarian award, 1998. Fellow Acad. Dentistry Internat., Am. Soc. Dentistry for Children, Am. Assn. Hosp. Dentists (regional v.p. 1993—, sec.), Acad. Gen. Dentistry, Am. Soc. Geriatric Dentistry, Acad. Dentistry for Handicapped (pres. 1992), Am. Coll. Dentistry, Pierre Fauchard Acad.; mem. ADA, Internat. Assn. Dentistry for Handicapped (pres. 1994-96, past pres. 1996-98, editor 1998—), Mo. Dental Assn., Internat. Assn. Dental. Handicap, Greater Kansas City Dental Soc., Fedn. Spl. Care Orgns. in Dentistry (chmn. 1992-93), Southwest Oncology Group, Internat. Soc. for Oral Oncology, Ohio Dental Assn. (Humanitarian award 1998). Club: Magna Charta Barons. Avocations: photography, skiing, scuba diving, swimming, horses. E-mail: jolly.4@osu.edu. Home: 1326 Glenn Ave Columbus OH 43212-3281 Office: Ohio State U Coll Dentistry 305 W 12th Ave Columbus OH 43210-1267

JOLLY, RICHARD STEPHEN, engineering executive; b. Birmingham, West Midlands, England, June 29, 1953; s. Reginald and Cathlen (Edwards) J.; m. Gillian Noreen Alderton, Dec. 31, 1976; children: Simon, Stephen, Sarah. BS, U. Coll. Swansea (Wales), 1975. Mgr. R.M. Douglas, Eng., 1975-86, Howard Assocs., Eng., 1986-93; dir. Howard Assocs., 1993—. Steward Aldridge Meth. Ch., Eng., 1997-99; exec. mem. Jesus 2000, Walsall, Eng., 1999. Mem. M.I.C.E., M.I.O.S.H., Europanie Ingenieur. Methodist. Avocations: flying, golf, badminton, sailing. Home: 6 Widney Ave, Aldridge WS9 8HF, England Office: Howard Assocs, 67 The Avenue, Northampton NN1 5BT, England

JOLOS, ROSTISLAV VLADIMIROVICH, physicist, researcher; b. Vladivostok, Russia, Jan. 11, 1942; s. Vladimir Fedorovich and Julia Mikhailovna (rovkah) J.; m. Liubov Valerianovna Kozlova, Jan. 28, 1967; children: Elena, Eugeny. PhD, Joint Inst. for Nuclear Rsch., Dubna, Russia, 1968, DS, 1977. Jr. scientist Joint Inst. for Nuclear Rsch., 1965-68, sr. scientist, 1968-86, leader sci. group, 1986—, prof., 1994—. Contbr. articles to profl. jours. Office: Joint Inst Nuclear Rsch, 141980 Dubna Russia

JOLY, HUBERT BERNARD, management executive; b. Laxou, France, Aug. 11, 1959; s. Jean-Louis and Denise (Grandjean) J.; m. Nathalie Christiane Motte, Sept. 19, 1981; children: Stanislas, Agathe. MBA, Ecole des Hautes Etudes Comml., Jouy-en-Josas, France, 1981; MPA, Inst. d'Etudes Politiques, Paris, 1983. Asst. to chmn. and CEO Sacilor, Paris, 1981-82; assoc. McKinsey & Co., Paris, 1983-84, San Francisco, 1984-85; mgr. McKinsey & Co., Paris, 1985-89, prin., 1990-91; prin. McKinsey & Co., N.Y.C., 1992-93; prin. McKinsey & Co., Paris, 1993-96, co-leader European electronics practice, 1994-96; pres. EDS-France, Paris, 1996-99; chmn. bd. dirs. EDS Progical, 1996-99; v.p. EDS Europe, 1998-99; CEO Havas Interactive Inc, 1999—; Mem. World European Forum, Global Leaders for Tomorrow, 1996. Author: Excellence in Electronics, 1993, Wake Up Europe!, 1999; contbr. articles to profl. jours. Bd. mem. Am. C. of C. in France, 1998—. Mem. Ctr. d'Etude Prospective es Stratègique. Office: Havas Interactive Inc 19840 Pioneer Ave Torrance CA 90503-1690

JOLY, JACQUES, humanities educator; b. Boussois, Nord, France, Dec. 1, 1948; arrived in Japan, 1987; s. Edmond and Evelyne (Agostini) J.; m. Zhen Wei, Feb. 5, 1990. MA in Philosophy, U. Lille III, France, 1972; PhD in Far Eastern Studies, U. Paris VII, 1991. Tchr. h.s. France, 1968-73, 77-87, Japan, 1973-77; rschr. Waseda U., Tokyo, 1987-88; prof. Notre Dame Women's Coll., Kyoto, Japan, 1988-91, Eichi U., Amagasaki, Japan, 1991—. Author: Le Naturel Selon Ando Shoeki, 1996; co-author: Cent ans de Pensée au Japon, 1995, Ebisu-Etudes Japonaises No 13, 1996; translator: Essais Sur L'Histoire de la Pensée, 1996. Home: Takano Kamitakeya cho 10-4, Sakyo ku Kyoto 606-8105, Japan Office: Eichi U Nakoji 2-18-1, 661 Amagasaki Shi, Hyogo-ken Japan

JONAH, JAMES O. C., UN official. Under-sec. gen. dept. polit. affairs UN, N.Y.C.; min. fin. and econ. planner Ministry of Fin, Freetown, Sierra Leone. Office: Secretariat Bldg, George St, Freetown Sierra Leone*

JONAKAIT, GENE MILLER, developmental neurobiologist; b. Evanston, Ill., May 15, 1946; d. William Cleveland and Mary Gene (Herren) Knopf; m. Randolph N. Jonakait, Mar. 21, 1970; 1 child, Amelia. AB, Wellesley (Mass.) Coll., 1968; MA, U. Chgo., 1969; PhD, Cornell U. Med. Coll., 1978. Postdoctoral fellow Cornell U. Med. Coll., N.Y.C., 1978-81, asst. prof., 1981-85; asst. prof. Rutgers U., Newark, N.J., 1985-90, assoc. prof., 1990-94, prof., 1994—, chmn. dept. biol. scis., 1994-96, 2000—, assoc. dean, 1996-98; chmn. conf. com. N.Y. Acad. Scis., N.Y.C., 1991-92; chmn. summer conf. neuroimmunology Fedn. Am. Socs. Exptl. Biology, Bethesda, Md., 1994, 96. Author: Neuropeptides and Immunopeptides, Messengers in a Neuroimmune Axis, 1990, Substance P and Related Peptides, Cellular and Molecular Physiology, 1991; editor NeuroImmunoModulation; contbr. articles to profl. jours. including Neuron, Jour. Neurosci., Exptl. Neurology, Jour. Neurosci. Rsch., Jour. Neuroimmunology, Trends in Neurosci., Devel. Biology, Adv. Pharmacol., others. Recipient award for Excellence in Rsch., Rutgers U. Bd. Trustees, 1990; Wellesley scholar, 1968; grantee NIH, 1982-84, 86-89, 93-96, BRSG, 1986-90, Rutgers U. Busch grantee, 1990—, grantee Johnson & Johnson, 1987-89, NIMH, 1990-93, Office Naval Rsch., 1990-93, NSF, 1993—, Merck Rsch. Labs., 1994-95. Fellow AAAS; mem. Soc. Neurosci. Achievements include research in regulation of cholinergic differentiation, interleukin-1 induction of substance P in sympathetic ganglia via the induction of leukemia inhibitory factor. Office: Rutgers U 101 Warren St Newark NJ 07102-1811

JONAS, PETER MICHAEL, physiology educator; b. Darmstadt, Germany, May 10, 1961; s. Horst and Elisabeth (Ullrich) J.; m. Karin Pilawa, Dec. 30, 1991; children: Anne, Christian. MD, U. Giessen, Germany, 1987. Rsch. asst. U. Giessen, Germany, 1988-89, Max Planck Inst. for Med. Rsch., Heidelberg, Germany, 1990-94; prof C3 Tech. U., Munich, Germany, 1994-95; prof. C4 U. Freiburg, Germany, 1995—. Contbr. articles to profl. jours. including Sci., Jour. Neurosci., Jour. Physiology, Neuron, Jour. of Membrane Biology and others; contbr. single channel recording, 1995; editor: Ionotropic Glutamate R Receptor in the CNS. Recipient Franz Vogt award Giessen U., 1991, Heinz-Maier-Leibnitz award, Ministry Sci. and Tech., Germany, 1994, Medinfar Europ. prize in physiology Pres. of Portugal, Lisbon, 1997, Max Planck Rsch. prize for Internat. Coop., 1998. Roman Catholic. Office: Physiol Inst, Hermann-Herder Str 7, D-79104 Freiburg Breisgau, Germany

JONAS, RUTH HABER, psychologist; b. Tel Aviv, Aug. 24, 1935; d. Fred S. and Dorothy Judith (Bernstein) Haber; m. Saran Jonas, Sept. 16, 1956; children: Elizabeth, Frederick. AB, Barnard Coll., 1957; MA, New Sch. for Social Rsch., 1977, PhD, 1987; grad. psychotherapy and psychoanalysis, NYU, 1996. Lic. psychologist, N.Y. 1st and 2d yr. intern clin. psychology NYU Med. Ctr.-Bellevue Hosp., N.Y.C., 1985-87; postdoctoral rsch. fellow NYU Med. Ctr., N.Y.C., 1987-88; clin. instr. psychiatry NYU Sch. Medicine, N.Y.C., 1987, clin. asst. prof. psychiatry, 1991; sr. psychologist forensic svc. Bellevue Hosp., N.Y.C., 1988—; pvt. practice psychology N.Y.C., 1988—. Fellow Am. Orthopsychiat. Assn.; mem. APA, N.Y. State Psychol. Soc., Manhattan Psychol. Assn., Am. Heart Assn. (fellow stroke coun.). Office: 200 E 33d St Ste 10B New York NY 10016-4827

JONAS, SARAN, neurologist, educator; b. N.Y.C., June 24, 1931; s. Myron and Margaret (Wurmfeld) J.; m. Ruth Haber, Sept. 16, 1956; children: Elizabeth Ann, Frederick Jonathan. B.S., Yale U., 1952; M.D., Columbia U., 1956. Diplomate Am. Bd. Psychiatry and Neurology, Am. Bd. Internal Medicine. Intern Bellevue Hosp., N.Y.C., 1956-57; resident and fellow in medicine and neurology Bellevue Hosp., 1957-62; practice medicine specializing in neurology N.Y.C., 1964—; from clin. instr. to assoc. prof. clin. neurology NYU Sch. Medicine, 1964-77, prof. clin. neurology, 1977—, acting chmn. dept. neurology, 1987-91; assoc. dir. neurology NYU Hosp., 1970-87, dir., 1987-91, dir. electroencephalography, 1969-94; acting dir. neurology Bellevue Hosp., N.Y.C., 1987-91, assoc. dir., 1991—, dir. electroencephalography, 1994—. Served with USN, 1962-64. N.Y. State fellow in rheumatic diseases, 1962-64. Mem. Am. Acad. Neurology, Assn. for Rsch. in Nervous and Mental Diseases, Am. Heart Assn. (Stroke Coun., Epidemiology Coun.), Am. Epilepsy Soc. Office: 530 1st Ave New York NY 10016-6402

JONAS, SIR PETER, opera company director; b. London, Oct. 14, 1946; s. Walter Adolf and Hilda May J.; m. Lucy Hull, Nov. 1989 (sep. 1998). BA with honors, U. Sussex, Eng., 1968; postgrad., Royal No. Coll Music, Eng., 1968-71; lt., Royal Coll. Mus., London, 1971; student, Eastman Sch. Music, Rochester, N.Y., 1973-74; DMus (hon.), U. Sussex, U.K., 1994. Asst. to music dir., artistic adminstr. Chgo. Symphony Orch., 1974-76; dir. artistic adminstrn. Orchestral Assn. Chgo., Chgo. Symphony Orch., Chgo. Civic Orch., Chgo., 1977-85; gen. dir. English Nat. Opera, London, 1985-93; staatsintendant Bavarian State Opera, Munich, 1993—; bd. mgmt. Nat. Opera Studio, London, 1985-93; mem. coun. Royal Coll. Music, 1988-95; mem. adv. bd. Bayerische Vereinsbank, 1994—; bd. govs. Bayerische Rundfunk, 1999—; fellow Royal No. Coll. Music, Manchester, 2000. Co-author: Powerhouse, 1993, Elite und Demokratie, 1999. Created knight, 1999; decorated comdr. Brit. Empire. Fellow Royal Soc. Arts, Royal Coll. Music. Club: Athenaeum (Pall Mall), PEGS (London). Avocations: cinema, cricket, Twentieth Century Architecture. Home: Frundsbergstr 13, D-80634 Munich Germany Office: Bayerische Staatsoper Nat Theatre, Max-Joseph-Platz 2, D-80539 Munich Germany

JÓNASDÓTTIR, ANNA GUDRÚN, political science educator; b. Akureyri, Iceland, Dec. 2, 1942; 3 children by previous marriage; m. Bo Jonsson, 1989. Fil. kand., U. Uppsala, Sweden, 1974; PhD in Polit. Sci., U. Gothenburg, Sweden, 1991. Part-time lectr. dept. women's studies U. Gothenburg, 1989—; sr. lectr. polit. sci. U. Örebro, Sweden, 1990—, dir. rsch. ctr. for women's studies, 1992—; hon. reader polit. sci. U. Gothenburg, 1997. Author: Why Women Are Oppressed, 1994; editor: (with Kathleen B. Jones) The Political Interests of Gender, 1988, (with Dride von der Fehr & Bente Rosenbeck) Is There a Nordic Feminism?, 1998; contbr. articles to profl. jours. Office: U Örebro Sect Politics, Dept Social Sci, S-701 82 Örebro Sweden

JONASSEN, THOR MAGNE, biologist, consultant; b. Lyngdal, Norway, Mar. 16, 1967; s. Magne and Ester (Hansen) J. Høyskolekandidat Aquaculture, Sogs og Fjordane Dist., Sogndal, Norway, 1990; cand. sci., U. Bergen, Norway, 1994; PhD, U. Bergen, 2000. Rsch. fellow U. Bergen,

1996-99; cons. Akvaplan-Niva, Tromsø, Norway, 1999—. Contbr. articles to profl. jours. Grantee Norwegian Rsch. Coun., 1996-99, 98. Office: Akvaplan-Niva AS, Polar Environ Ctr, N-9296 Tromsø Norway

JONASSON, KERSTIN MARIA, romance languages educator; b. Stockholm, Aug. 29, 1941; d. Rune and Lisbeth (Werner) Olsson; m. Stig Jonasson, Apr. 10, 1978; 1 child, Gösta. MA, Stockholm U., 1965, PhD, 1977. Asst. Dept. Romance Langs. Stockholm U., 1966-68, rschr., 1977-85, lectr., 1985-94; tchr. French, English Adult Coll., Stockholm, 1973-76; translator Interpol Bd. Police, Stockholm, 1975-77; prof. Uppsala U., Sweden, 1994—, deputy dean faculty langs., 1999—. Author: La construction verbe+objet direct + complément prédicatif en français, 1976, Le nom propre: Constructions et interpretations, 1994; co-author: (textbook) Chacun son goût, 1974; editor Stockholm Studies i Modern Philology, 1990-94, Studia Neophilogica, 1994—. Mem. Stockholm Modern Philology Assn. (chmn. 1989-94), Swedish Soc. Richard Wagner (bd. dirs. 1995—). Avocations: opera, classical music, film, biking, cooking. Home: Sveavägen 119, S-11349 Stockholm Sweden Office: Uppsala U, Dept Romance Langs, S-75120 Uppsala Sweden

JONDAHL, TERRI ELISE, importing and distribution company executive, medical equipment company executive; b. Ukiah, Calif., May 6, 1959; d. Thomas William and Rebecca (Stewart) J. AA in Bus. Adminstrn., Mendocino Coll., 1981; BA in Adminstrn. and Mgmt., Columbia Pacific U., 1993. Sec. to planning commn. County of Mendocino, Ukiah, Calif., 1977-80; office systems analyst County of Mendocino, Ukiah, 1980-83; micro systems analyst Computerland of Annapolis, Md., 1983-84; controller Continental Mfg. Inc., Nacogdoches, Tex., 1984-87; mktg. mgr. Continental Mfg. Inc., Nacogdoches, 1987-89, dir. sales and mktg., 1989-95; exec. v.p. CAB Inc., Oakwood, Ga., 1995—; pres., CEO Innovatec Med. Corp., Duluth, Ga., 1998—. Co-author: National Federation of Business & Professional Women Local Organization Revitalization Plan, 1989. Mem. NAFE, Tex. Fedn. Bus. and Profl. Women (state pres. 1994-95), Nacogdoches Bus. and Profl. Women (pres. 1987-88), Ukiah Bus. and Profl. Women (pres. 1981-82), Nacogdoches County C. of C. (small bus. adv. com. 1990), Decatur Bus. and Profl. Women, Peachtree Corners/Norcross Rotary, Gwinnett County C. of C. (CEO exec. roundtable). Home: 6344 Green Oak Rdg Flowery Branch GA 30542-6630 Office: CAB Inc 4161 Chamblee Rd Oakwood GA 30566-3518

JONDEAU, GUILLAUME, cardiologist, educator; b. Metz, France, Apr. 20, 1959; s. Roland and Francoise (Lafargue) J.; m. Katayoun Mansour, June 1, 1991; children: Camille, Bernard, Mathilde. PhD, U. RenéDescartes, Paris, 1995. Intern Hosps. of Paris, Pub. Assistance, 1984-89; rsch. asst. A. Einstein Coll. Medicine, Bronx, N.Y., 1989; asst. chief clinic Hopital Ambroise Pare, Boulogne, France, 1989-94; mem. staff Univ. Hosps., Boulogne, 1994—, prof. cardiology, 1999—. Contbr. articles to Circulation, Nature Genetics and other profl. jours. Fellow Am. Coll. Chest Physician, Am. Coll. Cardiology, Soc. Francaise de Cardiologie. Office: Hopital Ambroise Pare, 9 av Charles de Gaulle, 92100 Boulogne France

JONE, WEN-BEN, computer scientist, researcher; b. Taipei, Taiwan, May 18, 1956; s. Fu and Fun-Ing (Wong) J.; m. Li-Fen Tseng, Dec. 25, 1986; children: Alice, Alan. BS, Nat. Chiao-Tung U., Hsinchu, Taiwan, 1979, MS, 1981; PhD, Case Western Reserve U., 1987. R&D officer Mil. 206 Arsenal, Taiwan Armed Forces, Sanhsia, Taiwan, 1981-83; teaching asst. Case Western Reserve U., Cleve., 1983-87; asst. prof. N. Mex. Tech. Inst., Socorro, 1987-92, assoc. prof., 1992-93; prof. Nat Chung-Cheng U., Chiayi, Taiwan, 1993—; dir. Very Large Scale Integrated Circuits Design and Test Lab., Nat. Chung-Cheng U., Chiayi, 1994—; mem. program com. Integrated Cirs. Testing Confs. Contbr. articles on computers to profl. jours. 2d lt. Taiwan Armed Forces, 1981-83. Recipient Best Thesis award Chinese Inst. Elec. Engring., Taipei, Taiwan, 1981; grantee Sandia Nat. Lab., Albuquerque, N. Mex., 1989-91, Nat. Sci. Coun, Taipei, 1993-96. Mem. IEEE, IEEE Computer Soc. (test tech. tech. com.). Avocations: swimming, jogging, singing, travel. Office: Nat Chung Cheng U, Computer Sci & Info Engring, Chia-Yi 62107, Taiwan

JONEKEN, BERTIL, economist, consultant; b. Laholm, Halland, Sweden, July 9, 1944; s. Harald Edvin and Märta Lilian (Martinsson) J.; m. Anneli Sirkka Nilanko, May 30, 1970; 1 child, Jorvi. Student, Emory U., 1964-65, Cranfield (Eng.) U. Sch. Mgmt., 1992; BA, U. Lund, 1969, M of Polit. Sci., 1970. Adminstr. Nat. Bd. Pub. Bldg., Stockholm, Sweden, 1970-77, head of sect., 1977-93, head dept., 1993; economist Nat. Property Bd., 1993—; pvt. practice cons., Stockholm, 1993—. Cashier Nat. Kidney Assn. Sweden, 1982—; auditor Swedish Coop. Body Orgns. of Disabled Persons, 1995—. Home: Kistavägen 7, 19267 Sollentuna Sweden

JONES, ALAN PORTER, JR., food manufacturing executive; b. Milw., Feb. 27, 1925; s. Alan Porter and Eleanor Pratt (Bright) J.; m. Jean Drummond, Sept. 12, 1953; children: Richard, Susan, Cynthia, Alexandra. BA, Harvard U., 1948, MBA, 1950. With Jones Dairy Farm, Ft. Atkinson, Wis., 1950—, asst. treas., 1953-61, treas., 1961-74, v.p., treas., 1974-93, also bd. dirs.; pres. Uncle Josh Bait Co., 1978—; bd. dirs. Johnson Bank, PDQ Corp. Dir. Dwight Foster Pub. Libr., 1952-87, Wis. Livestock and Meat Coun., 1981-97, Ft. Atkinson C. of C., 1985-88; mem. Ft. Atkinson Sch. Bd., 1968-69, Wis. Gov.'s Adv. Com. on Internat. Trade, 1981-97, Wis. Internat. Trade Coun., 1997—, Wis. Citizens Environ. Coun., 1980-84, Wis. Radioactive Waste Policy Coun., 1984-87; trustee Ripon Coll., Wis., 1974-77; bd. dirs. Wis. Nature Conservancy, 1992-95. With Inf. U.S. Army, 1943-45. Decorated Bronze Star, Combat Inf. Badge. Mem. Nat. Audubon Soc., Sierra Club, Nature Conservancy, Wilderness Soc., Am. Legion, Internat. Crane Found., Ft. Atkinson Wisconservation Club. Republican. Home: 433 Adams St Fort Atkinson WI 53538-1401 Office: Jones Dairy Farm PO Box 808 Fort Atkinson WI 53538-0808

JONES, ARTHUR STANLEY, agricultural consultant; b. Belfast, Northern Ireland, May 17, 1932; s. John and Anne (Hamilton) J.; m. Mary Margaret Smith, 1962; children: Graeme, Roland, Nathan, Camilla. BSc in Nutritional Biochemistry, U. Durham, Eng., 1955; PhD, U. Aberdeen, Scotland, 1960. Rsch. officer Rowett Rsch. Inst., Aberdeen, 1959-66, head applied nutrition, 1966-75, head applied sci. divsn., 1975-83, dep. dir., 1983-86; Strathcona-Fordyce prof. agr., head Sch. Agr. U. Aberdeen, 1986-90; prin. North Scotland Coll., 1986-90, Royal Agrl. Coll., Cirencester, Eng., 1990-97; cons. to agr. food industries; chmn. Scottish Beef Devels. Ltd., Aberdeen, 1988-99; vis. prof. U. Praque. Gov. Aberdeen Ctr. for Land Use, 1986-90, Rowett Rsch. Inst., Aberdeen, 1986-90; trustee Trehane Trust, 1993—, Geoffrey Cragghill Meml. Scholarship Trust, 1993-97, Ceres Found., 1996—, Gov. Henley Coll. Mgmt., chmn. acad. adv. bd., 1996—. Lt. Brit. Army, 1955-57, officer RAF Res., 1958-62. Decorated Comdr. Most Excellent Order Brit. Empire, 1997. Fellow Inst. Biology, Bris. Inst. Mgmt., Royal Soc. Art Mfrs. and Commerce, Inst. Agr. Mgmt.; mem. Royal Agrl. Soc. Eng. (mem. coun. 1990-98), Rural Economy Group, Farmer's Club, Assn. Royal Agrl. Socs. Avocations: yachting, flying, gardening. Home: Begsdell Caskieben Kinellar, Aberdeenshire AB21 OTB, England

JONES, BARBARA DEAN, substance abuse and family relations counselor; b. Taunton, Mass., Dec. 11, 1931; d. Laurance Franklin and Amy Laura (Harrington) Dean; m. Rial Cooper Jones, Aug. 31, 1957 (div. July 1987); children: Dean Michael, Mark Jackson, Amy Winifred. Student, Duke U., 1952; BA, U. Mass., 1953; MEd in Human Svcs., Boston U., 1983. Cert. in alcohol education and prevention, Fla., 1981; lic. real estate agt., Va., 1979, Calif., 1984. Psychiat. social worker Alcohol Rehab. Ctr., Butner, N.C., 1953-55; social case worker Granville County Dept. Pub. Welfare, Oxford, N.C., 1955-56; dist. dir. Bright Leaf Girl Scout Coun., Durham, N.C., 1956-57; kindergarten tchr. Sasebo, Japan, 1961; social worker Assn. for the Blind, Charleston, S.C., 1962-63; tchr. Am. Studies Ctr., Naples, Italy, 1980-82; alcohol rehab. counselor Navy Regional Med. Ctr., Naples, 1982-83; family counselor Parkside Recovery Ctr., Oceanside, Calif., 1987-89; human rels. cons. Decorating Den, Anaheim, Calif., 1989-90; alcohol facilitator Navy Alcohol Safety Action Program, Naples, 1980-83. Bd. dirs. Fairfax (Va.) Ballet Co., 1978, YWCA, Glendora, Calif., 1972; pres. Naval Officers Wives Club, Charleston, 1964; lay min. St. Michael's Episcopal Ch., Carlsbad, Calif., 1966; chmn. alcohol and drug abuse com. Self Esteem Task Force of San Diego County, 1990; mem. San Diego Mus. Art, Mingei Mus. World Folk Art; v.p. Camino Real Assn., 1996-97, pres., 1997-98. Recipient cert. of appreciation U.S. Navy, 1983; Yale U. Summer Sch. of Alcohol Studies fellow, 1955. Mem. AAUW, Latin Am. Arts Assn., Women's Internat. Ctr., Oceanside Newcomer's Club (chmn. cultural arts 1996, 97, pres. elect 1997-98, pres. 1998-99, 99-2000). Republican. Avocations: travel, golf, arts, bridge. Home and Office: 3421 Summerset Way Oceanside CA 92056-3208

JONES, BERNARD ALAN, retired educator; b. Newcastle-Under-Lyme, Eng., Jan. 13, 1931; s. Alfred and Mary Ellen (Tompkin) J.; m. Gwenda Stafford, Oct. 6, 1956 (div. 1979); children: Carolyn Lesley, Elizabeth Helen; m. Hanna Kaarina Pietilä, June 22, 1985; children: Aino Maria Tuulikki, Petri Alan Väinö, Laura Suvi Orvokki. BA in Classics, Leeds U., Yorkshire, Eng., 1957. Cert. tchr. Eng., 1957, Finland, 1984. Tchr. pvt. prep. sch., Harrogate, Eng., 1955-58; tchr., dep. head Burley-in-Wharfedale (Eng.) Sch. West Riding County Coun., Yorkshire, 1958-70; head integrated studies West Riding County Coun., Ilkley, Yorkshire, 1970-72; English tchr. Eurolez Opisto, Tampere, Finland, 1972-74; English and history tchr. Bradford (Yorkshire) City Coun., 1974; head 4th yr. classes Hereford & Worcester (Eng.) Schs., Redditch, 1975-80; tchr., dir. studies P.L.P./Habil Pvt. Lang. Consultancy, Helsinki, Finland, 1980-83; tchr. EFL English Hartola (Finland) Coll., 1983-88, Peräpohjolan Coll., Tornio, Finland, 1988-90; pvt. tchr. Lappland, 1990-93; founder, local sec., examinations officer Cambridge U., Hartola, 1983-88, Tornio,.... Contbr., translator articles to profl. jours. Grantee Tchrs. Union-Finland, 1992. Mem. Internat. Biog. Ctr. Cambridge (hon. fellow 1996—, adv. coun. 1997—), Am. Biog. Inst., Kemi-Tornio English Club (founding mem., chmn. 1990—). Avocations: art, photography, archeology, calligraphy, computers. Home: Tervolantie 1511B, 95365 Maula Suomi Finland

JONES, BOB, journalist, educator; b. Wolverhampton, U.K., Jan. 18, 1934; s. William Skinner and Violet (Hughes) J.; m. Janet Mary Wilkinson, June 10, 1967; children: Holly, Katharine. BA in Geography with honors, U. Birmingham, Eng., 1955. Reporter Investor Chronicle, London, 1955-59; assoc. editor Forbes Mag., N.Y.C., 1959-61; asst. editor The Statist, London, 1961-67; bus. features editor The Times, London, 1967-73; reporter The Economist, London, 1975; sr. rsch. fellow London Bus. Sch., 1976-79; sr. lectr. journalism City U., 1979—, emeritus fellow. Office: City U Dept Journalism, Northampton Sq, London EC1V 0HB, England

JONES, BONNIE BILLICK, university administrator; b. Cleve., Oct. 13, 1952; d. Anthony Jr. and Mildred Ann Billick; m. Paul H. Jones, Aug. 13, 1977; children: Paul II, Tiffany, Cameron. BS in Edn., Miami U., Oxford, Ohio, 1974; MEd, Kent State U., 1977, PhD, 1986. Tchr. Kent (Ohio) City Schs., 1974-78; adminstr. admissions dept. U. Akron, Ohio, 1978-80; adminstr. student affairs, admissions, instnl. rsch. Northeastern Ohio Univs. Coll. of Medicine, Rootstown, 1980—. Trustee Ravenna (Ohio) Twp., 1986-91. Office: Northeastern Ohio Univs Coll of Medicine 4209 State Route 44 Rootstown OH 44272-9698

JONES, BRUCE ALLEN, pathologist; b. Indpls., Feb. 23, 1953. BS, U. Mich., 1975; MD, Wayne State U., 1979. Diplomate in anat. and clin. pathology and cytopathology Am. Bd. Pathology. Resident in internal medicine Harper Hosp., Detroit, 1979-80; fellow in diagnostic electron microscopy William Beaumont Hosp., Royal Oak, Mich., 1984-85; resident in pathology St. John Hosp., Detroit, 1980-84, assoc. pathologist, 1985-94, dir. pathology residency program, 1992—, dir. clin. pathology, 1994—; dir. St. John Clin. Pathology Labs., Romeo Plank br. St. John Health Sys., Clinton Twp., Mich., 1997—; bd. dirs. Joint Venture Hosp. Labs., Detroit. Contbr. articles to profl. jours. Mem. Coll. Am. Pathologists (chmn. quality practices com.), Detroit Acad. Medicine, Am. Soc. Clin. Pathologists, Am. Coll. Physician Execs. E-mail: bruce.jones@stjohn.org. Office: St John Hosp 22101 Moross Rd Detroit MI 48236-2172

JONES, C. PAUL, lawyer, educator; b. Grand Forks, N.D., Jan. 7, 1927; s. Walter M. and Sophie J. (Thorton) J.; m. Helen M. Fredel, Sept. 7, 1957; children—Katherine, Sara H. BBA, U. Minn., 1950, JD, 1950; LLM, William Mitchell Coll. of Law, 1955. Assoc. Lewis, Hammer, Heaney, Weyl & Halverson, Duluth, Minn., 1950-51; asst., chief dep. Hennepin County Atty., Mpls., 1952-58; asst. U.S. atty. U.S. Atty's. Office, St. Paul, 1959-60; assoc. Maun & Hazel, St. Paul, 1960-61; ptnr. Dorfman, Rudquist, Jones, & Ramstead, Mpls., 1961-65; state pub. defender Minn. State Pub. Defender's Office, Mpls., 1966-90; adj. prof. law William Mitchell Coll. of Law, St. Paul, 1953-70, prof. law, 1970—, assoc. dean for acad. affairs, 1991-95; adj. prof. U. Minn., Mpls., 1970-90; mem. adv. com. on rules of criminal procedure Minn. Supreme Ct., 1970—. Author: Criminal Procedure from Police Detention to Final Disposition, 1981; Jones on Minnesota Criminal Procedure, 1955, 64, 70, 75; Minnesota Police Law Manual, 1955, 67, 70, 76. Mem. Minn. Gov.'s Crime Commn., St. Paul, 1970s, Minn. Fair Trial-Free Press Assn., Mpls., 1970s, Citizens League, Mpls., 1955—, Mpls. Aquatennial Assn., Mpls., 1955-60, Minn. Coun. on Crime and Justice, 1991—. Recipient Reginald Heber Smith award Nat. Legal Aid and Defender Assn., 1969. Fellow Am. Coll. Trial Lawyers; mem. Am. Bd. Trial Advs., ABA, Minn. State Bar Assn., Hennepin County Bar Assn., Ramsey County Bar Assn., Nat. Legal Aid & Defender Assn. Democrat. Lutheran. Clubs: Suburban Gyro of Mpls., Mpls. Athletic. Lodge: Rotary. Avocations: fishing; hunting; golfing; desert watching. Home: 5501 Dewey Hill Rd Edina MN 55439-1906 Office: William Mitchell Coll Law 875 Summit Ave Saint Paul MN 55105-3030

JONES, CARROLL JEAN JOHNSTON, special education educator; b. June 29, 1944. BA, U. Ariz., 1966, MEd, 1970; PhD, Kans. State U., 1983. Tchr. Lineweaver Elem. Sch., Tucson, Ariz., 1986-70, Tecumseh (Kans.) North Elem. Sch., 1972-74; reading specialist Shawnee Heights Elem. Sch., Tecumseh, 1976-80; acting dir., instr. Ea. Ill. U., Charleston, 1983; chair Spl. Sch. Dist. St. Louis County, Town and Country, Mo., 1983-85; asst. prof. spl. edn. Associated Colls. Ctrl. Kans., McPherson, 1985-86, Fayetteville (N.C.) State U., 1986-88; dir. divsn. edn., phys. edn. Meth. Coll., Fayetteville, 1988-89; assoc. prof. spl. edn. Lander Coll., Greenwood, S.C., 1989-91; mgr. faculty coord. City Colls. Chgo., 1992; assoc. prof. spl. edn. Lander U., 1993-96, State U. West Ga., Carrollton, 1996-97, Clarke Coll., Dubuque, Iowa, 1998—; cons. and presenter in field. Author: Evaluation and Educational Programming of Deaf, Blind.Severly Multihandicapped Students: Sensorimotor Stage, 1988, Enhancing Self-Concepts and Achievement of Mildly Handicapped Students: Learning Disabled, Mildly Mentally Retarded and Behabior Disordered, 1992, Human Figure Drawings of Mildly Handicapped Students: Learning Disabled, Mildly Mentally Retarded, Emotionally Disturbed and Speech/Language Impaired, 1992, Social and Emotional Development of Exceptional Students: Handicapped and Gifted, 1992, Case Studies of Mildly Handicapped Students: LEarning Disabled, Mildly Mentally Retarded and Behavior Disordered, 1992, Case Studies of Severly/Multihandicapped Students, 1993, Case Studies of Exceptional Students: Handicapped and Gifted, 1993, Introduction to the Nature and Needs of Students with Mild Disabilities: Mental Retardation, Behavior Disorders, Learning Disabilities, 1996, Curriculum-Based Assessment: The Easy Way, 1998, Curriculum Development for Students with Mild Disabilities: Academic and Social Skills for Writing Inclusion IEPs, 2000; contbr. articles to profl. jours. Mem. S.C. Assn. Tchr. Educators, Internat. Assn. Spl. Edn., Coun. Exceptional Children, Delta Kappa Gamma, Kappa Delta Pi, Phi Delta Kappa. Office: Clarke Coll 1550 Clarke Dr Dubuque IA 52001-3117

JONES, CHRISTOPHER ANDREW, applied mathematics educator; b. London, Apr. 29, 1949; s. Harry and Frances Molly (O'Neill) J.; m. Phillis Bicknell, Mar. 31, 1973; children: Timothy, Nicholas, Rachel. BSc, Cambridge (Eng.) U., 1972, PhD, 1975, ScD, 1991. Rsch. fellow U. Sussex, Eng., 1975-76; rsch. fellow U. Newcastle-upon-Tyne, Eng., 1976-89, sr. lectr., 1989-91; prof. applied math. U. Exeter, Eng., 1992—, organizer math. master classes, 1993—; cons. for Brit. Gas (Transco Ltd.), 1978-96; external examiner Cambridge U., 1987-89, U. Bristol, Eng., 1993-95; vis. rsch. prof. UCLA, 1997, 89; vis. fellow commoner Trinity Coll., Cambridge U., 1998. Contbr. over 50 articles to sci. jours., including Nature, Sci., Jour. Fluid Mechanics, Procs. Royal Soc. Fellow Royal Astron. Soc.; mem. Am. Geophys. Union. Avocations: hill walking, cycling. Home: 8 Mill Rd Countess Wear, Devon Exeter EX2 6LH, England Office: U Exeter, Sch Math Scis, Devon Exeter EX4 4QE, England

JONES, CHRISTOPHER DON, lawyer; b. Longview, Tex., Jan. 23, 1964; s. Donald and Audrey Gale Jones; m. Michelle McCullough, Feb. 16, 1991; children: Catherine Abigail, Christopher Andrew. BBA, Baylor U., 1987, JD, 1989. Bar: Tex. 1989. Assoc. Worsham, Forsythe, Sampels & Wooldrige, Dallas, 1989-92, Misko, Howie & Sweeney, LLP, Dallas, 1992-95, Howie & Sweeney, LLP, Dallas, 1995-96, Erskine, McMahon & Stroup, LLP, Longview, Tex., 1996-97; ptnr. Stroup & Jones, LLP, Longview, Tex., 1997-2000, Jones & Jones, LLP, Longview, Tex., 2000—. Asst. mng. editor Baylor Law Rev., 1989. Mem. Leadership Longview, 1998-99. Named Kiwanian of Yr., Kiwanis Club Dallas, 1993. Mem. ABA, Tex. Bar Assn., Tex. Trial Lawyers Assn. (sustaining). Democrat. Avocations: golf, hunting, running. Office: Jones & Jones LLP 420 N Green St Ste C Longview TX 75601-6443

JONES, CLIFFORD AARON, SR., lawyer, international businessman; b. Long Lane, Mo., Feb. 19, 1912; s. Burley Monroe and Arlie (Benton) J.; children: Clifford A. Jones II, Joni Lee Jones Ryan; m. Marilyn T. Hayes, May 1, 1995. LL.B., U. Mo., 1938, J.D., 1969. Bar: Nev. 1938, U.S. Dist. Ct. Nev. 1939, D.C. 1982, U.S. Ct. Appeals (9th and D.C. cirs.) 1983, U.S. Supreme Ct. 1983. Founder, sr. ptnr. Jones Vargas (formerly Jones, Jones, Close & Brown), Las Vegas, Nev., 1938-93, retired, 1993; majority leader Nev. Legislature, 1941-42; judge 8th Jud. Dist., Nev., 1945-46; lt. gov. State of Nev., 1946-54; owner, builder, chmn. bd. Thunderbird Hotel, Inc., Las Vegas, 1948-64; founder Valley Bank of Nev., 1953; founder, sec., bd. dirs. First Western Savs. and Loan Assn., 1964-66; pres., chmn. bd. Caribbean-Am. Investment Co., Inc., 1960-78; pres., bd. dirs. Income Investments, Inc., 1963-65; sr. v.p., bd. dirs. Barrington Industries, Inc., 1966-70; chmn. bd., pres. Cen. African Land Co. Mem. Clark County (Nev.) Democratic Central Com., 1940-80, chmn., 1948; nat. committeeman from Nev. Dem. Party, 1954; mem. Nev. Dem. State Central Com., 1945-60; 4 time del. Dem. Nat. Conv. Served as lt. col. F.A. U.S. Army, 1942-46, ETO. Mem. ABA (past mem. tax sect.), Am. Coll. Trust and Estate Counsel, Nev. Bar Assn., D.C. Bar Assn., Am. Legion, VFW, Phi Delta Phi, Kappa Sigma. Clubs: United Nations Lions (N.Y.C.); Elks (Las Vegas), Lions (Las Vegas) (past pres.).

JONES, CLYDE ADAM, art educator, artist; b. Cobleskill, N.Y., Nov. 10, 1924; s. Lester L. and Myra (Karker) J.; BFA, Syracuse U., 1948, MA, 1954; EdD, Pa. State U., 1961. Tchr. art North High Sch., Binghamton, N.Y., 1948-49, 1950-56; instr. ceramics Jr. League of Binghamton, 1950-53; guest instr. ceramics Rehab. Guild, Saranac Lake, N.Y., 1951-54; asst. prof. art edn. Edinboro (Pa.) State Coll., 1956-58; instr. Creative Arts Workshop, Cornell U., Ithaca, N.Y., summer, 1958; asst. prof. child devel. U. Conn., Storrs, 1961-66, asst. dean Sch. Home Econs. and Family Studies, 1976-79, trustee Syracuse U. Libr. Assocs., 1970, assoc. prof. human devel. and family rels., 1966—; prof. emeritus, 1985—; cons. Head Start program, Conn., 1965-66. Mem. Gov.'s Commn. on Status or Women, 1965-67; bd. dirs. Greater Mansfield Arts Coun., 1986—, mem. adv. bd., 1989—; mem. governing bd. Nat. Assn. for Creative Children and Adults, 1986—; mem. Cobleskill (N.Y.) Hist. Soc., dir. bd. dirs. newsletter editor, 1993. With AUS, 1943-45. Recipient Honorable Mention Ceramic Nat. Exhbn., 1954. Mem. Conn. Assn. for Edn. of Young Children (v.p. 1970-72), New Eng. Assn. for Edn. of Young Children (publs. com. 1980—, editor newsletter 1963-65), Hartford Assn. for Edn. of Young Children (pres. 1967-69), Nat. Assn. for Edn. of Young Children, Soc. for Rsch. in Child Devel., Nat. Soc. for Study of Edn., Nat. Art Edn. Assn. (rsch. trainee 1965), Internat. soc. for Edn. thru Art, Assn. for Childhood Edn. Internat., Conn. Home Econs. Assn. (del., dir. 1978-82, newsletter editor 1984—, named Home Economist of Yr. 1992), Am. Home Econs. Assn., Phi Delta Kappa. One man shows: Rehab. Guild, Saranac Lake, N.Y., Windham Hosp., Willimantic, Conn., Art Bldg, Pa. State U., Student Union U. Conn.; group shows include: Roberson Meml., Binghamton, N.Y., Erie (Pa.) Art Mus., Munson-Williams-Proctor Inst., Utica, N.Y., Mus. of Fine Arts, Syracuse, Norwich (Conn.) Art Mus., Schoharie County Arts Coun., Albany Inst. of History and Art, Essex (Conn.) Art Assn., Rochester (N.Y.) Meml. Art Gallery; illustrations for history volumes of Sch. of Home Econs. and Family Studies and Sch. of Nursing, U. Conn. Home: 52 Storrs Heights Rd Storrs Mansfield CT 06268-2322 Office: U Conn Sch Family Studies Storrs Mansfield CT 06269-0001

JONES, CLYDE WILLIAM, anesthesiologist; b. Barbados, West Indies, Sept. 29, 1929; came to U.S., 1947; s. Lewis F. and Albertha B. (Lewis) J.; m. Norma Anita, Sept. 14, 1963; children: Michael W., Ronald C., Stephen T. BS, City Coll., N.Y.C., 1954; MD, Howard U., 1958. Diplomate Am. Bd. Anesthesiology. Capt. U.S. Navy, 1959-79, med. officer, 1959-63; resident in anesthesiology U.S. Naval Hosp., San Diego, 1963-66; staff anesthesiologist U.S. Naval Hosp., Camp Pendleton, Calif., 1966-67, chief of anesthesiology, 1967-69; chief of anesthesiology 1st Hosp. Co., Danang, Vietman, 1968, U.S. Naval Hosp., Marianas Island, Guam, 1969-71; staff anesthesiologist Naval Regional Med. Ctr., San Diego, 1971-73, chief of anesthesiology, 1973-79; staff anesthesiologist Kaiser Permanente Med. Ctr., San Diego, 1979-81, 87—, chief of anesthesiology, 1981-87. Contbr. articles to profl. jours. Acolyte lay reader, sub Deacon All Sts. Episcopal Ch., San Diego, 1971—; bd. dirs. Bishop's Sch., San Diego, 1980-81, San Diego Civic Light Opera, Inc., 1980-83. Recipient Meritorious Svc. medal, certificate of merit Surgeon Gen. U.S. Navy, 1979. Fellow Am. Coll. Anesthesiologists; mem.Am. Soc. Anesthesiologists (delegate), Assn. Mil. Surgeons of U.S., Am. Soc. Clin. Hypnosis, Internat. Anesthesia Rsch. Soc., Naval Inst., Sigma Pi Phi. Democrat. Avocations: hypnosis, coin collecting, medical volunteer. Home: 5201 Countryside Dr San Diego CA 92115-2136 Office: Kaiser Permanente Med Ctr 4647 Zion Ave San Diego CA 92120-2507

JONES, DAN THOMAS LLEWELLYN, medical physicist; b. Cape Town, South Africa, Feb. 14, 1943; s. Thomas Henry and Nora Joyce (Kingwill) J.; m. Diana Thelma Goedhals, Oct. 2, 1982. BSc, U. Cape Town, South Africa, 1964, MSc, 1967, PhD, 1972, MSc in Medicine, 1977. Cert. med. physicist South Africa Med. and Dental Coun., profl. natural scientist South Africa Coun. Natural Scientists. Rsch. assoc. U. Wis., Madison, 1972-74; sr. scientist Atomic Energy Bd., Pelindaba, South Africa, 1974-75; sr. med. physicist Groote Schuur Hosp., Cape Town, South Africa, 1975-78; chief med. physicist Nat. Accelerator Ctr., Faure, South Africa, 1978-85, head med. radiation group, 1985—. Recipient Radie Kotze Gold medal for med. physics Ebrahim Found., 1994. Fellow Inst. Physics (London); mem. South Africa Assn. Physicists in Medicine and Biology (treas. 1988—), South Africa Inst. Physics, South Africa Soc. Nuclear Medicine. Avocations: reading, walking, travel, sport. Home: 13 Gilmour Cir, 7800 Constantia Western Cape, South Africa Office: Nat Accelerator Ctr, Old National Rd PO Box 72, Faure 7131 Western Cape, South Africa

JONES, DAVID ALWYN, geneticist, botany educator; b. Colliers Wood, Surrey, Eng., June 23, 1934; came to U.S., 1989; s. Trefor and Marion Edna Jones; m. Hazel Cordelia Lewis, Aug. 29, 1959; children: Catherine Susan, Edmund Meredith, Hugh Francis. BA, MA in Natural Scis., U. Cambridge, Eng., 1957; DPhil in Genetics, U. Oxford, Eng., 1963. Chartered biologist, UK. Lectr. genetics U. Birmingham, Eng., 1961-73; prof. genetics U. Hull, Eng., 1973-89, head dept. plant biology and genetics, 1983-88; prof. botany U. Fla., Gainesville, 1989—, chmn. dept. botany, 1989-98; chmn. membership com. Inst. of Biology, London, 1982-87. Co-author: Variation and Adaptation in Plant Species, 1971, Analysis of Populations, 1976, What is Genetics?, 1976, Zmiennosc i przystosowanie roslin, 1977; contbr. over 100 articles to profl. jours. Fellow Linnean Soc., Inst. Biology; mem. AAAS, Am. Soc. Naturalists, Bot. Soc. Am., Internat. Soc. Chem. Ecology (coun. 1983-84, 89-91, keynote spkr. ann. meeting 1984, pres. elect 1986-87, pres. 1987-88, past pres. 1988-89, co-editor Jour. Chem. Ecology 1994—), Brit. Assn. Advancement of Sci. (chmn. coord. com. for cytology and genetics 1974-87), Genetical Soc. Gt. Britain (convenor ann. meetings profs. of genetics 1983-88), Ecol. Genetics Group, Population Genetics Group, Soc. for Study of Evolution, Gamma Sigma Delta, Sigma Xi (pres. U. Fla. chpt. 2000—). Achievements include research in practical population biology especially in ecological genetics and chemical ecology of cyanogenic plants. Home: 7201 SW 97th Ln Gainesville FL 32608-6378 Office: U Fla Dept Botany 220 Bartram Hall Gainesville FL 32611-8526

JONES, DONALD KELLY, state agency executive; b. Fresno, Calif., Aug. 9, 1944; s. Chester Henry and Helen Edith (Summers) J.; m. Carolyn Wray Dolly, Mar. 23, 1979. BA in History, Stanford U., 1966; M Internat. Affairs, Johns Hopkins U., 1968. Asst. prof. Davidson (N.C.) Coll., 1973-75; sr. economist GM Corp., N.Y.C., 1975-84; dir. internat. trade Am. Paper

Inst., N.Y.C., 1984-86; sr. mgr. bus. devel. Nissho Iwai Am. Corp., N.Y.C., 1986-95; dep. commr., sr. v.p., chief adminstrv. officer, bd. dirs. Empire State Devel. Corp., N.Y.C., 1995—; mem. U.S. bus./industry adv. com. OECD, N.Y.c., 1977-84; bd. dirs. Infosys Corp. Author: Structure of American Government, 1975. Rep. Party candidate for N.Y. State Assembly, 1992; chmn. Change-N.Y., Albany, 1992-95; pres. Taxpayers' Alliance of N.Y., Hartsdale, N.Y., 1994—; bd. dirs. Columbia Sch. Internat. Bus., N.Y.C., 1995—, N.Y.-Israel Econ. Devel. Partnership, 1999—; mem. Westchester County Budget Adv. Com., White Plains, N.Y., 1995—; apptd. mem. N.Y.C. Dist. Export Coun., 1996—. Recipient Recognition of Svc. award UN Internat. Bus. Coun., 1984, Outstanding Svc. award Cleve. World Trade Assn., 1993. Mem. Am. Enterprise Inst., Heritage Found., Cato Inst., Johns Hopkins U. Alumni Assn. (bd. dirs. 1994—), Eastside Conservative Club. Republican. Avocations: classical music, politics, travel. Home: 10 Hawthorne Way Hartsdale NY 10530-3005

JONES, DORIS (ANNA DORIS JONES), apparel buyer; b. Woodstock, Mich., Oct. 31, 1917; d. Lowren Orville and Lela Irene (Gallatin) Vogel; m. Verl Richard Huntley, April 13, 1946 (dec. 1966); 1 child, Karyl Lynn Huntley; m. Donald R. Jones, April 28, 1957 (dec. 1989). BA in Psychology, U. Mich., 1939. Salesperson J.L. Hudson Dept. Store, Detroit, 1939-40, Bullocks, L.A., 1940; asst. store mgr. Elaine Shop, Jackson, Mich., 1940-48; store mgr. Joseph Magnin, Sacramento, Calif., 1949-52; women's sportswear buyer Steinfelds Dept Store, Tucson, 1952-57; pvt. practice spiritual counselor Tucson, 1977-82; religious sci. practitioner, tchr. Golden Gate Ch. of Religious Sci., Corde Madero, Calif., 1982—, Santa Rosa (Calif.) Ch. of Religious Sci., 1992—; adv. bd. United Ch. of Religious Sci., L.A., 1994-98, practitioner emeritus religious sci., 1977. Recipient Meritorious Practitioner award United Ch. of Religious Sci., 1997. Home and Office: 284 Mockingbird Cir Santa Rosa CA 95409-6240

JONES, E. STEWART, JR., lawyer; b. Troy, N.Y., Dec. 4, 1941; s. E. Stewart and Louise (Farley) J.; m. Constance M., Dec. 28, 1968; children: Christopher, Brady, Erin. BA, Williams Coll., 1963; JD, Albany Law Sch., 1966. Bar: N.Y. 1966, U.S. Dist. Ct. (no. dist.) N.Y. 1966, U.S. Dist. Ct. (so. and ea. dist.) N.Y. 1994, U.S. Dist. Ct. (we. dist.) N.Y. 1987, U.S. Claims Ct. 1991, U.S. Ct. Appeals (2d cir.) 1976, U.S. Supreme Ct. 1976. Asst. dist. atty. Rensselaer County (N.Y.), 1968-70, spl. prosecutor, 1974; ptnr. E. Stewart Jones, Troy, 1974—; lectr. in field; mem. com. on profl. standards of 3d jud. dept. State of N.Y., 1977-80, mem. 3d jud. screening com., Albany County; mem. merit selection panel for selection and appointment of U.S. magistrate for No. Dist. N.Y., 1981, 91; bd. dirs. Univ. Found. at Albany, trustee Troy Savs. Bank. Contbr. numerous articles to profl. jours. Trustee The Albany Acad., Albany Law Sch.; active Nat. Alumni Coun. Albany Law Sch. With USNG. Fellow Am. Bar Found., Am. Inns Ct., Internat. Acad. Trial Lawyers, Am. Bd. Criminal Trial Lawyers (Upstate N.Y. chmn. 1998—), Am. Coll. Trial Lawyers, Inner Circle of Advs., Am. Bd. Profl. Liability Attys. (diplomate), Internat. Soc. Barristers (chmn. upstate N.Y. 1998—); mem. N.Y. State Bar Assn. (Outstanding Practitioner award 1980, mem. exec. com. of criminal justice sect. 1977-90, mem. exec. com. trial lawyers sect. 1981-94, mem. spl. com. med. malpractice, other coms.), N.Y. State Trial Lawyers Assn. (bd. dirs. 1982-91, dir. emeritus 1991), Capital Dist. Trial Lawyers Assn. (bd. dir. 1973-76), ABA (numerous coms.) Calif. Attys. for Criminal Justice, Practising Law Inst., Am. Judicature Soc. (sustaining), Rensselaer County Bar Assn., Am. Soc. Law and Medicine, Albany County Bar Assn., N.Y. State Defenders Assn., Am. Arbitration Assn. (nat. panel of arbitrators), Dispute Resolutions, Inc. (nat. panel of arbitrators), Fed. Bar Coun., Upstate Trial Attys. Assn., Inc., Nat. Bd. Trial Advocacy (diplomate), Nat. Assn. Criminal Def. Lawyers, N.Y. State Assn. Criminal Def. Lawyers, Am. Bd. Trial Advocates (advocate), Inst. for Injury Reduction (founder), Trial Lawyers for Pub. Justice (founder), Civil Justice Found. (founding sponsor), Schuyler Meadows Club, Troy Country Club, Troy Club, Steuben Athletic Club, Ft. Orange Club, Stone Horse Yacht Club (Harwich Port, Mass.), Equinox Country Club (Manchester, Vt.), Williams Club (N.Y.C.). Home: 46 Schuyler Rd Loudonville NY 12211-1447 Office: 28 2nd St Troy NY 12180-3986

JONES, EDWARD ALLEN, engineer; b. Piqua, Ohio, Nov. 28, 1946; s. Thomas Loya and Bessie Faith (Coffman) J.; m. Angeliki Athanasiou, Oct. 4, 1969; children: Faith H., Thomas A. BSME, Union Coll., 1978, postgrad., 1985—. Toolmaker GE, Schenectady, N.Y., 1970-74, foreman, 1974-75, instr., 1976-78, project engr., 1978-84, mfg. engr., 1984-92; sr. project engr. Westinghouse Electric, Schenectady, 1992-95; engring. tech. writer, 1995-99, tech. manual support engr., 1999—; exec. officer Advance Base Functional Component, Albany, 1988-92; cons. to GE. Author: Reactor Equipment Cost Estimating Manual, 1989, Steam Generator and Reactor Servicing Equipment Technical Manual, 1996. Co-provider Family Care Home for Adults, Schenectady, 1972—. With USN, 1966-70, ret Res., 1992. Mem. Soc. Mfg. Engrs., Naval Enlisted Res. Assn. (v.p. 1984-85), GE Apprentice Alumni Assn. Eastern Orthodox Ch. Avocations: wood working, reading, computer software and hardware. Office: Bechtel Nat 600 Liberty St Schenectady NY 12305-2105

JONES, ELSE SUSAN, journalist; b. Watertown, N.Y., Oct. 30, 1947; arrived in Germany, 1970; d. Emlen Howell and Else (Singer) J. BS, LeMoyne Coll., 1968; MA, SUNY, Binghamton, 1971. Tchg. asst. SUNY, Binghamton, 1968-70; acad. asst. U. Tuebingen, Germany, 1977-81; stringer Schwabishes Tagblatt, Tuebingen, 1980-83, editor, 1984-91; freelance writer, translator and musician Germany, 1992—; presenter workshops and seminars in field, 1994—. Co-author, editor, translator: Creating Community Voices, 1999-2000; musician/actor: (children's musical) Adventures of A.J. Kwak, 1992-95, Chamber Orch. Horb, 1994—, Madame Furiosa, 1995-96; writer/dir.: (radio play) Deines Glueckes Schmied, 1996; translator: Das Zwergen-Zerwuerfnis, 1998; musical dir. Cold Heart at Black Forest Summer Theater, 1999-2000. Founding mem., mgr. Pub. Access Radio, Germany, 1995—; campaign reporter Green Party, Baden-Wurttemburg, 1992, 94, 96; coord. radio tng. camp, Lake of Constance, 1999. Fellow Bd. of Regents, N.Y., 1968-70, German Acad. Exch. Svc., Tubingen, 1970-72. Mem. Media Union Germany.

JONES, EVAN ANTHONY, hepatologist; b. Yeovil, England, Apr. 5, 1938; arrived in The Netherlands, 1995; BSc, U. Birmingham, England, 1959, MB.ChB, 1962, MD with honors, 1969, DSc, 1991. Sr. lectr. medicine U. Liverpool, England, 1972-74; chief liver diseases sect. NIH, Bethesda, Md., 1977-92; chief hepatology Acad. Med. Ctr., Amsterdam, The Netherlands, 1995—; vis. scientist NIH, 1974-77. Contbr. articles to profl. jours. Fellow Royal Coll. Physicians London; mem. Am. Soc. Clin. Investigation, Assn. Physicians Great Britain and Ireland. Office: Acad Med Ctr, Meibergdreef 9, 1105 AZ Amsterdam The Netherlands

JONES, EVAN BENJAMIN GARETH, microbiologist, educator; b. Carmarthen, South Wales, Jan. 27, 1937; s. William Morgan and Mary Jane (Rees) J.; m. Marion Patricia Garton; children: Huw Patrick, Alun Rhys. BSc, U. Wales, Aberystwyth, 1958, MSc, 1960; PhD, U. Leeds, Eng., 1963; DSc, U. Wales, Cardiff, 1972. Lectr. Coll. Tech., Portsmouth, Eng., 1963-68; sr. lectr. Coll. Tech., Portsmouth, 1968-72; reader Portsmouth Polytech., Portsmouth, 1972-80; prof. Portsmouth Polytech. (later Portsmouth U), 1980-97; dir. rsch. Portsmouth U., 1980-97; vis. prof. BIOTEC, 1998—; cons. Cyanamid, U.S., 1992—, NCGEB, Thailand, 1994—; vis. prof. Hong Kong U. Editor: (books) Marine Borers, Fungi and Fouling Organisms of Wood, 1971, Recent Advances in Aquatic Mycology, 1976, Aspects of Marine Microbiology, 1988; contbr. over 245 articles, revs. and abstracts to profl. jours. Mem. Royal Soc. Kan Tong Po, Brit. Mycological Soc. (pres. 1992, com. mem., hon. centenary fellow), Com. Internat. Permanent pour la Recherche sur la Preservation des Materiaux en Mileu Marin (chmn.). Avocations: opera prodn. and listening, stamp collecting, travel, gardening. Office: Vis Prof City U Dept Biology & Chemistry, Tat Chee Ave, Kowloon Hong Kong China

JONES, EVELYN GLORIA, medical technologist, educator; b. Roanoke, Va., Aug. 13, 1940; d. William Darnell and Elizabeth (Harris) Powell; m. Theodore Joseph Jones, Aug. 21, 1965. BS in Biology, Tenn. State U., 1973; cert. in med. tech., Vanderbilt U., 1974; MEd in Adminstrn. and Supervision, Tenn. State U., 1993. Cert. clin. lab. scientist Nat. Cert. Agy. Med. Lab Pers. Med. technologist Metro Gen. Hosp., Nashville, 1974-78, Vanderbilt Med. Ctr., Nashville, 1978-97; microbiologist Tenn. Dept. Health Lab. Svcs., Nashville, 1997—; tech. cons. Vanderbilt Point of Care Program, 1993-96; lectr. St. Thomas Program Med. Tech., Nashville, 1991-94, Tenn. State U./Meharry Med. Tech. Program, Nashville, 1991—; instr. tchg. faculty Pub. Health Lab. Svcs., State Tenn., Nashville. Bd. dirs. Tenn. Valley Region ARC Blood Svcs., 1996—; asst. sec. The Links, Inc., 1997—. Mem. AAAS, Am. Soc. Clin. Pathologist (assoc., cert. med. technologist), Phi Delta Kappa, Alpha Kappa Alpha. Roman Catholic. Home: 1003 Cross Bow Dr Hendersonville TN 37075-9403 Office: Tenn Dept Health Lab Svcs Dept Microbiology Nashville TN 37202

JONES, FRANK STUART, economist, educator; b. Manchester, England, Mar. 29, 1933; s. John Brockley and Sarah Ellen (Riley) J. BA, MA, Oxford U., 1955; PhD, U. B.C., 1968. Lectr., sr. lectr., head dept. U. Witwatersrand, South Africa, 1969-93; prof. U. South Africa, 1993—. Author: The Great Imperial Ranks in South Africa, 1996; co-author: The South African Economy 1910-1990, 1992. Mem. Econ. History Soc. So. Africa (pres. 1986-88, 93-95). Anglican. Avocations: swimming, dog walking, history of architecture, politics, international affairs. Home: 82 6th St Parkhurst, Johannesburg 2193, South Africa

JONES, FRANKLIN ROSS, education educator; b. Charlotte, N.C., Jan. 3, 1920; s. William Morton and Olive Ruth (Moser) J.; divorced; children: Franklin Ross, C. Morton, Susan Noel. AB, Lenoir Rhyne Coll., 1941; MA, U. N.C., 1951; DEd, Duke U., 1960. Tchr. schs. N.C., 1944-48; prin. Jr. High Sch., Henderson, N.C., 1948-54; dist. sch. prin. Wake County, N.C., 1954-56; dist. supt. Roxboro (N.C.) schs., 1956-58; chmn. dept. edn. Randolph-Macon Coll., Ashland, Va., 1959-64; interim dean U. Richmond (Va.), 1962; dean Sch. Edn. Old Dominion U., 1964-69; Eminent prof. Old Dominion U., 1974-94; founder Child Study Center, 1965, disting. prof., 1969—, social founds. program leader, 1973-77, doctoral program liaison rep., 1974-77, faculty chmn., 1981—; dir. Forest Ridge Corp., 1985; vis. rsch. scholar Duke U., 1967; cons. HEW, State Sch. Sys. and Colls.; lectr. in field; mem. com. White house Conf. Children and Youth, 1968-71, Ea. regional chmn., 1968-71; mem. Va. Gov.'s Com. Implementation, 1971-73; spkr. 25th Internat. Congress of Psychology, Brussels, 1992; symposium chmn. European Congress of Psychology, Athens, Greece, 1995; cons. to dean on test score stats., Old Dominion U., 1995—. Author: Psychology of Human Devel., 1969, 2d edit. 1985, 3d edit. 1992, Handbook on Testing, 1972, Understanding the Middlescent Years, 1978, Theory of Adult Development, 1980, Radio series Sta. WTAR, Norfolk, 1973-75; test item writer for N.Y. Regency exams, 1987, Ednl. Testing Svc., 1989; guest editor of Education, 1990—. Mem. Norfolk Urban Coalition, 1969-73; chmn. March of Dimes, Person County, N.C., 1956-57; mem. adv. bd. Tidewater Rehab. Ctr., 1967-69; chmn. Hull Scholarship Fund, 1983-85; coord. U. Joy Fund Drive, 1974-95; univ. chmn. United Fund, 1982, 84; chmn. assessment com. Va. Reading to Learn Program, 1990-91; cons. to sch. systems, ETS, HEW, Coll. 1966—; dir. Praxis Ctr., 1993—; adminstr. Nat. Bd. for Cert. Counselors Ctr.; chmn. scholarship fund Brewton Parker Coll., Mt. Vernon, Ga., 1999-2000. Recipient Dean's Svc. award Old Dominion U., 1984, Univ. award for Fund RAising, 1994, Heritage Found. award, 1996, Football recognition and scholar Brewton Parker Coll., Ga., 1999. Mem. Am. Psychol. Soc. (charter), S.E. Psychol. Assn., Va. Assn. U. Profs. (dir. 1962-64), South Atlantic Philosophy Edn. Soc. (pres. 1966-69, dir. 1969—), Va. Assn. Rsch. in Edn. (Disting. Rsch. awards 1972, 73, 78),N.C. Edn. Assn. (pres. North Cen. chpt. 1951, pres. North Cen. Prins. 1956), Ea. Ednl. Rsch. Assn., Nat. Urban Edn. Assn., Bicycle Relay Jr. Marathon World's Record Team, 1933, Alpha Tau Kappa, Kappa Delta Pi, Phi Delta Kappa, Phi Kappa Phi, Pi Gamma Mu (sec. 1962-64). Club: Harbor (Norfolk). Lodges: Lions, Rotary. Home: 1026 Manchester Ave Norfolk VA 23508-1243

JONES, GAVIN WILLIS, demography educator; b. Armidale, NSW, Australia, Nov. 21, 1940; s. Alwyn Willis and Edna Joyce (Birch) J.; m. Margaret Helen Donaldson, Aug. 24, 1963; children: Andrew, Tanya, Gregory. BA with honors, U. New Eng., Armidale, NSW, 1961; PhD, Australian Nat. U., Canberra, 1966. Staff assoc. The Population Coun., N.Y.C., 1966-69; advisor Nat. Econ. Devel. Bd., Bangkok, 1969-72; rep. The Population Coun., Jakarta, Indonesia, 1972-75; sr. fellow demography dept. Australian Nat. U., Canberra, 1975-85, prof. demography dept., 1985—; cons. World Bank, Ford Found., UN orgns., others; pres. Australian Population Assn., 1991-92; leader missions for UN's Population Fund, Thailand, 1991, The Philippines, 1993, Indonesia, 1994, Cambodia, 1996, Laos, 1996; bd. trustees Internat. Ctr. for Diarrhoeal Disease Rsch., Bangladesh, 1979-83. Author: Population Growth and Educational Planning in Developing Nations, 1975, Marriage and Divorce in Islamic South-East Asia, 1994; co-author: Indonesia Assessment: Population and Human Resources, 1997, others. Mem. Australian nat. com. UN Internat. Conf. on Population and Devel., Cairo, 1994; chmn. com. econ. consequences of alt. demographic patterns Internat. Union for Sci. Study of Population, 1985-89. Fellow Acad. Social Scis. Australia. Avocations: running, tennis, gardening. Home: 7 Gidja Pl, Giralang 2617, Australia Office: Demograph Program Rsch Sch Social Sci, Australian National U PO Box 4, Canberra 0200, Australia

JONES, GEORGE FLEMING, international consultant; b. San Angelo, Tex., June 27, 1935; s. George Fleming and Cora (Brewer) J.; m. Maria Rosario Correa, Apr. 23, 1960; children: George III, Robert, Michael, Mary Louise. AB magna cum laude, Wabash Coll., 1955; AM, Tufts U., 1956; MA, Stanford U., 1967; LLD, Wabash Coll., 2000. Joined Fgn. Svc., Dept. State, 1956; with Econ. Bur., Dept. State, Washington, 1956-58; with Am. Embassy, Ecuador, 1958-60, Ghana, 1961-63, Venezuela, 1963-66; officer in charge Venezuelan affairs Dept. State, Washington, 1967-69, officer in charge Colombian affairs, 1969-71; polit. advisor U.S. Mission to IAEA, Vienna, Austria, 1971-74; counselor for polit. affairs Am. Embassy, Guatemala, 1974-77; student Nat. War Coll., Washington, 1977-78; Latin Am. adviser U.S. del. U.S.-Soviet Conventional Arms Talks, 1978; dep. dir. office Latin Am. regional polit. affairs Dept. State, 1978-80, dir., 1980-82; dep. chief of mission Am. Embassy, Costa Rica, 1982-85, Chile, 1985-89; sr. adviser for Latin Am. and Caribbean affairs U.S. del. UN Gen. Assembly, N.Y.C., 1990, 95; amb. to Republic of Guyana Georgetown, 1991-95; dir. programs for the Ams., Internat. Found. for Election Sys., Washington, 1996-99; cons. on internat. bus. and democracy issues, 1999—. Recipient Superior Honor award Dept. State, 1987. Mem. Am. Fgn. Svc. Assn. (v.p. 1989-90, bd. dirs. 1999—), Sr. Fgn. Svc. Assn. (bd. dirs. 1990-92). Home: 3804 Acosta Rd Fairfax VA 22031-3804

JONES, GERALD EDWARD, religion educator; b. Gettysburg, S.D., June 20, 1933; s. Otis Clinton and Alma May (Gorman) J.; m. Joyce Nadine Lindstrom; children: Eric Otis, JanEtta, Angela, Nadine, Sylvia, Gerald. BS, Brigham Young U., 1957, MA, 1960, PhD, 1972; postgrad., U. Minn., U. Iowa. Seminary prin. LDS Ch. Ednl. System, St. Johns, Ariz., 1957-59, Grantsville, Utah, 1960-63, Rexburg, Idaho, 1964-66, Pocatello, Idaho, 1966-67; dir. Inst. Religion U. Wyo., Laramie, 1967-70, U. Calif., Berkeley, 1971-85, Stanford U., Palo Alto, Calif., 1985-92, Yale U., New Haven, Conn., 1992-95; tour dir. Brigham Young U., Provo, Utah, 1978-80; lectr., cons. various orgns. Utah, Calif., Idaho, 1970-90; bd. dirs. Internat. Network for Religion and Animals, No. Wales, Pa. Author: Animals and the Gospel, 1980; contbg. editor: Between the Species Jour., Berkeley, 1984—; contbr. articles to profl. jours. Bd. govs. Nat. Coun. of Christians and Jews, San Franciscio, 1986-92, nat. trustee, N.Y.C., 1988-92; pub. policy expert Heritage Found., Washington, 1982-94. Recipient commendation Merritt Hosp., Oakland, Calif., 1984. Mem. S.D. Hist. Soc. (life), Utah Hist. Soc. (life), U. Wyo. Sch. Religion (pres. 1969-70). LDS. Avocations: world travel, book collector, church activities. Home: 1311 Edinburgh Ct Concord CA 94518-3918

JONES, GERALD PAUL, software educator; b. South gate, Calif., July 11, 1946. AB, U. So. Calif., L.A., 1968, MSEd, 1978, PhD, 1985. Mem. staff U. So. Calif., L.A. Contbr. articles to profl. jours. Mem. Phi Beta Kappa. Home: PO Box 18425 Los Angeles CA 90018-0425 Office: Univ of Southern Calif JEF 214 1020 W Jefferson Blvd Los Angeles CA 90089-0029

JONES, GLYN DAVID, publishing company executive/association executive; b. Glenboig, Lanarkshire, Scotland, Mar. 15, 1946; s. Clifford Crossley and Annie (Murphy) J.; m. Anne Doreen Muir, Apr. 1, 1970; children: Kirsty, Guy. B of Laws, U. Aberdeen, Scotland, 1966. Lectr. Coll. Commerce, Aberdeen, Scotland, 1968-69; mgr. Chamber of Shipping, London, 1969-75; from. asst. dir. to dir. Nat. Assn. Brit. and Irish Millers, London, 1975-84; CEO The Biochem. Soc., London, 1984—; chmn. Assn. Learned and Profl. Soc. Pub., London, 1993-95; dir. Pubs. Licensing Soc., 1996-2000, chmn. STM serials com., 1999—. Fellow Inst. Mgmt., Soc. of Assn. Execs., Internat. Assn. Sci., Tech. and Med. Pubs. Avocation: golf. Office: The Biochemical Soc, 59 Portland Pl, W1N 3AJ London England

JONES, GREGORY PERCY, barrister; b. Dartford, Eng., Jan. 4, 1968; s. Colin Frederick and Jeannette Bridget (McDonald) J.; m. Rosali Margareta Pretorius, Oct. 18, 1997. MA, New Coll. Oxford U., Eng., 1989; LLM, Univ. Coll. London U., 1995. Bar: London 1991, Dublin, 1997. Assoc. Chambers of Gerard Ryan QC, London, 1993—; Bd. dirs. European Inst. South Bank Univ., 1996—. Asst. editor Planning & Environ. Law Bull.; editor Edn. Case Reports, 1998—. Dir., trustee Lothian Found., London, 1996—; mem. internat. affairs com. The English Speaking Union, 1994—. Brit. debating scholar English Speaking Union, 1989, Jean Pierre Warner scholar European Ct. Justics, 1995; named stagiaire European Commn., 1990. Mem. U.K. Environ. Law Assn. (dir. 1997—), European Bar Assn., Oxford & Cambridge Club. Office: Chambers Gerard Ryan QC, 2 Harcourt Bldgs Temple, London EC4Y 9DB, England

JONES, HARRY GORDON, electronics company executive; b. New Orleans, Nov. 1, 1950; s. Harry G. and Jessie Mae (Alexis) J.; m. Judith D. Pitts, April 16, 1971 (dec. Feb. 1982); children: Kristina, Kimberly. AA, Pensacola Jr. Coll., 1981; student, Southeast La. U., 1975-78. Engr. Xerox Corp., New Orleans, 1975-78, Lear Siegler, Inc., Denver, 1978-81; pres., chief exec. officer Spectrum Systems, Inc., Pensacola, Fla., 1981—; mem. engring. adv. coun. U. West Fla. Past chmn. adv. bd. Small Bus. Devel. Ctr., U. West Fla. Coll. Bus. Mem. Instrument Soc. Am. (emissions monitoring stds. com.), Air Pollution Control Assn., Am. Mgmt. Assn., Pensacola C. of C. (cluster industry task force). Republican. Assembly of God. Office: Spectrum Systems Inc 3410 W Nine Mile Rd Pensacola FL 32526-7808

JONES, HARVEY ROYDEN, JR., neurologist; b. Plainfield, N.J., Nov. 18, 1936; m. Mary Elizabeth Norman, Mar. 18, 1961; children: Roy, Kathryn, Frederick, David. BS, Tufts U., 1958; MD, Northwestern U., 1962. Diplomate in Neurology and Clin. Neurophysiology Am. Bd. Psychiatry and Neurology; diplomate Am. Bd. Electroencephalography, Am. Bd. Electrodiagnostic Medicine. Intern Phila. Gen. Hosp., 1962-63; resident in internal medicine Mayo Grad. Sch. Medicine, Rochester, Minn., 1963-65; resident in neurology Mayo Grad. Sch. medicine, Rochester, Minn., 1965-66; chief neurology svc. U.S. Army Hosp., Bad Cannstatt, Germany, 1966-70; resident in neurology/clin. neurophysiology Mayo Grad. Sch. medicine, Rochester, Minn., 1970-72; from clin. instr. to clin. prof. neurology Harvard Med. Sch., Boston, 1972—; staff neurologist, Jaime Ortiz-Patino chair neurology Lahey Clinic, Burlington, Mass., 1972—; assoc. in neurology, assoc. divsn. neurophysiology Children's Hosp. Med. Ctr., Boston, 1977—; bd. dirs. Am. Bd. Psychiatry and Neurology, 1997—. Contbr. numerous articles to profl. jours.; editor, author: CIBA Collection, Nervous System Part II, 1986, Pediatric Clinical Electromyography, 1996. Fellow Am. Acad. Neurology; mem. Am. Neurol. Assn. E-mail: Royden.Jones@Lahey.org. Home: 22 Woodridge Rd Wellesley MA 02482-7033 Office: Lahey Clinic 41 Mall Rd Burlington MA 01805-0002

JONES, HELEN MARY, secretary; b. Rangoon, Apr. 28, 1955; m. Andrew Bass, May 13, 1999. Chartered sec., 1976. Grad. trainee Coventry Climax, 1976; with Ernst & Whinney, 1976-79; asst. co. sec. Guiness plc, 1979-87; asst. co. sec. Kingfisher plc, London, 1987-90, fin. ops. mgr., 1990-91; various positions including mktg., buying and logistics Woolworths plc, London, 1991-95; group co. sec. Kingfisher plc, London, 1995—. Fellow Inst. Chartered Secs. and Adminstrs. (chmn. co. secs. forum). Office: Kingfisher North West House, 119 Marylebone Rd, London NW1 5PX, England

JONES, HERMAN OTTO, JR., corporate professional; b. Jacksonville, Fla., Dec. 1, 1933; s. Herman Otto Sr. and Esther (Powell) J.; m. Marjorie Seaver, June 4, 1955 (dec. June 1996); two children (dec.); m. M. Beth Seaver, May 10, 1997. BSA, U. Fla., 1956. V.p. Oak Crest Hatcheries, Inc., Jacksonville, 1956-71; exec. v.p. Oak Crest Enterprises, Inc., Jacksonville, 1958-71; dir. sales Diversified Imports, Inc., Lakewood, N.J., 1971-73, BEC Ltd., Winchester, Eng., 1973-78; sales rep. Paul Revere Ins. Co., Jacksonville, 1978-81; v.p. Anitox Corp., Buford, Ga., 1981-85; pres. Gateway Suppliers, Inc., Jacksonville, 1986-98; v.p. Sales Agritek Bio Ingredients Corp., Montreal, Quebec, Can., 1993-97; pres. Gateway Bio-Nutrients, Inc., 1998—. Contbr. articles to profl. jours. Vice chmn. bd. deacons Riverside Bapt. Ch., 1988-89, deacon, 1991-94, sec. of deacons, 1991-92, dir. Sunday Sch., 1992-93; bd. dirs. South Shore Condos, 1998—, treas., 1998—. Named Outstanding Mem., Fla. Poultry Fedn., 1965, Southeastern Poultry and Egg Assn., 1963, State Outstanding Young Farmer, Fla. Jaycees, 1968; recipient Disting. Service award, Jacksonville Jaycees, 1970. Mem. Greater Jacksonville Fair Assn., Rotary (bd. dirs. South Jacksonville 1989-91), Masons (master), Shriners, Jesters, Order Ea. Star (past patron). Republican. Avocations: golf, travel. Home: CND #703 1551 1st St S Jacksonville FL 32250-6360

JONES, HOWARD JAMES, educator; b. June 19, 1944. BA, So. U., Baton Rouge, La., 1966; MA, Howard U., 1968; PhD, Washington State U., 1975. Asst. prof. U. So. Miss., Hattiesburg, 1974-76; instr. Prarie View (Tex.) A&M U., 1976-78, prof., 1985—; asst. prof. Tex. So. U., Houston, 1978-82. Home: 6747 Ridgeway Dr Houston TX 77087-5937

JONES, J. GILBERT, research consultant; b. San Francisco, June 1, 1922; s. Enoch Roscoe L. Sr. and Remedios (Ponce de Leon) J.; student U.S. Mcht. Marine Acad., 1942-44, San Francisco City Coll., 1942-44, 46-47; AB, U. Calif., Berkeley, 1949, MA, 1952. Lic. pvt. investigator. Ins. insp. Ins. Cos. Insp. Bur., San Francisco, 1959-62; pub. rels. cons., San Francisco, 1962-67; ins. insp. Am. Svc. Bur., San Francisco, 1967-72; propr., mgr. Dawn Universal Internat. San Francisco, 1972—, Dawn Universal Security Svc., San Francisco, 1983—. Mem. SAR, Libr. of Congress Assocs., Sons. Spanish-Am. War Vets. Soc., World Affairs Coun. N. Calif., U. Calif. Alumni Assn., Commonwealth Club of Calif. Republican. Office: PO Box 424057 San Francisco CA 94142-4057

JONES, JAMES ALLEN, secondary education educator; b. Detroit, May 2, 1925; s. David and Cornelia (Lula) J. BS, Wayne State U., 1946; MA, Oakland U., 1949; PhD in Bibl. Studies, Am. Coll. Metaphysical Theology, Mpls., 1998. Tchr. Detroit Pub. Schs., 1949-87; prin., tchr. Roman Catholic Archdiocese, Detroit, 1987-93; supervisor student tchrs. Wayne State U., Detroit, 1993-97; tchr. Loyola Jesuit H.s., Detroit, 1997—; instr. U. Mich., Dearborn, 1981—; ind. distributor seminar workshop in wellness Nikken, 1999. Author: A Guide to Teens Who Take Their Own Lives, 1987. Mem. English Speaking Union, Mich. Assn. Mid. Sch. Educators. Fax: 313-873-2299. Office: PO Box 2097 Detroit MI 48202-0097

JONES, JAMES EDWARD, mathematician, educator; b. Neath, Wales, Aug. 10, 1944; s. Edward Haydn and Mary Jane (Cockwell) J.; m. Carole Walsh, July 31, 1972; children: Rebecca Frances, James Peter Henry. BSc, Manchester U., 1964, MSc, 1966, PhD, 1971, DSc, 1995. Tchg. asst. U. Manchester, U.K., 1969; lectr. math. UWIST, U.K., 1969-88; lectr. math. U. Wales Coll. Cardiff, 1988-91, sr. lectr. math, 1991-96, reader math, 1996—. Contbr. articles to profl. jours. Home: Great House Ct, Welsh Saint Donats, Cowbridge CF71 7SS, Wales Office: Univ Wales Cardiff, Inst Math PO Box 926, Cardiff CF24 4YH, Wales

JONES, JAMES EDWARDS, SR., religion educator; b. Balt., Apr. 9, 1946; s. Temple and Rosemary (King) J.; m. Emma Pettway, Oct. 1976 (div. May 1994); children: James Jr., John, Tracy, Malik; m. Matiniah Yahya, Sept. 11, 1995; children: Shakoor, Abdul-Nur, Mustafah, Kabeerah, Muhammad, Abdul hakim, Haneefah, Ibraheem. BS in Secondary Edn., Hampton U., 1968; MA in Religion, Yale U., 1983; DMin, Hartford Seminary, 1989. Exec. dir. Black Coalition of Greater New haven, 1974-79; assoc. dir. NARCO Inc., New Haven, 1968-73; dir., assoc. prof. N.H. Coll., New Haven, 1979-89; ednl. coord. ADT Found., Yale U., New Haven, 1989-90; assoc. prof. religion and church Manhattanville Coll., Purchase, N.Y., 1990—; cons. New Haven Housing Auth., 1999—; Al Bashaer Schs., Cairo,

1998—. Mem. New haven Bd. Edn., 1975-79; Islamic chaplain New Haven Jail, 1980—. Mem. Nat. Tng. Labs. Inst., Assn. Muslim Social Scientists. Muslim. Home: 153 Greenwood St New Haven CT 06511-5310 Office: Manhattanville Coll 2900 Purchase St Purchase NY 10577-2131

JONES, JAMES REES, retired oil company executive; b. Britton, S.D., Nov. 26, 1916; s. Buell Fay and Florence (Bockler) J.; m. Betty Jane Preston, May 28, 1943; children—Quentin Buell, Newton James, Preston Lee. B.S. in Accountancy, U. Ill., 1938. From accountant to sr. accountant Ernst & Ernst (C.P.A.'s), Detroit and Kalamazoo, 1938-41, 46-48; auditor, then div. auditor, chem. plant office mgr. Pan Am. Petroleum Corp., 1948-56; comptroller Amoco Chems. Corp., Chgo., 1956-62; mgr. auditing Standard Oil Co., Ind., 1962-63; controller Murphy Oil Corp., El Dorado, Ark., 1963-74; v.p. Murphy Oil Corp., 1974-75; also dir.; chmn., mng. dir. Canam Offshore Ltd., Hamilton, Bermuda, 1975—; pres., dir. Mentor Ins. Ltd., Hamilton, 1975—; controller Ocean Drilling & Exploration Co., El Dorado, 1963-66, also; dir.; controller, dir. Deltic Farm & Timber Co., Inc., El Dorado, 1963-72, v.p., 1963-75. Past mem. El Dorado Water Utilities Commn.; past pres., bd. dirs. United Campaign El Dorado. Served to capt. AUS, 1941-46. Mem. Fin. Execs. Inst., Am. Petroleum Inst., Mid-Continent Oil and Gas Assn., Phi Kappa Psi. Home: 905 Kings Ct Russellville AR 72801-5719

JONES, JAMES THOMAS, JR., tobacco company executive; b. Beverly Manor, Va., June 14, 1946; s. James Thomas and Irene Celestine (Baldwin) J.; m. Vionia Ann Fisher, July 5, 1966; children: James T. III, Vionia Jr., Veronica. Field sales rep. R.J. Reynolds Tobacco Co., Camden, N.J., 1973-76; asst. div. mgr. R.J. Reynolds Tobacco Co., Phila., 1976-80; div. mgr. R.J. Reynolds Tobacco Co., Newark, 1980-84; regional tng. and devel. mgr. R.J. Reynolds Tobacco Co., N.Y.C., 1984-88; nat. trade rels. mgr., minority markets R.J. Reynolds Tobacco Co., Winston-Salem, N.C., 1988-90; chain accounts mgr. R.J. Reynolds Tobacco Co., Edison, N.J., 1990-95; regional mgr. air purification equipment Plymovent, Edison, 1996-2000; v.p. nat. sales Modular Ventilation Products, Inc., 2000—; cons., Sioux IndianTribe, Marty, S.D., 1989—. Mem. Internat. Platform Assn., S.C. Legis. Black Caucus, S.C. Legis. Corp. Roundtable. Republican. Baptist. Avocations: model railroading, gardening, swimming, tennis. Office: MVP Modular Ventilation Products Inc PO Box 6356 Freehold NJ 07728-6356 also: J & V Consulting Group 80 Highland Ridge Rd Manalapan NJ 07726-8640

JONES, JEFFREY DAVID, lawyer; b. U.S., June 7, 1952. BA, Brigham Young U., 1975, JD, 1978. Lawyer Baker & McKenzie, Tokyo, 1978-79, Chgo., 1979-80; lawyer Kim & Chang, Seoul, 1980—. Mem. Am. C. of C. in Seoul (v.p. 1980-99, pres. 1999—). Office: Seyang Bldg, 223 Nae-ja dong, Chongro-ku, Seoul Korea

JONES, JERRY C., special education educator, counselor; b. Memphis, June 7, 1962; s. Jimmy Lee and Dorothy Helen Jones. BSW, Freed-Hardeman U., 1983; MS in Edn., U. Memphis, 1985; PhD, Columbus U., Metairie, La., 2000. Cert. modified and comprehensive spl. edn. tchr. Correctional alcohol and drug counselor Wilder Youth Devel. Ctr., Sommerville, Tenn., 1988-89; vocat. rehab. counselor Tenn. Dept. Human Svcs., Jackson, 1989-91; coord. svs. for students with disabilities Tchrs. Coll. Columbia U., N.Y.C., 1991-94; fed. probation alcohol and drug counselor Jackson Area Coun. on Alcoholism, 1994-95; interim spl. edn. tchr. Sumner County Bd. Edn., Gallatin, Tenn., 1996; funding and policy analyst Tech. Access Ctr., Nashville, 1996-97; spl. edn. tchr. L.A. County Office of Edn., Downey, Calif., 1997-98, N.Y.C. Bd. Edn., 1999—; cons. WMC-TV, Memphis, Tenn. Dept. Youth Svcs.; spkr. in field. Jerry Jones award named in his honor Freed-Hardeman U., Henderson, Tenn., 1984—; sr. h.s. yearbook dedicated in his honor Chester County H.S., Henderson, 1980. Mem. Nat. Assn. Student Pers., Am. Coll. Pers. Assn., Coun. Exceptional Children, Jaycees. Home: 215 Saddle Club Rd Reagan TN 38368-1835

JONES, JOHN CLIFFORD, engineering educator; b. Rossendale, Eng., Apr. 4, 1952; s. Jack Bryan and Amelia (Camps) J. BSc with honors, Leeds (Eng.) U., 1974, PhD, 1977. Chartered chemist, Australia; chartered engr., U.K., chartered physicist, U.K. Tutor in chemistry Macquarie U., Sydney, Australia, 1978-82; scientific officer Herman Rsch. Lab., Melbourne, Australia, 1983-87; lectr. to sr. lectr. chem. engring. U. NSW, Sydney, 1987-95; sr. lectr. engring. Aberdeen (Scotland) U., 1995—; vis. rsch. assoc. in math., Massey U., Palmerston N., New Zealand, 1991; guest spkr. U. Mont., Missoula, 1996, U. Witwatersrand, Johannesburg, South Africa, 1997, U. Politech. Madrid, 1998. Author: Combustion Science: Principles and Practice, 1993, Topics in Environmental and Safety Aspects of Combustion Technology, 1997, The Principles of Thermal Sciences and their Application to Engineering, 1999; mem. editl. bd. Jour. Fire Scis., 1993—; contbr. over 150 articles to profl. jours. and conf. procs., including Jour. Fire Scis., Fuel, Jour. Loss Prevention in the Process Industries, Jour. Chem. Tech. and Biotech. Travel grantee Royal Soc. London, 1997, Royal Acad. Engring., 1997, 2000. Mem. Combustion Inst., Royal Australian Chem. Inst., Inst. Energy. Episcopalian. Avocations: motoring, reading, travel, fitness. Home: 86 Lord Hays Grove, Don St, Aberdeen AB24 1WT, Scotland Office: U Aberdeen Dept Engring, King's Coll Fraser Noble Bl, Aberdeen AB24 3UE, Scotland

JONES, JOHN CONWAY, construction educator, surveyor; b. London, Apr. 4, 1949; s. John Henry Conway Jones and Doris Hilda Emma (Bird) Percy; m. Susan Rosemary Angel, Oct. 11, 1974; children: Emma Natasha, Katrina Louise, Charlotta Marie. BSc in Geography with honors, London Sch. Econs., 1970; MSc in Constrn. Mgmt., Reading (Eng.) U., 1989; MA in Edn., Open U., 1997. Chartered surveyor, Fellow Royal Instn. Chartered Surveyors, Mem. Zimbabwe Instn. Quantity Surveyors. Trainee surveyor Greater London Coun., 1971-74; sr. quantity surveyor asst. U.K. Overseas Devel. Adminstrn., Gaborone, Botswana, 1974-80; asst. quantity surveyor Brit. Rwys. Bd., London, 1980-82; quantity surveyor Qatar Armed Forces, Doha, 1982-84; prin. quantity surveyor U.K. Overseas Devel. Adminstrn., Honiara, Solomon Islands, 1984-88; advisor/trainer U.K. Overseas Devel. Adminstrn., London and Harare, Zimbabwe, 1990-92; lectr. in constrn. Coll. North West London, 1995—; mem. Ctrl. Tender Bd. Ministry Fin. Honiara, 1985-87; tech. coop. officer U.K. Overseas Devel. Adminstrn. Fgn. Office, London, 1990; lectr. surveying, Robert Gordon U., Aberdeen, Scotland, 1994. Treas. Windsor and Maidenhead Constituency Labour Party, 1972-74. Mem. Labour Party. Avocations: geographic reading, travel, current affairs, politics, education. family life. Home: Llwyncelyn Victoria Rd, Powys Llanwrtyd Wells LD5 4SY, Wales Office: Coll North West London, 105 Brook Rd, London NW2 7BZ, England

JONES, JOHN HARDING, photographer; b. Pitts., Apr. 28, 1923; s. John F. and Emma Eleanor (West) J.; 1 child, Blair Harding; m. Teresa Watras, June 23, 1999. BFA, Rochester Inst. Tech., 1949; MBA, Pepperdine U., 1978; PhD, U. London, 1983; M in Photography (hon.), Brantridge Forest, Eng.; DLitt (hon.), Ky. Christian U.; EdD, St. John's U. Seaman U.S. Naval Air, 1940, advanced through grades to comdr., 1948; ret., 1963; chief photographer U.S. Steel Corp., Pitts.; mgr. art & photo dept. Magnavox Corp., Urbana, Ill.; chief photographer rehab. medicine sect. U.S. Vet. Adminstrn., L.A.; coord. rehab. medicine domiciliary sect. Wadsworth VA Hosp., L.A.; tchr. Carnegie Mellon Inst., Pitts., Earl Wheeler Schs., Pitts., Seattle U., Art Inst. Pitts.; dir., owner The Little Studio, Panorama City, Calif., 1989—, The Little Studio West, Panorama City, 1994—; owner The Little Studio, Pitts., The Little Studio West, The Howling Publ. Author: Photography, 1972, The Correspondence Educational Directory, 1976, 79, 84, 94, Correspondence Courses for High School Credit & GED Preparation, 1994. Comdr. USNR, ret. Recipient award Writers Guild, 1977, Merit award Cooking, 1986; elected to Am. Police Hall of Fame, 1996. Mem. Profl. Photographers Am., Masons, Shriners, Order of the Eastern Star (worthy patron 1986). Presbyn. Avocations: bowling, writing, travel, civic activities, stamp collecting, publishing. Home: 5320 Zelzah Ave Apt 203 Encino CA 91316-2214

JONES, JOHN HARRIS, lawyer, banker; b. New Blaine, Ark., Apr. 9, 1922; s. Ira Burton and Byrd (Harris); m. Marjorie Crosby Hart, 1983. A.B., U. Central Ark., 1941; postgrad., George Washington U. Law Sch., 1941-42; LL.B., Yale, 1947. Bar: Ark. 1946, U.S. Supreme Ct. 1963. Comms. clk. FBI, 1941-42; practice in Pine Bluff, 1947—; spl. judge Circuit Ct., 1950; spl. chief justice Ark. Supreme Ct., 1997; chmn. bd. Pine Bluff Nat. Bank, 1964-77, pres., 1966-76; Mem. Ark. Bd. Law Examiners, 1953-59; Republican nominee for U.S. Senate, 1974; Rep. presdl. elector, 1980; v.p., dir. John Rust Found., 1953-60. Served to 1st lt. USAAF, 1943-45. Decorated Purple Heart, Air medal. Mem. Ark. Bar Assn., Jefferson County Bar Assn. (pres. 1959-60). Mem. Christian Ch. (elder 1963-65, trustee 1965-71, 78-84). Clubs: Eden Park (Pine bluff), Little Rock Club. Home: 4001 S Cherry St Pine Bluff AR 71603-7156 Office: 104 S Main St Pine Bluff AR 71601-4320

JONES, JOHN IDRIS, publishing executive; b. Llanrhaiadr-Y-M, Wales, Mar. 9, 1938; s. Gwilym Idris and Margaret Maude J.; m. Denise Woodrow, July 17, 1986; 1 child, William Idris. Edu, U. Keele, Eng., 1961; Cert. in Edn., Leeds (Eng.) U., 1963; MA, Cornell U., 1965. Mng. dir. John Jones Pub. Ltd., Ruthin Denbighsire, Wales, 1980—. Author, translator: Feet in Chains, 1991, poems. Fellow Royal Soc. Arts. Mem. Labour Party. Office: John Jones Publ, Clwydfro Bus Ctr, Ruthin Denbigshire Wales

JONES, JOHN PAUL, probation officer, psychologist; b. Blanchard, Mich., July 23, 1944; s. Lawrence John and Thelma Blanche (Eldred) J.; m. Joan Margaret Bruder, Aug. 18, 1972; children: Jason John, Justin John, Jessica Joan-Margaret. BS, Cen. Mich. U., 1970, MA, 1974; PhD, Wayne State U., Detroit, 1980. Diplomate Am. Bd. Forensic Medicine, Am. Bd. Cert. Forensic Examiners, Am. Bd. Psychol. Specialties, Am. Acad. of Experts in Traumatic Stress; diplomate in psychotherapy; cert. addictions counselor. Mgr. F. W. Woolworth Co., Bay City, Mich., 1970; probation officer Oakland County Cir. Ct., Pontiac, Mich., 1970-74, probation officer supr., 1974-78, dir. spl. probation program, 1978-80; chief probation officer County of Oakland, Pontiac, 1980-93; outpatient clin. dir. Auro Med. Ctr., Bloomfield Hills, 1993—; lectr. Oakland U., Rochester, Mich., 1978-82; lic. psychologist Psychol. Svcs. of Bloomfield Hills, Mich., 1980-82, Family Treatment Ctr., Pontiac, Mich., 1983-84, Associated Profls., Bloomfield Hills, 1984-85, Auro Med. Ctr., Bloomfield Hills, 1985—. Pres. Pontiac Lions Club, 1986-87; study subcom. Oakland County Jail, 1982-84; mem. Oakland County Child Sexual Abuse Task Force, 1982-83. With U.S. Army, 1966-68. Mem. APA (bd. govs.), Internat. Neuropsychol. Assn., Am. Correctional Psychologist Assn., Am. Acad. Experts in Traumatic Stress, Am. Coll. Forensic Examiners (BCFE, BCFM), Am. Psychotherapy Assn., Mich. Corrections Assn., Mich. Assn. Probation Officers Svcs., Mich. Psychol. Assn., Fraternal Order of Police, Cen. Mich. U. Alumni Assn. (bd. dirs. Mt. Pleasant chpt. 1989-93), Mich. Neuropsychol. Soc., Am. Psychol. Assn. Republican. Avocations: travel, horseback riding, reading, fencing. Home: 2915 Masefield Dr Bloomfield Hills MI 48304-1951 Office: Auro Med Ctr Ste 102 1711 S Woodwood Ave Bloomfield Hills MI 48302

JONES, JOHN T., ceramics engineer, writer; b. Salt Lake City, Jan. 14, 1932; s. Lawrence A. and Alice Taylor J.; m. Patricia Arlene Wilcox, Sept. 15, 1953; children: Mark W., Mathew Barry, Alice Hauser. BS in Ceramic Engring., U. Utah, 1957, PhD in Ceramic Engring. and Metallurgy, 1965. Rsch. engr., prodn. supt. Coors Porcelain Co., Golden, Colo., 1962-65; asst. dir. R&D, Vesuvius Crucible Co., Pitts., 1965-66; assoc. prof. ceramic engring. and engring. Iowa State U., Ames, 1966-74; corp. dir. process devel. Interpace Corp., Glendale, Calif., 1974-75; dir. R&D, prodn. mgr. Pfaltzgraff Co., York, Pa., 1975-79; v.p. R&D, Lemox China, Inc., Pomona, N.J., 1979-96; writer, cons. TJ Books of Ariz., Payson, Ariz., 1996—. editor, cons. editor Ceramic Industry Mag., 1994-98; co-author: (with M.F. Berard) Ceramics: Industrial Processing and Testing, 1972, 2d edit., 1993; author: Engineering for You: A Career Guide, 1991, (novels) Bone China, In No Way Guilty, Bull, Revenge on the Mogollon, Rim. Cons. on toxic materials State of Iowa, 1972-74. Sgt. 1st class U.S. Army, 1950-52, Korea. Named Man of Yr., Ceramic Assn. N.J., 1990, Phila. Sect. Am. Ceramic Soc., 1993, Mt. Man of Yr., U. Utah Ceramic Engring. Alumni, 1993. Fellow Am. Ceramic Soc. (chmn. govt. liason com. 1993-95). Mem. LDS Ch. Avocations: oil painting, fishing, amateur radio. Fax: 520-742-7729. E-mail: kk7id@netzone.com.

JONES, JOHN WESLEY, entrepreneur; b. Wenatchee, Wash., Nov. 15, 1942; s. Richard F. and Hazel F. (Hendrix) J.; m. Melissa L. Meyer, June 22, 1968 (div. 1982); children: John E., Jennifer L.; m. Deborah G. Matthews, Apr. 24, 1993. BA in Bus./Econs., Western Wash. U., Bellingham, 1966. Trainee Jones Bldg., Seattle, 1967-69; mgr. Jones Bldg., 1969-78; owner/mgr. N.W. Inboards, Bellevue, Wash., 1974-78, Jones Bldg., Seattle, 1978-86; pvt. investor Bellevue, 1987—; owner/mgr. J. Jones Enterprises, 1994—; trustee BOMA Health & Welfare Trust, 1982-86, chmn. 1986; mem. Seattle Fire Code Adv. Bd., 1979-86. With USMCR, 1966-72. Mem. Seattle Bldg. Owners and Mgrs. Assn. (trustee 1979-86), Bldg. Owners and Mgrs. Internat., N.W. Marine Trade Assn., Am. Assn. Individual Investors, Composite Fabricators Assn., Soc. Naval Architects and Marine Engrs., Boat U.S., Seattle Yacht Club, NRA, Internat. Show Car Assn., Nat. Street Rod Assn., Specialty Equipment Mktg. Assn. Republican. Avocations: boating, water skiing, snow skiing, automobiles, photography. Home: 61 Skagit Key Bellevue WA 98006-1021 Office: PO Box 52745 Bellevue WA 98015-2745

JONES, KENNETH VAN LEER, psychologist, medical educator; b. Port Arthur, Tex., Aug. 25, 1942; Arrived in Australia, 1972; s. Harold Hunter and Ophelia (Wilcox) J.; m. Aileen Fairweather Fleming, Feb. 7, 1976; children: Caroline Urquhart, Michael Winning. AB, Northwestern U., 1964; MA, U. Mo., 1967, PhD, 1970. Registered psychologist, Victoria, Australia. Asst. prof. Office Med. Edn., U. Mo., Kansas City, 1971-72; from lectr. to assoc. prof. Monash U., Clayton, Victoria, Australia, 1972—; dir. clin. tchg. adminstrv. unit Faculty of Medicine Monash U., Clayton, 1997—; vis. rsch. assoc. Tulane U., New Orleans, 1978-79; vis. scholar Edinburgh (Scotland) U., 1988. Assoc. editor Focus on Health Profl. Edn., 2000—; contbr. articles to profl. jours. Named in top 5% of Univ. Tchrs., CAUT, Australia, 1995, ANZAME Achievement in Edn., 1999. Mem. Australasian New Zealand Assn. for Med. Edn., The Assn. for Health Profl. Edn. (v.p. 1986-88, pres. 1988-90, mem. sec. 1994-2000), Soc. for Behavioral Medicine (U.S.), Melbourne Chamber Choir. Avocations: choral singing, musical theatre, carpentry. Home: 9 Dundonald Ave, Victoria East Malvern 3145, Australia Office: Monash Med Ctr, Dept Psychol Medicine, Clayton Victoria 3168, Australia

JONES, LAMAR BABINGTON, educator; b. Moss Pt., Miss., Aug. 24, 1935; s. Alton Lamar and Dorothy (Babington) J.; m. Frances McMahen Jones, Aug. 17, 1959; children: Dorothy, Ellen, Janet. BA, La. Tech U., 1959; MA, La. State U., 1961; PhD, U. Tex., 1965. Asst. prof. Kans. State U., Manhatten, 1965-66, Va. Poly. U., 1966-67; assoc. prof. La. State U., Baton Rouge, 1967-71, prof., 1971—. Contbr. articles to profl. jours. Named Fellow H.B. Earhart Found., 1961-62, Ford Found., 1965. Office: Dept Econs 2107 Ceba La State U Baton Rouge LA 70803-0001

JONES, LARRY DARNELL, tax specialist; b. Birmingham, Ala., Feb. 21, 1959; s. Ron Shephard and Londene Jones. Student, Rutgers U., 1980-84, Camden County Coll., 1982. Tax specialist LDJ Inc., Camden, N.J., 1983-95, AMA, 1993—, GAU, 1995—. Home: 500 N 7th St Apt 204 Camden NJ 08102-2231 Office: LDJ Inc 655 Line St Camden NJ 08103-1452

JONES, LAURA MEAD, religion educator; b. Bucharest, Romania, Apr. 11, 1931; came to US, 1931; d. Joseph Atticus and Laura Caldwell (Mead) Morris; m. Gordon Leonard Jones, June 9, 1952; children: Martha Baird, Gordon Leonard Jr., Laura Caldwell, Hulda Wolf, Mary Keeny, John Sanders, Elizabeth Reid. BA in Philosophy, Dunbarton Coll., 1952; MA in Philosophy, Georgetown U., 1960. Organizer, supervisor spl. needs ednl. program Mt. Hope (N.Y.) Found., 1964-69; also bd. dirs., 1965-80; syss. analyst, translation sys. developer Logos Corp., Middletown, N.Y. and Mt. Arlington, N.J., 1969-86; pres. Lingualinks, Ltd., Milford, Pa., 1991-92; curriculum cons. Mt. Hope Day Sch., Middletown, N.Y., 1980. Contbr. articles to religious jours. and websites. Bd. dirs. Orthodox Christian Laity USA, 1995—; del. task force to support Orthodox Christians Jerusalem Patriarchate, 1995, 96. Russian Orthodox. Avocations: travel in Russia, Israel, Palestine, Haiti. Home: 508 W Harford St Milford PA 18337-1212

JONES, LAWRENCE DAVID, insurance and medical consultant; b. Cloquet, Minn., Mar. 4, 1928; s. Ellsworth D. and Opal I. Jones; m. Mary; children: David, Greta, Donald, Christopher, Laura, Sharon. B in Pharmacy, U. Utah, 1954; postgrad., U. N.D., 1960-62; MD, U. Minn., 1964. Bd. cert. ins. medicine. Owner, operator drug ctrs. Kemmerer (Wyo.), Big Piney, Trading Post and Sugar Bowl, 1955-60; intern St. Marys Hosp., Mpls., 1964-65; family practice physician Harlowton, Mont., 1965-69, Arcadia, Calif., 1969-74; med. dir. TransAmerica Occidental Life, 1969-79, Teledyne Life Ins., L.A., 1974-79, Gt. Am. Life, L.A., 1977-79; sr. med. dir. Sentry Ins., A Mut. Co., Stevens Point, Wis., 1979-80; assoc. med. dir. First Colony Life Ins. Co., 1981-83; v.p., assoc. med. dir. First Colony Life Ins. Co., Lynchburg, Va., 1983-85; v.p., med. dir., 1985-90, ind. cons. in ins. medicine/underwriting, 1990—; mem. faculty Bd. Ins. Medicine Triennial Course, 1979, 82, 85, 88, 91; mem. adv. bd. Lab. Corp. Am., Cons. Physicians Network; mem. NIH coordinating com. Nat. Heart Attack Alert Program; chmn. NIH-Nat. Heart Alert Program Task Force on Emergency Access to Med. Care in Managed Care; former mem. bd. dirs. Life and Health Ins. Rsch. Fund; former mem. adv. bd. Lifetime Corp. Am. Svc.Bur.-Meditest, others. Past chmn. utilization rev. com. Santa Teresita Hosp., Duarte, Calif.; past city health officer Harlowton; past county health officer Judith Basin County, Mont; past mem. bd. dirs. Health Sys. Agy., L.A., Deaconess Hosp. Sch. Nursing, Billings, Mont., past asst. scoutmaster, past. asst. dist. scout commr., past dist. scout commr., past scoutmaster. Sgt. U.S. Army, 1952-53, USAR, 1950-53. Mem. AMA, Med. Soc. Va., Calif. State Med. Assn., Am. Acad. Ins. Medicine (chmn. profl. and pub. rels. com.), Am. Coll. Cardiology (co-chmn. liaison com., others), Assn. Life Ins. Med. Dirs. Am. (past pres., past chmn. ethics com., past chmn. profl. and pub. rels. com., past chmn. mortality and morbidity com., others), So. Med. Assn. (chmn. sect. on cardiovascular disease 1994-95), Med. Soc. Va., others. Office: PO Box 6395 Diamondhead MS 39525-6008

JONES, LAWRENCE TUNNICLIFFE, lawyer; b. Mineola, N.Y., Jan. 20, 1950; s. Carroll Hudson Tunnicliffe and Florence Virginia (Greene) J. BA, U. Va., 1972; JD, U. Richmond, 1975. Bar: Va. 1975, D.C. 1976, N.Y. 1976, U.S. Dist. Ct. (ea. and so. dist.) N.Y. 1976, U.S. Supreme Ct. 1986. Bus. mgr. law review U. Richmond, Va., 1974-75; ptnr. Carroll Hudson Tunnicliffe Jones and Lawrence Tunnicliffe Jones Attys. at law, Mineola, 1976-91. Trustee Nassau County Hist. Soc., 1976—, pres., 1983-89; bd. dirs. Friends of Hist. St. George's Ch., Hempstead, N.Y., 1982—, v.p., 1990-92, pres., 1992-94; bd. dirs. St. Mary's Devel. Fund, Garden City, N.Y., 1983-89, pres., 1987-89; pres. coun. Cathedral Sch. St. Paul Alumni Fund, Inc., Garden City, 1984—; bd. govs. Cathedral Sch. St. Mary, Garden City, 1983-86. Mem. ABA, Nat. Acad. Elder Law Attys., Va. State Bar Assn., N.Y. State Bar Assn., Nassau County Bar Assn., Nassau County Tax and Estate Planning Coun., Univ. Club (N.Y.C.), Univ. Club (L.I., pres. 1986-87, 93-94, bd. dirs. 1983-86, 89—), Mineola C. of C. (dir. 1993—), Garden City Golf Club, Mineola-Garden City Rotary (dir. 1991-94), Garden City Fellowship (pres. 1993-94, dir. 1994—), Cathedral Club (Garden City) (pres. 1993-95), Garden City C. of C. Episcopalian. Avocation: historic building preservation. Home: 158 Cathedral Ave Hempstead NY 11550-1140 Office: Jones & Jones 1000 Franklin Ave Ste 302 Garden City NY 11530-2910

JONES, LAWRENCE WORTH, poet, editor, performance art producer, songwriter; b. Norman, Okla., Jan. 5, 1950; s. Walter Neil and Jane Elizabeth (McCauley) J. BA in English with deptl. honors, CUNY, 1991. Supr. Fidelity Svc. Co., Boston, 1978-83; compliance dir. Alliance Fund Svcs., N.Y.C., 1985-88; dir. Cafe Nico, artists, writers, photographers collective, N.Y.C., 1991—; advisor ABC No Rio, N.Y.C., 1991—. Author: We Become a Picnic, 1994; contbr. poetry to Downtown Poets, 1999. Coord. Gay Liberation Front, N.Y.C., 1970; plaintiff Gay Cmty. Alliance, Norman, Okla., 1972; campaign coord. Nader NYC '96, 1996. Mem. Poets and Writers, Poetry Project. Avocations: art history, watercolors, collage. Home: 101 Avenue A New York NY 10009-6103

JONES, LEON HERBERT, JR. (HERB JONES), artist; b. Norfolk, Va., Mar. 25, 1923; s. Leon Herbert and Edna May (Curling) J.; student William and Mary Coll., 1942-44; m. Barbara Dean, Sept. 14, 1947; children: Robert Clair, Louis Herbert. Marine structural draftsman and designer Norfolk (Va.) Shipbuilding & Dry Dock Co., 1944-46; free-lance comml. artist, 1946-49; prin. Herb Jones Realty, Norfolk, 1949-58; owner, mgr. Herb Jones Art Studio, Norfolk, 1958—; one-man shows: Norfolk Mus., 1968, Potomac Gallery, Alexandria, Va., 1979, Salisbury Gallery, 1979, Walter C. Rawls Mus., Courtland, Va., 1967, Virginia Beach Maritime Mus., 1983 Village Gallery, Virginia Beach, Va., 1984, Va. Mus. Marine Scis., 1986-87, Olde Towne Gallery, 1987, Amoco Oil, 1989, Petersburg Area Art League (affiliate Va. Mus.), 1990, Surrey Borger Lions Club, Surrey, Eng., 1990, Sr. Showcase Creative Living Cen. Libr., Virginia Beach, Va., 1990, Norview Lions Club Sponsored Show for Handicapped, Norfolk, Va., 1991, Surrey (Eng.) Border Lions Club, 1990, Lions Internat., 1991, 93, Cypress Point Lions sponsored show to benefit handicapped, Va. Beach, 1993, Harborfest, 1995, 96, Janaf Art Show, 1997, Jones Art Gallery, Dominion Tower & Waterside, Norfolk, 1998; 45 year retrospective: Louis and Susan Jones Art Gallery, Norfolk, Va., 1994, The Best of Herb Jones, 98; group shows include: Chrysler Mus., Norfolk, 1973, 74, SUNY, Buffalo, 1966, Springfield (Mass.) Mus. Fine Arts, 1966, Mariners Mus., Newport News, Va., 1967-73, Va. Mus., Richmond, 1969, 71, Columbia (S.C.) Mus. Art, 1972, Winston-Salem (N.C.) Gallery Contemporary Art, 1970, 72, Norfolk Mus., 1963-69, Vladimir Arts, Winsbach, West Germany, 1978, 79, Chesapeake Bay Maritime Mus., Md., Mobile Mus. Traveling Show, 1983, Knoxville World's Fair in Fine Arts, 1982, Art Buyers Caravan, Atlanta, 1982, Colonial Wild Fowl Festival, Williamsburg, Va., 1983, Chesapeake Jubilee (Va., Excellence award) 1984, Peninsula Fine Arts Festival, Newport News, 1984, Currituck Wildlife Show, N.C., 1984, Medley of Arts, Hampton (Va.) Coliseum, 1984 (6 awards 1986-87), Easton Nat. Wildfowl and Art Exhibit, Easton, Md., 1984; Mid-Atlantic Art Exhibit, Virginia Beach, Va., 1985, Chincoteague Island Easter Festival, Va., 1985, (2 awards) 1989 (1st and 2d Pl. award), Harborfest Norfolk, Va., 1985-96, Mid-Atlantic Wildfowl Festival, 1986-93 (1st and 3d award), Hampton Wildlife Festival, 1986 (award 1989), Medley of the Arts, 1986, 87, Mid Atlantic Art Exhibits, 1986, 87, Hampton Fall Festival, (award) 1989, Sr. Showcase Creative Living Art Exhibit, Va. Beach, 1990, River Gallery, Chesapeake, Va., 1992, MidAtlantic Waterfowl Festival, Va. Beach, 1993; represented in permanent collections: Chrysler Mus., wardroom USS Skipjack, USS Iwo Jima, USS John F. Kennedy, USS Dwight D. Eisenhower, USS Seattle, USS Raleigh, USS Biddle, USS Whidby Island Commn., 1992, U. Va., Charlottesville, U.S. Treasury Dept., Library of Congress, Washington, Edenton Hist. Commn. (N.C.), USS Whidby Island, 1994, USS Hayler, 1995, also pvt. collections; commd. ltd. edit. print series Ducks Unltd., also Va. Beach Maritime Mus., Boy Scouts Am., Va. Mus. Marine Scis., Wavy TV affiliate of Lin Broadcasting Co., Judy Boone Real Estate, Official Harborfest Poster, 1993—, Harbor Fest Poster, 1993-95, Official Urbanna (Va.) Oyster Festival print, 1993, plaque Chesapeake Bay Bridge and Tunnel Commn., two spl. print edits. Letton Gooch Printers Inc. Recipient diploma di merito Universita delle Arti, 1981, Gold Centaur award 1983, three Awards of Excellence Printing Industries of the Virginias, 1987, 1st and 2d Pl. Awards of Excellence, 1989, Oscar d'Italia, Acad. Italia Calvatore, 1985, award Mid-Atlantic Waterfowl Festival, 1986, 1st and 3d Place awards, 1993, Great Citizen of Hampton Roads award Cox Cable TV, 1991, Best Art Print in Show award Printing Industries Va., 1995; named Cavalier of Arts, Acad. Bedriacense Calvatore, Italy, 1985, Hampton Roads Original, WTAR-AM Radio, 1990, Granby Hall of Fame, 1997; selected as one of 100 leaders to judge "Best of Am.", U.S. News & World Report, 1990. Mem. Nat. Soc. Arts and Lit., Tidewater Artists Assn., Internat. Platform Assn., Virginia Beach Maritime Mus. (charter), Corr. Academie Europeene, Nat. Am. Film Inst., Lion's Internat. (hon., Melvin Jones fellow for dedicated humanitarian svcs. 1994, Disting. Svc. award for dedication to cmty. and Lions, 1997). Methodist. Home and Office: 238 Beck St Norfolk VA 23503-4902

JONES, LESLIE NICOLE, psychologist, educator; b. St. Paul, Minn., Sept. 2, 1968; d. Larry Wayne and Ruth Ann Weiss; m. Scott Kevin Jones, Aug. 12, 1999. AA, AS, Marshalltown Cmty. Coll., 1989; BA in Psychology, U. Iowa, 1991, MA in Psychology, 1996. Caseworker Tri-County Mental Health, Kansas City, 1997-98; mental health therapist Mental Health Ctr., Marshalltown, Iowa, 1997-98; tchg. asst. U. Mo., Kansas City, 1999—. Scholar U. Mo., Kans. City, 1999. Mem. Am. Psychological Assn. (student liason 1999—, student affiliate group 1999—). Lutheran. Avocations: gourmet cooking, travel, crafts. E-mail: lnicolejones@hotmail.com. Home: 5116 N Smalley Ave Kansas City MO 64119-4155

JONES, LESLIE NORMAN, microbiologist, research scientist; b. Melbourne, Victoria, Australia, Apr. 18, 1947; s. Frederick Leslie and Edna Florence (Piper) J. Degree in med. sci., Royal Melbourne Inst. Tech., 1972; MS, Victoria Inst. of Colls., Melbourne, 1978; PhD, U. Melbourne, 1987.

Rsch. asst. U. Melbourne, 1965-66; exptl. scientist Commonwealth Sci. and Indsl. Rsch. Orgn., Australia, 1967-88, sr. rsch. scientist, 1988-92, prin. rsch. scientist, 1993—. Author: (books) Dermatologic Clinics, 1966, Handbook of Fibre Chemistry, 1997, (ency.) Kirk Othmer Encyclopedia, 1997. Rsch. fellow Karolinska Inst., Stockholm, 1991. Fellow Australian Hair and Wool Rsch. Soc. (pres. 1997—). Home: 35 Brougham St. 3051 Melbourne Victoria, Australia Office: CSIRO Divsn Wool Tech, PO Box 21, 3216 Belmont Victoria, Australia

JONES, LEWIS ARNOLD, JR., physician, radiologist, consultant; b. Detroit, Sept. 16, 1950; s. Lewis Arnold, Sr. and Berlene (Irish) J.; m. Pamela Denise Jennings, Nov. 14, 1992; children: Jennifer Tiffany, Alicia Dawn, Lewis Alexander. Student, Highland Park Coll., 1968-69, Wayne State U., 1969-72; MD, U. Mich., 1978. Diplomate Am. Bd. Radiology. Radiology residency Providence Hosp., Southfield, Mich., 1978-82; diagnostic radiologist Tri-County Radiology, P.C., West Bloomfield, Mich., 1983-84; clin. instr. of radiology Wayne State U. Sch. of Medicine, Detroit, 1984-91, clin. asst. prof. radiology, 1991-97; physician cons. Mich. Dept. Cmty. Health, Lansing, 1997—; mem. cmty. adv. com. Karmanos Cancer Inst., Detroit, 1994—; adv. bd. African Am. anti-platelet stroke prevention Wayne State U., 1996-97; co-investigator Women's Health Initiative, Detroit, 1996-97; co-chmn. 1997 Mich.'s Year of Women's Health, Mich. Dept. Cmty. Health, Lansing, 1997—. Vol. spkr. Am. Cancer Soc., 1986—. Co-creator, co-presenter seminars Ptnrs. for Life, A women's health empowerment program, Mich., 1996—; bd. dirs. Oakland County Am. Cancer Soc., 1988—, Hospice of Mich. Recipient Life Saver award Am. Cancer Soc., Southfield, Mich., 1990, Frederick Douglass award Nat. Assn. Negro Bus. and Profl. Women's Clubs, New Met. Detroit Club, 1996; winner "What a Man" contest, Essence Mag./ Preferred Stock Cologne, N.Y.C., 1995. Mem. AMA, Mich. State Med. Soc., Wayne County Med. Soc., Am. Coll. Radiology, Assn. Univ. Radiologists. Avocations: women's health advocacy spkr., jazz and classical music collector. Home: 4951 Champlain Cir West Bloomfield MI 48323-3529

JONES, LOUIS WORTH, retired management analyst, journalist; b. St. Louis, Jan. 8, 1908; s. Ed C. and Vida Pearl (Wrather) J.; m. Pauline Marie Ernest, May 24, 1947; children: David Worth, Roger Louis, Ethan Ernest, Faye, Arthur Carlyle. Student, Washington U., St. Louis, 1925-27. Trainee, adminstrv. officer Farm Security Adminstrv., USDA, Washington, 1934-46; mgmt. analyst War Assets Adminstrn., San Francisco, 1946-48, US AEC, Los Alamos, N.Mex., 1948-50, USN Radiol. Def. Lab., San Francisco, 1950-68; ret., 1968; co-founder, trustee emeritus The World U., Benson, Ariz.; founder, exec. dir. Intergroup Rels. of No. Calif., 1966-73. Editor, pub. Lou Jones Newsletter, 1959-70; author: (scripts) Meet Mary Wollstonecraft, 1977, Meet Alexander Meiklejohn, 1978, So You Think We Have Democracy?, 1988. Vol. alt. coord. Civil Def., San Mateo County, 1957-58; pres. Mid-Peninsula Coun. Civic Unity, 1959-60; co-founder Bi-County Commn. Human Rels.; trustee Unitarian-Universalist congregation, 1958. Hon. Soc. scholar Washington U., 1925-27; recipient Mem. of Yr. award Unitarian-Universalist, 1977. Mem. Nat. Assn. Ret. Fed. Employees, Intergroup Rels. Assn. No. Calif. (founder). Avocations: piano, photography. E-mail: LouisWJ@aol.com. Fax: 650-344-0334. Home: 511 Verano Ct San Mateo CA 94402-3261

JONES, LUCINDA (CINDY JONES), oncology nurse; b. Sept. 17, 1950; m. Scott W. Kunkel, Jan. 11, 1997. BSN, U. Tenn., 1973; MSN, Tex. Woman's U., 1979. Advanced oncology cert. nurse. Staff nurse VA, San Antonio, 1973-76, San Diego, 1976-77; oncology clin. nurse specialist San Diego VA Health Care Sys., 1980-2000; cons. oncology nursing, 1980—; dir. Oncology Nursing Found., 1996-99; asst. prof. nursing UCLA, 1990—, San Diego State U., 1997—. Mem. Oncology Nursing Soc. (Nat. Oncology Cert. Nurse of the Yr. 1995). Home and Office: 2512 Clairemont Dr Apt 317 San Diego CA 92117-6610

JONES, MALLORY See **DANAHER, MALLORY MILLETT**

JONES, MARION, track and field athlete; b. L.A., Oct. 12, 1975. Major meets include placing 11th in the Long Jump, USA, 1995, 4th place, Long Jump, NCAA, 1995, 2d place, 1994, 6th place 200m, 1994, 4th place 100m, 1994, numerous others; 5th place Olympic Trials, 1992. Office: c/o USA Track & Field 1 Rca Dome Ste 140 Indianapolis IN 46225-1023

JONES, MARK ALLEN, structural engineer; b. Battle Creek, Mich., June 29, 1966; s. Earnest Stanley Jones and Patricia Ann (Potzner) O'Connell. BSCE, Walla Walla Coll., 1991. Naval architect Puget Sound Naval Shipyard, Bremerton, Wash., 1987-95; structural engr. Wharry Engring., Battle Creek, Mich., 1996-99, Jacobs Engring., Battle Creek, Mich., 2000—; lectr. Andrews U., Berrien Springs, Mich., 1997. Tour guide Adventist Hist. Ministries, Battle Creek, 1996—, cons. Jr. Achievement, Battle Creek, 1996—; vol. Adventist Devel. and Relief Agy., Sabah, Malaysia, 1995. Mem. ASCE, Kiwanis. Seventh Day Adventist. Home: 255 1/2 North Ave Battle Creek MI 49017-3430

JONES, MARK ELLIS POWELL, museum director; b. Bogota, Colombia, Feb. 2, 1951; s. John Ernest Powell-Jones and Ann Elizabeth (Murray) Paludan; m. Ann Camilla Toulmin, Sept. 25, 1983; children: Sarah, Luke, Agnes, William. BA, Oxford (U.K.) U., 1972; MA, Courtauld Inst., London, 1974. Asst. keeper Brit. Mus., U.K., 1974-90, keeper of coins and medals, 1990-92; dir. Nat. Mus. of Scotland, U.K., 1992—; founder, bd. dirs. Scottish Cultural Resources Access Network. Author: Art of the Medal, 1979, Catalogue of French Medals, 1982, 88; editor: Fake, 1990, Why Fakes Matter, 1992, Designs on Posterity, 1994. Fellow Royal Soc. Edinburgh. E-mail: m.jones@nms.ac.uk. Address: Nat Museums of Scotland, Royal Mus Chambers St, Edinburgh EH1 1JF, Scotland

JONES, MARLENE ANN, superintendent, school administrator; b. Bluffton, Ohio, Nov. 22, 1936; d. Waldo J. and Blanche M. (Criblez) Wilkins; m. Marvin O. Jones, July 3, 1965; children: John O., Dianne M. BS, Bowling Green State U., 1958, EdS, 1978; MA, Ohio State U., 1962. Cert. family and consumer scis. Vocat. home econs. tchr. 7-12 Liberty Ctr. (Ohio) Bd. of Edn., 1958-61; asst. state supr. Ohio Dept. of Edn., Columbus, 1962-65; chairperson of home econs. technologies Owens Cmty. Coll. (formerly Penta Tech. Coll.), Toledo, Ohio, 1965-71; supr. Penta County Vocat. Sch., Perrysburg, Ohio, 1965—. Past pres. United Meth. Women, Colton, Ohio, 1967—. Named 1 of 10 Outstanding Women in Toledo Jaycees, 1971-72; recipient Disting. Centennial Svc. award Ohio Agrl. and Home Econs. Rsch. and Devel. Ctr., 1982, Home Econs. Grad. fellowship award Am. Vocat. Assn., 1990; named Alum of Yr. Coll. of Edn., Bowling Green State U., 1990. Mem. ASCD, Am. Ohio Vocat. Assn., Am. Family and Consumer Svcs. Assn. (past state pres.), Ohio Vocat. Family and Consumer Svcs. Suprs. Assn. (treas.), N.W. Ohio FHA/HERO Alumni Assn. (sec.), Phi Delta Kappa, Phi Upsilon Omicron (past pres. Alumni chpt. 1965—). Methodist. Home: 5-212 US Hwy 24 Liberty Center OH 43532

JONES, MARY TRENT, endowment fund trustee; b. Durham, N.C., July 15, 1940; d. Josiah Charles Trent and Mary Duke (Biddle) Semans; m. James Parker Jones, June 27, 1964; children: James Trent, Benjamin Parker, Jonathan Edmund. AB, Duke U., 1963. Trustee The Duke Endowment, Charlotte, N.C., 1988—; chmn. Josiah Charles Trent Found., Durham, 1978-83; bd. dirs. Mary Duke Biddle Found., Durham, 1983—, Concert Artists Guild, N.Y.C., 1996-00. Mem. Va. Perinatal Svcs. Adv. Bd., Richmond, 1986-91; sec. Va. Arts Commn., Richmond, 1989-92; trustee Va. Intermont Coll., Bristol, Va., 1986-91, 98—; mem. State Coun. Higher Edn. Va., Richmond, 1991-95; trustee Va. Mus. of Fine Arts, Richmond, 1992-97; mem. bd. Washington County Pub. Libr. Found., 1997—; trustee Va. Intermont Coll., 1998—, William King Regional Arts Ctr., 1998—, Emory and Henry Coll., 1999—. Recipient outstanding alumni award Durham Acad., 1991. Mem. Va. Highlands Festival Bd. Episcopalian. Avocations: reading, walking, hiking. Home: 107 Hillside Dr NE Abingdon VA 24210-2013

JONES, MICHAEL JAMES, publisher; b. Swansea, Wales, Mar. 29, 1962; s. Abraham and Mary Patricia (Coffey) J.; m. Jill Jones, Sept. 24, 1995. BA in Human Geography with honours, U. London, 1985. Dep. editor Design mag., London, 1989-93, Architect's Jour., London, 1992-93; editor Broadcast mag., London, 1993-96; editor-in-chief Emap Media, London, 1996-97, pub., 1997-99, pub. dir., 1999—. Contbr. numerous articles to mags. Mem. Broadcast Writers Guild. Avocations: equestrianism, hill walking, photography, rugby. Office: Emap Media, 33-39 Bowling Green Ln, London EC1R 0DA, England

JONES, MICHAEL LYNN, financial consultant, branch operations manager; b. Tulsa, Okla., Aug. 24, 1967; s. Leonard A. and Loretta F. (Howard) J.; m. Renee D. Carter, Aug. 2, 1986; 1 child, Jonah Jacob. Student, U. Okla., 1985-88, Am. Coll., 1997-98. CFP, Internat. Bd. Cert. Fin. Planners. Retail mgr. The Finish Line, Broken Arrow, Okla., 1985-88; stockbroker Stuart James Co., Tulsa, 1988-89; rep. Am. Bank and Trust, Tulsa, 1989-91; fin. advisor Am. Express Fin. Advisors, Tulsa, 1991-97; fin. cons. PrimeVest Fin. Svcs., Tulsa, 1997-98, First Union Securities, Tulsa, 1998—. Mem. Young Dems., Tulsa, Promise Keepers, Tulsa; vol. Soc. for Prevention of Cruelty to Animals, Salvation Army, Boys Club, Broken Arrow, 1987-92; mem. Jr. C. of C., Tulsa. Mem. Internat. Assn. for Fin. Planning (regional chpt. v.p. 1995—), Inst. of CFP, Okla. U. Alumni Assn., Tulsa Running Club, Green Country Classic Mustangs, Tulsa Optimist Club, Toastmasters Internat. Tulsa, Mensa, Forest Ridge Country Club, Jr. C. of C. Democrat. Avocations: reading, music, physical fitness, family activities. Home: 9226 S Maplewood Ave Tulsa OK 74137-4123 Office: c/o First Union Securities 6120 S Yale Ave Ste 1650 Tulsa OK 74136-4218

JONES, NEIL DEATON, computer scientist, educator; b. Centralia, Ill., Mar. 22, 1941; s. Neil Haddon Jones and Serma Udine (Deaton) Ray; m. Shirley Irene Twente, Feb. 24, 1961 (div. Mar. 1978); children: Warren Russell, Melanie Eva, Katherine Laura; m. Lene Lise Rold, Jan. 10, 1981. BS in Math., So. Ill. U., 1962; MS in Math. and Computer Sci., U. Western Ontario, London, Can., 1965, PhD in Math. and Computer Sci., 1967. Lectr. U. Western Ont., London, Can., 1962-64, asst. prof., 1964-67; asst. prof. Pa. State U., State College, 1967-69, assoc. prof., 1969-73; assoc. prof. U. Kans., Lawrence, 1973-75, prof., 1975-81; guest prof. Aarhus (Denmark) U., 1976, 79-81; lectr. in computer sci. U. Copenhagen, 1981-87, prof., 1987—; bd. mem. Ctr. for Rsch. and Exploitation; adv. bd. Advanced Software Tech., Sweden; lectr. in field at various univs. and rsch. insts. Author: Computability Theory, 1973; co-author: Tempo: Binding Time Concepts, 1981, Partial Evaluation and Automatic Program Generation, 1993, Computability and Complexity From a Programming Perspective, 1997; editor: Logic, Language, and Computation, 1994; editor 7 books, numerous conf. procs.; mem. editl. bd. ACM Trans. Program Langs. Sys.; Jour. Functional Programming, 1990—, Nordic Jour. Computing, 1993—, Jour. Universal Computer Sci., 1993—. Conf. organizer and program com. at various univs. Invited conf. lectr., 1985—; named Best Computer Sci. tchr. U. Copenhagen, 1992. Fellow Assn. for Computing Machinery (editl. bd. 1998—); mem. Internat. Fed. Info. Proc. (functional programming 1990—, math. found. programming langs. 1986-92), European Assn. Programming Langs., European Assn. Theoretical Comp. Sci., Acad. Europaea, Knight of Dannebrog Order (Denmark). Office: Diku U of Copenhagen, Universitetsparken 1, 2100 Copenhagen Denmark

JONES, NIGEL VINCENT, psychologist; b. Cardiff, Wales, June 10, 1964; arrived in Australia, 1974; s. John Emrys and Beryl (Robinson) J.; m. Anita Fay Avery, Mar. 23, 1996; children: Claire Alexandra, Diana Jane. BSc with honors, U. Western Australia, Perth, 1986, M in Clin. Psychology, 1989; PhD, ECU, Perth, 1996. Sr. ptnr. N.V. Jones and Assocs., Warwick, Australia, 1988—. Recipient Postgrad. Course award Fed. Govt., 1986, Postgrad. Rsch. award Fed. Govt., 1988. Mem. APS, IPCPA (pres. 1997-99), Am. Psychol. Soc. Avocation: snow skiing. Office: N V Jones and Assocs, 316 Warwick Rd, Warwick WA 6024, Australia

JONES, NORMAN, mechanical engineer, educator; b. Farnham, Surrey, Eng., Mar. 18, 1938; s. Edward Valentine and Mary Alice (Collins) J.; m. Jenny Schofield, July 11, 1964; children: Alison Elizabeth, Catherine Ann. BS in Tech., U. Manchester, Eng., 1961, MS in Tech., 1962, PhD, 1965, DSc, 1980. Chartered engr. Asst. lectr. U. Manchester, 1963-65; asst. prof. Ga. Inst. Tech., 1965-66, Brown U., 1966-68; from asst. prof. to assoc. prof. to prof. MIT, Cambridge, 1968-79; A.A. Griffith prof. mech. engring. U. Liverpool, Eng., 1979—, head dept., 1982-90, dir. Impact Rsch. Ctr., 1985—; chmn. European Solid Mechanics Com., 1995—; mem. European Mechanics Coun., 1990—, Safety in Mines Rsch. Adv. Bd., 1985—; mem. activities com. Hazards Forum, 1990-98; hon. prof. Huazhong U. Sci., Wuhan, China, 1987, Taiyuan U. of Sci., 1988. Co-author: Structural Crashworthiness, 1983, Structural Impact, 1989, Structural Failure, 1989, Structural Crashworthiness and Failure, 1993; editor-in-chief Internat. Jour. Impact Engring., 1988—. Recipient Eminent Scientist award Wessex Inst. Tech., 1998. Fellow ASME, Royal Instn. Naval Archs. (Bronze medal 1998), Inst. Mech. Engrs. (William Sweet Smith prize 1989, Ludwig Mond prize 1992), Royal Acad. Engring. (elected 1998). Avocations: walking, music. Office: U Liverpool Dept Mech Engr, Brownlow St, Liverpool L69 3GH, England

JONES, OSCAR CALVIN, minister, dean; b. San Antonio, Sept. 1, 1932; s. Oscar Sr. and Nonnie Lee (Cunningham) Jones Simpson; m. Peggy Ann Helm, June 12, 1977; children: Dennis Ray, Shawntelle Janora. BTh, Am. Sch. Divinity, 1968, ThM, 1971; PhD, Trinity Theol. Sem., 1981, DMin, 1982, postgrad., 1982—. Ordained to ministry Am. Bapt. Chs., 1957. Pastor, counselor St. John Bapt. Ch., Long Beach, Calif., 1965-69; exec. dir. M.A.T.E., Inc., L.A., 1969-71; area rep. ABC, N.Y.C., 1971-83; pastor, counselor Shiloh Bapt. Ch., Sacramento, 1983-85; pres. Guardalupe Coll., San Antonio, 1995-97; dean Am. Internat. Theol. Inst. & Sem., San Antonio, 1996—, acad. dean, 1998—; pastor Corinthian Bapt. Ch., Fairbanks, Ak., 1998; interim pastor New Union Missionary Bapt. ch., San Antonio, 1999; prof. Calif. State U., Sacramento, 1985; western rep. M&M benefit bd. Am. Bapt. Chs. U.S.A., N.Y.C., 1985-95; mem. suprr. com. Am. Bapt. Credit Union, 1986-95; mem. Western Commn. on Ministry, Oakland, 1986-94. Author: The Preacher's Dilemma, 1978, The 10 Crowns of the Bible, 1974, The Psychological View-Point on Counseling The Black American, 1982, Motifs for Ministry, The Call to the Ministry. Mem. exec. com. Am. Bapt. Black Chs., Valley Forge, Pa., 1969-84; mem. exec. bd. Inter-Faith Svc. Bur., Sacramento, 1983-84; trustee Am. Bapt. Sem. West, Oakland, Calif., 1985—, Am. Bapt. Homes of West, pastoral clin. edn., fellow, 1982-84. Mem. Alpha Phi Alpha. Democrat. Office: New Union Missionary Bapt Ch 818 N Mittman San Antonio TX 78202-1507

JONES, OWEN DONALD, law educator; b. Glen Ridge, N.J., May 29, 1963; s. Donald Irvine and Margaret Rosalind Jones; m. Lydia Alyce Clougherty, Dec. 8, 1996. BA, Amherst Coll., 1985; JD, Yale U., 1991. Bar: Pa. 1991, D.C. 1992. Jud. clerk to Judge Thomas Penfield Jackson U.S. Dist. Ct. D.C., 1991-92; assoc. Covington & Burling, Washington, 1992-94; assoc. prof. law Ariz. State U., Tempe, 1994-98, prof., 1998—. Editor-in-chief Jurimetrics: The Jour. of Law, Sci. and Tech., 1997-98. Mem. Soc. Evolutionary Analysis in Law (pres. 1998—). Avocations: skiing, scuba, whitewater kayaking. Office: Ariz State U Coll Law Tempe AZ 85287

JONES, PAUL WILLIAM, metallurgist; b. Sutton Coldfield, England, Apr. 6, 1924; s. William Alfred and Kathleen Irene J.; m. Doreen Turner, Jul. 9, 1955; 1 child, Miranda. BSc, Univ. Birmingham, Eng., 1944, diploma, 1951, MSc, 1958. Metallurgist Magnesium Elektron, Manchester, Eng., 1943-45, McKechnie Bros Ltd., Birmingham, Eng., 1945-50; lectr. County Tech. Coll., Wednesbury, Eng., 1951-53; sr. rsch. officer British Welding Rsch. Assn., London, 1953-57; rsch. engr. Marshall's Flying Sch., Cambridge, 1957-61; engr. Gen. Elec. Co., Gainesville, Fla., 1961-73; chem. engr. Motorola Inc., Ft.Lauderdale, Fla., 1973-74; tech. sales engr. Selectrons Ltd., Redditch, United Kingdom, 1975-76; se. metallurgist United Glass Ltd., St. Albans, England, 1976-83; financial advisor, 1984-94. Contbr. articles to profl. jours.; patentee in field. Mem. Birmingham Metallurgical Assn. Avocations: foreign travel, gambling statistics, DIY, personal finance. Home: 1 Longfellow Rd, Birmingham B30 1BN, England

JONES, PETER DOMINIC, paediatrician, researcher; b. Orange, Australia, Apr. 17, 1965; s. Brian Edmund and Judith Isabel (Lyons) J.; m. Therese Elizabeth Mary Keenan, Dec. 8, 1990; children: Dominique, Harrison, Bethany, Hunter. MB BS, Sydney U., 1988; DCH, London Coll. Physicians, 1992; postgrad., Newcastle U. Intern Royal Canberra Hosp., 1988; lectr. in child health London U.; registrar in paediatrics Sydney, 1989-91, 93; sr. registrar in paediatrics John Hunter Hosp., Newcastle, 1994; lectr. in child health Newcastle U., 1995-99, sr. lectr., 1999—; mem. organizing com. for diploma of paediatrics, Newcastle; dir. residents registrars John Hunter Children's Hosp. Contbr. articles to profl. jours. Fellow Royal Australasian Coll. Physicians (coord. advanced physician tng.); mem. AMA, Coll. Paediatrics, Swansea Surf Club. Roman Catholic. Office: John Hunter Hosp, Dept Paediatrics, New Lambton 2305, Australia

JONES, RACHEL M., former educator, real estate agent; b. Ahoskie, N.C., July 1, 1929; d. George Washington and Lollie Eldo (Gatling) Manly; m. Edward Thomas Jones, Aug. 22, 1970 (dec. 1996); children: Antonio, Julie, Mark, Kimberely. BS, Agrl. and Tech. Coll., 1953; MA, Bklyn. Coll., 1976, M in Adminstrn. and Supervision, 1980. Tchr. home econs. Jr. High Sch. 265, Bklyn., 1962-64; dean girls med. program Jr. High Sch. 117, Bklyn., 1968-79, tchr. reading, sci., 1980-81, asst. prin., 1980-86; realtor Bklyn., 1987—; owner variety store, 1985-87. Pres. East 56th St Block Assn., 1975—. Recipient Cert. Community Planning Bd., 1985. Mem. Bklyn. Coll. Alumni, Am. Home Econs. Assn., Bklyn. Assn. Supervision and Curriculum Devel., N.Y. Nat. Assn. Black Educators. Lodge: Order Eastern Star. Home: 47 E 56th St Brooklyn NY 11203-2607

JONES, RAYMOND MOYLAN, strategy and public policy educator; b. Phila., Dec. 28, 1942; s. Raymond and Elizabeth (Shaw) J.; m. Barbara Ann Donaghue, May 22, 1965; children: Andrea Marie, Audra Marie. BS, U.S. Mil. Acad., 1964; MBA, Harvard U., 1971; JD, U. Tex., 1973; PhD, U. Md., 1993. Bar: Tex. 1973, U.S. Supreme Ct. 1993. Commd. 2d lt. U.S. Army, 1964, advanced through grades to capt., 1966, ret., 1969; legal asst. to chmn. Occidental Petroleum Corp., L.A., 1973-75; pres. Oxy Metal Industries Internat., Geneva, 1975-77, Occidental Resource Recovery Corp., Irvine, Calif., 1978-81; v.p. Hooker Chem. Corp., Houston, 1977-78; pvt. practice cons. Austin and Irvine, 1981-86; lectr. Calif. State U., Long Beach, 1986, U. Md., College Park, 1986-90, Loyola Coll., Balt., 1990—; cons. to multinational and domestic orgns. Author: Strategic Management in a Hostile Environment: Lessons from the Tobacco Industry, 1998; contbr. articles, book rev. to profl. publs. Mem. Friends of Austin Symphony Orch.; mem. Ludwig Von Mises Inst., Burlingame, Calif., 1987—, Intercoll. Studies Inst., Bryn Mawr, Pa., 1987—; mgmt. con. ARC, Balt., 1988—. Grantee U. Md. 1987, Loyola Coll. 1993. Mem. Am. Econ. Assn., Acad. Internat. Bus., Strategic Mgmt. Soc., Acad. Mgmt., State Bar Tex., Harvard Club. Roman Catholic. Home: 305 Kerneway Baltimore MD 21212-4714 Office: Loyola Coll Sellinger Sch Bus Mgmt Baltimore MD 21210-2699

JONES, RENEE KAUERAUF, health care administrator; b. Duncan, Okla., Nov. 3, 1949; d. Delbert Owen and Betty Jean (Marsh) Kauerauf; m. Dan Elkins Jones, Aug. 3, 1972. BS, Okla. State U., 1972, MS, 1975; PhD, Okla. U., 1989. Diplomate Am. Bd. Sleep Medicine. Statis. analyst Okla. State Dept. Mental Health, Okla. City, 1978-80, divisional chief, 1980-83, adminstr., 1983-84; assoc. dir. HCA Presbyn. Hosp., Okla. City, 1984—; adj. instr. Okla. U. Health Sci. Ctr., 1979—; assoc. staff scientist Okla. Ctr. for Alcohol and Drug-Related Studies, Okla. City, 1979—; cons. in field. Assoc. editor Alcohol Tech. Reports jour., 1979-84; contbr. articles to profl. jours. Mem. assoc. bd. Hist. Preservation, Inc., treas. 1994. Mem. APHA, NAFE, Assn. Health Svcs. Rsch., Alcohol and Drug Problems Assn. N.Am., Am. Sleep Disorders Assn., N.Y. Acad. Scis., So. Sleep Soc. (sec.-treas. 1989-91), Phi Kappa Phi. Democrat. Methodist. Avocations: skiing, scuba diving, racewalking, bicycling, painting. Home: 401 NW 19th St Oklahoma City OK 73103-1911 Office: Columbia Presbyn Hosp NE 13th at Lincoln Blvd Oklahoma City OK 73104

JONES, RICHARD WALLACE, interior designer; b. Canandaigua, N.Y., Dec. 6, 1929; s. William Wallace and Maybelle Louise (Smith) J.; m. Patricia Hardwick, June 24, 1957 (div. 1973). Student, Hobart Coll., 1946-47; tchr.'s cert., Longy Sch., Cambridge, Mass., 1952; postgrad., Yale U. Sch. Music, 1952-53. Owner, operator Richard W. Jones studios, Boston, Hartford, Conn., 1954-63; designer, mgr. House of Good Taste Pavilion, N.Y. World's Fair, 1963-66; design editor Redbook Mag., N.Y.C., 1967-72; sr. design editor Better Homes & Gardens mag., Des Moines, 1972-76; pres., dir. Circanow Interior Design Firm, Des Moines, N.Y.C., 1974-90; designer, mgr. D.H. Hershel Inc., Nantucket, Mass., 1978-81; ptnr., designer, buyer Portobello, Nantucket, 1981-83; dir. design Laura Ashley Inc., Ridgewood, N.J., 1989-90; interior designer Godfrey & Assocs., Naples, Fla., 1994-97; prin. Richard W. Jones Designs, Naples, Fla., 1997—; curator Hammond Mus., Gloucester, Mass., 1950-60, Hill-Stead Mus., Farmington, Conn., 1962; del. Internat. Fedn. Interior Designers, Amsterdam, The Netherlands, 1975-76. Editor in chief Interiors mag., Residential Interiors, 1976-78. Mem. Pres.' Com. on Barrier Free Design, Washington, 1972-74. Recipient Dorothy Dawe award Sr. Design Editor, 1974. Fellow Am. Soc. Interior Designers (nat. pres. 1976. Disting. Svc. medal 1977); mem. Nat. Soc. Interior Designers (nat. pres. 1972-74), Nantucket C. of C. (bd. dirs. 1980-82, sign approval com. 1982-84). Presbyterian. Avocations: collecting contemporary and African art, travel. Home and office: 292 14th Ave S Naples FL 34102-7254

JONES, ROBERT ALONZO, economist; b. Evanston, Ill., Mar. 15, 1937; s. Robert Vernon and Elsie Pierce (Brown) J.; m. Ina Turner Jones; children: Lindsay Rae, Robert Pierce, Gregory Alan, William Kenneth. AB, Middlebury Coll., 1959; MBA, Northwestern U., 1961, LLD (hon.) Middlebury (Vt.) Coll., 1992. Economist Hahn, Wise & Assoc., San Carlos, Calif., 1966-69; sr. rsch. officer Bank of Am., San Francisco, 1969-74; v.p., dir. fin. forecasting Chase Econometrics, San Francisco, 1974-76; chmn. bd. Money Market Svcs., Inc., Belmont, Calif., 1974-86; chmn. bd. MMS Internat., Redwood City, Calif., 1986-89, chmn. emeritus, 1989—; chmn. bd. dirs. Market News Svc., N.Y.C.; chmn. emeritus Geonomics Inst., Middlebury, 1995—, chmn. bd., 1986-95; chmn. bd. Jones Internat., 1989—; chmn. bd. Market News Svc., Inc., N.Y.C., 1993—; chmn. bd. Jones Fin. Network, Inc., Incline Village, N.Y.; dean coun. Harvard U. Div. Sch., Cambridge, Mass., 1991—; mem. Kellogg Alumni Adv. Bd., Northwestern U., 1993—; instr. money and banking, Am. Inst. Banking, San Francisco, 1971, 72; councilman, City of Belmont (Calif.), 1970-77, mayor, 1971, 72, 75, 76; dir. San Mateo County Transit Dist., 1975-77; chmn. San Mateo County Coun. of Mayors, 1975-76; trustee Incline Village Gen. Improvement Dist., Nev., 1984-85,Carlmont United Meth. Ch., 1978-81, Middleburg Coll., 1997—. Author: U.S. Financial System and the Federal Reserve, 1974, Power of Coinage, 1987. 1st lt. USAR, 1961-68. Named Hon. Life Mem. Calif. PTA, ordo honorum Kappa Delta Rho Nat. Fraternity; recipient Ernst & Young Entrepreneur of the Yr. award, 1986; John Harvard fellow Harvard U., 1996, Stanton Recognition award North Shore Country Day Sch., 1996. Mem. Nat. Assn. Bus. Economists, San Francisco Bond Club. Republican. Methodist. Office: Jones Internat Inc PO Box 7498 Incline Village NV 89452-7498

JONES, ROBERT CLAIR, middle school educator; b. Norfolk, Va., Apr. 9, 1949; s. Leon Herbert and Barbara Dean (Jones) J.; m. Geri Lee Siebels, Feb. 13, 1977; children: Adam, Matthew, Aaron, Lee. BS, Old Dominion U., 1971, MS, 1981. Tchr. Virginia Beach (Va.) Jr. High Sch., 1971-73, Kempsville Jr. High Sch., Virginia Beach, 1973—; adj. faculty Old Dominion U., Norfolk, Va., 1990—; co-chmn. faculty coun. Kempsville Mid. Sch., 1992-93, curriculum coord., grade level chair, 1993—; program devel. com. for mid. schs., Virginia Beach City Schs., 1990-91, chmn. social studies curriculum adv. com., 1990-91, instr. staff devel., 1989-91; speaker in field. Contbr. articles to profl. jours.; featured in Oasis mag. Baseball coach Pony Colt League, Virginia Beach, 1991-92; vol. Make A Wish Found., Virginia Beach, 1990-92. Named Tchr. of Yr., Va. Coun. Social Studies, 1987—. Mem. ASCD, NEA, Nat. Coun. Social Studies, Va. Edn. Assn., Va. Coun. Social Studies, Virginia Beach Edn. Assn. Avocations: profl. musician, collecting records, Beatles memorobilia. Home: 812 Yearling Ct Virginia Beach VA 23464-3214 Office: Kenpsville Mid Sch 260 Churchill Dr Virginia Beach VA 23456

JONES, ROBERT GRIFFITH, lawyer, mayor; b. State Coll., Pa., Mar. 25, 1936; s. Edward H. and Dorothy (Griffiths) J.; m. Carolyn E. Hazard, Aug. 29, 1959; Robert Griffith Jr., Chester H. AB, Davidson (N.C.) Coll., 1958; MDiv, Yale U., 1961; PhD, Duke U., 1966; JD, U. Va., 1974. Bar: Va. 1974, U.S. Supreme Ct. 1977. Asst. prof. Davidson (N.C.) Coll., 1964-65; assoc. prof. Lehigh U., Bethlehem, Pa., 1965-71; prof. U. Va., Charlottesville,

1971-74; mayor City of Virginia Beach, Va., 1986-88; chmn. Jones, Marcari, Russotto, Walker & Spencer, P.C., Virginia Beach, 1991—; adv. bd. mem. Princess Ancenit Bank, 1997—. Vice-chmn. Tidewater Transp. Dist. Commn., 1987-88, chmn., 1988; councilman City Council of Virginia Beach, 1982-88, sec. Va. Beach Econ. Devel. Authority. Mem. ABA, Va. Bar Assn., Virginia Beach Bar Assn. Democrat. Presbyterian. Home: 2716 Robin Dr Virginia Beach VA 23454-1814 Office: 128 S Lynnhaven Rd Virginia Beach VA 23452-7417

JONES, ROBERT HOWARD, government official; b. Melbourne, Australia, May 11, 1937. Diploma in mech. engring., Monash U., Melbourne, 1961, diploma in elec. engring., 1962; MS, Brunel U., U.K., 1985, PhD, 1991. Cert. engr., tchr., Australia. Computer engr. Amalgamated Wireless Australasia, Australia, 1959-62, Internat. Computers Ltd., U.K., 1962-68; math master West Sussex County Coun., Steyning, U.K., 1969-70; math. tchr. Inner London Edn. Authority, London, 1970-75; lectr. Westminster City Coun., London, 1980-90; pub. servant Ministry of Defense, Australia, 1990—; cons. Hobson Design, Geelong, Australia, 1992, Invision, Melbourne, 1993; tchr. Wodonga Tafe, 1998. Chmn. Austrian Alpine Club, 1966; coord. Nat. Trust, 1994, Geelong Hosp. Gala Day, 1994. Recipient honorarium, Nat. U. Singapore, 1990. Roman Catholic. Avocations: music, literature, swimming, mountaineering.

JONES, ROGER CLYDE, retired electrical engineering educator; b. Lake Andes, S.D., Aug. 17, 1919; s. Robert Clyde and Martha (Albertson) J.; m. Katherine M. Tucker, June 7, 1952; children: Linda Lee, Vonnie Lynette. B.S., U. Nebr., 1949; M.S., U. Md., 1953; Ph.D. U. Md., 1963. With U.S. Naval Research Lab., Washington, 1949-57; staff sr. engr. to chief engr. Melpar, Inc., Falls Church, Va., 1957-58; cons. project engr. Melpar, Inc., 1958-59, sect. head physics, 1959-64, chief scientist for physics, 1964; prof. dept. elec. engring. U. Ariz., Tucson, 1964-89; dir. quantum electronics lab. U. Ariz., 1968-88, adj. prof. radiology, 1978-86, adj. prof. radiation-oncology, 1986-88, prof. of radiation-oncology, 1988-89, prof. emeritus, 1989—; guest prof. of exptl. oncology Inst. Cancer Research, Aarhus, Denmark, 1982-83; tech. dir. H.S.C. and A., El Paso, 1989-96. Patentee in field. Served with AUS, 1942-45. Fellow AAAS; mem. IEEE, NSPE, Am. Phys. Soc., Optical Soc. Am., Internat. Soc. Optical Engring., Bioelectromagnetics Soc., NSPE, Am. Congress on Surveying and Mapping, N.Mex. Acad. Sci., N.Y. Acad. Sci., Eta Kappa Nu, Pi Mu Epsilon. Home: 5809 E 3rd St Tucson AZ 85711-1519

JONES, ROGER H., mechanical engineer, music educator; b. Charlestown, W.Va., Aug. 12, 1963; s. Benjamin Roger and Nancy Ellen Jones; m. Carolyn Rebecca, May 18, 1996. Diploma in design drafting tech., York Tech. Inst., 1984; A in Engring. Tech., Pa. State U., 2000. Detail drafter Allis Chalmers Hydro, Inc., York, Pa., 1984-85, Westinghouse Elevator, Gettysburg, 1985-86; tech. illustrator Byrnes Group, Gen. Def. G-P Contract Staffing, York, 1986; detail drafter CAM Industries, Hanover, Pa., 1986-87; CAD designer P.H. Glatfelter Co., Spring Grove, Pa., 1987-97, project maintenance project engr., 1997—. Republican. Avocations: scuba diving, drawing, painting, history, music. E-mail: drumZZZticks@aol.com. Office: PH Glatfelter Co 228 S Main St Spring Grove PA 17362-1000

JONES, ROGER WAYNE, electronics executive; b. Riverside, Calif., Nov. 21, 1939; s. Virgil Elsworth and Beulah (Mills) J.; m. Sherill Lee Bottjer, Dec. 28, 1975; children: Jerrod Wayne, Jordan Anthony. BS in Engring., San Diego State U., 1962. Br. sales mgr. Bourns, Inc., Riverside, 1962-68; sales and mktg. mgr. Spectrol Electronics, Industry, Calif., 1968-77, v.p. mktg., 1979-81; mng. dir. Spectrol Reliance, Ltd., Swindon, England, 1977-79; sr. v.p. S.W. group Kierulff Electronics Corp., L.A., 1981-83; v.p. sales and mktg. worldwide electronic techs. div. Beckman Instruments, Fullerton, Calif., 1983-86; pres., ptnr. Jones & McGeoy Sales, Inc., Newport Beach, Calif., 1986—. Author: The History of Villa Rockledge, A National Treasure in Laguna Beach, 1991, California From the Conquistadores to the Legends of Laguna, 1997. Republican. Office: 5100 Campus Dr Newport Beach CA 92660-2101

JONES, ROSEMARY, college official; b. Washington, Pa., Aug. 15, 1951; d. Roy F. and Grace Vivian (Beton) J. BA in Sociology, Ohio State U., 1974, MA in Pub. Adminstrn., 1977. Mgmt. analyst office planning studies Ohio State U., Columbus, 1974-76; staff assoc., edn. rev. com. Ohio Gen. Assembly, Columbus, 1977-78; from adminstr. to asst. dir. info. systems and rsch. Ohio Bd. Regents, Columbus, 1978-90; from project dir. instl. rsch. to dir. rsch. planning Lakeland C.C., Mentor, Ohio, 1990-93; dist. dir. instl. planning evaluation Cuyahoga C.C., Cleve., 1994—; NPECSS planning com. Dept. Edn., 1994-96, NPEC student outcomes data working group, 1996, NCES coop. sys. fellows program, 1996; com. on revising info. sys. for higher edn. Ohio Bd. Regents, Columbus, 1994-96, subsidy consultation com., 1996, cons., 1990-91, com. on resource analysis revision, 1994-96, vice-chair higher edn. info. adv. com., 1996-98, chair, 1999-2000, chair subcom. on data access and reporting, 1998-99; mem. Ohio Awards for Excellence Coun., 1999-2000; com. on performance Ohio Bd. Regents, 2000. Consumer adv. bd. United Health Plan, Columbus, 1978-82, chair, 1980-82; vol. Ronald McDonald House, Columbus, 1989, operating bd. mem., 1989; bd. dirs. Netcare Found., Columbus, 1988; state and regional conf. chair ASPA, Columbus, 1981, 83-84; steering com. Ctrl. Ohio Salute to Pub. Employees, Columbus, 1983; mem. strategic planning com. Mentor Pub. Libr., 1998-99. Mem. Assn. Instl. Rsch., Ohio Conf. for Coll. and Univ. Planning (two-yr. campus coun. rep. 1997-99), Ohio Assn. Instl. Rsch. (two-yr. campus coun. rep. 1994-96), Cleve. Planning Forum, Soc. for Coll. and Univ. Planning, Cleve. Commn. on Higher Edn. Strategic Planning Com. (temp. chair 1991), Ohio Assn. C.C.s (performance measurement study team 1999). Office: Cuyahoga CC 700 Carnegie Ave Cleveland OH 44115-2833

JONES, RUPERT JAMES LIVINGSTON, lawyer; b. London, Sept. 2, 1953; s. Walter Herbert and Dorothy Jocelyn (Dignum) J.; m. Sheila Carol Kertesz, June 24, 1978; children: Oliver, Philippa, Stephen, Michael. LLB with honours, U. Birmingham, Eng., 1975. Solicitor Supreme Ct. Articled clk. Allen & Overy, London, 1976-78, solicitor, 1978-85, ptnr., 1985-97; ptnr. Sonnenschein Nath & Rosenthal, London, 1997-99, Buchanan Ingersoll, London, 2000—. Barber scholar U. Birmingham, 1975. Mem. Law Soc. Eng. and Wales, City of London Solicitors Co. (liveryman), London Young Solicitors Group (sec. 1985, treas. 1986, chmn. 1987), City of London Law Soc. (Whittington Com. chmn. 1992-94, planning and environ. law subcom. 1998—). Avocations: gardening, cinema, motoring. Home: Pincotes, Plaistow Rd Dunsfold, Godalming GU8 4PF, England Office: Buchanan Ingersoll, 25 Old Broad St Tower 42, London EC2N 1HQ, England

JONES, SCHUYLER, museum director, anthropologist; b. Wichita, Kans., Feb. 7, 1930; s. Schuyler and Ignace (Mead) J.; m. Lis Margit Søndergaard Rasmussen, Dec. 20, 1955; children: Peter R., Hannah L.; m. Lorraine da'Luz Vieira, Aug. 4, 1998. MA in Anthropology with honors, Edinburgh (Scotland) U.; MA in Anthropology, Oxford (Eng.) U., DPhil in Anthropology. Asst. curator Pitt Rivers Mus., U. Oxford, 1970-71, asst. curator, univ. lectr. ethnology, 1971-85, dir., 1985-97; fellow Linacre Coll., Oxford U., 1970-97; Anthropol. expdns. to Atlas Mountains, So. Algeria, French West Africa, 1951-52, Morrocco High Atlas, Algeria, Sahara, Niger River, 1954, East Africa, 1953, Turkey, Iran, Afghanistan, Pakistan, India, Nepal, 1958-59; ten expdns. to Nuristan in the Hindu Kush, 1960-70, Chinese Turkestan, 1985, Tibet and Gobi Desert, 1986, So. China, Xinjiang and Pakistan, 1988, Western Greenland, 1991, Greenland and East Africa, 1993; mem. coun. Royal Anthropol. Inst., 1986-89. Author: Sous le Soleil Africain, 1955, Annotated Bibliography of Nuristan (Kafiristan) and the Kalash Kafirs of Chitral, part 1, 1966, part 2, 1969, The Political Organization of the Kam Kafirs, 1967, Men of Influence in Nuristan, 1974, Tibetan Nomads: Environment, Pastoral Economy & Material Culture, 1996; co-author: Nuristan, 1979, Afghanistan, 1992; contbr. numerous articles to profl. jours. Trustee Horniman Mus., 1989-95. Decorated comdr. Brit. Empire. Avocations: travel in remote areas, browsing in second-hand bookstores. Office: Wichita State U Anthropology Dept Anthropology Dept Wichita KS 67260

JONES, SHELDON ATWELL, lawyer; b. Melrose, Mass., Apr. 20, 1938; s. Sheldon Atwell and Hannah Margaret (Andrews) J.; m. Priscilla Ann Hatch, Sept. 10, 1966; children: Sarah Percy, Abigail Atwell. BA, Yale U., 1959; LLB, Harvard U., 1965. Bar: Mass. 1965, U.S. Dist. Ct. Mass. 1967. Assoc. Gaston, Snow, Motley & Holt, Boston, 1965-72; ptnr. Gaston Snow & Ely Bartlett, Boston, 1972-87, Dechert Price & Rhoads, Boston, 1987—; past sec. H&Q Healthcare Investors, Boston. Contbr. articles to profl. jours. Lt. (j.g.) USN, 1959-62. Mem. ABA (past chmn. subcom. on investment cos., state regulation of securities com.), Mass. Bar Assn., Boston Bar Assn. (past co-chmn. subcom. on investment cos. and investment advisers), Yale Club, Harvard Club. Congregationalist. Avocations: skiing, sailing. Home: 70 Indian Spring Rd Concord MA 01742-5512 Office: Dechert Price & Rhoads 12th Fl Ten Post Office Sq Boston MA 02109

JONES, SHELINA JANE, exhibition company owner and executive; b. Farnham, Surrey, Eng., June 28, 1966; d. Bernard Walter and Gulzar (Rawji) Hobbs; m. David Richard Jones, July 14, 1995. Apprentice engr. Brit. Aerospace, 1982-86, market analyst, 1986-88; mktg. analyst MEL, 1988-90; product planner Gen. Instrument, 1990-91; media contr. Brit. Aerospace, 1991-94; promotional sales mgr. BAe, 1994—; mng. dir. Cirrus Event Mgmt. Office: Cirrus Event Mgmt Ltd, 34 Foxhurst Rd Ash Vale, Aldershot Hants GU12 5DY, England

JONES, SHERYL LEANNE, retail sales executive; b. Burlington, Iowa, Jan. 5, 1959; d. Leo F. and Mary E. (Hudson) Wallace; m. Paul W. Jones, July 14, 1984. BA in Spanish Lit. and Lang., U. Kans., 1981, BSBA, 1982; cert. legal asst., S.W. Mo. State U., 1989; AS in Legal Asst. Studies, Drury Coll., 1991. Legal sec. Pratt & Fossard, Springfield, Mo., 1984-87; paralegal Pratt, Fossard & Rahmeyer, Springfield, Mo., 1987-97; owner, mgr. tHIS Way Up, LLC, Springfield, Mo., 1997—; mem. adv. com. dept. office systems & tech. Ozark Tech. Coll., Springfield, 1992-93; mem. adv. bd. dept. paralegal studies Drury Coll., Springfield, 1988-90; lectr. seminar Mo. Bar Assn., 1990. Contbr. articles to legal jours. Mem. S.W. Mo. Paralegal Assn. (chmn. various coms. 1987-96, bd. dirs. 1993-96), Springfield Mo. Alumnae Panhellenic (v.p., sec., treas., pres. 1994—), Sigma Kappa (pres., v.p., panhellenic rep., various coms., alumnae Springfield chpt. 1984—, coord. dist. housing 1992-93, corp. fin. coord. 1993-95, corp. coord. 1995—, v.p., sec., dir. nat. housing corp. 1993—, pres. Springfield Kappa Corp. Springfield, Inc. 1997—). Avocations: antiquing, collecting Hull pottery, juke-boxes and Band-Boxes, traveling. Home: 1149 E Greenwood St Springfield MO 65807-3714

JONES, STEPHEN, lawyer; b. Lafayette, La., July 1, 1940; s. Leslie William and Gladys A. (Williams) J.; m. Virginia Hadden (dec.); 1 child, John Chapman; m. Sherrel Alice Stephens, Dec. 27, 1973; children: Stephen Mark, Leslie Rachael, Edward St. Andrew. Student, U. Tex., 1960-63; LLB, U. Okla., 1966. Sec. Rep. Minority Conf., Tex. Ho. of Reps., 1963; personal asst. to Richard M. Nixon N.Y.C., 1964; adminstrv. asst. to Congressman Paul Findley, 1966-69, legal counsel to gov. of Okla., 1967; spl. asst. U.S. Senator Charles H. Percy and U.S. Rep. Donald Rumsfeld, 1968; mem. U.S. del. to North Atlantic Assembly NATO, 1968; staff counsel censure task force Ho. of Reps. Impeachment Inquiry, 1974; spl. U.S. atty. No. Dist. Okla., 1979; spl. prosecutor, spl. asst. dist. atty. State of Okla., 1977; judge Okla. Ct. Appeals, 1982; civil jury instrn. com. Okla. Supreme Ct., 1979-81; adv. com. ct. rules Okla. Ct. Criminal Appeals, 1980; now mng. ptnr. Stephen Jones & Assoc., Enid, Okla.; adj. prof. U. Okla., 1973-76; instr. Phillips U., 1982-90; bd. dirs. Coun. on the Nat. Interest Found. Author: Oklahoma and Politics in State and Nation, 1907-62, 1974, Others Unknown: The Oklahoma City Bombing Case and Conspiracy, 1998; co-author: France and China, The First Ten Years, 1964-74, 1991, Vernon's Oklahoma Forms 2d Criminal Practice & Procedure Vols. I, II, 1999; contbr. articles to various jours. Bd. dirs., coun. mem. Nat. Interest Found.; acting chmn. Rep. State Com., Okla., 1982; Rep. nominee Okla. atty. gen., 1974, U.S. Senate, 1990; spl. counsel to Gov. Okla., 1995; apptd. chief def. counsel by U.S. Dist. Ct., Oklahoma City, U.S. vs. Tim McVeigh, Oklahoma City Bombing Case, 1995-97; mem. vestry St. Matthews Episc. Ch., 1974, sr. warden, 1983-84, 89-90. Mem. ABA, Okla. Bar Assn., Garfield County Bar Assn., Beacon Club, Petroleum Club (Oklahoma City), Oakwood Country Club (Enid). Office: PO Box 472 Enid OK 73702-0472

JONES, STEPHEN WITSELL, lawyer; b. Honolulu, Aug. 12, 1947; s. Allen Newton Jr. and Maude Estelle (Witsell) J.; m. Judy Kaye Mason, Aug. 13, 1977; children: MaryAnn, Adam, Kathleen. Student, Hendrix Coll., 1965-66; AB with high honors, U. Ill., 1969; JD with highest honors, U. Ark., Little Rock, 1978. Bar: Ark. 1978, U.S. Dist. Ct. (ea. and we. dists.) Ark. 1978, U.S. Ct. Appeals (7th and 8th cirs.) 1978, U.S. Supreme Ct. 1984. Rsch. statistician Ark. Dept. Parks and Tourism, Little Rock, 1971-72, dir. tourist info. ctr., 1972-74; affirmative action specialist Office of the Gov., Little Rock, 1974-75; dir. pers. Ark. Social Svcs. Div., Little Rock, 1975-77; mgmt. info. specialist Ark. Health Dept., Little Rock, 1977-78; assoc. House, Holmes & Jewell, Little Rock, 1978-84; ptnr. House, Wallace, Nelson & Jewell, Little Rock, 1984-86; mng. ptnr. Jack, Lyon & Jones, P.A., Little Rock, 1986—; adj. instr. div. lifelong edn. U. Ark., Little Rock, 1992-95. Co-author: Employment Law Deskbook for Arkansas Employers, 1997; editor-in-chief U. Ark. Little Rock Law Rev., 1977; editor Ark. Employment Law Letter, 1996—; contbg. author: Employment Discrimination Law, 2d edit., 1983; editor. Bd. dirs. United Cerebral Palsy of Ctrl. Ark., Little Rock, 1978—; bd. dirs. Ark. Ice Hockey Assn., 1992—. With U.S. Army, 1969-71. Recipient Svc. Recognition award United Cerebral Palsy of Ctrl. Ark., 1986, 95. Fellow Coll. Labor's Employment Lawyers, Greater Little Rock C. of C.; mem. ABA (labor/litigation law practice mgmt. sect.), Ark. Bar Assn., Def. Rsch. Inst. Episcopalian. Avocations: photography, golf. Home: 1724 S Arch St Little Rock AR 72206-1215 Office: Jack Lyon & Jones PA 3400 TCBY Tower 425 W Capitol Ave Little Rock AR 72201-3405

JONES, SYDNEY, youth organization administrator; b. London, Feb. 1, 1937; s. George and Emily (Lowes) J.; m. Patricia Kathleen Gaines, Oct. 22, 1960; children: Michael Stephen, Timothy Paul. Tchg. cert., Westminster Coll., London, 1959; BA, Open U., Eng., 1977. From tchr. to dep. headmaster Approved Schs., Birmingham, Eng., 1960-73; prin. Cmty. Homes/Sch., Leicestershire, Eng., 1973-84; mgr. Local Authority Social Svcs., Aldridge, Eng., 1984-85; prin. Nat. Children's Home, Congleton, Cheshire, 1985-88; CEO, dir. Boys Brigade, Inc., Hertfordshire, Eng., 1988—; bd. dirs. Anchor Tng. Editor Boys Brigade Gazette. Mgr., treas. Cmty. Homes Gazette, 1975-81. Decorated Officer of the British Empire. Baptist. Avocations: music, reading, church. Home: 9 Brook Ln, Berkhamsted HP4 1SX, England Office: The Boys Brigade, Felden Lodge, Hemel Hempstead HP3 0BL, England

JONES, SYLVANUS BENSON, adjudicator, consultant, lawyer; b. Southport, N.C., Nov. 21, 1928; s. Thomas Henry and Katie Mable J.; m. Karen Ann Charbonneau, Aug. 10, 1970 (div. May 1975); 1 child, Donovan; m. Brenda Castleyoung-Jones, Sept. 9, 1999. Student, Howard U., 1945-48; AD in Fin., Peter's Bus. Coll., Washington, 1955; postgrad., Fgn. Svc. Inst., Arlington, Va., 1956, George Washington U., 1959-60, Bibliothèque de la Sorbonne U. de Paris, Paris, 1962, Georgetown U., Washington, 1962, Am. U., Washington, 1966-68. Lic. real estate agt.; lic. gen. contractor, Md.; lic. ins. agt., Md., D.C. Enumerator, IBM computer operator U.S. Census Bur., Suitland, Md., 1950-51; clk. typist, claims div. VA, Washington, 1951-52; rsch. clk. Bur. Security and Consular Affairs, U.S. Dept. State, Washington, 1952-53, supr. passport processing sect., 1953-56, from jr. to sr. adjudicator domestic adjudication div., 1956-61, consular affairs officer adv. opinions div., 1961-63, chief pvt. bill staff, office of dep. dir. for ops., 1963-68, chief fraud and investigation unit, 1968-72; adjudicator, gen. cons., 1972—; editor-in-chief The Washington Press, 1957-63; founder, dir. Mut. Fund Investment Program for Govt. Employees, Washingotn, 1969-73; instr. Tennis U. Puebla (Mex.), 1973-75; editor-in-chief The Annapolis (Md.) Press, 1989—; chmn. ad hoc com. to repeal the utilities tax, Annapolis, 1992—. Contbr. articles to profl. jours; grantee hub cap locking device. Treas. Annapolis City Dem. Ctrl. Com., 1992, 97; Dem. candidate for mayor, Annapolis, 1993, 97; chmn. trans. adv. bd., Annapolis, 1992-98. Recipient Cert. of Disting. Citizenship, City of Annapolis, 1987, 97, Gov.'s Citation for Outstanding Svc. to Citizens, State of Md., 1997, Red Cross Citizenship award, Trailblazer award U.S. Dept. State, 1998; numerous meritorious svc. awards; Howard U. scholar. Home: 16 Bausum Dr Annapolis MD 21401-4309

JONES, THOMAS OWEN, computer industry executive; b. Phila., Apr. 6, 1932; s. Paul John and Katharine (McCahey) J.; m. Mary Louise Russell, Sept. 19, 1959 (div. Aug. 1979); children: SusanR., Thomas H., Andrew S. BS in Engring., U. Pa., 1954, MBA, 1958. Account mgr. IBM Corp., Phila., 1958-66; asst. to sec. HEW, Washington, 1966-67; v.p. Donaldson, Lufkin & Jenrette, Inc., N.Y.C., 1967-72; pres. Jones/Hosplex Sys., N.Y.C., 1973-84, Carnegie-Madison Inc., N.Y.C., 1984-87, Fifth Generation Computer Corp., N.Y.C., 1987—, Golden Enterprises, Inc., Melbourne, Fla., 1999; cons. to sec. HEW, Washington, 1967-68; mem. Edn. Commr.'s Adv. Coun. on Copyright Policy, Washington, 1967-70. Mem. N.Y. State Adv. Coun. on Edn., Albany, 1970-75; mem. N.Y.C. #4 Cmty. Planning Bd., 1973-75. With U.S. Army, 1954-56. White House fellow U.S. Commn. on White House Fellows, Washington, 1966-67; named Outstanding Young Man of the Main Line, Jr. C. of C., Bryn Mawr, Pa., 1966. Mem. IEEE, N.Y. Acad. Scis., N.Y. Athletic Club, Union League Club Phila., Wharton Alumni Assocs. (exec. bd. 1993—), Am. Legion. Avocations: tennis, travel. Office: Fifth Generation Computer Corp 232 E 68th St New York NY 10021-6001

JONES, THORNTON KEITH, research chemist; b. Brawley, Calif., Dec. 17, 1923; s. Alfred George and Madge Jones; m. Evalee Vestal, July 4, 1965; children: Brian Keith, Donna Eileen. BS, U. Calif., Berkeley, 1949, postgrad., 1951-52. Research chemist Griffin Chem. Co., Richmond, Calif., 1949-55; western product devel. and improvement mgr. Nopco Chem. Co., Richmond, Calif., 1955; research chemist Chevron Research Co., Richmond, 1956-65, research chemist in spl. products research and devel., 1965-1982; product quality mgr. Chevron USA, Inc., San Francisco, 1982-87, ret. Patentee in field. Vol. fireman and officer, Terra Linda, Calif., 1957-64; mem. adv. com. Terra Linda Dixie Elem. Sch. Dist., 1960-64. Served with Signal Corps, U.S. Army, 1943-46. Mem. Am. Chem. Soc., Forest Products Research Soc., Am. Wood Preservers Assn., Alpha Chi Sigma. Republican. Presbyterian. Avocations: music, gardening, wine and food.

JONES, TINA CHARLENE, music educator, genealogy and law researcher; b. Washington, May 27, 1961; d. Charles Timothy Jones and Tiney Ruth (Marion) Haynie; James H. Haynie (stepfather). Cert. paralegal, George Washington U., Washington, 1986. Music educator Creative Music Melodies Co., Silver Spring, Md., 1984—; freelance geneal. and legal rschr., Silver Spring, 1986. Contbr. articles on geneal. rsch. to The Afro-American Newspaper, 1994-95. Recipient grants Delta Sigma Theta, 1979, Nat. Christian Choir, 1986. Mem. Am. Coll. Musicians, Nat. Piano Found., Music Educators Nat. Conf., Internat. Ctr. Rsch. in Music Edn. Avocations: singing, travel, reading. Email: jones61@bellatlantic.net. Home: 13810 Carter House Way Silver Spring MD 20904-4854 Office: Creative Music Melodies Co 6611 Gude Ave Silver Spring MD 20912-4828

JONES, TOM GEORGE, lawyer; b. Defiance, Ohio, Oct. 21, 1934; s. Russell George and Edith (Guinn) J.; m. Annette Huttmacher, June 14, 1959 (div. Mar. 1979); children: Amy Jones Rogers, Mary Margaret, Russell Nicholas, Jennifer Jones Auger; m. Susan Lee Crawford Whitacre, Sept. 17, 1981; stepchildren: Robert Parker Whitacre, James Alan Whitacre, Elizabeth Lee Whitacre. BS in Mktg., Ind. U., 1956; JD, Ind. U., Indpls., 1961. Bar: Ind. 1961, U.S. Dist. Ct. (so. dist.) Ind. 1961, U.S. Ct. Appeals (7th cir.) 1961. Ptnr. Jones, Hoffman, Franklin, Ind., 1961—; dep. pros. atty. Johnson County, 1960-61; lectr. Ind. Continuing Legal Edn. Forum, Indpls., 1982—; mem. faculty Nat. Inst. Trial Adv., Washington, 1985—; lectr. U. Mich. Ann. Advocacy Inst., 1991-92. Contbr. articles to profl. jours. Atty. Johnson County Planning Commn. and Zoning Bd., Ind., 1961-66. Fellow Ind. Trial Lawyers Assn. (chmn. criminal law sect. 1981-83, bd. dirs., 1982-95), Roscoe Pound Found.; mem. ABA, Indpls. Bar Assn., Johnson County Bar Assn.(sec. 1962, pres. 1974), Am. Bd. Trial Advocates (pres. Ind. chpt. 1990-95, nat. bd. dirs. 1990-96), Internat. Soc. Barristers, Nat. Assn. Criminal Def. Lawyers, Assn. Trial Lawyers Am. (sustaining), Tex. Trial Lawyers Assn., Melvin N. Bellie Soc., Phi Kappa Psi, I-Mans Assn. Mem. Disciples of Christ. Lodges: Elks, Shriners, Masons, Scottish Rite. Fax: 317-736-4440. E-mail: tommygjones@hotmail.com. Home: 200 N Water St Franklin IN 46131-1725 Office: Jones Hoffman & Admire 150 N Main St Franklin IN 46131-1721

JONES, TRACY L., insurance underwriter; b. Morrisville, Vt., Dec. 26, 1974; d. Elroy Clarence Jones and Margaret Lee Berry; m. Timothy S. Russell, Apr. 18, 1998 (div. Nov. 1999). BS, Gordon Coll., 1996; A in Ins. Svcs., Ins. Inst. of Am., Malvern, Pa., 1999. Sec. H.A. Manosh Corp., Morrisville, 1996; rating technician Acadia Ins., South Burlington, Vt., 1997-98; bus. analyst Acadia Ins., South Burlington, 1998-99, assoc. underwriter, 1999—. Mem. Nat. Assn. Ins. Women, Champlain Valley Assn. Ins. Women. Avocations: reading, writing poetry, watching old movies, biking. Home: 124A Mountain View Dr Swanton VT 05488-3010 Office: Acadia Ins 1775 Williston Rd South Burlington VT 05403

JONES, TREVOR OWEN, company executive; b. Maidstone, Kent, Eng., Nov. 3, 1930; came to U.S., 1957, naturalized, 1971; s. Richard Owen and Ruby Edith (Martin) J.; m. Jennie Lou Singleton, Sept. 12, 1959; children: Pembroke Robinson (dec.), Bronwyn Elizabeth. Higher Nat. Cert. in Elec. Engring., Aston Tech. Coll., Birmingham, Eng., 1952; Ordinary Nat. Cert. in Mech. Engring., Liverpool (Eng.) Tech. Coll., 1957. Registered profl. engr., Wis.; chartered engr., U.K. Student engr., elec. machine design engr. Brit. Gen. Electric Co., 1950-57; project engr., project mgr. Nuc. Ship Savannah, Allis-Chalmers Mfg. Co., 1957-59; with GM, 1959-78, staff engr. in charge Apollo computers, 1967, dir. electronic control sys., 1970-72, dir. advanced product engring., 1972-74; dir. GM Proving Grounds, 1974-78; v.p. engring., automotive worldwide TRW Inc., Cleve., 1978-80, v.p. transp. electronics group, 1980-87; chmn. bd. dirs. Libbey-Owens-Ford Inc., 1987-94; chmn., CEO Internat. Devel. Corp., 1987—; from vice chmn. to chmn. Echlin Inc., 1995-98, chmn. bd. dirs., interim pres. and CEO, 1997; chmn., CEO Biomec Inc., 1998—; vice chmn. Motor Vehicle Safety Adv. Coun., 1971; chmn. Nat. Hwy. Safety Adv. Com., 1976. Author, patentee automotive safety and electronics. Trustee Lawrence Inst. Tech., 1973-76; mem. exec. bd. Clinton Valley coun. Boy Scouts Am., 1975; mem. bd. govs. Cranbrook Inst. Sci., 1977; mem. Sec. of Def. Def. Sci. Bd. Task Force on Internat. Arms Devel. Cooperation, 1995-98; chmn. Nat. Rsch. Coun. Com. Partnership for a New Generation Vehicle, 1994—. Officer Brit. Army, 1955-57. Recipient Safety award for engring. excellence U.S. Dept. Transp., 1978. Fellow Brit. Instn. Elec. Engrs. (Hooper Mem. prize 1950), IEEE (life, exec. com. vehicle tech. soc. 1977-81), Royal Soc. of the Arts, Mfg. and Commerce, Soc. Automotive Engrs. (Arch T. Colwell paper award 1974, 75, Vincent Bendix Automotive Electronics award 1976, Edward N. Cole award 1988), Engring. Soc. Detroit, Engring. Soc. Cleve.; mem. NAE, Union Club, Kirtland Country Club, Bloomfield Hills Country Club. Republican. Episcopalian. Home: Two Bratenahl Pl Bratenahl OH 44108

JONES, VERNON KEITH, minister, educator; b. Augusta, Ga., Mar. 19, 1960; s. Frank Vernon and Susie Mae (Golden) J.; children: Jennifer Brandice, Justin Keith. BA, Morehouse Coll., 1982; MDiv, Howard U., 1993, postgrad., 1997—. Ordained to Ministry Bapt. Ch., 1993. Exec. sec. bicentennial commn. Office of the Mayor, Washington, 1987-91; counselor The Sidwell Friends Sch., Washington; state police officer State of Ga., Augusta, 1985-86; pres., CEO, counselor V. Keith Jones & Assoc., Inc., Silver Spring, Md., 1990—; counselor, asst. prof., acad. advisor to athletic programs Montgomery Coll., Germantown, Md., 1998-2000; pres., CEO The Vernon Jones Group, Gaithersburg, Md., 2000—; founder, presiding bishop African-Am. Bapt. Conv., Inc., Washington, 1991—; who's who review bd. Howard U., Washington, 1992, grad. asst. to dean of chapel, 1991-93; prof., counselor, mentor program coord. Montgomery Coll., Takoma, Md. Founder, pastor King Meml. Ch., Silver Spring, 1997—. Howard U. Div. Sch. scholar, 1988-93. Mem. Am. Sch. Counseling Assn., Am. Counseling Assn., Nat. Am. Mus. and Archives (bd. govs. 1996—), Am. Psychol. Assn., Am. Coll. Counselors Assn., Am. Assn. Pastoral Counselors, Nat. Assn. Talented Tenth, Inc. (founder, chmn. 1991—), Omega Psi Phi. Democrat. Baptist. Avocations: sports, writing, reading, collecting wrist watches and fountain pens. Home: 2716 Margate Dr Augusta GA 30909-3640 Office: King Meml Ch 711 Ritchie Ave Silver Spring MD 20910-5242 also: Montgomery Coll Office Student Devel Rm 124 7600 Takoma Ave Takoma Park MD 20912-4141 also: The Vernon Jones Group PO Box 3122 Gaithersburg MD 20885-3122

JONES, VERNON QUENTIN, surveyor; b. Sioux City, Iowa, May 6, 1930; s. Vernon Boyd and Winnifred Rhoda (Bremmer) J.; student UCLA, 1948-50; m. Rebeca Buckovecz, Oct. 1981; children: Steven Vernon, Gregory Richard, Stanley Alan, Lynn Sue. Draftsman III Pasadena (Calif.) city engr.,

1950-53; sr. civil engring. asst. L.A. County engr., L.A., 1953-55; v.p. Treadwell Engring. Corp., Arcadia, Calif., 1955-61, pres., 1961-64; pres. Hillcrest Engring. Corp., Arcadia, 1961-64; dep. county surveyor, Ventura, Calif., 1964-78; propr. Vernon Jones Land Surveyor, Bullhead City, Ariz., 1978—; city engr. Needles (Calif.), 1980-87; instr. Mohave Community Coll., 1987—. Chmn. graphic tech. com. Ventura Unified Sch. Dist., 1972-78, mem. career adv. com., 1972-74; mem. engring. adv. com. Pierce Coll., 1973; pres. Mgmt. Employees of Ventura County, 1974. V.p. Young Reps. of Ventura County, 1965. Pres., Marina Pacifica Homeowners Assn., 1973. Mem. League Calif. Surveying Orgns. (pres. 1975), Am. Congress on Surveying and Mapping (chmn. So. Calif. sect. 1976), Am. Soc. Photogrammetry, Am. Pub. Works Assn., County Engr. Assn. Calif. Home: PO Box 20761 Bullhead City AZ 86439-0761

JONES, WALTER HARRISON, chemist, educator; b. Griffin, Sask., Can., Sept. 21, 1922; s. Arthur Frederick and Mildred Tracy (Walter) J.; BS with honors, UCLA, 1944, PhD in Chemistry, 1948; m. Marion Claire Twomey, Oct. 25, 1959 (dec. Jan. 1976); m. Dorothy-Lynne Byrne, 1979 (div. 1981, remarried 1994). Rsch. chemist Dept. Agr., 1948-51, Los Alamos Sci. Lab., 1951-54; sr. rsch. engr. N.Am. Aviation, 1954-56; mgr. chemistry dept. Ford Motor Co., 1956-60; sr. staff and program mgr., chmn. JANAF-ARPA-NASA Thermochem. panel Inst. Def. Analyses, 1960-63; head propulsion dept. Aerospace Corp., 1963-64; sr. scientist, head advanced tech. Hughes Aircraft Co., 1964-68; prof. aero. systems, dir. Corpus Christi Center, U. West Fla., Pensacola, 1969-75, prof. chemistry, 1975-95; vis. rsch. chemist UCLA, 1994—; vis. prof. U. Toronto, 1979, 92, U. Queensland 1998; cons. pvt., fed. and state agys. Mem. Gov.'s Task Force on Energy, Regional Energy Action Com., Fla. State Energy Office, adv. com. Tampa Bay Regional Planning Coun.; judge regional and state sci. fairs. Fed. and state grantee; rsch. corp. grantee; Fellow ASEE/ONR, NATO, Am. Inst. Chemists; mem. AIAA, AAUP, AAAS, Am. Astron. Soc. (propulsion com.), Am. Chem. Soc. (chmn. Pensacola sect.), N.Y. Acad. Scis., Am. Phys. Soc., Internat. Solar Energy Soc., Combustion Inst. World Assn. Theoretical Organic Chemists, Am. Ordnance Assn., Air Force Assn., Philos. Soc. Washington, Pensacola C. of C., Phi Beta Kappa, Sigma Xi (pres. local chpt.), Pi Mu Epsilon, Phi Lambda Upsilon (sec. local chpt.), Alpha Mu Gamma, Alpha Chi Sigma (pres. local chpt.). Author: (fiction) Prisms in the Pentagon, 1971; contbr. numerous articles tech. jours., chpts. in books. Patentee in field. Home and Office: 355 Calle Loma Norte Santa Fe NM 87501-1256

JONES, WILLIAM GEORGE, oncologist, consultant; b. Widnes, Eng., Dec. 26, 1945; s. Arthur Constable and Edna May (Rickart) J.; m. Anthea Jane Heesterman; children: Penelope Jane, Karen Anne. MB ChB, U. Birmingham, 1969; Diploma in Med. Radiotherapy, London, 1972. Cons. radiotherapist, oncologist West Glamorgan Health Authority, Swansea, Wales, 1975-78; lectr., sr. lectr. in radiotherapy U. Leeds, 1978-92; cons. clin. oncologist Leeds Teaching Hosps. Cookridge Hosp., Leeds, 1992—; mem. med. rsch. coun. working party on testicular tumors, London, 1981-99. Editor: Germ Cell Tumours III, IV, 1994, 98, Prostate Cancer and Testicular Cancer, 1990. Fellow Royal Coll. Radiologists (editor Clin. Oncology 1994-99, examiner for part II 1988-96, sr. examiner 1994, Rohan Williams medal 1974), Brit. Inst. Radiologists, Royal Soc. of Medicine; mem. Brit. Med. Assn., Radiol. Soc., European Orgn. for Rsch. and Treatment of Cancer, Salmon and Trout Assn., Rotary. Anglican. Avocations: game fishing, gardening, reading, travel. E-mail: billjonesleeds@compuserve.com; wgjones@ulth.northy.nhs.uk. Home: 32 Adel Towers Ct Adel, Leeds LS16 8ER, England Office: Cookridge Hosp, Hospital Ln, Leeds LS16 6QB, England

JONES, WILLIAM KINZY, materials engineering educator; b. Miami, Fla., July 23, 1946; s. Harold Grover and Josephine (Kinzy) Jones; m. Sharon Mattingly, June 6, 1981; children: Kelli, Kinzy, Brent. BS, Fla. State U., 1967, MS, 1968; PhD, MIT, 1972. Mgr. engring. Cordis Corp., Miami, 1977-87; group head C.S. Draper Lab., Cambridge, Mass., 1972-77; assoc. prof. engring. Fla. Internat. U., Miami, 1987-91; prof., assoc. dean for rsch. Fla. Internat. U., Miami, 1991—; adv. bd. Nat. Elec. Packaging and Product Conf., Des Plaines, Ill., 1988—; cons. in field; chmn. advanced rsch. workshop NATO, 1994-95; gen. chair Internat. Microelectronics Conf., 1992, Multi-Chip Module Conf., 1995; tech. co-chair Electronic Packaging Conf., China, 1996, 98. Contbr. articles to profl. jours.; patentee in field. Recipient Rsch. award Fla. Internat. U., 1991. Fellow Internat. Soc. Hybrid Microelectronics (chmn. materials divsn. 1990, pres. 1992-93, v.p. membership 1998, Tech. Achievement Wagnon award 1991, Hughes award 1996); mem. IEEE (sr.). Republican. Home: 75550 Overseas Hwy # 534 Islamorada FL 33036-4005 Office: Fla Internat U University Park Campus Coll Of Engring Eas 2441 Miami FL 33199-0001

JONES, WILLIAM RICHARD, microbiologist, educator; b. Seattle, Apr. 29, 1959; s. Dan Lewis and Daisy Regina Jones; m. Diane Auer, Jan. 9, 1988; children: Patrick, Logan. BA, Towso U., 1982; PhD, U. Md., 1990. Asst. to v.p. Towson (Md.) U., 1983-84; rsch. asst. U. Md., Balt., 1985-90; postdoctoral fellow Ctr. for Vaccine Devel., U. Md. Sch. Medicine, Balt., 1991-93; rsch. assoc. Naval Med. Rsch. Inst., Nat. Naval Med. Command, Bethesda, Md., 1991-93; rsch. asst. prof. Uniformed Svcs. Univ. Health Scis., Bethesda, Md., 1992-94; rsch. assoc. faculty Ctr. Marine Biotech., U. Md. Biotech. Inst., Balt., 1993-96; grad. faculty Marine and Estuarine Environ. Scis., U. Md., College Park, 1997—; sr. scientist, head ednl. programs Ctr. Marine Biotech., U. Md. Biotech. Inst., 1997—; dir. Applied Biotech Consortium, Balt., 1993—; pres. Athena Environ. Scis., Inc., Balt., 1994—. Editor: Marine Microbial Ecology, 2000; contbr. articles to profl. jours. Mem. adv. com. U.S. Pavilion, World Exposition, Lisbon, Portugal, 1997; pres. bd. Relay Sch. and Children's Ctr., Balt., 1998—; internat. rsch. program reviewer NAS, Washington, 1998—. Fellow AAAS; mem. Internat. Soc. Environ. Biotech. (session chair 1998), Am. Soc. Microbiology, Nat. Marine Educators Assn. Avocations: gambling, juggling. E-mail: jones@umbi.umd.edu. FAX: 410-234-8898. Office: Ctr Marine Biotech 701 E Pratt St Baltimore MD 21202-3101

JONES DAVIES, MARIE-THÉRÈSE LOUISE, educator; b. Lyon, France, June 16, 1920; d. Louis and Louise (Chaput) Robelin; 1 child, Margaret. Doctorat d'Etat, U. Sorbonne, 1957. Prof. agrégée Lycees and Univ., Nancy and Lyon, France, 1943-46; English tchr. Llandovery Grammar Sch., U. Cardiff, 1947-48; prof. agrégée U. Lyon, 1948-52; prof. agrégé, rsch. worker CNRS, King's Coll., London, 1953-54; prof. U. Rennes, France, 1957-66, U. Sorbonne, Paris, 1966-87; prof. emeritus U. Sorbonne, 1987-92; lectr. U. Exeter, Keele, Poznan (Poland), Valencia, Stratford on Avon, Lisbon and Coimbra, Madrid, Rome; invited lectr. Merton Coll., Oxford, 1981, Barnard Coll., Columbia U., N.Y., 1987, Tokyo; examiner for competitive entrance exam. Ecole Normale Superieure, Paris, 1966-75. Author: Un Peintre de la vie londonienne, Thomas Dekker, 1958 (Prix A. Rocheron, Acad. Française Bronze Medal CNRS), Beaumont et Fletcher, Le Chevalier de l'Ardent Pilon, 1958, Inigo Jones, Ben Jonson et le Masque, 1967, Ben Jonson, collection SEGHERS, 1973, 2d edit., 1980, Victimes et Rebelles, L'ecrivain dans la Societe élisabéthaine, 1980, Shakespeare le theatre du Monde, 1987, Prix Biguet Acad. Française, 1988 (Silver medal); editor 25 vols. Studies on the Renaissance. Named Officier dans l'Ordre des Palmes Académiques. Mem. Etudes Anglaises (exec. com.), Internat. Shakespeare Assn. (hon. v.p.), N.Y. Acad. of Scis., Soc. Française Shakespeare (pres. 1978-84, 87-93, hon. pres.), Soc. Internat. Recherches sur la Renaissance (pres.). Avocations: travelling, theatre going. Office: U Paris Sorbonne, 1 Rue Victor Cousin, Paris 75005, France

JONG, KIM, II, government official; b. Mt. Paektu, Feb. 16, 1952; married; four children. Grad., Kim Il Sung U., Pyongyang. Sec.-gen. The Workers' Party of Korea, Pyongyang, 1972—. Office: Korea Workers Party, Polhburo of Cen Com, Pyongyang Korea

JONGEN, JOHANNES, surgeon; b. Maastricht, The Netherlands, Feb. 4, 1956; s. Johannes and Anna Maria Jongen; m. Karin Fischer, Feb. 2, 1996. MD, State U. of Utrecht, The Netherlands, 1981. Cert. surgeon, Drztekammer Westphalen-Lippe, Muenster, Germany. Resident in surgery Christliches in Krankenhaus, Quakenbrück, Germany, 1982-84, St. Elisabeth Hosp., Iserlohn, Germany, 1984-86, 87-88, Proctol. Office Dr. Bock and Park-Klinik, Kiel, Germany, 1986-87; surgeon, cons. surgeon Park-Klinik, Kiel, 1988—; surgeon Office Dr. Bock and Jongen, Kiel, 1988—. Contbr. articles to profl. jours. Lt. Dutch Infantry, 1981-82. Fax: 49 431 56 28 56. E-mail: karinjanjongen@t-online.de. Office: Office Dr Bock and Jongen, Beselerallee 67, 24105 Kiel Germany

JONIKIS, ARVIDAS ANTHONY, psychologist; b. Bad Aibling, Bavaria, Germany, July 21, 1945; arrived in Australia, 1949; s. Antanas and Bronislava (Grinkevičius) J.; m. Helene Ilze Pudovskis, Jan. 28, 1967; children: Martin Anthony, Simon Alexander. BA, U. Western Australia, Perth, 1971, diploma in Edn., 1972, B in Psychology, 1976, M in Psychology, 1983; grad. diploma in Psychol. Counselling, Curtin U. of Tech., Perth, 1980. Registered clin. psychologist, Western Australia. Counselling psychologist Tech. and Further Edn., Perth, 1974-82, clin. psychologist, 1983-87; sr. clin. psychologist Corrective Svcs. Dept., Perth, 1987-89, Graylands Hosp., Perth, 1989—. Mem. West Australian Ice Skating Assn. (judge, referee, hon. life mem., councillor 1979-82), Ice Skating Australia (championship judge, referee, councillor, hon. cons. psychologist, coord. internat. synchronized skating) Internat. Skating Union (championship judge, referee), Personal Construct Psychology Assn. West Australia (chair 1990-92, hon. treas. 1992—, lectr. 1992—), Australian Psychol. Soc. (hon. treas. West Australian Bd. Clin. Psychologists 1986-87), N.Y. Acad. Scis. Avocations: amateur astronomy, computing, science fiction. Home: 73 Williams Rd, Nedlands 6009, Australia Office: Graylands Hosp, Brockway Rd, Mount Claremont 6010, Australia

JONK, WILHELM, soccer player; b. Volendam, Dec. 10, 1966. Formerly with Ajax, Amsterdam, Inter Milan; midfielder PSV Eindhoven, Netherlands, 1995-98, Sheffield Wednesday, Eng., 1998—. Named English Champ, 1998, 2000. Address: SWFC, Hillsborough, NL-3700 Sheffield S6 1SW, England*

JONNA, SAINDRANATH, civil engineer; b. Gudiwada, A.P., India, Aug. 7, 1960; s. Naraiah and Krishnaveni (Vemana) J.; m. Ramani Katragadda, Apr. 3, 1988; 1 child, Saisankalp. BSc in Engring., Regional Engring. Coll., Calicut, India, 1982; ME, Karnataka Regional Engring. Coll., 1985. Cert. civil engr. Lectr. Chaitanya Bharathi Inst. Tech., Osmania U., Hyderabad, India, 1985-86; engr. 'SC' Dept. Space, Nat. Remote Sensing Agy., Hyderabad, 1986-90, engr. 'SD', 1991-95, engr. 'SE', 1996—, team leader irrigation, 1991—; mem. team of cons. World Bank, Internat. Irrigation Mgmt. Inst., Colombo, Sri Lanka, 1995-96. Contbr. articles to profl. jours., chpts. to books. Mem. Instn. Engrs. India (life), Indian Soc. Tech. Edn. (life), Indian Water Resources Soc. (life), Indian Assn. Hydrologists (life), Indian Soc. for Remote Sensing (life), Am. Geophys. Union, Nat. Remote Sensing Agy. (pres. officers' assn.). Avocations: reading, games, yoga, research on life in the universe and supernatural powers, remote sensing image processing for natural resources monitoring. E-mail: jonnasai@yahoo.com. Home: Plot No 226, SR Nagar PO, Klynngr Hyderabad 500 038, India Office: Nat Remote Sensing Agy, Balanagar, Hyderabad 500 037, India

JONSDOTTIR, ASLAUG, illustrator, author; b. Akranes, Melaleiti, Iceland, Mar. 31, 1963; d. Jon Kristofer Magnusson and Kristjana Höskuldsdottir; m. Vilhjalmur Svansson, Aug. 29, 1992; 1 child, Kristjana Vilhjalmsdottir. Grad., Hamrahlid Coll., Reykjavik, 1983; student, Myndlista-og Handidaskoli Islands, Reykjavik, Iceland, 1984-85; grad., Skolen for Brugskunst, Copenhagen, 1989. Tchr. art and illustration Hofsos Elem. & Middle Sch. Myndlista-og Handidaskoli Islands, Reykjavik, 1992; freelance illustrator, painter, writer. Author, illustrator: (children's books) Gullfjödrin, 1991, Fjölleikasyning Astu, 1992, Stjörnusiglingin, 1992, A Bak Vid Hus—Visur Önnu, 1993, Einu sinni var raunamaeddur risi, 1995, Prakkarasaga, 1996, Sexaevintyri, 1998. Recipient Haystack award Am.-Scandinavian Found.'s Icelandic Crafts Fund and Thor Thors Spl. Contbns. Fund, 1992, Children's Books Acknowledgment Barnabokaradid, I.B.B.Y., Iceland. Avocations: art, crafts, literature, nature. Home: Melhagi 7, 107 Reykjavik Iceland

JONSDOTTIR, GUDRUN SIGRIDUR, retired social worker; b. Vik, Iceland, June 16, 1931; d. Jon and Jonina (Magnusdottir) Palsson; m. Olafur Thorlacius, June 16, 1959; 1 child, Ragneidur. Diploma in social work, Social Inst., Gothenbourg, 1957; diploma in social work education, Nat. Inst. Social Work, London, 1973; PhD in Social Scis., U. Sheffield, England, 1992. Social worker various agys., Reykjavik, Iceland, 1957-75; tchr. Sch. Presch. Tchrs., Reykjavik, 1975-81; lectr. Tchrs. Coll., Reykjavik, 1975-81; dir. sch. social work U. Iceland, Reykjavik, 1981-92; coord., counsellor Counselling Ctr. Survivors of Sexual Violence, Reykjavik, 1992-98; ret., 1998. Author: Surviving Incest, 1992; co-author: (chpt.) Together, 1989, Descriptions of Social Work Education, 1986. Founding mem. Women's Shelter, Reykjavik, 1982; rep. women's party Reykjavik City Coun., 1982-86. Icelandic Ministry Edn. grantee, 1973, British Coun. grantee, 1987, 88, Forum Women's Studies grantee, Iceland, 1988. Mem. Icelandic Assn. Social Workers (hon., chmn. 1976-78). E-mail: gisi@isl.is.

JÓNSDÓTTIR, THÓRGUNNUR, writer, poet; b. Reykjavik, Iceland, Dec. 22, 1948; d. Jón Steingrimsson and Thórgunnur Ársaelsdóttir; m. Carl Jeffrey Fehlandt (div. 1985); m. Thórarinn Sveinbjörnsson; 1 child, Matthias. Grad., Menntaskólinn á Akureyri, 1969; postgrad., U. Iceland, 1973-74. Translator Joint Publs. Research Service, Arlington, Va., 1976-82; freelance creative writer, translator, 1982—. Contbr. poetry Great Poems of Western World, 1980, World's Great Contemporary Poems, 1981, Am. Poetry Anthology, 1987, The Wheel of Time, 1997. Avocations: swimming, Tai Chi Chih, reading, hiking.

JONSEN, RICHARD WILIAM, retired educational administrator; b. San Francisco, Mar. 29, 1934; s. Albert Rupert and Helen Catherine (Sweigert) J.; m. Ann Margaret Parsons, Nov. 20, 1955; children: Marie Wood, Eric, Gregory, Stephen, Matthew. BA, U. Santa Clara, 1955; MA, San Jose (Calif.) State U., 1970; PhD, Stanford U., 1973. Pub.'s rep. Hearst Advt. Service, San Francisco, 1955-58; alumni dir. U. Santa Clara, Calif., 1958-70; dir. admissions, asst. dean. Sch. Edn., asst. prof. Syracuse (N.Y.) U., 1972-76; project dir. Edn. Commn. States, Denver, 1976-77; project dir. Western Interstate Commn. Higher Edn., Boulder, Colo., 1977-79, dep. dir., 1979-90, exec. dir., 1990-99; ret., 1999; vis. prof. U. Tamaulipas, Mex., 1996, 97; cons. Consortium for N.Am. Higher Edn. Collaboration. Author: State Policy and Independent Higher Education, 1975, Small Liberal Arts Colleges, 1978, Lifelong Learning: State Policies, 1978, The Environmental context for Postsecondary Education, 1986; editor: Higher Education Policies in the Information Age, 1987. Roman Catholic. E-mail: dickjonsen@uswest.net. Home: 363 Troon Ct Louisville CO 80027-9592

JONSSON, ERNST OSSIAN, economics educator, researcher; b. Härnösand, Västernorrland, Sweden, Nov. 15, 1935; s. Lorentz Isidor and Elin Elisabeth (Hedstrom) J.; m. Ulla Bergheden; children: Michael, Jonas, Erika. B in Pub. Adminstrn., Stockholm Sch. Social Work, Sweden, 1960; B in Econs., Stockholm Sch. Econs., Sweden, 1962, Licentiate in Econs., 1964, D in Econs., 1972. Assoc. prof. bus. adminstrn. Stockholm U., 1973-87, prof. econs. in pub. adminstrn., 1988—; vis. prof. econs. Glasgow Caledonian U., Scotland, 1992; dir. Inst. Local Govt. Econs. Stockholm U., 1989—. Author: Effects of Competition Within Health Care, 1996; contbr. articles to profl. jours. Recipient award 3M/Nat. Soc. Road Safety, 1983. Avocations: antiques, climbing, classical music, art. Home: Bellmansgatan 6, 11820 Stockholm Sweden Office: Stockholm U, Universitetsvägen 10, 106 91 Stockholm Sweden

JONSSON, HELGI See JOHANNES, HELGI

JONSSON, LARS OLAV, microbiologist, infectious disease physician; b. Råneå, Sweden, June 7, 1948; s. Karl and Marta (Wikberg) J. BA, U. Gothenburg, Sweden, 1971, B in Medicine, 1978, MD, 1984, cert. for infectious diseases, 1988, cert. for microbiology, 1996. Physician, dept. infectious diseases Borås (Sweden) Lasarett, 1984-94; mgr. Clin. Microbiology, Borås, Sweden, 1994—. Office: Clinical Microbiology, Borås Lasarett, 501 82 Borås Sweden

JONSSON, MARITA LAILA, research administrator; b. Linkoping, Sweden, Mar. 12, 1943; d. Bror George and Maria Matilda (Sjoo) Ericsson; m. Jon Anders Jonsson, Oct. 12, 1973; children: Gustav, Nanna, Helga, Agnes. MA, U. Uppsala, 1967, PhD, 1976. Antiquarian Cen. Bd. Antiquities, Stockholm, 1975-79, Regional Mus. Visby, Sweden, 1979-85; dir. culture & environ. County of Gotland, Sweden, 1985-95; project leader Sesam Open Mus. Collections Dept. of Culture, 1995-97, head rsch., 1998—; Chmn. Home and Sch., Visby; chmn. Acad. Art, Visby. Author: Inizi di Restauro, 1979, Vagen Till Kulturen, 1987, Medieval Week in Gotland, 1990, (children's book) Visit William Shakespeare, 1993, Venice, 1994, Från Prästgårdar till Strandbodar Gotlandska hus och rum om hus på Gotland, 1996, Handens Verk, 1998, Stockholms Själ, 1998, Stockholm's Soul, 1999, Venice, 2000, Visty, ett hordiskt världsarv, 2000. Active Culture Tourism Sweden, 1992—; mem. h.s. bd. edn., Gotland, 1992; bd. dirs. Pub. Rels. Mus., Sweden, 1992. Mem. Orgn. Regional Antiquarians (chmn.), Royal U. Coll. Fine Arts (chmn. bd. 1998—). Avocations: art, architecture, nature, reading. Home: Klosterbrunnsgatan 6, Visby 62156, Sweden Office: Lansstyrelsen, Visby 62185, Sweden

JONSSON, NILS INGE EINAR, academic administrator; b. Stockholm, Nov. 7, 1928; s. Einar and Elsa (Adolfsson) J.; m. Ritva Jacobsson, April 1, 1953 (div. 1982); children: Mikaela, Magdalena, Gabriel, Matilda; m. Kerstin Fredga, Aug. 11, 1990. BA, Stockholm U., 1953, PhD, 1961. Rsch. fellow Swedish Rsch. Coun. Humanities, Stockholm, 1968-73, sec. gen., 1987-88; asst. prof. Stockholm U., 1961-68, prof. comparative lit., 1973-94, dean faculty of arts, 1978-84, prorector, 1984-88, pres., 1988-94; chmn. Rsch. Coun. Higher Edn., Stockholm, 1988-93; mem. Swedish Govt.'s Adv. Bd. Rsch., Stockholm, 1983-85. Author: Swedenborgs De Cultu et Amore Dei, 1961, Swedenborgs Korrespondenslära, 1969, Emanuel Swedenborg (N.Y.), 1971, I symbolens hus, 1983, Den sköna lögnen 1986, Humanistiskt credo, 1988, Visionary Scientist, rev. edit., 1999. Chmn. Magnus Bergvall's Found., Stockholm, 1983—; mem. Henrik Granholm's Found., Stockholm, 1988—, chmn., 1997—; mem. Natur & Kultur Pubs., Stockholm, 1990-98, chmn., 1995-98; mem. Marianne and Marcus Wallenberg Found., Stockholm, 1991—; chmn. The Swedish Nat. Bank's Tercentenary Found., 1992-98, Def. Coll., 1994—, The Baltic Rsch. Found., 1997-99; mem. Wenner-Gren Rsch. Found., 1997—; chmn. Stockholm Cultural Capital Europe 1998, 1997-99. Recipient Hirsch's prize Swedish Acad., 1970, Schück's prize, 1987, Kellgren's prize, 1995. Mem. Swedish Acad. Letters, History and Antiquities (Warburg's prize 1963, pres. 1994—), Swedish Acad. Sci., Samfundet De Nio, Academia Europaea. Avocations: music, skiing. Office: Stockholm U, S-106 91 Stockholm Sweden

JONSSON, OLOF KNUT, urologist; b. Torsby, Varmland, Sweden, May 12, 1941; s. Knut Theodor and Doris Elisabeth Jonsson; m. Marianne Ingrid Hulten, Oct. 25, 1969; children: Ann, Martin, Karin. PhD of Physiology, U. Göteborg, 1972, MD, 1972, PhD of Surgery, 1980, PhD of Urology, 1986. Gen. surgeon Sahlgrenska Hosp., Göteborg, Sweden, 1972-84; sr. urologist Sahlgrenska Hosp., Göteborg, 1984—. Contbr. articles to profl. jours. Home: Gertruds Gata 25, 42167 Västra Frolunoa Sweden Office: Dept Urology, Sahlgrenska Hosp, 41345 Göteborg Sweden

JÖNSSON, STEN ARNE, business administration educator; b. Mariestad, Sweden, Dec. 12, 1940; s. Thure and Inga Jönsson; m. Bozena Plukajtys, June 27, 1965; children: Richard, Henrik. M Social Scis., U. Gothenburg, Sweden, 1964, Lic in Econs., 1968, D Econs., 1971; PhD (hon.), U. Turku, 1995. Asst. prof. bus. adminstrn. U. Gothenburg Sch. Econs., 1968-74, assoc. prof., 1974-76; prof. Sch. Econs., Gothenburg, 1976—; com. mem. Jan Wallander's Found. for Social Rsch., Stockholm, 1985-99, Ctr. for Rsch. on European Acctg., Brussels, 1991-97. Author: Accounting Regulation and Elite Structures, 1988; editor-in-chief Scandinavian Jour. Mgmt., 1988—. Recipient prize for rsch. accomplishment Gothenburg Stock Exch. Assn., 1992. Mem. Sci. and Lit. Soc. (Gothenburg). Avocation: mountain climbing. Office: Sch Econs, Vasagatan 3, S-411 24 Gothenburg Sweden

JOOMMAL, ALI SARFARAZ KHAN, retired religious studies educator; b. Durban, South Africa, May 9, 1929; s. Goolam Mohammed Khan and Amina (Bakash) J.; m. Fatima Seedat, Oct. 15, 1952 (dec. May, 1997); 1 child. BA, U. Witwatersrand, Johannesburg, South Africa, 1953. Lectr. Damelin Coll., Johannesburg, 1955-94; ret. Damelin Coll., 1994. Author, editor: The Path of Islam, 1960, The Bible: Word of God or Word of Man?, 1974; editor (quar. jour.) Al-Balaagh, 1978. Active social, charitable works, Johannesburg, 1978—. Avocations: philately, tennis, table tennis, gardening, jogging. Home: 28 Lark St Ext 1, Lenasia 1827, South Africa Office: Al-Balaagh, PO Box 1925, Lenasia 1820, South Africa

JOONDEPH, MARCIA, diplomat; b. N.Y.C., Mar. 3, 1930; d. Isadore Horowitz and Bess Benenson Starfield; m. Norman H. Joondeph; children: Wendy, Michael. BA, Columbia U., 1952. Office mgr. dr.'s office Stamford, Conn., 1974-84; sculptor Pietra Santa, Italy, 1991; UN del. Promoting Enduring Peace, Milford, Conn., 1991—; bd. dirs., chmn. exec. bd. dirs., v.p., v.p. fin. com. Promoting Enduring Peace, Milford, 1991—. Exhibited in several juried shows, 1991—. Bd. dirs. Peace Action Internat., Geneva, 1992—; del. 4th World Conf. on Women in Beijing, China; mem. disarmament com. UN-Non-Govtl. Orgns. Avocations: sculpting, tennis, bridge, music. Home: 3250 S Ocean Blvd # 407 South Palm Beach FL 33480-5604

JOOS, FELIPE MIGUEL, mechanical engineer, researcher; b. Montevideo, Uruguay, Sept. 4, 1952; came to U.S., 1973; s. Carlos Jose and Alma Elena Joos; m. Caroline Rose Crocker, Aug. 28, 1982 (div.); children: Carolina Lucia, Catrina Aneliese, Celina Maria. BS in Applied Sci. and Engring., Calif. Inst. Tech., 1976; MSME, MIT, 1978, PhDME, 1982. Cert. engr., Uruguay. Engr. Ingenieros Consultores Latinoamericanos Limitada, Montevideo, Uruguay, 1978-79; mech. engr. research and devel. div. Gen. Electric Corp., Schenectady, N.Y., 1982-85; project engr. Creare, Inc., Hanover, N.H., 1985-87; tech. assoc. Eastman Kodak Co., Rochester, N.Y., 1987—; indsl. fellow Ctr. for Interfacial Engring., U. Minn., Mpls., 1991-92. Contbr. articles to profl. jours.; presenter at internat. symposium and conf. in field; patentee in field. Mem. ASME, Internat. Soc. Coating Sci. and Tech. (tech. session chair 1994, 98), Soc. Hispanic Profl. Engrs. (award 1993, v.p. 1989-90, treas. 1990-92, treas. Ea. Tech. and Career conf. 1991), Tau Beta Pi. Avocation: scuba diving. Home: 75 Wood Creek Dr Pittsford NY 14534-4415 Office: Eastman Kodak Co Kodak Park Rochester NY 14652-0001 Address: Le Trefle, Chemin De Thiere, 1272 Genolier Switzerland

JOOS, ULRICH KLAUS, oral and maxillofacial surgeon, educator; b. Wangen, Germany, Dec. 26, 1947; s. Alois and Alice (Vollmer) J.; m. Regine Joos. DDS, U. Freiburg, Germany, 1972, MD, 1974, DSc, 1978; DSc, U. Freiburg, Germany, 1992; DSc (hon.), U. Budapest, Hungary, 1994. Diplomate German Bd. Maxillofacial Surgery, Bd. Plastic and Reconstructive Surgery. Assoc. prof. U. Nantes, France, 1979-80; assoc. prof. U. Freiburg, 1980-83, prof., 1983-92; chmn., prof. U. Muenster, Germany, 1992—; v.p. German Coun. Cleft, Lip and Palate. Contbr. numerous articles to internat. profl. textbooks. Med. Adv. Orgn. Parents of Children with Congenital Craniofacial Malformations. Mem. European Assn. Cranio-Maxillofacial Surgery (pres. 2000—); hon. mem. French, Hungarian and Chile Cranio-Maxillofacial Surgery Assns. Roman Catholic. Address: Waldeyerstrasse 30, 48129 Münster Germany

JOOSTE, JOHANNA ALIDA, business executive; b. Pretoria, Gauteng, South Africa, Aug. 24, 1955; d. Gert Petrus and Engela Levina (Kruger) Eloff; m. Lorenz Dawid Jooste (div. Oct. 1999); children: Christian, Cornelius. B in Commerce, UNISA, South Africa, 1995. DP mgr. AUBOB, South Africa, 1975-86; pvt. practice farming South Africa, 1986-89; analyst programmer Momentum, South Africa, 1990-91; info. tech. mgr. Sterns Jewellers, South Africa, 1991-95; account dir. EDS (SA) Pty. Ltd., South Africa, 1995—. Avocations: playing keyboards, bass guitar and saxophone, singing. Office: EDS SA Pty Ltd, Private Bag X4, Sunninghill 2157, South Africa

JOOSUB, EBRAHAM HAJEE, executive; b. Pretoria, South Africa, Aug. 8, 1921; s. Mohamed Hajee and Homera Hajee (Aboobaker) J.; m. Hava Carrim, May 17, 1941 (dec. Oct. 1984); 2 children: m. Roshan Thaianall Pillay, Dec. 6, 1957; 1 child. D of Commerce, U. Durban, South Africa, 1981. Mng. dir., chmn. M H Joosub Group Cos., Pretoria, South Africa, 1983—; dir. M H Joosub & Sons., Associated Textiles, Amjo Distbrs., Ne WNat. Assurance Co., Ltd. Author: Bitterness Towards Indiana, 1958, South African Adventure Story, 1983. Chmn. Laudium Local Coun., South Africa, 1963; v.p. South African Found., Johannesburg, 1993; trustee World Wild Life Fund, Cape Town, South Africa, 1973, green Trust, johannesburg,

1992; mem. exec. coun. U. Durban-Westville, 1964-84. Recipient Indian Bus. Man's award, 1968. Avocations: fishing, bird watching, stamp collecting, art collection. Office: M H Joosub Group, PO Box 40, Pretoria 0001, South Africa

JOPPEN-HELLWIG, SANDRA, linguist, researcher; b. Krefeld, Germany, Jan. 22, 1965; d. Werner Wilhelm and Ingeborg Maria (Fercho) Joppen; m. Joerg Olaf Hellwig, June 4, 1994; children: Naomi, Lennart. MA, Heinrich-Heine-U., Duesseldorf, Germany, 1991; Dr.phil., Heinrich-Heine-U., Duesseldorf, 2000. Rsch. asst. Heinrich-Heine-U., 1991—. Author: Causatives in Basque, 1993, Case Alternation and Its Conceptual Basis, 1995, Structural Arguments with Semantic Case: The Case of Causees and Recipients in 4-Place Verbs, 1999, Verbclasses and Argument Linking-Non-Canonical Arguments, Expletives, and 4-Place Causatives in Ergative Versus Accusative Languages, 2000; co-author: Argument Linking in Basque, 1994, The Representation of Argument Linking in a Unification Based Formalism, 1996, First Steps in the Acquistion of German Phonology, 1998. Scholar German Acad. Exch. Svc., 1990. Mem. Deutsche Gesellschaft fuer Sprachwissenschaft. Office: HH-Uni Sprachwiss, Universitaetsstr 1, 40225 Düsseldorf Germany

JORDAAN, BAREND DANIEL, management educator; b. Beaufort West, South Africa, Mar. 2, 1954; s. Barend Daniel and Cecilia (Spies) J.; m. Marietjie Van der Ryst, Dec. 15, 1979; children: Daniel, Annelize. B of Commerce, U. Pt. Elizabeth, 1975, B of Commerce with honors, 1979, M of Commerce, 1987. Tchr. H.S. Framesby, South Africa, 1977-79; lectr. U. Ft. Hare, South Africa, 1979-91; sr. lectr. U. Ft. Hare, 1992, head of dept., 1993—. Contbr. articles to profl. jours. Sgt. South African Infantry, 1981-86. Fellow So. Africa Inst. Indsl. Engrs.; mem. Nat. Productivity Inst., So. Africa Inst. for Mgmt. Scientists. Nat. Party. Dutch Reform Ch. Avocations: music, singing. Home: 16 Pedlar St, Fort Beaufort 5720, South Africa Office: U of Fort Hare, 5700 Alice 5700, South Africa

JORDAN, AMOS AZARIAH, JR., foreign affairs educator, retired army officer; b. Twin Falls, Idaho, Feb. 11, 1922; s. Amos Azariah and Olive (Fisher) J.; m. MarDeane Carver, June 5, 1946; children: Peggy Jordan Hughes, Diana Jordan Paxton, Keith, David, Linda Jordan Mabey, Kent. BS, U.S. Mil. Acad., 1946; BA, Oxford U., Eng., 1950, MA, 1955; PhD, Columbia U., 1961. Commd. 2d lt. U.S. Army, 1946, advanced through grades to brig. gen., 1972; instr. U.S. Mil. Acad., 1950-53, prof. social scis., 1955-72; arty. battery comdr. U.S. Army, Korea, 1954-55; asst. S-3 7th Divsn. Arty. Korea, 1955; adviser econ. and fiscal policy U.S. Econ. Mission to Korea, 1955; ret. U.S. Army, 1972; dir. Aspen Inst., 1972-74; prin. dep. asst. sec. for internat. security affairs Dept. Def., Washington, 1974-76; dep. undersec. and acting undersec. for security assistance Dept. State, Washington, 1976-77; with Ctr. for Strategic and Internat. Studies, Washington, 1977-94, pres, chief exec. officer, 1983-88, vice chmn., 1988-94; pres. Pacific Forum Ctr. for Strategic and Internat. Studies, Honolulu, 1990-94; sr. adviser CSIS, 1994—; counselor Pacific Forum, 1994—; mem. staff Pres.'s Com. to Study Fgn. Assistance Program, 1959; staff dir. Adv. Com. to Sec. Def. on Non-Mil. Instrn., 1962; spl. polit. advisor to U.S. amb. to India, 1963-64; cons. NSC, 1979; mem. Nat. Com. on Security and Econ. Assistance, 1983; Henry Kissinger rsch. chair in nat. security policy CSIS, 1988-92; mem. Pres.'s Intelligence Oversight Bd., 1989-93; internat. co-chmn. Coun. on Sec. Coop. in the Asia Pacific, 1993-96, chmn. U.S. com., 1993-98; co-chmn. Korean-Am. Wisemen Coun., 1991-98; Asia area adminstr. Latter Day Saint Charities, 1998-99; mem. bd. dirs. Pacific Forum, Ctr. for Strategic and Internat. Studies. Author: Foreign Aid and the Defense of Southeast Asia, 1962, Issues of National Security in the 1970's, 1967; co-author: American National Security Policy and Process, 1981, 5th edit., 1999; contbr. chpts. to books and articles to profl. jours. Decorated D.S.M., Legion of Merit with oak leaf cluster, Disting. Civilian Svc. medal Dept. Def. Mem. Coun. Fgn. Rels., Assn. Am. Rhodes Scholars, Pacific Coun. Internat. Policy, Bretton Woods Com. Office: Pacific Forum CSIS Pauahi Tower 1001 Bishop St Ste 1150 Honolulu HI 96813-3407

JORDAN, ANDRE FRANCISCO, real estate developer; b. Lwow, Poland, Sept. 10, 1933; s. Henryk A. Spitzman and Faustyna J. (Scherman) J.; m. Princess Monica von Lichtenstein; m. Anna Milcetic; children: Gilberto Frederico, Constantino Pedro, Sarah Jordan do Botelho. Grad. high sch., Rio de Janeiro, 1952. Exec. Jordan Group, Rio de Janeiro, 1952-60, Buenos Aires, 1960-66; exec. Levitt & Sons, Lake Success, N.Y., 1967-69; pres. Planal S.A., Quinta do Lago, Portugal, 1971-87; mng. dir. Bovis Abroad Ltd., London, 1988-89, La Manga Club, Murcia, Spain, 1988-89; pres. Invesplano S.A., Lisbon, 1986—, Planbelas S.A., Lisbon, 1990—, Monte da Quinta Ltd., Quinta do Lago, 1994—, Vilar do Golfe Ltd., Quinta do Lago, 1994—; pres. Cofipsa Sociedade de Gestão de ParticipaÃões Sociais, 1996—, Lusotur-Vilamoura, Algarve, 1996—; v.p. global adv. coun. Chase Manhattan Pvt. Bank. Contbr. articles to Portuguese and Brazilian press. Founder Algarve (Portugal) Internat. Music Festival, 1983-84; v.p. Nova Filarmonica Portuguesa, Lisbon, 1989-93; chmn. Premio Infante D. Henrique, Portugal, 1993—, European Cmty. Chamber Orch., 1989—; hon. consul of Brazil in the Algarve, 1986—; mem. World Travel and Tourism Coun. Decorated Order of Tamandare, comdr. Order of Rio Branco (Brazil); recipient Gold Medal of Merit,, Portuguese Tourism, 1995, Fellow Duke of Edinburgh's award; named Comdr. of Order of Merit, Portugal. Mem. Assn. Real Estate Developers (chmn. accounts com. 1992—), Quinta do Lago Golf Club (pres. 1984-87), Lisbon Sports Club, Duke of Edinburgh's Award Fellowship. Office: InvesPlano SA, Av Marques de Tomar 35, 1000 Lisbon Portugal

JORDAN, BERNICE BELL, retired elementary education educator; b. Calvert, Tex.; d. Ocie Wade and Nannie B. (Westbrook) Bell; m. William B. Jordan, Sept. 28, 1956; children: Beverly, Terrence, Keith Jordan. BA, San Jose State Coll., 1959, MA, 1985; student, Prairie View A and M, Tex. Western Coll. Cert. elem. edn., fine arts, multi-cultural tchr., specially designed acad. instrn. in English. Writer curriculum guide, fine arts Alum Rock Union Elem. Sch. Dist., San Jose, Calif.; writer sch. plan Goss Elem.; elem. tchr. Alum Rock Union Elem. Sch. Dist., San Jose; adv. com., tchr.-cons. San Jose Area Writing Project, San Jose U., 1992—. Mem. ASCD, NEA, Alum Rock Edn. Assn., Calif. Tchrs. Assn., Calif. Reading Assn., Calif. Elem. Edn. Assn., Santa Clara County Reading Coun., Alpha Delta Kappa, Delta Kappa Gamma. Home: 3282 Fronda Dr San Jose CA 95148-2015

JORDAN, BRYCE, retired university president; b. Clovis, N.Mex., Sept. 22, 1924; s. W. Joseph and Kittie (Cole) J.; m. Patricia Jonelle Thornberry, June 10, 1948, (div.); children: Julia Cole, Christopher Joseph. Student, Hardin-Simmons U., 1941-42; MusB, U. Tex., 1948, MusM, 1949; PhD, U. N.C., 1956; LLD, Juniata Coll., 1985, Milliken U., 1990. Asst. prof. music Hardin-Simmons U., 1949-51; from asst. prof. to prof. music U. Md., 1954-63; prof. music, chmn. dept. U. Ky., 1963-65, U. Tex., 1965-68; v.p. student affairs U. Tex., Austin, 1968-70, pres. ad interim, 1970-71; pres. U. Tex., Dallas, 1971-81; exec. vice chancellor for acad. affairs U. Tex. System, 1981-83; pres. Pa. State U., 1983-90; mem. faculty Salzburg (Austria) Seminar Am. Studies, 1960, 62, 98; occasional lectr. Fgn. Svc. Inst., Dept. State, 1962-63; mem. Yale Coun. on Music, 1971-73, Nat. Commn. on Higher Edn. Issues, 1982-83. Author: (with Homer Ulrich) Student Manual for Music: A Design for Listening, 1957, Designed for Listening, 1962, also articles, revs.; assoc. editor: Coll. Music Symposium, 1961-66. Bd. dirs. Dallas Grand Opera Assn., 1973-75, Pa. Econ. Devel. Ptnrship, 1987-90; trustee St. Marks Sch. Tex., 1973-81, Dallas Symphony Assn., 1972-81, Presbyn. Hosp., Dallas, 1976-83; v.p. Dallas Civic Music Assn., 1978-79, pres., 1979-80, exec. com. 1980-81; bd. dirs. Dallas County chpt. ARC, 1976-79; div. chmn. United Way of Met. Dallas, 1979; Pa. state chmn. Am. Heart Assn., 1983-84; trustee Com. on Econ. Devel. 1988-90; mem. adv. bd. comml. programs NASA, 1988-90; nat. chmn. higher edn. U.S. Treasury Savs. Bond Programs, 1988-89, 89-90; presiding elder Presbyn. Ch.; chmn. Austin Lyric Opera, 1991-94; mem. vis. com. Eastman Sch. Music U. Rochester, 1991-94; chmn. fine arts adv. coun. U. Tex., Austin, 1994-96; chmn. adv. bd. U. Tex. Press, 1997-99. Recipient Hon. Alumni award Pa. State U., 1987, medal, 1990, Doty medal U. Tex., 1996; named Disting. Alumnus, U. N.C., 1985, Hardin-Simmons U., 1987, U. Tex., Austin, 1991. Mem. Coll. Music Soc. (v.p. 1963-65, coun. mem. 1968-70), Am. Musicol. Soc. (chmn. greater Washington chpt. 1958-60), Music Educators Nat. Conf. (pres. Md. br. 1963), Music Tchrs. Nat. Assn., Philos. Soc. Tex., Dallas C. of C. (dir. 1979-82), So. Assn. Colls. and Schs. (commn. on colls. 1981-83), Pa. Assn. Colls. and Univs. (chmn. 1988-89), Phi Kappa Phi, Pi Kappa Lambda, Phi Mu Alpha, Golden Key. Home: 7801 Comfort Cove Austin TX 78731-1471

JORDAN, CHARLYN LASKEY, computer systems and information executive; b. Grand Rapids, Mich., Nov. 25, 1948; d. Donald and Helen Laskey; m. Patrick Michael Jordan, Sept. 1, 1984. BA, Mich. State U., 1972. Cert. tchr., tchr. vocat. edn., Mich., N.J. Mgr. typography Touche Ross & Co., N.Y.C., 1977-79; founder, owner, pres. Laskey Word Processing, Inc., N.Y.C., 1979-85; mgr. software quality assurance Wang Labs., 1985-91; cons., spkr. quality control, info. tech., program mgmt., 1991—. Mem. Wang Labs. Photocomposition Users Group (v.p.), Pi Omega Pi. Office: 14 Schoolhouse Rd Amherst NH 03031-1601

JORDAN, DEIRDRE FRANCES, university chancellor; b. Loxton, Australia, Sept. 18, 1926; d. Clement John and Helena Frances (Roberts) J. BA, U. Adelaide, South Australia, 1947, diploma in Edn., 1948, MEd, 1967; MA in Sociology, U. London, England, 1974; PhD, U. London, 1983; HonDLitt, Flinders U. South Australia, 1986. Headmistress St. Aloysius Coll., 1954-68; sr. lectr. dept. edn. U. Adelaide, 1968-88, dep. chmn., 1975-82, acting chmn., 1979, chmn., 1982-84; chancellor Flinders U. South Australia, Adelaide, 1988—; ednl. cons., 1988—; found. mem. coun. Flinders U., 1966—, chmn. com. to inquire into access for aboriginal students, 1985—; internat. advisor Madinat Al-Hikmat, Karachi, 1995—. Contbr. articles to profl. jours. Pres. Flinders U. Found., 1991—; trustee SA Bus. Vision 2010, 1996—; patron Australian Nat. Youth Performing Arts Group, 1997—, Notre Dame Inst. Edn., Karachi, Pakistan, 1992—; trustee St. Francies Xavier's Sem., 1993—; mem. governing bd. Notre Dame Inst. Edn., Karachi, 1991—; chair bd. govs. Mercedes Coll., 1994—; dir. South Australian Lang. Ctr., 1994—; hon. life mem. Flin U of the 3rd Age; vice patron Flin U. Choral Soc., 1993—. Named Companion of Order of Australia, 1989, Mem. Brit. Empire, 1969, Zonta Woman of Yr. 1989, Pub. Sector Exec. Woman of Yr. Women's Network Australia, 1998; fellow Australian Coll. Edn., 1970. Mem. Flinders U. Alumni Assn. (pres. 1991—). Roman Catholic. Avocations: bush walking, camping, reading, theatre. Office: Flinders U South Australia, Sturt Rd, Bedford Park 5042, Australia

JORDAN, JAMES LOWELL, educator, writer; b. Mpls.; s. Lowell Stephen Jordan and Rose Mary Servatius; m. Deovina Bicarme Nasis, July 25, 1992. BA, U. Calif., Riverside, 1976; grad. cert. in administrn., U. Calif., 1982; M in Adminstrn., U. Calif., Riverside, 1983; cert. mfg. engring., U. Calif., L.A., 1990; PhD, Iowa State U., 1981, U. Iowa, 1987. Asst. prof. Ctrl. Wash. U., 1986-94, dir. ungergrad. bus. program, 1986-87; lectr. U. Calif., Riverside, 1988-92; prof. So. Calif. U., 1994—; prof. U. Lethbridge, Can., 1994—, pres. Jordan Rsch. Inst., 1994—. Reviewer, contbr. articles to profl. publs.; author: sci. and rel. books.

JORDAN, JAMES WALLACE, JR., trade association administrator; b. Orlando, Fla., Dec. 25, 1952; s. James and Catherine (Douvres) J.; m. Lynne Miller, Oct. 8, 1977; children: Brian, Scott. BBA, U. Notre Dame, 1974. Field svc. rep. Florists Transworld Delivery Assn., Southfield, Mich., 1974-78; mgr. mem. rels. Florists Transworld Delivery Assn., Southfield, 1978-80, dir. Mercury Network, 1980-85, dir. spl. svcs., 1985-87, group dir. mem. svcs., 1987-93; mng. exec. Florists Transworld Delivery Assn., Livonia, Mich., 1993—. Contbr. Sorin Soc., 1990—; treas., troop leader Cub Scout pack 755, 1981-84; coach Northville Travel baseball team, 1985-91; mem. Cath. Central Dad's Club, 1999—. Mem. Notre Dame Club of Detroit. Republican. Roman Catholic. Avocations: golf, reading. E-mail: jjordan@ftdassociation.org. Home: 574 Morgan Cir Northville MI 48167-2725 Office: FTD Assn 33031 Schoolcraft Rd Livonia MI 48150-1618

JORDAN, JOSEPH ANTHONY, writer, editor, retired academic administrator; b. N.Y.C., Mar. 31, 1932; s. William Henry Jordan and Anna O'Connor; m. Erica Judith Diem, May 7, 1960. AA, SUNY, Albany, 1981. Asst. mgr. Am. Savs. BAnk, N.Y.C., 1953-63; stock clk. Bergen Pines County Hosp., Hackensack, N.J., 1963-64; libr. The Record, Hackensack, 1964-67; proofreader West Shore Pub., Teaneck, N.J., 1967-68, Passaic (N.J.) Herald News, 1968-69; editor Maritime Reporter & Engring. News, N.Y.C., 1969, Discount Store News, N.Y.C., 1969-75, Avant-Garde Media, N.Y.C., 1975; fin. aid officer Phoenix Coll., 1975-88; ret., 1988. Author: Lebhar-Friedman Manual of Style and English Usage, 1973; editor (cmty. newspaper) Black Canyon City (Ariz.) Cmty. Assn., 1977, (newsletter) Homeowners and Taxpayers Assn., Black Canyon City, 1978; contbr. articles, book revs., poetry and short stories to publs. Chmn. Meals on Wheels Survival, Black Canyon City, 1999. Sgt. 1st class N.Y. Nat. Guard, 1948-58. Recipient Canyon Culture Guild Svc. award Canyon Culture Guild, Black Canyon City, 1997. Mem. ACLU, Ariz. Civil Liberties Union, Ariz. Assn. Ret. Persons, Black Canyon Cmty. Libr. Roman Catholic. Avocations: writing, reading, classical music.

JORDAN, JUDITH VICTORIA, clinical psychologist, educator; b. Milw., July 28, 1943; d. Claus and Charlotte (Backus) J.; m. William M. Redpath, Aug. 11, 1973. AB, Brown U., 1965; MA, Harvard U., 1968, PhD, 1973. Diplomate Am. Bd. Profl. Psychology. Psychologist Human Relations Service, Wellesley, Mass., 1971-73; assoc. psychologist McLean Hosp., Belmont, Mass., 1978-93, psychologist, 1993—, dir. women's studies program, 1988—, dir. tng. in psychology, 1991, dir. Women's Treatment Network, 1992—; vis. scholar Stone Ctr. Wellesley Coll., 1985—; asst. prof. psychiatry Harvard Med. Sch., 1988—; co-dir. Jean Baker Miller Tng. Inst., Wellesley Coll. 1998; adv. bd Fox TV Network, Women First healthcare., 1998; disting. prof. Menninger Clinic, 1999. Author: Empathy and Self Boundries, 1984, Women's Growth in Connection, 1991, (with others) The Self in Relation, 1986; editor, author: Relational Self in Women; editor: Women's Growth in Diversity, 1997. Fellow Am. Psychol. Assn.; mem. Mass. Psychol. Assn. (bd. dirs. 1983-85, Career Achievement award for outstanding contbns. to advancement of psychology as a sci. and a profession), Phi Beta Kappa. Office: McLean Hosp 114 Waltham St Lexington MA 02421-5415

JORDAN, MARCUS, insurance consultant; b. Bridgetown, St. Michael, Barbados, Mar. 2, 1929; s. Marcus Eglinton and Millicent (Payne) J.; m. Grace Enid Tudor, Sept. 10, 1960; children: David de Lambert, Alies Irene. Student, Harrison Coll.; BA, U. London, 1949. cert. life ins. Subeditor Barbados Advocate; sch. tchr. Combermere H.S.; life underwriter Mfrs. Life Ins. Co., Barbados, branch mgr.; mng. dir. Wildey Shopping Plz. Ltd., Barbados, Lamberts Ltd., Bank of Nova Scotia-Internat. Barbados Ltd. Former chmn. Barbados Tourist Bd.; pres. Jr. Chamber of Commerce; founding mem. Kiwanis Club; hon. consul of Cyprus to Barbados; justice of the peace Govt. Barbados; pres. Senate of Barbados. Mem. Dist. Grand Lodge Barbados S.C. (treas.), Lodge Pelican 1750 S.C. (master). Mem. Dem. Labour Party. Methodist. Avocations: golf, bridge, classical music, drama. Office: Lamberts Ltd, Wildey Shopping Plz, Saint Michael Barbados

JORDAN, MICHAEL A.P. (SPANKY JORDAN), elementary and secondary education educator; b. Palmerton, Pa., July 28, 1966; s. Anthony and Lillian (Johnson) J.; m. Kelly J. Heimbach, July 7, 1984 (div. July 1997); children: Michael II, Sydni; m. Christine N. Renaldi, July 1997; 1 child, Kasey. BS, Lehigh U., 1991, MEd, 1993; cert. adminstrn ., Eastroudsburg U., 1998; postgrad., Pa. State U. Social studies tchr. Saucon Valley Sch. Dist., 1993-94, East Stroudsburg Area Sch. Dist., 1994-98; asst. prin. Susquehanna Twp. Sch. Dist., 1998-99; prin. Ctrl. Dauphin Sch. Dist., Harrisburg, Pa., 1999—. Mem. NEA, Pa. State Edn. Assn. Democrat. Roman Catholic. Avocations: wrestling, weightlifting, reading, computers. Home: 5828 Barnsley Dr Harrisburg PA 17111-4756 Office: East Stroudsburg Area Sch Dist N Courtland St East Stroudsburg PA 18301-8549

JORDAN, MICHAEL JEFFREY, professional sports team executive, retired professional basketball player, retired baseball player; b. Bklyn., Feb. 17, 1963; s. James and Deloris Jordan; m. Juanita Vanoy, Sept., 1989; children: Jeffrey Michael, Marcus James, Jasmine. Student, U. N.C., 1981-84. Basketball player Chicago Bulls, 1984-93, 95-98; ret., 1998; baseball player Chicago White Sox AA Team, 1994-95; pres. basketball ops. Washington Wizards, 1999—; mem. NCAA Championship Team, 1982, U.S. Olympic Team (received Gold Medal), 1984, 92; holder record for most points in an NBA playoff game with 63. Author: RareAir: Michael on Michael, 1993. Recipient Naismith award, 1984, Wooden award, 1984, Rookie of Yr. award, NBA, 1985, IBM award, 1985, 89, Schick Pivotal Player award, 1985, 89; named Seagram's NBA Player of Yr., 1987, Slam-Dunk Championship winner, 1987, 88; named to Sporting News All-Am. first team, 1983-84, NBA All-Star team, 1985-93, 96-98, All NBA First Team, 1987-93, 96-98, NBA All-Def. Team, 1988-93, 96-98, NBA All-Star Game Most Valuable Player, 1988, 96, 98, NBA Def. Player of Yr., 1988, NBA Most Valuable Player, 1988, 91, 92, 96-98, NBA Finals MVP 1991-93, 96-98; mem. NBA championship team, 1991-93, 96-98. Mem. NCAA divsn. 1 championship team, 1982; NBA Scoring Leader, 1986-93, 96-98. Office: Washington Wizards 718 7th St NW Washington DC 20001-3716

JORDAN, NEIL PATRICK, film director; b. County Sligo, Ireland, Feb. 25, 1950. BA, Univ. Coll., Dublin, Ireland, 1968. Dir. feature films Angel, 1982, Company of Wolves, 1984, Mona Lisa, 1986 (nomiated Golden Globe Best Screenplay-Motion Picture 1987, nominated BAFTA Film awards Best Direction, Best Film, Best Original Screenplay 1987), High Spirits, 1988, We're No Angels, 1989, The Miracle, 1990, The Crying Game, 1992 (Alexander Korda award Best British Film, N.Y. Film Critics Cir. award Best Screenplay, 1992, Writers Guild Am. Screen award Best Screenplay Written Directly for Screen, 1993, L.A Film Critics award, Best Fgn. Film, 1993, Oscar Best Writing, Screenplay Written Directly for Screen 1993, nominated Oscar Best Dir. 1993, nominated BAFTA Film awards, Best Original Screenplay, 1993, nominated Edgar award Best Motion Picture Edgar Allen Poe Awards 1993), Interview with the Vampire, 1994, Michael Collins, 1996 (Golden Lion award Venice Film Festival 1996), The Butcher Boy, 1997 (nomiated CFCA award Best Dir., Best Picture, Chgo. Film Critics Assn. Awards 1999), In Dreams, 1999 (Silver Raven award Brussels Internat. Festival Fantasy Film 1999), The End of the Affair, 1999 (BAFTA Film award 2000); author: (fiction) The Past, 1979, A Night in Tunisia, 1976 (Guardian Fiction prize 1979), The Dream of a Beast, 1983 (Acad. Award Best Original Screenplay), Sunrise With Sea Monster, 1994. Recipient Crystal Isis award Brussels Internat. Film Festival, 1998. Office: ICM c/o Jeff Berg 8942 Wilshire Blvd Beverly Hills CA 90212 Office: Jenne Casarotto Casarotto Co Ltd, Nat House 60 66 Wardour St, London WIV 3HP, England*

JORDAN, PAMELA CAROLE, librarian; b. New Haven, Jan. 13, 1949; d. Arthur Sumner and Mary Theresa (Zarnowski) J. BA, Albertus Magnus Coll., 1972. Subject and lang. specialist Sterling Library Yale U., New Haven, 1973-76, librarian Drama Library, 1976—. Mem. Ams. for Arts, New Eng. Theater Conf., Theater Library Assn., U.S. Inst. for Theater Tech. Office: Yale U Drama Libr 222 York St Box 208244 New Haven CT 06520-8244

JORDAN, PETER, atlas editor, researcher; b. Hermagor, Austria, Nov. 15, 1949; s. Wilhelm and Hedwig (Ressi) J.; m. Charlotte Newerkla, Aug. 9, 1975; children: Christof, Veronika. PhD, U. Vienna, 1979; habilitation, U. Klagenfurt, 1998. Map editor Austrian Inst. East and S.E. European Studies, Vienna, 1977-79, dep. head dept. geography, 1979-89, editor-in-chief, head dept. geography, 1989—, dep. dir., 1997—; mem. UN Group of Experts on Geog. Names, 1986—. Author: Possibilities of a better representation of Slovenian place names in Austria's current topographic maps, 1988, Contributions to the tourism geography of the northern Croatian coast, 1997; editor: Atlas of Eastern and Southeastern Europe, 1989—; project mgr. Resources and Environment--World Atlas, 1998; mem. editl. bd. Turizam, 1996—, Tourism and Hospitality Mgmt., 1995—. Recipient Promotion award Dr. Adolf-Scharf-Fonds, Vienna, 1977. Mem. Croatian Geog. Soc. (hon.), Austrian Geog. Soc. (exec. bd. 1989—), German Cartographic Soc., Assn. Am. Geographers. Roman Catholic. Avocations: travel, skiing, collecting maps and atlases. Home: Lacknergasse 73/2/6, A-1180 Vienna Austria Office: Josefsplatz 6, A-1010 Vienna Austria

JORDAN, RITA RUTH, university lecturer, researcher, writer; b. Red Ruth, Eng., Oct. 10, 1941; d. Robert and Eda (Barazani) Tupper; m. Richard George Joseph Jordan, Nov. 11, 1962 (widowed Oct. 18, 1993); three children. BSc in Psychology, Univ. Coll., Eng., 1964; MSc in Child Development, Inst. Edn., London, 1972; MA in Applied Linguistics, CNAA (Eng.) Hatfield Poly., 1982; PhD in Autism, Birmingham U., 1998. Registered tchr., 1968; chartered psychologist for rsch., 1990. Tchr., tutor various schs., Hertfordshire, Eng., 1964-71; rsch. officer Thomas Coram Rsch. Unit, London, 1973-77; tchr. Sch. for Children with Severe Learning Difficulties, Hemel Hempstead, Eng., 1976-77; deputy prin. Sch. for Children with Autism, Radlett, Eng., 1977-85; prin. lectr. U. Hertfordshire, Eng., 1985-93; sr. lectr. U. Birmingham, Eng., 1993; chair Nat. Accreditation in Autism Network, Eng., 1994, Assn. for Heads and Tchrs. of Adults and Children with Autism, Eng., 1992-94, Monitoring Group for Profl. Tng. in Autism, Eng., 1995; spl. councillor Nat. Autistic Soc., Eng., 1990; chair BPS working party ASD's. Co-author: Starting Off, 1978, Understanding and Teaching Children wuth Autism, 1995; co-author: Autism and Learning: A Guide to Good Practice, 1997, Meeting the Needs of Children with Autistic Spectrum Disorders, 1999; author: Autistic Spectrum Disorders: A Handbook, 1999; contbr. articles to profl. jours. and acad. and chpts. to books. Leader Opportunity Group, Helem Hempstead, Eng., 1968-72; organizer Dacorum Toy Libr., Hemei Hempstead, Eng., 1969-78; sec. Dacorum Play Coun., Hemei Hempstead, Eng., 1969-72; adviser West Midlands Autistic Soc., Birmingham, Eng., 1993; chair BPS Working Party on ASDs; advisor Irish Soc. for Autism, Belgium and Budapest Autism Rsch. Ctr. Recipient Rsch. grant SOEID, Scotland, 1995-96, rsch. grant Nat. Autistic Soc., Eng., 1990-91, Option Trust, Eng., 1990, DFEE, Eng., 1997-98, Shirley Found., Egn., 2000—. Mem. Nat. Assn. Spl. Ednl. Needs, Assn. Heads and Tchrs. of Adults and Children with Autism, British Psychol. Soc., Assn. of Child Psychologists and Psychiatrists. Avocations: theatre, concerts, walking, dining, bridge. E-mail: rrjordan@bham.ac.uk. Office: U Birmingham Sch Edn, Edgbaston, West Midlands, Birmingham B15 2TT, England

JORDAN, ROBERT SMITH, political science educator; b. Los Angeles, June 11, 1929; s. Ralph Burdette and Mary Wright (Smith) J.; m. Sara Jane Hatch, Sept. 19, 1961; children: Sara Jane, Mary Rebecca Leming, Robert Hatch, David Thomas. AB, UCLA, 1951; MS, U. Utah, 1955; MA (E.I. DuBois fellow), Princeton U., 1957, PhD, 1960; DPhil (Fulbright scholar), St. Antony's Coll., Oxford U., Eng., 1960. Asst. to v.p. academic affairs U. Utah, 1954-55; budget examiner internat. div. U.S. Bur. Budget, 1956; instr. dept. politics Princeton U., 1956-57; asst. prof. pub. and internat. affairs, exec. asst. to dean Grad. Sch. Pub. and Internat. Affairs, U. Pitts., 1959-60; asso. professorial lectr. George Washington U., 1960-62; asst. dir. Army War Coll. Center, 1960-61; dir. Air U. Center, 1961-62, assoc. prof. polit. sci. and internat. affairs, 1962-70, asst. to pres., 1962-64; assoc. dir. internat. orgn. and internat. security studies Program of Policy Studies, 1964-65; dir. Fgn. Affairs Intern Program, Sch. Pub. and Internat. Affairs, 1968-70; dean faculty econ. and social studies, head dept. polit. sci. U. Sierra Leone, 1965-67; prof. polit. sci. State U. N.Y. at Binghamton, 1970-76, chmn. dept., 1970-74; dir. research UN Inst. for Tng. and Research, N.Y.C., 1975-79; Dag Hammarskold vis. prof. internat. relations U. S.C., Columbia, 1979-80; prof. polit. sci., rsch. prof. internat. instns. U. New Orleans, 1980—, dean Grad. Sch., 1980-82; adj. prof. polit. sci. Columbia U., 1978-79; Disting. vis. prof. Naval War Coll., 1984-86; Fulbright prof. Cen. Study of Arms Control and Internat. Security, U. Lancaster, Eng., Jan.-June, 1988; vis. prof. internat. rels. U.S. Air War Coll., 1992-94. Author/co-author, editor/co-editor: The NATO International Staff/Secretariat, 1967, Problems in International Relations, 1970, Government and Power in West Africa, 1970, rev. edit., 1977, Europe and the Superpowers, 1971, rev. edit., 1990, International Administration, 1971, Multinational Cooperation, 1972, Basic Issues in International Relations, 1974, Political Handbook of the World, 1975, The World Food Conference and Global Problem Solving, 1976, Political Leadership in NATO, 1979, Changing Role and Concepts in the International Civil Service, 1980, Dag Hammarskjold Revisited: The UN Secretary-General as a Force in World Politics, 1983, International Organizations: A Comparative Approach, 1983, 3d rev. edit., 1994, The U.S. and Multilateral Resource Management, 1985, Europe in the Balance: The Changing Context of European International Politics, 1986, Generals in International Politics: NATO's Supreme Allied Commander, Europe, 1987, Maritime Strategy and the Balance of Power: Britain and America in the Twentieth Century, 1989, Alliance Strategy and Navies: The Evolution and Scope of NATO's Maritime Dimension, 1990, Norstad: Cold War NATO Supreme Commander, 2000, International Organizations and the Manaagement of Cooperation, 2001. Mem. Commn. to Study Orgn. of Peace; bd. dirs. Scarsdale-Hartsdale chpt. UN Assn., 1976-79. Served with USAF, 1951-53. Decorated Bronze Star; named Disting. Alumnus Hinckley Inst., U. Utah, 1964; NATO

research fellow, 1969-70; fellow African Studies Assn.; Vice Adm. Edwin L. Hooper postdoctoral fellow U.S. Naval Hist. Ctr., 1987, 97; Ctr. Rsch. Assoc. USAF Hist. Rsch. Ctr., 1988, U.S. Army Mil. History Inst., 1990, Consortium for the Study of Intelligence. Mem. Assn. Princeton Grad. Alumni (pres.), Am. Polit. Sci. Assn., Internat. Studies Assn. (v.p.), Am. Soc. Pub. Adminstrn. (chmn. sect. on internat. and comp. adminstrn.), Am. Soc. Internat. Law, Acad. Coun. UN, Internat. Inst. Strategic Studies (London), Royal Inst. Internat. Affairs (London), Cosmos Club (Washington), Plimsoll Club (New Orleans),. Mormon.eans). Office: U New Orleans Dept Polit Sci New Orleans LA 70148-0001

JORDAN, RUTH ANN, physician; b. Oct. 12, 1928; d. Willard and Esther (Fouts) J.; children: Diane M., Linda J. AB, Ind. U., 1950; MD, Columbia U., 1957. Intern St. Luke's Hosp., N.Y.C., 1957-58, asst. resident, 1958-59; physician Met. Life Ins. Co., N.Y.C., 1960-62, Standard Oil Co. of N.J., N.Y.C., 1962, MIT, Cambridge, Mass., 1963-71; physician New Eng. Mut. Life Ins. Co., Boston, 1963-66, asst. med. dir., 1971-74; fellow internal medicine Mass. Gen. Hosp., Boston, 1974-75; physician Simmons Coll., Boston, 1975-78, Northeastern U., Boston, 1976-78; assoc. med. dir. New Eng. Telephone Co., Boston, 1978, med. dir. clin. svcs., 1978-86; dir. occupl. medicine Gen. Med. Assn., Boston, 1986-91; assoc. med. dir. Allmerica, Worcester, Mass., 1991-97; physician Health Resource, Woburn, Mass., 1996—; therapeutic dietitian Meth. Hosp., Indpls., 1951-53, Presbyn. Hosp., N.Y.C., part-time 1954-57; nat. coord. com. on cholesterol, 1986—, Mass. Adv. Coun. for Workers Compensation, 1986-89. Fellow Am. Coll. Occupl. and Environ. Medicine (membership com. 1985-88, health edn. com. 1984—, bd. dirs. 1986-92); mem. AMA, DAR, PEO, New Eng. Occupl. Med. Assn. (bd. dirs. 1980-89, pres. 1981-84), Mass. Med. Soc. (mem. Ho. of Dels., 1984—, chmn. environ. and occupl. health com. 1985-88, mem. interspecialty com. 1985-88), Norfolk County Med. Soc. (v.p., pres 1999—, edn. com., exec. com., alt. to Mass. Med. Soc. nominating com.), Columbia U. Club of New Eng. (v.p. 1981-84, pres. 1989-91), Roxbury Clin. Records Club, The Country Club, Alpha Chi Omega. Home: 105 Rockwood St Brookline MA 02445-7408

JORDAN, SHARIE CECILIA, small business owner; b. Grand Rapids, Mich., Sept. 12, 1961; d. Erwin Francis and Ardis Jean (Gilbert) Schmuker; m. Thomas William Jordan, Dec. 4, 1982. Registered well drilling contractor, Mich., 1996. Fashion cons. Mullberry Bush, Houghton Lake, Mich., 1982-84; freelance artist Houghton Lake, Mich., 1984-90; owner Jordan Illustration and Design, Houghton Lake, Mich., 1991-96; co-owner Jordan Well Drilling, Houghton Lake, Mich., 1994—; cons. Buyers Guide Weekly, Houghton, 1988-90. Founding chmn. Annual Meml. Day Parade, Houghton Lake, 1992—. Recipient Emily Hilton-Janice Reeney Art award, 1979. Mem. Mich. Ground Water Assn., Mich. Environ. Health Assn., Tri-Lakes Builders Assn., Eagle Aux. (chaplain 1991-92, activity chmn. 1991-92, trustee 1992-94, v.p. 1992-94, Mrs. Eagle award 1991-92, Outstanding Vol. Work and Svc. award 1991-92). Avocations: boating, horticulture, music.

JORDAN, WILLIAM, international organization administrator; b. Jan. 28, 1936; s. Walter and Alice J.; m. Jean Ann Livesey; 3 children. Diploma, Secondary Modern Sch., Birmingham, 1958; DSc (hon.), U. Cranfield, 1995; D. Univ. (hon.), U. Cen. Eng., 1993. Convenor of shop stewards Guest Keen & Nettlefolds, 1966-76; elected full-time divsnl. organizer Amalgamated Union of Engring. Workers, 1977-86; pres. Amalgamated Engring. Union, 1986-95, European Metalworkers' Fedn., 1986-95; pres British sect. Internat. Metalworkers' Fedn., 1986-95; now gen. sec. ICFTU; gov. London Sch. Econs., BBC, 1988-98, Ashridge Mgmt. Coll. Recipient City & Guilds Insignia award in Technology, 1989. Office: ICFTU, Bd du Roi Albert II 5, Btel, B-1210 Brussels Belgium

JORDANOV, VALERI MARINOV, chemistry educator; b. Sofia, Bulgaria, Feb. 9, 1959; s. Marin Angelov and Dimka Petrova (Tzambova) J.; m. Ivanka Todorova Andonova, July 21, 1985; children: Rossen Valeriev, Elitza Valerieva. MSc, U. Chem. Tech., Sofia, 1984, PhD, 1990. Lic. engr. Engr. Ctrl. Inst. Chemistry and Industry, Sofia, 1984-86; chemist U. Chem. Tech., Sofia, 1990-93, asst. prof., 1993—. Contbr. articles to profl. jours. Named Internat. Man of Yr., Internat. Biog. Ctr., Cambridge, Eng., 1997-98. Avocations: sports, music. Home: Complex Suha Reka Block 133, entr G Flat 72, 1517 Sofia Bulgaria Office: U Chem Tech and Metallurgy, 8 Kliment Okhridski Blvd, 1756 Sofia Bulgaria

JORGA, KARIN MONIKA, pharmacologist, researcher; b. Lübeck, Germany, Sept. 21, 1963; d. Horst and Edith Christa (Szebrowski) J. MSc in Pharmacy, Christian Albrechts U., Kiel, Germany, 1987, PhD in Pharm. Chemistry, 1990. Cert. pharmacist. Postdoctoral fellow U. Ky., Lexington, 1991; rsch. scientist Hoffmann-LaRoche, Basel, Switzerland, 1991-93; sr. rsch. scientist Hoffmann-LaRoche, Basel, 1993-2000, project leader exploratory drug devel., 2000—. Contbr. articles to profl. jours., confs. Mem. Am. Assn. Pharm. Scientists. Achievements includeresearch on neuropharmacology of Parkinson's disease; leading expert on the role of catechol-o-methylhaus-tuase in the human brain. Avocations: UNICEF, skiing, gardening, literature. Office: Hoffmann LaRoche, Grenzacher St 124, CH-4070 Basel Switzerland

JORGE, NUNO MARIA ROQUE, architect; b. Macao, Portugal, Feb. 9, 1947; s. Adolfo Adroaldo and Edith (Roque) J.; m. Maria de Fâtima da Costa Azevedo, Sept. 14, 1975; children: Edith Azevedo, Alexandra Azevedo, Filipa Azevedo. Cert Bus. Mgmt., Inst. Superior de Novas Profissoes, Lisbon, 1972; diploma in architecture, Higher Sch. Fine Arts, Lisbon (Portugal) U., 1974. Architect trainee Ministério do Ultramar, Lisbon, 1972-73; computer programmer, systems analyst Cen. Mecanografico de Exercito, Lisbon, 1973-75; pvt. practice architecture Macau, 1975—; pvt. practice bus. mgr., cons., Macau, 1981—; pvt. practice acct., Macau, 1981—; mng. ptnr. Gen. Soc. Commerce and Industry Ltd., Macau, 1983—. Pres. Macau Red Cross, 1990—; mem. Santa Casa de Misericordia, Macau, 1980—. With Portuguese Army, 1973-75. Decorated for profl. merit, 1984 (Macau), for valour, 1999, red cross Grand Order of Tai Geuk, 1995 (Republic of Korea); recipient spl. award for heritage preservation Pacific Area Travel Assn., 1982, Commendation award Portuguese Red Cross Nat. Soc., 1988, Merit award, 1990, Benemerit award, 1993, Plaque of Honor, 1999. Mem. WFO (treas. 1997-99, pres. Asia Pacific region 1999), Geog. Soc. Lisbon, Macau Assn. Archs. (founder, charter), Portuguese Assn. Accts.-Macau (founder, chmn. gen. meeting, 1989-97), Macau Mgmt. Assn. (charter, life, advisor 1985—), Assn. Portuguese Archs., Portuguese Assn. Mktg., Portuguese Assn. Quality Control, Alliance Francaise Macao (charter), Tenis Civil Club (pres. 1976-77), Skal, PATA (treas. Macau chpt. 1983-84), Elos Club (charter), Rotary (dist. gov. 1985-86, group leader internat. assembly 1991). Avocations: photography, tourism. Office: Cam Fai Coc Bldg, 255 Ave de Amizade 18th Fl C, Macau Macau

JØRGENSEN, CLAUS, investment company executive; b. Aarhus, Denmark, May 4, 1951; m. Karen Lund Jensen; 1 child, Jesper. Student, U. Aarhus, 1979. Chief of equities dept. Jyske Bank, Silkeborg, Denmark, 1979-85, Aage Philip, Copenhagen, 1985-86; mng. dir. Uni-invest Mgmt., Copenhagen, 1986—. Home: Sangsvanevej 42, 2970 Hørsholm Denmark Office: Uni invest Mgmt, Nr Voldgade 19, 1358 Copenhagen Denmark

JORGENSEN, GERALD THOMAS, psychologist, educator; b. Mason City, Iowa, Jan. 15, 1947; s. Harry Grover and Mary Jo (Kollasch) J.; m. Mary Ann Reiter, Aug. 30, 1969; children: Amy Lynn, Sarah Kay, Jill Kathryn. BA, Loras Coll., Dubuque, 1969; MS, Colo. State U., Ft. Collins, 1970, PhD, 1973; Juris Canonici Licentiae, Cath. U. Am., 1998. Lic. psychologist, Iowa; cert. health svc. provider Nat. Register, Iowa; ordained to ministry Roman Cath. Ch. as deacon, 1979. Psychology intern Counseling Ctr., Colo. State U., Ft. Collins, 1971-72, VA Hosp., Palo Alto, Calif., 1972-73; psychologist Loras Coll., Clarke Coll., Dubuque, 1973-76; asst. prof. psychology Loras Coll., 1976-80, assoc. prof., 1981-93, dir. Ctr. for Counseling and Student Devel., 1977-86, assoc. dean of students, 1985-86, dean of students, v.p. for student devel., 1986-93; cons. and supervising psychologist Gannon Ctr. for Cmty. Mental Health, 1977—; assoc. med. staff Mercy Med. Ctr., 1989—; asst. dir. for formation Office of Permanent Diaconate, Archdiocese of Dubuque, 1979-93, dir., 1993-96, auditor, 1993-98; cons. psychologist Met. Tribunal, 1993—, judge, 1998—; chairperson Iowa Bd. Psychology Examiners, Des Moines, 1984-90, continuing edn. coord., 1983; sec.-gen. First Internat. Congress on Licensure, Certification and Credentialing of Psychologists, New Orleans, 1995. Contbr. articles to profl. jours. Treas. Dubuque County Assn. Mental Health Inc., 1975-82. NDEA fellow, 1969-72. Fellow Assn. State and Provincial Psychology Bds. (exec. com. 1986-89, pres. 1989-92, Morton Berger award 1996); mem. Am. Coll. Pers. Assn. (chmn. com. VII 1980-82), Am. Assn. Counseling Devel., Am. Psychol. Assn., Iowa Psychol. Assn. (treas. 1976-80, mem. exec. coun. 1980-83, highest honors 1990), Nat. Assn. Diaconate Dirs. (sec. 1983-85, treas. 1985-90, award 1991), Canon Law Soc. Am., Iowa Student Pers. Assn., Fedn. Assns. Reg. Bds. (v.p. 1993-94, 96-97, pres. 1994-96), Delta Epsilon Sigma, Phi Kappa Phi, Sigma Tau Phi. Democrat. Roman Catholic. Home: 2183 St Celia St Dubuque IA 52002-2742 Office: Archdiocesan Ctr 1229 Mount Loretta Ave Dubuque IA 52003-7826

JØRGENSEN, KURT, physiologist; b. Copenhagen, Dec. 4, 1937; s. Hans and Gurli Rita (Ernst) J.; m. Lone Boesen, June 22, 1964; children: Jesper, Pernille. BSc, U. Copenhagen, 1962, MSc, 1964, ScD, 1997. Physiologist Polio Inst., Copenhagen, 1964-73; assoc. prof. physiology Aug. Krogh Inst., U. Copenhagen, Copenhagen, 1973—. Contbr. articles to profl. jours., chpts. to books. Recipient Danish Spine prize Soc. Manual Medicine, Denmark, 1990. Mem. Internat. Biomech. Soc., Nordic Soc. for Physiology. Office: U Copenhagen, Lab Human Physiol IESS, DK 21000 Copenhagen Denmark

JORGENSEN, PAUL ALFRED, English language educator emeritus; b. Lansing, Mich., Feb. 17, 1916; s. Karl and Rose Josephine (Simmons) J.; m. Virginia Frances Elfrink, Jan. 3, 1942; children: Mary Catherine, Elizabeth Ross Jorgensen Howard. A.B., Santa Barbara State Coll., 1938; M.A., U. Calif. at Berkeley, 1940, Ph.D., 1945. Instr. English Bakersfield (Calif.) Jr. Coll., 1945-46, U. Calif., Berkeley, summer 1946, U. Calif., Davis, 1946-47; mem. faculty UCLA, 1947—, prof. English, 1960-81, prof. emeritus, 1981—; vis. prof. U. Wash., summer 1966; mem. editorial com. U. Calif. Press, 1957-60; mem. Humanities Inst. U. Calif., 1967-69; mem. acad. adv. council Shakespeare Globe Ctr. N.Am. Author: Shakespeare's Military World, 1956, (with Frederick B. Shroyer) A College Treasury, rev. edit, 1967, (with Shroyer) The Informal Essay, 1961, Redeeming Shakespeare's Words, 1962; editor: The Comedy of Errors, 1964, Othello: An Outline- Guide to the Play, 1964, (with Shroyer) The Art of Prose, 1965, Lear's Self-Discovery, 1967, Our Naked Frailties: Sensational Art and Meaning in Macbeth, 1971, William Shakespeare: The Tragedies, 1985; mem. bd. editors Film Quar, 1958-65, Huntington Library Quar, 1965-83, Coll. English, 1966-70; mem. adv. com. Publs. of MLA of Am, 1978-82. Guggenheim fellow, 1956-57; Regents' Faculty fellow in humanities, 1973-74. Mem. Modern Lang. Assn., Shakespeare Assn. Am. (bibliographer 1954-59), Renaissance Soc. Am., Philol. Assn., Pacific Coast (exec. com. 1962-63), Internat. Shakespeare Assn. Episcopalian. Home: 234 Tavistock Ave Los Angeles CA 90049-3229

JORGENSEN, PETER LETH, physiologist, physician, researcher; b. Copenhagen, Denmark, Jan. 31, 1938; s. Kristian Leth and Esther Leth (Clausen) J.; m. Inge Sorensen, Oct. 14, 1961; children: Steen, Jens. MD, Aarhus U., 1964, DMS, 1976. Intern, resident Aarhus County Hosp., Denmark, 1964-65; asst. prof. physiology Aarhus U., 1967-72, assoc. prof. physiology, 1973-89; prof. physiology Copenhagen U., 1989—; vis. prof. physiology Vanderbilt U., Nashville, 1980. Mem. editl. bd. Biochimica et Biophysica Acta, 1983-86, Jour. Membrane Biology, 1993—; contbr. articles to profl. jours. Lt., Danish Army, 1965-66. Recipient Novo Nordic prize Novo Found., 1991, Vissing award Danish Rsch. Coun., 1989. Fellow Royal Danish Acad. Scis., Danish Acad. Natural Scis.; mem. Soc. Molecular Biology and Biochemistry. Avocations: biology, sailing, golf. Office: Copenhagen U/A Krogh Inst, Universitetsparken 13, 2100 Copenhagen OE, Denmark

JORGENSEN, ROBERT WILLIAM, product engineer; b. Allegan, Mich., Jan. 8, 1946; m. Deborah Ann Geiger; children: Linda, Eric, Laura, Lisa. BS in Aerospace Engring., U. Mich., 1969; AS, Radio Electronics Tech. Sch., South Bend, Ind., 1971. Engr. Kawneer Corp., Niles, Mich., 1970-80; tech. dir. Raco, Inc., South Bend, Ind., 1980—; mem. adv. coun. Underwriter's Assn. Holder 43 patents on elec. boxes and fittings. Mem. Underwriters Labs., Nat. Elec. Mfrs. Assn., Nat. Fire Protection Assn., Internat. Assn. Elec. Insps., Can. Stds. Assn. Avocations: private pilot, amateur radio, gardening. Home: 1353 Thompson Rd Niles MI 49120-9332 Office: Raco Inc PO Box 4002 South Bend IN 46634-4002

JORGESON, BRENT WILSON, management executive; b. Atlanta, Aug. 29, 1950; s. Charles Milton and Arleen Irma (Marshall) J.; m. Mary Elizabeth House, June 9, 1973. BS, Ga. Inst. Tech., 1973; MBA, Harvard U., 1973. With Advance Mortgage Corp., Southfield, Mich., 1975-76; v.p. ops. Hosp. Investors, Inc., Atlanta, 1977-80; sr. assoc. Booz, Allen & Hamilton, Inc., Atlanta, 1980-81; v.p. devel. Healthcare Internat., Inc., Austin, Tex., 1981-83, v.p. ops., 1984-88; pres. Regent Health Group, Inc., Austin, 1988-95; chmn. bd. Home Health Care Affiliates Inc., Austin, 1995—. Served 1st lt. U.S. Army, Mil. Intelligence, 1975. Clubs: Harvard Bus. Sch., Harvard. Home: 4505 Spicewood Rd Ste 304 Austin TX 78759-4505 Office: 4505 Spicewood Springs Rd Austin TX 78759-8584

JORRITSMA-LEBBINK, ANNEMARIE, Dutch government official; b. Hengelo, The Netherlands, June 1, 1950. Grad., Tourism Tng. Sch., Breda, 1969. Employee travel agy., export mgr.; mem. home ownership com. of steering com. Exptl. Housing; mem. exec. bd. Nieuwspoort Press Centre; mem. Berie foar ir Frysk; mem. bd. govs. Thorbecke Akademie; bd. mem. Assn. High-Rise Bldg.; People's Party for Freedom and Democracy mem. Mcpl. Coun., Bolsward, 1978-89; mem. Parliament Lower House, 1982-92; sec. People's Party for Freedom and Democracy Provincial Women's Orgn.; dep. mem. People's Party for Freedom and Democracy Adv. Coun. on Women; min. transport, pub. works and water mgmt. Dutch Govt., The Hague, 1994-99, vice prime min., 1999—, min. econ. affairs. Office: Office of Prime Minister, Binnenhof 20, 2513 AA The Hague The Netherlands*

JORTNER, JOSHUA, physical chemistry scientist, educator; b. Poland, Mar. 14, 1933; s. Arthur and Regina Jortner; m. Ruth Sanger, 1960; 2 children. PhD, Hebrew U. Jerusalem; hon. degree, Ben Gurions U. of Negev, Israel, 1985, Pierre and Marie Curie U., Paris, 1986; D (hon.), Tech. U. Munich, 1996. Instr. dept. phys. chemistry Hebrew U. Jerusalem, 1961-62, sr. lectr., 1963-65; assoc. prof. Tel Aviv U., 1965-66, prof., 1966—, Heinemann prof. chemistry, 1973—, Heinemann chair phys. chemistry Sch. Chemistry, head Inst. Chemistry, 1966-72, dep. rector, 1966-69, v.p., 1970-72; rsch. assoc. U. Chgo., 1962-64; vis. prof. U. Chgo., 1965-71, H.C. Orsted Inst., U. Copenhagen, 1974, 78, U. Calif., Berkeley, 1975. Author: (with M. Bixon) Intramolecular Radiationless Transitions, 1968; editor: (with Bernard Pullman) The Jerusalem Symposia on Quantum Chemistry and Biochemistry, 1982-95; contbr. over 650 articles to profl. jours. Recipient award Internat. Acad. Quantum Sci., 1972, Weizmann prize, 1973, Rothschild prize, 1976, Kolthof prize, 1976, Israel prize in Chemistry, 1982, Wolf prize, 1988, The Hon. J. Heyrovsky Gold medal, 1993, August-Wilhelm-von-Hofmann medal, 1995, R.S. Mulliken medal, 1998, J.O. Hirschfelder prize, 1999. Mem. Israel Acad. Scis. and Humanities (v.p. 1980-86, pres. 1986-95), Internat. Acad. Quantum Molecular Scis., Am. Philos. Soc., Danish Acad. Scis. and Letters (fgn. mem.), Polish Acad. Scis., Russian Acad. Scis. (fgn.), European Acad. Scis. and Arts, Romanian Acad. Scis., German Acad. Scis. Leopoldina, Indian Acad. Sci., U.S. Nat. Acad. Scis., (fgn. assoc.), Learned Soc. of Czech Repub., Royal Netherlands Acad. Arts and Scis. (fgn.), Internat. Union Pure and Applied Chemistry (v.p. 1996-97, pres. 1998-99). Avocation: science policy. Office: Tel Aviv U Sch Chemistry, Ramat-Aviv, 69978 Tel Aviv Israel also: Israel Acad Scis-Humanities, Einstein Sq PO Box 4040, 91040 Jerusalem Israel

JOSEFF, JOAN CASTLE, manufacturing executive; b. Alta., Can., Aug. 12, 1922; naturalized U.S. citizen, 1945; d. Edgar W. and Lottie (Coates) Castle; BA in Psychology, UCLA; widowed; 1 son, Jeffrey Rene. With Joseff-Hollywood, jewelry manufacture and rental, Burbank, Calif., 1939—, chmn. bd., pres., sec.-treas. Numerous TV appearances including CBS This Morning, Australia This Morning, Am. Movie Channel. Mem. Burbank Salary Task Force, 1979—, L.A. County Earthquake Fact-Finding Commn., 1981— ; bd. dirs. San Fernando Valley area chpt. Am. Cancer Soc., treas., Genesis Energy Systems, Inc., 1993—; mem. Rep. Cen. Com.; del. Rep. Nat. Conv., 1980, 84, 88, 92, 96; voting mem. Calif. Rep. Party; chmn. Women Legis.: active Beautiful People Award Com. Honoring John Wayne Carcer Clinic; appointed by Gov. Wilson to Barber and Cosmotology Bd; appointed br Pres. Clinton to Selective Svc. System. Recipient Women in Achievement award Soroptimist Internat., 1988. Mem. Women of Motion Picture Industry (hon. life), Nat. Fedn. Rep. Women (bd. dir., Caring for Am. award 1986), Calif. Rep. Women (bd. dir., treas. 1986-90), North Hollywood Rep. Women (pres. 1981-82, parliamentarian), Nat. Fedn. of Rep (voting mem., program chair, 1994—, bylaws chair 1998—), Calif. Fedn. of Rep. Women (chaplain, Americanism chmn. so. div., regent chmn. Women of Achievement award 1988), L.A. County Fedn. of Rep. Women (scholarship chmn.), Home: 10060 Toluca Lake Ave Toluca Lake CA 91602-2924 Office: 129 E Providencia Ave Burbank CA 91502-1922

JOSEFSON, HANS EINAR, lawyer; b. Gothenburg, Sweden, Dec. 13, 1940; s. Einar and Solvind (Lundgren) J.; m. Kerstin Kuusekänd, Feb. 14, 1981; children: Gustaf, Ebba, Hedvig. Undergrad. degree, Hvitfeldska, Gothenburg, 1959; LLB, Lund (Sweden) U., 1969. Judge apprentice Dist. Ct. Stockholm, 1969-72; asst. Jörgensen & Samzelius Lawfirm, 1972-73; legal counsel Investment AB Beijer, 1973-74, Sjöförsäkrings AB Hansa, 1974-75, Investment AB Asken, Gothenburg, 1975-78; chief legal counsel Kema Nobel AB, Stockholm, 1978-81; ptnr. Advokatfirman Carler, Gothenburg, 1981-90; owner Advokatfirman Cicero AB, Gothenburg, 1990—. Author: Royal Navy Minesweepers, 1996, Gothenburg Tramways, 1967, Gothenburg Tramways 100 Years, 1979. Cmdr. Royal Swedish Navy Res., 1985—. Recipient medal of honor RSwNR Officers' Assn., Stockholm, 1975. Mem. Royal Bachelors' Club of 1769, Naval Officers Soc. in Gothenburg (chmn. 1995—). Avocations: tramway models, sailing. E-mail: cicero@swipnet.se. Office: Advokatfirman Cicero 53043, Södra Hamngatan 11, S-400 14 Göteborg Sweden

JOSEFSSON, GÖRAN ERIK, orthopedic surgeon, administrator; b. Ljusne, Sweden, Dec. 26, 1933; s. Georg Axel and Helga Cecilia (Norén) J.; children: Torun, Jonatan, Maria, Fredrik; m. Anna Margareta Edlund, Aug. 5, 1989. MD, Royal Karolinska Inst., Stockholm, 1963; PhD, U. Lund, Sweden, 1980. Cert. specialist in gen. and orthopedic surgery. Asst. chief surgeon dept. orthopedic surgery Gävle (Sweden) Hosp., 1972-78, chief surgeon dept. orthopedic surgery, 1978-98, head dept. orthopedic surgery, 1986-95; ret., 1998; assoc. prof. orthopedic surgery U. Lund, 1991; asst. med. chief of staff Gävel, 1983-85; med. advisor to gen. ins., Gävleborg; apptd. mem. Ct. Commons. Author: The Hip, The Hip Society, 1977, Acta Orthop Scand, 1990, Excerpta Medica Amsterdam, 1983. Capt. Naval M.C., 1955-65. Recipient fin. support King Gustav V:s Found., 1978, Ulla and Gustaf af Ugglas Found., 1979, Swedish Med. Rsch. Coun., 1979. Mem. European Bone and Joint Inf. Soc., European Hip Soc., Rotary. Lutheran. Avocations: country life, music, dogs. Home: Sanna 1042, 82040 Jarvso Sweden Office: Gävle Hosp, Dept Orthopedic Surgery, S-801 87 Gävle Sweden

JOSEFSSON, TORGNY WILHELM EMANUEL, physicist, researcher; b. Stockholm, Jan. 27, 1965; arrived in Australia, 1970; s. Roland Stig Josefsson and Yvonne (Leijon) Kedzior; m. Alison Louise Moran, Apr. 23, 1994; 1 child, Michael William. BSc with honors, Monash U., Melbourne, Australia, 1989, PhD, 1993. Tutor Monash U., 1990-93; postdoctoral rsch. fellow U. Melbourne, Australia, 1993-97; rsch. scientist Def. Sci. and Tech. Orgn., Rockingham, Australia, 1997-98, sr. rsch. scientist, 1998-99; sr. rsch. scientist Air Ops. Divsn., Melbourne, 1999—. Contbr. articles to profl. jours. Mem. Am. Phys. Soc., Australian Inst. Physics. Office: Air Ops Divsn, PO Box 4331, Melbourne 3001, Australia

JOSEKUTTY, PUTHIYAPARAMBIL CHACKO, science firm administrator, researcher, educator; b. Koodathai, Kerala, India, May 24, 1964; arrived in Micronesia, 1998; s. Puthiyaparambil Varghese Chacko and Puthiyaparambil Chacko Mariam; m. Ruby Mathew, Jan. 14, 1994. BSc, U. Calicut, India, 1984, MSc, 1986; PhD, MS U. Baroda, India, 1993. Jr. and sr. rsch. fellow MS U. Baroda, 1987-91; cons. tissue culture Biotech. Biotype Pvt. Ltd., Baroda, 1991-92; lectr. MS U. Baroda, 1991-93; sr. sci. officer M.S. Swaminatham Rsch. Found., Chennai, India, 1993-95; rsch. assoc. U. Transkei, South Africa, 1996-98; rschr., scientist Coll. Micronesia, Kosrae, 1998—. Contbr. chpt. to book; articles to profl. jours. Recipient Award for Best Paper in Micropropagation, CFTRI, 1995. Mem. IAPTC, SBCI, SAAB. Roman Catholic. Avocations: sport fishing, volleyball, reading, movies. Home: Tofol Kosrae Box 1000, FM 96944 Kosrae Micronesia Office: MPPRC/COM-FSM, Tofol, FM 96944 Kosrae Micronesia

JOSEPH, CHRISTOPHER ARTHUR, ear, nose, and throat surgeon; b. Tredegar, Wales, Dec. 11, 1953; arrived in South Africa, 1965; m. Gail Symington, Dec. 10, 1977; children: Dylan, Adrian, Megan, Rhys. MBBCh, U. Witwatersrand, Johannesburg, South Africa, 1977, MMed, 1985. Hon. cons. U. Witwatersrand/JHG Gen., 1985—; lectr., part-time head dept. ear/nose/throat U. Medunsa, Garankua, South Africa, 1986-89, lectr., chief specialist dept. ear/nose/throat, 1989—; pvt. practice Morningside Clinic, Johannesburg, 1992—; bd. dirs. Audiology Inst., Johannesburg, 1993—. Contbr. articles to profl. jours., chpt. to book. Fellow Royal Coll. Surgeons, Coll. Surgeons South Africa; mem. South African Ear Nose Throat Soc. (exec. com. 1993—), South African Head and Neck Soc. (founding mem., sec.-treas. 1985—), Ear, Nose and Throat Inst. Johannesburg (founding mem.). Avocations: reading, art, antiques, squash. Office: Rochester Med Ctr, 173 Rivonia Rd, Morningside Johannesburg South Africa

JOSEPH, FREDERIC-GILLES, advertising executive; b. Paris, Jan. 12, 1967; s. Benoit Claude and Arlette Blanche (Stempler) J. Baccalaureat, Ecole Active Bilingue, Paris, 1984; LLM, U. Paris-Sorbonne, 1988; M in Polit. Scis., Inst. d'Etudes Polit. of Paris, Paris, 1989. Asst. to the media account mgr. Havas Dentsu Marsteller, 1989-90; media account mgr. EUROCOM, 1990-93; media acct. exec., 1993-95; media account mgr. EURO RSCG, 1995; media dir. Saatchi and Saatchi Advt., 1995-99; brand comm. dir. Saatchi & Saatchi, London, 1999-2000; gen. mgr. Zenith Interactive Solutions, Clichy, France, 2000—; prof. mktg. and comm. Inst. d'Etude Politiques de Paris. Mem. Racing Club France. Avocation: modern art. Home: 40 Rue Pascal, F-75013 Paris France Office: Zenith Interactive Sols, 31-33 Rue Mme de Sanzillon, F-92586 Clichy Cedex France

JOSEPH, JEFFREY ALAN, lawyer; b. Chgo., Aug. 3, 1947; s. Bryan Kenneth Joseph and Carol Maxine Cummings; m. Valerie Ann Pearson, Sept. 12, 1981; children: Adriana, Bryan. BA, U. Calif., Berkeley, 1969; JD, U. Calif., Davis, 1972. Bar: Calif. 1972, U.S. Dist. Ct. (ea. dist.) Calif. 1972, U.S. Dist. Ct. (so. dist.) Calif. 1973. Dep. atty. Calif. Atty. Gen.'s Office, Sacramento and San Diego, 1972-79; prin. atty. spl. prosecuting unit Calif. Atty. Gen.'s Office, San Diego, 1979-80; dep. chief counsel Calif. Dept. Transp., San Diego, 1980—; arbitrator, mediator San Diego Superior Ct., 1983—, superior judge pro tem, 1992—; adj. prof. law Thomas Jefferson Sch. of Law, San Diego, 1990—; bd. dirs. Assn. Calif. State Attys., 1982-83. Pres. Stella Maris Sch. Bd., La Jolla, Calif., 1996-97. Mem. San Diego County Bar Assn. Roman Catholic. Avocations: music, flute, guitar, basketball, history. Office: Calif Dept Transp Legal Divsn 610 W Ash St Ste 805 San Diego CA 92101-3373

JOSEPH, JOHN E., linguistics educator; b. Monroe, Mich., Oct. 30, 1956; arrived in Scotland, 1996; s. John and Glenlyn Pauline (Creason) J.; m. Jeannette Pascale Muñoz, Aug. 17, 1991; children: Julian, Crispin. BA with honors, U. Mich., 1977, MA, 1978, PhD, 1981. Lectr. U. Paul Valéry, Montpellier, France, 1980-81; from asst. to assoc. prof. Oklahoma State U., Stillwater, 1981-85, U. Md., College Park, 1986-92; prof. U. Hong Kong, 1993-96, U. Edinburgh, Scotland, 1997—; vis. assoc. prof. U. Maine, Orono, 1986. Author: Eloquence and Power, 1987, Limiting the Arbitrary, 2000; co-editor: Ideologies of Language, 1990, Linguistic Theory and Grammatical Description, 1991, The Emergence of the Modern Language Sciences, 1999. Nat. Endowment for the Humanities fellow, 1993, Camargo Found. fellow, 1993, Rsch. fellow Leverhulme Trust, 1999-2000. Fellow Royal Soc. Arts; mem. Philological Soc. (coun. mem. 1997—), Henry Sweet Soc. for the History of Linguistic Ideas (coun. mem. 1997—). Home: 3 Ann St, Edinburgh EH4 1PL, Scotland Office: Univ Edinburgh, Adam Ferguson Bld George Sq, EH8 9LL Edinburgh Scotland

JOSEPH, JOSEPH SAVVA, political science educator; b. Tsada, Cyprus, Nov. 16, 1952; s. Eleni Neocleous Socratous, 1986; children: Lina Mary, Savina Rita. BA, Panteion U., Greece, 1975; MA, U. Stockholm, 1979; PhD, Miami U., 1985. Postdoctoral fellow Harvard U., Cambridge, Mass.,

1988-90; min. plenipotentiary Ministry of Fgn. Affairs, Cyprus, 1993-95; prof. internat. rels. U. Cyprus; vis. prof. Miami U., 1986-87, Gustavus Adolphus Coll., 1987-88, U. Ala., 1989-91. Author: (book) Cyprus: Ethnic Conflict and International Politics, From Independence to the Threshold of the EU, 1997; contbr. articles to profl. jours. Recipient scholarship Govt. of Sweden, 1977-80; grantee Fulbright Commn., 1997, Salzburg Seminar, 1996. Mem. Am. Polit. Sci. Assn., Internat. Studies Assn., Brit. Internat. Studies Assn. Avocations: chess, travel, lecturing. Home: 13 Alfios St, 2313 Lakatamia Cyprus Office: Univ of Cyprus, PO Box 20537, 1678 Nicosia Cyprus

JOSEPH, MATHEW, physicist; b. Madras, India, July 7, 1958; s. Mathew and Mary Antony; m. Prema Mary, Apr. 5, 1991; 1 child, Antony Gautham. PhD, U. Madras, 1996. Scientist C Indian Dept. Atomic Energy, Kalpakkam, 1983-86, scientist D, 1986-88; guest scientist Nat. Inst. for Stds. and Technology, Gaithersburg, Md., 1989-90, 97; scientist E, F Indian Dept. Atomic Energy, Kalpakkam, 1991-95, 96; Japanese Soc. for Promotion of Sci. fellow Osaka (Japan) U., 1998—. Contbr. articles to profl. jours.; patentee in field. Mem. Matls. Rsch. Soc. Roman Catholic. Avocations: games, swimming. Office: IGCAR (RCL), Materials Chemistry Divsn, Kalpakkam 603102, India

JOSEPH, MICHAEL THOMAS, broadcast consultant; b. Youngstown, Ohio, Nov. 23, 1927; s. Thomas A. and Martha (McCarius) J.; m. Eva Ursula Boerger, June 21, 1952. BA, Case Western Res. U., 1949. Program dir. Fetzer Broadcasting, Grand Rapids, Mich., 1952-55; nat. program dir. Founders Corp., N.Y.C., 1955-57; program cons. to ABC, CBS, NBC, Capital Cities, Infinity, Cox, Gannett, Greater Media, N.Y. Times, 1958—; v.p. radio Capital Cities, N.Y.C., 1959-60; v.p. owned radio stas. NBC, N.Y.C., 1963-65. Mem. Internat. Radio and TV Soc., Nat. Assn. Broadcasters. Roman Catholic.

JOSEPH, RODNEY RANDY, artist, arts society executive; b. Providence, July 13, 1945; s. Sidney Wilson and Philomena Joseph; m. Rumiko Antoinette Joseph, Jan. 29, 1971; children: Randy P., Reiner Scott. Student, Sch. Practical Art, Boston, 1964-67, Boston Conservatory Music, 1972-73; BFA, Art Inst. Boston, 1994. With Joseph Art Studio, Plymouth, Mass., 1973-76; arbitrator Better Bus. Bur., Fair Haven, Mass., 1977-79; prodr. Cape 11-Cable, Yarmouth, Mass., 1980-81; pres. Creative Life for Humanitary Arts Soc., Plymouth, 1992—; pres. Creative Life Inc., Plymouth, 1976-92; cons. Creative Life Rsch., 1979—; program designer Office for Children of Boston, Plymouth, 1978-79; legal rsch. pres., 1976; cons. to govtl. policy on social welfare programs without the cost of taxation, 1994—; cons. svcs. to Pres. Clinton's Program, 1994—. Prodr. children's video: Captain Randy and Scott Terrific Adventures; author: (video) Saga of Old Plimoth Indians Cat the First Thanksgiving, 1999. Designed programs and campaigned for revitalization policies, talent laws; authored Act Naturally Talented Children, Mass., Nat. Campaign "Joseph Universal Welfare Act," Proposal for Resolution Article to cover local real estate tax cost and protection of hist. lands, Old Plymouth/Plymouth, Ma., Program of the Joseph Univ. Welfare Act proposal for constnl. programs for U.S. Sec. of Interior and Pres. Clinton Joint Social Pilot Project, recognized by Mass. State Senate for dedication and commitment in establishing Nov. 13 as Massasoit Compact Day, 1997; campaign for World Peace by C-Life Inc.; mem. Sandwich Hist. Soc. Recognized by Pres. Reagan Pvt. Sector Initiatives, 1982, Internat. Bio Ctr. Eng. Man of Yr. award, 1992-93, 93-94; recognized by House of Commons, London, Prime Min. John Major, Social Security divsn., leader of the opposition Tony Blair for the Joseph Universal Welfare Act, 1995. Mem. Internat. Platform Assn. (arts presentation 1993, nat. conv., presenter of poetry, theatre, works of art, speech), Boston Social Libr. (life), Sandwich Hist. Soc. Republican. Avocations: painting, antique collecting, art exhibitions. Home: 558 Wareham Rd Plymouth MA 02360-3239

JOSEPH, STEPHEN, nephrology and dialysis nurse; b. Bombay, India; came to U.S., 1991; s. Pottoore Chandy and Marykutty Joseph; m. Simi Simon. BSN, Coll. Nursing, Trivandrum, India, 1988; MBA in Internat. Bus., Pace U., 1996; grad. in Personal Fin. Planning, CUNY, 1998. RN, India, New Zealand, N.Y. Staff nurse Hinduja Nat. Hosp. and Med. Rsch. Ctr., Bombay, 1989-90; specialist nurse Ministry of Health, Baharain, 1990; nursing instr. Am. Inst., Kottayam, India, 1991; staff nurse/charge nurse Hemodialysis Unit, St. Barnabas Hosp., Bronx, N.Y., 1991-99; mgr. hemodialysis St. Luke's--Roosevelt Hosp., N.Y.C., 1999—. Mem. Dialysis Patient Assn. (organizer), Servas Internat., Trained Nurses Assn. of India. Roman Catholic. Avocations: training dogs, playing guitar and harmonica, stamp collecting, travel. Home: 2531 Holland Ave 2d Fl Bronx NY 10467-8703 Office: St Luke's--Roosevelt Hosp 114th St and Amsterdam New York NY 10025

JOSEPH, STEVEN W., real estate executive, lawyer; b. Cleve., Aug. 7, 1946; m. Linda E. Joseph; children: Jamie, Keith, Hallie, Lisa. BA in Polit. Sci., U. Pa., 1968; JD, U. Mich., 1972. Atty. Jones, Day, Reavis & Pogue, Cleve., 1972-74; real estate broker Klarreich, Wald, Fisher, Cleve., 1975; atty. Eaton Corp., Cleve., 1977-78; real estate atty. Burke, Haber & Berick, Cleve., 1978-84; co-founder, prin. Voinovich Co., Cleve., 1985-94; prin. Cleve. Real Estate Ptnrs., 1994-98; ptnr. Deloitte & Touche, Cleve., 1999—. Office: Deloitte & Touche 127 Public Sq Ste 2500 Cleveland OH 44114-1303

JOSEPH, THANGAM, pharmacology educator; b. Chennai, Tamil Nadu, India, July 21, 1935; d. Chulliparambil and Eva Vareed; m. Pulikottil Ittoop Joseph, May 22, 1960; children: Vinod, Anish. MB BS, Christian Med. Coll., Vellore, India, 1960; MD in Pharmacology, Med. Coll., Trivandrum, India, 1970. Lectr. in Physiology Med. Coll., Bangalore, India, 1960-67; tutor St. John's Med. Coll., Bangalore, 1967-70, asst. prof., 1970-75, assoc. prof., 1975-77, prof., head of dept., 1977-99; prof. emeritus, 1999—; vice prin. St. John's Med. Coll., Bangalore, 1985-89; Brit. Coun. fellow RVI, Newcastle, Eng., 1975-76; mem. ethical com. Nat. Inst. Mental Health & Neuroscis., 1989-98; mem. selection com. Union Pub. Svc. Commn., Govt. of India, 1982-83; editl. bd. Indian Jour. Pharmacology,. Contbr. 70 articles to profl. jours. Mem. Assn. Physiologists and Pharmacologists of India (life), Indian Pharmacol. Soc. (life), Indian Soc. for Clin. Pharmacology & Therapeutics (life). Avocations: painting, embroidery, sports, cooking. Home: 845 15th Main 3rd Block, Korarmangala, Bangalore 560 034, India Office: St Johns Med Coll, Johnnagara, Bangalore 560 034, India

JOSEPH, THOMAS ERINJERY, priest, religious organization administrator; b. Trissur, Kerala, India, Jan. 11, 1941; s. Erinjery Thomas Joseph and Palathinkal Varunny Kunjethy. BSc, St. Thomas Coll., Trissur, India, 1964; MA in Sociology, Loyola Coll., Thiruvananthapuram, India, 1966; BPh, Sacred Heart Coll., Shembaganur, 1968; BTh, Jna Deepa Vidhya Peeth, Pune, 1974; PhD in Sociology, U. Bombay, 1982. Lectr. Soc. Jesus, Thiruvananthapuram, 1968-69, 84-85, vice-prin., 1977-82; prin. Soc. Jesus, Lunglei, India, 1983-84; prin. Soc. Jesus, Thiruvananthapuram, 1985-86, rector, 1988-94; pastor Diocese of Silchar, Lunglei, 1982-83; pres. Loyola Ext. Svcs., Kerala, 1985-96; project dir. Jesuit Refugee Svcs., Adjumani, Uganda, 1996-98; dir. Samshviti, Parayaram, Kanmur, 1999—. Author: Coalition Game Politics in Kerala After Independence, 1982, Mizo Bamboo Hills Murmer Change, 1987, Ethnic Diversity and Public Policy, 1993; editor Loyola Jour. Social Scis., 1987-96. Mem. All Kerala Sociol. Soc. (pres. 1993-95). Avocations: political analysis, writing, reading, movies. Home: Christ Hall, PO Malaparamba, Kozhikode 673 009, India

JOSEPH, WILLIAM NATHANIEL, mechanical engineer, marine engineer; b. Georgetown, Guyana, Mar. 17, 1958; s. Ethellene Adella (Amsterdam) J. B of Engring., U. Guyana, 1987; MSc in Marine Engring., World Maritime U., 1991. From clk. to chief mech. engr. Transport and Harbours Dept., Georgetown, Guyana, 1976-96, dep. gen. mgr., 1996—; ship surveyor Govt. of Guyana, 1993—. Mem. Soc. Naval Archs. and Marine Engrs. (assoc.), Inst. Marine Engrs. (U.K.). Fax: 592-2-78545. Home: 2879 N Ruimveldt, Greater Georgetown Guyana Office: Transport and Harbours Dept, Battery Rd, Georgetown Guyana

JOSEPHSEN, JYTTE, food science educator; b. Elsinore, Denmark, Mar. 13, 1947; d. Povl and Stina Viola (Jönsson) J.; children from previous marriage: Andrei Bjarke Moskvitin Josephsen, Alexander Moskvitin Josephsen; m. Franz Berg, Sept. 12, 1987; 1 child, Nanna Lea Berg. MSc, Copenhagen (Denmark) U., 1973, PhD, 1982. Cert. biochemist. Vacancy for asst. prof. Copenhagen (Denmark) U., 1977-78; postdoctoral staff Danish Tech. U., Lyngby, Denmark, 1982-84; asst. prof. The Royal Vet. and Agrl. U., Frederiksberg, Denmark, 1984-89; assoc. prof. The Royal Vet. and Agrl. U., Frederiksberg, 1989—. Patentee in field. Mem. Danish Biochem. Soc. Avocations: literature, gardening. Home: Magnoliavej 34, 2000 Frederiksberg Denmark Office: KVL, Rolighedsvej 30, 1958 Frederiksberg C, Denmark

JOSEPHSON, BRIAN DAVID, physicist; b. Jan. 4, 1940; s. Abraham and Mimi Josephson; m. Carol Anne Olivier, 1976; 1 dau. BA, Cambridge U., 1960, MA, PhD, 1964; DSc (hon.), U. Wales, 1974, Exeter U., 1983. Asst. dir. research in physics Cambridge U., 1967-72, reader, 1972-74, prof. physics, 1974—, dir. Mind-Matter Unification Project, Cavendish Labs.; vis. faculty Maharishi European Res. U., 1975; vis. prof. dept. computer sci. Wayne State U., 1983; vis. prof. Indian Inst. Sci., Bangalore, 1984, U. Mo.-Rolla, 1987. Author: The Paranormal and the Platonic Worlds, 1997; author papers on physics and theory of intelligence; co-editor: Consciousness and the Physical World, 1980. Recipient Nobel prize in physics, 1973, New Scientist award, 1969, Guthrie medal, 1972, van der Pol medal, 1972, Elliott Cresson medal, 1972, Hughes medal, 1972, Holweck medal, 1973, Faraday medal, 1982, Sir George Thompson medal, 1984; fellow Trinity Coll., Cambridge, 1962—. Fellow Royal Soc.; mem. IEEE (hon.), Am. Acad. Arts and Scis. (fgn., hon.). Office: U Cambridge Cavendish Lab, Madingley Rd Dept Physics, Cambridge CB3 OHE, England*

JOSEY, DONNA PEARSON, art gallery director; b. Lynchburg, Va., Nov. 21, 1942; d. Gordon Trout and Eloise Virginia (Seabolt) Pearson; m. Joseph Oscar Neuhoff, May 1, 1965 (div. Mar. 1990); children: Laurel Neuhoff Page, Donna Ann, Emily Pearson, Joseph Oscar III, Virginiaa Folsom; m. Jack Smyth Josey, Jan. 16, 1992. Cert. in letters, U. Paris, 1963; BA, Sweet Briar Coll., 1964; postgrad., Rice U., 1997. Tchr. French, St. Mark's Sch., Dallas, 1964-65, Jesuit Coll. Prep. Sch., Dallas, 1981-83; pres. Neuhoff Galleries, Dallas, 1983-98, Houston, 1998—; aesthetic advisor The Crescent Devel., Dallas, 1984-85; v.p., art curator Josey Oil Co., Houston, 1992-96; pvt. art dealer, 1994—. Bd. dirs. Cath. Charities, Dallas, 1980—, Nat. Wildflower Found., Austin, Tex., 1995—, Am. Hosp. Paris, 1994—, Strake Jesuit Coll. Prep, Houston, 1998; mem. arts adv. bd. U. Tex., Austin, 1995—, Sweet Briar (Va.) Coll., 1995—. Mem. Met. Club (N.Y.C.), Crescent Club (Dallas), James River Country Club (Va.), River Oaks Country Club, Eldorado Country Club. Roman Catholic. Avocations: painting, horseback riding. Home: 1537 Kirby Dr Houston TX 77019-3301 Office: Neuhoff Galleries 2001 Kirby Dr Ste 1002 Houston TX 77019-6033

JOSHI, AMITABH, evolutionary biologist; b. Agra, India, Mar. 4, 1965; s. Devi Datt and Nirmala (Pande) J.; m. Vani Akella, Nov. 9, 1991; 1 child. BSc in Botany with honors, U. Delhi, India, 1986, MSc in Genetics, 1988; PhD in Genetics, Wash. State U., 1993. Postdoctoral rschr. U. Calif., Irvine, 1994-96; assoc. prof. Jawaharlal Nehru Ctr. for Advanced Sci. Rsch., Bangalore, India, 1996—; reviewer manuscripts and proposals Indian Dept. Sci. and Tech., Coun. for Sci. and Indsl. Rsch. Assoc. editor Resonance jour.; contbr. numerous articles to profl. jours. Mem. Indian Acad. Scis. (assoc.). Avocations: music, reading and writing poetry in Urdu and English, history, philosophy. Office: J Nehru Ctr Adv Sci Rsch, Biology Unit Jakkur PO, Bangalore Karnataka 560064, India

JOSHI, GIRISH PREMJI, anesthesiologist; b. Pune, India, Mar. 7, 1959; came to U.S., 1992; s. Premji Punja and Shanta Premji J. MB, BS, U. Pune, 1981, MD in Anesthesiology, 1985; MD, U. Coll. Dublin, Ireland, 1994. Diplomate Am. Bd. Anesthesiology. Lectr. King Edward Meml. Hosp., Pune, 1986-87; registrar Regional Gen. Hosp., Limerick, Ireland, 1988-89, Beaumont Hosp., Dublin, 1990; cons. anesthetist Cappagh Hosp. & mater Misericordia Hosp., Dublin, 1991; asst. prof. Oreg. Health Scis. U., Portland, 1992; asst. prof. U. Tex. S.W. Med. Ctr., Dallas, 1993-97, assoc. prof., 1997—; dir. perioperative medicine & ambulatory anesthesia Parkland Health & Hosp. Sys., Dallas, 1999—, chmn. pain com., 1998—; vice-chmn. clin. rsch. com. U. Tex. S.W. Med. Ctr., Dallas, 1997—. Editor: Anesthesia for Oscopies of the Abdominal and Thoracic Cavities, 2000; mem. editl. bd. Jour. Evaluation in Clin. Practice. Nat. Merit scholar Govt. India, Pune, 1980-81; named Man of Yr., B.J. Med. Coll. Students Assn., 1980; recipient Cost-Effectiveness award Anesthesiology News & Stuart Pharm., 1993, 96. Fellow Royal Coll. Surgeons; mem. Am. Soc. Anesthesiologists (subcom. mem. 1999—), Internat. Anesthesia Rsch. Soc., Soc. for Ambulatory Anesthesia (vice-chmn. publ. 1999—), Tex. Soc. Anesthesiologists, Dallas County Anesthesiology Soc. (pres. 1998). Hindu. Avocation: travel. E-mail: girish.joshi@email.swmed.edu. Office: Univ Tex SW Med Ctr 5323 Harry Hines Blvd Dallas TX 75390-7208

JOSHI, HARI HAR, medical microbiologist; b. Khalte Village, Tanahu, Nepal, Jan. 4, 1963; s. Cheta Raj and Ishwori Kumari (Mishra) J.; m. Bobby Pant, June 5, 1995; children: Shreedhar, Shreehar. B of Commerce, Tribhuvan U., Kathmandu, Nepal, 1983, BSc in Med. Lab. Tech., 1989; MSc in Med. Microbiology, Mahidol U., Bangkok, 1997; postgrad., Mahidol U., 1998—. Microbiologist Tchg. Hosp. Tribhuvan U., Kathmandu, 1983—. Author: Haematology, 2000. Treas. Nepal Health Profls. against AIDS, Kathmandu, 1994. USAID scholar Mahidol U., 1994, WHO/Tropical Disease Rsch. scholar, 1999. Avocations: fishing, hiking, Internet, reading, playing with kids. Home: Mali Gaon, GPO Box No 5427, Kathmandu Nepal

JOSHI, HARIHAR S., medical laboratory executive; b. Manjarkhed, India, Aug. 20, 1931; came to U.S., 1962; s. Sopandeo Waman and Manakarnika Narayan J.; m. Vaijayanti Pushpa Laxman Kukade, June 6, 1957; children: Chandrashekhar, Wandana, Sharad. B in Vet. Sci., M.P. Vet. Coll., 1954; MS, U. Hawaii, 1964; PhD, U. Guelph, 1971. Vet. officer Dept. Vet. & Animal Husbandry, India, 1954-58; rsch. assoc., lectr. Bombay Vet. Coll., India, 1958-62; asst. prof. U. Guelph, Ont., Canada, 1964-69; rsch. fellow Worcester Found. Exptl. Biology, Shrewsbury, Mass., 1971-75; tech. supervisor, dir. Ind. Med. Labs., Worcester and Cambridge, Mass., 1975-80; pres. Omega Med. Labs, Oxford, Mass., 1980-95. Head religious matters India Soc. Worcester, Shrewsbury, 1972-95; Hindu priest, 1972—. Mem. Am. Assn. Clin. Chemists. Home: 65 Locust Ave Worcester MA 01604-1129

JOSHI, HEMCHANDRA VINAYAK, electronic engineer, consultant; b. Hyderabad, India, Jan. 7, 1946; s. Vinayak Chintaman and Sarojini (Godbole) J.; m. Pratima Hemachandra Damale, Feb. 20, 1976; children: Shantanu, Anish. B Elec. Engring., COEP, Pune, India, 1966. Installation and commissioning engr. Western India Erectors, Pune, 1962-72; prodn. mgr. McNeil Magor Ltd., Madras, India, 1972-83; pvt. practice engr. Pune, 1983-85; dir. Inventa Electronics, Pune, 1986—; mng. dir. Vistar Electronics, Pune, 1989—, also bd. dirs.; bd. dirs. Inventa Electronics, Pine; cons. in field. Designer, developer charge controller, inverter for solar appliance, motor rotation tester. With Nat. Cadet Core, 1961-63. Mem. IEEE (sr.), Inst. Econ. Studies (Udyog Rattan award 1993). Hindu. Avocations: travel, watching cricket, Indian classical music, reading, teaching. Home: 2036 Sadashiv Peth Tilak Rd, Pune Maharashtra 411 030, India

JOSHI, JYESHTHARAJ BHALCHANDRA, chemical engineering educator, researcher; b. Masur, India, May 28, 1949; s. Bhalchandra Shivram and Shrada Bhalchandra (Akku) J.; m. Rujuta Jyeshtharaj Marathe, June 9, 1978; 1 child, Aniruddha. B in Chem. Engring., U. Mumbai, India, 1971, PhD in Tech., 1977. Assoc. lectr. U. Mumbai, India, 1972-79, lectr., then asst. prof., 1979-81, reader, assoc. prof., 1981-86, prof., 1986—; dir. dept. chem. tech. U. Mumbai, 1999—; cons. Bombay Oil Industried Ltd., Reliance Industries Ltd., Alkyl Amines and chems. Ltd., Deepak Nitrite Ltd., others, 1975—. Contbr. over 240 articles to profl. jours.; patentee in field. Recipient S.S. Bhatnagar prize Coun. Sci. and Indsl. Rsch./Govt. India, 1991; recipient Young Scientist medal Indian Nat. Sci. Acad., 1981, Vasvik Prize, 1992; named Achiever of yr. Chemtech Found., 1997, Goyal Found. awards, 1998. Mem. Maharashtra Acad. Scis., Indian Acad. Scis., Indian Nat. Sci. Acad. Avocation: yoga. Home: 33 Jaimangal Soc Shivsrushti, Mumbai 400024, India Office: U Mumbai Dept Chem Tech, Matunga 400019, India

JOSHI, MURLI MANSHAR, administrator. Elected to Lok Sabha, India, 1977; joint sec. Janata Party, India, 1977-80; founder, mem. BJP, India, 1980, pres., 1991-93; min. Ministry Home Affairs, India, 1996, Ministry Human Resources Devel., 1998—, Ministry Sci. & Tech, 1998—. Office: Ministry Human Resources, Shastri Bhawan-1, New Delhi 110 011, India

JOSHI, NIK M., consultancy company executive, educator, writer; b. Kampala, Uganda, Feb. 16, 1955; arrived in Eng., 1970; m. Maganlal and Prabha Joshi; m. Urmi Vachhrajani, Dec. 11, 1981; children: Guderian, Anushka, Bradley. BSc in Econs. with honors, U. London, 1977, MA in History, 1988. Econ. advisor Brit. Govt., London, 1977-80; mktg. mgr. Indsl. Oxygen Co. Ltd., New Delhi, India, 1980-84, Carless PLC, London, 1984-89; European mktg. dir. Brammer PLC, London, 1989-90; head mgmt. Kent Coll. Higher Edn., Chatham, 1990-95; dir. NJ Mgmt. Consultancy, London, 1995—; vis. lectr. London Guildhall U., 1995—; assoc. lectr. Bus. Sch., Open U., London, 1990—. Author: Supervision & Sales Management, 1996, Principles & Practice of Management in Insurance, 1996, Accounting and Finance for Managers in Insurance, 1996. Office: 251 Tiptree Crescent, Clayhall, Ilford, Essex 1GS 0SS, England

JOSHI, RAJENDRA PRASAD, political science educator, researcher; b. Nathdwara, Rajasthan, India, Aug. 1, 1949; s. Durga Shankar and Sushila Devi Joshi; m. Prem Lata, May 6, 1971; children: Yogita, Meenakshi, Manish. BA, U. Udaipur, India, 1968, MA, 1970; PhD, U. Rajasthan, Jaipur, India, 1986. Lectr. U. Rajashihan, 1970-85, reader, 1986-90; dir. Kota Open U., Jaipur, 1988-90; reader pub. adminstrn. Lal Bahadur Shastri Acad., Mussoralie, India, 1985-86; prof. pub. adminstrn. Hcm State Inst., Jaipur, 1994-95; prof. polit. sci. Maharshi Dayanand Saraswati U., Ajmer, India, 1990—; dean social scis. MDS U., Ajmer, 1998-2000. Author: Participation in Management, 1987, Police Training in Community Relations, 1993; editor: Nehru's Vision of Secularism, 1991, Whither Indian Politics, 1996, Constitutionalization of Panchayati Raj—A Reassessment, 1998, Panchayati Raj Ke Navin Aayam (Hindi), 1998, International Relations, 1999, Bharat Mein Panchayati Raj, 2000. Recipient Career award U. Grant Commn., New Delhi, 1987. Mem. Indian Inst. Pub. Adminstrn., Rajasthan Soc. for Consumer Edn. and Rsch. (sec. 1985—). Home: D-63 Chomu House, Jaipur 302001, India Office: MDS U, Ghoogra, Ajmer 305009, India

JOSHI, RAJINDER KUMAR, command and information systems company executive; b. Jullundur, Punjab, India, Feb. 21, 1959; arrived in Eng., 1966; s. Rattan Chand and Krishna Rani (Bhardwaj) J.; m. Anju Bala Sharma, Sept. 14, 1994; 2 children, Raam Chandra, Radha Aarti. BSc with honors, Lanchester Poly., Coventry, Eng., 1980; MSc, Cranfield Inst. Tech., Bedfordshire, Eng., 1982, PhD, 1988. Cert. engring. exec. Devel. test engr. Eddystone Radio Ltd., Birmingham, Eng., 1978-79; project systems engr. Serck Controls Ltd., Leamington Spa, Eng., 1979-80; sr. systems design/devel. engr. Radamec Def. Systems, Ltd., Chertsey, Surrey, Eng., 1982-83; projects mgr. Radamec Def. Systems, Ltd., Chertsey, Eng., 1983-84, tech. projects mgr., 1984-88; tech. quality assurance exec. Radamec Group Plc, Chertsey, Eng., 1988-91; chief systems engr. GQ Parachutes Ltd., Woking, Surrey, Eng., 1991-94; systems engring. mgr. GQ Parachutes Ltd., Blackmill, Bridgend, Wales, 1994-97; advanced sys. applications and techs. dept. mgr. GEC-Marconi Command & Info. Systems Divsn., Frimley, Eng., 1997-99; bus. devel. mgr. Integrated Systems divsn. Alenia-Marconi Systems, Frimley, 1999—. Author: A Computer-Aided Design Facility for System Identification, 1982, Control and Estimation Algorithms for Automating an Existing Fire Control System, 1988; contbr. tech. papers to profl. jours. Mem. IEEE, Inst. Elec. Engrs. U.K. (assoc.), N.Y. Acad. Scis. Avocations: still/video photography, painting and drawing, travel, squash, badminton, golf.

JOSHIPURA, BHUSHIT PRADYUMNA, engineering executive; b. Junagadh, Gujarat, India, Feb. 22, 1971; s. Pradyumna Jaysukhray and Avrutti Pradyumna (Nanavaty) J.; m. Vaishalee Bhushit Chhaya; child, Muktaka. BEng, Gujarat U., 1992; M.Tech., Indian Inst. Tech., Kanpur, 1995. Jr. engr. R&D Gujarat Hi-Rel Controls Ltd., Gandhinagar, 1992-93; engr. R&D CMC Ltd., Hyderabad, 1995-96, sr. engr. R&D, 1996—. Contbr. articles to profl. jours.; author: (poetry, prose) Ghazals and Poetries and Essays, 1997. Avocations: music, philosophy, yoga, cycling. Home: Asmakam Shakti Nagar, Kalawad Rd, Rajkot 360 005, India

JOSIFOVSKI, VANJA, engineering educator; b. Skopje, Macedonia, June 21, 1970; came to U.S. 2000; s. Georgi Josifovski and Svetlana Pendarovska. Diploma engring., U. Ljubljana, Slovenia, 1994; MSc, U. Fla., 1996; PhD, U. Linköping, Sweden, 1999. Rsch. asst. U. Fla., 1994-96; rsch. U. Linköping, Sweden, 1996-99; asst. prof. U. Uppsala, Sweden, 1999-2000; rschr. IBM Almaden Rsch. Ctr., 2000—. Contbr. articles to profl. jours. Avocation: skydiving. Office: 650 Harry Rd San Jose CA 95120-6001

JOSKOWICZ, LEO, computer scientist; b. Paris, Apr. 13, 1961; s. Alfredo and Esther (Seligson) J. BSc, Israel Inst. Tech., 1983; MSc, NYU, 1985, PhD, 1988. From rsch. staff leader to project leader IBM T.J. Watson Rsch. Ctr., Yorktown Heights, N.Y., 1988-95; assoc. prof. inst. computer sci. The Hebrew U., Jerusalem, 1995—. Editl. bd. Artificial Intelligence in Engring. Jour., 1992—, Jour. Computer Aided Surgery, Med. Image Analysis Jour., Annals of Maths. and Artificial Intelligence; contbr. articles to profl. jours. Mem. IEEE, ASME, AAAI. Office: The Hebrew U, Inst Computer Sci, Jerusalem 91904, Israel

JOSLYN, H. DAVID, turbomachinery research specialist, technology systems manager, consultant; b. Rochester, N.Y., Apr. 29, 1944; s. Howard David and Marjorie Ruth (Pembroke) J.; m. Sandra Marilyn Weiner. BS in Aeronautics and Aerospace, NYU, 1966, MS in Aeronautics and Aerospace, 1967. Grad. rsch. scientist dept. aeros. NYU, N.Y.C., 1966-67; assoc. rsch. engr. Boeing Co., Cape Kennedy, Fla., 1967-68; rsch. engr. United Techs. Rsch. Ctr., East Hartford, Conn., 1973-83, sr. rsch. engr., 1984-94; prin. coord. tech. and methods devel. BMW Rolls-Royce Aero Engines, Berlin, 1994-99; tech. acquisition mgr. Rolls-Royce Germany, Dahlewitz, 2000—; tech. cons. edn. and tng. program United Techs. Corp., Hartford, Conn., 1993-94; cons. German Ministry for Reunification, Dresden, 1991. Contbr. articles to sci. jours., including AIAA Jour. Propulsion and Power, ASME Jour. Engring. for Gas Turbines and Power, ASME Jour. Turbomachinery. Mem. ASME (tech. jour. reviewer 1978—, turbo machinery com. 1993—, best tech. paper award 1989), AIAA (tech. jour. reviewer 1978—). Avocations: windsurfing, sailing, skiing, tennis, bicycling. Office: Rolls Royce Germany GmbH, Eschenweg 11, 15827 Dahlewitz Germany

JOSLYN, ROBERT BRUCE, lawyer; b. Detroit, Jan. 9, 1945; s. Lee Everett, Jr. and Juanita Constance (McGonegal) J.; m. Karen Sue Glenny, July 8, 1967; children: Gwendolyn Constance, Robert Bruce. B.A., Fla. State U., 1967; J.D., Emory U., 1970. Bar: Mich. 1970. Law clk. Gurney, Gurney & Handley, Orlando, Fla., summer 1969; asso. Joslyn & Keydel, Detroit, 1970-74; ptnr. Joslyn, Keydel & Wallace, 1975-95; pvt. practice Robert B. Joslyn, PC, 1996—; vis. instr. Oakland U., Rochester, Mich., 1974-75; faculty Inst. Continuing Legal Edn., Ann Arbor, Michl, 1975—; guest instr. U. Mich. Law Sch. Co-author: Manual for Lawyers and Legal Assistants: Probate and Trust Administration, 1977, Manual for Lawyers and Legal Assistants: Taxation of Trusts and Estates, 1977, 3d edit., 1980. Mem. U.S. All Am. Prep. Sch. Swim Team, 1963. Mem. ABA, Detroit Bar Assn. (chmn. taxation com. 1985-87), State Bar Mich. (chairperson probate and estate planning sect. 1992-93), Am. Coll. of Trust and Estate Counsel (state chmn. 1987-92, bd. regents 1994—), Internat. Acad. Estate and Trust Law, Fin. and Estate Planning Coun. Detroit (bd. dirs. 1988-92, pres. 1992), Grosse Pointe Yacht Club, Phi Delta Phi, Phi Kappa Psi. Home: 286 Hillcrest Ave Grosse Pointe MI 48236-3123 Office: 200 Maple Park Blvd Ste 201 Saint Clair Shores MI 48081-2211

JOSPIN, LIONEL, prime minister of French Republic; b. Meudon, Hauts-de-Seine, France, July 12, 1937; s. Robert Jospin and Mireille Dandieu; m. Sylviane Agacinski, 1994; 3 children. Ed., Inst. Etudes Politiques, Paris, Ecole Nat. Administration. Sr. civil servant econs. French Fgn. Office, 1965-70; prof. econs. Tech. U. Inst. Paris-Sceaux, 1970-81; nat. sec. French Socialist Party for Tng., 1973-75, Third-World Affairs, 1975-79, Internat. Affairs, 1979-81; 1st sec. French Socialist Party, 1981-88; mem. French Parliament, 1981-88, European Parliament, 1984-88; ministre d'Etat in charge of nat. edn. and sports, 1988-92, mem. Haute-Garonne Conseil général, 1988—, mem. Midi-Pyrénées Conseil régional, 1992-97; plenipotentiary min. Fgn. Office, 1992—; 1st sec. Socialist Party, 1995-98; prime min. France, 1997—. Author: L'Invention du Possible, 1991, 1995-2000: Propositions pour la

France, 1995. Recipient Grand-Croix Ordre Nat. du Mérite, Commandeur Palmes Académiques. Avocations: basketball, tennis. Address: Hôtel de Matignon, 57 rue de Varenne, 75700 Paris France

JOST, JEAN-PIERRE, molecular biology researcher; b. Avenches, Vaud, Switzerland, Oct. 10, 1937; naturalized American citizen, 1970; s. Emile and Frida (Gerber) Jost; m. Yan-Chim Tse, Dec. 24, 1968; children: Isabelle King-Yi, Alain King-Ho. Engr. Agronomy, Swiss Fed. Inst. Tech., Zurich, 1961, PhD in Biochemistry, 1964. Postdoctoral fellow McArdle Cancer Rsch., Madison, Wis., 1964-66; rsch. assoc. molecular biology Univ. Wis., Madison, 1966-68; asst. prof. biophysics Med. Sch., Denver, 1968-71; group leader Nat. Jewish Hosp., Denver, 1968-71; sr. team leader Friedrich Miescher Inst., Basel, Switzerland, 1971—; industry cons. Co-author: Laboratory Guide to Genomic Sequencing, 1987, Laboratory Guide to In Vivo Studies of DNA Methylation and Protein/DNA Interactions, 1990; editor, co-author: Laboratory Guide to In Vitro Studies of Protein/DNA Interactions, 1991, DNA Methylation: Molecular Biology and Biological Significance, 1993; contbr. more than 200 articles to profl. jours.; patentee in biotech. field. Avocation: wildlife, photography for internat. competitions and exhibitions. Fax: (4161) 721 4091. E-mail: jpjost@datacomm.ch. Home: Fichtenrains 9, CH-4106 Therwil/Basel Land Switzerland Office: Friedrich Miescher Inst, PO Box 2543, CH-4002 Basel Switzerland

JÓSVAY, JÁNOS, plastic surgeon, consultant; b. Miskolc, Hungary, Sept. 14, 1958; s. János Jósuay and Erzsébet Szászfai. MD, U. Debrecen, Hungary, 1983; gen. surgeon, Semmelweis U., Budapest, Hungary, 1987, plastic surgeon, 1991. Qualified gen. surgeon, cons. surgeon; qualified plastic surgeon, cons. plastic surgeon. Resident traumatology County Hosp., Miskolc, 1983-86; resident gen. surgery Ctrl. Mil. Hosp., Budapest, 1986-87, cons. dept. burns, vice dir. dept. burns, 1987-89, cons. dept. plastic surgery, 1989—. Mem. Internat. Confedn. for Plastic, Reconstructive and Aesthetic Surgery, Hungarian Confedn. for Plastic, Reconstructive and Aesthetic Surgery, Hungarian Burns Assn. Office: Ctrl Mil Hosp, 1553 Budapest Pf1, Hungary

JOSYULA, ESWAR, aerospace engineer; b. Kakinada, India, Apr. 26, 1956; s. Govinda Rao and Umasundari J.; m. Santha Kumari Dinavahi; May 9, 1987; children: Krishnapriya, Srirama. BS, U. Mysore, India, 1978; MS, Wichita State U., 1985. Rsch. fellow Morgantown Energy Tech. Ctr., W.V., 1985-86; rsch. aerospace engr. USAF Rsch. Lab., Wright-Patterson Air Base, Ohio, 1986—. Contbr. articles to profl. jours. Fellow Am. Inst. Aeronautics and Astronautics. Avocations: yoga, classical music. Fax: 937-656-7867. E-mail: Eswar.Josyula@wpafb.af.mil. Office: USAF Rsch Lab Wright Patterson Air Base 2130 Eighth St AFRL/VAAC Wright Patterson AB OH 45433

JOTANIA, KANTI RAVAJIBHAI, physics educator; b. Botad, Gujarat, India, Sept. 19, 1965; s. Ravajibhai Tulshibhai and Gituben (Katudia) J.; m. Rajshree Bhagavandas, June 11, 1997. BSc, Gugarat U., Ahmedabad, India, 1987, MSc, 1989; PhD in Physics, U. Pune, India, 1995. UGC rsch. fellow Inter-Univ. Ctr. Astronomy and Astrophysics, Pune, 1989-95, vis. fellow, scientist, 1997, rsch. assoc., 1998—; postdoctoral fellow Raman Rsch. Inst., Bangalore, India, 1995-97; lectr. in physics St. Xavier's Coll., Ahmedabad, 1997—; lectr. govt. svcs. Gujarat Pub. Svc. Commn., 2000. Mem. Indian Assn. Gen. Relativity and Gravitation (life). E-mail: nlavingia@icenet.net. Office: St Xavier's Coll, Navrangpura, Ahmedabad Gujarat 380 009, India

JOTCHAM, THOMAS DENIS, marketing communications consultant; b. Llandudno, Wales, Feb. 21, 1918; s. George James and Marion (Brand) J.; m. Margaret Jean Thirlwell, Aug. 10, 1940 (dec.); children: Patricia, Douglas, Joy, Candace (dec.). Student, Lower Can. Coll., 1929-36, McGill U., 1937-39. Sales rep. Montreal Lithographing Co., Ltd., Montreal, 1945-47; sales mgr. Wesco Waterpaints Can., Ltd., Montreal, 1947-48; advt. mgr. Pepsi-Cola Co. Can., Ltd., Montreal, 1948-52, mgr., 1952-54; asst. advt. mgr. Reader's Digest Assn., Ltd., Montreal, 1954-56; mgr., v.p. Foster Advt. Ltd., Montreal, 1956-73, exec. v.p., 1973-75, pres., 1977-81, vice chmn., 1981-83; pres. Sherwood Communications Group Ltd., Toronto, 1977-81, vice chmn., 1981-83; mem. coun. Montreal Bd. Trade, 1973-75, v.p., 1977-78, pres., 1979, hon. chmn., 1980-81. Bd. dirs. Grace Dart Hosp., 1973-83, pres., 1979-83; bd. dirs. Can.Coun. Christians and Jews, 1978-81, Les Grands Ballets Canadien, 1976-77; mem. Venetion Condominium, Inc., pres. 1984, 88-92; treas. Freedom Found.-Broward, 1999-2000. Maj. Can. Army, 1940-45. Recipient ACA Gold medal, 1978; charter recipient McGill Mgmt. Achievement award, 1981. Fellow Inst. Can. Advt. (pres. 1976-77); mem. Can. Advt. and Sales Assn. (pres. 1960-61), Advt. and Sales Execs. Club (pres. 1956-58), Advt. and Sales Assocs. Montreal (pres. 1948-49), Advt. Agy. Coun. Que. (pres. 1975-76), Can.-South African Soc. (bd. dirs. 1980-89, chmn. 1983-86), Internat. Swimming Hall of Fame (bd. dirs., chmn. 1998 99), Mount Stephen Club (pres. 1967-68), St. James Club (com. chmn. 1979-81), Royal Montreal Golf Club, Ont. Club, Thistle Curling Club (pres. 1977-78), Ft. Lauderdale Golf and Country Club (dir. 1990-92), Coral Ridge Yacht Club (gov. 1993-97, commodore 1997), Psi Upsilon. Home and Office: 1 Las Olas Cir Apt 1101 Fort Lauderdale FL 33316-1637

JOUBERT, STANLEY, protective services official; b. Port Elizabeth, South Africa, May 24, 1955; s. Quartus Daniel and Thelma Elaine (Coltman) J.; m. Yvonne Elizabeth Christopher, Dec. 13, 1980; children: Pierre Daniel, Candice Michelle. Student, Queens Coll., Queenstown, U. of South Africa. Nat. diploma police adminstrn.; cert. chem. weapons conv. inspector, bomb disposal operator and explosive ordnance disposal, radiation worker, shooting range officer. Chief lifeguard Municipality, East London, South Africa, 1970-71; sect. head spl. guard unit South African Police Svc., Pretoria, 1979-80, counter insurgency and riots trainer and rschr., 1980-88, bomb disposal trainer and rschr., 1988-98, nat. comdr. bomb disposal, 1995-98, nat. coord. and investigator illegal firearms, 1998—. Coun. mem. Meth. Ch., Pretoria, 1990—; group chmn. Boy Scouts, Pretoria, 1994-97, 99. Mem. Internat. Assn. Bomb Technicians and Investigators, Nat. Inst. Explosive Tech., Inst. Small Arms Rsch. in Internat. Security, Police Sci. Assn. South Africa. Avocations: cooking, watching rugby, gardening. Home: 309 Ivor Ave Mountain View, Pretoria 0082, South Africa Office: Illegal Firearm Invest Unit, South African Police Svc, Pretoria 0001, South Africa

JOUDRIE, H. EARL, oil and gas manufacturing executive; b. Mar. 27, 1934; children: Neale, Carolyn, Colin, Guy. BA, U. Alta, 1957. Chief landman, office mgr. United Producing Co., 1961-63; Can. divsn. mgr. Ashland Oil and Refining Co., 1963-65; pres., CEO Ashland Oi Can. Ltd., 1965-68; chmn., CEO Ashland Oil Can. Ltd., 1968-76; sr. vice pres., grp. operating ofcr. Ashland Oil, Inc., KY, 1976-78; chmn. bd. dirs. Ashland Oil Can. Ltd., 1976-78; pres., CEO Nu-West Group Ltd., 1979-85; CEO Dome CAn. Ltd., 1985-88; chmn. bd. Algoma Steel Inc., 1991—; chmn. Rayrock Yellowknife Resources Inc., 1990-92, Gulf Can. Resources, 1993—; chmn. bd. dirs. Can. Tire Corp., Ltd.; dir., pres. A&G Resources Corp.; dir. Abitibi-Price Inc., Can. Ins. Group Ltd., Can. Utilities Ltd., Consolidated Carma Corp., Dorset Exploration Ltd., Rayrock Yellowknife Resources Inc., Trenton Works Inc., Unitel Comm. Inc., Unitel. Comm. Holdings, Inc., Zargon Oil & Gas Ltd.; chmn. emeritus Pub. Policy Forum, Ottawa; mem. prime min.'s adv. com. Govt. Restructuring; pres., CEO Voyager Petroleums Ltd., 1979-85, Encor Energy Corp., Inc., 1985-88. Home: #4106 1 Palace Pier Court, Toronto, ON Canada M8V 3W9 Office: Gulf Canada Resources Limited, 141 Adelaide St W Ste 310, Toronto, ON Canada M5H 3L5

JOUHKI, JUHA HEIKKI, healthcare executive; b. Helsinki, Finland, Sept. 12, 1966; s. Lauri Juhani and Soili Marjatta J.; m. Elina Tellervo Kajamaa, July 2, 1992; children: Mia, Ida, Oskar. MSc, Helsinki U. Technology, 1992. From project engr. to sales mgr. Finncarriers Oy Ab, Helsinki, 1992-96; CEO ContrAl Clinics Oy, Espoo, Finland, 1996-99; ptnr. Thominvest Oy, Helsinki, 1999—; bd. dirs. Dreadnought Fin. Oy, Helsinki, Thominvest Oy, Helsinki, ContrAl Clinics Oy, Espoo, Oy Control Pharma Ltd., Espoo. Avocations: golf, squash. Home: Lansilinnake 8 A, 02160 Espoo Finland 02160 Office: Thominvest Oy, PO Box 132, 00211 Helsinki Finland

JOUKOWSKY, ARTEMIS A. W., private investor; b. Shanghai, China, Dec. 26, 1930; s. Artemis M.W. and Helen (Skvorzov) J.; m. Martha Content Sharp, June 9, 1956; children: Nina Lydia Koprulu, Artemis W. III, Michael A. AB, Brown U., 1955, LLD (hon.), 1985. Dep. to dir. Am. Internat. Underwriters, Milan, 1960-66, dep. to regional dir. for Europe, 1963-66, dir. Italian div., 1963-65; regional v.p. for Middle East, North Africa Am. Internat. Underwriters, Beirut, 1966-72; pres., regional dir. S.E. Asia Am. Internat. Underwriters, Hong Kong, 1972-74; v.p. Am. Internat. Underwriters, N.Y.C., 1974-77; mng. dir. Middle East Assurance and Reinsurance Co., Beirut, 1966-72; dir. Tam Sigorta, Istanbul, Turkey, 1967-72, Union Atlantique de Reassurance SA, Brussels, 1979-88, European Am. Underwriters, Vienna, Austria, 1979-87; dir., shareholder's rep. AIG Joint Ventures with Govt. Agencies, N.Y.C., 1979-87, pres. socialist countries div. and spl. world markets div., 1977-87. Founder, chmn. Brown U. Sports Found., 1983—; trustee Brown U., Providence, 1985—, vice chancellor 1988-97, chancellor, 1997-98, chancellor emeritus, 1998—; mem. bd. overseers Thomas J. Watson Inst. for Internat. Studies, 1981—, Ctr. for the Study Fin. Markets and Insts., 1987-89, Ctr. for Old World Archaeology and Art, 1981-92; vice chmn. bd. govs. John Carter Brown Libr., 1988—; trustee Lawrenceville Sch., N.J., 1984—, pres. bd. trustees, 1997—; chmn. Lawrenceville Trustees Com., 1994-97, Archaeol Inst. Am., 1992—; pres. bd. trustees Am. Ctr. Oriental Rsch., Amman, Jordan, 1992—; mem. vis. com. Boston Mus. Fine Arts, 1985-92; dir. Clear Pool Camp, 1976-85; co-founder Am. Sch. Milan, 1962, bd. govs., 1961-65, pres. 1963-64, fin. com. 1962-65; trustee St. Croix Landmark Soc., Fredericksted, U.S. V.I., 1995—; trustee Internat. Rsch. and Exchs. Bd., 1998—. Mem. U.S. C. of C. (gov. Hong Kong chpt.), U.S.-USSR Trade and Econ. Coun. (tourist and travel com. 1974-77), Hungarian-Am. Trade and Econ. Coun. (vce chmn. 1984-87), Explorer's Club (N.Y.C.), India House (N.Y.C.), Hong Kong Club (life), Brown Club (N.Y.C.), Larchmont (N.Y.) Yacht Club, St. Croix Yacht Club (U.S. V.I.) Univ. Club (Providence), Hope Club (Providence), Knickerbocker Club (N.Y.C.). Office: Brown U 5 Benevolent St Providence RI 02912-9018

JOUN, MAN SOO, educator; b. Euiryung, Korea, Oct. 15, 1961; s. Yong Jung and Sulri (Hwang) J.; m. Hyang Im Ryu; children: Saang Yoon, Soung Hun. BS, Seoul Nat. U., Korea, 1983; MS, Korea Inst. Sci. & Tech., Seoul, 1985; PhD, Pohang Inst. Sci. & Tech., Korea, 1992. Rsch. team leader Samsung Aerospace Inc., Changwon, Korea, 1985-89; rsch. asst. RIST, Pohang, Korea, 1989-92; head dept. Gyeongsang Nat. U., Chinju, Korea, 1996-97, asst. prof., 1992-98, assoc. prof., 1998—; vis. prof. Ohio State U., Columbus, 1997-98; pres. Advanced Forming Rsch. Cons. Corp., 1998; leader Consortium Advanced Forging Tech., 1998; cons. in field. Mem. KSME, KSPE, KSTP. Avocations: fishing, golf, mountain climbing, Oriental chess. Office: Gyeongsang Nat U, 900 Kajoadong, Chinju 660-701, Korea

JOURA, ELMAR ARMIN, gynecologist; b. Graz, Austria, Sept. 7, 1962; s. Ignaz and Edith (Muller) J.; m. Eva Maria Berger, Apr. 21, 1993; children: Isolde, Lukas, Antonia, Alexandra. MD, U. Graz, 1987; Specialist OBGyn, U. Vienna, 1994. Rsch. fellow Inst. Pathology U. Graz, Austria, 1988; intern urology, surgery, medicine Regional Hosp., Leoben, 1989-90; registrar dept. ObGyn U. Vienna, 1991-96, cons. gynecologist, 1997, assoc. prof., 1998; clin. rsch. fellowship, dept. gynae-oncology, Nat. Women's Hosp., Auckland, New Zealand, 1996-97. Contbr. articles to profl. jours. Mem. Internat. Soc. for Study of Vulvovaginal Disease, European Coll. Study Vulval Diseases (councillor), Am. Soc. Reproductive Medicine, Austrian Soc. Colposcopy (bd. dirs.). Avocations: classical music, scuba diving. Office: Univ Vienna/Dept Gynecology, Wahringer Gurtel 18-20, A-1090 Vienna Austria

JOURDREN, MARC HENRI, investment banking company executive; b. Paris, Dec. 28, 1960; s. Pierre Auguste Jourdren and Berthe Augustine Dubois. Diploma in econs. and fin., Essec, Paris, 1983; MBA, Harvard U., 1987. Pres., founder Essec Enterprises Internat., Paris, 1982-83; econ. cooperant French Ministry of Economy and Fin., N.Y.C., 1983-85; assoc. Goldman Sachs & Co., N.Y.C. and Tokyo, 1987-88; assoc. Goldman Sachs Internat., London, 1988-91, v.p., exec. dir., 1991-99, mng. dir., 2000—, head Japanese product sales, 1996-99, head global products group, 1999—; fgn. advisor Harvard U., Cambridge, Mass., 1989—. Mem. Amis du Couserans, Mensa London. Avocations: piano, Russian art, gastronomy, oenology, skiing. Home: 48 Macready House, Crawford St, London W1H 5LP, England Office: Goldman Sachs Internat, Peterborough Ct 133 Fleet St, London EC4A 2BB, England

JOURNEY, DREXEL DAHLKE, lawyer; b. Westfield, Wis., Feb. 23, 1926; s. Clarence Earl and Verna L. Gilmore (Dahlke) Journey Gilmore; m. Vergene Harriet Sandsmark, Oct. 24, 1952; 1 child, Ann Marie. BBA, U. Wis., 1950, LLB, 1952; LLM, George Washington U., 1957. Bar: Wis. 1952, U.S. Dist. Ct. (we. dist.) Wis. 1953, U.S. Supreme Ct. 1955, U.S. Ct. Appeals (4th cir.) 1960, U.S. Ct. Appeals (5th cir.) 1961, U.S. Ct. Appeals (D.C. cir.) 1965, U.S. Ct. Appeals (7th and 9th cirs.) 1967, U.S. Ct. Appeals (1st cir.) 1969, D.C. 1970, U.S. Dist. Ct. D.C. 1970, U.S. Ct. Appeals (2d, 3d, 6th, 8th and 10th cirs.) 1976, U.S. Ct. Appeals (11th cir.) 1981. Counsel FPC, Washington, 1952-66, asst. gen. counsel, 1966-70, dep. gen. counsel, 1970-74, gen. counsel, 1974-77; ptnr. Schiff, Hardin & Waite, Washington, 1977—; mem. mediation program U.S. Dist. Ct. (D.C. cir.), 1989—, early neutral evaluation program, 1989-95; mem. case evaluation program D.C. Superior Ct., 1991—. Author: Corporate Law and Practice, 1975; contbr. articles to profl. jours. Pres. Am. U. Park Citizens Assn., Washington, 1970-72; trustee Lincoln-Wesmoreland Housing Project, Washington, 1978-79. With Mcht. Marine Res., USNR, 1944-46, USNG, 1948-50. Knapp scholar U. Wis., 1952. Mem. ABA, FBA, Fed. Energy Bar Assn., Masons, Army and Navy Club, Phi Kappa Phi, Phi Eta Sigma, Theta Delta Chi. Republican. Congregationalist. Home: 4540 Windom Pl NW Washington DC 20016-2452 Office: Schiff Hardin & Waite 1101 Connecticut Ave NW Ste 600 Washington DC 20036-4390

JOUSILAHTI, PEKKA JUHANI, medical researcher; b. Nilsiä, Finland, Sept. 1, 1955; s. Aleksanteri and Liisa (Nivalainen) J.; m. Marjo Peltonen, Aug. 28, 1987; children: Julia, Jukka-Pekka, Anna. MD, U. Kuopio, Finland, 1979, PhD, 1997. Specialist in gen. medicine. Special competence in Internat. Health. Gen. practitioner Uppsala (Sweden) Läns Landsting, 1979-80; med. officer Ctrl. Finlands Gen. Hosp., Jyväskylä, Finland, 1980-83; gen. practitioner Helsinki (Finland) Health Ctr., 1984-87; assoc. expert WHO, Pt. Moresby, Papua New Guinea, 1987-89; sr. rschr. Nat. Pub. Health Inst., Helsinki, 1989-92, 96—; rsch. assoc. Finnish Acad. Scis., Helsinki, 1993-95; sr. med. adviser Provincial State Office So. Finland, 1999—. Contbr. articles to sci. publs. on epidemiology and prevention of cardiovascular and other non-communicable diseases. Avocations: health-related issues in developing countries, Red Cross activities. Phone: 358-40-5124353. Home: Pihlajatie 24 A 1, FIN00270 Helsinki Finland Office: Nat Pub Health Inst, Mannerheimintie 166, FIN00300 Helsinki Finland

JOUSSON, OLIVIER, biologist, researcher; b. Geneva, May 12, 1972; s. Jean-Pierre and Maren Jousson; m. Burghardt Jousson. Lic., U. Geneva, 1995, diploma, 1997, postgrad., 1997—. Asst. U. Geneva, 1997—. Contbr. articles to profl. jours. Avocations: music, sports. E-mail: jousson2@c-s2a.unige.ch. Fax: 4122 3492647. Office: U Geneva Zool Sta, Rte de Malagnou 154, 1224 Chene-Bougeries Switzerland

JOUSTEN, KARL JOSEPH, physicist, researcher; b. Lörrach, Germany, Jan. 22, 1960; s. Rainer and Elisabeth (Leibbach) J.; m. Magda Barbara Krausche, June 5, 1985; children: Johanna, Laura, Lena. Diploma in physics, U. Heidelberg, Germany, 1984, PhD in Physics, 1987. Scientific asst. Max-Planck-Inst. for Nuc. Physics, Heidelberg, 1987-88; postdoctorand Oreg. Grad. Inst., Beaverton, 1988-89; sr. asst. Fritz-Haber-Inst., Berlin, 1990; sr. asst. Physikalisch-Technische Bundesanstalt, Berlin, 1990-92, sect. leader Vacuum Metrology, 1992—; cons. Deutsches Inst. Normung/Normenausschuss Maschinenbau, Frankfurt, Germany, 1996—, chair of sect. Vacuumphysics and Vacuumtechnology in the German Phys. Soc., 1998—. Contbr. articles to internat. scientific jours.; patentee in field. With German Army., 1978-79. Mem. German Phys. Soc. (bd. dirs. 1998—), German Vacuum Soc. (adv. bd. 1998—). Avocations: canoeing, swimming, hiking. Office: Physik-Tech Bundesanstalt, Abbestr 2-12, D-10587 Berlin Germany

JOUVE, BERNARD ALEXANDRE, public works researcher; b. Bordeaux, France; s. Rene and Yvette (Capit) J.; m. Catherine Labeaumont, Oct. 3, 1992; children: Alice, Benjamin. M in Geography, U. Bordeaux, 1987; PhD in Urban Planning, ENPC, 1992. Rschr. Min. of Pub. Works, Lyon, France, 1992—. Editor: In Search of Gargantuas, 2000, Villes Metropoles, 1999, Que gouvernent les rÉgions d'Europe, 1998; author: Urbanisme et frontières, 1994. Mem. Les Verts, Lyon, 1999. Avocations: yachting, cooking. Office: Ecole Nat Travaux Pub Etat, Rue Maurice Audin, 69518 Vaulx en Velin France

JOUVE, DANIEL GABRIEL, corporate government and executive search company executive; b. Paris, Oct. 12, 1938; s. Pierre A. and Jeanne (Daude) J.; m. Alice Higgins; children: Christine, Patrick, Alexandre. Diploma, Inst. D'Etudes Politiques, Paris, 1960; Lic. en Droit, Faculte de Droit, Paris, 1960; cert. d'aptitude, Inst. d'Adminstrn. des Entre, Paris, 1960; MBA, Harvard U., 1963. Lending officer The Chase Manhattan Bank, N.Y.C., 1965-68; gen. mgr., pres. Expansion Group, Paris, 1968-74; pub. founder Le Nouvel Economiste, Paris, 1974-78; gen. mgr. Russell Reynolds Assocs., Inc., Paris, 1978-86; mng. ptnr. founder Jouve & Assocs., Paris, 1986-97, chmn., 1997-99; pres. Directorship (France) S.A., 1999—; prof. Inst. D'Etudes Politiques, Paris, 1970-87; mem. adv. com. Prime Minister, Paris, 1971-74; pres. Harvard U. Bus. Sch. Club de France, Paris, 1985-89. Author: Votre Carriere Conseils pour la piloter, 1984, Capitaines d'enterprises, 1987, Dix Conseils Pour Reussir dans Votre Premier Job, 1989, Dix Conseils Pour Vos Relations Publiques Personnelles, 1992, La Methode Jouve, 1994, Paris Birthplace of the USA, 1995, Le Recrutement, 1996, A Chaque poste le meilleur, 1999; translator: Men, Money and Motivation, 1964. Mem. Harvard Bus. Sch. Alumni Coun., Boston, 1987-90; bd. dirs. Am. Ctr., Paris, 1991, Friends of Franklin, Inc., Phila.; pres. Friends of Chantilly Mus., 1996-97. Named Hon. Citizen, Vergennes, Vt., comdr. du Tastevin; recipient medal Vermeil Ville de Paris. Home: 9 Pl Vauban, 75007 Paris France Office: Directorship, 16 Place Vendôme, 75001 Paris France

JOUVIN, JOSE-VERNAZA, paper products engineer; b. Guayaquil, Guayas, Ecuador, June 7, 1948; s. Ernesto and Maria Olinda (Vernaza) J.; m. Maria Leonor Savinovich, Sept. 1, 1973; children: Jose, Arianna. Degree in comml. engring., Cath. Y., Guayas, 1974, degree in law, 1976. V.p. La Reforma, Guayaquil, 1980-85, pres., 1995; dir. Camara de Comercio, Guayaquil, 1980-86, Banco la Previsora, Guayaquil, 1980-82, Fin. Amerafin, Guayaquil, 1980-82; gen. mgr. Ecuapel, Guayaquil, 1985—; Convepel, Guayaquil, 1992-94; gen. mgr. Banco Consolidado, Guayaquil, 1993-95, Convepel, Guayaquil, 1994—; pres. ANPACE, 1995-97; pres. Indsl. la Reforma, Guayaquil, 1993—; bd. dirs. Cour Industries, Condor SA; pres. Grupo Indsl. Jouvin, 1999—. Dir. Camara de Industrias, 1992-94. Mem. ANPACE (pres. 1995—), Club de la Union, Guayaquil Tennis Club, Guayaquil Country Club, Club Metropolitano. Roman Catholic. Avocations: jogging, racquetball. Home: Circunvalacion sur # 211, Guayaquil Ecuador Office: Ecuapel and Convepel, PO Box 9678, Guayaquil Ecuador

JOVANOVIC, VLADISLAV, Serbian government official, diplomat; b. 1933. Student, Faculty of Law, Belgrad, Yugoslavia. With Fed. Ministry of Fgn. Affairs, Belgrade, Brussels, Ankara, London; min. of fgn. affairs Govt. of Yugoslavia, Serbia, 1991-95; permanent rep. to UN Govt. of Yugoslavia, N.Y.C., 1995—. Office: Permanent Mission of Yugoslavia to UN 854 5th Ave New York NY 10021-5802

JOVIĆ, TOMISLAV, economist; b. Mostar, Bosnia-Herzegovina, Apr. 22, 1954; s. Slavko and Šima (Kozina) J.; m. Ljiljana Trkalja, Mar. 24, 1990; children: Ivana, Andrea, Ines. Degree in econs., Econ. Faculty, Sarajevo, Bosnia-Herzegovina, 1976; postgrad., Econ. Faculty, 1991, Coopers and Lybrand, Croatia, 1993. Dep. dir. Energoinvest Inst. Econs., Sarajevo, 1984-85; v.p. Energoinvest Enercobanka, Sarajevo, 1985-93, gen. mgr., 1993-95; owner Andiv, Split, Croatia, 1993-95; dir. Kraš Econs. Dept., Zagreb, Croatia, 1995-99; v.p. Kraš Econs. Dept., Zagreb, 1999—; pres. supervisory bd. NPP Budget d.d., Split, 1993-98, Re-Final, Dubrovnik, Croatia, 1994-97. Recipient Gold medal Winter Olympic Games, Sarajevo, 1984. Mem. Croma, Assn. Croatian Accts., Assn. Auditing Cos. Avocations: jogging, tennis, swimming, bridge. Office: Kraš, 48 Ravnice, 10000 Zagreb Croatia

JOWELL, NEIL IAN, company executive; b. Springbok, South Africa, May 23, 1933; s. Joseph and Rebecca (Berelowitz) J.; m. Bertha Herschler, Mar. 18, 1956 (div.); children: David, Paul, Michael; m. Kathleen Bowman, Oct. 8, 1972; children: Justine, Nicola. BComm, U. Cape Town, South Africa, 1954, LLB, 1954; MBA, Columbia U., 1962. Exec. Trencor, Cape Town, 1965-72, chmn., 1972—. Avocations: squash, cycling.

JOWKO, ANTONI STEFAN, chemistry educator, researcher; b. Biala Podlaska, Poland, Mar. 14, 1947; s. Franciszek and Paulina J.; m. Grazynka Zofia Grabowska, Dec. 26, 1968; children: Jaroslaw, Arkadiusz. MSc, U. Maria Sklodowska-Curie, Lublin, Poland, 1970; PhD, Warsaw U., 1976; DSc, Tech. U., Lodz, Poland, 1984. Dept. dep. Textil Factory Karo, Siedlce, Poland, 1970-72; asst. Agrl. and Tchrs. U., Siedlce, 1972-76, adj., 1976-84, prof., 1984—, vice rector, 1987-90, 99—, dean chemistry dept., 1994-99. Contbr. articles to profl. jours. Recipient MEN award Polish Ministry Edn., 1985. Mem. European Photochemistry Assn., Polish Assn. Radiation Rsch. (dist. dept. 1992—). Avocations: skiing, fishing. Office: U Podlasie, 3 Maja 54, 08-110 Siedlce Poland

JOY, KEERIKKATTIL PAILY, zoologist, educator; b. Ernakulam, India, Feb. 18, 1950; s. Keerikkattil Mathai Paily and Elamma Paily; m. Vettikkattil Kuriakose Deena, Feb. 15, 1981; children: Eldo, Anupa. BSc, U. Kerala, India, 1971, MSc, 1973; PhD, Banaras Hindu U., Uttar Pradesh, India, 1977. From lectr. to reader Banaras Hindu U., Uttar Pradesh, 1977-95, prof., 1995—; rschr. Banaras Hindu U., Uttar Pradesh, 1981—. UNESCO/IBRO fellow U. Utrecht, 1985-86. Mem. Soc. Reproductive Biology and Comparative Endocrinology (life), India Comp. Endocrinol. Soc., Indian Coun. Agrl. Rsch. (Jawaharlal Nehru award 1979). Avocations: gardening, reading, stamp collecting. Office: Banaras Hindu Univ, Dept Zoology, 221005 Uttar Pradesh India

JOYCE, DONNA MARIE, lawyer, freelance graphic artist; b. New Haven, Oct. 16, 1965; d. Wallace Landon and Rose Marie Joyce. BA in Polit. Sci. with honors in polit. sci. and gen. scholarship, Trinity Coll., Hartford, Conn., 1987; JD, Georgetown U., 1991. Bar: Pa., D.C. Legal intern Conn. Conf. Municipalities, New Haven, 1989, Energy and Commerce Com., U.S. Congress, Washington, 1989; law clk. Arch. of the U.S. Capitol, U.S. Congress, Washington, 1990; legal paraprofl. Brown & Welsh, P.C., Meriden, Conn., 1993-95; legal advt. specialist, cons. and trainer Shore Line Newspapers, New Haven, 1995-97; advt. coordinator The Wall Street Journal, 1999-2000. Legis. intern State Rep. Michael Rybak, Hartford, 1985; press intern Senate Caucus Media Office, Hartford, 1986; campaign aide Conn. Senate, Hartford, 1986. Recipient Conn. Gen. Assembly citation for contbn. to legis. process, Conn. House of Reps., 1985, President's Fellow in Polit. Sci., Trinity Coll., 1986, Ferguson Prize in Govt., Trinity Coll., 1987. Mem. Fed. Am. Inn Ct., Amnesty Internat., Georgetown Club at the Chemists' Club N.Y., Pi Gamma Mu, Phi Beta Kappa. Roman Catholic. Avocations: antiques, studying Native American Indian culture, shamanism and theopneusty. Home: 506 Quinnipiac Ave North Haven CT 06473-3760

JOYCE, JOSEPH JAMES, lawyer, food products executive; b. Chgo., Sept. 28, 1943; s. Edward R. and Mary E. (Jordan) J.; m. Suzanne M. Sheridan, Aug. 26, 1967; children: Joseph, Michael, Peter, Kevin, Edward. BS, Xavier U., 1965; JD, Loyola U., 1968. Bar: Ill. 1968. Mem. Hill, Sherman, Meroni, Gross & Simpson, Chgo., 1968-72; atty. Pepsico, Inc., Purchase, N.Y., 1972-74, trademark counsel, 1974-77, asst. gen. counsel, 1977-86, v.p., asst. gen. counsel, 1986-98, v.p., assoc. gen. counsel, 1998—. Contbr. articles to profl. jours. Bd. mgrs. Lincoln Hall Found., Inc., 1989—. Mem. ABA, Ill. Bar Assn., U.S. Trade Assn., Assn. Internationale pour la Protection de la Propieté Industrielle (bd. dirs.), Licensing Execs. Soc., Westchester-Fairfield Corp. Counsel Assn., Inc., Assn. Inter-Am. de la Propriedad Industrial, IIPA (exec. com. 1989—, bd. dirs.). Roman Catholic. Office: Pepsico Inc Anderson Hill Rd Purchase NY 10577

JOYE, FREDERIC, emergency medicine physician, researcher; b. Tours, France, Mar. 6, 1970; s. Jean-Pierre and Therese (Gervais) J.; m. Fabienne Marion; 1 child, Clément Joye-Marion. MD, U. Tours, 1997, emergency medicine cert., 1999. Cert. in catastrophe and collective emergencies. Physician emergency dept. CHU, Tours, 1997-98, Chateauroux, France, 1998, Svc. d'Aide Medicale Urgente, Carcassonne, France, 1998—; mem. faculty Centre d'Enseignement des Soins d'Urgence, Carcassonne, 1999; med. and clin. rschr. in toxicology and primary outhosp. emergency care. Contbr.

articles to profl. jours. Mem. Société de Réanimation de Langue Francaise (consensus and guidelines com.), Société Francophone des urgences Medicales, Société Francaise de Toxicologie, Société de Toxicologie Clinique, Société Francaise de Médecine de Catastrophe, Société Francaise d'Anesthesie et Rénimation. Avocations: photography, mountain climbing, sports, music. Office: SAMU 11 CHG Antoine Gayraud, Rte de St Hilaire, 11890 Carcassonne Cedex 09, France

JOYNER, WILLIAM DAVID, mathematics educator, researcher; b. Phila., July 23, 1959; s. William Eppie and Beverley Louise (Brower) J. BS in Math., Ga. Inst. Tech., 1981; PhD in Math., U. Md., 1983. Rsch. instr. U. Md., College Park, 1983-84; asst. prof. U. Calif., San Diego, 1984-85; instr. Princeton (N.J.) U., 1985-86; mem. Inst. for Advanced Study, Princeton, 1986-87; asst. prof. U.S. Naval Acad., Annapolis, Md., 1987—. Contbr. revs. to Math. Revs., 1988-98, Zentralblatt fuer Mathematik, 2000—; author: Distribution Theorems for L-Functions, 1986; co-author: (with George Nakos) Linear Algebra with Applications, 1998; tech. editor: Cryptologia, 1999-2000; contbr. articles to Canadian Jour. Math., Israel Jour. Math., Math. Zeitschrift. NSF fellow, 1984-87, grantee, 1978. Mem. Am. Math. Soc. Office: US Naval Acad Dept Math Annapolis MD 21402

JOYNER KERSEE, JACQUELINE, track and field athlete; b. East St. Louis, Ill., Mar. 3, 1962; d. Alfred and Mary Joyner; m. Bob Kersee, Jan. 11, 1986. BA in History, UCLA, 1985; LLD (hon.), Washington U., St. Louis, 1992, Iona Coll., 1994; DHL (hon.), Harris-Stowe State Coll., 1993, Fontbonne Coll., St. Louis, 1998, Spelman Coll., 1998, Howard U., 1999, George Washington U., St. Louis, 1999. Winner 4 consecutive Nat. Jr. Pentathlon Championships; winner heptathlon Goodwill Games, Moscow, 1986, U.S. Olympic Festival, 1986; winner USA/Mobil Outdoor Track and Field Championship, 1987; winner, long jump and heptathlon World Track and Field Championships, 1987; winner Grand Prix Indoor Championships, winner indoor world record 55m hurdlers 7:37 seconds, 1989; winner heptathlon Goodwill Games, St. Petersburg, Russia, 1994; pres., founder JJK & Assocs., Inc. Author: (autobiography) A Kind of Grace: the Autobiography of the World's Greatest Female Athlete, 1997; co-author: A Woman's Place Is Everywhere. Founder JJK Cmty. Found. (name now JJK Found.); chmn. St. Louis Sports Commn., 1996—; Barbie Amb. of Dreams. Recipient Silver medal for heptathlon L.A. Summer Olympic Games, 1984, Sullivan award, 1986, Jesse Owens award, Am. Black Achievement award Ebony mag., 1987, Gold medal for long jump at 24 ft. 3 1/2 in. and heptathlon Seoul Summer Olympic Games, 1988, 1st Female Athlete of Yr. award Sporting News, 1988, Gold medal for heptathlon Barcelona Summer Olympic Games, 1992, Bronze medal for long jump Barcelona Summer Olympic Games, 1992, Gold medal for heptathlon World Track and Field Championships, 1993, Bronze medal in long jump in Atlanta, 1996, Jim Thorpe award, 1993, Jackie Robinson "Robie" award, 1994, Grand Prix Outdoor Champion, 1994, Parenting Leader award Parenting mag., Jesse Owens Humanitarian award, 1999, Humanitarian award Women Sports and Fitness, Pres.'s award Nat. Conf. Black Mayors; named Athlete of Yr., Track & Field News, 1986, Female Athlete of Yr., AP, 1987, Female of Yr. IAAF, 1994, St. Louis Ambassadors Sportswoman of Yr., Hon. Harlem Globetrotter, Goodwill Game heptathlon champion, 1986, 90, 94, 98, Woman Athlete of Century, Sports Illustrated, 1999; inductee Nat. Boys and Girls Club Hall of Fame. Achievements include setting world record of 7161 points at U.S. Olympic Festival, 1986; set world record of 7291 points at Seoul Summer Olympic Games for heptathlon, 1988; holder Am. record in long jump, 1994, 50 meter hurdles, 60 meter hurdles. Office: Elite Internat Sports Mktg and Mgmt 1034 S Brentwood Blvd Ste 1530 Saint Louis MO 63117-1215

JÓŹWIAK, IRENEUSZ JÓZEF, science educator; b. Poddębice, Łodź, Poland, Mar. 10, 1951; s. Czesław and Stanisława (Hajduk) J.; m. Elżbieta Łesak, Dec. 26, 1981; children: Piotr, Karol, Marianna, Alicja. MSc, Tech. U. Wroclaw, Poland, 1975, Doctorate degree, 1979; Dr. Habilitation, Polish Acad. Scis., 1994; prof., Tech. U. Wroclaw, 1998. Cert. in engring. With dept. informatics and mgmt. Tech. U. Wroclaw; sec. gen. Internat. Conf. RELCOMEX, Ksi—ż Castle, Poland, 1979-89. Author: Application of the Weibull Proportional Hazards Model to the Engineering System Reliability Assessment, 1991, (with W. Wrzaskala) OS/2 3.0 Warp Operating System Architecture and Function, 1998; contbr. over 100 articles to profl. publs.; editor: (with W. M. Barański and W. Zamojski) Performance Evaluation, Reliability and Exploitation of Computer Systems, 1989. Dir. Cath. Secondary Sch., Wrocław, 1996—; councilor City Coun. of Wrocław, 1994-98. Mem. Soc. Polish Informatics (dir. 1995—). Roman Catholic. Avocation: history, Reliability of systems. Home: ul Osiedlowa 7, 54-614 Wroclaw Poland Office: Tech U Dept Informatics, Wybrzeze Wyspianskiego 27, 50-370 Wroclaw Poland

JÓŹWIAK, LECH, technology educator; b. Grójec, Poland, May 14, 1952; arrived in The Netherlands, 1986; s. Roman and Anna (Swiecka) J.; m. Urszula Kalbarczyk, Oct. 2, 1975; children: Katarzyna, Marta, Izabela. MSc in Engring. and Electronics, Warsaw (Poland) U. Tech., 1976, PhD in Tech. Scis., 1982. Cert. in engring. Sci. asst. Warsaw U. Tech., 1976-79; asst. prof., head of R&D team Rsch. Inst. Computers, Warsaw, 1979-86; assoc. prof. Eindhoven (The Netherlands) U. Tech., 1986—; cons. UN Indsl. Devel. Orgn., Warsaw, 1983-86, Ministry of Industry, Warsaw, 1996, Ministry of Economy, Warsaw, 1997—, also various indsl. enterprises, Warsaw, 1979-86. Author: (book) Hardware Component Modeling, 1996; contbr. over 100 papers to profl. jours. and confs. Translator, interpretor Found. for Coop. Eindhoven-Bialystok, Eindhoven, 1990—. Mem. IEEE, EUROMICRO (dir. 1995—). Avocations: music, theater, touring, cycling, swimming. Home: Wildeman 65, 5629 KH Eindhoven The Netherlands Office: Eindhoven U Tech Fac Electrical Engring, Den Dolech 2 PO Box 513, 5600 MB Eindhoven The Netherlands

JU, DONG-YING, material scientist, researcher; b. Jinan, Shandong, China, July 17, 1954; s. Ming and Zun (Fang) Xiang; m. Ling An, Mar. 9, 1954; 1 child. BC, Hebei Inst. Mech./Elec. Tech., Shijiazhuang, China, 1980; postgrad., Tsinghua U., Beijing, 1985-86; ME, Kyoto (Japan) U., 1989, PhD, 1992. Asst. Hebei Inst. Mech. and Elec. Tech., Shijiazhuang, 1980-84; lectr. Saitama Inst. Tech., Okabe, Japan, 1992-96, assoc. prof., 1997—; hon. prof. Hebei Inst. Mech. and Elec. Tech., 1994—, Anshan I&S Inst. Tech., 1998—. Author: Advances in Continuum Mechanics, 1991; contbr. articles to profl. jours. Recipient Matsukawa award Saitama Inst. Tech., 1993. Mem. ASME, Japan Soc. Mech. Engrs., Japan Soc. Material Scientists. Avocation: swimming. Office: Saitama Inst Tech, 1690 Fusaiji, Okabe Saitama 369-02, Japan

JU, HUANGXIAN, chemistry educator; b. Jingjiang, Jiangsu, China, Nov. 10, 1964; s. Shunqiang Ju and Meifang Guo; m. Guifeng Yan, Feb. 5, 1989; 1 child, Yan Ju. BS, Nanjing (China) U., 1986, MS, 1989, PhD, 1992. Lectr. Nanjing U., 1992-93, assoc. prof., 1993-99, prof., 1999—, dir. sect. analytical chemistry, 1999—; postdoctoral rschr. Montreal (Can.) U., 1996-97. Editor Jour. Analytical Sci., 1999; contbr. articles to sci. publs., including The Analyst, Jour. Electroanalytical Chemistry, others. Grantee Royal Soc. Chemistry, London, 1999; recipient Sci. and Tech. Progress prize, State Edn. Com. China, 1995, Edn. Ministry China, 1998. Mem. Chinese Chemistry Soc. (Outstanding Young Chemist award 1996). Avocations: photography, travel. Fax: +86-25-3317761. E-mail: hxju@jlonline.com. Office: Dept Chemistry, Nanjing U, Jingsu Nanjing 210093, China

JUAN, I-JONG, photographer, publisher, editor; b. Toucheng, Taiwan, July 20, 1950; s. Yuan-Shun and Yuan-Yang (Wu) J.; m. Yao-Shu Yuan, June 13, 1977; 1 child, Sea. Grad. h.s., Toucheng. Editor Yu-Shih Lit. Mag., Taipei, Taiwan, 1968-69; photographer Echo Mag., Taipei, Taiwan, 1972-75; photo editor Family Mag., Taipei, Taiwan, 1975-81; TV prodr. Taiwan TV Cultural Co., Taipei, 1981-87; dir. Juan's Darkroom Workshop Co., Taipei, 1987—, Photographers Publs., Taipei, 1990—, Photographers Internat. Mag., Taipei, 1992—; assoc. prof. Nat. Inst. Arts, Taipei, 1988—. Author: Twenty Eye Witnesses of Humanity, 1985, Pei Pu, 1985, Pa chih Men, 1985, Man and Land, 1987, Taipei Rumor, 1988, Szu Chi, 1990, Retrospectiv, 1994, Seventeen Contemporary Photographers, 1987, The Secrets of Hands, 1999, The Known and the Unknown, 1999, The Square of Nostalgia, 1999, The Lost Grace, 1999; editor Photographers Internat. Mag., 1992—. With Taiwan Nat. Navy Force, 1969-72. Avocations: readings, musics, photography, movies, swimming. Office: Photographers Internat Mag, PO Box 39-1265, Taipei Taiwan

JUAN CARLOS, HIS MAJESTY I (JUAN CARLOS DE BORBÓN Y BORBÓN), King of Spain; b. Rome, Jan. 5, 1938; s. Don Juan de Borbón y Battenberg and Dona Maria de las Mercedes de Borbón y Orleans; m. Princess Sophia of Greece, May 14, 1962; children: Crown Prince Felipe, Princess Elena, Princess Cristina. Student, Inst. San Isidro, Madrid, Colegio del Carmen, Gen. Mil. Acad., Zaragoza, U. Madrid; Dr. h.c. (hon.), Strasbourg, 1979, Madrid, 1984, Harvard, 1984, Sorbonne, 1985, Oxford, 1986, Trinity Coll., Dublin, 1986, Bologna, 1988, Cambridge, 1988, Coimbra, 1989, Tokyo, 1990, Bogatá, 1990, Limerick, 1990, Tufts, 1990, Chile, 1990, Toronto, 1991, Jerusalem, 1993; D in Polit. Sci. (hon.), Chulalongkorn U., Bangkok, 1987. Commd. into three armed forces and undertook tng. in each, 1957-59; studied orgn. and activities various govt. ministries; named by Gen. Franco as future King of Spain, 1969; King of Spain, 1975—; commdr.-in-chief Armed Forces, 1975—; head Supreme Coun. of Defense, 1975—. Recipient Charlemagne prize, 1982, Bolivar prize UNESCO, 1983, Candenhove Kalergi prize Switzerland, 1986, Nansen medal, 1987, Elie Wiesel Humanitarian award, 1991, FÉlix Houphouët-Boigny Peace prize UNESCO, 1995, Franklin D. Roosevelt Four Freedoms award, 1995. Address: Office of King, Palacio de la Zarzuela, 28071 Madrid Spain*

JUANG, MIIN-HORNG, electrical engineer, educator, researcher; b. Pin-Tong, Taiwan, Aug. 12, 1964; s. Kwun-Tin Juang and Chin-Er Cheng. BS in Elec. Engring., Nat. Chiao-Tung U., Tawain, 1987, PhD in Elec. Engring., 1992. Sr. engr. Mosel-Vitelic Inc., Taiwan, 1994-96; assoc. prof. Nat. Taiwan U. Sci. Tech., Taipei, 1996—. Patentee in field. Recipient Good Rsch. award Nat. Sci. Coun. Taiwan, 1996, 97, 98. Avocations: singing, investing, internet, sports, tv. Home: 44-3 Yuan-Hou St, Hsin-Chu 300, Taiwan Office: Nat Taiwan U Sci Tech, Kee-Lung Rd, Taipei 106, Taiwan

JUAREZ, MARETTA LIYA CALIMPONG, social worker; b. Gilroy, Calif., Feb. 14, 1958; d. Sulpicio Magsalay and Pelagia Lagotom (Viacrusis) Calimpong; m. Henry Juarez, Mar. 24, 1984. BA, U. Calif., Berkeley, 1979; MSW, San Jose State U., 1983. Lic. clin. social worker; cert. in eye movement desensitization and reprocessing; registered play therapist; cert. alcohol and drug studies. Mgr. Pacific Bell, San Jose, Calif., 1983-84; revenue officer IRS, Salinas, Calif., 1984-85; social worker Santa Cruz (Calif.) County, 1985, Santa Clara County, San Jose, 1985-2000; field instr., mem. adj. faculty San Jose State U., 1994-2000, pvt. cons. 2000—; co-chair Inter-Agy. Coun. of South Santa Clara County. Recipient award Am. Legion, 1972. Mem. NASW, Nat. Coun. on Alcoholism, Assn. Play Therapists, No. Calif. Sandplay Soc., EMDR Network, Sandplay Therapists Am., Calif. Assn. Play Therapy, South County Multidisciplinary Team (co-founder), Calif. Alumni, U. Calif. Club of Santa Clara County. Democrat. Roman Catholic. Avocations: snow skiing, reading, writing, arts and crafts.

JUAREZ, MARTIN, priest; b. Kansas City, Kans., Mar. 23, 1946; s. Martin Huerta and Hermelinda (Rocha) J. AS, Colby Community Coll., 1971; BA in sociology, U. Mo., Kansas City, 1974; MDiv, St. Thomas Sem., Denver, 1985; cert. in Hispanic ministry, Oblate Sch. of Theology, San Antonio, 1991, Mexican-Am. Cultural Ctr., 1991. Priest Archdiocese of Kansas City, Kans., 1981—. Bd. dirs. Pioneer Village, Topeka, 1983-88; co-dir. El Centro, Topeka, 1989. Mem. Kans. Registered Animal Hosp. Techs. Assn., N.Am. Veterinary Tech. Assn., U. Mo. Alumni Assn., KC. Office: PO Box 410695 Kansas City MO 64141-0695

JUAREZ OLGUIN, HUGO, pharmaceutics educator; b. Mexico City, Sept. 21, 1959; s. Gervacio Juarez Palafox and Julia Olguin Monroy; m. Graciela Tapia Reyes, Mar. 9, 1991; children: Belen, Victor. Student, Colegio de Bachilleres, Mex., 1978; MS, U. Autonoma Met. Mex., 1983. Paramedic coord Inst. Nat. Perinatologia, Mexico City, 1987-91; assoc. prof. U. Nacional Autonoma Mex., Mexico City, 1988—; assoc. rschr. Inst. Nacional Pediatria, Mexico City, 1991—, chief dept. pharmacology, 1998—. Contbr. articles to profl. jours. Recipient award Inst. Nat. Perinatology, 1988-90, 93-99, U. Nat. Autonoma Mex., 1996-99. Mem. N.Y. Acad. Scis., Assn. Mex. Pharm., Assn. Mex. Med. Inst. Nat. Avocations: family, concerts, soccer, travel. Fax: 525 606 8058. E-mail: juarezol@yahoo.com. Home: Emiliano Zapata No 25, Col Malinche, Mexico City 10310, Mexico Office: Inst Nacional Pediatra, Av Iman No 1 Col Cuicuilco, Mexico City 04530, Mexico

JUCEAM, ROBERT E., lawyer; b. N.Y.C., June 16, 1940; s. Benjamin T. and Amelia B. (Spatz) J.; m. Eleanor Pam, May 24, 1970; children: Daniel, Jacquelyn, Gregory. AB cum laude, Columbia U., 1961, LLB, 1964, JD, 1972; LLM, NYU, 1966. Bar: N.Y. 1965, U.S. Dist. Ct. (so. and ea. dists.) N.Y. 1966, U.S. Tax Ct. 1968, U.S. Ct. Appeals (2d cir.) 1967, U.S. Supreme Ct. 1971, U.S. Ct. Appeals (5th cir.) 1978, U.S. Ct. Appeals (D.C. cir.) 1980, U.S. Ct. Appeals (11th cir.) 1987, U.S. Ct. Appeals (7th cir.) 1989, U.S. Ct. Appeals (9th cir.) 1999. Law clk. U.S. Dist. Ct., N.Y., 1964-66; assoc. Fried, Frank, Harris, Shriver & Jacobson, N.Y.C., 1966-73, ptnr., 1974—; bd. dirs. Nat. Network Def. of the Right to Counsel, Inc., 1985-89, Lawyers Com. for Human Rights, 1986-94, Bar Assurance and Reins. Ltd., 1991—, Am. Immigration Law Found., 1987—, pres., 1991-2000; gen. counsel U.S. Supreme Ct. Hist. Soc., 1995—, trustee, mem. exec. com., 1999—; mem. arbitration panel U.S. Dist. Ct. (ea. dist.) N.Y., 1986—; mem. comml. and constrn. panels Am. Arbitration Assn., 1972-94; dir. civil rights Washington Lawyers Com., 1996-99; mem. bd. advisors D.C. Bar Found., 1996—; treas., bd. dirs. Pro Bono Inst., 1997—. Contbr. articles to legal jours. Trustee Mex.-Am. Legal Def. and Edn. Fund, 1986-90, chmn. program and planning com., 1988-90; adv. com. to task force on racial, gender and minority discrimination U.S. Ct. Appeals for 2d Circuit, 1994-96; bd. dirs. Appleseed Found., Inc., 1997-99. Recipient Lester Zazuly medal, 1958, Columbia Coll. Alumni Achievement award, 1961, Edward Foxx prize Columbia Coll., 1961, Maldef Corp. Responsibility award, 1993, Valerie J. Kantor award for extraordinary achievement, 1997, Am. Immigration Law Found. hon. fellow and Founder's award, 1989, Lifetime Achievement award Ctr. for Human Rights and Constl. Law, 1993. Fellow Am. Bar. Found. (life), ABA (ho. of dels. 1983—, chmn. com. on immigration sect. litigation 1985-90, immigration pro bono adv. task force, 1992-98, vice chmn., 1995-96, mem. coordinating com. on immigration law 1984-87, chmn. 1989-92, mem. com. environ. controls sect. banking, 1983-86, vice chmn. com. on constrn., sec. gen. practice 1989-90, mem. standing com. lawyers pub. svc. responsibility 1993-96, mem. coun. fund justice & edn. 1994-99, chmn. major gifts com. 1997-98, Pro Bono award 1992); mem. Internat. Bar Assn. (chmn. Sect. Gen. Practice com. bus. migration 1987-88), N.Y. State Bar Assn., Assn. Bar City of N.Y. (com. on trademarks and unfair competition 1983-86, com. immigration 1986-89, com. on profl. and jud. ethics 1989-92, com. Human Rights Law 1994-96), Nat. Assn. Criminal Def. Lawyers (co-chmn. com. on immigration 1988-90), Am. Judicature Soc. (life), Am. Bar Endowment, Nat. Conf. Bar Presidents (assoc.), Am. Immigration Lawyers Assn. (pres. 1982-83, bd. govs. 1971—, chmn. N.Y. chpt. 1971-72, gen. counsel 1986-91, liaison to ABA commn. on nonlawyer practice 1993-94, editor Ann. Symposium Handbook 1985-88, assoc. editor 1989-90, Edith Lowenstein Meml. award 1981, Pro Bono award 1992), Am. Mgmt. Assn., Fed. Bar Assn., Fed. Bar Coun., N.Y. County Lawyers Assn. (reporter N.Y. Equitable Distribution Law Proposals 1968, bd. dirs. 1996-98), Def. Rsch. Inst., N.Y. Criminal Bar Assn., N.Y. State Trial Lawyers Assn., Assn. Profl. Responsibility Lawyers, Assn. Fed. Def. Lawyers, Cow Neck Peninsula Hist. Soc. (life), Italy and Colonies Philatelic Soc. of Gt. Brit. (life), Jack Knight Soc. (life), L.I. Postal History Soc. (life), Am. Helvetia Philatelic Soc. (life), City Club (Washington), Columbia Club, India House Club, Continental Club, Alpha Epsilon Pi. Home: 106 Hemlock Rd Manhasset NY 11030-1214 Office: Fried Frank Harris Shriver & Jacobson 1 New York Plz Ste 2500 New York NY 10004-1901

JUCHEM, ROBERT STANLEY, JR., product development manager, educator; b. Rahway, N.J., Aug. 26, 1951; s. Robert Stanley Sr. and Nancy Ann (Whittian) J.; m. Constance Ann Effertz, Aug. 5, 1972 (div. May, 1992); children Robert, Ben, Bethany, Brittany; m. Jane Ann Butler, Dec. 24, 1993; children Steve Ryan, Michael Ryan, Luke Deforest. Student, Com. College USAF, 1976; BS in Personal and Labor Rels., U. Md., 1978, BS in Bus. and Mgmt., 1978; MBA, Webster Coll., 1980. Missile sys. tech. USAF, 1972-81; aerospace application engr. AMP Inc., Harrisburg, Pa., 1981-82, mgr. new business devel., 1984-90; regional sales mgr. Northern Precision Labs, Morristown, N.J., 1982-83; v.p. bus. devel. Liberty Electronics, Franklin, Pa., 1990-91; v.p. sales and mktg. Pytronnic Industries, Lansdale, Pa., 1991-92; mgr. new product devel. Amphenol Aerospace, Sidney, N.Y., 1992-97; v.p. sales and mktg. Valdor Fiber Optics, Reno, 1997—; mktg. adv. bd. Valdon Fiber Optics, San Jose, Calif., 1996—. Contbr. articles to profl. jour. Mem. Congl. adv. bd. Aberdeen, Md. 1981-85; adv. bd. Catholic Ch., Aberdeen, Md.1982-84. With USAF, 1972-81. Mem. AIAA, IEEE, Tech. Mktg. Assn. Rebuplican. Achievements include contributions to the design and deployment of all air-to-air and air-to-ground missiles introducted into service between August 1972 and February 1981. Avocations: weight lifting, golf, basketball, soccer, fencing. Home: 5404 Tappan Dr Reno NV 89523-2253

JUCKER, HANS KONRAD, retired economist; b. Zurich, Nov. 3, 1927; m. Ursula Dorothea Wehrli, Aug. 23, 1963; children: Verena, Thomas, Barbara, Christian. MS, Swiss Fed. Inst. Tech., Zurich, 1951, PhD in Natural Sci., 1953. Analytical chemist Ciba, Ltd., Basel, Switzerland, 1955-56; head of rsch. and devel. Elesta Ltd., Bad Ragaz, 1956-60, Mettler Ltd., Greifensee, 1961-68; v.p., head R&D Swiss Aluminium Ltd., Zurich, 1969-72, sr. v.p., mem. exec. com., 1973; exec. v.p. Alusuisse, 1974, pres., CEO, 1986; pres., CEO Lonza Ltd., Basel, 1974, chmn. bd. dirs., 1986; chmn. bd. dirs. Alusuisse-Lonza Holding Ltd., 1991-97; retired. Swiss Ramsay fellow King Coll., London. Mem. ASM Internat. (disting. life mem.), Materials Info. Soc.

JUDD, DENIS, historian, educator; b. Byfield, Eng., Oct. 28, 1938; m. Dorothy Woolf; 4 children. BA with honors, Oxford U., 1961; PhD, London U., 1967. Prof. history U. North London. Author: Balfour and the British Empire, 1988, The Victorian Empire, 1972, The Evolution of the Modern Commonwealth, 1982, The Boer War, 1981, 91, The British Raj, 1972, Prince Philip: a Biography, 1977, 93, Radical Joe: a Life of Joseph Chamberlain, 1972, Livingstone on Africa, Edward VII, George V, King George VI, 1982, The House of Windsor, The Crimean War, Lord Reading, 1982, Jawaharlal Nehru, 1993, Alison Uttley, 1986, Empire: the British Imperial Experience From 1765 to the Present, 1996, Empire, 1997; editor Travellers' History series, A British Tale of Indian Foreign Service; the Memoirs of Sir Ian Scott; contbr. articles to profl. jours. and newspapers; cons., writer BBC TV and Radio, Overseas TV and Radio; mem. adv. panel BBC History Mag. Fellow Royal Hist. Soc. Home: 20 Mount Pleasant Rd, London NW10 3EL, England

JUDD, DENNIS L., lawyer; b. Provo, Utah, June 27, 1954; s. Derrel Wesley and Leila (Lundquist) J.; m. Carol Lynne Chilberg, May 6, 1977; children: Lynne Marie, Amy Jo, Tiffany Ann, Andrew, Jacquelyn Nicole. BA in Polit. Sci. summa cum laude, Brigham Young U., 1978, JD, 1981. Bar: Utah 1981, U.S. Dist. Ct. Utah 1981. Assoc. Nielson & Senior, Salt Lake City and Vernal, Utah, 1981-83; dep. county atty. Uintah County, Vernal, 1982-84; ptnr. Bennett & Judd, Vernal, 1983-88; county atty. Daggett County, Utah, 1985-89, 91-99; pvt. practice Vernal, 1988—; county atty. Daggett County, 2000—; prosecutor City of Naples, Naples, 1996-99; legal counsel Uintah County Sch. Dist., 1996—; city atty. Naples City, Utah, 1999—, Vernal City, Utah, 2000—; atty. City of Vernal, 2000—; mem. governing bd. Uintah Basin applied Tech. Ctr., 1991-95, v.p., 1993-94, pres., 1994-95. Chmn. bd. adjustment Zoning and Planning Bd., Naples, 1982-91, 94—; mem. Naples City Coun., 1982-91; mayor pro tem City of Naples, 1983-91; legis. v.p. Naples PTA, 1988-90; sec. Friends of Utah Field House of Natural History, 2000—; v.p. Uintah Dist. PTA Coun., 1990-92; mem. resolution com. Utah League Cities and Towns, 1985-86, small cities com., 1985-86; trustee Uintah Sch. Dist. Found., 1988-97, vice chmn., 1991-93; mem. Uintah County Sch. Dist. Bd. Edn., 1991-95, v.p., 1991-92, pres., 1992-95; chmn. Uintah County Rep. Conv., 1998. Hinkley scholar Brigham Young U., 1977. Mem. Utah Bar Assn., Uintah Basin Bar Assn., Statewide Assn. Prosecutors, Vernal C. of C. Republican. Mormon. Avocations: hunting, photography, lapidary. Home: 460 E 1555 S Naples UT 84078 Office: 461 W 200 S Vernal UT 84078-3049

JUDELL, HAROLD BENN, lawyer; b. Milw., Mar. 9, 1915; s. Philip Fox and Lena Florence (Krause) J.; m. Maria Violeta van Ronzelen, May 5, 1951 (div.); m. Celeste Seymour Grulich, June 24, 1986. BA, U. Wis., 1936, JD, 1938; LLB, Tulane U., 1950. Bar: Wis. 1938, La. 1950. Mem. Scheinfeld Collins Durant & Winter, Milw., 1938; spl. agt., adminstrv. asst. to dir. FBI, 1939-44; legal attache U.S. Embassy Peru, 1942-44; ptnr. Foley & Judell, LLP, New Orleans, 1950—; v.p., dir. Dauphine Orleans Hotel Corp., 1970—, chmn. bd., 1999—; mem. Tulane U. Bus. Sch. Coun.; trustee Greater New Orleans YMCA, 1981—; dir. Sizeler Property Investors, Inc., 1986—. Fellow Am. Coll. Bond Counsel (founding); mem. ABA, La. Bar Assn., Nat. Assn. Bond Lawyers (bd. dirs., pres. 1984-85), New Orleans Country Club, Lawn Tennis Club, Met. Club (N.Y.C.). Office: Foley & Judell 365 Canal St New Orleans LA 70130-1112

JUDGE, SIR PAUL (RUPERT), management professional; b. London, Apr. 25, 1949; s. Rupert Cyril and Betty Rosa Muriel (Daniels) J.; children: Christopher Paul, Michael James. MA, Trinity Coll. U. Cambridge, 1971; MBA, U. Pa., 1973; LLD (hon.), U. Cambridge, 1995. Fin. mgr. Cadbury Schweppes plc, London, 1973-78, dep. fin. dir., 1978-80, group planning dir., 1984-86; mng. dir. Cadbury Schweppes Kenya Ltd., Nairobi, 1980-82, Cadbury Typhoo, Birmingham, United Kingdom, 1982-84; mng. dir. Premier Brands Ltd., Birmingham, 1986-87, chmn., 1987-89; chmn. Food From Britain, London, 1990-92; dir. gen. Conservative Party, London, 1992-95; ministerial advisor U.K. Govt. Cabinet Office, 1995-96; chmn. Isoworth Ltd., Luton, U.K., 1989—; bd. dirs. Schroder Income Growth Trust plc., 1995—. Chmn. adv. bd. Inst. Mgmt. Studies, Cambridge, United Kingdom, 1990—, Assn. MBAs, 1997—, Understanding Industry, 1999—, Wharton European Exec. Bd., 2000—; trustee Cambridge Found., 1991—, Brit. Food Trust, 1997—, Royal Instn., 1999—, Am. Mgmt. Assn., 2000—; dep. chmn. Globe Theatre Devel. Coun., 2000—. Decorated knight bachelor, 1996; Freeman City of London. Fellow Royal Soc. Arts, Inst. Dirs., Mktg. Soc.; mem. Royal Agrl. Soc. (coun. 1991-96), Am. Mgmt. Assn., Worshipful Co. Marketors (liveryman 1993), Athenaeum Club, Carlton Club. Mem. Ch. of England. Avocation: family activities.

JUDGE, RAJINDER, psychiatrist; b. Jullundur, India, Mar. 22, 1961; came to U.K., 1964; d. Sadhu and Parkash Judge. MD, U. Birmingham, Eng., 1984. Intern Wordsley Hosp. and Russells Hall Hosp., Dudley, 1984-85; sr. house officer psychiatry Midland Nerve Hosp., Birmingham, 1985-86; physician Riyadh, Saudi Arabia, 1986-87; psychiatry registrar North Worcester, 1987-89; assoc. med. dir. Smith Kline Beecham, U.K., 1991-96; dir., global physician for Prozac Lilly, 1997—; psychiatrist Nat. Health Svc., 1991-94; registrar, sr. registrar London Charing Cross Rotation, 1989-91; forensic med. examiner London Met. Police Force, 1991—. Contbr. articles to profl. jours. Mem. Royal Coll. Psychiatrists, ENCP. Avocations: cars, movies, travel. Office: Eli Lilly & Co Corporate Ctr Indianapolis IN 46285-0001

JUDKINS, KEITH CHARLES, anesthetist; b. Watford, Herts., Eng., Aug. 23; s. Edgar S.C. and Lilian (Barr-Armstrong) J.; m. Mary Hayden, Mar. 29, 1951; children: Miriam, Matthew. M.B.Ch.B., U. Bristol, Eng., 1973. House officer medicine Royal Hosp., Weston-Super-Mare, Eng., 1973; house officer surgery Bristol Royal Infirmary, 1974; sr. house officer medicine Frenchay Hosp., Bristol, 1974-75; registrar tng. programme anesthetics Bristol, 1975-78; sr. registrar programme anesthetics Cardiff, 1978-83; cons. anesthetist Queen Victoria Hosp., East grinstead, 1983-94; med. dir. Pinderfields Burn Ctr., Wakefield, 1994-99; trust med. dir. Pinderfields & Pontefract Hosps., NHS Trust, Wakefield, 2000—; chmn. S.E. Thames Intensive Care Specialty Com., S.E. Thames N.H.S. Regional Health Authority, 1988-94. Contbr. articles to profl. jours., chpts. to books; editor: Bailliere's Clinical Anaesthesiology: Burns and Plastic Surgery, 1987. Fellow Royal Coll. Anesthetists; mem. Internat. Soc. Burn Injury (chmn. internat. burn care com. 1994-98, hon. sec. 1998—), Brit. Burn Assn. (pres. 1994-99), European Burn Assn. (asst. sec.-treas. 1995—), Plastic Surgery Soc. Romania (hon.), Australia and N.Z. Burn Assn. (hon.). Anglican. Avocations: skiing, books, sailing, music. Office: Pinderfields Burn Ctr, Pinderfields Hosp, Wakefield West Yorkshire WF1 4DG, England

JUDYCKI, JOZEF, civil engineer, educator; b. Czaplino, Poland, Sept. 4, 1945; s. Jozef and Eugenia (Lul) J.; m. Grazyna Wojciechowska, July 6, 1968; children: Agnieszka, Katarzyna. MSc, Tech. U. Gdansk, 1968, PhD, 1975. From asst. to prof. hwy. engring. Tech. U. Gdansk, Poland, 1968—;

chief inspector Energopol, Warsaw, 1975-77; from lectr. to asst. prof. U. Basrah, Iraq, 1979-90; sr. rschr. U. Oulu, Finland, 1991, 93; cons. in field. Author: Fatigue of Asphalt Mixes, 1991, Structural Characterization of Bases Treated with Hydraulic Binders, 1991; co-author: New Methods of Asphalt Pavements Renovations, 1986, Full-Scale Pavement Testing, 1993; contbr. articles to profl. jours. Mem. Internat. Soc. Asphalt Pavements, Assn. Asphalt Paving Technologists, Assn. Engrs. & Techs. Transportation. Roman Catholic. Office: Tech U Gdańsk, Narutowicza 11, 80-952 Gdańsk Poland

JUE, TSWEN-CHYUAN, vehicle engineering educator; b. Keelung, Taiwan, China, Dec. 9, 1960; m. Wen-Chuan Lung, May 7, 1989; children: I-Der Jue, Sing-I Jue. BS, Cheng Kung U., Tainan, Taiwan, 1983, MS, 1985; PhD, Rice U., Houston, 1992. Asst. engr. Aero-Industry Devel. Ctr., Tai-Chung, Taiwan, 1987-89; assoc. prof. Nat. Huwei (Taiwan) Inst. Tech., 1992—, chmn., 1993-96. 2d lt. Ordnance, 1985-87, Taiwan. Mem. ASME, Chinese Soc. Mech. Engring, CSAE. Buddhist. Avocations: travel, stamp collecting, basketball, singing, reading.

JUENGER, FRIEDRICH KLAUS, lawyer, educator; b. Frankfurt am Main, Germany, Feb. 18, 1930; came to U.S., 1955, naturalized, 1961; s. Wilhelm and Margarete J.; m. Baerbel Thierfelder, Sept. 15, 1967; children: J. Thomas, John F. Referendarexamen (Studienstiftung des deutschen Volkes scholar), J.W. Goethe-U., 1955; MCL, U. Mich., 1957; JD (Harlan-Fiske-Stone scholar), Columbia U., 1960. Bar: N.Y. 1962, Mich. 1970, U.S. Supreme Ct. 1970. Assoc. Cahill, Gordon & Reindel, N.Y.C., 1960-61, Baker & McKenzie, N.Y.C., Chgo., Madrid,, Frankfurt am Main, 1961-66; assoc. prof. law Wayne State U., Detroit, 1966-68; prof. Wayne State U., 1968-75; prof. U. Calif., Davis, 1975-93, Edward L. Barrett, Jr. prof., 1993—; vis. prof. Max-Planck-Inst. für ausländisches und internationales Privatrecht, Hamburg, Germany, 1981-82, U. Jean Moulin, Lyon, France, 1984; lectr. Hague Acad. Internat. Law, 1983, Uruguayan Fgn. Rels. Inst., 1987; Eason-Weinmann vis. prof. comparative law Tulane U., 1989; vis. prof. J. W. Goethe U., Frankfurt am Main, 1992; Allen Allen and Hemsley fellow U. Sydney, Australia, 1993; vis. prof. U. Française du Pacifique, Tahiti, 1993, U. Mich., 1994, Victoria U., Wellington, N.Z., 1998; sec. State Adv. Commn. Pvt. Internat. Law; advisor U.S. del. 5th Inter-Am. Specialized Conf. on Pvt. Internat. Law, Mexico City, 1994. Author: German Stock Corporation Act, 1967, (with L. Schmidt) Zum Wandel des Internationalen Privatrechts, 1974, Choice of Law and Multistate Justice, 1993; editor Columbia Law Rev., 1959-60; bd. editors Am. Jour. Comparative Law, 1977—, Revue Internat. Droit Comparé, Comité Patronage; contbr. articles on conflict of laws, fgn. and comparative law to legal jours. Recipient Faculty Rsch. award Wayne State U., 1971, Disting. Teaching award U. Calif., Davis, 1985, Gen. Reporter on Judgments Recognition 12th Internat. Congress of Comparative Law, Australia, 1986, Fulbright scholar, 1953-55; Rsch. grantee Volkswagen Found., 1972-73, Humboldt Found. Rsch. grantee Albert-Ludwigs-U. Freiburg, Fed. Republic Germany, 1990; Fulbright sr. rsch. fellow, 1981-82. Mem. ABA, Assn. of Bar of City N.Y., Am. Fgn. Law Assn., Am. Law Inst., Am. Soc. Internat. Law, Am. Soc. Comparative Law (past pres., past hon. pres.), Assn. Can. Law Tchrs., Gesellschaft für Rechtsvergleichung, Internat. Acad. Comparative Law (titular mem., pres. common law group), Internat. Law Assn. (com. on internat. litigation), Soc. Pub. Tchrs. of Law, Academia Mexicana de Derecho Internacional Privado y Comparado (hon.). Office: U Calif Sch Law King Hall Davis CA 95616

JUESCHKE, RAINIE BISHOP, non-profit organization administrator; b. Dover, N.H., July 25, 1960; d. Harold Green and Georgiana Julia (Slade) Bishop; m. Chris Lynn Jueschke, Apr. 4, 1998. BA, Trinity U., San Antonio, 1982. Devel. asst. San Antonio Zool. Gardens and Aquarium, 1983-86; devel. coord. The Nature Conservancy, San Antonio, 1986-89; pvt. practice life underwriter San Antonio, 1989-93; dir. devel. Planned Parenthood San Antonio and South Ctrl. Tex., 1993-96, Global Health Action, Atlanta, 1996—. Mem. Grey Forest (Tex.) City Coun., 1989-91; sec., bd. dirs. Friends of Freidrich Wilderness Park, San Antonio; chmn. income and devel. com., chmn. planned giving and maj. gifts sub-com. Am. Cancer Soc., San Antonio, 1991-96; bd. dirs. Govt. Canyon Natural History Assn., Helotes, Tex., 1995-96. Mem. Nat. Soc. Fund Raising Execs. (cert., v.p. greater Atlanta chpt.). Avocations: birding, hiking. Fax: 404-634-9685. E-mail: rainicj@dialupnet.com.

JUHAN-VAGUE, IRENE SUZANNE, hematologist, educator, biologist; b. Marseille, France, Jan. 8, 1945; d. Jean and Denise (Jouve) Vague; m. Claude Michel Juhan, Sept. 23, 1967; children: Valerie, Emmanuelle, Jean Luc. MD, U. Marseille, 1970; PhD in Biology, U. Paris VII, 1984. Asst. prof. Univ. Ctr. Scis. and Health, Yaounde, Cameroun, 1972-74; chief Nat. Transfusion Ctr. and Lab. Hematology Ctrl. Hosp., Yaounde, 1971-74; asst. prof. hematology Univ. Hosp., Marseille, 1974-84; prof. hematology Faculty of Medicine, Marseille, 1984—; chief hematology lab. Univ. Hosp. Timone, Marseille, 1985—, chief. Ctr. Thrombotic and Hemorrhagic Disorders, 1985—; creator, dir. Nat. Transfusion Ctr., Yaounde, 1972-74. Mem. editorial bds. Thrombosis and Haemostasis, Current Opinion in Cardiology, others; contbr. articles to profl. jours. Mem. adminstrv. coun. of pub. assistance Hosps. of Marseille, 1990—. Mem. Internat. Soc. Thrombosis and Haemostasis, European Thrombosis Rsch. Orgn., French Soc. Haematology, Internat. Soc. Fibrinolysis and Thrombolysis (pres.). Achievements include identification of thrombogenic risk factors for myocardial infarction. Home: 326 chemin du Roucas Blanc, 13007 Marseille France Office: Hematologie Lab, Univ Hosp Timone, 13385 Marseille 5, France

JUHASZ, CSABA, communications executive, researcher; b. Szeged, Hungary, July 18, 1966. MS, Tech. U., Budapest, Hungary, 1988; PhD, Acad. Scis., Budapest, Hungary, 1998. Dir. info. tech. Montel Telecomm. Ltd., Budapest, 1992-96, CEO, 1996—; lectr. Tech. U., Budapest, 1992-96. Contbr. articles to profl. jours. Scholar Brit. Coun., 1992. Mem. IEEE, EMBS, Scientific Soc. Measurement Automation Informatics. Office: Montel Telecomm Ltd, Mezeskalacs Ter 18, H-1155 Budapest Hungary

JUHASZ, GEORGE, engineer; b. Mako, Hungary, Oct. 17, 1965; s. Gyorgy and Gyorgyne (Sule Etelka) J.; m. Judith Herczku, March 26, 1993; children: Eniko, Adam, Botond, Akos. MSc, U. Agrl. Scis., Godollo, Hungary, 1993; MBA, U. Econs., Budapest, 1999; PhD, U. Godollo, 1999. Lectr. People's U. China, Beijing, 1991-93; mng. dir. Golden Dragon Ltd., Budapest, 1993-95, Sinoimpex Ltd., Budapest, 1995-97; rep. mgr. Sinopharm, Beijing, 1995-97; chmn. bd. dirs. Dragon Holding, Godollo, 1996—; bd. dirs. Coffee, Tea and Spice Bd. Hungary, Budapest, 1997; mem. Herb Com. Hungary, Budapest, 1996, Codex Alimentarius, Budapest, 1997. Author: The Tea The Plant Which Has Changed the World, 1999; contbr. articles to profl. jours. Mem. Swissair Travel Club, Golf Club, Wine Soc. Club. Avocations: traveling, fishing, martial arts, books. Fax: 36 28 430747. E-mail: george@dragon.hu. Home: Rakoczi f u 10, 2100 Godollo Hungary

JUHÁSZ, IMRE, mathematics and computer sciences educator; b. Balmazujváros, Hungary, Feb. 17, 1954; m. Éva Ormándlaky Juhászné; children: Ági, Kinga. Grad., Kossuth Lajos U., Debrecen, Hungary, 1978, Doctorate, 1982. Rsch. asst. U. Miskolc, Hungary, 1978-80, rsch. fellow, 1980-85, sr. lectr., 1985-99, assoc. prof., head dept., 1999—. Author: Computer Graphics and Geometry, 1993; co-author: Computer Aided Mechanical Design, 1996. Mem. Eurographics. E-mail: agtji@gold.uni-miskolc.hu. Office: Univ Miskolc, Egyetemváros, H3515 Miskolc Hungary

JUHÁSZ, ZOLTÁN ANDOR, chemistry educator; b. Kispest, Hungary, June 4, 1929; s. Jozef J. and Katalin (Berán) J.; m. Zoltanne Eva Hollos, Nov. 4, 1953; 1 child, Zoltan. MSc in Chemistry, U. Sci. Elte, Budapest, Hungary, 1951; D in Tech., U. Tech. of Vesprém, Hungary, 1959; PhD, Hungarian Acad. Scis., Budapest, 1971, DSc, 1982. Rschr. Rsch. Inst. of Mining, Budapest, 1951-56; head rsch. lab. Ore Mining Co., Eger, Hungary, 1956-70; cons. Tech. U. Budapest, 1970-82; head professorship U. Veszprém, 1982-95, prof. emeritus, 1995—. Author: (with L. Opoczhy) Mechanical Activation of Minerals By Grinding, 1990, Szilikátok Mechanikai Aktiválása, 1982. Mem. Hungarian Acad. Scis. (mem. or chmn. various coms., 1960—, award 1995, Acad. prize winner, 1996). Home: Szölö Köz 5, 1032 Budapest Hungary Office: Univ Veszprém, Egyetem U 10, Veszprém Hungary

JUHL, MAGNE, orthopedic surgeon, consultant; b. Jernved, Denmark, Nov. 1, 1947; s. Svend Bollerup and Karen (Beck) J.; m. Margrit Andresen, Aug. 15, 1970; children: Lene, Helle. MD, U. Aarhus, Denmark, 1975; PhD, U. Aarhus, 1985. Registrar various hosps., Odense, Haderslev, Denmark, 1975-82, Graasten, Denmark, 1975-82; sr. registrar Holstebau (Denmark) Hosp., 1982-84, Aarhus County Hosp., 1984-86, Orthop. Hosp., Aarhus, 1986-88; cons. Viborg (Denmark) Hosp., 1988—, head dept., 1998—. Contbr. articles to profl. jours.; contbr. articles to genealogy jours. Mem. Danish Soc. Traffic Medicine (sec. 1984-895), Scandinavian Soc. Traffic Medicine (sec. gen. 1985-89), Danish Orthop. Soc. (rep. in Nat. Bd. Health, Denmark 1990-99), Nordic Orthop. Fedn., Esska. Mem. Danish Ch. Avocations: genealogy, local history. Home: Raevehoejen 2, DK-8800 Viborg Denmark Office: Viborg Hosp, DK-8800 Viborg Denmark

JUHOLA, MARTTI, computer science educator; b. Pori, Finland, Oct. 6, 1956; s. Ilmari and Marja (Raekivi) J.; m. Katariina Koivisto, June 16, 1989; children: Martina, Henriikka, Henrik. MS, U. Turku, Finland, 1982; lic. in philosophy, U. Turku, 1985, PhD, 1987. Asst. U. Turku, 1980-85, lectr., 1986, sr. asst., 1989-92, rschr. Acad. Finland, 1987-91; prof. U. Kuopio, 1992-97, U. Tampere, 1997—. Contbr. articles to profl. jours. Recipient Innovation award High Tech. Found., 1991. Mem. IEEE, Barany Soc., Finnish Artificial Intelligence Soc., Finnish Computer Sci. Soc. Home: Kuupellonkatu 2, 33730 Tampere Finland Office: U Tampere Dept Comp Sci, Dept Computer/Info Scis, 33104 Tampere Finland

JULIANO, BIENVENIDO OCHOA, cereal chemist; b. Los Baños, Laguna, The Philippines, Aug. 15, 1936; s. Jose Buencamino and Teodora Canicosa Ochoa J.; m. Linda Cancisio Alvarez, Apr. 10, 1965; children: Bienvenido Jose Jr., Carmelinda, Benedict Deo. BS in Agr. magna cum laude, U. The Philippines, Los Baños, 1955; MS in Organic Chemistry, Ohio State U., 1958, PhD in Organic Chemistry, 1959. Registered chemist, The Philippines. Project chemist, head lab. and devel. sects. Philippine Refining Co., Inc., Manila, 1959-61; assoc. chemist Internat. Rice Rsch. Inst., Los Baños, 1961-67; asst. instr. Coll. Agr., U. The Philippines, 1955-56; vis. prof. U. The Philippines Los Baños, 1962-93; rsch. fellow AEC-Plant Rsch. Lab., Mich. State U., East Lansing, 1968; chemist Internat. Rice Rsch. Inst., Los Baños, 1968-93; vis. prof. dept. botany U. Durham, Eng., 1975; professorial lectr. Inst. Chemistry U. Philippines at Los Baños, 1993—; sr. rsch. fellow Rice Chemistry and Food Sci. divsn. Philippine Rice Rsch. Inst., Los Baños, 1993—; rsch. assoc. dept. nutritional scis. U. Calif., Berkeley, 1983. Author: Rice in Human Nutrition, 1993; author, editor: Rice Chemistry and Technology, 2d edit., 1985; 1st author: Grain Quality Evaluation of World Rices, 1993. Recipient Ayala Award in Phys. Sci., Filipinas Found., Inc., 1975, J. Rizal Pro Patria award Pres. of Republic of The Philippines, 1976, Medal of Merit, Japanese Soc. Starch Sci., 1982. Mem. Am. Assn. Cereal Chemists (T.B. Osborne medal 1988, fellow 1990), Soc. for Advancement of Rsch. (pres. 1965-66), Nat. Acad. Sci. and Tech. (Manila, mem. exec. coun. 1989-92, chmn. divsn. phys., math. and engring. sci. 1989-92), Nat. Rsch. Coun. of The Philippines (divsn. head 1977-78, Achievement award in Cereal Chemistry 1985, Nat. Rschr. award 1993), Chem. Soc. of The Philippines (pres. 1982-83), Gamma Sigma Delta (v.p. Los Baños chpt. 1964-65). Roman Catholic. Office: Inst Chemistry 4031 College, Laguna The Philippines also: PhilRice Los Baños, UPLB Campus, 4031 College, Laguna The Philippines

JULICHER, KATHLEEN HOOPER, publisher, educational administrator; b. Beaumont, Feb. 12, 1950; d. John and Constance Maude (Smith) Hooper; m. Mark Robert Julicher, May 13, 1972; children: Joseph, Esther, Daniel, Sarah. BS in Zoology, Tex. A&M U., 1972; MA in Polit. Sci., U. Dayton, 1985; postgrad., U. Ark., 1986-87, Ga. Inst. Tech., 1999—. Cert. tchr., Tex., N.C., Ohio, Ark., Ill.; cert. pvt. pilot. Rsch. asst., 1971-72, tchr., 1973-87; founder, owner Castle Heights Press, Inc., Marietta, Ga., 1988—; co-founder, prin. Westbridge Acad., Ltd., Chgo.; nat. spkr. and seminar leader, 1989—; sci. editor Homeschooling Today Mag., Ft. Collins, Colo., 1993—; columnist Family Times Mag., Gray, Maine, 1998—. Author: Experiences in Chemistry for Small Schools, 1991, Experiences in Biology for Small Schools, 1992, Survival Tools for Homeschooling Teens, 1994, Science for Young Catholics, 1995, Pathways in Science, 1996, Modern History, 1997, Ancient History, 1997; (with J. Baker and M. Hogan) Gifted Children at Home: Practical Helps for Homeschooling, 1999; editor: The Scientist's Apprentice (H. Welliver); also articles. E-mail: julicher@aol.com. Home and Office: 2578 Alexander Farms Dr SW Marietta GA 30064-2584

JULLENS, JOHN, management consultant; b. Onstwedde, Groningen, The Netherlands, Aug. 25, 1966; s. Johannes and Aaltje Lamke (De Jonge) J.; m. Melody Ran-Ja McKeehan, Dec. 15, 1998. BSc in Mktg. and Internat. Bus., NYU, 1991; MBA, Nyenrode U., Breukelen, The Netherlands, 1997. With Ford Motor Co., Detroit, 1992-96; sr. mgr. strategic svcs. Andersen Cons., Amsterdam, The Netherlands, 1997—. Office: Andersen Cons, Apollolaan 150 PO Box 75797, 1070 AT Amsterdam The Netherlands

JUMA, OMAR ALI, government executive; b. Chake Chake, Zanzibar, Tanzania, June 26, 1941; s. Ali and Fatma (Bakari) J.; m. Salma Mwalimu Ali, Oct. 10, 1967; children: Issa, Fatma, Mwalimu, Khalid, Zuhura, Ali, Hafsa, Khairatzakia. B Veterinary Medicine and Surgery, Moscow Veterinary Acad., 1967; postgrad. cert. Animal Prodn. & Health, Cairo U., 1970; postgrad. diploma Tropical Vet. Medicine, Edinburgh U., 1977; short course on diseases, U. Fla., 1977; course in Livestock Econs., Reading U., U.K., 1982. Veterinary officer Ministry of Agr., Zanzibar, 1967, asst. veterinary officer, field svcs., 1967-69, veterinary officer, Pemba Region, 1969-70; sr. veterinary officer Minstry of Agr. and Livestock Devel., Zanzibar, 1970-71, livestock officer, Govt. Farms, 1971-72, chief veterinary officer, 1972-78, dir. dept. of livestock devel., 1978-84, prin. sec., 1984-87; chief min. Zanzibar Revolutionary Govt., Zanzibar, 1988-95; v.p. United Republic of Tanzania, 1995—. Author: Zanzibar in Perspective, 1990; editor: Agricultural Policy in Zanzibar, 1984. Mem. nat. exec. com. NEC (CCM), 1987—, ctrl. com., Tanzania, 1988—; mem. Afro-Shirz Party (ASP), Zanzibar, 1958-77; mem. Chama Cha Mapinduzi, Tanzania, 1977—. Mem. Tanzania Veterinary Assn., Tanzania Animal Prodn. Soc. Sunni Muslim. Avocations: watching football, movies. *

JUMAN, MARIAM AHMED, electrical engineer; b. Muharraq, Bahrain, Oct. 10, 1960; d. Ahmed Mohammed and Dana Yousif (Obaidli) Juman; m. Omar Mohammed Mattar, Sept. 9, 1992; children, Abdulla, Dana. B of Engring., McGill U., Montreal, Can., 1982, M in Engring., 1983. Grad. engr. Ministry of Works, Power and Water, Manama, Bahrain, 1983-85, elec. engr., 1985-87, sr. elec. engr., 1987-95; elec. engring. specialist Ministry of Electricity and Water, Manama, Bahrain, 1995-99, head system studies, 1997-99; mgr. transmission planning Ministry of Electricity and Water, 1999—. Contbr. articles to profl. publs. Mem. IEEE (sr.), Inst. Elec. Engr., Internat. Conf. on Large High Voltage Elec. Systems, Bahrain Soc. Engrs. Muslim. Avocations: reading, interior design, working on the PC. Office: Ministry Electricity & Water, PO Box 2, Manama Bahrain

JUN, BYUNG HWAN, computer engineering and pattern recognition educator; b. Seoul, Apr. 18, 1966; s. Jong Kwon Chun and Young Sook Hwang; m. Soo Ah Sohn, Oct. 11, 1992; children: Je Eun, Chae Youn. BSc, Yonsei U., Seoul, 1989, MSc, 1991, PhD in Electronic Engring., 1996. Prof. divsn. info. and comm. engring. Kongju (Republic of Korea) Nat. U., Chungnam, 1997-2000; head R&D Ctr. Moriah Tech. Inc., 2000—. Contbr. articles to sci. jours. With Republic of Korea Army, 1989-90. Mem. IEEE, Korea Info. Processing Soc., Korea Info. Sci. Soc. (dir. Choongchung Br. 1999—). Avocation: tennis. Fax: 82-41-850-8479. E-mail: bhjun@knu.kongju.ac.kr. Office: Kongju Nat U, 182 Shinkwan-Dong, Kongju 314-701, Republic of Korea

JUN, CHEN, chemical engineer, researcher; b. Anqing, People's Republic of China, Sept. 28, 1967; s. Bao-Zhen Chen and Wang-Ying Gao; m. Jun Liu, Nov. 1, 1991; 1 child, Xin-Yi Chen. BS, Nankai U., China, 1989, MS, 1992; PhD, U. Wollongong, Australia, 1999. Assoc. rsch. fellow Nankai U., Tianjin, 1992-94, rsch. fellow, 1995-96; supr. Sino-Am. BTU, Tianjin, 1993-94, mgr. prodn., 1994-95; rsch. assoc. U. Wollongong, Australia, 1998-99; rsch. fellow ONRI-MITI, Japan, 1999—. Patentee in field of Ni/MH batteries. Mem. IES, JES, IEA. Avocations: cooking, sporting. Fax: 81-727-519-9629. Office: NEDO Rschr Osaka Nat Rsch Inst, 1-8-31 Midorigaoka, Ikeda Osaka 563-8577, Japan

JUN, DUK BIN, science educator; b. Seoul, Jan. 6, 1959; parents Tae Joon Jun and Sam Soon Park; children: Hyoungwoo Brian, Hyounglak David; m. Lee Yeonhee, May 6, 2000; 1 child, Jihyeon Brian. BS, Seoul Nat. U., 1981; D of Engring., U. Calif., Berkeley, 1985. Asst. prof. Kyoung Hee U., Seoul, 1985-89; from asst. prof. to assoc. prof. Grad. Sch. Mgmt. Korea Advanced Inst. Sci. and Tech., Seoul, 1989—; vis. rschr. Inst. Transp. Studies, U. Calif., Berkeley, 1991-92; dir. telecomms. MBA Korea Advanced Sci. and Tech., Seoul, 1999; cons. Korea Telecom, SK Telecom, LG, Samsung Cos., Seoul, 1993-99. Contbr. papers to profl. jours. Mem. Korea Ops. Rsch. and Mgmt. Soc. (bd. dirs. 1998-99), Korean Indsl. Engring. Soc. (bd. dirs. 1996-97, 85-99), Internat. Inst. Forecasters, Royal Statis. Soc. Avocation: skiing. Fax: 02-958-3604. E-mail: dbjun@kgsm.kaist.ac.kr. Home: Apt G-1 Hoeki-Dong, Dongdaemoon-Ku, Seoul Korea Office: Korea Adv Inst Sci & Tech, 207-43 Cheongryangri-Dong, Seoul 130-012, Korea

JUN, JAE-SHIK, physics educator; b. Seoncheon, Pyung-Buk, Korea, Oct. 17, 1936; s. Keun-Young and Heung-Pae (Yun) J.; m. Kyoung-Ok Shin, Oct. 12, 1963; children: Ji-Seon, Ji-Hie, Ji-Su. BSc, Sung Kyun Kwan U., Seoul, Korea, 1959, MSc, 1977, PhD, 1980. Lic. radiation safety officer, Korea; cert. profl. engr. radiation control, Korea. Researcher, sr. researcher Korea Atomic Energy Rsch. Inst., Seoul, 1961-78; rsch. fellow Centro Studi Nucleari, Casaccia, Rome, 1966-67, Oak Ridge (Tenn.) Nat. Lab., 1974; head radiation lab. Korea Stds. Rsch. Inst. (now Korea Rsch. Inst. Stds./Scis.), Taejeon, 1978-81; prof. physics Chungnam Nat. U., Taejeon, 1981—; dir. radioactivity measurement lab. Taejeon Area Min. Sci. and Tech./Korea Inst. Nuclear Safety, Taejeon, 1989—; guest researcher Nat. Bur. Stds. (NIST) Radiation Rsch. Ctr., Gaithersburg, Md., 1978-79, Nat. Inst. Radiation Protection, Stockholm, 1988, Japan Atomic Energy Rsch. Inst., Tokaimura, 1990-91, 94 Institut für Strahlenhygiene-BfS, Neuherberg, Germany, 1995-96, 97; mem. spl. com. nuclear safety AEC, Republic of Korea, Seoul, 1991-97. Contbr. more than 120 articles to profl. jours. With Korean inf., 1959-60. Recipient Prime Minister's Citation Republic of Korea, Seoul, 1963, Order Nat. Svc. merit Pres. Republic of Korea, Seoul, 1981. Fellow Korean Phys. Soc.; mem. Korean Nuclear Soc. (life), Korean Assn. Radiation Protection (life, pres. 1985-87, Disting. Contbn. award 1995), Korea Radioisotope Assn. (bd. dirs.), Health Physics Soc. (plenary mem.), Internat. Radiation Physics Soc. Avocations: mountaineering, tennis, reading. Home: 101-501 Mujike Apt, Wolpyong-Dong, Seo-Ku, Taejon 302-280, Republic of Korea Office: Chungnam Nat U, 220 Kung-Dong Yousong-Ku, Taejon 305-764, Republic of Korea

JUN, JONG-GAB, chemist, educator; b. Taegu, Korea, May 4, 1953; s. In-Kee Jun and Jun-Ok Kim; m. You-Kyung Ha; children: Se-Young, Ji-Young. BS, Sogang U., Seoul, 1979; PhD, Mont. State U., 1985. Rschr. KIST, Seoul, 1979-82; postdoctoral rschr. U. Minn., Mpls., 1985-86; vis. prof. chemistry Princeton (N.J.) U., 1994-95; prof. chemistry Hallym U., Chunchon, Republic of Korea, 1986—; cons. KRICT, Taejun, 1992-93. Contbr. articles to Jour. Heterocyclic Chemistry (KOSEF award, 1996), Tetrahedron Letters (Hallym award 1997), Synthetic Comms. (Korea Ministry Edn. award 2000). Corporal, Air Force, 1973-76, Suwon. Recipient rsch. award Japan Soc. Promotion Sci., Kochi, 1991; vis. scholar Korea Ministry Edn., Seoul, 1994, Ilsong Faculty award Hallym U., 2000. Mem. Korean Chem. Soc. Christian. Avocations: tennis, hiking. Home: 104-1303 Dong-A apt, Hoopyung-dong, Chunchon Kangwondo 200-163, Republic of Korea Office: Hallym U Dept Chemistry, 1 Okchon-dong, Chunchon Kangwondo 200-702, Republic of Korea

JUN, MOO-HYUNG, veterinary, educator; b. Taejon, Chungnam, Republic of Korea, May 8, 1944; s. Hak-Chul Jun and Chil-Sun Kim; m. Kwang-Ok Tae, May 27, 1972; children: Hae-Sung, Bo-Sung, Chan-Hyuk. B in Vet. Sci., Kyungbuk Nat. U., Taegu, Korea, 1967; M in Vet. Sci., Seoul (Korea) Nat. U., 1974; MSc, James Cook U., Townsville, Australia, 1976, PhD. Jr. rschr. Inst. Vet. Rsch., Office Rural Devel., Anyang, Korea, 1967-80; sr. rschr. Inst. Vet. Rsch., Office Rural Devel., Anyang, 1980-83; asst. prof. Coll. Agr. Chungnam Nat. U., Taejon, 1983-88, asst. prof. Coll. Vet. Medicine, 1988-93, full prof., 1993—, dean Coll. Vet. Medicine, 1995-97, dir. Vet. Tchg. Hosp., 1997-99, dir. Inst. Biotech., 1999—; spl. advisor Korean Nat. Examination Bd. for Vet., Seoul, 1980—. Advisor Korean Racing Assn., Seoul, 1980-82, Chungnam Provincial Govt., Taejon, 1994. Sub lt. Korean Artillery, 1967-69. Rsch. grantee Ministry Edn., Seoul, 1984-86, 97-99, Korean Sci. and Engring. Found., Taejon, 1992-94, 97-98. Mem. Korean Soc. Vet. Sci. (v.p. 1989-91, editor-in-chief 1993-95). Roman Catholic. Avocations: mountain climbing, golfing. E-mail: mhjun@cnu.ac.kr. Fax: 82-42-8216753. Home: 22/303 Samsung Apt, Oryudong Junggu, Taejon 301-120, Republic of Korea Office: Chungnam Nat Univ, 220 Gungdong Yousung-gu, Taejon 305-764, Republic of Korea

JUNCKER, JEAN-CLAUDE, Luxembourg government official; b. Redange-sur-Attert, Dec. 9, 1954. Attended, U. Strasbourg. Parliament sec. Christian Social Party, 1979-82, sec. of state for labour and social affairs, 1982-84, min. of labour, min. in charge of budget, 1984-89, min. of labour, of fin., 1989-95, party chmn., 1990-95; prime min., min. state, of fin., of labour and employment Luxembourg, Luxembourg, 1995-99, prime min., min. state, min. fin., 1999—. Office: Ministry of State, 4 rue de la Congrégation, L-2910 Luxembourg Luxembourg*

JUNCOS, LUIS ISAIAS, internal medicine educator; b. Cordoba, Argentina, Sept. 20, 1939; s. Isaias and Maria C. (Allende) J.; m. Norma Carmen Cherini, Dec. 26, 1959; children: Rossana, Luis A. Jr., Gabriela, Andrea. BS, Alejandro Carbó U., Cordoba, 1956; MD, Nat. U. Cordoba, 1963, D Medicine, 1975; MS, U. Minn., 1973. Diplomate Am. Bd. Internal Medicine, Am. Bd. Nephrology. Intern Stanford (Calif.) Hosp., 1964-65; resident in internal medicine VA Hosp., Dayton, Ohio, 1965-67; fellow in nephrology Mayo Sch. Medicine, Rochester, Minn., 1969-71; assoc. cons. Mayo Clinic, Rochester, 1971-72; asst. prof. U. Fla., Gainesville, 1972-76, assoc. prof., 1976-78; rschr. Nat. U. Cordoba, 1978-80, prof. internal medicine, 1980—, plenary prof., 1998, chmn. dept., 1983-98, plenary prof., 1998; med. dir. Pvt. Inst. Med. Spltys., Cordoba, 1984—. Maj. M.C., U.S. Army, 1967-69. Office: Pvt Inst Med Spltys, Av Colon 4154, 5003 Cordoba Argentina

JUNEBY, HANS BERTIL, medical consultant, health counselor, educator; b. Jönköping, Sweden, July 22, 1947; s. Ernst Josef and Maria Margareta (Lindahl) J.; m. Vilma Ester Coello Rivera, Dec. 30, 1987; children: Anna Rebeca, Hans Elias. BS, SUNY, Albany, 1977; MB, Uppsala (Sweden) U., 1978; BA, Thomas Edison State Coll., 1980; PhD, Clayton U., 1981; ScD, Columbia Pacific U., 1984. Cert. in reality therapy, Inst. for Reality Therapy. Med. cons. Swedish Consulate, Chgo., 1969-70; tchr. biology and chemistry area h.s., Jönköping, 1970-71; lectr. phys. medicine various colls., Europe and U.S.A., 1973-77; lectr. preventive medicine Dansville (N.Y.) Health Inst., 1980-84; ind. health counselor, educator Sweden and U.S.A., 1969—; lectr. physiology and hygiene Coll. Med. Arts, Jönköping, 1972—; corr. Swedish radio and newspapers, London, 1964-67; cons. nutrition Scan Products Internat., Stockholm, 1967-68; cons. natural products and drugs Swedish Health Food Coun., 1976—; cons. natural drugs Swedish Med. Products Agy., Uppsala, 1977—; health and sci. reporter, 1997—. Author: Connective Tissue Massage (Physical Medicine), 1976, Handbook of Medicinal Plants, 1977, Herbs and Public Health, 1982, Juneby's Medicinal Plants, 1984, Natural Drugs Registered in Sweden, 1988, Natural Drugs, 1992, Phytomedicine, 1999. Grantee, Ekhaga Found., Stockholm, 1966, 67. Fellow Swedish Soc. Medicine; mem. Swedish Med. Assn., World Med. Assn., Am. Assn. Sex Educators, Counselors and Therapists (life), N.Y. Acad. Scis. (life), Adventist Internat. Med. Soc. (life). Seventh-Day Adventist. Avocation: amateur radio. E-mail: juneby@juno.com. Home: Box 56, S-563 22 Gränna Sweden

JUNFENG, XIAO, Olympic athlete. Winner Gold medal gymnastics Sydney, 2000. Office: Chinese Gymnastics Assn, 9 Tiyuguan Rd, 100763 Beijing China*

JUNG, DORANNE, public relations, marketing and advertising consultant; b. Los Angeles, June 11, 1948; d. Harry Gordon and Frances (Wong) J. BA, Mills Coll., 1970; postgrad., U. Calif., Berkeley, 1969, Fla. Presbyn. Coll., London, 1970; MS, Boston U., 1972. Media asst. Young & Rubicam Internat., N.Y.C., 1970; comms. coordinator New Eng. Spl. Edn. Instrnl. Materials Center, Boston, 1972-73; media dir./account exec. Harcomm As-

socs., Cambridge, Mass., 1973-76; promotion, advt. and pub. rels. mgr. Westinghouse Broadcasting, SBA Radio, Boston, 1976-79; pres. Corcoran & Doranne, Inc., Cambridge, 1979-84; asst. prof. Boston U. Sch. Pub. Comm., 1980-89; prodr./dir. video TV and radio shows; cons. mem. pub. affairs com. Boston chpt. ARC, 1979-88, CHIAT/DAY, San Francisco, 1988, FCB/IMPACT, L.A., 1989; dir. mktg. original programming MCA Home Video/MCA, Inc., 1989-94; v.p. Vineyard Prodns., 1994-95; owner Jung & Assocs., 1995-98, 99—; v.p. creative svcs. DIVX Entertainment, 1998-99. Contbg. author: Teaching About Funerals, 1980; author/dir. radio series Fishing and Our Law, 1979-80. Mem. pub. rels. com. Am. Heart Assn., 1978; mem. Hale House/Back Bay Aging Concerns Benefit Com., 1981-83; mem. pub. rels. com. Family Service Assn. Greater Boston, 1983—. Recipient award Ohio State Inst. Edn. by Radio/TV award, 1978, Broadcast Promotion Assn., 1978; Clarion award Women in Communications, 1978. Mem. Press Club Boston, Broadcast Promotion Assn., New Eng. Broadcasters Assn., Nat. Assn. TV Program Execs., Women in Direct Mktg. Assn. So. Calif., Coalition Pacific Asians Entertainment, Direct Mktg. Club of So. Calif., Venice Interactive. E-mail: djungles@aol.com.

JUNG, HAI RYUN, ophthalmologist, educator; b. Osaka, Japan, June 23, 1941; came to U.S., 1975; s. Kun Jung and Kwe Y. Shin; m. Bo K. Lee, Oct. 21, 1972; children: Alice, Joseph, Richard. MD, Korea U., Seoul, 1965, MS, 1969, PhD, 1973. Diplomate Am. Bd. Ophthalmology, Korean Bd. Ophthalmology. Intern, resident Korea. U. Hosp., Seoul, 1965-70; chmn. ophthalmology Seoul Naval Hosp., 1970-73; instr. Korea U. Coll. Medicine, Seoul, 1973-75, chmn., prof., 1983-93, prof., 1993—; dean Korea U. Coll. Medicine, 1998—; intern St. John's Episcopal Hosp., Bklyn., 1975-76; resident St. Luke's Hosp. Ctr., N.Y.C., 1977, NYU Med. Ctr., N.Y.C., 1977-78, Hahnemann U. Hosp., Phila., 1978-80; cons. Mercy Cath. Med. Ctr., Phila., 1980-82. Author: Advanced Therapy of Glaucoma, 1985, Glaucoma, 1996. Fellow Am. Acad. Ophthalmology, Korean Ophthalmology Soc. (chmn. exec. bd. trustees 1998—); mem. Korean Glaucoma Study (pres. 1996-98). Office: Korea U Med Ctr, 126-1 Anamdong 5-Ka, 136-705 Seoul Republic of Korea

JUNG, HEE KON, veterinarian, educator; b. Kwangju, Chonnam, Republic of Korea, Oct. 10, 1938; s. Koo Rhe and Ill Soon (Phark) J.; m. Hyo Duk Jin, Nov. 11, 1979; 3 children. DVM, Chonnam Nat. U., 1961; MPH, Seoul Nat. U., Republic of Korea, 1968. Asst. Med. Sch. Chonnam Nat. U., Kwangju, Republic of Korea, 1969-72, instr., 1973-76; from asst./assoc. prof. to prof. dept. food and nutrition Songwon Coll., Kwangju, 1978—; joint rschr. dept. vet. pub. health Agrl. Coll. Osaka (Japan) Prefecture U., Sakai, 1993; mem. com. for dietitian exam. Nat. Inst. Pub. Health Orgn., Seoul, 1990. Author textbooks on food hygiene, nutrition edn., health sci., physiology. With Republic of Korea Army, 1961-64. Recipient Superior Thesis prize Korean Fedn. Sci. Tech., 2000. Mem. Korean Environ. Health Soc. (bd. dirs. 1986—), Korean Soc. Food and Nutrition (bd. dirs.), East Asian Dietitians (life, bd. dirs.), Am. Assn. Adv. Sci. Home: Whajung dong, 102-403 Daeju Apt, Kwangju 502-242, Republic of Korea Office: Songwon Coll, 199-1 Kwangcheong Dong, Kwangju 502-742, Republic of Korea

JUNG, HOI-SOO, marine geochemist; b. Ok-Ku, South Korea, June 15, 1961; s. Dong-Seok Jung and Bok-Nyu Kim; m. Hyun-Sook Ra. Apr. 24, 1991; children: Ha-Neul, Hai-Sung. BA, Seoul Nat. U., 1985, MA, 1987, PhD, 1994. Jr. scientist Korean Ocean R&D Inst., An-San City, 1989-94, sr. scientist, 1994—; guest investigator Woods Hole (Mass.) Oceanographic Instn., 1997-98; guest prof. Kun-San (South Korea) U., 1994-95. Contbr. articles to profl. jours. 2d lt. Korean 3d Mil. Acad., 1987-88. Avocations: Chinese chess, tennis. Office: Korea Ocean R&D Inst, An-San PO Box 29, 425-600 An-San City South Korea

JUNG, JAE HAK, engineering educator, consultant; b. Tae-gu, South Korea, Apr. 24, 1962; s. Kuk-won Jung and Soon-Hee Park; m. Hyun Jung Oh, Jan. 9, 1988; children: Jung, Jin. BS, Yonsei U., Seoul, 1988; MS, Postech, Pohang, South Korea, 1991, PhD, 1994. Rschr. Automation Rsch. Ctr., Pohang, 1989-94; postdoctoral assoc. Postech, 1994; lectr. Yeungnam U., Kyongsan, South Korea, 1994-96, asst. prof., 1997—; postdoctoral fellow MIT, Cambridge, 1996-97; reviewer I & EC Am. Chem. Soc., 1998-99; founder Chunma Data Sys., 1999; presenter in field. Author 3 books; contbr. articles to profl. jours. Mem. Assn. Protection Environment, Tae-gu, 1994—. Korea Sci. & Engring. Found. postdoctoral grantee, 1996. Mem. AIChE, Korean Inst. Chem. Engring., Inst. Control, Automation & Sys. Engrs. (cons. 1998-99). Avocations: paintings, swimming, movies, golf. Home: Nam-gu, 1883-2 Daemyong 2 dong, 705-032 Tae-gu South Korea Office: Yeungnam U Sch Chem Engring & Tech, 214-1 Dea-dong, 712-749 Kyongsan South Korea

JUNG, JEAN-LUC, surgeon; b. Metz, France, Oct. 10, 1951; s. Francois and Madeleine (Ibos) J.; m. Francoise Monchablon, Sept. 2, 1978; children: Nicholas, Nathalie, Mathiew, Francois. MD, Besancon Med. Sch., France, 1982. Resident Besancon, France; chief resident U. Hosp., Besancon, France, 1983-85; cons. Diaconat Clinics, Colmar, France, 1985-94; head urology svc. Pasteur Hosp., Colmar, France, 1994—. Contbr. articles to profl. jours. Mem. N.Y. Acad. Scis. Home: 21 Rue De St Pierre, 68000 Colmar France Office: Pasteur Hosp, 39 Ave De Liberté, 68000 Colmar France

JUNG, MUN YHUNG, chemistry educator; b. Seoul, Korea, Mar. 7, 1958; s. Chull Hwa Jung and Young Sook Lee; m. Jung Sun Cha; children: Hyun Hee, Hyun Jung, Hyun Jin. BS, Chungnam Nat. U., Taejeon, Korea, 1984; MS, Ohio State U., 1986, PhD, 1989. Rschr. Nhongshim Food Co., Seoul, Korea, 1983-84; postdoc. rschr. Tex. A&M U., Coll. Sta., 1989-91; asst. prof. Woosuk U., Jeonbuk, Korea, 1991-96; assoc. prof. Woosuk U., 1996—; tech. cons. Am. Soybean Assn., Seoul, Korea, 1996—. Assoc. editor, Korean Jour. of Food Nutrition, 1998—, editl. bd. mem., Food Sci. and Biotech., 1999—. Contbr. articles to profl. jours. With Korean Army, 1979-83. Recipient Outstanding paper Presentation Awd., Amer. Oil Chemist's Soc., 1990, Honored Stud. Awd., Amer. Oil Chemist's Soc., 1989, Stud. Rsch. Awd., Inst. Food Technologists, Ohio Valley Sect., 1988, Grad. Stud. ALumni Rsch. Awd., The Ohio State U., 1988. Mem. Inst. Food Technologists, Am. Oil Chem. Soc., Korean Soc. Food Sci. & Tech. Roman Catholic. Developed a rameon (oriental instant noodle) fried with 100% hydrogenated soybean oil for the first time, 1998. Avocations: hiking, badmitton, music. Home: Dong-Ah Apt 105-802 561-24, 621 1 Songchon Dong II Ga, Jeonju Jeonbuk 561300, Korea Office: Dept Food Sci Woosuk U, 490 Hoojeonghi Samrae Up, 565701 Jeonbuk Wanju Kun Korea

JUNG, OTMAR, political scientist, researcher; b. Würzburg, Germany, Jan. 22, 1947; s. Walther and Elisabeth (Schenk) J.; m. Ulrike Geissler, Sept. 28, 1970; children: Raphael, Merlin, Berenike. JD, U. Würzburg, 1973; habilitation in polit. sci. and history, Free U. Berlin, 1985. Cert. state exam. in law, 1970, assessor, 1974. Rsch. asst. Free U. Berlin, 1989-91; substitute prof. legal history U. Bremen, Germany, 1990-91, 92; univ. lectr. polit. sci. Free U. Berlin, 1992—; rsch. asst. Rsch. Ins.t Pub. Adminstrn. German Postgrad. Sch. Adminstrv. Scis., Speyer, 1999. Author: Direkte Demokratie in der Weimarer Republik, 1989, Senatspräsident Freymuth, 1989, Volksgesetzgebung, 1990, Grundgesetz und Volksentscheid, 1994, Plebiszit und Diktatur, 1995. Mem. Assn. Peace Rsch. in History. Home: Altonaer Str 10, D-10557 Berlin Germany Office: Freie Univ Berlin, FB 15 Ihnestrasse 21, D-14195 Berlin Germany

JUNG, PETER, electrical engineering researcher, educator; b. Kaiserslautern, Germany, Mar. 15, 1964; s. Wilhelm Heinrich and Hilde (Plocher) J. MSc in Physics, U. Kaiserslautern, 1990, PhD in Elec. Engring., 1993, DSc in Elec. Engring., 1996. Freelance cons. dept. profl. equipment Yamaha Europe GmbH, Rellingen, Germany, 1985-90; mem. acad. staff dept. elec. engring. microelectronics ctr. U. Kaiserslautern, 1990-92, vice dir. rsch. group radio frequency dept. elec. engring., 1992-98; dir. sgt. cellular innovation Infineon Techs. (formerly Siemens AG Semiconductors), Munich, 1998-99; sr. dir. concept engring. wireless baseband Infineon Techs. (formerly Siemens AG Semiconductors), 1999-2000; prof. comms. U. Duisburg, 2000—; mem. bd. govs. Fraunhofer-Inst. of Microelectronics Sys., Duisburg, 2000—; mem. senate commn. for data processing U. Kaiserslautern, 1994-98, commn. for edn. dept. elec. engring., 1996-98, mgr. ACTS project team, project coordination com. Future Radio Wideband Multiple Access Sys., 1995-98, vice mgr. several industry-univ. collaborative projects, 1991-98. Contbr. articles to profl. jours. Mem. fire brigade, Otterberg, Germany, 1982-91. Mem. IEEE (sr., sec. tech. program com., co-organizer 4th Symposium on Spread Spectrum Technologies and Applications 1996, sec. Comm. Soc. chpt. Germany 1996-98), German Assn. Elec. Engrs. (Best Paper award Info. Tech. 1995), Audio Engng. Soc., Soc. Mobile Radio Conf. (Johann-Philipp-Reis prize 1997). Avocations: dancing, swimming, choral singing. Home: Im Rabental 28, D-67697 Otterberg Germany

JUNG, PHILIPPE, aerospace executive, historian; b. Metz, Moselle, France, July 1, 1947; s. Jacques and Monique (Antier) J.; m. Renee Reiss, Feb. 10, 1979. MS, Metz U., France, 1976. Sup aero engr., 1978; design bur. Aerospatiale, Cannes, 1978-80; TVsat/TDF sys. Aerospatiale, Munich, 1980-81; tele-X term leader Aerospatiale, Linkoping, Sweden, 1981-82; tele-X structure mgr. Aerospatiale, Cannes, 1982-86; Hermes airframe mgr. Aerospatiale, Toulouse, 1986-91; program mgr. Aerospatiale, Cannes, 1991—; v.p. space edn. Parsec, Nice, 1996—; dir. Inst. Scis. de l'Espace, Cannes, 1995-97.; prof. Cannes U., Internat. Space U. Editor Internat. Acad. Astronautics Proceedings; contbr. articles to profl. jours. Student del. Metz U., 1972-76. Mem. Assn. Aero. and Astronautique de France (pres. history commn. 1995—), Internat. Acad. Astronautics (coord. history 1994—), Brit. Interplanetary Soc., Air Britain, Nat. Geog., Inst. des Hautes Etudes de Défense Nationale, 1999. Avocations: light aircraft/glider pilot, pole vaulting, ice skating, skiing. Home: 150 Rt de Pegomas, 06130 Grasse France Office: Aerospatiale, BP 99, 06322 Cannes la Bocca Cedex, France

JUNG, ROLAND TADEUSZ, physician; b. Glasgow, Scotland, Feb. 8, 1948; m. Felicity Helen, 1974; 1 child. BA, Cambridge U., England, 1969, MA, 1972, MD, 1980. Clin. scientist MRC Dunn Nutrition Unit, Cambridge, England, 1977-79; sr. registrar endocrinology Hammersmith Hosp., London, 1980-92; cons. physician, specialist endocrinology, diabetes, obesity Ninewells Hosp., Dundee, Scotland, 1982—; dir. R&D Tayside (Scotland) Nat. Health Svc. Consortium, 1997—; hon. prof. metabolic medicine, U. Dundee Med. Sch., Scotland, 1998—; chmn. Scottish Hosp. Endowments Rsch. Trust, 2000—. Author: Color Atlas of Obesity, 1990; editor: Endocrine Problems in Oncology, 1984. Mem. Assn. Physicians Gt. Britain, Scottish Soc. Physicians. Avocation: gardening. Office: Diabetes Ctr, Ninewells Hosp, Dundee DD1 9SY, Scotland

JUNGBLUT, PETER ROMAN, biochemist, researcher; b. Zürs, Vorarlberg, Austria, June 18, 1953; arrived in Germany, 1964; s. Armin Gottfried and Liane (Mück) J.; m. Elisabeth Caritas Drese, June 22, 1987; children: Jonas, Elisa. Diploma in chemistry, Tech. U., Berlin, 1978, D of Natural Scis., 1982. Sci. asst. Tech. U., Berlin, 1978-82, Free U., Berlin, 1982-91; group leader German Heart Ctr., Berlin, 1991-92; founder, sci. mgr. WITA GmbH, Teltow, Germany, 1992-96; group leader Max-Planck-Inst. for Infection Biology, Berlin, 1996—; lectr. U. Innsbruck, Austria, 1994-98; guest scientist Max-Delbrück Ctr., Berlin, 1994-96. Mem. editl. bd.: (jour.) Electrophoresis, 1997—; contbr. articles to profl. jours. Mem. German Electrophoresis Soc. (adv. bd. 1992—), Gesellschaft Biochemie und Molekularbiologie, Am. Soc. Mass Spectrometry. Avocations: mountain climbing, biking, ornithology. Office: Max-Planck-Inst Infect Biol, Monbijoustr 2, D-10117 Berlin Germany

JUNGHANS, HELMAR PAUL, pastor, theology educator; b. Geyer, Germany, Oct. 19, 1931; s. Paul and Elly (Günther) J.; m. Thekla Müller, June 6, 1960; children: Reinhard, Eckhard, Sieghard, Katharina, Burghard. Abitur, Kirchliches Oberseminar, Potsdam, Germany, 1955; Staatsexamen, U. Leipzig, Germany, 1960, ThD, 1964, Dr. habil. theol., 1981; LHD (hon.), Valparaiso U., 1981; DD (hon.), Wittenberg U., 1991. Wiss. mitarbeiter Sächsische Akademie der Wissenschaften, Leipzig, 1961-62; wiss. mitarbeiter Theologische Fakultät Leipzig, 1962-69, wiss. oberassistent, 1969-71, hochschuldozent, 1971-82, ao. prof., 1982-90, prof., 1990-97. Author: Ockham im Lichte der neueren Forschung, 1968, Der junge Luther und die Humanisten, 1984, Martin Luther in Two Centuries, 1992, Martin Luther und Wittenberg, 1996; editor Lutherjahrbuch, 1972—. Mem. Mitglied Sächsische Akademie der Wissenschaften. Lutheran. Home: Ludolf-Colditz-Str 22, D-04299 Leipzig Germany

JUNGKIND, WALTER, design educator, writer, consultant; b. Zurich, Switzerland, Mar. 9, 1923; came to Can., 1968; s. Oskar and Frieda (Leuthold) J.; m. Jenny Voskamp, 1953; children—Christine, Stefan, Brigit. Nat diploma, Kunstgewerbeschule, Zurich, 1943; nat diploma, Regent Street Poly tech., London, 1953. Freelance designer London, 1955-68; lectr. London Coll. Printing and Graphic Arts, 1960-65, sr. lectr., 1965-68; assoc. prof. dept. art and design U. Alta., Edmonton, Can., 1968-72, prof., 1972-90, prof. emeritus, 1990—; Design cons. pub. works Province of Alta., 1972-75; chmn. Canadian Adv. Com. Standards Council Can., 1978—. Initiator and curator internat. exhbn. Graphic Design for Pub. Service, 1972, Language Made Visible, 1973. Recipient Design Can. award Nat. Design Council Can., 1979, 1984; Chmns. award Nat. Design Council Can., 1982. Fellow Soc. Chartered Designers Gt. Britain, Soc. Graphic Designers Can. (pres. 1978-82); mem. Internat Coun. Graphic Design Assns. (pres. 1974-76, Design for Edn. award 1972.). Home: 6304 109th Ave, Edmonton, AB Canada T6A 1S2

JUNGMANN, RAUL, Brazilian government official. Minister land reform Govt. of Brazil, Brasilia, 1996—. Mem. Popular Socialist Party. Office: Ministry Land Reform, Esp Dos Ministerios Bloco D, 8 andar Brasilia DF 70043900, Brazil*

JUNGNICKEL, BERND-JOACHIM, physicist, educator; b. Gleiwitz, Silesia, Germany, Aug. 27, 1943; s. Rudolf and Jutta (Harasim) J.; m. Ingrid Steudel Siegeris, Aug. 26, 1966 (div. May 1973); children: Sven, Constanze. PhD, German Acad. Sci., Berlin, 1973. Group leader Inst. Polymer Chemistry, Teltow, Germany, 1968-78, German Plastics Inst., Darmstadt, 1978—; lectr. physics U. Ulm, Germany, 1987-92, Tech. U., Darmstadt, 1992—. Author, editor: Polymer Blends, 1990, Solid State Forming of Plastics, 1992; author: Measurement and Information in Experimental Physics--Theory and Applications, 1994. Mem. German Phys. Soc. Avocation: piloting. E-mail: bjungnickel@dki.tu-darmstadt.de. Home: Beethovenring 35, D-64342 Seeheim-Jugenheim Germany Office: German Plastics Inst, German Plastics Inst, Schlossgartenstr 6, D-64289 Darmstadt Germany

JUNOD, ALAIN RENÉ, physicist, researcher, educator; b. Geneva, Mar. 25, 1945; s. René Pierre and Aline Hélène (Michot) J.; m. Anne Claire Jullien, Sept. 3, 1965; children: Olivier, Jean-Michel. Diploma in Physics, U. Geneva, 1968, PhD in Physics, 1974. Cert. pedagogical studies. Lab. head U. Geneva, 1974-79, lectr., 1979-82, lectr., sr. rschr., 1982-92, master in tchg. and rsch., 1992-98, prof., 1999—; asst. conservator Mus. History Sci., Geneva, 1979-82; temporary fgn. collaborator Commissariat à l'Energie Atomique, Grenoble, France, 1991-92. Contbr. chpts. in books and articles to profl. jours. Achievements include research in superconductivity and development of low temperature calorimetry. Avocations: sailing, history of science. Home: Bourg-de-Four 32, CH-1204 Geneva Switzerland Office: U Geneva, 24 quai E Ansermet, CH-1211 Geneva 4, Switzerland

JUNQUEIRA, IVAN NOBREGA, editor; b. Rio de Janeiro, Brazil, Nov. 3, 1934; s. Roberto Lago Diniz and Horencia Nobrega J.; m. Maria Cecilia Barata Costa, May 4, 1987; children: Rafael, Suzana, Raquel, Octavio; m. Maria Celina Whately, June 11, 1960 (div. Apr. 1985). Diploma, Melo E Sousa, Rio de Janeiro, 1954. Dep. dir. UN Info. Ctr., Rio de Janeiro, 1970-77; editor UERJ, Rio de Janeiro, 1977-79, Expressao e Cultura, Rio de Janeiro, 1977-80; sub-editor O Globo, Rio de Janeiro, 1983-85, Jour. do Brasil, Rio de Janeiro, 1984-87; editor Funarte, Rio de Janeiro, 1987-97; cons. Ency. Britannica, Rio de Janeiro, 1962-66, Ency. Delta Larousse, Rio de Janeiro, 1966-69, Ency. Mirador, Rio de Janeiro, 1970-73, Nat. Libr., Rio de Janeiro, 1991-97. Author poetry and essays in jours. Ofcl. rank cpl. Brazilian Army, 1953-54. Named Intellectual of the Yr., Uniao Brasileira de Escritores, Rio de Janeiro, 1984, Translator of Yr. APCA, Sao Paulo, 1991, Nat. Libr., Rio de Janeiro, 1993, awards Jabuti Book Nat. Inst. and Pen Club Brazil. Mem. Pen Club of Brazil, Brazilian Acad. Letters. Avocations: archaeology, movies, theatre, TV, classical music. Home: Praça Xavier de Brito, 30/AP 102, 20530520 Rio de Janeiro Brazil

JUNXIAN, MA, research educator; b. Beijing, Aug. 29, 1961; s. Ma and Li (Shulan) Fengquan; m. Zhang Yanfang, Mar. 8, 1986; 1 child, Jie Ma. B Physics, Wuhan (China) Engring. Coll, 1982; M in Electronics, Sci. & Tech. U. China, Chengdu, 1988. Asst. prof. Survey and Mapping Coll., Zhengzhou, China, 1982-86; lectr. Shenzhen (China) U., 1988-93, assoc. prof., 1994—; cons. Sci. and Tech. Com., Guangdong Province, China, 1995-97, Econ. Devel. Com., Shenzhen, China, 1991-97; vice dir. Info. Engring. Coll., 1997—. Contbr. articles to profl. jours.; inventor in field; patentee in field. Named Best 10 Youth in Sci. and Tech., Assn. Sci. & Tech., Shenzhen, 1994, Best 20 Youth in Sci. and Tech., Govt. of City, Shenzhen, 1997. Fellow Electronics Assn. (Guangdong province 1997—); mem. Electronics Assn. China (sr.). Office: Shenzhen U, Advanced Tech Rsch Ctr, Shenzhen 518060, China

JUODKA, BENEDIKTAS, biochemist; b. Utena, Lithuania, Jan. 13, 1943; s. Antanas Juodka and Eugenija (Limanauskaite) Juodkiene; m. Tiina Pusse, Feb. 2, 1968; 1 child, Robert. MS, Moscow State U., 1965, PhD, 1968. Lectr. Vilnius U., Lithuania, 1968-69, sr. lectr., 1969-71, head of biochemistry dept., 1971—, prof., 1982—, vice-rector, 1991—; pres. Lithuanian Acad. of Scis., Vilnius, 1992—; adviser for rsch. and edn. Lithuanian Govt., Vilnius, 1993-94; mem. sci. coun., Vilnius, 1991-93. Author: (monograph) Chemical modelling of covalent Nucleic Acid-Protein complexes, 1985, Natural Covalent Mononucleotide-Protein Complexes, 1995, (textbook) Chemistry and Biochemistry of Nucleic Acids, 1988. Mem. World Commn. on the Ethics of Sci. Knowledge and Tech. Mem. Lithuanian Acad. Scis., Latvian Acad. Scis., European Acad. Scis. and Arts. Home: Antakalnio 95-1, Vilnius 2040, Lithuania Office: Lithuanian Acad of Scis, Gedimino pr 3, Vilnius 2600, Lithuania

JUODVALKIS, EGLE, writer; b. East Chicago, Ind., Jan. 28, 1950; d. Antanas and Ona (Norkus) J.; m. Henryk Skwarczynski, Sept. 2, 1989. BA, U. Chgo., 1973. Sr. editor Radio Free Europe/Radio Liberty, Inc., Munich, 1976-95. Author: (poetry) If You Touch Me, 1972, Who Has the Ring?, 1983, The Necklace of Mnemosine, 1996, Sugar Mountain or The Adventures of a Lithuanian Diabetic in America and Other Exotic Places, 2000. Mem. PEN Lithuanian Ctr., Lithuanian Writers' Union, Santara-Sviesa, Korp! Neo-Lithuania. Avocation: touring Greece. Home: 8608 Sayre Ave Burbank IL 60459-2260

JURADO, FABRICE MARCEL, physics educator; b. Lyon, France, Aug. 15, 1965; s. Francois and Colette (Dufour) J. BS in Physics, U. Montpellier II, France, 1986, MS in Physics, 1987, DEA Theoritical Physics, 1988, PhD, 1992. Postdoctoral fellow Politecnico Di Milano, Italy, 1993; rschr. IFP, France, 1994—. Contbr. articles to profl. jours. Avocation: chess. Office: IFP/BP311, Inst Francais du Petrole, 92506 Rueil-Malmaison France

JURCZYSZYN, ARTUR JAN, hematologist; b. Przemysl, Poland, June 17, 1971; s. Mieczyslaw and Elzbieta (Dudek) J. MD, Jagiellonian U., Cracow, Poland, 1996. Asst. dept. hematology Jagiellonian U., Cracow, 1996—. Mem. European Hematology Assn., Polish Soc. Organ Transplantation, Polish Assn. Internal Medicine, Polish Soc. Hematology and Blood Transfusion, N.Y. Acad. Sci., Internat. Soc. Nematology. Home: Szafrana 4/26, 30-401 Cracow Poland Office: Jagiellonian U Dept Hematol, Kopernika 17, 31-501 Cracow Poland

JUREWICZ, JOHN THOMAS, university dean, engineer; b. Wilkes-Barre, Pa., Mar. 16, 1945; s. Benjamin Urevitch and Sophia (Blotski) J.; m. Kathleen C. Vander Heyden, June 10, 1978; 1 child, Joseph; stepchildren: Stephen Unmuth, Elizabeth Unmuth. BA in Math., King's Coll., 1968; BS in Aero. Engring., Pa. State U., 1968; MS in Mech. Engring., Wash. State U., 1973, PhD in Engring. Sci., 1976. Rsch. engr. Pratt & Whitney Aircraft, E. Hartford,, Conn., W. Palm Beach, Fla., 1968-70; tchr. Bishop Hoban H.S., Wilkes-Barre, Pa., 1970-71; asst. prof. Inst. Paper Chemistry, Appleton, Wis., 1976-78; asst. prof. W. Va. U., Morgantown, 1978-79, from asst. prof. to prof., 1981-86, assoc. dean of engring., 1986-91, interim dean of engring., 1991-92; rsch. engr. Kimberly Clark Corp., Neenah, Wis., 1979-81; dean of grad. studies and rsch. Fla. Atlantic U., Boca Raton, Fla., 1993—; acting dean of engring. Fla. Atlantic U., Boca Raton, 1996—; dir. W. Va. Space Grant Consortium, Morgantown, 1989-91; bd. dirs. W. Va. Rsch. Corp., 1989-92, Fla. Atlantic Univ. Rsch. and Devel. Authority, Boca Raton, 1994-97; pres. Fla. Atlantic Rsch. Corp., Boca Raton, 1993-97. Editor (4 books) Gas-Solid Flows, 1986-91; assoc. editor ASME Jour. of Fluids Engring., 1984-86; contbr. articles to 10 profl. jours. Home: 2712 NW 27th Ter Boca Raton FL 33434-6001 Office: Fla Atlantic U 777 Glades Rd Boca Raton FL 33431-6424

JURGENS, GERMAN NICKOLAEVICH, microbiologist, researcher; b. Leningrad, Russia, July 24, 1966; s. Nickolai Mickhailovich Rebachuk and Ina Leopoldovna Jurgens; m. Olga Vjaeheslavovna Tarakanova, Oct. 28, 1989 (div. Sept. 1996); m. Natalia Vasiljevna Zhiganova, Aug. 29, 1997; 1 child, Kristina Germanovna. MSc, St. Petersburg Tech. U., 1989; postgrad., U. Helsinki, Finland, 1994—. Microbiologist All-Russian Rsch. Inst. for Agrl. Microbiology, St. Petersburg, 1989-93; microbiologist, rschr. U. Helsinki, 1994—. Office: U Helsinki Applied Chem, Viikinkaari 9 PO Box 56, 00014 Helsinki Finland

JÜRGENSEN, FRANK DIETRICH WALTER, museum educator; b. Gronau/Han, Germany, Apr. 22, 1943; s. Emil and Christa (Bunner) J.; m. Gisela Sell, June, 1971; children: Lena, Ulla, Peter Hinrich. PhD, U. Hamburg, Germany, 1972. Wiss. Oberrat im Verwaltungsdienst Kulturbehörde, Hamburg, Germany, 1977—. Home: Minsbekweg 10, 22399 Hamburg Germany Office: KZ-Gedenkstaette Neuengamme, Jean Dolidier Weg, 21039 Hamburg Germany

JURICIC, DAVOR, mechanical engineering educator; b. Split, Croatia, Aug. 2, 1928; came to U.S., 1968; s. Mate and Slavka (Franceschi) J.; m. Milesa L. Harris, Mar. 10, 1984; 1 child, Ivanna Albertin. Dipl.Ing., U. Belgrade, Yugoslavia, 1952, DSc, 1964. Stress analyst Icarus Aircraft Industries, Zemun, Yugoslavia, 1953-58; rsch. engr. Inst. Aeronautics, Belgrade, 1958-63; asst. prof. U. Belgrade, 1963-65, assoc. prof., 1965-68; assoc. prof. S.D. State U., Brookings, 1968-73, prof., 1973-75; vis. prof. Stanford (Calif.) U., 1975-78; prof. mech. engring. U. Tex., Austin, 1978-98, prof. emeritus, 1998—. Contbr. numerous articles to profl. jours. Rsch. grantee various agencies, 1962—. Mem. ASME, Am. Soc. Engring. Edn. (Chester F. Carlson award 1993), Sigma Xi. Achievements include research in suspension system for railway vehicles (patent). Office: Univ of Texas Dept Mech Engring Austin TX 78712

JURICSKAY, ZSUZSANNA TÜNDE, physicist, researcher; b. Pécs, Baranya, Hungary, Apr. 9, 1942; d. Pál and Ilona (Szabó) Dávid; m. István Juricskay; 1 child, Zoltán. M. Physics, Eötvös Lóránd, Budapest, Hungary, 1969; PhD, Med. U. Pécs, Hungary, 1978; B.Computer Sci., Computer Teaching Ctr., Pécs, 1985. Rsch. fellow Med. U. Pécs, 1969-78, postdoctoral fellow, 1978-95, assoc. prof., 1995—. Contbr. articles to profl. jours. Grantee Found. for Rsch. and High Edn. of Hungary, 1992, Nat. Found. for Sci. Rsch., 1993-94. Mem. Hungarian Biophys. Soc. Avocations: reading, gardening, knitting. Office: POTE Ctrl Rsch Lab, Szigeti ut 12, 7643 Pécs Baranya, Hungary

JÜRIMÄE, JAAK, physiologist, researcher; b. Tartu, Estonia, May 16, 1968; s. Arnold and Aino (Tamm) J.; m. Maria Herodes, Jan. 16, 1998. BSc, U. Tartu, 1990, MSc, 1992; PhD, U. Queensland, Brisbane, Australia, 1996. Rsch. asst. U. Queensland, 1992-95; rschr. U. Tartu, 1996—. Avocations: reading, theater, movies, basketball, rowing. Office: U Tartu, 18 Ulikooli St, EE51014 Tartu Estonia

JURIMAE, TOIVO, physical education educator, researcher; b. Tartu, Estonia, May 9, 1949; s. Arnold and Vaike (Parv) J.; m. Tiiu Matto, Apr. 27, 1978 (div. 1984); 1 child, Kadri. Diploma, U. Tartu, 1973, PhD in Phys. Edn. and Sports, 1980. Tchr. phys. edn. 5th Secondary Sch., Tartu, 1973-77; asst. U. Tartu, 1977-80, lectr. phys. edn., 1980-87, assoc. prof., 1987-92, prof., 1992—, head Inst. Sport Pedagogy, 1992—. Mem. Fedn. Internationale d'Education Physique (exec. bd.), Internat. Soc. for the Advancement of Kinanthropometry (bd. dirs.), N.Y. Acad. Scis. Avocation: sports. Office: U Tartu, 18 Ülikooli St, 51014 Tartu Estonia

JURISIC, M., scientist, educator; b. Cerna, Croatia, Oct. 26, 1961; s. Auro Mariaan Matuzovic and Mariga Agata Zurisic; married; 2 children. Grad., U. Strossmayer, Osijek, Croatia, 1986; BSc (hon.), Zagreb, Croatia, 1991. Dir. Agrl. Soc. Co., Croatia, 1987-89; aspirant faculty agr. U. Stossmayer, 1989-92, prof., 1992—; pres. mgmt. Agrl. Co. Mednik, Croatia, 1992-99; cons. in field. Author: Machine for Sugar Beet, 1999, Silage and Silage Machine, 1999. Mem. Govt. of County, Croatia, 1990-92. Mem. European Soc. for Agronomy, ESNA. Avocation: art. Home: B Bartok 61, 31000 Osiecko Croatia Office: U Strossmayer Faculty Agr, TRG Sv Trojstva 3, 31000 Osijek Croatia

JURKĀNS, JANIS, government official; b. Riga, Latvia, Aug. 31, 1946; s. Antons and Marianna (Zaharevič) J.; m. Ilze Auzere Grace, June 8, 1992; children: Janis, Dāvid. Degree in philology, Latvian State U., Riga, 1974. Lectr. Latvian State U., 1974-77; head dept. Enterprise Decorative Art, Riga, 1977-79; various positions, 1980-87; dep. chmn. fgn. rels. com. Latvian Popular Front, Riga, 1988-90; fgn. min. Ministry Fgn. Affairs, Riga, 1990-92; pres. Latvian Support Fund, 1992—; mem. Parliament, 1993—; chmn. Nat. Harmony Party, 1994—; parliamentary deputy Government of Latvia, Riga. Roman Catholic. Avocations: tennis, cycling, books, music. Office: Latvian Parliament, Jēkaba Iela 11, LV-1811 Riga Latvia*

JURKIEWICZ, STANISLAS, chemical engineer; b. Cagnac, Tarn, France, May 13, 1944; s. Ludwig and Czeslawa (Niemczyk) J.; m. Anne Marie Marcelle Massy; children: Pascal, Elsa. BS, U. Besançon, France, 1966. Area mgr. Flopetrol Schlumberger, various locations, 1968-85; tech. mgr., chmn. Flopetrol Schlumberger, Paris, 1986-87; gen. mgr. TNT IPEC, Paris, 1988-89, Air Liquide Polska, Warsaw, Poland, 1990-92; gen. mgr., chmn. bd. dirs. Air Liquide Polska, Cracow, Poland, 1996—; gen. mgr. Air Liquide Med., Paris, 1993-95; mgr. French C. of C. and Industry, Cracow; conseiller du commerce exterieur French Ambassy Warsaw. Avocations: golfing, swimming, rock and mineral collecting, bridge. Office: Air Liquide Poland, Ul Bora Komorowskiego 13, 31 476 Cracow Poland

JURKOWSKI, MAREK KAJETAN, neuroimmunologist, educator; b. Bydgoszcz, Poland, Jan. 1, 1951; s. Zygmunt and Irena Urszula (Ziółkowska) J.; m. Ewa Maria Krawczyk, Mar. 30, 1974; children: Anna, Marta. MSc, U. Gdansk, Poland, 1973; PhD, Med. Acad. Gdansk, 1985, clin. analyst, 1990. Asst. Med. Acad. Gdansk, 1973-85; adj. U. Gdansk, 1985—; asst. Clin. Hosp. #3, Gdansk, 1985-90. Contbr. articles to profl. jours. Fellow Internat. Soc. for Neuroimmunomodulation, Internat. Soc. for Neuroimmunology, Polish Physiol. Soc. Roman Catholic. Avocations: gardening, fishing. E-mail: marjur@biotech.univ.gda.pl. Office: Dept Animal Physiology, Kładki 24, 80-822 Gdańsk Poland

JURUKOVA, ZANKA BORISSOVA, pathologist, educator; b. Plovdiv, Bulgaria, Mar. 18, 1931; d. Boris Vassilev Jurukov and Rouja Todorova Jurukova; m. Velko Velkov, Sept. 6, 1961 (div. 1968); m. Peter Georgiev, Apr. 4, 1969; children: Nijagul, Ava. MD, H.S. Medicine, Sofia, Bulgaria, 1957; PhD, Med. Acad., Sofia, Bulgaria, 1968, DSc, 1978. Med. diplomate. Rsch. fellow Bulgarian Acad. Scis., Sofia, 1964-73; assoc. prof. pathology Med. Acad., Sofia, 1974-85, prof. pathology, 1986—; cons. pathologist State Hosp., Blagoevgrad, Bulgaria, 1981-88; mem. Superior Med. Certifying Commn., Sofia, 1987-92; pres. Sci. Coun. Morphology, Sofia, 1992-95, 97. Author: Cellular Pathology of the Arterial Wall, 1981; mem. adv. bd. Gen. Pathology/Pathol. Anatomy, 1990-95. Active Union Bulgarian Women. Recipient Best Monography of the Yr., Med. Acad. Sofia, Bulgaria, 1981. Mem. Internat. Soc. Artherosclerosis, European Soc. Pathology, Bulgarian Soc. Pathology (bd. mem. 1993—), N.Y. Acad. Scis. Roman Catholic. Avocations: classical music, skiing. Home: Boul Vitosha 28, 1000 Sofia Bulgaria Office: Med Acad Dept Pathology, G Sofiiski str 1, BG-1431 Sofia Bulgaria

JURZYSTA, MARIAN LUDWIK, biochemist; b. Wisznice, Poland, Aug. 19, 1932; s. Jan and Maria (Szpilewicz) J.; m. Aleksandra Ludwika Zyzik, June 8, 1964; children: Slawomir, Grzegorz. MS in Chemistry, U. Maria Curie-Sklodowska, 1955; PhD, U. Agriculture, Lublin, Poland, 1970, habilitation in biochemistry, 1983. Chemistry asst. U. Agriculture, 1955-64; biochemistry asst. Inst. Soil Sci. and Plant Cultivation, Pulawy, Poland, 1964-70, asst. prof., 1970-83, head lab. phytochemistry, 1973-91, assoc. prof., 1983-91, prof., 1991—; vis. prof. U. Ottawa, Canada, 1986-87, Okla. State U., Stillwater, 1987-88. Contbr. articles to profl. jours. Active Solidarity, Pulawy, 1980—. Recipient Outstanding award for saponin investigation Polish Acad. Scis., 1983, Outstanding award for chemotaxonomic studies, 1989, Worthy of Merit in Agriculture Warsaw, 1984, Golden Cross of Merit Pres. of Poland, 1990, Prof.'s Nomination, 1991. Mem. Polish Biochem. Soc., Phytochem. Soc. Europe, Sigma Xi. Roman Catholic. Avocations: horticulture, fishing. Home: Krancowa 21/2, 24-100 Polawy Poland Office: Inst Soil Sci Plant Cultiva, 24-100 Pulawy Poland

JUŠKA, ALFONSAS, biophysicist, researcher; b. Marijampole, Lithuania, July 9, 1937; s. Antanas and Zuzana (Kvietelaityte) J. Degree in electronics engring., Moscow Power Engring. Inst., 1965; PhD, Ukrainian Acad. Scis., Kiev, 1984. Deported to Siberia, 1948-58; joiner apprentice, then joiner Ust'-Abakan (Russia) Timber Plant, 1951-58; joiner Marijampole (Lithuania) Dist. Bldg. Enterprises, 1958-59, Moscow Plant Med. Electric Instruments, 1959; rsch. probationer, sr. engr., jr. rsch. assoc. Inst. Zoology and Parasitology, Vilnius, Lithuania, 1966-76; sr. engr., jr. rsch. assoc., rsch. assoc., sr. rsch. assoc., head sector informatics Inst. Biochemistry, Vilnius, 1976—; participant internat. sci. meetings and confs. Contbr. articles to sci. jours. Participant countryside folklore expdns., Lithuania, 1969-89; mem. Sajudis Lithuanian Reform Movement, 1988-92, advisor Sajudis Faction of Supreme Coun. of Republic of Lithuania, Vilnius, 1992. Travel grantee Internat. Sci. Found., 1994, 95. Avocations: folklore, travel. Home: Gyneju 4-213, LT-2001 Vilnius Lithuania Office: Inst Biochemistry, Mokslininku 12, LT-2600 Vilnius Lithuania

JUSKAITIS, RIMVYDAS, biologist, researcher; b. Sakiai, Lithuania, Nov. 27, 1959; s. Antanas and Antanina (Rubikaite) J.; m. Jurate Kalinauskaite, Aug. 4, 1984; children: Milda, Aiste, Rimantas, Ramunas. MSc, Vilnius U., 1982; PhD, U. Leningrad, 1990. Sr. lab. asst. Inst. Zoology and Parasitology, Vilnius, 1982-85, jr. rsch. fellow, 1985-90; chief zoologist Environ. Protection dept., Vilnius, 1990-91; sr. biologist Ctrl. Environ. Rsch. Lab., Vilnius, 1991-94; rsch. fellow Inst. of Ecology, Vilnius, 1994-98, sr. rsch. fellow, 1998—. Co-author: Fauna of Lithuania Mammals, 1988, Fauna of Lithuania Birds, 1991, Red Data Book of Lithuania, 1992, Atlas of Lithuanian Mammals, Amphibians and Reptiles, 1997, 2d edit., 1999; contbr. articles to profl. jours. Grantee Fauna & Flora Internat., Cambridge, 1997, The Mammal Soc., London, 1997. Mem. Soc. Europaea Mammalogica, Lithuanian Theriological Soc., Lithuanian Ornithological Soc. E-mail: juskaitis@takas.lt. Office: Inst of Ecology, Akademijos 2, LT-2600 Vilnius Lithuania

JUSKO, MARIÁN, banker; b. Prešov, Slovakia, Mar. 24, 1956. Engring. Degree, U. Econs., Bratislava, 1979, PhD in Fin., 1989. Lectr., sec. Dept. Fin., U. Econs., Bratislava, 1979-90; expert advisor Slovak Nat. Coun., 1990; head banking analyses and prognoses State Bank of Czechoslovakia, 1991; dep. minister Min. Adminstrn. and Privatisation of Nat. Property, Slovak Republic; chmn. bd. Nat. Property Fund; with State Bank of Czechoslovakia for Slovak Republic, Bratislava, 1992; vice gov. Nat. Bank of Slovakia, 1993-99, gov., 1999—; gov. of bd. govs. Internat. Monetary Fund; alt. gov. Slovak Republic to World Bank, European Bank for Reconstrn. and Devel.; mem. band bd. Internat. Bank for Econ. Coop., Internat. Investment Bank; rep. Nat. Bank of Slovakia at Bank of Internat. Settlements. Office: Nat Bank of Slovakia, Šturova 2, 813 25 Bratislava Slovakia

JUSOFF, KAMARUZAMAN, educator; b. Kota Bharu, Kelantan, Malaysia, Mar. 28, 1958; s. Jusoff Taib and Che Wook Abdullah; m. Rohaita Abdul Fathel, Aug. 24, 1985; children: Nur Syazana, Nur Atirah, Nur Afifah, Nur Amira. PhD in Forest Survey Engring., Cranfield U., Silsoe, Eng., 1992. Lectr. U. Putra Malaysia, Serdang, Malaysia, 1989-93, assoc. prof. forest survey engring., 1994-99; prof. U. Putra Malaysia, Serdang, 1999—; dep. dir. Ministry Sci., Tech. & Environ., Kuala Lumpur, Malaysia, 1996-97; fellow Inst. Multimedia, program head Inst. Biosci., Kuala Lumpur, Malaysia, 1997—; chmn. Remote Sensing/GIS Group, U.P.M., 1993—, co. comdr. Pasukan Latihan Pegawai Simpanan, 1992—, dep. dir. R & D, Malaysian Ctr. Remote Sensing, Ministry of Sci., Tech. and Environ., 1995-96. Contbr. articles to profl. jours. Environ. adviser Malaysian Parliamentarian Assn., Kuala Lumpur, 1995. Capt., comdr. Vol. Armed Forces, Regimen Askar Wataniah, Kuala Lumpur, 1984—. Rsch. grantee Brit. High Commn., U.K., 1996, Vice Chancellor Assn., U.K., 1989-92. Mem. Malaysian Assn. Remote Sensing (sec. 1996-97). Mem. United Malay National Organization (UMNO). Moslem. Avocations: travel, driving, sports. Home: No 22 Jln Indah 1/3, Taman U, Seri Kembangan 43300, Malaysia Office: Inst Bioscience UPM, Silicon Ave, Serdang Selangor 43400, Malaysia

JUST, JULIA BARNETT, newspaper editor; b. Chgo., Feb. 23, 1961; d. Ward Swift and Jean Ramsay (Bower) J.; m. Tom Reiss, May 19, 1996; 1 child, Lucy Madeline. BA, Columbia U., 1983. Editl. asst. The New Yorker, N.Y.C., 1983-90; asst. editor N.Y. Rev. Books, N.Y.C., 1991-93; staff editor op-ed page N.Y. Times, N.Y.C., 1993-95, story editor N.Y. Times Mag., 1996-97, dep. editor N.Y. Times Book Rev., 1998—; mem. N.Y. Book Critics Cir., 1990-97. Office: NY Times 229 W 43d St New York NY 10036

JUST, TOM, chemist, researcher; b. Copenhagen, Oct. 9, 1968; s. Ejner and Anne Betty (Larsen) J.; m. Lis Rasmussen, Dec. 12, 1995; children: Laurits Arthur, Terese Vera. BSc, U. Roskilde, Denmark, 1993; MSc, U. Copenhagen, 1996. Rsch. scientist DAKO, Glostrup, Denmark, 1996—. Author: (with others) Peptide Nucleic Acids, 1999; contbr. articles to profl. jours. Mem. Internat. Soc. Analytical Cytology. Office: DAKO A/S Immunocytochem, Produktionsvej 42, DK-2600 Glostrup Denmark

JUSTICE, ORA LYNN, chemical company executive; b. Milan, Ind., Aug. 6, 1942; s. Leo Edgar and Sarah Edna (Stacy) J.; m. Bonita Hedrick, June 30, 1963; children: Chrissan, Jennifer, Vanessa, Rebecca, Aaron, David, Sarah, Florence. BA, Ind. U., Bloomington, 1966. Store mgr. Western Auto Supply Co., Ponce, Puerto Rico, 1965-67; mgr. Argentine div. Nat. Chemsearch Corp., Buenos Aires, 1967-74; owner, mgr. Equity Labs., Fairfield, Ohio, 1974-77; gen. mgr. Arco de Centro Am., S.A., Tegucigalpa, Honduras, 1977-81; dir. temporal affairs, Cen. Am. Ch. of Jesus Christ of Latter-day Saints, Salt Lake City, 1981-90; founder, chief exec. officer Equilab, S.A., Guatemala City, Guatemala, 1990-99, UltraChem de Guatemala, S.A., Guatemala City, 1991-99; founder, CEO Club Mundo Magico S.A., Guatemala City, 1996—; franchiser cons. Equity Group, Mex., C.Am., Uruguay, Argentina, Chile, 1981—. Inventor aerosol can adaptor. Scoutmaster, Guatemala area Boy Scouts Am., 1988-90. Avocations: aviation, woodworking. Office: Club Mundo Magico SA, 15 Av 29-01 Zona 13, Guatamela City Guatemala

JUSTICE-MALLOY, RHONA JEAN, educator, theatrical artist; b. Boston, May 22, 1954; d. Joseph Miller and Regina Lucille (Burge) J.; m. James Kevin Malloy, Apr. 21, 1979; 1 child, Amanda Katherine. BS, U. Evansville, 1974; MFA, U. Ga., 1979, PhD, 1994. Profl. performer freelance, 1979-89; instr. Truman Coll., Chgo., 1986-89, South Suburban Coll., South Holland, Ill., 1989-90, Ind. Univ. N.W., Gary, Ind., 1989-90, U. Ga., Athens, 1994-95; co-producer, dir. Highlands (N.C.) Playhouse, 1996—; asst. prof. Ctrl. Mich. U., Mt. Pleasant, 1995—; adjudicator Am. Coll. Theatre Festival, Region III, 1995—; mem. U. Ga. Alumni Network, Athens, 1995—, U. Evansville Alumni Network, 1996—; v.p. Mid-Am. Theatre Conf., 1997—; adv. coun. to the Sch. Classical Studies Am. Acad. Rome, Nat. Theatre Conf. Contbr. articles to profl. jours. and chpts. to books. Mem. Highlands Assn. for Religious Thought, N.C., 1996—, Highlands Women's Discussion Group, 1996—, PTA, Mt. Pleasant, Mich., 1996—. Recipient Mortar Bd., U. Evansville, 1976. Mem. Actor's Equity Assn., Screen Actor's Guild, Am. Fedn. Radio and Television Artists, Congress of European Theatre, Internat. Fedn. for Theatre Rsch., Soc. for Sci. and Lit., Am. Soc. for Theatre Rsch., Mid-Am. Theatre Conf. (v.p.), Popular Culture Assn., Performance Studies Internat., Phi Beta Kappa. Home: 1425 E Gaylord St Mount Pleasant MI 48859 Office: Central Mich U 333 Moore Hl Mount Pleasant MI 48859-0001

JUSTON-COUMAT, DENIS EUGENE, engineering executive, educator; b. Algiers, Algeria, May 8, 1960; s. Fridal Desire and Maryse (Duburg) Juston-C.; m. Catherine Maitreau, Nov. 3, 1990; children: Pauline, Clementine. MSc, U. Paul Sabatier, 1981; engr., Ecole des Mines de Paris, 1983, Inst. Reinforced Cemente, 1984; PhD, Ecole des Ponts Chaussees, 1986. Clk. works Bouygues, Jeddah, Saudi Arabia, 1984-86; exec. mgr. SIT, Le Chesnay, France, 1990-92; gen. mgr. EMSL-France, Garches, 1996-98, Eurolab, Montreuil, France, 1998—, SEC Group, Paris, 1986—, SPI, Dakar, Senegal, 1999—. Mem. N.Y. Acad. Scis. Home: 23 Blvd de la Republique, 92210 Saint-Cloud France

JUSYS, OSKARAS, former ambassador; b. Anykščiai, Northeastern, Lithuania, Jan. 13, 1954; married; 1 child. JD, Vilnius U., 1977; LLD, V. Lomonosov U. Faculty of Law, 1981. Asst.; sr. lectr. law Vilnius U., 1985, acad. law prof., 1985-90; head legal dept. Lithuanian Ministry Fgn. Affairs, 1990-93, counsellor to fgn. minister, 1993-94; dir. Lithuanian branch McDermott, Will & Emery, 1993-94; amb. extraordinary and plenipotentiary UN, 1994, perm. rep. of Lithuania, 1994. Office: Permanent Mission of Lithuania to the UN 420 5th Ave Fl 3 New York NY 10018-2729*

JUTEAU, MICHEL HILAIRE, communications engineer; b. Landerneau, Brittany, France, Oct. 3, 1943; s. Roland Berthe (Tricot) J.; m. Marie-Josephe Le Fur, July 23, 1968; children: Olivier, Valerie. Degree in electronic/telecomm. engring., Ecole Nat. de l'Aviation Civ., Paris, 1967. Engr. ODA Rsch. Lab., Paris, 1970-72; network engr. Telesys., Paris, 1973-76; head R&D Sfena, Paris, 1976-81; engring. mgr. Ordoprocesseur, Paris, 1981-87; project chief Integrated Automation, Grenoble, France, 1988-90; mgr. TRT-Experdata (Philips), Paris, 1990-96; ATM network cons. Philips, Paris, 1992-95; electronic document engr. EDF Nuclear Power Plant, France, 1988-90; network expert Rsch. Ctr., Rennes, France, 1975-76, INRIA Rsch. Ctr., Paris, 1974-75. Developer, rschr. first data transmission network, 1974, multipurpose terminal, 1980. Mem. IEEE. Avocations: fishing, teaching volleyball, modern dance, theater. Home and Office: Impasse Amiral Courbet, 44510 Le Pouliguen France

JUTET, MONIQUE FRANCOISE JANET, interpreter, international business consultant; b. Asnieres sur Seine, France, Feb. 4, 1945; d. Jean Leon and Margaret Alexander Stevenson (Pottie) J. Degree as Interpreter, Sorbonne, Paris, 1964; Degree in Bus., Paris C. of C., 1964, Brit. C. of C., 1964. Translator Internat. Civil Aviation Orgn., UN, Neuilly, France, 1991-92; supernumerary Internat. Maritime Orgn., UN, London, 1966; interpreter, exec. sec. aircraft constrn. industry, London, Paris, Switzerland, 1964-70; exec. sec., legal asst. Payne Hicks Beach & Co., London, 1970-71; exec. sec., internat. trade asst. ACLI Internat., London, 1971-73; exec. sec., adminstrv./mgmt. asst. Grand Met. Ltd., London, 1973-76; interpreter, internat. bus. cons. Bizbox Internat., Paris, 1977—. Author tech. translations and corp. lit.; fashion designer. Mem. Armed Forces Comms. and Electronics Assn. Avocations: ballet, design, research. E-mail: bizboxintl@yahoo.fr. Office: Bizbox Internat, 37 rue des Mathurins, Paris 75008, France

JUUSELA, JYRKI TAPANI, business executive; b. Helsinki, Finland, Nov. 15, 1943; m. Leena Aro; 3 children. D in Tech., Helsinki U. Tech., 1971. Rsch. metallurgist Outokumpu Rsch. Ctr., Pori, Finland, 1971-73; head R&D Outokumpu, Harjavalta, Finland, 1974-77; gen. mgr. Outokumpu Nickel Plant, Harjavalta, 1978-82, Outokumpu Rsch. Ctr., Pori, 1983-87; exec. v.p., mem. exec. bd. Outokumpu Oy, Espoo, Finland, 1988-91, bd. dirs., chmn. group exec. bd., pres., CEO, 1992—. Contbr. articles to profl. publs.; patentee in field. Mem. AIME, Can. Inst. Mining, Metallurgy, Petroleum. Office: Outokumpu Oyj, PO Box 140, Riihitontuntie 7 B, FIN-02201 Espoo Finland*

JUVANEC, BORUT, architecture educator, researcher; b. Sept. 30, 1944. DS, Ljubljana U., 1969, PhD, 1985; postgrad., Zagreb U., 1980. Asst. FA Ljubljana U., 1971-90; lectr., 1990-94, prof., 1994—; mem. Working Cmty. Alps-Adria, Muenchen, 1989—; coord. Ceepus Network, Vienna, 1995—, Internat. Staedteforum Graz, 1995—; rschr. Hayrack, 2000. Editor: Proceedings-Conference on Vernacular Architecture Alps-Adria; author: Arhitektura Pri Lenartu/Architecture in NE Slovenia, 1998, Kozolec/Hayrack, 1997, Stone by Stone, 1999, Stone Shelters, 1999; inventor: elements in electrical equipment and indsl. design, 1980, 81, 85, 90; contbr. articles to profl. jours. Mem. Soc. Arch. Historians. Office: Ljubljana U Faculty Arch, Zoisova 12, Ljubljana 1000, Slovenia

JUVET, RICHARD SPALDING, JR., chemistry educator; b. L.A., Aug. 8, 1930; s. Richard Spalding and Marion Elizabeth (Dalton) J.; m. Martha Joy Myers, Jan. 29, 1955 (div. Nov. 1978); children: Victoria, David, Stephen, Richard P.; m. Evelyn Raeburn Elthon, July 1, 1984. BS, UCLA, 1952, PhD, 1955. Research chemist Dupont, 1955; instr. U. Ill., 1955-57, asst. prof., 1957-61, assoc. prof., 1961-70; prof. analytical chemistry Ariz. State U., Tempe, 1970-95, prof. emeritus, 1995—; vis. prof. UCLA, 1960, U. Cambridge, Eng., 1964-65, Nat. Taiwan U., 1968, Ecole Polytechnique, France, 1976-77, U. Vienna, Austria, 1989-90; mem. air pollution chemistry and physics adv. com. EPA, HEW, 1969-72; mem. adv. panel on advanced chem. alarm tech., devel. and engring. directorate, def. sys. divsn. Edgewood Arsenal, 1975; mem. adv. panel on postdoctoral associateships NAS-NRC, 1991-94; mem. George C. Marshall Inst., 1998—. Author: Gas-Liquid Chromatography, Theory and Practice, 1962, Russian edit., 1966; editl. advisor Jour. Chromatographic Sci., 1969-85, Jour. Gas Chromatography, 1963-68, Analytica Chimica Acta, 1972-74, Analytical Chemistry, 1974-77; biennial reviewer for gas chromatography lit. Analytical Chemistry, 1962-76. Deacon Presbyn. Ch., 1960—, ruling elder, 1972—, commr. Grand Canyon Presbytery, 1974-76; moderator, communion com. Valley Presbyn. Ch., Scottsdale, Ariz., 1999—. NSF sr. postdoctoral fellow, 1964-65; recipient Sci. Exch. Agreement award to Czechoslovakia, Hungary, Romania and Yugoslavia, 1977. Fellow Am. Inst. Chemists; mem. AAAS, Am. Chem. Soc. (nat. chmn. divsn. analytical chemistry 1972-73, nat. sec.-treas. 1969-71, divsn. com. on chem. edn., subcom. on grad. edn. 1988—, councilor 1978-89, coun. com. analytical reagents 1985-95, co-author Reagent Chemicals, 7th edit. 1986, 8th edit. 1993, 9th edit. 2000, chmn. U. Ill. sect. 1968-69, sec. 1962-63, directorate divsn. officers' caucus 1987-90), Internat. Union Pure and Applied Chemistry, Internat. Platform Assn., Am. Radio Relay League (Amateur-Extra lic.), Sigma Xi, Phi Lambda Upsilon, Alpha Chi Sigma (faculty adv. U. Ill. 1958-64, Ariz. State U. 1975-95, profl. rep.-at-large 1989-94, chmn. expansion com. 1990-92, nat. v.p. grand collegiate alchemist 1994-96). Achievements include rsch. on gas and liquid chromatography, instrumental analysis, computer interfacing, plasma desorption mass spectroscopy. Home: 4821 E Calle Tuberia Phoenix AZ 85018-2932 Office: Ariz State U Dept Chem and Biochem Tempe AZ 85287-1604

JUZWA, WITOLD JULIAN, medical educator; b. Lwów, Poland, Feb. 16, 1938; s. Kazimierz and Olga (Wychopień) J.; m. Alicja Zalewska, may 13, 1961; 1 child, Agnieszka. MD, Med. Univ., Wrocław, Poland, 1962; PhD, Med. Univ., 1968, Habilitation, 1975. Asst. Med. Univ., Wrocław, 1962-68, from asst. prof. to prof., 1968-90, prof., 1990—, head dept. bioanalysis, 1978-80, vice dean nursery faculty, 1976-79; mem. com. basic med. scis. Polish Acad. Scis., 1974-78; head dept. physiology Med. U., Gdańsk, Poland, 1980—, vice dean med. faculty, 1987-90. Contbr. articles to profl. jours. Recipient Scientific award Min. of Health, 1975. Mem. Polish Physiol. Soc. (pres. Wrocław divsn. 1975-78, pres. Gdańsk divsn. 1978-90, 93-96), Polish Pharmacol. Soc. Roman Catholic. Avocations: prehistory of man. Home: Junony 8, 80 299 Gdańsk Poland Office: Dept Physiology, Med U Gdańsk Debinki 1, 80 211 Gdańsk Poland

JYOO, SAMUEL YEONG-HEUM, physics educator, researcher; b. Seoul, Korea, Mar. 3, 1934; s. Soo-Kyeom and O-Am Jyoo. BSc in Physics, Seoul Nat. U. Coll. Edn., 1956; MSc in Physics, Korea U., Seoul, 1959; DSc in Physics, Kon-Kuk U., Korea, 1973. Lectr. Seoul Nat. Normal Sch., 1956-57; asst. Korea U., 1957-59; prof. of physics Kon-Kuk U., Seoul, 1960-99, emeritus prof., 1999—; lectr. Korea U., 1969-70, Seoul Nat. U., 1977-80; rsch. fellow Eindhoven U. Tech., The Netherlands, 1980-81; lectr. Chong-Shin U. Grad. Sch. Theology, 1990-95, Inst. Calvinis. Studies Korea, 1997—; planning mem., charter mem. Specialists Com. Korean Sci. and Tech. Info. Ctr., 1961-64; mem. Higher Civl Svc. Exam. Com. Engring., 1979, 81;mem. Coun. Curriculum, 1981. Author: Second Coming of Jesus Christ, 1991, The Genesis Creation of the Heavens and Earth, 1991, The Creation of God - The Bible and Natural Science, 1993, The Proper Course of the Bible Translation, 1976. Fellow Ctr. Rsch. Sci. Azusa Pacific U.; mem. AAAS, Korean Phys. Soc. (life, editl. sec. 1970-71), Phys. Soc. Japan, Am. Phys. Soc. (life), European Phys. Soc., Am. Math. Soc., Japan Soc. Plasma Sci. and Nuclear Fusion Rsch., Soc. Bibl. Lit., Nat. Assn. Profs. Hebrew, Ctr. Theology and Nat. Sci., Am. Sci. Affiliate. Presbyterian. Fax: 82-351-845-4642. Office: Kon-Kuk U Dept Physics, PO Box 26, Euijeongbu 480-600, Republic of Korea (South)

JYOT, GURDARSHAN, counselor, researcher; b. Hoshiarpur, Punjab, India, Mar. 3, 1968; d. Narinder Singh and Kamaljit Bagga. Grad., Guru Nanak Dev U., Amritsar, India, 1988, postgrad., 1990; PhD in Psychology, Jamia Millia Islamia, New Delhi, 1997. Lectr. K.M.V. Coll., Jalandhar, India, 1990-91; counseling psychologist Assn. U. Adminstrs., New Delhi, 1991-97; counselor All India Women's Conf., New Delhi, 1997-98, Lott Carey Bapt. Mission, New Delhi, 1998—. Contbr. articles to profl. jours. Mem. APA, Indian Sci. Congress (life). Avocations: reading, traveling. Home: 200 Green Pk, Jalandhar 144001, India

JYRKILA, FAINA, sociology educator; b. Impilahti, Finland, Sept. 1, 1917; d. Stephan and Outi (Iija) J. MA, Sch. of Social Scis., Helsinki, Finland, 1948, PhD, 1960; postgrad., Cornell U., 1952-53. Rsch. asst. Sch. of Social Scis., 1948-64; prof. U. Jyvaskyla, Finland, 1964-84, prof., researcher, 1984—, head dept. sociology, 1964-84. Author: Activities of the Finnish Youth, 1958, Adaptation of the Karelian Displaced and Resettled Persons, 1952-84, 90, 92, 94—, Recipients of Social Relief, 1963, 65, Society and Adjustment to Old Age, 1960, 63. With Finnish Army, 1941-44. Decorated Order of Finland; recipient Social Worker Found. prize, 1965. Mem. AAAS, Societas Gerontologica Fennica, European Soc. for Rural Sociology, Westermarck Soc. Avocations: art, painting. Home: Gummeruksenkatu 3A 19, Fin-40100 Jyväskylä Finland Office: U Jyvaskyla, Seninaarinkatu 15, Fin-40100 Jyväskylä Finland

KA, IBRA DEGUENE, diplomat. Rep. to UN Govt. of Senegal, 1996—. Office: Permanent Mission of Senegal 238 E 68th St New York NY 10021-6001*

KAASE, MAX WILLI, political science educator; b. Krefeld, Germany, May 14, 1935; s. Walter and Elisabeth (Eicker) K.; m. Christine Dorscht, June 20, 1961 (div. 1972); m. Petra Maria Bauer, Dec. 30, 1991; 1 child, Dominic. Grad. economist, U. Cologne, Germany, 1959, PhD in Polit. Sci., 1964; venia legendi, U. Mannheim, 1972. Cert. prof. polit. sci. and comparative social rsch. Market rschr. McCann Erikson, Düsseldorf, Germany, 1960-61; rschr. U. Cologne, 1962-64; asst. prof. U. Mannheim, 1965-73; dir. Zentrum für Umfragen, Methoden und Analysen Mannheim, 1974-80; prof. U. Mannheim, 1980-93; rsch. prof. Wissenschaftszentrum Berlin für Sozialforschung, 1993-2000; dean social scos. & humanities, v.p. Internat. U. Bremen, 2000—; mem. German Sci. Coun., Cologne, 1987-92; head of bd. Zentrum für Umfragen, Methoden und Analysen Mannheim, 1981—. Co-author: (books) Political Action, 1979, Politische Gewalt und Repression, 1990, Beliefs in Government, 1995, Estranged Friends, 1996. Mem. Internat. Polit. Sci. Assn. (exec. com. 1998-2000, 1st v.p. 2000—), European Sci. Found. (v.p. 1999—). Avocations: arts, literature, tennis. E-mail: petmaka@aol.com. fax: 49-421-200494451. Home: Bassermannweg 14B, D-12207 Berlin Germany Office: Internat U Bremen, Campus Ring 1, D-25759 Bremen Germany

KAASIK, AIN ELMAR, neurology educator; b. Tallinn, Estonia, Aug. 2, 1934; s. Aleksander and Ellen (Ahluhn) K.; m. Aidula Taie Aadla, Nov. 22, 1958; 1 child, Arne. MD, U. Tartu, Estonia, 1959, PhD, 1967, DS, 1972. Resident Tartu U. Hosp., Estonia, 1959-64, asst. prof., 1967-72, prof., 1972-84, prof., chmn. dept. neurology & neurosurgery, 1984-96, prof. neurology, 1996-99; prof. emeritus Tartu U. Hosp., 1999. Contbr. articles to profl. jours. Fellow Royal Soc. Medicine, Am. Acad. Neurology (corr.); mem. Estonian Acad. Scis., N.Y. Acad. Scis. Avocations: jogging, skiing, bicycling, gardening. Home: 14 Ylase St, 50412 Tartu Estonia Office: U Tartu Dept Neurology, 2 Ludvig Puusepp, 51014 Tartu Estonia

KAASIK, MARKO, environmental scientist; b. Tartu, Tartumaa, Estonia, July 25, 1966; s. Ago-Heikki and Maie (Burenkov) K.; m. Helle Laas, July 8, 1989; children: Laila, Alo. MS, U. Tartu, 1995, PhD, 2000. Jr. rschr. U. Tartu, 1989-92; rschr. Tartu Obs., 1993-97; head specialist Municipality of Tartu, 1997-98. Grantee Rsch. Coun. Norway, 1994, 96, Nessling Found., 1999, 2000. Mem. Estonian Phys. Soc., Group of Activists for Improving All Around. Avocations: hiking, skiing, shamanism. Home: Ringtee 3-46, 50105 Tartu Estonia Office: Tartu Obs, 61602 Tõravere, Tartumaa Estonia

KAASIK, TAIE AIDULA, health promotion and medical sociology educator, researcher; b. Tartu, Estonia, Dec. 9, 1934; d. Mihkel Kelus and Pauline (Singa) Aadla; m. Ain Elmar Kaasik, Nov. 22, 1958; 1 child, Arne. MD, U. Tartu, 1960, BA, 1980, PhD, 1990. Tchr. Tartu Med. Sch., 1960-81; rschr. U. Tartu, 1981-91, sr. asst., 1991-93, assoc. prof. pub. health, 1993-98, prof. pub. health, chair health promotion, 1998-2000, project mgr. on injury prevention, 2000—; cons. social and health care, Office of Tallinn, Estonia, 1996, injury prevention Estonian Health Edn. Ctr., 2000-; guest rschr. on injury prevention Karolinska Inst., Stockholm, 1997. Contbr. numerous articles to profl. jours. Recipient rsch. grants Estonian Sci. Found., Tallinn, 1992-99, Karolinska Internat. Rsch. and Tng. Program Com., Stockholm, 1996-97, Svenska Inst., Stockholm, 1997. Mem. Soc. Estonian Physiologists, Soc. Estonian Physicians, World Fedn. Mental Health, Internat. Univ. Women, Soc. Female Univ. Students, STAR Soc. Lutheran. Avocations: piano, gymnastics, skiing. Fax: 372 7 374192. E-mail: taie@ut.ee. Office: U Tartu Dept Pub Health, Ravila 19, 50411 Tartu Estonia

KABACIK, PAWEL, research electrical engineer; b. Wrocław, Poland, Jan. 1, 1963; s. Tadeusz and Maria (Kozdeba) K. MSEE with distinction, Tech. U. Wroclaw, 1986, postgrad., 1989-93; postgrad., Ctrl. Conn. State U., Tech. U. Wroclaw, 1993; PhD in Elec. Engring. with award, Tech. U. Wroclaw, 1996. Jr. design engr. Tech. U. Wroclaw, 1987, jr. rsch. asst., 1987-88, rsch. asst., 1988-96, asst. prof., 1996; vis. fellow Tech. U. Denmark, Lyngby, 1991-92; expert in European Union Cost 245 project, expert in European Union Cost 260 project, 1997—; vis. scholar U. Queensland, Brisbane, 1997. Co-author: Microstrip Antennas, 1992; contbr. articles to profl. publs. Pres. civic com. Solidarity, Wroclaw, 1990-91. Recipient Inst. Dir.'s award for rsch. Tech. U. Wroclaw, 1989, award for the Young Scientist 7th Nat. URSI Symposium, Gdansk, Poland, 1993; TEMPUS Program grantee European Community, 1991. Mem. IEEE (Harold A. Wheeler applications prize hon. mention 2000), Planetary Soc., N.Y. Acad. Scis., Antenna Measurement Technique Assn. Avocations: economics, management, architecture, touring, sailing. Home: Kilinskiego 32/6, 50-264 Wroclaw Poland Office: Wroclaw U Tech Telecom Ac, Wybrzeze Wyspianskiego 27, Wroclaw 50-370, Poland

KABACK, DAVID BRIAN, molecular biologist; b. N.Y.C., May 4, 1950; s. I. and R. (Silverman) K. BS, SUNY, Stony Brook, 1971; PhD, Brandeis U., 1976. Asst. prof. N.J. Med. Sch., Newark, 1979-85, assoc. prof., 1985-94, prof., 1994—. Postdoctoral fellow Damon Runyon-Walter Winchell, 1976-77, Calif. Inst. Tech., 1976-79; recipient Nat. Rsch. Svc. award, NIH, 1977-79. Mem. Am. Soc. Microbiologists, Genetic Soc. Am., Harvey Soc. Office: NJ Med Sch Dept Microbiology and Molecular Genetics Newark NJ 07103

KABAKCHIEVA, GERGANA ANGELOVA, archaeology researcher; b. Kustendil, Bulgaria, Apr. 6, 1952; d. Angel Aleksiev and Todorka Petrova (Jovcheva) Gochev; m. Yurii Skarlatov Kabakchiev, Dec. 29, 1974. Assoc. Inst. Archaeology, Sofia, Bulgaria, 1976-87, rsch. assoc., 1987-97, sr. rsch. assoc., 1997—. Author: Pottery from the Roman Villa by Ivajlovgard, 1986, Castra Oescensia, The Earlyroman Militarycamp at the Mouth of River Oescus, 1997; editor: Ancient Villa Armira, 1991; contbr. articles to profl. jours. Mem. Bulgarian-Germanian Scientific Soc., European Assn. Archaeologists, Rei Cretariae Romanae Fautorum. Home: Nadejda Bl 220 B 19, 1220 Sofia Bulgaria Office: Inst Archaeology, Saborna Str 2, 1000 Sofia Bulgaria

KABANE, SIPHO, general medical practitioner, business consultant; b. Johannesburg, South Africa, Sept. 4, 1959; s. Lockington Goira and Busisiwe Grace (Mathonsi) K.; m. Tankiso Lorraine Xaba, Dec. 7, 1989; children: Mpumi, Busisiwe, Zanele. BSc, Ft. Hare Coll, Alice, South Africa, 1980; MB ChB, Med. U. South Africa, Pretoria, 1986; DTM&H, U. Witwatersrand, Johannesburg, 1988; MBA, Heriot-Watt U., Edinburgh, 1997. Med. intern South African Govt., Krugersdorp, 1986-87; med. officer Gencor-Mine, Welkom, South Africa, 1987-89; gen. practitioner in pvt. practice, Welkom, 1989—. Mem. Mothusi Ind. Practitioner Assn. (chmn. 1994—). Avocations: television, reading, soccer, snooker, fishing. E-mail: kabane@masa.co.za. Home: 4 Europa St, Riebeeckstad, 9459 Welkom South Africa

KABANOV, MODEST MIKHAILOVICH, health facility administrator; b. St. Petersburg, Russia, Mar. 19, 1926; s. Mikhail Stepanovich and Vera Leonidovna (Shiller) K.; m. Lydia Victorovna Soloviyova, July 23, 1955. MD, PhD, Pavlov Med. U., St. Petersburg, 1948. Head physician Dist. Psychoneurol. Dispensary, St. Petersburg, 1958-60, IVth City Psychiat. Hosp., St. Petersburg, 1960-64; dir. The V.M. Bekhterev Psychoneurol. Rsch. Inst., St. Petersburg, 1964—; city head psychiatrist, St. Petersburg, 1960-64. Contbr. over 250 articles to profl. jours., 6 monographs. Mem. City Human Rights Com., St. Petersburg, 1996—. Named Honoured Scientist of Russia, 1982. Mem. WHO (dir. Sci. Rsch. Ctr. 1993—), World Assn. for Dynamic Psychiatry (pres. 1995—), World Assn. for Psychosocial Rehab., World Assn. Social Psychiatry. Avocations: tourism, ancient architecture, fine arts, literature. Home: Apt 115, 13 Reshetnikov St, St Petersburg Russia Office: The Bekhterev Inst, 3 Bekhterev St, 193019 St Petersburg Russia

KABASAWA, UKI, physicist; b. Namerikawa, Japan, Jan. 21, 1965; s. Ikuo and Yasuko (Shimasaka) K. Bachelor, Osaka U., 1988, Master, 1990. Rschr. ctrl. rsch. lab. Hitachi, Ltd., Kokubunji, Japan, 1990-96; engr. electronic device mfg. equipment and engring. divsn. Hitachi, Ltd., Tokyo, 1996-99; engr. Hitachi, Ltd. Instruments, Beam Tech. Ctr., Ibaraki, Japan, 1999—. Author: (with others) Studies of High Temperature Superconductors, Vol. 6, 1990, Studies of High Temperature Superconductors, Vol. 1, 1989, Advances in Superconductivitity VI, Vol. 2, 1994; translator: Quantum Theory of Many-Body Systems: Techniques and Applications, 1999, Elements of Advanced Quantum Theory, 2000, Introduction to Mesoscopic Physics, 2000. Mem. AAAS, N.Y. Acad. Scis., Phys. Soc. Japan, Japan Soc. of Applied Physics. Office: Hitachi Ltd Instruments, 882 Ichige, Hitachinaka-shi, Ibaraki ken 312-8504, Japan

KABAT, EDUARDO ESTEBAN, actuary; b. Madunice, Slovakia, Oct. 5, 1936; arrived in Argentina, 1937; s. Esteban and Cecilia (Vanco) K.; m. Clara Elena Macek, Feb. 17, 1966; children: Ludmila Maria Pia, Vlastimila Alexandra Marta. Degree in acctg., Faculty Econ. Scis., Buenos Aires, 1964. Cert. actuary, pub. translator. Auditor La Inmobiliaria Ins., Buenos Aires, 1966-79, tech. mgr., 1980-81; tech. mgr. Cosmos Ins. Co., Buenos Aires, 1982-85; dir. Flor de Lis, Buenos Aires, 1985-86; actuary San Cristobal Ins. Co., Buenos Aires, 1988—; hon. consul Slovak Republic, 1994—. Mem. governing body Actuarial Inst., 1985-87, 91-92, Argentine Naval League; counsellor Econ. Scis. Coun., 1975-81. Mem. Slovak Assn. (mem. governing body 1980-98), Actuarial Inst., Argentine Naval League. Roman Catholic. Avocation: numismatics. Office: Av Córdoba 952, Buenos Aires Argentina

KABBAH, AHMED TEJAN, government official. Pres. Sierra Leone, 1996—. Office: Embassy of Sierra Leone 1701 19th St NW Washington DC 20009-1699*

KABBAJ, OMAR, bank executive; married; four sons. Chmn. bd., CEO African Devel. Bank, 1995—; mem. exec. bd. IMF, World Bank; former min. econ. affairs Prime Min.'s Office, Morocco. Decorated Knight of the Order of Throne of Morocco. Office: African Devel Bank, 01 BP 1387, Abidjan 01, Côte d'Ivoire*

KABDEBÓ, LÓRÁNT, historian; b. Budapest, Hungary, Aug. 9, 1936; s. János and Jánosné (Farkas Magda) K.; m. Lórántné Dobos Marianne) K., July 18, 1964; children: Tamás, György. LittD, ELTE, Budapest, 1962, PhD, 1968. Prof. Grammar Sch. of Miskolc, 1958-70; dept. head Petőfi Mus., Budapest, 1970-90; prof., dept. head Janus Pannonius U., 1990-93; prof., dept. head, dean Miskolc U., 1993—. Author: Ten Years of Revolt, 1970, Searching for a Solution and Separate Peace, 1974, Time for Conclusion, 1980, Between Poets, 1980, After the War, 1983, The Workshop Secrets, 1985, Historical Moments in the Life of Writers, 1993, Poetry and Prose, 1996; contbr. articles to profl. jours. Mem. PEN, Hungarian Writers Union, Soc. Literary Historians of Hungary (gen. sec. 1991-92), N.Y. Acad. Scis. Avocation: dogs. Home: Dózsa György Str 19, H-1146 Budapest Hungary Office: Miskolc Univ, H-3515 Miskolc Hungary

KABDEBO, THOMAS GEORGE, library director; b. Budapest, Hungary, Feb. 5, 1934; arrived in U.K., 1956; s. Bela and Klara (Kelen) K.; m. Agnes Wohl, June 29, 1959 (div. 1984); children: Lilian, Andrea; m. Anna Kane, Dec. 22, 1986; 1 child, Istvan. BA, U. Wales, 1959; diploma in Libr., U. London, 1960, MPhil, 1968; PhD in History, U. Manchester, 1983. Asst. libr. U. Wales, 1959, U. London, 1960-69; libr. U. Guyana, 1969-72, U. Westminster, 1973-74; sublibr. U. Manchester, 1975-82; libr. Nat. U. Ireland, Maynooth, 1983—. Author 43 books in English, Hungarian and Welsh including Amonnan, 1993 (quality prize 1994), The Danube Trilogy, 1992-97 (award 1995), Dictionary of Dictionaries, 1992, Attila Jozsef (Fust Prize award), 1997. Decorated Order of Merit (Hungary); recipient Rakoczi essay prize Hungarians of N.Am., Ottawa, Pro Patria Hungarica, Hungarian Republic, Budapest, 1992, Arany Janos prize for Lit., 1998, Nagy Imre plaque for 1956 Activities, 1999. Fellow Libr. Assn.; mem. P.E.N. Roman Catholic. Avocations: fishing, swimming, chess. Home: 92 Aylmer Rd Newcastle Co, Dublin Ireland Office: Nat U Ireland, Meynooth, County Kildare Ireland

KABELE, JIRI, sociologist; b. Prague, Apr. 3, 1946; s. Jiri and Ludmila (Nachtikalova) K.; m. Anna Borkovcova, July 6, 1973; children: Stephan, Ruth, Christine. M Stats., Charles U., 1969, M Sociology, 1973, assoc. prof., 1996; PhD in Sociology, Masaryk's U., Brno, 1988. Rschr. Nat. Libr., Prague, 1973-76, Inst. of Indsl. Design, Prague, 1977-79, Sport Propag, Prague, 1980-83; clin. sociologist Faculty Hosp. in Motol, Prague, 1984-86, Inst. of Med. and Pharm. Postgrad. Study, Prague, 1987-89; tchr. faculty of social scis. Charles U., Prague, 1990—; rschr. Nat. Galery, Prague, 1980-86; journalist, Prague, 1992-94; adviser of minister Health Care Ministry, Prague, 1991-92. Co-author: (books) Morphology of Child Books, 1981; author: Transitions: Principles of Social Construction of Social World, 1998; editor: (book) The Integration of Methods In Social Forecasting, 1982. Co-founder: Civic Democratic Alliance, Prague, 1989-95, Film and Sociology, Prague, 1991—. Mem. Lipa. Roman Catholic. Avocation: fine arts. Home: Kaderakovska 7, 16000 Prague Czech Republic Office: Charles U/Social Scis Fac, Smetanoud Nabrezi 6, 11000 Prague Czech Republic

KABERGER, TOMAS ARNE, engineering researcher; b. Jonsered, Sweden, Jan. 16, 1961; s. Dage Robert and Margit Violett (Haglund) K.; m. Karin Astrid Wallstrom, Dec. 1, 1990; children: Bjorn, Axel. Internat. baccalaureat, UWC of the Atlantic, Wales, 1979; MSc, Chalmers U. Tech., Goteborg, Sweden, 1983, PhD, 1999. Lectr. Chalmers U. Tech., Goteborg, Sweden, 1985-89; rschr. Chalmers U. Tech., Goteborg, 1993—; energy campaigner Swedish Soc. Nature Conservation, 1989-92; sr. cons. Ecotraffic, Sweden, 1992-93; rschr. Chalmers U. Tech., 1993—; Mem. Swedish Govt. Energy Commn., Stockholm, 1994-95; expert pub. investigation on fin. nuclear waste mgmt. Govt. Sweden, 1993-94; bd. dirs. TPS Thermal Processes, Ltd., 1999—. Author: Act Electricity Efficient, 1991; editor: Linking the Natural Environment and the Economy, 1991; contbr. articles to profl. jours. Eexec. com. European Environ. Bur., Brussels, 1993—. Mem. Swedish Soc. Nature Conservation (v.p. 1995-2000), Swedish Bioenergy Assn. (bd. dirs. 1990—). Home: Krokslattsbacken 5, S-431 38 Molndal Sweden Office: Inst Phys Resource Theory, Chalmers U Technology, S-412 96 Göteborg Sweden

KABERUKA, WILLIAM, Ugandan government official; b. Kabale, Uganda, Jan. 20, 1949; s. Emmanuel Burugutira; m. Jane Mukagatare, May 8, 1976; children: Geraldine, William, Caroline, Emmanuel, Anita, Victor, George. BSc, Makerer U., Kampala, Uganda, 1975, MSc, 1978; PhD in Econs., La Trobe U., Melbourne, Australia, 1983. Rsch. economist East African Cmty., Arusha, Tanzania, 1975; lectr. Makerere U., Kampala, 1976-79; sr. lectr. U. Papua New Guinea, Port Moresby, 1983-86; advisor to Pres., Republic of Uganda, Kampala, 1986—. Author: The Political Economy of Uganda, 1990, Quantitative Technique, 1993. Mem. Presdl. Econ. Coun., Kampala, 1987—; mem., chmn. select com. III Constituent Assembly, Kampala, 1994. Avocation: Scrabble. Home and Office: PO Box 7168, Kampala Uganda

KABILA, LAURENT DESIRE, president Democratic Republic of the Congo; b. Jadotville, 1939. Student, U. Dar Es Salaam, Tanzania. Head of state, pres. Dem Republic of Congo, 1997—. founder People's Revolutionary Party. Office: Office Pres, Mont Ngaliema, Kinshasa-Gombe Zaire*

KABINGUE, KEN, biochemist; b. Tacloban, Leyte, The Philippines, Jan. 17, 1976; came to U.S., 1992; s. Ben and Virginia Kabingue. BS in Biochemistry, La Sierra U., 1997. Sr. rsch. asst. Baxter Healthcare Corp., Duarte, Calif., 1997—. Mem. AAAS, Am. Chem. Soc., Internat. Union Pure and Applied Chemistry. Avocations: music, sports. Office: Baxter Healthcare Corp 1710 Flower Ave Duarte CA 91010-2923

KABIR, ANWARA KHATOON, zoology educator; b. Dinajpur, Bangladesh, Jan. 15, 1940; d. Abdur and Asia (Khatoon) R.; m. Syed Mohammad Humayun Kabir, June 4, 1961; children: Mahbub Ara, Shamima Sultana, Nigar Sultana, Shabiul Ahsan. BS with honors, U. Dhaka, 1959, MS, 1960, PhD, 1986. Prof. biology Women's Coll., Mymensing, Bangladesh, 1968-70; lectr. Dhaka U., 1973-78, asst. prof., 1978-79, assoc. prof., 1987-93, prof., 1993—. Fellow Zoological Soc. of Bangladesh; mem. Bangladesh Assn. for Advancement of Sci., Bangladesh Entomological Soc. (life). Home: 20 E Fuller Rd, Dhaka 1000, Bangladesh Office: Dhaka Univ, Dept Zoology, Dhaka 1000, Bangladesh

KABIR, HUMAYUN, ambassador; b. Sept. 25, 1938; married; 3 children. BA, Dhaka U., 1957, MA in English Lit., 1959; postgrad., Harvard U., Tufts U., 1962. 1st sec. Pakistan Embassy, Algiers and Spain, 1965-70; dir. Ministry Fgn. Affairs, Islamabad, Pakistan, 1970-71; dir. UN & Econ. Coord. Affairs and Fgn. Min.'s Office Ministry Fgn. Affairs, Dhaka, Bangladesh, 1971-72, chief protocol, dir. gen. external info. divsn., 1973-74; dep. permanent rep. Bangladesh to UN and Consul Gen. N.Y., 1975-76; min., dep. chief of mission Bangladesh Embassy, Washington, 1976-79; amb. Bangladesh to Islamic Rep. of Iran, 1979-83; prin. Fgn. Affairs Tng. Acad., 1985-88; Bangladesh high commr. to Zimbabwe, 1988-91, Bangladesh rep. to UN, Bangladesh amb. to Chile and Nicaragua, sec. to Govt. of Bangladesh, 1991-93; amb. of Bangladesh to U.S. Washington, 1994-96; mem. Internat. Civil Svc. Commn., UN, N.Y.C., 1996—; dep. chief coord. 14th Islamic Fgn. Min.'s Conf., Dhaka, 1983; min. comm. Jamuna River Multipurpose Bridge Project, 1984. Decorated Order of Civil Merit (Spain). Office: Internat Civil Svc Commn UN Plz New York NY 10017*

KABIR, JUNAED, chemical company executive; b. Dhaka, Bangladesh, Mar. 10, 1964. BBA, George Washington U., 1987; MBA, Webster U., 1989. Sales exec. Otis Elevators, Singapore, 1988; customer svc. rep. Monsanto PLC, Basingstoke, U.K., 1989-91, strategic accounts rep., 1991-94; mgr. bus. redesign Monsanto Svcs. Internat., Brussels, 1994-96, mgr. strategic change, 1997; comml. devel. mgr. Solutia Europe NV, Brussels, 1997-98, comml. mgr., 1998—. Under officer U.K. Army Res., 1989-93. Avocations: shooting, fishing, traveling, learning languages. E-mail: jjkabi@solutia.com. Office: Solutia Europe NV, Rue Laid Burniat 3, B-1348 Louvain La Neuve Belgium

KABIR, SHAHJAHAN, immunologist, biomedical researcher, consultant; b. Jessore, Bangladesh, Jan. 24, 1943; s. Shamsuz Zuha and Ayesha Khanam; m. Ingrid Birgitta Sterner, Aug. 12, 1971. BS, Rajshahi (Bangladesh) Coll., 1961; MS, Rajshahi U., 1963, U. B.C., Vancouver, Can., 1970; PhD, U. B.C., Vancouver, Can., 1971. Rsch. assoc. NIH, Bethesda, Md., 1974-76; rsch. scientist Johns Hopkins U., Balt., 1977-78; scientist Internat. Ctr. for Diarrhoeal Disease Rsch., Bangladesh, 1979-82, Nat. Inst. Pub. Health and U. Groningen, Bilthoven, The Netherlands, 1983-85; scientist dept. immunology Karolinska Inst., Stockholm, 1986-90; rsch. cons. Sultan Qaboos U. Coll. Medicine, Oman, Muscat, 1990-95; cons. U. Sci. and Tech., Chittagong, Bangladesh, 1996-97; CEO Acad. Rsch. and Info. Mgmt. Ltd., Stockholm, 1998—. Contbr. articles to sci. jours., including Jour. Bacteriology, Infection and Immunity, Jour. Gen. Microbiology, Biochim. Biophys. Acta, Soc. for Gen. Microbiology Quar.; sci. invention related to cholera bacteria. Pres. Bangladesh Assn. B.C., 1971-72; mem. governing com. Bangladesh Assn., Washington, 1974-75. Mem. Am. Soc. for Microbiology, N.Y. Acad. Scis. Avocations: literature, music, travel, photography. Home and Office: Tobakspinnargatan 5, 117 36 Stockholm Sweden

KABIR, SYED MOHAMMAD HUMAYUN, zoologist; b. Sirajgong, Bangladesh, Nov. 24, 1939; s. Mohammad Nazabat Ali and Hyatun (Nessa) Ali; m. Anwara Khatoon, June 4, 1961; children: Mahbub Ara, Shamima Sultana, Nigar Sultana, Shabiul Ahsan. BS with honors, U. Dhaka, 1959, MS, 1960; PhD, Tex. A&M U., 1966; PhD (hon.), World Devel. Parliament, India, 1983. Assoc. prof. U. Dhaka, Bangaldesh, 1974-78, prof., 1978—; lectr. U. Dhaka, Bangladesh, 1961-62; sr. lectr. Agrl. U., Bangladesh, 1962-70; resident biologist Inst. for Advancement of Sci., Bangladesh, 1970-74; cons. planning commn., Govt. Bangladesh, 1984-85; mem. evaluation com. Bangladesh Agrl. Rsch. Coun., 1976-78; team leader Nat. Com. for Devel. Curriculum and Textbook, 1995; cons. editor Bangladesh Nat. Ency., 1999—. Author: General Zoology, 4th edit., 2000; editor: Environmental Crisis in Bangladesh, 1993, Dhaka U. Jour. Biol. Scis., 1999—; editor-in-chief Bangladesh Jour. Zoology, 1992—. Samshad professorship World Devel. Parliament, India, 1983. Fellow Zool. Soc. Bangladesh (pres. 1988-89); mem. Bangladesh Assn. for Advancement of Sci. (treas. 1984-85), Bangladesh Entomol. Soc. (v.p. 1992-93), Internat. Geosphere Biosphere Program (nat. com.). Office: Dept Zoology, Univ Dhaka, Dhaka 1000, Bangladesh

KABIRAJ, MOHAMMAD MUSLIM UDDIN, neurophysiologist; b. Rajshahi, Bangladesh, Dec. 30, 1945; came to U.S., 1997; s. Mohammad Jasimuddin and Moriom (Bibi) K.; m. Monower Sultana Chowdhury, Sept. 10, 1972; children: Tanzima Taskin, Shazia Mahrin, Naila Tasnim. MBBS with honors in pathology, Rajshahi Med., Bangladesh, 1969; MPhil with honors in Physiology, Dhaka U., Bangladesh, 1974. Demonstrator physiology Govt. Bangladesh, 1970-74, lectr., 1974-77; rsch. fellow Swedish Assn., 1977-80; asst. prof. King Saud U., Saudi Arabia, 1980-99; cons. Saudi Arabia, 1984-99, Riyadh Armed Forces Hosp., Ministry Def. and Aviation, Saudi Arabia, 1999—; rsch. fellow U. Lund, Sweden, 1980; cons. King Saud U. Hosp., 1984-99, RKH, Tiyada, 1999. Contbr. articles to profl. jours. Hon. mem. Bangladesh Family Planning Assn., 1974—. Recipient scholarships Japanese Govt., Tokyo, 1976. Swedish Nat. Assn. Against Heart and Lung Diseases, 1977. Mem. AAEM, Riyadh neurosci. Club. Avocations: playing cards, watching TV, research, public lecturing and teaching students. Office: Riyadh Armed Forces Hosp, PO Box N 641 Neurosci Dept, 1159 Riyadh Saudi Arabia

KABIRU, EPHANTUS WANJOHI, parasitologist, educator; b. Nyeri, Central, Kenya, Oct. 20, 1949; s. Naftaly Gathiti and Peninah Gathoni (Kabiru) Wanjohi; m. Pamela Nyawira Gituku, Dec. 31, 1977; three children. Diploma, U. Nairobi, 1971, higher diploma, 1975, PhD, 1995; MS, U. Columbia, 1983. Technologist Ministry Health, Kenya, 1971-76, lectr., 1977-83, rschr., 1984-96; sr. lectr. Kenyatta U., Kenya, 1996—; examiner Ministry Edn., Kenya, 1986-90; mgr. Ministry Health, Kenya, 1989, 92-95. Contbr. articles to profl. jours. Elder Presbyn. Ch. Mem. Lab. Scientists (chmn. 1986-89), Ngong 10 Welfare Group (chmn. 1995—). Avocations: athletics, reading, site seeing, soccer, watching documentaries. Home: PO Box 20921, Nairobi Kenya Office: Kenyatta Univ, PO Box 43844, Nairobi Kenya

KABIR-UD-DIN, KABIR, chemistry educator; b. Village Kolhi Gharib, India, July 15, 1945; s. Mohammad Naseer and Hajira Khatoon; m. Maria Bilquis Kabir, June 9, 1969; children: Huma Kabir, Hena Kabir. PhD, Aligarh Muslim U., India, 1969. Lectr. Aligarh Muslim U., 1969-82; UNESCO fellow Charles U., Prague, 1973-74; postdoctoral rsch. asst. U. Keele, U.K., 1975-77; postdoctoral rsch. fellow U. Tex., Austin, 1977-78; reader Aligarh Muslim U., 1983-93, prof., 1993—. Contbr. articles to profl. jours. Mem. Indian Coun. Chemists (life), Indian Sci. Congress Assn. (life), Indian Soc. for Surface Sci. and Tech. (life), Indian Assn. for the Cultivation Sci. (life). Home: 4/1227 Sir Syed Nagar, 202002 Aligarh India Office: Chemistry Dept, AMU, 202002 Aligarh India

KABORÉ, JOSEPH, government official; b. Ouagadougou, Burkina Faso, Aug. 16, 1951; married; 2 children. Degree in geometric tech., 1972, degree in engring., applied sci., 1976, degree in engring., cartography, 1979. Dir. cartography Geog. Inst. Burkina, 1980-85; ofcl. cartographer Govt. of Burkina Faso, 1985-86, sec. gen. Ministry of Equipment, 1986-88, tech. advisor to pres. of Faso, 1988-89, sec. of state for housing and urban affairs, 1989-91, minister of housing and urban affairs, 1991-92, minister of pub. works, housing and town planning, 1992-99; min. of infrastructure, housing and urban planning Govt. of Burkina Faso, Ouagadougou, 1999—. Dep. Nat. Assembly, Govt. Burkina Faso, 1992—. Mem. Orgn. for Popular Democracy/Labor Movement. Office: Ministry of Infrastructure, 03 BP 7011, Ouagadougou 03, Burkina Faso*

KABURLASOS, VASSILIS GEORGE, electrical engineer, researcher; b. Pylea, Greece, Sept. 24, 1963; s. George and Evangelia (Kontoulis) K. Diploma in electronics/computer engring., Nat. Tech. U. Athens, Greece, 1986; MS in Electronics/Computer Engring., U. Nev., 1989, PhDEE, 1992. Registered profl. engr., Greece; engr.-in-tng., U.S.A. Instr. U. Nev., Reno, 1987, 90; rschr. Computerized Thermography Ctrs., IFEX, Inc., N.Y.C., 1988-89; software developer Washoe Med. Ctr., Reno, 1991; rschr./developer/contractor intelligent surg. tools Aristotle U. Thessaloniki, Greece, 1994-97, rsch. assoc. robotics and automation lab., 1997—, developer hypertext software for ednl. use, 1998-2000; instr. labs., computational rschr. Aristotle U. Thessaloniki, 1999—; engr.-in-tng. U. Tel Aviv, summer 1985; computer programmer Nat. Tech. U. Athens, spring 1987; mem. program com. Internat. Sci. Confs., 1998—; presenter and spkr. in field. Contbr. articles to profl. jours. including IEEE Transactions, New Methods for International Journal of Computers and Their Application, Neural Networks, Philosophical Perspectives Regarding Modern Technology for Journal of Liberal Arts; tchg. material for labs. at Aristotle U. Thessaloniki. With signal corps Greek mil., 1992-93. Mem. IEEE (sci. soc., vice-chmn. student chpt. in No. Nev. 1990-91), Tech. Chamber Greece, Internat. Neural Network Soc., Assn. for Computing Machinery, Internat. Neural Network Soc., Sigma Xi (Swiss chpt.), Phi Kappa Phi, Tau Beta Pi, Eta Kappa Nu, Delta Phi Alpha. Greek Orthodox. Avocations: wind surfing, skiing, horseback riding, foreign languages and cultures. Office: Aristotle U Thessaloniki, Sch Engring, Dep El/Comp En, 540 06 Thessaloniki Greece

KABUZI, FELICITY SARAH BATEBE (PRINCESS FELICITY SARAH BATEBE KABUZI OF TORO), motivational speaker, screenwriter, film producer; b. Fort Portal, Toro, Uganda, Sept. 11, 1955; arrived in U.K., 1976; d. Jotham Rukiidi and Marjorie Marian (Kamuhiigi) K.; m. Olujide Onyechi Obonyo, Aug. 8, 1983 (div. Dec. 1995); children: Muganzi Obonyo, Isimbwa Obonyo, Olimi Obonyo. Tech. translator's diploma, Bradford (Eng.) Coll., 1978. Cert. tech. translator/legal interpreter (French, German, English, Rutoro, Luganda); film prodrs.'/dirs' diploma Hollywood Film Inst., L.A., London, 1993; stress mgmt./staff motivation instr.'s diploma SM&M Ltd., London, 1990. Administr. Trans World Metals Ltd., London, 1979-82; dir. Primary Mgmt. and Holding Co., Ltd., London, 1982-85; sr. ptnr., mgmt. cons., conf. planner and presenter FJO Mgmt. Svcs., London, 1985—; dir. FJO Prodns. Ltd., London, 1993—. Screenwriter: (feature film) Life Beyond Time, 1993, (short film) Sacred Spirits, 1998, (TV plays) Many Wives One Mother, 1992, The Other Side of the Moon, 1975, The Slum, 1975, The Ring of Life, 1997, Dream Team, 1998. Mem. Inst. Linguists, Brit. Mensa Soc. Avocations: writing music and poetry, personal growth/esoteric reading, painting, sailing, travel.

KACELNIK, ALEJANDRO, ethologist, zoology educator; b. Buenos Aires, Argentina, Dec. 14, 1946; s. Meyer and Lisa (Kogan) Kacelnik; m. Lidia Estela Rapaport, Dec. 3, 1971; 1 child, Oliver. Lic. in Biology, Buenos Aires U., 1969; DPhil, Oxford U., 1979. Rsch. scholar Nat. Inst. Pharmacology, Argentina, 1971-73; British coun. scholar Oxford (Eng.) U., 1974-76, rsch. asst., 1976-79; vis. prof. zool. lab Groningen U., The Netherlands, 1980-82;

rsch. assoc. dept. zool. Oxford U., 1982-86; Van der Klaauw prof. biology dept. zool. Leiden U., 1988-89; sr. rsch. fellow Kings Coll., Cambridge, England, 1986-90; lectr. animal behavior dept. zool. and EP Abraham fellow Oxford U., 1990-96, prof. behavioral ecology, 1997—; prof. behavioral ecology Buenos Aires U., 1999—; mem. bd. Faculty of Biol. Scis.; chmn. Sub-Faculty Biol. Scis.; mem. internat. sci. adv. bd. Max-Planck Inst. Verhaltensphysiologie, Seewiesen/Starnberg; mem. editl. bd. Behavioural Processes, 1990—, Behavioural Ecology, 1990-96; assoc. editor Quarterly Jour. Experimental Psychology, 1990-93, The American Naturalist, 1991-95, Behavioral Ecology and Sociobiology, 1998—, Ethology, 1999—. Editor: (book) Quantitative Analyses of Behaviour, Vol. VI, 1987; contbr. articles to profl. jours. Mem. Assn. Study of Animal Behaviour, Internat. Soc. Behavioral Ecology, British Ecological Soc., Experimental Psychology Soc., Soc. Quantitative Analyses Behavior, Psychonomics Soc. Avocations: Latin-American fiction, science related books, cycling, squash, outdoor pursuits. Office: Dept Zoology, Dept Zoology, Oxford University, OX1 3PS Oxford England

KACHAN, ALEXANDER SEMIONOVICH, physicist; b. Zaporozhye, Ukraine, Nov. 18, 1947; s. Semion Alexandrovich and Evdokiya Emelyanovna (Degtiaryova) K.; m. Tatiana Alekseevna Fiodorova, Apr. 6, 1968; children: Aleksei, Ol'ga. PhD in Physics and Math., Inst. Physics and Tech., Kharkov, Ukraine, 1985. Rsch. scientist Inst. Physics and Tech., Kharkov, 1971-92, sr. rsch. assoc., 1992-95, head of lab., 1995—. Contbr. articles to profl. jours. Avocations: viticulture, fisherman. Home: 5 Valter St Ap 69, 61108 Kharkov Ukraine Office: Inst Physics and Tech, 1 Akademicheskaya St, 61108 Kharkov Ukraine

KACHERGIS, JOYCE W., designer; b. Omaha, Feb. 9, 1925; d. Lawrence Benjamin Webster and Olga Agnes Olsen; m. George J. Kachergis, July 6, 1946 (dec. Aug. 1974); children: Peter W., Karl George, Anne Olga; m. Jess G. Bell, 1986. AA, Stephens Coll., 1945; BFA, Sch. of the Art Inst., Chgo., 1947. Prodn. design mgr. U. N.C. Press, Chapel Hill, 1963-77; prodn. and design mgr. Stanford U. Press, Palo Alto, Calif., 1977-80; founder, pres., designer Kachergis Book Design, Pittsboro, N.C., 1980—; vis. prof. Radcliffe Sch. Pub., Cambridge, Mass., 1979-82. Mem. Am. Assn. Univ. Presses (bd. dirs. 1978-80). E-mail: jwkb@mindspring.com. Office: Kachergis Book Design 14 Small St N Pittsboro NC 27312-5453

KACHIN, SERGEY VASSILYEVICH, dean, chemistry educator; b. Novogeorgyevka, Kuraginsky, Russia, Sept. 1, 1951; s. Vassily Ivanovich and Nadezhda Stepanovna (Belonogova) K.; m. Antonina Gavrilovna Olennicova, Nov. 26, 1973 (div. Oct. 1994); 1 child, Olga Sergeyevna; m. Veronica Adolfovna Robova Razumovskaya, Nov. 15, 1994. Specalist, Krasnoyarsk (Russia) State U., 1973; Candidate of Scis., Moscow State U., 1979; PhD, U. Fla., 1984. Asst. prof. Krasnoyarsk State U., 1974-80, sr. lectr., 1980-82, head of the chair analytical chemistry, 1982—, dean dept. chemistry, 1988—; dir. sci. ednl. ctr. Khimpribor, Russia, 1989-99. Author: Solid-phase Colorometry, 1997; contbr. articles to profl. jours. Sgt. Mil. Space Troops, 1973-74. Grantee Ministry Edn., Russia, 1997-2000, Regional Fund Sci., Russia, 1998, U.S. Civilian R & D Found., 1999. Mem. IUPAC (affiliate), Sci. Coun. Analytical Chemistry and Russian Acad. Scis. Russian Orthodox Church. Avocations: fishing, swimming, beach volleyball. Office: Krasnoyarsk State U, Svobodny Ave 79, 660041 Krasnoyarsk Russia

KACHOS, GEORGE, financial analyst; b. Athens, Greece, July 18, 1963; s. Anastasios and Panagoula (Karalivanos) K.; m. Nicki Gerente; 1 child, Anastasios. BS in Physics, U. Patra, Greece, 1986; MBA in Fin., U. Pacific Western, L.A., 1988; PhD in Econs., U. Pacific Western, 1990. Chartered cons. in econs. Advisor Itea (Greece) Paper Products SA, 1989-90; assoc. Eurospace Ltd., Athens, 1991-93; mng. dir., ptnr. Mentor Ltd., Athens, 1993-94; dir. internat. mktg. divsn. Kalcom Group SA, Athens, 1994-97; dir. bus. ops. Frans Maas Hellas S.A., Athens, 1997—; cons. Technometriki Ltd., Athens, 1992—. Mem. gov. bd. Found. Fil d'Ariane, Brussels, 1993. Recipient Diploma, Organizing Com. of the 1980 Olympic Games, Moscow, 1980; hon. diploma Hellenic Ministry of Health and Social Ins., Athens, 1993. Fellow Fin. Planners Assn.; mem. Am. Consultants League, Inst. of Mgmt. (assoc.), Oxford Club. Avocations: art, classic music, archeology, studying ancient civilizations.

KACHURIN, OLEG IVANOVICH, chemist, researcher; b. Sumy, Ukraine, June 27, 1928; s. Ivan Alexandrovich and Alexandra Ananievna (Syrosh) K.; m. Anna Yurievna Lyukhnich, Aug. 26, 1952; children: Galina, Olga, Ivan, Yurii. Diploma in chemistry, U. Uzhgorod, 1951; MS in Chem. Scis., Chem. Technol. Inst., Ivanovo, 1959; D of Chem. Scis., U. Odessa, 1976. Head sci. worker Technol. Inst. Ivanovo, 1960-65; head sci. worker Inst. Physics, Organic Chemistry and Coal, Donetsk, Ukraine, 1965-75, head of dept., 1976-96, chief sci. worker, 1996—. Contbr. articles to profl. jours; patentee in field. Recipient medal for valiant labor, Govt. of Ukraine, 1970. Avocation: mountaineering. Home: ul Tsusimskaya 63 Apt 29, 83052 Donetsk Ukraine Office: Inst Phys Organic Chemistry, Coal Chem 70 R Luxembourg, 83114 Donetsk Ukraine

KACZANOWSKA, LAURIE HYSON SMITH, lawyer; b. Palmerton, Pa., July 7, 1953; d. James Donaldson and Mary Ann (Hyson) Smith; m. Donald James Gerber, Aug. 1976 (div. May 1981); m. Witold-K, Dec. 11, 1993; 1 child, Wit Thomas Kaczanowski. BS, Pa. State U., 1975; MSW, U. Denver, 1981; JD, Northeastern U., 1989. Adminstrv. staff, resource coord., vol. coord., counselor Women in Crisis, Lakewood, Colo., 1977-79; program adminstr. Big Sis. of Colo., Life Choices Program, Denver, 1979-80; legis. coord., lobbyist Common Cause, Denver, 1980-81; social work advocate Denver Legal Aid Soc., 1982-86; legis. analyst Nat. Conf. State Legis., Denver, 1987; mediator, intake coord. Harvard Law Sch., Cambridge, Mass., 1988; law clk. Supreme Jud. Ct. State Mass., Boston, 1988-89; legis. staff Rep. Patricia Schroeder, U.S. Congress, Washington, 1989; dir., ptnr. Pfaff & Smith Family Law Clinic, Denver, 1990-91; asst. city atty., sr. atty. unit leader, dir. alternative resolution program Denver City Attys. Office, Denver, 1991—; Co-owner, Arte Gallery, Inc.; pres., Apollon, Inc. Mem. Colo. Women's Bar Assn., Colo. Bar Assn., Colo. Lawyers for the Arts, Denver Bar Assn. Presbyterian. Home: 3216 E 6th Ave Denver CO 80206-4407 Office: Denver City Attys Office 303 W Colfax Ave Ste 500 Denver CO 80204-2623

KACZMARCZYK, ANDRZEJ DARIUSZ, information technology educator; b. Siedlce, Poland, Dec. 19, 1934; s. Wladyslaw and Aleksandra (Mlynarczyk) K.; m. Anna Krystyna Jastrzebska, Apr. 2, 1955; children: Katarzyna, Jaroslaw. MSME, Warsaw U. Tech., 1956, PhD in Tech., 1966. Engr. Inst. of Fine Mechs., Warsaw, 1955-64; dept. mgr. Ctrl. Lab. Measuring Instruments and Optics, Warsaw, 1964-65; vice dir., dept. mgr. Indsl. Inst. Automation and Measurements, Warsaw, 1965-84; prof. Guanajuato U., Salamanca, Mex., 1984-86; dept. head. Bialystok (Poland) U. Tech., 1989-95; sci. sec., dept. mgr. Inst. Math. Machines, Warsaw, 1987-89, 95—; lectr. Wroclaw (Poland) U. Tech., 1981, Warsaw U. Tech., 1982-84. Author: Technology Around You, 1966, Industrial Robots of Eighties, 1984; co-author: Elements of Modern Technology, Robots, Factory of the Future, 1987; contbr. articles to profl. jours. Mem. IEEE (sr.), Polish Soc. Informatics, Polish Soc. Measurements, Automation and Robotics. Avocations: gardening, hiking, bicycling, electronic classical music. Office: Inst Math Machines, Krzywickiego 34, 02-078 Warsaw Poland

KACZMAREK, ZDZISLAW, environmental engineer, scientist, educator; b. Poznan, Poland, Aug. 7, 1928; s. Edward and Klara K.; m. Imelda Kaczmarek, 1950; 3 children. D. Tech. Scis., Poly. U., Warsaw, Poland, 1958. Sci. worker Poly. U., Warsaw, 1947-78, assoc. prof., 1961-67, extraordinary prof., 1967-72, ordinary prof., 1972—, prof. Warsaw Tech. U., 1969—, former dir. Inst. Environ. Engring. dept. water and san. engring.; chief of div. State Hydro-Meteorol. Inst., Warsaw, 1957-60, gen. dir. Hydro-Meteorol. Inst., 1963-66; dir. Inst. for Meteorology and Water Economy, Warsaw, 1976-80; chmn. water resources div. Inst. Geophysics, 1981—; former chmn. com. water economy Polish Acad. Scis.; first dep. min. of sci. higher edn., and tech., 1972-74; project leader Internat. Inst. Applied Systems Analysis, Austria, 1974-76, 89-91; chmn. State Coun. for Environ. Protection, 1981-87. Author numerous sci. publs. Decorated Silver and Gold Cross of Merit, Knight's and Officer's Cross, Order of Polonia Restituta and other decorations. Mem. Polish Acad. Scis. (dep. sci. sect. 1971-72, sec. VII dept. 1978-80, sec.-gen. 1981-88).*

KACZYNSKI, LECH, federal official; b. June 18, 1949; married; 1 child. Degree, U. Warsaw, 1971; D, Gdansk U., 1980. With Lech Wales's Team of Assocs., 1982; adviser Temporary Coordinating Commn., 1983-84, sec., 1986; sec. solidarity Nat. Exec. Commn., 1988-90; mem. Solidarity Nat. Commn., 1989; 1st dep. chmn., 1990-91; senator Republic of Poland, 1989-91; dep. to First Sejm, 1991-93; chmn. Commn. for Adminstrn. and Internal Affairs, 1991-92, Supreme Chamber of Control, 1992-95; min. of justice Warsaw, Poland, 2000—. Office: Ministry of Justice, Al Ujazdowskie 11, 00-950 Warsaw Poland*

KAD, SURINDER KUMAR, physician, educator, researcher; b. Patiala, Punjab, India, Nov. 17, 1950; s. Ram Lall and Sarla Rani (Bhala) K.; m. Joan Mary Peters, Apr. 16, 1977; children: Robert Steven, Elizabeth Mary. Grad., Punjabi U., India, 1968, MB, BChir, 1974; MS in Healthcare Mgmt. and Policy, New Sch., N.Y., 1998; MPH, U. South Fla., 1998; postgrad., Syracuse U., 1999—. Diplomate Command and Gen. Staff Officers' Course, U.S. Army Reserves, 1995, Am. Acad. Pain Mgmt., Am. Coll. Forensic Examiners, ABQAURP; cert. in internal medicine, nephrology AAPS; sr. diplomate Am. Coll. Disability Analysts. Resident med. officer Phila. Hosp., Ambala City, India, 1975-77; sr. house officer Royal N. Infirmary, Raigmore, Inverness, Scotland, 1977; clin. instr. phys. medicine and rehab. Med. Coll. Wis., Milw., 1978-79; resident in internal medicine Kingsbrook Jewish Med. Ctr. affiliate SUNY Downstate Med Ctr, Bklyn., 1979-82; fellow in nephrology SUNY, Stony Brook, 1982-84; internist, nephrologist PHP Health Ctr. East, Syracuse, N.Y., 1984—; med. dir. UM HSMC, 1998; chmn. dept. medicine HSA, 1999; clin. instr. Med. Coll. Wis., Milw., 1978-79; asst. clin. instr. internal medicine SUNY-Stony Brook, 1982-84, clin. instr. dept. medicine SUNY Upstate Med. Ctr., Syracuse, 1984-88; clin. asst. prof. SUNY Health Sci. Ctr., 1988—. Vol. med. officer in rural/underdeveloped area in India, 1973-74; lector, eucharistic min., choir. Lt. col. M.C., USAR, 1998. Fellow ACP, Royal Soc. Health, Am. Soc. Internal Medicine; mem. N.Y. Acad. Scis., Am. Soc. Hypertension, Am. Diabetes Assn., Am. Heart Assn., Am. Soc. Nephrology, Internat. Soc. Nephrology, Am. Fedn. Clin. Rsch. (assoc.), Limestone Harmonizers Club, Rotary, Kiwanis, Sigma Xi (assoc.). Avocations: reading, traveling, music, swimming, tennis, jogging. Home: 100 Cedar Heights Dr Fayetteville NY 13066-9757 Office: PHP Health Ctr E 2803 Erie Blvd E Syracuse NY 13224-1396

KADA, MORIHIRO, electronic company executive; b. Kawachinagano, Osaka, Japan, May 5, 1947; s. Takeo Tanaka and Ai Kada; m. Takako Hayama, Oct. 25, 1974; children: Wataru, Shiho. B of Applied Physics, Fukui U., Japan, 1970. Cert. engr. Mgr. assembly engring. Sharp Corp., Japan, 1985-87; factory mgr. Sun-S Corp., Japan, 1987-90; gen. mgr. assembly engring. dept. Sharp Corp., Japan, 1991-94, gen. mgr. dept. VLSI devel. lab., 1994-98; gen. mgr. dept. System LSI Devel. Ctr., 1998—. Co-author: (books) Examples of Reliability Design, 1984, Latest Semiconductor Process and Automation, 1986, VLSI Manufacturing and Testing Equipment Guide Book, 1987, CSP/BGA Technology, 1998, CSP/MCM Jisso Tschnology, 1999. Mem. Electronic Industries Assn. of Japan, Semiconductor Equipment and Materials Internat., Inst. Advanced Microsys. Integration, Surface Mount Tech. Assn. Avocations: computers, golf. Home: 25-9 Higashikatazoe, Kawachinagano Osaka 586-0045, Japan Office: 2613-1 Ichinomoto, Tenri Nara 632-8567, Japan

KADANTSEV, VASSILIJ NIKOLAEVICH, physicist, researcher; b. Taganrog, Rostov, Russia, Oct. 6, 1941; s. Nikolay Vassilievich and Ekaterina (Kazimirova) K.; m. Galina Michailowna Abramova, Sept. 24, 1976; 1 child, Vassilij Vassilievich. Diploma in Physics, Moscow State U., 1964; PhD, Moscow State Pedagogical Inst., 1972; DSc, State Inst. Physics & Tech., Moscow, 1991. Sci. rschr. Inst. for Optico-Phys. Rsch., Moscow, 1964-71; asst. prof. Moscow Automobile Engring. Inst., 1971-80; sr. sci. rschr. Inst. Control Scis., Russian Acad. Sics., Moscow, 1980-83; head sci. dept. State Inst. Physics and Tech., Moscow, 1984; asst. prof. Moscow Automobile Engring. Inst., 1980-86; prof. dept. cybernetics Moscow Inst. for radio-Electronics and Automatics, 1986—. Co-author: The Thermodynamics of Biological Systems, 1997; patentee in field. Grantee Internat. Sci. Found., 1993, 94-95, Internat. Sci. and Tech. Ctr., 1999—. Mem. Internat. Acad. Noosphere, Russian Ecol. Acad., N.Y. Acad. Scis., European Bio-Electromagnetics Assn. Home: Vilnusskaya str 4 Apt 170, 117574 Moscow Russia Office: State Inst Physics and Tech, Prechistenka str 13/7, 119034 Moscow Russia

KÁDÁR, ANNA, pathologist, educator; b. Budapest, Hungary, Aug. 15, 1935; d. Miklós Kádár and Sarolta Várady; m. Gábor Krakovits, Feb. 10, 1958. MD, Semmelweis U. Medicine, Budapest, 1959; specialist in pathology, Postgrad. Med. Sch., Budapest, 1963; specialist PhD, Hungarian Acad. Sci., Budapest, 1971, DMSc, 1982. Cert. in gen. medicine. Asst. prof. Semmelweis U. Medicine, Budapest, 1959-71, adjunct. prof., 1971-72, dep. dir., 1972-74, assoc. prof., 1974-81, apptd. chmn., 1981-82, prof. pathology, 1982—; assoc. dean Semmelweis Med. U., Budapest, 1989-94, head electron microscope labor, 1973—, head dept. pathology, 1993—, dir. fgn. student sec., 1994—. Author: (book chpt.) New Concepts in Elastic Tissue Disorders, 1980, Pathobiology and Aging of Elastic Tissue, 1984; contbr. articles to profl. jours. Mem. IAP (v.p. 1992-96, pres. Hungarian divsn. 1997, pres.-elect 1996-98), Internat. Acad. Pathology (pres.-elect 1997-98, pres. 1998-00). Avocations: traveling, music, reading, swimming, gardening. Office: Semmelweis Med U Dept Path, Üllői-Str 93, 1450 Budapest Hungary

KADAR, AVRAHAM, immunologist; b. Rishon Le Zion, Israel, Nov. 13, 1950; s. Yosef and Amalia (Hayon) K.; m. Naomi Carol Prawer, Sept. 2, 1976; children: Maya, Nadav, Einat. BS in Physics, Hebrew U., Jerusalem, 1972; MD, Sackler Sch. Medicine, Tel Aviv, Israel, 1983. Diplomate Am. Bd. Pediatrics, Am. Bd. Diagnostic Lab. Immunology, Am. B. Allergy and Immunology, Am. Bd. Medicine. Intern Tel-Hashomer, Ramat Gan, Israel, 1982; intern Albert Einstein Coll. of Medicine, N.Y.C., 1983, resident, 1984-86, asst. prof., 1989-92, asst. clin. prof., 1992—; fellow NIH, Bethesda, Md., 1986-89; immunology cons. Pediatric HIV Primary Care, N.Y.C., 1989—. Mem. AAAS, N.Y. Acad. Scis. Avocations: classical music, literature. Home: 5 Woodland Ct Bedford NY 10506-2034 Office: 530 Park Ave New York NY 10021-8015 also: 666 Lexington Ave Mount Kisco NY 10549-3632

KADER, HOWARD AARON, pediatrician; b. Montreal, Canada, May 31, 1965; s. Fred J. and Sarah K.; m. Lori Joy, Oct. 10, 1993; children: Joseph, Emily. MD, U. Nebr., 1992. Intern in surgery Washington Hosp. Ctr., 1992-93; resident in pediatrics U. Nebr. Med. Ctr., Omaha, 1993-96; fellow in pediatric gastroenterology Children's Hosp. Phila., 1996-99; asst. prof. pediats. Duke U. Med. Ctr, Durham, N.C., 1999—. Author: Clinical Pediatric Gastroenterology, 1998. Fellow Am. Acad. Pediats.; mem. Am. Gastroenterology Assn., N.Am. Soc. Pediat. Gastroenterology & Nutrition, Crohn's & Colitis Found. Am. Office: Duke U Med Ctr PO Box 3009 Durham NC 27715-3009

KADHOM, NOMAN, veterinarian, cell biologist; b. Misan, Iraq, July 1, 1944; arrived in France, 1981; s. Jawad Kadhom and Kadija Mousa; m. Doco Isabelle, July 27, 1996; children: Sarah, Nadia. BVMS, Coll. of Vet. Medicine, Baghdad, 1969, MS in vet. Clin. Pathology, 1977; PhD in Animal Biology and Physiology, U. Paris 7, 1990. Vet. Instr./vet. U. Baghdad, 1969-77; chief Vet. Lab., Baghdad, 1978-81; rschrs. Nat. Inst. for Agrl. Rsch., Paris, 1982-83, Nat. Inst. for Health and Med. Rsch., Paris, 1984-91; head of tissue culture sect. Nat. Inst. for Health and Med. Rsch., 1995—; rschrs. Nat. Ctr. for Sci. Rsch., Paris, 1992-94; com. chmn. Vet. Hosp., Anbar, Iraq, 1977-78; chmn. sci. bd., Agr. Regional Direction, Anbar, 1977-79; cons. Cen. lab. of Biochem., Bicetre, France, 1988-89; advisor Nat. Ctr. for Sci. Rsch., Paris, 1993-94. Editor: Jour. of Vet. Med. Coll., Iraq, 1969; author: (govtl. study) Poultry Management in Anbar District, 1978 (Ministerial prize 1979); contbr. articles to profl. jours. and publs. Fellow nat. Ctr. of Blood Transfusion, Paris, 1984, Ctr. Nat. d'Assurance Maladie, Paris, 1986; grantee Soc. d'Etudes et de Soins pour Enfants atteints de Rhumatologie Articulaire et de Cardiopathie, Paris, 1990. Mem. Iraqi Vet. Assn., N.Y. Acad. Scis. Avocations: travel, music, theater, photography, movies. Office: Inserm U393 Med Genetic Rsch Unit, 149 Rue de Sevres, 75015 Paris France

KADIATA, BAKACH DIKAND, agriculture educator; b. Luputa, Republic of Congo, Aug. 18, 1956; s. Alexis Hian Bakul and Marie (Sula) B.; m. Esther Tshiala, Nov. 25, 1986. Diploma, I.T. of Agrl., Tshibashi, Congo, 1975; ingenieur technicien, I.S.E.A., Bengamisa, Congo, 1979; ingenieur agronome, I.F.A., Yangambi, Congo, 1987; PhD, R.S.U.S.T., Portharcourt, Nigeria, 1995. Lectr. I.S.E.A., Bengamisa, Congo, 1979-82; asst. lectr. I.F.A., Yangambi, 1987-89, dept. sec., 1988-89; rsch. fellow I.I.T.A., Ibadan, Nigeria, 1989-95, rsch. collaborator, 1995-97; assoc. prof. U. Kinshasa, Congo, 1998—; Advisor Ministry of Reconstruction, Kinshasa, Congo, 1999—; reviewer AB Academic Publs., U.K., 1997; cons. Genagro, Ibadan, Nigeria, 1995; interpreter, IIRSBA, 1992. Recipient scholarship Zairean Govt., ISEA Bengamisa, 1976-79, IFA Yangambi, 1982-87; rsch. grant Internat. Inst. Tropi Agrl., Ibadan, Nigeria, 1989. Fellow ARSAF; mem. African Assn. Biology, N.Y. Acad. Sci. Avocations: reading, football, tourism, singing. Office: Faculty of Agronomy, U Kinshasa, BP 866 Kinshasa Republic Congo

KADIR, DJELAL, literature educator, writer, translator, editor; b. St. Theodoros, Larnaca, Cyprus, Jan. 21, 1946; m. Juana Celia Cohen, May 24, 1969; 1 child, Aixé. BA, Yale U., 1969; PhD, U. N.M., 1972. Prof., chair comparative lit. Purdue U., West Lafayette, Ind., 1973-91; Disting. prof. lit. U. Okla., Norman, 1991-95, Neustadt prof. comparative lit., 1995-97; E.E. Sparks prof. of comparative lit. Pa. State U., 1998—; dir. Coun. on Inter-Am. Literary Cultures, 1998—, Internat. Sch. Theory in humanities, 1999—; founding pres. Internat. Am. Studies Assn., 2000; editor World Literature Today, U. Okla., Norman, 1991-96; cons. Libr. Congress, Washington, 1975—; vis. scholar Russian Acad. Scis., Moscow, 1992; lectr. in field; sr. rsch. assoc. U. Leipzig, 1994—, Borges Ctr., Aarhus U. Denmark; bd. dirs. Coun. on Nat. Lits., Internat. Writers Ctr.; sr. rsch. fellow, mem. exec. bd. Internat. Sch. of Theory in the Humanities, Santiago, Spain, 1997-99. Author: Juan Carlos Onetti, 1977, Questing Fictions, 1986, Columbus and the Ends of the Earth, 1992, The Other Writing, 1993; editor, translator selected poetry of Joao Cabral de Melo Neto, 1994; editor: Oxford History of Latin American Literature, Longman Anthology of World Literature; mem. editl. bd. PMLA 1998—. Mem. State Arts Coun. Okla., Oklahoma City, 1991-96; cons. Indpls. Mus. Art. Resident fellow Rockefeller Found., Bellagio, Italy, 1993. Mem. MLA (chmn. Del. Assembly 1999-2000), Internat. Comparative Lit. Assn. (exec. bd. com. Lit. Histories, 1992—, chmn. com. on theory 1998—), Am. Comparative Lit. Assn., Internat. Found. Global Studies (sec. 1998-2000), Internat. Coll. Global Studies (v.p. 1998-2000). Avocations: music (cello), hiking, horseback riding, polo. E-mail: dxk50@psu.edu. Office: Dept Comparative Lit Pa State U 311 Burrowes Bldg University Park PA 16802-6203

KADIRGAMAR, LAKSHMAN, minister of foreign affairs. LLB, Ceylon U.; BLitt, Oxford U. Barrister U.K.; dir. World Intellectual Property Orgn., Geneva, 1983; min. fgn. affairs Pres.'s Counsel, Sri Lanka, 1991; M.P., hon. bencher Inner Temple, U.K., 1995. Office: Ministry Fgn Affairs, Ministry of Fgn Affairs, Republic Bldg PO Box 583, Colombo 1, Sri Lanka*

KADKADE, DATTARAM GOPAL, construction company executive; b. Bicholim, Gao, India, Feb. 20, 1931; s. Gopal Damodar and Ramabai Gopal (Vijay) K.; m. Suman Dattaram Virjinker, July 24, 1931; children: Sudhir, Sunil. BCE, Pune (India) U., 1953. Design engr. Hindustan Constrnl. Co. Ltd., Bombay, 1954-55; Kyona Hydroproject project mgr. Hindustan Constrnl. Co. Ltd., 1958-60; DBK RLY project mgr. Hindustan Constrnl. Co. Ltd., Vizag, India, 1960-63; zonal mgr. Hindustan Constrnl. Co. Ltd., Bombay, 1963-66; asst. gen. mgr. Hindustan Constrnl. Co. Ltd., Dehradun, India, 1966-75; dir. Jaipraksy Industries, Ltd., New Delhi, 1975—; mng. dir. Internat. Design Assn., New Delhi, 1995—; mng. dir. J.P.T.C., New Delhi, 1984—. Contbr. articles to profl. jours. Fellow Inst. Engrs.; mem. ISRMTT (pres. 1996-98), ITA, IWRS, IRC, ISCS, ISRMTT, MICE, MICI, BITS, ICA, ICOLD, IHA. Avocations: reading papers, writing, indoor games. home: B3/23 Vasant Vihar, New Delhi 110057, India Office: Jaiprakash Industries Ltd, 63 Basant Lok Cmty Ctr, New Delhi 110057, India

KADMENSKY, STANISLAV GEORGIEVICH, physics educator; b. Voronezh, Russia, Sept. 30, 1937; s. Georgy Dmitrievich and Taisiya Ivanovna (Shiryaeva) K.; m. Raisa Grigorievna Ryaguzova, Oct. 1, 1972; children: Elena, Svetlana, Stanislava, Stanislav. D of Phys. Math. Scis., Joint Inst. Nuclear Rsch., 1973. Lectr. Voronezh (Russia) U., 1962-68, asst. prof., 1968-76, head nuclear physics dept., 1976—; prorector Internat. U. Computer Techs., Voronezh, 1992—. Author: Alpha-Decay and Relative Nuclear Reactions, 1985; contbr. articles to profl. jours. (two articles named as Best on Theory of Atomic Nucleis by Jour. Phys. Atom. Nucl.); patentee in field. Deputy People Deputies Congress, Moscow, 1990-93; gov.'s cons. Voronezh Region Adminstrn., 1994-96. Russian Found. Fundamental Investigations grantee, Moscow, 1994-2000. Mem. Med. Physics Found. (pres. 1995—), Russian Acad. Natural Scis., N.Y. Acad. Scis., Soros. Avocations: nature studies, book collecting. E-mail: kadmensky@cd.vsu.ru. Home: Plekhanovskaya St 22 360, 394030 Voronezh Russia Office: Voronezh State U, Universitetskaya Ploschad 1, 394000 Voronezh Russia

KADOKAWA, JUN-ICHI, chemist, scientist; b. Matsuyama, Ehime, Japan, Mar. 29, 1964; s. Shin-ichi and Kumiko K. BSc in Applied Chemistry, Tohoku U., Sendai, Japan, 1987, MSc in Materials Chemistry, 1989, PhD in Materials Chemistry, 1992. Asst. prof. applied chemistry Yamagata U., Yonezawa, Japan, 1992-99, assoc. prof. applied chemistry, 1999—. Mem. Am. Chem. Soc., The Chem. Soc. Japan, Soc. of Polymer Sci., Japan (award for encouragement of rsch. in polymer sci. 1998), Soc. Synthetic Organic Chemistry, Japan. Office: Yamagata U Faculty Engring, 4-3-16 Jonan, Yonezawa 992-8510, Japan

KADOMA, YOSHIHITO, chemist; b. Chinan City, China, Jan. 11, 1943; s. Yoshiaki and Momoko (Tamai) K.; m. Noriko Asano, Jan. 6, 1975. BS, Osaka City U., 1967, MSc, 1969, PhD, 1973. From mgr. to gen. mgr. NOF Corp., Tokyo, 1980-2000; dir. Japan Chem. Innovation Inst., Tokyo, 2000—; guest rschr. Tsukuba Advanced Rsch. Assn., 1995-97; guest prof. Gunma U., Japan, 1994-95; chmn. Food Forum Tsukuba, 1995-99; chmn. Internat. Symposium Com., Tokyo, 1998—. Mem. Japan Chem. Soc. (dir. 2000—), Tsukuba Chem. Sci. Club. Avocations: personal computing, gardening, reading. Office: Japan Chem Innovation Inst, 1-3-5 Kanda-Jinbochu, Chiyoda-ku Tokyo 101-0051, Japan

KADOTA, EIJI, pathologist, researcher; b. Osaka-city, Osaka, Japan, Apr. 20, 1949; s. Toyomi and Noboruko (Enokura) K.; m. Fukuko Jinnouchi, May 26, 1975; children: Mitsuru, Aiko. MB, Tottori (Japan) U., 1974; MD, Kinki U., Osaka, 1989. Lic. pathologist. Intern Osaka Univ. Hosp., 1974-75; neuropsychiatrist Kansai-Rosai Hosp., Osaka, 1975-78; physician Hanwa Hosp., Osaka, 1978-82; tchg. asst. Kinki U., 1982-90, lectr., 1990-92; chief pathologist Kishiwada City Hosp., Osaka, 1992—; part-time lectr. Kinki U., Osaka, 1992—. Fellow Japanese Soc. Pathology; mem. Internat. Neurtrauma Soc., Internat. Soc. for Brain Edema. Avocations: referee and judge of amateur boxing, social dancing, photography. Home: 1-5-11 Ebaraji-cho, 593-8304 Sakai-city Osaka, Japan Office: Kishiwada Hosp Div Pathol, 2 Gakuhara-cho, 596-8501 Kishiwada-city Osaka, Japan

KADOTA, KOICHI, pathologist, veterinarian; b. Ochi-cho, Kochi, Japan, Mar. 25, 1957; s. Michiaki and Hisako (Yokobatake) K.; m. Eri Kobayashi, Mar. 31, 1991. MA, Hokkaido U., 1981, PhD, 1990. Chief veterinarian Nat. Inst. Animal Health, Sapporo, 1993—. Contbr. articles to profl. jours. Avocation: gardening. Office: Nat Inst Animal Health, 4 Hitsujigaoka Toyohira, Sapporo 062-0045, Japan

KADYK, FOLKERT HERPEL, music educator; b. Tulsa, Okla., June 25, 1932; s. Jacob Merion and Elizabeth (Herpel) K.; m. Jean Erickson, Sept. 1, 1956; children: Charles C., Winona Kadyk Smith. BA, Coll. of Wooster, Ohio, 1955; MEd, Temple U., 1961; MA, Villanova U., 1978; D.Mus. Art, Temple U., 1987. Music therapist Phila. State Hosp., 1956-58; tchr. music grades 8-10 Pennsbury Schs., Yardley, Pa., 1958-60; tchr. music K-12 Bridgeport (Pa.) Schs., 1960-62, Great Valley Schs., Malvern, Pa., 1962-86; adj. faculty Delaware County C.C., Media, Pa., 1987-2000, Pa. State U., Media, 1989—; adj. faculty Immaculata Coll., Immaculata, PA, 1976—; hymnal coord. Friends Gen. Conf., Phila., 1996-97. Editor: (hymnal) Worship in Song, 1997. Bd. dirs. Main Line Symphony Orch., Wayne, Pa., 1974—. Mem. Am. Fedn. Musicians. Soc. of Friends. Avocations: woodworking, carpentry, walking, computers. Home: 945 Conestoga Rd Berwyn PA 19312-1305

KAELBLE, HARTMUT, social history educator; b. Göppingen, Germany, Apr. 12, 1940; s. Fritz and Hilde (Schühle) K.; m. Brigitte Müller; children: Hendrik, Martin. PhD, Free U. Berlin, 1966, Habilitation, 1971; Dr h.c., U. Paris I, 1997. Prof. social and econ. history Free U. Berlin, 1971-91; prof. social history Humboldt U. Berlin, 1991—. Author: (in German) Social Mobility in the 19th and 20th Centuries, 1985 (also English and Spanish edits.), (in German) Industrialization and Social Inequality in 19th Century Europe, 1986 (also English and Spanish edits.), (in English) A Social History of Western Europe 1880-1980, 1989 (also German, French, Italian and Japanese edits.), Nachbarn am Rhein (Social History of France and Germany), 1991, The Historical Comparison, 1999. Mem. com. of sages European Commn., 1995-96. Decorated chevalier Order des Palmes Académiques (France). Office: Humboldt U Berlin History, Sci, Unter den Linden 6, 10099 Berlin Germany

KAELIN, EUGENE FRANCIS, philosophy educator; b. St. Louis, Oct. 14, 1926; s. Albert Aloysius and Bertha (Earni) K.; m. Pierrette Nicole Demartini, Dec. 30, 1952; children: Valérie Chantal, Carolyne Pascale, Martine Laurence. BA with distinction, U. Mo., 1949, MA, 1950; diploma of higher studies, U. Bordeaux, France, 1951; PhD, U. Ill., 1954. Instr. philosophy U. Mo., 1952-53; fellow philosophy U. Ill., 1953-54, post-doctoral fellow, 1954-55; instr. philosophy U. Wis., 1955-57, asst. prof., 1957-61, assoc. prof., 1961-65; assoc. prof. Fla. State U., 1965-67, prof., 1967-96, ret., 1996; mem. nat. adv. bd. aesthetic edn. program Central Midwestern Regional Ednl. Lab., 1968-76. Author: An Existentialist Aesthetic, 1962, Art and Existence, 1970, The Unhappy Consciousness, 1981, Heidegger's Being and Time: A Reading for Readers, 1988, An Aesthetics for Art Educators, 1989, Texts on Texts and Textuality, 1999. With USMC, 1945-46. Recipient William Henry Kiekhofer Meml. Teaching award U. Wis., 1959. Mem. Am. Philos. Assn., Am. Soc. Aesthetics, Am. Soc. Phenomenology and Existential Philosophy, Fla. Philos. Assn. (pres. 1977-78). Home: 1910 Atapha Nene Tallahassee FL 32301-5851

KAELIN, WILLIAM GEORGE, JR., physician, oncologist; b. Nov. 23, 1957. BA, Duke U., 1979, MD, 1982. Diplomate Am. Bd. Internal Medicine, Am. Bd. Med. Oncology. Assoc. prof. Dana Farber Cancer Inst. Harvard Med. Sch., Boston, 1997—; asst. investigator Howard Hughes Med. Inst., 1998—. Office: Dana Farber Cancer Inst 44 Binney St Boston MA 02115-6013

KAEMPEN, CHARLES EDWARD, manufacturing company executive; b. Quincy, Ill., Mar. 10, 1927; s. Charles Herman and Margo (Gochicoa) K.; m. Inger Margareta Nystrom, Aug. 5, 1951; children: Charles Robert, Donald Michael, Annette Earline, Laura Inger. BS in Aeron. Engring., U. Ill., Urbana, 1950; DSc in Astronautics, Internat. Acad. Astronautics, Paris, 1964. Registered profl. engr., Calif., Conn. Sr. designer Saab Aircraft Co., Linkôping, Sweden, 1950-52; design analyst Sikorsky Helicopter United Aircraft, Stratford, Conn., 1952-56; space mission analyst Missle div. N.Am. Rockwell, Downey, Calif., 1957-60; staff scientist Hughes Aircraft, Fullerton, Calif., 1961-63; lunar systems analyst Northrop Space Lab., Hawthorne, Calif., 1963-64; pres. Am. Space Transport Co., Tustin, Calif., 1964-66; transport systems analyst Dashaveyor Co., Venice, Calif., 1966-67; pres. Kaempen & Assocs., Orange, Calif., 1967-68; sr. rsch. engr. Baker Oil Tools Inc., L.A., 1968-69; pres. Kaempen Industries, Inc., Santa Ana, Calif., 1969-82, Kaempen & Assocs., 1982—; pres., CEO Kamepen Composite Products, Inc., 1996-2000. Author papers on fiberglass composites and filament winding; patentee in field. With U.S. Army, 1944-47. Reciepient Cert. of Merit Pictionary of Internat. Biography, London, 1965,. Fellow AIAA; mem. ASME, ASTM, Soc. Aerospace Materials and Process Engring., Soc. of Plastics Industry, Nat. Soc. Profl. Engrs., Mason. Republican. Lutheran. Home: 3202 E Larkstone Dr Orange CA 92869-5546 Office: Kaempen Composite Products Inc 681 S Tustin St Ste 110 Orange CA 92866-3345

KAESEMEYER, WAYNE HARRY, internist, hypertension specialist; b. Cincinnati, Ohio, Oct. 12, 1947; s. Harry and Grace (Sanker) K.; m. Dorothy Jean Kaesemeyer, Nov. 3, 1978 (div. Feb. 1984); 1 child Kelly Ann. BS, BA, Wilmington Coll., 1969; MD, Wake Forest U., 1978. Diplomate Nat. Bd. Med. Examiners, Am. Bd. Internal Medicine. Intern in internal medicine N.C. Baptist Hosp., Winston Salem, N.C., 1978-79; residency internal medicine Washington (D.C.) Hosp. Ctr., 1979-80; residency internal medicine Med. Coll. Ga., Augusta, 1980-81, chief resident, 1981-82; clinical attending, internal medicine Med. U. S.C., Charleston, 1983-86, Univ. Hosp., Augusta, Ga., 1987-90; clinical attending, Hypertension Clinic Univ. Hosp., Augusta, 1987-94, Summerville Profl. Ctr. St. Joseph Hosp., Augusta, 1993—; pres., sr. sci. officer NitroSys. Inc., Augusta; hosp. appts. Talmadge Hosp., Augusta, 1981-82, VA Hosp., Augusta, 1981-82, Univ. Hosp., Augusta, 1987—, St. Joseph Hosp., Augusta, 1987—, Humana Hosp., Augusta, 1990—; speaker Pfizer Pharms., Calcium Antagonists in Hypertension, Cardiovascular Diseases, 1988—, speaker Knoll Pharms., Calcium Antagonists in Hypertension Cardiovascular diseases, 1989—, speaker for Parke Davis, Med. Edn. programs on Angiotensin Mediated Hypertension and cardiovascular diseases, 1991-92, speaker Hoechst Pharms. ACE Inhibition in Hypertensive and Cardiovascular diseases, 1993— speaker Bristol Myers Squibb Pharms ACE Inhibition in Hypertensive and Cardiovasculardiseases, 1993—; organic chemist Richardson Merrill Pharms., Phillipsburg, N.J., 1970-73; prin. investigator Parke-Davis ADPOt1, 2 segments, Hoechst Pharms, Altace Care Program, Pfizer Pharms., Abbott Labs. Renin inhibitor, Sankyo U.S. A. Corp., Temocapril alone or in combination with hydrochlorothiazide, 1987—. Inventor: Method and Formulation of Stimulating Nitric Oxide Synthesis, U.S. patent, 1994, Method and Formulation for Treating Vascular Disease, patent pending, applied 04/05/97; contbr. more than 15 articles to profl. jours. including New Eng. Jour. Medicine, Am. Jour. Hypertension, Archives Internal Medicine and others. With U.S. Army Reserves, 1969-75. Grantee: Bristol Myers Squibb, Merck & Co., Pfizer. Mem. ACP, Richmond County Med. Soc., Med. Assn. Ga., Am. Soc. Hypertension, Am. Coll. Clin. Pharmacology, Am. Heart Assn., Inter-Am. Soc. Hypertension. Home: 2433 Mcdowell St Augusta GA 30904-4682 Office: NitroSys Inc 512 Telfair St Augusta GA 30901-5863

KAESLER, DIRK RUDOLF, sociologist, educator; b. Wiesbaden, Germany, Oct. 19, 1944. Diploma in Sociology, Ludwig-Maximilians U., Munich, 1972, Dr.rer.pol., 1976, Dr.rer.pol.habil., 1983; student, London Sch. Econs., 1968-69. Asst. prof. U. Munich, 1972-83, assoc. prof., 1984; prof. sociology U. Hamburg, 1984-95; sr. prof. sociology U. Marburg, 1995—; vis. scholar dept. sociology and com. on social thought U. Chgo., 1981; vis. prof. Seminar for Sociology, U. Cologne, 1988-89; dist. vis. prof. Ctr. Interdisciplinary Studies in Culture and Soc., U. South Fla., Tampa-St. Petersburg, 1989-90; vis. scholar Inst. Germanic Studies and Inst. for Advanced Study, Ind. U., Bloomington, 1994-95; dir. d'Etudes Invité Ecole des Hautes Etudes in Social Scis., Paris, 1995, Inst. Sozial Wissen-schaften, Humboldt U., Berlin, 1999. Author: Klassiker der Soziologie, 1999, Sociology als Berufung, 1997, Max Weber, 1995, 2nd edit., 1998, Aushandeln and (proto-)politische Communication, 1994, Sociology Responds to Fascism, 1992, 2d edit., 1996, Der politische Skandal, 1991, Sociology Abenteuer, 1985, Klassiker des sociology Denkens, vol. 2, 1978, Revolution and Veralltäglichung, 1977, Wege in die Sociology Theory, 1974, Sociology and Ethology, 1971, others; contbr. articles to profl. jours.; referee, spl. reader Am. Jour. Sociology, Am. Sociol. Rev., Internat. Rev. Social History, Sociol. Quar., Sociol. Theory, Internat. Sociology, Kölner Zeitschrift for Sociology and Socialpsychology; editl. bd. Sociol. Theory, 1989-93, Jahrbuch for Soziologiegeschichte, 1990—. German Nat. Scholarship Found. fellow, 1967-72. Mem. Internat. Sociol. Assn. (rsch. com. on history of sociology, sec., newsletter editor, program coord. 1983-92, v.p. 1992-98, pres. 1998—), German Soc. Sociology (mem. Konzil 1999—, mem. coun. of sect. polit. sociology 1995-98, com. for code of ethics of German sociology 1989-92), Am. Sociol. Assn., Deutscher Hochschulverband, European Assn. for Study of Sci. and Tech. Office: Philipps U Marburg/Sociol, Ketzerbach 11, D-35032 Marburg Germany

KAFARSKI, ERIK MICHAEL, chemical processing company executive, lawyer; b. Detroit, Mar. 31, 1968; s. Mitchell I. Kafarski and Zofia J. F. Drozdowska. BS, U. Mich., 1991; JD, Mich. State U., 1994. Bar: Mich. 1995. Law clk. Miller, Canfield, Paddock & Stone, Bloomfield Hils, Mich., 1992; jud. clk. Wayne County Cir. Ct., Detroit, 1992-93; program mgr. Aactron, Inc., Madison Heights, Mich., 1993-95, pres., 1995—; bd. dirs. Straith Hosp. Spl. Surgery. Rsch. assoc., contbr. Nerve Regeneration and Palsies, 1989-91. Asst. campaign dir. Com. Retain Supreme Ct. Justice Boyle, Detroit, 1990. Mem. U.S. Tennis Assn. (area champion 1998, 2000, state champion 1999), Soc. Mfg. Engrs./Assn. Electroplaters and Surface Finishers, Mich. Assn. Metal Finishers. Avocations: tennis, skiing, squash, biking. Fax: 248-543-6847. Office: Aactron Inc 29306 Stephenson Hwy Madison Heights MI 48071-2394

KAFELINKOV, YEVGENY, tennis player; b. Sochi, Russia, Feb. 18, 1974. Profl. tennis player, 1992—; participant French Open, 1996, Australian Open, 1999, semi-finalist U.S. Open, 1999. Avocations: fishing, soccer, hockey, basketball. Office: c/o ATP Tour Internat Hdqrs 201 Atp Tour Blvd Ponte Vedra Beach FL 32082*

KAFFENBERGER, WALTER, biologist, radiobiologist; b. Fraenkisch-Crumbach, Germany, May 17, 1950; s. Friedrich and Margarete Kaffenberger; m. Christel B. Hofmann, Mar. 7, 1975; 1 child, Jessica N.Y. D Natural Scis., U. Heidelberg, Germany, 1979; Habilitation in Radiobiology, Tech. U. Munich, 1997. Head radiobiology sect. Fed. Armed Forces Def. Sci. Agy., Munster, Germany, 1979-88; group leader Inst. Radiobiology Fed. Armed Forces Med. Acad., Munich, 1988-98; program dir. divsn. sci. and environ. affairs NATO, Brussels, 1998—; vis. scientist Armed Forces Radiobiology Rsch. Inst., Bethesda, Md., 1985-86, chmn. selection panel for supervisory radiol. physicists, 1986; vis. scientist U. Chgo., 1993. Contbr. articles to profl. jours. Mem. Deutsche Gesellschaft fuer Radioonkologie, Strahlenbiologie und Medizinische Physik (founding), Gesellschaft für Preventive Onkologie (chmn.). Lutheran. Avocations: travel, hiking, cross-country skiing, gardening. E-mail: w.kaffenberger@hq.nato.int. Fax: 0032-2-707-4232. Home: Av de l'Optimisme 99 bte 52, Brussels 1140, Belgium

KAFKA, VRATISLAV, research scientist; b. Hevlín, Moravia, Czech Republic, July 3, 1929; s. Karel and Helena (Jarošová) K.; m. Dagmar Hechtová, Jan. 31, 1953 (div. Nov. 1956); m. Jiřina Fediuková, June 14, 1958; children: Solarik Eva. Degree in engring., Czech Tech. U., Prague, 1953; PhD, Czech Acad. Scis., Prague, 1957, DSc, 1981. Rsch. asst. Inst. Theoretical and Applied Mechanics Acad. Scis. of Czech Republic, Prague, 1953-57, rsch. scientist Inst. Theoretical and Applied Mechanics, 1957-79, head of dept. Inst. Theoretical and Applied Mechanics, 1979-99; v.p. sci. com. Inst. Theoretical and Applied Mechanics, Prague, 1990-92, pres., 1992-94. Author: Foundations of Theoretical Microrheology, 1984, Inelastic Mesomechanics, 1987, (book chpts.) Biomechanics, 1993, Ligaments and Ligamentoplasties, 1996. Recipient prize Czech Acad. Scis., 1976, 92. Fellow Czech Soc. Mechanics (medal 1990); mem. Czech Soc. Biomechanics (pres. 1994-97), N.Y. Acad. Scis. (active). Avocations: hiking, swimming, skiing, music. Home: Ružinovská 10, 14200 Prague Czech Republic Office: Inst Theoretical and Applied Mechanics, 76 Prosecká, 19000 Prague 9, Czech Republic

KAFOUROS, GEORGE, physical therapist, consultant; b. Pireas, Greece, May 6, 1972; s. Stelios and Maria (Vladitsi) K. BSc in Phys. Therapy with honors, Leeds (Eng.) Met. U., 1994, Postgrad. Diploma in Health Scis., 1996, MSc in Health Mgmt., 1997. Phys. therapist St. James's Hosp., Leeds, 1994-96; adminstrn. mgr. Natl Health Svc. Exec., Leeds, 1997-98. Coauthor: Physiotherapy Treatment of Spina Cord Injuries, 1998. Christian Orthodox. Avocations: piano, cinema, reading, music. Home: Leoforos Irinis 271, 18863 Perama, Pireas Greece

KAFRI, YARIV, physicist; b. Haifa, Israel, Dec. 9, 1970; s. Oded and Hava Kafri; m. Galit Kafri, Aug. 26, 1997; 1 child, Yael. BSc in Physics, Tel Aviv U., 1994; MSc in Physics, Weizmann Inst. Sci., Rehovot, Israel, 1996. Physicist Weizmann Inst. Sci., Rehovot. Contbr articles to profl. jours. E-mail: fekafri@wisemail.weizmann.ac.il. Office: Weizmann Inst Sci, Rehovot Israel

KAGAN, CONSTANCE HENDERSON, philosopher, educator, consultant; b. Houston, Sept. 16, 1940; d. Bessie Earle (Henderson) Davis; m. Morris Kagan, May 27, 1967. BA, Baylor U., 1962; MSSW, U. Tex. Austin, 1966; PhD, U. Okla., 1979. congl. fellow, 1981-82. Mem. NASW, Am. Philos. Assn.

KAGAN, SIOMA, economics educator; b. Riga, Russia, Sept. 29, 1907; came to U.S., 1941, naturalized, 1950; s. Jacques and Berta (Kaplan) K.; m. Jean Batt, Apr. 5, 1947 (div. 1969). Diplom Ingenieur, Technische Hochschule, Berlin, 1931; M.A., Am. U., 1949; Ph.D. in Econs, Columbia U., 1954. Sci. asst. Heinrich Hertz Inst., Berlin, 1931-33; partner Laboratoire Electro-Acoustique, Neuilly-sur-Seine, France, 1933-48; chief French Mission Telecom. French Supply Council in N.Am., Washington, 1943-45; mem. telecom. bd. UN, 1946-47, econ. affairs officer, 1947-48; econs. cons. to govt. and industry; assoc. prof. econs. Washington U., St. Louis, 1956-59; staff economist Joint Council Econ. Edn., N.Y.C., 1959-60; prof. internat. bus. U. Oreg., Eugene, 1960- 67; prof. internat. bus. U. Mo., St. Louis, 1967-87, prof. emeritus, 1987—; faculty leader exec. devel. programs Columbia, Northwestern U., NATO Def. Coll., Rome, others. Contbr. numerous articles profl. publs. Served with Free French Army, 1941-43. Decorated Legion of Honor (France). Recipient Thomas Jefferson award U. Mo., 1984. Fellow Latin Am. Studies Assn.; mem. Am. Econ. Assn., Acad. Polit. Sci., Assn. Asian Studies. Clubs: University (St. Louis); Conanicut Yacht (Jamestown, R.I.). Home: 8132 Roxburgh Dr Saint Louis MO 63105-2436 Office: U Mo Sch Business Saint Louis MO 63121

KAGAN, VAL ALEXANDER, engineer, researcher, educator; b. Odessa, Ukraine, Aug. 24, 1940; came to U.S., 1991, naturalized, 1999; m. Rina V. Kaplan, July 5, 1969; children: Atalia, Anna. BS, MS in Mech. Engring., Tech. U. Kaunas, Lithuania, 1964, PhD in Engring., 1970, DSc, Acad. Scis., Moscow, 1985. Design engr. R&D Co. Priekalas, Kaunas, 1965-66; postgrad. course scientist Tech. U. Kaunas, 1967-69, postdoctoral fellow, 1970-71, asst. prof., 1971-72; assoc. prof. Tech. U., Vilnius, Lithuania, 1972-84, prof., rsch. fellow, head ctr., 1984-91; engr., sr. engr. Honeywell Internat. (formerly Allied Signal, Inc.), Morristown, N.J., 1992-95, sr. prin. scientist, 1996-98, applied technology leader, 1998—; sr. cons. Acad. Sci., Vilnius, 1984-91; mem. sci. coun. Russian Acad. Sci., Moscow, 1986-91; mem. adv. bd. Vilnius U., 1983-91. Editor Applied Mechanics, 1986-91; author 4 monographs; contbr. more than 230 articles to profl. jours. Mem. ASTM, AIAA, ASME, Soc. Plastics Engrs. Achievements include 11 U.S., Russian and Lithuanian patents. Home: 122 Edgefield Dr Morris Plains NJ 07950-1960 Office: Honeywell Internat 101 Columbia Rd Morristown NJ 07960-4658

KAGAN, YURI MOISEEVICH, physicist; b. Moscow, July 6, 1928; s. Moisey Alexandrovich and Rachill Solomonovna (Chazrevina) K.; m. Tatjana Nikolaevna Virta, Nov. 1958; 1 child, Maxim. Candidate of sci., Kurchatov Inst., Moscow, 1954, DSc, 1959; D (hon.), Munich Tech. U., 1990, Uppsala (Sweden) U., 1996. Rschr. Kurchatov Inst., 1950-54, sr. scientist, 1954-62, head theory divsn., 1962—; full prof. physics Phys. Engring. Inst., Moscow, 1962—; Morris Loeb lectr. Harvard U., Boston, 1988, 96; hon. van der Waals prof. Amsterdam (The Netherlands) U., 1990, Emil Warburg lectr. Bayreuth (Germany) U., 1992, Jacob Wallenberg lectr. Uppsala (Sweden) U., 1992; vis. prof. Coll. de France, Paris, 1993. Contbr. articles to Jour. Theoretical and Exptl. Physics (Lomonosov prize 1975, State prize 1976, Lenin prize 1986); contbr. numerous articles to profl. jours. Recipient award Alexander von Humboldt Found., Germany, 1994, Karpinskii award Toepfer Found., Germany, 1994—. Mem. Am. Phys. Soc., Russian Acad. Scis., Acad. Europaea, Hungarian Phys. Soc., Hungarian Acad. Scis. (fgn. mem.). Avocations: the arts, tennis. Office: Kurchatov Inst, Kurchatov Sq 46, 123182 Moscow Russia

KAGAWA, KOJI, naval architectural engineering educator; b. Nakama City, Japan, Oct. 18, 1939; s. Masaichi and Matsue (Nakagawa) K.; m. Keiko Kawaguchi, Nov. 30, 1967; children: Onta Junko, Kagawa Takashi. B of Engring., Kyushu U., Fukuoka, Japan, 1962, M of Engring., 1964, DEng, 1987. Rsch. engr. vibration lab. Mitsubishi Heavy Industries Ltd., Nagasaki, Japan, 1964-73, sr. rsch. engr., 1973-80, rsch. project mgr., 1980-93; prof. Kyushu U., Fukuoka, Japan, 1993—; cons. Internat. Maritime Orgn. dispatched by UN Devel. Program, 1981; instr. Technopolis Found., Nagasaki, 1990-91; analyst Indsl. Property Cooperation Ctr. of Japan, 1990-92; taskmaster The Shipbuilding Rsch. Assn. of Japan, 1997—. Author: (book) Vibration Control Handbook, 1992 . Recipient Pres. award of Japan, Ship Promotion Found., 1971, Pres. award Japan Classification Soc. of Shipping, 1971, Outstanding Paper award Soc. Naval Arch. of Japan, 1971, Outstanding Paper award ASME, 1983, Disting. Invention award Bd. of Sci. & Tech. of Japan, 1993, Pres. Encouraging award Patent Bur. Japan, 1996, Pres. Grand prize Japan Inst. Invention and Innovation, 1997. Mem. Soc. Naval Architects of Japan (judging com. mem. 1992—), West Japan Soc. Naval Architects (mem. editl. bd. 1991—), Archtl. Inst. Japan, Marine Engring. Soc. Japan. Home: 3-16-16 Sakurayamate, Shingumachi, Kasuyagun Fukuoka 811-0113, Japan Office: Kyushu U Faculty Engring, 6-10-1 Hakozaki Higashiku, Fukuoka 812-8581, Japan

KAGAWA, NOBORU, physics educator, researcher; b. Tokyo, July 26, 1957; s. Masateru Ohkado and Hiroe Kagawa; m. Madoka Hashimoto, June 2, 1981; children: Nagisa, Ko. BS, Keio U., Tokyo, 1980, MS, 1982, PhD, 1989. Rschr. Toshiba, Yokohama, Japan, 1982-89, dep. mgr., 1989-91; lectr. Nat. Def. Acad., Yokosuka, Japan, 1991-92, assoc. prof., 1992—; guest rschr. Nat. Inst. Stds. and Tech., Boulder, Colo., 1995-97; mem. staff gen. affairs Japan Symposium Thermo. Props, Tokyo, 1998-99. Author: JARef JAR Thermodynamic Tables, Vol. 1, 1994, Theory and Design of Stirling Engines, 1999, Regenerative Thermal Machines (Stirling and Vuilleumier Cycle Machines) for Heating and Cooling, 2000; patentee in field; contbr. articles to profl. jours. Recipient Best Paper award ASME, 1992. Mem. Japan Soc. Mech. Engring. (Contbn. award Internat. Conf. Stirling Cycle 1995), Japan Soc. Reintegration and Air Conditioning Engrs., Japan Soc. Thermophysical Protevties. E-mail: kagawa@cc.nda.ac.jp. Office: Nat Def Acad Dept Mech Engr, 1-10-20 Hashirimizu, Yokosuka 239-0811, Japan

KAGAWA, SOHEI, internist, anesthesiologist; b. Hiroshima, Japan, Jan. 9, 1948; s. Kunikichi and Eiko K.; m. Sachiko Kagawa, Feb. 2, 1972; children: Osamu, Hiroshi. MD, Jikei U. Sch. Medicine, Tokyo, 1972, PhD, 1982. Cert. Japanese Bd. Internal Medicine, Japanese Bd. Anesthesiology; med. diploma. Resident physician The Jikei U. Sch. Medicine, Tokyo, 1972-81, Albert Einstein Coll. Medicine, N.Y.C., 1974-75; asst. rsch. physiologist U. Calif., San Francisco, 1979-81; instr. St. Marianna U. Hosp., Kawasaki, Japan, 1983-85, The Jikei U. Sch. Medicine, Tokyo, 1982—; dir. Aiwa Clinic, Tokyo, 1985—; med. cons. Nerima Home Med. Divsn., Tokyo, 1985-93; sch. physician Chofu Med. Assn. Nursing Sch., 1996—. Author: (book) Cardiopulmonary Resucitation, 1979; contbr. articles to profl. jours. Bd. trustees Chofu-city Med. Assn., 1994-96, PTA of The Jikei U. Sch. Medicine, 1997—; dir. Jikokai Inc. Med. Instn. Mem. N.Y. Acad. Sci., Japan Med. Assn. Avocations: golf, classic car racing. Office: Aiwa Clinic, 1-15-47 Sengawa, Chofu 1820002, Japan

KÅGE, JONAS, ballet company artistic director; b. Stockholm; m. Deborah Dobson; 1 child, Isabelle. Student, Royal Swedish Ballet Sch. Mem. Royal Swedish Ballet; mem. Am. Ballet Theatre, 1971-75, soloist, 1972-75, prin. dancer, 1973-75; prin. dancer Stuttgart (Germany) Ballet, 1975-76, Geneva (Switzerland) Ballet, 1976-78, Zürich (Switzerland) Ballet, 1978-88; artistic dir. Malmo (Sweden) Opera Ballet, 1988-95; freelance guest artist, master tchr., 1995-97; artistic dir. Ballet West, Salt Lake City, 1997—; Guest artist Am. Ballet Theatre, 1977—, Frankfort (Germany) Ballet, Basel (Switzerland) Ballet, Royal Swedish Ballet, 1980-81, Deutsche Opera Berlin, 1982, Pitts. Ballet, 1984-85, Nat. Ballet of Can., 1984-85, 85-86, Milw. Ballet, 1984-85, NAPAC Dance Co., 1985-86, Munich Opera Ballet, 1985-86, Nat. Ballet of Portugal, 1986-87, Ariz. Ballet, 1987-88,. Prin. dancer Swan Lake, Coppélia, La Bayadere, Tales of Hoffmann, Lander's Etudes, Shadowplay, Leaves are Fading, Balanchine's Theme and Variations, Gemini, Some Times, Intermezzo, Les Noces, Am. Ballet Theatre, 1971-75, Swan Lake, Don Quixote, Sphinx, Voluntaries, 1977; prin. dancer The Taming of the Shrew, Romeo & Juliet, Onegin, Gemini, La Sacre de Printemps, Greening, Stuttgart Ballet, 1975-76, Apollo, The Four Temperaments, Agon Symphony in C, Who Cares?, Geneva Ballet, 1976-77, Romeo & Juliet, The Sleeping Beauty, Sphinx, Rosalinda, London Festival Ballet (now English Nat. Ballet), 1977, La Sylphide, Cinderella, Swan Lake, Giselle, Romeo & Juliet, 1982-83; prin. dancer Swan Lake, Frankfort Ballet, Giselle, Basel Ballet, Don Quixote, Vienna Ballet, The Taming of the Shrew, Manon, Royal Swedish Ballet, 1980-81, La Sylphide, Deutsche Opera Berlin, 1982, Coppélia, Giselle, Greening, Apollo, Spoleto and Naples, 1982, Swan Lake, Pitts. Ballet Theatre, 1984-85, Romeo & Juliet, Nat. Ballet of Can., 1984-85, Swan Lake, 1985-86; prin. dancer The Merry Widow, Milw. Ballet, 1984-85, Apollo, NAPAC Dance Co., 1985-86, Romeo & Juliet, Munich Opera Ballet, 1985-86, Apollo, Nat. Ballet of Portugal, 1986-87, The Nutcracker, Ariz. Ballet, 1987-88; creator prin. role Chopin Pas de Deux, Malmo Opera Ballet, 1993-94; choreographer Swedish TV, 1983, Simple Symphony, Zurich Ballet, 1984, Baroque Variations, Malmo Opera Ballet, 1988, Swan Lake, 1992-93 (Thalia prize 1993); master of ceremonies dance competition, Swedish TV, 1997. Bd. dirs. Swedish Dance U., Stockholm, Dalhalla amphitheater, Rattvik, Sweden. Recipient Carina Ari Found. for Dance medal, 1994. Avocations: photography, skiing, mountain climbing, horseback riding, wilderness guide training. *

KAGEMORI, NORIKO, geologist, wood anatomist; b. Toyama, Japan, Jan. 9, 1940; d. Tokio Kuroda and Hanae (Okaki) Kuroda; m. Yutaka Kagemori, Apr. 29, 1967; 1 child, Shigeko. BA, Nara (Japan) Woman's U., 1962; MS, Osaka City U., 1964, DSc, 1971. Tchr. Kadoma (Japan) H.S., 1971-74, Katano (Japan) H.S., 1974-92; rschr. Wood Rsch. Inst. Kyoto U., Uji, 1992—; lectr. Nara Woman's U., 1994-97; rschr. Wood Rsch. Inst. Kyoto U., Uji, 1992—; mem. editl. staff City History, Katano City, 1981-86, councilor to cultural properties enterprise, 1993—; expert mem. Com. Counter Measures for Highlands Reservation, Katano City, 1997—. Mem. editl. bd., co-author: Guide Book for Nature Study Around Osaka and Kobe, 1979; editor, author: History of Katano City, Vol. II, Geology and Geography, 1986; co-author: The Plains of Japan, 1987, The Osaka Group, 1993. Mem. Geology Tchrs. Assn. Osaka (founder), Geol. Soc. Japan (Encouragement prize 1972), Internat. Assn. Wood Anatomists, Japan Assn. for Quaternary Rsch. Avocations: chanting of Noh texts, singing Japanese folk songs, playing violin. Office: Kyoto U Wood Rsch Inst, Gokasho, Uji, Kyoto 611-0011, Japan

KAGESON, PER O.R., environmental science consultant; b. Trollhattan, Sweden, Apr. 14, 1947; s. Sven K.O. and Anna-Britta (Edbäck) K.; m. Ann-Marie Lidmark; children: Anna, Lena. Grad., U. Stockholm, 1970; PhD, U. Lund, Sweden, 1997. V.p. Swedish Writer's Union, Stockholm, 1982-84, pres., 1984-87; v.p. Swedish Soc. Nature Conservation, Stockholm, 1987-91; pres. European Fedn. Transport and Environment, Brussels, 1992-96; dir. Nature Assocs., Stockholm, 1996—; mem. Environ. Adv. Coun., Sweden, 1983-94, European Forum on Environment and Sustainable Devel., Brussels, 1997—. Author: Economic Instruments in European Environmental Policy, 1993, Getting The Prices Right, 1993, Growth Versus The Environment—Is There a Trade-off?, 1998. Social Democrat. Avocations: sailing, canoeing, long-distance skating. Office: Nature Associates, Vintertullstorget 20, S-116 43 Stockholm Sweden

KAGEYAMA, TARO, theoretical linguist, educator; b. Kobe City, Japan, Feb. 13, 1949; s. Masao and Shizu (Uragami) K.; m. Reiko Jinnaka Kageyama, Mar. 21, 1978; children: Yoko, Tomoko. BA, Osaka (Japan) U. Fgn. Studies, Japan, 1971; MA, Osaka (Japan) U. Fgn. Studies, 1973; PhD, U. So. Calif., 1977. Lectr. Kobe Gakuin U., Japan, 1973-74; asst. prof. Osaka U., 1978-80, assoc. prof., 1980-87; prof. Kwansei Gakuin U., Japan, 1987—; exec. com. The Linguistic Soc. Japan, 1988-91, 97-2000; editl. bd. The Linguistic Soc. Japan, 1991-96, The English Linguistic Soc. Japan, 1989-93, The English Literary Soc. Japan, 1992-96. Author: Lexical Structures, 1980, Grammar and Word Formation, 1993, Verb Semantics, 1996, Word Formation and Conceptual Structure, 1997; contbr. articles to profl. jours. Recipient 3rd prize Tokyo Inst. for Advanced Studies of Lang., 1973, Ichikawa award Inst. for Rsch. in Lang. Tchg., 1980, Kindaichi award Dr. Kyosuke Kindaichi Meml. Found., Tokyo, 1994. Mem. Linguistic Soc. Am., English Literary Soc. Japan (auditor 1996-98), English Linguistic Soc. (councilor 1998—). E-mail: tkage@sannet.ne.jp. Office: Kwansei Gakuin U, Uegahara 1-1-155, Nishinomiya 662-8501, Japan

KAGGEN, LOIS SHEILA, non-profit organization executive; b. N.Y.C., Jan. 2, 1944; d. Elias and Sylvia (Muntner) K.; m. Harold Jay Burns, June 29, 1969 (div. June 1975); 1 child, David Henry (dec.); m. Michael Francis McCann, Sept. 26, 1984. BS in Fine Arts, Skidmore Coll., 1964; postgrad.,

Cooper Union, 1967-70; MA in Art Edn., CCNY, 1973; PhD in Art Edn., NYU, 1997. Tchr. fine arts grades 7-9 Jr. H.S. 149, Bronx, N.Y., 1967-74; founder, pres. Resources for Artists With Disabilities, N.Y.C., 1987—; Traumatic Brain Injury Consumer Adv., 1977—; mem. adv. bd. com. Art in Edn. Project, N.Y. State Coun. on the Arts, Ctr. for Safety in the Arts, N.Y.C., 1987; cons. Ea. Paralyzed Vets. Assn., Guggenheim Mus. Art, N.Y.C., 1990; mem. bd. advisors Ind. Arts Gallery, Queens Ind. Living Ctr., Jamaica, N.Y., 1987-97, 98; mem. steering com. Ann. Disability Independence Day March, 1992-93, mem. Media Outreach, 1992; provider written and oral testimony in field to orgns. including N.Y. City Coun., 1992, 93, Nat. Coun. on Disability, N.Y.C., 1994, Washington, 1995, N.Y. State Assembly mems. and N.Y. State senators, 1994, 99, N.Y. State Standing Com., 1996, mem. citizens adv. coun. Andrew Heiskell Libr. for the Blind and Physically Handicapped, N.Y.C., 1997—; bd. dirs. Ctr. for Independence of the Disabled of N.Y., Inc., N.Y.C., 1996—, Gov.'s appt. to Traumatic Brain Injury Svcs. Coordinating Coun., Albany, 1997-98, 98—, others; presenter NIH Consensus Devel. Conf. on Rehab. of Persons with Traumatic Brain Injury, Bethesda, Md., 1998, 5th Ann. Conf., Traumatic Brain Injury Program, N.Y. State Dept. Health, Albany, 1998; originator, conf. com. co-organizer, consumer panelist NYU Moses Ctr. for Students with Disabilities and Ctr. for Independence of Disabled of N.Y., Loeb Student Ctr., NYU, N.Y.C., 1998; panel organizer, moderator, presenter Inst. for Rsch. on Women's 16th Ann. Celebration of Our Work Conf., Douglass Coll., Rutgers U., New Brunswick, N.J., 1998; mem. N.Y.C. coun. planning com. info. subcom. Dept. for the Disabled, 2000—; art presenter in field. Photography exhbns. include 80 Washington Sq. East Galleries, N.Y.C., 1977, Soho Photo Gallery, N.Y.C., 1978, 4th St. Photo Gallery, N.Y.C., 1979, Womanart Gallery, N.Y.C., 1979, Leslie-Lohman Gallery, N.Y.C., 1980, 81, Window Gallery, Met. Savs. Bank, N.Y.C., 1980, Cathedral St. John-the-Devine Gallery, N.Y.C., 1980, Donnell Libr. Gallery, 1981; originator, organizer various exhbns. African-Am. Artists with Disabilities, Artists with Phys. Disabilities; contbr. articles, photographs to profl. jours. Mem. disability rights steering com. 504 Dem. Club for Persons with Disabilities, 1987-88, mem. exec. com., 1990—; active Disabled in Action of Greater N.Y., 1989—, Manhattan Borough Pres. Disability Adv. Coun., 1988-98, 99—, access subcom., 2000—, Mayor's Adv. Com. on People with Disabilities, N.Y.C., 1991-93, Citywide Coalition on Disability, N.Y.C., 1994-95, Nat. Inst. on Disability and Rehab. Rsch., Office Spl. Edn. and Rehab. Svcs., U.S. Dept. Edn., Washington, mem. peer rev. registry, 1995—; mem. New York County Dem. Com. 102ED, 1995—; active in assistive signage needs Planning Meeting NYC Coun./Dept. for Disabled, 2000; mem. information sub. com. NYC Coun. Planning Com. Dept. for Disabled, 2000—. Grantee Whitney Mus. Am. Art and the Smithsonian Instn., summer 1967, summer film inst. Stanford U., 1968; Cooper Union scholar, 1967-70; recipient Appreciation cert. Manhattan Borough Pres., 1991, Dean's Disting. Alumni Achievement award NYU, N.Y.C., 1998. Mem. Coll. Art Assn. (com. mems. with disabilities for accessible programs and places 1990—), N.Y.C. Coun. dept. for disabled. Office: Resources for Artists with Disabilities 77 7th Ave Ste PH-H New York NY 10011-6645

KAGI, JEREMIAS H.R., biochemist, educator; b. Winterthur, Zürich, Switzerland, Mar. 2, 1930; s. Rudolf W. and Anna (Moser) K.; m. Birte Ostergaard, July 25, 1963; children: Anne Marie, Karen Elisabeth, Ellen Margrit. MD, U. Zürich, 1956. Rsch. fellow Harvard Med. Sch., Boston, 1957-59, rsch. assoc., 1959-63, assoc. medicine, 1964-68, asst. prof. medicine, 1968-70; assoc. prof. biochemistry U. Zürich, 1970-73, full prof. biochemistry, 1973-97, prof. biochemistry emeritus, 1997—; guest investigator Carlsberg Lab., Copenhagen, 1961-63. Recipient Raulin award Ind. Soc. for Trace Element Rsch. in Humans, Stockholm, 1992; named hon. prof. Med. U. Beijing, 1993. Mem. Swiss Reformed Ch. Office: U Zürich Biochem Inst, Winterhurerstrasse 190, CH-8057 Zürich Switzerland

KAHALAS, HARVEY, business educator; b. Boston, Dec. 3, 1941; s. James and Betty (Bonfeld) K.; m. Dianne Barbara Levine, Sept. 2, 1963; children: Wendy Elizabeth, Stacy Michele. BS, Boston U., 1965; MBA, U. Mich., 1966; PhD, U. Mass., 1971. Data processing coord. Ford Motor Co., Wayne, Mich., 1963-66; lectr. Salem (Mass.) State Coll., 1966-68; asst. prof. bus. Worcester (Mass.) Poly. Inst., 1970-72; asst. prof. Va. Poly. Inst. and State U., Blacksburg, 1972-75, assoc. prof., 1975-77; assoc. prof. SUNY, Albany, 1977-79, assoc. dean, 1979-81, prof., 1979-89, dean, 1981-87; pres. HKE Inc., 1987-97; prof. U. Mass., Lowell, 1989-94, dean, 1989-94, exec. dir. Ctr. Indsl. Competitiveness, 1990-94; Commonwealth disting. prof. U. Mass., 1994-97; dir. Ctr. for Bus. Rsch. and Competitiveness, U. Mass., Dartmouth, 1994-97; prof., dean Wayne State U., 1997—; program dir. Aspen Inst., 1994-97; cons. Aspen Inst./Fund for Corp. Initiatives, N.Y.C., 1980-94, GE, Schenectady, N.Y., 1981-85, GM, Tarrytown, N.Y., 1987-89; bd. dirs. Lumigen Inc., Southfield, Mich. Contbr. articles to profl. jours. Bd. dirs. Fund for Corp. Initiatives, N.Y.C., 1980—, Nat. Found. Ileitis and Colitis, Albany, 1982-89, Blue Cross Northeastern N.Y., Albany, 1983-89, Capital Dist. Bus. Rev., Albany, 1984—, Greater Detroit Area Health Coun., 1998—. Named Disting. Alumni, U. Mass., 1982, Disting. Lectr. USIA, 1985, Am. Participant USIA, 1989; Fulbright scholar, 1987, 88, Aspen Inst. scholar, 1997. Mem. Fulbright Assn. (life), Acad. Mgmt. (treas. 1971-73, mem. exec. com.), Human Resource Planning Soc. (hon.), Human Resource Systems Profls. (hon.), Pers. Accreditation Inst. (life), Beta Gamma Sigma, Sigma Iota Epsilon, Delta Tau Kappa. Office: Wayne State Univ Sch Bus Adm 226 Prentis Bld 5201 Cass Ave Detroit MI 48202-3930

KAHÁN, LLONA LASZLO, biochemist; b. Budapest, Hungary, Feb. 9, 1923; d. Arpad and Margit (Szauer) Laszlo; m. Agost Kahán, May 5, 1942 (div. 1977); 1 child, Zsuzsanna; m. Imre Molnar, Feb. 8, 1994 (dec. 1996). Dr. nat. scis., Eotvos Lorand U., 1952, PhD, 1968; DSc, Semmelweis Med. U., 1996. Chem. rsch. worker Rsch. Lab. Chinoin Pharm. Factory, Budapest, 1952-54; head lab. dept. internal medicine Szentgyorgyi Albert U., Szeged, Hungary, 1955-60, head. rsch. lab. dept. ophthalmology, 1960-77; head. rsch. lab. dept. ophthalmology Semmelweis U., Budapest, 1977—; lectr. ophthal. biochemistry Szentgyorgyi Albert Med. U., Semmelweis Med. U. Author: Zur Biochemie des Auges, 1982, Studies of Urobilinoids, 1961, Biochemistry of Vision, 1986; contbr. chpt. to book; patentee in field. Travel grantee King's Coll. Hosp., 1962, grantee, 1965, Dry Eye Inst., 1984. Mem. Assn. for Eye Rsch., Joint European Rsch. Meetings on Ophthalmology and Vision. Office: Semmelweis Med U, Dept Ophthalmology, 1068 Budapest Hungary

KAHANE, SIMONA ESTHER, virology researcher; b. Bucharest, Romania, May 6, 1945; d. Heinrich and Ena (Reischer) K. BSc, Technion-Chemistry, Israel, 1967, MSc, 1969; PhD, Hebrew U., Jerusalem, 1977. Asst. Technion-Chemistry, Haifa, 1967-69, Molecular Biology, Jerusalem, 1971-77; rsch. faculty health scis. Ben Gurion U., Beer Sheva, Israel, 1977—. Grantee Israel Office Sci., 1991-94, 94-96, Ministry Health Israel, 1995-97, US.-Israel BSF, 1996-99, Kenen Kajemet, 1999-00. Office: Soroka Hosp, Dept Virology, 84367 Beer Sheva Israel

KÄHÄRÄ, VEIKKO JOHANNES, physician, researcher; b. Mikkeli, Savo, Finland, Dec. 28, 1953; s. Onni Pellerro Kähärä and Sulvi Lyytikäinen; m. Aira Irmeli Etelämäki; 1 child, Otso. BA, Helsinki (Finland) U., 1974; MD, Tampere (Finland) U., 1980, PhD, 1999. Neuroradiologist Helsinki U., 1970-94, Tampere U., 1994—. Author: Angiographie Results and Patient Outcome of Neurovascular Embolotherapy, 1997.

KAHILL, ARMAND GEORGE, mechanical engineer; b. Alexandria, Egypt, Dec. 23, 1928; s. George Joseph and Linda (Accaoui) K. Grad., Victoria Coll., Alexandria, Egypt, 1946, British Inst. Engring. Tech., London, 1957. Clk. Barclays Bank, Alexandria, Egypt, 1946-50; tech. sales mgr. Ch. Geahel Fils, Alexandria, Egypt, 1950-57; self-employed Alexandria, Egypt, 1958-64; mng. dir. Zenith Internat., Beirut, Lebanon, 1965-75, Alexandria, Egypt, 1976—. Mem. Old Victorian Assn. (editor mag. and newsletter 1978-96, hon. sec. gen.), Club Alexandria. Avocation: art collecting. Office: Zenith Internat, 7 Greek Patriarchate St, 21131 Alexandria Egypt

KAHIRSKY, VLADIMIR GRIOGRIEVICH, energetics specialist, educator; b. Lopatino, Penza, Russia, June 3, 1914; s. Grigoriy Pavlovich and Alexandra Vasilyevna (Zemskova) K.; m. Nina Ivanovna L., June 29, 1939; children: Elena, Irena. Student, Electro-Mech. Coll., Saratov, USSR, 1933; engr.-technologist, Inst. Steel and Alloys, Moscow, 1941, Candidate of Scis., 1950; DSc, Chem.-Tech. Inst., Dnepropetrovsk, USSR, 1966. Technician chem. factory, Rybenzonye, Ukraine, USSR, 1933-36; engr. power sta., Saratov, USSR, 1944-45; engr.-controller State Planning Orgn., 1945-49; dir. Chem. Inst. Saratov State U., 1949-59; chief chair of power energetics Saratov Tech. U., 1958-85; prof. Tech. U. Saratov, 1959-99. Author: Experimental Basis of Complex Energy-Technological Use of Fuels, 1981, Thermal Processing of Shales and Their Energy-Technological Use, 1987; contbr. articles to profl. jours. Recipient Order of Honor Govt., 1986, Gold Medla Exhibn. Econ. Achievements, 1989; named Honored Scientist of Russia, 1980, Honored Inventor, Moscow. Mem. Soc. Spreading Scientific and Polit. Knowledge (bd. dirs. 1972-76). Communist. Avocations: collecting memoirs. Home: Sovetskaya 72/82, 410056 Saratov Russia Office: Saratov Tech U, Politechicheskaya 17, 410016 Saratov Russia

KAHN, ALAN EDWIN, lawyer; b. N.Y.C., Aug. 9, 1929; s. Joseph and Harriet Rose (Rubel) K.; m. Regina Wolf, Aug. 7, 1960 (div. Jan. 1978); 1 child, Jolie Galen; m. Patricia Ann Dugan, June 4, 1978. BBA, CCNY, 1950; JD, Bklyn. Law Sch., 1956. Bar: N.Y. 1956, U.S. Dist. Ct. (so. and ea. dists.) N.Y. 1978, U.S. Tax Ct. 1978; CPA, N.Y. Staff asst.-acct. Feinberg, Jacobs & Furman, N.Y.C., 1956-57; pvt. practice N.Y.C., 1957-96, 98—; prin. Law Office of Alan E. Kahn, N.Y.C., 1957-99; sr. ptnr. Kahn, Boyd, Levychin CPAs, N.Y.C., 1993; pvt. practice, 1998—; tax cons. to various nonprofit orgns., N.Y.C., 1977—. Cons. Vol. Lawyers for the Arts, N.Y.C., 1978—. Sgt. U.S. Army, 1951-52. Mem. ATLA (mem. com. 1990—), N.Y. State Bar Assn. (elder law com.), N.Y. State Trial Lawyers Assn. (chmn. subcom. on legis. estate and trusts 1979, spkr. bd. 1990—, mem. com. 1991—, chair 2000—), N.Y. County Lawyers Assn. (taxation com. 1988—, sec. com. on taxation 1996-2000, chair com. on taxation 2000—), Spkr.'s Bur., Assn. Trial Lawyers City N.Y., Jewish Lawyers Guild, N.Y. State Soc. CPAs, Nat. Sculpture Soc. (patron mem.), Odd Fellows (grand adv. bd. N.Y. chpt. 1979-80, gen. counsel grand lodge 1989—), Mchts. Club (bd. govs., asst. treas., treas. and gov. 1992—, award chmn. legal com. 1995—). Democrat. Avocation: collecting prints, paintings and oriental ceramics. Home: 370 1st Ave New York NY 10010-4923 Office: 67 Wall St New York NY 10005-3101

KAHN, DAVID MILLER, lawyer; b. Port Chester, N.Y., Apr. 21, 1925; m. Barbara Heller, May 9, 1952; children: William, James, Caroline. BA, U. Ky., 1947; LLB cum laude, N.Y. Law Sch., 1950. Bar: N.Y. 1951, U.S. Dist. Ct. (ea. and so. dists.) N.Y. 1953, U.S. Supreme Ct. 1958. Sole practice White Plains, N.Y., 1951-60; ptnr. Kahn & Rubin, White Plains, 1960-66, Kahn & Goldman, White Plains, 1967-80; sr. ptnr. Kahn & Landau, White Plains, Palm Beach, Fla., 1980-88, Kahn and Kahn, Fla., N.Y., 1988-95, Kahn, Kahn & Scutieri Esq., Palm Beach Gardens, 1995—; lectr. N.Y. Law Sch., 1982—; spl. counsel Village Port Chester, N.Y., 1960-63; commr. of appraisal Westchester County Supreme Ct., 1973-77; counsel Chemplex Industries, Inc., BIS Communications Corp., Bilbar Realty Co. Chmn. Westchester County Citizens for Eisenhower, 1950-52; pres. Westchester County Young Reps. Clubs, 1958-60; founder, chmn. bd. dirs. Port Chester-Rye Town Vol. Ambulance Corps, 1968-77; pres. Driftwood Corp., Amagansette, L.I., N.Y., 1984-91. Served with Counter Intelligence Corps USAF, 1942-46. Recipient John Marshall Harlan fellow N.Y. Law Sch., 1990-93. Fellow Am. Acad. Matrimonial Lawyers (bd. govs. N.Y. chpt. 1976-79); mem. ABA, N.Y. State Bar Assn., Westchester County Bar Assn., White Plains Bar Assn., N.Y. Law Sch. Alumni Assn. (bd. dirs. 1970-80), Elmwood C.C. (legal counsel), Eastpointe Country Club. Home and Office: 6419 Eastpointe Pines St Palm Bch Gdns FL 33418-6906 also: 175 Main St White Plains NY 10601-3105

KAHN, ELLIS IRVIN, lawyer; b. Charleston, S.C., Jan. 18, 1936; s. Robert and Estelle Harriet (Kaminski) K.; m. Janice Weinstein, Aug. 11, 1963; children: Justin Simon, David Israel, Cynthia Kahn Nirenblatt. AB in Polit. Sci., The Citadel, 1958; JD, U. S.C., 1961. Bar: S.C. 1961, U.S. Ct. Appeals (5th cir.) 1963, U.S. Ct. Appeals (4th cir.) 1964, U.S. Supreme Ct. 1970, D.C. 1978, U.S. Claims Ct. 1988; diplomate Nat. Bd. Trial Advocacy, Am. Bd. Profl. Liability Attys. (trustee 1989—). Law clk. U.S. Dist. Ct. S.C., 1964-66; prin. Kahn Law Firm, Charleston; adj. prof. med.-legal jurisprudence Med. U. S.C., 1978-87; mem. rules com. U.S. Dist. Ct., 1984-96. Chmn. campaign Charleston Jewish Fedn., 1986-87, pres., 1988-90, S.C. Organ Procurment Agy., 1987-94, chmn. bd. 1989-94, mem. nat. coun. Am. Israel Pub. Affairs Com., 1982-88, Hebrew Benevolent Soc., pres., 1994-96; mem. Hebrew Orphan Soc. Capt. USAF, 1961-64. Fellow Internat. Soc. Barristers; mem. S.C. Bar, ABA, ATLA (state committeeman 1970-74), S.C. Trial Lawyers Assn. (pres. 1976-77), 4th Cir. Jud. Conf. (permanent mem.). Home: 316 Confederate Cir Charleston SC 29407-7431 Office: PO Box 898 Charleston SC 29402-0898

KAHN, FREDRICK HENRY, internist; b. L.A., Aug. 26, 1925; s. Julius and Josephine Leone (Langdon) K.; m. Barbara Ruth Visscher, Feb. 14, 1952; children: Susan, Kathryn, William. AB, Stanford U., 1947, MD, 1951. Diplomate Am. Bd. Internal Medicine. Rotating intern San Francisco Gen. Hosp., 1950-51, fellow pathology, 1951-52; resident medicine Los Angeles VA Hosp., 1954-57, sr. resident, 1956-57; asst. clin. prof. medicine UCLA Sch. Medicine, 1957-91; attending physician Cedars Sinai Med. Ctr., L.A., 1957-96, attending physician emeritus, 1996—; attending physician UCLA, 1957-95; med. advisor Vis. Nurse Assn., Los Angeles, 1957-87. Contbr. articles to med. jours.; inventor blow-through high altitude chamber; promoter iodine method of personal water disinfection for travelers and hikers. Served with USNR, 1943-46; lt. (M.C.), USNR, 1952-54. Fellow ACP; mem. AMA, Los Angeles County Internal Medicine Soc., Am. Handel Soc., Sierra Club. Avocations: hiking, collecting and listening to baroque music. Home: 3309 Corinth Ave Los Angeles CA 90066-1312

KAHN, HERTA HESS (MRS. HOWARD KAHN), retired stockbroker; b. Wuerzburg, Germany; came to U.S., 1939, naturalized, 1944; d. Ferdinand and Lilly (Suesser) Hess; m. Herbert Levy, Jan. 4, 1947 (dec. 1966); 1 dau., Linda; m. Howard Kahn, 1970 (dec. 1997). Student, Northwestern U. Sch. Commerce, 1947-49, 51-56. Joined Paine, Webber, Jackson & Curtis, Inc., Chgo., 1941; registered rep. Paine, Webber Inc., 1955-94; acct. v.p., 1955-86; v.p. investments Paine, Webber Inc., 1986-94, ret., 1994; mktg. cons., 1995—. Author: What Every Woman Should Know About Investing Her Money, 1968. Hon. life mem. nat. commn., hon. life mem. Chgo. exec. com. Anti-Defamation League B'nai B'rith; bd. dirs. Found. Hearing and Speech Rehab. at Northwestern U., Chgo. Mem. N.Y. Soc. Security Analysts, Investment Analysts Soc. Chgo., Assn. for Investment Mgmt. and Rsch., Chgo. Fin. Exch. Chgo Crime Commn. Clubs: Northmoor Country (Highland Park, Ill.); Standard, Economic, Execs. (Chgo.); Tamarisk Country (Rancho Mirage, Calif.).

KAHN, J. MEYER, brewery company executive; b. Pretoria, Gautene, South Africa, June 29, 1939; s. Ben and Sarah (Feinbuum) K.; m. Wynette Sandra Asmer, Dec. 1, 1968; children: Deanne, Maywey. BA in Law, U. Pretoria, South Africa, 1962, MBA, 1966, D.Comm. (hon.), 1981. Exec. chmn. O.K. Bazaars Ltd., South Africa; group mng. dir. S.A.B. Ltd., South Africa, exec. chmn.; chief exec. S.A. Powice Svc., 1997-99; chmn. S.A.B. plc, U.K., 1999—. Mem. State Pres. Econ. Adv. Coun.; pres. South Africa Found. Fellow Assn. of Marketers. Avocation: golf. Office: SAB plc Box 1099, 2 Jan Smuts Ave Braameonten, Gauten JHB 2000, South Africa

KAHN, JAMES STEVEN, retired museum director; b. N.Y.C., Oct. 14, 1931; 3 children. BS in Geology, CCNY, 1952; MS in Minerology, Pa. State U., 1954; PhD in Geol. Sci., U. Chgo., 1956. Instr. U. R.I., Kingston, 1957, asst. prof., 1958-60, research assoc. Narragansett Marine Lab., 1957-60; group leader U. Calif., Livermore, 1960-70; dept. head Physics Internat. Co., San Leandro, Calif., 1970-71; div. head geophysics U. Calif., Livermore, 1971-75; dep. assoc. dir. human resources U. Calif., 1975-78, assoc. dir. nuclear testing, 1978-80, dep. dir. lab., 1980-87; pres., chief exec. officer, dir. Mus. Sci. and Industry, Chgo., 1987-97; retired, emeritus; trustee Mus. Sci. and Industry; mem. math. scis. edn. bd. NAS, 1991-94; chmn. sci. adv. com. Gov. Ill., 1994-98; IMAX Corp. Co-author: Statistical Analysis in Geological Sciences, 1962, Microstructure, 1968; contbr. articles to scientific jours. Bd. dirs. Franklin and Eleanor Roosevelt Inst., Dubuque (Iowa) Art Inst., 1999—; rector sci. and medicine Lincoln Acad. Ill.; mem., vice-chmn. Bd. Natural Resources and Conservation, State of Ill. Centennial fellow Pa. State U. Coll. Earth and Mineral Scis., 1996. Fellow Geol. Soc. Am.; mem. Quadrangle Club, Missions Hills (Calif.) Country Club, Sigma Xi. Unitarian.

KAHN, KALJU, biochemist, researcher; b. Tallinn, Estonia, Jan. 9, 1970; s. Harry and Leida Kahn; m. Iiris Aavaksaar, Dec. 14, 1992; 1 child, Karoli. Jr. scientist inst. Chem. and Biol. Physics, Tallinn, 1988; rsch. scientist Inst. Exptl. Biology, Tallinn, 1992-94; sci. advisor U. Tartu, Estonia, 1994; postdoctoral rschr. U. Calif., Santa Barbara, 1998—; mentor, translator Internat. Chemistry Olympiad, Oslo, 1994. Contbr. articles to profl. jours. Mem. AAAS, Am. Chem. Soc., Sigma Xi. E-mail: kalju@bioorganic.ucsb.edu. Office: U Calif Chemistry Dept Santa Barbara CA 93106

KAHN, MARC LESLIE, orthopedic surgeon; b. Phila., Mar. 12, 1956; s. Sigmund and Joanne (Pokras) K.; divorced; two children. AB, Lafayette Coll., 1978; MD, Hahnemann Med. Coll., 1982. Resident in orthopedics Monmouth Med. Ctr., Long Branch, N.J., 1987; surgeon, maj. U.S. Army, Ft. Dix, N.J., 1987-91; orthopedic surgeon Garden State Orthopedics, Pennsauken, N.J., 1991—. Fellow Am. Acad. Orthopedic Surgeons; mem. AMA, N.J. Med. Soc., Camden County Med. Soc., N.J. Orthopedic Soc. Home: 6 Regan Ct Voorhees NJ 08043

KAHN, RONALD N., investment researcher; b. Schenectady, N.Y., Aug. 6, 1956; s. Ernest H. and Gloria K. Kahn; m. Bonnie Menes, Sept. 2, 1984. AB in Physics, Princeton U., 1978; PhD in Physics, Harvard U., 1985. Dir. rsch. Barra, Inc., Berkeley, Calif., 1991-98; mng. dir. Barclay Global Investors, San Francisco, 1998—. Editorial adv. bd. Jour. Portfolio Mgmt., N.Y.C., 1998—, Jour. Investment Cons., Denver, 1998—; author: Active Portfolio Management, 1995, 2d edit., 2000; contbr. articles to profl. jours. Recipient Journalism award Investment Mgmt. Cons. Assoc., Denver, 1995; Mass Media Sci. fellow AAAS, Washington, 1983. Avocations: travel, reading. E-mail: ron.kahn@barclaysglobal.com. Office: Barclays Global Investors 45 Fremont St San Francisco CA 94105-2204

KAHRE, RAGNAR E., engineering executive; b. Stockholm, Dec. 30, 1963; s. Bjorn R. and Eva J. (Basch) K. MSc, Royal Inst. Tech., Stockholm, 1997. Rsch. engr. Ericsson, Stockholm, 1988-90; systems engr. Telia, Malmo, Sweden, 1990-93; tech. attaché Swedish Consulate, San Francisco, 1993-94; project mgr. Telia, Stockholm, 1994-96; engring. mgr. Ericsson, Stockholm, Sweden, 1996-98; dir. engring. UPC Sweden, Stockholm, 1998-99; v.p. tech. Bredbandsbolaget, Stockholm, 1999—. Patentee in field. 2d lt. Swedish Army, 1984-85. Mem. IEEE, Soc. Cable TV Engrs. Home: Asogatan 133, 11624 Stockholm Sweden Office: Bredbandsbolaget, Smalanelsgatan 12, 11146 Stockholm Sweden

KAHUMBA, RICHARD KARIUKI WANYOIKE, sales and marketing executive; b. Maranga, Kenya, Sept. 1953; s. Wilfred Karume and Edith Njeri (Kahumba) Wanyoike; m. Beatrace Waitaga Mburu, Oct. 1962; children: Edith Njeri, Wilfred Kungu, Kevin Kamau. Diploma in salesmanship, Nat. Sch. Salesmanship, 1984; diploma in retail salesmanship, Mng. and Mktg. Sales Assn., 1990, higher diploma in sales mktg., 1992. Debt collector, credit contr. Chermered Flag Ltd., Touring, Kenya, 1981-83; sales and mktg. staff Farmer's Choice Ltd., Kenya, 1985-87, Procter and Gamble, Kenya, 1987-95; sales coord. Hatabor Rainbow Blooms Ltd., Kenya, 1998-99; regional sales mgr. Population Svcs. Internat., Kenya, 1999-2000; sales and mktg. exec. Roshni Distbrs. Ltd., Kenya, 2000—; market rschr. Proctor & Gamble, Kenya, 1993-95. Mem. Inst. Profl. Sales U.K. Democrat. Avocations: traveling, watching football, reading professional journals, public speaking. Home: PO Box 50147, Nairobi Kenya Office: PO Box 43937, Nairobi Kenya

KAI, MASAAKI, pharmacist, educator, researcher; b. Taketa, Ohita, Japan, Oct. 1, 1951; parents Sadamu and Sadako (Misaka) K.; m. Mayumi Imahuku, Apr. 17, 1977; children: Anna, Natsumi. BS, Kyushu U., Fukuoka, Japan, 1974, MS, 1977, PhD, 1981. Cert. pharmacist, clin. inspector, radiol. inspector. Postdoctoral rsch. assoc. U. Tenn., Memphis, 1981-83; from asst. prof. to assoc. prof. Kyushu U., Fukuoka, 1983-98; prof. Nagasaki (Japan) U., 1998—. Author: (book) Experimental Chemistry, 1991; contbr. articles to profl. jours. Mem. Pharm. Soc. Japan, Japan Soc. for Analytical Chemistry (Analytical Chemistry award for Young Rschrs. 1986), Japan Soc. for Clin. Chemistry, Am. Chem. Soc., Soc. Neurosci. E-mail: ms-kai@net.nagasaki-u.ac.jp. Office: Nagasaki U Sch Pharm Scis, Bunkyo-Machi, 852-8521 Nagasaki Japan

KAI, SHOICHI, physics educator; b. Ohita, Japan, Oct. 31, 1947; s. Katumi and Misaho (Inoue) K.; m. Keiko Nishimura, Apr. 23, 1978; children: Masayoshi, Kazuki, Satoru. BS, Miyazaki U., Japan, 1970; MS, Kyushu U., Fukuoka, Japan, 1974, PhD, 1977. Asst. prof. Kyushu U., Fukuoka, 1977-79; postdoctoral fellow Stanford (Calif.) U., 1979-82; assoc. prof. physics and electronics Kyushu Inst. Tech., Kitakyushu, Japan, 1982-88, prof. physics and electronics, 1988-93; prof. applied physics Kyushu U., Fukuoka, Japan, 1994—. Author: Noise in Nonlinear Dynamical Systems, 1989, Liquid Crystal Dictionary, 1988, Pattern Formation, 1991; editor: Pattern Formation in Complex Dissipative Systems, 1992; contbr. more than 160 articles to profl. jours. Cons. Kitakyushu City, Japan, 1986-87. Grantee Yamada Sci. Found., Osaka, 1985, Kajima Found., Tokyo, 1991, Shimadzu Sci. Found., Kyoto, 1991. Mem. Am. Phys. Soc., Phys. Soc. Japan, Soc. Applied Physics Japan, Inst. of Elec. Engring. (councilor 1989-91), Soc. of Sci. on Form (councilor 1985—), Inst. of E.I.C.E., Japanese Liquid Crystal Soc. (councilor 1998-2000). Avocations: fishing, archaeology. Home: Kokura Wakazono 1-25-24, Kitakyushu 802-0816, Japan Office: Kyushu U, Dept Applied Physics, Fukuoka 812-8581, Japan

KAI, TATSUYA, cardiologist; b. Osaka, Japan, Oct. 24, 1966; s. Kohzou and Noriko (Yamashita) K.; m. Rieko Furuya, Oct. 22, 1995; 1 child, Sh iori K. BM, Kinki U., Osaka-sayama, 1992, MD, 1998. Trainee Kinki U. Hosp., Osaka-sayama, 1992-94, asst., 1998—. Contbr. articles to profl. jours. Fellow Japanese Soc. Internal Medicine; mem. Am. Soc. Hypertension, Japanese Soc. Hypertension, Japanese Circulation Soc., Japanese Coll. Cardiology. Avocations: playing instruments, movies, museums. Office: Kinki U Sch Medicine, 377-2 Ohno-higashi, Osaka-sayama, Osaka 589-8511, Japan

KAID, LYNDA LEE, communications educator; b. Harrisburg, Ill., Aug. 22, 1948; d. Billy Cameron and Leona Elizabeth (Oglesby) K.; m. Clifford Alan Jones. BA, So. Ill. U., 1970, MS, 1972, PhD, 1974. Prof. dept. comm. U. Okla., Norman, 1974—, dir. Polit. Comm. Ctr., 1984—; mem. adv. bd. Mus. of Broadcast Comm., Chgo., 1990—. Co-author: Political Campaign Communication: A Bibliography and Guide to the Literature, 1974 (Outstanding Reference Book of 1974, Choice mag.); co-editor Political Communication Yearbook 1984, 1985, Political Campaign Communication: A Bibliography and Guide to the Literature, Vol. 2, 1973-1982, 1985, New Perspectives on Political Advertising, 1986, The Political Commercial Archive: A Catalog and Guide to the Collection, 1991, Mediated Politics in Two Cultures: Presidential Campaigning in the United States and France, 1991, Die Massenmedien im Wahlkampf, 1993, The Lynching of Language: Gender, Politics and Power in the Hill-Thomas Hearings, 1996, Political Advertising in Western Democracies: Parties and Candidates on Television, 1995, The Electronic Election, 1999; contbr. numerous articles to profl. jours. Recipient Rsch. award on Polit. Advt., NSF & Nat. Endowment for Humanities, 1992—; Fulbright scholar USIA-Fulbright Commn., Western Europe, 1987-88, 1997. Mem. Am. Film Inst., League of Women Voters, Internat. Comm. Assn. (pres. polit. comm. divsn. 1979-81). Avocation: internat. travel. Office: U Okla Polit Comm Ctr 610 Elm Ave Norman OK 73019-2080

KAIER, EDWARD JOHN, lawyer; b. Sewickley, Pa., Sept. 23, 1945; s. Edward Anthony and Mary Patricia (Crimmins) K.; m. Annette Thomas, July 31, 1976; children: Elizabeth Anne, Charles Crimmins, Thomas Edward. AB, Harvard U., 1967; JD, U. Pa., 1970. Bar: D.C. 1970, Pa. 1970, U.S. Dist. Ct. (ea. dist.) Pa. 1971, U.S. Ct. Appeals (3rd and D.C. cirs.) 1971, U.S. Dist. Ct. D.C., 1971. Law clk. to presiding justice U.S. Dist. Ct. for D.C., Washington, 1970-71; assoc. Dechert Price & Rhoads, Phila., 1971-74; ptnr. Kaier and Kaier, Phila., 1974-77, Hepburn Willcox Hamilton & Putnam, Phila., 1977—; pres. Savoy Co., Phila., 1978-80; bd. dirs. Mgrs. Funds, Norwalk, Conn., Mgrs. AMG Funds, Boston. Vice chmn. Rosemont (Pa.) Sch. of Holy Child, 1981-90. Mem. ABA, Phila. Bar Assn. (chmn. office practice com. probate sect. 1987-90, exec. com. 1990-92), Merion Cricket Club, Phila. Club, Phila. Country Club, Avalon Yacht Club (trustee

1987-90, 92-93, treas. 1990-92), Harvard-Radcliffe Club (Phila., sec. 1989—). Republican. Roman Catholic. Avocations: sailing, golf. Home: 111 N Lowrys Ln Rosemont PA 19010-1408 Office: Hepburn Willcox Hamilton & Putnam 1100 One Penn Ctr Philadelphia PA 19103

KAIFU, NORIO, astronomer; b. Niigata, Japan, Sept. 21, 1943; s. Yasuyoshi and Kiyoko K.; m. Shigemi, May 3, 1968; children: Yohsuke, Kohji, Kenzoh, Takeshi. Grad., U. Tokyo, 1962, PhD, 1972. Rsch. assoc. Dept. Astronomy, U. Tokyo, Japan, 1969-79; assoc. prof. Tokyo Astron. Obs., U. Tokyo, 1979-88; prof., dir. Nobeyama (Japan) Radio Obs., Nat. Astron. Obs., 1988-90; vice dir. Nat. Astronomy Obs., Mitaka, Japan, 1992-96, dir. Subaru Telescope project, 1996-2000; nat. gen. dir. Astronomy Obs., Mitaka, Japan, 2000—. Co-author: Cosmic Radio Astronomy, 1988, Molecular Processes in Space, 1990; author 10 books; contbr. numerous papers to profl. jours. Recipient Nishina Meml. award, 1987, Japan Acad. award, 1998. Mem. Nat. Astron. Obs. (bd. dirs 1988—), Astron. Soc. Japan (bd. dirs. 1980—), Internat. Astron. Union (v.p. 1997—), Royal Astron. Soc. (assoc.). Achievements include construction of 45-mm-wave telescope at Nobeyama Radio Observatory, 8.2 Subaru telescope at Manna Kea; detection of many new interstellar molecules in dark clouds. Office: Nat Astron Obs, Osawa 2-21-1, Mitaka Tokyo Japan

KAIHO, TAKASHI, bank executive. CEO Daiwa Bank, Osaka, Japan, 1996—. Office: Daiwa Bank, 2-2-1 Bingomachi, 541 Osaka Japan

KAIJSER, GÖRAN FRITZ, aviations products marketing, consultant; b. Stockholm, 1934; s. Rolf and Ingrid (Kjellin) K.; m. Ulla B.E. Kaijser, 1963; children: Mats, Malin, Anna. Grad., Karlstad Högre Allmänna Läroverk, Karlstad, Sweden, 1953; MS in Physics, Royal Inst. of Tech., 1960; post-grad., U. Stockholm, Sweden, 1979. Asst. tchr. Royal Tech. Inst., 1958-60; rschr. AB Atomenergi, Stockholm, 1959-60; system devel. dir. guided weapons SW Def. Materiel Adminstrn., 1960-76; mktg. dir. Swedair AB, 1976-88; mng. dir. Aerotech Trade AB, 1989-91, Kaitech Trade AB, 1992—. Officer Swedish Air Force Res., 1956-99. Mem. Assn. of Old Crows, The Mil. Tech. Assn., Rotary Internat. Home: Rinkebyvägen 21, SE-17237 Sundbyberg Sweden Office: Kaitech Trade AB, Ekovägen 12, 172 37 Sundbyberg Sweden

KAIKURANTA, TERHO OTSO TAPIO, physicist, researcher; b. Kangasniemi, Finland, May 5, 1966; s. Ahti Tapio and Leena Kaarina Kaikuranta; m. Heli Talvikki Pusa, Nov. 16, 1996; 1 child, Teemu Matias. MSc in Physics, U. Oulu, Finland, 1991. Rsch. asst. Acad. Finland, Oulu, 1989; rsch. asst. dept. physics U. Oulu, 1989-91; physicist DCA Instruments Ltd., Turku, Finland, 1991-95; project mgr. Nokia Mobile Phones, Salo, Finland, 1995-98; rsch. mgr. Nokia Mobile Phones, Salo, 1998—. Safety officer Finnish Assn. Sport Diving, Helsinki, 1996-99. Cpl. Finland Army Engrs., 1987-88. Mem. Internat. Soc. for Optical Engring., Finnish Optical Soc. Achievements include several patent applications. Avocations: sport diving, diving instructing. E-mail: terho.kaikuranta@nokia.com. Fax: 358-10-5053068. Office: Nokia Mobile Phones, Joensuunkatu 7 E, 24101 Salo Finland

KAIL, KONRAD, physician; b. Iowa City, July 7, 1949; s. Joseph Andrew Kail and Jean Lucille (Peterson) Tienan; m. Jane Marie Petersen, Jan. 5, 1973. BS in Biology, U. Houston, 1974; BS in Medicine, Baylor Coll. Medicine, 1976; ND, Nat. Coll. Naturopathic Medicine, 1983; DACNFM, Am. Coll. Naturopathic Family, Medicine, 1995. Lic. naturopathic physician. Cardiac-catherization technician St. Luke's/Tex. Children's Hosp., Houston, 1972-75; physician's asst. various clinics, Silver City, N.Mex., 1976-80; dir. Naturopathic Wheeling and Healing Around Country Bike Tour, 1983-84; chmn. bd. dirs. U.S. Complementary Health, Inc., Phoenix, 1995—; bd. dirs., co-founder, mem. faculty S.W. Coll. of Naturopathic Medicine, Phoenix, 1996—; owner, operator Naturopathic Family Care, Inc., Phoenix, 1990—; cons. Ins. Cos., Nutrient Supplement Cos., Govt. Agys., 1985—; mem. adv. bd. NIH Nat. Ctr. for Complementary and Alternative Medicine, 1999—. Editor: Alternative Medicine, 1994; contbr. articles to profl. jours. Mem. adv. bd. Inst. for Natural Medicine; v.p. SCAVE-USA, Inc.; pres. MIC-USA, Inc. With USN Res., 1971-76. Fellow Am. Assn. Naturopathic Physicians (chmn. scientific affil. 1986-97, pres. 1992-94, Physician of Yr. 1997), Am. Coll. Naturopathic Family Practice (chmn., pres. 1995—). Green Party. Avocations: ultimate frisbee, bicycling, skiing, golf. Office: Naturopathic Family Care 13832 N 32nd St Ste C2-4 Phoenix AZ 85032-5616

KAILA, LAURI JAAKKO, entomologist, curator, researcher; b. Helsinki, Finland, Feb. 20, 1967; s. Sakari Yrjäna and Marja Leena (Itkonen) K.; m. Sari Sinikka Timonen, May 20, 1998. MS, U. Helsinki, 1992, PhD, 1998. Curator Finnish Mus. Natural History, Helsinki, 1996—. Recipient prize Best Lepidopterol. Study in Finland Lepidopterol. Soc. Finland, 1995, 2000, Risto Tuomikoski prize for best rsch. in biol. taxonomy, 1998. Home: Mannerheiminte 120 A 16, FIN00270 Helsinki Finland Office: Finnish Mus Natural History, P Rautatiekatu 13 PO Box 17, FIN00014 University Helsinki Finland

KAILAS, LEO GEORGE, lawyer; b. N.Y.C., May 28, 1949; s. George and Evanthia (Skoulikas) K.; m. Merle S. Duskin; children: Arianne, George, Shirley. AB, Columbia U., 1970, JD, 1973. Bar: N.Y. 1974. Assoc. Olwine, Connelly, Chase, O'Donnell and Weyher, N.Y.C., 1973-77; ptnr. specializing in internat., comml.-admiralty litigation Milgrim Thomajan Jacobs & Lee, PC (now Piper & Marbury LLP), N.Y.C., 1977-2000, mem. internat. trade and litigation group, until 2000; ptnr. Rock Silverstein, N.Y.C., 2000—. Mem. ABA, Assn. Bar City N.Y. (chmn. admiralty com. 1985-88). Office: Rock Silverstein 800 3d Ave 21st Fl New York NY 10022*

KAIMSTHORN, LORD RENFREW OF See RENFREW, ANDREW COLIN

KAINBERGER, FRANZ M., radiologist, researcher; b. Salzburg, Austria, Dec. 22, 1957. MD, U. Innsbruck, Austria, 1983. Prof. radiology U. Vienna, 1994—. Mem. Austrian Soc. Radiation Protection (acting v.p. 1995—), Austrian Roentgen Soc. (mem. exec. com. 1998—). Office: U Vienna, Dept Diagnostic Radiology, A-1090 Vienna Austria

KAINTHLA, RAMESH CHAND, manufacturing company executive; b. Shimla, India, Feb. 18, 1954; came to U.S., 1983; s. Hira Nand and Belku (Devi) K.; m. Neetu Dua, Aug. 9, 1981; children: Priyanka, Radhika. BS, HP Univ., Shimla, 1973, MS in Physics, 1975; PhD in Physics, IIT Delhi, India, 1980. Rsch. assoc. IIT Delhi, 1980-81, U. NSW, Sydney, Australia, 1981-83; rsch. assoc. Tex. A&M U., College Station, 1984-86, sr. rsch. assoc., 1986-88, rsch. scientist, 1988-89; v.p. Rechargeable Battery Corp., College Station, 1989—; dir. Rechargeable Battery Corp., 1990—. Contbr. articles to profl. jours.; patentee in field. Mem. Electrochem. Soc. Avocations: music, movies, gardening, Web creation. E-mail: kainthla@tca.net. Office: Rechargeable Battery Corp 809 University Dr # 100E College Station TX 77840-1431

KAINZ, CHRISTIAN, physician, educator; b. Linz, Austria, July 31, 1962; s. Adolf and Brigitte Kainz. MD, Vienna U., 1987. Resident Upper Austria Hosp., 1987-89; intern Vienna U. Hosp., 1989-94, cons., 1994—, assoc. prof., 1995. Editor Jour. Gynecol. Endoscopy. Grantee Major of Vienna, 1994, 96. Mem. Austrian Gynecol. Endoscopy Soc. (bd. mem. 1994). Avocations: skiing, tennis. Home: Antonig 39/5, A-1180 Vienna Austria Office: Vienna U Hosp, Waehringer Guertel 18-20, A-1097 Vienna Austria

KAIS, TONU, management consultant; b. Tallinn, Estonia, Nov. 2, 1942; arrived in Sweden, 1944; s. Karl and Armide Luise (Erikson) K.; m. Irene Birgitta Eriksson, Jan. 24, 1970; children: Carl Tomas, Anna Karin Madeleine. BS in Civil Engring., Boras (Sweden) Tech. Sch., 1962; MS in Econ., Stockholm (Sweden) U., 1970. Design engr. Blomgren & Co. Engring. Co. AB, Stockholm, Sweden, 1963-71; planning specialist Planab AB, Stockholm, Sweden, 1971-72; project mgr. Hifab AB, Stockholm, Sweden, 1972-79; sr. mgmt. cons. Projekstyrning AB, Stockholm, Sweden, 1979—; mem. bd. Hifab AB, Stockholm, Sweden, 1977-79, Projekstyrning AB, Stockholm, Sweden, 1986—; lectr. Project Mgmt. internat. tng. programs, 1982—. Co-author: Project Manager, 1982; contbr. articles to profl. jours. Sgt. Swedish Army, 1963-89. Mem. The Swedish Project Mgmt. Soc., The Swedish Assn. for Graduated Bus. Adminstrs., The Stockholm Golf Club. Avocations: golf, tennis, motorboating, country-housing. Home: Ekplan 1, S-18238 Danderyd Sweden Office: Projektstyrning AB, Box 17500, S-11891 Stockholm Sweden

KAISER, FLORIAN GABRIEL, psychologist, researcher, educator; b. Lohn, Switzerland, Aug. 27, 1959; s. O. Florian and Maria-Magdalena (Gwerder) K.; m. Marianne Münger, Oct. 20, 1994; 2 children. MA, U. Zürich, Switzerland, 1986; PhD, U. Bern, Switzerland, 1992. Rsch. asst. U. Zürich, Switzerland, 1986-87, U. Bern, Switzerland, 1987-92; rsch. fellow U. Calif., Berkeley, 1994-96, U. Trier, Germany, 1996-97; postdoctoral asst. U. Fribourg, Switzerland, 1997-98; asst. prof. Swiss Fed. Inst. Tech., Zürich, 1998—; lectr. U. Zürich, 1998—. Author: Mobility as a Dwelling Problem—Place Attachment as Emotional Regulation, 1993; co-author: Multilocal Dwelling-Psychological Aspects of Leisure Time Mobility, 1994. Mem. APA, Environ. Design Rsch. Assn., German Psychol. Assn., Internat. Assn. Applied Psychology, Soc. Personality and Social Psychology. Office: Swiss Federal Inst Tech, ETH Zentrum HAD, CH-8092 Zürich Switzerland

KAISER, GABRIELE, educator; b. Lambrecht, Germany, Apr. 2, 1952; d. Fritz and Hildegard (Kern) K.; m. Ullrich Messmer, Nov. 2, 1984 (div. Nov. 1997); 1 child, Sarah. Master Degree, U. Kassel, Germany, 1978, PhD, 1986, habilitation, 1997. Tchr. diplomate. Rsch. asst. U. Kassel, 1984-92; rschr. German Rsch. Soc., 1992-96; guest prof. U. Potsdam, Germany, 1996-98; full prof. U. Hamburg, Germany, 1998—. Author: Anwendungen im Mathematikunterricht, 1986; editor: (with P. Rogers) Equity in Mathematics Education, 1995; chief editor: International Comparisons in Mathematics Education, 1998, Unterrichtswirklichkeit in England und Deutschland, 1999. Mem. German Soc. for Didactics Maths. Avocation: sports. Office: U Hamburg Dept Edn Inst 9, Von-Melle-Park 8, 20146 Hamburg Germany

KAISER, MARC AUREL, human resource specialist; b. Stolberg, Rheinland, Germany, July 15, 1968; s. Hans Joachim and Ulrike (Fleischhauer) K. Grad., U. Duisburg, Germany, 1991; student Polit. Sci./Econs., Simon Fraser U., Vancouver, 1993-94; diploma in Bus. Adminstrn., U. Konstanz, 1995, diploma in Jap. Mgmt. Cult. and Soc., 1996. Cons., rschr. TRW, Radolfzell, Germany, 1995, Mitsui, Dusseldorf, Germany, 1995; asst. Diht, Bonn, Germany, 1996; jr. cons. European Commn. Leonardo da Vinci, Brussels, 1996-97; mgmt. asst. Citibank, Bremen, Germany, 1997-98; human resource asst. Citibank, Duesseldorf, 1998-99, human resource specialist, 1999—; human resource specialist Deutsche Boerse, Frankfurt, 1999—. Co-author: W.I.S.-Further Training, 1996. Pub. rels. asst. Junge Union, Stolberg, 1987-89; chmn. Ring Christian Dem. Student Orgn., U. Duisburg, 1990-91. With German Air Force, 1987-88. Mem. Christian Fraternity. Mem. Christian Democratic Party. Avocations: reading, sports, travel. Home: PF 1343, 52249 Eschweiler Germany

KAISER, ROBIN, researcher; b. Esch/Alzette, July 2, 1963; p. Joseph Kaiser and Regine Sinner. PhD, Ecole Normale Supérieure, Paris, 1990. Staff Harvard U., Cambridge, Mass., 1990-91; head of rsch. Ctr. Nat. Rsch. Sci., Paris, Orsay, France, 1991-96, Nice, France, 1996—; presenter in field. Author: Petits Problèmes de Physique, 1999; contbr. articles to profl. jours. Founder, pres. Eurye-Paris, 1987, Plafond Ouvert, Paris, 1996; founder, sec. Bosnie 14th of Sept., Paris, 1997; founder, mediator Euryca, 1986. Avocations: travel, art. Fax: 33 (0) 4 92 93 65 25 17. E-mail: kaiser@inln.cnrs.fr. Office: Inst Non Linéaire Nice, 1361 route des Lucioles, 06560 Valbonne France

KAISER, RUDOLF ERNST, analyst, analytical chemistry educator; b. Teplitz, Czechoslovakia, Feb. 12, 1930; s. Ernst F. and Anny (Goebel) K.; m. Annemarie Woelfel, Apr. 15, 1954 (dec. Feb. 1990); children: Annette, Andrea; m. Olga Katkova, Oct. 12, 1990. Diploma in chemistry, U. Leipzig, Germany, 1952, Dr.rer.nat., 1954; prof. chemistry, Lamar U., 1990. Head dept. Inst. Indsl. Chemistry, Leipzig, 1954-60; analyst BASF, Ludwigshafen, Germany, 1960-72; head Inst. Chromatography, Bad Duerkheim, Germany, 1973—. Author 30 books on chromatography, including Computer Chromatography (Vol. 1), 1983, High Pressure Planar Liquid Chromatogrpahy, 1985, others; editor: Recent Advances in Capillary Gas Chromatography (Vol. 3), 1982, Instrumental High Performance Thin-Layer Chromatography, 1983, Instrumental Thin-Layer Chromatography/Planar Chromatography, 1989, Chromatography: Celebrating Michael Tswett's 125th Birthday, 1997, others; author and editor numerous monographs in field; editor Analytical Book Series; founder Internat. Jour. Chromatography and Computer Application; founder, editor-in-chief Chromatographia, 1968-78, Jour. High Resolution Chromatography, 1978-88. Recipient Tswett medal Chromatographic Soc. USSR, Moscow, 1978, Tswett medal II, 1995, gold medal Chinese Acad. Sci., Duerkheim, 1988, M.J.E. Golay award Riva del Garda, 1989, A.J.P. Martin award Chromatographic Soc., Brighton, 1989, Verdienstorden D. Bundesrepublik Deutschland Bundes President, Berlin, 1996. Avocations: teaching computers, electronic books, computer learning, computer programming. Office: Inst F Chromatography, PO Box 1141, D-67085 Bad Duerkheim Germany

KAISER, WERNER ALOIS, radiology educator; b. Buehl, Germany, Oct. 5, 1949; m. Ursula Kaiser; children: Clemens, Simon, Daniel, Birgit, Ulrich. MS in Chemistry, U. Freiburg, 1975. Resident in internal medicine Hosp., Offenburg, Germany, 1980-82; resident in pediat. U. Hosp., Freiburg, Germany, 1982-83; resident in radiology Hosp. Nürnberg, Germany, 1983-90; asst. prof. radiology U. Hosp., Bonn, Germany, 1990-93; assoc. prof. U. Hosp. Wuerzburg, Germany, 1993-94; prof., dept. chmn. U. Hosp. Jena, Germany, 1994—. Author: MR Mammography, 1993; contbr. articles to profl. jours. Recipient European Magnetic Resonance award, Zurich, 1991. Mem. Radiol. Soc. N.Am., Germany X-Ray Soc. Avocations: surfing, skating. E-mail: werner.kaiser@med.uni-jena.de. Office: Univ Hosp Jena, Bachstr 18, D-07740 Jena Germany

KAISSLING, KARL-ERNST, zoophysiologist, researcher; b. Duisburg, Germany, Apr. 26, 1933; s. Karl Walter and Traute (Ackermann) K.; m. Roswitha Koschnick (div.); children: Helgi Bugula K., Karl Tillmann K. PhD, Munich U., 1962. Asst. Dept. Comp. Neurophysiology MPI Psychiatry, Munich, Germany, 1963-65; sci. asst. MPI Verhaltensphysiologie-Seewiesen, 1966-72; Sci. mem. Max-Planck Soc., 1972—; apl prof. Munich U. Author: R.H. Wright Lectures on Insect Olfaction, 1987; contbr. articles to profl. jours. Recipient R.H. Wright award in Olfactory Rsch., Simon Fraser U., Burnaby, Can., 1985. Mem. Assn. Phys. Biology, European Chemo Reception Rsch. Orgn., Assn. Deutsch Zoology. E-mail: kaissling@mpi-seewieseu.mpg.de. Home: Nixenweg 3, 82319 Starnberg Germany Office: Max-Planck Inst Verhaltens, 82319 Seewiesen Germany

KAITERA, JUHA ANTERO, forest pathologist, researcher; b. Oulu, Finland, Oct. 8, 1962; s. Yrjö Anton and Kaiho Maiju (Mattila) K.; m. Erja Maaria Ruuhela, May 8, 1993; children: Jasmin, Oona. MSc in Forestry, Helsinki (Finland) U., 1990, D of Forestry, 1997. Rsch. asst. Finnish Forest Rsch. Inst., Sounenjoki, 1987, Vantaa, 1988-89; rsch. asst. dept. entomology Helsinki U., 1989-90; sr. rschr. Finnish Forest Rsch. Inst., Rovaniemi, 1990—. Contbr. articles to sci. jours., including Mycological Rsch., Can. Jour. Botany, others. Avocations: floorball, movies. Office: FFRI Rovaniemi Rsch Sta, Etelaranta 55, 96301 Rovaniemi Finland

KAIXI, ZHANG, physicist, educator; b. Jinmen, Hubei, China, Nov. 25, 1937; s. Zhang and Li (Suzhen) Lang; m. Wang Shumian, Dec. 25, 1967; children: Dazheng Zhang, Daguang Zhang. BS, Lanzhou (China) U., 1958. Asst. prof. Lanzhou U., 1958-63; assoc. prof. Hebei U., Baoding, 1963-81, prof., 1983—; vis. scholar Northwestern U., Evanston, Ill., 1981-83; chmn. dept. physics Hebei U., 1991-95. Author: Electrostatics, 1976 (Hebei Province prize 1979); contbr. articles to profl. jours. Standing com. mem. Chinese People's Polit. Cons. Com. Hebei Province, 1993—. Sci. scholar Hebei U., Baoding, China, 1978; recipient Higher Edn. prize Chinese People's Govt., Hebei, 1993. Mem. Optics Soc. Hebei Province (com. mem. 1978—), Optic Soc. China (com. mem. 1991—, Sci. prize 1991). Avocations: biology, walking. Office: Hebei Univ, Dept Physics, 071002 Baoding China

KAIZAKI, YOICHIRO, automotive executive; b. 1933. BA in Econs., Kyoto U., 1956. With Bridgestone Tire Co., Ltd. (now Bridgestone Corp.), 1962-85, dir., 1985-86, v.p. chem. and indsl. products, 1986-90, sr. v.p. chem. and indsl. products, 1990-91; chmn., CEO Bridgestone/Firestone Inc., 1991-93; pres. Bridgestone Corp., 1993—. Office: Bridgestone Corp, 10-1 Kyobashi 1-chome, Chuo-ku Tokyo 104-8340, Japan also: Bridgestone Firestone Inc 50 Century Blvd Nashville TN 37214-3672*

KAJANDER, RICHARD EMIL, chemical engineer; b. Mich., Dec. 10, 1951. BS in chem., Mich. Tech. Univ., 1974, Mich. Tech. Univ., 1975; MS in chem., Mich. Tech. Univ., 1976. Process engr. Proctor and Gamble Co.; rsch. engr. Am. Can Co.; sr. devel. engr. Dexter Corp.; project mgr. Tambrands, Inc.; sr. rsch. engr. Johns Manville Corp. Patentee in field. Named Vol. of Yr. Cmty. Living Options, Inc., 1996. Mem. ACS, Tech. Assn. Pulp and Papper Industry. E-mail: kajander@jm.com. Office: Johns Manville Corp 7500 Dutch Rd Waterville OH 43566-9731

KAJANTI, MIKAEL JOHANNES, radiotherapy and oncology specialist; b. Helsinki, Finland, July 20, 1951; s. Caius Filip and Anna Liisa (Niskanen) K.; m. Beatriz Maria Garcia Arribas, June 28, 1978; 1 child, Alexander. Licentaite of Medicin, U. Helsinki, 1977, DMS, 1984. Diplomate Finnish Bd. Radiotherapy and Oncology. House officer Helsinki U. Ctrl. Hosp., 1981-83, specialist dept. radiotherapy and oncology, 1984—; sr. lectr. radiotherapy and oncology U. Helsinki, 1993. Contbr. over 150 articles to profl. jours. Treas. Nordic Com. Radiotherapy, Helsinki, 1986-89. Mem. European Soc. for Therapeutic Radiology and Oncology (Belgium), Finnish Coll. Physicians, Radiol. Soc. Finland, Am. Soc. Therapeutic Radiology and Oncology. Home: Topeliuksenkatu 7 A 14, 00250 Helsinki Finland Office: Helsinki U Ctrl Hosp Dept Radiotheraphy & Oncol, Haartmaninkatu 4, 00290 Helsinki Finland

KAJIMA, SHOICHI, general contractor executive; b. 1930. Grad., U. Tokyo, 1953, Harvard U., 1957. Dir. Kajima Corp., Tokyo, 1953, now dir., sr. advisor to the bd. Office: Kajima Corp, 2-7 Motoakasaka 1-chome, Minato-ku Tokyo 107-8388, Japan Office: Kajima USA Inc 55 E 52d St 32d Fl New York NY 10022-5907*

KAJINO, AKIHIDE, orthopedist; b. Sapporo, Hokkaido, Japan, Jan. 29, 1955; s. Kazuhiko and Masa (Kazehaya) K. MB, Nippon Med. Sch., Tokyo, 1982; MD, Nippon Med. Sch., 1989. Orthopedist Tokyo, 1982—; hon. lectr. Nippon Med. Sch., 1993. Contbr. articles to profl. jours. Mem. Japanese Orthopaedic Assn., Japan Rheumatism Assn., Assn. Rehab. Medicine. Fax: 81-3-3871-5696. Office: Shitaya Hosp Orthopaedics, 3-12-40 Negishi Taito-ku, 110-0003 Tokyo Japan

KAJITANI, MOTOHISA, sociology educator; b. Kamioka, Gifu, Japan, May 8, 1937; s. Miyokichi and Nui (Taguchi) K.; m. Yoko Shimizu, Nov. 1969; 1 child, Kuri. BA, Tokyo U. Fgn. Studies, 1961; Diploma in Social Sci., U. Tokyo, 1961; MA, Kyoto (Japan) U., 1964. Lectr. Meijo U., Nagoya, Japan, 1964-69, assoc. prof., 1970-76, prof., 1976—, chmn. Libr., 1991—; joint lectr. Tokyo U. Fgn. Studies, 1965-72; vis. prof. dept. sociology UCLA, 1990; non-resident mem. Queen Elizabeth House, Oxford, 1972-74; guest prof. U. Klagenfurt, Austria, 1996; guest lectr. Nagoya City U., 1997—. Assoc. editor History of Sociology, 1981-87; author: Shakaigaku to Nippon, A Step to Internatl. Sociology, 1999; Press and Empire, 1981; author, editor: Shakaigaku no Rekishi: A History of Sociology, 1982, 89; editor: (with Hisao Naka) Sociologie Globale, 1987; editor: (with J. Langer) Shakaigatu to Europa, 1994; contbr. articles to Global, 1984-87. Recipient prize of social thought Akegarasu Fund, Tokyo and Kanazawa, 1964, Outstanding Achievement award in edn., Cambridge, Eng., 1999; over 10 grants in Japan. Mem. Internat. Sociol. Assn. (life), European Sociol. Assn., others. Avocations: operas, concerts, major league baseball viewing. Fax: (52) 833-7247. Office: Meijo U, 1-501 Shiogamaguchi, Nagoya 468, Japan

KAJIWARA, KAGEMASA, neuroscientist, researcher; b. Tokyo, Oct. 5, 1958; s. Kageyuki and Hiroko (Takashina) K.; m. Shiori Sugita, Oct. 29, 1988; 1 child, Ayaka. B of Dentistry, Kanagawa Dental Coll., Yokosuka, Japan, 1984, PhD, 1988. Rsch. asst. Kanagawa Dental Coll., Yokosuka, 1988-90; rsch. worker Tokai U., Isehara, Japan, 1988-90, lectr., 1996—; lectr. Keio U., Tokyo, 1990-95, 1993-96. Kanagawa Acad. Sci. and Tech. grantee, 1992-94. Mem. AAAS, N.Y. Acad. Sci., The Physiol. Soc. Japan, The Molecular Biology Soc. Japan. Office: Inst Med Sci Tokai U, Bohseidai, Isehara 259-1193, Japan

KAJIYAMA, FUMIO, corrosion scientist, researcher; b. Niigata, Japan, Mar. 20, 1953; s. Aiko and Katsukiyo (Kato) K.; m. Midori Nakamura, Mar. 22, 1981; children: Keisuke, Hiroaki. Bachelor, Yokohama (Japan) Nat. U., 1977; Master, Tokyo Inst. Tech., 1979, DEng, 1989. Rschr. Fundamental Tech. Rsch. Lab., Tokyo Gas Co. Ltd., 1979-88, sr. rschr., 1989—. Author: Environmental Oriented Electrochemistry, 1994; contbr. articles to profl. jours. Mem. Nat. Assn. Corrosion Engrs. Avocations: walking, philately. Fax: 03-3453-7583. Office: Tokyo Gas Co Ltd, 16-25 1-Chome Shibaura, Minatoku Tokyo 105-0023, Japan

KAKABADSE, ANDREW PANAJOTIS, international management development educator; b. Athens, Mar. 3, 1948; s. George and Elfrieda (Meissner) K.; m. Nada Korac, Dec. 27, 1995. BSc, Salford U., 1970; MA, Brunel U., 1973; PhD, U. Manchester, 1977, diploma in psychiat. social work, 1972. Mental welfare officer Derbyshire County Coun., 1970-71; psychiat. social worker, child guidance officer Liverpool City Coun., 1971-72; rsch. fellow in mgmt. devel. dept. mgmt. Manchester Polytechnic, 1973-77, lectr. orgn. behavior, dir. orgn. R&D unit dept. mgmt., 1975-77; pers. cons. WS Atkins Group Internat. Cons., 1977-78; chmn. mgmt. devel. forum, chmn. human resources group Cranfield Sch. Mgmt., Cranfield U., 1978—, prof. internat. mgmt. devel., dep. dir., 1978—; lectr., cons. in field. Author: Success in Sight: Visioning, 1999, Essence of Leadership, 1999, Leadership in Government: A Study of the Australian Public Service, 1998, Japanese Business Leaders, 1996, Cases in Human Resource Management, 1994, Sabotage: How to Recognise and Manage Employee Defiance, 1991, Creating Futures: Innovative Application of IS/IT, Ashgate, 2000, others; contbr. numerous articles to profl. jours. Fellow Internat. Acad. of Mgmt., Brit. Psychol. Soc., Brit. Acad. Mgmt., Royal Soc. of Arts. Avocations: walking, travel. Office: Cranfield Univ, Cranfield MK43 OAL, England

KAKANIS-CHRYSSOVERGIS, PELAGIOS, nuclear physicist, researcher; b. Thessaloniki, Macedonia, Greece, Sept. 16, 1951; s. Konstantinos and Eleni (Matrakalidou) K.; m. Olga Popova, Mar. 27, 1990; 1 child, Konstantinos. PhD in Physics, U. Athens, Greece, 1981. Instr., rschr. Nat. Tech. U., Athens, 1979-80; health physicist Ministry of Labour, Athens, 1981-96; collaborator Greek Atomic Energy Com., Athens, 1989-90; part-time collaborator Nat. Rsch. Ctr. Demokritos and Greek Atomic Energy Commn., Athens, 1994—; part-time collaborator N.R.C. Demokritos, Athens, 1981-90; vis. prof. Tech. Edn. Inst., Thessaloniki, Greece, 1987-88. Mem. Greek Physicists Assn. Avocation: collecting match-boxes. Home: 56 Ipirou Str, GR-15341 Aghia Paraskevi Attica, Greece Office: Greek Atomic Energy Commn, GR-15310 Aghia Paraskevi Attica, Greece

KAKAR, DAISY ADARSH, nutrition educator, consultant; b. Ambarnath, India, Jan. 23, 1960; d. Krishna Prakash and Kamlesh Krishnaprakash (Seth) Sagar; m. Adarsh Satinderlal Kakar, Nov. 28, 1986; children: Asmish, Aksnay. BSc in Food Sci. and Nutrition, S.N.D.T., Bombay, 1980, MSc in Food Sci. and Nutriton, 1982, PhD in Nutrition, 1995. Lectr. S.N.D.T., 1982-83; asst. prof. nutrition Bombay Vet. Coll., 1985—; cons., Bombay, 1995—. Contbr. articles to sci. jours., including Indian Jour. Dairy Sci., Jour. Food Sci. and Tech. Mem. Nutrition Soc. India (lie), Assn. Food Scientists and Technologists India (life), Indian Dietetic Assn. (life), ACASM (life). Avocations: reading, Indian classical music, gardening, travel. Office: Bombay Vet Coll, Parel Village, Mumbai 400 012, India

KAKIGI, AKINOBU, otolaryngologist; b. Onomichi, Hiroshima, Japan, Jan. 13, 1963; s. Hyozo and Yoshiko (Sato) K.; m. Michi Takeshima, Jan. 15, 1996; 1 child, Teruyo. Med. degree, Kochi Med. Sch., Nankoku, Japan, 1988. Resident Kochi Med. Sch., Nankoku, 1988-90; staff Inan Hosp., Tosashimizu, Japan, 1990-91, Kochi Mcpl. Hosp., 1991-92, Kochi Med. Sch., Nankoku, 1992; rsch. fellow Hosp. for Sick Children, Toronto, Ont., Can., 1994-97; asst. Kochi Med. Sch., Nankoku, 1992—. Contbr. rsch. articles to profl. jours. Avocations: snow boarding, soccer, traveling, motor

sports. Home: 1568 Otsu Osone, 783-0005 Nankoku Kochi, Japan Office: Kochi Med Sch, Kohasu Oko, 783-8505 Nankoku Kochi, Japan

KAKINUKI, JOHN C., lawyer; b. San Francisco, June 20, 1956; s. John Leo Countouriotis and Nobuko Kakinuki; m. Ikuyo Ito, Jan. 5, 1982; children: Junichi John, Joji George, Maria Nobuko. Student, U. Calif., Berkeley, 1974-77; BA, Internat. Christian U., Tokyo, 1979; JD, U. Calif., San Francisco, 1984. Bar: Calif. 1985, D.C. 1988, Japan (as atty. at fgn. law) 1994, N.Y. 1996, U.S. Dist. Ct. (no. dist.) Calif. 1986, U.S. Ct. Appeals (Fed. cir.) 1990, U.S. Dist. Ct. (ctrl. dist.) Calif. 1991, U.S. Dist. Ct. (so. dist.) Calif. 1993, U.S. Dist. Ct. (so. dist.) N.Y. 1996, U.S. Dist. Ct. (ea. dist.) N.Y. 1997. Assoc. Tokyo Aoyama Law Office, 1984-89, Baker & McKenzie, Palo Alto, Calif., 1989-91; ptnr. Baker & McKenzie, San Francisco, 1992-94; of counsel Tokyo Aoyama Law Office, 1994-96; ptnr. Baker & McKenzie, Tokyo, 1996—. Contbr. articles to profl. jours. Mem. IEEE, ABA, Internat. Trademark Assn., Am. C. of C. in Japan (chair IP com.), State Bar Calif., D.C. Bar, Tokyo Bar Assn. (chair lawyers subcom., internat. rels. com.), N.Y. State Bar Assn., Am. Intellectual Property Law Assn., Japan Fedn. Bar Assns., Fed. Cir. Bar Assn. Avocation: karate. Office: Baker & McKenzie GJBJ, 1-2-3 Kita Aoyama, Minato-ku Tokyo 107-0061, Japan

KAKITANI, SATORU, mineralogist, material scientist, educator; b. Nakamura, Japan, Feb. 24, 1924; s. Yukiji and Matsuki (Kamioka) K.; m. Haruka Kadota (dec. 1960); children: Hitoshi, Makoto; m. Harumi Watanabe, June 25, 1962. BS, Kyoto (Japan) U., 1947, MSc, 1950; DSc, Hiroshima U. Lit. and Sci., Japan, 1961. Lectr. Osaka City (Japan) U., 1956-63; asst. prof. Kobe (Japan) U., 1963-65, Hiroshima U., 1975-87; prof. Okayama (Japan) U. Sci., 1987—; chmn. Hot Spring Coun. of Hiroshima, 1986-87. Contbr. articles to profl. jours. Recipient Maj. Achievement prize Clay Sci. Soc. Japan, 1994, Contbn. prize Ceramic Soc. Japan, 1996. Avocation: Japanese mythology. Office: Okayama U Sci, 1-1 Ridaicho, Okayama 700-0005, Japan

KAKIZOE, SABURO, surgeon; b. Fukuoka, Japan, June 6, 1958; s. Shinobu and Tamako (Shimura) K.; m. Yumiko Hironaga, May 27, 1990; children: Showtaro, Mayuco. MD, Kurume U., Fukuoka, 1983; PhD, Kyushu U., Fukuoka, 1988. Surg. resident Kyushu U., Fukuoka, 1983-84; vis. fellow dept. pathology Kurume U., Fukuoka, 1984-86; rsch. fellow dept. pathology Wis. U., Madison, 1987-88; fellow dept. pathology Pitts. U., 1988-89, fellow dept. surgery, 1989; staff surgeon Ctrl. Fukuoka Nat. Hosp., 1989-90; fellow surgeon Kyushu U., Fukuoka, 1990-91; staff surgeon Kakizoe Hosp., Hirado, Nagasaki, Japan, 1991-93, chief dept. surgery, 1993—. Contbr. articles to profl. jours. Mem. Japan Soc. for Endoscopic Surgery (councilor), Japan Surg. Soc., Am. Assn. for Study Liver Disease, Transplantation Soc., Internat. Gasto-Surg. Club, Smithsonian Instn., Porsche Club Japan. Office: Ilikai Med Inc/Kakizoe Hosp, Kagamigawa 278, Nagasaki 859-5152, Japan

KAKKAR, VIRENDER KUMAR, scientist, researcher; b. Okara, Montgomery, India, Aug. 1, 1940; s. Kuljas Rai and Ram Piari (Achhreja) K.; m. Veena Chhabra, Apr. 27, 1971; children: Poonam, Neeraj, Pakaj. BSc in Biochemistry with honors, Panjab U., Chandigarh, India, 1965, MSc in Biochemistry with honors, 1967, PhD in Animal Nutrition, 1977. Rsch. asst. Punjab Agrl. U., Ludhiana, 1968-76, asst. nutritionist, 1976-83, nutritionist, 1983-91, sr. nutritionist, 1991-2000; lectr. in field. Contbr. over 150 articles to profl. publs.; inventor in field. Nat. Merit fellow, 1985-90. Mem. Am. Chem. Soc. (hon.), Animal Nutrition Soc. India (life, mem. editl. bd., publ. com. 1996-2000), Dairy Herd Improvement Assn. Chennai India (life, mem. tech. adv. com. 1997-2000). Avocations: reading, writing, mentoring, social work. Office: Civil Lines Dept Animan Nut, Punjab Agrl U, Punjab Ludhiana 141 004, India

KAKOSY, TIBOR, physician, consultant; b. Budapest, Hungary, May 15, 1936; s. Karoly and Ilona (Vamos) K.; m. Zita Konczer, Oct. 21, 1967; children: Csaba, Zsolt. Degree Tuberculosis and Pulmonary Diseases, 1963; degree Internal Diseases, Hungary, 1969; PhD, Hungarian Acad. Scis., 1975. Med. diplomate. Jr. surgeon Inst. TBC, Szentgotthard, 1960-65; rsch. fellow Inst. Occupational Health, Budapest, Hungary, 1965-86; head dept. geriatrics St. Stephen Hosp., Budapest, Hungary, 1986-92; head intern dept. Inst. Occupational Health, Budapest, Hungary, 1992—; dir. Hosp. Kun of St. Stephen Hosp., 1991-92; cons. Occupational Health Found. for Healthy Heart, 1995-97. Author: X-ray Morfology of Occupational Locomotor Diseases, 1980, Occupational Rheumatic Diseases, 1989; contbr. articles to profl. jours. Recipient award for excellent work Min. Health of Hungary, 1982. Mem. Hungarian Angiological Soc., Hungarian Gerontological Soc. Roman Catholic. Avocations: theater, football, photography, travel, reading. Home: Csaba u 34/a, 1122 Budapest Hungary Office: Nat Inst Occup Health, Nagyvarad ter 2, 1096 Budapest Hungary

KAKOUROU, TALIA TSIVITANIDOU, pediatric dermatologist; b. Cyprus, Apr. 19, 1952; d. George and Melanie (Efthymiou) Tsivitanidou; m. Stavros Kakouros, Aug. 24, 1975; children: Nick, Melanie, Georgia. Med. diploma, U. Athens, 1975, specialized pediatrician, 1980, MD, 1988. House officer in internal medicine Tzanion Hosp. Pireaus, 1976-77; registrar in pediatrics Aghia Sophia Children's Hosp., U. Athens, 1978-80, sr. registrar in pediatrics fellow, 1980-85; clin. asst. pediatrics dermatology St. Thomas Hosp., London, 1986-87, Hosp. for Sick Children, London, 1986-87; clin. asst. dermatology Syngros Hosp. for Skin Diseases, Athens, 1988-89; cons. in pediatric dermatology Aghia Sophia Children's Hosp., U. Athens, 1990—. Author: Pediatric Dermatology, 1995; contbr. articles to profl. jours. Grantee A. Onassis Found., 1986-87. Mem. Dowling Club for Dermatologists, British Soc. for Pediatric Dermatology, European Soc. for Pediatric Dermatology. Office: U Athens Dept Pediatrics, Aghia Sophia Children's Hosp, 11527 Athens Greece

KAKUDA, NAOYUKI, neurologist; b. Takaoka, Toyama, Japan, June 24, 1960; s. Masao and Fusae (Kaji) K.; m. Tomoko Namie, Oct. 10, 1989; 1 child, Akiyoshi. MD, Kanazawa (Japan) U., 1985, PhD, 1993. Physician Kanazawa Univ. Hosp., 1985-93, Tokyo Met. Neurol. Hosp., 1987-90; scientist Göteborg (Sweden) U., 1993-95; rschr., physician Nat. Rehab. Ctr. for the Disabled, Tokorozawa, Japan, 1995—. Contbr. articles to profl. jours. Mem. Soc. for Neurosci. Office: Nat Rehab Ctr for Disabled, Namiki 4-1, 359-8555 Tokorozawa Japan

KAKUDOH, KENICHI, bank company executive. CEO Norinchukin Bank, Tokyo, 1996—. Office: Norinchukin Bank, 1-13-2 Yuraku-cho Chiyoda-Ku, 100-8420 Tokyo Japan*

KAKUHATA, HIROSHI, physicist; b. Kitami, Japan, Jan. 16, 1956; s. Giichi and Eiko (Kajita) K.; m. Akiko Matsuo, July 25, 1992; children: Kazunari, Susumu, Minoru. DSc, Nihon U., Tokyo, 1986. Rsch. fellow Nihon U., 1984-91; asst. prof. Tsuruga (Japan) Jr. Coll., 1992—. Contbr. articles to profl. jours. Mem. Phys. Soc. Japan. Avocation: hiking. Office: Tsuruga Jr Coll, Kizaki 78-2-1, Tsuruga 914-0814, Japan

KALA, MIROSLAV MICHAEL, neurosurgeon; b. Novy Jičín, Moravia, Czech Republic, Apr. 30, 1958; s. Miroslav and Anna (Černochová) K.; m. Marta Forejtková, Apr. 24, 1981 (div. June 1993); 1 child, Irena; m. Vladimíra Lachmanová, Dec. 10, 1994; 1 child, Vojtěch. MD, Faculty of Medicine, Olomouc, Czech Republic, 1983; postgrad., Hradec Kralove, Czech Republic, 1990; PhD, Faculty of Medicine, Olomouc, Czech Republic, 1991; postgrad., Vienna, Austria, 1992. Med. diplomate, postgrad. diploma in surgery I. grade, postgrad. diploma in neurosurgery. Surgeon Faculty Hosp., Olomouc, 1983-86, neurosurgeon, 1986—, asst. prof., 1998; referee Commn. for State Examinations of Surgery, Faculty Medicine, Olomouc, 1993; referee Jour. Czech and Slovak Neurology and Neurosurgery, Olomouc. Author (monographs): Pyogenic Diseases of the Brain, 1997, How Neurosurgeon Works and What He Thinks About, 1998, Malignant Brain Tumors in Adults, 1999, The Thirteen Apartment-Miracles and Chances in Health and Illness, 1999, Hospital-guidebook for curious patient, 2000; contbr. articles to profl. jours: Recipient prize for eminent results in studies Min. Edn., Prague, 1983;. Mem. Czech Med. Assn. J.E. Purkinje, Congress Neurol. Surgeons. Roman Catholic. Avocations: classical music, family. Home: Nešverova 1, 77200 Olomouc Czech Republic Office: Clinic Neurosurgery, I P Pavlova 6, 77520 Olomouc Czech Republic

KALABUKHOVA, TATYANA NIKOLAEVNA, biophysician, writer; b. Moscow, Apr. 19, 1939; d. Nikolay Ivanovich Kalabukhov and Olga Ilyinichna Barsova. Diploma, Moscow State U., 1962; BS, Inst. Biophysics, USSR Acad. Sci., Pushchino, 1971. Stager, rschr. USSR Acad. of Sci., Inst. Biophysics, Moscow, 1962-64, jr. scientist, collaborator, 1964-65, postgrad., 1965-68; scientist, collaborator USSR Acad. of Sci., Inst. Biophysics, Pushchino, 1968-90; scientist, collaborator USSR Acad. Sci., Inst. of Cell Biophysics, Pushchino, 1991, sr. scientist, collaborator, 1992—; lectr. Pushchino br., chair physiochem. biology Moscow State U.,, 1972-80; chmn. Pushchino br. of ultraviolet radiation sect. Sci. Coun. on Biophysics Problems, USSR Acad. Sci., 1976-80. Editl. bd. Nauka, 1975; contbr. articles to profl. jours. Recipient Medal Vet. of Labor Presidium of Supreme Soviet of USSR, 1988, Medal Pres. of Russian Fedn. B.N. Yeltzin, 1997; grantee Russian Found. for Basic Rsch., 1996-98. Home: Mukpop uoh AOM 25, Kb 116, 142290 Pushchino-on-Oka Russia Office: Inst Cell Biophys, Russian Acad Sci, 142292 Pushchino Russia

KALAČ, PAVEL, chemist, educator, researcher; b. Novy Knín, Czech Republic, June 24, 1943; s. Josef and Marie (Brejchová) K.; m. Marie Kubísková, Aug. 6, 1966; children: Pavel, Martin. MSc, Inst. Chem. Tech., Prague, Czech Republic, 1965, PhD, 1979. Technologist South Bohemian Meat Enterprise, České Budějovice, Czech Republic, 1965-71; sr. lectr. U. South Bohemia, České Budějovice, 1971-83, asst. prof. chemistry, 1983-99, prof. agrl. chemistry, 1999—. Sr. author: Natural Toxicants in Feeds, 1988, 2nd edit., 1997; contbr.: (book) Natural Toxic Compounds of Foods, 1995; contbr. articles to profl. jours. Avocations: gothic architecture, history of the Middle Ages. E-mail: kalac@zf.jcu.cz. Office: Univ of South Bohemia, Studentská 13, 370 05 Ceske Budejovice Czech Republic

KALAGA, WOJCIECH HENRYK, literature educator; b. Cracow, Poland, July 27, 1949; s. Henryk and Longina Kalaga; m. Lucyna Malik, Aug. 28, 1974; children: Tomasz, Maciej. MA, Jagellonian U. Cracow, 1972, PhD, 1979; Habilitation, Adam Mickiewicz U., Poznań, Poland, 1986. Dozent, assoc. prof. U. Silesia, Katowice, Poland, 1987-94; chair of comparative lit. Murdoch (Australia) U., 1992-94; prof. U. Silesia, Katowice, 1995—, head dept. lit. theory, 1998—; Fulbright vis. prof. Yale U., New Haven, 1983-84; vis. prof. U. Queensland, Brisbane, Australia, 1987; dep. dir. Inst. English, Katowice, 1981-84; head dept. lit. theory and English lit., Katowice, 1984-89; rsch. mgr. Murdoch U., 1993-94; dir. Inst. Brit. and Am. Culture and Lit., Katowice, 1995—. Author: Mental Landscape: The Novel of Samuel Beckett, 1981 (Rector's award 1981), The Literary Sign, 1986 (Min. of Sci. award 1987), Nebulae of Discourse, 1997 (Min. of Edn. award 1988); editor: Discourses/Texts/Contexts, 1990, Memory/Remembering/Forgetting, 1998; gen. editor Peter Lang Verlag, 1997—; editor-in-chief Jour. ER(R)GO. Fulbright grantee, 1983-84, Alexander von Humboldt grantee, 1988, Australian Rsch. Coun. grantee, 1994. Mem. Internat. Assn. for Semiotic Studies, Charles S. Peirce Soc., Polskie Towarzystwo Semiotyczne, Internat. Comparative Lit. Assn. Avocations: fishing, sailing, martial arts, wine. Office: Inst Brit and Am Culture and Lit, ul Żytnia 10, 41-205 Sosnowiec Poland

KALAGIN, IGOR, physicist; b. Penza, USSR, Aug. 8, 1963; s. Vladimir and Svetlana (Mukhaeva) K.; m. Ludmila Vikhreva; children: Anton, Ilya. Engr. Physicist, Engring.-Phys. U., Moscow, 1986; PhD, Joint Inst. Nuclear Rsch., Dubna, Russia, 1997. Engr. Joint Inst. Nuclear Rsch., Dubna, 1986-89, sr. engr., 1989-91, leading engr., 1991-96, scientific collaborator, 1996-98, acceleramor chief, 1999—. Contbr. articles to profl. jours. Travel grantee Soros Found., 1994, European Orgn. Nuclear Rsch., 1996. Office: JINR FLNR, Joliot Curie 6, RU141980 Dubna Moscow, Russia

KALAI, EHUD, decision sciences educator, researcher in economics and decision sciences; b. Tel Aviv, Dec. 7, 1942; came to U.S., 1963; s. Meir and Elisheva (Rabinovitch) K.; m. Marilyn Lott, Aug. 24, 1967; children: Kerren, Adam. AB with distinction, U. Calif. at Berkeley, 1967; MS, Cornell U., 1971, PhD in Applied Math., 1972. Asst. prof. dept. statistics Tel Aviv U., 1972-75; vis. asst. prof. decision scis. J.L. Kellogg Grad. Sch. Mgmt. Northwestern U., Evanston, Ill., 1975-76, assoc. prof. decision scis., 1976-78, prof. managerial econs. and decision scis., 1978-82, The Charles E. Morrison Chair prof. decision scis., 1982—; prof. math. Northwestern U., Evanston, 1990—; IBM rsch. chair managerial econs. Northwestern U., Evanston, Ill., 1980-81, J.L. Kellogg rsch. chair in decision theory, 1981-82, chmn. meds. dept., 1983-85; dir. Ctr. for Strategic Decision-Making Kellogg Sch. Mgmt., Northwestern U., 1995—; Oskar Morgenstern rsch. prof. game theory NYU, 1991; expert testimony in ct. cases, 1982—; cons. Israeli Def. Forces, 1974-75, 1st Nat. Bank Chgo., 1987, Arthur Anderson, 1990, Kaiser Permanente, 1995, Nath Sonnenschein and Rosenthal, 1999, Baxter Healthcare Corp., 1999—. Founder, editor Games and Econ. Behavior Jour., 1988—; editl. bd. Math. Social Scis., 1980-90, Jour. Econ. Theory, 1980-88, Internat. Jour. Game Theory, 1984—; contbr. numerous articles on game theory and econs. to profl. jours. Sgt. Israeli Def. Forces, 1960-63. NSF grantee, 1979—; Sherman Fairchild Disting. scholar, Calif. Inst. Tech., 1994-95. Fellow Econometrics Soc.; mem. Am. Math. Soc., Pub. Choice Soc., Game Theory Soc. (founder, exec. v.p. 1998—), Beta Gamma Sigma. Home: 1110 N Lake Shore Dr Apt 23S Chicago IL 60611-1023 Office: Kellogg Grad Sch of Mgmt Northwestern Univ Evanston IL 60208-0001

KALAIDJIAN, BERJ BOGHOS, civil engineer; b. Jerusalem, Mar. 7, 1936; s. Boghos Hovhanes and Shoghagat Kevork (Sahakian) K.; B.C.E., Am. U., Beirut, Lebanon, 1958; m. Sonia Kouyoumdjian, Aug. 19, 1963; children: Shahe, Vatche. Site engr. Consol. Contractors Co., Beirut, 1958-62, project mgr., 1962-64, asst. area mgr., jr. partner, 1964-69; mng. dir., partner Acmecon, Jeddah Saudi Arabia, 1969—, also dir. Club: Armenian Benevolent Union. Home: 35 Blvd du Larvotto, MC 98000 Monaco Monaco

KALANDARISHVILI, ARNOLD GALAKTIONOVICH, physicist, researcher; b. Tbilisi, Georgia, Mar. 1, 1939; s. Galaktion Grigorevich Kalandarishvili and Anna Iakovlevna Azatiane. Diploma, State U., Tbilisi, 1962; candidate of tech. sci., Sukhumi Inst. Physics and Engring, Moscow, 1971; D of Tech. Sci., I. Vecua Sukhumi Inst. Physics and Engring., Moscow, 1983. Sr. technician Sukhumi (Georgia) Inst. Physics and Engring., 1962-66, mem. jr. sci. staff, 1966-72, mem. sr. sci. staff, 1972-73; head of lab. I. Vecua Sukhumi Inst. Physics and Engring., 1973-94; program mgr. Russian Rsch. Ctr. Kurchatov Inst., Moscow, 1992-95, chief specialist, 1996-98, leading scientist, 1998—; sci. cons., physicist Space Exploration Assocs., Cedarville, Ohio, 1992, 93; sci. cons. INERTEK Russian/U.S. Joint Venture, Moscow, 1993; prof., lectr. Abkhazian State U., Sukhumi, 1984-91. Author: Working Medium Sources for Thermioc Power Converters, 1986 (State prize of sci. and engring. Republic of Georgia 1989), 2d edit., 1993; contbr. articles to profl. jours.; inventor in field. Named Meritorious Inventor and Innovator of Georgian Soviet Socialist Republic, Tbilisi, 1990; recipient diploma Coun. of Supreme Soviet of SSR, Tbilisi, 1990, diploma of Coun. of Supreme Soviet of Abkhazian Autonomous SSR, Sukhumi, 1983. Mem. Russian Fedn. Acad. of Scis. (rsch. coun.), Internat. Thermionic Soc. Avocations: tennis, chess. Fax: (095) 196 89 71. Home: Raspletina 4-2-73, 123002 Moscow Russia Office: Kurchatov Inst, Kurchatov Sq 1, 123182 Moscow Russia

KALANTARI, ISA, Iranian government official; b. Marand, Azarbyejan, Iran, Apr. 10, 1952; s. Mohammad Hossein Kalantari and Kobra Esfandi; m. Effat Ejtehadi, 1982; children: Mohsen, Fereshte. BSc in Agronomy and Plant Breeding, U. Urumia, Iran, 1975; MSc in Agronomy and Physiology, U. Nebr., 1978; PhD in Crop Physiology, Iowa State U., 1981. Pres. Agrl. Ext. Orgn., Iran, 1982, Plant & Seed Improvement Rsch. Ins., Iran, 1983-88; dep. min. Rsch. & Tng. Dept., Iran, 1983-86; head dept. hort. and plant breeding Tarbiat Moddares U., Iran, 1984-88; dir.-gen. Moghan Agro-Indsl. Complex, Iran, 1985-88; min. Ministry of Agr., Iran, 1988—. Author: Agri-Econ & Development, 1994. Mem. bd. regents North Western Univs., Iran, 1991; head Iranian Olympic Com., 1991-93; pres. World Food Coun., 1991-94. Mem. Am. Soc. Agronomy, Am. Soc. Crop Sci., Iranian Soc. Crop Breeding and Prodn. Home: No 26-Morshed # sh, Sheidai-Yakhchal-Shariati Ave, Tehran Iran*

KALANTZOPOULOS, GEORGE COSTAS, food microbiologist; b. Athens, Greece, Mar. 31, 1936; s. Costas Spyros and Angellic Maria (Joannidou) K.; m. Sofia Stayros Lardi, Oct. 5, 1967; children: Costas, Angela. Diploma in agrl. scis., Agrl. U. Athens, 1960, PhD, 1970, fellow, 1975. Asst. Agrl. U. Athens, 1962-70, sr. asst., 1970-75, asst. prof., 1975-90, full prof., 1990—, head dept. food sci. and tech., 1996, dir. lab. food quality control and hygiene; internat. expert French Govt. and of the Internat. Dairy Fedn.; pres. Francohellenic Assn. Author: Dairy Microbiology, 1986; mem. editl. bd. Food Sci. and Tech.; mem. internat. editl. bd. Food Sci. and Tech. Internat., 1998; mem. adv. editl. bd. Ency. Food Microbiology, 1999. Lt. Greek Artillery, 1960-62. Recipient Chevalier de Merite Agricole de la Republique Francaise, 1988. Mem. Internat. Dairy Fedn. (chmn. group A7 1998), French Microbiology Soc., Am. Dairy Sci. Assn., Greek Soc. Nutrition and Food, Greek Inst. Food Technologists (pres.), Club Lactic Acid Bacteria. Home: El Venizelou 8, 17235 Athens Greece Office: Agrl Univ Athens, Botanikos, 11855 Athens Greece

KALAS, FRANK JOSEPH, JR., financial, information systems consultant; b. Stafford Springs, Conn., Dec. 31, 1943; s. Frank Joseph and Margaret Mary (LaPanne) K.; m. Minh Tran, June 24, 1972; children: Jennifer Ann, Joanne Catherine. BBA, U. N.Mex., 1966; MS, U. Ark., London, Eng., 1974. Sr. auditor Knox & Scott, CPAs, Albuquerque, 1963-66; commd. officer USN, 1967, advanced through grades to capt., 1987; dir. fin. mgmt. office Naval Sea Systems Command, Washington, 1988-93; ret., 1993; mgr. material and prodn. svcs. Intermarine USA, Savannah, Ga., 1993-95; adj. prof. acctg. R.I. Coll., 1978-80, Far East divsn. U. Md., 1980-82. Author: Food Service Operations and Contracting, 1987. Decorated Meritorious Svc. medal, Legion of Merit. Mem. Am. Soc. Naval Engrs., Soc. Logistics Engrs. (pres. 1979-80), Profl. Picture Framer's Assn. (cert.), Am. Soc. Mil. Comptrs. (Outstanding Mem. award 1985), Nat. Amateur Press Assn., Inst. of Mgmt. Accts., Am. Prodn. and Inventory Control Soc. Roman Catholic. Avocations: amateur journalism, clocks, Russian History, competition dancing. Office: Am Mgmt Systems Inc 4114 Legato Rd Fairfax VA 22033-4002

KALASHNICK, MAXIM VALENTINOVICH, geophysicist; b. Kremenchug, USSR, Apr. 14, 1961; s. Valentin Timotheevich and Nina Alexandrovna (Brueva) K.; m. Olga Stanislavovna Belyaeva, Jan. 10, 1987; 1 child, Alexei. Diploma in Geophysics, Hydrometeorological Inst., Odessa, Ukraine, 1983; PhD, Inst. Exptl. Meteorology, Obnisk, USSR, 1991. Engr. Inst. Exptl. Meteorology, Obnisk, USSR, 1985-86; scientist Inst. Exptl. Meteorology, Obnisk, 1986-93, sr. scientist, 1993—. Contbr. articles to profl. jours. Grantee, The Internat. Scientific Found., The Russian Found. Fundamental Rschrs., 1997, 98, Internat. Soros Sci. Edn. Program, 1998, 99. Avocations: fishing, running, football. Phone: 7 (08439) 52317. Office: Inst Exptl Meteorology, Prosp Lenina 82, 249030 Obnisk Russia

KALASHNIKOV, SERGEI, Russian federal official; b. 1951. Student, Leningrad State U., 1975; postgrad. Inst. of Psychology, USSR Acad. of Sci., 1979. Head social-psychol. svc. Rsch. Inst. USSR Ministry of Def. Industry; chair Inst. of Advanced Studies USSR Ministry of Oil and Chem. Industry, Moscow, 1998—; dir. intermanager State Enterprise; chmn., bd. dirs. Europian-Asian Bank; chmn. com. on labor and social policy State Duma, dep.; com. on social policy Interpaliamentary Assembly of CIS. Mem. Assn. of Def. Against Unemployment and Poverty, Internat. Acad. of Informatics, Russian Acad. of Sci. Liberal Democratic Party. Office: Ministry of Labor, 1-y Basmannyi per 3, Moscow 103706, Russia

KALASHNIKOV, VLADIMIR LEONIDOVICH, physicist, educator; b. Minsk, Belarus, Apr. 7, 1965; s. Leonid Vladimirovich and Nadezhda Petrovna (Shevkoplias) K.; m. Marina Nikolaevna Morozova, July 3, 1987; children: Andrej, Anastasija. CSc in Physics, Belorussian U., Minsk, 1992. Jr. rschr. Belarus U., Minsk, 1989-92, sr. rschr., 1992-93; sci. sec. Internat. Laser Ctr., Minsk, 1993-96, head lab., 1996—; lectr. Belarus Tech. U., Minsk, 1996—. Contbr. articles to sci. jours., including Optics Comm., Jour. Optical Soc. Am., Optical and Quantum Electronics, Quantum Electronics, lit. jour. Don. Grantee Meyer Found., 1993, Soroc, 1993, DAAD, 1996. Avocations: philosophy, literature, art, design. Home: 21/3 Kozirevskaja Apt 37, 220028 Minsk Belarus Office: Internat Laser Ctr, 65 F Skorina Ave 17 Bld, 220027 Minsk Belarus

KALASINSKY, VICTOR FRANK, chemist; b. Columbus, Ohio, Dec. 30, 1949; s. Frank and Waleria (Kozicka) K.; m. Kathryn Schade, June 15, 1974; children: Victoria, Nicholas. SB, MIT, 1972; PhD, U. S.C., 1975. Postdoctoral fellow U. S.C., Columbia, 1975-76; prof. dept. chemistry Furman U., Greenville, S.C., 1976-77, Miss. State (Miss.) U., 1977-90; chief divsn. environ. toxicology Armed Forces Inst. Pathology, Washington, 1989—; vis. scientist Nat. Inst. Diabetes and Digestive and Kidney Diseases NIH, Bethesda, Md., 1987-88. Contbr. 4 chpts. to books and 90 articles to profl. jours.; mem. editl. bd. Jour. Raman Spectroscopy, 1980-96, Vibrational Spectroscopy, 1988-99, editor, 1999—. Mem. Am. Chem. Soc. (Outstanding Chemist award Miss. chpt. 1982), Am. Phys. Soc., Am. Assn. Clin. Chemistry, Soc. Applied Spectroscopy. Office: Armed Forces Inst Pathology Divsn Environ Toxicology Rm M093 Bldg 54 Washington DC 20306-0001

KALAUS, GYÖRGY, chemical engineer, educator; b. Újpest, Hungary, Dec. 15, 1939; s. Endre and Margit (Szöke) K.; m. Éva Fenyőváry, Aug. 18. 1967; 1 child, Valter; m. Beáta Boruzs, Jan. 16, 1988. Chem. Engr., Tech. U., Budapest, Hungary, 1963, PhD, 1968; C. Sc., Hungarian Acad. Scis., Budapest, Hungary, 1977, D. Sc., 1989. Chem. engr. Asst. Tech. U. Inst. Organic Chemistry, Budapest, Hungary, 1963-70, first asst., 1970-78, lectr., reader, 1978-92, prof., 1992—. Contbr. chpts. to books, articles to scientific jours. Fellow Hungarian Scientific Rsch. Found.; mem. Organic and Bioorganic Chemistry Hungarian Acad. (com. sec. 1996-99, alkaloid chemistry working com. sec. 1986-99, chmn. 1999—). Avocations: swimming, touring. Home: Mártonhegyi u 38/b, H-1124 Budapest Hungary Office: Tech U Inst Organic Chem, Gellért tér 4, H-1111 Budapest Hungary

KALAVROUZIOTIS, GEORGIOS, cardiothoracic surgeon; b. Kerkyra, Greece, Jan. 15, 1964; s. Nickolaos G. and Pipitsa A. (Barbatsi) K. Med. diploma, Athens (Greece) U., 1988, PhD, 1993. Resident Apostolos Pavlos Hosp., Athens, 1988-91, Evangelismos Hosp., Athens, 1994-98; physician Astypalea (Greece) Med. Sta., 1993-94; guest physician Charite Hosp., Berlin, 1998; cardiothoracic surgeon Apollonion Hosp., Athens, 1998-99; pediatric cardiac surgeon Aghia Sophia Children's Hosp., Athens, 1999—. Author: Blunt Pancreatic Trauma, 1993; contbr. articles to profl. jours. With Greek Med. Corps, 1991-93. Mem. European Soc. Thoracic Surgeons, Hellenic Trauma Soc., Hellenic Surg. Soc., European Assn. of Cardiothoracic Surgery, Internat. Soc. of Surgery, Internat. Orgn. Correspondence Chess (mem. Chess in Friendship). Avocations: chess, music, travel, collecting stamps and coins. Home: 119 Papagou Ave, Zografou Attica 15773, Greece

KALAY, GURHAN, project engineer, materials scientist; b. Kirkagac, Manisa, Turkey, July 26, 1966; arrived in U.K., 1991; s. Ismail and Hatice Kalay; m. Claudia Bachner, May 22, 1999. BS, Mid. East Tech. U., Ankara, Turkey, 1988, MS, 1990; PhD, Brunel U., Uxbridge, U.K., 1994. Rsch. asst. Mid. East Tech. U., 1989-91; rschr. Brunel U., 1991-92, postdoctoral rsch. fellow, 1994-95, sr. project engr. Wolfson Ctr. for Materials Processing, 1995-98, quality mgr., 1998—; specialist in polymer processing and biomaterials. Co-editor: Wagner Jour., 1999—; contbr. articles and papers to profl. jours. Fgn. and Commonwealth Office scholar Brit. Coun., 1991; Shell Rsch. SA sponsorship Shell Chems., 1992-95. Mem. The Wagner Soc. Avocations: photography, classical music, opera, ballet, theater. Office: Brunel U Wolfson Ctr for Materials Processing, Dept Materials Engring, Uxbridge UB8 3PH, England

KALE, VIVEK SHIVARAM, geologist, educator; b. Pune, India, Apr. 12, 1959; s. Shivaram Shreedhar and Sadhana Shivaram (Oak) K.; m. Rajashree Vivek Gawankar, Jan. 16, 1986; 1 child, Athang Vivek. SSc, Loyola, Pune, India, 1975; BSc (hons.), Fergusson Coll., Pune, India, 1979; MSc in geology, Poona Univ., Pune, India, 1981, PhD in geology, 1986. Geologist Dubon Proj. Engr., Bombay, 1981-82; rsch. fellow geology dept. Pune Univ., 1982-86, lectr. geology dept., 1986-87, rsch. assoc., 1987-93, rsch. scientist, 1994-96, reader, 1996-99; coord. Geoscan Digital, Pune, 1999—. Author: Bhima Basin, 1995; contbr. over 100 articles to profl. jours. Chmn. Chaitranagari Coop. Housing Soc., 1993-96; founder Advanced Ctr. for Water Resources Devel. and Mgmt. Recipient rsch. scientistship Univ. Grants Commn., 1994. Fellow Geol. Soc. India, Indian Soc. Remote Sensing (sec. 1995—), Remote Sensing Soc., Indian Sci. Congress Assn. (Young Scientist award 1987), Indian Assn. Sedimentologists, Internat. Assn. Structural and Tectonic Geologists, Assn. Geoscientists for Internat. Devel., Indian Geophys. Union.

Avocations: trekking, chess, stamps. E-mail: vivekale@pn2.vsnl.net.in. Home: 917/11 Ganeshwadi, 411004 Pune India Office: Geoscan Digital CTPL, 48A Parvati Indsl Estate, 411009 Pune India

KALEGAEV, VLADIMIR VLADIMIROVICH, physicist, researcher; b. Bezrechnaya, Chita, USSR, Nov. 22, 1958; s. Vladimir Petrovich and Zoya Nikiforovna (Novozhilova) K.; m. Natalia Vladimirovna Gorshkova, Sept. 17, 1988; 1 child, Nastya. MSc in Math., Moscow State U., 1980, PhD in Space Physics, 1992. Engr., mathematician Inst. Nuc. Physics, Moscow State U., 1980-84, jr. rschr., 1984-93, rsch. scientist, 1993-94, sr. rschr., 1994—. Contbr. articles to profl. jours. Grantee Am. Astron. Soc., 1992, Internat. Sci. Found., 1993. Mem. Am. Astron. Soc., Am. Geophys. Union. Avocations: basketball, tourism, guitar, computers. Office: Inst Nuc Physics, Moscow State Univ, 119899 Moscow Russia

KALELI, SEMIH, obstetrician-gynecologist, educator; b. Yerköy, Yozgat, Turkey, Jan. 1, 1962; s. Remzi and Mediha (Ülgener) K.; m. Ayse Özlem Cokar, June 19, 1993 (div. 1998). Physician, Hacettepe U., Ankara, Turkey, 1985. Physician Ministry of Health, Kars, Turkey, 1986-87; resident physician in neurosurgery Ministry of Health, Ankara, 1987-88; resident physician in ob-gyn. Istanbul (Turkey) U., 1988-93, specialist and fellow in ob-gyn. and gynecologic oncology, 1993-97, assoc. prof. ob-gyn., 1997—. Author: (books) Gynecologic Oncology, 1996, 2d edit., 1998, Gestational Trophoblastic Diseases, 1997, Teratology, 1999; mng. and exec. editor Turkish Jour. Ob-Gyn., 1989—. Lt. Harita Genel Komutanligi, 1993. Recipient Prize of Cancer Rsch., Turkish Cancer Soc., 1994, Best Study award Turkish Soc. Gynecologic Oncology, 1996, Best Study of Yr. award Turkish Fertility Soc., 1997. Home: Senlikköy Mahallesi, Çekmece Sokak # 14/1, Istanbul Murat Villa Florya, Turkey Office: Istanbul U Dept Ob-Gyn, Kocamustafapasa, Istanbul Turkey

KALÉN, JOHAN GUNNAR INGEMAR, internist, endocrinologist; b. Säby, Småland, Sweden, Dec. 21, 1946; s. Ingemar Johan Eskil and Inger Elsa (Cars) K.; m. Bodil Elisabeth Hansen, July 1, 1972; children: Peter, Mikael, Markus, Marie. Med. Candidate, U. Upsala, Sweden, 1967, Med. Lic., MD, 1972; Specialist Internal Medicine, U. Upsala, 1979, Specialist in Endocrinology, 1993. Internship X-ray dept. Ctrl. Hosp., Västerås, Sweden, 1969; anesthesia dept. Löwenströska Lasarettet, Uplands Väsby, 1970; surgery County Hosp., Sala, Sweden, 1971; resident gen. hosp. and psychiatry St. Maria Hosp., Helsingborg, Sweden, 1972-73; gen. practice County Dists. Helsingborg, Landskrona, Höganäs, Sweden, 1973; gynecology dept. Helsingborg Hosp, Sweden, 1974; pediatric dept. Ängelholm Hosp., 1976, internal medicine, 1975-82; internist U. Hosp., Lund, 1978-79; consulting internist Helsingborg Hosp., 1983—. Contbr. articles to profl. jours., posters to med. soc. meetings. Fellow Swedish Soc. Medicine; mem. Swedish Med. Assn., Swedish Diabetes Assn., European Soc. for Study of Diabetes. Avocations: golf, travel, classical music. Home: Höganäsvägen 68, S-26040 Viken Sweden Office: Med Clin, Helsingborg Hosp, S-25187 Helsingborg S, Sweden

KALFF, PETER JAN, former banker; b. Amsterdam, May 12, 1937; married; 3 children. LLD, U. Leiden. With Algemene Bank Nederland N.V., 1964-91, authorized signatory Arnhem br., 1966-67; authorized signatory head office Treasury Dept. Algemene Bank Nederland N.V., Amsterdam, 1967-70; mgr. Rotterdam br. Algemene Bank Nederland N.V., 1970-73, regional mgr. Rotterdam/Zeeland Dist., 1973-74, gen. mgr. directorate Netherlands, 1974-77, mng. bd., 1977-91; mng. bd., chmn. internat. divsn. ABN AMRO Holding N.V./ABN AMRO Bank N.V., Amsterdam, 1991-94, chmn. mng. bd., 1994-2000; nque ABN AMRO Holding N.Y./ABN AMRO Bank N.Y., Amsterdam; dir. Bankraad (De Nederlandsche Bank N.V.), Beleggingsmaatschappij Calvé-Delft N.V.; Hagemeyer N.V., G.U.S. Holland B.V., Kondor Wessels Groep N.V., others; mem. internat. capital markets adv. com. Fed. Res. Bank N.Y.; mem. bd. HAL Trustee Ltd., Rochester Erasmus Exec. MBA Program; chmn. exec. bd. Netherlands Bankers Assn., 1994—. Office: ABN-AMRO Holding NV, PO Box 283, 1000 EA Amsterdam The Netherlands*

KALICKI, JAN H., federal official, banker, political scientist; b. London, Aug. 5, 1948; s. Jan and Mireya (Jaimes-Freyre) Kalicki; m. Jean Ellen Engelmayer, Oct. 22, 1989; children: Jan Harlan, Alexander Van, Peter Daniel. AB with honors, Columbia Coll., 1968; PhD, London Sch. Econ., 1971. Rsch. assoc., lectr. Princeton (N.J.) U., 1971-72, Harvard U., Cambridge, Mass., 1972; Fgn. Svc. officer U.S. Dept. State, Washington, 1972-75, mem. policy planning staff, 1974-77; chief fgn. policy advisor to Senator Edward Kennedy, U.S. Senate, Washington, 1977-84; adj. prof. Georgetown U., Washington, 1983-85; adj. prof., asst. to pres. Brown U., Providence, 1985-88, exec. dir. Ctr. Fgn. Policy Devel., 1985-88, sr. advisor, 1988-94, sr. fellow Watson Inst. Internat. Studies, 1994—; v.p. Lehman Bros., N.Y.C., 1984-88, sr. v.p., 1988-93; U.S. ombudsman for energy and comml. cooperation with NIS, 1994—; counselor U.S. Dept. Commerce, Washington, 1994—; mem. coun. fgn. rels. Internat. Inst. Strategic Studies, Royal Inst. Internat. Affairs, London. Author: The Pattern of Sino-American Crises, 1975; contbr. chpts. to books and articles to profl. jours. Sr. fellow Watson Inst. Internat. Studies Brown U., 1994—. Office: US Dept Commerce Washington DC 20230

KALIHER, MICHAEL DENNIS, librarian, historian; b. Santa Monica, Calif., Nov. 7, 1947; s. Eugene Charles and Phyllis Joan (McCrary) K. BA, U. Ariz., 1990. Pres. Klamath County (Oreg.) Hist. Soc., 1985; founder Native Am. History Week, Klamath County Mus., 1985-86. Contbr. articles to various hist. jours. Mem. Ariz. Libr. Assn., Pi Lambda Theta, Phi Alpha Theta. Roman Catholic. Avocations: backpacking, trout fishing. Home: PO Box 634 Winslow AZ 86047-0634

KALIKHMAN, IGAL, oceanographer, researcher; b. Moscow, USSR, Apr. 28, 1947; arrived in Israel, 1990; s. Leonid and Valentina (Spindler) K.; m. Tatiana Mereino, Apr. 5, 1975; 1 child, Dinah. MS, Moscow Inst. Energetics, USSR, 1971; PhD, Inst. Fisheries and Oceanog., USSR, 1983. Sr. scientist Inst. Fisheries and Oceanography, Moscow, 1973-90, Israel Oceanographic and Limnological Rsch., Haifa, 1990—. Author: Manual of Acoustic Surveys, 1984, Multidisciplinary Surveys of Fishing Conditions, 1988; contbr. papers in field. Office: Israel Oceanog Rsch, Tel Shikmona, Haifa 31080, Israel

KALIMAN, PAVLO AVKSENTIYOVICH, biochemist, researcher; b. Litvyaki, Ukraine, May 7, 1930; s. Avksentij Semenovich and Nastya Phedorivna (Bobkha) K.; m. Valentina Alekseevna Lukina, Sept. 24, 1957; 1 child, Victor. Degree, Kharkiv (Ukraine) State U., 1951, DS in Biology, 1967. Asst. lectr. Kharkiv Med. Sch., 1952-60, asst. prof., 1960-68, prof., 1968-73; chief dept. biochemistry Kharkiv State U., 1973—. Mem. editl. bd. Ukrainian Biochem. Jour. Mem. Biochem. Soc. Ukraine (mgmt. bd., chief Kharkiv br.). Home: Apt 35, Av L Svobody 39-B, 61077 Kharkiv Ukraine Office: Kharkiv Nat U, Pl Svobody 4, 310077 Kharkiv Ukraine

KALIMO, ESKO ANTERO, research institute administrator, educator; b. Helsinki, Finland, July 9, 1937; s. Yrjö Edvard and Hilma (Hiltunen) K.; m. Raija Vuokko Moilanen, Dec. 20, 1964; children: Anna, Antti. D in Social Scis., U. Helsinki, 1969. Lic. psychologist. Asst. tchr. U. Helsinki, 1961-64; sr. sci. Social Ins. Inst., Helsinki, 1964-73; chief sci. WHO, Geneva, 1974-75, sci., 1981-83; dir. rsch. inst. Social Ins. Inst., Helsinki, 1973—, prof., 1999—; lectr. psychometrics, U. Helsinki, 1964-69; rsch. assoc. Johns Hopkins U., Balt., 1969-70; assoc. prof. U. Helsinki, 1971—; prof. Nordic Sch. Pub. Health, Gothenburg, Sweden, 1989-92; chmn. adv. commn. rsch. Internat. Social Security Assn., Geneva, 1985-93, mem., 1993—; mem. expert panel WHO, Geneva, 1977-81, 1983—; cons. in social security and health UN agys., 1976—. Contbr. articles to profl. jours. Mem. Med. Rsch. coun. of Acad. in Finland, Helsinki, 1976-79; chmn. Finnish Coun. for Health Edn., Helsinki, 1981-87; vice chmn. Finland Com. for the Club of Rome, Helsinki, 1985—. 2d lt. Finland Mil., 1963-64. Decorated knight's cross 1st class Order of the Lion, Order of the White Rose (Finland). Mem. Internat. Sociol. Assn., Internat. Epidemiol. Assn., European Soc. Med. Sociology, Found. for Internat. Studies on Social Security (gov. 1987—), Club of Rome, Rotary (sec. Helsinki 1985—). Avocation: tennis. Home: Kilonkallionkuja 6, 02610 Espoo Finland Office: Social Ins Inst, PO Box 450, 00101 Helsinki Finland

KALININ, VICTOR ALEXANDROVICH, engineering educator, researcher; b. Podolsk, Russia, Jan. 15, 1956; arrived in England, 1996; s. Alexander Semionovich and Zoya Pavlovna (Kutiumina) K.; m. Elena Nikolaevna Chernousova, Feb. 11, 1983; 1 child, Tanya. MS, Moscow Power Engrng. Inst., 1978, PhD, 1983; docent in radio engrng., 1991. Rsch. engr. Moscow Power Engrng. Inst., 1978-80, asst. prof., 1984-89, assoc. prof., 1989-96; sr. lectr. comm. Oxford Brookes U., Oxford, Eng., 1996—; cons. Transense Technologies plc, Banbury, Eng., 1998—. Contbr. articles to profl. jours. Rsch. fellow Belgian Sci. Policy Office, Brussels, 1994, Cath. U. Leuven, Belgium, 1994-96, U. Oxford, 1996; rsch. grantee Oxford Brookes U., 1997. Avocations: reading, classical music. Office: Oxford Brookes U Sch Engrin, Gypsy Lane Campus, Headington OX3 OBP, England

KALINKOVA, GALINA NIKOLOVA, chemistry educator, researcher; b. Sofia, Bulgaria, Aug. 8, 1938; d. Nikola Ganchev and Valentina Nikolova (Kaleskova) K.; life ptnr. Kristan Dimov Denchev; 1 child, Victor Kristanov Denchev. Degree, U. Sofia, Bulgaria, 1968, U. Sofia, Bulgaria, 1969. Analyst, microbiologist Ministry Agr., Sofia, 1958-59; analyst, chemist Pelikan Industry, Sofia, 1959-65, Pure Chemicals and Reagents, Vladaia, Bulgaria, 1965-67; chemist Faculty Pharmacy, Sofia, 1968-73; rsch. assoc. IR-Spectroscopist, Sofia, 1973-93; sr. asst. prof. Faculty Pharmacy, Sofia, 1993—; cons. Med. Acad. Med. U., Sofia, 1973. Co-author: Encyclopedia of Pharmaceutical Technology, 2d edit., 2000; contbr. articles to profl. jours.; inventor in field. Mem. Union Dem. Forces, 1994. Named Internat. Woman of Yr. Internat. Biog. Ctr., 2000-2001. Mem. Bulgarian-Austrian Sci. Soc., Bulgarian Pharm. Soc., N.Y. Acad. Scis. Avocations: philosophic books, music, investigations and laboratory research, picture gallery, excursions. Home: 24 Krakra St, 1504 Sofia Bulgaria Office: Faculty of Pharmacy, 2 Dunav St, 1000 Sofia Bulgaria

KALINOWSKI, JAN, physicist, educator; b. Grodno, Poland, Mar. 9, 1938; s. Antoni and Wiktoria (Sienkiewicz) K.; m. Krystyna Wierzbowska, July 29, 1978; children: Sebastian Jan, Artur Kamil. MS in Physics, U. Gdańsk, Poland, 1962; PhD, Nicolaus Copernicus U., Toruń, Poland, 1968; Habilitation, U. Wrocław, Poland, 1978. Rsch. and tchg. scientist Tech. U. Gdańsk, 1962-75, assoc. prof., 1975-83, prof. physics, 1983—; guest scientist NYU, 1970-71; vis. prof. Consiglio Nazionale Delle Ricerche, Bologna, Italy, 1990-96, Inst. Molecular Sci., Okazaki, Japan, 1993; dir. Inst. Physics, Tech. U. Gdańsk, 1981-83, dir. faculty applied physics and math., 1985-90. Author: Molecular Structure of Matter, 1983, Organic Electroluminescent Materials and Devices, 1996; editor: Procs. of the 6th Internat. Conf. on Elec. and Related Properties of Organic Solids, 1993. Recipient award Ministry of Sci. and Higher Edn., 1975, award Sci. Sec. of Polish Acad. of Scis., 1984, award Czechoslovak and Polish Acads. of Scis., 1987. Avocations: classical music, garden plants, yachting. Office: Tech U Gdańsk, G Narutowicza 11/12, 80-952 Gdańsk Poland

KALINOWSKI, KONSTANTY, art historian; b. Wilno, Poland, Mar. 26, 1935; s. Anatol and Zofia (Janowicz-Czaińska) K.; m. Izabella Anna Sankiewicz; 1 child, Olga. MA, A. Mickiewicz U., Poznań, Poland, 1957, PhD, 1963, PhD Disseration and veniam legendi, 1971. Asst. Nat. Mus., Poznań, Poland, 1957-61; asst. Inst. of Art History A. Mickiewicz U., Poznań, Poland, 1961-71, asst. prof., 1971-80, full prof. Inst. of Art History, 1980—; vis. prof. U. Kiel, Germany, 1990; gen. dir. Nat. Mus., Poznań, 1990—. Author: (book) Glorification of a Ruler and Dynasty in the 17th and 18th Century, 1973, Baroque Architecture in Silesia, 1986, Baroque Art in Silesia, 1990. Recipient Golden Cross of Merit, Pres., Poland, 1973; named to Order of Polonia Restituta, Pres., Poland, 1982, Knight Comdr. Constantinian Order of St. Georg C. Bourbon Neapol, 1995. Mem. Assn. Polish Art Historians (v.p. 1981-91), Com. Internat. d'Histoire de L'art, Polish Nat. Com. of Internat. Coun. Mus. (pres. 1996—), Polish PEN Club. Orthodox. Avocations: collecting of Russian Orders and Badges. Home: Augustowska 28, 61-051 Poznań Poland Office: A Mickiewicz U Inst Art History, Niepodległości 4, 61-874 Poznań Poland

KALINOWSKI, MAREK WOJCIECH, physicist, mathematician, philosopher; b. Lublin, Poland, 1950; s. Jozef Henryk and Maria (Myszka) K. MSc in Theoretical Physics, U. Lublin, 1972, MSc in Math. and Computer Sci., 1973; PhD in Physics, U. Warsaw, Poland, 1978; MA in Philosophy, U. Lublin, 1979. Asst. prof. Polish Acad. Scis., Warsaw, 1978-82, Inst. Nuclear Rsch., Warsaw, 1979-82; rsch. assoc. dept. physics U. Toronto (Can.), 1982-86; assoc. prof. Tech. U., Warsaw, 1987-93, U. Lódź, 1993—; cons. Canada's Tomorrow, Toronto, 1984-86, Oyster Noise Reduction, Toronto, 1985-86, Warsaw Car Factory, 1987-90. Author: Nonsymmetric Fields Theory and Its Applications, 1990, Riemann Waves and Their Applications, 1992, O Teorii i Projektowaniu Nadwozi Samochodowych, 1994, Holizm a Geometryzacjai Unifikacja Oddzialywan Fizycznych, 1995; contbr. articles, papers to profl. pubs. Mem. Am. Phys. Assn., Polish Assn. Physicists, Polish Philos. Assns., IEEE, JAMP.

KALISIŃSKA, ELŻBIETA, biologist, educator; b. Szczecin, Poland, June 29, 1954; d. Eugeniusz and Janina (Terechowicz) Mazurek; m. Marek Michał Kalisinski, Jan. 30, 1982; 1 child, Dawid. MSc, Adam Mickiewicz U., Poznań, Poland, 1978, PhD, 1996; DSc, Agrl. U., Szczecin, Poland, 1989. Tchg. asst. dept. environ. protection Agrl. U., Szczecin, 1978-80, rsch. asst. dept. zoology, 1980-83, sr. rsch. asst. dept. zoology, 1983-89, asst. prof. dept. zoology, 1989-97, assoc. prof., head dept. zoology, 1998—, vice dean Faculty Biotechnology and Animal Breeding, 1999—; cons. in zoology TV Sta., Szczecin, 1989. Contbr. articles to profl. jours. Mem. Polish Zool. Soc., Polish Ornithopathology Soc., World's Poultry Sci. Assn. (Polish br.). Roman Catholic. Avocations: bicycling, nature traveling, bird watching. Office: Dept Zool Univ Agrl, Doktora Judyma 20, 71466 Szczecin Poland

KALISKI, MARY, psychologist; b. Bratislava, Czechoslovakia, Dec. 9, 1938; came to U.S., 1950; d. Frank and Margaret (Fleischman) Reichenthal; m. Thomas Kaliski, Sept. 21, 1957; children: Karen, Kenneth. BS summa cum laude, C.W. Post Coll., 1978; MS, profl. diploma, St. John's U., 1980, PhD, 1987. Psychologist North Shore Schs., L.I., 1977-79, Herricks Schs., L.I., 1979—; speaker in field. Chief psychologist Stepfamily Found. L.I., 1987-92; bd. dirs. Nassau Psychol. Svcs. Inst., 1989—. Mem. Am. Psychol. Assn., Nassau County Psychol. Assn.

KALIŠNIK, MIROSLAV, medical educator; b. Videm/Krško, Slovenia, Apr. 8, 1927; s. Ivan and Ivanka (Bukovnik) K.; m. Nevenka Oražem, July 16, 1955; children: Metka, Matjaž. MD, U. Med. Faculty, Ljubljana, Slovenia, 1952, PhD, 1960. Demonstrator U. Med. Faculty, Ljubljana, 1947-52, provisory asst., 1952-54, asst., 1954-61, asst. prof., 1961-67, assoc. prof., 1967-72, prof., 1972-95, emeritus prof., 1996—; vis. prof. U. Benghazi, Libya, 1981, external examiner, 1982; head of dept. U. Ljubljana, 1991-94, prorector, 1991-93; sci. coworker Slovenian Acad. Scis. and Arts, 1963—. Editor: Med. Jour. Slovenia, 1967-80, chief, responsible editor, 1980-88; editor-in-chief: Acta Stereologica, Ofcl. Jour. of Internat. Soc. for Stereology, 1982-ii, hon. editor, 2000—; author: (textbooks) Navodila za vaje iz histologije z embriogijo, 1972, 80, 95, Oris histologije z embriologijo, 1976, 90, 92, Osnove stereologije, 1976, 82, Croatian transl., 1984, (with L. Lah) Uvod v Znarstvenoraziskovalno Metodogijo, 1998, (with J. Zabavnik-Piano) Uvodv Znanrtvenoraziskovalno Metodologijo na Področju Veterinarstva, 1999, (with J. Zabavnik-Piano and A. Rozic-Hristovski) Uvod u Znanrstvenozaziskovalno Metodologijo na Področju Biomedicine, 2000. Roman Catholic. Home: Prijateljeva 9, 1000 Ljubljana Slovenia Office: Histology and Embryology Dept, Korytkova 2/1, 1105 Ljubljana Slovenia

KALITKAR, KISHAN RAO, engineering educator; b. Gadwal, Andhra Pra, India, Apr. 5, 1943; s. Laxman Rao and Laxmi (Bai) K.; m. Rukmini Bai Jhade, June 29, 1967; children: Praveen Kumar, Pradeep Kumar. BEngring., Osmania U., Hyderabad, India, 1965, MEngring., 1967; PhD, Indian Inst. Tech., Kanpur, 1973. Sr. rsch. asst. Indian Inst. Tech., Kanpur, 1967-72; lectr. Regional Engring. Coll., Warangal, India, 1972-74, asst. prof., 1974-79, prof., 1979—, head Electronics and Computer Sci. dept., 1983-88, dean students, 1991-92, dean acad., 1993-96; chief warden Regional Engring. Coll. Hostels, 1989-91. Recipient gold medals (2), Osmanian U., 1966, Disting. Leadership award Am. Biog. Inst., 1993, Best Tchr. award Govt. Andhra Pradesh, 1999. Mem. IEEE (sr.), Indian Soc. Tech. Edn. (life), Instrument Soc. India (life). Hindu. Achievements include research in digital signal processing; microprocessors and microcontrollers. Avocations: music, reading, watching games. Home: Principals Banglow REC, Warangal 506004, India Office: Regional Engring Coll, ECE Dept, Warangal 506004, India

KALIYAMURTHY, KRISHNASWAMY, engineer, educator, researcher, consultant; b. Pathirakottai, Tamil Nadu, India, Feb. 6, 1944; s. Krashnaswamy Arumugam and Mangathal (Krishnaswany) K.; m. Jula Sundaramurthy, June 15, 1973; children: Jaya Chaumndeshwari, Ashok Kumar. B in Engring., Anna U., Madras, India, 1967; M in Engring., Indian Inst. Sci., Bangalore, 1969. Test engr. Crompton Creaves Ltd., Bombay, 1969; dep. mgr. N.G.E.F. Ltd., Bangalore, 1969-74, mgr., 1975-79, works mgr., 1980-92, dep. gen. mgr., 1992-96; gen. mgr. Mangalam Electricals, New Delhi, 1996; assoc. prof. Vellore Engring. Coll., Tamil Nadu, 1996-99, prof., 1999—; cons. 515 Army Base Workshop, Bangalore, 1996-97, Meher Capacitors, Ltd., Bangalore, 1997-98. Inventor protective device for closed tube diffusion ampule and a new improved diffusion process. Pres. Resident's Welfare Assn., Bangalore, 1988-96, Prasanna Ganapathy Seva Trust, Bangalore, 1982—. Mem. IEEE, Indian Soc. for Tech. Edn. Avocations: yoga, swimming. Office: Vellore Engring Coll, Vellore-14, Tamil Nadu 632014, India

KALKHOF, THOMAS CORRIGAN, physician; b. Wellsville, N.Y., Aug. 12, 1919; s. Arthur Albert and Evelyn (Corrigan) K.; m. Mary E. Jones, Mar. 3, 1946 (dec. 1955); children: Thomas E., Susan A., Mark A., Patricia D.; m. 2d Constance N. McCarthy, Apr. 19, 1958 (dec. 1998); children: Christopher J., Constance M., Craig Alan. B.S., Gannon U., 1943; M.D., Marquette U., 1946. Intern, resident St. Vincent's Hosp., Erie, Pa., 1946-47; pvt. practice in holistic medicine, nutritional problems, continued breast cancer rehab. and thermography, gen. geriatrics and psychosomatic, Erie, 1947—; pvt. practice holistic medicine Erie, 1947—; med. dir. Twinbrook Med. Ctr., 1960-84; dir. Iroquois Med. Centre, Erie; staff mem. St. Vincent's Health Ctr., Hamot Med. Ctr., Erie; pres., dir. Small Hosp. Cons., Inc., Erie, 1954—. Past chmn. Pa. Bd. Accreditation Nursing Homes and Related Facilities; past pres. Cath. Social Svcs., Erie; past pres. Erie County Ind. Coun. on Aging.; bd. dirs. Cath. Charities USA Commn. on Aging. With M.C., AUS, 1943-44. Fellow Am. Coll. Health Care Adminstrs., Am. Geriatric Soc., Am. Acad. Family Physicians, Acad. Psychosomatic Medicine (past pres.); mem. AMA, Pa. Health Care Assn. (past pres.), Acad. Psychomatic Medicine (past pres.), Pa. Acad. Family Physicians (past pres. Erie chpt.), Assn. Physicians in Chronic Disease Facilities (past pres.), Am. Soc. Clin. Hypnosis, Pa., Erie County Med. Socs., Nat. Geriatric Soc. (pres.), Soc. Prospective Medicine, Ind. Coun. on Aging (past pres.), KC (4 deg.), Internat. Transactional Analysis Assn. Republican. Roman Catholic. Office: PO Box 7265 3749 E Lake Rd Erie PA 16511-1346

KALKREUTH, WOLFGANG DIETER, geology educator; b. Bad Polzin, Germany, July 24, 1944; arrived in Brazil, 1996; s. Werner Barsikow and Gisela Kalkreuth; m. Sabine Beckmann-Kalkreuth; children: Sophie, Johanna. Diploma in geology, Free U., Berlin, 1973, Habilitation, 1989; PhD in Geology, Rheinisch Westfälische Technische Hochschule Aachen, Germany, 1976. Rsch. assoc. Rheinisch Westfälische Technische Hochschule Aachen, Germany, 1977-78, U. Sherbrooke, Can., 1979-80; rsch. scientist Geol. Survey Can., 1980-91, 92-96; prof. geology U. Cologne, Germany, 1991-92; vis. prof. U. Fed. do Rio Grande do Sul, Porto Alegre, Brazil, 1996-99, prof., 1999—; hon. adj. prof. Dalhousie U., Halifax, N.S., 1993—, U. Calgary, Alta., 1994—. Mem. editl. bd. Can. Soc. Petroleum Geologists Bull., Can., 1994-96, Internat. Jour. Coal Geology, Amsterdam, The Netherlands, 1994—, Latin Am. Assn. Organic Chemistry, Rio de Janeiro, 1994—. Fellow Geol. Survey Am.; mem. Internat. Com. for Coal and Organic Petrology (chmn. commn. II 1993—), The Soc. for Organic Petrology, Can. Soc. Petroleum Geologists (medal of merit 1984). Office: Inst Geociências, Ave Bento Gonçalves 9500, 91501-970 Porto Alegre RSI, Brazil

KALLA, SHYAM LAL, mathematician, educator; b. Jodhpur, India, Jan. 4, 1938; s. Dau Lal and Fateh Kor (Bohra) K.; m. Kamla Devi Vyas, May 5, 1960; children: Raj Kumar, Sharda Vyas. BS, Rajasthan U., Jaipur, India, 1957, MS, 1959, PhD, 1968, DSc, 1976. Sr. rsch. fellow Jodhpur U., 1967-70; prof. Nat. U. Tucuman, Argentina, 1970-76, Zulia U., Maracaibo, Venezuela, 1976-87, 88-92, Kuwait U., 1987-88, 92—; prin. investigator Conicit, Caracas, Venezuela, 1990-94, v.p., 1990-92; dir. Rsch. Ctr. CIMA, Maracaibo, 1991-92; chmn. Workshop-TMSF, Sofia, Bulgaria, 1994, Varna, 1996. Chief editor Revista Technica, 1978-92; editor: Hadronic Jour., 1993, Integral Transform and Sp.Fun., 1991; contbr. more than 260 articles to profl. jours. Fellow Nat. Acad. Sci.; mem. Am. Math. Soc., N.Y. Acad. Scis. Achievements include research in fractional calculus and special functions. Office: Kuwait U Dept Math, PO Box 5969, 13060 Safat Kuwait

KALLAKIS, ACHILLEAS MICHALIS S., shipping company executive; b. London, Sept. 3, 1968; s. Michalis and Erinoula (Angelinakis) K.; m. Pamela Anne Stachowsky, Sept. 1995; children: Erinoula, Michalis and Aristotelis (twins). BSc in Econs. with honors, Buckingham (Eng.) U., 1989. Dir. Global Transport, Del., N.Y., 1989-91; chmn., CEO The Pacific Group of Cos., London, N.Y.C., 1991—, 1991—, Pacific Risk Corp., 2000—; dir. U.S. C. of C., London, 1997—, Ocean Group USA, 1989—, Pacific Maritime, N.Y., 1991—, Bernouli Trust Corp., N.Y., 1994—, South Pacific Adv. Bd., Sydney, Australia, 1994—; chmn., CEO Pacific Coffee Corp., Hellenic Capital Mgmt.; chmn. Pacific Vending Group; chmn. & CEO, Hellenic Capital Mgmt.; chmn., CEO Atlas Alliance Group. Author: Maritime Registers of the World, 1994, Transport Economics, 1996; co-editor: The Wonders of Italy, 1996. Pres. Youth Anglo-Hellenic Soc. U.K., London, 1986-88; dir. Friends of Florence, Italy, 1997—; mem. com. Youth Enterprise Initiative, London, 1989-92; mem. Royal Opera, London, Met. Opera Guild, N.Y., Navy League. Recipient Churchill award for Excellence Churchill Enterprise Found., 1993, Pres.'s Golden Honor award South Pacific Action, Foru, 1995, Prime Min.'s award South Pacific Action Forum, 1996, Outstanding Emerging Leader award Office of Maritime Affairs, 1997. Fellow Inst. Dirs., Inst. Transport and Tourism; mem. Friends of Conservation, Cliveden Club, Queen's Club, U.S. C. of C. Japan, Met. Opera Guild (N.Y.C.), Met. Club (N.Y.C.), Nat. Trust (London), Soc. for the Protection of Ancient Bldgs. (London), The Landmark Trust (Eng.). Greek Orthodox. Avocations: travel, Italian studies, Back-gammon, fencing, tennis, antiques. Office: Pacific Group Cos, 42 Berkeley Sq, Mayfair London WIJ 5AW, England also: 1st Fl 50 Hans Crescent, Knightsbridge, London SW1X 0NA, England

KALLAS, SIIM, government official; b. Tallinn, Estonia, Oct. 2, 1948; s. Udo and Rita (Alver) K.; m. Kristi Kartus, may 6, 1972; children: Ülo, Kaja. Diploma, Tartu (Estonia) U., 1972. Lectr. Tartu U., 1972-75; head specialist Ministry of Fin., Tallinn, 1975-79; gen. mgr. Estonian Savs. Bank, Tallinn, 1979-86; dep. editor in chief (Estonian daily newspaper) Rahva Hääl, Tallinn, 1986-89; pres. Bank of Estonia, Tallinn, 1991-95; min. fgn. affairs Tallinn, Estonia, 1995-96, min. of finance, 1999—; lectr. Estonian Bus. Sch., Tallinn; chmn. Assn. Trade Unions, 1989. Contbr. over 100 articles to profl. jours. Mem. Supreme Council of the USSR, Moscow, 1989-91, Riigikogu-Parliament Republic of Estonia, 1995—; founder, chmn. Reform Party. Office: Estonian Ministry Fin, 1 Suur-Anneerikaa, 15006 Tallinn Estonia*

KALLEE, EKKEHARD ALBERT HERMANN, physician, educator; b. Stuttgart-Feuerbach, Germany, Jan. 30, 1922; s. Albert and Helene (Schmolz) K.; m. Barbara Weigmann, Sept. 23, 1941; 1 child: Stephan. MD, U. Tuebingen, Germany, 1950. Head clin. radioisotope lab. med. clinic U. Tuebingen, 1951-87, asst. prof., dozent, 1961, assoc. prof., 1967; prof. emeritus, 1987; fellow Max Kade Found., N.Y.C., 1955-56; with dept. radiology Strong Meml. Hosp., U. Rochester, N.Y., 1955-56; with Med. U. Klinik, Tuebingen, Germany; founder, chief of Radioisotope Lab., U. Tuebingen, 1951. Inventor direct detection of protein traces (insulin) using paper electrophoresis; first descriptions of (a) some details of Bennhold's analbuminemia, (b) passive transport by means of adsorptive distribution equilibria, (c) binding ability of subcellular proteins, (d) disruption of antigen-antibody bonds by antirheumatics, (e) pyramidal lobe in hyperthyroidism; contbr. articles to profl. jours. Mem. Student Fraternity Tuebinger Königsgesellschaft "Roigel", European Thyroid Assn. (emeritus), Deutsche Gesellschaft fuer Endokrinologie, Deutsche Gesellschaft fuer Innere Medizin. Avocations: gardening, foreign languages. Office: Medizinische Universitaetsk, Otfried-Mueller-Strasse 10, D-72076 Tuebingen Germany

KALLIOKOSKI, PENTTI JUHANI, engineering educator, dean; b. Helsinki, Finland, Aug. 2, 1947; s. Lauri Johannes and Lydia Miljana (Kujanpaa) K.; m.Maijaleena Annikki Rouvinen, June 1970; children: Antti, Laura, Tuomo. MSc in Chemical Engring., Helsinki U. of Tech., 1970, Lic. Sc. in Chemical Engring., 1976; PhD, U. Minn., Mpls., 1979. Cert. Occpl. Hygenist, 1974. Rsch. asst. Helsinki U. of Tech., 1970-71; chemist Inst. Occupational Health, Helsinki, 1971-74, occpl. hygenist, 1974-77, spl. rschr., 1978-79; acting prof. U. Kuopio, Finland, 1979-80; prof. environ. hygiene U. Kuopio, 1980—, dean, 1984-2000; vis. prof. U. Mich., Ann Arbor, 2000—. Editor: (book) Industrial Hygene, 1992; contbr. over 500 articles to profl. jours. Mem. Internat. Soc. Indoor Air Quality and Climate (mem. task force and chmn.), Am. Indsl. Hygiene Assn. (Yant award 1999), Internat. Commn. on Occupl. Health, Internat. Acad. Indoor Air Scis. Avocation: skiing. Office: Mich Environ Hlth Scis 109 Observatory Dr Ann Arbor MI 48109-2029

KALLIONTZIS, CONSTANTINE, civil engineer, consultant; b. Athens, Dec. 1, 1954; s. Nicolaos and Helen (Philippides) K. BS, Univ. Leeds, Leeds, Eng., 1977, D in philosophy, 1981. Owner Computational Hydraulics Office, Athens, 1982—. Contbr. articles to profl. jours. Greek Orthodox. Avocations: swimming, driving, listening to classical music. Fax: 301 93 15 196. Office: Computational Hydraulics, 70 Omirou St, 17121 Athens Greece

KALLITHRAKAS-KONTOS, NIKOLAOS GEORGE, chemistry educator; b. Athens, Attiki, Greece, Oct. 10, 1957; s. George Dimitrios Kallithrakas and Adamantia Nikolaos (Samartzi) Kallithraka; m. Roubini Dimitrios Moschochoritou, Sept. 12, 1987. BS in Chemistry, U. Athens, 1981, PhD in Chemistry, 1988. Rschr. Numismatic Mus. Athens, 1987-89, Nat. Ctr. Demokritos, Athens, 1990-91; lectr. Tech. U. Crete, Athens, 1992—, asst. prof., 1995—. Avocation: chess. Home: Melidoniou 11, 73100 Chania Greece Office: Tech U Crete, Lab of Chemistry, 73100 Chania Greece

KALLÓ, DÉNES, chemist, educator; b. Nyíradony, Szabolcs, Hungary, Aug. 6, 1931; s. Sándor Ferenc and Izabella Klára (Schlett) K.; m. Aranka Gizella Unger, May 11, 1958. BSc, U. Veszprém, Hungary, 1953; Cand.Chem. Sci., Hungarian Acad. Sci., Budapest, 1962, DSc, 1979; Doctorate (hon.), Veszprém U., 1999. Scientist Hungarian Oil and Gas Rsch. Inst., Veszprém, 1953-56; scientist Ctr. Rsch. Inst. for Chemistry, Hungarian Acad. Scis., Budapest, 1956-65, sr. scientist, 1966-74, head of dept., 1974-95, sci. advisor, 1995—; mem. Commn. of Sci. Qualification, Budapest, 1987-94; expert Nat. Com. Tech. Devel., Budapest, 1992—; mem. accreditation com. U. Veszprém, 1994—; mem. DSc coun. Hungarian Acad. Sci., 1995-99; mem. Nat. Sci. Rsch. Found., Budapest, 1995-99. Author/editor: Contact Catalysis, 1976 (Medal of Acad. Sci. 1978). Recipient Prize of Hungarian Acad. Sci., 1983, J. Varga Medallion, 1995; Golden Order of Labour, Presidium of Hungarian People's Rep., 1985. Mem. Internat. Zeolite Assn., Internat. Com. on Natural Zeolites. Presbyterian. Avocations: tourism, gardening, photography, carpeting. Home: Frankel Leó u 2-4, 1027 Budapest Hungary Office: Ctrl Rsch Inst Chemistry Hungarian Acad Scis, Pusztaszeri u 59-67, 1025 Budapest Hungary

KÁLMÁN, ALAJOS, chemistry educator, researcher; b. Rákoskeresztur, Pest, Hungary, June 26, 1935; s. Peter and Peterne (Kaproncai) Maria; m. Alajosne Eva Borbala Kiss, Nov. 10, 1961 (div. 1991); children: Csaba Péter, András Pal; m. Julia Albrecht, Aug. 10, 1991. Diploma in chemistry, Eotvos Lorand U., Budapest, Hungary, 1958, PhD, 1968; DSc, Hungarian Acad. Scis., Budapest, Hungary, 1975. Rsch. asst. Ctrl. Rsch. Inst. for Chemistry Hungarian Acad. Scis., Budapest, 1958-61, rsch. fellow, 1961-69, sr. rsch. fellow, 1969-72, head rsch. group, 1972-76, head rsch. dept., 1976—; dir. Hungarian Affiliated Ctr. to the Cambridge Crystallographic Database, Budapest, 1979; bd. dirs. Chem. Rsch. Ctr. Itas. Recipient golden medal Hungarian Govt., 1986, Hungarian State prize bearing the name Count István Széchenyi, 1994; named Hon. Citizen, XVIIth Dist. Budapest, 1997. Mem. Hungarian Acad. Scis. (corr.), Hungarian Chem. Soc. (v.p. 1990-96, pres. 1996—), Internat. Union Crystallography (v.p. 1990-93), F. Vigyázó Cultural Soc. (pres. 1989-99). Avocations: fine art, cathedrals, music, gardening. E-mail: akalman@cric.chemres.hu. Home: Zsuzsanna Tér 5, 1174 Budapest Hungary Office: Hungarian Acad Scis Chem Rsch Ctr, Pusztaszeri ut 59-67, 1025 Budapest Hungary

KÁLMÁN, BÉLA, solar astronomer; b. Ersekujvar, Hungary, Dec. 5, 1944; s. Béla and Gabriella (Farkas) K.; m. Gyöngyi Gyertyános, Aug. 12, 1969. Diploma of astronomer, Lomonosov Univ., Moscow, 1969; candidate of scis., Pulkovo Observatory, Leningrad, USSR, 1980. Rsch. scientist Heliophysical Observatory Hungarian Acad. Sci., Debrecen, Hungary, 1969—, head of observatory, 1982-97. Co-author: Astronomy, 1989; contbr. articles to profl. jours. Mem. Internat. Astronomical Union. Office: Heliophysical Observatory, P O Box 30, H 4010 Debrecen Hungary

KALMAN, PETER, cardiologist; b. Feb. 26, 1928; s. Alexander and Ilona (Balog) K.; m. Susan Horanyi, July 7, 1951. MD, Med. U. Budapest, 1952. Dir. non-invasive lab. Nat. Inst. Cardiology, Budapest, 1956-70; head dept. Nat. Med. Inst. Sports, Budapest, 1970-77; head dept. internal medicine and cardiology Tetenyi Hosp., Budapest, 1977—; fellow cardiology Hahnemann Med. Coll., Hosp. Cardiovascular Sect., Phila., 1963; vis. prof. Hahnemann U., Likoff Cardiovascular Inst., Phila., 1981-82. Author: Atlas in Phonocardiography, 1973; textbook chpt. on cardiac auscultation. Fellow Am. Coll. Cardiology; mem. Am. Fedn. Aging Rsch., Internat. Assn. Olympic Med. Officers, European Soc. Cardiology, Hungarian Soc. Cardiology (bd. dirs.), Hungarian Soc. Atherosclerosis (bd. dirs.). Home: 29 Hidasz, 1026 Budapest Hungary

KÀLMÀN, PÈTER, physicist, educator; b. Budapest, Hungary, June 3, 1951; s. Pèter and Csilla (Sàndor) K.; m. Àgnes Horvàtth, Dec. 30, 1973; children: Kristòf, Bence. MSc in Physics, Roland Eötvös U., Budapest, Hungary, 1974, DSc in Physics, 1977; 1st degree, Hungarian Acad Scis., 1991. Doctorand Ctrl. Rsch. Inst. for Physics, Budapest, 1975-77, rsch. worker, 1977-79; asst. lectr. Tech. U. Budapest, 1980-91, assoc. prof., 1991—; adj. lectr. Semmelweis Med. U., Budapest, 1985-97; vis. prof. Tech. U. Wien, Austria, 1992-93. Contbr. articles to profl. jours. Mem. Roland Eötvös Phys. Soc., Budapest. Roman Catholic. Avocations: Viola da Gamba artist (17 records and CDs from Hungarian early music). Office: Tech U of Budapest, Budafoki ut 8 F 1 1 10, 1521 Budapest Hungary

KALMAN, RUDOLF EMIL, research mathematician, system scientist; b. Budapest, Hungary, May 19, 1930; s. Otto and Ursula (Grundmann) K.; m. Constantina Stavrou, Sept. 12, 1959; children: Andrew E.F.C., Elisabeth K. SB, MIT, 1953, SM, 1954; DSc, Columbia U., 1957; DEng (hon.), U. Bologna, 1988; DSc (hon.), U. Kyoto, Japan, 1990; PhD (hon.), Heriot Watt U., Edinburgh, Scotland, 1990, Tech. U. Crete, 1993, Budapest Tech. U., 1999. Staff engr. IBM Research Lab., Poughkeepsie, N.Y., 1957-58; research mathematician Research Inst. Advanced Studies, Balt., 1958-64; prof. engring. mech. and elec. engring. Stanford U., 1964-67, prof. math. system theory, 1967-71; grad. rsch. prof. Ctr. for Math. System Theory U. Fla., 1971-92; dir. Center for Math. System Theory, U. Fla., 1971-92, prof. emeritus, 1992—; prof. math. sys. theory Swiss Fed. Inst. Tech., Zurich, 1973-97; sci. adviser Ecole Nationale Superieure des Mines de Paris, 1968—; mem. sci. adv. bd. Laboratorio di Cibernetica, Naples, 1970-73. Author: Topics in Mathematical System Theory, 1969, over 150 sci. and tech. papers.; editorial bd. Internat. Jour. Math. Modelling, Jour. Computer and Systems Scis., Jour. Nonlinear Analysis, Jour. Optimization Theory and Applications, Applied Math. Letters, Math. of Control, Signals and Systems, Jour. Forecasting, Revue Internationale de Systemique. Named outstanding young scientist Md. Acad. Sci., 1962; recipient IEEE medal of honor, 1974, Rufus Oldenburger medal ASME, 1976, Centennial medal IEEE, 1984, 1st Kyoto prize Inamori Found., 1985, Steele prize Am. Math. Soc., 1987, Bellman prize Automatic Control Coun., 1997; Guggenheim fellow IHES Bures-sur-Yvette, 1971. Fellow Am. Acad. Arts and Scis.; mem. NAE (U.S.), NAS (U.S.), Hungarian Acad. Scis. (fgn.), Académie des Scis., Inst. de France (fgn.), Russian Acad. Scis. (fgn.). Office: ETH Zentrum, CH-8092 Zurich Switzerland

KALMAZ, ERROL EKREM, environmental scientist; b. Turkey, Jan. 2, 1940; came to U.S., 1962, naturalized, 1979; s. Memet and Ayse Sarah K.; m. Grace G. Durusoy, Oct. 3, 1974; children: Phyllis, Denise. Student, Queens Coll., 1962-63; BA in Chemistry, Okla. State U., 1969, MS in Environ. Sci. and Engring., 1972, PhD in Engring., 1974. Rsch asst. Okla. Med. Rsch. Found., Oklahoma City, 1969-72, rsch. assoc., 1972-74; postdoctoral fellow Duke U., Durham, N.C., 1974-76; asst. prof. dept. engring. sci. and mechanics U. Tenn., Knoxville, 1976-79; sr. environ. sci. Hennington, Durham & Richardson, Inc.; engring. cons. Santa Barbara, Calif., 1979-83; sr. rsch. scientist NASA Johnson Space Ctr., Houston, 1983-87; sr. rsch. scientist Walls Med. Found. U. Tex., Galveston, 1987-90; assoc. prof. U. S. Fla. Coll. Pub. Health, Tampa, 1990-94; v.p. Caltex Internat. Inc., Houston, 1994—; sr. rsch. assoc. NRC., Houston; cons. to industry, engrs., and govt. agys.; bd. dors. Advance Environ. Studies; adj. assoc. prof. dept. civil engring. U.S. Fla. Coll. Pub. Health div. environ. engring. Contbr. articles to profl. jours., chpts. to books; patentee in field. Mem. AAAS, Am. Chem. Soc., Am. Coll. Toxicology, Inst. Environ. Scis. (tech. chmn. water quality impact), Internat. Soc. Ecol. Modeling, N.Y. Acad. Scis., Soc. Computer Simulation, Am. Inst. Chemists, Sigma Xi. Home: 7036 N Holiday Dr Galveston TX 77550-3028 Office: PO Box 580629 Houston TX 77258-0629

KALMAZ, GULGUN DURUSOY, physician, scientist; b. Ankara, Turkey; came to U.S., 1974; d. Avni H. and Nazime A. (Ipari) Durusoy; BA in Biochemistry, Am. Coll. for Women, Turkey, 1965; MD, U. Istanbul, Turkey, 1974; postgrad. Duke U. Med. Center, 1974-76; m. Ekrem E. Kalmaz, Oct. 3, 1974; children: Phyllis, Denise. Intern in pediatrics and surgery U. Istanbul Sch. Medicine, 1972-73, resident, 1973-74; practice medicine specializing in hematology, 1973—; rsch. assoc. pediatric hematology Zeynep Kamil Children's Hosp., Istanbul, 1973-74; vis. scientist U. Tenn. Meml. Research Center, Knoxville, 1976-78, research asso. dept. med. biology Sch. Medicine, 1978-80; fellow NIH, 1980-83, hematology Shriners Burn Inst., 83-85, dept. internal medicine, div. hematology and oncology U. Tex. Med. Br., Galveston, 85—, asst. prof. medicine, sci. staff mem. Shriners Burns Inst.. Recipient Nat. Svc. award NIH, 1980-83. Mem. AAAS, Am. Chem. Soc., Am. Soc. Hematology, Assn. Exptl. Hematology, Internat. Soc. for Exptl. Hematology, N.Y. Acad. Scis., Tissue Culture Assn., Sigma Xi. Contbr. articles on hematology to profl. jours. and books. Home: 7036 N Holiday Dr Galveston TX 77550-3028 Office: U Tex Med Br Dept Internal 45135 Galveston TX 77555-0001

KALMS, IAN CHARLES, plant company executive; b. Taree, NSW, Australia, June 14, 1962; s. Raymond Edward Victor and Laurel Gwendolyn Ann Kalms; m. Margaret Lynda Van Klaveran, Oct. 1, 1983; children: Melissa, Gavin. Trainee ginner Namoi Cotton Co-op, Moree, 1979-83; ginner Auscott, Moree, 1983-84; mgr. Darling River Cotton, Bourke, 1984-86; mgr. seed coating Heritage Seeds P/L, Toowoomba, 1986—; designer/commr. trial plant in China; cons. in field. Inventor high tipping coating pan, coating pan stirrer, and continuous flow buffel coater. Mem. SME (sr., chmn.), Austrlaian Soc. Nitrogen Fixation. Avocations: golf, fishing. Home: 9 Jane Ct, Toowoomba QLD 4350, Australia Office: Heritage Seeds P/L, CNR Indsl Ave Orford Ct, Toowoomba QLD 4350, Australia

KALMS, STANLEY, industrialist; b. Nov. 21, 1931; s. Charles and Cissie Kalms; m. Pamela Jimack; 3 children. Student, Christ's Coll., Finchley, Eng.; DLitt (hon.), Coun. for Nat. Acad. Awards, Eng., 1991; D (hon.), U. North London, 1994. With Dixons Group, 1948—, mng. dir., 1962-72, chmn., 1972—; vis. prof. Bus. Sch. U. North London, 1991—. Chmn. King's Healthcare Nat. Health Svc. Trust, 1993-96; bd. dirs. Ctr. for Policy Studies, 1991—; mem. Funding Agy. for Schs., 1994-97; gov. Dixons Bradford City Tech. Coll., 1988—; trustee Industry in Edn., 1993—; chmn. Jewish Ednl. Devel. Trust, 1978-89, Jews' Coll., 1983-89; co-founder, sponsor Immanuel Coll.; founder Stanley Kalms Found.; founder, sponsor Ctr. for Applied Jewish Ethics in Bus. and the Professions, Jerusalem. Named Knight Brit. Empire, 1996. Fellow City and Guilds of London Inst. (hon.);. Avocations: opera, ballet. Office: Dixons Group PLC, 29 Farm St, London W1X 7RD, England

KALNINS, OJARS ERIKS, Latvian diplomat; b. Munich, Oct. 22, 1949; came U.S., 1951; s. Eizens and Matilde Marija (Silkalns) K.; m. Irma Ferlins; children: Dagmara, Richard, Christopher, Ingrida. BA in Philosophy, Roosevelt U., Chgo., 1972. Mgr. advt. Osco Drug, Inc., Oakbrook, Ill., 1974-79; creative dir. Semel-Kaye & Co., Chgo., 1979-84; dir. pub. rels. Am.-Latvian Assn., Rockville, Md., 1985-91; min.-counselor Latvian Embassy, Washington, 1991-92, amb. to U.S. and Mex., 1993-2000; permanent observer OAS, 1996; dir. Latvian Inst., Riga, 2000—; commn. mem. U.S.-Baltic Partnership Fund, 2000—; bd. mem. The Kids First Fund. Author: Chautauqua-Jurmala, 1986; editor Chgo.-Latvian Newsletter, 1981-91; contbr. articles to newspapers and mags. Cons. United Latvian Assn. Chgo., 1981-84; advisor World Fedn. Free Latvians, Rockville, 1985-91, Popular Front Latvia, Riga, 1988-91; chmn. Joint Baltic-Am. Nat. Com., Rockville, 1988. Recipient Baltic Freedom award Baltic Youth Conf., 1988, Order of Three Stars, Latvia, 1998. Office: The Latvian Inst, Smilsu 1E 1/3 7th Fl, LV 1050 Riga Latvia

KALNINS, ULDIS, economist; b. Riga, Latvia, July 24, 1967; s. Ivars and Rasma (Svárpstone) K.; m. Agate Sliede, June 15, 1996; one child: Mārtiņš. B in Engring., Tech. U. Riga, Latvia, 1992, diploma in prodn. adminstrn., 1993. Cert. engr. Divsn. head Ministry Fin., Latvia, 1991-93, Latvian Privatization Agy., 1993—; bd. dirs. Riga Stock Exch., Latvia, 1994—; supr. bd. dirs. Latvian Ctrl. Depository, Riga, 1998—. Supt. bd. dirs. State Social Welfare Agy. Avocation: hiking. Office: Privatization Agy, K Valdemāra Iela 31, LV 1887 Riga Latvia

KALO, ZAIA MARBINA, managing director; b. Nineveh, Iraq, Mar. 23, 1942; came to Australia,; s. Marbina and Sarah (Odisho) Pithyou; m. Mabel Yacob Mikhael, Nov. 8, 1958; children: Alexander, Demetrius, Susan, Rosan, Sylvana. Diploma in voice of prophecy, Beirut, 1962; diploma, Bennett Coll., London, 1960; cert., Royal Soc. Arts, London, 1964, London Sch. Journalism, 1961; cert. in tert. studies, Catholic Coll., Sydney, 1990; cert. in profl. devel., U. NSW, Sydney, 1995; cert. in tchng. lang., U. Sydney, 1995; cert. in orientation, Ethnic Affairs Commn., 1995; cert., Conf. Lang. Svcs., Sydney, 1997. Clerk, typist in English/Arabic Iraq Petroleum Co. Ltd, Kirkuk, Iraq, 1955-65; supervisor Min. of Oil and Minerals, Baghdad, Iraq, 1966-68; typing pool supr. Min. of Econs., Baghdad, Iraq, 1968-71; gen. clerk Guardian Royal Exchange Assurance Group, Sydney, Australia, 1971-74; plant operator Fairfield City Coun., New South Wales, 1974-81; tchr. Hurstville Bus. Coll., New South Wales, 1983-87; mng. dir. Zacsam Pty. Ltd., 1995—; translator/interpreter Ethnic Affairs Commn. Panel, 1995—, chairperson Assyrians Examiner's Panel Nat. Accreditation Authority for Translators & Interpreters, 1996—, translator/interpreter Panel for On-Call Translation and Interpreters Agy. Pty., Ltd., Panel for Translation Express Pty. Ltd., New South Wales, 1995—; translator, intrepreter Panel for Assoc. Translators & Linguists, 1995—; del. Internat. Annual Congress Assyrian Universal Alliance, Sydney, 1978, 84, U.S., 87; del. Coun. of Assyrian Ch. of The East to USA, 1988, Ancient Ch. of the East Inc. to New Zealand, 1991, 92, Fedn. Ethnic Cmty. Coun. of Australia Inc. Congress, 1994. Author: Torment, 1996, Is The Bible True?, 1996. Active Assyrian Universal Alliance, 1971, amb. in Australia, 1986-89; sec. Coun. of the Assyrian Ch. of the East Inc., 1972-77, pres. 1977-80; mem. Assyrian Literary Com., 1976-84; justice of peace, Australia, 1979—; sec. Assyrian Sports and Cultural Club, Inc., 1982-84; pres. Coun. of the Ancient Ch. of the East Inc., 1988-93; sec., coord. Assyrian Nissibin Sch., 1988-94; bd. dirs. NSW Fedn. Ethnic Schs., 1991-92; del. to New Zealand for Ancient Ch. of the East Inc., 1992—, Assyrian Universal Alliance Polit. Arm to U.S., 1997; founder, sec. Assyrian Fedn. of Australia, Inc., 1992-93; mem. Immigration and Refugees Com., 1992-95; pres. Assyrian Fedn. of Asutralia, Inc., 1993-95. Recipient Italian Oil Refinery Co. medal, 1968, Citizen of Yr. Australia Day Cmty. Award, 1993. Mem. Assyrians Nation Assn. Inc. (pres. 1993—), Mt. Prichard Club. Avocations: reading, writing, sports, social entertainment. Home: Greenfield Park, 17 Mistral St, 2176 New South Wales Australia Office: Zacsam Pty Ltd, PO Box 123A, 2165 Fairfield Heights Australia

KALOF, LINDA HENRY, sociologist, educator; b. Norfolk, Va., Dec. 17, 1946; d. William Douglas Henry and Mary Elizabeth Bailey; m. Thomas Michael Dietz; children: Alexandra, Adam. BA, U. Fla., 1975; PhD, The Am. U., 1989. Asst. prof. SUNY, Plattsburgh, 1989-95, assoc. prof., 1995-96; assoc. prof. George Mason U., Fairfax, Va., 1996—. Co-author: Evaluating Social Science Research, 1996; author: (with others) Discourses of Animal Concern, 2000; contbr. articles to profl. jours. E-mail: lkalof@gmu.edu. Office: George Mason U Dept Sociology and Anthro Fairfax VA 22030

KALPAKAM, SARASWATHI, mathematician, researcher; b. Madras, Tamil Nadu, India, May 9, 1947; s. Saraswathi and Venkata (Lakshni) Venkataramiah; m. Arun Kumar Subrahmanyan, May 16, 1976; children: A.K. Shyam, A.K. Shiva. BSc, Andhra (India) U., 1965; MSc, Indian Inst. Tech., Madras, 1967, PhD, 1973. Postdoctoral fellow dept. math. Indian Inst. Tech., Madras, 1973-74, lectr., 1974-79, asst. prof., 1979-88, assoc. prof., 1988-91, prof. math., 1991—; lectr. in field. Referee jours. incl. European Jour. Ops. Rsch., Jour. Operational Rsch. Soc., Opsearch, others; reviewer Math. Revs., Zentralblatt für Mathematik; contbr. articles to profl. jours. Recipient Best Paper award Indian Soc. theoretical and Applied Mechanics, 1975. Mem. Am. Math. Soc., Indian Soc. Probability and Stats. (life), Operational Soc. India (life). Avocations: reading, solving crossword puzzles, music. E-mail: kalpakam@acer.iitm.ernet.in. Office: Indian Inst Tech, Dept Math, Madras 600 036, India

KALRA, ALOK, plant pathologist; b. Hisar, Haryana, India, Apr. 16, 1959; s. Dharam Sarup and Pushpa (Gauba) K.; m. Meenu Sikka, May 21, 1988; children: Pulkit, Saumya. BSc with honors, Haryana Agrl. U., Hissar, India, 1980, PhD in Plant Pathology, 1986; MSc in Plant Pathology, Punjab Agrl. U., 1982. Scientist Coun. Sci. and Indsl. Rsch., Bangalore, India, 1986-94, Pantnagar, India, 1994-99, Lucknow, India, 1999—; rschr. in field. Contbr. articles to profl. jours.; contbr. to patents. Sr. rsch. fellow Indian Coun. Agrl. Rsch. Fellow Indian Phytopathol. Soc.; mem. Indian Virolog. Soc. (councillor 1991), Asian Agri-History Found. Home: 1523 U E II, Hissar Haryana 125005, India Office: Divsn Mycol & Plant Path CIMAP, PO CIMAP, Lucknow 226015, India

KALRAH, NIDHAN SINGH, biochemist; b. Bareilly, India, July 2, 1942; s. Budh Singh and Sheela Wanti; m. Jag Mohini Gulati, Feb. 13, 1972; children: Guneet, Tanumeet. BSc with Honors, G.B. Pant U. Agr. and Tech., India, 1963, MSc in Biochemistry, 1965, PhD in Biochemistry, 1972. Jr. biochemist LHMC, New Delhi, 1973-80; biochemist R.M. Lohia Hosp., New Delhi, 1980-89, sr. biochemist, 1989—; jr. rsch. fellow UGC, 1966-72. Contbr. articles to prof. jours. Fellow Inst. Chemists; mem. ASCB, Assn. Non-Med. Scientists (sec. 1972—), Assn. Gazzetted Officer Ctrl. Hosps. (pres.). Avocations: bioelectronics, religious discourse, educating and counseling,. Home: E 6/16 Municipality Bldg, Mumbai Maharashtra India Office: Dr R M Lohia Hosp, Babakharak Singh, New Delhi India

KALTENBACH, MARTIN HANS, cardiologist, educator; b. Lörrach, Baden, Germany, Sept. 23, 1928; s. Hans Berthold and Lise Agnes (Maurer) K.; m. Dorothee Elisabeth Edelmann, Feb. 20, 1960. MD, U. Marburg, Germany, 1955; priv. dozent, U. Frankfurt, Germany, 1966, prof. medicine, 1972. Physician Hosp. Lörrach, Germany, 1955-58, Hosp. Frankfurt, Germany, 1958-62; MD Univ. Hosp., Frankfurt, 1958-66; med. rschr. Frankfurt, Cleve., Zürich, 1966-72; prof. medicine, head dept. cardiology U. Frankfurt,, 1972-93; cons. Heart Ctr., Frankfurt, 1993—. Author: (books) Research Medicine, 1978, (Morawitz prize German Cardiology Soc., 1978), Medical Research Cardiology, (Albert Knoll prize 1981), Research Interventional Cardiology (A Grünzig award European Soc. Cardiology 1988). Founding mem. German Heart Found., 1970, Rockenberg-Verein for Juvenile Convicts, 1977. Recipient Bundesverdienst Kreuz 1st Class, Pres. of Germany, 1993. Fellow Am. Heart Assn., European Heart Assn.; mem. German Cardiac Soc. (pres. 1990). Mem. Free Dems. Germany. Home: Falltorweg 8, D 63303 Dreieich Hessen, Germany

KALTSCHMID, JOCHEN HORST, writer, science educator; b. Apr. 17, 1933; s. Karl August and Margot (Silberhorn) K.; m. Helga Schumann, Aug. 11, 1961; children: Astrid, Gerd. Dipl. Hdl., U. Mannheim, 1958, Dr. Pol. Sci., 1962. Wiss. asst. U. Mannheim, 1962-68; dozent, prof. Paedagogische Hochschule Reutlingen, 1968-73; prof. ednl. sci. U. Heidelberg, 1973-98. Author: Menschsein i.d.ind. Gesellschaft, 1965, (with A.F. Caspers) Projektstudien zur Arbeitslehre, 1974, Die SchÜlerrolle zwischen Anpassung und Emanzipation, 1978, Didaktik d.Erwachsenbildung, 1986, Biographie und PÜdagogik, 1988, Bildung und Lebenslanges lernen, 1988, Biographische und lebenslauftheoretische AnsÜtze und Erwachsenenbildung, 1999; editor: (with B. Goetz) Erziehungswiss, u. Soziologie, 1977, Sozialisation und Erziehung, 1978, (with R. Arnold) Erwachsenensozialisation und Erwachsenenbildung, 1986. Mem. Deutsche Gesellschaft fuer Erziehungswissenschaft, Ges.z. Foerd.paed. Forschung, Arbeitskreis Univ. Erwachsenenbildung, Deutsche Schiller-Gesellschaft, Gutenberg-Gesellschaft, Weinfreundeskreis Hochheim a.M. Home: Danziger Strasse 20, D-65462 Gustavsburg Hessen, Federal Republic of Germany Office: Univ Heidelberg, Akademiestrasse 3, D-69117 Heidelberg Federal Republic of Germany

KALTSOS, ANGELO JOHN, electronics executive, educator, photographer; b. Boston, Aug. 19, 1930; s. John Angelo and Rita Thomas (Goudas) K.; m. Verna Kay Wilson, June 30, 1952 (dec. Jan. 1973); children: Pamela, Elaine, Gregory, Stephanie, Lenora, Demetra, Dana. Student, Mass. Radio and TV Sch., Boston, 1955-57, Harvard Coll. Extension, 1964, Boston State Coll., 1965-67, U. N.M., 1976, Fitchburg State Coll., 1977. Clk. U.S. Postal Svc., Boston, 1954-57; electronic rsch. technician Crosley div. Avco, Cin., 1957; electronic technician Raytheon Mfg. Co., Waltham, Mass., 1957-63; educator Cambridge (Mass.) Sch. Dept., 1961-81; ind. ethnology rsch. N.Mex., 1969—; mgr. Pampas, Inc., Boston, 1987-90; bd. dirs. Expansion Dance Co., Boston; cons. 5 P.I.E., Albuquerque, 1976—, Indian Tribal Group, N.Mex.; lectr. S.W. Indian Culture in Boston, Cambridge area, 1990—; pres., treas. Spartan Enterprises, Inc., 1965-69. Author: Southwest Indian, 1986; one-man photo exhibits: Christmas Tree Gallery, Manteo, N.C., 1977, The 4th St. Photo Gallery, N.Y.C., 1980, Cambride Rindge and Latin Sch., Mass., 1981, Jay's, Cambridge, Mass., 1983, Here Today Gallery, Boston, 1984, Andover (Maine) Town Hall, 1984, 86, Piedmont Art Assn., Martinsville, Va., 1985-86, Cambalache Gallery, Boston, 1986-87, The 4th St. Gallery, N.Y.C., 1990, Andover (Maine) Pub. Libr., 1997, 98; contbg. journalist in field. Chmn. No Thank Q Hydro Quebec, Andover, Maine, 1988-91, coord., Dryden, Maine, 1991—; regional and media coord. N.E. Alliance to Protect James Bay, 1990-91, mem. exec. bd., mem. adv. bd., treas., 1991—, project dir., 1995; mem. senate faculty Cambridge Sch. Dept., 1980-81; sec. New Eng. Model Car Assn. of Raceways, 1966-69; educator Cambridge Adult Ctr., 1990-97, Paulist Ctr., Boston, 1991-92. Recipient Robert Sweeney award Rindge Alumni Assn., 1996. Mem. Appalachian Mountain Club. Greek Orthodox. Avocations: ethnography, entomology, cooking, gardening, hiking. Home: PO Box 33 Andover ME 04216-0033

KALUGER, GEORGE, clinical psychologist, educator; b. Tataria, Alba Iulia, Romania, Sept. 20, 1921; s. Niculae and Valeria (Suteu) K.; m. O. Meriem Fair, June 11, 1947. BS in Edn., Slippery Rock (Pa.) U., 1946; MEd, U. Pitts., 1948, PhD, 1950; postdoctoral, Pa. State U., Univ. Park, 1955. Lic psychologist, Pa., tchr., Pa. Tchr. science and math. Butler (Pa.) City Schs., 1946-49, guidance counselor, 1949-53; prof. edn. and psychology Shippensburg (Pa.) U., 1953-72, prof. psychology, 1972-89, chair dept. psychology, 1972-76; part time pvt. practice in clin. psychology, 1954-93; cons. rsch. learning disabilities Capital Area Inter. Unit, Camp Hill, Pa., 1960-74, Lincoln Intermediate Unit, Cross Keys, Pa., 1970-76; psychol. cons. Bur. Vocat. Rehab., Harrisburg, Pa., 1954-64; cons. perceptual devel. ctr. Shippensburg Area Schs., 1970-74. Co-author: (books) Clinical Aspects of Remedial Reading, 1963, 5th printing; Psychology and Sociology, 1969, Profiles in Human Development, 1976, Reading and Learning Disabilities, 1969, 78 (2 edits.), Human Development: Span of Life, 1974, 79, 84 (3 edits.). Pres. Tuesday Club, Shippensburg, 1958, Shippensburg Hist. Soc., 1961, Rotary Club, Shippensburg, 1963; nat. co-chmn. Shippensburg Univ. Found., 1987. 1st Lt. USAAF, 1942-45. Recipient Commonwealth Disting. Chair award Commonwealth of Pa., 1978-79, Commonwealth Disting. Tchg. Fellow award, 1978-79, Citation for Humanitarian Svc. Pa. Cerebral Palsy, 1964, Shippensburg U. Alumni Exceptional Svc. award, 1996. Fellow Pa. Psychol. Assn. (pres. acad. divsn. 1972); mem. Am. Psychol. Assn., Cumberland Valley Masonic Lodge, Ancient Order of Scottish Rites, Phi Delta Kappa (Educator of the Yr. award 1990). Avocations: adventure travelling, cultural photography, workshops in neuropsychology, writing. Home: 625 Brenton St Shippensburg PA 17257-2113

KALVODA, ROBERT, chemist, researcher; b. Sumperk, Czech Republic, Mar. 28, 1926; s. Robert and Marie (Grolig) K.; m. Hana Flegrova, June 6, 1951; 1 child, Dagmar. MS in Pharmacy, Charles U., Prague, 1948, PhD in Chemistry, 1950; DSc, Inst. Tech. Chemistry, Prague, 1974. Cert. in polarography and chem. instrumentation. Asst. prof. Charles U., 1950-54, prof. analytical chemistry, 1992—; rsch.scientist Polarographic Inst., Acad. of Sci., Prague, 1954-74; sr. scientist Inst. Phys. Chemistry, Czech Acad. Sci., Prague, 1974—, dep. dir., 1974-89, dir., 1990; chmn. UNESCO Lab. Environ. Electrochemistry, 1990. Author sci. books; contbr. more than 150 articles to profl. jours. Recipient Heyrovsky Golden medal Czechoslovak Acad. Scis., 1986-93. Mem. Internat. Union Pure and Applied Chemistry (analytical divsn.). Avocation: polarography. Home: 643 Alzirska, 16000 Prague 6, Czech Republic Office: J Heyrovsky Inst Phys Chem, Czech Acad Scis, Dolejskova 3, 18223 Prague 8, Czech Republic

KALWARA, JOSEPH JOHN, engineer; b. Syracuse, N.Y., June 4, 1953; s. Stanley W. and M. Bonita (Caraglin) K; m. Edith Ann Doust, 1980; children: John C., Joseph S., James V. BS in Forestry, Syracuse U., 1977; BS in Wood Products Engring., SUNY, Syracuse, 1977; AAAS in Archtl. Tech., Onondaga County C.C., 1980. Asst. engr. Firestone Bldg. Products, Carmel, Ind., 1983-84; regional tech. coord. Firestone Bldg. Products, Carmel, 1984-86, product assurance engr., 1986-88, sr. engr., 1988—. Contbr. articles to profl. jours. Mem. Single-Ply Roofing Inst., Riviera Club (Indpls.). Achievements include research in the development and engineering of building products, insulations and adhesives, sealants, and tapes relative to single-ply roofing membranes and systems; patentee in field. Avocations: Olympic style competitive weightlifting, photography, astronomy, Rolleiflex twin lens cameras. Home: 6050 Broadway St Indianapolis IN 46220-1808 Office: Firestone Bldg Products 525 Congressional Blvd Carmel IN 46032-5644

KALYANARAMAN, SHIVKUMAR, computer engineering research and educator; b. Chenmai, Tamil Nadu, India, Apr. 30, 1971; came to the U.S., 1993; s. K. and Geetha Kalyanaraman; m. Sharanya Shivkumar. B in Tech., Indian Inst. Tech., Madras, 1993; MS, PhD, Ohio State U., 1997. Asst. prof. Rensselaer Poly. Inst., Troy, N.Y., 1997—; mem. adv. bd. Packeeter, Inc., Cupertino, Calif., 1997-99, Expeditrix.com, Austin, Tex., 1999—. Mem. IEEE, Assn. Computing Machinery. Achievements include author of three inventions. E-mail: skalyanl@nycap.rr.com. Office: Rensselaer Poly Univ 110 8th St Rm Jec6003 Troy NY 12180-3522

KALYANARAMAN, SUBRAMANYAM, space scientist; b. Mudikondan, Tamilnadu, India, June 10, 1942; s. Natesan Subramanyam and SNS Savithiri; m. Kalyanaraman Meenakshi Mahaganapathy, July 4, 1965; children: Rama, Mythili. BSc, U. Madras, Madurai, India, 1962; diploma, Madras Inst. Tech., 1965; MSc, U. Fla., 1970; MA, U. Madras, 1986. Project mgr. Indian Space Rsch. Orgn., Bangalore, 1972-80, dep. project dir., 1980-88; project dir. Indian Remote Sensing Satellite Project 1-C, Bangalore, 1989-95, program dir., 1996—. Guest editor: Jour. Spacecraft Tech., 1995; contbr. articles to profl. jours. Fellow Indian Nat. Acad. Engring., Instn. Electronics and Telecomm. Engrs. India; mem. Vol. Assn. Relief to Poor (pres. 1994—), Indian Soc. Remote Sensing (life), Astron. Soc. India (life), N.Y. Acad. Scis. Avocations: music, gardening, social work. Home: 26 8th Cross ISRO layout, Bangalore 560078, India Office: ISRO Satellite Ctr, Airport Rd, Bangalore 560017, India

KALYANASUNDARAM, N. KRISHNAMURTHY, educator; b. Sathambadi, India, June 19, 1945; s. Krishamurthy and Meenakshi K.; m. Sukanya Kalyanasundaram, Sept. 1, 1977; children: Bhuvana, Bharathi. BS in Chemistry, A.M. Jain Coll., Madras, India, 1966; MS, Inst. Agrl., Anand, India, 1970; PhD, Gujarat Agrl. U., Anand, India, 1980. Sr. rsch. asst. Inst. Agrl., Anand, India, 1970-75; asst. rsch. scientist G.A.U., Anand, India, 1975-81; assoc. rsch. scientist G.A.U., S.K. Nagar, India, 1981-91; prof. G.A.U., India, 1991—. Co-editor: Potassium in Gujarat Agriculture, 1993, Crop Sequence Research, 1997; editor: Vermitechnology, 1997. Mem. Indian Soc. Soil Sci., Arid Zone Assn. India. Avocation: reading. Office: Gujarat Agrl U BA Coll Agr, Dept Soil Sci, Anand 388110, India

KALYUZHIN, OLEG VITALIEVICH, education educator; b. Kaunas, Russia; s. Vitaly Vasilievich and Mariya Ivanovna (Belash) K. MD, Sechenov Moscow Med. Acad., 1993; PhD, Human Morphology Rsch. Inst., Moscow, 1999. Sr. project rschr. Human Morphology Rsch. Inst., Moscow, 1995-99; asst. prof. Sechenov Moscow Med. Acad., 1999—; gen. dir. Krystal-Med Ltd., Moscow, 1997—; sci. dir. Ctr. Modern Medicine Medicor, Moscow, 1997-99. Author: Cerebro-vascular Disorders in Therapeutic Pracice, 1993; patentee immunomodifier and pharmaceutical composition with antitumor activities, food additive. Mem. Internat. Soc. Immuno., N.Y. Acad. Scis. Home: Angarskaya Str 22-1-46, 127635 Moscow Russia Office: Human Morphology Rsch Inst, Tsurupa 3, 117918 Moscow Russia

KAM, JIN G., artist, educator; b. Shanghai, China, July 10, 1953; came to U.S., 1989; s. Hong Kam and Xue Yu Li; m. Adeline J. Fu, May 25, 1997. BA, China Nat. Acad. Fine Art, Hangzhou, 1982; postgrad., U.S. Internat. U., San Diego, 1989-91. Instr. Coll. Fine Arts Shanghai U., 1983-87; designer, artist Oh-Ami Inc., Tokyo, 1987-89; artist Symphony Fine Art Inc, San Diego, 1990—. Oil paintings include Roots, 1981, Ballade, 1990. Bd. dirs. Shanghai Tech. Art Inst., 1986-90. Grantee Leonard Berstein Edn. Through the Arts Fund, N.Y.C., 1991, Louis Armstrong Ednl. Found., N.Y.C., 1992, U.S. Post Office, 1995, Miles Davis Estate, N.Y.C., 1995. Avocations: piano, violin, sports, travel. Home: 1324 Elm Ave Apt J San Gabriel CA 91775-3082

KAM, MOSHE, electrical and computer engineering educator; b. Tel Aviv, Oct. 3, 1955; s. Chanina and Sara Kam. BSc, Tel Aviv U., 1977; MS, Drexel U., 1985, PhD, 1987. Asst. prof. Drexel U., Phila., 1987-90, assoc. prof., 1990-96, prof., 1996—. Mem. Choral Arts Soc. Phila., 1992-99, Mendelssohn Club Phila., 1999—; mem. sci. working group document examination U.S. Dept. Justice, Washington, 1997—. Tech. officer Israeli Def. Forces, 1976-83. Recipient Presdl. Young Investigator award NSF, 1990, C. Holmes MacDonald award Eta Kappa Nu, 1991, Engring. Achievement award Del. Valley Engrs. Week Coun., 1996. Mem. IEEE (sr., assoc. editor 1993—, chmn. Phila. sect. 1998, Pa. area rep. region 2 1999—), Pattern Recognition (assoc. editor 1993—), Internat. Neural Network Soc. Office: Drexel U Data Fusion Lab 3141 Chestnut St Philadelphia PA 19104-2875

KAMABE, HIROSHI, engineering educator; b. Ayabe, Kyoto, Japan, Feb. 24, 1960; s. Yoshio and Yasuko (Sakata) K. BS, Toyohashi U., 1982; MS, Toyohashi U. of Tech., 1984; PhD, Nagoya U., 1994. Rsch. asst. Mie U., Tsu, Japan, 1984-94, asst. prof., 1994—; vis. rschr. Tech. U. of Eindhoven, The Netherlands, 1996; asst. prof. Gifu (Japan) U., 1996—. Author: (with others) Stochastic Process, 1994; contbr. articles to profl. jours. Mem. IEEE, Inst. Elecs., Info. & Comm. Engrs. Avocations: painting, drumming. Home: 6-34 Daifuku, Gifu 502-0934, Japan Office: Gifu U, 1-1 Yanagido, Gifu 501-1193, Japan

KAMADA, MASARU, engineering educator; b. Hitachi, Ibaraki, Japan, Mar. 19, 1962; s. Hiroshi and Kyoko (Hanazono) K.; m. Toshie Shiina, Nov. 3, 1988; children: Chie, Hisashi. BE, U. Tsukuba, 1984, ME, 1986, DEng, 1988. Rsch. assoc., asst. prof. U. Tsukuba, Japan, 1988-92; assoc. prof. Ibaraki U., Hitachi, Japan, 1992—; acad. guest Swiss Fed. Inst. Tech., Zurich, 1993-95; reviewer Math. Rev., 1990—. Reviewer Inst. Electronics, Info. and Comm. Engrs. Trans. on Engring. Sci., 1992—, assoc. editor, 1997-2000, publs. sec., 1998-99; contbr. articles to profl. jours. Mem. IEEE, Cirs. and Sys. Soc. of IEEE (treas. Japan chpt. 2000—), European Assn. Signal Processing. Achievements include invention in analog/digital conversion systems. Avocation: blues guitar. Office: Ibaraki U Computer Dept, Hitachi Ibaraki 316-8511, Japan

KAMAKURA, MITSUHIRO, epidemiologist, educator, researcher; b. Tokyo, Feb. 15, 1954; s. Nakanari and Sachiko (Wada) K. MD, Keio U., Tokyo, 1979; PhD, Keio U., 1984. Trainee in surgery Keio U. Hosp., Tokyo, 1979-80, asst. dept. preventive medicine and pub. health, 1984-88, asst. prof., 1988—; mem. steering com. Clinic for Infectious Diseases, Keio U. Hosp., 1995—; mem. rsch. group HIV epidemiology Min. Health and Welfare, Japan, 1992—; mem. AIDS panel Japan-U.S. coop. med. sci. program Min. Fgn. Affairs, 1995—; mem. AIDS task force overseas med. coop. com. Japan Internat. Coop., 1995; mem. Monitoring AIDS Pandemic network, 1996—; group leader Internat. Epidemiology HIV infection, Min. Health and Welfare, Japan, 1998—; mem. AIDS annual report drafting com., Japan, 1997-98. Author: AIDS-A Basic Guide, 1987; editor: (Japanese edit.) The Status and Trends of the Global HIV/AIDS Pandemic, 1996; mem. editl. staff (Japanese edit.) AIDS in the World II, 1997. Grantee Uehara Fund, 1987. Mem. Japanese Soc. Genetics (leading doctor). Avocations: classical music, painting, traveling. Office: Dept Prevent Medicine/Pub Health, Keio U 35 Shinano Machi, Tokyo 1608582, Japan

KAMAL, MARWAN RASIM, chemistry educator; b. Anabta, Palestine, June 27, 1933; s. Rasim Kamal and Amnah Massoud (Abu Hadba) K.; m. Maha Marwan Hamzeh, June 21, 1963; children: Rhonda, Lisa, Iyad, Omar. BSc, Roosevelt U., 1955; MSc, DePaul U., 1958; PhD, U. Pitts., 1961; MBA, U. Minn., 1969. Rschr., adminstr. Gen. Mills, Mpls., 1961-67; faculty mem. U. Petroleum and Minerals, Dhahran, Saudi Arabia, 1967-77; faculty mem., dean, v.p. U. Jordan, Amman, 1977—; pres. U. Bahrain, 1987-91; min. of agr. Amman, 1993; pres. Yarmouk U., Irbid, Jordan, 1994-98; sec. gen. Assn. of Arab U., 1998—. Contbr. articles to profl. jours.; patentee in field. Mem. Nat. Soc. Civil Def. (pres. 1990—), Assn. Am. Univ. Grads. (v.p. 1991—). Avocations: reading, sports, writing, travel. Home: PO Box 13118, Amman Jordan

KAMAL, MOHAMMAD AMJAD, biochemist, researcher; b. Dera Ismail Khan, Pakistan, Apr. 4, 1962; arrived in Australia, 1998; s. Khadim Mohammad Hussain Khan and Bashir-un-Nissa; m. Maimoona Kamal, Sept. 13, 1989; children: Farda, Warda, Sundus, Hanan. BSc, Gomal U., Pakistan, 1983, MSc, 1986; postgrad., Islamia U., Pakistan, 1999. Lectr. Gomal U., Pakistan, 1987-90; rsch. asst. dept. biochemistry Coll. Sci. King Saud U., Riyadh, Saudi Arabia, 1990-2000. Contbr. over 37 articles to profl. jours., over 38 abstracts to internat. confs. Recipient merit scholarships Govt. Pakistan, 1978-80, 84-86, awd. of a prestigious U2000 postdoctoral fellshp., Univ. of Sydney, Dept. Biochem. Fellow Internat. Soc. Neurochemistry; mem. (1999) Can. Soc. Pharm. Scis., European Soc. for Toxicology in Vitro, Internat. Soc. for Neurochemistry, Soc. Exptl. Biology and Medicine. E-mail: makamal.saddozai@mailcity.com. Office: Dept Biochemistry G08, U Sydney, Sydney NSW 2006, Australia

KAMAL, SYED ARIF, mathematical physicist, educator; b. Hyderabad, Sind, Pakistan, May 23, 1956; s. Syed Ishtiaq and Asia (Khatoon) Raza; m. Khadija Ghufran Kamal, Jan. 4, 1990; 1 child, Iqra Ahmed. MSc, U. Karachi, Pakistan, 1978, PhD, 1993; MS, Ind. U., 1982; MA, Johns Hopkins U., 1986. Asst. master, head physics dept. Karachi Grammar Sch., 1979; coöp. tchr. physics U. Karachi, 1978-79, 86-88, asst. prof. physics, 1988-90, assoc. prof. math., 1995—, head Nat. Growth and Devel. Stds. for Pakistani Children, 1998—; asst. prof. math. Defence Housing Authority Degree Coll., Karachi, 1991-92; sr. sci. officer SUPARCO, Karachi, 1992-95; vis. rsch. fellow Albert Einstein Coll. Medicine, N.Y.C., 1990; vis. assoc. prof. Malmö (Sweden) Gen. Hosp., U. Lund, 1988; tchg. asst. physics Johns Hopkins U., Balt., 1983-84; assoc. instr. physics Ind. U., Bloomington, 1979-82. Author: The Early Childhood Integrated Developmental Examination for 3-8 Years Old Children, Version 1.0, 1998. Rsch. grantee U. Karachi, 1995-96, Sir Syed U. Engring. and Tech., 1994-95. Islam. Avocations: travel, learning languages, elementary science education, nature photography. E-mail: drakamal@hotmail.com. Office: U Karachi, PO Box 8406, Karachi 75270, Pakistan

KAMALAKAR, KADALI VENKATA NAGARAJA, cardiologist, consultant; b. Hyderabad, Andrapradesh, India, June 4, 1963; s. Chandraiah and Priyamvada Kadali; m. Suryalata Kadali, June 1, 1990; children: K. Chandra Kiran, K. Mounika. MBBS, Rangaraya Med. Coll., Kakinada, India, 1987; MD in Gen. Medicine, Andhra Med. Coll., Visakhapatnam, India, 1993; DM in Cardiology, Nizams Inst. Med. Scis., Hyderabad, India, 1998. Asst. prof. cardiology Nizams Inst. Med. Scis., Hyderabad, 1998; cons. cardiologist Yasoda Super Splty. Hosp., Hyderabad, 1998—. Contbr. articles to profl. jours. Avocations: reading, watching tv. Home: Kirthi Apts F-108, Yellareddyguda, Hyderabad 500073 Andhrapradesh, India Office: Yashoda Super Splty Hosp, Somajiguda Rajbhavan Rd, Hyderabad Andrapradesh, India

KAMALAKSHAPPA, RAVI BHUSHAN, physical therapist; b. Shimoga, Karnataka, India, Dec. 2, 1973; s. Kukkalli and Jaya Kamalakshappa. Student, Deshiya Vidya Shala Jr. Coll., Shimoga, 1990; B in Physiotherapy, MVST Coll. Physiotherapy, Mangalore, Karnataka, 1995; diploma in sports physiotherapy, Alagappa U., Karaikudit, Tamil, Nadu, India, 1998. Cert. phys. therapist. Phys. therapist Nanjappa Hosp., Shimoga, 1997—; part-time phys. therapist Ravi Orthopaedic Clinic, Shimoga, 1997—. Mem. Indian Assn. Physiotherapists (life), Indian Assn. Grad. Physiotherapists. Avocations: reading, playing, workouts, driving. Home: # 1905 1350 W Bethune St Apt 1905 Detroit MI 48202-2667

KAMALI, HOSSAIN, Iranian government official; b. Dorood, Lurestan, Iran, 1953. Worker cement factories; founder Coordination Ctr., Islamic Coun. of Factories; mgr. Moslem Worker Langs.; mem. Ctrl. Coun., Labor House; alt. mem. Ctrl. Coun. Islamic Rep. Party; mem. People's Consultative Assembly (Majlis), Tehran, 1981-89; min. labor and social affairs Iranian Cabinet, Tehran, 1989—. Mem. Islamic Republican Party. Address: pr Jibek Jolu 356, Bishkek 720000, Iran Office: Min Labor/Social Affairs, Azadi Ave, Tehran Iran*

KAMALI, MOHAMMAD HASHIM, law educator; b. Lalpur, Afghanistan, Feb. 7, 1944; s. Muhammad Shirin and Tabarruk Bibi K.; m. Susannah Abdullah, Apr. 2, 1999; children: Leila Francesa, Russell William. BA Sch. of Law, Kabul U., Afghanistan, 1965; LLM, London U., 1972; PhD, U. London, 1976. Asst. prof. Kabul U., 1965-66, McGill U., Montreal, Que., 1980-84; pub. atty. Ministry of Justice, Kabul, 1966-68; lang. monitor BBC, Reading, Eng., 1975-80; rsch. assoc. Can. Coun. Social Sci., Ottawa, Ont., 1984-85; prof. dept. law Internat. Islamic U., Kuala Lumpur, Malaysia, 1985—; dir. pub. atty.'s office, Faryab, Afghanistan, 1967-68. Author: Principles of Islamic Jurisprudence, 1991 (Isma'il al-Faruqi award 1995), Freedom of Expression in Islam, 1994 (Isma'il al-Faruqi award 1997); editor Shari'ah Law Jour., 1987-90. Chmn. Assn. of Afghans in Que., 1983-85; active Afghanistan Refugee Info. Network, London, 1978-80. Rsch. grantee Can. Coun. Social Sci., 1984. Fellow Internat. Inst. Islamic Thought; mem. The Islamic Found. U.K. (gen. editor). Muslim. Avocations: swimming, music, travel, arts. Home: Apt 165-1 Jalan Ara, Sri Wangsaria Condominium, Bangsar Kuala Lumpur 59100, Malaysia Office: Internat Islamic U Malaysia, 53100 Kuala Lumpur Malaysia

KAMALI, NORMA, fashion designer; b. N.Y.C., June 27, 1945; d. Sam and Estelle (Mariategui) Arraez. Grad., Fashion Inst. of Tech., 1965. Established Kamali Ltd., N.Y.C., 1967-78; owner, designer On My Own Norma Kamali, N.Y.C., 1978—. Designer costumes for Emerald City in The Wiz, 1978; for Twyla Tharp dance In the Upper Room, 1986; Parachute Designs displayed Met. Mus. of Art, N.Y.C., 1977; prodr., dir. (video) Fall Fantasy; dir. (video) Fashion Aid, 1985. Recipient CFDA award, 1982, 1985, Coty award, 1981, 82, 83, Ernie awards Earnshaw Rev., 1983, Fashion Inst. Design and Merchandising award, 1983, Annual Interiors award Interiors Mag., 1985, Salute to Women award N.Y. Fashion Group, 1986, Disting. Arch. award N.Y. chpt. AIA, 1986, Outstanding Grad. award Pub. Edn. Assn. N.Y., 1988, Award of Merit, Internat. Video Culture Competition, 1988, Am. Success award Fashion Inst. Tech., 1989, Youth Friends award Sch. Art League, 1997, Pencil award, 1999, Willow award Lower East Side Girls Club, 1999, Fashion Outreach Style award, 1999. Office: 11 W 56th St New York NY 10019-3902

KAMALIPOUR, YAHYA R., communications educator; b. Ravar, Kerman, Iran, Nov. 29, 1947; came to U.S., 1972; m. Gholam-Reza and Robabeh (Yazdanpanah) K.; m. Margaret Tighe, Mar. 3, 1973 (div. May 1986); 1 child, Daria; m. Mah Zarei, Aug. 12, 1988; children: Shirin, Niki. AA, Marshalltown (Iowa) C.C., 1975; BA, Minn. State U., 1977; MA, U. Wis., Superior, 1978; PhD, U. Mo., Columbia, 1986. Instr. Franciscan U., Steubenville, Ohio, 1979-82; asst. prof. Quincy (Ill.) U., 1982-86; asst. prof. Purdue U. Calumet, Hammond, Ind., 1986-91, assoc. prof., 1991-96, prof., dir. grad. studies, 1996-99; prof., head dept. communication Purdue U. Calumet, Hammond, 1999—; mem. KMSU-FM Radio Staff, Minn. State U., Mankato, Minn., 1976-77; dir. Sta. WSSU-FM, U. Wis., Superior, 1977-78. Editor: The U.S. Media and the Middle East, 1995 (Book of Yr. 1996), Images of the U.S. Around the World, 1999; co-editor: Mass Media in the Middle East: A Comprehensive Handbook, 1994, Cultual Diversity and the U.S. Media, 1998, Religion, Law and Freedom: A Multicultural Perspective, 2000. Recipient Disting. scholarship Nat. Comm. Assn., San Diego, 1996. Mem. Broadcast Edn. Assn., Internat. Comm. Assn., Cultural Environ. Movement (bd. mem. 1995—), Comm. N.W. Ind. (bd. mem. 1988-91, outstanding svc. to comm. award 1996). Avocations: reading, writing, walking, travel, swimming. Office: Purdue U Calumet Comm Dept, 2200 169th St Hammond IN 46323

KAMALVAND, KAYVAN, physician; b. Tehran, Iran, Aug. 5, 1963; arrived in U.K., 1976; s. Ali and Amireh (Shiri) K.; m. Isik Kale, July 30, 1984; children: Shabnam, Shirin, Meltem. BSc, St. Georges Hosp. Med. Sch., London, 1984, MB BS, 1987. House officer St. James Hosp., London, 1987, St. Helier Hosp., London, 1988; sr. house officer Royal Sussex County Hosp., Brighton, Eng., 1988-89, Kings Coll. Hosp., London, 1989; registrar in transplant medicine Harefield Hosp., Eng., 1990-92; registrar William Harvey Hosp., Ashford, Kent, Eng., 1992-93; cardiac registrar Guy's Hosp., London, 1993-96; sr. registrar Eastbourne (U.K.) Hosp., 1996—; cons. Cardiologist and Physician William Harvey Hosp., Ashford, Kent, 1997; presenter at confs. in field. Contbr. articles, revs. to profl. publs. Mem. Royal Coll. Physicians, Brit. Cardiac Soc. Avocations: poetry, backgammon, chess, music, tennis.

KAMAN, JIŘÍ FRANTIŠEK, veterinary morphology educator, researcher; b. Dolní Loučky, Czech Republic, Mar. 31, 1926; s. Božena Kamanová Žáková; m. Anna Brunthalerová, Oct. 22, 1954; 1 child, Dagmar. DVM, U. Med. Vet., Brno, Czech Republic, 1954, Candidatus Sci., 1962, DSc, 1990. Asst. lectr. Anat. Inst. Vet. U., Brno, 1954-63, docent, reader Anat. Inst., 1964-65, head Anat. Inst., 1965-70, rschr. Inst. Pathol. Morphology, 1971-75, head rsch. team Inst. Pathol. Morphology, 1975-89, prof. Anat. Inst., 1990-93; prof. postgrad. study Inst. Postgrad. Study Vet. Drs., Brno, 1972-92; cons. Transplantation Ctr., Med. Faculty U., J.E. Purkyně, Brno, 1969-89, State Pigs Farm, Králuv Dvur, Czech Republic, 1975-89, State Breeding Farm, Bílovec, Czech Republic, 1975-89. Co-author: (textbooks) Veterinary Anatomy I, 1973 (Prague State Agrl. Pub. H. award 1973), Veterinary Anatomy II, 1982 (Czech Found. Tech. award, Prague Czech Ministry Edn. award 1982), Pathological Anatomy Domestic Animals, 1987 (Czech Found. Tech. award 1987), further numerous textbooks of normal and pathological veterinary anatomy, (sci. books) Nomina Anat. Vet., 1974, Nomina Anat. Avium, 1979, Encyclopedia of Microscopy and Microtechnique, 1973; contbr. numerous articles to sci. jours. Mem. city com. Acad. Assn. Polit. Discr. Higher Schs., 1948-89, Brno, 1989-93. 1st lt. Vet. Svc., 1954. Mem. Internat. Com. Avian Anat. Nom., World Assn. Vet. Anat., European Assn. Vet. Anatomists. Roman Catholic. Avocations: cycling, skiing, gardening. Home: Šumavská 25, 602 00 Brno Czech Republic Office: U Vet and Pharm Scis, Dept Pathol Morphology, 612 42 Brno Czech Republic

KAMANDA, KAMA, poet, writer, novelist, lecturer; b. Luebo, Congo, Nov. 11, 1952; s. Malaba Kamenga and Kony Ngalula Kamanda. State Diploma in Literary Humanities, 1968; degree in journalism, Journalism Sch., Kinshasa, Congo, 1969; degree in polit. scis., U. Kinshasa, 1973; JD, U. Liège, 1981, U. Strasbourg, 1988. lectr. various univs., schs. and cultural ctrs. Lit. critic various newspapers; author: Les Contes des Veillées Africaines, 1967, 85, Chants de Brumes, 1986, 97, Les Résignations, 1986, Eclipse d'Etoiles, 1987, 97, Les Contes du Griot, 1988, La Somme du Néant, 1989, L'Exil des Songes, 1992, Les Myriades des Temps Vécus, 1992, Les Vents de l'Epreuve, 1993, Quand dans l'Âme les Mers s'Agitent, 1994, La Nuit des Griots, 1997, Lointaines sont les Rives du Destin, 1994, L'Étreinte des Mots, 1991, 96, Le Sang des Solitudes, 1995, La Joueuse de Kora, 1995, Oeuvre Poétique, 1999. Recipient Paul Verlaine award French Acad., 1987, Thèophile Gautier award, 1993, Silver medal French Inst., 1987, 93, Louise Labé award Jury, 1990, Lit. award Black Africa Assn. French-Speaking Writers, 1991, Spl. Poetry award Acad. Inst. Paris, 1992, Silver Jasmin for Poetical Originality, 1992, Spl. prize French-Speaking Countries Gen. Coun. Agen, 1992; subject of Kama Kamanda au Pays du Conte (M.C. De Coninck), 1993, Kama Kamanda Poète de l'Exil (Pierrette Sartin), 1994. Mem. Soc. French Poets, French Soc. Men of Letters, Assn. African Writers, Internat. PEN Club, Assn. French-Speaking Writers, Internat. Coun. French-Speaking Studies. Humanist. E-mail: kamanda@pt.lu. Home: 18 Am Moul, L-7418 Buschdorf Luxembourg

KAMANINA, NATALIA VLADIMIROVNA, physicist, researcher; b. Kaliningrad, Russia, Mar. 19, 1957; d. Vladimir Grigor'evich and Mariya Fiodorovna (Oksimets) Yarosh; m. Alexander Vadimovich Kamanin, Oct. 17, 1978; children: Alexey, Tatyara. Honors diploma, Poly. Inst., Leningrad, Russia, 1981; PhD, Vavilov State Optical Inst., St. Petersburg, Russia, 1995. Engr. Vavilov State Optical Inst., Leningrad, 1981-87, jr. rsch. assoc., 1987-93, rsch. assoc., 1993-97, sr. rsch. assoc., 1997—; sci. sec. Conf. Non-Resonant Laser Matter in Interaction, St. Petersburg, 1996, PhD Degree Coun. Vavilov State Optical Inst., St. Petersburg, 1994—. Contbr. articles to profl. jours. Recipient individual grant Internat. Sci. Found., 1993. Mem. Internat. Liquid Crystal Soc. Avocations: books, theatre. Office: Vavilov State Optical Inst, 12 Birzhevaya Line, 199034 Saint Petersburg Russia

KAMARCK, MITCHELL DAVID, lawyer; b. Rye, N.Y., July 15, 1960; s. Lawrence and Caroline Kamarck; m. UnJu Paik, Oct. 20, 1990. BA, Colgate U., 1982; JD, Cornell U., 1987. 010Bar: Mass. 1987, U.S. Ct. Appeals (1st cir.) 1990, U.S. Dist. Ct. Mass. 1990, Calif. 1991, U.S. Dist. Ct. (cen. dist.) Calif. 1994, U.S. Ct. Appeals (9th cir.) 1994, U.S. Dist. Ct. (no. dist.) Calif. 1995, U.S. Dist. Ct. (so. dist.) Calif. 1998. Assoc. Hale and Dorr, Boston, 1987-89; ptnr. Rosenfeld, Meyer & Susman, LLP, Beverly Hills, Calif., 1989—; adj. prof. Calif. State U., L.A., 1996; bd. editors Calif. Causes of Action, James Pub.; presenter in field. Author: Detours, Misdirections and False Starts on the Information Super Highway: The Hidden Dangers in Marketing Your Web Site, 1999; contbr. numerous articles to profl. jours. Mem. L.A. Bar Assn., Beverly Hills Bar Assn. E-mail: mKamarck@rm-slaw.com. Office: Rosenfeld Meyer & Susman LLP 9601 Wilshire Blvd Fl 4 Beverly Hills CA 90210-5288

KAMATA, KATSUO, pharmacologist; b. Kagoshima, Japan, Nov. 10, 1947; s. Utako Kamata; m. Michiru Uge; children: Takeshi, Saori, Kaori. BS, Kumamoto U., Japan, 1971, MA, 1973; PhD, Tokyo U., 1977. Asst. prof. Mejo U., Japan, 1978-92; prof. Hoshi U., Tokyo, 1993—. Mem. Soc. Pharmaceutical Sci., Soc. Pharmacology (Japan), Soc. Neurosci. (U.S.). Avocations: fishing, reading, painting. Office: Hoshi Univ, Shinagawa-ku, Tokyo 142, Japan

KAMATA, KAZUO, computer scientist, educator; b. Izumo, Shimane, Japan, Mar. 27, 1947. B in Engring., Yamanashi U., 1969, M in Engring., 1971; D of Engring., Tokyo Inst. Tech., 1977. Rsch. assoc. Tokyo Inst. Tech., 1971-78; assoc. prof. Utsunomiya (Japan) U., 1978-90, prof., 1990—. Author: Digital Signal Processing, 1990. Home: 2980 Ishii-machi, Tochigi Utsunomiya 321-0912, Japan Office: Utsunomiya Univ, 7-1-2 Yoto, Tochigi Utsunomiya 321-8585, Japan

KAMATA, MICHISADA, electric power industry executive. Former CEO, Kyushu Electric Power Co., Fukuoka, Japan, now sr. v.p. Fax: 81-92-7610-6498. Office: Kyushu Elec Power Co, 2-1-82 Watanabe-dori Chuo, Fukuoka 810-8720, Japan*

KAMATA, YOSHIRO, food scientist; b. Sendai, Miyagi-ken, Japan, Feb. 23, 1952; s. Tetsuro and Michiko (Sakai) K.; m. Samiko Miyazaki, Apr. 29, 1978; children: Yumiko, Mayuko. B of Agr., Tohoku U., Sendai, 1975, M of Agr., 1977, PhD, 1981. Rsch. assoc. Tohoku U., 1977-88; assoc. prof. food sci. Miyagi U. Edn., Sendai, 1988-97, prof. food sci., 1998—. Author: Biotechnology, 1987, Soybean Science, 1992, Food Proteins and Lipids, 1997. Mem. Japan Soc. Biosci. Biotech. and Agrochemistry, Japanese Soc. Food Sci. and Tech., The Soc. Rheology, N.Y. Acad. Scis. Home: 12-10-305 Ohkaji, Miyagino-ku, Sendai 983-0835, Japan Office: Miyagi U Edn, Aramaki-aza-Aoba Aoba-ku, Sendai 980-0845, Japan

KAMATH, PATRICK SEQUEIRA, physician, educator, researcher; b. Bassein, India, Sept. 4, 1953; came to U.S., 1991; s. James Alexis and Fifine Sequeira; m. Janine Remela Ann Kamath, July 23, 1989; children: Marielle, Amika. MB BChir, Bangalore (India) U., 1976; MD in Internal Medicine, Inst. Med. Edn. and Rsch., Chandigarh, India, 1980, DM in Gastroenterology, 1982. From asst. prof. to assoc. prof. gastroenterology St. John's Med. Coll. Hosp., Bangalore, 1983-90, prof., chair gastroenterology, 1990-91; asst. prof. medicine Mayo Med. Sch., Rochester, Minn., 1991-96, assoc. prof., 1996—; cons. Mayo Clinic and Found., Rochester, 1991—. Mem. Am. Gastroenterology Assn., Am. Soc. Gastrointestinal Endoscopy, Am. Assn. Study Liver Diseases, European Assn. Study Liver Diseases. Avocations: travel, high altitude trekking, tennis. Office: Mayo Clinic and Found 200 1st St SW Rochester MN 55905-0002

KAMBA, WALTER JOSEPH, university administrator; b. Zimbabwe, Sept. 6, 1931; s. Joseph Mafara and Hilda Kamba; m. Angeline Saziso Dube, 1960; children: Dennis (dec.), Mark, Julian. BA, U. Cape Town, Rep. of South Africa, 1954, LLB, 1957; LLM, Yale U., 1963; LLD (hon.), U. Dundee, Scotland, 1982. Legal practitioner High Ct. Zimbabwe, 1957-63, 64-67; rsch. fellow Inst. Advanced Legal Studies U. London, 1967-69; lectr., sr. lectr. U. Dundee, Scotland, 1969-80, dean faculty of law, univ. orator, 1977-80; prof. law U. Zimbabwe, Harare, 1980—, pro vice chancellor, 1980-81, vice chancellor, 1981-92; prof. law, founding dean U. Namibia, 1994—, legal advisor, 1995—; bd. dirs. Kingstons Booksellers, Zimbabwe, Internat. Devel. Rsch. Ctr., Canada; bd. govs. Zimbabwe Inst. Devel. Studies; chmn. bd. govs. Zimbabwe Broadcasting Corp. Mem. council U. Zambia, 1981—, UN U., Tokyo, 1983—; mem. Nat. St. John's Ambulance Council, Zimbabwe, 1982-87; trustee Conservation Trust of Zimbabwe, 1981-87; bd. dirs. Electoral Supervisory Commn., Zimbabwe, 1984—; patron Commonwealth Legal Edn. Found., 1986—; bd. govs. Commonwealth of Learning, 1988; mem. Bd. Internat. Com. for Study of Ednl. Exch., 1988—; former legal advisor Zimbabwe African Nat. Union-Patriotic Front. Decorated Officer dans l'Ordre des Palmes Academiques France, 1982; named Mgr. of Yr. Zimbabwe, 1985. Mem. Internat. Assn. Univs.-Internat. Univs. Bur. (v.p. 1985—, pres.), Legal Resources Found. (trustee 1984—), Zimbabwe Inst. of Devel. Studies (bd. dirs. 1981—), Assn. of African U. (exec. bd. dirs. 1984—). Roman Catholic. Avocations: tennis, theatre. Office: U Namibia Faculty Law, Fac Officer, Pvt Bag 13301, Windhoek Zimbabwe also: Intl Assn Univs/Internat Univs Bur, 1 rue Miollis, 75732 Paris Cedex 15, France*

KAMBHATO, PHUMCHAI, investment banker; b. Bangkok, Thailand, July 26, 1968; s. Tamchai and Orasa Kambhato; m. Pattama Jittalan, July 22, 1999. Student, Eton Coll., 1986; MA in Engring., Econs. and Mgmt., Oxford U., 1990, MPhil. in Mgmt. Studies, 1992. Exec. J. Henry Schroder Wagg & Co. Ltd., London, 1992-94; mgr. Robert Fleming & Co. Ltd., London, 1994-98; first v.p. Jardine Fleming Thanakom Securities Ltd., Bangkok, 1998—. Co-author: Privatization and Emerging Equity Markets, 1998. Mem. Royal Bangkok Sports Club. Buddhist. Avocations: golf, badminton, squash, food and fine wine, travel. Office: 29th Fl 191 Silom Rd, Silom Complex Office Bldg, Bangkok 10500, Thailand

KAMBOURIS, MANOUSOS, journalist, biologist; b. Athens, Attiki, Greece, June 25, 1971; s. Emmanouil and Dimitra (Glystra) K. Cert. of Proficiency in English, Cambridge, 1988; BS, Athens U., 1992; diplôme des etudes, Sup. Inst. Francais Athens, 1992; PhD, Athens U., 2000. Journalist Modern Army mag., Athens, 1993-97, Defence & Diplomacy mag., Athens, 1996-99, Strategy mag., Athens, 1999—. Author: Marina, 1996, Training Improvement of Greek Army, 1995 (1st prize of Hellenic Army 1996), Ancient Greek Warriors, 2000; contbr. articles to profl. jours. 2d lt. Hellenic Army, 1993-95. Avocations: Aikido, Tae Kwon Do, scuba diving, Warefare in Ancient Greece.. Home: 89 3 Septemvriou St, 104 34 Athens Greece

KAMEDA, HISAO, science educator; b. Gifu City, Gifu, Japan, Apr. 15, 1942. BS, U. Tokyo, 1965, MS, 1967, DSc, 1970. From asst. prof. to assoc. prof. to prof. U. Electro-Comms., Tokyo, 1971-92, chmn. dept. computer sci., 1986-87, chmn. dept. computer sci. and info. math., 1990-91; prof. U. Tsukuba, Japan, 1992—; vis. scientist IBM T. J. Watson Rsch. Ctr., Yorktown Heights, 1973-74; vis. rsch. fellow U. Toronto, Can., 1974-75. Author: (book) Optimal Load Balancing in Distributed Computer Systems, 1997; contbr. articles to profl. jours. Recipient Best Paper award 49th Nat. Aerospace and Electronics Conf., 1997. Mem. Info. Processing Soc. Japan (chmn. SIGOS 1986-90, jour. editor 1971-85), Assn. for Computer Machinery (profl. mem.), Inst. Electronics, Info., and Comm. Engrs. Tokyo, Ops. Rsch. Soc. Japan. Avocation: hiking.

KAMEDA, TATSUYA, psychologist, educator; b. Tokyo, Feb. 19, 1960; s. Takashi and Fumiko (Fukushima) K.; m. Yumi Hagiwara, June 21, 1986. BL, U. Tokyo, 1982, MA, 1984; PhD, U. Ill., 1989. Instr. U. Tokyo, 1989-90; asst. prof. Toyo U., Tokyo, 1991-93; assoc. prof. Hokkaido U., Sapporo, Japan, 1994-99, prof., 2000—; vis. prof. U. Colo., Boulder, 1997, Northwestern U., Evanston, Ill., 1998. Author: (book) Group Decision Making: Toward a Theory of Collaborative Intelligence, 1997; co-author: (book) Understanding Group Behavior, vol. 1, 1996; contbr. articles to profl. jours. Recipient Young Psychologist award Japanese Psychol. Assn., 1992; Fulbright fellow, 1997. Mem. APA, Japanese Social Psychol. Assn. (dir. 1996—), Soc. Exptl. Social Psychology. Office: Hokkaido U Dept Behav Sci, N10W7 Kita-ku, 060-0810 Sapporo Hokkaido, Japan

KAMEI, CHIAKI, pharmacology educator; b. Kyoto, Japan, Feb. 15, 1945; s. Taiga Nakahara and Kyoko Kamei.; m. Setsuko Kitayama, Oct. 30, 1950; children: Haruhiko, Tomohiko. BS, Osaka (Japan) U. Pharm. Scis., 1968; MS, Kyushu U., Fukuoka, Japan, 1971, PhD, 1976. Assoc. prof. pharmacology Okayama (Japan) U., 1978-94, prof. pharmacology, 1994—. Home: 2-7-6 Jotodai-Nishi, Okayama 709-0624, Japan Office: Okayama U, 1-1-1 Tsushima-Naka, Okayama 700-8530, Japan

KAMEI, HIDEO, surgeon, medical educator; b. Takatoh, Japan, May 31, 1930; s. Soh and Tamaki (Toyoshima) K.; m. Keiko Hirano, Dec. 9, 1932; children: Keitaro, Sohtaro, Yohtaro, Rentaro. MD, Nagoya (Japan) U., 1955; PhD, Nagoya U. Sch. Medicine, 1965. Intern Nagoya U. Br. Hosp., Japan, 1955-56, West Jersey Hosp., Camden, N.J., 1956-57; resident Bradford (Pa.) Hosp., 1957-58, Sacred Heart Hosp., Allentown, Pa., 1958-60; cancer rschr. Roswell Park (N.Y.) Meml. Inst., 1965-68; assoc. prof. dept. surgery Nagoya U., 1983-85; prof. dept. surgery Aichi-Gakuin Univ. Hosp., Nagoya, 1985—. Contbr. cancer rsch. articles to profl. jours. including Nature, Jour. Immunology, Jour. Nat. Cancer Inst., others. Home: 4-214 Uedayama Tenpaku, Nagoya 468, Japan Office: Aichi-Gakuin Hosp Surgery, 2 Suemori-dori Chikusa, Nagoya 464, Japan

KAMEI, TAMIO, physician; b. Kasukawa, Japan, Jan. 2, 1933; s. Kazuo and Shizu (Takai) K.; m. Yoshiko Tokuoka Kamei, Oct. 18, 1960; children: Takako, Tokuko. MD, Gunma U., Maebashi, Japan, 1957, DMS, 1962. Diplomate of Bd. Otolaryngology, Japan, 1984. Asst. Gunma U. Sch. Medicine, Maebashi, Japan, 1962-64, instr., 1965-79, assoc. prof., 1980-83, dir., prof., 1984-98; cons. Japan Otorhinolaryng Soc., Tokyo, 1979-98; pres. Gunma Otolaryng. Soc., Maebashi, Japan, 1985-98, Soc. for Afternystagmus Study, Maebashi, Japan, 1992-98; cons. Gunma Pref. Welfare Coun., Maebashi, Japan, 1987-98. Author: Vestibular Mechanisms in Health and Disease, 1978, CT-Diagnosis of Head and Neck Diseases, 1985, From Neuron to Action, 1990; chief editor, author: Illustrated Neurotology, 1995. Recipient Rsch. scholarship Taito-Pfizer Co., Japan, 1958, Alexander von Humboldt, Germany, 1972, 77. Mem. The Barany Soc., The Japanese Soc. for Equilibrium Rsch., The Prosper Meniere Soc. Home: 1-20-9 Otonemachi, Maebashi 371-0825, Japan

KAMEI, TSUTOMU, medical researcher; b. Shimabara, Japan; s. Hiroshi and Yoko (Honda) K. MD, Nagasaki U., 1985, PhD, 1989. Postdoctoral fellowship U. Mich., Ann Arbor, 1988-89; physician Saitama Children's Med. Ctr., Iwatsuki, Japan, 1989-90; rschr. Shimane Med. U., Izumo, 1990-94; dir. Shimane Inst. Health Sci., Izumo, 1994—; adminstrv. doctor Shimane Inst. Health Sci., Izumo, 1994—; part-time lectr. Kanazawa Med. U., 1998—, Ochanomizu U., 1999—. Contbr. articles to profl. jours.; patentee in field. Grantee Illuminating Engring. Inst., Japan, 1993, Shimane Med. U. Edn. and Rsch. Found., Japan, 1993, Rsch. Found. Traffic Preventive Medicine, Japan, 1994, Japan Rsch. Found. for Chronic Disease and Rehab., 1998. Mem. World Fedn. for Mental Health, Internat. Union for Health Promotion and Edn./France, Physiol. Soc. Japan, Japanese Soc. for Complementary and Alternative Medicine (bd. dirs.). Office: Shimane Inst Health Sci, 223-7 Enya-cho, 693 0021 Izumo Shimane, Japan

KAMÉL, LARS, astronomer, programmer; b. Hudiksvall, Sweden, June 7, 1960; s. Lennart and Gunborg (Wounder) K. BSc, Uppsala (Sweden) U., 1983, PhD, 1991. Astronomer Astron. Observatory, Uppsala; freelance astronomer Uppsala, 1991-98, software engr., 1998—. Author: The Comet Lightcurve Catalogue/Atlas, 1990. Mem. Upsala Pub. chess Soc. (rating officer 1993—). Home: Fälhagsleden 4D, S-753 24 Uppsala Sweden Office: Astronomical Observatory, Box 515, S-751 20 Uppsala Sweden

KAMEL, OSMAN MOSTAFA, astronomy educator, consultant, researcher; b. Cairo, Dec. 9, 1935; s. Mostafa Osman Kamel; married. BSc, Cairo U., 1957, MSc, 1971, PhD, 1974. Demonstrator faculty scis. Cairo U., 1957-71, instr. faculty scis., 1971-74, asst. prof. faculty scis., 1974-82, assoc. prof. faculty scis., 1982-87, prof. faculty scis., 1987—; vis. prof. in aerospace Engrng. Dept. U. Tex., Austin, 1981-83, L'Obs. de la Côte d'Azur, Grasse, France, 1994, 96, BDL, Paris, 1991; vis. prof. Paris U., 1997, 98; cons. JPL, Pasadena, Calif., 1989, Inst. of Astronomy Cambridge U., Eng., 1997. Contbr. articles to sci. jours. Fulbright grantee, 1981-83, 89, Bur. Des Longitudes grantee, Paris, 1991; recipient Rsch. award French govt., 1979-80. Mem. AAAS, Am. Astron. Soc., Egyptian Astron. Soc., Internat. Astron. Union, Div. Dynamical Astronomy, N.Y. Acad. Scis., Henry Poincaré Inst. Home: 31 Eskandar Akbar St, Heliopolis 11341 Cairo Egypt

KAMENAR, BORIS, chemistry educator; b. Susak-Rijeka, Croatia, Feb. 20, 1929; s. Vitomir and Katarina (Skitarelic) K.; m. Maja Perusko, Sept. 16, 1953; 1 child, Vedrana. Diploma in Chem. Technology, U. Zagreb, Croatia, 1953, PhD in Chemistry, 1960; Postdoctoral fellow, U. Oxford, U.K., 1964. Head of testing lab. Metal Factory and Foundry, Rijeka, Croatia, 1953-56; rsch. scientist Rudjer Boskovic Inst., Zagreb, 1956-62; prof. U. Zagreb, 1972-99, prof. emeritus, 1999—; vis. fellow All Souls Coll., Oxford, 1971, 72; vis. prof. U. Auckland, New Zealand, 1980, Massey U., Palmerston North, New Zealand, 1989-90, 95; head chemistry dept. Faculty of Sci., Zagreb, 1965-66, univ. postgrad. study in chemistry, 1972-80, dean faculty of sci., 1976-78, head lab. of gen. and inorganic chemistry, 1982-84. Contbr. more than 130 articles to profl. jours. With Croatian partizans, 1943-45. Recipient Scientific award of Republic of Croatia, Parliament of Croatia, Zagreb, 1970, Scientific award of City of Zagreb, City Coun., 1980, Life Achievement prize Parliament of Croatia, Zagreb, 2000. Mem. Croatian Chem. Soc. (pres. 1976-80), European Crystallographic Com. (pres. 1978-81), Croatian Crystallographic Assn. (pres. 1992—), Croatian Acad. of Scis. and Arts. Avocation: travel. Fax: "5-1-4611191. Office: Faculty of Sci, Ulica kralja Zvonimira 8, 10000 Zagreb Croatia

KAMENETSKII, EUGENE (OSIP), physicist, research scientist; b. Tashkent, USSR, Aug. 25, 1946; arrived in Israel, 1992; s. Josef Kamenetskii and Nina Chertkov-Kamenetskii; m. Rozalia Shrabman (div. 1985); children: Natalia, Ilya; m. Elena M. Fainstein, Spet. 28, 1991; 1 child, Michal. Diploma in elec. engring., Elec. Engring. Inst., Leningrad, USSR, 1969, PhD, 1986. Engr. "Svetlana", Leningrad, 1969-74; sr. engr., adj. asst. prof. North-Western Polytechnic Inst., Leningrad, 1974-83; sr. engr. Elec. Engring. Inst., Leningrad, 1983-87; sr. rsch. fellow, adj. assoc. prof. Elec. Engring. Inst., 1987-92; rsch. scientist Tel-Aviv U., 1994-97, sr. rschr., 1997—; vis. prof. Yamaguchi U., Japan, 1998-99; lectr. in field. Contbr. articles to profl. jours. Grantee Min. Sci., Tel-Aviv, 1994-97. Mem. N.Y. Acad. Scis. Avocations: history and philosophy physics, long-distance running. Office: Tel-Aviv U, Dept EE-Phys Electronics, 69978 Tel Aviv Israel

KAMENETSKII, VALENTINE ROBERTOVICH, engineering educator, researcher; b. Odessa, Ukraine, USSR, Apr. 11, 1938; s. Robert Borisovich Kamenetskii and Raisa Arkadievna (Puritz) Kamenetskaya; m. Larisa Georgievna Vinogradskaya, Nov. 9, 1961; children: Helen, Robert. Engr., Polytech. Inst., Odessa, 1960; candidate, Sci. Tech. Inst., Odessa, 1969. Cert. engring. Foreman Sevzapenergomontage, Leningrad, Russia, 1960-63; sr. engr. Tech. Inst., Odessa, 1964-69; sr. sci. collaborator Refrigerator Inst., Odessa, 1969-79; instr. State Econ. U., Odessa, 1979—. Author: Transport Properties of Real Gases, 1976, General Theory of Statistics, 1985; contbr. articles to profl. jours. Mem. N.Y. Acad. Scis. Avocation: electronics. Home: 43 Koblevskaya str, Apt 6, 65045 Odessa Ukraine

KAMENIR, YURY GREGORY, scientist, researcher; b. Kursk, USSR, May 17, 1949; arrived in Israel, 1996; s. Gregory Pinhas and Helena Moses (Kaz) K. MSc in Radioelectronics, Moscow Aviation Inst., 1972; PhD in Biology, Inst. Biology South Seas, Sevastopol, USSR, 1991; English Lang. grad., Tchrs. Inst. at Volgograd. Head programming dept. Parus Factory, Sevastopol, 1978-81; sr. engr. Inst. Biology South Seas, Sevastopol, 1981-92, rsch. fellow, 1992-93, sr. rsch. fellow, 1993-96; rsch. fellow Haifa U., Kazrin, Israel, 1996-98; sr. rsch. fellow Bar-Ilan U., Ramat-gan, Israel, 1999—. Contbr. articles to profl. jours. Mem. N.Y. Acad. Scis., Societas Internat. Limnologicae, Israel Soc. Water Rsch. Avocations: history of culture, poetry, music, travel, languages. Home: t Nave 28b/5, 12900 Kazrin Israel Office: Bar-Ilan U, 52900 Ramat-Gan Israel

KAMERMAN, SHEILA BRODY, social worker, educator; b. Jan. 7, 1928; d. S. Lawrence and Helen (Golding) Brody; m. Morton Kamerman, Sept. 11, 1947; children: Nathan Brody, Elliot Herbert, Laura Kamerman-Katz. BA, NYU, 1946; MSW, Hunter Coll., 1966; D in Social Welfare, Columbia U., 1973; PhD (hon.), York U., Eng., 1998. Social worker N.Y.C. Dept. Social Svcs., 1966-68; social work supr. Bellevue Psychiat. Hosp., 1968-69; assoc. prof. social work Hunter Coll., 1977-79; from rsch. assoc. to sr. rsch. assoc. Columbia U. Sch. Social Work, 1971-79, assoc. prof. social policy and planning, 1979-81; prof. Sch. Social Work Columbia U., 1981—, Compton Found. Centennial prof., 1996—; dir. Columbia U. Inst. for Child and Family Policy, 1998—; chair NAS-NRC panel on work, family and community, 1980-82; mem. Com. Child Devel. Rsch. and Pub. Policy, 1983-88; mem. com. on prenatal care Inst. Medicine, 1986-88; cons. in field; mem. numerous social welfare coms. and adv. bds.; mem. Gov. Cuomo's Task Force on Poverty and Welfare Reform, 1986-87, adv. com. on Work and Family, 1987-88, UN Expert groups on social welfare and family policies; mem. Inst. Medicine/Nat. Rsch. Coun. bd. on children and families, 1998—. Author: (with Alfred J. Kahn) Not for the Poor Alone, 1975, Social Services in the United States, 1976, Social Services in International Perspective, 1977, Family Policy: Government and Families in Fourteen Countries, 1978, Child Care, Family Benefits and Working Parents, 1981, Parenting in an Unresponsive Society, 1980, Maternity and Parental Benefits and Leaves, 1980, Helping America's Families, 1982, Maternity Policies and Working Women, 1983, Income Transfers for Families with Children, 1983, Child Care: Facing the Hard Choices, 1987, The Responsive Work Place, 1987, Child Support: From Debt Collection to Social Policy, 1988, Mothers Alone: Strategies for a Time of Change, 1988, Privatization and the Welfare State, 1989, Social Services for Children, Youth and Families in the United States, 1990, Child Care, Parental Leave, and the Under 3's, 1991, A Welcome for Every Child, 1994, Starting Right: How America Neglects Its Youngest Children and What We Can Do About It, 1995, Children in big Cities, 1996, Confronting the New Politics of Child and Family Policies, (series of 6 reports), 1997, Family Change and Family Policies in Britain, Canada, New Zealand and the United States, 1998, Big Cities in the Welfare Transition, 1998; contbr. over 200 articles to profl. jours. Recipient Hexter award Hunter Coll. Sch. Social Work, 1977, Nat. Leadership award in Social Policy, Heller Sch. Brandeis U., 1989; named to Hunt Coll. Hall of Fame, 1981; fellow Ctr. Advanced Study in Behavioral Scis., 1983-84. Mem. NASW, Am. Pub. Human Svcs. Assn., Assn. Policy Analysis and Mgmt., Phi Beta Kappa. Home: 1125 Park Ave New York NY 10128-1243 Office: Columbia U Sch Social Work 622 W 113th St New York NY 10025-7982

KAMEYAMA, OSAMU, orthopaedic surgeon, educator; b. Osaka, Japan, July 14, 1950; s. Susumu and Yoshiko (Eguchi) K.; m. Hinako Shimazu, Sept. 2, 1984; children: Tadashi, Akira. MD, Kansai Med. U., 1978, PhD, 1982. Asst. prof., assoc. prof. Kansai Med. U., Osaka, Japan, 1993—; chief surgeon Otokoyama Hosp., 1982-85; dir. Rakusai NT Hosp., Kyoto, 1995—; Olympic Sports Dr., Tokyo, 1988—; chief sports dr. Japan Canoe Assn., Tokyo, 1988—. Author: Neural and Mechanical Control of Movement, 1984, Minimum Orthopaedics, 2000; contbr. articles to profl. jours. Recipient Arukea award Japan Orthopaedics and Traumatology Found., 1994, Osaka Gas award Osaka Gas Group Found., 1995, Barrier Free award Barrier Free Sys. Found., 1996. Office: Kansai Med Univ, 10-15 Fumizono, Osaka 570, Japan

KAMH, SANAA ABD EL-TAWAB, physicist; b. Cairo, June 15, 1949; d. Abd El-Tawab Abd El-Halim and Zinab Mahmoud Hafiz (Wahbi) K.; m. Zakaria Meshrif Omran Kamh, Feb. 20, 1975; children: May, Mohammed, Yasmin. BS, Ain-Shams U., Cairo, 1971, PhD, 1985. Demonstrator Ain-Shams U., Cairo, 1971-75, asst. tchr., 1975-85, asst. prof., 1996—. Regional mng. editor Asian Jour. Physics, 1996, mem. adv. bd. 1996; contbr. articles, papers to profl. jours. Mem. Egyptian Assn. Crystallographic Sci., N.Y. Acad. Scis. Major field of interest: physics; special field of interest: electronics. Home: 35 Khalifa El-Radi St, Nasr City, Cairo 11471, Egypt Office: Ain Shams U, Asma Fahmi St, Cairo 11757, Egypt

KAMIENSKA-CARTER, EVA HANNA, designer, artist; b. Warsaw, Feb. 19, 1960; came to U.S., 1987; d. Witold and Kamilla (Karwowska) K.; m. Bernard Owen Carter, July 25, 1992; children: Lisa Camille, Maya Lee. MArch, Warsaw Tech. U., 1983; grad. with honors, Art Inst. Pitts., 1991. Certificate to practice art Ministry of Culture. Freelance artist, design cons. Warsaw, 1983-87, N.Y.C., Detroit, Boston, Pitts., 1987-92; design cons., ptnr. Carter-Kamienska Design, Pitts., 1992—; freelance set designer in motion picture prodn., Pitts., 1994—; art tchr. Carnegie Mus. Art, Pitts., 1991-92, Pitts. Ctr. Arts, 1991-92. Storyboard illustrator: (software) The Ripper, 1995; one woman shows include Zdzisiaj Gallery, Warsaw, Poland, 1981, Na Brechta Gallery, Warsaw, 1984. At 700 PArker, Detroit, 1988; group exbhns. include Manfred Schuller Gallery, Zurich, 1985, Zdzisiaj Gallery, 1985, Tripoli Gallery, Phila., 1987, Pitts. Ctr. Arts, 1989. Birmingham Loft, Pitts., 1989, Mendelson Gallery, Pitts., 1989, Monroeville (Pa.) Libr. Gallery, 1989, IUP Gallery, Indiana, Pa., 1998, Carnegie (Pa.) Libr., 1992, Associated Artists Pitts. Gallery, 1993, ZPAP Gallery, Warsaw, 1998. Mem. Assoc. Artists Pitts., Pitts. Soc. Artists, Pitts. Ctr. Arts. Avocations: attending cultural and social events, hiking, canoeing, computers. Home and Office: Carter-Kamienska Design 853 Phineas St Pittsburgh PA 15212-8026

KAMIN, WILLIAM STEPHEN, food company executive, photographer; b. Chgo., Feb. 3, 1930; s. Emil Zola and Berta Magid; m. Adrienne Bloomberg, Aug. 28, 1955; children: Steven B., Andrew G. PhB, U. Chgo., 1947; BS, U. Ill., 1952. CPA, Ill. Staff acct. D. Himmelblau & Co., Chgo., 1955-57; budget analyst Westinghouse Electric Co., West Mifflin, Pa., 1957-63; contr. Std. Fruit Co., La Ceiba, Honduras, 1963-68; gen. mgr. Std. Fruit Co., Guayaquil, Ecuador, 1968-70; v.p. fin. Dole Fruit Co., Honolulu, 1970-72; v.p. ops. Castle & Cooke, Inc., San Francisco, 1972-78, v.p. strategic planning, 1978-82; pvt. practice photography Menlo Park, Calif., 1985—; cons. William S. Kamin Cons., Atherton, Calif., 1982-85; adj. prof. Coll. Notre Dame, Belmont, Calif., 1984-85, U. Santa Clara, Calif., 1986, Golden Gate U., San Francisco, 1987. Author, photographer: Tenderloin, 1989. Bd. dirs., fin. cons. Valley Inst. of Theatre Arts, Saratoga, Calif., 1986-87; docent Coyote Point Mus., San Mateo, 1992-95, Fitzgerald Marine Res., Pacifica, Calif., 1995-97. Mem. Sons in Retirement. Avocation: tennis, travel. Home and Office: 169 Stone Pine Ln Menlo Park CA 94025-3050

KAMINS, BARRY MICHAEL, lawyer; b. Oct. 3, 1943; s. Abe and Evelyn Bertha (Goffen) K.; m. Fern Louise Kamins, Mar. 30, 1968; 1 child, Allyson. BA, Columbia U., 1965; JD, Rutgers U., 1968. Bar: N.Y. 1969, U.S. Dist. Ct. (ea. and so. dists.) N.Y. 1973, U.S. Supreme Ct. 1974. Asst. dist. atty., 1969-73; dep. chief Criminal Ct. Bur., 1971-73; ptnr. Flamhaft, Levy, Kamins & Hirsch, 1973—; chmn. grievance com. 2d and 11th Jud. Dist., 1994-98; adj. prof. Fordham Law Sch., Bklyn. Law Sch., Bklyn. Law Sch.; adj. asst. prof. in criminal law N.Y. Tech. Coll.; apptd. spl. prosecutor, Kings County, 1990-92; adj. assoc. prof. N.Y. criminal procedure, law sch. Fordham U., 1994—. Author: The Social Studies Student Investigates the Criminal Justice System, 1978, New York Search and Seizure, 1991; contbr. numerous articles on criminal law to profl. jours. Mem. ABA, N.Y. State Bar Assn. (mem. ho. dels., chair com. prof. discipline 1999—), Bklyn. Bar Assn. (past pres., chair jud. com. 1994—), Kings County Criminal Bar Assn. (past pres.), Nat. Dist. Attys. Assn., Assn. of Bar of City of N.Y. (chair jud. com. 1998—, chairperson oversight com. for criminal def. orgns., 2d appellate divsn. 1997—). Office: 16 Court St Brooklyn NY 11241-0102

KAMINSKA, TERESA, federal official; b. Kraśnik Fabryczny, Jan. 25, 1956; married; 1 child. Grad. Acad. Agr., Olsztyn, 1980; postgrad., 1982, 96. Worker Health Care Ctr., Gdansk-Zaspa, 1985, Dept. Mcpl. Hygiene, Voivodship Sanitary Epidemiology Sta., 1986-95; dir. Voivodship Ctr. Analyses Promotion Health, Gdansk, 1995-97; min. Social Reforms, Warsaw, 1997-99, pres. health ins. supervisory office, 1999—. Solidarity Election Action. Office: Chmn Coun Mins, Aleje Ujazdowskie 1/3, 00-583 Warsaw Poland

KAMINSKI, FRANCISZEK, science educator; b. Warsaw, Poland, Oct. 9, 1930; s. Antoni Lipski and Helena (Starewicz) Kaminska; m. Jadwiga Szymanska, Jan. 6, 1968; children: Ewa, Agnes, Olga. MSc in Electronics, Warsaw U. Tech., 1956; DSc in Electronics, Polish Acad. Scis., 1966; DHabil, Warsaw U. Tech., 1978. Scientist Inst. Tele- and Radiotech., Warsaw, 1956-62; scientist Polish Acad. Scis., Warsaw, 1962-66, asst. prof., 1967-85; assoc. prof. Inst. Telecomm., Warsaw, 1985—; mem. sci. coun. Min. Comms., Warsaw, 1996-98. Author: (book) Linear Distributed Circuit Synthesis Appropriate to the Polynomial Electromechanical Filter and Microwave Network Design, 1976, The State and the Telecommunications Market, 1995; contbr. articles to sci. jours. Avocations: books, good movies. Home: Litewska 10 m 17, 00-581 Warsaw Poland Office: Inst Telecomms, Szachowa 1, 04-894 Warsaw Poland

KAMINSKI, JANUSZ, cinematographer; b. Ziembice, Poland, June 27, 1959; came to U.S., 1981; s. Marian Kaminski and Jadwiga Celner; m. Holly Hunter, May 20, 1995. BA in Film, Columbia Coll., 1987. Dir. photography film Lisa, 1988 (Line Eagel award Ill. Film Festival), Absence, 1988, Selling Short, 1988, Grim Prairie Tales, 1989, All The Love in The World, 1989, Rain Killer, 1990, The Terror Within II, 1991, The Adventures of Huck Finn, 1992, Cool As Ice, 1992, Mad Dog Coll, 1992, Trouble Bound, 1993, Schindler's List, 1993 (Academy Award, Best Cinematography), How to Make an American Quilt, 1995, Jerry Maguire, 1996, Lost World, 1997, Amistad, 1997, Saving Private Ryan, 1998 (Academy Award, Best Cinematography). Office: 1223 Wilshire Blvd # 645 Santa Monica CA 90403-5400

KAMINSKI, WŁODZIMIERZ, economist, researcher; b. Skierniewice, Poland, Apr. 16, 1924; s. Stanisław and Stanisława (Zielinska) K.; m. Krystyna Tyszkowska, Dec. 27, 1947; 1 child, Andrzej. MS, Jagiellonian U., 1947, D of Law, 1948; D of Agrl. Econs., Agrl. U., 1961, D honoris causa, 2000. Prof. Agrl. U. Warsaw, 1973-92; prof., mem. senate, prorector Warsaw Coll. Econs., 1997—; vis. prof. various univs. and instns., Liege, Belgium; Plovdiv, Bulgaria; Angers, Massy, Paris, and Montpellier, France; Berlin and Essen, Germany; Szeged, Hungary; Zurich, Switzerland. Editl. bd. Internat. Jour. of Refrigeration, 1975-99; author: Regional Aspects of Food Economy (1st Scientific award 1989, Min. of Agrl. 1991), 18 Books Concerning Food Economy, 1972-2000 (5 awards Min. of Edn. 1975-85), (booklet) Refrigeration and the Worldwide Food Industry on the Threshold of the 21st Century, 1995 (award Internat. Inst. Refrigeration 1999). Recipient Comdr. Cross of Polonia Restituta, 1987, Croix d' Officier du Merite Agricole French Govt., 1995, Cross Nat. Army Govt. of Poland, 1994. Mem. Polish Acad. Scis. (hon. mem. agrl. econs. com., spatial mgmt. com.), Polish Sci. Soc. Food Industry (hon.), Hungarian Sci. Soc. Food Industry (hon.), Internat. Inst. Refrigeration (hon., v.p. sci. coun. 1971-79, mgmt. com. 1979-87, v.p. exec. com. 1987-95), N.Y. Acad. Scis., French Acad. Agr. (fgn.). Achievements include research on theoretical analysis and scientific aspects concerning, systems of food economy, regional aspects of agriculture and food economy, refrigeration and food economy. Home: Smolna 15 RM 11, 00375 Warsaw Poland Office: Warsaw Coll Econs, Abramowskiego 4, 02-667 Warsaw Poland

KAMINSKY, ANATOL, educator, writer; b. Ukraine, May 17, 1925; came to U.S., 1960; s. Gregory and Eudokia Kaminsky; m. Tatjana Kripacky; 1 son, Taras. PhD, Ukrainian Free U., Munich, 1990; cert. in internat. rels., London Sch. Econs./Polit. Sci., 1958. Editor Ukrainian Ind., Munich, 1953-

58; v.p. rsch. Prolog Assocs., N.Y.C., 1960-81; sr. editor Suchasnist, N.Y.C., 1962-83; dir., chief editor Ukrainian svc. Radio Free Europe/Radio Liberty, Munich, 1983-89; prof. internat. rels. Ukrainian Free U., 1993—, dean faculty of law and socio-econ. scis., 1996-98; guest prof. Lviv (Ukraine) State U., 1993—. Author; 12 books in Ukrainian. Chmn. polit. coun. Rep. of Ukrainian Supreme Liberation Coun., N.Y.C. and Munich, 1996—; assoc. mem. nat. coun. Dem. Party of Ukraine, 1996—. Recipient Internat. Orlyk prize Dem. Party of Ukraine, 1994. Mem. Orgn. Ukrainian Nationalists (chmn. 1991—). Home: 68 The Rise Warwick NY 10990-4234

KAMINSKY, RICHARD ALAN, lawyer; b. Toledo, Nov. 15, 1951; s. Jack and Sally (Kale) K. BA, Johns Hopkins U., 1973; JD, U. Mich., 1975. Bar: Ill. 1976, U.S. Dist. Ct. (no. dist.) Ill. 1976. Assoc. Vedder, Price, Kaufman & Kammholz, Chgo., 1976-83; atty. Borg-Warner Corp., Chgo., 1983-89; v.p., assoc. gen. counsel CNA Ins. Cos., Chgo., 1989—. Contbr. chpt. to book. Mem. ABA, Chgo. Bar Assn., Ill. State C. of C. Home: 47 Williamsburg Rd Evanston IL 60203-1813 Office: CNA Ins Cos Cna Pla Chicago IL 60685-0001

KAMISAKO, TOSHINORI, physician, educator; b. Osaka, Japan, Jan. 7, 1961; s. Keinosuke and Terumi (Fujinaga) K.; m. Hitomi Hirano, May 1, 1994. MD, Kinki U., Osakasayama, Japan, 1985, PhD, 1991. Resident Kinki U. Hosp., Osaka, 1985-86, Toranomon Hosp., Tokyo, 1986-87; asst. Kinki U., Osakasayama, 1991-93, lectr., 1993—. Contbr. articles to profl. jours. Fellow Japanese Soc. Internal Medicine, 1991—. Office: Kinki U Sch Medicine, 377-2 Ohnohigashi, Osakasayama 589, Japan

KAMIYA, YOSHIO, research chemist, educator; b. Ofuna, Kanagawa, Japan, Mar. 25, 1930; s. Minoru and Kimi (Moro) K.; m. Masuko Nakamura, Mar. 18, 1957; children: Shoshi, Yoshiko, Mari. B in Engring., U. Tokyo, 1953, PhD, 1960. Postdoctoral fellow Nat. Rsch. Coun. Canada, Ottawa, Ontario, 1962-64; assoc. prof. U. Tokyo, 1964-75, prof., 1975-90, prof. emeritus, 1990—; head dept. reaction chemistry U. Tokyo, 1975, 80, 85; chmn. com. coal energy MITI, Tokyo, 1985-99. Author: Autoxidation of Organic Compounds, 1974, Chemistry of Fuel and Combustion, 1987, Chemistry of Petroleum and Coal, 1973, Process Organic Chemistry, 1981, Aspects of Degradation and Stabilization of Polymer, 1978; published 300 scientific papers. Recipient Award for Progressive Rsch. Chem. Soc. Japan, 1961, Award for Disting. Rsch. Fuel Soc. Japan, 1979, Japan Petroleum Inst., 1988. Mem. Inst. Energy Japan (v.p. 1992, pres. 1993-95), Engring. Acad. Japan. Achievements include research in catalysis in organic oxidation reaction, effects of solvent and catalyst in coal liquefaction, autoxidation of organic compounds. Home: 590-96 Ozenji Aso-ku, Kawasaki 215, Japan Office: Sci U Tokyo Dept Ind Chem, 1-3 Kagurasaka Shinjuku, Tokyo 162, Japan

KAMIYAMA, SHINICHI, engineering educator; b. Tochigi, Japan, Mar. 5, 1935; s. Juudou and Chiyo K.; m. Eiko Izumi, May 3, 1963; 1 child, Keiichi. BS, Tohoku U., Sendai, 1957; MS, Tohoku U., 1959, PhD, 1962. Lectr. Inst. of High Speed Mechanics, Tohoku U., 1962-63, assoc. prof., 1963-75, prof., 1975-88, dir., 1988-89; dir. Inst. Fluid Sci., Tohoku U., 1989-93, 95-97, prof., 1993-95; prof. emeritus Tohoku U., 1998—; dean sys. sci. and tech. Akita (Japan) Prefectural U., 1999—. Author: Introduction to Magnetic Fluid, 1989, Fluid Machinery, 1980. Recipient Paper award Japan Soc. Mech. Engrs., 1985, Contbn. award Fluid Engring. Divsn. Japan Soc. Mech. Engrs., 1995, Acad. Achievement award Fluid Engring. Divsn. Japan Soc. Mech. Engrs., 1997. Mem. Engring. Acad. Japan. E-mail: kamiyama@akita-pu.ac.jp. Fax: 81-184-27-2180. Office: Fac Systems Sci and Tech, Akita Prefectural Univ, Tsutiya Honjyo Akita, Japan

KAMIYAMA, YASUSHI, humanities educator; b. Ashiya City, Hyogo, Japan, Nov. 14, 1927; s. Hisanosuke and Kumi (Ikeda) K.; m. Emiko Nakamura, Nov. 28, 1960; children: Mariko Hamano, Hiroshi. BA, Osaka U., 1953. Lectr. Shimonoseki City (Japan) U., 1962-65, asst. prof., 1965-67; asst. prof. Mukogawa Women's U., Nishinomiya, Japan, 1967-70, Kansai U., Suita, Japan, 1970-75; prof. Kansai U., Suita, 1975-98, hon. prof., 1998—. Author: English Novels and Morality, 1978, English Humanism Novels, 1982, The Background of English Literature, 1993, Thomas Hardy and Novelists, 1996, Some Studies of English Literature, 1998; translator: A Group of Noble Dames, 1983. Mem. Japan Hardy Soc. Tokyo, Thomas Hardy Soc., Japan Brontë Soc., Japan George Eliot Soc., Japan Virginia Woolt Soc. Avocations: travel, photography. Home: 3-19-12 Shinsenri-Nishimach, Yoyonaka Toyonaka Osaka 560-0083, Japan Office: Kansei U, 3-3-35 Yamatecho, Suita Osaka 564-8680, Japan

KAMJORN, SIRI PATNA, pharmaceutical executive, consultant; b. Tarua, Ayudhya, Thailand, Nov. 4, 1923; s. Rew Kamjorn and Syn Bodharam; m. Vilaivan Ternvises, Aug. 12, 1952; children: Kanokwan, Ponpich, Sisda. BSc, Chulalongkorn U., Thailand, 1943; MD, Siriraj Sch. Medicine, Thailand, 1947; cert. in pediatrics, U. Pa., 1954. Resident Siriraj Hosp. & Med. Sch., Thailand, 1947-50; rschr. Israves Clinic, Bangkok, 1955-60; dir. Israves Clinic, 1961-71, 73-90; mem. People's Reps., Thailand, 1972-73; mng. dir. Israves Inc., Bangkok, 1991-94; lectr. poisons and drug abuse Faculty of Sci. Chulalongkorn U., Thailand, 1961-90. Author: Wonder of the Mind, 1961, Passion and Crimes, 5 vols., 1962-65, Werewolf, 1986, Man-Eater in Southern Thailand, 1992, Behavior of Thai Woodcutters, 1995, The Fate of Thai Elephants, 1998. Mem. Med. Assn. Thailand, N.Y. Acad. Scis. Buddhist. Avocations: psychological research, meditation, writing. Home: 261 Soi-Mit-Anan Rajvat, 10300 Bangkok Thailand

KAMLAGE, BEATE, microbiologist; b. Meppen, Germany, Feb. 2, 1966; d. Karl-Heinz and Margret Bernhardine (Altevers) K.; m. Stefan Gommlich, Oct. 30, 1998. PhD in Microbiology, U. Göttingen, Germany, 1994. Microbiologist German Inst. Human Nutrition, Potsdam, Germany, 1995—. Contbr. articles to profl. jours. Mem. VAAM. Office: German Inst Human Nutrition, Arthur-Scheunert Allee 114, 14558 Potsdam Germany

KAMM, CHRISTIAN PHILIP, manufacturing company executive, writer, investment company executive; b. Lakewood, Ohio, Oct. 30, 1967; s. Jacob and Judith (Steinbrenner) K. BA cum laude, Ohio Wesleyan U., 1990; MBA, Baldwin Wallace Coll., 1992. Cert. investment mgmt. analyst. Chief fin. analyst, asst. treas. Electric Furnace Co., Salem, Ohio, 1992-93; v.p., treas. Wilkinson Co., Inc., Stow, Ohio, 1993-94; pres. Ostalden Corp., Cleve., 1994—; pres., COO Wilkinson Co., Inc., Stow, Ohio, 1994-97; vice chmn., CFO EFCO Inc., Salem, Ohio, 1995—; pres. Kamm Investment Co., Cleve., 1995—; chief, rep. office Kamm Investment, Inc., Ho ch'i Minh City, Vietnam, 1998—; bd. dirs., exec. com. Electric Furnance Co., Inc., Salem; bd. dirs. Canefco, Ltd., Toronto, Can., Turner Machine Co., Kamm Investment Co.; adj. prof. U. Econs., Ho Chi Minh City, Vietnam. Author: The Dream of the Dragon, 2000; inventor recycle bin system, home recycle chute system. Mem. Cleve. Athletic Club, Akron City Club. Office: Kamm Investment Co 526 Superior Ave E Ste 1250 Cleveland OH 44114-1900

KAMM, THOMAS ALLEN, air transportation company executive; b. Lynden, Wash., June 10, 1925; s. Charles J. and Teena I. (Kampen) K.; m. Geraldine V. Leek, Sept. 4, 1948; children—Kristine E., Thomas A. Jr. B.S., U. Wash., 1947; J.D., U. Detroit, 1957; LL.M., George Washington U., 1973. Bar: Mich. 1957, Calif. 1980, D.C. 1981. Commd. ensign U.S. Navy, 1945, advanced through grades to rear adm., 1975; various assignments antisubmarine warfare, transport squadrons, res. units, 1947-62; assigned (Transport Squadron 21), Japan; in support (7th Fleet), 1962-65; mgr. antisubmarine program, officer flight tng. (Naval Air Res. Unit), Alameda, Calif., 1965-67; mem. staff (Chief of Naval Air Reserve Tng.), Glenview, Ill., 1967-69; asst. naval air reserve coordinator (Office of Dep. Chief Naval Ops.), 1969-71; asst. dir. (Office of Dep. Asst. Sec. Def.), 1971-72; comdg. officer (Naval Air Res. Unit), Alameda, 1972-75; asst. dep. to dir. (Naval Res., Office Chief of Naval Ops.), Washington, 1975-76; dep. chief (Naval Res.), New Orleans, 1976-78; dep. dir. (Naval Res.), Washington, 1978-80; pvt. practice, Calif., 1980-95; pres. Kamm Air, Inc., Santa Rosa, Calif., 1991—; v.p. Ralph C. Wilson Agy., Detroit, 1952-59; gen. assoc. John M. Grubb Co., Oakland, Calif., 1959-61; adj. asst. prof. internat. law Golden Gate U. Law Sch., San Francisco. Decorated Legion of Merit, Meritorious Service medal. Mem. ABA, Naval Res. Assn., Res. Officers Assn., Assn. Naval Aviation, Phi Delta Theta, Delta Theta Phi, Bohemian Club, N.Y. Yacht Club, Army-Navy Country Club, Ironwood Country Club. Home: 11000 Chalk Hill Rd Healdsburg CA 95448-9649

KAMMAN, CURTIS WARREN, retired ambassador; b. Chgo., Jan. 15, 1939; s. Glenn Forrest and Mildred Isabel (Merry) K.; m. Mary Glasgow Curtis, Feb. 10, 1962; children: Edward, John, W. Stephen. BA, Yale U., 1959; postgrad., U. Washington, 1964-65. Joined Fgn. Service, U.S. Dept. State, 1960-2000; various diplomatic positions Am. embassies, Washington, Mexico City, Hong Kong, Moscow, Nairobi, 1960-80; dir. East African Affairs, Washington, 1980-82; polit. counselor Am. embassy, Moscow, 1982-84, minister, counselor, 1984-85; prin. officer U.S. Interests sect. Swiss embassy, Havana, Cuba, 1985-87; dep. asst. sec. U.S. Dept. State, Washington, 1987-91; amb. to Chile Santiago, 1991-94; amb. to Bolivia, 1994-97, amb. to Colombia, 1997-2000, ret., 2000. Bd. dirs. Fgn. Students Sch., Havana, 1985-87. Mem. Phi Beta Kappa. Episcopalian. Avocation: choral singing. Address: 2236 Lakeshore Dr Fennville MI 49408-9715 also: 5102 US Embassy APO AA 34038

KAMOI, KYUZI, physician, researcher; b. Tokyo, Aug. 28, 1945; s. Taro and Kimiko Kamoi; m. Keiko Matsuki. MD, Niigata U., 1970, D in Med. Scis., 1982. Diplomate Japanese Bd. Diabetes Mellitus, Japanese Bd. Endocrinology, Japanese Bd. Cons. Diabetes Mellitus. Resident in internal medicine Niigata U. Hosp., Japan, 1970-72; rsch. fellow endocrinology and metabolism Niigata U. Sch., 1972-77; postdoctoral fellow endocrinology and metabolism Ind. U., 1977-79; chief internal medicine Nagaoka (Japan) Red Cross Hosp., 1980—; lectr. Niigata U., 1987—. Mem. Internat. Diabetes Fedn., Japanese Soc. Internal Medicine, Japan Endocrine Soc., Am. Soc. Hypertension, N.Y. Acad. Scis. Avocations: tennis, mountain hiking. Home: 3-4-6 Hanazono, Nagaoka Niigata 940, Japan Office: Nagaoka Red Cross Hosp, 299-1 Terajima, Nagaoka Niigata 940 2085, Japan

KAMOTHO, JOSEPH, minister of education; b. Kangema, Kenya, Dec. 5, 1941. BS, Syracuse U., 1968; MA in Econs., U. Birmingham, 1970. Lectr. Kenya Inst. Adminstrn., 1971; manpower planning officer E. African Airways, 1971-72; dir. Kenya Inst. Mgmt., 1972-74; MP Kangema, Kenya, 1974; min. higher edn. Govt. of Kenya, 1979-83, asst. min. office of pres., 1988, min. transport and comms., 1988, min. edn., 1993-98, min. trade, 1998—; min. local govt. Govt. Kenya, Nairobi. Mem. Kenya African Nat. Union. *

KAMP, JOHANNES LEONARDUS, telecommunications specialist, consultant; b. Breda, The Netherlands, Aug. 8, 1945. Ingenieur, Tech. U. Eindhoven, The Netherlands, 1970. Lic. elec. engr. Developer Dr Neherlab, Leidschendam, The Netherlands, 1972-75; group leader transmission Dutch PTT, The Hague, The Netherlands, 1975-86; transmission specialist Nepostel, Indonesia, 1985; mgr. E-mail product Philips, Eindhoven, 1986-94; telecomm. cons. Origin, Eindhoven, 1994-98; telecom. cons. Philips Corp. IT, Eindhoven, 1998—. Home: Heytvelden 6, 5673 KJ Nuenen The Netherlands

KAMPE, CAROLYN JEAN, elementary art and special education educator; b. Chicago Heights, Ill., July 8, 1943; d. Fred H. and Harriet (Bobrowski) K. Student, Mt. St. Clare Jr. Coll., Clinton, Iowa, 1966-68; BA in Art, St. Ambrose U., 1970; MA in Cultural Studies, Gov. State U., 1974; EdD in Art Edn., Ill. State U., 1990. Cert. art tchr.; cert. spl. edn.; cert. K-12 specialist. Art supr., coord., and elem. art tchr. Dist. 170, Chicago Heights, 1970-87; grad. asst. art dept. Ill. State U., Normal, 1987-90; spl. edn. tchr. Hugh Jr. H.S., Matteson, Ill., 1990-91, Burr Oak, Calumet Park, Ill., 1991-92; homebound tchr. Dist. 162, Matteson, 1991-98; art edn. for spl. edn. Dist. 170, Chicago Heights, 1992—; art tchr. Field Sch. Dist. 152, Harvey, Ill., 1994-00, Vogt Visual Art Ctr., Tinley Park, Ill., 1996-99; spl. edn. tchr. Hufford Jr. H.S., Joliet, Ill., 1996-98; vis. faculty and adaptive art specialist St. Norbert Coll., DePere, Wis., 1990-92; active in Put Your Heart Illinois Youth Art Month, 1985-86 and 1993-94, spl. edn. "Earth Day" Art Exhbn. (200 works on display); homebound tchr. Dist. 162 and 227, 1991-98; bd. dirs. Very Spl. Arts, Ill. State U., Normal, 1992-96. Group exhbns. include Chicago Heights Libr., Chicago Heights Mcpl. Bldg., 1993-94, Wash. Jr. H.S., Chicago Heights, 1994; contbr. articles to profl. jours. Bd. dirs. Very Spl. Arts Ill., Ill. State U., Normal, 1992-94; Ill. Coalition for Disabilities, Normal, 1985-86; pres. Self Help for Hard of Hearing, Ill., 1984-86; mem. White House Exhbn. Com., Chgo., 1992-93; vol. Chgo. Pub. Libr., 1993; mem. Put Your Heart in Month, Ill. Youth Art Month, 1985-86; art judge Girl Scout Art Contest, 1982, Chicago Heights Jaycees, 1982-83. Named One of 5 Best and Brightest Outstanding Disabled Coll. Grads., Mainstream Mag. and Am. Bus. Women's Assn., 1990, to Hall of Fame for Outstanding Achievement, Mt. St. Clare Coll., 1996, to Hall of Fame for Fine Art, Marian Cath. H.S. Alumni Assn., 1997; recipient Kohl Internat. Tchg. award 1993. Mem. Nat. Assn. Art Edn., Ill. Art Edn. Assn. (Best Art Tchr. award 1984), South Surburban Spl. Recreation Assn. Roman Catholic. Achievements include: first deaf female doctoral graduate from Ill. State Univ. Avocations: fishing, sports, visiting museums, oil painting, reading.

KAMPF, HENNING ERNST WILHELM, food company executive; b. Athens, Greece, July 6, 1933; arrived in Germany, 1944; s. Erich Carl and Ilse H. (Hercksen) K.; m. Antje A. Jenautzke, Mar. 26, 1982; children: Markus, Melanie. Asst. to gen. mgr. Elektroholmen A.B., Stockholm, 1959; sales mgr. no. Europe G. Johnson Internat., Gloucester, G.B., 1959-63; mktg. dir., mng. dir. McCormick GmbH, Frankfurt, Germany, 1963—; mng. dir. McCormick Gewuerzvertrieb GmbH & Co. KG, Eschborn, Germany, 1987—; dep. chmn. supervisory bd. Black & Decker GmbH, Idstein, Germany, 1974—. Hon. comml. judge State Ct., Frankfurt, 1973—; pres. Henning & Antje Kampf Found., 1998—; mem. Sr. Expert Svc., Bonn, 1998—; fin. advisor German C. of C. Recipient Merit award West London C. of C., 1959. Mem. Union Magistrats Europeenne Commerciaux (bd. dirs.), Assn. Hon. Comml. Judges Germany, German Spice Assn./Packers (chmn. 1978-95, pres. 1995—), European Spice Assn. (pres. 1989-94), Internat. Assn. Hon. Comml. Judges, U.S. C. of C. (Frankfurt), Mktg. Execs. Club Germany. Avocations: classical music, long-distance skying, history research, golf. Home and Office: Sperberstrasse 45, D65812 Bad Soden Germany

KAMPIK, MARIAN PAUL, engineering educator, scientist; b. Rydultowy, Poland, Dec. 8, 1964; s. Adolf and Zofia (Fojcik) K. MS, Silesian Tech. U., Gliwice, Poland, 1988, PhD, 1996. Cert. elec. engr. Vis. scientist Phys. Tech. Inst., Braunschweig, Germany, 1993-95; jr. asst. dept. elec. engring. Silesian Tech. U., 1988-89, asst., 1989-93, asst. lectr., 1995-96, asst. prof., 1996—. Contbr. articles to profl. jours. Scholar, German Acad. Exchange Svc., 1993-95. Mem. IEEE, Polish Acad. Scis. (mem. metrology commn.), Polish Assn. Theoretical and Applied Electrotechnics, Polish Soc. Sensor Technology. Roman Catholic. Avocations: books, mountain trekking, electronics. Home: ul Krasickiego 18, 44 370 Pszow Poland Office: Silesian Tech U, ul Akademicka 10, 44 100 Gliwice Poland

KAMPS, JACOB, computer science educator; b. Kampen, Overijssel, The Netherlands, Oct. 23, 1967; s. Lukas and Henny (Boer) K.; m. Anne-Rose Brinkuis. M in Computer Sci., U. Twente, Enschede, The Netherlands, 1990; M in Artificial Intelligence, Free U., Amsterdam, The Netherlands, 1993; PhD in Applied Logic, U. Amsterdam, 2000. Asst. prof. U. Amsterdam, The Netherlands, 1993—. Contbr. articles to sci. jours. E-mail: kamps@ccsom.uva.nl. Home: Van Rensselaerstraat 13hs, NL1058XR Amsterdam NHolland, The Netherlands Office: U Amsterdam, Sarphatistraat 143, NL1018GD Amsterdam NHolland, The Netherlands

KAMSO-PRATT, JIMMY MICHAEL, physician, administrator; b. Freetown, Sierra Leone, Feb. 15, 1951; came to U.S., 1972; s. Josiah Pratt and Namina Kargbo; 1 child, Santigi. BS magna cum laude, Cumberland Coll., 1975; MS in Microbiology, McNeese State U., 1982; PhD in Microbiology, Plant Pathology, La. State U., 1985; MD, U. Tenn., 1993. Rsch. assoc. Ministry Health, Sierra Leone, 1969-72, 75-80; lab. technician Patrick's Hosp., Lake Charles, La., 1980-82; grad. rsch. asst. McNeese State U., Lake Charles, 1980-82; grad. rsch. fellow plant pathology/molecular biology La. State U., Baton Rouge, 1982-85; postdoctoral rsch. fellow Dept. Microbiology Meharry Med. Coll., Nashville, 1985-86; postdoctoral rsch. fellow Dept. Pathology Vanderbilt U. Med. Ctr., Nashville, 1987-89; internat. health cons. U. Tenn., Memphis, 1993-94; resident family medicine U. Tenn. Med. Ctr., Knoxville, 1993-96; emergency physician Southeastern Emergency Physicians, Knoxville, 1994-95; med. dir. East Jackson Family Med. Ctr., Jackson, Tenn., 1996—. Contbr. articles to profl. jours. Mem. AMA, Nat. Med. Assn., Am. Acad. Family Physicians, Am. Med. Student Assn., Tenn. Acad. Family Physicians, Tenn. Med. Assn., Sigma Xi. Avocations: soccer, reading. Office: East Jackson Family Med Ctr 655 Lexington Ave Jackson TN 38301-5075

KAMYSHANCHENKO, NIKOLAI VASILYEVICH, university administrator; b. Chaikovka, Kharkov, Ukraine, Feb. 5, 1937; s. Vasili Afanasyevich Kamyshanchenko and Praskovya Petrovna Zakurdayeva; m. Lidiya Mikhailovna Mischenko, Oct. 4, 1962; 1 child, Elena. Diploma, Pedagog. Coll., Volchansk, Kharkov, 1955, Pedagog. Inst., Kharkov, 1960; prof., Belgorod (Russia) U., 1991. Cert. in solid body physics. Tchr. secondary sch. Secondary Sch., Lozovaya, Ukraine, 1961; engr. boiler bldg. plant/telephone plant Belgorod, 1961-64; sr. instr. Mining Inst., Belgorod, 1964-68; dean, vice-dean Extra-mural Inst. Bldg. Inst., Belgorod, 1968-74; dean Inst. Bldg. Materials, Belgorod, 1974-78; pro-rector Pedagog. Inst., Belgorod, 1978-90; rector U. Belgorod, 1990—. Author: (textbook) Basics for Physics of Metals Resiliency and Plasticity, 1988; patentee in field (Bronze medal 1982, Inventor of USSR 1980). Dep. City Coun., Town of Belgorod, 1984-87, 87-89, 95-99. Named Honored Specialist in Field of Higher Edn. in Russia, 1996; recipient medal for labor valor Ministry of Edn. of USSR, 1970, medal for distinction in labor, 1972, badge of honor, 1996. Mem. Internat. Acad. Pedagog. Scis. Academician, Acad. Pedagog. and Social Scis. Academician, Acad. Engring. Scis. Acad., Petrovskaya Acad. Arts and Scis. Academician. Avocations: computer, reading classical literature. E-mail: kamysh@bsu.egu.ru. Home: 70 Krasin St Apt 114, Belgorod 308017, Russia Office: Belgorod State U, 12 Studencheskaya St, Belgorod 308007, Russia

KAMZARI, HAMIM, government executive; b. Singapore, May 2, 1946; s. Kamzari Bin Sasmito and Hasnah Binte Hassan; m. Zainab Binte Aboul Aziz, Dec. 22, 1974; children: Mohamed Saidil Helmy, Rasyiqah Hamim. BSc, Pacific western U., L.A., 1989; PhD, Brantridge Forest Sch., Sussex, Eng., 1990. Cert. in edn. Singapore. Edn. officer in tng. Min. of edn., Singapore, 1964-67, edn. officer, 1968-69; edn. officer Vocat. Inst. Min. of edn., Geylang Serai, 1969-72; acad. edn. officer Min. of edn., Singapore, 1972—; homeopathic cons., lectr. Wisma Perubatan Homeopathy Tutorial, Singapore, 1981—; homeopathy study advisor Pesantren Al Hidayah, Padang-Sumbar, Indonesia, 1995—. Author: Repertory Homoeopathy, 1990, Panduan Biokemik, 1986; asst. editor/author Generasi Jour.; contbr. articles to profl. jours. Com. mem. Citizen Cons. Com., Singapore, 1967-75; vol. aftercare officer Singapore Anti-Narcotic Assn., 1978-84. Recipient Pingat Bakti Setia award Min. of Edn., 1997; Brantridge U. fellow, 1994, Am. Biog. Inst. fellow, 1999. Mem. Singapore Malay Tchr. Union, U.S. Homeopathic Assn., Royal Soc. Health, N.Y. Acad. Sci., The Planetary Soc. Avocations: translating books, cartoon work. Home: Blk 867, Tampines St 83 #02-247, Singapore 520867, Singapore Office: Wisma Perubatan Homeopathy, Blk-1 03-1013 Joo Chiat Comp, Singapore 420001, Singapore

KAN, CHU-CHENG, electronics company executive; b. Hsiu Jen County, China, Oct. 19, 1924; arrived in South Africa, 1985; s. Chung Shan and Liang Jei Yuan Kan; m. Man Chih; children: Rachel, David, Edwin. MPA, Century U., 1978. Rsch. assoc., fellow Inst. Internat. Rels., Taiwan, 1967-77; chief dir. Rsch., Devel. and Evaluation Commn., Taiwan, 1977-82; counsellor Ministry Fin., Taiwan, 1982-84, Ministry Econ. Affairs, Taiwan, 1984-85, Embassy China, South Africa, 1985-89; chmn. Mustek Ltd. (formerly Mustek Electronics Pty Ltd.), Johannesburg, South Africa, 1990—; chmn., CEO Continental Weapons (Pty) Ltd., Johannesburg, South Africa, 1994—. Mem. Assn. Chinese Industrialists South Africa (chmn. 1992—), Confedn. Employers South Africa (mem. exec. com. 1994—). Office: Continental Weapons Pty Ltd, 322 15th St Randjespark, Midrand South Africa

KAN, ELIZABETH KA YEE, investment company executive; b. Hong Kong, July 17, 1957; d. Pun Shui and Helen Wai Ying (Yeung) K.; m. Sammy Kai Kong Chiu, Dec. 28, 1985; children: Jeremy Ho Hei Chiu, Jeffrey Ho Jun Chiu. BSBA, U. Minn., 1981. CPA, Calif. Dir., adminstr. Arthur Andersen & Co., Hong Kong, 1981-88; dir. fin. and adminstn. Victor Chu & Co., Hong Kong, 1988—; mng. dir. First East Investment Group, Hong Kong, 1988—; dep. mng. dir. China Merch. China Investment Mgmt. Ltd., Hong Kong, 1993—; bd. dirs. Guang Lee Securities Ltd., Hong Kong, Pres. Securities Internat., Ltd., Pres. Asset Mgmt. Internat. Ltd., Equity Fin. Press Ltd., Hong Kong, Ctrl. Lang. Svcs. Ltd., Hong Kong, Ctr. Comms. Consultancy Ltd., Hong Kong, Asia House Hong Kong Ltd., Siam Select Fund, Cayman Is. Mem. AICPA, Hong Kong Soc. Accts., Rotary Club Admiralty (charter). Avocations: music, reading. Fax: (852) 2956-1162. Office: First Ea Investment Group, The Gateway Tower II 19th F, Hong Kong Hong Kong

KAN, LAI-BING, librarian. BSc, U. Hong Kong, 1957; MA, MLS, U. Calif., Berkeley, 1959; PhD, U. Hong Kong, 1968, ALAA; DLitt (hon.), Charles Stuart U., 1994. Various adminstrv. positions U. Hong Kong, 1959-70, dep. libr., 1970-72; univ. libr., dir. univ. libr. sys. Chinese U. Hong Kong, 1972-83; libr. U. Hong Kong, 1983-99, dir. libr. and info. sci. programs, 1964-90, fellow Ctr. Asian Studies, 1996—, mem. standing com. of the convocation, 1996-99; library cons., U. Macau, 1980-82; hon. cons., U. East Asia, Macau, 1983-88. Author 8 books; contbr. articles on library edn., libr. and info. sci. to numerous profl. publs. Vice chmn. Patients Concern and Libr. Svc. com., Hong Kong Red Cross, 1982—. Hon. fellow Charles Stuart U., Australia, 1990—, U. Hong Kong, 1997; recipient badge of hon. Brit. Red Cross, 1992. Mem. Australian Libr. Info. Assn., Inst. Info. Scientists U.K., Internat. Assn. Orientalist Librarians, Hong Kong Library Assn., Hong Kong Assn. Univ. Women, Hong Kong Inst. Chinese Culture (adviser 1984—), Assn. S.E. Asian Inst. Higher Learning (hon. libr. 1976-78), Soroptimist. Office: Univ Hong Kong Libr, Pokfulam Rd, Hong Kong Hong Kong

KANAAN, OUSSAMA, economist; b. Beirut, Lebanon, May 11, 1965; s. Taher and Ilham Yeihia (Kahwaji) K. BA, BSc, Swarthmore Coll., 1986; M Phil, Trinity Coll. Cambridge Univ., 1987; PhD, Yale Univ., 1993. Cons. World Bank, Washington, 1988; economist Internat. Monetary Fund, Washington, 1993—; teaching fellow Yale Univ., New Haven, Conn., 1991-93; lectr. on the economy of the West Bank and Gaza Ctr. for Policy Analysis on Palestine, Middle East Inst., Washington, 1998-99. Contbr. articles to profl. jours. Recipient Sasakawa award for Internat. Econ. Sasakawa Fund for Outstanding Young Leaders Yale Univ., 1992-93, scholarship Cambridge Univ., fellow Yale Univ., 1989-93. Mem. IEEE, Am. Econ. Assn., Tau Beta Pi. Avocations: swimming, poetry, cinema. E-mail: okanaan@imf.org Fax number: 202 589-4001. Office: Internat Monetary Fund 700 19th St NW Washington DC 20431-0001

KANAI, HIROSHI, electrical engineering educator; b. Tokyo, June 1, 1930; s. Izumi and Fumiko Kanai; m. Masako Nakazawa, May 1, 1959; children: Naoaki, Masaaki. B of Engring., Tokyo U., 1953, DEng, 1967. Assoc. prof. elec. engring. Sophia U., Tokyo, 1962-71, prof., 1971—, dean of students, 1977-79, dir. grad. sch., 1979-81. Contbr. articles to profl. publs. Mem. IEEE, Internat. Fedn. for Med. and Biol. Engring., Japan Soc. Med. and Biol. Engring. (pres. 1987-89, paper award 1971, 86), Japan Soc. Elec. Engring., Japan Soc. Measurement and Control (paper award 1967). Buddhist. Home: 5-13-2 Minamizawa, Higashikurume, Tokyo 203-0023, Japan Office: Sophia U Dept Elen Engring, 7-1 Kioicho, Chiyoda-ku, Tokyo 102-0094, Japan

KANAI, KIMIO, engineering educator; b. Nagano, Japan, June 12, 1936; s. Morishige and Ichi (Sato) K.; m. Seiko Shizume, May 5, 1961; children: Shuichiro, Shihoko. B in Engring., Nat. Def. Acad., Yokosuka, Japan, 1960; M in Engring., Nagoya (Japan) U., 1965, D in Engring., 1971. Lectr. dept. aero. engring. Nat. Def. Acad., Yokosuka, 1969, assoc. prof. dept. aerospace engring., 1972-77, prof. dept. aerospace engring., 1977—, dept. head dept. aerospace engring., 1993-95, dean, 1996-2000, v.p., 2000—; postdoctoral fellow dept. mech. engring. U. Sask., Saskatoon, Can., 1971-73, vis. prof., 1977, 79, 81, 84, 85, 88, 90. Author: Control System Design, 1982, Adaptive Control, 1984, Flight Control, 1985, Robust Adaptive Control, 1989, Digital Control System, 1992, Guidance and Control for Aerospace, 1995, Fundamental of Digital Control, 2000. Recipient Kelvin prize Instn. Elec. Engrs., U.K., 1993. Fellow AIAA (assoc.), Soc. for Instrument Control Engrs. (bd. dirs. 1993-95, Author's prize 1992); mem. Japan Soc. for Aero. and Space Sci. (v.p. 1994-96). Avocation: tennis. Home: 2-18-33 Shirayuri Izumi-ku, Yokohama 245, Japan Office: The Nat Def Acad, 1-10-20 Hashirimizu, Yokosuka 239, Japan

KANAI, SHIGEHIKO, lawyer; b. Tokyo, May 5, 1952; s. Shigeoki and Kinuko (Shiina) K.; m. Yoshiko Tomioka, Mar. 6, 1988. LLM, Rikkyo U., Tokyo, 1980. Lawyer Ogawa Law Office, Tokyo, 1983-84, Yanase Law Office, Tokyo, 1984-85; mgr. mergers and acquisitions divsn. Daiwa Security Co., Tokyo, 1985-86; pres. Kanai Law and Patent Office, Tokyo, 1988—; patent atty. J.P.A.A., Tokyo, 1992. Author: Copyright Law, 1992, Criminal Procedure, 1995; editor: Practice of M&A, 1989, Handbook of Products Liability, 1990, Handbook of M&A, 1986. Mem. Japan Law Assn., Japan Bar Assn. (v.p. intellectual property com., vice chmn.), Japan Patent Atty. Assn., Tokyo Bar Assn (v.p. libr. com. 1994), Lawasia, Rotary. Mem. Episc. Ch. Japan. Avocations: travel, cycling, art, history. Office: Nagatani Ryudo Roppongi, #510 8-25 Rappongi 7 chome, Minato-ku Tokyo 106, Japan

KANAI, TSUTOMU, electronics executive; b. Feb. 26, 1929. Student, Tokyo U., 1958. Mng. dir. Hitachi Seisakujo Co. Ltd., Tokyo; pres.and ceo Hitachi Ltd., Tokyo, chmn. Office: Hitachi Ltd 4-6 Kanda-Surugadai, Shin-Juko-ku, 101-8010 Chiyoda Tokyo, Japan*

KANAKOUDI-TSAKALIDOU, FLORENCE, pediatrician, immunologist educator; b. Thessaloniki, Greece, Jan. 27, 1940; d. Sterianos and Hellen (Kouyoumtzi) Kanakoudi; m. Dimitrios Tsakalides, Apr. 24, 1971; children: Maria, Venetia. DCH, Thessaloniki U., Greece, 1968, MD, 1970, PhD, 1980. Lectr. Aristotle U., Thessaloniki, Greece, 1970-80, sr. lectr., 1980-86, assoc. prof., 1986-2000, prof., 2000—; rsch. fellow Royal Infirmary, Edinburgh, 1970-71; head immunology lab. Hippokration Hosp., U. Thessaloniki, 1972—, cons. for chronic rheumatic diseases, 1982—. Organizer, leader League Against Pediatric Rheumatism in No. Greece, Thessaloniki, 1989—. Recipient Rotary Club award, 1990, 95, Internat. Women's Orgn. of Greece award, 1991, Acad. of Athens award, 1998. Mem. Pediat. Soc. No. Greece (v.p. 1982-84), Greek Soc. Pediatrics (adminstrv. bd. 1996-98), Med. Soc. No. Greece, Greek Soc. Immunology (v.p. 1988-91), Brit. Soc. Immunology, Friends Assn. Children with Rheumatic Diseases (pres. 1989—, rep. of Greece in European League Against Rheumatism standing com. on pediatric rheumatology 1990-99), Pediatric Soc. No. Greece (pres. 1998—). Greek Orthodox. Avocations: supporting financially and socially children with rheumatic diseases. Office: Hippokration Hosp 49 Konstantinoupoleos, 1st Dept of Pediatrics, 546 42 Thessaloniki Greece

KANAL, ARNO, soil scientist, educator; b. Paide, Estonia, Jan. 29, 1964; s. Aare and Viivi (Tomberg) K. Degree in agronomy, Estonian Agrl. U., Tartu, 1987, PhD, 1996. Trainee, lectr. Estonian Agrl. U., 1988-91, assoc. prof., 1997—. Contbr. articles to profl. jours. O. Hallik scholar Estonian Agrl. U., 1986, 87; recipient award Young Scientist Estonian Acad. Agrl. Soc., 1997. Mem. European Soc. Soil Conservation, Estonian Acad. Agrl. Soc. Lutheran. Avocation: tennis. Fax: 370 7 313 535. E-mail: kanal@.eau.ee. Home: Tammsaare 2-3, Tartu 50006, Estonia Office: Dept Soil Sci Agrochemistry, Estonian Agrl U, Tartu 50412, Estonia

KANAMORI, HIROSHI, constructions company executive; b. Hoya-city, Tokyo, Japan, Jan. 22, 1958; s. Yoshiyuki and Taeko (Takagi) K.; m. Tomoko Uenishi, Dec. 24, 1997. B Engring., Waseda U., Tokyo, 1980, M Engring., 1982, D Engring., 1995. Lic. 1st class civil engr., prin. concrete engr. Rsch. engr. Shimizu Corp., Tokyo, 1982-96, sect. mgr., 1996—, cons. civil engr., 1982-87, rschr., 1987-96, rschr., rsch. mgr., 1996—. Co-author: New-Frontier Construction Concepts and New Materials, 1995, Handbook for Civil Engineering, 1995; contbr. articles to profl. jours. Mem. Am. Concrete Inst., Japan Soc. Civil Engrs., Japan Concrete Inst. Avocations: ceramics art, musical composition. Home: No 902 1-5-10 Imai Chuo-ku, Chiba City 2600834, Japan Office: Shimizu Corp, Seavans-S 1-2-3 Shibaura, Minato-ku Tokyo 1058007, Japan

KANAMORI, JUNJIRO, physicist, educator; b. Osaka, Japan, Mar. 7, 1930; s. Kenji and Humie Kanamori; m. Sachiko Kuno, Nov. 1, 1961; children: Yoshio, Takeshi. BS, Osaka U., 1953, DSc, 1957. Asst. prof. Osaka U., 1958-65; prof. Osaka U., Toyonaka, Osaka, 1965-91, dean faculty of sci., 1981-85, 89-91; pres. Osaka U., Suita, Osaka, 1991-97; prof. emeritus Osaka U., Suita. Editor: Solid State Comms., Oxford, Eng., 1979-90; assoc. editor: Advances in Physics, London, 1979-88, Jour. Magnetism and Magnetic Materials, The Netherlands, 1980-91. Recipient Asahi Cultural prize Asahi Newspaper Co., 1962, Yamaji prize Yamaji Found., 1975, Japan Acad. prize, 1996, Honda prize Honda Meml. Soc., 1999, Fujiwara prize Fujiwara Found., 1999. Mem. Phys. Soc. Japan. Avocation: gardening. Home: 3-1-1 Hyakurakuen, Nara 631-0024, Japan

KANATAS, ATHANASIOS GEORGE, electrical engineer, researcher; b. Agrinion, Greece, Mar. 31, 1968; s. George Alexios and Heleni Athanasios (Xirotsopanos) K.; m. Theodora Constantinos Farmaki, May 14, 1994; 1 child, Heleni. Diploma, Nat. Tech. U. Athens, 1991, PhD, 1997; MSc, U. Surrey, Guilford, Eng., 1992. Elec. engr. Nat. Documentation Ctr., Athens, 1993-94; tech. project mgr. SpaceTec Ltd., Athens, 1994-95; rsch. fellow Nat. Tech. U. Athens, 1995-97, rsch. assoc., 1998—; rep. European COST programs Nat. Tech. U. Athens, 1993-97; seminar instr. Ol Pliroforiki Ltd., Athens, 1993-94. Contbr. articles to profl. jours. English C. of C. scholar U. Surrey, 1991-92. Mem. IEEE (elected chmn. comm. chpt. Greek sect.), Hellenic Elec. and Electronic Engrs. Soc. Avocations: guitar, music, basketball. Home: 252 Akti Themistokleous Str, 185 39 Piraeus Greece Office: Nat Tech U Athens, 9 Iroon Polytechniou Str, 157 73 Zografos Greece

KANAZAWA, MASAKATA, musicologist; b. Tokyo, Jan. 6, 1934; s. Tsuneji and Fumiko (Nakamura) K.; m. Chizuko Yasukawa, Jan. 6, 1979; 1 child. BA, Internat. Christian U., 1957; AM, Harvard U., 1961, PhD, 1966. Lectr. various instns., Tokyo, 1966-82; prof. Internat. Christian U., Tokyo, 1982—; rsch. fellow Inst. Renaissance Studies, Florence, Italy, 1970-71; vis. prof. Antioch Coll., Yellow Springs, Ohio, Earlham Coll., Richmond, Ind.; dir. Internat. Christian U. Sacred Music Ctr., 1982—; nat. advisor The New Grove Dictionary of Music and Musicians, 1980—. Author: Invitation to Early Music, 1998 (Japan Music Pen Club grand prix 1998); co-author: The Musical Manuscript Montecassino 871, 1978 (ASCAP award 1980). Trustee Christian Music Sch., Tokyo, 1985—. Mem. Musicol. Soc. Japan, Internat. Musicol. Soc. (dir.-at-large 1997—), Japan Clavichord Soc. (pres. 1996-99), Internat. Assn. Music Librs. (Japanese rep. 1999—), Japan Organ Soc. (pres. 1999—). Avocations: theatre, travel. Home: 2-2-7 Nishikata, Bunkyo, Tokyo 113-0024, Japan Office: Internat Christian U, 3 Osawa, Mitaka 181, Japan

KANAZAWA, SATOSHI, sociologist; b. Tokyo, Nov. 16, 1962; s. Makoto and Hiroko Kanazawa. BA, Sophia U., 1985; MA, U. Wash., 1987; PhD, U. Ariz., 1994. Asst. prof. Cornell U., Ithaca, N.Y., 1994-98, Ind. U. Pa., 1999—; vis. asst. prof. U. Ill., Urbana, 1988-99. Co-author: (with A. Miller) Order By Accident: The Origins and Consequences of Contormity in Contemporary Japan, 2000; contbr. articles to profl. jours. Rsch. grantee NSF, 2000. Mem. Am. Sociol. Assn., Human Behavior and Evolution Soc., Am. Econ. Assn., Am. Polit. Sci. Assn. Fax: 724-357-4842. Home: 114 Saddlebrook Dr Indiana PA 15701-9712 Office: Ind U Pa Dept Sociology Indiana PA 15705-0001

KANAZAWA, YASUNORI, medical facility administrator; b. Hongo/Tokyo, May 31, 1935; s. Masayasu and Moto (Mikami) K.; m. Kazuko Kugimoto, May 14, 1968; children: Taro, Jiro, Yasushi. MD, U. Tokyo, 1961, Dr Med. Sci., 1968. Lic. phys., Japan. Assoc. clin. instr. U. Tokyo, 1972-79, lectr. medicine, 1979-85, asst. prof. medicine, 1985-88; prof. medicine Jichi Med. Sch., Tochigi, Japan, 1988-89; vice-dir. Omiya Med. Ctr. Jichi Med. Sch., Japan, 1989-90, dir., 1990-99; head affiliated clin. rsch. lab. Omiya Med. Ctr. Jichi Med. Sch., 2000—. Author: (book) Diabetes Mellitus, 1995; contbr. articles to profl. jours. and publs. Bd. dirs. Japan Diabetes Found., Tokyo, 1990. Rsch. awardee Japan Med. Assocs., Tokyo, 1976, Belz award, 1984, Hargedorn award Japan Diabetes Soc., Tokyo, 1994. Mem. Japan Soc. Internal Medicine, European Assn. for Study of Diabetes, Am. Diabetes Assn. Avocations: oil paintings, classic music, audiophile. Office: Omiya Med Ctr Jichi Med Sch, Amanuma-cho 1-847, Omiya Saitama 330-8503, Japan

KANBARGI, RAMESH RAGHAVENDRA, researcher, educator; b. Belgaum, India, May 1, 1940; s. Raghavendr Ramachandra and Ambabai (Kulkarni) K.; m. Shanta Ramarao Hukerikar, May 10, 1966; 1 child, Prasad. BA, Lingaraj Coll., 1961; MA in Sociology, Karnatak U., 1969, PhD in Econs., 1990. Postdoctoral fellow Johns Hopkins U., Balt., 1992-93; dir. Child Labor Project, Bangalore, India, 1980-83; asst. prof. Inst. for Social and Econ. Change, Bangalore, 1983-95, assoc. prof., 1996—; dir. Karl Kuebel Stiftung, Dehradun, India, 1995-96, Ctr. for Social Devel., 2000; cons. Population Coun., USAID, ILO, NORAD, others, 1980-91. Editor: Child Labor in India, 1991; author: Induced Abortions in Bangalore City, 1972-74, 1978, Medical Terminations, 1984, Widow-Remarriages in India in Population Studies, 1984. Grantee Pop Council, N.Y., 1980, 84, ILO, Geneva, 1985. Mem. Internat. Union for Study of Population, Indian Assn. for Study Population. Office: Inst for Social-Econ Change, Nagarbhavi Post, Bangalore 560072, India

KANDA, TATSUO, physician, surgeon; b. Tagami, Japan, Aug. 20, 1960; s. Takuji and Fumie (Hirota) K.; m. Eriko Nakano Kanda, Apr. 14, 1991; children: Mutsuo, Marie. MD, Niigata U. Sch. Medicine, Japan, 1985; PhD, Grad. Sch. Niigata U., Japan, 1991. Cert. Nat. Bd. for Med. Lic. Resident U. Hosp. Niigata (Japan) U., 1985-86; jr. surgeon Prefectual Cancer Ctr., Niigata, Japan, 1991-92; postdoctoral fellow Nat. Superior Biology Application and Nutrition, Dijon, France, 1992-93; rsch. fellow Japan Soc. for Promotion of Sci., Niigata, 1993-94; assoc. dept. surgery Niigata (Japan) U. Sch. Medicine, 1997—. Contbr. articles to profl. jours. Mem. Japan Surgical Soc., The Japanese Soc. for Gastroenterology, The Japanese Soc. of Gastroenterological Surgery. Buddhism. Avocation: Japanese chess. Home: 202 President-Yorii, Niigata 951, Japan Office: Niigata Sch Medicine, 1 Asahimachi-dori, Niigata 951, Japan

KANDA, YOZO, electronics educator; b. Gifu, Japan, June 7, 1932; s. Kingo Yamaoka and Shigeo Kanda; m. Ikuko Kataoka, Oct. 25, 1957; children: Mizuho, Rika, Hiroshi. B Engring., Waseda U., Tokyo, 1957, DSc, 1968. Rschr. Aichi Tokei Denki Co., Nagoya, Japan, 1957-61, Hitachi Ctrl. Rsch. Lab., Kokubunji, Japan, 1961-74; vis. rschr. NASA Langley Rsch. Ctr., Hampton, 1970-72; prof. Hamamatsu (Japan) U. Sch. Medicine, 1974-92; prof. electronics Toyo U., Kawagoe, Japan, 1992—, Bio-Nano Electronics Rsch. Ctr., 1999—; vis. prof. Tech. U. Berlin., 1990; Japanese head IMEKO TC 16; mem. program com. MSM. Contbr. articles to profl. publs. Recipient Takayanagi Meml. prize Hamamatsu Electronic Rsch. Found., 1987. Mem. Phys. Soc. Japan, Japan Soc. Applied Physics, Inst. Elec. Engrs. Japan, Japan Soc. Med. Electronics and Biol. Engring., Soc. Instruments and Control Engrs., N.Y. Acad. Scis. Avocations: swimming, go, yachting. Home: 3-31-20 Nishimoto-machi, Kokubunji 185-0023, Japan Office: Toyo U Faculty Engring, 2100 Kujirai, Kawagoe 350-8585, Japan

KANDEL, CHRISTOPHER NELSON, lawyer; b. Balt., May 11, 1960; s. Nelson Robert and Brigitte Kleemaier; m. Tanya Marie Neill Cox, 1994; 1 child, Edward Neill Alexander. BA magna cum laude with distinction, Yale U., 1982; JD cum laude, Cornell U., 1985. Bar: Calif. 1985, Md. 1986, D.C. 1987, Eng. and Wales 1999. Assoc. O'Melveny and Myers, L.A., 1985-88, London, 1988-90, 92-94; spl. counsel O'Melveny & Myers, London, 1994-97, ptnr., 1998-2000; assoc. Piper and Marbury, London, 1990-92; ptnr. Fried, Frank, Harris, Shriver & Jacobson, London, 2000—; panelist Bond Atty.'s Workshop, Chgo., 1987, SMI conf., 1994, Euroforum conf., 1994, Internat. Bar Assn. Conf., 1997. Former assoc. editor Cornell Internat. Law Jour.; contbr. articles to profl. jours. Former dir. Yale Alumni Schs. Com., Eng. and Wales. Democrat. Lutheran. Avocation: mountain climbing.

KANDEL, DONALD HARRY, financial analyst; b. Phila., Jan. 20, 1956; s. Lawrence Harold and Carol Ethel (Dettelbach) K.; m. Bonnie Susan Daduk, Aug. 1, 1982; children: Ian Alexander, Michael Andrew. BA, Franklin and Marshall U., 1978; MBA, LaSalle U. Fin. affairs adminstr. United Cerebral Palsy Assn., Phila., 1979-84; contr., dir. data processing and control Dow Jones and Co., Princeton, N.J., 1984-87; v.p. ops. Pvt. Industry Coun., Phila., 1987-95; dep. exec. dir., dep. exec. dir., CFO Crime Prevention Assn., Phila., 1995—. Bd. dirs. Valley Athletic Assn., Riverside, New Directions for Women, fin. chair; treas. Bnai Brith Phila. Region. Avocations: coaching baseball, soccer, basketball. Home: 9 Auburn Dr Richboro PA 18954-1269 Office: Crime Prevention Assn 230 S Broad St Philadelphia PA 19102-4121

KANDEL, ERIC RICHARD, neuroscience educator; b. Vienna, Austria, Nov. 7, 1929; arrived in U.S., 1939; married, 1956; two children. BA, Harvard Coll., 1952; MD, NYU, 1956. Intern Montefiore Hosp., N.Y.C., 1956-57; rsch. assoc. neurophysiology lab. NIH, Washington, 1957-60; rsch. psychiatrist NIH, 1960-62, 63-64; dir. Mass. Mental Health Ctr., Boston, 1960-65; assoc. prof. physiology, psychiatry to prof. NYU Sch. Medicine, 1965-74; prof. physiology and psychiatry Howard Hughes Med. Inst. Columbia U. Coll. Physicians and Surgeons, N.Y.C., 1974-83, Univ. prof. Howard Hughes Med. Inst., 1983—. Recipient Harvey Prize, Technion, 1993, Nobel Prize, 2000. Fellow AAAS; mem. NAS, Am. Acad. Arts and Scis., Soc. Neuroscis. (pres. 1980-81), Internat. Brain Rsch. Orgn, NY Acad. of Scis. (Mayor Awd. Excellence in Sci. & Tech., 1994). Office: Columbia U Coll Physicians & Surgeons Howard Hughes Med Inst 722 W 168th St New York NY 10032-2603

KANDEL, JOAN ELLEN, osteopath; b. L.A., Apr. 6, 1963; d. William Isadore Kandel and Helen Sylvia (Cutler) Abraham; m. Kristin Graziano, July 13, 1996. BA, U. Calif., 1985; DO, Coll. Osteo. Med. Pacific, 1993. Vol. health educator U.S. Peace Corps, Nuapua, Paraguay, 1986-88; resident, chief resident family practice Cmty. Hosp., Santa Rosa, Calif., 1993-96. Mem. Am. Acad. Family Physicians, Am. Acad. Osteopathy, Physicians for a Violence-Free Soc., Gay and Lesbian Med. Assn. Democrat. Jewish. Avocations: ultimate frisbee, bicycling, gardening, music, dancing.

KANDEL, ROBERT SAMUEL, climate and earth scientist, writer, lecturer; b. N.Y.C., Dec. 27, 1937; arrived in France, 1974 (dual nat.); s. Max and Netty N. (Kanner) K.; m. Danielle M.C.A. Béguin, June 24, 1967; children: Maya Tamar, Tania Myriam, Arielle Tamina. AB, Harvard U., 1958; Lic. Sci., U. Paris, 1961, DSc, 1967. Rsch. attache at obs. Nat. Ctr. Sci. Rsch., Meudon, France, 1961-67, sr. rschr., 1974-78; NAS rsch. assoc. NASA Goddard Inst. Space Studies, N.Y.C., 1967-69; asst. prof. astronomy Boston U., 1969-74; sr. rsch. aero. svc. Nat. Ctr. Sci. Rsch., Verrieres le Buisson, France, 1978-85; dir. rsch. Lab. Dynamic Meteorology, Nat. Ctr. Sci. Rsch., Palaiseau, France, 1985—; prin. Scanner for Radiation Budget scientist Nat. Ctr. Sci. Rsch., Paris, 1986-98; mem. nat. com. sci. rsch. Nat. Ctr. Space Rsch., Paris, 1987-91; sci. advisor European Space Agy., Paris, 1992—; vis. prof. Va. Poly. Inst. and State U., Blacksburg, spring 1998; mem. Internat. Radiation Comm., 1988—, French Nat. Com. Geodesy and Geophysics, 1984—; assoc. Com. for Space Rsch. (COSPAR), 1984—. Author: Earth and Cosmos, 1980, Le Devenir des Climats, 1990 (Prix Roberval Grand Pub. award 1990), L'Incertitude des Climats, 1998, Les Eaux du Ciel, 1998 (prize of sci. and tech. culture Nat. Ctr. Sci. Rsch. 1999). Colloquium organizer Universal Movement Sci. Responsibity, Paris, 1979, 89. A.C. Tower fellow Harvard U., Paris, 1958-59, fellow Alliance Française, Paris, 1960. Mem. Internatl Astron. Union, Am. Geophys. Union, Am. Meteor. Soc.. Office: CNRS Lab Meteor Dynamique, Ecole Poly, 91128 Palaiseau Cedex, France

KANDEL, WILLIAM LLOYD, lawyer, educator, writer; b. N.Y.C., Apr. 25, 1939; s. Morton H. and Lottie S. (Smith) K.; m. Joyce Roland, Jan. 27, 1974; 1 child, Aron Daniel (Ari). AB cum laude, Dartmouth Coll., 1961; JD, Yale U., 1964; LLM in Labor Law, NYU, 1967. Bar: N.Y. 1965, U.S. Dist. Ct. (ea., so. and no. dists.) N.Y., U.S. Ct. Appeals (2d cir.), U.S. Dist. Ct. (no. dist.) Calif. 1988, U.S. Ct. Appeals (3rd cir.), (5th cir.) 2000. Assoc. Lorenz, Finn & Giardino, N.Y.C., 1964-66; labor atty. NAM, N.Y.C., 1966-68; with Singer Co., N.Y.C., 1968-79, asst. v.p. pers. dept., 1973-76, mng. counsel pers. office of gen. counsel, 1976-79; assoc. Skadden, Arps, Slate, Meagher & Flom, N.Y.C., 1979-85; ptnr. Finley, Kumble, Wagner, Heine, Underberg, Manley, Myerson & Casey, N.Y.C., 1985-87, Myerson & Kuhn, N.Y.C., 1987-89, McDermott Will & Emery, 1989-97, Orrick, Herrington & Sutcliffe, 1997—; lectr. to Law and bus. groups, 1974—; adj. prof. employment law Fordham U., 1983-86; lectr. Practising Law Inst.'s Ann. Inst. on Employment Law, 1980—, co-chair, 1995, chair, 1996—; mem. adv. panel Am. Arbitration Assn., 1996—; mem. adv. com. employment law City Coun. N.Y., 1996—. Contbg. editor Employee Rels. Law Jour., 1975—; contbr. articles to profl. jours. V.p., bd. dirs. Assn. for Integration Mgmt., 1979-85; bd. dirs. N.Y. chpt. Am. Jewish Com., 1980-82; mem. human resources com. N.Y. YMCA, 1994—. Recipient award of Merit, Nat. Urban Coalition, 1979. Democrat. Jewish. Office: Orrick Herrington & Sutcliffe 666 5th Ave Rm 203 New York NY 10103-1798

KANDIAH, SUNDARALINGAM, physicist, seismologist; b. Jaffna, No., Sri Lanka, Jan. 15, 1942; arrived in Australia, 1990; s. Kandiah and Kanakamma (Murugesu) K.; m. Sivmalar Thambiyiah, Aug. 23, 1972; children: Aravinthan, Ananth. BS with honors, U. Colombo (Sri Lanka), 1965; MS, U. Durham (Eng.), 1969, PhD, 1971; postdoct., UCLA, 1978. Advanced cert. in micro computer tech. Asst. lectr. U. Sri Lanka, Peradineyia, 1965-71, lectr., 1971-75; lectr. U., Lae, Png., 1975-78, sr. lectr., 1978-82; sr. lectr. U. Suva, Fiji, 1982-89, reader, 1989-90; academic U. Melbourne, Australia, 1990—; chief examiner Edn. Dept., Colombo, Sri Lanka, 1972-74; cons. PWD, Suva, Fiji, 1984; vis. scientists AGSO, Canberra, 1985-89; liaison officer ILP IV-II, U.S., 1993-98. Editor: (scientific mag.) Oortu, 1972—; contbr. articles to profl. jours. Sr. treas. Hindu temple, Peradeniya, Sri Lanka, 1973; chmn. constitutional com. HSV, Melbourne, Australia, 1993; sports coord. CTA, Melbourne, 1994-95. Fellow Geol. Soc. London; mem. AIP, ASEG, ACS, ICTP (assoc.), Old Boy's Assn. (pres. 1990—). Avocations: tennis, badminton, cricket, reading and writing scientific articles. Home: 77 Camelot Dr, 3150 Glen Waverley Victoria, Australia Office: Dept Applied Physics, Swinburne U, 3168 Hawthorn Victoria, Australia

KANDIL, AHMED AMINE, international financial consultant, entrepreneur; b. Casablanca, Morocco, Dec. 1, 1964; s. Driss and Aicha (Zhiri) K.; m. Laila Tazi-Hemida, Jan. 25, 1992; children: Aida, Alia. MSc in Ops. Rsch., Fla. Inst. Tech., 1988; diploma, Ecole Internat. Scis., 1988; MBA, U. Chgo., 1998. Cons., info. specialist Paris, 1986-88; commodities option specialist Melbourne, Fla., 1988; cons., auditor capital markets Soc. Generale, Paris, 1989-90; sr. salesman, account mgr. Software AG, Paris, 1990-92; sr. salesman, sr. account mgr. Promodata, Group Suez, Paris, 1992-93; gen. mgr. BTB Express, Sevres, France, 1993-95; CFO Charaf Corp., Casablanca, 1995-97, COO, 1997—. Mem. Royal Golf Anfa, The Round Table, Maroc 2020. Muslim. Avocations: travel, third world development. Office: Charaf Corp, 278 Bd Zerktouni, Casablanca 20 000, Morocco

KANDIL, MAHMOUD SABER, electrical power engineering educator; b. Damanhour, Behera, Egypt, Jan. 27, 1938; s. Saber Ahmed Kandil and Naggia Ahmed Elbesoomy; m. Fatma Ahmed Fouad Saad, Aug. 15, 1968; children: Tarek, Hanan, Ahmed, Mohammed. BSEE, Alexandria (Egypt) U., 1961; MSc in Tech., U. Manchester, Eng., 1964, PhD, 1967. Cert. in elec. engring. Demonstrator Assuit (Egypt) U., 1961-63; from asst. to assoc. prof. Alfateh U., Tripoli, Libya, 1968-76; assoc. prof. Mansoura (Egypt) U., 1976-79, prof., head of dept., 1980-81, 85; prof., head of dept. Kuwait U., 1981-84; prof. Mansoura U., 1985—; vice dean faculty of engring. Mansoura U., 1985-88, 92-94, dean faculty engring., 1994-98, dir. Ctr. Consultations, 1994-98, dir. Ctr. Tech. Svcs., 1994-98; prin. investigator PI, AI. Contbr. sci. papers to profl. jours. including IEEE, IEE. Recipient Sci. Mission award Egyptian Govt., 1963-67. Fellow Instn. Elec. Engrs.; mem. Egyptian Instn. Engrs. Avocations: literature, music, tennis. Home: 18 Shaarawy Pasha St, Loran Alexandria Egypt Office: Mansoura U Faculty Engring, Algomhoria St, Mansoura Dakahlia, Egypt

KANDIL, NASSER FATHY, sales executive; b. Washington, June 1, 1958; s. Fathy Abdel-Halim and Fawkia Hussein (Ahmed) K.; m. Maha Mostapha Bahgat, Oct. 28, 1982; children: Seif, Farah. BA in Polit. Sci., Am. U., Cairo, 1981. arrived in Egypt, 1981;. Pub. rels. and mktg. mgr. BMW, Cairo, 1981-88, mktg. mgr., 1986-89; chief of protocol His Royal Highness Prince Turki Bin Abdul Aziz Al-Saud, Jeddah, 1989-92; gen. mgr. sales and mktg. Al Alam Al-Youm Newspaper & Kolenas Mag., Cairo, 1992—. Named Best Automobile Editor, Adam Mag., Egypt, 1999. Avocations: horseback riding, car racing.

KANDLE, SURESH KALLAPPA, microbiologist; b. Solapur, India, Mar. 9, 1961; s. Kallappa and Gajarabai (Kasar) K.; m. Jyoti Sagare, June 9, 1987; children: Kaustubh, Rutuja. BSc, Dayanand Coll., Solapur, India, 1982; MSc, PhD, Dr. V.M. Med. Coll., Solapur, India, 1985. Lectr. Rural Med. Coll., Ahmednagar, India, 1985-88, Dr. V.M. Med. Coll., 1988—. Authored numerous rsch. publs. Mem. Indian Assn. Med. Microbiologists, Indian Assn. Pathologists & Microbiologists, Assn. Microbiologists of India. Home: 190/191 Paparamnagar, Sanskriti Vijapur Rd, Solapur 413 004, India

KANDO, NORIKO, information science researcher; b. Tokyo, Japan, Sept. 2, 1960; d. Shigeki and Kaneko (Ohyachi) Matsuyama; m. Takashi Kando, Oct. 10, 1987. MA, Keio U., Tokyo, 1991, PhD, 1995. Rsch. assoc. NACSIS, Tokyo, 1994-97, assoc. prof., 1998-2000; assoc. prof. NII, Tokyo, 2000—; rsch. fellow Japanese Soc. for promotion of sci., Tokyo, 1993-94; vis. scholar Syracuse (N.Y.) U., 1995-96; vis. rsch. fellow Lancaster (Eng.) U., 1997; mem. Database Standardization Com., Tokyo, 1994—, Japanese Com. for Internat. Standardization Orgn./Tech. Com. 37, Tokyo, 1995—. Mem. editorial bd. Jour. of Info. Processing Soc. of Japan. Mem. Assn. Computer Machinery/Spl. Interest Group Info. Retrieval, Am. Soc. Info. Sci., Assn. for Natural Lang. Processing (coun. mem.). Office: Nat Inst Informatics, 2-1-2 Hitotsutashi, Bunkyo-ku Chiyodu-ku Tokyo 101-8430, Japan

KANDRA, JOSEPH, retired federal agency administrator; b. North Braddock, Pa., Aug. 5, 1927; s. John and Susana (Ruzbarsky) K.; m. Dorothy Maxine Eller, Aug. 26, 1950; children: Joel Christopher, Robert Andrew, Susan Dorothea. BS, Southeastern U., Washington, 1953; MS, Southeastern U., 1955; postgrad., U.S. Dept. Agr. Grad. Sch., 1961-62. Budget analyst U.S. War Claims Commn., Washington, 1950-54; chief, acctg. and fiscal br. Fgn. Claims Settlement Commn., Washington, 1954-58; budget examiner U.S. Civil Svc. Commn., Washington, 1958-60, adminstrv. officer, 1960-63; budget officer Fed. Crop Ins. Corp., USDA, Washington, 1963-81, comptroller, 1981-82; ret., 1982. Instnl. rep. Boy Scouts Am.,Hyattsville, Md., 1965-70. With USN, 1945-49, ETO. Recipient scholarship Carnegie Inst. Tech., Pitts., 1944. Mem. Nat. Assn. Retired Fed. Employees, Profl. Employees of USDA, Ea. Shore Threshermen Assn., Am. Legion Post 455, DAV Comdrs. Club, VFW Post 7046, Stewartstown Hist. Soc. Avocations: reading, painting and sketching, gardening, small wood projects, collecting old and new tools. Home: 18184 Ridge Meadow Rd Stewartstown PA 17363-7552

KANE, ARTHUR O., lawyer; b. Chgo., Jan. 16, 1918; s. Henry L. and Bertha Y. Kane; m. Bernice Estelle Levine, June 14, 1942 (dec. Aug. 1984); m. Esther Steinback, Apr. 21, 1985. AB, U. Chgo., 1937, JD, 1939. Bar: Ill. 1939, U.S. Dist. Ct. (no. dist.) Ill. 1940, U.S. Ct. Appeals 1961. Ptnr. Henry L. Kane & Arthur Kane, Chgo., 1939-63; sole practitioner Kane, Doy & Harrington, Chgo., 1965-81; pres., CEO Kane, Doy & Harrington, Chgo., 1981-98; chmn. bd. Kane, Doy & Harrington, Chgo., 1998—; instr. Ill. Inst. Continuing Legal Edn., Springfield, Ill., 1990. Capt. J.A.G., U.S. Army, 1947-52. Mem. ABA, Workers Compensation Lawyer Assn. Ill. (pres. 1957-58), Ill. Bar Assn. (chair workers compensation com. 1967-68), Chgo. Bar Assn. (chmn. workers compensation com. 1957-61). Avocations: reading, teaching. Office: Kane Doy & Harrington Ltd One N LaSalle St Chicago IL 60602

KANE, GORDON LEON, physics researcher and educator; b. St. Paul, Jan. 19, 1937; m. Lois Elizabeth Kliffer; children: Hal, Mollie. BA, U. Minn., 1958; MS, U. Ill., 1961, PhD, 1963. Postdoctoral scholar Johns Hopkins U., Balt., 1963-65; asst. prof. U. Mich., Ann Arbor, 1965-69, assoc. prof., 1969-72, prof. physics, 1972—; mem. sci., policy com. Stanford Linear Accelerator Ctr., 1988-90; mem. program adv. com. Brookhaven Nat. Lab., 1983-87; mem. exec. com. user's orgn. of Superconducting Supercollider, 1988-91; mem. Stanford Linear Accelerator Ctr. program adv. com., 1993—; mem. U.S.-Japan Joint Working Group on Superconducting Supercollider, 1992; Delphasus lectr. U. Santa Cruz, 1988. Author: Modern Elementary Particle Physics, 1988, The Particle Garden, 1995, Supersymmetry, 2000; editor: Perspectives on Higgs Physics II, 1997, Perspectives on Supersymmetry, 1997; contbr. over 100 articles to profl. jours. Recipient Rsch. Excellence award U. Mich., 1997; J.S. Guggenheim Found. fellow, 1971-72; Dozor fellow Ben-Gurion U., 1999.. Fellow Am. Phys. Soc. (nominating com. 1990-93, Centennial spkr. 1998-99), Mich. Soc. Fellows (sr.); mem. Johns Hopkins U. Soc. Scholars, Particles and Fields Soc. (exec. com. 1986-88). Office: Univ Mich Randall Physics Lab Ann Arbor MI 48109

KANE, JAY BRASSLER, banker; b. Bklyn., June 4, 1931; s. Arthur Ferris and Margaret (Brassler) K.; m. Marian Albertson, Oct. 15, 1960 (dec. 1993); children: Lisa Kane Brown, James Brassler. Grad., Poly. Prep. Sch., 1949; AB, Columbia, 1953; MBA, NYU, 1961. With Met. Life Ins. Co., N.Y.C., 1954-55; with Bankers Trust Co., N.Y.C., 1955—, asst. v.p., 1965-68, v.p., 1968-88; v.p. BT Brokerage Corp., 1988-90; regional dir. Frank Russell Trust. Co., N.Y.C., 1990-97; assoc. P.P.I. Internat., 1997—; also mgr. corp. pension funds, mktg. dir. trust svcs.; spkr. Am. Bankers Assn.; lectr. New Sch. for Social Rsch., Attach bd. dirs. Contbr. articles to profl. jours. Mem. N.Y. Soc. Security Analysts, Fin. Analysts Fedn., Am. Pension Conf., Riverside (Conn.) Yacht Club, N.Y. Yacht Club. Home and Office: Hilton Heath Cos Cob CT 06807

KANE, JOSEPH PATRICK, lawyer, financial planner, educator; b. Phila., Dec. 5, 1957; s. James Thomas Jr. and Rita Margaret (Pergolese) K.; m. Lynn Marie Danesi, May 6, 1989. BS in Econs. cum laude, U. Pa., 1979; JD, U. Va., 1982; CFP, Coll. for Fin. Planning, Denver, 1988. Bar: Pa. 1982, U.S. Dist. Ct. (ea. dist.) Pa. 1983, U.S. Ct. Appeals (3d cir.) 1983, U.S. Dist. Ct. (mid. dist.) Pa. 1993, U.S. Supreme Ct. 1993. Assoc. Obermayer, Rebmann, Maxwell & Hippel, Phila., 1982-85, Kleinbard, Bell & Brecker, Phila., 1985-86, O'Donnell, Weiss & Mattei PC, Pottstown, Pa., 1989-92, Liebert, Short & Hirshland, Williamsport, Pa., 1992-93; fin. and pension cons. PACS, Inc., Phila., 1986-89; pvt. practice, Williamsport, 1993-99; asst. prof. mgmt. and bus. law Pa. Coll. Tech., Williamsport, 1998-99; lectr. Bucknell U., Lewisburg, Pa., 1999-00. Bd. dirs., com. mem. Lycoming United Way, Williamsport, 1994-99; bd. dirs. Pa. Coll. Tech. Found., Williamsport, 1995-97, Lycoming County Health Improvement Coalition, Inc., Williamsport, 1995-97, Cmty. Theatre League, Inc., Williamsport, 1996—, Lycoming Mediation Project, Inc., Williamsport, 1997-99. Mem. Penn. Bar Assn., Lycoming Law Assn., Williamsport-Lycoming C. of C. (com. mem., chmn. subcom. 1992-99), Eagles Mere Country Club, Ross Club (bd. dirs. 1997-99). Avocations: choral and barbershop singing, community theatre, golf, tennis, hiking. Office: PO Box 55 Muncy Valley PA 17758-0055

KANE, KEVIN PATRICK, economist; b. Oil City, Pa., Apr. 20, 1974; s. William Richard and Arlene Fae Kane; m. Tabitha Gibson, Aug. 15, 1998. BS in Econs. and Math., St. Vincent Coll., 1996; MA in Econs., Washington U., 1997, postgrad., 1997—. L. René Gaiennie fellow Washington U., Ctr. for the Study of Am. Bus., St. Louis, 1998—. Chmn. Coll. Reps. at St. Vincent Coll., Latrobe, Pa., 1993-95; parish coun. mem. Christ the King Cath. Ch., University City, Mo., 2000. Mem. Am. Econ. Assn., Regional Sci. Assn. Internat., Soc. Cath. Social Scientists. Republican. Roman Catholic. E-mail: kane@wueconc.wustl.edu. Home: 6820 Delmar Blvd Apt 305 Saint Louis MO 63130-3155 Office: Washington Univ Ctr for the Study Am Bus Campus Box 1027 One Brookings Dr Saint Louis MO 63130

KANE, LORIE, professional golfer; b. Prince Edward Island, Can., Dec. 19, 1964; d. Jack Kane. Student, Acadia U. Mem. Can. Internat. Team, 1989-92, Can. World Amateur Team, 1992; golfer LPGA, 1993—; du Maurier Ltd. Series champion, 1994, 95, series event winner, 1993-95; 2d place Toray Japan Queens Cup, 1997. Recipient Heather Farr award, 1998. 1 LPGA career hole-in-one. Office: c/o LPGA 100 International Golf Dr Daytona Beach FL 32124-1082

KANE, MICHAEL BARRY, social science research executive; b. Taunton, Mass., July 2, 1944; s. Julius J. and Dorothy M. (Moscoff) K.; children: Jared E., Stacy E., Matthew D. BA in Polit. Sci., NYU, 1966; MA in Ednl. Adminstrn., Columbia U., 1968, MEd in Ednl. Adminstrn., 1970, EdD in Ednl. Adminstrn., 1974. Tchr. Roosevelt Sch., Stamford, Conn., 1966-67; asst. to dir. New Lincoln Sch., N.Y.C., 1969; spl. asst. to dep. commr. for devel. U.S. Office of Edn., Washington, 1970-71; headmaster Downtown Community sch., N.Y.C., 1971-73; coord. program for situational analysis and program for ednl. leadership Columbia U. Tchrs. Coll., N.Y.C., 1970-73; group mgr., project dir. Abt Assocs., Inc., Cambridge, Mass., 1973-79; asst. dir., assoc. dir. Nat. Inst. Edn., U.S. Dept. Edn., Washington, 1979-82; pres. MCK Assocs., Inc., Tallahassee, Fla., and Annapolis, Md., 1982-87; prin. Pelavin Assocs., Inc., Washington, 1988-94; v.p. Am. Inst. for Rsch., Washington, 1995—, sr. v.p., dir. Washington Rsch. Ctr., 1998—; chmn. Profl. Tchr. Career Devel. Coun., Fla.; vis. scholar Fla. State U.'s Ctr. for Needs Assessmtn and Planning; pres. Citizen's Coun. Edn., Fla.; chmn. Fla. Bus. and Edn. Coalition; lectr. numerous workshops. Author, co-author or editor: Minorities in Textbooks: A Study of Their Treatment in Social Studies Texts, Improving Schools: Using What We Know, Changing the Odds: Factors Increasing Access to College, Implementing Performance Assessments: Promises, Problems, and Challenges, Principles and Practices of Performance Assessment; contbr. articles to profl. jours. Avocations: boating, photography, scuba diving. Home: 2921 Garfield Ter NW Washington DC 20008-3507

KANE, MICHAEL JOSEPH, director; b. N.Y.C., July 9, 1922; s. Max and Sophie (Kuznets) Cohen; m. Winifred June Fay, Oct. 1, 1947 (div. 1972); children: Amy Lynn, Jennifer Ann. Student, King-Smith Playhouse and Sch. of Theatre Arts, 1939-41. Actor, stage mgr. in Mister Roberts Leland Hayward Prodns., N.Y.C., 1947-51; stage mgr., assoc. dir. CBS-TV, Hollywood, Calif., 1951-53; freelance dir. Art Linkletter's House Party, Hollywood, 1953-70; dir., producer various commls., Hollywood, 1957-85; producer, dir. Can You Top This?, Hollywood, 1969-70; lectr. TV/film writing, cable TV prodn., directing for the camera Calif. State U., Fullerton, 1987-92; mem. Radio and TV Dirs. Guild, 1952-58; co-founder The Fullerton Acting Lab., 1992. Dir.: (stage prodn.) Happy Birthday, Wanda Jane, 1970, (TV prodns.) Gilligan's Island, Hawaiian Eye, The Brady Bunch, Quincy, Hardcastle and McCormick. Served as staff sgt. USAAF, 1942-46. King-Smith Playhouse and Sch. Theatre Arts scholar, 1939-41. Mem. AFTRA, SAG, Soc. Stage Dirs. and Choreographers, Actors Equity Assn., Dirs. Guild Am. (trustee DGA producers pension and health plans).

KANE, PATRICK J., elementary school educator; b. Cleve., June 14, 1955; s. Eugene F. and Elizabeth A. Kane; m. Heidi C. Kane, Oct. 9, 1982; children: Erin E., Jacqueline A. BS in Edn., Kent State U., 1977; MS in Athletic Adminstrn., Seattle Pacific U., 1989, cert. adminstrn., 2000. Cert. elem. tchr., Wash. Spl. edn. instr. Mentor (Ohio) Sch. Dist., 1977-78, Browning (Mont.) Sch. Dist., 1978-79; elem. tchr. Cut Bank (Mont.) Sch. Dist., 1979-81; mem. collections staff Ford Motor Credit, Portland, Oreg., 1981-84; tchr. Port Angeles (Wash.) Schs., 1984—; track coach Port Angeles H.S., 1984-93, soccer coach, 1993—; intern Sport for Understanding, Washington, summer 1989, West Seattle YMCA, summer 1988. Pres. Port Angeles Jr. Soccer, 1986-91, North Olympic Soccer Referees, 1986-92; tournament dir. Jr./Sr. Babe Ruth, Port Angeles, 1990-92. Mem. Nat. Soccer Coaches Assn. Am. Avocations: hiking, weight lifting, reading. Home: 350 Viewcrest St Port Angeles WA 98362-6979 Office: Port Angeles HS 304 E Park Ave Port Angeles WA 98362-6934

KANE, STEPHANIE C., social anthropologist, educator; b. N.Y.C., Jan. 24, 1951; d. Bernard David and Gerry Kane. BA in Biology, Cornell U., 1972; MA in Zoology, U. Tex., 1981, PhD in Social Anthropology, 1986. Tchg. asst. Biology and Physiology Labs, Dept. Zoology, U. Tex., Austin, 1981, Dept. Anthropology, U. Tex., Austin, 1985-86; resident faculty Sch. for Field Studies, Virgin Islands, 1987; adj. asst. prof. Dept. Anthropology, Ind. U., 1992—; asst. prof. Dept. Criminal Justice, Ind. U., 1992-99, assoc. prof., 1999—. Author: The Phantom Gringo Boat, 1994, AIDS Alibis: Sex, Drugs and Crime in the Americas, 1998; contbr. to profl. papers and jours. Recipient rsch. grant Inst. Latin Am. Studies U. Tex., Austin, 1979-80, 84-85, Fulbright rsch. grant Coun. for Internat. Exch. of Scholars, 1989-90, rsch. grant Rural Ctr. for Study and Promotion of HIV/STD Prevention, Ind., 1995, rsch. grant Wenner-Gren Found. for Anthropol. Rsch., 1995-96, 99-2000; scholarship U. Tex., Austin, 1979-83; Lang. and Area Studies fellowship Inst. Latin Am. Studies, U. Tex., Austin, 1982-83, Tng. fellowship Orgn. Am. States, 1984-85, Rockefeller Humanities fellowship rsch. grant SUNY, Buffalo, 1991-92, Coll. Arts and Scis. Summer Faculty fellowship Ind. U., Bloomington, 1994. Mem. NOW, AAUW, Am. Anthropol. Assn. (mem. task force on AIDS, 1991-93), Am. Soc. Criminology, Acad. Criminal Justice Scis., Law and Soc. Assn., Am. Jail Assn., Midwestern Criminal Justice Assn., Amnesty Internat. Avocations: art, gardening, traveling. Office: U Ind Dept Criminal Justice 302 Sycamore Hall Bloomington IN 47405

KANE, STEVEN EDWARD, human resources executive; b. Milw., Sept. 7, 1949; s. Edward Thomas and Marion Jean (Regan) K.; m. Jacqueline Peacock; children: Clifford, Stacy. BS in Indsl. Relations, Cornell U., 1972, MBA, 1973; JD, U. Akron, 1977. Bar: Ohio 1977, Tex. 1977. Labor relations staff BF Goodrich, Akron, Ohio, 1973-77; cons. Modern Mgmt., Bannockburn, Ill., 1978; dir. employee relations Am. Hosp. Supply, Evanston, Ill., 1979-85; v.p. human resources adminstrn. Baxter Internat. (formerly Baxter Travenol Labs.), Deerfield, Ill., 1986-87, v.p. human resources, corp. groups, 1987-89, v.p. human resources hosp. and alternate site group, 1989-90, v.p. human resources alternate site group, chief labor counsel, 1990-91, v.p. employee rels., assoc. gen. counsel, 1992-94, v.p. compensation, 1995-96, v.p. govt. affairs, 1996-98; cons. StevenKane.com, Hillsborough, Calif., 1999; sr. v.p. human resources, legal, comm. Neoforma, Inc., 2000—. Mem. ABA, Ohio Bar Assn., Tex. Bar Assn. Home: 1425 San Raymundo Rd Hillsborough CA 94010-6658

KANE, THOMAS JAY, III, orthopaedic surgeon, educator; b. Merced, Calif., Sept. 2, 1951; s. Thomas J. Jr. and Kathryn (Hassler) K.; m. Marie Rose Van Emmerik, Oct. 10, 1987; children: Thomas Keola, Travis Reid, Samantha Marie. BA in History, U. Santa Clara, 1973; MD, U. Calif., Davis, 1977. Diplomate Am. Bd. Orthopaedic Surgery. Intern U. Calif. Davis Sacramento Med. Ctr., 1977-78, resident in surgery, 1978-81; resident in orthopaedic surgery U. Hawaii, 1987-91; fellowship adult joint reconstruction Rancho Los Amigos Med. Ctr., 1991-92; ptnr. Orthop. Assocs. of Hawaii, Inc., Honolulu, 1992—; asst. prof. surgery U. Hawaii, Honolulu, 1993—, chief divsn. implant surgery, 1993—. Contbr. articles to profl. jours. Mem. AMA, Am. Assn. Hip and Knee Surgeons, Hawaii Med. Assn., Hawaii Orthop. Assn., Am. Acad. Orthop. Surgery, Western Orthopedic Assn., Alpha Omega Alpha, Phi Kappa Phi. Avocations: tennis, golf, skiing, music, surfing. Office: Orthopaedic Svcs Co LLP 1380 Lusitana St Ste 608 Honolulu HI 96813-2442

KANEDA, YASUHIRO, neuropsychiatrist; b. Ayauta-Gun, Japan, Apr. 5, 1963; s. Nobuharu and Aiko (Sako) K.; m. Ikumi Yoshida, May 27, 1990; children: Makito, Taiki. MD, U. Tokushima, Japan, 1992, PhD, 1997. Lic. physician, Japan; qualified psychiatrist, Japan. Intern, resident U. Tokushima Sch. Medicine, 1992-93, lectr., 1997-99, med. dir., 2000—; neuropsychiatrist Pvt. Health Facility for Old Men, Komatsushima, Japan, 1996—, Pvt. Psychiatric Hosp., Anan, Japan, 1997—; cons. Pub. Psychiat. Hosp., Tokushima, 1993-97, Pub. Health Care Ctr., Tokushim , 1995-97, 2000—; with Coll. Welfare, Tokushima, 1998—. Recipient award Tokushima Med. Assn., 1999, European Cert. award World Fedn. Soc. Biol. Psychiatry, 2000. Mem. Internat. Soc. Psychoneuroendocrinology, Internat. Psychogeriatric Assn., Internat. Brain Rsch. Orgn., Internat. Behavioural Neural Genetics Soc., Internat. Soc. Neuroimaging in Psychiatry, Interdisciplinarian Soc. Biol. Psychiatry, Am. Neuropsychiatric Assn. (Japanese chpt.), Am. Orthopsychiatric Assn., Am. Assn. Cmty. Psychiatrists, British Assn. Psychopharmacology, Am. Psychopathological Assn., Am. Assn. General Hosp. Psychiatrists, Japanese Soc. Psychiatry Neurology, Japan Soc. EEG and EMG, Kyushu Assn. Neuropsychiatry, Japanese Soc. Neurology, Japanese Soc. Psychosomatic Medicine, Japan Epilepsy Soc., Japanese Soc. Biological Psychiatry, Japan Medical Assn., Japanese Soc. Clinical Neuropsychopharmacology, Japan Psychogeriatric Soc., Japanese Soc. Occupational Mental Health, Japanese Soc. Psychiatric Diagnosis, Japanese Soc. Sleep Rsch., Soc. Psychophys. Rsch., Soc. Biol. Psychiatry, Internat. Neuropsychol. Soc., Internat. Pharm.-EEG Group, Internat. Soc. Psychiatric Genetics, German Soc. Biol. Psychiatry, Am. Psychosomatic Soc., European Sleep Rsch. Soc., Assn. European Psychiatrists, Am. Acad. Clin. Psychiatrists, Coll. Internat. Neuropsychopharmacology, Can. Coll. Neuropsychopharmacology, Japanese Coll. Neuropsychopharmacology, Internet Assn. for Biomed. Scis. Avocations: watching movies, listening to music, travel, reading books. Fax: 81-886-32-3214. Home: 2 89 501 Minami Shimada, Tokushima 770 0053, Japan Office: U Tokushima Sch Medicine, Dept Neuropsychiat 3-18-15, Kuramoto Tokushima 770-8503, Japan

KANEFF, STEPHEN, electrical engineer, researcher, consultant, educator; b. Broken Hill, Australia, June 19, 1926; s. Dimo and Nedela (Mitev) K.; m. Lillian Semcheff, Jan. 24, 1959; children: Deema, Llyana. BEE with first class honors, U. Adelaide, South Australia, 1949, PhD, 1956. Elec. engr. Brit. Thomson Houston Co., Rugby, Eng., 1952-54; lectr., sr. lectr., reader in elec. engring. U. Adelaide, 1955-65; professorial fellow Australian Nat. U., Canberra, 1966-70, prof. engring., physics, head Energy Rsch. Ctr., 1971—; guest researcher Nat. Physical Lab., Teddington, 1961, Stanford Rsch. Inst., Manlo Pk., Calif., 1970; cons. in renewable energy various industries and govt., 1979—. Contbr. numerous articles to profl. jours. Named Carnegie fellow Carnegie Found., 1960-61; recipient numerous grants for energy rsch. from govts. and pvt. industry, 1979—. Fellow Instn. Engrs. Australia; mem. Internat. Solar Energy Soc. (dir. 1994-97). Achievements include development and introduction of means for the mass utilization of solar energy via solar thermal/thermochemical systems; recent realisation of large cost effective solar concentrating collectors for producing many solar driven energy conversion processes thus enabling the early commercialization of solar-fossil combined systems and solar only systems of subsantial size; received government and industrial support for the first multimega watt solar thermal dish based generator working with a coal-fired power station to reduce greenhouse gas emissions. Recent developments have made practicable large systems of solar paraboloidal concentrating collectors to produce via steam turbogenerators and gas tubine combined cycle systems, electricity and viable waste-heat-driven desalination of value to many cuntries currently lacking in electricity and potable water. Office: Australian Nat U, Rsch Sch Phys Scis and Engr, Canberra ACT 0200, Australia

KANEGAONKAR, HARI BHAGWAN, structural engineer; b. Solapur, India, Feb. 28, 1955; arrived in Norway, 1988; s. Bhagwan Ramachandra Kanegaonkar and Indira Bhagwan (Honap) K.; m. Vidya Subramanian, Oct. 12, 1987; 1 child, Suryaprakash. B in Engring., Shivaji U., Kolhapur, India, 1976; M in Tech., Indian Inst. Tech., Bombay, 1979, PhD, 1984. Rsch. fellow Indian Inst. Tech., Bombay, 1978-79, project engr., 1980-82; owner, dir. Oriental Tech. Cons., Bombay, 1983-84; chief engr. Aker Offshore Ptnr., Stavanger, Norway, 1988—; vis. prof. Høgskolen i Stavanger, Norway, 1995, 97. Contbr. articles to profl. jours.; inventor in field. Coord. Student Orgn., Bombay, 1981-82. Post-doctoral fellow Ga. Inst. Tech., Atlanta, 1984-87, Internat. fellow Norwegian Coun. for Sci. and Indsl. Rsch., 1987. Hindu. Avocations: philosophy, education and social development activities. Home: Donevikstraen 5, 4048 Hafrsfjord Norway Office: Aker Maritime/Aker Offshore Ptnr, PO Box 589 Badehusgt 39, 4001 Stavanger Norway

KANEHARA, YU, publishing company executive; b. Tokyo, Jan. 3, 1949; s. Hajime and Kimiko Kanehara. B of Engring., Seikei U., Tokyo, 1991. Pres. Igaku-Shoin Ltd., Tokyo, 1987—. E-mail: y kanehara@lgaku-shoin.co.jp. Office: Igaku-Shoin Ltd, 5-24-3 Hongo Bunkyo-ku, Tokyo 113-8719, Japan

KANEHIRO, KENNETH KENJI, insurance educator, risk analyst, consultant; b. Honolulu, May 10, 1934; s. Charles Yutaka and Betty Misako (Hoshino) K.; m. Eiko Asari, June 23, 1962; 1 child, Everett Peter. BA in Counseling Psychology, U. Hawaii, 1956, grad. cert. in Counseling Psychology, 1957; grad. cert. in ins., The Am. Inst., 1971. CPCU; cert. continuing profl. devel. Claims adjustor Cooke Trust Co., Honolulu, 1959-62, underwriter, 1962-66; account supr. Alexander & Baldwin, Honolulu, 1966-68; spl. risk exec. Hawaiian Ins. & Guaranty, Honolulu, 1968-71; br. mgr. Hawaiian Ins. & Guaranty, Hilo, Hawaii, 1971-72; chief officer Marsh & McLennan, Inc., Hilo, 1972-78; sr. mktg. rep. Occidental Underwriters, Honolulu, 1978-87; pvt. practice Honolulu, 1987—; coord. Ins. Sch. of Pacific, Honolulu, 1978—; lectr. ins. Hawaii State Cts., 1986—; cons. Dai Tokyo Royal State Ins. Co., 1992—; mem. arbitration panel, ct. observer panel Hawaii State Cts., 1993-96, Hawaii Criminal Ct., 1994—; proctor Hawaii State Bar Exam., 1994—; ins. expert witness, 1995—; instr. ins. agt.'s lic. course, 1995—. Adult leader Boy Scouts Am., Hilo and Honolulu, 1956—, risk mgr. Aloha coun., Honolulu, 1980—; edn. chmn. Gen. Ins. Assn., Hawaii, Hilo, 1971-77; ins. cons. Arcadia Retirement Residence, Honolulu, 1987—; cons., Waikole Cmty. Assn.; bd. govs. U. Hawaii Founders Alumni Assn., Honolulu, 1993—, scholarship chmn., 1993—. With U.S. Army, 1957-59. Recipient First Lady's Outstanding Vol. award First Lady/State of Hawaii, 1990; recipient Pres.'s award Boy Scouts Aloha Coun., 1997. Mem. Soc. CPCU (pres. 1986-87, nat. publs. com., 1996—, nat. ethics com. 1999—, contbr. jour.), Soc. Ins. Trainers and Educators. Avocations: art, photography, music. Home: 1128 Ala Napunani St Apt 705 Honolulu HI 96818-1606

KANEKI, TADASHI, electronics company executive; b. Tokyo, Apr. 18, 1944; m. Sumiko Kaneki, Nov. 10, 1973; children: Michiko, Etsuko. BS, Tokyo U., 1967, MS, 1969. Design engr. compressor design dept. Tsuchiura (Japan) Works Hitachi, Ltd., 1969-80, mgr. design sect., 1980-86, dep. mgr. compressor and fan design dept., 1986-91, mgr. dept., 1991-94, gen. mgr. environ. sys. and plant engring. divsn., 1996—; spkr., presenter Design Automation of Centrifugal Compressor, Turbo Machinery Symposium, 1978. Mem. ASME. Home: Ibaraki Prefecture, 1-11-18 Tsuwa, Tsuchiura T300, Japan Office: Hitachi Ltd, 6 Kanda surugadai 4 Chome, Chiyoda Tokyo T101, Japan

KANEKO, HISASHI, engineering executive; b. Tokyo, Nov. 19, 1933; came to U.S., 1989; s. Shozo and Toshi K.; m. Motoko Washino; children: Satoshi, Makoto, Hajime. BSEE, U. Tokyo, 1956, PhD in Engring., 1967; MSEE, U. Calif., 1962. Rsch. asst. U. Calif., Berkeley, 1960-62; mem. tech. staff Bell Tel. Labs., Holmdel, N.J., 1968-70; rsch. staff NEC Corp., Tokyo, 1956-60, rsch. mgr., 1962-68, gen. mgr. transmission div., 1970-85, v.p., 1985-89, sr. v.p., 1989-93; pres., CEO NEC America, N.Y.C., 1991-93; exec. v.p. NEC Corp., Tokyo, 1993-94, pres., 1994-99; CEO NEC Corp, Tokyo, counselor, mem. be., 1999-2000, counselor, 2000—; mem. Sci. Coun. Japan, 2000—. Author 4 books in communications; contbr. 100 articles to profl. jours. Holder 70 patents in Japan, 5 in U.S.A. Recipient Kajii Meml. prize Elec. Comm. Assn., Japan, 1979. Fellow IEEE (life, E.H. Armstrong award 1992, Internat. Comm. award 1999); mem. NAE (fgn. assoc.), Inst. Electronics, Info. and Comm. Engrs. (Achievement award 1985), Engring. Acad. Japan. Office: NEC Corp, 5-7-1 Shiba Minatoku, Tokyo 1088001, Japan

KANEKO, ISAO, air transportation executive. CEO Japan Airlines, Tokyo. Office: 2-4-11 Higashi Shinagawa, Shinagawa-ku, Tokyo 140, Japan*

KANEKO, RYOJI LLOYD, human resources specialist; b. L.A., Apr. 11, 1951; s. Hayao and Yoshiko (Kawaguchi) K.; m. Marie Antoinette Bawany, June 29, 1985; 1 child: Laura Shigemi. BA in English, Calif. State U., Long Beach, 1974. Marching instr. Third Generation Drum and Bugle Corps., L.A., 1973-75; trainer, supr. Teledyne-Geotronics, Long Beach, 1975-79; tng. coord., supr. tng. and procedures, tng. adminstr. Hughes Aircraft Co., El Segundo, Calif., 1980-87; sys. analyst, trainer Great Western Bank, Chatsworth, Calif., 1987-97; cons. Great Western Bank, Chatsworth, 1997-99; tng. mgr. Thinque Sys. Corp., North Hollywood, Calif., 1999—; guest lectr., spkr., cons. in field. Columnist Drum Corps. News; contbr. articles to various gen. interest publs. Elder, mem. chancel choir Chorale Bel Canto; mem. Cornerstone Vocal Ensemble Bellflower (Calif.) First Christian Ch. Recipient Profl. Designation award UCLA. Mem. Am. Soc. Tng. and Devel. (cert. outstanding svc. 1982, editor L.A. Interchange newsletter), So. Calif. Judges Assn., Assn. Disciple Musicians, All-Am. Judges Assn., Western States Judges Assn., Calif. State U., Long Beach Alumni Assn., Nanka Hiroshima Kenjinkai Club. Home: 13707 La Cuarta St Whittier CA 90602-2516 Office: 11755 Victory Blvd Ste 250 North Hollywood CA 91606-3423

KANEKO, RYOTARO, insurance company executive. Pres. Meiji Life Ins. Co., Tokyo. Office: Meiji Life Ins Co, 2-1-1 Maronouchi Chiyoda-ku, Tokyo 100-0005, Japan*

KANEKO, TAKASHI, medical educator; b. Yamanashi, Japan, July 15, 1962; s. Fumio and Fujiko)Wakasugi) K.; m. Miki Sawanobori, Mar. 14, 1993. MD, Med. U. Yamanashi, Japan, 1987, PhD, 1991. Assoc. prof. Med. U. Yamanashi, Japan, 1996—; dir. occupational health Matsushita Elecs. Corp. Co., Ltd., Japan, 1989—. Contbr. articles to profl. jours. Med. U. Yamanashi fellow, 1991-96. Mem. Internat. Diabetes Fedn. (life), Internat. Commn. Occupational Health. Avocation: Japanese chess. Office: Med U Yamanashi, Shimokato 1110 Tamaho, Yamanashi 409-3898, Japan

KANEKO, TETSUO, physicist; b. Matsudo-shi, Chiba-ken, Japan, Nov. 3, 1953. BS, Chuo U., Tokyo, 1977, 80; MS, Chuo U., 1984. Mem. tech. survey staff Japan NUS Co., Ltd., Tokyo, 1985-87; tech. asst. Tokyo Food Sanitation, 1987-93; exptl. asst. Seikei U., Tokyo, 1990-93; mem. tech. staff IAI Co., Ltd., Tokyo, 1993-97; PC operator DIS Sys. Trading Co., Ltd., Tokyo, 1997—. Contbr. articles to profl. jours. Mem. Am. Phys. Soc., Chem. Soc. Japan, Phys. Soc. Japan. Fax: 047-341-0638. E-mail: kanekous@ppp.bekkoame.ne.jp. Home: Kogane Kazusa-cho 16-1, Matsudo-shi 270-0015, Japan Office: DIS Sys Trading Co Ltd, Shiba 3-14-2, 105-0014 Minato-ku Tokyo, Japan

KANEKO, YOSHIHIRO, cardiologist, researcher; b. Shizuoka, Japan, Jan. 22, 1922; s. Rokurohei and Yoshino (Momochi) K.; m. Toyo Nozaki, Apr. 8, 1962; children: Kyoko, Eriko, Hiroko. MD, Tokyo U. Med. Sch., Japan, 1945, DMS, 1951. Clin. assoc. dept. internal medicine Tokyo U. Hosp., Japan, 1945-53, instr., 1953-70; rsch. fellow Cleve. Clinic Found., 1958-61, 1962-63; asst. prof. 2d dept. internal medicine Tokyo U. Med. Sch., 1971-73; prof. medicine, chmn. dept internal medicine Yokohama City (Japan) U. Med. Sch., Japan, 1973-87, emeritus prof., 1987—; dir. Yokohama Hypertension Rsch. Ctr., 1987—; prof. emeritus Yokohama City U., 1987—; hon. dir. Nishi-Yokohama Internat. Hosp., 1987-93. Contbr. articles to profl. jours. Com. mem. Pharm. Bur. Japan Ministry Health & Welfare, Tokyo, 1974-87, Med. Affairs Bur., Tokyo, 1976-79. Grantee NIH, 1965-67; recipient award Japanese Kidney Found., 1986, Internat. Soc. Hypertension, 1988. Fellow High Blood Pressure Coun.; mem. Japanese Soc. Hypertension (1st pres. 1978-79, dir. 1978-89), Japanese Soc. Internal Medicine (councilor), Japan Circulation Soc., Japan Soc. Nephrology (dir. 1974-87), Am. Heart Assn. (coun. mem.), Internat. Soc. Hypertension, (coun. 1982-90, chmn. 1988). Avocations: reading, gardening. Home: 2-27-14 Nishishiba, Kanazawa-ku, Yokohama 236-0017, Japan Office: Yokohama Hypertension Rsch Ctr, Deiki 2-8-19-402 Kanazawa-k, Yokohama 236-0021, Japan

KANEKURA, TAKURO, physician; b. Kagoshima, Japan, June 26, 1958; s. Teruo and Shoko (Jifuku) K.; m. Shoko Ohno, May 8, 1988; children: Kyoko, Yuko. MD, Kagoshima U., 1983, PhD, 1991. Instr. dept. dermatology Kagoshima U., 1985-91, asst. prof. dept. dermatology, 1993—; chief dr. dept. dermatology Miyakonojo (Japan) Nat. Hosp., 1991-93; vis. researcher dept. rheumatology U. Tenn., Memphis, 1996-98. Contbr. articles to profl. jours. Scientific rsch. grantee Ministry Edn., Sci. and Culture, Japan, 1999. Office: Kagoshima U Sch Medicine, 8-35-1 Sakuragaoka, 890-8520 Kagoshima Japan

KANEMATSU, HIDEYUKI, materials science and engineering researcher; b. Sakai, Osaka, Japan, Nov. 21, 1957; s. Shoji and Reiko Komori, Apr. 30, 1988; children: Hitomi, Hiroyuki. B of Engring., Nagoya (Japan) U., 1981, M of Engring., 1983, D of Engring., 1989. Rsch. assoc. Nagoya U., 1986-90, Osaka U., 1990-92; rsch. assoc. Suzuka (Japan) Nat. Coll. Tech., 1992-94, asst. prof., 1994-97, assoc. prof., 1997—. Contbr. articles to profl. jours. Mem. Internat. Soc. Electrochemistry, Am. Electroplaters and Surface Finishing Soc., Minerals, Metals and Material Soc., Japanese Inst. Metals. Shinto Buddhist. Avocations: German literature, playing piano. Home: 5-3-1 Sakurajima-cho, Suzuka 513-0817, Japan Office: Suzuka Nat Coll Tech, Shiroko-cho, Suzuka 510-0294, Japan

KANEOKA, KOJI, orthopedic surgeon; b. N.Y.C., Apr. 13, 1962; parents Tsuyoshi and Fumiko K.; m. Kiyoko Nagasaka, Aug. 29, 1992; children: Natsuki, Yuji. PhD, U. Tsukuba, 1998. Resident in orthopedic surgery U. Tsukuba, Ibaraki, Japan, 1988-94; lectr. dept. orthopedic surgery, 2000—; chief physician dept. orthopedic surgery Tokyo Kosei-Nenkin Hosp., Tokyo, 1998-2000. Grantee Marine & Fire Ins. Assn. Japan, 1996, 97, 99. Mem. Japan Orthopedic Assn., Japan Spine Rsch. Soc., Japanese Orthopedic Soc. Sports Medicine, Soc. Japan Clin. Biomechs., N.Y. Acad. Scis., Orthopedic Rsch. Soc. Avocation: swimming. Office: U Tsukuba Dept Ortho Surger, 1-1-1 Ten-nohdai, Tsukuba Ibaraki 3058575, Japan

KANESTRØM, INGOLF, geophysicist, educator; b. Molde, Norway, May 16, 1933; s. Otto and Jenny (Lillebostad) K.; m. Olaug Laland, June 1, 1963; children: Odd Egil, Anita, Tor Ivar. MS, U. Oslo, 1963, PhD, 1967. Rsch. scholar Inst. Physics, Oslo, 1962-63, univ. fellow, 1965-70, asst. prof., 1970-92, prof., 1993—, vice dean faculty math. and natural scis., 1978-80, 90-93,

dean faculty math. and natural scis., 1994-97; rsch. scholar NORDITA, Copenhagen, 1963-65; mgr. Inst. Geophysics, Oslo, 1985-87. Author: Drivhuseffekten, U. Oslo, 1990, Energi-klima-natur-miljö, Gyldendal, Oslo, 2000; contbr. articles to profl. jours. Vol. collaborator Norwegian Luth. Missionary Soc. Mem. European Geophys. Soc., Norwegian Geophys. Soc. (chmn. 1984-87), Oslo Geophys. Soc. (chmn. 1976-77). Lutheran. Home: Syrenveien 16, 0870 Oslo Norway Office: U Oslo Inst Geophysics, Box 1022 Blindern, 0315 Oslo Norway

KANE-VILLELA, GRACE MCNELLY, maternal, women's health and pediatrics nurse; b. Auburn, Ill., Mar. 31, 1939; d. Irving Benjamin and Ruby Louise (Stinnett) McNelly; m. Robert John Kane, July 23, 1960 (dec. 1994); children: Scott Robert, Timothy Phillip, Pamela Collette, Glenn Randall, Andrew Keith, Bruce Ryan; m. Carlos Albert Villela, Mar. 21, 1998. Diploma, Mem. Hosp. Sch. Nursing, Springfield, Ill., 1960; BS in Profl. Arts, St. Joseph's Coll., North Windham, Maine, 1985. RN, Ill.; cert. in occupational hearing conservation, fetal monitoring I and II; cert. ACLS. Staff nurse nursery-newborn units Walther Meml. Hosp., Chgo., 1962-67; staff nurse rooming-in nursery Luth. Gen. Hosp., Park Ridge, Ill., 1977-85; staff nurse med.-surg. unit Swedish Covenant Hosp., Chgo., 1989; staff nurse occupational clinic Rush-Presbyn-St. Luke's, Elk Grove Village, Ill., 1988; nurse various hosps., Arlington Heights, Ill., 1989-93; staff nurse couplet care St. Joseph's Hosp., Phoenix, 1997—. Address: 5821 E Acoma Dr Scottsdale AZ 85254-2413

KANEVSKY, MIKHAIL BORISOVICH, physicist, researcher; b. Gorky (Nizhnii Novgorod), Russia, Nov. 3, 1940; s. Boris Moisseyevich and Sophiya Marcovna (Eizenberg) K.; m. Helena Borisovna Bougaieva, Aug. 12, 1967; children: Yekaterina (now Katrin), Victor. PhD, U. Gorky, Russia, 1975; DSc, Inst. Gen. Physics, Moscow, 1993. Cert. radiophysics and electronics. Jr. scientist Radiophys. Rsch. Inst., Gorky, 1962-65, sr. engr., 1965-77; sr. scientist Inst. Applied Physics, Gorky, 1977-94; head scientist Inst. Applied Physics, Nizhnii Novgorod, 1994—; sci. supr. PhD students, parent inst., 1994—; sci. supr. grad. students, lectr. Nizhnii Novgorod State U., 1990, 93, 94, 97, 99, 2000; expert Sci. Counsel on Hydrophysics at Presidium of Russian Acad. Sci., Moscow, 1977-93. Co-editor: Remote Sensing of the Ocean, 1987; contbr. articles to profl. jours. Grantee Russian Found. Basic Investigations, Moscow, 1995-2000, Internat. Sci. Found., 1994, Internat. Ctr. Advanced Studies, Nizhnii Novgorod, 1997, Internat. Assn. Promotion of Cooperation with Scientists from Ind. States of Former Soviet Union, 1999; recipient Charter of Honour Presidium of Russian Acad. Scis., 1999. Mem. N.Y. Acad. Scis. Avocation: communication with nature (trips). Home: 4-104 Ussilov Str, 603093 Nizhnii Novgorod Russia Office: Inst Applied Physics, 46 Ulyanov St, 603600 Nizhnii Novgorod Russia

KANEYOSHI, TAKAHITO, physicist; b. Otaru, Hokkaido, Japan, Aug. 24, 1940; s. Chukichi and Ine (Yoshikawa) K.; m. Yoshiko Yamashina, Mar. 24, 1968; children: Yoshitaka, Akihiro, Yukako. B Tech., Waseda U., Tokyo, 1963; MS, Kyoto (Japan) U., 1965, DSc, 1969. Rsch. assoc. Nagoya (Japan) U., 1968-92, assoc. prof., 1992-93, prof. physics, 1993—. Author: Amorphous Magnetism, 1984, Introduction to Surface Magnetism, 1991, Introduction to Amorphous Magnets, 1992. Mem. Phys. Soc. Japan, Applied Magnetic Soc. Japan, Am. Phys. Soc. Office: Nagoya U, Furoucho, Chikusaku, Aichi Nagoya 464-8601, Japan

KANG, BANN C., immunologist; b. Kyungnam, Korea, Mar. 4, 1939; d. Daeryong and Buni (Chung) K.; came to U.S., 1964, naturalized, 1976; A.B., Kyungpook Nat. U., 1959, M.D., 1963; m. U. Yun Ryo, Mar. 30, 1963. Intern, L.I. Jewish Hosp.-Queens Hosp. Center, Jamaica, N.Y., 1964-65, resident in medicine, 1965-67; teaching assoc. Kyungpook U. Hosp., Taegu, Korea, 1967-70; fellow in allergy and chest Creighton U., Omaha, 1970-71; fellow in allergy Henry Ford Hosp., Detroit, 1971-72; clin. instr. medicine U. Mich. Hosp., Ann Arbor, 1972-73; asst. prof. Chgo. Med. Sch., 1973-74; chief allergy-immunology Mt. Sinai Hosp., Chgo., 1975—; asst. prof. Rush Med. Sch., Chgo. 1975-84, assoc. prof., 1984-86; assoc. prof. U. Ky. Coll. Medicine, 1987-92, prof., 1992—; cons., 1976—, Nat. Heart, Lung, Blood Inst., 1979—; mem. Exptl. Transplantation Adv. Bd., Ill., 1985-86, Diagnostic and Therapeutic Tech. Assessment (AMA), 1987—, Gen. Clin. Rsch. Com. (NIH), 1989-93; adv. com. Ctr. for Biologics and Rsch., FDA, 1993-96; counselor Chgo. Med. Soc., 1984-86, mem. policy com., adv. com. to health dept. Chgo. and Cook County, 1984-86. Recipient NIH award U. Mich., 1972-73. Diplomate Am. Bd. Internal Medicine, Am. Bd. Allergy-Immunology. Fellow ACP, Am. Acad. Allergy; mem. Am. Fedn. Clin. Research, AMA, Inter-Asthma Assn. Contbr. over 50 articles to profl. jours. Home: 2716 Martinique Ln Lexington KY 40509-9509 Office: U Ky Coll Medicine K528 Albert B Chandler Med Ctr 800 Rose St Lexington KY 40536-0001

KANG, BYUNG KYU, association administrator; b. Kengnam, Republic of Korea, July 19, 1931; s. Taek Sun and Myung (Soo) K.; m. Jou Il Hee; children: In Soo, Sang Mook. BA, Chungang U., Seoul, 1954, MA, 1956; LLD, Pusan Nat. U., 1971; PhD (hon.), William Penn U., 1983. Prof. Chungang U., Seoul, 1956-70; sec.-gen. Aspac Culture Ctr., Seoul, 1968-71, Korea-Japan Coun., Seoul, 1986-89; congressmen Nat. Assembly, Seoul, 1971-81, chmn. Edn. and Culture Cmty., 1979-81; pres. Hansung U., Seoul, 1981-85, Korean World Peace Assn., Seoul, 1990—; prof. Damul Nat. Sch., Seoul, 1995—; vis. prof. Grad. Sch. Social Devel., Changang U., 1995—; advisor Claremont Inst., Calif.; rsch. assoc. Inst. Internat. Studies, U. Calif., Berkeley. Author: Contemporary Foreign Policy, 1965, Political Environment of the Korean War, 1970, Selection of Dr. Kang's Writings, 1991; contbr. articles to profl. jours. Chmn. Yongdongpo Ku, Drp. Party, Seoul, 1971-81; pres. Korean Legitimate Congress, Seoul, 1991—, Nat. Coun. for Prevention of War on the Korean Peninsula, Seoul, 1997—. Rsch. Officer Nat. Def. Coll., 1956-61. Decorated Hon. Comdr. Knight, Malta Knight Coun.; recipient prize KBS, 1968. Mem. Nat. Union Korean Ufologists (pres. 1997—), Internat. Studies Assn., Internat. Inst. Strategic Studies. Avocations: golf, travel, tracking, fishing, boating. Fax: 822-323-6464. E-mail: bklkang@shimbiro.com. Home: 476-2 Seokyodong Mapoku, Seoul 476-53, Korea Office: Korean World Peace Assn, 476-53 Seokyodong Mapo, Seoul 121-211, Korea

KANG, CHANG IL, physician, educator; b. Hobu, Yamaguchi, Japan, May 5, 1943; arrived in Korea, 1945; s. Sang Jo and Keum Soon (Won) K.; m. Soo Young Kim, Dec. 20, 1995; children: Min Joung, Min Young. MB, Pusan (Korea) Med. Coll., 1967. Diplomat Korean Bd. Internal Medicine, Korean Bd. Endocrine and Metabolism, Am. Bd. Internal Medicine. Med. resident Wyckoff Heights (N.Y.) Hosp., 1973-76; staff physician Internat. Lady Garment Worker's Union Health Ctr., N.Y.C., 1976-77, Menorah Home and Hosp., N.Y.C., 1977-78, Beth Israel Hosp., N.Y.C., 1978-79; from asst. to assoc. prof. internal medicine Inje Med. Coll., Pusan, 1979-86; prof. internal medicine Inje Med. Coll., 1986—; chief internal medicine Pusan Paek Hosp., 1986-96; chief med. staff Inje Med. Coll., 1994-96, chief, 1997-98. Editor: (textbook) Endocrine and Metabolism, 1997, 98, 99. Capt. Korean Army, 1967-70. Mem. Korean Physicians Assn., Korean Internist Assn., Korean Endocrinology Assn. Avocation: reading geography and history books. Office: Pusan Paek Hosp, Inje Med Coll Kaekeum dong, Pusan City Korea

KANG, CHIL-YONG, virology, immunology educator; b. Hadong, Kyung-Nahm, South Korea, Nov. 28, 1940; came to Can., 1966, naturalized, 1971; s. Whashik and Ungee (Song) K.; m. Myung-Ja Oh Kang, Dec. 17, 1966; children: Julie, Rosanne, Matthew. Dipl. Vet. Sci., Malling Agrl. Coll., Denmark, 1963; BSA, Kon-Kuk U., Korea, 1965; PhD, McMaster U., Hamilton, Ont., 1971; DSc, Carleton U., 1991. Postdoctoral fellow U. Wis.-Madison, 1971-74; asst. prof. Southwestern Med. Sch. U. Tex., Dallas, 1974-78, assoc. prof. Southwestern Med. Sch., 1978-82; prof., chmn. dept. microbiology and immunology U. Ottawa, Ont., 1982-92; dir. U. Ottawa Biotech. Inst., 1987-92; dean sci., prof. medicine U. Western Ont., 1992-99, prof. virology, 1992—. Contbr. articles to profl. jours. Office: U Western Ont Siebens-Dranke Inst Rm 129, 1400 Western Rd, London, ON Canada N6G 2V4

KANG, CHIN HUAT, minister; b. Taiping Perak, Malaysia, Oct. 12, 1953; s. Chooi Tit and Siew Mooi (Chong) K.; m. Wai Chee Muck, May 20, 1982. BA, William Jewell Coll., 1982; MDiv, MA, Golden Gate Bapt. Theol. Sem., 1983-84; DMin, San Francisco Theol. Sem., 1986. Ordained to ministry Gashland Bapt. Ch., 1982. Assoc. pastor Southbay Chinese Bapt. Ch., San Jose, 1982-83; pastor Chinese Mission, 1st Bapt. Ch., Rancho Cordova, Calif., 1983-84; lectr. Bapt. Theol. Sem., Penang, 1986-88; adv. pastor Penang Bapt. Ch., 1986-88, Emmanuel Bapt. Ch., Petaling Jaya, 1988; chaplain Hong Kong Bapt. U., 1989—; sr. pastor Acad. Community Ch., Hong Kong, 1989-94; adv. pastor Univ. Bapt. Ch., 1995, Christ Bapt. Ch., 1995—; adv. pastor Pui Ching Rd. Bapt. Ch., 1999; mem. bd. dirs. Hong Kong Bapt. Theol. Sem., 1990-93, 95-98; speaker Malaysia Bapt. Conv. Ann. Messagers' Conf., Port Dickson, Malaysia, 1986, Malaysia Bapt. Conv. Youth Conf., Port Dickson, 1987. Contbr. articles to profl. jours. Mem. Fedn. of Chinese Univ. and Coll. Chaplincies (pres. 1998), Pi Gamma Mu. Baptist. Avocations: swimming, classical music, table tennis, badminton. Office: Hong Kong Bapt Univ, Kowloon Hong Kong

KANG, DER-KUAN, optical scientist; b. Ping-Tong, Taiwan, Dec. 25, 1956; came to the U.S., 1996; s. Chiang-Yen and Fenging (Hwang) K. B in Engring., Feng-Chia U., Taichung, Taiwan, 1979; M in Engring., Kyoto (Japan) Inst. Tech., 1987; PhD in Engring., Tokyo Inst. Tech., 1991. Optical scientist Am. Banknote Holographics Co., Elmsford, N.Y. Author: Image Processing for Holography, 1990, Holographic Security System, 1996. Recipient Display Hologram Developing award Toppan Printing Co., Tokyo, 1995. Mem. Internat. Soc. for Optical Engring. Office: Am Banknote Holographics 399 Executive Blvd Elmsford NY 10523-1205

KANG, HIE CHAN, mechanical engineering educator; b. DaeJeon, Republic of Korea, Jan. 8, 1962; s. Young Sik Kang and Young Bae Moon; m. Mi Kyung Kim, Sept. 3, 1962; children: Nam Kyoo, Hyeon Kyoo, Janice. BS, Kyunghee U., Seoul, 1984; MS, Yonsei U., Seoul, 1986; PhD, POSTECH, Pohang, 1992. Post-doctoral POSTECH, Pohang, Korea, 1992; assoc. prof. Kunsan Nat. U., Kunsan, 1992—; head faculty mech. engring. Kunsan Nat. U., 1999—; post-doctoral vis. scholar Penn. State U., University Park, 1996—; cons. Kunsan City, 1990-96. Contbr. articles to profl. jours. Second lt. 3d Military Acad., Korea, 1986-87. Recipient Changyongshil award Min. Sci. & Tech., 1995, Korean Technology award, 1995. Mem. Korean Soc. Mech. Engrs., Soc. Air Conditioning & Refrigerating Engrs. Avocations: reading, invention, tennis. Office: Sch Mech Engring, Kunsan Nat U Miryoungdon, 573-701 Kunsan Republic of Korea

KANG, HONG SEOK, chemist, educator; b. Kwangju, Korea, July 14, 1957; s. Joongwon Kang and In Kum Hwang; m. Kyung Hyung Kim, June 15, 1986; children: Choonhye, Seung Ku. BS, Seoul Nat. U., Republic of Korea, 1979; MS, Korea Advanced Inst Sci. Tech., Daejon, Republic of Korea, 1982, PhD, 1986. Rsch. assoc. U. Pitts., 1986-87; vis. fellow NIH, Bethesda, Md., 1988-91. Contbr. articles to scientific jours. Mem. Korean Phys. Soc., Korean Chem. Soc. Home: Green Pk # 310, 2 Cha Donga Apt 204-306, 560-240 Chonju Seoshin-dong Republic of Korea Office: Jeonju U Sch Applied Sci, Hyoja-Dong, 560-170 Chonju Chonbuk, Republic of Korea

KANG, JIAN, architectural acoustician; b. Shanxi, China, Aug. 2, 1964; s. Zhao-ming and Huan-yun (Fan) K.; m. Mei Zhang, Oct. 22, 1987; 1 child, Zheng-yu Joe. BArch, Tsinghua U., Beijing, 1984, MS, 1986; PhD, U. Cambridge, England, 1996. Asst. Tsinghua U., Beijing, 1987-90, lectr., 1990-92; sr. rsch. assoc. U. Cambridge, Eng., 1997-99; univ. lectr. U. Sheffield, Eng., 1999—; cons. for various constrn. projects. Contbr. articles to profl. jours. Vis. scholar Fraunhofer-Inst. Bauphysik, Stuttgart, Germany, 1992-93; Humboldt fellow, 1997; fellow Wolfson Coll., Cambridge U. Mem. Acoustical Soc. Am. (R. Newman medal 1996, tech. com. on noise), Deutsche Gesellschaft Akustik, Inst. Acoustics, Acoustical Soc. China, Internat. Inst. Acoustics and Vibration. Fax: 0044-114-2798276. Office: U Sheffield, Sch Arch, Western Bank Sheffield S10 2TN, England

KANG, JUAN, pathologist; b. Chang-Young, Kyung-Nam, Republic of Korea, Aug. 10, 1935; came to U.S., 1965; s. Bugon and Umchun (Chung) K.; children: Angie, Alex, Erik. PreMed, Kyung-Pook U., Taegu, Republic of Korea, 1955; MD, Kyung-Pook U., 1959. Diplomate Am. Bd. Pathology, Am. Bd. Radioisotopic Pathology, Am. Bd. Hematology, Am. Bd. Dermatopathology. Capt. Med. Corps Republic of Korea Army, 1959-65; intern Watts Hosp., Durham, N.C., 1965-66; resident St. Louis U. Hosp., 1968-70; pathologist Allen Pathology Group, St. Louis, 1971—; clin. asst. prof. St. Louis U. Med. Sch., 1979—. Mem. AMA, Am. Soc. Clin. Pathologists, Coll. Am. Pathologists, Internat. Acad. of Pathologists, Am. Soc. Dermatopathology, Soc. for Hematopathology. Home: 12939 Banyan Town Dr Saint Louis MO 63146-4300 Office: Christian Hosp NE 11133 Dunn Rd Saint Louis MO 63136-6192

KANG, KE WON, molecular geneticist; b. Andong, Kyungbook, S. Korea, July 3, 1934; s. Doo Hyun Kang and Myung Hee Choe; m. Hyun Suk Kim; children: Peter H., Henry H. BS, Seoul Nat. U., 1957, MS, 1960; PhD, N.C. State U., 1966. Prof. Ind. U. Med. Sch., Indpls., 1968-83; Fulbright fellow Korea Inst. Sci. and Tech., 1983-84; prof. Korea Nat. Edn. U., Chungju, Korea, 1985-86; dean, acad. affairs KIT, Taejon, Korea, 1989-98; dir. gen. KOSEF, Taejon, 1990-92; dean Korea Advanced Inst. Sci. and Tech., Taejon, 1992-95; prof. Korea Advanced Inst. Sci. and Technology, Taejon, 1987—; dir. Human Biomed. Rsch. Ctr., Taejon, 1992-96; dir. gen. Korea Sci. Found., Taejon, 1990-92; dir. internat. corp. rsch. com., 1993. Author: (book) Biomedical Research of Leeches, 1994; patentee in field; contbr. over 150 articles to profl. jours. and publs. Recipient Internat. Cooperative award Korean Min. Sci., Seoul, 1994; named chief del. Korea-U.K. Coop. Rsch. Progam, 1993. Mem. Korea Genetic Soc. (pres. 1993-94), Korean Biol. Sci. Assn. (bd. dirs. 1995—), Korea Acad. Scis. Tech. (life).

KANG, LEEN-SEOK, engineering educator; b. Seoul, Dec. 2, 1960; parents Bong-Su Kang and Bong-Rae Chu; m. Jin-Hee Jang, Sept. 29, 1984; 1 child, Min-Su. BA, Chungang U., Seoul, 1984, MS, 1986, PhD, 1990. Sr. rschr. Korea Nat. Housing Inst., Seoul, 1991; lectr. Gyeongsang Nat. U., Chinju, Korea, 1991-93, asst. prof., 1991-97, assoc. prof., 1997—, divsn. head divsn. constrn., 1997-99; vis. prof. Chungang U., Seoul, 1994-95, U. Salford, Eng., 1999; postdoctoral fellow dept. civil engring. Stanford U., Palo Alto, Calif., 1995-96; mem. adv. bd. Korea Inst. Constrn. Tech., Seoul, 1999—, Ministry of Constrn. and Transp., Seoul, 1999—. Author: (book) National Standard Specifications for General Civil Works, 1998, New Construction Engineering and Management for Civil Engineering Project, 1999; contbr. articles to profl. jours. Mem. ASCE, Korean Soc. Civil Engrs. (editl. bd. 1998—, Award for Paper Work 1999), Korea Inst. Constrn. Engring. & Mgmt. (dir. 2000—). Fax: 0 55 753 1713. E-mail: lskang@nongae.gsnu.ac.kr. Office: Gyeongsang Nat U, Dept Civ Eng 900 Gajoa-dong, Chinju Gyeongnam 660-701, South Korea

KANG, MANJIT SINGH, geneticist, plant breeder; b. Punjab, India, Mar. 3, 1948; came to U.S., 1969, naturalized, 1976; s. Gurdit Singh and Parminder Kaur (Brah) K.; m. Georgia Anna Crocker, Feb. 13, 1971 (div. May 2000). BS in Agr. with honors, Punjab Agrl. U., Lunhiana, India, 1968; MS, So. Ill. U., Edwardsville, 1971; MA in Botany, So. Ill. U., Carbondale, 1977; PhD, U. Mo., Columbia, 1977. Tchg. asst. So. Ill. U., Edwardsville, 1969-71; rsch. asst. plant and soil sci. So. Ill. U., Carbondale, 1971-72, preceptor plant and soil sci., 1972-74; grad. rsch. asst. agronomy U. Mo., Columbia, 1974-77; rsch. assoc. Ctr. Biology of Natural Sys. Washington U., St. Louis, 1977; sr. plant breeder hybrid corn rsch. sta. Cargill, Inc., St. Peter, Minn., 1977-78, rsch. sta. mgr., 1979—; rsch. assoc. agronomy U. Mo., 1980; asst. prof. genetics U. Fla. Everglades Rsch. and Edn. Ctr., Belle Glade, 1981-85; assoc. prof. agronomy La. State U., Baton Rouge, 1986-90, prof., 1990—; cons. Malaysia, Palm Oil Rsch. Inst., Malaysia, 1997; apptd. bd. invited disting. jurors Internat. Jour. Scholarly Acad. Intellectual Diversity, 1997, appt. bd. editl. advs. Food Products Press, 1999. Author: Applied Quantitative Genetics, 1994; editor: Genotype-By-Environment Interaction, 1990, Genotype-By-Environment Interaction: New Perspectives, 1996; editor-in-chief: Crop Improvement for 21st Century, 1997—; contbr. Ency. Genetics, 1999; contbr. articles to profl. jours. Fulbright Sr. scholar Coun. for Internat. Exch. of Scholars and Malaysian-Am. Commn. on Edn1. Exch., 1999. Fellow Am. Soc. Agronomy (elected), Crop Sci. Soc. Am. (elected); mem. AAAS, Am. Genetic Assn., Am. Soc. Sugar Cane Technologists, Internat. Soc. Plant Molecular Biology, Coun. Agrl. and Sci. Tech., Sigma Xi (treas. Sci. Rsch. Soc. La. State U. chpt. 1998-99, v.p. La. State U. chpt. 1999-2000, acting pres. 2000, pres. 2000—), Gamma Sigma Delta. Achievements include research on developing resistance to Aspergillus flavus and the carcinogen aflatoxin in maize grain. Home: 2477 Creekside Dr Baton Rouge LA 70810-6966 Office: La State U Dept Agronomy MB Sturgis Hall Baton Rouge LA 70803

KANG, MING-CHANG, mathematics educator; b. Tainan, Taiwan, Apr. 20, 1948; s. Tien-Teh and Shui-Lien (Lee) K.; m. Shu-San Yu, Nov. 17, 1979; children: Chi-Yun, Chi-Hung. BS, Nat. Taiwan U., 1971; MS, U. Chgo., 1974, PhD, 1977. Assoc. prof. Nat. Taiwan U., Taipei, 1977-81, prof., 1981—, chmn. dept. math, 1987-90, dean, Coll. of Sci. Mem. Am. Math. Soc. Office: Nat Taiwan U Dept Math, Gl Roosevelt Rd, Sec 4 Taipei 10617, Taiwan*

KANG, MING-YUAN, dentist, researcher, educator; b. Tainan, Taiwan, Sept. 3, 1963; s. Mu-Choan and Chun-Chu (Luo) K. BS, Taipei (Taiwan) Med. U., 1988; postgrad., Yamanashi Med. Sch., Kofu, Japan, 1991-93; PhD in Med. Sci., Kochi Med. Sch., Nankoku, Japan, 1996. Dental diplomate. Asst. lectr. Kochi Med. Sch., Nankoku, 1996-97; head dept. dentistry Pei-Kang (Taiwan) Hosp., China Med. Coll., 1997—; lectr. Kaohsiung (Taiwan) Med. U., 1998—; asst. prof. China Med. Coll., Taichung, Taiwan, 1998—. Contbr. articles to profl. jours. Scholar Rotary Yoneyama Meml. Found., Japan, 1994-96. Mem. Japanese Soc. Dentistry for the Handicapped, Japan Soc. Anesthesiology, Japanese Dental Soc. Anesthesiology. Avocations: reading, researching, enjoying opera, playing tennis. Home: 53 Sec 2 Min-Sheng Rd, Tainan 703, Taiwan Office: Pei-Kang Hosp China Med Col, 123 Shin-Dou Rd, Pei-Kang Yun-Lin 651, Taiwan

KANG, MOON WON, physician, medical educator; b. Seoul, Rep. of Korea, June 26, 1948; s. Il Young and Woo Soon (Yoon) K.; m. Hye Kyung Lee, Nov. 29, 1978; children: Kyoung-Hoon, Tae-Hoon. MD, Cath. U. Seoul, 1973, Med. Diploma, 1983, PhD, 1988. Intern St. Mary's Hosp., Seoul, 1973-74, resident, 1974-78; instr. Med. Coll. Cath. U., Seoul, 1981-86, asst. prof. Med. Coll., 1986-90, assoc. prof. Med. Coll., 1990-97, prof., 1997—. Editor: Jour. Korean Soc. Chemotherapy, 1990-94, Korean Jour. Infectious Diseases, 1992-94; mem. exec. bd. Jour. Korean Med. Sci., 1994—. Maj. Korean Army, 1978-81. Fellow Korean Soc. Nosocomical Infection Ctrl.; mem. Korean Soc. Infectious Diseases (v.p. 1984-88, pres. 1988—), Korean Assn. Internal Medicine (dir. scientific bd. 1995-98, dir. tng. bd. 1998—), Am. Soc. Microbiology, Internat. Soc. Chemotherapy. Roman Catholic. Avocations: golf, driving. Home: 102-104 hansung Apt, Shin-Gil 7-Dong, 150-057 Young-deung Do Ku Seoul, Republic of Korea Office: Kang Nam St Mary's Hosp, # 505 Banpo-Dong Seocho-ku, 137-701 Seoul Republic of Korea

KANG, SEONG, lawyer; b. Puyeo, Chungnam, Korea, Jan. 13, 1969; s. Dayhyeon Kang and Cheongsoon Lee; m. Heesun Kim, Oct. 10, 1993; 2 children: Hyeongmim, Hyeonhee. Bachelor's, Seoul Nat. U., 1990. Atty. Kim & Chang Law Office, Seoul, 1995—; mem. Korea Info. Ethics Com., Seoul, 1995—. Mem. Korea Bar Assn. Home: 714-1901 Kangchonsun-kyeong, Madu-dong Ilsan-ku, Koyang Korea Office: Kim & Chang Seyang Bldg 223, Naeja-Dong Chongro-ku, Seoul 110-053, Korea

KANG, SEONG-WOO, acoustical engineer; b. Wonju, Korea, Mar. 3, 1968; s. Jae-Won Kang and Jung-Ye Kim; m. Ahn Seong-Hee, Nov. 7, 1998. BS, Yonsei U., Seoul, Korea, 1990; MS, Korea Advanced Inst. Sci. Tech., Taejon, Korea, 1992; PhD, Korea Advanced Inst. Sci. Tech., 1996. Sr. rschr. Samsung Electronics Co., Suwon, Korea, 1996, project leader, 1997—; tchg. asst., rschr. Korea Advanced Inst. Sci. Tech., 1990-95. Contbr. articles to profl. jours.; reviewer Transactions on Signal Processing-IEEE, 1998—. Mem. IEEE, N.Y. Acad. Sci., Acoustical Soc. Am. Avocation: classical guitar. Home: 38-11 In-Dong, Wonju 220 070, Korea Office: Samsung Corp R&D Ctr, 416 Maetan-3Dong Paldal-Gu, Suwon 442 742, Korea

KANG, SHIN IL, economist; b. Seoul, Korea, Jan. 7, 1955; s. Min Chang and In Suk (Cha) K.; m. Kyong Ok Chon; children: Young Suk, Kun Suk. BA, Hankuk U. Fgn. Studies, Seoul, 1980; MA, Ohio State U., 1984, PhD, 1986. Rsch. fellow Korea Devel. Inst., Seoul, 1986-89; rsch. coord. Korea Econ. Rsch. Inst., Seoul, 1989-93; assoc. prof. Hansung U., Seoul, 1994-99; assoc. editor Korean Jour. Indsl. Orgn., 1999—; cons. Asian Devel. Bank, Manila, 1988. Author: Privatization in Korea, 1988, Role of R&D in Public and Private Sector in Korea, Analysis of Changes in Korean Firms' Growth and Size, 1990, A Study on the Business Group, 1991, A Style of Entrepreneurship and its Effects on the Firm Growth in Korea: Analysis of Leadership of Owners and CEOs in Top 30 Business Groups, 1998, Corporate Culture in Korea, 1999. Home: Yongsanku Subingodong, Shindongah Apt # 7-107, Seoul Republic of Korea Office: 389-2GA Samsun-Dong Sungbuk gu, Seoul 150-756, Republic of Korea

KANG, SHIN-SUNG, biologist, educator; b. Seoul, Korea, Feb. 11, 1945; m. Young-Hee Min, Nov. 11, 1969; children: Min-Suk, Yoo-Lee. BS, Seoul Nat. U., 1969, MS, 1971; PhD, Cath. Med. Coll., Seoul, 1976; postgrad., Med. U. S.C., 1980-81. Lectr., assoc. prof. Kyungpook Nat. U., Taegu, Korea, 1976-90; prof. Kyungpook Nat. U., Taegu, 1990—, chmn. dpet. premedicine, 1990-92, chmn. dept. biology, 1993-96, dir. rsch. inst. genetic engring., 1996-97, vice-dean acad. affairs, 1997-98, dean, planning coord., 1998-99; asst., lectr. Cath. Med. Coll., Seoul, 1971-76; rsch. assoc. U. Ky., Lexington, 1982-84; vis. scientist NCI, Frederick, Md., 1995. Author: Biological Sciences, 1987, College Biology, 1991; contbr. articles to profl. jours. Mem. Zool. Soc. Korea (dir., editor 1988—, v.p. 1998-99), Korean Soc. Molecular Biology (dir. 1991—, v.p. 2000—), Genetic Soc. Koea (v.p. 1997-99, pres. 1999-2000). Avocations: swimming, tennis, golfing. Office: Kyungpook Nat U, Taegu 702701, Korea

KANG, WON HO, engineering educator, researcher; b. Kyoung-Ki, Rep. of Korea, Mar. 18, 1945; s. Soon Keun Kang and Won Ja Lee; m. Choon Kang Lee; children: Eun Ha, Eun Sil, Eun Young, Shin Ae, Shin Woong. B in Engring., Han Yang U., Seoul, 1971, M in Engring., 1973, PhD in Engring., 1985. Profl. engr. ceramic. Tchr. Induk Pvt. Inst., Seoul, 1974-76; dir. mgr. SamSung Corning Co. Ltd., Suwon, Rep. of Korea, 1976-89; asst. prof. Dankook U., Cheon An, 1989-91, assoc. prof., 1991-96, prof., 1997—; lectr. Han Yang U., Seoul, 1985-89, Myoung Ji U., Seoul, 1985-89; engr. cons. Samsung Corning Co. Ltd., Suwon, 1989-90; cons. Pacific Devel. Co. Ltd., Suwon, 1990-94; cons. Ministry Commerce, Industry & Energy, Seoul. Mem. Choong Nam Techno Park, Cheon An, 1997-99. Sgt. 38 Brigade, 1967-68. Recipient Award of Advanced Sci. Korean Ceramic Soc., 1988, Scientific award Korean Ceramic Assn., 1997. Fellow Profl. Engr. Assn. Avocations: HAM radio, badminton. Home: # 1-707 Misung Apt, 161 Song Pa dong, Seoul Kyoung Ki Republic of Korea Office: Dankook U, # 29 Anseo dong, Cheon An Choong Nam 330-714, Republic of Korea

KANG, YOOGOO, anesthesiologist; b. Seoul, Korea, Apr. 10, 1946; s. Kiduk and Samkum (Koh) K.; m. Young H. Kim, Nov. 9, 1972; children: Michael N., David H. BS, Seoul (Korea) Nat. U., 1967, MD, 1971. Diplomate Am. Bd. Anesthesiology. Intern St. Raphael Hosp., New Haven, Conn., 1974-75; resident in surgery Albert Einstein Med. Ctr., Phila., 1975-76; resident in anesthesiology Thomas Jefferson U. Hosp., Phila., 1976-78; fellow in obstetric anesthesia Magee Women's Hosp., Pitts., 1978-79; asst. prof. U. Pitts., 1979-88, dir. hepatic transplantation anesthesiology, 1984-98, assoc. prof., 1989-93, prof., 1994-98; prof., chmn. dept. anesthesiology Tulane U. Med. Ctr., New Orleans, 1998—; head Internat. Symposium in Liver Transplantation, Pitts., 1984-88. Editor: Hepatic Transplantation: Anesthetic Management and Perioperative Care, 1985, Anesthesia and Intensive Care for Patients with Liver Disease, 1995; assoc. editor Liver Surgery and Transplantation, 1993—; mem. editl. bd. Current Opinions in Organ Transplantation, 1996—. Med. officer Korean Army, 1971-74. Mem. Am. Soc. Anesthesiologists, Internat. Soc. Rsch. in Anesthesiology, Internat. Liver Transplantation Soc. (pres. 1989-93, mem. exec. coun. 1993-95, adv. bd. 1995—), Liver Intensive Care Group Europe. Avocations: woodwork, photography. Office: Tulane Univ Sch Medicine Dept Anesthesiology 1430 Tulane Ave New Orleans LA 70112-2699

KANG, YOUNG WOO, special education educator; b. Kyonggi, Korea, Jan. 16, 1944; came to U.S., 1972; naturalized; s. Myung Ki Kang and Lin Hee Lim; m. Kyoung Sook Suk, Feb. 26, 1972; children: Paul, Christopher. BA, Yonsei U., Seoul, Korea, 1972; MEd, U. Pitts., 1973, PhD, 1976. Cert. tchr. ESL, spl. edn.; cert. rehab. counselor. Spl. edn. cons. Gary (Ind.) Sch.

Corp., 1976—; adj. prof. Northeastern Ill. U., Chgo., 1979—; prof., dean Taegu (Korea) U., 1978—; pres. EREF (Edn. Rehab. Exch. Found.) Internat., 1993—; vice-chmn. World Com. on Disability, 1995—; dir. Nat. Orgn. on Disability, 1995—, Goodwill Industries Internat., 1998—; sr. advisor Roosevelt Inst., 1996. Author: A Light in My Heart, 1987, Love, Light, Liberty, 1989, (with Kyoung Sook Kang) Two Candles Shining in the Darkness of the World, 1990, Secrecy to Success Through Education, 1995, Dreams of a father and his sons, 1998. First blind Korean to earn a PhD. Mem. Internat. Coun. for Exceptional Children, Edn. Rehab. Exch. Found. Internat. (founding pres. 1992—), Rotary (bd. dirs., trustee Munster, Ind. chpt. 1982—, chmn. internat. svc. and youth svc. coms. dist. 6540 1983-85, presenter confs. 1983, 87, 88, one of 75 candles in 75th anniversary celebration 1992, Meritorious Svc. citation 1982, Paul Harris fellow 1987, scholar 1973). Presbyterian. Avocations: public speaking, writing, reading, travel, advocating rights of disabled. Home: 8912 Chestnut Ln Munster IN 46321-3224 Office: Gary Community Sch Corp 1988 Polk St Gary IN 46407-2443

KANGDA, ZHANG, educator, researcher; b. Hangzhou, Zhejiang, China, June 18, 1935; s. Zhanhua Zhang and Jin Yua ha; m. Hu Britian, Jan. 17, 1971; 1 child, Chengping. Student, Zhejiang Sch. Tech., 1952; bachelor, Dalian Inst. of Tech., 1956. Tchr. Zhejiang Inst. Chem. Tech., Hangzhou, China, 1956-77, assoc. prof., 1978-83, prof. head of dept., 1984-91, prof., editor Zhejiang Gongxua Yuan Xuebao, 1992-97, prof., 1997—. Author: The Equipment of Chemical Engineering, 1961, Fatigue of Pressure Vessel, 1987 (award Ministry of Labor 1990); inventor in field. Recipient 2d prize sci. and tech. Zhejiang Province, 1995, Ministry of Machinery Ind. of China, 1996. Mem. Chinese Mech. Engring. Soc. (sr.), Nat. Stds. Com. of Pressure Vessels (commr.), Zheijiang Mech. Engring. Soc. (sr.). Avocation: football. Home: 6 Dist Zhoahui 72 #2-502, Hangzhou 310014, People's Republic of China Office: Zhejiang U of Tech, 6 Dist Zhaohui, Hangzhou 310032, People's Republic of China

KANIAS, GEORGE DIMOSTHENIS, radiochemist; b. Piraeus, Greece, Nov. 15, 1944; s. Dimosthenis and Zoy (Mengelou) K.; m. Marianna Eleni Margariti, Sept. 21, 1975; children: Zoy, Angela. Diploma, U. Athens, 1974, PhD, 1983. Rschr. Nat. Ctr. for Sci. Rsch. "Demokritos", Athens, 1975—; reviewer grant orgn., Prague, 1994; PhD thesis reviewer Pune U., India, 1997. Reviewer Jour. Analytical Chemistry, 1994—, Jour. Radioanalytical and Nuclear Chemistry, 1995-96, 99, Jour. Traces and Microprobe Techniques, 1998—. Mem. Inst. Phys. Chemistry (sci. bd. 1996—), Greek Pharm. Assn. Home: Xenofontos 20 Kallithea, 176 73 Athens Greece Office: NCSR Demokritos, Aghia Paraskevi, 15310 Athens Greece

KANIM, LINDA ELIE ALIEA, medical researcher; b. L.A.; d. Elie Sab and Margaret Lucille K. Student, U. Calif., Santa Barbara, 1975, UCLA, 1975; BA, Calif. State U., L.A., 1975; MA, Am. U. Beirut, Lebanon, 1983; postgrad., U. Mich., 1986. Rsch. asst. dept. behavioral scis. Am. U. Beirut, 1977-79; rsch. asst. coronary care unit Am. U. Beirut Hosp., 1978-80, rsch. asst. dept. anesthesiology, 1978-82; rsch. assoc. Sch. Pub. Health UCLA, 1982-84, rsch. assoc. Jonsson Comprehensive Cancer Ctr., 1982-84, rsch. assoc. dept. orthopedic surgery Sch. Medicine, 1986-91; rsch. assoc. UCLA Comprehensive Spine Ctr. and West Coast Spine Inst., 1991-93, UCLA Comprehensive Spine Ctr. and Univ. Spine Assocs., 1993—; rsch. cons. in design and statistics Am. U. Beirut Hosp., 1978-83; statis. programmer Sch. Pub. Health UCLA, 1996-97. Contbr. articles to profl. jours., chpts. to books; artist book cover. Recipient award Internat. Soc. Study of the Lumbar Spine, 1999; co-recipient Russell Hibbs award Scoliosis Rsch. Soc., 1999. Avocations: swimming, gymnastics, skiing, white water rafting, scuba diving. E-mail: kanim@ucla.edu. Office: Spine Inst at St Johns Hlth Ctr UCLA Comprehen Spine Ctr 1301 20th St Ste 400 Santa Monica CA 90404-6990

KANIN, DORIS MAY, political scientist, consultant; b. Somerville, Mass., Mar. 28, 1928; d. Sidney J. and Ida Gail (Gelbsman) Small; m. Irving L. Kanin, June 11, 1944; children: Dennis, Erik, Lisa Hochheiser. BA in Govt., Boston U., 1966; MA in Govt., 1970; postgrad., Boston U., 1970-74. Dir. cultural activities Staff of George McGovern, 1972; legis. dir. to congressman Joe Moakley, 1972-74; nat. polit. dir. Frank Church for Pres., 1975-76; spl. asst. Paul Tsongas U.S. Senate campaign, Boston, 1977-78; dir. Human Svcs. Dept. Fed. State Rels., Mass., 1979-81; nat. dir. pub. affairs Physicians for Social Responsibility, 1981-82; exec. of Pub. Rels. and Comms. Lynwood Labs. Inc., 1982—; polit. adv. Paul Tsongas for pres. campaign, Mass., 991-92. Inventor, creator: Spray-n-Starch aerosol, 1968; editor: Quincy Mass. Cmty. Ctr. Newsletter, 1956-58, Mass. Liberal Citizens of Mass. Bulletin; journalist Boston Daily Record, 1944; reporter Boston Daily Record-Am. Pres. LWV, Norwood, Mass., 1956-59; Mass. Citizens for Participation in Politics, Boston, 1973-74; chair, bd. mem., mem., state bd. Mass. Civil Liberties Union, Boston, 1976-81; elected del. to all Nat. Nominating Conventions, 1972-92; dir. Mass. Cultural Affairs for Pres. Campaign, George McGovern; elected Dem. Nat. Committeewoman, Mass., 1972-76, mem. women's caucus, 1972-76; mem. steering com. Capitol Hill Women's Polit. Caucus; elected edn. and tng. coun. Dem. Nat. Com., 1976-80; chair Mass. Citizens for Participation in Politics, 1973-74; bd. dirs. Mass. Ams. for Dem. Action, 1978-80, Mass. Pax; del. Dem. Nat. Conv., 1972, 76, 80, 82, 86, 92. Named: Woodrow Wilson Semi-Finalist, 1972-76, Mass. Spelling Bee Champion, Boston Herald Traveler, 1939. Mem. Internat. Aerosol Congress. Democrat. Avocations: travel, painting, poetry writing, opera, ballet. Home: 511 Boylston St Brookline MA 02445-5701 also: 1289 Breakers West Blvd West Palm Beach FL 33411-1881

KANINSKI, PAVEL SERGEYEVICH, research scientist; b. Yaroslavl, Russia, Oct. 29, 1954; s. Sergey Ivanovich and Serafima Ivanovna (Raskumandrina) Koninski; m. Galina Nikolayevna Grizodub, Dec. 18, 1976; 1 child, Sergey. Grad. in electro chemistry, Polytech. Inst., Yaroslavl, 1977; postgrad. in organic chemistry, Polytech. Inst., 1981-84; D in Chem. Scis., Moscow's Inst. Thin Chemical Tech., 1987. Engr.-technologist diplomat. Engr. Polytechnic Inst., Yaroslavl, 1977-82, sr. engr., 1982-85, sci. collaborator, 1985-87, sr. sci. collaborator, 1987-89, head dept., 1989-91; chief of rsch. Ctr. Spectrum, Yaroslavl, 1991—. Patentee in field. Dept. chief Voluntary People's Brigagde, Yaroslavl Polit. Inst., 1988; mem. direcktorate Music Likers Orgn., Yaroslavl, 1996. Recipient medal USSR Econ. Achievement Exhbn., Moscow, 1986; named Premium of Leninsky's Komsomol of Region, Yaroslavl, 1986. Mem. Acad. Natural Scis. Russian Fedn. (corr.), N.Y. Acad. Scis. Avocations: music, reading, movies, tennis, swimming. Office: Centre Spektrum, 62 Bolshaya Oktyabrskaya St, 150000 Yaroslavl Russia

KANIOR, MARIAN, historian; b. Rudnik, Cracow, Poland, Nov. 29, 1929; s. Konstanty and Karolina (Kosałka) K. Student, Comml. Acad., Cracow, 1948-52, Superior Diocesan Sem., Wloclawek, Poland, 1955-61; M of Econ. Studies, Acad. Economy, Cracow, 1963; D of Humane Studies, U. Breslau, Poland, 1969; Habilitation, Papal Acad. Theology, Cracow, 1985. Ordained priest, 1961; monk Benedictine Abbey, Cracow 1968, libr., 1969-83. Lectr. history of ch. Inst. Theology of Lasaristes, Cracow, 1983-86; lectr. history of ch. Papal Acad. Theology, 1984-89, reader history Christian spirituality, 1989-95, prof. history ch. and Christian spirituality, 1995—. Editor Ossolineum, 1990, Unum, Cracow, 1993, Papal Acad. Theology, 1998, Abbey Staniatki, 1999, Abbey Tyniec, 2000. Recipient scholarship Cath. U. Louvain, Belgium, 1976-77, scholarship Cath. U. Washington, 1988, scholarship Janineum, Wien, Austria, 1993. Mem. Polish Assn. Theology (editor 1993, 98), Polish Assn. History. Home: The Benedictine Abbey, Benedyktynska 37, 30-375 Cracow Poland Office: Papal Acad Theology, Franciszkanska 1, 31-004 Cracow Poland

KANJILAL, PARTHA PRATIM, systems engineer, researcher; b. Jamshedpur, India, Nov. 14, 1952; s. Gopal and Bina K.; m. Sagarika Banerjee; children: Debayan, Sreyashi. B in Tech., Indian Inst. Tech., Kharagpur, 1974; M in Engring., U. Sheffield, 1980, PhD, 1983. Instrument foreman Tata Steel, India, 1975-79; postdoctoral rsch. fellow U. Oxford, England, 1983-86; pool officer CSIR, India, 1987-88; from asst. prof. to prof. Indian Inst. Technology, Kharagpur, 1988—. Author: Adaptive Prediction and Predictive Control, 1995; contbr. numerous papers to profl. jours., chpt. to book: Neural Network Systems Techniques and Applications, 1997. Fellow IEE; mem. IEEE. Office: USARIEM Biophysics & Biomedical Modeling Dvsn 5 Kansas St Natick MA 01760-2623

KANKARE, JYRKI HEIKKI ANTERO, orthopedic and trauma surgeon, spine consultant; b. Helsinki, Mar. 29, 1959; s. Antero and Tuulikki K.; m. Kaisa Liisa Raittila, Feb. 2, 1980; children: Lotta, Johannes, Tuomas, Reetta, Elsa. MD, U. Helsinki, 1986, Specialty Gen. Surgery, 1992, Specialty in Orthopedics and Traumatology, 1994, PhD, 1999. Med. diplomate. Asst. surgeon City Hosp., Helsinki, 1987-90, cons. in orthopedics and traumatology, 1994-95; asst. surgeon U. Hosp., Helsinki, 1990-94, cons. in orthopedics and traumatology, 1995—; med. cons. Ins. Co. Ilmarinen, Helsinki, 1994-96. Contbr. articles to profl. jours. Mem. Finnish Med. Assn., Finnish Surg. Soc., Finnish Orthopedic Assn. Lutheran. Office: Helsinki U Ctrl Hosp, PO Box 266, FIN00029 HUS Finland

KANKOFER, MARTA ELIZABETH, veterinary biochemist, educator; b. Lublin, Poland, May 15, 1963; d. Waldemar and Danuta Kankofer. Degree in vet. surgery, Agrl. U., Lublin, 1987, D of Vet. Medicine, 1994. Asst. Inst. Biochemistry Faculty of Vet. Medicine, Lublin, 1987-95, dr. of vet. medicine, 1995—. Contbr. articles to profl. jours. Scholar Tempus, Hannover, Germany, 1990-91, Deutscher Akademiescher Austaudienst, Hannover, 1991-92, Polish Ministry Higher Edn., Utrecht, 1994-95. Mem. Internat. Fedn. Placental Assns. Home: Krakowskie Przedmiescie 51/10, 20-076 Lublin Poland Office: Inst Biochemistry Agrl U, Ul Lubartowska 58a, 20-123 Lublin Poland

KANN, HANS, concert pianist, composer, educator; b. Vienna, Feb. 14, 1927; s. Emil and Karoline (Jelinek) H.; m. Kue Hee Ha, Jan. 19, 1978; 1 child, Johann Sebastian. Grad. h.s., Vienna. Prof. piano U. of Arts, Tokyo, 1955-58, State Acad. Music, Darmstadt, Germany, 1962-67; prof. piano U. of Music, Vienna, 1977-95, prof. emeritus, 1995—. Contbr. articles to mus. publs., Austria and Japan. Avocations: collecting antique musical prints, historical musical instruments, ceramics, furniture. Fax: (43 1) 512-01-474. Home: Sonnenfelsgasse 11/14, A-1010 Vienna Austria

KANN, ISABEL, artist; b. Kingston, India, 1921; parents English citizens; Ed., Bournemouth Art Sch., 1942, Edinburgh Coll. Art, 1942-43, 46-48; BA, U. Toronto, 1974. Solo exhbns. at Nancy Poole's Studio, Silverstone Gallery, Montreal; group shows include RCA House, Cambridge Pub. Gallery, Lynwood Arts Ctr., Simcoe, Ont., NewEnglish Art Club, London; represented in collections at Can. Coun. Art Bank, Imperial Oil, Mary Kay Cosmetics, Shell Can., Union Gas, Royal Bank, Vanguard Trust, Gen. Electric Can., Inc., others; subject of articles. Address: Nancy Poole's Studio, 16 Hazelton Ave, Toronto, ON Canada M5K 2E2

KANN, KONSTANTIN BORISOVITCH, physics educator, physicist, researcher; b. Kherson, Ukraine, USSR, Apr. 23, 1936; s. Boris Isaakovitch and Zelda Tevelevna (Medvedeva) K.; m. Valentina Petrovna Bojandina, Sept. 15, 1969 (div. July 1974); 1 child, Nataly; m. Larissa Iljinitchna Podstrelova, Oct. 1957; children: Sergey, Vladimir, Dmitry. Degree in mining engring., Mining Inst., Dnepropetrovsk, USSR, 1958. Constrn. engr. Chem. Factory, Severodonezk, Ukraine, 1958-62; rsch. engr. Inst. Nuc. Physics, Novosibirsk, USSR, 1962-67; scientist Inst. Non-Organic Chemistry, Novosibirsk, USSR, 1967-71, Inst. Thermophysics, Novosibirsk, USSR, 1971-85; sr. scientist Inst. Northern Problems, Tyumen, USSR, 1985-92; chair physics dept. Stat Oil & Gas Univ., Tyumen, Russia, 1992—. Author: Capillary Hydrodynamic of Foams, 1989; contbr. articles to profl. jours. Mem. N.Y. Acad. Scis. Home: Scherbakova St 112/211, 625022 Tyumen Russia Office: Tyumen Stat Oil & Gas Univ, Volodarskogo St, 38625000 Tyumen Russia

KANN, PETER ROBERT, journalist, newspaper publishing executive; b. N.Y.C., Dec. 13, 1942; s. Robert A. and Marie (Breuer) K.; m. Francesca Mayer, Apr. 12, 1969 (dec. 1983); m. Karen Elliott House, 1984; children: Hillary Francesca, Petra Elliott, Jason Elliott, Jade Elliott. BA, Harvard U., 1964. With The Wall St. Jour., 1964—; journalist N.Y.C., 1964-67, Vietnam, 1967-68, Hong Kong, 1968-75; pub., editor Asian edit., 1976-79, assoc. pub., 1979-88; formerly asst. to chmn. and mem. exec. com. Dow Jones & Co., 1986-89, pres. internat. and mag. groups, 1986-89, also chmn. bd. dirs.; chmn. CEO, pub. Wall St. Jour., 1989—; pres. Dow Jones & Co., N.Y.C., 1989-91, chmn., CEO, 1991—; chmn. bd. Far Ea. Econ. Rev., 1987-89; mem. Pulitzer Prize Bd., 1987-96. Trustee Asia Soc., 1989-94, Inst. for Advanced Study, Princeton, N.J., 1990—, Aspen Inst., 1994—, Spelman Coll., 1994-97. Recipient Pulitzer prize for internat. reporting, 1972. Mem. Spee Club (Cambridge, Mass.). Office: Wall Street Journal Dow Jones & Co Inc 200 Liberty St New York NY 10281-1003

KANNAN, ANUPAMA, pathologist, consultant; b. Apr. 8, 1960. MD in Pathology, B.J. Med. Coll., Pune, India, 1986. Med. officer Ardeer Hosp., Gomia; pathologist Inlaks Genl. Hosp., Chembur, 1987, Bhikubai C. Jalundwala Genl. Hosp., Mumbai, 1988, Lakshmi Diagnostic Ctr., Chembur, 1989-92; cons. Niriksha Computerised Pathology Lab., Navi, Mumbai; pathologist Prerna Hopsp.; hon. lectr. Modern Coll., Vashi. Office: Niriksha Comp Pathol Lab, 31 Prabhat Ctr Sect 6, Navi Mumbai, India

KANNAN, V., math educator, researcher; b. Thanjavur, Tamil Nadu, India, Oct. 24, 1946; s. Varadachariar N. and V. (Rajalakshmi) K.; m. K. Manipaduka, May 10, 1971; chidlren: Rangarajan, Srinathan. MSc, Nat. Coll., Trichy, Madras, India, 1967; MPhil, Madurai (India) U., 1968, PhD, 1971. Lectr. Madurai U., 1972-76, reader, 1976-78; reader U. Hyderabad, 1978-85, prof., 1985—, dean, 1990-95. Recipient Career award for young scientists U. Grants Commn., 1981, nat. lectr. award, 1985. Fellow Indian Acad. Scis., Indian Nat. Sci. Acad.; mem. Indian Math. Soc. (pres. 1992-93), Indian Sci. Congress Assn. (sect. pres. 1994). Hindu. Avocations: Sanskrit literature, Hindu philosphy. E-mail: vksm@uhyd.ernet.in. Office: U Hyderabad, Ctrl Univ Post, Andhra Pradesh 500046, India

KANNER, DAN, communications executive, journalist; b. Petach Tikva, Israel, Dec. 4, 1945; s. Israel Zvi and Miriam Gertrude (Gutter) K.; m. Daphna Elizabeth Web, July 4, 1976 (div. 1992); children: Inbal, Anat. BA in Hebrew Lit., Art History, The Hebrew U., Jerusalem, 1972, MA in Comm., Journalism, 1997. Radio announcer Mil. Broadcasting Svc., Tel Aviv, Jaffa, 1964-65; presenter, anchorman of youth program Israel Broadcasting Authority TV, Jerusalem, 1970-89, announcer, anchorman (radio) Sta. KOL Israel,, 1966—; head dept. ops. Israel Broadcasting Authority, Jerusalem, 1970-94; spl. asst. to dir. Sta. KOL Israel, Israel Broadcasting Authority, 1994—; Master of Ceremony, numerous nat. and state ceremonies. Active Israel-Austria Friendship Assn., Mejtar Jewish Culture Assn. Sgt. Edn. Corps., Israeli Army, 1963-65. Home: 17 Mevo Horkanya, Maale Adumim 98 421, Israel Office: IBA Kol Israel, 21 Heleni Hamalka, Jerusalem 91 010, Israel

KANNER, GIDEON, lawyer; b. Lwów, Poland, Apr. 15, 1930; came to U.S., 1947; s. Stanley and Claire Kanner; children: Jonathan, Jesse. B of Mech. Engring., The Cooper Union, 1954; JD, U. So. Calif., 1961. Bar: Calif. 1962, U.S. Supreme Ct. 1967. Rocket engr. USN, N.J., 1954-55, Rocketdyne, Calif., 1955-64; assoc. Fadem & Kanner, L.S., 1964-74; prof. law Loyola U., L.A., 1974-90; assoc. Crosby, Heafey, Roach & May, L.A., 1990-95; lawyer Berger & Norton, Santa Monica, Calif., 1995—; cons. Calif. Law Revision Commn., 1968-77, 97—. Co-editor: Nichols on Eminent Domain, Compensation for Expropriation-A Comparative Study, Vol. II, 1990, After Lucas: Land Use Regulation and the Taking of Property Without Compensation, 1993; editor, pub. Just Compensation, 1974—; contbr. articles and revs. to profl. law jours. Recipient Shattuck prize Am. Inst. Real Estate Appraisers, 1973, Harrison Tweed Spl. Merit award for continuing legal edn. Am. Law Inst.-ABA, 1999. Home: PO Box 1741 Burbank CA 91507-1741 Office: Berger & Norton 1620 26th St Ste 200 Santa Monica CA 90404-4059

KANNIAH, JAGANNATHAN, engineering educator; b. Manalmedu, India, Jan. 6, 1945; arrived in Singapore, 1985; s. Nellore J. Kanniah Naidu and Bahirathi Ganthi (Kuppuswamy) K.; m. Gunasundari Purushotham, Sept. 6, 1972; children: Lakshminarayan, Priya, Reka. BE, Annamalai (India) U., 1969, MS in Engring., 1971; PhD, U. Calgary, Can., 1982. Assoc. lectr. S.V.U. Coll. Engring., Tirupati, India, 1971-74, U. Madras Coll. Engring., 1974-77; lectr. A.C. Coll. Engring. and Tech., Karaikudi, India, 1977-78; rsch. asst., vis. scientist U. Calgary, 1978-83; asst. prof. NBKR Inst. Tech., Vidyanagar, India, 1983-85; from lectr. to sr. lectr. dept. engring. Singapore Poly., 1985-94, head sect. robotics and digital control, 1991—, prin. lectr., 1994—. Contbr. articles to profl. jours. Mem. IEE, IEEE, Robotics and Automation Soc. of IEEE (mem. internat. bd. dirs. 1996-97), Robotics Game Soc. Singapore (founding). Hindu. Avocation: writing poetry. Home: 124 Jurong E ST 13 No 10-05, Singapore Singapore Office: Singapore Poly EC Dept, 500 Dover Rd, Singapore 139651, Singapore

KANNINEN, MARKKU TAPANI, ecologist; b. Jyväskylä, Finland, Oct. 22, 1952; s. Hugo Armas and Aili Helena (Karjalainen) K.; children: Perttu, Ohto. MSc in Forestry, U. Helsinki, Finland, 1977, PhD, 1985. Asst., part-time lectr. U. Helsinki, 1978-84, acting assoc. prof. silviculture, 1983-84; rsch. mgr. Found. Rsch. of Natural Resources in Finland, 1985-90; project mgr. Finnish Rsch. Programme on Climate Change/Acad. Finland, Helsinki, 1990-95; rsch. dir. Centro Agronomica Tropical de Investigation y Ensenanza, Turrialba, Costa Rica, 1996—; Editor-in-chief Jours. of Silva Fennica and Acta Forestalia Fennica, 1985-90; contbr. articles to profl. jours. Mem. Soc. Forestry in Finland (sec. 1985-90), Brit. Ecol. Soc., Internat. Soc. Tropical Foresters, Ecol. Soc. Am. Office: Acad Finland, CATIE, Turrialba Costa Rica

KANNO, AKIRA, professional society administrator; b. Tokyo, Dec. 1, 1932; s. Sokichi and Kiyoko (Hatta) K.; m. Yasuko Matsumoto, Nov. 15, 1957; children: Yaeko Tomita, Yuta Kanno. BA, Tokyo U., 1955; MA, Yale U., 1963. Exec. dir. Bank of Japan, Tokyo, 1986-92; dep. gov. Export-Import Bank, Tokyo, 1992-94; vice chmn. Japanese Bankers Assn., Tokyo, 1994—. Home: Kouyama 4-12-14, Nerima-ku 176-0022, Japan Office: Tokyo Bankers Assn Inc, 3-1 Marunouchi 1-chome, Chiyoda-ku Tokyo 100-8216, Japan

KANNO, HIROSHI, neurosurgeon; b. Yokosuka, Japan, Sept. 12, 1955; s. Tatsuo and Kazuko (Matsunaga) K.; m. Yoko Morita, Nov. 4, 1984; children: Yumi, Ryo, Shu. MD, Hirosaki U., Japan, 1983; PhD, Yokohama City U., Japan, 1987. Neurosrugeon Kanagawa Children Med. Ctr., Yokohama, Japan, 1987, Odawara Mcpl. Hosp., Japan, 1987-88, Kanagawa Rehab. Ctr., Atsugi, Japan, 1988-90, Nishiarai Hosp., Tokyo, 1990-92; neurosrugeon Yokohama City U. Hosp., 1992—, asst. prof., 1997—; dir. depot. neurosrugery Yokohama City U. Hosp., 1999—. Contbr. articles to profl. jours. Grantee Min. Edn. Sci. & Culture, Japan, 1994-96, 97-98. Avocations: golf, tennis. Home: 2-7-8Nagata-higashi, Yokohama 232-0072, Japan Office: Yokohama City U Sch Med, Dept Neurosurgery 3-9 Fukuura, Kanazana-ku Yokohama 236-0004, Japan

KANNO, YOSHINORI, material scientist, educator; b. Tokiwamachi, Fukushima, Japan, June 12, 1950; s. Yoshichika and Tori K.; m. Mikiko Hirose, Dec. 26, 1981; 2 children. Bachelor, Tokyo U. Agr. and Tech., 1975, Master, 1977; PhD, Tokyo Inst. Tech., 1982. Rschr. Govt. Indsl. Rsch. Inst., Nogoya, Japan, 1982-87; assoc. prof. Nantes (France) U., 1990-92, Okayama (Japan) U., 1994; prof. Yamanashi U., Kfu, Japan, 1997—. Avocations: jazz, boxing. Home: 2-23-10 Myojincho, Tokyo Hachiouji 400-8511, Japan Office: Yamanashi U Dept Mech Sys, Takeda 4-3-11, Yamanash Kofu 400-8511, Japan

KANNOURAKIS, GEORGE, pediatrician, hematologist, oncologist, medical researcher; b. Sianna, Greece, Aug. 16, 1954; arrived in Australia, 1961; s. Triantafillos and Maria (Hagioglou) K.; m. Trudi Christine Martin; children: Joshua, Rebecca. MB, BS, Monash U., 1978, BSc, 1978; PhD, U. Melbourne, 1989. Resident in pediatrics Queen Victoria Hosp., Melbourne, Australia, 1979-81; pediat. registrar Royal Children's Hosp., Melbourne, 1981-83; rsch. fellow Walter and Eliza Hall Inst., Melbourne, 1984-88, Nat. Health & Med. Rsch. Coun., Melbourne, 1988-96; rsch. fellow in medicine Childrens Hosp./Dana-Farber Cancer Inst., Boston, 1988-89; rsch. fellow Harvard U., Boston, 1988-89; head hematology/oncology rsch. Royal Children's Hosp., 1990-96; adv. bd. Internat. Severe Chronic Neutropenia Registry, 1994—; cons. AMGEN, 1994—; dir. cancer rsch. U. Ballarat, 1996—. Fellow Royal Australian Coll. Physicians, Coll. Pediat.; mem. Internat. Soc. Hematology, Am. Soc. Hematology, Am. Soc. Microbiology, Clin. Oncol. Soc. Australia, Am. Assn., Cancer Rsch. Avocations: tennis, gardening, bush walking. Home: Marion House, 1002 Mair St, Ballarat Victoria 3350, Australia Office: St John of God Hosp, Cancer Rsch Ctr-1002 Mair St, Ballarat 3350, Australia

KANNUS, VELI PEKKA, sports medicine physician, educator; b. Kangasala, Tampere, Finland, July 29, 1959; s. Pauli Aulis and Pirkko Amalia (Ulvinen) K.; m. Johanna Maarit Vihervuori, July 22, 1989; children: Katariina, Kristian. MD, Med. Sch. Tampere, 1984, PhD, 1988; assoc. prof., U. Jyväskylä, Finland, 1991, U. Tampere, 1995. Resident physician Rsch. Ctr. Sports Medicine, Tampere, 1987-91; rsch. fellow physician U. Vt., Burlington, 1989-90; specialist in sports medicine Rsch. Ctr. Sports Medicine, Tampere, 1991-92; sr. rsch. fellow Accident and Trauma Rsch. Ctr. UKK Inst., Tampere, 1992, chief physician, head Accident and Trauma Rsch. Ctr., 1993—; vis. prof. U. Vt. Sch. Medicine, Burlington, 1994; cons. to several nat. orgns. in field of sports, exercise and osteoporosis; keynote lectr. IV World Congress on Sports Sci., Monaco, 1997. Author: Human Tendons, 1997; sect. editor Scandinavian Jour. Medicine and Sci. in Sports; fgn. cons. editor Clin. Exercise Physiology; mem. editl. bd. Isokinetics and Exercise Sci., Sports Medicine Digest, Phys Sportsmed, Brit. Jour. Sports Medicine, Clin. Jour. Sport Medicine; contbr. numerous articles to profl. jours.; patentee in field. Recipient Vince Higgings Keynote Lectr. award Australian Conf. of Sci. and Medicine in Sport, 1995. Mem. Finnish Soc. Sports Medicine (pres. 1992-98), Scandinavian Found. Medicine and Sci. in Sports (pres. 1997-98), N.Y. Acad. Sci. Lutheran. Avocations: jogging, cross-country skiing, gardening, playing with kids. Office: UKK Inst Accident and Trauma Rsch Ctr, Box 30, FIN33501 Tampere Finland

KANNUSAMY, GANESH GANI (GANESH GANI, GANI GANESH), industrialist, software company executive; b. Srirangam, Trichy TN, India, Mar. 12, 1941; s. Peria Kannusamy and Alamelu Kannusamy; m. Jane Janaki, Aug. 24, 1961; children: Vijaya Krishnamoorthi, Rajesh Kavitha, Guruprasad, Shweta, Kiran. B Commerce, St. Joseph's U., Bangalore, India, 1960; M Commerce, U. Mysore, 1961; DSc, Sci. Inst., Bangalore, 1963. Proprietor Ganesh Silk Factory; mng. ptnr. Kannusamy & Co., Bangalore, 1963-65; sales mgr. Vickers Plc, London, 1965-75; dir. Paperodex Shreepack, Shreekailash Dairy Farm, Krishnagiri, India, Jayalakshmi Silk Mills, SRI, Ambal Silk Stores, Vijayapuram Tiravarur, Shreekalilash Shreepack, Kailashagiri; mng. dir. Ganeshwari Group, Bangalore, 1975-85; chmn., CEO Ganeshwar Inficons, Bangalore and Washington, 1985—; fin. mgmt. cons. Pub. Rels. Soc. India; vis. faculty mem. govt. of India Sci. and Tech. Exec. Devel. Program. Author: Packaging Management, Quality Control & Waste Management, Crew Education and Training, Agile Management System. Dist. commr. World Scouts Meet, 1975; leader Indian delegation Youth Camp Cairo, 1964, Indian Delegation Family Exch., 1984, Group Study Exch., Perth, Western Australia, Toronto, Ont., Can., 1983, Asia-Pacific Boy Scouts Jamboree, Colombo, Ceylon, 1995; hon. Traffic Warden, Karnataka Police Dept.; hon. Wildlife Warden, Worldwide Fund for Nature; hon. Inspector, Soc. Prevention for Cruelty to Animals, Indian Red Cross. Paul Harris fellow Rotary Found., Evanston, Ill., 1983, Baden-Powell fellow World Scouts Found., Geneva, 1986; recipient Rotary Youth Leadership award Rotary Found., 1953. Fellow Inst. Mgmt. (Lifetime Achievement award), Inst. Packaging Profls.; mem. U.S.-India Bus. Coun., Washington, 1994, Inst. Dirs. Quality Assurance U.K., Inst. Quality Assurance (lead assessor), All India Mgmt. Assn. (bd. dirs.), Am. Bus. Coun., Am. Chamber, South India Coun. (chmn.), Indo-Am. C. of C. (chmn.), Bangalore Mgmt. Assn. India (dir.), Am. Mgmt. Assn., Non Resident Indians Assn., Indian Nat. Congress, Mysore Pradesh Youth Congress, Dist. Industries Assn. (pres.), Dist. Devel. Coun. (adv.), Bombay Natural History Soc., Nat. Geog. Soc., Bangalore Freemasons Soc., Discharged Life Prisoners Aid Soc., Internat. Soc. Krishna Consciousness, Ramakrishna Mission Rural Devel. Swami Vivekananda U., Swami Vivekananda Trust (pres.), Hindu Mission Hosp. (v.p.), U.S. C. of C. (dir. bus. coun.), Jr. Chamber Internat. (dist. chmn. 1965), Rotary Internat. (dist. chmn. 1985, counselor), Masons. Kailash Ashram. Avocations: collecting coins, stamps, miniature bottles and dolls., tennis, golf. Home: PO Box 12 GaneshCenter, Multiplex Kailashagiri, Krishnagiri 635001, India Office: Ganeshwar Inficons, 45 Basappa Rd, Shanthinagar, Bangalore 560027, India

KANONOWICZ, ROBERT PETER, obstetrician, gynecologist; b. Warsaw, Masovia, Poland, Jan. 19, 1956; s. Peter and Ursula (Hubicka) K.; m. Margareth Maria Ciołkowska, Dec. 29, 1979; children: Martin, Peter. MD, Warsaw Ned. Acad., 1979. Med. diplomate. Asst. Warsaw, 1979-81; intern in gynecology, internal medicine, surgery and pediat., 1980-81; asst. Zurich, Switzerland, 1981-82; asst. I Ob-Gyn., Warsaw, 1982-84; sr. asst. II Warsaw, 1984-92; sr. asst. Pretoria, South Africa, 1992; sr. asst. Cancer Inst., Warsaw, 1992-94, cons.; cons. Saint Family Hosp, Warsaw, Lot, Polish airline, Warsaw; mem. Ob-Gyn. Coun., Warsaw, Menopause and Andropausa Coun., Poland. Inventor H Replacement Therapy. Mem. N.Y. Acad. Scis. Roman Catholic. Avocations: yachting, skiing, music, art. Home: 2 Grottgera St 29-30, 00785 Warsaw Poland Office: 16/22 Elektoralna St Apt 9, 00139 Warsaw Poland

KANORIA, MRIDULA, physicist; b. Calcutta, India, Mar. 22, 1955; d. Manohar and Gyan (Jain) K. BSc, Bethune Coll., 1974; MSc, Calcutta U., 1976, PhD, 1984. From jr. rsch. fellow to sr. rsch. fellow Calcutta U., 1978-82; rsch. assoc., then vis. scientist Indian Statis. Inst., Calcutta, 1984—. Mem. Indian Statis. Inst., Indian Soc. Theoretical & Applied Mechs., Calcutta Math. Soc. Avocations: books, music, gardening. Home: 2/1 A Nando Mullick Ln, 700 006 Calcutta W Bengal, India

KANT, KRISHNAN, Indian vice president; b. Kot Mohammed Khan, Punjab, Amritsar Dist., India, Feb. 28, 1927; married. MSc in Tech., Banaras Hindu U. Past scientist Coun. Sci. and Indsl. Rsch.; mem. Congress Party Govt. of India, until 1975, mem. Rajya Sabha, 1966-71, elected to Lok Sabha, 1971, nat. exec. mem. Janata Party, 1977-88, v.p., 1997—; journalist; writer. Mem. Janata Party. Avocation: Urdu poetry. Office: Office VP Bharat Ka Up Rashtrapati, 6 Maulana Azad Rd, New Delhi 110 011, India*

KANTARELLI, NURETTIN, apparel company executive; b. Istanbul, Turkey, Oct. 18, 1953; s. Nazim and Nezihe (Ural) K.; m. Ursula Prusak, Feb. 15, 1982; children: Can Atilla, Defne Selma. BA, Bosphorus U., Istanbul, 1981. Cert. in bus. adminstrn. Procurement mgr. Nasas A.S., Istanbul, 1983-85; gen. mgr. Internas S.A., Geneva, Switzerland, 1985-88; fin. dir. Essex Metals Ltd., Chelmsford, Eng., 1988-91; CFO Ascott A.S., Istanbul, 1992-94; dep. gen. mgr. Mavi Giyim A.S., Istanbul, 1994-96, CEO, 1996—. Named one of 50 Top Successful Mgrs. in Turkey, 1997. Mem. Bosphorus U. Alumni, Ortakoy Sports Club (dir. 1994-95), Galatasaray Sports Club. Avocations: reading, basketball, soccer, computers. Office: Mavi Giyim San Ve Tic AS Gumussuyu Cad Faith, Sehitleri Sk 3/2, Topkapi Istanbul 34020, Turkey

KANTAWALA, SURESHACHANDRA GOVINDLAL, humanities educator, researcher; b. Vadodara, India, July 14, 1930; s. Govindlal Harilal and Kesarben Govindlal K.; m. Virbala Jariwala, May 2, 1955; children: Bhavana, Pragna, Amita. BA with honors, U. Baroda, Vadodara, India, 1951, MA, 1953, PhD, 1959, cert. in German, 1962, cert. in French, 1966, cert. in linguistics, 1968. Tutor in Sanskrit, U. Baroda, 1951-57, lectr., 1957-70, reader, 1970-80, prof., 1980-90, dir. Oriental Inst.,, 1982-87, dean Faculty of Arts,, 1988-90, Shastra Chudamani scholar, 1995-97; nat. lectr. Univ. Grants Commn., New Delhi, 1985-86. Author: Research Study: Cultural History from the Matsya Purana, 1964, Research Study: Legends in Puranas, 1995, Studies in Puranas, 1999; contbr. over 170 articles to profl. jours. Recipient Silver Jubilee award All India Kashiraj Trust, 1983, Pres. award of Cert. of Honor, 1998. Mem. All India Oriental Conf. (pres. Vedic sect. 1985, 89, pres. Indian linguistics sect. 1993, treas.). Avocation: listening to music. Home: Shri Ram, Kantareshwar Mahadev's Pole, Bajwada Vadodara Gujarat 390 001, India

KANTER, DONALD RICHARD, pharmaceutical executive; b. Detroit, Jan. 22, 1951; s. Harry Richard and Dorothy May (Kelch) K.; m. Diane Lynn Fickert, July 9, 1971 (div. Sept. 1993); children: Sean Richard, Donald Mathew, Lauren Marie. BA, Oakland U., Rochester, Mich., 1976; MS, Eastern Mich. U., 1979; PhD, U. Cin., 1983. Instr., lectr. U. Cin., 1978-84; health scis. officer VA med. Ctr., Cin., 1980-85; supr. med. affairs Genetic Systems, Seattle, 1985-88; dir. stats. and clin. rsch. Solvay Pharm.; pres., CEO PharmData, Inc.; cons. in field. Author: (with Karoly et al) Child Health Psychology, 1982; (with Daniel B. Berch) Sustained Attention in Human Performance, 1983; contbr. med. articles to profl. jours. Oakland U. grantee, 1976, NIMH grantee, 1984, VA merit grantee, 1984, Outstanding Contbn. award, 1985. Mem. AAAS, Sigma Xi. Roman Catholic. Home: 2034 Kinridge Trl Marietta GA 30062-1828 Office: Bldg E 205 1000 Johnson Ferry Rd Ste E205 Marietta GA 30068-2175

KANTHRAJ, GAREHATTY RUDRAPPA, dermatologist; b. Chitradurga, India, June 29, 1968; s. Garehatty and Garehatty (Leelavathy) R. MBBS, J.S.S. Med. Coll., Mysore, India, 1993; MD, Kasturba Med. Coll., Manipal, India, 1997. Jr. resident Kasturba Med. Coll., Manipal, India, 1994-97; sr. resident GOA Med. Coll., Bambolim, India, 1997-98; with Govt. Med. Coll. Hosps., Bellary, Karnataka, India, 1998—. Contbr. articles to profl. jours. Mem. (life) Indian Assn. Dermatologists, Venereologists and Leprologists. Avocations: reading, travel, writing, music. Home: No 254 I Stage Brindavan, 570 020 Mysore India Office: Dept Skin & STD, Govt Med Coll & Hosps VIMS, 583 104 Bellary, Karnataka India

KÁNTOR, LAJOS, writer, editor-in-chief; b. Kolozvâr (Cluj), Transylvania, Romania, Aug. 7, 1937; s. Lajos K. and Irén Hantos; m. Erzsébet Nagy, Dec. 21, 1963; children: László, István. Literary diplomate, Bolyai U., Kolozsvâr, Romania, 1959; D in Literary Scis., Babes-Bolyai U., Cluj, Romania, 1979. Editor Korunk, Kolozsvâr, Romania, 1959-90; editor-in-chief Korunk, Kolozsvâr, 1990—. Author: Hungarian Literature in Romania, 1971, A Journey Around the Modern Arts, 1972, Attila Jozsef in Transylvania, 1980, Lyrical Poetry and short Story, 1981, A Literary Debate (1929-1930), 1984, Hamlet in Transylvania, 1990, Transylvanian Chronicle (1911-1959), 1992, My Hungarian-Romanian Relations, 1993, Hungarian Theatre in Romania, 1994, Who Was Domokos Szilagyi?, 1996, László Szabédi and the History, 1999; contbr. short stories, descriptions of journeys to Hungarian Literature in Romania, articles to literary jours. Pres. Union of Hungarian Democrats in Kolozsvar, Cluj, Romania, 1989-90. Decorated officer's cross Order of Hungarian Republic, 1997; recipient Timoter Ciparíu prize Acad. Romania, 1975, Pulitzer prize, 1992. Mem. Assn. Hungarian Journalists in Romania (pres. 1993-97), Assn. Romanian Writers, Assn. Hungarian Writers, Internat. Soc. Hungarian Lang. and Culture (co-pres. 1993-2000), PEN Club. Home: 15 str Croitorilor, 3400 Cluj-Napoca Cluj, Romania Office: Rev Korunk, 14 str Iasilor, 3400 Cluj-Napoca Cluj, Romania

KANTOR, LEV YAKOVLEVICH, communications company executive, researcher; b. Minsk, Belorussia, USSR, Mar. 6, 1928; s. Yakov Jesekilevich and Debora Faivushevna (Lurie) K.; m. Elisaveta Mikhailovna Goldberg, July 25, 1952; 1 child, Eugenia. Engr., Moscow State Tech. Comms. U., 1950, MSc, 1962, DSc, 1974. Rschr. Radio Rsch. Inst., Moscow, 1959-62, sr. rschr., 1962-70, head satellite comms. dept., 1970-95, chief rschr., 1995—; dir. for R&D, CJSC BONUM-1, Moscow, 1995—; chmn. com. R.F. Ministry of Comms. Sci. and TEch. Coun., Moscow, 1997—. Author: Satellite Broadcasting, 1981; author, editor: Handbook of Satellite Telecommunication and Broadcasting, 1983, 3d edit., 1997; chief designer Orbita, Gorizont, Mars. Recipient USSR State award, 1968, 81. Mem. Internat. Informatisation Acad. Home: Nicolo-Yamsky 3a-2-56, 109004 Moscow Russia Office: CJSC BONUM-1, Kazakova 16, 103064 Moscow Russia

KANTOR, TIBOR, chemistry researcher, educator; b. Mesztegnyo, Somogy, Hungary, Nov. 3, 1930; s. Bela and Franciska (Deak) K.; m. Margit Bobinac, May 10, 1954 (div. 1957); 1 child, Kornel; m. Barbara Kormany, June 15, 1966; children: Tibor, Bela. Bachelor's degree, Tech. U. Budapest, Hungary, 1953, Master's degree, 1965; PhD, Hungarian Acad. Scis., Budapest, 1975, D of Chem. Sci., 1987. Cert. in engring. Rsch. chemist Rsch. Inst. Physics, Budapest, 1953-69; sr. rsch. chemist Tech. U. Budapest, 1969-90; prof. Eötvös U., Budapest, 1991—. Author: Emission Spectroscopy in Comprehensive Analytical Chemistry, 1974; contbr. numerous sci. papers to internat. jours. Rsch. grantee Hungarian Sci. Found., 1991-97. Office: Lorand Eötvös U Dept Inorganic & Analytical Chemistry, PO Box 32, H-1518 Budapest Hungary

KANTOROWICZ-TORO, DONALD MANUEL, investment banker; b. Cali, Colombia, Aug. 4, 1945; arrived in Eng., 1980; s. Rodolph Kantorowicz and Livia Toro; m. Chantal Lancrenon, Sept. 15, 1974 (div. 1984); children: Melanie Tatina, Joanna Joy; m. Laura Puyana Bickenbach, July 1999. B, Gen Sch. Cali, 1965; MBA, Welthandel Coll., Vienna, Austria, 1969; PhD in Econs., U. Paris, 1972. V.p., mgr. Bank of Am., Madrid and Paris, 1973-80; CEO Consolidado Banking Group, London, 1980-95; 1st v.p. Merrill Lynch, London, 1995—; rep., agt. Vesteocpartners, London, 1987-93. Mem. Societe Francaise d'Analistis Financieres, Club Interallie Paris. Roman Catholic.

KANWAR, NEERAJ SINGH, manufacturing executive; b. Delhi, India, Sept. 6, 1971; s. Onkar Singh and Taru (Kapoor) K.; m. Simran Marwah; 1 child, Jaikaran O.S. BS in Indsl. Engring., Lehigh U., 1993. Cert. indsl. engring. in mfg. sys. Mgmt. trainee Am. Express Bank, N.Y., 1993-94; exec. trainee Apollo Tyres Ltd., New Delhi, 1994-95, gen. mgr., 1996-97; mgr. Global Fin. Ltd., New Delhi, 1995-96, chief mfg. and strategic planning and whole time dir., 1997—. Mem. Confedn. Indian Industry, Young Entrepreneurs Orgn. (co-chmn. 1999). Avocations: tennis, swimming, music, reading, traveling. Home: Apt A-301, 6 Aurangzeb Rd, New Delhi 110011, India Office: Apollo Tyres Ltd, 7 Inst Area Sec 32, Gurgaon Haryana 122 001, India

KANYA, MARY MADZANDZA, diplomat; m. Leo L. Kanya. Amb. AE&P to U.S. Govt. of Swaziland, D.C., 1994—. Office: Embassy of the Kingdom 3400 International Dr NW Washington DC 20008-3006

KANZER, LARRY, small business owner, food service director; b. Albany, N.Y., June 13, 1942; s. Sanford and Beatrice Helen (Strick) K.; m. Ginger Sherman, July 13, 1966 (div. 1983); 1 child, Glen Harris; m. Lynn Karen Trost, June 2, 1985. AAS in Culinary Arts, N.Y.C. Community Coll., 1962; Cert. Food Service supr., Auburn U., 1982-83; Master Locksmith, Foley Belsaw Inst., 1985. Food beverage controller Longchamps Restaurants, N.Y.C., 1962-65; dir. food service Laurelcrest Prep. Sch., Bristol, Conn., 1965-69; owner, operator Anze's Place Restaurant, Nashua, N.H., 1969-73; dir. food service Servend-Seilers, Waltham, Mass., 1973-76, Service Systems, Cambridge, Mass., 1976-78, ARA Services, White Plains, N.Y., 1978-88; owner Lots of Lock, Etc., 1988—. Com. chmn. Cub Scouts Am., Nashua, 1977-80; umpire Little League, Nashua, 1978-81. Served to sgt. USMCR, 1963-69. Recipient Otto Klitgord Meml. award N.Y.C. Community Coll., Bklyn., 1962, Student Govt. Service award, 1962, Cert. of Merit Jewish War Vets. of U.S., Bronx, N.Y., 1982, Cert. and Publ. Locksmith Ledger, Nat. Locksmith, Cert. Cmty. Svc., Pike County Sheriff's Office. Mem. Rte. 739 Bus. Coun. (treas. 1999, 2000), Pike County C. of C. Democrat. Avocations; gunsmithing, clock repair, woodworking, antiques, gardening. Office: Lots of Lock Etc Locksmith Shop Hemlock Plz Rt 739 Hawley PA 18428

KAO, CHARLES KUEN, electrical engineer, educator; b. Shanghai, China, Nov. 4, 1933; s. Chun-Hsien and Tisung Fong K.; m. May Wan Wong, Sept. 19, 1959; children—Simon M.T., Amanda M.C. B.Sc. in Elec. Engring., U. London, 1957, Ph.D. in Elec. Engring., 1965. Devel. engr. Standard Telephones & Cables Ltd., London, 1957-60; prin. research engr. Standard Telecommunications Lab. Ltd., Harlow, Eng., 1960-70; prof. electronics, chmn. dept. Chinese U. Hong Kong, 1970-74, vice chancellor, 1987-96; chief scientist Electro Optical Products div./ITT, Roanoke, Va., 1974-81; v.p., dir. engring. Electro Optical Products div./ITT, Roanoke, VA, 1981-83; exec. scientist, dir. research ITT Advanced Tech. Ctr., Shelton, Conn., 1983-87; chmn., CEO Transtech Svcs. Group Ltd., Hong Kong, 1996—. Author: Optical Fiber Technology II, 1981, Optical Fibers Systems: Technology, Design and Applications, 1982, Optical Fibre, 1988, A Choice Fulfilled--The Business of High Technology, 1991; contbr. articles to profl. jours.; patentee in field. Decorated Commdr. Brit. Empire, 1993; recipient Morey award Am. Ceramic Soc., 1976, Stewart Ballantine medal Franklin Inst., 1977, Rank prize Rank Trust Funds, 1978, LM Ericsson Internat. prize, 1979, gold medal Armed Forces Comm. and Electronics Assn., 1980, Internat. C & C prize Found. for C & C Promotion, Japan, 1987, New Materials prize Am. Phys. Soc., 1989, Gold medal Internat. Soc. for Optical Engring., 1992, Japan prize The Sci. and Tech. Found. Japan, 1996; Marconi Internat. fellow, 1985. Fellow IEEE (Morris Liebmann Meml. award 1978, Alexander Graham Bell medal 1985, Faraday medal 1989), Inst. Elec. Engring. (U.K.), Chinese Acad. Scis., Royal Soc. (U.K.), Royal Acad. Engring. (U.K.), Royal Swedish Acad. Engring. Scis. (fgn. mem.), Academia Sinica (Taiwan); mem. NAE (U.S., Charles Stark Draper prize 1999). Office: 1-9 ON Hing Terrace, 20/F ON Hing Bldg, Central Hong Kong China

KAO, CHIANG, management educator; b. Taipei, Taiwan, Dec. 4, 1952; s. Run Wu and Hui Chin (Liu) K.; m. Min Fuh, Sept. 16, 1984; children: Wei-Kan, Wei-Han, Wei-Fan. BS, Nat. Taiwan U., 1975; MS, Oreg. State U., 1977, PhD, 1979. Head dept. indsl. mgmt. Nat. Cheng Kung U., Tainan, Taiwan, 1981-86, dean univ. librs., 1994-96, dean coll. mgmt., 1996—; vis. prof. Purdue U., West Lafayette, Ind., 1986-87; prof. S.W. Tex. State U., 1989-90; guest prof. Aachen (Germany) U. Tech., 1994. Editor-in-chief Jour. of Chinese Inst. Indsl. Engrs., 1992-94; contbr. articles to profl. jours. Recipient Disting. Rsch. award Nat. Sci. Coun., Taiwan, 1994, 96, 98; named Disting. Instr., Ministry of Edn., Taiwan, 1993. Mem. Assn. Mgmt. Sci., Assn. Chinese Inst. of Indsl. Engrs. Office: Nat Cheng Kung Univ, 1 University Rd, Tainan 701, Taiwan

KAO, MING-CHIEN, neurosurgeon; b. Taipei, Taiwan, Jan. 3, 1939; m. Chung-Mei Tsai; children: Laurence, Frances. MD, Nat. Taiwan U., 1964; DMS, Tokyo Med. and Dental U., 1973. Clin. fellow in neurosurgery Tokyo U., 1972-73; neurosurg. resident Harvard Med. Sch., Cambridge, Mass., 1974-75; prof. neurosurgery Nat. Taiwan U. Hosp., 1983—, chmn. divsn. neurosurgery, 1995—; dir. laser medicine rsch. ctr. Nat. Taiwan U., 1987; cons. Neurosurg. Soc. China, 1996. Mem. Laser Medicine Soc. (pres. 1984-90), Internat. Soc. Laser Surgery and Medicine (pres. 1987-89), Chinese Assn. Endoscopic Surgery (pres. 1994), China Med. Assn. (editor-in-chief 1995—), Taipei Med. Assn. (editor-in-chief 1994—), China Med. Assn. (bd. dirs. 1995—), Taipei Med. Assn. (standing dir. 1993—), Internat. Coll. Surgeons (bd. dirs. 1996), Taiwan Neurosurg. Soc. (pres. 1999—), Cardiovasc. Disease Prevention and Treatment Found. (pres. 2000—). Office: Nat Taiwan U Hosp, #7 Chung-Shan S Rd, Taipei Taiwan

KAO, TSAIR, biomedical engineering educator, researcher; b. Tienchin, China, Sept. 6, 1948; s. Hong-Yu Kao and Shyan-Te Cheng; m. Chien-Chiou Liu, Oct. 7, 1974; children: Yii-Leh, Yii-Lin. BS, Chung Cheng Inst. Tech., Taoyuan, Taiwan, 1970; MS, Northwestern U., 1976; PhD, U. Mich., 1984. Assoc. prof. Chung Cheng Inst. Tech., 1984-88; prof. biomed. engring. Nat. Yang-Ming U., Taipei, Taiwan, 1990—, chmn. Inst. Biomed. Engring., 1989-94, dean gen. affairs, 1994-96; mem. med. devices subcom. Nat. Bur. Stds., Taipei, 1985—; cons. dept. med. engring. Tri-Svc. Gen. Hosp., Taipei, 1987-91; presenter Biomed. Engring. Conf., 1997. Co-Author: Introduction to Computer Science, 1991; editor-in-chief Chinese Jour. Med. and Biol. Engring., 1990-94; contbr. articles to sci. jours. Sect. dir. Sun Yat-sen Inst. on Policy R & D, Taipei, 1994-97. Capt. Taiwan Navy, 1970-88. Recipient Hai-Feng medal Ministry Nat. Def., Taipei, 1986, Hai-chi medal, 1987, Chung-chin medal, 1991. Mem. IEEE, Biomed. Engring. Soc. Home: PO Box 16-16, Taipei 112, Taiwan Office: Nat Yang-Ming U Inst Biomed, Engring 155, Sec 2 Li-Lung, Taipei 112, Taiwan

KAPADIA, YEZAD SAM, retired engineering executive, consultant; b. Bombay, India, Oct. 12, 1934; s. Sam Sohrabji and Perin Sam (Madon) K.; m. Rati Yezad Keravalla, Jan. 11, 1962; children: Jeroo, Rukshna. BS, Bombay U., 1954; diplom ingenieur, Tech. U., Aachen, Germany, 1958. Supt. blast furnaces Tata Steel, Jamshedpur, 1970-76, asst. gen. supt. iron and steel, 1976-78, dep. gen. supt., 1978-79, gen. supt., 1979-86, gen. mgr., 1986-87; mng. dir. Lurgi India, New Delhi, 1987-95; ret., 1995; mng. dir. Kapadia Cons. (P) Ltd., India, 1987—; dir. FAG (India), 1995—; chmn. Tata Korf, India, 1997—. Contbr. articles to profl. jours. Trustee Jamshedpur Parsi Agiari, 1980—, Delhi Parsi Anjuman, Delhi, 1987—. Recipient Metallurgist's award Min. Mines and Steel, Govt. India, Delhi, 1976. Mem. German Iron and Steel Inst., Indian Iron and Steel Inst., India Internat. Ctr. (assoc.). Zoroastrian. Avocations: sports, reading. Home and Office: 9 Silver Oaks Ave, Dlf City Phase I, Gurgaon 122002, India

KAPANGA, ANDRE, diplomat. Dem. Republic of Congo rep. UN, N.Y.C. Office: Permanent Rep Dem Republic of Congo to UN 866 U N Plz Rm 511 New York NY 10017-1822

KAPASI, FAIYAZ MOHAMED, urologist; b. Mahuva, Bhavnagar, India, Nov. 10, 1960; s. Mohamed Fidahusein and Khairunnissa Mohamed (Rajani) K.; m. Sukaina Faiyaz Peerbhoy, Apr. 11, 1988; children: Kamil Ali, Anam. MBBS, M.P. Shah Med. Sch., India, 1983, M in Surgery, 1983. House officer Sir. T. Hosp., Bhavnagar, 1983-84; sr. house officer Irwin Hosp., Jamnagar, India, 1984-85, registrar, 1985-87, sr. registrar, 1987; asst. surgeon Habib Hosp., Bombay, 1988; registrar Liverpool/North Wales Hosp., United Kingdom, 1988-93; staff urologist Yeovil (United Kingdom) Dist. Hosp., 1994-96, Medway Hosp., Gillingham, 1996-98, Princess Alexandra Hosp., Harlow, 1998—; cons. urologist Huntington Hosp., 1998. Fellow Internat. Coll. Surgeons, Assn. Surgeons of India, European Bd. of Urology. Avocations: current affairs, cricket, photography. Office: Princess Alexandra Hosp, St Margaret Hosp/Epping, Bishops Stortoford 5, United Kingdom

KAPDI, MOHAMMED NOOR, investment company executive; b. Cape Town, South Africa, Mar. 28, 1961; s. Mohammed Ali Gadlta (Balla) K.; m. Minaxie Trueshane Gihwala (div. Mar. 1988); m. Fatima Ismail Timol, Dec. 20, 1993; children: Khatija, Ammaarah, Isra. B Proc., U. Cape Town, 1984. Prosecutor Dept. Justice, South Africa, 1985-87; sr. mgr. Village Reef, South Africa, 1988-89; candidate atty. Bodensteins, 1990-92; dir. Kapdi & Daniels, Cape Town, 1992—; dir., dep. chairperson Wesgro SA, Cape Town, 1995—; dir. Mnyama, 1997; cons. Merctor Cons., 1996, Malawi Investment, 1997; dir. Western Cape Bus. Forum, 1996. Author: Legislation-Informac Sector. Trustee Islamic Coun., 1995; cons. Dept. Econ. Affairs, Western Cape, 1996, Dept. of Sport, Western Cape, 1996, Dept. Transport, Western Cape, 1996. Mem. Dutch Club. Mem. African Nat. Congress. Muslim. Office: Kritzinger & Co, 33 Church St 5th fl, Cape Town 8001, South Africa

KAPFER, MIRIAM BIERBAUM, technical documentation and training specialist; b. Atlantic, Iowa, May 8, 1935; d. Roy C. and Alma L. Bierbaum; m. Philip G. Kapfer, Aug. 21, 1960 (dec. 1988); children: Paul, Stephanie. B in Music Edn., Drake U., 1956; M in Music Edn., U. Kans., 1958; postgrad., U. Aberdeen, Scotland, 1958-59; PhD, Ohio State U., 1964. Tchr. cert. Iowa, Calif. Instr. Concordia Coll., Seward, Nebr., 1958, St. John's Coll., Winfield, Kans., 1959-61; tchr. Hamilton Local Sch., Columbus, Ohio, 1962-64; tchr., libr., curriculum staff Clark County Sch. Dist., Las Vegas, 1964-70; prof. project adminstrn. U. Utah, Salt Lake City, 1970-77; prof., tchr. U. North Iowa, Cedar Falls, 1977; tchr., analyst Arabian Am. Oil Co., Dhahran, Saudi Arabia, 1978-88; instrnl. designer Usertech, Chgo., 1989—. Author, editor: Behavioral Objectives in Curriculum Development, 1971, Behavioral Objectives: Position of Pendulum, 1978; co-editor, author: Learning Packages in American Education, 1972; co-author: Inquiry ILPs, 1978, Project ILPs, 1978; contbr. articles to profl. jours. Mem. Soc. for Tech. Commn. (sr.), Music Educators Nat. Conf. (life), U. Kans. Alumni Assn. (life), Ohio State U. Alumni Assn. (life), Phi Delta Kappa (life). Avocations: traveling, hiking, reading. Office: Usertech Inc 150 S Wacker Dr Ste 2515 Chicago IL 60606-4202

KAPIČKA, ALEŠ, physicst, research scientist; b. Pardubice, Czech Republic, June 24, 1945; s. Ludvík and Jarmila (Brodská) K.; m. Olga Smolíková, July 10, 1970; children: Marek, Jana. Degree in physics, Charles U., Prague, Czech Republic, 1963-68, RNDr, 1972; PhD, Acad. Scis., Prague, Czech Republic, 1979. Fellow Inst. Physics Acad. Sci., Prague, 1968-72; rschr. Inst. Geophysics Acad. Sci., Prague, 1972-79, sr. scientist, 1979—; tchr. Tech. U., Prague, 1988-94; orgn. com. European High Pressure Rsch. Group Conf., Brno, Czech Republic, 1994; convener European Geophysics Soc. Symposium, The Hague, The Netherlands, 1996, 99. Editor: Physical Properties of the Earths Int., 1985; co-author: Magnetic Anisotropy of Rocks, 1993. Recipient award Czechoslovak Acad. Scis., 1986; grantee Grant Agy. Czech Republic, 1993. Mem. Am. Geophys. Union (regional adv. com. 1994-96), Czech Union Math. and Physicists (chmn. geophys. sect. 1988—, hon. award 1991), European Geophys. Soc. Avocations: literature, skiing. Office: Geophys Inst Acad Sci, Boční II, 141 31 Prague 4, Czech Republic

KAPILA, KUSUM ANGRISH, cytopathologist, pathologist, educator; b. Jullundar, Punjab, India, Dec. 29, 1952; d. Pran Nath and Padma (Kalia) Angrish; children: Supriya, Veeranwali, Gauri. MB, BChir, Lady Hardinge Med. Coll., Delhi, 1974; MD in Pathology, All Indian Inst. Med. Scis., Delhi, 1978. Med. diplomate. Fellow cytopathology Meml. Sloan Kettering Inst., N.Y.C., 1980-81; asst. prof. All India Inst. Med. Scis., Delhi, 1982-85, assoc. prof., 1985-89, additional prof., 1989-96, prof., 1996—; cons., assoc. prof. Kuwait U., 1993-95. Fellow Internat. Acad. Cytologists; mem. Royal Coll. Pathologists U.K., Indian Acad. Cytologists (sec. 1997-99). Avocations: painting, embroidery, reading, cooking. Office: All India Inst Med Scis, Dept Pathology Ansari Nagar, New Delhi 110029, India

KAPITOLA, JIRI, endocrinologist; b. Pisek, Czech Republic, Apr. 12, 1928; s. Bernard and Jarmila (Knoflikova) K.; m. Jaroslava Pluhovska, Aug. 21, 1939; two children. MD, Charles U., 1952. Staff physician City Hosp. Ostrava, Czech Republic, 1953-55; from staff physician to sr. lectr. 3d Med. Clinic, Prague, 1955-63; sr. rschr. Lab. for Endocrinology & Metabolism, Prague, 1963-94. Author: Magnesium, Metabolism and Clinical Significance, 1968, Blood Flow Through the Thyroid Gland in Rats, 1974, Local Blood Flow in Rats, 1975. Mem. Czech Med. Soc.

KAPITZA, SERGEY PETROVICH, physicist, educator; b. Cambridge, Eng., Feb. 14, 1928; arrived in USSR, 1935; s. Peter L. and Anna A. (Kriloff) K.; m. Tatiana A. Damir, Oct. 11, 1949; children: Feodor, Maria, Barbara. Grad., Moscow Aero. Sch., 1949; PhD, Inst. Geophysics, Moscow, 1953; DSc, Joint Inst. Nuclear Physics, Dubna, USSR, 1961. Engr. Ctrl. Aerohydrodynamic Inst., Jukovskii, USSR, 1949-51; rschr. Inst. Geophysics, Moscow, 1951-53; sr. scientist Inst. Phys. Problems, Moscow, 1953—; assoc. prof. Moscow Inst. Physics and Tech., 1956-65, prof., 1965—; Moderator (nat. TV) Science and Technology, Moscow, 1973—; participant Pugwash confs. on science and world affairs, 1970—. Author: Life of Science, 1973, General Theory of Growth of Humankind, 1999; co-author: The Microtron, 1968, Between the Obvious and Incredible, 1980, Synergetics and the Foreseeable Future, 1997; editor (Russian edition) Scientific American, 1982-93; mem. editorial adv. bds. Classics of Science, 1974—, Public Understanding of Science, 1991—, Skeptical Inquirer, 1992—, New Technologies for 21st Century, 1997—; contbr. over 100 articles to profl. jours.; patentee in field. Mem. Presdl. Com. on Culture and Arts, Moscow, 1996, Internat. Coun. on Culture and Devel. UNESCO, 1996—. Recipient Oppenheimer medal Los Alamos Nat. Lab., 1993, Prize Russian Acad. Sci., 1996, Kalinga Prize, State prize UNESCO, 1980; minor planet N5094 Seryozha named in hon. Internat. Astronomy Union. Mem. Internat. Fedn. Aeronautical Scis., Euro Asian Phys. Soc. (pres. 1993—), Assn. Learned and Engring. Socs. (v.p. 1993), Acad. Natural Scis. (v.p. 1990—), planetary Soc. (adv. coun. 1992), Acad. Europaea, Union of Sci. Socs. (v.p. 1999), Club of Rome, World Acad. Arts and Scis., Manchester Literary and Phil. Soc., Internat. Acad. Humanism. Avocations: underwater sports and exporation, tennis. E-mail: sergey@kapitza.ras.ru. Home: 13 Leninsky Prospekt Apt 103, 117071 Moscow Russia Office: Inst Phys Problems, 2 Kosygina St, 117334 Moscow Russia

KAPLAN, ALAN I., film producer; b. Balt.; s. Emmanuel and Dora (Yanigee) K.; m. Gina Chiao, Feb. 17, 1991 (div. May 1994); 1 child, Daniel Victor. BA, U. Md., MA; postgrad, Md. Inst. Art. Freelance photographer N.Y.C., 1968-70; chmn. media dept. Antioch Coll., Balt., 1970-76; pres./owner Alan Kaplan Prodns., L.A., Calif., 1976-91; pres. Wavecrest, L.A., 1991-96, Cine L.A., 1998—. Co-prodr./dir./writer (films) including Harold Clurman: A Life of Theater (Cine Golden Eagle award 1989), (TV cable) What's Up America?; prodr. (film) Bad Manners, 1996, Felons, 1997, Lucky 13, 1998, Touched By a Killer, 1999. Fax: 310-820-4415. Office: Cine LA 11693 San Vincente Blvd # 321 Los Angeles CA 90049-5105

KAPLAN, ALEXANDER EFIMOVICH, physics educator, engineering educator; b. Kiev, Ukraine, USSR, June 9, 1938; came to U.S., 1979; s. Efim S. and Anna A. K. MS in Physics, Moscow Phys. Tech. Inst., 1961; postgrad., USSR Acad. Scis., Moscow, 1963-66; PhD in Physics and Math.,

Gorkii State U., USSR, 1967. Rsch. scientist Radio R & D Lab., Moscow, 1961-63; rsch. staff mem. USSR Acad. Scis., 1963-79, MIT, Cambridge, 1979-82; prof. elec. engring. sch. Purdue U., West Lafayette, Ind., 1982-87; prof. elec. and computer engring. dept. Johns Hopkins U., Balt., 1987—; cons. Bell Labs, Homdell, N.J., 1980-81, Los Alamos (N.Mex.) Nat. Lab., 1981, Honeywell Rsch. Ctr., Mpls., 1982; guest scientist Max-Planck-Inst. Quantenoptik, Garching, Fed. Republic Germany, 1981; Alexander-von-Humboldt prof. quantum physics dept. U. Ulm, Germany, 1996. Contbr. more than 100 articles to profl. jours. and 3 books. Recipient Alexander von Humboldt award for sr. U.S. scientists Alexander von Humboldt Found. Germany, 1996. Fellow Optical Soc. Am.; mem. Am. Phys. Soc., Laser & Electro-Optic Soc. Achievements include patent in field. Office: Johns Hopkins U Elec and Comp Engring Dept 34th & Charles Sts Baltimore MD 21218

KAPLAN, ANDREA EDITH, dental educator; b. Capital Federal, Argentina, Nov. 23, 1963; d. Marcos Kaplan and Hilda Marta Craimowicz Craimowicz. Cert. technician in chemistry, Hipolito Yrigoyen, Buenos Aires, 1982; degree in dentistry, U. Buenos Aires, 1987, DDS, 1992. Tchr. dental materials U. Buenos Aires, 1985-94, student rschr. Sch. Dentistry, 1987-88, asst. prof. dental materials, 1994—; asst. prof. dental materials Sch. Dentistry Maimonides U., Buenos Aires, 1991-92. Recipient Prof. Dr. Fernando Pinto award Soc. Operative Dentistry and Dental Materials, Argentina Dental Assn., Elida Pond's award for young rschrs. Argentine divsn. Internat. Assn. Dental Rsch., 1994. Jewish. Avocation: photography. Fax: (5411) 4508-3958. E-mail: mater@odon.uba.ar. Home: JA Pacheco de Melo 3056 3 C, 1425 Capital Federal Argentina Office: Dept Dental Materials, M T de Alvear 2142, 1122 Capital Federal Argentina

KAPLAN, CLAUDETTE S. (CLAUDIA KAPLAN), civic leader, philanthropist, volunteer; b. Chgo., June 4, 1931; d. Jacob and Celia (Lopaty) Mirotsnic; m. Saul M. Kaplan, Nov. 28, 1953 (div. Mar. 1980); children: Allan, Laurie K., David. Grad., Chgo. City Coll., 1951; student, Coll. Jewish Studies, 1951-53. Pres. Hadassah, Memphis, 1970-72, So. region, 1978-81, nat. svc. com., 1981-83, mem. nat. pres.'s coun., 1984—, founder major and big gifts event, 1974, area founders chair nat. major gifts dept. Nat. Israel Edn. Svcs. Com., chpt. cons., 1999; bd. dirs. NCCJ, Memphis Jewish Cmty. Rels. Coun., Memphis Jewish Fedn./Unite Jewish Appeal, 1972-80; mem. So. Poverty Law Ctr. Recipient 25th Anniversary award State of Israel Bonds, 1973, Guardian of the Dream Founder award Hadassah, 1995, donor award, 1974. Mem. Am. Israel Pub. Affairs Com. (exec. com. Memphis coun.), Nat. Coun. Jewish Women, World Jewish Congress, Am. Soc. for Yad Vashem Simon Wiesenthal Ctr., Hadassah Women's Zionist Orgn. of Am. (life), City Hope (life), Memphis and Mid-South Jewish Hist. Soc., B'nai B'rith. Home: 408 River Oaks Pl Memphis TN 38120-2538

KAPLAN, DAVID LOUIS, lawyer, investment banker; b. Lakeland, Fla., Jan. 10, 1961; s. Donald David and Jane Zelda Kaplan; m. Katherine Ann Gibbons, Jan. 4, 1992. BA, Emory U., 1983, MA, 1983; JD, U. Fla., 1986. Bar: Fla. 1987, D.C. 1999, U.S. Supreme Ct. 1992; registered rep., mcpl. fin. prin. Dir. Cegmark Internat., N.Y.C., 1986-87; sr. assoc. Kubicki Draper, Miami, Fla., 1987-94; shareholder, ptnr. Adorno & Zeder, P.A., Miami, 1994-97; mng. dir. Prudential Securities, Coral Gables, Fla., 1997—. Chair devel. com. Girl Scouts U.S., 1997; bd. dirs. ARC Zool. Soc. Fla.; exec. bd. dirs. Swithboard Miami; bd. dirs. ARC Greater Miami and The Keys, Fla. Zool. Soc., Switch Bd. Miami. Republican. Jewish. Avocations: riding, sailing, travel, reading. Office: Prudential Securities Inc 2800 Ponce De Leon Blvd Coral Gables FL 33134-6913

KAPLAN, FRANCIS, philosophy researcher; b. Mulhouse, France, June 13, 1927; s. Jacob and Fanny (Dichter) K.; m. Helene Miakotine, July 15, 1970. Lic. in Philosophy, Sorbonne, France, 1950, Diplome D'Etudes Superieures, 1950, Doctorat D'Etat, 1971. Prof. Lycee, 1956-67; asst. U. Tours, France, 1967-69, maitre asst., 1969-73, maitre de conferences, 1973-78, prof. d'univ., 1978-95, dir. du dept. de philosophie, 1984-95, prof. emeritus, 1995—. Author: La Verite et ses Figures, 1977, Les Pensees de Pascal classement et annotations, 1982, Marx Antisemite, 1990, Le Paradoxe de la Vie, 1995, Les trois Communismes de Marx, 1996, La Verité, le Dogmatisme et le Scepticisme, 1998, L'Ethique de Spinoza et la méthode géométrique, 1998, Pascal, 1998; editor: Alain Propos sur les Pouvoirs, 1985; author, editor: Introduction a la Philosophie de la Religion, 1989. Home: 31 Rue Cavendish, 75019 Paris France

KAPLAN, HOWARD BERNARD, sociologist, educator; b. N.Y.C., Mar. 17, 1932; s. Samuel and Esther K.; m. Diane S. Kaplan, Aug. 9, 1970; children: Samuel Charles, Rachel Esther. AB, NYU, 1953, MA, 1954, PhD, 1958. Asst. prof. sociology NYU, N.Y.C., 1957-58; prof. sociology Baylor Coll. Medicine, Houston, 1958-88; disting. prof. sociology Tex. A&M U., College Station, 1988—; cons. VA Hosp., Houston, 1961-88. Author: Patterns of Juvenile Delinquency, 1984, Social Psychology of Self-Referent Behavior, 1986; editor: Drugs, Crime, and Other Deviant Adaptations: Longitudinal Studies, 1995, Psychosocial Stress: Perspectives on Structure, Theory, Life Course and Methods, 1996; editor Jour. of Health and Social Behavior, 1979-81. Recipient Sr. Scientist award Nat. Inst. Drug Abuse, Rockville, Md., 1985—, Outstanding Mental Health Rsch. award Mental Health Assn. Houston, 1986. Mem. Internat. Sociological Assn., Am. Sociological Assn., Soc. Life History Rsch. E-mail: h-kaplan@tamu.edu. Office: Texas A&M Univ Dept Sociology College Station TX 77843-0001

KAPLAN, ILYA GRIGORIEVICH, physicist; b. Kiev, Ukraina, USSR, Sept. 22, 1932; s. Gregory E. and Rachel I. (Savitskaya) K.; m. Larissa Vasilievna Popova, May 26, 1959; children: Gregory, Vasily. MS, State U., Saratov, USSR, 1955; PhD, Physics Inst. Acad. Scis., Moscow, 1962; D Scis. Phys-Math., Inst. Chem. Phys. Acad. Scis., Moscow, 1969; Prof. Chem. Physics, Min. of H.S. Edn., Moscow, 1979. Rsch. scientist Inst. Chem. Physics Acad. of Scis., Moscow, 1960-61; rsch. scientist Karpov Inst. Phys. Chemistry, Moscow, 1961-69, head theoretical dept., 1969-94; prof. Inst. de Fisica/U. Nacional Autonoma Mexico, 1992-99, Inst. Investigation Materials/U. Nacional Automa Mexico, 2000—; vis. prof. Napole U., Italy, 1990, Sussex U., Eng., 1995-99, Jackson U., 1999; mem. coord. rsch. program, IAEA, Vienna, 1988-94. Author: (books) Symmetry of many-electron systems, 1975, Theory of Molecular Interactions, 1986; mem. internat. adv. bd. for Handbook of Molecular Physics and Quantum Chemistry (J. Wiley & Sons); inventor in field. Recipient Nat. State prize Govt. USSR, 1985, Academician, Russian Acad. Natural Scis., Moscow, 1991, The Kapitza Fellowship, Royal Soc., London, 1995; mem. Mexican Acad. Scis., Mex., 1997. Mem. Internat. Radiation Physics Soc., Am. Phys. Soc., Mexican System of Nat. Investigators. Achievements include introduction of the transformation matrices of permutation group (the Kaplan matrices), development of so-called quantum chemistry without spin, prediction of interference phenomena in photoionization of molecules in X-ray region, stats. of quasi-particles in a crystal lattice. Avocations: collecting modern painting, music. Office: Inst Investigation Mat UNAM, Ciudad Universitaria, 70-360 Mexico City Mexico

KAPLAN, ISAAC RAYMOND, chemistry educator, corporate executive; b. Baranowicze, Poland, July 10, 1929; came to U.S., 1957; s. Morris and Anny (Chait) K.; m. Helen Fagot, Sept. 4, 1955; children: Debora, David Joel. BS, Canterbury U., Christchurch, New Zealand, 1951, MS, 1953; PhD, U. So. Calif., 1961. Rsch. scientist Commonwealth Sci. and Indsl. Rsch. Orgn., Sydney, Australia, 1953-57; postdoctoral fellow Calif. Inst. Tech., Pasadena, 1961-62; guest lectr. Hebrew U., Jerusalem, 1962-65; assoc. prof. UCLA, 1965-69, prof., 1969-93, prof. emeritus, 1993—; pres. Global Geochemistry Corp., Canoga Park, Calif., 1977—; cons. city, county, state and fed. regulatory agys., L.A. Contbr. and co-contbr. over 300 sci. rsch. articles to profl. jours. Guggenheim Found. fellow, Sydney, 1970-71. Fellow AAAS, Am. Inst. Chemists, Geol. Soc. Am.; mem. Russian Acad. Natural Sci. (fgn., Kapitsa medal 1998), Am. Chem. Soc., Geophys. Union, Geochem. Soc. (Alfred Treibs medal for organic geochm. 1993). Office: U Calif ESS Dept Plaza Circle Dr Los Angeles CA 90024

KAPLAN, JOEL STUART, lawyer; b. Bklyn., Feb. 1, 1937; s. Abraham Larry and Phayme (Moses) K.; m. Joan Ruth Katz, June 19, 1960; children: Andrea Beth, Pamela Jill. BA, Bklyn. Coll., 1958; LLB, NYU, 1961. Bar: N.Y. 1962, U.S. Dist. Cts. (ea. and so. dists.) N.Y. 1964, U.S. Ct. Appeals (2d cir.) 1966, U.S. Supreme Ct. 1979, Fla. 1982, D.C. 1987. Asst. town atty. Town of Hempstead, Nassau County, N.Y., 1962-67; ptnr. Jaspan, Kaplan, Levin & Daniels and predecessors, Garden City, N.Y., 1970-83; sole practice Garden City, 1983-95; counsel Levin Belsky Ross and Daniels, Garden City, 1995—. Chmn. Hempstead Town Pub. Employment Rels. Bd., 1973-81; pres. dist. 1 B'nai B'rith, 1986-87, mem. internat. bd. govs., 1987—; internat. program chmn., 1999—; mem. B'nai B'rith Found. U.S., 1989-90; Rep. candidate for N.Y. State Senate, 1974. Mem. ABA, N.Y. State Bar Assn., Nassau County Bar Assn. Home: 973 E End Woodmere NY 11598-1005 Office: 585 Stewart Ave Ste 700 Garden City NY 11530-4785

KAPLAN, JOHN, photojournalist, educator, consultant; b. Wilmington, Del., Aug. 21, 1959; s. Ralph Benjamin and Ruth Jillya (Denkin) K. BJ cum laude, Ohio U., Athens, 1982; MS in Journalism, Ohio U., 1998. Photojournalist, designer Spokesman Rev./Chronicle, Spokane, Wash., 1983-84; photojournalist, picture editor Pitts. Press, 1984-90; photojournalist Pitts. Post-Gazette, 1990-92; spl. corr. Block Newspapers, 1992-94; dir. Media Alliance, cons., Pitts., 1990—; vis. lectr. Bradley U., Peoria, Ill., 1989; tchr., lectr. numerous univs., seminars, profl. groups, U.S., Can., 1984—; adj. prof. Syracuse U., London campus, 1993; mem. Pulitzer Prize jury, 1994, 95; Knight fellow U. Ohio, 1997—; photojournalism mem. Ball State U., Muncie, 1998-99; assoc. prof. U. Fla., Gainesville, 1999—. Author: Mom and Me, 1996; contbr. to book series The Best of Photojournalism, Vols. 6, 7, 9, 10, 11, 14, 18, 1981-93. Recipient Golden Quill Journalism award Pitts. Press Club, 1986, 89, Pitts. Photographer of Yr. News Photographers Assn. Greater Pitts., 1986, 89, 92, Robert F. Kennedy Journalism award Kennedy Found., 1989, Pulitzer Prize for feature photography, 1992, Matrix Mag. award Women in Comm., 1992, Ohio U. Disting. Grad. award, 1993; named Photographer of Yr. Pa. Press Photographers Assn., 1989, No. Photographer of Yr., 1992, Ohio U. Coll. Comm. Hall of Fame, 1993; work in permanent collection Carnegie Mus. of Art, Pitts.; named Knight fellow Ohio U., 1997-98. Mem. Nat. Press Photographers Assn. (contest chmn. Region 3, 1987-89, Regional Photographer of Yr. awards 1985, 86, 87, 89, Nat. Newspaper Photographer of Yr. award 1989, Nikon Documentary Sabbatical award 1990, other awards), Soc. Newspaper Design (Gold award 1989), Amnesty Internat. Avocations: racquet sports, furniture design, wines. Address: 3067 Weimer Hall Gainesville FL 32611-8400

KAPLAN, KENNETH EDWARD, public relations specialist, writer; b. San Leandro, Calif., Mar. 26, 1968; s. Steve and Yolanda Kaplan. BA, Calif. State U., Chico, 1986-91. Publicist Sta. KRON-TV, San Francisco, 1992-2000; broadcast pub. rels. mgr. Intel Corp., Santa Clara, Calif., 2000—. Columnist North Beach Now newspaper, 1992-96; mng. editor Cue mag., 1999-2000. Democrat. Roman Catholic. Avocations: travel, writing, reading, cooking, Italian culture. E-mail: kkaplan@jps.net. Home: 424 Chestnut St San Francisco CA 94133-2302 Office: Intel Corp 2200 Mission College Blvd Santa Clara CA 95054-1549

KAPLAN, LEV, mathematician, researcher; b. Moscow, Oct. 11, 1953; arrived in Israel, 1992; s. Isaac and Seina (Krazer) K.; m. Alla Portnov, Dec. 30, 1978; children: Evgenia, Alexander. MSc in Math., Moscow Pedagogical Inst., 1975, PhD in Math., 1983. Rsch. fellow Inst. Electronic Control Machines, Moscow, 1981-92, Technion, Haifa, Israel, 1992-95, Tel Aviv U., 1995-96; algorithm developer MicroSpec Techs. Ltd., Yokneam, Israel, 1996—. Author: Programming Contests for Schoolchildren, 1985; contbr. articles to profl. jours. Mem. AAAS. Avocation: chess. Home: Harel 18 Apt 6, 34555 Haifa Israel Office: MicroSpec Techs Ltd, 20692 Yokneam Israel

KAPLAN, MARSHALL MYLES, gastroenterologist, researcher, educator; b. Boston, Feb. 20, 1935; s. Harold and Ginda (Braverman) K.; m. Nancy Proger, June 5, 1960; children: Ginda, William, Thomas, Deborah. BS summa cum laude, Yale U., 1956; MD cum laude, Harvard U., 1960. Intern, resident Columbia-Presbyn., N.Y.C., 1960-62; clin. assoc. NIH, Bethesda, Md., 1962-65; trainee liver disease Yale U., New Haven, Conn., 1965-66; asst. prof. medicine Tufts-New England Med. Ctr., Boston, 1966-69, assoc. prof. medicine, 1969-75, prof. medicine, 1975—, chief divsn. gastroenterology, 1972—; chmn. merit rev. com. VA Hosps., Washington, 1975-77; mem. gastroenterology bd. Am. Bd. Internal Medicine, 1983-89, chmn., 1987-89, bd. govs., 1987-89; manuscript reviewer Annals Internal Medicine, Am. Jour. Medicine, Archives of Internal Medicine, Gastroenterology, Hepatology, Digestive Diseases and Sci., Am. Jour. Gastroenterology, Jour. Hepatology. Assoc. editor New Eng. Jour. Medicine, 1993—; editor Tufts Family Health Guides, 1979-82; mem. editl. bd. Hepatology, 1988-92; contbr. chpts. to books and more than 200 articles to profl. jours. Lt. comdr. USPHS, 1962-65. Master ACP (chair sci. program com. 1990-93, gastroenterology med. knowledge self-assessment program); mem. Assn. Am. Physicians, Am. Soc. Clin. Investigation, Am. Gastroenterology Assn., Am. Assn. for Study of Liver Disease (com. chair 1984-86), Phi Beta Kappa, Alpha Omega Alpha (dir. 1983-89). Democrat. Jewish. Avocations: tennis, squash, golf, gardening, music, theatre, history. Home: 30 Oakridge Rd Wellesley MA 02481-2504 Office: New England Med Ctr 750 Washington St Boston MA 02111-1526

KAPLAN, MITCHELL ALAN, sociologist, researcher; b. Bklyn., Jan. 26, 1954; s. Murray Robert and Claire (Meshnick) K. BA in Sociology and Psychology cum laude, L.I. U., 1976; MA in Sociology, New Sch. for Social Rsch., 1979; PhD in Sociology, CUNY, 1987. Cert. social rsch. specialist; cert. profl. sociol. practitioner Am. Acad. Profl. Sociol. Practitioners. Rsch. fellow Narcotic and Drug Rsch. Inc., N.Y.C., 1986-89, cons., 1989-90; cons. Am. Found. for AIDS Rsch., N.Y.C., 1989-90; rsch. scientist Rsch. & Tng. Inst. Nat. Ctr. for Disability Svcs., Albertson, N.Y., 1991-92; acad. rsch. cons. Acad. Rsch. Consulting Svcs., Bklyn., 1993—; project mgr. dept. pain medicine and palliative care Beth Israel Med. Ctr., N.Y.C., 1999—; evaluations cons. office rsch. and ednl. assessment Bklyn. divsn. N.Y.C. Bd. Edn., 1992-93; acad. rsch. cons. Acad. Rsch. Consulting Svcs., Inc., 1993—; devel. rschr. Am. Heart Assn. N.Y.C. Affiliate, 1994; sr. rsch. assoc., program evaluator Office Acad. Affairs, CUNY, Kennedy Fellows Program, 1994-95; evaluation cons. Mayor's Office on AIDS Policy Coordination, 1996. Co-author: (chpt.) Days with Drug Distribution Which Drugs? How Many Transactions? With What Returns? 1990; contbr. articles to profl. jours. Nat. Inst. on Drug Abuse fellow, 1986-89. Mem. APHA, Nat. Rehab. Assn., Soc. for Disability Studies, N.Y. Acad. Scis., Am. Sociol. Assn. (cert. med. sociologist, social policy & evaluation rschr. law & social control rschr.), N.Y. State Sociol. Assn., Am. World Health Assn., Am. Assn. Sex Educators, Counselors and Therapists, Am. Assn. for Pub. Opinion Rsch., Nat. Rehab. Counseling Assn., Nat. Rehab. Assn. (job placement div. 1991), Pi Gamma Mu, Psi Chi, Phi Theta Kappa. Democrat. Jewish. Achievements include research in the areas of Aids and intravenous drug use, the relationship between drug use and criminal behavior, drug treatment methods, and vocational rehabilitation and the physically and emotionally disabled. Home and Office: 2560 Batchelder St Apt 8K Brooklyn NY 11235-1558

KAPLAN, PHYLLIS, computer artist, painter; b. Bklyn.; d. Abraham and Ida (Heller) K. BFA, Cooper Union, 1972; postgrad., Domus Acad., Milan, 1985. curator art exhibit Orgn. Ind. Artists, N.Y.C., 1995-96, Westside Arts Coalition, N.Y.C., 1997; lectr., presenter in field. Exhibited paintings at Lever House, N.Y.C., 1968, Berkshire Mus., Pittsfield, Mass., 1970, L.I. U., N.Y.C., 1975, Biola U., La Mirada, Calif., Nat. Mus. Women in the Arts, Beijing, China, 1995, Three Rivers Arts Festival, Carnegie Mus., Pitts., 1995-96, Fine Arts Mus. L.I., Hempstead, 1996-97, Halpert Biennial, Boone, N.C., 1997, Cork Gallery, Lincoln Center, N.Y., 1997, Blue Mountain Gallery Invitationals, N.Y.C., 1996-98, World Artists for Tibet at Blue Mountain, 1998, Trevi Flash Art Mus., Italy, 1998; contbr. paintings to various publs. including Kings Courier, 1974, The Villager, N.Y.C., 1994, CPM News, 1994, Bklyn. Graphic, 1996, Adell McMillan Gallery, U. Oreg., Eugene, 2000, Coll. Visual Arts Gallery, St. Paul, 2000, Open Space Gallery, Allentown, Pa., 2000, Blue Mountain Gallery, 2000; contbr. ann. calendar Orgn. Ind. Artists. Recipient award for patriotism U.S. Savs. Bond Dr., 1987, hon. mention award Internat. Female Artist's Art Biennial, Stockholm, 1994, Halpert Biennial, Boone, N.C., 1999, Sharjah Art Mus., United Arab Emirates, 2000, Open Space Gallery, 2000, hon. mention award Mayfair, Allentown, Pa., 2000, Art Environ. Advocacy U. Oreg., Eugene, 2000, Virtue Coll. Visual Arts Gallery, St. Paul, Minn., 2000, Mayfair Open Space Gallery, Allentown, Pa., 2000, Snapshot Contemporary Mus., Balt., 2000, Small Works Invitational Painting, 2000, Blue Mountain Gallery, N.Y.C., 2000; grantee Artists Space/Ind. Project, 1999. Mem. Nat. Mus. Women in the Arts, Guggenheim Mus., Greene County Coun. on Arts, The New Mus. Avocations: travel, collecting antique tin toys, classical music. Home: 98 Park Ter E New York NY 10034-1417

KAPLAN, RICHARD N., broadcast executive, cable; married; 2 children. Prodr. The CBS Evening News with Walter Cronkite, N.Y.C.; sr. prodr. World News Tonight, ABC, N.Y.C., 1979; exec. prodr. World News This Morning, Good Morning Am., Nightline, ABC, N.Y.C., 1984-89, Viewpoint, The Koppel Report; creator, exec. prodr. Capitol to Capitol; coord. ABC News; exec. prodr. PrimeTime Live, 1989-94, World News Tonight with Peter Jennings, 1994-96; exec. prodr. spl. projects ABC Television Network, 1996-97; pres. Cable News Network, Atlanta, 1997-. Recipient 32 Emmy awards, 4 Overseas Press Club awards, 3 George Foster Peabody awards, 2 George Polk awards, 4 Alfred I. du Pont-Columbia U. awards, 2 Gold Batons. Office: Cable News Network One CNN Ctr PO Box 105366 Atlanta GA 30348-5366

KAPLAN, STEVEN MARK, accountant; b. Bklyn., June 22, 1952; s. Irwin and Ruth (Lieberman) K.; m. Susan Lynn Rosenberg, Nov. 19, 1972; children: Eric, Corey, Shannon. BS in Acctg., Bklyn. Coll., 1973. CPA, N.Y. Staff acct. Morris Sherwood & May, N.Y.C., 1973-74; sr. acct. Slater & Slater, Rockville Centre, N.Y., 1974-75; ptnr. Kaplan and Roberts CPA, East Rockaway, N.Y., 1975-95; prin. Steven M. Kaplan, CPA, P.C., Merrick, N.Y., 1995—; dir. investor rels. Healthaxis, Inc., East Norriton, Pa., 2000—. Treas. Temple Beth Am., Merrick, 1989-94, Merrick-North Merrick Little League, 1984-97, v.p., 1989, treas., 1990-92, pres. 1993-97; bd. dirs. Merrick-North Merrick Police Athletic League, 1984-88. Mem. AICPA, N.Y. State Soc. CPA's, Nat. Soc. Pub. Accts. Avocations: baseball, photography. Office: 25 Merrick Ave Ste 8 Merrick NY 11566-3433

KAPLANOGLU, HALUK, film company executive; b. Istanbul, Turkey, Aug. 25, 1957; s. Necdet and Nevzat Kaplanoglu; m. Soil Kaplanoglu, July 7, 1999. BA, Ind. U., 1985. Sales mgr. Pars AS, Istanbul, 1986-88; gen. mgr. Vikom AS, Istanbul, 1988-90; mng. dir. Warner Bros. Turkey, Istanbul, 1990—. Pres. Film Bd., Istanbul, 1998—. Avocations: sports, films, reading. E-mail: haluk kaplanoglu@warnersbros.com. Office: Warner Bros Turkey, Topcu Cd No 2/6 Taksim, Istanbul Turkey

KAPLANOV, VASILY ILLICH, metal press treatment educator, researcher; b. Mariupol, Ukraine, Jan. 4, 1934; s. Ilia Georgievich and Vera Vasilievna Kaplanov; m. Lidia Alexandrovna Kuznetsova, June 25, 1964; children: Elena, Natalia. Diploma in Engring., Mariupol Metall. Inst., 1957, Candidate of Scis., 1968, DSc, 1987. Registered prof. engr., metallurgist. Head cold rolling shop Beloretsk (Russia) Metall. Plant, 1957-59; head technol. office cold rolling steel works shop Illich Iron and Steel Works, Mariupol, 1959-64; postgrad. rolling prodn. dept. Mariupol Metall. Inst., 1964-80, asst. prof. rolling prodn. dept., 1980-82, head rolling prodn. dept., 1982-89; v.p. sci. work Azov State Tech. U., Mariupol, 1989—. Recipient medals Exhbn. of Nat. USSR, 1975-85, Badge of Honor, USSR Supreme Soviet, 1986. Avocations: music, football, fishing. Home: Kuprina St 13 Apt 58, 341037 Mariupol Ukraine Office: Priazovskyi State Tech U, Republik Lane 7, 341000 Mariupol Ukraine

KAPLIN, YURY MICHAILOVICH, physical chemist, researcher; b. Vladivostok, Russia, May 12, 1937; s. Michail Andreyevich and Ulyana Efimovna (Mislivets) K.; m. Ekaterina Mitrofanovna Rogova, Oct. 14, 1967; 1 child, Konstantin Yurevich. Ship repair mech. engr. diploma, Far Ea. Higher Engring. Marine Sch., Vladivostok, 1960; D Tech. Sci. in Phys. Chemistry, Acad. Scis. USSR, Moscow, 1970. Sr. engr., head Lab. Corrosion, Far Ea. br. Ctrl. Sci. Rsch. Marine Inst., Leningrad (Vladivostok), 1961-71; sr. sci. worker, prof. tech. maerials Far Ea. Higher Engring. Marine Sch., 1970-71; sr. sci. worker, organizer, head Far Ea. Corrosion Sta., Inst. Phys. Chemistry, Acad. Scis. USSR, Moscow, Vladivostok, 1971-81; prof. material corrosion Far Ea. Poly. Inst., Vladivostok, 1980-82; orgnizer, head Far Ea. Marine Corrosion Sta., Vladivostok; sr. sci. worker, head Lab. Marine Corrosion Inst. Chemistry, Far Ea. br. Russian Acad. Scis., Vladivostok, 1981—, mem. acad. coun., 1984-90, 94—; chmn. local trade union com. Inst. Chemistry, Far Ea. br. Russian Acad. Scis., Moscow, 1993—; mem. acad. coun. Prob. Biodamages Russian Acad. Scis., Moscow, 1998—. Editor: The Questions of Marine Corrosion and Biofouling, 1985; contbr. articles to profl. jours. Mem. town com. Communist Party Russian Fedn., Vladivostok, 1999—; mem. mcpl. election com. Town of Vladivostok, 1999—. Officer Russian Naval Res., 1961—. Decorated 50 Yr. medal Soviet People in Great Patriotic War, Adm. of Fleet N.G. Kusnetsov. Mem. Soc. Water Transport Pacific Basin, All Union D.I. Mendeleev Chem. Soc., Far Ea. Assn. Corrosions (mem. leadership 1989-94). Achievements include patent for method of receipt from toxic on basis of lignin's derivatives; inventor chamber for electrochemical cut metal constructions. Avocations: photography, travel, literary creative work. E-mail: chemi@online.ru and kym@mail.primorye.ru. Home: 14/2 Kirov St 49, 690068 Vladivostok Russia Office: Inst Chem Russian Acad Scis, 159 Pr Stoletiya, 690022 Vladivostok 25, Russia

KAPLOWITZ, LISA GLAUSER, physician, educator; b. Phila., Apr. 18, 1951; d. Felix E. and Charlotte (Gordy) Glauser; m. Paul Bernard Kaplowitz, Dec. 28, 1970; children: Joshua Michael, Daniel Steven. BS, U. Mich., 1970; MD, U. Chgo., 1975; student, Hahnemann U., 1999—. Diplomate Am. Bd. Internal Medicine, Am. Bd. Infectious Diseases. Resident U. N.C., Chapel Hill, 1976-78, postgrad. fellow, 1978-80, instr. dept. medicine, 1980-82; asst. prof. dept. medicine Med. Coll. Va., Richmond, 1982-89; assoc. prof. Med. Coll. Va., 1989—; dir. HIV/AIDS Ctr., Va. Commonwealth U., Richmond, 1993—, asst. v.p. fed. health policy; bd. dirs. AIDS Action Coun., Washington, 1995-96; mem. 1999-2000 class Exec. Leadership in Acad. Medicine Program for Women, MCP-Hahnemann U. Contbr. (book chpt.) Conn's Current Therapy, 1985, 2d rev. edit., 1988, 3d edit., 1998, Principles of Critical Care Medicine, 1992. Mem. adv. bd. Va. League for Planned Parenthood, Richmond, 1993—, Richmond AIDS Ministry, 1988-92, Leadership Metro Richmond, 1992-93; grad. Exec. Leadership in Acad. Med. for Women, MCP-Hahnemann U., 2000. Named Woman of Year Va. Commonwealth U., 1995, mem. Va. Women's Hall of Fame Va. Coun. on Status of Women, 1992; health policy fellow Inst. Medicine, 1996-97, fellow Office of Senator Jay Rockefeller, 1997. Fellow ACP, Infectious Disease Soc. Am.; mem. APHA, Am. Soc. Microbiology. Avocation: piano. Office: HIV AIDS Ctr Va Commonwealth U 1001 E Broad St Ste 125 Richmond VA 23219-1928

KAPNICK, RICHARD BRADSHAW, lawyer; b. Chgo., Aug. 21, 1955; s. Harvey E. and Jean (Bradshaw) K.; m. Claudia Norris, Dec. 30, 1978; children: Sarah Bancroft, John Norris. BA with distinction, Stanford U., 1977; MPhil in Internat. Rels., U. Oxford, 1980; JD with honors, U. Chgo., 1982. Bar: Ill. 1982, N.Y. 1993. Law clk. to justice Ill. Supreme Ct., Chgo., 1982-84; law clk. to Justice John Paul Stevens U.S. Supreme Ct., Washington, 1984-85; assoc. Sidley & Austin, Chgo., 1985-89, ptnr., 1989—. Mng. editor U. Chgo. Law Rev., 1981-82. Trustee Chgo. Symphony Orch., 1995—, governing mem., 1988-95; chmn. bd. dirs. Civic Orch. Chgo., 1999—, bd. dirs., 1997—; bd. dirs. Cabrini Green Legal Aid Clinic, 1990-94, chmn. bd., 1991-93; mem., advisor, bd. dirs. Stanford Inst. for Econ. Policy Rsch., 1999—; vestryman Christ Ch., Winnetka, Ill., 2000—. Marshall scholar, 1978-80; fellow Leadership Greater Chgo., 1989-90. Mem. Order of Coif, Chgo. Club, Econ. Club Chgo., Law Club Chgo., Phi Beta Kappa. Republican. Episcopalian.

KAPNICK, S. JASON, oncologist; b. Providence, Mar. 28, 1949; s. I.H. and Martha (Shaulson) K.; children: Senta Marie-Rose, Isrel Berndt-Stefan, Sesselja Edda. BLS summa cum laude, boston U., 1974; MD, Harvard Med. Sch., 1981. Surg. rsch. assoc. Harvard Med. Sch., Boston, 1976-77, assoc. in ob/gyn., lectr., 1981-85, instr. in gynecology, 1985-87; cons. in gynecologic oncology Dana Farber Cancer Inst., Boston, 1985-87; clin. fellow Am. Cancer Soc., Boston, 1985-87; attending gynecologic oncologist West Palm Beach, Fla., 1989—; asst. cons. prof. gynecol. oncology Duke U. Med. Ctr., Durham, N.C., 1994—; reviewer of rsch. submissions Cancer med. jour., Bethesda, Md., 1995—; invited lectr., 1995, Palm Beach County Hosps., 1990—, Am. Cancer Soc., Bethesda, 1995, also Switzerland, Germany, France and Eng., 1990—. Contbr. articles on colon, breast, and female

pelvic cancers to profl. jours. Vol., contbr. Ctr. for Family Svcs., West Palm Beach, 1992—; active Cath. Diocese children's programs, 1998—; mem., religious edn. tchr. First Unitarian Ch., North Palm Beach, Fla., Bullfinch Soc., Mass. Gen Hosp.; mem. dean's coun. Med. Sch. Harvard U.; bd. dirs. Palm Beach Opera, 1992—. Henry Merritt Wriston scholarship Brown U. Mem. Harvard Club of Palm Beach. Avocations: philosophy, music. Office: Farris Bldg Gynecol Oncology 1411 N Flagler Dr Ste 5000 West Palm Beach FL 33401-3410 Address: PO Box 30053 Palm Bch Gdns FL 33420-0053

KAPOOR, DEEPAK, electronics executive; b. Peshawar, Punjab, India, Oct. 25, 1944; s. Om Prakash and Shakuntla (Dandona) K.; m. Krishna Batra, Nov. 16, 1969; children: Payal Sharma, Manav. BA, Delhi U., 1967; MBA, Delhi Sch. Econs., 1969. Sales exec. Kapoor Lamps, Delhi, 1962-68, mgr., 1968-79, dir., 1979-84; mng. dir. Kapoor Lamp Shades, Delhi, 1985—. Mem. exec. com. Faridabad Indsl. Assn., 1980, Okhla Indsl. Assn., New Delhi, 1997. Recipient Best Catalogue award Pres. of India, 1981, Highest Exports award Min. of Commerce, 1985-97. Mem. Indo-German C. of C. Avocations: designing lamps, traveling, old coins, yoga. Fax: 91-11-6841448. E-mail: kis@vsnl.com. Home: R-31 GK 1, New Delhi 110048, India Office: Kapoor Lamp Shades, A66 Okhla Phase II, New Delhi 110020, India

KAPOOR, JAGDISH R. (JACK KAPOOR), marketing educator, writer; b. Amritsar, Punjab, India, Sept. 13, 1937; came to the U.S., 1958; s. Ram Prasad Kapoor and Susheela Mehra; m. Theresa M. Kapoor, Feb. 11, 1961; children: Karen Tucker, Kathryn Thumme, Dave. BA, San Francisco State U., 1964, MS, 1966; EdD, No. Ill. U., 1977. Cert. std. tchg. credential, Calif. Lectr. San Francisco State U., 1967-69; prof. mktg. Coll. DuPage, Glen Ellyn, Ill., 1969—; adj. prof. indsl. mktg. Ill. Inst. Tech., Chgo., 1970-71; adj. prof. internat. bus. Northwood U., Lisle, Ill., 1995—; internat. trade cons. Bolting Mfg. Co., Bombay, 1981-89; mem. adv. bd. The Bus. File Video Course, Dallas County C.C. Dist., 1990-96. Co-author: Business: A Practical Approach, 1980, Business, 1985, 6th edit., 1999, Personal Finance, 5th edit., 1999. Republican. Hindu. Avocations: swimming, walking, music, PBS, world travel. E-mail: kapoorj@cdnet.cod.edu. Office: Coll DuPage 425 22nd St Glen Ellyn IL 60137-6784

KAPOOR, MALTI, librarian; b. Nowshera, India, Mar. 3, 1938; d. Sher Knarayan and Savitri Dev; m. Prakash Chandra Kapoor, Nov. 17, 1959 (dec. Jan. 1979); children: Gauri, Ashok. BSc with honors, Delhi U., India, 1957. Reference libr. U.S. Libr., New Delhi, 1958-59; libr. St. Xaviers, Ahmedabad, 1968-71, Calcutta Boy's Sch., 1975-78; sr. libr. Delhi Pub. Sch., New Delhi, 1979—; cons. in field. Co-author: Guidelines for School Libraries, 1995. Home: 132 Jorbagh, 110003 New Delhi 3, India Office: Delhi Pub Sch, Sector 12 R K Puram, 110 022 New Delhi India

KAPOOR, VIJAY KUMAR, medical educator; b. Saharanpur, India, July 10, 1943; s. Ram Narain and Raj Dulari Lal; m. Shashi Prabha Wahi, Mar. 9, 1970; 2 children. BPharm, Panjab U., 1962, MPharm, 1966, PhD, 1974. Lic. pharmacist. Pharmacognosist Med. Coll. Amritsar, India, 1963-64; sr. rsch. fellow Panjab U., Chandigarh, India, 1966-68, lectr. in pharm. chemistry, 1968-77, reader in pharm. chemistry, 1977-88, prof. pharm. chemistry, 1988—, sec. faculty of pharm. scis., 1996-97, dean faculty pharm. scis., 1997-98, chmn. Univ. Inst. Pharm. Scis., 1997-2000; mem. working group Indian Pharmacopoeia, 1996. Contbr. articles to profl. jours. Commonwealth fellow U. Bath, 1983-84, Acad. Staff fellow Commonwealth Univs. London. Mem. Indian Pharm. Assn. (sec. 1982—), Indian Pharm. Congress (chmn. sci. com. 1994—), Assn. Pharm. Tchrs. India, Indian Soc. Tech. Edn. Avocations: music, gardening. Office: Univ Inst Pharm Scis, Panjab Univ, Chandigarh 160014, India

KAPOSTA, IOSIF, dean; b. Bucharest, Romania, Jan. 1, 1955; s. Emerich and Ileana (Hidyed) K.; m. Hajnalka Emilia Kelemen, July 23, 1977; children: Victor Sevastian, Adrian. MSEE, U. Polytech., Timisoara, Romania, 1980, PhD in Engring., 1995. Rschr. S.C. ARIS S.A., Arad, Romania, 1980-82; asst. lectr. U. Polytech., Timisoara, Romania, 1982-90, lectr., 1990-95; prof. U. Aurel Vlaicu, Arad, 1995—, dean, 1996—; cons. in field. Inventor in field. Mem. Romanian Robot Assn., Romanian Tribology Assn, Pannonian Applied Math. Meetings Interuniv. Network. Office: U Aurel Vlaicu, B-Dul Revolutiei No 81, 2900 Arad Romania Address: PO Box 140 Arad 2, 2900 Arad Romania

KAPP, GERALD BERNHARD, agrosilviculturist, researcher; b. Freiburg, Breisgau, Germany, Mar. 12, 1956; s. Rudolf and Ingeborg (Möhler) K.; m. Helen Wong, Mar. 27, 1987; 1 child, Rolf-Gerrit. Student, Oxford (Eng.) U., 1976-77; diploma, Freiburg (Germany) U., 1980, Dr.rer.nat., 1986, postgrad., 1997. Sci. asst. Göttingen (Germany) U., 1980; forestry advisor Ministry Environ., Ouagadougou/Burkina Faso, 1981-83; rschr., lectr. Centro Agronomico Tropical de Investigacion y Enseñanza, Turrialba, Costa Rica, 1987-92, Freiburg U. Silvic Inst., 1992-97; project coord., cons. GFA-Agrar, Hamburg, 1998—; cons. German Agy. for Tech. Cooperation, various tropical countries, 1985—; lectr. German Found. for Internat. Devel., 1996, 2000; external lectr. Freiburg U. Silvic Inst.; sci. advisor Internat. Found. Sci., Stockholm, 1996—. Author: Agroforstliche Landnutzung in der Sahel-Sudanzone, 1987, Perfil Ambiental de la Zona Baja de Talamanca, Costa Rica, 1989; Bäuerliche Forst und Agroforstwirtschaft in Zentral-Amerika, 1997. Recipient Habilitationsstipendium German Rsch. Soc., 1992-94. Mem. Internat. Soc. Tropical Foresters, Internat. Union Forest Rsch. Orgns., German Forest Soc. (com. for internat. cooperation). Office: GFA-Agrar, Eulenkrugstr 82, 22359 Hamburg Germany

KAPP, MICHAEL KEITH, lawyer; b. Winston-Salem, N.C., Nov. 28, 1953; s. William Henry and Betty Jean (Minton) K.; m. Mary Jo Chancy McLean, Aug. 13, 1977; 1 child, Mary Katherine. AB with honors, U. N.C., 1976, JD with honors, 1979. Bar: N.C. 1979, U.S. Dist. Ct. (ea. dist.) N.C. 1980, U.S. Ct. Appeals (4th cir.) 1982, U.S. Dist. Ct. (mid. dist.) N.C. 1986, U.S. Supreme Ct. 1988. Law clk. to presiding justice N.C. Ct. Appeals, Raleigh, 1979-80, N.C. Supreme Ct., Raleigh, 1980-81; assoc. Maupin, Taylor & Ellis, Raleigh, 1981-85; ptnr. Maupin, Taylor & Ellis, P.A., Raleigh, 1985—. Research editor U. N.C. Jour. Internat. Law and Comml. Regulation, 1978-79; editor Survey of Significant Decisions of North Carolina Court of Appeals and North Carolina Supreme Court, 1979-81, 2d vol., 1981-82. N.C. teen Dem. advisor, 1983-85; mem. exec. council N.C. Dem. Party, 1983-85; founding dir. N.C. Vol. Lawyers for Arts, Raleigh, 1982-85; counsel Moravian Music Found., Winston-Salem, 1982-85, trustee, 1985-90, pres., 1990-92; counsel Raleigh Little Theatre, 1996-98, bd. dirs., 1998—; bd. dirs. Moravian Ch. Archives, Wiston-Salem, 1984-89, Soc. for Preservation of Historic Oakwood, Raleigh, 1981-83, Carolina Charter Corp., 1990—, dir. 1995—. Morehead scholar U. N.C., 1972. Mem. ABA, N.C. Bar Assn. (chmn. young lawyer div. continuing legal edn. 1980-82, membership 1984-86, bd. govs. 1983-86), N.C. State Bar (ethics com. 1981-91, com. on professionalism 1986-87), Wake County Bar Assn. (bd. dirs. 1988-90, pres.-elect 1995, pres. 1996), Kiwanis (Raleigh Kiwanis Found. dir., 1996-98), Raleigh Execs. Club (pres. 1998-99), Phi Beta Kappa, Phi Delta Phi, Pi Lambda Phi. Avocation: historic preservation, hiking, gardening. Home: 1615 Craig St Raleigh NC 27608-2201 Office: Maupin Taylor & Ellis Highwoods Tower One 3200 Beech Leaf Ct Ste 500 Raleigh NC 27604-1670

KAPPACHER, WALTER, writer; b. Salzburg, Austria, Oct. 24, 1938; s. Sebastian and Barbara (Rohrmoser) K. Author: Tomorrow, 1975, The Workshop, 1975, 81, Rosina, 1978, The Long Letter, 1982, Plaster Head, 1984, Cerreto, 1989, Touristomania, 1990, An Amateur, 1993, The One Who Laughs First, 1997, Silverarrows, 2000. Recipient Staatspreis (Förderpreis) Lit., 1978, Prize cultural group of Germany Industry, 1986, Baden-Württemberg state scholar, 1982, Hermann-Hesse scholar, 1997. Home: Thaddäus Zauner Str 12/7, A-5162 Obertrum Austria

KAPPATOS, KONSTANTINOS NICHOLAS, engineering executive; b. Ceffalonia, Greece; came to U.S., 1969; s. Nicholas Kappatos and Denise Kavadias; married, Dec. 4, 1988; children: Nicole, Christos. BSEE, Va. Poly. Inst. and State U., 1974; MSEE, George Washington U., 1977. Registered profl. engr. Va., Del. Sys. planning engr. Potomal Electric Power Co., Washington, 1974-77; elec. engr. Rural Electrification Adminstrn., Washington, 1974-77; sr. cons. Dalton Assocs. P.C., Fairfax, Va., 1982-84; v.p. engring. and ops. Old Dominion Elec. Coop., Glen Allen, Va., 1984—; mem. several coms. relating to electric utility coop. bus. Old Dominion/Va., Md. and Del. Assn./Nat. Rural Electric Coop. Assn., Richmond and Washington, 1984—. Registered lobbyist Va., Md. and Del. Assn., Richmond, 1984—. Officer Merchant Marines, Eng., 1961-67; officer Greek Royal Navy, 1967-69. Recipient Superior Achievement award USDA, 1980. Mem. NSPE. Achievements include research in electric power contracting; siting, contracting and constructing state of the art coal fired electric power plant in Virginia. Avocations: reading, fishing, hunting. Home: 11516 Bridgetender Dr Richmond VA 23233-1782 Office: Old Dominion Elec Coop 4201 Dominion Blvd Glen Allen VA 23060-6743

KAPPE, C. OLIVER, chemist, researcher; b. Graz, Austria, June 18, 1965; s. Thomas and Elfriede (Hotter) K. M of Natural Scis., U. Graz, 1989, D of Natural Scis., 1992, univ. dozent, 1998. Cert. in chemistry. Rsch. assoc. U. Queensland, Brisbane, Australia, 1993-94, Emory U., Atlanta, 1994-96; rsch. asst. U. Graz, 1991-92, sr. rsch. assoc., 1996-99, assoc. prof., 1999—. Mem. editl. bd.: Molecules, Arkivoc, 1998—; contbr. 70 articles to profl. jours. Recipient Rsch. award Govt. Styria, 1998; Erwin Schrödinger fellow Austrian Sci. Fund, 1995, Apart fellow Austrian Acad. Scis., 1996. Mem. AAAS, Internat. Soc. Heterocyclic Chemistry (adv. bd. mem. 1998—), Am. Chem. Soc., Austrian Chem. Soc. (Dissertation award 1993), German Chem. Soc.

KAPPENBERG, MARILYN KASCIUS, library director; b. Hicksville, N.Y., July 19, 1948; d. Adolf A. and Mary T. Kascius; m. Richard L. Kappenberg, Apr. 5, 1975; children: Neal, Glenn. BA, Molloy Coll., 1970; MLS, L.I. U., 1972. Children's libr. Hicksville (N.Y.) Pub. Libr., 1972-90; head ref. Hicksville Pub. Libr., 1990-95, asst. libr. dir., 1992-95; libr. dir. Wantagh (N.Y.) Pub. Libr., 1995—. Sec. Hicksville Lions Club, 1990-95. Mem. ALA, Nassau County Libr. Assn., Wantagh C. of C. (mem.-at-large 1995—). Avocations: writing, volunteering. Home: 2873 Janet Ave N Bellmore NY 11710-2026 Office: Wantagh Pub Libr 3285 Park Ave Wantagh NY 11793-3356

KAPPES, PHILIP SPANGLER, lawyer; b. Detroit, Dec. 24, 1925; s. Philip Alexander and Wilma Fern (Spangler) K.; m. Glendora Galena Miles, Nov. 27, 1948; children: Susan Lea, Philip Miles, Mark William. Bar: Ind. 1948. Assoc. Armstrong and Gause, 1948-49, C.B. Dutton, 1950-51; ptnr. Dutton, Kappes & Overman, 1952-85, of counsel, 1983-85; ptnr. Lewis Kappes Fuller & Eads, Indpls., 1985-89, Lewis & Kappes, Indpls., 1989-92, Lewis & Kappes PC, Indpls., 1993—, Labeco Properties, Creston Group, Indpls.; pres., dir. K&K Realty, Inc., Indpls.; sec., dir., mem. exec. com. Lab. Equipment Corp., Mooresville, Ind.; instr. bus. law Butler U., 1948-49, chmn. bd. govs., 1965-66, bd. trustees, 1987-90; chmn. Ovid Butler Soc., 1982-83. Life bd. dirs. Crossroads Am. coun. Boy Scouts Am., 1965—, v.p. fin., mem. exec. com., pres., 1977-79, chmn. trustees endowment fund, 1987-92, trustee, 1987—, chmn. Gathering of Eagles dinner, 2000; bd. dirs. Fairbanks Hosp., Indpls., 1986-94, chmn. bd., 1988-91, exec. com., 1987-94, mem. audit and fin. com., 1992-94, life dir. emeritus, 1994—, chmn. nominating com., 1991; trustee Butler U., 1987-90, Children's Mus., Indpls., 1969-88, pres. bd. trustees, 1984-85, bd. disting. advisors, 1990—; mem. First Meridian Heights Presbyn. Ch., 1933—, chmn. bd. trustees, 1958-61, 69-72, 1996— ruling elder 1982-85, 94-99, deacon, 1950-58; mem. planning com. and dir. 32-Degree Scottish rite Children's Learning ctr., 1997—. Recipient Paul H. Buchanan award of excellence Indpls. Bar Found. Mem. ABA (ho. of dels. 1970-71), Ind. State Bar Assn. (ho. dels. 1959—, chmn. pub. rels. exec. com. 1966-69, sec. 1973-74, bd. mgrs. 1975-77, chmn. law practice mgmt. com. 1991-92), Indpls. Bar Assn. (treas., 1st v.p. 1965, pres. 1970, bd. mgrs. 1968-71, 75-77, chmn. law day com. 1991-92, settlement week com. 1989-95, co-chair Family Law Study Commn., co-chair ct. liaison com. 1992-93, family law implementation com. 1993-97, mem. exec. com. bd. mgrs. 1994-96, counsel bd. mgrs. 1994, chmn. sr. lawyers divsn. 1999—), Am. Judicature Soc., Indpls. Legal Aid Soc., Indpls. Jr. C. of C. (past 1st v.p., dir. ct. unification implementation com., chmn. 1995-98), Butler U. Alumni Assn. (past pres.), Mich. Alumni Assn., Meridian Hills Country Club, Lawyers Club, Gyro Club (pres. 1966), Masons (worshipful master 1975), Valley Scottish Rite Found. (33d degree, most wise master 1982-84, trustee 1996—, chmn. bd. trustees 1998-99, pres. Indpls. Scottish Rite Cathedral Found., dir. 1997—, chmn. 1998-99, dir. Indpls. Scottish Rite Found., Inc., dir. Scottish Rite Learning Ctr. 1998—), Shriners, Phi Delta Theta (chpt. advisor 1950-82), Tau Kappa Alpha. Republican. Presbyterian. Home: 624 Somerset Dr W Indianapolis IN 46260-2924 Office: 1 American Square PO Box 82053 Indianapolis IN 46282-2053

KAPS, PETER, mathematics educator, researcher; b. Feldkirch, Austria, Apr. 7, 1947; s. Ernst and Anna (Alber) K. MSc, U. Innsbruck, Austria, 1972, PhD, 1979, Habilitation, 1986. Assoc. prof. math. U. Innsbruck, 1972—. Office: Dept Math and Geometry, Technikerstr 13, A-6020 Innsbruck Austria

KAPSAMBELIS, VASSILIS, psychiatrist, psychoanalyst; b. Nicosia, Cyprus, July 13, 1955; s. Stavros and Toula (Mandari) K.; m. Sophie Kecskemeti, Oct. 31, 1993; children: Dorothee, David. MD, Med. Sch. of Athens, 1980. Psychiatrist MGEN, Paris, 1985-91; hosp. practitioner in psychiatry U. Amiens, 1991-94; chief dept. of psychiatry Mental Health Assn. XIII, Paris, 1995—. Author: The Drugs of Narcissism, 1995, Psychiatric Terms of Greek Origine, 1997; editor: Chemical Treatment in Psychiatry, 1996. Mem. Evolution Psychiatry, CPNLF, Helenic Soc. of Social Psychiatry. Home: 40 Blvd de Montparnasse, 75015 Paris France Office: Assoc Sante Mentale, 11 rue Albert Bayet, 75013 Paris France

KAPTEIN, ADRIAN AREND, psychologist; b. Beverwijk, The Netherlands, June 27, 1949; s. Jan A. and Catharina A.M. (Frankfort) K. BA in Psychology, Leiden U., 1973, MA, 1977; PhD, Free U., 1982. Rschr. dept. social medicine Leiden (The Netherlands) U., 1976-82, asst. prof. dept. family medicine, 1983-92, assoc. prof. dept. psychiatry, 1992—; cons. Dutch Asthma Ctr., Davos, Switzerland, 1986-91, various govtl. orgns., The Netherlands, 1985—. Author: Living With Respiratory Illness, 1988, 2d edit., 1991; editor: Behavioural Medicine, 1990; editor-in-chief: Psychology & Health, 1992—. Vol., bd. dirs. SOS Telephone Crisis Intervention Svc., Leiden, 1970-92. Rsch. grantee Asthma Found., 1979—, Med. Rsch. Coun., 1986—. Mem. European Health Psychology Soc. (sec. 1986—, pres. 2000—), European Respiratory Soc. (sec. sect. health edn. 1985-96). Avocations: playing bridge, bicycling. Fax: (071) 527 5240. E-mail: akaptein@pobox.leidenuniv.nl. Home: Maredijk 58, 2316 VN Leiden The Netherlands Office: Leiden U Dept Psychiatry, PO Box 1251, 2340 BG Oegstgeest The Netherlands

KAPTEYN, PAUL JOAN G., judge; b. Laren, The Netherlands, Jan. 31, 1928; s. Paulus Johannes and Picaine (Schröder) K.; m. Hendrina Johanna Streef, Mar. 20, 1956; children: Marina, Paul. LLM, Law Faculty, Leiden, The Netherlands, 1950, LLD, 1960. Asst. prof. internat. law Law Faculty, Leiden, 1953-60; prof. law internat. orgns. Law Faculty, Utrecht, The Netherlands, 1963-74; idem Law Faculty Law Faculty, Leiden, 1974-76; official fgn. office The Hague, The Netherlands, 1960-63, mem. coun. of state, 1976-90, pres. jud. div. coun. of state, 1984-90; mem. Ct. of Justice European Communities, Luxembourg, 1990—, now judge. Author: The Common Assembly of the European Coal and Steel Communities, 1960,; co-author: Introduction to the Law of the European Communities, 1987, rev. edit., 1989. Mem. Com. on Elimination Racial Discrimination UN Conv., 1974-78, past chmn. Decorated comdr. Order Orange-Nassau (Netherlands), 1983. Mem. Royal Dutch Acad. Scis., Netherlands Assn. Internat. Law (pres. 1988—), Internat. Com. of Jursits (Geneva). Mem. Dutch Labour Party. Office: Ct Justice European Cmtys, Palais la Cour Justice, L-2925 Luxembourg Luxembourg*

KAPUR, SUMAN OMPRAKASH, psychology educator; b. Rawalpindi, Pakistan, Aug. 23, 1943; arrived in India, 1947; d. Wazirchand Kishinchand and Janakidevi Wazirchand (Kapur) Khanna; m. Omprakash Madan Lal Kapur, Jan. 24, 1977; 1 child. BA with honors, Jai Hind Coll., Bombay, 1965; MA, Dept. Applied Psychology, Bombay, 1967, MPhil, 1988, PhD, 1998. Registered clin. rehab. Coun. India. Lectr. Gordhandas Sunderdas Med. Coll., King Edward Meml. Hosp., Bombay, 1967-68; lectr. Topiwalla Nat. Med. Coll., Nair Hosp., Bombay, 1968-71, assoc. prof., 1971—; in charge Nair Hosp. Sch. for Deaf, Bombay, 1997—; vis. prof. Nat. Assn. for the Blind, India, 1996—; hon. chief advisor Om Shanti Coll. Alternative Medicine, India, 1999—; hon. counselor Lala Lajpat Rai Coll. of Commerce and Econs., Bombay, 1998—; v.p. Staff Soc., T.N. Med. Coll., 1996, pres. Staff Soc., 1998; condr. workshops, spkr. in field. Contbr. chpts. to books including Child Psychology and Child Guidance, 1978, Psychological Testing, 1990, Psychology of Exceptional Children, 1990. Recipient Disting. Svc. award Heart Care Found. and Govt. Delhi, 1998, Appreciation award World Congress-Alternative Therapies, 1999, 2000; grantee Univ. Grants Commn., 1987. Mem. APA (internat. affiliate), Internat. Coun. Psychologists, Indian Speech and Hearing Assn. (life), Bombay Psychol. Assn. (life). Mem. Yogoda Satsang Soc. Avocations: painting, swimming, gardening, music. E-mail: suman kapur@yahoo.com/ sumankapur@im.eth.net. Home: 1/22 Nair Hosp Staff Flats, Haji Ali Bombay 400 034, India

KAPUSCINSKI, RYSZARD, journalist; b. Pinsk, Poland, Mar. 4, 1932; s. Jozef and Maria (Bobka) K.; m. Alicja Mielczarek; 1 child. MA Faculty History, Warsaw U.; D honoris causa, U. Silesia, Katowice, 1997. With Sztandar Mlodych, 1951, Polityka, 1957-61; corr. Polish Press Agy., Africa, Latin Am., 1962-72; with Kultura, 1974-81; vis. prof. Temple U., Phila.; vice chmn. com. rsch. and prognosis Polish Acad. Scis. Author: Busz po polsku, Czarne gwiazdy, Kirgiz schodzi z konia, Gdyby cala Afryka..., Dlaczego zginal Karl von Spreti, Chrystus z karabinem na ramieniu, Jeszcze dzien zycia, Cesarz, Wojna futbolowa, Szachinszach, Notes, Lapidarium, Laidarium II, Lapidarium III, Lapidaria, Imperium Heban. Decorated Golden Cross of Merit, Knight's Cross, Order Polonia Restituta; recipient B Prus, 1975, Internat. prize Internat. Journalists Orgn., 1976, State prize (2d class), 1976, German prize for European Understanding, 1994, Lit. award Alfred Jruzykowski Found., 1994, Prix d'Astrolab, 1995, Jan. Parandowski PEN Club prize, 1996, Lit. award Truzanski Found., 1996, Joseph Conrad Lit. award J. Pilsudski Inst. Am., 1997, Hansische Goethe-Preis, 1999, S.B. Linde lit. award Twin Cities Toruń-Götingen, 1999. Mem. Nat. Coun. Culture, European Acad. Sci. and Art, Polish Acad. Sci. and Art.

KAR, RAMESH CHANDRA, mechanical engineer, educator; b. Cuttack, India, Nov. 9, 1942; s. Lambodar and Ichha Lata (Dash) K.; m. Charubala Acharya, May 27, 1966; children: Jyotiranjan, Saswati, Bratati. BSc (Engring.), Utkal Univ., Orissa, India, 1964; M Tech, I.I.T., Kharagpur, India, 1970, PhD, 1979. Assoc. lectr. Regional Engr. Coll., Rourkela, India, 1964-66; scientist B Regional Rsch. Lab., Bhubaneswar, India, 1966-67; assoc. lectr. mech. engr. dept. I.I.T., Kharagpur, 1967-70, lectr. mech. engr. dept., 1970-79, asst. prof. mech. engr. dept., 1979-90, assoc. prof. mech. engr. dept., 1990-96, prof. mech. engr. dept., 1996—; vis. prof. Regional Engr. Coll., Silchar, India, 1985-86; bd. studies, Rourkela, India, 1990-92, 94-96. Recipient rsch. fellow Alexander von Humboldt Stiftung, Germany, 1980-81, 1991. Mem. Inst. of Engrs., Bureau of Indian Standards, Indian Nat. Scientific Documentation Ctr. (translator). Office: Indian Inst Tech dept mech engring, 721302 Kharagpur India

KAR, SUPRIYA, research scientist; b. Balasore, India, June 10, 1967; s. Sripati Charan and Ira (Sen) K.; m. Shraboni Dutta, May 10, 1996; 1 child, Prakriti. BS with honors, F.M. Coll., Balasore, India, 1987; MS in Physics, Utkal U., Bhubaneswar, India, 1990; PhD, Inst. Physics, Bhubaneswar, India, 1995. Vis. fellow Mehta Inst. Rsch., Allahabad, India, 1995-96; jsps post doctoral fellow Tokyo U., 1996-98; post doctoral fellow Chalmers U., Goteborg, Sweden, 1998-2000. Contbr. articles to profl. jours. Recipient fellowship, Japan Soc. for Promotion of Sci., 1996-98, FNR fellowship, Swedish Natural Sci. Rsch. Coun., 1998—. Avocations: cyber games, sci. fiction, reading, music, travel. E-mail: supriya kar@hotmail.com.

KARA, AYSUN, chemical engineer; b. Eskisehir, Turkey, Feb. 10, 1972; d. Ahmet and Hadiye (Dinger) K. Degree in Chem. Engring., Hacettepe U., Ankara, Turkey, 1994, MSc, 1997. Cert. specialist chem. engr. Rsch. asst. chem. engring. dept. Hacettepe U., Ankara, 1995-97, specialist pharmacol. dept., 1997—, lab. specialist, 1997—. Mem. Turkish Pharmacol. Soc. Avocations: Turkish Ebru art, riding, bicycling, theatre. Office: Hacettepe Univ, 06100 Ankara Sihhiye, Turkey

KARAALI, ARTEMIS FATMA, food engineering educator; b. Kutahya, Turkey, June 16, 1948; d. Sitki and Mualla (Goktan) Tuncer; m. Atok Karaali, Aug. 7, 1970; children: Dide, Gizem. BS in Chem. Engring., Robert Coll., Istanbul, Turkey, 1969; PhD in Food Sci., Ege U., Izmir, Turkey, 1981. Analyst Ministry of Health, Ankara, Turkey, 1970-72; researcher Tubitak, Gebze, Turkey, 1973-89; rsch. dir. Meyna, Istanbul, 1989-91; assoc. prof. Istanbul Tech. U., 1991-93, prof., 1993—, dept. head, 1993—. Contbr. numerous articles to profl. jours. Home: Sahrayicedit Intas Sitesi, E Blok D1 Erenkoy, Istanbul 81080, Turkey Office: Istanbul Tech U, Dept Food Engring, Istanbul 80626, Turkey

KARABACHEV, IVAN, otolaryngologist; b. Sofia, Bulgaria, Sept. 10, 1947; came to U.S., 1976; s. Dimitri and Anna K.; m. Jane Aimme Karabachev, May 24, 1989; children: Anna, Alexander. MD, U. Sofia, 1972; grad., U. Vt., 1980. Surgeon Ear, Nose and Throat Clin., Las Vegas, 1981—. Mem. Am. Acad. Otolaryngology and Head and Neck Surgery, Am. Coll. Surgeons, Rotary. Republican. Office: 3201 S Maryland Pkwy Ste 500 Las Vegas NV 89109-2427

KARABULUT, ABDULHALIK, atom and molecular physicist, educator; b. Erzurum, Turkey, Jan. 5, 1968; s. Refik and Latife (Turan) K.; m. Feyza Mualla Aggül, Sept. 20, 1972; children: Yaser, Ömer, Nursima. PhD, Atatürk U., Erzurum, 1996, Arts and Sci. Faculty, 1989, M, 1992, PhD, 1996. Asst. Atatük U., Erzurum, 1990-97, asst. prof., 1997—. Office: Atatürk Univ, Faculty Arts and Scis, 25240 Erzurum Turkey

KARAFFA, STEVEN WILLIAM, telecommunications equipment executive; b. Bitburg, Germany, June 23, 1961; came to U.S., 1963; s. William Steve and Ingrid Margarete Karaffa; m. Anja Leiter, Dec. 5, 1986; children: Max Alexander, Nikolas Xaver, Johannes Bensiek, Willem Wolf. BA in Govt., U. Notre Dame, 1983, MBA in Fin. and Internat. Bus., 1985. Sales engr. Siecor Corp., Hickory, N.C., 1989-93, nat. account and Western area sales mgr. cable TV, 1993-96, mgr. strategic planning, 1996-99; v.p. pub. network sales and mktg. Ams. Corning Inc., Hickory, N.C., 1999—. Editor Competitive Info. Newsletter, 1996—; contbr. articles to profl. jours. Capt. USAR, 1985-95. Decorated Meritorious Svc. medal. Mem. Soc. Cable TV Telecom. Engrs. Avocations: downhill skiing, whitewater rafting, travel, European history, family. E-mail: steve karaffa@siecor.com. Office: Corning Inc 489 Siecor Park Hickory NC 28601-3394

KARAGEORGHIS, VASSOS, archaeologist; b. Trikomo, Cyprus, Apr. 29, 1929; s. George Georghiou and Panayiota Georghiou; m. Jacqueline Girard, Mar. 21, 1953; children: Clio, André. Student, Nicosia U. Coll., Inst. Archaeology, London U.; D (hon), U. Lyon, U. Göteborg, U. Athens, Birmingham (Eng.) U., Toulouse U., France, Brock U., Can., Oxford (Eng.) U., U. Brussels. Asst. curator Cyprus Mus., 1952-60, curator, 1960-63; acting dir. Dept. Antiquities, Cyprus, 1963-64, dir., 1964-89; advisor to Pres. of Republic of Cyprus, 1989-93; prof. archaeology U. Cyprus, 1992-96; vis. rsch. fellow Merton Coll., Oxford U., 1979, sr. rsch. fellow, 1980; vis. fellow All Souls Coll., 1982, Merton Coll., 1988, Inst. for Advanced Study, Princeton U., 1989-90. Author books in English and French on Cypriot archaeology; archaeol. excavations at Salamis, Kition and several other sites in Cyprus. Decorated Chevalier de la Légion d'Honneur (France), Order Merit 1st Class (Fed. Republic of Germany), Comdr. Royal Order of Polar Star (Sweden), Order of Merit Republic of Italy, Order of Arts and Letters, France, Order of Honour for Sci. and Art, Austria, Officier de la Légion d'Honneur, France, 1998; recipient Prix de la Soc. des Études Grecques, Sorbonne, 1966, R.B. Bennett Commonwealth prize, 1978, Onassis prize Olympia, 1991, I Cavalli d'oro San Marco, 1996, Arts and Letters award Rep. of Cyprus, 1997; fellow Univ. Coll., London. Fellow Soc. Antiquaries London (hon.), Brit. Acad. (corr.); mem. Soc. Cypriot Studies, Archaeol. Soc. Athens, Acad. Athens (fgn.), Royal Swedish Acad. (fgn.), Archaeol. Inst. Am., Acad. des Inscriptions et Belles Lettres (fgn.), Acad. dei Lincei (fgn.), Inst. Berlin (ordentliches mem.), Austrian Acad. Scis. (corr.), Royal Acad. Spain. Office: PO Box 22543, 40 Gladstonos St, Nicosia 1095, Cyprus

KARAGODOVA, TAMARA YAKOVLEVNA, physics educator; b. Saratov, Russia, Apr. 25, 1945; d. Yakov Efimovich and Anastasiya Alexandrovna (Goryachena) Gindelis; m. Alexander Ivanovich Karagodov, Sept. 19, 1964; children: Olga Alexandrovna, Alla Alexandrovna. DSc, Saratov State U., 1997. Asst. Saratov State Tech. U., 1972-75, assoc. prof., 1976-97,

prof., 1997—. Contbr. articles to profl. jours. Grantee Internat. Sci. Found., 1993, Internat. Soros Sci. Edn. Program, 1998. Mem. Assn. of Spectroscopists. Avocations: travels, swimming, basketball. Office: SSTU, Politechnicheskaya 77, 410054 Saratov Russia

KARAK, ASIS KUMAR, pathology educator, consultant; b. Calcutta, India, Sept. 13, 1955; s. Kashi Nath Prem Sakhi Karak; m. Dipali Ghosh, July 20, 1997. MB, BChir, N.R.S. Med. Coll., Calcutta, 1980; MD, All India Inst. Med. Scis., New Delhi, 1984, PhD, 1990. Asst. prof. pathology All India Inst. Med. Scis., New Delhi, 1988-92, assoc. prof. pathology, 1993—; cons. in histopathology All India Inst. Med. Scis., New Delhi, 1988—. Mem. Indian Assn. Pathologists and Microbiologists. Avocations: reading, net surfing, computer games. Office: Dept Pathology All India Inst Med Scis, Ansari Nagar, New Delhi 110029, India

KARAKAS, UCAN NURAY, microbiologist; b. Eskisehir, Turkey, Apr. 1, 1969; d. Sabahattin and Aytac (Cetin) K. BS, Anadolu U.; MS, U. East Anglia; PhD, Anadolu U., Turkey. Rsch. asst. Anadolu U., 1993—, rschr., 1994-96. Contbr. articles to profl. jours. Mem. Turkish Biologists Soc. (gen. sec. 1995—), Turkish Phytopathology Soc., Turkish Found. for Combatting Soil Erosion, for Reforstation and Protection Natural Habitats, Soc. Culture Collections, Indsl. Microbiology and Biotech. Avocations: reading, travel, walking, music. Office: Anadolu U, Fen Fak Biyoloji Bol, Eskisehir 26470, Turkey

KARAKAYA, SIBEL, food engineer, researcher; b. Izmir, Turkey, Dec. 23, 1959; d. Kadri Erol and Nurten (Gundogmus) Eroğlu; m. Ismail Mesut Karakaya, Oct. 30, 1981; 1 child, Beste. MS, Ege U. Inst. Scis., Izmir, Turkey, 1991, PhD, 1997. Assoc. prof. faculty engring., dept. food engring. Ege U., Izmir, Turkey, 1997—. Contbr. articles to profl. jours. Mem. Sports Internat. Office: Ege U Faculty Engring, Dept Food Engring, 35100 Izmir Turkey

KARAKITSOS, ELIAS, economist; b. London, Apr. 28, 1948; s. Demosthenes and Anastasia (Strouza) K.; m. Chloe Despotopoulos, Dec. 6, 1972; children: Nepheli, Eliza. BSc, Athens (Greece) Sch. Econs., 1972; MSc, U. Surrey, Eng., 1975; PhD, U. Surrey, 1977. Demonstrator U. Surrey, 1976-77; econ. cons. Econ. Models Ltd., London, 1977-79; rsch. fellow Imperial Coll., U. London, 1979-82, sr. rsch. fellow, 1982-86, lectr. econs., 1986-89, reader in econs., 1989-93; prof. econs. Mgmt. Sch., Imperial Coll., U. London, 1993—, Nestle, 1997-98, Allianz, 1997-99, Abbey Nat. Bank, 1992-95, Kredit Bank, 1994-95; cons. Brit. Airways, 1988-89, Citibank-Citicorp, 1988—, Banque Indosvez, 1994—, Oppenheimer, N.Y., 1994-98; advisor DGII European Commn., 1992-95. Contbr. over 60 articles to econs. publs. Mem. Am. Econ. Assn., Royal Econ. Soc. Office: Mgmt Sch Imperial Coll, 52/53 Princes Gate, London England

KARAKUZU, RAMAZAN, mechanical engineer, educator; b. Konya, Turkey, Feb. 10, 1964; s. Fettah and Teslime (Abukan) K.; m. Asuman Erdogan, Jan. 14, 1995. MSc in Mech. Engring., Dokuz Eylul U., Izmir, 1988, PhD in Mechanics, 1992. Rsch. asst. engring. Dokuz Eylul U., Izmir, 1986-93, asst. prof., 1993-96, assoc. prof., 1996—. Author: Strength of Materials, 1997; contbr. articles to profl. jours. including Computers and Structures and Composites Scis. and Tech.; co-editor Jour. Engring. and Applied Scis., 19986. Grantee NATO, 1998, Turkish Rsch. Coun., 1991. Avocations: golfing, fishing, travel, camping, reading. Office: Dokuz Eylul U, Dept Mech Engring, 35100 Bornova-Izmir Turkey

KARAM, ANWAR G., construction engineer; b. Lebanon, Jan. 10, 1969; s. George Anouar and Rosemary Michel (Daher) K. BCE, Am. U., Beirut, Lebanon, 1991, M of Engring. Mgmt., 1993. Rsch. asst. The Am. U., Beirut, 1993; project financing engr. Byblos Bank Sal, Beirut, 1993; constrn. engr. Eastern Bechtel Corp., Abu Dhabi, United Arab Emirates, 1993-95; design engr. Bechtel Ltd., London, 1996—; area engr. (gas oil separation plant) Saudi Arabian Bechtel Co., Shaybah, Empty Quarter, Saudi Arabia, 1997—; lead civil/bldg./structural engr. (onshore gas development project) Eastern Bechtel Co. Ltd., Habshan, United Arab Emirates, 1998-99, area supt., 1999—. Contbr. articles to profl. jours. Mem. ASCE, Project Mgmt. Inst., Instn. Civil Engrs., Alumni Assn. of Am. U. Beirut. Achievements include contributions in the area of spares provisioning. Address: Eastern Bechtel Co Ltd, PO Box 2661 OGD2 Project, Abu Dhabi United Arab Emirates

KARAM, VANIA JOSE, engineer, researcher, educator; b. Rio de Janeiro, Brazil, Apr. 26, 1959; s. Jose and Victoria (Abrao) K. Engr., State U. Rio de Janeiro, 1982; MSc, Fed. U. Rio de Janeiro, 1986, PhD, 1992. Auxiliar rschr. Army Technol. Ctr., Rio de Janeiro, 1985-86, asst. rschr., 1987; collaborate prof. Fed. U. Rio de Janeiro, 1991-92; assoc. prof. State U. Norte Fluminense, Campos, Brazil, 1995—, chair structures divsn., 1996-97, civil engring. course coord., 1996-99, grad. coord. Technology and Sci. Ctr., 1997-99. Contbr. chpt. to book; contbr. articles to profl. jours. Mem. Brazilian Assn. Mech. Scis., Brazilian Soc. Computational and Applied Math, Internat. Soc. for Boundary Elements. Avocations: music, plastic arts, reading. Office: UENF, Av Alberto Lamego 2000, Campos Rio de Janeiro 28015, Brazil

KARAMAGIOLIS, SOTIRIS, consultant; b. Thiva, Viotia, Greece, Jan. 12, 1964; s. Padelis and Asimina (Andrianos) K.; m. Maria Kyriazis, Aug. 25, 1966; 1 child, Padelis. BS, Athens (Greece) Sch. Econs. and Bus. Sci., 1987; MPhil in Mktg., U. Strathclyde, U.K., 1989. Cert. trainer, GMA. Product mgr. Credin Hellas Ltd., Greece, 1991-92; asst. mktg. mgr. Optima S.A., Greece, 1992-93; project mgr. Eurospace Ltd., Greece, 1993-95; mng. dir. S. Karamagiolis & Co. Ltd., Thiva, Greece, 1995—; advisor Prefecture of Viotia, 1996-98; trainer Export Greek Orgn., 1998-99. V.p. Econ. Chamber of Greece, 1998-99. Mem. Greek Mgmt. Assn., Greek Union of Industries, Greek Inst. Mktg. Office: SKC Ltd, 17 Drakou Str, 322 00 Thiva Viotia Greece

KARAMANOS, ANDREAS J., agriculture educator, agronomist; b. Athens, Greece, Sept. 13, 1946; s. John S. and Ephrosyne (Nefeloudis) K.; m. Georgia Xanthakis, Dec. 16, 1971; children: Joanna, John-Constantine. MSc, Agrl. U. Athens, 1969; PhD, U. Reading, Eng., 1976. Asst. lectr. U. Athens, 1973-78; lectr. Agrl. U. Athens, 1978-81, prof., 1981—, head dept. plant sci., 1988-89, vice-rector, 1991-97, chmn. rsch. com., 1991-97. Author: Water Stress on Plants, 1981, Sage, 1999. Greek State scholar, 1964-69; Stathatos scholar U. Athens, 1973-75. Mem. Am. Soc. Agronomy, Crop Sci. Soc. Am., European Soc. Agronomy. Avocations: music, cinema, theatre. Office: Agrl Univ, 75 Iera Odos, 11855 Athens Greece

KARAMATSU, YOSHIKAZU, mathematics educator; b. Matsuyama, Ehime, Japan, Feb. 8, 1937; s. Yoshimasa and Yoshiko (Miyanishi) K.; m. Keiko Inoue, Jan. 5, 1966; children: Michiko, Hironori, Yoko. BS, Sci. U. Tokyo, 1964, MS, 1966. Instr. Sci. U. Tokyo, 1965—; instr. Utsunomiya U., Japan, 1968-70, assoc. prof., 1970-81, prof., 1982—, councilor, 1988-92. Author: On Fermat's Last Theorem and the First Factor of the Class Number of the Cyclotomic Fields, 1968, 80, Introduction to Linear Algebra, Kyoritsu Shuppan, 1983, Introduction to Differential and Integral Calculus, 1994; editor: Collected Papers of Taro Morishima, Queen's Papers in Pure and Applied Mathematics, 1990. Mem. Math. Soc. Japan., Math. Soc. Am., Am. Indsl. and Applied Math. Soc. Clubs: Ijikai (Shinjuku), Risokai. Avocations: Go-game, Kendo, Aikido. Home: 842-1 Hiramatsu-honcho, Tochigi Utsunomiya 321-0932, Japan Office: Utsunomiya U, 350 Minemachi, Tochigi Utsunomiya 321-8505, Japan also: Utsunomiya U Dept Math Fac, 7-1-2 Youto Utsunomiya, Tochigi 321-8585, Japan

KARAMOUN, NICOLAS, international marketing executive; b. Beirut, Lebanon, Feb. 6, 1953; s. Assaad and Antonia (Jirikez) K.; m. Julia Jabre, Jul. 10, 1982; children: Sandra, Natasha, Cynthia, Elsa. B in engring., American Univ., Beirut, 1974. Sales engr. Kettaneh Bros., Beirut, 1974-76; project mgr. Lahoud Engring., Syria, Qatar, 1976-78; country mgr. Sogelerg, Riyadh, Saudi Arabia, 1978-81; regional mgr. Gen. Elec., Zeddah, Saudi Arabia, 1981-84; mgr. bus. devel. Gen. Elec., Rye, N.Y., 1984-90; dir. internat. mktg. Hubbell Lighting, Inc., Christiansburg, Va., 1990—. E-mail: nkaramaour@hubbell ltg.com. Office: Hubbell Lighting Inc 2000 Electric Way Christiansburg VA 24073-2500

KARAMYCHEV, VALERI NIKOLAEVICH, radiochemist, biochemist; b. Petropavlovsk, Kazakhstan, USSR, Dec. 1, 1961; came to US, 1996; s. Nikoali Ivanovich and Valentina Ivanovna K.; m. Svetlana Alexandrovna Karamycheva, Apr. 28, 1984; children: Anastasiya, Denis. MD, Novosibirsk State U., USSR, 1984; PhD, Novosibirsk Inst. Bioorganic Chemistry, 1993. Radiochemist Inst. Nuclear Physics Tashkent (Uzbekistan), 1984-90; sr. scientist Inst. Bioorganic Chemistry, Novosibirsk, Russia, 1990-96; vis. fellow NIH, Bethesda, Md., 1996—. Author: Delivery and Strategies, 1995; contbr. article to profl. jours. Fogarty postdoc. fellow NIH, 1996; recipient Fogarty awards for rsch. excellence NIH, 1998. Mem. AAAS, Radiation Rsch. Soc. Avocations: volleyball, skiing, badminton, tennis. Home: 12907 Crookston Ln Apt 35 Rockville MD 20851-2005

KARAN, DONNA (DONNA FASKE), fashion designer; b. Forest Hills, N.Y., Oct. 2, 1948; m. Mark Karan; 1 child, Gabrielle. BFA, Parsons Sch. Design, 1987. With Addenda Co., to 1968; with Anne Klein & Co., N.Y.C., 1968-84; co-designer Anne Klein & Co., 1971-74, designer, 1974-84; owner, designer, ptnr. Donna Karan Co., N.Y.C., 1984-96, chmn. bd., chief designer, 1996—. Showed first complete collection for Anne Klein & Co. in 1974; collaborator on Anne Klein collections with Louis dell'Olio; author: DKNY: NYC, 1994. Bd. dirs. Design Industries Found. for AIDS; co-chair Kids for Kids, 1993, Ovarian Cancer Rsch. Super Saturday, East Hampton, N.Y, summers 1998, 99. Recipient Coty award, 1977, Awards Coun. of Fashion Designers of Am., 1985, 86, 92, Frontrunner award Sara Lee Corp., 1992; co-recipient (with Louis dell'Olio) Coty Return award, 1981, Coty Hall of Fame citation, 1982, Coty award, 1984; named Menswear Designer of Yr. Coun. Fashion Designers Am., 1992. Mem. Fashion Designers Am. (bd. dirs.). Office: Donna Karan Co 15th Fl 550 7th Ave New York NY 10018-3203

KARANDE, SUNIL, pediatrician, researcher; b. Bombay, July 29, 1961; s. Chandrakant and Swarooprani (Bhatt) K. MBBS, Seth GS Med. Coll., Bombay, 1984, MD in Pediat., 1989. House physician in pediat. Seth GS Med. Coll. and Bai Jerbai Wadia Hosp. for Children, Bombay, 1986-87, Seth GS Med. Coll. and Dr. RN Cooper Hosp., Bombay, 1987-88; registrar in pediat. Seth G.S. Med. Coll. and KEM Hosp., Bombay, 1988-90, med. officer (adverse drug reaction monitoring project), 1990-91, lectr. in pediat., 1992-98; assoc. prof. pediat. Lokmanya Tilak Mcpl. Med. Coll., Bombay, 1998—; cons. KEM Hosp., 1989-98, Lokmanya Tilak Mcpl. Gen. Hosp., 1998—; med. tchr. U. Bombay, 1988—, examiner pediat. Third MBBS exam., 1998—; mem. tech. com. WHO, 1997-99; expert for essential drug list, Indian Pharmacol. Soc. Clinicians & Pharmacologists, 1994; postgrad. guide Diplomate Nat. Bd. pediat. dissertation Nat. Bd. Exams., New Delhi, 1999—; postgrad. guide Fellow Coll. Physicians and Surgeons pediat. dissertation Coll. Physicians and Surgeons Bombay, 1999—; postgrad. guide MD pediat. dissertation, Univ. Bombay, 1998—; facilitator Mother and Child Friendly Hosp. Initiative, UNICEF, 2000—. Contbr. articles to profl. jours., chpts. to books; joint editor Pediatric Pulmonology Update, 1993-97; reviewer Jour. Indian Pediatrics, 2000—. Trainer, breastfeeding mgmt. course, Maharashtra State Breastfeeding Promotion Initiative, Bombay, 1994—; nodal person for surveillance of acute flaccid paralysis cases, Greater Bombay Mcpl. Corp., 1996-98. Surgeon lt., Indian Navy, 1991-92, INHS Asvini, Bombay. Mem. N.Y. Acad. Scis., Indian Acad. Pediat. (life mem.), Indian Acad. Pediat.—Respiratory Chpt. (life mem.; treas. 1997, coord. seminars, confs. and continuing med. edn. 1993-99). Avocations: swimming, music, computers, novels, cricket. Home: Fl 24 5th fl Joothica, 22A Naushir Bharucha Rd, Bombay 400 007, India Office: LTM Med Coll & LTMG Hosp, Dept Pediatrics, Bombay 400 022, India

KARANTOKIS, NICOLAS GEORGIOU, contractor, developer; b. Nicosia, Cyprus, Jan. 13, 1917; s. Georgios Nicola and Panayiota Georgiou (Karantoki) K.; student Pancyrprian Gymnasium Nicosia, 1929-35, Athens U., 1935-39; m. Lella Phisentzides, Apr. 27, 1947; 3 children. Interpreter, recruiting office, 1941-42; contractor Brit. Army, 1943-60; chmn. Medcon Constrn. Ltd., Nicosia, 1956—; chmn., mng. dir. Medcon Group. Chmn. com. Tripiotis Ch., Nicosia. Home: 1 Kalamatas, Nicosia Cyprus Office: Medcon Constrn Ltd, 24 Voulgaris, Nicosia Cyprus

KARAPANCHEV, GEORGI LUBOMIROV, treasurer; b. Samokov, Bulgaria, Oct. 21, 1965; s. Lubomir Georgiev Karapanchev and Nina Ilieva Kostova; m. Assia Ananieva Apostolova, July 17, 1988; children: Alex, Nadine. BA, U. Econs., Budapest, Hungary, 1992. Sr. asst. KPMG Hungary, Budapest, 1991-93; regional fin. controller Oriflame Internat., Brussels, 1993-97, treas., 1997—. Mem. Assn. Chartered Certified Accts. Mem. Bulgarian Orthodox. Avocation: gardening. Fax: 36-1-457-3833. Office: Oriflame KFT, Florian Ter 1, 1033 Budapest Hungary

KARAPETSAS, ARGYRIS, neuropsychologist; b. Neochorion, Greece, Jan. 7, 1952; s. Vasileios and Maria (Rarra) Karapetsas; m. Maria Babou, July 6, 1985; children: Vasileios, Aikaterini. DSc, U. Paris, 1979, PhD, 1980. Vis. prof. dept. psychology Aristotle U., Thessaloniki, Greece, 1982-84; dir. Ctr. Mental Health, Athens, Greece, 1984-86; lectr, asst. prof. Dept. Primary Edn., Crete, Volos, 1989-98; assoc. prof. Dept. Pre-Sch. Edn., Volos, 1994-98; prof. Dept. Spl. Edn., Volos, 1998—. Author: Neuropsychology of the Developing Man, 1988, Child's Language: Development, Pathology, and Treatment, 1989, Child Dyslexia: Diagnosis and Treatments, 1991; contbr. articles to profl. jours. Sgt. Greek infantry, 1981-82. Mem. Internat. Neuropsychol. Soc., French Neuropsychol. Soc., APA, Hellenic Psychol. Assn. Christian Orthodox. Avocations: driving, swimming, climbing, snow skiing. Office: U Thessaly, Argonafton D Filellinon, 382 21 Volos Thessaly, Greece

KARAS, VLADIMIR, astrophysicist; b. Praha, Czech Republic, Feb. 1, 1960; s. Vladimir and Milada Karasova (Zlabova) K.; m. Jana Chasakova, Aug. 9, 1985; children: Ondrej, Ladislav. PhD, Charles U. Prague, Praha, 1989. Vis. scientist Internat. Sch. for Advanced Studies, Trieste, Italy, 1993-94; asst. prof. Charles U. Prague Astronomical Inst., Praha, 1995-97, assoc. prof., 1998—. Translator: The Brief History of Time (S.W. Hawking), 1991; contbr. articles to profl. jours. Fellow Royal Astronomical Soc. London; mem. Internat. Astronomical Union, European Phys. Soc. Fax: 420-2-6885095. E-mail: karas@mbox.troja.mff.cuni.cz. Office: Charles U Prague Astron Ins, V Holesovickach 2, Praha CZ180 00, Czech Republic

KARASAWA, SHINJI, electrical engineer, educator; b. Minowa Town, Nagano, Japan, Nov. 30, 1942; s. Tutayuki and Masa (Ozawa) K.; m. Junko Uchida, Oct. 8, 1967; children: Yashiko Sato, Munehiko. BEE, Tohuku U., Sendai, Japan, 1965, MEE, 1967, PhD, 1993. Asst. Miyagi Nat. Coll. Tech., Natori, Japan, 1967-72; from lectr. to prof. Miyagi Nat. Coll. Tech., Natori, 1972-88, prof., 1988—; dean Miyagi N. Coll. Tech., Natori, 1995-98; long term expert Japan-Internat. Coop. Agy., Tech. U. of The Philippines, 1985-86; exec. staff summer sch. Internat. Comm. Found., 1994-2000. Contbr. articles to profl. jours.; inventor in field. Mem. Inst. Elec. Info. Comm. Engrs., Japan Soc. Applied Physics, Acoustical Soc. Japan. Home: 1 3 6 Oyama, Natori shi 981 1233, Japan Office: Miyagi Nat Coll Tech, Nodayama Medeshima, Natori shi 981 1239, Japan

KARÁSEK, JIŘÍ, mathematician, educator; b. Brno, Moravia, Czech Republic, Jan. 10, 1938; s. Antonín and Marie (Pospíchalová) K.; m. Ivana Kubová, Feb. 8, 1963; 1 child, Iveta Klimešová. MSc, Masaryk U., Brno, 1960, PhD, 1969. Asst. Tech. U., Brno, 1960-63, lectr., 1963-71; lectr. Mil. Tech. Coll, Cairo, 1971-72; lectr. Tech. U., Brno, 1972-81, assoc. prof. math., 1981—. Mem. Union of Czech Mathematicians and Physicists, Am. Math. Soc. Roman Catholic. Avocations: traveling, geography, languages, railway history. Home: Slavíčkova 11, 638 00 Brno Czech Republic Office: Dept Math Tech U, Technická 2, 616 69 Brno Czech Republic

KARASEV, ANDREJ L'VOVITCH, physical chemist, researcher; b. Moscow, Feb. 13, 1940; s. Lev Vasil'evitch and Tatiana Vasil'evitch (Kostileva) K.; m. Luidmila Grigorevna Nazarienko, Sept. 9, 1961; children: Alexander, Peter. Engr.-Technologist, Mendellev Inst. Chem. Tech., Moscow, 1963; PhD in Chemistry, Russian Acad. Scis., Moscow, 1969; Tech. Bus. Specialist, Acad. Nat. Economy, 1996. Cert. engring. tech. in radiation chemistry. Rschr. Russian Acad. Scis., Frumkin Inst. Electrochemistry, Moscow, 1963-77, sr. rschr., 1977—; chief technologist Latent Image Tech. Ltd., Jerusalem, 1997—; cons. Volcanological Expedition, Kamchatka, Russia, 1964, 67, Geochem. Expedition, Chabarovik, Russia, 1966, Byelorussian State U., 1976-80, Plant Info. Techs., Pereslovl, Russia, 1992-93. Contbr. articles to profl. jours. Mem. N.Y. Acad. Scis., Nat. Geog. Soc. Achievements include co-inventor of polymer material with latent images visible in polarized light. Office: Latent Image Tech Ltd, PO Box 23946, 91237 Jerusalem Israel

KARASIN, F. BANU, bank executive; b. Istanbul, Turkey, Mar. 18, 1958; d. Orhan L. and Hayret U. Karasin. BA in sociology, Bosphorus U., 1980, MA in Sociology, 1984. Project asst., dept. asst. Bosphorus U., Istanbul, 1975-82; journalist Turkish Daily News, Ankara, 1982-83; cons., sales rep. Kopiteknik Corp., Ankara, 1984-85; supr., translator State Investment Bank, Ankara, 1985-87; account mgr. Iktisat Bank T.A.S., Istanbul, 1987-90; sr. account mgr. corp. and corr. banking dept. Credit Lyonnais, Istanbul, 1990-98, dep. asst. gen. mgr. corp. and corr. banking dept., 1999—. Contbr. articles to profl. jours. Mem. Ankara Coll. Alumni Assn., Bosphorus U. Alumni Assn., Mid. East Tech. U. Alumni Assn. Avocations: playing guitar, movies, reading, attending concerts and exhibitions. E-mail: banu.karasin@creditlyonnais.fr.

KARATHANASSIS, ATHANASSIS, research center administrator, educator; b. Volos, Greece, July 7, 1946; s. Eufthimios and Vassiliki K.; m. Helene Papaemmanouil, July 14, 1974; children: Vassiliki, Erasmie. Faculty Letters, U. Thessaloniki, 1969; Masters, Scuola Paleografia e Diplomatica, Venezia, Italy, 1971; Doctorate, U. Thessaloniki, 1976, Faculty Theology, 1987. Assoc. researcher Inst. Ellenico di Venezia (Italy), 1969-72, Inst. Balkan Studies, Thessaloniki, 1974-87; assoc. prof. U. Thessaloniki, 1985-87, U. Athens, 1987-89; prof. U. Thessaloniki, Greece, 1989—. Author: The Phlanginian School, 1976, The Greek Scholarships, 1982, The Unity of Hellenism, 1985, L'Hellenisme en Transylvanie, 1987, The Metropolitan of Neurokopi, 1987; editor: Fiori di Pietà, 1978, Thrace, 1996, Thessalonikia, 1996, Greece and Balkan, 1999; contbr. articles and book revs. to profl. jours. Sec. Dimitria, Thessaloniki, 1987. Mem. Soc. Greek Historians, Soc. Macedonian Studies Inst., Patristik Studies. Avocations: classical music, folklore. Home: Harissi 86, 54639 Thessaloniki Greece

KARATSU, OSAMU, research company executive; b. Tokyo, Apr. 25, 1947; s. Hajime and Sumako (Narumi) K.; m. Yoko Endo Sakai; children: Ken Endo, Yumiko Endo. BS, Tokyo U., 1970, MS, 1972, PhD in Physics, 1975. Researcher Musashino Labs. Nippon Telegraph and Telephone Pub. Corp., Tokyo, 1975-79, staff researcher, 1979-83; sr. staff researcher Atsugi (Japan) Labs. Nippon Telegraph and Telephone Corp., 1983-86; rsch. group leader LSI Labs. Nippon Telegraph and Telephone Corp., Atsugi, 1987, sr. rsch. mgr., 1989-90, exec. mgr., 1991-96; v.p., dir. ATR-I, Kyoto, Japan, 1997-98; sr. mgr. Nippon Telegraph and Telephone Corp. Hdqrs., Tokyo, 1988-89; chmn. LSI design lang. standardization com., Tokyo, 1987-95; prin. Stanford Rsch. Inst. Cons., Tokyo, 1999—; chief exec. dir. Stanford Rsch. Inst. Internat, Tokyo, 2000—. Author: Introduction to Very Large Scale Integration Design, 1983; Microelectronics Series, 1985, Encyclopedia of Information Science, 1990, Electronics Revolution in Everyday Life, 1999. Mem. IEEE, Japan Soc. Applied Physics, Am. Phys. Soc., Inst. Electronic, Info. and Communication Engrs. Japan, Inst. Elec. Engring. Japan. Avocations: playing and listening to classical music. Home: 2-3-34 Mita #208, Minatoku Tokyo 108-0073, Japan Office: SRI Internat Daito Bldg 2F, 3-7-1 Kasumigaseki, Tokyo 100-0013, Japan

KARATZAS, BASIL MICHAEL, holding company executive, consultant; b. Mytilene, Greece, June 5, 1968; s. Michael Basil and Vassiliki Karatzas. Student in med. sch., Athens (Greece) U., 1986-90; BS in Chemistry and Biology, Houston Bapt. U., 1996; MBA, Rice U., 1999. Pres. Platinum Holdings Internat., Houston, 1995—; adv. bd. Earth Telecomm. Internat., Houston, 1999—. Subject several articles Houston Bus. Jour., Brazzil. Greek Orthodox. Avocations: sailing, languages. E-mail: karatzas@rice.edu. Office: Platinum Holdings Internat PO Box 130064 Houston TX 77219-0064

KARAVANIĆ, IVOR, archaeologist; b. Zagreb, Croatia, June 27, 1965; s. Antun and Ružica (Lincender) K.; m. Snježana Vrdoljak, June 19, 1999. BA in Archaeology, U. Zagreb, 1990, MA in Archaeology, 1993, PhD in Archaeology, 1999. Rsch. asst. U. Zagreb, 1991—, sr. asst., 1999—. Mem. editl. bd. MI Youth Cath. Monthly, 1989-92, Opuscula Archaeologica, 1993-95; contbr. articles to profl. jours. Scholar French Govt., 1995; Constantin-Jireček scholar Austrian Inst. E. and S.E. European Studies, 1995, Fulbright scholar U.S. Info. Agy., 1996-97. Mem. Nat. Geographic Soc., Croatian Archeol. Soc., Serra Internat. Roman Catholic. Avocations: stamp collecting, coin collecting, running, swimming. Office: U Zagreb Dept Archaeology, Ivana Lučića 3, 10000 Zagreb Croatia

KARAYALÇIN, ÜMIT, internist, endocrinologist, educator; b. Ankara, Turkey, Apr. 7, 1958; s. Yasar and Melek (Durusoy) K.; m. Binnur Ercan, Apr. 9, 1982; children: Can, Cem. MD, Ankara U., 1981, specialist in internal medicine, 1985. Asst. prof. dept. internal medicine Akdeniz U., Antalya, Turkey, 1987-92, assoc. prof., 1992-97, prof., 1998—; head divsn. endocrinology Akdeniz U., Antalya, 1988—; fellow in endocrinology Kanazawa (Japan) U. Sch. Medicine, 1990-91; mem. Com. for Edn., Antalya, 1989-93, Com. for Postgrad. Edn., Antalya, 1987. Mem. editorial bd. Med. Jour. Akdeniz U., 1988-97; contbr. articles to profl. jours. With Turkish Army, 1985-86. Recipient award Japanese Internat. Cooperation Agy., 1990-91. Mem. Nat. Soc. Diabetes, Nat. Soc. Endocrinology, Akdeniz U. Sports Club (bd. dirs. 1992-97). Avocations: tennis, bridge, chess, archeology, interior decorating. Home: Gursu Mahallesi 310 Sokak, 14/1 Antalya Turkey Office: Akdeniz U Sch Medicine, Dept Endocrinology, 07058 Antalya Turkey

KARAYAN, HARRY J., electrical engineer; b. Nicosia, Cyprus, Can., Jan. 22, 1944; s. John and Karmella K.; divorced; children: Alex, Aliki. Grad. IERE, U. North London, 1971. Chartered engr. Project engr. Paging Co., London, 1972-74; lectr. Telecom. Ctr., Kingston, Jamaica, 1974-78; founder, officer Indsl. Tng. Authority, Nicosia, Cyprus, 1978-82; acad. dean Devry Inst. of Tech., Toronto, 1982-86; chairperson elec. engring. dept. Centenial Coll., Toronto, 1986-91; dir. Karayan and Assocs., Cyprus and Can., 1991—; cons. in field for Cyprus Govt. Cand. Cyprus Green Party, 1996, internat. rels. officer, 1996—. Mem. IEEE, Instn. Elec. Engrs., Inst. of Elec. and Electronic Engrs. Avocations: skiing, tennis. Office: 30 K Matsi Ave, Agios Dometios Nicosia 2368, Cyprus

KARAYIANNAKIS, ANASTASIOS IOANNIS, surgeon; b. Komotini, Rodopi, Greece, May 3, 1960; s. Ioannis Anastasios and Maria Ioannis (Doudaki) K.; m. Georgia George Makri, Dec. 18, 1994; 1 child, Ioannis. Med. diplomate, Med. Acad., Sofia, Bulgaria, 1985; MD, U. Athens, Greece, 1994; MS, U. London, 1996. Resident surgery U. Athens, 1987-93; sr. specialist First Ika Hosp., Athens, 1993—; clin. asst. St. George's Hosp., London, 1995-97; rsch. fellow Royal Postgrad. Med. Sch. Hammersmith Hosp., London, 1996-97. Contbr. articles to profl. jours. Scholar in surg. oncology Greek State Scholarship Found., Athens, 1995-97. Mem. AAAS, N.Y. Acad. Scis., Internat. Gastro-Surg. Club, Greek Soc. Laparoscopic Endoscopic Surgery, Hellenic Surg. Soc. Avocations: scuba diving, music, theatre. Home: 47 Peloponisou St, 153 41 Aghia Paraskevi Athens, Greece Office: First Ika Hosp, Terma Zaimi, 151 27 Melissia Athens, Greece

KARA-ZAITRI, CHAKIB, engineering educator; b. Tlemcen, Algeria, Sept. 2, 1960; s. Ghouti and Nafissa (Iles) K.-Z.; m. Lesley Jayne Storey, July 20, 1985; children: Ryad, Lula. B in Engring., U. Bradford, United Kingdom, 1983, PhD in Indsl. Tech., 1994. Rsch. asst. U. Bradford, 1983-88, rsch. asst., lectr., 1988-90, lectr., 1990—; engring. cons. Ventures and Consultancies Bradford, Ltd., 1985—. Asst. editor: Internat. Jour. on Quality and Reliability Mgmt.; contbr. articles to profl. jours. Grantee NATO, 1995, 96, NASA, 1993, European Commn., 1996, Dept. of Trade and Industry, 1996. Fellow Royal Statis. Soc. Avocations: travel, computing, sports, satellites. Office: U Bradford Dept Indsl Tech, West Yorkshire BD7 1DP, United Kingdom

KARAZIJA, ROMUALDAS, physicist, writer; b. Subačius, Lithuania, May 18, 1942; s. Jonas and Ona (Gužinskaite) K.; m. Aldona Degutyte; 1 child, Gita. PhD, Vilnius (Lithuania) U., 1968; DSc, Phys.Inst. Vilnius, 1993. Sr. sci. rschr. Inst. Physics, Vilnius, 1970-90; prin. sci. rschr. Inst. Theoretical

Physics and Astronomy, Vilnius, 1991—; prof. Vilnius Pedagogical U., 1995—; mem. Sci. Coun. Lithuania, Vilnius, 1991-93. Author: Joyful Physics, 1982 (Soc. for Dissemination of Sci. Knowlege of USSR award 1983), Sums of Atomic Quantities, 1991, Introduction to the Theory of X-Ray Spectra, 1996, (manual) Physics for Humanitarians, 1996 (Ministry of Edn. award 1997), Riddles of Physics, 1999. Recipient Nat. Sci. award, Lithuania, 1995. Mem. Lithuanian Phys. Soc. (sci. sec. 1972-79). Avocations: traveling, gardening, collection of physical toys. Home: Architektu 25-65, 2043 Vilnius Lithuania Office: Inst Theoretical Physics & Astronomy, Gostauto 12, 2600 Vilnius Lithuania

KARBANOVSKI, VALERI, physicist, educator; b. Noril'sk, Russia, Apr. 3, 1960; s. Victor K. and Raisa G. (Oleinich) K.; m. Ekaterina I. Kozlova, Nov. 30, 1958; children: Ivan, Roman. Degree in Physics, Kuban U., Krasnodar, Russia, 1982; PhD, Moscow Pedagogical U., 1993. Tchr. Pedagogical Inst., Komsomol'sk-on-Amur, Russia, 1983-86; aspirant Moscow Pedagogical U., 1986-91; sr. tchr. Pedagogical Inst., Murmansk, Russia, 1991-98, docent, 1998—; supernumerary employee Russian Inst. Info., Moscow, 1995—. Contbr. articles to profl. jours. Sr. lt. Russian Mil., 1987. Avocations: chess, football, walking. Home: Severni pr 1 1, 183038 Murmansk Russia Office: State Pedagogical Inst, Egorova 15, 183720 Murmansk Russia

KARCHEV, TODOR, otorhinolaryngologist; b. Ljubimetz, Bulgaria, May 28, 1945; s. Violeta Stefanova Doncheva, Sept. 16, 1973; children: Vessela, Maria. MD, Med. U. Sofia, 1969, PhD, 1983, DSc, 1997. From asst. to assoc. prof. Med. U. Sofia, Bulgaria, 1970-99, prof., 1999—. Co-author: Lympoid Throat Ring in Normal and Pathological State, 1978, Textbook of Pediatric Otorhinolaryngology, 1981, 89, Textbook of ENT Diseases, 1994, 2d edit., 1999; contbr. articles to profl. jours. Mem. European Soc. Pediat. ORL, European Soc. Rhinology, N.Y. Acad. Scis., European acad. Otology and Neuro-Otology, 1998—. Achievements include detection of M cells in human adenoid. Avocations: football, tennis, boxing, violin. Home: Tzar Peter 12, 1463 Sofia Bulgaria

KARCZEWSKI, JAN ANTONI, engineering educator, researcher; b. Drobin, Poland, June 12, 1937; m. Teresa Irena Karczewska; children: Dominika, Zuzanna. MS in Civil Engring., Warsaw U. Tech., 1961, PhD, 1971, DSc in Theory of Structures, 1976; postdoctoral student, U. Liverpool, Eng., 1976-77; prof., Polish State Coun., 1987. Designer various orgns., 1960-64; from lectr. to assoc. prof. Faculty of Civil Engring. Warsaw U. Tech., 1964-87, prof., 1987—, dep. dir. Inst. of Bldg. Industry, 1984-85, 93—, vice dean civil engring., 1987-93; assoc. prof. Moscow Engring. and Bldg. Inst., 1980; engr. sports ctr., car factory, airport terminal, others, Poland; cons. in field; mem. com. of mechanics engring., com. civil engring. & hydraulic engring, steel structure divsn. Polish Acad. of Sci., 1974—. Contbr. numerous articles to profl. jours. Mem. Polish Soc. Civil Engring. (mem. sci. com. 1964—), Internat. Assn. Shell and Spatial Structures, Internat. Assn. for Bridges and Structural Engring., Internat. Soc. Structural and Multidisiplinary Optimization, Euromech. E-mail: jkab@siwy.il.pw.edu.pl. Office: Warsaw U Tech of Civil Engring, Armii Ludowej 16, 00 637 Warsaw Poland

KARCZMARZYK, STANISŁAW, research scientist, educator; b. Zabełcze, Lublin, Poland, Jan. 2, 1954; s. Wiktor and Maria (Krowisz) K.; m. Regina Chmielewska, Jan. 18, 1984; 1 child, Konrad. M in Engring., Warsaw (Poland) U. Tech., 1978, PhD, 1989. Cert. mech. engring.-mechanics of layered structures. Designer Harvester Machinery Factory, Płock, Poland, 1978-80; tchr. Sch. Engring., Radom, Poland, 1980-82; rschr. Inst. Machine Design Fundamentals, Warsaw, 1983—. Contbr. articles to profl. publs. Active Trade Union Solidarity, Radom, 1981. Recipient award Polish Min. Edn., Warsaw, 1999. Roman Catholic. Avocations: history, belles-lettres. Office: Inst Machine Design Fund, Narbutta 84, 02-524 Warsaw Mazovia, Poland

KARDAR, ABDUL HAFEEZ, urologist; b. Faisalabad, Pakistan, Apr. 6, 1956; s. Muhammad Tufal and Aziza Begum; m. Nuzhat Rasheed, Dec. 22, 1985; children: Ahmed, Maria, Iman, Reem. MBBS, Punjab Med. Coll., 1980. Registrar King Khalidy Univ. Hosp., Riyadh, Saudi Arabia, 1985-88; clin. fellow Western Gen. Hosp., Edinburgh, U.K., 1989-90; asst. cons. King Faisal Hosp., Riyadh, 1991—. Fellow Royal Coll. Surgeons; mem. Internat. Urology Assn., Br. Med. Coun., Pakistan Med. Coun., Brit. Assn. Urol. Surgeons, N.Y. Acad. Scis. Avocations: swimming, cricket, basketball. Office: King Faisal Spec Hosp, King Faisal Spec Hosp, Surg Dept MBC #83, 11211 Riyadh Saudi Arabia

KARDASHIAN, JANE FLORA, dermatologist; b. Paterson, N.J., May 24, 1951; d. John Charles and Florence (Tashjian) Kardashian; m. Vatche Soghomonian, Aug. 8, 1981. Student, Mich. State U., 1969-71; BS in Pharmacy, Rutgers U., 1974; MD, U. Medicine and Dentistry of N.J., 1979. Diplomate Am. Bd. Dermatology. Resident in internal medicine U. Medicine and Dentistry of N.J., 1979-80, in dermatology, U. Calif., San Francisco, 1980-83; practice medicine specializing in dermatology, Fresno, 1983—; mem. dermatology faculty Valley Med. Ctr. (div. U. Calif.), Fresno; cons. staff Valley Children's Hosp., Fresno Community Hosp., St. Agnes Hosp. Recipient Cert. of Recognition, Am. Med. Women's Assn., 1979. Fellow Am. Acad. Dermatology; mem. AMA, Am. Med. Women's Assn., Calif. Med. Assn., Am. Soc. Dermatologic Surgery, Armenian Women's League, Alpha Omega Alpha, Rho Chi, Alpha Lambda Delta. Club: Fresno Women's Trade. Home: PO Box 3825 Fresno CA 93650-3825 Office: 728 E Bullard Ave Fresno CA 93710-5445

KARDASSIS, DIMITRIOS, physician; b. Freiburg im Breisgau, Germany, Oct. 22, 1970; s. Stergios and Eva-Maria (Beckmann) K.; m. Panagiota Sarischouli, June 20, 1998; 1 child, Maria Nepheli. MD, Humboldt U., Berlin, 1997. Rsch. fellow Virchow Clinic, Humboldt U., Berlin, 1997—, clin. study investigator and med. theses supr., 1997—. Contbr. articles to profl. jours. Donor German Red Cross, 1994—, SOS Children Villages, 1996—. Mem. WWF. Greek Orthodox Ch. Avocations: basketball referee, stamp collecting, travel. E-mail: dimitrios.kardassis@charite.de. Home: Westfaelische Str 70, 10709 Berlin Germany Office: Humboldt U Virchow Clinic, Augustenburger Platz 1, 13353 Berlin Germany

KARDO-SYSOEV, ALEXEI FEDOROVICH, physicist, researcher; b. Leningrad, Russia, June 7, 1941; s. Fedor Stepanovich Ignatiev and Elena Constantinovna Kardo-Sysoev; m. Elena Pavlovna Tenyakova; children: Constantin, Alexander, Natalia, Maria. Master's degree, Electrotech. inst., Leningrad, 1964; PhD, Ioffe Phys.-Tech. inst., Leningrad, 1973. Cert. in engring. Engr. TV Inst., Leningrad, 1964-67; jr. rschr. Ioffe Phys.-Tech. Inst., Leningrad, 1967-77, sr. rschr., 1977-90, lab. head, 1990; gen. mgr. Pulse Sys. Group, St. Petersburg, Russia, 1997—; prof. Ioffe Phys.-Tech. Inst., Leningrad, 1987. Recipient Soviet State prize USSR State Prize Com., 1987. Mem. Orthodox Church. Avocations: sports, amateur radio. Home: Bldg 75/2 Flat 3 M Toresa, 194214 Saint Petersburg Russia

KAREKIN, II, religious leader. Patriarch Armenian Apostolic Orthodox Ch., Beirut. Office: Armenian Catholicosate of Cilicia, Antelias POB 70317, Beirut Lebanon

KAREKLAS, PETROS MICHAEL, economist, association administrator; b. Kythrea, Nicosia, Cyprus, Apr. 19, 1949; s. Michael and Xenia (Panayi) K.; m. Ursula-Margarete Vallo; children: Melina, Christina. Diploma in econs., U. Freiburg, Fed. Republic of Germany, 1977; MA in Econs., U. S.C., 1983; PhD in Econs., U. S.C., Columbi, S.C., U.S., 1986. Stats clk. Stats. & Rsch. Dept. Ministry Fin. Govt. of Cyprus, Nicosia, 1969-86, sr. stats. asst., 1983, stats. officer, 1986; adviser to dir. dept. inland revenue Govt. of Cyprus, Nicosia, 1986; dir. Econ. Dept. Employers & Industrialists Fed. of Cyprus, Nicosia, Cyprus, 1987-98; permanent sec. Ministry Def., 1999-2000, Ministry Edn. and Culture, 2000—; co-researcher, cons. Bank of Jamaica, 1985-86; lectr. econs. Intercollege. Contbr. articles and reviews to profl. jours. Pres. Cyriot-German Assn., Nicosia, 1978-82, 1989-99; mem. Adv. Com. on Tertiary Edn., Nicosia, Cyprus, 1988-98. Decorated officer's cross Order of Merit (Fed. Republic Germany); scholar German Acad. Exchange Svc., 1972-77, CASP, 1982-83; prize winner European composition competition Coun. Europe, 1979. Mem. Am. Econ. Assn., Cyprus Econ. Assn., Cyprus Soc. Scis., Cyprus Popular Bank Club. Greek Orthodox. Avocations: reading, football, swimming, classical music. Home: Archbishop Makarios Ave 46, 2107 Algandjia Cyprus Office: Ministry Edn & Culture, Thoukididou & Kimonos Str, 1434 Nicosia Cyprus

KARELIN, ALEXANDER VITAL'EVICH, physicist, researcher; b. Berdichev, Zhitomir, Ukraine, Aug. 24, 1962; s. Vitalii Anan'evich and Liliya Fedorovna (Kokurkina) K.; m. Olga Alexandrovna Bondina, July 3, 1982; children: Tanya, Anna. Diplomate, MEPhI Moscow, 1985; PhD, Gen. Physics Inst., 1989, Dr. Sci., 1999. Rschr. Gen. Physics Inst., Moscow, 1988-90, sr. rschr., 1991-98, assoc. prof., 1993—, leading rschr, head lab., 1999—. Contbr. articles to profl. jours. Home: Savvinskoe Shosse 4-50, 143980 Zheleznodorozhny Moscow, Russia Office: General Physics Inst, Vavilov Str 38, 117942 Moscow Russia

KARELIN, ARTHUR ANANIEVICH, biochemistry educator; b. Nov. 15, 1935. PhD, The First Moscow Med. Sechenov, Moscow, Russia, 1963. Sr. lab. asst. Inst. Biochemistry and Physiology Microbes, Moscow, 1966; jr. rsch. worker Siberian Vet. Inst., Omsk, USSR, 1967, The Skliphosophsky Inst. First Aid, Moscow, 1967-68, Inst. Biol. Chemistry of Acad. Med. Scis. of USSR, Moscow, 1968-72; sr. rsch. worker Acad. Med. Sci. USSR, Moscow, 1972-77; head biochemistry dept. The Vishnevsky Inst. Surgery, Moscow, 1977—. Contbr. over 200 publs. in field. Mem. Organizing Com. First All-Union Symposium on Med. Enzymology, Odessa, USSR, 1969, Organizing Com. Second All-Union Symposium on Med. Enzymology, Dushanbe, USSR, 1969; scientific sec. Problem Com. on Med. Enzymology of Acad. Med. Scis. of USSR, 1981-86; vice chmn. Organizing Com. of Symposium of States-Members of Cmty. of Ind. States, Moscow, Russia, 1993. Recipient Medal in honor Pres. of Russian Acad. Med. Scis. N.M. Burdenko, 1994. Mem. Moscow Med. Inst. on Biochem., Vishnevsky Inst. Surgery Moscow. Office: The Vishnevsky Inst Surgery, Bolshaya Serpuhovskaya 27, 113093 Moscow Russia

KAREM, KEVIN LEE, microbiologist, educator; b. Louisville, June 20, 1965; s. Victor Michael and Minnie Naiser Karem; m. Karen S. Weldon, June 13, 1992; 1 child, Christina Nicole. BA in Biology, U. Louisville, 1988; PhD in Med. Scis., U. South Ala., 1993. Rsch. technician Pharmacology and Toxicology Rsch. Labs., Lexington, Ky., 1986; rsch. asst. U. Louisville, 1987-88; grad. asst. U. South Ala., Mobile, 1988-90, grad. rschr., 1990-93; postdoctoral fellow U. Tenn., Knoxville, 1993-96; rsch. microbiologist HESKA Corp., Ft. Collins, Colo., 1996-99; sr. microbiology fellow Ctrs. for Disease Control and Prevention, Atlanta, 1999—; vis. guest microbiologist Ctrs. for Disease Control and Prevention, Atlanta, 1996-99; continuing med. edn. lectr. So. Crescent Pers., Inc., Atlanta, 1997-99; grad. faculty U. Ala., Birmingham, 1999. Contbr. med. rsch. articles to profl. publs. Mem. Internat. Soc. Muscosal Immunology, Am. Soc. for Microbiology, Am. Soc. for Rickettsilogy, Order Ky. Cols. Achievements include patents pending for novel Bartonella proteins, nucleic acid molecules and uses thereof, use of Bartonella antigens as skin test reagent for diagnosis of Bartonella infections. Avocations: martial arts, golf, painting, fitness, home distilling. E-mail: kkarem@mindspring.com and kdk6@cdc.gov. Fax: 404-639-0049. Office: Ctrs for Disease Control MS-G18 1600 Clifton Rd Atlanta GA 30333

KARETZKY, JOANNE LOUISE, librarian; b. San Francisco, Apr. 20, 1952; d. Anthony Joseph and Augustina Clara (Armanino) Ballestrasse; m. Norman Martin Kunz, Dec. 28, 1975 (div. June 1984); m. Stephen Karetzky March 17, 1985. BA, U. San Francisco, 1972; MLS summa cum laude, San José State U., 1984; MA in Humanities summa cum laude, Calif. State U., Dominguez Hills, 1994. Cert. Calif. standard secondary tchr. Libr. dir. St. Paul H.S., San Francisco, 1977-85; spl. project libr., head tech. svc. Mercantile Libr., N.Y.C., 1986-89; head tech. svc., catalogue libr. Felician Coll., Lodi, N.J., 1989—. Author: The Mustering of Support for World War I by the Ladies Home Journal, 1998. Mem. Nat. Trust Hist. Preservation, Victorian Soc. Am., William Morris Soc., Found. for Study the Arts and Crafts Movement at Roycroft, Phi Alpha Theta. Avocations: music, needlework, collecting books, vintage needlework/textiles, antiques. Office: Felician Coll Libr 262 S Main St Lodi NJ 07644-2117

KARETZKY, STEPHEN, library director, educator, researcher; b. Bklyn., Aug. 29, 1946; s. Harry and Lillian Dorothy (Abrams) K.; m. Deborah Ann Shaw, Apr. 12, 1970 (div. July 1972); Joanne Louise Ballestrasse, Mar. 17, 1985. BA, CUNY, Flushing, 1967; MLS, Columbia U., 1969, DLS, 1978; MA, Calif. State U., Dominguez Hills, 1991. Libr. Bklyn. Pub. Libr., 1969-70; asst. prof. SUNY, Buffalo, 1974-76, Geneseo, 1977-78; assoc. prof. U. Haifa, Israel, 1978-81, San Jose (Calif.) State U., 1982-85; researcher, editor Shapolsky/Steimatzky Pub., N.Y.C., 1981-82; sr. editor Shapolsky Pubs., N.Y.C., 1985-86; libr. dir. Felician Coll., Lodi, N.J., 1986—. Author: Reading Research and Librarianship: A History and Analysis, 1982 (2d place award for Best Book of Yr. Am. Soc. Info. Sci 1983), The "Cannons" of Journalism, 1984; editor: The Media's War Against Israel, 1985, The Media's Coverage of the Arab-Israeli Conflict, 1989, Not Seeing Red: American Librarianship and the Soviet Union, 1999; bd. advisors Directory of American Scholars, 1999—; contbr. articles to profl. jours. Exec. dir. Ams. for a Safe Israel, N.Y.C., 1985-86. Mem. Am. Soc. Info. Sci., Am. Hist. Assn., Orgn. Am. Historians, Assn. for Libr. and Info. Sci. Edn. Jewish. Avocation: book collecting. Office: Felician Coll Libr 262 S Main St Lodi NJ 07644-2117

KARHU, JUHA ANTERO, geochemist, researcher; b. Helsinki, Finland, Oct. 25, 1951; s. Esko Antero and Marja Helena (Vesa) K.; m. Mirja Helena Kivisto, Apr. 25, 1974; children: Toni, Antti Juhani. MS, U. Helsinki, 1981, PhD, 1993. Rsch. scientist Geol. Survey Finland, Espoo, 1980-82; vis. assoc. Calif. Inst. Tech., Pasadena, 1983-85; sr. rsch. scientist Geol. Survey Finland, Espoo, 1986—; docent U. Helsinki, 1998—. Contbr. articles to profl. jours. Mem. Geol. Soc. Finland, Am. Geophys. Union. Home: Otsonkallio 4B, 02110 Espoo Finland Office: Geological Survey Finland, Betonimiehenkuja 4 PO Box96, 02151 Espoo Finland

KARI, JOUKO, education educator; b. Lehtimäki, Finland, Mar. 18, 1939; s. Väinö and Lyyli Wilhelmiina (Saarenpää) K.; m. Pirkko Kaarina Hautamäki, June 25, 1960; children: Tuulikki, Hannu, Aila, Elina. PhD, U. Jyväskylä, 1972. Headmaster of secondary sch. Soini, Finland, 1966-70; rschr. Inst. of Edn., Jyväskylä, 1970-76, prof., 1980-93; assoc. prof. U. Jyväskylä, Finland, 1977-80, prof. dept. tchr. edn., 1993—; docent U. Tampere, Finland, 1980—. Editor Scandinavian Jour. of Ednl. Rsch., 1983-91; author: Opetus-ja kasvatustyö ammattina, 1986, Opettajan ammatti ja kasvatustietoisuus, 1996. Mem. Finnish Assn. of Ednl. Rsch. (head 1978, 86). Home: Korkeakatu 7, SF-40630 Jyväskylä Finland Office: PO Box 35, SF-40351 Jyväskylä Finland

KARIKAS, GEORGE ALBERT, pharmacist, educator; b. Piraeus, Attica, Greece, Aug. 12, 1950; s. George Karikas and Maria (Gravinger) Scordianos; m. Kyriaki Savva, July 26, 1981; 1 child, Vasilios. Degree in pharmacy, Athens U., 1976, PharmD, 1980, PhD, 1986. Cert. hosp. pharmacist. Rschr. Biochemistry Dept., Athens, 1977-81, 87-88, Pharmacology Dept., Athens, 1981-82; rschr., tutor in medicinal chemistry and pharmacognosy Manchester (Eng.) U., 1983-86; quality control dir. MED-HELLAS, Attica, Greece, 1988-89; clin. pharmacist Children's Hosp., Athens, 1989—; dir. Nat. Health Sys.; vis. prof. U. Panama, 1992-95, U. Athens, 1998—; postdoctorate U. Salamanca, Spain, 1995; rschr. Organic Chem. Dept., Athens, 1995—. Inventor in field. Pres. Union Greek-Panamenians, 1996—. Mem. AAAS, Balkan Union of Ongology, N.Y. Acad. Scis., Phytochem. Soc. Europe. Avocations: athletics, football, traveling. Home: Kallergi 273, 18546 Piraeus Attica, Greece Office: Childrens Hosp Aghia Sophia, Pharma/Parenteral Nutrition, Athens 11527, Greece

KARIM, ABBAOUI, mathematician; b. Setif, Algeria, May 6, 1961; arrived in France, 1992; s. Abbaoui and Djilani (Ouarda) Djelloul; m. Meriane Djamila, Aug. 26, 1985; children: Intissar, Mohamed Abdoul Djalil. MA, U. Setif, Algeria, 1985, U. Paris, 1992; PhD, U. Paris, 1995. From asst. to prof. Algeria, 1984-93; tchr., rschr. Medimat, Paris, 1993—; dept. head U. Setif, 1984-87, sub. dir. 1987-91; rsch. dir. Medimat, Paris, 1993-97. Contbr. articles to profl. jours. Recipient Excellence award, 1997, Norbert Wiener award, 2000. Mem. AAAS, N.Y. Acad. Scis. Moslem. Home: 20 Rue Colonel Haoues, 19000 Setif Algeria Office: Medimat, 15 Rue de l'Ecole Medicine, 75270 Paris France

KARIM, HABIBULLAH NEYAMUL, computer company executive, consultant; b. Kushtia, Bangladesh, Nov. 9, 1962; s. Abu Nayeem and Sultana Zabinda (Choudhury) Jahed. BSEE, Yale U., 1984. Mktg. exec. CIPROCO Computers Ltd., Dhaka, 1985-86; pres. Technohaven Co., Dhaka, 1986—; exec. dir. Masharro & Co., Dhaka, 1990—; cons. WHO, Bangladesh, 1994-95, The Asia Found., Bangladesh, 1987-88, Capital Devel. Authority, Bangladesh, 1992-95; chmn. tech. com. fair election monitoring alliance FEMA, 1996; sec. gen. Bangladesh Assn. Software and Info. Svcs. (BASIS), 1998-99. Editor Bichayan--a social rsch. jour., 1999—; contbr. articles to profl. jours. including The Computer Jagat. Grantee ITC/UNCTAD, 1995. Mem. IEEE, Remians Bus. and Profl. Forum (hon. sec. 1993-95). Avocations: political history, psychology, philosophy. E-mail: hnkarim@bangla.net. Office: Technohaven Co House 37, Rd 6 Dhanmondi R/A, Dhaka 1205, Bangladesh

KARIM, JANET ZEENAT, broacasting professional; b. Blantyre, Malawi, Nov. 18, 1954; d. Nyemba Wales and Lois (Chikankheni) Mbekeani; m. Adam Karim, Nov. 3, 1984; children: Chiza, Adam Jr., Moses. BA, Chancellor Coll., Zomba, Malawi, 1978, BA with honors, 1979. Tutorial asst. Chancellor Coll., 1978-79; tchr. secondary sch. various govt. schs., Malawi, 1979-82; sr. journalist, sect. editor Daily Times, Blantyre, 1982-87; dep. editor Malawi News, Blantyre, 1987-89; founding editor Woman Now, Blantyre, 1989—; founding editor-in-chief Independent, Blantyre, 1993-99. Author: ABC The Alphabet, 1988, Mau Otsutsana, 1988; co-author: How to Make a Boat, 1989, Slap Me Five! God is Alive! - The Christmas Collection, 2000. Trustee Save the Children's Fund, Malawi, 1982-84; mem. Mayor's Christmas Cheer Fund Com., Blantyre, 1985-87, Malawi Broadcast Corp. Bd., 1994-96; founder, trustee Cmty. Media Found., 1997; co-founder DZIMWE Women's Cmty. Radio, 1996, project mgr., 1998—; founder Padangokhala Children's Pub. Found. Press fellow, nuffield Found. award Wolfson Coll., Cambridge, Eng., 1996. Mem. Journalists Assn. Malawi (founder, publicity sec. 1991-94), Pubs. Assn. Malawi (founder, sec. 1992-96), Malawi Media Women's Assn. (founder, chairperson 1994-97, com. mem. 1998—). Pentecostal. Avocations: reading novels and religious books, bicycling, swimming, jigsaw puzzles with family.

KARIM, MOHAMMED MOHIBUL, ophthalmologist; b. Comilla, Bangladesh, Apr. 5, 1954; s. Mohammed Rezaul and Ashia (Khatun) K.; m. Sultana Begum, Oct. 12, 1984; children: Saad, Maisha. Diploma, Intermediate Coll., Rajshahi, Bangladesh, 1971; MBBS, Mymensingh Med. Coll, Bangladesh, 1978; diploma in ophthalmology, Nat. Inst. Ophthalmology, Dhaka, Bangladesh, 1988; PhD, Kobe U., 1997. House surgeon Islamia Eye Hosp., Dhaka, 1983-85; sr. med. officer Lions Eye Hosp., Dhaka, 1985-88, cons. eye surgeon, 1988-91; vis. fellow Kobe U., Japan, 1992-93, asst. prof., 1995-96; cons. and head dept. ophthalmology Gono U., Dhaka, 1997-99; dept. head Z.H. Sikder Med. Coll., Dhaka, 1999—; med. dir. Cmty. Devel. Bureau, Dhaka, 1984-92. Author: (books) Disorders of the Eye and Thier Treatment, 1999, Phacoemulsifications and It's Technique, 1999; contbr. articles to profl. jours. Mem. Kalabagan Welfare Soc., Dhaka, 1995—. Grantee Pfizer Labs., Ltd., 1987. Mem. (life) AMA, (life) Ophthalmological Soc. Bangladesh, Bangladesh Acad. Ophthalmology. Avocation: travel, sports. Home: 44/1 Kalabagan N Dhanmondi, 1205 Dhaka Bangladesh

KARIMOV, ISLAM ABDUGANIYEVICH, Uzbek government official; b. Samarkand, Samarkand, Jan. 30, 1938; M. Karimova Tatiana; 2 children. Educated, Cen. Asian Poly. and Tashkent Econs. Inst.; D of Econs. (hon.), Univ. Seoul, 1992, Univ. Al-Azhar, Cairo, 1992, Univ. New Delhi, 1994; academician, Acad. of Uzbekistan. With Tashkent aviation constrn. factory, 1960-66; sr. specialist, head of sect., vice-chmn. Uzbekistan Gosplan, 1966-83; min. of fin., dep. chair Coun. of Mins. Uzbek SSR, 1983-86; 1st sec. Kashkadarya Dist. Communist Party, 1986-89; 1st sec. Cen. Com. Uzbek Communist Party, 1989—; mem. Cen. Com., People's Dep., mem. Politbureau Communist Party, USSR, 1990—; pres. Uzbekistan, Tashkent, 1990—; chmn. Cabinet of Mins.; pres. 2000—. Author: Uzbekistan - Own Way of Renovation and Progress, 1992, Uzbekistan - a State With a Great Future, 1992, On the Priorities of the Economic Policy of Uzbekistan, 1993, Uzbek Model of Deepening Econ. Reforms, 1995, Stability and Reforms, 1996, Uzbekistan on the Threshold of the 21st Century, 1997, Uzbekistan Striving Towards the 21st Century, 1999, The Spiritual Path of Renewal, 2000. Named Hero of Uzbekistan the Mustakillik and Amir Temur awards; many fgn. awards. Address: Office of Pres, Uzbekiston shohkochasi 43, 700163 Tashkent Uzbekistan

KARINO, KENJI, educator; b. Mito, Ibaraki, Japan, Nov. 15, 1963; s. Mamoru and Katsuko Karino. BS, Ibaraki U., 1986; MS, U. Ryukyus, 1988; D of Agrl., Kyushu U., 1994. Postdoctoral fellow U. Ryukyus, Okinawa, 1995-97; lectr. Tokyo Gakugei U., 1997-2000, asst. prof., 2000—. Author: Reproductive Strategies in Fishes, Vol. 1, 1996; contbr. articles to profl. jours. Home: Nukui kita 3-3-31-45, Koganei 184-0015, Japan Office: Dept Biol Tokyo Gakugei U, Nukui-kita 4-1-1, Koganei 184-8501, Japan

KARIOTAKIS, EMMANUEL, surgeon; b. Iraklion, Greece, Jan. 21, 1941; came to France, 1961, naturalized, 1974; s. Constantin and Iokasti (Toupoyanni) K.; m. Regine Loisel, May 22, 1971. M.D., Faculte de Medicine de Paris, 1967, laureat, 1975. Head dept. veinous surgery American Hosp. Paris, Neuilly-sur-Seine, 1980—; cons. French Red Cross, Paris, 1979-87. Contbr. articles to profl. jours. Fellow Association Francaise de Chirurgie, College Francais de Pathologie Vasculaire. Office: Hopital Americain de Paris, 63 Blvd Victor Hugo, 92202 Neuilly-sur-Seine France

KARIVALIS, DAMIANOS GEORGE See DIODOROS, I

KARIYA, PAUL, professional hockey player; b. Vancouver, Oct. 16, 1974. Forward/hockey player Anaheim (Calif.) Mighty Ducks, 1994—. Winner Lady Byng Meml. Trophy for sportsmanship and gentlemanly conduct, 1995-96; mem. silver-medal-winning Can. Olympic team, 1994. Office: Anaheim Mighty Ducks PO Box 61077 2695 E Katella Ave Anaheim CA 92803-6177

KARJALA, EDUARDO DANIEL, management consultant; b. Buenos Aires, Sept. 7, 1955; s. A. Le Roy and Edelmira C. (Marin) K.; m. Kathleen Marie Kayser, June 25, 1978 (div. July 1999); children: Maria, Rebekah. BS, U. Minn., 1980; MBA, Regis U., 1995. Computer ops. lead Kodak, Greeley, Colo., 1982-84; supr. AT&T, Denver, 1984; mgr. Ford Aerospace, Colorado Springs, Colo., 1984-91; mgmt. developer Intergraph Corp., Huntsville, Ala., 1991-94; dir. Townsends, Inc., Millsboro, Del., 1994-96; cons. Williams Cos., Houston, 1996-98; regional practice mgr. Shell Svcs. Internat., Houston, 1998-99; pres., owner EDK Cons., Houston, 1999—. Vol. fund raiser Senator R. Armstrong, Denver, 1984. Mem. ASTD (dir. fund raising 1990), ODN. Avocations: artistic photography, drawing, architecture. E-mail: edkarjala@yahoo.com. Office: EDK Cons Internat 2222 Maroneal St Unit 125 Houston TX 77030-3237

KARK, RUTH, geographer, historian, educator, writer; b. Petach Tiqwa, Israel, Mar. 28, 1941; d. Avraham and Shoshana (Motchan) Kleiner; m. Jeremy David Kark; children: Ronit, Salit, Guy. BA, Hebrew U., Jerusalem, 1964, MA cum laude, 1972, PhD, 1977. Prof. Hebrew U., Jerusalem, 1988—. Sgt. Israel Def. Force, 1958-60. Office: Hebrew U Dept Geography, Mt Scopus, 91905 Jerusalem Israel

KARLBERG, BARBARA MARY, retired translator, educator; b. Halifax, Eng., Dec. 1, 1927; arrived in Sweden, 1965; d. John and Amy (Brook) Greene; m. Jägmästare Åke Gunnar Karlberg, Apr. 2, 1965 (dec. 1991); children: Knut Kåre Joakim, Måns Olof Ingemar. First Class Diploma in Edn., U. London, 1947, Art Diploma with distinction, 1948; Diploma in Spl. Edn., U. Oxford, Eng., 1965; postgrad., U. Coll. Arts, Crafts, Design, Stockholm, 1989. Tchr. Kent Edn. Com., 1948-50, Slepe Hall, Cambridge, Eng., 1950-51; woman police constable Met. Police, London, 1951-56; tchr. English British Ctr., Stockholm, 1956-58; tchr. Approved Sch. Delinquents, Devon, Eng., 1958-59; headmistress Spl. Sch. Disturbed Children, Guildford, Eng., 1959-65; tchr. Spl. Sch., Gavle, Sweden, 1970-87; lectr. Univ. Coll., Kalmar, Sweden, 1988-92; tchr. People's Univ., Kalmar, —; retired, 1992. Translator: Öland, Substance & Shadow, 1995, The Castle on Kalmar Sound, 1998. Avocations: painting, writing, table tennis. Home: Klunkens Backe 1, 39352 Kalmar Sweden

KARLE, JEROME, physicist, researcher; b. N.Y.C., June 18, 1918; married, 1942; 3 children. B.S., CCNY, 1937; A.M., Harvard U., 1938; M.S., U.

Mich., 1942, Ph.D. in Phys. Chemistry, 1943. Rsch. assoc. Manhattan project, Chgo., 1943-44, U.S. Navy Project, Mich., 1944-46; head electron diffraction sect. Naval Rsch. Lab., Washington, 1946-58, head diffraction br., 1958-68, now head lab. for structure matter, 1968—; mem. NRC, 1954-56, 67-75, 78-87; chmn. U.S. Nat. Com. for Crystallography, 1973-75. Recipient Nobel prize in chemistry, 1985. Fellow Am. Phys. Soc.; mem. NAS (chairperson chemistry sect. 1988-91), AAAS, Am. Chem. Soc., Am. Math. Soc., Crystallograph Assn. (treas. 1950-52, pres. 1972), Internat. Union Crystallography (mem. exec. com. 1978-87, pres. 1981-84). Office: US Naval Rsch Lab Lab for Structure of Matter Code # 6030 Washington DC 20375-0001

KARLEMO, ROLF WALDEMAR, naval architect, consultant; b. Helsinki, Finland, Aug. 30, 1931; s. Waldemar Adolf and Hildur Amanda (Ekblom) K.; m. Clary Maud Elisabeth Lonnstrom, Feb. 21, 1960; children: Ben, Tom, Pontus, Filip. Degree in naval arch., Tech. U., Helsinki, 1956. Mgr. Wartsila Shipyard, Helsinki, 1956-62, Finland Steamship Co., Helsinki, 1962-81; dir. Effoa Ltd., Helsinki, 1981-85, Finncarriers Ltd., Helsinki, 1985-89; v.p. FG-Shipping Ltd., Helsinki, 1990-91; pres. Karlemo-Consulting Ltd., Helsinki, 1991—. Chmn. Finnish Sailship Found., Helsinki, 1987-97. Sub. lt. Finnish Navy, 1955-56. Decorated Order of the Lion of Finland. Mem. Finnish Shipowners Assn. (bd. dirs. 1990-91), Soc. Naval Archs. and Marine Engrs. Avocations: rowing, boating, bridge. Home and Office: 11 Marcus Collinsgr, FIN02700 Grankulla Finland

KARLICKY, MARIAN, astrophysicist; b. Frydek Mistek, Czech Republic, Oct. 20, 1949. RNDr, Charles U., Prague, Czech Republic, 1976; PhD, Acad. Scis., Prague, 1981, DSc, 1992. Scientist Astron. Inst., Acad. Scis., Ondrejov, Czech Republic, 1981-90, head solar dept., 1990-96, dep. dir., 1996—, dir. Ondrejov observatory, 1996—. Contbr. over 130 sci. articles to internat. jours. and conf. procs. Mem. Internat. Astron. Union (mem. commn. 10 1991-95). Avocation: poetry. Office: Acad Sci Astron Inst, 25165 Ondřejov Czech Republic

KARLIN, GARY LEE, insurance executive; b. Chgo., Jan. 18, 1934; s. Jack and Pearl (Malin-Weiss) K.; children: David, Paige; m. Cheryl Daneman; stepchildren: Chad, Brooke. Student, U. Ill., 1951-52, Roosevelt U., 1952. With Mut. of N.Y., 1956-62; sales mgr. Mut. of N.Y., Chgo., 1958-62, regional trainer, 1962-63; pres. Exec. Motivation, Inc., Chgo., 1964—; fin. planner, 1980—; chmn. field underwriters benefits/contracts com. MONY, 1974-85; v.p. Exec. Planning Svcs. divsn. Alexander & Alexander, Inc., 1990-96; dir., chmn. audit and compensation coms. Vasocor, Inc., Miami, Fla., 1990—; dir., chmn. audit com. Perception, Inc., Miami, 1993-98; v.p., treas. Exec. Fin. Group divsn. F.P.I.S., Inc., 1993-99; pres. Karlin Bus. Group, 1998—; cons. in field; speaker numerous ins. seminars. Contbg. editor Profl. Mgmt. mag., 1965-67; subject of poem There Are No Heroes Anymore; contbr. articles to profl. jours.; subject of ins. film Impressions of Life. Named to MONY Hall of Fame, 1966; featured in Time mag., 1967. Mem. Internat. Assn. Fin. Planners, Chgo. Assn. Life Underwriters, (past bd. dirs.) Nat. Assn. Life Underwriters (life), Million Dollar Round Table (Top of Table), Ill. Leaders Round Table (past pres.), Emil Verban Soc., Carolina Club, Gov.'s Club (Chapel Hill). Home: 55230 Broughton Govs Club Chapel Hill NC 27514

KARLOS, GEORGE EFTHIMIOS, chemical engineer, consultant; b. Athens, Greece, Mar. 31, 1938; s. Efthimios Ioanis and Sekka E. (Economou) K. Chem. Engr., Athens Nat. Tech. U., 1963. Cert. chem. engr. Asst. Nat. Tech. U., Athens, 1966-72; cons. salt prodn. C. Kalamarakis Salt Industries, Athens, 1967-69, Messolongi Chems. S.A., Athens, 1969-73; free lance cons. on water pollution control Athens, 1970—. Author: The Alumnina Industry and the Environment, 1976; co-author: Conservation in the Existing Buildings and in the Tomato Paste Industry, 1977, 78; 8 patents on wastewaters aeration and 2 patents on salt purification; contbr. articles to newspapers. Sgt. Greek Air Forces, 1963-66. Mem. Tech. Chamber Greece. Home and Office: 1 Yannopoulou Str, 157 73 Zografou Athens, Greece

KARLS, JOHN SPENCER, lawyer, accountant; b. Saginaw, Mich., Feb. 26, 1942; s. Harold M. and Mary Ellen (Spencer) K.; m. Andrea Lisbeth Berens, Dec. 23, 1967; children: Michael Berens, Hilary Marie. BA in Econs., U. Mich., 1964; JD, Harvard U., 1967; LLM in Taxation, NYU, 1973; MS in Acctg., Northwestern U., 1971. Bar: N.Y. 1967, Conn. 1978. Acct. Arthur Young & Co., N.Y.C., 1969-74; sr. tax atty., dir. tax planning Texaco Inc., White Plains, N.Y., 1974-87; tax ptnr. Ernst and Young, N.Y.C., 1987—; prof. taxation Fordham U. MBA program, N.Y.C., 1988—; lectr. NYU Law Sch. Tax Inst., 1994—. Deacon First Congregational Ch., Greenwich, Conn. Adv. bd. Jour. International Taxation. Editor: Effective Tax Strategies for International Corporate Acquisitions; assoc. editor Federal Income Taxation of Oil and Gas. Pres. I Have A Dream Found. of Stamford Inc., 1991—; treas. Nat. I Have a Dream Found.,1995—. Served to lt. USN, 1967-69. Recipient Elijah Watt Sells Silver medal Am. Inst. CPA's, 1971. Mem. ABA (tax sec. fgn. tax com., chmn.), Tax Execs. Inst., Westchester-Fairfield County Corp. Counsel Assn., YMCA, Harvard (N.Y.C.). Editorial asst. Oil and Gas: Federal Income Taxation (CCH), 1971-74. Home: 27 W 44th St New York NY 10036-6613 Office: 75 Wall St New York NY 10005-2833

KARLSSON, CHRISTER B., academic administrator, educator; b. Sweden, Oct. 25, 1944; s. Gustav and Ingeborg (Bengtsson) K.; m. Ingrid Hanell, July 16, 1988; 1 child, Joakim Karlsson. MS, Chalmers U. Tech., Goteborg, Sweden, 1970, D in Tech., 1975. Dir. Inst. for Mgmt. of Innovation and Tech., 1979-83; prof. European Inst. for Advanced Studies in Mgmt., Brussels, 1984-95, 99—; dir. Inst. for Foretagsledning S.A./Mgmt. Rsch. Internat. S.A., Brussels, 1984-94; prof. Stockholm Sch. Econs., 1994—; dir. Inst. for Mgmt. of Innovation & T., 1994—; v.p. of bd. European Inst. for Advanced Studies in Mgmt., Brussels, 1996—. Author: Components in Organization Analysis, 1975, Energy Decisions, 2 vols., 1983; author: chpt. Creation of New Business, 1986, Japanese Production Management in Sunrise or Sunset, 1999; editor: Management and New Production Systems, 1987, 90, 92, 94; editl. bd., author articles in various jours. Mem. IEEE, Engring. Mgmt. Soc. IEEE, Royal Swedish Acad. Engring. Scis., European Operation Mgmt. Assn. (bd. dirs.), Prodn. and Opers. Mgmt. Soc. (v.p.). Office: Stockholm Sch Econs, PO Box 6501, 11383 Stockholm Sweden

KARLSSON, GUDLAUGUR TRYGGVI, academic administrator; b. Reykjavík, Iceland, Sept. 9, 1943; s. Karl I. Jónasson and Guony Guolaugsdóttir; m. Margrét Ingibjörg Valdimarsdóttir, Sept. 19, 1964 (div. Dec. 1970); children: Valdimar Karl, Karl Höskuldur; m. Vigdís Bjarnadóttir, Aug. 9, 1975; children: Bjarni Karl, Guony Marta. Grad. music history and singing, Reykjavík Sch. Music, 1964; BA in History, U. Iceland, Reykjavík, 1964; BA in Econs. with honors, U. Manchester, Eng., 1967. Economist Statis. Bur. Iceland, Reykjavík, 1967, Ctrl. Bank Iceland, Reykjavík, 1968, Rd. Constrn. Authority, Reykjavík, 1969, The Econ. Bur. Iceland, Reykjavík, 1970-72; mgr., editor The Social Dem. Party Iceland, 1973; dep. Main Office U. Iceland, Reykjavík, 1974—. Editor The Students Rev.-U. Iceland, 1963-64, 68-69, The Social Dem. Bull., 1970-82; editor, mgr. The Univ. News Bull., 1978-81, The Daily Albyoublaoio Bus. Rev., 1983-88; co-editor: The Historic Genealogy of the Icelandic People, 1999; contbr. articles to profl. jours.; dir., prodr. (documentary films) Landmannaleitir, Sheep Roundup in Volcanic Mountains, 1980, World Championships in Riding Icelandic Horses, 1983, 85, 87, 89, 91, 93, 95. Coun. mem. Soc. for Western Alliance, Varoberg, Reykjavík, 1967-69; asst. Fgn. Min. of Iceland in the European Econ. Area Discussions, Portugal, 1992; sec. Social Dem. Party, Reykjavík, 1970-82, Coun. Univ. Tchrs., Reykjavík, 1978-82. Named Hon. Citizen, City Balt., 1997. Mem. Econ. Soc. Iceland, Social Dem. Club Reykjavík (hon. Rose fellow 1995), Reykjavík Riding Club. Avocations: riding, singing, skiing, soccer, fencing. Office: Univ Iceland, PO Box 1162, Reykjavík 121, Iceland

KARLSSON, GUNNAR, hotel executive; b. Akureyri, Iceland, Mar. 29, 1952; s. Karl Liljendal and Lilja (Randoversdóttir) Frimannsson; m. Dec. 26, 1983 (div. July 1987); children: Gunnar Már, Ragnheiour Diljá. Grad., Norwegian Sch. Hotel Mgmt., Stavanger, Norway, 1975; grad. in Bus. Adminstrn., Icelandic U., Reykjavík, 1981. From asst. mgr. to mng. dir. Hotel KEA, Akureyri, Iceland, 1976-83, mng. dir., 1986—; tchr. Akureyri Tech. H.S., 1986-96; tax dir. Akureyri N.E. Iceland, 1996—; lectr. U. Akureyri, 1987—; rschr. Hotel Industry, Iceland, 1990—. Bd. dirs. Icelandic Hotel and Restaurant Assn., Reykjavík, 1980-83, Akureyri Tourist Soc., 1981-92. Mem. Rotary. Home: Reykjasida 1, 603 Akureyri Iceland

KARLSSON, INGMAR AXEL, ambassador; b. Hestra, Smaland, Sweden, Jan. 16, 1942; s. Axel Karl Karlsson and Lisa Anna Classon; m. Margareta Samekova; 1 child, Andrea. BA, B of Econs., U. Gothenburg, 1967. Head of sect. Ministry of Fgn. Affairs, Stockholm, 1974-78; chargé d'affaires Swedish Embassy, Damascus, 1979-83; min. Swedish Embassy, Beijing, 1984-86, Bonn, 1987-91; amb. Ministry Fgn. Affairs, Stockholm, 1992-95, Swedish Embassy, Prague, 1996—. Author: (books) The Cross and the Crescent, 1991, Germany and the New Europe, 1991, Islam and Europe, 1994, Europe and the Peoples, 1996. Fellow Internat. Inst. Strategic Studies; mem. Swedish Fgn. Policy Assn. Avocations: golf, tennis. Home: Prästgärden, 330 26 Burseryd Sweden Office: Embassy of Sweden, Uvoz 13 PO Box 35, 160 12 Prague 612, Czech Republic

KARLSSON, NILS GÖRAN, medical director; b. Vimmerby, Sweden, Jan. 23, 1948; s. Nils Einar and Anna Lisa K.; m. Ingrid Margareta Lindberg, Sept. 28, 1974; children: David, Karin. MD, U. Göteborg, Sweden, 1973, PhD, 1986. Asst. prof. ear, nose and throat U. Hosp., Göteborg, Sweden, 1981-84; cons., surgeon Mölndal Hosp., Sweden, 1984-95; assoc. prof. U. Hosp., Göteborg, Sweden, 1988—; med. dir. Glaxo Wellcome, Mölndal, Sweden, 1997—; vis. assoc. prof. Dept. Allergy U. Va., Charlottesville, 1988-89. Contbr. several book chpts., books and many articles to profl. jours. Mem. Swedish Assn. Otolaryngol. Head and Neck Surgery (pres. 1993-97), Swedish Assn. Allergology (v.p. 1995-97), Rotary. Avocations: golf, tennis. Office: Glaxo Wellcome, Box 263, S-43123 Mölndal Sweden

KARLSTROM, ANDERS ROLF, laboratory professional, educator; b. Eskilstuna, Sweden, Oct. 27, 1956; s. Rolf Gunnar Emanuel and Anna Inga-Brita Karlstrom; m. Helena Anna Linnea Wiman, June 20, 1997; 1 child, Fanny Anna Linnea. BS, U. Uppsala, Sweden, 1983, MSc, 1986, PhD, 1989. Cert. med. virology Faculty Medicine, Uppsala U. Scientist KabiGen, Stockholm, 1987-89; head dept. biochemistry KabiPharmacia, Stockholm, 1992-94; head biochemistry Pharmacia, Stockholm, 1994-95, Parmacia & Upjohn, Stockholm, 1995-96; dir. Biotech Lab. AstraZeneca, Sodertalje, Sweden, 1996—; assoc. prof. U. Uppsala, 1993—; mem. Indsl. Rsch. Com., Royal Swedish Acad. Engring. Scis., Stockholm, 1998—. Contbr. articles to profl. jours.; performer (CD) Mark's Brothers-On a Coconut Island, 1998. Lt. Swedish Army, 1976-78. Recipient Fogarty Fellowship stipend NIH, Bethesda, Md., 1989-91, Postdoctoral stipend Nat. Swedish Bd. for Tech. Devel., Stockholm, 1989, Postdoctoral stipend The Swedish Inst., Stockholm, 1989, Postdoctoral stipend Swedish Med. Rsch. Coun., Stockholm, 1980. Mem. JuvenalOrden. Avocations: music, diving, skiing, wining and dining. E-mail: anders.karlstrom@astrazeneca.com. Fax: 46 8 552 531 89. Home: Tryffelgrand 2, 112 63 Enskede Sweden

KARMAKER, RATNESWAR, mathematics educator; b. Barisal, Bangladesh, Jan. 22, 1938; s. Satish Chandra and Abala Bala K.; m. Monika Rani, Feb. 13, 1969; children: Mallika, Kanika, Subir. ISc, B.M. Coll., Barisal, 1956, BSc, 1958; MSc, Dhaka U., Bangladesh, 1961; PhD, U. Bergen, Norway, 1974. Lectr. math. Bangladesh Agrl. U., Mymensingh, 1963-68, asst. prof., 1968-77, assoc. prof., 1977-89, prof. math., 1989—. Author: Agricultural Mathematics, 1987; contbr. articles to profl. jours. Mem. Bangladesh Math. Soc., Bangladesh Assn. for Advancement Sci. Avocations: music, gardening, travel. Home: Vil-Wzirpur PO Wazirpur, Barisal Bangladesh Office: Agrl Univ, Dept Math, Mymensingh Bangladesh

KARNAD, GIRISH RAGHUNATH, playwright, filmmaker, actor; b. Matheran, India, May 19, 1938; s. Raghunath Krishna and Krishnabai (Mankikar) K.; m. Saraswathy K. Ganapathy, Sept. 15, 1980; children: Shalmali Radha, Raghu Amay. BA in Math., Karnatak U., 1958; MA, Oxford (Eng.) U., 1963; LLD, Karnatak U., India, 1994. Asst. mgr. Oxford U. Press, Madras, India, 1963-69, mgr., 1969-70; dir. Film & TV Inst. of India, Pune, 1974, 75; vis. prof., Fulbright scholar in residence U. Chgo., 1987-88; chmn. Sangeet Natak Acad. Nat. Acad. Performing Arts, New Delhi, 1988-93; Indian co-chair Joint Media Com. of Indo-U.S. Subcommn. on Edn. and Culture, 1984-93; dir. The Nehru Ctr., London, 2000—. Author numerous plays including Hayavadana, 1971 (Kamaladevi award 1972), Anjumallige, 1977, Hittina Hunja, 1980, Naga-Mandala, 1988, Taledanda, 1990, Agni Mattu Male, 1995 (Nat. Acad. of Letters award 1994), Tipu Sultan Kanda Kanasu, 2000; dir. (films) Vamsha Vriksha, 1971 (Best Dir. award 1971), Tabbaliyu Neenade Magane, 1977, Ondanondu Kaaladalli, 1978, Utsav (in Hindi), 1984, Kanaka-Purandara (in English), 1989 (Nat. award 1989), Kanooru Heggadithi, 1999. Recipient Padma Sri award Pres. of India, 1974, Padma Bhushan award, 1992. Fellow Nat. Acad. for Performing Arts. (Jnanapith award 1999). Home and Office: JP Nagar Phase II, 697 15th Cross Rd, Bangalore 560078, India

KARNANDA, BOPANNA, pharmacist; b. Bangalore, Karnataka, India, Apr. 28, 1972; s. Nanaiah Kunjappa Karnanda and Bollamma Nanaiah Pandianda; m. Latha Bopanna, Nov. 1, 1998. B in Pharmacy, U. Mysore, India, 1994; M in Pharmacy, M.S. U., Baroda, India; advanced diploma mktg. mgmt., Nat. Sch. Mgmt. Studies, Chennai, India, 1998; postgrad. diploma in tng. and devel., Inst. Health Care Adminstrs., Chennai, 1998. Cert. Pharmacy Coun. India. Product specialist ASTRA-IDL Ltd., Bangalore, 1997, sr. exec. med. and regulatory affairs, 1997-98, asst. mgr. med. svcs., 1998—, mem. new product bench marking com. Referee Indian Jour. Pharmacology, 1998-2000; contbr. articles to profl. jours. Recipient Outstanding Achievement awad MSPI, Delhi, 1999, Mgmt. Excellence award MSPI, New Delhi; Mgmt. Rsch. Program fellow DASPI, 1999. Fellow United Writers Assn. (Excellence award 2000); mem. IPA, N.Y. Acad. Scis. (v.p. 2000), Toastmasters Internat. (v.p. membership comm. and leadership track 1999-2000, Competent Toastmasters award, Competent Leader award). Avocations: reading, music, traveling. E-mail: krathishbopanna@yahoo.com. Fax: 91-080-2252894. Home: 325 ii fl II Stage, Malleswaram 8th A Main Rd, Bangalore Karnataa 560055, India Office: ASTRA-IDL Ltd, 32/1-2 Crescent Rd, Bangalore Karnataka 560001, India

KARNAVAT, SUMATILAL CHHAGANLAL, educator, consultant; b. Maharashtra, India, Mar. 11, 1941; s. Chhaganal Hirachand and Bugalbai Chhaganlal Karnavat; m. Jyoti Sumatilal, May 7, 1966; children: Sandeep Sumatilal, Deepa Sumatilal, Sachin Sumatilal. B in com., Pune Univ., 1964, M in com., 1966. Prof. N.G. Bedekar Coll. Commerce, Bombay, 1966-80, head of dept., 1966-80, dir. inst. mgmt., 1975-78; bd. of studies in commerce Univ. Bombay, 1977-80; prin. Karnavat Classes, Thane, Bombay, 1980—; mem. acad. coun. Univ. Pune, 1967-72. Author 20 books on commerce; contbr. articles to profl. jours. Recipient Samaj Ratna award Jain Ekata Maha Mandal. Home: Opp Hariniwas Circle, 504 Monalisa Apt, Bombay 400 602, India Office: Lohar Ln, Near Railway Station, Thane 400 601, Bombay

KARNER, IVAN, physician, researcher, medical educator; b. Osijek, Slovania, Croatia, Sept. 24, 1951; s. Stjepan and Katarina (Madar) K.; m. Nelica Kornelia Tomljanovic, Nov. 2, 1978. MD, Zagreb, Croatia, 1975; postgrad., Faculty Med. Studium, Zagreb, Croatia, 1983. Head of dept. Clin. Hosp., Osijek, Croatia, 1991-96; head pathophysiology Chatedra Med. Faculty, Osijek, Croatia, 1997, vice dean of med. faculty, 1998—. Mem. Croatian Med. Assn., Croatian Assn. Nucelar Medicine, European Assn. of Nuclear Medicine. Roman Catholic. Avocations: photography, philatelia, traveling. Office: Clinical Hosp, Huttlerova 4, 31000 Osijek Slavonia, Croatia

KARNES, EVAN BURTON, II, lawyer; b. Chgo.; s. Evan Burton and Mary Alice (Brosnahan) K.; m. Bridget Anne Clerkin, Oct. 9, 1976 (dec. June 1994); children: Kathleen Anne, Evan Burton III, Molly Aileen, Lauren Jean; m. Janet Ann Pioli, Nov. 2, 1996. AB, Loyola U., Chgo., 1975; JD, DePaul U., 1978; grad. civil trial advocacy program, U. Calif., 1979. Bar: Ill. 1978, U.S. Dist. Ct. (no. dist.) Ill. 1978, U.S. Ct. Appeals (7th cir.) 1978, U.S. Dist. Ct. (no. dist.) Ind. 1995, U.S. Supreme Ct. 1983. Trial atty. Chgo. Milw. St. Paul & Pacific R.R., Chgo., 1978-81; litigation dept. Baker & McKenzie, Chgo., 1981-87; sr. litigation counsel Levin & Ginsburg Ltd., Chgo., 1987-89; of counsel Oppenheimer, Wolff & Donnelly, 1989-91; prin. Law Offices of Evan B. Karnes ((& Assocs., 1992-99; mng. ptnr. O'Connor & Karnes, Chgo., 2000—; bd. dirs. Triad Communications Inc, Albuquerque, chmn. bd., 1988. Trustee Village of Northfield, Ill., 1999—, mem. fin. com., mem. planning and zoning commn., 1990-99, vice chmn., 1994-99. Mem. ABA, ATLA, Ill. Bar Assn., Fed. Bar Assn. (bd. dirs. Chgo. chpt. 1995—), Chgo. Bar Assn., Def. Rsch. Inst., Nat. Assn. R.R. Counsel (chmn. sci. evidence com. 1995—, nat. exec. com. 1995—, v.p. Midwest region 2000—), Ill. Trial Lawyers Assn., Blue Key (sec. Loyola U. chpg. 1974-75), Phi Sigma Alpha, Phi Alpha Delta. Office: Xerox Centre 55 W Monroe St Fl 32 Chicago IL 60603-5001

KARNEY, IRVING HYMAN, construction company executive; b. Bklyn., Dec. 1, 1923; s. Meyer and Lena (Feldman) K.; m. Reba Krell, June 21, 1947; children: Robert Lloyd, Mark Howard. BS in Constrn. Mgmt., Columbia U., 1956. Archl. draftsman Kahn & Jacobs, Archs., N.Y.C., 1946-52; asst. arch. N.Y.C. Bd. Edn., 1952-54; constrn. adminstr. Uris Bldgs. Corp., N.Y.C., 1954-63; v.p. constrn. Goodrich Constrn. Corp., N.Y.C., 1963-67; constrn. project mgr. Tishman Realty & Constrn. Corp., N.Y.C., 1967-69; v.p. constrn. The Frouge Corp., N.Y.C., 1969-72; constrn. project mgr. Litwin & Swarzman, Owner-Builders, N.Y.C., 1972-75; v.p. constrn. Cohen Bros. Realty & Constrn., Inc., N.Y.C., 1975-77, 79-91; constrn. project mgr. Rose Assocs., Inc., N.Y.C., 1977-79; adv. bd. The Frouge Corp., N.Y.C., 1970-72. With U.S. Army, 1943-46. Recipient Master Builder award Builders Assn. Greater N.Y., 1960, Excellence in Constrn. award N.Y. Soc. Archs., 1977; completion of tallest apt. building in N.Y.C., Park Ave. Assn., 1979. Avocations: tennis, biking, swimming, arts and crafts, handball. Home: 1317 E 23rd St Brooklyn NY 11210-5112

KARNIG, MICHAEL ANDREW, media specialist; b. N.Y.C., Dec. 10, 1956; s. Andrew Marvin and Joanne (McCoy) K.; m. Maria Lena Hultgren, June 10, 1985; children: Nathalie, Alexandra, Michaela. BA, Lund U., Sweden, 1978; degree, U. Sorbonne, Paris, 1979. Sales mgr. Benn Bros., London, 1980-81; sales mgr. Andrew Karnig Assocs., Stockholm, 1981-86, pres., 1987—; mng. dir. Nordic region Publicitas Promotions Network, 1997—; bd. dirs. Gerd:n Media Mktg., Stockholm, Planit Media, Malmoe, Sweden, Media House, Stockholm; bd. chmn. e-licious.com., adwyze.com., Stockholm. Founding mgr. Tovio Daycare Ctr., Gustausberg, Sweden, 1987-90, Parlan Daycare Ctr., Saltsjobaden, Sweden, 1990-95. Mem. Sallskapet. Office: Andrew Karnig Assocs, Finnbodavagen 29, 131 31 Nacka Sweden

KARNOFSKY, MOLLYNE, artist, poet, art educator; b. New Orleans, July 19, 1932; d. Nick Samuel and Lena (Gaethe) Finegold; m. Dave E. Winston, Sept. 17, 1952 (div. Sept. 1975); children: Craig T. Winston, Janelle R. Winston Lewis. BBS in Bus. Adminstrn., Tulane U., New Orleans, 1966; student in Art Studio Courses, Tulane, Newcomb Coll., New Orleans, 1966-70; MAT in Painting and Teaching, Tulane U., New Orleans, 1972. Lic. teaching La., 1972, N.Y.C. Bd. Edn., 1986. Dir., owner La. Lic. Art Sch., New Orleans, 1972-77; art tchr., art workshops N.Y.C., 1977—; mem. self-study com. Tulane U., 1952; panelist Artists Talk on Art, N.Y.C., 1993, 94; guide to internat. artist, Mid. Am. Arts Alliance, N.Y.C., 1994. One-woman shows include Vincent Mann Gallery, New Orleans, 1971, Viridian Gallery, N.Y.C., 1977, 79, 99, PS1 Inst. Art and Urban Resources, Long Island City, N.Y., 1978, Contemporary Art Ctr., New Orleans, 1978, Galerie Forum, Stockholm, 1980, Satellite gallery Bronx Mus. Art, N.Y., 1980, Galerie Leger, Malmö, Sweden, 1980, Ave. B Gallery, 1985, Asphalt Green Cmty. Ctr., N.Y.C., 1988, N.Y. Pub. Libr., 1988, NYU, 1994, (Site Specific: Found Spaces in Other Places) Eclectic Properties, 1979, Rudolph Bass Power Tool Co., N.Y.C., 1982; exhibited in group shows at Judson Poets Theater, N.Y.C., 1977, World Trade Ctr., N.Y.C., 1979, Ear Inn, N.Y.C., 1979, Atlantic Ave. Galleries, Bklyn., 1979, Bklyn. Arts Cultural Assn., 1981, Emily Harvey Gallery, N.Y.C., 1983, WPA Gallery, Washington, 1983, Jack Tilton Gallery, N.Y.C., 1983, Jon Leon Gallery, N.Y.C., 1984, Franklin Furnace, N.Y.C., 1984, Minor Injury Gallery, Williamsburg, Bklyn., 1989, World Congress Arts and Medicine, N.Y.C., 1992, Tribeca 148, N.Y.C., 1993, 94, Printmaking Workshop, N.Y.C., 1997, Chuck Levitan Gallery, N.Y.C., 1998, Broome St. Gallery, N.Y.C., 2000; permanent collections include Cigna, Insurance Co. of N.Am., Anthology Film Archives, N.Y.C., 1996, Chuck Levitan Gallery, N.Y.C, 1998; subject of art Coll. Art Assn., N.Y.C., 1980; documentary video of art ehbn. Vesteras Mus., Sweden, 1981; documentary video of art ehbn. and interview Fuji Network, Japan, 1981; contbr. articles to profl. jours. Pres. Tulane Commerce Women's Club, New Orleans, 1951; publicity dir. Chevra Thilim Sisterhood, New Orleans, 1960-63; com. mem. Coun. of Jewish Women, New Orleans, 1965-70; tour dir. Spring Fiesta Assn., New Orleans, 1965. Grantee for performance poetry, Poets and Writers, N.Y.C., 1982, 92, 98; named Artist in Residence Avenue B. Gallery, N.Y.C., 1985, honorarium, spl. project, Coal Bin PSI Inst. for Arts and Urban Resources, Queens, N.Y., 1978, Contemporary Art Ctr., New Orleans, 1978. Mem. Tulane Alumni Assn. (bd. dirs. 1970-71, editor bus. review 1971), Artists Equity, Mcpl. Art Soc. Avocations: writing, music, urban archaeology. Fax: 212-423-5706.

KARO, TAMAS ANDRAS, investment banker, financial-economic adviser; b. Isaszeg, Budapest, Hungary, Nov. 28, 1932; came to U.S., 1959; s. Janos Görgy and Anna Maria (Godor) K.; m. Malgorzata Maria Sobanska, Feb. 14, 1975; 1 child, Sophie-Anna. LLD, Eötvö Lorand U. Budapest, 1955; postgrad., Econs. U. Rotterdam, The Netherlands, 1956-58, State U. Leiden, The Netherlands, 1958-59, NYU, 1964-65, U. Paris Sorbonne, 1978-80. Cert. br. mgr. N.Y. Stock Exch.; cert. prin. Nat. Assn. Securities Dealers. Area exec. for Europe, Mfrs. Hanover Trust N.Y., N.Y.C., 1960-65; regional v.p. Dominick & Dominick, Inc., N.Y.C., 1966-71; sr. European rep. Dominick & Dominick, Ltd., London, 1966-71; mgr. fgn. dept. N.Y. Securities Co., Inc., N.Y.C., 1972; CEO, Tamas A Karo, fin. counselor, Paris, 1973—; fin. adminstr. PHARE program European Cmty., Brussels and Budapest, 1991-92; spl. adviser Cabinet of Prime Min., Republic of Hungary, Budapest, 1992-94; mem. adv. bd. Arthur D. Little Internat., Cambridge, Mass. and Brussels, 1992. Contbr. articles to various publs. Active Reps. Abroad, N.Y.C., 1964-70, London, 1970-71, Paris, 1973-89, Budapest, 1989—, amb. of the Rep. Nat. Com., Washington, 1990. Mem. The Travellers (Paris), Wall Street Club (N.Y.C.). Roman Catholic. Avocations: collecting rare books, opera, travel, reading, sailing. Home: 28 rue du Champ de Mars, 75007 Paris France

KARON, BERTRAM PAUL, psychologist, educator; b. Taunton, Mass., Apr. 29, 1930; s. Harold Banny and Celia (Silverman) K.; m. Mary Kathryn Mossop, Oct. 17, 1957; 1 son, Jonathan Alexander. AB, Harvard U., 1952; MA, Princeton U., 1954, PhD (USPHS fellow), 1957; grad. Social Sci. Research Council Inst. Maths. for Social Scientists, Dartmouth, summer 1953. Diplomate in clin. psychology and psychoanalysis Am. Bd. Profl. Psychology. Rsch. fellow psychometrics Ednl. Testing Svc. and Princeton, 1952-55; intern in direct analysis John N. Rosen, M.D., Gardenville, Pa., 1955-56; sr. clin. psychologist Annandale (N.J.) Reformatory, 1958; psychologist, dir. rsch. Akron (Ohio) Psychol. Cons. Ctr., 1958-59; rsch. psychologist Phila. Psychiat. Hosp., 1959, USPHS fellow, 1959-61; practice clin. psychology Phila., 1961-62; asst. prof. psychology Mich. State U., 1962-63, assoc. prof., 1963-68, prof., 1968—; vis. lectr. Calif. Sch. Profl. Psychology, L.A., 1972; vis. scholar Wright Inst., L.A., 1979; rsch. cons. U.S. Naval Hosp., Phila., 1962, U. Pa., 1962; lectr. psychiatry Ypsilanti (Mich.) State Hosp., 1964-65; cons. VA Hosp., Allen Park, Mich., 1966-75, Ann Arbor, Mich., 1971-72. Author: The Negro Personality: A Rigorous Investigation of the Effects of Culture, 1958, rev. edit., Black Scars, 1975, (with others) Psychotherapy of Schizophrenia: The Treatment of Choice, 1981; contbg. author: Projective Techniques in Personality Assessment, 1968, Techniques for Behavior Change, 1971, The Schizophrenic Syndrome: An Annual Review, 1971, The Construction of Madness, 1976, Assessment with Projective Techniques: A Concise Introduction, 1981, Comprehensive Textbook of Psychotherapy, 1994, Dynamic Therapies for Psychiatric Disorders (Axis I), 1995; editor: Affects, Imagery, and Consciousness (Silvan S. Tomkins), vols. 1 and 2, 1962, 63; contbr. numerous articles on schizophrenia and psychoanalysis to profl. jours. Recipient Fowler award for disting. grad. tchg. APA Grad. Students, 1990; named disting. psychoanalyst Soc. for Psychoanalytic Tng., N.Y., 1988; NIMH grantee, 1966-71. Fellow APA (divsn. psychotherapy, clin. psychology, divsn. psychoanalysis, pres. 1990-91); mem. Soc. Psychotherapy Rsch., Am. Statis. Assn., Psychologists Interested in Study Psychoanalysis (pres. 1987-89), Mich. Psychoanalytic Coun. (pres. 1993-95). Home: 420 John R St East Lansing MI 48823-3710 Office: 108 Psychology Research East Lansing MI 48824-1117

KARP, GERALD CHARLES, biologist, educator, writer; b. L.A., Dec. 24, 1942; s. Harry and Sally Karp; m. Patrice Marie Patrick, Nov. 21, 1973; 1 child, Jennifer. BS, UCLA, 1964; PhD, U. Wash., 1970. Postdoctoral rschr. U. Colo. Med. Ctr., Denver, 1970-71; prof. biology U. Fla., Gainesville, 1971-84; vis. scientist U. Iowa, Iowa City, 1984, U. Calif., San Francisco, 1988-89; freelance writer Cin., 1990—; mem. ad hoc com. med. grants rsch. NIH, Bethesda, Md., 1976; cons. Morrison and Foerster, San Francisco, 1988, Wiley and Sons Publs., N.Y.C., 1990—. Author: Development, 1976, 2d edit., 1981, Cell Biology, 1979, 2d edit., 1984, Cell and Molecular Biology, 1996, 2d edit., 1999. Predoctoral fellow NSF, 1964-69, Postdoctoral fellow NIH, 1970-71. Mem. AAAS, Phi Beta Kappa.

KARP, JORDAN PAUL, lawyer; b. Huntington, N.Y., May 24, 1966; s. Richard Gordon and Nita Eileen (Gadaver) K.; m. Alice Lucinda Wilkenfeld, Sept. 22, 1998. BA, Johns Hopkins U., 1988; JD, Yale U., 1991. Law clk. U.S. Ct. Appeals (3rd cir.), Phila., 1991-92; assoc. Hogan & Hartson LLP, Balt., 1992-95; atty. MCI Comms. Corp., Washington, 1995-96; sr. counsel, asst. sec. Guilford Pharms. Inc., Balt., 1996—. Contbr. article to 100 Yale Law Jour. Beneficial-Hudson merit scholar Beneficial-Hudson Trust, 1986. Mem. Am. Soc. Corp. Lawyers, JHV 2nd Decade Soc., Phi Beta Kappa. Office: Guilford Pharms Inc 6611 Tributary St Baltimore MD 21224-6515

KARP, PETER SIMON, marketing executive; b. New City, N.Y., Dec. 9, 1935; s. Joseph Bernard and Esther (Wexler) K.; m. Mona Leea Pecheux; children: Matthew Henry, Mark Andrew. BA, Hobart Coll., 1954; MFA, Columbia U., 1957. Rschr. Bur. Advt., Am. Newspaper Pubs. Assn., N.Y.C., 1954-56; media dir. Smith, Hagl & Knudsen, Inc., N.Y.C., 1957-59; media and rsch. dir. CAG Advt., Inc., N.Y.C., 1960-62; exec. v.p. Bennett-Chaiken, Inc., N.Y.C., 1963-66; founder, CEO BSI/Bus. Sci. Internat., N.Y.C., 1967—; mng. dir. The Concept Testing Inst., N.Y.C., 1972—; N.Y.C., 1976—; co-dir. The Genesis Group, N.Y.C., 1983—. Co-author: Customer Satisfaction: How to Maximize, Measure and Market your Company's Ultimate Product, 1989, Competing on Value, 1991; creator BSI Tech. Value Assessments, 1989-90; editor BSI Newsletter, 1976—. Pollster Ken Keating Campaign, State of New York, 1964; vol. Grand Cen. YMCA, N.Y.C., 1964-82. Fellow Inst. Dirs. (London); mem. Am. Mktg. Assn., Advt. Rsch. Found., Artificial Intelligence Assn., N.Y. Acad. Scis., Palisades Tennis Club. Jewish. Avocations: art, sculpture, travel, music. Home: 159 Tweed Blvd Upper Grandview NY 10960-4913

KARP, ROSANNE, oncology and women's health nurse; b. Lynn, Mass., Oct. 8, 1946; d. Max and Dorothy (Cohen) Sidman; children: Stacy, Matthew. ADN, Northeastern U., 1967; postgrad., Lesley Coll., 1990—. RN, Mass. Staff nurse Holy Family Hosp., Methuen, Mass., 1969-90; staff nurse Mass. Gen. Hosp., Boston, 1990-96, case mgr. gynecology svc., 1996—; chair, prof. edn. Greater Lawrence unit Am. Cancer Soc., bd. dirs. Mass. div., 1990-92. Recipient Excellence in Med./Surg. Nursing award Merrimack Valley Area Health Edn. Ctr., 1988, Award for Disting. Vol. Leadership Greater Lawrence unit ACS, 1995, nat. leadership award Hadassah, 1997, Ptnrs. award Ptnrs. Healthcare Sys., Inc., 1999.

KÁRPÁTI, PÁL, cardiologist; b. Budapest, Hungary, Oct. 23, 1936; s. Imre Quitt and Magda Földe; m. Márta Frisch, Sept. 07, 1964; children: Róbert, Judit. MD, Semmelweis U., Budapest, 1961; degree in splty. of internal medicine, Postgrad. Med. Sch., Budapest, 1971, degree in splty. of cardiology, 1973, PhD, 1975. Intern Postgrad. Med. Sch., 1961-63, resident, 1963-66; asst. Nat. Inst. Cardiology, Budapest, 1961-65; docent Postgrad. Med. Sch., 1965-80; head internal medicine Merényi Gen. Hosp., Budapest, 1980-96; cardiologist St. Stewen Hosp., Budapest; prof. cardiology Budapest Postgrad. Med. Sch., 1981. Author: Myocardial Infarction, 1980; contbr. many articles to med. jours. Home: 26 Wesselényi Str, 1075 Budapest Hungary Office: St Stewen Hosp Dept Cardiology, Nagyvarad sq 1, 1097 Budapest Hungary

KARPE, FREDRIK, physician, researcher; b. Stockholm, Sweden, June 24, 1962; s. G and Birgitta (Rhodin) K. MD, Karolinska Inst., Sweden, 1988; PhD, 1992. Houseman Danderyd Hosp., Stockholm, Sweden, 1990-91; registrar Karolinska Hosp., Stockholm, Sweden, 1992-98; assoc. prof., 1995; sr. clin. rsch. fellow, hon. cons. physician Ctr. Diabetes, Endocrinology and Metabolism U. Oxford. Contbr. over 60 articles in peer-reviewed med. jours. Mem. The European Atherosclerosis Soc. Office: Oxford Lipid Metabolism, Radcliff Infirmary, OX2 6HE Oxford United Kingdom

KARPEL VEL LEITNER, NATHALIE, chemistry researcher; b. Chatellerault, Vienne, France, Sept. 23, 1966. Grad. engr., Ecole Superieure d Ingenieurs de Poiters, Poitiers, France, 1989, PhD in Chemistry-Microbiology of water, 1991. Instr. chemistry dept. U. Poitiers, 1991-92; rschr. Nat. Ctr. Sci. Rsch., Poitiers, 1992—. Mem. French Groupement de Recherche U. su les Techniques de Tractement et d'Epuration des Eaux, Soc. Française de Chimie. Office: Lab Chimie Eau et Environ, 40 ave du Recteur Pineau, 86022 Poitiers Cedex, France

KARPENKO, LARISA IVANOVNA, molecular biologist, researcher; b. Kokui, Chita, USSR, May 9, 1959; d. Ivan Pavlovich and Vera Nikolaevna (Astafurova) K.; m. Nikolai Andreevich Chikaev, Apr. 24, 1986; 1 child, Anton. M, U. Novosibirsk, USSR, 1981; PhD, Inst. Molecular Biology, Koltsovo, Novosibirsk, Russia, 1993. Jr. rsch. scientist Inst. Biol. Active Substance, Berdsk, Russia, 1981-89; rsch. scientist Inst. Bioengring., Koltsovo, 1989-93, sr. rsch. scientist, 1994-96, sr. rsch. scientist, leader group, 1997-99; sr. rsch. scientist Inst. Molecular Biology, Koltsovo, 1997. Contbr. articles to profl. jours.; patentee in field. Grantee Ministry Pub. Health, 1998, Ministry Sci., 1999, Internat. Sci. and Tech. Ctr., 1999. Fellow Mendelev All Union Chem. soc., Biotech. Soc. Russia. Russian Orthodox. Avocations: classical music, playing piano, tourism, mountaineering, boating. Home: 14/85, 633159 Koltsovo Russia Office: Inst Bioengring, State Rsch Ctr Virology and, 633159 Koltsovo Russia

KARPINSKI, HUBERTA ELAINE, library trustee; b. Cato, N.Y., Jan. 4, 1925; d. Alfred Raymond and Lena Margaret (Fuller) Tuxill; m. Edward Karpinski, Nov. 17, 1956; children: Susan Tanielian, Rebecca Hitch, Amy Jaward. Student, U. Mich., 1943-45, Wayne U., 1949-50; grad., N.Y. Art Acad. Design, 1972. Operator to svc. observer supr. Mich. Bell Telephone Co., Detroit, 1946-57; tchr. art Birmingham (Mich.) Pub. Sch., 1977-87; libr. trustee Redford (Mich.) Twp. Dist. Libr., 1971—. Chmn. Lola Valley Civic Assn., Redford, 1960-70; vice chmn. Redford Twp. Coun. Civic Assn., 1967-71; bd. dirs. 17th Dist. Mich. Dem. Party, Redford, 1968-71. Mem. Nat. Mus. Women in arts (charter), Mich. Porcelain Artists, Internat. Porcelain Art Tchrs. Avocations: portrait painting in pastel, oil or on porcelain. Home: 17418 Macarthur Redford MI 48240-2241

KARPINSKI, STANISLAW, biologist; b. Poznan, Poland, Nov. 5, 1960; s. Franciszek and Danuta Regina (Karasinska) K.; m. Barbara Okoniewska, Oct. 5, 1985; children: Stanislaw, Ann Maria. MS, Agriculture U., Poznan, Poland, 1984; PhD, Agriculture U., Umea, Sweden, 1994, Docent, 1999. Asst. prof. dept. biochemistry Agriculture Acad., Poznan, Poland, 1985-88; postgrad. Swedish U. Agricultural Scis., Umea, Sweden, 1989-94; rschr. Swedish U. Agricultural Scis., Umea, 1994-95; postdoctoral fellow John Innes Cen., Norwich, U.K., 1995-97; asst. prof. Swedish U. Agricultural Scis., Umea, 1997-98; assoc. prof./sr. lectr. dept. botany Stockholm U., 1999—. Contbr. articles to profl. jours. Recipient rsch. project, Swedish Found. Strategic Rsch., Swedish Coun. Forestry and Agricultural Rsch., Swedish Found. Natural Scis., others. Mem. Soc. Free Radical Rsch., Internat. Soc. Photosynthesis Rsch. Roman Catholic. Avocations: astromony, stamp/coin collection, weight lifting. Office: Stockholm U Dept Botany, SE-10691 Stockholm Sweden

KARPISCAK, JOHN, III, engineer, army officer; b. Teaneck, N.J., Nov. 11, 1957; s. John and Norma Lina (Alfano) K.; m. Linda Sue Anderson, June 11, 1983. AS, Mercer County Coll., 1977; BArch, Kans. State U., 1981; MBA, Rider Coll., 1983. Commd 2d lt. U.S. Army, 1983, advanced through grades to capt., 1986; platoon leader D Co. 52nd Battalion, Ft. Bliss, Tex., 1984, 43rd Engr. Co. 3rd Armored Cav., Ft. Bliss, Tex., 1984-85; exec. officer 43rd Engr. Co. 3rd Armored Cav., Ft. Bliss, 1985; architect Directorate Engring. and Housing., Ft. Bliss; battalion adj. 169th Engr. Battalion, Ft. Leonard Wood, Mo., 1987-88; commdr. Hdqrs. Co. 1st Engr. Brigade, Ft. Leonard Wood, 1988-89; space action officer U.S. Army Engr. Sch., Ft. Leonard Wood, 1989-91; bn. motor officer 802d Engr. Bn., Camp Humphreys, Republic of Korea, 1991-92; naval spl. ops. officer Naval Space Command, Dahlgren, Va., 1992-94; sr. engr. Allied Signal Tech. Svcs. Corp., Washington, 1994-95; scientist with U.S. Army Topographic Engring. Ctr., Alexandria, Va., 1995—. Fellow Explorer's Club; mem. AIAA, Brit. Interplanetary Soc., Armed Forces Comm. and Electronics Assn., Planetary Soc. Republican. Lutheran. Avocations: space science, model railroading, running. Home: 1802 Genther Ln Fredericksburg VA 22401-5207 Office: US Army Topographic Engring Ctr Alexandria VA 22315

KARPISEK, LADISLAV STEPHAN, engineering company executive, researcher; b. Sabinov, Czechoslovakia, June 20, 1924; arrived in Australia, 1952, naturalized, 1957; s. Ladislav and Stepanka (Knapikova) K.; Helena Erna Kutena, Jan. 20, 1962; 1 child, Andy Ladislav. Student, Tech. Coll., Prague, Czechoslovakia, 1943-45, Charles U., Prague, 1945-49. Mgr. A & A Industries, Sydney, Australia, 1952-55; devel. engr., R&D Chep Australia, Sydney, 1956-72; mng. dir., R&D LSK Industries P/L, Sydney, 1973—. Rschr., inventor, patentee in field. Avocations: diving, bushwalking, gardening. Home: PO Box 2352, Taren Point NSW 2229, Australia Office: LSK Industries P/L, 92 Woodfield Blvd, Caringbah NSW 2229, Australia

KARPLUS, MARTIN, chemistry educator; b. Vienna, Austria, Mar. 15, 1930; came to U.S., 1938; s. Hans and Isabella (Goldstern) K.; m. Marci Anne Hazard. BA, Harvard U., 1950; PhD, Calif. Inst. Tech., 1953; DSc (hon.), U. Sherbrooke, Que., Can., 1998. NSF fellow Oxford (Eng.) U., 1953-55; asst. prof. chemistry U. Ill., 1957-60, assoc. prof., 1960; prof. Columbia U., N.Y.C., 1960-66; prof. Harvard U., Cambridge, Mass., 1966—, Theodore William Richards prof. chemistry, 1979-99, Theodore William Richards rsch. prof., 1999—; prof. U. Paris VII, 1974-75, Coll. de France, Paris, 1980; prof. associé U. Paris-Sud, 1980-81, U. Louis Pasteur, Strasbourg, France, spring 1992, 94-95, prof. conventionné, 1995—; Eastman prof. Oxford U., 1999-2000. Author: (with R.N. Porter) Atoms and Molecules: An Introduction for Students of Physical Chemistry, 1970, (with C.L. Brooks III and B.M. Pettitt) Proteins: A Theoretical Perspective of Dynamics, Structure and Thermodynamics, 1988; also articles. Westinghouse scholar, 1947; recipient Fresenius award Phi Lambda Epsilon, 1965, Harrison Howe award Am. Chem. Soc., 1967, Outstanding Contbn. award Internat. Soc. Quantum Biology, 1979, Disting. Alumni award Calif. Inst. Tech., 1986, Irving Langmuir award Am. Phys. Soc., 1987, Theoretical Chemistry award Am. Chem. Soc., 1993, Joseph O. Hirschfelder prize in theoretical chemistry U. Wis. Theoretical Chemistry Inst., 1995; nat. lectr. Biophys. Soc., 1991. Mem. NAS, Am. Acad. Arts and Scis., Internat. Acad. Quantum Molecular Sci., Netherlands Acad. Art and Scis. (fgn.). Office: Harvard U Dept Chemistry 12 Oxford St Cambridge MA 02138-2902

KARPMAN, DIANA ORA, pediatrician, researcher; b. N.Y.C., July 29, 1957; arrived in Sweden, 1987; d. Itzhak J. and Esther (Goldfinger) Karpman; m. Anders T. Övermark, Aug. 9, 1983; children: Reuben B., Hanna B. MD, Sackler Sch. Medicine, Tel Aviv, Israel, 1987; PhD in Med. Microbiology, Lund (Sweden) U., 1997. Cert. in pediatrics and pediatric nephrology. Fellow in pediatric nephrology Children's Hosp., Phila., 1997-98; pediatrician Lund U. Hosp., 1991-97, pediatric nephrologist, 1998—; sr. rschr., asst. prof. Lund U., 1998—. Contbr. articles to Jour. INfectious Disease, Kidney Internat., Infection and Immunity, others. Wallenberg Found. grantee, 1998. Mem. Internat. Pediatric Nephrology Assn., Swedish Med. Soc. Office: Univ HOsp, Dept Pediatrics, 22185 Lund Sweden

KARPMAN, VLADIMIR IOSIPHOVICH, physicist, educator; b. Gomel, Belorussia, USSR, Feb. 28, 1928; arrived in Israel, 1992; s. Iosiph Borisovich and Bella Abramovna (Rosenberg) K.; m. Raissa Naumovna Kaufman, July 11, 1954; 1 child, Irene. M, Belorussian U., Minsk, USSR, 1949; PhD, USSR Acad. Sci., Moscow, 1954, DSc, 1966. Lectr., prof. Pedagogical Inst., Minsk, 1952-61; sr. rschr. Inst. Nuclear Physics, Novosibirsk, Russia, 1961-69; prof. Novosibirsk U., 1961-69; head theoretical dept. Inst. Ionosphere and Radiowave Propagation, Moscow, 1969-92; prof. physics Hebrew U., Jerusalem, 1992—; co-chmn. working group Waves and Instabilities in Space Plasmas Internat. Assn. Geophysics and Aeronomy-Union Radio Sci. Internat., 1976-79; mem. sci. coun. on plasma physics Acad. Sci. USSR, 1978-92. Author: Nonlinear Waves in Dispersive Media, 1975, Nichtlineare Wellen, 1978; co-author: (with B.B. Kadomtsev) Nonlinear Waves, 1972; contbr. articles to profl. jours. Grantee Danish Acad. Scis., Denmark, 1991-92, Ministry of Sci. and Arts, Israel, 1996-98; recipient Lady Davis fellowship, Jerusalem, 1992. Mem. Am. Geophys. Union, N.Y. Acad. Scis. Office: Hebrew U, Rach Inst Physics, 91904 Jerusalem Israel

KARPOV, DMITRI ALEXEEVICH, physicist, researcher; b. Leningrad, Russia, Aug. 5, 1956; s. Alexey Fiodorovich and Nina Alexeevna (Matveeva) K.; m. Valentina Alexandrovna Rybalko, Sept. 13, 1985; 1 child, Alexandra. Degree in physics, Phys. Engring. Inst., Moscow, 1979; PhD in technics, D.V. Efremov Inst., 1990. Engr., rschr. D.V. Efremov Inst., St. Petersburg, 1979-84, sci. collaborator, 1984-89, head of lab., 1989—. Co-author: Handbook of Vacuum Arc Science and Technology, 1995; patentee in field; contbr. articles to profl. jours. Mem. N.Y. Acad. Scis. Avocations: art, travels. Office: DV Efremov Inst, Sovietskiy Prospect 1, 189631 Saint Petersburg Russia

KARPPANEN, HEIKKI OLAVI, pharmacology educator; b. Kitee, Finland, Oct. 9, 1944; s. Heikki Jalmari and Tyyne Ester (Savolainen) K; m. Laelia Pirjo Anthoni, June 2, 1968; children: Mari, Pasi. MD, U. Helsinki, Finland, 1971, PhD, 1974. Rsch. fellow Alexander von Humboldt Found., Hannover, Germany, 1972-73; sr. lectr. U. Oulu, Finland, 1973-76, assoc. prof., 1977-78; rsch. project dir. U. Helsinki, 1978-80, prof., 1981—; cons. Astra Corp., Stockholm and Helsinki, 1978—, Parke-Davis, Morris Plains, N.J. and Sweden, 1974-77. Patentee in field, including imidazole/imidazoline receptors, cholesterol reducing and weight reducing MultiBebe food compositions, salt alternatives; contbr. articles to profl. jours. Rsch. grantee Assn. Finnish Life Ins. Cos., 1976, Ctr. for Advancement of Tech., 1997, 98, 99; named Best Cardiology Rschr. of Yr., Finnish Cardiol. Soc. Mem. Finnish Hypertension Soc. (pres.), Internat. Soc. Hypertension, Danish Soc. Hypertension, Royal Soc. Medicine U.K., Am. Heart Assn. (coun. for high blood pressure rsch.), N.Y. Acad. Scis., Lions. Avocations: tennis, fishing, travel, arts. Home: Riippakoivunkuja 5, FIN02130 Espoo Finland Office: U Helsinki Inst Biomedicine, POB 8 Dept Pharmacology/Toxicology, FIN00014 Helsinki Finland

KARPUKHIN, OLEG YUREVICH, surgery educator; b. Kazan, Russia, Jan. 15, 1961; s. Yury Matveevich and Ludmila Vladimirovna (Trofimova) K.; m. Tatyana Sergeevna Varlamova, Oct. 2, 1992; 1 child, Anna Olegovna. Med. diploma, Kazan State Med. U., 1984, physician probationer, 1984-86, postgrad., 1986-89. Instr. dept. surgery Kazan State Med. U., 1990-96, reader dept. surgery, 1996—; editor, transaltor Geotar Medicina, Moscow, 1995-99. Translator: Stedmans Medical Dictionary, 1995, Atlas of Gynecologic Surgery, 1997; translator, editor chpts.: Textbook for Physician and Students Surgery, 1996. Fellow Assn. Coloproctologists Russia, Surgeons Sci. Soc. Tatarstan. Avocations: photography, drawing, hiking, fishing, growing vegetables and fruits. Office: Kazan State Med Univ, Butlerov St 49, 420012 Kazan Russia

KARPUZOV, DIMITRE STOIANOV, physicist, educator; b. Bourgas, Bulgaria, Dec. 13, 1940; s. Stoian Stojkov and Irina Dimitrova (Tzerova) K.; m. Plouma Kirova Kostova, July 14, 1977; children: Stefan Dimitrov, Irina Dimitrova. MSc, Moscow State U., 1966, PhD, 1970; DSc, Sofia State U., 1980. Rsch. fellow Inst. Electronics, Bulgarian Acad. Sci., Sofia, 1970-76, 79-80, prof. physics, 1984-92, 95; prof. physics Inst. Electronics, Bulgarian Acad. Sci. Electr., 1997—; rsch. fellow U. Salford, Eng., 1977-78, 81-83, 1993; vis. prof. U. Houston, 1993-94, U. Western Ont., London, Can., 1996-97, U. Newcastle, NSW, Australia, 1998-99; adv. bd. Vacuum internat. jour., 1981—, Rsch. Trend Series. Editor: Ion Implantation and Ion Beam Equipment, 1991, Vacuum Electron and Ion Technologies, 1996; co-author: Modern Problems of Surface Physics, 1981. Leverhulm Ltd. grantee, 1977, Fulbright grantee USIA, 1993, NATO grantee, 1992, 95, Copernicus grantee, European Union, 1995; sr. vis. fellow Ctr. for Chem. Physics, U. Western Ont., 1996, 99-2000. Mem. IEEE. Avocations: violin, gardening. E-mail: karpuzov@emeie.ie.bas.bg. Home: Block 524-2 Apt 38, Mladost 1A, 1784 Sofia Bulgaria Office: Bulgarian Acad Sci, Blvd Tzarigradsko Chaus 72, 1784 Sofia Bulgaria

KARRAKER, LOUIS RENDLEMAN, retired corporate executive; b. Jonesboro, Ill., Aug. 2, 1927; s. Ira Oliver and Helen Elsie (Rendleman) K.; m. Patricia Grace Stahlheber, June 20, 1952; children: Alan Louis, Sharon Elaine Cohen. BA, So. Ill. U., 1949, MA, 1952; postgrad., U. Wis., 1951-52, Washington U., St. Louis, 1954-56. V.p. personnel Am. Appraisal Assocs., Inc., Milw., 1969-73, v.p. adminstrn., 1973-74, group v.p., dir., 1974-77, exec. v.p., dir., 1977-79, pres., dir., 1979-82; bus. mgr. Concordia Coll., Ann Arbor, Mich., 1986-91; cons. in field, 1982-86; asst. to chmn. Parker Pen Co., Janesville, Wis., 1967-69, personnel mgr., 1964-67; asst. to pres. Augustana Coll., Sioux Falls, S.D., 1962-64, acting chmn., dept. social scis., 1960-61, asst. prof. history, 1956-60. Columnist The Jour. Times, Racine, Wis., 1993-99; speaker Rep. and civic groups, Wis., 1993—. Trustee Better Bus. Bur., Milw., 1979-82, Citizens Govtl. Rsch. Bur., Milw., 1979-82; speaker, canvasser Rep. Party, S.D., 1956-60. With USNR, 1952-53, Korea. Mem. The Heritage Found., Hoover Presdl. Libr. Assn., Am. Legion. Lutheran. Avocation: church activities, travel, family activities, fishing. Home: 217 S 7th St Apt 11 Waterford WI 53185-4500

KARRER, CAROL CONVERSE, nurse educator; b. Columbus, Ohio, Dec. 10, 1940; d. Edward Beck and Elma Louise (McClain) Converse; m. George Henry Karrer, Aug. 26, 1961; children: Andrew (dec.), Matthew, James. Dipl. Nursing, Grant Hosp. sch. Nursing, Columbus, 1961; BSN, Ohio State U., 1963, MSN, 1964, PhD in Family Rels. and Human Devel., 1984. RN, Ohio. Nurse Grant Hosp., Columbus, 1961-63; instr., rsch. assoc. Ohio State U. Sch. Nursing, Columbus, 1964-67; organist and presch. music tchr. St. Andrew Presbyn. Ch., Columbus, 1967-71; instr. nursing Grant Hosp. Sch. Nursing, Columbus, 1971-72; nursing coord. Ohio State U. Sch. Nursing, Columbus, 1973-75; asst. prof. nursing Ohio Wesleyan U., Delaware, 1976-80; prof. nursing Franklin U., Columbus, 1981—; cons. evaluator North Cen. Assn. Colls. and Schs., Commn. on Instns. of Higher Edn., Chgo., 1991—. Contbr. articles to profl. jours., chpt. to book. Ohio State U. Home Econs. Alumni Assn. rsch. grantee, 1978. Mem. Mid-Ohio Nurses Assn. (pres. 1986-90), Ohio Bd. Nursing (chmn. ednl. adv. com. 1989-90). Home: 13887 Robinson Rd Plain City OH 43064-9028

KARSH, YOUSUF, photographer; b. Mardin, Armenia, Dec. 23, 1908; emigrated to Can., 1924; s. Amsih and Bahia K.; m. Estrellita Nachbar, Aug. 28, 1962. Pupil, John H. Garo; numerous hon. degrees including; LL.D., Queen's U., Kingston, Ont., Carleton U.; D.H.L., Dartmouth Coll., Ohio U., Mt. Allison U.; D.C.L., Bishop's U., Lennoxville, Que.; D.H.L., Emerson Coll.; B in Profl. Arts, Brooks Inst.; D.F.A., U. Mass., 1979; DFA, U. Hartford, 1980; MFA, Tufts U., 1981, Dawson Coll., Montreal, Can., 1981; DFA (hon. degree), Syracuse U., 1986, Yeshiva U., N.Y.C., 1989, Columbia Coll., Chgo., 1990, U. Victoria, B.C., Can., 1990, U. B.C., Can., 1991, Salisbury Coll., 1998. Opened photog. studio Ottawa, Ont., Can., 1932; vis. prof. photography Ohio U., Emerson Coll.; lectr in field. Author: Faces of Destiny, 1946, Portraits of Greatness, 1959, This Is the Mass, 1958, This Is Rome, 1959, This Is the Holy Land, 1960, These are the Sacraments, 1962, In Search of Greatness (autobiography), 1962, The Warren Court, 1965, Karsh Portfolio, 1967, Faces of Our Time, 1971, Karsh Portraits, 1976, Karsh Canadians, 1978, Karsh: A Fifty-Year Retrospective, 1983, paperback edit., 1986, Karsh: American Legends, 1992, Karsh: A Sixty-Year Retrospective, 1996; portrait photographer leading nat. and internat. statesmen, corporate execs., polit. and govtl. ofcls., religious leaders including royal families of, Eng., Monaco, Norway, Greece, Pope John Paul II, also leading intellectual and entertainment figures; first one-man show, Nat. Gallery Can., 1959, one man shows Men Who Make Our World, Expo 67, Internat. Ctr. Photography, N.Y.C., 1983, Mus. Photography, Bradford, Eng., 1983, Nat. Portrait Gallery, London, 1984, Edinburgh, Scotland, 1984, People's Republic China, 1985, Helsinki, 1985, Muscarelle Mus. Art, 1987, William and Mary Coll., Williamsburg, Va., 1987, Barbican Ctr., London, 1988, Palais de Tokyo, Paris, 1988, Geneva Inst. Photography, Mus. für Gestahlung, Zürich, Switzerland, 1988, Huntington Library and Art Gallery, San Marino, Calif., 1988, 1988—, Frankfurter Kunstverein, Frankfurt, 1989, Internat. Ctr. Photography, 1992, Nat. Gallery, Copenhagen, Buda Castle Palace, Budapest, Hungary, Gulbenkian Found., Lisbon, Portugal; retrospective Nat. Gallery Ottawa, Karsh: The Art of the Portrait, 1989; one-man retrospective exhbn. Vancouver (B.C.) Art Gallery, 1990, Glenbow Mus., Calgary, 1990, Art Gallery N.C., 1992, Montreal Mus. Fine Arts, 1992, Halifax, Nova Scotia, 1992, Toronto, Ont., Can., 1992; exhbn. of gift of portraits Nat. Portrait Gallery, London, 1991, one man retrospective Nat. Gallery, Nova Scotia, 1992, Montreal Mus. Fine Arts, 1992, McMichael Mus., Toronto, 1992, exhbn. Am. Legends Internat. Ctr. of Photography, 1992, Corcoran Gallery, Washington, 1993, Mint Mus. Charlotte, 1993, 10th anniversary inaugural retrospective, 85th birthday tribute exhibition Mus. Photography Film and TV, Bradford, Eng., 1993, Art Gallery Can. Embassy, Washington, 1994, Mus. Fine Arts, Boston, 1996, Mus. of Fine Arts, Montgomery, Ala., 1996, Detroit Art Inst., 1996—, Tower Gallery, Yokahama, Japan, 1997, Canada House, London, 1998, Charlottetown (Canada) Festival, June-Sept. 1998, Nat. Portrait Gallery of Australia, Canberra, 1999, Boston/Nagoya (Japan) Mus. Fine Arts, 2000, BankBoston Internat. Hdqs., Sao Paulo, Brazil, 2000, Sherbrooke (Que., Can.) Mus., 2000, Deutsche Historisches Mus., Berlin, 2000—; exhibited throughout Can., U.S., Europe, Australia, TV appearances; works represented in permanent collections: Mus. Modern Art, N.U.C., Met. Mus. Art, N.Y.C., Detroit Inst. of Arts; Internat. Ctr. of Photography, N.Y., Montgomery Mus. of Art. Montgomery, Art Inst. Chgo., St. Louis Art Mus., George Eastman House, Rochester, N.Y., Nat. Portrait Gallery, London, Nat. Gallery Can., Mus. Fine Arts, Boston, Can. House, London numerous others; photographer ann. poster child: Muscular Dystrophy Assn. Am; 25 photographs used on postage stamps in 15 countries. Decorated Order of Can., Companion of Can., 1990; recipient Centennial medal, Can. Council medal, U.S. Presdl. citation for service to handicapped, 1971, Achievement in Life award Ency. Brit., Silver Shingle award Boston U. Sch. Law, 1983, America's Soc. medal, 1989, Creative Edge award Time Inc. and NYU, 1989, 90, Gold medal of merit Nat. Soc. Arts and Letters, 1991, Jerusalem prize in the arts, Bezalel Acad., Israel, 1997, Fox Talbot award, Eng., 1998, Key to City of Ottawa, Can., 2000; named Master Photog. Arts Profl. Photographers Assn. Can. (Infinity award), Master Photographer Internat. Ctr. Photography, Person of the Week, World News Tonight-ABC, 1997, 60 Minutes update on 1977 segment, 1999-2000, documentary film The Searching Eye, 1983; annual Karsh Lectureship, Karsh prize in photography established Sch. of the Mus. Fine Arts, Boston, 1998; portraits of med. and scientific luminaries gift Harvard Med. Sch., 1998; established Karsh Med. fellowship Brigham & Women's Hosp., Boston, 1998, Mary Fay Essence of Nursing fellowship, 1999, Gift of Artists Pretholtz Family Ctr., 2000. Fellow Royal Photog. Soc. Gt. Britain; mem. Royal Can. Acad. Arts, Dutch Treast Club (N.Y.C.), Century Club (N.Y.C.), Rideau Club (Ottawa). E-mail: karshphoto@aol.com. Office: c/o Jerry Fielder PO Box 430 Monterey CA 93942-0430

KARSHIKOFF, ANDREY DIMITROV, physicist, researcher; b. Sofia, Bulgaria, Sept. 8, 1952; s. Dimitar Borisov and Rosa (Georgieva) K.; m. Danuta Lewandowicz, July 28, 1974; children: Milena, Aleksander. MS, U. Sofia, 1977; PhD, Bulgarian Acad. Sci., Sofia, 1985. Rsch. assoc. Bulgarian Acad. Sci., 1978-86; fellow Tech. U. Aachen/Max-Planck-Inst. Biochemie, Munich, 1986-91; lectr. Karolinska Inst., Stockholm, 1992-94, assoc. prof., 1994—; coord. European Biotech. Program, Stockholm, 1998—; organizer internat. meeting Understanding Electrostatics, Stockholm. Contbr. over 30 articles to sci. publs. Chmn. election com. Bulgarian Embassy, Sweden, 1995—. Alexander von Humboldt Found. fellow, 1986. Christian Orthodox. Home: Solskensvägen 15, 14646 Stockholm Sweden Office: Karolinska Inst, Dept Bioscis, 14157 Stockholm Sweden

KARTAL-OZER, NESRIN, biochemistry educator; b. Adapazari, Turkey, Aug. 29, 1955; d. Ramazan and Yuksel (Tokbay) K.; m. Ali-Fahir Özer, July 7, 1980; children: Onur Can. MS in Biochemistry, Hacettepe U., Ankara, Turkey, 1980, PhD in Biochemistry, 1983. Instr. Hacettepe U., Ankara, Turkey, 1977-86; assoc. prof. biochemistry Marmara U., Istanbul, Turkey, 1986-94, prof., 1994—; exec. com. health edn. faculty Marmara U., senate mem., 1996—; Turkey rep. UNESCO-Global Molecular and Cell Biology Network, 1994—. Co-author: Antioxidents in Nutrition and Health, 1998; contbr. chpts. to books and articles to profl. publs. Recipient Rsch. award

Turkish Toxicology Soc., 1992, Chamber of Medicine, 1997. Mem. Soc. for Free Radical Rsch. (com. mem. 1999—), European Acad. of Nutritional Sci., Soc. for Free Radical Rsch. Europe (com. mem.). Avocation: golf. Home: Fener Yolu Sokak No 37 A/22, 81040 Istanbul Turkey Office: Marmara U Fac Medicine, Dept Biochem Haydarpasa, 81326 Istanbul Turkey

KARTAVENKO, VLADIMIR GRIGORY, nuclear physicist, researcher; b. Kraskino, Russia, Aug. 19, 1947; s. Grigory Dmitry and Alexandra Jackov (Kurchenkova) K.; m. Anna Grigiry Mel'nikova, Mar. 16, 1976; 1 child, Serge. Degree, Far East State U., Vladivistok, Russia, 1970; DSc in Theoretical Nuc. Physics, Joint Inst. Nuc. Rsch., Dubna, Russia, 1975. Investigator Joint Inst. Nuc. Rsch., 1970-72, jr. rschr., 1977-82, sr. rschr., 1982—; guest prof. CENBG and U. Bordeaux 1, France, 1995, 2000; guest rschr. Inst. Theoretical Physics-JWG U., Frankfurt, Germany, 1994-2000. Avocations: soccer, gardening, bicycling, french wine. E-mail: kart@thsun1.jinr.cu. Office: Joint Inst Nuc Rsch, Joliot Courie 6, 141980 Dubna Moscow, Russia

KARTHA, CHANDRASEKHARAN CHERANELLORE, medical educator; b. Ernakulam, India, Dec. 14, 1951; s. Janardanan Kartha and Bharathy Kunjamma; m. Mira Mohanty, June 18, 1981. MB, BChir, Trivandrum (India) Med. Coll., India, 1974; MD, All India Inst Med. Scis., New Delhi, 1979. Lectr. in pathology Sree Chitra Tirunal Inst. Med. Scis. and Tech., Trivandrum, 1979-82; asst. prof. Sree Chitra Tirunal Inst. Med. Scis. and Tech., 1982-85, assoc. prof. pathology, 1986-88, additional prof. pathology, 1988-93, prof. divsn. cell molecular cardiology, 1993—. Author: Modern Medicine-Transitions and Promises, 2000; contbg. author: India's Environment: Problems and Perspectives, 1986, Wound Healing in Cardiovascular Disease, 1995; editor: Endomyocardial Fibrosis, 1993; mem. editl. bd. Current Sci., India, 1991—; editl. advisor Indian Heart Jour., 1995—; sect. editor Jour. Basic and Applied Biomedicine, India, 1994. Vice chmn. Health Action by People, Trivandrum, 1994—. Nat. Merit scholar Govt. India, 1966-74. Fellow Indian Coll. Pathology, Nat. Acad. Scis. (India), Indian Acad. Scis. Avocations: writing popular science articles, gardening, classical music. Home: Drisia TC 39-1796, Kesavan Nair Rd, Trivandrum 695012, India Office: Sree Chitra Tirunal, Inst Med Scis and Tech, Trivandrum 695011, India

KARTHA, RAVINDRANATHAN K.P., research scientist; b. Panthalloor, Kerala, India, Dec. 2, 1952; s. Raman Kartha and Bharathy K.P. Elayanna; m. Jayalakshmi Poduval, Aug. 3, 1989; 1 child, Vinayak. BSc, Calicut U., India, 1973, MSc, 1975; PhD, Gujarat U., India, 1984. Jr. rsch. fellow coun. scientific and indsl. rsch. Indian Coun. Agrl. Rsch., Ahmedabad, India, 1976-80; sr. rsch. fellow coun. scientific and indsl. rsch. Indian Coun. Agrl. Rsch., Ahmedabad, 1980-84; sci. officer Ctrl. Food Technol. Rsch. Inst., Mysore, India, 1984-86; vis. scientist Gifu (Japan) U., 1986-88, 94-95; rsch. assoc. NRC Can., Ottawa, 1988-92; scientist fellow Regional Rsch. Lab., Jammu, India, 1992-94; post-doctoral rsch. assoc. St. Andrews (Scotland) U., 1995—; presenter in field. Contbr. chpts. to books and articles to profl. jours. Mem. AAAS, Am. Chem. Soc., Assn. Carbohydrate Chemists and Technologists (life), Brit. Assn. for Advancement of Sci., Royal Soc. Chemistry. Avocations: sightseeing, hill walking, reading. Home: 27 Greenside Ct, St Andrews KY16 9UG, Scotland Office: U St Andrews, 308 Biomolecular Scis Bldg, St Andrews KY16 9ST, Scotland

KARTHIKEYAN, JANAKIRAM, engineering educator; b. Chittoor, India, Feb. 10, 1957; s. Karnam Janakiraman and Chittoor Ramaswamy Rajeswari; m. Chittoor Sesha Nagalakshmi, Aug. 17, 1984; children: Tanuja, Rahul. BTech, Sri Venkateswara U., Tirupati, India, 1980; MTech, Indian Inst. Tech., Kanpur, India, 1982, PhD, 1990. Cert. engring. Lectr. Sri Venkateswara U., Tirupati, 1983-86, reader, 1990—; cons. Indo Nat. Ltd., Chennai, India, 1990-95, advisor on environment, 1996—. Author: (book chpts.) Pollution Management in Industries, 1990, Advances in Wastewater Treatment, 1998; contbr. articles to profl. jours. Recipient Devel. Project award Ministry of Human Resources Devel., Govt. India, 1992, Rsch. Project award All India Coun. Tech. Edn., Govt. of India, 1995; rsch. scholar Indian Inst. Tech., 1986-89, Inidan Water Works Assn. prize, 1998. Fellow Instn. Engrs. India (Nawab Jain Yar Jang Bahadur award 1994-95); mem. Indian Soc. for Tech. Edn., Indian Assn. for Environ. Mgmt. Avocations: reading, social/advisory work. Office: Sri Venkateswara U, Dept Civil Engring, 517502 Tirupati India

KARTIGANER, JOSEPH, retired lawyer; b. Berlin, June 5, 1935; came to U.S., 1939; s. Harold and Lilly (Wolkowitz) K.; m. Audrey Gertsmun Amdursky; children: Deborah Lynn, Alison Beth. A.B., CCNY, 1955; LL.B., Columbia U., 1958. Bar: N.Y. 1960, Fla. 1978, D.C. 1979. Assoc. White & Case, N.Y.C., 1960-69, ptnr., 1969-88; ptnr. Simpson Thacher & Bartlett, N.Y.C., 1988-99; ret., 1999; lectr. law Columbia Law Sch., N.Y.C., 1973-80; vis. lectr. Sch. Law Yale U., 1997-99; mem adv. com. N.Y. Estates, Powers and Trust Law-Surrogate's Ct. Procedure Act, 1997-99. Fellow Am. Bar Found., Am. Coll. Trust and Estate Counsel (regent 1978-84), Am. Coll. Tax Counsel, N.Y. State Bar Found.; mem. ABA (chmn. real property, probate and trust law sect. 1986-87), N.Y. State Bar Assn., Assn. of Bar of City of N.Y. (chmn. com. on trusts, estates and surrogate's cts. 1990-92), Nat. Conf. Lawyers and Corp. Fiduciaries (co-chair 1991-93), Am. Law Inst., Internat. Acad. Estate and Trust Law (exec. coun.), Scarsdale Golf Club (Hartsdale, N.Y.). E-mail: joekart@yahoo.com. Home: 812 5th Ave # 5B New York NY 10021-7253 Office: Simpson Thacher & Bartlett 425 Lexington Ave Fl 15 New York NY 10017-3954

KARTSOUNIS, LOUCAS DEMOS, clinical neuropsychologist, consultant; b. Chios, Greece, Jan. 9, 1945; arrived in Eng., 1970; s. Adamantios and Argyro (Vafiades) K. BSc, Brunel U., London, 1978; MSc, Plymouth (Eng.) U., 1984; PhD, London U., 1982. Clin. neuropsychologist Nat. Hosp. for Neurology/Neurosurgery, London, 1984-96; cons. neuropsychologist Oldchurch Hosp., Romford, Eng., 1996—; hon. lectr. Inst. Neurology, London, 1993-96. Contbr. chpts. to books, articles to profl. jours. Fellow Brit. Psychol. Soc. (assoc.), Royal Soc. Medicine; mem. AAAS, Internat. Neuropsychol. Soc., N.Y. Acad. Scis. Office: Dept Neurology, Oldchurch Hosp, Romford RM7 0BE, England also: 10 Harley St, London W1N 1AA, England

KARU, TIINA, biophysicist; b. Tartu, Estonia, Apr. 19, 1947; d. Johannes and Leida Täpsi; m. Vladilen Letokhov, Nov. 30, 1979; 1 child, Inga. PhD, Moscow, 1974; DSc in Physics, St. Petersburg, 1990. Rsch. fellow Inst. Chemistry Acad. Sci., Tallinn, Estonia, 1974-75; rsch. fellow Inst. Physics Acad. Sci., Tartu, 1976-79; head of lab. Laser Tech. Rsch. Ctr. Russian Acad. Scis., Troitsk, Russia, 1980—; academician, Russian Acad. of Laser Scis., 1998—, prof., 1990—. Author: Photobiology of Low Power Laser Therapy, 1989, The Science of Low Power Laser Therapy, 1998; contbr. over 200 articles to profl. jours.; mem. editl. bd. Lasers in Surgery and Medicine, 1988-95, Lasers in the Life Sciences, 1986—, Laser Therapy, 1992—, Laser and Technology, 1991—. Fellow European Soc. Photobiology (nat. rep. 1986-96), Am. Soc. Photobiology; mem. Internat. Assn. Photobiology (v.p. 1996—), Am. Soc. Lasers in Surgery and Medicine, Academician of Russian Acad. of Laser Scis. Avocations: classical music, opera, gardening, writing Chinese characters. Home: Puchkovo 66, 142092 Troitsk Russia Office: Laser Tech Rsch Ctr, Acad Sci, 142092 Troitsk Russia

KARUNAKARAN, NAIR VENUGOPAL, viral oncologist, researcher; b. Vaikom, Kerala, India, Feb. 5, 1955; arrived in U.K., 1989; s. Karunakaran Nair and Thankamma Lakshmiamma; m. Geetha Vasudevamenon, Mar. 17, 1960; 1 child. B in Vet. Sci., Kerala U., 1976, M in Vet. Sci., 1978; diploma in med. virology, Pune (India) U., 1981; PhD, Madras (India) U., 1987. Asst. prof. Vet. Sch., Trichur, India, 1978-89; postdoctoral rschr. Inst. Virology, Oxford, Eng., 1989-94; project leader Inst. Animal Health, Compton, U.K., 1994—. Contbr. articles to profl. jours. Mem. Am. Soc. for Virology. Home: 78 Derwent Ave, Headington OX3 0AS, England Office: Inst Animal Health, Compton, Newbury RG20 7NN, England

KARUS, AVO, biochemist, educator; b. Rakvere, Estonia, Jan. 12, 1963; s. Leo and Helja (Plöks) K.; m. Virge Mets, Jan. 29, 1983; children: Siim, Kärt, Kaur. PhD, Moscow Vet. Acad., 1990; DSc in Agr., Estonian Agrl. U., Tartu, 1995. Vis. lectr. Moscow Vet. Acad., 1987-88; sr. lectr. Estonian Agrl. U., 1991-95, asst. prof. biochemistry, 1995-97, prof. biochemistry, 1997—; prin. dir. HTI Labs. Ltd., Tartu, 1994-97; head chemistry dept. Estonian Agrl. U., 1997—. Author: Basic Chemistry Manual, 1995, Biochemistry Manual, 1997. Grantee Estonian Sci. Found., Tallinn, 1993-95, 96-98, 99—. Mem. N.Y. Acad. Scis., Acad. Soc. Agriculture (Tartu). Avocation: chess. Office: Inst Animal Sci EAU, Kreutzwaldi 1, 51014 Tartu Estonia

KARYONO, TRI HARSO, architect, researcher, educator; b. Yogyakarta, Indonesia, Dec. 15, 1956; s. Lilik Soeparto and Sutinah Wirjosudjojo. B in Architecture, Bandung Inst. Technology, Indonesia, 1983; MA, U. York, 1989; PhD, U. Sheffield, 1996. Asst. architect Gita Rancana, Bandung, 1983-84; freelance architect, rschr. Agy. Assessment Technology, Jakarta, 1985-96, rschr. thermal comfort, 1993—; lectr. dept. architecture, U. Tarumanagara, U. Mercu Buana; vis. lectr. U. Bina Nusantara, U. Indonesia, U. Trisakti, U. Soegijapranata, U. Jakarta. Contbr. numerous articles to sci. and profl. jours., and short stories in mags. Home: Pondok Benda Indah N1/35, 15416 Tangerang Indonesia

KASA, PETER, medical educator; b. Ujkigyos, Hungary, June 19, 1934; s. Janos and Veronika (Krucsai) K.; m. Janina Soltysiak, Dec. 27, 1958; children: Peter, Katalin. MD, U. Szeged, Hungary, 1959, PhD, 1969, DSc, 1982. Asst. Med. U., Szeged, Hungary, 1962, asst. prof., 1962-73, assoc. prof., head, 1973-99, Szechenyi prof., 1999—; vis. prof. NYU, 1989. Contbr. articles to profl. jours. The Wellcome Trust rsch. fellow, Cambridge, 1967-*68, 69-70. Mem. IBRO, ISN, ENA. Avocations: reading, gardening. Home: Hargitai u 49/A, 6726 Szeged Hungary Office: Univ Szeged, Somogyi u 4, 6720 Szeged Hungary

KASAHARA, YASUSHI, chemist; b. Tokyo, Oct. 1, 1941; s. Sadao and Mitsuyo (Hashimoto) K.; m. Keiko Morisawa; children: Kyoko, Ayako. BA in Chemistry, Tokyo Sci. U., 1966; PhD in Chemistry, Tokyo Inst. Tech., 1977; DMS, Showa U., 1994. Chief chemist tech. rsch. labs. Toa Doro Industries, Inc., Tokyo, 1966-77; sr. rschr. ctrl. rsch. labs. Fujirebio Inc., Tokyo, 1977-79, gen. mgr. clin. chemistry divsn., 1979-88, dir ctrln. rsch. labs., 1986—, mng. dir., 1990-99; pres., CEO BIC Inc., Tokyo, 1999—; lectr. clin. lab. medicine Chiba (Japan) U. Med. Sch., 1985-91; lectr. biochemistry Kyorin U. Med. Sch., 1994—; vis. prof. Sch. Pub. Health, Kyorin U., 1998—; vis. specialist basic clin. rsch. Scripps Clinic and Rsch. Found., La Jolla, Calif., 1983. Co-author: Progress in Clinical Enzymology, Vol. 2, 1983, Selected Topics in Clinical Enzymology, Vol. 2, 1984, Dictionary of Biotechnology, 1986, Testing Values Ranging between Normal and Abnormal, 1987, Manual for Clinical Laboratory Testing, 1988, Clinical Laboratory Test for Sexually Transmitted Disease Using Advanced Technology, 1989; co-author, editor: Laboratory Reagents of Biotechnology, 1989; editor, co-author: Immunochemical Assays and Biosensor Technology in the 1990s, 1992; bd. editors Jour. Clin. Lab. Analysis, Clinical Diagnosis and Management by Laboratory Methods, 1996; contbr. articles to sci. jours. Recipient Best Tech. Report award Asphalt Soc. Japan, 1977, Best Tech. Paper award Japan Cement Assn., 1978, Best Scientific Paper award Jour. of Japan Petroleum Inst., 1979. Mem. AAAS, Am. Assn. for Clin. Chemistry, Nat. Acad. Clin. Biochemistry, Japanese Soc. Clin. Chemistry (bd. dirs.). Avocations: oil painting, skiing, go. Home: 4-24-6 Hijirigaoka, Tama-shi 206-0022, Japan Office: BIC Inc Settle Bldg, 3-5-4 Jingumae, Shibuya-ku, Tokyo 150-0001, Japan

KASAI, KAZUHIKO, banking executive; b. Takamatsu-shi, Kagawa Prefecture, Japan, Jan. 16, 1937; m. Naoko Kasai. Econs. degree, Kagawa U., 1959; postgrad. in mgmt., Harvard U., 1983. With The Fuji Bank, Ltd., Tokyo, 1959-78, from mgr. fgn. exch. dept. fgn. bus. devel. div. to asst. gen. mgr. internat. money desk internat. treasury div., 1978-83; gen. mgr. Chgo. br. The Fuji Bank, Ltd., 1983-86, gen. mgr. N.Y.C. br., 1986-87, dir., gen. mgr. N.Y.C. br., 1987-88; from dir. and gen. mgr. head office corp. banking div. II to mng. dir. in charge of internat. banking activities The Fuji Bank, Ltd., Tokyo, 1988-90, sr. mng. dir., 1991—; Chmn. Yasuda Trust & Banking, Tokyo, Japan; bd. dirs. The Fuji Bank, Ltd. Avocations: golf, drawings. Office: The Yasuda Trust and Banking Co Ltd, 1-2-1 Yaesu, Chuo-ku Tokyo 103-0028, Japan*

KASAI, KOHEI, surgeon; b. Sapporo, Hokkaido, Japan, Nov. 26, 1937; s. Takemi and Suzu (Isobe) K.; m. Haruko Fujimura, Oct. 30, 1972 (div. Oct. 1995); children: Takatoshi, Aki. MB, Showa Med. Coll., Tokyo. Surgeon Maruyama Meml. Hosp., Saitama-Ken, Japan, 1946, Tokyo Isuzumorter Hosp., Tokyo, 1947, Oomiya Cen. Hosp., Saitama-Ken, 1948; cardiologist Hakodate Mcpl. Hosp., Hokkaido, Japan, 1949-53; surgeon Orissa State U. Host, India, 1946. Mem. Hakodate Unesco Assn. (v.p. 1975), Lions (41st pres. Hakodate Higasi club). Japan Democratic Party. Avocations: aerophotographica, mountaineering, philatelist. E-mail: dr kasai@d1.dion.ne.jp. Home: 5-10 Honcho, 0400011 Hakodate/Hokkaido Japan Office: 5-10 Honcho Hakodate, Hokkaido 0400011, Japan

KASAI, MAKIKO, psychologist; b. Nagaya, Aichi, Japan, Oct. 22, 1964; d. Michiki and Fusa (Kimura) K. MA, Osaka U., 1990; PhD, U. Mo., 1997. Cert. clin. psychologist, Japan. Intern U. Iowa, Iowa City, 1995-96; instr. Naruto (Japan) U. Edn., 1997-2000, assoc. prof., 2000—. Mem. APA, Kappa Delta Pi. Office: Naruto U of Edn, 748 Nakajima Takashima, Naruto 772-8502, Japan

KASAI, NAOKI, electronics engineer; b. Niigata, Japan, June 16, 1957; s. Shoichi and Chiyomi (Kobayashi) K.; m. Yuriko Takamiya, Oct. 10, 1985; 1 child, Hikaru. B of Engring., Waseda U., Tokyo, 1980, M of Engring., 1982, D of Engring., 1999. Rschr. NEC Corp., Kawasaki, Japan, 1982-88; engr. NEC Corp., Sagamihara, Japan, 1989—; vis. rschr. Stanford U., 1988-89. Contbr. articles to profl. jours. Mem. IEEE. Office: NEC Corp, 1120 Shimokuzawa, Sagamihara 229-1198, Japan

KASAI, YOSHIYUKI, rail transportation executive. CEO Ctrl. Japan Railway, Nagoya, Japan, pres. *

KASAIKINA, OLGA TARASOVNA, scientist, health facility administrator; b. Drogobych, Lvov, Ukraine, Jan. 19, 1947; arrived in Russia, 1964; d. Taras Nikolaevich and Elena Anatolèvna (Shevchuk) Torbyak; m. Victor Alexandrovich Kasaikin; children: Alexandr, Marina. D in Chem. Scis., Moscow State U., 1964-69. Jr. rschr. Inst. Chem. Physics, Moscow, 1969-76; PhD rschr. Inst. Chem. Physics, 1976-84, sr. rschr., 1984-92, doctor of scis., 1992—, head lab., 1995—; participant Antarctic Sea Expedition, 1977-78. Contbr. articles to profl. jours. Grantee Internat. Sci. Found., 1994-95, Russian Fundamental Sci. Found., 1996-98. Mem. Internat. Electron Paramagnetic Soc. Roman Catholic. Avocations: classical music, opera. Home: Uralskaya St 6-4-96, 107207 Moscow Russia Office: RAS Inst Chem Physics, Kosygin St 4, 117977 Moscow Russia

KASAL, ALEXANDER, organic chemist, researcher; b. Prague, Czechoslovakia, June 4, 1934; s. Henry and Martha (Netvalova) K.; m. Hana Hanusova, July 6, 1971; 1 child, Barbara. RNDr, Charles U., Prague, 1957; PhD, Acad. Sci., Prague, 1962, DSc, 1990. Rschr. Inst. Organic Chemistry and Biochemistry, Prague, 1962-83, head of divsn., 1983—; mem. coun. fgn. affairs Acad. Sci., Prague, 1991—, mem. sci. coun. Inst. Organic Chemistry and Biochemistry, 1990—; mem. orgn. com. of a series of isoprenoid confs., Prague and Warsaw, 1970—. Author some 100 sci. papers and 10 patents. Recipient Hon. medal Polish Chem. Soc., Cracow, 1997. Mem. Czech Chem. Soc., Czech Biotech. Soc. Roman Catholic. Avocations: tennis, skiing, theatre. Office: Inst Organic Chemistry and Biochemistry, Fleming Sq 2, 16610 Prague Czech Republic

KASAMI, TADAO, information science educator; b. Kobe, Hyōgo, Japan, Apr. 12, 1930; m. Fumiko Okada, May 9, 1964; children: Yuuko, Ryuichi. B in Engring., Osaka (Japan) U., 1958, M in Engring., 1960, D in Engring., 1963. Assoc. prof. engring. Osaka (Japan) U., 1963-66, prof. engring. sci., 1966-94, dean engring. sci., 1990-92, prof. emeritus, 1994—; prof., Grad. Sch. Info. Sci. Nara (Japan) Inst. Sci. and Tech., 1992-98, dean, Grad. Sch. Info. Sci., 1992-94, dir. libr., 1994-98, prof. emeritus, 1998—; prof. Hiroshima (Japan) City U. Sch. Info. Sci., 1998—; adj. prof. Grad. Sch., U. Hawaii, Honolulu, 1992-97. Author: Coding Theory, 1978, Discrete Structure II, 1983, Formal Language Theory, 1988, Introduction to Information and Coding Theory, 1989, Trellises and Trellis-based Decoding Algorithms for Linear Block Codes, 1998. Fellow IEEE (life). Inst. Electronics, Info. and Comm. Engrs. (Achievement award 1987); mem. Soc. Info. and It's Applications (pres. 1993), IEEE Info. Theory Soc. (Claude E. Shannon award 1999). Office: Hiroshima City U, Ozukahigashi 3-4-1, Hiroshima 731-3194, Japan

KASANDA, PETER LESA, ambassador; b. Kasama, No., Zambia, Aug. 24, 1938; came to U.S., 1994; s. Anderson Chusa and Kaela (Makwaya) K.; m. Dorothy Chilombo Nalutongwe, Aug. 29, 1970; children: Kaela, Mwamba, Chilombo, Lesa, Luse. BSc in Econs., U. Rhodesia and Nyasaland, Harare, Zimbabwe, 1965; diploma in internat. rels., London Sch. Econs., 1967. Pvt. sec. to resident State House, Lusaka, Zambia, 1970-76; amb. to USSR Moscow, 1976-79; permanent sec. Ministry Fgn. Affairs, Lusaka, 1979-86; amb. to Fed. Rep. Germany Bonn, 1986-87; amb. to France Paris, 1987-89; amb. to China Beijing, 1989-94; amb. and permanent rep. of Zambia to the UN Permanent Mission of Zambia, N.Y.C., 1994—. Office: Mission of Zambia 800 2nd Ave Fl 9 New York NY 10017-4709*

KASANO, HIDEAKI, mechanical engineering educator; b. Tokyo, Nov. 30, 1946; s. Tomeko (Moriyama) K.; m. Yoko Gomyo; children: Hideyuki, Hidehiro. M of Engring., Tokyo Inst. Tech., 1973, D of Engring., 1985. Rsch. assoc. Tokyo Inst. Tech., 1973-88; assoc. prof. Takushoku U., Tokyo, 1988-93, prof. mech. engring., 1993—. Contbr. articles to profl. jours. Mem. Japan Soc. for Composite Materials (bd. dirs. 1998—). Office: Takushoku U, Hachioji, Tokyo 193-0985, Japan

KASAP, ERGUN, physics educator; b. Mucur, Kirsehir, Turkey, Sept. 2, 1961; p. Mahmut and Aliye (Akalin) K.; children: Aliye, Ulker. Degree in Engring., Ankara (Turkey) U., 1983; MSc, Gazi U., Ankara, 1986, PhD, 1992. Cert. engring. Rsch. asst. Gazi U., Ankara, 1984-92, rsch. fellow, 1992-97, asst. prof., 1997—, dep. head dept. physics, 1996—, head computing unit Arts and Scis. Faculty, 1994—. Contbr. articles to profl. jours. Cons. Nat. Movement Party, Ankara, 1998. Sgt. Turkish Artillery, 1994. Avocations: fishing, hunting, computer programming. E-mail: ergun@quark.fef.gazi.edu.tr. Fax: (312) 2122279. Office: Gazi U Arts & Scis Faculty, Teknikokullar, 06500 Ankara Turkey

KASARI, LEONARD SAMUEL, quality control professional, concrete consultant; b. Los Angeles, Sept. 22, 1924; s. Kustaa Adolph and Impi (Sikio) K.; m. Elizabeth P. Keplinger, Aug. 25, 1956; children: Lorraine Carol, Lance Eric. Student, Compton Coll., 1942-43, UCLA, 1964-70. Registered profl. engr., Calif. Gen. construction Los Angeles, 1946-61; supr. inspection service Osborne Labs., Los Angeles, 1961-64; mgr. customer service Lightweight Processing, Los Angeles, 1965-77; dir. tech. service Crestlite Aggregates, San Clemente, Calif., 1977-78; quality control mgr. Standard Concrete, Santa Ana, Calif., 1978-92. Camp dir. Torrance YMCA, High Sierras, Calif., 1969-80, mem. bd. mgrs., 1970—. Served with USN, 1943-46. Recipient Sam Hobbs Svc. award ACI-So. Calif., 1992; named Hon. Life Mem. Calif. PTA, 1983. Mem. Am. Concrete Inst. Democrat. Lutheran. Avocations: skiing, hunting, fishing, backpacking. Office: 2450 W 233rd St Torrance CA 90501-5730

KASARSKIS, EDWARD JOSEPH, neurologist; b. Chgo., Oct. 9, 1946; s. Edward Joseph Sr. and Valeria T. (Krauchunas) K.; m. Mary Baron Lenroot, Aug. 9, 1969; children: Andrew, Peter, Larisa, Irina. BA, Coll. St. Thomas, St. Paul, 1968; MD, U. Wis., 1974, PhD, 1975. Intern internal medicine U. Wis., Madison, 1974-75, resident internal medicine, 1975-76; resident neurology U. Va., Charlottesville, 1976-79; asst. prof. La. State U., Shreveport, 1979-80; asst. prof. U. Ky., Lexington, 1980-85, assoc. prof., 1985-92, prof., 1992—; chief neurology VA Hosp., Lexington, vice-chmn., 1998—. Author 150 articles, abstracts and book chpts. Recipient awards NIH, Muscular Dystrophy Assn., ALS Assn., VA. Office: U Ky Dept Neurology Lexington KY 40536-0001

KASATKIN, ANATOLII VLADIMIROVICH, metallophysicist, researcher; b. Moscow, July 10, 1947; s. Vladimir Nicolaevich and Barbara Timopheevna (Rodionova) K.; m. Oxana Ivanovna Mitrohina, Feb. 21, 1970; 1 child, Veronika Anatolievna. Degree in Engring.-Phys., U. Moscow, 1972. Sr. engr. Inst. Phys. Chemistry, Moscow, 1972-78, jr. rschr., 1978-81, sr. rschr., 1981-90, head lab., 1990—; cons. Inst. Info., Moscow, 1975-95, Inst. Patent Info., Moscow, 1980-99. Contbr. articles to profl. jours. Recipient Bronze medal Exhbn. VDNH, Moscow, 1987, Silver medal Exhbn. VDNH, Moscow, 1989. Mem. Inst. Phys. Chemistry (sci. coun. 1990-99). Avocation: translating from Japanese to Russian. Office: Inst Phys Chemistry, Leninskii pr 31, 117071 Moscow Russia

KASEMO, BENGT HERBERT, physics educator; b. Amal, Apr. 21, 1942; s. Carl Herbert and Anna Lena (Boquist) K.; m. Lena Kristina Sjovall, Apr. 5, 1969; children: Andreas, Jonas, Anna, Katarina. BS Physics, Goteborg U., 1966, MS Physics, 1969, PhD Physics, 1974. Rsch. assoc./asst. prof. Chalmers Univ. Tech., Goteborg, 1974-82, docent/assoc. prof., 1982-83, prof., 1983—; bd. dirs. Chalmers Indsl. Tech., 1985—, SKF Nova, Quartz Pro Instrument; founder, bd. dirs. Q-Sense AB; initiator, chmn. Ctr. Basic Combustion Rsch., Chalmers, 1985-87; mem. sci. bd. Volvo Rsch. Found., 1986-94, Perstorp Rsch. Found., 1986-93; mem. steering com. Interdisciplinary Rsch. Ctr. Surface Sci., U. Liverpool, 1988-95; mem. steering com. ESF Assoc. Program, 1990-96; consortium leader Biomaterial Consortium, program dir. SSF Edn. and Rsch. Program, 1990—; chmn. engring. physics Swedish Rsch. Coun. for Engring. Sci., Sweden, 1991-95; mem. Swedish Govt. Com. on Rsch., 1995-96; initiator, bd. dirs. Competence Ctr. for Catalysis, Chalmers Univ. Tech., 1995—; expert evaluator The Acad. of Finland, 1995; mem. adv. bd. Swedish Nat. Bd. for Tech. Devel., 1985-99. Contbr. over 200 articles to profl. jours. Fulbright scholar Fulbright Commn., Cornell U., 1988, 89. Mem. Am. Phys. Soc., Am. Chem. Soc., Am. Vacuum Soc., Biomaterials Soc., Swedish Acad. of Engrings. Scis., Royal Swedish Acad. Engring. Scis. (v.p. 1999—). Avocations: wildlife, gardening, reading. Office: Applied Physics, Chalmers Univ Tech, Göteborg 41296, Sweden

KASEMSUWAN, LALIDA, medical educator, otolaryngologist; b. Bangkok, May 21, 1958; d. Yong and Pisawong Watana; m. Piya Kasemsuwan, May 18, 1985; children: Panote, Punyavee. BS, Mahidol U., Bangkok, 1981; Med. Diplomate, Mahidol U., 1983. Diplomate Thai Bd. Otolaryngology. Fellow in otolaryngology Ramathibodi Hosp., Bangkok, 1989-92; instr. Mahidol U., Bangkok, 1992-95, asst. prof., 1995-99, assoc. prof., 1999—. Contbr. articles to profl. jours. Office: Ramathidodi Hosp Dept Otolaryngology, Rama 6 Rd, 10400 Bangkok Thailand

KASHAEV, RINAT MAVLYAVIEVICH, physicist, researcher; b. Chekmagush, Bashkiria, USSR, May 24, 1964; s. Mavlyavi Shaihetdinovich and Lena Makmunovna (Urazaeva) K.; m. Guljihan Rafisovna Biktimirova, Aug. 20, 1994; children: Danish, Camilla. MSc in Physics, U. Moscow, 1987; PhD, Inst. High Energy Physics, Protvino, USSR, 1992. Spl. rschr. Joint Inst. for Nuclear Rsch., Dubna, 1987-89; rsch. scientist Inst. for High Energy Physics, Protvino, 1992-93, Petersburg Nuclear Physics Inst., Gatchina, 1992-93, Rsch. Inst. for Theoretical Physics, Helsinki Inst. Physics, Helsinki, Finland, 1993-94, 96-97, 1999; rsch. scientist Ecole Normale Superieure, Lyon, France, 1995-96; sr. rsch. scientist Petersburg divsn. Steklov Math. Inst., St. Petersburg, Russia, 1997—; lectr. Helsinki U. Tech., Finland, 1999. Contbr. articles to profl. jours. including Comms. in Math. Physics, Letters in Math. Physics, Modern Physics Letters A, Nuclear Physics B. Mem. St. Petersburg Math. Soc. Avocation: jogging. Home: Sadovaya 128-48, 190008 Saint Petersburg Russia Office: Steklov Math Inst, Fontanka 27, 191011 Saint Petersburg Russia

KASHERININOV, PETER GEORGIEVICH, physicist; b. Leningrad, Russia, Apr. 14, 1938; s. George Orestovich Kasherininov and Olga Fedorovna Piaid; m. Ruslana Sergeevna Stezuk, Aug. 9, 1945. Degree in engring., Electrotech. Inst., Leningrad, 1962; postgrad. student, Inst. Semiconductors, Leningrad, 1964-66; PhD, A.F. Ioffe Phys. Tech. Inst., Leningrad, 1971. Engr. Svetlana, Leningrad, 1962-64; jr. rschr. A.F. Ioffe Phys. Tech. Inst., Leningrad, 1966-86, sr. rschr., 1986—. Contbr. articles to profl. publs.; patentee in field. Inco Copernicus grantee European Commn., Brussels, 1996. Fellow Scholars Club (St. Petersburg). Avocations: scuba diving, skiing, tennis. Home: Elisarova 12 Ap 57, 193029 Saint Petersburg Russia Office: AF Ioffe Phys Tech Inst, Politechnicheskaya 26, 194021 Saint Petersburg Russia

KASHIDA, JEFFREY SHINJI, amusement company executive; b. Kyoto, Japan, Dec. 2, 1947; s. Kiyoshi and Yukiko (Noguchi) K.; m. Emily F. takagi, Apr. 15, 1972; children: Eugene, Leilani, Richard. BA, Kansai U., Japan, 1970; AA, Southwest Coll., L.A., 1974; MIA, Columbia U., 1976. Pres. T.L.I. Inc., N.Y.C., 1989-92; pres., CEO ACE USA, Inc., Bellevue, Wash., 1996—; treas. Systemland U.S.A., Inc., Honolulu, 1996—; pres. Den Internat., Honolulu, 1996—; chmn. Complete Kitchen Inc., Honolulu, 1996—; mng. dir. ACE Co., Ltd., Tokyo, 1996—; pres., CEO Landmark Corp., Honolulu, 1998—, Ace Shoji Co. Ltd., Tokyo, 1999—, Pacific Angel Capital Corp., Honolulu, 2000—; com. mem. UNLV Internat. Gaming Inst., 1997—. Co-author: Challenge of Las Vegas. Mem. Am. Mgmt. Assn. Democrat. Buddhist. Avocations: movies, walking, golf, fishing, reading. Home: 107 Higuchi-Cho, Nishino-kyo, Nakagyo-ku, Kyoto 604, Japan Office: ACE Company Ltd, 3-12-9 Higashi-Ueno, Taito-ku Tokyo 110, Japan

KASHIMOTO, SATOSHI, anesthesiologist; b. Shinjuku, Tokyo, Japan, Oct. 6, 1955; s. Shirou and Sachiko (Mitsuno) K.; m. Junko Suzuki, Jan. 24, 1982; 2 children. MD, Tokyo Med. and Dental U., 1981. Resident Tokyo Met. Hiroo Hosp., 1981-82; clin. staff Yamanashi (Japan) Med. U., 1982-89, asst. prof., 1989-90, assoc. prof., 1992—. Contbr. articles to profl. jours. Mem. Am. Soc. Anesthesiologists, Internat. Soc. Heart Rsch., N.Y. Acad. Scis. Avocations: computor, music, movies, tennis. Home: Tamaho-cho Wakamiya 40-3, Nakakoma-gun 409-3803, Japan Office: Yamanashi Med Univ, Shimokato 1110 Tamaho-cho, Nakakoma-gun 409-3898, Japan

KA-SHING, LI, finance company executive; b. 1928; children: Victor, Richard. Degree (hon.), U. Cambridge, England, Beijing U., U. Hong Kong, Hong Kong U. Sci. & Tech., Chinses U. Hong Kong, City U. Hong Kong, Open U. Hong Kong, U. Calgary, Can. Founder Cheung Kong Industries, 1950; chmn. Cheung Kong Holdings. Offic: Cheung Kong Holdings Ltd, 2 Queens Rd, Hong Kong Hong Kong*

KASHIO, KAZUO, computer company executive; b. Jan. 9, 1929. Grad., Nihon U., 1949. Dir. Casio Lease Co. Ltd., Tokyo, 1949; dir. Casio Seisakusho, 1950, pres.; pres. Casio Computer Co., Ltd., Tokyo. Avocations: golf. Office: 6-2 Hon-machi 1-chome, Shibuya-ku, Tokyo 151-8543, Japan*

KASHIO, TOSHIO, electronics company executive; b. Jan. 1, 1925; m. Masako. Mng. dir. Casio Computer Co., Ltd., Tokyo, chmn. bd. Office: Casio Computer Co Ltd, 6-2 Hon-machi 1-chome, Shibuya-ku Tokyo 151-8543, Japan*

KASHIWAGI, NAOYA, pediatric orthopedic surgeon; b. Kobe, Japan, Sept. 14, 1960; s. Takeyoshi and Misako (Hirai) K.; m. Miki Yanaga, Sept. 14, 1988; children: Yuuka, Ayaka. Physician, Kyoto U., 1986. Jr. resident Kyoto U., 1986-87; sr. resident Kokura Meml. Hosp., Kitakyusyu, Japan, 1987-89; staff Koga Public Hosp., Minakuchi, Japan, 1989-93; chief orthopedic surgeon Med. Ctr. for Children, Moriyama, Japan, 1993—. Contbr. articles to profl. jours. Office: Shiga Med Ctr for Children, 5-7-30 Moriyama, Moriyama Shiga 524-0022, Japan

KASHIWAGI, YUSUKE, bank executive; b. Dalian, China, 1917; s. Hideshige and Kiyo (Yamada) K.; married; 4 children. LLB, Tokyo Imperial U., 1941. Dir. gen. internat. fin. bur. Japan Ministry Fin., Tokyo, 1966-68, vice minister fin., 1968-71, spl. advisor to the minister, 1971-72; dep. pres. Bank Tokyo, 1973-77, pres., 1977-82, chmn. bd., 1982-92, sr. advisor, 1992-96; sr. advisor Bank of Tokyo-Mitsubishi, Ltd., 1996—; mem. bus. adv. coun. European Bank for Reconstrn. and Devel., 1991—. Author: Gekidohki no Tsuuka Gaikon (Monetary Diplomacy in Turbulent Times), (1972, Watashi no Rirekisho (My Hometown-Dalian-New York-Tokyo), 1987. Named to Grand Cordon of the Order of the Sacred Treasure, Emperor of Japan, 1989. Mem. Rotary (Tokyo), Tokyo Club. Avocations: travel, golf. Home: 11-16 Nishi-Azabu 1 chome, Minato-ku Tokyo 106, Japan Office: Bank Tokyo-Mitsubishi Ltd, 3-2 Nihombashi Hongokucho, 1 chome Tokyo 103, Japan

KASHIWAZAKI, HIROSHI, human sciences educator; b. Tokyo, Apr. 10, 1946; s. Shoichi and Kazue (Takanashi) K.; m. Sachiko Shishido, Feb. 22, 1976; children: Atsuko, Koichi. BS, U. Tokyo, 1970, MS, 1972; PhD, Tohoku U., Sendai, Japan, 1978. Rsch. assoc. Tohoku U., Sendai, Japan, 1973-81; rsch. assoc. U. Tokyo, 1981-84, asst. prof., 1984-92, assoc. prof., 1992-97; prof. U. Occupl./Environ. Health Kytakyushu, Japan, 1997—. Contbr. articles to profl. jours. Mem. Population Assn. Am., N.Y. Acad. Sci., Japanese Assn. Pub. Health. E-mail: h-kashiw@health.uoeh-u.ac.jp. Office: U Occupl Environ Health 1-1, Iseigaoka Yahatahishi-ku, Kitakyushu, Fukuoka 80708555, Japan

KASHLEV, YURI ALEXANDROVICH, physicist; b. Nizhniy Tagil, Russia, Apr. 23, 1935; s. Alexandr Dmitrievich and Antonina Sergeevna (Serova) K.; m. Lidiya Konstantinovna Skolysheva, Aug. 30, 1978; 1 child, Sergei Yurievich. D of Physics & Math., Russian Acad. Scis., Moscow, 1982. Rsch. scientist A.A. Baikov Inst. Metallurgy, Russian Acad. Sci., Moscow, 1963-86, chief lab., 1986—, prof., 1995—. Author: (periodicals) Physica, 1984, Physica Status Solidi, 1995, 96, Teoreticheskaya i Matematicheskaya Fizika, 1973, 76, 77, 81, 83, 95, 97, 99; co-author: Diffusion Processes in Nuclear Materials, 1992. Internat. Sci. Found. grantee, Moscow, 1993. Avocation: classical music. Home: Lyapidevski Str 8, Bldg 1 Apt 53, 125581 Moscow Russia Office: AA Baikov Inst Metallurgy, Leninski Prospekt 49, 117334 Moscow Russia

KASHURNIKOV, VLADIMIR ANATOLIEVICH, physicist, educator; b. Khrabrovo, Russia, Dec. 13, 1958; s. Anatoliy Semenovich and Ida Muchailovna (Podzunskaya) K.; m. Galina Petrovna Arvacheva, June 11, 1983; 1 child. Diploma in engring., physics, Moscow State Engring. Inst., 1982; M in Physics, Math. Scis., High Test Com. USSR, Moscow, 1988, D of Physics, Math. Scis., 1997. Engr. Moscow Engring. Physics Inst., 1982-86, sr. engr., 1986-87, rschr., 1987-90, sr. rschr., 1990-99, prof. asst., 1993-99, prof., 1999—. Contbr. articles to profl. jours. Avocations: mountain travels, tourism. Office: Moscow Engring Physics Inst, Kashirskoe shosse 31, 115409 Moscow Russia

KASHYAP, AJIT SINGH, endocrinologist; b. Palwal, Haryana, India, June 6, 1959; s. Bhupendra Pal Singh and Chand Rani Lanba Kashyap; m. Surekha Gandhi, Nov. 20, 1989; 1 child, Aseem. B Medicine B Surgery, Armed Forces Med. Coll., Pune, India, 1980, MD, 1986; DM in Endocrinology, Postgrad. Inst., Chandigarh, India, 1998. Commd. Indian Army Med. Corps, 1981, advanced through grades to lt. col., med. specialist, 1986-96; sr. resident postgrad. Inst. Med. Edn. and Rsch., Chandigarh, 1996-98; assoc. prof. endocrinology Armed Forces Med. Coll., Pune, India, 1998—; clin. tutor Armed Forces Med. Coll., 1986-88. Contbr. articles to profl. jours. Mem. Assn. Physicians of India, Endocrine Soc. India. Hindu. Avocation: trekking. Office: Armed Forces Med Coll, Sholapur Rd, Pune Mahrashtra 411040, India

KASHYAP, BHAGWATI PRASAD, metallurgical, materials educator, researcher; b. Akhara, India, Oct. 5, 1948; s. Keshaw Ram and Dewa Bai (Verma) K.; m. Laxmi Bai Nayak, Aug. 12, 1983; 1 child, Priyanka. BE in Metallurgy, Govt. Coll. Engring. & Tech., Raipur, India, 1971; MTech, Indian Inst. Tech., Kanpur, India, 1975, PhD, 1980. Trainee Bhilai Steel Plant, India, 1972-73; rscg. engr. Steel Auth. India Ltd., Ranchi, India, 1980, U. Calif., Davis, 1981-84; rsch. assoc. U. Manitoba, Winnipeg, Can., 1984-87; asst. prof. Indian Inst. Tech., Bombay, 1987-90, assoc. prof., 1990-95, prof., 1995—. Contbr. articles to profl. jours. Recipient Fellowship award Assn. Commonwealth Univs., 1998. Mem. Indian Inst. Metals (sec. 1996), Inst. Engrs. India (Disting. Metallurgist award 1995), Materials Rsch. Soc. India. Avocations: yoga, literature. Home: B-5 Central Area, Mumbai 400 076, India Office: Indian Inst Tech, Dept Met Engring/Matl Sci, Mumbai 400 076, India

KASHYAP, SUDHIR KUMAR, communications executive, researcher, engineer; b. Patna, Bihar, India, Jan. 15, 1964; s. Mithila Sharan Singh and Shakuntala Devi; m. Nutan Kashyap, May 17, 1993; children: Shashank, Snigdha. Intermediate of sci., Sindri Coll., Sindri Dhanbad, India, 1981; BS in Engring., Bihar Inst. Tech. Sindri, Dhanbad, 1987, postgrad., 1999—. Chartered engr. Inst. Engrs.; cert. quality engr.; internal quality auditor. Lectr. part-time Bihar Inst. Tech. Sindri, Dhanbad, 1987-90; scientist B Ctrl. Mining Rsch. Inst. Dhanbad, 1990-95, scientist C, 1995-99, scientist in-charge, 1999—; presenter tech. papers in field. Mem. Inst. Engrs. (assoc.), Mining, Geol. and Metallurg. Inst. India, Indian Soc. Non-Destructive Testing, Indian Soc. Mech. Engrs., ASME. Avocations: reading newspapers, entertaining with Hindi filmi song, social service, reading technical articles. Office: Ctrl Mining Rsch Inst, Barwa Rd, 826001 Bihar India

KAŠIČKA, VÁCLAV, chemist; b. Nymburk, Czech Republic, Oct. 10, 1952; s. Václav and Libuše (Stuchlová) K.; m. Rosina Simeonova, July 27, 1983; children: Rosina, Václava. MSc, Charles U., Prague, Czech Republic, 1977, RNDr, 1979; PhD, Czech Acad. Sci., Prague, 1985. Cert. chemist, phys. chemist, biochemist. Postgrad. Inst. Organic Chemistry & Biochemistry Czech Acad. Sci., Prague, 1980-83, jr. scientist Inst. Organic Chemistry & Biochemistry, 1983-88, rsch. scientist Inst. Organic Chemistry & Biochemistry, 1989-96, sr. scientist Inst. Organic Chemistry & Biochemistry, 1997—. Author: (with others) Encyclopedia of Analytical Science, 1995, Progress in HPLC-HPCE, 1997, Analytical and Preparative Separation Methods of Biomacromolecules, 1999; editor Jour. Chromatography, 1996; mem. editl. bd. internat. jour. Electrophoresis; contbr. articles to profl. jours. 1st lt. Czech Army, 1977-78, Karlovy Vary. Recipient young scientist award Czech Acad. Sci., Prague, 1984, young investigator award World Exhbn. Young Investigators, Plovdiv, Bulgaria, 1985. Mem. Internat. Coun. Electrophoretic Socs., Internat. Soc. for Molecular Recognition, Czech Chem. Soc. (sec. Chromatography and Electrophoresis Group 1990, chmn. 1996, young analytical chemist award 1988), Czech Biochemistry Soc. Avocations: sports, culture. Office: Czech Acad Sci Flemingovo 2, Inst Organic Chem Biochem, 166 10 Prague 6 Czech Republic

KASIPATHI, CHINTA, geologist, educator, consultant, researcher; b. Rajahmundry, India, Oct. 17, 1955; s. Chinta Veerabhadra Rao and Chinta M. Viyyuri Manikyamba; m. Chinta Hemalatha, May 9, 1979; children: Anand Chinta, Pramod Chinta. BS, Andhra U., Visakhapatnam, India, 1973, MS, 1976, PhD, 1981. Rsch. assoc. Andhra U., 1981-84, officer, 1984, lectr., 1984-86, reader, 1986-94, prof., 1994—, dir. rsch., 1984—; rschr., Andhra U., 1976—, tchr., 1980—, cons., 1981—, pres., 1983—; expert India Bur. Mines, 1995—. Contbr. articles to profl. jours. Gemologist, Visakhapatnam, 1992—; geoscientist, Visakhapatnam, 1976—; vol. Helpless Pub., Andhra Pradesh, 1973—. Recipient Young Scientist award Wadia Inst. Himalian Geology, Dept. Sci. and Tech., India, 1985. Fellow Indian Sci. Congress (life), Internat. Geol. Congress; mem. Instn. Geoscientists India (life), Soc. Geoscientists and Allied Techs. (life). Avocations: tourism, scientific pursuits, music, games, TV. Home: P8 Andhra Univ Quarters, Sivajipalem Visakhapatnam 530017, India Office: Andhra Univ, Dept Geology, 530 003 Visakhapatnam India

KASKARELIS, IOANNIS ALKIVIADES, economist, educator; b. Piraeus, Greece, Jan. 21, 1962; s. Alkiviadis I. and Asimina A. (Mbouris) K. BA in Econs., U. Athens, 1983; MA, Athens Sch. Econs., 1985; PhD, Birkbeck Coll., U. London, London, 1990. Rsch. asst. Athens Sch. Econs., 1985-86; part-time rsch. asst. U. London, 1987-88, rsch. asst., 1988-90; lectr. U. Macedonia, Thessaloniki, Greece, 1992-95, asst. prof., 1995—. Author: Cyclical Fluctuations and Economic Policy, 1996, Private Investment in Greece, 1996, Eleven Lectures in Econometrics, 1996, 2d edit., 1999, Exercises in Econometrics, 1999; contbr. articles to acad. and profl. jours. With Greek Navy, 1990-92. Grantee Greek Scholarships Found., 1979, 80, 81, 82, 86-90, Athens Sch. Econs., 1983-85. Mem. N.Y. Acad. Sci., Inst. Econ. Policy Rsch., Royal Econ. Soc., European Econ. Assn., Am. Econ. Assn. Home: 2 Kadmou Str, GR175-61 Paleo Phaliro Greece Office: U Macedonia Dept Econs, 156 Egnatia St, GR540-06 Thessaloniki Greece

KASKARELIS, VASSILIS, Greek diplomat to NATO; b. Athens, Nov. 26, 1948; married; 2 children. Degree in econs. and polit. sci., U. Thessalonoki; degree in law, U. Athens. Attaché of embassy Ministry of Fgn. Affairs, Greece, 1974-76; 3d sec. Greek Embassy, Ankara, Turkey, 1976-79; consul of Greece Office of Greek Consulate, Venice, 1979-83; counsellor Greek Embassy, Nicosia, Cyprus, 1984-87; head of mil. mission of Greece Berlin, 1987-90; dep. dir., Turkish Desk Ministry for Fgn. Affairs, 1991-93, minister plenipotentiary, Head of Cabinet of Sec. Gen., 1993-95; dep. perm. rep. of Greece to UN, N.Y.C., 1995-2000; perm. rep. from Greece to NATO Brussels, 2000—. Office: NATO Hdqrs, Blvd Leopold III, 1110 Brussels Belgium*

KASMAI, HAMID SALEH, chemistry educator, researcher, consultant; b. Tabriz, Azarbaijan, Iran, May 28, 1939; came to U.S., 1962; s. Hoseinguli Saleh-Kasmai and Aameneh Aalemrajabi; m. Roselyn Mae Senior, July 18, 1971; children: Armon, Nikoo. BSc in Chemistry, Tchrs. Coll., Tehran, Iran, 1961; PhD in Chemistry, U. Wis., 1969; postdoctoral, Syracuse U., 1973-74, 78-79. Asst. prof. Pahlavi U., Shiraz, Iran, 1968-74, assoc. prof., 1974-80; adj. prof. Syracuse U., 1980-82; asst. prof. Hamilton Coll., Clinton, N.Y., 1982-87; asst. prof. East Tenn. State U., Johnson City, 1987-91, assoc. prof., 1991-99, prof., 1999—; cons. chem. industries, 1987—; spkr. in field. Author: (with others) Advances in Heterocyclic Chemistry, 1978, Trends in Organic Chemistry, 1993; contbr. articles to profl. jours. Fulbright-Hays travel grant Fulbright Found., 1973; Cottrell Coll. Sci. grant Rsch. Corp., 1982-84, type B grants Am. Chem. Soc., 1986-88, 89-91, various grants Hamilton Coll. and East Tenn. State U., 1982-94. Mem. AAAS, AAUP, Am. Chem. Soc. (type B grant 1986-88, 89-91, Spkr. of Yr. N.E. sect. 1994), Internat. Soc. of Heterocyclic Chemistry, Tenn. Acad. of Scis., Sigma Xi. Avocations: woodworking, swimming, hiking, music, stamp and coin collecting. Office: East Tenn State U PO Box 70695 Johnson City TN 37614-1710

KASPARAITIS, DARIUS, hockey player; b. Elektrenai, Russia, Oct. 16, 1972; married. Ice hockey player N.Y. Islanders, 1992-97; def. player Pitts. Penguins, 1997—. Recipient ice hockey Silver medal Olympic Games, Nagano, Japan, 1998. Avocations: fishing, tennis. Office: Pitts Penguins Civic Arena 66 Mario Lemieux Pl Pittsburgh PA 15219-3501*

KASPAREK, MAX, biologist; b. Landshut, Germany, Nov. 21, 1956; s. Max Udo and Marianne (Eberle) K.; m. Aygün Kilic, Aug. 5, 1985; children: Nathalie, Laura. Diploma in biology, Heidelberg U., 1984; PhD in Biology, Darmstadt U., 1986. Project leader World Wide Fund for Nature, 1988; expert World Bank, 1996; team leader UN Environ. Program, 1993; project mgr. GTZ German Devel. Cooperation, 1995—; expert UN Devel. Program, 1997—. Author: Nature Guide to Turkey, 1990, Directory for Medicinal Plants Conservation, 1996; contbr. articles to profl. jours. Mem. World Conservation Union (species survival commn.), Mediterranean Assn. to Save the Sea Turtles (sci. com.), Ornitholog. Soc. of Mid. East. Fax: 49-6221-471858. Home and Office: Kasparek Verlag, Monchhofstr 16, 69120 Heidelberg Germany

KASPER, ERICH ALEX, electrical engineering educator; b. Eisenerz, Styria, Austria, Mar. 6, 1943; arrived in Germany, 1971; s. Franz and Hedwig (Keplinger) K.; m. Anna Christine Aschacher, Apr. 8, 1971; children: Wolfgang, Sebastian, Johannes. PhD, U. Graz, Austria, 1971. Scientist AEG-Telefunken, Ulm, Germany, 1971-80; lab. head AEG, Ulm, 1980-90; dept. head Daimler Benz, Ulm, 1990-93; dir. Inst. Halbleiter Tech., Stuttgart, Germany, 1993—; prof. U. Stuttgart, 1993—; curator Physikalisch Blaetter, Weinheim, 1990-99. Editor: Silicon Molecular Beam Epitaxy, 1988, Properties of Strained and Relaxed Silicon Germanium, 1995; inventor coplanar transciever, 1991. Beirat Inst. Schicht und Ionen Technik, Juelich, Germany, 1989-95, Beirat Inst. Halbleiter Physik, Frankfurt, Germany, 1992-96. Mem. IEEE, AAAS, Electrochem. Soc., Deutsche Physikal Gesellschaft, Verein Deutscher Elektrotechnik. Avocations: astronomy, skiing. Home: Osterholz Str 16, D-89284 Pfaffenhofen Germany Office: Pfaffenwaldring 47, D-70569 Stuttgart Germany

KASPER, HORST MANFRED, lawyer; b. Dusseldorf, Germany, June 3, 1939; s. Rudolf Ferdinand and Lilli Helene (Krieger) K.; 1 child, Olaf Jan. Diploma in chemistry, U. Bonn, 1963, D. in Natural Scis., 1965; JD, Seton Hall U., 1978. Bar: N.J. 1978, U.S. Patent Office 1977. Mem. staff Lincoln Lab., MIT, Lexington, 1967-69; mem. tech. staff Bell Tel. Labs., Murray Hill, N.J., 1970-76; assoc. Kirschstein, Kirschstein, Ottinger & Frank, N.Y.C., 1976-77; patent atty. Allied Chem. Corp., Morristown, N.J., 1977-79; pvt. practice Warren, N.J., 1980-83; with Kasper and Weick, Warren, 1983-85, Kasper and Laughlin, 1985—. Contbr. numerous articles to profl. jours.; patentee semicondr. field. Mem. ABA, AAAS, N.J. Bar Assn., Internat. Patent and Trademark Assn., Am. Patent Law Assn., N.J. Patent Law Assn., Am. Chem. Soc., Electrochem. Soc., Am. Phys. Soc., N.Y. Acad. Scis. Home and Office: 13 Forest Dr Warren NJ 07059-5832 Office: ul Na Grzgdkach 9, 30421 Cracow Poland

KASPERCZAK, HENRY, professional soccer coach, former player. Defender Poland Nat. Team, World Cup Finals, 1974, 78, Stal Mielec Football Club; coach Metz Football Club, St. Etienne Football Club, Strasbourg Football Club, Racing Paris Football Club, Montpellier Football Club; winner French Cup; coach Ivory Coast Nat. Team, Tunisian Nat. Team, 1995-98, World Cup, France, 1998, Sporting Club Bastia, 1998—, Moroccan Nat. Team, 2000S. *

KASPERCZYK, JÜRGEN CHRISTIAN, business executive, government official, educator; b. Pitschen, Germany, Mar. 4, 1941; arrived in Luxembourg, 1980; s. Gerhard Max and Edith Clara (Utta) K.; m. Katrin Schimbke, Apr. 25, 1968 (div.); children: Martin, Kristina; m. Le Ngoc Nguyen, Jan 30, 1997. MSc in Mining Engring., Tech. U., Berlin, 1968, PhD in Chem. Engring., 1970. Rsch. scientist Bergbauforschung GmbH., Essen, Germany, 1968-72; mgr. coking plant Rhodesian Iron and Steel Co., Ltd., Redcliff, Rhodesia, 1972-74; project mgr. Exploration und Bergbau GmbH., Düsseldorf, Germany, 1974-76; tech. mgr. Hansen Neuerburg GmbH., Essen, Germany, 1976-78; mng. dir. CARBOMINA Rohstoffhandel GmbH., Essen, Germany, 1978-82; pres., CEO ENSCH, Luxembourg, 1980-90, ENSCH Internat. S.A., Luxembourg, 1990-96; dir. Entec Computer Taiwan Ltd., Taipei, 1985—; hon. prof. Institut des Hautes Etudes Economiques et Sociales, Brussels; pres. Entex Intl. S.A., Luxembourg, 1996-2000; ptnr. Dr. Jürgen Kasperczyk Cons., Luxembourg, 2000—; pres. Lux Commodities S.A., Luxembourg; vice chmn. S.P. Otema, Moscow, 1988-92, Implus Internat., Vinnitsa, Ukraine, 1989—; pres. Entex Ltd., Sofia, Bulgaria, 1994—; bd. dirs. Tino Commodities Ltd., Nicosia, Cyprus, 1999—. Contbr. papers on coal and cokemaking rsch. to tech. mags., internat. confs. Dep. Internat. Parliament for Safety and Peace, 1993-98. Mem. Inst. Mining and Metallurgy, Verein Deutscher Eisenhüttenleute, Deutsche Wissenschaftliche Gesellschaft für Erdöl, Erdgas and Kohle, Gesellschaft Deutscher Metallhütten-und Bergleute, Am. Iron and Steel Soc., Golf Grand-Ducal Club, Old Tablers Club (Essen), Order of the Knight Templars of Jerusalem (Great Prior). Office: Lux Commodities SA, 241 Route D Arlon, L-2150 Luxembourg Luxembourg

KASPERKOWIAK, STANISLAW KAZIMIERZ, career officer; b. Szelejewo, Poland, Jan. 16, 1942; s. Stanislaw and Jadwiga (Kaczmarek) K.; m. Ursula Maria Piechocka Kasperkowiak, June 10, 1967; children: Waldemar, Agnieszka, Magdalena. Degree, Naval Acad., Gdynia, Poland, 1961-65, Military Study, Warsaw, Poland, 1978-79. Commanding officer of war ship Navy, Swinoujscie, Poland, 1967-69, staff officer, 1969-82; chief of staff 8th Coastal Def. Flotilla, Swinoujscie, Poland, 1982-87; dept. dir. Maritime Office, Warsaw, Poland, 1987-93; commr. 8th Coastal Def. Flotilla, Swinoujscie, Poland, 1993—. Rear Admiral Polish Navy, 1993, Poland. Recipient Hon. Cross of Bundeswehr in gold, Min. of Def. of Germany, 1997, Award for the Best Naval Unit Min. of Def., 1998, Pres. of Rep. of Poland, 1999. Avocations: yachting, tourism. Office phone: 48 91 324 2221. Office: 8th Coastal Def Flotilla, Bohaterow Wrzesnia 31, 72-600 Swinoujscie Poland

KASPERLIK-ZALUSKA, ANNA ANTONINA, medical educator, consultant, researcher; b. Warsaw, Poland, Aug. 16, 1933; d. Stanisław and Waleria (Zakrzewska) Kasperlik; m. Józef Roman Załuska, Feb. 8, 1964; 1 child, Andrzej. Grad., Acad. Medicine, Warsaw, 1957, D Med. Scis., 1967. Intern in surgery Inst. Hematology, Warsaw, 1957-58; intern in pediatrics Pediatric Hosp. Nr 1, Warsaw, 1957-58; intern in obstetrics and gynecology Hosp. Gynecology and Obstetrics, Warsaw, 1957-58; intern in internal medicine Inst. Postgrad. Med. Edn., Warsaw, 1957-58, fellow in internal medicine, 1958-60; jr. asst. Bielanski Hosp., Warsaw, 1960-62; jr. asst. Postgrad. Med. Sch., Acad. Medicine, 1963-66, asst. lectr., 1966-69; asst. prof. medicine Ctr. Postgrad. Med. Edn., 1970-80, assoc. prof., 1981-89, prof., 1989—; dist. endocrinology cons. Dept. Health, Warsaw, 1992-99. Contbr. numerous articles to sci. jours. Recipient award Ministry Health, 1977, 87, 92, 96, 98; grantee Com. Sci. Rsch., 1992, 94, 96. Fellow Polish Endocrinology Soc. (pres. Warsaw sect. 1990—). Roman Catholic. Avocations: classical music. Home: Gabinska 18/35, 01-703 Warsaw Poland Office: Ctr Postgrad Med Edn, Ceglowska 80, 01-809 Warsaw Poland

KASPROW, BARBARA ANNE, biomedical scientist, writer; b. Hartford, Conn., Apr. 23, 1936; d. Stephen G. and Anna M. Kasprow. AB cum laude, Albertus Magnus Coll., 1958; postgrad., Laval U., 1958, Yale U., 1958-61; PhD, Loyola U., Chgo., 1969. Staff microbiology dept. Conn. State Dept. Health, 1957; lab. asst. dept. microbiology Yale U., New Haven, 1958-59; tng. scholar USPHS, 1959-60; asst. rsch. and editl. dept. anatomy Yale U., New Haven, 1961; rsch. assoc. N.Y. Med. Coll., 1961-62; from rsch. assoc. to sr. rsch. and adminstrv. assoc., asst. to dir. grad. med. edn., asst. dir. adminstrn. grad. rsch. endocrinology Inst. for Study Human Reprodn. St. Ann Ob-Gyn. Hosp., Cleve., 1962-67; sr. rsch. assoc. dept. anatomy Stritch Sch. Medicine, Chgo., Hines, Ill., 1967-69; asst. prof. anatomy Loyola U., Chgo., 1969-75; asst. to v.p. University Rsch. Sys., 1975-79, v.p. med. topics, 1979—; asst. to pres. Internat. Basic and Biol.-Biomed. Curricula, Lombard, Ill., 1979—; lectr. in field; invited U.S. del. on reprodn. to Vatican, 1964; round table leader Brazil-Israel Congress on Fertility and Sterility, Brazil Soc. Human Reprodn., São Paulo, 1972. Editl. asst. vol. VIII/3 Handbuch der Histochemie, Gustav Fischer Verlag, 1963; prodn. aide ednl. med. film The Soft Anvil, 1965-66; co-editor: Biology of Reproduction, Basic and Clinical Studies, 1973; contbr. articles to profl. jours. Recipient Certificate of Outstanding Achievement and Scholarship award Am. Assn. German Tchrs. and New Britain German Assn., 1954; named Honorary Citizen São Paulo, 1972. Mem. AAAS (life), Am. Assn. Anatomists, Am. Soc. Zoologists-The Soc. Integrative and Comparative Biology, Pan Am. Assn. Anatomy (co-organizer symposium on reproduction New Orleans 1972), Midwest Anatomists Assn. (program officer ann. meeting Chgo. 1974), Sigma Xi (life). Roman Catholic. Achievements include biological elucidation of growth horizons in uterine development, growth, and maturity; perfection of a hormonal model-system in highly controlled (surgerized) animals to ascertain quantitative relationships of purified estradiol-17beta and progesterone required for promotion of and duplication of these uterine growth horizons; development of experimental paradigms for the biomorphological elucidation of hormonally stimulated growth responses in endocrine target organs, and cyto- and histochemical elucidation of growth stimulants. Office: 607 E Wilson Ave Lombard IL 60148-4062

KASPROWSKI, ZYGMUNT JAN, engineering executive, consultant; b. Mikolow, Poland, Dec. 28, 1958; s. Wojciech and Eryka Maria (Piorecka) K.; m. Bozena Glombik Kasprowska, Jan. 17, 1985; children: Daniela, Krzysztof, Marek. MS in Engring., Tech. Inst., Gliwice, Poland, 1982. IT specialist Laziska Power Station, Laziska Gorne, Poland, 1982-88; deputy mgr. of R&D, 1989-97; with Elektro Ltd., Laziska Gorne, Poland, 1998—. Mem. European Oracle Users Group. Avocation: climbing mountains. Office: Elektro Ltd, Wyzwolenia 30, 43-170 Laziska Gorne Poland

KASPRZAK, WACŁAW ANTONI, engineering educator, researcher; b. Golina, Poland, Sept. 26, 1932; s. Antoni Klemens and Helena (Makowska) K.; m. Krystyna (Wycichowska), Apr. 26, 1958; 1 child, Cezary Pawel. MSc, Tech. U., Wrocław, Poland, 1956, PhD in Mechanics, 1962, DSc, 1967. Designer Mech. Engring. Design, Wrocław, 1954-58; asst. prof. Tech. U., Wrocław, 1958-67, assoc. prof., 1967-71, prof., 1971—; dir. devel. Tech. U., Wrocław, 1963-69, v.p., 1969-81, pres., 1982-84; head lab. Dynamics, Tech. U., Wrocław, 1974. Co-author: (books) Dimensional Analysis and Mathematical Models, 1988, Dimensional Analysis, 1990 (Ministry Sci. award 1991), Computer Aided Data Processing, 1991; editor Proceedings of 1989 Cosmex Meeting, Stochastic Methods in Exptl. Scis. E-mail: kasprzak@immt.pwr.wroc.pl. Home: ks K Damrota 41 m 3, 50-306 Wroclaw Poland Office: Tech U, Wyb Wyspianskiego 27, 50-370 Wroclaw Poland

KASS, JEROME ALLAN, writer; b. Chgo., Apr. 21, 1937; s. Sidney J. and Celia (Gorman) K.; children from previous marriage: Julie, Adam; m. Delia

Ephron, May 21, 1982. BA, NYU, 1958, MA, 1959. instr. Colulmbia U. Film Sch. Playwright: Monopoly, 1965, Saturday Night, 1968, (mus.) Ballroom, 1978 (Tony nomination), (TV) A Brand New Life, 1973, Queen of the Stardust Ballroom, 1975 (Writers Guild Am. award, Emmy nomination), My Old Man, 1979, The Fighter, 1982, Scorned and Swindled, 1984, Crossing to Freedom (aka Pied Piper), 1989, Last Wish, 1991, The Only Way Out, 1993, Secrets, 1995; screenwriter: The Black Stallion Returns, 1981, (miniseries) Evergreen, 1985; author: Four Short Plays by Jerome Kass, 1966, Saturday Night, 1969; adapted to concert form Finian's Rainbow, L.A., 1997, Pajama Game, L.A., 1998, Fiorello, L.A., 1999; musical version Queen of the Stardust Ballroom, Chgo., 1998. Mem. Dramatists Guild, Writers Guild Am., Phi Beta Kappa.

KASSA, JIŘÍ, toxicologist, researcher, educator; b. Vimperk, Czechoslovakia, May 21, 1956; s. Štefan and Ružena (Hejzlarová) K.; m. Iva Fousková, June 25, 1983; children: Šárka, Martin. MD, Mil. Med. Acad., Hradec Králové, Czechoslovakia, 1981; PhD, Mil. Med. Acad., Hradec Králové, Czechoslovakia, 1991. Asst. dept. toxicology Mil. Med. Acad., 1985-92, head biochem. group, 1992-97, assoc. prof., 1996, dep. head dept. toxicology, 1997—. Seed grantee Internat. Soc. Neurochemistry Com. for Aid for Neurochemistry, 1996. Avocations: playing piano, travel, playing chess. Office: Purkyně Mil Med Acad, PO Box 35/T, 500 01 Hradec Kralové Czech Republic

KASSAI, TIBOR, parasitologist; b. Miskolc, Hungary, Sept. 5, 1930; s. József K. and Mária Farkas; m. Ilona Dávid (div. 1987); children: Tibor, Tamás. DVM, Vet. Sch., Budapest, Hungary, 1952, PhD, 1956; DSc, Acad. Sci., Budapest, Hungary, 1991. Lectr. U. Vet. Sci., Budapest, Hungary, 1955-60, rsch. assoc., 1960-68, gen. rsch. assoc., 1968-80, u. prof., 1980—, head dept., 1981-94, prof. emeritus, 1995—; expert, project mgr. UN Devel. Programme FAO, Baghdad, Iraq, 1970-72, cons., Aden, Yemen, 1988. Author: Handbook of Nippostrongylus brasiliensis, 1982, Veterinary Helminthology, 1999; first editor: Parasitologia Hungarica, 1968. Decorated K.A. Rudolphi medal German Soc. Parasitologists, Berlin, 1987, Order of Merit Republic of Hungary, 1995. Mem. Hungarian Soc. Parasitologists (pres. 1972-99), European Fedn. Parasitologists (pres. 1980-84), Serbian Acad. Sci. and Arts, World Assn. Advancement Vet. Parasitology (hon. 1999). Avocations: aphorisms. Home: Rözse utca 19, H-1125 Budapest Hungary

KASSAM, AMIRALI HASSANALI, agricultural scientist; b. Zanzibar, Tanzania, June 30, 1943; s. Hassanali Mohamed Saleh and Roshan Fazal (Bhanji) K.; m. Parin Suleman, May 3, 1968; children: Zahra, Shireen, Laila, Salman. BSc in Agrl. Sci., Reading U., 1966, PhD in Agrl. Botany, 1971; MS in Irrigation Sci., U. Calif., Davis, 1967. Rsch. demonstrator Reading (Eng.) U., 1968-71; rsch. fellow Inst. for Agrl. Rsch., Ahmadu Bello U., Samaru, Nigeria, 1971-74; internat. scientist Internat. Crops Rsch. Inst. for Semi-Arid Tropics, Hyderabad, India, 1974-76; dir. Echemess Ltd., mgmt. and devel. cons., London, 1978-90; sr. cons. FAOUN, Rome, 1977-90, sr. agrl. rsch. officer, tech. adv. com. to consultative group on internat. agrl. rsch., FAOUN, Rome, 1990-98; deputy dir. gen. West Africa Rice Devel. Assn., Bouake, Ivory Coast, 1998—; mem. WHO/FAO/UNEP panel of experts on Environ. Mgmt. of Vector Control, 1983-85; chmn. Aga Khan Found. (U.K.), 1985-89; mem. adv. com. Overseas Devel. Inst., London, 1988-91; referee Directorate Gen. for Sci., Rsch. and Tech., Commn. for European Cmty., Brussels, 1984-91; mem. sci. adv. com. Ctr. World Food Studies, Free U. Amsterdam, 1993-96; mem. adv. bd. interuniv. programme water resources engring. Katholieke U. Leuven and Vrije U. Brussels, Belgium, 1994—; chmn. FOCUS Humantarian Assistance Europe Found., 1995-98; coconvenor World Faiths Devel. Dialogue Engagement Group on Hunger and Food Security, 1998—. Author: Agricultural Ecology of Savanna, 1978, Yield Response to Water, 1979, Agroecological Zones Project Reports, 1978-81, Potential Population Supporting Capacities of Lands in the Developing World, 1982, Assessment of Land Resources for Rainfed Crop Production in Mozambique, 1982, Land Resources Appraisal of Bangladesh for Developing Planning, 1988, Land Resource Inventory and Productivity Evaluation for National Development Planning, 1990, Agroecological Land Resources Appraisal for Development Planning in Kenya, 1991, Agroecological Assessments for National Planning, 1993; co-editor Irrigation Sci. Jour., 1976—; mem. editl. bd. Exptl. Agrl. Jour., 1998—. English Speaking Union King George VI Meml. fellow, 1966; Hon. Prin. Rsch. fellow U. Reading, Eng, 1995—. Fellow Inst. Biology (London). Muslim. Home: 88 Gunnersbury Ave, Ealing London W5 4HA, England

KASSEM, ABIR ABD-EL-MOHSEN, archaeologist, construction company official; b. Alexandria, Egypt, Dec. 30, 1968; d. Abd-El Mohsen Ibrahim and Aicha Shaeban Kassem; m. Ayman Hassan Habiba, June 27, 1989; 1 child, Esrae. Lic., U. Alexandria, 1990, diploma in archaeology, 1992, MA in Graeco-Roman Archaeology, 1998, postgrad., 1998—; postgrad., Goethe Inst., Alexandria, 1990--94. Prof. Tourism and Hotelerie Inst., Alexandria, 1990-91; exec. sec., quality assurance supr. MAS Engring. & Constrn., Alexandria, 1994—. Author: Geographical Tourism, 1990, History of Pharaonic Egypt, 1991, Roman Mosaic, 1998. With Egyptian Pub. Svc., 1990-91. Mem. Archaeol. Soc. Alexandria, Sporting Club, Ethad Club. Muslim. Avocations: reading, playing music, computers, Internet, designing. Home: 14 Aly Zuel Fakkar St, Roushdy app 9, Alexandria 21311, Egypt

KASSEM, MOUSTAPHA SAAD EL-DEEN, endocrinologist, educator; b. Giza, Egypt, July 21, 1959; S. Saad El-Deen Kassem and Fatma Salama; m. Mette Kaltoft, Mar. 23, 1986; children: Sarah, Anders, Laura-Amira. B Medicine B Surgery, Cairo Med. Sch., 1983; PhD, U. Aarhus, Denmark, 1994, DSc, 1997. Resident in endocrinology and internal medicine U. Aarhus, 1988-90, rsch. fellow, 1990-93, asst. prof. dept. endocrinology, 1995-98, assoc. prof. medicine, 1998—; postdoctoral fellow Mayo Clinic, Rochester, Minn., 1993-95. Contbr. over 60 articles to profl. publs. Mem. Danish Com. on Med. Ethics. Home: Kvedemarken 21, 8520 Lystrup Denmark Office: Aarhus Amtssygehus, Dept Endocrinology/Int Med, DK-8000 Århus Denmark

KASSIANOS, GEORGE, physician, educator, editor; b. Lysi, Famagusta, Cyprus, Sept. 30, 1948; s. Christopher and Eleni (Poullaidou) K.; m. Karen Anne Hewison-Phillips, July 3, 1976; children: Alexander, Nicholas, Juliana. Med. diploma with honors, Med. Acad., Lodz, Poland, 1974. Cert. in med. hypnosis, acupuncture; diplomate Royal Coll. Ob-Gyn.; licentate Edinborough, Glasgow. Sr. house officer in medicine Hammersmith Hosp., London, 1976, sr. house officer in ob/gyn., 1977; sr. house officer in pediat. St. Mary's Hosp., London, 1977; sr. house officer in accidents and emergencies Hammersmith Hosp., 1978; registrar in gen. practice Grove Health Ctr., London, 1978-79; gen. practitioner, exec. ptnr. Ringmead Med. Practice, Bracknell, Eng., 1979—; gen. practitioner tutor for East Berkshire, Eng., 1989—. Author: Immunisation-Precautions and Contraindications, 1990, 3d edit. now titled Immunization Childhood and Travel Health, 1998; editor (jour.) Audit in General Practice, 1993—; co-editor (jour.) Managing Heart Failure in Gen. Practice, 1996—; med. editor (jour.) Care of the Elderly, 1995; mem. editl. bd. Brit. Jour. Cardiology, 1996—, Healthy Practice, 1995—, Travel Medicine in Practice, 1999—; editl. cons. Guidelines In Gen. Practice, 1998. V.p. Windsor and West of London Greek Orthodox Cmty. Recipient 1st Rsch. prize Med. Acad. Lodz, Poland, 1973, Dr. of Yr. award Brit. Migraine Assn., 1995. Fellow Royal Coll. Gen. Practitioners; mem. Brit. Med. Journalists' Assn., Br. Travel Health Assn. (hon. sec.). Avocations: reading, music, gardening. Office: Dr Kassianos and Ptnrs, Birch Hill Med Ctr, Bracknell Berkshire RG12 7WW, England

KASSIN, SAUL, psychology educator; b. N.Y.C., Apr. 25, 1953; s. Mordy and Betty (Ashear) K.; m. Carol Beth Goldner, Sept. 19, 1952; children: Briana Rachel, Marc Joseph. BS, Bklyn. Coll., 1974; MA, U. Conn., 1976, PhD, 1978. NIH postdoctoral fellow U. Kans., Lawrence, 1978-79; asst. prof. Purdue U., West Lafayette, Ind., 1979-81, Williams Coll., Williamstown, Mass., 1981-84; rsch. assoc. Fed. Jud. Ctr., Washington, 1984-85; NIH postdoctoral fellow Stanford (Calif.) U., 1985-86; from assoc. to full prof. Williams Coll., Williamstown, 1986—; jury cons., expert witness. Author: Psychology, 1995, 3d edit., 2001; co-author: The American Jury on Trial, 1988, Confessions in the Courtroom, 1993, Social Psychology, 1990, 4th edit., 1999; co-editor: Developmental Social Psychology: Theory and Research, 1981, The Psychology of Evidence and Trial Procedure, 1985, On The Witness Stand: Controversies in the Courtroom, 1987, In the Jury Box: Controversies in the Courtroom, 1987; cons. editor Jour. Exptl. Social Psychology, 1982-87, Jour. Personality and Social Psychology: Attitudes and Social Cognition, 1992-94; editl. cons. Law and Human Behavior, 1986—; ad hoc reviewer in field; contbr. articles to profl. jours. Rsch. grantee Found. Child Devel., 1984-85; Jud. fellow U.S. Supreme Ct., Washington, 1984-85. Mem. APA, Am. Psychol. Soc., Am. Psychology-Law Soc., Soc. for Exptl. Social Psychology, Phi Beta Kappa. Office: Williams Coll Bronfman Sci Ctr Williamstown MA 01267

KASSLER, HASKELL A., lawyer; b. Boston, Feb. 8, 1936; s. Harry and Natalie (Steinberg) K.; m. Mary Elizabeth Kelligrew, May 30, 1965; children: Marion Adelaide, Sarah Elizabeth. BA, Tufts U., 1957; JD, Boston U., 1960. Bar: Mass. 1960, U.S. Dist. Ct. Mass. 1961, U.S. Dist. Ct. (no. dist.) Miss. 1964, U.S. Dist. Ct. (so. dist.) La. 1965, U.S. Ct. Appeals (5th cir.) 1965, U.S. Ct. Appeals (1st cir.) 1969, U.S. Supreme Ct. 1967. Assoc. Poster, Wilinsky & Goldstein, Boston, 1960-64; pvt. practice law Boston, 1964-66, 69-71; asst. dir. Vol. Defenders Com., Inc., Boston, 1967-68; ptnr. Kassler & Feuer (formerly Richmond, Kassler, Feinberg & Feuer), Boston, 1971-99, Casner & Edwards, LLP, Boston, 1999—; regional counsel New Eng. Region, Am. Jewish Congress, 1965-67; counsel Civil Liberties Union Mass., 1968-70; asst. prof. criminal justice Northeastern U., Boston, 1969-76; chmn. Mass. Jud. Nominating Coun., 1987-90; mem. Lawyers Constl. Def. Commn., 1964-65. Trustee U. Mass., 1977-81, U. Mass. Bldg. Authority, 1980-81, Mus. Transp., 1981—; selectman Town of Brookline, 1971-74, elected town meeting mem., 1959-84; mem. Local Redistricting Rev. Commn., 1976—. Fellow Am. Acad. Matrimonial Lawyers (chpt. bd. mgrs. 1980-90, v.p. 1981-82, pres. 1984-86, Judge Haskell Freedman award Mass. chpt. 1984, Mass. Jurisprudence award 1999); mem. ABA, Mass. Bar Assn., Norfolk County Bar Assn., Tufts U. Alumni Coun. Office: Casner & Edwards LLP 1 Federal St Boston MA 02110-2012

KASSMAN, ANDREW LANCE, orthodontist; b. N.Y.C., Nov. 14, 1950; s. David and Phyllis Ivy (Einhorn) K.; children: Stacey Arielle, Alexandria Devin; m. Laurie Ann Kassman, July 7, 1997; 1 child, Dylan Nathaniel. BS in Engring., Tulane U., 1972; DMD, Tufts U., 1975; cert. orthodontics, Columbia U., 1978. Lab. technician Tufts Med. Ctr., Boston, 1973-75; resident VA Hosp., Northport, N.Y., 1975-76; pvt. practice Astoria, N.Y., 1976-78, Phila., 1978-79, East Pathogue, N.Y., 1979-80; pvt. practice dentistry specializing in orthodontics Tucson, 1980—; chief orthodontia Crippled Children's Ctr., Tucson, 1980—; assoc. staff Tucson Med. Ctr., 1980—. Bd. dirs. Comstock Found., Tucson, 1980—; active Congregation Or Chadash, Tucson, 1996—, Alta Vista Assn., 1996—, Tucson Boys Club, 1988—, Jewish Cmty. Ctr., Tucson, 1988—. Mem. ADA, Am. Assn. Orthodontists, Pacific Coast Soc. Orthodontists, Tucson Orthodontist Soc., Tucson C. of C. Avocations: baseball, football, tennis, travel. Home: 6501 N Placita Alta Reposa Tucson AZ 85750-4204 Office: 6700 N Oracle Rd Ste 327 Tucson AZ 85704-7740

KASSNER, HERBERT SEYMORE, lawyer; b. N.Y.C., Dec. 3, 1931; s. Abraham and Rose (Rosenblatt) K.; m. Sheilah Goodwin, 1957 (div. 1965); children: Andrew, Kenneth; m. Marjorie Fern Golding, 1974 (div. 1992); children: Robin, Jeffrey; m. Linda Rubinstein Finder, 1993. BA (hon.), Franklin and Marshall U., 1952; cert., Hague (Netherlands) Acad. of Internat. Law, 1953; MA, NYU, 1955; LLB (hon.), Harvard U., 1955. Bar: N.Y. 1955, Conn. 1986. Atty. Gallap, Climenko & Gould, N.Y.C., 1955, Otterbourg, Steindler, Huston & Rosen, N.Y.C., 1956; pvt. practice law N.Y.C., 1957-65, 1969; atty. Dryer & Traub, N.Y.C., 1966-68, Kassner & Detsky, N.Y.C., 1970-80, Kassner & Haigney, N.Y.C., 1981-90; instr. Ohio State U., Columbus, 1956-57; asst. prof. Ark. State U., Pine Bluff, 1965. Contbr. articles to profl. jours. on 1st amendment law. Mem. Phi Beta Kappa. Home: 7221 Montrico Dr Boca Raton FL 33433-6931

KASSNER, JAY EDWARD, small business owner; b. San Diego, July 6, 1943; s. Ewald George and Thelma Marie (Ernster) K.; m. Mary Lou Ness, Dec. 10, 1963; 1 child, Adam Wayne; m. Tammy Lynn Peden, Dec. 31, 1982; children: Brittany Michelle, Courtney Marie. BA in Bus. Adminstrn., U. Wash., 1971. Cert. mgmt. specialist, Wash. Acct. Sites & Co., Inc., Seattle, 1971-73; ptnr. Arctic World Ltd., Anchorage, 1972-75; owner Kassner & Assocs., Anchorage, 1976—; pres. Alaska Fishing Charters, Inc., Anchorage, 1990—; v.p. Interior Plant Designs, Inc., Anchorage, 1982—; pres. Norton Sound Constrn., Inc., Anchorage, 1992—; chmn., CEO K & R Enterprises, Inc., Anchorage, 1981—; bd. dirs. Trans-Pacific North, Inc., Kenai, Alaska, TLC Flooring, Inc., Anchorage. Editor: Who's Available, 1969; newspaper editor Jet City News, 1969. 1st lt. inf. U.S. Army, 1966-69; Vietnam. Decorated Bronze Star, Purple Heart; NSF scholar, 1960. Mem. Am. Legion, Elks, Eagles, Moose, Amvets, Mil. Order of Purple Heart. Republican. Lutheran. Avocations: skiing, fishing, hunting, collecting baseball cards and memorbilia.

KASSUBEK, JAN RAINER, physician, researcher; b. Herne, Germany, Feb. 12, 1969. Med. diploma, Essen Med. Sch., Germany, 1995, MD, 1996. Rsch. assoc. Erlangen-Nuremberg Med. Sch., Germany, 1995-96; rschr. U. Minn., Mpls., 1996; physician, rschr. U. Hosp. Freiburg, Germany, 1997—. Contbr. articles to profl. jours. Mem. Deutsche Gesellschaft fuer Neurologie. Office: U Hosp Freiburg, Breisacher Str 64, 79106 Freiburg Germany

KAST, W. MARTIN, microbiology and immunology educator; b. Haarlem, The Netherlands, Mar. 24, 1958; came to U.S., 1996; s. Hendrikus Martinus Kast and Dina Scholte; m. Sylvia Martha Helene Ferkranus, Oct. 7, 1983; children: Dieuwertje Jasmijn, Hinde Rozemarijn, Harold Martin. BS, U. Amsterdam, 1980, MS, 1983, PhD, 1987. Cert. immunologist, The Netherlands. Postdoctoral fellow immunology The Netherlands Cancer Inst., Amsterdam, 1987-90, asst. prof. immunology, 1990-91; assoc. prof. immunohematology Leiden (The Netherlands) U. Med. Ctr., 1991-96; prof. microbiology and immunology and pharmacology Loyola U., Chgo., 1996—; vis. sr. scientist immunochemistry Cytel Corp., San Diego, 1992-93; vis. prof. molecular genetics Pitts. Cancer Inst., 1994; cons. Wyeth Lederle Vaccines and Pediats., Pearl River, N.Y., 1996—; mem. NIH Study Sect. Exptl. Immunology, Washington, 1998—; cons. Nat. Gynecol. Oncology Group, 2000—. Editor: (book) Peptide Based Cancer Vaccines, 2000; sect. editor: Leukemia, 1999—, YourDoctor.com, 2000; contbr. numerous sci. articles to profl. jours. Recipient Career award Royal Netherlands Acad. Arts and Scis., 1991-96, Antoni Van Leeuwenhoek Rsch. award, 1991. Mem. Am. Assn. Immunologists, Am. Assn. for Cancer Rsch., Dutch Soc. Immunology, Chgo. Assn. Immunology (pres. 1997—). Avocation: long distance swimming. E-mail: mkast@luc.edu. Office: Loyola U Chgo 2160 S 1st Ave Maywood IL 60153-3304

KASTANAKIS, SERAFIM, hospital administrator; b. Chania, Greece, Dec. 25, 1936; s. George and Ariadni (Loupasaki) K.; m. Maria Vittoraki, Nov. 5, 1978. BSc in Medicine, Athens (Greece) U., 1963, spl. diploma in internal medicine, MD, 1969, specialist in infectious diseases, 1997. Cert. prof. physician. House officer in medicine Alexandra Hosp., Athens, 1967-69; registrar in medicine King Paul Hosp., Athens, 1969-74; sr. registrar in medicine Gen. Hosp., Athens, 1974-75; dir. 1st med. dept. St. George Hosp., Chania, 1976—, dir. med. sector, 1987-93, gen. dir. med. svcs., 1999—; hon. registrar in cardiology Queen Elizabeth Hosp., Birmingham, 1972-73; pres. infection control com. St. George Hosp., Chania, 1987—. Contbr. numerous articles and papers to profl. jours. Pres. Julius Tsivakis Cultural Found., Crete, Greece, 1995—. Mem. Internat. Soc. Chemotherapy, Internat. Soc. for Infectious Diseases, Am. Soc. for Microbiology. Avocations: hill walking, traveling, swimming. Home: Xirouhaki str 1 koube, Chania 73100, Greece Office: Saint George Hosp, 73700 Chania Greece

KASTANIAS, ISIDOROS, surgeon; b. Vrontados, Greece, Mar. 9, 1941; s. Edameinondas and Maria (Vassilakis) K.; m. Anna Perris, Aug. 24, 1975; children: Maria, Artemis, Edameinondas, Stamatis. MD, Med. Sch. Thessaloniki, Greece, 1967. Sr. house officer Chios Gen. Hosp., Greece, 1967-71, Warwick Hosp., England, 1972-73; sr. house officer Solihull Hosp., England, 1973-74, registrar, 1974-76; registrar E.B.H., Birmingham, England, 1976-78; med. supt. Zoodohos Pighi Gen. Clinic, Chios, 1979—. Fellow Internat. Coll. Surgeons; mem. Senologic Hellenic Soc., Soc. Angiology Athens, Internat. Union Angiology. Avocation: collecting books. Home: 93 Panagia Moutsena, 92200 Vrontados Greece Office: Gen Clinic, 10 Evangelistrias Str, 82100 Chios Greece

KASTE, LINDA MARIE, medical educator, researcher; b. Havre de Grace, Md., Mar. 19, 1955; d. Orrin Charles and Elsie Louise K. BS in Biochemistry, Albright Coll., 1977; DDS, U. Md., 1985; MS in Epidemiology, Harvard U., 1986; PhD in Epidemiology, U. N.C., 1996. Diplomate Am. Bd. Dental Pub. Health. Lab. scientist U. Md., Balt., 1978-81; instr. Harvard U., Boston, 1988-89; assoc. prof., divsn. dir. Med. U. S.C., Charleston, 1996—; cons. in field. Contbr. articles to profl. jours. Vol. dentist Dominican Dental Mission, San Jose de Ocoa, 1985—. Rsch. fellow Harvard U., Boston, 1985-88, U. N.C., Chapel Hill, 1989-92, sr. staff fellow Nat. Inst. Dental Rsch., Bethesda, Md., 1992-96. Mem. ADA, Am. Assn. Dental Schs., Am. Assn. Dental Rsch., Am. Assn. Pub. Health Dentistry, Am. Pub. Health Assn., Internat. Assn. Dental Rsch. (behavioral sci. and health svcs. rsch. group, symposium coord. 1997-98, program chair 1998-99, pres.-elect 1999-2000, pres. 2000—), Nat. Acads. Practice, Soc. Epidemiologic Rsch. Office: MUSC CDM 173 Ashley Ave PO Box 250507 Charleston SC 29425-0507

KASTE, SUE CREVISTON, pediatric radiologist, researcher; b. Lakewood, Ohio, Feb. 25, 1952; d. Donald P. and Marion S. Creviston; m. Ronald H. Kaste, Apr. 28, 1984; children: Rebecca, Steven, Matthew. BA, Lake Erie Coll., 1974; AAS Physicians Asst., Cuyahoga C.C. and Cleve. Clin., 1977; DO, Chgo. Coll. Osteo. Medicine, 1981. Diplomate Am. Bd. Radiology cert. added qualifications pediat. radiology; cert. osteopath Osteo. Nat. Bd. Med. Examiners. Intern Chgo. Coll. Osteo. Medicine, 1981-82; diagnostic radiology U. Hosps. Cleve., 1982-86, fellow pediat. radiology, 1986-87; officer in charge pediat. radiology KTTCMC, Keesler AFB, Biloxi, Miss., 1987-90, chief diagnostic radiology, 1990-91; cons. dept. radiology LeBonheur Children's Med. Ctr., Memphis, 1991—; assoc. prof. dept. radiology U. Tenn. Coll. Medicine, Memphis, 1991—; assoc. mem. dept. diagnostic imaging St. Jude Children's Rsch. Hosp., Memphis, 1991—. Reviewer Am. Jour. Roentgenology, 1994—, Pediat. Radiology, 1997—, Cancer, 1997—; contbr. articles to profl. jours. Leader/asst. leader Girl Scouts Am., Cordova, Tenn., 1992-99; youth club asst. Advent Presbyn. Ch., Cordova, 1993-98, mem. ch. orch. Maj. USAF Med. Corps, 1977-91. Recipient grant Soc. Pediat. Radiology, 1998. Mem. Pediat. Oncology Group, Am. Coll. Radiology, Radiologic Soc. N.Am., Midwest Soc. Pediat. Radiology. Avocations: flute, painting, drawing, swimming. E-mail: sue.kaste@stjude.org. Fax: 901-495-4398. Home: 8796 Wood Mills Cv N Cordova TN 38018-6133 Office: St Jude Childrens Rsch Hosp Dept Diagnostic Imaging 332 N Lauderdale St Memphis TN 38105-2729

KAŠTELAN-MACAN, MARIJA, chemist, educator; b. Dubrovnik, Croatia, May 23, 1939; d. Mladen Kaštelan and Marija Oriental; m. Trpimir Macan, Sept. 5, 1964; children: Darko, Tvrtko, Jelena. Diploma, U. Zagreb, Croatia, 1962, Master's degree, 1968, PhD, 1973. Asst. faculty tech. U. Zagreb, 1963-75, asst. prof. faculty tech., 1975-82, assoc. prof. faculty tech., 1982-87, univ. prof. faculty chem. engring. and tech., 1987—, dean faculty chem. engring. and tech., 1991-93. Author: Analytical Chemistry, 1985, 90; editor: Technical Faculty 1919-94, 1994 (J.J. Strossmayer award 1995), National Program of Island Development, 1997, Vukovar-Reconstruction Challenge, 1997. Asst. min. Ministry Reconstrn. and Devel., Zagreb, 1994-2000. Recipient Order of Danica Hrvatska, Pres. Republic of Croatia, 1996, 98. Fellow Alma Mater Alumni Chem. Engring. U. Zagreb (founder); mem. Internat. Assn. Water Quality, Croatian Soc. Chem. Engring. Roman Catholic. Avocation: choir singing. E-mail: mkastela@public.srce.hr. Home: Bozidara Magovca 16c, 10010 Zagreb Croatia Office: U Zagreb Fac Chem Engring, Marulicev trg 19, 10000 Zagreb Croatia

KASTEN, WENDY CHRISTINA, literacy educator, writer, consultant; b. Neptune, N.J., Jan. 13, 1951; d. Henry and Mary H. Overeem; 1 child, Tiara Denise. BA, Rowan U., 1973; MEd, U. Maine, 1981; PhD, U. Ariz., 1984. Tchr. St. Mary's Sch., Bangor, Maine, 1974-76, Searsport (Maine) Elem. Sch., 1977-80; asst. prof. U. So. Fla., Sarasota, 1984-90, assoc. prof., 1990-94; assoc. prof. Kent State U., Kent, Ohio, 1995-99, prof., 1999—; pres. Ctr. for Expansion of Lang. and Thinking, 1996-01; bd. dirs. Children's Lit. Spl. Interest Group of Internat. Reading Assn., Newark, Delaware. Co-author: The Multi-age Classroom: Implementing Multiage Education, 1998. Mem., bd. dirs. Friends of Selby Libr., Sarasota, Fla., 1987-89. Recipient Literacy award Sarasota Reading Coun., 1986. Mem. Internat. Reading Assn. (editorial review bd. 1995—), Nat. Coun. Tchrs. English (editorial review bd. 1999—), Nat. Reading Conf. (mem. ethics com.). Democrat. Buddhist. Avocations: travel, walking, pets, craft shows, music. E-mail: wkasten@kent.edu. Office: Kent State U 402 White Hall Kent OH 44242-0001

KASTENING, BORIS MANUEL, physicist; b. Bamberg, Bavaria, Germany, Jan. 10, 1964; s. Bertel and Hiltraud K. Diplom, Hamburg (Germany) U., 1988; M in Physics, UCLA, 1990, PhD in Physics, 1992. Postdoc. Utrecht (The Netherlands) U., 1992-94, Purdue U., West Lafayette, Ind., 1994-96, Freiburg (Germany) U., 1996-98; postdoctoral rschr. Heidelberg (Germany) U., 1998-2000, Berlin Free U., 2000—. Contbr. articles to profl. jours. With German Army, 1982-83. Mem. German Physical Soc. Avocations: traveling, skiing, hang gliding. Office: Inst Theoretical Physics, U Arnimallee 14 Berlin Free, 14195 Berlin Germany

KASTIA, RAVINDRA, power equipment company executive; b. Jodhpur, India, June 12, 1955; s. Johari Mal and Anand Kanwar Jain; m. Madhu Mehta, Nov. 30, 1980; children: Ankita, Anika. B of Commerce with honors, Jai Narayan Vyas U., Jodhpur, 1974, MBA, 1976, diploma in labor laws, 1979. Chartered acct., Inst. Chartered Accts. India, 1979; cert. co. sec., Inst. Co. Secs. India, 1981. Fin. mgr., sec. Suraj Diamond and Nihon Nirman, Bombay, 1981-87; gen. fin. mgr., sec. Dalmia Group, Delhi, India, 1987-90; gen. mgr., comml. JK Singhania Group, JK Tyre, Banmore, India, 1990-91; sr. v.p. AV Birla Group, Vikram Ispat, Bombay, 1991-94; joint exec. pres. AV Birla Group, Bombay, 1994-96; exec. pres. AV Birla Group, Grasim Cement, Raipur, India, 1996-99; sr. pres. Jaya Shree Insulators, Calcutta, 1999—; sr. cons. K. Singhvi & Co., Jodhpur, 1977-79; asst. prof. Jodhpur Mgmt. Program, Jai Narayan Vyas U., 1979-81. V.p. Indian Red Cross Soc., Raipur, 1996—. Fellow Inst. Chartered Accts. India, Inst. Co. Secs. India; mem. Cement Mfrs. Assn. India (mem. apex com. 1997—), Rajasthan Mitra Parishad (life), Jodhpur Assn. (life), Indian Inst. Mgmt. Alumni (Ahmedabad), Dept. Mgmt. Sci. Alumni Assn. (Jodhpur), Chhattisgarh Club. Mem. Indian National Congress. Hindu. Avocations: photography, reading, travel. Home: 64 Satnam Apartments, Cuffe Parade, Mumbai 400 005, India Office: Jaya Shree Insulators, 15A Hemanta Basu Sarani, Calcutta 700001, India

KASTNER, MICHAEL JAMES, dentist; b. Huntington, Ind., Oct. 20, 1954; s. James H. and Barbara A. (Bartrom) K.; m. Kimberly A. Ricke, June 18, 1983; children: Kevin Michael, Ryan James, Derek Edward. BS in Biology and Chemistry, Manchester Coll., 1977; DDS, Ind. U., Indpls., 1981; postgrad., Armed Forces Inst. Pathology, 1989. Gen. practice dentistry Toledo, 1981—; asst. dentist Toledo Zoo, 1991—; mem. Ohio Mass Disaster Team, 1995—; asst. Lucas County Coroner's Office, 1987—. Bd. trustees Dental Ctr. Northwest Ohio, 1995-2001, nominating com., 1995-2001, long range planning com., 1999-2001, dental com., 1995-2001. Recipient Alumni Honor award Manchester Coll., 1997, Recognition for Honor award Ohio State Senate Resolution, 1997. Mem. ADA (Recognition for Vol. Svc. Fgn. Country award in Dominican Republic 1984, 87, in Costa Rica 1990, in Nepal 1994), Ohio Dental Assn. (state del. 2000, statewide subcom. on peer rev. 2000—, Humanitarian of Yr. 1995), Toledo Dental Soc. (bd. dirs. 1996-99, peer rev. com. 1998—, nominating com. 1999—, program and continuing edn. com. 1999—, fin. com. 2000, exec. office com. 2000, exec. bd. sec.-treas. 2000—, long range planning com. 2000—), Am. Acad. Cosmetic Dentistry, Am. Soc. Forensic Odontology, Am. Coll. Oral Implantology, Am. Soc. Osseointegration Internat. Congress Oral Implantologists, Mensa. Roman Catholic. Avocations: photography, basketball, tennis, travel, outdoor activities. Home: 4616 Waterford Ct Toledo OH 43623-2988

KASTOVSKY, DIETER, English language educator; b. Freudenthal, Dec. 26, 1940; s. Heinrich and Christiane (Ulrich) K.; m. Ursula Becker, Mar. 21, 1970 (div. 1990); m. Barbara Kryk, July 17, 1992. PhD, U. Tübingen, Fed. Republic Germany, 1967. Rsch. asst. English dept. U. Tübingen, 1967-73; prof. English Wuppertal, Fed. Republic Germany, 1973-81, U. Vienna, Austria, 1981—. Author: Studies in Morphology, 1971, Word-formation and Semantics, 1982; contbr. articles to profl. publs. Recipient medal of honor Ministry of Edn., Poland, 1989, Order of Merit, Commdr. Cross, Republic of

Poland, 1990. Mem. Soc. Linguistica Europaea (sec.-treas. 1991—), Linguistic Soc. Am., Linguistic Assn. G.B., Deutsche Gesellschaft fur Sprachwissenschaft, Deutscher Anglistentag, Internat. Cognitive Linguistics Assn., Internat. Pragmatics Assn. Home: Perlhofgasse 17, A-2372 Giesshuebl Austria Office: Inst Anglistik Amerikanistk, Inst Angl Amerikan/U Altes, AKH, Spitalgasse 2-4 H of 8, A-1090 Vienna Austria

KASTRUP, DIETER, diplomat. Mem. German permanent mission to UN, N.Y.C.

KASTURI, SITAPATI ROW, biophysics educator; b. Amalapuram, India, Oct. 4, 1942; s. Satyanarayana and Subbayamma (Sripati) K.; m. Lakshmi Manchiraju, Oct. 12, 1973; children: Niraja, Satyavikas. BS, Andhra U., Visakhapatnam, India, 1961; MS, Andhra U., 1963, U. Wis., 1968; PhD, U. Wis., 1971. Rsch. asst. U. Wis., Madison, 1966-71; pool officer (CSIR), 1972-73; vis. fellow Tata Inst., Bombay, 1973-75, fellow, 1975-84, reader of fundamental rsch., 1984-90, assoc. prof., 1990-96, prof., 1996—. Author: NMR Data Handbook for Biomedical Applications, 1984; contbr. articles to profl. jours. Fulbright scholar U.S. Ednl. Found. in India, 1966-71. Mem. Indian Physics Assn. (life), Indian Biophys. Soc. (life), Nat. Magnetic Resonance Soc. (life). Avocations: listening to music, reading. Home: 7 D Everest Anushaktinagar, Bombay 400094, India Office: Tata Inst Fundamental Rsch, Homi Bhabha Rd, Bombay 400005, India

KASULKA, LARRY HERMAN, management consultant; b. Wagner, S.D., Apr. 5, 1940; s. Alfred E. and Lillian J. (Gasper) K.; m. Susan A. Smart, Sept. 8, 1962; children: Shawn L., Christine A. BS in Electronics, Northrop U., 1961; grad. cert. in bus. adminstrn., UCLA, 1969; grad. cert., Brookings Inst., 1986, Harvard U., 1989; PhD in Bus. Adminstrn., LaSalle U., 1995. Registered profl. engr., Calif. Electronic engr. Douglas Aircraft Co., 1962-77; unit chief avionics McDonnell Douglas Astronautics Co., 1977-81, br. chief avionics, 1981-84; dir. design engr. McDonnell Douglas Electronic Systems Co., 1984-87, dir. program mgmt., 1987-89, dir. new bus., 1989-91; spl. asst. U.S. Dept. Commerce, Office of the Dep. Sec., 1990-91; v.p., dep. gen. mgr. Kennedy Space Ctr. McDonnell Douglas Space Systems Co., 1991-93; v.p., gen. mgr. McDonnell Douglas Aerospace N.Mex. Ops., 1993-94; program mgr. McDonnell Douglas Aerospace, Huntingtron Beach, Calif., 1994-96; pres. L.H. Kasulka & Assocs., 1996—; presenter in field; bd. dirs. Ctr. Info. Tech. Rsch. PLC, Brisbane, Australia, Ctr. Info. Tech. Rsch. Inc., Boulder, Colo. Contbr. articles to profl. jours. Bd. dirs. Brevard Achievement Ctr., Rockledge, Fla., 1991-93; mentor Sci. Engrin. and Rsch. Career Help; mem. Pres. Commn. Exec. Exch. Alumni U. Calif.-L.A. Alumni. Recipient Dir.'s Safety award NASA KSC Ctr., 1992, Group Achievement award NASA JSC Ctr., 1995, Sr. Exec. Svc. award Dept. Commerce, 1990, commendation Inst. Soc. Am., 1983, White House Pres. Bush, 1990; named Outstanding Cadet, CAP-Internat. Aviation Cadet Exch.; named to Hon. Order Ky. Cols. Assoc. fellow AIAA; mem. Armed Forces and Comm. Elec. Assn., Nat. Man. Assn., Assn for Quality Participation, Am. Soc. Quality Control, UCLA Alumni Assn. (mem. Goal/QPC Pres.' Commn. on Exec. Exch. Alumni). Achievements include patent for new low-cost temperature measurement.

KASUYA, SUSUMU, law educator; b. Tokyo, June 23, 1937; s. Kumazo and Ito Kasuya; m. Shizuho Okuyama, 1964; children: Gen, Atsushi. LLB, Nihon U., 1961, LLM, 1964. Lectr. Teikyo U., Tokyo, 1967-72, asst. prof., 1972-74; asst. prof. Nihon U., Tokyo, 1974-77, prof., 1977—. Author: Contemporary Legal Problems, 1979, Article IX of the Japanese Constitution and the Right of Self-Defence, 1985, The Security Controversy in Postwar Japan-Origin of Article IX of the Japanese Constitution and the Japan-U.S. Security Treaty, 1992. Exec. dir. Coun. of Intellectuals for Peace and Democracy, Tokyo, 1980; ombudsman Nat. Adminstrn. Supr. Com., Tokyo, 1993; mem. Japanese com. to promote establishment of Internat. Space Law, Tokyo, 1996; rep. Japanese Com. on Human Rights Involved in TV Broadcasting, Tokyo, 1997. Mem. Japan Assn. Interant. Rels. (trustee 1974—), Japanese Assn. Internat. Law. Avocations: swimming, cycling, travel, walking. Home: 3-23-20 Umezono, Kiyose City Tokyo 204 0024, Japan Office: Nihon U, 1-3-2 Misaki-Cho, Tokyo 101 8360, Japan

KASUYA, TOSHIO, whale biologist; b. Kawagoe, Saitama, Japan, Nov. 1, 1937; s. Ichiro and Shizuko (Iino) K.; m. Kazuko Akasaka, Oct. 28, 1962; children: Akiko, Atsuko. B of Agrl., U. Tokyo, 1961, D of Agrl., 1972. Staff Whales Rsch. Inst., Tokyo, 1961-66; rsch. assoc. Ocean Rsch. Inst., U. Tokyo, 1966-83; project leader Nat. Inst. Rsch. on Far Seas Fisheries, Shimizu, 1983-91, divsn. dir., 1991-97; prof. faculty bioresources Mie U., Tsu, Mie, Japan, 1997—; mem. sci. com. Internat. Whaling Commn., Cambridge, Eng., 1982—; mem. cetacean specialist group Species Survival Commn., Gland Switzerland, 1985—, mem. sirenia specialist group, 1994—. Assoc. editor Marine Mammal Sci., 1985-95, Sci. Rep. Whales Rsch. Inst., 1981-88. Mem. Mammalogical Soc. Japan, Soc. for Marine Mammaloy (com. sci. advisors 1995-2000), Soc. for Conservation Biology (Disting. Achievement award 1994). Achievements include assessment of stocks for the conservation of small cetaceans and dugongs killed by Japanese fisheries, and finding of extended post-reproductive lifetime and its significance in the community of short-finned pilot whales. Home: 5-30-32-3 Nagayama, Tama Tokyo 206-0025, Japan Office: Faculty of Bioresources, Mie U, Tsu 514-8507, Japan

KAS'YANOV, DMITRY AL'BERTOVICH, radiophysicist, researcher; b. Nizhny Novgorod, Russia, Feb. 12, 1964; s. Al'bert Borisovich and Olga Il'inichna (Mamaeva) K. MSc, State U., N. Novgorod, Russia, 1986, PhD in Physics and Math., 1997. Engr. Radioph. Rsch. I, N. Novgorod, 1986-90, rschr., 1990-93, sr. rschr., 1993; sr. rschr. Sci. Ctr., Diaton, N. Novgrod, 1992-97; sr. cons. Sci. Ctr. Optimum, N. Novgorod, 1995. Contbr. articles to internat. jours; patentee on nonlinear acoustics. Grantee Internat. Sci. Found., 1992, Russian Found. Fundamental Investigation, 1998—. Mem. N.Y. Acad. Scis., The Planetary Soc. Avocations: philosophy, mineralogy, gem cutting. E-mail: kasd@nirfi.sci-nnov.ru. Home: PO Box 17, 603074 Nizhny Novgorod Russia Office: Radiophys Rsch I, 25/14 Bolshaya Pecherskya, 603600 Nizhny Novgorod Russia

KASYANOV, MIKHAIL M., federal official. Min. of fin. Govt. of the Russian Fedn., 1999-2000, chmn., 2000—. Office: Office Prime Min, Krasnopresneska nab 2, Moscow 103274, Russia*

KASYANOV, VLADIMIR LEONIDOVICH, biologist; b. Leningrad, Russia, Jan. 4, 1940; s. Leonid Pavlovich and Zlata Meyerovna (Dynkina) K.; m. Valeria Vasilievna Isaeva, Mar. 1977; 1 child, Nikolai. PhD, U. Leningrad, 1969; DSc, Inst. Evolutionary Morphology, Moscow, 1985. Jr. scientist U. Leningrad, 1966-71; jr. scientist Inst. Marine Biology, Vladivostok, 1971-72, sr. scientist, 1972-73, head lab., 1973—, dep. dir., 1977-79, 86-88, dir., 1989—; v.p. Otto Kinne Found., Germany, 1995—; chair Temp. East Asia Com., 1998—; dir. Acad. Marine Biology, U. Far Eastern, 1999. Author: (with C.A. Kruychkova, V.A. Kulikova and L.A. Medvedeve) Larvae of Marine Bivalve a.Echinoderms, 1998, Reproductive Strategy of Bivalues a.Echinoderms, 1989; contbr. articles to profl. jours. Chair expert coun. Far East Marine Fund, Vladivostok, 1997. Recipient Kovalevsky award Russian Acad. Scis., 1994, Order of Friendship, 1999; grantee Leading Russian Sci. Sch., 1996. Mem. Russian Acad. Scis. (v.p. hydrobiology 1995), Ecology Inst. (Germany). Office: Inst Marine Biology FEB RAS, Palchevskogo Str 17, 690041 Vladivostok Russia

KASZUBOWSKI, LESZEK JOZEF, coastal and marine geologist; b. Twarda Edvgorka, Pomerania, Poland, Mar. 19, 1954; s. Aleksander and Wanda (Piyontek) K.; m. Evgrazyna Kaszubowska, Oct. 4, 1980; 1 child, Dariusz. MS, Gdansk U., 1979; PhD, Maria-Curie Sktodowska U., 1988. Marine geologist Meteorological and Water Mgmt. Inst., Gdynia, Poland, 1980-82, Geol. Inst., Sopot, Poland, 1983-84; lectr. Tech. U. of Szczecin, Poland, 1983-84, sr. lectr., 1988—; leader Polish working group IGCP Project 437, 2000—. Contbr. articles to profl. publs. Mem. Internat. Geograph. Union. Avocations: astronomy, archaeology. Home: Bolwtenow Warszawy St 91/8, 70-343 Szczecin Poland Office: Tech U of Szczecin, Piastow 50a St, 70-310 Szczecin Poland

KATABUCHI, HIDETAKA, obstetrician/gynecologist, researcher; b. Tosu, Saga, Japan, Nov. 30, 1955; s. Yoichi and Masako (Shigematsu) K.; m. Miwako Oka, Sept. 25, 1983; children: Koki, Kanako, Yuko, Misako. MD, Kumamoto U., Japan, 1982, PhD, 1988. Med. diplomate oB-gyn. Resident Kumamoto U. Hosp., Japan, 1982-84, rsch. fellow, 1988-89; instr. Kumamoto U., Japan, 1989-96, asst. prof., 1997—. Author: Recent Advances in Microscopy of Cells, Tissues and Organs, 1997; contbr. articles to profl. jours. Sci. rsch. grantee Japanese Ministry Edn., 1991, 92, 93, 99, 2000; rsch. fellow Johns Hopkins U., Balt., 1993-95. Mem. Internat. Soc. Gynecologic Pathology, Japanese Soc. Ob-Gyn., Am. Assn. for Cancer Rsch. Home: Higashihonmachi 1-27-1, Kumamoto Prefecture, Kumamoto 862-0902, Japan Office: Kumamoto Univ Dept Ob-Gyn, Honjo 1-1-1, Kumamoto 860-8556, Japan

KATAJA, MIRJA BIRGITTA, psychologist; b. Helsinki, Finland, Apr. 28, 1961; d. Taisto Aatos and Sirkka Liisa (Luukkanen) Kaartinen; m. Pekka Kullervo Kataja, May 17, 1996; 1 child, Adele. M in Psychology, Jyvaskyla U., 1987. Cert. profl. lic. psychology in edn., specialization in children's learning problems and Montessori. Psychologist Family Ctr., Imatra, Finland, 1988-89, Nilsia, Finland, 1989-94; psychologist Social Office, Juankoski, Finland, 1995-97, Children's Psychiat. Clinic, Ctrl. Hosp. of Mikkeli, Finland, 1998—; sec. Psychol. Assn. Nort Savo, Finland, 1992-94, chmn., 1995-97; coun. mem. Finnish Psychol. Assn., 1994-97. Mem. com. Children and Youth of Mannisto Parish, 1996-97. Lutheran. Avocations: church choir, cultural activities, skiing. Home: Louhenkatu 7, 50130 Mikkeli Finland

KATAKIS, CHARIS, psychologist; b. Kavala, Greece; d. Philip and Archontoula (Mylondakis) A.; children: Leto, Fotis. MA, U. Calif., San Jose, 1969; PhD, U. Thessaloniki, Greece, 1975. Dir. Lab. for Study of Human Rels., 1982—. Author: The Three Identities of the Greek Family, 8th edit., 1984, The Purple Liquid, 5th edit., 1995; contbr. over 50 articles to profl. jours. Office: Lab Study Human Rels, Konitsis 33, Maroussi Athens, Greece

KATAOKA, HIROSHI, patent lawyer, chemist; b. Nara, Japan, Jan. 25, 1931; s. Choji and Tatsuko K.; m. Michiru Uotani, Nov. 1, 1953; children: Ruriko, Tsukasa. B in Pharm. Scis., Kyoto (Japan) U., 1953; student in patent law, Acad. of Japanese Patent Assn., Osaka, 1953-55. Patent counsel Nippon Shinyaku Co., Ltd., Kyoto, Japan, 1953-92; pres. Kataoka Internat., Kyoto, Japan, 1992—; com. mem. Invention Examining Com. Kyoto Prefectural Govt., 1984—, Technique Award Com., 1994—; mem. Am. NGO Congress WIPO UN, Geneva, Switzerland, 1987-92, arbitrator, mediator, WIPO, 1994—. Author: (books) Patent Laws for Chemists and Chem. Engrs., 1961, Dictionary for Writing Chemical Papers in English, 1999; contbr. articles to profl. jours. Recipient award for contbns. Kyoto Prefectural Govt., 1985, award for contbns. patent system, Japanese Govt., Tokyo, 1989;. Mem. Japan Patent Assn. (bd. dirs., v.p. 1971-87, award for contbns. 1992), Osaka Pharm. Mfrs. Assn. (chmn. patent com., 1990-92), Kyoto Invention Soc. (mng. dir. 1982—), Japan Assn. for Chem. Info., (bd. dirs. 1985—), Internat. Assn. for Protection Intellectual Property, Internat. Fedn. for Patent Attys., Rotary Club. Avocations: classical music, travel, writing essays. Home and Office: Kataoka Internat, 33 Yoshida Kami-oji-cho, Sakyo-ku Kyoto 606-8312, Japan

KATAOKA, MASATAKA, electric company executive; b. June 30, 1946; m. Kuniko Kataoka. Student, Waseda U., Japan, 1971. With Sharp, 1971, Alps Electric, 1988; now pres. Alps Electric Co., Ltd., Tokyo, also bd. dirs. Avocations: golf, skiing, travel, reading. Home: 4-11-3 Minamiyukigaya, Ota-ku Tokyo 145-0066, Japan Office: Alps Electric Co Ltd, 1-7 Yukigaya-Ohtsuka-cho, Ohta-ku Tokyo 145-8501, Japan

KATAYAMA, FUMIHIKO, physician; b. Moriguchi, Osaka, Japan, Sept. 28, 1956; s. Yozo and Fusako (Tsutada) K.; m. Noriko Ochiai, July 11, 1982; children: Erina, Taiga, Daichi. LLB, Hitotsubashi U., Tokyo, 1980; BA, Williams Coll., 1983; BMed, Juntendo U., Tokyo, 1992. Officer Fgn. Ministry of Japan, Tokyo, 1980-85; physician Kitasato U. Hosp., Sagamihara, Japan, 1992-97; vice dir. Ochiai Med. Clinic, Atsugi, Japan, 1997—; lectr. Sch. Nursing, Ebina (Japan) Gen. Hosp., 1996—. Contbr. articles to profl. jours. Mem. Japan Pediatric Soc. (bd. cert.), Japan Soc. Internal Medicine. Avocations: reading, travel. Office: Ochiai Med Clinic, 1016 Nurumizu, Atsugi, Kanagawa 243-0033, Japan

KATAYAMA, ISAO, pathology educator; b. Mishima-shi Shizuoka-ken, Japan, June 13, 1930; s. Koji and Kachi Katayama; m. Yukiko Yanai, Mar. 30, 1961; children: Ken, Taul, Makoto. BS, Keio U., 1950, MD, 1954. Mem. dept. of surgery Keio U. Sch. Medicine, Tokyo, 1958-63; resident East Tenn. Bapt. Hosp., Knoxville, 1963-64; resident, jr. staff mem. Mallory Inst. of Patholoty, Boston, 1964-68; assoc. pathologist Monmouth Med. Ctr., Long Branch, N.J., 1968-69, U. Hosp., Boston, 1972-73, St. Vincent Hosp., Worcester, Mass., 1973-74; staff dept. pathology U. Mass. Med. Ctr., Worcester, 1974-76, chief surg. pathology, 1976-79; prof. Saitama (Japan) Med. Sch., 1979—. Contbr. articles to profl. jours.; rschr. in hematopathology. Fullbright scholar 1955; Am. Cancer Soc. grantee, 1979. Mem. Am. Assn. Pathologists, Japanese Soc. Pathologists, Japanese Soc. Hematology, Japanese Soc. Clin. Heamtology. Avocations: reading, fishing. Home: 5-6-17 Higashicho, Koganeishi, Tokyo 184-0011, Japan Office: Saitama Med Sch, 38 Moro-Hongo Moroyamamachi, Saitama-ken 350-0495, Japan

KATAYAMA, MASAAKI, information electronics educator, researcher; b. Kyoto, Japan, Jan. 6, 1959; s. Shozo and Takako (Umezono) K.; m. Hiroko Sano, May 24, 1987; children: Takashi, Akari. BS, Osaka U., Suita, Japan, 1981, MS, 1983, PhD in Engring., 1986. Asst. prof. Toyohashi (Japan) U. Tech., 1986-89; lectr. Osaka U., 1989-92; assoc. prof. info. electronics Nagoya (Japan) U., 1992—. Author: COMA and Next Generation Mobile Communication, 1995. Mem. IEEE, Inst. Electronics Info. and Comm Engrs. (Shinohara Meml. Young Engr. award 1986). Avocations: amateur radio, esperantisto. Office: Nagoya U Dept Info Electron, Furo-chio, Aichi Nagoya 464-8603, Japan

KATAYAMA, TAKESHI, physicist; b. Sasaho, Japan, Dec. 9, 1943; s. Asakazu and Kinue (Fujiwara) K.; m. Hatsume Ueda, May 2, 1969; children: Hika, Daiichiro. BS in Pure and Applied Sci., U. Tokyo, 1965, M in Pure and Applied Sci., 1967, PhD, 1972. From rsch. assoc. to prof. physics Ctr. Nuclear Study U. Tokyo, 1975—; chief scientist, dir. Beam Physics and Engring. Lab., Riken, Japan, 1998—. Editor: Procs. of Cooler Rings and Their Applications, 1990; contbr. articles to profl. jours. Mem. Japanese Phys. Soc. Office: U Tokyo Ctr Nuclear Study, 7-3-1 Hongo Bunkyo, 113-0033 Tanashi Tokyo, Japan

KATCHALSKI-KATZIR, EPHRAIM, biophysicist, educator; b. Kiev, Russia, May 16, 1916; arrived in Israel, 1922; s. Yehuda and Tsila Katchalski; m. Nina Gotlieb, Feb. 14, 1938 (wid. Mar. 1986); children: Nurith (dec.), Meir, Irit (dec.). MS summa cum laude, The Hebrew U., Jerusalem, 1937; PhD, The Hebrew U., 1941. Rsch. fellow Polytechnic Inst./Bklyn. and Columbia U., N.Y.C., 1946-48; head dept. biophysics The Weizmann Inst. of Sci., Rehovot, Israel, 1951-73; sr. fgn. scientist fellowship UCLA, 1964; chief scientist Israel Def. Ministry, 1966-68; elected 4th Pres. State of Israel, 1973-78; head dept. biotechnology Tel-Aviv U., Ramat Aviv, 1980-88, prof. emeritus, 1987—; vis. prof. biophysics Hebrew U., Jerusalem, 1953-61, Rockefeller U., N.Y., 1961-65, U. Mich., Ann Arbor, 1961-65, Battelle Seattle Rsch. Ctr., Wash., 1971; guest scientist Harvard U., Cambridge, Mass., 1957-59; Regents prof. U. Calif., San Diego, 1979; pres. Cobiotech, 1990-95. Recipient Tchernikhovski prize, 1948, Weizmann prize, Mcpl. of Tel-Aviv, 1950, Israel prize in Natural Scis., 1959, Rothschild prize in Natural Scis., 1961, Linderstrom Lang Gold medal, Copenhagen, 1969, Hans Krebs medal Fedn. of European Biochem. Socs., 1972, Japan prize Sci. and Technol. Found., 1985, Underwood Prescott award MIT, 1982, Enzyme Engring. award Engring. Found. and Genencor, Inc., USA, 1987; first incumbent of Herman Mark Chair in Polymer Sci., Polytechnic Inst. of N.Y., 1979; apptd. to Order of Legion of Honor, France, 1990; numerous hon. doctorates. Mem. AAAS, NAS (U.S.), Am. Acad. Arts and Scis., Acad. des Scis./ France, Am. Chem. Soc., Am. Philos. Soc., Am. Soc. Biol. Chemists, Assn. Franco-Israelienne pour la Recherche Scientifique et Technologique (v.p. 1985-86, pres. 1987), Assn. of Harvard Chemists, Biophys. Soc., Ciba Found., European Molecular Biology Orgn., Fedn. of Am. Socs. for Exptl. Biology, Royal Instn. of Gt. Britain, Royal Soc./London, World Acad. of Art and Sci., Am. Acad. of Microbiology, others. Office: Weizmann Inst Sci, PO Box 26, Rehovot 76100, Israel

KATEMOPOULOS, MILDRED JOSEPHINE, executive secretary; b. Shanghai, China, Apr. 29, 1925; came to the U.S., 1977; d. James Jeremiah and Camille Helmana (Barradas) O'Leary; m. Theodore Demetrius Katemopoulos, Apr. 29, 1946; children: Maureen, Eileen, Kathryn, Paul, Anne-Marie. Grad., Loretto H.S., Shanghai. Pvt. sec. Royal Netherlands Embassy, Shanghai, 1946-49; sec. to mng. dir. Dairy Farm Co., Hong Kong, 1949-58; confidential sec. H.K. Land Co., Hong Kong, 1958-66; writer Children's Page H.K. Sunday Std., Hong Kong, 1966-71; pub. rels. staff Mandarin Hotel, Hong Kong, 1970-73; asst. to CEO Regent Internat. Hotels, Hong Kong, 1974-77; sr. sec. Stanford Rsch. Inst., Menlo Park, Calif., 1977-79; asst. to CEO Cath. Charities, San Jose, Calif., 1981-89, Econ. and Social Opportunities, San Jose, 1989-94; adminstrv. asst. Christ United Presbyn. Ch., San Jose, 1995—; Author: Loretto School, 1990, Born in Shanghai, 1996, (book of poems) When Silver Turns to Gold, 1996. Chmn. Loretto Internat. in the Far East, Hong Kong, 1966-77; founder, pres. Tuesday Club of Hong Kong, 1970-77; pres. Little Flower Club, Hong Kong, 1972-77. Recipient resolution for decade of svc. to Cath. Charities, Bishop of San Jose, 1989. Roman Catholic. Avocations: writing, editing, gardening, crafts and doll collecting. Home: 6330 Blackberry Ct Gilroy CA 95020-3422

KATER, VICTOR RICARDO, marketing professional; b. Tucuman, Argentina, June 19, 1944; came to U.S., 1973; s. David and Sonia M. (Zimmerman) K.; m. Kathryn Holt, Oct. 4, 1975; 1 child, Andrew Alexander. Licenciado Economia, Nat. U. Tucuman, 1972; MA in Econs., Washington U., St. Louis, 1975. Econ. advisor Social Welfare Ministry, Tucuman, 1969-73; prof. econs. U. Santo Tomas de Aquino, Tucuman, 1970-73, St. Louis Community Coll., 1976-78; mgr. area Brauner Export Co., St. Louis, 1977-86, sr. mgr. area, 1986-88, mgr. internat. mktg., 1988-90; dir. mktg., Latin Am. and Caribbean Brauner Export Co., 1990-92; pres. Portal-Mundo, Inc., 1992—. Author (poem) " Him", 1972 (1st prize 1972); editor: (quar. mag.) Ecos del Sur, 1991-94. Chmn. adult edn. Congregation Kol Am, 1991—; pres. Devel. Party Youth, Argentina, 1965. Scholar Am. Field Svs., 1962-63, Fulbright Hays, 1973-75. Mem. Am. Econ. Assn. Reform Judaism. Avocations: writing humor stories and poetry, jazz pianist. E-mail: vicmundo@aol.com. Home: 13309 NW 16th St Pembroke Pines FL 33028-2730

KATERNDAHL, PAUL DAVID, financial consultant; b. Pontiac, Mich., Feb. 18, 1964; s. Richard Hanley Katerndahl and Estella Marie Rivera-Katerndahl; m. Piezhi Wu-Katerndahl, Sept. 13, 1999. BA, U. of the Pacific, 1986; JD, Golden Gate U., 1989; LLM, Nottingham U., 1990. Bar: Calif., 1989; registered investment advisor. Assoc. Leach, McGreevy & Ellassen, San Francisco, 1989-92; investment advisor Dean Witter Reynolds, Corte Madera, Calif., 1992-94; sr. portfolio mgr. Brindenberg Securities, Copenhagen, 1994-96; fin. cons. Salomon, Smith, Barney, San Francisco, 1996—; arbitration judge NASD, San Francisco, 1998—. Mem. ABA, Calif. Bar Assn., Internat. C. of C. - San Francisco. Republican. Roman Catholic. Avocations: Lacrosse, paintball. Office: Salomon Smith Barney One Sansome St 38th Flr San Francisco CA 94104

KATES, BRIAN C., newspaper editor; b. N.Y.C., Mar. 15, 1946; s. Charles Oliver Kates and Elmyra Van Winkle; 1 child, Elizabeth. BA, Pa. Mil. Coll., 1968. Tchr. English and French Gunning-Bedford High, Delaware City, Del., 1968-69; reporter, editor Herald Statesman, Yonkers, N.Y., 1972-74; reporter Daily News, N.Y.C., 1974-87, night city editor, 1987-91, regional editor, 1991-93, spl. projects editor, 1993-96, dep. editl. page editor, 1996—; adj. prof. NYU, 1976-83, Columbia Grad. Sch. Journalism, N.Y.C., 1980-83. Author: The Murder of a Shopping Bag Lady, 1985 (Spl. Edgar Allan Poe award Mystery Writers of Am. 1985, named one of 25 Books to Remember, N.Y. Pub. Libr. 1985). Capt. mil. police, 1968-72. Recipient 1st pl. prize deadline reporting AP, N.Y. State, 1983, 1st prize editl. writing, 1998; Gold Typewriter award N.Y. Press Club, 1985, 89, Pulitzer prize Columbia U., 1999, George Polk award L.I. U., 1999. Office: NY Daily News 450 W 33d St New York NY 10001

KATHIRGAMANATHAN, POOPATHY, chemist; b. Inuvil, United Kingdom, Aug. 27, 1952; s. Muthuthamby and Sellappa (Luxumy) Poopathy; m. Jayanthy Kathirgamanathan, Oct. 20, 1980; children: Janany, Ganesh. BS with honors, U. Colombo, 1976; PhD, U. Exeter, 1980. Postdoctoral fellow U. Exeter, United Kingdom, 1980-82; sr. demonstrator U. Newcastle, United Kingdom, 1982-85; teaching fellow U. Southampton, United Kingdom, 1985-86; prin. scientist Cookson Group plc, Oxford, United Kingdom, 1986-92; mgr. USEP Univ. Coll., London, 1992—; sr. lectr. South Bank U., London, 1993-95, prof., 1995—; exec., dir. tech. ELAM-T Ltd., London, 2000—; com. mem. British Standards Inst., London, 1990—. Contbr. articles to profl. jours. Recipient Sir Monty Finniston award Eureka Engrng. Materials and Designs, 1991. Fellow Royal Soc. of Chemistry, Inst. of Physics; mem. Materials Chemistry Group (chmn.), Electrochem. Soc. Inc., Soc. Chem. Industries. Achievements include numerous patents in field; inventor microwave welding of plastics and light emitting crystals, and molecular rare earth chelates. Office: South Bank U, 103 Borough Rd, London SE1 0AA, England

KATHJU, SHYAM, plant physiologist; b. Bikaner, India, May 4, 1947; s. Jitendra and Sushila (Wali) K.; m. Sarita Bhan; children: Archana, Shashi. BSc, Jodhpur U., 1965, MSc, 1967, PhD, 1971. From scientist to divsn. head Ctrl. Arid Zone Rsch. Inst., Jodhpur, India, 1972—. Mem. Arid Zone Rsch. Assn. India, Indian Soc. Plant Physiology, Soc. Plant Physiology & Biochemistry. Home: 49-E PWD Colony, Jodhpur India 342 001 Office: Ctrl Arid Zone Rsch Inst, Head Divsn, Jodhpur India 342 003

KATHURIA, NIRMAL BHATIA, psychiatrist; b. New Delhi, India, May 23, 1948; came to U.S., 1973, naturalized, 1980; d. Banarsi Das and Chander (Kanta) Bhatia; m. Mineshwar Kathuria, Jan. 14, 1973. MD, Lady Hardinge Med. Coll., New Delhi, 1969. Diplomate Am. Bd. Psychiatry and Neurology; cert. adminstrv. psychiatrist. Intern Lady Hardinge Med. Coll. and Hosp., 1970-72; resident in psychiatry Fairfield Hills Hosp., Newtown, Conn., 1974-77, staff psychiatrist, 1977-78; resident in psychiatry Yale-New Haven Hosp., also Stamford (Conn.) Hosp., 1974-77; dir. outpatient clinic Charlotte Hungerford Hosp., Torrington, Conn., 1978-80, dir., chmn. psychiat. svcs., 1980-95; bd. govs., cons. Country Place, Litchfield, Conn., 1979-86; mem. adv. bd. Regional Health Svcs., Winsted, Conn., 1979—; sole practitioner Torrington; program chmn., mem. exec. com. Assn. Psychiat. Clinics Conn., 1981-82. Mem. Am. Psychiat. Assn., Conn. Psychiat. Assn. Home: 200 Beach St Goshen CT 06756-2213 Office: 778 E Main St Torrington CT 06790-3902

KATIBAH, DANIEL DAOUD, surgeon, administrator; b. Nabk, Syria, July 5, 1916; s. Daoud Ibrahim and Emilie Mushrik (Haddad) K.; m. Lily Ramez Sarkis, Dec. 19, 1947; children: Aida, Walid, Nabil. BA, Am. U. Beirut, 1938, MD, 1943. Intern and resident Kennedy Meml. Hosp., Am. Presbyn. Mission Hosp., Mina Hosp., Tripoli, Lebanon, 1948-50; gen. surgeon, ob/gyn. physician Pvt. Hosp., Syria, 1949; founder, dir. family health ins. Iraq Petroleum Co., Syria, 1950-60; surgeon New Assi Hosp., Homs, Syria. Pres. med. com. Nat. Evangelical Synod Syria and Lebanon, 1961-96. Mem. Internat. Rotary (pres. dist. 195 Homs Syria 1964-65), Order Physicians Homs Syria (pres. 1965-66). Presbyterian. Home: PO Box 959, Homs Syria Office: New Assi Hosp, Dablan, Homs Syria

KATILA, MARJA LEENA, medical educator; b. Kuopio, Finland, Oct. 26, 1939; d. Edvart and Ida Raatikainen; m. Touko Katila; m. 1963; children: Päivi, Lisbeth, Antti-Jussi. MD, Turku U., Finland, 1966; PhD, Kuopio U., Finland, 1979. Cert. respiratory diseases and clin. microbiology. Cons., asst. head Dept. Respiratory Diseases Kuopio U. Hosp., 1972-77; asst. head. Dept. Clin. Microbiology U. Hosp., Kuopio, Finland, 1980-98; head dept. clin. microbiol. U. Hosp., Kuopio, 1999—; bd. dirs. Tb Control Group, Finland, 1994—, Finnish Microbiologist Finnish Med. Assn., 1992-95; mem. adv. com. communicable diseases Ministry of Social Affairs and Health, Finland, 1995—; program sec. Internat. Union Against Tb and Lung Disease, Paris, 1994-97, vice chair sect. bacteriology and immunology, 1998-99, 1st chair section bacteriology and immunology; specialist in respiratory diseases Med. Bd. Finland, 1972—, specialist in clin. microbiology, 1980; assoc.

prof. Kuopio U., 1991—; Thematic Working Grp. for TB Info. Network & QC, WHO - Ministry of Health, Russian Fedn., 1999—, cons. Nat. TB progs., Estonia, 1998—, Karelia, Russian Fedn., 1999—. Mem. Zonta Internat. Club, European Soc. Microbiology, Internat. Union Against TB and Lung Diseases, Am. Soc. for Microbiology, European Soc. for Clin. Microbiology and Infectious Diseases (European coun.), European Soc. Chemotherapy and Infectious Diseases (European coun.). Avocations: scientific writing, gardening, literature. Home: Isokaari 12, Kuopio Finland Office: Dept Clinical Microbiology, Kuopio University Hospital, 70211 Kuopio Finland

KATIN, PETER ROY, pianist; b. Nov. 14, 1930; m. Eva Zweig, 1954;2 children. Ed., Royal Acad. Music.; DMus (hon.), De Montfort U., 1994. Prof. Royal Acad. Music, 1956-60; prof. piano U. Western Ont., Can., 1978-84; prof. Royal Coll. Music, 1992—. Made 1st London appearance Wigmore Hall, 1948; leading interpreter of Chopin; concerts include Europe, Africa, Japan, Can., U.S., Hong Kong, India, New Zealand, Singapore, Malaysia; rec. artist for Athene, Decca, Everest, Unicorn, HMV, Philips, Lyrita, MFP, Carlton, Simax, Claudio, Olympia; formed The Katin Piano Trio, 1997. Pres. London Camerata; v.p. Bridgwater Arts Centre. Recipient Chopin Arts award, N.Y.C., 1977. Fellow Royal Acad. Music; assoc. Royal Coll. Music; mem. Inc. Soc. Musicians, Royal Soc. Musicians. Avocations: reading, writing, theatre, tape recording, photography. Office: Transart, 8 Bristol Gardens, London W9 2JG, England

KATIYAR, ANAND S., mathematics educator; b. Kanpur, India, Mar. 10, 1938; s. Shanti Swa Roop and Jam Vati K.; m. Prem Lata, Sept. 8, 1970; children: Manju, Kiran, Seema. MS, Agra U., India, 1959, 61; BS, U. Southwestern La., Lafayette, 1989; PhD, Tex. A&M U., 1969. Chemist/supr. Kashipur Sugar Factory, 1957; assoc. prof. Dav Coll., Muzaffarnagar, India, 1961-66; asst. prof. McNeese State U., Lake Charles, La., 1969-76, prof., 1977—; vis. prof. Va. Polytechnic Inst. and State U., Blacksburg, 1976-77; dir. Compu Conault, Lake Charles, 1988—; phys. sci. divsn. dir. La. Acad. of Sci., 1984—. Laser grantee State of La., Baton Rouge, 1992, Shearman fellow McNeese State U., Lake Charles, 1997. Mem. India Assn. (pres. 1977-86, 89-91, 97-98), Pi Mu, Mu Sigma Rho. Democrat. Hindu. Avocations: fishing, travel.

KATO, FUMIHIKO, English and American literature educator; b. Kobe, Hyogo, Japan, May 15, 1947; s. Yasushi and Fumiko (Okazaki) K.; m. Yoko Suizu, Nov. 21, 1971; children: Yasuhiko, Nobuko. Student, Palmore Inst., Kobe, 1966-69; BA, Kwansei Gakuin U., Nishinomiya, Japan, 1970; postgrad., Yale U., New Haven, Conn., 1970-71; MA, Kobe U., 1975. Lectr. Kyoto (Japan) Women's U., 1976-79, asst. prof., 1980-90, prof., 1991—; vis. scholar Keble Coll., Oxford, England, 1986-87. Author: Bungakushi to Tekusuto (Literary History and the Text), 1996, Always Already: Some Aspects of Intertextuality, 2000; co-author: The World of Walter Pater, 1995; co-translator: Selected Poems of Wallace Stevens, 1986. Mem. Internat. Assn. for Study of Irish Lit., British Soc. Aesthetics, Semiotic Soc. Am., English Literary Soc. Japan. Home: 3-9-4 Kofudai, Toyono, Osaka 563-0104, Japan Office: Kyoto Womens Univ, 35 Kitahiyoshicho Imakumano, Higashiyamaku Kyoto 605-8501, Japan

KATO, FUMINORI, pharmaceutical researcher; b. Seto, Aichi, Japan, Feb. 17, 1955; s. Isohachi and Shiki (Inoue) K.; m. Yukiko Mizoguchi, Apr. 6, 1986; children: Taichi, Ryuma, Honami. PhD, Nagoya (Japan) City U., 1983. Rschr. Ishihara Sangyo Kaisha Ltd., Kusatsu, Shiga, Japan, 1983-97, chief rschr., 1997—. Contbr. articles to profl. jours.; patentee in field. Avocations: swimming, skiing. Office: Ishihara Sangyo Kaisha Ltd, 2-3-1 Nishi-shibukawa, Kusatsu 525, Japan

KATO, HARUO, electronics engineer, researcher; b. Osaka, Japan, Jan. 8, 1955; m. Taiju and Michiko (Shimaya) K.; m. Akiko Kitaichi, Oct. 30, 1986; children: Kazuma, Gensei, Shiko. BS, Hokkaido U., Sapporo, Japan, 1977, MS, 1979, PhD, 1982. Rsch. scientist Toshiba Corp., Otawara, Japan, 1982-88; rsch. mgr. Advantest Corp., Otaru, Japan, 1988-96; mgr. R & D, C's Lab. Ltd., Sapporo, 1996—. Contbr. articles to sci. jours., including English Jour. Inst. Electronics, Info. and Comm. Engrs.; patentee in Japan, U.S., Europe. Mem. IEEE, Inst. Electronics, Info. and Comm. Engrs. Avocations: swimming, skiing. Office: C's Lab Ltd, Hokuen Bldg N-7 W-6, Sapporo 060-0807, Japan

KATO, HIDEO, insurance company executive. Chief fin. officer Sumitomo Life Ins. Co., Osaka, Japan. Office: Sumitomo Life Ins Co, 2-2-5 Nakanoshima Kita-ku, Osaka 530-8220, Japan*

KATO, HIROHISA, biochemist, researcher; b. Tokushima City, Japan, June 29, 1950; s. Tadayuki and Hiroko (Minato) K.; m. Michiko Mitsuhashi, July 8, 1979; children: Akiko, Kumiko, Junko. Bachelor, U. Tokyo, 1974, PhD, 1979. Postdoctoral fellow U. Colo., Denver, 1979-82, Cancer Inst., Tokyo, 1982-83; rsch. assoc. U. Tokushima, Japan, 1983-87; chief NIH Japan, Tokyo, 1988-98; prof. Iwate Med. U., Morioka, Japan, 1998—. Contbr. articles to profl. publs. Buddhist. Home: 3-15-1-404 Honchoudori, Morioka 020-0015, Japan Office: Iwate Med U Sch Dentistry, 1-3-27 Chuodori, Morioka 020-8505, Japan

KATO, IHACHI, dentist, periodontology educator; b. Nishio, Japan, July 10, 1934; s. Iroku and Kiyoko K.; m. Kato Fukiko, Mar. 24, 1965; children: Miya Iwao, Yuko Tsurusako, Kana Matsumoto. DDS, Tokyo Med. and Dental U., 1967; PhD, Tohoku U., 1977. Assoc. prof. Tohoku U. Sch. Dentistry, Sendai, Japan, 1978, Tokyo Med. and Dental U., 1982; prof. dept. periodontology Sch. Dentistry Nagasaki (Japan) U., 1989-93; dir. Sch. Dentistry Nagasaki U. Hosp. Dentistry, 1993-97; dean, dir. Grad. Sch. Dentistry Nagasaki U., 1997—. Contbr. articles to med. jours. Postdoctoral fellow in microbiology and periodontology Forsyth Dental Ctr., Boston, 1981. Mem. Japanese Soc. Periodontology (bd. dirs. 1982—), Japanese Soc. Conservative Dentistry (bd. dirs. 1982—), Stomatol. Soc., Internat. Acad. Periodontology, Internat. Assn. Dental Rsch., Japanese Assn. for Dental Edn. (bd. dirs. 1996—). Home: 2-43-7 Kakido, Nagasaki 851-0115, Japan Office: Nagasaki U Sch Dentistry Dept, Periodontology 1-7-1 Sakamoto, Nagasaki 852-8588, Japan

KATO, KENJI, plant breeding educator; b. Nagoya, Japan, Jan. 2, 1958; s. Mikio and Nobuko Kato; m. Hiroko Naito, Dec. 15, 1984; 1 child, Omoi. BSc, Kyoto (Japan) U., 1981, MSc, 1983, PhD, 1992. Lectr. Kochi (Japan) U., 1983-92, asst. prof. plant breeding, 1992-95; assoc. prof. plant breeding Okayama (Japan) U., 1995—. Author: Experimental Protocols for Plant Genetics and Breeding, 1995; contbr. articles to profl. jours., including Hereditas, Euphytica, Theoretical and Applied Genetics; mem. editl. bd. Internat. Jour. Wheat Info. Svc., 1993-97. Recipient Ryobi-Teien Found. acad. award, 1995. Mem. Japanese Soc. Breeding (gen. sec. 1996—), Genetics Soc. Japan, Japanese Soc. Plant Cell and Molecular Biology. Home: 112-8 Takashima, Shinyashiki, Okayama 703-8241, Japan Office: Okayama U Fac Agr, 1-1-1 Tsushima-Naka, Okayama 700-8530, Japan

KATO, KIYOSHI, civil engineering educator, researcher; b. Iwanai Town, Hokkaido, Japan, Sept. 1, 1934; s. Masuzo and Yoshino Kato; m. Hisayo Suhara, Mar. 30, 1959; 1 child, Naoki. B Engring., Hokkaido U., Sapporo, 1958, DEng, 1973. Rsch. fellow Nat. Def. Acad., Yokosuka, Japan, 1958-64, lectr. civil engring., 1964-67, assoc. prof., 1967-77, prof., 1977-2000, prof. emeritus, 2000—. Author: Advances in Fracture, 1982, Introduction to Reinforced Concrete Engineering, 1994, Essential Surveying, 1995; also articles. Appraiser Shizuoka Dist. Ct., Numazu City, Japan, 1990. Recipient award dept. indsl. engring. Nihon U., Narashino City, Japan, 1996. Avocations: photography, cinema, reading history books, visiting ancient temples. Home: 272 Nagae, Hayama Town 240-0113, Japan Office: Nihon U Indsl Engring Dept, 1-2-1 Izumi-cho, Narashino 275-8575, Japan

KATO, MICHINOBU, chemistry educator; b. Hiroshima, Japan, July 26, 1926; s. Sadao and Kosen (Yamada) K.; m. Michiko Itahashi, 1953. BS, Hiroshima U., 1950, DSc, 1960. Asst. Aichi (Japan) Gakugei U., Nagoya, 1950-60; lectr. Aichi Prefectural U., 1960-61, asst. prof., 1961-67, prof., 1967-92, emeritus prof., 1992—, chief kindergarten, 1982-85. Contbg. author: Chelate Chemistry (Magnetism), 1976; contbr. articles to profl. jours. Avocations: writing poetry and Japanese verse (Tanka). Home: 6-5-603 Kamezaki 4 chome, Asakita-ku, Hiroshima 739-1742, Japan Office: Aichi Prefectural U, Nagakute-cho, Aichi-gun, Aichi 480-1198, Japan

KATO, MORIHIRO, business educator; b. Tokyo, May 20, 1936; s. Yozo and Roku (Ikeda) K.; m. Hisako Nishina, Jan. 8, 1962; children: Hirofumi, Koichi. BA, Doshisha U., Kyoto, 1959, MBA, 1961, PhD, 1994. Instr. Doshisha U., 1961-64, asst. prof., 1964-67, assoc. prof., 1967-73, prof., 1973—, dean grad. sch. of bus. adminstrn., 1995-2000. Author: Logics of Accounting, 1973, Accounting Theories Supporting GAAPs, 1980, Contemporary GAAPs, 1985, Generally Accepted Accounting Principles, 1994; transl. Making Accounting Policy, 1990; editor: Future Events Accounting, 2000. Mem. Am. Acctg. Assn., Acad. Acctg. Historians, Assn. Internat. Acctg. Studies, Acctg. History Assn., Japan Mgmt. Assn., Japan Acctg. Assn. (bd. dirs. 1997-2000, editor jour. 1999—). Avocation: fishing. Office: Doshisha U Hagashiiru, Karasuma Imadegawa dori, Kamigyo-ku Kamigyoku Kyoto 602-8580, Japan

KATO, MORIYUKI, governor; b. Yawatahama, Ehime, Japan, Sept. 18, 1934; m. Michiko Uchida, May 5, 1964; children: Hidemi, Masami, Tamami. B, Tokyo U., 1957. Dep. commr. Agy. for Culture, Japan, 1983-86; dir. gen. Adminstrn. Bur., sec. gen. Ministry of Edn., Japan, 1986-89; pres. Mut. Aid Assn. Pub. Tchrs., Japan, 1989-92, Nat. Theatre, Japan, 1992-95, JASRAC, Japan, 1995-98; gov. Ehime (Japan) Prefecture, 1999—; bd. dirs. Found. for Welfare of Tchrs., Tokyo, Edni. Rsch. Inst., Tokyo. Author: Commentary on Copyright Law, 1974; editor Bunkyo, 1989—. Bd. dirs. Tokyo-Kioicho Rotary Club, 1995. Recipient Copyright Merits Copyright Coun., 1992. Mem. Copyright Law Acad. (bd. dirs.). Avocations: go, music, karaoke. Office: 4-4-2 Ichibancho, Matsuyama City, Ehime 790-8570, Japan Address: Governor of Fhime Prefecture, 122 Kitamochidacho, Matsuyama City EHIME 790-0873, Japan

KATO, NOBUO, bacteriology educator; b. Nagoya, Aichi, Japan, Jan. 25, 1930; s. Kiyoshi and Mieko Kato; m. Shoko Kato, Nov. 18, 1958; children: Katsuhiko, Masako, Yoshiro. MD, Nagoya U., 1955, D Med. Sci., 1959. Intern Tosei Hosp., Seto City, Japan, 1954-55; assoc. prof. Aichi Gakuin U. Sch. Dentistry, Nagoya, 1963-70; rsch. assoc. dept. bacteriology Nagoya U. Sch. Medicine, 1959-63, asst. prof. to prof., 1970—, dean, 1976-78, 81-85, dir. Rsch. Inst. for Germfree Life, 1977-79, dir. Rsch. Inst. for Disease Mechanism and Control, 1983-84; pres. Nagoya U., 1992-98; pres. emeritus Aichi Arts Ctr., Nagoya, 1998—; pres. Aichi Med. U., Nagoya, 2000—. Mem. Japanese Soc. Bacteriology (bd. dirs. 1983—, chmn. edn. com. 1988—). Home: 1-17 Shumoku-cho Higashi-ku, Nagoya 461-0014, Japan Office: Aichi Med U, Nagakute, Aichi 480-1195, Japan

KATO, PETER EIICHI, political scientist, journalist, educator, university dean; b. Osaka, Japan, Mar. 13, 1934; s. Sakae and Yukik0 (Masunaga) K.; m. Masako Nagatani, Apr. 16, 1961; children: Momoko, Yuri. LL.B., Tokyo U., 1959. Dep. div. head Ministry Home Affairs, Tokyo, 1970-73; fellow Japanese Govt., Sacramento, Calif., 1974-75; prof. Local Autonomy Coll., Tokyo, 1973-76; sr. staff researcher Nat. Inst. Research Advancement, Tokyo, 1976-78; assoc. prof Tsukuba U., Tsukuba, Japan, 1978-84, prof., 1985-97, dean Coll. Internat. Rels., 1985-88; dir. Chusu Inst. Govtl. Studies, Tsukuba, 1978—; prof. Tokiwa U., Mito, Japan, 1997—; dean Coll. Applied Internat. Studies, 2000—; mem. bd. dirs. Doshikai, Tokyo, 1981-85, Japan Ctr. for Internat. and Strategic Studies, Tokyo, 1988—. Author: Better Week, 1973; Correspondence From the Source, 1977; The Japanese Public Adminstration, 1980; Meet Us Kanryo, 1983; Administrator's Information Collecting, 1983, The Revenge of Cities, 1983; Information: The New Wealth of Nations, 1985, Full of Geniuses, 1992, The Brain Business, 1993, From Religions to Wa-ism, 1995; editor Chishiki mag., 1982-84. Councillor, Ministry of Home Affairs, Tokyo, 1978. Mem. Japanese Polit. Sci. Assn., Gakushikai (Tokyo). Home: 9-1-2802 Yamatocho, Tsuchiura 300-0036, Japan

KATO, SHUNSAKU, retired educator; b. Tokyo, Feb. 27, 1923; s. Fuyusaku and Fumiko (Adachi) K.; m. Chizuko Uozumi, Oct. 16, 1958; children: Mariko, Masako, Mamiko. BA, Keio Gijuku U., Tokyo, 1946. With liaison sect. Cen. Labor Coll., 1946-48, asst. prof., 1948-51, prof., 1951-66; rsch. fellow Keio Gijuku U., Tokyo, 1961-62; vis. fellow Australian Nat. U., Canberra, 1965-66; dean Coll. Econs. Kanto Gakuin U., Yokohama-Shi, Japan, 1967-68, dean Coll. Humanities, 1972-76, dir. Internat. Ctr., 1976-86, prof. internat. rels., prof. emeritus; dean Kyoai Gakuen Women's Jr. Coll., Maebashi-Shi, Japan, 1988-92; acting pres. Kyoai Gaken Women's Jr. Coll., Maebashi-Shi, Japan, 1989-92. Mem. Japanese Assn. Internat. Rels. (coun. 1980-94), Peace Study Assn. Japan (v.p. 1981-83), Keio Assn. Law Politics and Sociology (adviser 1978—), Internat. Peace Assn. (coun. 1973-96), World Federalist Movement (exec. com. 1991-95, coun. 1983—), World Federalist Movement of Japan (v.p. 1986—). Methodist. Home: 4-2-15 Jomyoji, Kamakura 248-0003, Japan

KATO, TERRI EMI, elementary school and gifted and talented educator; b. Gardena, Calif., Sept. 1, 1953; d. Shunji James and Ruby Miyo (Sumi) K. BA, Calif. State U., Long Beach, 1976; MA, U.S. Internat. U., 1987. Cert. tchr. multiple subjects, learning handicapped, severely handicapped, resource specialist, lang. devel. specialist, c.c.'s, Calif. Learning disabled group specialist Montebello (Calif.) Unified Sch. Dist., 1979-81; resource specialist ABC Unified Sch. Dist., Cerritos, Calif., 1981-82; spl. day class tchr. Santa Ana (Calif.) Unified Sch. Dist., 1982—; math. resource tchr., 1990-98; 1st and 2nd grade tchr. Santa Ana (Calif.) Unified Sch. Dist., 1996-98, kindergarten tchr., 1999—. Mem. NEA, Calif. Tchrs. Assn., Santa Ana Educators Assn. (mem. spl. edn. task force rules and election com., bldg. rep. 1992—, mem. supt.'s cabinet 1995—), Coun. for Exceptional Children, Orange County Math. Coun. Avocations: travel, reading, hiking, dog grooming, golf. Office: James Monroe Elem 417 E Central Ave Santa Ana CA 92707-3501

KATO, TOMIKO, artist; b. Tokyo, Nov. 16, 1936; d. Seiji and Yae Suzuki; m. Yasuo Kato, Mar. 7, 1958; 1 child, Yuka. BFA, Tokyo Nat. U. Fine Arts/Music, 1959. Cert. secondary and univ. tchr. Artist in Nihon-ga (Japanese style painting). Solo exhbns. of works at Shiseido Ginza Gallery, Tokyo, Matsuya Ginza Gallery, Tokyo, 1983, 86, 90, 93, Bill Hodges Gallery, N.Y.C., 1996-98, Takashimaya Art Gallery, Tokyo, 1997; group exhbns. at Yamatane Art Mus., Tokyo, 1977, 79, 81, Saitama Prefectural Modern Art Mus., 1988, Takashimaya Gallery, Tokyo, 1981-98, Mitsukoshi Gallery, Tokyo, 1992-96, numerous others; author: Sakura no mori no mankai no shita (Beneath Blossoming Cherry Trees), 1993; dancer, choreographer Performance Art: Dances of My Paintings in Real Space, 1986; guest on TV program; subject of numerous revs. Recipient honorable mention Yamatane Art Mus. Award, 1981. Avocations: Japanese dance, shamisen, theater, music. Home: 1184-63 Hamanogo, Chigasaki-Shi, Kanagawa 253-0086, Japan

KATO, YUKO, company executive; b. Seto, Aichi, Japan, Mar. 29, 1957; d. Matsuro and Noriko Kato. BBA, Nanzan U., Japan, 1977. Dir. mgr. In Rock Co., Ltd., Seto, Japan. Editor monthly publs. In Rock, Movie Star. Office: In Rock Bldg 2d Fl, 1-86 Nichihara cho, Seto Aichi 489-8567, Japan

KATODRITOU, ANGELA NICOLAS, radiologist; b. Limassol, Cyprus, Aug. 23, 1960; d. Andreas and Thekla (Mani) Limnatitis; m. Nicolas Antonis Katodritis, Aug. 30, 1986; 1 child, Stephany. MD, U. Goettingen, 1991. Physician Hosp. Limassol, 1985; scientific rschr. Anatomic Inst. Goettingen, Germany, 1986-87; asst. radiol. dept. Univ. Clinic, Goettingen, 1987-92; radiologist pvt. MRI practice, Nicosia, Cyprus, 1992-94, Limassol, 1994-96; radiologist, dir. pvt. MRI practice, Nicosia, 1997—. Mem. Cyprus Radiol. Soc., Meridien Sports Club, German Radiol. Soc., European Soc. of Musculosceletal Radiology. Greek Orthodox. Avocations: theatre, music, cooking, sports. Home: 4 Sapfous Str App 301, 2007 Strovolos/Nicosia Cyprus

KATOH, SHUJI, internist; b. Gifu City, Japan, July 29, 1947; s. Shuzoh and Nobuko (Ohno) K.; m. Yohko Kuga, Dec. 21, 1975; children: Shusuke, Sachiko. MD, Kyoto Prefectural U. Medicine, Kyoto City, Japan, 1972. Jr. resident Kyoto Prefectural U. Medicine, Kyoto City, 1972-74, sr. resident, 1975-79; physician Ohmihachiman City (Japan) Hosp., 1974-75, Shakaihoken Kobe Ctrl. Hosp., Kobe City, 1979-83; asst. medicine Murakami Meml. Hosp./Asahi U., Gifu City, 1983-86, assoc. prof., 1986-98, prof., 1998—. Author: Internal Medicine for Dentistry, 1997; contbr. articles to profl. jours. Office: Murakami Meml Hosp/Asahi U, 3-23 Hashimoto-cho, Gifu 500-8856, Japan

KATOH, YOSHIMITSU YUKI, anatomist, educator; b. Miyoshi, Aichi, Japan, Oct. 3, 1953; s. Genichiro and Yukie (Kasai) K.; m. Keiko Suzuki, Mar. 12, 1978; children: Yasuyo, Taihei, Tomomi, Naoki. B of Health Scis., Fujita Health U., Toyoake, Japan, 1976, PhD, 1986. Med. technologist Fujita Health U. Hosp., Toyoake, 1976-78; asst. dept. anatomy Fujita Health U., 1978-88; asst. prof. physiology Albert Szent (Hungary)-Györgyi Med. U., 1988-90; asst. dept. anatomy Fujita Health U., 1990-93, asst. prof. anatomy, 1993-98, assoc. prof. anatomy, 1998—; part-time instr. Chiiki-Iryo Acad. Nursing, Toyota, Aichi, 1985, Yokkaichi U. Jr. Coll., Yokkaichi, Japan, 1992-95, Toyota Acad. Nursing, Toyota, 1995—, Aichi Women's Jr. Coll., 1998—. Fujita Health U. grantee, 1994—; grantee Min. Edn., Sci., and Culture Japan, 1996-98. Buddhist. Achievements include work with staining method, distribution, and quantitative changes of nucleolus-like inclusion bodies in the mouse brain; direct projections from the cerebellar fastigial nucleus to the thalamic suprageniculate nucleus in the cat; bilateral projections from the superior colliculus to the thalmic suprageniculate nucleus in the cat. Home: 34-7 Maehara Nishiishiki, Miyoshi Nishikamo 470-02-26, Japan Office: Fujita Health U Anatomy Dept, 1-98 Dengaku-Gakubo, Aichi Toyoake 470-11-92, Japan

KATOVIĆ, DRAGO, chemistry educator, researcher; b. Zagreb, Croatia, Dec. 24, 1941; s. Nine and Elza (Brkić) K.; m. Branka Vukić, May 25, 1974; children: Darko, Tonko. BS, Faculty of Tech., Zagreb, 1977, MS, 1982, DSc, 1985. Cert. in textile engring. Asst. Faculty of Tech., Zagreb, 1977-82, rsch. asst., 1982-86, from asst. prof. to assoc. prof., 1986-97, prof., 1997—; head of dept., vice dean Faculty of Textile Tech., Zagreb, 1995-98, dean, 1998. Co-author: (textbook) The Basis of Textile Finishing, 1992; contbr. rsch. articles to profl. jours. Fellow The Textile Inst. (internat. governing coun. 1998—); mem. Croatian Acad. Tech. Sci., N.Y. Acad. Sci. Avocation: sailing. Home: Goljak 38, 10 000 Zagreb Croatia Office: Faculty of Textile Tech, Pierottijeva 6, 10 000 Zagreb Croatia

KATOW, SHIGETAKA, virologist; b. Amagasaki, Hyogo, Japan, Jan. 8, 1942; s. Toshio and Taeko (Nakamura) K.; m. Nobuko Ueda, Dec. 18, 1976; children: Shinsuke, Asuka, Sayaka. BS, U. Tokyo, 1964, MS, 1966, DSc, 1989. Rschr. NIH, Tokyo, 1969-78, sr. rschr., 1978-97; sr. rschr. Nat. Inst. Infectious Diseases, Tokyo, 1997-2000, head, 2000—; expert Japan Internat. Cooperation Agy., Tokyo, 1984-89; sec. gen., editl. com. Vaccine Handbook, Tokyo, 1991-96; task force Inst. for Internat. Cooperation, Tokyo, 1989-90. Author: Clinical DNA Diagnostics, 1995, Modern Application of DNA Amplification Techniques, 1997; editor, author: Vaccine Handbook, 1996. Nat. com. World U. Svc., Tokyo, 1962-63; instr. Tachikawa Swimming Assn., 1998—. Mem. Tachikawa Swimming Assn. (dir. 1989-91), Tokyo Myojo Card Club (v.p. 1992-93), Japanese Soc. for Virology, Japanese Soc. for Clin. Virology. Buddhist. Avocations: swimming, archaeology, drawing, jogging, poetry. Home: 2-19-10 Sunagawa Tachikawa, Tokyo 190-0031, Japan Office: Nat Inst Infectious Diseases, 4-7-1 Gakuen Musashi-Murayama, Tokyo 208-0011, Japan

KATRANA, DAVID JOHN, plastic and reconstructive surgeon; b. Moline, Ill., Oct. 16, 1945; s. Nicholas John and Marilyn Ann Katrana; children: Nicole Elaine, Kimberly Ann. BA in Biology, Northwestern U., Evanston, Ill., 1967; DDS, Northwestern U., Chgo., 1971, MD, 1974. Diplomate Am. Bd. Plastic and Reconstructive Surgery. Resident oral surgery Northwestern U. Dental Sch., Chgo., 1971-72; intern surgery Northwestern U. McGraw Med. Ctr., Chgo., 1974-75, resident gen. surgery, 1975-77, resident plastic and reconstructive surgery, 1977-79; assoc. Houston Plastic Surgery Assocs., 1979-91; pvt. practice plastic surgery, 1991—; asst. clin. prof. plastic surgery Baylor Coll. Medicine, Houston, 1980—; pres. Hyperbaric Mgmt. Assocs. Inc., 1997—; dental cons. The Chgo. Bulls, 1977-79; instr. surgery, dental cons. Northwestern U. Med. Sch., Chgo., 1978-79; dir. burn unit Humana Hosp. Southmore, Pasadena, Tex., 1982-88; div. chief surgery Rosewood Hosp., Houston, 1984-86, pres. med. staff, 1988-89; plastic surg. cons. Houston Gamblers Profl. Football Team, 1984; mem. courtesy staff St. Luke's Episcopal Hosp., West Houston Med. Ctr., Meml. Hosp. at Memorial City, also others; lectr. various univs. and hosps. Contbr. articles to profl. jours. Trustee Rosewood Med. Ctr., Houston, 1989—, chmn. bd., 1993-95; dir. Ctr. for Wound Care and Hyperbaric Medicine, Spring Br. Med. Ctr., 1999—. Fellow ACS; mem. Undersea and Hyperbaric Med. Soc., Internat. Soc. Burn Injuries, Am. Burn Assn., Am. Soc. Plastic and Reconstructive Surgeons, Tex. Soc. Plastic Surgeons, Tex. Med. Assn., Harris County Med. Soc., Houston Soc. Plastic Surgeons, Wound Healing Soc. Home: 5035 Tangle Ln # A Houston TX 77056-2113 Office: 9034 Westheimer Rd Ste 320 Houston TX 77063-3614

KATSAS, ARISTOTELES GREGORY, surgeon; b. Athens, Attica, Greece, Sept. 13, 1932; s. Gregory George and Anastasia (Laubou) K.; m. Theochari Vassilakaki, Jan. 27, 1960; children: Gregory, Helen. MD, Nat. U. Athens, 1957, MSc, 1966. Diplomate Am. Bd. Surgery; cert. gen. surgery, Greece. Intern, resident surgery Am. Hosps., Balt. Burlington & Bklyn., N.Y., 1957-62; chief resident surgery Coney Island Hosp., Bklyn., 1962-63; assoc. surgery Evangelismos Hosp., Athens, 1963-81, dir. surgery, 1982-2000. Author: Basic Surgery, 1973; contbr. articles to profl. jours., chpts. to books. Bd. mem. Soc. Doctors for Environ. (bd. mem. 1994-95). With Hellenic Air Force, 1951-53. Study grantee Brit. Coun., London, 1969. Fellow ACS; mem. Soc. Med. Studies (bd. mem. 1971-74, pres. 1980-82), Hellenic Surg. Soc. (bd. mem., v.p. 1986, 90-92), Hellenic Soc. Med. Ethics (bd. mem., v.p. 1990-95). Avocations: history, music, travel. Home: 7-9 Vrasida St, GR 11528 Athens Greece

KATSCHINSKI, MARTIN KURT, gastroenterologist, researcher; b. Eschwege, Hessen, Germany, Nov. 19, 1958; s. ERwin and Annemarie (Beissert) K. MD, U. Goettingen, Germany, 1983. Bd. cert. internal medicine and gastroenterology. Clin. rsch. fellow internal medicine Philipps U., Marburg, Germany, 1983-85; rsch. fellow gastrointestinal motility Erlangen (Germany) U., 1985-86; clin. and rsch. fellow internal medicine & gastroenterology U. Marburg, 1986-95, staff mem. dept. gastroenterology, 1995—, prof. internal medicine and gastroenterology, 2000—; reviewer European Pancreatic Club, 1996-98, European Digestive Disease Week, 1995, 97, German Soc. Gastroenterology and Metabolism. Reviewer Digestive Diseases and Scis., Life Scis., Jour. Clin. Investigation, Digestion, others; contbr. articles to profl. jours. Mem. German Soc. Gastroenterology, German Motility Club (pres. 1997). Office: U Marburg, Dept Gastroent, Baldingerstr 1, 35033 Marburg Germany

KATSIFIS, SPIROS PANAGIOTIS, biological sciences educator, researcher; b. Athens, Greece, Feb. 2, 1949; s. Panagiotis Spiros and Kalliope Katsifis. BS in Toxicology and Chemistry, St. John's U., Jamaica, N.Y., 1983, MS in Toxicology, 1987; PhD in Environ. Medicine, NYU, 1993. Diplomate Am. Bd. Forensic Toxicology-Medicine. Tchg. asst. St. John's U., 1984-86; rsch. toxicologist Am. Health Found., Valhalla, N.Y., 1985-87; rsch. assoc. Adelphi U., Garden City, N.Y., 1988-89; rsch. fellow NYU, Tuxedo, 1989-92; adj. asst. prof. CUNY, N.Y.C., 1993-98; asst. prof. biol. scis. Sch. Arts and Scis., U. Bridgeport, Conn., 1998—, prof. Coll. Naturopathic Med., 1999—; dir. Toxiconsult Assoc., N.Y., N.J., 1995—; adj. assoc. prof. St. Francis Coll., Brooklyn Heights, N.Y., 1993-98; prof. Contbr. articles, abstracts to profl. jours., chpts. to books. Fellow Nat. Inst. Occupl. Safety and Health, 1989-91. Fellow Am. Coll. Forensic Examiners; mem. Soc. Toxicology, Northeastern Assn. Forensic Sci., Met. Assn. Coll. and Univ. Biologists. Greek Orthodox. Avocations: fishing, travel. E-mail: skatsif@bridgeport.edu. Office: U Bridgeport Dana Hall of Sci Bridgeport CT 06601

KATSIKAS, MICHAEL D., air transportation executive; b. Thessaloniki, Greece, July 18, 1950; s. Dimitri M. and Maria D. (Tsakonas) K.; m. Sophie G. Lykourinou, Nov. 4, 1978; children: Maria, Olga, Dimitri. Math. and physics, U. Thessalonik, 1973, bus. adminstrn. and econs., 1977. Cert. mktg. analyst, bus. planner, corp. planner, computer analyst. From sales, bus. accounts to comml. planning Olympic Airways, Athens, Greece, 1976-89; corp. planning, rsch. Olympic Airways, Athens, 1990-97, gen. mgr. mktg., 1998—; mem., del. various coms. Assn. European Airlines, 1982—; cons.

various orgns., Greece, 1990-94; chmn. Bd. Airlines Reps., Greece, 1998—; spkr. in field. Mem. Parents Assn., Glyfada, Athens, 1992—, Glyfada's Ch. com., 1993—. Greek Orthodox. Avocations: music, mountain climbing, photography, gardening. Home: Nymfon 52, 16561 Athens Greece

KATSNELSON, BORIS ALEXANDROVITCH, environmental and occupational health researcher, consultant; b. Lugansk, Ukraine, Oct. 20, 1926; s. Alexandr Borisovitch and Sarah Adolfovna (Levina) K.; m. Myrah Ilyinichna Fridjeva, May 6, 1947; 1 child, Leonid. MD, Med. Inst., Cheljabinsk, Russia, 1949; PhD, Acad. Med. Scis., Moscow, 1957; DSc, USSR High Commn. Attestation, Moscow, 1969. Labor hygiene insp. various state agencies, Cheljabinsk, 1949-59; head lab. pneumocomioses Med. Rsch. Ctr., Ekaterinburgh, Russia, 1959-72, head dept. toxicology and bioprophylaxis, 1972—; expert Fed. Commn. Hygienic Stds.-Setting, Moscow, 1962—; cons. Dept. Environ. Epidemiology, Environ. Mgmt. Project in Russian Fedn., Ekaterinburgh, 1996—; chief rschr. Ural Regional Ctr. Environ. Epidemiology, Ekaterinburgh, 1998—. Bd. editors Toxicol. Review, 1993; contbr. over 270 articles to profl. jours.; author of sci. books. Fellow Russian Soc. Toxicology (bd. dirs. 1995); mem. N.Y. Acad. Scis. Avocations: reading English and French detective novels. Home: Apt 382, 69 Lenins Prosp Bld 7, 690075 Ekaterinburgh Russia Office: Med Rsch Ctr, 30 Popov Str, 620014 Ekaterinburgh Russia

KATSOULIS, BASIL D., meteorology and climatology educator; b. Neraida, Karditsa, Greece, Mar. 3, 1940; s. Dimitrios K. and Konstantia D. (Katsabrias) K.; m. Dimitra Zarafonitis, Apr. 23, 1977; children: Dimitris, Konstantia. BSc in Math., Athens, Greece, 1963; PhD, Physicomath., Athens, 1970, diploma in meteorology, 1972; MSc, Imperial Coll., London, 1971. Asst. U. Athens, 1966-72; sr. rschr. Nat. Obs. of Athens, 1972-85; chief asst. Meteorol. Inst., Athens, 1972-85; prof. Nat. Acad. Air Force, Athens, 1974-85, U. Ioannina, Greece, 1985—; dir. divsn. astro-geophysics U. Ioannina, 1989-94. Author: Fluid Mechanics, 1985, General Meteorology and Climatology, 1993, Physics of the Environment. Served with Greek mil., 1964-65. Scholar NATO, 1970, 73; grantee European Union, 1993-2000. Mem. Royal Meteorol. Soc., Hellenic Meteorol. Soc., European Geophys. Union, European Wind Energy Assn. Mem. Liberal Party. Greek Orthodox. Avocations: tennis, climbing, swimming. Office: Dept Physics, U Ioannina Campus, 45110 Ioannina Greece

KATSURA, ISAO, molecular biologist; b. Kamakura, Kanagawa, Japan, Aug. 20, 1945; s. Itsumi and Chieko Katsura; m. Masae Takahara, Mar. 10, 1972; 2 children. BSc, U. Tokyo, 1968, MSc, 1970, DSc, 1973. Postdoctoral fellow U. Basel, Switzerland, 1973-76; rsch. assoc. U. Tokyo, 1976-88, assoc. prof., 1988-91; prof. Nat. Inst. Genetics, Mishima, Japan, 1991—; head structural biology ctr. Nat. Inst. Genetics, Mishima, 1996—. Contbr. articles to profl. jours. Office: Nat Inst Genetics, 1111 Yata, Mishima 411-8540, Japan

KATSURAJIMA, NOBUHIRO, educator; b. Tokyo, Oct. 11, 1953; s. Yuzo and Tei (Takatsu) K; m. Hidemi Kanazu, Nov. 18, 1996. PhD, Ritsumeikan U., Kyoto, 1994. Assoc. prof. Japanese intellectual history Hinomoto Jr. Coll., Himeji, Japan, 1983-94; assoc. prof. Ritsumeikan U., Kyoto, 1995-96, prof., 1997—. Author: Bakumatsu-Minshu-Shiso-no-Kenkyu, 1992, Shisoshi-no-19-seiki, 1999. Office: Ritsumeikan U, 56-1, tojiin-kitamachi kita-ku, Kyoto 603-8577, Japan

KATSURINIS, STEPHEN AVERY, lawyer; b. Houston, Aug. 4, 1966; s. Ted and JoAnn Katsurinis. BA, Southwestern U., 1988; JD, Franklin Pierce Law Ctr., 1991. Bar: Va. 1992, D.C. 1999, U.S. Ct. Appeals (4th cir.) 1992, U.S. Dist. Ct. (ea. dist.) Va. 1995. Legis. counsel to Rep. Dana Rohrabacher Washington, 1991-94; policy analyst Dept. of Planning and Budget, Richmond, Va., 1994-95; of counsel Magenheim, Bateman, Houston, 1995-97; staff atty. McGuireWoods LLP, Washington, 1997—. Alt. del. Rep. Nat. Conv., San Diego, 1996; election judge State of Tex., Georgetown, 1986; mem. Alexandria City Rep. com.; Alexander city chair Bush for Pres., 2000. Recipient Am. Citizenship award DAR, 1980. Mem. Am. Hellenic Progressive Assn. (chpt. sec. 1990-91), Federalist Soc. for Law and Pub. Policy, Charles Fahy Am. Inn of Cts. (barrister). Republican. Greek Orthodox. Office: McGuireWoods LLP # 1200 1050 Connecticut Ave NW Washington DC 20036-5317

KATSUTA, SHOICHI, chemist, educator; b. Nagoya, Japan, Aug. 23, 1964. DSc, Tohoku U., Sendai, Japan, 1993. JSPS rsch. fellow Tohoku U., Sendai, Japan, 1993-95; part time rsch. assoc. Sci. U. Tokyo, 1995-96; rsch. assoc. Chiba (Japan) U., 1996—. Author: Current Topics in Solution Chemistry, 1997; contbr. articles to profl. jours. Mem. The Chem. Soc. Japan, The Japan Soc. for Analytical Chemistry, Japan Chemistry Program Exchange. Office: Chiba U Faculty Sci, 1-33 Yayoi-cho Inage-ku, Chiba 263-8522, Japan

KATTAN, MOHD IMAD, architect; b. Amman, Jordan, Sept. 3, 1951; s. Mahmoud Kamal Kattan and Ilham Hamzah Malas; m. Leen Mohd Halawa, 1983 (div. 1985); 1 child, Ramsey; m. Nawal Radi Abdullah, 1987. BS in Architecture with hons., Bath U., Eng., 1975; MA in Civic Design, Liverpool U., Eng., 1977. Architect, planner CH2M Hill, Portland, Oreg., 1977-81; lectr., prof. Jordan U., Amman, 1981-84; mng. dir. UBMC, Amman, 1982-95; chmn., mng. dir. Union Distbrs. Co., Amman, 1987—. Chmn. SOS Childrens Village Assn. Jordan, 1999—. Mem. Jordanian Engrs. Assn. Avocations: tennis, jogging, photography, scuba diving. Office: UDC, PO Box 182185, Amman 11118, Jordan

KATTENBECK, KLAUS, cardiologist; b. Emsdetten, Germany, Aug. 17, 1968; s. Paul August and Mathilde Josephine (Feld) K. MD, U. Luebeck, Germany, 1995, Ednl. Commn. Fgn. Med. grads., Phila., 1996. Fellow U. Med. Ctr., Bonn, Germany, 1995-96, U. Bochum, Germany, 1997, U. Limburg, Maastricht, Netherlands, 1997-98; with dept. cardiology Univ. Bochum, Germany, 1997—. Author: Das Herz Buch, 1997. Mem. Deutsche Gesellschaft fuer Kardiologie-Herz und Kreislaufforschung, Deutsche Gesellschaft fuer Innere Medizin. Avocation: running marathons. Office: U Klinik Marien Hosp Herne, Hoelkeskampring 40, 44625 Herne Germany

KATTI, MURALIDHAR KOTLESHACHAR, microbiologist, researcher, consultant; b. Gulbarga, India, Apr. 15, 1959; s. Kotleshachr Subbannachar and Shakuntala Kotleshachar (Huilgol) K.; m. Ashwini Muralidhar Kakhandaki Katti, June 25, 1992; children: Meghana, Vasudha. BS, Nat. Coll., Bangalore, India, 1978; MS, Karnataka U., Dharwad, India, 1981; PhD, Nat. Inst. Mental Health, Bangalore, India, 1991. Rsch. asst. Kidwai Meml. Inst. Oncology, Bangalore, India, 1982-85; rsch. scholar Nimhans, Bangalore, India, 1985-90; postdoctoral scientist Bangalore (India) Genei, 1990; postdoctoral assoc. Ind. Inst. Sci., Bangalore, India, 1990-93; asst. prof. Sdu Med. Coll., Kolar, India, 1993-95, Sree Chitra Tirunal Inst., Trivandrum, India, 1995—; vis. faculty Bangalore U., 1994-95, Rajiv Gandhi Ctr. for Biotech., Trivandrum, 1995-96. Inventor: Serodign, Immunotherapy Infectious Disease, 1995; author: J Clin Microbiology, 1996, Jour. Infectious Disease, 2000. Grantee Dept. Sci. and Tech. Govt. Kerala State, 1996. Fellow Ind. Soc. Malaria and Other Communicable Diseases; mem. Ind. Assn. Biomed. Sci., Ind. Immunologists' Soc., Assn. Microbiologists of India, Biotech. Soc. India. Avocations: reading, walking, listening to music, quizzing and discussions. Home: No 32 Kamadhenu, 4 Cross 5 Main, Srinidhi Layout Bangalore 560062, India Office: Tirunal Inst Med Sci and Tech, Sree Chitra, Kerala, Trivandrum 695011, India

KATTIDENIOS, GEORGIOS DIMITRIOS, computer science educator, pilot; b. Simi, Dodecanese, Greece, June 30, 1968; p. Dimitrios G. and Sevasti (Katris) K. B in Engring., U. Salford, Manchester, Eng., 1991; MS, U. Manchester Inst. Sci. Tech., 1993. Lic. to practice the profession of radio-electrician class A, Greek Dept. Comm. and Transports. Computer sci. coord. U. of the Aegean, Rhodes, Dodecanese, Greece, 1995-96, Oaed Tech. Inst., Rhodes, 1995-97; computer sci. lectr. Coll. Advanced Tourist Profession, Rhodes, 1996-97, Greek Lyceum, Rhodes, 1998—; airline pilot Cronus Airlines, 1999—; computer cons. Diagoras Maritime Ltd., Rhodes, 1996, 97, 98. Pres. Rhodes Aeroclub, 1997. Greek Orthodox. Avocations: flying, sailing, swimming, amateur radio. E-mail: gkattidenios@hotmail.com. Fax: 30 241 25049. Home: 107 Lindou St, GR 85100 Rhodes Greece

KATZ, ABRAHAM, retired foreign service officer; b. Bklyn., Dec. 4, 1926; s. Alexander and Zina (Rabinowitz) K.; children: Tamar, Jonathan, Naomi; m. Marion Scheinberger, July 29, 1996. B.A. cum laude, Bklyn. Coll., 1948; M.I.A., Columbia U., 1950; Ph.D., Harvard U., 1968. Commd. fgn. service officer Dept. State, 1951; 1st sec. U.S. missions to NATO, OECD, Paris, 1959-64; counselor Am. Embassy, Moscow, 1964-66; dir. office of OECD European Communities and Atlantic Polit. Econ. Affairs, Washington, 1967-74; dep. chief of mission OECD, Paris, 1974-78; dep. asst. sec. for internat. econ. policy and research Dept. Commerce, Washington, 1978-80; asst. sec. internat. econ. policy Dept. Commerce, 1980-81; U.S. rep., ambassador OECD, Paris, 1981-84; pres. U.S. Coun. Internat. Bus., 1984-99, pres. emeritus, 1999—; employer mem. gov. body Internat. Labor Orgn., 1984-99; v.p. Internat. Orgn. Employers, 1984-99. Author: The Politics of Economic Reform in the Soviet Union, 1972. Decorated grand officier Ordre National du Merite (France); recipient U.S. Coun. Internat. Bus. Internat. Leadership award. Mem. Am. Polit. Sci. Assn., Assn. Advancement Slavic Studies, Am. Fgn. Svc. Assn., Am. Assn. Comparative Econ. Studies, Coun. of Fgn. Rels., Cosmos Club, Harvard Club, B'nai Brith, Century Assn. Office: US Coun Internat Bus 1212 Avenue Of The Americas New York NY 10036-1602

KATZ, ALFRED, pharmacognosist; b. Basel, Switzerland, Aug. 9, 1916; s. Ernst Georg and Klara (Straus) K.; m. Hannah Alice Straus, July 17, 1951; children: Katharina, Georg. MPharm, U. Basel, 1941; PhD, Basel U., 1943. Assoc. researcher Pharm. Inst. U. Basel, 1943-52, Chem. Inst. U. Basel, 1950-57; owner pharmacy, Basel, 1957-87; owner, chief researcher Natural Products Rsch. Lab., Basel, 1978—. Contbr. articles to profl. jours. Named hon. prof. U. Basel, 1993. Mem. Swiss Pharm. Soc., Sci. Pharm. Soc., Swiss Soc. Preventive and Social Medicine, New Swiss Chem. Soc., Am. Soc. Pharmacognosy, Internat. Pharm. Fedn., Phytochem. Soc. Europe. Avocations: skiing, hiking. Home: Riedbergstr 21, CH-4059 Basel Switzerland Office: Natural Products Rsch Lab, Oberwilerstr 9, CH-4054 Basel Switzerland

KATZ, ARNON, management consultant; b. Urmston, U.K., Mar. 13, 1955; s. Dov and Edith (Geitheim) K.; m. Pnina Schwartz, July 11, 1984; children: Amit, Lior, Maya. BSc, Technion, Haifa, Israel, 1978, MSc in Indsl. Mgmt., 1993; MBA in Engring. Project leader RAFAEL, Haifa, 1987-90; sr. design engr. USC, Mahwah, N.J., 1990-92; group leader RAFAEL, Haifa, 1992-95, project mgr., 1996-98, contracts mgr., 1998—; mktg. dir. ORNET, Carmiel, Israel, 1995-96; cons. KCL, Haifa. Contbr. articles to profl. jours. Maj. IDF, 1978-82.

KATZ, SIR BERNARD, physiologist; b. Leipzig, Germany, Mar. 26, 1911; s. Max and Eugenie (Rabinowitz) K.; m. Marguerite Penly, Oct. 27, 1945; children: David, Jonathan. MD, U. Leipzig, Germany, 1934; MD (hon.), U. Leipzig, German Dem. Republic, 1990; PhD, U. London, 1938, DSc, 1943; DSc (hon.), U. Southampton, 1971, U. Melbourne, 1971, Cambridge U., 1980; PhD (hon.), Weizmann Inst. Sci., 1979. Beit Meml. Research fellow, 1938-39; Carnegie Research fellow Sydney, Australia, 1939-42; asst. dir. biophys. research U. Coll., London, 1946-50, reader, 1950, prof., head biophysics dept., 1952-78, prof. emeritus, 1978—; lectr. univs., socs. Author: Electric Excitation of Nerve, 1939; Nerve, Muscle and Synapse, 1966; The Release of Neural Transmitter Substances, 1969; also articles. Mem. Agrl. Research Council, 1967-77. Recipient Feldberg award, 1965, Copley medal Royal Soc., 1967, Nobel prize in medicine-physiology, 1970, Cothenius medal Deutsche Akademie der Naturforscher Leopoldina, 1989; created knight, 1969. Fellow Royal Soc. (council 1964-65, v.p. 1965, biol. sec. 1968-76), Royal Coll. Physicians (Baly medal 1967); fgn. mem. Royal Danish Acad. Scis. and Letters, Acad. Nat. Lincei, Am. Acad. Arts and Sci., Nat. Acad. Scis. U.S. (fgn. assoc.), Order Pour le Mérite für Wissenschaften und Künste (fgn.). Achievements include research on nerve and muscle function especially transmission of impulses from nerve to muscle fibers. Office: U Coll Dept Physiology, Gower St, London WC1E 6BT, England

KATZ, DAVID, gastroenterologist, educator; b. Harrisburg, Pa., Nov. 28, 1928; s. William Meyer and Fanny (Zwick) K.; m. Judith Lynn Zimmerman, June 18, 1961 (div. Aug. 1977); children: Jonathan, Peter, Jeremy; m. Shirley Eileen Love, Sept. 17, 1987. BS, Tulane U., 1946, MD, 1950. Intern Kings County Hosp., Bklyn., 1950-52; resident in internal medicine VA Hosp., Newington, Conn., 1952-53, West Haven, Conn., 1955; fellow in gastroenterology VA Hosp., West Haven, 1955-56; asst. prof N.Y. Med., N.Y.C., 1958-62, assoc. prof., 1962-68, prof., 1968—; prof. N.Y. Med., Valhalla, 1974—. Home: 100 E Hartsdale Ave Apt 6jw Hartsdale NY 10530-3846

KATZ, KENNETH ARTHUR, lawyer, accountant; b. N.Y.C., Apr. 4, 1955; s. Bernard and Shirley Anne (Schachter) K.; m. Gillian Lynn Bagg, Nov. 29, 1986; children: Melissa Lee, Ashley Dawn. AB in Econs. cum laude, Harvard U., 1976; JD, Yeshiva U., 1980; MBA in Pub. Acctg., Pace U., 1987. Bar: N.Y. 1994, U.S. Tax Ct. 1994, D.C. 1995; CPA, N.Y. Legal asst. Law Offices of Jerome A. Wisselman, Manhasset, N.Y., 1980-81, Law Offices of S. Mac Gutman, Forest Hills, N.Y., 1981-82; asst. contr. Tauck Tours, Inc., Westport, Conn., 1982-84; pvt. practice acct. Eastchester, N.Y., 1984-87; tax specialist KPMG Peat Marwick, White Plains, N.Y., 1987-88; atty., acct., ptnr. Bernard Katz & Co, P.C., Eastchester, 1988—. Mem. ABA (taxation and internat. law sects.), N.Y. State Bar Assn. (tax sect.), D.C. Bar Assn. (taxation and sect. on corps., fin. and securities law), Westchester County Bar Assn. (tax and trusts and estates coms.), N.Y. State Soc. CPAs, Nat. Tax Assn.-Tax Inst. Am. (com. on internat. pub. fin.), Harvard-Radcliffe Club of Westchester. Avocations: sports, music, personal investing. Office: Bernard Katz & Co PC 1 Mayfair Rd Eastchester NY 10709-2701

KATZ, MICHAEL JESSE, orthopedic surgeon; b. N.Y.C., Mar. 7, 1956; s. Walter and Thea Katz; m. Sherry Falk, July 4, 1979; children: Jonathan, Judith, Ezra, Daniel. BA, Queens Coll., N.Y.C., 1976; MD, Albert Einstein Coll. Medicine, N.Y.C., 1980. Diplomate Am. Bd. Forensic Examiners, Am. Bd. Orthopedic Surgery. Intern Hosp. U. Pa., 1980-81; resident in orthopedic surgery U. Pa. Hosp., Phila., 1981-85; pvt. practice Flushing, N.Y., 1985—; cons. U.S. Fed. Cts., N.Y., 1994—. Jonas Salk scholar, 1976; faculty fellow U. Pa., 1981. Fellow Am. Acad. Orthopedic Surgeons, Am. Bd. Forensic Examiners; mem. AMA, Nassau County Med. Soc. Jewish. Home: 170 Pond Xing Lawrence NY 11559-2022

KATZ, ROBERT IRWIN, retired physician; b. Springfield, Mass., Dec. 16, 1924; s. Julius Louis and Florence (Greenburg) K. Student, Tufts Coll., 1942-44; MD, Tufts U., 1948. Diplomate Am. Bd. Surgery, Am. Bd. Thoracic Surgery, Nat. Bd. Med. Examiners. Intern Charity Hosp. of La., New Orleans, 1948-49, resident in pathology, 1949-50; resident in gen. surgery Boston City Hosp., 1953-56; asst. in surgery Boston U. Sch. Medicine, 1955-56; resident in surg. oncology Anderson Cancer Ctr. U. Tex., Houston, 1956-57; resident in thoracic surgery VA Hosp., L.A., 1960-61, Children's Hosp., L.A., 1961; chief thoracic surgery V.A. Hosps., Sepulveda/San Fernando, Calif., 1962-70; pvt. practice gen. and thoracic surgery L.A., 1970-86; head gen. surgery Naval Hosp., Corpus Christie, Tex., 1987; head dept. surgery Naval Hosp., Cherry Point, N.C., 1988-90; surgeon USS New Jersey WES PAC, 1986, 88; ret., 1990; clin. asst. prof. UCLA Med. Ctr., 1969-89, U. So. Calif., L.A., 1964-96. Contbr. articles to profl. jours. Tournament ofcl. So. Calif. Tennis Umpires Assn., L.A., 1972—; commr. Med. Bd. of Calif., Sacramento, 1980-98. With USN, 1944-45, surgeon USMC, 1950-52, US Merchant Marines, 1953. Recipient clin. fellowship Am. Cancer Soc., Houston, 1957-58. Fellow Am. Coll. Chest Physicians; mem. AAAS, AMA, Soc. Thoracic Surgeons (founding), So. Med. Assn., So. Assn. Oncologists, Assn. Mil. Surgeons U.S., Marine Corps Heritage Soc., 2nd Marine Divsn. Assn. (life), Nat. Wildlife Fedn. (life), USTA (life), Naval Res. Assn., M.D. Anderson Assocs. Republican. Jewish. Avocations: tennis, physical fitness. Home and Office: 1733 Centinela Ave Santa Monica CA 90404-4238

KATZ, RUTH, musicology educator; b. Duisburg, Germany, Aug. 5, 1927; arrived in Israel, 1934; d. Zecharia and Risse (Ganger) Torgovnik; m. Elihu Katz, Sept. 16, 1951; children: Matthew Joseph, Nathaniel Zvi. BS, Columbia U., 1954, MA, 1956, PhD, 1963. Lectr., sr. lectr., assoc. prof. musicology Hebrew U. Jerusalem, 1964-80, Emanuel Alexandre prof. musicology, 1980-96, prof. emeritus, 1996—, chair grad. faculty of humanities, 1983-86, chair excellence program in humanities, 1989-95, co-dir. Electronic Lab. for Musicology, 1957—; adv. com. Min. Edn. on Higher Musical Edn., Jerusalem, 1968-75; mus. com. Israel Broadcasting Authority, 1966-78. Author: Divining the Powers of Music, 1986, 2d edit. (The Powers of Music) 1994, (with Carl Dahlhaus) Contemplating Music, 4 vols., 1987-91, (with Dalia Cohen) The Israeli Folksong, 1977, (with Ruth HaCohen) Tuning the Mind, 2000, (with Dalia Cohen) A Maqam Tradition in Theory and Practice, 2000; music editor Ency. Hebraica, 1969—. Inst. Advanced Study fellow, Berlin, 1986-87, Ctr. for Judaic Studies, U. Pa., fellow, Phila., 1995. Mem. Israel Musicol. Soc. (past chair), Internat. Musicol. Soc., Gesellschaft fur Musikforschung. Jewish. Home: Hagdud Haivri 15, Jerusalem 92344, Israel Office: Hebrew U Jerusalem, Dept Musicology Mt Scopus, Jerusalem 91905, Israel

KATZ, STANLEY NIDER, law history educator; b. Chgo., Apr. 23, 1934; s. William Stephen and Florence (Nider) K.; m. Adria Holmes, Jan. 16, 1960; children: Derek Holmes, Marion Holmes. AB, Harvard U., 1955, MA, 1959, PhD, 1961; LLD (hon.), Stockton State Coll., 1981; DHL (hon.), U. Puget Sound, 1994, C.W. Post/L.I. U., 1997, Sacred Heart U., 1997; LLD, Ohio State U., 1998, U. Hartford, 1998. Asst. prof. history Harvard U., 1961-65, U. Wis., Madison, 1965-71; prof. legal history Law Sch. U. Chgo., 1971-78; Class of 1921 Bicentennial prof. history Am. law and liberty Princeton U., 1978-86, sr. fellow Woodrow Wilson Sch., 1986-97, lectr. with rank of prof. Woodrow Wilson Sch., 1997—; pres. Am. Council Learned Socs., N.Y.C., 1986-97; dir. Ctr. for Arts and Cultural Policy Rsch./Woodrow Wilson Sch., 1998—; vis. prof. law U. Pa., 1978-86; mem. Oliver Wendell Holmes Devise, Washington, 1976-84; bd. govs. Inst. European Studies, Chgo., 1976—; chmn. Coun. on Internat. Exchange Scholars, Washington, 1981-85; adj. prof. Cardozo Law Sch., 1999-2000. Author: Newcastle's New York, 1968; editor: The Case and Tryal of John Peter Zenger, 1963, rev. edit., 1972, Oliver Wendell Holmes Devise History of U.S. Supreme Court, 1984—, Colonial America, 1971, 76, 83, 92, 2000, American History: Promise and Progress, 1983, Constitutionalism and Democracy, 1993, The Life of Learning, 1994, Philanthropy in the World's Traditions, 1998. Active N.J. Com. for Humanities, 1978-84, 96—; trustee So. Meth. U., 1988-2000, Nat. Cultural Alliance, 1990-97, chmn., 1997—; trustee Rsch. Librs. Group, 1991-93, 1997-99, Brit.-Am. Arts. Assn., 1991—, Newberry Libr., Chgo., ind. sector, 1990-95, chmn. rsch. com. ind. sector, 1989-92, Toynbee Prize Found., 1994-97, pres. 1995-97; Nat. Faculty, 1995—, Fulbright Internat. Ctr., 1995—, Copyright Clearance Ctr., 1997—, civic edn. project, 1997—; v.p. Friends of the Law Libr., Libr. of Congress, 1991—, Supreme Ct. N.J., disciplinary oversight com., 1994—, N.J. Ethics Commn., 1991-94, com. model rules of profl. conduct, 1982-83, com. sale of law practices, 1983-84, 89. Fellow Am. Soc. Legal History (pres. 1978-81); mem. AAAS, Papers of the Founding Fathers (chair 1985—), Inst. Early Am. History and Culture (coun. 1974-76, 90-93, 97-98), Am. Hist. Assn. (v.p. rsch. 1997-2000), Orgn. Am. Historians (exec. com. 1976-79, pres. elect 1986-87, pres. 1987-88), Am. Antiquarian Soc., Mass. Hist. Soc., Am. Philos. Soc., Soc. Am. Historians, Coun. Fgn. Rels., Phi Beta Kappa. Democrat. Jewish. Clubs: Princeton (N.Y.C.). Office: Princeton U Woodrow Wilson Sch Princeton NJ 08544-0001

KATZ, STEVEN BARRY, English educator, writer; b. Albuquerque, Oct. 27, 1953; s. Elliot Saul and Leona Katz; m. Alison Burns, Sept. 27, 1980; 1 child, Jason Michael. BA, Mich. State U., 1977; MA, U. R.I., 1980; PhD, Rensselaer Poly. Inst., 1988. Tchg. asst. U. R.I., Kingston, 1978-81; tchg. asst. Rensselaer Poly. Inst., Troy, N.Y., 1981, 82-83, writing instr. Ctr. for Urban and Environ. Studies, 1982, instr. lang., lit. and comm., 1983-85; instr. English N.C. State U., Raleigh, 1986-87, asst. prof., 1988-94, assoc. prof., 1994—; dir. MS program in tech. comm. N.C. State U., 1995-98, dir. profl. writing cert. program, 1995-97, cons. Ctr. for Comm. in Sci., Tech. and Mgmt., 1998; manuscript reviewer Tech. Comm. Quar., 1991—, others; spkr. 4th Internat. Conf. Global Lang. and Literacy, 2000. Author: The Epistemic Music of Rhetoric, 1996; co-author: Writing in the Sciences, 1998; contbr. articles to profl. jours., poetry to mags. and lit. jours.; recordings include (CD) InSight and Vision, 1999; mem. Jewish musical group Mishpacha. Vol. Against End of World benefit; panelist, lectr. in field; judge various poetry competitions. Grantee N.C. State U., 1992-93, Am. Coun. Learned Socs., 1995. Mem. MLA, Internat. Soc. for History of Rhetoric (grantee 1999), Rhetoric Soc. Am., Nat. Coun. Tchrs. English (award 1993), Assn. for Expanded Perspectives in Learning, Sci. Fiction Poetry Assn., Assn. for Tchrs. of Tech. Writing, Soc. for Literature and Sci., Assn. Tchrs. Tech. Writing, Nat. Comm. Assn., Popular/Am. Culture Assn. Jewish. Avocations: classical guitar, songwriting, performing, Jewish studies, languages. E-mail: sbkeg@unity.ncsu.edu. Office: NC State U Dept English PO Box 8105 Raleigh NC 27695-0001

KATZ, WILLIAM MICHAEL, writer; b. N.Y.C., Mar. 18, 1940; s. Herbert and Sylvia (Dulberg) K.; m. Jane Louise Reckseit, Dec. 11, 1966; children: Sharon Elizabeth, Abigail Eve. BA, U. Chgo., 1961; MS, Columbia U., 1962. Officer CIA, Washington, 1962-63; asst. to dir. Hudson Inst., Harmon, N.Y., 1964-65; mem. editl. staff N.Y. Times, N.Y.C., 1965-70; staff editor N.Y. Times Mag., 1968-70; adj. instr. writing and speech SUNY, Westchester. Author: North Star Crusade, 1976, Death Dreams, 1979, Ghostflight, 1980, Visions of Terror, 1981, Copperhead, 1982, Surprise party, 1984, Open House, 1985, Facemaker, 1988, After Dark, 1988, Double Wedding, 1990; TV dramas include Nicky's World, 1974, Nightmare at 43 Hillcrest, 1974, Death Dreams, 1991, Please Forgive Me, 1996. Mem. Soc. Singers East (bd. dirs.).

KATZIN, CAROLYN FERNANDA, nutritionist, consultant; b. London, July 21, 1946; came to U.S., 1983; d. John Mourier and Shelagh B. A. (Tighe) Lade; m. Anthony Arthur Speelman, Mar. 18, 1968 (div. Dec. 1984); 1 child, Zara Jane; m. David Brandeis Katzin (div. Mar. 1999). BS with honors, U. London, 1983; MS in Pub. Health, UCLA, 1988. Nutritionist L.A., 1985—; cons. HerbaLife Internat., L.A., 1986—; chair dean's adv. bd. UCLA Sch. Pub. Health, 1997—; mem. profl. adv. bd. The Wellness Community, L.A., 1998—; pres. Am. Cancer Soc., L.A., Coastal Cities U., 1999—. Author: (books) The Advanced Enegy Guide, 1994, The Good Eating Guide and Cookbook, 1996. Democrat. Jewish. Office: 12011 San Vicente Blvd Ste 402 Los Angeles CA 90049-4946

KATZMAN, HARVEY LAWRENCE, lawyer, educator; b. Youngstown, Ohio, Sept. 2, 1948; s. Abraham and Elsie Katzman; m. Elizabeth Viola Ball, Dec. 27, 1980. BA, Ohio No. U., 1971; JD, Glendale U., 1976. Bar: Calif. 1978, U.S. Dist. Ct. (cen. dist.) 1978, U.S. Ct. Appeals (9th cir.) 1979. Pvt. practice L.A., 1978-97; prof. law Glendale (Calif.) U., 1979—; lawyer La Casella & Katzman, Pasadena, Calif., 1997—; cons. to newly admitted attys., so. Calif., 1990—; legal advisor Calif. Inst. Baseball Acad., Riverside, 1995—. Mem. L.A. County Bar Assn. (family law com. 1997-99), Delta Theta Phi. Avocations: gardening, baseball, traveling, writing. Office: La Casella & Katzman LLP 234 E Colorado Blvd Ste 800 Pasadena CA 91101-2208

KATZMANN, ROBERT ALLEN, judge; b. N.Y.C., Apr. 22, 1953; s. John and Sylvia Edith (Butner) K. AB summa cum laude, Columbia U., 1973; MA in Govt., Harvard U., 1975, PhD in Govt., 1978; JD, Yale U., 1980. Bar: Mass. 1982, U.S. Ct. Appeals (1st cir.) 1983, D.C. 1984, U.S. Dist. Ct. Mass. 1984, N.Y. Law clk. to judge U.S. Ct. Appeals (1st cir.), Concord, N.H., 1980-81; rsch. assoc. Brookings Instn., Washington, 1981-85, fellow, 1985-99; adj. prof. law, pub. policy Georgetown U., Washington, 1984-92; William J. Walsh prof. govt., prof. law Georgetown U., 1992-99; pres. Governance Inst., Washington, 1986-99; acting dir. govt. studies Brookings Instn., Washington, 1998; judge U.S. Ct. Appeals (2nd cir.), 1999—; vis. prof. polit. sci. UCLA, Washington program, 1990-92; vis. chair, Wayne Morse prof. law and politics U. Oreg., 1992; cons. Fed. Cts. Study Com., 1990. Author: Regulatory Bureaucracy: The Federal Trade Commission and Antitrust Policy, 1980, Institutional Disability, 1986, Courts and Congress, 1997; co-editor: Managing Appeals in Federal Courts, 1988; editor: Judges and Legislators, 1988, The Law Firm and the Public Good, 1995; article and book editor Yale U. Law Jour., 1979-80. Mem. ABA (adminstrv. law sect. vice chair com. on govt. ops. and separation of powers 1991-94, pub. mem. adminstrn. conf., 1992-95), Am. Judicature Soc. (bd. dirs. 1992-98), Am. Polit. Sci. Assn., Assn. Pub. Policy Analysis and Mgmt., Phi Beta Kappa. Office: US Ct Appeals 2d Cir 40 Foley Sq New York NY 10007-1502

KATZNELSON, DAVID, recording company executive; b. San Francisco, May 11, 1969; s. Gordon and Doris Katznelson. B.English, U. Calif.,

Berkeley. Intern CD Presents, San Francisco, 1986-89; disc jockey KUSF, San Francisco, 1986-88; usher, promotion aide Bill Graam Presents, San Francisco, 1985-90; disc jockey KALX, Berkeley, 1989-91; intern Warner Bros. A&R, Burbank, Calif., 1988-91, v.p., 1991—; CEO Birdman Records, Burbank, 1996—, v.p., 1996-2000. Prodr. (record/CD): Muffs, 1993, Blacktop, 1995, Tarnation, 1996, Bassholes, 1999, Cheaterslicks, 1999. Mem. Friars Club. Jewish. Avocations: reading, tennis, yoga, hiking, road-tripping and grooving.

KAUFER, SHIRLEY HELEN, artist, painter; b. Bklyn., Oct. 3, 1920; m. Bernard Goldberg, Apr. 18, 1943; children: Alice, Marjorie. Student in srt studies, Pratt Inst.; student, Bklyn. Mus., Art Students League, N.Y.C. Art dir. Advt. Agys., N.Y.C., 1938-63; cons. N.Y.C., 1964-73; sculptor Vero Beach, Fla., 1973-77; graphic designer Jewish Fedn. Coun., L.A., 1977-82; with Haystack Mt. Art Colony, Deer Isle, Maine, summers 1959-65; instr. advt., design, illustration Pels Art Sch., N.Y.C., 1968-71; instr. painting Indian River C.C., Vero Beach, 1973-77. Represented in permanent art collection pf UCLA Med. Ctr., L.A.; exhibited in numerous nat. and internat. galleries; 2 films produced on her life and works. Home: 1029 Via De La Paz Pacific Palisades CA 90272-3534

KAUFFELD, MICHAEL, engineer, researcher; b. Darmstadt, Hessen, Germany, May 18, 1962; s. Jürgen and Bärbel (Köhler) K.; m. Henriette Kristensen, May 21, 1994; children: Rasmus Martin, Sophus Jonathan. MSc, U. Hannover, Germany, 1988, PhD in Engring., 1992. Rsch. asst. U. Hannover, 1985-86, rschr., 1989-92; vis. rschr. Nat. Bur. Rsch. Standards, Gaithersburg, Md., 1986-87; devel. engr. Hydro Aluminium, Tønder, Denmark, 1992-94; project mgr. Danish Technol. Inst., Aarhus, Denmark, 1994—; tech. journalist Promotor Verlag, Karlsruhe, Germany, 1989-92; vice-chmn. Internat. Inst. Refrigeration Working Group on Ice Slurry, 1999—. Author: Air Cycle Refrigeration, 1993; co-author: Compression Cycles for Environmentally Acceptable Refrigeration A/C, 1993, Thermophysical Properties of Liquid Secondary Refrigerants, 1997; editor: Applications for Natural Refrigerants, 1996. With German Navy, 1981-83. Mem. ASHRAE, German Refrigeration Assn., Ry Yacht Club (vice-chmn. 1995-98), Danish Refrigeration Assn., UNEP Refrigeration, Air Conditioning and Heat Pumps (mem. tech. options com.). Avocations: sailing, skiing, horseback riding. Office: Danish Technol Inst, Teknologiparken, 8000 Århus C, Denmark

KAUFMAN, CHARLES DAVID, controller; b. N.Y.C., Apr. 17, 1931; s. M. Laurence and Anna (Goldberg) K.; m. Elvira Sampere Camps, Mar. 1, 1955; children: John, Janet. BS, Northwestern U., 1952; MBA, NYU, 1958. CPA, N.Y. Fin. analyst Nestle Co., Stamford, Conn., 1958-61; area contr. IBM World Trade Corp., Mexico City, 1967-69; dir. fin. controls ITT Corp., Brussels and N.Y.C., 1974-85, controller's dept., 1985-94; ret., 1994. Bd. dirs. Scottsdale League for The Arts, Valley Acad.; vol. cons. Exec. Svc. Corps Ariz., Svc. Corps Ret. Execs. Cpl. U.S. Army, 1952-54. Mem. AICPAs, N.Y. Soc. CPAs, Ariz. Soc. CPAs.

KAUFMAN, CHARLOTTE S., communications executive; b. Bridgeport, Conn., Mar. 8, 1918; d. Samuel N. and S. Elizabeth (Cohen) Schnee; m. William Kaufman, May 9, 1940. BA, U. Mich., 1938. Med. office assoc., 1941-63; dir. pub. rels. Parents and Friends of Retarded Children, Bridgeport, 1965-66; founder, exec. dir. Family Life Film Ctr. of Conn., Fairfield, Conn., 1967-74; exec. producer Topic '69/WNHC-TV, New Haven, Conn., 1969; project dir. pilot project with Social/Rehab. Svc. U.S. Dept. HEW, 1969-70; pub. rels. chmn. Friendship Fair of Aux./Bridgeport Regional Ctr. Retarded, 1979; founder CAT-TV, pub. access channel, Winston-Salem and Forsyth County, 1994; coord. five annual Film Day Workshops, Fairfield U., 1967-71; coord. coms. of jurors for Am. Film Festival, N.Y.C., 1968-74; chmn./mem. planning and adv. bd. Bridgeport Regional Ctr. for the Retarded; exec. bd. Bd. of Assocs., U. Bridgeport, others; film use cons. to many local and state orgns. Author: Film Discussion: A Technique to Communicate Information About Rehabilitation, 1970; exec. producer: A Day in the Life of P.T. Barnum, 1971; author publs. in field. Vol. patient advocate for nursing homes, Southwestern Conn. Area Agy. on Aging, 1976-78; v.p. Oronoque Village Improvement Assn., 1986-88. Home: 3180 Grady St Winston Salem NC 27104-4008

KAUFMAN, DAVID GRAHAM, construction company executive; b. North Canton, Ohio, Mar. 20, 1937; s. DeVere and Josephine Grace (Graham) K.; m. Carol Jean Monzione, Oct. 5, 1957 (div. Aug. 1980); children: Gregory Allan, Christopher Patrick. Student, Kent State U., 1956; grad., Internat. Corr. Schs., 1965, N.Y. Inst. Photography, 1983; postgrad., Calif. Coast U. Cert. constrn. insp., constrn. project mgr., asbestos insp., lead insp., lead risk assessor, asbestos project designer, lock-out/tag-out. Machinist apprentice Hoover Co., North Canton, Ohio, 1955-57; draftsman-designer Goodyear Aircraft Corp., Akron, Ohio, 1957-60, Boeing Co., Seattle, 1960-61; designer Berger Industries, Seattle, 1961-62, Puget Sound Bridge & Drydock, Seattle, 1963, C.M. Lovsted, Seattle, 1963-64, Tracy, Brunstrom & Dudley, Seattle, 1964, Rubens & Pratt Engrs., Seattle, 1965-66; founder, owner Profl. Drafting Svcs., Seattle, 1965, Profl. Take-Off Svcs., Seattle, 1966, Profl. Representation Svcs., Seattle, 1967; pres. Kaufman Inc., Seattle, 1967-83, Kaufman-Alaska Inc., Juneau, 1975-83, Kaufman-Alaska Constructors, Inc., Juneau, 1975-83; constrn. mgr. U. Alaska, 1979-84; constrn. cons. Alaskan native and Eskimo village corps., 1984—; prin. Kaufman S.W. Assocs., N.Mex., 1984—, Graham Internat., 1992—; trustee, advisor Kaufman Internat., The Kaufman Group, Kaufman Enterprises. Mem. Constrn. Specifications Inst., Assn. Constrn. Insps., Associated Gen. Contractors Seattle Constrn. Coun., Producers Coun. Oreg., Wash., Idaho, Hawaii, Alaska, Portland C. of C., Nat. Eagle Scout Assn., Toastmasters (past gov.), Lions. Republican. Roman Catholic. Home: PO Box 1781 Santa Fe NM 87504-1781 Office: PO Box 458 Haines AK 99827-0458 also: PO Box 915 Crownpoint NM 87313-0915

KAUFMAN, DAVID JOSEPH, lawyer; b. Harrisburg, Pa., Apr. 7, 1931; s. S. Herbert and Bessie (Claster) K.; m. Virginia Stern, Aug. 30, 1959; children: David J. Jr., James H. BS in Econs. cum laude, Franklin and Marshall Coll., 1952; JD cum laude, U. Pa., 1955. Bar: Pa. 1955. First assoc., to ptnr., then of counsel Wolf, Block, Schorr & Solis-Cohen, Phila., 1957—; chmn., exec. com., 1979, 83. Trustee Abington (Pa.) Meml. Hosp., 1981—, chmn. bd. trustees, 1992-94; pres. Congregation Rodeph Shalom, Phila., 1983-86. Fellow Am. Coll. Trust and Estate Counsel; mem. ABA, Pa. Bar Assn. (chmn. real property, probate and trust sect. 1986-87), Phila. Bar Assn. (chmn. probate sect. 1977). Republican. Home: 2191 Paper Mill Rd Huntingdon Valley PA 19006-5817 Office: Wolf Block Schorr & Solis-Cohen LLP 1650 Arch St Fl 20 Philadelphia PA 19103-2029

KAUFMAN, JAMES JAY, lawyer; b. Newark, N.Y., Jan. 23, 1939; s. Joseph Julius and Ann Gertrude (Quick) K.; m. Patricia Ann Patterson, Sept. 3, 1966; children: Kristine, Jeffrey. BA, Bucknell U., 1960; LLB, JD, Union Coll., Albany, 1964. Bar: N.Y. 1965, U.S. Ct. Appeals (2nd cir.) 1966, U.S. Dist. Ct. (we. and no. dists.) N.Y. 1968, N.C. 1985, Pa. 1985, U.S. Supreme Ct. 1985, U.S. Dist. Ct. (ea. dist.) N.C. 1991, U.S. Ct. Appeals (4th cir.) 1991, U.S. Ct. Appeals (7th cir.) 1992, U.S. Dist. Ct. (mid. dist.) N.C. 1993. Legal counsel, legis. and adminstrv. asst. Rep. Theodore R. Kupferman, U.S. Congress, Washington, 1965-67; assoc. Houghton, Pappas & Fink, Rochester, N.Y., 1967-70; ptnr. Culley, Marks, Rochester, 1970-75; sr. ptnr. James J. Kaufman, P.C., Newark, 1975-84, Kaufman & Forsyth, Rochester, 1984-91, Barefoot & Kaufman, Wilmington, N.C., 1991-93, Kaufman, Barefoot & Green, Wilmington, 1993-94; of counsel Hancock & Estabrook, Syracuse, N.Y., 1994-96; sr. ptnr. Kaufman & Green, L.L.P., Wilmington, 1994—; V.p. Fed. Bar Coun., 1968; mem. 7th Jud. Dist. Grievance Com., 1983-89; del. U.S./China Joint Session on Trade, Investment and Econ. Law, Beijing, 1987; strategic planning cons., Rochester, 1994-95; panel mem. Commerce Tech. Adv. Bd. on Noise Abatement, Washington, 1968; chmn. noise task force Genesee Region Health Planning, Rochester, 1970-71, mem./counsel noise task force, mem./counsel environ. health planning com., 1972-73. Author: What to Do Before the Money Runs Out—A Road Map for America's Automobile Dealers, 1993; contbr. articles to profl. publs. Justice Town of Arcadia, Newark, 1976-89. Mem. N.Y. State Bar Assn. (mem. spl. com. on environ. law 1974-77, mem. com. on profl. discipline, mem. com. on ct. in cmty. banking com. 1986—), Wayne County Bar Assn. (pres. 1986-87, v.p. 1985-86, chmn. family law sect. 1975-80, chmn. com. on profl. discipline 1975-89), N.C. Bar Assn., Pa. Bar Assn., New Hanover County Bar Assn., Monroe County Bar Assn., Wilmington Inns of Ct. (pres. 1994-97). Republican. Presbyterian. Avocations: boating, scuba diving, fishing. Office: Kaufman & Green LLP 1985 Eastwood Rd Ste 200 Wilmington NC 28403-7208

KAUFMAN, JONATHAN REED, journalist; b. N.Y.C., Apr. 18, 1956; s. H. George and Bernice (Rosenblatt) K. B.A., Yale U., 1978; M.A., Harvard U., 1982. Reporter South China Morning Post, Hong Kong, 1978-79, Wall St. Jour., Chgo., 1979-80, Boston Globe, 1982-94; nat. reporter Wall St. Jour., West Medford, Mass., 1995—. Author: Broken Alliance: The Turbulent Times Between Blacks and Jews in America, 1988. Henry Luce Found. fellow, 1978; recipient Pulitzer prize, 1984, award New Eng. UPI, 1984, Nat. Jewish Book award, 1988; Alicia Patterson fellow, 1986. Jewish. Office: Wall Street Jour PO Box 364 Boston MA 02258

KAUFMAN, JOYCE JACOBSON, chemist, educator; b. N.Y.C., June 21, 1929; d. Abraham and Sarah (Seldin) Deutch; m. Stanley Kaufman, Dec. 26, 1948; 1 child, Jan Caryl. B.S. with honors, Johns Hopkins U., 1949, M.A., 1959, Ph.D. in Chemistry, 1960; D.E.S. with honors in Theoretical Physics, Sorbonne, Paris, 1963. Analytical research chemist Army Chem. Ctr., Md., 1949-52; mem. chemistry rsch. staff Johns Hopkins U., Balt., 1952-60; mem. quantum chemistry group Rsch. Inst. Advanced Studies, Balt., 1960-69, staff scientist, 1965-69, head, 1963-69; prin. rsch. scientist dept. chemistry Johns Hopkins U., Balt., assoc. prof. dept. anesthesiology Sch. Medicine, 1969—; mem. sci. adv. com. Dept. Def., 1977; mem. rev. panel for undergrad. chemistry edn. NSF, 1977; Fogarty Internat. Exchange specialist NIH-USSR Ministry of Health, 1978. Mem. editorial adv. bd.: John Wiley and Intersci. Pubs., 1965-80; Molecular Pharmacology, 1970-80; Internat. Jour. Quantum Chemistry, 1967-85; Jour. Computational Chemistry, 1980—; editor Benchmark Book Series in phys. chemistry-chem. physics, 1975-77, overall chemistry editor, 1977-80. Contbr. articles to profl. jours. Recipient Garvan medal as outstanding woman chemist Am. Chem. Soc., 1974; Md. Chemist award Am. Chem. Soc. Md. sect. 1974. Fellow Am. Phys. Soc., Am. Inst. Chemists; mem. Am. Chem. Soc. (chmn. Md. sect. 1972, councilor phys. chemistry div. 1971-94, budget and fin. com. 1981-91, pubs. com. 1992—), Am. Soc. Pharmacology and Exptl. Therapeutics, European Acad. Scis., Arts and Letters (corr. mem.), Internat. Soc. Quantum Biology, Phi Beta Kappa, Sigma Xi. Office: Johns Hopkins U Dept Chemistry Baltimore MD 21218

KAUFMAN, LUNA AMALIA, musicologist; b. Nov. 28, 1926; came to U.S., 1952; Musicologist, Jagellonain U., Cracow, Poland, 1949. Pres. Temple Sholom, Plainfield, N.J., 1980-82; chmn. Liberty State Park (N.J.) Monument, 1982-85; pres., mgr. N.J. State Opera, Newark, 1987-94; exec. bd. mem. endowment for Judeo-Christian edn. Seton Hall U., West Orange, N.J., 1984—; pub. spkr. on the Holocaust, 1976—; exec. bd. Anti-Defamation League of N.Y. Charter mem. Gov.'s Coun. on Holocaust Edn., 1982-92, Trenton, N.J.

KAUFMAN, PAULA T., librarian; b. Perth Amboy, N.J., July 26, 1946; d. Harry and Clara (Katz) K.; m. L. Ratner, 1989. AB, Smith Coll., 1968; MS, Columbia U., 1969; MBA, U. New Haven, 1979. Reference libr. Columbia U., N.Y.C., 1969-70, bus. libr., 1979-82, dir. libr. svcs., 1982-86, dir. acad. info. svcs., 1986-87, acting v.p., univ. libr., 1987-88; dean of librs. U. Tenn., Knoxville, 1988-99; univ. libr. U. Ill., Urbana Champaign, 1999—; reference coord. McKinsey & Co., N.Y.C., 1970-73; founder, ptnr. Info. for Bus., N.Y.C., 1973-76; prin. reference libr. Yale U., New Haven, 1976-79; bd. dirs. Ctr. Rsch. Librs., 1994-2000, chmn., 1996-97; bd. dirs. CAUSE, 1996-98; bd. dirs. Assn. Rsch. Librs., 1997—. Contbr. articles to mags., 1983—. Bd. dirs. Cmty. Shares, Knoxville, 1993-97. Mem. ALA, Soc. for Scholarly Pub., Solinet (bd. dirs., chmn. 1992-93).

KAUFMAN, SAMUEL LEOPOLD, dentist, educator; b. Secureni, Cernowitz, Ukraine, Sept. 8, 1944; arrived in Israel; s. Leopold Haim and Fani Samuel (Bain) K.; m. Liliane Herscovici, Jan. 23, 1982; children: Elia, Lior. D in Med. Dentistry, Med. Inst. Timisoara, Romania, 1972; Cert. Implant Dentistry, Sch. Dental Medicine/U. Pitts., Pitts., 1992. Diplomate Internat. Congress of Oral Implantology, Am. Soc. Osseo Integration. Cons. Franch Hosp. and Policlinics, N.Y., 1976; asst. Clinic, Dusseldorf, Germany, 1977, Berlin, 1978-79; head Dental Clinic, Kiriat Bialik, Israel, 1980—; clin. assoc. prof. dept. prosthodontics Pitts. U., 1991; assoc. academician Internat. Info. Acad., Moscow, 1996; assoc. mem. UN, 1996. Contbr. articles to profl. jours. V.p. ICOI Israeli Sect., 1988; chmn. bd. Israeli Linkow Implant Assn., Israel, 1988. Recipient KCM, Knights of Malta, 1987, Cert. of Achievement, Allegheny County, Pitts., 1996. Master Am. Acad. Implant Prosthdontics (Hall of Fame Celebrated Pioneer 1996). Achievements include patent for quick hardening of bone substitutes with soft laser. Home: 60 Weitzman Rd, 26350 Kiriat Motzkin Israel Office: Dental Ctr, Ben Gurion Blvd 63 5, Kiriat Bialik Israel

KAUFMAN, STEVEN MICHAEL, lawyer; b. Spokane, Wash., July 2, 1951; s. Gordon Leonard and Terri (Thal) K.; m. Connie Hoopes, June 7, 1973; children: Kristopher, Shana. BS magna cum laude, U. Utah, 1973; JD cum laude, Gonzaga U., 1977. Bar: Utah 1977, U.S. Dist. Ct. Utah 1977, U.S. Ct. Appeals (10th cir.) 1977, U.S. Supreme Ct. 1985. Founding ptnr. Farr, Kaufman, and Hamilton, 1979-89; mng. ptnr. Farr, Kaufman, Sullivan, Gorman, Jensen, Medsker, Nichols & Perkins, 1989—; judge pro tem, 1981-98; bar commr. Farr, Kaufman, Sullivan, Gorman, Jensen, Medsker, Nichols, 1991-98; chmn. Commn. on Pub. Defenders, Ogden, 1984. Mem. ATLA, ABA, Utah Bar Assn. (pres.-elect 1995-96, pres., 1996-97, bar commr. 1992-98, rep. Utah Jud. Coun. 1998-99), Weber County Bar Assn. (pres. 1981-82), Rex E. Lee Inn of Ct. (master), Utah Jud. Coun. Jewish. Home: 5878 S 1050 E Ogden UT 84405-4959 Office: Farr Kaufman Sullivan Gorman Jensen Medsker Nichols & Perkins 205 26th St Ste 34 Ogden UT 84401-3109

KAUFMAN, TEODORO SAUL, chemistry researcher, chemistry educator; b. Sunchales, Santa Fe, Argentina, July 24, 1958; s. Samuel and Fanny (Schliserman) K.; m. Miriam Rosa Hazan-Barki, Mar. 21, 1991; children: Gabriela Judith, Uriel Jeremías, Cintia Daniela. Biochemist, Nat. U. Rosario, Argentina, 1982, Pharmacist, 1985, PhD in Chemistry, 1987. Diplomate biochemistry, pharmacy. Tchg. asst. Nat. U. Rosario, 1978-87, adj. prof., 1989-99, assoc. prof., 1999—; fellow Nat. Sci. and Tech. Rsch. Coun., Argentina, 1982-87; asst. rsch. scientist NRC, Argentina, 1990-95, adj. rsch. scientist, 1995-99; ind. rsch. scientist NRC, 2000—; postdoctoral rsch. assoc. U. Miss., 1987-89; mem. dept. bd. Sch. Pharmacy Nat. U. Rosario, 1990—, dir. prof. capacitation, 1995—. Contbr. articles to profl. jours.; patentee in field. Recipient award Fulbright Found., 1987, King Baoudouin award Internat. Found. for Sci., Sweden, 1994. Fellow Sociedad Argentina de Investigations en Química Orgánica (dist. dep. 1989-91, 93-95, auditor 1989-90, sci. adv. com. 1999—); mem. Japanese Pharm. Soc., Am. Assn. Pharm. Scientists. Avocations: collecting stamps, jogging, reading sci fi books, building exotic devices. Home: San Lorenzo 2826, 2000 Rosario Santa Fe, Argentina Office: Inst Química Orgánica de Síntesis, Suipacha 570, 2000 Rosario Santa Fe, Argentina

KAUFMANN, CHARLES ARTHUR, psychiatrist, neuroscientist, educator; b. N.Y.C., Mar. 10, 1951; s. Harold Joseph and Martha Marcia (Martel) K.;m. Joan Ruth Zoldessy, Apr. 25, 1980; children: Sasha Zoldessy, Amelia Maude, Samuel Aslan. SB, MIT, 1971; MD, Columbia U., 1977. Lic. physician medicine and surgery, N.Y., D.C.; diplomate Am. Bd. Psychiatry and Neurology. Intern dept. medicine Meml. Sloan Ketterin Cancer Ctr., 1977; intern N.Y. Hosp., N.Y.C., 1977-78; resident psychiatry Payne Whitney Psychiat. Clinic, N.Y. Hosp., N.Y.C., 1977-81; sr. staff fellow adult psychiatry br. NIMH, Washington, 1981-85; postdoctoral fellow Lab. Molecular Neurobiology Ctr. Neurobiology and Behavior, Columbia U., N.Y.C., 1986-88; ward adminstr. William A. White divsn. St. Elizabeths Hosp., Washington, 1981-82, attending psychiatrist, 1981-85; attending psychiatrist George Washington U. Hosp., Washington, 1982-85; asst. attending psychiatrist Presbyn. Hosp., N.Y.C., 1986-90, assoc. attending psychiatrist, 1990—; psychiatrist II N.Y. State Psychiat. Inst., N.Y.C., 1986—, head Lab. Molecular Neurobiology, dept. med. genetics, 1988—, sci. dir. Schizophrenia Rsch. Unit, 1989—; guest investigator neuropsychiatry br. NIMH, Washington, 1986—; dir. Diagnostic Ctr. for Schizophrenia Linkage Studies Columbia U., N.Y.C., 1989-97; rsch. asst. Neal E. Miller Lab. Physiol. Psychology, The Rockefeller U., N.Y.C., 1977, guest investigator Mary Jeanne Kreek Lab. Biology of Addictive Diseases, 1979-81, D. Carleton Gajdusek Lab. Ctrl. Nervous Sys. Studies, Nat. Inst. Neurol. and Communicative Disorders and Stroke, Bethesda, Md., 1982-85; vis. assoc. physician Rockefeller U. Hosp., N.Y.C., 1981; instr. clin. psychiatry Cornell U. Med. Coll., N.Y.C., 1980-81; asst. clin. prof. psychiatry and behavioral scis. George Washington U., Washington, 1982-85; asst. prof. clin. psychiatry Columbia U., N.Y.C., 1986-90, assoc. prof., 1990—; vis. lectr. Cornell U. Med. Coll., N.Y.C., 1992—; examiner Am. Bd. Psychiatry and Neurology, 1985—; pvt. practice psychiatry Columbia Presbyn. Med. Ctr., N.Y.C., 1986—; spl. reviewer psychopathology and clin. biology rsch. rev. com. NIMH, Washington, 1987—; spl. reviewer Ont. Mental Health Found., 1992—; mem. epidemiology and genetics rev. com. NIMH, 1992-96; mem. residency selection com. dept. psychiatry Columbia U., N.Y.C., 1994—, qualifying examiner dept. genetics and devel., 1995; mem. mental health task force Coalition for the Homeless, Washington, 1982-85, chair, 1982-83; mem. Task Froce on Homeless Mentally Ill, Am. Psychiat. Assn., 1983-84; cons. Sarah House Women's Shelter, Washington, 1983-85; mem. Working Group on Mental Health Svcs. to Homeless, D.C. Mental Health Sys. Reorgn. Project, Washington, 1985. Mem. editl. bd. Schizophrenia Bull.; editor: (with others) The American Psychiatric Press Review of Psychiatry Volume 9, 1990, Schizophrenia: New Directions for Clnical Research and Treatment, 1996; contbr. articles to profl. jours., chpts. to book. MIT nat. scholar, Cambridge, 1967; recipient Physician Scientist award NIMH, 1987-92, Judith Silver Meml. Young Scientist award Nat. Alliance for Mentally Ill, 1990, Scientist Devel. award NIMH, 1992-97, Disting. Investigator award NARSAD, 1997; grantee NIMH, 1989—, G. Harold and Leila Y. Mathers Charitable Trust, 1994-96, Scottish Rite Schizophrenia Rsch. Program, 1995-97, NARSAD, 1997-98. Fellow Am. Psychiat. Assn. (Falk fellow 1979-81), Am. Psychopath. Assn., N.Y. Acad. Medicine; mem. AAAS, Soc. Biol. Psychiatry (membership com. 1993), Am. Soc. Clin. Psychopharmacology, Am. Soc. Human Genetics, Assn. Rsch. in Nervous and Mental Disease, Internat. Brain Rsch. Orgn., Internat. Soc. Psychiat. Genetics, N.Y. Acad. Scis., Physicians for Social Responsibility, Soc. Neurosci., Psychiat. Soc. Westchester County, Phi Beta Kappa, Sigma Xi, Alpha Omega Alpha. Jewish. Avocations: hiking, sea kayaking. Office: NY State Psychiat Inst 1051 Riverside Dr New York NY 10032-1013

KAUFMANN, HENRY MARK, mortgage banker; b. Basel, Switzerland, May 23, 1929; came to U.S. 1940; s. Ferdinand and Carola (Levy) K.; m. Barbara Lurie, Dec. 23, 1961; children: Frederic, Nancy. Student, Univ. Geneva, Switzerland, 1948; BA in Economics, Oberlin Coll., 1951; JD, Harvard U., 1954. Bar: N.Y. 1957, U.S. Ct. Appeals 1960, U.S. Supreme Ct. 1960, U.S. Tax Ct. 1974. V.p. Pearce Mayer & Greer, N.Y.C., 1958-70, I.F.C. Capital Resources, N.Y.C., 1970-75, Smith Barney Real Estate Corp., N.Y.C., 1975-80; pres., chmn. Henry Kaufmann Assocs., Larchmont, N.Y., 1980—. With Mil. Intelligence Europe 1955-57. Mem. New Rochelle Bar Assn., N.Y. Bar Assn., New York County Lawyers Assn., Harvard Club. Avocations: numismatist, world travel. Home: 64 Greentree Dr Scarsdale NY 10583-7029 Office: Henry Kaufmann Assocs 2 East Ave Larchmont NY 10538-2462

KAUFMANN, MARK STEINER, banker; b. N.Y.C., Dec. 3, 1932; s. Milton L. and Elsa S. (Steiner) K.; m. Carole Richard, June 16, 1957; children: Jon Richard, Susan Helen. BS cum laude in Bus. Adminstrn., Lehigh U., 1953. V.p., dir. mktg. Standard Fin. Corp., N.Y.C., 1958-64; sr. v.p., dir. Milberg Factors, Inc., N.Y.C., 1964-73; dir. corp. devel. Chase Manhattan Bank, N.Y.C., 1973-87, sr. v.p., 1987-96; chmn. Kaufman & Ptnrs., LLC, N.Y.C., 1996—; chmn. banking div. UJA/Fedn.; chmn. bd. dirs. Industry Leaders Fund. Hon. trustee Calhoun Sch., N.Y.C.; hon. dir. Lower Manhattan Cultural Coun.; chmn. bd. Temple Israel, N.Y.C.; mem. bus. adv. coun. Lehigh U. Served as 1st lt. USAF, 1953-55. Recipient human rels. award Anti-Defamation League, 1973, Am. Jewish Com., 1987. Mem. Harmonie Club, Old Oaks Country Club, Beta Gamma Sigma, Lambda Mu Sigma, Pi Gamma Mu, Omicron Delta Kappa. E-mail: mskaufmann@aol.com. Home: 124 W 79th St New York NY 10024-6446 Office: Kaufmann and Ptnrs LLC 712 5th Ave 22d Fl New York NY 10019-4108

KAUFMANN, STEFAN HUGO ERNST, immunologist; b. Ludwigshafen, Germany, June 8, 1948; s. Otto and Annelore (Niemeyer) K.; m. Elke Pamp, Dec. 18, 1980; children: Moritz, Felix. Diploma in Biology, U. Mainz, Germany, 1973, PhD, 1977; Habilitation, U. Berlin, 1981. Sci. asst. U. Bochum, Germany, 1976-78; asst. prof. U. Berlin, 1978-81, docent, 1981-87; staff scientist Max-Planck Inst., Freiburg, Germany, 1982-87; prof. U. Ulm, Germany, 1987-91, full prof. and chair dept. immunology, 1991-98, chair Collaborative Rsch. Ctr., 1992-97; dir. Max-Planck Inst., Berlin, 1993—; advisor German Rsch. Soc., Bonn, 1992-99, WHO, Geneva, 1992-95; E. Neter Meml. lectr. ASM, 1996. Editl. bd. more than 20 sci. jours.; contbr. over 300 sci. articles to jours. Recipient Pettenkofer prize City of Munich, 1992, Aronson prize State of Berlin, 1988, Krupp Found. prize, 1987, Smith Kline Beecham prize, 1991, Sasse prize, 1981, Merckle prize, 1991, Pfleger prize, 1992. Mem. European Fedn. Immunol. Socs. (sec.-gen. 1992-95), German Soc. Med. Microbiology and Hygiene (Ann. award 1983, 93), German Soc. Immunology (mem. sci. bd. dirs. 1999—), Am. Acad. Microbiology, Am. Soc. Microbiology, Berlin-Brandenburg Acad. Sci. Office: Max-Planck Inst Infect Biol, Schumann Strasse 21/22, 10117 Berlin Germany

KAUFMANN, SYLVIA, economics educator, researcher; b. Sion, Valais, Switzerland, Nov. 14, 1965; d. Hansruedi and Maria Magdalena (Popp) K.; lifetime companion Stefan Gmünder; children: Jeanne, Julie. Lic. in polit. econs., U. Berne, Switzerland, 1990, D Polit. econs., 1993. Asst. rschr. U. Berne, 1990-93; asst. prof. econs. U. Vienna, Austria, 1994—; cons., Austria, 1995—. Author: Permanent Components in Swiss Macroeconomic Variables, 1994. Office: U Vienna Dept Econs, Hohenstaufengasse 9, 1010 Vienna Austria

KAUHANEN, JUSSI HEIKKI, physician; b. Kuopio, Finland, July 23, 1958; s. Juho Olavi and Aino (Laatunen) K.; m. Paula M. Suominen, Mar. 7, 1980; children: Okko, Otso, Sofia. MD, U. Kuopio, Finland, 1986, PhD, 1993, MPH, 1995. Physician Ea. Finland, 1986-88; rsch. assoc., lectr. U. Kuopio, 1988-91, 97-98; sr. rsch. scientist The Acad. of Finland, 1992—; physician chief Kuopio Occupl. Rehab. Clinic, Finland, 1996-98; vis. scholar/vis. rsch. scientist U. Calif., Berkeley, 1991-93; lectr. pub. health and epidemiology various schs. in Finland, 1988—. Author: (textbook) Public Health, 1998; contbr. articles to profl. jours. Mem. city coun., City of Kuopio, 1989—, bd. dirs., 1995-96, 2000; mem. Coun. of Social and Health Affairs, Kuopio, 1997-99. 2d lt. Finnish Def. Forces, 1978-79. Mem. Soc. of Behavioral Medicine, Finnish Med. Assn., Soc. Epidemiologic Rsch. Mem. Green Party. Greek Orthodox. Avocations: writing, hiking, music. E-mail: jussi.kauhanen@uku.fi. Office: U Kuopio/Dept Pub Health, PO Box 1627, 70211 Kuopio Finland

KAUKINEN, LIISA MARJATTA, anesthesiologist, educator; b. Pori, Finland, Apr. 4, 1941; d. Uuno Edvard and Lahja Raakel (Mäkelä) Mäkinen; m. Seppo Antero Kaukinen, Dec. 14, 1969; 1 child, Ulla. MD, U. Turku, Finland, 1967; D Med, U. Tampere, Finland, 1985. Staff anesthesiologist Kuopio (Finland) U. Hosp., 1974-75; staff anesthesiologist dept. anesthesiology intensive care Tampere U. Hosp., 1975-85, asst. chief dept. anesthesiology intensive care, 1985—; assoc. prof. faculty medicine U. Tampere, 1985—. Contbr. articles to profl. publs. Mem. Soc. Cardiovascular Anesthesiologists, Scandinavian Soc. Anesthesiologists. Avocation: skiing. Home: Inkerink 14, FIN33730 Tampere Finland Office: Tampere U Hosp Dept, Anesthesia & Intensive Care, FIN33521 Tampere Finland

KAUKINEN, SEPPO ANTERO, anesthesiologist, educator; b. Viipuri, Finland, Feb. 16, 1939; s. Eino and Marja-Liisa (Riikonen) K.; m. Liisa Marjatta Mäkinen, Dec. 14, 1969; 1 child, Ulla. MD, U. Helsinki, 1966; DMed, U. Tampere, Finland, 1979. Staff anesthesiologist Kuopio (Finland) U. Hosp., 1974-75; staff anesthesiologist intensive care Tampere U. Hosp., 1975-84, asst. chief anesthesiology intensive care, 1984-87, chmn. dept. anesthesiology intensive care, 1987—; assoc. prof. medicine U. Tampere, 1981—; vis. prof. anesthesiology Sun Yat-Sen U. Med. Scis., Guangzhou, China, 1999—. Contbr. articles to profl. jours. Mem. European Assn. of Cardiothoracic Anaesthesiologists, Soc. of Cardiovascular Anesthesiologists, Anesthesia Rsch. Soc., Scandinavian Soc. of Anesthesiologists. Avocations: alpine skiing, orienteering, fishing. Home: Inkerinkatu 14, 33730 Tampere Finland

Office: Dept Anes Intensive Care, Tampere Univ Hosp POB 2000, 33521 Tampere Finland

KAUL, CHAMAN LAL, science administrator; b. Srinagar, India, Oct. 10, 1936; s. Dinanath and Dhanwati Kaul; m. Krishna Bujoo, Nov. 6, 1959; children: Anuradha, Adarsh. BSc, Panjab U., Amritsar, India, 1956; B. Pharm., Gujarat U., Ahmedabad, India, 1959; PhD, Glasgow (U.K.) U., 1964. Postdoctoral fellow Glasgow U., 1964; rsch. scientist CIBA-GEIGY, Bombay, 1965-77, group leader, 1977-79; rsch. mgr. Boots Pharms., Bombay, 1979-84, dir. rsch., 1984-87, dir. R&D, 1987-94; dir. NIPER, Sas Nagar, India, 1994—; mem. governing bd. Punjab Health Corp., Chandigarh, India, 1995—. Editor Indian Jour. Pharm. Scis., 1990-96; contbr. articles to profl. jours. Recipient award Indian Pharmacol. Soc., Jammu, 1998. Mem. Indian Pharm. Assn. (pres. 1994-96). Avocations: reading, music, photography. Home and Office: NIPER, Phase X, Sas Nagar Punjab 160062, India

KAUL, DEEPAK, biomedical scientist, educator; b. Srinagar, India, May 21, 1953; s. Shambunath and Sarla Kaul; m. Usha Jalali, Aug. 13, 1982; 1 child, Gargi. BSc, Jammu & Kashmir U., Srinagar, 1972; MSc, Indian Inst. Tech. Kharagpur, Calcutta, India, 1974; PhD, All India Inst. Med. Scis., New Delhi, 1978. Sr. rsch. fellow Indian Coun. Med. Rsch., New Delhi, 1975-78; tutor All India Inst. Med. Scis., New Delhi, 1978-81; rsch. assoc. WHO, India, 1981-83; lectr., asst. prof. Postgrad. Inst. Med. Edn. and Rsch., Chandigarh, India, 1983-92; assoc. prof. Postgrad. Inst. Med. Edn. and Rsch., Chandigarh, 1992-94, prof., 1994—; pres. Indian Soc. Atherosclerosis Rsch., 1996-98; chmn. Leukemia Rsch. Found., India, 1998—. Contbr. articles to profl. jours. Fellow Internat. Coll. Angiology; mem. Assn. for Promotion of DNA Figure Pointing and Tech. (life), Biotechnol. Soc. India (life), Internat. Atherosclerosis Soc. (life). Avocations: poetry, philosophy. Home: H No 1153 Sector 24B, Chandigarh 160023, India Office: Postgrad Inst Med Edn Rsch, Sector 12, Chandigarh 160012, India

KAUL, DHANANJAYA KUMAR, physiologist; b. Etawah, India, July 23, 1943; came to U.S., 1974; s. Gopal K. and Kamla (Devi) K. MS, Agra U., Nainital, India, 1963; PhD, Rajasthan U., Jaipur, India, 1969. Lectr. Rajasihan U., Jaipur, 1966-74; staff assoc. Columbia U., N.Y.C., 1974-77; assoc. Albert Einstein Coll. Medicine, Bronx, N.Y., 1978-81, asst. prof. medicine, 1981-88, assoc. prof., 1988-94, prof., 1994—. Fellow WHO, Lyon, France, 1974; rsch. grantee Am. Heart Assn., 1986-93, NIH, Bethesda, Md., 1990—. Mem. Am. Soc. Hematology, Microcirculatory Soc. USA, N.Am. Soc. Biorheologists. Achievements include elucidation of microcirculatory and hemodynamic behavior of pathologic human red cells in situ and ex vivo microvascular preparations; mechanisms of cell adhesion and vascular obstruction in cerebral malaria and sickle cell anemia. Office: Albert Einstein Coll Med Dept Medicine Rm U-917 1300 Morris Park Ave Bronx NY 10461-1926

KAUL, PRAN NATH, veterinarian; b. Srinagar, Kashmir, India, Mar. 1, 1942; s. Janki Nath and Janak Rani (Hastu) K.; m. Manorma Sharma, Feb. 16, 1968; 1 child, Aarti. BS, U. Jammu & Kashmir, India, 1960; BVSc and AH, Punjab Agrl. U., India, 1964; MS, Punjab Agrl. U., 1967, PhD, 1970. Registered vet. Tchg. asst. Punjab Agr. U., India, 1964-67, lectr. in ext., 1967, asst. prof. ext. edn., 1969-70; scientist S-2, agr. ext. Indian Vet. Rsch. Inst., India, 1970-78; scientist S-3 Cen. Inst. of Fisheries Tech., India, 1978-86, Cen. Inst. for Rsch. on Goats, India, 1986-89; prin. scientist Ind. Vet. Rsch. Inst., India, 1989—. Contbg. author: Research in Extension Education, 1970, Studies in Extension Education, 1972, Women in Agriculture: Their Status and Role, Vol. 1, 1991, Advances in Veterinary Research and Their Impact on Animal Health and Production, 1994; contbr. articles to profl. jours. Recipient award Nat. Seminar on Vet. Edn., Haryana Agr. U., India. Mem. Indian Soc. Ext. Edn., Indian Assn. Advancement of Vet. Rsch., Bharatiya Manovigyan Parishad. Hindu. Avocation: instrumental music (Sitar). Office: Divsn Ext Edn, Indian Vet Rsch Inst, Izatnagar Bareilly 243122, India

KAUL, VICTOR, veterinarian, researcher; b. Srinagar, India, Feb. 3, 1959; s. Pushker Nath and Raj Dulari Kaul; m. Rita Ganjoo, Jul. 5, 1987; children: Vishesh, Vaibhav. BVSc, AH, Ranchi Vet. Coll., Ranchi, India, 1982; MSc in animal biotech., Nat. Dairy Rsch. Inst., Karnal, India, 1992. Vet. asst. surgeon Animal Husbandry Dept, India, 1982-87; rsch. asst. Biological Products Inst., Kashmir, India, 1987-90; scholar Biotechnology Divsn. Regional Rsch. Lab., Jammu, India, 1994-99. Contbr. articles to profl. jours. Recipient Dir. Gold medal Nat. Dairy Rsch. Inst., 1990-91. Mem. N.Y. Acad. Scis., Assn. Microbiologists of India, J&K Vet. Doctors Assn., Nat. Geog. Soc. USA. Hindu. Avocations: painting, sports, music. Home: Behind 159 Jawahar Nagar, Talab Tillo, 180 002 Jammu India Office: Dir of Animal Husbandry, Gole Pully Talab Tillo, 180 002 Jammu India

KAULAKYS, BRONISLOVAS, physicist, researcher; b. Kupiskis, Lithuania, Nov. 12, 1951; s. Povilas and Ona (Zulonaite) K.; m. Laima Gailiute, July 8, 1978; children: Tomas, Mantas. Degree, Vilnius (Lithuania) U., 1974; cert. engring. physicist, Moscow Inst. Physics and Tech., 1977; PhD, Vilnius (Lithuania) U., 1980; DSc, Inst. Theoretical Physics AND Astronomy, Vilnius, 1994. Jr. rschr. Lithuania Acad. Scis., Vilnius, 1977-84, sr. rschr., 1977-94; prof. Vilnius U., 1996—; head dept. Inst. Theoretical Physics and Astronomy, 1990—, coun. chmn., 1992—; expert Sci. Coun. Lithuania, 1999—. V.p. Lithuanian Edn. and Sci. Instn., 1994-97, pres., 1997—. Home: Taikos 239-20, 2017 Vilnius Lithuania Office: Inst Theoretical Physics & Astronomy, Gostauto 12, 2600 Vilnius Lithuania

KAUP, ENN, limnologist, researcher; b. Võrnu, Virumaa, Estonia, May 22, 1946; s. Bruno and Alvine (Kreisman) K.; m. Raili Seping, Apr. 28, 1973; 1 child, Pille-Riin. BSc in Physics of Atmosphere, Tartu U., Estonia, 1969, PhD in Biology, 1981. Engr. Tallinn Tech. U., Estonia, 1969-72, Soviet Antarctic Expdn., 1972-73; engr., jr. and sr. rsch. assoc. Inst. Thermophysics and Electrophysics, Tallinn, 1973-84; sr. rsch. assoc. Tallinn Bot. Garden, 1984-93, Inst. of Geology, Estonia, 1993—; guest rschr. Uppsala (Sweden) U., 1992-95; hon. vis. fellow U. NSW, Canberra, Australia, 1993-94; rsch. assoc. Soviet Antarctic Expdns., 1976-77, 83-84, 86-87, 88-89, Australian Nat. Antarctic Rsch. Expdns., 1993-94, 97-98; vis. prof. Nat. Inst. Polar Rsch., Tokyo, 2000; limnologist, cons. Estonian Ministry Environment, U.S. AID, 1994-95; mem. steering com. BIOTAS, 1996-98. Editor, author: Polar Letters, 1992; author monographs and articles. Bd. dirs. Estonian Polar Found., Tallinn, 1997—; mem. Estonian Popular Front, Tallinn, 1988-90. Mem. Internat. Assn. Theoretical and Applied Limnology, N.Y. Acad. Scis., Estonian Polar Club (pres. 1991—). Avocations: popularization of science, foreign languages, amateur cross-country skiing. Office: Tallinn Tech U, Inst Geology 7 Estonia Ave, 10143 Tallinn Estonia

KAUPUŽS, JEVGENIJS, physicist, researcher; b. Ludzas, Latvia, Dec. 24, 1960; s. Daniels and Anna Kaupužs. Physicist, Latvian State U., 1984; M in Physics, Latvia U., 1994, D of Physics, 1995. Engr. Latvia Acad. Scis., Riga, 1984-91; rschr. Riga Tech. U., 1991-96, Latvia U., Riga, 1997—. Contbr. articles to profl. jours. Avocations: orientation sport, bicycling. Home: Miera str 16/7-410, LV 2169 Salaspils Latvia Office: Univ Latvia Inst Math, U Latvia Inst Math, Rainja Blvd 29, LV 1459 Riga Latvia

KAUR, JASJEET, chemistry educator; b. Meerut, India, Nov. 19, 1964; d. Gurcharan S. and Gurnam K.; m. Gurvinder Singh Sodhi; children: Kirandeep Sodhi, Harjas Sodhi. BS, Meerut U., India, 1984, MS, 1986; PhD, Punjabi U., Patiala, India, 1992. Project asst. Defense Rsch. Devel. Orgn., New Delhi, 1988-91; rsch. assoc. Coun. Scientific &Indsl. Rsch., New Delhi, 1995-98; lectr. Coll. Applied Scis. for Women, Delhi, India, 1996—; prin. investigator Scheme for Young Scientists, Dept. Scis. Tech., New Delhi. Patentee in field. Sr. rsch. fellow Coun. Scientific & Indsl. Rsch., 1991-94. Mem. Indian Sci. Congress Assn. (Young Scientist award 1997), Indian Acad. Forensic Scis. Avocations: reading, painting, gardening. Home: 38 Jagriti Enclave, I P Extension II, 110 092 Delhi India Office: Coll Applied Scis Women, Jhilmil Colony Vivek Vihar, 110 095 Delhi India

KAURA, SUSHIL KUMAR, physicist; b. Ambala, Indai, Mar. 7, 1952; s. Hari Kishan and Staya (Wati) K.; m. Nimrta Chhabra, Sept. 19, 1985; children: Amit, Anuj. BS with honors in Physics, Punjabi U., India, 1971; MS in Physics, Punjabi U., 1973; M in Tech., Indian Inst. Tech., 1975. Scientist Cen. Scientific Instruments Orgn., Chandgarh, India, 1976—. Recipient fellowship German Acad. Exchange Svc., 1982-83, Govt. India, New Delhi, 1978. Fellow (life) IETE, OSI, CSI, IPA. Avocations: driving, movies, sight seeing. Home: House No 2815 Sector 22-C, 160022 Chandigarh India Office: Cen Scientific Instruments, COS, SCIO Sector 30, Chandigarh 160020, India

KAUS, EBERHARD JOSEF ERWIN, secondary school educator; b. Frankfurt, Germany, Sept. 17, 1956; s. Helmut Friedrich Wilhelm and Josefine Gertrud (Hey) K. Aux. in letters Inst. of Classical Philology, Giessen, 1979-82; student tchr. Landgraf-Ludwig Secondary Sch., Giessen, 1982-84; tchr., master Hoelty-Gymnasium, Wunstorf, Germany, 1984—; chmn. of Latin group Hoelty-Gymnasium, Wunstorf, Germany, 1997. Translator Polykarp Leyser, Geschichte der Grafen von Wunstorf, 2000; contbr. articles to profl. jours. Mem. German Philologists Assn., German Assn. of Classical Philologists. Roman Catholic. Fax: 05031-71864. Home: Am Bruche 2, D-31515 Wunstorf Germany

KAUSHAL, JAGDISH MITRA, editor-in-chief; b. Dasuya, Punjab, India, Aug. 29, 1932; Immigrated to U.K., 1966.; s. Perma Nand and Khem Kaur (Sharma) Pandit; m. Shobha Rani Subhash Sharma, Apr. 16, 1962; children: Balram, Krishan, Amardeep, Neelam. BA, DAV Coll., Jalandhar, 1953; ABMS, Benaras Hindu U., 1959. Prof. DAV Coll., Jalandhar, 1960-64; editor Amar Deep Hindi Weekly, London, 1971—; pres. 4th Tulsi Ramayan Centenary Celebration, 1974; sec. Hindi Sahitya-Sahha U.K., 1968-84; pres. Hindi Kendra U.K., 1984-96. Author: (book) United We Stand-Asians in Britain, 1979; editor Punjabi Darpan U., 1985-93. Sec.-gen. Anglo Asian Soc., 1980. Recipient Pulic Work award Vishwa Hindu Kendra, 1995, Cmty. Svc. award Overseas Congress U.K., 1996. Mem. Internat. Soc. Krishna Consiousness (hon. life). Avocations: swimming, gardening, meditation. Home: 2 Chepstow Rd-Hanwell, W72BG London England Office: 36 Trent Ave, W56TL London England

KAUSHAL, RADHEY SHYAM, theoretical physicist, researcher; b. Aligarh, India, June 30, 1944; s. Khem Karan and Ram Devi Kaushal; m. Shashi Rajoria, June 26, 1972; children: Shraddha, Medha, Mukta, Govind. BSc, Agra (India) U., 1963; MSc, Aligarh Muslim U., 1965; PhD in Physics, Indian Inst. Tech., Kanpur, 1970; PhD in Philosophy, Delhi U., 2000. Lectr. Ramjas Coll., Delhi, 1971-82; lectr. reader grade Ramjas Coll., 1983-85, reader, 1986-88; rsch. scientist dept. physics and astrophysics Delhi U., 1988—; Av. H. fellow U. Kaiserslautern, Germany, 1978-80, vis. fellow, 1984; del. conf. ICTP, Trieste, Italy, 1979, 84, 93, IOP, Birmingham, Eng., 1979, Asia Pacific Conf., Seoul, Republic of Korea, 1990, 4th Internat. Wigner Symposium, Guadalajara, Mex., 1995, 13th Internat. Cong. Math. Physics, London, 2000, EPS HEP Conf., Brussels, 1995, others; visitor European Ctr. Nuc. Rsch. (CERN), Geneva, Switzerland, 1979, 91. Author: The Philosophy of the Vedanta: A Modern Scientific Perspective, 1994, Classical and Quantum Mechanics of Noncentral Potentials: A Survey of Two Dimensional Systems, 1998; co-author: Advanced Methods of Mathematical Physics, 2000; contbr. numerous articles to profl. jours. Mem. Indian Physics Assn. (life), Soc. for Sci. Values (life), Internat. Assn. Math. Physics, N.Y. Acad. Scis., Nat. Acad. Sci. (India) (life). Office: Dept Physics and Astrophys, U Delhi, Delhi 110007, India

KAUSHIK, RAJIV, information systems specialist, consultant; b. Nangal, Punjab, India, Sept. 30, 1959; arrived in N.Z., 1987; s. Amrit Lal and Renu (Sharma) K.; m. Ashla Cecilia Lochan, May 30, 1987; children: Rahul Amrit, Meera Ambika. MSc in Physics, Bangalore (India) U., 1983; PhD, Indian Inst. Tech., Madras, 1988; diploma in bus., Auckland (N.Z.) U., 1992. Electronics engr. Lucas Industries, Auckland, 1987-89; mgr. product devel. Yuasa Batteries, Auckland, 1989-92; dir. mktg. Amren Bus. Sys., Auckland, 1992-93; tech. dir. Propad 2000 Ltd., Auckland, 1993-94, mng. dir., 1994-96; contract mgr. Andrews Ptnrs., Auckland, 1996-97; gen. mgr. Newcall Comms. Ltd., Auckland, 1997—; mng. dir. Mgmt. Info. Sys. and Tech., Auckland, 1992-94. Author (software) Perfect Practice, 1989-94; inventor rechargable thin film solid state battery; contbr. articles to profl. publs. Intrepreter Ministry Immigration, Auckland, 1987—, Dept. Justice, Auckland, 1987—. Mem. N.Z. Software Exporters Assn., Planetary Soc. Labour Party. Hindu. Avocations: reading, guitar, writing software, mountaineering, sky diving. Home: 308 Hillsborough Rd, Hillsborough Auckland New Zealand Office: Online Software Ltd, PO Box 24307, Royal Oak Auckland New Zealand

KAUSIKAN, BILAHARI, Singapore government official. Singapore rep. to UN, N.Y.C.; dep. sec. for S.E. Asia, Singapore Ministry Fgn. Affairs, 1998—. Office: 07-00 Raffles City Tower, 250 N Bridge Rd, Singapore 179101, Singapore*

KAUSTOVÁ, JARMILA, microbiologist; b. Vsetin, Czech Republic, Mar. 8, 1945; d. Leopold and Vlasta (Pščolková) Hrazdil; m. Boleslav Kausta, Apr. 9, 1966; 1 child, Peter. MD, Charles U., Prague, Czech Republic, 1969, postgrad. 1st grade med. sch., 1972, postgrad. 2d grade med. sch., 1975. Head dept. diagnostics of mycobacteria Regional Inst. Hygiene, Ostrava, Czech Republic, 1976—, head Nat. Reference Lab. for M. Kansasii, 1986—, head microbiol. divsn., 1986-91, regional specialist in microbiology for North Moravia, 1987-90. Co-author: Czechoslovac Standard Methods in Microbiology of Tuberculosis and Leprosy, 1975, 80, 90, 98; Czechoslovac Informative System of Bacillary Tuberculosis, 1980. Recipient grants Ministry Health Czech Republic, 1986-90, 93-95. Mem. N.Y. Acad. Scis., Czech Soc. Epidemiology and Microbiology, Czech Med. Soc. of J.E. Purkyne, Czech Soc. Pneumology and Physiology (head com. 1987—). Office: Regional Inst Hygiene, Partyzanske Namesti 7, 728 92 Ostrava N Morav, Czech Republic

KAUTMAN, FRANTIŠEK, library historian, writer; b. České Budějovice, Czech Republic, Jan. 8, 1927; s. František and Stanislava (Skálová) K.; m. Zina Liňkovová, July 2, 1955; 1 child, František. PhD, Inst. of Lit., Moscow, 1956. Editor-in-chief Československy Spisovatel, Prague, Czechoslovakia, 1949-52; editor Kultura jour., Prague, 1957-58; expert documentalist Encyclopedic Inst. Czechoslovak Acad. Scis., Prague, 1959-61; mem. staff Inst. Czech Lit., Prague, 1961-71; salesman Klenoty, Prague, 1973-74, invalid pensioner, 1974—. Author: The World of Franz Kafka, 1990, Dostoyevski—The Eternal Problem of Mankind, 1992, Backwater, 1992, Hopes and Obstacles of Czech Nationalism, 1992, The Polarity of Our Age in the Works of E. Hostovsky, 1993, On the Typology of Literary Criticism and Literary Science, 1996, How Jack and I Found Freedom, 1996, The Novel for You, 1997. Home: Jabloňová 55, 10600 Prague Czech Republic

KAUTZNER, JOSEF, physician, cardiologist, researcher; b. Vlasim, Czech Republic, Nov. 9, 1957; s. Josef and Miloslava (Jaklova) K.; m. Dana Brozkova, Apr. 11, 1981; children: Jakub, Marketa. MD, Charles U., Prague, 1983, PhD, 1998. Med. diplomate, specialist in internal medicine. Resident Charles U. Gen. Hosp., Prague, 1985-87, fellow in internal medicine, 1987-90, fellow in internal medicine and cardiology, 1990-92; asst. prof. Charles U. Med. Sch., Prague, 1992—; rsch. fellow in cardiology St. George's Hosp. Med. Sch., London, 1994-96; cons. electrophysiologist Inst. for Clin. and Exptl. Medicine, Prague, 1996—. Brit. Coun. Travelling fellow, 1992-93; Tex.-Czech Physicians Exch. Program vis. fellow, Houston, 1993; Wellcome Trust Travelling fellow, London, 1994-96. Fellow European Soc. Cardiology; mem. NASPE, Purkinje Czech Soc. Physicians. Avocations: photography, music, fine arts, squash. Home: Hurbanova 1305, 14200 Prague Czech Republic Office: Inst Clin & Exptl Medicine, Videnska 1958/9, 14021 Prague Czech Republic

KAUZLARICH, RICHARD DALE, ambassador, retired foreign service officer; b. Moline, Ill., Aug. 18, 1944; s. Victor and Eva Marie (Kronfeld) K.; m. Anne Elizabeth Bregstone, Aug. 26, 1967; children—Richard Dale Jr., Terri Lynne. AA, Black Hawk Coll., Moline, Ill., 1964; BA, Valparaiso U., 1966; MA, Ind. U., 1967, U. Mich., 1976. 2d sec. U.S. Embassy, Addis Ababa, Ethiopia, 1973-75; fin. economist Office Devel. Fin. Dept. State, Washington, 1976-77; dep. office dir. Office Investment Affairs Dept. State, Washington, 1977-80; counselor for econ. affairs U.S. Embassy, Tel Aviv, Israel, 1980-83; office dir. ops. ctr. Dept. State, Washington, 1983-84, dep. asst. sec. Internat. Orgn. Affairs, 1984-86, dep. dir. policy planning staff, 1986-89, office dir. Regional Polit.-Econ. Affairs, 1989-91, dep. asst. sec. Bur. European Affairs, 1991-93; prin. dep. to the amb.-at-large and spl. adviser Dept State, S/NIS; U.S. amb. Republic of Azerbaijan, 1994-97, Bosnia and Herzegovina, 1997-99; sr. advisor to undersec. state econ., bus. & agrl. affairs U.S. Dept. State, 1999—. Mem. Am. Internat. Sch. Bd., Tel Aviv, Israel, 1981-83. Recipient Presl. Meritorious Svc. award, 1993, Hall of Fame award Black Hawk Coll. Alumni Assn., 1993, Valparaiso U. Disting. Alumnus award, 1999; named Internat. Person of Yr. Dnevi Avaz, 1997. Lutheran. Home: 7019 Ted Dr Falls Church VA 22042-3943

KAVADIA, KISHORE MURARJI, cement company executive; b. Mandvi, Kutch, India, Apr. 26, 1947; s. Murarji Mavji and Mridula Murarji (Joshi) K.; m. Krupa Kishore Mehta, Mar. 5, 1976; children: Hemali, Nishita. B-Tech in Chem. Engring., Nagpur (India) U., Nagpur, India, 1969; M of Chem. Engring., U. Bombay, 1972; postgrad., Indira Gandhi Nat. Open U., Delhi, 1993—. Mgr. Excel Industries, Ltd., Mumbai, 1972-87; gen. mgr. Bhagwati Assocs., Mumbai, 1987-92; sr. mgr. environment The ACC Ltd., Mumbai, 1992-98, Gujarat Ambuja Cements, Ltd., Mumbai, 1998—; rsch. mgr. C.C. Shroff Rsch. Inst., Mumbai, 1978-80; vis. prof. environment S.B.M. Poly., Mumbai, 1980—, U. Bombay, 1988—. Contbr. articles to profl. jours. U.S. AID fellow, 1995; Ministry of I.T.I. scholar, Yokohama, Japan, 1996. Mem. Indian Inst. Chem. Engrs. (life), Nat. Soc. for Air Pollution Control (life), Mensa. Mem. Hindu Brahmin religion. Avocations: mountaineering, ecology studies, environmental extension, bridge. Home: F-418 Bussa Apts, B M Bhargava Rd, Santacruz Mumbai 400054, India Office: Gujarat Ambuja Cements Ltd, CST Rd Near Vidyanagari, Santacruz, Mumbai 400098, India

KAVALDZHIEV, TODOR, Bulgarian government official. V.p. Govt. of Bulgaria, 1997—. Office: Office of VP, 2 Dondoukov Blvd, 1000 Sofia Bulgaria*

KAVALENKO, KONSTANTIN VASILIEVICH, physicist, researcher; b. Moscow, Apr. 1, 1961; m. Nonna Alexandrovna Kovalenko; children: Anna, Andrei. Diploma engring., Mephi, Moscow, 1984. Engr. Astrophysics, Moscow, 1984-87; physicist Fian Sci., Moscow, 1987-99. Avocations: mountaining, alpinism. Office: PN Lebedev Physics Inst, Leninsky prospect, 53, 117924 Moscow Russia

KAVAN, LADISLAV, chemist, educator; b. Jilemnice, Czech Republic, Aug. 17, 1951; s. Ladislav and Drahomíra (Pertlíčková) K.; m. Jarmila Jašková, June 24, 1977; children: Ladislav, Mojmír. CSc, Charles U., Prague, 1978, teaching qualification, 1992. Rsch. asst. Charles U., 1978-79; scientist J. Heyrovsky Inst., Prague, 1979—, group leader, 1990—, dep. head dept. electrochemistry, 1996—; vis. prof. Swiss Fed. Inst. Tech., Lausanne, 1988. Author: Methods of Electron Spectroscopy, 1986; co-author: Chemistry and Physics of Carbon, vol. 23, 1991, (with J. Koryta and J. Dvorak) Principles of Electrochemistry, 1993; co-editor: Carbyne and Carbyne-like Structures, 1999. Recipient academic award Czechoslovak Acad. of Scis., 1988; rsch. grantee Grant Agy. of the Czech Republic, 1993-2000. Mem. Czech Chem. Soc. (mem. electrochemistry com. 1994—), European Cmty. Commn. for Cooperation in Sci. (mem. mgmt. com. D4/14 1994—, rsch. grantee 1995-2000). Avocation: classical music. Home: Na Slovance 34, CZ-18200 Prague 8, Czech Republic Office: JH Inst Physical Chemistry, Dolejškova 3, CZ182 23 Prague 8, Czech Republic

KAVANAGH, JOHN JOSEPH, medical educator; b. Phila., Aug. 7, 1947; s. John and Christine Kavanagh; m. Teresa Ann Brown. BA, Sch. Internat. Svc., Washington, 1969; MD, Jefferson Med. Coll., 1975. Clin. asst. prof. U. Nebr., Omaha, 1980-81; instr., asst. internist M.D. Anderson Cancer Ctr., Houston, 1981-82; asst. prof., chief sect. gynecologic med. oncology M.D. Anderson Cancer Ctr., 1983-85, assoc. gynecologist, 1987—, assoc. prof., chief sect. gynecologic med. oncology, 1987—; assoc. prof. H. Lee Moffitt Cancer Ctr., Tampa, Fla., 1985-87; assoc. prof. ob-gyn. and reproductive scis. U. Tex. Health Sci. Ctr., Houston, 1991—, prof. dept. clin. investigation, 1996—; cons. S.W. Oncology Group, San Antonio, 1994—; mem. faculty European Sch. Oncology. With USAR, 1969-71. Grantee ASTA Medica, Inc., Hackensack, N.J., 1994, Hoffman-LaRoche, Nutley, N.J., 1994. Fellow ACP, European Soc. Gynecol. Oncology (assoc.); mem. Internat. Gynecologic Cancer soc. (chmn. membership com., exec. com.), So. Oncology Assn. (pres. 1991-92), So. Med. Assn. (Presdl. com. on endowments 1993—), Tex. Soc. Med. Oncology (founding). Avocations: fishing, boating, reading. Office: M D Anderson Cancer Ctr 1515 Holcombe Blvd # 39 Houston TX 77030-4009

KAVANAGH, JOHN JOSEPH, naval officer; b. Cobh, Cork, Ireland, July 22, 1941; s. Dennis Joseph and Norah (Daly) K.; m. Pauline Mary Healy, June 18, 1970; children: Hilary, Michele. Student, Naval Staff Coll., 1974; Master's Degree, Naval Command Coll., 1982. Commd. Irish Naval Svc., 1960—, advanced through grades to commodore, 1993—, flag commanding officer, 1993—; mem. Marine Emergency Adv. Group, Dublin, 1993—. Mem. Nat. Sail Trg. Orgn. (dir. 1993—), Ballina Golf Club, Howth Yacht Club (hon.), Royal St. George Yacht Club (hon.). Roman Catholic. Avocations: golf, reading, gardening.. Office: Naval Hdqrs, Naval Base, Haulbowline Cork, Ireland

KAVANAUGH, KEVIN PATRICK, research analyst, consultant; b. Worcester, Mass., Apr. 29, 1959; s. Roger Patrick and Frances Marie K. BA, Norwich U., 1981; MA, Monterey Inst. English Studies, 1993; PhD, Johns Hopkins U., 1999. Commd. 2nd lt. U.S. Army, 1981, advanced through grades to lt. col., 2000; rsch. scientist Fedn. Am. Scientists, Washington, 1997-99; rsch. analyst Def. Intell Agy., Washington, 1999—; cons. landmine UN, Cambodia, 1999. Mem. Am. Legion, Assn. Old Crows. Democrat. Avocations: black and white photography, SCUBA diving.

KAVISHE, FESTO PATRICK, nutritionist; b. Mkuu-Rombo, Tanzania, May 5, 1951; s. Patrick Lemama and Celina Ali-Maskoi (Swai) K.; m. Mwagombeani Juma, Dec. 18, 1982; children: Patrick, Lulu-Lucy. MD, U. Dar-Es-Salaam (Tanzania), 1978; MSc, U. London, 1982; postgrad. cert., U. Brussels, 1987, U. Lubeck, Germany, 1991. Registered gen. med. practitioner. Dist. med. officer Ministry of Health, Mafinga, Tanzania, 1979-80; head med. nutrition Tanzania Food and Nutrition Ctr., Dar-Es-Slaam, 1980-85, dir. med. nutrition, 1985-89, mng. dir., 1989-93; regional nutrition advisor UNICEF Eastern and Southern Africa Regional Office, Nairobi, Kenya, 1993-96; chief of Cmty. Action for Social Devel. Program UNICEF, Phnom Penh, Cambodia, 1996-99; rep. UNICEF, Asmara, Eritrea, 1999—; bd. dirs., sr. advisor Internat. Coun. Control of Iodine Deficiency Disorders, Adel;aide, Australia, Brussels, 1986-98; rsch. attachment U. Uppsalla, Sweden, 1989-93; cons. WHO, UNICEF, FAO, World Bank, USAID, UN-Adminstrv. Coordinating Com./Sub-Com. on Nutrition, various cities, 1985-93; v.p., bd. dirs. Ctr. Biol. and Oncol. Studies, Lyon, France, 1991-95; rep. Internat. Vitamin A Consultative Group, 1992-93. Contbr. articles to profl. jours. Recipient Med. Assn. Tanzania award, 1978; UN Univ. fellow, 1981. Mem. British Nutrition Soc., UNICEF Staff Assn. (1st dep. chair 1997, chair Cambodia and the East Asia and Pacific region 1999), Am. Inst. Cancer Rsch./World Cancer Rsch. Fund (mem. internat. panel), Opportunities for Micronutrient Intervention (tech. adv. group 1993-99), World Health Policy Forum. Roman Catholic. Avocations: table tennis, basketball, writing, photography, reading. Home: PO Box 621, Dar-Es-Salaam Tanzania Office: UNICEF, PO Box 2004, Asmara Eritrea

KAVSAN, VADIM MOISEEVICH, molecular biologist; b. Donetsk, Ukraine, June 17, 1939; s. Moisey A. Kavsan and Vera P. Kovalenko; m. Alla Rynditch, Mar. 16, 1977; 1 child, Dmitry. MD, Kiev Med. U., 1964; PhD, Inst. Biochemistry Kiev, 1969; DS, Inst. Genetics Moscow, 1985. Rschr. Inst. Microbiology and Virology, Kiev, Ukraine, 1967-73; rschr., head lab. Inst. Molecular Biology and Genetics, Kiev, 1973-83, dept. head Biosynthesis of Nucleic Acids, 1983—; vis. rschr. UCLA, 1990, NIH, Bethesda, Md., 1993, Lineberger Cancer Ctr. U. N.C., Chapel Hill, 1994; vis. prof. U. Canterbury, Christchurch, New Zealand, 1995, Paul Sabatier U., Toulouse, France, 1996-98, Colo. U., Denver, 2000. Inventor in field; editl. bd. mem. Folia Biologica, 1992—, Biopolymers and Cell, 1990—, Cytology and Genetics, 1990—. Recipient Laureate in Sci. and Tech. Coun. Ministers, 1979; grantee Utrecht U., 1994, Johannes Gutenberg U., 1994, Internat. Union Against Cancer, 1994, Internat. Sci. Found., 1994, 95, HUGO, 1995. Mem. AAAS, NAS Ukraine, European Assn. Cancer Rsch., Human Genome Orgn., N.Y. Acad. Scis., Internat. Union Biol. Scis. (reproductive biology in aquaculture program bd.).

KAVUSSANOS, MANOLIS GEORGE, applied shipping economics educator, finance educator, researcher, consultant; b. Rethimno, Crete, Greece, Dec. 2, 1963; arrived in Eng., 1981; s. George Emmanuil Kavussanos and Erofili Ioannis Kourinou; m. Rhoda Triantafillidou, Aug. 24, 1997; children: Dimitra, George. BSc in Econs., U. London, 1986, MSc in Econs., 1987; PhD in Applied Econs., City U., London, 1993. Rschr. City U. Bus. Sch., London, 1987-90, lectr. scale A, Econ. and Social Rsch. tchg. fellow, 1990-93, lectr. in applied econs. scale B, 1993-97, sr. lectr. in applied econs., 1997—; dir. MSc in trade, transport and fin. City U. Bus. Sch., 1997—; apptd. evaluation expert for transp. and shipping by the European Commn. and Cen. Rsch. Agy. of Hong Kong. Contbr. articles to jours. in field; mem. editl. adv. bd. of transp. rsch. (The Logistics and Transportation Review). Mem. Internat. Assn. Maritime Economists, WCTR Soc. Avocations: soccer, travel. E-mail: m.kavussanos@city.ac.uk. Office: City U Bus Sch, Barbican Ctr, London EC2Y 8HB, England

KAWABATA, HIDETAKA, surgeon, oncologist; b. Hojo, Ehime, Japan, Mar. 15, 1963; s. Yutaka and Kyoko (Takahasi) K.; m. Kazuko Yagi, Aug. 8, 1996; 1 child, Rina. MD, U. Tokyo, 1988. Resident Tokyo Univ. Hosp., 1988-89, asst., 1992-98; sr. resident Tokyo Met. Police Hosp., 1990-92; dir. dept. surgery JR Tokyo Gen. Hosp., 1998—. Author: Current Cancer Treatment, 1997, Standard Treatment for Cancer, 1999; contbr. articles to profl. jours. Mem. Japan Surg. Soc., Japanese Breast Cancer Soc. Avocations: golf, baseball. Home: 2-14-15-102, Meguro-ku Tokyo 152-0001, Japan Office: JR Tokyo General Hosp, 2-1-3 Yoyogi, Sibuya-ku Tokyo 151-0053, Japan

KAWABATA, KEISHI, engineering educator; b. Omuta, Fukuoka, Japan, Oct. 31, 1942; s. Shigeo and Shizu Kawabata; m. Yukiko Nakagawa, Nov. 5, 1972; children: Fumie, Eri, Takashi. B in Engring., Hiroshima (Japan) Inst. Tech., 1967, D in Engring., 1994. Asst. Hiroshima (Japan) Inst. Tech., 1967-71, lectr., 1971-81, assoc. prof., 1981-91, prof., 1991—. Contbr. articles to profl. jours. Mem. IEEE, Am. Vacuum Soc., Japan Soc. Applied Physics. Avocations: driving, collecting pipes, photography. Home: 4-2-9 Kuba, Otake Hiroshima 739-0651, Japan Office: Hiroshima Inst Tech, 2-1-1 Miyake Saeki-ku, Hiroshima 731-5193, Japan

KAWABATA, KIYOSHI, astrophysicist, educator; b. Hisai-shi, Mie, Japan, Oct. 27, 1940; s. Sotaroh and Masu (Ubukata) K.; m. Hideko Miyazaki, June 24, 1978; 1 child, Shino. BS, U. Kyoto, 1964, MS, 1966; PhD, Pa. State U., 1973; DSc, U. Kyoto, 1981. Rsch. scientist Columbia U., N.Y.C., 1974; rsch. scientist Goddard Inst. Space Studies NASA, N.Y.C., 1974-82; from assoc. prof. to prof. Sci. U. Tokyo, 1982—, dean Coll. Sci. divsn. II, 1999—. Co-author: Observing the Universe, 1991, Physics Laboratory: Advanced Course, 1991, Physics Laboratory: Basic Course, 1993; contbr. articles to profl. jours. Grantee Fulbright Found., 1967. Mem. Am. Astronomical Soc., Astronomical Soc. Japan, Internat. Astronomical Union. Avocations: drawing, paperfolding, football, baseball, reading. E-mail: kawabata@rs.kagu.sut.ac.jp. Home: #E2-906, Katsuse 3369 Fujimi-shi, Saitama 354-0031, Japan Office: Sci U Tokyo Dept Physics, 1-3 Kagurazaka Shinjuku-ku, 162-8601 Tokyo Japan

KAWABATA, NARIYOSHI, chemistry educator; b. Yokohama, Kanagawa, Japan, July 13, 1935; s. Naotaro and Koyuki (Araki) K.; m. Akiko Usutani, Apr. 15, 1962; children: Etsuko, Haruko Ogawa, Hiromi. B in Engring., Kyoto (Japan) U., 1958, M in Engring., 1960, D in Engring., 1963. Staff asst. Kyoto U., 1963-69; assoc. prof. Kyoto Inst. Tech., 1969-76, prof., 1976-99; prof. U. Shiga Prefecture, 1999—; dir. student affairs office Kyoto Inst. Tech., 1992-94. Active amateur symphony orch. Achievements include functional polymers that capture micro-organisms and viruses alive, control of soil born plant diseases using functional polymer, method for making synthetic polymers biodegradable by partial modification of the chemical structure. Home: 4-5-6 Kitahorie, Nishi-ku Osaka 550-0014, Japan Office: U Shiga Prefecture, Hassako-cho, Hikone Shiga 522-8533, Japan

KAWADA, JANET HANSEN, artist, educator; b. Newton, Mass., June 20, 1953; m. Charles V. Kawada; children: Taylor Hansen, Russell Hansen. AS, Lasell Jr. Coll., Newton, Mass., 1973; BFA, Mass. Coll. Art, 1992; MFA, Vermont Coll., 1998. Studio mgr. Mass. Coll. Art., Boston, 1992—; mem. adj. faculty Mass. Coll. Art, 1996—, New Eng. Sch. Art and Design, Boston, 1997—; dir. Kingston Gallery, Boston, 1999—; tech. dir. Devotion Pub. Sch., Brookline, Mass., 1985-92. Martin Godine fellow Mass. Coll. Art, 1992. E-mail: hansenj@massart.edu. Home: 197 Fuller St Brookline MA 02446-5774

KAWAGOE, KOH, physician; b. Yamaguchi, Japan, May 11, 1947; s. Kenzo and Shizue (Miyana) K.; m. Hiromi Lucia Matsusaka, Apr. 29, 1973; children: Shin, Makiko. MD, U. Tokyo, 1981. Chief of ob-gyn. Ibaragi Prefectural Gen. Hosp., 1981-86; asst. prof. U. Tokyo, 1986-89; med. dir. Life Care System, Tokyo, 1989-94; dir. San-ikukai Gen. Hosp., Tokyo, 1994-2000; rep. of group pallium Tokyo, 2000—. Author: Gynecologic Oncology (Japanese), 1990, Want to Die At Home (Japanese), 1992; editor: Introduction of Home Hospice (Japanese), 1991, For Those Who Begin to Learn Home Hospice Care (Japanese), 1996. Recipient Med. Rsch. award Tokyo Met. Med. Assn., 1996. Mem. Home Hospice Assn. (cons. advisor 1995—). Avocations: travelling, classic music, Japanese chess, fishing. Office: Home Care Clinic Kawagoe, Midori 1-14-4, Sumida 130-0021, Japan

KAWAGUCHI, KAZUKO HIROSE, sociology of international law educator; b. Setagaya, Tokyo, Japan, June 22, 1941; d. Yoshiki and Kikue (Asaba) Hirose; m. Minato Kawaguchi, May 5, 1971 (dec. Sept. 1995); children: Ginga, Mari. BA, U. Tokyo, 1964, MA, 1966, PhD, 1969. Rsch. assoc. U. Tokyo, 1969-71; lectr. sociology of internat. law Sophia U., Tokyo, 1971-75, assoc. prof., 1975-85, prof., 1985—, dir. Inst. Internat. Rels., 1994-96; vis. scholar MIT, Boston, 1982-84, Harvard U., Cambridge, Mass., 1998-99. Author: Disputes and Law, 1970 (Adachi Mineichiro award and Kido Kotaro award 1971), Theory of Sociology of International Law, 1998; contbg. author: Reconstruction of Study of International Law, 1978, Convention on the Elimination of All Forms of Discrimination against Women: A Commentary, 1995; editor, author: New International Studies: Change and Order, 1995. Mem. Japanese Assn. Internat. Law (coun.), Japan Sociol. Soc., World Law Assn. Avocations: piano, social dancing, handicrafts, cooking. Home: 3-30-11 Miyasaka, Setagaya-ku, Tokyo 156-0051, Japan Office: Sophia U Inst Internat Rels, 7-1 Kioi-cho Ciyoda-ku, Tokyo 102-8554, Japan

KAWAHIRA, YOUICHI, cardiovascular surgeon, researcher; b. Hiroshima, Japan, Oct. 29, 1962; s. Hitoshi and Yasuko Kawahira; m. Yuka Nakamura, Apr. 8, 1988; children: Yosuke, Tomomi. MD, Hiroshima U., 1988. Med. lic., Japan. Cardiovasc. surgeon Nat. Cardiovasc. Ctr., Suita, Osaka, Japan. Contbr. articles to profl. jours. Recipient Best Presentation award Japanese Soc. Gastroenterol. Surgery, 1993, 6th World Congress in Ultrasound, 1993. Avocation: golf. E-mail: youichi@x.age.ne.jp and ykawahir@hsp.ncvc.go.jp. Office: Nat Cardiovasc Surgery, 5-7-1 Fujishirodai, Suita Osaka 565, Japan

KAWAI, CHUICHI, medical educator, cardiologist; b. Kyoto, Japan, Mar. 31, 1928; s. Takashi and Yae K.; m. Toshiko Matsumura, Apr. 24, 1959; children: Hiroko, Ken, Junko, Makoto. MD, Kyoto U., Japan, 1953, D of Med. Sci., 1959. Prof. medicine Kyoto (Japan) U., 1974-91, dir., 1989-91, prof. emeritus, 1991—; mem. Sci. Coun. Japan, Tokyo, 1994-97. Author: Textbook of Cardiomyopathy, 1985, Textbook of Cardiology, 1986, (with others) Atlas of the Heart, 1995, Cardiovascular Medicine, 1995. Recipient Japan-U.S. Vis. Med. Scientist Program award Phila. Coll. Physicians, 1987, Med. award Japan Med. Assn., 1993. Mem. Internat. Soc. and Fedn. Cardiology (pres. 1987-88, Asia-Pacific rep. 1995-98), Japanese Circulation Soc. (pres. 1986-87, chief dir. 1988-94). Office: Goshomae Sky-Mansion Rm 503, 419 Kusuriyacho Ichijo-sagaru, Muromachi-dori Kamikyo-ku Kyoto 602-0918, Japan

KAWAI, JUN, chemist, educator; b. Gifu, Japan, Dec. 14, 1957; s. Saburo and Kaoru (Fujiwara) K. D of Engring., U. Tokyo, 1989. Rsch. asst. U. Tokyo, 1986-89; spl. rschr. RIKEN, Wako, Japan, 1989-93; rsch. assoc. Kyoto (Japan) U., 1993-94, assoc. prof., 1994—. Author: Instrumentation Chemistry, 1997; editor: Advances in Quantum Chemistry Vol. 29, 1997. Mem. Japan Soc. for Analytical Chemistry. Office: Kyoto U Dept Materials Sci & Engring, Sakyo-ku, Kyoto 606-8501, Japan

KAWAI, KOICHI, endocrinologist; b. Maebashi, Gumma-ken, Japan, Feb. 22, 1943; s. Toshihiko and Reiko (Umeyama) K.; s. Kazuko Aoyama, Mar. 20, 1971 (dec. Mar. 1985); children: Makiko, Masako; m. Noriko Matsuhashi, Mar. 31, 1988; 1 child, Tomoko. MD, Tokyo Med. Dental U., 1968, PhD, 1973. Rsch. assoc. of biochemistry Tokyo Med. Dental U., 1973-74, clin. fellow, 1974-76; clin. fellow Tokyo Women's Med. Coll., 1976-77; asst. prof. medicine Inst. of Clin. Medicine, U. Tsukuba, Japan, 1977-95; dir. Tsukuba Diabetes Ctr. Kawai Clinic, 1996—. Contbr. articles to profl. jours. Mem. Japan Diabetes Soc. (coun.), Japan Endocrine Soc. (coun.), Am. Diabetes Assn., Am. Endocrine Soc., European Assn. for Study of Diabetes. Avocations: golf, skiing, soccer, arts. Fax: 0298-54-1883. Home: Namiki 3-22-14, Tsukuba Ibaraki 305-0044, Japan Office: Tsukuba Diabetes Ctr Kawai Clinic, Higashi-Hiratsuka 715-1, Tsukuba Ibaraki 305-0812, Japan

KAWAI, MASAO, chemistry educator; b. Hirakata, Osaka, Japan, Sept. 6, 1942; s. Kenjiro Shima and Shizue Kawai; m. Mitoko Hirai, Sept. 12, 1942; children: Kumi, Kiyohiko. B, Kyoto (Japan) U., 1965, M Engring., 1967, D Engring., 1970. Instr. Kwansei-Gakuin U., Nishinomiya, Japan, 1970-72; rschr. Mitsubishi-Kasei Inst. Life Scis., Machida, Japan, 1972-83; assoc. prof. Nagoya (Japan) Inst. Tech., 1983-89, prof. chemistry, 1989—. Mem. Chem. Soc. Japan. Avocations: amateur magician, jogging. Office: Nagoya Inst Tech, Gokiso-cho Showa-ku, Nagoya 466-8555, Japan

KAWAI, TOKUHARU, philosophy educator; b. Osaka, Japan, Jan. 17, 1935; s. Shozo and Hisako Maki; m. Tatsumi Kitabayashi, May 25, 1966; children: Harumi Matsushita, Mariko. BA, Osaka U., 1960, MA, 1962; postgrad., U. Heidelberg, Germany, 1975-76; PhD habilitated, Tsukuba U., Ibaragi, Japan, 1993. Lectr. philosophy Osaka Sangyo U., 1967-70, asst. prof., 1970-77, prof., 1977—, curator libr., 1970, 96—, dean liberal arts, 1986-88; lectr. Osaka U., 1969-89, Nara (Japan) Women's U., 1989-98, Kobe Coll., 1995—. Author: Understanding Philosophy, 1980, A Study of Spinoza's Philosophy, 1994; translator numerous German works of Georg Picht and C.F. von Weizsäcker into Japanese. Mem. Philos. Assn. Japan (mem. editl. com. 1997—), Kansai Philos. Assn., Kansai Ethical Soc. (com. 1985-87, 89-93, 95—), Spinoza Soc. Japan (com. 1995—). Avocation: listening to classical music. Home: 99 Akaiyama, Takata, Kamo-cho 619 1144, Japan

KAWAI, YASUHITO, engineering educator; b. Osaka, Japan, May 18, 1950; s. Yoshio and Shizuko (Sato) K.; m. Yasuko Toda, Oct. 25, 1981; children: Masashi, Atsushi. BEng, Kansai U., Osaka, 1973, MEng, 1975; DEng, Kyoto (Japan) U., 1992. Cert. noise control engring. Rsch. asst. Osaka Inst. Tech., 1978-83, lectr., 1983-92, assoc. prof., 1992-98; assoc. prof. Kansai U., Osaka, 1998—; acoustic cons. City of Osaka, 1987, City of Kyoto, 1991-92. Contbr. chpt. to book: BEM Applications in Architectural Acoustics, 1991; contbr. articles to profl. jours. (Insentive award 1991). Mem. INCE-Japan, Archtl. Inst. Japan, Acoustical Soc. Japan. Avocations: hiking, reading, fishing, travel, cooking. Fax: 81-6-6339-7720. E-mail: kawai@ipcku.kansai-u.ac.jp. Office: Kansai U Faculty Engring, 3-35 Yamate-cho 3, Suita Osaka 564-8680, Japan

KAWAKAMI, MASAYA, medical educator; b. Tokyo, Apr. 27, 1929; s. Shoichiroh and Kimiko (Hasegawa) K.; m. Noriko Tsuchida, Oct. 1, 1957; children: Kyoko, Toshiya, Eriko. MB, Hokkaido U., Sapporo, Japan, 1953; D of Med. Sci., Gunma U., Maebashi, Japan, 1960. Diplomate Med. Bd. Japan. Lectr. Gunma U., Maebashi, 1958-60; rsch. assoc. Georgetown U., Washington, 1964-66; assoc. prof. Gunma U., Maebashi, 1960-72; prof. Kitsako U., Sagamihara, Japan, 1972-96; dir. dept. molecular biology Kitasato Univ. Sagamihara, 1972—, Kitasato Inst., Tokyo, 1987—. Author: Immune Response, 1978; editor, author: Genetic Engineering in Medicine, 1992; (textbooks) Medical Molecular Biology, 1984, Human Medical Genetics, 1991. Mem. com. of Bioethics Japan Med. Assn., Tokyo, 1986-92, Gene Therapy, Japan. Govt.; bacteriology divsn. Japan del. Internat. Union of Microbiol. Socs., Washington, 1991—. Recipient Asahi Sci. award Asahi Co., Tokyo, 1959, Naito award Naito Meml. Found., Tokyo, 1975; grantee: Japanese Govt., Tokyo, 1960-92. Mem. Japanese Soc. for Bacteriology (trustee, Asakawa award 1999), Molecular Biology Soc. of Japan, Japanese Biochem. Soc., Am. Soc. Microbiology. Avocations: painting, rose culture. Home: 2-3-3 Kamitsuruma, Sagamihara Kanagawa 228-0802, Japan Office: Kitasato U Sch Medicine, 1-15 Kitasato, Sagamihara Kanagawa 228, Japan also: Kitasato Inst, 5-9-1 Shirokane, Minato-ku Tokyo 108, Japan

KAWAKAMI, SHOGO, civil engineering educator; b. Okayama, Japan, Nov. 10, 1938; s. Katsuma and Harumi (Bouno) K.; m. Hideko Kawai, Oct. 10, 1964; children: Kyoko, Aya. BCE, Kyoto U., 1961, postgrad., 1961-66, DEng., 1969. Prof. Nagoya U., 1979—, asst. prof. dept. civil engring., 1966, assoc. prof., 1967-79. Mem. transp. policy com. Japanese Ministry Transport, 1990-92; mem. nat. devel. planning com. Nat. Land Agy., 1996-2000; pres. Japan sect. Regional Sci. Assocs. Internat., 1997-98. Recipient Disting. Svcs. prize Minster Nat. Environ. Agy., 1999, Disting. Svcs. prize Nagoya Mcpl. Office, 1989; Humboldt Found. fellow, 1978. Fellow Japan Soc. Civil Engrs. Buddhist. Home: Sekobo 1-1004, Meito-ku, Nagoya 465-0055, Japan Office: Nagoya U Dept Civil Engring, Chikusa-ku, Nagoya, Aichi 464-8603, Japan

KAWAKAMI, TETSURO, electric industry executive; b. Aug. 3, 1928; m. Naomi Kawakami. Student, Tokyo Comm., 1952. With Sumitomo Denki Kogyo, 1952, pres., 1982; pres. Sumitomo Electric Industries Ltd., Osaka, Japan, now chmn., CEO, cons., sr. advisor; bd. dirs. Semb Corp. Industries. Office: Sumitomo Electric Indust, 5-33 Kitahama 4-chome, Chuo-ku Osaka 541-0041, Japan*

KAWAKAMI, YUTAKA, biomedical researcher, hematologist, educator; b. Osaka, Japan, Jan. 27, 1956; came to U.S., 1985; s. Kiichi and Etsuko Kawakami; m. Masako Abe, Apr. 29, 1982; children: Yuko, Tadashi, Kazuki. MD, Keio U, Tokyo, 1980, PhD, 1996. Resident Keio U. Hosp., 1980-82; mem. med. staff Nat. Okura Hosp., Tokyo, 1982-84; instr. med. div. hematology Keio U., 1984-85; rsch. assoc. dept. med. microbiology U. South Fla., Tampa, 1985-87; vis. fellow surgery br. Nat. Cancer Inst., NIH, Bethesda, Md., 1987-90, vis. assoc. surgery br., 1990-92, vis. scientist surgery br., 1992-97; prof. Inst. for Advanced Med. Rsch. Keio U. Sch. Medicine, 1997—. Contbr. articles to sci. jours. Keio U. Rsch. grantee, 1985; Fogarty Internat. fellow NIH, 1987-90. Mem. Am. Assn. Immunologists, Am. Assn. for Cancer Rsch. Home: 757 Katakuracho Kanagawa-ku, Yokohama-Shi, Kanagawa 221-0861, Japan

KAWAKATSU, HEITA, economic history educator; b. Kyoto, Japan, Aug. 16, 1948; s. Hiromu and Kuniko (Nakajima) K.; Kimi Kamiyama, Oct. 13, 1980. BA in Econs., Waseda U., Tokyo, 1972, MA in Econ. History, 1975; DPhil in Modern History, Oxford U., U.K. Jr. rsch. fellow Waseda U., 1975-82, lectr., 1982-85, assoc. prof., 1985-90, vice dir. libr., 1990-94, prof., 1990-98; rsch. prof. Internat. Rsch. Ctr. for Japanese Studies, Kyoto, 1998—; guest prof. Nat. Ethnological Mus., Osaka, 1993-95, Ctr. Southeast Asian Studies Kyoto U., 1993-95; spl rsch. fellow Ministry Fin., Tokyo, 1995—; adviser Nat. Land Agy., Tokyo, 1996—, Tokyo Met. Govt., 1996—; mem. ex-prime min. Obuchi's adv. body, 1998—. Author: Japanese Civilization and the Modern West, 1991, A Treatise on Wealth & Virtue, 1995, A Maritime View of History of Civilizations, 1997; co-editor: Japanese Industrialization and the Asian Economy, 1994, The Evolving Structure of a World Economy, 1994. Recipient Ishizaka Meml. award Japanese Fedn. Econ. Orgns., 1977, 10th Ann. Essay award Japan Found., Tokyo, 1982, Asia-Pacific Spl. award Mainichi Daily Newspaper, Tokyo, 1996, 8th Yomiuri Essay prize, 1998. Mem. Oxford Soc. Avocations: violin, low mountain climbing. Fax: 0267-45-0492. Office: Internat Rsch Ctr Japan Std, 3-2 Oeyama-Cho Goryo, Kyoto Nishikyo-ku 610-1192, Japan

KAWAKATSU, MASAHARU, zoology educator; b. Kameoka, Japan, Jan. 20, 1929; s. Masakazu and Tei (Okajima) K.; m. Kazuko Hatano, Jan. 5, 1959; children: Tetsuya, Miyuki. DS, Hokkaido U., Sapporo, Japan, 1961. Asst. Kyoto (Japan) Gakugei U., 1953-61; asst. prof. Fuji Women's Coll., Sapporo, Japan, 1961-66, prof. biology, 1966-99, ret.; vis. prof. UNISINOS, Sao Leopoldo, Brazil, 1979; attending com. Red Data Book Japan, Tokyo, 1988—. Author: Red Data Book Japan, Tokyo, 1991, 98; contbr. articles to profl. jours. Mem. protective com. environ. agy. Prime Min. Office of Wild Plants and Animals Japan, Tokyo, 1994—. Mem. Zool. Soc. Japan, Soc. Sys. Zool. Japan, Speleol Soc. Japan, Biogeography Soc. Japan (2d prize 1993). Home: 9jô 9chôme 1-8, Shinkotoni, Kita-ku Sapporo, Hokkaidô 001-0909, Japan

KAWAKUBO, REI, fashion designer; b. Tokyo, 1942; m. Adrian Joffe. Degree in fine arts and lit., Keio U., Tokyo, 1964. With dept. advt. Asahi textile co.; freelance stylist; founder, owner, operator Comme des Garçons Ltd., Tokyo, 1973—. Named one of leading women in 20th century design N.Y.'s Fashion Inst. Tech., 1987; recipient Tokyo's Mainichi Newspaper award, 1983, 87. Office: Comme des Garçns, 16 Place Vendome, 75001 Paris France*

KAWALEY, IAN ROWE CHUKUDINKA, lawyer; b. Paget Parish, Bermuda, Aug. 20, 1955; s. Solomon Reginald Chukudinka and Beatrice Elizabeth (Musson) K.; m. Janet Cynthia Ferguson, Apr. 8, 1980; 1 child, Christopher William Chukudinka. LLB with honors, U. Liverpool, Eng., 1977; LLM, U. London, 1979, PhD, 1999. Barrister-at-law Mid. Temple, 1978; barrister Bermuda, 1980. Crown counsel Atty.-Gov.'s Chambers, Bermuda, 1980-83; sr. state counsel Atty.-Gov.'s Chambers, Seychelles, 1983-85; assoc. atty. Browne & Wade Chambers, Hamilton, Bermuda, 1985-89; barrister-at-law Sibghat Kadri's Chambers, London, 1987-89; assoc. atty. Milligan Whyte & Smith, Hamilton, 1989-99, ptnr., 1999—; acting magistrate Bermuda Govt., Hamilton, 1992—; bd. dirs. Venturilla Found., Bermuda, Montessori Edn. Trust, Bermuda; pres. Seaton Found., 1995—. Co-editor: (jour.) Bermuda Bar Rev., 1989-99; contbr. articles to profl. jours. Justice of the peace, 1998. Fellow Ctr. for Internat. Legal Studies, 1994. Mem. Bermuda Bar Assn. (v.p.), Brit. Inst. Internat. Comparative Law. Avocations: soccer, writing, photography. Home: Ste 747, 48 Par-La-Ville Rd, Hamilton HM 11, Bermuda Office: Millligan Whyte & Smith, 12 Par-La-Ville Rd, Hamilton HM 11, Bermuda

KAWAMITSU, ISAO, publishing company executive; b. Tokugun, Taiwan, July 12, 1944; s. Takeji and Mitsuyo (Sawada) K.; m. Sachiko Katayama, Mar. 3, 1983. LLB, Toyo U., Tokyo, 1967. Assoc. mgr. adminstrv. dept. Reader's Internat. Co., Tokyo, 1968-69; with sales dept. Nikkel Sales Ctr. Inc., Tokyo, 1969-73; with sales dept. Nikkel-McGraw-Hill Subscription Sales Co., Tokyo, 1973-90, assoc. mgr., 1981-90, mktg. dir. fgn. publs. dept., 1991—. Avocations: reading, lure and fly fishing, deep-sea fishing. Home: 1-1-ME-1201, Oguradai Inzai-shi, Chiba-ken 270-1356, Japan Office: Nikkei Bus Pub Sub Sales Co, Sanbancho 1, Chiyoda-ku Tokyo 102-0075, Japan

KAWAMOTO, HIROHISA, manufacturing company executive; b. Tokyo, June 18, 1938; s. Yoshiyuki and Yuri (Sawai) K.; m. Yasuko Yoshioka, Mar. 3, 1968; children: Eugene, Hanna, Naomi. BS in Electronics, Kyoto U., 1961; MS in Elec. Engring., U. Calif., Berkeley, 1966; PhD, U. Calif., 1970. Mem. tech. staff RCA, Princeton, N.J., 1970-80; gen. mgr. Sony Consumer Elec. Lab., Paramus, N.J., 1981-83; chmn. Internat. Conf. Consumer Electronics, Chgo., 1984; gen. mgr., dir. image sensors group Sony Component Products Divsn., 1983-85; gen. mgr. CCD project Sharp IC Group, Tenri, Nara, Japan, 1985-88; gen. mgr. planning & devel. Sharp Corp. R&D Group, Kashiwa, Chiba, Japan, 1988-92; v.p., divsn. gen. mgr. Sharp Tech. Info. Ctr., Tenri, 1992—; del. Internat. Electrotechnical Commn., Com. of Action, 1996—. Co-author: Carbon Black Polymer Composites, 1982; contbr. articles to profl. jours.; patentee in field. Chmn. bd. dirs. Princeton Cmty. Japanese Lang. Sch., 1980-85. Fulbright Exchange scholar, 1964. Fellow IEEE (chmn. Princeton sect. 1980, Centennial award 1984, Third Millennium medal 2000), Consumer Electronics Soc. IEEE (editl. bd.). Presbyterian. Office: Sharp Tech Info Ctr, Tenri Nara 632-8567, Japan

KAWAMOTO, HIROSHI, maritime safety educator; b. Matsuyama, Japan; s. Kenji and Fumiko (Inoue) K.; m. Mayuko Sakuta, Mar. 1977; 1 child, Naoko. DSc, Kyoto U., 1984. Asst. prof. Kyoto U., 1977-85. Contbr. articles to profl. jours. Recipient Internat. Order of Merit, Britain., 2000. Mem. AAAS, N.Y. Acad. Scis., Planetary Soc. Office: Maritime Safety Acad, 5-1 Wakaba-cho, Kure-shi 737, Japan

KAWAMOTO, NOBUHIKO, automotive executive; b. Mar. 3, 1936. Student, Tohoku U., Japan, 1963. Dir. Honda Motor Co., Tokyo, 1981, mng. dir., 1983—; pres., CEO Honda Motor Co., Ltd., 1990-98, dir., advisor, 1998—. Named Comdr. of the Order of the Crown of Belgium, 1999. Office: Honda Motor Co Ltd, 1-1 Minami-Aoyama 2-chome, Minato-ku Tokyo 107, Japan*

KAWAMOTO, PAULINE NAOMI, information engineering educator; b. L.A., Feb. 11, 1966. BS in Gen. Engring., Harvey Mudd Coll., 1988; MS in Info. Engring., Shinshu U., Japan, 1993, PhD in System Devel. Techs., 1996. Engr. Gen. Instrument, San Diego, 1988-90; software cons. San Diego, 1990; assoc. prof. info. engring. Shinshu U., Nagano-shi, Japan. Scholar Japanese Ministry of Edn., 1993. Mem. IEEE, Mizar Soc. Avocations: sports, writing, reading. Home: Kami-takada 1121-1 Shiny, Gurenji Oka A-105, Nagano-shi Nagano-ken 381-0034, Japan Office: Shinshu U Faculty Engring, Wakasato 4-17-1, Nagano-shi 380-8553, Japan

KAWAMURA, AKIRA, lawyer; b. Kyoto, Japan, May 9, 1941; s. Ushinosuke and Sumie (Yamamoto) K.; m. Masako Kodama Kawamura, Nov. 10, 1968; children: Ikuka, Naoko. LLB, Kyoto (Japan) U., 1965; LLM, Sydney U., 1979. Bar: Japan. With Daini Tokyo Bar Assn., 1967; assoc. Anderson Mori, Tokyo, 1967-75, ptnr., 1975-99; exec. v.p. Japan Fedn. Bar Assns., 1987; chmn. Fgn. Lawyers Commn., 1993-97; dir. Borg Warner Automotive, 1980-2000, Warner Mycal Corp. Tokyo, 1989-2000. Editor-in-chief: Law and Business in Japan. Mem. ABA, Daini Tokyo Bar Assn. Home: Apt 1102 Kudan-Kita, 2-3-25 Chiyoda-ku, Tokyo 102-0037, Japan Office: Anderson Mori AIG Bldg, 1-3 Marunouchi Chiyoda-ku, 1-chome Tokyo 100-0005, Japan

KAWAMURA, HARUKI, science educator; b. Tokyo, Feb. 9, 1944; s. Hajimu and Sachiko (Komura) K.; m. Akiko Tanaka, May, 1974; 1 child, Akito. DSc, U. Tokyo, 1973. Rschr. Nat. Rsch. Inst. Metal, Tokyo, 1973-79, sr. rschr., 1979-86; prof. faculty sci. Himeji Inst. Tech., Kamigori, Japan, 1986-90, prof. dept. material sci., 1990—. Home: 9-2-34 Kasugadai Nishi-ku, Kobe 651-2276, Japan Office: Himeji Inst Tech, Kouto 3-2-1, Kamigori 678-1297, Japan

KAWAMURA, HIDETO, medical scientist, educator; b. Sakai City, Osaka, Japan, July 4, 1949; s. Toshita and Tsunako (Tanaka) K.; m. Michiko Ito; children: Hidekatsu, Masato. BS, Osaka City U., 1973, MS, 1975; PhD, Aichi Med. U., 1987. Rsch. assoc. Aichi Med. U., Aich-Gun, Japan, 1975-93, lectr., 1994—. Home: 7 36 12 Wakinoshima-Cho, Tajimi City 507-0826, Japan Office: Aichi Med U, Yazako Nagakute-cho, Aichi gun Aichi-ken 480 11, Japan

KAWAMURA, HIROYUKI, structural engineer, educator; b. Shizuoka, Japan, Nov. 1, 1936; s. Iich and Kane (Norizuki) K.; m. Hiroko Tazima, Apr. 1, 1966; 3 children. MS in Engring., Kyusyu U., Fukuoka, Japan, 1972, PhD in Engring., 1985. Engr. Ministry of Constrn., Govt. of Japan, Tokyo, 1959-60, Taisei Corp., Tokyo, 1962-65; assoc. prof. Kyushu Sangyo U., Fukuoka, 1965-85, prof., 1986—. Grantee Fukuoka Indsl. Sci. and Tech. Found., 1990-92. Mem. Japan Concrete Inst. (bd. dirs. 1997—), Japan Archtl. Inst., Japan Prestressed Concrete Engring. Assn. Buddhist. Avocations: travel, photography, ballroom dancing. Home: 2-35-7 Wakamiya, Higashi-ku, Fukuoka 813-0036, Japan Office: Kyusyu Sangyo U, 2-3-1 Matsukadai, Fukuoka 813-8503, Japan

KAWAMURA, YOYA, retired diplomat, correspondent, writer; b. Kokura, Japan, Aug. 28, 1932; s. Shinichi and Shigeno (Kojima) K.; m. Yoko Masuda, June 10, 1959; children: Maya, Yuniya. Grad., Fgn. Svc. Inst. Japan, 1952. Tchr. Shimizugaoka H.S., Muroran, Japan, 1950-52; ofcl. Min. Fgn. Affairs, Japan, 1952-96, mem. policy planning staff, 1969-73; diplomatic trainee Russian Inst. Columbia U., N.Y.C., 1956-59; 3d sec. Embassy, Prague, Czechoslovakia, 1963-65; 2d sec. Embassy, Moscow, USSR, 1965-69; consul Embassy, Sydney, Australia, 1973-75, Madras, India, 1975-78; minister-counsellor Embassy, Bucharest, Romania, 1978-83; chargé d'affaires

Embassy, Honiara, Solomon Islands, 1983-85; curator Diplomatic Archives, 1985-96; freelance writer, 1996—; civilian employee U.S. Occupation Forces 8th Army, Japan. Contbr. articles to profl. jours., newspapers, mags. Mem. U.S. Naval Inst. (Life Silver mem.). Avocations: adventure travel, cruises, photography. Home: 6-54-10 Higashi-Mukojima, Sumidaku Tokyo 131-0032, Japan

KAWAMURA, YUTAKA J., coloproctologist; b. Suginami, Tokyo, Japan, Jan. 26, 1962; s. Shogo and Takako Kawamura; m. Yuki Izumi, m. Sept. 19, 1997; 1 child, Miki. MD, U. Tokyo, 1987, PhD, 1997. Resident Tokyo U. Hosp., 1987-88; surgeon Tokyo Wellfare Pension Hosp., 1988-91, Tokyo U. Hosp., 1991-92; asst. prof. dept. surgery Med. Sch. U. Tokyo, 1997—. Author: (book) Laparoscopic Assisted Colorectal Surgery, 1998; contbr. articles to profl. jours. Recipient Germany-Japan Young Surgeon award Deutsche Gesellschaft fuer Chirurgie, 1995. Mem. Japanese Soc. Surgery (cert. surgeon), Japanese Soc. Gastrointestinal Surgery (cert. gastrointestinal surgeon), Japanese Soc. Coloproctology (cert. coloproctologist), Japanese Soc. for Endoscopic Surgery. Avocation: guitar. Fax: 81 3 3811 6822. E-mail: kawamura-1su@h.u-tokyo.ac.jp. Office: U Tokyo Dept Surgery, Hongo 7-3-1, Bunkyoku Tokyo 113-8655, Japan

KAWANISHI, HIDENORI, opto-electronics researcher; b. Higashiosaka, Osaka, Japan, Mar. 17, 1961; s. Akira and Toshie (Takashima) K.; m. Harumi Iizumi, Oct. 25, 1991; children: Yosuke, Taiyo. BS, Kyoto (Japan) U., 1983, MS, 1985, D of Engring., 1995. Researcher Sharp Corp., Tenri, Japan, 1985-89, 93—, Optoelectronics Tech. Rsch. Lab., Tsukuba, Japan, 1990-92. Avocation: sailing. Home: 3-413, 6-6-1 Jingu, Nara 631-0804, Japan Office: Sharp Corp, 2613-1 Ichinomoto-cho, Tenri Nara 632-8567, Japan

KAWANISHI, TETSUYA, government official, researcher; b. Moriguchi, Osaka, Japan, July 22, 1969; s. Hiroaki and Mitsuko (Kondo) K. B of Engring., Kyoto (Japan) U., 1992, M of Engring., 1994, PhD, 1997. Engr. Prodn. Engring. Lab., Matsushita Electric Indsl. Co., Ltd., Osaka, 1994-95; postdoctoral fellow Venture Bus. Lab., Kyoto U., 1997-98; rschr. Comm. Rsch. Lab., Ministry of Posts and Telecom., Tokyo, 1998—; instr. Nishizawa Acad., Osaka, 1996-97, Ritsumeikan U., Otsu, Japan, 1997-98. Contbr. articles to profl. jours. Recipient Young Scientist award Union Radio-Scientifique Internat., Can., 1999. Office: Comm Rsch Lab Photonic Tech, 4-2-1 Nukuikitamachi, Koganei Tokyo 184-8795, Japan

KAWANO, ARNOLD HUBERT, lawyer; b. Phila., Mar. 27, 1948; s. James Tadao and Shigeko (Sakamoto) K.; m. Sandra K. Lee, July 1, 1970; children: Thomas L., Mark L. BS magna cum laude, Columbia U., 1975, JD, 1977. Bar: N.Y. 1978, D.C. 1979, Pa. 1981, U.S. Dist. Ct. (ea. and so. dists.) N.Y. 1978, U.S. Ct. Appeals (fed. cir.) 1992, U.S. Ct. Internat. Trade 1992, U.S. Supreme Ct. 1981. Assoc. Reid & Priest, N.Y.C., 1977-80, Weil, Gotshal & Manges, N.Y.C., 1980-81; counsel Sumitomo Corp. of Am., N.Y.C., 1981-84; pvt. practice N.Y.C., Mineola, N.Y., 1984-87; v.p. J.P. Morgan, N.Y.C., 1987-91; ptnr. Inouye & Ogden, N.Y.C., 1992-93; sr. v.p., gen. counsel ORIX USA Corp., N.Y.C., 1993-98; mng. dir. Harold L. Lee & Sons, Inc., N.Y.C., 1999—; bd. dirs. Harold L. Lee & Sons, Inc., N.Y.C. Bd. dirs. Asian-Am. Legal Def. and Edn. Fund, N.Y.C., 1977-88, N.Y. Civil Liberties Union, 1992-94. Harlan Fiske Stone scholar Columbia Law Sch., 1976, Internat. fellow Columbia U. Sch. Internat. Affairs, 1976. Fellow Am. Coll. Investment Counsel; mem. ABA, NAACP, N.Y. State Bar Assn., D.C. Bar, Assn. of Bar City N.Y., Asian Pacific Am. Bar Assn. N.Y. (bd. dirs. 1992-93), Am. Corp. Counsel Assn., Am. Intellectual Property Law Assn., Computer Law Assn., Assn. for Computing Machinery, Internat. Assn. for Artificial Intelligence and Law, Nat. Press Photographers Assn., Evidence Photographers Internat. Coun., Japanese Am. Citizens League, Phi Beta Kappa. Avocations: camping, canoeing, photography, skiing. Office: 31 Pell St New York NY 10013-5148

KAWANO, HIDEAKI, space physicist; b. Nobeoka City, Miyazaki, Japan, Sept. 1, 1964; s. Shohachirou and Sumako (Hamada) K. BS, U. Tokyo, 1987, MS, 1989, PhD, 1992. Postdoctoral fellow U. Tokyo, 1993-95, UCLA, 1994-95, 95-97; rschr. Ctr. of Excellence Solar-Terrestrial Environment Lab., Nagoya U., Toyokawa, Japan, 1997; assoc. prof. Kyushu U., Fukuoka, Japan, 1998—. Contbr. papers to profl. jours. Mem. Am. Geophys. Union, Soc. Geomagnetism and Earth, Planetary and Space Scis. Office: Kyushu U Dept Earth/Planet, 6-10-1 Hakozaki Higashi-ku, 812-8581 Fukuoka City Japan

KAWANO, KENJI, physicist; b. Nichinan, Miyazaki, Japan, June 16, 1967; s. Yutaka and Toshiko (Oowaki) K. B Physics, Hokkaido U., Sapporo, Japan, 1991, M Physics, 1993; D Engring., Toyohashi (Japan) U. Tech., 1998. cert. material sci. Rschr. Rlwy. Tech. Rsch. Inst., Tokyo, 1994-96, Toyohashi U. Tech., 1996-99, U. Birmingham, Eng., 1999—. Office: Univ Birmingham, Sch Metallurgy & Material, Edgbaston Birmingham B15 2TT, England

KAWANO, MASATERU, dean, law educator. Dean faculty law Kyushu U, Fukuoka, Japan. Office: Kyushu U Faculty Law, 6-19-1 Hakozaki, Fukuoka 812-8581, Japan*

KAWANO, MICHIO MOTTO, hematologist, physician; b. Sanyo-cho, Yamaguchi, Japan, Jan. 12, 1953; s. Ikuta and Fumi Kawano; m. Yumie Keshi, Mar. 22, 1981; children: Yawara, Haruka. MB, Yamaguchi U., 1977; DMS, Kyoto U., 1982. Rsch. assoc. Rsch. Inst. Radiation Biology Medicine Hiroshima U., 1983-92, asst. prof. faculty of medicine, 1992—; prof. immuno-hematology faculty of medicine Yamaguchi U., 1996—. Author: (jour.) Nature. Mem. AAAS, Am. Soc. Hematology. Achievements include finding that interleukin-6 (IL-6) is a major growth factor for human myeloma cells; revealed difference of normal plasma cells from mature myeloma cells, altered expression of Pax-5 gene in human myeloma cells, IL-6 signalling in human myeloma cells; research in field of multiple myeloma. Avocations: tennis, baseball. E-mail: mkawano@po.cc.yamaguchi-u.ac.jp. Home: 358-89 Nakayama, Ube Yamaguchi 755-0058, Japan Office: Yamaguchi U Sch Medicine, 1-1-1 Minami-Kogushi, Ube 755-8505, Japan

KAWANO, TOSHIAKI, economics educator; b. Shintomi-machi, Miyazaki, Japan, Jan. 25, 1933; s. Yoshimatsu and Kesazuru (Hiezima) K.; m. Miho Kanai, Dec. 8, 1967 (dec. May 1979); children: Chiho, Toshihide, Toshifumi. Bachelor, Miyazaki (Japan) U., 1955; M in Agr., U. Tokyo Grad. Sch., 1958, PhD in Agr., 1982. Rsch. fellow Internat. Christian U., Tokyo, 1955-56; rschr. Nat. Inst. of Agrl. Sci., Tokyo, 1960-73, chief mktg. lab., 1974-80; prof. economic geography Hitotsubashi U., Tokyo, 1983-96; prof. agrl. econ. Ryutsu Keizai U., Ryugasaki, Japan, 1996—; vis. lectr. Chiba U. Sch. Horticulture, Matsudo, Japan, 1980-98, Tokyo U. Agr. and Engring., 1988-91; cons. Nat. Rural Devel. Assn., others, Tokyo, 1960-1990; del. to internat. congresses Asian Productivity Orgn., Tokyo, 1970-90; sec. gen. Farm Mgmt. Assn. Japan, Tsukuba, 1982-83' lectr. in field. Author, editor books; editor Agrl. Econ. Soc. of Japan, 1976-77; contbr. articles to profl. jours. FAO fellow UN, Mich. State U., 1964-65. Mem. Internat. Soc. Horticultural Sci. (corr. economic newsletter 1970-80), Internat. Assn. Agrl. Economists. Buddist. Avocations: fishing, folkmusic. Home: 381-13 Myojin Kukizaki, Inashiki-gun, Ibaraki 300-1257, Japan Office: Ryutsu Keizai U Sch Economy, 120 Hirahata, Ryugaski Ibaraki 301-8555, Japan

KAWASAKI, TOSHISUKE, biochemistry educator; b. Okayama, Japan, Dec. 5, 1941; s. Hiroyuki and Mutsuko (Kanda) K.; m. Nobuko Miyajima, Mar. 20, 1972; children: Keisuke, Yousuke. BSc, Kyoto (Japan) U., 1964, MSc, 1966, PhD, 1971. Instr. biochemistry Kyoto U., 1971-82, assoc. prof., 1982-89, prof., 1989—, dean Grad. Sch. Pharm. Scis., 1998—; vis. fellow NIH, Bethesday, Md., 1974-76; vis. prof. Chest Disease Rsch, Inst., 1992-94; rsch. dir. Core Rsch. Evolutional Sci Tech. (CREST) project, Japan Sci. Tech. (JSP), 1997—. Mem. editl. bd. Glycoconjugate Jour., 1990—, assoc. editor, 2000—; mem. editl. bd. European Jour. Biochemistry, 1998—; editor Jour. Biochemistry, 1997—, Jour. Biol. Chemistry, 1998—, Jour. Biochemistry, Molecular Biology and Biophysics, 2000—. Mem. Japanese Cancer Assn. Mem. Japan Biochemistry Soc. (Young Investigator award 1979), Am. Soc. Biochemistry and Molecular Biology, Pharm. Soc. of Japan, Japanese Soc. Carbohydrate Rsch (v.p. 1997-97, pres. 1998—), Molecular Biology Soc. Japan, Japan Neurosci. Soc., Japanese, Soc. Cell Biology, Soc. Glycobilogy (U.S.A.). Office: Kyoto U Dept Pharm Scis, Yoshida, Sakyo-ku, Kyoto 606-8501, Japan

KAWASHIMA, KOHEI, history scholar; b. Jujo, Tokyo, Japan, Aug. 29, 1961; s. Isamu and Kayoko Kawashima; m. Akiko Haruyama, Mar. 20, 1994; children: Rinako, Takayuki. BA, U. Tsukuba, 1985, MA, 1987; PhD, Brown U., 1992. Postdoctoral rschr. Kyoritsu Women's U., Hachioji, Tokyo, 1992-94; asst. prof. Kanda U. Internat. Studies, Chiba, Japan, 1994-98; assoc. prof. Musashi U., Nerima, Tokyo, 1998—; pres. Japanese Assn. of Am. Historians, Kunitachi/Tokyo, 1994-95. Co-author: America: A Geographical Introduction, 1992, The Nation State and Archives, 1999; co-editor: 60 Chapters on Contemporary America, 1998, Atlas of American History and Society, 1999; editor-in-chief Japanese Jour. Am. History, 1995-96. Fulbright scholar, Tokyo, 1987, Melon scholar Mass. Hist. Soc., Boston, 1990. Mem. Am. Hist. Assn., Orgn. Am. Historians, Am. Studies Assn., Japanese Assn. Am. Studies. E-mail: kokoharu@cc.musashi.ac.jp.

KAWASHIMA, TAKESHI, artist; b. Takamatsu, Japan, Jan. 13, 1930; came to U.S., 1963; s. Tsuneichi and Mizue (Tada) K.; m. Junko Kuruma, Feb. 5, 1973; 1 child from previous marriage, Kokoro. Student Musashino Art U., Tokyo, 1951-56, Art Students League, N.Y.C., 1965-66. One man shows include Nantenshi Gallery, Tokyo, 1984, 89, Gallery Internat. 57, N.Y.C., 1988, Takamatsu City Mus. of Art, 1989, Yamaso Art Gallery, Kyoto, Japan, 1990, 93, 96, 99, Ryoko Art Gallery, Kyoto, 1991, Magna Gallery N.Y.C., 1992, JAL Gallery, N.Y., 1992, TSK Exhibition Hall, Matsue, 1993, Haenah-Kent Gallery, N.Y.C., 1995, Kaibundo Gallery, Kobe, Japan, 1996, 98, Walter Wickiser Gallery Inc., N.Y.C., 1998; exhibited in group shows at Bergen Mus. Art and Sci., N.J., 1983, Sande Webster Gallery, Phila., 1983, Mus. Modern Art, Guuma, Japan, 1984, Fire House Gallery of Nassau C.C., Garden City, N.Y., 1985, Gallery Internat. 57, 1988, Gallery Internat. 52, N.Y.C., Ise Art Found., N.Y., 1992, Mita Copy, N.J., 1992, Fukuyama Mus. Art, Hiroshima, 1993, Park Ryu Sook Gallery, Seoul, 1993, Seoul Arts Ctr., 1993, Haena-Kent Gallery, 1993, 94, Walter Wickiser Gallery, N.Y.C., 1993, Taipei Gallery, N.Y.C., 1994, Hachioji Art Cutural Ctr., Tokyo, 1994, Takamatsu City Healthcare Ctr., Koshindo Gallery, Tokyo, 1997; works represented in collections at The Mus. Modern Art, N.Y.C., 1965, Chase Manhattan Bank, N.A., N.Y.C., 1966, SUNY, Postdam, 1970, 73, Kyoto Nat. Mus. of Art, 1976, Edwin A. Ulrich Mus. Art, Wichita (Kans.) State U., 1976, Ohara Mus. Art, Kurashiki, Japan, 1984, 87, 89, Frederick R. Weisman Art Found., L.A., 1985, Tokyo Met. Mus. Art, Kushiro Uoichiba Corp., Hokkaido, Japan, Takamatsu Mcpl. Mus. Art, 1987, Tokushima Mus., 1986, 87, Toyama Prefectural Mus. of Art, Toyama-ken, 1989, Takamatsu City Libr., 1992, Kawachi-Nagano City Cultural Ctr., Osaka, 1992, Conv. Ctr. Kunibiki Messe, Matsue City, 1993, Hiroshima (Japan) Mus. Contemporary Art, 1999, Okazaki City Mus., Aichi, Japan, 2000; commd. by Okinoshima Island, Shimane, 1996, Kagawa Sangyo Zunoka Ctr., Takamatsu City, 1996, San-In Godo Bank, Matsue, Kansai TV Broadcasting Co., Osaka, 1997, Tokushima (Japan) U., 1998, Takamatsu Technol. High Sch., 1998; organizer Kshionoe Internat. Young Artist Festival, 1993, 95, 98. Daniel Schnakenberg scholar, 1965; Bd. of Control scholar, 1966; recipient Silvermine award, 1967. Home: 11 Mercer St # 2 F New York NY 10013-2579

KAWASOE, KATSUHIKO, automotive company executive; b. 1936. CEO Mitsubishi Motors Corp., Tokyo. Office: Mitsubishi Motors Corp, 5-33-8 Shiba Minato-ku, Tokyo 108-8410, Japan*

KAWATA, TADASHI, academic administrator, educator; b. Tochigi-ken, Japan, June 22, 1925; s. Junichiro and Tei (Mitsugi) K.; m. Sadako Niimura, May 22, 1952; children: Atsushi, Shin, Chiharu. BA in Econs., U. Tokyo, 1948, PhD, 1968. From lectr. to prof. internat. rels. U. Tokyo, 1951-72, prof. emeritus, 1987—; prof. internat. rels. Sophia U., Tokyo, 1972-96, dean Faculty Fgn. Studies, 1981-84, prof. emeritus, 1996—; vis. scholar Harvard U., 1955-57, 85; vis. prof. U. Nacional Federico Villarreal, Lima, Peru, 1969, El Colegio de Mex., 1973-74; lectr. Internat. Seminar Fgn. Svc., Salzburg, Austria, 1971; vis. fellow U. Essex, 1985. Author: International Relations, 1958, Modern International Economics, 1967, The North-South Problem, 1977, Political Economy of International Relations, 1980, Economic Friction, 1982, A Series of (Kawata's) International Studies (Vol. I International Relations, Vol. II Power Politics, Vol. III Peace Research, Vol. IV North-South Relations, Vol. V International Economics, Vol. VI International Political Economy), 1998; mem. editl. com. The Developing Economies, 1965-83; editor: (with Hideki Ohata) Encyclopedia of International Political Economy, 1993. Served with Japanese Army, 1945. Decorated grand cordon Order of the Sacred Treasure (Japan). Mem. Internat. Peace Rsch. Assn. (coun. 1965-71), Assn. Asian Social Sci. Rsch. Couns. (pres. 1991-93), Peace Studies Assn. Japan (pres. 1975-77), Japan Peace Rsch. Group (dir. 1966-72), Japan Assn. Internat. Econs. (exec. com. 1965-93), Japan Assn. Internat. Rels. (pres. 1982-84), Sci. Coun. Japan (v.p. 1991-94), Japan Acad. Home: 1-15-11 Arima Miyamae-Ku, Kawasaki Shi 216-0003, Japan

KAWIAK, JERZY WLADYSLAW, cell biologist, educator; b. Bielsko-Biala, Poland, Aug. 1, 1928; s. Wladyslaw and Maria (Grodzinska) K.; m. Halina Sabina Saracen, Dec. 8, 1952; children: Anna, Jan. MD, Jagiellonian U., Krakow, Poland, 1952; D in Med. Sci., Med. Acad., Warszawa, Poland, 1958, Habil D in Med. Sci., 1963. Asst., adj. instr., assoc. prof. Med. Acad., Warszawa, 1952-58, 60-69; rsch. assoc. U. Gothenburg, Sweden, 1959; assoc. prof. SUNY, Buffalo, 1966-67; assoc. prof., prof. Med. Ctr., Warszawa, 1970-79; prof. Med. Acad., Warszawa, 1977-78, Pomeranian Med. Acad., Szczecin, Poland, 1980-86; vis. prof. McGill U., Montreal, Can., 1986-87; prof. Med. Ctr., Warszawa, 1987—; vis. prof. U. Ulm, Germany, 1986. Author, editor: Cytophysiology, 1990, Basic Cytophysiology, 1985; editor (jour.): Advances in Cell Biology, 1974—. Grantee Polish Acad. Sci. 1980, 1989. Mem. Polish Histo & Cytochem. Soc. (pres. 1970-76, v.p. 1977-87), Polish Acad. Sci. Cell Biology Com. (pres. 1981-87), Fedn. Soc. Histo & Cytochemistry, Gesellschaft f. Topochemie u. Elektronenmikroskopie Lipzig, European Tissue Culture Soc., N.Y. Acad. Sci. Avocations: walking, canoeing. Office: Med Ctr Postgrad Edn, Marymoncka 99, 01813 Warsaw Poland

KAY, BERNARD SAMUEL, theoretical physicist; b. Guildford, England, Nov. 13, 1951; s. Max and Freda (Pearl) K.; m. Wanda Andreoni, Sept. 29, 1980 (div. 1995); 1 child, Michael Max. BA, U. Cambridge, 1972; PhD, London U., 1977. Postdoctoral rsch. fellow Internat. Ctr. Theoretical Physics, Trieste, Berne, London, 1977-83; McCormick fellow Fermi Inst., Chgo., 1983; asst. Inst. Theoretical Physics, U. Zurich, 1983-89; SERC advanced fello U. Cambridge, England, 1989-92; lectr. dept. maths. U. York, England, 1992-99, sr. lectr. dept. maths., 1999—; vis. prof. dept. maths. U. Rome, Italy, 1982, 95; vis. rschr. Inst. Advanced Study, Princeton, N.J., SUNY, Buffalo, U. N.C., Chapel Hill, U. Berne, Switzerland. Mem. Internat. Soc. Gen. Relativity and Gravitation, Internat. Assn. Math. Physics. Office: U York, Dept Maths, Y010 5DD York England

KAY, JAMES FRANKLIN, religion educator; b. Kansas City, Mo., May 18, 1948; s. Bob Burton and Mary Lenore (Branstetter) K. BA, Pasadena (Calif.) Coll., 1969; MDiv, Harvard U., 1972; MPhil, Union Seminary, N.Y.C., 1984, PhD, 1991. Pastor No. Lakes Parish, Beltrami County, Minn., 1974-78; campus minister United Ministries, Bemidji, Minn., 1977-79; cons. PHEWA, N.Y.C., 1980-82; instr. Princeton (N.J.) Theol. Seminary, 1988-91, asst. prof., 1991-95, assoc. prof., 1995-97, Joe R. Engle assoc. prof., 1997—; Warrack lectr. St. Andrews U., Scotland, 1997. Author: Christus Praesens, 1994, Seasons of Grace, 1994; editor: Women, Gender, and Christian Community, 1997; book rev. editor The Princeton Sem. Bull., 1991-94, editor, 1994-2000. Vice-pres. Bemidji Home Loan Improvement, 1978. Mem. Am. Acad. Religion, Acad. Homiletics, Duodecim Theol. Soc., Karl Barth Soc. of N.A., Phi Delta Lambda. Office: Princeton Theol Seminary PO Box 821 Princeton NJ 08542-0803

KAYA, AKIRA, association executive, real estate executive; b. Kyoto, Japan, Mar. 20, 1930; s. Tohru and Kiyoe (Shinoda) K.; m. Itsko Kitano, Apr. 25, 1958; children: Satoshi, Takako Tone. BS, Kyoto U., 1953. With Bur. Budget, Japan, 1953-55; sec. Japanese Embassy, Washington, 1960-64, counselor, 1971-75; dir. Hokkaido (Japan) Fin. Bur., 1969-70; dir. Vice Min.'s Office, Ministry Fin., Japan, 1971, dir. investment divsn., 1975-77; dir. gen. Nagoya (Japan) Customs Bur., 1977-78; dir. Tokyo Office, World Bank, 1978-80; asst. vice min. Ministry Fin., Japan, 1982; exec. v.p. Japan Nat. Tourist Orgn., 1982-85; spl. advisor to pres. Tokai Bank, Japan, 1985-98; pres. Japan-Libya Friendship Assn., 1998—; exec. dir. Japan Traffic Safety and Edn. Assn., 1998—; dir. Suginami Sr. and Jr. H.S.s, 2000—; chmn. Fgn. Bankers Conf., Japan, 1982-86. Author: International Development Finance, 1977. Mem. Okbridge Worldwide Assn., Japan Contract Bridge League. Avocations: duplicate bridge, Go game. E-mail: kaya@mxg.mesh.ne.jp. Home: 1-22-18 Higashi-Tamagawa, Setagaya-ku, Tokyo 158-0084, Japan Office: Tokyo Bay Hotels Co Ltd, 1-7 Maihama, Urayasu-City 279-0031, Japan

KAYA, NUSRET, psychiatrist; b. Antalya, Turkey, June 11, 1943; s. Kazim and Pakize (Mericboyu) K.; m. Semra Hatice Bayrakdaroglu, Mar. 12, 1971 (div. Jan. 1996); children: Aral, Artun; m. Yasemin Gesit, Aug. 3, 1998. Degree, Istanbul (Turkey) Med. U., 1968, Gulhane Med. U., Ankara, Turkey, 1973. Commd. Turkish Navy, 1969, advanced through grades to col.; med. officer T.C.G. Istanbul Destroyer, Golcuk, Turkey, 1969-70, Manire Sinif Sch., Derince, Turkey, 1970-73; asst. dir. Gulhane Med. Acad., Ankara, 1973-77; rsch. fellow in sleep disorders Baylor Coll., Houston, 1977-79; psychiatry clinic dir. Istanbul Navy Hosp., 1979-86; psychol. clinic dir. Haydarpasa Mil. Acad., 1986-89; dir. Psiko-Estetik Ltd., Istanbul, 1989—; cons., spkr. in field. Author: Intstitions of National Knowledge, 1987, Special Obsessions for Anatolian People, 1992, Psycho-Estetic, 1999. Dir. ATV TV, Istanbul, 1997-98. Mem. Istanbul Med. Prof. Assn., Turkish Neuro-Psychiat. Assn., BEMEV Med. Orgn. Avocations: guitar, bridge, chess, tennis, bowling. Home: Fener Kalamis # 96/19, 81030 Istanbul Turkey Office: Psiko-Estetik Ltd, Fener-Kalamis # 96/18, 81030 Istanbul Turkey

KAYAALP, N(ESIBE) MEHLIKA, public health engineer; b. Ankara, Turkey, Mar. 21; arrived in Australia, 1982; d. Huseyin and Havva (Nalic) Islam; m. Ahmet Sadik Kayaalp, 1981; children: Pelin, Yeliz. BSCE, Mid. East Tech. U., Ankara, 1974; postgrad. diploma in san. engring., Internat. Inst. Hydraulic and Environmental Engring., Delft, The Netherlands, 1979; MPhil in Environ. Sci., Murdoch U., Perth, Australia, 1990. Engr. Provincial Bank, Ankara, 1974-76, specialist wastewater engr., 1976-78, supervising environ. engr., 1979-82; grad. rsch. asst. Murdoch U., 1984-85; project officer Dept. Resources Devel., Perth, 1985-86; sr. environ. engr. Maunsell and Ptnrs., Adelaide, Australia, 1987; environ. engr. South Australian Water (Engring. and Water Supply Dept.), Adelaide, 1988-90; sr. environ. engr. South Australian Water (then Engring. and Water Supply Dept.), Adelaide, 1990-94; sr. pub. health engr., mgr. environ. waste unit South Australian Health Commn., Adelaide, 1994—; curriculum developer South Australian Secondary Sch. Bds., Adelaide, 1992-93, examiner, 1992—. Contbr. articles on environ. sci. and engring. to profl. jours. Organizer Children's Festival; tchr. of account Turkish Assn. South Australia, 1990-93; dep. chmn. Camden Cmty. Ctr., Adelaide, 1991-92. Postgrad. scholar WHO, Delft, 1978-79; grantee South Australia Edn. Dept., 1992, rsch. grantee South Australian Health Commn., 1995-96. Mem. Australian Water Works Assn. (co-editor South Australian br. seminar 1988). Muslim. Avocations: voluntary teaching of Turkish language, swimming, gardening, spending time with her children. Office: SA Health Commn Environ, Health Br POB 6 Rundle Mall, Adelaide SA 5000, Australia

KAYANE, ISAMU, science educator; b. Niigata, Japan, Nov. 1, 1932; s. Shigekichi and Matsuo (Washio) K.; m. Hide Gocho, Oct. 22, 1961; children: Shino, Mari. BSc, Tokyo Kyoiku U., 1957, MSc, 1957, DSc, 1965. From rsch. assoc. to assoc. prof. Tokyo Kyoiku U., 1962-75; from assoc. prof. to prof. U. Tsukuba, Japan, 1976-96; prof. Aichi (Japan) U., 1996—; v.p. Internat. Commn. on Groundwater, 1980-87. Author: Hydrology, 1980, Water Cycle in Bali Island, 1992; mem. editl. bd. Hydrological Processes, 1986—. Mem. AAAS, Am. Geophys. Union, Japanese Assn. Hydrological Scis. (pres. 1992-94), Sci. Coun. Japan (chmn. nat. com. 1994—). Home: Kariya 3-123, 300-1235 Ushiku Japan

KAYE, ALAN DAVID, anesthesiologist, researcher; b. L.I., N.Y., Mar. 21, 1962; s. Joel and Florence Susan (Feldman) K.; m. Kim Sutker, May 26, 1990; children: Aaron, Rachel. BS in Biology, U. Ariz., 1984, BS in Psychology, 1985, MD, 1989; PhD in Pharmacology, Tulane U., 1997. Diplomate Am. Bd. Anesthesiology, Nat. Bd. Med. Examiners; lic. physician, La.; cert. ACLS. Intern Alton Ochsner Med. Found. and Clinic, New Orleans, 1989-90; resident in anesthesiology Mass. Gen. Hosp., Boston, 1990-91; resident in anesthesiology Tulane Med. Ctr., New Orleans, 1991-93, asst. prof. anesthesiology/attending staff, 1993-97, assoc. prof., 1997-99; attending staff/vice med. dir. Greater New Orleans Surg. Ctr., 1995-97, med. dir., 1997-2000; chmn., prof. dept. of anesthesia Tex. Tech U. Med. Ctr., Lubbock, 1999—, prof. dept. pharmacology, 1999—; lectr. in field. Contbr. articles and abstracts to profl. jours., chpts. to books; mem. editl. adv. bd. OR Reports, 1997—; co-editor: JASA Mfg. Book, 1986—, JASA Contractor's Book, 1986—; mem. editl. bd. Current Drugs, Anesthesia News. Capt. U.S. Army Med. Res., 1990—, maj., 1997. Recipient Nat. Student Rsch. Forum 1st place Roche Labs. award for excellence in basic sci. rsch., 1992, Baxter Clin. Rsch. award of Excellence, 1999; Ariz. Med. Assn. scholar, 1987-89, U. Utah Joshua Millbank Scholars Program scholar, 1987, E. Blois du Bois scholar, 1981-89; Tulane Sch. Medicine grantee, 1993-94, 94, 95—, 97—. Fellow N.Y. Acad. Sci., Am. Physiol. Soc.; mem. Bd. Examiners in Anesthesia (nat. assoc.), Am. Soc. Anesthesiology (pres. 1992-93), Am. Heart Assn., Mass. Gen. Hosp. Anesthesia Alumni Assn., Soc. Critical Care Medicine, Soc. Cardiovascular Anesthesiologists, Internat. Anesthesia Rsch. Soc., La. Soc. Anesthesiologists, New Orleans Anesthesia Soc., Tulane Med. Ctr. Anesthesia Alumni Assn., Golden Key, Blue Key, Phi Beta Kappa, Phi Eta Sigma (pres. 1982-83, Baxter award of appreciation 1999). Fax: 806-743-2984. E-mail: aneadk@ttuhsc.edu. Office: Tex Tech U Health Sci Ctr Sch Medicine 3601 4th St Rm 1c282 Lubbock TX 79430-0001

KAYE, GEORGES SABRY, physician; b. Nice, France, May 21, 1949; s. Georges and Claire (Cases) K.; m. Georgina Margaret Knott Kaye, 1980 (div. 1989); children: Charles Edwin, Alice Georgina, Olivia Sarah. BSc, Kings Coll., London, 1971; MB BS, Westminster Hosp., London, 1973. Co. physician Claris Intrnat., U.K., Air France, U.K.; European med. dir. GE; co. physician Salomon Bros. Internat.; physician-in-charge O.H. Cromwell Hosp., London. Author: The Thirst, 1973. Recipient scholarship Clev. Clinic, 1973. Mem. Internat. Commn. on Occupational Health, Royal Soc. Medicine, Soc. Occupational Health, Reform Club. Avocations: novels, psychological writing, music. Home: Braco Castle, By Dunblane Perthshire, Scotland Office: Cromwell Hosp, Cromwell Rd, London SW50TU, England

KAYE, GERALD CYRIL, physician, consultant; b. Luton, Bedfordshire, Eng., Apr. 5, 1955; s. Henry Kawalgk and Sally Berenholtz Kaye; m. Conor Jane Brolhy, Jan. 6, 1990; 1 child, Avi Cuo. MB ChB, Manchester U., 1978, MD, 1988. Rsch. registrar London, 1984-87; cardiology registrar Leeds, U.K., 1987-89; lectr. U. Leeds, U.K., 1987-92; cons. cardiologist East Yorks Trust, U.K., 1992—. Jr. rsch. fellow British Heart Found., 1984-86. Mem. Royal Coll. Physicians. Avocations: saxophone, guitar. Office: Castle Hill Hosp, Dept Cardio Castle Rd, Cottingham HU16 5JN, United Kingdom

KAYE, LORI, actress, news reporter, producer; d. Eldin Bert and Katherine Angeline Onsgard. Student, Detroit Inst. Art, 1951, 56, U. N.Mex., 1960. Actress, radio and TV commls., 1951-82, Warner Bros., 1960-64; dir., v.p. John Robert Powers Schs., L.A., 1961-71; v.p. Electron Industries, Torrance, Calif., 1963-65; pres. Lori Kaye Cosmetics, Hollywood, Calif., 1964-70; co-owner, v.p. K and S Employment, Calif. Fashion Mart, 1965-67; dir. Caroline Leonetti Ltd. Sch., Hollywood, 1976-79; pres. Lori Kaye's Internat. Travel Acad., North Hollywood, Calif., 1980-98, Global Image Prodns., Studio City, Calif., 1999—; internat. cons. Internat. Career Acad., Van Nuys, 1978—; pres. Molori Publs., Studio City, Calif., 1981—; cons. A&T Inst. Travel and Tourism, 1982; lectr. in field, 1969—. Paintings include in UNICEF collection, 1967; hostess TV talk show The New You, Sta. KTTV, Hollywood, 1964-65; hostess TV show Lori Kayes Week-End Escape, Sta. KCBS, 1997—; travel expert, live travel TV show hostess, spl. assignment TV reporter U-Team, Sta. CBS-2, 1997—; instr. travel tourism UCLA, 1997—. Dir. project Camarillo State Hosp., 1963-69; cons. Job Corps; dir., instr., adminstr. Calif. Pvt. Postsecondary Edn. Instns., 1995; instr. travel tourism U. So. Calif., 1997—. Recipient Mental Health Achievement award, 1967. Mem. NAFE, Assn. for Promotion of Tourism Africa, AAU, SAG, AFTRA, Smithsonian Assocs., Am. Soc. Travel Agts., Internat. Airline Travel Agts. Network, Internat. Air Transport Assn., Soc. Travel Agts. in

Govt., Calif. Assn. Pvt. Postsecondary Schs., Nat. Geog. Soc., Internat. Platform Assn., Better Bus. Bur. (arbitrator), L.A. World Affairs Coun., Universal City-No. Hollywood C. of C. Office: Lori Kayes Internat Travel Ctr 12723 Ventura Blvd Studio City CA 91604-2430

KAYLOR, JEFFERSON DANIEL, JR., marketing manager; b. Birmingham, Ala., Dec. 10, 1947; s. Jefferson Daniel and Mary Charlye (Montague) K.; m. Terry Frances Hill, June 13, 1970; children: Christopher Robert, Laure Danielle. BS, USN Acad., 1970; MBA, Fla. Inst. Tech., 1981, MS, 1983. Sr. electronic systems engr. E-Systems, Garland, Tex., 1977-79; sr. staff engr. Sperry, Clearwater, Fla., 1979-83; program mgr. Amecom div. Litton Systems, College Park, Md., 1983-85, program dir., 1985-87, dir. program devel., 1989-94; v.p. ops. Micro-Tel div. Adams-Russell, Hunt Valley, Md., 1987-88, div. mgr., 1988-89; sr. program mgr. AEL Industries, Inc., Lansdale, Pa., 1994-96; mgr. advanced devel. SCI Sys., Huntsville, Ala., 1996-98, mktg. mgr., 1997; dir. Miltope Corp., Huntsville, 1998-99; mgr. program devel. GroupTechs. Corp., Tampa, Fla., 2000—. Lt. USN, 1970-77, capt. USNR, ret. 1997. Republican. Methodist. Avocations: golf, sailing, motorcycling. Home: PO Box 47106 Tampa FL 33647-0110 Office: Group Tech 10901 Malcolm McKinley Dr Tampa FL 33612-6455

KAYMAZ, ZEREFSAN, educator; b. Samsun, Turkey, Jan. 15, 1963; d. Cemal and Meliha (Köse) K. BSc, Istanbul (Turkey) Tech. U., 1984, MSc, 1988; MSc, UCLA, 1991, PhD, 1993. Rsch. asst. Istanbul Tech. U. UUBF, 1984-88, asst. prof., 1995-96, assoc. prof., 1996—; grad. student asst. dept. atmospheric sci. UCLA, 1991-93; postdoctoral rschr. Boston U. CSP, 1993-94; rsch. fellow Boston U./CSP, 1996, 97; vis. rschr. Johns Hopkins U./APL, Balt., 1998, cons., 1999. Contbr. articles to profl. jours. Recipient Young Scientist award Turkish Sci. and Tech. Rsch. Coun., Istanbul, 1999; scholar Turkish Higher Edn. Coun., Istanbul, 1988. Mem. Am. Geophys. Union, Am. Meteorol. Soc., European Geophys. Soc. Avocations: tennis, volleyball, traveling, photography, reading. Office: Istanbul Tech U, Faculty Aero and Astron, 80626 Maslak Istanbul, Turkey

KAYNAK, GÖKAY ZEKI, nuclear physicist, researcher; b. Ankara, Turkey, June 3, 1952; s. Akif and Hesna (Erdal) K.; m. Gönül Mutel, Aug. 22, 1974; children: Isin, Gigdem. PhD, Dicle U., Turkey, 1980. Asst. U. Diyarbakir, Turkey, 1974-80, lectr., 1980-84; asst. prof. U. Bursa, Turkey, 1984-86, assoc. prof., 1996—; head Sci. Inst., U. Diyarbakir, 1982-84. Mem. European Phys. Soc., Turkish Physics Soc. E-mail: kaynak@uludag.edu.tr. Home: Uludag Univ Lojmanlori 5/8, 16059 Bursa Turkey Office: Uludog Univ, Faculty Sci and Arts, 16059 Bursa Turkey

KAYNE, JON BARRY, industrial psychologist; b. Sioux City, Iowa, Oct. 20, 1943; s. Harry Aaron and Barbara Valentine (Daniel) K.; m. Bunee Ellen Price, July 25, 1965; children: Nika Jenine, Abraham; m. Sandra Kay Fossbender, Jan. 5, 1985; 1 child, Shay-Marie Kathryn. BA, U. Colo., 1973; MSW, U. Denver, 1975; PhD, U. No. Colo., 1978. With spl. svcs. Weld County Sch. Dist. 6, Greeley, Colo., 1975-77; forensic diagnostician Jefferson County (Colo.) Diagnostic Unit, 1977-78; assoc., dir. mktg. 1 Dow Ctr., assoc. prof. psychology Hillsdale (Mich.) Coll., 1978-87; pres. Jon B. Kayne, P.C., Hillsdale, 1980-87; pres. bd. dirs. Lang. Learners in Partnership of Omaha, 1989-93; chmn. bd. dirs., CEO Am. Internat. Mgmt. Assocs., Ltd., Denver, 1984-87; prof. bus. adminstrn. and psychology Bellevue (Neb.) U., 1987—, v.p. profl. and continuing edn. studies, 1987-93, v.p. acad. affairs, 1993—. Chmn. bd. dirs. Domestic Harmony, 1979-82; bd. dir. religious sch., Greeley, 1975-77; candidate for sheriff of Boulder County, 1974. With USAR, 1962. Mem. Am. Psychol. Assn., Am. Soc. Clin. Hypnosis, Am. Statis. Assn., Internat. Neuropsychol. Soc., Mich. Soc. Investigative and Forensic Hypnosis (chmn. bd., pres. 1982), N.Y. Acad. Scis., Phi Delta Kappa, Psi Chi, Alpha Gamma Sigma. Office: Bellevue U 1000 Galvin Rd S Bellevue NE 68005-3098

KAYODE, OYEWUMI ABIWONLEKO, military officer, aircraft technician; b. Ile-Ife, Osun State, Nigeria, July 1954; s. Salami Gbadamosi Salami and Ayoka Jimoh Wulemoth Oyewumi; m. Ose Ogumakinwa Yemi, Dec. 12, 1982; children: Saheed, Kazeem, Funmilayo. Secondary, Oduduwa Coll., 1999; primary, Nigeria Airforce Sch., 2000. Lic. aircraft technician. Engrng. control officer Presdl. Fleet, Abuja, Nigeria, 1999, Nigeria Air Force, Benin, Nigeria, 1999-2000; aircraft technician Nigeria Air Force, 1995-2000. Local govt. task force supr. IKEJ Local Govt., 1981. Flight sgt. Air Force, 1974-2000. Avocations: table tennis, film, flying, music, traveling. Home: Ikeja Lagos, Nafpmbikj, Lagos Nigeria Office: Nigeria Air Force PMB 1145, 81 Air Centry Edo State, Benin City Nigeria

KAYSER, PAUL, judge. Pres. Superior Ct. Justice Luxembourg. Office: Cour Superiéure de Justice, Rue d'Eich, Luxembourg Luxembourg*

KAZAKEVITCH, OLGA ANATOLIEVNA, linguist, researcher; b. Moscow, Feb. 6, 1948; d. Anatoly Alexandrovich Bylin-Lubertsev and Julia Petrovna Kazakevitch; m. Leonid Markovich Chachko, Mar. 17, 1973 (div. Feb. 1977); 1 child, Alexei; m. Alexander Alexandrovich Malinovsky, May 18, 1977 (div. 1999); 1 child, Sergei. MA, Lomonosov U., Moscow, 1971, PhD, 1989. Jr. rschr. Rsch. Computational Ctr. Lomonosov U., 1976-91, sr. rschr., 1992—; lectr. Lomonosov U., 1991-93; sr. rschr. Rsch. Ctr. Ethnic and Lang. Rels. Inst. Linguistics Russian Acad. Scis., 1992—. Author: Using Computers in Studies of Unwritten and New Written Languages, 1990; co-author: The Selkup Language, The Taz Dialect, vol. 1, 1980, vol. 2, 1993; contbr. articles to profl. jours. Expert working group on minorities UN, Geneva, 1997. Grantee Internat. Found. Cultural Initiative, 1993, Internat. Found. Sci., 1994, Assn. of Univs. and Colls. of Canada, 1997; Rsch. Support Scheme Open Soc. Support Found., 1998; recipient Medal to the 850th Anniversary of Moscow. Mem. Internat. Sociol. Assn. (rsch. com. 1998—), Internat. Assn. Quebec Studies. Office: Russian Acad Sci Inst Linguistics, B Kislovsky Per 1/12, 103009 Moscow Russia

KAZAMA, TOSHIO, humanities educator; b. Tokyo, Jan. 2, 1924; s. Kiichi and Mume (Yamana) K.; m. Kazuyo Shimomura, May 10, 1955; children: Keiichi, Shinjiro, Naoto. BA, Tokyo U., 1947, grad., 1949; grad., Tokyo U., 1952. Instr., asst. prof. liberal arts Hosei U., Tokyo, 1969-74, prof. liberal arts, 1974-94; bd. dirs. Japanese Assn. Indian and Buddhist Studies. Author: A New Interpretation of Bi-Yan-Ji, 1978. Cadet Japanese Shipping Engr., 1945. Avocation: seal engraving. Home: Shimorenjaku 6-4-23, Mitaka 181-0013, Japan

KAZAMA, YASUHIRO, communications executive; b. Yamanashi, Japan, Aug. 2, 1950; s. Yasunori and Fukuyo (Kunugi) K.; m. Harumi Hirose, Oct. 22, 1981; children: Yuichiro, Shingo. B Engring, Hosei U., Tokyo, 1976, M Engrng., 1978; D Engrng. (hon.), Chiba (Japan) Inst. Tech., 1999. Engr. Hitachi Device Engrng., Chiba, 1978-80; engr. Japan Radio Co., Ltd., Tokyo, 1980-85, sr. engr., 1985-91, assoc. mgr., 1991-95, mgr., 1995—. Inventor antenna element, parabola antenna, rhombic antenna. Avocations: music, painting, art. Home: 4-13-33 Hiyoshi, Kokubunji 185-0032, Japan Office: Labs Japan Radio Co Ltd, 5-1-1 Shimo-Renjaku, Mitaka-shi Tokyo 181-8510, Japan

KAZAN, ELIA, theatrical, motion picture director and producer, author; b. Constantinople, Turkey, Sept. 7, 1909; s. George and Athena (Sismanoglou) K.; m. Molly Day Thacher, Dec. 2, 1932 (dec.); children: Judy, Chris, Nick, Katharine; m. Barbara Loden, June 5, 1967 (dec.); 1 child, Leo; m. Frances Rudge, June 28, 1982. A.B., Williams Coll., 1930; postgrad., Yale U., 1930-32; M.F.A., Wesleyan U., Middletown, Conn., 1955. Co-founder Actors Studio. Actor with Group Theatre, 1932-39; dir. stage plays, 1940-55, including Skin of Our Teeth, Harriet, Jacobowsky and the Colonel, All My Sons, Deep Are the Roots, A Streetcar Named Desire, Death of a Salesman, Camino Real, Tea and Sympathy, Cat on a Hot Tin Roof, The Dark at the Top of the Stairs, J.B (Antoinette Perry award for direction 1958), Sweet Bird of Youth, After the Fall, But for Whom Charlie, The Changeling; numerous motion pictures, 1944—, including A Tree Grows in Brooklyn, Boomerang, Gentlemen's Agreement (Acad. award for best direction 1947), Pinky, Panic in the Streets, A Streetcar Named Desire, Zapata, Man on a Tight Rope, On the Waterfront, (1954 Acad. Award for best direction), East of Eden, Baby Doll, A Face in the Crowd, Wild River, Splendor in the Grass, America, America, The Arrangement, The Visitors, The Last Tycoon; author: America, America, 1962, The Arrangement, 1967, The Assassins, 1972, The Understudy, 1974, Acts of Love, 1978, The Anatolian, 1982, Elia Kazan-A Life, 1988, Beyond the Aegean, 1994. Recipient D.W. Griffith award Dirs. Guild Am., 1987, hon. Oscar (for Long, Disting. and Unparalleled Career), 1999.

KAZAN, ROBERT PETER, neurosurgeon; b. Chgo., Mar. 29, 1947; s. Peter Joseph and Genevieve (Pauga) K.; m. Janet Rae Hoiland, June 21, 1975. BS, Loyola U., Chgo., 1969, MD, 1973. Diplomate Am. Bd. Neurol. Surgeons; lic. physician Ill., Minn. Intern Mayo Clinic, Rochester, Minn., 1973-74, resident in neurosurgery, 1974-78; neurosurg. cons. West Suburban Neurosurg. Assocs., Hinsdale, Ill., 1978-92; med. dir. neurosci. dept. Hinsdale Hosp., 1992; clin. asst. prof. neurosurgery U. Ill., Chgo., 1983—; various teaching appointments West Suburban Hosp. Dept. Surgery, Chgo. Med. Soc. Midwest Conf., Northwestern U.; staff neurosurgeon Hinsdale Hosp., vice-chmn. surgery, 1988-90, chmn. dept. surgery, 1990—, med. dir. neurosci., 1992. Contbr. articles to profl. jours. Fellow ACS; mem. AMA, DuPage County Med. Soc., Ill. Med. Soc., Mayo Clin. Neurosurg. Soc., Congress Neurosurg. Surgeons, Am. Assn. Neurol. Surgeons, Cen. Neurosurg. Soc., Soc. Med. Cons. Armed Forces U.S., Am. Assn. Neurol. Surgeons (joint sec. trauma and disorders of spine and peripheal nerves), Congress Neurol. Surgeons (joint sect. trauma and disorders of spine and peripheral nerves), Internat. Skullbase Soc., Ill. State Neurosurg. Soc. (membership chmn. 1995, treas. 1996, sec.-treas. 1997, v.p. 1998, pres. 1999-2000). Republican. Roman Catholic. Office: West Suburban Neurosurg Assocs 20 E Ogden Ave Hinsdale IL 60521-3543

KAZANDJIEV, ROBERT FLAVY, mechanical engineer, mathematician, researcher; b. Sofia, Bulgaria, Apr. 30, 1948; s. Flavy Georgiev and Elena Angelova (Guleva) K.; m. Elena Radeva Tomova, May 2, 1980; 1 child, Bogdan Robertov. BS in Mechanics, Tech. U., Sofia, 1970, MS in Mechanics, 1972; BS in Math., U. Sofia, 1986. Charterted engr. metal plant, Kremikovtsi, Bulgaria, 1972-77; 3d degree rsch. fellow Inst. Mechanics and Biomechanics, Bulgarian Acad. Sci., Sofia, 1977-80, 2d degree rsch. fellow, 1980-85, 1st degree rsch. fellow, 1985—; head project Nat. Fund Sci. Rsch., Sofia, 1995-98. Author, editor: Laboratory Book on Mechanics I: Elasticity, Plassticity, Structure of Solids, 1987, II, Elasticity, Plasticity, Fracture of Solids, 1989, III, Elasticity, Plasticity, Non-Destructive Tests of Solids, 1991; also articles. Head local coordinating coun. Union Dem. Forces, 1990. With inf. Bulgarian Army, 1972-74. Avocations: angling, fly fishing. Home: 23 Fr Nansen St, 1000 Sofia Bulgaria Office: Inst Mechanics, Bl 4 G Bonchev St, 1113 Sofia Bulgaria

KAZANTSEVA, TATAYANA IVANOVNA, English educator; b. Volgograd, Russia, Nov. 8, 1950; d. Ivan Alexeevich and Elizaveta Grigorievna (Krukova) K.; 1 child, Kirill Vladimirovich. MS in Pedagogy, Pedagogical Inst. Fgn. Langs., Moscow, 1975. Asst. Russian Friendship U., Moscow, 1975-80, prof. English, 1980-84, sr. prof. English, 1984-93, lectr. Am. studies, 1993-96, master prof. English, 1996—; lang. cons. Tuborg Beer Co., Moscow, 1997-98; bus. lang. cons. Zeneca Co., Moscow, 1998-99. Fulbright grantee USIA, Washington, 1995. Mem. Am. Studies Assn., Russian-Am. Acad. Exch. Assn. Russian Orthodox. Avocations: gardening, painting, ornithology, dog training. Home: Fasadnaya St 5A-70, 143080 Lesnoy Gorodok Russia

KAZARYAN, MISHIK A., physics educator; b. Hrazdan, Armenia, Feb. 28, 1948; s. Haerazat G. Kazaryan and Serine M. Vanuni; m. Arpik A. Asratyan, March 4, 1975; children: Serine, Haerazat. Degree in physics and engrng., Moscow Physico-Tech. Inst., 1970, postgrad., 1975; D Phys.-Math., Lebedev Phys. Inst., Moscow, 1989. Engr. Lebedev Physics Inst., 1970—, head active optical sys. group, 1978—. Patentee in field. Recipient State prize USSR Govt., 1980. Mem. Euro-Asian Phys. Soc. (mem. coun. 1992), Armenian Phys. Soc., N.Y. Acad. Scis. Office: Lebedev Phys Inst, Leninsky Prospect 53, 117924 Moscow Russia

KAZAZIS, MARIO A., brand manager; b. Athens, July 26, 1969; s. Alexander and Catherine Kazazis; m. Cathy Hassapogianni, July 10, 1999. BA, U. Athens, 1992; cert., Athenian Ctr. of Comm., 1994; honors degree, Hellenic Productivity Ctr., 1994; MBA, U. Indpls., 1996. Acct. mgr. Greta Promotion, Athens-Salonica, 1994-96; brand mgr. Daewoo, Athens-Seoul, 1997-98; sr. brand mgr. Reckitt & Colman, Athens, 1998—; cons. in field, Athens. Mem. European Mktg. Confedn., Am. Mktg. Assn., Hellenic Mgmt. Assn. Avocations: sailing, movies, literature. Fax: 30 1 81 61 591. E-mail: mario.kazazis@reckittbenckiser.com. Home: 5 Aminiou St, 116 31 Athens Greece Office: Reckitt & Colman, 23d klm Athens-Lamia, 145 68 Attica Greece

KAZEMIAN, HOSSEIN, scientist, researcher; b. Bahabad, Iran, Sept. 23, 1968; s. Hassan Kazemian and Fatemeh Maleki Nedjad; m. Youshita Gashtil, Mar. 1, 1994; 1 child, Ali Seena. BSc, Isfahan (Iran) U., 1990, MSc, 1993, PhD, 1999. Mem. staff Isfahan (Iran) U., 1991-95, Payame noor U. Ardakan, Iran, 1993-95; mem. staff, rschr. Atomic Energy Orgn. Iran, Tehran, Iran, 1995—. Muslim.

KAZEN, JULIUS SIDNEY, hotel faculty executive; b. Bklyn., Dec. 24, 1956; s. Robert and Muriel (Edelstein) K.; m. Susan Fazen, Oct. 15, 1990; children: Thomas, Christopher. BFA, U. Las Vegas, 1980. Desk clk. Las Vegas (Nev.) Hilton, 1982-84, chief rm. clk., 1984-85, asst. hotel mgr., 1985-87, asst. dir. to dir. front office, 1987-95, exec. asst. mgr., 1995-99, asst. v.p. hotel ops., 1999—. Office: Las Vegas Hilton 3000 Paradise Rd Las Vegas NV 89109-1283

KAZI, ASADULLAH, engineering geologist; b. Nasarpur, Sindh, Pakistan, Nov. 1, 1943; s. Khudabakhsh and Kamul Kazi; m. Khurshaid Kazi, Oct. 27, 1968; children: Abdul Samad, Abdul Ahad, Abdul Subhan. BSc with honors, U. Sind, Hyderabad, Pakistan, 1963; MSc, Imperial Coll., London, 1965, PhD, 1968. Student demonstrator Imperial Coll., London, 1965-68; dep. dir. rsch. Engring. U., Lahore, Pakistan, 1969-70; assoc. prof. Sind U., Hyderabad, 1970-73; prof. Mehran U., Jamshoro, Pakistan, 1973-87; chmn. engrng. geology Asian Inst. Tech., Bangkok, Thailand, 1973-75; UNESCO expert (P-5) Ministry of Edn., Jeddah, Saudi Arabia, 1975-80; prof. King Abdulaziz U., Jeddah, 1980-88; tech. advisor Ministry of Petroleum and Mineral Resources, Jeddah, 1988-97; vice chancellor Isra U., Hyderabad Sindh, Pakistan, 1997—; postdoctoral rsch. fellow Norwegian Geotechnical Inst., Oslo, 1971-72; dir. rsch. Nat. Book Found., Islamabad, 1972; mem. Senate Asian Inst. Tech., Bangkok, 1973-75; engrng. geology advisor Centre for Applied Geology, Jeddah, 1975-80; mem. bd. studies Faculty of Earth Scis., Jeddah, 1980-87, mem. com. for grad. studies, 1987-88; supr. more than 35 master and doctoral theses, 1973—. Contbg. author: Studies in Abnormal Pressures, 1994; contbr. over 50 articles to profl. jours. Recipient Vice Chancellors medal U. Sind, 1963, Chancellors medal, 1964, Pride of Performance award King Abdul Aziz U., 1981, 82. Mem. ASCE, S.E. Asian Geotech. Soc., Internat. Assn. Engrng. Geologists, Internat. Soc. Rock Mechanics, Internat. Soc. Soil Mechanics and Found. Engrng. Muslim. Achievements include research in site characterization techniques in engineering geology; engineering assessment of earthquakes and other geohazards; abnormal pressures and accumulation of hydrocarbons; fabric of clays and its influence on engineering properties of soils; engineering geological aspects of Sabkhas, dams, tunnels, highways and geological materials; occurence movement and exploration of ground water; environmental assessment of landfills and hazardous waste disposal; fractal characterization of geological features and processes. Avocations: Oriental music, readings on creation of universe. Home: 69 St 5 N Gulistan-e-Sajjad, Hyderabad Sindh, Pakistan Office: Isra U, Hala Rd PO Box 313, Hydrabad Sindh Pakistan

KAZI, KAROLY, microwave engineer; b. Kiskunhalas, Bacs-Kiskn, Hungary, Sept. 24, 1955; s. Janos and Erzsebet (Papdi) K.; m. Erzsebet Kazine Budai; children: Agnes, Andrea. Diploma Elec. Engrng., Tech. U., Budapest, 1980, PhD, 1986. Jr. rsch. fellow Rsch. Inst. for Tech. Physics of Hungarian Acad. Scis., Budapest, 1980-83; asst. head microwave dept. Rsch. Inst. for Tech. Physics of H.A.S., Budapest, 1983-88, asst. head of microwave dept., 1988-90; rsch. fellow Rsch. Inst. for Tech. Physics of H.A.S., 1992-93, Yokogawa Elec. Corp., Tokyo, 1990-92; tech. dir. Bonn Hungary Electronics, Budapest, 1993-96, mng. dir., 1996—; mem. state examination bd., Tech. U., Budapest, 1994—. Devel. mgr.: Microwave Range Finder Development, 1983-86 (Pres. award of Hungarian Acad. of Sci. 1986); patentee in field (Gold prize of Inventors 1988). Mem. IEEE (founder, chmn. MTT/AP/ED/COM 1987—), Scientific Soc. for Telecomm. (vice-sec.-gen. 1981—). Avocations: taking video-films, skiing, rowing, outing, music. Office: Bonn Hungary Electronics, PO Box 164/Foti u 56, H-1325 Budapest Hungary

KAZI, SHAHNAZ, science educator; b. Hyderabad, Sindh, Pakistan, Aug. 18, 1959; parents Waqfullah and Mehmooda Kazi. MSc, U. Sindh, Jamshoro, 1981; MPhil, NCEAC, Jamshoro, 1992; PhD in Chemistry, NCEAC, U. Sindh, 1998. Lectr. Govt. Girls Coll., Jamshoro, 1983-85, Hyderabad, Sindh, 1985-89; lectr. Govt. K.B.M.S. Coll., Hyderabad, 1989-99, asst. prof., 1999—; head dept. chemistry Govt. K.B.M.S. Coll., Hyderabad, 1989—. Mem. ACS, CSP. Avocations: computer programming, reading books. Home: B/99 Tilak-in-Cline, 71000 Hyderabad Sindh, Pakistan Office: Govt K B M S Coll, Sakhi Peer Rd, 71000 Hyderabad Sindh, Pakistan

KAZIAE, NIKOLA, veterinarian, beekeeper; b. Banja Luka, Bosnia, Croatia, Jan. 14, 1946; s. Franjo and Rubica (Kneeviae) K.; m. Janja; m. Dubravka Stavljeniae, Feb. 28, 1977; 1 child, Dubravko. Asst., Inst. Rudjer Boškoviae, Zagreb, Croatia, 1985; Asst. Prof., Faculty Agr., Zagreb, Croatia, 1988, Prof., 1997. Jr. asst. beekeeping and fish pathology Vet. Faculty, Zagreb, 1972-78; asst. Inst Rudjer Bošsilviae, Zagreb, 1978-88; asst. prof. beekeeping Faculty Agr. U. Zagreb, 1988-97, prof. beekeeping Faculty Agr., 1997—; head katedra Faculty Agr. Vice-editor: Agr. conspectus scientificus. Mem. Apimondia (mem. economy commn. 1991). Avocations: hunting, surfing. Office: Faculty Agr, Svetosimunska 25, Zagreb HR-10000, Croatia

KAZIMEE, BASHIR AHMAD, educator, architect; b. Kandahar, Afghanistan, Apr. 20, 1947; came to U.S., 1981; s. Mohammad Kazim and Mehr Negar K.; m. Parveen B., Mar. 23, 1978; children: Maryam, Reshad, Dawoud. BA in Architecture with honors, Kabul (Afghanistan) U., 1973; MArch, MIT, 1977; diploma (hon.), Mich. State U., 1977, Internat. Acad. Architecture, 1996. Lic. architect, Tex. Rschr. Harvard U., Cambridge, Mass., 1977; asst. prof. Kabul U., 1977-80; lectr. Tex. Tech U., Lubbock, Tex., 1981-84; asst. prof. King Faisal U., Dammam, Saudi Arabia, 1984-89, Wash. State U., Pullman, Wash., 1990-95; architect self-employed, Wash., 1990—; assoc. prof. Wash. State U., 1995—; architect Memar Collaborative, Kabul, 1977-79; Noon Qayum & Co., Lahore, Pakistan, 1980-82; Harsen & Johns Architects, Rochelle Park, N.J., 1989; lectr. in field. Contbr. over 34 articles to profl. jours. Recipient IAA/U.N. Gold Medal, 1996; edn. and rsch. grantee U.S. AID, Kabul U., 1976, U.S. Internat. Devel. Mich. State U., 1977, HUD, 1994, Sch. Architecture. Mem. AIA (coun. archtl. rsch. nat. award, 1998). Avocations: travel, chess player, poetry, philosophy. Office: Wash State Sch Architecture Carpenter Hall Pullman WA 99163

KAZINCZI, GABRIELLA, horticulturist; b. Salgotarjan, Hungary, Mar. 15, 1964; d. Ferenc and Ilona (Fodor) K.; m. Istvan Pacseszak, May 15, 1988; children: Dora Pacseszak, Eszter Pacseszak. Aspirant, Hungarian Acad. Scis., Keszthely, 1987-90, Pannon U. Agrl. Scis., Keszthely, Hungary, 1995; PhD, Pannon U. Agrl. Scis., Keszthely, Hungary, 1996. Rsch. asst. Pannon U. Agrl. Scis., 1996—; rschr. Georgikon Faculty Agrl. Scis. U. Veszprem, Keszthely. Contbr. over 100 articles to sci. pubis. Bolyai rsch. scholar Hungarian Acad. Scis., 1998—; recipient medal Hungarian Agrarian Soc., Budapest, 1998. Mem. European Weed Rsch. Soc. (Hungarian divsn.), IOBC (mem. WPRS working group 2000—). Avocations: travel, swimming. Home: Balogh F U 5/A, 8360 Keszthely Hungary Office: Univ Veszprem GMK, Deak F 16, 8360 Keszthely Hungary

KAZMAIER, ULI, chemist, educator; b. Boennigheim, Germany, Jan. 17, 1960; s. Eberhard and Gudrun (Beck) K. PhD, U. Stuttgart, Germany, 1989; Habilitation, U. Heidelberg, Germany, 1997. Postdoctoral rschr. Manfred T. Reetz, Marburg, Germany, 1990-91; postdoctoral rschr. Barry M. Trost Stanford (Calif.) U., 1991-92; private docent Organisch-Chem. Inst., Heidelberg. Mem. German Soc. Chemists, Am. Chem. Soc. Office: Organisch-Chemisches Inst, Im Neuenheimer Feld 270, 69120 Heidelberg Germany

KAZMER, WILLIAM JAMES, retired traffic and distribution manager; b. Kenosha, Wis., May 29, 1914; s. Max Kazmer and Gertrude Alice McManus; m. Mary Kazmer, June 29, 1940; 1 child, Mary Kathleen. Student, Union Grove Tchrs. Coll., 1933-36; Interstate Commerce Commn. practitioner, U. of Wis., Milw., 1962. Rate clk. C & NW Rlwy., Waukegan, Ill., 1936-46; traffic mgr. Snap On Inc., Kenosha, Wis., 1946-66; mgr. traffic and distbn. Borg Inc., Delavan, Wis., 1966-77; exec. dir. Wis. Movers Assn., Kenosha, 1968-84; pres. Wisdel Traffic Bur., Kenosha, 1968-90; practitioner Interstate Commerce Commn., Washington, 1962, Fed. Maritime Commn., Washington, 1962. Pres. Middlewest Shipper-Motor Carrier Conf., 1966-67; gen. traffic com., chmn. Wis. Mfrs. Assn., 1971-72. Recipient Founder plaque Am. Soc. Traffic and Transp., Emeritus award, 1977, Cert. of Appreciation, 1996. Mem. U. Wis. Mgmt. Inst. (spkr., plaque), U. Marquette (spkr. Packaging Inst., plaque), S.W. Traffic Club (pres. 1971-72). Republican. Roman Catholic. Avocations: golf, walking. Home: 8835 42d Ave Kenosha WI 53142-5003

KAZOR, WALTER ROBERT, statistical process control and quality assurance consultant; b. Avonmore, Pa., Apr. 16, 1922; s. Steven Stanley and Josephine (Lestic) K.; m. Gloria Rosalind Roma, Aug. 10, 1946; children: Steven Edward, Christopher Paul, Kathleen Mary Jo. BS in Mech. Engrng., Pa. State U., 1943; MS, U. Pitts., 1953, M of Letters in Econs. and Indsl. Mgmt., 1957. Registered profl. engr., Pa. Rsch. engr. Gulf Oil Corp., Pitts., 1946-57; with Westinghouse Electric Corp., Tampa, Fla., 1957-84, quality assurance mgr. breeder reactor components project, 1977-81, mgr. nuclear svc. ctr., 1981-84; pres. Integrated Quality Systems Corp., Mgmt. Quality Assurance Cons., St. Petersburg, Fla., 1984-86; quality assurance specialit in nuclear waste mgmt. Sci. Applications Internat. Corp., Las Vegas, 1986-88; sr. cons. statis. process control and quality assurance Fischbach Tech. Svcs., Inc., Dallas, 1988-89; sr. cons. Savannah River site Gen. Physics Corp., Aiken, S.C., 1990-91; chmn., bd. dirs. ABB Fed. Tech. Svcs., Aiken, S.C., 1990-91; prin. engr. Applied Stats. Reynolds Elec. Engrng. Co., Las Vegas, Nev., 1992—; cons., guest lectr. in field. Author; patentee in field. Bd. dirs. New Kensington (Pa.) coun. Boy Scouts Am., 1958-62. With USNR, 1944-46. Mem. ASME, Am. Soc. Quality Control, Lions (past pres.). Republican. Roman Catholic. Home: 1120 88th Ave N Saint Petersburg FL 33702-2966

KAZUMA, NORIO, pediatrician; b. Haramachi-shi, Japan, Aug. 25, 1954; s. Haruhisa and Tsuneko (Watanabe) K.; m. Masako Watanabe, June 17, 1986; children: Hiroki, Takaki. BS, Juntendo U., Tokyo, 1982; MD, Tokyo Women's Med. Coll., 1990. Asst. prof. Tokyo Women's Med. Coll., Daini Hosp., 1985—. Contbr. articles to profl. jours. Mem. Internat. Soc. Chronobiology. Avocations: reading, music, swimming. Home: Higashi Nakacho 14-13, Urawa-shi Saitama-ken 336-0005, Japan Office: Tokyo Women's Med Coll 116-8567, Daini Hosp Dept Pediatrs, Nishioku Arakawa-ku 2-1-10, Japan

KAZUMASA, TAKEI, manufacturing and quality management engineer, consultant; b. Nagano, Japan, Dec. 7, 1950; m. Miwako Takei, May 25, 1980; 3 children. M in Engrng., Keio U., Yokohama, Japan, 1976. Registered lead auditor Inst. Quality Assurance, London. Chief engr. Nittan Valve Co., Hatano, Japan, 1976-84; chief cons. JMA Consulting, Tokyo, 1984-94; mgr. Shindengen Elec. Mfg., Hanno, Japan, 1994—; cons. heavy industry co., Korea, 1987-88, elec. co., Korea, 1988-90, automotive co., Korea, 1992-93, air conditioner co., Japan, 1984-87. Author: A New Engineering Management and Production Technology, 1993, (text for corr. course) Introduction to ISO 9000, 1994. Mem. Children's Internat. Summer Village, Japan, 1992—. Avocations: camping, agricultural work, travel, carpentry. Home: 1-7-17 Tsukimino, Yamato-City Kanagawa 242-0002, Japan

KAZUYA, TETSUJI, business educator; b. Kure, Japan, Mar. 20, 1944; s. Kengiro and Yotsue (Tatebe) K.; m. Keiko Matsushita, Nov. 11, 1973. MEcon, U. Osaka Prefecture, Japan, 1969. Lectr. Osaka Shogyo U., Higashi, Japan, 1973-78, assoc. prof., 1973-90, prof. bus. orgn., 1990—. Author: Organization Theory of Business, 1980, Organization Theory of Modern Business, 1985. Mem. mediation com. Higashi-Osaka Ct., 1992;

adminstrv. monitor Nara Prefecture, Japan, 1993-94l mem. com. adminstrv. change Haibara, Japan, 1997—. Mem. Assn. Organizational Sci. (bd. dirs. 1993-96). Home: Akanedai 2-13-8, Nara Haibara 633 0256, Japan Office: Osaka Shogyo U Fac Commerce, Mikuriya Sakae Machi 4-1-10, Osaka Higashi-Osaka 577 8505, Japan

KAŽYS, RYMANTAS JONAS, electronics educator; b. Skuodas, Lithuania, Feb. 3, 1943; s. Juozas and Barbora (Strakšyte) K.; m. Saule Marija Čepaityte, Dec. 26, 1964; 1 child, Elena. Degree in engring., Kaunas (Lithuania) Poly. Inst., 1965, PhD, 1970, DSc, 1981, prof., 1982. Rschr., assoc. prof. Kaunas Poly. Inst., 1965-81, chief dept., 1982-91, sci. dir. lab., 1991-93, 95-96, dir. ultrasound rsch. ctr., 1996—; vis. rschr. U. Tokyo, 1977-78; prof. Nat. Inst. Applied Scis., Lyon, France, 1991; sr. scientist Lorentzen & Wettre AB, Kista, Sweden, 1993-95; vis. prof. Uppsala U., Sweden, 1994-96. Author: Piezoelectric Transducers for Measuring Devices, 1975, Ultrasonic Information Measuring Systems, 1986, Imaging and Automation of Non-Destructive Testing, 1993, Measurements of Non-Electric Quantities, 1997; contbr. over 120 articles to profl. jours.; over 90 patents in field. Recipient Lithuanian State Prize, 1975, prize Ministry Coun. of Lithuania, 1988, prize Acad. of Scis. of Lithuania, 1994, Lithuanian Sci. prize, 2000. Mem. IEEE, Acoustical Soc. Am. Home: Saules 39-12, 3031 Kaunas Lithuania Office: Kaunas U Tech, Studentu 50, 3031 Kaunas Lithuania

KDOLSKY, RICHARD K., surgeon; b. Vienna, Austria, Nov. 5, 1964; s. Leopold and Cornelia (Kollwentz) K. MD, U. Vienna, 1989. Rsch. scientist dept. traumatology U. Vienna, 1989, asst. dept. traumatology, 1990—, lectr. dept. traumatology, 1994—; resident Lorenz Böhler-Trauma Ctr., Vienna, 1990, specialist in traumatology, 1996. Contbr. articles to profl. jours. Lorenz Böhler Found. grantee, 1991. Mem. European Soc. Sports Traumatology, Knee Surgery and Arthroscopy, Orthopaedic Rsch. Soc., N.Y. Acad. Scis. Roman Catholic. Avocation: violin. Home: Dachensteingasse 4, A-2700 Wr Neustadt Austria Office: U Vienna Dept Traumatology, Währinger Gurtel 18-20, A-1090 Vienna Austria

KE, CHIH-MING, engineer, semiconductor company official; b. Hsin-Chu, Taiwan, Nov. 18, 1964; s. Lien-Fu Ke and Pau-Feng Huang; m. Juchien Chao, Apt. 13, 1997; 1 child, Howard. BS, Nat. Tsing-Hua (Taiwan) U., 1988; MS, Northwestern U., 1994, PhD, 1995. Cert. engr. Prin. engr. etching process sect. Taiwan Semicondr. Mfg. Co., Ltd., Hsin-Chu, 1996-98, team leader, 1998-99, tech. mgr. advanced lithography divsn., 1999—. 1d lt. arty. Taiwan Army, 1988-90. Fax: 886-3-5790298. E-mail: cmke!tsmc.com.tw. Home: Hsin-Chu PO Box 2-26, Hsin-Chu Taiwan Office: Taiwan Semicondr Mfg Co Ltd, 9 Creation Rd, Hsin-Chu Taiwan

KE, WEIZHONG, chemist, educator; b. Poyang, Jiangxi, China, July 30, 1947; s. Zhi and Minsheng (Jiang) K.; m. Qinfen Xia; 1 child, Lin. BS, Nanjing Normal U., 1982, MS, 1986. Asst. engr. Nanjing Normal U., 1982-87, engr., 1987-94, assoc. prof. and dir. Laser Raman Spectroscopy Lab., 1994—. Recipient 3d prize sci. advance Govt. of Province of Jiangsu, 1995. Fellow Raman Spectroscopy Soc.; mem. Optical Soc., Phys. Soc. Office: Nanjing Normal U, Physics/Chemistry Ctrl Lab, Nanjing 210097, People's Republic of China

KEAN, JOHN VAUGHAN, retired lawyer; b. Providence, Mar. 12, 1917; s. Otho Vaughan and Mary (Duell) K. AB cum laude, Harvard U., 1938, JD, 1941; grad., U.S. Army War Coll., 1970. Bar: R.I. 1942. With Edwards & Angell, Providence, 1941—, ptnr., 1954-87, of counsel, 1987—. Bd. dirs. The Robbins Co., Attleboro, Mass., Greater Providence YMCA, 1964-76; chmn. Downtown Providence YMCA, 1964-67. Capt. AUS, 1943-46, 50-52, brig. gen. Decorated Legion of Merit. Mem. ABA, R.I. Bar Assn., N.G. Assn., Res. Officers Assn., Assn. U.S. Army, R.I. Army N.G. (brig. gen. 1964-72), Harvard R.I. Club (pres. 1964-66), Soc. Cin. (R.I. hon.), Agawam Hunt Club, Hope Club (v.p. 1996—, bd. govs. 1996—), Providence Art Club, Army and Navy Club (Washington), Sakonnet Golf Club (Little Compton, R.I.). Home: 518 W Main Rd Little Compton RI 02837-1121 Office: Edwards & Angell 2800 Bank Boston Plz Providence RI 02903-2499

KEANE, JOHN PATRICK, retired secondary education educator; b. N.Y.C., Nov. 28, 1931; s. John and Mary (Walsh) K.; m. Lucille Ann Dunn, Apr. 3, 1976. BA in English, Iona Coll., 1954; JD, Fordham U., 1963, MS in Edn., 1965; EdM, Columbia U., 1973; MA in English, CUNY, 1984. Cert. secondary tchr. (English), adminstr., N.Y.C., N.Y. State. Tchr. area jr. h.s., N.Y.C., 1962-65; tchr. h.s. English N.Y.C. Bd. Edn., Bklyn., 1965-93; dean of boys W.H. Taft H.S., Bronx, 1969-72; reading, writing coord. John F. Kennedy H.S., Bronx, 1985-91; tchr. English advanced placement John F. Kennedy H.S., Manhattan Coll., Bronx, 1991-93, retired, 1993. Editor, compiler: (manual) Handbook for Teachers of Reading and Writing, 1987, Writing Sampler (student's work), 1989-91 biannual. Founder Hamilton Heights Dems., 1965-69; candidate N.Y. State Assembly, 1965; Dem. candidate 1st Selectman, North Stonington, 1997; mem. North Stonington, Conn. Bd. Edn; justice of peace North Stonington; chmn. North Stonington Dem. Town Com. MA thesis placed on permanent display as model, Lehman Coll., CUNY, Bronx, 1984. Mem. NEA (del. local 2), Am. Fedn. Tchrs. (del. local 2), United Fedn. Tchrs. (del N.Y. State, chpt. leader, unity com.), N.Y. State United Tchrs., Delta Kappa Pi, Phi Delta Kappa. Roman Catholic. Avocations: poetry, drama, environmentalist. Home: 6 Wyassup Lake Rd North Stonington CT 06359-1124

KEANE, PHILIP VINCENT, investment company executive; b. London, Aug. 11, 1940; s. Bernard Vincent and Brenda Ellen (Ford) K.; m. Kathleen Winifred Thomson, Sept. 18, 1965; children: Angelina Teresa, Noelle Francesca. BSc in Econs., London Sch. Econs., 1963. Equity fund mgr. Prudential Pensions, London, 1976-78; dir. Rea Bros Plc, London, 1978-82, Wardley Investment Svcs, London, 1982-88, HK Unit Trust Co., London, 1982-88, CS Investments, London, 1989-92, IBJ Asset Mgmt. Internat., Plc, London, 1992-99; cons. Bluestone Capital Ptnrs. (U.K.) Ltd., London, 2000—. Assoc. mem. Inst. Investment Mgmt. and Rsch. Roman Catholic. Avocations: travel, photography, literature, music. Home: 70 Pine Grove, Off Lake Rd, Wimbledon, London SW19 7HE, England Office: Bluestone Capital Ptnrs Ltd, 12 Berkeley St, London W1X 5AD, England

KEARNEY, MARIANNE, biologist, researcher; b. Providence, Dec. 13, 1964; d. William Francis and Alice Miriam Kearney. BA in Biology, R.I. Coll., 1990. Rsch. assoc., lab. supr. St. Elizabeth's Med. Ctr., Boston, 1990—. Author: Atherosclerosis: Pathology of the Vasculature in Live Patients, 1999; contbr. numerous articles to sci. jours. Vol. Boston Cares, 1997—. Mem. AAAS. Avocations: skiing, golf, sculpting, volunteering, reading. E-mail: marianne77@aol.com.

KEARNS, ROBERT WILLIAM, manufacturing engineer, inventor; b. Gary, Ind., Mar. 10, 1927; s. Martin William and Mary Ellen (O'Hara) K.; m. Phyllis Joan McElwee, Aug. 1, 1953 (annulled Oct. 1980); children: Dennis M., Timothy B., Patrick S., Kathleen A., Maureen M., Robert M. Student, U.S. Army Fin. Sch., Ft. Atterbury, Ind., 1945-46; BME, U. Detroit, 1952; MS in Engring. Mechanics, Wayne State U., 1957; cert. Internat. Sch. Nuclear Sci., Argonne Nat. Labs., Chgo., 1958; PhD, Case Inst. Tech., 1964. Registered profl. mech. and elec. engr., Mich.. Rsch. engr. Bendix Rsch. Labs., Detroit, 1952-57; assoc. prof. engring., faculty advisor SPE student br. Wayne State U., Detroit, 1957-67; commr. Dept. Bldgs. & Safety Engring., Detroit, 1967-71; prin. investigator for fed. hwy. Nat. Inst. Sci. & Tech., Gaithersburg, Md., 1971-76; trial litigator U.S. Cts.- Auto U.S. Detroit Dist. Ct., 1978—. Inventor intermittent windshield wiper systems; holder numerous patents. Bd. dirs. Vets. of Office of Strategic Svcs. and William J. Donovan Meml. Found., Inc., 1994—, Office of Strategic Svcs. Soc., 1999—, sr. v.p., 2000—; bd. dirs. Queen Anne's County (Md.) Hist. Soc., 1995—; cand. Comptroller for State of Md., 1998—. With U.S. Army, 1945-47. Mem. OSS Soc. (sr. v.p. 2000—). Roman Catholic. Avocation: violinist. Office: Kearns Trust 301 Houghton Lab Ln Queenstown MD 21658-2500

KEATING, MARGARET MARY, entrepreneur, business consultant; b. Chgo., Feb. 18, 1950; d. Jeremiah Joseph and Margaret Mary (Donnelly) K. Cert. in law, U. Mass., 1993; BS, Emmanuel Coll., 1994; MBA, Simmons Coll., 1996. Sr. merchandiser J.C. Penney Co., Chgo., 1971-73, dist. mgr. fashions, 1973-75, regional mgr., 1976-78; gen. mgr. merchandise J.C. Penney Co., Aurora, Ill., 1978-82; co-founder, exec. v.p., dir. mktg. The Pres. Mgmt. Group, Inc., Hingham, Mass., 1984-88; pres., dir. Keating Konsult, Inc., Scituate, Mass., 1988—; v.p., co-founder Video Tours, Inc., Hartford, Conn., 1986-87. Founder Advocates for Moral and Ethical Treatment by Divorce Attys., Accord, Mass., 1991—. Mem. NAFE, LWV, Nat. Assn. for Women in Careers, Nat. Womens Polit. Caucus, Am. Mgmt. Assn., Ctr. for Entrepreneurial Mgmt. Democrat. Avocations: political and community drives. Home and Office: Keating Konsult 55 Richfield Rd Scituate MA 02066-3425

KEATINGE, ROBERT REED, lawyer; b. Berkeley, Calif., Apr. 22, 1948; s. Gerald Robert and Elizabeth Jean (Benedict) K.; m. Katherine Lou Carr, Feb. 1, 1969 (div. Dec. 1981); 1 child, Michael Towne; m. Cornelia Elizabeth Wyma, Aug. 21, 1982; 1 child, Courtney Elizabeth. BA, U. Colo., 1970; JD, U. Denver, 1973, LLM, 1982. Bar: Colo. 1974, U.S. Dist. Ct. Colo. 1974, U.S. Ct. Appeals (10th cir.) 1977, U.S. Tax Ct. 1980. Ptnr. Kubie & Keatinge, Denver, 1974-76; pvt. practice Denver, 1976; assoc. Richard Young, Denver, 1977-86; counsel Durham & Assoc. P.C., Denver, 1986-89, Durham & Baron, Denver, 1989-90; project editor taxation Shepard's/McGraw-Hill, Colorado Springs, Colo., 1990-96; of counsel Holland & Hart, LLP, Denver, 1992—; lectr. law U. Denver, 1982-92, adj. prof. grad. tax program, 1983-94. Author, cons. (CD-ROM) Entity Expert, 1996; co-author: Ribstein and Keatinge on Limited Liability Companies, 1992; contbr. articles to profl. jours. and treatises. Spkr. to profl. socs. and univs. including AICPA, ALI-ABA, U. TEx., 1984—. Recipient Law Week award U. Denver Bur. Nat. Affairs, 1974. Mem. ABA (chmn. subcom. ltd. liability cos. of com. on partnerships 1990-95, 2000—, chmn. com. on taxation 1995-99, mem. ho. of dels. 1996—, editl. bd. ABA/BNA Lawyer's Manual on Professional Conduct 1998—, chair 2000—, joint editl. bd. ABA/NCCUSL on unincorporated orgns. 1996—), Colo. Bar Assn. (ethics com., corp. code revision com., co-chmn. ltd. liability co. revision com., taxation sect. exec. coun. 1988-94, sec.-treas. 1991-92, chmn. 1993-94), Denver Bar Assn. Home: 460 S Marion Pky # 1904 Denver CO 80209-2544

KEATON, DIANE, actress; b. Santa Ana, Calif., Jan. 5, 1946. Student, Neighborhood Playhouse, N.Y.C., 1968. Appeared on N.Y. stage in Hair, 1968, Play It Again Sam, 1969, The Primary English Class, 1976; appeared in numerous films including Lovers and Other Strangers, 1970, Play It Again Sam, 1972, The Godfather, 1972, Sleeper, 1973, The Godfather Part II, 1974, Love and Death, 1975, I Will, I Will...For Now, 1975, Harry and Walter Go To New York, 1976, Annie Hall, 1977 (Best Actress Acad. award 1978, Brit. Acad. Best Actress award 1978, N.Y. Film Critics Circle award 1978, Nat. Soc. Film Critics award 1978), Looking for Mr. Goodbar, 1977, Interiors, 1978, Manhattan, 1979, Reds, 1981 (Acad. award nominee), Shoot the Moon, 1982, Little Drummer Girl, 1984, Mrs. Soffel, 1984, Crimes of the Heart, 1986, Radio Days, 1987, Baby Boom, 1987, The Good Mother, 1988, The Lemon Sisters, 1990, The Godfather Part III, 1990, Father of the Bride, 1991, Manhattan Murder Mystery, 1993, Look Who's Talking Now, 1993 (voice), Father of the Bride 2, 1995, Marvin's Room, 1996, First Wives Club, 1996, The Only Thrill, 1997, The Other Sister, 1999, Town and Country, 1999, Hanging Up, 1999; (TV movie) Running Mates, 1992, Amelia Earhart, 1994; dir. film: Heaven, 1987, Wildflower, 1991, Unstrung Heroes, 1995; accomplished artist and singer; author book of photographs: Reservations, 1980; editor: (with Marvin Heiferman) Still Life, 1983, Mr. Salesman, 1994; prodr.: The Lemon Sisters, 1990; exec. prodr.: Northern Lights (TV), 1997. Recipient Golden Globe award, 1978. Office: John Burnham William Morris Agy 151 S El Camino Dr Beverly Hills CA 90212-2704

KEATON, LAWRENCE CLUER, safety engineer, consultant; b. Gainesville, Tex., Nov. 24, 1924; s. William Lenard and Lettie (Phipps) K.; m. Emalee Prichard, Feb. 22, 1947; children: Lawrel Larsen, L.C. Jr., T.E. BSME, U. Okla., 1945; MS in Safety Mgmt. (hon.), Western States U., 1989, PhD in Bus. Adminstrn. (hon.), 1989. Registered profl. engr., Tex.; cert. lightning protection inspector; diplomate Coun. of Engring. Specialty Bds. In various engring. positions Phillips Petroleum Co., Borger, Tex., 1946-65; project devel. engr. Phillips Petroleum Co., N.Y.C., 1964-65; mng. dir. Nordisk Philback AB, Malmo, Sweden, 1965-73; dir. carbon black ops. Europe and Africa Phillips Petroleum Co., 1973-74, world-wide dir. carbon black ops., 1974-76; mng. dir. Sevalco Ltd., Bristol, Eng., 1976-81; ind. cons., 1981-85; mng. ptnr. System Engring. and Labs. Northwest Tex., Amarillo, 1985—. 5 patents in petrochem. processes. Lt. (j.g.) USN, 1943-45, PTO. Mem. ASME, Am. Soc. Safety Engrs., Lightning Protection Inst., Nat. Assn. Corrosion Engrs., Nat. Acad. Forensic Engrs., Nat. Assn. Fire Investigators, Nat. Assn. Profl. Accident Reconstruction Specialists, Nat. Soc. Profl. Engrs., Soc. Am. Mil. Engrs., Tex. Soc. Profl. Engrs., Amarillo Rotary, Shriners, Masons, Amarillo Club, Am. Legion, Tenn. Squires. Methodist. Avocations: gourmet cooking, gardening. Home: 7720 Baughman Dr Amarillo TX 79121-1752 Office: System Engring and Labs NW Tex PO Box 1506 Amarillo TX 79105-1506

KEATS, GLENN ARTHUR, manufacturing company executive; b. Chgo., July 1, 1920; s. Herbert J. and Agnes H. (Streich) K.; m. Olga Maria Loor Hurtado, Feb. 13, 1946; children: Maria Susana Keats Eggemeyer, Allwyn Dolores Keats Gustafson. BS in Commerce, Northwestern U., 1941. Sales exec. Keats-Lorenz Spring Co., Chgo., 1947-56; controller, auditor Plantaciones Ecuatorianas, S.A., Guayaquil, Ecuador, 1956-58; co-founder Keats Mfg. Co., Wheeling, Ill., 1958—. Sec. Hispanic Soc. Chgo., 1965—. Lt. comdr. USN, 1941-47. Mem. Spring Mfrs. Inst., Northwestern U. Alumni Assn., Sigma Nu. Republican. Lutheran. Club: Evanston Golf, Amelia Island (Fla.). Home: 368 Woodland Rd Highland Park IL 60035-5055 Office: 350 Holbrook Dr Wheeling IL 60090-5812

KEBEDE, BEREKET, economist, educator; b. Addis Ababa, Ethiopia, Oct. 26, 1963; s. Kebede Desta and Gebayanesh A.; m. Etalem Aberra; children: Mintewab B., Aklile Bereket. BA in Econs., Addis Ababa U., 1986; MSc, Oxford U., 1993, postgrad., 1997—. From grad. asst. lectr. to lectr. dept. econs. Addis Ababa U., Ethiopia, 1986—. Mem. Ethiopian Econs. Assn. (v.p. 1996-97), Oxford Soc., Ethiopan Wildlife and Natural History Soc., Am. Econs. Assn., Game Theory Soc., African Energy Policy Rsch. Network. Ethiopian Orthodox Christian. Avocations: literature, swimming, tennis. Fax: 44-01865-516973/554465. Home: 117 Summertown House, 369 Banbury Rd, Oxford OX2 7RD, England Office: Addis Ababa U Dept Econs, PO Box 1176, Addis Ababa Ethiopia Office: St Antonys Coll, Oxford OX2 6JF, England

KEBUDI, REJIN, pediatric oncologist, educator; b. Izmir, Turkey, Nov. 1, 1958; d. Israel and Coya Akyüz; m. Abut Kebudi, Aug. 24, 1986; children: Eli Erol, Izzet. MD, Aegean U., Izmir, 1982. Lic. physician, pediatrician, pediatric oncologist. Physician Ctr. for Fighting Against Tb, Istanbul, 1983-85; resident dept. pediatrics U. Istanbul Sch. Medicine, 1985-90; fellow U. Istanbul Oncology Inst., 1990-93, assoc. prof. pediatrics and pediatric oncology, 1993-2000, prof., 2000—; clin. observer Meml. Sloan Kettering Cancer Ctr., N.Y.C., 1992; vis. fellow UCLA, 1992; cons. tchg. staff U. Istanbul (Turkey) Oncology Inst., 1993; tchg. staff U. Instanbul Sch. Medicine, 1996. Contbr. articles to profl. jours. Recipient Rsch. award Turkey's Sci. and Tech. Rsch. Coun., Ankara, 1980, 81, 82, Sci. Publ. award, 1994, 95, 96, 97, 2000, Short term fellowship grant Bobst Internat. Cancer Edn. Fund, N.Y.C., 1992,, Sci. Meeting grant Internat. Soc. Pediatric Oncology, 1992, 93, 95, Best Poster prize Internat. Soc. Pediat. Oncology, 1999, Successful Investigator award U. Istanbul Rsch. Fund, 1995, 96, 97, 99. Mem. Internat. Soc. Pediatric Oncology, European Soc. Med. Oncology, Turkish Oncology Soc., Am. Soc. Clin. Oncology, Clin. Microbiology and Infectious Diseases Soc. Avocations: travel, archaeology, learning foreign languages. Office: U Instanbul Oncology Inst, Capa, 34390 Istanbul Turkey

KECHROUD, AMMAR TAYEB, psychologist, educator; b. Tebessa, Algeria, July 1, 1952; s. Tayeb Aissa and Djemaa Ibrahim K.; m. Soraya Med Lakhdar Attia, Sept. 14, 1989; children: Nabil, Amine. BA, Oran (Algeria) U., 1977; MSc, Queens U., Belfast, Northern Ireland, 1980; PhD, U. Wales, Cardiff, U.K., 1986. Asst. prof. Garyounis U., Benghazi, Libya, 1986-94, assoc. prof., 1994—; Author: Contemporary Indust/Organiz Psychology, vol. 1 & 2, 1995, Dictionary of Indust/Organiz Terms, 1994, Dictionary of Statistics & Methodology, 1998, Research Methods in Social & Behavioral Sciences, 1999. Fellow British Psychol. Soc. (assoc.); mem. APA (affiliate), N.Y. Acad. Sci. Avocations: reading, sports, theater, travel, writing. Fax: (00)(218)(61) 9098484. Home: PO Box 32535, Omar Mokhtar St, Benghazi Libya Office: Garyounis U Dept Psychology, Faculty of Arts PO Box 1308, Benghazi Libya

KECK, ERNST WILHELM, pediatric cardiologist; b. Hamburg, Germany, Aug. 30, 1927; s. Karl Heinrich and Margot (Specht) K.; m. Helen Beryl Spoerri, June 11, 1960; 1 child, Pascal. MD, U. Hamburg, 1954; MS, U. Minn., 1961. Fellow Mayo Clinic, Rochester, Minn., 1958-61; asst. prof. U. Hamburg Clinic, 1963-68; dir., prof. pediat. cardiology U. Hamburg, 1968-93. Author: Kardiologie, 5th edit., 2000; co-author: Kinderheilkunde, 9th edit., 1994. With German Air Force, 1945. Mem. Assn. European Pediatric Cardiology (hon.), Mayo Found. Alumnus. Lutheran. Avocations: playing cello, sailing. Home: Papenkamp 6, D 22607 Hamburg Germany

KECK, LOIS T., anthropology educator; b. Bklyn., Jan. 19, 1947; d. Joseph Francis and Madeline Teresa (Donnelly) K.; m. Thomas Gregory Raslear, Aug. 7, 1971. BA in Anthropology, CUNY, 1969, MA in Anthropology, 1974; PhD in Anthropology, SUNY, Binghamton, 1986; MPH in Internat. Health, Johns Hopkins U., 1992; cert. health edn. specialist, Nat. Commn. for Health Edn., 1994. Reader in anthropology and archaeology undergrad. program Queens Coll., CUNY, 1968-70, rsch. asst. Archaeology Lab., 1968-69, field instr. archaeology Summer Field Sch., 1969; tchg. asst. dept. anthropology Brown Univ., Providence, 1969-70; assoc. prof. dept. anthropology George Washington U., Washington, grad. advisor for students in women and disability; chief rsch. scientist Nat. Coun. on Disability, Washington; cons. D.C. Women's Coun. on AIDS, 1989-95; mem. study group for peer rev. panel on grants Nat. Inst. on Disability Rsch. and Rehab.-Dept. Edn.; mem. Montgomery County (Md.) Com. on Ethnic and Minority Affairs; adj. asst. prof. CUNY-Kingsborough C.C., fall 1974; vis. asst. prof. Howard U., Washington, fall 1988; guest lectr. U. Md., fall 1988, Am. U., 1994; adj. prof. U. Md.-Univ. Coll.; sr. rsch. assoc. LTG Assocs., Inc., Turlock, Calif., 1993-94. N.Y. State Regents Nursing scholar, 1964, N.Y. State Regents scholar, 1964; Mary Switzer fellow Nat. Inst. for Disability Rsch. and Rehab., 1995-96. Fellow Am. Anthropol. Assn. (commn. on disability, advisor for students with disabilities); mem. AAAS, APHA, Am. Ethnol. Assn., Soc. for Applied Anthropology, Ctr. for Women's Policy Studies, Soc. for Med. Anthropology, Washington Evaluators Assn., Washington Assn. Profl. Anthropologists (pres. 1996-97, sec. 1993-96, 1999—), Anthropol. Soc. Washington, Washington Assn. Profl. Anthropologists (sec. 1999—), Nat. Assn. Practicing Anthropologists, Md. Pub. Health Assn., N.Y. Acad. Scis., Middle East Inst. Home: 1408 Woodman Ave Silver Spring MD 20902-3905 Office: Nat Coun on Disability 1331 F St NW Ste 1050 Washington DC 20004-1138

KECKLER, STEPHEN WILLIAM, computer science educator; b. Palo Alto, Calif., July 11, 1968; s. William George and Joyce Brodovsky Keckler. BSEE, Stanford U., 1990; MS in Computer Sci., MIT, 1992, PhD in Computer Sci., 1998. Circuit design engr. Intel Corp., Santa Clara, Calif., 1989-90; rsch. assoc. MIT, Cambridge, Mass., 1990-97, Stanford (Calif.) U., 1997-98; asst. prof. dept. computer scis. U. Tex., Austin, 1998—; cons. Equator Techs., Inc., Seattle, 1995. Patentee multiprocessor coupling system, memory systems. Intel Corp. Found. grad. fellow, 1996; recipient Faculty Partnership award IBM, 1999. Mem. IEEE, Assn. for Computing Machinery, Phi Beta Kappa, Sigma Xi, Tau Beta Pi. Avocations: sailboat racing, hiking, skiing, backpacking. E-mail: skeckler@cs.utexas.edu. Office: U Tex Dept Computer Scis Taylor Hall 2.124 Austin TX 78712-1188

KEDING, REINHARD CHRISTIAN, bishop; b. Salzhausen, Germany, Sept. 5, 1948; arrived in Namibia, 1993; s. Max Paul and Lieselotte (Kröselberg) K.; m. Margarete Gremels Frauke, Dec. 12, 1943; children: Achim, Andreas, Angela, Olaf, Holger. Ordained to ministry Evang. Luth. Ch., 1977. Pastor in Natal and Transvaal, Luth. Ch. in South Africa, Dundee, 1977-82; sch. chaplain Luth. Ch. in South Africa, Hermannsburg, 1982-89; head adult edn. desk Evang. Luth Mission Lower Saxony, Her, Germany, 1989-93; bishop Evang. Luth. Ch. in Namibia (German Evang. Luth. Ch.), Windhoek, 1993—. Chmn. Red Cross, Her, 1992-93. Office: Evang Luth Ch in Namibia, Box 233 12 Peter Muller St, Windhoek Namibia

KEDVES, MIKLÓS JÓZSEF, biologist, researcher; b. Szeged, Hungary, Mar. 21, 1933; s. Miklós Jás and Teréz (Mihály) K.; m. Jolán Erzsébet Schneider, July 31, 1962 (div. Dec. 1975). Diploma in biology and chemistry, Szeged U., 1955, PhD, 1958, D Biol. Sci., 1974; Candidate Biol. Sci., Hungarian Acad. Sci., Budapest, 1965. Tchr. P.M. Secondary Sch., Siófok, Hungary, 1955-58; asst. J.A. U., Szeged, 1958-63, 1st asst., 1963-65, lectr., 1965-75, rsch. councillor, 1975—, hon. prof., 1984—, head Cell Biol. and Evolutionary Micropalentol. Lab., 1990—. Author: Palynological Studies on Early Tertiary Deposits of Hungary, Paleogene Fossil Sporomorphs of the Bakony Mountains I-IV, Introduction to the Palynology of Pre-Quaternary Deposits, I, II. Recipient medal univ. con el sello del estudio U. Salamanca, 1986, Birbal Sahni Centenary medal Birbal-Savitri Sahni Found., 1995, Lucknow Silver medal Birbal-Savitri Sahni Meml. Mus., 1995, Internat. Man of Yr. award Internat. Biographical Ctr., Cambridge, Eng., 1995, 96, Citation of Meritorious Achievement, Internat. Biographical Ctr., 1995, Internat. Cultural Diploma on Honor Am. Biographical Inst., 1995, Man of Yr. Commemorative medal Am. Biographical Inst., 1995, 20 Century award for achievement, Silver medal of Honor Internat. Biographical Ctr., 1995, Intenrat. Leader in Achievement award IBC Cambridge, 1997, Internat. Order of Ambassadors award Am. Biog. Inst., 1997, Man of Yr. award Am. Biog. Inst., 1997, 2000 Outstanding People of 20th Century award IBC, 1998. Mem. N.Y. Acad. Scis., Hungarian Acad. Scis. (pres. paleontol. coun. 1996—), Am. Assn. Stratigraphic Palynologists. Avocations: swimming, travel. Home: PO Box 993, Vitéz u 13-15 19, 6722 Szeged Hungary Office: JA U Dept Botany, Egyetem u 2, 6722 Szeged Csongrad, Hungary

KEE, LEE SHAU, real estate developer; married; 5 children. With Henderson Land Devel., Hong Kong; chmn. Hong Kong & China Gas. Avocation: golfing. Office: 23d Fl, 363 Java Rd Northpoint, Hong Kong China*

KEE, WALTER ANDREW, former government official; b. Phila., July 12, 1914; s. Walter Leslie and Regina Veronica (Corcoran) K.; m. Genevieve O'Hair, Dec. 2, 1943; children: Kathleen, Sheila. B.S., Purdue U., 1949; M.L.S., Columbia U., 1950. Engring. and phys. sci. librarian N.Y. U., N.Y.C., 1950-51; librarian E.I. DuPont de Nemours, Savannah River Lab., Aiken, S.C., 1951-55; head library and documents sect. Martin Co., Balt., 1955-59; chief library br. AEC, Washington, 1959-74; librarian ERDA, Washington, 1975-76; asst. to dir. div. adminstrv. services ERDA, 1976-77, also Freedom of Info. and Privacy Act officer, 1975-77; dir. div. publs. mgmt. Dept. Energy, 1977-78; ret., 1978; chmn. AEC-Dept. of Def. Joint Atomic Weapon Tech. Info. Group, 1962-72. Contbr.: chpt. to Special Librarianship: A New Reader (Eugene Jackson), 1980. Asst. to chief So. Shores Fire Dept.; sec. Dare County Firemen's Assn., 1980-83; historian So. Shores Civic Assn.; legis. officer Alamance County, N.C. fedn. Nat. Assn. Ret. Fed. Employees, 1994-99, 2000; bd. dirs. Friends Alamance County Librs. Served with USNR, 1942-45. Mem. Fed. Library Com., Com. on Sci. and Tech. Info., Spl. Libraries Assn. (cons., pres. nuclear sci. divsn. and info. tech. divsn., pres. Balt. chpt.), Am. Soc. Info. Sci. Home: 1652 Wycliff Ct Burlington NC 27215-8739

KEECH, ANN MARIE, training design and multimedia consultant; b. Salt Lake City, July 25, 1951; d. Stanley Michael and Rose Elma (Migliore) Bachmurski; m. Michael Ross Keech, July 21, 1972 (div. 1983); 1 child, Jason Michael. BA in English, Christopher Newport Coll., 1976. Mgr. publs. Newport News (Va.) Shipbuilding, 1981-84; office mgr. Computer Scis. Corp., Newport News, 1984-86; mgr. Comsell, Atlanta, 1986-87, Crawford Comms., Inc., Atlanta, 1988-91; cons. Coastal Video Comms., Inc., Virginia Beach, 1991-93; project mgr. Star Mountain, Inc., Alexandria, Va., 1991-96; v.p. D&A World Wide, Inc., Atlanta, 1996-97; owner, cons. AMK, Newport News, 1997—. Writer, developer: (tng. materials) BTOS FSA Programming Guide, 1988 (Soc. for Tech. Comm. Cert. of Achievement 1989); developer: (multimedia tng. program) Confined Space Entry, 1993; mgr., editor, developer: (internat. tng. materials) International Technical Training for Telecommunications, 1996-97; developer, editor: (tng. program) Family Violence Prevention Program, 1997; developer Web-based Training Style Guide, 2000. Vol. Newport News Police, Cmty. Svc. Dept.; aux. mem. 106th Infantry Divsn. Assn., 76th Infantry Divsn. Assn., 2d Divsn. Assn.

13th Airborne Divsn. Assn., 18th Airborn Corps Assn., 1st Infantry Divsn. Assn., 3d Infantry Divsn. Assn. Avocations: music, horseback riding, pleasure reading. Fax: (757) 988-0448. E-mail: amkeech@mindspring.com. Office: AMK 824 Cascade Dr Newport News VA 23608-3223

KEEFE, CAROLYN JOAN, tax accountant; b. Huntington Park, Oct. 11, 1926; d. Paul Dewey and Mary Jane (Parmater) K. AA, Pasadena (Calif.) City Coll., 1947; BA, U. So. Calif., 1950. Tax acct. Shell Oil Co., L.A., 1950-71; tax acct. Shell Oil Co., Houston, 1971-91, ret., 1991. Advisor Midwest Mus. of Am. Art, 1993—; vol. Houston Mus. of Fine Arts, 1991—; vol. docent Houston Mus. of Natural Sci., 1991—, Theatre Under the Stars, 1991—, Houston Pub. TV Channel 8, Houston, 1989—; donor 2 ann. coll. scholarships in memory of Paul Dewey and Mary Jane Keefe. Mem. LWV, Inst. Mgmt. Accts. (emeritus life mem.), Desk and Derrick Club (bd. dirs. 1994-95), Houston Alumni Club of Alpha Gamma Delta, USC Houston Alumni Club. Christian Scientist. Avocation: travel. Home: 1814 Auburn Trl Sugar Land TX 77479-6333

KEEFE, DEBORAH LYNN, cardiologist, educator; b. Oklahoma City, Nov. 23, 1950; d. Stanley William and Gloria Jean (Kelsoe) Denton; m. Richard Alan Keefe, May 14, 1971; children: Jennifer, Colin, Corwin. BA, Rice U., 1973; MD, N.Y. Med. Coll., 1976; MPH, Columbia U., 1990. Diplomate Am. Bd. Internal Medicine, Am. Bd. Cardiovascular Disease, Am. Bd. Critical Care, Am. Bd. Clin. Pharmacology. Intern and resident St. Vincent's Hosp., N.Y.C., 1976-79; fellow in cardiology Stanford (Calif.) Univ. Hosp., 1979-81; dir. CCU Bronx (N.Y.) Mcpl. Hosp., 1981-87; assoc. dir. Am. Cyanamid, Pearl River, N.Y., 1987-88; assoc. mem. Sloan-Kettering Meml. Hosp., N.Y.C., 1988-94, mem., 1994—; asst. prof. medicine Albert Einstein Coll. Medicine, Bronx, 1981-87; assoc. prof. medicine Cornell U., N.Y.C., 1988-95, prof. medicine, 1995—; regent Am. Coll. Clin. Pharmacology, 1985-89, 92-96, treas., 1992-94. Assoc. editor Jour. Clin. Pharmacology, 1985-94, editor, 1994—; contbr. articles to Clin. Pharm. Therapeutics, Jour. Cardiovascular Pharmacology, Am. Jour. Cardiology. Fellow Am. Coll. Cardiology, Am. Coll. Chest Physicians, Am. Coll. Angiology; mem. Am. Bd. Clin. Pharmacology, Inc. (sec.-treas. 1994-96). Office: Sloan-Kettering Meml Hosp 1275 York Ave New York NY 10021-6094

KEEFFE, JOHN ARTHUR, lawyer, director; b. Bklyn., Apr. 5, 1930; s. Arthur John and Mary Catherine (Daly) K.; m. Frances Elizabeth Rippetoe, July 24, 1952; children: Virginia Frances, Cynthia Louise, Amy Marie. AB, Cornell U., 1950; JD, U. Va., 1953. Bar: Va. 1953, N.Y. 1956. Asst. U.S. atty. so. dist. State of N.Y., 1955-57; assoc. Rogers, Hoge & Hills, N.Y., 1957-63; of counsel Havens, Wandless, Stitt & Tighe, N.Y., 1963-65; ptnr. Keeffe & Costikyan, N.Y.C. and Washington, 1965-74, Keeffe Bros., N.Y.C. and Washington, 1974-77; sec., mng. dir. Saud Al-Farhan Inc., N.Y.C., 1979-80; pres., dir. J.A. Keeffe, P.C., Eastchester, N.Y., 1981—. Bd. dirs., sec. The Street Theater, White Plains, N.Y., 1973—. 1st lt. USAF, 1953-55. Mem. ABA, ATLA, N.Y. State Bar Assn., Va. Bar Assn., Westchester County Bar Assn. (dir. 1989-90, chmn. com. on fed. courthouse plans and procedures 1994—), N.Y. State Trial Lawyers Assn., Eastchester Bar Assn. (v.p. 1988-89, pres. 1989-90, dir. 1990—), Rotary (bd. dirs. 1991—, sec. 1991-92, pres.-elect 1992-93, pres. 1993-94, co-chair Eastchester Rotary Gift of Life 1993-94, co-chair dist. 7230 Gift of Life 1995-97). Republican. Congregationalist. Avocations: golf, reading. Home and Office: PO Box 855 Katonah NY 10536-0855

KEEGAN, JAMES JOSEPH, financial executive; b. Phila., Sept. 6, 1947; s. George Washington and Kathryn Margaret (Eckels) K.; m. Martha Jana Pettinga, Apr. 27, 1984. BBA in Acctg. cum laude, Tex. Christian U., 1969; MBA in Internat. Fin., U. Mich., 1970. CPA, Colo. Supervising sr. acct. Peat Marwick Mitchell, Denver, 1974-79; pvt. practice acctg. Englewood, Colo., 1979-81; pres. Trinity Securities, Englewood, 1981-83, Keegan Capital Devel., Englewood, 1983-89; chmn. bd. Fairway Sys., Inc., Englewood, 1989—. CPA Small Bus. Adv. Coun., 1984-85; vol. Internat. Golf Tournament, 1986; mem. rules and course rating coms. Colo. Golf Assn., committeeman, 1986-2000; mem. sectional affairs com. USGA, 1996-97; mem. Fellowship Christian Athletes. Capt. USAF, 1971-74. Mem. AICPA's, Colo. Soc. CPA's, Colo. C. of C. (mem. pres. coun. 1981-82), Rockies Venture Club (pres. 1989), Beta Gamma Sigma, Beta Alpha Psi, Delta Sigma Pi. Republican. Roman Catholic. Home: 8101 E Dartmouth Ave Apt 36 Denver CO 80231-4259 Office: Fairway Systems Inc 6 Inverness Ct E Ste 120 Englewood CO 80112-5517

KEEHN, NEIL FRANCIS, investment banker, engineer, technologist; b. Massillion, Ohio, Oct. 24, 1948; s. Russell Earl and Mary (Danner) K. BS in Math., Ariz. State U., Tempe, 1970, postgrad. in elec. engring., 1970. Mem. tech. staff Tech. Service Corp., Santa Monica, Calif., 1972-74, Hughes Aircraft, El Segundo, Calif., 1974-77; program mgr. TRW, Inc., Redondo Beach, Calif., 1977-79; mgr. advanced concepts Mil. Space Sys. divsn. Sci. Applications, Inc., El Segundo, Calif., 1979-80; pres. Strategic Systems Scis., Santa Monica, Calif., 1980-91, Engr.'s Toolbox, El Segundo, Calif., 1992—, Tech. Brokers Internat., El Segundo, Calif., 1994—, Knowledge Trust, El Segundo, Calif., 1998—, Acad. Intangible Asset Mgmt., El Segundo, Calif., 1995—. Contbr. articles to profl. jours.; patentee in digital signal processing; pub. ednl. materials. Mem. IEEE (vice chmn. aerospace def. sys. panel 1972-76, chmn. 1976-79), AIAA, Brit. Internat. Studies Assn., U.S. Strategic Inst., Internat. Inst. for Strategic Studies.

KEEHNER, MICHAEL ARTHUR MILLER, investment bank executive; b. Cedar Rapids, Iowa, Nov. 15, 1943. BS in Nuclear Physics, MIT, 1965; MBA in Fin. with high distinction, Harvard U., 1971. Registered securities rep. Engring. mgr. Gen. Dynamics Corp., Quincy, Mass., 1965-69; investment banking mgr. Kidder Peabody & Co., 1971-89; exec. mng. dir. individual investor svcs. Kidder Peabody & Co., N.Y.C., 1991-94; chmn., dir. Kidder Peabody Internat. Corp., N.Y.C., 1989-91; pres., chief exec. officer K P Exploration, Inc., N.Y.C., 1982-88; mng. dir., mem. exec. com., bd. mem. Kidder Peabody Group, Inc., N.Y.C., 1987-94; mng. ptnr. The Keehner Group, LLC, N.Y.C., 1994—; bd. dirs. Cross Border LLC, LDMI Com., Inc., Brownstone Pub. LLC. Trustee Bklyn. Mus. Baker scholar Harvard U.; Loeb Rhodes fellow Harvard U. Mem. India House (N.Y.C.), Heights Casino, Rembrandt Club (Bklyn.), Long Island Wyandanch Club (N.Y.), Lake Waramug Country Club.

KEEL, KEITH GARNETT, economist; b. Richmond, Va., Dec. 1, 1961; s. Paul L. Sr. and Lois Alma Keel; m. Lysiane Godart, Aug. 12, 1997; children: Corinne, Keith Garnett Jr., Phillip. BA in Econs., Hampton U., 1985. Account rep. Ford Motor Credit Co., McLean, Va., 1985-87; economist U.S. Dept. Labor, Bur. Labor Stats., Washington, 1987—; mem. recruitment team U.S. Dept. Labor. Mem. Air Force Officers Club. Baptist. Avocations: sport fishing, skiing, tennis, coin collecting. E-mail: keel k@bls.gov. Home: 17239 Nugent Ln Dumfries VA 22026-3339 Office: US Bur Labor Stats PSB Bldg Rm 2930 2 Massachusetts Ave NE Washington DC

KEELE, LYNDON ALAN, electronics company executive; b. Clyde, Tex., Nov. 3, 1928; s. Theadore Fannin and Zada (Sikes) K.; B.B.A., U. Tex., 1951; m. Muriel Alice Murphy, June 1, 1968; children—Carolyn Chase, Tiffany Ames. With York div. Borg-Warner Co., York, Pa., 1953-58, asst. gen. plant mgr., 1956-58; program mgr. Sylvania Elec. System div. Gen. Telephone & Electronics Co., Needham, Mass., 1958-62; program mgr. ITT Fed. Labs., Nutley, N.J., 1962-68; exec. v.p. TeleScis., Inc., Moorestown, N.J., 1968-73; chmn. Sci. Dynamics Corp., Cherry Hill, N.J., 1973—. Served with AUS, 1946-47, USAAF, 1951-53. Mem. IEEE. Club: Riverton Country. Office: Sci Dynamics Corp 1919 Springdale Rd Cherry Hill NJ 08003-1603

KEELER, BRADFORD RICHARD, surgeon; b. Kansas City, Kans., Jan. 6, 1964; s. William Robert and Shirley Anne (Ward) K.; children: Gabrielle, Molika. MD, U. Kans., 1990. Diplomate Am. Bd. Surgery. Intern U. N.C. Hosps., Chapel Hill, 1990-91, resident, 1991-95; attending physician McKee Med. Ctr., Loveland, Colo., 1995—. Fellow ACS. Office: Loveland Surg Assocs 1900 Boise Ave Ste 210 Loveland CO 80538-5004

KEELER, CARDINAL WILLIAM H., archbishop; b. San Antonio, Mar. 4, 1931; s. Thomas Love and Margaret T. (Conway) K. BA, St. Charles Borromeo Sem., 1952; STL, Pontifical Gregorian U., Rome, 1956, JCD, 1961; DD (hon.), Lebanon Valley Coll., 1984, Gettysburg Coll., 1986, Susquehanna U., 1989; LHD (hon.), Mt. St. Mary's Coll., 1985; LLD (hon.), Gannon U., 1993; LHD (hon.), Loyola Coll., 1995, Shippensburg State U., 1995; DD (hon.), St. Mary's U., Winona, Minn., 1995, Elizabeth Coll., 1996, Western Md. Coll., 1996, St. Vincent Sem., 1996, Coll. of Notre Dame of Md., 1997, U. Notre Dame, 1998, Ateneo de Manila U., 1998. Ordained priest Roman Catholic Ch., 1955, consecrated bishop, 1979. Asst. pastor Our Lady of Good Counsel Ch., Marysville, Pa., 1956-58; sec. diocesan tribunal Diocese of Harrisburg, Pa., 1956-58, defender of the bond, 1961-66, vice-chancellor, 1965-69, chancellor, 1969-79, aux. bishop and vicar gen., 1979-83, bishop of Harrisburg, 1984-89; archbishop of Balt., 1989-94, cardinal, 1994—; chmn. Md. Cath. Conf., 1989—; co-chmn. Pa. Conf. Inter-Ch. Coop., 1981-89; pres. Pa. Cath. Conf., 1983-89; chmn. com. on ecumenical and inter-religious affairs Nat. Conf. Cath. Bishops, 1984-87, mem., 1984—, Episcopal moderator for Cath.-Jewish Rels., 1988-92, 95—, sec., 1988-89, v.p., 1989-92, pres., 1992-95, chmn. World Youth Day Celebration, Denver, 1993, cons. Com. Comm., 1995—, chair Com. Pro-Life Activities, 1998—; former pastor Marysville parish; former titular bishop Ulcinium (Dulcigno); mem. Internat. Joint Com. for Cath.-Orthodox Theol. Dialogue, 1986—; mem. Internat. Liaison Com. Caths. and Jews, 1987—; sec., spl. advisor 2nd Vatican Coun., 1962-65; mem. staff Coun. Digest, 1963-65; mem. Synod of Bishops for Africa, 1994, World Synod of Bishops for the Consecrated Life, 1994, Synod of Bishops for Am., 1996; apptd. mem. Coun. for Assembly of Synod Bishops, 1997—. Pub. The Cath. Rev. newspaper. Mem. Interreligious Forum Greater Harrisburg, 1968-89; mem. exec. bd. Keystone Area coun. Boy Scouts Am., 1979-89; mem. Pontifical coun. Promoting Christian Unity, 1994—; mem. Congregation for the Oriental Chs., 1994—; trustee Cath. U. Am.; chmn. bd. trustees Associated Cath. Charities, 1989—; chancellor, chmn. bd. trustees St. Mary's Sem. and Univ., 1989—; chancellor Mount St. Mary's Sem., 1989—; trustee Basilica of Nat. Shrine of Immaculate Conception, Washington, 1989—; chmn. bd. trustees Basilica of Nat. Shrine of Assumption of the Blessed Virgin Mary, 1989—; mem. Black and Native Am. Missions Bd.; v.p. Cath. Near East Welfare Assn.; vice chair North Am. Coll. Bd. Govs., 1998—. Recipient Gold medal Pope John XXIII, 1961, John Baum Humanitarian award Dauphin County unit Am. Cancer Soc., 1984, Anti-Defamation League Americanism award, 1985, De Tocqueville Soc. award, 1988, Nat. award Boy Scouts of Am., 1990, Disting. Citizen award, 1998, Weil medallion Jewish Chataqua Soc., 1993, award Salvation Army, 1995, Shaw award Rotary Internat., 1995, Mahmoud Abu Sand Excellence award Am. Muslim Coun., 1995, Nostra Aetate award Inst. Christian Jewish Understanding, 1997, Silver St. George medal Nat. Cath. Com. Scouting, 1998, Lifetime Achievement award Shaare Zedek Med. Ctr., Jerusalem, 1999, Disting. Citizens award Balt. coun. Boy Scouts Am., 1999; named papal chamberlain Pope Paul VI, 1965, prelate of honor Pope Paul VI, 1970, Marylander of Yr., Md. Colonial Soc., 1986, The Balt. Sun, 1994, Media Person of Yr., Md. Press Assn., 1994. Mem. Canon Law Soc. Am., Am. Cath. Hist. Soc., Cath. Extension Soc. Govs.

KEELEY, MICHAEL GLENN, arbitrator, mediator, consultant; b. Memphis, Jan. 8, 1953; s. Lerman and Benneta (Thompson) K.; m. Sandra Virginia Hughes, Oct. 6, 1978 (div. Aug. 1992); m. Karen Bonner, Dec. 31, 1993; 1 child, Kim. BA, UCLA, 1975; JD, U. Calif., Hastings, 1978; A in Risk Mgmt., Ins. Edn., 1999. Negotiator for NFL players Profl. Sports Mgmt. Inc., 1979-81; sr. rep. Employers Benefits Ins., 1981-85; claims supr. Claims Mgmt. Svcs., 1985-86; sr. litigation specialist Reliance/United Pacific Ins Co, Rancho Cordova, Calif., 1986-96; ptnr. JKP Mgmt. Svcs. Inc., Sacramento, 1996-97; broker, risk mgmt. cons. J&K Risk and Ins. Svcs., Inc., 1997—; cons. to 3rd party adminstr. in workers' compensation, casualty and auto claims; lic. ins. broker's specializing in mcpl. entities and sch. dists. and spl. dists. Mem. Black Ins. Profls. Assn. (pres. 1991-92, student mentor program 1991-93, LINK program 1991), Charles Houston Bar Assn. Avocations: golf, baseball, football, racquetball.

KEELING, JOE KEITH, religion educator, college official and dean; b. Muskogee, Okla., Apr. 21, 1936; s. William Lytle and Anna Madge (Watts) K.; m. Marjorie Ann Brotherton, 1957; children: Kara Kay, William Kent. BA in History, Northeastern State U., 1958; BD in Theology, So. Meth. U., 1962; MA in Theology, U. Chgo., 1967, PhD, 1974. Ordained to ministry United Meth. Ch., 1962. Dir. orientation, acad. advisor U. Chgo., 1964-68; asst. prof. religion Augustana Coll., Sioux Falls, S.D., 1968-72; from asst. to assoc. prof. philosophy and religion Rockford (Ill.) Coll., 1972-86, dean of spl. acad. programming, assoc. dean of coll., 1981-86; adj. assoc. prof. dept. medicine U. Ill. Coll. of Medicine at Rockford, 1984-86; provost, dean, prof. religion and philosophy Baker U., Baldwin City, Kans., 1986-96; v.p., dean Ctrl. Meth. Coll., Fayette, Mo., 1996—; mem. bd. ordained ministry Kans. Ea. Conf. United Meth. Ch., 1987-96; cons., evaluator, mem. accreditation rev. coun. North Ctrl. Assn. Colls. and Schs., Am. Conf. Acad. Deans, Midwest Bioethics Ctr. Author and lectr. in field. Mem. Kansas City Regional Coun. Higher Edn., 1986-94; mem. instnl. rev. com. Swedish-Am. Hosp., Rockford, 1981-86. Mem. Am. Acad. Religion (v.p., program chmn. Midwest region 1981-82, pres. 1982-83), Rockford C. of C. (bd. dirs. 1983-86), AAUP (Ill. state coun. mem. 1979-81), Archael. Inst. Am. (bd. dirs. Rockford chpt. 1984-86), Rotary. Democrat. Avocations: fishing, camping, canoeing. Home: PO Box 429 878 Highway 5 And 240 Fayette MO 65248-9509 Office: Ctrl Meth Coll Office of Vice Pres 411 Central Methodist Sq Fayette MO 65248-1129

KEELING; ADYTUM, E. B. See CURL, JAMES STEVENS

KEELY, GEORGE CLAYTON, lawyer; b. Denver, Feb. 28, 1926; s. Thomas and Margaret (Clayton) K.; m. Jane Elisabeth Coffey, Nov. 18, 1950; children: Margaret Clayton, George C. (dec.), Mary Anne, Jane Elisabeth, Edward Francis, Kendall Anne. BS in Bus, U. Colo., 1948; LLB, Columbia U., 1951. Bar: Colo. 1951. Assoc. Fairfield & Woods, Denver, 1951-58, ptnr., 1958-86, sr. dir., 1986-90, of counsel, 1990-91, ret., 1991; v.p. Silver Corp., 1966-86; mem. exec. com. Timpte Industries, Inc., 1970-78, dir., 1980-89. Mem. Colo. Commn. Promotion Uniform State Laws, 1967—; regional planning adv. com. Denver Regional Coun. Govts., 1972-74; bd. dirs. Bow Mar Water and Sanitation Dist., 1970-74; trustee Town of Bow Mar, 1972-74; trustee, v.p. Silver Found., 1970-90, mem. bd., 1983-90; trustee, v.p. Denver Area coun. Boy Scouts Am., 1985-90; bd. dirs. Pub. Broadcasting of Colo., Inc., 1986-90, St. Mus. KCFR. With USAF, 1944-47. Fellow Am. Bar Found., Colo. Bar Found.; mem. ABA (ho. of dels. 1977-79), Denver Bar Assn. (award of merit 1980), Colo. Bar Assn., Nat. Conf. Commrs. Uniform State Laws (sec. 1971-75, exec. com. 1971-79 , chmn. exec. com. 1975-77, pres. 1977-79, co-chmn. com. U.S.-Can. Transboundary Pollution Reciprocal Access Act 1979-82, chmn. com. Determination of Death Act 1979-80), Am. Law Inst., Cath. Lawyers Guild of Denver (dir. 1965-67), Denver Estate Planning Coun., U. Club of Denver, (dir. 1966-75, pres. 1973-74), Law Club of Denver (pres. 1966-67, Lifetime Achievement award, 1994), Pinehurst Country Club, Hundred Club, Cactus Club, Rotary, Phi Delta Phi, Beta Theta Pi, Beta Gamma Sigma. Home: 5220 W Longhorn St Littleton CO 80123-1408

KEEM, MICHAEL DENNIS, veterinarian; b. Buffalo, July 29, 1950; s. Sanford Joseph and Clara C. (Chmiel) K.; m. Mary Beth Fix, June 1, 1973 (div. 1993); children: Chelsey, Erin, Daniel, Ryan. BS, Niagara U., 1972; MS, U. Wyo., 1974; DVM, Cornell U., 1979. Assoc. veterinarian Spink Vet. Assn., Attica, N.Y., 1979-80; assoc. veterinarian Cheektowaga (N.Y.) Vet. Hosp., 1980-1984, vet., owner, pres., 1985—; vet., owner, pres. Amclare Vet. Hosp., P.C., Williamsville, N.Y., 1987—; ptnr. Greater Buffalo Vet. Emergency Svcs., P.C., 1985—, also bd. dirs. Com. chmn. pack 601 Boy Scouts Am., 1989-91, Webelos den leader, 1991-92, asst. scoutmaster troop 601, 1992-96, com. mem. 1996—. Mem. AVMA, Animal Birth Control Soc. (bd. dirs. 1981—), N.Y. State Vet. Med. Soc., Am. Animal Hosp. Assn., Western N.Y. Vet. Med. Assn. (pres.-elect 1988, pres. 1989, past pres. 1990, bd. dirs. 1991-94), Niagara Frontier Vet. Soc. (bd. dirs. 1986-96, 00—), Buffalo Acad. Vet. Medicine (sgt.-at-arms 1995-96, sec./treas. 1996-97, v.p. 1997-98, pres. 1998-99), Phi Kappa Phi, Phi Zeta, Omega Tau Sigma. Republican. Roman Catholic. Office: Cheektowaga Vet Hosp PC 957 Dick Rd Buffalo NY 14225-3554 also: Amclare Vet Hosp PC 895 Hopkins Rd Williamsville NY 14221-1728

KEENAN, RETHA ELLEN VORNHOLT, retired nursing educator; b. Solon, Iowa, Aug. 15, 1934; d. Charles Elias and Helen Maurine (Konicek) Vornholt; m. David James Iverson, June 17, 1956; children: Scott, Craig; m. Roy Vincent Keenan, Jan. 5, 1980. BSN, State U. Iowa, 1955; MSN, Calif. State U., Long Beach, 1978. Cert. nurse practitioner adult and mental health. Pub. health nurse City of Long Beach, 1970-73, 94-96, cons., 1998, 99, 2000, coord. continuing edn., 1999, 2000; pub. health nurse Hosp. Home Care, Torrance, Calif., 1973-75; patient care coord. Hillhaven, L.A., 1975-76; mental health cons. InterCity Home Health, L.A., 1978-79; instr. C.C. Dist., L.A., 1979-87; instr. nursing El Camino Coll., Torrance, 1981-86; instr. nursing Chapman Coll., Orange, Calif., 1982, Mt. St. Mary's Coll., 1986-87; cons., pvt. practice, Rancho Palos Verdes, Calif., 1987-89, 98, 99. Contbg. author: American Journal of Nursing Question and Answer Book for Nursing Boards Review, 1984, Nursing Care Planning Guides for Psychiatric and Mental Health Care, 1987-88, Nursing Care Planning Guides for Children, 1987, Nursing Care Planning Guides for Adults, 1988, Nursing Care Planning Guides for Critically Ill Adults, 1988. Mem. Assistance League of Temecula Valley, Calif. NIMH grantee, 1977-78. Mem. Sigma Theta Tau, Phi Kappa Phi, Delta Zeta. Republican. Lutheran. Avocations: traveling, writing, reading. Home: PO Box 205 Temecula CA 92593-0205

KEENE, MARY ELLEN, federal agency executive; b. Washington, July 30, 1955; d. William Charles and Doris Eva (Springer) Keene; m. Randy Duane Ferryman, Dec. 4, 1982. BS in Edn. with honors, George Mason U., 1977; MPA, Harvard U., 1992. With CIA, Washington, 1974—, imagery analyst specializing mil. assessments, 1979-84, mgr., sr. departmental requirements officer, 1984-86, first-line mgr., later middle mgr. planning/programming unit, 1986-87, first-line mgr. imagery analytic unit, 1987-88, with Intelligence Cmty. Staff, Com. Imagery Requirements and Exploitation, 1988-90, mid. mgr. customer svcs., 1990-93, mid. mgr. imagery analytic element, 1993-95, mgr. comptr. function, 1995-98, mid. mgr. all-source analytic unit, 1998—. Mem. Kappa Delta Pi. Avocations: reading, gardening, collecting Hummels, dogs.

KEENEY, STEVEN HARRIS, lawyer; b. Phila., Oct. 1, 1949; s. Arthur Hail and Virginia (Tripp) K.; m. Jean Ashburn, May 10, 1974 (div. Oct. 1986); 1 child, Christian Jeffrey. BA, Trinity Coll., Hartford, Conn., 1971; MA, Hartford Sem. Found., 1973; JD, U. Conn., 1980. Bar: Ky. 1980, U.S. Dist. Ct. (we. dist.) Ky. 1981, U.S. Dist. Ct. (ea. dist.) Ky. 1983. Staff reporter/edn. editor The Hartford Courant, 1971-74; asst. to supt. Hartford Pub. Schs., 1974-77; assoc. Igor Sikorsky & Assocs., Hartford, 1979-80, Brown, Todd & Heyburn, Louisville, 1980-82; ptnr. Barnett & Alagia, Louisville, 1982-88, Keeney & Willock, Louisville, 1988-90; prin. Amerilaw, Louisville, 1990-93; pres. LawTech Svcs. Co., Louisville, 1993—; mng. mem. Trautwein & Keeney PLLC, Louisville, 1993—. Co-author/editor: Death Benefit: A Lawyer Uncovers A 20 Year Pattern of Seduction, 1993, 94, Reader's Digest Today's Best Non-Fiction Vol. 24, 1994; contbr. articles to profl. jours. Bd. dirs. Hospice of Louisville, Inc., 1984-86; exec. dir. Juvenile Justice Pub. Edn. Project, West Hartford, Conn., 1978-80; pres. bd. dirs. Stage One: Louisville Children's Theatre, 1982-83; founding bd. dirs. Ky. Citizens for Arts, Frankfort, 1983; mem. Lebanon (Conn.) Bd. Edn., 1975-80; campaign mgr. Mazzoli 3d C.D. Ky., Jefferson County, 1982, 84; elder 2d Presbyn. Ch., Louisville, 1984-86. Recipient Disting. Contbn. award Nat. Com. for Prevention of Child Abuse, Ky. chpt., 1982, Disting. Svc. award Conn. Assn. Bds. of Edn., 1976, Profl. Achievement for Gen. Reporting Series award Soc. Profl. Journalists, Sigma Delta Chi, Conn. chpt. 1974. Mem. ABA (editl. com. The Tax Lawyer 1984-89), Assn. Trial Lawyers of Am., Nat. Assn. Criminal Def. Lawyers, Ky. Acad. Trial Atty's., Ky. Bar Assn., Louisville Bar Assn., Million Dollar Advocates Forum, Jefferson Club, Hon. Order of Ky. Cols. Democrat. Presbyterian. Avocations: bibliophile, marksman, golf. Office: Trautwein & Keeney PLLC 1 Riverfront Plz Ste 510 Louisville KY 40202-2923

KEERTHIPALA, WICKRAMAARACHCHIGE WEEBADDA LIYANAGE, electrical engineering educator; b. Pimbura, Sri Lanka, Oct. 21, 1961; s. Wickramaarachchige Weebadda Liyanage Erolis and Jayaneththi-Koralalage Joselin Thilakaratne; m. Palandapathirage-Gangasri Tamarasi Dias, Nov. 20, 1992. BSc in Engring. with 1st class honors, Peradeniya U., Sri Lanka, 1984; PhD, Cambridge (Eng.) U., 1989. Asst. lectr. Peradeniya U., Sri Lanka, 1985-86; rsch. scholar Cambridge (Eng.) U., 1986-89; vis. scholar, tchg. asst. U. Manitoba, Can., 1988-89, post-doctoral rsch. fellow, lectr., 1989-92; lectr. Nanyang Technol. U., Singapore, 1992-97, rschr., cons. in charge of lab., 1992-96; sr. lectr. Curtin U. Tech., Australia, 1997—; rschr. in photo-voltaics; cons., advisor in sys. stimulation; lab. demonstrator Cambridge (Eng.) U., 1986-88; rschr., sessional lectr. Manitoba (Can.) Power Systems Rsch. Lab., U. Manitoba, 1989-92. Contbr. articles to profl. jours. Recipient Overseas Rsch. Students award, Cambridge, 1986-89; Cambridge (Eng.) Commonwealth Trust scholar Cambridge U., 1986-89. Fellow Cambridge Commonwealth Soc.; mem. IEEE, Internat. Neural Network Soc., Cambridge Soc. (life) Planetary Soc., N.Y. Acad. Scis. Avocations: cricket, tennis, squash, swimming, walking. Home: 3/90 Robert St, Como WA 6152, Australia Office: Curtin U Tech Sch Elec Engr, GPO Box 01984, Perth WA 6845, Australia

KEESLING, JAMES EDGAR, mathematics educator; b. Indpls., June 26, 1942; s. Fred Edgar and Martha Belle (Grimes) K.; m. Marian Ellen Calley, Jan. 26, 1963; children: James Jr., Marian Esther, Timothy Carl, Ruth Emily. BS in Indsl. Engring., U. Miami, 1964, MS in Math., 1966, PhD in Math., 1968. Asst. prof. math. U. Fla., Gainesville, 1967-71; assoc. prof. math. U. Fla., 1971-75, prof. math., 1975—; pres. pro-tempore Coll. of Liberal Arts and Scis., U. Fla., 1989-90; vis. faculty U. Ga., 1976-77, U. Utah, 1991-92; vis. lectr. Soc. Indsl. and Applied Math., 1992—; lectr. numerous nat. and internat. conf. in math., 1969—. Contbr. articles to math. jours.; mng. editor Topology and its Applications. Elder, ch. chmn. Creekside Community Ch. (Evangelical Free Ch. of Am.), Gainesville, 1987-90, 94-97. Recipient Tchg. award U. Fla., 1994, 98. Mem. Am. Math. Soc., Math. Assn. Am., Soc. Indsl. and Applied Math., Tau Beta Pi, Phi Kappa Phi. Home: 710 NE 6th St Gainesville FL 32601-5566 Office: U Fla Dept Math Gainesville FL 32611-8105

KEESOM, CORNELIS H.A., translator; b. Bussum, The Netherlands, Jan. 19, 1917; s. Petrus Cornelis and Carolina CSM Batenburg; m. Jeannetta LC Pennarts, Apr. 11, 1942; children: Pierre, Annie, Tilly, Ria, Cor. Tchg. lic., Pabo, Alkmaar; sworn transl. Portuguese, Spanish. Chancery officer H.M. Legation, Lisbon, 1938-39; interpreter USAF, Venlo, The Netherlands, 1945; purser 1st grade KLM Royal Dutch Airlines, Schiphol, 1946-68; tchr. St. Hubertus Sch., Amsterdam, 1970-82; freelance transl., 1965—; chmn. bd. Keesom & Hendriks N.V., The Hague, The Netherlands, 1973-89. Author: (book) Wine Book, 1988, (dictionary) Portuguese-Dutch Dictionary, 1997. Decorated Knight Officer Orange-Nassau, Queen Beatrix of the Netherlands, 1996, Knight St. Sylvester by Pope John Paul II, 1981; recipient Pro Ecclesia et Pontifice Cross of Honor by Pope Paul VI, 1966, St. Jerome Nat. Translation prize 1995, Netherlands Translators Assn. Roman Catholic. Avocations: gardening, reading. Fax: 0031703504996. E-mail: tm law@keesom.nl. Home: Mozartstraat 48, Heemskerk NL 1962, The Netherlands Office: Keesom & Hendriks NV, Delistraat 45, The Hague 2585 VX, The Netherlands

KEESOM, PIERRE HENRI MARIE, business executive, trademark lawyer, translator; b. Heerlen, Limburg, The Netherlands, Aug. 21, 1943; s. Cornelis Hendrikus Anthonius Keesom and Jeannetta Leonarda Catharina Pennarts; m. Xiaodu Liu, Apr. 9, 1990; children: Cor, Hans, Joseph. JD, Cath. U., Nijmegen, The Netherlands, 1988. Sworn trademark broker Ct. of Appeal, 1973; sworn translator, English, 1975, French, 1981. Trademark atty. Markgraaf, Amsterdam, 1965-75; prin. Keesom & Hendriks N.V., The Hague, Netherlands, 1973—; collaborator BMM Bull., 1990—. Author: The New Benelux Trademarks Act, 1986; contbr. articles to profl. publs. Pvt. Telecomms. regiment, 1963-65. Named Knight 6th grade Order of Orange-Nassau Her Majesty Queen Beatrix of the Netherlands, 1999. Fellow Inst. of Linguists, Royal Soc. for the Encouragement of Arts, Mfrs., and Commerce; mem. Netherlands Soc. of Translators (treas. 1992), Royal Netherlands Soc. for Geneology and Heraldry (treas. 1992-97), Benelux Trademark Law Assn., Netherlands Soc. Translators. Roman Catholic. Avocations: genealogy, history. Office: Keesom and Hendriks NV, POB 85533, 2585VX The Hague Netherlands

KEETH, BETTY LOUISE, geriatrics nursing director; b. Hayward, Okla., Nov. 15, 1931; d. Harley Enoch and Violet Verona (Space) George; m. Melvin L. Gillham, May 4, 1951 (div. July 1969); children: Melvin L., Dennis Ray, Debra Lynne Gillham; m. William D. Keeth, Nov. 19, 1976 (dec. Aug. 1992). ADN, Carl Albert Jr. Coll., 1984. LPN, Ark. DON MENA Manor, Mena, Ark., 1987-89, Living Ctrs. of Am., Oklahoma City, 1989-90, Westlake Sq. Ctr., Oklahoma City, 1990-91, Bethany Village, 1991-94, East Moore Nursing, Moore, Okla., 1994-95; dir. Ctrl. Okla. Christian Home, Oklahoma City, 1995-98, ret., 1999; with Mariner Health of Bethany, Okla.; cons. Precision Home Health, Oklahoma City. Registrar Lefiore County, Poteau, Okla., 1989; sec. Dem. Women, 1984-90. Avocations: crocheting, bowling, fitness. Home: HC 62 Box 185A Stidham OK 74461-9801 Office: Mariner Health of Bethany 6900 NW 39th Expy Bethany OK 73008-2514

KEETON, J. E., retired psychiatrist; b. Brilliant, Ala., Oct. 8, 1925; s. James Willie and Mary Etta (Dodd) K.; m. Mary Ann Trantham, May 31, 1953 (dec. Dec. 1989); children: Jonathan Eric, David Wright, Adam Blake. BS, Birmingham So. U., 1951; MD, U. Ala., 1955. Intern U. Chgo. Clinics, 1955-56; resident psychiatry Inst. Living, Hartford, Conn., 1956-59; dir. day hosp. Vets. Hosp., Washington, 1960-61, asst. chief psychiatry, 1961-64; pvt. practice psychiatry Bethesda, Md., 1964-78; staff psychiatrist Vets. Med. Ctr., Tuscaloosa, Ala., 1978-97; ret., 1998; dir. clozapine rsch. Vets. Hosp., Tuscaloosa, 1991-97. Pharmacist mate USN, 1944-46. Mem. Am. Psychiat. Assn. (life). Home: 4324 Stonehill Ln Tuscaloosa AL 35405-5441

KEETS, JOHN DAVID, JR., insurance company executive; b. Atlantic City, N.J., Apr. 1, 1948; s. John D. and Doris F. (Fleiss) Keets; m. Julianne Zellers, Nov. 3, 1973; children: J. David, Brian. BA, High Point Coll., 1970. CLU., cert. fin. planner, chartered fin. cons. Account exec. Mgmt. Recruiters, Phila., 1972-75; sales mgr. Cigna Fin. Svc., Miami (Fla.), Balt., 1975-82; agy. mgr. Fidelty Mut., Balt., 1983-85, Provident Mut. Ins. Co., Phila., 1985-88; regional v.p. Equitable Ins. Co., Mpls., 1988-90; prin. Keets & Assocs., Mpls., 1991-93, 97—; mgr. Prudential Ins. Co., Mpls., 1993-94; v.p. bus. devel. Carlson Mktg. Group, Mpls., 1994—; gen. mgr. Mut. of Omaha Cos., Mpls., 1998—. With U.S. Army, 1970-72, Germany. Mem. Mpls. Assn. Life Underwriters, Gen. Agts. and Mgrs. Assn, Internat. Assn. Fin. Planners, Am. Soc. CLU, Chartered Fin. Cons. Avocations: golf, boating. Home: 2420 Comstock Ln N Minneapolis MN 55447-2303

KEEVIL, CHARLES WILLIAM, microbiologist, researcher; b. Kingston Upon Hill, Eng., Sept. 15, 1951; s. Harold Ernest and Nancy (Hogben) K.; m. Margaret Jane Peddie, Apr. 12, 1980; children: James, Helen, Timothy. BSc in Biochemistry, Birmingham U., Eng., 1973; PhD in Biochemistry, 1976. Rsch. fellow Southampton U., Eng., 1976-78; head of small scale polysaccharide rsch. Tate and Lyle Ltd., Reading, Eng., 1978-79; sr. grade microbiologist Pub. Health Lab. Svc., Salisbury, Eng., 1979-84; prin. grade microbiologist, 1984-90, cons. clin. scientist, 1990-94; head of microbial tech. dept. Microbial Rsch. Authority, Salisbury, Eng., 1994-98, sci. leader, 1998—; mem. adv. bd. Fermentech Ltd., Edinburgh, Eng., 1984-86; mem. standing com. of analysts Dept. of Environment. Co-editor: Carbon Substrates in Biotechnology, 1987, Microbial Growth Dynamics, 1990, Detection Methods for Cyanobacterial Toxins, 1994, Biofilms in Aquatic Environment, 1999; contbr. over 120 rsch. papers in microbiology and biochemistry to profl. jours. Chmn. Joint Staff Consultative Com., CAMR, Salisbury, 1989-94. Recipient scholarship Brewers Soc., Eng., Birmingham, 1973, vis. rsch. fellowship Canadian MRC, Winnipeg, Can., 1983, Colgate prize British Soc. for Dental Rsch., 1985. Fellow Am. Acad. Microbiology, Inst. of Biology; mem. Soc. for Gen. Microbiology, Am. Soc. Microbiology, Soc. Applied Bacteriology, European Fedn. of Biotech., Internat. Assn. Water Quality. Anglican. Avocations: hockey, golf, cycling, reading, pub quizzes. Office: Ctr Applied Microbiology, Porton Down, Salisbury SP4 0JG, England

KEFFER, MARIA JEAN, environmental auditor; b. Sacramento, Dec. 10, 1951; d. George Edwin and Genevieve Nellie (Babuska) Scott; m. Gerry Craig Keffer, Nov. 6, 1971; children: Annemarie, Gregory, Margaret. AA in Liberal Arts, San Bernardino Valley Coll., Calif., 1973; BS in Natural Scis., U. Alaska, 1988, MS in Environ. Quality, 1995. Cert. environ. auditor Nat. Registry of Environ. Profls., prin. environ. auditor/EARA - U.K.; registered environ. health specialist, Nat. Environ. Health Assn. and State of Calif. Rsch. lab. assoc. VA/Loma Linda (Calif.) Hosp., 1988-90; environ. health specialist San Bernardino County, Calif., 1990-91, S&S Engring., Eagle River, Alaska, 1991-92; regulatory specialist ENSR Consulting and Engring., Anchorage, 1992-94; quality assurance environ. specialist Alyeska Pipeline Svc. Co., Anchorage, 1994-98; ISO 14001 project mgr. Hoefler Consulting Group, Anchorage, 1998—. Mem. Environ. Auditing Roundtable, Nat. Environ. Health Assn. Office: Hoefler Consulting Group 701 Sesame St Ste 200 Anchorage AK 99503-6641

KEFFLER, KARL JOSEPH, investment company executive, lawyer; b. St. Louis, July 1, 1943; s. Karl Leopold and Dorothea Agnes (Lucas) K. Student, U.Notre Dame, 1961-62; BA cum laude, Regis U., 1965; JD, St. Louis U., 1968; postgrad., Northwestern U., Chgo., 1972, Oxford (Eng.) U., 1995. Bar: Mo. 1969, U.S. Dist. Ct. D.C. 1970, Ill. 1987. Spl. agt. FBI, Washington, Mpls., San Francisco, 1968-71; asst. pros. atty. Office Pros. Atty. St. Louis County, Clayton, Mo., 1971-74; pvt. practice, St. Louis, 1974-81; trust officer Merc. Trust Co., NA, St. Louis, 1981-85; trust exec., head trust dept. People's Bank & Trust Co., Waterloo Iowa, 1985-86, Ill. Nat. Bank, Springfield, 1987-88, 1st Comml. Bank, Little Rock, 1988-89; pvt. investor St. Louis, 1989-97; exec. v.p., chief investments officer St. Louis Capital Mgmt., LLC, 1997—. Author investment newsletter Capital Idea, 1998. Bd. dirs. Springfield Symphony, 1987. Mem. Mo. Bar, Soc. Former Spl. Agts. FBI, Am. Mensa, Phi Delta Phi. Avocations: sports, art collecting, music. Home: 155 N Hanley Rd Apt 105 Saint Louis MO 63105-4106 Office: St Louis Capital Mgmt LLC 9845 Northbridge Rd Saint Louis MO 63124-1025

KEGLEVICH, GYÖRGY, chemistry educator; b. Budapest, Hungary, Mar. 13, 1957; s. László and Mária (Schirilla) K.; m. Rita Rochlitz, July 4, 1981; children: Kristóf, Péter, Laura, András. MS, Tech. U. Budapest, 1981, PhD, 1990, Habilitation, 1995; DSc, Hungarian Acad. Sci., Budapest, 1994. Asst. prof. Tech. U., 1983-92, assoc. prof., 1992-96; prof. chemistry Budapest U. Tech. and Econs., 1996—, head dept. organic chem. tech., 1999—. Contbr. more than 125 articles to profl. jours. Mem. Coms. of Hungarian Acad. Scis. (Géza Zemplén prize 1991, mem. various coms.), Internat. Coun. Main Group Chems., Inc. Roman Catholic. Avocations: music, swimming, bicycling. Home: B Bartok ut 53, 1114 Budapest Pest Megye Hungary Office: Budapest U Tech and Econs, Muegyetem PO Box 91, H-1521 Budapest Hungary

KEGLEVICH, NICOLAS, travel assistance company executive; b. Budapest, Hungary, June 8, 1939; arrived in Argentina, 1968; s. Count Peter and Countess Marka (Pejacsevich) K.; m. Marina Rusconi, June 29, 1963 (div. 1970); children: Flavia, Alexia; m. Countess Maria Khevenhüller Metsh, June 1974 (div. 1996); 1 child, Maximilian. Grad. h.s., Porto Alegre, Brazil, 1956. Sales, area mgr. I.O.S., Geneva, 1962-67, Alicante, Spain, 1967-68; area rep. France Secours Internat., Paris, 1968-70, Assist Card Internat., Geneva, 1970-72; dir. Latin Am. Assist Card Internat., 1972—. Mem. SKAL (pres. 1989-91), SKAL Internat. (dir. 1984-89). Avocation: boating. Home: 1541 Brickell Ave Miami FL 33129-1213

KEGLEY, CHARLES WILLIAM, JR., political science educator, author; b. Evanston, Ill., Mar. 5, 1944; s. Charles William and Elizabeth Euphemia (Meck) K.; m. Ann Curry Taylor, Apr. 1, 1966 (div.); 1 child, Suzanne Taylor; m. Pamela Ann Holcomb, July 6, 1975 (div.). BA, Am. U., 1966; PhD, Syracuse U., 1971. Asst. prof. Sch. Fgn. Svc., Georgetown U., 1971-72, prof., chmn. dept. govt. and internat. studies, 1981-85; dir. Byrnes Internat. Ctr. U. S.C., 1986-88, holder Pearce chair internat. studies, 1985—; vis. prof. U. Tex., 1976; Moses Back Peace prof., Rutgers U., New Brunswick, N.J., 1989. Author: A General Empirical Typology of Foreign Policy Behavior, 1973; co-author, co-editor (with William Coplin): A Multi-Method Introduction to International Politics: Observation, Explanation and Prescription, 1971, Analyzing International Relations: A Multi-Method Introduction, 1975; co-author: (with Eugene R. Wittkopf) American Foreign Policy: Pattern and Process, 1979, 5th edit., 1996, World Politics: Trend and Transformation, 1981, 7th edit., 1999; (with Gregory A. Raymond) A Multipolar Peace? Great-Power Politics in the 21st Century, 1994, How Nations Make Peace, 1999; co-editor: (with Robert W. Gregg) After Vietnam: The Future of American Foreign Policy, 1971; (with Gregory A. Raymond, Robert M. Rood, Richard A. Skinner) International Events and the Comparative Analysis of Foreign Policy, 1975; (with Patrick J. McGowan) Challenges to America: U.S. Foreign Policy in the 1980's, 1979, (with Patrick McGowan) Threats, Weapons, and Foreign Policy, 1980, The Political Economy of Foreign Policy, 1981, Foreign Policy: USA/USSR, 1983; (with Eugene R. Wittkopf) Perspectives on American Foreign Policy, 1983, The Global Agenda: Issues and Perspectives, 1984, 6th edit., 1999 (with Patrick McGowan) Foreign Policy and the Modern World System, 1983; (with Eugene R. Wittkopf) The Nuclear Reader: Strategy, Weapons, War, 1985, 2d edit., 1989; (with Charles F. Hermann and James N. Rosenau) New Directions in the Study of Foreign Policy, 1987, (with Eugene R. Wittkopf) The Domestic Sources of American Foreign Policy, 1988 (with Gregory A. Raymond) When Trust Breaks Down: Alliance Norms and World Politics, 1990, (with Kenneth Schwab) After the Cold War: Questioning the Morality of Nuclear Deterrence, 1991, (with Eugene R. Wittkopf) The Future of American Foreign Policy, 1992; editor: The Long Postwar Peace: Contending Explanations and Projections, 1990, International Terrorism: Characteristics, Causes, Controls, 1990, Controversies in International Relations Theory: Realism and the Neoliberal Challenge, 1995; contbr. chpts. to books, articles to profl. jours. Bd. trustees Carnegie Coun. Ethics & Internat. Affairs, 1992-98, 2000—. Recipient Disting. Alumni award Am. U., 1984; R.M. Davis scholar, 1962-66; Maxwell fellow, 1968-69, 70-71; N.Y. State Regents fellow, 1969-70; Fulbright sr. scholar, 1978, Russell rsch. awardee in humanities and social scis., 1982. Mem. Am. Polit. Sci. Assn., Am. Soc. Internat. Law, Am. Soc. Advancement Sci., Internat. Polit. Sci. Assn., Internat. Studies Assn. (assoc. dir. 1980-84, pres. 1993-94), Midwest Polit. Sci. Assn., Peace Sci. Soc., Peace Rsch. Soc., So. Polit. Sci. Assn., Pi Sigma Alpha, Omicron Delta Kappa, Delta Tau Kappa. Home: 1829 Senate St Apt 4B Columbia SC 29201-3837 Office: U SC Dept Govt & Internat Studies Columbia SC 29208-0001

KEH, HUAN JANG, chemical engineering educator, researcher; b. Chang-Hwa, Republic of China, Nov. 3, 1955; s. Chan-Wu and Chen-Lan (Yen) K.; m. Sue-Jean Chen Keh, Apr. 2, 1989; children: Eileen, Pei-Chong. BS, Nat. Taiwan U., Taipei, 1978; MS, U. Fla., Gainesville, 1980; PhD, Carnegie Mellon U., Pitts., 1984. Teaching asst. Nat. Taiwan U., Taipei, 1978-79; rsch. asst. U. Fla., Gainesville, 1979-80; rsch. and teaching asst. Carnegie Mellon U., Pitts., 1980-84; assoc. prof. Nat. Taiwan U., Taipei, 1984-88; vis. assoc. prof. U. Wis., Madison, 1989-90; prof. Nat. Taiwan U., Taipei, 1988—; assoc. dean Coll. of Engring., 1992-99; dir. rsch. ctr. petrochem. industry, 1998—, Nat. Taiwan U., Taipei. Contbr. articles to profl. jours. Mem. acting chmn. adminstrv. com. Roman Roland Cmty., Taipei, 1991-98. Recipient Excellence in Teaching award Min. of Edn., Republic of China, 1993, Outstanding Teaching award Nat. Taiwan U., 1999, Outstanding Rsch. awards Nat. Sci. Coun., Republic of China, 1992-99. Mem. Chinese Inst. of Chem. Engrs., J.Ch.I.Ch.E (editl. bd.), Internat. Assn. Colloid Interface Sci. Avocations: swimming, travel, bridge, music. Office: Dept of Chemical Engring, National Taiwan University, Taipei Taiwan 106-17, China

KEHAL, HARBHAJAN SINGH, economics educator; b. Sandaur, Punjab, India, June 25, 1942; s. Harkishan Singh and Harnam Kaur K.; m. Harbans Kaur, June 11. 1959; children: Harjinder Singh Kehal, Parminder Kaur Kehal, Harcharan Singh Kehal. BA in Econs., Punjab U., Chandigarh, 1961, MA in Econs., 1963; PhD in Econs., U. Western Australia, Nedlands, 1984. Econ. investigator, statis. asst. Punjab Pub. Svc., 1963-64; dist. family planning edn. officer Directorate of Health Svcs., Punjab, 1965-66; postgrad. tchr. econs. Cen. Sch., Chandigarh, 1966-70; asst. prof. econs., rsch. asst. Punjab Agr. U., 1970-77; rsch. scholar U. Western Australia, Nedlands, WA, 1977-84; sr. fin. officer Dept. Fin./Commonwealth Govt., 1986-87; lectr. in econs. U. Western Sydney, 1987-91, sr. lectr. in econs., 1992—, head econ. group, faculty mgmt.; vis. prof. econs. Fukuoka U., Japan, 1992, Chulalongkorn U., Bangkok, Thailand, 1996, Inst. Econ. Growth, Delhi U., 1996, Punjabi U., Patiala, India, 1996; vis. fellow econs. U. Durham, U.K., 1992; postgrad. studies coord. Faculty of Mgmt., Richmond, U. Western Sydney, 1991, 93, head econs. group, 1999; vis. fellow Inst. S.E. Asian Studies, Singapore, 1996; founder, mem. Indian Ocean Rsch. Network; presenter, panelist Internat. Conf. Info. Resources Mgmt. Assn., Anchorage, 2000. Contbg. author: Globalisation, Flexibility and Competitiveness: A Technology Management Perspective, 1998, Overseas Trading Sourcebook, 1995-96, Proceedings of the First World Congress on a Holistic Approach to Business/Management, 1995, National Strategies for Australasian Countries: The Impact of the Asian/Pacific Economy, 1993, Proceedings of the International Conference in Economics in Business and Govern ment, 1992, Development with Social Justice, 1974, Market Towns and Spatial Development, 1972, Twenty-Point Economic Programme, 1976; contbr. articles to profl. jours. Pres. PTA, Govt. Model Sch., Punjab Agr. U., Ludhiana, 1975-76. Recipient univ. scholarship U. Western Australia, Nedlands, 1977-81; rsch. grantee U. Western Sydney, 1990, 91, 97, 98. Mem. Internat. Assn. Agrl. Econs. (chmn. discussion group opener, rapporteur), Econ. Soc. Australia (exec. coun. mem. N.S.W. br. 1994-95, 95-96), Pacific Rim Coun. on Urban Devel. (spkr. internat. confs. Japan 1992, San Francisco 1993), Australia-Japan Soc., Australia-China Friendship Soc., Australian Inst. Internat. Affairs (coun. 1997-2000), Internat. Food and Agribus. Mgmt. Assn., Info. Resources Mgmt. Assn. Office: U Western Sydney, Bourke St, Richmond NSW 2753, Australia

KEHAYIAS, GEORGE, marine biologist, researcher; b. Ioannina, Ipiros, Greece, Dec. 16, 1967; s. Achilleas and Anthoula (Priovolou) K. Diploma of Biology, U. Patras, Greece, 1990, PhD, 1996. Instr. marine biology U. Patras, 1996-2000; lectr. U. Agrinio, Greece, 2000—. Contbr. articles to profl. jours. Mem. Chaetognath Group. Home: Kimonos and Leonidou 1, 36 100 Agrinio Greece Office: U Agrinio, 30 100 Agrinio Greece

KEHEW, GEORGE MANSIR, artist; b. Harvey, Ill., Aug. 17, 1923; s. George Henry and Blanche Willard (Holt) K.; m. Dolores Smith, Mar. 21, 1947; children: Eric Wayne, Roger Mark, Jai Lynne. Student, Chouinard Art Sch., L.A., Art Ctr. Coll. of Design, L.A. Cert. indsl. edn. tchr. Calif., Calif. C.C. tchr. in art, design and photography. Various positions in field to illustrator Northrop Aircraft Corp., Hawthorne, Calif., 1957-59; lead man, tech. illustrators Cannon & Sullivan, San Diego, 1959-61; art dir. applied oceanog. group Scripps Inst. Oceanography U. Calif., San Diego, 1961-66, illustrator, photographer Office Learning Resources, 1966-67; artist Complete Art Svc., San Diego, Calif., 1966-68; illustrator, tng. visuals Grumman Aerospace, NAS Miramar, Calif., 1972-73; visual info. specialist Naval Edn. and Tng. Support Ctr., San Diego, 1973-85; alt. mem. Equal Employment Opportunity Com., San Diego, 1983. Artist/author: Mac Goes to the Hospital, Best Friends Animal Coloring and Activity Book; creator ofcl. Squadron patch (Red Wolf) for VF-1 Mira Mar Naval Air Sta., logo for Scripps Applied Oceanographic Group, Point Loma, Calif., (game) Bushwacker; syndicated cartoon strip Hamalot; exhibiting cartoonist 1968 Terre Des Hommes, Man and His World, Pavilion de L'Humor, Montreal; designer, dir. TV show packaging for Art Around Us, San Diego Area Instrnl. TV Authority, 1965, others; paintings represented in Ariz., Calif. and Utah gallerys; represented in Vincent Price Sears travel show, 1965-67, also others; contbr. articles to Desert Mag. Sgt. U.S. Army, PTO, 1942-46. Recipient numerous art awards, including Bicentennial First Ann. Best of Show award, 1976, Merit award in publs. San Diego C.C., 1972, award for best painting 3d Ann. Juried Exhbn., St. George Art Mus., 1999, Sweepstakes award Washington County Fair Juried Show, 1999, 2000; grantee in field. Mem. San Diego Watercolor Soc. (pres. 1967-68). Democrat. Avocations: mountain biking, cross country skiing, sailing, classic guitar.

KEHL, RANDALL HERMAN, executive, consultant, lawyer; b. Furstenfeldbruck, Fed. Republic Germany, May 18, 1954; came to U.S., 1955; s. Raymond Herman and Annabelle (Fair) K.; m. Sharon Kay Barnes; children: Lindsey Elizabeth, Jessica Anne, Austin Randall, Ky Randall. BS, USAF Acad., 1976; MBA, U. N.D., 1980; JD, Pepperdine U., 1983. Bar: N.D. 1983, D.C. 1988, U.S. Supreme Ct. 1990. Commd. 2d lt. USAF, 1976, advanced through grades to maj., 1986, chief civil law, 1983-84, chief criminal law, 1984-85; squadron commdr. Alaska Air Command, Anchorage, 1985, chief def. counsel, 1985-86; dep. base atty. Kirtland AFB, Albuquerque, 1986-89; spl. asst. U.S. atty. U.S. Dept. Justice, Albuquerque, 1986-89; chief energy litigation Office of USAF JAG, Washington, 1989-90; White House fellow, 1990-91; chmn., CEO POD Assocs., Inc., 1992-97; cons., counsel to DESA-office of sec. of def. U.S. Dept. Def., Albuquerque, 1993; prin. Randall H. Kehl Consulting, Albuquerque, 1993-98; chmn. RHK Capital Group Internat., San Antonio, 1997—; pres., CEO Safe Zone Sys., Inc., 1998-99; CEO Optomec, Inc., 2000—; mem. staff Pres.'s Coun. on Competiveness, 1990-91; vice chmn. White House Working group on Commercialization of Fed. Lab. Tech., 1991; chmn. Candeli, Ltd., Kerorioni, Ltd., Rep. of Georgia, 1992-96; adj. instr. law U. Alaska, 1985-86; bd. dirs., counsel Kirtland Fed. Credit Union, Albuquerque; bd. dirs., sec. Triad Comm., Inc., Albuquerque; chmn. bd. POD Assocs., Inc., 1988-90. Asst. scoutmaster Boy Scouts Am., Minot, N.D., 1977-80; tchr. Officers Christian Fellowship, Minot, 1977-80; civic arbitrator Mediation and Conciliation Svc., 1983-86; mem. pvt. sch. bd. Anchorage, 1984-85; mem. Gov.'s Task Force for Utility Corp. Restructuring, 1987; vice-chmn. N.Mex. Gov.-Elect Transition Team, 1994, Gov.'s Bus. Adv. Coun., 1995—; mem. steering com. Rep. Campaigns, 1995—; co-chmn. N. Mex. Character Counts in the Workplace, 1996—; bd. dirs. Kirtland Partnership Com., 1995—, N.Mex. Ctr. for Civic Values, 1997—; dir. Albuquerque Character Counts, 1998—. Mem. ABA, AMA, Albuquerque Acad. Capital Devel. Com. and Assoc. Trustee, The Forman Sch. (capital devel. com.), Tanoan Country Club, Phi Delta Phi. Republican. Presbyterian. Avocations: swimming, skiing, scuba diving, sailing, golf. Office: Ste 415 5100 John D Ryan Blvd San Antonio TX 78245-3534

KEHOE, THOMAS FRANCIS, curator; b. Janesville, Wis., Nov. 29, 1926; s. Robert Bartholomew Kehoe and Ada Stevens; m. Alice Eve Beck, Sept. 18, 1956 (div. Nov. 1993); children: Daniel Miles, Thomas David, Cormac Joel; life ptnr. Mary Anne Siderits. BA in Anthropology, Beloit Coll., 1950; MA in Anthropology, U. Wash., 1957; postgrad., Harvard U., 1957-62. Dir., curator U.S. Dept. Interior, Mus. Plains Indian, Browning, Mont., 1952-59; curator, provincial archaeologist Mus. Nat. History, Regina, Can., 1959-65; dir. Nebr. State Hist. Soc. Mus., Lincoln, 1965-66; asst. clin. prof. anthropology U. Wis., Milw., 1968-82; curator anthropology Milw. Pub. Mus., 1968-90, curator emeritus, 1991—; coord. ethnology working groups Internat. Coun. Mus., Paris, 1974-83; Fulbright prof., rschr. U. Tubingen, Germany, 1978-83; lectr. Groningen (The Netherlands) Inst. Archeology, 1979, U. Leicester (Eng.), 1981; U.S. corr. ArchaeoZoologia, Internat. Coun. Archaeozoology, Bordeaux, France, 1986-90; rschr., spkr. in field. Author: Stone Tipi Rings in North-Central Montana and the Adjacent Portion of Alberta, Canada, 1960, The Boarding School Bison Drive, 1967, The Gull Lake Site, 1973, Solstice-Aligned Boulder Configurations in Saskatchewan, 1979; contbr. articles and revs. to profl. jours., chpts. to books. Mem. Boy Scouts Am., 1944 (Eagle Scout). With U.S. Army, 1945-46. Rsch. Travel grantee NEA, 1972, Nat. Mus. Can., 1972-73, 75, 77, Am. Coun. Learned Socs., 1974-75, 77-78, NSF, 1982. Fellow Am. Anthrop. Assn. (mus. tng. and profl. standards com. 1975, bd. dirs. 1987, exec. bd. gen. anthropology divsn. 1987-89, mus. symposium organizer and chair 1988); mem. Am. Mus. Assn., Soc. Am. Archaeology, Am. Ethnological Soc., Coun. Mus. Anthropology, Wis. Archeol. Survey, Sask. Archeol. Soc. (charter), Sask. Assn. Profl. Archaeologists. Avocation: cross country skiing. Office: Milw Pub Mus 800 W Wells St Milwaukee WI 53233-1404

KEICHER, WILLIAM EUGENE, electrical engineer; b. Pitts., Dec. 28, 1947; s. William John and Gina Rina (Magrini) K.; m. Barbara Marie Gurgacz, Aug. 12, 1972; children: Lisa Anne, Kathy Marie, William Michael. BSEE, Carnegie-Mellon U., 1969, MSEE, 1970, PhD in Elec. Engring., 1974. Sr. elec. engr. CBS Labs., Stamford, Conn., 1974-75; mem. tech. staff Lincoln Lab., MIT, Lexington, Mass., 1975-83, asst. group leader, 1983-85, group leader, 1985-93, 2000—, assoc. group leader, 1993-2000; cons. Sci. and Engring. Support Group for Strategic Def. Initiative, Arlington, Va., 1988; co-chair for numerous confs. in field. Editor: Millimeter Wave Technology, 1982, Applied Laser Radar Technology, 1993, Industrial Applications of Laser Radar, 1994; contbr. articles to profl. publs.; patentee spatial filter sys. Capt. U.S. Army, 1974. Mem. IEEE (sr.), Optical Soc. Am., Nat. Rsch. Coun. (Air Force sci. and tech. com. on rev. of Air Force hypersonic tech. program 1997-98), Assn. Old Crows. Roman Catholic. Avocations: history, snorkeling, travel, microcomputers. Home: 6 Winn Valley Dr Burlington MA 01803-4727 Office: MIT Lincoln Lab 244 Wood St Lexington MA 02421-6426

KEIGER, JOHN FREDERICK VICTOR, history educator; b. London, Middlesex, Eng., Dec. 7, 1952; s. Frederick Granville Middleton and Anna Isabella Carmina (Iseppi) K.; m. Victoria Ann McQuillan; children: Emma, Laura, Edward. Diploma in Polit. Sci., Inst. D'Etudes Politiques, Aix-en-Provence, France, 1974; PhD, U. Cambridge, 1980. Lectr. Salford U., Manchester, Eng., 1978-89, sr. lectr., 1989-93, reader, 1993-95, prof., 1995—; vis. prof. Inst. D'Etudes Politiques, Aix-en-Provence, 1985, U. Clermont Ferrand, France, 1990-91; external examiner, U. Leeds, Eng., 1995-99, London Sch. Econs., 1999—; cons. BBC, London, 1995-96. Author: (books) France and the Origins of First World War, 1983; editor: British Documents on Foreign Affairs, 19 Vols., 1989-92, Raymond Poincaré, 1997; author: (nat. radio broadcasts) BBC Patriotic Money, Etc., 1995-96. Major Bursary, Leverhulme Trust, London, 1988; rsch. grantee Brit. Acad., London, 1989. Mem. Assn. Study Modern France (editl. bd.). Avocations: swimming, tennis, ornithology, langs.

KEII, TOMINAGA, academic administrator; b. Takikawa, Hokkaido, Japan, Dec. 10, 1920; s. Yosaku and Matsu (Endo) K.; m. Kuniko Utsunomiya, Dec. 24, 1959; 1 child, Hiroshi. BS, Kyusyu Imperial U., Japan, 1945; DSc (hon.), Hokkaido U., Japan, 1956. Assoc. Inst. Sci. (Riken), Tokyo, 1945-46; assoc. Hokkaido U., Sapporo, Japan, 1946-51, assoc. prof., 1951-57; assoc. prof. Tokyo Inst. Tech., 1957-60, prof., 1960-81, prof., inst. senator, 1970-77; prof. emeritus Tokyo Sci. U., 1981-82; pres. Numazu Nat. Coll. Tech., Japan, 1982-89; prof. emeritus Japan Advanced Inst. Sci. and Tech., Hokuriku, Japan, 1990-98; founding pres. alumni sci. U. Tokyo, 1999—; vis. scientist NRC Can., Ottawa, 1962; mem. Univ. Chartering Coun. Ministry Edn., 1975-81; bd. dirs. Inst. Dem. Edn., Tokyo, 1970—, Inst. Higher Edn., Tokyo, 1980—. Author: Kinetics of Ziegler-Natta Polymerization, 1972 (Tejima award 1975); editor: Academic Assessment, 1984. Govtl. vis. fellow Ministry Edn. Japan, 1967, 68, Japan Sci. Promotion Soc., 1975, 78. Fellow Engring. Acad. Japan; mem. Am. Chem. Soc., Japan Chem. Soc. (bd. dirs. 1966-68), Japan Catalysis Soc. (hon., bd. dirs. 1959-78, v.p. 1978-79, pres. 1979-80), Assn. Nat. Colls. (hon., pres. 1984-89). Buddhist. Avocations: kenndo (black belt), studying science philosophy. Home: Tamagawa-Gakuen 4-12-4, Tokyo, Machida 194, Japan Office: Japan Advanced Inst Sci & Tech, Tatsunokuck, Ishikawa 923-12, Japan

KEIL, CHARLES GEORGE, public relations executive; b. London, Mar. 7, 1933; s. George and Jane Dryburgh (Grieve) K.; m. Janette Catherine Loder, Apr. 23, 1960; children: Fiona, Duncan, Ewan. BS in Engring., U. London, 1959. Chartered engr. Flt. lt. Royal Air Force, 1951-55; editor tech. mag. Aircraft Engring., London, 1959-65; London editor Indian Aviation, Calcutta, 1962-67; group editor Thomas Reed Publs., London, 1965-66; dir. John Fowler & Ptnrs., Ltd., London and Birmingham, 1966-73; mng. dir., CEO Harrison Cowley Pub. Rels., Birmingham, 1974-94; chmn. Harrison Cowley Group, 1987—. Editor, joint translator: Aerodynamics, 1964. Chmn. Birmingham Readers and Writers Festival, 1992-96, Brumhalata Intercultural Storytelling Co., 1995-2000; mktg. advisor Arts and Bus., Birmingham, 1992—; mktg. lectr. Understanding Industry, Birmingham, 1992-2000; mktg. dir. Birmingham Ctr. for Drama, 1994-95. Avocations: skiing, water skiing, walking, reading, writing. Home: Illyria, 536 Streetsbrook Rd, Solihull B91 1RD, England Office: Harrison Cowley, 154 Great Charles St, Birmingham B3 3HU, England

KEIL, FRERICH JOHANNES, chemical engineer; b. Esens, Germany, Sept. 24, 1947; s. Karl and Wilma Gerhardine (Graalfs) K.; m. Anke Hemsath, Aug. 29, 1980; 1 child, Vera-Catharina. MS in Chemistry, Tech. U., 1973, PhD in Quantum Chemistry, 1976; D (hon.), U. Chem. Tech., Sofia, 2000. Sr. rschr. UHDE Ltd., Dortmund, Germany, 1977-81, authorized agt., 1981-85, chief engr., 1985-89; prof. chem. engring. Tech. U., Hamburg, Germany, 1989-90, dean, 1990—, head of rsch. coun., 1990—; cons. Beiersdorf Ltd., Hamburg, 1995—, Deutsche Airbus, Hamburg, 1996—, SOLVAY, Ltd., Hannover, 1996—, ICP, Bucaramanga, Columbia, 1997; lectr. in field. Editor: Scientific Computing in Chemical Engineering, 1999, Hungarian Jour. Indsl. Chemistry; contbr. articles to profl. jours. Referee Jugend forscht, Hamburg, 1993—. Fellowship Gartow Found., 1995—.

Fellow DECHEMA; mem. AIChE, N.Y. Acad. Sci., Assn. of German Engrs. Avocations: history, philosophy. Office: Tech U of Hamburg, Eissendorferstr 38, D-21073 Hamburg Germany

KEIL, GUNDOLF, medical historian, medievalist, Germanist; b. Wartha, Niederschl, Germany, July 17, 1934; s. Walther and Lucie (Bremer) K.; m. Annemarie Flach, June 1, 1968. PhD, U. Heidelberg, Germany, 1961; MD, U. Bonn, Germany, 1969; Privat-Dozent, U. Freiburg, Germany, 1971. Asst. prof. med. faculty U. Göttingen, Germany, 1962-64; asst. prof. med. faculty U. Bonn, 1964-69, assoc. prof., 1970; prof. German U. Stockholm, 1969; assoc. prof. med. faculty U. Freiburg, 1971; head dept. med. history U. Marburg, Germany, 1971-73; prof. and head dept. med. history U. Würzburg, Germany, 1973—, mng. dir. Gerhard-Möbus-Institut für Schlesienforschung, 1986—; pres. coun. Stiftung Kulturwerk Schlesien, Würzburg, 1991—. Co-editor: (ency.) Die deutsche Literatur des Mittelalters. Verfasserlexikon, 10 vols., 1977—, (series of studies) Texte und Wissen, 4 vols., 1995—; editor: (series of studies) Würzburger medizinhistorische Forschungen, 69 vols., 1974—; (textbook) Ein teutsch puech machen, 1993; co-editor Sudhoffs Archiv, 1972-73, 85—; chief editor Würzburger medizinhistorische Mitteilungen, 1983—. Decorated Knight of Order of Holy Sepulchre of Jerusalem; recipient Scheffel prize Volksbund für Dichtung, Karlsruhe, 1954, Avicenna medal Med. Faculty, U. Istanbul, Turkey, 1989, Friedrich-Behn medal City of Lorsch, Germany, 1990. Fellow N.Y. Acad. Scis.; mem. Medieval Acad. Am., Historische Kommission für Schlesien, Historische Kommission für Hessen, Darmstadt, Physikalisch-Medizinische Gesellschaft Würzburg (pres. 1974-75, 76), Deutsche Gesellschaft für Geschichte der Medizin, Naturwissenschaft und Technik (v.p. 1982-85), Verein für Geschichte Schlesiens (pres. 1989—), Würzburger Medizinhistorische Gesellschaft (bd. dirs. 1982—), Istituto Veneto Scienze, Lettere Arti (socio straniero 1999—), Akademik gemeinnütziger Wiss. zu Erfurt. Mem. Christlich-Soziale Union. Roman Catholic. Avocations: botany, walking, ornithology, Silesia travels. Home: #44, Walther-von-der-Vogelweide-Str, D-97074 Würzburg Germany Office: Inst Geschichte der Medizin, Oberer Neubergweg 10a, D-97074 Würzburg Germany

KEIL, HAROLD H. (BILL KEIL), writer; b. Portland, Oreg., Apr. 11, 1926; s. Harry G. and Elizabeth M. K.; m. Gloria T. Trantanella, Feb. 27, 1959; children: Richard T., Gregory H. BS in Forestry, Oreg. State Coll., 1950. Ski editor The Oregonian newspaper, Portland, 1959-75, KOIN-TV, Portland, 1968-75; city forester Portland Park Bur., 1952-56; assoc. editor, logging & forestry editor The Timberman, The Lumberman, and Forest Industries mags., Portland, 1956-60; editor World Wood mag., Portland, 1960-71; pub. affairs officer U.S. Bur. Land Mgmt., Portland, 1975-88; U.S. corr. Wood-Based Panels Internat. Mag., Tonbridge, Kent, England, 1988—; freelance writer numerous newspapers and mags., 1950—; adv. bd. mem. Mt. Hood Nat. Forest, Portland, 1985-87. Author: Trails & Roads of Forest Park, 1973; editor: American Ski Annual, 1956, World Forestry Statistical Yearbook, 1961-71. Tax increment adv. com. Clackamas County, Oreg., 1988-90; com. chmn. U.S. Ski Assn., Denver, 1953-65. Staff sgt. U.S. Army, Philippines, 1944-46. Mem. Soc. Am. Foresters (publicity chmn. 1959-60), N.Am. Ski Journalists Assn Outdoor Writers Assn. Am., Nat. Press Photographers Assn. Avocations: skiing, hiking, photography.

KEILMANN, ANNEROSE, pediatric otolaryngologist, phoniatrician; b. Tuttlingen, Germany, June 1, 1960; d. Ignaz and Marianne (Weggler) Schmid; m. Christoph Keilmann, June 19, 1986; 1 child, Lucia. Med. state exam., U. Freiburg, Germany, 1985; MD, U. Saarlandes, Homburg, Germany, 1985; privatdozent, U. Heidelberg, Mannheim, Germany, 1995. Asst. doctor U. Heidelberg Clinic, Mannheim, 1986-94, sr. physician, 1994-96; sr. physician Comm. Clinic, U. Mainz, Germany, 1996—. Recipient Geers-Stiftung prize, 1996. Mem. German Soc. Ear, Nose, and Throat, German Soc. Phoniatrics and Pediatric Audiology (Annelie-Frohn prize 1996), German Soc. Lang. and Voice Medicine. Office: Clinic for Comm Disorders, Langenbeckstr 1, D-55101 Mainz Germany

KEIM, DANIEL ANDREAS, computer science educator, researcher; b. Gelsenkirchen, Germany, Nov. 30, 1965; s. Walter and Nelly (Mogck) K.; m. Ilse Stetter, Sept. 24, 1988; children: Lydia, Hanna, Johannes, Damaris. Diploma, Univ. Dortmund, 1990; PhD, Univ. Munich, 1994, habilitation, 1997. Instr., rsch. assoc. Naval Postgrad. Sch., Monterey, Calif., 1990-91; asst. prof. Univ. Munich, 1994-97; assoc. prof. Univ. Halle, Germany, 1997-2000, prof., 2000—. Author: Datenbankmaschinen: Performance by Parallelism, 1992, Visual Support of Querying and Mining Large Databases, 1995; contbr. articles to profl. jours. Recipient scholarship German Scholarship Found., 1986-90, 90-91. Mem. ACM, IEEE, German Computer Soc. Avocations: music, swimming, hiking. Office: Inst of Computer Sci, Kurt Mothes Str 1, 06120 Halle Germany

KEIM, DONALD BRUCE, finance educator; b. Bethlehem, Pa., Feb. 7, 1953; s. Elwood Benjamin and Doris Mae (Wanamaker) K.; m. Susan Langshaw, July 10, 1976; children: Sarah Elizabeth, Julia Diane. BSBA, Bucknell U., 1975; MBA, U. Chgo., 1980, PhD, 1983; MS (hon.), U. Pa., 1988. Rsch. assoc. Fed. Deposit Ins. Corp., Washington, 1978; lectr. Loyola U. of Chgo., 1981-82; asst. prof., fin. U. Pa., Phila., 1982-88, assoc. prof. fin., 1988-94, prof. fin., 1994—; vis. prof. INSEAD, Fontainebleau, France, 1994, 96-98; vis. scholar Dimensional Fund Advisors, Santa Monica, Calif., 1990, 1995-96; mem. acad. adv. bd. Brandywine Asset Mgmt., Wilmington, Del., 1993—. Assoc. editor Jour. of Fin. and Quant. Analysis, 1993—; co-editor European Fin. Rev., 1998—; contbr. articles to profl. jours. Rsch. grantee Inst. for Quantitative Rsch., 1984, 92, 99; recipient Graham and Dodd award Fin. Analysts Fedn., 1987, 99, N.Y. Stock Exch. award, 1996. Mem. Am. Fin. Assn., Western Fin. Assn. (program com. 1992-96), European Fin. Assn. (program com. 1996-99). Avocations: music, photography, golf, gardening. Office: Univ Pa The Wharton Sch 2300 Steinberg Hall Philadelphia PA 19104

KEISEL, MAURINE LILLEY, rehabilitation nurse; b. Corry, Pa., Oct. 31, 1939; d. Maurice D. and Violet S. (Vettenburg) Lilley; m. Glenn L. Keisel, Apr. 7, 1962; children: G. Adam, Glenda (Sunny), Mark. Diploma in nursing, Hamot Hosp. Sch. Nursing, 1961. RN; CRRN, Rehab. Nursing Certification Bd. RN Bethesda Childrens Home, Meadville, Pa., 1961-62; staff RN Ashtabula (Ohio) Gen. Hosp., 1969-71; coord., supr. restorative nursing program Ashtabula Medicare Ctr., 1975-87; co-owner, cons. Keisel Phys. Therapy, Ashtabula, 1989—; parish nurse, health ministries coord. Bethany Luth. Ch., Ashtabula, 1992—; cons. in field; coord. Faith and Health Partnership Ashtabula County, 1995—; bd. dirs. Faith and Health Partnerships/Interfaith Vol. Caregiver Ashtabula County, Ohio, 1996—. Mem. ANA, Ohio Nurses Assn., Assn. Rehab. Nurses, Health Ministries Assn., Nurses Christian Fellowship. Lutheran. Avocations: singing gospel music, playing piano and guitar, gardening. Home: 3016 S Ridge W Ashtabula OH 44004-9061 Office: Keisel Phys Therapy 416 W 27th St Ashtabula OH 44004-4968

KEISLER, RON S., oil company executive; b. Camden, Ark., 1947. M.Geology, U. Ark., 1971. With Marathon Oil Co., 1971—; head exploration for Vietnam, Thailand, Philippines Marathon Oil Co., Singapore, 1974-79; with Marathon Oil Co., Findlay, Ohio, 1979-80, coord. mgr. prodn. internat., 1980-82; regional exploration mgr. Europe and North Africa Marathon Oil Co., Houston, 1982-87; prodn. mgr. Marathon Oil Co., Bridgeport, Ill., 1987-89; prodn. mgr. Mid-Continent region Marathon Oil Co., Midland, Tex., 1989-91; v.p. domestic prodn. continental U.S. Marathon Oil Co., Houston, 1991-94, v.p. worldwide exploration, 1994-95, bd. dirs., 1995—, sr. v.p. worldwide exploration, 1998—. Office: Marathon Oil Co PO Box 3128 5500 San Felipe Rd Houston TX 77253

KEITH, BRAD ALLEN, rector; b. Kansas City, Mo., Aug. 20, 1966; s. Charles Michael and Joyce Sue (Davidson) K. BA in Internat. Rels., Webster U., St. Louis, 1989; MA in Internat. Rels., Webster U., 1989. Internat. trade specialist State of Mo., Kansas City, 1994-98; rector Webster U. Thailand, Cha-am, 1998—; dir. State of Mo. Internat. Trade Office, Bangkok, 1998—. Democrat. Avocations: reading, travel. E-mail: keithb@webster.ac.th. Office: Webster U Thailand, 518/5 Ploenchit Rd 7th Fl, Bangkok 10330, Thailand

KEITH, BRIAN THOMAS, automobile executive; b. Houston, Aug. 2, 1951; s. Thomas Ross and Elsie Ann (Carden) K.; m. Anna Lee Rogers, Nov. 17, 1973; children: Kevin Patrick, Lindsay Rogers. BSBA, Samford U., 1973. Educator installation IBM, Birmingham, Ala., 1971-73; salesman Albeco-Ala. Bus. Equipment Co., Birmingham, 1973-74; pres., owner Walter S. White Auto Parts, Inc., Birmingham, 1974—; bd. dirs. Ala. Power Co. Vendor Rels. Bd., Birmingham; trustee Automotive Wholesalers Ins. Trust, Montgomery, 1985—, treas. investment com., 1992—, chmn. trust, 1996-99; industry spkr. Automotive Market Rsch. Coun., 1995, Automotive Wholesalers Assn. Ala. and Ga., Automotive Aftermarket Industry Assn. Pub. mag. Auto Svc. and Repair, 1988—; contbr. articles to publs. and mags. V.p. Park Bd. Patriot Baseball, Homewood, Ala., 1985-89; celebrity fundraiser Am. Cancer Soc., 1993; mem. canvass com. All Sts. Ch., Homewood, 1986-90, youth com., 1992-99; active St. Andrews Soc. of the Middle South. Named Outstanding Young Men in Am., U.S. Jaycees, 1983; recipient Tech. Tng. award Arvvin Industries, 1983-88. Mem. Automotive Wholesalers Assn. Ala. (bd. dirs. 1985—, chmn. 1986-91, treas. 1992-95, 98—, polit. action com. 1992-99, exec. com. 1991—, Leadership award 1991), Automotive Svc. Industry Assn. (bd. dirs. 1992-98, nat. polit. action com. 1993-99, co-chmn. automotive com. 1994-98), Birmingham C. of C., U.S. C. of C., Young Exec. Forum, Assn. Enterprises (pres. 1991-92), Jr. Achievement, Nat. Fedn. Ind. Bus. Episcopalian. Avocations: family, golf, travel.

KEITH, KENT MARSTELLER, academic administrator, corporate executive, government official, lawyer; b. N.Y.C., May 22, 1948; s. Bruce Edgar and Evelyn E. (Johnston) K.; m. Elizabeth Misao Carlson, Aug. 22, 1976. BA in Govt., Harvard U., 1970; BA in Politics and Philosophy, Oxford (Eng.) U., 1972, MA, 1977; JD, U. Hawaii, 1977; EdD, U. So. Calif., 1996. Bar: Hawaii 1977, D.C. 1979. Assoc. Cades, Schutte, Fleming & Wright, Honolulu, 1977-79; coord. Hawaii Dept. Planning and Econ. Devel., Honolulu, 1979-81, dep. dir., 1981-83, dir., 1983-86; energy resources coord. State of Hawaii, Honolulu, 1983-86, chmn. State Policy Coun., 1983-86; chmn. Aloha Tower Devel. Corp., 1983-86; project mgr. Mililani Tech. Park Castle and Cooke Properties, Inc., 1986-88, v.p. pub. rels. and bus. devel., 1988-89; pres. Chaminade U., Honolulu, 1989-95; v.p. devel. and comm. YMCA Honolulu, 1998—; bd. dirs. Grove Farm Co., Inc., 1990-93. Author: Jobs for Hawaii's People: Fundamental Issues in Economic Development, 1985, Hawaii: Looking Back from the Year 2050, 1987, For the Love of Students, 1992; contbr. articles on ocean law to law jours. Pres. Manoa Valley Ch., Honolulu, 1976-78; mem. platform com. Hawaii Dem. Conv., 1982, 84, 86; trustee Hawaii Loa Coll., 1986-89, vice chmn., 1987-89; mem. Diocesan Bd. Edn., 1990-95, chmn., 1990-93; bd. dirs. St. Louis Sch., 1990-95, Hanahauoli Sch., 1990-98; chmn. Manoa Neighborhood Bd., 1989-91. Rhodes scholar, 1970; named one of 10 Outstanding Young Men of Am., U.S. Jaycees, 1984; recipient Disting. Alumni award U. Hawaii, 1993. Mem. Am. Assn. Rhodes Scholars, Internat. House of Japan, Nature Conservancy, Pla. Club, Pacific Club, Harvard Club Hawaii (Honolulu, bd. dirs. 1974-78, sec. 1974-76), Rotary (Honolulu Sunrise). Home: 2626 Hillside Ave Honolulu HI 96822-1716

KEITH, PAULINE MARY, artist, illustrator, writer; b. Fairfield, Nebr., July 21, 1924; d. Siebelt Ralph and Pauline Alethia (Garrison) Goldenstein; m. Everett B. Keith, Feb. 14, 1957; 1 child, Nathan Ralph. Student, George Fox Coll., 1947-48, Oreg. State U., 1955. Illustrator Merlin Press, San Jose, Calif., 1980-81; artist, illustrator, watercolorist Corvallis, Oreg., 1980-94. Author 6 chapbooks, 1980-85, including Christmas Thoughts Retelling the Story, 1985, Poems, 1999; editor: Four Generations of Verse, 1979; contbr. poems to anthologies and mags. and articles to mags.; one-woman shows include Roger's Meml. Libr., Forest Grove, Oreg., 1959, Corvallis Art Ctr., 1960, 98-99, Human Resources Bldg., Corvallis, 1959-61, Chintimini Sr. Ctr., 1994—, Corvallis Parteral Counseling Ctr., 1992-94, 96, Hall Gallery, Sr. Ctr., 1993, 94, 95-96, 97, 98, 99, 2000, Consumer Power, Philomath, Oreg., 1994, Art, Etc., Newburg, Oreg., 1995, 96, 97, 98, 99, 2000; exhibited in group shows at Hewlett-Packard Co., 1984-85, Corvallis Art Ctr., 1992, Chintimini Sr. Ctr., 1992. Co-elder First Christian Ch. (Disciples of Christ), Corvallis, 1988-89, co-deacon, 1980-83, elder, 1991-93; sec. Hostess Club of Chintimini Sr. Ctr., Corvallis, 1987, pres., 1988-89, v.p., 1992-94; mem. Luth. Ch. Coun., 1998, 99—. Recipient Watercolor 1st price Benton County Fair, 1982, 83, 88, 89, 91, 2d prize, 1987, 91, 3d prize, 1984, 90, 92. Mem. Oreg. Assn. Christian Writers, Internat. Assn. Women Mins., Am. Legion Aux. (elected poet post II Covallis chpt. 1989-90, elected sec. 1991-92, chaplain 1992-93), ArtVine. Republican. Avocations: nature walks, singing in church choir. Office: 304 S College St Newberg OR 97132-3114

KEITHLEY, BRADFORD GENE, lawyer; b. Nov. 23, 1951; s. Sanderson Irish and Joan G. (Kenneday) K.; m. Ginger W. Wilhelmi, Mar. 26, 1994; children: Paul Michael, Rachel Austin Bernstein. BS, U. Tulsa, 1973; JD, U. Va., 1976. Bar: Va. 1976, Okla. 1978, D.C. 1979. Atty. Office of Gen. Counsel to Sec. USAF, Washington, 1976-78; ptnr. Hall, Estill, Hardwick, Gable, Collingsworth and Nelson, Tulsa, 1978-84; sr. v.p. gen. counsel Arkla, Inc. (now NorAm Energy Corp. divsn. Reliant Energy, Inc.), Shreveport, La., 1984-90; ptnr. head global oil, gas and power practice team Jones, Day, Reavis and Pogue, Dallas, 1990—. Mem. ABA, Fed. Energy Bar Assn., Va. State Bar, Okla. Bar Assn., D.C. Bar Assn., Am. Gas Assn. (mem. legal sect.), Dallas Petroleum Club. Home: 12652 Sunlight Dr Dallas TX 75230-1856 Office: Jones Day Reavis & Pogue 2727 N Harwood Dallas TX 75201-1856

KEKÄLE, JOUNI ILMARI, personnel specialist, researcher, consultant; b. Kokkola, Finland, Aug. 1, 1963; s. Teuvo Einari and Airi Inkeri (Kauppinen) K.; m. Leea Helena Keskitalo, July 8, 1995; children: Jere, Toni, Henrikki. M in Psychology, U. Joensuu, Finland, 1991; Lic. in Psychology, U. Joensuu, 1993, D of Psychology, 1997. Rschr. U. Joensuu, 1991-95, 97-98, personnel dir., 1998—, docent higher edn. studies, 1999—; rschr. U. Sussex, Brighton, U.K., 1995-96; external cons. U. Helsinki, Finland, 1997-99; cons. Finnish ednl. orgns., 1991-96. Author: Developing Lecturing, 1994, Climates of Discussion Within Three Fields of Study, 1991, Leadership Cultures in Academic Departments, 1997, Quality and Assessment in Diverse Disciplines, 2000; contbr. articles to profl. jours. Rsch. grant Ministry of Edn., Finland, 1991-97. Avocation: music. Office: Univ Joensuu PO Box 111, Tulliportinkatu 1, 80101 Joensuu Finland

KEKRE, SHREEKANT H., dean; b. Nagpur, India, Dec. 12, 1938; s. Harishchandra G. and Taramati H. (Rege) K.; m. Smita S. Mahajan, Dec. 12, 1969; children: Pallavi, Shital. BE with honors, Govt. Coll. Engring., Jabalpur, India, 1961; MSc with Engring., Birla Inst. Tech., Ranchi, India, 1968. Cert. engr. Lectr. Govt. Coll. Engring. & Tech., Raipur, India, 1961-64; asst. prof. Birla Inst. Tech., Ranchi, 1964-74; assoc. prof. Birla Inst. Tech., Mesra, Ranchi, 1974-84, prof., 1984-94, head dept. elec. & electronics engring., 1994-96, dean U.G. studies, 1996—; adj. prof. dept. indsl. rsch. Birla Inst. Tech., Ranchi, 1968-74, coord. continuing edn. program, 1977-87; sr. sci. officer Small Indsl. Rsch. Orgn., Ranchi, 1974-75. Patentee in field. Avocations: Indian music, photography, reading.

KELAIDITIS, ANESTIS, construction company executive; b. Cairo, Feb. 28, 1948; s. Stylianos and Anastasia (christodoulou) K.; m. Stefania Zaglaras, July 2, 1977; children: Stylianos, Nicolaos, Anastasia. Diploma in Civil Engring., Nat. Tech. U., Athens, 1971; student, Mgmt. Ctr., London, 1985; MBA, U. de la Romande, 1987. Site engr. Edok S.A.-Eter S.A., Agrinion, Greece, 1972-73, GETEM S.A., Pireasu, Greece, 1973-74; market survey and tenders staff Hydrotechnic S.A., Athens, Greece, 1974-75; site engr. Odon & Odostro Maton S.A., Saudi Arabia, 1975-79, bridge engr., 1979-80, project mgr., 1980-85; comml. mgr. Itihad Al Tatwir Wal Tanmia Al Saoudia Ltd., Saudi Arabia, 1986-89, pvt. practice, Athens, 1990-94, Christiani & Nielsen-TCGC S.A., Joint Venture, Preveza, Greece, 1995-97; comml. dir. TCGC S.A., Athens, 1997—. Greek Orthodox. Avocations: boy scouts, photography, painting. Home: 50 Vitsi Str Ilioupolis, 16346 Athens Greece

KELDMANN, ERIK CHRISTIAN VILHELM, innovation company executive; b. Naestved, Sealand, Denmark, Feb. 7, 1940; s. Charles Johannes and Karen Rigmor (Hansen) K.; m. Annelise Keldmann, Apr. 6, 1963; children: Troels, Linda. BSc in Mech. Engring., Odense Teknikum, 1965. Devel. engr. Motorfabriken Bukh, Kalundborg, Denmark, 1965-67; mgr. R&D Carmen-Clairol, Kalundborg, 1967-71; pres. Ve-va Cons., Jerslev, Denmark, 1971-85, Elpan-Wanpan, Odense, 1974-85; v.p. R&D Superfos Bldg. Components, Vebaek, Denmark, 1985-86; pres. E.K. Innovation, Odense, 1985—; bd. dirs. Servodan, Direct-Haler A/S, E.K. Innovation A/S; co-founder High Performance Inst. Co-author: The Innovation-Tree; patents include heat embracement, zone impregnation and direct inhaler. Recipient Initiative Diploma for Entrepreneurship Nat. Soc. Danish Work, 1977. Mem. Acad. Using Philosophy, Soc. Exec. Engrs., Rotary. Avocations: classic cars. Office: EK Innovation, Aaloekken 44, 5250 Odense Denmark

KELEKIAN, LENA, painter, art restorer, geologist, researcher; b. Beirut, Lebanon, May 18, 1959; d. Krikor and Maxim (Mosditchian) K. BSc in Geology, Am. U. Beirut, 1981; DSTheology, Religious Inst., Beirut, 1992; Diploma Conservation/Restoration Murals, U. London, Florence and Andalusia, 1992, 95; Diploma Conservation/Restoration Icons, U. London, Macedonia, 1993. Artist and restorer of murals and icons, 1992—; artist representing Lebanon, Ministry of Culture, Ministry of Tourism, 1995-98; pvt. expo at Museu Ses Voltes in Palma de Mallorca, 1998; artist at Internat. Art Expo, Ont. and Man., Can., Madrid; pres. Accdemia Intl. Greci-Marino for the Mid. East & Lebanon, 2000. Exhibited in group shows at Espace Culturel Oud-Sint-Jan, Bruges/Mechellin, Belgium, Biennal of Women Artists, Stockholm, London and Samlesbury, Eng., Anderson Gallery, Billy Graham Mus., N.Y. Art Expo, U.S.A., Grand Palais Salon d'Automne and others in France, 1992-98, Am. U. Beirut Aumni Assn. and others, Lebanon, Muscat, Kuwait City; represented in permanent collections at Billy Graham Mus., Nicholas Suksock Mus., others; work on icons and murals at Archives of Nat. Mus. for Women in the Arts, others. Coord., Embellishing the Cities and Roundabouts with Monuments in Lebanon, Beirut, 1997; chmn. exhbn. Assn. Beyrouth Patrimoine, 1992-2000; mem. Beirut Cultural Coun., 1996-2000; vol. mem. UN (RSRD), 1997; mem., profl. artist UNESCO, Paris, 1992-97. Recipient La Toile d'Or, Nat. Fedn. French Culture, 1995, Hon. Gold medal Biennal of Women Artists, Stockholm, 1995, medaille d'Or de Prestige,European Art Group, 1996, 1st prize winner of Joudraniyat, othrs. Mem. Am. U. Beirut Alumni Assn. (chmn. social com. 1992-2000), Artiste de la Communaute Europeene. Avocations: mineral and fossil collecting, designing ceramic tiles, tennis, skiing, dancing. Fax: 00961-1264002; e-mail: lena@kelekian.com. Home: Portemilio, 3504C Kaslik Lebanon Office: Sacred Art Studio, Garnet Bldg 1st Fl, Zalka Beirut Lebanon

KELEMEN, ENDRE, hematologist, researcher; b. Szekszard, Hungary, Jan. 17, 1921; s. József and Klára (Kardoss) K. MD, Pazmany Peter U., Budapest, Hungary, 1945; degree in Hematology, Min. Health, Budapest, Hungary, 1960; DSc, Hungarian Acad. Sci., 1966. Resident to assoc. prof. Med. U. Szeged, Hungary, 1945-58; assoc. prof. Postgrad. Sch. Medicine, Budapest, Hungary, 1958-67; scientific leader Semmelweis U. Budapest, Hungary, 1967-92; head Bone Marrow Transplantation unit Nat. Inst. Hematology, Budapest, Hungary, 1992-95; pres. Nat. Coll. Hematology, 1991-95, mem. com. for degree hematologist, 1992—. Author: Inflammatory Oedema: Salicylates, 1960, Physiopathology and Therapy of Human Blood Diseases, 1969, Atlas of Human Hemopoietic Development, 1979; contbr. 300 articles to profl. jours. Pres. Bone Marrow Transplantation Found., Budapest, Hungary, 1991; mem. Pub. Welfare Found. Hungarian Nat. Bank, Budapest, Hungary, 1991—; freeman of Szekszard, 1989. Recipient Exptl. Haematology fellow Paterson Labs., Manchester, U.K., 1966, 67, Marshalko Grand prize Hungarian Haematological Soc., 1989; fellow Internat. Union Contra Cancer, Lyon, France, 1974, 75. Mem. European Soc. Haematology, Hungarian Soc. Hematology (pres. 1976-82, hon. life pres. 1997—), German Soc. Hematology and Oncology (hon.), Internat. Soc. Exptl. Haematology (Szècheny prize 1992, Laureatus Academiae 1995, Szent-Györgyi prize 1996), Hungarian Acad. Sci. (rep. gen. assembly 1998). Achievements include discovery of thrombopoietin. Home: Pasareti ut 115, 1026 Budapest Hungary Office: Nat Inst for Haematology & Immunology, Daroczi ut 24, 1519 Budapest Hungary

KELEMEN, JANOS, philosopher, educator; b. Kassa, Hungary, June 8, 1943; s. Janos and Ilona (Franck) K.; m. Gabriella Klimo, Oct. 16, 1965 (dec. 1983); 1 child, Balazs; m. Judit Bardos, Apr. 7, 1989; 1 child, Agnes. Degree in Italian and Russian Philology, U. JATE, Szeged, Hungary, 1966; Degree in Philosophy, U. ELTE, Budapest, Hungary, 1969. Diplomate in Italian and Russian langs., diplomate in philosophy. Lectr. in philosophy U. ELTE, 1970—, prof. philosophy, 1980—, head dept. philosophy, 1986-90, 96—; dir. Hungarian Acad. in Rome, 1990-95; head dept. Italian studies U. JATE, 1995-97. Author: Profili ungheresi e altri saggi, 1994, Idalismo e storicismo nell'opera di Benedetto Croce, 1995 (Premio Valitutti 1996); editor: Atti del congresso internazionale Benedetto Croce, 1993, (with others) Reading su Ferruccio Rossi-Landi, 1994. Recipient Premio Sabetia Ter, Municipality of Naples, 1992, Premio Valitutti, Univs. Salerno and Naples, 1996. Home: Veres Palne U 33, H-1053 Budapest Hungary Office: Elte Btk Filosofia, Piarista Koz 1, 1052 Budapest Hungary

KELEMEN, JOHN, neurologist, educator; b. Nyíregyháza, Hungary, Apr. 28, 1948; s. Ignac and Anna (Hartman) K. BA, SUNY, Binghamton, 1970; MD, Georgetown U., 1974. Cert. Am. Bd. Psychiatry and Neurology-Neurology, Am. Bd. Electrodiagnostic Medicine. Med. intern Nassau County Med. Ctr., East Meadow, N.Y., 1974-75; neurology resident Nassau County Med. Ctr., East Meadow, 1975-78, staff neurologist, 1980-85, dir. MDA clinic, 1980-85, chief neuromuscular program, 1981-85; neuromuscular fellow Tufts U.-New Eng. Med. Ctr., Boston, 1978-80; pntr. Island Neurol. P.C., Plainview, N.Y., 1985—; clin. asst. prof. neurology NYU Sch. of Medicine, 1996—; clin. asst. prof. neurology Cornell U. Med. Coll., N.Y.C., 1986-95; tchg. residents and med. students Stony Brook U., Cornell U., NYU, Manhasset, East Meadow, 1980—; lectr. in field. Contbr. chpts. to books and articles to profl. jours. Rsch. grantee Muscular Dystrophy Assn., Boston, 1979, Nassau Heart Assn., East Meadow, 1984. Fellow Am. Acad. Neurology. Avocations: tennis, sailing, skiing, computers, cinema. Office: Island Neurol PC 824 Old Country Rd Plainview NY 11803-4935

KELEMEN, JOZEF, computer scientist; b. Nove Zamky, Slovakia, Mar. 16, 1951; s. Viktor and Julia (Marczibanyi) K.; m. Alice Piricka, Apr. 12, 1975; children: Eduard, Robert. Diploma in Math., Comenius U., Bratislava, 1974, DrRerNat, 1976; Cand Scis, USSR Acad. Scis., Moscow, 1984; DSci, Slovak Tech. U., 1998. Asst. lectr. Comenius U., Bratislava, 1974-89, asst. prof., 1990-92; assoc. prof. U. of Econs., Bratislava, 1992-97; prof. U. of Econs., Bratislava, Czech Republic, 1997—; assoc. prof. Silesian U., Opava, Czech Republic, 1994-97; prof. Silesian U., Opava, 1997—; vis. lectr. Eotvos U., Budapest, 1987-88; vis. scientist MIT, Cambridge, 1992; cons. Rsch. Inst. Med. Bionics, Bratislava, 1984-87, Glass Svc., Ltd., Vsetin, Czech Republic, 1994-97; rsch. fellow Slovak Acad. Scis., Bratislava, 1988-89. Co-author: (In Slovak lang.) Expert Systems, 1989, Expert Systems for Practice, 1996, Building Expert Systems, 1999, Fundamentals of Artificial Intelligence, 1992, (in English) Grammar Systems, 1994; co-editor: (in English) Fundamentals of Artificial Intelligence, 1991. Mem. Am. Assn. for Artificial Intelligence, N.Y. Acad. Scis. Avocations: collecting fine art, writing essays, reading contemporary philosophy. Home: Zacpalova 29, 74601 Opava Czech Republic Office: Silesian U Inst Computer Sc, Bezruc Sq 13, 74601 Opava Czech Republic

KELEMEN, JOZSEF, consultant neuropathologist; b. Reghin, Mures, Romania, Nov. 9, 1934; s. József and Piroska (Bojtás) K.; married; children from previous marriage: Katalin, Eva. Diploma, Med. U., Tg. Mures, Romania, 1958. Physician Batos (Romania) Village Med. Cabinet, 1958-62; rsch. fellow Rsch. Sta. of Romanian Acad., Tg. Mures, 1962-69; sr. rsch. fellow Med. Rsch. Sta. of Med. Acad., Tg. Mures, 1969-75; head dept. pathology State County Hosp., Miercurea Ciuc, Romania, 1975—; vis. rsch. fellow Nat. Inst. Neurology-Psychiatry, Budapest, Hungary, 1969, Med. U. Pecs, Hungary, 1969; lectr. on med. edn. various civic orgns., TV, radio, 1987—. Contbr. articles to profl. jours. Fellow Alexander von Humboldt Found., 1971-72, 91-92. Mem. Romanian Med. Assn. (pres. Hargita County br. 1992—), Romanian Soc. Morphology, Hungarian Soc. Neuropathology, Internat. Soc. Neuropathology-Internat. Brain Rsch. Orgn., N.Y. Acad. Scis., Humboldt Club of Romania. Roman Catholic. Avocations: mountain excursions, photography. Home: Apt 25, Str Libertatii Nr 12 Etj VI, RO-4100 Miercurea Ciuc Romania Office: Hargita County Ctrl Hosp, Str T Vladimirescu Nr 50, RO-4100 Miercurea Ciuc Romania

KELEPECZ, BETTY PATRICE, protective services official, lawyer; b. Santa Monica, Calif., Nov. 13, 1955; d. Andrew J. and Doris L. Giba; m. Steve T. Kelepecz, Sept. 3, 1983. AS, Antelope Valley Coll., 1975; BS in

Biology, U. So. Calif., L.A., 1977; JD, Southwestern U., 1990; grad., FBI Nat. Acad., 1992. Bar: Calif. 1990, U.S. Dist. Ct. (ctrl. dist.) Calif. 1991. Microbiologist Rachelle Labs., Long Beach, Calif., 1978-80; police officer I, II, III, background investigator L.A. Police Dept., 1980-85, detective I S.W. Cmty. Police Sta., 1985-86, sgt. I Pacific, 77th and West L.A. patrol divsn., 1986-88, sgt. I ops. South Bur., 1988-89, sgt. II planning and rsch. divsn., 1989-90, lt. I Harbor Cmty. Police Sta., 1990-91, lt. II Ops.-South Bur., 1991, lt. II Office of the Chief of Police, 1991-93, capt. I Harbor Cmty. Police Sta., 1993-95, capt. I Pacific Cmty. Police Sta., 1995-96; owner, ptnr. Law Offices of Pheil & Kelepecz, Long Beach, Calif., 1995-96; capt. II West Traffic divsn. L.A. Police Dept., 1996, capt. III Sci. Investigation divsn., 1996-97, comdr. Cmty. Policing Group, 1997, comdr. Ops.-West Bur., 1997-98, comdr. Pers. Group, 1998—; spkr., trainer and cons. in field. Recipient Am. Jurisprudence Book award, 1987, Congratulatory cert. Mayor Riordan, 1997, Affirmative Action Assn. Women Recognition for women leaders and pacesetters, 1997, Congress Racial Equality Calif. commendation, 1997; named Outstanding Young Women of Am., 1988. Mem. ABA, FBI Nat. Acad. Assocs., Internat. Assn. Chiefs Police (com. mem. major city chiefs human resources), Nat. Assn. Women Law Enforcement Execs. (past pres., charter), Calif. Bar Assn., L.A. County Bar Assn., L.A. County Police Officer's Assn., L.A. Police Command Officer's Assn. (com. mem.), L.A. Women Police Officer's Assn., Police Exec. Rsch. Forum, Rotary Club Westchester, Delta Theta Phi.

KELETI, GEORG, retired microbiologist, researcher; b. Michalovce, East Slovakia, Czechoslovakia, May 30, 1925; s. Louis and Lilly (Silberstein) K.; m. Martha Helene Maxian, July 28, 1956; children: Eva, Daniel. Degree in pharmacy, Comenius U., Bratislava, Czechoslovakia, 1950, PhD in Microbiology, 1952; candidate of sci. in biology, Acad. Scis., Bratislava, 1961; cert., Continuing Edn. Physicians, Bratislava, 1963. Asst. prof. microbiology Comenius U., 1950-53, prof.'s asst., 1953-63, assoc. prof., 1963-68; sr. fellow Max-Planck Inst., Freiburg, Fed. Republic of Germany, 1968-70; asst. rsch. prof., then assoc. prof. U. Pitts., 1970-96; sr. scientist Bactex Pitts., 1979-81; cons. in field, 1986—; adj. assoc. prof. occupational environ. health Grad. Sch. Pub. Health, U. Pitts., 1986-96, ret., 1996; adj. assoc. prof., U. Pitts. Author: Handbook of Micromethods for the Biological Sciences, 1974; contbr. articles to profl. jours. Patentee Anti-tumor process using a Brucella Abortus preparation, 1989. Served to 1st lt. Czech. Army, 1951-54. Mem. Am. Soc. Microbiology. Avocation: swimming. Fax: (412) 420-4088. Home: 5831 Nicholson St Pittsburgh PA 15217-2309

KELKAR, JAYANT V., petrochemical company executive; b. Pune, India, Jan. 23, 1947; s. Vishnu and Kamal V. Kelkar; m. Chhaya J. Gokhale, May 10, 1973; children: Amit, Gauri. B of Tech., Indian Inst. Tech., Bombay, 1968; PhD, U. Salford, 1972. From chem. engr. to sr. project mgr. Indian Petrochems. Corp. Ltd., Vadodara, Nagothane, India, 1972-88; from head technology to olefins plant mgr. Nat. Organic Chem. Industries Ltd., Bombay, 1988-91; from gen. mgr. to sr. v.p. group mfg. tech. Reliance Industries Ltd., Mumbai, 1991—.

KELLAR, WILLIAM OWEN, business owner, writer; b. Omaha, Jan. 3, 1922; s. Clyde Amos and Agnes (Connolly) K.; widowed; children: Juan, Carmen, Philip, William. BS, U.S. Naval Acad., 1944; MA, U. So. Calif., 1946; PhD, U. Mo. Unity Campus, 1978. Commd. ensign USN, 1944, advanced through grades to vice adm., 1994, ret., 1975; pres. Kelco Internat. Inc., Ashland, Oreg., 1979—. Decorated Congressional medal of honor, 2 Navy Cross, Silver Star, Bronze Star, 4 Purple Hearts, 3 Disting. Crosses. Avocations: fishing, hunting, camping, flying.

KELLE, UDO, social science lecturer, researcher; b. Hannover, Germany, June 1, 1960; s. Gerd and Marianne K.; m. Ruth Fruehwald Kelle, Apr. 21, 1989; 1 child, Lisa. Diploma in Psychology, U. Bremen, Germany, 1988, PhD in Sociology, 1993. Rsch. asst. Spl. Rsch. Unit 186 U. Bremen, 1989-92, sr. rschr., 1993-97; lectr. U. Vechta, 1997—; vis. rsch. fellow Dept. Sociology, U. Surrey, Great Britain, 1996; organizer Internat. Conf., The Qualitative Rsch. and Computing in Bremen, 1993. Author: Empirisch begruendete Theoriebildung, 1994, 2d edit., 1998, (with S. Kluge) Vom Einzelfall zum Typus, 1999; editor: Computer-aided Qualitative Data Analysis, 1995; edtl. bd.: Social Research Methods, 1997. Recipient Bremer Studienpreis, U. Bremen, 1993. Mem. German Sociol. Assn. Office: U Vechta, Driverstr 22, 49377 Vechta Germany

KELLEHER, GRAEME GEORGE, natural resources manager, civil engineer; b. Sydney, Australia, May 2, 1933; s. Richard and Joyce (Illidge) K.; m. Fleur Meachen, Nov. 21, 1959; children: Wade, Melanie, Serena. B of Civil Engring., U. Sydney, Australia, 1955. Civil engr. project mgr., 1955-74; dep. chmn. nuclear nonproliferation task force Dept. Prime Minister and Cabinet, Canberra, Australia, 1977-78; chmn., CEO Gt. Barrier Reef Marine Park Authority, Canberra, 1979-94; vice-chair World Commn. Protected Areas (WCPA), Gland, Switzerland, 1986-98; sr. advisor WCPA, 1999—; prof. sys. engring. James Cook U., Townsville, Australia, 1992-94; pres. Graeme Kelleher & Assocs., Canberra, 1995—; co-chair panel Coop. Rsch. Ctr., Canberra, 1996—; commr. Ranger Uranium Inquiry Dept. of Environment, Canberra, 1976-77; examiner New Zealand OECD, Paris, 1980; cons. World Bank, Washington, 1996-99. Co-author (2-vol. book) Ranger Uranium Environmental Inquiry, 1976; co-author, editor: Guidelines for Establishing Marine Protected Areas, 1992, Guidelines for Marine Protected Areas, 2000; co-editor (4-vol. book) A Global Representative System of Marine Protected Areas, 1995, PARKS, Vol. 2, No. 8, 1998; contbr. numerous articles to profl. jours. Mem. sci. and religious com. Religion, Sci. and the Environment, Athens, 1995—; chmn. adv. com. marine sector Commonwealth Sci. and Indsl. Rsch. orgn., Hobart, Australia, 1995-99. Decorated mem. Order of Australia, 1988, officer Order of Australia, 1996; recipient Monash medal, 1986, Fred Packard Internat. Parks Merit award, 1998; Winston Churchill Meml. Trust fellow, 1972. Fellow Acad. Technol. Scis. and Engring., Instn. Engrs. Australia, World Commn. Protected Areas (steering commn. 1986—). Avocations: science, bushwalking, scuba diving, tennis, skiing. Home: 12 Marulda St Canberra Aranda ACT 2614, Australia

KELLEHER, KATHLEEN, financial services marketing specialist; b. Suffern, N.Y., May 3, 1951; d. John James and Carol (Re) K. BA, Fairleigh Dickinson U., 1973. CLU, chartered fin. cons., chartered mut. fund counselor. Ins. sales adminstr. Blyth Eastman Dillon & Co., 1977-79; product mktg. assoc. Dean Witter Reynolds, N.Y.C., 1980-82; mgr. product mktg. annuities and ins. dept. Kidder, Peabody & Co., 1982-85; v.p. nat. sales mgr. ins. Paine Webber, 1985-88; v.p., dir. mktg. and sales support Landmark Fin. Corp., Oklahoma City, 1988-91; cons. fin. svcs., 1991—; dir. Mktg. Svcs. Protective Life investment product divsn., Cin., 1993-94; mktg. cons. fin. svcs. Mktg. Svcs. Protective Life investment product divsn., 1995—; dir. mktg. Prudential Annuity Svcs.; v.p. mut. funds and annuity tng. Prudential Investments, 1996, v.p. edn. strategy and integration, 2000; corp. v.p., dir. ins. mktg. Paine Webber, 2000—. Mem. Am. Mgmt. Assn., Internat. Fin. Planners, Am. Soc. CLU and ChFC. Republican. Office: 3 Gateway Ctr Newark NJ 07102-4000

KELLEHER, RICHARD CORNELIUS, marketing and communications executive; b. Buffalo, Nov. 21, 1949; s. Cornelius and Lucile Norma (White) K.; m. Sherri Fae Anderson, Mar. 17, 1981 (div. 1991); children: Erin Marie, Shawn Michael. BA, U. New Mex., 1975; MBA, U. Phoenix, 1984. Reporter, photographer Daily Lobo, Albuquerque, 1973-75; mgn. editor News Bulletin, Belen, New Mex., 1975-77; various corp. mktg. titles AT&T Mountain Bell, Denver, 1978-84; exec. editor Dairy Mag., Denver, 1984-86; communications dir. Am. Heart Assn., Phoenix, 1987-90; cons. Kelleher Communications & Mktg., Phoenix, 1990—; spl. writer Denver Post, 1977-82, Denver Corr. Billboard Mag., 1977-82. Mem. Gov.'s Roundtable on Employee Productivity, Gov. of Ariz., 1990-91; vol. communications Am. Cancer Soc., 1990-92. Recipient Harvey Communications Study award, 1986. Mem. Pub. Rels. Soc. Am., Toastmasters.

KELLER, ARTHUR MICHAEL, computer science researcher; s. David and Luba Keller. BS summa cum laude with honors, Bklyn. Coll., 1977; MS, Stanford U., 1979, PhD, 1985. Instr. computer sci. Stanford (Calif.) U., 1979-81, rsch. asst., 1977-85, acting asst. chmn. dept. computer sci., 1982, rsch. assoc., 1985, 89-91, vis. asst. prof., 1987-89, rsch. scientist, 1991-92, sr. rsch. scientist, 1992-99; sr. rsch. scientist Advanced Decision Systems, Mountain View, Calif., 1989-92; chief tech. advisor Persistence Software, San Mateo, Calif., 1991-99; co-founder, COO, CFO Mergent Sys. Inc., Palo Alto, Calif., 1996-99; chief tech. advisor ccRewards.com Corp., Los Altos, Calif., 1998—; also bd. dirs. CCRewards.com Corp., Los Altos, Calif.; co-founder, mng. ptnr. Minerva Cons., Palo Alto, Calif., 1999—; sys. analyst Bklyn. Coll. Computer Ctr., 1974-77; summer rsch. asst. IBM, Thomas J. Watson Rsch. Ctr., Yorktown Heights, N.Y., 1980; acad. assoc. IBM San Jose Rsch. Lab., 1981; asst. prof. U. Tex., Austin, 1985-88, adj. asst. prof., 1988-89; mem. program com. Internat. Conf. on Data Engring., L.A., 1986, 87, 89, Internat. Conf. on Very Large Data Bases, Amsterdam, The Netherlands, 1989; mem. program com. Internat. Workshop on Advanced Transaction Models & Architectures, Goa, India, 1996, Internat. Conf. on Info. & Knowledge Mgmt., Rockville, Md., 1996. Author: A First Course in Computer Programming Using Pascal, 1982. Bd. dirs. Congregation Kol Emeth, Palo Alto. Grad. fellow NSF, 1977-80. Mem. IEEE (vice chmn. com. database engring. Computer Soc. 1986-87), Assn. Computing Machinery, TeX Users Group (fin. com. 1983-85, internat. coord. 1985-87), Chai Soc. (communications officer 1987-89, v.p. publicity 1989-90). Avocations: singing, travel. Home: 3881 Corina Way Palo Alto CA 94303-4507 Office: Minerva Cons Dept Computer Sci PO Box A-G Stanford CA 94309-9424

KELLER, EGON HEINRICH JOSEF, surgeon; b. Remagen, Rheinland, Germany, May 2, 1950; s. Anton Josef and Elsbeth Maria (Louen) K.; m. Angela Anna Pauline Kratzig, May 20, 1978; children: Andrea, Michael, Martin. DrMed, U. Bonn, 1971; MD, Joh.Gutenberg-U. Mainz, 1979. Resident Borromäerinnen-Hosp., Trier, Germany, 1977-78; sr. house officer dept. surgery Vincenz-Hosp., Mainz, Germany, 1978-80; acad. asst. dept. surgery U. Mainz, 1980-87; asst. med. dir. dept. surgery Gen. Hosp. Heidberg, Hamburg, Germany, 1987-93; sr. surg. dept. vascular surgery Gen. Hosp. Harburg, Hamburg, 1994-95; asst. med. dir. Gen. Hosp. Ochsenzoll, Hamburg, 1993-94, 96—. Co-author: Therapie des Magenkarzinoms, 1984, Therapie Gastroenterologischer Erkrankungen, 1986; contbr. articles to profl. jours. With Med. Corps, 1970, 71. Mem. Deutsche Gesellschaft für Chirurgie AG Onkologie, European Soc. Surg. Oncology, Deutsche Krebsgesellschaft, Deutsche Gesellschaft für Gefässchirurgie. Roman Catholic. Avocations: church music, mountaineering, skiing. Office: Klinikum Nord Heidberg, Tangstedter Landstr 400, D-22417 Hamburg Germany

KELLER, HARRY ALLAN, electronics technician; b. Columbus, Nebr., Dec. 19, 1943; s. Guy and Charlotte (Cameron) K. Degree in electronic technology, Radio Engring. Inst., Omaha, 1965; cert. of tng., Sears Ext. Inst., Dallas, 1969. Lead electronic technician Dale Electronics, Columbus, 1965-70; electronic mech. technician Sears & Roebuck, Columbus, 1969-70; electronic technician Ed's TV, North Bend, Nebr., 1970-73, P&K Electronics, Columbus, 1973-77; electronic mechanic Wards, Columbus, 1977-79; electronic mech. technician Becton Dickinson, Columbus, 1979—. Active State of Nebr. R.A.C.E.S., Civil Def. Nebr. Races Network, Colfax County, 1992. Recipient Speech Craft Cert. Toastmasters Internat., 1970. Mem. Inst. Electronics Engrs. Inc., Am. Radio Relay League (v.p. local club 1976-79). Republican. Methodist. Avocations: amateur radio, car club. Home: 410 Center St Rogers NE 68659-2803 Office: Becton-Dickinson PO Box 987 Columbus NE 68602-0987

KELLER, HEIDI, psychologist, educator; b. Talling, Trier, Germany, Dec. 8, 1945; d. Hans Heinz and Marianne (Oder) K.; 1 child, Ulrich Voss. PhD, U. Mainz, Germany, 1970; Habil, Tech. U. Darmstadt, Germany, 1984. Asst. U. Mainz; asst. prof. Tech. U. Darmstadt; prof. psychology U. Osnabrück, Germany. Editor handbook on infant devel., textbook on developmental psychology. Office: U Osnabrück, Seminarstr 20, 49069 Osnabrück Germany

KELLER, JACKIE LEE, paper industry executive; b. Nowata, Okla., Oct. 29, 1951; s. William Claude Keller and Lilie Mae Richards; m. Rebecca Joanne Francisco, Nov. 13, 1986. BSBA, Rockhurst Coll., 1981. Various positions Westvaco, Kansas City, Mo., 1972-85; prodn. mgr. Westvaco, Detroit, 1985-89; sys. application mgr. Westvaco, Charleston, S.C., 1989-95; mgr. projects Weyerhauser, Tacoma, Wash., 1995—. E-mail: jack.keller@weyerhauser.com. Home: 32617 7th Ave SW Federal Way WA 98023-4901 Office: Weyerhauser # Tb-701 Tacoma WA 98477-0001

KELLER, J(AMES) WESLEY, credit union executive; b. Jonesboro, Ark., Jan. 6, 1958; s. Norman Grady and Norma Lee (Ridgeway) Patrick; m. Patricia Marie Delavan, July 7, 1979. Student, U. Miss., 1976-78; BS in Bus. and Mgmt., Redlands U., 1991, MBA, 1994. Sr. collector Rodkwell Fed. Credit Union, Downey, Calif., 1978-79; acct. Lucky Fed. Credit Union, Buena Park, Calif., 1979-84; pres., chief exec. officer Long Beach (Calif.) State Employees Credit Union, 1984—. Mem. Credit Union Exec. Soc., Calif. Credit Union League (bd. govs. Long Beach chpt., treas. 1985-86), So. Calif. Credit Union Mgrs. Assn., U. Redlands Whitehead Leadership Soc., Nat. Assn. State Charted Credit Unions (chmn. 1995—), Kiwanis. Republican. Baptist. Avocations: photography, skiing, woodworking, biking. Office: Long Beach State Employees Credit Union 3840 N Long Beach Blvd Long Beach CA 90807-3312

KELLER, JOHANNA BEALE, writer, editor. MusB, U. Colo., 1977; MA in Lit., Antioch U., 1996. Editor Chamber Music mag., N.Y.C., 1997—. Author: The Skull: North Carolina, 1961, 1998; contbr. articles, revs., translations, essays, and poetry to The New York Times, S.W. Rev., Chelsea, Hudson Rev., others. Recipient Arts fellow in poetry N.Y. Found. for the Arts, 1997; grantee Ludwig-Vogelstein Found., 1997; recipient Editor's award in poetry Fla. Rev., 1997.

KELLER, JOHN WARREN, lawyer; b. Niagara Falls, Aug. 6, 1954; s. Joseph and Edith Lillian (Kilvington) K.; m. Sandra D. Hubbard, Dec. 18, 1981; children: Sean, Christopher. BA, Rider U., 1976; JD, Coll. William and Mary, 1979. Bar: Ky. 1980, U.S. Dist. Ct. (ea. dist.) Ky. 1985, U.S. Ct. Appeals (6th cir.) 1988, U.S. Dist. Ct. (we. dist.) Ky. 1988. Staff atty. Appalachian Rsch. & Def. Fund Ky., Inc., Barbourville, 1979-82; assoc. F. Preston Farmer Law Offices, London, Ky., 1982-88; ptnr. Farmer, Keller & Kelley, London, 1988-91, Taylor, Keller & Dunaway, London, 1991—; mem. Fla. Adv. Com. on Arson Prevention, 1990—; chair bd. dirs. Appalachian Rsch. & Def. Fund Ky., 1994-96; founder, chmn. bd. dirs. Ky. Lawyers for Legal Svcs. to the Poor; mem. editl. adv. bd. Ky. West Publ. Group, 1997; bd. mem. Nat. Soc. Ins. Investigators. Contbg. editor: ABA Annotations to Homeowner's Policy, 3rd edit., 1995, ABA Bad Faith Annotations, 2d edit., 1997. Bd. dirs. Christian Ch. in Ky., 1994-98; elder First Christian Ch., London, 1994-97; pres. Access to Justice Found., 1996—. Recipient Access to Justice award Ky. Legal Svcs. Programs, 1995. Mem. ABA (vice chair property ins. law com. 1992-97), Laurel County Bar Assn. (pres. 1992-93), Ky. Bar Assn. (mem. bd. govs. 1996—), Ky. Bar Found. (bd. dirs. 2000—), The Honorable Order of Ky. Cols. Office: Taylor Keller & Dunaway 1306 W 5th St London KY 40741-1615

KELLER, NADYA CLARK, biochemistry educator, researcher; b. St. Francis, Kans., July 28, 1933; d. Albert Vernon and Lois Beatrice (Needles) Clark; m. Karl Ernest Keller, Feb. 13, 1954 (div. Oct. 1965); children: Karen Sue Keller Searight, Kevin Dean. AB, Ft. Hays U., 1965; PhD, U. Okla., 1970. Dir. metabolic lab. Cornell U. Med. Ctr./N.Y. Hosp., N.Y.C., 1970-73; prof. Northwestern State U., Natchitoches, La., 1973—, Richard Lounsbery prof., 1994—. Contbr. articles to profl. jours. Mem. AAAS, Am. Chem. Soc., La. Acad. Scis. (pres-elect 1992-93, pres 1993-95, editor newsletter 1995-97), Sigma Xi (pres. local chpt. 1974). E-mail: keller@alpha.nsula.edu. Office: Northwestern State Univ La Scholars Coll Natchitoches LA 71497-0001

KELLER, PAUL RAYMOND, health facility administrator; b. Hibbing, Minn., Dec. 28, 1951. BA, St. Cloud State U., 1975, AS, 1983. Asst. group supr. Fergus Falls (Minn.) Regional Treatment Ctr., 1983—. Mem. Am. Atheists, Minn. Atheists, Freedom from Religion Found.

KELLER, ULRICH OTTO, dentist, consultant; b. Nürnberg, Germany, 1954. DDS, U. Erlangen, Germany, 1979, DMD, 1981, PhD, 1990. Assoc. prof. Dental Sch., U. Ulm, Germany, 1982—, oral surgeon, 1983—, Univ. lectr., 1990—, prof., 1996—. Author: Die ablative Wirkung des Erbium: YAG Lasers an oralen Hartgeweben und Weichgeweben, 1990 (Merckle Rsch. award). Recipient Cooperation award Found. Sci.-Economy, 1997. Mem. German Assn. Dentistry, Internat. Soc. Laser Dentistry, European Soc. Biomed. Optics. Office: U Ulm Dental Sch Dept Oral Surgery, Albert-Einstein-Allee 11, 89081 Ulm Germany

KELLERMAN, FAYE MARDER, writer, dentist; b. St. Louis, July 31, 1952; d. Oscar and Anne (Steinberg) Marder; m. Jonathan Seth Kellerman, July 23, 1972; children: Jesse Oren, Rachel Diana, Ilana Judith, Aliza Celeste. AB in Math., UCLA, 1974, DDS, 1978. Author: The Ritual Bath, 1986 (Macavity award best 1st novel 1986), Sacred and Profane, 1987, The Quality of Mercy, 1989, Milk and Honey, 1990, Day of Atonement, 1991, False Prophet, 1992, Grievous Sin, 1993, Sanctuary, 1994, Justice, 1995, Prayers for the Dead, 1996, Serpent's Tooth, 1997, Moon Music, 1998, Jupiter's Bone, 1999, Stalker, 2000; contbr. short stories to Sisters in Crime vols. 1 and 3, Ellery Queen Mag., A Woman's Eye, Women of Mystery, the year's 2d finest crime: mystery stories, The Year's 25 Finest Mystery and Crime Stories, A Modern Treasury of Great Detective and Murder Mysteries, Mothers, Murder for Love, Mothers and Daughters. UCLA rsch. fellow, 1978. Mem. Mystery Writers of Am. (So. Calif. bd. dirs.), Womens' Israeli Polit. Action Com., Sisters in Crime. Jewish. Avocations: fencing, gardening, music.

KELLERMANN, PETER FELIX NATAN, psychologist; b. Stockholm, Aug. 21, 1953; arrived in Israel, 1980; s. Kurt and Livia (Frishmann) K.; m. Rachel Yehoshua, June 26, 1984; children: Yuval, Ofir, Michal. MA, U. Stockholm, 1979, PhD in Psychology, 1986. Clin. psychologist Kupat Cholim Meuchedet, Jerusalem, Israel, 1993-96; chief psychologist AMCHA, Jerusalem, Israel, 1996—; spkr., lectr. in field. Author: Focus on Psychodrama, 1992; co-editor: Trauma & Psychodrama, 2000; contbr. articles to profl. jours. Lt. Israeli Army, 1992. Fellow Am. Soc. Group Psychotherapy and Psychodrama (Zerka T. Moreno award 1993); mem. Fedn. European Psychodrama Tng. Orgns. (founding), Internat. Assn. Group Psychotherapy (elected chair psychodrama sect. 1998-2000). Home: Burla Str 23/4, 93714 Jerusalem Israel Office: AMCHA, 23 Hillel St, 91029 Jerusalem Israel

KELLEY, ANDY, information technology executive; b. Methuen, Mass., Oct. 1, 1960; s. Guy Franklin Kelley and Mary Corinne; children: Andrew, Emma. BS, Boston Coll., 1983; Cert. of Studies, Bently Coll., 1993. Dir. mktg. and sales Boston U. Corp. Edn., Tyngsboro, Mass., 1992-96; exec. dir. Boston U. Corp. Edn., Tyngsboro, 1998, acting exec. dir., 1999—; v.p. mktg. and sales SyberWorks.com, Cambridge, Mass., 1996-98. Recipient award Microsoft New Eng., Waltham, Mass., 1988. Mem. Internat. Tech. Tng. Assn., Direct Mktg. Assn. Roman Catholic. Avocations: hiking, web surfing, technogadgets. E-mail: andykelley@hotmail.com. Office: Boston U Corp Edn Ctr 72 Tyng Rd Tyngsboro MA 01879-2044

KELLEY, CHRISTOPHER DONALD, lawyer; b. Manhasset, N.Y., Nov. 6, 1957; s. Donald Kelley and Audrey (Wuestman) Raebeck; m. Nancy Nagle, June 27, 1981. BA in History with high honors, Coll. William and Mary, 1978; JD cum laude, N.Y. Law Sch., 1981. Bar: N.Y. 1982, U.S. Dist. Ct. (ea. dist.) N.Y. 1984. Assoc. Twomey Latham & Shea, Riverhead, N.Y., 1981-85; ptnr. Twomey Latham Shea & Kelley, Riverhead, N.Y., 1985-99, mng. ptnr., 1999—. Chmn. East Hampton (N.Y.) Dem. Com., 1982-86, 87-88, 92—, East Hampton Town Zoning Bd. Appeals, 1986-87. Mem. N.Y. Bar Assn. (environ. law sect.), Suffolk County Bar Assn., N.Y. County Bar Assn., Am. Trial Lawyers Assn. Episcopalian. Home: 727 Accabonac Rd East Hampton NY 11937-1807 Office: Twomey Latham Shea & Kelley 33 W 2nd St Riverhead NY 11901-2701

KELLEY, EDWARD ALLEN, publisher; b. Clinton, Mass., June 28, 1927; s. Edward Francis Kelley and Lillian Marion (Keigwin) French; m. Margaret Jordan Talbott, Feb. 24, 1962; children: Catherine, Edward, Michael. BA, Trinity Coll., Hartford, Conn., 1950; STM, Gen. Theol. Sem., N.Y.C., 1953. Prodn. asst., customer svc. rep. Colonial Press, Clinton, 1953-57; mgr. bookstore Morehouse-Barlow Co. Inc., N.Y.C., 1957-61, v.p., editorial dir., 1961-74; sr. v.p. Oxford U. Press, N.Y.C., 1974-83; pres. Kelley Assocs., Ridgefield, Conn., 1983-87; pres., pub. Morehouse Pub. Co., Ridgefield, 1988-97; pvt. practice pub. cons. Ridgefield, 1997—. Editor The Episcopal Ch. Ann., 1967-74, 87-97. With USNR, 1945-47, World War II. Democrat. Episcopalian. Avocations: golf, reading.

KELLEY, EDWARD WATSON, JR., federal agency administrator; b. Eugene, Oreg., Jan. 27, 1932; s. Edward Watson and Allie (Autry) K.; children: Kinsloe K. Queen, James M., Michael; m. Janet H. Kelley. BA, Rice U., 1954; MBA, Harvard U., 1959. Pres., chief exec. officer Kelley Industries, Inc., Houston, 1959-81; chmn. bd. Investment Advisors, Inc., Houston, 1981-87; gov. FRS, Washington, 1987—. Lt. (j.g.) USNR, 1954-56. Mem. Houston Country Club (bd. dirs. 1984-87), Bayou Club. Methodist. Office: FRS Office of Chmn 20th & C Sts NW Washington DC 20551-0001

KELLEY, JOSEPH FRANK, retired allergist; b. Salem, Ohio, Dec. 3, 1927; s. Joseph Martin and Ella (Smith) K.; m. Ann Higley, June 22, 1957; children: David Martin, Elizabeth Smith. AB, Dartmouth Coll., 1948; MD, Case Western Res. U., 1953. Intern Univ. Hosp., Cleve., 1953-54, resident, 1956-58, 59-60; allergies and immunology fellow Univ. Hosp., Ann Arbor, Mich., 1958-59; gen. practice medicine Univ. Hosps., Cleve., 1960-67; staff Cleve. Clinic Found., 1967—, chmn. dept. allergy and immunology, 1977-87, sr. physician dept. allergy and immunology, 1987-90; ret., 1990. Served to capt. USAFR. Fellow Am. Acad. Allergy and Immunology, Am. Assn. Cert. Allergists; mem. Ohio Soc. Allergy and Immunology (pres. 1981-82), Cleve. Allergy Soc. (pres. 1973-74, 80-81). Republican. Home: 10 Prescott Pl 2950 Warrensville Center Rd Shaker Hts OH 44122-2689

KELLEY, LARRY DALE, retired army officer; b. Geary, Okla., Sept. 1, 1944; s. Cecil and Myrtle Irene (Burch) K.; m. Ellen Elizabeth Neeley; children: Sara M., Rebecca I., Lynette C., Stacey A. BS, Cameron U., 1974; M in Criminal Justice, Okla. City U., 1977; MBA, Ctrl. State U., 1980. Enlisted U.S. Army, 1964, advanced through grades to lt. col., 1990; ret., 1992; pers. officer/spl. forces officer, capt. U.S. Army, 1964-79; asst. sales mgr. Pacesetter Corp., Oklahoma City, 1980; acctg. mgr. Hertz Corp., Oklahoma City, 1981-84; systems mgr. U.S. Army, 1985-92; exec. dir. Sanctuary, Inc., 1994-95; bd. dirs., treas. Muskogee Fed. Credit Union. V.p. student senate Cameron U., Lawton, pres. student senate; pres. chpt. 32 Spl Forces Assn., 1984, chpt. 95 Res. Officers Assn., 1988. Decorated Bronze Star, Vietnamese Cross of Gallantry, Combat Infantryman's badge. Mem. VFW (life), DAV (life), Res. Officers Assn. (life), Ret. Officers Assn. (life), Spl. Forces Assn. Avocations: model railroading, geneal. rsch., travel.

KELLEY, LYNNE DHIONIS, language educator; b. Newton, Mass., Jan. 5, 1947; d. Kosta and Theodora (Lambert) Dhionis; m. Richard Gerard Kelley, Oct. 17, 1971. BS, Boston U., 1969. Cert. ESL tchr., Mass. Tchr. ESL, curriculum developer Greek bilingual program Cambridge (Mass.) pub. schs., 1970-78, tchr. ESL, curriculum developer Haitian bilingual program, 1978-84, tchr. ESL, curriculum developer Korean bilingual program, 1984-90, tchr. ESL, curriculum developer Chinese bilingual program, 1990-98; tchr., coord. ESL Korean Bilingual Program, 1998—; coord. Chinese Bilingual Multicultural Com., Cambridge, Mass., 1990-98. fundraiser New Eng. Albanian Relief Orgn., Worcester, Mass., 1996; vol., polit. activist Coastal Coalition, Scituate, Mass., 1990—; vol. Friends of Scituate, 1992—. Grad. fellow Haitian Creole Ind. U., 1980. Mem. NEA, ASCD, TESOL, Mass. Tchrs. Assn., Mass. Assn. Bilingual Educators, Cambridge (Mass.) Tchrs. Assn. Mem. Albanian Orthodox Ch. Home: 10 Orchard Rd Scituate MA 02066-2524

KELLEY, PAUL LEWIS, retired educator; b. Englewood, Tenn., Jan. 13, 1928; s. Lewis Edgar Kelley and Iva Pearl Webb; m. Norma Anne Sawyer, Dec. 21, 1958; children: Michael, John. BS, Tenn. Poly. Inst., 1949; MA, Northwestern U., 1955; EdD, U. Tenn., Knoxville, 1971. Tchr. Christenberry Jr. H.S., Knoxville, 1949-59, Fulton H.S., Knoxville, 1959-65; prin. South H.S., Knoxville, 1965-70, West H.S., Knoxville, 1971-73; asst. supt. Knoxville City Schs., 1973-82; prof. edn. Knoxville Coll., 1983-94; ret. Author: Historic Fort Loudoun, 1958. Pres. Knoxville Tchrs. League, 1958-60, Child and Family Svcs., Knoxville, 1967-68, Ft. Loudoun Assn.,

Knoxville, 1982-84; mem. Knox County Bd. Edn., Knoxville, 1991—. Cpl. U.S. Army, 1950-52. Recipient Silver Beaver award Boy Scouts Am., 1983. Mem. Tenn. Sch. Bd. Assn., Phi Delta Kappa. Republican. Methodist. Avocations: reading, gardening, hiking. E-mail: kelley1928@aol.com. Home: 1009 E Churchwell Ave Knoxville TN 37917-4422

KELLEY, WILLIAM, author, screenwriter; b. Staten Island, N.Y., May 27, 1929; s. Edward Thomas and Alethea Waldegrave (Mulligan) K.; m. Cornelia Ann Chamberlin, Sept. 18, 1954; children: Maura Alethea Kelley Deering, Shaun Kelley Jahshan. AB, Brown U., 1955; AM, Harvard U., 1957. West Coast editor Doubleday & Co., N.Y.C., 1958-61; fiction editor McGraw Hill Co., N.Y.C., 1961-62. Author: Gemini, 1959, The God Hunter, 1965, The Tyree Legend, 1979, (feature film) Witness, 1985 (Academy Award 1986), The Sweet Summer, 2000, Ah, Bright Wings, 2000. Sgt. USAF, 1947-50. Recipient Edgar award Mystery Writers Assn., 1986, Best Script award for Witness, W.G.A., 1986, Western Writers, 1972, 77. Home: 864 Rocking K Rd Bishop CA 93514-3704

KELLGREN, GEORGE LARS, manufacturing company executive; b. Boras, Sweden, May 23, 1943; came to U.S., 1979; s. Lars Anders and Ann-Marie (Fröberg) Kjellgren; m. Rubi Caridad Godoy, Nov. 6, 1982; children: Adrian Anders, Derek Lars, Viveka Victoria. BS, Umea U., Sweden, 1967. Researcher, developer Husqvarna (Sweden) Arms Factory, Husqvarna, 1968; tech. officer Council for Sci. and Industrial Research, Pretoria, Republic of South Africa, 1969-74; mng. dir. Interdynamic Forsknings AB, Stockholm, 1975-79; tech. dir. Intratec U.S.A., Inc., Miami, 1979-83; pres. Grendel, Inc., Cocoa, Fla., 1983-95; CEO Kel-Tec CNC Industries, Inc., Cocoa, 1995—. Contbr. articles to profl. jours.; inventor firearms. Republican. Lutheran.

KELLIS, MICHAEL JOHN, osteopathic physician; b. Wheeling, W.Va., Dec. 2, 1958; s. John George and Mary (Moskos) K. BS magna cum laude, Bethany (W.Va.) Coll., 1981; DO, Ohio U., 1985. Resident Brentwood Hosp., Cleve., 1985-86, fellow, 1986-87; pvt. practice, Chardon, Ohio, 1987—; dir. sports medicine Geauga Hosp., 1987—; team physician Berkshire High Sch., Burton, Ohio, 1987—, Notre Dame-Cath. Latin High Sch., Chardon, 1989—. Basketball coach, speaker on drug abuse Sts. Constantine and Helen Green Orthodox Ch., Cleveland Heights, Ohio 1987—; mem. leadership com. Geauga County unit Am. Heart Assn., Chardon, 1990—; ch. bd. mem. Sts. Constantine and Helen Greek Orthodox Ch., 1996-98; founder, pres. Friends of St. Michael non-profit orgn., 1996—; dir. summer camp Monastery of St. Michael, Rhodes, Greece; active Hunger Task Force, Geauga County, 1998-99. Named one of Cleve.'s 50 Most Interesting People, Cleve. Mag., 1997. Fellow Am. Osteopathic Acad. Sports Medicine (bd. dirs. 1996—, dir. nat. conv. 1999); mem. Am. Coll. Osteo. Sports Medicine, Am. Coll. Gen. Practitioners, Am. Osteo. Assn. Republican. Avocations: biking, weightlifting, stamp collecting. Office: 13207 Ravenna Rd Chardon OH 44024-7032

KELLOGG, C. BURTON, II, financial analyst; b. Plainfield, N.J., June 22, 1934; s. Chester M. and Alice L.; m. Dorothy E. Harasty, July 31, 1954; children: Katharine E., Patricia A., Peter B. BA in Econs., Dartmouth Coll., 1956; MBA in Fin., Columbia U., 1958. With A.M. Best Co., N.Y.C., 1958-68; v.p. A.M. Best Co., Oldwick, N.J., 1968-81, sr. v.p., 1981—, corp. sec. bd. dirs. Editor: Best's Insurance Reports, 1963-94. Sec. Westfield, N.J. YMCA, 1972-76. Mem. Assn. Ins. and Fin. Analysts, Echo Lake Country Club (trustee 1985-90). Office: AM Best Co Ambest Rd Oldwick NJ 08858

KELLOGG-SMITH, PETER, sculptor; b. N.Y.C., Apr. 21, 1920; s. Jewell and Margaret (Shearer) Kellogg-Smith; children by guardianship: Peter von Pein, Lee von Pein Schreitz, Ruth Bueneman, Cynthia Taylor Dax; grad. Putney Sch., Vt., 1939; studied yacht design with Franz Plunder, 1940-43; AB, St. John's Coll., Annapolis, Md., 1943; MA in Philos. Edn., Putney-Antioch Grad. Sch. Tchr. Edn., 1962; postgrad. U. Md., 1968. Tchr. Ojai (Calif.) Valley Sch., 1944-47; founding dir.-tchr. Happy Valley Sch., Ojai, 1948; yacht designer, broker, Chestertown, Md. 1949-57; asst. head, tchr. Gunston Sch., Centerville, Md., 1950-57; tchr. Grapho-English, Abana, Turkey, 1956; founding dir., tchr. Key Sch., Annapolis, Md., 1958-62; founding dir., hands-on tchr. oceanography Bay Country Sch., Arnold, Md., 1963-72; tchr. stone carving Acad. Arts, Easton, Md., 1972-76. Prin. works include marble carving under Etienne Desmet, Carrara, Italy, 1972, under Kenneth Davis, Carrara, 1974, drawing and modeling with Reuben Kramer, modeling and bronze casting with Arthur Benson, 1975-79; patentee new type engine and marine hardward. Bd. dirs. Fairhaven "free" sch.; ind. counselor students and parents on ednl. problems. Westinghouse Sci. fellow MIT, 1952; recipient Best in Show award Chestertown Arts League Show, numerous awards for sculpture. Avocations: traveling, playing music, sailing. Address: 202 Divinity Ln Arnold MD 21012-1301

KELLS, LYMAN F., scientist theoretical generalist, consultant; b. Seattle, May 19, 1917; s. Lucas Carlisle and Edith Rosetta (Stefani) K.; divorced; children: Leila S. Newcomb, Christina V. Cohen. PhD, U. Wash., 1944. Rsch. scientist Manhattan project Kellex Corp., Carbide Carbon, N.Y.C., 1944-46; rsch. chemist Std. Oil Devel., N.J., 1946-48; mem. faculty Hunter Coll., N.Y.C., 1948-49; asst. prof. Iona Coll., New Rochelle, N.Y., 1949-51; rsch. chemist Gen. Chem. Divsn., Allied Chem., Morristown, N.J., 1951-61; spl. lectr. Newark Coll. Engring., 1961; assoc. prof. chemistry East Tenn. State U., Johnson City, 1962-64; prof. chemistry Westmar Coll., LeMars, Iowa, 1964-74; ind. theoretical rschr. Seattle, 1974—. Author: Collected Works: Physical Chemistry, Physics and Astronomy, 1972, Reaction Mechanisms, Kinetics, Molecular Bonding, 1973, Supplement Number Two: Variable Stars, Velocity of Light, Nature of Theories, 1978, Binary Theory of Variable Stars and the Velocity of Light, 1984, Astrometry, Binary Theory and Observations, 1990, Variable Stars, Relativity, Nature of Science, 1992. Fellow AAAS; mem. Am. Astron. Soc., Am. Chem. Soc., Astron. Soc. Pacific, N.Y. Acad. Scis. Democrat. Unitarian. Achievements include electrostatic reaction mechanisms, kinetics and molecular bonding, variable stars and the velocity of light, the relationships between classical and relativity theories and the history and philosophy of science; revised method for analysis of measurements in determination of stellar distances by astrometry. Avocations: art, music, interpersonal relationships, alternative and complementary health treatments, reading. Home: 13716 12th Ave SW Apt 47 Seattle WA 98166-1143

KELLS, MELVIN RICHARD See ROBERTS, MEL

KELL-SMITH, CARLA SUE, federal agency administrator; b. Highland Park, Mich., Sept. 15, 1952; d. Carl William and Margie May (Cannon) Bodner; m. Joseph Mark Kell, Oct. 10, 1971 (div. Dec. 1980); m. Richard Charles Smith, Jan. 28, 1989; Student, Anderson Coll., 1970-71, Glendale Coll., 1976-77, Ariz. State U., 1978-79, Mesa Coll., 1979-80. Private tutor English, Fed. Republic of Germany, 1971-74; office mgr. Bell & Schore, Rochester, Mich., 1974-75, COL Press, Phoenix, 1978-80; publicity mgr. O'Sullivan Woodside & Col, Phoenix, 1980-81, gen. mgr., 1982-84; pub. relations/promotion cons. GPI Publs., Cupertino, Calif., 1985; pub. cons., 1985-88; project adminstr. FAA, 1986—; account coord. Bernard Hodes Advt., Tempe, Ariz., 1981; cons. freelance mktg., Phoenix, 1983. Vol., Fiesta Bowl Parade Com., Phoenix, 1983, FAA Airport Improvement Project. Office: 1200 Bayhill Dr Ste 224 San Bruno CA 94066-3006

KELLUM, BETSY M., artist, educator; b. Sheffield, Ala., Oct. 20, 1943; d. DeWitt O'Kelly and Emily (Weigel) Myatt; m. Joseph W. Kellun, Apr. 3, 1965; children: Trisha K. Smith, Tracy L. BA, Coll. William and Mary, 1965. Tchr. Pub. Schs., Fairfax, Va., Rockville, Md., Henrico, Va., 1965-74; artist Midlothian, Va., 1993—. Exhibited pastels in show at Cudahy Gallery, Richmond, Va., 1997, Pastel Soc. Am., N.Y., 1999, Degas Pastel Soc., New Orleans, 1999, Hermitage Found. Mus., Norfolk, Va., 1999, Southeastern Pastel Soc., Atlanta, 1998, LaFord Galleries, Pitts., 1998, Pastel Soc. West Coast, Calif., 1998, Fort Walton Beach (Fla.) Mus., 1998; pastels published in various publs. Recipient awards for pastels. Mem. Vienna (Va.) Arts Soc. (pres. 1993-94), Assoc. Pastellists On The Web (signature mem.), Pastel Soc. West Coast (Disting. Mem., awards of excellence 1996, 97, 98), Am. Artist Profl. League, Pastel Soc. Am. (assoc.). Avocations: golf, fitness, stained glass. Address: 2808 Sugarberry Ln Midlothian VA 23113-1198

KELLY, ABESIE OGAIL, psychologist; b. Muskegon, Mich., July 18, 1968; d. Ellis Dogan and Ruther Mae K. BA, Mich. State U., East Lansing, 1990; MA, Ind. State U., Terre Haute, 1992; MA, PhD, DePaul U., Chgo., 1996. Psychologist, cons. scientist U. Ark. for Med. Scis., Little Rock, 1996—; co-owner Psychology in the Cmty., Little Rock, 1998—. Bd. dirs. Little Rock Sch. Dist., 1998—, Drug Prevention, Little Rock, 1998—. Recipient Co-PI Ill. Dept. Children and Family Svcs., 1995, Ctr. for Disease Control, 1999. Mem. Am. Psychol. Assn., Psi Chi. Democrat. Pentecostal. Avocations: reading, dancing. E-mail: kellyabesie@exchange.vams.edu. Home: #382W 1912 Green Mountain Dr Apt 382W Little Rock AR 72212-4055

KELLY, ANGELINE AGNES, writer; b. London, Feb. 28, 1924; d. Patrick Joseph and Katherine Russell (Thompson) Kelly; m. George Hughan Hampton, Dec. 1944; children: Clare, Lalage, Sharne, Fergus. BA, U. London, 1965; LLD, U. Geneva, 1973. Editl. work British Embassy, Cairo, 1947-49; sec. various offices, London, 1950-55; tchr. English Geneva, 1965-73; curriculum devel. officer Internat. Baccalaureate Office, Geneva, 1972-76; free-lance writer, editor England, 1977—. Author: Liam O'Flaherty The Storyteller, 1976, Mary Lavin Quiet Rebel, 1980, Joseph Campbell, 1879-1944, 1988; editor: The Pillars of the House, 1987, Wandering Women, 1995, The Letters of Liam O'Flaherty, 1996, Collected Short Stories of Liam O'Flaherty, 1999; contbr. articles to profl. jours. Founder, chmn. English-Speaking Cath. Women's Group, Geneva, 1966-70. With Women's Royal Naval Svc., 1942-46. Rsch. grantee British Acad., London, 1987. Mem. Soc. Authors London, Royal Overseas League. Roman Catholic. Avocations: travel, literature, swimming, drama.

KELLY, ANNE-MAREE, emergency physician, medical educator; b. Melbourne, Victoria, Australia, Dec. 18, 1959; d. William Graeme and Kathleen Emily (McCarthy) K. MBBS, U. Melbourne, 1983, MD, 1999; M Clin. Edn., U. NSW, Australia, 1996. Lic. med. specialist. Emergency physician The Queen Elizabeth Hosp., Adelaide, Australia, 1990-91, Western Hosp., Melbourne, 1993—; sr. lectr. emergency medicine U. Otago, New Zealand, 1991-93; clin. sub-dean dept. medicine U. Melbourne, 1993-97, sr. lectr. dept. medicine, 1995-97, assoc. prof., 1998-99, prof., dir., 1999—; keynote spkr. New Zealand Emergency Nurses Conf., Hamilton, 1993, St. John (New Zealand) Conf., Christchurch, 1993. Author: Study Guide in Emergency Medicine, 1995, 2d edit., 1997, rev., 2000; co-editor: Textbook of Adult Emergency Medicine; mem. editl. bd. Emergency Medicine, 1991—; contbr. over 60 articles to med. jours. Med. Edn. fellow Glaxo Found. for Med. Edn., 1992. Fellow Australasian Coll. Emergency Medicine (convenor conf. 1993, ACEM Victoria rsch. prize 1995); mem. Australasian Soc. Emergency Medicine (pres. 1991-93, Tom Hamilton lectr. 1995). Office: Western Hosp Footscray, Dept Emer Medicine Pvt Bag, Footscray Vic 3011, Australia

KELLY, ARTHUR LLOYD, management and investment company executive; b. Chgo., Nov. 15, 1937; s. Thomas Lloyd and Mildred (Wetten) K.; m. Diane Rex Cain, Nov. 25, 1978; children: Mary Lucinda, Thomas Lloyd, Alison Williams. BS with honors, Yale U., 1959; MBA, U. Chgo., 1964. With A.T. Kearney, Inc., 1959-75; mng. dir. A.T. Kearney, Inc., Dusseldorf, Germany, 1964-70; v.p. for Europe A.T. Kearney, Inc., Brussels, 1970-73; internat. v.p. A.T. Kearney, Inc., London, 1974-75; ptnr., dir. A.T. Kearney, Inc., 1969-75, mem. exec. com., 1972-75; pres., COO, dir. LaSalle Steel Co., Chgo., 1975-81; pres., CEO, dir. Dalta Corp., Chgo., 1982—; mng. ptnr. KEL Enterprises L.P., Chgo., 1983—; chmn. bd. dirs. ARCH Devel. Corp., Chgo.; dir. BMW A.G., Munich, DataCard Corp., Minnetonka, Minn., Deere & Co., Moline, Ill., HomePlace of Am. Inc., Myrtle Beach, S.C., mpct Solutions Corp., Chgo., No. Trust Corp., Chgo., Snap-On, Inc., Kenosha, Wis., Thyssen-Krupp Industries A.G., Essen, Germany, HSBC Trinkaus & Burkhardt KGaA, Dusseldorf, S.C. Trustee U. Chgo., chmn. vis. com. div. phys. scis.; mem. adv. coun. Ditchley Found., Oxford, Eng.; bd. dirs. Chgo. Coun. Fgn. Rels. Fellow Royal Geog. Soc. (life, London); mem. World Pres.' Orgn., Econ. Club, Comml. Club, Racquet Club, Casino Club, Brook Club, Yale Club, Beta Gamma Sigma. Office: 20 S Clark St Ste 2222 Chicago IL 60603-1805

KELLY, BRIAN L., lobbyist; b. New Orleans, Oct. 9, 1965; s. Earl and Amanda Harding Kelly; m. Karen Vance, Aug. 4, 1990; children: Connor, Emma. BS, Sanford U., 1987. Polit. analyst Rep. Nat. Conv., Washington, 1988-95; asst. to gov. Office Gov. Don Sundquist, Nashville, 1995-96; dir. govt. rels. Nat. Assn. Broadcasters, Washington, 1996-99, Walt Disney Co., Washington, 1999—. Republican. Southern Baptist. Office: Walt Disney Co 1150 17th St NW Ste 400 Washington DC 20036-4622

KELLY, CURTIS HARTT, publishing executive; b. Ft. Atkinson, Wis., May 17, 1935; s. Curtis and Edna (Guenther) K. BA, Yankton Coll., 1957. With fin. divsn. Scott Foresman Co., Glenview, Ill., 1962-86; with info. sys. divsn. Scott Foresman Co., Glenview, 1986-97. Home: 1409 W Farwell Ave Apt G1 Chicago IL 60626-3488

KELLY, EAMON MICHAEL, university president emeritus; b. N.Y.C., Apr. 25, 1936; s. Michael Joseph and Kathleen Elizabeth (O'Farrell) K.; m. Margaret Whalen, June 22, 1963; children: Martin (dec.), Paul, Andrew, Peter. BS, Fordham U., 1958; MS, Columbia U., 1960, PhD, 1965. Officer in charge Office of Social Devel., Ford Found., N.Y.C., 1969-74; officer in charge program related investments Ford Found., 1974-79; exec. v.p. Tulane U., New Orleans, 1979-81, pres., 1981—; dir. policy formulation div. Econ. Devel. Adminstrn., Dept. Commerce, Washington, 1968; spl. asst. to adminstr. SBA, Washington, 1968-69; spl. cons. to sec. Dept. Labor, 1977; bd. dirs. So. Edn. Found., La. Land and Exploration Co., Nat. Captioning Inst., Assn. Gov. Bds. Colls. and Univ., Econ. Devel. Commn. State of La.; mem. Nat. Sci. Bd., Nat. Security Edn. Bd., Humphrey Fellows Nat. Adv. Bd., Bus. Higher Edn. Forum, com. econ. devel. Gabelli Enterprises Inc., exec. com. Assn. Am. Univs.; pres. Commission NCAA, Found. for Biomed. Rsch., Nat. Sci. Bd., 1996; former chair Presidential Adv. Bd.; chair Nat. Sci. Bd. Pres. city coun., councilman-at-large City of Englewood, N.J., 1974-77; bd. advocates Planned Parenthood of La. Mem. AAUP, La. Conf. Univs. and Colls., La. Assn. Ind. Colls. and Univs., Bus. Coun. New Orleans, City Club, Inc., Met. Area Com., New Orleans Ednl. Telecom. Consortium. Democrat. Roman Catholic. Home: 3122 Octavia St New Orleans LA 70125-4936 Office: Tulane U Payson Ctr Bldg 7 Rm 300 6823 Saint Charles Ave New Orleans LA 70118-5698

KELLY, ERIC DAMIAN, lawyer, educator; b. Pueblo, Colo., Mar. 16, 1947; s. William Bret and Patricia Ruth (Ducy) K.; children: Damian Charles, Eliza Jane, Valissitie Christina Heeren, Douglas Ray Heeren; m. Sandra Walker, 1996. BA, Williams Coll., 1969; JD, U. Pa., 1975, M of City Planning, 1975; PhD, Union Inst., 1992. Bar: Colo. 1975, U.S. Dist. Ct. 1976, U.S. Tax Ct. 1976, U.S. Ct. Appeals (10th cir.) 1986. Chief citizens' participation unit Region III EPA, Phila., 1971-72; project planner Beckett New Town, N.J., 1972-73; v.p., project mgr. Rahenkamp Sachs Wells & Assocs., Inc., Denver and Phila., 1973-76; sole practice Pueblo, 1976-83; pres. Kelly & Potter, P.C., Pueblo, Albuquerque and Santa Fe, 1983-90; adj. prof. U. Colo. Coll. Architecture and Planning, 1976-90; chmn., prof. Dept. cmty. and regional planning Iowa State U., 1990-95; adj. asst. prof. grad. sch. bus. U. So. Colo., 1986-90; dean coll. architecture and planning Ball State U., 1995-98, prof. urban planning, 1999—; mem. city devel. bd. State of Iowa, 1991-95; bd. trustees Common Assocs. Inst., 2000—. Gen. editor Zoning and Land Use Controls, 1995—; author: Enforcing Zoning and Land Use Codes, 1988, Managing Community Growth: Policies, Techniques and Impacts, 1993, Selecting and Retaining Consultants, 1993, Planning, Growth and Public Facilities: A Primer for Public Officials, 1994; editor, prin. author: The Roadtripper, 1969; contbr. articles to profl. planning and legal jours. Mem. adv. bd. Mcpl. Legal Studies Ctr., S.W. Legal Found., 1989—; mem. nat. adv. bd. Rocky Mountain Land Use Inst. Coll. Law U. Denver, 1992—; bd. dirs. Broadway Theatre League, Pueblo, 1976-77, Pueblo Beautiful Assn., 1978-82, Better Bus. Bur., 1988-89; trustee Sangre de Cristo Arts and Conf. Ctr., 1981-87, chmn. 1986; trustee Christ Congl. Ch., 1982-83. With U.S. Army, 1969-71; mem. Ind. Land Resources Coun., 1999—. Named Outstanding Student, Am. Inst. Planners, 1976; recipient Outstanding Faculty award Order of Omega, 1992. Mem. ABA, Am. Inst. Cert. Planners (charter, elected Coll. of Fellows 1999), Am. Planning Assn. (nat. pres., 1997—, chair planning & law divsn. 1996-97, pres. Iowa chpt. 1994-95, amicus curiae com. 1988-94, 95-97, legis. & policy com. 1993-97, Colo. chpt. excellence award 1989), Williams Coll. Alumni Assn. (class sec. 1969-74, regional sec. 1980-82, class agt. 1985-89), Rotary (local dir. 1988-90, dir., pres. Pueblo Rotary Found. 1988-89, v.p. 1988-89, pres. 1989-90, area rep. for dist. gov. 1991-92), Phi Kappa Phi. Democrat. Home: 2312 W Audubon Dr Muncie IN 47304-2003 Office: Ball State U Coll Architecture Planning Muncie IN 47306-0001

KELLY, HENRY CHARLES, scientist; b. Boston, July 10, 1945; s. Harry Charles and Irene Ermina (Andes) K.; m. Ann Elizabeth Clind, May 10, 1969; children: Sophia Elizabeth, Alice Bridget. BA, Cornell U., 1967; PhD, Harvard U., 1971. With U.S. ACDA, 1970-74; Congl. sci. fellow AAAS, 1974-75; project mgr. Office Tech. Assessment, Washington, 1975-77, program mgr., 1977-78, assoc. dir. solar energy rsch. inst., 1978-81, sr. assoc., 1981-92; asst. dir. White House Office of Sci. and Tech. Policy, Washington, 1993-2000; pres. Fedn. Am. Scientists, 2000—. Contbr. articles to profl. jours., also books. Fellow Am. Phys. Soc.; mem. AAAS, Fedn. Am. Scientists. Home: 2210 N Nelson St Arlington VA 22207-3841 Office: OSTP Old Exec Office Bldg Washington DC 20500

KELLY, JAMES MICHAEL, lawyer; b. Pitts., May 24, 1947; s. James M. and Catherine C. Kelly; m. Mary J. Armstrong, Dec. 20, 1980; children: Lea Day, Heather Marie. AB, Princeton U., 1969; JD, U. Pitts., 1978. Bar: Mich. 1978, Fla. 1982, U.S. Supreme Ct. 1985, U.S. Ct. Appeals (6th cir.), Ga. 1990. Atty. Chrysler Corp., Highland Park, Mich., 1978-81; corp. counsel Harris Corp., Melbourne, Fla., 1981-87; v.p., gen. counsel, corp. sec. Lanier Worldwide, Inc., Atlanta, 1987—. Editor U. Pitts. Law Rev., 1978. Capt. U.S. Army, 1969-75. Mem. ABA, Am. Corp. Counsel Assn., Am. Assn. Corp. Secs., Fla. Bar Assn., Ga. Bar Assn., Atlanta Bar Assn., DeKalb County Bar Assn., Assn. 82d Airborne Divsn., Cannon Club. Office: Lanier Worldwide Inc 2300 Parklake Dr NE Atlanta GA 30345-2902

KELLY, JOHN JOSEPH, chemical engineer, educator; b. Newry, Ireland; s. James and Rita (Curran) K.; m. Nora Doyle, May 24, 1968; children: James, Mary Louise, Michael, John. B in Engring., Univ. Coll. Dublin, 1957, PhD, 1969. Process engr. Esso Co., Southampton, England, 1957-58; plant supervisor Irish Refining Co., Cork, 1958-63; lectr., assoc. prof. chem. engring., dean Univ. Coll. Dublin, 1963-86, registrar, 1986-95, prof., dir. internat. office, 1995-97; vis. Fulbright prof. U. Md., College Park, 1969-70; exec. dir. The Ireland-U.S. Commn. for Ednl. Exch. or Fulbright Commn., 1997—. Author, co-editor: Gas Cleaning for Air Quality Control, 1975. Exec. dir. Ireland Can. Univ. Found. Grantee European Union, 1982, 85. Fellow Inst. Engrs. Ireland., Instn. Chem. Engrs. (U.K.), Irish Fulbright Assn. (pres.). Roman Catholic. Avocations: tennis, golf, sailing. Home: 6 Mount Eden Rd Donnybrook, Dublin 4, Ireland Office: Univ Coll, Sch Engring, Dublin 4, Ireland

KELLY, JOHN JOSEPH, JR., government executive; b. Paterson, N.J., Dec. 28, 1940; s. John Joseph Sr. and Helen C. (Ebersach) K.; m. Brenda Ruth Miller, July 1, 1966; children: Elizabeth Ann, Kathleen Anne, John J. BS in Chemistry, Seton Hall, 1963; MS, Pa. State U., 1969; MPA, Auburn U., 1976. Commd. 2d lt. USAF, 1963, advanced through grades to brig. gen., 1989; dir. spl. projects, HQ USAF, Scott AFB, Ill., 1978-80; comdr. 15 WEA Squadron USAF, McGuire AFB, N.J., 1980-81; dep. dir. programs/policy Air Force info. systems USAF, Washington, 1981-84; vice comdr. 7th Weather Wing Scott AFB, 1984-85; comdr. 5th Weather Wing Langley AFB, Va., 1985-88; comdr. Air Weather Svc. Scott AFB, 1988-91; dir. weather AF/XOW Washington, 1991-94; dir. Nat. Weather Svc., 1998—; cons. Dept. Commerce, 1991. Fellow Am. Meteorol. Soc., Air Force Assn., Nat. Weather Assn. Roman Catholic. Avocations: golf, reading. Office: NWS 1325 E West Hwy Silver Spring MD 20910-3280

KELLY, KARLA ROSEMARIE, lawyer; b. Newcastle, Wyo., Jan. 16, 1954; d. Carl Elvin and Elvera Marie (Pettis) Denning; children: Scharlet Lee, Jennifer Lynn. BA in Nursing, Coll. St. Katherine, 1976, RN, 1976; JD, George Washington U, Washington, D.C., 1984. Bar: Va. 1984, U.S. Dist. Ct. (ea. dist.) Va. 1984, U.S. Ct. Appeals (4th cir.) 1984, Calif. 1986, U.S. Dist. Ct. (so. dist.) Calif. 1986, U.S. Ct. Appeals (9th cir.) 1986. Charge nurse Bayshore Comm. Hosp., Pasadena, Tex., 1976-78; lt. USNR, San Diego, 1978-81; assoc. atty. Hirschkop & Grad, Alexandria, Va., 1984-86, Gray, Cary Ames & Frye, San Diego, 1987-92; asst. gen. counsel Scripps Health, San Diego, 1992—; bd. dirs. Gluck Child Care Ctr., La Jolla, Calif., 1993—, Campfire Coun., San Diego, 1995—. Contbr. articles to profl. jours. Mem. ABA, San Diego Bar Assn., Nat. Health Lawyers Assn., Calif. Soc. Healthcare Attys. Republican. Avocation: classical pianist. Office: Luce Forward Hamilton and Scripps 600 W Broadway San Diego CA 92101-3311

KELLY, KATHLEEN DENNIS, international government affairs consultant; b. Ann Arbor, Mich., Aug. 20, 1952; d. Edward Wimberly and Beatrice Forrest Dennis; children: Charlotte, John. BA in Polit. Sci., U. Tex., 1974. Pres. Interisk, Inc., Houston, 1981-85, Internat. Protocol Advisors, Houston, 1994—; cons. Russell Reynolds & Assoc., Houston, 1985-88; exec. dir., pres. Houston Internat. Protocol Alliance, 1988-94; chair Houston Com. Fgn. Rels., 1997, mem. exec. com., 1997—. Author booklet: consular Ball, 1993. Bd. dirs. Houston World Affairs Coun., 1996—, Bolivian Charity Found., Houston, 1997—; bd. dirs. world trade divsn. Greater Houston Partnership; mem. internat. rev. bd. Park Plz. Hosp., Houston, 1993-95; mem. exec. com. Consular Corps of Houston, 1994—. Recipient Cert. of Appreciation, U.S. Dept. State, 1992, U.S. Secret Svc., 1992, Cert. Merit, Bolivian Govt., 1994. Mem. Bus. Coun. for Internat. Understanding. Republican. Presbyterian. E-mail: Kathleen-Kell@earthlink.com.

KELLY, KEITH JOHN, journalist; b. Bklyn., Sept. 10, 1954; s. John Joseph and Virginia (O'Connell). Student, SUNY, Stony Brook, 1972-74; BA in English Lit., SUNY, Oneonta, 1976. Reporter Smithtown News, L.I., N.Y., 1976-77; asst. editor McGraw-Hill, Inc., N.Y.C., 1977-79; journalist Belfast, No. Ireland, 1980; editor McGraw-Hill Inc., 1981-87; bur. chief Mag. Week, N.Y.C., 1988-92; chief editor Folio: First Day, editor-at-large Folio: Mag. Cowles Bus. Media, N.Y.C., 1992-94; sr. editor Advt. Age mag. Crain Comm., N.Y.C., 1994-97; reporter, columnist N.Y. Daily News, N.Y.C., 1997-98; columnist New York Post, N.Y.C., 1998—; spl. corr. The Irish Press, Dublin, Ireland, 1980-89. Mem. Deadline Club (v.p.). Roman Catholic. Home: 300 1st Ave Apt 8C New York NY 10009-1844 Office: New York Post Ste 900A 1211 Avenue Of The Americas New York NY 10036-8790

KELLY, MAURA ANNE, reporter; b. Bridgeport, Conn., Apr. 2, 1971; d. Richard Francis and Margaret Mary Kelly. BA, Boston Coll., 1993; MS in Journalism, Northwestern U., 1994. Intern The Patriot Ledger, Quincy, Mass., 1993; corr. Conn. Post, Bridgeport, 1993; reporter Naugatuck bur. Waterbury (Conn.) Rep.-Am., 1994-95, edn. reporter, 1995, city hall reporter, 1995-96, state capitol reporter, 1996-99; reporter Chgo. Tribune, 2000—; mem. reporters' roundtable discussion Conn. Jour. on Conn. Pub. TV, Hartford, 1998-99 and WFSB's CT '97, CT '98, Ct '99 in Hartford. Mem. Soc. Profl. Journalists (Reporting awards Conn. chpt. 1998, 99, 2000), Investigative Reporters and Editors, Boston Coll. Alumni Assn., Northwestern U. Alumni Club Conn. Roman Catholic. Avocations: photography, travel, skiing, tennis, swimming. E-mail: makelly@tribune.com. Home: 633 W Deming Pl Apt 205 Chicago IL 60614-2671 Office: Chgo Tribune 435 N Michigan Ave Chicago IL 60611-4066

KELLY, MAURICE PAUL, internist, gastroenterologist, researcher; b. Workington, Eng., June 3, 1961. BA, MA, Oxford (Eng.) U., 1983; MBBS, London U., 1986, MD, 1997. Cert. in internal medicine and gastroenterology. Sr. lectr. St. Bartholomew's/The Royal London Sch. Medicine, 1993—. Contbr. articles to profl. jours., including The Lancet, Jour. Infectious Diseases, Gut, Brit. Med. Jour. Gastroenterology. Fellow Royal Soc. Tropical Medicine; mem. Royal Coll. Physicians Edinburgh, Brit. Soc. Gastroenterology. Anglican. Avocations: singing, mountaineering. Office: St Bart's/Royal London Sch, Digestive Diseases Rsch Ctr, London E1 2AD, England

KELLY, MICHAEL HOWARD, education educator; b. Hull, U.K., Nov. 19, 1946; s. Kenneth and Kathleen (Lucas) K.; m. Josephine Ann Doyle, Jan. 3, 1975; children: Thomas, Paul. BA, Warwick U., Eng., 1969; PhD,

Warwick U., 1975; MBA, U. Southampton, Eng., 1995. Lectr. U. Coll., Dublin, Ireland, 1972-86; prof. U. Southampton, 1986—; dir. U.K. Subject Ctr. for Langs., 2000—; chair U. Coun. Modern Lang., 1993-97. Author: Pioneer of the Catholic Revival, 1979, Modern French Marxism, 1982, Hegel in France, 1992; editor: France: Nation & Regions, 1993, French Cultural Studies, An Introduction, 1995, Pierre Bourdieu, Language, Culture and Education, 1999. Chmn. Irish Coun. for Civil Liberties, Dublin, 1981-86; pres. Assn. U. Prof. French, 1990-93. Fellow Royal Soc. Arts, 1992. Mem. Labour Party. Avocations: tennis, golf. Office: Univ Southampton, Highfield, Southampton S017 1BJ, England

KELLY, MICHAEL THOMAS, educator; b. Easton, Pa., Feb. 1, 1961; s. Thomas B. and Marion E. (Beers) K. BA, Westchester U., 1983; EdS, Coll. William & Mary, 1989, EdD, 1991. Dean students Northeastern Ill. U., 1999—. Mem. Nat. Assn. Student Personnel Adminstrs., Assn. Student Jud. Affairs, Coll. William & Mary Alumni Assn., Kappa Delta Pi, Theta Xi. Democrat. Roman Catholic. Avocations: music, civic involvement. Home: 1039 N Harlem Ave Apt 1sd Oak Park IL 60302-1569 Office: 5500 N Saint Louis Ave # B-108 Chicago IL 60625-4679

KELLY, PAUL DONALD, lawyer; b. Rochester, N.Y., Sept. 20, 1955; s. Gerard D. and Ruth A. K.; m. Anne E. Alfieri, Nov. 30, 1985; children: Thomas, Alexander, Raymond, John. BA in English, LeMoyne Coll., 1977; JD, U. Albany, 1980. Bar: N.Y. 1981, U.S. Dist. Ct. (no. dist.) N.Y. 1986, U.S. Dist. Ct. (we. dist.) 1988, U.S. Ct. Claims 1989. Asst. counsel N.Y. State Sen. Mary Goodhue, Albany, 1980-81; asst. pub. defender Monroe County Pub. Defender, Rochester, N.Y., 1981-85; assoc. Davidson, Fink, Cook & Gates, Rochester, N.Y., 1985-91; ptnr. Davidson, Fink, Cook, Kelly & Galbraith, Rochester, N.Y., 1992—. Mem. Assn. Trial Lawyers Am., N.Y. State Trial Lawyers Assn., Genesee Valley Trial Lawyers Assn. (pres.), N.Y. State Bar Assn., Monroe County Bar Assn. (plaintiff's personal injury sect.). Democrat. Roman Catholic. Avocations: family activities, athletics. Office: Davidson Fink Cook Kelly & Galbraith 28 Main St E Ste 1700 Rochester NY 14614-1915

KELLY, PAUL KNOX, investment banker; b. Boston, Feb. 18, 1940; s. Thomas Joseph and Rita Patricia Kelly; m. Nancy Lee Belden, July 17, 1978; 1 child, 3 stepchildren. AB in English, U. Pa., 1962; MBA in Fin., Wharton Sch., 1964. Investment analyst bond dept. Prudential Ins. Co. Am., 1964-65; asst. treas. Comml. Credit Co., 1965-68; v.p. First Boston Corp., N.Y.C., 1968-75; ptnr., mem. mgmt. com., dir. Prescott, Ball & Turben, Cleve., 1975-77; sr. v.p., dir. Butcher & Singer, Inc., 1977-78; exec. v.p., mem. exec. com., dir. Blyth Eastman Dillon & Co., N.Y.C., 1978-80; mng. dir. Merrill Lynch White Weld Capital Markets Group, N.Y.C., 1980-82; exec. v.p., dir. Dean Witter Reynolds, Inc., 1982-84; pres., dir. Quadrex Securities Corp., 1984-85, Peers & Co., N.Y.C., 1985-90, PH II, Inc., Westport, Conn., 1988—, Knox & Co., N.Y.C., 1992—; trustee U. Pa.; bd. dirs. THT, Inc. Mem. Union Club (Cleve.), Chagrin Valley Hunt Club, Penn Club N.Y., The LInks, Union League (Phila.), The No. Club (Auckland, New Zealand). Office: Knox & Co 33 Riverside Ave Westport CT 06880-4223

KELLY, PETER JOHN, computer scientist; b. N.Y.C., Dec. 4, 1957; arrived in Australia, 1975; s. Peter John and Edith Elizabeth (Rocks) K.; m. Sharon Anne Reeves, Aug. 15, 1981; children: Blaise, Merryn. Degree, Waverly Coll., 1975; BS, U. NSW, 1989. Rsch. officer Arrawana Sapphires, Sydney, Australia, 1980-82; tech. officer C.S.I.R.O., Sydney, 1982-89, ACIRL, Sydney, 1989-91; cons. RJE, Sydney, 1991-94; project mgr. Bankers Trust, Sydney, 1994-96; chief architect Optus Comms., 1996-99, IBM GSA, North Sydney, 1999—; cons. Dept. Tech. Edn. Sydney, 1992-94. Grantee Fed. Dept. Indsl. R&D, 1982. Master Masons; mem. AAAS, Australian Computer Soc., N.Y. Acad. Scis. Avocations: scuba diving, tree planting, wilderness regeneration. Home: 1/39 Moira Crescent, Randwick 2031, Australia

KELLY, RALPH WHITLEY, emergency physician, health facility administrator; b. Hernando, Miss., Oct. 13, 1949; s. Leslie Athrel and Nina Earline (Christopher) K.; m. Janet Sue Evans Burns, May 15, 1971 (div. May 1991); children: Rochelle, Angela, Melanie, Christopher; m. Virginia Markle Alfson, Mar. 13, 1993. BS, U. Tex., Arlington, 1972; DO, Tex. Coll. Osteo. Medicine, Ft. Worth, 1976. Diplomate Am. Bd. Emergency Medicine, Am. Bd. Pediat. Emergency Medicine, Am. Bd. Pediat., Am. Bd. Quality Assurance and Utilization Rev. Physicians, Nat. Bd. Med. Examiners; subsplty. bd. cert. in risk mgmt.; cert. physician exec. Mem. staff pediat. USAF, Wichita Falls, Tex., 1979-82; med. dir. emergency dept. Fischer-Mangold Group, Pleasanton, Calif., 1982-90, EmCare, Inc., Dallas, 1990-91; chmn. emergency dept. Hillcrest Bapt. Med. Ctr., Waco, Tex., 1990-91; dir. EMS tng. programs Vernon Regional Jr. Coll., Wichita Falls, 1991-95; dir. emergency svcs. Wichita Gen. Hosp., Wichita Falls, 1991-95; pres. Texoma Emergency Assn., Wichita Falls, 1991-95; dir. practice mgmt. MEPA, Dallas, 1995-98; chmn. emergency dept. Trinity Med. Ctr., Carrollton, Tex., 1995—, also chmn. QA Ctr.; chmn. emergency dept. RHD Meml. Med. Ctr., 1996—; bd. dirs. Foster Child Advocacy Svcs., Wichita Falls, 1983-85; mem. faculty Tex. affiliate Am. Heart Assn., Austin, 1985—, course dir. ACLS, 1982—; mem. exec. com. Wichita Gen. Hosp., 1991-95; physician advisor for quality Trinity Med. Ctr., 1996—. Rev. editor Tex. Emergency Bulletin of Tex. Coll. Emergency Physicians, 1987-89. Mem. pre-med. adv. com. Midwestern State U., Wichita Falls, 1987-89; mem. child mortality com. DA's Office, Wichita Falls, 1994-95; EMS med. dir. Lifeline EMS, Wichita Falls, 1992-94, AMT EMS, Waco, 1990-91. Major USAF, 1976-82. Recipient Physician Recognition award AMA, 1985. Fellow Am. Coll. Emergency Physicians, Am. Acad. Pediat.; mem. Tex. Med. Assn., Tex. Osteo. Med. Assn., Group Mgmt. Sect. (charter), Pediat. Emergency Med. Sect. Republican. Avocations: cycling, downhill skiing, numismatics, hiking, computers. Home: 2405 Winding Hollow Ln Plano TX 75093-4108 Office: Trinity Med Ctr 4343 N Josey Ln Carrollton TX 75010-4603

KELLY, RAYMOND BOONE, III, lawyer; b. Ft. Worth, Oct. 12, 1947; s. Raymond Boone Jr. and Martha (Morehead) K.; children: Alice Katherine, Anne Rowan. BA, Tulane U., 1970; JD, So. Meth. U., 1974. Bar: Tex. 1974. Ptnr. Decker, Jones, McMackin, McClane, Hall and Bates, Ft. Worth, 1974—; v.p., trustee William E. Scott Found., Ft. Worth, 1978—. Bd. dirs., past pres. Goodwill Industries Ft. Worth, 1975-97; bd. dirs. Arts Coun. Ft. Worth and Tarrant County, 1980-91, 95-97, Conf. of S.W. Founds., Dallas, 1986-89, 97—, Big Bros./Bis Sisters, Ft. Worth, 1987-94, Intercultura, Inc., Ft. Worth, 1989-96, chmn., 1992-94, Funding Info. Ctr., 1993-97, Ft. Worth Dallas Ballet, 1996-97, Cmty. Found. North Tex., 1996—, All Saints Health Sys., 1997—; trustee Modern Art Mus. Ft. Wroth, 1981—, Fort Worth Country Day Sch., 1996—; chmn. All Saints Health Found., 1989—, Goodwill Industries Ft. Worth Found., 1997—, Ft. Worth Club, 1999—. Mem. ABA, State Bar Tex., Tarrant County Bar Assn., Tarrant County Young Lawyers Assn. (v.p., sec. 1976-77), Ft. Worth Club, Exchange Club, Rivercrest Country Club, Steeplechase Club, Ind. Prodrs. Assn. Am., Tex. Oil and Gas Assn. Republican. Episcopalian. Home: 301 Virginia Pl Fort Worth TX 76107-1611 Office: Decker, Jones, McMackin, McClane, Hall 500 Throckmorton St Ste 2500 Fort Worth TX 76102-3812

KELLY, REID BROWNE, lawyer; b. Kingston, Ont., Can., June 19, 1960; came to U.S., 1965; s. William Browne and Betty Lou (Rowland) K.; m. Debra Lee Carpenter, July 11, 1987. BA magna cum laude, Colo. Coll., 1982; JD, U. Colo., 1985; cert., U. San Diego Inst., Oxford U., Eng., 1985. Bar: Colo. 1986, U.S. Dist. Ct. Colo. 1987, U.S. Ct. Appeals (6th cir.) 1997. Assoc. LaFrance & Assoc., Durango, Colo., 1986-87, Warren, Mundt, Martin & O'Dowd, Colorado Springs, Colo., 1987-93; ptnr. Warren, Mundt & Martin, Colorado Springs, 1993-95; mem. The Kelly Law Firm, L.L.C, Pagosa Springs, Colo., 1996—; co-chair employment law com. El Paso County Bar Assn., Colorado Springs., 1992-94. Named Outstanding Young Men of Am., 1987-96. Mem. S.W. Colo. Bar Assn. (sec. local chpt. 1997-99), Pi Gamma Mu. Avocations: Tae Kwon Do, yoga, running, skiing, chess. Office: The Kelly Law Firm LLC 4440 N Pagosa Blvd Pagosa Springs CO 81147-8312

KELLY, ROBERT VINCENT, JR., metal company executive; b. Phila., Sept. 29, 1938; s. Robert Vincent and Catherine Mary (Hanley) K.; m. Margaret Cecilia Taylor, Feb. 11, 1961; children: Robert V. III, Christopher T., Michael J., Tasha Marie. BS in Indsl. Mgmt., St. Joseph's U., Phila., 1960; postgrad., Roosevelt U., 1965-66. Gen. foreman prodn. Republic Steel Corp., Chgo., 1963-68; supt. prodn. Phoenix Steel Corp., Phoenixville, Pa., 1969-73; gen. supt. ops. Continental Steel Corp., Kokomo, Ind., 1973-77; gen. mgr. MACSTEEL div. Quanex Corp., Jackson, Mich., 1977-81; corp. v.p. Quanex Corp., Houston, 1979—; pres. MACSTEEL group Quanex Corp., Jackson, 1982—; pres. La Salle Steel Co., Hammond, Ind., 1985-87, Arbuckle Corp., Jackson, 1984-88. Leader, com. mem. Boy Scouts Am., Jackson. Lt. USN, 1960-63. Mem. Am. Mgmt. Assn. (pres.), Inst. Indsl. Engrs., Assn. Iron and Steel Engrs., Am. Soc. for Metals, USN Inst., Jackson C. of C. Clubs: Jackson Country. Avocations: hiking, camping, sailing, scouting. Home: 1734 Metzmont Dr Jackson MI 49203-5379 Office: Macsteel, Quanex Corp 1 Jackson Sq Ste 500 Jackson MI 49201-1446

KELLY, SOPHY, principal; b. Bombay, Mar. 12, 1917; d. Khadoorie Barukh Hayeem and Sally K.; m. Emile Vanura, Oct. 16, 1946 (div. Feb. 1951); 1 child, Marcelle V. Bonchek. Tching. cert., St. Mary's Tng. Coll., Bombay, 1937, Maria Grey Tng. Coll., London, 1938; student in speech tng. and elocution, Trinity Coll. of Music, London; student in Russian Classical Ballet, Trinity Coll. Music in Ballet, London; student in European character dancing, Prague, Czechoslovakia, student in Indian dance and vocal music; student in Yoga Asanas, Bombay; PhD, Zoroastrian Coll., India, 1998. Founder Hill Grange Nursery and Kindergarten Sch., Bombay, 1939—, founder primary sect., 1942—; founder lower secondary sect. Hill Grange Sch., 1943—; founder Urvashi Nrittya Art Acad., Urvashi Nrittya Ballet, Bombay; founder Cambridge sect. Hill Grange Sch., 1956—; Indian del. World Confedn. Orgn. of Tchg. Profn. in Dublin, Ireland, 1968, London; . Author: Souvenir, 1985. Apptd. Justice of the Peace by Brit. gov. of Bombay Presidency, 1942; apptd. Hon. Sec. for establishment of Bombay State Parents Assn., 1954; assisted in initiating litigation in High Ct. of Bombay for retention of English lang.; established secondary sch. cert. exam., Maharashtra Bd. Edn., 1956; organized All India 3 Day Music and Dance Festival, 1958, and numerous other festivals and entertainment programs; established Charity Schs. Fund Com., 1960; re-organized E.E.E. Sassoon Sch.; apptd. Justice of Peace, Govt. of Maharashtra, 1965; organized 1st conf. Soc. Justices of Peace and Hon. Presidency Magistrates, 1965; apptd. Hon. Sec. for establishment of Indo Israel Friendship League, 1967, which eventually had 74 brs. throughout India; trustee E.E.E. Sassoon Sch., Bombay, Sir Jacob Sassoon Charity Trust, Jacob Sassoon Sch. Feeding Fund, Fort Synagogue, Byculla Synagogue, Poona Synagogue, Lady Rachael Sassoon Dispensary, Bombay and Poona Passover Food Trust Funds for the Poor, Bombay and Poona Jewish Burial Grounds, R.A. Coll. Engring. (Pune and Bombay), D.Y. Patil Coll. Engring., Kohapur; appted. Spl. Exec. Magistrate, Govt. Maharashtra; mem. Maharashtra State Women's Coun.; organizer Centenary Celebrations of Kenesseth Eliyahu Synagogue, 1985; numerous other civic activities. Recipient Silver sheild of merit for excellence in edn. and Mahila Shiromani award, Govt. of India, 1991, Rajiv Gandhi Gold Medal for excellence in edn., 1992; recipient Bal Sahyog award, Govt. of India, 1994. Mem. Indian Coun. Mgmt. Execs. (v.p., pres., named Samajshree 1992, Order of merit for edn. 1992), All India Assn. Heads of Schs. (bd. govs., pres. 1971—), Indo-Israel C. of C. (gen. sec., chmn.), B'nai B'rith Women's Auxiliary (organizer Lodge 2626, pres.), Willingdon Sports Club, Royal Western Indian Turf Club of Poona, Jewish Club of Bombay (pres.), Western India Automobile Assn. Jewish. Avocations: reading, writing, Jewish Kabbalah and contemporary religions, psychology. Office: Hill Grange HS Ednl Instns, 13-A Peddar Rd, Mumbai 400026, India

KELLY, THOMAS CAJETAN, archbishop; b. Rochester, NY, July 14, 1931; s. Thomas A. Kelly and Katherine Eleanor (Fisher) Conley. A.B., Providence Coll., 1953; S.T.L., Dominican House of Studies, Washington, 1959; D.Canon Law, U. St. Thomas, Rome, 1962; S.T.D. (hon.), Providence Coll, 1979; D.H.L. (hon.), Spalding Coll., 1983. Ordained priest Roman Cath. Ch., 1958. Sec. Dominican Province, N.Y.C., 1962-65; sec. Apostolic Del., Washington, 1965-71; assoc. gen. sec. Nat. Conf. Cath. Bishops-U.S. Cath. Conf., Washington, 1971-77; gen. sec. U.S. Cath. Bishops Conf. Washington, 1977-82, ordained Roman Cath. aux. bishop, 1977; archbishop Archdiocese of Louisville, 1982—; chmn. Cath. Conf. Ky., Louisville, 1982—. Chancellor Bellarmine Coll.; bd. dirs. St. Luke Inst. Recipient Veritas medal St. Catharine Coll., 1984. Mem. Canon Law Soc. Am., Nat. Cath. Edn. Assn. (chmn. bd. dirs. 1991-94). Home and Office: 212 E College St Louisville KY 40203-2334

KELLY, TIMOTHY WILLIAM, lawyer; b. Apr. 27, 1953; s. George Raymond and Mary Therese (Kelly) K.; m. Mary Teresa Harms, May 24, 1980; children: Ryan Timothy, Colin Patrick, Kaitlynn Elizabeth. BS in Bus. Adminstrn., U. Dayton, 1975, JD, 1978. Bar: Ill. 1978, U.S. Dist. Ct. (cen. and no. dists.) Ill. 1979. Staff counsel Prairie State Legal Aid, Bloomington, Ill., 1978-81; felony asst. McLean County Pub. Defenders, Bloomington, 1981-83; assoc. Jerome Mirza & Assocs., Bloomington, 1983-88; asst. prof. polit. sci. Ill. State U., Normal, 1980-83; faculty mem. Ill. Inst. Continuing Legal Edn.; lectr. in field. Contbr. articles to profl. jours. Bd. dirs. Bloomington/Normal Day Care Assn., 1982-83; civil actions arbitrator and mediator McLean County, 1996—. Named one of Top Three Attys. in McLean, Bus. to Bus. Mag., 1997. Fellow Ill. Bar Found.; mem. ATLA, Ill. State Bar Assn. (mem. civil practice and procedure sect. coun. 1992—, chmn. 1998, Allerton house steering com. 1994, 96, 98, tort law sect. coun. 1995—, assembly mem. 1995—), Ill. Trial Lawyers Assn. (mem. bd. mgrs. 1992—, continuing legal edn. com. 1995-96, exec. com. 1996, chmn. ins. law com. 1996-98), Chgo. Bar Assn., McLean County Bar Assn. (sec. 1984-85), McLean County Inns of Ct., IICLE (bd. dirs. 2000—). Democrat. Roman Catholic. Office: 205 N Williamsburg Dr Ste A Bloomington IL 61704-7721

KELLY, WILLIAM E., psychoanalyst; b. Nashville, Mar. 17, 1914; s. Charles Peck and Alice (Eager) K.; m. Martha L. Parks, June 6, 1953; children: Susie Eager Kelly Sayegh, Penelope Ellen Bayley, Benjamin Alexander Kelly. Student, Antioch Coll., 1932-34; B.S. in Edn., U.Va., 1938, M.D., 1945. Diplomate Am. Bd. Psychiatry and Neurology. Intern Kings County Hosp., Bklyn., 1945-46; resident psychiatrist U. Va. Hosp., 1946, Pa. Hosp., Phila., 1948-50; sr. rsch. psychiatrist VA Hosp., Coatesville, Pa., 1950-51; asst. vis. physician Phila Gen. Hosp., 1951-59; staff psychiatrist Lakeland Mental Hosp., Camden, N.J., 1951-55; pvt. practice specializing in psychiatry Phila., 1951-83; mem. staff Jefferson Hosp., 1951-71; sr. attending staff Inst. Pa. Hosp., 1951-78, pres. staff, 1968-70; asst. neurologist Wills Eye Hosp., Phila., 1959-71; staff psychiatrist Coatesville (Pa.) Hosp., 1974-77, dir. profl. edn., 1977-79, assoc. chief of staff for edn., 1979-83; staff psychiatrist Western State Hosp., Staunton, Va., 1985-89; cons. Pa. Hosp., 1978-97 (hon. cons. 1987—), cons. neuropsychiatrist Graterford Penitentiary, 1954-58; asst. cons. neuropsychiatrist Devereaux Schs., 1956-58; cons. psychiatry Valley Forge Gen. Hosp., 1965-74. Editor: Barriers to the Efficacy of Psychiatric Treatment, 1981, The Changing Role of Rehabilitation Medicine in the Management of the Psychiatric Patient, 1983; Alheimer's Disease and Related Disease Disoroders, 1984, Posttraumatic Stress Disorder and the War Veteran Patient, 1985. Capt. M.C., AUS, 1946-48. Fellow AMA, ACP, Am. Psyciat. Assn., Phila. Psychiat. Soc., Phila. Coll. Physicians, Am. Coll. Psychiatrists, Am. Coll. Psychoanalysts, Am. Psychoanalytic Assn., Internat. Psychoanalytic. Assn. Home and Office: 5320 Patriots Colony Dr Williamsburg VA 23188-1393

KELLY, WILLIAM HENRY, computer company executive, mayor; b. Kingston, N.Y., June 27, 1940; s. William Aloyishus Kelly and Jeanette Wilhelm; m. Ann Kelly, Nov. 9, 1996; 1 child, Morgan Sarah. BSE, Villanova U., 1962; MA in Econ., Georgetown U., 1970. Sales engr. Allis-Chalmers, Milw., 1962-64; regional mgr. Electronic Assocs., West Long Branch, N.J., 1964-69, Honeywell Inc., Mpls., 1969-70; v.p. Leasco Computer, Great Neck, N.Y., 1971-76; pres. WHK Leasing, Northport, N.Y., 1976—; dir. N.Y. Conf. Mayors, Albany, 1985—; outside dir. N.Y. Partnership Cultural Flagship, Troy, 1998—; bd. dirs. 5B Techs., Inc. Contbg. editor: Empire State Report, 1994-98. Pres. N.Y. Conf. of Mayors, 1988-89, Tri-County Village Ofcls., 1989, Suffolk County Village Ofcls., 1988-90. Mem. Phila. Soc. (v.p. 1994), Kiwanis (pres. Norport chpt. 1982). Roman Catholic. Avocations: currency collecting, flying, real estate, reading, writing. Home: 220 Asharoken Ave Northport NY 11768-1160 Office: WHK Leasing 136 Woodbury Rd Woodbury NY 11797-1411

KELMAN, LORRAINE MACELLARO, biology educator, molecular biology researcher; b. N.Y.C., May 16, 1960; d. Charles John and Eleanor (Cacace) M.; m. Zvi Kelman, May 18, 1996. AB in Biochemistry, Mt. Holyoke Coll., 1982; MS in Biology, St. John's U., 1984; PhD in Molecular Biology, Cornell U., 1994; MBA in Mgmt., Iona Coll., 2000. Yeast molecular geneticist Sloan-Kettering Inst., N.Y.C., 1986-95; asst. prof. biology Iona Coll., New Rochelle, N.Y., 1991-96, assoc. prof., 1996—. Editor Bios, 1998—. Mem. AAUW (chair So. Westchester chpt. 1994-97), AAAS, Am. Women in Sci., Genetics Soc. Am., N.Y. Acad. Scis. (chair biol. scis. sect. 1994-96). Office: Iona Coll Dept Biology 715 North Ave New Rochelle NY 10801-1830

KELMANSON, IGOR, pediatrics educator; b. St. Petersburg, Russia, Dec. 6, 1962; s. Alexander and Margarita (Turetskaya) K. Pediatrician, Leningrad (USSR) Med. Inst., 1985, candidate of Scis. in Medicine, 1989; DScis., State Pediatric Med. Acad., St. Petersburg, Russia, 1995. Postgrad. trainee Leningrad Pediat. Med. Inst., 1985-87, postgrad. student, 1987-89, asst. prof. pediatrics, 1989-91; asst. prof. pediatrics St. Petersburg State Pediat. Med. Acad., 1991-95, assoc. prof. pediatrics, 1995-97, prof. pediatrics, 1997—. Translator (book) Nelson Textbook of Pediatrics, 1989-91; inventor (with others); respiratory monitor, 1993; author: (book) Breathing Disturbances in Children in Sleep, 1997, Low Birth Weight Infant and Postponed Risk of Cardiovascular Pathology, 1999, Evaluation of Temperament in the Infants under One Year Old, 2000; co-author: Sudden Infant Death Syndrome, 1995, 2d edit., 1997. Recipient award for young scientists of The Commonwealth of Ind. States, European Acad., 1996.; grantee: Rsch. Coun. Norway, Oslo, 1997, Free U. Brussels, 1997, 99, 2000. Mem. All Russian Union of Pediatricians, European Soc. for Study and Prevention of Sudden Infant Death (nat. sec. Russia 1992—), Sudden Infant Death Syndrome Internat. Office: State Ped Med Acad, Litovskaya 2, 194100 Saint Petersburg Russia

KELOHARJU, MATTI RAIMO, economics researcher; b. Espoo, Uusimaa, Finland, June 20, 1965; s. Raimo Jyrki and Elina Martta (Saloheimo) k.; m. Liisa Pirkko Kananen, July 18, 1992; 1 child, Roope. BSc, MSc, Helsinki Sch. Econs. & Bus., Finland, 1987, PhD in Fin., 1993. Vis. scholar Stern Sch. NYU, N.Y.C., 1989; asst. Helsinki Sch. Econs. and Bus. Adminstrn., 1992-94, acting asst. prof., 1994-96, acting prof., 1996-97, sr. rschr., 1997-98; vis. scholar Anderson Sch., UCLA, 1997-98, vis. asst. prof., 1998-99; prof. Helsinki (Finland) Sch. Econs. and Bus. Adminstrn., 1999—. Mem. European Fin. Assn., Am. Fin. Assn. Avocation: chess.

KELSEY, JEFFREY EASTON, psychiatrist, educator; b. Toronto, Ont., Can., May 18, 1958; s. Easton Trowbridge and Joanne Elizabeth Kelsey; m. Marlene Rodriguez, Sept. 10, 1988; children: Stephen, Lauren. BS, St. Lawrence U., 1980; PhD, U. Mich., 1986; MD, U. Miami, 1988. Diplomate Am. Bd. Neurology and Psychiatry. Resident psychiatry Stanford U. Sch. Medicine, Palo Alto, 1988-92; asst. prof. Bowman Gray Sch. Medicine, Winston-Salem, N.C., 1992-96, Emory U. Sch. Medicine, Atlanta, 1996—. Avocations: bicycling, cooking. Office: Emory U Sch Medicine 1841 Clifton Rd NE Rm 402 Atlanta GA 30329-4021

KELTON, ARTHUR MARVIN, JR., real estate developer; b. Bennington, Vt., Sept. 12, 1939; s. Arthur Marvin and Lorraine (Millington) K.; m. Elaine White, Nov. 1, 1986; 1 child, Ashley. BA, Dartmouth Coll., 1961; postgrad., U. Vt., 1963. Ptnr. Kelton and Assocs., Vail, Colo., 1966-77; pres. Kelton, Garton and Assocs. Inc., Vail, 1977-84, Kelton, Garton, Kendall, Vail, 1984-93, Christopher, Denton, Kelton, Kendall, Vail, 1993—. Head agt. Dartmouth Alumni Fund, Hanover, N.H., 1985-90, class pres., 1990-96; Dartmouth Alumni Coun., 1996—; pres. Vail Valley Med. Ctr. Found., 1991—. Republican. Congregationalist. Avocations: skiing, golf, wingshooting. Fax: 970-476-7994. Home: 1034 Homestake Cir Vail CO 81657-5111 Office: Christopher Denton Kelton & Kendall 225 Wall St Ste 210 Vail CO 81657-3615

KELTZ, AMY LYNN, foundation administrator; b. New Haven, Apr. 11, 1966; d. David Irwin and Sondra Lois (Ofstrock) Marshall; m. Ira Richard Keltz, July 13, 1991; children: Jennifer, Samuel. BA in French Lit., Johns Hopkins U., 1988; student, Am. Coll. Paris, 1986, Gallaudet U., 1988. Cert. Fund Raising Exec., Nat. Soc. Fund Raising Execs. Dir. devel. Friendship Ho., Washington, 1990-92; sr. devel. assoc. Econ. Policy Inst., Washington, 1993-95; v.p., dir. devel. Inst. Women's Policy Rsch., Washington, 1996-98; exec. dir. Frederick B. Abramson Meml. Found., Washington, 1998—; columnist The Daily Jour., 1999—; fundraising cons. Ben Lomond Manor Ho., Manassas, Va., 1995—; profl. fundraising spkr., AAUW, Prince William, Va., 1997-98. Chair grants panel, Prince William County Arts Coun., 1994-98; bd. mem., pub. rels., Prince William Chorale, Manassas, 1993-99; participant Cmty. Leadership Inst., Prince William County, 1994; bd. mem., sec. Prince William Com. of 100, 1995—, bd. dirs., pres. Vpstart Crow, Manassas, 1999—; bd. dirs., sec. Manassas Dance Co., 1999—; mem. 2d Decade Soc., Johns Hopkins U., 1998—. Mem. Nat. Soc. Fund Raising Execs., Am. Soc. Assn. Execs., Ind. Sector, Washington Regional Assn. Grantmakers, Nat. Ctr. Responsive Philanthropy. Office: The Frederick B Abramson Meml Found 1025 Connecticut Ave NW Ste 400 Washington DC 20036-5423

KEMAL, YASAR, author; b. Adana, Turkey, 1923; s. Sadik and Nigar Gokceli; m. Thilda Serrero, 1952; 1 child, Rasit. Student primary sch.; D honoris causa, Strasbourg U., 1991, Akdeniz U., Antalya, Turkey, 1992, Free U., Berlin, 1998. Works include novels, short stories, articles; author: (novels translated into English) Memed My Hawk, 1961, The Wind from the Plain, 1963, Anatolian Tales, 1968, They Burn the Thistles, 1973, Iron Earth, Copper Sky, 1974 (1st prize 14th Internat. Theatre Festival 1966), The Legend of Ararat, 1975, The Legend of the Thousand Bulls, 1976, The Undying Grass, 1977, The Lords of Akchasaz, Part 1: Murder in the Ironsmiths Market, 1979 (Madarali award Best Turkish Novel 1973), The Saga of a Seagull, 1981, The Sea-Crossed Fisherman, 1985, The Birds Have Also Gone, 1987, To Crush the Serpent, 1991, Salman The Solitary, 1997. Journalist, imprisoned for polit. views, 1971, later released without being charged. Recipient Prix Mondial Cino del Duca, Paris, 1982, The Sedat Simavi award for Lit., Istanbul, 1985; named Comdr. de la Légion d'Honneur de France, Paris, 1984, Internat. Catalonie prize, 1996, hellman/Hammett award, 1996, Nonino prize for lit., 1997, Kenne Font Found. award, Uppsala, 1997, Frankfurt Peace prize, 1997. Mem. Turkish Writers Union (past pres.). Home: PK 14 Basinkoy, Istanbul 34820, Turkey

KEMBLE, JAMES RICHARD, engineering services executive, retired; b. Mishawaka, Ind., Sept. 28, 1935; s. Richard Ralph and Lucille Marie (Wickey) K.; m. Dorothy Faye Millican, Oct. 1960 (div. 1961); m. Anne Duval, Oct. 6, 1962; children: Dawn Marie, Joseph James, Lisa Marie, Theresa Marie. Student, Notre Dame U., 1953-54, Purdue U., 1954-59; B in Gen. Studies, U. Nebr., Omaha, 1969. Clk. stock rm. Powell Tool Supply, Inc., South Bend, Ind., 1952-54; truck driver South Bend Supply Co., 1959; commd. 2d lt. U.S. Army, 1959, advanced through grades to maj., 1967, ret., 1979; tech. writer VSE Corp., Alexandria, Va., 1979-80, sr. logistic engr., 1980-82, div. mgr. plans and programs, 1982-84, mgr. air launched missile group, 1984-86; asst. v.p., mgr. Systems Engring. Group, Washington, 1986-94; v.p., mgr. air systems ops. divsn. Value Sys. Svcs., Arlington, Va., 1994-95; ret., 1995. Decorated Bronze Star, Meritorious Svc. medal with 3 oak leaf clusters, Joint Svc. Commendation medal, Army Commendation medal with 1 oak leaf cluster. Mem. Am. Def. Preparedness Assn., KC. Roman Catholic. Avocations: reading, personal computing, writing, volksmarching. Home: 5300 Holmes Run Pkwy Alexandria VA 22304-2834

KEMELHOR, ROBERT E(LIAS), mechanical engineer; b. N.Y.C., May 19, 1919; m. Shirley P. Tennen; children: Judith Ellen, Joel Martin, Barry Alan. Student Pre-Law, Bklyn. Coll., 1936-38; BSME, George Washington U., 1949. Registered profl. engr., Washington. Sr. draftsman Bur. Ships Navy Dept., Washington, 1940-43, design engr. Bur. Ordnance, 1943-46, sr. engr. head weapon launching sect. Bur. Aeros., 1946-53; chief engr. design, devel. prodn. McLean Devel. Labs., Copiague, N.Y., 1953-58; dir. rsch. and devel. Pesco Products div. Borg-Warner Corp., Bedford, Ohio, 1958; with applied physics lab. Johns Hopkins U., Laurel, Md., 1958-91; program mgr. John Hopkins U., Laurel, 1982-85, chief engr. tech. svcs. dept., 1986-91; pvt. practice cons. Bethesda, 1991—; cons. Advanced Tech. and Mfg. Enterpirse Programs, Nat. Inst. Stds. and Tech., U.S. Dept. Commerce, Aeronautics Indsl. Tech. Program, NASA/JPL. Numerous patents in field; contbr. articles to profl. jours. U.S. del. Internat. Standards Orgn. Subcom., Mfg. Automation. Fellow AIAA (assoc.); mem. AAAS (sr. sci. and engr.'s), Soc.

Mfg. Engrs. (sr. mem., chmn. Washington chpt. No. 48), Sigma Tau, Tau Beta Pi. Home: 6211 Redwing Ct Bethesda MD 20817-5914

KEMENT, ISABELLA VINICONIS, retired construction company executive; b. Sept. 9, 1923; d. Paul and Mary (Karsokas) Viniconis; married Stanley J. Kement, Feb. 6, 1943 (dec. Dec. 1998); children: Stanley J. Jr., Joan Kement Turbie. Owner, mgr. tobacco farm, 1943-45; bookkeeper, dispatcher, sec., owner Kement Constrn. Co. Inc., Broad Brook, Conn., 1945-70; owner, bookkeeper, mgr., builder E-Z Living Suites, Broad Brook, 1959-84; owner restaurant and hotel, 1959-65; ptnr. Kement Park Landfill and Gravel, Broad Brook, 1947—; sec. Kement Devel. Corp.; mgr., pres., bookkeeper Apt. Complex, Broad Brook, 1959-84; ptnr. Depot St. Gravel Pit; pres. Manor House, Inc., 1959-84, E-Z Living Suite, 1959-84; ptnr. Kement Ltd. Partnership, Inc., Kement Investment Corp. Mem. bd. North Cen. Health Dist.; mem. ch. coun. and social coms., Broad Brook, 1985-87; Cath. Christian Doctrine tchr. Recipient First Place trophy East Windsor Bicentennial Parade, 1968. Mem. Tobacco Valley Art Assn., Univ. of Third Age, East Windsor Garden Club. Roman Catholic. Avocations: line dancing, traveling, art, craft design, gardening. Home: 307 North Rd Broad Brook CT 06016-9642

KEMILÄINEN, AIRA TELLERVO, historian, educator, researcher; b. Kuopio, Finland, Aug. 4, 1919; d. Juho Arvi and Aino Tyyne (Hyvärinen) K. MA, U. Helsinki., Finland, 1943; PhD, U. Helsinki, Finland, 1956. H.S. tchr. Helsinki, 1945-50, 57-62; asst. Nat. Archives of Finland, Helsinki, 1950, archivist, 1952-57; sr. lectr. U. Helsinki, 1961-86; sr. lectr., assoc. prof. U. Jyväskylä, Finland, 1962-70, prof. world history, 1971-86, prof. emerita, 1986—. Author: Nationalism. Problems Concerning the Word, the Concept and Classification, 1964, Die Historische Sendung der Deutschen in Leopold von Rankes Geschichtsdenken, 1968, L'Affaire d'Avignon (1789-91) from the Viewpoint of Nationalism, 1971, Finns in the Shadow of the Aryans. Race Theories and Racism, 1998; contbr. articles to profl. jours. Mem. vol. female orgn. def. Lotta Svärd, 1938-44. Johann Gottfried Herder scholar, 1954-55, ASLA-Fulbright rsch. scholar, 1958-59, Finnish State scholar, 1974; decorated Chevalier Order White Rose Finland 1st class. Mem. Finnish Hist. Soc., Finnish Acad. Sci. and Letters, Swedish History of Sci. Soc., Internat. Soc. for Study of European Ideas, Assn. for Study of Ethnicity and Nationalism, Finnish Fedn. Univ. Women (br. pres. 1970-82). Avocation: summer cottage. Home: Raiviosuonmäki 5 B 23, 01620 Vantaa Finland Office: U Jyväskylä, Dept History, Jyväskylä Finland

KE MING, WANG, retired engineer, researcher; b. An Shun, Guizhou, China, Dec. 1, 1939; s. Wang Liang Cai Shu Fan and Du Ying Huai; m. Luo Ping, Aug. 6, 1988; 1 child, Run Ze. Student, Guizhou Post & Telecom. Sch., Guiyang, China, Nanjing Post & Telecom. Sch., China; grad., Beijing Post & Telecom. U. Tech. pers. An Shun (China) Post and Telecom. Office, 1957-58, 59, Guizhou Post and Telecom. Equipment Factory, Guiyang, 1974-84, Guiyang Post Office, 1984-95; ret., 1995. Participant Chinese Guizhou Inst. Comm., An Shun, 1985, Chinese Exhibit Sales Invention Patent and New Products Meeting, Shen Zhen, 1991, IEEE Internat. Reliability Workshop, Calif., 1995. Mem. AAAS,IEEE, Chinese Inst. Natural Scis., N.Y. Acad. Scis. Achievements include patent in field. Avocatiosn: swimming, physical training, reading, researching and solving problems. Home: 24 Xu Dong Xiang, Guiyang 550001, China

KEMKIN, IGOR VLADIMIROVICH, geologist, researcher; b. Vladivostok, Russia, Aug. 16, 1959; s. Vladimir Gavrilovich and Valentina Alekseevna (Seliphonova) K.; m. Raisa Anatol'evna Mescheryakova, Dec. 20, 1980; children: Aleksey Igorevich, Il'ya Igorevich. Student, Far Eastern State Tech. U., Vladivostok, Russia, 1981; PhD, Far Eastern Geol. Inst., Vladivostok, 1989. Cert. engr.-geologist. Rschr. on probation Far Eastern Geol. Inst., Vladivostok, 1981-83, engr., geologist, 1983-86, jr. rschr., 1986-90, rschr., 1990-93, sr. rschr., 1993-98, leading rschr., 1998—. Contbr. articles to profl. jours. and books. Judge assessor Ct. of Law, Vladivostok, 1983. Avocation: tourism. E-mail: i-kemkin@mail.ru, fegi@on-line.marine.su. Home: Chkalova St 8-4, 690068 Vladivostok-68 Russia Office: Far Eastern Geol Inst, Prospekt 100-letiya, 690022 Vladivostok-22 Russia

KEMM, KELVIN RICHARD, nuclear physicist, consultant; b. Durban, South Africa, Mar. 13, 1950; s. Claude Vincent and Gloria (de Kock) K.; m. Diana Gail Richardson, May 10, 1974; children: Warren, Steven. BSc, U. Natal, Durban, 1970, BSc with honors, 1971, MSc in Nuclear Physics, 1973, PhD in Nuclear Physics, 1976. Rsch. scientist Atomic Energy, Pretoria, 1977-79; project mgr. CSIR, Pretoria, 1979-80; head of dept. systems devel Armscor, Pretoria, 1980-86; head of divsn. ednl. systems Learning Technologies Pty. Ltd., Pretoria, 1986-89; CEO Tech. Strategy Cons., Pretoria, 1989—; bd. dirs. European Sci. and Environ. Forum, London; bd. advisors Com. for a Constructive Tomorrow, Washington, 1992—; dir. Green and Gold Forum, Pretoria, 1990—. Author: Techtrack: A Winding Path of South African Development, 1995, A New Era for Nuclear, 1999, (with others) Environmental Health: Third World Problems-First World Preoccupations, 1999; prodr., writer (TV series) Curiosity Feeds the Cat, 1981, Halleys Comet, 1985, Impact, 1988, The Environment and Packaging, 1992; author (newspaper column) Techtrack, 1991—. Chmn. Round Table, Pretoria, 1987. Corporal Infantry, 1968. Named Spkr. of Yr. Round Table South Africa, 1987, SA Def. Force Coll., 1996, 98, Toastmasters, 1997. Mem. Inst. of Nuclear Engrs., South Africa Inst. of Physics. Anglican. Avocations: philatilist, oil painting, model building, nature hiking, TV commentator. Home: 56 Grace Ave, Murrayfield, Pretoria 0184, South Africa Office: Stratek, PO Box 74416 Lynnwood Ridge, Pretoria 0040, South Africa

KEMMIS, ROBYN, academic administrator; b. Grafton, Australia, Sept. 3, 1943; d. Arthur Scott and Muriel Beryl (Sabine) K. BA in Econs. with honors, U. New Eng., Armidale, Australia, 1965; MA in Econs. with distinction, U. Essex, Colchester, Eng., 1969. Computer programmer dept. math. and agrl. econs. U. New Eng., Australia, 1964-66; rsch. officer Internat. Wool Secretariat, London, 1967; rsch. asst. dept. econs. U. Essex, U.K., 1967-70; tech. rep. Honeywell Time-Sharing U.K. Ltd., London, 1970-71; self-employed guide/lectr. Eng. and Spain, 1972; advt. mgr. Time-Out Pub. Party, Ltd., London, 1973-74; mgmt. analyst Mgmt. Consultancy Divsn. Pub. Svc. Bd. of NSW, Australia, 1975-78, asst. dir. Personnel and Job Opportunity Divns., 1978-81; dir. Corp. Svc., dir. Affirmative Action Dept. of Lands, NSW, 1981-87; asst. dir. Dept. Water Resources, NSW, 1987-90; dep. vice-chancellor, adminstr. U. Tech., Sydney, 1991—. Office: Univ of Technology, Sydney No 1/PO Box 123, Broadway NSW, Australia

KEMNITZ, KLAUS DIETER KARL, laser spectroscopist; b. Nürnberg, Germany, Sept. 18, 1948; s. Hans and Martha (Budszinsky) K. D Natural Scis. in Chemistry, U. Erlangen-Nürnberg, 1981. Postdoctoral fellow Inst. for Molecular Sci., Okazaki, Japan, 1982-84, rschr., 1986-89; postdoctoral fellow Columbia U., N.Y.C., 1984-86; rschr. Exploratory Rsch. of Advanced Tech., Kyoto, Japan, 1989-91, Govt. Indsl. Rsch. Inst. Osaka, Japan, 1991-92; sr. rschr. Bioquant, Ltd., Berlin, 1992-94; mng. dir. HoshKem, Kyoto, Japan, 1990-92, Klaus Kemnitz Cons., Berlin, 1992—, EuroPhoton Ltd., Berlin, 1994—; coord. EC projects, 1994—. Contbr. articles to sci. jours. Rotschild-Mayent fellow Inst. Curie, Paris, 1997. Mem. AAAS. Avocations: painting, travel, music, literature, natural sciences.

KEMP, DAVID, JR., administrator; b. Melbourne, Australia, Oct. 14, 1941; married; 3 children. B of Law, Melbourne U., 1966; PhD in Polit. Sci., Yale U., 1975. Sr. advisor Office of Leader of Opposition & Office Prime Min., Australia, 1975-76; dir.advisor Pvt. Office of Prime Min.ition & Office Prime Min., Australia, 1981; cons. acting as dir. strategy, state dir. Liberal Party, Victorian Divsn., Australia, 1987-88; elected mem. Ho. of Reps., Australia, 1990; shadow min. Dept. Edn., Australia, 1990-93, Dept. Sci., Tech. & Export Devel., Australia, 1993-94, Dept. Employment, Tng. & Family Svcs., Australia, 1994-96; min. Assisting Min. for Fin. & Privatization, Australia, 1996-97, Assisting Prime Min. Pud Svcs. Matters, Australia, 1996—, Dept. Schs., Vocat. Edn. & Tng., Australia, 1996-97, Dept. Employment, Edn., Tng. & Youth Affairs, Australia, 1997-98, Dept. Edn., Tng. & Youth Affairs, Australia, 1998—; prof. politics Monash U., Australia, 1979-90. Office: Dept Edn Tng & Youth Affair, Parliament House Ste MG 61, Canberra ACT 2600, Australia*

KEMP, HUBERT BOND STAFFORD, orthopaedist; b. Cardiff, Glamorgan, Gt. Britain, Mar. 25, 1925; s. John Stafford and Cecilia Isabel (Bond) K.; m. Moyra Ann Margaret Odgers, June 22, 1947; children: Sian Amanda, Sarah Marilyn, Louise Kirsten. MRCS, St. Thomas' Hosp. U., London, 1947; BS, London U., 1949, MS, 1969. Hon. cons. orthopaedic surgeon Royal Nat. Orthopaedic Hosp., London, 1945-74, cons. orthopaedic surgeon, 1974-92; hon. cons. orthopaedic surgeon Royal Nat. Orthopaedic Hosp. Trust, London, 1992—; sr. cons. Inst. Orthopaedics U. London, 19665-74; hon. cons. orthopaedic surgeon St. Luke's Hosp. for Clergy, 1975-90; cons. orthopaedic surgeon Middlesex Hosp., London, 1984-90. Contbr. chpts. in books and articles to profl. jours. Med. Rsch. Coun. com. mem. Tuberculosis of the Spine, 1974—, Osteosarcoma, 1985-94; chmn. London Bone Tumour Svc., 1985-91. Recipient Robert Jones Gold medal, 1964, Brit. Orthopaedic Assn. prize, 1969. Fellow Royal Coll. Surgoens. Avocations: oil painting, fishing. Home: 55 Loom Ln, Radlett WD7 8NX, Great Britain Office: Royal Nat Ortho Hosp Trust, 45 Bolsover St, London W1P 8AQ, Great Britain

KEMP, JACK FRENCH, association director, former United States secretary of housing and urban development, former congressman; b. L.A., July 13, 1935; m. Joanne Main; children: Jeffrey, Jennifer, Judith, James. B.A., Occidental Coll., 1957; postgrad., Long Beach State U., Calif. Western U. Spl. asst. to gov. Calif., 1967; spl. asst. to chmn. Republican Nat. Com., 1969; mem. 92d-100th congresses from 31st N.Y. Dist., 1971-89; former sec. Dept. of Housing and Urban Development, 1989-92; co-dir. Empower America, Washington, D.C., 1993—; profl. football player for 13 years; pub. relations officer Marine Midland Bank, Buffalo; candidate for Rep. Presdl. nomination, 1987-88; Rep. nominee for v.p., 1996. Mem. Pres.'s Council on Phys. Fitness and Sports; mem. exec. com. player pension bd. NFL. Recipient Disting. Service award N.Y. State Jaycees; Outstanding Citizen award Buffalo Evening News, 1965, 74. Mem. Nat. Assn. Broadcasters, Engrs. and Technicians, Buffalo Area C. of C., Sierra Club, Am. Football League Players Assn. (co-founder, pres. 1965-70). Republican. Office: Empower America STe 900 1701 Pennsylvania Ave NW Washington DC 20006-5807

KEMP, JAMES WILLIAM, graphic artist; b. Alliance, Ohio, Aug. 7, 1950; s. Albert William and Ethel Jean (Bricker) K. BA, U. Pa., Phila., 1972. Project editor Random House, Inc., N.Y.C., 1972-78; prin. designer, ptnr. Compass Projections Design Studio, Bklyn., 1978—; map, lettering designer Random House, N.Y.C., 1978—, Harcourt Brace, San Diego, 1982—, Franklin Libr., N.Y.C., 1978-85, Doubleday, N.Y.C., 1985—, Simon and Schuster, N.Y.C., 1992—, Rolling Stone Mag., N.Y.C., 1980-81, 89-93, N.Y. Times, 1988—, Kirshenbaum & Bond, N.Y.C., 1997, 98, Romann Group, N.Y.C., 1998. exhibited in group shows at Art Dirs. Club, N.Y.C., 1981, 90, 91, 95, Master Eagle Gallery, N.Y.C., 1981, 83-84, 87, 90, Donnell Libr., N.Y.C., 1987, ITC Gallery, N.Y.C., 1987, 90-93, Berthold Type Ctr., Toronto, Ont., Can., 1988, 90, Cooper-Hewitt Mus., N.Y.C., 1996, AIGA Gallery, N.Y.C., 1999; contbr. articles to profl. jours.; artwork appearing in books and anns. Co-founder Summer Mus. Theater for Young Adults, Bennington, Vt., 1985-96. Recipient certs. of excellence Am. Inst. Graphic Arts, N.Y.C., 1987, Type Dirs. Club, N.Y.C., 1989-94, merit award Art Dirs. Club, N.Y.C., 1991, 94. Avocations: writing, drawing. Home and Office: 20 Henry St Apt 5E Brooklyn NY 11201-1348

KEMP, MARTIN JOHN, art history educator, history of science educator; b. Windsor, Eng., Mar. 5, 1942; s. Frederick Maurice and Violet Anne (Tull) K.; m. Jill Lightfoot, Aug. 27, 1966; children: Joanna Lynn, Jonathan Andrew. BA, Cambridge (Eng.) U., 1963, MA, 1965; postgrad., Courtauld Inst. Art, London, 1963-65; DLitt (Hon.), Heriot Watt, 1995. Lectr. Dalhousie U., Halifax, N.S., Can., 1965-66, U. Glasgow, Scotland, 1966-81; prof. history and theory of art U. St. Andrews, Scotland, 1981-95, assoc. dean, 1983-87; provost St. Leonards Coll., U. St. Andrews, Fife, 1991-94; prof. Brit. Acad. Wolfson Rsch., Fife, 1993-98; prof. history of art U. Oxford, England, 1995—; mem. Inst. Advanced Studies, Princeton, N.J., 1984-85; vis. prof. Inst. Fine Arts, NYU, N.Y.C., 1988, U. N.C., Chapel Hill, 1993; Slade prof. U. Cambridge, 1987-88; bd. dirs. Mus. Tng. Inst.; hon. fellow Domingo Coll., Cambridge, 1999—. Author: Leonardo da Vinci, The Marvellous Works of Nature and Man, 1981 (Mitchell prize 1981), The Science of Art, 1989, Behind the Picture, 1998, Immagine e Verita, 1999, Oxford History of Western Art, 2000, Visualizations. The Nature Book of Art and Science, 2000; contbr. articles to art and sci. jours. Trustee Nat. Galleries of Scotland, Edinburgh, 1982-87, Victoria & Albert Mus., London, 1985-89, Brit. Mus., 1995—, Ashmolean Mus., 1995—, Nature; mem. visual arts adv. bd. Arts Coun. Eng., 1995—. Fellow Royal Soc. Arts, Brit. Acad., Am. Acad. Arts and Scis., Royal Soc. Edinburgh; mem. AAAA (fgn. hon.); Royal Scottish Acad. (hon. prof. history 1985—), Brit. Soc. History of Sci., Asn. Art Historians (chair 1989-92), Leonardo da Vinci Soc. Avocations: sports, hockey. Office: U Oxford, Dept History Art, Oxford England

KEMP, SARAH (SALLY LEECH), developmental psychologist, neuropsychologist; b. Bryn Mawr, Pa., Sept. 13, 1940; d. Thomas Bailey and Mary Elizabeth (Veasey) Leech; m. G. Philip Fritz, June 18, 1960 (dec. May 1968); 1 child, Mary Elizabeth Fritz Fitch; m. Garry Colquhoun Kemp, July 25, 1970; children: Sarah, Hannah. BA, Calif. State U., Sacramento, 1963; MA, U. Tulsa, 1970; EdM, Columbia U., 1989, PhD, 1991. Tchr., counselor, psychometrist various cities, 1968-85; program asst. for neuroscience and edn. program Tchrs. Coll., Columbia U., 1985-88; neurodevelopmental specialist Tulsa Devel. Pediatrics and Ctr. for Family Psychology, 1988—; developmental psychologist Tulsa, 1990—; instr. ednl. and devel. neurosciences Tchrs. Coll., Columbia U., fall 1987, summer 1988; adj. asst. prof. pediatrics U. Okla. Med. Sch., Tulsa, 1991—; pres. Neuropsychoednl. Svc. PC; presenter in field. Co-author: (with Ursula Kirk and Marit Korkman) NEPSY, a Developmental Neuropsychological Assessment, 1998. Lay reader Trinity Episc. Ch., 1990—; bd. mem. Magic Empire Coun. Girl Scouts U.S.A., 1993—. Mem. Internat. Neuropsychological Soc., Assn. for Children and Adults With Learning Difficulties, Rodin Remediation Soc., Orton Soc. Episcopalian. Achievements include neuropsychological test development and research on attention deficit disorder, autism, and school-related problems. Office: Tulsa Devel Pediatrics 4520 S Harvard Ave Ste 200 Tulsa OK 74135-2919

KEMP, TORBEN PETER, philosopher, educator; b. Vindum, Jutland, Denmark, Jan. 24, 1937; s. Svend Carl Hartvig and Brigitte-Augusta (Cotzsche) K. Grad. in Theology, U. Aarhus, Denmark, 1964; D in Theology, U. Copenhagen, 1973; grad. in philosophy, U. Gothenberg, 1991. Prof. philosophy U. Copenhagen, 1972—, dept. head, 1979-81, vice chmn. dept., 1981-84, head Ctr. Philosophy Tech., 1986-87; U. Copenhagen del. Inter-Univ. Ctr., Dubrovnik, Yugoslavia, 1979-93; pres. Nordic Inst. for Philosophy, 1980-89, Acad. Applied Philosophy, 1986-88; mem. collective bd., co-founder Filosofisk Forum, Copenhagen, 1980—; dir. Ctr. Ethics and Law, 1993—; sec.-gen. Fédération Internat. Des Socs. de Philosophie, 1998—; Waerner-prof. U. Gothenburg, Sweden, 1987-88. Author: Sprogets Dimensioner, 1972, Theorie de l'Engagement, 2 vols., 1973, Track af Nutidens Taekning, 1977, Marxism i Frankrig, 1978, Doden og Maskinen, 1981; co-author: (with P. Ph. Druet and G. Thill) Technologies et Societes, 1980, Ethique et Medecine, 1987, L'irremplacable, une ethique de la technolgie, 1997, Levinas une introduction philosophique, 1997. Recipient Rosenkjaerprisen, Danish Radio, 1972. Mem. Academie Internationale de Philosophoe des Sciences, Institut Internationale de Philosophie (bd. dirs.), Fedn. Inst. Soc. Philosophie (gen.). E-mail: ethiclaw@inet.uni2.dk. Office: Ctr for Ethics and Law, Valkendorfsgade 30, DK 1150 Copenhagen Denmark

KEMPCKE, GÜNTER RUDOLF, linguist; b. Vorbeck, Germany, Mar. 9, 1931; s. Karl and Johanna (Witte) K.; m. Gerda Dedow, Sept. 27, 1956; 1 child, Birgit. Diploma in German, U. Leipzig, Germany, 1954, PhD, 1963. Lic. lexicographer. Head rsch. project (lexicography) Acad. Sci., Berlin, 1970-96. Co-editor: Dictionary of German Synonyms, 1973, new edit., 1999, Dictionary of Linguistic Norms, 1984; editor: Dictionary of Current German, 1984, Learner's Dictionary of Current German, 2000. Recipient Nat. award of scis. II class, Berlin, 1979. Home: Waldstr 2, 12527 Berlin Germany

KEMPE, FREDERICK SCHUMANN, newspaper editor, author; b. Salt Lake City, Sept. 5, 1954; s. Fritz Gustav and Johanna Irmgardt (Schumann) K. BA in Comm. magna cum laude, U. Utah, 1976; MA in journalism, Columbia U., 1977; LLD (hon.), U. Md., 1995; HD (hon.), Queen Coll., 1999; LHD (hon.), Queens Coll., 1999. Copy editor Salt Lake Tribune, Salt Lake City, 1974-76; free-lance writer Chgo. Daily News, Christian Sci. Monitor, Rome, 1977-78; Frankfurt corr. AP-Dow Jones, Germany, 1978-79; Bonn corr. Newsweek, Germany, 1979-81; London corr. The Wall St. Jour. (USA), 1981-84; Vienna bureau chief The Wall St. Jour. (USA), Austria, 1984-86; chief diplomatic corr. The Wall St. Jour. (USA), Washington, 1986-89; founder, mng. editor Cen. European Econ. Rev., 1993-94, editor, 1995-96; mng. editor Wall St. Jour. Europe, Brussels, 1992-96; editor, assoc. publ. Wall St. Jour. Europe, 1998—. Author: Divorcing the Dictator: America's Bungled Affair with Noriega, 1990, Siberian Odyssey: A Voyage Into the Russian Soul, 1992, Father/Land: A Personal Search for the New Germany, 1999; contbr. Das Neue Europa, 1992. Recipient Quentus Wilson award U. Utah, 1987; named Top Young Alumnus of Yr. U. Utah, 1987. Mem. Coun. Fgn. Rels., Internat. Inst. Strategic Studies. Avocations: tennis, skiing, basketball. Office: Wall Street Jour Europe, Blvd Brand Whitlock 87, 1200 Brussels Belgium

KEMPE, PETER BENJAMIN, solicitor; b. Cologne, Rheinland, Germany, June 16, 1961; s. Herbert Ernst and Victoria (Lane) K.; m. Julia Margaret Kenyon, Apr. 19, 1986; children: Max, Harry, Jack. BA with honours, Cambridge (Eng.) U., 1983, MA, 1986. Solicitor of the Supreme Ct. Articled clk. Joynson-Hicks, London, 1984-86; solicitor Taylor Joynson Garrett, London, 1986—, ptnr., 1990—; bd. dirs. Huntsmoor Ltd., London, Huntsmoor Nominees Ltd., London, TJG Secretaries Ltd., London, TJG Process Svc. Ltd., London. Author: (children's book) Otto and the Secret Passage, 1994. Mem. Law Soc., Adrian Com., Old Chigwellians Football Club, Hawks Club, Idlers, P.S.I.C., Epping Golf Course. Anglican. Avocations: family activities, golf, football, game fishing, viticulture. Office: Taylor Joynson Garrett, 50 Victoria Embankment, London Blackfriars EC4Y 0DX, England

KEMPER, DIRK HARRY, executive; b. Gottingen, Germany, Jan. 12, 1952; s. Wolfgang and Wilma (Haepe) K.; m. Katrin Krogmann, July 7, 1990; children: Julia, Leonard, Elena, William. Dipl.klm., U. Gottingen, Germany, 1976, Dr.rer.pol., 1980. Asst. to main bd. Beiersdorf, Germany, 1976-80; pres. CFB, Paris, 1980-84, Knipping Internat. GmbH, Brunen, 1984-86; with Filtrona Filter GmbH, Germany, 1986—; dir. Filtrona Internat., England, 1988—, Bunzi Fibre GmbH, Germany, 1988—. Author: Imponderabilien im Investitions Kalkul, 1980. Chmn. Med. Ctr., Reinbek, 1996—. Avocations: tennis, sailing, golf, Bordeaux wines. Office: Filtrona Tilhona Filter, Gutenbergstr 5-9, 21465 Reinbek Germany

KEMPERS, ALEXANDER JACOBUS, environmental chemist, researcher; b. Amsterdam, The Netherlands, Oct. 11, 1939; s. Jacobus Johannes and Jacoba Emma (van Lobberegt) K.; m. Albertine Eveline Vos, May 27, 1967; children: Ingeborg, Else. MSc in Phys. Geography, U. Amsterdam, 1967. Asst. editor Elsevier Sci. Publ. Co., Amsterdam, 1967-69; profl. UNESCO, Paris, 1969-71; rschr. Nijmegen (The Netherlands) U., 1971—. Contbr. articles to profl. jours. Avocations: classical piano, rowing. E-mail: lexk@sci.kun.nl. Home: Kastanjelaan 7, 6584 CN Molenhoek The Netherlands Office: U Nijmegen Fac Scis, Toernooiveld, 6525 ED Nijmegen The Netherlands

KEMPF, DAVORIN, composer, educator; b. Virje, Croatia, Aug. 21, 1947; s. Branimir and Barbara (Markov) K.; m. Bosiljka Perić, Dec. 26, 1970. Acad. musician, Acad. Music, Zagreb, Croatia, 1973, Hochschule für Musik und Darstellende Kunst, Stuttgart, Fed. Republic of Germany, 1975-76, Musikhochschule Cologne, Fed. Republic of Germany, 1976-77; MA, U. Iowa, 1990. Instr. Acad. Music, Zagreb, 1972-73, asst. prof., 1977-88, assoc. prof., 1988-95, prof., 1995—. Compositions: Spectrum for orch. and electronics, 1984-85 (Josip Slavenski Ann. award 1986, Vladimir Nazor Ann. award 1986), Five Haikus for mezzo-soprano and piano, 1988, Fantasy for organ, 1991, Fiat lux for tape, 1994. Mem. Croatian Composers' Soc., Am. Biographical Inst. Rsch. Assn. (lifetime mem., dep. gov.), German Soc. Electroacoustic Music. Avocations: reading, chess, walking. Home: Rudina 2a, 10000 Zagreb Croatia Office: U Zagreb Acad Music, Gundulićeva 6, 10000 Zagreb Croatia

KEMPKEN, FRANK, molecular biologist; b. Moers, Germany, Mar. 3, 1960; s. Karl-Heinz and Kaete (Olyschlaeger) K.; m. Renate Radzio Kempken. BS, Ruhr U., 1985, PhD, 1988. Rsch. assoc. Ruhr U., Bochum, Germany, 1987-89; postdoctoral rsch. assoc. U. Fla., Gainesville, 1989-90; from rsch. assoc. to asst. prof. Ruhr U., 1991—. Pvt. German air force, 1979-80. Recipient Bennigsen Foerder award, 1991, Klaus Marquardt award, 1996. Mem. German Botanical Soc., German Genetical Soc., German Soc. Gen. and Applied Microbiology. Avocation: photography. Office: Ruhr U, Dept Gen & Molecular Botany, 44780 Bochum Germany

KEMPNER, MARVIN A., broadcasting corporation executive; b. Albany, N.Y., July 7, 1921; s. Marvin William and Anna K.; m. Aileen Juvelier, Aug. 20, 1950 (div. 1974); children: Candice Ann, Daniel Henry; m. Jeanne Kay Cantor, Aug. 26, 1976 (dec. 1990). Student, U. Buffalo, 1941. Acct. exec. Louis G. Cowan Inc., N.Y.C., 1946-48; v.p. Richard H. Ullman Inc., Buffalo, N.Y., 1949-60; pres. Richard H. Ullman Inc., N.Y.C., 1960-62, Mark Century Corp., N.Y.C., 1962-68; pres. broadcasting divsn. Music Makers Inc., N.Y.C., 1968-71; v.p. Music Makers Pub. Co., N.Y.C., 1968-71; prin., owner M.A. Kempner Inc., N.Y.C., 1971—; bd. dirs. So. Fla. RR Mus., Deerfield Beach. Author: Can't Wait Till Monday Morning, 1998. Treas. Scleroderma Found., Watsonville, Calif., 1992-98. Corp. USAF, 1943-46. Mem. Friars Club (book warming award 1999). Republican. Avocations: golf, photography, modeling and building railroad diaramas, public speaking. E-mail: mksand@earthlink.net. Home: 11820 Fountainside Cir Boynton Beach FL 33437-4921

KEMPSTON DARKES, V. MAUREEN, transportation company executive; b. Toronto, Can.. BA in History and Polit. Sci., U. Toronto, LLB; D in Commerce (hon.), St. Mary's U., Halifax, 1995; LLD (hon.), U. Toronto, 1996, U. Victoria, 1996, McMaster U., 1997. Bar: Ont. Mem. legal staff GM Can. Ltd., 1975-79; asst. counsel GM Can. Ltd., Detroit, 1979-80; head tax staff GM Can. Ltd., 1980-84; mem. treas. office GM Can. Ltd., N.Y.C., 1985-87; acting treas. GM Can. Ltd., gen. dir. pub. affairs, 1987-91, v.p. corp. affairs, 1991, bd. dirs., 1991, gen. counsel, sec., 1992; pres., gen. mgr., v.p. GM GM Can. Ltd., Oshawa, Ont., 1994—; appointed Free Trade Agreement Automotive Select Panel, 1989, Transp. Equipment Sectoral Adv. Group on Internat. Trade, 1994; bd. dirs. CAMI Automotive, CN Rail, Noranda Inc., Thomson Corp. Active Ont. Govt. Edn. Accountability Bd.; mem. arts and sci. adv. bd. U. Toronto; bd. govs. U. Waterloo; mem. adv. com. U. We. Ont.'s Richard Ivey Sch. Bus.; bd. dirs. Women's Coll. Hosp. Found., New Directions; chair major gifts fundraising campaign Women's Coll. Hosp.; mem. coun. adv. govs. YMCA Greater Toronto. Recipient Order of Ont., 1997. Mem. Bus. Coun. on Nat. Issues, Can. Vehicle Mfrs. Assn., Natural Resources Can. Min. Adv. Coun. on Indsl. Energy Efficiency, Automotive Adv. Com. Office: 1908 Colonel Sam Dr, Oshawa, ON Canada L1H 8P7

KENAWI, MOHAMMAD, surgeon, educator; b. Cairo, Feb. 16, 1946; s. Mohammad Metwalli Kenawi and Ehsan Moustafa Hedayat; m. Heba Salah Hedayat, Mar. 3, 1977. MBBCh, Cairo U., 1967, Diploma of Surgery, 1969, MD in Surgery, 1972; Diploma in Computer Programming, 1992. FRCS. presenter confs. in field. Author: (textbook/10 vols.) Spotlights on Surgery; co-author booklets in field and texts in field; mem. translation team The World Book Ency.; contbr. articles to profl. jours. Recipient Scientific Rsch. prize in gen. surgery Acad. Scientific Rsch., Cairo, 1991, Scientific Rsch. prize in oncotherapy, 1994, State Rsch. award, 1998, others. Mem. Egyptian Soc. Plastic and Reconstructive Surgeons, Egyptian Surg. Soc., Internat. Soc. Plastic and Reconstructive Surgeons, Brit. Assn. Urol. Surgeons, N.Y. Acad. Scis. Avocations: swimming, jogging, tennis, aerobics, travel. Office: 13 Sherif Pasha St, Cairo 11111, Egypt

KENCE, AYKUT, biologist, educator; b. Istanbul, Turkey, Aug. 27, 1946; s. Hacibay and Hayriye (Sukru) K.; m. Meral Savasan; children: Ozlem, Kutay. Diploma in sci., Istanbul U., 1968; PhD, SUNY, Stony Brook, 1973. Rsch. asst. SUNY, Stony Brook, 1972-73; postdoctoral fellow U. Houston, 1973-74; instr. Mid. East Tech. U., Ankara, 1974-75, asst. prof., 1975-80, assoc. prof., 1980-88, prof., 1989—, chmn. biology dept., 1977-79, 88-94; exec. sec. basic scis. group Sci. and Tech. Rsch. Coun. Turkey, Ankara,

1988-89. Editor: Biological Diversity in Turkey, 1987, Biological Diversity and Development, 1988, Check-List of Vertebrates of Turkey, 1996; editor Turkish Jour. Zoology, 1991—. Recipient Young Scientist award Sci. and Tech. Rsch. Coun. Turkey, 1986, Pub. Health Svc. award Ankara Chamber of Medicine, 1987. Mem. Soc. for Biologists of Turkey (pres. 1988-92). Office: Mid East Tech U, Dept Biology, 06531 Ankara Turkey

KENDAL, FELICITY, actress; b. Sept. 25, 1946; d. Geoffrey and Laura K.; 2 children. Edn. at 6 convents in India. First stage appearance in A Midsummer Night's Dream, 1947; grew up touring with parents' theatre co., appearing in such plays as Midsummer Night's Dream, Twelfth Night, The Merchant of Venice, Hamlet, India and Far East; London debut as Carla in Minor Murder, Savoy Theatre, 1967; other stage appearances include: Henry V, The Promise, Leicester, Eng., 1968, Back to Methuselah, Nat. Theatre, A Midsummer Night's Dream, Much Ado About Nothing, Regent's Park, London, 1970, Kean, Oxford, Eng., 1970, London, 1971, Romeo and Juliet, 1972, 'Tis Pity She's a Whore, 1972, The Three Arrows, 1972, The Norman Conquests, London, 1974, Once Upon a Time, Bristol, Eng., 1976, Arms and the Man, Greenwich, Eng., 1978, Clouds, London, 1978, Amadeus, Othello, On the Razzle, 1981, The Second Mrs. Tanqueray, The Real Thing, 1982, Made in Bangkok, 1986, Hapgood, 1988, Much Ado About Nothing, 1989, Ivanov, 1989, Hidden Laughter, 1990, Tartuffe, 1991, Heartbreak House, 1992, Arcadia, 1993, An Absolute Turkey, 1994, Indian Ink, 1995, Mind Millie for Me, 1996, Waste, 1997, The Seagull, 1997, Alamrs & Excursions, 1999; TV appearances include: four series of The Good Life, Solo, Twelfth Night, 1979, The Mistress, Camomile Lawn, 1991, Honey for Tea, 1994; also plays, serials; films include: Shakespeare Wallah, 1965, Valentino, 1976, Parting Shots, 1999; author: (book) White Cargo, 1999. Named Most Promising Newcomer, Variety Club, 1974, Best Actress, 1979; recipient Clarence Derwent award, 1980, Evening Standard Best Actress award, 1989. Office: 123A Kings Rd, London SW3 4PL, England*

KENDALL, HARRY OVID, internist; b. Eugene, Oreg., Nov. 29, 1929; s. Edward Lee and Jessie Avis (Giem) K.; m. Katherine Alexander, June 20, 1951 (div. 1957); 1 child, Jessica Gail Gress; m. Barbara Ann Matt, Jan. 21, 1961 (div. June 1, 1977); children: David Lee, Brian Padraic; m. Wanda Eve Helmer, July 2, 1993. AB, U. Redlands, 1952; MD, Yale U., 1955. Diplomate Am. Bd. Internal Medicine, Am. Bd. Pulmonary Disease. Intern in internal medicine UCLA Med. Ctr., 1955-57; resident in internal medicine West L.A. VA Med. Ctr., 1957-59; staff physician U.S. Naval Regional Med. Ctr., San Diego, 1959-62, Tulare-Kings Counties Hosp., Springville, Calif., 1962-63; staff physician, ptnr. So. Calif. Permanente Med. Group, Fontana, Calif., 1963-67, Kaiser Hosp. and So. Calif. Permanente Med. Group, San Diego, 1967—; dir. respiratory care Kaiser Hosp., San Diego, 1967—; attending physician San Bernardino County Hosp., 1964-67; asst. clin. prof. medicine U. Calif. San Diego Med. Ctr., 1976—; com. mem. numerous hosps. and med. clinics. Mem. NAACP, Amnesty Internat., ACLU. Lt. USNR, 1954-56, lt. comdr. 1961, comdr. 1973. Mem. Am. Thoracic Soc., cAlif. Thoracic Soc., San Diego Pulmonary Soc. Avocations: western history, paleontology, geneology, book collecting.

KENDALL, KATHERINE ANNE, social worker; b. Muir-of-Ord, Scotland, Sept. 8, 1910; came to U.S., 1920, naturalized, 1940; d. Roderick and Annie Scott (Walker) Tuach; m. Willmoore Kendall, June 22, 1935 (div. Apr. 1950). BA, U. Ill., 1933; MA, La. State U., 1939; PhD, U. Chgo., 1950; D Public Service (hon.), Syracuse U., 1981; DSW (hon.), U. Pa., 1985, La. State U., 1987, U. Ill., 1989. Asst. prof. Richmond Sch. Social Work, 1941-42; asst. dir. home service A.R.C., 1942-44; lectr. U. Chgo. Sch. Social Service Adminstrn., 1944-45; asst. dir., tng. supr. Inter-Am. and Internat. Tng. units U.S. Children's Bur., 1945- 47; social affairs officer UN Secretariat, 1947-50; exec. sec. Am. Assn. Schs. Social Work, 1950-52; ednl. sec. Council on Social Work Edn., 1952-58, assoc. dir., 1958-63, exec. dir., 1963-66, dir. internat. edn., 1966-71; Carnegie vis. prof. U. Hawaii, 1960-61; mem. exec. bd. Internat. Assn. Schs. Social Work, 1954-66, sec.-gen., 1966-78, hon. pres., 1978—; ofcl. non-govtl. rep. UN, 1954-94; Moses prof. Hunter Coll. Social Work, 1983-84; dir. Internat. Conf. on Social Work Edn., Population and Family Planning, East-West Ctr., Hawaii, 1970; exec. sec. Coun. of Advisors to Hunter Coll., Hunter Coll. Sch. Social Work and Lois and Samuel Silberman Fund, 1985-87. Author: Reflections on Social Work Education, 1950-1978, Social Work Education: Its Origins in Europe, 2000; UN reports International Exchange of Social Welfare Personnel, 1949, Training for Social Work: First International Survey, 1950; editor: Social Work Values in an Age of Discontent, 1970, Population Dynamics and Family Planning: A New Responsibility for Social Work Education, 1971, World Guide to Social Work Edn., 1984, Eileen Blackey; Pathfinder for the Profession, 1986; co-editor: Gerontological Social Work: International Perspectives, 1988; compiler: Social Casework—Cumulative Index 1920-1979, 1981. Mem. UN Internat. meeting experts on social work tng., Munich, 1956; faculty mem. UN Seminar, Keeru, Finland, 1952; assignment by UN mission social work edn., Guatemala, 1949, UN, Brazil, 1952, Paraguay, 1954; dir. 1st seminar Schs. Social Work in Central Am., 1963. Mem. Mortar Bd., Nat. Assn. Social Workers, Nat. Conf. Social Welfare, Internat. Assn. Schs. Social Work, Council on Social Work Edn., Internat. Council on Social Welfare, Phi Beta Kappa, Chi Omega. Home: Collington # 2003 10450 Lottsford Rd Mitchellville MD 20721-2734

KENDALL, LEIGH WAKEFIELD, surgeon; b. Brattleboro, Vt., Mar. 8, 1937; s. Irwin Samuel and Laura Eliza (Walbridge) K.; m. Grace Eleanor Fullarton, July 1, 1961; children: William Leigh, Bradley Edward. AB, U. Pa., Phila., 1959; D of Medicine, U. Vt., 1963; MS, U. Ill., Chgo., 1965. Diplomate Nat. Bd. Med. Examiners, Am. Bd. Surgery; cert. ACLS. Intern then resident surgery U. Ill. Hosp., Chgo., 1963-69; rsch. fellow Am. Cancer Soc., Chgo., 1964-65; clin. fellow Am. Cancer Soc., 1968-69; staff surgeon USN Hosp., Great Lakes, Ill., 1969; surgeon USN Hosp. Ships, Vietnam, 1969-70; pvt. practice Lancaster, Pa., 1971-93; med. dir. Alliance Health Plan, Lancaster, 1995—; assoc. med. dir. St. Joseph Regional Health Network, Lancaster and Reading, 1999—; med. dir. St. Joseph Hosp., Lancaster, 2000—; instr. surgery U. Ill. Hosp., Chgo., 1968-69; active staff St. Joseph Hosp., Lancaster, 1971—, sect. chief gen. surgery, 1981-88, chmn. dept. surgery, 1989-93; mem. courtesy staff Lancaster Gen. Hosp., 1971—; cons. surgery Franklin & Marshall Coll., Lancaster, Masonic Homes, Elizabethtown, Pa., staff physician, Millersville, U., 1993—; staff physician cardiac rehab., Lancaster Gen. Hosp. Health Campus, 1995-98. Lt. comdr. USNR M.C., 1959-71, Vietnam. Decorated 1st Class Mil. Honor medal Republic of Vietnam. Fellow ACS, Internat. Soc. Surgeons; mem. AMA, Pa. Med. Soc., Warren H. Cole Soc. (pres. 1994-95), Royal Soc. Medicine (Eng.), Am. Coll. Physician Execs., Intrepids Club, Sigma Nu. Republican. Episcopalian. Avocations: photography, travel. Home: 1314 Quarry Ln Lancaster PA 17603-2424 Office: Med Affairs Office St Joseph Hosp Lancaster PA 17604-0302

KENDALL, PHILLIP ALAN, lawyer; b. Lamar, Colo., July 20, 1942; s. Charles Stuart and Katherine (Wilson) K.; m. Margaret Roe Greenfield, May 2, 1970; children: Anne, Timothy. BS in Engring., Stanford U., 1964; JD, U. Colo., Boulder, 1969; postgrad., U. Freiburg (Germany), 1965-66. Engr. Siemens Halske, Munich, 1965; ptnr. Kraemer, Kendall & Benson, Colorado Springs, Colo., 1969—; gen. counsel Peak Health Care, Inc., Colorado Springs, 1979-87; bd. dirs. Norwest Banks Colorado Springs. Pres. bd. Colorado Springs Symphony Orch. Assn., 1977-80; bd. dirs. Penrose Hosps., Colorado Springs, 1982-88; pres. bd. Citizen's Goals, Colorado, 1984-86; bd. dirs. Legal Aid Found., Denver, 1988-94, chmn., 1991-93; bd. dirs. Colo. Nature Conservancy, 1996—. Recipient Medal of Distinction-Fine Arts, Colorado Springs C. of C., 1983. Mem. ABA, Colo. Bar Assn. (bd. govs. 1985-88, outstanding young lawyer 1977), El Paso County Bar Assn. (bd. trustees 1983-85), Colorado Springs Estate Planning Coun. Avocations: triathlons, helicopter skiing, marathon swimming, windsurfing, sailing. Home: 1915 Wood Ave Colorado Springs CO 80907-6714 Office: Kraemer Kendall & Benson PC 430 N Tejon St Ste 300 Colorado Springs CO 80903-1167

KENDALL, SUSAN HAINES, library director; b. Greenville, Ohio, Nov. 5, 1952; d. Kenneth Edward and Zelda Lucille (Delk) Haines; m. John Leroy Sweigart, May 25, 1974 (div. 1986); m. Patrick William Kendall, Nov. 28, 1986. BS in Edn., Wright State U., 1977; MLS, Ball State U., 1981. Cert. tchr., Ohio; cert. libr., Ohio. Libr. clk. Greenville (Ohio) Pub. Libr., 1971-77; libr. asst. Flesh Pub. Libr., Piqua, Ohio, 1977-78, Amos Meml. Pub. Libr., Sidney, Ohio, 1978-81; libr. dir. Preble County Dist. Libr., Eaton, Ohio, 1981—; mem. tech. task force Ohio Pub. Libr. Info. Network, Columbus, 1993-95, bd. dirs., 1995—. Editor Preble's Pride quar., 1986—. Bd. dirs. Preble County Hist. Soc., 2000—. Mem. ALA, Ohio Libr. Assn. (mem. S.W. chpt. mem. coun. 1984-86, asst. coord. 1986-87, coord. 1988-89), Commodore-Preble DAR, Preble County Genealogy Soc., Eaton/Preble County C. of C. Republican. Methodist. Avocations: genealogy, motorcycling. Office: Preble County Dist Libr 450 S Barron St Eaton OH 45320-2402

KENDIG, EDWIN LAWRENCE, JR., pediatrician, educator; b. Victoria, Va., Nov. 12, 1911; s. Edwin Lawrence and Mary McGuire (Yates) K.; m. Emily Virginia Parker, Mar. 22, 1941; children: Anne Randolph (Mrs. R.F. Young), Mary Emily Corbin (Mrs. T.T. Rankin). BA magna cum laude, Hampden-Sydney Coll., 1932, BS magna cum laude, 1933, DSc (hon.), 1971; MD, U. Va., 1936. House officer Med. Coll. Va. Hosp., Richmond, Bellevue Hosp., N.Y.C., Babies Hosp., Wilmington, N.C., Johns Hopkins Hosp., Balt., 1936-40; instr. pediatrics Johns Hopkins U., 1944; pvt. practice Richmond, 1940-94; dir. child chest clinic Med. Coll. Va., 1944-94, prof. pediatrics, 1958-99; chief of staff St. Mary's Hosp., Richmond, 1966-67; cons. on diseases of chest in children, 1944-94, William P. Buffum orator Brown U., 1978; Abraham Finkelstein Meml. lectr. U. Md., 1983; Derwin Cooper lectr. Duke U., 1984; Renato Ma Guerrero lectr. U. Santo Tomas, Manila, 1984; Bakwin Meml. lectr. NYU-Bellevue Hosp., 1986. Contbr. numerous articles on disease of chest in children to profl. publs.; editor: Disorders of Respiratory Tract in Children, 1967, 72, 77; co-editor: (with V. Chernick) Disorders of Respiratory Tract in Children, 4th edit., 1983, cons. editor to V. Chernick, 5th edit, to V. Chernick and T. Boat, 6th edit., pub. as Kendig's Disorders of the Respiratory Tract in Children, 1990, 97; (with C.F. Ferguson) Pediatric Otolaryngology, 1972; contbg. editor: Gellis and Kagan Current Pediatric Therapy, 12 edits., 1993, Burg, Ingelfinger, Wald Current Pediatric Therapy, 14th edit., Antimicrobial Therapy, Kagan, 3 edits., Practice of Pediatrics, Kelley, Practice of Pediatrics, Maurer, Allergic Diseases of Infancy, Childhood and Adolescence, Bierman and Pearlman, Sarcoidosis and Other Granulomatous Diseases, James, 1994; former mem. edit. bd. Pediat. Pulmonology, Pediat. Annals, Pediat., Alumnews U. Va., 1988. Chmn. Richmond Bd. Health, 1961-63; bd. visitors U. Va., 1961-72; former mem. bd. dirs. Va. Hosp. Svc. Assn.; former ofcl. examiner Am. Bd. Pediatrics; mem. White House Conf. on Children and Youth, 1960; pres. alumni adv. com. U. Va. Sch. Medicine, Charlottesville, 1974-75; past bd. dirs. Maymont Found., Richmond; bd. dirs. Children's Hosp., 1985-97, Children's Hosp. Found., 1997—, Sheltering Arms Hosp.; former mem. adv. bd. Ctr. for Study of Mind and Human Interaction, U. Va. Sch. Medicine, 1988; mem. steering com. One Hundred Twenty Fifth Anniversary, Med. Coll. of VA Hosps., 1986; bd. dirs. St. Mary's Health Care Found., 1990. Recipient resolution of recognition Va. Health Commr., 1978, Obici award Louise Obici Hosp., 1979, Bon Secours award St. Mary's Hosp., 1986, Keating award Hampden-Sydney Coll., 1989, Disting. Citizen award Boy Scouts Am., R.E. Lee chpt., 1996, Disting. Svc. to Cmty. award Richmond Acad. Medicine, 1999; named an Outstanding Alumnus Sch. Medicine U. Va., 1986; The Edwin Lawrence Kendig Jr. Disting Profesorship in Pediatric Pulmonary medicine named in honor Med. Coll. Va. Commonwealth U., also Edwin Lawrence Kendig Jr. Med. Edn. Rm. at St. Mary's Hosp., 1999. Mem. AMA (pediat. residency rev. com., Disting. Svc. award 2000), Am. Acad. Pediat. (past pres. Va. sect., chmn. sect. on diseases of chest, mem. exec. bd. 1971-78, nat. pres. 1978-79, Abraham Jacobi Meml. award with AMA, 1987, cons. com. on internat. child health, Lifetime Achievement award Va. chpt. 1999), Am. Acad. Pediat. for Latin Am. (ofcl. adv. to exec. bd. 1988), Va. Bd. Medicine (former pres.), Richmond Acad. Medicine (pres. 1962, chmn. bd. trustees 1963), Va. Pediat. Soc. (past pres.), Am. Pediat. Soc., So. Med. Assn., So. Soc. Pediat. Rsch., Internat. Pediat. Assn. (cons., standing com., medal 1986), Med. Soc. Va. (editor Va. Med. Quarterly 1982-98, resolution of recognition), Soc. Cin., Raven, Commonwealth, Country Club of Va., Farmington Club, Phi Beta Kappa, Alpha Omega Alpha, Tau Kappa Alpha, Kappa Sigma, Omicron Delta Kappa. Episcopalian. Home: 5008 Cary Street Rd Richmond VA 23226-1643 Office: Laburnum House 1300 Westwood Ave Richmond VA 23227-4624

KENDRICK, BONNIE ANN, educational diagnostician, educator; b. Miami, Fla., Sept. 18, 1954; d. John L. and Elizabeth A. (Taylor) Harborn; m. Rodney L. Kendrick, Apr. 11, 1981; children: Melanie E., Rhett L. BSED, U. Ga., 1976, MEd, 1979; ednl. specialist degree, State U. West Ga., Carrollton, 1998. Cert. elem. tchr., spl. edn. tchr., instrnl. supervision, Ga. Elem. tchr. Sea Pines Acad., Hilton Head, S.C., 1976-77; spl. edn. tchr. Charleston (S.C.) County Schs., 1978-79, Biloxi Sch. Dist., Miss., 1979-80; spl. edn. tchr. Cobb County Pub. Schs., Marietta, Ga., 1981-84, ednl. diagnostician, 1984—. pres. Cheatham Homeowners Assn., Marietta, 1984, social chmn., 1985-99; bible sch. dir. 1st United Meth. Ch., Marietta, 1998; leader Boy Scouts Am., Girl Scouts U.S. Mem. Coun. Exceptional Children (Support Person of Yr. 1999, editor newsletter 1999—, Chpt. Mem. of Yr. 2000). Methodist. Avocations: reading, travel. E-mail: bahk72@aol.com. Home: 745 Cannon Crse SW Marietta GA 30064-2843 Office: Cobb County Pub Schs Cheatham Hill Elem 1350 John Ward Rd SW Marietta GA 30064-3816

KENDRICK, JAMES EARL, business consultant; b. Indpls., Sept. 12, 1940; s. John William and Mab.e E. (Coleman) K.; m. Carrie L. Fair, July 19, 1969; children: Carrie F., Leslie F., John F. BA, Butler U., 1963; postgrad., Ind. U., 1963-65. Exec. dir. Knox County Econ. Opportunity Coun., Barbourville, Ky., 1965-66; rsch. scientist NYU, 1967-68; mgr. Volt Info. Scis., Washington, 1968-71, Nat. Urban Coalition, 1972-74; pres. Kendrick & Co., Washington, 1974-91; sr. v.p. Kendrick & Co., 1992-93; pres. P2C2 Group, Silver Spring, Md., 1994—; devel. cons. Coppin State Coll., Balt., 1995-99, Exec. Office of the Pres. of The U.S., 1999-2000. Author: Community Energy Workbook, 1974; National Urban Agenda Survey, 1974; (video) Americans on the Move, 1984; (software) Help for PC DDS, 1985, Children of 2010, 1999; contbr. articles to profl. jours. and newsletters. Mem. Fellowship Merry Christians. Recipient Rural Svc. award OEO, 1968; citation Washington chpt. Am. Soc. Tng. and Devel., 1971; named one of Outstanding Young Men of Am., 1974, Ranked Among the Best 100 Mgmt. Firms in N.Am. by Consulting News, 1993. Mem. Inst. Mgmt. Consultants, Assn. Proposal Mgmt. Profls., Sigma Delta Chi. Office: P2C2 Group 2402 Darrow St Silver Spring MD 20902-4919

KENDRICK, JOSEPH TROTWOOD, former foreign service officer, writer, consultant; b. Pryor, Okla., Feb. 5, 1920; s. Joseph Trotwood and Anne (Williams) K.; m. Loreine York, July 18, 1942 (div. 1954); m. Elise Fleager Simpkins, Aug. 20, 1955 (div. 1977); children: Pamela York, Drew Trotwood (dec. 1970), Juliette Simpkins, Katherine Mary. Student, U. Okla., 1938-40; B.S., Georgetown U., 1948; M.A., Columbia, 1951; Ph.D., George Washington U., 1979; postgrad., Cambridge (Eng.) U., summer 1998. Joined Fgn. Svc., U.S. Dept. State, 1941; assigned Nicaragua, Poland, USSR, Germany, 1941-54; spl. asst. to dir. Office Ea. European Affairs, U.S. Dept. State, Washington, 1954-57, pub. affairs adviser, 1958; 2d sec., consul Am. Embassy, Kabul, Afghanistan, 1959-61; dep. polit. adviser SHAPE, Paris, 1962-64; polit. counselor Am. Embassy, Oslo, 1964-68; dep. dir. Office Atomic Energy and Aerospace, U.S. Dept. State, 1968-70, dir., 1970-71, spl. asst. to dir. Bur. Pol. Mil. Affairs, 1971-72; detailed to Dept. Def., 1972-73; dean, Center for Area and Country Studies, Fgn. Svc. Inst., U.S. Dept. State, 1974-75; writer, cons., 1975—. Author: Executive-Legislative Consultation on Foreign Policy: Strengthening Executive Branch Procedures. Served to lt. (jg.) USNR, 1944-46. Recipient Outstanding Civilian Service medal Dept. Army, 1974. Mem. Am. Assn. Advancement Slavic Studies, Am. Fgn. Service Assn., Am. Polit. Sci. Assn., Inst. Strategic Studies (London), Delta Chi.

KENDRICK, LAURIE LYNN, artist; b. Inglewood, Calif., Apr. 15, 1969; d. R. Davis and Evelyn (Grace) K. BA, Lycee Francais, L.A., 1987. Poet Enright House, County Kerry, Ireland, 1992-95. Contbr. poems to anthologies: Best New Poems, 1995 (award), Amherst Soc. Anthology, 1995 (award), Iliad Press' Anthology, 1996, A Lasting Mirage, 1997. Vol. Beyond Baroque Lit. Ctr., Venice, Calif., 1991-92. Recipient Editor's award for photography Nat. Libr. Photography, 1998. Mem. Nat. Preservation Soc., Wilson Quar., Smithsonian Inst. Avocations: jewelry making, volunteer work, linguistics, travel, reading. Home: 2200 S Coast Hwy Laguna Beach CA 92651-3669 Office: PO Box 34991 Los Angeles CA 90034-0991 Address: 268 Bush St San Francisco CA 94104-3503

KENDZIOR, ROBERT JOSEPH, marketing executive; b. Mar. 24, 1952; s. Joseph W. and Josephine R. Kendzior. BArch, Ill. Inst. Tech., 1975. Account supr. Burger King Corp. Rogers Merchandising, Inc., Chgo., 1975-77; account exec. Walgreen Corp. Eisaman, Johns & Laws Advt., Inc., Chgo., 1977-78; v.p. mktg. Dunkin Donuts Am., Inc., Randolph, Mass., 1978-95; v.p., chief mktg. officer Factory Card Outlet Am., Inc., Chgo., 1995-98; v.p. internat. mktg. Allied Domecq Retailing, 1999—; v.p. Internat. Mktg. and Retail Concepts, Randolph. Recipient Most Valuable Promotion award PepsiCo, 1984. Mem. Triangle Fraternity.

KENEN, PETER BAIN, economist, educator; b. Cleve., Nov. 30, 1932; s. Isaiah Leo and Beatrice (Bain) K.; m. Regina Horowitz, Aug. 21, 1955; children: Joanne Lisa, Marc David, Stephanie Hope, Judith Rebecca. AB, Columbia U., 1954; MA, Harvard U., 1956, PhD, 1958. Mem. faculty Columbia U., 1957-71, prof. econs., 1964-71, chmn. dept., 1967-69, provost univ., 1969-70; prof. econs. and internat. fin. Princeton (N.J.) U., 1971—, dir. internat. fin. sect., 1971-99; Ford rsch. prof. U. Calif., Berkeley, 1979-80; Res. Bank Australia professorial fellow Australian Nat. U., 1983-84; rschr. on internat. monetary theory and policy; cons. Coun. Econ. Advisors, 1961, U.S. Treasury, 1962-68, 77-80, 95-98, Bur. Budget, 1964-68, IMF, 1990, 92. Author: British Monetary Policy and the Balance of Payments (1951-57), 1960, Giant Among Nations, 1960, (with A.G. Hart and A. Entine) Money, Debt and Economic Activity, 4th edit., 1969, (with R. Lubitz) International Economics, 3d edit., 1971, A Model of the U.S. Balance of Payments, 1978, (with P.R. Allen) Asset Markets, Exchange Rates, and Economic Integration, 1980, Essays in International Economics, 1980, Managing Exchange Rates, 1988, Exchange Rates and Policy Coordination, 1989, International Economy, 4th edit, 2000, Exchange Rates and the Monetary System, 1994, Economic and Monetary Union in Europe, 1995; editor: International Trade and Finance, Frontiers for Research, 1975, (with others) The International Monetary System Under Flexible Exchange Rates, 1982, (with R.W. Jones) Handbook of International Economics, 1984, Managing the World Economy, 1994, Understanding Interdependence, 1995, (with M. Mussa and A.K. Swoboda) Key Issues in Reform of the International Monetary and Financial System, 2000; contbr. articles to profl. jours. Recipient David A. Wells prize Harvard U., 1958-59, Univ. medal Columbia U., 1977; Ctr. Advanced Study Behavioral Scis. fellow, 1971-72, John Simon Guggenheim Found. fellow, 1975-76, Royal Inst. Internat. Affairs fellow, 1987-88, German Marshall Fund fellow, 1987-88, Houblon-Norman fellow Bank of Eng., 1991-92. Mem. Am. Econ. Assn., Coun. Fgn. Rels., Royal Econ. Soc., Group of Thirty. Home: 176 Western Way Princeton NJ 08540-7208 Office: Princeton U Dept of Econs Fisher Hall Princeton NJ 08544-1021

KENESEI, ISTVÁN, linguist, educator; b. Budapest, Hungary, Mar. 29, 1947; s. Tibor and Ilona (Szücs) K.; children: Réka Zsuzsanna, Tamás Gábor. BA, U. Budapest, 1967, MA, 1970, PhD, 1974. Asst. prof. English U. Szeged, Hungary, 1971-82, assoc. prof. English, 1982-93, prof. English, 1993—, dir. PhD program in linguistics, 1993—, vice rector, 1997-99; vis. prof. U. Venice, Italy, 1995; Fulbright prof. U. Del., Newark, 1992-93, vis. lectr., 1987-88. Editor/author: Approaches to Hungarian, vols. 1-7, 1985-2000, Introduction and Overview to/of Linguistics Languages and Language, 1984, 89, 95, 2000, Hungarian Descriptive Grammar, 1998, Crossing Boundaries, 1999; mem. edit. bd. Acta Linguistica Hungarica, 1991—; contbr. articles to profl. jours. Grantee Ford Found., 1973, Fulbright Commn., 1992-93, Hungarian Nat. Sci. Found., 1993-95, 95—. Mem. Generative Linguists of the Old Worlds (bd. dirs. 1994-96), Linguistic Soc. Am., Linguistic Assn. G.B., Nat. Bd. Accreditations. Office: U of Szeged Dept of English, Egyetem U2, 6722 Szeged Hungary

KENESI, CLAUDE, orthopedic surgeon; b. Paris, June 4, 1930; s. Andre Jules and Louise Marie (Pasqueron) K.; m. Marie Claude Cherest, Aug. 1, 1959; children: Marie-Anne, Laurent, Francois. MD, U. Paris, 1965. Externe, then intern Paris hosps., 1953, 1960; prosecutor Faculty Medicine, Paris, 1965-70; pvt. practice specializing in orthopedic surgery Paris, 1970-; assoc. prof. anatomy faculty medicine Univ. Paris, 1970,, 1980—; chief svc. Hosp. Henri Mondor, Creteil, France, 1980—, chmn. in anatomy, hon. prof., 1999. Author: Atlas de'Anatomie Clinique, 1981, Rehabilitation of Hand, 1984; contbr. articles to med. publs. Served to lt. French armed forces, 1957-59. Recipient Chevalier award Palmes Academiques, 1987. Mem. Acad. Surgery, Soc. Orthopedic Surgery, Soc. Rheumatology, Guepar Group (pres. 1970-84). Roman Catholic. Avocations: opera, hunting, painting. Home: 10 Ave Constant Coquelin, 75007 Paris France

KENG, TAY BOON, surgeon, consultant, health facility administrator; b. Malaysia, Johore, Malaysia, Jan. 28, 1949; s. Tay Chye Huat and Yap Al Chu; m. Quek Swee San; children: Darren, Sherilyn, Stacie. MBBS, U. Singapore, 1978. Registrar Singapore Gen. Hosp., 1977-80, sr. registrar, 1980-85, cons., 1985-95, sr. cons., 1989-95, head dept., 1995—, chmn. divsn. surgery, 1999—; assoc. prof. Nat. U. Singapore, 1998—. Contbr. articles to profl. jours. Major Singapore Army, 1974-76. Health Manpower Devel. Plan fellow Ministry Health, 1988; Travelling fellow Asean Orthop. Assn., 1994. Fellow ACS, Royal Coll. Surgeons Edinburgh, Royal Coll. Orthop. Surgeons Edinburgh, Acad. Medicine; mem. Singapore Med. Assn. (sec. 1973), Singapore Orthop. Assn. (pres. 1977), Knee Soc. (mem. coun. 1989). Avocations: golfing, reading, travelling, video, surfing.

KENGYEL, MIKLÓS, law educator; b. Kaposvar, Hungary, Aug. 15, 1953; s. Istvan and Emma (Harmatos) K.; m. Marta Buzas, May 27, 1977; children: Andras, Peter. BA in Law, U. Pecs, 1977, PhD, 1985, habilitation, 1994. Asst. U. Pecs, Hungary, 1977-83, asst. lectr., 1983-87, asst. prof., 1987-94, prof., 1994—; prodean U. Pecs, 1991-93, dean faculty of law, 1993-99. Author: Evidence by Witnesses in Civil Procedure, 1988, Culture of Litigation, 1993, Civil Procedural Law I-III, 1993-95, Handbook on Civil Procedure, 1995, Hungarian Civil Procedural Law, 1998, Ungarisches Zivilverfalneusrecht, 1999. Mem. Internat. Assn. Procedural Law. Avocation: opera. Home: 20 Golya dulo, 7635 Pecs Hungary Office: U Pecs, 1 48-as ter, 7622 Pecs Hungary

KENJI, UENO, electrical engineer; b. Hokkaido, Japan, Dec. 13, 1949; s. Teruo and Masae Ueno; m. Yumiko Hayashi, Oct. 2, 1977; children: Shiori, Koutaro, Takuya. BSEE, Hokkaido U., 1972, PhD, 1988. Cert. in engring. Sr. rsch. engr. NTT, Yokosuka, 1999; head ASC, Tokyo. Mem. IEEE, Inst. Electronics, Info. and Comm. Engrs. Avocations: tennis, skiing. Fax: 81358215096. E-mail: ueno@asc.co.jp. Office: ASC, 2-12-5 Iwamoto-cho, Tokyo 101-0032, Japan

KENKEL, JEROME BERNARD, civil engineer; b. Cin., May 14, 1950; s. Lawrence Joseph and Mildred Henrietta (Schmidt) K.; m. Sharon Ann Adams, June 21, 1985; children: Angela, Andrea. BSCE, U. Cin., 1973, MSCE, 1975. Registered profl. engr., Ohio, Ind., Ky., W.Va. Engr.-in-tng. hwys. Vogt-Ivers Engrs., Cin., 1969-71; engr.-in-tng. sewers Met. Sewer Dist. Cin., 1971-72; rsch. asst. hwys. U. Cin./Ohio Dept. Transp., 1973-75; staff geotech. engr. H.C. Nutting Co., Cin., 1975-78, project geotech. engr., 1978-83, sr. geotech. engr., 1983-93, prin. geotech. engr., 1993—, also bd. dirs.; br. mgr. H.C. Nutting Co., Lawrenceburg, Ind., 1999—; adj. assoc. prof. geotech. engring. U. Cin. Coll. Civil Engring., 1995, 96, 97, 98, 99. Contbr. articles to profl. jours. Univ. scholar U. Cin., 1968-69, 73-75. Mem. ASCE, Am. Soc. Hwy. Engrs., Engrs. and Scientists Cin., ASCE Geotech. Group Cin. (chmn. geotech. tech. group 1996-97). Roman Catholic. Avocations: softball, basketball, snow skiing. Home: 5596 Picardy Ln Cincinnati OH 45248-5026 Office: HC Nutting Co 611 Lunken Park Dr Cincinnati OH 45226-1813 also: HC Nutting Co Walnut St Lawrenceburg IN 47025

KENNAN, STEPHANIE ANN, legislative staff member; b. Frankfurt am Main, Germany, Oct. 25, 1958; d. Ralph Hyde and Loretta (Pumphrey) K. BA in Am. Govt. and Fgn. Affairs, U. Va., Charlottesville, 1980; MA in Creative Writing, Johns Hopkins U., Balt., 1997. Legis. asst. Rep. Larry Smith, Washington, 1983-85; asst. dir. edn. Group Health Assn. Am., Washington, 1985-86; legis. rep. Am. Assn. Ret. Persons, Washington, 1986-89, Am. Coll. Emergency Physicians, Washington, 1989-94; dir. fed. rels. Md. Dept. Health, Balt., 1995-97; sr. policy advisor U.S. Senator Ron Wyden, Washington, 1998—; mem. Montgomery County (Md.) Commn. on Aging, 1983-86. Co-author: Health Care Playbook, 1994; contbr. articles to profl. jours., books. Mem. Nat. Press Club. Episcopalian. Office: Senate Office Bldg 516 Hart Senate Office Bldg Washington DC 20510-0001

KENNARD, EDWARD TREVOR, construction consultant; b. Worthing, Sussex, Eng., Oct. 25, 1930; s. Edward John and Ellen Kathleen (Trevor) K.; m. Pamela Florence Tucker, Oct. 17, 1955 (div. 1982); children: Susan Baldwin, Simon, Trevor John. Student, Brighton Coll., 1946-51. Bldg. surveyor London, 1950-57, Her Majesty's Overseas Civil Svc., Uganda, 1957-60; bldg. surveyor Hong Kong Govt., 1961-69, sr. bldg. surveyor, 1969-72, chief bldg. surveyor, 1972-74, prin. govt. bldg. surveyor, 1974-81; mng. dir. Kenward Svcs. Ltd., Hong Kong, 1983-98, Kenward Consultancy Ltd., Hong Kong, 1988—; chmn. Viva Racing Ltd., Hong Kong, 1999—. Mem. coun. St. John's Cathedral. Sgt. Brit. Army, 1951-53. Fellow Royal Instn. Chartered Surveyors. Mem. Citizen's Party. Avocations: kart racing, golf, reading. Office: 6 Upper High Street, Worthing West Sussex BN11 1DL, England

KENNEDY, CHARLES, retired medical educator; b. Buffalo, N.Y., Aug. 27, 1920; m. Eulsum Kennedy, Aug. 27, 1968; 3 children from previous marriage. BA in Chemistry cum laude, Princeton U., 1942; MD, U. Rochester, 1945. Diplomate Am. Bd. Pediats., Am. Bd. Psychiatry and Neurology; lic. N.Y., Pa., D.C., Maine, Md. Intern in pathology New Haven (Conn.) Hosp., 1945-46; instr. pathology Sch. Medicine Yale U., New Haven, 1945-46; fellow in child psychiatry Children's Hosp., Buffalo, N.Y., 1948-49; resident pediatrician Children's Hosp., Buffalo, 1949-51; fellow in physiology Grad. Sch. Medicine U. Pa., Phila., 1951-53, assoc. pediats. Sch. Medicine, 1952-55, assoc. in neurology Sch. Medicine, 1955-58, asst. prof. neurology in pediats. Sch. Medicine, 1958-61, assoc. prof. neurology in pediats. Sch. Medicine, 1961-67; prof. pediats., neurology Sch. Medicine Georgetown U., Washington, 1971-90, prof. emeritus, 1990—; chief divsn. neurology, dir. child neurology Children's Hosp., Phila., 1959-67; vis. fellow in neurology Neurol. Inst. Columbia Presbyn. Med. Ctr., 1957-58; guest researcher Lab. Clin. Sci. Nat. Inst. Mental Health, 1967-68, Lab. Cerebral Metabolism, 1968-90;, sr. rsch. scientist, 1979-80, med. officer, spl. expert Lab. Cerebral Metabolism, Bethesda, Md., 1990-96; cons. Pa. Hosp., Phila., 1960-69, Hosp. U. Pa., Phila., 1961-67, Bd. Edn. City of Phila., 1962-64; lectr. U.S. Naval Hosp., Phila., 1962-68, Found. Advanced Edn. in Scis., 1978-87; mem. adv. com. on dyslexia State of Tex., 1965; guest lectr. Nat. Naval Med. Ctr. Uniformed Svcs. U. Health Scis., 1977-87; mem. faculty spl. courses Am. Acad. Neurology, 1978, 80; mem. NIMH AIDS rsch. rev. com., 1988; mem. ad hoc com. evaln. of program project rsch. in learning disabilities NICHHD, 1989, planning com., moderator workshop, Rockville, Md., 1989; researcher in field. Mem. editl. bd. Pediat. Rsch. 1978-84, Brain Rsch., 1980-96, Jour. Cerebral Blood Flow and Metabolism, 1981-88. Lt. jg USNR, 1946-48. Fellow Life Ins. Med. Rsch. Fund, 1951-53. Fellow Coll. Physicians Phila.; mem. Am. Pediat. Soc., Am. Acad. Pediats., Am. Neurol. Assn., Am. Acad. Neurology (chmn. sect. child neurology 1964-66, com. problems of mental retardation 1965-67), Am. Soc. Neurochemistry, Nat. Bd. Med. Examiners (mem. pediat. com. 1960-64), Internat. Soc. Neurochemistry, Internat. Soc. Cerebral Blood Flow and Metabolism (dir. 1989-93, chmn. fin. com. 1992-96), Phila. Pediat. Soc. (pres. 1964), Phila. Neurol. Soc. (v.p. 1967), Assn. Rsch. in Nervous and Mental Disease, Soc. Neurosci., Child Neurology Soc., Profs. of Child Neurology.

KENNEDY, CHESTER RALPH, JR., former state official, art director; b. Middleboro, Mass., Apr. 22, 1926; s. Chester Ralph and Mary Carmen (Mello) K.; m. Barbara Ann Partridge, June 27, 1953; children: Karen Brooke, Scott Douglas. BFA, Mass. Coll. Art, 1951; postgrad., New Eng. Adult Edn. Inst., 1959, Boston U., 1966, Brandies U., 1985. Supr. pub. health edn. Mass. Dept. Pub. Health, Boston, 1953-56, coordinator health edn., 1956-74, asst. dir. health edn., 1974-81, dir. health edn., 1981-84, dist. health officer, 1984-89; ret., 1989; asst. art dir. Barchét Studios, Middleboro, 1949-59, art dir., co-owner, Sherborn, Mass., 1959—; cons. USPHS, Assn. State and Territorial Health Officers; lectr., instr. Harvard, Boston U., Mass. Coll.; mem. Acad. Master Plan Adv. Commn., Mass. State Coll. System; exhibit chmn. 22nd World Health Assembly. Editor: Commonwealth of Mass. Secretarial Reference Manual, 1969; designer blue ribbon exhibit New Eng. Hosp. Assembly, 1969; designer five pvt. homes. Pres. Pub. Health Museum in Mass., 1991-93, mem. exec. bd., 1993—; pres. Reach Out, Inc., 1970-74, bd. dirs., 1974—; bd. dirs. Greater Framingham Mental Health Assn., 1974-76; elected to Sherborn Bd. Health, 1974-86; mem. Solid Waste Recovery Tech. Com., 1975-84; co-chair Coalition Organized for Health Edn. in Schs., 1982-89. Served with USN, 1944-46. Recipient Boy Scouts Am. Organizer award, 1941, Commonwealth Mass. Disting. Svc. citation, 1971, Health Edn. citation New Eng. Consortium Health Edn. Assn., 1975, Coalition Organized for Health Edn. in Schs. citation, 1989, Reach Out award, 1977, Southeastern Assn. Health Bds. award, 1989, Michael Dukakis Gov.'s award, 1989, Mass. Dept. Pub. Health award, 1989, Pub. Health Museum Organizer award Mass. Ho. of Reps., 1993, Gov. William Weld Museum Founder award, 1993. Mem. New Eng. Health Edn. Assn. (pres. 1971-72), Mass. Health Coun., New Eng. Health Promotion Coun., Soc. Pub. Health Edn., Mass. Audubon Soc., Mass. Archeol. Soc., Mass. Coll. Art Alumni (pres. 1968-72), Assn. Mass. State Colls. Alumni (pres. 1973-75), Mass. Pub. Health Assn. (health edn. chmn. 1974-76, 25 yr. award 1986, Paul Revere award 1990), Mass. Health Officers Assn. (emeritus, Curtis M. Hillard award 1989, exec. sec. 1992-98), Mass. Assn. Health Bds. (hon., exec. bd. 1990-94), New Eng. Pub. Health Assn. (pres. 1984-85, Ira Hiscock award 1980, 25 yr. award 1989, pres. com. pub. health mus. in Mass. 1991-93, exec. bd. 1993—). Office: Barchét Studios 178 Washington St Sherborn MA 01770-1022

KENNEDY, CLIVE RUSSELL, zoologist, educator; b. Liverpool, England, June 17, 1941; s. Thomas Kennedy and Victoria Alice (Russell) Wallwork; m. Beryl Pamela Jones, Feb. 23, 1963 (dec. 1978); children: David Aidan, Katherine Anne; m. Patricia Broughton, Sept. 4, 1999. BSc, Liverpool U., 1961, PhD, 1964, DSc, 1978. Asst. lectr. zoology U. Coll., Dublin, Ireland, 1963-64, Birmingham (Eng.) U., 1964-65; lectr. zoology Exeter (Eng.) U., 1965-76, reader zoology, 1976-86, prof. parasitology, 1986—; dean sci. Exeter U., 1990-93, head biology, 1996-2000. Author: Ecological Animal Parasitology, 1975, Ecological Aspects of Parasitology, 1976; contbr. over 160 articles to profl. jours. Recipient E.N. Pavlovski medal Acad. Sci., Leningrad, USSR, 1984. Mem. British Soc. Parasitology (hon., pres. 1994-96), Russian Soc. Parasitology (hon.), Fisheries Soc. British Isles (hon., sec. 1974-77), Scandinavian Soc. Parasitology. Avocations: glass, churches, walking, rugby. E-mail: c.r.kennedy@exeter.ac.uk. Home: 2 Marsh Mill Ct, Newton, St Cyres EX5 5AB, England Office: Dept Biol Scis, Hatherly Lab Exeter Univ, Exeter EX4 4PS, England

KENNEDY, DAVID BOYD, foundation executive, lawyer; b. Ann Arbor, Mich., Sept. 2, 1933; s. James Alexander and Elizabeth (Earhart) K.; m. Sally Martin Pyne, 1964; children: Jane Elizabeth, Douglas Earhart. Student, McGill U., 1951-52, U. Mich., 1952-54; AB, Ind. U., 1958; LLB, U. Mich., 1963. Bar: Mich. 1964, Wyo. 1965. Pvt. practive law Sheridan, Wyo., 1964-84; pres., trustee Earhart Found., Ann Arbor, Mich., 1985—; trustee Citizens Rsch. Coun. of Mich.; chmn., bd. dirs. Inst. for Justice, Washington; mem. bd. overseers Hoover Instn./Stanford U. Mem. Wyo. Ho. Reps., 1967-72; chmn. Wyo. Rep. State Ctrl. Com., 1971-73; Rep. nat. committeeman, 1976-80, vice chmn., 1978-80; atty. gen. State of Wyo., 1974-75; mem. Mont Pelerin Soc.; apptd. mem. Pres.'s Com. on Arts and Humanities, Washington, 1990-93; bd. dirs. Philanthropy Roundtable, Washington; bd. dirs. Univ. Music Soc., 1986-90, pres., 1990. With U.S. Army, 1954-57. Mem. Wyo. Bar Assn., Mich. Bar Assn. Republican. Office: Earhart Found 2200 Green Rd Ste H Ann Arbor MI 48105-1569

KENNEDY, DONALD, editor, environmental science educator, former academic administrator; b. N.Y.C., Aug. 18, 1931; s. William Dorsey and Barbara (Bean) K.; children: Laura Page, Julia Hale; m. Robin Beth Wiseman, Nov. 27, 1987; stepchildren: Cameron Rachel, Jamie Christopher. AB, Harvard U., 1952, AM, 1954, PhD, 1956; DSc (hon.), Columbia U., Williams Coll., U. Mich., U. Ariz., U. Rochester, Reed Coll., Whitman Coll. Mem. faculty Stanford (Calif.) U., 1960-77, prof. biol. scis., 1965-77, chmn. dept., 1965-72, sr. cons. sci. and tech. policy Exec. Office of Pres., 1976, commr. FDA, 1977-79, provost, 1979-80, pres., 1980-92; prof. emeritus, Bing prof. environ. sci. Stanford U., 1992—; bd. overseers Harvard U., 1970-76; bd. dirs. Health Effects Inst., Nat. Commn. on Pub. Svc., Carnegie Commn. on Sci., Tech. and Govt. Author: Academic Duty, 1997; mem. editl. bd. Jour. Neurophysiology, 1969-75, Science, 1973-77, editor-in-chief, 2000—; contbr. articles to profl. jours. Bd. dirs. Carnegie Endowment for Internat. Peace. Fellow AAAS, Am. Acad. Arts and Scis.; mem. NAS, Am. Philos. Soc. Office: Stanford U Inst for Internat Studies Encina Hall 401 Stanford CA 94305-6055

KENNEDY, EDWARD MOORE, senator; b. Boston, Feb. 22, 1932; s. Joseph Patrick and Rose (Fitzgerald) K.; m. Joan Kennedy (div.); children: Kara Anne, Edward Moore, Patrick Joseph; m. Victoria Anne Reggie, 1992. A.B., Harvard U., 1956; postgrad., Internat. Law Sch., The Hague, Netherlands, 1958; LL.B., U. Va., 1959. Bar: Mass. 1959, U.S. Supreme Ct. 1963. Asst. dist. atty. Suffolk County, Mass., 1961-62; U.S. senator from Mass., 1962—, chmn. judiciary com., 1979-81, ranking Dem. mem. labor and human resources com., 1981—, also mem. armed service, joint econ., labor and human resources (chmn. full com., chmn. subcom. on health 1971-80) and judiciary coms., also mem. Dem. steering & coordination com. Author: Decisions for a Decade, 1968, In Critical Condition: The Crisis in America's Health Care, 1972, Our Day and Generation, 1979, (with Mark O. Hatfield) Freeze: How You Can Help Prevent Nuclear War, 1979. Pres. Joseph P. Kennedy, Jr. Found., from 1961; trustee Children's Hosp. Med. Ctr., Boston, John F. Kennedy Library, Boston Symphony (emeritus), John F. Kennedy Ctr. for Performing Arts, Robert F. Kennedy Meml. Found., Boston Coll., Mass. Gen. Hosp. Served with AUS, 1951-53. Decorated knight comdr. Order of Phoenix (Greece), grande croce Al Merito della Republica Italiana (Italy), Order el Sol (Peru); named One of 10 Outstanding Young Men, U.S. Jaycees, 1967; recipient meritorious svc. citation U.S. Com. for Refugees and Am. Immigration and Citizenship Coun., Solidarity award Nat. Conf. on Soviet Jewry, award Nat. Mil. Family Assn., 1985, Homeric award Chian Fedn., Scopus award Am. Friends Hebrew U., Hubert H. Humphrey award Leadership Conf. on Civil Rights, others. Mem. Tech. Assessment Bd., Congl. Friends of Ireland, Biomed. Ethics Bd., Arms Control Observer Group, Commn. on the Bicentennial of the U.S. Constitution, Martin Luther King Jr. Fed. Holiday Commn., NAACP. Office: US Senate 315 Russell Senate Bldg Washington DC 20510-0001

KENNEDY, ELIZABETH LEVINE, public relations executive; b. N.Y.C., Sept. 16, 1963; arrived in Australia, 1987.; d. Stephen Maxwell and Rhea Joy (Cotler) Levine; m. Robert William Kennedy, Aug. 30, 1987; 1 child, Zoe Isabella. BA, Smith Coll., 1985; BS, U. New South Wales, 1986; MBA, Fordham U., 1996. Dep. mgr. Macy's, N.Y.C., 1988-89; mgr. Saks 5th Avenue, N.Y.C., 1989-90; buyer, merchandise mgr. Galeries Lafayette, N.Y.C., 1992-94; v.p. Fordham U. Mktg. Club, N.Y.C., 1995-96; sec. UN Internat. Sch. Parents Assn., 1997-98; dir. pub. rels. and mktg. Nine West Watches, Anne Klein Watches, Armitron Watches, Joseph Abboud Watches, 1998—; dir. pub. rels. E. Gluck Corp., 1998—. V.p. Fordham U. Mktg. Club, N.Y.C., 1995-96; v.p. UN Sch. Parents Assn., 1996-98. Mem. Am. Mktg. Assn., Shipley Sch. Alumni Assn., Smith Coll. Alumni Assn., Australian Am. Assn. Avocations: sailing, skiing, epicurean pursuits, surfing the internet.

KENNEDY, HARVEY JOHN, JR., lawyer; b. Barnesville, Ga., Apr. 9, 1924; s. Harvey John and Marisu (Reeves) K.; m. Jean McRitchie King, Apr. 8, 1950; children: Marisu, Jean Gay. LLB, U. Ga., 1949, JD, 1969; diplomate of psychology, Colo. Christian Coll., 1973. Bar: Ga. 1948. Atty. Lamar Electric Membership Corp., Barnesville, Ga., 1948—; county atty. Lamar County, Barnesville, Ga., 1950-52, 58-60; mem. Ga. Indigent Def. Coun., 1958, Ga. Bar Assn. Bd., 1958-59, State Bar of Ga. Bd. Govs. 1980-92; agt. Govt. Appeal Local Bd. 89, 1958; city atty. City of Barnesville, Ga., 1958-65, 83, City of Milner, Ga., 1963-68. Past pres. Barnesville (Ga.) Rotary Club, 1959-60. Capt. U.S. Army, 1942-46, ETO, PTO. Decorated Bronze Star medal and Combat Infantry badge. Mem. ABA, Ga. Trial Lawyers Assn. (v.p. 1972), State Bar Ga., Ga. Assn. Plaintiff's Trial Attys. (v.p. 1968), Am. Legion (comdr. post #25), Moose (32d degree shriner). Democrat. Presbyterian. Avocations: amateur radio, fishing. Office: PO Drawer B 217 Zebulon St Barnesville GA 30204-1126

KENNEDY, J. JACK, JR., court administrator, lawyer; b. Abingdon, Va., June 11, 1956; s. J. Jack Sr. and Bobbie Lee (Porter) K.; m. Susan Maura Muir, June 30, 1979; children: J. Jack III, Jillian Susanne. BS, U. Va., Wise, 1978; cert. in internat. study, U. London, 1977; MA in Polit. Sci., East Tenn. State U., 1982; JD equivalent, Va. State Bar, 1982; BA in Orgnl. Mgmt., Va. Intermont Coll., 1994. Bar: Va. 1982, U.S. Dist. Ct. (we. dist.) Va. 1982, U.S. Ct. Appeals (4th cir.) 1982, U.S. Tax Ct. 1982, U.S. Ct. Claims 1982, Supreme Ct. Va. 1982, U.S Internat. Ct. Trade 1992. Mem. Va. Ho. of Dels., Richmond, 1988-91, Va. State Senate, Richmond, 1991-92; clk. Cir. Ct. for Wise County and City of Norton, Va., 1995—; dir. Coalition for Open Govt., 2000-01; bd. dirs. Black Diamond Savs. Bank, E-Commerce Today, Ltd., Kennedy & Kennedy Investment Corp., Turkey Gap Coal Co., Inc., Southwestern Va. Tech. Coun. State pres. Young Dems. Va., 1984-85; nat. sec. Young Dems. Am., 1985; chmn. Norton (Va.) Dem. Com., 1982-92, 95-99, 9th Congl. Dist. Dem. Com., 1985-89; del. Dem. Nat. Conv., 1976, 84, 88, 92, 2000; state chmn. Va. Assn. Local Dem. Chairmen, 1986-87; bd. dirs., chmn. Va. Land Records Mgmt. Task Force, 1997-2000. Named Outstanding Young Dem. Va., 1985; recipient Tech. Innovation award Va. Supreme Ct., 1997; fellow Nat. Ctr. for State Cts., 1999. Fellow Inst. for Ct. Mgmt.; mem. ABA, Nat. Assn. for Ct. Mgmt., Va. State Bar, Va. Bar Assn., Wise County and City of Norton Bar Assn. (pres. 1997), Wise County C. of C. (v.p.), Va. Cir. Ct. Clks. Assn., Kiwanis, Phi Sigma Kappa. Baptist. Avocations: international travel, reading, Internet technology, space exploration. E-mail: jkennedy@naxs.com. Home and Office: 699 Fox Run Rd SE Norton VA 24273-2722 also: Court House PO Box 1248 Wise VA 24293-1248

KENNEDY, JERRIE ANN PRESTON, public relations executive; b. Quanah, Tex.. Student, Sunset Sch. Preaching, Lubbock, Tex., 1975-78, Jo-Susan Modeling Sch., Nashville, 1984, Film Actors Lab., 1986. Co-prodr. Vincent Cirrincione & Assocs., N.Y., 1986; freelance internat. mktg. and public rels. exec. U.S., and Papua, New Guinea, 1988—; military del. NATO Allies for The French Liaison, Ft. Hood, Tex., 1992. Asst. prodr. film Legend of Johnny Kahota, 1997; author screenplay, fed. and comty. pub. spl. events prodn. U.S.A. Recipient 1st and 3d pl. awards Modeling Assn. Am., N.Y.C., 1985.

KENNEDY, LINDA MANN, neuroscience educator, researcher; b. Malden, Mass., July 29, 1939; d. Alfred William Mann and Etta May (Maglue) Stenquist; m. Richard Dearman Kennedy, Apr. 15, 1961; children: Pamela Lee, Ruth Alexander. Diploma in nursing, New England Deaconess Hosp., 1959; AB, Simmons Coll., 1975; PhD, Harvard U., 1980. RN, Mass. Staff nurse Lahey Clinic, Boston, 1959-61, various hosps., Mass., Ga., 1962-72; tchg. asst. Simmons Coll., Boston, 1972-75; vis. rsch. fellow Cornell U., Ithaca, N.Y., 1978-81; rsch. assoc. Worcester (Mass.) Found. Exptl. Biology, 1980-83; rsch. asst. prof. Clark U., Worcester, 1983-84, asst. prof., 1984-91, assoc. prof., 1991—; assoc. prof. U. Mass. Med. Sch., 1995—; vis. scientist Weizmann Inst. Sci., Rehovot, Israel, 1991-92; co-founder, co-dir., dir. interdisciplinary neurosci. program Clark U., Worcester, 1984-91, 94-98; mem. adv. panel sensory sys. program and ILI program NSF, Washington, 1993-94; mem. area grant study sects. NIH, Nat. Inst. for Neurol. and Comm. Disorders and Stroke, Nat. Inst. for Deafness and Other Comm. Disorders, Washington, 1988-89; vis. program dir. sensory systems program, NSF, 2000—. Mem. editl. com. Univ. Press New England, 1989-91; contbr. articles to profl. jours. Mem. conservation com. Town of Framingham, Mass., 1973-74. Recipient Grad. fellowship for women Danforth Found., 1975-79, Rsch. Svc. award NIH, 1980-83, multiple Rsch. grants NSF, NIH, 1978—. Mem. New Eng. Psychol. Assn. (hon.), Assn. Chemoreception Scis. (exec. bd. councilor 1986-88), Soc. for Neurosci., Soc. for Values in Higher Edn., European Chemoreception Orgn., Internat. Brain Rsch. Orgn., Assn. for Women in Sci., Assn. Univ. Profs. Unitarian. Avocations: scuba diving, classical and jazz concerts, travel, reading mysteries. Home: 98 Waterford Dr Worcester MA 01602-3512 Office: Clark Univ Dept Biology Worcester MA 01610

KENNEDY, MARLA CATHERINE, psychologist; b. Milw., June 28, 1935; d. Raymond G. and Catherine (Wimmer) Mueller; m. William Robert Kennedy, Mar. 2, 1957; children: Joseph, Timothy, Kristin, William, Daniel. BS, Alverno, Milw., 1956; MA, U. Minn., 1983, postgrad., 1983-1989. Lic. psychologist, lic. marriage and family therapist. Intern with mentally ill and mentally retarded Met. Clin., Mpls., 1984-85; pvt. practice psychology, marriage and family therapy Mpls., 1985—; spkr. in field; part-time at Family Svc. Greater St. Paul, 1989-98; dir., co-counselor Adlerian Family Edn. Ctr., 1983-85. Contbr. articles to profl. jours. Bd. dirs. Books for Africa, 1997-98; co-founder Community Line (now First Call for Help); pres. Legions of PTAs; active YWCA Shelter for Women, St. Paul; vol. Rams Juvenile Justice, 1985—. Mem. Am. Acad. Nurology Aux. (bd. dirs.), Minn. Assn. Marriage and Family Therapists, Minn. Assn. Group Psychotherapists (pres. 1998-00), Alfred Adler Assn. (bd. dirs. 1965-80), AAUW (bd. dirs.), New Century (bd. dirs.), Mensa, Phi Lambda Theta. Unitarian. Avocations: swimming, tennis, reading.

KENNEDY, MARY SUSSOCK, artist; b. Liverpool, Eng., Oct. 29, 1926; came to U.S., 1951; d. Charles Archibald and Maria (Mullin) Sussock; m. Rogers Jack Kennedy, May 18, 1946 (dec. Jan. 1987); children: Jacollyn Fenny-Maria, Beverley Gillian, Kimberley Tara. AAS with highest honors, Fashion Inst. Tech., 1975; BA summa cum laude, Montclair State Coll., 1977, postgrad., 1977-78. Portrait, stage and wedding photographer Wilkinson and Kennedy, Liverpool, 1943-47; freelance artist Montville, N.J., 1956-73, Key Largo, Fla., 1984—; grad. asst. in sculpture Montclair State Coll., Upper Montclair, N.J., 1977-78; diamond stylii maker Rogers Kennedy Inc., Saddle Brook, N.J., 1978-84. One woman show at Fashion Inst. Tech., 1974; exhibited in group shows at Smithsonian Instn., Washington, 1963, Montclair Art Mus., 1964, U.S. Custom House, N.Y.C., 1979, also exhibit opened by Princess Grace of Monaco, 1960; sculpture exhibited in two person show at Montclair State Coll., 1977. Mem. Phi Kappa Phi. Democrat. Episcopalian. Avocations: anthropology, reading, travel, gardening, sewing. Home: PO Box 2560 Key Largo FL 33037-7560

KENNEDY, MICHAEL PETER, engineering educator, researcher; b. Dublin, Apr. 25, 1963; s. Michael Joseph and Hilda K. BE in Electronics, U. Coll. Dublin, 1984; MSEE, U. Calif., Berkeley, 1987, PhD in Elec. Engring., 1991. Test engr. Philips, Dublin, 1980-85; tchg. asst. U. Calif., Berkeley, 1986, postgrad. researcher, 1986-91, postdoc. rsch. engr., 1992; lectr. Univ. Coll. Dublin, 1992-96, sr. lectr., 1996-99, assoc. prof., 1999-2000; prof., head dept. Univ. Coll. Cork, 2000—; vis. prof. Swiss Fed. Inst. of Tech., Lausanne, Switzerland, 1992, 1997, BME, Tech. U. of Budapest, 1995, 98, 99; cons. U. Calif., Berkeley, 1996. Author: (software) ABC-Adventures in Bifurcation and Chaos, 1993; contbr. articles to profl. jours.; inventor in field. U. Calif. Regents fellow, 1988; scholar Semiconductor Rsch. Corp., USA, 1990; recipient bursary in elec. engring. Nat. U. Ireland, 1984. Fellow IEEE, IEE, European Cirs. Soc. Avocations: reading, walking, singing, travel. Office: Dept Microelectronic Engrng, Univ Coll, Cork Ireland

KENNEDY, RICARDO IGNACIO, lawyer; b. Buenos Aires, May 5, 1969; s. Ricardo Ignacio Kennedy and María Angélica Puelles. Grad. in law, Cath. U. Argentina, Buenos Aires, 1994. Trainee Cleary Gottlieb Steen & Hamilton, N.Y.C., 1994; assoc. Brons & Salas, Buenos Aires, 1995-97, Kennedy & Assocs., Buenos Aires, 1997—; prof. law Nat. U. Buenos Aires, 1997—. Mem. Internat. Bar Assn., Buenos Aires Bar Assn., Jockey Club. Roman Catholic. Avocations: music, painting, soccer, golf, boxing. Office: Kennedy & Assocs, Av Cordoba 1215, 1055 Buenos Aires Argentina

KENNEDY, ROBERT, international affairs educator; b. Newark, Sept. 20, 1939; s. Cecil L. (stepfather) and Marie E. (Rega) Smith; m. Vevonna M. Clark, Nov. 4, 1966; children: Shaun C., Teague C. BS, USAF Acad., Colorado Springs, Colo., 1963; MA, Georgetown U., 1964, PhD, 1978. With USAF, 1963-71; fgn. affairs officer U.S. Arms Control and Disarmament Agy., Washington, 1974; sr. researcher strategic studies inst. U.S. Army War Coll., Carlisle, Pa., 1974-83; Dwight D. Eisenhower prof. nat. security studies U.S. Army War Coll., 1983-85; dep. comdt. NATO Def. Coll., Rome, 1985-88; prof. dept. nat. security studies U.S. Army War Coll., 1988-89; prof. sch. internat. affairs Ga. Inst. Tech., Atlanta, 1989-97; dep. dir., co. dir. Ctr. for Internat. Strategy, Tech. and Policy, Atlanta, 1990-97; dir. Marshall European Ctr. for Security Studies, Garmisch, Germany, 1997—; cons. Inst. for Pub. Policy Devel., Washington, 1977-78. Author, editor: The Defense of the West: Strategic and European Security Issues, 1984, U.S. Policy Towards the Soviet Union: A Long Term Western Prospective 1987-2000, 1988, Alternative Conventional Defense Postures for the European Theater, Vol. I, 1990, Vol. 2, 1992, Vol. 3, 1993; mem. editl. bd. Atlantic Community Quarterly, 1987-89, ORBIS, 1982-87; contbr. articles to profl. publs.; founding gen. editor The Atlanta Papers, 1996—. Mem. adv. bd. Notre Dame Internat. Sch., Rome, 1986-88, Cumberland Valley High Sch., Mechanicsburg, Pa.; mem. exec. com., chmn. joint chiefs of staff Process for Accreditation of Joint Edn., Washington, 1991-97; acad. assoc. Atlantic Coun. U.S., 1989—. With USAFR, 1971-86. Recipient Superior Civilian Svc. award, U.S. Army, 1989; named Oustanding Young Men of Am., U.S. Jaycees, 1972; Fulbright scholar, 1965-66; Georgetown U. fellow, 1974, Atlantic Coun. U.S. non-resident sr. fellow, 1983-84. Mem. Internat. Inst. for Strategic Studies, Internat. Studies Assn. (chmn. sect. on mil. studies 1985-87). Avocations: water and snow skiing, surf boarding, woodworking, furniture making. Home: Riessersee Strasse 20, 82467 Garmisch Germany Office: Marshall Ctr Unit 24502 Box 42 APO AE 09053-4502

KENNEDY, ROGER I.L., psychoanalyst, child psychiatrist; b. London, Jan. 12, 1949; s. Philip and Trudy S. (Summer) K.; m. Elizabeth C. Jessett (div. 1995); 1 child, Tom; m. Jennifer Boost; children: Sarah, George; stepchildren: Rose, Jack. BSc, U. London, 1970, MBBS, 1973. Cert. psychoanalyst, 1981. Cons. child psychiatrist Cassell Hosp., Family Unit, London, 1982—. Author: The Works of J. Lacan, 1986, Freedom to Relate, 1994, Child Abuse, Psychotherapy and the Law, 1997, The Elusive Human Subject, 1998; editor: The Family as In-Patient, 1987. Fellow Royal Coll. Psychiatry; mem. Brit. Psychoanalytical Soc. (tng. analyst 1994—). Avocations: football, the arts, fatherhood. Office: Cassel Hosp, 1 Ham Common, Richmond TU10 7JF, England

KENNEDY, THOMAS PATRICK, financial executive; b. N.Y.C., Oct. 13, 1932; s. Andrew Francis and Marie P. (Scullen) K.; m. Mary P. Drennan, Jan. 14, 1956 (dec.); children: Thomas Patrick, Kevin M. (dec.), Michael J., Mary P. Kennedy Handsman, Deborah A. Kennedy Carter. BS, St. Peter's Coll., 1958; postgrad., Seton Hall U., 1959. Accountant Haskins & Sells CPAs, N.Y.C., 1953-54; staff Emerson Radio & TV, N.Y.C., 1957-58; various exec. positions CBS, N.Y.C., 1958-67; with Ford Found., N.Y.C., 1967; dir. fin. Pub. Broadcasting Lab., N.Y.C., 1967-69; with Children's TV Workshop (Sesame St.), N.Y.C., 1969-80, v.p. fin. and adminstrn., 1969-78, treas., 1969-78, sr. v.p., 1978-80; exec. dir. Ctr. Non-Broadcast TV, 1980-85; pres. Tomken Mgmt., Ltd., 1980—, chmn. bd., 1983—; chmn. bd., chief exec. officer Effie Techs., Inc., 1984—; v.p., corp. fin. Jersey Capital Mkts Group, Inc., 1987-88; chief exec. officer, chmn. bd. Corp. Strategies Group, Inc., 1988-89; v.p. Vantage Securities, Inc. (co-venture with Whitehall Fin. Group), 1991-94; cons. in field; bd. advisers Franciscan Comm. Ctr.; bd. dirs., exec. dir. Ctr. for Non-Broadcast TV, 1980-85. With C.E., U.S. Army, 1954-55, Korea. Mem. Fin. Execs. Inst., Internat. Radio and TV Soc., Inst. Broadcast Fin. Mgmt., Nat. Assn. Accts., Internat. Broadcast Inst., Internat. Inst. Comm., Internat. Assn. Fin. Execs., Am. Assn. Individual Investors, Am. Legion, Korean War Vets., N.Y. Athletic Club, KC. Republican. Roman Catholic. Fax: 321-799-0812. E-mail: tompk@worldnet.att.net.

KENNEDY, X. J. (JOSEPH KENNEDY), writer; b. Dover, N.J., Aug. 21, 1929; s. Joseph Francis and Agnes (Rauter) K.; m. Dorothy Mintzlaff, 1962; children: Kathleen, David, Matthew, Daniel, Joshua. BSc, Seton Hall U., 1950; MA, Columbia U., 1951; cert., U. Paris, France, 1956; LHD (hon.), Lawrence U., 1988; DFA (hon.), Adelphi U., 1998. Teaching fellow U. Mich., Ann Arbor, 1956-60; instr. English U. Mich., 1960-62; lectr. English Woman's Coll., U. N.C., Greensboro, 1962-63; asst. prof. English Tufts U., Medford, Mass., 1963-67; assoc. prof. Tufts U., 1967-73, prof., 1973-79; vis. lectr. Wellesley Coll., 1964, U. Calif., Irvine, 1966-67. Author: Nude Descending a Staircase, 1961, 2d edit., 1994, Introduction To Poetry, 1966, 9th edit., (with Dana Gioia) 1997, Growing into Love, 1969, Breaking and Entering, 1971, Emily Dickinson in Southern California, 1974, Celebrations After the Death of John Brennan, 1974, (with J.E. Camp, Keith Waldrop) Three Tenors, One Vehicle, 1975, One Winter Night in August, 1975, Introduction to Fiction, 1976, (with Dana Gioia) 7th edit., 1998, Literature, 1976, (with Dana Gioia) 7th edit., 1998, The Phantom Ice Cream Man, 1979, (with Dorothy M. Kennedy) The Bedford Reader, 1982, (with Dorothy M. Kennedy and Jane Aaron) 7th edit., 2000, Did Adam Name the Vinegarroon?, 1982, French Leave: Translations, 1983, Hangover Mass, 1984, (with Dorothy M. Kennedy) Knock at a Star: a Child's Introduction to Poetry, 1982, revised edit., 1999, The Owlstone Crown, 1983, The Forgetful

Wishing-Well, 1985, Cross Ties: Selected Poems, 1985, Brats, 1986; (with Dorothy M. Kennedy) The Bedford Guide for College Writers, 1987, 5th edit., (with Dorothy M. Kennedy and Sylvia A. Holladay) 1999, Ghastlies, Goops and Pincushions, 1989, Fresh Brats, 1990, Winter Thunder, 1990, The Kite That Braved Old Orchard Beach., 1991, (with Dorothy M. Kennedy) Talking Like the Rain, 1992, The Beasts of Bethlehem, 1992, Dark Horses: New Poems, 1992, Drat These Brats!, 1993, The Minimus Poems, 1996, Uncle Switch, 1997, The Eagle as Wide as the World, 1997, Elympics, 1999; poetry editor: Paris Rev., 1961-64; editor: (with J.E. Camp) Mark Twain's Frontier, 1963, (with J.E. Camp, Keith Waldrop) Pegasus Descending, 1971, Messages, 1973, Tygers of Wrath: poems of hate, anger and invective, 1981; editor, pub. (with Dorothy M. Kennedy) Counter/Measures mag, 1971-74. Judge Nat. Coun. on Arts poetry book selections, 1969, 70, T.S. Eliot prize Thomas Jefferson Univ. Press, 1998, X.J. Kennedy poetry award Tex. Rev., 1998, 99. With USN, 1951-55. Recipient Lamont Poetry award Acad. Am. Poets, Bess Hokin prize Poetry mag., 1961; Golden Rose award New Eng. Poetry Club, 1974; Los Angeles Times book award for poetry, 1985, Michael Braude award for light verse Am. Acad. and Inst. Arts and Letters, 1989, Aiken-Taylor award U. of the South, 1999, Excellence of Poetry for Children award, Nat. Coun. Tchrs. of English, 2000; grant Nat. Council Arts and Humanities, 1967-68; Shelley Meml. award, 1970; Bread Loaf fellow in poetry Middlebury Coll., 1960; Guggenheim fellow, 1973-74; Bruern fellow in Am. civilization U. Leeds, 1974-75. Mem. Assn. Lit. Scholars and Critics, John Barton Wolgamot Soc., PEN (mem. coun. New Eng. 1996—), MLA, Poetry Soc. Am., Nat. Coun. Tchrs. English, Authors Guild, Phi Beta Kappa, Sigma Tau Delta (hon.). Home: 22 Revere St Lexington MA 02420-4424

KENNETT, KEITH FRANKLIN, psychologist, educator; b. Adelaide, Australia, July 18, 1935; s. Ernett Franklin and Olive Myrtle (Bowes) K.; m. Barbara Eileen Henderson, 1957; children: Elizabeth, Paul, James; m. Gaile Louise Hanson, Jan. 4, 1992. Diploma in Tchg., Adelaide Tchr.'s Coll., 1955; Diploma in Edn., U. Adelaide, 1965, BA in English and History, 1967, Assoc. Univ. Adelaide Pub. Adminstrn., 1968, MEd, 1976; MA in Psychology, U. Saskatchewan (Can.), 1969, PhD in Psychology, 1972. Registered psychologist, New South Wales and Australia. Prin., owner Oxford Coaching Coll., Adelaide, 1962-68; pvt. clin. practice, vocat. guidance Can., 1970-77; pvt. clin. practice New South Wales, Australia, 1977—; tchr., prin. South Australia Edn. Dept., 1955—; head dept. psychology Salisbury Tchrs. Coll., South Australia, 1970; asst. prof. St. Francis Xavier U. and U. Coll. Cape Breton (N.S.), Can., 1970-72; assoc. prof. St. Francis Xavier U. and U. Coll. Cape Breton (N.S.), 1973-77; prof., dean edn. U. We. Sydney, Nepean, Australia, 1977-91; prof. U.S. Sports Acad., 1984—; mng. dir. Excelsior Coll. Pty. Ltd., Sydney, 1998—; co-owner, co-creator Cape Breton Playventure Way; exec. dir. Jeffries Industries Ltd., 1993-94; past dep. chmn., internat. coord. Kampala (Uganda) Heart and Gen. Hosp., 1996; mng. dir. R.R.C.S. Employment Svcs. Pty. Ltd.; non-exec. chmn. Australian Wine & Living, First Oceania Securities, 1997; chmn., mng. dir. various cos.; assessor, counselor work adjustment tng. programs Province of N.S., Can.; vocat. assessor Dept. Manpower Govt. Can.; prin. asst., lectr. Univ. Sarkatchewm, 1968-69;expert witness Supreme Ct.; cons., lectr., presenter, spkr. in field. Author: Cash In Your Career: Making the Move, 1999, Cash In Your Career: Setting-Getting Goals, 1999; co-author: English Language Communication Skills: Basic Phonics, 1997; contbr. chpts. to books, numerous articles to profl. jours. Active various sr. bds., Can. Can. doct. fellow. Fellow Inst. Chartered Secs. and Adminstrs.; mem. Australian Inst. Co. Dirs., Australian Psychol. Soc., Inst. Pvt. Clin. Psychologists Australia, Am. Coll. Forensic Examiners (Diploma 1996), Internat. Coun. Psychologists (past exec. dir.), Assn. Psychologists N.S. (Can.) (past pres.), Nat. Assn. Autisim (pres. 1985). Home: 157 B Old Northern Rd, 2154 Castle Hill NSW, Australia Office: Excelsior Coll, Level 8 540 George St, 2000 Sydney NSW, Australia

KENNEY, CHRISTOPHER SAYLES, adult education educator; b. Fall River, Mass., Aug. 27, 1962; s. Daniel M. Kenney and Carol S. Smith. MusB, DePauw U., 1988; MusM, Ohio State U., 1989, Mus D, 1992. Tchg. assoc. Ohio State U., Columbus, 1990-92; vis. asst. prof. U. Rio Grande, Ohio, 1993-00. Composer: Symphony No. 1; Winding an Exiles' Rd., 1987, Trilmalchio, 1989, Concerto for Soprano Saxophone and Brass Quintet, 1991, Symphony No. 2: Night Piece, 1992. Bd. dirs. Valley Artist Series. Mem. Broadcust Music, Coll. Music Soc. Avocations: cycling, bonsai. Office: U Rio Grande Fine & Performing Arts Ctr Rio Grande OH 45674

KENNEY, DION PATRICK, business strategist, entrepreneur; b. Middletown, N.Y., Apr. 26, 1962; s. John Michel Kenney and Joan Elizabeth (Bennett) Klein. BS in Physics, Fla. State U., 1984; MS in Physics, Tex. A&M U., 1989; MBA, U. Pa., 1995. Engr. Navair-Dept. of Navy, Lakehurst, N.J., 1985-86, Stratford, Conn., 1986-87; software engr. Unisys, Houston, 1990-93; mktg. and bus. planning profl. Health Care Devel. Internat., Tarrytown, N.Y., 1993-97; founder, pres. Cybernet Info. Systems, Yorktown Heights, N.Y., 1994—; COO AHSC Group, LLC, Tarrytown, N.Y., 1997—. Home: 8 Parkway Dr Yorktown Heights NY 10598-6407 Office: 777 Old Sawmill River Rd Tarrytown NY 10591

KENNEY, DONNA DENISE, accountant; b. Bklyn., Oct. 4, 1960; d. Donald and Sherry Sheila (Nedol) Yules; m. Eugene L. Kenney, Jr., May 31, 1981; children: Kyle Asher, Graham Stewart. BBA in Bus. Mgmt., Adelphi U., 1981, MBA with distinction, 1989. CPA, N.Y. Grad. asst. dept. acctg. and law Adelphi U., Garden City, N.Y., 1984-89; mgr. Susnick and Harris, CPAs, Cedarhurst, N.Y., 1994-98, David Berdon & Co., LLP, Jericho, N.Y., 1998-99; tax mgr. Bertelsmann, Inc., N.Y.C., 1999—. Mem. N.Y. State Soc. CPAs (com. mem. acctg. and auditing Suffolk chpt. 1991-92, award of honor 1989), Delta Mu Delta, Eta Chi Alpha. Office: Bertlesmann Inc 1540 Broadway New York NY 10036-4039

KENNEY, JOHN MICHEL, architect; b. N.Y.C., Oct. 22, 1938; s. John Peter and Madeline Loretta (Fuller) K.; children: John Michel, James Brian, Dion Patrick. AAS, Orange County Community Coll., 1966; student, Columbia U., 1969. Registered arch., N.Y., N.J., Conn., Ill., Pa., Del., Ill., S.C., N.C., Ga. V.p., ptnr., dir. health facilities Perkins & Will Architects, White Plains, N.Y., 1968-81; mng. mem. AHSC Archs. P.C., Tarrytown, N.Y., 1981—, AHSC/Melellan, Copenhagen; mng. mem. AHSC Group LLC; co-chmn. AHSC/Destefano and Ptnrs., Chgo.; pres. ArquInter-AHSE Europe, Madrid. Vice chmn. Orange County Dem. Coms., N.Y., 1968; chmn. Dem. Com., Middletown, N.Y., 1966-68; co-chmn. Robert Kennedy Presdl. Election Primary, Orange/Sullivan County, 1968; mem. United Hosp. Fund; bd. mem. Aging in Am. Found. Mem. AIA, Nat. Coun. Archtl. Registration Bds., N.Y. Soc. Hosp. Planning, Am. Assn. Hosp. Planners, N.Y. Acad. Scis. Democrat. Avocations: skiing, sailing, travelling. Office: AHSC Architects 777 Old Saw Mill River Rd Tarrytown NY 10591-6717

KENNTEMICH, WOLFGANG, television editor; b. Koln, Germany, Oct. 28, 1946; s. Hans August and Liesel Maria (Boisseree) K.; m. Anita Margarete Eschweiler (div. 1992); children: Bastian, Saskia, Alexander, Christopher, Maximilian. Abitur, Gymnasium, Coesfeld, Germany, 1966. Officer, lieutenant Bundeswehr, Germany, 1966-70; editor Westf. Nachrichten, Munster, 1970-73, News Agy. DDP, Germany, 1973-83; buero chief Bild Bild Am Sonntag, Bonn, 1983-90; chief corres. Gruner & Jahr, Hamburg, 1990; editor in chief MDR/ARD TV, Dresden, 1991—; lectr. Fachhochschule, 1994—. Author: Das War Die DDR, 1993, Helmut Kohl, 1994, Die Neue Republik, 1995, Aktien-Fieber, 1997; anchor radio-show: Around the World, 1964. With Luftwaffe, 1966-70. Avocations: golf, tennis. Office: Mitteldeutscher Rundfunk, Kant Str 71-73, D 01169 Dresden Germany

KENNY, ALAN DENNIS, international sales executive, computer educator; b. Quebec City, Quebec, Can., Nov. 12, 1963; s. Thomas Geer and Charlene Mae (Hecker) K. Student, U.S. Naval Acad., 1982, U. Minn., 1983-89. Engring. technician Honeywell, Inc., Hopkins, Minn., 1984-89; sales acct. mgr. Gen Rad, Inc., Chgo., 1989-90, Milpitas, Calif., 1990-2000; internat. sales mgr. Spectral Dynamics, Inc. (formerly Gen Rad, Inc.), Santa Clara, Calif., 1994—; v.p. ops., bd. mem. Transworld Trading Co. Inc., Windsor, Calif., 1996—; internat. bus. mgr. Vibro-Acoustic Scis., San Diego, 2000—. Joint contbr. disk drive mounting patent. With USN, 1982. Recipient Spl. Achievement award Honeywell, Inc., 1985, 87, 88, Creative Sci. award 3M, Inc., 1981, Honeywell Math and Sci. Excellence scholarship, 1982. Mem. Ins. Environ. Scis. Office: 12555 High Bluff Dr Ste 310 San Diego CA 92130-2056

KENRICK, PAUL, botanist; b. Bath, England, Oct. 20, 1960; s. Michael Ernest and Pauline (Murray) K.; m. Ann Joachimowicz, Sept. 22, 1990; childre; Carole, Julien. BS, U. Wales, Cardiff, 1982, PhD, 1988. Rsch. assoc. Field Mus., Chgo., 1989-92; asst. Swedish Mus. Natural History, Stockholm, 1992-93, sr. curator, 1993-98; palebotanist The Natural History Mus., London, 1998—; guest rschr. Swedish Mus. Natural History, 1992. Author: The Origin and Early diversification of Land Plants, 1997. Recipient Michael A. Cichan award Botanical Soc. Am., 1991; rsch. fellow U. Liege, Belgium, 1988-89. Fellow Linnean Soc. London; mem. Systematics Assn. (coun. mem.), Palaeontological Assn. Office: The Natural History Mus, Cromwell Rd, London SW7 5BD, England

KENT, HOWARD, health foundation director; b. London, Apr. 2, 1919; s. James John Adam and Marion May (Battishall) Pittock-Buss; m. Evelyn Olive Marchant, Nov. 15, 1946; children: Rosemary Jane, Julian David, Jennifer Marion, James Edward, Elisabeth Alice. Ed., Whitgift, Surrey, Eng. Editor North London Observer, 1941-55; chief picture editor News Chronicle, London, 1955-60; picture editor Lawrence of Arabia, Amman, Jordan, 1961-62; prodr. for film, stage and TV London, 1962-72; founding dir. Yoga for Health Found., Bedfordshire, Eng., 1972—; advisor Internat. Integrated Health Assn., Winchester, Eng., 1994—, Internat. Assn. Yoga Therapists, L.A., 1993—. Author: Day-By-Day Yoga, 1973, Key Facts: Yoga, 1979, Yoga for the Disabled, 1985, Complete Yoga Course, 1994, Breathe Better--Feel Better, 1997, Complete Illustrated Guide to Yoga, 1999. Mem. com. Indian Freedom Campaign, London, 1942-45; mem. Parliamentary Group for Complementary and Alternative Medicine, London, 1993—. Recipient Lifetime award Unity in Yoga, U.S., 1995. Mem. N.Y. Acad. Scis. Avocations: cinema, music. Home: Highfields Norfolk Rd, Turvey MK43 8DU, England Office: Yoga for Health Found, Ickwell Bury, Biggleswade SG18 9EF, England

KENT, JAN GEORG, computer consultant; b. Oslo, Norway, Nov. 23, 1942; s. Rolf and Ragna Katarina (Kent) Nielssen; m. Elisabet Bigset, Mar. 20, 1973; 1 child, William. MS, U. Oslo, 1966, PhD, 1979. Lectr. U. Waterloo, Ont., Can., 1967; system programmer Stanford (Calif.) U., 1967; researcher Norwegian Def. Rsch. Est., Norway, 1968-69; stipendiat IBM Norway, Oslo, 1969-72, systems engr., 1977-79; researcher Norwegian Computing Ctr., Oslo, 1972-77; chief cons. Tandberg Data, Oslo, 1979-81; chief engr. Norwegian Def. Command, Norway, 1981-85; chief cons. Christiania Bank, Oslo, 1985-92; sr. quality assurance engr. Sci. Project Contractors, Oslo, 1992-93; IT dept. advisor Directorate of Customs and Excise, Oslo, 1993—. Contbr. articles to profl. publs. Mem. IEEE, ACM (Norwegian chpt. chair 1973—). Lutheran.

KENT, JEANNE YVONNE, artist; b. Lawrence, Mass., Feb. 6, 1947; d. Gerard George and Cecile Fecteau Galarneau; m. Martin Joseph Kent, Dec. 4, 1971; children: Nicole Michelle, Sarah. Student, Lowell State Tchr.'s Coll., 1966-68, Northea. U., 1970-73; BFA, Mass. Coll. Art, 1989. Resident asst., slide lectr. Elderhostel Mass. Coll. Art, Boston, 1988; slide lectr. Weymouth North H.S., East Weymouth, Mass., 1990, 93; instr. art Lee Wards Arts and Crafts Store, Quincy, Mass., 1990, Roslindale Comm. Ctr., Roslindale, Mass., 1996. One-woman shows include Rubin O'Barry's Coffee Shop, Jamaica Plain, Mass., 1989, Brookline Pub. Libr., Brookline Art Soc., 1995, West Roxbury (Mass.) Pub. Libr., 1995, Boston Publ. Libr. Jamaica Plain Branch, 1998, Jamo's Restaurant, Roslindale, Mass., 1998; exhibited in group shows at Mass. Coll. Art, Boston, 1988-89, 95, Arts in the Pks., Boston, 1989, Brookline (Mass.) Art Soc., 1989-97, Boston Visual Artist's Union, 1990, Arnold Arboretum of Harvard U., Jamaica Plain, 1992, West Roxbury Pub. Libr., 1996, Picture This Gallery, West Roxbury, 1996, West Roxbury Pub. Libr., 1996-97, Greater Roslindale Art Assn., 1997, Boston City Hall, 1997, State House, Boston, Jamaica Plain Art Assn., 1998, Lowell St. Gallery, Cambridge Art Assn., 1998, Eliot Sch. Fine and Applied Arts, Jamaica Plain, 1998; contbr. poems to various publs. Recipient Silver medal World of Poetry, 1989, Intergenerational Poetry hon. mention award West Roxbury Pub. Libr., 1989, 4th Pl. painting award Dedham (Mass.) Arts and Crafts Fair, 1990, Calendar Illustration painting award 1st ann. Dedham Cmty. Art Competition, Dedham Cmty. Ho. Gallery, 1993, Juror's Choice award Cambridge Art Assn. image and verse show, 1998; poems named Best Poems of the '90s, Nat. Libr. Poetry. Mem. Cambridge Art Assn., Greater Roslindale Arts Assn. Jehovah's Witness. Avocations: reading, poetry, tennis, walking, diary-keeping. Home: 5 Eastland Rd Jamaica Plain MA 02130-4616

KENT, JULIE, ballet dancer, actress, model; b. Bethesda, Md., July 11, 1969; d. Charles Lindbergh and Jennifer Elsie (Machirus) Cox; m. Victor Barbee, 1996. Grad. high sch., Potomac, Md. Apprentice Am. Ballet Theatre, N.Y.C., 1985-86, mem. corps de ballet, 1986-1990, soloist, 1990-93, prin. dancer, 1993—. Starring role (film) Dancers, 1986; performed as a guest artist nationally and internationally. Recipient Prix de Lausanne Internat. Ballet competition, 1986, 1st prize at Erik Bruhn Competition in Toronto, 1993; named one of 50 Most Beautiful People, People Mag., 1993. Office: Am Ballet Theatre 890 Broadway Fl 3 New York NY 10003*

KENT, MARTIN, biogeography educator; b. Newcastle, Eng., Feb. 10, 1950; s. Paul and Joan (Keyworth) K.; m. Susanna Mary Kulisa (div. 1982); 1 child, Jonathan Paul; m. Gabrielle Ann Blamey, 1997. BSc in Geography with honors, U. Sheffield, Eng., 1970, PhD in Landscape Arch., 1979; MSc in Conservation, U. Coll. London, 1971, Diploma in Conservation, 1971. Lectr. in biogeography Plymouth (Eng.) Poly., 1973-82; sr. lectr. in biogeography Poly. South West, 1982-90; prin. lectr. in biogeography U. Plymouth, 1990-95, reader in biogeography, 1995-98, prof. biogeography, 1998—; cons. Didcot Instrument Co., 1977-78, Dept. Environment-Water Rsch. Ctr./ENSIS, U. Coll. London, 1988-95, Joint Nature Conservation Com., 1995-96. rschr., examiner, presenter in field. author: Practical Ecology for Geography and Biology, 1985, Vegetation Description and Analysis: A Practical Approach, 1992; editor: (with D.D. Gilbertson) Nutrient Cycling and Land Use Management, 1987, (with A.R. Jones and R.E. Weaver) Geographical Information Systems and Remote Sensing in Land Use Planning, 1993, (with D. Gilbertson and J. Grattan) The Outer Hebrides: The Last 14000 Years, 1996; mem. editl. bd. Jour. Applied Geography, 1987-96; contbr. chpts. to books and articles to profl. jours. Grantee Natural Environ. Rsch. Coun., 1992, Brit. Ecol. Soc., 1992, HEFC/DevR, 1994. Mem. Brit. Ecol. Soc., Internat. Assn. Vegetation Sci., Inst. Brit. Geographers (biogeography study group). Avocations: violinist, botanist, naturalist, walking, music. Office: Dept Geog Scis U Plymouth, Drake Circus, Plymouth Devon PL4 SAA, England

KENT, MOLLIE, writer, publishing executive, editor; b. Abilene, Tex., July 21, 1933; d. Henry Lee and Clyde Radia (Free) Summers; m. Paul Raymond Kintzinger, June 15, 1954 (div. July 1982); children: Katrina, Alice, Sarah. Student, Tulsa (Okla.) U., 1962-64, U. N.Mex., 1970-72. Lic. insurance and real estate agt., N.Mex. Owner, pub. Jemez Pub. Co., Jemez Springs, N.Mex., 1976-81, Albuquerque and Bernalillo, N.Mex., 1976-81; pub., editor S.W. Chronicle mag., La Plata, 1999—; pub., editor Jemez Mountain Views, 1976-80, Sandoval County Rev., 1977-80, Sandia Sun, 1979-81; assoc. editor, advt. mgr. Aztec (N.Mex.) Local News, 1993-98. Republican. Avocations: writing, travel, music, art, family. Home: PO Box 360 La Plata NM 87418-0360

KENT, PAULA, public relations, marketing and management consultant, lecturer; b. N.Y.C.; d. John and Estelle (Frye) Smith; BS, State Tchrs. Coll., Worcester, Mass., 1939; MS, Boston U., 1941; m. Stanley J. Lloyd, Jan. 23, 1943; children: Diane Adrienne Noel, Robin Michele Cheri, Kevin Christopher Kent, Gisele Nicolette Jolie. Methods engr. Internat. Bus. Machines, 1941-42; personnel dir., fashion editor Daily Jour., San Diego, also radio sta. KSDJ, 1946-48; fashion and beauty editor, columnist The San Diego Union, 1949-64; promotion dir. The San Diego Union and the Evening Tribune, 1948-71, also UCLA Extension Div. Faculty, 1961-63; pub. relations, mktg. and mgmt. cons., 1970—; v.p. La Jolla Clin. Labs., Inc., 1970-81. Lectr. mktg. workshop tour, speaker at seminars, Brussels, London, Paris, Madrid, 1972; speaker nat. and regional confs. in maj. U.S. cities; del. Nat. Fedn. Press. Women Touring Russia, 1973. Formerly active ARC, Am. Cancer Soc., Med. Aux. San Diego. Officer USN; lt. (sr.g.) USCG, 1942-45. Recipient over 158 awards 1950—, including: 39 nat., 18 western states, over 100 Calif. state awards, 13 Lulus L.A. Advt. Women's Assn., 1 local award, resulting from ann. competitions sponsored by Los Angeles Advt. Women's Club, Nat. Newspaper Publs. Assn., Calif. Press Women, Los Angeles Sales Promotion Execs. Assn., Nat. Fedn. Press Women, Editor and Pub. Mag.; recipient Outstanding Service award Boy Scouts Am., 1962, 65; civic awards City of San Diego, Distinguished Service award Investment Edn. Inst., Detroit, 1969, Golden Spear award Twin Cities Sales Promotion Execs. Assn., Mpls., 1965; Outstanding Service thru Annual Investment Clinics N.Y. Stock Exchange, 1964, L.A. Theta Sigma Phi Walter O'Malley Unique Coverage award, 1968; named Woman of Achievement San Diego, 1958, 59, 64, Woman of Valor, 1958, Woman of Year, San Diego, 1965, Woman of Achievement, Nat. Fedn. Bus. and Profl. Women's Clubs, 1966; Advt. Man of Distinction, San Diego, 1970, Don award, Legion of Portola, 1968.; fellow Boston U. 1940-41. Mem. Advt. and Sales Club San Diego (dir. 1951-71), Sales and Marketing Execs. Club San Diego (pres. 1970-71), Personnel Mgmt. Assn. (hon. mem., plaque 1963), Sales and Mktg. Execs. Internat. (dir. at large 1971-73), Sales Promotion Execs. Assn. Los Angeles (Man of Year 1965), Am. Advt. Fedn. (western region chmn. edn. com., mem. nat. edn. com. 1971-72) Nat. Newspaper Promotion Assn. (pres. Western region 1964, dir. 1968-70, chmn. western regional conv. 1964), Calif. Assn. Press Women, Nat. Fedn. Press Women, Internat. Newspaper Promotion Assn. (bd. dirs. 1971-73), Am. Mgmt. Assn. (San Diego pres's coun. bus., profl. womens' clubs outstanding svc. plaque 1969). Roman Catholic. Editor: Monthly Bull., Personnel Mgmt. Assn., 1955-59, monthly bull., Sales Execs. Club. Chmn. San Diego's Ann. Giant Sales Rally, 1953-55, 70-71, co-chmn., 1964, 65; chmn. Advt. Recognition Week Campaign, 1953-54, Nat. Unltd. Hydroplane Races, San Diego, 1953-54, sponsor rep. Evening Tribune; pub. relations advisor Nat. Mrs. Am. Pageant, honored by London Press Club Members Luncheon, 1970, San Diego 200th Anniversary celebration; producer, emcee ann. Holiday for Housewives, San Diego, 1955-60; producer, co-ordinator U. Calif., Today's World, San Diego, 1962; exec. dir., producer, dir. San Diego Ann. Golden Gloves Boxing Tournament, 1961-68; producer San Diego Ann. Metrotennis Championships, 1952-70; dir. Ann Power Boat Regatta, 1950-62; exec. dir. Ann Jr. Golf Championships; dir. Ann. Hole-in-One Tournament, 1951-70; master ceremonies, producer, emcee Gentlemen of Distinction Awards, 1967, 68, 69; producer/dir. San Diego Advt. Salesrama, 1971; producer, dir. master ceremonies San Diego Ann. Woman of Yr. Awards, 1967, 68, 69; producer/designer 34 exhibits for convs. and fairs; developed and produced A Day in San Diego for European Travel Commn., 1964; produced and emceed Ann. Boy Scout Jamboree Stage Show, 1967. Del. Nat. Fedn Press Women touring Russia. Commd. ensign, Women's Reserve, USNR, 1942, transferred USCG, served from ensign to lt. (sr.g.), 1943-46. Avocation: world travel. Office: PO Box 2243 La Jolla CA 92038-2243

KENT, SERGEI, electrical engineer. BA in Econs., Columbia U., 1982; BSEE, N.J. Inst. Tech., 1985. Cons. Rsch. Devices, Berkeley Heights, N.J., 1985; design engr. Lockheed Electronics, Plainfield, N.J., 1985-89; project engr. U.S. Army CECOM, Ctr. for EW/RSTA, Ft. Monmouth, N.J., 1989-90; sr. staff engr. Anadigics, Warren, N.J., 1990—; equipment automation cons. Berkeley Heights, N.J., 1999—. Active Zoning Bd., Berkeley Heights, 1992—. Recipient Svc. award Internat. Conf. Consumer Electronics, 1993. Mem. IEEE (sr.), Assn. Old Crows. Home: 125 Kent Dr Berkeley Heights NJ 07922-2331 Office: Anadigics Inc 35 Technology Dr Warren NJ 07059-5197

KENT, SUSAN, library director, consultant; b. N.Y.C., Mar. 18, 1944; d. Elias and Minnie (Barnett) Solomon; m. Eric Goldberg, Mar. 27, 1966 (div. Mar. 1991); children: Evan, Jessica, Joanna; m. Rolly Kent, Dec. 20, 1991. BA in English Lit. with honors, SUNY, 1965; MS, Columbia U., 1966. Libr., sr. libr. N.Y. Pub. Libr., 1965-67, br. mgr. Donnell Art Libr., 1967-68; reference libr. Paedergaat br. Bklyn. Pub. Libr., 1971-72; reference libr. Finkelstein Meml. Libr., Spring Valley, N.Y., 1974-76; coord. adult and young adult svcs. Tucson Pub. Libr., 1977-80, acting libr. dir., 1982, dep. libr. dir., 1980-87; mng. dir. Ariz. Theatre Co., Tucson and Phoenix, 1987-89; dir. Mpls. Pub. Libr. and Info. Ctr., 1990-95; city libr. L.A. Pub. Libr., 1995—; tchr. Pima C.C., Tucson, 1978, grad. libr. sch. U. Ariz., Tucson, 1978, 79; panelist Ariz. Commn. Arts, 1981-85; reviewer pub. programs NEH, 1985, 89, panelist challenge grants, 1986-89, panelist state programs, 1988; cons. to librs. and nonprofit instns., 1989-90, 92—; mem. bd. devel. and fundraising Child's Play, Phoenix, 1983; bd. dirs., mem. organizing devel. and fundraising com. Flagstaff (Ariz.) Symphony Orch., 1988; cons., presenter workshops Young Adult Svcs. divsn. ALA, 1986-88; bd. advisors UCLA Grad. Sch. Edn. and Info. Scis., 1998—; presenter in field. Contbr. articles to profl. jours. Chair arts and culture com. Tucson Tomorrow, 1981-85; bd. dirs., v.p. Ariz. Dance Theatre, 1984-86; bd. dirs. women's studies adv. coun. U. Ariz., 1985-90, Arizonans for Cultural Devel., 1987-89, YWCA Mpls., 1991-92; commr. Ariz. Commn. on Arts, 1983-87; participant Leadership Mpls., 1990-91. Fellow Sch. Libr. Sci., Columbia U., 1965-66. Mem. ALA (membership com. S.W. regional chair 1983-86, com. on appts. 1986-87, planning and budget assembly del. 1991-93, gov. coun. 1990-98, chair conf. com. 1996-97), Pub. Libr. Assn. (nominating com. 1980-82, v.p. 1986-87, pres. 1987-88, chair publs. assembly 1988-89, chair nat. conf. 1994, chair legis. com. 1994-95), Calif. Libr. Assn., Urban Librs. Coun. (exec. bd. 1994—, treas. 1996-98, vice chair/chair elect 1998, 99, chair 1999-2000, immediate past chair 2000—), Libr. Adminstrn. and Mgmt. Assn. (John Cotton Dana Award com. 1994-95). Office: LA Pub Libr 630 W 5th St Los Angeles CA 90071-2002

KENT, THOMAS J.R., editor; b. Cleve., May 31, 1950. BA, Yale U., 1972. Corr. AP, Brussels, 1978-79; chief ops. AP, Tehran, Iran, 1979; bur. chief AP, Moscow, 1979-81; dep. editor World Svc. News AP, N.Y.C., 1981-85, editor World Svc. News, 1985-90, internat. editor, 1990-99, dep. mng. editor, 1999—; juror Pulitzer Prize. Recipient Cert. of Merit Overseas Press Club of N.Y. Office: AP 50 Rockefeller Plz New York NY 10020-1605

KENTERIS, KONSTANTINOS, Olympic athlete; b. Mytilene, Greece, July 11, 1973. Phys. edn. tchr. Athens; winner Gold medal 200 meters Sydney, 2000. Set nat. record over 200 meters. Office: Assn Héllenique d'Athlet, 137 Ave Syngrou, Athens 1712, Greece*

KENTON, MARY JEAN, artist, writer; b. Fayette County, Pa., 1946; m. Jim Rosenberg, 1969. BA cum laude, Pomona Coll., Claremont, Calif., 1968; MFA, San Francisco Art Inst., 1974. Editor (for Pitts.) New Art Examiner, 1986-94. Contbr. to Sculpture mag., Washington, 1996-99; one woman shows include Allegheny Coll., Meadville, Pa., 1990, Mattress Factory, Pitts., 1992, 98, Westminster Coll., New Wilmington, Pa., 1992, Seton Hill Coll., Greensburg, Pa., 1999; group exhbns. include: Carnegie Mellon U. Art Gallery, 1986, Carnegie Mus. Art, 1991, Tweed Mus. of Art, 1999, Duluth, Minn., 1990' works in permanent collections at Mus. of Contemporary Art, L.A.; environ. art includes: The Geometry of Color, 1989, Every Twig to Product a Shining Thriving, 1999; others; author: (novel) Hay Fields, Fields of Silk: The Woodland Gales The Listening, 1999. Pa. Coun. on the Arts fellow in art criticism, 1987, 91, 94. Home and Office: PO Box 42 Merrittstown PA 15463-0042

KENWAY, IAN MICHAEL, clergyman, researcher; b. Fareham, Hampshire, Eng., May 13, 1952; s. John and Hazel (Rothery) K.; m. Wilgress Audrey Case. BA, U. Leeds, Eng., 1974; postgrad., Coll. of the Resurrection, Mirfield, Eng., 1974-76; PhD, U. Bristol, Eng., 1986. Ordained deacon Ch. of Eng., 1976, priest, 1977. Asst. curate Coventry East Team Ministry and Parish, 1976-79, St. Stephen's, Southmead, Eng., 1979-81; priest-in-charge St. Mary and St. John, Alum Rock, Birmingham, 1982-88; asst. bd. sec. Ch. of Eng. Bd. for Social Responsibility, 1988-93; dir. studies Ctr. for Study of Theology, U. Essex, Eng., 1993-99; Archbishop of Canterbury's chaplain to the Ch. House, Westminster, 1989-93; chaplain gen. Cmty. of St. John the Divine, 1991-99; mem. coun. Royal Found. of St. Katharine, London, 1993-96; mem. com. Soc. for Study of Christian Ethics, 1997—. Editor jour. Crucible, 1988-93; cons. jour. Foundations, 1997—; contbr. articles to Theology, Contact, Ministry, Sobornost, other profl. jours. Sec., No. Ireland Children's Holiday Scheme, 1974-75; mem. coun. William Temple Found., 1997-99. Avocations: swimming, walking, music, poetry, computing. Home: 9501 W Sahara Ave Apt 1100 Las Vegas NV 89117-5309

KENYHERCZ, THOMAS MICHAEL, pharmaceutical company executive; b. Youngstown, Ohio, Jan. 6, 1950; s. William Stephen and Goldie Elizabeth (Matica) K.; m. Linda Jane Kostyshak, Mar. 20, 1973; 1 child, Craig Thomas. BS, Youngstown State U., 1971; MS, U. Cin., 1973, PhD in Analytical Chemistry (Lowenstein Schubert Twitchell fellow), 1975; postdoctoral fellow in bioanalytical chemistry, Kissinger fellow, Purdue U., 1975-77. Cert. regulatory affairs profl. Scientist, sr. scientist, mgr. prodn. support labs. Ortho Pharm. Corp., Raritan, N.J., 1977-80; dir., product devel., quality assurance and regulatory affairs Janssen Pharmaceutica Inc., Piscataway, N.J., 1980-85; pres. KROSS, Inc., Hillsborough, N.J., 1985—; founder KROSS Coatings, Inc., 1987—; Telluride Pharm. Corp., 1994—; founder, pres. Telluride Analytical Svcs. Corp., 1996—; owner Telluride Devel. Corp., 1997—; participant FDA approved Orphan Drug Devel. program, IND Treatment of Cachexic AIDS Patients, 1996. Mem. editorial bd. Jour. Automated Chemistry, 1975—. Coach basketball St. Mary's Sr. H.S., 1979-83. Recipient SBIR Rsch. award EPA Phase I and II for studies of marine contamination, 1987, 88, FDA Orphan Drug designation, 1994. Active Ctr. for Creative Living, Religious Sci. Ch. Princeton. Mem. Am. Mgmt. Assn., Am. Assn. Clin. Chemists, Am. Assn. Anti Aging Med., Am. Chem. Soc., Am. Assn. Pharm. Scientists, Am. Soc. for Quality Control, U.S.-N.I.S. C. of C., Electrochem. Soc., Parenteral Drug Assn., Pharm. Mfrs. Assn., Drug Info. Assn., Regulatory Affairs Profl. Soc., Am. Soc. Pharmacognosy, We. Electroanalytical Theoretical Soc., Licensing Execs. Soc., Aquinas Inst., Controlled Release Soc., Soc. for Biomaterials. Byzantine Catholic. Office: Telluride Compound 300 Valley Rd Bldg 278 Hillsborough NJ 08876-4059

KENYON, ARNOLD OAKLEY, III, lawyer; b. Creston, Iowa, Aug. 15, 1952; s. Arnold O. II and Joy L. (Lawrence) K.; m. Mary Ann Clendenen, Dec. 23, 1972; children: Angela, Joseph, Arnold O. IV. BS, Iowa State U., 1974; JD with honors, U. Iowa, 1977. Bar: Iowa 1977. With Kenyon & Kenyon PC, Creston, 1977-89; ptnr. Steffes Kenyon & Nielsen PC, Creston, 1989-98, Kenyon & Nielsen PC, Creston, 1998—; county atty. Union County Atty.'s Office, Creston, 1979-87, asst. county atty., 1987-89; city atty. City of Creston, 1992—. Chmn. Crestland Betterment Found., 1983-95. Mem. Iowa Trial Attys. Assn. (bd. govs. 1989-91). Avocation: sailing. Home: 1403 Orchard Dr Creston IA 50801-1035 Office: 211 N Maple St Creston IA 50801-2311

KENYON, DAPHNE ANNE, economics educator; b. Augusta, Ga., Aug. 14, 1952; d. Lawrence Austin and Shirley (Knaus) Kenyon; m. Peter George Kachavos, Oct. 22, 1988. BA, Mich. State U., 1974; MA in Econs., U. Mich., 1976, PhD in Econs., 1980. Asst. prof. Dartmouth Coll., Hanover, N.H., 1979-83; sr. analyst U.S. Adv. Commn. on Intergovt. Relations, Washington, 1983-85; fin. economist U.S. Treasury Dept., Washington, 1985-87; sr. research assoc. Urban Inst., Washington, 1987-88; Lincoln fellow Lincoln Int. of Land Policy, Cambridge, Mass., 1988-89; asst. prof. econs. Simmons Coll., Boston, 1989-90, assoc. prof. econs., 1991-98, chair dept. econs., 1996-99, prof. econs., 1998-2000; pres. The Josiah Bartlett Ctr. for Pub. Policy, 1999—; cons. U.S. IRS Adv. Panel, Washington, 1987-99; appt. to Mass. Dept. of Revenue Adv. Group, 1991; bd. dirs. New Eng. Econ. Project, v.p., 1997-98, pres., 1999. Assoc. editor Urban Studies, 1988-93, mem. U.S. editl. adv. com., 1993—; co-editor: Coping with Mandates, 1990, Competition Among States and Local Governments, 1991; N.H. corr. State Tax Notes, 1990-93; mem. editl. bd. Mass. Benchmarks, 1997-99; contbr. articles to profl. jours. Mem. N.H. Gov.'s Revenue Adv. Com., Concord, 1982, 98. NSF grad. fellow, 1974. Mem. Am. Econ. Assn. (mem. com. on the status of women in econs. profession 1995-98), Nat. Tax Assn. (bd. dirs. 1996-99, chair intergovernmental fiscal rels. com. 1996-98, program chair 1999), Nat. Tax Jour. (referee Ea. Econ. Jour.). Episcopalian.

KENYON, ROSEMARY GILL, lawyer; b. Syracuse, N.Y., May 3, 1954; d. Harry Paul and Josephine McCullough (Sullivan) Gill; m. Douglas Wayne Kenyon, Mar. 15, 1980; children: Mary Patricia, Katharine Anna, Sarah Rose. Student, Saginaw Valley State Coll., 1972-74, U. Mich., 1974; BA magna cum laude, St. Mary's Coll., Notre Dame, Ind., 1976; JD, U. Notre Dame, 1979. Bar: State Bar Mich. 1979, Va. 1980, N.C. 1986. Law clk. to Hon. W. Earl Britt U.S. Dist.; assoc. Christian, Barton, Epps, Brent & Chappel, Richmond, Va., 1979-85; assoc. gen. counsel legal dept. Carolina Power & Light Co., Raleigh, N.C., 1986-98, dep. gen. counsel, 1998-98; of counsel Smith, Anderson, Blount, Dorsett, Mitchell & Jernigan, Raleigh, 1999—. Co-editor: Desk Book on Alternative Dispute Resolution in North Carolina, 1991. Chair nominating com. Commonwealth Girl Scout, Richmond, 1982-83, bd. dirs., 1983-85; bd. dirs. Pines Carolina Girl Scout Coun., 1986-90, 1st v.p., 1990-92, pres., 1992-95; mem. Exec. Women for Healthier Babies Campaign, March Dimes, 1993. Mem. ABA (mem. dispute resolution sect., mem. labor and employment law sect., mem. lit. sect.), N.C. State Bar, N.C. Bar Assn. (mem. coun. corp. counsel sect. 1989-96, chmn. pro bono com. 1991—, mem. commn. status women in legal profession 1991-92, 99—, dispute resolution com. 1988-92, dispute resolution sect., mem. coun. 1992-94, mem. Susie M. Sharp Inn Ct. 1992—, vice chair 1994-95, chair 1995-96), Va. State Bar, Va. Bar Assn., Metro. Richmond Women's Bar Assn. (pres. 1983-84), State Bar Mich., Wake County Bar Assn. Democrat. Roman Catholic. Avocations: running, photography, spectator sports, gardening. Home: 2105 Royal Oaks Dr Raleigh NC 27615-7122 Office: Smith Anderson et al PO Box 2611 Raleigh NC 27602-2611

KEOBOUNPHAN, SISAVATH, prime minister of Laos; b. Houaphanh, Laos, May 1, 1928. Min. of interior Govt. of Laos, 1975-91, min. agriculture and forestry, 1991-96, v.p., 1996—, prime minister, 1998—. Mem. Lao People's Revolutionary Party. Office: Office of the President, Lane Xang Ave, Vientiane Laos*

KEOGH, ANNE MARGARET, clinical cardiologist, researcher; b. Broken Hill, NSW, Australia, June 18, 1957; d. James Edwards and Heather Patricia (Bowden) White; m. Andrew Potter. MBBS, U. NSW, Sydney, Australia, 1979, MD, 1984. FRACP. Intern Royal North Shore Hosp., Sydney, 1990-92; cardiologist heart and lung transplant unit St. Vincent's Hosp., Sydney, 1993—; assoc. prof. U. NSW. Mem. Internat. Heart and Lung Transplant Soc. (exec. coun. 1994-98, pres.), Cardiac Soc. Australia and New Zealand (fed. councillor 1996-99). Office: St Vincent's Hosp delacy 14, Heart-Lung Transplant Unit, Sydney Darlinghurst 2010, Australia

KEOGH, DAMIAN T., marketing executive; b. Melbourne, Australia, Feb. 1, 1962; s. Michael M. and Margaret M. (Keenan) K.; m. Maree B. White, Nov. 1, 1986; children: Maddison, Sam, Isabella. B Commerce, Melbourne (Australia) U., 1984. Basketball player Australian Nat. League, 1981-95; mktg. cons. Sydney Olympic COm., 1996-97; mktg. cons. Seven Network, Australia, 1997-98, gen. mgr. sport mktg., 1998—; dir. Basketball Australia, Sydney, 1997—, New South Wales Australia Day Coun., 1995—, Wyralla Rd. Kindergarten, 1997—, Damien Keogh & Assocs., P/C. Author: Making A Dream Come True, 1993, Money for Jam, 1996. Liberal. Mem. Australian Olympic Basketball Team, 1984, 88, 92. Roman Catholic. Avocations: sports, music, reading. Home: 28 N East Crescent, Lilli Pilli NSW 2029, Australia Office: Seven Network Australia, Leve 13 1 Pacific Hwy, North Sydney NSW 2060, New Zealand

KEOUGH, DONALD RAYMOND, investment company executive; b. Maurice, Iowa, Sept. 4, 1926; s. Leo H. and Veronica (Henkels) K.; m. Marilyn Mulhall, Sept. 10, 1949; children: Kathleen Anne, Mary Shayla, Michael Leo, Patrick John, Eileen Tracey, Clarke Robert. BS, Creighton U., 1949, LLD (hon.), 1982; LLD (hon.), U. Notre Dame, 1985, Emory U., 1993, Trinity U., Dublin, Ireland, 1993, Clarke U., 1994. With Butter-Nut Foods Co., Omaha, 1950-61; with Duncan Foods Co., Houston, 1961-67; v.p., dir. mktg. foods div. Coca-Cola Co., Atlanta, 1967-71, pres. div., 1971-73; exec. v.p. Coca-Cola USA, Atlanta, 1973-74; pres. Coca-Cola USA, 1974-76; exec. v.p. Coca-Cola Co., Atlanta, 1976-79, sr. exec. v.p., 1980-81, pres., COO, dir., 1981-93; chmn. bd. dirs. Coca-Cola Enterprises, 1986-93; advisor to bd. Coca-Cola Co., Atlanta, 1993-98; bd. dirs. Washington Post Co., H.J. Heinz Co., McDonald's Corp., USA Networks, Inc., YankeeNets LLC; chmn. bd. Allen & Co., Inc., Atlanta, 1993—, Excalibur Technologies, Inc., 1996—. Mem. president's coun. Creighton U.; trustee emeritus U. Notre Dame and Lovett Sch. With USNR, 1944-46. Mem. Capital City Club, Piedmont Driving Club, Commerce Club, Peachtree Golf Club. Office: 200 Galleria Pky NW Ste 970 Atlanta GA 30339-5945

KEOWN, LAURISTON LIVINGSTON, JR., consulting psychologist; b. Balt., Feb. 24, 1942; s. Lauriston Livingston and Gladys May (Dykes) K.; m. Patje Alexandra Susemihl, Aug. 7, 1962 (div. 1977); children: Christina, Cassandra, Lauriston, Clayton; m. Nancy Ann Hastie, Mar. 18, 1978 (div. 1990). BA cum laude, U. Balt., 1965; MS, U. Alta., 1970, PhD, 1977. Chartered psychologist, Alta.; Can. Register Health Svc. Providers in Psychology. Lectr. Nippissing Coll., Laurentian U., North Bay, Ont., Can., 1968-69; chief sys. analyst Dept. Youth, Edmonton, Alta., Can., 1969-71; rsch. dir. Dept. Youth, Edmonton, 1971-72; dir. planning and rsch. Dept. Culture, Youth and Recreation, Alta., 1972-74; dir. planning and devel. Dept. Recreation, Pks. and Wildlife, Edmonton, Alta., 1974-75; asst. dir. Transp. Safety Alta. Transp. Dept., 1975-87; dir. Motor Transp. Planning and Bus. Analysis Alta. Transp. and Utilities, 1987-93; sr. psychologist Wainwright Cmty. Mental Health Svcs. Project, Alberta Hosp., Ponoka, 1993-95; regional mental health mgr. East Ctrl. Health Region, 1995-99; psychologist The Family Ctr., 1999—; cons. R. Dehaas Assocs., Edmonton, 1979-80, Draherin Group, Edmonton, 1980-82, Denlaur Assocs., 1990-92. Author: (with others) Evaluation of Traffic Safety Programs, 1980, Strategic Management of The Motor Transport Industry, 1989, The Obsessive Compulsive Organization, 1993; contbr. articles to profl. jours. Mem. Alta. Planning Bd., 1974-82; bd. dirs. Alta. Royal Can. Mounted Police Hist. Celebrations Commn., 1974-75; exec. bd. Traffic Records Commn., Nat. Safety Coun., 1978-93; Minister's Adv. Com. on Traffic Safety, 1992-93. Indsl. psychology scholar Lamond Dewhurst & Assocs., U. Alta., 1966. Mem. EMDR (Eye Movement Desentization and Reprogramming) Assn. Can., Alta. Psychologists Assn. Episcopalian. Home: 26 Donaldson Park, Sherwood Park, AB Canada T8C 1H3 Office: The Family Ctr, 20-9912 106 St, Edmonton, AB Canada T5K 1C5

KEOWN, WILLIAM ARVEL, minister, educator; b. Clinton, Ind., June 4, 1920; s. James Edward and Lula Nettie (Jackson) K.; m. Jewel Cook, Mar. 25, 1950; children: Evelyn Jewel, Deborah Anne, William S., A. Duane, Wayne A. ThB cum laude, God's Bible Sch. and Coll., Cin., 1949; MA, Butler U., Indpls., 1956; cert. in edn., Ind. State U., 1961. Ordained to ministry, 1956, Holiness, later transferred to Ch. of God (Anderson affiliation), 1957. Dean of men God's Bible Sch. and Coll., Cin., 1948-49; pastor ch. Evansville and Clinton, Ind., 1950-52; tchr. Frankfort (Ind.) Coll., 1954-57, dean of men, 1954-55; tchr. jr. high sch. Clinton, 1957-79; pastor 1st Ch. of God, Terre Haute, Ind., 1970-80, interim pastor, 1980-81, assoc. min., 1981—; basketball coach, 1967-70; instr. Ind. State Dept. Corrections, Anderson, 1979-82. With Civilian Conservation Corps., 1938-40; with U.S. Army, 1942-46. Fellow Internat. Platform Assn.; mem. Nat. Ret. Tchrs. Assn, Ind. Ret. Tchrs. Assn., Ind. Ministerial Assembly. Home and Office: 18820 S Rhodes Cir Clinton IN 47842-7208

KEPÁK, FRANTIŠEK, chemist, educator; b. Brno, Czech Republic, Feb. 11, 1931; m. Jana Kopelentová, July 27, 1957; 1 child Martina. MSc, U. Chem. Tech., Prague, Czech Republic, 1954, Dr.Sc., 1991; PhD, Czech Acad. Scis., Prague, 1964. Rsch. worker ČKD-Dukla, Prague, 1954-58; sr. scientist Nuclear Rsch. Inst., Rez, Czech Republic, 1958-95; assoc. prof. faculty of environment J.E. Purkyně U., Ústí nad Labem, Czech Republic, 1996—. Author: Sorption and Colloidal Properties of Radionuclides in Water Solutions, 1985, Separation of Radionuclides from Gas, 1989. Mem. Czech Chem. Soc. Home: Na Chobotě 1343, 163 00 Prague Czech Republic Office: JE Purkyne U, Fac of Environment, Na okraji 1001, 400 01 Usti nad Labem Czech Republic

KEPHART, LARRY ROBERT, architect; b. Clearfield, Pa., Sept. 1, 1949; s. Robert Joseph and Nora Elizabeth (Livergood) K. Student, Pa. State U., 1967-69. Registered architect, D.C. Drafter RCP Architects, Johnstown, Pa., 1970-72; office mgr. R. William Clayton Jr., Ft. Lauderdale, Fla., 1972-80; project architect C.F. McKirihan, Ft. Lauderdale, 1980-81, A. Nicholas Hosking, Ft. Lauderdale, 1981-82, Randall F. Keller, Ft. Lauderdale, 1982-83; architect, mgr. info. systems Vander Ploeg & Assocs., Boca Raton, Fla., 1983—; propr. Laroke Microcomputer Cons., 1993—; vis. lectr. Ft. Lauderdale Art Inst., 1983—. Avocations: computer programming, reading, wargames. Mem. Rotary (bd. dirs. 1981), Masons. Home: 772 Tivoli Cir Apt 204 Deerfield Bch FL 33441-8137 Office: Vander Ploeg & Assocs 155 E Boca Raton Rd Boca Raton FL 33432-3911

KEPLINGER, BRUCE (DONALD KEPLINGER), lawyer; b. Kansas City, Kans., Feb. 4, 1952; s. Donald Lee and Janet Adelheit (Viets) K.; children: Mark William, Lisbeth Marie, Kristen Michelle, Kailyn Emily, Courtney Nicole; m. Carol Ann Heinz, Apr. 12, 1991. BA with highest distinction, U. Kans., 1974; JD cum laude, So. Meth. U., 1977. Bar: Kans. 1977, U.S. Dist. Ct. Kans. 1977, Mo. 1980, U.S. Ct. Appeals (10th cir.) 1985, U.S. Supreme Ct. 1989. Assoc. Clark, Mize & Linville, Salina, Kans., 1977-79, Blackwell, Sanders et al, Kansas City, Mo., 1979-82; ptnr. Payne & Jones, Overland Park, Kans., 1982-94, Norris, Keplinger & Herman, LLC, Overland Park, 1994—; master Kansas Inns of Ct.; chmn. Kansas Lawyer Svcs Corp. Contbr. articles to profl. jours. V.p. Friends of Library, Johnson County, Kans., 1980-85; deacon Village Presbyn. Ch., 1982-86. Mem. ABA, Internat. Assn. Def. Counsel, Assn. Def. Trial Attys. (state chmn. 1996—, exec. coun., 1999—), Kans. Bar Assn. (chmn. Kans. lawyer svc. corp. 1992—), Mo. Bar Assn., Kans. Assn. Def. Counsel (bd. dirs. 1990—, pres.-elect 1992-93, pres. 1993-94), Def. Rsch. Inst., Rotary Internat., Hallbrook Country Club. Republican. Avocations: reading, golf. Office: Norris Keplinger & Herman LLC 6800 College Blvd Ste 630 Overland Park KS 66211-1556

KEPPELMAN, NANCY, lawyer; b. Abington, Pa., June 28, 1950; d. H. Thomas and Helene A. (Harrow) Keppelman; m. Michael E. Smerza, Sept. 9, 1978. Student, Oberlin (Ohio) Coll., 1968-70; BA, U. Mich., 1972, JD, 1978; Cert., Inst. for Paralegal Tng., Phila., 1972. Bar: Mich. 1978, U.S. Dist. Ct. (ea. dist.) Mich. 1978, U.S. Tax Ct. 1986. Legal asst. Dykema, Gossett et al, Detroit, 1972-75; assoc. Butzel, Keidan et al, Detroit, 1978-80, Law Offices of Brook McCray Smith, Ann Arbor, Mich., 1980-82, Miller, Canfield et al, Detroit, 1982-89, Stevenson Assocs., Ann Arbor, 1989-90; shareholder/lawyer Stevenson Keppelman Assocs., Ann Arbor, 1991—; condr. seminars in field. Chpt. author, co-editor QDROs, EDROs and Retirement Benefits: A Guide for Michigan Practitioners, 1994; contbr. articles to profl. jours. James B. Angell scholar, U. Mich., 1972. Fellow Mich. State Bar Found.; mem. ABA, State Bar Mich. (mem. taxation coun. 1991-94), Washtenaw County Bar Assn., Women Lawyers Assn. Mich. (bd. dirs., pres. Washtenaw region 1990-93). Avocations: birdwatching, music, hiking. Office: 444 S Main St Ann Arbor MI 48104-2304

KER, IAN TURNBULL, priest, scholar; b. Naini Tal, India, Aug. 30, 1942; s. Charles Murray and Joan May (Knox) K. BA, Balliol Coll., Oxford, 1964; PhD, Trinity Coll., Cambridge, 1969. Lectr. in English lit. U. York, 1969-74; endowed chair in theology and philosphy U. St. Thomas, Minn., 1987-89; tutor in theology Campion Hall, Oxford, 1996—; vis. prof. humanities Franciscan U., Steubenville, Ohio, 1993; Cath. chaplain Southampton U., 1982-87; sr. Cath. chaplain Oxford U., 1989-90. Author: The Achievement of John Henry Newman, 1990, (biography) John Henry Newman: A Biography, 1988; editor: Newman: Idea of a University, 1976, (with T. Gornall) Newman: Letters and Diaries, vols. 1-4, 1978-80. Mem. Cath. Theol. Assn. Avocations: walking, listening to music. Home: 171 The Hill, Burford OX18 4RE, England Office: Campion Hall, Brewer St, Oxford OX1 1QS, England

KERAMANE, ABDELOUAHAB, banker. Gov. Bank of Algeria. Office: Bank of Algeria, 38 Ave Franklin Roosevelt, Algiers Algeria*

KERBER, MICHAIL LEONIDOVICH, chemistry educator; b. Sebastopol, Krimea, Russia, July 4, 1932; s. Leonid Lvovich Kerber and Elisaveta Michailovna Schischmareva; m. Natalia Ivanovna Skripchenko, Feb. 8, 1964; children: Michael, Sergei. Engr., Mendeleevs' Inst. Chem. Tech., Moscow, 1954, PhD in Chemistry, 1962, DS in Chemistry, 1982. Engr. Inst. Polymer Tech., Moscow, 1954-58, 61-65; aspirant Mendeleer Inst., Moscow, 1958-61, docent, 1965-83, prof., 1984—. Grantee Soros Found., 1997. Mem. Mendeleev's Chem. Soc., Vinogradov's Rheological Soc. Avocations: yachting, travel, skiing. Home: Chajanov St N20 apt 13, 125047 Moscow Russia Office: Mendeleev U Chem Tech Russi, Misskaja-Sq 9/Polym Dept, 125190 Moscow Russia

KERBRAT, PIERRE, medical educator; b. Quimder, France, June 22, 1949; s. Yves and Jeanne (Chevallereau) K.; m. Martine Guerin; children: Denis, Antoine. Pharmacist degree, Nantes, France, 1971; MD, U. Rennes, France, 1981. Asst. prof. Comprehensive Cancer Ctr., Rennes, 1981-93; prof. med. oncology U. Rennes, 1993—; head of dept. Centre Eugene Marquis, Rennes, 1996—; treas. early clin. study group European Orgn. for Rsch. on Treatment of Cancer, Europe, 1997-99. Mem. Soc. Clin. Oncology, European Soc. Clin. Oncology Brussels. Office: Centre Eugene Marquis, U Pontchaillou, CS4429 Rennes Cedex, France

KERBS, WAYNE ALLAN, transportation executive; b. Hoisington, Kans., Mar. 21, 1930; s. Emanuel and Mattie (Brack) K.; m. Patricia Ann Aitchison, Dec. 5, 1953; children: Jacqueline Lee Kerbs Kepler, Robert Wayne. BSEE, U. Kans., 1952; MSEE, Ohio State U., 1960; M Engring., UCLA, 1968; postgrad., Calif. State U., Long Beach, 2000—. Test engr. Mpls.-Honeywell, 1952-54; sr. engr. Booz Allen & Hamilton, Dayton, Ohio, 1957-60; program mgr. Hughes Aircraft Co., L.A., 1960-74; pres., bd. dirs. Kerbs Industries, Inc., Los Alamitos, Calif., 1975—. Developer spacecraft devel. surveyor, 1960's, transit plan, 1996; patentee in field. Vol. PTA, Boy Scouts Am., Meth. Ch., 1952—; organizer Am. Mature Vols., L.a., 1994—; active Orange County Transp. Authority, 1994—. Lt. USN, 1954-57. Fellow Inst. for the Advancement of Engring.; mem. Soc. Automotive Engrs. (sec.), Inst. of Transp. Engrs., Elec. Automobile Assn., Advanced Transit Assn., Transp. Rsch. Bd., Am. Legion, Sigma Tau, Eta Kappa Nu, Kappa Eta Kappa. Republican. Avocations: sports, building, inventing, writing, investing.

KERC, JANEZ, pharmacist; b. Podrecje, Slovenia, May 22, 1962; s. Ivan Janez and Kristina (Sorn) K. BSc, U. Ljubljana, 1987, MSc, 1990, PhD, 1995. Rschr. LEK d.d., Ljubljana, 1988-94, sr. rschr., 1994-96, group leader, 1996—; asst. prof., U. Ljubljana, 1990-96, assoc. prof., 1996—. Mem. editl. bd. Farmacevtski Vestnik, 1998—; contbr. articles to profl. jours.; patentee in field. Fellow Sect. for Pharm. Scis.; mem. Slovenian Pharm. Soc. (pres. editl. coun. 1995-97), Controlled Release Soc. Avocations: stamps, jogging, cycling. Home: Ulica Bratov Ucakar 86, 1000 Ljubljana Slovenia Office: LEK dd Rsch and Devel Divsn, Celovska 135, 1526 Ljubljana Slovenia

KERCH, GARRY, physicist; b. Riga, Latvia, May 26, 1947; s. Michael and Valentina (Svencicka) K.; m. Tatyiana Nesova, June 2, 1979. Dr.sci.eng., Inst. of Polymer Mechanics, 1975. Sr. rschr. Inst. of Polymer Mechanics, Riga, Latvia, 1969-89; head of sector Ctr. of Engring. and Tech., Riga, 1990-91; dir. Ctr. of Sci. and Engring. Ekotra, Riga, 1991—. Editor Advertising Catalogs, 1995-97; contbr. articles to profl. publs. Office: Ekotra Ctr Sci and Engring, Nicgales Str 4-235, LV-1035 Riga Latvia

KERCKAERT, PIERRE, engineering executive; b. Brugge, Belgium, May 3, 1943; d. Theo and Julie Creps Kerckaert; m. Rita Helewaut, May 4, 1968; children: Koen, Luc, Annelies, Hans. Diploma cum laude, St. Leo Coll., Brugge, 1961, State U., Ghent, Belgium, 1966. Engr. bridges and rds. Office for Rds. of the Ministry of Pub. Works at Bruges, 1967-71, sr. engr., 1972; counsellor cabinets of J. De Saeger and A. Califice Minister of Pub. Works, Brussels, 1972-74; sr. engr., head dept. of waterways Office of the Coast of Ministry of Pub. Works, Ostend, 1974, chief engr., mgr. bridges and rds., 1977-89, inspector-gen. bridges and rds., head, 1989-92; counselor cabinets L. Dhoore and M. Eyskens Secs. of State Flemish Regional Economy/Environl. Planning, Brussels, 1974-76; gen. mgr. Bruges-Zeebrugge Port Authority, 1992—, also bd. dirs.; personal tech. counsellor Gov. Province of West-Flanders; tchr. math. Mcpl. Acad. of Bruges, 1970-75. Contbr. articles to profl. publs. Mem. Interurban Assn. for Motor Hwys. in West-Flanders (chmn. 1973-76). Office: Port Authority Bruges, Zeebrugge Isabellalaan 1, 8380 Zeebrugge W-Vl, Belgium

KERCKHOFFS, EUGENE JULES HUBERT, science educator; b. Heerlen, Limburg, The Netherlands, Sept. 7, 1942; s. Eugene J. H. Kerckhoffs and Désirée Lièbin; m. Alida J. M. de Heij, Nov. 22, 1968. MS in Phys. Engring., Delft U. Tech., The Netherlands, 1970; PhD in Computer Sci., U. Ghent, Belgium, 1986. Asst. prof. Delft U. Tech., 1970-89, assoc. prof., 1989—; part-time adj. prof. U. Ghent, 1993—; co-chmn. EU Esprit Working Group Simulation in Europe, Ghent, 1993-96; exec. dir. SCS Europe Ltd., 1994—. Co-editor 10 books in field; contbr. more than 225 articles and papers to profl. jours. and Congress procs. Sec. Parish Coun., The Hague, The Netherlands, 1992-96; vice chmn. Cath. Parish Fedn., The Hague, Netherlands, 1999—. Recipient Internat. Order of Merit, 1993. Fellow Soc. for Computer Simulation Internat. (v.p. Europe 1992-94, gen. chmn. European simulation symposium 1993, Disting. Svc. award 1996); mem. Internat. Assn. for Math. and Computers in Simulation, Internat. Neural Network Soc., Dutch Benelux Simulation Soc. (founding). Roman Catholic. Avocations: playing piano, spiritual activities. Home: Jacob van Campenlaan 55, 2321 GB Leiden The Netherlands Office: Delft U Tech Fac Info Tech, Zuidplantsoen 4, 2628 BZ Delft The Netherlands

KEREKOU, MATHIEU (AHMED), president People's Republic of Benin; b. Natitingou, Sept. 2, 1933; ed. Saint Raphael Mil. Sch., France, other French mil. schs., 1968-70. Served in French Army until 1961; joined Dahomey Army, 1961; aide-de-camp to Pres. Maga, 1961-63; participant mil. coup d'état which removed Pres. Christophe Soglo, 1967; chmn. Mil. Revolutionary Council, 1967-68; comdr. Ouidah paratroop unit, dep. chief of staff, 1970-72; leader mil. coup d'état which ousted Pres. Ahomadegbe, 1972; pres., Benin, 1972—, prime minister, min. nat. def., 1972-90, also head Mil. Revolutionary Govt.; former minister planning, former minister coordination of fgn. aid, info. and nat. orientation. Address: Office of President, BP 1288, Cotonou Benin*

KEREM, YITZCHAK, historian, researcher; b. Cleve., Dec. 7, 1956; arrived in Israel, 1977; s. Harvey Weingarten and Louise Orkin (Merlin) Spiro; m. Viviane Sabason Kerem, Dec. 1985 (div. 1991); 1 child, Orit Kerem; m. Julie Abby Smerling, May 25, 1997. BA, Macalester U., 1977; MA, Hebrew U., Jerusalem, 1984; PhD, Aristotle U., Thessaloniki, Greece, 1986. Lectr. Yad Vashem, Jerusalem, 1986, Sephariz Ednl. Ctr., Jerusalem, 1987-88; jr. adminstr. Gilat Psycho-Ednl. Project, Jerusalem, 1987-89; rschr. Hebrew U., Jerusalem, 1991—; bd. dirs. Inst. Hellenic-Jewish Studies, U. Denver, Casa Shalom Inst. Marrano Studies, Gan Yavnae, Israel, H-Judaic; cons. Film Salonika-Auschwitz, Jerusalem, 1986-87, Hebrew Union Coll., N.Y.C., 1994. Sgt. Israeli Def. Force, 1979-81. Editor Sefarad, The Sephardic Newsletter, Jerusalem, 1996—; prodr., dir. (films) The Burla Family, Ioannina, Athens, 1996, Arraham Franco, Hebron-Jerusalem, 1998; prodr. (film) David Benvenisti, Salonika-Jerusalem, 1997. West Bank com. mem. Assn. for Civil Rights in Israel, Jerusalem, 1982-84; com. mem. Peace Now, Jerusalem, 1982-84; treas. Laor Ednl. Movement, Jerusalem, 1991-93; activist Student Action Com. for Soviet Jewry, Mpls., 1994-96; founder Internat. Forum for Tolerance and Peace, Jerusalem, 1997—. Doctoral grantee Greek Govt. Ministry Edn., Athens, 1982-84, rsch. grantee Jewish Nat. Fund, Jerusalem, 1995, U.S. Holocaust Meml. Mus., Washington, 1999. Mem. European Assn. Jewish Studies, Assn. Jewish Studies, Com. des Etudes Ottomans et Pre-Ottomanes. Jewish. Avocations: collecting postcards, playing Scrabble, basketball, traveling, playing Trombone. Home: PO Box 10642, 91102 Jerusalem Israel Office: Dept Romance Langs, Hebrew Univ, Jerusalem Israel

KERFANT, HERVÉ, retired oil and gas company administrator; b. Guingamp, France, May 12, 1938; s. René and Ann (Ollivier) K.; m. Christa Anna, Nov. 28, 1965; children: Corinna, Nicolas, Tania, Daniela, Vanessa. Bachelor, Inst. N.D., Guingamp, 1956; grad. in Mech. Engring., Cesti U., Stoven, France, 1963. Engr. Entrepose, The Netherlands, 1965-68; dep. project mgr. Sadepose, Abudhabi, United Arab Emirates, 1968-69; dep. agy. mgr. Entrepose, Bordeaux, France, 1970-74; dep. project mgr. Entrepose, Paris, 1974-91; procurement mgr. Stolt Offshore SA, Nanterre, France, 1991-2000; ret., 2000. Author pushing boring machine, project estimating software. Treas. Lycee Internat. Asst. Parent Eleves, St. Germain, France, 1982-86; pres. Apeli, St. Germain, 1986-89. 2d lt. German Army, 1963-64. Mem. Oenologie Club (purchaser 1985-89). Roman Catholic. Avocation: computer. Office: Stolt Offshore SA, 32 Ave Pablo Picasso, 92754 Nanterre France

KERGOMARD, JEAN DUPLESSIS, researcher; b. Paris, Mar. 24, 1951; s. Alain and Genevieve (Sachet) K.; m. Joelle Gaultier; children: Alice, Pauline, Zoe. DS in Physics, U. Paris, 1981. Rschr. CNRS, Paris, 1973-81, LeMans, France, 1982—; head lab. U. Maine, LeMans, France, 1993—; Author, editor: Mechanics of Musical Instruments, 1996; contbr. articles to profl. jours.; patentee in field. Mem. Soc. French Acoustique. Avocation: music. Home: 20 Bd Philippon, 13004 Marseille France Office: LMA-CNRS, 31 Chemin J Aiguier, 13402 Marseille Cedex 20, France

KERH, TIENFUAN, civil engineer, educator; b. Tainan, Taiwan, Nov. 1, 1956; came to U.S., 1984; s. Chinchi and Guayfah (Huang) K.; m. Huiming Wang, Feb. 6, 1988; children: Rhoann, Hanley, Onttim. BS, Nat. Cheng Kung U., Tainan, 1979, MS, 1981; PhD, U. So. Calif., 1989. Engr.-in-tng., Calif. Rsch. asst. Found. for Cross-Connection Control and Hydraulic Rsch., L.A., 1985-89; civil engr. Leedco Engrs., A&E Co., Alhambra, 1990; assoc. prof. Nat. Pingtung U. Sci. and Tech., 1991-96; prof., 1996—; vis. scholar UCL, U. London, 2000-2001; spkr. in field. Reviewer Internat. Jour. of Modelling and Simulation, U.S., Can., Switzerland, 1992, Chinese Jour. Mechanics, Jour. of Chinese Inst. Transp.; contbr. articles to profl. jours. 2d lt. Chinese Army, 1981-83. Recipient Ann. award Nat. Sci. Coun., NPPI & NPUST, 1994-98. Mem. Internat. Assn. of Sci. and Tech. for Devel. (mem. tech. com. 2000—), Chinese Inst. of Engrs., N.Y. Acad. of Scis. Avocations: traveling, mountaineering, camping, swimming, ball games. E-mail: tfkerh@mail.npust.edu.tw. Office: Dept Civil Engring, Nat Pingtung U Sci/ Tech, Pingtung 91207, Taiwan

KERIMOV, AZER ALI OGLU, mathematician, educator; b. Baku, Azerbaijan, Jan. 5, 1961; s. Ali and Elza (Rasulova) K.; m. Fatima Mamedova, Aug. 20, 1993; children: Suleyman, Nergis. BS, MS, Moscow State U., 1983, PhD, 1988. Rschr. Landau Inst. Theoretical Physics, Moscow, 1983-85; rschr. Acad. Scis. Azerbaijan, Baku, 1985-88, sr. rschr., 1988—; asst. prof. math. Bilkent U., Ankara, Turkey, 1991—. Contbr. articles to profl. jours. Home: 29/3 Ctrl Campus Bilkent U, 06533 Ankara Turkey Office: Dept Math, Bilkent U, 06533 Ankara Turkey

KERIN, JOHN CHARLES, company director; b. Bowral, NSW, Australia; s. Joseph Sydney Kerin and Mary Louise Fuller; m. Barbara Elizabeth Taber Large (div. Jan. 1982); children: Tracy, Suellen, Andrew, Heidi; m. June Raye Verrier, June 7, 1983. BA, U.N.E., Armidale, Australia, 1967; B of Econs., Australian Nat. U., Canberra, 1977; Hon. D. Rur. Sci., U.N.E., 1992; Hon. DLitt, UWS, Campbelltown, Australia, 1994. Axeman Yerrinbool, Australia, 1953-57; bricksetter Bowral Brickworks, 1957-59; farmer Yerrinbool, 1959-71; econ. res. officer Bur. Agrl. Econs., Canberra, 1971-72; M.P. C'th Parliament, Canberra, 1972-75, 78-93; econ. res. officer Bur. Agrl. Econs., Canberra, 1976-78; dir. various cos. Australia, 1993—; min. for primary industry, 1983, min. for industries and energy, 1987, treas., 1991, min. for transport and comm., 1991, min. for trade and overseas devel., 1991-93; chair bd. NSW State Forests, 1998, NSW Water Adv. Coun., 1995, Queensland Fisheries Mgmt. Authority, 1999, NSW Crawford Fund, 2000; mem. bd. UNICEF, Australia, 1999. Part author: (books) Economic and Rural Policy Statement, 1986, Primary Industries and Resources—Policies for Growth, 1988, Research Innovation and Competitiveness, 1989. Dep. chancellor UWS, 1999; chair UWS MacArthur Coun., 1994. Fellow Australian Inst. Agrl. Scientists and Technologists. Mem. Australian Labor Party. Avocations: reading, walking, golf, live arts. Home: 26 Harpur Pl, 2605 Garran ACT, Australia

KERIS, VALDIS, neurosurgeon, consultant; b. Riga, Latvia, Jan. 26, 1961; s. Vilnis and Asja (Taukule) K.; m. Sandra Mihalenoka, July 20, 1985; children: Janis, Ieva. MD, Med. Acad. Latvia, 1985; PhD, 1991, DSc, 1996. Rsch. fellow Med. Acad. Latvia, Riga, 1985-87; cons. 7th Clin. Hosp., Riga, 1987—; cons. Clin. Emergency Hosp., Riga, 1988-89; lectr. 5th Med. Sch., Riga, 1990-93; asst. dir. Latvian Neuroangiological Ctr., Riga, 1995—; cons. rschr. Med. Acad. Latvia, Riga, 1997-98; asst. prof. Med. Acad. Latavia, 1998-99, assoc. prof., 1999—. Author: Transluminal Angioplasty of Precerebral and Cerebral Arteries: Experimental and Clinical Aspects, 1996; inventor in field; contbr. articles to profl. jours. Mem. World Fedn. Neurosurg. Socs., European Fedn. Neurol. Socs., European Assn. Neurosurg. Socs., Baltic Neurosurg. Assn. (pres.), Latvian Neurol. Assn. Avocations: basketball, darts, painting, poetry. Office: Clin Hosp Gailezers, 2 Hipokrata St, LV-1038 Riga Latvia

KERKHOF, MAXIMILIAAN PAUL ADRIAAN, Spanish language and philology educator; b. Boirle, Brabant, Holland, Jan. 26, 1944; s. Anton and Cornelia (Van Erven) K.; m. Maria Cecilia Correia Castilho, Feb. 7, 1945; children: Guido, Karin. MA, Cath. U., Nijmegen, Holland, 1967; doctorate, State U., Groningen, Holland, 1976. Univ. tchr. State U., Groningen, 1967-78; prof. Cath. U., Nijmegen, 1978—. Editor: La Comediета de Ponza, 1976, La Defunsion, 1977, Bias contra Fortuna, 1983, Pregunta de nobles, 1984, The Sonetos, 1985, Marques de Santillana, Obras completas, 1988, Laberinto de Fortuna, 1995; contbr. numerous articles to profl. jours. Home: Okapistraat 47, 6531 RJ Nijmegen Gelderland Holland Office: Catholic University, Erasmusplein 1, Nijmegen, Gelderland 6500 HD, Holland

KERKYASHARIAN, STEPAN, foundation executive; b. Nicosia, Cyprus, Sept. 2, 1943; arrived in Australia, 1967; s. Manuel and Zarouhi (Karaian) K.; m. Hilda Kayik, Aug. 2, 1998; m. Brenda Jean Anabel Arratoon (dec. June 1988); children: Massis, Karyne, Emmanuel. Head of radio Spl. Broadcasting Svc., Australia, 1980-89; chmn., CEO Ethnic Affairs Commn., Artarmon, NSW, Australia, 1989—; chmn. multicultural adv. com. Sydney Organizing Com. of Olympic Games, 1997-00. Recipient Gold Cross Order of Merit, Poland, 1990; named to Order of Australia, 1992; fellow U. Tech., 1995. Office: Ethnic Affairs Commn, C-8 Weedon Rd, Artarmon 2064, Australia

KERMAN, DAVID D., judge; b. Durham, N.C., Jan. 8, 1944. BA, Duke U., 1965; JD, Syracuse U., 1970. Bar: N.Y., Mass., other various courts. Exec. dir. Neighborhood Legal Svcs., 1973-90; judge N.E. Housing Ct., Lawrence, Mass., 1990—; mem. faculty Nat. Inst. Trial Advocacy, 1985—, Hofstra U. Law Sch., 1986—, Mass. CLE, Inc., 1991—. Mem. ABA, Mass. Bar Assn., Essex County Bar Assn., Lynn Bar Assn., Lawrence Bar Assn. Office: Northeast Housing Ct 2 Appleton St Lawrence MA 01840-1573

KERMANI, ABDY, structural engineering educator; b. Ardebil, Iran, Mar. 19, 1958; arrived in the U.K., 1976; s. Ali Asghar and Batoul (Memarzadeh) K.; m. Dawn Anderson, June 9, 1990; 1 child, Roman. BSc with honors, U. Teesside, Eng., 1982, PhD, 1990; MSc with distinction, U. Manchester, Eng., 1984. Cert. civil and structural engring. Educator U. Manchester, Eng., 1983-84; rschr., cons. U. Teesside, Eng., 1984-86; educator Loughborough U., Eng., 1988-90, Napier U., Scotland, 1990—; structural engring. cons. in field, 1984—. Author: Structural Timber Design, 1998; contbr. articles to profl. jours.; inventor in field. Grantee Sci. and Engring. Rsch. Coun. U.K., 1995, Engring. Phys. Sci. Rsch. Coun. U.K., 1997. Fellow Inst. Wood Sci.; mem. Instn. Structural Engrs. (chartered). Avocations: football, hill walking, chess. Office: Napier Univ, 10 Colinton Rd, Edinburgh EH10 5DT, Scotland

KERMODE, FRANK (JOHN KERMODE), literary critic, educator; b. Douglas, Isle of Man, U.K., Nov. 29, 1919; s. John Pritchard and Doris (Kennedy) K. B.A., Liverpool U., 1940, M.A., 1947, D.Litt. (hon.), 1981; D.H.L. (hon.), U. Chgo., 1975; PhD (hon.), Amsterdam U., 1988, Newcastle U., 1993, Yale, 1995, U. Wesleyan, 1997, U. London, 1997, U. Sewanee, 1999. J.E. Taylor prof. English Manchester U., Eng., 1958-65; Winterstoke prof. English Bristol U., Eng., 1965-67; Lord Northcliffe prof. English Univ. Coll. London, 1967-74; King Edward VII prof. English Cambridge U., 1974-82; vis. prof. humanities Columbia U., N.Y.C., 1983, 85; Charles E. Norton prof. Harvard U., 1977-78; Henry Luce prof. Yale Y., 1994. Author numerous books including Romantic Image, 1957, Wallace Stevens, 1960, The Sense of an Ending, 1967, D.H. Lawrence, 1973, The Classic, 1975, The Genesis of Secrecy, 1979, The Art of Telling, 1983, Forms of Attention, 1985, History and Value, 1988, An Appetite for Poetry, 1989, The Uses of Error, 1991, Not Entitled, 1995, (with Anita Kermode) The Oxford Book of Letters, 1995, Shakespeare's Languages, 2000; co-editor Encounter, 1965-67, (with Robert Alter) The Literary Guide to the Bible, 1987; editor Modern Masters Series, 1969—, Oxford Authors, 1984—. Served to lt. Royal Navy, 1940-46. Decorated officier Ordre des Arts et Sciences (France), 1973; named Knight Bachelor granted by the Queen of Eng., 1991; King's Coll. hon. fellow, 1987—. Fellow Brit. Acad., Royal Soc. Lit.; mem. Am. Acad. Arts and Scis. (hon.), Am. Acad. Arts and Letters (hon.). Home: 9 The Oast House, Pinehurst Grange Rd, Cambridge CB3 9AP, England

KERN, ALFRED M., English language educator, writer; b. Alliance, Ohio, Aug. 8, 1924; s. Harry and Mollie Cohen; m. Carole Ellen Franklin; children: Sheridan, Pamela, Stephen. AB, Allegheny Coll., 1948; MA, NYU, 1952. Prof. english Allegheny Coll., Meadville, Pa., 1948-86; vis. prof. USAF Acad., Colo. Springs, Colo., 1979-80; cons. United Steelworkers, Pitts., 1955-70, Pa. AFL-CIO, Phila., 1958-68. Author: The Width of Waters, 1958, Made in U.S.A., 1966, The Trial of Martin Ross, 1971. Active Democratic Party, Western Pa., 1950-80. Sgt. USAF, 1942-45.

KERN, HEINZ ERNST, ceramics company executive, researcher, consultant; b. Rochlitz, Sachsen, Germany, Dec. 30, 1919; s. Erich Ernst and Frieda Anna (Stelzer) K.; m. Elfriede Jaeglin, Apr. 13, 1946; 1 child, Ulrich. Dir. Tonwerke Kandern, 1961-83, Astrecent, Kandern, 1982—, Astrecent Consulting, Kandern, 1985—. Author: Diotimas Rückkehr, 1986, Besuch bei Scardanelli, 1986, (under pseudonym Enzio Enrici) Mars in Libra, 1984, Moon in Aries, 1982, Venus in Scorpio, 1987. Sgt. German mil., 1942-45. Recipient Bundesverdienstkreuz award Pres. of Fed. Republic of Germany, 1979. Mem. Rotary (pres. 1972-73). Avocation: writing. Office: Astrecent Consulting, Postfach 1168 Sitzenkircherstr12, 79400 Kandern Germany

KERN, MANFRED JAKOB, biologist, researcher; b. Bodenheim, Germany, Feb. 25, 1952; s. Ludwig Johann and Anna (Streichsbier) K.; m. Ursula Dorothee Schoenfeld, Apr. 14, 1978; children: Verena, Laura. Diploma in biology, Johannes Gutenberg U., Mainz, Germany, 1979, Doctor Rerum Naturalium, 1982; postgrad., So. Meth. U., 1983. Scientifical auxiliary German Rsch. Assn., Mainz, 1980-81; scientifical collaborator Johannes Gutenberg U., Mainz, 1982-84; scientist biol. rsch. Hoechst Ag, Frankfurt, Germany, 1984-93; sr. scientist biol. rsch. Agrevo GmbH, Frankfurt, 1994-98, head sci. comm., 1998-99; mem. tech. com. Aventis Crop Sci., 1999—; global head tech. comm. in tech. strategy and resources Aventis Crop Scis., 2000—, global head tech. comm. in tech. safety and resources, 2000—; coord. Forum Village and Agr. Expo 2000, Hannover, 1998—; mem. internat. adv. coun. Soc. for Sustainable Agr. and Resource Mgmt., Haryana, India, 1998; expert for life sci. panel for agro/food European Commn., Seville, Spain, 1998—; participant Internat. Food Policy Rsch. Inst., Washington, 1998; co-convenor XXI Internat. Congress Entomology, Foz de Iguazu, Brazil, 1998-2000; bd. mem. Coun. for Tropical and Agrl. Rsch., Stuttgart, Germany, 2000—; mem. adv. svc. for devel. Oriented Agrl. Rsch.; mem. German delegation Global Forum on Agrl. Rsch., Dresden, Germany, 2000. Mem. editl. bd. Pest Mgmt. Sci., 1994—, Internat. Jour. Biotech., 1999—; contbr. chpts. to books and articles to profl. jours.; inventor in field. Lt. col. German Army Res., 1971-73. Decorated Silver medal German Army, 1989. Roman Catholic. Avocations: handball, Russian literature, meeting people, insect brains, global future development and socioeconomy. Office: Aventis Crop Sci, Indsl Park K 607 Höchst, D-65926 Frankfurt Hessen, Germany

KERN, MATTHIAS, dentistry educator; b. Obergrenzebach, Hessen, Germany, July 11, 1958; s. Karlheinz and Ruth (Petri) K.; m. Kathrin Christa Schroeder, Nov. 2, 1979; children: Jan Stephen, Lena Marie, Jonas Henrik, Nils Valentin, Nora Charlotte. DMD, U. Freiburg, 1985, Dr.med.dent., 1987, PhD, 1995. Dentist dept. prosthodontics U. Freiburg, 1985-89, sr. lectr., 1989-91, 94-95, vice-chmn. dept., 1995-97; prof., chmn. dept. U. Kiel, Germany, 1997—; vis. rsch. assoc. prof. Dental Sch., U. Balt., 1991-93. Mem. editl. bd. Quintessenz, Berlin, 1989—, Clin. Oral Investigations, 1998—, German Zahnärztliche Zeitschrift, Jour. Adhesive Dentistry, 1999—; assoc. editor Internat. Jour. Prosthodontics, Chgo./Germany, 1999—; contbr. articles to profl. jours. Com. activist Red Cross, Schwalmstadt, Germany, 1977-79. Rsch. grantee German Soc. Rsch., Bonn, 1991-93. Mem. Internat. Assn. Dental Rsch., Acad. Dental Materials, German Soc. Dentistry. Office: U Kiel Dental Sch, Arnold-Heller-Strasse 16, 24105 Kiel Germany

KERN, WILLIAM BLIEM, JR., minister; b. Phila., Nov. 24, 1943; s. William Bliem Kern and Helen Elizabeth Kennedy; m. Ellen Evjen, Dec. 13, 1968 (div. Dec. 1972). BA, Wilmington Coll., 1967; MSc, MST, The New Seminary, 1990. Ordained min. N.Y. State Bd. Regents. Graphic design cons. to chief arch. Gibbs & Hill, N.Y.C., 1976-77; art dir. spl. projects The N.Y. Times Mag. Group, N.Y.C., 1979-80; design dir. Moving House and Home Mag., N.Y.C., 1981; assoc. art dir. Weight Watchers Mag., N.Y.C., 1982-83; market analyst The Comex Commodity Exch., N.Y.C., 1987-89; tv host, satellite psychic Internat. Satellite Nework, N.Y.C., 1991-92; min., pvt. practice spiritual counseling N.Y.C., 1990—. Author: MeditationsMeditationsMeditations, 1973, Sound Poetry: A Statement of My Poetics, 1976, George Washington Kern was My Grandfather, 1976, Hymn to America, 1976, Nuclear Prayes, 1978, Pharoah on the Ferry, 1981, Ode to the Foot, 1981, So it Was Written Thus it is Fulfilled, 1983, Astrologers Prayer, 1984, Hail Jupiter, 1994, The Temple of Sound, 1995, The Jewel in the Lotus, 1999; performer poetry/prayer Nuc. Prayer The UN Hdqrs., 1994, Text of Amen The Great Pyramid Egypt, 1995, Meditations, Text of Amen, Amon Chapel in Temple of Osiris, Egypt, 1980, Word Farm, Temple of Dendur at the Met. Mus. of Art, 1979; (CD with Allen Won Quartet) The Jewel in the Lotus, 2000. Mem. Masonic edn. com. Mem. Am. Rsch. Ctr. in Egypt, Nat. Coun. for Geosomic Rsch., Soc. for Sci. Exploration, The Rosicsucian Soc. Am. (dir. astrology 1985—), Chakrasambara Buddhist Ctr., George Washington Lodge (treas. lodge #285 1993-98). Avocations: watercolor landscape painting, Masonic education committee, Vajrayana Buddhist meditation. E-mail: wbk@idt.net. Home: 230 Riverside Dr New York NY 10025-6105

KERNEL, GABRIJEL, physicist; b. Koce, Slovenia, Sept. 14, 1932; s. Franc and Franciska (Bole) K.; m.Irena Maver, Oct. 25, 1958; 1 child, Igor. MS, U. Ljubljana, Slovenia, 1965, D, 1965. Asst. J. Stefan Inst., Ljubljana, Slovenia, 1959-65; rsch. assoc. U. Oxford, England, 1965-67, J. Stefan Inst., 1967-70; docent U. Ljubljana, 1970-76, assoc. prof., 1976-81, prof., 1981—; head physics dept. J. Stefan Inst., 1972-73, head nuclear physics divsn., 1982-86; collaboration spokesman CERN, Geneva, 1980-82; group leader DESY, Hamburg, Germany, 1985-94. Editor: Low-Energy Antiproton Physics, 1995; contbr. articles to profl. jours. (Nat. Sci. awards 1960, 70, 91). Mem. Slovenian Acad. Scis. and Arts. Achievements include initiation of particle physics rsch. in Slovenia, determination of photonuclear cross sections, measurement of low energy pion production, measurement of two-photon reactions. Home: Bicevje 2, SI-1000 Ljubljana Slovenia Office: U Ljubljana, Jadranska 19, SI-1000 Ljubljana Slovenia

KERNER, FRED, book publisher, writer; b. Montreal, Can., Feb. 15, 1921; s. Sam and Vera (Goldman) K.; m. Jean Elizabeth Somerville, July 17, 1945 (div. Apr. 1951); 1 son, Jon Fredrik; m. Sally Dee Stouten, May 18, 1959; children: David, Diane. BA, Sir George Williams U. (now Concordia U.), Montreal, 1942. Mem. editl. staff Saskatoon (Can.) StarPhoenix, 1942; Asst. sports editor Montreal Gazette, 1942-44; news editor Can. Press, Montreal, Toronto, N.Y.C., 1944-50; asst. night city editor A.P., N.Y.C., 1950-57; editor Hawthorn Books, Inc., N.Y.C., 1957-58, pres., 1964-68; exec. editor Crest-Premier Books, Hall House, Fawcett World Libr., N.Y.C., 1958-63; editor-in-chief Crest-Premier Books, Fawcett World Libr., N.Y.C., 1963-64; pres. Centaur House, Inc. (pubs.), 1964-80, Paramount Securities Corp., 1965-67, Veritas Internat. Pubs., 1976—, Publishing Projects, Inc., 1967—, Communications Unltd., 1968—; editorial dir. book and ednl. divs. Reader's Digest, Can., 1968-75; v.p., pub. dir. Harlequin Enterprises Ltd., 1975-83, sr. cons. editor, 1984-96, editor emeritus, 1983—; v.p. Publitex Internat. Corp. (pubs.), 1968-75; pres. Athabaska House, 1975-77; dir. Nat. Mint, Inc., various other corps.; panelist various profl. confs.; chmn. Internat. Affairs Conf. Coll. Editors, 1965; drama festival adjudicator, 1940-48; Broadway theatrical script cons., 1948-56; speechwriter Adlai Stevenson, 1952, 56; ghostwriter Dr. Joyce Brothers, Anita Colby, Enid Haupt, and others; mem. nat. negotiating com. Am. Newspaper Guild, 1949-54, Wire Svc. Guild, 1954-57, chmn. grievance com., 1955-57; instr. Insider's Guide to Writing and Pub., U. Toronto, 1999—. Author: (with Leonid Kotkin) Eat, Think and Be Slender, 1954, 2d edit., 2000, (with Walter M. Germain) The Magic Power of Your Mind, 1956, (with Joyce Brothers) Ten Days to a Successful Memory, 1957, Stress and Your Heart, 1961, 2d edit., 2000; pseudonym Frederick Kerr: Don't Count Calories!, 1962, 2d edit., 2000, (with Walter M. Germain) Secrets of Your Supraconscious, 1965, (with David Goodman) What's Best for Your Child and You, 1966, (with Jesse Reid) Buy High, Sell Higher, 1966; (pseudonym M.N. Thaler) It's Fun to Fondue, 1968, (with Ion Grumeza) Nadia, 1977, Careers in Writing, 1985, Mad About Fondue, 1986, (with Andrew Willman) Prospering Through the Coming Depression, 1986, Home Emergency Handbook and First-Aid Guide, 1990, Fabulous Fondues, 2000; contbg. author: Successful Writers and How They Work, 1958, Words on Paper, 1960, Overseas Press Club Cookbook, 1964, The Senior's Guide to Life in the Slow Lane, 1986, The Writer's Essential Desk Reference, 1991, 96, Lifetime: A Treasury of Uncommon Wisdoms, 1992, Chambers's Ency.; books transl. into French, German, Japanese, Portuguese, Spanish and Italian; editor: Love is a Man's Affair, 1958, 2d edit., 2000, Treasury of Lincoln Quotations, 1965, new edit. 1996, The Canadian Writer's Guide, 9th edit., 1985, 10th edit., 1988, 11th edit., 1992, Selling Your Short Fiction, 1992. Mem. local sch. bd., N.Y.C., 1967-68; chmn. sch. com. Westmount High Sch., 1970-72; mem. sch. com. Roslyn Sch., 1973; chmn. publs. com. Edward R. Murrow Meml. Fund; judge Dr. William Henry Drummond Nat. Poetry Contest; trustee Gibson Lit. Awards, C.A.A. Lit. Awards, Benson & Hedges Lit. Awards, CA&B Student Creative Writing Awards; bd. govs. Concordia U., 1975-79; hon. life mem. Can. Pubs. Coun.; founding mem. exec. com. Pub. Lending Rights Commn., 1986-89, vice chmn., 1988-89; founding dir. Toronto Book and Mag. Fair, bd. dirs., 1990-94. Recipient Queen's Silver Jubilee medal for contbns. to internat. pub., 1977, Allan Sangster award, 1982, Internat. Pub. award Air Can., 1982, 2 internat. awards for advertorial writing, 1990, Apex' 92 award for newsletter editing. Fellow Can. Copyright Inst. (vice chmn. 1995, chmn. 2000), Acad. Can. Writers (vice chmn., bd. govs. 1986—); mem. European Acad. Arts, Scis. and Humanities, Orgn. Can. Authors and Pubs. (founding dir.), Can. Authors Assn. (v.p. 1972-80, founding dir. Lit. Luncheons, pres. Montreal br. 1974-75, nat. pres. 1982-83, founding editor Nat. Newsline 1982, pub. Can. Author 1982-95, hon. life, chmn. editl. adv. com. Can. Author 1978-94, chmn. grievance com. 1983-93, pub. com. 1986-92), Periodical Writers' Assn. Can. (chmn. grievance com. 1990, contracts com.), Can. Writers' Found. (bd. govs. 1982—), Assn. Am. Pubs. (hon. life), Mystery Writers Am. (editor Third Degree, co-chmn. awards com.), Writers' Union Can. (hon. life, chmn. grievance com. 1990-99, contracts com. 1990—), Soc. Profl. Journalists' Pres.'s Club, Book and Periodical Coun. (bd. govs. 1983-94), Authors Guild, Authors League Am., Internat. P.E.N., Nat. Spkrs. Assn., Am. Acad. Polit. and Social Sci., Can. Assn. Restoration of Lost Positives (pres.), Can. Soc. for Preservation of the Natural Bowtie (pres.), Sir George Williams U. Alumni Assn. (founding pres. N.Y.C. br., exec. com. 1970-75, pres. 1971-73), Georgi Antiques (founding dir.), Avodah Honor Soc., Advt. Club, Deadline Club, Overseas Press Club, Dutch Treat Club (N.Y.C.), Toronto Press Club, Author's Club (London), Sigma Delta Chi. Home: 1405-1555 Finch Ave E, Willowdale, ON Canada M2J 4X9 Office: 55014 Fairview Mall, Willowdale, ON Canada M2J 5B9

KERNERMAN, LIONEL JACOB, publisher; b. Toronto, Ont., Can., Apr. 13, 1929; arrived in Israel, 1950; s. Samuel Charles and Sara (Jessel) K.; m. Ahuva Levy, Aug. 12, 1957; children: Ilan, Yair, Ronen. BA in Eng. Lit. and Polit. Sci., Tel Aviv U., 1969, secondary sch. English tchr. degree, 1970. Cellist Toronto Philharm. Symphony, 1945-49; founding mem. Kibbutz Kissufim, Negev, Israel, 1950-55; H.S. English tchr. Tel Aviv, 1956-76; English tchr. Tel Aviv U., 1977-87; founder, dir., pub. Kernerman Pub., Ltd., Tel Aviv, 1986—; founder, dir. Internat. Sci. Publs., Ltd., Israel, 1972-86, Password Pubs., Ltd., 1995—, K Dictionaries, 2000—; presenter in field. Editor various internat. sci. jours., 1970-86; founding editor Pub. Health Revs.; pub. numerous books; contbr. articles to profl. jours. Founder, sec. Can. Rocket Soc., Toronto, 1945-48; founding mem. Com. for a Just Peace Between Israel and the Arab States; active in various left-wing movements and orgns. for peace. Recipient 1st prize for strings Stratford Music Festival, Can., 1942. Mem. Internat. Assn. Tchrs. English as a Fgn. Lang., European Assn. for Lexicography, English Tchrs.' Assn. Israel, Royal Can. Astronomical Soc. Avocations: playing cello and viola da gamba in non-professional chamber music ensembles, swimming, walking, astronomy. Fax: 972-3-6493712. E-mail: kernermn@internet.zahav.net. Home: 44/4 Levi Eshkol St, 69361 Tel Aviv Israel Office: Kernerman Pub Ltd, 46 Hagolan St, 69718 Tel Aviv Israel

KERNS, DAVID VINCENT, lawyer; b. Jan. 29, 1917; s. Clinton Bowen and Ella Mae (Young) K.; m. Dorothea Boyd, Sept. 5, 1942; children: David V., Clinton Boyd. BPh, Emory U., 1937; JD, U. Fla., 1939. Bar: Fla. 1939, U.S. Dist. Ct. (mid. dist.) Fla. 1939, (so. dist.) Fla. 1978, (no. dist.) Fla. 1981, U.S. Ct. Appeals (11th cir.) 1981, U.S. Supreme Ct. 1988. Assoc. Sutton & Reeves, Tampa, Fla., 1939-41, Fowler & White, Tampa, 1945-47; ptnr. Moran & Kerns, Tampa, 1948-49; resident atty. Fla. Road Dept., 1949-53; rsch. asst. Supreme Ct. Fla., 1953-58; dir. Fla. Legis. Reference Bur., 1958-68, Fla. Legis. Svc. Bur., 1968-71, Fla. Legis. Libr. Svcs., 1971-73; gen. counsel Fla. Dept. Adminstrn., 1973-82; mem. Fla. Career Svc. Commn., 1983-86; spl. master Fla. Senate, 1987-96; legal cons. chief inspector gen. Fla. Gov. Office, 1995-98. Contbr. articles to profl. jours. Served with U.S. Army, 1941-45. Mem. Fla. Govt. Bar Assn. (pres. 1956, J. Ernest Webb Meml. award 1982), Fla. Bar (bd. govs. 1978-84), Tallahassee Bar Assn. (spl. dir. 1993-95). Democrat. Methodist. Home: 418 Vinnedge Ride Tallahassee FL 32303-5140

KERNSTOCK, ELWYN NICHOLAS, political science educator, author; b. Bronx, N.Y., Dec. 24, 1917; s. Charles Henry and Irene (Paollilo) K.; m. Peggy Giles, Dec. 20, 1947; children: Stephan Giles, Nicholas Charles, Christopher John, Wendy Kernstock Robinson. BS in Edn., Ctrl. Conn. State Coll., 1963, MS, 1965; PhD, U. Conn., 1972. Commd. 2d lt. U.S. Army, 1943, advanced through grades to maj., 1962, ret., 1962; instr., chmn. social studies various secondary schs., Conn., 1962-70; faculty St. Michael's Coll., Winooski, Vt., 1971-88, prof. emeritus, 1988—; prof. Acad. Sr. Profls. U. West Fla., 2000—; political science educator, author; b. Bronx, N.Y., Dec. 24, 1917; s. Charles Henry and Irene (Paollilo) K.; m. Peggy Giles, Dec. 20, 1947; children: Stephan Giles, Nicholas Charles, Christopher John, Wendy Kernstock Robinson. BS in Edn., Ctrl. Conn. State Coll., 1963, MS, 1965; PhD, U. Conn., 1972. Enlisted in U.S. Army, 1942, commd. 2d lt., 1943, advanced through grades to maj., 1962, ret. 1962; instr., chmn. social studies, various secondary schs., Conn., 1962-70; faculty St. Michael's Coll., Winooski, Vt., 1971-88, prof. emeritus, 1988—; mem. Acad. Sr. Profls., U. West Fla., 2000—. Advisor to chmn. Vt. Dem. Com., 1974-76; del. Conn. Dem. Conv., 1970, Vt. Dem. Conv., 1972, 74, 76, 80, 84, 86, 92, 94. Dem. candidate for Congress from Vt., 1978; elected committeeman Santa Rosa County, Fla., 1996; pres. New Britain Unitarian Universalist Soc., 1962, New Britain Edn. Assn., 1964. Co-recipient Ninth Ann. Freedom of Choice award Pro Choice Vermont, 1994. Mem. AAUP, Am., New Eng. Polit. Sci. Assns., Americans United for Separation Ch. and State (mem. nat. adv. bd. 1987-93, 98—, pres. N.W. Fla. chpt.), Ret. Officers Assn. Author: How New Migrants Behave Politically: Puerto Ricans in Hartford, 1970, Rx Political Party, 1987.. Author: How New Migrants Behave Politically: Puerto Ricans in Hartford, 1970, Rx Political Party, 1987. Pres. New Britain Unitarian Universalist Soc., 1962, New Britain Edn. Assn., 1964; del. Conn. Dem. Conv., 1970, Vt. Dem. Conv., 1972, 74, 76, 80, 84, 86, 92, 94; advisor to chmn. Vt. Dem. Com., 1974-76; Dem. candidate for Congress from Vt., 1978; elected committeeman Santa Rosa County, Fla., 1996. Co-recipient 9th Ann. Freedom of Choice award Pro Choice Vt., 1994. Mem. AAUP, Am. Polit. Sci. Assn., New Eng. Polit. Sci. Assn., Americans United for Separation Ch. and State (mem. ant. adv. bd. 1987-93, 98—, pres. N.W. Fla. chpt.), Ret. Officers Assn. Home: 10100 Hillview Dr # 2105 Pensacola FL 32514-5436

KERPA, GARY J., computer science consultant; b. Derby, Conn., Apr. 20, 1958; s. George B. and Marcia J. (Tiano) K. Cert., Tech. Careers Inst., West Haven, Conn., 1978. Auto. tech. Racebrook Auto., Orange, Conn., 1974-77; computer system integration cons. Lawson & Assocs., Ansonia, Conn., 1980—. Regional coord. Ams. for Perot, Dallas, 1992. Mem. ABA, Assn. Trial Lawyers Am., Aircraft Owners and Pilots Assn. Republican. Roman Catholic. Avocation: flying. Home and Office: 18 Fairview St Ansonia CT 06401-2707

KERR, ALEXANDER DUNCAN, JR., lawyer; b. Pitts., May 6, 1943; s. Alexander Duncan Sr. and Nancy Greenleaf (Martin) K.; m. Judith Kathleen Mottl, May 25, 1969; children: Matthew Jonathan, Joshua Brandon. BS in

Bus., Northwestern U., 1965, JD, 1968. Bar: Ill. 1968, Pa. 1969, U.S. Dist. Ct. (ea. dist.) Pa. 1969, U.S. Dist. Ct. (no. dist.) Ill. 1969, U.S. Ct. Appeals (3rd and 7th cirs.) 1969, U.S. Supreme Ct. 1969. Assoc. Clark, Ladner, Fontenbaugh & Young, Phila., 1968-69, 73-74; asst. U.S. atty. U.S. Dept. Justice, Chgo., 1974-79; assoc., ptnr. Keck, Mahin & Cate, Chgo., Oak Brook, Ill., 1979-90; shareholder Tishler & Wald, Ltd., Chgo., 1990—. Staff atty. Park Dist. La Grange, Ill., 1985—; active Ill. St. Andrew Soc., North Riverside, 1982—, pres., 1995-97; vestryman, lay reader, chancellor, chalice bearer Emmanuel Episcopal Ch., 1980-99; mem. Pack 177, Troop 19, Order of the Arrow, Boy Scouts Am., La Grange, 1980—. With USN, 1969-75. Mem. Am. Legion, DuPage Club, Atlantis Divers. Fax: 708-354-1208. E-mail: adkerrjr@aol.com. Home: 709 S Stone Ave La Grange IL 60525-2725

KERR, ALLEN STEWART, retired psychologist; b. Evanston, Ill., Nov. 13, 1928; s. Charles Allen and Mildred (Latham) K.; m. Charlyn Floyd, July 19, 1952; children: Betsy Kerr Hedding, Chet, Peggy Kerr Ihinger, Cindy Kerr Levesque. BA, Brown U., 1950; D of Psychology, Forest Inst. Profl. Psychology, 1988. Lic. psychologist, Ga. Salesman Sleepeck Printing Co., Bellwood, Ill., 1953-68, v.p. sales, 1968-83; staff psychologist The Bradley Ctr., Columbus, Ga., 1988-94; sr. psychologist The Pastoral Inst., Columbus, Ga., 1994-99; ret., 1999. Lt. (j.g.) USN, 1950-53. Recipient Bell Ringer award Mental Health Assn. Columbus (Ga.), 1995. Mem. APA, Ga. Psychol. Assn., Columbus Area Psychol. Assn., Rotary (Muscogee charter mem., pres. 1997-98). Methodist. Avocations: golf, photography, writing, travel. Home: 887 Oakwood Dr Columbus GA 31904-2483

KERR, BAINE PERKINS, oil company executive; b. Rusk, Tex., Aug. 24, 1919; s. James Herman and Myrta Blake (Perkins) K.; m. Mildred Pickett Caldwell, June 13, 1942; children: Baine Perkins, John Caldwell, James Robinson, Mary Blake Kerr Winters. B.A., LL.B., U. Tex. at Austin, 1942. Bar: Tex. 1942. Practiced in Houston, 1945-77; partner firm Baker & Botts, 1955-77; dir. Pennzoil Co., Houston, 1964-94, chmn. exec. com., 1972-94, pres., 1977-85, dir. emeritus, 1994—. Served with USMCR, 1942-55. Mem. Chancellors, Order of Coif, Phi Beta Kappa. Office: Esperson Bldg 808 Travis St Ste 2200 Houston TX 77002-5704

KERR, DIANA PATRICIA, lawyer, consultant; b. Ipswich, Suffolk, Eng., Aug. 16, 1949; d. Henry Neville and Jessica Irene (Guppy) Sneezum; m. Michael Kerr, Jan. 29, 1983; children: Lucy Jessica, Alexander Michael. BSc in Linguistic and Internat. Studies, Surrey U., Eng., 1971. Solicitor Supreme Ct. Eng. and Wales 1974. From articled clk. to solicitor Theodore Goddard (Law Firm), London, 1972—, ptnr., 1979-87, cons., 1987—; assoc. lectr. in German legal translation U. Surrey, 1974-76. Mem. coun. U. Surrey, 1997—; mem. various charitable orgns. Mem. Brit. German Jurists' Assn. (com. 1974-95, chmn. 1994-95, v.p. 1995—), City of London Solicitors' Co. (Freeman 1976—), Hurlingham Club. Avocations: tennis, theatre, gardening. Office: Theodore Goddard, 150 Aldersgate St, London EC1A 4EJ, England

KERR, DONALD CRAIG, retired minister; b. Pitts., July 29, 1915; s. Hugh Thomson and Olive (Boggs) K.; m. Nora Minetta Lloyd, Sept. 12, 1942; children: Donald Jr., Elizabeth, Douglas. BA, Princeton U., 1937; MDiv, Princeton Theol. Sem., 1940; ThD, U. Toronto, Ont., Can., 1942. Ordained to ministry Presbyn. Ch. (U.S.A.), 1940. Min. East Kiskacoguillas Presbyn. Ch., Reedsville, Pa., 1942-47, 1st Presbyn. Ch., New Haven, 1947-48; min. Roland Pk. Presbyn. Ch., Balt., 1948-80, pastor emeritus, 1980; pastoral assoc. Presbyn. Ch., Sarasota, Fla., 1980-87; chaplain Plymouth Harbor, Sarasota, 1982-91; moderator Presbytery of Balt., 1960-61, mem. bd. pensions, exec. com., 1963-66. Author: How the Church Began, 1953, What the Bible Means, 1954, History of Religion in America, 1975; editor: Design for Christian Living, 1952. Bd. advisors Presbyn. Home of Md. Recipient 50-yrs. in ministry plague Lake Joseph Community Ch., 1989, 50-yr. Ordination Recognition, 1992; honored for being 50 yr. mem. Balt. Presbytery. Mem. St. Andrew's Soc. (trustee, chaplain 1980-91, cert. appreciation 1990), Ivy League Club (v.p. 1991, pres. 1992-93), Princeton Club (pres. 1988-90), Univ. Club Sarasota, Sarasota Yacht Club, Sara Bay Club, Gibson Island Club, The Johns Hopkins Club, Shriners, Masons (32 degrees). Home: 830 W 40th St Apt 409 Baltimore MD 21211-2126

KERR, DUNCAN, Australian government official; b. Hobart, Australia, Feb. 26, 1952. B of Law, U. Tasmania, BA social work. Atty. gen. Commonwealth of Australia, 1993, min. for justice, 1993-96; chmn. intergovtl. com. Nat. Crime Authority, 1993-96; mem. parliament for Denison, 1987—; chmn. aboriginal affairs com., 1990-93; opposition spokesman for Arts, Justice and Customs. Mem. Australian Labor Party. Office: GPO Box 32A, Hobart Tasmania, Australia

KERR, GARY ENRICO, lawyer, educator; b. Kewanee, Ill., Feb. 8, 1948; s. Roy Harrison and Marietta (Dani) K.; m. Eileen Elizabeth Straeter, Aug. 18, 1978; 1 child, Victoria Elizabeth. BA, No. Ill. U., 1970; JD, Northwestern U., Chgo., 1973. Bar: Ill. 1974, U.S. Dist. Ct. (cen. dist.) Ill. 1982, U.S. Ct. Appeals (7th cir.) 1983, U.S. Supreme Ct. 1983. Adminstrv. asst. Office Supt. Pub. Instrn. State Ill., Chgo., Springfield, 1971-74; asst. legal advisor Ill. State Bd. Edn., Springfield, 1974-78; spl. counsel Ill. State Comptroller, Springfield, 1978-79; pvt. practice Springfield, 1979—; adj. faculty Sangamon State U. (now Ill. State U.), Springfield, Ill., 1994; pres., dir. counsel Kerr Products, Inc., Kewanee, Ill., 1980—; instr. paralegal program Robert Morris Coll., Springfield, 1992. atty. South County Democrats, Sangamon County, Ill. Fellow Ednl. Policy program Inst. Ednl. Leadership, George Washington U., 1976-77. Mem. ABA, Ill. State Bar Assn. (chmn. sch. law sect. coun. 1983-84), Sangamon County Bar Assn., Automotive Parts and Accessories Assn. (mem. govtl. affairs and internat. trade com. 1997). Avocations: snow skiing, tennis, fishing. Office: Gary Kerr Ltd 1020 S 7th St Springfield IL 62703-2417

KERR, GERALD LEE, III, lawyer, paralegal educator; b. Mpls., July 7, 1944; s. Gerald L. Kerr Jr. BS, U.S. Naval Acad., 1966; JD, Cath. U., 1972; MPA, Golden Gate U., 1976. Bar: D.C., Va. Atty. Kelberg & Childress, Virginia Beach, Va., 1977-78, Gerald L. Kerr III, P.C., Virginia Beach, 1978—; asst. prof. Tidewater C.C., Virginia Beach, 1977—. Pres., Norfolk Sister City Assn., 1979-81. Served to comdr. JAGC Corps, U.S. Navy, 1966-87. Named to Outstanding Young Men of Am., 1979, 80, 81. Office: 3634 S Plaza Trl Virginia Beach VA 23452-3351

KERR, JAMES WILSON, engineer; b. Balt., May 21, 1921; s. James W. and Laura Virginia (Wright) K.; m. Mary Thomas Montgomery, Feb. 25, 1945 (div., dec.); children: April Kerr Miller, Catherine Kerr Wood (dec.), Wilson, Andrew; m. June Walker, Dec. 27, 1977 (div.); m. Janice White Bain, Jan. 19, 1985. BS with honors, Davidson Coll., 1942; MS, NYU, 1948; postgrad., Freiburg U., 1957-60, Brookings Inst., 1970, 758; PhD, Kennedy Western U., 1989. Registered profl. engr., Calif. Commd. 2d lt. U.S. Army, 1942, advanced through grades to lt. col., 1964, with inf., World War II, Korea; electronics staff U.S. Army, Ft. Bragg, N.C., 1948-51; weapons rsch. U.S. Army, N.Mex., 1953-57; adviser French Army U.S. Army, 1957-60; staff electronics U.S. Army, Ft. Monroe, Va., 1960-62; rsch. mgr., divsn. dir. CD U.S. Army, Pentagon, 1962-64, as civilian, 1964-81; asst. assoc. dir. Fed. Emergency Mgmt. Agy. for Rsch., 1981-85; sr. staff Michael Rogers, Inc., Winter Park, Fla., 1986—; dr. Mt. St. Helen's Tech. Office, 1980; v.p. Latherow & Co., Arlington, Va., 1965-86; radiol. officer Talbot County, Md., 1997—. Author: Korean-English Phrase Book, 1951, 19th Century Korea Postal Handbook, 1965, 2d edit., 1990; editor Korean Philately mag., 1971-80, 85-95; contbr. articles to profl. jours. Advanced English instr. French Army, 1957-60; cons. Am. Nat. Red Cross Mus., 1968-85, Smithsonian Instn. Dept. Postal History, 1966-85, NSF, 1976-85; vol. firefighter N.Y. State, 1946-48, Fairfax County, Va., 1969—; fire commr. Fairfax County, 1975-81, chmn., 1977-81, Orange County, Fla., 1986—; pres., 1987-90, Pike County, Ala., 1994-98, Talbot County, Md., 1997—; active Boy Scouts Am., in U.S., Asia, Europe, 1933—; chmn. libr. bd. Orangeburg, N.Y., 1946-48. Decorated bronze star with three oak leaf clusters, Purple Heart; recipient silver beaver award Boy Scouts Am., 1956, James E. West award, 1994; Fulbright selectee, Japan, 1986. Fellow AAAS (life), Explorers Club; mem. NAS (various coms. 1962-87), IEEE (life, sr.), NSPE, Internat. Assn. Fire Chiefs (chmn. rsch. com. 1969-88, chief sci. adviser 1982-86), Fed. Fire Coun., Nat. Fire Protection Assn. (chmn. hosp. disaster com. 1973-86), Presdl. Nat. Def. Execs., SAR (fire safety medal 1995), Black Forest Mardi Gras (Germany), Nat. Comms. Club, Pentagon Officers Athletic Club, Univ. Club Fla., Korean War Vets. Assn. (nat. bd. dirs. 1999), Elks, Phi Beta Kappa, Gamma Sigma Epsilon, Delta Phi Alpha. Presbyn. (elder 1963—). Home: PO Box 1537 Easton MD 21601-8929 Office: MR Inc 199 E Welbourne Ave Winter Park FL 32789-4365

KERR, SIR JOHN, diplomat; b. Feb. 22, 1942; s. Dr. and Mrs. J.D.O. Kerr; m. Elizabeth Kalaugher; 5 children. Student, Glasgow Acad., Pembroke Coll. Oxford, 1991. With diplomatic svc. Brit. Govt., 1966—; with Fgn. Office and Fgn. Commonwealth Office Brit. Govt., Moscow and Rawalpindi; pvt. sec. to permanent under sec. Fgn. Commonwealth Office Brit. Govt., 1974-79; head DM1 divsn. Her Majesty's Treasury, 1979-81; prin. pvt. sec. Chancellor of the Exchequer, 1981-84; head of chancery Washington, 1984-87; asst. under-sec. of state Fgn. and Commonwealth Office, 1987-90; amb., U.K. permanent rep. European Union, Brussels, 1990-95; amb. Brit. Embassy, Washington, 1995-97; permanent under sec. of state, head diplomatic svc. Fgn. and Commonwealth Office, London, 1997—. Hon. fellow Pembroke Coll. Oxford U., 1991. Office: Fgn and Commonwealth Office, King Charles St, 1040 London SW1A 2AH, England

KERR, KLEON HARDING, former state senator, educator; b. Plain City, Utah, Apr. 26, 1911; s. William A. and Rosemond (Harding) K.; m. Katherine Abbott, Mar. 15, 1941; children: Kathleen, William A., Rebecca Rae. AS, Weber Coll., 1936; BA, George Washington U., 1939; MS, Utah State U., Logan, 1946. Tchr. Bear River H.S., Tremonton, Utah, 1940-56; prin. jr. high sch. Bear River H.S., Tremonton, 1956-60, prin., 1960-71; city justice Tremonton, 1941-46; sec. to Senator Arthur V. Watkins, 1947. Author: (poetry) Open My Eyes, 1983, We Remember, 1983, Trouble in the Amen Corner, 1985, Past Imperfect, 1988, A Helping Hand, 1990, Sound of Silence, 1991, Power Behind the Throne, 1992, Unreachable Goal?, 1993, The Only Difference, 1994, Please Boss, 1995, Beach Comber, 1995, Under the Hood, 1999; (history) Those Who Served Box Elder County, 1984, Those Who Served Tremonton City, 1985, Diamond in the Rough, 1987, Facts of Life, 1987, Gettin' and Givin', 1989, Wells Without Water, 1998, Hand in Pocket, 1998, I Want to Come Home, 1997, No Days Off, 1999. Mayor Tremonton City, 1948-53; mem. Utah Local Govt. Survey Commn., 1954-55; mem. Utah Ho. of Reps., 1953-56; mem. Utah State Senate, 1957-64, chmn. appropriation com., 1959—, majority leader, 1963; mem. Utah Legis. Coun.; dist. dir. vocat. edn. Box Elder Sch. Dist. Recipient Alpha Delta Kappa award for outstanding contbn. to edn., 1982, award for outstanding contbrs. to edn. and govt. Theta Chpt. Alpha Beta Kappa, 1982, Excellence Achieved in Promotion of Tourism award, Allied Category award Utah Travel Coun., 1988, Merti award, 1993, Andy Rytting Cmty. Svc. award, 1991; named Tourism Ambassador of Month, 1986. Mem. NEA, Utah Box Elder edn. assns., Utah Sheriff's Assn. (hon.), Bear River Valley C. of C. (sec., mgr. 1955-58), Lions, Kiwanis, Phi Delta Kappa. Mem. Ch. of Jesus Christ of Latter-day Saints. Home: PO Box 246 Tremonton UT 84337-0246

KERR, NANCY KAROLYN, pastor, mental health consultant; b. July 10, 1934; d. Owen W. and Iris Irene (Israel) K.; m. Richard Clayton Williams, June 28, 1953 (div.); children: Richard Charles, Donna Louise. Student, Boston U., 1953; AA, U. Bridgeport, 1966; BA, Hofstra U., 1967; postgrad. in clin. psychology, Adelphi U. Inst. Advanced Psychol. Studies, 1968-73; MDiv, Associated Mennonite Bibl. Sems., 1986. Ordained pastor Mennonite Ch., 1987; apptd. pastor Kamloops Presbyn. Ch., Can., 1992. Pastoral counselor Nat. Coun. Chs., Jackson, Miss., 1964; dir. teen program Waterbury (Conn.) YWCA, 1966-67; intern in psychology N.Y. Med. Coll., 1971-72, rsch. cons., 1972-73; coord. home svcs., psychologist City and County of Denver, 1972-75; cons. Mennonite Mental Health Svcs., Denver, 1975-78; asst. prof. psychology Messiah Coll., 1978-79; mental health cons., 1979-81; called to ministry Mennonite Ch., 1981; pastor Cin. Mennonite Fellowship, 1981-83, mem. Gen. Conf. Peace and Justice Reference Coun., 1983-85; instr. Associated Mennonite Bibl. Sems., 1985; tchg. elder Assembly Mennonite Ch., 1985-86; pastor Pulaski Mennonite Ch., 1986-89; exec. dir., pastoral counselor Bethesda Counseling Svcs., Prince George B.C., 1989-99; pvt. practice, 1999—; spl. ch. curriculum Nat. Coun. Chs., 1981; mem. Cen. Dist. Conf. Peace and Justice Com., 1981-89; mem. exec. bd. People for Peace, 1981-83. Bd. dirs. Tri-County Counselling Clinic, Memphis, Mo., 1980-81, Boulder (Colo.) ARC, 1977-78, PLURA, B.C. Synod, 1995-98, Prince George Neighbor Link, 1995—, Davis County Mins. Assn., v.p., 1988-89 active Prince George Ministerial Assn., chmn. edn. and airport chapel coms., 1990-92; mem. Waterbury Planned Parenthood Bd., 1964-67; mem. MW Children's Home Bd., 1974-75; elder St. Giles Presbyn. Ch., 1996—; mem. Mennonite Disabilities Respite Care Bd., 1981-86; Prince George Children's Svcs. com., 1992-94; adv. com. Prince George Planning Coun., 1997-98; mem. housing Prince George adv. bd. Mennonite Cen. Com., 1998-99. Mem. APA (assoc.), Can. Psychol. Assn., Soc. Psychologists for Study of Social Issues, Christian Assn. Psychol. Studies, Soc. Bibl. Lit. & Exegesis. Office: Nancy Kerr Counselling Svcs, 110-154 Quebec St, Prince George, BC Canada V2L 1W2

KERR, WALTER BELNAP, retired missile instrumentation engineer, English language researcher, consultant; b. Salt Lake City, Oct. 14, 1926; s. Walter Affleck and Marion Adeline (Belnap) K.; m. Raida Nebeker, May 2, 1952 (dec. Mar. 1992); children: Valerie Jean Kerr Lynch, Grant Mercer, Janice Arlene Kerr Hahn, Marilyn, m. Lillian Hamilton Nelson Ettinger, Oct. 1, 1992; children: Edgar Nelson Jr., James Nelson, Patricia Nelson Hardwick, Douglas Nelson. BA in French, U. Utah, 1951, BSEE, 1955; MBA in Internat. Bus., U. So. Calif., 1972. Electrical engr. Hughes Aircraft Co., L.A., 1955-61, 67-69; missile instrumentation engr. Hercules Inc., Salt Lake City, 1961-66, 84-89, Rockwell Internat., Anaheim, Calif., 1969-70; investment broker Titan Capital Corp., L.A., Ogden, Utah, 1970-79; electrical engr. White Motor Corp., Ogden, 1979-84; tax examiner IRS, Ogden, 1990-91, ret., 1991; cons. Soc. for the Advancement of Good English, Pittsford, N.Y., 1985-86. Author: (book) Instrumentation Methods, 1963, (card) Pocket Guide to Good English, 1984; columnist Correct Corner, Cherokee Scout newspaper, 1996-99; inventor. Juggler St. Benedict's Hosp., and various nursing homes, grade schs., h.s., univs., shopping ctrs. and chs., 1947—. With USN, 1945-46, 1st lt. U.S. Army, 1951-53. Mem. IEEE, The Planetary Soc., World Wildlife Fund, Soc. for the Preservation of English Lang. and Lit., Soc. Alphanumeric Improvement, Sierra Club, Soc. for Alpha Numeric Improvement. Republican. LDS. Avocations: tennis, juggling, planetoid research, kite flying, computing, astronomical model building. Home: 395 Messer Rd Murphy NC 28906-9197

KERRES, BERNHARD HUGO HELMUT, management consultant; b. Vienna, Austria, Dec. 9, 1966; arrived in Eng., 1996; s. Helmut and Erika (Purschke) K.; m. Nicole A. Tury. Student, Acad. Music & Performing Arts, Vienna, 1987-92; MBA, London Bus. Sch., 1998. Mgr. IKEA, Vienna, 1987-92; dir. Die Wiener Taschenoper, Vienna, 1988-90; project mgr. Jeunesse, Vienna, 1991-92; prin. opera singer, 1992-95; dir. Musikwerkstatt, Vienna, 1992-95; mgmt. cons. AEA Ltd., London, 1996-97; assoc. Booz Allen & Hamilton, Munich, Vienna, 1997—; guest lect., European Bus. Sch., London, 1997. Mem. adv. coun. London Mozart Players. Mem. Round Table Austria (chmn. 1994-96), fell., Royal Soc. for the Encouragement of Arts, Manufacture & Commerce. Avocations: classical music, literature, philosophy. Office: Booz Allen & Hamilton, Kaerntner Ring 5-7, A-10103 Vienna Austria

KERRIGAN, NANCY, professional figure skater, former Olympic athlete; b. Woburn, Mass., Oct. 13, 1969; d. Daniel and Brenda Kerrigan; m. Jerry Solomon, 1995; 1 child, Matthew Eric Solomon. Bronze medalist World Championships, 1991, 92, Olympic Games, Albertville, France, 1992; U.S. nat. champion, 1993; silver medalist Olympic Games, Lillehammer, Norway, 1994; owner, choreographer Halloween on Ice, 1995—. Numerous commercials and product endorsements including Walt Disney Co., Reebok, Northwest Airlines, Frosted Cheerios, Ray Ban, Revlon, Aetna U.S. Healthcare, Salvino Bammers, AquaTrend, Tostitos; author: In My Own Words, 1996; choreographer Halloween on Ice, (video) Fairy Tales on Ice; performer: Champions on Ice Tour, 1992—; star TV spls. incl.: Dreams on Ice, Breaking the Ice, Nancy Kerrigan and Friends, Holiday Celebration on Ice, One Enchanted Evening; host Nancy Kerrigan's World of Figure Skating; released Shining Through as part of Reflections Off the Ice Co., 1999; starred as Sandy in Grease on Ice, 1998-99, Broadway on Ice, Branson, Mo., 2000; appeared in various TV movies and shows, including Boy Meets World, 1995, The Journey of Allen Strange, 1998, Ice Angel. Spokesperson Lions Club, 1994, Children's Trust Fund, 1997, Spalding Rehab. Hosp., MADD; founder, benefactor Nancy Kerrigan Found.; hon. chairwoman Nancy Kerrigan Golf Classic, Sept. 2000. Recipient Bronze medal World Figure Skating Championships, 1991, Silver medal, 1992, Bronze medal U.S. Pro Championships, 1997. Office: care of StarGames Bldg 1 40 Salem St Lynnfield MA 01940

KERR-JARRETT, MARK NEWTON, mechanical engineer; b. Kingston, Jamaica, Nov. 10, 1960; s. Peter Francis and Janet Eleanor (Hesselbrock) K.; m. Paula Kay Bovell, Dec. 29, 1990; children, Joshua Francis, Rebecca Michelle. BS in Mech. Engring., Va. Tech., 1987. Mech. engr. NTSB, Washington, 1988-89; gen. mgr. Barnett Ltd., Montego Bay, Jamaica, 1989—; pres., mng. dir. Barnett Ltd., Montego Bay, 1992—; dir. Greater Montego Bay Redevel. Co., Ltd., 1991-94, 96—, Campus Crusade for Christ, Jamaica, 1996—. Justice of the Peace, Govt. Jamaica, 1997; chmn. St. James Parish Devel. Com., Flankers Jr. H.S., New Life Discipleship Ministries; trustee Teamwork Trust and Christian Ctr. Mem. Montego Bay C. of C. (dir. 1997-98, 2d v.p. 1998—, 1st v.p., 1999-2000, pres. 2000—). Avocations: scuba diving, horseback riding, sailing. Home: Tamarind Barnett Estates, Montego Bay Jamaica Office: Barnett Ltd, PO Box 876, Montego Bay Jamaica

KERRY, JOHN FORBES, senator; b. Denver, Dec. 11, 1943; s. Richard John and Rosemary (Forbes) K.; m. Teresa Heinz, May 25, 1995; children from previous marriage: Alexandra, Vanessa. BA, Yale U., 1966; MA, JD, Boston Coll., 1976. Bar: Mass. 1976. Nat. coordinator Vietnam Vets. Against The War, 1969-71; asst. dist. atty. Middlesex (Mass.) County, 1976-79; ptnr. firm Kerry & Sragow, Boston, 1979-82; lt. gov. State of Mass., 1982-84; U.S. senator from Mass., 1985—; chmn. Dem. Senatorial campaign com., 1986-88; mem. Fgn. Rels. Com., Fgn. Rels. subcom. Internat. Ops., Sen. Dem. Steering & Coordination Com.; mem. Com. Banking, Housing & Urban Affairs, ranking minority mem. Com. Small Bus., Select Com. on Intelligence; ranking minority mem. Commerce, Sci. & Transp. subcom. on Oceans & Fisheries. Author: The New Soldier, 1971, The New War, 1997. Democratic candidate for Congress from 5th Mass. Dist., 1972; bd. vistors Walsh Sch. Fgn. Service, Georgetown U. Served to lt. (j.g.) USNR, 1966-69. Decorated Silver Star; decorated Bronze Star with oak leaf cluster, Purple Hearts (3). Mem. Vietnam Veterans Am. (founder). Roman Catholic. Office: US Senate 304 Russell Senate Bldg Washington DC 20510-0001

KERSCHBAUM, FRANZ J.H., astronomy scientist and educator; b. Zwettl, Austria, Dec. 5, 1963; s. Franz and Irmtraud (Redl) K.; m. Christiana Maria Riedl Kerschbaum, June 22, 1991; children: Christoph, Nikoloius. M in Natural Scis., U. Vienna, 1988, PhD in Natural Scis., 1993. Univ. asst. U. Vienna, Austria, 1988-89, rsch. asst., 1990-91; astronome adjoint DESPA, Paris-Meudon, France, 1991; rsch. asst. U. Vienna, Austria, 1993-97; org. of exhibitions, Austria, 1988—; coinvestigator FIRST-PACS Space Mission, ESA, 1997—; cons. for space projects Austrian Min. Sci., 1995—. Contbr. articles to profl. jours. Coord. interdisciplinary rsch. group PRO Scientia, Austria, 1996—. Recipient Sci. grant Austrian Min. Sci., Vienna, 1990, 93, APART grant Austrian Acad. Scis., Vienna, 1997. Mem. Deutsche Astronomiesche Gesellschaft, European Astronomy Soc. (astr. working group), Internat. Astronomy Union. Roman Catholic. Avocations: tennis, skiing, diving, singing, theater. Office: Inst Astronomy, Turkenschanzstrasse 17, A-1180 Wien Austria

KERSTEN, MICHAEL, geochemist, educator; b. Bad Homburg, Germany, Feb. 14, 1956; s. Wassily Matjukov and Eleonore (Delbat) K.; m. Sibylle Hielscher, Oct. 10, 1995; children: Anna Neissa, Paul Joel. Diploma in Engring., Tech. U., Darmstadt, Germany, 1983; D in Engring., Tech. U., Hamburg-Harburg, Germany, 1989, D in Engring. habilitation, 1996—. Rsch. asst. Tech. U. Hamburg-Harburg, Germany, 1983-92; rsch. assoc. Swiss Fed. Inst. for Environ. Sci. and Tech. (EAWAG), Dübendorf, Switzerland, 1993-94; sr. scientist Baltic Sea Rsch. Inst., Rostock, Germany, 1995-97; assoc. prof. Gutenberg U., Mainz, Germany, 1997—; chmn. Internat. coun. for Exploration of the Sea (ICES-WGMS), Copenhagen, 1996—. Contbr. articles to profl. jours. Habilitation fellow German Sci. Found., Bonn, Germany, 1992-93. Office: Gutenberg U Geosci Inst, Becherweg 21, D-55099 Mainz Germany

KERSTEN, ROBERT C., ophthalmic plastic surgeon; b. Ft. Dodge, Iowa, July 28, 1952; s. John and Jeanne M. (Montgomery) K.; m. Jennifer L. Lee, May 21, 1977; children: Charles, Andrew, Elizabeth, Cal. BA, U. Notre Dame, 1974; MD, U. Iowa, 1978. Diplomate Am. Bd. Ophthalmology. Intern U. Hawaii, 1978-79; resident U. Iowa, 1980-84; chief ophthalmic plastic surgery K.K.E.S.H., Riyadh, Saudi Arabia, 1984-86; asst. prof. U. Cin., 1987-90, assoc. prof., 1990-97, prof. ophthalmic plastic surgery, 1997—. Contbr. over 100 articles to profl. jours. Recipient P.J. Linefelder award U. Iowa, 1982. Fellow Am. Soc. Ophthalmic Plastic and Reconstructive Surgery; mem. Am. Acad. Ophthalmology (honor award 1995), Phi Beta Kappa, Alpha Omega Alpha. Office: Cincinnati Eye Inst 10494 Montgomery Rd Cincinnati OH 45242-5207

KERTESZ, ANDRAS LAJOS, linguist; b. Debrecen, Hungary, Mar. 8, 1956; s. Andor and Ilona (Toth) K.; m. Ildiko Toth, Jan. 26, 1983; children: Mate, Annamaria. MA, U. Debrecen, 1981, Dr.univ., 1983, PhD, 1991, habilitation, 1995; DSc, Hungarian Acad. Sci., Budapest, 1996. Asst. prof. U. Debrecen, 1981-87, assoc. prof., 1987-96, prof., 1996—, head. dept., 1994—, dir. Inst. German Studies, 1996-99. Author: Die Modularität der Wissenschaft, 1991, Artificial Intelligence and the Sociology of Knowledge, 1993, Heuristik der Deutschen Phonologie, 1993, Die Ferse und der Schild, 1995, Metalinguistik, 1999; editor: Sprache als Kognition--Sprache als Interaktion, 1995, Metalinguistik im Wandel, 1997; mem. editl. bd. LOGOS and Lang.: Jour. Gen. Linguistics and Lang. Theory, 1998—, Officina Textologica, 1997—, Acta Linguistica Hungarica, 1999—; editor-in-chief Metalinguistica, 1994—, Sprachtheorie und germanistische Linguistik, 1994— (Hungarian Rsch. Fund award 1996). DAAD fellow, Tubingen, Germany, 1987-88, Humboldt fellow A.V. Humboldt Found., Bielefeld, Germany, 1992-93, Tubingen, Germany, 1997-98, Telegdi fellow Ctr. Advanced Studies, Stanford, Calif., 1995; recipient Kanyo award, 1988. Mem. Hungarian Rsch. Fund (bd. dirs. 1994-99), Internat. Pragmatic Assn., Internat. Soc. Semiotic Studies, Soc. Linguistica, Found. Theoretical Linguistics (bd. dirs. 1994-99), Sci. Coun. U. Debrecen, Hungarian Acad. Sci. (linguistics bd. 1997), Hungarian Accreditation Coun. (linguistics bd. 1998—). Avocations: jogging, swimming, aquatics. Home: Nemeth Laszlo 4, H-4032 Debrecen Hungary Office: U Debrecen, Pf 47, H-4010 Debrecen Hungary

KERUR, BASAVARAJ RACHAPPA, physicist; b. Aluvandi, Koppal, India, Oct. 17, 1965; s. Rachappa Fhakirappa and Drakshayani Rachappa Kalamma K.; m. Rajeshwari Basavaraj Mahanand, May 25, 1994. BS, Karnatak Coll., Dharwad, India, 1985; MS, Karnatak U., 1987, PhD, 1992. Jr. rsch. fellow UGC/New Delhi, Dharwad, 1988-91; sr. rsch. fellow CSIR/New Delhi, Dharwad, 1991-93; rsch. assoc. DRDO/New Delhi, Jodhpur, 1994; lectr. Karnatak U., 1993-94, Gulbarga U., India, 1995—; panel mem. Nat. Assessment and Accreditation Coun., Bangalore, India, 1995—; project investigator Univ. Grants Commn. maj. rsch. project, New Delhi, 1997-2000, univ. project Gulbarga U., 1997-98; project co-investigator Nuclear Sci. Ctr., New Delhi, 1995-98; jr. assoc. Internat. Ctr. Theoretical Physics, Trieste, Italy, 1997-2000, visitor, 1993, 99. Inventor in field; contbr. articles to profl. jours. Pres. Karnatak U. Rsch. Forum, Dharwad, 1990-92. Mem. Inst. Physics, Internat. Soc. for Radiation Physics, Instrument Soc. India Bangalore, Indian Assn. Physics Tchrs., Gulbarga U. Post-Grad. Tchrs. Assn. (exec. mem.). Hindu. Avocations: fundamental rsch., study of physics, adventure films. Home: s/o RF Kerur Basaveshwar Ng, 582 101 Gadag Karnatak, India Office: Dept Physics/Jhana Ganga, Gulbarga Univ, 585 106 Gulbarga Karnatak, India

KERVÉGAN, JEAN-FRANÇOIS, philosophy educator, researcher; b. Algiers, Algiera, Dec. 5, 1950; s. Ernest and Lucie (Richard) K.; m. Argyriadis Caroula, Sept. 17, 1993; children: Lucas Armand, Paul Hector. Agregation, Superior Normal Sch., St. Cloud, France, 1975; PhD, U. Lyon (France) III, 1990. Tchr. France, 1977-86; rschr. Nat. Ctr. for Sci. Rsch., Paris, 1987-89; vis. rschr. Max Planck Inst. for European Legal History, Frankfurt, Germany, 1989-91; prof. philosophy U. Cergy-Pontoise, France, 1992-99, dir. Rsch. Ctr. German Philosophy, 1993—, mem. sci. coun., 1995; dir. rsch. ctr. 456 Nat. Ctr. Sci. Rsch., 1995-98, mem. philosophy jury of agregation; prof. philosophy U. Paris 1 Sorbonne, 1999—. Co-author: In-

troduction a la Lecture de la Logique de Hegel 1986 (bronze medal Nat. Ctr. for Sci. Rsch. 1986), Hegel, Notes and Fragments, 1993; author: Hegel, Carl Schmitt, Le Politique entre Speculation et Positivite, 1992 (Crouzet prize Inst. France 1993),. Hegel, Principes de la Philosphie du Drsit, 1999. Mem. Internat. Soc. for Hegelian Studies, French Soc. Philosophy. E-mail: kerve-gan@u-cergy.fr. Fax: 01 40 46 31 57. Home: 16 rue du Parc de Noailles, F-78100 Saint-Germain-en-Laye France Office: Paris I Dept Phil, 17 rue de la Sorbonne, F-75231 Paris cedex 05 France

KERWIN, LARKIN, retired physics educator; b. June 22, 1924; m. Maria Guadalupe Turcot, 1950; 8 children. Cert. engrng. studies, St. Francis Xavier U., 1943, BSc summa cum laude, 1944; MSc magna cum laude, MIT, 1946; DSc magna cum laude, U. Laval, 1949; LLD (hon.), St. Francis Xavier U., 1970, U. Toronto, 1973, Concordia U., Montreal, 1976, U. Alta., 1983, U. Dalhousie, 1983, U. Moncton, 1985; DSc (hon.), U. B.C., 1973, McGill U., 1974, Meml. U. Newfoundland, 1978, U. Ottawa, 1981, Royal Mil. Coll. Can., 1982, U. Winnipeg, 1983, U. Windsor, 1984, U. Montreal, 1991; DCivil Law (hon.), Bishop's U., 1978. Tchg. asst. St. Francis Xavier U., 1944; lab. demonstrator U. Toronto, 1945; rsch. physicist Geotech. Corp., Cambridge, Mass., 1945; lab. asst. physics dept. U. Laval, Que., 1946-48, from asst. prof. to assoc. prof., 1948-56, prof., chair atomic physics, 1956; dir. Mass Spectrometry Lab. U. Laval, 1955-66, chmn. dept. physics, 1961-67; dir. Van de Graaf Accelerator Lab., 1961-72, vice-dean faculty of scis., 1967-68, acad. vice-rector, 1969-72, rector, 1972-77, prof. emeritus, 1991; pres. Assn. Univs. and Colls. Can., 1975-75, Nat. Rsch. Coun. Can., 1980-89, Can. Space Agy., 1989-92, Can. Acad. Engrng., 1989-90. Author: Atomic Physics, An Introduction, 1963; mem. editl. bd. Interdisciplinary Sci. Revs. Mag., 1981—; contbr. numerous articles to profl. jours. Trustee Nat. Museums of Can., 1980-89; adv. coun. Ottawa chpt. Can. Soc. Weizmann Inst. Sci., 1981; Can. rep. Versailles conf. on tech. and employment, 1982; bd. govs. Carleton U., 1983-86. Recipient Centenary medal, 1967; knight Equestrian Order of Holy Sepulchre of Jerusalem, 1970, knight comdr., 1972, comdr. with star, 1974, knight grand cross, 1980; Jubilee medal, 1977; Centenary medal of Roumania, 1977; officer Order of Can., 1978, companion, 1980; medal of Laval Alumni, 1978; Ordre du Merite, Sociète Saint-Jean Baptiste de Que., 1979; Gold medal, Can. Coun. Profl. Engrs., 1982, Officer Order of Que., 1987, officier Legion Honor, France, 1989; Outstanding Achievement award Govt. Can., 1987. Fellow AAAS, Royal Soc. Can. (pres. 1977-78), Royal Soc. Arts, Am. Inst. Physics; mem. Internat. Union Pure and Applied Physics (pres. 1987-91), Assn. Canadienne Française pour l'Avancement des Scis. (Pariseau medal 1965, Jacques Rousseau medal 1983), Am. Phys. Soc., Corp. Profl. Engrs. Que., Sociedad Mexicana Fisica, Can. Assn. Physicists (pres. 1954, Gold medal 1969), Acadèmie des Grands QuÂbecois.

KERWIN, WALTER THOMAS, JR., career officer, consultant; b. West Chester, Pa., June 14, 1917; s. Walter Thomas and Mary Joseph (Farra) K.; m. Barbara Walker Connell, July 10, 1940 (dec. 1980); children: Bruce Richard, Ann Walker; m. Marion Thompson McCutcheon, Oct. 27, 1984. BS, U.S. Mil. Acad., 1939; postgrad., Command and Gen. Staff Coll., 1948, Armed Forces Staff Coll., 1953, U.S. Army War Coll., 1957, Nat. War Coll., 1960; LLD (hon.), U. Akron, 1976; M in Mil. Art and Sci., Command and Gen. Staff Coll., 1978. Commd. 2nd lt. U.S. Army, 1939, advanced through grades to gen., 1973; commdg. gen. 3d armored divsn. arty. U.S. Army, Hanau, Germany, 1961-63; chief nuclear activities SHAPE NATO U.S. Army, Paris, 1963-65; commdg. gen. 3d armored divsn. U.S. Army, Frankfurt, Germany, 1965-66; asst. dep. chief staff ops. gen. staff U.S. Army, Washington, 1966-67; chief staff mil. asst. command U.S. Army, Saigon, Vietnam, 1967-68; commdg. gen. II field force Vietnam U.S. Army, Bien Hoa, 1968-69; dep. chief staff pers. gen. staff U.S. Army, Washington, 1969-72; commdg. gen. continental army command U.S. Army, Norfolk, Va., 1973; commdg. gen. forces command U.S. Army, Atlanta, 1973-74; vice chief staff U.S. Army, Washington, 1974-78; cons. Martin Marietta Corp., Bethesda, Md., 1978-94, Lockheed-Martin, 1994-97; assoc. dir. ops. Los Alamos (N.Mex.) Sci. Lab., 1953-56; bd. dirs. Gen. Employment Enterprises, Oakbrook, Ill., 1984—; mem. bd. mgrs. Army Emergency Relief, 1982—. Chmn. Army Air Force Mut. Aid Assn., Arlington, Va., 1982-97, chmn. emeritus 1997—; mem. strategy com. Army Hist. Found., 1995-97, bd. dirs., 1997—. Recipient Disting. Svc. medal Commonwealth of Pa., 1975, Outstanding Alumnus award U.S. Army War Coll., 1997, numerous mil. awards and decorations; named to Henderson Hall of Fame, West Chester, Pa., 1991, Res. Officers Assn. of U.S. Minute Man Hall of Fame, 1978. Fellow Nat. Def. U. Capstone Program (emeritus); mem. Am. Def. Preparedness Assn. (comdr. Chief award 1984), West Point Soc. (Castle-Duty Hon. Country award 1993), U.S. Field Arty. Assn. (pres. 1981-96). Avocations: fishing, wilderness hiking.

KERYCZYNSKYJ, LEO IHOR, county official, educator; b. Chgo., Aug. 8, 1948; s. William and Eva (Chicz) K.; m. Alexandra Irene Okruch, July 19, 1980; 1 child, Christina Alexandra. BA, DePaul U., 1970, BS, 1970, MS in Pub. Svc., 1975; JD, No. Ill. U., 1979; postgrad., U. Ill., Chgo., 1980-82. Bar: Ill. 1981, U.S. Dist. Ct. (no. dist.) Ill. 1981, U.S. Ct. Appeals (7th cir.) 1981, U.S. Tax Ct. 1981, U.S. Ct. Claims 1982, U.S. Ct. Mil. Appeals 1982, U.S. Ct. Appeals (fed. cir.) 1983, U.S. Supreme Ct. 1984. Condemnation awards officer Cook County Treas.'s Office, Chgo., 1972-75, adminstrv. asst., 1975-77, dep. treas., 1977-87, chief legal counsel, 1987-96, dir. fin. svcs., 1988-96; pvt. practice, 1996-98; adv. Office of Profl. Stds. Chgo. Police Dept., 1998—; adj. prof. DePaul U., Chgo., 1979-95; elected chmn. bd. dirs., 1st Security Fed. Savs. Bank Chgo., 1992-93. Capt. Ukrainian Am. Dem. Orgn., Chgo., 1971. Recipient Outstanding Alumni award Phi Kappa Theta, 1971. Mem. ABA, Ill. State Bar Assn., Ill. Trial Law Assn., Ukrainian Am. Bar Assn., Chgo. Bar Assn., Ill. Assn. County Ofcls., Internat. Assn. Clerks, Recorders, Election Ofcls. and Treas., Shore Line Interurban Hist. Soc. (bd. dirs., legal counsel 1987—, pres. and chmn., 1993-98), Theta Delta Phi. Ukrainian Catholic. Home: 2324 W Iowa St Apt 3R Chicago IL 60622-4720 Office: Office Profl Stds 1130 S Wabash Ave Chicago IL 60605-2372

KERZHENTSEV, ANATOLY SEMENOVICH, ecologist; b. Chapaevsk, Russia, May 2, 1936; s. Semen Stepanovich and Klavdia Mikhailovna (Tsapaeva) D.; m. Valentina Stepanovna Shviratskaya, June 20, 1959 (div. Feb. 1968); 1 child, Alexandr Anatolevich;m. Vera Vasilevna Kolesnikova, Feb. 12, 1970. MSc in Agronomy, Agrl. Inst., Saratov, 1959; PhD in Soil Sci., Moscow State U., 1972; DSc in Soil Sci., Inst. Soil Sci. Agr., Novosibirsk, 1993. Engr. of soil mapping Inst. Rosgiprozen, Saratov, 1959-62; engr. of soil mapping Rosgiprozem, Nalchik, 1962-65, Kuybishev, 1965-67, Novosibirsk, 1967-68; head of lab. Inst. of Agrochemistry and Soil Sci., Russian Acad. Sci., Pushchino, 1971—; head of dept. and soil sci. Russian Acad. Sci., Moscow; prof. ecology Pushchino State U., 1994—, Internat. U., , Moscow, 1995—; v.p. Univ. Life Keeping Problem Acad., Moscow, 1991—; pres. Ecol. Found. of Oka Region, Pushchino, Russia, 1989—. Author, editor: Regional Ecological Monitoring, 1983; author: Soil Variability in Space and Through Time, 1992, Eurasian Soil Science, 1996; contbr. articles to profl. jours. Deputy Town Soviet, Pushchino, 1982-87. Recipient Gov. Prize for Sci. and Tech. of Russian Fedn., 1996. Avocations: singing, automobile traveling. Home: Micro-rn 27 dep 54, 142292 Pushchino Russia Office: Inst of Soil Sci, Institutskaya Str 2, 142292 Pushchino Russia

KESAVADAS, THENKURUSSI, mechanical engineering educator, researcher; b. Palghat, Kerala, India, Apr. 17, 1962; came to U.S., 1990; s. Marayil Tharkdas and Nalini T. Narayan; m. Mini P. Kesavadas, Aug. 12, 1995; 1 child, Tushar N. B of Tech., U. Calicut, India, 1985; M of Tech., Indian Inst. Tech., Madras, 1987; PhD, Pa. State U., 1995. Engr. Hindustan Aero. Ltd., India, 1987-90; rsch. asst. Pa. State U., State College, 1992-95; assoc. scientist Iowa State U., Ames, 1995-96; asst. prof. U. Buffalo, 1996—, dir. Virtual Reality Lab., 1997—. Editor: ASME Industrial Virtual Reality, 1999; contbr. articles to profl. jours. Mem. ASME (Leadership Devel. Internship award 1997), IEEE. Avocations: music, tennis, travelling. E-mail: kesh@eng.buffalo.edu. Office: Univ Buffalo Dept Mech Engring 1006 Furnas Hall Buffalo NY 14260-4200

KESAVAN, SUNDARARAJO, sociology educator; b. Madurai, India, May 19, 1949; s. Ramasamy Sundararaju and Kunjammal Subbanaidu; m. Uttarah Govindarajulu, June 8, 1978; 1 child, K. Vikraman. BA in Social Sci., Madura Coll., Madurai, India, 1971; MA in Sociology, Madras (India) U., 1973; AMA in Sociology, M.K. U., Madurai, 1980, PhD in Sociology, 1990. Lectr. Gandhigram (India) Rural Inst., Deemed U., 1976-85, sr. lectr., 1986-90, reader in rsch., 1990—. Author rsch. monograph. Avocations: reading, writing, table tennis. Office: Gandhigram Rural U, 624 302 Tamil Nadu India

KESEL, ANDREAS JOHANNES, pharmacist, researcher; b. Munich, Germany, Jan. 21, 1967; s. Günther and Hildegard (Aumüller) K. Chem Tech. Asst., 1993; student, Ludwig-Maximilians U., Munich, 1995—. Tech. asst. Max-Planck-Institut für Biochemie, Martinsried, Germany, 1993-95. Contbr. articles to profl. jours.; patentee in field. Mem. N.Y. Acad. Scis. Avocations: music, skiing, art, philosophy, history.

KESEY, KEN, writer; b. La Hunta, Colo., Sept. 17, 1935; s. Fred and Geneva (Smith) K.; m. Norma Faye Haxby, May 20, 1956; children: Shannon, Zane, Jed (dec. 1984) Sunshine. BS, U. Oreg., 1957; postgrad., Stanford U., 1958-60. Pres. Intrepid Trips, Inc., 1964; editor, pub. mag. Spit in the Ocean, 1974—. Author: One Flew Over the Cuckoo's Nest, 1962, Sometimes a Great Notion, 1964, Garage Sale, 1973, Demon Box, 1986, Little Tricker the Squirrel Meets Big Double the Bear, 1988; co-author: Caverns, 1989, The Further Inquiry, 1990, The Sea Lion, 1991, Sailor Song, 1992; (with Ken Babbs) Last Go Round: a Real Western, 1994; author, prodr.: (play) Twister, 1995; (video and script) Twister, 1998. Address: 85829 Ridgeway Rd Pleasant Hill OR 97455-9627

KESHAVAN, MATCHERI, psychiatrist; b. Belur, Karnataka, India, May 23, 1953; came to U.S., 1985; s. Matcheri Sannaiyengar and Rama Matcheri Srinivasamurthy; m. Asha Keshavan, June 5, 1981; children: Meghana, Vidya. MB BS, Mysore Med. Coll., Karnataka, India, 1977; MD, Nat. Inst. of Mental Health, Bangalore, India, 1979. Asst. prof. psychiatry St. Johns Med. Coll., Bangalore, 1979-80; lectr. in psychiatry NIMH, Bangalore, 1980-82; IBRO rsch. fellow Internat Brain Rsch. Orgn., Vienna, Austria, 1982-83; registrar Maudsley Hosp., London, 1984-85; asst. prof. of psychiatry Wayne State U., Detroit, 1986-87; asst. prof. of psychiatry U. Pitts., 1987-91, assoc. prof., 1991—; med. dir. schizophrenia unit Western Psychiat. Inst. and Clinic, Pitts., 1988—, prof. psychiatry, 1998—. Contbr. over 100 articles to profl. publs.; author 3 books. Recipient Silver Jubilee prize Mysore U., 1977, Young Investigator award NIMH, 1989, Rsch. Scientist Devel. award, 1995—; Schizophrenia Rsch. grantee Scottish Rite Found., 1989; Internat. Brain Rsch. Orgn. scholar, 1982-83. Mem. Royal Coll. Psychiatrists (Gaskell medal 1985), Indian Psychiat. Soc. (Jayaram award), IndoAm. Psychiat. Assn. (Sci. award 1996). Hindu. Avocation: paintings and sketches. Home: 2570 Mt Royal Rd Pittsburgh PA 15217-2542 Office: Western Psychiat Inst 3811 Ohara St Pittsburgh PA 15213-2593

KESSEL, BRINA, ornithologist, educator; b. Ithaca, N.Y., Nov. 20, 1925; d. Marcel and Quinta (Cattell) K.; m. Raymond B. Roof, June 19, 1957 (dec. 1968). BS (Albert R. Brand Bird Song Found. scholar), Cornell U., 1947, PhD, 1951; MS (Wis. Alumni Research Found. fellow), U. Wis.-Madison, 1949. Student asst. Patuxent Research Refuge, 1946; student teaching asst. Cornell U., 1945-47, grad. asst., 1947-48, 49-51; instr. biol. sci. U. Alaska, summer 1951, asst. prof. biol. sci., 1951-54, assoc. prof. zoology, 1954-59, prof. zoology, 1959-96, head dept. biol. scis., 1957-66; dean U. Alaska (Coll. Biol. Scis. and Renewable Resources), 1961-72, curator terrestrial vertebrate mus. collections, 1972-90, curator ornithology collection, 1990-95, adminstrv. assoc. for acad. programs, grad. and undergrad., dir. acad. advising, office of chancellor, 1973-80; sr. scientist U. Alaska, 1996-99, prof. emeritus, dean emeritus, curator emeritus, 1999—; project dir. U. Alaska ecol. investigation for AEC Project Chariot, 1959-63; ornithol. investigations NW Alaska pipeline, 1976-81, Susitna Hydroelectric Project, 1980-83. Author books, monographs; contbr. articles to profl. jours. Fellow AAAS, Am. Ornithologists' Union (v.p. 1977, pres.-elect 1990-92, pres. 1992-94), Arctic Inst. N.Am.; mem. Wilson, Cooper ornith. socs., Soc. for Northwestern Vertebrate Biology, Pacific Seabird Group, Assn. Field Ornithologists, Sigma Xi (pres. U. Alaska 1957), Phi Kappa Phi, Sigma Delta Epsilon. Office: U Alaska Mus PO Box 80211 Fairbanks AK 99708-0211

KESSEL, HUMBERTO DOMINGO, physician; b. Güines, Habana, Cuba, Nov. 14, 1952; s. Domingo Kessel and Sirgelina Sardiñas; m. Marcia Torriente, June 20, 1976; 1 child, Ilay; m. Emilia Moya-Angeler, July 19, 1989; 1 child, Emilio. MD, Havana U., Cuba, 1975; PhD in Geriatric Medicine, Ministry of Edn. and Scis., Spain, 1989. Physician 10 of Oct. Hosp., Habana, Cuba, 1976-77; dir. Amancio Rodriguez Hosp., Tunas, Cuba, 1977-79, Marianao Nursing Home, Habana, 1979-83; resident Red Cross Hosp., Madrid, 1983-88; prof. Geriatric Nursing Sch., Almeria, Spain, 1986-98, Almeria U., 1991—; invited prof. Cadiz (Spain) U., 1998—. Contbr. articles to profl. jours. Vol. Red Cross, Almeria, 1997—. Recipient 1st Accesit Subvention, Cordoba, Spain, 1994, Malaga, Spain, 1998. Mem. Spanish Soc. Geriatricians, N.Y. Acad. Scis., Andalucian Soc. Geriatrics. Roman Catholic. Avocations: music, computers, sports. Home: Melilla 17 2o A, 04007 Almeria Spain Office: Torrecardenas Hosp, Paraje Torrecardenas s/n, 04008 Almeria Spain

KESSELER, MATTHEW JOHN, librarian; b. Mt. Lebanon, Pa., Oct. 21, 1969; s. Robert Charles and Georgia Ellen Kesseler. AA in Univ. Parallel Tchr. Edn., C.C. Allegheny County, Pitts., 1990; BA in History, U. Pitts., 1993, MLS, 1994. Libr. grad. intern Hillman Libr. U. Pitts., 1994-95, libr. specialist III Chemistry/Computer Sci. Libr., 1998-99; part-time reference libr. Gumberg Libr. Duquesne U., Pitts., 1995-97; asst. libr. Pfeiffer Libr. Tiffin (Ohio) U., 1997-98; asst. libr. N. Libr. Cambria County Area C.C., Ebensburg, Pa., 1999—. Democrat. Roman Catholic. Avocations: reading, computers, piano, travel. Office: Cambria County Are CC PO Box 68 Johnstown PA 15907-0068

KESSELER, MICHAEL EDWARD, physician; b. Birmingham, Eng., Dec. 18, 1946; s. Sydney Joseph and Edith Maud (Smith) K.; m. Gale Narbett, Apr. 15, 1978. MBChB, Birmingham (Eng.) U., 1970. Registrar in Dermatology Liverpool (Eng.) Royal Infirmary, 1977-78; sr. registrar Royal S. Hants Hosp., Southampton, Eng., 1978-83; cons. dermatologist Rotherham (Eng.) Gen. Hosp., 1983—, clin. dir., 1991-99, dep. med. dir., 1999—; hon. lectr. U. Sheffield (Eng.), 1983—; tutor Rotherham Gen. Hosp., 1993-97. Contbr. articles to profl. jours. Fellow Royal Coll. Physicians (London,), Royal Soc. Medicine, St. John's Hosp. Dermatology Soc.; mem. Brit. Med. Assn. (chmn. Rotherham divsn. 1994). Avocations: walking, wine, theater. Home: The Beeches, 236 Doncaster Rd Thrybergh, Rotherham 565 4NU, England Office: Rotherham Dist Gen Hosp Dep, Dermatol Moorgate Rd, S6O 2UD Rotherham England

KESSLER, DANIEL SOLOMON, biologist, educator; b. Manhassett, N.Y., Feb. 28, 1964; s. Milton and Sonia Berer Kessler; m. Karen Zedeck, May 3, 1993; children: Aaron, Jonah. BS, Cornell U., 1986; PhD, Rockefeller U., 1990. Postdoctoral fellow NYU Med. Ctr., N.Y.C., 1990-91, Harvard U., Cambridge, Mass., 1991-95; asst. prof. U. Pa. Sch. Medicine, Phila., 1995—; vis. scientist Rockefeller U., N.Y.C., 1990-91; grant reviewer NIH, Washington, 1997-2000, Israel Acad. Scis., 1997-98. Contbr. articles to profl. jours. Cornell Tradition scholar Cornell U., Ithaca, N.Y., 1985, Am. Gastroenterol. Assn. and Schering-Plough Corp. Rsch. scholar Am. Digestive Health Found., Washington, 1996, Pew scholar Pew Charitable Trusts, Phila., 1997. Mem. Am. Soc. for Cell Biology, Soc. for Developmental Biology, John Morgan Soc., N.Y. Acad. Sci. Jewish. E-mail: kesslerd@mail.med.upenn.edu. Fax: 215-573-7601. Office: U Pa Sch Medicine 1110 BRB2/3 421 Curie Blvd Philadelphia PA 19104-6160

KESSLER, JURGEN, academic administrator. Chancellor Rheinisch-Westfalische Technische Hochschule, Aachen, Germany; dir.-gen. Rheinisch-Westfalische Technische Hochschule, Aachen, 1999. Office: Rheinisch-Westfallische Tech, Hoschschule Aachen, 52056 Aachen Germany*

KESSLER, RICHARD PAUL, JR., lawyer; b. Latrobe, Pa., July 11, 1945; s. Richard Paul Sr. and Dorothy Henrietta (Comp) K.; m. Kathleen Jane Parker, June 17, 1973 (dec. May 11, 1996); 1 child, Grace Elizabeth. BA, Fairfield (Conn.) U., 1968; JD, Emory U., 1971. Bar: Ga. 1971, U.S. Dist. Ct. (no. dist.) Ga. 1973, U.S. Ct. Appeals (5th cir.) 1974, U.S. Ct. Appeals (11th cir.) 1981, U.S. Supreme Ct. 1995. Law clk. to presiding justice U.S. Dist. Ct. (no. dist.) Ga., 1971-73; ptnr. Macey, Wilensky, Cohen, Wittner & Kessler, Atlanta, 1973—; lectr. Practising Law Inst., 1981, 83, Fin. Svc. Corp. Career Conf., Atlanta, 1986, Ga. and Ala. Insts. of Continuing Legal Edn., 1993-95; panelist Credit Union Nat. Assn., Inc. League Attys. Conf., 1980-82, 87, 88-93, ABA, 1990-91; participant Nat. Conf. Commrs. on Uniform State Laws Drafting Com. on U.C.C. Articles, 3, 4, 4A, 1985-90; chair corp. and banking law sect. State Bar Ga., 1995-96. Author: What You Should Know About the New Bankruptcy Code, 1979, Guide to the Bankruptcy Laws: The Bankruptcy Reform Act of 1978, 79, Guide to the Bankruptcy Laws: The Bankruptcy Reform Act of 1978 (Bankruptcy Code) as Amended by the Bankruptcy Amendments and Federal Judgeship Act of 1984, The Bankruptcy Judges, U.S. Trustees and Family Farmer Bankruptcy Act of 1986; contbr. articles to profl. jours. E-mail: rkessler@maceywilensky.com. Office: Ste 600 285 Peachtree Center Ave NE Atlanta GA 30303-1234

KESSLER, ROBERT ALLEN, data processing executive; b. N.Y.C., Feb. 2, 1940; s. Henry and Caroline Catherine (Axinger) K.; m. Marie Therese Anton, Mar. 17, 1967; children: Susanne, Mark. BA in Math., CUNY, 1961; postgrad., UCLA, 1963-64. EDP analyst Boeing Aircraft, Seattle, 1961-62; computer specialist System Devel. Corp., Santa Monica, Calif., 1962-66; mem. tech. staff Computer Scis. Corp., El Segundo, Calif., 1966-67, sr. mem. tech. staff, 1971-72, computer scientist, 1974-81; systems mgr. Xerox Data Systems, L.A., 1967-71; prin. scientist Digital Resources, Algiers, Algeria, 1972-74; sr. systems cons. Atlantic Richfield, L.A., 1981-94; computer cons., 1994—. Mem. Big. Bros. L.A., 1962-66; precinct capt. Goldwater for Pres., Santa Monica, 1964; mem. L.A. Conservacy, 1987. Mem. Assn. Computing Machinery. Avocations: racquetball, theatre, gourmet dining. Home: 6138 W 75th Pl Los Angeles CA 90045-1634 Office: Pfizer Health Solutions 2400 Broadway Santa Monica CA 90404-3030

KESSLER, VADIM G., chemist, educator; b. Moscow, Jan. 22, 1966; arrived in Sweden, 1997; s. Hermann E. and Galina Ya (Saxonova) K.; m. Gulaim A. Seisenbaeva; children: Alexandra, Irene. Grad. in Chemistry, Moscow State U., 1987, PhD, 1990. Rsch. asst. dept. chemistry Moscow State U., 1989-90, tchg. asst. dept. chemistry, 1990-92; postdoctoral U. de Nice, France, 1992-93; assoc. prof. dept. chemistry Moscow State U., 1994-95; postdoctoral Stockholm U., 1995-96; assoc. prof. dept. chemistry Moscow State U., 1996-97, Swedish U. Agrl. Sci., Uppsala, 1997—. Contbr. articles to profl. jours. Lutheran. Avocations: history of Sweden, Scandinavian languages. Home: Bergslagsresan 45, 75755 Uppsala Sweden Office: Swedish U Agrl Sci, Arrheniusplan 8, 75007 Uppsala Sweden

KESTENBAUM, RICHARD, clinical and school psychologist, consultant adolescent, family and child psychology, biofeedback; b. N.Y.C., Nov. 16, 1955; s. Ralph and Evelyn (Rose) K. B.S., SUNY-Buffalo, 1977; M.A., U. Colo., Boulder, 1979, Ph.D., 1983. Cert. sch. psychologist, Colo.; lic. clin. psychologist, Colo. Staff psychologist San Luis Valley Bd. Coop. Ednl. Services, Alamosa, Colo., 1980-81; staff psychologist Jefferson County Schs., Lakewood, Colo., 1981-86; instr. U. Colo., Boulder, 1982-83; pvt. practice clin. and counseling psychology, Denver, 1983-86; staff clinician, postdoctoral intern Jefferson County Mental Health Ctr., Arvada, Colo., 1984-85; inpatient psychologist Mercy Med. Ctr., Denver, 1985, Horizon Hosp., Denver, 1985-86; instr. U. So. Maine, 1988; workshop lectr. nat., state, local confs. Mem. Rocky Flats Conversion Campaign, 1978-79; bd. dirs. Boulder County Youth Planning Council, 1979-80. Recipient Henry S. Loeb Brotherhood award, 1973; N.Y. State Regents scholar, 1973-77; State of Colo. grad. grantee, 1981-83, fellow, 1981-82. Mem. Colo. Soc. Sch. Psychologists. Home: 2882 S Gray Way Denver CO 80227-3854

KESTILA, MATTI SEPPO, radiologist; b. Helsinki, Finland, Sept. 23, 1956; s. Pekka Veijo J. and Brita Anna-Liisa (Helin) K.; m. Tuija Leena Heininen, Feb. 18, 1984 (div. July 1992); children: Hans, Sven, Lisa; m. Aysel Azize Mersinli, Nov. 24, 1995; children: Nadim, Carlo. MD, Medizinische Hochschule, Hannover, West Germany, 1982; Radiologist, U. Helsinki, 1990. Resident Helsinki U. Hosp., 1986-90; asst. chief radiologist Forum Med. Office, Helsinki, 1991-96; chief of staff, CEO UltraRontgen, Inc., Helsinki, 1996—; cons. Turunmaa Regional Hosp., Turku, Finland, 1991-93; cons., chief of mammography screening, Lulea, Sweden, 1991; cons. Lycksele Hosp., Sweden, 1992. Contbr. articles to profl. jours. Recipient full scholarship DAAD, Germany, 1976-83. Mem. Medici Practici (bd. dirs. 1998—). Lutheran. Avocations: family life, business, badminton, music. Home: Maarinrannantie 11, 02320 Espoo Finland Office: UltraRontgen, Aleksanterinkatu 21 A, 00100 Helsinki Finland

KESTLMEIER, RALPH, physician, researcher; b. Wasserburg, Germany, Oct. 13, 1966; s. Erwin and Ingeborg (Frank) K. MD, Tech. U. Munich, 1996. Med. diplomate. Physician dept. orthop. surgery Kliniken Harthausen, Bad Aibling, Germany, 1994; physician dept. orthop. surgery Tech. U. Munich, 1994-95, physician dept. neurosurgery, 1996—; instr. Ctr. Orthop. Scis. Munich/Berne, U. Witten/Herdecke, Munich, 1990-94. Contbr. articles to profl. jours. Mem. Red Cross, Germany, 1996. Mem. N.Y. Acad. Scis., Fedn. Friends of Tech. U. Munich (jr. scientists award 1996), Deutsche Gesellschaft für Chirotherapie. Office: Tech U Munich Dept Neurosur, Ismaningerstrasse 22, 81675 Munich Germany

KESTY, ROBERT EDWARD, chemical manufacturing company executive; b. Camden, N.J., Dec. 11, 1941; s. Edward Adam and Helen Dorothy (Maciejko) Krzysztanowicz; m. Louise Marie Kesty, June 12, 1976; children: Nicole Christina, Alicia Anne, Christopher Edward, Robert Edward Jr. Student, Purdue U., 1960-63. Tech. rep. E.F. Houghton & Co., Phila., 1963-67; rsch. chemist H. Miller Corp., Phila., 1968-72; owner, founder R.E. Kesty Inc., Medford, N.J., 1977—; semi-ret., 1993; cons. Air Products and Chems. Inc., Middlesex, N.J., 1973, Monsanto, St. Louis, 1994, Crown Tech. Inc., 1994—, Wuhan Chem. Industries, China, 1996—, Solutia Inc., St. Louis, 1997; tech. advisor EPA, Indpls., 1974-76. Contbr. articles to profl. jours.; patentee in field. Recipient Franklin and Marshall Alumni award Franklin & Marshall Coll., 1959; recipient Hearst Trophy William Randolph Hearst Found., 1959. Mem. Nat. Assn. of Corrosion Engrs., South Jersey C. of C., Delta Sigma Kappa. Roman Catholic. Avocations: sailing, skydiving, bird watching. Home: 1 Country Club Dr Medford NJ 08055 Office: RE Kesty Inc 125 Eayrestown Rd Medford NJ 08055-9505

KESZEI, ERNO, chemist educator; b. Jakfa, Hungary, Jan. 26, 1951; s. Kalman and Karolina (Liszta) K.; m. Maria Julia Grim, Sept. 10, 1979 (div. 1994); children: Janos Farkas, Julia Piroska, Zsofia Dorottya. MS, Eotvos U., Budapest, Hungary, 1975; PhD, 1978. Asst. prof. to prof. chemistry Eotvos U., 1978-99, prof., 1999—, head dept. phys. chemistry, 1993—; vis. scientist Sherbrooke (Que., Can.) U., 1985-87, 89-91. Contbr. papers in scientific jours. Mem. Hungarian Chem. Soc., Budapest, 1976, Hungarian Acad. Scis., Budapest, Hungary, 1992, N.Y.Acad. Scis., 1993, European Molecular Liquid Group, London, 1995. Grantee Nat. Rsch. Found, Budapest, Hungary, 1991—, NATO Linkage, Brussels, Belgium, 1993-94. Avocations: antique literature, fgn. langs., hiking. Email: keszei@chem.elte.hu. Home: 30 Ugron Gabor, 1118 Budapest Hungary Office: Eotvos U Dept Phys Chem, PO Box 32, 1518 Budapest 112, Hungary

KESZTHELYI, LAJOS, science educator; b. Kaposva'r, Hungary, Feb. 15, 1927; s. Jozsef and Terez (Virth) K.; m. Sa'ra La'ndori, Aug. 23, 1951. Grad. in physics and math. edn., Eötvös Lorand Univ., Budapest, Hungary, 1950; D in Physics, Hungarian Acad. Sci., 1962. Sci. coworker Ctrl. Rsch. Inst. Physics, Budapest, 1954-63, head lab., 1963-70, dep. head dept., 1970-73; dep. dir. Inst. Biophysics, Szeged, Hungary, 1973-75; dir. Inst. Biophysics, Szeged, 1975-93; titular prof. Eötvös Lorand U., Budapest, 1978; dir. gen. Biol. Rsch. Ctr., Szeged, 1989-93, rsch. prof., 1994—. Author: Atoms and Atomic Particles, 1959, Scintillation Counters, 1962. Recipient Szechenyi prize Pres. Hungary, 1993. Mem. Hungarian Acad. Phys. Scis., European Acad. Arts, Scis. and Letters, Hugarian Biophys. Soc. (pres. 1990-98, hon. pres. 1999—). Home: 79 Fillér, H-1022 Budapest Hungary Office: Inst Biophysics, 62 Temesva'ri, H-6701 Szeged Hungary

KETCH, TINA, writer; b. Des Moines, June 19, 1952; d. Clifford and Dorothy (MacCaughey) Ketch; m. Michael Bennett, Sept. 18, 1990; children: Richard, Christopher, Timothy, Thomas James. PhD in Religious Scis., U. Strasbourg, France, 1987; grad., World Christian Ministries, Fresno, Calif., 1996, Profl. Career Devel. Inst., Atlanta, 1997. Writer Ketch Prodn., Lilburn, Ga., 1972—; founder Ketch Inst. Metaphysics, 1999. Author: Candle Lighting Calendar, 1992—; Candle Lighting Encyclopedia, Vol. I,

1991, Vol. II, 1992, Candle Lighting Workbook, 1996, Candle Lighting Feng Shui, 1999.

KETCHAM, RALPH, history and political science educator; b. Berea, Ohio, Oct. 28, 1927; s. Sherman G. and Laura (Murphy) K.; m. Julia Stillwell, Nov. 30, 1958; children: Benjamin, Laura Lee. AB, Allegheny Coll., 1949, DLitt (hon.), 1985; MA, Colgate U., 1952; PhD, Syracuse U., 1956, D.Litt. (hon.), 1999; D.Litt. (hon.), McKendree Coll., 1988. Rsch. assoc. U. Chgo., 1956-60; lectr. history Yale U., New Haven, 1961-63; prof. history and polit. sci. Syracuse (N.Y.) U., 1963-97, prof. emeritus, 1997—; Fulbright lectr., Japan, 1965, India, 1974, Netherlands, 1987. Author: James Madison, 1971 (Nat. Book nominee 1972), From Colony to Country, 1974, Presidents Above Party, 1984, Individualism and Public Life, 1987, Participation in Government: Making a Difference, 1988, 3d edit., 1996, Framed for Posterity, 1993. Mem. U.S. framework com. Civitas, 1988-90, Hungarian com., 1992-93, Russian com. 1993-94. With USCG, 1945-47. Named Prof. of Yr., Council for Advancement and Support Edn., 1987. Mem. Orgn. Am. Historians, Am. Studies Assn., Am. Antiquarian Soc., Inst. Early Am. History and Culture (coun. 1986-88). Avocation: skiing, sailing. Home: 1420 Salt Springs Rd Syracuse NY 13214-1434 Office: Syracuse U Maxwell Sch Syracuse NY 13244-0001

KETCHAM, RICHARD SCOTT, lawyer; b. Columbus, Ohio, Jan. 8, 1948; s. Victor Alvin and Dorothy Eloise (Becher) K.; m. Kim Michelle Haliburton, Apr. 7, 1984 (div. 1989); 1 child, Kate Erin; m. Christy M. Canaday, Sept. 9, 1990 (div. 1994). BS, Bowling Green (Ohio) State U., 1970; JD cum laude, Capital U., Columbus, 1974. Bar: Ohio 1974, U.S. Dist. Ct. (so. dist.) Ohio 1979. Asst. pros. atty. Franklin County (Ohio) Pros., Columbus, 1974-79; sr. asst. pros. atty. Franklin County (Ohio) Pros., 1979-84; ptnr. Ketcham & Ketcham, Columbus, 1984—; mem. task force Legal Aid Referral Project, Columbus Bar Assn. Homeless Project, 1989—. Mem. Gov.'s Task Force on Family Violence, 1984-86. Mem. Nat. Assn. Criminal Def. Lawyers, Ohio Assn. Criminal Def. Lawyers (bd. dirs. 1989—, v.p. CLE, sec.), Ctrl. Ohio Assn. Criminal Def. Lawyers (pres. 1994-95), Ohio State Bar Assn., Columbus Bar Assn. (chmn. criminal law com. 1994-95, 95-96), Franklin County Trial Lawyers. Avocations: fishing, basketball, model railroads. Home: 1937 Elmwood Ave Columbus OH 43212-1112 Office: Ketcham & Ketcham 755 S High St Columbus OH 43206-1908

KETCHAM, WARREN ANDREW, psychologist, educator; b. Manistee, Mich., June 28, 1909; s. Perry Warren and Anna Ella (Ulrich) K.; m. Edna May Wearne, Nov. 23, 1962 (dec. Mar. 1991). BM, U. Mich., 1932, MA, 1947, PhD, 1951. Lic. psychologist Mich., Tex. Tchr. Reed City (Mich.) Pub. Schs., 1934-36, Melvindale (Mich.) Pub. Schs., 1936-38; supr. Dearborn (Mich.) Pub. Schs., 1938-43; sch. psychologist Ferndale (Mich.) Pub. Schs., 1950-53; prof., sch. psychologist U. Mich., Ann Arbor, 1953-77, prof. emeritus, 1978—; pvt. practice clin., indsl., orgnl. psychology Mich. and Tex., 1964—; cons. Am. Sch., Guatemala City, Guatemala, 1958-80. Sgt. U.S. Army, 1943-45, PTO. Fulbright scholar Leeds U., 1959, Hinsdale scholar U. Mich., 1951. Fellow Am. Psychol. Assn.; mem. Am. Soc. Clin. Hypnotists, Mich. Soc. Clin. Psychologists, Mich. Psychol. Assn., Nat. Registered Health Svc. Providers in Psychology. Home and Office: 608 E Lake Rd Harbor Springs MI 49740-1220

KETCHLEDGE, KATHLEEN A., nurse; b. Reading, Pa., May 12, 1956; d. Charles C. and Arlene M. (Krommes) T. AS, Reading Area Community Coll., 1977. Staff nurse Community Gen. Hosp., Reading, Leigh Valley Hosp. Ctr., Allentown, Pa.; nurse mgr. skilled unit Laurel Nursing and Rehab. Ctr., Hamburg, Pa., medicare coord. infection control, 1995—, case mgr. coord., 1997-98; coord. medicare unit, coord. staf devel. Orwigsburg (Pa.) Ctr., 1998—. Home: 30 E William St Apt 2 Schuylkill Haven PA 17972-1715

KETELAAR, FREDERICK CORNELIS JOHANNES, archivist, educator; b. Amsterdam, The Netherlands, Jan. 31, 1944; s. Jan A. A. and Helena J. (Wehlburg) K.; m. Elizabeth A. De Vries Reilingh, May 23, 1972; children: Titia, Willemyn Anne. LLM, Leiden U., 1967, LLD, 1978. Asst. lectr. legal history Leiden U., 1967-69; sec. Archives Coun., 1969-74; dir. State Sch. Tng. of Archivists, 1969-75; deputy gen. state archivist, 1975-84; state archivist Groningen, 1985-88; gen. state archivist The Netherlands, 1989-97, gen. counsel state archives, 1997—; prof. Leiden U., 1992—; prof. Amsterdam U., 1997—; Netherlands vis. prof. U. Mich., 2000—. Mem. Royal Soc. Dutch Archivists (pres. 1983-86, Hendrik Van Wijn medal 1987), Hollandsche Maatschappy Wetenschappen, Soc. Am. Archivists. Home: Rusthoekstr 9, 2584 CP The Hague The Netherlands Office: U Amsterdam Dept Archive, Oude Turfmarkt 147, 1012 GC Amsterdam The Netherlands

KETS DE VRIES, MANFRED FLORIAN, psychoanalyst, educator; b. Huizen, Holland, Aug. 19, 1942; s. Jonas and Henriette (Houtman) Kets de V.; m. Elisabet Engellau, Aug. 9, 1973; children: Eva, Fredrik, Oriane. Econ. Drs. (M.Sc.), U. Amsterdam, 1966; MBA, Harvard U., Cambridge, Mass., 1968, DBA, 1970; Psychoanalytic Cert., Can. Psychoanalytic Inst., Montreal, 1982. Rsch. fellow Harvard Bus. Sch., Cambridge, 1968-71, 73-74; asst. prof. INSEAD, Fontainebleau, France, 1971-73; prof. orgnl. behavior INSEAD, Fontainbleau, France, 1974-85; prof. McGill U., Montreal, 1974-85, H.E.C. Montreal, 1980-81, Harvard Bus. Sch., Cambridge, 1983-84; Raoul de Vitry d'Avaucourt prof. human resource mgmt. INSEAD, 1992—. Columnist NRC/Algemeen Handelsblad (daily newspaper), Holland, 1990—; author: Power and the Corporate Mind, 1975, Organizational Paradoxes, 1980, The Neurotic Organization, 1984 The Irrational Executive, 1984, Unstable at the Top, 1988, Prisoners of Leadership, 1989, Handbook of Character Studies, 1991, Organizations on the Couch, 1991, Leaders, Fools and Impostors, 1993, Life and Death in the Executive Fast Lane, 1995, Family Business: Human Dilemmas in the Family Firm, 1996, The New Global Leaders, 1999, Struggling with the Demon: Essays in Individual and Organizational Irrationality, 2000. Mem. APA, Canadian Psychoanalytic Soc., Internat. Psychoanalytic Assn., Canadian Psychol. Assn., Internat. Soc. of Polit. Psychology, Internat. Soc. for Psychoanalytic Study of Orgns. Avocations: fly fishing, hunting. Office: INSEAD, Fontainebleau France 77305

KETTEL, EDWARD JOSEPH, oil company executive, retired; b. N.Y.C., Sept. 13, 1925; s. Harold J. and Evelyn M. (Melbourne) K.; student St. John's U., 1943; BA, St. Francis Coll., 1949; MA, Columbia U., 1953; m. Janet M. Johnson, Nov. 27, 1952; children: Dorothy A., David A. Ins. mgr. Arabian Am. Oil Co., 1950-56, Ethyl Corp., 1956-65; asst. treas. Atlantic Richfield Co., L.A., 1965-85, asst. treas., Chevron Corp., San Francisco, 1985-94; expert witness, 1994—; chmn. bd. Oil Ins., Ltd.; pres. Greater Pacific, Ltd.; dir. Am. S.S. Owners Mut. Protection and Indemnity Assn., Inc., Internat. Tanker Indemnity Assn., Ltd. With inf. AUS, 1943-46. Decorated Bronze Star, Purple Heart with oak leaf cluster. Mem. Am. Petroleum Inst., Mfrs. Chem. Assn., Nat. Fire Protection Assn., Risk and Ins. Mgmt. Soc., N.Y. Athletic Club, L.A. Athletic Club, Palos Verdes Country Club, Jonathan Club, Comml. Club, Ocean Colony Golf Club, Westhampton Beach Yacht Squadron, Ltd.

KETTEMBOROUGH, CLIFFORD RUSSELL, computer scientist, consultant, manager; b. Pitesti, Arges, Romania, June 8, 1953; came to U.S., 1983; s. Petre and Constanta (Dascalu) I. MS in Math., U. Bucharest, Romania, 1976; MS in Computer Sci., West Coast U., L.A., 1985; MS in Mgmt. Info. System, West Coast U., Los Angeles, 1986; PhD in Computer and Info. Sci., Pacific We. U., 1988; MBA, U. LaVerne, 1992; PhD in Bus. Adminstrn., U. Santa Barbara, 1996; EdD in Computer Tech. in Edn., Nova Southeastern U., 1998. Lic. mathematician. Mathematician, programmer Nat. Dept. Chemistry, Bucharest, 1976-80; sr. programmer, analyst Nat. Dept. Metallurgy, Bucharest, 1980-82; sr. software engr. Xerox Corp., El Segundo, Calif., 1983-88; task mgr. Rockwell Internat., Canoga Park, Calif., 1989-91, cons., 1991-93; mgr. micro devel. Transam. Corp., L.A., 1993-95; MIS dir. Maxicare Health Plans, L.A., 1995-96; computer and info. scientist Jet Propulsion Lab.-NASA, Pasadena, Calif., 1988-89, project mgr., 1996—; adj., asst. prof. W. Coast U., Chapman U., U. Redlands, Nat. U., U. Phoenix, Union Inst., Pepperdine U., UCLA Ext., Keller Grad. Sch., 1991—. Contbr. articles to profl. jours. Sec. Romanian Nat. Body Bldg. Com., Bucharest, 1980-82; pres., chmn. Bucharest Mcpl. Body Bldg. Com., 1978-82. Served to lt. Romanian Army, 1978. Mem. IEEE, Assn. for Computing Machinery. Republican. Avocations: soccer, body building, traveling. Home: 6004 N Walnut Grove Ave San Gabriel CA 91775-2530

KETTERLING, HANS-PETER ALFRED, electrical engineer; b. Berlin, Germany, Apr. 30, 1941; s. Heinz and Ursula (Schaffrath) K.; m. Heide Meyer, Mar. 11, 1969; children: Bianca, Corinna. Diploma in telecomms. engrng., Tech. U., Berlin, 1969. Engr. SEL AG, Berlin, 1969-70, head of lab., 1970-80, dept. head, 1981-82; dept. head Bosch GmbH, Berlin, 1983-95, sr. mgr., 1996-97; sr. mgr. Motorola Betriebsfunk, Berlin, 1997; sr. cons. Mobile Radio Cons., Berlin, 1998—; chmn. ZVEI AK Radio, Frankfurt, Germany, 1988-97, ECTEL MRSG, London, Brussels, 1991-97, vice chmn. ECTEL PMRWG, London, Brussels, 1986-97; tech. project leader, DMCS 900, Nuremberg, Germany, 1988-90. Author: Wege zum digitalen Betriebsfunk, 1998; co-author: Schach dem Computer, 1980, 2d edit., 1983; contbr. numerous articles to profl. pubs. Chmn. Schachklub Tempelhof, Berlin, 1975-79; owner Chess Shop, Berlin, 1981—. Mem. IEEE. Achievements include over 30 patents in field of radio transmission, 1976—. Fax: 49 30 785 4569. E-mail: h.-p.ketterling@t-online.de. Home and Office: Boelckestr 74, D-12101 Berlin-Tempelhof Germany

KETTLE, DOUGLAS STEWART, tertiary educator, researcher; b. London, Jan. 28, 1918; arrived in Australia, 1969; s. Christopher James and Theresa Frances (Beyer) K.; m. Gladys Emily Horne, July 7, 1945 (dec. 1973); children: Stephen, St. John, Anna; m. Ada Dora Harthoorn, Dec. 11, 1974. BSc, London U., 1939; MSc, U. London, 1946, DSc, 1952. Cert. biologist. Rsch. scientist Cooper Tech. Bur., Berkham, Eng., 1946-47; scientist in charge Midge Control Unit, Glasgow (Scotland) U., Scotland, 1947-51; lectr. U. Edinburgh, Scotland, 1952-61; dir. sandfly control unit U. Montego Bay, Jamaica, 1959-60; prof. zoology U. Nairobi, Kenya, 1961-69; prof. entomology U. Queensland, Brisbane, Australia, 1969-83, prof. emeritus, 1983—. Author: Medical and Veterinary Entomology, 1984, 2d edit., 1995. Capt. Royal Army Med. Corps., 1940-46. Carnegie Found. fellow, 1951-52. Fellow Inst. of Biology, Royal Entomol. Soc.; mem. Australian Entomol. Soc., Birds Australia. Anglican. Avocations: bird watching, photography. Home: PO Box 313, Mount Ommaney QLD 4074, Australia Office: Dept Zoology/Entomology, U Queensland, St Lucia QLD 4072, Australia

KEUM, JONG-HAE, mathematician, educator; b. Kunsan, Korea, Apr. 5, 1957; s. Ki-Soo and Jeong-Gyo (Kwon) K.; m. Soonyiel Park, June 13, 1984; children: Yong-Yeon, Goo-Tag. BS, Seoul Nat. U., 1980, MS, 1982; PhD, U. Mich., 1988. Cert. in math. Asst. prof. U. Utah, Salt Lake City, 1988-90; assoc. prof. Konkuk U., Seoul, 1991-96, prof., 1997-2000; prof. Korea Inst. Advanced Study, Seoul, 2000—; vis. prof. U. Mich., Ann Arbor, 1996-97; vice chmn. Korea Nat. Com. for Univ. Entrance Exam., Seoul, 1997-99; dept. head Konkuk U., Seoul, 1998-2000. Contbr. articles to profl. jours. Lt. Korean Army, 1982. Recipient Best Paper award in sci. and tech. Korean Fedn. Sci. and Tech., 1998; rsch. fellow Math. Scis. Rsch. Inst., 1993, Japan Soc. for Promotion of Sci. fellow Nagoya U., 1998, fellow Korea Inst. for Advanced Study, 1998—. Mem. Korean Math. Soc., Am. Math. Soc., Math. Assn. Am. Avocation: golf. Office: Korea Inst Adv Study 203-43, Cheongryangri-dong Dongdaemun-gu, 130-012 Seoul Korea

KEUNE, WERNER, applied physics educator; b. Saarbruecken, Germany, June 11, 1939; s. Kurt August and Dora Ida (Lange) K.; m. Ingeborg Hermine Krummel, June 27, 1973; children: Peter (dec.), Christina E., Philipp M. Diploma in physics, Tech. U. Munich, 1965, PhD, 1969; Habilitation, U. Saarland, Saarbrücken, Germany, 1975. Cert. physicist. Staff assoc. N.Am. Aviation Sci. Ctr., Thousand Oaks, Calif., 1967-69; rsch. asst. U. Saarland, Saarbrücken, 1969-72, asst. prof., 1972-75; prof. applied physics U. Duisburg, Germany, 1975—, chmn. dept. physics, 1986-88; tech. expert Internat. Atomic Energy Agy., Vienna, Austria, 1972; vis. rschr. Kyoto (Japan) U., 1979; vis. assoc. divsn. engrng. and applied sci. Calif. Inst. Tech., Pasadena, Calif., 1991; vis. scholar Argonne (Ill.) Nat. Lab., 1996. Contbr. articles to profl. jours. Recipient rsch. scholarship Volkswagen Found., Hannover, Germany, 1996. Mem. German Phys. Soc., German Soc. Materials Sci. Avocation: tennis. Office: Gerhard-Mercator U, Lotharstr 65, D-47048 Duisburg Germany

KEUTGEN, HENRI ANTOINE, pediatrician; b. Eupen, Liege, Belgium, Aug. 13, 1942; s. Henri and Josephine (Roderburg) K.; m. Christine Troisfontaines, Sept. 7, 1967; children: Thierry, Patrick, Olivier. MD, U. Liege, 1967. Lic. paediatrician, Belgium. Resident in microbiology U. Liege, 1964-66, resident in internal medicine, 1966-67, asst. in paediatrics, 1967-71; paediatrician Civil Hosp., Verviers, Belgium, 1973-79, head dept. paediatrics, 1979—; tng. master medicine, postgrad. training U. Liege, 1979—; faculty nurses sch. CPAS, Verviers, 1973-84. Med. comdr. Belgian Army, 1971-72. Home: 14 rue du Parc, 4800 Verviers Belgium Office: CHR La Tourelle, 29 rue du Parc, 4800 Verviers Belgium

KEVANISHVILI, ZURAB SHAMSHE, audiologist, researcher, educator; b. Tbilisi, Georgia, Mar. 15, 1941; s. Shamshe Ivan and Natalia Iosiph (Lobzhanidze) K.; m. Buciko Vladimir Chkhartishvili, July 15, 1970; children: Ivan, Lasha. Cert., Tbilisi, Georgia, 1958; diploma, Medical Inst., Tbilisi, Georgia, 1965; MD, Inst. of Physiology, Tbilisi, Georgia, 1968; PhD, Med. Inst., Leningrad, Russia. Jr. rschr. Inst. Physiology, Tbilisi, 1968; jr. rschr. Ctr. Audiology, Tbilisi, 1968-69, sr. rschr., 1969-75, head dept., 1975-89, dir., 1989—; lectr. otorhinolaryngology Med. Acad., 1979-83, prof., 1983—. Co-author: The Split Brain, 1973, Human Auditory Evoked Potentials, 1985; editor-in-chief Jour. Georgian Medicine, 1992—; contbr. articles to profl. jours. Recipient George Soros award, 1993. Mem. Otorhinolaryngological Soc. Georgia, IBRO, Medico-Physical Soc. Erlangen (assoc.), Collegium ORL Amicitiae Sacrum (assoc.), ORL, Head and Neck Surgery Soc. Germany (corr. mem.). Avocations: football, table tennis, chess, fishing, gardening. Home: I, Khvichia str 31, 380060 Tbilisi Georgia Office: Centre of Audiology, Chavchavadze ave 33, 380079 Tbilisi Georgia

KEVDINA, IRINA BORISOVNA, physicist; b. Moscow, Jan. 21, 1948; d. Boris Mikhailovich and Maria (Maximovna) Stepanov; m. Oleg Petrovich Kevdin; 1 child, Luidmila Olegovna. Degree in engrng., Phys. Inst. Moscow, 1972. Lic. engr.-scientist. Engr. N.N. Semenov Chem. Phys. Inst., Moscow, 1972-73, dr., scientist, 1973—; lectr. in field. Contbr. articles to sci. jours. Avocation: classical music. Home: St Gorohovskii 8 Art 79, 103064 Moscow Russia Office: NN Semenov Chem Phys Inst, ul Kosygina 4, 117977 Moscow Russia

KEVELAITIS, EGIDIJUS, physiologist, educator; b. Kaunas, Lithuania, July 27, 1961; s. Zigmantas and Grasilda (Staneviciute) K.; m. Sigita Zemaitytė, Aug. 26, 1983; children: Mantas, Rytis. MD, Med. Inst., Kaunas, 1985, PhD, 1988; D in Med. Sci., Med. Acad., Kaunas, 1993. Asst. prof. Med. Inst., Kaunas, 1985-88, sr. lectr., 1988-92; assoc. prof. Med. Acad., Kaunas, 1992—; local coord. Jep Tempus, Kaunas, 1992-95; vis. rschr. INSERM U-127, Paris, 1993, 94, 97, 98, 99, Dept. Pharmacology, Århus, Denmark, 1993-94, Royal Sch. Pharmacy, Copenhagen, 1997. Editor: Human Physiology, 1998; contbr. articles to profl. jours. Grantee Lithuanian Acad. Scis., 1983; European Soc. Cardiology fellow, 1997. Mem. N.Y. Acad. Scis., Lithuanian Physiol. Soc., Nat. Geog. Soc. Avocations: basketball. Office: Dept Physiology Med Acad, Mickeviciaus 9, 3000 Kaunas Lithuania

KEVENHÖRSTER, PAUL JOHANNES, political scientist, educator, consultant; b. Schwerte, Germany, June 5, 1941; s. Walter and Elfriede (Schäfer-Tusch) K.; m. Gisela Drerup, May 25, 1966; children: Uta, Eva, Ina. Diploma in Econs., U. Cologne, Germany, 1965, Diploma in Bus. Adminstrn., 1966, DrRerPol, 1968; Habil. in Polit. Sci., U. Bonn, Germany, 1973. Rsch. fellow Konrad-Adenauer-Found., 1967-69, Socioecon. Inst., Bad Godesberg, Germany, 1969-71, Inst. for Comm. Planning, 1972-74; prof. Tech. U. Braunschweig/U. Edn., Münster, 1974-82; dir. gen. German Found. for Internat. Devel., Berlin, 1982-88; Univ. prof. polit. sci. U. Münster, 1988—, dir. Inst. Polit. Sci., 1998—, vice dean faculty edn., 1976-79; cons. Konrad-Adenauer-Found., St. Augustin, Germany, 1988-97; cons. Fed. Ministry for Rsch., Bonn, 1982-83; mem. com. UNESCO, Germany, 1983-89; mem. adv. com. UNCRD, Nagoya, Japan, 1986-93; vis. prof. Sophia U., Tokyo, 1994, Nihon U., Tokyo, 2000; vis. fellow Princeton U., 1999. Author: Das politische System Japans, 1969, Computerized Policy in Japan, 1982, Development through Dialogue and Training, 1984, Japan. Aussenpolitik im Aufbruch, 1993, Politikwissenschaft fur Entschidungen und Strukturen der Politik, 1997. Mediator, Internat. Mediation Group, Johannesburg, South Africa, 1994. Mem. Internat. Polit. Sci. Assn., Am. Polit. Sci. Assn., Rotary Club Burgsteinfurt (pres. 1996-97). Mem. CDU Party. Roman Catholic. Avocations: chamber music, tennis. Office: U Munster Inst Polit Sci, Scharnhorststr 100, 48151 Münster Germany

KEVORKOV, DMYTRO, chemist, researcher; b. Kiev, Ukraine, Apr. 17, 1973; s. Georgij Kevorkov and Natalia Chugaeva; m. Olha Tsysnetska, June 14, 1997. Grad., Lviv (Ukraine) State U., 1995, PhD in Chem. Scis., 1999. Assoc. rschr. Tech. U., Clausthal-Zellerfeld, Germany, 1997—. Tech. editor: Red Book, vol. 39, 1997. Grantee Internat. Soros Sci. Found., 1995, 96, 97, INTAS, Brussels, 1998; German Acad. Exchange Svc. fellow, 1997. Avocation: studying languages.

KEVREKIDIS, THEODOROS, marine biologist, researcher; b. Florina, Greece, Apr. 19, 1958; s. Dimitrios and Fanie (Bogdanou) K.; m. Paraskevi Malea, Sept. 14, 1961; children: Dimitrios-Phaedon, Alkestis. Degree in biology, U. Thessaloniki, Greece, 1980, PhD, 1988. Head master tchr. Post High Sch. Ctr., Thessaloniki, 1988-90; tchr. Experimental H.S., Thessaloniki, 1990-92; lectr. Democritus Univ. of Thrace, Alexandroupoli, Greece, 1992-96, asst. prof., 1996-2000, assoc. prof., 2000—. Author: Biology, Structure and Function of Organisms, 1996; contbr. articles to profl. jours. With Air Forces, 1986-88. Recipient grant Athens Acad., 1981. Mem. Panhellenic Union of Biologists, Greek Biological Soc., Greek Ecologists Union. Avocation: music. Office: Democritus Univ of Thrace, N Hili, 68100 Alexandroupolis Greece

KEY, HELEN ELAINE, accountant, consulting company executive, educator; b. Cleve., Jan. 16, 1946; d. Maud and Helen (Key) Vance. B.S., W.Va. State Coll., 1968; M.Ed., Cleve. State U., 1977, postgrad., 1998. Prin. Cleve. Bd. Edn., 1968—; instr. Cuyahoga Community Coll., Cleve., part-time, 1969-78, Dyke Coll., Cleve., part-time, 1979—; pres. H.E. Key & Assos., Cleve., 1983—; treas. BK4W Inc., Cleve., 1981; sec. Progressive Pioneers, Inc. Mem. Am. Assn. Notary Pubs., Women Bus. Owners Assn., AAUW, NAACP, Cleve. Area Bus. Tchrs., NEA, Pi Lambda Theta, Alpha Kappa Alpha. Democrat. Baptist. Club: Toastmistress (sec. 1978) (Cleve.). Home: 564 Wilkes Ln Cleveland OH 44143-2622

KEYDAR, IAFA, virology educator; b. Yassy, Romania, July 6, 1923; arrived in Israel, 1941; d. Zeev and Sara (Rosenzweig) Pomerliano; m. Abraham Tiberius Keydar Klein, July 9, 1942 (dec. 1982); 1 child, Yael. Degree in nursing, Nurses Tng. Coll., Tel Aviv, 1950; BSc in Zoology, Tel Aviv U., 1956, MSc in Microbiology, 1958; PhD, Hebrew U., 1967. Nurse Kibbutz Maagan, Israel, 1950-53; rsch. assoc. Inst. for Cancer Rsch., Columbia U., N.Y.C., 1969-71; sr. lectr. microbiology Tel Aviv U., 1971-74, assoc. prof., 1974-82, prof., 1982—, prof. emeritus, 1993—; chair dept. microbiology, Tel Aviv U., 1974-76, dean faculty of life scis., 1984-89; dir. Moise and Frida Eskenasy Inst. for Cancer Rsch., 1990-92; vis. prof. Inst. for Cancer Rsch., Columbia U., N.Y.C., 1976-78. Mem. editl. bd. Jour. of Women's Cancer, 2000. Mem. N.Y. Acad. Sci, Internat. Assn. Breast Cancer Rsch. (pres. 1989), Israel Cell Biology Assn., Israel Microbiology Assn. Office: Tel Aviv U Dept Cell Rsch, and Immunology, 69978 Tel Aviv Israel

KEYES, DAVID ELLIOT, scientific computing educator, researcher; b. Bklyn., Dec. 4, 1956; s. Elliot Fuller and Edna (Corsini) K.; married; 2 children. BSME, Princeton U., 1978; MS in Applied Math., Harvard U., 1979, PhD in Applied Math., 1984. Rsch. assoc. dept. computer sci. Yale U., New Haven, 1984-85, asst. prof. dept. mech. engrng., 1986-90, assoc. prof. dept. mech. engrng., 1990-94; assoc. prof. dept. computer sci. Old Dominion U., 1993—, teletechnet broadcast instr., 1996—, Richard F. Barry Chair prof., chmn. dept. math. and stats., 1999—; dir. Program in High Performance Computing and Comm., Va. Inst. for Computer Applications and Sci. Engrng., Langley Rsch. Ctr., 1994—; acting dir. Inst. Sci. Computer Rsch. Lawrence Livermore Nat. Lab., 1999—; vis. scientist Inst. Computer Applications in Sci. and Engrng., Hampton, Va., 1990, sr. rsch. assoc., 1993—. Editor: Domain Decomposition Methods in Partial Differential Equations, 1991, Domain-based Parallelism and Problem Decomposition Methods, 1995, Domain Decomposition Methods in Scientific and Engineering Computing, 1995, 98, Parallel Numerical Algorithms, 1996; mem. editl. bd. Internat. Jour. for Supercomputer Applications, 1994—, Lecture Notes in Computational Sci. and Engrng., 1996—, Soc. for Indsl. and Applied Math. Jour. Sci. Comput., 1999—; contbr. articles to profl. jours. Named Presdl. Young Investigator, NSF, Washington, 1989, Gordon Bell prize winner IEEE Supercomputing '99, Portland, 1999. Mem. ASME, AIAA (coun. mem. 1991-93, chair 1992-93)), IEEE Computer Soc., Soc. Indsl. and Applied Math. (sec. 1991-93, vis. lectr. 1992—, coun. 1999—), Assn. for Computing Machinery, The Combustion Inst., Tau Beta Pi, Sigma Xi, Phi Beta Kappa. Office: ICASE NASA Langley Rsch Ctr Ms 132 C Ctr Hampton VA 23681-0001

KEYES, MARION ALVAH, IV, manufacturing company executive; b. Bellingham, Wash., May 11, 1938; s. Marion Alvah and Winnefred Agnes (Nolte) K.; m. Loretta Jean Mattson, Nov. 17, 1962; children: Marion A., Zachary Leigh, Richard. BS in Chem. Engrng., Stanford U., 1960; MSEE, U. Ill., 1968; MBA, Baldwin Wallace Coll., 1981. Registered profl. engr., Calif., Wis., N.Y., Ill., Ohio. Tchg. asst. dept. math. Stanford U., 1958-59; tech. Stanford Aerosol Labs., 1957-59; chem. engr. Ketchikan (Alaska) Pulp Co., 1960-63; dir engrng. Control Sys. divsn. Beloit (Wis.) Corp., 1963-70; gen. mgr. digital sys. divsn. Taylor Instrument Co., Rochester, N.Y., 1970-75; sr. v.p., group exec. Indsl. Products and Svcs. Group; mem. exec. operative bd. McDermott Internat. Inc., 1985-89; v.p. engrng., pres. Bailey Controls Co., Wickliffe, Ohio, 1975-85, pres., CEO, 1989-90; chmn. Dcom Corp., Eastlake, Ohio, 1990-93; sr. v.p. tech. and bus. devel. process group, pres. rosemount Analytical Inc. divsn. Emerson Electric Co., St. Louis, 1993—; bd. dirs. Fibermark Corp. Author: Offshore Platform Automation, 1990; editor: A Glossary of Automatic Control Terminology, 1970; contbr. articles to profl. jours.; holder 54 U.S. and more than 100 fgn. patents. Past bd. advisors Fenn Coll. Engrng., Cleve. State U.; bd. dirs. Baldwin Coll., United Cerebral Palsy, Cleve.; past pres., mem. exec. bd. N.E. Ohio coun. Boy Scouts Am.; past pres. Area 5 Boy Scouts Am. Fellow ISA (hon. life), TAPPA (Pioneer award), IEEE, Am. inst. Chemists, Instrument Soc. Am. (life hon.); mem. AIChE, Ohio Acad. Scis. (life; bd. dirs., Centennial honoree 1991, fellow), Cleve. Engrng. Soc. (bd. dirs.), Soc. Am. Mil. Engrs. (life), Am. Assn. Artificial Intelligence (charter), Am. Mgmt. Assn., U.S. Automation Rsch. Coun., Am. Automatic Control Coun. (past. sec. and bd. dirs., Am. Chem. Soc., Wis. Acad. Arts, Scis. and Letters, Cleve. World Trade Assn. (Man of Yr. 1984), Canterbury Golf Club. Republican. Roman Catholic. E-mail: bud@keyes.org. Home: 8 Washington Terr Saint Louis MO 63112-1914 Office: 8000 Maryland Ave Ste 600 Clayton MO 63105-3752

KHABAROVSKY, BARON See DRUTCHAS, GERRICK GILBERT

KHACHADURIAN, AVEDIS, physician; b. Aleppo, Syria, Jan. 6, 1926; s. Khachadur and Aznive (Demirjian) K.; m. Laura Hadidian, July 27, 1961; children: Cynthia, Linda. BA, Am. U. of Beirut, 1949, MD, 1953. Resident internal medicine Am. U. of Beirut, 1953-56; fellow Postgrad. Sch. Medicine, London, 1956-57, Harvard Med. Sch., 1957-59; asst. prof. biochemistry and medicine Am. U. of Beirut, 1959-64, assoc. prof., 1964-71, prof., 1971; prof. pediatrics, dir. Clin. Research Center, Northwestern U. Med. Sch., 1971-73; prof. medicine, head div. endocrinology metabolism and nutrition U. Medicine and Dentistry N.J.-R.W. Johnson Med. Sch., Piscataway, N.J., 1973; mem. staff pediatrics Children's Meml. Hosp., Chgo.; cons. U. Chgo. Sch. Medicine. Mem. Am. Diabetes Assn., N.Y. Acad. Sci., Am. Fedn. Clin. Rsch., Am. Heart Assn., Am. Inst. Nutrition, Endocrine Soc., N.Y. Lipid Rsch. Club, Sigma Xi, Alpha Omega Alpha. Achievements include rsch. in genetics; natural history, pathogenesis and treatment of hereditary hyperlipidemias; diabetes; studies on various inborn errors of metabolism; osteoporosis.

KHADDAM, ABD AL-HALIM IBN SAID, Syrian government official; b. Lattakia, Syria, 1932. LL.B., Damascus U. Gov. of Damascus, 1964. Minister of economy and fgn. trade Govt. of Syria, 1969-70, v.p. Fgn. Affairs; dep. prime minister and minister of fgn. affairs, 1970-84, v.p. for mil. and polit. affairs, 1984, v.p., 1984—. Mem. Regional Command, Baath

Party, 1971-84. Address: Office of Pres/Muhajreen, Abu Rumanch, al Rachid St, Damascus Syria*

KHADEM, RAMIN, satellite company executive; b. Teheran, Iran, Jan. 21, 1945; Can. citizen; arrived in Eng., 1981; s. Zikrullah and Malektaj (Javidi) K.; m. Faraneh Vargha, Sept. 20, 1969; children: Paryssa, Varga, Ryyan. BSEE, U. Ill., 1967; MA in Econs., McGill U., Montreal, Can., 1970, PhD in Econs., 1975. Lectr. McGill U., Montreal, 1970-72; cons. Bell Can., Montreal, 1972-74; mgr. economy and mktg. Teleglobe Can., Montreal, 1975-78, dir. mktg., 1979-80; mgr. fin. Inmarsat, London, 1981-84, dir. fin., 1985-88, dir. fin. and adminstrn., 1989-93, CFO, 1993—; cons. Pub. Utility Power and Telephone, Vancouver, Ottawa, 1972-75, Inmarsat, London, 1980-81, team mem. privatization, 1st dir., London, 1999; Can. Nat. Rlwy., Montreal, 1989; cons., dir. KMK, Inc., Montreal, 1975-80; 1st dir. ICO Ltd., London, leader pvt. placement of shares internationally, 1995; lectr. Internat. Telecom. Union Seminars, Hong Kong, 1976; trustee Internat. Space U., Strasbourg, France, 1998-00; bd. dirs. Inmarsat Holdings, Ltd., INVSAT Ltd., Merasis Ltd., Airia Ltd. Co-prodr.: (satellite program) Second Baha'i World Congress, 1992; contbr.: Computer Simulation in Business, 1980; contbr. articles to profl. jours. Mem. Am. Mgmt. Assn., Internat. Telecom. Soc., Inst. Dirs. (Eng.), European Baha'i Bus. Forum. Mem. Baha'i Ch. Avocations: jogging, film making, tennis. Office: Inmarsat, 99 City Rd, London EC1Y 1AX, England

KHADILKAR, BHUSHAN MADHUKAR, chemistry educator; b. Satara, Maharashtra, India, Dec. 19, 1957; s. Madhukar Pandurang and Padma Madhukar (Dixit) K.; m. Sujata Vidyasagar Menon, Feb. 17, 1984; 1 child, Aditi Bhushan. BSc, Ruia Coll., Mumbai, India, 1979, MSc, 1981; PhD, U. Mumbai, 1986. Rsch. chemist Alembic Chem. Works Co., Ltd., Baroda, India, 1981-82; lectr. dept. chem. tech. Mumbai Univ., 1987-92, sr. lectr. dept. chem. tech., 1992—. Contbr. articles to profl. jours. Fellow Indian Chem. Soc.; mem. Indian Pharm. Assn., Indian Soc. Surface Sci. and Tech. Avocations: hypnotherapy, ednl. psychology, Indian classical music, Yoga. E-mail: bhushank@vsnl.com. Home: RA Kidwai Rd, University Quarters, 400019 Mumbai 400019, India Office: Dept Chem Tech/Mumbai Univ, Nathalal Parikh Marg, 400019 Mumbai 400019, India

KHAFAGY, MOHAMED ABDFEL MONEIM, poet, educator, writer; b. Egypt, 1915; s. Abdel Moneim and Shouk Khafagy; married, 1943; 1 child. Lic. in Lit., Azhar U., Egypt, DLitt. Tchr. Arabic lang. and lit. Azhar U., 1948-74, dean faculty, 1974-78. Chmn. al-Hadara Mag., 1986; author over 500 books on lit., poetry, history and Islamic writings. Recipient 1st class Medal of Sci. and Arts, Pres. Mubarak, Egypt. Avocations: reading, writing, music. Office: PO Box 46, Mohamed Farid Post Office, Cairo Egypt Home: 290 Faisal St Al haram, Giza Egypt

KHAIROUN, IBRAHIM, materials engineer; b. Tangier, Morocco, Nov. 8, 1971; s. Mohamed and Zahra (Belhaj) K. BS, 1989; PhD in Physics, U. Politech. Catalunya, Barcelona, Spain, 1998. With Materials Sciene/ETSEIB, Barcelona, indsl. engr., 1995—. Author: Bioceramics, 1997; contbr. articles to profl. jours. With Morocco Mil., 1994-95. Avocations: lectures, sports, music, travel, collecting stamps. Home: Tnin Sidi Lyamani, Asilah Morocco Office: Materials Sciene/ETSEIB, Diagonal 647, 08028 Barcelona Spain

KHAIRULLINA, ALPHIJA YAGPHAROVNA, physicist; b. Kazan, USSR, Sept. 22, 1936; s. Yagphar Khairullovich and Amina Ibatullovna (Enikejeva) K.; m. Mr. Yusupov, Dec. 2, 1959 (dec. 1962); 1 child, Lira Yusupova; m. Mr. Vlasov, Dec. 25, 1964 (dec. Jan. 1976); 1 child, Vadim Vlasov. Student, State U., Tatarstan, 1954-59; postgrad. student, Nat. Acad. Scis. Belarus, 1963-66, D in Phys. and Math. Scis., 1998. Engr. State Optical Inst., Kazan, Tatarstan, 1959-60; asst. Aviation Inst., Kazan, Tatarstan, 1960-63; sr. engr.-designer Inst. Physics Nat. Acad. Scis. Belarus, Minsk, 1966-70, jr. rsch. worker Inst. Physics, 1970-72, sr. rsch. worker Inst. Physics, 1972-88, leading rsch. worker Inst. Physics, 1988—. mem. Inst. of Physics, Nat. Acad. Scis. of Belarus (mem. problems coun.), Biomechanics Soc. Russia, BIOS Europe. Achievements include the foundation of blood optics; new optical diagnostic methods of blood and biological tissues, including tumors; methods of determination of sizes, real and imaginary parts of refractive indices in dispersed media at multiple scattering; dynamic spectroscopy of erythrocytes; peculiarities of interference in scattering media; new possibilities in investigations of scattering of smooth surfaces. Avocations: reading of art literature, concerts of classical music. Home: Glebky 18-3, Minsk Belarus 220121 Office: Inst Physics/Nat Acad Scis, Scorina 70, Minsk Belarus 220072

KHALADJAN, NIKOLAI NIKOLAEVICH, university president; b. Sevastopol, USSR, Feb. 23, 1931; s. Tigran Avanesovich and Anna Karlovna (Vaivads) K.; m. Tamara Mihkailovna Doroshenko, Sept. 22, 1954; children: Dubrova Ludmilla Nikolaevna, Mikhail Nikolaevich. M of Culture, Leningrad Inst. Culture, 1960; Cand Philosophy, Moscow State U., 1971; D of Pedagogy, Moscow External U. Humanities, 1992. Sr. lectr. Inst. Structural Engring. and Architecture, Dnepropetrovsk, Ukraine, 1976-79, Moscow State U., 1980s, Inst. Civil Aviation, Moscow, 1984; dean of faculty Moscow Vet. Acad., 1984, Moscow State Acad. Pub. and Design, 1984-91; pres. Moscow External U. Humanities, 1991—; bd. dirs. Horizont Zentrum der Internationalen Freundschaft und Cultur, Cologne, Germany, 1996—; co-chair I.C.A.E., Inc., Beverly Hills, Calif., 1992—. Author: Manifesto of Authorized Education, 1993, Manifesto of the Authorized Revival of Secondary Education, 1996, The Autoengineering, 1995, Legenda-Kovalenda Art of Ironworks, History of Krasnodar Region, 1992; editl. dir. Megu Herald, Moscow, 1994—; pub. The Intellectual newspaper, Moscow, 1991—. Dir. Dept. Aesthetical Devel. of Children and Youth, Krasnodar Region, 1960s; founder Inst. of Design in No. Caucasus, Krasnodar, 1975; organizer mass movement in higher edn. for rsch. and study of Slavonic langs., USSR, 1980s; founder Inst. Civil Edn. of the Armed Forces, Moscow, 1995. Recipient medal USSR Nat. Achievement Exhbn., 1979, Eileen Tosney award for excellence in prractice of higher edn., 1996; The Nikolai N. Khaladjan Internat. award established in his name Am. Asn. Univ. Adminstrs., 1997. Mem. AAAS, Internat. Coun. on Edn. for Tchg. (life), N.Y. Acad. Scis., Am. Assn. Univ. Adminstrs. Avocations: music, singing and songwriting, history of philosophy and education. Office: Pres/Moscow External U Hum, 37 Perovskaya Str, 111141 Moscow Russia also: PO Box 17211 Beverly Hills CA 90209-3211

KHALAF, FOUAD MOHAMMED, civil engineer, educator; b. Baghdad, Iraq, Oct. 8, 1950; s. Mohammed Khalaf Al-Sumidaie and Sabria Abdual-Salame Al-Rawie; m. Abeer Ibrahim Al-Izzi, Apr. 22, 1985; children: Senna, Maysem, Wissam. Diploma in surveying, Inst. Tech., Baghdad, 1972; BEng in Bldg. and Constrn., U. Tech., Baghdad, 1976; MSc in Civil Engring., U. Man., Can., 1981; PhD in Civil Engring., U. Edinburgh, Scotland, 1991. Porject mgr. Ministry of Housing, Baghdad, 1976-78; demonstrator U. Tech., Baghdad, 1978-79, asst. lectr., 1981-86; rsch. assoc. U. Man., 1980-81, U. Edinburgh, 1986-91; lectr. Napier U., Edinburgh, 1992—; cons. Telling Lime, Ltd., Edinburgh, 1996-99. Patentee in field; contbr. numerous tech. articles to profl. publs. Fellow Brit. Masonry Soc. (liaison group for masonry rsch. 1992); mem. ASCE, Am. Concrete Inst. Achievements: include research on properties of civil engineering materials, plain and reinforced masonry, recycling of building materials, electrical properties of concrete, electrical curing of concrete, and properties of hydraulic lime mortar; invention of new design patterns for cavity walls entitled "Tradbond." Avocations: reading, computing, swimming. Office: Napier U Sch Built Environ, 10 Colinton Rd, Edinburgh EH10 5DT, Scotland

KHALEEFA, OMAR HAROON, psychologist, researcher; b. Al-rahad, Sudan, Jan. 1, 1962; s. Haroon Khaleefa and Hayat Al-Sharief (Ali) K.; m. Ikhlas Hassan Ashria, Oct. 5, 1992; children: Qabas, Karmal. BA, U. Khartoum, Sudan, 1985, MA, 1987; PhD, U. Newcastle, Eng., 1995. Tchg. asst. U. Khartoum, 1986-91; asst. prof. U. Bahrain, 1996—; lectr. Omdurman U., Sudan, 1990-91, Faculty of Edn., Sudan, 1989-90, Coll. of Prison Officers, 1988-89, Inst. of Extramural Studies, 1987-88; Bahrain del. WCGTC, North Africa and Mid. East rep. to IAACP. Contbr. articles to profl. jours. Recipient Best Arab Rschr. in Psychology award Shoman Found., 1996, First Prize in Rsch. Oxford Acad. for Advanced Studies, 1995, scholarship Sudan Gov., 1991. Mem. APA (affiliate), Internat. Coun. Psychologists, Sudanese Assn. for Gifted Children (pres. 1990-91). Avocations: travel, watching documentaries, listening to music, writing. Office: Coll Edn Univ Bahrain, PO Box 32038 Dept Psycholog, Manama Bahrain

KHALEELI, ALI MOHAMMAD, retired consulting engineer; b. Madras, India, Nov. 25, 1935; arrived in Pakistan.; s. Abbas and Gouher Begum Shirazi Khaleeli; m. Zahra Shirazi, Aug. 6, 1963 (seperated); children: Wusooq, Safiyeh, Hussain, Nusrat. Diploma, Ingeneur Eidg. Tech., Hochshule, Zurich, 1962. With Ea. Refinery, Chittagong, 1963-71; trainee Nat. Iranian Oil Co., Tehran, 1964; instrumentation engr. Jovan Cons., Tehran, 1972; mech. engr. cons. Con. Mecon, Tehran, 1973; installation engr. Iranlaup, Tehran, 1978; air conditioning counsel Tehran, 1979; chief engr. Iran Gooshi, Qazvin, 1980; exec. dir. Ace Testing Lab., Karachi, Pakistan, 1974-77, 81-84; cons. engr. Assoc. Cons. Engring. Ltd., Karachi, 1984-95; adviser Petrochem Project EPIDC, Dacca, 1969. Muslim. Avocation: reading or current affairs.

KHALEF, BACHIR, physician, physicist, educator; b. Constantine, Algeria, Jan. 2, 1937; arrived in France, 1954; s. Mohand Khalef and Zahra Belmoufok; m. Nicole Auge, July 8, 1962 (div.); children: Francois, Anne, Emmanuelle; m. Evelyne Ritaine. Lic. in Math., Faculte des Scie, Bordeaux, France, 1960, Lic. in Physique, 1961, Diplôme d'Etudes Approfondies, 1966; MD, Faculte de Medecine, 1973. Intern Inst. des Scis. & Techniques Nuclaires, Saclay, France, 1964, Hosp. Pellegrin, 1969-71; resident Hosp. Haut Leveque, 1971-73; math. monitor Faculte des Scie, Bordeaux, 1960-62; prof. physics Lycee Montaigne, Bordeaux, 1962-73; chargé d'enseisnement d'anatomie et d'electrologie Institute Des Carrieres de Sante, 1973-78; prof. acupuncture U. Bordeaux, 1979-88; dir. Cabinet Med., Talence, France, 1973-97, Societe SERI, 1997-98, Etude de Medicine Legale, 1998—. Author: Approche Mathematique et Thermodynamique de l'Acupuncture, 1978, Vitesse de Reactions Photo Chimique, 1966, Laser en Medecine, 1984, Acupuncture Medecine de L'Energie, 1984, Energie en Medecine Acupuncture Medecine D'Avant-Garde, 1993, Hypnose Renouveau, 1994, Energie Perception Sensorielle Dans La Relation Medecin Malade, 1996, Hypnose Clinique, Approche Medico-Legale, Laboratoire Demedecineiegale, U. de Bordeaux, 1999. Mem. Milton H. Erickson Inst. Paris. Avocation: tennis.

KHALEQUZZAMAN, MOHAMMAD, zoology educator; b. Rajshahi, Bangladesh, Sept. 16, 1952; m. M. Azimuddin Ahmed and Khadiza Begum; m. Ismat Ara Chowdhury, May 25, 1976; children: Riffat Zaman, Rashed Zaman. BSc with honors, Rajshahi U., 1972, MSc, 1973, PhD, 1985; postdoc., U. Newcastle, U.K., 1992-93. Lectr. in zoology Rajshahi U., 1976-79, asst. prof., 1979-86, assoc. prof., 1986-91, prof., 1991—, chmn. dept. zoology, 1995-98; project dir. Rangpur U. Sci. & Tech., 1999—; guest mem. staff U. Newcastle, 1992-93. Exec. editor Univ. Jour. Zoology, 1996. Mem. Rajshahi Cancer Shelter, 1990—, Rajshahi Old People's Svc. Ctr., 1990—; chmn. Rajshahi Lions Eye Hosp., 1995—. Commonwealth fellow Assn. Commonwealth Univs., U.K., 1992-93. Fellow Royal Entomol. Soc., Bangladesh Zool. Soc.; life mem. Bangladesh Entomological Soc., Asiatic Soc. Bangladesh; mem. Bangladesh Assn. for the Advancement of Sci., Lions Club Rajshali. Avocations: traveling, swimming, listening to music, computer modelling. Home: House 384 Road 9 Padma R/A, Rajshahi 6204, Bangladesh Office: Rangpur U Sci & Tech, PO Box 49, Rangpur 5400, Bangladesh

KHALESSI, MOHAMMAD R., structural engineer, researcher; b. Yazd, Iran, Nov. 18, 1952; came to U.S., 1976; s. Mohammad-Ali and Farangis (Bahadorani) K.; m. Fariba Touhidi, Aug. 14, 1977 (div. 1984); 1 child, Ahoo; m. Mercedeh Rusty, Oct. 25, 1986; 1 child, Bobak. BS, Arya Mehr U., Tehran, Iran, 1976; MS, UCLA, 1978, PhD, 1983. Engr. C.F. Braun, Alhambra, Calif., 1980-81; rsch. engr. UCLA, 1981-83; sr. engr. Allied Signal, Torrance, Calif., 1983-87; sr. engring. splst. Boeing N.Am., Downey, Calif., 1987-97; chief technologist Mitratech Probabilistic, Fountain Valley, Calif., 1997-99; chief product devel. officer Unipass Techs., Inc., Irvine, Calif., 1999—; also bd. dirs. Unipass Techs., Inc., Irvine; bd. dirs. Advanced Probabilistic Rsch., Inc.; adv. Unicorp, VanNuys, Calif., 1995—. Contbr. articles to profl. jours. Recipient Outstanding Engring. Merit award Orange County (Calif.) Engring. Coun ., 1994. Fellow Inst. Advancement Engring.; mem. AIAA, SAE (chair subcom. probabilistic method, comm. 1994—, tech. adv. leadership coun. for probabilistic methods 1995—, Disting. Probabilistic Methods Implementations award 1996). Republican. Muslim. Achievements include pioneering work in practical application of probabilistic methods, integration of probabilistic methods with finite element technique, identification of most-probable-failure point in original space. Office: Unipass Techs 18008 Sky Park Cir Ste 125 Irvine CA 92614-6470

KHALID, GHULAM HAIDER, physician, educator, consultant; b. Zhob, Pakistan, Dec. 15, 1956; s. Din Mohammed Chaudry and Rabia Umer Din Din Mohammad; m. Nayyer Azim, June 7, 1990; children: Qurat Ul A'in, Khawla, Hafsa, Rabia. DTCD, Punjab U., Lahore, Pakistan, 1983; FCPS, CPSP, Karachi, Pakistan, 1989, 95; MB, BCh, BMC, Quetta, Pakistan, 1982. Ho. officer Bolan Med. Coll., Quetta, 1981-82, registrar, 1982-84, asst. prof., 1990-96, assoc. prof., 1996-99, prof., head med. unit, 1999—; med. officer Sandeman Hosp., Quetta, 1984-90; cons. physician Ministry of Health, Saudi Arabia, 1991-93. Contbr. articles to profl. jours. Mem. Acad. Coun., Nat. Geog. Soc. Avocations: computers, internet, cricket, travel. Office: 45 Saleem Med Complex, Jinnah Rd, Quetta Balochistan 87300, Pakistan

KHALID, MUHAMMAD WASIM, engineering executive; b. Fasalabad, Punjab, Pakistan, Sept. 5, 1953; s. Muhammad Ashraf Khan and Sadiqa Sultana; m. Farrukh Wasim, Oct. 16, 1981; children: Muhammad Farid, Sana Wasim, Anum Wasim, Muhammad Anas. BSc in Engring., U. Engring. and Tech., Lahore, Pakistan, 1974; MSc in Engring., U. Birmingham, Eng., 1980. Chartered mfg. and elec. engr., U.K.; registered profl. engr., Pakistan Engring. Coun. Jr. engr. Pakistan Indsl. Tech. Assistance Ctr., Lahore, 1975-79; dep. mgr., mgr. Millat Tractors Ltd., Lahore, 1981-88; dir. works Mecas Engring. (Pvt.) Ltd., Lahore, 1989-97, CEO,, 1997—; external examiner U. Engring. and Tech., Lahore, 1990-95. Exec. mem. Assn. Overseas Tech. Scholarship Alumni Soc. and Asia Bunka Kaikau Dosokai, Lahore, 1988-90. Mem. Inst. Engrs. Pakistan. Home: 104-G Model Town, Lahore Punjab, Pakistan Office: Mecas Engring Pvt Ltd, 0.6 km Katar Bund Rd, Lahore Punjab, Pakistan

KHALIFA, MOHAMED MOUSTAFA, chemical company manager; b. Cairo, Apr. 23, 1962; s. Moustafa Mohamed Khalifa and Bouthina Aly El Makhzangi; m. Amany Mohamed Wahba, July 25, 1993; children: Sonaila, Khalid. BSc, Ain Shams U., Cairo, 1983, MSc in Biochemistry, 1990, PhD in Biochemistry, 1996. Asst. med. dir. SOS, Cairo, 1985-86; med. rep. Pfizer Egypt, Cairo, 1987-93, dist. sales mgr., 1993-95, product mgr., 1995—. Soldier Chem. Wars, 1984-85. Avocations: football, swimming, reading. Home: 62 Sakr Korish Bldgs, Cairo Egypt Office: Pfizer Egypt, 47 Ramsis St, Cairo Egypt

KHALIFA, YASER, engineering educator; b. Cairo, July 1, 1970; came to U.S., 1998; s. Mohammed Agami and Adiba (Kamel) K.; m. Hala Mahfouz, July 22, 1994; 1 child, Doaa. BSc, Alexandria U., Egypt, 1992; PhD, U. Wales, Cardiff, 1997. Maintenance engr. Specific Sci. Components, Cairo, 1992-93; rschr. U. Wales Cardiff, 1993-97; asst. prof. engring. Girne Am. U., Turkey, 1997-98, U. N.D., Grand Forks, 1998—; referee conf: Artificial Neural Networks Engring., Rolla, Mo., 1999, Newnes Pub. House. Recipient Indsl. Contbn. award Veribest Inc., Grand Forks, N.D., 1998. Mem. IEEE, Internet Soc., Egyptian Engring. Syndicate. Avocations: chess, horse riding. Fax: 701-777-5253. E-mail: yaserma@mail.nodak.edu. Office: U ND U Ave Grand Forks ND 58202

KHALIL, ABDEL-RAHMAN MOHAMMED, chemist; b. Fariskour, Domiat, Sept. 5, 1946; s. Mohammed Abdel-Aal and Hafiza Mohammed (Mai) K.; m. Anwaar El Sayed Khalil, July 6, 1973; children: Rafik, Mohammed, Heba. BSc in Chemistry, Ain Shams U., Cairo, 1967, MSc in Surface Chemistry, 1971, PhD in Surface Chemistry, 1976; diploma, Oslo U., 1980. Demonstrator faculty sci. Ain Shams U., Cairo, 1967-72, asst. lectr., 1972-76, lectr. phys. chemistry, 1976-80, asst. prof., 1980-86, prof., 1986—. Reviewer Jour. Thermal Analysis Cairo/Budapest, 1991-94; mem. editl. bd. Am. Biog. Inst., 1995; contbr. articles to profl. jours. Recipient Author and Editors card El-Sevier, Amsterdam, 1977, State prize in chemistry Egypt Acad. Sci., Cairo. Mem. Syndicated Sci. Profls. Cairo, Egyptian Chem. Soc., Ain Shams Univ. Staff. Avocations: listening to classical music, free walks and one day trips. Home: 31 Dr Ahmed Zaki St, El-Nozha El-Gedida 11769, Egypt Office: Ain Shams U Faculty Sci, Dept Chemistry Ramsis St, Abbassia 11566, Egypt

KHALIL, AHMAD KHALIL, ophthalmologist, educator; b. Cairo, Sept. 15, 1962; s. Khalil Ibrahim and Safwat Abdalla (Mekkawi) K.; m. Nouran Amal Aref Mostafa, Aug. 22, 1996; children: Hassan, Omar. MB, Cairo U., 1985, M Ophthalmology, 1989; PhD, Kyushu U., Fukuoka, Japan, 1998. Med. diplomate. House officer Cairo U. Hosp., 1986-87, resident ophthalmology, 1987-90; asst. lectr. Rsch. Inst. Ophthalmology, Ciaro, 1991-98, lectr., 1998—; clin. rsch. fellow Kyushu U., Fukuoka, Japan, 1993-98, editor in chief Web Site dept. ophthalmology, 1996-98; bd. dirs. Egyptian Soc. Cataract Corneal Disease, Cairo, 1992-93, 1999—. Contbr. articles to profl. jours. and books. Recipient 1st prize All Egyptian Univs., Supreme Coun. Youth and Sports, 1985; grantee Ministry Edn., Japan, 1993-98. Mem. Egyptian Ophthal. Soc., Japanese Ophthal. Soc. Avocations: travel, photography, book collecting, golf. Home: PO Box 397 Embaba, Giza Cairo, Egypt Office: Rsch Inst Ophthalmology, 2 Al-Ahram St, Giza Cairo, Egypt

KHALIL, HUSSEIN MOHAMMAD, engineering company executive, electrical engineer; b. Tulkarm, Palestine, Apr. 22, 1950; s. Hussein Khalil Al-Araj Mohd and Fatima Saeed Qaroot; m. Ibtisam Ragheb Sulaibi; children: Mohammad, Hazem, Hisham, Reem, Bashar. BE(E), Karachi (Pakistan) U., 1974; MBA, Washington Internat. U., Pa., 2000. engr. Nat. Kharafi, Kuwait, 1984-87; sr. engr. Al-Hani Bur., Kuwait, 1975-84; head elec. dept. Khamis & Aryan Co., Kuwait, 1987-90; sr. supervision engr. PMC, Kuwait, 1991-93; elec. contracting in-charge Al-Dar Establishment, Kuwait, 1993; head supervision, design engr. Dirwaza Cons. Engrs., Kuwait, 1994-96; elec. supervision in-charge A. Al-Fulaji & Mashhour Cons. Engrs., Kuwait, 1996; project mgr. Arcan Co., Kuwait, 1996-97; v.p. for electromech. svcs. PROJACS (Project Analysis & Control Sys.), Kuwait, 1997—. Contbr. articles to profl. jours. Mem. IEEE, Kuwait Soc. Engrs., N.Am. Soc. Illumination, Jordan Soc. Engrs. Avocations: reading, photography, travel, cinema. Office: PROJACS, PO Box 25 944, Kuwait City 13120, Kuwait

KHALIL, SYED MOZAFFAR, geologist, geophysicist, researcher; b. Gaya, Bihar, India, Mar. 30, 1950; s. S. Khalil Ahmad and S. Kanizun Nisa; m. Farzana Mozaffar, Dec. 15, 1976; children: S. Musab, S. Muaz, S. Muasir. BS in Geology, Patna (India) U., Bihar, 1966; MS in Geology, Patna (India) U., 1969; MS in Geology (Coastal), Fla. Atlantic U., 1999. From asst. geologist to geologist Hindustan Gen. Electric Co., Barbil, Orissa, India, 1969-72; sr. tech. asst. mineral econs. Indian Bur. Mines, Nagpur, 1972-74; geologist, marine geologist Geol. Survey India, Bhopal and Patna, 1974-85; sr. marine geologist Geol. Survey India, Calcutta, 1985-94; co-chief scientist Geol. Survey India, 1986-92, chief scientist, 1992-94; grad. studies/marine geoscientist Fla. Atlantic U., Boca Raton, 1995—, Coastal Planning and Engring. Inc., 1995—, C & C Tech., 1995—. Contbr. articles to profl. jours. Fellow UN, 1985-86. Mem. Am. Geophys. Union, S.W. La. Geophys. Soc., Coastal Rsch. Edn. Found., Phi Kappa Phi. Achievements include discovery of approximately 10 million tons of bauxite in parts of eastern India; pioneer in submarine geomorphological mapping of inner continental shelf off Broward County, Florida. Avocations: reading, travel. Home: 200 Oakcrest Dr Lafayette LA 70503-2701

KHALILOV, ERKIN, Uzbek government official. Chmn. supreme nat. assembly Govt. of Uzbekistan, Tashkent. Office: Oliy Majlis (Parliament), Pr Drujby Narodov, 1 700035 Tashkent Uzbekistan

KHALILOVA, ALIYA ZUFAROVNA, chemistry researcher; b. Nasibash, Russia, June 14, 1950; d. Zufar Alfafovich and Fatkiya Akhmetovna Gainanov; m. Leonard Mukhibovich Khalilov, Aug. 9, 1974; children: Asiya, Zulphiga. Degree in Biology, Baskirian State U., Ufa, Russia, 1975; PhD, Inst. Petrochem. & Catalysis, Ufa, Russia, 1999. Engr. Mechnikov Inst. Vaccine, Ufa, 1975-78, Bashkortostan Rsch. and Project Inst. of Oil Industry, Ufa, 1978-92; rchr. Inst. Petrochemistry and Catalysis, Ufa, 1993—. Contbr. articles to profl. jours. Achievements include patent for remedy for potato protection. Avocation: medicinal herbs. Office: Inst Petrochem & Catalysis, 141 Prospekt Oktyabrya, 450075 Ufa Russia

KHALKA, JETSUN DHAMPA, head of religious order; b. Lhasa, Tum se khang, Tibet, Jan. 10, 1932; arrived in India, 1960; s. Phenpo Lhundup Khangsar Losang Jampel and Yangchen Lhamo; m. Pema Choedon, 1957 (dec. 1994); children: Tukse Tulku, Jampa Namgyal, Tsering Choedon; m. Rinzin Dolma, 1958 (dec. 1993); children: Thupten Sherap, Tashi Dhondup (dec.), Sonam Gyatso (dec.), Choephel Yonten. Studied and ordained, Drepung Gomang Monastery, 1939-53. Head lama Phuntsok Ling Monastery, Tibet, 1953-60; acting lama in exile various Tibetan refugee cmtys., India, 1960-92; 9th Jetsun Dhampa, head of Buddhism Dharamsala, India, 1992—. Home: Tak Tan House Jogibara Rd, PO McLeod Ganj 176219, Dharamsala Kangra, India

KHAMBANONDA, CHALERMRATH, dean, educator, author; b. Angthong, Thailand, Dec. 5, 1933; s. Iam and Chamniansook (Samitasiri) K.; m. Chaveevan Kosolawat, Mar. 8, 1965; children: Chaichanok, Chantharath. BS in Commerce, Thammasat U., Bangkok, Thailand, 1957, BS in Acctg., 1957; M of Pub. Adminstrn., Ind. U., 1967, PhD, 1972. Econ. planner Nat. Econ. Coun., Bangkok, 1959-62; lectr. Inst. of Pub. Adminstrn., Thammasat U., Bangkok, 1962-65; dean, asst. prof. Sch. of Pub. Adminstrn. Nat. Inst. of Devel. Adminstrn., Bangkok, 1975-76; rsch. fellow Environ. and Policy Inst./East-West Ctr., Honolulu, Hawaii, 1979-80; assoc. prof. faculty of bus. adminstrn. Ramkhamhaeng U., Bangkok, 1980-94; dean grad. sch. Vongchavalitkul U., Nakhon Ratchasima, Thailand, 1994—; mem. Internat. Coun. of Environtl. Law, Bonn, Germany, 1981—; adv. UN Ctr. for Human Settlement Tng., Nairobi, Kenya, 1983. Author: Thailand's Public Law and Policy for Conservation and Protection of Land: With Special Attention to Forests and Natural Areas, 1972; contbr. articles to profl. jours. Advisor to Prime Min. Govt. of Thailand, 1976-77; spl. asst. to Prime Min.'s Sec.-Gen., 1977-79; mem., advisor Senate's Com. on Environ., 1992-93. 2d lt. Royal Thai Army, 1957-58. Fellowship Ind. U.-Ford Found., 1965-67, 67-71. Fellow East-West-Ctr.; mem. World Future Soc. (coord. 1980—), Thailand Future Soc. (pres. 1989—), Soc. for Conservation of Nat. Treasure and Environ., Assn. of Profl. Acct. and Auditor of Thailand, Profl. Guide Assn. of Thailand. Buddhist. Avocations: traveling, sightseeing, jogging, classical music, golf. Home: 13 Ln 19 Seree 1 Huamark, Bangkapi, Bangkok 10250, Thailand Office: Vongchavalitkul U, Mitrapab Hwy, Nakhon Ratchasima 30000, Thailand

KHAMENEI, AYATOLLAH ALI HOSEINI, religious leader Islamic Republic of Iran; b. Meshed, Khorassan, 1940; married, 1964; 4 sons, 2 daugs. Ed. in Qom, studied under Ayatollah Khomeini. Imprisoned 6 times, 1964-78; former personal rep. of Ayatollah Khomeini to Supreme Def. Council; mem. Revolutionary Council until its dissolution, 1979; Friday prayer leader Teheran, 1980—; sec.-gen., mem. central com. Islamic Republican Party, 1980-87; pres. of Iran, 1981-89, supreme religious leader, 1989—. Address: Secretariat of the Imam, Pastor Ave, Tehran Iran*

KHAMISOV, OLEG VALERIEVITCH, mathematician; b. Elantsy, Russia, May 8, 1963; s. Valerii Innokentievitch Khamisov and Taisia Ivanovna Aksenova; m. Natalia Vassilievna Masterskiku, Aug. 7, 1992; 1 child, Oleg. Degree, State U. of Irkutsk, 1985, PhD in Math., 1993. Jr. rschr. Inst. of Energy Systems, Irkutsk, 1985-91, sci. rschr., 1991-93, sr. rschr., 1993, head of ops. rsch. lab., 1993—. Recipient Lev kantorovitch prize Siberian br. Russian Acad. Scis., 1995. Home: Lezmontov St 333B-289, 664033 Irkutsk Russia Office: Inst Energy Systems, Lezmontov St 130, 664033 Irkutsk Russia

KHAMOUAN BOUPHA, Laotian government official. Min. Ministry of Justice, Loas. Office: Ministry of Justice, Lane Xang Ave, Vientiane Laos*

KHAMOUNA, MO, communicatons associate, consultant; b. Casablanca, Morocco, Jan. 6, 1959; came to U.S., 1988; s. Ahmed and Malika (Katim)

K.; m. Lori McNutt, July 20, 1990; children: Jasmine, Zackary. Diploma d'Etudes U. Gen./ Am. Studies, U. Paris, France, 1988; BS in Tourism & Recreation, U. Nebr., Kearney, 1993; MS in Tourism & Recreation, Black Hills State U., 1996. Proficiency cert. travel & tourism McCook C.C. Dir. recreation Spearfi Parks & Recreation Dept., Spearfish, S.D., 1995; comm. assoc. Nebr. Coll. Tech. Agr., Curtis, 1996—; v.p., cons. U.S. Hwy 83 Trade & Tourism Assn., Nebr., 1997—; pres. Prairie Lakes Country Travel Coun., McCook, Nebr., 1999—. Author : (with others) Profile of American Tourists, 1996. Named Hon. Citizen of Tanyang Municipality Magistrate, South Korea, 1198. Mem. Internat. Peace Acad., Rotary, Nat. Recreation and Park Assn. (nat. certification bd. 1994-95). Avocations: book collecting, wilderness vision quest, travelling, low impact camping. Fax: 367-5209. E-mail: mkhamouna1@unl.edu. Home: 307 Pope Ave Curtis NE 69025 Office: Nebr Coll of Tech Agr RR 3 RR 3 Box 23A Curtis NE 69025-9525

KHAMZAYEV, ALMAZ N., diplomat; b. Dec. 18, 1955; m. Gulistan Miyazbayeva; children: Anar, Asel, Asem. Diploma, U. Fgn. Languages, Almaty Diplomatic Acad., Moscow, U. Fgn. Languages, Almaty Diplomatic Acad., Moscow. Ministry fgn. affairs Kazakhstan Govt., Almaty, 1978-92; counsellor, charge d'affaires Embassy to U.S., Washington, 1992-96; min.-counsellor, charge d'affaires Embassy to U.K., London, 1996-97; vice-minister foreign affairs Kazakhstan Govt., Astana, 1997-98; amb. to Spain Kazakhstan Govt., Madrid, 1998—. Office: Kazakhstan Embassy to Spain, C/Cascanueces, 25/28043 Madrid Spain

KHAN, ABU SAYED SERAJUL ISLAM, neonatologist; b. Baragram, Mymensingh, Bangladesh, Jan. 3, 1937; s. Saad Uddin and Sophia Billah (Khandokar) K.; m. Lakshmi Bhargava, Oct. 10, 1975; 1 child, Sophia Seraj. MBBS, Dacca (Bangladesh) Med. Coll., 1962; diploma of Child Health, London Royal Coll., 1967. Rotating intern Dacca Med. Coll., 1962-64; med. officer Mitford Med. Hosp., Dacca, 1964-65; sr. house officer Doncaster Royal Infirmary, Eng., 1967-69; pediatric registrar Kettering Hosp., Eng., 1969-73; registrar Pontefract Infirmary, Eng., 1973-74, Luton Dunstable Hosp., Eng., 1974-75; sr. specialist neonatology Hamad Med. Corp., Doha, Qatar, 1975-80, sr. cons. neonatology, 1980—, chief sect., 1985-90, sr. cons. neonatology, 1990—; established first neonatal unit, Doha, 1975, commissioned new maternity and neonatal unit, 1988, established B.C.G. & Hepatitis B vaccination, 1978, 90. Contbr. articles to profl. jours. Fellow Royal Coll. Physicians (London), Royal Coll. Pediatric and Child Health; mem. Royal Coll. Physicians (England), Brit. Pediatric Assn., Nat. Geog. Soc., Nat. Biog. Soc. Avocations: reading political history, swimming. Office: Hamad Med Corp, PO Box 3050, Doha Qatar

KHAN, AFTAB MOHAMMED, retired geophysics educator; b. Rio Claro, Trinidad and Tobago, Oct. 31, 1933; arrived in Eng., 1956; s. Abrahim and Ayesha (Mohammed) K.; m. Audrey Diana Bates, Oct. 22, 1958; children: Rebecca, Richard. BSc with honors, U. Birmingham, Eng., 1956; PhD, U. Birmingham, 1958. Rsch. fellow in geophysics U. Birmingham, 1958-63; lectr. in geophysics U. Leicester, Eng., 1963-73; sr. lectr. in geophysics U. Leicester, 1973-93, prof. geophysics, 1993—; internat. coord. Kenya Rift Internat. Seismic Project, 1985-99; co-leader UNESCO IGCP 400 on continental rifts, 1996—. Author: Global Geology, 1976; contbr. over 100 articles to profl. jours.; mng. editor Geophys. Jour. Internat., 1992—. Chmn. governing bd. Sch. Cosmic Physics, Dias, Ireland, 1995—. Over 20 grants for geophys. rsch. Fellow Royal Astron. Soc. (v.p. 1989-90), Geol. Soc. London, Brit. Geophys. Assn. (chmn. 1990-93), Am. Geophys. Union. Mem. Labour Party. Avocations: golf, cricket, gardening, opera, wine. Home: 144 Evington Ln, Leicester LE5 6DG, England Office: Dept Geology, The University, Leicester LE1 7RH, England

KHAN, AFZAL HUSSAIN, information scientist; b. Karachi, Sindh, Pakistan, July 8, 1950; s. Mehmood Hassan and Rehana (Khatoon) K.; m. Fareeda Parveen, Apr. 30, 1980; children: Jahanzeb, Nazia Afzal. M in Polit. Sci., U. Karachi, 1990. Asst. mgr., programmer State Life Ins., Karachi, 1972-78; asst. mgr., programmer Enar Petrotech Svcs., Karachi, 1978-79, mgr., analyst programmer, 1979-84, mgr., sys. analyst, 1984-94; sr. mgr. State Petroleum, Karachi, 1994-98; sr. mgr. MIS Nat. Refinery Ltd., 1998—; cons. in field. Contbr. articles to profl. jours. Mem. Computer Soc. Pakistan (life), Karachi Ideal Club (sec. 1989-90, treas. 1990-91). Avocations: collecting coins, chess, music. Home: 1340/2 Azizabad, 75950 Karachi Pakistan Office: Nat Refinery Ltd, 7-B Korangi Industrial Zone, 74900 Karachi Pakistan

KHAN, AHMED MUKHTAR MOHAMED, geotechnical engineer; b. Tamewali, Bahawal Pur, Punjab/Pakistan, Jan. 1, 1948; s. Mohamed Hayat Khan and Bakhtawar Ali Begum; m. Sabiha Haji, Feb. 23, 1969; children: Kashif A., Asif A., Farina A., Saad M. BSCE, U. Engring. and Technology, Lahore, Pakistan, 1968, MSc in Engring., 1974; M Engring., Asian Inst. Technology, Bangkok, 1976; PhD, U. Birmingham, Eng. Registered profl. engr. Design engr. structures and head pub. health engring. Illeri and Assoc., Lahore, 1968-69; design engr. ZDK and Assocs., Lahore, 1969-70; lectr. in civil engring. U. Engring. and Technology, Lahore, 1970-73, asst. prof. of civil engring., 1973-79, head soil mechanics and found. engring., 1979-80; lectr., geotech. group sec. King Abdulaziz U., Jeddah, Saudi Arabia, 1980—; sec., grad. com. civil engring. dept. King Abdulaziz U., Jeddah, 1990—; chief cons. engr. Chishty Bros., Lahore, 1970-72. Inventor in field. Vol. project engr. for relief housing Cooperative for Am. Relief Everywhere, Pakistan, 1972-73; prin. trainer low-cost housing, People's Works Programme, Pakistan, 1973-74. Rsch. grantee CARE, Lahore, 1974; recipient scholarship Internat. Telegraph and Telephone, Bangkok, 1974-76. Fellow Instn. Engrs. Pakistan; mem. ASCE, Internat. Soc. for Soil Mechanics and Found. Engring., S.E. Asian Geotech. Soc., Pakistan Engring. Coun. (life). Avocations: travel, tourism, sports/badminton and swimming. Home: 284-A Rivaz Garden, Lahore/Punjab 54000, Pakistan Office: King Abdulaziz U Civil Engring Dept, Univ St PO Box 9027, Jeddah 21413, Saudi Arabia

KHAN, AHMED QASIM, computer software company executive; b. Lahore, Pakistan, Jan. 18, 1950; arrived in Norway, 1974; s. Abdul Azim and Amtullah (Khan) K.; m. Mehnaz Faridi, Apr. 21, 1991; 1 child, Emad. Grad. Engr., Elec. Comm. Engring., Lahore, Pakistan, 1967; post-grad., Møre Romsdale Ingeniør H, Ålesund, Norway, 1978. Chartered engr. Jr. engr. Telephone Industries Pakistan, Haripur, 1967-74; devel. engr. Elektrisk Bur., Oslo, 1979-81; chief cons. Haukeland Sykehus, Bergen, Norway, 1981-82; head of indsl. projects dept. U. Bergen, 1982-84; mng. dir. SCS, 1984-87; pres. SCS, Islamabad, Pakistan, 1987—. Mem. IEEE, Norwegian Soc. Chartered Engrs., N.Y. Acad. Scis. Avocations: tennis, music, literature, cosmology, theoretical physics. Office: SCS Scand Computer Sys Ltd, 6-A Street 51, F/84 Islamabad Pakistan

KHAN, ALI YAR, mechanical and industrial engineer; b. Hyderabad, India; came to U.S., 1967; s. Sayeed Yar and Sayeeda (Bano) K.; m. Tehniat Jehan, Sept. 4, 1967; children: Azam Yar, Asif Yar. BE in Mech. Engring., Osmania U., Hyderabad, 1965; MSc in Indsl. Engring., Miss. State U., 1970. Instr. Miss. State U., State College, 1969-70; indsl. engr., prodn. supt., plant mgr. Burlington Industries, N.C., Va., 1970-88; jr. engr. AEP Bd., Hyderabad, 1988-99; plant mgr. Precision Fabrics Group, Inc., Vinton, Va., 1988—. Bd. dirs. United Way, Roanoke, Va., 1990-97, campaign chmn. maj. firms, 1991-92. Mem. IIE (chpt. v.p. programs 1976-77), Lions Club (pres. 1990-91), Mgmt. Assn. (bd. dirs. 1995-99, chmn. 1995-96). Home: 1305 Winston Dr Salem VA 24153-7739

KHAN, AMANULLAH, physician; b. Jullundhar, India, Mar. 2, 1940; came to U.S., 1964; s. Ahmad Ali and Qamar (Nisa) K.; m. Fran Elise Austin, Dec. 9, 1972; children: Roxanna, Sabrina, Amanda. Licentiate state med. faculty, West Pakistan Med. Sch., 1959; MBBS, King Edward Med. Coll., Lahore, 1963; PhD, Baylor U., 1968. Diplomate: Am. Bd. Allergy and Immunology, Am. Bd. Lab. Immunology. Rotating intern Samaritan Hosp., Troy, N.Y., 1965-66; fellow in hematology and oncology Wadley Insts. of Molecular Medicine, Dallas, 1966-69, chief research fellow, 1969-70, chmn. dept. immunotherapy, 1970-91; mem. staffs HCA Plano Med. Ctr., Doctor's Hosp., Dallas, Richardson Med. Ctr., St. Paul Med. Ctr., North Central Med. Ctr., McKinney. Author: Immune Regulators in Transfer Factor, 1979, Inteferon: Properties and Clinical Uses, 1980, Experimental Hematology Today, 1980, Human Lymphokines, 1982; editor: Jour. Clin. Hematology and Oncology, 1971-87; mem. editorial bd.: Exptl. Hematology, 1973-75; patentee in field; contbr. articles to sci. jours. Bd. dirs. St. vincent Med. Found., St. Paul Med. Found., Tex. Healthxare Info. Coun. Recipient Pres. of Pakistan Gold medal Pakistan Acad. of Med. Scis., 1992. Fellow ACP, Am. Coll. Allergists; mem. Am. Assn. Immunologists, Am. Soc. Clin. Oncology, Am. Soc. Hematology, AMA, Dallas County Med. Soc., Tex. Med. Assn., King Edward Med. Coll. Alumni Assn. (pres. 1974-75, 78-79), Assn. Pakistani Physicians N. Am. (pres. 1983-84). Office: Cancer Ctr Assocs 5959 Harry Hines Blvd Ste 620 Dallas TX 75235-5328

KHAN, EAKALAK, civil engineering educator; b. Chiang Mai, Thailand, Aug. 20, 1968; came to U.S., 1991; s. Zafar and Ploenchit Khan. B in Engring., Chiang Mai U., 1990; MS in Agrl. Engring., U. Hawaii, 1993; MS in Civil Engring., UCLA, 1994, PhD in Civil Engring., 1997. Engr.-in-tng. Calif.; registered profl. civil engr., Thailand. Engr. Envirtech Cons. Co. Ltd., Bangkok, Thailand, 1990; jr. expert U. Hawaii, Honolulu, 1993; postdoctoral rsch. assoc. UCLA, 1998; asst. prof. civil engring. Bklyn. Poly. U., 1999—. Inventor in field. Rsch. grantee Ahmanson Found., 1994, 95, Santa Monica Bay Restoration Project, 1995, 96, EarthShell Corp., Inc., 1997, State of Calif., 1998. Mem. ASCE, Am. Water Work Assn., Assn. Environ. Engring. and Sci. Profs., Internat. Assn. Water Quality, Water Environment Fedn. E-mail: ekhan@poly.edu. Office: Bklyn Poly U 6 Metrotech Ctr Brooklyn NY 11201-3840

KHAN, EJAZ AHMED, pediatrician consultant; b. Mansehra, Pakistan, Dec. 27, 1964; s. Haroon Mohammad Khan and Khurshid Begum; m. Lubna Ejaz Iqbal, Sept. 26, 1990; 1 child, Hamza Khan. MB, BS, Aga Khan Med. Sch., Karachi, Pakistan, 1988. Diplomate Am. Bd. Pediatrics. Assoc. cons. Shifa Internat. Hosp., Islamabad, Pakistan, 1997-99, cons. in pediatrics, acting chmn. pediat. dept., 1999—. Author: Current Therapy in Pediatrics, 1998; contbr. articles to profl. jours. Mem. Pakistan Med. and Dental Coun., Pakistan Acad. Pediatrics, Am. Acad. Pediatrics. Islam. Avocations: sports, sightseeing. Home: Village and PO Battal, Tehsil Mansehra NWFP, Pakistan Office: Shifa Internat Hosp, H 8/4, Islamabad Pakistan

KHAN, FIDA MOHAMMAD, company executive; b. Banda Piran, Pakistan, Feb. 20, 1938; s. Mohammad Usman Khan and Taj Nisa. MSc in Geography, U. Peshawar, Pakistan, 1959. Lectr. in geography Govt. Colls., Pakistan, 1959-61; commd. officer Pakistan Army, 1962, advanced through grades to lt. col., resigned, 1980; mgr. Trading and Indenting and Mfrs. Representation, Abu Dhabi, United Arab Emirates, 1982—. Office: PO Box 43185, Abu Dhabi United Arab Emirates

KHAN, HAFIZ TAREQ ABDULLAH, statistics educator; b. Chandpur, Bangladesh, Sept. 3, 1966; s. Hafizullah and Nurunessa (Begum) K.; m. Rehana Bari, Apr. 10, 1992; 1 child, Rifah Binte Abdullah. BS with honors in Statistics, U. Chittagong, Bangladesh, 1986, MS in Statistics, 1987; PhD in Statistics, Napier U., Edinburgh, Scotland, 1996. Asst. prof. U. Dhaka, Bangladesh, 1996—; lectr. U. Dhaka, 1991-96, Napier U., Edinburgh, U.K., 1993-96. Avocations: travel, TV. Home: 678/5C N Kafrul, Dhaka 1206, Bangladesh Office: Dept Statistics, U Dhaka, Dhaka 1000, Bangladesh

KHAN, HAFIZ WASI, agronomist, consultant; b. Jhang, Punjab, Pakistan, Jan. 13, 1950; s. Hafizali Mohd Khan and Ahmadi Mohd Khanam; m. Khalida Wasi Khanam, Mar. 18, 1977; children: Sara, Ahmed Hisham, Umara, Ahmed Hassan, Umer Khayam. MSc in Agronomy with honors, U. Agr., Pakistan, 1975; LLB, U. Karachi, Pakistan, 1981. Agr. credit officer Habib Bank Ltd., Karachi, Pakistan, 1974-75; agronomist Dawood Corp. Ltd., Lahore, Pakistan, 1975-79; farm mgr. Islamic Found., Nairobi, Kenya, 1979-86; project mgr. Alemar Group, Riyadh, Saudi Arabia, 1988—; wheat cons. Alemar Group, Riyadh, 1990—. Pres. Islami Jamiat Tulaba, Faisal Abad, Pakistan, 1969-74; mem. Hope, Jhang, Pakistan, 1998—; patron Agr. Policy Studies Inst., Lahore, 1999—. Named Best Farmer FAO/UNO, Isiolo, Kenya, 1983, 84, 86. Mem. Kenya Energy Non-Grant Orgn., Kenya Farmers Assn., Kisan Bd. Avocations: reading, forestry. Home: 169/B Setlite Town, Jhang Sadar Punjab, Pakistan Office: Alemar Group, PO Box 22181, Riyadh 11495, Saudi Arabia

KHAN, IJAZ JAMIL, microbiologist; b. Bahawalpur, Punjab, Pakistan, Jan. 10, 1957; s. Abdul Jamil Khan and Iqbal Fatima; m. Fouzia Ijaz, Mar. 7, 1991; children: Asad, Tuba. MB, BChir, Punjab U., 1982, MPhil in Microbiology, 1992; diploma in clin. pathology, Islamia U., Pakistan, 1988. Med. diplomate. Blood transfusion officer Bahwal Victoria Hosp., Bahawalpur, Pakistan, 1983-84; demonstrator, med. lectr. Quaid-i-Azam Med. Coll., Bahawalpur, 1984-90, 92-95, asst. prof. microbiology, 1995-96; cons. microbiologist, pathology lab. dir. Armed Forces Hosp., Najran, Saudi Arabia, 1996—. Mem. Am. Soc. for Microbiology. Avocation: swimming. Home: Armed Forces Hosp, PO Box 1002, Najran Saudi Arabia Office: Dept Pathology, Armed Forces Hosp, Najran Saudi Arabia

KHAN, ISHTIAQ RASOOL, electrical engineer, researcher; b. Daska, Punjab, Pakistan, Sept. 10, 1969; arrived in Japan, 1995; Cert. in engring., U. Sci. and Tech., Lahore, 1992; M in Sys. Engring., Quaid-i-Azam U., Islamabad, Pakistan, 1994; M in Info. Engring., Hokkaido U., Sapporo, Japan, 1998, postgrad., 1998—. Prin. City Computer Coll., Daska, 1992; sr. engr. Informatic Complex, Islamabad, 1995—. Contbr. papers to profl. jours. Recipient S&T Postgrad. award Ministry of Sci. and Tech., Govt. Pakistan, 1995-00; Merit scholar Govt. Pakistan, 1987-91. Mem. Inst. Elec. Engrs., Engring. Coun. Fax: 81 11 751 7034. E-mail: ir khan@hotmail.com. Home: Adamke Cheema Tehsil Daska, District Sialkot 51031, Pakistan Office: Hokkaido U, Applied Physics Divsn, Sapporo Hokkaido 060-8628, Japan

KHAN, KAMRUL ALAM, physicist, educator; b. Dhaka, Bangladesh, Oct. 9, 1965; s. Abul Hossen Khan and Amena Khanam; m. Nayar Sultana, June 6, 1974; children: Farhana Alam, Fazana Alam. BSc with honors in Physics, Dkaha U., 1985, MSc in Physics, 1986, MPhil in Physics, 1990, PhD in Physics, 1999. Lectr. Uttara Anwara Model Degree Coll., Dhaka, 1989-93, Nagarpur Govt. Coll., Tangail, Bangladesh, 1993-94, Dhaka Coll., 1994-98; asst. prof. Gazarza Govt. Coll., Munshigoni, Bangladesh, 1998—. Contbr. articles to profl. jours. ISESCO rsch. grantee, 1998—. Mem. Bangladesh Phys. Soc., UNESCO Club. Avocations: research, gardening, teaching. Home: Vill Habla South Para, Tangail Bangladesh Office: RERC Energy Park, Dhaka 1000, Bangladesh

KHAN, KHALID SAEED, clinical epidemiologist, obstetrician-gynecologist; b. Muzapfargarh, Punjab, Pakistan, Sept. 22, 1965; s. Muhammad Saeed Khan and Zarina (Danish) S.; m. Heinke Kunst, Feb. 28, 1996. MBBS, Aga Khan U., Karachi, Pakistan, 1989; MSc, McMaster U., Hamilton, Canada, 1995; diploma in med. edn., U. Dundee, Scotland, 2000. Resident Aga Khan U. Med. Ctr., Karachi, 1990-94; fellow McMaster U. Internat. Program, Hamilton, 1994-95; registrar Ninewells Hosp. & Med. Sch., Dundee, Scotland, 1995-97; lectr. U. Birmingham, Eng., 1997—. Nishan E. Haider scholar Edn. Ministry, Pakistan, 1983-88, family planning scholar Organon, The Netherlands, 1993, Internat. Develop. scholar Aga Khan Found., Canada, 1994. Fellow Coll. Physicians and Surgeons (Karachi, Pakistan); mem. Royal Coll. of Ob.-Gyn. (U.K.). Avocations: squash, swimming. Home: 39 Queens Dr Finsbury Pk, London N4 2SZ, England Office: Acad Dept Ob-gyn, Birmingham Women's Hosp, Birmingham B15 2TG, United Kingdom

KHAN, MAHBUBAR RAHMAN, microbiologist, educator; b. Shamashpur, Faridpur, Bangladesh, Sept. 1, 1937; s. Majed Ali Khan (dec.) and Musammat Anwara Begum; m. Mufti Nurunnessa Khatun, Jan. 17, 1963 (dec.); children: Nurur Rahman, Motiur Rahman (dec.). BS, Dhaka (Bangladesh) U., 1959, MS, 1961; PhD, Liverpool (Eng.) U., 1972. Fellow dept. botany Dhaka U., 1962-63, lectr., 1963-73, asst. prof., 1973-76, assoc. prof., 1976-85, prof., 1985-93, selection grade prof., 1993—, chmn. dept. microbiology, 1984-86, chmn. dept. botany, 1987-90. Author: Udvid Bigyan Part I, Jib Bigyan Part I. Founding mem. Bangladesh Nat. Rose Soc., 1982. Mem. Bangladesh Soc. Microbiologists (founder, life), Bangladesh Bot. Soc. (life), Soc. for Applied Microbiology Eng. Avocations: education research, gardening, scientific photography. E-mail: Khan mr@bangla.net. and Khan mr@ducc.agni.com. Home: 20/B Fuller Rd, Dhaka 1000, Bangladesh Office: Dept Botany Curzon Hall, Dhaka Univ, Dhaka 1000, Bangladesh

KHAN, MOHAMMAD ASAD, geophysicist, educator, former energy minister and senator of Pakistan; b. Aima, Lahore, Pakistan, Aug. 13, 1940; came to U.S., 1964; s. Ghulam Qadir and Hajira (Karim) K.; m. Tahera Pathan, Jan. 4, 1974; 1 dau., Shehzi Samira. B.S., U. Punjab, Lahore, Pakistan, 1957, M.S., 1963; postgrad., Harvard U., 1964-65; Ph.D. (East West Center scholar), U. Hawaii, 1967. Lectr. in geophysics U. Punjab, 1963-64; asst. prof. geophysics and geodesy U. Hawaii, 1967-71, assoc. prof., 1971-74, prof., 1974-96, prof. emeritus, 1996—; minister of petroleum and natural resources Govt. Pakistan, 1983-86, senator, 1984-86; cabinet mem. Eonc. Coordination Commn. of the Cabinet, Govt. of Pakistan, 1983-86; chmn. internat. advisors, 1987—; chmn. Hydrocarbon Devel. Inst., Pakistan, 1984-86, Attock Oil Refinery, Pakistan, 1984-86; cabinet mem. Nat. Econ. Council, Govt. Pakistan, 1984-86; NSF and NASA fellow Summer Inst. Dynamical Astronomy at MIT, 1968-69; cabinet mem. Econ. Coord. Com. Cabinet Govt. Pakistan, 1983-86; sr. vis. scientist geodynamics Goddard Space Flight Ctr., NASA, Greenbelt, Md., 1972-74; sr. scientist Computer Scis. Corp., Silver Spring, Md., 1974-76, sr. cons., 1976-77; diplomatic minister/adviser Resource Survey and Devel. Pakistan, 1974-76; sr. resident assoc. Nat. Acad. Scis., 1972-74; leader Am. Asian Studies and Contemporary Social Problems Seminar Series, Honolulu, 1968-69. Contbr. articles to profl. publs. Chmn. East and West: A Perspective for the 80's; mem. Hawaii Environ. Council, 1979-83, chmn. exec. com., 1979-83, vice chmn., 1981-83; chmn. Pakistan Relief Fund, Honolulu, 1971. Recipient Gold medal Rawalpindi Union of Journalists, 1985, Pakistan Engring. Coun., 1985, Pakistan Assn. of Minorities, 1984, 85, Disting. Alumnus award for pofl. excellence and leadership U. Hawaii, 1995. Fellow Explorers Club; mem. Geol. Soc. U. Punjab (pres. 1962-63), Am. Geophys. Union, Pakistan Assn. Advancement Sci., Am. Geol. Inst., Am. Geophys. Union, East West Ctr. Alumni Assn. (dir. 1976-80), Internat. Alumni of East West Ctr. (exec. com., chmn. 1977-80, Disting. Alumnus award for Outstanding Career Achievements and Leadership 1984). Achievements include research in geophysics, geodetic and oceanographic applications of satellites, geodynamics, planetary interiors, global tectonics, global correlations, core-mantle boundary problems, equilibrium figures, gravity, isostasy, satellite altimetry, geodesy, earth models, geophysical exploration, ocean dynamics. Office: U Hawaii-Hawaii Inst Geophysics Planetology Post 602 Honolulu HI 96822-2219

KHAN, MOHAMMAD HUSSEIN GAMERYANI, physician, consultant; b. Peshawar, Pakistan, Feb. 2, 1933; arrived in Germany, 1955; s. Mohammad Umar Gameryani and Chuhara Muhmand; m. Helga Schenk, Nov. 11, 1964; children: Mansur Umar, Almas, Mohammad Kareem. MD, U. Heidelberg, Germany, 1962; DSc, U. Hokkaido, Japan, 1969. Cert. hematologist. Pvt. practice Frankfurt, Germany; prof. medicine U. Frankfurt, 1972—. Contbr. articles to profl. jours. Office: Clinic, Gerauer Str 15, 60528 Frankfurt Germany

KHAN, MOHAMMAD KHAIRUL ALAM, science educator; b. Bainchaitala, Jessore, Bangladesh, Sept. 13, 1949; s. M. Moksed Ali and Saleha Begun Khan; m. Nurun Nahar, June 9, 1974; children: Ummul Khair Nazia, Naheemul Alam. BS, Michel Modhusudan Coll., Jessore, 1970; MS in Applied Physics, Rajshahi (Bangladesh) U., 1972, PhD, 1990; MSc in Physics, Regina U., Can., 1982; profl. cert. internat. scis. program, Uppsala (Sweden) U., 1987-88, 89. From lectr. to asst. prof. to assoc. prof. U. Rajshahi, 1974-91, prof., 1991—; house tutor Motihar Hall, U. Rajshahi, 1985-87, chmn. dept. applied physics and electronics, 1992-95, provost Madar Bux Hall, 1997—. Co-author: (book) Solid State Physics, 1995; contbr. rsch. articles to nat. and internat. jours. and confs. Life mem. Rajshahi unit Bangladesh Heart Found., 1989—. Grad. rsch. scholar U. Regina, Can., 1980-83. Fellow N.Y. Acad. Scis.; mem. Bangladesh Phys. Soc. (life), Bangladesh Electronic Soc. (life). Muslim. Avocations: music, sports, documentary films, traveling, driving. Home: W/77/D University Campus, 6205 Rajshahi Bangladesh Office: U Rajshahi, Dept Applied Physics/Elec, 6205 Rajshahi Bangladesh

KHAN, MOHAMMAD MOHABBAT, public administration educator; b. Dhaka, Bangladesh, Jan. 16, 1949; s. Mohammad Azhar and Musammat (Shamsunnessa) K.; m. Rokeya Chowdhury, May 28, 1977; children: Asheq, Imran. MA, U. Dhaka, Bangladesh, 1969; MPA, Syracuse (N.Y.) U., 1974, U. So. Calif., 1976; PhD, U. So. Calif., 1976. Vis. assoc. prof. U. Benin, Nigeria, 1981-82; assoc. prof. U. Dhaka, Bangladesh, 1978-81, 82-83, prof., 1983-89; sr. Fullbrign fellow Cornell U., U. Tex. at Austin, 1989-90; prof. Yarmouk U., Jordan, 1990-91, U. Dhaka, 1991-99; mem. Bangladesh Pub. Svc. Commn., 1999—; project dir., team leader USAID, Bangladesh, 1989; cons. UNDP, Bangladesh, 1991-92, 93, World Bank, Bangladesh, 1994. Author: (books) Bureaucratic Self-Preservation, 1980, Politics of Administrative Reforms, 1991, Administrative Reforms in Bangladesh, 1998; co-author: (book) The Decentralized Planning Process in Bangladesh, 1988, Urban Governance in Bangladesh and Pakistan, 1997; contbr. chpt. to books. Mem. exec. com. Dhaka U. Tchr. Assn., 1983, 88, 92, treas., 1989; mem. Dhaka U. Senate, 1988—; mem. Dhaka City Mayor's Expert Team, 1995. Recipient Grad. scholarship U. Dhaka, 1968-69, Grad. fellowship Asia Found., 1972-76, Teaching assistantship U. So. Calif., 1976. Mem. ASPA, Commonwealth Assn. for Pub. Adminstrn. and Mgmt., Internat. Polit. Sci. Assn. Avocations: jogging, reading books, listening to commentaries of games, watching television, talking to friends. Home: House 09 Apt 201 Rd 03, Dhawarondi Residential Area, Dhaka 1205, Bangladesh Office: U Dhaka, Bangladesh Pub Svc Commn, Tejgaon, Dhaka 1215, Bangladesh

KHAN, MUKHLESUR RAHMAN, agricultural educator, researcher; b. Shibpur, Narsingdi, Bangladesh, Mar. 15, 1969; s. Lutfur Rahman and Amena Akhter (Khaton) K.; m. Salma Binte Shams, Sept. 26, 1995. BS in Fisheries, Bangladesh Agrl. U., 1990, MS, 1995; M in Philosophy, Hiroshima (Japan) U., 1998. Asst. prof. Bangladesh Agrl. U., Mymensingh, 1995—; doctoral fellow Hiroshima (Japan) U., 1998-2001; Contbr. articles to profl. jours. including Jour. Fisheries Sci., Jour. Agrl. Rsch., Bangladesh Jour. Agrl. Sci., Bangladesh Jour. Life Sci., Bangladesh Jour. Bio Sci., Japan Jour. Fish Genetics and Breeding Sci. Mem. social welfare com. Muslim Assn., Hiroshima, 1998. Recipient Nat. Sci. and Tech. award Bangladesh U., 1994, grantee, 1998. Mem. N.Y. Acad. Scis., Libr. Sci. Club. Islam. Avocations: gardening, reading Islamic books, computers, playing football, travel. Home: Vill Ashrafpur (Girza Para), Shibpur Narsingdi 1620, Bangladesh Office: Hiroshima U Lab Aquaculture, Fac Applied Biol Scis, Higashi Hiroshima 739-8528, Japan

KHAN, NIAZ AHMAD, environmental affairs executive, consultant; b. Punjab, Pakistan, Apr. 24, 1954; s. Fazal Ahmad and Alam (Bibi) K.; m. Perveen Akhtar, Nov. 2, 1984; children: Zuhaib N., Haneen N., Samreen N. BS in Chemistry with honors, Punjab U., 1975; BSChemE, U. Engring. and Tech., Lahore, Pakistan, 1980; cert. air pollution, USEPA-Air Pollution Tng. Inst., Research Park Triangle Park, N.C., 1990. Registered environ. profl. U.S. Registry Environ. Profls. Environ. specialist Am. Arabian Techs., Jubail, Saudi Arabia, 1982-87; environ. coord. Al-Jubail Fertilizer Co., Jubail, 1987-89; head environ. affairs Royal Commn. for Jubail and Yanbu, Jubail, 1989—; cons. engr. Amartech, Ltd., Jubail, 1982-87; trainee engr. Ravi Rayon, Ltd., Lahore, 1979, Dawood Hercules Chems., Lahore, 1980; RC rep. IPIECA, Manama, Bahrain, 1990. Sub-editor Auditing bull., 1979-80; contbr. articles to profl. jours. Chief prefect hostel adminstrn. Sci. Coll., Lyallpur, Pakistan, 1975-76, pres. coll. hostel, 1973-74. Ministry of Edn. scholar, 1981. Mem. Am. Inst. Chem. Engrs., Soc. Environ. Engrs. (U.K), Am. Soc. Safety Engrs., Pakistan Engring. Coun. (profl. engr., life mem.), Nat. Geog. Soc., Jubail Environ. Engring. Orgn. Avocations: jogging, swimming, reading, collecting antiques. Office: Royal Commn Jubail & Yanbu, PO Box 10001 HSD, Jubail 31961, Saudi Arabia

KHAN, RAFEEQ ALAM, pharmacology educator; b. Karachi, Pakistan, Sept. 9, 1959; s. Iqbal Alam and Waheeda (Khatoon) K.; m. Hajra Khan, Nov. 22, 1986; children: Umair, Najiya, Sohaib, Muneeb, Sarah. BPharm, U. Karachi, 1983, MPharm, 1986, PhD, 1996; DSc (hon.), Open Internat. U., 1996. Quality control officer Hoechst Pakistan Pvt., Karachi, 1986-88; lectr. dept. pharmacology U. Karachi, 1988-97; lectr. Umm Ul Qura U., Makkah, Saudi Arabia, 1997-98; asst. prof. U. Karachi, 1998—. Contbr. articles to profl. jours. Gold medal U. Karachi, 1986, 97. Mem. Pakistan Pharmacol. Soc. (life), N.Y. Acad. Sci. Avocations: reading Islamic literature. Home: R-275 15 A 5 Buffer Zone, 75850 Karachi Pakistan Office: Univ Karachi, Faculty Pharm Dept Pharm, 75270 Karachi Pakistan

KHAN, RAHMATTULLAH, psychologist, educator; b. Bangkok, Thailand, June 4, 1952; s. Abdul Wahab Khan and Fatimah Bee; m. Yasmin Anum Mohamed Yusof, Aug. 14, 1980; children: Omar, Nuur. AS in Agriculture, Abraham Baldwin Agrl. Coll., 1978; BS, U. Ill., 1982; M in Psychology, Flinders U., 1988; D in Psychology, Murdoch U., 1998. Trainee clin. psychologist U. Sains Malaysia Sch. Psychology, Penang, 1982-85; lectr. in clin. psychology U. Sains Malaysia Sch. Med. Scis., Kota Bharu, 1988-93; asst. prof. dept. psychology Internat. Islamic U., Kuala Lumpur, Malaysia, 1993—, dean student affairs, 1998—; cons. Hosp. U. Sains Malaysia, Kota Bharu, 1990-94. Mem. APA (fgn.), Malaysian Psychol. Assn., Australian Psychol. Soc. Islam. Avocations: stamp collecting, coin collecting, travel. Home: 50 Jalan Cempaka SD 12/4C, 52200 Kuala Lumpur Malaysia Office: Internat Islamic U, Jalan Gombak, 53100 Kuala Lumpur Malaysia

KHAN, SAGHIR AHMED, publishing company executive; b. Karachi, Sind, Pakistan, Oct. 28, 1952; s. Nisar Ahmed and Zahida (Begum) K.; m. Shakila Bano, Sept. 7, 1978; children: Sara, Sameer Ahmed, Salman Ahmed, Shumail Ahmed. BS, D.J. Sind Govt. Sci. Coll., Karachi, 1972; BBA with honors, Inst. Bus. Adminstrn., Karachi, 1975, MBA, 1976; cert. Grad. Sch. Pub. & Internat. Sch., U. Pitts., 1988. Asst. mgr. fin. Pakistan Automobile Corp., Karachi, 1976-79; fin. exec. A.R.E. Galadari & Bros. Liaison Office, Karachi, 1979-82; fin.mgr. Galadari Cement (Gulf) Ltd., Karachi, 1982-89; mgr. planning and devel. Galadari Printing & Pub., Dubai, United Arab Emirates, 1989, mgr. fin. and adminstrn., 1990-94, gen. mgr. fin. and adminstrn., 1994—; trustee, sec. Galadari Cement (Gulf) Ltd., Karachi, 1982-89; founder trustee Khatija Bibi Trust, Karachi, 1985—; sec. Sci. Soc. D.J. Sind Govt. Sci. Coll., Karachi, 1971-72, sec. Bot. Soc., 1972-73. Mem. Inst. Cost and Mgmt. Accts. U.K., Internat. Assn. for Newspaper and Media Tech. (cert. Delhi 1994, cert. Hong Kong 1995), Karachi Gymkhana Club, Mbaians (life). Avocations: swimming, listening to music, reading, indoor sports, chess. Home: Murjanet Al Khaleej #604, PO Box 11243, Dubai United Arab Emirates Office: Galadari Printing & Pub, Sheikh Zayed Rd PO Box 11243, Dubai United Arab Emirates

KHAN, SALAHUDDIN KASEM, industrialist, diplomat; b. Chittagong, Bangladesh, Sept. 12, 1947; s. A.K. and S.N. Khan; m. Farhat Ahmed Khan, Oct. 15, 1981; children: Mustafa, Murteza, Mujtaba. BA, Punjab U., Lahore, Pakistan, 1968; postgrad., London, 1972-75. Mng. dir. A.K. Khan Co. Ltd., 1991—; chmn. Coats (BD) Ltd., Dhaka, 1992-94; bd. dirs. Bengal Fisheries Ltd., Chittagong, Telekom Malaysia Internat. (BD) Ltd.; mem. Nat. Coun. for Indsl. Devel., 1988-90; mem. cons. comms. Ministry of Labor, Textile, Commerce, 1988-90; chmn. adv. coun. UCEP, Chittigong, 1991—; proposed formation of IFTA, Commn. Islamic Common Market, formation of Bay of Bengal Growth Triangle, 1994, formation of SEACO. Contbr. articles to profl. publs. Mem. task force on indsl. policy Ministry of Planning, Govt. of Bangladesh, Dhaka, 1990; chmn. Underprivileged Children's Ednl. Programs, 1992—; mem. bd. govs. Chittagong Eye Infirmary and Tng. Complex, 1999; mem. governing coun. Inst. Cmty. Ophthalmology, 1995-97. Named Hon. Consul-Gen. Republic of Turkey, Bangladesh, Chittagong, 1984. Mem. Bangladesh Employers Assn. (mem. exec. com. 1989—), Bangladesh Assn. for the Blind, Textile Coun. Islamic Countries (chmn. 1993-95), Bangladesh Textile Mills Assn. (chmn. 1988-90), Chittagong C. of C. (mem. exec. com. 1984-88). Islam. Avocations: reading, writing, classical music. Home: Shama Batali Hills, Chittagong Bangladesh Office: AK Khan Group, Batali Hills, Chittagong Bangladesh

KHAN, SHAH WAZIR, water and power development authority professional; b. Swat, Pakistan, July 9, 1949; s. Faridoon and Shahimran Khan; m. Bibi Sadia; children: Abdul Qadir, Bibi Zainab, Zubeda Bibi, Rabia Bibi, Abdul Raziq. BSEE, U. Peshawar, Pakistan, 1973; postgrad., CUNY. Operational elec. engr. Water and Power Devel. Authority, Pakistan, 1977—. Mem. IEEE, I.E. (assoc. mem.). Islam. Home: Lalazar St, Arbab Rd Tehkal Bala, Peshawar Pakistan Office: Office of RDIC AEB WAPDA, House Shami Rd, Peshawar Pakistan

KHAN, SHAHANA SALEEM, psychologist; b. Lahore, Punjab, Pakistan, June 15, 1966; d. Saleem and Iqbal Khan; m. Zahid Haleem; children: Sidra Haleem, Momina Haleem, Sulqarnain Zahid. BA, Lahore Coll. for Women, 1986; MSc, Punjab U., Lahore, 1998, advanced diploma in clin. psychology, 1991. Supr. Punjab U., 1992. Mem. Pakistan Assn. Clin. Psychologists, Pakistan Psychol. Assn. Home: 52-A Block M, Model Town Extension, Lahore Pakistan

KHANANI, NAEEM ILYAS, engineering executive; b. Karachi, Sindh, Pakistan, Nov. 25, 1970; s. Ilyas Aba Hussain Khanani and Ameena Suleman Rathore; m. Fazila Naeem Koylanawala, Aug. 10, 1997. BEE, Nadir Shah Eduljee Dinshaw U. Engring., Karachi, 1992; MA in Econs., U. Karachi, 1995; LLB, Sindh Muslim Law Coll., Karachi, 1995; MBA, Newport U., Karachi, 1996. Trainee engr. Tajik Elec. Engring. Plant, Hujand, Tajikistan, 1993; project engr. Fahim, Nanji & Desouza Consulting Engrs., Karachi, 1993-96; prin. engr. Chartered Consulting Engrs., Karachi, 1996—; joint sec. Memon Profl. Forum, 1996—. Author: Memon Vision-2005 Restructuring & Reengineering of Priorities in the Next Millenium, 1998. Mng. trustee Memon Profl. Forum Ednl. Trust, Karachi, 1998—. Mem. IEEE, Inst. Engrs. (asst.), Pakistan Engring. Coun., Mktg. Assn. Pakistan, Mgmt. Assn. Pakistan, Mktg. Rsch. Soc. Pakistan, Shehri, Amnesty Internat. Avocations: reading, writing, sightseeing. E-mail: n khanani@yahoo.com. Home: Sharfabad, 305 Classic Heights 67/3, Karachi Sindh, Pakistan

KHANDELWAL, CHIRANJIVA, gastroenterologist; b. Rajnagar, India, Oct. 8, 1952; s. Sitaram and Manbhari K.; m. Poonam Jalan, May 19, 1977; children: Manish, Piyush. BSc, Patna U., 1971, MBBS, 1977. Sr. rsch. fellow ICMR, India, 1979-82; pool officer CSIR, India, 1989-92; prof. gastrointestinal surgery, head of dept. Indira Ghandi Inst. Med. Scis., Patna, India, 1995—; cons. Indian Cancer Soc., Bihar, 1987. Fellow Cleve. Clinic. Fellow Internat. Coll. Surgeons, Internat. Union Against Cancer; mem. Indian Acd. Med. Specialists, Indian Soc. Gastroenterology. Home: 6 Nehru Nagar, 800013 Patna Bihar, India

KHANJANASTHITI, PRIYA, physician; b. Bangkok, May 31, 1930; d. Luang Prakoonvichasnong. MD, Mahidol U., Bangkok, 1956; cert. in radiology, U. Pa., 1960; cert. in neurology, U. Oslo, 1972; cert. neuroradiology, U. Calif., San Francisco, 1985. Straight intern medicine Siriraj Hosp., Bangkok, 1956-57, resident in radiology, 1957-58; grad. student in radiology U. Pa., Phila., 1959-60; resident in radiology, 1960-64; asst. prof. radiology Siriraj Hosp., 1973-75, assoc. prof. radiology, 1976-80, prof. radiology, 1980—, chmn. dept. radiology, 1987-90; cons. in radiology Mahidol U. Siriraj Hosp., Bangkok, 1990—. Recipient fellowship NORADS, 1971-72, Takeda Scis. Found., 1979, Utretch U., 1980. Fellow AAUW; mem. Radiological Soc. Thailand (mem. com. 1980-91, vice chmn. 1987-91), Med. Assn. Thailand, Women Med. Assn. Thailand, Neurological Soc. Thailand, Royal Coll. Radiologists Thailand. Buddhist. Avocations: reading, swimming, photographing. Home: 15 Issaraparp Rd Soi 17/1, 10600 Bangkok Thailand Office: Mahidol U Faculty Medicine, Dept Radiology, 10700 Bangkok Thailand

KHANNA, AJAY KUMAR, surgeon, educator; b. Dibai, India, Oct. 14, 1954; s. Bijay Narain and Radha Devi (Tandon) K.; m. Anuradha Singh, May 26, 1979; children: Divya, Soumya. MB, BChir, Banaras Hindu U., Varanasi, India, 1975, MS in Surgery, 1980; Cert. in Surgery, Nat. Acad. Med. Scis., Delhi, 1982. Lectr. in surgery Banaras Hindu U., Varanasi, 1981-85, sr. lectr., 1986-92, reader in surgery, 1993—; cons. surgeon Sir Sunderlal Hosp., Varanasi, 1981; hon. sec. Indian Med. Assn., Banaras Hindu U., Varanasi, 1989-90; organizing sec. Uttar Pradesh chpt. Indian Soc. Gastroenterology, Varanasi, 1992; sci. sec. Indian Med. Assn., Varanasi, 1995-96; organizing sec. Internat. Workshop on Hernia, Varanasi, 1996. Author: Current Trends in Surgery, 1991, Immunology Update, 1992; contbr. articles to profl. jours. Fellow Internat. Coll. Surgeons; mem. Nat. Acad. Med. Scis., N.Y. Acad. Scis. Hindu. Avocations: reading, watching tv, international travel. Fax: (0542) 367568. Home: N8-180/AK-1 Rajendra Vihar, Newada Sunderpur DLW-BHU Rd, Varanasi 221005, India Office: Dept Surgery Inst Med Scis, Banaras Hindu Univ, Varanasi 221005, India

KHANNA, RAJENDRA PALL, marine services company executive; b. New Delhi, India, Sept. 18, 1926; s. Ram and Kartar (Devi) K.; m. Nirmal Chopra. BSc, IMMTS Dufferin, Bombay, 1944. Commodore Indian Navy, 1946-86; mng. dir. Techno Marine Svcs., New Delhi, 1986—. Avocations: golf, bridge, writing, reading. Home: A/15-33 Vasant Vihar, New Delhi 110057, India

KHANNA, RAMESH KUMAR, hotel executive; b. Lahore, Pakistan, Nov. 30, 1938; s. Mahadev Prasad and Shashi Prabha (Mehra) K.; m. Andree Prade, July 30, 1964; children: Ramesh Kumar Jr., Manish P. BA in Econs., St. Stephens Coll., New Delhi, 1959; BS in Hotel Mgmt., Cornell U., Ithaca, N.Y., 1962. Mgmt. trainee Queen Elizabeth Hotel, Montreal, Que., Can., 1960, Internat. Conv. Hotel, Dutch Antilles, 1961; f & b mgr. Caribe Hilton Hotel, P.R., 1964-65, Tunis Hilton, Tunisia, 1965-66; owner Maharani Restaurant, Montreal, Que., Can., 1968; gen. mgr. Claridges Hotel, New Delhi, 1969-71; owner Expo '70 Maharani Restaurant, Osaka, Japan, 1970; mng. dir. Eastern Internat. Hotels Ltd., Bombay, 1971-91, exec. dir., 1991—. Recipient medal of honor Pres. Finland Tunisia, 1965. Mem. Delhi Golfer, Bombay Presidency Golf Club. Avocations: gardening, orchid growing, reading, golf. Home: 3 Rvia Park, Juhu, Mumbai 400049, India Office: Holidy Inn, Balraj Sahani Marg, Mumbai 4000 049, India

KHANNA, SUDHI RANJAN, business director; b. Calcutta, W. Bengal, India, Dec. 28, 1976; s. Chitta Ranjan and Suvra Mehra. BComm (hons.), Bhawanipore Edn., India, 1998. Dir. Artistique Internat Ltd., India, 1996—; chmn. Status Welfare and Cultural Soc., 1994-97. Social organiser of com. Status Welfare and Cultural Soc., Calcutta, 1994-97.

KHANNA, YASH KUMAR, family practice physician, pediatrician; b. Lahore, India, Dec. 28, 1941; came to U.S., 1970; s. Sohan Lal and Savitri (Mehra) K.; m. Christine Anne Warren, Sept. 22, 1972; children: Rajan Yash, Nisha, Dev Yash. MBBS, King George Michael Coll., Lucknow, India, 1964. Diplomate Am. Bd. Pediat., Am. Bd. Forensic Examiners, Child Health Royal Coll. Physicians and Surgeons, London. Sr. house officer Monsall Hosp., Bouth Hall Children's Hosp., Manchester, Eng., 1966-68, Joyce Green Hosp., Dastford, Eng., 1969-70; house officer, emergency physician St. Mary's Hosp., Orange, N.J., 1971-87, resident in pediat., 1971-73; pvt. practice physician Orange, N.J., 1973—; med. dir. Quick Med.-West Essex Med. Group, West Caldwell, N.J., 1983—; asst. surgeon Ctrl. Health Svcs., New Delhi, 1965-66; house physician and surgeon Irwin Hosp., New Delhi, 1964-65; mem. med. staff Hosp. Ctrs. at Orange, N.J., 1973—, pres. med. staff, 1986-87, pres.-elect med. staff, 1997—. Mem. adv. com. to the handicapped Twp. of Livingston, N.J.; trustee Hosp. Ctr. at Orange, 1986-96. Recipient Med. Outreach award Grace Reformed Bapt. Ch., Newark, 1997. Mem. AMA, Am. Assn. Physicians from India, N.J. Med. Soc., Essex County Med. Soc., Orange Mountain Med. Soc., Asian Music Acad. (founder, pres. 1999—). Democrat. Hindu. Avocations: music, antiques. Home: 112 Shrewsbury Dr Livingston NJ 07039-3404 Office: Family Medicine/Pediat 280 Henry St Orange NJ 07050-3422 also: Quick Med-West Essex Med Group 607 Bloomfield Ave West Caldwell NJ 07006-7504

KHANUJA, SUMAN PREET SINGH, molecular biologist and biotechnologist; b. New Delhi, India, Aug. 13, 1958; s. Narinder and Pritpal (Kaur) Singh; m. Archana Suman, Dec. 9, 1986; children: Joyce, Grace. BSc in Agr. with honors, GP Pant U. Agr. and Tech., Pant Nagar, India, 1980, MSc in Plant Breeding, 1982; PhD in Genetics, Indian Agrl. Rsch. Inst., New Delhi, 1986. Scientist NYRI, New Delhi, 1986-91; sr. scientist IARI, New Delhi, 1991-96; prin. scientist, head divsn. Ctrl. Inst. Medicinal and Aromatic Plants, Lucknow, India, 1996—, dep. quality mgr., 1998—; workshop coord. Recipient awards in field. Avocation: reading. E-mail: root@cimap.sirnetd.ernet.in. Office: CIMAP, PO CIMAP, Lucknow UP India 226 015

KHANUM, FARHATH, biochemist, researcher; b. Tiptur, India, Nov. 29, 1959; d. Sattar and Amtuz (Zaher) Khan; m. Riaz Ahmed, Jan. 7, 1990; children: Faraaz Ahmed Riaz, Faiza Riaz. MSc, Kasturba Med. Coll., Manipal, India, 1983; PhD, Nat. Inst. Mental Health, Bangalore, India, 1995. Rsch. scholar Nat. Inst. Mental Health and Neuroscis., Bangalore, India, 1984-88; scientist Inst. Nuclear Medicine and Allied Scis., Delhi, India, 1988-91, Def. Food Rsch. Lab., Mysore, India, 1991—. Govt. of Karnataka scholar, 1975-79; Nat. Merit scholar, 1981-83. Mem. Assn. Food Sci. and Tech. (India), Indian Photobiology Soc. (life), indian Soc. for Radiation Biology (life), Soc. Biol. Chemistry. Home: DNO 114, 570 019 Mysore Karnataka, India Office: Def Food Rsch Lab, Siddartha Nagar, 570 011 Mysore Karnataka, India

KHANZHINA, HELEN P., English educator, translator; b. Perm, Russia, Aug. 28, 1954; came to U.S., 1995; d. Pavel L. and Dina B. Wexler; m. Yevgenii A. Khanzhin, Dec. 4, 1975 (div. Jan. 1984); 1 child, Dmitri. MA in English Lit., U. Perm, 1976; PhD in World Lit., U. St. Petersburg, 1985; assoc. prof. diploma, USSR State Com. Nat. Edn., Moscow, 1991. Asst. prof. dept. world lit. U. Perm, 1976-95; lectr. dept. English div. then assoc. prof. dept. world lit. U. Va., Charlottesville, 1996-98; interpreter Lang. Learning continuing edn. U. Va., Charlottesville, 1996-98; interpreter Lang. Learning Enterprises, Washington, 1996—; libr. joint state govt. commn. gen. assembly Commonwealth Pa., Harrisburg, 1998—; lectr. divsn. Comm. and Arts, Harrisburg Cmty. Coll., 1998—, lectr. Sch. of Humanities Pa. State U., Harrisburg, Pa., 1999—. Author: The Making of the National Tradition in American Romantic Poetry and William Cullen Bryant's Creative Work, 1987, Genre, Mode and Style in American Romantic Poetry, 1998; editor: Problems of Method and Poetics in World Literature of the Nineteenth and Twentieth Centuries, 1995, 97; contbr. articles to profl. jours. Vis. scholar grantee USIA, 1993-94, Brit. Coun. Beatrice Ward Found., 1990. Mem. MLA, Am. Assn. Tchrs. Slavic and E. European Langs., Pa. Libr. Assn., Spl. Librs. Assn. Avocations: classical music, ballet, painting, sculpture. E-mail: ykhanzhina@legis.state.pa.us. Office: Joint State Govt Commn 108 Fin Bldg Harrisburg PA 17120

KHARADIA, VIRABHAI CHELABHAI, economist, educator, researcher; b. Laxmipura, Gujarat, India, Jan. 21, 1939; came to U.S., 1969; s. Chelabhai Manabhai and Joitiben Chelabhai K.; m. Kokila Virabhai, Apr. 26, 1961; children: Shanta, Geeta, Bharat. B in Commerce, Maharaja Sayajirao U. Baroda, Gujarat, 1964, M in Commerce, 1966; MS, U. Ill., 1971, PhD in Econ. and Fin., 1973. Lectr. banking and fin. Maharaja Sayajirao U. of Baroda, Gujarat, 1966-69; from asst. to assoc. prof. N.W. Mo. State U., Maryville, 1973-77, prof., 1977—, chmn. dept. econ., 1979-93; vis. prof. Internat. U. Bus. and Econ., Beijing, 1985. Contbr. articles to profl. jours. Recipient Acctg. prize H.L. Coll. of Commerce, 1960; fellow U. Ill., 1969-70, 71, 72-73. Avocations: racquetball, biking, jogging, gardening, traveling. E-mail: vkharad@mail.nwmissouri.edu. Office: NW Mo State U Dept Econ Maryville MO 64468

KHARAKOZ, DMITRI PETROVICH, biophysicist; b. Frunze, USSR, July 7, 1949; s. Petr Ivanovich and Olga Mikhailovna (Badikova) K.; m. Elena Gurtovaia, 1973 (div. 1980); 1 child, Alexei; m. Lyuba Arutiunova, Nov. 30, 1985; 1 child, Zoia. M degree, Moscow State U., 1973; PhD, Russian Acad. Scis., 1984, DSc, 1995. Probationer, rschr. Inst. Theoretical and Exptl. Biophysics Russian Acad. Scis., Pushchino, 1973-75, jr. scientist, 1975-85, rsch. scientist, 1985-91, sr. scientist, 1991—. Contbr. articles to profl. jours. including Jour. Physical Chemistry, Jour. Acoustical Soc. Am., Biochemistry, among others. Grantee Internat. Sci. Found., 1994-95, Russian Found. for Basic Rsch., 1995-97, 98-2000; recipient Fellowship award Pres. of R.F., 1997-2000. Mem. Russian Biochem. Soc. Avocation: music. Office: Inst Theoret & Exptl Biophy, Russian Acad Scis, 142290 Moscow Russia

KHARAZIPOUR, ALIREZA, biotechnologist; b. Tabriz, Iran, Feb. 6, 1947; s. Sadeg Kharazipour and Raffaela Mortazawi; m. Karin Warnecke, Apr. 5, 1983; children: Darius, Daniel. MS, U. Göttingen, Germany, 1980, PhD, 1983, DSc, 1995. Scientist U. Göttingen, 1981-85, head divsn. biotech. Inst. Forest Botanics, 1988-92; indsl. rschr. Pfleiderer AG, Neumarktlopfz, Germany, 1985-88, head divsn. biotech., 1992—. Contbr. articles to profl. jours.; patentee in field. Mem. Mycological Assn. Germany. Office: U Göttingen, Büsgenweg 2, 37077 Göttingen Germany

KHARB, SIMMI, physician, consultant; b. Jhajjar, Haryana, India, June 12, 1966; d. Chander Bhan and Kalawati (Kadian) K. BSc, DAV Coll., Ambala, India, 1985; MBBS, Govt. Med. Coll., Rohtak, India, 1989, MBBS, MD in Biochemistry, 1995. Sr. resident PT. B.D.S. PGIMS, Rohtak, 1994-99, lectr., 1999—. Fellow N.Y. Acad. Scis.; mem. Soc. Exptl. Medicine & Biology. Avocations: music, painting. Home: HNO: 1447, Sector 1, Rohtak 124001, India

KHARCHENKO, VALENTINA GRIGORIEVNA, chemist; b. Kalininsk, Russia, Sept. 27, 1920; d. Grigory Safonovich and Anna Petrovna (Podgainova) K.; m. Ivan Andreevich, Aug. 8, 1939 (dec. 1944); 1 child, Boris. MS, Saratov State U., 1946, PhD, 1955, DSc, 1969. Asst. Saratov (Russia) Poly. U. Dept. Organic Chemistry, 1946-59, reader, 1959-71, prof., 1971, dept. head, 1971-92, prof., 1992—. Author: Thiopyrans, Thiopyrylium Salts and Related Compounds, 1986; contbr. articles to profl. jours.; patentee in field. Mem. Russian Chem. Soc. Avocation: art. Office: Saratov State U, Astrakhanskaya St 83, 410026 Saratov Russia

KHARCHENKO, VIKTOR NIKOLAI, physicist, educator; b. Chaldovar, Kirgizia, Oct. 18, 1936; s. Nikolai Alexander and Anna Ilyiya (Budyanskaya) K.; m. Tatiana Alexey Lensina; children: Elena, Galina, Nikolai. Degree, Moscow Forestry Inst., 1959, PhD, 1963, PhD in Mech. Engring., 1963; DSc, Acad. Scis. USSR, Novosibirsk, Siberia, 1975. Researcher Ctrl. Aeorhydrodynamical Inst., Zukovski, USSR, 1964-77; head of phys. dept. Moscow State Forestry U., 1977—. Contbr. articles on thermophysics, physics of plasma, lasers to sci. and profl. jours. Mem. Russian Acad. Natural Scis., Internat. Higher Edn. Acad. Scis., Acad. Mil. Scis., Acad. Energoinformation Scis. Office: Moscow State Forestry U, Mytischi-5, 141005 Moscow Russia

KHARCHILAVA, AVTANDYL IRODION, physicist, researcher; b. Tsalejikha, USSR, Mar. 21, 1955; s. Irodion Anton Kharchilava and Guli Philippe Gvadzabia; m. Ia Tamaz Iashvili, Jan. 14, 1995. Diploma in physics, Moscow State U., 1978, MS, 1978; PhD, Tbilisi State U., USSR, 1990. Rsch. assoc. Inst. Physics Acad. Scis., Tbilisi, 1978-90, sr. rsch. assoc. Inst. Physics, 1990—; vis. scientist Inst. High Energy Physics, Serpukhov, USSR, 1978-84, Joint Inst. Nuc. Rsch., Dubna, USSR, 1980-90, Deutsche Electronen Synchrotron, Hamburg, Germany, 1994-95, 97-98, Ctr. Nuc. Rsch., Strasbourg, France, 1995-97; cons. Inst. Nuc. Rsch., Sofia, Bulgaria, 1990—; High Energy Physics Inst., Vienna, Austria, 1993; invited rschr. European Lab. Nuc. Rsch., Geneva, 1992-94, 97-99; exch. visitor Fermi Lab. U. Notre Dame, Batvia, Ill., 2000—. Contbr. articles to profl. jours. Cofounder Coll. Natural Scis. Inst. Physics, Tbilisi, 1992—. Named Laureat in Sci. Ministry Sci., 1983; grantee Internat. Sci. Found., 1994. Mem. Georgia Phys. Soc. (sect. leader 1993—). Avocations: chess, music, literature, soccer. Office: U Notre Dame Fermilab, MS352 PO Box 500 Batavia IL 60510-0500

KHARE, MUKESH KUMAR, environmental engineer, educator; b. Varanasi, India, Jan. 1, 1956; s. Amar Nath and Chandra Khare; m. Lekha Khare, Feb. 12, 1992; 2 children. B Engring., U. Roorkee, India, 1977, M Engring., 1979; PhD, U. Newcastle Upon Tyne, Eng., 1989. Asst. engr. Irrigation Dept., Lucknow, India, 1979-81; asst. environ. engr. Pollution Control Bd., Lucknow, 1981-84; rsch. fellow U. Newcastle Upon Tyne, Eng., 1984-89; fellow CSIR Nat. Environ. Engring. Rsch. Inst., Nagpur, India, 1989-90; asst. prof., then assoc. prof. Indian Inst. Tech., Delhi, 1990-97, 99—; lectr. II U. Tech., Lae, Papue New Guinea, 1996-97; cons. Nat. Smokeless Fuels Ltd., Newcastle, 1987-89, Assocs. in Rural Devel., Vt., 1990—; prin. reviewer Found. Rsch. Devel., Pretoria, South Africa, 1995—; prin. cons. Ednl. Cons. (India) Ltd., New Delhi, 1993—; cons. Nuclear Power Corp., Narora, India, 1992—; prin. coord. Internat. Tng. on Pollution Control for South Asean Nations, New Delhi, 1992; author water monitoring program Indian Inst. Tech. Delhi, 1993—. Vol. V.S.O. U.K., Newcastle upon Tyne, 1985-89, Nat. Svc. Scheme, Roorkee, India, 1973-77. Recipient univ. grant fellowship Univ. Grant Commn., New Delhi, 1977-79, nat. scholarship Ministry Edn., Govt. of India, Delhi, 1984-89, overseas rsch. student award Com. Prins. and Vice-Chancellor, Eng., 1987-89; Nat. Merit scholar, 1973-77. Fellow Indian Water Works Assn. (life); mem. Indian Assn. Environ. Mgmt. (life), Indian Soc. Wind Engrs. (life), Indian Soc. Environ. Mgmt. (life), Indian Assn. Air Pollution Control (life). Mem. Baba Muktanand Ashram. Avocations: singing (Indian, Western, pop), wildlife, bird watching, reading general periodicals, watching and playing cricket, table tennis. Office: Indian Inst Tech, Civil Engr Dept Hauz Khas, New Delhi 110016, India

KHARIN, VLADIMIR MICHAYLOVICH, engineering educator; b. Voronezh, Russia, Sept. 11, 1940; s. Michail Eleazarovich and Evgenya Ivanovna Kharin; m. Margarita Fedorovna Parinova, July 4, 1969; 1 child, Michail. Degree in Mech. Engring., Voronezh Technol. Inst., 1962. Prof. Voronezh Technol. Acad., 1982—. Contbr. articles to profl. jours. Fellow Internat. Acad. Refrigeration. E-mail: mmtc@vgta.comch.ru. Home: Morozov Str 10-42, 394043 Voronezh Russia Office: Voronezh State Technol Acad, pr Revolutsii 19, 394017 Voronezh Russia

KHARISSOV, BORIS ILDUSOVICH, inorganic chemist, educator, researcher; b. Uglegorsk, Sakhalin, USSR, Jan. 19, 1964; arrived in Mexico, 1994; s. Ildus Khabitovich Kharissov and Galina Arsenievna Chekalova; m. Oxana Vasilievna Khablenko, Feb. 1, 1991; children: Alena, Sofia. MSc, Moscow State U., 1986, PhD, 1993. Engr. Inst. Chem. Tech., Moscow, 1986-89; rschr. Moscow State U., 1989-94; prof., rschr. U. Autónoma de Nuevo Leon, Monterrey, Mexico, 1994—. Co-author: Direct Synthesis of Coordination Compounds, 1997; co-editor: Direct Synthesis of Coordination and Organometallic Compounds, 1999; co-author, co-editor: Synthetic Coordination & Organometallic Chemistry; contbr. articles to profl. jours.; patentee in field. Subdir. Assn. Chernobyl Participants, Moscow, 1990-99; co-chmn. VII Iberoamerican Congress on Inorganic Chemistry, 1999. Grantee Soros Found., 1993; named Nat. Rschr. of Mex., 1999—. Mem. Mexican Chem. Soc., Mexican Acad. Inorganic Chemistry. Office: U Autonoma Nuevo Leon, San Nicolas de los Garza, NL 66450 Monterrey Mexico

KHARJRULLIN, RADIK MAGSINUR, physician, researcher; b. Ufa, USSR, Aug. 2, 1958; s. Magsinur Nurligajan and Shakira Wildan (Mohammetjan) K.; m. Gulnara Magan Ahmed, Apr. 26, 1986; children: Farhad, Kamilla. Diploma, Bashkir State Med. U., Ufa, 1981; MD, PhD, Acad. Med. Scis., 1986. Asst. prof. dept. human histology & embryology Bashkir State Med. U., Ufa, 1986-91; asst. prof. dept. common biology & histology Lomonosov M. V. Moscow State U., 1991-92; head dept. human anatomy Ulyanovsk State U., 1993—. Contbr. articles to profl. jours. Mem. All Russian Sci. Soc. Anatomists, Histologists and Embryologists (bd. dirs. 1998—). Avocations: photography, gardening, classical music, philosophy, journalism. Home: Sozidatelej Ave, 2, Apt 31, 432072 Ulyanovsk Russia Office: Ulyanovsk State U, Leo Tolstoj St 42, 432700 Ulyanovsk Russia

KHARLAMOV, ALEXANDER ALEXANDROVITCH, physics educator; b. Moscow, June 13, 1953; s. Alexander Alexandrovitch and Eugenia Petrovna (L'vova) K.; m. Vera Ivanovna Barteneva, Sept. 7, 1979; children: Daria, Alexander. MS in Physics, Moscow State U., 1976; PhD, Inst. Solid State Physics, 1982. Rschr. Inst. Solid State Physics, 1976-83; sr. rsch. scientist Inst. Chem. Physics, Moscow, 1983—; prof. physics U. Aveiro, Portugal, 1995—; cons. in field. Contbr. articles to profl. jours. Mem. Russian Biomech. Soc. Avocations: travel, target shooting. Home: Rua da Saudade 106, Gafanha da Encarnaçao, 3830 Ilhavo Portugal

KHARRAZI, KAMAL A., diplomat; b. Tehran, Iran, Dec. 1, 1944; s. Mehdi and Kobra K.; m. Mansoureh, July, 1973; children: Mehdi, Ali. BA, U. Tehran, 1969, MEd, 1972; EdD, U. Houston, 1976. Dep. mgr. Nat. Radio and TV, Tehran, 1979; dep. fgn. min. Ministry of Fgn. Affairs, Tehran, 1979-80; mng. dir. Ctr. Intellectual Devel. Children and Young Adults, Tehran, 1979-81; prof. U. Tehran, 1980-89; head War Info. Hdqs. Supreme Defence Coun., Tehran, 1980-88; mng. dir. Islamic Republic News Agy., Tehran, 1980-89; permanent rep. to UN Govt. of Islamic Republic of Iran, N.Y.C., 1989-97; fgn. min. Govt. of Islamic Republic of Iran, Tehran, 1997—. Office: Office Min Fgn Affairs, Imam Khomeini Ave, Tehran Iran*

KHASAINOV, BORIS ABIDULOVICH, physics researcher; b. Moscow, Apr. 10, 1948; s. Abidulla Arifzhanovich and Zeitunia Nezametdinovna (Sadretdinova) K.; m. Marina Sergeevna Baskakova, June 28, 1969; 1 child, Alexey. Diploma in physics of fast processes, Moscow Phys.-Tech. Inst.,

1972; PhD in Physics and Math., Semenov Inst. Chem. Physics, Moscow, 1981. Jr. scientific rschr. Semenov Inst. Chem. Physics, Russian Acad. Scis., 1972-83, sr. scientific rschr., 1983—; expert All-Union Inst. Scientific and Tech. Info., Moscow, 1980-88; scientific editor Chem. Physics Reports, Moscow, 1987-94; invited vis. prof., ENSMA, 1995-99. Contbr. articles to profl. jours. and internat. conf. procs.' Grantee Russian Found. Basic Rschs., 1996-98. Avocations: fishing, chess, gardening. Fax: (7-095) 9382156. E-mail: khasainov@usa.net, khasain@center.chph.ras.ru. Home: 12-125 Kravchenko St, 117331 Moscow Russia Office: Semenov Inst Chem Phys, 4 Kossyguine St, 117977 Moscow Russia

KHASGIWALE, UPENDRA VIJAYSINH, manufacturing and transportation executive; b. Rajkot, Gujrat, India, June 2, 1928; s. Vijaysinh Vithalrao and Indumati Gupte; m. Malati Ishwerprasad Pathak, Nov. 2, 1953; 1 child, Aparna Upendra. Degrees in engring., mech. engring., St. Xaviers U., Bombay, 1950. Owner Rajkamal Transp. Co., Bombay and Ahmedabad, India, 1947—; mng. dir. Unimac Corp., Ahmedabad, 1975—; owner Vijayager Properties, Western India, 1947—. With RAF, 1943-45. Award recipient Pres. of India, New Delhi, 1998. Avocations: travel, fishing, aviation, stamp and coin collecting. Home: Udhyan, Satellite Rd, Ambavadi, Gujrat Ahmedabad 380 015, India

KHASNABISH, BHUMIP, telecommunications engineering executive, information scientist, educator. MS in Engring., Bangladesh U. Engring. Tech., 1984; MA in Sci., U. Waterloo, Can., 1986; PhD, U. Windsor, Can., 1992. Lectr. elec. and electronic engring. dept. Bangladesh U. Engring. and Tech., Dhaka, 1982-84; rsch. and tchg. asst. U. Waterloo, Ont., Can., 1984-86, McMaster U., Ont., 1986-89, U. Windsor, Ont., 1989-92; mem. sci. staff NorTel Tech., 1992-95; prin. mem. tech. staff Verizon Labs., 1995—, sr. prin. mem. tech. staff. Mem. bd. editors Jour. Network and Sys. Mgmt., 1999—. Mem. IEEE (sr.), Assn. Computing Machinery. E-mail: bhumip@acm.org. Office: Verizon Labs Waltham MA 02451

KHATAMEE, MASOOD AHMAD, obstetrician, gynecologist; b. Mashhad, Iran, Feb. 12, 1936; s. Ahmad and Cobra (Tadbir Kashani) K.; married, Mar. 11, 1966; children: Pira, Neda, Yalda. MD, Shiraz U., Iran, 1961. Diplomate Am. Bd. Ob-Gyn. Intern Nemazee Hosp., 1960-61; resident in ob-gyn. Bellevue Hosp. Ctr., N.Y.C., 1962-66, fellow in infertility, 1966-67; exec. dir. Fertility Rsch. Found., N.Y.C.; mem. staff Lenox Hill Hosp., N.Y.C., Beth Israel-North Divsn., N.Y.C., NYU Med. Ctr., N.Y.C.; clin. prof. NYU Sch. Medicine; pres. Iranian Am. Med. Assn., 1998-2000; founder Soc. Prevention Human Infertility; founder, pres. Shiraz U. Sch. Medicine Alumni Assn. USA, Inc., 1988-89. Pres. Iranian Am. Rep. Party, N.Y.c., 1994—. Fellow ACOG; mem. Am. Fertility Soc., Fertility Rsch. Found. E-mail: frfbaby@msn.com. Home: 23 Church St Alpine NJ 07620 Office: Fertility Rsch Found 877 Park Ave New York NY 10021-0341

KHATAMI-ARDAKANI, HOJJAT OL-ESLAM ALI MOHAMMAD, president of Iran; b. Ardakan, Yazd, Iran, Sept. 29, 1943; s. Saied Rohollah Khatamee; married; 2 children. BA in Philosophy, Coll. Lit. and Human Scis., Esfahan, Iran. Tchr., then prof. Theol. Ctr., Qum, Iran; dir. Hamburg Islamic Ctr., 1978-80; mem. parliament Islamic Consultative Assembly Iran, Tehran, 1980-81; minister Ministry Culture and Islamic Guidance, Tehran, 1982-92; elected pres. of Iran, 1997—; supr. Keyhan Inst., Tehran, 1980—. Contbr. articles to profl. jours. Served with Iranian Army, 1968-70. Avocations: studying and research, ping-pong. Office: Office of Pres, Palestine Crossrd/Pastor Av, Tehran Iran*

KHATIB, RUSTOM ATFAT, endocrinologist, researcher, consultant; b. Beirut, Lebanon, Sept. 3, 1962; s. Atfat Rustom and Samia Ibrahim (Jannoun) K.; m. Mona Adnan Tabbara, Feb. 11, 1993; children: Samia Karla, Ryan Atfat. BS with honors, Am. U. Beirut, 1984, MD, 1988. Resident in ob-gyn. Am. U. Beirut, 1992-94; fellow in reproductive endocrinology Mich. State U., Saginaw, 1994, clin. instr., 1992-94; clin. cons. Rizk Hosp., Beirut, 1994—; clin. cons. European Heart Ctr., Saida, 1994-96; chmn. ob-gyn. United Med. Group, Beirut, 1996—; sci. cons. Beirut Fertility Ctr., 1994—; dir. fertility unit European Heart Ctr., Saida, 1994-96, United Med. Group, Beirut, 1997; dir. fertility svc. Jubeily Hosp., Saida, 1996-99. Contbr. articles to profl. jours. including Gynecologic Oncology, Fertility and Sterility, European Jour. Obstets., Clin. Consultation in Ob-Gyn. Advisor Lebanese Environmentalist Group, Beirut, 1996. Recipient Physician's Recognition award AMA, 1994, Ob-Gyn. Rsch. award Saginaw Coop. Hosps., 1994. Mem. Am. Soc. for Reproductive Medicine, N.Y. Acad. Scis., European Soc. for Human Reproduction and Embryology, Am. Soc. for Reproductive Medicine, Greenpeace. Office: United Med Group, Abdul Aziz St Al Mabani Ctr, 14-5354 Beirut Lebanon

KHATIM MOHD, SALAH SIR, hematologist; b. Shendi, Sudan, Jan. 1, 1949; s. Sir Khatim and Saraiti Hassan (Saraiti) M.; m. Shadia Mohammed Ali; children: Waleed, Walla, Waeel, Waad. MBBS, Khartoum U., Sudan, 1974; diploma clin. pathology, London U., U.K., 1981. House med. officer Ministry of Health, Sudan, 1974-78; registrar pathology Ministry of Health, Khartoum, 1978-80; student dcp London U., 1980-81; sr. registrar Bradford & Leeds, U.K., 1981-85; head lab. Armed Forces, Sharjah, 1995-98, Ministry Health, Khorfakkan, 1998—; hematologist Armed Forces Hosp., Abu Dhabi, 1985-98; assoc. mem. Thalassaemia, Cyprus, 1999—. Muslim. Office: Khorfakkan Hosp, PO Box 19427, Khorfakkan United Arab Emirates

KHATRI, MUHAMMED JAWED, executive secretary; b. Karachi, Sindh, Pakistan, May 4, 1959; s. Wali Muhammed and Fatima Khatri; m. Seema Muhammed Jawed Seema, Apr. 24, 1992; children: Qurat-Ul-Ain, Sidrat-Ul-Muntaha. B of Commerce, U. Karachi, 1987. Factory worker M/S Swiss Screens Aust. Pty. Ltd., Melbourne, Australia, 1989-91; steno-typist Mustafa Industries, Hyderabad, Pakistan, 1992-95; confidential sec. to sr. v.p. ops. New Jubilee Ins. Co. Ltd., Karachi, 1995—. Avocations: collecting stamps and antique coins, pen-friendships, traveling. Home: B/26 Khatri Colony, FMD Khan Rd Usmanabad, 75660 Karachi Sindh, Pakistan

KHATRI, TIKAM CHAND, zoology educator; b. Mohan Garh, India, Feb. 12, 1950; s. Jeth Mal and Sita Devi Khatri; m. Kanta Kharti; children: Jyoti, Rakhee, Tripta, Priyanka, Kanak. BSc, Rajasthan Univ., Jaipur, India, 1971, MSc, 1973; PhD, Jodhpur Univ., Jodhpur, India, 1981. Lectr. in zoology Maharahi Sri Jaya Coll., Rajasthan, India, 1974-75, Gov. Coll., Rajasthan, India, 1978; rsch. assoc. Zoological Survey of India, Kerala, India, 1982-85, Tamil Nadu, India, 1985-87; lectr. Jawaharhal Nehru Gov. Coll., A&N Islands, India, 1987—; reader in zoology Jawaharhal Nehru Gov. Coll., A&N Islands, 1996; participated in numerous confs. and seminars; coord. Indo-US Primate Project on Crab Eating Macaque, 1999. Editor: Environmental Protection and Toursim Development in Adnoman and Nitobar Islands, 1992; contbr. numerous articles to profl. jours. Pres. Andaman Coll. Tchr. Assn., 1991-92, 93. Recipient Gold Record of Achievements Am. Biographical Inst., 1996; Gov. Merit scholarship, 1966; STA fellow Japan Internat. Sci. Tech. Exch. Ctr., 2000. Fellow The Royal Entomological Soc.; mem. Entomological Soc. India, Andaman Sci. Assn., Indian Sci. Congress. Avocations: environmental conservation, faunal, writing scientific articles. Home: Gc 3 Gov Coll Colony Post, 744104 Andamans India Office: J N Gov Coll, 744104 Post Blair India

KHATTAK, NAZIR SHAH, physicist; b. Karak, Pakistan, Nov. 15, 1949; s. Khan Shah and Janat (Begum) K.; m. Khurshid Begum, Aug. 8, 1977; children: Abid, Samina, Huma, Seema, Majid. BSc, U. Peshawar, Pakistan, 1970, MSc, 1972; MA, Temple U., 1982, PhD, 1985. Lectr. NWFP Govt. Edn. Dept., Kohat, Pakistan, 1972-74; lectr. U. Peshawar, 1974-78, asst. prof. to assoc. prof., 1985-92, 92-96, prof. physics, 1996—; grad. asst. Temple U., Phila., 1978-85; prof. Indsl. Coll. Yanbu, Saudi Arabia, 1997-99; chmn., head elect. dept. U. Peshawar, 1992-93, bd. studies, 1985—. Contbr. articles to profl. jours. Sec. Peshawar U. Tchrs. Assn., 1995-96. Merit scholar NWFP, 1967-72, Ctrl. Oversea Tng. scholar, 1978-83. Mem. Am. Phys. Soc., Phys. Soc. Pakistan. Office: Univ Peshawar, Dept Physics, Peshawar Pakistan

KHATTER, PRITHIPAL SINGH, radiologist; b. Ferozepore Cant, Punjab, India, Feb. 1, 1936; came to U.S., 1976; s. Harnam Singh and Jagjit Kaur; m. Kamal Jit Kaur Chahal; children: Avinash, Boldy. MB BChir, Med. Coll., Amritsar, Punjab, 1959; diploma in radiology, GSVM Med. Coll., Kanpur, 1961, diploma in clin. pathology, 1962, MD in Radiology, 1965. Diplomate Am. Bd. Radiology. Resident in diagnostic radiology VA Med. Ctr., Dallas, 1976-78; radiologist, clin. pathologist Jit & Pal X-Rays (P) Ltd., Moradabad, India, 1965-76; radiologist, chief VA Med. Ctr., Huntington, W.Va., 1978-90; clin. faculty radiology, from instr. to assoc. prof. Marshall U. Sch. Medicine, Huntington, 1978-90; radiologist Radiology, Inc., Huntington, 1980-90, Davis Meml. Hosp., Elkins, W.Va., 1990-96, Radiol. Cons. Assn., Fairmont, W.Va., 1996-98, Radiology Physicians Assocs., 1998—. Fellow Indian Med. Assn.; mem. Indian Radiology Assn. Avocations: reading, music, tennis, badminton. Home: 50 Eastridge Dr Elkins WV 26241-9585 Office: Davis Meml Hosp Gorman & Reed Elkins WV 26241-1484

KHATTRI, KAILASH NATH, seismologist, geophysicist; b. Varanasi, U.P., India, June 24, 1934; s. Baij Nath and Tara Devi (Seth) K.; m. Savita Kapoor, Feb. 25, 1959 (dec. Jan. 1989); children: Nidhi, Harsha. BS, Lucknow (India) U., 1953; BS with honors, Indian Inst. Tech., 1956; MS in geophysics, St. Louis U., 1968, PhD, 1969. Jr. geophysicist Oil and Natural Gas Commn., Dehradun, India, 1956-65, sr. geophysicist, 1965-72; reader U. Roorkee, India, 1972-76, prof., 1976-92; emeritus scientist Wadia Inst. Himalayan Geology, Dehradun, 1993-98; vis. fellow Coop. Inst. Environ. Scis., Boulder, Colo., 1976-77; vis. prof. Inst. Geophysics, Hamburg (Germany) U., 1982; chmn. dept. earth scis. Roorkee U., 1986-88; chmn. nat. com. Internat. Union of Geodesy and Geophysics, Indian Nat. Sci. Acad., New Delhi, 1983-87, vice chmn. Internat. Assn. Seismic Physics Eath's Interior work group on Seismic Patterns, 1987-91. Contbr. articles to profl. jours. Recipient Best Paper award Indian Soc. Eathquake Tech., 1981, 91, Nat. Lectureship, Univ. Grants Commn., New Delhi, 1983, rsch. award and Gold Medal Khosla, 1984, rsch. prize, 1984, rsch. award and Silver Medal, 1985, Decinnial Award, Indian Geophys. Union, 1990, Assn. Exploration Geophysicists award, 1997. Fellow Indian Nat. Sci. Acad., Nat. Acad. Sci. India, Sigma Xi. Hindu. Avocations: meditation, travel. Home: 100 Rajendra Nagar, Dehradun 248 001, India Office: Wadia Inst Himalayan Geol, 33 Gen Mahadeo Singh Marg, Dehradun 248 001, India

KHAVROSHKIN, OLEG BORISOVIC, geophysicist, educator, inventor; b. Voronezh, Russia, May 13, 1938; s. Boris Nikolaevich Khavroshkin and Valentina Petrovna Glotova; children: Aleksandr, Yulia. Diploma of mech. engring., Moscow State Tech. U., 1962; Candidate of Sci., Inpulse Rsch. Inst., Moscow, 1970; D in Physics and Math., 1999. Test engr. Jet Propulsion Ctr., Voronezh, 1962-64; chief engr. Inpulse Rsch. Inst., Moscow, 1969-70; sr. rschr. Inst. Measurements, Moscow, 1970-78; sr. rschr. Inst. Physics of Earth, Moscow, 1978-94, head lab., 1994—. Contbr. articles to profl. jours.; inventor and patentee in field. Recipient Diploma for Discover 282, State Com. on Cause of Discoveries and Inventiions USSR, 1983. Mem. Russian Acad. Natural Sci. (academician). Avocations: classical music, Russian nature. Home: Acad Millionshikova 15-36, 115487 Moscow Russia Office: Inst Phys Earth RAS, B Gruzinskaja St 10, 123810 Moscow Russia

KHAWAJA, XAVIER, biochemical pharmacologist; b. La Ferte sous Jouarre, S.et Marne, France, Mar. 6, 1960; came to U.S., 1995; s. Ishtiaque and Anne Marie (Bourgeois) K. BSc. with hons., Chelsea Coll., London, 1982, MSc, 1984; PhD, U. Sussex., Brighton, Eng., 1987. Post doctoral rsch. fellow Med. Rsch. Coun., Brighton, Sussex, Eng., 1987-88, Wellcome Trust, Brighton, Sussex, Eng., 1988-91; sr. rsch. scientist Wyeth Ayerst Rsch. Labs., Taplow, Berkshire, Eng., 1991-95; prin. rsch. scientist Wyeth Ayerst Rsch. Labs., Princeton, N.J., 1995—. Contbr. articles to profl. jours. including Diabetes, Jour. Neurochemistry, Brain Rsch., Peptides, Jour. Neurosci. Rsch. Achievements include contributions to the knowledge of opioids and opioid receptors involvement in the regulation of food intake, glucose homeostasis and their central and peripheral effects related to obesity and type 2 diabetes; contributions to the knowledge of G-protein coupled receptor characterization and signal transduction events in the central nervous system; contributions to the field of proteomics, functional genomics and neuroscience. Office: Wyeth-Ayerst Rsch CN 8000 Princeton NJ 08543

KHAWLIE, MOHAMAD RADWAN, national remote sensing center director; b. Accra, Ghana, Sept. 28, 1947; arrived in Lebanon, 1950; s. Radwan Mohamad Khawlie and Amneh Abdulmajid Bayakly; m. Sawsan Yehia Yamout, Feb. 27, 1985; 1 child, Elissa. BS, Am. U. Beirut, Lebanon, 1970; MS, U. Ill., 1972, PhD, 1975. Cert. geologist, environmentalist. Investigator Nat. Coun. for Sci. Rsch., Beirut, 1975; geologist Al-Rasheed Engring., Riyadh, Saudi Arabia, 1976, Dames & Moore Internat., London, 1977; from asst. to full prof. Am. U. Beirut, 1978-95, chmn. geology dept., 1986-95; dir. Nat. Ctr. for Remote Sensing, Beirut, 1995—; cons. Engring. Firms, Lebanon, 1980—, UN Devel. Program, Beirut, 1992—, UN Svcs., 1994—; bd. dirs. World Ecology Report, Beirut; chief phys. environmentalist Soc. Protection of Nature, Beirut, 1990—; chair Nat. Internat. Geosphere Biosphere Program Com., Beirut, 1992—; team leader Nat. Climate Change Com., Beirut, 1998—, Nat. Sci. Com. on Environment, Beirut, 1995; sec. gen. Devel. Studies Assn., 1999. Author: Desertification in the Arab World, 1985, 2nd edit., 1990, Beyond the Oil Era: Arab Minerals Resources and Future Development, 1990; co-author: Environment and Development in Lebanon, 1993; editor: The Role of Science and Technology in Developing Industry in Lebanon, 1983. Recipient Sci. Achievement award Higher Coun. of Scis., Syria, 1979. Mem. Internat. Assn. Impact Assessments, Geosci. Internat. Devel., World Information Transfer (dir. Mid-East). Avocations: swimming, mountain climbing, reading non-fiction. Office: Nat Ctr for Remote Sensing, PO Box 11-8281, Beirut Lebanon

KHAZANOV, EFIM ARCADIY, physicist, educator; b. Gorky, USSR, Nov. 12, 1965; s. Arcadiy Haim and Raisa (Grigoriy) K.; m. Sofia Vladivlav Stroganova, June 6, 1997; 1 child, Grigoriy. MD, Politech. U., Gorky, USSR, 1988; PhD, Inst. Applied Physics, Nizhny Novgorod, Russia, 1992. Scientist rschr. Inst. Applied Physics, Nizhny Novgorod, 1992-93, sr. scientist rschr., 1994-98, head lab., 1999—; asst. prof. State U., Nizhny Novgorod, 1997—; vice dir. Summer Physics and Math. Sch., Nizhny Novogorod, 1988—. Contbr. more than 25 articles to profl. jours. Recipient Lenin's State awards for students, 1986, 87, Russian Pres.'s award for young scientists, 1997-99, medal Russian Acad. Sci. Mem. Optical Soc. Am. Office: Inst Applied Physics, 46 Uljanov St, 603600 Nizhny Novgorod Russia

KHEDDAR, ABDERRAHMANE, research scientist, educator; b. Algiera, Algeria, Aug. 4, 1967; arrived in France, 1993; s. Mahmoud and Zohra (Attou) K. Engr., Inst. Nat. Informatique, Algiers, 1990; MSc, U. Paris 6, 1993, PhD, 1997. Rsch. asst. Haut Commisseriel Recherche, Algeria, 1990-92; rschr. Ctr. Robotique Integre Ile France, France, 1994-97; asst. prof. U. Versailles, France, 1995-97; assoc. prof. U. Evry, Paris, 1997—. Contbr. chpts. to books. Avocations: sports, reading, hunting.

KHEMKA, SHIV VIKRAM, investment company executive, venture capitalist; b. New Delhi, Aug. 19, 1962; s. Nand and Jeet (Nabha) K.; m. Urvashi Rajya Laxmi Rana, Jan. 25, 1996; children: Bhavani, Jayashree. BA, Brown U., 1985; MA, Lander Ins., 1990; MBA, U. Pa., 1990. With Sun Group of Cos., Moscow, 1985—. Author: (poetry) Offshore Breeze, 1995. Bd. govs. Lander Inst., 1997—; mem. adv. bd. Ctr. for Internat. Bus. and Mgmt., U. Cambridge, Eng., 1999—; mem. vis. com. Harvard U. Ctr. for Russian Studies, Cambridge, Mass., 1995—; mem. Brotn U. Internat. Young Alumni Coun., Providence, 1999—; chmn. Russian country com. Confedn. Indian Industries, Delhi, India, 1999—. Named one of Global Leaders for Tomorrow, World Econ. Forum, 1997. Mem. Young Pres.' Orgn. Avocations: Indian classical music, art collecting, writing. Office: SUN Group Cos 9th Fl, Paveletskaya Pl 2 Bld 2, 113054 Moscow Russia

KHER, SANJAY, scientist; b. Jhansi, India, July 23, 1960; s. Balkrishna and Shakuntala (Wakhle) K.; m. Neeta Sholapurkar, Nov. 30, 1986; 1 child, Tanvi. BSc, Bipin Bihari Degree Coll., Jhansi, 1980; MSc in Physics, Indian Inst. Tech., New Delhi, 1983. Cert. physicist. Sci. offcer (C) BARC, Bombay, 1984-88; sci. officer (D) Ctr. for Advanced Tech., Indore, India, 1988-93, sci. officer (E), 1993-99, sci. officer (F), 1994—; rsch. scholar U. Tokyo, 1994-96; Inst. fellow Indian Inst. Tech., Dehli, 1983. Sec. Paramanu Welfare Soc., 1998-99; sec. Staff Club, Ctr. for Advanced Tech., 1987-89. Mem. Indian Laser Assn. (treas. 1992-93), Indian Assn. Laser Surgery and Medicine, Assn. Internat. Edn. in Japan, Indian Laser Assn. Avocations: touring, teaching, gardening. Home: Ctr for Adv Tech Colony, 452013 Indore India Office: Ctr for Advanced Tech, PO-CAT, 452013 Indore India

KHERATI, RIZWAN ULLAH, accountant; b. Karachi, Sind, Pakistan, Sept. 19, 1974; s. Lutfur Rahman and Zamira Kherati; m. Erum Rizwan Aboobakar, Feb. 20, 1999. B of Commerce, St. Patricks Govt. Coll., Karachi, 1993; chartered acct., Ins. Chartered Accts. Pakistan, Karachi, 1997; cost and mgmt. acct., ICMAP, Karachi, 1997. Trainee A.F. Ferguson & Co. Chartered Accts., Karachi, 1994-98; v.p. Pakistan Kuwait Investment Co. (pvt.) Ltd., Karachi, 1998—; dir. Al-Mal Securities and Svcs. Ltd., Karachi. Author: (books) Kia Waseela Jaiz Hai, 1994, Ja-Al-Haq, 1995. Avocations: philosophy, comparative religion, health and medicine, theology. E-mail: pkic@yahoo.com. Home: 137 Block A SMCHS, 74400 Karachi Sind, Pakistan Office: Pakistan Kuwait Investment, FTC Bldg Sharah-e-Faisal, 74400 Karachi Sind, Pakistan

KHESIN, BORIS EMANUEL, geophysicist; b. Baku, Azerbaijan, Mar. 3, 1932; arrived in Israel, 1990; s. Emanuel Benzion and Miryam Mordeckai (Dreizin) K.; m. Vera Nikolai Kuptzov, Mar. 19, 1970; children: Sofia, Inna. MSc (hon.), Moscow Geol. Prospecting Inst., 1954, DSc, 1982; PhD, Azerbaijan Oil and Chem. Inst., 1964. Chief of geophys. works All-Union Geol. Inst., Leningrad, 1954-57; chief engr. Azerbaijan Geophys. Expedn., Baku, 1957-67; sr. scientist All-Union Inst. Geophysics, Baku, 1967-73, chief of the lab., 1973-90; sr. scientist, prof. Ben Gurion U., Beer-Sheva, Israel, 1991—; assoc. prof. Azerbaijan Oil and Chem. Inst., Baku, 1970-82, prof., 1982-90. Author: Ore Geophysics in Mountainous Regions, 1969, Prognosis and Localization of Hidden Mineralization in Mountainous Regions on the Basis of Geophysical Data, 1976; co-author: Interpretation of Geophysical Fields in Complicated Environments, 1996; editor: Interpretation of Magnetic Anomalies in the Conditions of Oblique Magnetization and Rugged Topography, 1983. Mem. presidium Israel Assn. Scientists-Immigrants, Jerusalem, 1993—, Scientists of the South Assn., Beer-Sheva, 1994—. Awarded Prospector, Min. Geology of the USSR, 1982; named USSR's Inventor, State Com. of Inventions and Discovers of the USSR, 1987. Mem. Azerbaijan Mining Soc. (head of geophys. sect. 1962-67), Israel Geol. Soc., Soc. Exploration Geophysicists. Home: 1/26 M Namir, 84483 Beer Sheva Israel Office: Ben Gurion U Dept Geol Sci, PO Box 653, 84105 Beer Sheva Israel

KHETAGUROV, VALERY NICKOLAEVICH, technology educator; b. Vladikavkaz, Russia, Sept. 7, 1953; s. Nickolaj Nesterovich Khetagurov and Zinaida Gavrilovna Murasheva; m. Irina Vasilievna Isakova, Jan. 13, 1958; children: George, Soslan. MA, U. Tech., Vladikavkaz, 1975, PhD, 1988. Cert. in engring. Engr. Inst. Giprozvetment, Vladikavkaz, 1975-79; rschr. U. Tech., Vladikavkaz, 1979-88, prof., 1988—. Author: (book) Development of Vertical Types of Mills, 1999; patentee in field. Recipient medal Exhbn. of Achievements, 1987; grantee Ministry of Edn., 1997. Avocation: chess. Home: 64/1 Kalinin St Apt 142, 362039 Vladikavkaz Russia Office: U of Tech, 44 Nicholaev St, 362021 Vladikavkaz Russia

KHIN-NWE-OO, microbiologist; b. Rangoon, Burma, Aug. 30, 1950; parents Myint-Thoung and Tin-Han. MBBS, Inst. Medicine, Rangoon, 1974, D Bacteriology, 1982, M Med. Sci., 1994. Asst. surgeon Aung San Tb Hosp., Rangoon, 1978-81; med. officer Nat. Health Lab., Rangoon, 1981-83; rsch. officer Dept. Med. Rsch., Rangoon, 1983-91, sr. rsch. officer, 1991-94, rsch. scientist, 1994-97, dep. dir., head, 1997—. Contbr. articles to profl. jours. Recipient fellowship Japanese Internat. Coop. Agy., Japan, 1991-92, Best Poster award Myanmar Health Rsch. Congress, 1993, 97, medal for pub. svc. Govt. Myanmar, 1995. Mem. Myanmar Med. Assn. (life), Microbiology Assn. (life). Avocation: reading. Home: 90 Sabaichan 2nd Ln, Hlaing, Yangon Myanmar Office: Immunology Rsch Divsn, Dept Med Rsch, 5 Ziwaka Rd, Yangon 11191, Myanmar

KHIRNYI, VITALII FILIPPOVITCH, physicist; b. Kharkov, Ukraine, Apr. 12, 1938; s. Filipp Vladimirovitch and Nadezhda Stepanovna (Solodovnikova) K.; m. Alevtina Aleksandrovna Smirnova, Aug. 8, 1968; children: Aleksandr, Vladimir. BS, Kharkov State U., USSR, 1965; D in Physics, Donetsk State U., USSR, 1982. Engr. Donetsk Physico-Tech. Inst., 1965-80, younger rschr., 1980-83, sr. rschr., 1983-89; sr. rschr. Inst. for Single Crystals of Nat. Acad. of Scis. Ukraine, Kharkov, 1989—. Author publs. in field. Grantee Internat. Sci. Found. Avocations: painting, agriculture. Office: Inst for Single Crystals, Lenin ave 60, Kharkov 310001, Ukraine

KHISAMUTDINOV, GILMUTDIN KHISAMUTDINOVICH, chemistry educator, researcher; b. Verkhny Kuyuk, Russia, July 24, 1935; s. Khisamutdin Salyakhovich and Sabira (Safargalievna) Salyakhova; m. Avgusta Ivanovna Mikryukova, Oct. 7, 1961; 1 child, Asia Gilmutdinovna. Degree in chem. engring., Chem. Engring. Inst., Kazan, Russia, 1958; PhD in chem. Scis., Inst. Organic Chemistry, Moscow, 1971. Engr. of sci. rsch. Inst. of Polymer Mater, Perm, Russia, 1958-59; chief section. Sci. Rsch. Inst. Chem. Tech., Biysk, Russia, 1959-64; chief of lab. Sci. Rsch. Chem. Pharmas. Inst., Novokuznetsk, Russia, 1964-67; docent Kuzbass Polytech. Inst., Kemerovo, Russia, 1971-81; chief of lab. Sci. Rsch. Inst. Chem. Products., Tashkent, Uzbekistan, 1981-83; rschr., chief lab. GosNII Kristall, Dzerzhinsk, Russia, 1983—; lectr. chemistry Altai Polytech. Inst., Biysk, 1962-64; cons. PO Khimprom, Kemerovo, Russia, 1978-80. Contbr. articles to profl. jours.; patentee in field. Mem. Knowledge Soc. (bd. dirs. reg. com. 1971-81), Mendeleev Chem. Soc. (bd. dirs. reg. com. 1970-80). Avocations: gathering mushrooms and berries, growing flowers and vegetables. Home: pr Chkalova 29 Apt 69, 606007 Dzerzhinsk Russia Office: GosNII Kristall, ul Zelionaya 6, 606007 Dzerzhinsk Russia

KHITRIN, SERGEI VLADIMIROVICH, chemistry educator; b. Kotelnich, Russia, May 16, 1950; s. Vladimir Ivanovich and Nadegda Aleksandrovna (Belykh) K.; m. Iraida Ilyinichna Rozhkova, Feb. 1, 1974; children: Elena, Kirill. Degree, St. Petersburg State U., 1969, Kirov Polytech. Inst., 1975; doctor, Gorky Polytech. Inst., 1981, Kazan State U., 1996. Lab. asst. Kirov Polytech. Inst., 1971-75, docent, 1986-96; sr. engr. Project Inst., Kiron, 1975-77; rsch. asst. GPI, Gorky, Russia, 1977-80; sr. rschr. GPI, KPI, Gorky, 1980-86; prof. Vyatka State Tech. U., Kirov, 1996—; chmn. commn. of com. on ecology Biochem. Plant, Kirov, 1996-97, Chmn. Plant, Kirovo-Chepetsk, 1997-2000; mem. Russian Acad. of Natural Scis., Moscow, 1998. Inventor, patentee in field, chemistry of amids, transformations of acrilic polymers, polyalkohols and biopolymers, polymeryzation lactams and lactons, organo-phosphorus compounds. Sgt. Soviet Army, 1969-71. Recipient Mendeleev prize Regional Soviet, 1981; grantee Internat. Soros Sci. Edn., 1995, 98. Mem. Russian Acad. Natural Scis., N.Y. Acad. Scis., Nat. Geographic Soc. Avocations: drawing, hunting, fishing, skiing, construction. E-mail: vgtu@vgtu.exel.direct.ru. Home: 111 Karl Libkneht str, 610027 Kirov Russia Office: Vyatka State Tech U, 36 Moskonskaya Str, 610601 Kirov Russia

KHIZHNYAK, N(ICOLAI) A(NTONOVITCH), physics researcher, educator; b. Kharkov, Ukraine, May 18, 1929; s. Anton Stepanovitch and Anna Nickolayevna (Minayva) K.; m. Nina Danilovna Ogdanetz, Sept. 23, 1951; children: Sergey, Alexander. Grad., Kharkov State U., Ukraine, 1952, DSc, 1969, PhD, 1958; academician, Acad. of Radioelectronics of Belorussia, Russia and Ukraine, 1993. Rsch. scientist Kharkov Inst. Physics and Tech., 1953-58, sr. rsch. scientist, 1959-69, lab. head, 1969-82, dept. head, 1983—; prof. radio phys. faculty Kharkov State U., 1970—; lectr. Kharkov Aviation Inst., 1959-69; lectr. Knowledge Soc., Kharkov, 1953-91. Author: Integral Equations of Macroscopical Electrodynamics, 1986; co-author: Modern Problems of Nonstationary Macroscopic Electrodynamics, 1991, Boundary Problems of Hydromagnetic Electrodynamics, 1992. Recipient Hon. State prize State Com. of Sci. and Tech., Russia, 1979, Hon. State prize State Com. of Sci. and Tech., Ukraine, Kiev, 1989, 96. Mem. IEEE, Ukranian Phys. Soc., Am. Phys. Soc., Russian Nuclear Soc. Avocations: reading, stamp collecting. Home: Pavel Morozov St 2, Apt 22, 61 108 Kharkov Ukraine Office: Nat Sci Ctr Kharkov Phys Tech Inst, Academicheskaya St 1, 61 108 Kharkov Ukraine

KHIZINDAR, TARIQ MOHAMMED, marketing educator; b. Mecca, Saudia Arabia, Nov. 2, 1954; s. Mohammed Abdul-Rahman and Sameeha Rabah Al-Ogeel K.; m. Leila Darwish Chahbar, Aug. 6, 1984; children: Huda, Sameeha, Abdul-Rahman, Darwish. BS, King Abdul Aziz U., Saudi

Arabia, 1973; MS, U. Wis., 1983; PhD, Lancaster U., 1992. Lectr. King Abdul-Aziz U., Jeddah, Saudi Arabia, 1985-88; asst. prof. King Abdul-Aziz U., Jeddah, 1992—; pres. New Trends for Mktg. and Managerial Consultancy, Jeddah, 1992—; dir. of recycling program Islamic Relief Orgn., Jeddah, 1993-94; v.p. rsch. and devel. Sanabal Al-Kayr Investment Co., Jeddah, 1993-94; head/advisor mktg. club King Abdul-Aziz U., 1990-99; v.p. cons. com. Jeddah C. of C., 1999—. Author: (books) Career Planning and Your CV, 1997, Practical Marketing, 1999, Consumer Behavior, 1999. CEO King Abdul-Aziz Coop Orgn., Jeddah, 1997-99. Mem. Am. Mktg. Assn., Saudi Coun. for Total Quality Mgmt. Avocations: weight lifting, reading, jogging, scuba diving. Office: King Abdul Aziz Univ, PO Box 52374, 21563 Jeddah Saudi Arabia

KHLGATIAN, SVETLANA VAGINAKOVNA, physiologist, researcher; b. Moscow, Nov. 1, 1962; d. Vaginak Egorovich and Genya Avetisovna (Vardanian) K. BS, Moscow State U., 1986, MS, 1987, PhD in Biol. Scis., 1990. Rschr. Mechnikov Rsch. Inst. Vaccine, Sera Russian Acad. Med. Scis., Moscow, 1991-93, sr. rschr., 1993—. Contbr. articles to profl. jours. Mem. N.Y. Acad. Scis. Avocation: painting. Home: Nagatinskaya Nab 70-160, 115407 Moscow Russia Office: Mechnikov Rsch Inst Vaccine, Sera RAM Mechnikov per 5a, 103064 Moscow Russia

KHLYAP, GALINA, physics educator, researcher; b. Drogobych, Ukraine, Nov. 13, 1961; d. Michail Khlyap and Klara Varshavskaya. Degree in tchg. physics, Pedagogical Inst., Drogobych, 1984; PhD, U. Chernivtsi, Ukraine, 1995. Lab. asst. Pedagogical Inst., Drogobych, 1984—, lab. asst. rsch. and devel. Contbr. articles to profl. jours. Mem. European Materials Rsch. Soc., N.Y. Acad. Sci. Avocations: foreign languages, lecturing, classical music, travel. Home: 117-1 Grushevsky St, 82106 Drogobych Ukraine Office: State Pedagogical U, 24 Franko St, 82100 Drogobych Ukraine

KHMELNITSKAYA, ANNA BORISOVNA, mathematician, researcher; b. St. Petersburg, Russia, Nov. 10, 1950; d. Boris Efimovich Chernomordick and Sima Davidovna Goldschteine; m. Peter Ehil'evich Khmelnitsky, May 10, 1973 (div. Apr. 1977); 1 child, Galperina Maria. MSc, Leningrad (Russia) State U., 1973, PhD, 1987. Jr. rsch. assoc. USSR Rsch. Inst. for Hydrolysis of Vegetative Materials, Leningrad, 1974-77; asst. prof. Leningrad State Poly. Coll., 1977-78; rsch. assoc. Inst. Socio-Econ. Problems, USSR Acad. Scis., 1978-90; sr. rschr. St. Petersburg Inst. Econs. and Math., Russian Acad. Sci., 1990—; adj. assoc. prof. St. Petersburg State Marine Tech. U., 1995-97, European U., St. Petersburg, 1995-97; vis. prof. Karl-Franz U., Graz, Austria, 1996; vis. fellow The Hebrew U. Jerusalem, 1998-99; vis. rschr. U. Twente, The Netherlands, 1999. Contbr. articles to profl. jours. Rsch. grantee Russian Found. for Basic Rsch., 1996-97, Internat. Assn. for Promotion of Cooperation with Scientists from New Ind. States of Former Soviet Union, Belgium, 1997-2000, Dutch Nat. Orgn., The Netherlands, 1999, 2000—. Mem. Internat. Game Theory Soc. Avocations: classical and jazz music, literature, mountain skiing, traveling. Home: 5/41 Lev Tolstoy St, 197022 St Petersburg Russia Office: SP6 Inst Econ & Math RAS, 1 Tchaikovsky St, 191187 St Petersburg Russia

KHMURCHIK, VADIM TARASOVICH, biologist, researcher; b. Perm, USSR, Jan. 24, 1965; s. Taras Semyonovich and Aleftina Anatol'evna (Khomyakova) K.; m. Tatyana Yur'evna Vedrova, Feb. 12, 1988; children: Julia, Mary. Grad., Perm State U., 1989; PhD in Biology, Russian Acad. Scis., Perm, 1997. Engr. Inst. Ecology and Genetics of Microorganisms Russian Acad. Scis., Perm, 1990-91, jr. rsch. scientist, 1991-93, rsch. scientist, 1993-98, sr. rsch. scientist, 1998—; sr. rsch. scientist Perm State Tech. U., 2000—. Chmn. Coun. Pub. Self-Govt. of Micro-Dist. Stakhanovsky, Perm, 1998—. Grantee Spl. Fund for Granting Talented Young Scientists, 1993. Christian Orthodox. Avocations: dacha, book-covering. Home: Karpinsky St 31-87, 614022 Perm Russia Office: Inst Ecology/Genetics RAS, Golev Str 13, 614081 Perm Russia

KHO, HING GWAN, anesthetist, researcher; b. Surabaja, East Java, Indonesia, Jan. 20, 1948; s. Sien Biauw and Swan Nio Kwee; m. Leng Nio The, Aug. 5, 1974; children: Kuan Hua, Ay Lin, Kuan Kun, Pau Lin. SMA, Canisius Coll., Jakarta, Indonesia, 1966; Degree in Acupuncture, Ludwig Boltzmann Inst., Vienna, 1977; MD, Cath. U., Nijmegen, Netherlands, 1974, PhD, 1991. Registered anesthetist, Netherlands. Gen. practitioner Volendam, Utrecht, Netherlands, 1975-79; resident in anesthesiology Univ. Hosp., Nijmegen, 1979-82, anesthetist, 1982—; rsch. fellow, Nanjing, China, 1987, Shanghai, China, 1994—. Author: Acupuncture, 1975, also articles. Mem. Dutch Com. of Med. Aid for Vietnam, 1968-75; mem. Frendship Assn. Dutch-China, 1970-76; chmn. Found. Sci. Study Chinese Medicine, 1995—; Dutch rep. Intern. Soc. Orient Medicine, 1995—. Fellow Royal Dutch Acad. Scis.; mem. Dutch Soc. Anesthetists, N.Y. Acad. Scis., Royal Inst. Linguistic & Anthropology, Austrian Soc. Acupuncture (Prof. Dr. Alfred Pischinger prize 1990, 92). Avocations: reading, sports. Home: Aldenhof 50-06, 6537 EC Nijmegen The Netherlands Office: Univ Hosp Nijmegen, Geert Grooteplein 10, 6500 HB Nijmegen The Netherlands

KHODIER, SORAYA ABD-EL-AZIZ, science educator; b. Cairo, July 17, 1948; d. Abd-El-Aziz Sayed Ahmed Khodier and Hameda Salem Amer; m. Ahmed Wahby Mohammed Amin Shalaby, Nov. 16, 1972; children: Aliaa, Mohammed, Mostafa, Moataz. BSc in Physics and Math., Ain Shams U., Cairo, 1970, MSc in Physics, 1976, PhD in Physics, 1991. Cert. physicist. Asst. rschr. Nat. Inst. for Stds., Giza, Egypt, 1971-76, asst. lectr., 1976-91, rschr., 1991-97, asst. prof., 1997—. Contbr. sci. articles to profl. jours. Office: Nat Inst for Stds, 12211 Giza Egypt

KHODJAMIRIAN, ALEXANDER, physicist; b. Yerevan, Armenia, Sept. 28, 1951; s. Yuri and Sousanna (Avsharova) K.; m. Noune Ambartsoumian, Aug. 4, 1984; children: Yuri, Sergey. PhD in Theoretical Phyusics, Yerevan Physics Inst., Armenia, 1980. Jr. rschr. Yeravan Physics Inst., Armenia, 1976-83, sr. rschr., 1983-88, leading rschr., 1988—; invited prof. U. Minn., Mpls., 1989-90; vis. rschr. U.Munich, Germany, 1994-96, U. Wuirzburg, Germany, 1996-97. Contbr. articles to profl. jours. Alexander von Humboldt fellow U. Munich, 1992-94. Mem. Armenian Ch. Avocation: music. Office: Yerevan Physics Inst, Yerevan Physics Inst, Alikhanian Br Str 2, 375036 Yerevan Armenia

KHODYKIN, SERGEY ALEXANDROVICH, physics educator; b. Izhevsk, Udmurtia, Russia, Apr. 17, 1957; s. Alexander and Nina (Kharkova) K.; m. Nina Krivkina, June 23, 1979; 1 child, Andrew. Astronomer, Moscow U., 1980, D in Physics and Math. (hon.), 1991. Asst. prof. math. Volgograd (Russia) Pedagogical Inst., 1980-81, asst. prof. physics, 1981-85, assoc. prof. physics, 1989—, sub-dean faculty physics, 1992—; rsch. asst. Sternberg Astron. Inst., Moscow, 1985-89. Author: Astronomy, 1997, Physics in Questions and Answers, 1997, Physics: Self-Education of Pupils, 1997; contbr. articles to profl. jours. Mem. N.Y. Acad. Scis. Avocations: foreign languages, children's education, sports, music, guitar playing. Home: Bukhantsev St 2-b 10, 400120 Volgograd Russia Office: Volgograd Pedagog U-Physics, Academicheskaja st 12, 400001 Volgograd Russia

KHOE, GIOK-DJAN, communications executive; b. Magelang, Jateng, Indonesia, July 22, 1946; arrived in The Netherlands, 1965; s. Gwan-tin and Tjiauw-len (Tjia) K.; m. Lilian Liem; children: Yung Han, Yu Li. Diploma in Engring., Tech. U. Eindhoven, The Netherlands, 1971. Profl. engr. Scientist Plasma Physics Inst. Rijnhuizen, Nieuwegein, The Netherlands, 1972-73; sr. scientist Philips Rsch. Labs, Eindhoven, 1973-93; prof. Tech. U., Eindhoven, 1983—; mem. program com. Ministry Econ. Affairs, Innovative Rsch. Programs, The Hague, 1989—; bd. mgmt. Cobra Rsch. Ctr., Eindhoven, 1994—; auditor, evaluator European Comty. Rsch. and Tech. Devel. in Advanced Comms. in Europe program, Brussels, 1988-91, project leader, 1993-95. Contbg. author: Advances in Low Temperature Plasmas, 1984, Optoelectronic Technology and Lightwave Communication Systems, 1989, Photonic Networks, 1997; assoc. editor Jour. of Lightwave Technology, 1990-95; mem. editl. bd. Optical and Quantum Electronics Jour., 1990-95; patentee in field; contbr. numerous articles to profl. jours. Recipient Microoptics award Japan Soc. Applied Physics, 1997. Fellow IEEE (mem. com. Benelux sect.), IEEE Lasers and Electro-Optics Soc. (European rep. 1993-95, v.p. 1996-98, bd. govs. 1999—); mem. European Conf. on Optical Comm. Tech. Program (com. mem. 1986-89, chmn. 1990, mgmt. com. mem. 1991—), Royal Inst. Engrs. (bd. dirs. telecom 1986-88, coun. for sci. and tech. 1996—), Microoptics Conf. Program. Avocations: tennis, gardening, music. Home: Luxemburglaan 23, 5625 NA Eindhoven The Netherlands Office: Tech U Eindhoven Bldg, EH-12 PO Box 513, 5600 MB Eindhoven The Netherlands

KHOI, NGUYEN THE, physics educator; b. Hanoi, Vietnam, Nov. 19, 1943; s. Nguyen Duc Thinh and Pham Thi Van Thuong; m. Nguyen Thi Thanh Hien; children: Nga Nguyen Quynh, Ngoc Nguyen Minh. Grad., Pedagogic U., Hanoi, 1965; PhD, U. Warsaw, 1979. Lectr. Pedagogic U., Hanoi, 1965-75, tchr., lectr., 1980-90, 98; doctoral fellow U. Warsaw, 1975-80, rsch. fellow, 1990-98; dep. dean dept. physics, Pedagogic U., Hanoi, 1986-89, dep. rector, 1989-90. Co-author: (books in Vietnamese) Electricity and Magnetism, 1970, Introduction to Physics of Solids, 1992; contbr. articles to profl. jours. Avocations: classical music, cello, painting. Office: Dept Physics Hanoi Ped U, XuanThuy Rd, 00-681 Hanoi Vietnam

KHOJASTEH, ALI, medical oncologist, hematologist; b. Shiraz, Pars, Persia, Nov. 10, 1947; came to U.S., 1974; s. Mostafa and Pari Jan (Azimi) K.; children: Artemis, Amitis. Degree, Pahlavi U., Shiraz, 1968, MD, 1974. Vice dean Sch. Medicine Shiraz U., 1980-82, chmn. med. dept. Sch. Medicine, 1982-83; chief med. oncology Ellis Fischel Cancer Ctr., Columbia, Mo., 1983-87, chmn. med. dept., 1987-90, chief of staff, 1988-89; med. dir. St. Mary Cancer Ctr., Jefferson City, Mo., 1993—; pres. Columbia Comprehensive Cancer Care Clinic and Rsch. Inst., 1990—; assoc. prof. U. Mo., Columbia, 1989—; prin. investigator Ellis Fischel CCOP, Columbia, 1988-90; chmn. Mo. Acad. Sci. Oncology, 1988-89, Mo. Cancer Pain Initiative, 1991-96; investigator Nat. Cancer Inst., 1990—; liaison Am. Coll. Surgeons, 1992—. Contbr. articles to New Eng. Jour. Medicine, Cancer, Am. Jour. Medicine, Am. Jour. Hematology, Jour. Clin. Oncol. Cancer Bull., Jour. Pain Sys. Mgmt., Can. Jour. Medicine; author: (with others) Pulmonary Medicine, Cancer and Heart, Chemotherapy Resource Book, Small Intestinal Disease. Rsch. grantee Purdue Fredrick Co., Conn., 1984—, Adria Lab., Columbus, 1988—, Glaxo Rsch. Lab., Research Triangle Park, N.C., 1988-91, Ciba-Geigy Co., 1990-93, Merrill Dow Co., 1991-95, Pfizer, 1995—, Matrix Pharm., 1996, Ross Lab., 1996, Aronex Pharm., 1997, Merck Rsch. Lab., 1997, Ligand Lab., 1997, Maxim-Pharm., 1998, Nat. Cancer Inst., 1998, Glaxo-Wellcome, 1998, Bayer Lab., 1999, Amgen, 1999, Arugon Lab., 1999, Pharmacia & Upjohn Lab., 2000, Hoffman-Roche Lab., 2000. Fellow ACP, Royal Soc. Medicine (Eng.); mem. Am. Soc. Clin. Oncology, Am. Soc. Internat. Medicine, Smithsonian Soc., N.Y. Acad. Sci., Mo. Acad. Scis. (chmn. oncology sect. 1988-89), So. Med. Assn., Am. Soc. Hematology. Zoroastrian. Home: 2801 Greenbriar Dr Columbia MO 65203-3663 Office: Columbia Comprehensive Cancer Care Clinic 500 Keene St Ste 202 Columbia MO 65201-8104

KHOKHLOV, ALEXEI REMOVICH, physics educator; b. Moscow, Jan. 10, 1954; s. Rem Viktorovich Khokhlov and Elena Mikhailovna Dubinina; m. Natalia Alexeevna Prokhorova, July 10, 1982; children: Olga, Marina. MSc, Moscow State U., 1977, PhD, 1979, DSc (hon.), 1983. Asst. prof. Moscow State U., 1979-86, assoc. prof., 1986-88, prof., 1988-93, head of chair, 1993—; head lab. Inst. Organoelement Compounds, Russian Acad. Scis., Moscow, 1991—; adj. prof. SUNY, Stony Brook, 1995—. Author: Statistical Physics of Macromolecules, 1994, Giant Molecules: Here and There and Everywhere, 1997. Recipient USSR award for young scientists, 1982, Humboldt rsch. award, 1992. Mem. UIPAC (titular mem. macromolecular divsn.), Polymer Coun. Russian Acad. Scis. (vice chmn. 1994—). Fax: 7-095-939-2988. E-mail: khokhlov@polly.phys.msu.su. Office: Moscow State U Physics Dept, Vorobievy Gory, 117234 Moscow Russia

KHOKHLOV, DMITRIY REMOVICH, physicist, researcher; b. Moscow, Dec. 26, 1957; s. Rem Viktorovich K. and Elena Mikhailovna Dubinina; m. Vera Aleksandrovna Kovrigina, Jan. 23, 1982; children: Tat'yana, Mariya. MS, Moscow State U., 1980, PhD, 1982, DSc, 1992. Jr. researcher physics dept. Moscow State U., 1982-88, asst. prof. physics dept., 1988-90, sr. researcher physics dept., 1990-92, leading researcher physics dept., 1992-98, prof. physics dept., 1998—; expert Supreme Attestation Commn., Moscow, 1997—. Recipient State Prize of Russia in Sci. Pres. of Russian Fedn., 1995. Mem. Materials Rsch. Soc. Avocations: jogging, skiing, windsurfing. Fax: 7-(095)-9328876. E-mail: khokhlov@mig.phys.msu.su. Home: L-14 Moscow State U, Moscow 117234, Russia Office: Moscow State U, Dept Physics, Moscow 119899, Russia

KHOKHLOV, VITALY SERGEYEVICH, banker; b. Moscow, Aug. 15, 1938. Grad., Moscow Inst. of Nat. Economy, All-Union Acad. of Foreign Trade. Sr. adviser Bank for Foreign Trade of USSR, Moscow, 1964-71; sr. economist Eurobank, Paris, 1971-74; v.p. East-West United Bank, Luxembourg, 1974-77; adviser Communist Party Cen. Com., Moscow, 1977-87; dep. chmn. Bank for Foreign Econ. Affairs of USSR, Moscow, 1987-88; chmn. bd. Internat. Bank for Econ. Co-operation, Moscow, 1988—. Office: IBEC, 11 Masha Poryvaeva St, 107815 GSP Moscow B-78, Russia

KHOKHLOV, VLADIMIR ABRAMOVICH, pianist, educator; b. St. Petersburg, Fla., May 25, 1943; s. Abram Mendelevich and Nina Dmitrievna Khokhlov; m. Aina Jana M. Kalnciema, July 14, 1974 (div. Sept. 1989); m. Irisa Voldemara M. Levica Kaupman, Nov. 4, 1989; children: Mark, Maya. BFA, St. Petersburg State Conserv., Russia, 1961, MFA, 1968. Tchr. Leningrad (Russia) Cmty. Coll., 1965-68; soloist, accompanist Karelian Philharmonic, Petrozavodsk, Karelia, 1968-70, Lenconcert Philharmonic Dept., Leningrad, 1970-74, Latvian State Philharmonic, Riga, 1974-91; tchr. Latvian Music Acad., Riga, 1985-91; piano performer, tchr. Tampa, 1991—; mem. artistic bd. Latvian Philharmonic, Riga, 1986-90; music dir., bd. dirs. Russian Heritage, St. Petersburg, Fla., 1997—; choir condr. Latvian Cmty. Choir, St. Petersburg, 1991—; coach, accompanist singers winning numerous awards in vocal competitions, Greece, 1983, Latvia, 1975, 79, Lithuania, 1977, Italy, 1984, 85, Japan, 1990. Composer: Piano Ensembles (Latvian folk songs), 1981, Compositions for Kokle, Xilophono, Voice, 1974-91, Music Book for Kokle, 1982, (record, CD) Jewish IImpressions, Jewish Folk Songs, 1989, 95. Mem., organizer People's Front, Latvian Philharmonic Group, Riga, 1988-91. Recipient honor award for best accompaniment Jury of E. Darzins Vocal Competition, Riga, 1975, honor diplomas for best accompaniment Jury of USSR Vocal Competition, Vilnius, Lithuania, 1977, Latvian State award, 1977, Jury of A. Kalnins Vocal Competition, Riga, 1979, honorable mention Jury of Internat. Pinaut Soc. Competition, N.Y.C., 1996. Mem. Nat. Music Tchrs. Assn., Fla. State Music Tchrs. Assn., Tampa Music Tchrs. Assn., Russian Heritage. Democrat. Avocations: gardening, travel, basketball. Home and Office: 14941 Old Pointe Rd Tampa FL 33613-1618

KHOKHLOVA, LUDMILA PETROVNA, biologist, physiologist, biology educator; b. Kalinin, Russia, Dec. 10, 1938; d. Peter and Nadejda Nikolaevna (Matveitzeva) Masurov; m. Valeriy Nikolaevich Khokhlov; 1 child, Nikolay Valerievich. Cand.Biol.Scis., Kazan U., 1966, D Biol. Scis., 1986. Jr. scientist Kazan U., 1964-67, asst. prof., 1967-90, prof., 1990—, head plant physiology chair, 1991—. Contbr. articles to profl. jours. Named Meritorious Sci. Worker, Parliament of Tatarstan, 1995; Russian Acad. Scis. sci. grantee, 1977—; Ministry for Edn., Sci. Rsch. and Tech. grantee, Bonn, Germany, 1996-98, grantee Kazan, Tatastan Sci. Acad., 1998-2000. Mem. Russian Acad. Scis. (sci. coun.),Soc. Plant Physiologists, Sci. Coun. of Russian Ministry for Edn. Christian. Avocations: reading of belles-lettres, gardening. Office: Kazan State U, Kremlyovskaya 18, Kazan, Tatarstan Russia

KHOLSHEVNIKOV, KONSTANTIN VLADISLAVOVICH, astronomer; b. Leningrad, Russia, Jan. 19, 1939; s. Vladislav and Olga (Lohman) K.; m. Galina Novojenina, Mar. 26, 1960; two children. Grad., Leningrad U., 1962, PhD, 1965, DSc, 1972. From asst. to prof., head chair astronomy dept. St. Petersburg U., Russia, 1964—. Author: Asymptotical Methods of Celestial Mechanics, 1985; co-author: History of Astronomy in Russia and USSR, 1999. Minor planet 3504 named in honor of Kholshevnikov. Office: Math Faculty St PetersburgU, Bibliotechnaya pl 2, 198504 Saint Petersburg Russia

KHOO, ANDREW KIAN MING, plastic/reconstructive surgeon, researcher; b. Penang, Malaysia, Oct. 6, 1963; Immigrated to Singapore, 1970.; s. Boon Seng and Peggy Sook Koo (Wong) K.; m. Chuen T'ng Lee, Apr. 27, 1996. MB, BChir, Nat. U. Singapore, 1987, M of Medicine, 1992. Diplomate Royal Coll. Surgeons, Royal Coll. Physicians & Surgeons; reg. med. practitioner. Med. officer Singapore Gen. Hosp., 1989-92, registrar, 1992-96, sr. registrar, 1998; microsurgical fellow MD Anderson Cancer, Houston, 1996-97; craniofacial fellow Providence Hosp., Southfield, Mich., 1997—. Capt. Singapore Armed Forces, 1988-90. Fellow Royal Coll. Surgeons Edinburgh, Royal Coll. Physicians and Surgeons Glasgow; mem. Singapore Med. Assn., Cleft Palate Lip & Palate Assn. of Singapore, Assn. Burn Injuries of Singpore. Methodist. Avocations: photography, scuba diving, skiing, film, travel. Office: Singapore Gen Hosp Pl Surg, Outram Rd, Singapore 169608, Singapore

KHOO, BENJAMIN CHENG CHOON, physicist, educator; b. Singapore, Aug. 18, 1962; s. Paul Peng Kim Khoo and Theresa Chwee Neo Ong; m. Sock Huay Chua, May 14, 1995. BSc with hons., U. Otago, Dunedin, New Zealand, 1987, MSc, 1989. Rsch. fellow Nat. U. Singapore, 1990-94; lectr. Nanyang Poly., Singapore, 1994—. Contbr. articles to Australasian Physical and Engring. Scis. in Medicine, Jour. Biomed. Engring., Clin. Orthopaedics Related Rsch., Med. Engring. and Physics. Recipient Lee Found. award U. Otago, 1985, 86, 87, U. Otago postgrad. award, 1988, 89, Japan Soc. Promotion Sci. fellow Nat. U. Singapore, 1991; recipient Kenneth Clarke award, 1990. Mem. IEEE Engring. in Medicine and Biology Soc., Australian Coll. Phys. Scientists and Engrs. in Medicine, Biomed. Engring. Soc. (mem. com. 1995—), Inst. of Physics, Chartered Physicists, Inst. of Physics and Engring. in Medicine. Roman Catholic. Home: 24 Evergreen Gardens, Singapore 468895, Singapore Office: Nanyang Poly Sch Health Sci, 180 Ang Mo Kio Ave 8, Singapore 569830, Singapore

KHOO, BOO CHEONG, engineering educator; b. Singapore, Singapore, May 6, 1958; s. Chin Sian and Imp Tee (Tan) K.; m. Peck Ha Tan; children: Ivan, Sonia. BA with honors, U. Cambridge, Eng., 1980; M.Engring., Nat. U. Singapore, 1984; PhD, MIT, 1989. Sr. tutor Nat. U. Singapore, 1982-88, lectr., 1988-92, sr. lectr. dept. engring., 1992-98, dept. dir. Ctr. Computational Mechanics, 1995-98, assoc. prof., 1998—; dep. dir. Inst. High Performance Computing, Singapore, 1998-99; program chair High Performance Computation for Engineered Systems MIT Alliance, Singapore, 1998—; lectr. numerous confs. Contbr. over 50 articles to profl. jours. Mgr. Bethesade (Ang Mo Kio) Kindergarten, Singapore, 1991—; mem. Marine Emergency Response Com., Singapore, 1998—. Capt. Singapore Armed Forces, 1997—. Recipient royal Aero. prize Royal Soc. London, 1980; Singapore Govt. Pres.'s scholar, 1977, Overseas Merit scholar, 1977. Mem. Engring. Alumni Singapore, Soc. of Loss Prevention in the Chem. and Process Industries (exec. com., asst. hon. sec.). Office: Nat Univ Singapore, Kent Ridge/Dept Mech Eng, Singapore 119260, Singapore

KHOO, FRANCIS KAH SIANG, journalist, writer, lawyer; b. Singapore, Oct. 23, 1947; arrived in Eng., 1977; s. Anthony Teng Eng and Dorothy Swee Neo (Chew) K.; m. Swee Chai Ang, Jan. 29, 1977. LLB with honors, U. Singapore, 1970; MA, U. London, 1980. Pvt. practice law Singapore, 1971-77; sr. journalist South Mag., London, 1980-87; gen. sec. War on Want, London, 1988-89; Solicitor England, 1996—. Author: And Bungarraya Blooms All Day, 1978, The Rebel and the Revolutionary, 1994; camera design patentee. Vice-chair Med. Aid for Palestinians, U.K., 1984—. Mem. Nat. Union Journalists, Singapore Law Soc. (adv. and solicitor). Roman Catholic. Avocations: cartooning, photography, swimming, singing, song writing. Home: Bethnal Green, 285 Cambridge Heath Rd, London E2 OEL, England

KHOR, KHIAM AIK, materials scientist, educator; b. Alor Star, Malaysia, Nov. 30, 1961; s. Teik Hooi and Boon Khim (Seow) K.; m. Ying King Wong. BS, Monash U., 1984, PhD, 1989. Chartered engr., England. Exptl. scientist CSIRO, Melbourne, Australia, 1988-89; lectr. Nanyang Tech. U., Singapore, 1989-93, sr. lectr., 1994—. Contbr. articles to profl. jours.; author: Surface Modification Technologies X, 1997, Processing and Fabrication of Advanced Materials VI, 1997. Mem. Inst. Materials (hon. sec. 1991-95, pres. 1996-97). Office: Nanyang Tech U Sch Material, Nanyang Ave, Singapore 639798, Singapore

KHOR, LIAN HUAT, auditor; b. Batu Ferringhi, Malaysia, Feb. 23, 1973; p. Soon Lai Khor and Phaik Gaik Tan. B of Comm. in Acctg. and Fin., Deakin U., Australia, 1996; MBA, Heroit-Watt U., Malaysia, 1998, Honolulu U., Malaysia, 1998. Sr. Moore Stephens, Penang, Malaysia, 1996—. Mem. Golden Key Nat. Hon. Soc. Avocations: reading, badminton, jogging, tennis, swimming. Home: 418 Batu Ferringhi, Penang 11100, Malaysia Office: Moore Stephens, 85 Beach St, Penang 10300, Malaysia

KHORANA, HAR GOBIND, chemist, educator; b. Raipur, India, Jan. 9, 1922; s. Shri Ganpat Rai and Shrimati Krishna (Devi) K.; m. Esther Elizabeth Sibler, 1952; children: Julia, Emilie, Dave Roy. BS, Punjab U., 1943, MS, 1945; PhD, Liverpool (Eng.) U., 1948; DSc (hon.), U. Chgo., 1967, Simon Fraser U., Vancouver, Can., 1969, U. Liverpool, Eng., 1971, U. Punjab, India, 1971, U. Miami, 1994; hon. degree, U. Bergen, Norway, 1996; others. Head organic chemistry group B.C. Rsch. Coun., 1952-60; vis. prof. Rockefeller Inst., N.Y.C., 1958—; prof. co-dir. Inst. Enzyme Rsch. U. Wis., Madison, 1960-70, prof. dept. biochemistry, 1962-70, Conrad A. Elvehjem prof. life scis., 1964-70; Alfred P. Sloan prof. biology and chemistry MIT, Cambridge, 1970-97, A.P. Sloan prof. emeritus, sr. lectr., 1997—; vis. prof. Stanford U., 1964; mem. adv. bd. Biopolymers; researcher chem. methods for synthesis of nucleotides, coenzymes and nucleic acids, elucidation on the genetic code, lab. synthesis of genes, biol. membrane and light-transducing pigments. Author: Some Recent Developments in the Chemistry of Phosphate Esters of Biological Interests, 1961; mem. editorial bd.: Jour. Am. Chem. Soc, 1963—; contbr. numerous articles to profl. jours. Recipient Merck award Chem. Inst. Can., 1958, Gold medal Profl. Inst. Pub. Service Can., 1960, Dannie-Heinneman Preiz Göttingen, Germany, 1967, Remsen award Johns Hopkins U., 1968, Am. Chem. Soc. award for creative work in synthetic organic chemistry, 1968, Louisa Gross Horwitz prize, 1968, Lasker Found. award for basic med. research, 1968, Nobel prize in medicine, 1968; elected to Deutsche Akademie der Naturforscher Leopoldina HalleSaale, Germany, 1968; Overseas fellow Churchill Coll., Cambridge, Eng., 1967. Fellow AAAS, Chem. Inst. Can., Am. Acad. Arts and Scis.; mem. NAS, Am. Philos. Soc., Indian Acad. Scis. (fgn.). Pontifical Acad. Scis. (Rome), Royal Soc. (London), Royal Soc. Edinburgh, Japanese Biochem. Soc. (fgn. hon.), Pharm. Soc. Japan (hon.), others. Office: MIT 77 Massachusetts Ave Rm 68-680 Cambridge MA 02139-4307

KHORKINA, SVETLANA, olympic athlete; b. Belgorod, Russia, Jan. 19, 1979. Mem. gymnastics team Russia; winner gold in uneven bars World Championship, 1995-97, 99, winner all-around, 1997, winner bronze in floor exercise, 1999; winner gold in uneven bars European Championship, 1996, 98; winner gold in uneven bars Olympics, Atlanta, 1996, Sydney, Australia, 2000. Four skills in the Women's Code of Points are named after Khorkina. Office: Fedn Gymnastique de Russie, Lujnetskaya Nabereynaya 8, 119 871 Moscow Russia*

KHOSA, HAFIZ MUHAMMAD ALI, federal investigator; b. D.G. Khan, Punjab, Pakistan, Sept. 11, 1963; s. Khurshid Ahmed Khosa and Ameer Bibi; m. Hina Ali Khosa, July 29, 1996; children: Zahra Ali, Khuda Dad Khan. MPA, Punjab U., Lahore, 1987; MBA in Fin., Oklahoma City U., 1995; LLM, Karachi (Pakistan) U., 1997. Preventive officer Pakistan Customs, Preventive Collectorate, Karachi, 1988-92, sr. preventive officer, 1992-98; sr. auditor sales tax dept. CBR Govt. of Pakistan, Karachi, 1998; inspector Fed. Investigating Agy., Crime Cir., Multan, Punjab, 1998—; mem. Common Pool Trust, Custom House, Karachi, 1996-98. Sub-editor: (mag.) Manager, 1986; contbr. rsch. papers to profl. jours. Sec. lit. cir. Govt. Comprehensive Sch., D.G. Khan, 1978; sec. gen. Pakistan Customs Preventive Svc. Officers Assn., Custom House, Karachi, 1996-98; pres. Pakistani Student Assn., Oklahoma City U., 1994-95. Janbaz N.G., 1976. Named Lt. Gov. for State of Okla., Lt. Gov. Jack Mildren, 1995; recipient Roll of Honor, Govt. Coll., 1983, Silver medal Nat. Celebrations Coun., 1983. Mem. Pakistan Inst. Mgmt. (assoc.). Avocations: traveling, music, reading. Home: House #93/24 Kehkashan St 3, New Gulgasht Colony, Multan Punjab, Pakistan

KHOSLA, ASHOK, association executive; b. Lahore, India, Mar. 31, 1940; m. Rekha Bery; 1 child. BA with honors in Natural Sci., U. Cambridge,

U.K., 1962; PhD in Physics, Harvard U., 1971. Lectr. phys. and environ. scis. Harvard Coll., 1964-70; dir. environ. divsn. Dept. Sci. & Tech. Govt. India, India, 1972-76; dir. INFOTERRA UN Environment Programme, Nairobi, India, 1976-82; pres. Soc. for Devel. Alternatives, New Delhi, 1982—, Tech. and Action for Rural Advancement, New Delhi, 1983—, People First, 1984—; participant at more than 200 internat. confs., meetings and seminars on behalf of Govt. of India, UNEP, Devel. Alternatives; spl. advisor Brundtland Commn., 1984-87; cons. ICSU/SCOPE, UNEP, UNU, World Bank, Internat. Devel. Rsch. Ctr., MacArthur Found., Dept. Environment, India, Royal Swedish Acad. Scis., others. Contbr. numerous articles to profl. jours.; co-editor: The Survival Equation. Chmn. Ctr. for Our Common Future; mem. governing body IUCN, World Wide Fund for Nature; mem. com. Internat. Inst. Sustainable Devel., Winnipeg, Expo 2000, Hannover; chmn. NGO Global Forum Earth Summit; pres. Indian Environ. Congress, New Delhi; chmn. Forum on Industry and Environment, India; mem. governing bodies Nat. Inst. Design, Ahmedabad, Environ. Protection and Coord. Orgn., Bhopal, Stockholm Environment Inst.; mem. Nat. Environ. Adv. Com., Delhi; adv. com. Risk Capital and Tech. Corp.; mem. Factor of 10 Club, Wuppertal, Delhi Urban Arts Commn., New Delhi; pres. UN Sec. Gen. Task Force Restructuring Environ. Programmes of UN. Mem. Club Rome (governing body). Hindu. Avocations: music, literature, philosophy of science. Home: 22 Palam Marg, Vasant Vihar, New Delhi 110057, India Office: B-32 Tara Crescent, Qutab Instnl Area, New Delhi 110 016, India

KHOSLA, MANOVIRAJ, fashion designer; b. Calcutta, India, Feb. 25, 1967; s. Rajendra Kumar and Gieta (Kapoor) K.; m. Vedika Chawla, Jan. 23, 1992; 1 child, Ahaana. B of Comm., St. Xavier Coll., Calcutta, 1987; diploma in fashion design, Am. Coll., London, 1989. Fashion designer in pvt. practice Bangalore, India; proprietor Kingfisher Line, Bangalore, 1995—. Avocations: horse riding, parties, music, squash, swimming. Home: 206 Express Apt, 135 Richmond Rd, Bangalore 560025, India Office: 27 Dickenson Rd, Bangalore 560042, India

KHOSLA, VED MITTER, oral and maxillofacial surgeon, educator; b. Nairobi, Kenya, Jan. 13, 1926; s. Jagdish Rai and Tara V. K.; m. Santosh Ved Chabra, Oct. 11, 1952; children: Ashok M., Siddarth M. Student, U. Cambridge, 1945; L.D.S., Edinburgh Dental Hosp. and Sch., 1950, Coll. Dental Surgeons, Sask., Can., 1962. Prof. oral surgery, dir. postdoctoral studies in oral surgery Sch. Dentistry U. Calif., San Francisco, 1968—; chief oral surgery San Francisco Gen. Hosp.; lectr. oral surgery U. of Pacific, VA Hosp.; vis. cons. Fresno County Hosp. Dental Clinic.; Mem. planning com., exec. med. com. San Francisco Gen. Hosp. Contbr. articles to profl. jours. Examiner in photography and gardening Boy Scouts Am., 1971-73, Guatemala Clinic, 1972. Granted personal coat of arms by H.M. Queen Elizabeth II, 1959. Fellow Royal Coll. Surgeons (Edinburgh), Internat. Assn. Oral Surgeons, Internat. Coll. Applied Nutrition, Internat. Coll. Dentists, Royal Soc. Health, AAAS, Am. Coll. Dentists; mem. Brit. Assn. Oral Surgeons, Am. Soc. Oral Surgeons, Am. Dental Soc. Anesthesiology, Am. Acad. Dental Radiology, Omicron Kappa Upsilon. Club: Masons. Home: 1525 Lakeview Dr Hillsborough CA 94010-7330 Office: U Calif Sch Dentistry Oral Surgery Div 3D Parnassus Ave San Francisco CA 94117-4342

KHOTUNTSEV, YURY LEONTIEVITCH, education educator, academic administrator; b. Podolsk, Moscow, July 30, 1937; s. Leontiy Leontievitch and Eya Vjatcheslavovna (Petrova) K.; m. Ljudmila Petrovna Legtchilina, Apr. 26, 1937; 1 child, Andrey Yurievich. BS, Radioengring./Electronics Inst, Moscow, 1965; MS, Moscow State Pedag. U., 1973. Jr. rsch. worker Radioengring. and Electronics Inst., Moscow, 1960-65; sr. rsch. worker Moscow State Pedagog. Inst., 1965-68, asst. prof., 1968-74, head dept., 1974—, pres. faculty tech. and mgmt., 1993-95; pro-rector Moscow Retng. Pedag. Inst., Moscow, 1995-97; head ednl. field tech. experiment, ednl. field scis. experiment Vocat. Ctr. Khomovniky, Moscow, 1995-97; prof. Ctr. Tech., Moscow, 1995-97. Author: Semiconductor UHF Systems, 1978; co-author: Regenerative Semiconductor Parametric Amplifiers, 1965, Semiconductor Synchronized Oscillators and Short Distance Radars, 1982, Transistor and Varactor Systems, 1995, Electrotechnics, 1998, Foundations of Radioelectronics, 1998. Active Moscow Tribune polit. club, 1988-97. Recipient Medal for putting virgin lands to plough Supreme Soviet USSR, Vet. of Labour medal Supreme Soviet USSR, 1986, 850 Yr. of Moscow medal Pres. Russian Fedn., 1997, Ushkinogo medal Ministry Gen. Profl. Edn., 1997. Mem. Internat. Acad. Scis. High Sch. (academician), Moscow House of Scientists, N.Y. Acad. Scis. Buddhist. Avocations: lawn tennis, reading, mushroom gathering, Mozart, Oriental culture. Home: Ul Volgina dom 17 Kvart 125, 117485 Moscow Russia Office: ul Malaja Pirogovskaha, dom 1, Moscow 119435, Russia

KHOUW, BOEN TIE, retired biochemist; b. Tegal, Java, Indonesia, Sept. 4, 1934; came to Can., 1957; s. Bian Hin and Swan Nio (Liem) K.; m. Eugenia Yuen-Chi Yu, Sept. 29, 1967; children: Charlotte, Vivian. BSc, Mt. Allison U., 1960; MSc, U. Windsor, 1965, PhD, 1968. Technician, Fisheries Rsch. Bd., Ellerslie, P.E.I., 1959-62; rsch. scientist Can. Packers, Inc., Toronto, Ont., 1967-73, sr. scientist, 1973-80, tech. group mgr. pharms., 1980-87, sect. leader biochem. rsch., 1986-87; tech. mgr. Waitaki Internat. Biosciences, Toronto, 1987-92; tech. mgr. Intergen BioMfg. Corp., Toronto, 1992-96; ret., 1996; guest lectr. chem. engring. U. Toronto, 1980—. Contbr. articles to profl. jours.; patentee in field. Home: 52 Laurel Ave, Etobicoke, ON Canada M9B 4T2

KHOZEIMEH, ISSA, electrical engineer; b. Tehran, Iran, Dec. 25, 1939; came to U.S., 1959; s. Ismail and Zohreh (Alam) K.; m. Nahid Khozeimeh; children: Lili, Nini. BSEE, George Washington U., Washington, 1966; MSEE, 1973, D in Engring., 1984, DSc in Engring. Mgmt., 1993. Registered profl. engr. Jr. engr. Potomac Electric Power Co., Washington, 1967-68; substation engr., 1968-73, design standrads engr., 1973-79, sr. engr. substation design, 1979-80; dept. head, chief elec. engr. David Volkert and Assocs., Bethesda, Md., 1980-88; mgr. Util. Svcs. Metro. Washington Airports Auth. Dulles Internat. Airport, 1988—; prof. engring. and mgmt. U. Md., Balt., 1998—; prof. mgmt. U. Balt., 1999—; pres. Internat. Mktg. and Consulting Corp., Washington, 1980-82; v.p. Horizon Internat., Washington, 1982-88; pres. Forum Internat. Glen Echo, Md., 1988—; prof. U. Md., Balt., 1998—, U. Balt., 1999—. Author: An Automated Maintenance Management System for International Airports, 1993; contbr. articles to profl. jours. Recipient Sch. of Engring Svcs. award, 1976, Gen. Alumni Assn. Svc. award, 1971, George Washington U., 1976, Engr. Coun. Cert. of Appreciation, 1984, 85, Disting. Svc. award 1986, Disting. Alumni Svc. award George Washington U. Alumni Assn., 1998, Tech. Forum Leadership award, 1999, Outstanding Profl Efforts award Met. Washington Airport Authority, 2000. Mem. IEEE (sr.), NSPE, Instrument Soc. Am., Md. Soc. Profl. Engrs. (Disting. Sr. Engr. award 1997), Washington Soc. Engrs., pres. 1998-99. Republican. Moslem. Avocations: water skiing, snow skiing, hiking, reading, publishing, lecturing, travel. Home: PO Box 557 Glen Echo MD 20812-0557 Office: Metro Washington Airports Authority Dulles Internat Airport PO Box 17045 Washington DC 20041-7045

KHOZOUEI, HOMAYOUN, psychiatrist; b. Tehran, May 16, 1948; s. Ghodratollah and Tahereh (Roshan) K.; m. Mayreni Korkor, July 21, 1974; children: Golriz, Roshan, Anisa. MD, Istanbul U., Turkey, 1973; Bd. Eligible, Pahlavi U. Med. Sch., Shiraz, Iran, 1979. Med. diplomate. Registrar in psychiatry Pahlavi U., Shiraz, 1976-79, Cen. Hosp., Warwick, Eng., 1982-85; sr. registrar North Wales Hosps./U. Wales, Bangor, 1986-87; cons. psychiatrist, dir. psychiatry, dir. area mental health svcs. South Canterbury Health Svcs., Timara, New Zealand, 1987-96; cons. psychiatrist We. Bay Health, Tauranga, New Zealand, 1996-97; dir. psychiatry We. Bay Health, Tauranga, 1998—; with dept. psychiatry Geelong Hosp., Victoria, Australia, 1998—. Served with Iranian Army, 1974-76. Fellow Royal Australia and New Zealand Coll. of Psychiatrists; mem. Royal Coll. of Psychiatrists. Mem. Bahá'i Faith. Avocations: music, travel, gardening, philosophy, violin. Office: Geelong Hosp, Dept Psychiatry, Geelong 3220, Australia

KHRENOVA, NATALIA FJODOROVNA, English educator; b. Voronezh, Russia, Apr. 16, 1948; d. Fjodor Mikajlovich and Tatjana Illarionovna (Zadorozhnjaja) K. MA, Pedagogical U., Voronezh, 1971, degree, 1981; PhD, Moscow Pedagogical U., 1993; postgrad., NYU, 1995. Interpreter Voronezh State U., 1971-73; asst. prof. Pedagogical U., Voronezh, 1973-79, 81-89, assoc. prof., 1993—; cons. Comml. Coll., Voronezh, 1989-90, Bus. Sch., Voronezh, 1993-94, Regional Tchrs.' Tng. Inst., Voronezh, 1993—, Voronezh br. Moscow Humanitarian Econ. Inst., 1995—. Author: Semantics of Nominative Language Phenomena, 1985, Foreign Languages in Teaching University Students, 1995, The English Language at School and University, 1996, Communication Culture and Its Formation, 1999. Mem. Voronezh Assn. English Lang. Tchrs. Avocations: travel, knitting, design, reading faces, psychology.

KHRIACHTCHEV, LEONID YURIEVICH, physics researcher, chemistry researcher; b. Severomorsk, Russia, Jan. 21, 1958; arrived in Finland, 1993; s. Yuri Kapitonovich and Zoya Yulievna (Peshkova) K.; m. Anna Vadimovna Sokolova, Dec. 3, 1983; 1 child, Vera Leonidovna. MSc, St. Petersburg U., 1981, PhD, 1986. Rsch. scientist St. Petersburg U., 1981-93, U. Helsinki, Finland, 1994—; head program All-Russian Ecology Ctr., Moscow, 1988-92; asst. dir. Erfa Ltd., St. Petersburg, 1991-93; docent U. Helsinki, 1999. Contbr. numerous articles to profl. jours.; inventor in field. Office: U Helsinki Phys Chem Lab, PO Box 55, 00014 Helsinki Finland

KHUENL-BRADY, KARIN SIGRID, anesthesiologist, researcher; b. Vienna, Austria, Mar. 20, 1961; d. Hans Heinz and Dorothea (Mantler) K.-B.; 1 child, Arline. MD, U. Vienna, 1986; PhD, U. Innsbruck, Austria, 1994. Univ. asst. U. Innsbruck, 1987-93, asst. prof., 1994—, resident, 1987-92, intern, 1992-93; pvt. practice, 1992—. Avocations: basketball, music. Office: Clinic for Anesthesia, Anichstrasse 35, 6020 Innsbruck Austria

KHUGAEVA, VALENTINA KARGOEVNA, pathophysiologist, researcher; b. Reutovo, USSR, Jan. 25, 1947; d. Kargo Alexeevich and Tamara Agubeevna (Dzutseva) K.; m. Valery Nikolaevich Ardasenov, June 16, 1941 (div. 1976); 1 child, Alan Valerevich Ardasenov. B of Med. Sci., Acad. Med. Scis., Moscow, 1993, DMS, 1994. Lic. physician; cert. pathophysiologist. Jr. rschr. Inst. Normal and Pathol. Physiology, Acad. Med. Scis., Moscow, 1974-78, All-Union Cardiol. Sci. Ctr., Acad. Med. Scis., Moscow, 1978-81; sr. rsch. worker Inst. Gen. Pathology and Pathophysiology, Acad. Med. Scis., Moscow, 1981-92, leading sci. worker, 1992—; leader sci. group Inst. Gen. Pathology, Acad. Med. Scis., Moscow, 1981—, leader med. svc. of civil def., 1981-91; cons. expert Fed. Reestr. Experts in Sci.-Tech. Sphere, Moscow, 1996—; lectr. Moscow State Pedagog. U. of V.I. Lenin, 1985—. Inventor in field; contbr. articles to profl. jours. Dep. pres. Soc. of Knowledge, Moscow, 1983-86. Decorated Excellent Pupil Civil Def. of USSR, 1982; grantee State Sci. Grant, 1997-2000. Mem. Internat. Soc. Pathophysiology (Sign award 1991), Assn. Reologists, Am. Acad. Scis., Nat. Geographic Soc. (invited). Avocations: chess, philately, numismatics, volleyball, music. Home: 6 Parkovaya St 13-23, 105043 Moscow Russia Office: Inst Gen Pathol/Pathophys, Baltiyskaya str 8, 125315 Moscow Russia

KHULIL, MOHAMED MAGDY, chemist, educator, researcher; b. Beni-Suef, Egypt, Nov. 23, 1952; s. Khalil Mahmoud Khalil; children: Mona, Ahmed. MSc, U. Assiut, Egypt, 1978; PhD, Poly. Inst., Bucharest, Romania, 1984. Demonstrator chemistry dept. U. Assiut, 1975-78, asst. lectr., 1978-85, lectr., 1985-86; lectr. U. Beni-Suef, 1986-94, asst. prof., 1994-2000. Contbr. articles to profl. jours. Home: El-Gomhoria St. No. 5, Beni-Suef Egypt Office: U Beni-Suef, Faculty Sci, Beni-Suef Egypt

KHULLAR, KRISHAN, publisher; b. Lahore, Pakistan, Oct. 9, 1922; arrived in India, 1947; s. Karam Chand and Mela Devi Khullar; m. Prakash Wati Laroia, Nov. 27, 1946; children: Pramod Vijay, Harsha, Vinod Vijay. BA, Hindu Coll., Delhi, India, 1946. Proprietor Mfr., Sialkot, 1942-47; with Cen. Govt., New Delhi, 1948-74; proprietor in publishing/editorial Samkaleen Prakashan, New Delhi, 1974—. Author books; editor: Art and Poetry Today; translator poetry and lit. (Gold medals 1978, 82). Avocations: international art, poetry, religion, Indology. Home and Office: 2762 Rajguru Marg, 110055 New Delhi India

KHULLAR, SHELLEY GODTFREDSEN, oral surgeon, researcher; b. London, Jan. 21, 1963; arrived in Norway, 1993; d. Raj Paul and Meena Kumari Khullar; m. Tom Godtfredsen, Aug. 21, 1998. B in Dental Surgery, U. Manchester, Eng., 1986; PhD, U. Oslo, 1997. House officer Manchester Dental Hosp., 1987; sr. house officer, house officer Southampton (Eng.) Gen. Hosp., 1988; sr. house officer Eastman Dental Hosp./Univ. Coll., London, 1989; registrar Aberdeen (Scotland) Royal Infirmary, 1989-92; rsch. assoc. U. Oslo, 1993-97; dir. oral surgery Colosseum Klinikken A/S, Oslo, 1997—. Contbr. articles to profl. jours. Imperial Chems. Industry Pharm. Elective scholar Prince of Wales Hosp., Hong Kong, 1985, Wisdom Nomination scholar, 1987. Fellow Royal Coll. Surgeons Eng.; mem. Brit. Assn. Oral and Maxillofacial Surgeons, Norwegian Oral Surgery Assn. Hindu. Avocations: skiing, swimming, reading, French language. Home: Brygge Gate 16, 0250 Oslo Norway Office: Colosseum Klinikken, Sørkedals Veien 10C, 0369 Oslo Norway

KHURANA, ASHOK KUMAR, ophthalmologist, educator; b. Charkhi Dadri, Haryana, India, Dec. 28, 1953; s. Sat Pal and Krishan Kanta (Madan) K.; m. Indu Bala Bharti, Dec. 8, 1979; children: Aruj, Arushi. MB, BS, Kurukshetra U., India, 1976; MS in Ophthalmology, M.D. U., Rohtak, India, 1981; cert. in tropical ophthalmology, Inst. Ophthalmology, London, 1994. Eye specialist Civil Hosp., Rohtak, India, 1981-83; sr. resident Govt. Med. Coll., Rohtak, 1983-84, lectr. ophthalmology, 1984-89, reader ophthalmology, 1989-94; assoc. prof. ophthalmology Postgrad. Inst. Med. Scis., Rohtak, 1994—, head unit II dept. ophthalmology, 1995-96; cons. ophthalmologist Govt. Med. Coll. Hosp. Rohtak, 1984—; WHO fellow Moorfields Eye Hosp. Inst. Ophthalmology, London, 1994. Author: Ophthalmology, 1996, Practical Ophthalmology, 1996, Quick Revision and MCQs in Ophthalmology, 1997, Ophthalmology: Viva Questions and Answers, 1997, Anatomy and Physiology of the Eye, 1998, Theory and Practice of Squint and Orthoptics, 1999; editor North Zone Jour. of Ophthalmology Vol. IV-VII, 1994-96, Haryana Jour. Ophthalmology, 1998—; contbr. chpts. to books. Mem. North Zone Ophthalmol. Soc. (editor jour. 1993-96, joint sec. 1997-99), Haryana Ophthalmol. Soc. (joint sec. 1984-93, editor jour. 1997—), All India Ophthalmology Soc., Haryana Ophthalmic Acads. (acad. sec. 1992-95, v.p. 1999). Avocations: watching English movies, playing chess, playing table tennis, playing cards, listening to old classical songs. Home: 34/9J Medical Enclave, Rohtak 124001, India

KHURANA, ATUL, physician; b. Lucknow, India, Mar. 16, 1966; arrived in Russia, 1985; s. Krishanlal and Kiron (Mehrotra) K.; m. Madhavi Chitnis, Feb. 3, 1991; 1 child, Arun. EdB in Russian Lang., Minsk State Med. Inst., Belarus, 1992, MD, 1992. Asst. mgr. Dina Handels, Minsk, 1992-93; mgr. Dina Handels, Moscow, 1993-94; dir. Star Overseas Pte. Ltd., Moscow, 1994—. V.p. Fgn. Students Union, Minsk, 1990-92. Avocations: music, books, computers, travel. Home: Leninsky PR 148-68, 117 571 Moscow Russia Office: Star Overseas Pte Ltd, PR Vernadskogo 41/439, Moscow Russia

KHURANA, SATYENDRA MOHAN PAUL, food scientist, editor, researcher; b. Jalna, India, Dec. 31, 1944; s. Narsingh Dass and Veeranwali (V. Khetarpal) K.; m. Sumi (Suman) Batra, Apr. 20, 1974; 3 children. BSc, U. Gorakhphur, 1963, MSc in Plant Pathology-Botany, 1965, PhD, 1968. Rsch. pool officer Ctrl. Potato Rsch. Inst., Shimla, 1973-74, jr. aphidologist, 1974-76, virus pathologist, 1976-82, prin. scientist, 1982-88, 93-94, head dept., 1988-93; project coord. All India Coord. Potato Improvement Project, Shimla, 1994—; cons. Internat. Potato Ctr.-Helvatas, Thimpu, 1992; postdoctoral fellow Kyushu U., Fukuoka, Japan, 1970-72; vis. scientist U. Minn., 1987-88; convenor Global Conf. on Potato, New Delhi, 1999. Editor: Potato: Present & Future, 1994, Pathological Problems of Economic Plants and Management, 1996, Comprehensive Potato Biotechnology, 1998; contbr. articles to profl. jours. Recipient Hon. award Aphidological Soc., 1994, Best Exhibit award Amateur Artist's Assn., 1969, Silver Plaque Orissa U. of Agr. and Tech., 1997, Prof. R.K. Hegde Meml. award lecture, 1999. Fellow Indian Potato Assn. (disting. fellow, editor-in-chief 1985-86, 91-95, 98—, pres. 1996-97, Best Paper's award 1998), Indian Phytopathol. Soc. (pres. north zone 1990, editor 1991-93, Mundkur Meml. award 1992, Best Paper's award 1997-98); mem. Indian Virology Soc. (sect. editor 1993-95, editor-in-chief 1996—). Hindi. Avocations: photography, painting. Home: Type V/Set 3 Green Park, Shimla 171002, India Office: All India Coord Potato Improvement Project, CPRI, Shimla 171001, India

KHUSH, GURDEV SINGH, geneticist; b. Rurkee, Punjab, India, Aug. 22, 1935; arrived in Philippines, 1967; s. Kartar Singh and Pritam Kaur (Dosanjh) Kooner; m. Harwant Kaur Grewal, Dec. 31, 1961; children: Ranjiv, Manjeev, Sonia, Kiran. BS in Agr., Punjab U., India, 1955; PhD, U. Calif., Davis, 1960; DSc (hon.), Punjab Agr. U., 1987, Tamil Nrdu Agr. U., 1995, CS Azad U. Agr. & Tech., 1995, G.B. Pant U. Agr. and Tech., 1996, De Montfort U., 1998, Assam Agrl. U., 2000, U. Cambridge, 2000. Rsch. asst. U. Calif., Davis, 1957-60, asst. geneticist, 1960-67; plant breeder Internat. Rice Rsch. Inst., Manila, 1967-72, plant breeder, head dept. plant breeding, 1972-85, prin. plant breeder, head dept. plant breeding, 1986—; cons. rice breeding programs Burma, Bangladesh, China, India, Indonesia, Iraq, Egypt, Sri Lanka, Bhutan, Cambodia, Vietnam, Korea, Australia, Laos. Author: Cytogenetics of Aneuploids, 1973, Host Plant Resistance to Insects, 1995; editor: Rice Genetics Newsletter; contbr. articles to books and profl. jours. Recipient Borlaug award Coromandal Fertilizeers Ltd., Delhi, India, 1977, Japan prize Sci. and Tech. Found., Tokyo, 1987, Internat. Agronomy award Am. Soc. Agronomy, 1989, World Food prize World Food Prize Found., Des Moines, Iowa, 1996, Rank Prize, Rank Prize Found., London, 1998, Wolf prize Agrl., Wolf Found., 2000. Fellow Rice Genetics Coop. (elected, sec. 1985—); mem. Genetic Soc. Am., Am. Soc. Agronomy (fellows award 1987), Indian Soc. Genetics and Plant Breeding (fellows award 1988), Royal Soc. London, Crop Sci. Soc. Philippines (fellows award 1986), Indian Nat. Sci. Acad., U.S. NAS (fgn. assoc.), Third World Acad. Scis. Avocations: reading world history, jogging. Office: care Internat Rice Rsch Inst, MCPO Box 3127, Makati 1271, The Philippines

KHUSHU-LAHIRI, RAJYASHREE, English educator, researcher; b. Srinagar, J&K, India, June 23, 1959; d. Chunilal and Susheela (Wali) K.; m. Somdeb Lahiri, Oct. 12, 1987; children: Abhik, Pratik. BA with honors, H. P. Univ., Shimla, India, 1979; MA in English, Delhi U., 1981; PhD, Indian Inst. Tech., Kanpur, India, 1988. Lectr. M. G. Sci. Inst. Gujarat U., Ahmedabad, India, 1991-92; lectr. St. Xavier's Coll., Ahmedabad, India, 1992—. Contbr. articles to profl. jours.; author American Women Novelists. Postdoctoral fellow Univ. Grants Commn., 1991; recipient Fulbright fellowship. Mem. MLA, Am. Studies Assn., Indian Assn. Am. Studies (life), Forum Contemporary Theory (life), Rotary (dir. 1998-99). Hindu. Avocations: reading, writing, music. Home: 306 IIM Campus, Vastrapur, Ahmedabad 380 015, India Office: Saint Xaviers Coll, Navrangputa, Gujarat 380 009, India

KHUWEITER, ABDUL AZIZ ABDALLAH AL, Saudi Arabian government official; b. Onaizah, 1927; s. Abdullah and Moody K.; m. Fatima Khuwaytir, 1963; 4 children. Vice rector King Saud U., gen. auditor; former min. health, min. edn., min. edn. Govt. of Saudi Arabia, 1987-95, min. state, 1995—. Author: Fi Turuq Al-Bahth, Al-Maik Al-Zahir Bybars, Ibn Bishr, Min Hatab Allayl, Ayy Bunayy, Gira, Itlala Ala Al-Turath; editor: Fi Turuk al Bahth, Tarikh Shafi Ibn Ali, Al-Malik al-Zahir, Min Hatab al-Layl, Ayy-Bunayy, Qiraah Fi Diwan al Sha'ir Muh, Al-Rawd Al-Zahir, Al-Manaqib Al-Sariyyah, Tareekh Al-Mangloor. Recipient King Abdulaziz Order of Merit (second class), Rep. Order, Sudan (first class). Avocation, reading. Office: Royal Ct, Riyadh 11121, Saudi Arabia*

KHWAJA, ISKANKER SULTAN, apparel machinery executive; b. Peshawar, Pakistan, Oct. 20, 1958; s. Yousaf and Jan (Begum) K.; m. Kanwal Raana, Nov. 12, 1987; children: Tariq, Aaqib, Mustafa. BA, U. Karachi, 1978. Dir. Khwaja Usaf Corp., Pakistan, 1974-80; mng. dir. Al Zarooni & Al Khwaja Co. Ltd., Al Borj Garment Machinery Co. Ltd., United Arab Emirates, 1980—. Mem. Pakistan Bus. Coun., Marbella Club, Young Pres. Orgn. Avocations: cars, traveling, philanthropy. Office: Al Borj Garment Machinery Co Ltd, PO Box 4182, Sharjah United Arab Emirates

KIA, SEYED JALAL, computer company executive; b. Semnan, Iran, Sept. 11, 1958; s. Agha Hassan abd Akhtar K.; m. Marzieh Kazemi; children: Elahe, Layla. BSEE, Sharif U. Tech., Tehran, Iran, 1984, MS, 1987; PhD, U. Auckland, New Zealand, 1993. Design engr. Sharif U., Tehran, Iran, 1982-85; rsch. asst. IRan Telecomm. Rsch. Ctr., Tehran, Iran, 1985-88; rschr. U. Auckland, New Zealand, 1989-93, lectr., 1993; cons. rsch. & devel. Infomace Internat., Auckland, New Zealand, 1994-96; dir., cons. Intelligent Decision Support Solutions, Auckland, New Zealand, 1996—; leader info. mgmt. team Fletcher Challenge Forests, Auckland, New Zealand, 1997—; software engr. Prism Software, Auckland, 1998—; cons. Dairy U., Australia, 1995-96; cons. New Zealand Telecom, Wellington, 1992-93; co-chmn. World Automation Congress, 2000. Inventor in field; developer of software. Scholar Ministry Edn., Iran, 1988, 91. Mem. IEEE, Inst. Profl. Engrs. New Zealand, New Zealand Neural NEtwork Interest Group. Islam. Avocations: reading, classical music, home video. Home and office: 62A Vale Rd, Saint Heliers New Zealand

KIAM-SIEW, MICHAEL YAP, technology entrepreneur; b. Singapore, Feb. 23, 1961; s. Chin Huat and Ngak Ching (Ong) Y.; m. Big-Yee Wong, July 26, 1991; children: Timothee, Nicole. Degree in econs. and computer sci., U. Md., 1985, MS, 1987; postgrad., Stanford U., 1998. Mem. staff software engring. lab. Nat. Computer Bd., Singapore, 1987-90, mgr. rsch. planning, 1990, asst. dir. bus. devel. and planning, 1991, dir. planning and infrastructure, 1992-95, asst. chief exec. info. and infrastructure, 1995-97, dep. chief exec. infrastructure and sys., 1997-99, chief exec., 1999—; CEO Commerce Exch. PTE Ltd., Singapore, 1999—; CEO, Commerce Exch. Pte; chmn. Coolconnect, Spacedisk; venture ptnr. Venture TDF Pte. Editor-in-chief Internat. Jour. IT, 1994, 98, 99; contbr. chpts. to books. Founder, chair Singapore Student Assn., 1985-97; mem. Nat. Internet Adv. Panel, Singapore, 1997; insp. Singapore Police Force, 1980-82. Overseas undergrad. scholar Nat. Computer Bd., 1982; recipient Silver award Nat. Day Pub. Adminstrn., 1998; named one of 50 Stars of Asia, Bus. Week, 1999, Top 100 Future Global Leaders, World Econ. Forum. Mem. Assn. Muslim Profls. (panel of experts 1999), Singapore Computer Assn. (sr.), Nat. Info. Infrastructure Std. Com. (chair 1997-99), Working Gorup i=on ASEAN Info. Infrastructure (chair 1999), Inst. Sys. Sci. (chmn.), Singapore Sci. Coun. Avocations: architecture, tennis, golf.

KIANI, REZA, endocrinology and internal medicine educator; b. Iran, Feb. 23, 1939; came to U.S., 1969; s. Farjollah and Salamah Kiani; m. Mahshid Zameni, June 24, 1981; children: Mandy, Mary, Cyrus, Soroosh. D in Medicine, Shiraz Univ., Shiraz, Iran, 1966; F.A.C.P., Am. Coll. Physicians, 1981. Instr. in medicine Univ. Ill., Chgo., 1972-73, assoc. in medicine, 1973-74, asst. prof. medicine, 1974-79, assoc. prof. medicine, 1979-91, prof. medicine, 1991—; dir. medicine clinic, Univ. Ill., Chgo., 1983-88; cons. ophthalmology, urology, orthopeadics, surgery, 1989—, dir. diagnostic clinic, 1990—, dir. diabetes program, 1992—. Recipient Physician's Recognition award AMA, 1971, 73-76, Golden Apple award Univ. Ill., 1982-85, 90-93, C.G. Pilz award Univ. Ill., 1979. Fellow Am. Coll. Physicians; mem. Am. Fedn. Clinical Rsch., Am. Assn. Univ. Profs., Am. Soc. Internal Medicine, Am. Diabetes Assn. Avocations: gardening, fishing, boating, horseback-riding, reading. Home: 730 Bentwood Trce Alpharetta GA 30005-4144 Office: Univ Ill Dept Medicine 840 S Wood St Rm E123 Msa Chicago IL 60612-7317

KIATKAMJORNWONG, SUDA, engineering educator, polymer engineer, consultant; b. Bangkok, June 18, 1947; d. Lee Hong Siang and Lee Ngulang. BS in Chemistry, Chulalongkorn U., Bangkok, 1971, MS in Phys. Chemistry, 1973; Diploma in Photographic Sci., ETH, Zurich, 1977; PhD in Polymer Sci. and Engring., Lehigh U., 1983; Postdoct. Degree in Radiation Chemistry, U. New South Wales, Australia; postdoct., Osaka U., Chiba U., Japan, Korea Inst. Advanced Sci. and Tech, Korea, 1989. Lectr. Chulalongkorn U., Bangkok, 1971-77, asst. prof., 1978-89, assoc. prof., 1990-99, prof., 1999—, co-dir. Petroleum Coll., founder, 1987-90, bd. mem. Faculty of Sci., 1990—, bd. mem. faculty Grad. Sch., 1997—; cons. Thai Screen Printing Assn., Thai Plastic Assn., 1984—. Co-editor: Jour. Scientific Rsch. Chulalongkorn U., 1988-94; contbr. articles to profl. jours. Grantee Nat. Metal and Materials Tech. Ctr., 1991-93, 94-96, Govt. of Japan, 1997—, Internat. Atomic Energy Agy., 1998—, numerous others. Mem. Thailand Sci. Assn., Tech. Assn. of Pulp and Paper Industry I (assoc.), Jour. of Oil Chemist Color Assn., Radtech Asia (founder). Democrat. Buddhist. Avocations: jogging, cooking, gardening. Office: Chulalongkorn U Faculty Sci, Dept Imaging and Printing Tech, 10330 Bangkok Thailand

KIBA, TETSUJI, anesthesiologist, hospital administrator; b. Ohzu-shi, Ehime-ken, Japan, Aug. 26, 1933; s. Yoshikazu and Fumi (Okamoto) K.; m. Sachiko Takahashi, May 5, 1965; children: Shuh, Koh. MD, Tottori U., Yonago, Japan, 1958. Diplomate Am. Bd. Anesthesiology, Japanese Bd. Anesthesiology. Resident in anesthesiology George Washington U., Washington, 1961-63; rsch. fellow Univ. Hosps. Cleve., 1963-64; mem. staff Kyoto (Japan) U. Hosp., 1964-67; resident in ob-gyn. Kitano Hosp., Osaka, Japan, 1967-69; dir. Kiba Ob-Gyn. Hosp., Matsuyama-shi, Japan, 1969-82, Kiba Pain Clinic Hosp., Matsuyama-shi, 1982—. Author: Pain Clinic for Practitioners, 1992. Mem. Japan Soc. Anesthesiology, Japan Soc. Pain Clinicians (diplomate). Avocation: local modern history. Home and Office: 4-18 Sugacho, Matsuyama-shi, Ehime-ken 791-8052, Japan

KIBARDIN, ALEXANDER MIKHAILOVICH, chemist; b. Village Krasniy, Russia, May 23, 1948; s. Michail Andreevich and Yevgeniya Vasil'yena (Nehorochkova) K.; m. L'udmila Konstantinovna Ivanova, July 30, 1971; children: Natal'ya, Michail. Higher Edn., Kazan (Russia) State U., 1971; Kand. of Sci., Inst. Organic & Phys. Chemisty, 1994, DSc, 1994. Sr. lab. asst. Inst. Organic and Phys. Chemistry, Kazan, Russia, 1971-74, jr. rsch. worker, 1974-82, sr. rsch. worker, 1982-94, leading rsch. worker, 1994-96, head rsch. lab., 1996—; consulter LTD "FORSAT", Kazan, Tatarstan. Contbr. over 150 articles to profl. sci. jours. Dep. of dist. advice, Kazan, 1987-90. Capt. of chem. array, 1996—. Recipient Individual grant ISF, 1993, Long-Term Rsch. Program grant, 1994. Mem. Assn. Organophosphorus Chemistry. Avocations: electronic machines, chess. Home: Prospect Pobedy, apt 237 house 56, 420110 Kazan Russia Office: AE Arbuzov Inst, Arbuzov str 8, 420083 Kazan Russia

KIBBE, JAMES WILLIAM, real estate broker; b. Bound Brook, N.J., Oct. 5, 1926; s. Orlando A. and Anna Rose (Tomb) K.; m. Bettie Brooks Dailey, June 11, 1949; children: James William Jr., Linda Jean. BS, U. Md., 1951. Salesman real estate Eig & Mc Keever, Silver Spring, Md., 1955-57, Weaver Bros., Inc., Chevy Chase, Md., 1957-70; asst. v.p. sales, leasing dept. Weaver Bros., Inc., Chevy Chase, 1970-72, mgr. sales, 1972-89, v.p., 1973-82, sr. v.p., 1983-89; sr. v.p., dir. sales The Michael Co., Lanham, Md., 1989-95; sr. v.p., dir. indsl. Barrueta, Washington, 1995-96; sr. v.p. Carey Winston/Barrueta, Bethesda, Md., 1996-98, Transwestern Carey Winston, Bethesda, 1998—; lectr. in field; chmn. Brokers and Salesmen's council, 1968-69. With USNR, 1944-46. Mem. Soc. Indsl. Office Realtors (pres. Md. and Washington chpt. 1985-86, nat. bd. dirs. 1988-90), Nat. Assn. Indsl. Office Pks. (bd. dirs. 1987), Nat. Inst. Real Estate Brokers (state chmn. 1968-70), Nat. Assn. Realtors, New Am. Network (adv. bd. dirs. 1986-99, chmn. adv. bd. 1991-93), Md. Assn. Realtors, Washington Bd. Trade, Washington Builders Assn., D.C. Assn. Realtors, Montgomery County Bd. Realtors, Lions (started health fairs chmn. 25 yrs.). Republican. Methodist. Home: 1000 Ashland Dr Ashton MD 20861-9718 Office: Transwestern Carey Winston Ste 400A 7600 Rockledge Dr Bethesda MD 20817

KIBRIK, GRIGORY EUGENYEVICH, physicist; b. Kirovsk, Murmansk, Russia, June 12, 1947; s. Eugeny Grigoryevich and Elizaveta Alexandrovna (Lazareva) K.; m. Lyudmila Ivanovna Pugachyova, Sept. 5, 1969; 1 child, Anna. MSc, Perm U., Russia, 1970, PhD, 1990. Engr. Inst. Control Systems, Perm, 1970-72; sr. engr. Inst. Control Systems, Perm, 1972-73; jr. rschr. Perm U., 1973-74, sr. rsch. assoc., 1974-77, head lab., 1977-95; dir. gen. Ural Centre Info. Techs., Perm, 1995—; sr. rschr. Russian Cert. Com., Moscow, 1992. Contbr. articles to profl. jours. Grantee Russian State Com. High Edn., 1992, 94, Russian Fund Fundamental Investigation, 1995. Mem. N.Y. Acad. Scis. Home: Pushkina St 66 Apt 50, 614000 Perm Russia Office: Perm Univ, Bukireva St 15, 614 000 Perm Russia

KICE, JOHN EDWARD, engineering executive; b. Wichita, Kans., Sept. 11, 1949; s. Jack Wilbur and Anna Ruth (Jones) K.; m. Susan Pappas; children: Adam Wesley, Jason Mathew. BSBA and BS in Flour Milling Sci., Kans. State U., 1972; BS in Engring., Wichita State U., 1980; tech. diploma, Glasgow Caladonian U., 2000. Registered profl. engr., Kans. Design engr. Kice Industries, Wichita, 1973-84, v.p. engring., 1984—; lectr. Wichita State U., 1980-86. Recipient Disting. Svc. award Assn. Operative Millers, 1988, 90, 92, 94, 96. Mem. Soc. Mfg. Engrs. Republican. Presbyterian. Achievements include patents for Positive Displacement Air Pump, Reciprocating Airlock Valve, Rotary Mixing Damper, Blade Type Mixing Damper, Conveying Air Velocity Control, Pneumatic Conveying Injector. Office: Kice Industries Inc 5500 Mill Heights Dr Wichita KS 67219-2658

KICKISH, MARGARET ELIZABETH, elementary education educator; b. Atlantic City, N.J., Nov. 30, 1949; d. James Bernard and Margaret Elizabeth (Egan) Parlett; m. Robert Anthony Kickish, June 30, 1973; children: Eileen, Kathleen, Robert Jr. BS, Franciscan U., 1971; MEd, Coll. N.J., 1977. Cert. elem. educator, learning disabilities tchr. cons. Tchr. Our Lady Star of the Sea Sch., Atlantic City, N.J., 1971-75, Weymouth Twp. Elem. Sch., Dorothy, N.J., 1975-89; curriculum coord. Port Republic (N.J.) Sch., 1990-91; tchr. Brigantine (N.J.) Bd. Edn., 1991-94, supr. curriculum and instrn., 1995—; cognetics coach St. Joseph Sch., Somers Point, N.J., 1989—. Treas. PTA, Somers Point, 1987-89, pres., 1989-90; asst. coach Somers Point Softball Assn., 1991—; mem. St. Joseph Ch. Choir, Somers Point, 1985—. Mem. AAUW, NEA, ASCD, N.J. Edn. Assn. (treas. 1977-86), Prins. and Suprs. Assn., Coun. Exceptional Children, Assn. Learning Cons., Seashore Mother of Twins Club (pres. 1994-96), South Jersey Irish Cultural Soc., Kappa Delta Pi, Delta Zeta, Phi Delta Kappa. Democrat. Roman Catholic. Avocations: swimming, biking, reading, travel, crafts. Home: 526 9th St Somers Point NJ 08244-1458 Office: Brigantine Bd of Edn 301 E Evans Blvd Brigantine NJ 08203-3424

KICZKA, WITOLD, medical researcher, educator; b. Katowice, Poland, Apr. 21, 1924; s. Tomasz and Maria (Sznober) K.; m. Malgorzata Kulesza. MD, Univ. Sch. Medicine, Katowice, 1952, PhD, 1961. Assoc. prof. dept. infectious diseases Univ. Sch. Medicine, Katowice/Bytom, Poland, 1952-71; chmn. dept. infectious disease Univ. Sch. Medicine, Poznan, Poland, 1971-88; dir. Inst. Microbiology and Infectious Diseases Univ. Sch. Medicine, Poznan, 1980-85; sr. sci. advisor Nika Health Products, Inc., Lawrenceville, Princeton, N.J., 1989—; mem. Nat. Com. for Hygiene, Epidemiology and Infectious Diseases, 1975-88. Mem. editl. bd.: Internat. Jour. Thymology; contbr. rsch. to profl. jours. Grantee Claude Bernard Clinic for Infectious Diseases, 1962. Mem. AAAS, Am. Soc. Microbiology, Internat. Assn. for Thymus Rsch. (bd. dirs. 1983-88), Polish Assn. Epidemiologists and Drs. Specializing in Infectious Diseases (v.p. 1975-78), N.Y. Acad. Sci. Avocations: ethnography, archaeology, history. Office: Klin Chorob Zakaznych, Ul Wincentego 1, 61003 Poznan Poland

KIDA, HIROSHI, theater administrator; b. Onomichi, Hiroshima, Japan, Mar. 22, 1922; s. Soichiro and Yoshiko (Okazaki) K.; m. Saeko Hidaka, May 4, 1947 (dec. Aug. 1991); 1 child, Nozomu. Officer Ministry of Edn., Tokyo, Japan, 1946-78; vice min. Ministry of Edn., Japan, 1976-78; pres. Nat. Inst. Edn., Japan, 1978-85; dir. gen. Japan Soc. for Promotion of Sci., Tokyo, 1985-87; chancellor Dokkyo U., Soka-shi, Japan, 1987-91; pres. New Nat. Theatre, Tokyo, 1993-99; mem. presdl. adv. bd. U. Tsukuba, 1986-96; mem. adv. bd. Toyohashi U. Tech., Nara Inst. Sci. and Tech., 1991-99; part-time lectr., advisor Osaka (Japan) U., Kyoto (Japan) U., Tohoku U., Sendai, Ashiya U., Hanshin, U. South Fla., 1960-85; pres. Japan Cert. Bd. for Clin. Psychologist, Inc., Tokyo, 1988—, adv. New Nat. Theatre, Tokyo, 1999—. Author: Daigaku-eno-Kitai, 1991, others. Bd. councilors Nat. Mus. Ethnology, Osaka, 1980-98; trustee Internat. Rsch. Ctr. for Japanese Studies, Kyoto, 1987-95; chmn. Matsushita Audio-Visual Edn. Found., Tokyo, 1982—; pres. Japan Ednl. Administrn. Soc., Tokyo, 1982-88. Fellow honors course Coll. of Preceptors, London, 1985—. Mem. Japan Assn. for Cultural Econs. (pres. 2000—), Bus. Ctr. for Acad. Socs. (pres. 2000—). Home: 2-11-20 Miyakubo, Ichikawa Chiba 272-0822, Japan Office: New Nat Theatre Tokyo, 1-1-1 Honmachi Shibuya, Tokyo 151-0071, Japan

KIDD, DARLENE JOYCE, social services administrator, nurse; b. Clintonville, Wis., Feb. 3, 1935; d. Clarence Louis Julius and Elvira Norman (Horn) Krueger; m. Donny Ramon Kidd, Apr. 29, 1955 (dec. Mar. 1968); children: Andrew Louis, Kevin Hugh, Donny Ramon, Jr., Patrick Ozwald Michael. BBA, U. Okla., 1974; grad. student, Cen. State U., Milw., 1990. RN, Okla. Staff nurse Presby. Hosp. (Wesley Hosp.), Oklahoma City, 1955-56; emergency room supr. Stillwater (Okla.) Mcpl. Hosp., 1956-58; charge nurse Mercy Hosp., Dubuque, Iowa, 1958, Benton Harbor, Mich., 1959-61; charge nurse Winnebago (Wis.) State Hosp., 1963-65; adminstrv. staff, nurse Camp Classen, YMCA, Davis, Okla., 1968-72; billing mgr. Univ. Hosp. and Clinics, Oklahoma City, Okla., 1975-79; team leader Hillcrest Osteo. Hosp., Oklahoma City, 1979-80; dir. Health Care Profls., Oklahoma City, 1980-81; exec. dir. Big Bros./Big Sisters of Greater Oklahoma City, Inc., 1981-89, also bd. dirs., past. treas., past v.p.; dir. quality assurance Ctrl. Home Care, 1990-93; dir. quality assurance and billing Integrity Home Health Care, 1993—, dir. nurses, 1994-96; dir. nurses Managed Health Care Am., 1996-97. Bd. dirs. Neighborhood Devel. and Conservation Ctr., Oklahoma City, 1982; pres. Oklahoma City chpt. Gold Star Wives Am., 1984-85, regional pres. 1988-89; active Big Bros./Big Sisters, 1981-89. Kerr Found. fellow, 1982. Mem. U. Okla. Alumni Assn. (life), Women for Women Club (v.p. 1981-82), Soccer Bus. Tips Club (pres. 1983), Investment Club. Republican. Lutheran. Avocations: knitting, reading, walking, writing, bicycle riding.

KIDD, DAVID PAUL, investment manager; b. Falkirk, Scotland, Mar. 12, 1960; s. Lawrence and Henrietta Cooper Wilson (Anderson) K.; m. Ruth Mary Sinclair, Aug. 11, 1981. MA, U. St. Andrews, 1981; MPhil, U. Oxford, 1984. Internat. economist, investment mgr. Britannia Asset Mgmt. Ltd., London, 1984-86; from dir. to chief investment dir. Capital House Asset Mgmt., London, 1986-93; chief investment officer, dep. mng. dir. Chiswell Assocs. Ltd., London, 1993—. Mem. Inst. Investment Mgmt. & Rsch. Avocations: soccer, chess, gardening, current affairs. Office: Chiswell Assocs Ltd, #4 Chiswell St Finsbury Sq, EC1Y 4UP London England

KIDD, GARRY JOHN, psychology educator; b. Melbourne, Australia, Nov. 12, 1944; s. Henry Charles and Helen Courage (Paterson) K. BEdn, Melbourne CAE, 1983; MEdn, U. Melbourne, 1988, PhD, 1992. Cert. psychologist, Australia. Lectr. in psychology U. Ballarat, Australia, 1991-94; asst. prof. Bond U., Gold Coast, Australia, 1995—. Mem. Australian Psychol. Soc., Internat. Assn. Applied Psychology, Australian Assn. Rsch. in Edn. Office: Bond U, Dept Psychology, Gold Coast QLD 4229, Australia

KIDD, HILLERY GENE, educational publisher; b. Cin., May 8, 1945; s. Herbert Kidd and Amber L. (Smith) Reed; m. Sylvia Jean Smith, Dec. 21, 1971 (div. Nov. 1980); 1 child, Shane Thomas; m. Catherine Arnold Dec. 1980 (div. 1989). Student, Austin Peay State Coll., 1963-64. Owner KIDD Contrs., Cin., 1969-72; ptnr., v.p. So. Cemetaries Svcs., Inc., Fayetteville, N.C., 1972-73; state sales dir. Life Safety Inc., Clearwater, Fla., 1975; sales mgr. Jodean Water Conditioning, Lutz, Fla., 1973-78; owner Advanced Water Sys., Largo, Fla., 1978-83; regional v.p., securities broker A.L. Williams Corp., Largo, 1983-86; rep. Uniway of Mid-East Tenn., Knoxville, 1986-92; pres., CEO H.G. KIDD Corp., Boulder City, Nev., 1993—. Author: (textbooks) Human Growth and Development, 1992, Introductory Psychology, 1993, Introductory Sociology, 1993; editor: General Biology: Microbiology, Human Anatomy and Physiology, 1993, English Composition with Essay, American Literature, 1993—, Commonalities in Nursing Care—A, 1993, Commonalities in Nursing Care—B, 1993—, Differences in Nursing Care—A, 1993—, Differences in Nursing Care—B, 1993—, Differences in Nursing Care—C, 1993—, Occupational Strategies in Nursing, 1993—. Lt. col. mil. affairs Tenn. Def. Force, Nashville, 1989-94. 1st lt. 46th Spl. Forces Co. (Airborne), U.S. Army, 1965-68. Mem. Order of DeMolay (counselor 1961-62, life mem.). Republican. Avocations: aircraft piloting, scuba diving, sport parachutist. Office: PO Box 60067 Boulder City NV 89006-0067

KIDD, JAMES LAMBERT, retired minister; b. Fall River, Mass., June 12, 1933; s. Thomas W. and Elizabeth Ann (Buckley) K.; m. O. Joann Hamilton, Sept. 12, 1953; 1 child, Pamela Elizabeth. BA, U. Mass., 1955; MDiv, Andover Newton Theol. Sem., Mass., 1959; DDiv, Chgo. Theol. Sem., 1969. Ordained to ministry United Ch. of Christ, 1958. Pastor First Congl. Ch., Pelham, N.H., 1957-61, Wellington Ave. United Ch. of Christ, Chgo., 1961-69, First Congl. Ch., Wilmete, Ill., 1969-79; sr. pastor Asylum Hill Congl. Ch., Hartford, Conn., 1979-98; ret.; vice pres. bd. dirs. Chgo. Theol. Sem., 1969-79; bd. dirs. Andover Newton Theol. Sem., 1986-97, pres. alumni/ae, 1984-85. Author: Good News from Growing Churches, 1990; contbr. articles to profl. jours. Pres. Nat. Cystic Fibrosis Rsch. Found., Chgo., 1968-70; host TV talk show Wonderful World, Chgo., 1968-70; bd. dirs. Hartford Hosp., 1995—; pres. Hartford City Wide Clergy, 1993-97. Recipient Ch. Growth award, UCC Ann. Synod, 1985, 89, Humanities award St. Joseph's Coll., West Hartford, Conn., 1998, Humanitarian award NCCJ, 1998; named Hartford Citizen of Yr., 1998. Mem. Hartford Citywide Clergy Assn. (v.p. 1990-91).

KIDD, JAMES MARION, III, allergist, immunologist, naturalist, educator; b. Baton Rouge, Dec. 15, 1950; s. James Marion Jr. and Germaine Elizabeth (Hunt) K.; children: Mackenzie Elizabeth, Katherine Anne. MD, La. State U., 1976. Diplomate Am. Bd. Internal Medicine, Am. Bd. Allergy and Immunology; lic. physician, La., Fla., Wis. Resident physician La. State U. Sch. Medicine, New Orleans, 1977-79; rsch. fellow Med. Coll. Wis., Milw., 1980-82; pvt. practice in allergy and immunology Allergy, Asthma, and Immunology Clinic, Baton Rouge, 1982—; clin. asst. prof. medicine La. Sch. Medicine, New Orleans, 1982—; clin. assoc. prof. community medicine and pub. health Tulane U. Sch. Medicine, New Orleans, 1992—; dir. Baton Rouge Pollen Counting Sta., Nat. Allergy Bur. Fellow Am. Coll. Physicians, Am. Acad. Pediat., Am. Acad. Allergy and Immunology, Royal Soc. of Medicine (U.K.), La. Allergy Soc. (pres. 1989-90, exec. sec.-treas. 1992-96), Baton Rouge Allergy Soc. (pres. 1990-95), Rotary (Paul Harris fellow). Fax: 225-768-7642. E-mail: drjmkidd3@aol.com. Office: James M Kidd III MD 8017 Picardy Ave Baton Rouge LA 70809-3538

KIDD, JASON, professional basketball player; b. San Francisco, Mar. 23, 1973. Guard Dallas Mavericks, 1994-96, Phoenix Suns, 1996—. Active West Dallas Cmty. Ch.; formed Jason Kidd Found., Jason Kidd Basketball Scholarship Fund. Named Pac-10 Player of the Year, 1993-94; named nat. freshman of the yr. by The Sporting News and USA Today, 1993-94; voted Shick Rookie of the Year (with Grant Hill), 1994-95; tied for fourth on all-time NBA rookie impact list, 1994-95. Avocations: R&B music, movies, baseball. Office: Phoenix Suns 201 E Jefferson St Phoenix AZ 85004-2412

KIDD, MICHAEL RICHARD, medical educator, general practitioner; b. Melbourne, Victoria, Australia, Nov. 11, 1959; s. Richard Edward and Jill Dulcie (East) K. MB BS, U. Melbourne, 1983; diploma in cmty. child health, Flinders U., Adelaide, Australia, 1989; MD, Monash U., Melbourne, 1995. Sr. lectr. Monash U., 1990-95; prof. gen. practice U. Sydney, 1996—, head dept. gen. practice, 1999—. Editor: (book) Health Informatics, 1996. Fellow Royal Australian Coll. Gen. Practitioners; mem. World Orgn. Family Drs. (chair informatics working party 1995—), Australasian Soc. for HIV Medicine (treas. 1997-99), Australian Med. Assn., Australian Gen. Practice Computing Group (chair 1998—). Office: U Sydney Dept Gen Practice, 37A Booth St, Balmain Sydney NSW 2041, Australia

KIDD, ROBERT, science educator; b. Pt. Dickson, Malaya, Apr. 22, 1955; arrived in Australia, 1990; s. Hugh McPherson and Mary Lytle (Stewart) K.; m. Rosalind Margaret Hancock, July 19, 1975; children: Sarah Elizabeth, Joanna Clare. BA, Open U., Milton Keyens, Eng., 1986, BA with honors, 1989; PhD with distinction, U. Western Australia, Perth, 1995. Lectr. Salford (Eng.) Coll. Tech., 1980-87; sr. lectr. Nene Coll., Northampton, Eng., 1987-90; lectr. Curtin U., Perth, 1990-95; assoc. prof. U. Western Sydney-Macarthur, NSW, 1995—; external examiner Cen. Inst. Tech., Wellington, New Zealand. Contbr. articles to profl. jours. Mem. Australasian Soc. for Human Biology (sec.), Rotary Internat (Campbelltown br.). Avocations: sailing, scuba diving.

KIDDA, MICHAEL LAMONT, JR., psychologist, educator; b. Jackson, Miss., May 24, 1945; s. Michael Lamont and Annie Laurie (McKeithen) K.; m. Ellen Gordon, Aug. 23, 1977; children: Patrick Gordon, John McKeithen. BA in English, Centenary Coll., Shreveport, La., 1969; MDiv, U. South, Sewanee, Tenn., 1972; MS in Social Psychology, U. Ga., 1984, PhD in Social Psychology, 1987. Youth cons. Cathedral of St. Philip, Atlanta, 1974-76; counselor All Saints' Sch., Vicksburg, Miss., 1977-79; coord. of assessment J.C. Smith U., Charlotte, N.C., 1989-94, assoc. prof. psychology, 1985—, dept. head, 1987-89, 99—; corp. sec. Kidda Enterprises, 1999—; coord. Grad. Student Conf./Personality and Social Psychology, Athens, 1981; bd. trustees N.E. Ga. Area, Cmty. Resource Coun., Athens, 1980-83, v.p., 1982, tech. adminstrn., 1984; data analysis cons., Athens, 1980-85; presenter in field; corp. sec. Kidda Enterprizes, 1999-2000. Contbr. articles to profl. jours. and to On-line and CD-Rom data bases; author newsletter ETS Higher Edn. Assessment, 1993. Adv. bd. Washington Hghts. Project, Nat. Children's Def. Fund, Charlotte, 1994; chair evaluation com. Fighting Back Against Drugs, Charlotte, 1992-94; com. mem. cub scouts pack 19 Boy Scouts Am., Huntersville, N.C., 1994-97, Lions Club, 1997-99, Davidson, 1999—, membership com., 2000—; bd. dirs. Lions Svcs. for the Blind, Charlotte, N.C., 1999—. Recipient Nat. Retention Excellence award Noel-Levitz Ctrs., Cross of Nails award St. Michael's Cathedral, Coventry, Eng., cert. of appreciation Washington Hts. Youth Svcs. Acad., 1997; Retention and Performance grantee Pew Charitable Trusts, 1994, Equipment grantee AT&T Found., 1991, grantee APA, 1996, United Negro Coll. Fund, 1996; Inst. Non-Traditional Ministries rsch. fellow, 1994-99. Mem. Am. Statis. Assn., Soc. Southeastern Social Psychologists, Lions, Sigma Xi (site coord. celebration of undergrad. rsch. 1999), Sigma Tau Delta, Psi Chi. Achievements include empirical demonstration of superiority of college-level inquiry curriculum over remediation in post-secondary education; research on effects of social control on prosocial behavior; research on causal attribution on evaluation of people with disabilities; research on effects of accepting non-reciprocal aid; devel. of relationship mapping as a curriculum assessment tool. Home: 126 Kinderston Dr Davidson NC 28036-6947 Office: Johnson C Smith Univ 100 Beatties Ford Rd Charlotte NC 28216-5398

KIDO, EWA MARIA, architect, consultant; b. Gdansk, Poland, Mar. 29, 1957; d. Zbigniew and Helena (Wilczynska) Cywinska; 1 child, Linda Czernichowska; m. Makoto Kido, Apr. 12, 1993. MSc in Engring. Arch., Tech. U. Gdansk, 1984; PhD, U. Tokyo, 1995. Engr. Design Office Miastoprojekt, Gdansk, 1982-87; rschr., tchg. asst. Tech. U. Gdansk, 1987-90; engr. K. Kurokawa Archs. & Assocs., Tokyo, 1991-92, CTI Engring. Co., Ltd., Tokyo, 1995—. Designs include fountain plz. in Abiko City, 1995, surrounding of left side of Urayama Dam in Chichibu City, 1996, Community Road in Ashikagg City, 1998, Yomasegawa River Park, Nagano Pref., 1998-99; contbr. articles to profl. jours. Recipient Monbusho scholarship Japanese Govt., 1990-94. Mem. Internat. Assn. Bridge and Structural Engring., Am. Soc. Civil Engrs. Roman Catholic. Avocations: taking photographs of architecture and bridges, skiing, travel. Home: 11-304 1-1-17 Koyodai, Iruma-shi Saitama 358-0001, Japan Office: CTI Engring Co Ltd, 4-9-11 Nihonbashi Honcho, Chuo-ku Tokyo 103-8430, Japan

KIDO, TAKAHIKO, lawyer; b. Tokyo, Feb. 23, 1923; s. Koichi and Tusuruko Kido; m. Mieko Kido; children: Tomoko, Yumiko, Makiko. LLB, Tokyo U., 1946. Bar: First Tokyo Bar Assn., 1948. Atty. Internat. Mil. Trial for the Far East, Tokyo, 1946-48; statutory auditor Overseas Petroleum Corp., Tokyo, 1975—, Sunshine City Co. Ltd., Tokyo, 1979—, Fianuc Ltd., Yamanashi, Japan, 1982—; bd. dirs. Japan Automobile Fedn., Tokyo, v.p. 1989—; auditor Japan Auto Appraisal Inst., Tokyo, 1979—. Dir., v.p. Kiwanis Internat. Found. Trustees, 1996-98. Home: 10 2 3 Chome Nishi Azabu, Minato Ku, Tokyo 106, Japan Office: Kido & Harada Law Office, 828 New Kokusai Bldg 341 Makunouchi, Chiyoda-Ku Tokyo 100-0005, Japan

KIDO, TOMOYUKI, physician; b. Kyoto, Japan, Sept. 12, 1951; s. Tomosaburo and Miyuki (Takaoka) K.; m. Atsumi Sugimoto, Apr. 28, 1984; children: Yuya, Takashi, Yutaka. MD, Osaka (Japan) Med. Coll., 1977. Diplomate Am. Bd. Family Practice. Intern Osaka (Japan) Med. Coll. Hosp., 1977-79; resident Downstate Med. Ctr., Bklyn., 1980-83; staff physician, chief resident edn. Osaka Nat. Hosp., 1983-93; pvt. practice Osaka, 1993-95, 97—, Am. Hosp. Paris, 1995-97; chief Japanese Govt. Med. Team during Gulf Crisis, Ryad, Saudi Arabia, 1990; clin. prof. medicine Kyoto (Japan) U., 1998—. Author: Ideal Family Physician for Japan, 1991, American Medicine: Its Glory and Shadow, 1996. Recipient grant for new anticancer device Osaka Anticancer Soc., 1987, Poster award Internat. Conf. Advanced in Regional Cancer, Ulm, Germany, 1987, award for cooperation for govt. Ministry Health and Welfare, Tokyo, 1992. Fellow Japanese Assn. Internal Medicine; mem. Am. Acad. Family Physicians. Avocations: tennis, travel. Office: 3-3-61 Itakano, Higashiyodogawa-ku, Osaka 533, Japan

KIDWAI, ZUBAIR, chemical pathologist; b. Quetta, Pakistan, Aug. 14, 1952; s. Aqil and Salima (Fatima) K. MBBS, Liaquat Med. Coll., Hyderabad, 1977; D, U. Punjab, 1980; D in Clin. Chem., U. Vienna, 1986. Med. officer Sukkur Mcpl. Com., Pakistan, 1978-79; jr. pathologist Dr. Ziuddin Hosp., Karachi, Pakistan, 1981-82; from jr. pathologist to chem. pathologist Dr. Ehsanullah's Lab., Karachi, 1982—. Mem. Pakistan Assn. Pathologists, Am. Assn. Clin. Chemistry. Home: A-554 Block J N Nazimabad, 74700 Karachi Pakistan

KIEFER, FERENC, linguist, educator; b. Apatin, Yugoslavia, May 24, 1931; s. Márton and Margit (Till) K.; m. Julia Janczyszyn, Mar. 17, 1977; children: Tamás, Henrik. MA in Maths., U. Szeged (Hungary), 1956, MA in German Linguistics, 1962, MA in French Linguistics and Lit., 1965, PhD in German Linguistics, 1965; Candidate degree, Acad. Scis., 1971, D, 1977; PhD honoris causa, Stockholm U., 1992. Tchr. various high schs., 1956-62; rsch. fellow Computing Ctr. Hungarian Acad. Scis., 1962-73, sr. rsch. fellow Rsch. Inst. Linguistics, 1973-84, dep. dir. Rsch. Inst. Linguistics, 1984-91, dir. Rsch. Inst. Linguistics, 1992—; part-time tchg. appt. math. linguistics, morphology, semantics, pragmatics Budapest (Hungary) U., 1963—, part-time prof. theoret. linguistics, 1982—; vis. prof. Stockholm U., 1969-71, U. Paris/Vincennes, 1971-72, U. Stuttgart (Germany), 1972-73, Uppsala (Sweden) U., 1974, Aarhus (Denmark) U., 1977, La Sorbonne Nouvelle, France, 1977-78, U. Antwerp (Belgium), 1984, U. Vienna, 1984-85, 85-86, École Pratique Hautes Études Sorbonne, Paris, 1993-94; mem. exec. com. Com. Internat. Permanent des Linguistes, 1992—; presenter in field. Author: Ábrahám Samu: A Theory of Structural Semantics, 1966, On Emphasis and Word Order in Hungarian, 1967, Mathematical Linguistics in Eastern Europe, 1968, Bevezetés a generatív nyelvelméletbe, 1969, Studies in Syntax and Semantics (in Hungarian), 1970, Swedish Morphology, 1970, Generative Morphologie des Neufranzösischen, 1973, Essais de sémantique générale, 1974, The Theory of Presuppositions (in Hungarian), 1982, Magyar-svéd kéziszótár, 1984; assoc. editor Acta Linguistica Hungarica, 1982, editor, 1992; review editor Jour. Pragmatics, 1977-83, assoc. editor, 1983; mem. publs. com. Folia Linguistica; mem. editl. bd. Studies in Lang., 1976-96, Metalinguistica, 1994, Hungarian Lang., 1992, Corpus Linguistics, 1996—; cons. editor: Lingvisticae Investigationes, 1976, Linguistic Abstracts, 1985—; mem. adv. bd. Studies in Applied Linguistics, 1994; contbr. numerous articles to profl. jours. Mem. standing com. humanities European Sci. Found., 1997—. Vis. fellow Ford Found., 1965-66; vis. scholar Sloan Found., 1981, U. Paris VII, 1991; vis. prof. U. Paris XII, 1993, XIII, 1995. Mem. Hungarian Acad. Scis. (cons. 1984, corr. 1987, mem. com. linguistics 1990), Hungarian Linguistic Soc., Nat. Accreditation Com., Linguistic Soc. Am. (hon.), Philol. Soc. of Gt. Britain (hon.), Academia Europaea, Austrian Acad. Scis. (corr.), Societas Linguistica Europaea, European Acad. Arts, Scis. and Humanities, Internat. Pragmatics Assn. (pres. 1995—, mem. adv. bd.), Internat. Assn. Cognitive Linguistics (mem. adv. bd.). Roman Catholic. Avocations: music, gardening. Home: BERC UTCA 7, H-1016 Budapest Hungary Office: Rsch Inst Linguistics, Benczúr Utca 23, H-1068 Budapest Hungary

KIEFER, HELEN CHILTON, emergency/trauma neurologist; b. Washington; d. Frank McGlowing and Sue (Stanford) Chilton; m. John Harold Kiefer, Feb. 4, 1961 (div. July 1971); 1 child, Steven Chilton. AB in Chemistry magna cum laude, Cornell U., 1961; MS, U. Chgo., 1971, PhD in Biochemistry, 1971; MD with honors, Northwestern U., 1981. Lic. physician, Ill.; diplomate Nat. Bd. Med. Examiners. Intern psychiatry and internal medicine Michael Reese Hosp. and Med. Ctr., Chgo., 1981-82; resident neurology U. Ill. Med. Sch., Chgo., 1983-85; physicist, computer programmer physics div. Los Alamos (N.Mex.) Sci. Labs., 1965—; asst. prof. dept. biochemistry Northwestern U. Med. Sch., Chgo., 1972-78; editor Marcus Acad. Media, Chgo., 1978-81; clin. assoc. prof. dept. biochemistry Loyola Med. and Dental Sch., Chgo., 1978-81; med. staff Charter Barclay Neuropsychiat. Hosp., Chgo., 1983—; pvt. practice Chgo., 1983—; dir. med. rsch. for biotech., assoc. med. dir. high tech. Abbott Labs., Abbott Park, Ill., 1986-89; assoc. ctr. for biotechnology Northwestern U., 1992—; adj. assoc. prof. dept. biomed. engring. and grad. multidisciplinary program in neurosci. Northwestern U., Evanston, Ill., 1989-90, vis. prof., assoc. ctr. for biotech., 1992—; affiliate Internat. Human Genome Mapping Project, 1991—; vis.

prof. dept. bioengring. U. Wash., Seattle, 1982-83; mem. presdl. adv. com. NIH, 1976-80; CEO, pres. The Doctor Cooks, Inc., 1995—; mem. numerous program project rev. bds., 1978-80. Woodrow Wilson fellow, NSF fellow, Danforth Found. fellow, NIH postdoctoral fellow. Mem. Assn. Clin. Scientists, N.Y. Acad. Scis., Phi Beta Kappa, Alpha Omega Alpha.

KIEFER, RAYMOND HAROLD, computer systems design engineer; b. East Brunswick, Victoria, Australia, Dec. 29, 1965; s. Robert and Josyna Syke (Ramsteyn) K.; m. Julie Ann Rowett, May 6, 1989; 1 child, Gaston. AA in Engring., Footscray Inst. Technology, Victoria, 1986; B Engring. in Elec. Engring. with honors, U. South Australia, 1997. Profl. engr. Elec. engr. Vision Sys., Ltd., Technology Park, The Levels, South Australia, 1989-90; tech. officer U. South Australia, The Levels, 1990-94; sr. tech. officer dept. laser physics Australian Nat. U., Canberra, 1994-95; rsch. engr. U. South Australia, The Levels, 1996-98; project engr. Daronmont Techs. Pty Ltd., Mawson Lakes. Mem. IEEE. Avocations: scuba diving, photography, art. E-mail: RKiefer@Daronmont.com.au. Office: Daronmont Techs Pty Ltd, Tech Park, Mawson Lakes 5095, South Australia

KIEFER, RENATA GERTRUD, physician, epidemiologist, economist, international health management consultant; b. Lorrach, Baden, Germany, July 4, 1946; came to U.S., 1970; d. Friedrich W. and Gertrud Anna (Keller) K.; m. James C. Bridgman. BA, Stanford U., 1963; MA, U. Calif., Berkeley, 1967; MD, U. Geneva, Switzerland, 1982; MPH, U. Calif., Berkeley, 1990. Diplomate Am. Bd. Pediatrics; cert. in environ. health, Germany. Asst. instr. dissection lab. dept. morphology U. Geneva Sch. of Medicine, Switzerland, 1979-80; interim resident dept. diagnostic radiology Univ. Hosp., Geneva, 1980, intern physician, 1982-83; clin. fellow in pediatrics Harvard Med. Sch., Boston, 1983-85; resident physician Mass. Gen. Hosp., Boston, 1983-85; sr. resident dept. pediatrics U. Calif., San Francisco, 1985-86; attending physician emergency dept. Children's Hosp. Med. Ctr., Oakland, Calif., 1986-94; fellow dept. epidemiology and internat. health U. Calif., San Francisco, 1988-90; German tech. cooperation expert tropical medicine & internat. health Inst. for Health Sci. Rsch., Asuncion, Paraguay, 1990-94, vis. prof. epidemiol. and preventive medicine, 1992—; sci. methods advisor Nat. U. Asuncion, 1994—; chief adv. rsch. and human resource devel. Health Strategies Internat.; rep. of IICS/Internat. Orgns.; cons. and presenter in field; chief adviser on health projects, dir. internat. teams GTZ/Health Ministry of Colombia, 1997—. Contbr. numerous articles to profl. jours. Floyd Internat. fellow in medicine, 1999; co-winner nat. sci. prize Paraguay Parliament, 1994; ASSU scholar Stanford U., 1962-63, Fulbright scholar, 1962-64, Internat. scholar Swedish Inst., 1968, Internat. Health scholar U. Calif., 1990; fellow AAUW, 1968; recipient award USPHS Nat. Rsch. Svc., 1989-90. Address: 6 Locksley Ave San Francisco CA 94122-3854

KIEFER, STACY M., secondary education educator; b. Temple, Tex., Sept. 25, 1976; d. Joseph F. and Cathy O. Kiefer. BA in English, Austin Coll., 1997, MA in Tchg., 1998. English tchr. Berkner H.S., Richardson, Tex., 1998—; acad. decathlon coach U.S. Acad. Decathlon, Richardson, 1999—. Mem. PTA, Internat. Reading Assn., Nat. Coun. Tchrs. English. Republican. Baptist. Avocations: reading, hiking, snow skiing, home decorating. Office: Berkner HS 1600 E Spring Valley Rd Richardson TX 75081-5399

KIEHL, JUDITH E., pastoral associate; b. Rome, N.Y., June 12, 1941; d. M.F. and Eugenie Carpenter Eakins; m. James M. Kiehl, Aug. 24, 1963 (div. 1966). BA in English and Classics cum laude, Syracuse U., 1963; MA in Linguistics with distinction, U. Rochester, N.Y., 1972; MA in Theology with distinction, St. Bernard's Inst., Rochester, 1991. Tchr. Latin and English St. Agnes H.S., Rochester, 1966-70, head dept. Latin, 1972; care asst. Home and Family Svcs. of Rochester, 1983-87; pastoral assoc. Roman Cath. Diocese of Rochester, 1987—; editl. asst. Gannett Rochester Newspapers, 1973-74; freelance writer, Rochester area publs., 1974-80; publicity writer, coord. portable channel videocenter, Rochester, 1978. Author: (poetry) Advice for the Comfort Ministers, 1988. Chair Diocesan Human Life Commn., Rochester, 1980-85; mem. Diocesan Pastoral Coun., Rochester, 1982-83; advisor social ministry curriculum Finger Lakes Social Ministry, Geneva, N.Y., 1993; mem. Consistent Life Ethic Awards and Grants Com. Mem. Am. Classical League, Pax Christi, Thomas Merton Soc., Greenpeace, Bread for the World, Coalition to End the Death Penalty, PETA. Democrat. Avocations: writing, sketching, bicycling, theatre, photography. Home: 48 Kings Court Way Apt 8 Rochester NY 14617-5526 Office: Holy Trinity Ch 1460 Ridge Rd Webster NY 14580-3699

KIEHL, REINHOLD, chemist, biochemist, human biologist; b. Worms, Germany, Oct. 8, 1947; s. Heinrich Erwin and Katherina Hertha (Fuhr) K.; m. Ilse Gertraud Schoyerer, Apr. 11, 1974 (div. 1997); children: Christina, Stephanie. BEng, Engring. Sch., Mannheim, Germany, 1971; MS in Chemistry, U. Heidelberg (Germany), 1974, DSc, 1977; MEng, Fachhochschule, Mannheim, 1982. Registered eco-audit specialist. Rsch. fellow Max Planck Inst., Heidelberg, 1977; postdoctoral fellow Scripps Clinic, La Jolla, Calif., 1977-79; asst. prof. physiol. chemistry Ruhr U., Bochum, Germany, 1979-85; asst. prof. phys. and biophys. chemistry U. Bielefeld (Germany), 1985-87; head lab. and rsch. dept. Clinic Neukirchen (Germany), 1987-94; prof. and dir., freelance workshop and course instr. Furth, Germany, 1995—. Contbr. over 40 articles to profl. jours. Max Planck Soc. fellow, 1976-78, Am. Heart Assn. fellow, 1978-79. Fellow Royal Soc. Chemistry; mem. AAAS, Brit. Soc. Allergy and Clin. Immunology, Am. Assn. Clin. Chemistry, Internat. Fedn. Clin. Chemistry. World Assn. Sarcoidosis and other Granulomatous Disorders, Internat. Union of Pure and Applied Chemistry, N.Y. Acad. Sci. Achievements include work with mechanism of bioenergy, mechanism in patho-biochemistry and relation to the environment. Office: RKI-Lab Rsch Molecular Med/Biol, Saliterweg 1, 93437 Furth im Wald Germany

KIEHN, OLE, neurobiology educator, researcher; b. Nakskov, Lolland, Denmark, Sept. 30, 1958; s. Kaj and Kirsten Kiehn. MD, U. Copenhagen, 1985, DMSc, 1990. Postdoctoral assoc. sect. neurobiology Cornell U., Ithaca, N.Y., 1989-90; rsch. asst. dept. neurophysiology U. Copenhagen, 1983-85, rsch. assoc., 1985-88, sr. rsch. assoc., 1988-89, lab. leader, asst. prof., 1990-95; assoc. rsch. prof., 1995—, assoc. prof., 1997; mem. bd. Neurosci. Ctr. U. Copenhagen, 1992—; referee several internat. jours., 1990—. Contbr. articles to profl. jours. Mem. Danish Soc. for Theoretical Scis., European Neurosci. Assn., Am. Neurosci. Assn., Physiol. Soc. London, N.Y. Acad. Scis., Physicians Orgn. U. Copenhagen (pres. 1991-93). Office: U Copenhagen Sect Neurophys, Inst Med Physiology, Blegdamsvej 3, DK-2200 Copenhagen Denmark

KIEL, EWALD, education educator; b. Bad Pyrmont, Germany, Feb. 27, 1959; s. Ewald and Ursula (Hundertmark) K.; children: Constanze, Helene. Grad., U. Göttingen (Germany), 1985, doctorate, 1990. Vis. scholar UCLA, 1986-87; tchr. Gymnasium, Wolfsburg, 1988—; assoc. prof. Intercultural Inst., Göttingen, 1992—; cons., Germany, 1991—; pres. Göttingen Zentrum für didaktische Studien, Göttingen, 1992—. Author: Dialog und Handlung im Drama, 1992, Evlävn als didaktisches Handeln, 1999. Grantee govt. of Lower Saxony, 1990-92, 91-92, Deutsche Forschungsgemeinschaft, 1993-96. Mem. Internat. Soc. of Knowledge Orgn. (fin. auditor 1994—). Home: Auf der Lehmbuende 22, 37085 Göttingen Germany Office: Inst Interkulturelle Didaktik, Waldweg 26, 37075 Göttingen Germany

KIELBASA, WLADYSLAW, engineering consultant; b. Liza Stara, Bialystok, Poland, Apr. 5, 1954; s. Zygmunt and Maria (Kruk) K.; m. Barbara Koziejko, May 5, 1979; children: Katarzyna Anna, Ewa Alicja. Cert. technician, Tech. Sch., Lapy, Poland, 1974; MSc, Tech. U., Warsaw, Poland, 1979, M Engring., 1979. Rsch. engr. Zarnowiec (Poland) Nuclear Power Plant, 1982-85, head nuclear safety and reactor physics, 1985-95; devel. specialist Hydromex Ltd., Czymanowo, Poland, 1993-95; chief specialist Pumped-Storage Storage Plants Co., Warsaw, 1995-97, comml. mgr., 1997-99; chief cons. Energoprojekt-Cons., Warsaw, 1999—; expert witness Internat. Atomic Energy Agy., Vienna, Austria, 1993, 93; mem. UNIPEDE, Paris, 1989-90. Author: Energetyka, 1997. Mem. SEP. Office: Energoprojekt-Cons SA, ul Krucza 6/14, 00-950 Warsaw Poland

KIELCZYNSKI, WOJCIECH EDWARD, medical herbalist; b. Lodz, Poland, Apr. 26, 1952; arrived in Australia, 1983, naturalized, 1985; s. Edward Kielczynski and Krystyna (Sypniewska) Prekier; m. Irena Stylska, Apr. 16, 1988; 1 child, Thomas. MD, Med. Acad., Warsaw, Poland, 1975; PhD, Med. Ctr. Postgrad. Edn., Warsaw, 1982; cert. med. herbalist, Sch. Phytotherapy, Tunbridge Wells, U.K., 1986. Intern Med. Ctr. Postgrad. Edn., Warsaw, 1976-78, resident med. officer, 1978-82; postdoctoral fellow Royal Melbourne (Australia) Hosp., 1986-87; sr. scientist Walter and Eliza Hall Inst., Melbourne, 1988-93; pvt. practice med. herbalist Melbourne, 1993—; rsch. dir. Australian Coll. Herbal Medicine, 1997—; rsch. fellow Juvenile Diabetes Found. Internat., 1989-91; sr. lectr., clin. supr. So. Sch. Natural Therapies, Melbourne, 1988-93; govt. advisor Traditional Med. Evaluation Com., Canberra, Australia, 1990-97; tchr. RMIT U., Melbourne, 1996, Swinburne U., Melbourne, 2000—. Contbr. articles to profl. jours. Recipient Sci. award Polish Ministry of Health, 1979, award Apex/Diabetes Australia, 1988, award Kellion Diabetes, Australia, 1992; grantee Nat. Health and Med. Rsch. Coun., Australia, 1987. Mem. Nat. Inst. Med. Herbalists (Eng.), Nat. Herbalists Assn. Australia, Victorian Herbalists Assn. Avocations: music, golf. Home: 32 Gloria Ave, Dandenong Victoria 3175, Australia

KIELMEYER, WILLIAM HENRY, ceramic engineer, researcher; b. Columbus, Ohio, Jan. 6, 1943; s. Petr Henry and Dorothy Ruth (Potts) K.; m. Marjorie E. Kaufman, Oct. 5, 1968; children: Cheryl A., Thomas W. BS in Ceramic Engring., Ohio State U., 1966, MS, 1973. Project engr. Owens-Corning Fiberglas Corp., Granville, Ohio, 1968-72; rsch. engr. Johns-Manville Sales Corp., Littleton, Colo., 1973-78, sr. rsch. engr., 1978-86, rsch. assoc., 1987—. Mem. Am. Ceramic Soc. Republican. Lutheran. Achievements include 17 patents, including co-patentee process for making high-purity silica fiber for use in space shuttle reusable surface insulation; loose-fill residential insulation, commercial insulation materials and systems, manufacturing processes for dual glass and cladglass fibers. Home: 3374 W Chenango Ave Englewood CO 80110-6312 Office: 10100 W Ute Ave Littleton CO 80127-5002

KIELSMEIER, CATHERINE JANE, school system administrator; b. San Jose, Calif.; d. Frank Delos and Catherine Doris (Sellar) MacGowan; m. Milton Kielsmeier; children: Catherine Louise, Barry Delos. MS, U. So. Calif., 1964, PhD, 1971. Tchr. pub. schs., Maricopa, Calif.; sch. psychologist Campbell (Calif.) Union Sch. Dist., 1961-66; asst. prof. edn. and psychology Western Oreg. State Coll., Monmouth, 1966-67, 70; asst. rsch. prof. Oreg. Sys. Higher Edn., Monmouth, 1967-70; dir. spl. svcs. Pub. Schs., Santa Rosa, Calif., 1971-91; cons., 1991—. Author: Tibetan Language Pre-Primer, 1999. Mem. Sonoma County Coun. Cmty. Svcs., 1974-84, bd. dirs., 1976-82, Sonoma County Orgn. for Retarded/Becoming Ind., 1976-84, bd. dirs., 1978-82; bd. dirs. Gold Ridge Sangha, 1994-97, Hosp. Chaplaincy Svcs., 1996—. Office: 7495 Poplar Dr Forestville CA 95436-9671

KIELSTEIN, RITA, physician; b. Erfurt, Thuringia, Germany, Nov. 8, 1941; d. Alwin and Amalia Regina (Karsten) Buchholz; m. Volker Rudolf Kielstein, Sept. 21, 1968; 1 child, Jan Thomas. MD, Med. Acad. Magdeburg, Germany, 1969, internal medicine, 1975, nephrologist, 1978, habilitation in medicine, 1980; prof. medicine, Otto-von-Guericke U., Magdeburg, 1993. Sr. physician Med. Acad. Magdeburg, 1976-91, head dept. nephrology, 1991-93; head K&H Dialysis Ctr., Magdeburg, 1992—; bd. dirs. German AG Nephrologie, Germany; mem. ethics com. Fed. Ministry Health, Germany, 1995-99, Chamberphysians Saxoma-Auhalt, Magdeburg; mem. Kennedy Inst. Ethics, Georgetown U., 1992—. Author: Physical Training, Klinik, Ethik u Genetik of ADPKD, 2nd edit., 1997; co-author: Betreuung-Vertügung in der Praxis, 5th edit., 1999; editor: Ethik in der Nephrologie, 1996. Advanced Directives grantee Deutsche Forschungsgemeinschaft, 1991. Mem. European Dialysis and Transplant Assn., Internat. Assn. Artificial Organs (bd. dirs. 1994-98). Home: Hecklinger Str 25, D-39112 Magdeburg Germany Office: Otto von Guericke U, Leipziger Str 44, 39120 Magdeburg Germany

KIELY, GABRIEL MARTIN, social policy and social work educator, college dean, researcher; b. Ballinasloe, Co. Galway, Ireland, Oct. 22, 1940; s. Michael Kiely and Honoria Margaret Cahill; m. Linda Marie Mattison, Apr. 19, 1969; children: Kathleen, Marleen, Frank, Lindara. BA, Univ. Coll. Dublin, Ireland, 1965, grad. diploma in social sci., 1966; MSW, Fla. State U., 1968; PhD, Nat. U. Ireland, Dublin, 1979. Caseworker Cath. Social Svcs., L.A., 1968-71; lectr. social work Univ. Coll. Dublin, 1971—, dir. Family Studies Ctr., 1986—, head dept. social policy and social work, 1992-98, dean Faculty Philosophy and Sociology, 1992-98, Jean Monnet prof. family policies and European integration, 1998—; vis. prof. Calif. State U., Sacramento, 1981; mem. bd. family mediation svc. Dept. Equality and Law Reform, Dublin, 1986-99; chmn. nat. program adv. panel Irish Youth Found., Dublin, 1995—; Irish mem. obs. nat. family policies European Union, Brussels, 1989—; mem. panel assessors Nat. Social Work Qualifications Bd., Dublin, 1997—. Author: Finding Love: Counselling for Couples in Crises, 1989; joint author: Cost of a Child, 1994; joint editor: European Family Policy, 1990, Irish Social Policy in Context 1999, Contemporary Irish Social Policy, 1999; editor: In and Out of Marriage, 1992. Mem. Royal Irish Acad. (nat. com. for econs. and social scis. 2000—), Irish Assn. Social Workers (past v.p.), Internat. Sociol. Assn. (com. on family rsch. 1997—). Office: Univ Coll Dublin Dept, Social Policy-Social Work, Belfield Dublin 4, Ireland

KIENAST, HERMANN JOSEF, architect, archaeologist; b. Stätzling, Fed. Republic Germany, May 14, 1943; s. Josef and Therese (Lindermayr) K.; m. Birgitt Rösch, Jan. 10, 1969; 1 child, Markus. Diploma, Tech. U., Munich, Fed. Republic Germany, 1970, D in Engring., 1974. Asst. prof. Tech. U., Munich, 1971-72; referent German Archaeol. Inst., Athens, 1972-84; dir. Samos Excavation, Athens, Greece, 1984—, II dir., 1987—. Author: Ancient Walls of Samos, 1978, Der Nordbau, 1989, The Tunnel of Eupalinos, 1995. Office: German Archaeol Inst, Odos Pheidiou 1, 10678 Athens Greece

KIENING, CHRISTIAN WERNER, German literature educator; b. Munich, July 30, 1962. MA, U. Munich, 1987, PhD, 1989, Habilitation, 1996. Fellow Maison des Scis. de L'Homme, Paris, 1992-93; Heisenberg scholar Deutsche Forschungsgemeinschaft, 1996; prof. Medieval German lit. U. Munich, 1996-97; prof. German lit. U. Zürich, Switzerland, 2000—; vis. prof. U. Calif., Berkeley. Author: Reflexion-Narration, 1991, Anthropologische Zugänge zur mittelalterlichen Literatur, 1996, Schwierige Modernität, 1998, Johannes von Tepl, 2000. Office: Zürich Deutsches Seminar, Schönberggasse 9, 8001 Zürich Switzerland

KIENZLE, JOHN FRED, history educator; b. Allentown, Pa., Apr. 1, 1945; s. Fred John and Florence Mary K.; m. Patricia Catherine Evertsen, Aug. 22, 1970. BA in history, Albany State U., 1967; MA in History, NYU, 1969; PhD in History, Princeton U., 1972. Retail sales clk. Floyd Bennett Stores, Patchogue, N.Y., 1960-63; cafeteria worker Albany State Dorms, 1963-67; libr. aide NYU, N.Y.C., 1967-69, Firestone Libr.,Princeton (N.J.) U., 1969-70; tchr. history Maple Hill H.S., Castleton, N.Y., 1970—. Mem. Met. Mus. Art, 1987—, Lake Chaplain Maritime Mus., 1994—, Schodack Faculty Assn., 1970—; trustee Maple Hill H.S. Amateur Radio Club, 1975—; radio officer Rensselaer County (N.Y.) Civil Emergency Svcs., 1980—. Mem. Archaeol. Inst. Am. Republican. Roman Catholic. Avocations: sailing, flying, amateur radio, astronomy, photography. E-mail: jkienzle@albany.net. Office: Maple Hill H S 1216 Maple Hill Rd Castleton On Hudson NY 12033-1604

KIERDASZUK, BORYS, biophysics educator, researcher; b. Horostyta, Poland, Nov. 9, 1955; s. Pawel and Nina (Samczuk) K.; m. Ludmila Kalinowska, May 15, 1982; children: Biruta-Maria, Jacob. MSc, U. Warsaw, Poland, 1979, PhD, 1985, DSc, 1999. Asst. dept. biophysics U. Warsaw, 1981-85, rschr. asst. prof., 1986-99, assoc. prof., 1999—; postdoctoral fellow Karolinska Inst., Sweden, 1986-88, vis. prof., 1989, 91, 92, 97, 98; vis. prof. U. Md., Balt., 1994. Contbr. articles to sci. jours. Fulbright fellow, 1994; grantee Howard Hughes Med. Inst., 1995—. Fellow European Molecular Biology Orgn.; mem. Polish Biophys. Soc., Polish Phys. Soc., Internat. Soc. for Advancement Sci., N.Y. Acad. Scis. Mem. Solidarity. E-mail: borys@asp.biogeo.uw.edu.pl. Office: U Warsaw Dept Biophysics, 93 Zwirki i Wigury St, PL-02089 Warsaw Poland

KIERKEGAARD, ASBJOERN, physician; b. Aarhus, Denmark, Mar. 24, 1950; s. Christian and Anna (Stejlgaard Jensen) K.; m. Lena Kennevik, June 18, 1982; children: Marcus, Daniel, Andreas. Grad., Faculty of Medicine/U. Aarhus, Denmark, 1977; PhD, U. Lund, Sweden, 1993. Med. diplomate; specialist in internal medicine, cardiology. Asst. physician County Hosp., Boras, Sweden, 1977-82, U. Hosp., Lund, Sweden, 1982-87; cons. County Hosp., Halmstad, Sweden, 1987—. Author: (book) Deep Vein Thrombosis and Venous Function, 1993. Office: Laenssjukhuset, Medicinkliniken, 30185 Halmstad Sweden

KIERNAN, MATTHEW COLM, neurologist; b. Wollongong, Australia, June 18, 1966; s. Colm Patrick and Joan Louise (McKay) K.; m. Clare Elizabeth Caldwell, Oct. 1, 1999. MB, BS with honors, U. Sydney, Australia, 1990; PhD, U. N.S.W., Australia, 1997. Fellow Brain Found., Australia, 1994-95, Nat. Health and Med. Rsch. Coun., Australia, 1995-97; C.J. Martin fellow Nat. Health and Med. Rsch. Coun., London, 1999—; neurophysiology registrar Prince of Wales Hosp., Sydney, 1997, staff specialist, 1998; Australasian registrar Nat. Hosp. for Neurology and Neurosurgery, London, 1998-99; neurologist Prince of Wales Pvt. Hosp., Sydney, 1998—. Contbr. articles to profl. jours. Travelling fellow Internat. Fedn. EEG & Clinical Neurophysiology; recipient Young Investigar award Australian Assn. Neurologists, 1997. Fellow Royal Australian Coll. Physicians (Best Rsch. prize 1996). Avocations: golf, tennis, reading, history. Home: Mecklenburgh Sq Ap 939, William Goodenough House, WC1N 2AN London England Office: Inst Neurology, Sobell Dept Neurophysiology, WC1N 3BG London England

KIESER, ARND, molecular biologist; b. Bad Aibling, Bavaria, Germany, Aug. 27, 1965; s. Diethelm and Edith (Heidenreich) K. Diploma in biology, U. Freiburg, Germany, 1993; PhD, U. Munich, 1996. Rschr. U. Freiburg, 1992-93; guest rschr. Nat. Cancer Inst., Bethesda, Md., 1993; rschr. GSF Nat. Rsch. Ctr. Environ. Health, Munich, 1993-98, rsch. group leader, 1998—. Contbr. articles to profl. jours. Recipient award GSF-Nat. Rsch. Ctr. Environ. Health, 1997. Mem. Signa Transduction Soc. Office: GSF Inst Clin Molecular Biology, Marchioninistrasse 25, D 81377 Munich Germany

KIESER, MEINHARD, biostatistician, researcher; b. Buchen, Germany, Jan. 1, 1960; s. August and Hedwig (Wolf) K.; m. Yvonne Letzelter, Dec. 30, 1991. MSc with distinction, U. Heidelberg, Germany, 1986, PhD, 1991. Cert. Biometry in Medicine. Rsch. assoc. U. Mainz, Germany, 1987, U. Heidelberg, 1987-92; biostatistician Dr. Willmar Schwabe Pharm., Karlsruhe, Germany, 1992-93; head dept. biometry Dr. Willmar Schwabe Pharm., Karlsruhe, 1993—; lectr. U. Heidelberg, 1994—. Co-author: Statistische Auswertungssysteme, 1992; contbr. articles to profl. jours., including Biometrika, Stats. in Medicine, Internat. Jour. Clin. Pharmacology, Biometr. Jour., Drug Info. Jour., Method Info. Med. Jour., Pharmacopsychiatry, Dementia and Geriatric Disorders, Jour. Statis. Planning Infy. Scholar Studienstiftung des Dt. Volkes, Bonn, 1982-86. Mem. Internat. Biometric Soc., Drug Info. Assn., Soc. for Clin. Trials. Office: Willmar Schwabe Pharm, Willmar-Schwabe-Str 4, 76227 Karlsruhe Germany

KIESEWETTER, HOLGER HEINZ, physician, consultant; b. Varel, Germany, Nov. 4, 1947; s. Werner Rolf Gerhard and Käte Magdalena (Aschmann) K.; m. Elisabeth Müller, May 23, 1969; children: Thorsten, Svenja, Bianca, Annika, Signe. DEng, Tech. U., Berlin, 1976; diploma in engring., RWTH, Aachen, Germany, 1971, MD, 1980, habilitation, 1982. Med. diplomate. Asst. Reinisch Westfalische Technische Hochschule, Aachen, 1971-72, 76-83, Tech. U., Berlin, 1972-76; asst., vice dir. Homburg (Germany) U. Clin., 1983-94; dir. Charity U. Clin., Berlin, 1994—; cons. Freseuius, Bad Homburg, Germany, 1986—, Haemonetics, Ghent, Switzerland, 1997—. Office: Med Faculty Charity Clin, Humboldt U, 10098 Berlin Germany

KIESEWETTER, HUBERT, economist, historian, educator; b. Dessau, Anhalt, Germany, July 11, 1939; s. Erwin Max and Elisabeth (Brockmeier) K.; m. Renate Stiller, Sept. 21, 1984. MSc, London Sch. Econs., 1968; PhD, U. Heidelberg, Germany, 1973; Habilitation, Free U. Berlin, 1985. Journeyman German Railways, Frankfurt, 1954-60; mechanic TV Comp., Darmstadt, Germany, 1960-63; asst. prof. Free U., Berlin, 1975-89; prof. Cath. U., Eichstätt, Germany, 1990—; Konrad-Adenauer-Chair, Georgetown U., Washington, 1987-88; vis. prof. St. Anthony's Coll., Oxford, Engl, 1989-90. Author: Industrialization and Agriculture, 1988, From Hegel to Hitler, 2d edit., 1995, Industrial Revolution in Germany, 3d edit., 1996, The Unique Europe, 1996, Region and Industry in Europe, 1815-1995, 2000; editor Region, State and Industrialization, 1985, Karl R. Popper, 1992, (with Michel Hau) Chemins vers L'an 2000, 2000. U. Ill. fellow, 1986-87, Sorbonne U. fellow, 1994. Roman Catholic. Avocations: music, mountain climbing. Home: Schimmelleite 4, 85072 Eichstätt Germany Office: Cath Univ, Ostenstrasse 26, 85072 Eichstätt Germany

KIESLICH, KLAUS FRANZ, retired chemist; b. Breslav, Silesia, Germany, Oct. 29, 1929; s. Paul and Margarete (Just) K.; m. Dagmar Else Gross, Oct. 29, 1964 (div. Dec. 1986); 2 children. Diploma Chemist, Tech. U., Braundschweig, Germany, 1953, PhD, 1955; postgrad., Univ. Hamburg, Germany, 1955-57; hon. prof., Free U., Berlin, Germany, 1980. Chemist in pharm. rsch. Univ. Hosp., Hamburg, Germany, 1955-57; head rsch. dept. Schering AG, Berlin, Germany, 1957-79; sci. dir. Nat. Inst. for Biotech. Rsch., Braunschweig, Germany, 1979-84, head rsch. dept., 1984-94; guest lectr. Free Univ. Berlin, Germany, 1975—; ret., 1996. Author: (book) Biotransformations, 1974; mem. editl. bd. of several sci. jours.; editor: Biotransformations, 1984; author: (data file on CD-ROM) Biotransformations, 1996; contbr. over 100 articles to profl. jours. and over 70 patents in the field. With German Army, 1945. Mem. ACS, Dechema. Avocations: classical music, sailing, swimming, tennis, skiing. Home: Fischhausenweg 4, D 38124 Braunschweig Germany

KIESSLING, LAURA LEE, chemist; b. Milw., Sept. 21, 1960; d. William E. and LaVonne V. (Korth) K. SB, MIT, 1983; PhD, Yale U., 1989. Teaching asst. MIT, Cambridge, Mass., 1982-83; teaching asst. Yale U., New Haven, Conn., 1983-84, rsch. asst., 1984-89; rsch. fellow Calif. Tech. U., Pasadena, 1989-91; asst. prof. chemistry U. Wis., Madison, 1991-97, assoc. prof., 1997-99, prof. chemistry, prof. biochemistry, 1999—; cons. Ophidian, Inc., 1997-99, Alfred P. Sloan Fond. Fellowships, 1997—; mem. bioorganic and natural products study sect. NIH, 1997—; sci. adv. bd. Promega Corp., 1999—; selection com. for editor Jour. Organic Chemistry, 1999. Mem. editl. bd. Chemistry and Biology, 1997—, Organic Reactions, 2000—; contbr. articles to profl. jours. Recipient Dow Chems. New Faculty award, 1992, Shaw Scientist award, 1992-97, Nat. Young Investigator award NSF, 1993-98, Beckman Young Investigator award, 1994-96, Zeneca Excellence in Chemistry award, 1996, Dreyfus Tchr.-Scholar award Dreyfus Found., 1996; Postdoctoral fellow Am. Cancer Soc., 1989-91, MacArthur fellow John D. and Catherine MacArthur Found., 1999, Alfred P. Sloan Found. fellow, 1997. Mem. AAAS, Am. Chem. Soc. (Cope scholar 1999, Isbell award 2000), Soc. Glycobiology, Am. Soc. for Biochemistry and Molecular Biology, Sigma Xi, Phi Lambda Upsilon. Avocations: canoeing, rowing, running. Fax: 608-265-0764. Office: U Wis Dept Chemistry 1101 University Ave Madison WI 53706-1322

KIESSLING, WERNER WILLI, computer science educator, scientist; b. Schwarzenbach-Saale, Bavaria, Germany, Jan. 30, 1953; s. Walter Max and Doris Berta (Kirmse) K.; m. Elfriede Maria Nüssel, June 16, 1977 (div.); children: Michael, Julia; m. Jutta Trude Seidel, Mar. 16, 1996. Diploma in Informatics, Tech. U., Munich, 1978, D Natural Sci., 1983. Cert. computer sci. Asst. prof. Tech. U., Munich, 1983-86, assoc. prof., 1991-93; dir. R&D MAD Intelligent Systems, Munich and San Jose, Calif., 1986-89; prof. U. Munich, 1990, U. Augsburg, Germany, 1993—; co-founder Internet co. Database Preference Software GmbH, 1997. Author, chief designer deductive database system Declare, 1994; textbook author including multimedia software; contbr. articles to profl. jours. Postdoctoral grantee DAAD/Germany, U. Calif., Berkeley, 1984-85. Avocations: trekking, biking, chess, soccer. Office: U Augsburg Inst Informatik, Universitats Str 14, D-86135 Augsburg Bavaria, Germany

KIEU, TIEN DUNG, theoretical physicist; b. Saigon, Vietnam, Oct. 25, 1960; arrived in Australia, 1980; s. The Van and Thuy Ngoc Bui K.; m. Liem Thanh Hoang, 1980; children: Vi, Tu Mi. BSc (hons.), U. Queensland, Australia, 1984; PhD, U. Edinburgh, Scotland, 1988. Rsch. asst. U. Queen-

sland, Australia, 1982; rsch. fellow U. Edinburgh, Scotland, 1988, U. Oxford, Eng., 1988-91; rsch. fellow U. Melbourne, Australia, 1991-93, Queen Elizabeth II rsch. fellow, 1994-97; sr. rsch. scientist, project leader Commonwealth Sci. & Indsl. Rsch. Orgn., Melbourne, Australia, 1997—; jr. rsch. fellow Linacre Coll. Oxford, 1989-91; pres. sr. common room St. Hilda Coll., Melbourne, 1992-95; vis. scholar Inst. Advanced Study, Princeton U., U.S.A., 1994; Fulbright sr. fellow Columbia U., N.Y.C., 1996; rsch. fellow, Asia Pacific Ctr. Theoretical Physics, Seoul, Republic of Korea, 1997—. Contbr. numerous conf. proceedings and over 40 articles to profl. jours. Recipient The Commonwealth scholarship and fellowship plan, 1984, The Pamela Todd award St. Hilda's Coll., Melbourne, 1992, Sr. Fulbright award Fulbright Commn., 1996; grantee Australian Rsch. Coun. Avocations: reading, martial arts. Office: DMST CSIRO Pvt Bag 33, Normandy Rd, Clayton VIC 3168, Australia

KIFER, YURI I., mathematics educator; b. Moscow, Jan. 13, 1948; arrived in Israel, 1978; s. Isaak I. and Lubov I. Kifer; m. Ludmila V. Kifer, Dec. 30, 1975; children: Ilona, Iona. MA, Moscow U., 1971, PhD, 1974. Sr. lectr. Hebrew U., Jerusalem, 1978-82, assoc. prof., 1982-88, prof. math., 1988—; speaker Internat. Congress of Math., Berlin, 1998. Author: Ergodic Theory of Random Transform, 1986, Random Perturbations of Dynamical Systems, 1988; contbr. articles to profl. jours. Binat. US-Israel Sci. Found. grantee, 1982—; recipient Humboldt-Meitner Rsch. award, 1999. Mem. Am. Math. Soc., Israel Math. Union. Office: Hebrew Univ Inst of Math, Givat Ram, 91904 Jerusalem Israel

KIGOSHI, KUNIHIKO, geochemistry educator; b. Tokyo, July 7, 1919; s. Senpachi and Misao (Ito) K.; m. Noriko Hayashi, Oct. 14, 1944; children: Masako, Ikuko. MSc, U. Tokyo, 1942, DSc, 1954. Rsch. asst. Physics and Chemistry Rsch. Inst., Tokyo, 1942-46, Meteorol. Rsch. Inst., Tokyo, 1946-50; asst. prof. geochemistry Gakushuin U., Tokyo, 1950-54, prof., 1954-90, dir. Radiocarbon Lab., 1959—, dean Faculty Sci., 1969-71, 82-84, prof. emeritus, 1990—. Author: Radiochemistry, 1956, Age Determination, 1965. Recipient award Nishina Meml. Found., Tokyo, 1970. Mem. Chem. Soc. Japan, Geochem. Soc. Japan, Am. Geophys. Union, Japanese Assn. for Quaternary Rsch. Home: Shibuya-ku Higashi 3-8-4, Tokyo 150, Japan Office: Gakushuin U, Toshima-ku Mejiro 1-5-1, Tokyo 171, Japan

KIGUCHI, TAKASHI, electric power industry executive, educator; b. Tokyo, May 12, 1944; m. Yoshiko Takeuchi, Mar. 12, 1972; children: Manabu, Tomoko. BSc, Tokyo U., 1967, MS, 1969, PhD, 1975. Rsch. scientist ctrl. rsch. lab. Hitachi Ltd., Tokyo, 1969-71; rsch. scientist atomic energy rsch. lab. Hitachi Ltd., Kawasaki, Japan, 1971-78; sr. rsch. scientist, mgr. energy rsch. lab. Hitachi Ltd., Hitachi, Japan, 1978-91; mgr. ctrl. rsch. lab. Hitachi Ltd., Tokyo, 1991-93; dep. gen. mgr. energy rsch. lab. Hitachi Ltd., Hitachi, 1993-95, dep. gen. mgr. power and indsl. sys. rsch. and devel. divsn., 1995-99, gen. mgr. power and indsl. sys. R&D lab., 1999—; rsch. assoc. MIT, Cambridge, Mass., 1975-76; lectr. Tohoku U., Sendai, Japan, 1990-96, Osaka (Japan) U., 1990—, Tokyo U., 1996-98. Author: AI Application to 3-D Plant Design, 1986 (Okochi award 1989); contbr. articles to profl. jours. Mem. Atomic Energy Soc. (planning bd. 1986-90, dir. 1999—, awards 1972, 80, 84), Am. Nuclear Soc. Avocations: nature photography. Home: 2274-39 Senba, Mito 310-0851, Japan Office: Hitachi Ltd, 7-2-1 Omika, Hitachi 319-1221, Japan

KIGURE, TERUAKI, urologist, researcher; b. Isesaki, Gunma, Japan, Apr. 16, 1954; s. Yasui Yamada and Akino K.; m. Miwako Sasaki, Mar. 24, 1984; children: Naoko, Eriko, Saeko. MB, Akita (Japan) U., 1982, MD, 1989. Resident Akita (Japan) U. Hosp., 1982-92; asst. prof. Akita U., 1992-95; chief Nakadori Gen. Hosp., Akita, 1995—. Contbr. articles to Cancer, Brit. Jour. Urology, Ultrasound in Medicine and Biology, Internat. Jour. of Urology. Fellow Japanese Soc. Nephrology, Japan Soc. Ultrasonics in Medicine, Japanese Urol. Assn., Am. Urol. Assn. (corr. mem.). Avocations: classical music, reading. Office: Nakadori Gen Hosp Urology, 3-15 Misonocho Minamidori, Akita 010, Japan

KIHANA, TOSHIMASA, gynecological oncologist; b. Iyomishima, Japan, Sept. 17, 1955; s. Yoshio and Sumiko Kihana Terao; m. Mieko Kihana Daigen, July 3, 1988; children: Rieko, Toshiomi. MD, Ehime U., 1982, DSc, 1993. Physician Ehime Univ. Hosp., Shigenobu, Japan, 1982-83, Kurashiki Ctrl. Hosp., Japan, 1983-88; resident Nat. Cancer Ctr., Tokyo, 1988-91; physician Ehime Univ. Hosp., 1991-98, Ehime Prefectural Ctrl. Hosp., 1998—. Grantee Min. Edn., Sci., Sports & Culture of Japan, 1993, 95, 98. Avocations: golf, driving, cinema. Fax: 81-89-943-4136. Home: 617-21 Higashi-ishii, Matsuyama 790-0932, Japan Office: Ehime Prefectural Ctrl Hosp, 83 Kasuga-chou, Matsuyama 790-0024, Japan

KIHLE, DONALD ARTHUR, lawyer; b. Noonan, N.D., Apr. 4, 1934; s. J. Arthur and Linnie W. (Ljunngren) K.; m. Judith Anne, Aug. 18, 1964; children: Kevin, Kirsten, Kathryn, Kurte. BS in Indsl. Engring., U. N.D., 1957; JD, U. Okla., 1967. Bar: Okla. 1967, U.S. Dist. Cts. (we. and no. dists) Okla. 1967, U.S. Ct. Appeals (10th cir.) 1967, U.S. Supreme Ct. 1971. Assoc. Huffman, Arrington, Scheurich & Kincaid, Tulsa, 1967-71, ptnr., 1971-78; shareholder, dir., officer Arrington Kihle Gaberino & Dunn, Tulsa, 1978-97, pres., 1994-97; shareholder, dir. Gable & Gotwals, Tulsa, 1997-99, advisor, dir., 1999-2000. Dist. chmn. Boy Scouts Am., 1983-85, cubmaster, 1986-88, coun. coms., 1988-96, campiree chmn., 1990; mem. Statewide Law Day Com., 1982-86, chmn., 1983-85; trustee Brandon Hall Sch., Atlanta, 1991—, chmn., 1995-99. Lt. U.S. Army, 1957-59. Recipient Silver Beaver award Boy Scouts Am. Mem. ABA, Okla. Bar Assn. (chmn. constl. bicentennial com. 1986-89), Tulsa County Bar Assn., So. Hills Country Club, Q Club (scribe 1991—), Tulsa Club (bd. govs. 1987-94, pres. 1992), Order of Coif, Order of Arrow (vigil), Sigma Tau, Phi Delta Phi, Sigma Chi (Tulsa alumni pres. 1995-97). Republican. Home: 4717 S Lewis Ct Tulsa OK 74105-5135 Office: 1100 ONEOK Plz 100 W 5th St Tulsa OK 74103-4240

KIHLSTROEM, JAN ERIK, ecotoxicology educator, writer; b. Ovansjö, Sweden, Mar. 23, 1928; s. Gustaf Valdemar and Anna Margareta (Brodén) K.; m. Ingeborg Anna Linnéa Johansson, July 29, 1950; children: Ingemar, Staffan, Yngve. BSc, Uppsala (Sweden) U., 1953, PhD, 1956, DSc, 1958. Asst. prof. Swedish Nat. Sci. Rsch. Coun., Stockholm, 1973-79; asst. Uppsala U., 1951-58, lectr. ecotoxicology, 1958-72, prof., 1979-93; ret., 1993; mem. various rsch. couns., including natural sci. and agrl. sci., 1977-91. Author: Toxicants in Nature, 1986; co-author: Zoophysiology, 1966; sci. editor Ambio, 1976-83. Mem. Royal Swedish Acad. Scis. Lutheran. Avocation: music. Home: Vretgränd 17, S-753 22 Uppsala Sweden

KIHLSTROM, LARS LENNART GRAHL, neurosurgeon; b. Alingsas, Sweden, Mar. 29, 1957; s. Lennart Reinhold and Vanja Elisabeth (Grahl) K.; m. Linder Buenstam, Sept. 1, 1984; 1 child, Malcolm. MD, Karolinska Inst., Stockholm, 1984. Asst. prof. Karolinska Hosp., Stockholm, 1992, cons. neurosurgeon, 1992—, rschr. neurosci., 1992—. Contbr. articles to profl. jours. Councillor, Danderyd, 1994—. Lt. Swedish Navy, 1977-79. Mem. Royal Tennis Club, Djursholms Golf Club. Avocations: skiing, hiking, sailing, tennis, literature. E-Mail: goodlife@telia.com. Office: Dept Neurosurgery, Box 60 500, S-104 02 Stockholm Sweden

KIHM, HONG-CHUL, international relations educator; b. Jungup City, Korea, Apr. 5, 1930; s. Hyung Wan (dec.) and Kyu Sung (dec.) K.; m. Yang Ja Park, Jan. 21, 1955; 4 children. BA in Polit. Sci., Seoul Nat. U., 1957, MA in Polit. Sci., 1959, PhD in Polit. Sci., 1976. Lectr. war studies Seoul Nat. U., 1960-79; prof. Hankook U. Fgn. Studies, Seoul, 1963-65, Korean Nat. Def. U., Seoul, 1965-69; editl. writer Seoul Shinmun, 1969-71; prof. Hanyang U., Seoul, 1976-95, dir. Inst. Soviet Studies, 1976-79, dean Coll. Social Scis., 1985-88, dir. Audio-Visual Ctr., 1988-92, sr. lectr. war-peace studies and history diplomatic methods, 1995—. Author: A Study of War and Peace (in Korean), 1977, 93, History of Diplomatic Methods (in Korean), 1985, 94, On War Studies (in Korean), 1991, 94 (Publ. award), On Frontiers and Boundaries (in Korean), 1997; translator (into Korean) On War (von Clausewitz), 1977; co-translator (into Korean) Foreign Policy and the American Spirit (D. Perkins). Adv. mem. def. policy Ministry Nat. Def., Seoul, 1981-83; examiner State Exam. of Diplomatic Svc., Seoul, 1984; mem. consulting com. Dem. Peaceful Unification Consulting Com., 1995-99. Recipient Medal of Merit, Office of Prime Min. and Ministry of Gen. Affairs, Korea, 1995. Mem. Korean Polit. Sci. Assn., Korean Assn. Internat. Rels. (pres. 1983), Brit. Internat. Studies Assn., Internat. Polit. Sci. Assn. (bd. dirs. Korean nat. com. 1974-97), Korean Assn. Internat. Studies (adv. com. 1984—), Internat. Inst. for Strategic Studies. Avocations: mountaineering, golf. Home: 42-46 Bomoun-dong 6-Ga, Seongbouk-ku, Seoul 136-086, Korea Office: Hanyang U Coll Social Scis, 17 Haengdang-Dong Seoungdong-Gu, Seoul 133-791, Korea

KIJAK, JAROSLAW, astronomer; b. Zielona Gora, Poland, Jan. 22, 1965; s. Kazimierz and Elzbieta (Piskorz) K. MSc, Pedagogical U. Poland, 1990; PhD, Warsaw U., 1994. Rsch. asst. Pedagogical U. Poland, Zielona Gora, 1990-91; from rsch. asst. to rsch. assoc. Astronomical Ctr., Zielona Gora, 1991—. Mem. Internat. Astronomical Union. Avocations: tennis, chess. Office: Astronomical Ctr, Lubuska 2, 65265 Zielona Gora Poland

KIJLSTRA, AIZE, ophthalmology educator; b. Makassar, Indonesia, Nov. 10, 1950; s. Harke and Foekje (Dragstra) K.; m. Ellen Sluiters, Dec. 18, 1971; children: Harke, Rinse. MA, U. Leiden, The Netherlands, 1974, PhD in Immunology, 1977. Fellow U. Leiden, 1974-80; postdoctoral fellow Netherlands Ophthal. Rsch. Inst., Amsterdam, 1980-84, head dept. ophthalmology and immunology, 1984—; prof. exptl. ophthalmology U. Amsterdam, 1989—. Sect. editor Brit. Jour. Ophthalmology, 1992—; chief editor Ocular Immunological Inflammation, 1992—; contbr. over 150 articles to sci. jours. Office: Head Dept IP&E ID-Lelystad, Edelhertweg 15 PO Box 65, 8200 AB Lelystad The Netherlands

KIKAMA, YASUO, religion educator, translator; b. Tokyo, Oct. 14, 1932; s. Hanjiro and Setsu (Ishii) K.; m. Utako Yusa, Jan. 7, 1964; children: Setsuko, Yuichiro, Koichro. BA, Sophia U., Tokyo, 1955. Cert. tchr. Prof. Caritas Jr. Coll., Yokohama, Japan, 1970-85, chair acad. affairs, 1972-85; lectr. Senshuu U., Tokyo, 1977-85; prof. Eichi U., Amagasaki/Hyogo, Japan, 1985—; lectr. Kobe (Japan) Kaisei Coll., 1985—, Konan U., Kobe, 1986-94; dean acad. affairs Eich U., 1987-93, v.p., 1994-99; lectr. Kinki U., Osaka, Japan, 1994-98. Author: Thomas Merton A Life, 1992 (Joseph Roggendorf prize 1992), G.M. Hopkins's Case for Christianity, 1994, Catholics and America, 1996, Three Nuns of Quebec, 1998, The American Catholic Experience in Historical Perspective, 1999, American Catholics: Five People and Their Spirituality, 2000; editor Studies in Cath. Edn., 1984—. Mem. Internat. Comparative Lit. Soc., Internat. Thomas Merton Soc. (internat. adviser 1989-91), Conf. on Christianity and Lit., Am. Cath. Hist. Assn. Roman Catholic. Home: 1-8-18 Tsukimiyama, Takarazukashi 665, Japan Office: Eichi Univ, 2-18-1 Nakoji, Amagasaki 661, Japan

KIKAWA, KAZUHIKO, physician, educator; b. Yamaguchi, Japan, July 7, 1943; s. Kaoru Kawazoe and Matsuko K.; m. Naoko Higa, June 6, 1975; 2 children. BM, Kumamoto (Japan) U., 1970. Diplomate Japanese Soc. Internal Medicine. Intern Mercy Hosp., N.Y.C., 1974-75, resident in internal medicine, 1975-77; from physician-in-chief to asst. dir. Fukuoka Tokushukai Hosp., Kasuga, Japan, 1980-91, dir., 1991-98; prof. gen. medicine Kumamoto U. Hosp., Kumamoto, Japan, 1999—; chmn. Tokuwakai Social Welfare Corp., Fukuoka, Japan, 1995-99. Coun. mem. Japan-N.Am. Med. Exch. Found., 1997-99. Fellow ACP; mem. Japanese Soc. Internal Medicine (coun. Kyushu chpt. 1991-99), Japan Hosp. Assn., Japan Hosp. Quality Assurance Soc. Buddist. Avocation: Japanese archery. Home: 4-9-88-203 Nagamine-minami, Kumamoto 862-0932, Japan Address: Kumamoto U Med Sch, 1-1-1 Honjo Kumamoto-Shi, Kumamoto 8608556, Japan

KIKICHI, TATEKI, science association director; b. Sapporo, Hokkaido, Japan, Mar. 9, 1942; s. Shyuji and Masako (Sukegawa) K.; m. Fumiko Shinomi; children: Yoko, Michiko. BS, Tohoku U., Japan, 1966, PhD, 1974. Cert. animal anatomy, neurosci., neuropathology, molecular biology. Instr. Tohoku U., Sendai, Japan, 1967-84, assoc. prof., 1985-86; postdoctoral fellow U. Calif., Davis, 1975-77; vis. scholar U. Saarlandes, Homburg, Germany, 1981; dir. Nat. Inst. Neurosci., NCNP, Tokyo, 1987—. Contbr. articles to profl. jours. Grantee Muscular Dystrophy Assn., 1979-83. Avocations: water painting, tennis, book reading. Office: Nat Inst Neurosci NCNP, Kodaira, Tokyo 187-8502, Japan

KIKOLER, STEPHEN PHILIP, lawyer; b. N.Y.C., Apr. 24, 1945; s. Sigmund and Dorothy (Javna) K.; m. Ethel Lerner, June 18, 1967; children: Jeffrey Stuart, Shari Elaine. AB, U. Mich., 1966, JD cum laude, 1969. Bar: Ill. 1969, U.S. Dist. Ct. (no. dist.) Ill. 1969, U.S. Ct. Appeals (7th cir.) 1988, U.S. Ct. Appeals (11th cir.) 1994, U.S. Ct. Mil. Appeals 1970, U.S. Supreme Ct. 1994. Assoc. Rosenthal & Schanfield, Chgo., 1969-70, 73-77, shareholder, 1977—; capt. Judge Advocate Gen.'s Corps U.S. Army, 1970-73. Mem. ABA, Am. Land Title Assn., Ill. State Bar Assn., Chgo. Bar. Assn. (real property law com., mechanics' liens subcom.), Lake County Contractors/Devel. Assn. (govt. affairs com.). Home: 2746 Norma Ct Glenview IL 60025-4661 Office: Rosenthal & Schanfield PC 55 E Monroe St Fl 46 Chicago IL 60603-5713

KIKONYOGO, CHARLES NYONYINTONO, bank executive. Gov. Bank of Uganda, Kampala. Office: Bank of Uganda, 37-43 Kampala Rd PO Box 7120, Kampala Uganda*

KIKUCHI, KEN, infectious disease physician, educator; b. Sendai City, Japan, Feb. 3, 1961; s. Akira and Ikuko (Nakata) K.; m. Chizu Kassai, Jan. 27, 1991. MD, Shinshu U., 1985; PhD, Tokyo Women's Med. Coll., 1991. Asst. prof. Tokyo Women's Med. U., 1989-99, assoc. prof., 1999—; rsch. fellow Meml. Sloan-Kettering Cancer Ctr., N.Y.C., 1996; guest investigator Rockefeller U., 1996-97. Grantee Clin. Pathology Found., 1997, Sankyo Biol. Sci. Found., 1992, others. Mem. Am. Soc. Microbiology, Gen. Soc. Microbiology, Japanese Soc. Infectious Diseases (bd. dirs.). Avocations: minerals, model railroading. Office: Tokyo Women's Med U, 8-1 Kawada-cho Shinjuku-ku, 162-8666 Tokyo Japan

KIKUCHI, KIYOKATSU (KYOHSHA KIKUCHI), electrical engineering educator; b. Tokyo, Jan. 16, 1929; s. Tsuneo and Michi Kikuchi. BS, Nihon U., Tokyo, 1952; BA, Keio U., Tokyo, 1956, MA, 1973; BS, Defiance Coll., 1957. Lic. 1st class elec. engr., applied psychologist. Dir. Shakaizin Pub. Co., Tokyo, 1957-67; lectr. Rissho U., Tokyo, 1967-74, assoc. prof., 1974-85, prof., 1985-99; lectr. Tokyo Met. Adult Edn. Ctr., Saitama Prefecture Adult Edn. Ctr. Translator/essayst: Confirmed Bachelor, The Study of Language Laboratory System, 1974, Contemporary American Writers, 1979, Technology and Education in Future, 1972. Mem. Japanese Psychol. Assn., Applied Psychology Japan, Internat. House of Japan (acad.). Avocations: music, painting, coin and stamp collecting, photography. Home: 4-3-14 Akatsutsumi, Setagayaku Tokyo 156-0044, Japan

KIKUCHI, KOKICHI, pathologist, medical educator; b. Maoka, Karafuto, Japan, May 17, 1932; s. Toyokichi and Yoshi K.; m. Yuko Tsuji, Nov. 17, 1962; 1 child, Yuri. MD, Hokkaido U. Sch. Medicine, Sapporo, Japan, 1957, PhD in Medicine, 1962. Instr. Cancer Inst. Hokkaido U. Sch. Medicine, Sapporo, 1962-66, asst. prof. Dept. Pathology, 1966-69, assoc. prof., 1968-71; prof., chmn. Dept. Pathology Sapporo Med. U. Sch. Medicine, 1971-98, prof. emeritus, 1998—, v.p., dean, 1982-86, pres., 1986-92, pres. Sch. Allied Health Professions, 1986-92; vis. investigator Sloan-Kettering Cancer Inst., N.Y.C., 1966-68; dir. Japanese Cancer Assn., Tokyo; pres. Japanese Immunology Soc., Japan, 1993-94, Japan Pathol. Soc., Tokyo, 1997; dir. Sapporo Immunodiagnostic Lab., 1998—. Author, editor: Medical Immunology, 5th edit., 2000, Pathology,, 3d edit., 1984, New Spl. Pathology, 14th edit., 2000, New General Pathology, 16th edit., 1997, Immunology, Ann. Rev. edit., 1987-99. Recipient Hokkaido Med. prize Hokkaido Prefecture, Sapporo, 1974, Hokkaido Med. Assn. prize, 1974, Akiyama Found. prize, 1994, Hokkaido Press Culture Prize, 1995, Hokkaido Culture prize, 1996. Mem. Japan Med. Assn., Internat. Acad. Pathology, N.Y. Acad. Sci., Hokkaido Med. Cong. (pres. 1986-87), Hokkaido Cancer Soc. (v.p. 1998—). Home: Fushimi 3-7-1, Chuo-ku, Sapporo, 064 Hokkaido Japan Office: Sapporo Med U Sch Medicine, South 1 West 17 Chuo-ku Sapporo, 060 Hokkaido Japan

KIKUCHI, SHIGEAKI, architectural engineering educator; b. Tokyo, Jan. 27, 1944; s. Juro and Ikuko (Harada) K.; m. Toshiko Morimoto, Apr. 11, 1976; children: Shigeo, Tomoko, Akito. B in Engring., Meiji U., 1967, M in Engring., 1969, DEng, 1978. Cert. architect. Lectr. Nishinippon Inst. of Tech., Fukuoka, Japan, 1973-76, assoc. prof., 1976-80, prof., 1980—. Mem. Archtl. Inst. of Japan. Avocations: photography, painting, golf. Home: Kiyomizu 2-2-13 Kokurakita, Kitakyusyu Fukuoka, Japan 8030841 Office: Nishinippon Inst Tech, Aratsu 1633, Kanda Fukuoka, Japan 8000394

KIKUCHI, SOKA KAZUHIRO, marine consultant; b. Yokohama, Japan, Apr. 3, 1934; s. Kanehiro and Saki Kikuchi; m. Yukiko Gotoh; children: Yota, Akiko. B of Polit. Sci. and Econs., Waseda U., Tokyo, 1959; M of Edns., Waseda U., 1961. Cert. mktg. exec. With overseas mktg. Yokohama Rubber Co., Tokyo, 1962-71; chief Europe rep. Yokohama Rubber Co., London, 1972-77; overseas mktg. mgr. Yokohama Rubber Co., Tokyo, 1978-86; specific marine projects gen. mgr. Yokohama Rubber Co., 1987-94; pres. Marine Bus. Consultancy (MBC) Internat., Yokohama, 1994—; marine cons. Ship to Ship Transfer, ports and harbours, 1994—; tea master Enshu Tea Ceremony, 1961—. Profl. internat. tea master, Tea Ceremony, Tokyo, 1980. Mem. Internat. Assn. Ports & Harbours (life support mem.), Enshu Style Traditional Tea Ceremony (tea master profl.). Zen Buddhist. Avocation: tea ceremony. Fax: 81-45-741-6285. Home: 12 20 3 Chome Nagata Kita, Minami ku Yokohama 232 0071, Japan

KIKUCHI, YUJI, educator; b. Tokyo, Oct. 2, 1942; s. Tohru and Mieko K.; m. Yukie Kobayashi, June 17, 1973; children: Yoko, Yasushi. B of Law, Tokyo U.; D of Econs., Kobe U., Japan. Chief economist Bank of Tokyo, 1993-95; prof. econs. Teikyo U., Japan, 1996—. Author: A New Theory on International Financial Economy, 1995, Conditions of a Successful Financial "Big Bang", 1997, An International History of the Yen, 2000; co-author: Elucidation of International Finance, 1997. Mem. Japan Soc. Monetary Econs., Japan Soc. Internat. Econs., Japan Soc. East Asian Economy. Avocations: golf, birding, painting. Home: 10-85 Moegino Aobaku, Yokohama 227-0044, Japan Office: Teikyo U, 359 Otsuka, Hachioji 192-0395, Japan

KIKWETE, JAKAYA, Tanzanian government official. Min. energy, minerals and water Govt. Tanzania, Dar-es-Salaam, min. fin., min. fgn. affairs & coop. Office: Min Fgn Affairs & Coop, PO Box 9000, Dar es Salaam Tanzania*

KILANI, JOHN SHAIBU, environmental advisor, civil engineer; b. Okene, Nigeria, Feb. 26, 1954; arrived in South Africa, 1991; m. Ibrahim Kilani and Rekiyatu (Jimoh) Abdul; m. Nesther Pwaduluwi Myada, Aug. 8, 1981; children: Elizabeth, Lydia, Joshua. BEng in Civil Engring., Ahmadu Bello U., Nigeria, 1978, MEng. in Environ. Engring., 1981; PhD in Civil Engring., U. Birmingham, U.K., 1985. Registered profl. engr., South Africa. Asst. lectr. Ahmadu Bello U., 1979-81, lectr., 1985-87; lectr. U. Nairobi, Kenya, 1987-91; sr. lectr. U. Durban-Westville, South Africa, 1991-93, assoc. prof., faculty dean, 1993-94; environ. mgr. Chamber of Mines, Johannesburg, South Africa, 1994-96, environ. advisor, 1996—; faculty rsch. coord. U. Nairobi, 1989-91. Contbr. articles to profl. jours. Treas. U. Nairobi Staff Assn., 1990-91. Mem. South African Inst. Civil Engrs. Avocations: chess, reading biographies, movies, music, travel. Home: 57 Bamboes St, Constantiakloof, Reedeport 1709, South Africa Office: Chamber of Mines, 5 Hollard St, Johannesburg 2001, South Africa

KILANOWSKI, DANA MARCOTTE, historian, writer, filmmaker, archaeologist; b. Grand Forks, N.D., Aug. 30, 1946; d. Virgil Wallace and Lucille Hogan (Weidel) Marcotte; m. Samuel Joseph Kilanowski, Aug. 30, 1975; children: Kristen Marcotte, Samantha Marcotte. BA, U. N.D., 1975. Acting dir. non-acad. employment U. N.D., Grand Forks, 1968-71; historian, archaeologist Computer Scis. Corp., Edwards AFB, Calif., 1987-94; pres. Dana Marcotte Kilanowski Prodns., Palmdale, Calif., 1994—; guest historian The History Channel, N.Y.C., 1997. Co-author: The Quest for Mach One, 1997 (Best Book award Am. Libr. Assn. 1998, 99); contbr.: Our American Century: A Century of Flight, 1999; exec. co-prodr. (TV show and video) Mach One, 1997; prodr. (video documentary) The Happy Bottom Riding Club, 1994; contbr. articles to profl. jours. Pres. Officers Wives Club, Edwards AFB, 1985-86, PTA, Edwards AFB, 1986; dir. Flight Test Hist. Found., Lancaster Calif., 1991—; guest lectr. Antelope Valley (Calif.) Schs., 1987—. Recipient Commendation, Air Force Flight Test Ctr., 1989, Commendation, Jet Pioneers of Am., 1991, Key Rsch. Historian award Dept. of Def. and Ctr. Environ. Excellence, 1997. Mem. AAUW, Nat. Coun. Pub. History, Nat. Trust Hist. Preservation, South West Oral History Assn., Oral History Assn., Am. Film Inst. Republican. Roman Catholic. Avocations: reading, hiking, swimming, water skiing. E-mail: skilano@prodigy.net. Home and Office: Dana Marcotte Kilanowski Prodns 41445 Almond Ave Palmdale CA 93551-2843

KILARSKI, WINCENTY MICHAL, cytology educator, department chairman; b. Krakow, Poland, Jan. 22, 1931; s. Michal and Maria (Rams) K.; m. Maria Magdalena Brabanska, Oct. 25, 1963; children: Przemyslaw, Paulina. BSc, Jagiellonian U., Krakow, 1957; PhD, Jagiellonian U., 1961. Asst. dept. comparative anatomy Jagiellonian U., Krakow, 1955-63, asst. prof. dept. comparative anatomy, 1964-68, assoc. prof., 1968-74, prof., 1975-80, prof., chmn. dept. comparative anatomy, 1980-85, prof., chmn. dept. cytology and histology, 1985—; rsch. fellow dept. biology Harvard U., Cambridge, Mass., 1962-63; rsch. assoc. Pa. U., Wistar Inst., Phila., 1974-75. Author: Ultrastructure of Capillary Vessels in Vertebrate, 1978, Ultrastructure of the Cell, 1978, 85, Atlas of the Ultrastructure of Vertebrata's Cell, 1978; translator: Biology, 1966. Recipient Minister of Higher Edn. prize for sci. achievement, 1968, Sec. of Polish Acad. of Scis. prize, 1976, Jakub Karol Parnas prize Polish Biochem. Soc., 1979. Fellow Polish Acad. Sci., Polish Acad. Sci. Arts and Letters (sec. natural scis. divsn. 1989-93, dir. 1993-99), PAN (pres. commn. for electron microscopy 1974-84, pres. com. for cell biology 1980-85), Com. for Cell Pathophysiology, Commn. for Physiology and Pathology of Muscle, Polish Sterological Soc. (v.p. 1992-96), Polish Cell Biol. Soc. (pres. 1993-99). Avocations: music, sports, history. Home: Wiedenska 4b, 30-147 Krakow Poland Office: Jagiellonian U Dept Cytol, R Ingardena 6, 30-060 Krakow Poland

KILBOURN, FRANK WILFRED, corporate development executive; b. Ventersdorp, South Africa, Sept. 7, 1961; s. Frank W.J. and Alida H. (Roothman) K.; m. Elizabeth Swart, Sept. 26, 1987; children: Claudia-Ann, Frank Wilfred James. BComm, Rand Afrikaans U., Johannesburg, 1982, LLB, 1985, BA cum laude, 1988, diploma in tax law, 1990; LLM in Tax Law, U. South Africa, 1999. Profl. asst. Hofmeyer Attys., Johannesburg, 1988-91; dir. corp. fin. Std. Corp. & Merchant Bank, Johannesburg, 1991-96; dir. corp. devel. Safren Ltd., Johannesburg, 1996-99; exec. dir. Kersaf Investments Ltd., Johannesburg, 1996—, Sun Internat. Mgmt. Svdcs., 1996—, Royale Resorts Ltd., Bermuda, 1996—; dir. City Lodge Hotels Ltd., Johannesburg, 1996—, Rennies Grinaker Zimbabwe Ltd., 1997-99. Pres. Student Rep. Coun., 1984-85; chmn. Jr. C. of C., Johannesburg, 1993. Lt. Armoured Divsn., 1986-87. Recipient Pres.'s prize Transvaal Law Soc., 1988-89. Mem. Randpark Golf Club, Afrikaans C. of C. Avocations: golf, music, running, reading, birdwatching.

KILBOURNE, GEORGE WILLIAM, lawyer; b. Berea, Ky., Mar. 29, 1924; s. John Buchanan and Maud (Parsons) K.; m. Helen Spooner, Dec. 25, 1945 (div. 1968); m. Carole Marko, June 12, 1970 (div. 1984); children: Stuart (dec.), Charles; m. Anne F. Lavine, Aug. 19, 1996. Student, Berea Coll., 1941-42, Denison U., 1944; BS in Mech. Engring., U. Mich., 1946; JD, U. Calif., Berkeley, 1951. Bar: Calif. 1952, U.S. Dist. Ct. (no. dist.) Calif. 1952, Ind. 1957, U.S. Appeals (9th cir.). Sole practice Berkeley, 1952-57; assoc. Hays & Hays, Sullivan, Ind., 1957-59, Boyle & Kilbourne, Sullivan, 1961-63, Bernal, Rigney & Kilbourne, Berkeley, 1963-68, Sherbourne & Kilbourne, Pleasant Hill, Calif., 1968-75; sole practice Pleasant Hill and Martinez, Calif., 1975—; lectr. Lincoln Law Sch., San Francisco, 1956-57, John F. Kennedy Law Sch., Orinda, Calif., 1977-78. Served to 2d lt. USMC, 1942-46, PTO. Episcopalian. Lodge: Elks. Avocations: tennis, bowling, outdoors. Office: 661 Augusta Dr Moraga CA 94556-1035

KILBOURNE, KRYSTAL HEWETT, rail transportation executive; b. Sandersville, Ga., Apr. 7, 1940; d. John Ray and Kathleen (Perkins) Hewett; m. Alan Arden Kilbourne, July 1, 1961 (div. May 1972); children: Arden Alan, Keith Ray. A, U. Ga., 1960. Tchr. Massey Bus. Coll., Jacksonville, Fla., 1968-72, editor, reporter, photographer, 1968-72; asst. to pres. Luter Advt. Agy., Jacksonville, Fla., 1973-74; asst. to dir. Leukemia Soc., Jacksonville, Fla., 1975-76; asst. to pres. TeleCheck Corp., Jacksonville, Fla., 1979; mgr. customer svc. railroad ops. CSX Transp., Jacksonville, Fla., 1980—. Chair CSX Equal Employment Opportunity Coun., 1992-94. Tuition scholar U. Ga., 1958; recipient Transp. Workers Leadership award,

1995. Mem. Nat. Assn. Railway Bus. Women, Am. Coun. Railroad Women. Democrat. Presbyn. Avocations: oil painting, poetry, snorkeling, traveling, reading. Home: 4856 Deermoss Way S Jacksonville FL 32217-9306 Office: CSX Transportation 6737 Southpoint Dr S Jacksonville FL 32216-6177

KILBURN, PENELOPE WHITE, retired data processing executive; b. Freeport, N.Y., June 25, 1940; d. William Prescott and Marian (Churchill) White; m. Edwin Allen Kilburn, Feb. 7, 1964; children: Penelope Allen, Nancy Kitchen. BA, Barnard Coll., 1962. Elem. sch. tchr. Holmdel (N.J.) Bd. Edn., 1975-78; tech. writer Continental Data Ctr., Neptune, N.J., 1983-86; with Johnson & Higgins, N.Y.C., 1986-89; asst. v.p., 1989-91; v.p. Johnson & Higgins, N.Y.C., 1991-95, ret., 1995. Sustaining mem. Jr. League, Phoenix, 1980—; chmn. St. Georges refugee com., Rumson, N.J., 1981-83; dir. St. Lukes Altar Guild, mem. vestry, 1997—, Branch Port, N.Y., 1997—; trustee Keuka Coll., Keuka Park, N.Y., 1997—. Episcopalian. Avocation: gardening. Home: 513 E Bluff Dr Penn Yan NY 14527-8926

KILBY, JACK ST. CLAIR, electrical engineer; b. Jefferson City, Mo., Nov. 8, 1923; s. Hubert St. Clair and Vina (Freitag) K.; m. Barbara Annegers, June 27, 1948; children: Ann, Janet Lee. BEE, U. Ill., 1947; MS, U. Wis., 1950; DEng (hon.), U. Miami, 1982; DSc (hon.), U. Wis., 1990; DEng (hon.), Rochester Inst. Tech., 1986; DSc (hon.), U. Ill., 1988; DSc, Rensselaer Poly. Inst., 1990; DSc (hon.), Yale U., 1996. Program mgr. Globe-Union, Inc., Milw., 1948-58; asst. v.p. Tex. Instruments, Inc., Dallas, 1958-70; self-employed inventor Dallas, 1970—; disting. prof. elec. engring. Tex. A&M U., 1978-85; inventor monolithic integrated circuit, others; cons. to govt. and industry. Served with AUS, 1943-45. Recipient Nat. Medal of Sci., 1969, 90, Ballentine medal Franklin Inst., 1967, Alumni Achievement award U. Ill., 1974, Holley medal ASME, 1982, 89; inducted into Nat. Inventors Hall of Fame, U.S. Patent Office, 1981. Fellow IEEE (Sarnoff medal 1966, Brunetti award 1978, Medal of honor 1986); mem. NAE (Zworykin medal 1975, co-recipient Charles Stark Draper prize 1989, Kyoto prize for tech. achievement 1993). Home: 7723 Midbury Dr Dallas TX 75230-3211 Office: Ste 155 6600 Lyndon B Johnson Fwy Dallas TX 75240-6531

KILBY, THEODORE MORGAN, JR., auditor, educator; b. Washington, Mar. 2, 1948; s. Theodore Morgan Sr. and Doris Marie Kilby; m. Valerie Stamps, Aug. 18, 1974 (div. 1989); children: Stephanie Michelle, Eric Hamilton. BS, Columbia Union Coll., 1975; MPA, Southeastern U., 1984, MBA, 1985. Cert. fraud examiner, cert. govt. fin. mgr. Dialysis technician VA Hosp., Washington, 1971-75, sickle cell counselor, 1975-78; staff acct. Dept. Vet. Affairs, Washington, 1978-79; auditor office of inspector gen. Dept. Transp., Washington, 1979-93, audit project mgr. office of inspector gen., 1993—; chmn. supr. com. Transp. Fed. Credit Union, Washington. Chmn. adv. coun. Childrens Nat. Med. Ctr., 1996, mem., 1997. With U.S. Army, 1970-71. Mem. Nat. Soc. Accts., Assn. Govt. Accts. Avocations: golf, travel, music, arts. Home: 1108 Beatrice Ct Fort Washington MD 20744-3654 Office: Dept Transp OIG/JA-40 400 7th St NW Rm 9201 Washington DC 20590-0001

KILEY, THOMAS, rehabilitation counselor; b. Mpls., Aug. 28, 1937; s. Gerald Sidney and Veronica (Roberts) K.; m. Jane Virginia Butler, Aug. 25, 1989; children: Martin, Truman, Tami, Brian. BA in English, UCLA, 1959; MS in Rehab. Counseling, San Francisco State U., 1989. Cert. rehab counselor, nat. and Hawaii. Former rsch. profl., businessman various S.E. Asian cos., U.S. Army; sr. social worker Episcopal Sanctuary, San Francisco, 1986-88; dir. social svcs. Hamilton Family Ctr., San Francisco, 1988-89; rehab. specialist Intracorp, Honolulu, 1989-91; v.p. Heritage Counselling Svc., Honolulu, 1991—; pres. Hunter Employment Svcs., Yuma, Ariz., El Centro, Bakersfield and Salinas, Calif., 1995—, Algo Enterprises, Yuma, 1998—. Mem. Am. Counseling Assn., Nat. Assn. Rehab. Profls. in Pvt. Sector, Am. Rehab. Counselors Assn. (profl.), Nat. Rehab. Assn., Rehab. Assn. Hawaii, Rotary, Phi Delta Kappa. Office: Heritage Counselling Svcs PO Box 4699 Yuma AZ 85366-4699 also: 2450 S 4th Ave Ste 102A Yuma AZ 85364-8557

KILGORE, ATHERINE DELOIS ROSS, retired educator; b. Troup, Tex., Aug. 20, 1920; d. Bonnie Bass Ross and Fannie Bell Thompson; 1 child. Bachelor, Tex. Coll., 1950, masters, 1958. Primary tchr. Olney, Tex.; prin. tchr. Seymour, Tex.; prin. head tchr. Vernon, Tex.; primary tchr. music Dunbar Sch., Kermit, Tex.; tchr. Jr. H.S., Kermit; sec. Dist. 18 Social Studies Coun., W.C.T, Kermit, 1984. Tchr. Sunday Sch. Mission, 1952-90, V.B. Sch., 1980-84. Democrat. Baptist. Avocation: music. Home: 301 Entrada Ave Sebring FL 33875-5698

KILGORE, CAROLYN HARRELL (CAROLYN LAWTON HARRELL), writer; b. Macon, Ga., Apr. 10, 1911; d. Furman Dargon and Mary Elliott (Nottingham) Lawton; m. Glover Futch Harrell, June 17, 1933 (dec. Oct. 1983); children: Mary Elliott Harrell Reeves, Carolyn Harrell Foley; m. Morris Ward Kilgore, Jan. 13, 1991 (dec. Jan. 1995). BA, Wesleyan Coll., 1933; cert. tech. writing, Rensselaer Poly. Inst., 1962. Newswriter Marine Corps Supply Ctr., Albany, Ga., 1957-59; tech. writer Thiokol Chem. Corp., Huntsville, Ala., 1960-63; publs. engr. Lockheed Aerospace Rsch. and Engring. Ctr., Huntsville, 1964-72. Author: (history) Kith and Kin: A Portrait of a Southern Family (1630-1934), 1984, When the Bells Tolled for Lincoln: Southern Reaction to the Assassination, 1997; contbr. numerous articles to mags. and newspapers. Recipient citation for outstanding performance in writing, editing and prodn. of four book-length volumes of classified documents pertaining to R & D of space vehicles, Lockheed-Huntsville Rsch. and Engring. Ctr., 1965. Mem. DAR, Nat. Soc. Colonial Dames, XVIII Century Huguenot Soc. S.C., Soc. 1st Families of S.C., Macon, Ga., Writers' Club (pres. 1957). Avocations: classical music, family history. E-mail: CLHK@aol.com. Home: 7400 Clarewood Dr Apt 928 Houston TX 77036-4342

KILGORE, JOE EVERETT, JR., army officer; b. Chattanooga, Dec. 11, 1954; s. Joe Everett and Jewell Yvonne (Nunley) K.; m. Mary Nijhuis, Aug. 21, 1982. BA in Biology, U. Tenn., Chattanooga, 1976; MS in Systems Mgmt., U. So. Calif., 1980; MA in Internat. Rels., Salve Regina Coll., Newport, R.I., 1990; MS in Nat. Security, U.S. Naval War Coll., Newport, 1990; student, Army War Coll., 1998-99. Cert. diving officer and civilian diving instr. Commd. 2d lt. U.S. Army, 1976, advanced through grades to lt. col., 1987; platoon leader 101st Airborne Div., Ft. Campbell, Ky., 1976-79; detachment comdr. 1st bn. 7th Spl. Forces Group, Ft. Bragg, N.C., 1980-83, co. comdr. hdqs., 1983-84; plans and ops. officer U.S. Army Western Command, Ft. Shafter, Hawaii, 1985-89; comdr. A Co., 2d bn. 1st Spl. Forces Group, Ft. Lewis, Wash., 1990-91, exec. officer 2d bn., 1991-92; commander 1st bn. 7th SFGA U.S. Army, 1995-97; chief spl. forces divsn., dir. tng. and doctrine John F. Kennedy Spl. Warfare Ctr. and Sch., 1997-98; chief of staff, 2000—; comdr. combined joint spl. ops. Task Force Bosnia, 1999-00; exec. officer 1st Spl. Forces Group, 1992; inspector gen. US-SOCOM, 1993; dir. tng. Down Under Divers, Waipahu, Hawaii, 1985-89; instr. scuba diving Aquidneck Island Divers, Salve Regina Coll., 1989-90. Contbr. articles to mil. and diving publs. Advisor Explorer Post 5101, Boy Scouts Am., Chattanooga, 1972-76; dir. Explorer Olymics, U. Tenn., 1975; instr. oxygen first aid Divers Alert Network, Chapel Hill, N.C., 1991; instr., disaster vol. ARC; spkr. jr. ROTC program, Oahu, Hawaii, 1985-89. Mem. NRA (life), Nat. Assn. Underwater Instrs. (life, instr.), Spl. Forces Assn. (life, membership com. 1991-92), Assn. U.S. Army, Res. Officers Assn., Am. Legon, N.Am. Fishing Club (life charter), Army War Coll. Alumni Assn. (life), N.Am. Hunting Club (life), VFW, Beta Beta Beta. Methodist. Avocations: boating, fishing, teaching scuba diving. Home: 725 Stonington Dr Fayetteville NC 28311-0329

KILGUSS, ELSIE SCHAICH, artist, gallery owner; b. Manhattan, N.Y., Aug. 4. BS in Advt., Mktg., Bryant Coll.; studied with Charles Sovek, studied with Betty Cappelli, 1968, studied with Henry Hensche, Lois Griffel; grad., RISD; student, Cape Sch. Art. With Horton, Church & Goff, Advt. Agy., Providence; represented by Gallery at Chatham, Mass., 1990-99; owner, instr. Studio Zwei, Wickford, R.I., 1991—; art instr. Warwick Art Mus., 1998-2000. One-woman shows include Studio Zwei, Wickford, 1991—, Alfred Butler & Co., North Kingstown, 1992, Fleet Bank, North Kingstown, 1992, R.I. State House, Providence, 1993, Aszzo, 1998, Cafe Gallery, 1998-99, Dodge House Gallery, Providence, 1999; two-person shows include Providence Art Club, 1991, 93, 95, 97, 98; group exhibits include Warwick (R.I.) Art Mus., 1987, 89, 91, 97, 98, 99, Helme House, Kingston R.I., 1990, 93, 95, 97, Woods-Gerry Gallery, Providence, 1991, Wickford Art Assn. Gallery, North Kingstown, 1991, 93, 95, 97, 99, R.I. Sch. Design Mus., Providence, 1992, 94, Spring Bull Gallery, Newport, R.I., 1993, 99, Newport Art Mus., 1990, 93, 95, 97, 99, R.I. Watercolor Soc., Pawtucket, 1993, 95, 97, 2000; represented in permanent collections Alfred Butler & Co., Carribean Villas, others; catalog covers Providence Mag., R.I. Sch. Design, Cape Cod Mag., North Kingstown Villager. Mem. Providence Art Club, R.I. Watercolor Soc., Wickford Art Assn. (art instr. 1990-91, 98-99), South County Art Assn., Newport Artist's Guild, Creative Arts Ctr., Copley Soc. (Boston), Neport Mus., Attleboro Mus., RISD Mus., Boston Mus. Fine Arts, Warwick Mus., Nat. Mus. Women in Arts, North Kingstown C. of C. E-mail: ekilguss@aol.com. Studio: Studio Zwei Gallery 2 Main St North Kingstown RI 02852-5016

KILHAMN, JAN ERIK, physician, researcher; b. Goteborg, Sweden, Feb. 1, 1961; s. Erik and Marianne (Fredriksson) K.; m. Cecilia Nyberg, Sept. 26, 1987; children: Henrik, Jonatan, Naima. Student, Dickinson Coll., 1980-81; MD, Goteborg U., 1989. Cert. specialist in infectious diseases. Sec. Swedish Embassy, Moscow, 1982-83; intern Molndal (Sweden) Hosp., 1990-92; resident dept. infectious diseases Ostra Hosp., Goteborg, 1992-97; med. adviser Bayer, Med. Affairs Northern Europe, Goteborg, 1997-99; scientific mgr. Fujisawa Scandinavia, Goteborg, 1999—. Del. Swedish Red Cross, 1991, 92. Fellow Swedish Med. Soc.; mem. Goteborg Med. Assn. (treas. 1997-99, auditor 1999—).

KILIC, ALTEMUR, communications professional; b. Ankara, Turkey, Aug. 1, 1924; s. Ali Kilic and Humeyra Aykut; m. Asuman Yavuzer (div.); m. Guzide Ayse Esirgemez, Dec. 29, 1969; 1 child, Aysegul. BA, Robert Coll., Istanbul, 1944; MA, New Sch. for Social Rsch., N.Y., 1950. Various to editor and pub. Devir Newsmag., Istanbul, 1953-54, 72-73; press attache Turkish Embassy, Washington, 1954-59; dir. gen. Press and Info. Dept./ Prime Minister's Office, Ankara, Turkey, 1959-60; chief editor Gun Newspaper, Istanbul, 1961-62; spl. advisor on radio and TV affairs Minister of Tourism and Info., Ankara, 1962-63; info. counselor Turkish Embassy, Bonn, Germany, 1963, Washington, 1963-67; chief of radio and TV sect. UNICEF Hdqtrs., N.Y.C., 1967-68; chief European Info. Office UNICEF Hdqtrs., Paris, 1969; dir. gen. of info. Prime Minister's Office, Ankara, 1963-72; CEO Milliyet Publs., Istanbul, 1973-75; dep. permanent rep. of Turkey UN, N.Y.C., 1975-80; Bd. dirs. List 2000 Internet Co. Author: (book) Turkey and the World, 1957. Mem. Turkish Radio and TV Corp. (bd. govs. 1983-87), Supreme Coun. of Radio and TV, 1992-96; bd. govs. 1st Bank Ankara, 1989-92; mem. exec. bd. Nat. Action Party, 1994-97. Lt. Turkish Brigade, Korea, 1951-52. Decorated Comdr. of Victorian Order, HM the Queen, Crosse Verdienst Kreuz, Germany. Mem. Turkish Journalist Assn., Press Coun. of Turkey.

KILICKAN, LEVENT, physician, medical educator; b. Kutahya, Turkey, Oct. 20, 1966; s. Fevzi and Saide (Karakas) K.; m. Zisan Yardim, Sept. 26, 1990; 1 child, Berkan. MD, Edirne Sch. Medicine, Turkey, 1989. Intern in ob-gyn. Bristol Maternity Hosp., Eng., 1988; resident Istanbul Taksim State Hosp., 1990-94; practitioneer Sofular Sanitary Locality, Nigde, 1989-90; asst. physician Taksim State Hosp. Anesthesiology and Reanimation Svcs., Istanbul, 1990-94; speicalist physician Marmara U. Sch. Medicine, Istanbul, 1995-96; asst. prof. anaesthesiology Kocaeli U. Sch. Medicine, Izmit, 1996—. Avocations: swimming, running. Home: Sok Baris Ap, B Blok D6, 81110 Istanbul Bostanci, Turkey Office: Sopali Ciftligi Kocaeli, Universitesi tip Fakultesi, 41900 Kocaeli Turkey

KILLE, JOHN WILLIAM, JR., toxicology and biomedical product consultant; b. Tampa, Fla., June 17, 1943; s. John William and Myrtle Kille; m. Elaine Anderson; children: Amy, Lindsey, Thomas; m. Camille Ragazzo, Sept. 22, 1991; 1 stepchild, Richard. AB, Lafayette Coll., 1965; MS, Villanova U., 1968; PhD, U. Va., 1972. Diplomate Am. Bd. Toxicology. NIH rsch. trainee Worcester Found. for Exptl. Biology, 1970-72; rsch. fellow Cambridge (Eng.) U., 1972-73; lectr., rschr. Northwestern U., Evanston, Ill., 1974-78; group leader for drug safety Ortho Pharm. Co. divsn. Johnson & Johnson, Raritan, N.J., 1978-88; assoc. dir. product safety and regulatory affairs McNeil Splty. Products Co. divsn. Johnson & Johnson, New Brunswick, N.J., 1988-93; sr. toxicologist Cantox, Inc., Bridgewater, N.J., 1994-96; prin. J.W. Kille Assocs., Stanton, N.J., 1996—; cons. to various pharm., food and biotech. cos., and legal firms, 1994-96, Johnson & Johnson, Emisphere Techs., Inst. for Diabetes Discovery, Virus Therapeutics, Can., Genesoft, Medtox, Italy, various other internat. projects in Can., Mex., Europe and Australia, 1996—; advisor Office Tech. Assessment, U.S. Congress, 1984. Contbr. articles to sci. jours. Chmn. Family Life Edn. Com., Bloomsbury, N.J., 1985-86. Rsch. fellow Lalor Found., 1972-73, WHO, 1972-73. Mem. Genetic Toxicology Assn., Inst. Food Technologists, Regulatory Affairs Profls. Soc., Soc. Toxicology (program com. Mid-Atlantic chpt. 1996—, chmn. edn. and pub. comms. com. 1999—), Teratology Soc., Mid-Atlantic Reprodn. and Teratology Assn. (pres. 1986-87). Avocations: listening to music and singing in choral groups, camping, hunting, fishing, stained glass creations. Fax: 908-236-0921. E-mail: jwkille@blast.net. Office: PO Box 69 Stanton NJ 08885-0069

KILLEMAES, DAAN RICHARD, journalist; b. Aalst, Belgium, Dec. 19, 1973; s. Cyriel Killemaes and Erna De Dongker. Degree in econs., Cath. U., Leuven, 1996. Journalist Trends, Belgium, 1996—. Author: Crash of Boom, 1999. Praeses Thomas Rorus, Leuven, 1995. Avocation: soccer. Home: AAigemdorp 57, 9420 Erpe Mere Belgium Office: Trends, Raketstraat 50, 1130 Evere Belgium Address: Trends Mag, Rsch Park, 1731 Zellik Belgium

KILLHOUR, WILLIAM GHERKY, paper company executive; b. Phila., June 2, 1925; s. William Brelsford and Jean (Gherky) K.; AB in Econs., U. Pa., 1947; m. Josephine Quarrier Greenwood, July 12, 1947; children: Daphne S. (Mrs. John David Polys), William Brelsford II, Jean Gherky (Mrs. David Akers), Gilson Engel. Salesman, Quaker City Paper Co., York, Pa., 1947-50; co-founder W.B. Killhour & Sons, Inc., Phila., 1950, salesman, treas., mgr. printing paper div., 1950-61, pres., 1961-84; v.p. sales Killhour Comml. Paper Co., 1984—; mem. Paper Distbn. Coun. of U.S., 1977-81; past mem. mcht. adv. com. Sorg Paper Co., Scott Paper Co., Howard Paper Mills, Kimberly Clark. Pres., Stafford Sch. PTA, 1959; advisor Savannah Coll. of Arts and Designs; head coach, founder Hilton Head H.S. crew, 1989-94; mem. Land Bank Commn., Town of Hilton Head Island, 1994—; mem. U.S. Rowing Masters Com., rep. S.E. U.S.A. Region, 1994—. Served from ensign to lt. (j.g.) USNR, 1944-46; PTO. Mem. U.S. Rowing Assn. (cert., past chmn. Master's com., coach 1991) Paper Trade Assn. Phila. (pres. 1966), Nat. Paper Trade Assn. (regional dir. 1974—, mem. indsl. paper com. 1972-73, nat. treas. 1977-78, nat. v.p. 1978-80, pres. 1980-81), Susquehanna Litho Club (pres. 1970), Jr. Execs. Club Graphic Arts of Phila. (dir. 1955-60), St. Andrews Soc. Phila., York Club Printing House Craftsmen, Fearing Family Orgn., Mayflower Soc., Merion Cricket Club, Palmetto Rowing Club (founder, pres., head coach Hilton Head, S.C.), Philadelphia Racquet Club (chmn. squash racquets com. 1972-82), Country of York, Undine Barge Club, Spanish Wells Golf Club (Hilton Head, S.C.), Masons, S.C. Yacht Club (Hilton Head). Nat. age group champion double sculls, 1982, 85, 91, nat. single sculls champion, 1985, world single sculls champion, 1990, Can. Henley single sculls champion, 1985, world 8-oar crew champion, Toronto, 1985, world 4-oar crew champion, 1985, 87, 90-95, world double sculls bronze, 1985, world double sculls champion, 1990-92, nat. 8-oar crew age group champion, 1986, 88, 89-90, 92-93, nat. 4-oar crew age group champion, 1987-91, Nat. Quad champion, 1991, World Quad, 1993-94, world 8 champion 1985, 87-90, 92-93, 95, single scull winner Head of Chattahoochie Regatta, Atlanta 88, and numerous others.

KILLIAN, LAWRENCE HARDING, II (LARRY H. KILLIAN), sculptor; b. San Antonio, May 6, 1943; s. Lawrence Harding and Dorothy Louise (Wright) K.; m. Beverly Gayle Schlueder, Dec. 21, 1963 (div. 1979); children: Lawrence Harding III, Michael Ray; m. Janice Kay Nelson, June 18, 1981. Student, Tex. A&M, 1961; BS in Indsl. Arts, Southwest Tex. State, 1971, postgrad., 1971-72; postgrad., RIT Coll., 1981. Instr., job corps. and trade schs. Tex., 1971-75; owner of metal fabrication and welding bus. Austin, Tex., 1975-81; salesperson Hart Graphics, Austin, Times Printing, Random Lake, Wis., 1982-93; freelance metal sculptor Gainesville, Tex., 1991—. Exhibiting at World Trade Ctr., Dallas. Active Leadership Gainesville, 1999. Southwest Tex. State U. scholar, 1970. Mem. Tex. Sculpture Assn., Dallas Visual Arts, Gainesville Area Visual Arts, Dallas Mus. Art, Lions (pres. 1993), Rotary, Gainesville Rotary Club. Avocations: antiques, real estate, travel. Home and Office: 1605 W Hwy 82 Gainesville TX 76240-2003

KILLINGBECK, JANICE LYNELLE (MRS. VICTOR LEE KILLINGBECK), journalist; b. Flint, Mich., Nov. 11, 1948; d. Leonard Paul and Ina Marie (Harris) Johnson; B.A., Mich. State U., 1970; postgrad. Delta Coll., 1971-72; m. Victor Lee Killingbeck, Sept. 26, 1970; children: Deeanna Dawn, Victor Scott. Tourist counselor Mich. Dept. State Hwys., Clare, 1969; copy editor Mich. State News, East Lansing, 1969-70; gen. reporter Midland (Mich.) Daily News, 1970; tchr. Saginaw (Mich.) Public Schs., 1971; public relations teller 1st State Bank of Saginaw, 1971-75; crew leader spl. census in Buena Vista Twp., Detroit Regional Office, U.S. Bur. Census, 1976, interviewer ann. housing survey-standard met. statis. areas, 1977-78, interviewer on-going health surveys, 1979-85, Nat. Crime Survey, 1985-86; editor AMEN newsletter United Meth. Women, Saginaw, 1984-87, Bridgeport-Birch Run Weekly News, 1986-93; owner Have Camera Will Travel, 1993—; accelerated reader para-profl. A.A. Clayton Elem. Sch. Buena Vista Sch. Dist., Saginaw, Mich., 1997, libr., 1998—. Mem. Women in Communications, Sigma Delta Chi. Methodist. Home: 4946 Hess Rd Saginaw MI 48601-6809 Office: 3200 Perkins St Saginaw MI 48601-6563

KILLINGSWORTH, ELIZABETH ANN, special education educator; b. Longview, Tex., May 7, 1950; d. Carl and Martha Katherine (Brown) Rogers; m. Pascal Leroy Killingsworth, Nov. 24, 1972; 1 child, Pascal Leroy Killingsworth, Jr. AS, Kilgare Jr. Coll., 1970; BSin Edn., Stephen F. Austin U., 1971, MEd, 1980. Cert. speech pathologist all levels, cert. tchr. learning disabled, emotionally disturbed, mentally retarded, multi handicapped. Speech therapist Henderson (Tex.) Ind. Sch. Dist., 1971-74, Longview (Tex.) Ind. Sch. Dist., 1974-75; tchr. multi-handicapped Jacksonville (Tex.) Ind. Sch. Dist., 1975-83; tchr. mentally retarded, speech therapist Tyler (Tex.) Ind. Sch. Dist., 1983-85; tchr. mentally retarded, multi-handicapped Beaumont (Tex.) Ind. Sch. Dist., 1985-87; tchr. mentally retarded, learning disabled Brazosport (Tex.) Ind. Sch. Dist., 1987-90, cons. instructional materials support, 1990—. Leader Girl Scouts Am., Brazosport Area, 1990-98; scoutmaster, scout leader, Boy Scouts Am., 1990—, adv. explorer post, 1991—, cub master, Cub Scout leader, 1989—. Mem. Tex. State Tchrs. Assn., Nat. Edn.Assn., Brazosport Ednl. Assn., Brazonia County Aggie Mothers Club, Delta Kappa Gamma. Methodist. Avocations: sailing, reading, unusual crafts. Home: 219 Any Way St Lake Jackson TX 77566-4167 Office: Brazosport I S D P O Drawer Z Freeport TX 77541

KILLION, REDLEY, government official; b. Weno, Chuuk Stat, Micronesia, Oct. 23, 1951; m. Jacinta Antonio; nine children. BA in Econs., U. Hawaii, 1973; MA in Econs., Vanderbilt U., 1978. With Trust Territory Govt. Hdqtrs./Dept. Resources and Devel., Saipan, Micronesia, 1974-79; dir. Dept. Resources and Devel., Saipan, 1979-86; elected At-Large Four-Yr. Seat Chuuk State Congress, 1987—; elected 6th v.p. Federated State of Micronesia, 1999—; vice-chmn. com. on ways and means, mem. com. on resources and devel., health, edn. and social affairs, Congress of Fed. States of Micronesia. Office: Vice Pres FSM, Chuuk State, Weno Federated States of Micronesia

KILLORIN, EDWARD WYLLY, lawyer, tree farmer; b. Savannah, Ga., Oct. 16, 1928; s. Joseph Ignatius and Myrtle (Bell) K.; m. Virginia Melson Ware, June 15, 1957; children: Robert Ware, Edward Wylly, Joseph Rigdon. BS, Spring Hill Coll., Mobile, 1952; LLB magna cum laude, U. Ga., 1957. Bar: Ga. 1956. Pvt. practice in Atlanta, 1957—; ptnr. firm Gambrell, Russell, Killorin & Forbes, 1964-78; sr. ptnr. firm Killorin & Killorin, 1978—; lectr. Inst. Continuing Legal Edn. Ga., 1967—. Adj. prof. law Ga. State U., 1984-87. Chmn., Gov.'s Adv. Com. on Coordination State and Local Govt., 1973, Gov.'s Legal Adv. Council for Workmen's Compensation, 1974-76; bd. regents Spring Hill Coll., 1975-82, trustee, 1981-91. Served with AUS, 1946-47, 52-54. Recipient Disting. Alumnus award Spring Hill Coll., 1972. Mem. Internat., Ga. (chmn. jud. compensation com. 1976-77, chmn. legis. com. 1977-78), Atlanta Bar Assn. (editor Atlanta Lawyer 1967-70, exec. com. 1971-74, chmn. legislation com. 1978-80), D.C. Bar Assn., Am. Judicature Soc., Lawyers Club Atlanta, Atlanta Legal Aid Soc. (adv. com. 1966-70, dir. 1971-74), Nat. Legal Aid and Defender Assn., Internat. Assn. Ins. Counsel (chmn. environ. law com. 1976-78), Atlanta Lawyers Found., Ga. Bar Found. (life), Ga. Def. Lawyers Assn. (dir. 1972-80), Ga. C. of C. (chmn. govtl. dept. 1970-75, chmn. workmen's compensation com. 1979—, Disting. Svc. award 1970-75), Def. Research Inst. (Ga. chmn. 1970-71), Spring Hill Coll. Alumni Assn. (nat. pres. 1972-74), U. Ga. Law Sch. Assn. (nat. pres. 1986-87, Disting. Svc. Scroll 1989), Ga. Forestry Assn. (life, bd. dirs. 1969—, pres. 1977-79, chmn. bd. 1979-81), Am. Forestry Assn., Demosthenian Lit. Soc. (pres. 1957), Sphinx, Blue Key, Gridiron, Phi Beta Kappa, Phi Beta Kappa Assos., Phi Kappa Phi, Phi Delta Phi, Phi Omega. Clubs: Capital City, Peachtree Golf, Commerce, Oglethorpe (Savannah), Highland Country Club (LaGrange). Roman Catholic. Contbr. articles to legal jours. Home: 436 Blackland Rd NW Atlanta GA 30342-4005 Office: Killorin & Killorin 11 Piedmont Ctr NE Atlanta GA 30305-1769

KILLORIN, ROBERT WARE, lawyer; b. Atlanta, Nov. 12, 1959; s. Edward W. and Virgina (Ware) K. AB cum laude, Duke U., 1980; JD, U. Ga., 1983. Bar: Ga. 1984, U.S. Dist. Ct. (no. dist.) Ga. 1984, U.S. Ct. Appeals (11th cir.) 1984. Ptnr. Killorin & Killorin, Atlanta, 1984—. Mem. Atlanta Bar Assn., Ga. Def. Lawyers Assn., State Bar Ga. (chair SCOPE com. 1986, young lawyers sect. legis. affairs com. 1989-91, instr. mock trial program 1989—), Ga. C. of C. (govtl. affairs com.), Internat. Assn. Def. Counsel, 11th Cir. Hist. Soc., Assn. Trial Lawyers Am., Nat. Assn. Underwater Instrs., Nat. Speliological Soc., Mil. Order of Carabao, U. Ga. Pres.'s Club, Explorer's Club. Avocations: forestry, scuba diving, basketball, tennis. Office: Killorin & Killorin 5587 Benton Woods Dr NE Atlanta GA 30342-1308

KILMANN, RALPH HERMAN, business educator; b. N.Y.C., Oct. 5, 1946; s. Martin Herbert and Lilli (Loeb) K.; 1 child, Christopher Martin; m. Patricia C. Nalepa, Aug. 7, 1999. BS, Carnegie Mellon U., 1970; MS, Carnegie-Mellon U., 1970; PhD, UCLA, 1972. Instr. U. Pitts. Katz Grad. Sch. Bus., 1972, asst. prof., 1972-75, assoc. prof., 1975-79, prof., 1979—, George H. Love prof. orgn. and mgmt., 1991—, coord. orgnl. studies group, 1981-84, 86-89, dir. program in corp. culture, 1983—; pres. Organizational Design Cons., Pitts., 1975—. Author: Social Systems Design: Normative Theory and the MAPS Design Technology, 1977, Beyond the Quick Fix: Managing Five Tracks to Organizational Success, 1984, Managing Beyond the Quick Fix: A Completely Integrated Program for Creating and Maintaining Organizational Success, 1989, Escaping the Quick Fix Trap: How to Make Organizational Improvements That Really Last, 1989, Workbook for Implementing the Five Tracks: Vols. I and II, 1991, Logistics Manual for Implementing the Five Tracks: Planning and Organizing Workshop Sessions, 1992, Workbook for Continuous Improvement: Holographic Quality Management, 1993; co-author: Methodological Approaches to Social Science: Integrating Divergent Concepts and Theories, 1978, Corporate Tragedies: Product Tampering, Sabotage and Other Catastrophes, 1984, The Management of Organization Design: Vols. I and II, 1976, Producing Useful Knowledge for Organizations, 1983, Gaining Control of the Corporate Culture, 1985, Corporate Transformation: Revitalizing Organizations for a Competitive World, 1988, Making Organizations Competitive: Enhancing Networks and Relationships Across Traditional Boundaries, 1991, Managing Ego Energy: The Transformation of Personal Meaning into Organizational Success, 1994; mem. editorial bd. Jour. Mgmt., 1983-86, Acad. Mgmt. Exec., 1987-90, Jour. Organizational Change Mgmt., 1988—; developed Kilmann Insight Test, Learning Climate Questionnaire, Thomas-Kilmann Conflict-Mode Instrument in Ednl. Testing Svc., MAPS Design Tech. for Social Systems Design, Kilmann-Saxton Culture-Gap Survey, Kilmann's Organizational Belief Survey; contbr. chpts. to books, articles to profl. jours. Mem. Eastern Acad. Mgmt. (treas. 1975-76, dir. 1983-86), Am. Psychol. Assn., Inst. Mgmt. Scis. (1st prize Nat. Coll. Planning competition 1976), Beta Gamma Sigma, Sigma Xi. Home: 165 Millview Dr Pittsburgh PA 15238-1625 Office: U Pitts Jos M Katz Grad Sch Bus Roberto Clemente Dr Pittsburgh PA 15260

KILNER, URSULA BLANCHE, genealogist, writer; b. Chgo., Feb. 2, 1925; d. Frederic Russell and Blanche (Miller) Gamble; m. Glen Kilner, May 12, 1950. BA cum laude, Mt. Holyoke Coll., 1946; MA, Columbia U., 1947, postgrad., to 1951. Asst. to editor Grolier Pub., N.Y.C., 1947; mgr.

Magnamusic Inc., Garrison, N.Y., 1954-55; publicity and fundraising Little Guild of St. Francis Inc., Cornwall, Conn., 1957-68; lectr. U. Conn., Torrington, 1964-66; genealogist Bird Bottom Genealogy, Salisbury, Conn., 1979—; owner, mgr. The Tenth Muse, phonograph and stereo co., 1958-60; reporter The Comml. Record, 1960-61. Author, editor: A Revolutionary Cook Book, 1985, A Cook Book for All Seasons, 1994; columnist The Voice, 1993—; book reviewer Heritage Books; contbr. articles to profl. jours. Mem. Planning and Zoning Commn., Salisbury, Conn., 1981-82, N.Y. State Hist. Assn. Mem. DAR (chpt. registrar), Am. Coll. Genealogists (cert. genealogist; asst. nat. registrar 1990-91), New Eng. Hist./Geneal. Soc. (life), N.Y. Geneal./Biog. Soc. (life), N.H. Soc. Genealogists (life), Conn. Soc. Genealogists, Suffolk County Hist. Soc., Nat. Soc. Huguenots (mem. adv. bd. 1993—, life, Conn. registrar 1998—), Nat. Soc. Colonial Dames XVII Century (ret. Conn. state registrar 1995-99, organizing pres. Winthrop Fleet chpt. 1990, chpt. pres. 1999—), Nat. Soc. Colonial Dames XII Century (former Conn. state registrar), Vt. Genealogists Soc., Ea. Star, Nat. Soc. Daus. Am. Colonists (Conn. registrar), Assn. Gravestone Studies, Conn. Gravestone Studies, Soc. Genealogists, Nat. Geneal. Soc., Greyhound Friends West, Inc., Piscataqua Pioneers N.H. (life), Essex (Mass.) Soc. Genealogists, Morse Family Soc. (life), Seeley Family Soc., Van Voorhees Family Soc., Whitlock Family Soc., N.Y. Hist. Assn., Ill. Geneal. Soc., Sons and Dau. First Settlers Newbury, Kewanee (Ill.) Hist. Soc. (life), Salisbury Assn., Sheffield Hist. Soc. (life), Andover (Mass.) (life), Hist. Soc., N.Y. State Hist. Assn., Essex (Mass.) Soc. Genealogists, N.H. Genealogy Soc. (life). Avocations: knitting, lecturing, saving greyhounds, greenhouse plants. Home and Office: Bird Bottom Farm RR 1 Salisbury CT 06068-9802

KILPATRICK, CLIFTON WAYNE, book dealer; b. Pontiac, Mich., Nov. 16, 1949; s. Martin Laverne and Shirley Irene (Powell) Ball (dec.). Grad. high sch., Ortonville, Mich. With Royal Castle (restaurant), Miami, Fla., 1969-71, Yankee Clipper (restaurant), Ft. Lauderdale, Fla., 1971-73, Creightons (restaurant), Ft. Lauderdale, Fla., 1973-75; book collector Trivia King, Ft. Lauderdale, Fla., 1975-93. Author: Trivia Professor, 1980. Democrat. Methodist. Avocations: supplying info. to radio and TV programs. Home and Office: 2805 NW 30th Ct Oakland Park FL 33311-1331

KILPATRICK, DAVID, cardiologist, educator; b. Dunedin, Otago, New Zealand, June 27, 1945; s. John Alexander and Effie Forsyth (McKnight) K.; children: James, Rhys. BSc, U. Otago, New Zealand, 1968, MB ChB, 1972, MD, 1981. Hon. registrar Royal Postgrad. Med. Sch., London, U.K., 1974-78; fellow Victoria Gen. Hosp., Halifax, Can., 1978-79, U. Calif., San Francisco, 1979-81; sr. lectr. U. Tasmania, Hobart, Australia, 1981-89, reader, 1990-92, prof., 1993—. Fellow Royal Coll. Physicians (Australia and New Zealand); mem. Royal Coll. Physicians (U.K.). Office: U Tasmania, 43 Collins St, Hobart 7000, Australia

KILPELÄ, ARI JUHANI, electrical engineering researcher; b. Kemi, Finland, Dec. 14, 1960; s. Lalli Kullervo and Valma Irmeli Kilpelä; m. Sirpa Sylvia Rauhanen, July 11, 1991; children: Ellinoora, Helmi. MS, Oulu (Finland) U., 1985. Rschr. U. Oulu, 1985—. Home: Tokantie 34, FIN90800 Oulu Finland Office: U Oulu Electronics Lab, Linnanmaa, FIN90570 Oulu Finland

KILTY, JEROME TIMOTHY, playwright, stage director, actor; b. Balt., June 24, 1922; s. Harold Joseph and Irene (Zellinger) K.; m. Cavada Humphrey, May 11, 1956. B.A., Harvard U., 1949. prof. drama U. Okla., Norman, 1971, U. Tex., Austin, 1972, U. Kans., Lawrence, 1973; appointed to O'Conner Chair of Lit., Colgate U., Hamilton, N.Y., 1974-75, 91-92; instr. in drama Harvard U., Cambridge, Mass., 1983-85, 89. Co-founder, dir., actor Brattle Theatre Co., Cambridge, Mass., 1948-52; actor N.Y.C. stage and TV, 1952-57, including Relapse, 1951, Quadrille, 1952, Misalliance, 1953; played: Falstaff, Iago, City Centre, 1954; writer, actor Dear Liar, Chgo. and London, 1957 (Berlin Festival Critics award 1961, Baton Du Brigadier 1962-63, Palma D'Oro 1962-63, Stanislavsky Centenary medal 1963), dir. revival, Paris, 1974, 80, Rome, 1975, 85, for TV, Hallmark Hall of Fame, 1981, dir. Australian Premiere, 1993, Melbourne; writer, dir. for TV Ides of March, London, 1963, Long Live Life, San Francisco, 1967; dir. Marie Bell, Elisabeth Bergner, Maria Casares, Pierre Brasseur in various French, German, Italian prodns., 1962-65; assoc. dir., Am. Conservatory Theatre, San Francisco, 1966-68, Am. Shakespeare Co., Stratford, Conn., 1965-68; dir. Possibilities, N.Y.C., 1968, Sarah Ferrati in Mrs. Warren's Profession (in Italian), Rome, 1976; writer, dir. Don't Shoot Mable, It's Your Husband, 1968; writer, actor Dear Love, Boston, 1969, London, 1973, The Laffing Man, 1975; dir., actor Androcles and the Lion, 1985, Love's Labor's Lost, 1985; writer: The Little Black Book, N.Y.C., 1972, Look Away, N.Y.C.; musicals What the Devil, 1977, Barnum, 1978; play Hey Marie!, 1979; dir. Julius Caesar, San Diego Nat. Shakespeare Festival, 1979, Love's Labor's Lost, 1980, Misalliance, Denver, 1980, I, James McNeill Whistler, Hartford Stage Co., Peter Pan, Kansas City, Mo., 1985; appeared in play A Month in the Country, N.Y.C., 1979-80, Enter a Free Man, N.Y.C., 1984, Foxfire, Kansas City, Mo., 1985; mem., Hartman Theatre Co., 1981-82, 86-87, played the Doctor in Three Sisters and Ernest in Bedroom Farce; dir. Tammy Grimes in The Millionairess; star The Magistrate; mem., Am. Repertory Theatre Co., Cambridge, Mass., 1983—, created role: The King in Big River, 1983, directed, played Armado in Love's Labor's Lost, 1985, played Abel Bishop in Right You Are (If You Think So), 1988, played Don Antonio in Saturday, Sunday, Monday, 1988; played title role in King Lear, Col. Treletsky in Platonov, played James Tyrone with Claire Bloom in Long Day's Journey into Night, 1996, played Old Ekdal in Wild Duck, 1997; created role Chairman Bowman in Mastergate by Larry Gelbart, 1989, repeated role on Broadway, Criterion Theater, 1989; co-star: A Moon for the Misbegotten, Cort Theatre, N.Y.C., 1984; repeated role of Phil Hogan, Am. Repertory Theatre (Best Actor award Boston Theatre Critics 1984); mem. Hartford Stage Co., 1985-86, played in The Tempest, Twelfth Night, directed and acted in Androcles and the Lion; played Boss Mangan in Heartbreak House, Yale Repertory Theatre, 1986; dir. The Seagull, Am. Conservatory Theatre, San Francisco, 1987, The Man Who Was Peter Pan, Am. Repertory Theater, Cambridge, 1990, Arms and the Man, Alley Theater, Houston, 1995; co-star The Doctor's Dilemma, N.Y.C., 1990, played Harry Hope in The Iceman Cometh, Chgo., 1990 (Joseph Jefferson award 1991); author plays About to Begin, 1988, Margaret Sanger/Unfinished Business, 1989, The Hermit of Yalta, 1993; starred with Opera Co. of Boston in world premiere of The Balcony, 1990, Bolshoi Theatre, Moscow, 1991, starred in Gigli Concert, Court Theatre, Chgo., Spoleto Festival U.S.A., 1992, The Substance of Fire, Asolo Theatre, Sarasota, Fla., 1992, Stages Repertory Theatre, Houston, 1994, Love Letters, Asolo Theatre, 1993, King Lear, Asolo Theatre, 1993; played Horace Vandergelder in The Matchmaker, McCarter Theater, Princeton, N.J., 1994, Gov. Danforth in The Crucible, Alley Theater, Houston, 1994, King Lear, Nebr. Shakespeare Festival, 1995, Tobias in A Delicate Balance, Stages Repertory Theater, Houston, 1996, Athol Fugard's Valley Song, Arizona Theatre Co., 1997, Michael James in Playboy of the Western World, Steppenwolf Theatre, Chicago, 1998, Long Wharf Theatre, New Haven; guest starred as King Lear, Arizona State Univ., 1998; played Leo Tolstoy in world premiere of The Last Station, Vt. State Co., Burlington, 1999, Scrooge, Va. Stage Co., Norfolk, 1999, Inherit the Wind, Mo. Repertory Co., 2000. Served to capt. USAAF, 1942-46, ETO. Decorated D.F.C., Air Medal with seven clusters. Mem. Signet Soc. Club: Players (N.Y.C.). Home: PO Box 1074 Weston CT 06883-0074

KIM, BONG HWAN, veterinary educator, swine consultant; b. Taegu, Korea, Feb. 11, 1941; s. Sang-Dong and Dal-Yae (Kwon) K.; m. Kae-Sook Oh, Dec. 21, 1988; children: Won-Bae, Sung-Bae, So-Young, Ihn-Bae. DVM, Kyungpook Nat. U., Taegu, 1964; Diploma in Vet. State Medicine, U. Edinburgh, 1973, PhD, 1976. Rsch. assoc. Royal Sch. Vet. Studies, Edinburgh U., 1973-76; rsch. scientist Inst. Vet. Rsch., Ministry Agr. and Forestry, Anyang, Korea, 1967-72, sr. rschr., 1977-80; asst. prof. Kyungsang Nat. U., Jinjoo, Korea, 1980-83; assoc. prof. Kyungpook Nat. U., Taegu, 1984-90, prof., 1990—; vis. prof. U. Minn., St. Paul, 1995; chmn. nat. adv. com. for animal disease control Ministry of Agr. and Forestry, Seoul, 1996. Author: Care and Management of Pigs, 1998, Pork Production, 1999, Swine Diseases, 1999; inventor in field. Adviser Nat. Vet. Rsch. and Quarantine Svc., Anyang, 1998—; chmn. quality assurance com. Pig Testing Sta., Hadong, Korea, 1997—; chmn. tech. adv. com. Nat. Hog Cholera Eradication Campaign, Seoul, 1999-2000. Served to 2d lt. Korean Army, 1964-66. Recipient Ministerial award Ministry of Agr. and Forestry, 1999. Mem. Korean Soc. Vet. Sci. (v.p. 1991-93, steering com. 1999—), Korean Swine Assn. (adviser 1994—), Korean Soc. Vet. Pub. Health (v.p. 1999—), Korean Acad. Sci. and Tech. Presbyterian. Avocations: hiking, reading, Go-game. E-mail: bhkim@knu.ac.kr. Office: Kyungpook Nat U/Vet Med, 1370 Sangyuk-dong, Puk-gu, Taegu Korea 702-701

KIM, BYUNG SOO, physician, educator; b. Seoul, Korea, May 8, 1936; s. Young Kwan and Sun Le (Shim) K.; m. Mija Choi, Nov. 3, 1966; children: Helen, Ellen, George. MD, Yonsei U., Seoul, 1961; postgrad., Harvard Med. Sch., Boston, 1970; PhD, Okayama (Japan) U., 1985. Instr., staff mem. Harvard Med. Sch., 1970-74; assoc. prof. Yonsei U., 1974-78, prof., 1978—, also bd. dirs., pres.; cons. WHO, 1975-85. Editor: Current Status of Cancer Control and Immunobiology, 1987. Fellow Am. Pediatric Assn.; mem. Korean Med. Assn., Korean Cancer Assn. Methodist. Home: 95-48 Yonhi Dong, Seoul Republic of Korea Office: 134 Shinchon-dong, Sudaemoon-gu, Seoul 120-749, Republic of Korea*

KIM, BYUNG-DO, marketing educator; b. Seoul, South Korea, Aug. 13, 1958; s. Sang-Wook and Chang-Hee Kim; m. Je-Hee Kim, Dec. 28, 1986; 1 child, Soo-Bin. BBA, Seoul Nat. U., 1982; MBA, NYU, 1985; PhD, U. Chgo., 1992. Sr. v.p. Hasae Pub. Co., Seoul, 1985-87; vis. rsch. scholar U. Chgo., 1992; asst. prof. mktg. Carnegie Mellon U., Pitts., 1993-96; prof. Seoul Nat. U., 1996—. Contbr. articles to profl. jours. U. Chgo. fellow, 1988, Oscar Mayer Found. fellow, 1991; Korean Consulate Honor scholar, 1990. Mem. Am. Mktg. Assn., Am. Econ. Assn., Am. Statis. Assn., Inst. for Ops. Rsch. and Mgmt. Scis. Avocation: golf. Home: 129-1203 Samsung Apt, Seohyun-dong Boondang-ku, Sungnum South Korea Office: Seoul Nat Univ Sch Bus, 56-1 Shinlim-dong Kwanak-ku, 157-742 Seoul South Korea

KIM, BYUNG-DONG, molecular biology educator; b. Chunan, Choongnam, Republic of Korea, Dec. 10, 1943; s. Boong-Han and Eul-Soon Kim; m. Il-Young Yoo, Apr. 1, 1972; children: Jihyun Jenifer, Soohyun Sarah. BS, Seoul (Rep. of Korea) Nat. U., 1966, MS, 1970; PhD, U. Fla., 1974. Postdoctoral fellow Sch. Medicine, U. Fla., Gainesville, 1975-76, asst. rsch. scientist, 1978-80; rsch. assoc. Sch. Medicine, W.Va. U., Morgantown, 1976-78; assoc. in rsch. Fla. State U., Tallahassee, 1980-83; asst. prof. U. R.I., Kingston, 1983-87; prof. molecular biology Seoul Nat. U., 1987—; program devel. and rsch. com. R&D Promotion Ctr. for Agr., Forestry and Fishery, 1995—. Contbr. articles to profl. publs. R&D Promotion Ctr for Agrl. Forestry and Fishery (program dir. and rsch com, 1995s). Fellow AAAS, Internat. Soc. Plant Molecular Biology, Internat. Soc. Molecular Plant-Microbe Interactions, Biochem. Soc. Republic of Korea (chair organizing com. 7th, 8th Sorak conf. on gene expression and regulation, and protein structure and function 1993-95), Korean. Soc. Horticultural Sci. (editor 1991-95, sec. gen. 1995—), Genetics Soc. Korea, Korean Soc. Molecular Biology (assoc. editor 1990-93), Korea Sci. and Engring. Found. (program devel. and rsch. com. 1995-97), Nat. Instrumentation Ctr. for Environment Mgmt. (assoc. dir. 1993-94), N.Y. Acad. Sci. Baptist. Avocations: swimming, tennis, hiking, classical music. Office: Seoul Nat U Dept Horticultr, 103 Seodoon-dong, Suwon 441-744, Republic of Korea

KIM, CHANG-JIN, mechanical engineer; b. Taegu, Korea, Sept. 14, 1958; s. Hong Kon Kim and Bok Joo Lee; 1 child, Andrew J. BS, Seoul Nat. U., 1981; MS, Iowa State U, 1986; PhD, U. Calif., Berkeley, 1991. Mem. chmn.'s staff Tongkook Corp., Seoul, 1982; postdoctoral rschr. U. Calif., Berkeley, 1992; vis. postdoctoral fellow U. Tokyo, 1992-93; asst. prof. engring. UCLA, 1993-98, assoc. prof. engring., 1998-2000, prof. engring., 2000—. Contbr. articles to profl. jours.; patentee in field. Bd. dirs. Korean Am. Coalition, L.A., 1998—; mem. adv. coun. Dem. and Peaceful Unification of Korea, L.A., 1998—. Recipient Faculty Early Career Devel. award NSF, 1997. Mem. ASME (exec. com. MEMS divsn. 1999—), IEEE, AAAS, Tau Beta Pi. Office: UCLA 38 137 E4 Bldg Los Angeles CA 90095-0001

KIM, CHAN-KI, scientist; b. CHung-Ju, Korea, Dec. 17, 1968; s. Young-Gun and Bok-Sun K.; m. Seong-Jung Song, Feb. 18, 1995; children: Ryang-Kyu, Nam-Kyu. BD, Seoul Indsl. Nat. U., Korea, 1991; MD, Chung-Ang U., Seoul, 1993, PhD, 1996. Part-time prof. Chung-ang U., Seoul, 1993-95; sr. scientist Korea Elec. Power Rsch. Inst., Daejon, Korea, 1996—. Inventor in field. Fellow Korean Inst. Elec. Engring.; mem. IEEE. Avocation: reading. Home: Sam Sung Purun Apt 110-101, Junmin-Dong, Yusung-Gu 705-390, Korea Office: Korea Elec Power Rsch Inst, 103-16 Munji-Dong, Daejon 305-380, Korea

KIM, CHEOL GI, physicist; b. Yecheon, Korea, Feb. 27, 1961; s. Ki-Joo and Wol-Kim (Ko) K.; m. Lacky Han; children: Gee-Hye, Geie-Soo. BS, Seoul Nat. U., Korea, 1983; MS, KAIST, Korea, 1986, PhD, 1989. Sr. rschr. KRISS, Taejon, Korea, 1989-96; prof. Sun Moon U., Asan-Si, Korea, 1996—; cons. in field. Contbr. articles to profl. jours. With Korean Army, 1990-93. Mem. IEEE, Korean Phys. Soc., Korean Magnetics Soc. Office: Sun Moon U, Kalsan-ri, Chungnam 336-840, Korea

KIM, CHIN-SAM SAM-WOO, zen master, seminary president, publisher; b. Chinju, Korea, Mar. 3, 1941; came to U.S., 1967; s. Heechul Kim and Dogak Yi; m. Marianne Sasha Bluger, June 6, 1968 (div. Nov. 1986); children: Maji Kim, Agyong. Student, Namjang-Sa Monastery, Sangju, Korea, 1958-61, Pomo-Sa Monastery, Pusan, Kore, 1962-66. Dharma tchr. Pongun-Sa Sem., Seoul, 1964-66; founder, pres. Buddhist Soc. for Compassionate Wisdom, N.Y.C., 1967—; zen master Buddhist Soc. for Compassionate Wisdom, Chgo. and Toronto, Ont., Can., 1983—; pub. Spring Wind-Buddhist Cultural Forum, quar. mag., Chgo., 1981—; pres. Maitreya Buddhist Sem., Ann Arbor, Mich., 1985—, Toronto and Chgo., 1985—; co-chmn., organizer 1st Conf. on World Buddhism in Am., Ann Arbor, 1983; organizer 1st Zen Tchrs.' Conf. in Am., Ann Arbor, 1987; co-organizer, chmn. 1st Conf. on Buddhism in Can., Toronto, 1990; Buddhist rep. Gethsemani Encounter-Interreligious Monastic Encounter, Gethsemani Abbey, Ky., 1996. Author: Zen Lotus Society Handbook, 1986, Zen Buddhism in North America, 1986; contbr. articles to religious publs. Moderator, facilitator Buddhist Movement for Peace and Justice, Ann Arbor, 1987—. Recipient citation organizing com. for celebration 25th anniversary Zen Master Samu nim Dharma Tchgs. in N.Am., Toronto, 1992, Boundless Bodhisattva award Sangha coun. Buddhist Soc. for Compassionate Wisdom and Maitreya Buddhist Sem., 1997. Mem. Assembly Religious and Spiritual Leaders, Parliament of World's Religions (trustee of coun., 1995-98). Avocations: gardening, travel, reading, writing. Home and Office: 1710 W Cornelia Ave Chicago IL 60657-1219

KIM, CHUL GEUN, science educator; b. Yesan, Korea, Aug. 30, 1958; s. Young Wan and Soon Jeon (Chang) K.; m. Sookyeong Kim, June 25, 1984; children: Hyunjin, Hyun-Jee, Hyun Young. BS, Hanyang U., 1981; MS, Seoul Nat. U., 1983; PhD, Cornell U., 1990. Rsch. asst. Wash. State U., Pullman, 1984-85, Cornell U., N.Y.C., 1985-90; sr. fellow U. Wash., Seattle, 1990-91; rsch. assoc. Fred Hutchinson Cancer Rsch. Ctr., Seattle, 1991-93; lectr. Chonbuk Nat. U., Chonju, Korea, 1992-94; asst. prof. Hanyang U., Seoul, 1994-98, assoc. prof., 1998—; spl. lectr. The First Korean Sci. Award Rsch. Presentation, Seoul, 1992; spkr. in field. Editl. mem. Korean Soc. for Molecular Biology News, 1993, Korean Jour. Biol. Sci., 1997—, Mol. Cells, 1999—; contbr. articles to profl. jours. Scholarship Korean Embassy in U.S.A.; fellowship Cooley's Anemia Soc., 1991. Mem. ASM, AAAS, Korean Soc. for Molecular Biology (edn. mgr. 1997, internat. affairs com. 1999, acad. affairs mgr. 2000), Korean Genetics Soc. (fund sec. 1995-98, sec. internat. affairs 1999—), Zool. Soc. of Korea (editl. mgr. ZSK news 2000), Biochem. Soc. of the Republic of Korea. Office: Hanyang U Dept Life Sci, 17 Haengdang-Dong Sungdong, Seoul 133-791, Republic of Korea

KIM, CHULJOO, air transportation executive; b. Teagu, Republic of Korea, Jan. 15, 1954; s. Hooseok Kim and Hanie Woo; m. Miyeon Kim, Feb. 22, 1982; children: Yoonmi, Hyunho. BS, Inha U., Inchon, Republic of Korea, 1976. Quality control engr. Samsung Aerospace, Changwon, Republic of Korea, 1979-85; asst. mgr. Samsung Aerospace, Seoul, Republic of Korea, 1985-87, mgr., 1987-92; gen. mgr. Mando Machinery Corp., Kunpo, Republic of Korea, 1992-97, LG Internat. Corp., Seoul, 1998—. With Republic of Korea Air Force, 1976-79. Mem. Korean Soc. Aero. and Space (councilor 1998—), Ihna U. Alumni Assn. (dir. 1989—). Avocations: fishing, model aircraft, tennis. Fax: 82-2-662-8659. Office: LG Internat Corp, Yeoido, 11th Fl, LG Twin Tower, Seoul 150-721, Republic of Korea

KIM, CHUNG-KIL, Republic of Korea government official; b. Koje, Korea. Student, Pusan Nat. U. Former Dem. mem. Nat. Assembly; joined Nat. Congress for New Politics, 1997; min. govt. adminstrn., from 1998; now min. of justice Ministry Justice, Kwachon, Republic of Korea. Mem. Nat. Congress for New Politics. Office: Ministry of Justice, 1 Chungang-dong, Kyonggi Kwachon Republic of Korea*

KIM, DAE YOUNG, chemist, educator; b. Hongsung, Korea, July 15, 1961; s. Mansoo and Jumsoon (Oh) K.; m. Jong-Im Lee, Nov. 21, 1987; children: Jiwon, Dongwon. BSc, Chungnam Nat. U., Taejon, Korea, 1983; MSc, Korea Advanced Inst. Sci. Tech., Seoul, 1985, PhD, 1987. Rschr. Dyson Perrins Lab., Oxford, Eng., 1987-88; sr. rschr. Daewoong Ltd., Seoul, 1989-91, consulting prof., 1991—; asst. prof. Soonchunhyang U., Asan, Korea, 1991-96, assoc. prof. 1996—. Contbr. articles to profl. jours.; patentee in field. Mem. Korea Chem. Soc. Roman Catholic. Avocations: tennis. Home: Ssangyong-Dong Moran, Apt 5-1802, Chonan 330-090, Korea Office: Soonchunhyang U, Asan PO Box 97, Asan 336 600, Korea

KIM, DAE-JUNG, president of Republic of Korea; b. Hungwang-Ri, Korea, Dec. 3, 1925. Student, Korea U., Seoul, 1964; MA in Econs., Kyunghee U., Seoul, 1970; PhD in Polit. Sci., Diplomatic Acad. Fgn. Ministry, Moscow, 1992; LLD (hon.), Emory U., 1983, Cath. U. Am., 1993; D Polit. Sci. (hon.), Won-Kwang U., Korea, 1994. Spokesman ruling Dem. Party, 1960, 63, elected to 5th, 6th, 7th, 8th, 13th and 14th Nat. Assemblies, 1961; spokesman People's Party, 1965; spokesman, mem. exec. bd. New Dem. Party, 1967; fgn. exile, polit. prisoner during Yushin Sys. Korea, 1970-87; founder, pres. Party for Peace and Democracy, Korea, 1987-91, New Dem. Party, Korea, 1991; founder, co-chmn. Dem. Party, Korea, 1991; elected pres. Nat. Assembly, 1992, Republic of Korea, 1997—; vis. fellow Clare Hall Coll., U. Cambridge, Eng., 1993; hon. prof. Moscow U., 1992, Chinese Acad. Social Scis., Beijing, 1994, Nankai U., Tianjin, China, 1994, Fudan U., Shanghai, 1994; inaugurated Nat. Congress for New Politics, 1995; co-pres. FDL-AP, Seoul, 1994, permanent co-pres., 1995. Author: (in Korean) Letters from Prison, 1983, (also English and Japanese translations), Conscience in Action, 1985, (Japanese edit. 1987), Mass Participatory Economy, 1992, A New Beginning, 1993; (in English, Chinese, Japanese and Russian) Building Peace and Democracy, 1987, Three Stage Approach to Korean Reunification: Focusing on the South-North Confederal State, numerous others. Founder, chmn. bd. dirs. Kim Dae-jung Peace Found. for Asia-Pacific Region, 1994; advisor Robert F. Kennedy Meml. Fund., Washington, 1983; advisor internat. adv. coun. Union Theol. Sem., N.Y.C., 1984—; advisor Internat. Com. for Relief of Victims of Torture, Mpls., 1984—. Recipient Bruno Kreisky Human Rights award Austria, 1981, George Meany Human Rights award AFL-CIO, 1987, Union medal Union Theol. Sem., 1994, Nobel Peace Prize, 2000; named Hon. Citizen, City of Nashville, 1983; named Lifetime Mem. Clare Hall Coll., U. Cambridge, 1993. Mem. Internat. Ecol. Acad. Home: Chong Wa Dae, 1 Sejongno Chongno-gu, Seoul Korea*

KIM, DAE-KEE, medicinal chemist; b. Pusan, Korea, Sept. 20, 1956; s. Seon-Tae Kim and Bong-Ak Park; m. Seon-Hee Hwang, Nov. 1, 1981; children: Kyoung-Nam, Kyoung-Seok. BS, Seoul Nat. U., 1977, MS, 1982; PhD, SUNY Buffalo, 1986. Postdoctoral fellow Nucleic Acid Rsch. Inst., Costa Mesa, Calif., 1986-87; sr. rschr. Korea Rsch. Inst. Chem. Tech., Daejeon, 1987-88; rsch. assoc. Sunkyong Industries, Suwon, Korea, 1989-96; dir. R&D SK Chems., Suwon, 1997—. Inventor in field. Recipient Disting. Patent prize Jungang Daily News, 1995, Dasan Tech. Grand prize Korea Econ. Daily, 1999; Scientist of Mth. prize Seoul Econ. Daily/Korea Sci. & Engring. Found., 1999; New Drug Devel. Grand prize Maeil Bus. Newspaper, 1999. Mem. Am. Chem. Soc., Am. Soc. Microbiology, Korean Chem. Soc. (edit. bd., Tech. Progress prize 1995), The Pharmaceutical Soc. of Korea. Office: SK Chems Life Sci Rsch Ctr, 600 Jungja-Dong, Suwon 440-745, Korea

KIM, DAL SOO, medical educator; b. Chinju, Kyungnam, Republic of Korea, Sept. 5, 1943; s. Young Zo and Soon Zo (Park) K.; m. Chung Hee Nahm, Feb. 15, 1974; children: Choong Han, Jimin. MD, Cath. Med. Coll., Seoul, Republic of Korea, 1970; PhD, Cath. U., Seoul, 1985. Resident in neurosurgery St. Mary's Hosp., Seoul, 1971-75; chief neurosurgery Capital Armed Forces Hosp., Seoul, 1976-81; asst. prof. Cath. Med. Coll., Seoul, 1982-86, assoc. prof., 1987-92, prof., 1993—, dir., 1999—; cons. neurosurgery Capital Armed Forces Gen. Hosp., 1991. Contbr. rsch. papers to profl. jours. Lt. col. Korean Armed Forces, 1976-81. Mem. Korean Soc. for Cerbrovascular Disease (pres. 1998, exec. mem.), Korean Neurosurg. Soc. (acad. award 1989, 98—), Korean Brain Tumor Study Group. Avocations: tennis, golf, calligraphy. Office: Uijongbu St Mary's Hosp Cath U, Dept Neurosurg 65-1 Kumoh-dong, Uijongbu 480-130, Republic of Korea

KIM, DALWOO, physicist, researcher; b. Pusan, Korea, Sept. 16, 1949; s. Sang-Chul and Wol-Bo (Kim) K.; m. Myo-Rae Kim, Dec. 20, 1976; 1 child, Kwang-Youn. BS, Seoul Nat. U., 1973, MS, 1976; MS, La. State U., Baton Rouge, 1987, PhD, 1989. Tchr. Attached Mid. Sch. of Seoul Nat. U., 1973-77; sr. rschr. Pohang (Korea) Iron and Steel Co., 1978-84; rsch. asst. La. State U., 1985-87; jr. guest rschr. Brookhaven Nat. Lab., Upton, N.Y., 1988-89; rsch. head Rsch. Inst. Indsl. Sci. and Tech., Pohang, 1989—; adj. prof. Pohang U. Sci. and Tech., 1990—; guest prof. Jilin U. Tech., Changchun, China, 1995—, Changchun Inst. Optics and Fine Mechanics, 1996—; adj. prof. Chosun U., 2000—. Contbr. articles to profl. jours. Recipient Yangbak Tech. award The Korea Herald, 1995, Govt. award for sci. and tech. promotion Ministry of Sci. and Tech., 1997, New Tech. Korea '97 Ministry of Comml. Industry and Energy, 1997. Mem. Optical Soc. Am., Korean Phys. Soc., Optical Soc. Korea. Avocations: collecting stones, listening to music. Fax: (08) 9389 1906. Home: 1503-7 Profs Apt Jigok-dong, 790-390 Pohang Republic of Korea

KIM, DAVID SANG CHUL, publisher, evangelist, retired seminary president; b. Seoul, Republic of Korea, Nov. 9, 1915; came to U.S., 1959; m. Eui Hong Kang, Jan. 6, 1942; children: Sook Hee, Sung Soo, Hyun Soo, Young Soo, Joon Soo. BA in English Lit., Chosen Christian Coll., Seoul, 1939; postgrad., U. Wales, 1954-55, Western Conservative Bapt. Sem., 1959-61, U. Oreg., 1962-63; MA, U. Oreg., 1965; postgrad., Pacific Sch. Religion, Berkeley, Calif., 1965-66; PhD, Pacific Columbia U., 1988. Staff Chosen Rubber Industry Assn., Seoul, 1939-45; fin asst. U.S. Mil. Govt., Kunsan City, Republic of Korea, 1945-48; govt. official Ministry of Fin., Ministry of Social Affairs and Health, Ministry of Fgn. Affairs Govt. of Republic of Korea, Seoul, 1948-59; charter mem. Unification Ch., Seoul, 1954—; 1st missionary to Eng. Unification Ch., 1954-55; missionary, evangelist Unification Ch., U.S., 1959-70; supr. counseling Clearfield (Utah) Job Corps Ctr., 1966-70; founder, pres., owner The Cornerstone Press (name change to Rose of Sharon Press), 1978-85; charter mem., trustee World Relief Friendship Found., Inc. (now Internat. Relief Friendship Found., Inc.), 1974—; pres. Internat. One World Crusade Inc., 1975—; founder, United Faith, Inc., Portland, Oreg., 1970—, Global Edn. R & D Fund, Inc., 1981-96; pres. Unification Theol. Sem., 1974-94; charter mem., trustee Nat. Coun. Chs. and Social Action, 1976-96; adv. fin. supporter Global Congress of World Religions, Inc., 1978-96; charter mem. Internat. Religious Found., Inc., 1982—; v.p. Unification Thought Inst., 1989-97; founder, pres. Marriage and Family Inst. Am., 1994—; chmn. inauguration The Family Fedn. for Unification and World Peace, The Netherlands, 1996—. Author: Individual Preparation for His Coming Kingdom: Interpretation of the Principle, 1964, Victory Over Communism and the Role of Religion, 1972; editor: (book series) Day of Hope in Review, Part 1-1972-74, 1974, Part 2-1974-75, 1975, Part 3-1976-81, 1981; exec. prodr. (radio) The Unification Hour, 1975—, True Love Journey, 1993—; contbr. articles to profl. jours. Recipient Byzantine Golden medal Am. Inst. Patristic Byzantine Studies, Inc., 1992. Address: PO Box 1755 South Rd Sta Poughkeepsie NY 12601-0755

KIM, DEOK, government official; b. Kumi, Korea, May 25, 1935; s. Woodong and Kyeompil (Song) K.; m. Eunheh Park, Oct. 9, 1962; children: Jun, Hoh. LLB, Seoul (Korea) Nat. U., 1954; MA in Polit. Sci., Ind. U., 1962; PhD, Hankook U. Fgn. Studies, Seoul, 1975. Prof. Hankook U. Fgn. Studies, Seoul, 1967-93, dean grad. sch., 1986-89; dir. Agy. Nat. Security Planning, Seoul, 1993-94; dep. prime min., min. Bd. Nat. Unification, 1994-95; pres. Seoul Peace Prize Cultural Found., 1995-96; mem. nat. assembly Nat. Assembly Republic of Korea, Seoul, 1996-2000; mem. adv. coun. Ministry Nat. Unification, 1982-92, Ministry Fgn. Affairs, 1991-93, South-North Red Cross Talk, 1986-93; sr. advisor Com. for Inter-Korean Trade

and Investment, 1995-98. Author: Foreign Policy of Weak States, 1992, Path to Reunification of Divided Korea, 1997. pres. Korea-China Forum, 1996-98. With Korean Army, 1958. Recipient Order of Service Merit, Korean Govt., 1992. Mem. Korean Assn. Internat. Studies (pres. 1987), Korean Polit. Sci. Assn., Internat. Polit. Sci. Assn. Roman Catholic. Home: #203-202 Hyundai Apt 654, Kaepo-Dong, Seoul 135-240, Korea

KIM, DONG GYU, neurosurgeon; b. Seoul, Jan. 31, 1954; s. Young Sang Kim and Kang Hye Cho; m. In Ae Park, Dec. 13, 1981; children: Jung Ah, Yong Wook. BS, Seoul Nat. U., 1978, MS, 1982, PhD, 1989. Lic. med. doctor Govt. Korea, 1978, bd. neurosurgeon Govt. of Korea, 1983. Asst. prof. Gyeongsang Nat. U., Chinju, Korea, 1986-90; prof. Seoul Nat. U. Hosp., 1990—. Contbr. articles to profl. jours. Capt. Korean Army, 1983-86. Recipient awards for sci. papers Korean Neurosurg. Soc., 1992, 96, 98, 99. Office: Seoul Nat U Hosp/Neurosurg, 28 Yongon-dong, 110-744 Seoul Korea

KIM, DONG IK, surgeon, educator; b. Jeju, Korea, Dec. 12, 1959; s. Ki Su and Seo Bae Kim; m. Sung Hee Park, Mar. 20, 1988; children: Mu-Kun, Mu-Jun. BSc, Hanyang U., Seoul, 1980, MD, 1984, MS, 1988, PhD, 1996. Diplomate Nat. Bd. Medicine of Korea, Korean Bd. Surgery. Rotating intern Hanyang Univ. Hosp., Seoul, 1984-85, asst. resident, 1988-91, chief resident, 1991-92; fellow Osaka (Japan) Univ. Hosp., 1992-94; staff surgeon Samsung Med. Ctr., Seoul, 1994—; prof. surgery Sungkyunkwan U., Seoul, 1995—; dir. divsn. vascular surgery Samsung Med. Ctr., 1999—; mem. bd. Korean Soc. Vascular Surgery. Author: Handbook of Management of Thrombosis, 1993; editor: Handbook of Vascular Surgery, 1998; editor Newsletter for Cardiovascular Diseases, 1995—. Capt. Korean Army, 1985-88. Recipient Investigators award Samsung Med. Ctr., 1997, Korean Surg. Soc., 1997. Fellow Internat. Coll. Angiology; mem. European Soc. for Vascular Surgery, Internat. Union of Angiology. Avocation: golf. Office: Samsung Med Ctr/Vasc Surg, 50 Il Won-Dong Kangnam-ku, 135-710 Seoul Republic of Korea

KIM, DONG-KYOO, chemistry educator; b. Pusan, South Korea, May 20, 1953; s. Bong-Li and Deuk-Bun (Hah) K.; m. Jung-Won Bae, Feb. 23, 1983; children: Doh-Hyung, Nam-Hee. BSc, Pusan Nat. U., MSc, 1983; PhD, Seoul Nat. U., 1992. Instr. Inje U., Kimhae, 1985-88, asst. prof., 1988-92, assoc. prof. dept. chemistry, 1992-99; prof., 2000—; postdoctoral fellow St. Jude Children's Rsch. Hosp., Memphis, 1994-96. Contbr. articles to profl. jours. Office: Inje U Dept Chemistry, 607 Aubang-dong, Kimhae 621-749, South Korea

KIM, DOO HWAN, law educator; b. Cheongju, Korea, Feb. 28, 1934; s. Dong Beok and Dai Soon (Lee) K.; m. Yong Ok Lee, Mar. 29, 1961; children: So Hyeon, Ki Won. LLB, Seoul (Korea) Nat. U., 1957, LLM, 1959; JD, Kyong Hee U., Seoul, 1984. Assoc. prof. faculty econs. and commerce King Saejong U., Seoul, 1979-81; prof., dean Coll. Law Soong Sil U., Seoul, 1981-99, prof. emeritus, dir. Inst. Legal Studies, 1986-98; mgr. account dept., mng. dir. Korean Nat. Coal Corp., Seoul, 1959-76; exec. dir. Han Wha Group Korean Explosive Corp., 1976-79; vis. scholar Law Sch. UCLA, 1990, Inst. Air and Space Law, McGill U., Montreal, Que., Can., 1990-91, Washington Coll. Law, Am. U., 1990-91; mem. adv. com. Ministry Transp., Seoul, 1980-85, Prime Min., Seoul, 1980-83, Ministry Justice, Seoul, 1985-94; arbitrator Korean Comml. Arbitrator Bd., Seoul, 1992—; lectr. Coll. Law, Koockmin U., 1960-62, Keong Kuk U., 1960-62, Kyongki U., 1968-75, Fgn. Lang. U., 1972-73, Soongjeon U., 1976-77, Grad. Sch., Korea U., 1981-83, Seoul Nat. U., 1981-83, Seong Kyoon Kwan U., 1983-86, Coll. Law and Politics, Rhee Hwa Woman U., 1971-72; v.p. Korean Aerospace Rsch. Inst., 1979-81; vis. prof. Chuogakuin U., Japan, 2000—; spkr. many internat. confs., seminars, symposiums at Warsaw, Washington, Montreal, Buenos Aires, Tokyo, Beijing Taipei, Manila, Macau, Singapore, others, 1984—. Author: Accounting System of Corporation, 1992, The Law of International Relations, 1997; contbr. over 115 articles to profl. jours. Recipient gold medal Order Nat. Svc. Merit, Korean Govt., Seoul, 1994. Mem. Korean Maritime Law Assn. (dir. 1986-99), Korean Law Prof. Assn. (dir. 1989-93), Korean Assn. Air and Space Law (chmn., pres. 1993-99), Korea Comml. Law Assn. (dir. 1959-97), Internat. Law Assn. (London), Air Law Inst. Japan, Korea-Japan Law Assn. (dir., auditor 1984-97), World Jurist Assn., Japan Assn. Pvt. Law, Korean Assn. Air Law (v.p. 1989-93), Korean Inst. Internat. Pvt. Law (dir. 1994-97), Japan Assn. Internat. Econ. Law, Japan Assn. Econ. Law, Internat. Inst. Space Law. Presbyterian. Fax: 2-379-0627. E-mail: doohwank@nuri.net. Home: Jongro Ku, 174-5 Pyongchang Dong, Seoul 110-012, Korea

KIM, E. HAN, finance and business administration educator; b. Seoul, Korea, May 27, 1946; came to U.S., 1966; s. Chang Yoon and Young Ja (Chung) K.; m. Tack Han, June 14, 1969; children—Juliane H., Elaine H., Deborah H. BS, U. Rochester, 1969; MBA, Cornell U., 1971; PhD, SUNY-Buffalo, 1975. Asst. prof. Ohio State U., Columbus, 1975-77, assoc. prof., 1979-80; assoc. prof., then prof. fin. and bus. adminstrn. U. Mich., Ann Arbor, 1980-84, Fred M. Taylor Disting. prof., 1984—, chmn. dept. fin., 1988-91; dir. Mitsui Life Fin. Rsch. Ctr., 1990—; vis. assoc. prof. U. Chgo., 1978-79; vis. rsch. fellow Korea Devel. Inst., 1986-87; econ. cons. Govt. of Korea, 1985-87, 98; Cycle and Carriage vis. prof. Nat. U. Singapore, 1989; Yamaichi prof. econs. U. Tokyo, 1990-91; cons. Bank of Korea, 1985, U.S. Dept. Treasury, IRS, 1988-94, World Bank, 1989-91, 93, Posco, 1995-98, Korea Stock Exch., 1997-98; co-chair Citizens for Econ. Freedom, 1997—; bd. dirs. Found. Rsch. in Internat. Banking and Fin. Assoc. editor Jour. Fin., 1979-83, 88-92, Fin. Rev., 1982—, Internat. Jour. Fin., 1990—, Internat. Rev. Fin. Analysis, 1990-92, Rev. No. Am. Jour. of Econs. and Fin., 1990—, Rev. Quantitative Fin. and Acctg., 1990—, Pacific Basin Fin. Jour., 1991-96; edit. bd. Jour. Bus. Rsch., 1977—; adv. bd. Asia-Pacific Jour. Mgmt., 1990-96, Jour. Asian Bus., 1996—; contbr. articles to profl. jours. Mem. Korea-Am. Econ. Assn. (sec. gen. 1985, v.p. 1986, pres. 1996), Am. Econ. Assn., Am. Fin. Assn., Western Fin. Assn. Avocation: tennis, golf. Office: U Mich Sch Bus Adminstrn Ann Arbor MI 48109

KIM, E. KITAI, pathologist; b. Sangjoo, Kyungbook, Republic of Korea, June 5, 1933; came to U.S., 1966; s. Byung O. and Soon A. (Park) K.; m. Chung Ok Roh, Apr. 3, 1960; children: Steve Ho-Suk, David Hyun-Min. Pre-med., Seoul Nat. U., 1954, MD, 1958. Diplomate Am. Bd. Pathology. Resident, tchg. fellow Case-We. Res. U. Hosp., Cleve., 1968-72; asst. prof., assoc. prof. Med. Coll. Ohio, Toledo, 1972-89, prof. pathology, 1989—. Author: Surgical Pathology with Cytology Correlation, 1992, (book chpt.) Gastrointestinal Cancer, 1989. Capt. Korean M.C., 1958-64. Recipient Brilliant Citizens' award Seoul City Govt., 1995. Fellow Coll. Am. Pathologists, Internat. Acad. Pathology, Internat. Acad. Cytology; mem. Am. Soc. Cytology. Avocations: golf, indoor exercise, reading. Office: Med Coll Ohio 3000 Arlington Ave Toledo OH 43614-2595

KIM, EDWARD WILLIAM, ophthalmic surgeon; b. Seoul, Korea, Nov. 25, 1949; came to U.S., 1957; s. Shoon Kul and Pok Chu (Kim) K.; m. Carole Sachi Takemoto, July 24, 1976; children: Brian, Ashley. BA, Occidental Coll., Los Angeles, 1971; postgrad., Calif. Inst. Tech., 1971; MD, U. Calif., San Francisco, 1975; MPH, U. Calif., Berkeley, 1975. Diplomate Nat. Bd. Med. Examiners, Am. Bd. Ophthalmology. Resident in ophthalmology Harvard U.-Mass. Eye and Ear Infirmary, Boston, 1977-79; clin. fellow in ophthalmology Harvard U., 1977-79, clin. fellow in retina, 1980; practice medicine in ophthalmic surgery Laguna Hills, San Clemente, Calif., 1980—; vol. ophthalmologist Eye Care Inc., Ecole St. Vincent's, Haiti, 1980, Liga, Mex., 1989, Tonga, 1997; chief staff, South Coast Med. Ctr., 1988-89; assoc. clin. prof. dept. ophthalmology, U. Calif., Irvine. Founding mem. Orange County Ctr. for Performing Arts, Calif., 1982, dir. at large, 1991; pres. Laguna Beach Summer Music Festival, Calif., 1984. Reinhart scholar U. Calif.-San Francisco, 1972-73; R. Taussig scholar, 1974-75. Fellow ACS, Am. Acad. Ophthalmology, Internat. Coll. Surgeons; mem. Calif. Med. Assn., Keratorefractive Soc., Orange County Med. Assn., Mensa, Expts. in Art and Tech. Office: Harvard Eye Assocs 665 Camino De Los Mares Ste 102 San Clemente CA 92673-2840

KIM, ELAINE HAIKYUNG, humanities educator, writer; b. N.Y.C., Feb. 26, 1942; d. Sae Sun and Anne C. (Lee) K.; 1 child, Oliver Newman. BA, U. Pa., 1963; MA, Columbia U., 1965; PhD, U. Calif., Berkeley, 1976; LHD (hon.), U. Mass., Boston, 1995. Prof. Asian Am. studies U. Calif., Berkeley, 1974—. Author: Asian American Literature, 1982, With Silk Wings: Asian American Women at Work, 1983, Writing Self, Writing Nation, 1994; co-editor: Making Waves: Writings By and About Asian American Women, 1989, East to America: Korean American Life Stories, 1996, Making More Waves: New Writing by American Asian Women, 1997, New Formations, New Questions: Asian American Studies, 1997, Dangerous Women: Gender and Korean Nationalism, 1998. Co-founder Asian Women United of Calif., 1976, Korean Cmty. Ctr., Oakland, Calif., 1977, Asian Immigrant Women Advocates, 1985; active White House Commn. on Women in U.S. History, 1998—. Fulbright fellow, 1987-88, Rockefeller fellow, 1992. Mem. Am. Studies Assn. (nat. coun. 1992-95), Assn. Asian Am. Studies (pres. 1991-93). Office: UC Berkeley Asian Am Studies Berkeley CA 94720-0001

KIM, EUNSOOK, physics educator; b. Seoul, Korea, Dec. 24, 1958; d. Dukhwan Kim and Kiseok Seo; m. Jongsoo Kim; children: Sunhee, Hyewon, Jaehee. BA in Sci. Edn. in Physics, Seoul Nat. U., 1981; MS in Physics, Ohio State U., 1987, PhD in Physics, 1991, PhD in Sci. Edn., 2000. Postdoctoral rschr. Ohio State U., Columbus, 1991-93; lectr. Seoul Nat. U., 1994—, Kwangwoon U.; physics curriculum coord. Young Scholars Program, Ohio State U., 1992-93. Contbr. articles to profl. jours. Recipient Exemplary Svc. award Young Scholars Program Ohio State U., 1993. Mem. Am. Assn. Physics Tchrs., Korean Assn. Rsch. in Sci. Edn., Korean Elem. Sci. Edn. Soc. Office: Seoul Nat U, Physics Edn, 151-742 Seoul Republic of Korea

KIM, HAK YANG, gastroenterologist, educator; b. Seoul, Korea, June 6, 1956; s. Soon Kyung Kim and Won Yim Cho; m. You Jeon Lee, June 12, 1987; children: Min Ki, Pyung Ki. MD, Kyung Hee U., 1982, PhD, 1996. Intern, resident Kyung Hee U., Seoul, 1982-86; lectr., asst. prof. Hallym U., Seoul, 1988-97, assoc. prof., 1997—; rsch. fellow Baylor Coll. Medicine, Houston, 1992-93. Contbr. articles to profl. jours. Mem. Korean Soc. Internal Medicine, Korean Soc. Gastroenterology, Korean Soc. Gastrointestinal Endoscopy. Avocations: sports, travel. Office: Kangdong Sacret Heart Hosp, Seoul 134-010, South Korea

KIM, HAK-HOON, geographer, educator; b. Seoul, Korea, June 8, 1956; s. Insik and Imsik (Oh) K.; children: Eugene, Daniel. BA, Seoul Nat. U., 1981; MA, Calif. State U., L.A., 1986; PhD, U. Ariz., 1993. Tchr. geography Kumho Mid. Sch., Seoul, 1981-82; tchg. asst. U. Ariz., Tucson, 1987-92, rsch. specialist, 1992-93; prof. geography Chongju (Korea) U., 1994—. Contbr. articles to profl. jours. Cpl. Korean Army, 1978-80. Recipient Alumni Cert. of Honor, Calif. State U., L.A., 1986; U. Ariz. grantee, 1991. Mem. Korean Geog. Soc., Korean Regional Sci. Assn., Assn. Am. Geographers, Western Regional Sci. Assn. Avocations: tennis, classical guitar. Office: Chongju Univ, Dept Geography, Chongju 360-764, Republic of Korea

KIM, HAN PYONG, dentist, researcher; b. Seoul, Korea, May 2, 1945; s. Koe Jin and Jung Bok (Park) K.; m. Young Sook Yoon, Apr. 27, 1974; 1 child, Sung Mo. MA, DDS, Seoul Nat. U., 1975; PhD, Yonsei U., Seoul, 1982; MA, Monterey Inst. Internat. Study, 1996. Prof. Yonsei U., Seoul, 1977-84; vis. scholar UCLA, 1982; project rschr. for health care sys. Korea Dental Assn., Seoul, 1988-92; mem. bd. health ins. Nat. HIC, Seoul, 1990-92. Mem. Pres.'s Leadership Circle, Washington, 1995. Avocations: golf, fishing, photography. Home: 3125 Hermitage Rd Pebble Beach CA 93953-2812

KIM, HAN-DO, molecular biologist, educator; b. Hamchang, Republic of Korea, Dec. 3, 1939; s. Kye-Duk Kim and Bong-Nim Park; m. Sun-Ok Kim; 1 child, Byung-Soo. BS in Biology, Seoul (Korea) Nat. U., 1963, PhD, 1982; M in Agr., Dong A U., Pusan, Korea, 1967; postdoctoral, U. Pa. and U. Md., 1982-84. Instr. Pusan Nat. U., 1975-77, from asst. to assoc. prof., 1977-90, prof., 1990—, dir. Inst. for Genetic Engring., 1986-90, dean Coll. Natural Scis., 1993-95, dir. Ctrl. Lab., 1995-97, dean acad. affairs, 1997-98. Author: Origin of Life and Life Itself, 1990, Molecular Biology, 1991, Human Physiology, 1993, Animal Physiology, 1994. Trustee Korean Rsch. Inst. for Aging, 1988—; active Asian Game Attraction Com. to Pusan, 1994. Recipient Basic Sci. Rsch. award Korea Sci. and Engring. Found., 1995, Spl. Maline Rsch. award Korea Sci. and Engring. Found., 1996, Spl. Cancer Rsch. award Korea Sci. and Engring. Found., 1997. Mem. Korean Soc. Molecular Biology, Korean Acad. Sci. and Tech., Zool. Soc. Korea (v.p. 1993-95, 98—), Zool. Soc. Japan, Am. Assn. for Cancer Rsch. Roman Catholic. Home: Daedong Apt 503, 701 Haeundae New Town, Pusan 612-030, Republic of Korea Office: Pusan Nat U Dept Mol Biol, Jangjun-dong, Pusan 609-735, Republic of Korea

KIM, HEE CHAN, biomedical engineering educator; b. Daejeon, Republic of Korea, June 5, 1959; s. Ick Deok Kim and Shin Il Lee; m. Mee Rhan Kim, Oct. 22, 1984; 2 childen. BS, Seoul Nat. U., 1982, MS, 1984, PhD, 1989. Rsch. mem. Seoul Nat. U. Hosp., 1982-89; staff engr. Artificial Heart Rsch. Lab., U. Utah, Salt Lake City, 1989-91, vis. prof. dept. pharmaceutics, 1993-94; instr. biomed. engring. Seoul Nat. U., 1991-93, asst. prof., 1995—. Author: Biomedical Signal Processing, 1996; parentee for artificial heart (U.S.); inventor insulin pump. 2d lt. Republic of Korea Army, 1984-85. Mem. IEEE, Engring. in Medicine & Biology Soc., Korean Soc. Med. & Biol. Engring., Am. Soc. Artificial Organs. Presbyterian. Avocations: playing guitar, tennis. Office: Seoul Nat U Hosp Dept Biomed Eng, 28 Yongon Dong Chongno Gu, Seoul 110-744, Republic of Korea

KIM, HO GILL, poet; b. Sachon, South Korea, June 22, 1943; s. Jong Soo and Ul Soon (Lee) K.; m. Sherrie Chul Ja Park, Mar. 19, 1970; children: Brian Ki-Man, Eugene Yoo-Jin. BA, Gyeng Sang Univ., Jin-Joo, Korea, 1970; MS in Econs., Kun Kook Univ., Seoul, 1975. Airline pilot Korean Airlines, Seoul, 1972-81; columnist Korean Central Daily News, L.A., 1981-83; pres. Eveglobe Enterprises Inc. dba Sunflower Farms, L.A., 1984—. Editor: Literary realm, 1987-95, Korean American Literature, 1982-86, SiJo World, 1999—; author poetry. Capt. Korean Army, 1965-71, Vietnam. Decorated Military Merit Vietnam War Korean Army, 1971; recipient Anti-Communist Poetry award Korea Def. Ministry, 1969, Overseas Korean Literary award Chu Kang Literary Soc., 1997, Modern Si Jo Poetry award Modern SiJo Publ. Co., 1998. Mem. SiJo Soc. Am. (pres. 1995), Korean Literary Soc. Am. (pres. 1982—, adv.), Internat. Pen Club, Acad. Am. Poets, World Korean Writers Network (pres. 2000—). E-mail: hogill@aol.com. Office: 3065 Mt View Ave Los Angeles CA 90066

KIM, HO JIN, educator; b. Andong, Korea, Apr. 20, 1939; s. Jong Kyu Kim and Soon Yi Kwon; m. Woo Young Lee, Dec. 14, 1968; children: Suk Han, Joo Han, Hong Joon. BA, Korea U., Seoul, 1968; MA, Seoul Nat. U., 1974; PhD, U. Hawaii, 1979. Prof. Kookmin U., Seoul, 1979-80, Korea U., 1981—; dir. Inst. Labour Studies Korea U., Seoul, 1990-94; dean Grad. Sch. Labour Studies Korea U., 1994-98; vis. prof. Berlin U., 1999; chmn. presdl. com. Tripartite Com., 1999—; cons. Ministry of Unification, Seoul, 1995-98; vis. fellow U. Cambridge, 1985. Editor: Political Economy of the Third World, 1984, Korea: The State and Political System in Transition, 1990, Political History of Modern Korea, 1995. Standing mem. Presdl. Commn. Rebuilding Korea, 1998—. Pvt. 28th Divsn. Army, 1960-61, DMZ. Mem. Korean Polit. Sci. Assn. (pres. 1994). Avocation: hill walking. Home: 566-18 Soo Yoo Dong, Seoul 132-074, Republic of Korea Office: Korea U, 1 Anam-dong 5 Ga, Seoul 136-075, Republic of Korea

KIM, HONG NACK, polictical science educator; b. Youngchun, Korea, Aug. 20, 1933; came to U.S., 1956, naturalized, 1973; s. Sang Do and Nam Jo (Sung) K.; m. Boohi Suh, Mar. 26, 1967; children: Michael, Jeffrey, Brian Kim. BA, Seoul Nat. U., Korea, 1956; MA, Georgetown U., 1960, PhD, 1965. Lectr. Georgetown U., Washington, 1965-66; asst. prof. North Tex. State U., Denton, 1966-67, 1967-72, assoc. prof., 1972-77; prof. polit. sci. W.Va. U., Morgantown, 1977—. Author: Scholars Guide to Washington, D.C. for East Asian Studies, 1979; editor-in-chief: Internat. Jour. of Korean Studies, 2000—; editor: Asian Forum, 1972-74, Polit. Studies Rev., 1984-87; co-editor: Essays in Political Science, 1972, Korean Reunification: New Perspectives and Approaches, 1984; contbr. articles to various publs. Pres. Korean Assn. W.V., 1981-82; chmn. Assn. Korean Polit. Scientists N.Am., 1983-85. Fulbright-Hays Faculty Rsch. Abroad grantee U.S. Dept. Edn., 1979, 82; Fulbright Lecturing/Rsch. grantee U.S. Info. Agy., 1990; recipient Outstanding Rsch. award W.Va. U., 1985. Mem. Am. Polit. Sci. Assn., Assn. Asian Studies. Democrat. Presbyterian. Home: 614 Killarney Dr Morgantown WV 26505-3339 Office: W Va U Dept Polit Sci Morgantown WV 26505

KIM, HONGKEUN, neuropsychologist; b. Seoul, Korea, Aug. 19, 1959; s. Chonggu and Kyunghee (Kang) K.; m. Yongsook Kim, May 15, 1994; children: Kim, Euna. BA, Korea U., Seoul, 1985; PhD, U. Chgo., 1989. Postdoctoral rschr. U. Toledo, Ohio, 1990-91; prof. Taegu (Korea) U., 1992—. Contbr. articles to profl. jours. Mem. Internat. Neuropsychol. Soc., Korean Psychol. Assn. Office: Coll Rehab Sci, Taegu U, 2288 Taemyung-dong, Nam-gu, Taegu 705-714, Korea

KIM, HWAN-KYU, chemist, educator; b. Ulsan, Korea, Mar. 1, 1958; s. Sung-Kug Kim and Gil-Soon Lee; m. Jum-Ae Kwak, July 27, 1986; children: Jin-Yong, Eun-Jung. BS, U. Ulsan, Korea, 1980; MS, Korea Advanced Inst. Sci Tech., Seoul, 1982; PhD, Carnegie Mellon U., 1990. Rschr. Korea Rsch. Inst. Chem. Tech., Taejon, Korea, 1982-86; post doctoral assoc. Cornell U., Ithaca, N.Y., 1991-93; sr. rschr. Electronics Telecomm. Rsch. Inst., Taejon, Korea, 1993-94; assoc. prof. Hannam U., Taejon, Korea, 1994—. Contbr. articles to profl. jours. including Macromolecules and Chemical reviews; patentee in field. Mem. Korean Chem. Soc. (young scientist award 1998, sec. 1998-99), Korean Polymer Soc. (mem. editl. bd. 1996-97, assoc. editor 1999-2000), Am. Chem. Soc., The Optical Soc. Korea. Avocations: tennis, soccer, bowling, oriental chess, golf. E-mail: hwankkim@mail.hannam.ac.kr. Fax: 82-42-626-8841. Home: Taepyung-2-Dong Jung-Gu, Sambu Apt 403 64, Taejon 301-152, Republic of Korea Office: Hannam U Dept Polymer Sci, 133 Ojung Dong Daeduck Gu, Taejon 306-791, Republic of Korea

KIM, HYEONJAE, engineering educator; b. Muan, Korea, Jan. 6, 1935; m. Chun-Ja Kim, Feb. 9, 1965; children: Regina, Michael, Julia. B in Engring., Chonnam Nat. U., Kwangju, Korea, 1961, M in Engring., 1968; D in Engring., Junbuk Nat. U., Chonju, Korea, 1984. Teaching asst. Chonnam Nat. U., 1967-71, lectr., 1971-77, asst. prof., 1977-82, assoc. prof., 1982-87, prof., 1987—; dir. computing ctr. Chonnam Nat. U., 1990-92, dir. inst. info. and telecomm., 1997-99. Roman Catholic. Avocations: mountaineering, fishing, swimming, photography. Home: Daeju-Mansion 301-301, Munheung-Dong Puk-Gu, Kwangju Republic of Korea Office: Chonnam Nat U, Yongbongdong 300, 500-757 Kwangju Republic of Korea

KIM, HYO KATHERINE, oncologist; b. Seoul, Korea, Feb. 7, 1959; came to U.S., 1984; d. Byung Chul and Young Soon (Chung) K.; m. Sam Whan Lee, Oct. 15, 1988; 1 child, Kevin K. BS, Chung Ang U., Seoul, 1979, MD, 1983. Diplomate Am. Bd. Radiology, Am. Bd. Nuclear Medicine. Resident nuc. medicine U. Wis. Hosp. and Clinics, 1987-89; intern Boston VA Hosp., 1989-90; resident radiation oncology U. Chgo., 1990-91, U. Mich., 1992-93; fellow radiation oncology Harvard Med. Sch., Boston, 1993-94, instr., 1994-99; asst. prof. Brown U., Sch. Medicine, Providence, 1999—. Contbr. articles to profl. jours. Mem. Am. Soc. Therapeutic Radiology, Am. Radium Soc. Avocations: swimming, traveling, gardening, cooking. E-mail: KHKIM@lifespan.org.

KIM, HYO-SUNG, engineering educator; b. Seoul, Korea, Oct. 24, 1958; s. Cheol-Hee and Keum-Hong (Lee) K.; m. In-Oak Choi, Feb. 22, 1992; children: Gee-Eun, Do-Eun. B Engring., Seoul Nat. U., 1981, M Engring., 1983; DEng, Chungbuk U., Choengju, Korea, 1995. Cert. 1st class elec. engr., Korea. Chief engr. Tong-Yang Cement Mfg. Co. Ltd., Samchuck, Korea, 1982-86; prof. Cheonan (Korea) Nat. Tech. Coll., 1987—; Engring. cons. Samjin Precision Co., Cheonan, 1998-99, Dongbang Heavy Elec. Co., Cheonan, 1999—; vis. prof. Okayamo Univ.,m Japan, 1996-97. Mem. IEEE, Korean Inst. Elec. Engrs., Inst. Electronics Engrs. of Korea, Korean Soc. for Engring. Edn. & Tech. Transfer (sch. rep. 1999-2001). Avocations: swimming, tennis, choir, mountain trekking. Home e-mail: hyoskim@sbsmail.net. Office e-mail: hyoskim@dragon.cntc.ac.kr. Home: #6-502 Cheong-ho 5th Apt, Kun-seo Jik-san, Cheonan 330-810, Korea Office: Cheonan Nat Tech Coll, 275 Budae, Cheonan 330-717, Korea

KIM, HYUN, lawyer; b. Seoul, Korea, Jan. 17, 1956; s. Kyu-dong Kim and Chun-young Kang; m. Jyoung-mi Paik; children: Young-Hoon, Min-Hee. LLB, Seoul Nat. U., Korea, 1980; LLM, Cornell U., 1984, U. Wash., 1985; PhD in Law, U. Wash., 1990. Bar: Korea, N.Y. Fgn. legal cons. Bogle & Gates, Seattle, 1985; legal advisor Korea Min. Maritime Affairs, 1991—; lectr. Jud. Tng. Inst., Chungnam U., Korea; arbitrator Korea Comm. Arbitration Bd., 1999—; legal advisor Korea Min. Constrn. & Transp., 1999—; sr. ptnr. Sechang Law Offices, Seoul, Korea, 1992—. Co-author: Basic Text in Maritime Law in Korea, 1999. Recipient Pres.'s award, Seoul, 1997. Mem. Maritime Law Assn. U.S. Avocations: golf, skiing, mountain climbing. Home: Daechi-dong, Kangnam-gu, 207-502 Mido Apt 511, Seoul 135-282, Korea Office: 3d Fl Harim Bldg 1699-14, Seocho-4-dong Seocho-gu, Seoul 137-074, Korea

KIM, HYUN JIN, venture capitalist; b. Seoul, Korea, Jan. 21, 1948; s. Bong Chul Kim and Il Sun Bang; m. Hye Sook Kim, Nov. 25, 1978; children: Soo Yeon, Hyong Joon. BBA, Yonsei U., 1974, MBA, 1977. Credit analyst Seoul br. Bank of Am., 1973-77; credit-lending officer Seoul br. First Nat. Bank. Chgo., 1977; mktg. mgr., acct. officer Seoul br. Am. Express Internat. Banking Corp., 1977-82; gen. mgr., owner Evergreen Garden Restaurant, Seoul, 1983-89; CEO, owner Jin Hwa Trading Co., Seoul, 1990-94, Dong Jin Bldg., Seoul, 1990—; lectr. econ. Shin Gu Coll., Sungnam City, Korea, 1981-82; Pai Hwa Women's Coll. , Seoul, 1981-82; cons. H.S. Enterprises. With Air Force of Rep. of Korea, 1968-71. Recipient award Korea Food and Restaurant Assn., 1990. Mem. Nat. Geographic Soc., Internat. Airline Passengers Assn. Avocations: travel, music, swimming. E-mail: hjksr@yahoo.com. Home and Office: Ste 401 Dong Jin Bldg, 243 3-Ka Dongsun-Dong, Sungbuk-Ku Seoul 136-053, Korea also: 8468 Osler St, Vancouver, BC Canada V6P 4E4

KIM, HYUNG-IL, dental educator, metallurgist; b. Pusan, Korea, Apr. 11, 1953; s. Sook-Young Kim and Hwa-Young Park; m. Hyung-Sook Jee, Nov. 29, 1978; children: Min-Kyung, Young-Oh. B in Dentistry, Seoul U., 1978; M in Dentistry, Chosun U., Kwangju, Korea, 1985, PhD, 1989. cert. doctor of dental surgery. Instr. Pusan U., 1986-89, asst. prof., 1989-93, assoc. prof., 1993-98, prof., 1998-99, dean Coll. of Dentistry, 1999—; vis. rschr. Kyushu U., Fukuoka, Japan, 1991-92. Author: Dental Materials, 1995. Capt. Korean Army, 1978-81. Mem. Korea Rsch. Soc. for Dental Materials (v.p.), Japanese Soc. for Dental Materials and Devices, Internat. Assn. for Dental Rsch. Office: Pusan U Coll Dentistry, 1-10 Ami-Dong Seo-Gu, Pusan 602-739, Korea

KIM, HYUN-JOONG, scientist, educator; b. Daejeon, S. Korea, Apr. 22, 1963; m. Bok-Ja Lee, Apr. 20, 1991; children: Sun-Kyong, Timothy Sun-Woo. BS, Seoul Nat. U., 1987, MS, 1989; PhD, U. Tokyo, 1995. Postdoctoral fellow U. Tokyo, 1995; vis. rsch. scientist Va. Tech., Blacksburg, 1995-96; vis. asst. prof. SUNY, Stony Brook, 1996-98, rsch. scientist, 1998-99; mem. editl. bd. Internat. Jour. Adhesion and Adhesives, 2000—; asst. prof. Seoul Nat. U., 1999—. Contbg. author: Advanced Pressure Sensitive Adhesive Technology - 3, 1998; assoc. editor Soc. Adhesion and Interface Korea jour., 2000. Mem. The Adhesion Soc. (Peebles award 1995), Am. Phys. Soc., Am. Chem. Soc., Matl. Rsch. Soc., Soc. Adhesion and Interface Korea (chmn. internat. coop. 2000—). Home: 936-607 Bong-chun, Kwan-Ak Seoul 151, South Korea Office: Lab of Wood-based Materials & Adhesion Sci, Seoul National Univ, Suwon 441-744, South Korea

KIM, HYUN-MIN, chemistry educator, researcher; b. Seoul, Korea, Dec. 20, 1965; arrived in Japan, 1993; parents Kap-Jin Kim and Seung-Ho Choi; m. Hyun-Jung Ahn, June 10, 1995. BSc, Yonsei U., Seoul, 1989; MSc, Yonsei U., 1991; PhD, Kyoto (Japan) U., 1997. Rsch. scientist Korea Inst. Sci. and Tech., Seoul, 1992; rsch. assoc. Kyoto U., 1997-99, asst. prof., 1999—. Contbr. articles to profl. jours. Served with Korean Army, 1991-92. Scholar Japanese Govt., 1994; postdoctoral fellow Japanese Soc. Promotion of Sci., 1997; recipient award for Young Investigator Japanese Soc. for Biomaterials, 1998. Mem. Am. Ceramic Soc., Ceramic Soc. of Japan, Chem. Soc. of Japan. Roman Catholic. Avocation: yachting. Home: Minami 4-35-103 Sakyo-ku, Kyoto 606, Japan Office: Kyoto U Faculty Engring, Yoshida Sakyo-ku, Kyoto 606-8051, Japan

KIM, HYUN-SOO, urban planner, educator; b. Taegu, Republic of Korea, Oct. 17, 1962; s. Jung Yeop and Kyeong Suk Kim; m. Sue Yeon Kim, Nov. 17, 1989; 1 child, Seong-Dae. B of Engring., Seoul Nat. U., Republic of Korea, 1985, M of Engring., 1987, PhD, 1994. Rschr. Korea Rsch. Inst. Human Settlement, 1989; lectr. Kyeongwon U., Seongnam, Republic of Korea, 1990-92, Kyenggi U., Seoul, 1991-92, Seoul Nat. U., 1995—, U. Seoul, 1996-97; mem. city planning com. Dongducheon, Republic of Korea, 1994—, Yangju County, 196—, Dobong-Gu/Seoul, 1997—; vis. prof. dept. town and regional planning U. Sheffield, Eng.; sr. rschr. Seoul Devel. Inst., 2000. Co-author: Site Planning, 1997, Urban Planning: Theory and Practice, 1998, Urban Planning: Exercise and Explanation, 1998; contbr. articles to profl. jours. Mem. Citizens Coalition for Econ. Justice, Seoul, 1997—. With Korean Army, 1987-88. Mem. Korea Planners Assn., Assn. European Schs. of Planning, Korean Assn. North Korea Studies (dir.), Assn. Korean Regional Devel. (dir.). Avocations: climbing, swimming, reading, computers. E-mail: djkhs@road.daejin.ac.kr; fax: 82-357-539-1931. Office: Dept Urban Engring Daejin U, Pocheon-Gun, Kyeonggi-Do 487 711, Korea

KIM, JAE HO, government official; b. Hadong-gun, Kyungram-Do, South Korea, Feb. 4, 1947; s. Il Bong Kim and Myeong Geum Cheong; m. In Yob Kang, Feb. 1975; children: Cheong Ran, Hong Ki. BS, Kyungsang Nat. U., South Korea, 1970; MS, Seoul Nat. U., South Korea, 1977; MPS, U. of the Phillippines, 1980, PhD, 1995. Dir. Agrl. Tech. Ctr. Tongyong City, Korea, 1976-94; asst. dir. extension planning RDA, Korea, 1977-96, dir. tech. tng., 1976-77, asst. dir. expention planning, 1977-94; rsch. fellow Internat. Rice Rsch. Inst., Phillippines, 1981-85; asst. prof. Seoul Nat. U., Suwem, Korea, 1988-92. Author: Training Module for Home Advisor, 1998. 1st lt. Korean Army, 1970-72. Recipient Presdl. award Korean Govt., 1996. Mem. Korea Agrl. Extension Soc. (dir. 1997-99, assoc. prof. 1997-99), Korea Agrl. Info. Tech. Soc. (assoc. prof. 1997-99), Agrl. Edn. Soc. (bd. dirs. 1977-99). Avocations: Go-game, reading, music. Office: Rural Devel Adminstn, Suwen City 441-707, South Korea

KIM, JAI-BEOM, international business educator; b. Seoul, Mar. 17, 1964; s. Yonghyun and Hichung Kim; m. Ajung Kim, May 2, 1998; 1 child, Deho. BBA, Seoul Nat. U., 1986, MBA, 1988; MPhil, Cambridge (Eng.) U., 1991; PhD, Manchester Bus. Sch., Eng., 1997. Chief overseas strategic planning dept. Samsung Corp., Seoul, 1988-90; comml. officer Brit. Embassy, Seoul, 1991-92; ESRC rsch. fellow City U. Bus. Sch., London, 1996-97; lectr. internat. bus. U. London, 1997-98; prof. internat. bus., dir. Office Internat. Affairs Myongji U., Seoul, 1998—; exec. dir. Korean Acad. Internat. Bus., Seoul, 1998—; exec. v.p. ArtLifeShop.com., 1999—; mng. dir. Yeah Publ. Corp., 1999—. Contbr. papers to profl. jours. Bd. dirs. Gallery ArtLife, 1999—. Recipient Best Paper award Brit. Acad. Mgmt., 1996; scholar Seoul Nat. U., 1986-87. Mem. Acad. Internat. Bus., Strategic Mgmt. Soc., Marshall Soc. (life). Office: Myongji U, 50-3 Namkajwa-Dong, 120-728 Seoul Korea

KIM, JEONG DU, mechanical engineer, educator; b. Inchon, Kyoungido, Korea, Mar. 6, 1949; s. byoung Tea and Tae Im kim; m. Myoung Ja Huh, Sept. 17, 1977; children: Mi Suk, Mi Youl, Sang Kee. BSc, Dankook U., Seoul, Korea, 1973, MS, 1975, PhD, 1984; post Dr. grad., Darmstadt (Germany) U., 1986. Registered profl. engr., Korea. Mech. engr. Daewoo Heavy Industry Co.. Ltd., Inchon, 1966-69; rsch. asst. Dankook U., Seoul, 1973-75; prof. Chungkyung Tech. Coll., Taejon, Korea, 1975-79; vis. rschr. DSE, Mannheim, Germany, 1979-80; prof. mech. engring. Changwon Masters Coll., Taejon, 1978-84, Korea Advanced Inst. Sci. and Tech., Taejon, 1984-2000; prof. dept. mech. engring. Sejong U., Seoul, 2000—, pres. Advanced Inst. Sci. and Tech., 2000—; tech. cons. AJU Acshim, Seoul, 1997-98, Hwail Engring., Changwon, Korea, 1998—; chief expert Internat. Vocat. Tng. Competition, Zürich, Switzerland, 1985-97. Inventor in field; contbr. articles to profl. jours. Recipient HANBAT Econ. prize, Taejon City, 1994, Sci. prize KAIST, 1997, Tech. prize Korean Profl. Engrs. Assn., 1999; decorated of Nat. Pres., 1997. Mem. Korean Soc. Machine Tool Engrs. (v.p. 1998—), Korean Soc. Mech. Engrs. (Sci. prize 1993). Avocations: climbing, bowling, golf, tennis, swimming. E-mail: jdkim@sejong.ac.kr. Home: Hammaul Apt 114-502, Kaebong-dong Kurogu, 152-090 Seoul Korea Office: Sejong U, 98 Kunja-dong, Kwangjin-gu Seoul 143-747, Korea

KIM, JEONG-KYUN, metallurgist, researcher; b. Kwang-Ju, Korea, Aug. 29, 1960; came to U.S., 1992; s. Jae-Hoo Kim and Soon-Ja Jung; m. Eun-Young Jang, Jan. 9, 1988. BS, Chon-Nam U., Kwang-Ju, 1987; MS, Korea Advanced Inst. Sci. & Tech., Seoul, 1990; PhD, U. Wis., Milw., 1997. Rschr. Korea Atomic Energy Rsch. Inst., Tae-Jon, Korea, 1990-92; rsch. asst. U. Wis., Milw., 1992-97, postdoctoral fellow, 1997-98, rsch. assoc., 1998-2000; rsch. assoc. MER Corp., Tucson, Ariz., 2000—. Contbr. articles to profl. jours. Mem. Am. Foundrymen's Soc., Minerals, Metals and Materials Soc. Office: 7960 S Kolb Rd Tucson AZ 85706

KIM, JEONG-WON, chemist; b. Choengju, Korea, Oct. 20, 1968; s. Sook-Young and Jong-Ja (Lee) K.; m. Hyun-Sook Uhm, Jan. 8, 1995; children: Kuan, Joon. BS, KAIST, Taejon, Korea, 1991, MS, 1993, PhD, 1997. Sr. engr. Hyundai Micro Elecs, Cheongju, Korea, 1997—. Contbr. articles to profl. jours. Mem. N.Y. Acad. Scis. Avocations: tennis, Go. Office: Hyundai Micro Elecs, 1 Hyangjeong-dong, Choengju 361-725, Korea

KIM, JI YEUL, nuclear medicine physician, educator; b. Mokpo, Republic of Korea, Sept. 3, 1937; s. Oul Oak Kim and Ie Yere Oh; m. Soon Gum Kim, Mar. 29, 1943; children: Jun Seoing, Sun-Hee, Kyung-Ha, Min-Ha, Sang-Yoon. BS, Chosun U., Kangju, Republic of Korea, 1968; MS, Chonnam U., Kwangju, Republic of Korea, 1970; PhD, Seoul Cath. Med. Sch., 1980. Prof. nuc. medicine Chonnam U. Hosp., 1992—; chmn. 1st China-Korea Internat. Nuc. Medicine Conf., Beijing, 1998. Editor: Basic Radiobiology, 1987, Nuclear Medicine, 1992. Regional dir. Korea South Internat. Y's Men's Club, 1995-96, internat. coun. mem., 1997—; dir. Kwangju City YMCA, 1990-99. Named to honor roll of internat. men's clubs. Mem. Korean Soc. Nuc. Medicine (pres.-elect 1994-96, pres. 1996-98, Abbott Co. USA award 1991), Korea Chitin Chitosan Soc. (v.p. 1999—). Fax: 82-02-223-1666. Home: # 809 Cho-Own Park Apt, Seo-Gu Yang Dong, Kwangju Republic of Korea Office: Chonnam U Med Sch and Hosp, #8 Hak-Dong Donggu, Kwangju City 501-757, Republic of Korea

KIM, JIN YOUNG, telecommunications engineer; b. Seoul, Republic of Korea, Feb. 8, 1968; p. Sung Moon and Nak Soon Kim; m. Jin A Kim, Apr. 25, 1998; 1 child, Se Ho Kim. BS, Seoul Nat. U., 1991, MS, 1993, PhD, 1998. Registered profl. engr. Prin. rsch. engr. Seoul Nat. U., 1997-98; postdoctoral rsch. fellow Princeton (N.J.) U., 1998-99, rsch. assoc., 1999-2000; prin. rsch. engr. SK Telecom, Seoul, 2000—; cons. Korea Telecom. Contbr. articles to profl. jours. Korea Sci. and Engring. Found. fellow, 1998, NSF grantee, 1999. Mem. IEEE, Inst. Elec. Engrs. (London), Inst. Electronics Info. and Comm. Engrs., Inst. Elec. Engrs. Korea. Avocations: travel, sports, music, movies. Home: 180-34 Muk 1-Dong, Chungrang-Gu, Seoul 131-141, Republic of Korea Office: SK Telecom 9-1 Sunae-Dong, Pundang-Gu, Sungnam City 463-020, Republic of Korea

KIM, JIN-KEUN, engineering educator; b. Milyang, Kyungnam, Republic of Korea, May 21, 1952; s. Yong-Sul Kim and Kye-Ah Ha; m. Min-Hee Choi, Dec. 26, 1976; children: Kil-Soo, Jung-Soo, Che-Young. BS, Seoul Nat. U., Seoul, Republic of Korea, 1975, MS, 1978; PhD, Northwestern U., 1985. Cert. profl. engr. Lectr. Ulsan U., Korea, 1979-81; asst. prof. Korea Advanced Inst. Sci. and Tech., Taejon, Republic of Korea, 1985-89; vis. scholar Tohoku U., Sendai, Japan, 1991; assoc. prof. Korea Advanced Inst. Sci. and Tech., Seoul, 1989-94, prof., 1994—, dept. head, 1995—; cons. Dongyang Engring. Co., Taejon, 1989—, Daewoo Constrn. Co., Seoul, 1989-90, Rsch. Inst. of Korea Electric Power Co., Taejon, 1990, VSL Korea Co., Seoul, 1992—. Postdoctoral scholar Korea Sci. and Engring. Found., 1991. Mem. ASCE, Soc. Exptl. Mechanics, Am. Concrete Inst. (bd. dirs., sec. Korea chpt. 1988-89), Prestressed Concrete Inst., Korea Concrete Inst. (sec. 1989-90, editor 1993-94, dir. 1995-96), Japan Concrete Inst., Réunion Internationale des Laboratoires d'Essais et de Recherches. Office: Korea Advanced Inst Sci and Tech, Kusong 373-1, Yusong Taejon Republic of Korea

KIM, JINWOONG, pharmacist, educator; b. Seoul, Korea, Mar. 15, 1956; s. Wansik and Inhum (Yeon) K.; m. Young-Hee Choi, June 23, 1984. BS, Seoul Nat. U., 1979, MS, 1981; PhD, U. Ill., 1988. Registered pharmacist, Korea. Rsch. assoc. in chemistry U. Okla., Norman, 1988-89; asst. prof. Seoul Nat. U., 1989-93, assoc. prof., 1993-99, prof. pharmacy, 1999—. Mem. Korean Soc. Pharmacognosy (exec. com. 1990—), Pharm. Soc. Korea (coun. 1993—), Am. Soc. Pharmacognosy. Office: Seoul Nat U Coll Pharm, San 56-1, Sinlim-Dong, Kwanak-Ku, Seoul 151-742, Korea

KIM, JIYOUNG, materials engineering educator; b. Seoul, Korea, Sept. 13, 1963; s. Song Hak and Jungsim (Song) K.; m. Soon Yeon Park, July 21, 1990; children: Cheoljoon David, Myungjoon Eric. BS Seoul Nat. U., 1986, MS, 1988; PhD, U. Tex., Austin, 1994. Acad. contractor Motorola, Inc., Austin, 1993-94; process integration engr. Tex. Instruments, Dallas, 1994-96; prof. dept. materials engring. Kookmin U., Seoul, 1996—; project mgr. Korea Sci. & Engring. Found., Daejum, 1996—, Ctr. Advanced Materials Rsch., Seoul, 1996—; cons. Korea Gas Corp., Ansan, Korea, 1997—; prin. rschr. Inter-Univ. Semiconductor Rsch. Ctr., Seoul, 1997—. Contbr. articles to profl. jours. Recipient Korean Govt. oversea scholarship Korea Edn. Ministry, Seoul, 1989, grants for acad. conf. Korea Rsch. Found., Seoul, 1997, rsch. grants Korea Edn. Ministry, Seoul, 1997. Mem. IEEE, Am. Vacuum Soc., Korean Ceramic Soc. Avocation: swimming. E-mail: jiyoung@kmu.kookmin.ac.kr. Office: Kookmin U Sch Material Engr, 861-1 Jeong-Neung Dong, Seoul 136-702, Republic of Korea

KIM, JONG SHIK, manufacturing company executive; b. Jeonju, South Korea, Mar. 2, 1955; m. Wooyoung Chung, Sept. 27, 1989; children: Charles Kyungwuan, Edward Kyungjune. BS, Seoul Nat. U., 1977; MS, Ill. Inst. Tech., 1983; PhD in Mech. Engring., Purdue U., 1986. Sr. engr. tech. ctr. Cummins Engine Co., Columbus, Ind., 1986-89, tech. specialist, 1989, indsl. product planning mgr., 1989-90, mgr. Korean bus., 1990-91, Korea bus. dir., 1991-93, mng. dir. Korean bus., 1993—; gen. mgr. Cummins Korea, Seoul, 1993—; area mng. dir. East Asia/Korea Cummins Engine (China) Invest Co. Ltd., Beijing, 2000—. Contbr. articles to profl. jours. Recipient 1st Korean Honor Scholarship, 1984. Mem. ASME, Am. C. of C., Soc. Automotive Engrs. Avocations: golf, history, music. Office: Cummins Engine Invest Co, 1 Jian Guo Men Wai Ste 917, Beijing 100004, China

KIM, JONG-IL, leader of Democratic People's Republic of Korea; b. Dem. People's Republic Korea, Feb. 16, 1942; s. Kim Il Sung and Kim Jong Sug. Grad., Pyongyang Kim Il Sung U., Dem. People's Republic Korea. Officer, sect. chief, dep. dir., dir. dept. ctrl. com. Workers' Party Korea, 1964-73; mem. Ctrl. Com., 1972, sec. com., 1973, mem. polit. commn., 1974, mem. presidium polit. bur., 1980—; mem. Ctrl. Mil. Commn., 1980—; dep. Supreme People's Assembly Dem. People's Republic Korea, 1982, 1st vice chair Nat. Def. Commn., 1990-93, chmn. Nat. Def. Commn., 1993—, supreme comdr. Korean People's Army, 1991—, marshal, 1992—, gen. sec. Workers' Party Korea, 1997—. Author: Selected Works of Kim Jong Il (13 vols.), For the Completion of the Revolutionary Cause of Juche (10 vols.). Named Hero of Dem. People's Republic Korea (3 times), Kim Il Sung Order (3 times); recipient Kim Il Sung prize, other domestic and foreign orders, medals, titles, and doctorates. Office: Ctrl Com Workers' Party Korea, Pyongyang Dem People's Republic Korea*

KIM, JONG-KYU, architect, educator; b. Seoul, Feb. 8, 1960; s. Hyeong-Seong and Hyeon-Jip (Ahn) K.; m. Byeong-Ah Whang, Oct. 15, 1994. BSc in Arch., Yonsei U., Seoul, 1983; AA diploma, Archtl. Assn. Sch. Arch., London, 1989. Chartered arch. Arch. Dongwoo Archs., Seoul, 1983-85, Bldg. Design Partnership, London, 1989-91, Florian Beigel Archs., London, 1991-93; dir. Met. Arch. Rsch. Unit, Seoul, 1993—; prof. Korean Nat. U. of Arts, Seoul, 1998—; tutor diploma course design U. North London, 1990-92, rsch. reader, 1996-97; studio master Kyungi U., Seoul, 1993-94, Yonsei U., Seoul, 1993-97. Prin. works include Japanese Cultural Ctr., 1990 (Hon. mention 1990), Nara Conv. Hall, 1992 (Hon. mention 1992), Myung-Dong Cath. Redevel., 1996 (1st prize 1996), Clinic for People with Dementia, 1996-97. Recipient Eileen Gray award Eileen Gray Found., 1986. Mem. Archs. Registration Coun. of U.K. (registered), Royal Inst. Brit. Archs. (corp. mem.). Home: ga-203 Namseong Villa, Seocho-dong Seocho-gu, Seoul Korea Office: Met Arch Rsch Unit, 287-3 Yangjae-dong Seochogu, Seoul Korea

KIM, JULIAN ANTHONY, surgical oncologist; b. Brookline, Mass., Oct. 30, 1960; s. Byung Cho and Delores Carhart Kim; m. Amy Elizabeth Brunk, May 25, 1986; children: Elizabeth Anne, Justin Michael. BA, Miami U., Oxford, Ohio, 1982; MD, Med. Coll. Ohio, 1986. Diplomate Am. Bd. Surgery. Surg. resident U. Md. Hosps., Balt., 1986-91; surg. oncology fellow Ohio State U., Columbus, 1991-94, asst. prof. surgery Sch. Medicine, 1994-98; surg. oncologist, staff scientist Cleve. Clinic Found., 1998—; cons. in field. Contbr. articles to profl. jours.; patentee in field. Fellow ACS. Avocations: fishing, golf. Fax: (216) 445-7653. E-mail: kimj@ccf.org. Home: 21899 Parnell Rd Shaker Hts OH 44122-2722 Office: Cleve Clinic Found 9500 Euclid Ave Cleveland OH 44195-0001

KIM, KE BOM, stockbroker, financial planner; b. Seoul, Apr. 6, 1936; came to U.S., 1954; s. Doo B. and S.K. (Hahn) K.; m. Myung S. Chung, June 6, 1964; children: John, David. BS, U. Redlands, 1959; MS, Yale U., 1961, M in Indsl. Adminstrn., 1963. CFP. Asst. v.p. investments Merrill Lynch, N.Y.C., 1970-81; sr. v.p. investments Morgan Stanley Dean Witter & Co., L.A., 1982—. Office: Morgan Stanley Dean Witter 601 S Figueroa St 28th Fl Los Angeles CA 90017-5704

KIM, KEE YOUNG, economist, educator; b. Seoul, Oct. 7, 1937; parents Choon Kyoung Kim and Soon Young Kim; m. Hae Sook Kim; children: Ilho, Myoung-Sun, Joon Ho. BS in Commerce, Yonsei U., 1961, MS in Ops. Mgmt., 1966; MBA, Washington U., 1973, PhD, 1975. Prof. Coll. Bus. & Econs. Yonsei U., 1968—, Sangnam chair prof. mgmt., 1997—, v.p. info. tech., 1998—, dean grad. sch. info., 2000—; chair dept. bus. adminstrn. Yonsei U., 1975-79, dean grad. sch. bus. adminstrn., 1990-92, v.p., 1996-98, prof. mgmt., 1988—; rsch. fellow MIT, Boston, 1980-81; bd. dirs. Samsung Fire & Marine Ins. Co., 1998—, The First Bank, Seoul, 1998—; advc. coun. Korean Fedn. Industry, Seoul, 1995—; v.p. Decision Scis. Inst., 1994-97, fellow, 1999—. Mem. World Tae Kwon Do Fedn. (adv. coun. 1997—), Korean Acad. Soc. Bus. Adminstrn., Korean Soc. Ops. Rsch. Mgmt. Sci. (pres.). Methodist. Avocations: golf, travel, painting. Home: 746-17 Yoksam-dong, Kangnam ku, Seoul Korea 135-081 Office: 134 Shinchon-dong Yonsei U Sch Bus Admin, Sodaemoon-ku, Seoul Korea 120-749

KIM, KI YOUNG, engineering educator; b. Seoul, Korea, Oct. 13, 1955; s. In Whan Kim and Woon Hee Park; m. Tae Sook, Nov. 1, 1984; 1 child, Jee Eun. B of Engring., Yonsei U., Seoul, 1980, M of Engring., 1982; D of Engring., U. Tokyo, 1990. Cert. in metallurg. engring. Rschr. Korea Inst. Sci. and Tech., Seoul, 1982-83, Korea Inst. Machinery and Metals, Incheon, 1983-89; prin. rschr. Korea Inst. Indsl. Tech., Incheon, 1989-97; assoc. prof. Korea U. Tech. and Edn., Chonan, 1997—; com. mem. Korea Energy Mgmt. Co., Seoul, 1996—, Inst. Indsl. Tech. Policy, Seoul, 1993—, Small and Medium Bus. Adminstrn., Seoul, 1993—. Author: (transl.) Extending Methods of Die Life in Die Casting, 1997; mem. editl. com. Jour. Korean Foundrymen's Soc., 1994—; patentee in field. Sgt. Korean, 1976-78. Mem. Japan Foundry Engring. Soc. (Excellent Paper prize 1990), Korea Foundrymen's Soc. (Acad. prize 1996), N.Am. Die Casting Assn. Avocations: reading books, basketball, imagination. Home: Shinbangdong Sungji 102-402, 330-260 Chonan Chungnam, Korea Office: Korea U Tech and Edn, Gajeonri 307 Byungchunmyon, 330-860 Chonan Chungnam, Korea

KIM, KISEON, information and communications educator; b. Seoul, Aug. 27, 1956; s. Chang and Geum Kim; m. Jeong-A Lee, Sept. 15, 1988; children: Paul, Sara, Peter. BSc, Seoul Natl. Univ., 1978, MSc, 1980; PhD, U. So. Calif., L.A., 1987. Chartered engr., U.K. Prof. Korean Mil. Acad., Seoul, 1980-83; rsch. assoc. CSI, L.A., 1987-88; sr. devel. engr. Schlumberger, Houston, 1988-91; computer comm. specialist Superconducting Super Collider, Dallas, 1991-94; dir. Central Computing Ctr., Kwang Ju, Korea, 1994-97; prof. Kwang-Ju Inst. of Sci. and Tech., Kwang Ju, 1994—. Contbr. articles to profl. jours. Lt. Korean Army, 1980-83. Mem. IEEE (sr.), IEEK. E-mail: kskim@kjist.ac.kr. Home: K-JIST Faculty, Apt B-202, Kwang Ju 506-712, Korea Office: K-JIST, Kwang-San Kwang-Ju, Kwang-Ju 506-712, Korea

KIM, KWANG-IEL, psychiatrist, educator; b. Pyungyang, Dem. Peoples Rep. Korea, Dec. 6, 1936; s. Insong and Youngbok (Chie) K.; m. Haeshin Kim, May 10, 1965; children: Daeho, Sora, Yongho. MD, Seoul Nat. U., 1961, M in Med. Scis., 1963, PhD in Med. Sci., 1967. Clin. rschr., instr. neuropsychiatry Seoul Nat. U. Hosp., 1968-71; chief dept. psychiatry Seoul Mcpl. Hosp., 1969-71; chmn., assoc. prof. Kyung Hee U., Seoul, 1971-75; chmn., prof. Hanyang U., Seoul, 1975-97, pres. Mental Health Rsch. Inst., 1975-88, 97-99; supt. Kuri Hosp. Hanyang U., 1999—; cons. The Women's Hotline and Sexual Violence Hotline, Seoul, 1985—, Nat. Annuity Corp., Seoul, 1989—; med. advisor The Korean Automobile Accident Ins., Seoul, 1988—, Upjohn Pharmaceutica, Seoul, 1989—, Asiana Airline, Seoul, 1995—, Samsung Marine and Accident Ins., Seoul, 1995—. Author: Psychoanalytic Study of Korean Traditional Culture, 1983 (award 1984); editor: Family Violence: The Fact and Counteract, 1988; editor-in-chief Jour. Korean Neuropsychiat. Assn., 1989-95; mem. editl. bd. Children and Youth Svcs. Rev., 1990—; contbr. articles to profl. jours. Mem. deliberations com. Korean Broadcasting Comm., Seoul, 1988-91. Capt. Korean Army, 1961-66. Recipient Best Sci. Publ. prize Korean Med. News, 1973. Mem. Korean Neuropsychiat. Assn. (pres. 1985-86, trustee, chmn. 1986-87, Byokbong prize 1993), Korean Cultural Anthropology Assn., World Psychiat. Assn. (transcultural psychiat. com. 1983—, Wyeth-Ayerst award 1989), Coun. Korean Med. Inst. (deliberations com. 1989—), Korean Acad. Sci. Tech. (acting mem.). Fax: 82-346-565-2250. E-mail: kikim@email.hanyang.ac.kr. Home: Pyungchang-dong 175-7 1-106, Seoul 110-12, Republic of Korea Office: Hanyang U Kuri Hosp, Dept Neuropsychiatry, Kuri City 471-701, Korea

KIM, KYEONG-WON, economist; b. Seoul, Korea, Mar. 8, 1959; parents Byung-Sik Kim and Jung-Soon Seo; m. Jin-Won Moon, May 12, 1984; 1 child, Alex. BA, Seoul Nat. U., 1984; MBA, U. Wis., 1986; PhD, Columbia U., 1991. Sr. economist Samsung Econ. Rsch. Inst., Seoul, 1991-94; head of rsch. Samsung Securities, Seoul, 1995-97; chief economist Samsung Econ. Rsch. Inst., Seoul, 1998—, exec. dir., 2000—; pvt. econ. cons. Prime Min., Korea, 1993; dir. Samsung Econ. Rsch. Inst., 2000. Author: (book) Cross-Country Comparison of Financial Industry Structure, 1993; editor-in-chief: (weekly bull.) Korean Econ. Trend, 1998. Cpl. Korean Army, 1981-83. Roman Catholic. Avocations: golf, military history, gardening. Home: Jamwon-Dong Seocho-Gu, Hanshin Apt 306-904, Seoul Republic of Korea Office: Samsung Econ Rsch Inst, 191 Hangangro 2-Ka, Seoul Republic of Korea

KIM, KYU-JIN, research scientist; b. Jinan, Korea, June 15, 1946; d. Young-gil and Bok-Soon (Chang) K.; m. Alan Gilpin, Feb. 1984 (div. Dec. 1988); 1 child, Eun-Jee. BS, Hannam U., Taejon, Korea, 1968; PhD, U. New South Wales, Sydney, Australia, 1988. Rschr. Korea Tungsten Mining Co., Ltd., Seoul, 1969-76, Korea Inst. Sci. & Tech., Seoul, 1977-83; rsch. assoc. U. New South Wales, Sydney, Australia, 1988-90, rsch. fellow, 1991-93, sr. rsch. fellow, 1994—. Mem. Korean Profl. Engrs. Assn., Korean Acad. Sci. & Tech., Environ. Inst. Australia. Home: 86/3 Sorrell St, PO Box 2184 North Parramatta 2150, Australia Office: U New South Wales, Dept Chem Engring, Sydney 2052, Australia

KIM, LILLIAN G. LEE, retired administrative assistant; b. Toishan, Canton, China, June 17, 1919; came to the U.S., 1921; d. Yick You and Lucy Yu Oy (Louie) Lee; m. Herman Hom Kim, Oct. 12, 1941. Cert., Ea. U., 1941. Stenographer, sec. Peabody Book Shop, Balt., 1937-38; sec. Prisoners Aid Assn., Balt., 1938-41; sec. Civilian Def. Exec. Office Balt. Mcpl. Govt., 1942-44, sec. to safety dir., 1944-48; sec.-stenographer, asst. supr. stenography divsn. Ctrl. Payroll Bur., 1948-64, adminstrv. sec., supr. adminstrv. and stenographic sect., 1964-64; ret., 1977; ctrl. payroll councilwoman Classified Mcpl. Employee Assn., Balt., 1949-77, columnist Hall Light, 1950-77; chair ret. employee group CHICA-Combined Health/Industry Comb. Appeal and United Way, Balt., 1970-77; bd. dirs. Women's Civic League; pres., bd. dirs. AARP (Rodgers Forge Chpt. 2360), 1997-2000, publicity and pub. rels. officer, corr. sec. 2000—; lectr. in field. Author: (with Lee Yick You and Louie Yu Oy) Early Baltimore Chinese Families, 1976, Chinese Americans-A Part of America, 1977; Letters to the Editor: Tien Nien Poems, Lectures, and Speeches, Gnin-Gnin's China: Our Heritage, 1980, Grace and St. Peter's Chinese Church School (founders Frances L. and Florence M. "Daisy" Marshall), Chinese Traditions, Customs, and Festivals; edit. publ. Wah Kue Sim Mon (bilingual news bull.), 1998, Tien Nien Chatter; cmty. news columnist Towson Times, 1978—; freelance writer Senior Digest, 1990—; editor-pub. Tien Nien Chatter, 1946-60; contbg. writer Hall Light, 1950-77. organizor Chinese Young People's Fellowship, 1946-65; founder, exec. sec. Grace & St. Peter's Chinese Lang. Sch., Balt., 1954-73, dir., prin., 1974—; vestrywoman Grace & St. Peter's Ch., Balt., mem. parish activity planning, 1969—, sec. bd. trustees Grace & St. Peter's Sch., Balt., 1980-86, trustee, 1987-90; exec. bd. Boy Scouts Am., 1978-95; bd. dirs. Women's Civic League, 1979-82, exec. bd., 1999; mem. Bishop's Guild, Diocese of Md., 1960-99; mem. Holly Tour Com., Inc. of Balt., 1975-85, sec., 1978-82; sec., pub. rels. Chinese Women's Assn. Balt., 1937-46; Chinese interpreter of Am. laws, social security taxes, federal and state taxes to Chinese; represented Chinese immigrants in cts. as a vol.; participant Testimonial Dinner Tribute to Councilman Leon A. Rubenstein, Senator Charles McMathias Retirement Dinner; spkr. Tribute to Senator Barbara A. Mikulski; del. to Md. Diocesan Conv., selected lay reader Diocesan Conv. Holy Eucharist Svc., St. Anne's Ch., Annapolis, numerous other diocesan activities; cmty. advocate Dept Justice, Immigration and Naturalization Svc., 1997—; initator, coord. Grace and St. Peter's Chinese Lunar New Yr., Balt. Recipient Gold 13 medal WJZ-TV, Exec. Citation Humanitarian award Baltimore County, Golden Rule award JC Penney's, Best of Towson, 1998, First Place Best Vol. award Readers of Towson Times, 1998; Congratulatory Honors award Club 88 Tchrs. of Lyndhurst Elem. Sch. No. 88), 1999, award for outstanding svc. tchg. and promoting lang., culture, tradition, and history Coordination Coun. for N.Am. Affairs, Dist. Svc. to Balt. Chinese Cmty. award Balt. chpt. Orgn. Chinese Ams., Outstanding Achievement award Dorothy G. Reddick, 1999, Feast of the Dedication cert. of appreciation Grace and St. Peter's Parish, 1999, My Most Significant Memory of 20th Century award Dept. Aging, 2000. Mem. AARP (pub. rels. dir., bd. dirs.), Episcopal Asiamerica Ministry (parish rep. 1975-93, diocesan rep. 1994—), Nat. Soc. D.A.R. (medal of hon.), Walters Art Gallery, Balt. Mus. Art, Md. Hist. Soc., Stars Spangled Banner Assn., Johns Hopkins Alumni Assn., UCLA Alumni Assn. Democrat. Episcopalian. Avocations: community service, gardening, bowling, reading. Home: 524 Anneslie Rd Baltimore MD 21212-2009 Office: Grace & St Peters Chinese Lang Sch 707 Park Ave Baltimore MD 21201-4703

KIM, MICHAEL CHARLES, lawyer; b. Honolulu, Mar. 9, 1950; s. Harold Dai You and Maria Adrienne K. Student, Gonzaga U., 1967-70; BA, U. Hawaii, 1971; JD, Northwestern U., 1976. Bar: Ill. 1977, U.S. Dist. Ct. (no. dist.) Ill. 1977, U.S. Ct. Appeals (7th cir.) 1981, U.S. Supreme Ct. 1986. Assoc. counsel Nat. Assn. Realtors, Chgo., 1977-78; assoc. Rudnick & Wolfe, Chgo., 1978-83, Rudd & Assocs., Hoffman Estates, Ill., 1983-85; ptnr. Rudd & Kim, Hoffman Estates and Chgo., 1985-87; prin. Michael C. Kim & Assocs., Chgo. and Schaumburg, Ill., 1987-88; ptnr. Martin, Craig, Chester & Sonnenschein, Chgo. and Schaumburg, 1988-91; sr. ptnr. Arnstein & Lehr, Chgo. and Hoffman Estates, 1991—; gen. counsel Assn. Sheridan Condo-Coop Owners, Chgo., 1988—; adj. prof. John Marshall Law Sch., Chgo. Author column Apt. and Condo News, 1984-87; co-author Historical and Practice Notes; contbr. articles to profl. jours. Bd. dirs. Astor Villa Condo Assn., Chgo., 1987-91, treas. 1987-89. Mem. ABA, Chgo. Bar Assn. (chmn condominium law subcom. 1990-92, chmn. real property legis. subcom. 1995-97, vice chmn. real property law com., 1998-99, chmn. real proprty law com. 1999-2000), Ill. State Bar Assn. (real estate law sect. coun. 1990-94, corp. and securities law sect. coun. 1990-92), Asian Am. Bar Assn. Greater Chgo. Area (bd. dirs. 1987-88, 90-91), Cmty. Assns. Inst. Ill. (bd. dirs. 1990-92, pres. 1992), Coll. Cmty. Assn. Lawyers (bd. govs. 1994-98), Univ. Club (Chgo.). Avocations: squash, photography, travel. Office: Arnstein & Lehr 120 S Riverside Plz Ste 1200 Chicago IL 60606-3910

KIM, MIN-HUEI, electrical engineer, educator; b. Yhe-Chun-Koon, Kyoungbook, Republic of Korea, Aug. 25, 1951; s. Jae-Gook Kim and Soo-Bong Lee; m. Hyun-Jung Kim, Sept. 14, 1980; children: Ji-Eun Kim, Hyo-Eun (Sally) Kim. BA, Yeungnam U., Taegu, Republic of Korea, 1974, MA, 1980; PhD, Chung-Ang U., Republic of Korea, 1989. Instr. Pho-Hang (Republic of Korea) Jr. Coll., 1978-79; instr. Yeungnam Jr. Coll., Taegu, 1979-81, asst. prof., 1981-86, assoc. prof., 1986-91; prof. Yeungnam Coll., Taegu, 1991—; rsch. prof. U. Tenn., Knoxville, 1993-95. Author: Electric

Machinery, 1979, Electromagnetics, 1986, Power Electronics, 1993, Instrument Engineering, 1996. Advisor Indsl. Advancement Adminstrn. Korea Govt., Taegu, 1988-93. Sgt. Korean Army, 1974-76. Mem. IEEE, Korean Inst. Elec. Engring., Japanese Inst. Elec. Engring., Korean Inst. Power Electronics (org. com. dir. 1997—). Avocations: mountain climbing, traveling, Baduk. Home: Chung-San Town 101/301, 1269-1 Jisan-dong Susung-Gu, Tae-Gu Republic of Korea Office: Yeungnam Coll Sci & Tech, #1737 Taemyeng 7 Dong, Nam-Gu Tae-gu 705-037, Republic of Korea

KIM, MOON-JUNG, pianist; b. Seoul, Nov. 26, 1970; came to U.S., 1994; d. Jong-Sik Kim and Keum-Hee Youn. MusB, Seoul Nat. U., 1993, MusM, 1995; MusD, Ind. U., 1996—. Assoc. instr. piano Ind. U., Bloomington, 1996-99. Performer on CD's Bela Bartok Paino Concerto No. 3, 1999, Maurice Ravel Gaspard de la nuit. Scholar Seoul Nat. U., 1989-93. Mem. Coll. Music Soc., Pi Kappa Lambda. E-mail: mojkim@indiana.edu. Home: 364-5 Mapo-su Seokyo-dong, Seoul 121-210, Korea

KIM, NAM-KYOUNG, materials science and engineering educator; b. Kangneung, Korea, May 19, 1956; s. Young-Ki Kim and Jae-Young Choi; m. Hyunjoo Cho, Oct. 16, 1982; children: Seong-Hwan, Seong-Jun. BS in Engring., Seoul Nat. U., 1979, MS in Engring., 1981; PhD in Materials Sci. and Engring., U. Ill., 1988. Rschr. U. Ill., Urbana-Champaign, Ill., 1987-89; from lectr. to asst. prof. Kyungpook Nat. U., Taegu, Korea, 1989-95; vis. rsch. assoc. U. Ill., Urbana-Champaign, 1992-93; assoc. prof. Kyungpook Nat. U., 1995-2000, chmn. dept. inorganic materials engring., 1995-96, mem. planning com. Coll. of Engring., 1998—; prof. Kyungpook Nat. U., Sankyuk-Dong Buk-gu, Rep. of Korea, 2000—. Author: (with others) Ceramic Experiments, 1998; mem. editl. bd. Jour. Korean Ceramic Soc., 1994-95; contbr. more than 40 articles to internat. sci. jours. Recipient Best Paper award Jour. Am. Ceramic Soc., 1996. Mem. Korean Ceramic Soc. Avocations: fishing, mountain hiking, travel, climbing, classical music. Fax: 82-53-950-5645. E-mail: nkkim@kyungpook.ac.kr. Home: 1-302 Mirinae Apt, Bongduk-Dong Nam-Gu, 705-023 Taegu Republic of Korea Office: Kyungpook Nat U Dept Inorg Materials Engrs, 1370 Sankyuk-Dong Buk-gu, 702-701 Taegu Republic of Korea

KIM, PYUNG-SOO, martial arts educator; b. Seoul, Korea, Dec. 4, 1939; came to U.S., 1968; s. Chong Won and Duk In (Lee) Kim; m. Sonnya Park Kim; children: Sean Kim, Tasha Kim. BA in Russian Lang. and Lit., Han Kuk U. Fgn. Studies, Seoul, 1963. 10th degree Black Belt, 1994. Founder Kong Soo Do Club, Joong Ang H.S., Seoul, 1954, Kwon Bop Martial Arts Club, Han Kuk U. Fgn. Studies, Seoul, 1957-63; tchr. Spl. Police Detachment Korean Pres., 1958; tchr. hand-to-hand combat tng. Republic of Korea Army, 8th Divsn., 1961-63; founder Korean Tae Kwon/Karate Acad., Seoul, 1963; chief instr. Kang Duk Won Martial Arts Assn., Seoul, 1964, 8th U.S. Army and HQ I Corps, 1964-67; founder Kim Soo Coll. Tae Kwon-Karate, Houston, 1968, ChaYon-Ryu, Houston, 1970—; founding pres. Byung in Martial Arts Friendship Assn., Houston, 1994-97; lectr. in field; faculty martial arts instr. U. Houston and Rice U., 1970—; Tae Kwon Do coord. U.S. Olympic Festival '86, Houston; fight choreographer Houston Grand Opera, 1986; presdl. appt. to Com. on Unification of Korea, 1986-93; advisor World Martial Arts Coun., 1990. Editor, corr. Black Belt Mag., 1964-67; author: Palgue 1,2,3, 1973, Palgue 4,5,6, 1974, Palgue 7 & 8: Black Belt Requirements, 1976, History of ChaYon-Ryu, 1990, Chayon-Ryu, Taekwondo, 2000 (in Russian). Recipient citation for contbn. to elevating Korean nat. image in world Korean Govt., 1970, Leadership commendation Mayor Kathy Whitmire, 1987, commendation U.S. Pres. Bill Clinton, 1993, 98, Ednl. Leadership citation Gov. Ann Richards, 1993, Gov. G.W. Bush, 1998, Leadership commendation Mayor Bob Lanier, 1993, Lifetime Achievement award of honor World karate Union Hall of Fame, 1997; named Best Karate Instr. in Houston, Houston Press, 1990, Grandmaster of the Yr., Tex. Martial Arts Hall of Fame, Man of Yr. Am. All-Open Hall of Fame, 1991, World Karate Union Hall of Fame, Internat. Martial Arts Hall of Fame, 1997. Avocation: golf. Office: ChaYon-Ryu Internat Martial Arts Assn 1740 Jacquelyn Dr Houston TX 77055-3604

KIM, SANG-WOOK, industrial and engineering chemistry educator; b. Seoul, Korea, Mar. 24, 1952; s. Wan-Kyu Kim and Ki-Yul Choi; m. Mee-Sook Ahn, May 29, 1977; children: Bo-Sung Kim, Hyoung-Joon Kim. BS, Han Yang U., Seoul, Korea, 1974, MS, 1976, PhD, 1979. Prof. U. Seoul, Korea, 1979—, dir. Inst. Indsl. Tech., 1995-97, dir. Environ. Engring. Ctr., 1998—; chmn. com. recycling Korean Soc. Automotive Engrs., Seoul, Korea, 1997—; auditor The Korean Soc. Clean Tech., Seoul, Korea, 1995-97; asst. rsch. officer Nat. Rsch. Coun. Can., Ottawa, 1980-81; adv. SK Group, Seoul, Korea, 1986-95, Taekwang Chem. Co., Seoul, Korea, 1986-95, Shinyang Co., Seoul, 1986-95; columnist The Jeon-Buk Ilbo (daily newspaper), Korea, 1998—. Author: Methods of Instrumental Analysis, 1995, Experimental Organic Chemistry, 1995, Polymer Engineering, 1998; editor: Fabrication and Characterization of Advanced Materials, vols. 1,2,3, 1995, J. Indsl. and Engring. Chemistry, 1995, J. Korean Indsl. and Engring. Chemistry, 1994-95; contbr. articles to profl. jours. Adv. prof. Min. Commerce, Industry and Energy, Seoul, Korea, Min. Constrn. and Transp., Seoul, Korea, Agy. for Tech. and Stds., Kwacheon, Korea; mem. IBC Millennium Time Capsule Commn.; dep. gov. Am. Biograph. Inst. Rsch. Assn., 1999. Recipient The 6th Excellent Paper Prize of Sci. and Tech., The Korean Fedn. of Sci. and Tech. Soc., 1996, The 45th Seoul Cultural prize in field of sci., Seoul Metro. Govt., 1996. Mem. IEEE, Soc. Plastics Engrs. (sr. mem.), Nat. Acad. Engring. Korea, Korean Soc. Indsl. and Engring. Chemistry (chmn. com. process Eng. 1995—, v.p. 1998—, 1st Sci. prize 1999), Materials Rsch. Soc. Korea (editor 1993—, 1st Sci. prize 1993), Soc. of Plastics Engrs., Korean Inst. of Electrical Engrs., Korean Inst. Electrial and Electronic Material Engrs., Korean Soc. of Clean Technology, Korean Inst. of Chem. Engrs., Polymer Soc. of Korea, Korean Soc. Indsl. and Engring. Chemistry (chmn. process engring. com. 1995—). Fax: 82-2-2210-2310. E-mail: swkim@uoscc.uos.ac.kr. Home: A-401 Hyundai Riverville, 135-1 Kwangjang-Dong, Kwangjin-Ku Seoul 143-210, Republic of Korea Office: U Seoul, 90 Jeonnong-Dong, Dongdaemun-gu Seoul 130-743, Republic of Korea

KIM, SEOCK-HO, educator; b. Pusan, South Korea, Feb. 20, 1961; came to U.S., 1984; s. Duk-Joon Kim and Myung-Hwa Yoon; m. Mi-Ran Cho, Aug. 16, 1987; children: Naanhee Kristin, Yoonhee Kathleen. BA, Korea U., Seoul, 1983; MS, U. Wis., 1986, PhD, 1991. Asst. scientist U. Wis., Madison, 1991-95; asst. prof. U. Ga., Athens, 1995—. Contbr. articles to profl. jours. 2d lt. Korean Army, 1997-98. Fellow Ctr. for Future Human Resource Studies, Seoul, 1996—. Mem. APA, Am. Ednl. Rsch. Assn., Am. Statis. Assn., Inst. Math. Stats., Nat. Coun. Measurement in Edn., Psychometric Soc. E-mail: skim@coe.uga.edu. Home: 1180 Chaddwyck Dr Athens GA 30606-7004 Office: U Ga 325 Aderhold Hall Athens GA 30602

KIM, SEOCK-SAM, engineering educator; b. Kimchon, Rep. of Korea, Feb. 7, 1949; s. Mal-chool Kim and Duk-rim Bae; m. Moo-hyun Chang, Feb. 24, 1973; children: Joo-hae, Sung-hae, Jong-hyung. Bachelor, Kyungpook Nat. U., Taugu, Korea, 1973, Master, 1976; Doctor, Tohoku U., Sendai, Japan, 1987. Class I engr. in constn. equipment, precision measuring, heat consumption mgmt. Rschr. Korean Inst. Machine and Metal, Seoul, 1974-79; chmn. dept. mech. engring. Kyungpook Nat. U., 1994-96; dir. Engring. Tribology Rsch. Inst., Taegu, 1995—. Author: Processing Design, 1983, Precision Measurement Theory and Application, 1986. Recipient Excellent Paper award Korean Fedn. Sci. & Tech. Socs., 1997. Mem. Japanese Soc. Tribologists, Korean Soc. Tribologists and Lubrication Engrs. (pres.). Avocation: mountain climbing. Home: Sangin Chunggu Town 103-702, 1520 Sangin-dong Dalseo-ku, 704-370 Taegu Republic of Korea Office: Kyungpook Nat U Mech Engrin, 1370 Sankyukdong Puk-ku, 702-701 Taegu Republic of Korea

KIM, SHIN-KON, hospital administrator, surgeon, educator; b. Hwasun, Chonnam, South Korea, May 16, 1944; s. Yong-Il and Shin-Bang (Lee) K.; m. Chung-Woo Kim, Dec. 6, 1969; children: Yu-Jin, Jong-Seon, Jong-Jin. Diploma, Chonnam U., Kwangju, Korea, 1968, MS, 1982; PhD, Jeonbuk U., Chonju, Korea, 1985. Dir. emergency dept. Chonnam U. Hosp., Kwangju, 1983-85, dir. med. edn., 1988-90, chmn. dept. surgery, 1993-96, gen. dir., 1996-99; prof. surgery Chonnam U. Med. Sch., 1988—, assoc. dean acad. affairs, 1990-92. Editor textbooks: Nephrology, 1990, Emergency Medicine, 1991, A Guide to the Medical Fellowship in USA, 1997. 1st lt. Korean Air Force, 1968-71. Fellow Internat. Coll. Surgeons; mem. Aerospace Med. Assn., Collegium Internat. Chirurgiae Digestivae, Korean Surg. Soc. (bd. dirs. 1994—), Korean Hosp. Assn. (bd. dirs. 1996—), Kwangju City Med. Assn. (v.p. 1994-96), Chonnam Nat. U. Alumni Assn. (v.p. 1996—). Roman Catholic. Avocations: collecting stamps, collecting spoons, golf. Home: Kakhwadong Kumho Town, 101-501, Kwangju City 500-120, South Korea Office: Chonnam U Hosp Dept Surgery, Hakdong 8, Kwangju City 501-757, South Korea

KIM, SONG-HUN, federal official; b. Mokpo, Republic of Korea. Grad., Seoul Nat. U., 1963; D in Resource Econs., U. Hawaii, 1971. Prof., v.p. Chungang U., 1976—; min. Agr. and Forestry, Kyonggi, Republic of Korea, 1998—. Office: Min Agr and Forestry, 1 Chungang-dong Kwachon, Kyonggi Republic of Korea*

KIM, SOO JIN, mineralogy educator; b. Youngjoo, Kyungbugdo, Korea, Jan. 15, 1939; s. Seong Dae and Choon Ran (Hwang) K.; m. Young Hee; children: Hyo Eun, Hyo Jun, Hyo Jung, Hyo Won. BSc, Seoul (Korea) Nat. U., 1961, MSc, 1963, PhD, 1971; D of Natural Scis., U. Heidelberg, Germany, 1979. Asst. prof. Inha U., Inchon, Korea, 1966-68; prof. mineralogy Seoul Nat. U., 1968—; vis. prof. Harvard U., 1978, U. Chgo., 1978-79; advisor to Prime Min., Korea, 1981-83; dir. Rsch. Inst. Mineral Scis., 1990-92; vice dir. Korea Inst. Geology, Mining and Materials, 1991-98; councilor Korea Resources Corp., 1991—; mem. Cultural Property Com., Korea, 1995—. Author: (textbooks) Elements of Mineralogy, 1982, Mineral Sciences, 1996; contbr. numerous articles to profl. jours. Recipient award of Min. of Fgn. Affairs, Korean Govt., 1978, award for best rsch. 5th Internat. Congress on Applied Mineralogy, 1996. Mem. Nat. Acad. Scis. Republic of Korea (prize 1976), Mineral. Soc. Korea (pres.). Achievements include discovery of new mineral Janggunite. Avocation: mountain-climbing. Home: Banpo Apt 76-304, 137-049 Seoul Korea Office: Seoul Nat U, Dept Geol Scis, 151-742 Seoul Korea

KIM, SOOK CHA, artist; b. Choong-Joo, Korea, Mar. 30, 1940; came to U.S., 1973; d. Kyung Nam Chai and Choon Yi Lim; m. Myung Hak Kim, Dec. 5, 1967; 1 child, Young Kyoon. Student, Seoul Nat. U.; BFA, Hong-Ik U., 1965, MFA, 1967. Owner Morning Star Art Gallery, Washington, 1995—. Featured artist New Art Internat. 1997 Edit. Recipient Gold medal--Art Addiction Internat. prize Most Talented Artists Competition, Sweden, 1997, Cert. of Merit 6th Internat. Female Artist Art Exhbn. on Internet Art Mus., 1999. Home: 6540 Braddock Rd Alexandria VA 22312-2206 Office: Morning Star Art Gallery 600 T St NW Washington DC 20001-5117

KIM, SOU-HWAN STEPHEN, cardinal, retired archbishop; b. Taegu, Korea, May 8, 1922. BTh, Sophia U., Tokyo, 1944; ThM, Cath. Coll., Seoul, Republic of Korea, 1950; D of Sociology, Münster U., Fed. Republic Germany, 1964; hon. doctorate, Sogang U., Seoul, 1974, U. Notre Dame, 1977, Sophia U., Tokyo, 1988, Korea U., Seoul, 1990, Seton Hall U., 1990, Yonsei U., Seoul, 1994, Fu Jen U., Taiwan, 1995, Seoul Nat. U., 1999. Ordained priest Roman Cath. Ch., 1951, consecrated bishop of Masan, 1966, archbishop of Seoul, 1968, Cardinal, 1969. Pastor Andong Parish, Archdiocese of Taegu, Taegu, Korea, 1951-53; sec. to archbishop Archdiocese of Taegu, Republic of Korea, 1953-55; pastor Hwangkeumdong parish, Archdiocese of Taegu, Kimcheon, Republic of Korea, 1955-56; pres. Cath. Shibo weekly newspaper, Taegu, 1964-66; bishop Diocese of Masan, Republic of Korea, 1966-68; archbishop Archdiocese of Seoul, 1968-98, cardinal, 1969—; pres. Bishop's Conf. Korea, Seoul, 1970-75, 81-87, del. to synod, Vatican City, 1967, 71, 74, 80, 83, 85; pres. Follow-up Com. for Fedn. Asian Bishop's Conf., 1970-73. Home and Office: Cath U Bishop's House, 90-1 Hyehwa-Dong Chongno-ku, Seoul 110-758, Republic of Korea

KIM, SUK-JOON, political science educator; b. Seoul, South Korea, June 15, 1950; s. Yong-Won and Tae-Yon (Chang) K.; m. Jung-Sook Choi, Feb. 27, 1975; children: Dong-Wook, Yu-Kyung. BE, Seoul Nat. U., 1973, MPA, 1975; MA, UCLA, 1985, PhD, 1987. Prof. Ewha Woman's U., Seoul, 1979—, dean Grad. Sch., 1993—; mem. Presdl. Comm. on Policy Planning, Republic of Korea, 1996—; v.p. The Citizens' Coalition for Econ. Justice, Korea, 1997—; mem. Adminstrv. Reform Commn., Republic of Korea, 1997—; vis. prof. Harvard U./Yenching Inst., 1998-99, Balliol Coll., Oxford (Eng.) U., 1999. Author: Crisis in the Korean Capitalist States, 1991, The State, Public Policy and NIC Development, 1988, The Korean Industrializing State (Korean Pub. Adminstrn. Assn. Book award 1993), The State and Change: Dynamics of the Modern States and Strategies for the Twenty-First Century Korean State, 1995, The State and Public Administration under the American Military Government in Korea: A Semi-State Building and Administrative System Arrangement, 1996. Mem. Korean Assn. for Indsl. and Trade Policies (pres. 1995—), Korean Assn. for Policy Studies (chmn. rsch. com. 1992-94), Korean Polit. Sci. Assn. (chmn. 1998-99), Korean Assn. Pub. Adminstrn. (editor-in-chief 1995), Phi Beta Kappa. Home: 752-12 Sinbongri, Sujiup, Yonginsi, Seoul 449-840, South Korea Office: Ewha Womans U, 11-1 Daehyung-Dong, Seodaemun-ku, Seoul 120-750, South Korea

KIM, SUNG SOO, chemist, educator; b. Seoul, South Korea, May 11, 1945; s. Dong Ho and Jung Ja (Cha) K.; m. Ja Ae Koo; children: Sang Yeon, Sang Hwa, Sang Wook. BS, Seoul Nat. U., 1968; PhD, U. So. Calif., L.A., 1974. Postdoctoral fellow U. Utah, Salt Lake City, 1974-76, U. Alta., Edmonton, 1976-79; sr. rsch. fellow Korea Rsch. Inst. Chem. Tech., Dae Jeon, 1979-80; assoc. prof. dept. chemistry INHA U., Inchon, Korea, 1980-85, prof., 1985—. Contbr. articles to profl. jours. Mem. Korean Chem. Soc. (editor 1984, gen. dir. 1988, exec. dir. 1995), Am. Chem. Soc., Korea Chem. Engring. Soc. Avocations: jogging, hiking, swimming, skiing. Home: Apkujung Kangnam, 24-405 Hyundai Apt, Seoul South Korea Office: INHA Univ, Dept Chemistry, 402-751 Inchon South Korea

KIM, SUN-JANG, engineer, construction company executive; b. Taegu, Korea, May 28, 1946; s. Soo-Il and Myo-Yon (Park) K.; m. Seung-Ok Choi; children: Ki-Hyok, Mi-Kang, Eun-Hye. BS, Seoul Nat. U., 1969; MS, U. Calif., Berkeley, 1978. Engr. Namyang Engring. Cons., Seoul, 1971-72, Pub. Works Dept., Ipoh, Malaysia, 1972-76; gen. mgr. Hyundai Engring. & Constrn. Co. Ltd., Seoul, 1978-89; mng. dir. Woobo Engring. Cons., Seoul, 1989-90; v.p. Dongmyong Engring. Cons., Seoul, 1990-97; pres. Hyosung Ebara Environ. Engring. Co. Ltd., Seoul, 1997—; lectr. Chungju (Korea) Nat. U., 1996, Chungang U., Seoul, 1995-98. Mem. Korean Soc. Civil Engrs. (bd. dirs.), Korean Soc. Environ. Engrs. (bd. dirs.). Mem. Yoido Full Gospel Ch. Avocations: golf, swimming, mountain climbing, classical music. Office: Hyosung Ebara Environ Engrg, 1006-2 Bangbae-Dong, Seocho-ku Seoul 137-063, Korea

KIM, TAE-CHANG, public philosopher, educator; b. Cheong-ju, Chungbuk, Republic of Korea, Aug. 1, 1934; arrived in Japan, 1990; s. Kyoo-Ung Kim and Sun-Haeng Park; m. Hyo-Ae Oh, Mar. 1, 1970; 1 child, Christine M. Cepedas. BA in Polit. Sci., Yonsei U., Seoul, 1957, PhD in Polit. Sci., 1980; MA in Internat. Studies, U. S.C., 1970. Head dept. polit. sci. and internat. studies Chungbuk Nat. U., Cheong-ju, 1977-84, dir. social sci. rsch. ctr., 1982-84, dean Coll. Social Scis.,, 1984-86, dir. Inst. for Internat. Studies and Comparative Ideologies, 1986-90; rsch. fellow U. Tokyo Faculty Law, 1990-92; pres. Inst. for Integrated Study of Future Generations, Kyoto, Japan, 1992—; vis. prof. Chinese Acad. Social Sci., Beijing, Acad. Social Sci., Open U., Ho Chi Minh City, Republic of Vietnam; dean faculty of humanities Kyushu Women's U., Fukuoka, Japan; acad. advisor Hanbeck Rsch. Found., Seoul, Japanese Rsch. Ctr. of Taiwan Nat. U., Taipei; spkr. in field. Author: Philosophy of Happiness Together, 1992; editor: Creating a New History for Future Generations, 1994, Thinking About Future Generations, 1994, Why Future Generations Now, 1994, Why Generativity Now?, 1999, Self and Future Generations, 1999, Co-Creating a Public Philosophy for Future Generations, 1999. Recipient Award for Disting. Accomplishment Chungbuk Provincial Govt., 1989. Avocations: walking, meeting and talking with friends, traveling. Home: 302 St Paulia Kita Osaka, Shimoshinjo 5-26-10, Osaka 533-0021, Japan Office: Inst Integrated Study 88, Kankoboko-cho Shimogyo-ku, Kyoto 600-8009, Japan

KIM, TAEWHAN, physics educator, scientist; b. Euisung, Korea, June 25, 1957; s. Wansik and Jongleem (Lee) K.; m. Heesun Lee; children: Kim Shiyeon, Kim Seojean. BS, Kyungbuk Nat. U., 1979; PhD, SUNY, 1989. Asst. prof. physics Kwangwoon U., Seoul, 1989-93, assoc. prof., 1993-2000, chmn. dept. physics, 1993-95, prof., 2000—; collaboration rsch. staff Korea Inst. of Sci. and Tech., Seoul, 1993—, Semiconductor Physics Rsch. Ctr., Jeon Ju, Korea, 1993-99; proposal judge com. mem. Korea Sci. and Engring. Found., Tajeon, Korea, 1994—, Korea Ministry of Edn., Seoul, 1994—. Contbr. articles to profl. jours. Grantee Korea Sci. and Engring. Found., 1994, 96, 97, 98, 99, 2000. Fellow Korean Vacuum Soc.; mem. Korean Phys. Soc. (session chmn. 1993, 94, 96, 95-97, Honor award 1991, Young Investor Honor award 1991), N.Y. Acad. Sci. Avocations: tennis, mountaineer, soccer. Home: 181-7 Sung San Dong, Ma-Po-Ku, Seoul 120-250, Republic of Korea Office: Kwangwoon U Dept Physics, 447-1 Wolgye-dong Nowon-ku, Seoul 139-701, Republic of Korea

KIM, WON, architect; b. Seoul, Republic of Korea, Mar. 10, 1943; s. Jongsoo and Yong Kim; m. Joung-ai Park, May 20, 1967; children: Ji-young, Tae-yoon. BS in Arch., Seoul Nat. U., 1965; diploma, Bowcentrum Postgrad. Internat., Rotterdam, The Netherlands, 1973. Architect Kim Swoogeun Atelier, Seoul, 1965-70; prin. ptnr. Wondoshi Architects, Seoul, 1973-75; prin. Architects' Group Forum, Seoul, 1976—; prof. Grad. Sch. Architecture Konkuk U., 1998—; pres. Feng-shui/Geomancy Rsch. Ctr., Seoul, 1981-91; head cmty. planning Archtl. Inst. Korea, Seoul, 1984-96; chmn. mng. com. Seoul Archtl. Sch., 1997—. Prin. works include Master Plan Independence Hall, 1983, Nat. Theater for Traditional Performing Arts, 1984 (Korean Inst. Arch. spl. award 1991), Nat. Reunification Edn. Ctr., 1987 (Korean Inst. Arch. award 1992), Cath. Martyr's Monument and Memorial Chapel (Korean Inst. Architects award 1986), Kwang-ju Cath. U. (Korean Inst. Arch. award 1998), Seoul film complex Korean Motion Picture Promotion Corp., 1991, Russian Embassy to Korea, 1995; author: Mirror of Our Age, 1975, (essays on architecture) Light and Shadow, 1982, Let the River Run Through, 1999. Sec.-gen. Kim Swoo-geun Cultural Found., Seoul, 1986—; mem. Korean Cath. Bishop's Coun. for Arts, Seoul, 1995—; rep. Civilian Environ. Group Agains Dong River Dam Constrn., 1999. Recipient Order Indsl. Svc. merit, 1988. Mem. Soc. Nat. Modern Art Mus. (bd. dirs. 1995—), Nat. Mus. Soc. (bd. dirs. 1995—), Korean Inst. Architects (hon. bd. dirs. 1996—), Korean Soc. Interior Designers (pres. 1982-84, hon. bd. dirs. 1985—, hon. chmn. 1999), Korean Inst. Interior Designers (hon. bd. dirs. 1992—), Samsung Museum (bd. dirs. 2000). Roman Catholic. Office: Architects Group Forum 1-94, Dong Soong-dong Jongro-gu, Seoul 110-510, Republic of Korea

KIM, WOO-CHOONG, industrialist; b. Taegu, Republic of Korea, Dec. 19, 1936; s. Yong-Ha and In-Hang (Chun) Kim; m. Hrrja Chung, Apr. 4, 1964; children: Sun-Jeong, Sun-Jae, Sun-Hyup, Sun-Yong. BA in Econs., Yonsei U., Seoul, Republic of Korea, 1960; D in Econs (hon.), Yonsei U., 1985; DBA, Korea U., Seoul, 1986. Founder/chmn. Daewoo Group, Seoul, 1967—; mem. Pacific adv. council of United Technologies Corp. Author: It's a Big World, and There's a Lot to be Done. Vice-chmn. Fedn. Korean Industries, Seoul, 1979—, Korean Fgn. Trade Assn., Seoul, 1979—; bd. dirs. Korea-U.S. Econ. Council, Seoul, 1987—, Yonsei Cancer Ctr., Seoul, 1987—. Recipient Indsl. Order Gold Tower Korean Govt., 1972, Yonsei Mgmt. prize, 1976, Order of the Two Niles Sudanese Govt., 1979, Internat. Bus. award Internat. C. of C., 1984. Mem. Korean Fedn. Textile Industries (chmn. bd. dirs. 1986—), Korea Sports Assn. (vice-chmn. 1987—), Korea Baduk Assn. (chmn. bd. dirs. 1987—). Office: Daewoo Corp 541 Namdaemunno 5-Ga, Chung-ku, Seoul Republic of Korea also: Cen PO Box 2810, 541 Namdaemunno 5 Ga, Chung Qu Seoul Korea*

KIM, YANGHO, language educator; b. Seoul, S. Korea, Apr. 9, 1943; s. Kyoungsoon Han; m. Dongchoon Cho, Oct. 1, 1973; 1 child, Junghoon. B in Law, Dongguk U., Seoul, 1972, M in Bus. Adminstrn., 1987; PhD, LiaoNing U., Senyang, China, 1996. Instr. Ewha Women's U., Seoul, Korea, 1996—; hon. prof. LiaoNing U., Senyong, China, 1995—; vis. instr. Cen. Officials Tng. Inst., Seoul, 1984—; editor Indsl. Edn. 2000, Seoul, 1995-99; instr. Han Yang U., Seoul, 1983-93; editor Speech Culture Mag., Seoul, 1975-80; instr. Chung-ang U., Seoul, 1999—; cons. Korea Speech Club, 1984—, adv. com. Democratic Peaceful Unification, Seoul, 1999. Author: (books) Speech Encyclopedia, 1976, Psychological Tactics for Communication, 1975, Communication and Human Relationship, 1986, A Successful Man Thinks the Other Way, 1998. Exec. First Family Soc. Korea; mng. dir. Orgn. Promoting Economic and Cluture N.E. Asia, 1997—. Mem. Korea Speech Culture Acad. (pres. 1971—), Nat. Oratory Assn., Toastmasters Internat. Korea Speech Club (chmn.), Korean Edn. Assn. (dir.). Buddist. Avocations: climbing, reading, baseball, fishing. Home: RM 201 15-11 Haewha-dong, Chongno-gu, 110-530 Seoul S Korea

KIM, YONG-CHU, North Korean government official. V.p. Govt. of Democratic People's Republic of Korea, Pyongyang. Office: Office of the President, Pyongyang Dem Peoples Republic of Korea*

KIM, YONGMIN, electrical engineering educator; b. Cheju, Korea, May 19, 1953; came to the U.S., 1976; s. Ki-Whan and Yang-Whi (Kim) K.; m. Eunai Yoo, May 21, 1976; children: Janice, Christine, Daniel. BEE, Seoul Nat. U., Republic of Korea, 1975; MEE, U. Wis., 1979, PhD, 1982. Asst. prof. U. Wash., Seattle, 1982-86, assoc. prof., 1986-90, prof., 1990—, chair, 1999—; bd. dirs. Optimedx, Precision Digital Images, Redmond, Wash.; cons. MITRE Corp., McLean, Va., 1990, Lotte-Canon, Seoul, 1991, Seattle Silicon, Bellevue, Wash., 1990-93, U.S. Army, 1989-96, Neopath, Inc., Bellevue, 1989-90, Trinius Ptnrs., Seattle, 1989-91, Samsung Advanced Inst. Tech., Suwon, Republic of Korea, 1989-92, Daewoo Telecom. Co., Seoul, 1989-91, Intel Corp., Santa Clara, 1992, Aptec Sys., Portland, Oreg., 1992-93, Optimedx, Seattle, 1992-96, Precision Digital Images, Redmond, Wash., 1994-96, Micro Vision, Seattle, 1994-96, Hitachi, Tokyo, 1995, Fujitsu, Tokyo, 1995; bd. dirs. Image Computing Sys. Lab., 1984—, Ctr. for Imaging Sys. Optimization, 1991, Optimedx, 1993-96, U. Wash. Image Computing Libr. Consortium, 1995—; program evaluator Accreditation Bd. for Engring. and Tech., 1992—. Editor Procs. of the Annual Internat. Conf. of the IEEE EMBS, vol. 11, 1989, Procs. of the SPIE Med. Imaging Confs., vol. 1232, 1990, vol. 1444, 1991, vol. 1653, 1992, vol. 1897, 1993, vol. 2164, 1994, vol. 2431, 1995, vol. 2707, 1996, vol. 3031, 1997, vol. 3335, 1998, vol. 3658, 1999; mem. numerous editl. bds.; contbr. chpts. to books and numerous articles to profl. jours.; inventor in field. Mem. various nat. coms., chmn. steering com. IEEE TMI; chmn. numerous confs. Recipient Career Devel. award Physio Control Corp., 1982; grantee NIH, 1984—, NSF, 1984—, U.S. Army, 1986—, USN, 1986—; Whitaker Found. biomed. engring. grantee, 1986. Fellow IEEE (Early Career Achievement award 1988, Disting. Spkr. 1991), Am. Inst. Med. and Biol. Engring.; mem. Assn. Computing Machinery, Soc. Photo-Optical Instrumentation Engrs., Tau Beta Pi, Eta Kappa Nu. Presbyterian. Achievements include subspecialties in computer engineering, multimedia, high-performance media processors, image processing, computer graphics, medical imaging, and virtual reality. Home: 4431 NE 189th Pl Seattle WA 98155-2814

KIM, YONG-NAM, North Korean government official. Grad., Kim Il-Song U. Vice fgn. min., 1962; vice premier and min. fgn. affairs Govt. of Dem. People's Republic of Korea, Pyongyang, 1983—; pres. Supreme People's Assembly Presidium, Pyongyang; chmn. Com. for Cultural Rels. With Fgn. Countries. Mem. Korean Worker's Party, 1970—, sec. 1975, polit. commissar 1977, dir. internat. dept. and chmn. com. of peaceful reunification of fatherland; mem. Politburo, 1980—. Office: Supreme Peoples Assembly, Presidium, Pyongyang Dem Peoples Republic of Korea*

KIM, YONG-SUK, materials science educator; b. Seoul, Rep. of Korea, July 15, 1955; s. Yoon-Soo Kim and Soon-Hae Chung; m. Hye-Min Kim, Apr. 15, 1982; children: Hyun-Jung, Ji-Yoon. BS, Seoul Nat. U., 1978; MS, Korea Advanced Inst. Sci., Seoul, 1980; PhD, Stanford U., 1989. Rschr. Daewoo Motors Co., Ltd., Inchon, Rep. of Korea, 1980-83; rschr. Lewis Rsch. Ctr. (now Glenn Rsch. Ctr.) NASA, Cleve., 1989-90; prin. rschr. Rsch. Inst. Indsl. Sci. and Tech., Pohang, Rep. of Korea, 1990-95; asst. prof. Sch. Metallurgical and Materials Engring., Kookmin U., Seoul, 1995—. Contbr. articles to sci. jours. Mem. Minerals, Metals and Materials Soc., Korean Inst. Metals and Materials, Korean Soc. for Tech. Plasticity. Avocations: hiking, reading, trekking. E-mail: ykim@kmu.kookmin.ac.kr. Fax: 82-2-910-4320. Office: Kookmin U Sch Metal Mater, 861-1 Chongnungdong, Songbuk-ku Seoul 136-702, Republic of Korea

KIM, YONG-WOO, mechanical engineering educator; b. Pusan, Korea, Oct. 2, 1958; s. Guang Sik and Ae Soo Kim; m. Sun Young Ko, Oct. 29, 1991;

children: Hee Jung, Dowan. B in Engring., Yonsei U., 1982, M in Engring., 1984, PhD, 1991. Engr. Gold Star Telecommunication, Anyang, Korea, 1986-87; rschr. Yonsei U., Seoul, 1988-91; instr. Sunchon (Korea) Nat. U., 1992-93, asst. prof., 1994-98, chief dept. mech. engring., 1997-98, assoc. prof., 1998—; vis. prof. Ga. Inst. Tech., Atlanta, 1996. Contbr. articles to profl. jours. Recipient awards Comml. and Indsl. Resources Ministry, 1993, Korea Rsch. Found., 1993, L.G. Yonam Found., 1996. Mem. Korean Soc. Mech. Engrs., Computational Structural Engring. Inst. Korea. Avocations: mountaineering, collecting stamps, playing tennis, floriculture. Office: Sunchon Nat U Dept Mech Engring, 315 Maegok-dong, Sunchon 540-742, Republic of Korea

KIM, YOO YIK, law firm adviser; b. Ulsan, Korea, May 24, 1929; s. Sang Eon Kim and Won Seong Li; m. Sun Yong Chu, June 26, 1974 (div. Aug. 1978); 1 child, Han Yong. Student, Seoul Nat. U., 1946-51, Seoul Journalism Acad., 1952-53. Fgn. news reporter Kukje Newspaper Co., Pusan, Korea, 1953-55; fgn. news editor Sekye News Agy., Seoul, 1960-61, Chosun Ilbo Newspaper Co., Seoul, 1963-65, Orient Press Co., Seoul, 1965-70, Korea Herald, Seoul, 1970-73; spl. adviser Law Offices of Kim, Shin & Yu, Seoul, 1973—; rschr. Mass. Comm. Rsch. Inst., Seoul Nat. U., 1967-69; prof. Korea U. Fgn. Studies, Seoul, 1971-75. Sec. Korea League of World Fedn., 1976-85. Mem. Nat. Geog. Soc. Avocations: mountain climbing, skiing, partook game. Home: AID Apt 24-103, 50 Samseongtong 2, 135-092 Kangnamku Seoul, Korea Office: Kim Shin & Yu, 146-1 Susongtong Chongloku, Seoul 110-755, Republic of Korea

KIM, YOON BERM, immunologist, educator; b. Pyongnam, Korea, Apr. 25, 1929; came to U.S., 1959, naturalized, 1975; s. Sang Sun and Yang Rang (Lee) K.; m. Soon Cha Kim, Feb. 23, 1959; children: John, Jean, Paul. MD, Seoul Nat. U., 1958; PhD, U. Minn., 1965. Intern Univ. Hosp. Seoul Nat. U., 1958-59; asst. prof. microbiology U. Minn., Mpls., 1965-70, assoc. prof., 1970-73; mem., head lab. ontogeny of immune system Sloan Kettering Inst. Cancer Research, Rye, N.Y., 1973-83; prof. immunology Cornell U. Grad. Sch. Med. Scis., N.Y.C., 1973-83; chmn. immunology unit Cornell U. Grad. Sch. Med. Scis., 1980-82; prof. microbiology, immunology and medicine, chmn. dept. micorbiology and immunology Finch U. Health Scis., Chgo. Med. Sch., 1983—, acting dean Sch. Grad. and Postdoctoral Studies, 1994-95; mem. Lobund adv. bd. U. Notre Dame, 1977-88. Contbr. numerous articles on immunology to profl. jours. Recipient rsch. career devel. award USPHS, 1968-73, Morris Parker Rsch. award U. Health Scis., Chgo. Med. Sch., 1984. Fellow Am. Acad. Microbiology; mem. AAAS, Korean Acad. Sci. and Tech., Assn. Gnotobiotics (pres.), Internat. Assn. for Gnotobiology (founding), Am. Assn. Immunologists, Am. Soc. Microbiology, Am. Assn. Pathologists, Korean-Am. Med. Assn., N.Y. Acad. Scis., Soc. for Leucocyte Biology, Internat. Soc. Devel. Comparative Immunology, Harvey Soc., Internat. Soc. Interferon and Cytokine Rsch., Korean Acad. Sci. and Tech., Chgo. Assn. Immunologists (pres.), Assn. Med. Sch. Microbiology and Immunology Chairs, Internat. Endotoxin Soc. (charter), Soc. Natural Immunity (charter), Sigma Xi, Alpha Omega Alpha. Achievements include discovery of the unique germfree dolostrum-deprived immunologically "virgin" piglet model used to investigate ontogenic development and regulation of the immune system including T/B lymphocytes, natural killer/killer cells, and macrophages; research on ontogeny and regulation of immune system, immunochemistry and biology of bacterial toxins, host-parasite relationships and gnotobiology. Home: 313 Weatherford Ct Lake Bluff IL 60044-1905 Office: Finch U Health Scis Chgo Med Sch 3333 Green Bay Rd North Chicago IL 60064-3037

KIM, YOON SOO, wood biology educator; b. Kwangju, Korea, Aug. 11, 1949; s. Suck Hyun Kim and Soon Ihm Chung; m. Eun-Sook Lee, Aug. 1983; children: Nah-Ihm, Dah-Ihm. BS cum laude, Chonnam Nat. U., Kwangju, 1971, MS, 1976; Dr.rer.nat.tech., Bodenkultur U., Vienna, Austria, 1983. Assoc. dean acad. affairs Chonnam Nat. U., Kwangju, 1989-91, chmn. dept. forest products, 1991-93, v.p. planning and rsch., 1994-96; guest scientist Inst. for Holzforschung, Munich U., 1987-88, Dept. Forest Products, Swedish U. Agrl. Scis., Uppsala, 1991, Ctr. Rsch. Macromolecules Vegetables, Ctr. Nat. Rsch. Scis., Grenoble, France, 1993; vis. rsch. prof. Coll. Forest Resources, U. Maine, Orono, 1988-89; vis. sci., New Zealand Forest Rsch. Inst., Roturua, 1997-98; organizer 4th Pacific Regional Wood Anatomy Conf., 1994-98. Editor-in-chief Jour. of Korean Wood Sci. and Tech., 1998-2000; contbr. articles to profl. jours. Sgt. Korean Army, 1971-74. Recipient Outstanding Work award Korean Soc. Wood Sci. and Tech., 1989. Fellow Internat. Acad. Wood Sci.; mem. IUFRO (co-chair 1991-95), Internat. Wood Anatomist Assn. (coun. mem. and editorial bd. mem., 1997-99), Korean Wood Sci. & Tech. Soc. (v.p. 2000-2002). Avocations: travel, golf, opera. Office: Dept Forest Products & Tech, Chonnam Nat Univ, Kwangju 500-757, Republic of Korea

KIM, YOUNG HO, electrical engineer; b. DaeGu, Republic of Korea, May 16, 1961; s. Hai Gi and Hwa Ja (Park) K.; m. Mi Ran Jeong, Apr. 20, 1986; children: Jee Young, Yoon Soo. BS, Korea Mil. Acad., 1983; MS, U. Ctrl. Fla., 1988; PhD, U. Tex., 1997. Author: High-level Feedback Control with Neural Networks, 1998; contbr. articles to profl. jours. Lt. col. Republic of Korea, 1998—. Mem. Sigma Xi. Avocations: soccer game, climbing mountains.

KIM, YOUNG KIL, aerospace engineer; b. Pusan, Korea, June 18, 1956; came to U.S., 1984; naturalized, 1988; s. Tae Hyun and Myong Ok (Shin) K.; m. Susan Katherine Hong, July 16, 1981; children: Steven Charles, Christina Kay. BS, Seoul Nat. U., Rep. of Korea, 1979; MS, Ga. Inst. Tech., 1985, PhD in Aerospace Engring., 1991. Rsch. engr. Korean Inst. Aero. Tech. Korean Air Lines, Seoul, 1978-84; vis. rsch. engr. Agy. for Def. Devel., Daedog, Republic of Korea, 1981-82; rsch. assoc. Univs. Space Rsch. Assn., Huntsville, Ala., 1991-93; rsch. engr. U. Ala. Rsch. Inst., Huntsville, 1993-96; sr. rsch. engr. U. Ala. in Huntsville Rsch. Inst., 1996-2000; aerospace engr. NASA Marshall Space Flight Ctr., Ala., 2000—. Mem. AIAA. Roman Catholic. Avocations: tennis, golf. Home: 9010 Cannstatt Dr SE Huntsville AL 35802-3716 Office: TD55 NASA/MSFC Huntsville AL 35812

KIM, YOUNG KOO, international law educator, museum director; b. Seoul, June 26, 1939; s. Wan Tae Kim and Chae Kyong Won; m. Sung Sook Lee, Oct. 9, 1969; children: Eun Chung, Pu Kyum. BS, Korea Naval Acad., Chin Hae, 1962; LLB, Seoul Nat. U., 1971; LLM, Hanyang U., Seoul, 1978, JSD, 1984. Cert. 2d class navigator. Commd. officer Korean Navy, advanced through grades to capt., 1980, retired, 1989; staff judge adv. Republic of Korea Fleet, Chin Hae, 1971-75; dep. judge adv. gen. Navy Hdqs., Seoul, 1975-80; dean faculty Naval War Coll., Chin Hae, 1982-87, dir. Ctr. for Maritime Strategic Study, 1987-88, sr. prof., 1988-89; prof. internat. law Korea Maritime U., Pusan, 1989—, dir. Faculty Law, 1993-95, chief curator Mus., 1996—, dir. Ctr. for Social Sci. Rsch., 1997—. Author: Korea and the Law of the Sea, 1988. Confirmation mgr. Chin Hae Naval Ch. Recipient Best Working Scholar award Hyun Min Korean Assn. Internat. Law, 1997, Most Disting. Jurisprudence Work award Korea Legal Ctr., 1999, Letter of Commendation, Min. Edn., 2000; decorated Korean Navy; recipient medal of Samil, Pres. Republic of Korea, 1982. Avocations: playing tennis, hiking. Home: 202 Blvd 6 Whashin Villa, 213-35 Tongsamdong Youngdo, Pusan 606-080, Republic of Korea Office: Korea Maritime U Museum, 1 Tongsamdong Yongdoku, Pusan 606-791, Republic of Korea

KIM, YOUNGCHUL, publisher; b. Youngdong, Choungbook, Republic of Korea, July 13, 1936; s. Je-choon Kim and Byungsoon Lee; m. Jungja Kim, Apr. 15, 1966; children: Ki-Hyoung, KiHong, Hyoun Kyoung. Postgrad., Kyoungki U. Pres. Hakmun Pub., Inc., Seoul, 1962—. Mem. Alumni Assn. Kyoungki U. Grad. Sch. Nat. Security (chmn. 1998—). Fax: 02 733-8998. E-mail: hakmun97@soback.kornet21.net. Home: No 106 Rm 205 Hanyang Apt, Honje-2-Dong SeoDaeMun-Gu, Seoul Republic of Korea Office: Hakmun Pub Inc, 6th Fl, Sahak Hall 7-2 Sajik-Dong, Jongro-Gu, Seoul 110-054, Republic of Korea

KIM, YOUNG-WOOK, materials scientist, educator; b. Seoul, Korea, Sept. 25, 1958; s. Dong-Myeong and Eun-Shin (Park) K.; m. Ki-Young Lee, Dec. 25, 1987; children: Hyung-Seok, Eun-Seok. BS, Yonsei U., Seoul, 1981; MS, Korea Advanced Inst. Sci/Tech., Seoul, 1983, PhD, 1990. Rsch. scientist Korea Inst. Sci. and Tech., Seoul, 1983-96; vis. scientist Nat. Inst. for Rsch. in Inorganic Materials, Tsukuba, Japan, 1993-94; prof. Seoul City U., 1996-98, U. Seoul, 1998—. Contbr. articles to profl. jours.; patentee in field. Recipient Best Paper award Korea Inst. Sci. and Tech., 1990. Mem. Am. Ceramic Soc., Korean Ceramic Soc. Office: U Seoul Dept Material Sci, 90 Jeonnong-Dong Dongdaemoon-Gu, Seoul 130-743, Republic of Korea

KIM, YUNG KWON, electrical engineer, educator; b. Chawol, Inchon, Korea, Jan. 9, 1936; s. Eun Sung and Hui Boon Kim; m. Soon Ai Lee, Sept. 22, 1961; children: Jang Hwan, Ae Ryung. BA, Yonsei U., Seoul, 1958, ME, 1961, PhD, 1970. Asst. prof. Kwangwoon Inst. Tech., Seoul, 1966-68, pres., 1972-76; assoc. prof. Kyunghee U., 1968-71, Yonsei U., 1971-72; prof. elec. engring. Konkuk U., 1977—, dean Grad. sch. Engring., 1990-92. Recipient Nat. medal Pres. Korea, 1994; Konkuk U. Scholastic Rsch. award, 1985. Mem. Inst. Electronic Engrs. Korea (pres. 1992, Paper award 1970), IEEE (chmn. Korean Coun. 1996-97), KIEE. Office: Konkuk U Dept Elec Engring, 93-1 Mojin-Dong Kwangjin-Ku, 143-701 Seoul Republic of Korea

KIMBALL, DONALD ROBERT, food company executive; b. Anderson, Ind., Mar. 4, 1938; s. Robert Martin and Mary Lucille (Gibson) K.; m. Mari-Anne Talbot, Apr. 6, 1985; children: Randy, Rick, Sharon-Lee, Douglas, David. BS in Agr., Purdue U., 1960. Registered profl. sanitarian, Ind. Pub. health sanitarian Div. Dairy Products, Ind. Bd. Health, LaPorte, 1962-66; milk sanitation rating officer Div. Dairy Products, Ind. Bd. Health, Indpls., 1966-75; chief milk sanitation rating officer Div. Dairy Products, Ind. Bd. Health, 1973-75, dir., 1975-87; dir. regulatory affairs Dean Foods Co., Rockford, Ill., 1987—, dir. farm rels., 1990-98. Contbr. articles to profl. jours. Capt. U.S. Army, 1960-68. Recipient Disting. Svc. award, Midwest Dairy Products Assn., 1988. Mem. Internat. Assn. for Food Protection, Nat. Conf. Interstate Milk Shipments (single svc. containers com., drug residue program rev. com., methods for making ratings com., coun. III), Assn. Food and Drug Ofcls., Dairy Practices Coun., Conf. Food Protection (coun. I), Ill. Food Safety Task Force, Dairy Shrine. Methodist. Avocations: bicycling, hiking. Office: Dean Foods Co Technical Ctr PO Box 7005 Rockford IL 61125-7005

KIMBELL, MARION JOEL, retired engineer; b. McDonough, Ga., Sept. 7, 1923; s. Charles Marvin and Mary (McMillian) K.; BS in Civil Engring., U. Houston, 1949, MChem Engring., 1953; m. Judy Weidner, Dec. 18, 1946; children: Nancy, Susan, Candice. Civil engr. U.S. Dept. Interior, Lemmon, S.D., 1954; chief piping engr. M.W. Kellog Co., Paducah, Ky., 1955; nuclear engr. Westinghouse Atomic Power Div., Pitts., 1956-59; control systems prin. engr. Kaiser Engrs., Oakland, Calif., 1959-80; control systems supervising engr. Bechtel Inc., San Francisco, 1980-86; ret., 1986; control systems tchr. Laney Coll. cons. engr. NASA, Gen. Atomic Co.; advisory bd. Chabot Collage on radiation tech. Served as sgt. U.S. Army, 1943-46. Registered profl. nuclear engr., Calif.; control systems engr., Calif. Mem. Instrument Soc. of Am. (sr. mem. exec. com.). Clubs: Moose. Contbr. articles to profl. jours. Home: 22324 Ralston Ct Hayward CA 94541-3336

KIMBENG, COLLINS ANYE, research scientist; b. Bamenda, Cameroon, Mar. 2, 1964; arrived in Australia, 1998; s. William Nango Kimbeng and Cecielia Chayi Ngambong; m. Lucy Ayuk Eno, Dec. 18, 1999. BSc in Botany with honors, Ahmadu Bello U., Zaria, Kaduna State, Nigeria, 1987, MSc in Plant Breeding, 1992; PhD in Plant Breeding and Genetics, U. Wis., 1995. Rsch. asst. Ahmadu Bello U., 1988-92, U. Wis., Madison, 1992-95; territory mgr. Granulawn Lawn Care Co., Mpls., 1996; rsch. assoc., postdoctoral rsch. fellow U. Man., Winnipeg, Can., 1996-97; rsch. scientist Agr. Victoria, Hamilton, Australia, 1998; sr. rsch. scientist Bur. Sugar Experiment Stas., Mackay, Queensland, Australia, 1998—, mem. rsch. sta. exec. com., 1999—. Contbr. articles to profl. jours. Pres. Cameroon Students Assn., 1989, Grad. Student Assn., dept. agronomy U. Wis., Madison, 1994; vol. soccer coach Manona Grove H.S., Madison, 1994. Mem. Crop Sci. Soc. Am. Avocation: soccer. Fax: 61 7 4954 5167. E-mail: ckimbeng@bses.org.au. Home: 3/381 Bridge Rd, Mackay Queensland 4740, Australia Office: Bur Sugar Experiments Sta, PMB 57, Mackay Queensland 4741, Australia

KIMBLE, JAMES A., management consultant, accountant; b. Owosso, Mich., June 16, 1937; s. Gaylord Browning and Iva I. (Ansted) K.; children from previous marriage: Kim, Katherine, Kerri, Charles; m. Anne Park, June 13, 1970; 1 adopted child, Jeffrey. BBA, U. Toledo, 1959. With The PM Group Toledo Inc., 1961-99, v.p., 1964-90, pres., 1990-99; mem. Accreditation Coun. Accountancy, 1975, Accreditation Coun. Taxation, 1984; bd. dirs. Black and Skaggs Assocs., chmn. bd., 1994; bd. dirs. Nat. Assn. Health Care Cons., Inc., 1992-95. Pres. Citizens for Metroparks, Toledo, 1976-77; v.p., commr. Met. Park Dist., 1977-86; pres. Metroparks, Toledo, 1986-94; chmn. July spl. events Toledo Sesquicentennial, 1987; bd. dirs. Stone Oak Village, Ohio, 1998—, Assistance Dogs of Am., 1998-2000. Recipient Treasury Card IRS, 1976. Mem. Soc. Profl. Bus. Cons. (bd. dirs. 1977-80, cert.), Inst. Cert. Profl. Bus. Cons., Black & Skaggs Assocs. Republican. Avocations: fishing, travel, photography, genealogy. Office: Gilmore Jasion & Mahler 6591 W Central Ave Toledo OH 43617-1087

KIMEMIN, JOSEPH KANGARA, agronomist researcher; b. Limuru, Central, Kenya, Aug. 23, 1956; s. John Kimemia and Josephine Nungari (Mweru) K.; m. Lilian Nini Kironji, May 25, 1985; children: John, Ephraim, Samuel. BSc in Agriculture, Nairobi (Kenya) U., 1980; MSc in Agronomy, Andra Pradesh Agrl. U., Hyderabad, India, 1983; PhD in Agronomy, Nairobi (Kenya) U., 1997. Farming sys. agronomist Nat. Dryland Farming Rsch. Sta., Machakos, Kenya, 1980-86; officer in charge, maize agronomist Nyandarua Agrl. Rsch. Sta., Ol Joro Orok, Kenya, 1986-87; rsch. officer Coffee Rsch Found., Ruiru, Kenya, 1987-90, sr. rsch. officer, 1991—; officer in charge Nyandarua Agrl. Rsch. Sta., Oljoro Orok, 1986-87; head agronomy sect. Coffee Rsch Found., Ruiru, 1996-00; sec. gen. ASIC, Nairobi, 1996-97; mem. task force on coffee liberalisation Minister of Agriculture, Livestock Devel. and Mktg., 1996; mem. task force on strategies to enhance coffee productions in Kenya, 1998-99; mem. Ministeried Com. on the way forward for the coffee industry, 2000. Contbr. articles to profl. jours. Mem. African Coffee Rsch. Network, Eastern African Weed Sci. Soc., Weed Sci. Assn. Eastern Africa. Presbyterian. Avocations: reading, walking, gardening, ch. activities, photography. Office: PO Box 4, Coffee Rsch Found, Ruiru Kenya

KIMHI, SHAUL, psychologist, consultant, educator; b. Haifa, Israel, Nov. 22, 1948; s. Mordechai Kimhi and Gita Dizicer Ronen; m. Tovit Ilan; children: Naama, Yael, Michal. BA, Haifa U., 1975, MA, 1980; MS, Pacific Grad. Sch. Psychology, Palo Alto, Calif., 1988, PhD, 1991. Mgr. Regional Clinic, Kiriat Shemona, Israel, 1982-85; acad. lectr. Tel-Hai Acad. Coll., 1991—; rschr. Inst. Rsch. on Kibbutz-Oranim, 1991-94; cons. stress mgmt. Golan County, 1994-96; spl. cons. Govt. of Israel, 1992-95. Gen. sec. Kibbutz Shamir, Israel, 1979-81. Officer with Israeli Def. Force, 1967-70. Mem. APA, Israeli Psychol. Assn., Israeli Hypnosis Soc., Internat. Soc. for Polit. Psychology. Avocations: SCUBA diving, hiking. Home: Kibbutz Shamir, 12135 Shamir Israel

KIMISHIMA, AKIRA, finance company administrator, educator; b. Tokyo, July 10, 1934; s. Akira and Mie (Okina) K.; m. Noriko Ebihara, Sept. 23, 1962; children: Albert Tetsu, Margaret Hiro. BA in Econ., Keio U., Tokyo, 1957; Cert. of Grad., Harvard U., 1983. Asst. mgr. Daiwa Securities Co., N.Y.C., 1960-65; mgr. corp. planning Fuji Xerox Co., Tokyo, 1965-69; asst. to dir. planning Rank Xerox Co., London, 1969-74; dir. Mitsubishi France Co., Paris, 1974-79; pres. Altmann Sys. Internat. Co., Tokyo, 1979-83; exec. v.p. Dainana Securities Co., Tokyo, 1983-92; mng. dir. JP Capital Fin. Co. Ltd., Hong Kong, 1993—; bd. dirs. indsl. adv. bd. U. Bristol; bd. trustees Hollins Coll., Va. Ptnr. prodn. team (film) Sex Lies and Video Tape, 1989 (Grand Prix at Canne 1989), (film) Mr. Baseball, 1993. Mem. Anglican Ch. Avocations: travelling, reading. Home: 3-10-27 Higashicho, Kanagawa 255, Japan Office: JP Cap Fin Co Ltd, 1808 World Wide House Ctrl, Hong Kong China

KIMLIČKA, ŠTEFAN, information scientist, educator; b. Topoľčany, Czechoslovakia, Nov. 9, 1943; s. Stefan and Stefania (Davidova) K.; m. Zuzana Svitacova, May 18, 1968; 1 child, Matej. Diploma in engring., Slovak Tech. U., Bratislava, Czechoslovakia, 1968; postgrad., Inst. Sci. and Tech. Info., Moscow, 1969; D of Engring., Inst. Economy, Bratislava, 1978; postgrad., Comenius U., Bratislava, 1984. Research worker Cen. Economy Library, Bratislava, 1969-76; research worker Comenius U., 1976-78, vis. lectr. philosophy, 1980-84, head dept. info., 1985-87, mem. state examination commn. for grads., 1981-97, head dept. libr. and info. scis. on philosophy, faculty of arts, 1990-97; chief project Inst. Water Research, Bratislava, 1978-80; head rsch ctr. Matica Slovenska, Bratislava, 1987-90; assoc. prof. Comenius U., 1990, prof., 1996—; mem. Experts Commn., Ministry Edn., Bratislava, 1981-88; mem. sci. adv. bd. Info. Ctr., Slovak Acad. Scis., Bratislava, 1986—. Recipient Memory medal Matica Slovenska, 1986. Mem. Assn. Slovak Librs. and Informatists (exec. sec. 1976-85, v.p. 1976-89), Slovak Librs. Assn. (pres. 1990-92. Avocations: collecting stamps, painting, skiing. Home: Gessayova 23, 85103 Bratislava Slovak Republic Office: Comenius U, Gondova 2, 818 01 Bratislava Slovak Republic

KIMMEL, MARK, writer, retired venture capital company executive; b. Denver, Feb. 15, 1940; s. Earl Henry and Gerry Claire Kimmel; m. Gloria J. Danielewicz, Jan. 29, 1966 (div.); children: Kenton, Kristopher; m. Heidi J. Moller, Sept. 5, 1999. BSEE, U. Colo., 1963, BS in Mktg., 1963; MBA in Fin., U. So. Calif., 1966; MA in Psychology, Regis U., 2000. Sales engr., market rsch. analyst 3M Co., Calif. and Minn., 1963-70; mktg. mgr. Am. Computer and Comms., Calif., 1970-71; mgr. new bus. devel. Motorola, Inc., Schaumburg, Ill., 1971-76; v.p. corp. devel. Nat. City Lines, Denver, 1976-77; pres. Enervest, Inc., Denver, 1977-84; gen. ptnr. Columbine Venture Fund Ltd., 1983-91, Columbine Venture Fund II, 1983-91, Columbine Venture Mgmt. I, 1983-91, Columbine Venture Mgmt. II, 1983-91; pres. Columbine Venture Mgmt. Inc., 1983-91, Paradigm Ptnrs., Inc., 1992-96; writer Boulder, Colo., 1996—. Mem. Nat. Assn. Small Bus. Invesetment Cos. (past bd. govs.), Venture Capital Assn. Colo. (past chmn.). Home and Office: 61 Columbine Ln Ridgway CO 91432

KIMMEL, MORTON RICHARD, lawyer; b. N.Y.C., Nov. 10, 1940; s. Benjamin Bert and Sylvia (Alabaster) K.; m. Marcia Harriet LaPotin, Sept. 10, 1967; children: Wayne Douglas, Michelle Wendy, Karen Paige, Larry Keith. BA, Temple U., 1962; JD, George Washington U., 1965. Bar: Del. 1965, D.C. 1966. Law clk. Del. Superior Ct., Wilmington, 1965-66; ptnr. Kimmel, Carter, Roman & Peltz P.A., Wilmington, 1970—; supr. Del. Justices of the Peace, 1970-72; rep. State Farm Ins. Co., 1968-90, trustee lawyers' fund for client protection, 1985-97; arbitrator and mediator; lectr. in fields of criminal law, ins. law, personal injury law, law office mgmt., trial practice, ethics, professionalism, mediation and arbitration, 1970—. Author: You Can Do It, 1973, Emergency Medicine, 1982, Delaware Arbitration Manual, 1984, The Delaware Bar in the 20th Century, 1994. Mem. ATLA, Am. Bd. Trial Advs., Del. Trial Lawyers Assn., Fedn. Ins. Counsel, Def. Rsch. Inst. (chmn. Del. 1976-77). Democrat. Jewish. Avocations: sports, reading. Office: Kimmel Carter Roman & Peltz PA 913 N Market St Wilmington DE 19801-3019

KIMMEL, PAUL ROBERT, financial executive; b. Balt., Sept. 7, 1947; s. Walter William and Lisette Marie Elizabeth (Hasenzahl) K.; m. Cynthia Ann Bowers, Nov. 17, 1984; children: Elliott Paul, Charlotte Lisette Marie. BS in Engring. summa cum laude, Case Inst. Tech., 1969; MBA, Harvard Sch. Bus. Adminstrn., 1975. CPA. Mfg. mgr. Procter & Gamble Co., Cin., 1969-73; sr. acct. Arthur Andersen & Co., Boston, 1975-78; dir. mfg. and control Brilliant Seafood Co., Boston, 1978-79; sr. analyst Am. Cyanamid Co., Wayne, N.J., 1979-81; plant controller Shulton Inc., Mays Landing, N.J., 1981-83; mgr. acctg. and systems Am. Cyanamid Co. Med. Internat. Div., Wayne, N.J., 1983-85; dir. corp. acctg. Hartz Mountain Corp., Harrison, N.J., 1985-86; v.p. Citibank/Citicorp, N.Y.C., 1986-89; controller Airwick Industries, Wayne, N.J., 1989-90; dir. acctg. devel. Reckitt & Colman Inc., Wayne, N.J., 1990-94; v.p., CFO Eurostar Perfumes, Inc., Pleasanton, Tex., 1994-95; v.p., CIO Tristar Corp., San Antonio, Tex., 1995-98; CFO NBGS Internat., Inc., New Braunfels, Tex., 1998-99; v.p. of fin. McGhan Medical Corp., Santa Barbara, Calif., 2000—. Mem. AICPA, Fin. Execs. Inst., Inst. Mgmt. Acctg., Confrerie de la Chaine des Rotisseurs. Republican. Lutheran. Avocations: music, theater, food and wine. Home: 7929 Winchester Cir Goleta CA 93117-1069 Office: McGhan Medical Corp 700 Ward Dr Santa Barbara CA 93111-2936

KIMMICH, CHRISTOPH MARTIN, academic administrator, educator; b. Dresden, Jan. 16, 1939; s. Emil and Dora (Dreher) K.; m. Flora Graham Horne, July 10, 1965. BA, Haverford Coll., 1961; DPhil, U. Oxford, Eng., 1964. Asst. then assoc. prof. Columbia U., N.Y.C., 1965-73; assoc. then full prof. Bklyn. Coll., CUNY, 1973—, assoc. provost, 1984-88, provost, v.p. acad. affairs, 1988-97; interim chancellor CUNY, N.Y.C., 1997-99; pres. Bklyn. Coll., 2000—; v.p. bd. dirs. rsch. and devel. fedn. Bklyn. Coll., 1989—, chmn. bd. dirs. rsch. found. of CUNY, 1997—. Author: The Free City, 1968, Germany and the League of Nations, 1976, German Foreign Policy: 1918-1945, 1981, 2d edit., 1991. Trustee St. Antony's Coll. Trust, N.Y.C., 1978—; bd. dirs. Northeastern Sci. Found., Troy, 1987-98, Coll. Cmty. Svcs., Inc., Bklyn., 1988-95, bd. trustees Cranbury Pub. Libr., 1997—. Fulbright scholar, 1961; Internat. Affairs fellow, 1974; Guggenheim fellow, 1983. Mem. Phi Beta Kappa. Home: 183 Plainsboro Rd Cranbury NJ 08512-2603 Office: Bklyn Coll Office of the Pres 2900 Bedford Ave Brooklyn NY 11210-2814

KIMMICH, JON BRADFORD, computer science program executive; b. Lancaster, Pa., Aug. 8, 1964; s. John Howard and Alice (Ingram) K. BS in Computer Sci., Ind. U. Pa., 1986; MS in Computer Sci., Ohio State U., 1988; MBA, Seattle U., 1993. Developer Microsoft, Redmond, Wash., 1988-93, lead program mgr., sr. producer, 1993-97, lead product planner, 1997—; dir. PKT Found. Contbr. articles to profl. jours. Trustee PKT Found. Mem. IEEE (Computer Soc.), Assn. for Computing Machinery, Acad. Interactive Arts and Scis., Internat. Interactive Comms. Soc., Am. Film Inst. Achievements include 7 patents pending. Home: 1442 W Lake Sammamish Pkwy SE Bellevue WA 98008-5218 Office: Microsoft Corp 1 Microsoft Way Redmond WA 98052-8300

KIMMITT, ROBERT MICHAEL, executive, banker, diplomat; b. Logan, Utah, Dec. 19, 1947; s. Joseph Stanley and Eunice L. (Wegener) K.; m. Holly Sutherland, May 19, 1979; children: Kathleen, Robert, William, Thomas, Margaret. BS, U.S. Mil. Acad., 1969; JD, Georgetown U., 1977. Bar: D.C. 1977. Commd. 2d lt. U.S. Army, 1969, advanced through grades to maj., 1982, served in Vietnam, 1970-71; maj. gen. USAR, 1999—; law clk. U.S. Ct. Appeals, Washington, 1977-78; sr. staff mem. NSC, Washington, 1978-83, dep. asst. to Pres. for nat. security affairs and exec. sec. and gen. counsel, 1983-85; gen. counsel U.S. Dept. Treasury, Washington, 1985-87; ptnr. Sidley & Austin, Washington, 1987-89; undersec. for polit. affairs Dept. State, Washington, 1988-91, ambassador to Germany, 1991-93; mng. dir. Lehman Bros., Washington, N.Y.C., 1993-97; sr. ptnr. Wilmer, Cutler & Pickering, Washington, 1997-00; vice-chmn., pres. Commerce One, Pleasanton, Calif., 2000—; U.S. mem. Panel of Arbitrators, Internat. Ctr. for Settlement of Investment Disputes, 1988-89. Bd. dirs. Mannesmann AG, Siemens AG, Allianz Life Ins. Co. N.Am., United Def. Industries, German Marshall Fund, Atlantic Coun., Mike Mansfield Found., Am. Coun. on Germany, Am. Inst. for Contemporary German Studies, U.S. Group Coun., BMW AG. Decorated Bronze star (3), Purple Heart, Air medal, Vietnamese Cross of Gallantry, German Svc. Cross, German Army Cross in Gold; recipient Arthur Flemming award Downtown Jaycees, 1987, Alexander Hamilton award U.S. Dept. Treasury, 1987, Presdl. Citizens medal, 1991, Def. Disting. Civilian Svc. medal, 1993. Mem. Am. Acad. Diplomacy, Assn. Grads. U.S. Mil. Acad. (trustee 1976-82), Coun. Fgn. Rels. Roman Catholic. Office: Commerce One Inc 4400 Rosewood Ave Ste 200 Pleasanton CA 94588

KIMMONS, DONA L., writer; b. Ft. Worth, June 14, 1944; d. Wilbur Lewis Flloyd and Frankie Bess (Williams) Shelton; m. William E. Sanders, Aug. 1963 (div. 1968); m. Kenneth M. Kimmons Sr.; 1 child, Sheryl Lynn Garman. Degree in bus., U. Houston; degree, Sheltons Sch. Floral Design. Sec. Gulf Oil & Rsch., Houston, Judge Bustomonte, San Antonio, Judge Alvin Williams, Fairbanks, Alaska, Rowles Winston, Houston, Dean Witter, Houston. Author: Williams Family History, 1989, Searcher, 1989, Floyd Family History, 1996, Floyd Biography, 1996. Mem. DAR (registrar 1995). Home: PO Box 1544 Wimberley TX 78676-1544

KIMOTO, YASUHIKO, surgical oncologist; b. Nara, Japan, Oct. 28, 1953; s. Masatake and Hideko (Hiraka) K.; children from previous marriage: Yu Kimoto, Ko Kitaoka. Grad., Osaka (Japan) U., 1979. Surgeon Rsch. Inst. for Microbial Diseases Osaka U., 1979-84, 86-93; rsch. fellow Wistar Inst.,

Phila., 1984-86; asst. dept. surg. oncology Biomed. Rsch. Ctr. Osaka U., 1993-98; dept. Tanabe Seiyaku Co., Ltd., 1999—. Contbr. rsch. articles to profl. jours. Mem. N.Y. Acad. Scis. Avocations: painting, tennis. Home: Yamada-higashi 3-18-1-1020, Suita Osaka 565-0821, Japan Office: Tanabe Seiyaku Co Ltd, 3-16-89 Kashima Yodogawaku, Osaka 532-8505, Japan

KIMURA, ICHIRO, engineering educator; b. Nishinomiya, Japan, Feb. 19, 1946; s. Hiroji and Tomiko (Tani) K.; m. Yumiko Nakagawa, Apr. 1, 1973; children: Mayuko, Tomomi. BS, Kobe (Japan) U., 1968, MS, 1972; D of Engring., Osaka (Japan) U., 1983. Engr. Koyo-Seiko Co., Ltd., Osaka, 1968-69; rsch. assoc. Kobe U., 1972-84, assoc. prof., 1984-93; prof. Osaka Electro-Comm. U., Neyagawa, 1993—. Contbr. articles to sci. jours. Mem. ASME, Soc. Instrument and Control Engrs., Visualization Soc. Avocations: playing tennis, movies, art museums. Home: 12-4 Shinkoyo-cho, Nishinomiya 662-0013, Japan Office: Osaka Electro-Comm U, 18-8 Hatsu-cho, Neyagawa Osaka 572-8530, Japan

KIMURA, KATSUMI, molecular scientist, educator; b. Okazaki, Aichi, Japan, Aug. 31, 1931; s. Isaku and Kana (Kaneiwa) K.; m. Fumiko Goto, May 3, 1956; children: Keiko, Isao. BSc, Nagoya (Japan) U., 1954, MSc, 1956, PhD in Chemistry, 1959. Rsch. assoc. Tokyo U., 1959-60, 62-63, Cornell U., Ithaca, N.Y., 1960-62; assoc. prof. Osaka (Japan) U., 1963-68; prof. Hokkaido U., Sapporo, Japan, 1968-79; prof. Inst. for Molecular Sci., Okazaki, 1979-92, head dept. molecular assemblies, 1984-92, dir. Synchrotron Radiation Facility, 1987-92, prof. emeritus, 1992—; prof. Japan Advanced Inst. Sci. and Tech., Tatsunokuchi, Japan, 1992-98, dir. Ctr. of New Materials, 1992-93; dean Sch. Material Sci. Japan Advanced Inst. Sci. and Tech., Tatsunokuchi, 1993-95, presdl. advisor, 1995-96, prof. emeritus, 1998—; sr. rschr. Nat. Comm. Rsch. Lab., Nagoya, 1999—. Recipient award for young chemists Chem. Soc. Japan, 1966, award Chem. Soc. Japan, 1990, Purple Ribbon medal Govt. of Japan, 1998. Avocations: classical music, tennis. Home: 2-9-12 Tatsumi-Minami, Okazaki 444-0874, Japan Office: Prof Emeritus, Inst for Molecular Sci, Okazaki 444-8585, Japan

KIMURA, MASASHI, graphic design educator; b. Matsudo, Chiba, Japan, Nov. 29, 1955; s. Shigeto and Hiroko (Maruyama) K.; m. Rie Ueda, Oct. 15, 1988. BFA, Nihon U., Tokyo, 1978; MFA, Washi. State U., 1982. Intern Smithsonian Instn., Washington, 1985; pres. design co. Tokyo, 1987-98; lectr. Nihon U., 1993-98, assoc. prof. graphic design, scientific illustration, 1998—; illustrator Nat. Geog. Soc., Washington, 1986; graphic cons. U.S. Embassy, Tokyo, 1988—; exhbn. dir. Biohistory Rsch. Hall, Osaka, Japan, 1992—. Illustrator: Birth of Insect, 1997. Avocations: making model ship, bug hunting. Office: Nihon U Coll Art, 2-42 Asahigaoka, Nerima-ku Tokyo 176, Japan

KIMURA, MINEO, physics educator; b. Tokyo, Japan, Nov. 15, 1946; s. Shoichi and Tsugiko (Tada) K.; m. Keiko Arai, Dec. 2, 1973; children: Kana, Mari, Nao. BS, Waseda (Japan) U., 1970; MS, U. Tokyo, 1972; PhD, U. Alta., Edmonton, Can., 1981. Asst. prof. U. Mo., Rolla, 1981-84; scientist Joint Inst. for Lab. Astrophysics U. Colo., Boulder, 1984-86; physicist Argonne (Ill.) Nat. Lab., 1986-96; prof. physics Yamaguchi U., Ube, Japan, 1996—; adj. prof. Rice U., Houston, 1986—, Inst. Space and Astron. Sci., Kanagawa, Japan, 1997—; cons. Internat. Atomic Energy Agy., Vienna, 1991—, Nat. Inst. Fusion Sci., Nagoya, Japan, 1996—, Dept. of Energy, Washington, 1996—. Grantee NSF, 1991—, Ministry of Edn., Tokyo, 1996—. Mem. Am. Phys. Soc., Japanese Phys. Soc., Internat. Radiation Rsch. Soc. Fax: 81-836-35-9492. Office: Yamaguchi U, Grad Sch Sci and Engring, Ube 755-8611, Japan

KIMURA, MIYOSHI, statistics educator, researcher; b. Ena-shi, Gifu-ken, Japan, Aug. 22, 1947; s. Masaru and Toshiko (Kato) K.; m. Hiroko Nakatsuru, May 17, 1974; children: Shogo, Ayako. BSc, Nagoya U., 1970; MSc, Kyushu U., 1973, DSc, 1988. Asst. prof. Nanzan U., Nagoya, Japan, 1975-82, assoc. prof., 1982-90, prof., 1990—, course leader Grad. Sch., 1992-96, head dept. info. sys. and quantitative scis., 1999—, head dept. math. scis., 2000—; vis. rschr. Stanford (Calif.) U., 1980-81, U. Wash., Seattle, 1991, U. Sheffield, U.K., 1997-98. Contbr. articles to profl. jours. Avocation: tennis. Home: 22 1-Chome Ryokuen-nishi, Kakamigahara-shi, Gifu-Ken 509-0116, Japan Office: U Nanzan Dept Info Sys Quant Scis, 18 Yamazato-cho Showa-ku, Nagoya 466-8673, Japan also: U Nanzan Dept Math Scis, 27 Serei-cho, Seto-Shi Aich 489-0863, Japan

KIMURA, SHIGENOBU, art historian; b. Jōyō, Kyoto, Japan, Aug. 10, 1925; s. Jutako and Toyo Kimura; m. Yoshiko Tsuji, Dec. 2, 1954; children: Aya, Ake. BA, Kyoto U., 1949; LittD, Osaka (Japan) U., 1975. Lectr. Kyoto City U. of Arts, 1953-58, asst. prof., 1958-69, prof., 1969-74; prof. Osaka U., 1974-89, prof. emeritus, 1989—; prof. Nat. Mus. Ethnology, Osaka, 1976-89; dir. Nat. Mus. of Art, Osaka, 1992-98, Hyogo Prefectual Mus. of Modern Art, Kobe, 1998—. Author: On Primative Art, 1959, Beginning of Art, 1971, What Does Art Mean to Man?, 1976, Sources of the Beauty, 1984, S.Kimura's Selected Works, 8 vols., 1999—. Commr. Sci. Com. of Govt., Tokyo, 1976, Cultural Com. of Govt., Tokyo, 1978, Planning Com. of City, Osaka, 1980. Mem. Art History Soc. Japan (pres. 1978-90), Ethno-Arts Soc. Japan (pres. 1984—), Soc. for Aesthetics in Japan (standing com.), Soc. for African Studies in Japan (standing com.), Collegium Mediterranistarum in Japan (standing com.), Assn. Internat. Critic of Art. Home: 2-18-3 Shinsenri-Kitamachi, Toyonaka, Osaka 560-0081, Japan Office: Hyogo Prefectural Mus Art, Kobe 3-8-30 Harada-Dori, Kobe 657-0837, Japan

KIMURA, SHIGENOBU, microbiology educator, dentist; b. Osaka, Japan, Jan. 10, 1954; s. Jiro and Katsuko (Nagashima) K.; m. Chieko Okuda, Apr. 27, 1980; children: Yoshihito, Toru, Junya. DDS, Osaka U., 1979, PhD, 1983. Rsch. assoc. U. Ala., Birmingham, 1983-85; asst. prof. Osaka U., 1985-92, 94-97, assoc. prof., 1997-98; asst. prof. Fukuoka (Japan) Dental Coll., 1992-94; prof. Iwate Med. U., Marioka, Japan, 1998—. Co-author: (in Japanese) Strategy and Background in Periodontics, 1991, Standard Textbook of Peridontology, 1994, Periodontology, 1996; mem. editl. bd. Dictionary of Dental Technology, 1991—. Mem. Japanese Soc. Periodontology (coun. mem. 1987—), Japanese Assn.. Oral Biology (coun. mem. 1998—), Japanese Soc. Bacteriology (coun. mem. 1999—), Internat. Fedn. Dental Edn. Assn. (mem. coun. 1999), Am. Soc. Microbiology, Internat. Endotoxin Soc., Internat. Assn. Dental Rsch. Office: Iwate Med U Dept Oral Micro, 1-3-27 Chuodori, 020-8505 Morioka Japan

KIMURA, SHIGERU, surgeon, educator; b. Sendai, Miyagi, Japan, Jan. 23, 1931; s. Seiichi and Haru Kimura; m. Tomoko Endoh, May 16, 1961; 3 sons. MD, Tohoku U., Sendai, Japan, 1955, PhD, 1960. Instr. Tohoku U. Sch. Medicine, Sendai, 1960-67; assoc. prof. Iwate Med. Coll., Morioka, Japan, 1968-74; prof. surgery Ehime U. Sch. Medicine, Matsuyama, Japan, 1974—; chmn. dept. surgery Ehime U., Matsuyama, 1974—, dir. univ. hosp., 1990-93; cons. Ehime Med. Assn., Japan, 1988—; guest prof. Taisan (China) Med. Coll., 1992—. Author: Biliary Artresia, 1991, New Encyclopedia of Surgical Science, Vol. 30, Pediatric Portal Hypertension, 1992, Clinical Surgery, Vol. 2, Pediatric Abdominal Surgery, 1994; editor: Principle of Pediatric Surgery, 1989. Mediator Ehime Dist. Ct., Japan, 1976—. Fellow Internat. Coll. Surgeons; mem. Internat. Soc. Surgery, Japan Surg. Soc. (exec. mem.). Avocations: golf, skiing, classic music, historical novel. Home: Hiraicho ko 2172, Matsuyama 791-02, Japan Office: Ehime Univ Sch Medicine, Shigenobu, Matsuyama 791-02, Japan

KIMURA, TAKANORI, health facility administrator, family physician; b. Yawatahama, Ehime, Japan, Dec. 27, 1930; s. Masao and Shizuko (Koizumi) K.; m. Tomoko Inoh, Oct. 24, 1961; children: Takashi, Yoshiye, Hiromi. MD, Kyushu U., 1955. Resident in contagious disease Cook County Hosp., Chgo., 1958-59; resident in tuberculosis Sea View Hosp., S.I., N.Y., 1959-60; resident in gen. practice Louise Obici Meml. Hosp., Suffolk, Va., 1964-66; chief examiner Ministry of Health and Welfare, Tokyo, 1962-63; dep. dir. Nakamura (Japan)-shimin Hosp., 1972-73; chief family practice, dir. Benda Hosp., Pineland Center, Maine, 1976-77; dep. dir. Iyo (Japan) Hosp., 1982-83, Matsuyama (Japan) Bethel Hosp., 1983-86; dir. Tojima Clinic, Uwajima, Japan, 1987—. Co-author: Handbook of Everyday Practice, 1987; author: (mag.) The Den-den jidai, 1979; contbr. articles to profl. jours. Recipient Disting. Svc. cert. Japan Primary Care Assn., 1987, Disting. Svc. cert. Nat. Health Ins. Groups, 1993. Fellow Am. Acad. Family Physicians; mem. Japan Med. Assn. (cert. specialist in occupational health 1991). Buddhist. Avocations: writing, reading, photography, art. Home: 1983 Tojima, Uwajima Ehime, Japan Office: Tojima Clinic, 2014 Tojima, Uwajima Ehime, Japan

KIMURA, TAKEMUNE, automotive executive. Chmn. Mitsubishi Motors, Tokyo. Office: Mitsubishi Motors, 5-33-8 Shiba Minato-ku, Tokyo 108-8410, Japan*

KIMURA, TATSUO, mathematician, martial artist; b. Tokyo, Aug. 10, 1947; parents Masao (Honda) and Ineko K.; m. Kazuyo Kimura; 1 child, Sakiko. BA, U. Tokyo, 1970, MA, 1973; PhD, Nagoya (Japan) U., 1978. Rsch. asst. Nagoya U., Nagoya, 1973-80; with Inst. for Advanced Study, Princeton, N.J., 1975-77; asst. prof. math. U. Tsukuba, Ibaraki, Japan, 1980-85, assoc. prof., 1985-93, prof., 1993—; vis. assoc. prof. Johns Hopkins U., Md., 1986. Author: (with M. Kashiwara and T. Kawai) Foundations of Algebraic Analysis, 1986, Transparent Power, 1995, Prehomogeneous Vector Spaces, 1998. Mem. Japan Math. Soc., Am. Math. Soc. Office: Univ Tsukuba, Inst of Math, Ibaraki 305-8571, Japan

KIMURA, TOKIHISA, endocrinologist; b. Isawa, Yamanashi, Japan, June 1, 1940; s. Jishu and Chie Kimura; m. Ishimori Katsuko, Apr. 11, 1969; children: Kyoko, Osamu, Takako. MD, Tohoku U., Sendai, Miyagi, Japan, 1966, PhD, 1974. Diplomate internal medicine, endocrinology. Intern Mizusawa (Japan) Mcpl. Hosp., 1969-70; rsch. fellow dept. medicine Tohoku U. Sch. Medicine, Sendai, 1970-71, instr. dept. physiology, 1971-72, instr. dept. medicine, 1973-78, asst. prof. dept. medicine, 1981-92, assoc. prof., 1993-97, clin. prof.; adminstr., pres. Furukawa City (Japan) Hosp., 1988—; asst. prof. dept. physiology U. Tenn., Memphis, 1979-80; chief doctor dept. internal medicine Tohoku U., Sendai, 1992-94. Author: Annuals New York Academy Science, 1993; editorial bd. Advances in Neuroimmunology, 1991—; contbr. articles to profl. jours. Recipient Golden prize for established researcher Tohoku U., Sendai, 1991; rsch. grantee Ministry of Edn. Japan, Tokyo, 1989, 92. Mem. Am. Physiol. Soc., Am. Endocrine Soc., Japan Endocrine Soc., Japan Med. Soc., Japan Neuroendocrine Soc., N.Y. Acad. Sci., Am. Heart Assn. Avocations: jogging, reading, music. Home: Aobaku, Higashi-Katsuyama 3-33-8, Sendai 980, Japan Office: Furukawa City Hosp, 2-3-10 Senjujicho, Furukawa 989-61 Miyagi Prefecturu, Japan

KINABO, LUDOVICK DOMINICK BATI, adult education educator; b. Rombo, Tanzania, Apr. 23, 1954; s. Dominick Bati and Mariana Kinabo; m. Joyce Chisawillo, Dec. 21, 1983; children: Heri, Mariana. B in Vet. Sci., U. Dar Es Salaam, 1980; M Vet. Medicine, Sokoine U. Agr., 1984; PhD, U. Glasgow, 1989. Cert. vet., Tanzania Vet. Bd. Tutorial asst. U. Dar Es Salaam, Tanzania, 1980-82, asst. lectr., 1982-84; asst. lectr. Sokoine U. Agr., Tanzania, 1984-85, lectr., 1985-88, sr. lectr., 1988-91, assoc. prof., dir. rsch. and postgrad. studies, 1991-99, dir. rsch. and postgrad. studies, 1992-99, prof., 1999—, dir. Solomon Mahlangu campus, 1999—; external examiner vet. pharmacol. and toxicology, Makerere U., Uganda, masters degree students, U. Nairobi, Kenya. Designer emblem Tanzania Livestock Rsch. Orgn. (prize), emblem of Nat. Urban Water Authority, 1983, (prize), emblem Com. Vice-Chancellors and Principals of Tanzania, 1996 (prize), emblem Higher Edn. Accreditation Coun., 1997 (prize); sci. reviewer, mem. editl. bd. Toxicology Letters, 1993—; sci. reviewer Jour. Vet. Pharm. and Therapeutics. Mem. Nat. Agr. Rsch. Coun., Dar Es Salaam, 1993—, Agr. Rsch. Fund Mgmt. Team, Min. Agr., Dar Es Salaam, 1993—, R&D Agr. Commn. Sci. and Tech., Dar Es Salaam, 1993—, Nat. Animal Disease Rsch. Com., Dar Es Salaam, 1998—, Sci. Organizing Com., 6th Congress European Assn. Vet. Pharmacology and Toxicology, Edinburgh, 1994, Joint food and Agr. Orgn., WHO, expert com. on food additives, 1998—. Fellow Danish Agy. Internat. Devel., 1982-84, 86-89, Internat. Livestock Rsch. in Animal Diseases, 1989-90. Roman Catholic. Avocations: painting, drawing, badminton. E-mail: Alkinabo@suanet.ac.tz . Home: PO Box 3275, Chuo Kikuu Morogoro Tanzania Office: Sokoine U Agr, University Rd PO Box 3017, Morogoro Tanzania

KINAHAN, TIMOTHY CHARLES, priest, writer; b. London, England, Dec. 31, 1953; Immigrated to Northern Ireland, 1955.; s. Charles Henry and Kathleen Blanche (McClintock) K.; m. Jacqueline Elizabeth Irwin, Nov. 22, 1988; children: Michael, Katherine. Attended, Jesus Coll., Cambridge, 1972-75. Tchr. Asra Hawariat Sch., Addis Abeba, Ethiopia, 1971-72; cross cmty. worker Belfast, 1975-77; curate asst. St. Nicholas Ch., 1978-80; theol. lectr. Newton Coll., Papua, New Guinea, 1981-83; rector St. Columba's Ch., Belfast, 1984-90, St. Dorothea's Ch., Belfast, 1990—. Author: (book) Where Do We Go From Here: Protestants & The Future of Northern Ireland, 1995, A More Excellent Way: A Vision For Northern Ireland, 1997. Chair Faith & Politics Group, Northern Ireland, 1995—; mem. Cmty. Rels. Coun., Northern Ireland, 1995—. Fellow Royal Geographical Soc. Mem. Ch. Ireland. Avocations: woodcarving, photographing tropical butterflies, gardening, family, music. Home: 237 Lower Braniel Road, BT5 7NQ Belfast Northern Ireland

KINART, CEZARY MACIEJ, chemistry educator; b. Łódź, Poland, Jan. 1, 1949; s. Zdzisław and Wanda (Gawęcka) K.; m. Krystyna Florczak, Dec. 8, 1979; children: Zdzisław, Andrzej. MSc, U. Łódź, 1972, PhD, 1976, DSc habilitation, 1996. Asst. dept. inorganic chemistry U. Łódź, 1972-73, sr. asst. dept. inorganic chemistry, 1973-76, adj. dept. chem. edn., 1976—. Contbr. articles to profl. jours. Cpl. Compulsory Mil. Tng., 1976. Fellow Polish Soc. Chemistry, Sci. Soc. Łódź. Roman Catholic. Avocations: sports, travel, angling. Home: Sienkiewicza 147a m.45, 90-302 Łódź Poland Office: U Łódź Chem Edn, Pomorska 163, 90-236 Łódź Poland

KINAY, NADIR OSMAN, military officer; b. Hereke, Kocaeli, Turkey, Mar. 30, 1947; s. Seyfettin and Vesile Ayse (Çolak) K.; m. Ferda Gökçeer, Feb. 20, 1978 (dec. Aug. 1999); 1 child, Seçil. Grad. as ensign, Turkish Naval Acad., 1968; student, U.S. Naval Postgrad. Sch., 1969-70; MS in Mech. Engring. in Ocean Engring., MIT, 1973. Commd. officer Turkish Navy, 1968, advanced through grades to rear (LH) admiral, 1996; welding workshop supt. Gölcük (Turkey) Naval Shipyard, 1973-74, chief hull design sect., 1975-81, project officer submarine constrn., 1982-83, head planning, estimating and design dept., 1993-96; trainee for submarine constrn. Howaldtswerke Deutsche Werf Shipyard, Kiel, Germany, 1974-75; liaison officer submarine constrn. Howaldtswerke Deutsche Werf Shipyard, Kiel, 1981-82; frigate constrn. project officer ship constrn. dept. Turkish Navy Hdqrs., Ankara, 1983-85, 1987-90, head ship constrn. dept., 1990-93, navy chief tech. dept., 1996—; head liaison officer for frigate constrn. Blohm und Voss Shipyard, Hamburg, Germany, 1985-87. Mem. Soc. Naval Arch. and Marine Engrs. (assoc.). Office: Turkish Navy Chief Off Tech, Bakan Liklar, 06100 Ankara Turkey

KINCAID, STEVEN RANDALL, marketing professional; b. Oklahoma City, July 19, 1953; s. William Calvin Hoover and Mary Elizabeth (Cochran) K. BA, Okla. State U., 1975; MA, U. Ill., 1977, PhD, 1980. Rsch. analyst Gen. Foods Corp., White Plains, N.Y., 1980-82; rsch. assoc. Opinion Rsch. Corp., Princeton, N.J., 1982-85, rsch. dir., 1985-86, rsch. exec., 1986-87, account exec., 1989-91; cons. John Hancock Life Ins. Co., Boston, 1987-88, dir. rsch., 1988-89; dir. rsch. Prudential Ins. Co., Newark, 1991-93; sr. assoc. Abt Assocs., Cambridge, Mass., 1993-95; pres. Kincaid Assocs., Boxford, Mass., 1995-98; v.p. Fidelity Investments, Boston, 1998—. Named Eagle Scout Boy Scouts Am., 1968. Mem. Am. Assn. Pub. Opinion Research, Am. Polit. Sci. Assn., Applied Polit. Sci. Study Group. (charter), Mktg. Sci. Inst. (trustee), Phi Kappa Phi. Democrat. Methodist. Office: Fidelity Investments 100 Summer St Fl 18 Boston MA 02110-2106

KINCART, ROBERT OWEN, technological executive; b. Youngstown, Ohio, Feb. 8, 1949; s. Robert E. and Mary Louise (Briach) K.; children: Jeffrey, Jennifer, Michael. Student, Ohio U., 1967-70, U. Fla., 1970-72. Registered environ. profl., environ. property assessor, environ. lending analyst, Nat. Registry of Environ. Profls.; lic. radon measurement specialist, 1988; cert. hazardous materials mgr.; lic. pollutant storage sys. contr., Fla. Rsch. chemist Roux Labs., Inc., Jacksonville, Fla., 1972-73; sr. control chemist Kerr-McGee Chem. Corp., Jacksonville, 1973-77; ops. mgr. The UpJohn Co./Asgrow, Plant City, 1977-82; pres., founder Resource Recovery Am., Mulberry, 1980-87, Am. Compliance Tech., Lakeland, 1987—; bd. dirs. Fla. Spillage Com., Jacksonville, Fla. Author: Chemical Handling, 1986, Detection and Measurement of Radon Progeny, 1988, Radon Gas Information, 1988. Bd. dirs. Traviss Vo-Tech Inst., Lakeland, 1984, Goodwill Industries Fla., Lakeland, 1985, Polk County Disaster Com., 1988, Local Emergency Planning Coun., Polk County, 1989—, Habitat for Humanity; judge local sci. fair, Little Miss Am. Beauty contest, Fla. State Sci. and Engring. Fair. Named to Hon. Order of Ky. Cols., 1994. Mem. Am. Chem. Soc., U. Fla. Alumni Assn., Fla. Physics Soc., Polk County Transp. Soc., Tampa Com. of 100, Fla. Bar Assn., Fla. Petroleum Assn., Inst. Hazardous Material Mgmt., Am. Water Works Assn., Am. Soc. Safety Engrs., So. Environ. Bus. Coun., Propeller Club (bd. dirs.), Rotary (chartered; Paul Harris fellow), Bartow C. of C., Lakeland C. of C., Gator Boosters of U. Fla., U. Fla. Pres.'s Coun. Republican. Methodist. Avocations: family, golf, outdoor activities, community involvement, traveling, innovative business ventures. Office: Am Compliance Techs Inc 1875 W Main St Bartow FL 33830-7718

KINDER, EUGENE J(OSEPH), psychiatrist, psychoanalyst; b. Chgo., Mar. 5, 1926; s. Joseph Casimer and Helen (Lincoln) K.; m. Patricia N. Chambers, Sept., 1953; children—Jean Marie Kinder Zukowski, Thomas E. M.D., Loyola U., Chgo., 1952. Diplomate Am. Bd. Psychiatry and Neurology. Intern, St. Anne's Hosp., Chgo., 1952-53; resident in psychiatry, Georgetown U., Washington, 1957-60; clin. dir. Riveredge Hosp., Chgo., 1963-65; assoc. clin. prof. psychiatry U. Chgo., 1960-62; assoc. clin. prof. Rush Med. Sch., Chgo., 1960-70, U. Wis., Madison, 1975-79; grad. Inst. for Psychoanalysis, Chgo., 1972; pres. Ariz. Psychoanalytic Study Group, Phoenix, 1984—; med. staff Maricopa Med. Ctr., Phoenix, 1979—, Camelback Hosp., Scottsdale, Ariz., Meml. Hosp., Phoenix Baptist Hosp., Good Samaritan Hosp., Phoenix, 1979—. Served to lt. comdr. USNR, 1954-56. Fellow Am. Psychiat. Assn.; mem. Am. Psychoanalytic Assn., AMA, Chgo. Psychoanalytic Soc., Ariz. Med. Assn., Ariz. Psychiat. Soc.(v.p.), Denver Psychoanalytic Soc., Colo. Psychiatric Soc. Office: 832 Lincoln Pl Boulder CO 80302-7555

KINDERMANN, GERHARD WILHELM, internist; b. Berlin, May 28, 1926; s. Carl and Manalle (Caver) K.; m. Christa Hermann, Sept. 77, 1954; children: Christel, Katja, Peter. MD, U. Freiburg, 1954. Intern Danbury Hosp., 1954-55; resident DePaul Hosp., St. Louis, 1955-56, City Hosp., St. Louis, 1956-57; asst. Sanatorium Kuppelmuhle, Bad Orb, Germany, 1957-58, Knappselaftskraukerlaus, Dortmund, Germany, 1958-61, Univ. Clinic Kiel, Germany, 1961-62; head physician Stadt Kraukerhaus, Baden-Bauer, Germany, 1962-65, Dortmund, 1965-72; leading physician Kreiskraukerhaus, Bad Berlegorg, Germany, 1972-97; cons. internist Ode Gorn Clinic, Bad Berlegorg, 1997-98. Home: Franz von Winckel weg 1, 57319 Bad Berlegurg Germany

KINDERMANN, WILFRIED, physician, educator, researcher; b. Halle/Saale, Germany, Sept. 4, 1940; s. Friedrich and Erna (Ritter) K.; m. Ingrid Wittkowsky, Apr. 1, 1966; children: Michael, Petra. MD, U. Hamburg, 1967; Habilitation, U. Freiburg, 1977. Asst. lectr. Max-Planck-Inst., Bad Nauheim, Fed. Republic Germany, 1970-72; asst. lectr., sr. physician Med. Univ. Clinic, Freiburg, Fed. Republic Germany, 1972-77; attending physician Med. U. Clinic, Freiburg, 1977-78, physician internal medicine, cardiology, sports medicine, 1977—; prof. sports medicine U. Saarland, Saarbrücken, Fed. Republic Germany, 1978—, head Inst. Sports Medicine, 1978—; team physician German soccer nat. team. Mem. editorial bd. several nat. and internat. jours.; contbr. over 450 articles to nat. and internat. sci. jours. Recipient Carl Diem award Deutscher Sportbund, 1976, Ernst v. Bergmann medal Bundesärztekammer Fed. Republic Germany, 1989; European champion 4x400 meter relay, 1962. Mem. German Soc. Sports Medicine, German Soc. for Heart and Circulation Rsch. Office: U Saarland Inst Sports Med, Im Stadtwald, D-66041 Saarbrücken Federal Republic of Germany

KINDERMANS, JEAN-MARIE, international medical organization executive; b. Melun, France, 1950. Dir. Agence Europé Dévol. et la Santé, 1984-96; bd. dirs. Médecins Sans Frontières, Brussels, 1988-94, sec. gen., 1995—; tchr. Inst. médecine et épidémiologie tropicales U. Paris. Recipient Nobel Peace prize, 1999. Office: MSF Internat Office, Rue de la Tourelle 39, Brussels 1040, Belgium*

KINDERSLEY, LYDIA HELENA (LIDA) See LOPES CARDOZO KINDERSLEY, LYDIA HELENA (LIDA)

KINDLMANN, PAVEL, ecologist; b. Prague, Czech Republic, Nov. 29, 1954; s. Jaroslav and Karla (Škávová) K.; m. Dana Šindelková, Apr. 12, 1986; children: Lucie, Petr. BS, Charles U., Prague, 1979, MS, 1981; PhD, Inst. Entomology, Č. Budějovice, Czech Republic, 1984. Rschr. Inst. Entomology, Czech Acad. Sci., 1980-94; assoc. prof., vice-dean U. South Bohemia, Ceske Budějovice, 1993—; head sci. coun. Inst. Entomology, Czech Republic, 1994-95. Editor: Critical Issues in Aphid Biology; contbr. articles to sci. jours. Grantee European Sci. Found., Switzerland, 1994, Nat. Environ. Rsch. Coun. (U.K.), 1995, Grant Agy. of Czech Republic, 1995. Mem. Intecol, Am. Orchid Soc., Eastern and Ctrl. European Soc. on Math. Ecology (hon.), Brit. Ecol. Soc., Soc. Math. Biology. Avocations: horse breeding, mountaineering. Home: Frydova 11, 370 05 Ceske Budejovice Czech Republic Office: U South Bohemia Faculty Biology, Branisovska 31, 370 05 Ceske Budejovice Czech Republic

KING, ALMA JEAN, former health and physical education educator; b. Hamilton, Ohio, Feb. 28, 1939; d. William Lawrence and Esther Mary (Smith) K. BS in Edn., Miami U., Oxford, Ohio, 1961; MEd, Bowling Green State U., 1963; postgrad., Fla. Atlantic U., 1969, '92, Nova U., Ft. Lauderdale, Fla., 1979. Cert. elem. and secondry tchr., Ohio, all levels incl. coll., Fla. Tchr. health, physical edn. Rogers Middle Sch., Broward County Bd. Pub. Instrn., 1963-64; assoc. prof. health, phys edn., recreation, dance Broward C.C., Fort Lauderdale, Fla., 1964-94; ret., 1994; dir. Intramurals and Extramurals Boward C.C., Fort Lauderdale, Fla., 1964-67, chair person Women's Affairs, 1978, health and safety com., 1975, faculty evaluation com. 1980-85, mem. faculty ins. benefits com. 1993-94. Sponsor Broward County Fire Fighters, Police; active mem. Police Benevolent Assn.; Historical Soc. Grantee Broward C.C. Staff Devel. Fund, 1988. Mem. AAHPERD, NEA, Fla. Edn. Assn., Fla. Assn for Health, Physical Edn., Recreation and Dance, Am. Assn. for Advancement of Health Edn., United Faculty of Fla., Fla. Assn. of C.C., Order of the Eastern Star (past Worthy Matron), Order of Shrine. Avocations: concerts, theater, art, historic museums, recreational activities. Home: 4310 Buchanan St Hollywood FL 33021-5917

KING, AMBROSE YEO-CHI, sociology educator, university official; b. Zhejiang, People's Republic China, Feb. 14, 1935; s. Hsiang-chuan (Fan) King; m. Yuan-jan Tao; children: Ambrose Jun-shen Jr., Joseph Jun-chi, Daniel Jun-yu, Christopher Jun-ping. BA in Law, Nat. Taiwan U., 1957, MA in Polit. Sci., 1959; PhD in Pub. and Internat. Affairs, U. Pitts., 1970. Lectr. sociology New Asia Coll., Chinese U. Hong Kong, 1970-74; dir. social rsch. ctr. Chinese U. Hong Kong, 1972-73; head dept. sociology New Asia Coll., Chinese U. Hong Kong, 1972-75, sr. lectr. sociology, 1974-79; chmn. and dir. studies in sociology Chinese U. Hong Kong, 1976-89; head New Asia Coll., Chinese U. Hong Kong, 1977-85; reader in sociology Chinese U. Hong Kong, 1979-83, chmn., prof. sociology, 1983—; pro-vice chancellor Chinese U. Hong Kong, 1989—. Internat. cons. editor, contbr. Jour. Applied Behavioral Sci., 1980-90; mem. editorial bd. China Quar., 1982-92; author: The Historical Development of Chinese Democratic Thought, 1964, The Modernization of China and Intellectuals, 1977, From Tradition to Modernity, 1978, Some Reflections on Cambridge, 1977, Social Life and Development in Hong Kong, 1981, The Idea of the University, 1983, The Predicament and Development of Democracy in China, 1984, Some Reflections on Heidelberg, 1986, The Politics of the Three Chinese Societies, 1988, Salient Issues of Chinese Society and Culture, 1992, Salient Issues of Chinese Politics and Culture, 1997. Chmn., mem. community rsch. subcom. Independent Commn. Against Corruption, 1977-82; mem. Law Reform Commn., 1980-85, subcom. on homosexuality, 1980-82, subcom. on confession statements and their admissibility in criminal proceedings, 1981-84; mem. Cen. Policy Unit, 1989—. Avocation: tennis. Office: Chinese Hong Kong U Dept Soc, Shatin NT, Hong Kong Hong Kong

KING, ANTHONY CHARLES, archaeologist, researcher; b. London, Feb. 23, 1954; s. Geoffrey and Anne (Dayrell-Stenning) K. BA in Archaeology, U. London, 1975, PhD in Archaeology, 1985. Dir. excavations Hayling Island Temple, 1976-81, Monte Gelato, Lazio, Italy, 1986-91, Meonstoke Villa, Hants., Eng., 1986-91; lectr. King Alfreds Coll., Winchester, Eng.,

1980-91, head dept. archaeology, 1991—, prof. archeology, 1997—. Author: Archaeology of the Roman Empire, 1982, Roman Gaul and Germany, 1990, British and Irish Archaeology: A Bibliographical Guide, 1994; editor: The Roman West in the Third Century, 1981. Trustee Roman Rsch. Trust, Oxford, 1994—. Grantee Brit. Acad., 1976-79. Fellow Soc. Antiquaries; mem. Hampshire Field Club and Archaeol. Soc. (editor 1990—). Avocations: hill walking, gardening. Office: King Alfreds Coll, Dept Archaeology, Hants Winchester SO22 4NR, England

KING, BARBARA JEAN, nurse; b. Cape Girardeau, Mo., June 28, 1941; d. Otto Samuel and Goldie Elizabeth (Clover) Fowler; m. Charles Basil King, Jr., Sept. 4, 1972; children: Otto Samuel, Christopher Lee. Student, Weatherford Jr. Coll., 1965; nursing degree, John Peter Smith Hosp. Sch. Profl. Nursing, 1969. RN, Tex. Head nurse pediat. and isolation County Hosp.; also ICU and CCU, Small Gen. Hosp., Ft. Worth, 1969-72; dir. nursing svcs. Jarvis Hts. Nursing Ctr., Ft. Worth, 1976-77; dir. nursing svcs. Ft. Worth Rehab. Farm, 1978-80; staff nurse, asst. supr. shift Decatur (Tex.) Cmty. Hosp., 1983-85; staff nurse and supr. Burdgeport Hosp., Tex., 1986—; clin. supr., patient care coord. Hospice of Tejas; instr. vocat. nursing Cooke County Coll., Gainesville, Tex., 1981; clin. care supr. home health dept. Faith Community Hosp., 1992, assoc. dir. 1993—; patient care coord. Family Svcs. Home Health Svcs., Inc., 1994, adminstrn. for choice Choice Home Health Svcs., Inc., Nocona Gen. Hosp. Home Health, 1995, asst. dir., 1999; cons. convalescent centers and hosps. Chmn. child care com. Women of Moose, 1997—; ch. organist Bethel Bapt. Ch., assoc. pianist, 1996. Served with M.C., USN, 1962-65. Mem. Dirs. of Nursing Homes Assn. Tarrant County (v.p.). Democrat. Home: 202 S Trappier St Alvord TX 76225-6015

KING, BETSY, professional golfer; b. Reading, Pa., Aug. 13, 1955. Winner U.S. Open-Women, 1989, 1990, LPGA, 1992; 3d ranked woman LPGA Tour, 1992; LPGA tour victories include: Orlando Classic, 1984, Columbia Savings Classic, 1984, Henredon Classic, 1986, Rail Charity Classic, 1986, 88, Tucson Open, 1987, Dinah Shore Invitational, 1987, McDonald's Classic, 1987, Atlantic City Classic, 1987, Kemper Open, 1988, Cellular One-Ping Championship, 1988, Jamaica Classic, 1989, Nabisco Dinah Shore, 1990, U.S. Women's Open, 1989, 1990, Corning Classic, 1991, Mazda Championship, 1992, ShopRite Classic, 1995, Corestates Betsy King Classic, 1997, Solheim Cup, 1998. Inductee LPGA Hall of Fame, 1995. Achievements include LPGA leading money winner, 1984, 89, 93. Office: LPGA 100 International Golf Dr Daytona Beach FL 32124-1092

KING, DAVID PAUL, lawyer; b. Washington, June 20, 1956; s. Ivan Robert and Alice King. AB, Princeton U., 1977; JD, U. Pa., 1982. Bar: Ga. 1984, U.S. Dist. Ct. (no. and so. dists.) Ga. 1984, U.S. Ct. Appeals (11th cir.) 1984, D.C. 1985, U.S. Dist. Ct. Md. 1987, U.S. Ct. Appeals (4th cir.) 1987, Md. 1991, U.S. Dist. Ct. D.C. 1995. Law clk. to Hon. Alvin B. Rubin, U.S. Ct. Appeals for 5th Cir., Baton Rouge, 1982-83; assoc. Rogers & Hardin, Atlanta, 1983-85, Covington & Burling, Washington, 1985-87; asst. U.S. atty. Dept. Justice, Balt., 1987-90; assoc. Hogan & Hartson, L.L.P., Balt., 1990-92, ptnr., 1992—; adj. prof. U. Md. Law Sch., Balt., 1995—. Mem. ABA, Fed. Bar Assn. (Md. bd. govs.), Md. Bar Assn., D.C. Bar Assn., Ga. Bar Assn., Serjant's Inn. Office: Hogan & Hartson LLP 111 S Calvert St Ste 1600 Baltimore MD 21202-6106

KING, ELIZABETH MAUREEN, business systems executive; b. Bellefonte, Pa., Nov. 13, 1957; d. Richard A. and Joanne Sellers King. BA, Pa. State U., University Park, 1979. Sys. analyst R.H. Macy, Newark, Fla., 1979-81; mgr. applications Eckerd Corp., Clearwater, Fla., 1981-93; dir. retail sys. Rite Aid Corp., Camp Hill, Pa., 1993; mgr. applications devel. IBM Global Svcs. Corp., Clearwater, Fla., 1993-96; sr. cons. McCready, Manigold, Ray and Co., Dunedin, Fla., 1996-97; v.p. bus. sys. Starbucks Coffee Co., Seattle, 1997—. Active Tribute to Women and Industry, 1989. Betty J. Lockington scholar, Martin Marietta scholar. Mem. NAFE, Pa. State U. Alumni Assn., Phi Beta Kappa, Phi Kappa Phi, Pi Sigma Alpha. Home: 4601 174th Pl SE Bellevue WA 98006-6549

KING, FRANCIS HENRY, novelist; b. Adelboden, Switzerland, Mar. 4, 1923; s. Eustace Arthur Cecil and Faith Mina (Read) K. MA, Oxford U., 1948. Drama critic Sunday Telegraph, London, 1978-88. Author: To the Dark Tower, 1946, Never Again, 1947, An Air That Kills, 1948, The Dividing Stream (Somerset Maugham award), 1951, The Dark Glasses, 1954, The Widow, 1957, The Man on the Rock, 1957, So Hurt and Humiliated, 1959, The Custom House, 1961, The Japanese Umbrella (Katherine Mansfield Short Story prize), 1964, The Last of the Pleasure Gardens, 1965, The Waves Behind the Boat, 1967, The Brighton Belle, 1968, A Domestic Animal, 1970, Flights, 1973, A Game of Patience, 1974, The Needle, 1975, Hard Feelings, 1976, Danny Hill, 1977, The Action, 1978, Indirect Method, 1980, Act of Darkness, 1983, Voices in an Empty Room, 1984, One is a Wanderer, 1985, Frozen Music, 1987, The Woman Who Was God, 1988, Punishments, 1989, Visiting Cards, 1990, The Ant Colony, 1991, Secret Lives, 1991, The One and Only, 1994, Ash on an Old Man's Sleeve, 1996, A Hand at the Shutter, 1996, Dead Letters, 1997; (poetry) Rod of Incantation, 1952; (biography) E.M. Forster and His World, 1978; (autobiography) Yesterday Came Suddenly, 1993; gen. editor: Introducing Greece, 1956, Travel: Japan, 1970, Florence: A Literary Companion, 1991. Decorated comdr. Brit. Empire. Fellow Royal Soc. Lit.; mem. Soc. Authors Internat. PEN (pres. 1986-89, v.p. 1989—). E-mail: fhk@dircon.co.uk.

KING, FREDERIC, health services management executive, educator; b. N.Y.C., May 9, 1937; s. Benjamin and Jeanne (Fritz) K.; m. Linda Ann Udell, Mar. 17, 1976; children from previous marriage: Coby Allen, Allison Beth, Lisa Robyn, Daniel Seth Yehuda. BBA cum laude, CUNY, 1958. Dir. adminstrn. Albert Einstein Coll. Medicine, Bronx, 1970-72; assoc. v.p. health affairs Tulane Med. Ctr., New Orleans, 1972-77; dir. fin. Mt. Sinai Med. Ctr., N.Y.C., 1977-78; v.p. fin. Cedars-Sinai Med. Ctr., L.A., 1978-82; pres. Vascular Diagnostic Svcs., Inc., Woodland Hills, Calif., 1982-84; exec. dir. South Bay Ind. Physician's Med. Group, Inc., Torrance, Calif., 1984-98; ret., 1999; assoc. adj. prof. Tulane U. Sch. Pub. Health; asst. prof. Mt. Sinai Med. Ctr.; instr. Pierce Coll., L.A. Bd. dirs. Ohr Eliyahu Acad., chmn.; bd. dirs. AMHO Pacific Region, Milw. Kollel, Congregation Beth Jehudah; pres. Torah Learning Ctr. Young Israel Venice. With U.S. Army, 1959-62. Mem. Healthcare Forum, Am. Hosp. Assn., Pres.'s Assn., Calif. Assn. Hosps. and Health Systems. Republican. Home: W75n749 Tower Ave Cedarburg WI 53012-1024

KING, GEORGE RALEIGH, manufacturing company executive; b. Benton Harbor, Mich., May 13, 1931; s. Maurice Peter and Opal Ruth (Hart) King; m. Phyllis Stratton, Apr. 10, 1950; children: Paul King Zang, Angela King Young, Philip. Student, Adrian Coll., 1950-51. Cert. purchasing profl. exec. status. With Kirsch Co., Sturgis, Mich., 1951—, data processing trainee, 1951-53, data processing mgr., 1953-59, asst. purchasing agt., 1959-62, purchasing agt., 1962-68, asst. dir. purchasing, 1968-91. Author: Rods & Rings, 1972. Elder 1st Presbyn. Ch., Sturgis, 1970; pres. Sturgis Civic Players, 1972. Recipient citation Boy Scouts Am., 1966, Jr. Achievement, 1967; nominated candidate for adminstrn. Fed. Procurement Policy, Reagan Adminstrn., Washington, 1980. Mem. Am. Purchasing Soc. (pres. 1979-81), Nat. Assn. Purchasing Mgmt., southwestern Purchasing Assn., Exchange (pres. Sturgis 1959, dis. gov. dist. and nat. clubs 1961), Berrien Hills Country Club, Rotary (Lakeshore), Masons, Elks. Home: 1804 Lakeshore Dr Apt 16 Saint Joseph MI 49085-1616

KING, HAROLD, artistic director; b. Durban, South Africa. Student, U. Capetown Ballet Sch. From dancer to soloist Ballet Co. of Cape Town (South Africa) Performing Arts Bd., 1968-70; dancer, choreographer The Scottish Ballet (formerly The Western Theatre Ballet, England), Glasgow, Scotland, 1970, Royal Opera House, Covent Garden, National Ballet of Zimbabwe; guest artist, tchr. Ballet Co. Capetown Performing Arts Bd.; artistic coord. Victor Hochhauser Gala Ballet Season, Royal Festival Hall, 1978; assisted with 2 Rudolf Nureyev Seasons London Coliseum; producer Lunch Hour Concerts Arts Theatre, Leicester Sq., 1978; founder, dir. London City Ballet, 1978, City Ballet London, 1996. Producer numerous works including Dances from Napoli, Prince Igor; choreographed Carmen for London City Ballet, Strauss Galas series for Victor Hochhauser, Nutcracker Suite, The Lion, The Witch and The Wardrobe for London Studio Ctrs., Mrs. Harris Goes to Paris for London Children's Ballet, 1998. HRH The Princess of Wales became Patron of the London City Ballet Co. at his invitation, 1983, the Duke of York, 1998. Office: City Ballet London, 113 Leadenhall St 3rd Fl, Lloyds TSB Bank London EC3A 4AX, England also: City Ballet London, 71 Kingsway Holborn, London WC2B 6SX, England*

KING, HELEN EILEEN, service executive; b. Sunnyslope, Alberta, Can., June 3, 1920; d. Elvin Cyril and Pearl Marion (Archibald) White; m. Charles Lester King, Dec. 20, 1949; children: Gail, Carol, Laura. BEd, U. Alberta, 1947; postgrad., Pasadena Coll., 1948, U. Colo., 1979. Cert. elem. and secondary tchr., Can. Tchr. various sch. dists., Alberta, Can., 1941-45, C.N. Coll., Red Deer, Alberta, 1947-48; English tchr. Centro Boliviano Am., La Paz, Bolivia, 1954-56; forest fire lookout U.S. Forest Svc., Coeur d'Alene, Idaho, 1950, Grand Canyon, Ariz., 1974; mgr. Campus Natural Food Shoppe, Boulder, Colo., 1981-82; pres. Bus. and Postal Svcs., Boulder, 1982-98; pres. Neola, Inc., Boulder, 1992—; mem. Alberta Tchrs. Assn., Edmonton, 1941-48. Vol. coord. Boulder County Safe house, Boulder, 1979; bd. dirs. Images in Motion differently abled Dance Group, Boulder, 1985—. Named Eco Hero, Boulder Daily Camera, 1990, Colo. Recycler of Yr., Recycle Now, Denver, 1990. Mem. Nat. Fedn. Ind. Bus., Associated Mail Receiving Agy., Hill Merchants Assn., Nat. Health Fedn. Avocations: ecology, gardening, health rsch. counseling, drawing. Office: Bus and Postal Svcs 1085 14th St Boulder CO 80302-7309

KING, HENRY EDWARD ST. LEGER, solicitor; b. Oct. 11, 1936; s. Robert James and Dorothy Louisa Marie (Wickert) K.; m. Kathleen Bridget Wilcock, 1964 (dissolved 1989); 2 children (1 dec.); m. Margaret Empson Cox, 1996. MA, LLB, Cambridge (Eng.) U. Solicitor, Eng. 1964, Hong Kong 1977. Solicitor Denton Hall, 1964-67, ptnr., 1967-96, chmn., 1993-96; chmn. bd. dirs. Rentokil Initial PLC, City Centre Restaurants PLC, GKR Group Ltd.; bd. dirs. Brambles Investments PLC, Total Oil Marine PLC. Mem. Riverside Racquet Club. Avocations: travel, theatre, music. Office: Rentokil Initial PLC, 1 Fleet Place, London EC4M 7WS, England

KING, JAMES A., NATO official; b. Montreal, 1948; m. Barbara King. BS, McGill U., 1968. Commd. Royal Can. Navy, 1968, advanced through grades to vice-admiral, 1998, ops. specialist with Maritime Command and Nat. Def. Hdqrs., squadron ops. officer with USN ships and NATO Naval Force, comdr. destroyer HMCS Huron and 5th Can. destroyer squadron, 1984-89; dep. chief of staff readiness, Maritime Command Hdqrs. Royal Can. Navy, Halifax, N.S., Can.; chief of staff ops., Can.'s Naval Task Group to Persian Gulf Royal Can. Navy; chief of staff personnel & tng., Maritime Hdqrs. Royal Can. Navy, Halifax, 1992-93; dir. gen. Maritime Devel., Nat. Def. Hdqrs. Royal Can. Navy, 1993-95, rear-adm., assoc. asst. dep. minister of policy, 1995, dir. gen. internat. security policy; Can. mil. rep. to NATO Mil. Com. in Permanent Session Royal Can. Navy, Brussels, 1998—. Named Comdr. Order of Mil. Merit, 1997. Avocations: travel, skiing, sailing, reading, fishing. Office: NATO Hdqrs, Blvd Leopold III, 1110 Brussels Belgium*

KING, JOHN JOSEPH, manufacturing company executive; b. Toledo, Jan. 12, 1924; s. Walter and Frances (Gwozd) Kawecka; m. Joy G. Mohler, Jan. 28, 1950; children: Catherine M., Carolyn S., David J., Michael R., Mark A.R. BSME magna cum laude, U. Toledo, 1957, MS in Indsl. Engring., 1961. Registered profl. engr., Ohio. Draftsman, Tecumseh Products Co., 1941-42; die designer Bingham Stamping Co., 1942-46; tool designer Spicer Mfg. Co., 1946-47; product designer Am. Floor Surfacing Co., 1947-50; founder, mgr. engr. Kent Industries, 1950-52; mech. engr. Owens Ill. Inc., Toledo, 1953-63; mgr. rsch. and devel. Permaglass Inc., Genoa, Ohio, 1963-69; founder, pres. Ashur Inc., Rossford, Ohio, 1969—, also chmn. bd. dirs. Patentee in field. Mem. Am. Ceramic Soc., Soc. Mfg. Engrs., Phi Kappa Phi, Tau Beta Pi. Republican. Roman Catholic. Clubs: Devils Lake Yacht. Lodges: KC, Eagles. Home: 1111 W Elm Tree Rd Rossford OH 43460-1338 Office: Ashur Inc 28663 Glenwood Rd Perrysburg OH 43551-3011

KING, JOSEPH, JR., government administrator, educator, consultant; b. Charleston, W.Va., June 8, 1950; s. Joseph and Jessie Ree (May) K.; m. Linda Streeter, Sept. 4, 1986. BA, Ohio State U., 1972; MS, Xavier U., 1975; EdD, U. Cin., 1982; diploma, U.S. Army War Coll., 1999. Investigator U.S. EEOC, Cin., 1976-79; tng. officer U.S. EEOC, Washington, 1979-82; EEO advisor U.S. Army, Washington, 1982-84; EEO officer U.S. Army, Giessen, Germany, 1984-86, Nurenburg, Germany, 1986-89; dir. EEO U.S. Army, St. Louis, 1989-99; dir. The King Group, St. Louis, 1989—, command exec. officer, 1999—; prof. Boston U., 1984-89, Webster U., 1989—; cons. in field. Author: Discretionary Equality, 1982. Unit commr. Boy Scouts Am., St. Louis, 1990; congrl. intern. Congrl. Black Caucus, Washington, 1980. Sgt. USAF, 1979-82. Mem. ASTD, Am. Mgmt. Assn., Soc. Human Resource Mgmt., Soc. for Profls. in Dispute Resolution. Independent. Avocations: jogging, fitness, martial arts. Home: 4520 Chouteau Ave Saint Louis MO 63110-1518 Office: USAR Personnel Command 1 Reserve Way Saint Louis MO 63132-5299

KING, LEA ANN, community volunteer and leader; b. Elkhart, Ind., July 26, 1941; d. Lloyd Emerson and Mildred Salome (Hostetler) Hartzler; children: Thomas Ellsworth III, Alden Elizabeth. BA in History, DePauw U., 1963. Participant in Intensive Workshop in Intercultural Comm. U. Calif., Irvine, 1993, Study Tour of Ethnic Minorites of China, UCLA Extension, 1990; audited The Ethics of War and Peace, Ethikon Inst., Jerusalem, 1993; attended Three Intercultural Colloquia of Family Life, Cultural Diversity and Human Values, Ethikon Inst., 1989. Producer, hostess Pub. Access cable TV programs; travel writer, photographer. Bd. dirs., chair The Ethikon Inst. for Study of Ethical Diversity and Intercultural Rels.; pres. Vol. Ctr. S. Bay-Harbor-Long Beach, 1993-95; v.p. Comty. Assn. of the Peninsula, chair multicultural com., chair PV 2000; sec. Planned Parenthood L.A., 1991—; past pres. Jr. League; past chair San Pedro Peninsula Hosp. Found.; founding chair Forward-Looking Strategies for Women Coalition, 1985; co-chair United Way Sys. Wide Admissions Com.; mem. Nodrstrom's Com. for Salute to Cultural Diversity, L.A., 1993-95, diversity com. Planned Parenthood Fedn. We. Region, 1996-99; field rep. Congresswoman Jane Harman, Calif. 36th Dist., 1997—. Named Woman of Yr. Nat. Women's Polit. Caucus, San Fernando Valley, 1986, South Bay YWCA; recipient John Anson Ford award L.A. County Commn. on Human Rels., 1992, Spirit of Volunteerism award Jr. League L.A., 1991, Founders award Vol. Ctrs. Calif., 1996, commendations from L.A. Mayor Tom Bradley, L.A. County Bd. Suprs., Calif. State Sen. Robert Beverly, Congressmen Dana Rohrabcher and Howard Berman; mem. Los Angeles County Commn. on Human Rels., 1993, 96, pres., 1997. Home and Office: 229 17th St Manhattan Beach CA 90266-4633

KING, M. JEAN, association executive; b. Cleve., May 5, 1930. BS in Med. Tech., U. Del., 1960, MS in Microbiology, 1960. Med. technologist Del. Hosp., Wilmington, 1950-60; staff microbiologist Wilmington Gen. Hosp., 1960-61, Episcopal Hosp., Phila., 1961-68; mem. faculty dept. microbiology Temple. U. Med. Sch., 1966-68; staff microbiologist Crozier Chester (Pa.) Med. Ctr., 1969-71; pres., founder Ind. Dogs, Inc., Chadds Ford, 1984—; designer Parkinson's Walker Dog Pilot Program, U. Pa. Hosp., Phila., 1997; pres. Akbash Dogs Internat., 1987; speaker rehab. hosps., svc. orgns., self help groups, radio and TV. Theater pipe organ concert artist Longwood Gardens, Kennett Square, Pa., Dickenson Theater Organ Soc., Wilmington, Del., Sunnybrook Ballroom, Pottsdown, Pa., Marietta (Pa.) Theater, Phoenixville (Pa.) Theater. founder Parkinsans Walker Dog Pilot Program, U. Pa. Hosp. Recipient award Delta Soc., Am. Animal Hosp. Assn., Gaines Dog Food, 1987-88, Work with Handicapped Population citation Pres. George Bush, 1990, Poor Richard Pro Bono award, 1994; named to Hall of Fame, U. Del., 1988. Mem. Am. Akbash Dog Assn. (pres. emeritus), Delta Soc., Del. County C. of C., Beta Beta Beta. Home: 14 Maple Ln Chadds Ford PA 19317-9201 Office: Independence Knoll 146 Stateline Rd Chadds Ford PA 19317-9047

KING, MARGARET ANN, communications educator; b. Marion, Ind., Feb. 27, 1936; d. Paul Milton and Janet Mary (Broderick) Burke; m. Charles Claude King, Aug. 25, 1956; children: C. Kevin, Elizabeth Ann, Paul S., Margaret C. Student, Ohio Dominican, 1953-56, U. Kans., 1980-81; BA in Communication, Purdue U., 1986, MA in Pub. Communication, 1990. Regional rep. Indpls. Juv. Justice Task Force, 1984-85; vis. instr. dept. communication Purdue U., West Lafayette, Ind., 1992-96; v.p. King Mktg. Cons., Inc., 1996—; bd. mem. Vis. Nurse Home Health Svcs. Contbr. chpt. to book. Grad. mem. Leadership Lafayette, 1983. Purdue U. fellow, 1986-87. Mem. AAUW, Ctrl. States Comm. Assn. (conf. presenter 1989), Golden Key, Phi Kappa Phi. Republican. Roman Catholic. Avocations: poetry writing, vocal and piano music. Home: 7938 Wild Orchard Ln Cincinnati OH 45242-4309

KING, MARGARET ETUKUDO, educator in public policy and geography; b. Abak, Akwa Ibom, Nigeria, Dec. 12, 1970; came to U.S., 1988; d. Augustine Ibongedi and Nse Veronica Etukudo; m. Anietie James King, Nov. 4, 1989; children: James Akan, Ifreke Cynthia. BA in Geography and Regional Planning, Calabar, Nigeria, 1983; MA in Geography, Chgo. State U., 1992; PhD in Urban Planning, Policy, U. Ill., Chgo., 1998. Rsch. exec. Peril's Group of Cos., Lagos, Nigeria, 1983-85; project coord. Small Bus. Devel. Ctr. Moraine Valley C.C., Palos Hills, Ill., 1992-93; rsch. asst. CUED U. Ill., Chgo., 1993-94; exec. dir., founder Econ. Recovery Inst., Chgo., 1994-96; coop. edn. coord. Urban Planning and Policy Univ. Ill., Chgo., 1995-97; adj. faculty Malcolm X Coll., Chgo., 1997—, Chgo. State U., 1993—; cons. Parkview Metal Products, Chgo., 1994, Women Self-Employment Project, 1994-97, United Way Chgo., 1997; project assoc. planning dept. City of Country Club Hills, Ill., 1997. Editor Ann. News Review Update, 1996, (tech. report) Update, 1996. Founder and facilitator Women's Network for Entrepreneurial Devel., Chgo. S. Suburbs, 1993; leader Akwaibom Assn., Chgo., 1997-98; vice chair econ. devel. com. Summit on Africa, Washington and Chgo., 1998. Recipient KIZZY award, 1995; grantee: Hyde Park-Kenwood CDC, Chgo., 1991, U.S. Dept. Housing and Urban Devel., 1997. Mem. Nigerian Nat. Alliance (sec.-gen. 1997—, chair econ. devel. com. 1997—), Assn. Collegiate Schs. of Planning (presenter 1992—), Women for African Devel. (pres. 1994—, Revlon award 1995). Mem. Apostolic Faith Ch. Achievements include dissertation analysis of small and microenterprise programswith implications for urban economic development policy; lists components of effective microenterprise programs and assesses micro and small enterprise development models. Avocations: piano, violin, classical music, softball, photography. Office: Chgo State U SCI321 9501 S King Dr Chicago IL 60628-1501

KING, MARGARET RENÉ (PEGGY HARRIS), medical/surgical nurse; b. Chgo., June 4, 1959; d. Ludalph Edward and Josephine (Antoinette (Dinolfo) H. Diploma, Evang. Sch. Nursing, Oak Lawn, Ill., 1982; BSN, Elmhurst Coll., 1985. Staff nurse Christ Hosp. and Med. Ctr., Oak Lawn, 1982-88, Mercy Home Healthcare, Chgo., 1988-91, Ventilator Support Ctr., Hinsdale, Ill., 1988-89, North Ctrl. Dialysis Ctrs., Chgo., 1991-98, Merit Healthcare, 1998—, Dynacare, 1999—, RML Specialty Hosp., 1999—. Mem. Am. Lung Assn. Met. Chgo. (vol. RN Camp Action 1988-98, edn. chairperson 1993-95). Democrat. Roman Catholic. Avocations: reading, theatre, fine dining, bowling, bicycling.

KING, MERVYN ALLISTER, economist, educator; b. Chesham Bois, Eng., Mar. 30, 1948; s. Eric Frank and Kathleen Alice (Passingham) K. BA with first class honors, King's Coll., Cambridge U., Eng., 1969; postgrad., Harvard U., 1971-72. Jr. rsch. officer, dept. allied econs. Cambridge U., 1969-73, rsch. officer, 1973-76, lectr. faculty econs., 1976-77; Esmee Fairbairn prof. investment U. Birmingham, Eng., 1977-84; prof. econs. London Sch. Econs., 1984-95; exec. dir., chief economist Bank of Eng., 1990-97, dep. gov., 1998—; vis. prof. econs. Harvard U., 1982, MIT, 1983-84, LSE, 1996; rsch. assoc. Nat. Bur. Econ. Rsch., 1978—; rsch. fellow Centre for Econ. Policy Rsch., 1984—; mem. Econs. Policy Panel, 1985—; mem. CLARE Group of Economists, 1976-85; bd. dirs. LSE Fin. Markets Group; cons. to N.Z. Treasury, 1979, to OECD, 1982; sr. v.p. Aston Villa F.C., 1995—; pres. Inst. for Fiscal Studies, 1999—; founding mem. Monetary Policy Com., 1997. Author: Public Policy and the Corporation, 1977; (with J.A. Kay) The British Tax System, 1978, 5th edit., 1990, (with D. Fullerton et al) The Taxation of Income from Capital, 1984, 93; editor: (with T. Liesner) Indexing for Inflation, 1975; mng. editor Rev. Econ. Studies, 1978-83; assoc. editor Jour. Pub. Econs., 1982-99; asst. editor Econ. Jour., 1974-75; editl. bd. Am. Econ. Rev., 1985—, Jour. Indsl. Econs., 1977-83; contbr. numerous articles to profl. jours. Trustee Kennedy Meml. Trust, 1990-2000. Hon. fellow St. John's Coll., Cambridge, 1997, rsch. fellow Centre for Econ. Policy Rsch., 1984—; hon. sr. scholar King's Coll., 1969, Wrenbury scholar U. Cambridge, 1969, Kennedy scholar Harkness fellow, 1971; hon. rsch. fellow Univ. Coll. London, 1977-79; recipient Richards prize King's Coll., 1969, Stevenson prize U. Cambridge, 1970, medal U. Helsinki, Finland, 1982. Fellow Econometric Soc. (mem. Congress program com. 1974, 79, 85); mem. Soc. Econ. Analysis (chmn. 1984-86), Royal Econ. Soc. (mem. coun. and exec. com. 1981-86), Nat. Inst. Econ. and Social Rsch. (gov. 1985—), The Securities Assn. (bd. dirs. 1987—), European Econs. Assn. (pres. 1993). Office: Bank of England, Threadneedle St, London EC2R 8AH, England

KING, MICHAEL DENNIS, marketing professional, consultant; b. Johannesburg, South Africa, Aug. 28, 1970; s. Herbert and Colleen Diane (Clarkson) K.; m. Ginny Britt. BA, U. Witwatersrand, Johannesburg, South Africa, 1993, BA with honors, 1996. Diplomat South African Dept. Fgn. Affairs, 1993-96; market advisor Norwegian Trade Coun., Norwegian Embassy, Johannesburg, 1996—. Avocations: rowing, scuba diving, marathon running. Home: PO Box 652137, Benmore Guateng 2010, South Africa

KING, PETER TIAN-LUNG, physician; b. Shanghai, Republic of China, May 9, 1947; arrived in Hong Kong, 1958.; s. Gordon S. and Sunny (Moh) K. BS, Fordham U., N.Y.C., 1970; MD, Temple U., Phila., 1974. Diplomate Am. Bd. Internal Med., Am. Bd. Internal Med. subspecialty Cardiovascular Diseases. Intern Pacific Med. Ctr., San Francisco, 1974-75; resident UCLA and VA Med. Ctr., Sepulveda, Calif., 1975-78; fellow in cardiology UCLA and VA Med. Ctr., 1978-80; attending cardiologist and dir. Hong Kong Adventist Hosp. Heart Ctr., 1980—, dir. intensive care unit, cardiac rehab. program, cardiopulmonary lab., 1981—; CEO www.kingdoctor.com. Author, editor: Cardiac Rehabilitation for Nurses, 1982. Fellow ACP, Am. Coll. of Chest Physicians, Am. Coll. Cardiology. Club: Rotary. Office: Prince's Bldg Suite 1508, 10 Chater Rd, Hong Kong China

KING, POPPY, cosmetics executive. CEO Poppy Industries, Melbourne, Australia. Named Young Australian of the Yr., 1995. Office: Poppy Industries Pty Ltd, 23/521 Toorak Rd, Toorak VIC 3142, Australia

KING, PRESTON THEODORE, social science educator, writer, political philosopher; b. Albany, Ga., Mar. 3, 1936; s. Clennon Washington and Margaret (Slater) K.; children: Akasi Peter, Oona, Slater. BA, Fisk U., Nashville, 1956; DLitt (hon.), Fisk U., 1999; MS in Econ., London Sch. Econ., 1958, PhD, 1966. Tutor London Sch. Econ., 1958-60; lectr. Keele U., Eng., 1961-62, U. Ghana, 1963-66, U. Sheffield, Eng., 1966-68; reader U. East Africa, Nairobi, 1968-70; sr. rsch. fellow Acton Soc. Trust, London, 1970-72; prof. U. Nairobi, 1972-76, U. New South Wales, Sydney, Australia, 1976-86, Lancaster (Eng.) U., 1986—; vis. prof. McGill U., Montreal, Can., 1981, Auckland (New Zealand) U., 1995, Australian Nat. U., Canberra, 1997, others. Author: Fear of Power, 1967, The Ideology of Order, 1974, 2000, Toleration, 1976, 2d edit., 1998, Federalism & Federation, 1982, The History of Ideas: An Introduction to Method, 1983, An African Winter, 1986, Thomas Hobbes: Critical Assessments, 4 vols., 1993, Thinking Past a Problem, 2000; author, narrator documentary; editor Socialism and the Common Good: New Fabian Essays, Critical Rev. of Internat. Social and Polit. Philosophy. Past convenor Fabian Soc. Socialist Philosophy Group; trustee Nat. Museums and Galleries on Merseyside. Mem. Internat. Polit. Sci. Assn., Phi Beta Kappa. Mem. Labour Party. Avocation: walking. Office: Lancaster U, Bailrigg Cartmel Coll, Lancaster LA1 4YL, England

KING, RICHARD JOSLIN, librarian; b. Northfield, N.J., Feb. 18, 1942; s. Richard and Mary (Joslin) K. BA, Rowan Coll., 1965, MA, 1970; MS, U. Pa., 1975. Tchr., libr. Vineland (N.J.) H.S., 1965-66; asst. prof. Cumberland County Coll., Vineland, 1966-92; libr. Millville (N.J.) Pub. Libr., 1992—; biomed. cons. Kingdom of Saudia Arabia, Tabuk, 1991; video rschr. Inctr. Prodns., Luxor, Egypt, 1987. Co-author: Ware Chairs, 1966. Trustee Hist. Soc. Libr., Greenwich, N.J., 1995, Police Athletic League, Millville, 1995. Mem. N.J. Libr. Assn. Avocations: photography, Arabic. Home: 2000 Miller Ave Apt 7 Millville NJ 08332-1570 Office: Millville Pub Libr 210 Buck St Millville NJ 08332-3818

KING, RICHARD LEE, retired educator; b. Springfield, Mo., July 29, 1920; s. Charles Calvin and Clara Fredericka King; m. Eleanor B. King, Apr. 5, 1942; 1 child, Caroyn Jean McGowan. BSEd, S.W. Mo. State U., 1951; MEd, U. Mo., 1953, EdD, 1967; postgrad., Harvard U., 1964. Cert. tchr., sch. adminstr., Mo. Tchr., prin. Urbana (Mo.) H.S., 1947-50, Buffalo (Mo.) H.S., 1950-54; chief flight instr. Ohio State U., Columbus, 1955-56; asst. supt. Buffalo Sch. Dist., 1957-61, U.S. Dept. Def. Dependents Schs.-Europe, Karlsruhe, Germany, 1961-65; prof. No. Ariz. U., Flagstaff, 1967-71; coord. curriculum svcs. Mo. Dept. Edn., Jefferson City, 1971-91; ret., 1991; cons. Agt. for Instnl. Tech., Bloomington, Ind., 1978-91; v.p. Network for Quality Learning, Bear, Del., 1986-95. Author: Reclaiming Our Schools, 2000; editor jour. Focus on Learning, 1988-95. Pres. Rotary Club, Buffalo, 1960. Flight officer USAF, 1943-46. Named Hon. Officer, Chinese Air Force, 1991. Mem. AARP, Mo. Ret. Tchrs. Assn. (pres. 1998). Avocations: photography, flying, carpentry. Home: 4009 Cambridge Cir Jefferson City MO 65109-5735

KING, ROBERT AUGUSTIN, engineering executive; b. Marion, Ind., Sept. 3, 1910; s. Roy Melvin and Estella Bernice (Sheron) K.; m. Johanna A. Akkerman, July 19, 1975; children: Robert Alexander, Sharon Johanna, Estella Regina; children by previous marriage: Hugh Melbourne, Mary Elizabeth. BSChemE, U. Okla., 1935. Chief chemist Phillips Petroleum Co., Borger, Tex., 1935-43; sr. process engr. E. B. Badger & Sons, N.Y.C. and London, 1944-53; dist. mgr. Stone & Webster, N.Y.C., 1954-56; mng. dir. Badger Co., The Hague, Netherlands, 1957-64; pres. King-Wilkinson, Inc., Houston, 1965-84; also dir. King-Wilkinson, Inc.; pres. Robert A. King Inc., 1985—. Mem. Am. Inst. Chem. Engrs., Am. Chem. Soc., Inst. Petroleum (London). Democrat. Episcopalian. Clubs: Petroleum, Braeburn Country (Houston); Chemists (N.Y.C.). Home: 4 Tree Frog Dr Houston TX 77074-6617 Office: 8300 Bissonnet St Ste 260 Houston TX 77074-3993

KING, ROGER GRAHAM, pharmacology educator; b. Oxford, England, Dec. 3, 1950; s. Gareth Blackburn and Olwen Eva (Hughes) K.; m. Janet Margaret Empson, Aug. 2, 1978; children: Clare Ralda, Tessa Maria. BA (hons.), Cambridge Univ., England, 1971, MB B.Chir., 1974, MA, 1975; MSc, London Univ., England, 1979, PhD, 1981; MEd, Monash Univ., Australia, 1992, grad. diploma family medicine, 1997. Medical intern Hull A Group Hosps., England, 1975-76; ship doctor P&O, Oriana, England, 1976; medical practitioner & gen. practitioner Hull, London, England, 1976-81; rsch. fellow MRC, London, 1979-81; clinical asst. physician Prince Henry's, MMC Hosp., Melbourne, Australia, 1982-91; medical practitioner, dermatology Melbourne, Australia, 1994-95, gen. practitioner, 1995—; forensic physician Victorian Inst. of Forensic Medicine, Melbourne, 1995-96; assoc. prof. pharmacology Monash Univ., Clayton, Australia, 1995—; lectr. in pharmacology Monash Univ., Clayton, 1982-86, sr. lectr. in pharmacology, 1987-94; sr. rsch. assoc. Royal Women's Hosp., Melbourne, 1994—; dir. Internat. Diabetes Inst., Melbourne, 1995-96; cons. Optiscan, Melbourne, 1995—. Contbr. over 100 articles to profl. jours.; patentee in field. Recipient Open scholarship King's Coll., 1968, Glenn prize Richards Prize King's Coll., 1970, 71, Sigma Drug Delivery prize Sigma, 1990, over 25 rsch. grants NHMRC and others, 1985—. Mem. Australiasian Soc. of Clinical and Experimental Pharmacologists, Australian Physiological & Pharmacologists Soc., Australian Soc. Medical Rsch. Avocations: music, walking. Office: Monash Univ dept pharmacology, 3168 Clayton Australia

KING, RONALD LEE, accountant, government agency official; b. Scottsbluff, Nebr., Aug. 23, 1941; s. Fred and Dorothy Eldean (Lang) K.; m. Bouala Phannavong Oudomvilay Phasiboribounbane, Dec. 7, 1974; children: Donald, Naransra, Terry. Student, Oceanside-Carlsbad Coll., 1961-62; BS in Acctg., Golden Gate U., 1966. CPA, Calif. Office mgr. Nat. Auto Supply, San Francisco, 1963-66; acct. GAO, San Francisco, 1966-68; supervisory auditor GAO, Saigon, Vietnam, 1969-72, Bangkok, 1973-75; supervisory auditor GAO, Washington, 1975-80, GGAO evaluator, 1980-83, group dir., 1983-89, asst. dir. RTC issues, 1989-95, asst. dir. facility mgmt. issues, 1996—; agy. rep. constrn. sector Nat. Metric Council, Washington 1979-89, Fed. Constrn. Council, 1983-94; mem. conf. planning com. Adv. Bd. on Built Environment, Nat. Acad. Sci., Washington, 1981-83. Cpl. USMC, 1959-63. A.P. Giannini Found. scholar, 1965. Mem. AICPA, Assn. Govt. Accts., Internat. Facility Mgmt. Assn. Democrat. Lutheran.

KING, RONOLD WYETH PERCIVAL, physics educator; b. Williamstown, Mass., Sept. 19, 1905; s. James Percival and Edith Marianne Beate (Seyerlen) K.; m. Justine Merrell, June 22, 1937 (dec. Aug. 1990); 1 son, Christopher Merrell; m. Mary M. Govoni, June 1, 1991. A.B., U. Rochester, 1927, S.M., 1929; Ph.D., U. Wis., 1932; student, U. Munich, Germany, 1928-29, Cornell U., 1929-30. Asst. in physics U. Rochester, 1927-28; Am.-German exchange student, 1929-30; White fellow in physics Cornell U., 1929-30; U. fellow in elec. engring. U. Wis., 1930-32, research asst., 1932-34; instr. physics Lafayette Coll., 1934-36, asst. prof., 1936-37; Guggenheim fellow Berlin, Germany, 1937-38; with Harvard U., 1938—, successively instr., asst. prof., assoc. prof., 1938-46, prof. applied physics, 1946-72, prof. emeritus, 1972—; cons. electromagnetics and antennas, 1972—. Author: Electromagnetic Engineering, Vol. 1, 1945, 2d edit, Fundamental Electromagnetic Theory, 1963, Transmission Lines, Antennas and Wave Guides, (with A.H. Wing and H.R. Mimmo), 1945, 2d edit., 1965, Transmission-Line Theory, 1955, 2d edit., 1965, Theory of Linear Antennas, 1956, (with T.T. Wu) Scattering and Diffraction of Waves, 1959, (with R.B. Mack and S.S. Sandler) Arrays of Cylindrical Dipoles, 1968, (with C.W. Harrison, Jr.) Antennas and Waves: A Modern Approach, 1969, Tables of Antenna Characteristics, 1971, (with G.S. Smith et al) Antennas in Matter, 1981 (with S. Prasad) Fundamental Electromagnetic Theory and Applications, 1986, (with M. Owens and T.T. Wu) Lateral Electromagnetic Waves Theory and Applications to Communications, Geophysical Exploration and Remote Sensing, 1992; also articles in field. Guggenheim fellow Europe, 1937, 58, IBM scholar Northeastern U., 1985; recipient Disting. Service citation U. Wis., 1973, Pender award U. Pa., 1986. Fellow IEEE (Centennial medal 1984, Grad. Edn. award 1997), AAAS, Am. Acad. Arts and Scis., Am. Phys. Soc.; mem. IEEE Antennas and Propagation Soc. (Disting. Achievement award 1991), AAUP, Internat. Sci. Radio Union, Bavarian Acad. Sci. (contbg. mem.), Phi Beta Kappa, Sigma Xi. Home: 92 Hillcrest Pky Winchester MA 01890-1440 Office: Gordon McKay Lab 9 Oxford St Cambridge MA 02138-2901

KING, SHELDON SELIG, medical center administrator, educator; b. N.Y.C., Aug. 28, 1931; s. Benjamin and Jeanne (Fritz) K.; m. Ruth Arden Zeller, June 26, 1955 (div. 1987); children: Tracy Elizabeth, Meredith Ellen, Adam Bradley; m. Xenia Tonesk, 1988. A.B., NYU, 1952; M.S., Yale U., 1957. Adminstrv. intern Montefiore Hosp., N.Y.C., 1952, 55; adminstrv. asst. Mt. Sinai Hosp., N.Y.C., 1957-60, asst. dir., 1960-66, dir. planning, 1966-68; exec. dir. Albert Einstein Coll. Medicine-Bronx Mcpl. Hosp. Ctr., Bronx, N.Y., 1968-72; asst. prof. Albert Einstein Coll. Medicine, N.Y.C., 1968-72; dir. hosps. and clinics Univ. Hosp., assoc. clin. prof. U. Calif., San Diego, 1972-81; acting head div. health care scis., dept. cmty. medicine U. Calif. Sch. Medicine, 1978-81; assoc. v.p. Stanford U., 1981-85, clin. assoc. prof. cmty., family and preventive medicine; exec. v.p. Stanford U. Hosp., 1981-85, pres., 1986-89; pres. Cedars-Sinai Med. Ctr., L.A., 1989-94; exec. v.p., pres. ea. region Salick Health Care, Inc., L.A., 1994-99, pres. eastern region, 1996-98; interim dir. UCLA Med. Ctr., 1995; interim COO INFOHEALTH Mgmt. Cons. Corp., 1999-2000, bd. dirs., 2000—; mem. adminstrv. bd. coun. teaching hosps., 1981-86, chmn. adminstrv. bd., 1985; preceptor George Washington U., Ithaca Coll., Yale U., U. Mo., CUNY; chmn. health care com. San Diego County Immigration Coun., 1974-77; adv. coun. Calif. Health Facilities Commn., 1977-82; chmn. ad hoc bd. advs. Am. Bd. Internal Medicine, 1985-91; bd. dirs. Nat. Com. Quality Health Care, chmn., 1993-94; mem. exec. com. St. Joseph Health Sys., 1990-94; bd. dirs. Am. Health Properties, 1988-99, acting chmn. 1996—; nat. adv. com. Robert Wood Johnson Exec. Nurse Fellows Program, 1998—. Mem. editorial adv. bd.: Who's Who in Health Care, 1977; mem. editorial bd. Jour. Med. Edn, 1979-84. Bd. dirs. hosp. coun. San Diego and Imperial Counties, 1974-77, treas., 1976, pres., 1977; bd. dirs. United Way San Diego, 1975-80, B'rith Milah Bd., Vol. Hosps. Am., 1990-94, mem. exec. com., 1991-93; mem. Accreditation Coun. for grad. med. edn., 1987-90, Prospective Payment Assessment Commn., 1987-90, Inst. of Medicine, 1988—. With AUS, 1952-55. Fellow Am. Coll. Health Care Execs., Am. Pub. Health Assn., Am. Hosp. Assn. (governing coun. Met. sect. 1983-86, coun. on fin. 1987, ho. of dels. 1987-89), Calif. Hosp. Assn. (trustee 1978-81), Am. Podiatric Med. Assn. (project coun. 2000 1985-86), Healthcare Rsch. and Devel. Inst. (bd. dirs., chmn. 1993-97).

KING, STEPHEN EDWIN, novelist, screenwriter, director; b. Portland, Maine, Sept. 21, 1947; s. Donald and Nellie Ruth (Pillsbury) K.; m. Tabitha Jane Spruce, Jan. 2, 1971; children: Naomi Rachel, Joseph Hillstrom, Owen Phillip. B.S., U. Maine, 1970. Tchr. English Hampden (Maine) Acad., 1971-73; writer in residence U. Maine at Orono, 1978-79. Novels include Carrie, 1974, 'Salem's Lot, 1975, The Shining, 1976, The Stand, 1978, The Dead Zone, 1979, Firestarter, 1980, Danse Macabre, 1981, Cujo, 1981, Different Seasons, 1982, The Dark Tower: The Gunslinger, 1982, Christine, 1983, Pet Sematary, 1983, The Talisman, 1984, Cycle of the Werewolf, 1985, Skeleton Crew, 1986, It, 1986, The Eyes of the Dragon, 1987, Misery, 1987, The Dark Tower: The Drawing of the Three, 1987, The Tommyknockers, 1987, The Dark Half, 1989, The Stand (uncut), 1990, Four Past Midnight, 1990, The Dark Tower III: The Waste Lands, 1991, Needful Things, 1991, Gerald's Game, 1992, Dolores Claiborne, 1992, Insomnia, 1994, Rose Madder, 1995, Desperation, 1996, The Green Mile (serial), 1996, Bag of Bones, 1997, Wizard & Glass, 1997, The Girl Who Loved Tom Gordon, 1999, Storm of the Century, 1999; short story Night Shift (collection), 1978, Nightmares and Dreamscapes, 1993, Creepshow (comic), 1982, The Plant (self pub.), 1983, 1984, My Pretty Pony, 1988, Dolan's Cadillac, 1989, Six Stories, 1997; author numerous other short stories; (as Richard Bachman) Rage, 1977, The Long Walk, 1979, Roadwork, 1981, The Running Man, 1982, Thinner, 1984, Insomnia, 1993, The Regulators, 1996; author numerous short story screenplays; writer, creator TV program "Stephen King's Golden Years", 1991; film director: Maximum Overdrive, 1986; original screenplay: Sleepwalkers, 1991; actor: Knightriders, 1981, Creepshow, 1982, Maximum Overdrive, 1986, Creepshow II, 1988, The Shawshank Redemption, 1995 (USC Scriptor Awd. 1995); creator, writer (TV miniseries) The Stand, 1994, Storm of the Century, 1999 (mini-series). Mem. Author's Guild Am., Screen Artists Guild, Screen Writers of Am., Writer's Guild. Democrat. Office: 49 Florida Ave Bangor ME 04401-3005

KING, STEPHEN WILLIAM PEARCE, fine art dealer, journalist, writer; b. Worcester, Eng., Jan. 21, 1947; s. William Raymond Pearce and Edna Gertrude (Swannock) K.; m. Angela Denise Gammon, Sept. 22, 1973; children: Alexander, Jeremy. Student, King Edward Sch. Edgbaston, Birmingham. Lic. practising solicitor. Asst. solicitor George Mitchell, Colman & Co., Birmingham, Eng., 1973, Haynes Duffell Arnold & Co., Birmingham, 1973-74; prin. solicitor Stephen King & Co., Birmingham, 1974-97, Phoenix Fine Art, 1997—; freelance journalist, writer Sutton Coldfield, England, 1998—. Avocations: sports, music, charity work, travel, theater. Office: Phoenix Fine Art 258 High St, Erdington Birmingham B23 6SN, England

KING, SUE A., import company executive; b. Lansing, Mich., Nov. 18, 1946; d. George Edward and Cleo Belle King. Grad. h.s., Lakeview, Mich. Internat. supr. The Franklin Mint, Franklin Center, Pa., 1975-85; mgr. internat. Coleco Industries, Gloversville, N.Y., 1985-87; dir. distbn. Coleco Industries, Long Beach, Calif., 1987-89; dir. transp. Galoob Toys Inc., San Francisco, 1989-91; dir. worldwide logistics Eden LLC, Jersey City, N.J., 1991—. Mem. NAFE, Toy Shipper's Assn. (chmn. bd.), Toy Mfrs.'s of Am. Logistics (steering com.), Am. Exporter's and Importers Assn., Women in Internat. Trade. Avocations: golf, bowling, music, reading, dancing. Office: Eden LLC 812 Jersey City Jersey City NJ 07310

KING, (ROBERT) THOMAS, linguistics and computer science educator; b. Dallas, Nov. 15, 1944; s. Thomas Edward and Effie Dee (Chaffin) K. BA, Rice U., 1967, PhD, 1974. Tchr. Homburg, Fed. Rep. Germany, 1971-72; lectr. Johann-Wolfgang-Goethe U., Frankfurt, Fed. Rep. Germany, 1972-79, asst. prof., 1979-85; project dir. Gesellschaft fur Mathematik und Datenverarbeitung, Darmstadt, Fed. Rep. Germany, 1987-89; assoc. prof. U. Koblenz, Fed. Rep. Germany, 1989—; part time lectr. European br. U. Md., Frankfurt, 1977-85; adj. lectr. U. Heidelberg, Fed. Rep. Germany, 1985-87; cons. Kraftwerkunion, Offenbach, Fed. Rep. Germany, 1976-85; expert evaluator, cons. European Commn., Brussels, 1988—. Fellow NSF, 1967, NTSC, 1969. Mem. Gesellschaft für Informatik, Linguistic Soc. Am., Am. Assn. Artificial Intelligence, Cognitive Sci. Soc., Cognitive Linguistics Assn., Internat Pragmatics Assn., Phi Beta Kappa. Avocations: baroque music, piano, mountain hiking. Home: Bergweg 7, D-56179 Vallendar Germany Office: U Koblenz, Rheinau 1, D-56075 Koblenz Germany

KING, WALTER WING-KEUNG, plastic surgeon, head and neck surgery consultant; b. Hong Kong, Jan. 27, 1950; s. Albert Cheng and Josephine Shou-Fan (Chao) K.; m. May Kam-Wei Poon, June 8, 1985; children: Kenneth S. F., Spencer S. W. BA with honors, U. Wis., 1971; MD, Vanderbilt U., 1975. Diplomate Am. Bd. Surgery. Intern Vanderbilt U. Hosp., Nashville, 1975-76; resident surgeon SUNY, Stony Brook, 1976-80; clin. asst. in surgery Mass. Gen. Hosp., Boston, 1980-82; clin. fellow in surgery Harvard U., Boston, 1980-82; fellow, head and neck svc. Meml. Sloan-Kettering Cancer Ctr., N.Y.C., 1982-83; asst. prof. surgery SUNY, Stony Brook, 1983-84; vis. fellow otolaryngology Stanford (Calif.) U. Med. Ctr., 1984; lectr. head and neck surgery Chinese U., Hong Kong, 1984-88, sr. lectr. surgery, 1988-93, reader surgery, 1993-95, prof. surgery, 1995-98; dir. plastic and reconstructive surgery ctr. Hong Kong Sanatorium and Hosp., Happy Valley, Hong Kong, 1998—; asst. dir. Nutritional Support Unit, Mass. Gen. Hosp., Boston, 1981-82; cons. surgeon head and neck-plastic surgery Prince of Wales Hosp., Sha Tin, Hong Kong, 1988-98. Contbr. articles to profl. jours. Shriners Burn Inst. rsch. fellow, 1980-82; Am. Soc. for Head and Neck Surgery fellow, 1984, Royal Coll. Surgeons Edinburgh fellow, 1991. Fellow ACS, Royal Coll. Surgeons Can.; mem. Soc. Head and Neck Surgeons, Am. Burn Assn., Am. Soc. for Head and Neck Surgery, Internat. Assn. Endocrine Surgeons, Am. Acad. Facial Plastic and Reconstructive Surgery, Coll. Surgeons Hong Kong. Avocations: tennis, swimming, squash, computers. Office: Hong Kong Sanatorium & Hosp, Plas and Recon Surgery Ctr, Happy Valley Hong Kong China

KING, WAYNE EDGAR, journalist, educator; b. McDowell County, N.C., Mar. 31, 1939; s. Weldon Edgar and Mary King; m. Nina Davis, (div. June 1978); m. Paula Theodore Carroll, July 16, 1984. BA in Journalism, U. N.C., 1964. Reporter, editor The Detroit Free Press, 1964-69; editor, bur. chief, corr. The N.Y. Times, N.Y.C., 1969-93; dir. journalism program Wake Forest U., Winston-Salem, N.C., 1993—; working group on disability in U.S. Pres. The White House, 1996. Mem. editl. bd. Acad. Mag., Washington, 1996—. Recipient Pulitzer prize, 1968. Mem. AAUP, Torch Club. Home: 1901 Waycross Dr Winston Salem NC 27106-3416

KINGERY, SANDRA LYNN, Spanish language educator, translator; b. Urbana, Ill., Nov. 22, 1964; d. Ross Alan and Phyllis (May) Kingery Martin; m. Miguel Angel Delgado, June 19, 1992. BA in Polit. Sci., Philosophy, Lawrence U., Appleton, Wis., 1986; certificado, U. Barcelona, Spain, 1987; MA in Spanish, U. Wis., 1989, PhD in Spanish, 1996. Lectr., tchg. asst. U. Wis., Madison, 1987-94; asst. prof. Lycoming Coll., Williamsport, Pa., 1994-96, 98—, Wake Forest U., Winston-Salem, N.C., 1996-97; curriculum devel. com. Lycoming Coll., Williamsport, Pa., 1995-96, 99—, judicial bd., 1995-96, 98—, faculty exec. coun., 1998-99, freshman seminar com., substance abuse com., 1998—, mid. states task force, 1999—. Recipient Tchg. award Lycoming Coll., 1999. Mem. AAUW, MLA, Am. Assn. Tchrs. of Spanish and Portugese, Phi Sigma Iota, Spanish Club, Scholars Coun. Office: Lycoming Coll PO Box 2 Williamsport PA 17703-0002

KINGHAM, RICHARD FRANK, lawyer; b. Lafayette, Ind., Aug. 2, 1946; s. James R. and Loretta C. (Hoenigke) K.; m. Justine Frances McClung, July 6, 1968; 1 child, Richard Patterson. BA, George Washington U., 1968; JD, U. Va., 1973. Bar: D.C. 1973, U.S. Dist. Ct. D.C. 1974, U.S. Ct. Appeals (8th cir.) 1977, U.S. Supreme Ct. 1977, U.S. Ct. Appeals (5th cir.) 1980; registered fgn. lawyer Law Soc. Eng. and Wales, 1994. Editorial asst. Washington Star, 1964-68, 69-70; assoc. Covington & Burling, Washington, 1973-81, ptnr., 1981—, mng. ptnr. London office, 1996-2000; lectr. law U. Va., Charlottesville, 1977-90; mem. com. issues and priorities new vaccine devel. Inst. Medicine, NAS, 1983-86, Nat. Adv. Allergy and Infectious Diseases Coun. NIH, 1988-92, adv. bd. World Pharms. Report, 1990-96; mem. World Health Org. Coun. Internat. Orgns. Med. Scis. Working Party Comm. in Pharmacovigilance, 1997—. Articles editor U. Va. law rev., 1972-73; contbr. articles to profl. jours. Treas., mem. parochial ch. coun. St. Peter's Ch. Eaton Sq., London, 1998—. Mem. ABA, Brussels Pharm. Law Group, Drug Info. Assn., Food and Drug Law Inst., European Soc. Pharmacovigilance, Food Law Group (U.K.), Soc. Vertebrate Paleontology, European Forum for Good Clin. Practice, Order of the Coif, Reform Club (London). Republican. Episcopalian. Avocation: vertebrate paleontology. Home: 14 Chelsea Embankment, London SW3 4LA, England

KING HOOKHAM, ELEANOR, artist; b. Marlow, Okla., Apr. 5, 1909; d. William Frank Sr. and Sara Caroline (Smith) King; m. George Lawrence Salley, July 9, 1934 (div. Mar. 1940); 1 child, Jane King Salley; m. Robert Ernest Hookham, Nov. 5, 1943 (dec. Aug. 1989); children: Tarrant K., Robert Peyton. Student, Oklahoma City Coll.; Doctorate (hon.), Cultural Acad. de France, Paris, 1980; DA (hon.), Elmhurst Coll., 1987. Pvt. art tchr. Elmhurst, Ill., 1946-83; hon. chairperson Elmhurst Art Mus., 1997—. One-woman shows include Montross Gallery, N.Y.C., 1939, 41, Wheaton (Ill.) Pub. Libr., 1956, Concordia Sr. Coll., Fort Wayne, Ind., 1959, Galerie Internat., N.Y.C., yearly 1950-65, Pensacola (Fla.) Art Mus., 1969, Galerie Marcel Bernheim, Paris, yearly 1965-74, Galerie Bernheim-Jeune, Paris, yearly, 1985-92; works exhibited in group shows at Leonard Clayton Gallery, N.Y.C., 1938, Montross Gallery, N.Y.C., 1942, Johnson Gallery, Chgo., 1959, 60, 61, Ill. State Art Mus., Springfield, 1964, Internat. Fedns. Cultureelle Feminine Musée d'Art Moderne, Medaille D'Argent, 1968; author: Creative Art and the Subconscious, 1979, Complete Color Theory, 1979. Founder Elmhurst Fine Arts and Civic Ctr. Found., 1974, pres. 1974-92, chmn. bd., 1992-97; founder Elmhurst Art Mus., 1981, pres., 1981-91; cofounder Elmhurst Artist Guild. Recipient Nat. award Elmhurst Art Mus., 1998. Mem. Elmhurst Artists' Guild (co-founder, hon. life, pres. 1951-53), found. Elmhurst Art Mus. Episcopalian. Avocations: golfing, swimming. Home and Office: Eleanor King Studio 289 Adelia St Elmhurst IL 60126-3537

KINGMAN, ELIZABETH YELM, anthropologist; b. Lafayette, Ind., Oct. 15, 1911; d. Charles Walter and Mary Irene (Weakley) Yelm; m. Eugene Lingman, June 10, 1939; children: Mixie Kingman Eddy, Elizabeth Ann Kingman. BA, U. Denver, 1933; MA, 1935. Asst. in anthropology U. Denver, 1932-34; mus. asst. Ranger Naturalist Staff Mesa Verde Nat. Park, Colo., 1934-38; asst. to husband in curatorial work Indian art exhibits Philbrook Art Ctr., Tulsa, 1939-42, Joslyn Art Mus., Omaha, 1947-69; tutor humnaities dept. U. Omaha, 1947-50; cjhn. bd. govs. Pi Beta Phi Settlement Sch., Gatlinburg, Tenn., 1969-72, Joslyn Art Mus., Omaha, 1947-50; tutor humanities dept. U. Omaha, 1947-50; chmn. bd. govs. Pi Beta Phi Settlement Sch., Gatlinburg, Tenn., 1969-72; asst. to husband in exhibit design mus. Tex. Tech. U., 1970-75; bibliographer Internat. Ctr. ARid and Semi-Arid Land Studies, 1974-75; libr. Sch. Am. Rsch., Santa Fe, N.Mex., 1978-86; rsch. assoc., 1986-98. V.p. Santa Fe Corral of the Westerners, 1985-86. Mem. AAUW, LWV, Archeol. Inst. Am. (v.p. Santa Fe chpt. 1981-83), Santa Fe Hist. Soc. (sec. 1981-83). Home: 604 Sunset St Santa Fe NM 87501-1118

KING-NING, TU, materials science and engineering educator; b. Canton, China, Dec. 30, 1937; came to U.S., 1962; s. Ying-Chiang Tu and Sau-Yuk Chen; m. Ching Chiao, Sept. 25, 1964; children: Olivia, Stephen. BSc, Nat. Taiwan U., 1960; MSc, Brown U., 1964; PhD, Harvard U., 1968. Rsch. staff mem. IBM Watson Rsch. Ctr., Yorktown Heights, N.Y., 1968-93, sr. mgr. thin film sci. dept., 1978-85, sr. mgr. materials sci. dept., 1985-87; prof. dept. materials sci. & engring. UCLA, 1993—. Co-author: (textbook) Electronic Thin Film Science, 1992. Recipient Acta/Scripta Metallurgica Lecturer, 1990; grantee Alexander von Humboldt, 1996. Fellow Am. Phys. Soc., The Metall. Soc. (Applications to Practice award 1988), Churchill Coll. (U.K.). Achievements include 8 patents on thin film technology for microelectronics. Office: UCLA Boelter Hall 6532 B Los Angeles CA 90095-0001

KINGSBURY, MICHAEL BRYANT, organist, retired elementary and secondary education educator; b. Wilmington, N.C., Dec. 25, 1933; s. Walter Russell and Olga Loretta (Lewis) K. BA, Emory U., 1957; MA, Atlanta U., 1978. Cert. mid. sch. sci. tchr., sci. tchr. K-12, social studies tchr., Ga. Tchr. Bouldercrest Elem. Sch., Atlanta, 1958-62; sci. tchr. Northcutt Elem. Sch., College Park, Ga., 1962-66, G.P. Babb Jr. H.S., Forest Park, Ga., 1966-84, Pointe South Mid. Sch., Jonesboro, Ga., 1984-94; organist, choir master Episcopal and Cath. Chs., Atlanta and Decatur, Ga., 1955—; organist, dir. Cath. music Ft. McPherson/U.S. Army, Atlanta, 1994—. Author, editor: Laboratory Manual for Earth Science, 1970. Bd. dirs. Camelot Homeowners Assn., Jonesboro, 1978-84; patron Atlanta Symphony Orch., 1992—; lector St. Luke's Episcopal Ch. Recipient Ritter Music award Atlanta Pub. Schs., 1951, Cmty. Svc. award Clayton County Ret. Tchrs., 1998, Service Playing cert. Am. Guild Organists, Cert. of Appreciation, Clayton County Educators Assn., 1999, others; NSF grant, 1970. Mem. Clayton County Ret. Tchrs. Assn. (pres. 1996—), Clayton County Ret. Educators Assn. (pres. 1996-98, dir. 10th dist.), Ga. Ret. Tchrs. Assn. (10th dist. dir. 2000—), Am. Guild of Organists (membership com. 1958—), Atlanta Music Club. Democrat. Episcopalian. Avocations: walking, bicycle riding, collecting southern writings and Gone with the Wind memorabilia. Home: 2669 Lake Jodeco Dr Jonesboro GA 30236-5355 Office: Ft McPherson US Army Lee St Atlanta GA 30330

KINGSLEY, BEN, actor; b. Scarborough, Eng., Dec. 31, 1943; s. Rahimtulla Harji and Anna Lyna (Goodman) Bhanji; children: Edmund William Macaulay, Ferdinand James Macaulay, Thomas Alexis, Jasmin Anna. MA (hon.), Salford U. Assoc. artist Royal Shakespeare Co., Eng., 1968—. Appeared in plays including Hamlet, 1975-76, Othello, 1985-86, Edmund Kean, 1981-83; films include Gandhi, 1981 (Acad. award 1992), Betrayal, 1982, Turtle Diary, 1984, Sleeps Six, 1984, Harem, 1985, Maurice, 1987, Testimony, 1987, Pascali's Island, 1988, Without a Clue, 1988, Slipstream, 1989, The Children, 1990, Una Vita Scellerata, 1991, Bugsy, 1991, Sneakers, 1992, Dave, 1993, Innocent Moves, 1993, Searching for Bobby Fisher, 1993, Schindler's List, 1993, Death and the Maiden, 1994, Species, 1994, Twelfth Night: Or What You Will, 1996, The Assignment, 1997, Photographing Fairies, 1997, Parking Shots, 1998, Rules of Engagement, 1999, Sexy Beast, 1999, Spooky House, 1999, The Confession, 1999, What Planet Are You From, 1999; (TV movies) Camille, 1984, Murderers Among Us: The Simon Weisenthall Story, 1988 (Disting. Svc. award 1989), Joseph, 1995, Moses, 1996, Weapons of Mass Distraction, 1997, The Tale of Sweeny Todd, 1998, Alice in Wonderland, 1999; (TV series) Oxbridge Blues, 1986, Crime and Punishment, 1998; (TV spls.) Silas Marner, 1987. Recipient Padma Shri award Govt. of India, 1984, Grammy award, 1984, Oscar award, 1983; named Best Actor and Best Newcomer Brit. Acad. Film and TV Arts, 1982, Best Actor Standard Film Awards, London, 1983. Mem. Brit. Acad. Film and TV Arts, Acad. Motion Picture Arts and Scis. (Golden Camera Berlin award, Evening Standard Film award for Best Actor for Schindler's List 1995). Office: care ICM care ICM/Chris Andrews 8942 Wilshire Blvd Beverly Hills CA 90211-1934

KINGSLEY, CHARON, nurse practitioner; b. Miami, Fla., Jan. 29, 1960; d. Nelson T. and Beauty K. Harris; m. Emeka Dike Kingsley, Oct. 12, 1990. BSN, Fla. Internat. U., Miami, 1988; MSN, Barry U., Miami, 1990. Nurse I med./surg. Jackson Hosp., Miami, 1983-85; nurse II Jackson Meml. Hosp., Miami, 1985-90, nurse II MHER, 1990-92, assoc. head nurse, 1992-97, sch. health base ctr. nurse practitioner, 1999. Avocations: swimming, skiing, cooking. Office: Jackson Meml Hosp 1611 NW 12th Ave Miami FL 33136-1096 also: Annex 5 701 NW 57th Ave Ste 380 Miami FL 33126-2072

KINGSLEY, JUDITH, artist; b. N.Y.C.; d. Fred and Minna Evelyn (Weisman) Gladstone; m. Theodore Kingsley, Oct. 26, 1950 (dec. May 1964); children: Ellen Kingsley Hirschfeld, Melinda Kingsley Nester; m. John Fitting Jr., Apr. 9, 1976 (dec. Dec. 1997). Student, Syracuse U., 1948-49, Adelphi U., 1949-50, Pratt Inst., Art Students League, N.Y.C., Nat. Acad. Fine Arts, Positano Art Inst., Italy, 1972, China Inst., N.Y.C., 1977. One-woman shows include Galerie Internat., N.Y.C., 1969, Weiner Gallery, N.Y.C., 1970, Palm Beach Gallery, 1971, Lobster Pot Gallery, Nantucket, Mass., 1972, Crystal House Gallery, Miami Beach, Fla., 1973, Springfield (Ill.) Art Assn., 1975, East River Savs. Bank Gallery, Rockefeller Ctr., N.Y., 1976, Bergdorf Goodman Art Gallery, N.Y.C., 1977, Adelphi U. Art Gallery, Garden City, N.Y., 1978, Multiple Images Gallery, Palm Beach, Fla., 1982, Valand Gallery, Naples, Fla., 1983, La Galeria De Santa Fe, N.Mex., 1984, Reece Gallery, N.Y.C., 1979-80, Nelson Rockefeller Collection, N.Y.C., 1981-82, L'Atelier Gallery, Piermont, N.Y., 1991-92, Jain Maru-

nouchi Gallery, N.Y.C., 1995-96, G.G. Rein Gallery, Houston, 1995-96, The Darvish Collection, Naples, 1995-98, Hofburg Palace Exhibit, Vienna, Austria, 1993, No. Trust Bank, Naples, 1998, Naples Art Gallery, 1998-99, Artsforum Gallery, N.Y.C., 1998-2000, The Gallery at the Registry Resort, Naples, 1999-2000, Alpers Fine Art, Andover, Mass. Sec. bd. dirs. N.Y. Artists Equity, 1984-93. Recipient Morilla Oil award New Rochelle Art Assn., 1973. Mem. English Speaking Union, Marco Island Art Assn., Naples Art Assn., Nat. Arts Club N.Y., Collier Athletic Club, Island Country Club, Marco Island Yacht and Sailing Club, Dartmouth Club of S.E. Fla. Avocations: golf, tennis, swimming, yachting. Home and Office: 311 Nassau Ct Marco Island FL 34145-4013

KINGSNORTH, ANDREW NORMAN, surgery educator; b. Dartford, Kent, U.K., Nov. 20, 1948; s. John Norman and Kathleen Dorothy Bassett K.; m. Jane Mary Poulter, June 1, 1974; children: Edward Anthony, Bryony Jane, Peter John. BS with honors, U. London, 1970, MBBS, 1973, MS, 1982. Registrar in surgery John Radcliffe Hosp., Oxford, Eng., 1977-80; rsch. fellow Harvard U., Boston, 1980-81; lectr. in surgery U. Edinburgh, Scotland, 1982-86; jr. cons. Groote Schuur Hosp., Cape Town, South Africa, 1986-87; sr. lectr. in surgery U. Liverpool, Eng., 1987-95, reader in surgery, 1995-96; prof. surgery Derriford Hosp., Plymouth, Eng., 1996—. Co-editor: Management of Gastrointestinal Cancer, 1996, Fundamentals of Surgical Practice, 1998; co-author: Management of Abdominal Hernias, 2d edit. 1998, Incisional Hernia, 1999; mem. editl. Internat. Jour. Surg. Investigation, Hernia. Fellow ACS, Assn. Surgeons Gt. Britain and Ireland, Royal Coll. Surgeons (ct. of examiners 1994-2000, tutor telemedicine, 1999—); mem. Brit. Soc. Gastroenterology, Surg. Rsch. Soc. U.K. (mem. com. 1995-99). Avocations: hill walking, method bellringing. Office: Plymouth Postgrad Med Sch, Derriford Hosp, Plymouth PL6 8DH, England

KINGSON, ERIC ROGER, educator; b. N.Y.C., Mar. 13, 1946; s. Milton S. Kingson and Ethel (Schachtel) K.; m. Joan Fernbach, Apr. 29, 1979; children: Aaron, Johanna. BA, Boston U., 1968; MPA, Northeastern U., Boston, 1975; PhD, Brandeis U., 1979. Asst. prof. sch. social work U. Md., Balt., 1979-86; assoc. prof. Grad Sch. Social Work Boston Coll., Chestnut Hill, Mass., 1986-98; prof. social work, pub. adminstrn. Syracuse (N.Y.) U., 1998—; Advisor Nat. Commn. on Social Security Reform, Washington, 1982; sr. advisor Bipartison Commn. on Entitlement and Tax Policy, 1994. Author/co-author, co-editor 8 books and numerous jour. articles on population aging, social welfare and the baby boom generation; mem. editl. bd. Jour. Gerontol. Social Work, 1999—, Jour. Longterm Care, 2000—. Fellow Gerontol. Soc. Am. (dir. emerging issues in aging program 1984-85, chmn. pub. policy com. 1985); mem. Nat. Acad. Social Ins. (bd. dirs. 1986-96). Democrat. Jewish. Avocations: magic, coaching soccer. Office: Syracuse U Sch Of Social Work Syracuse NY 13244-0001

KINGSRITER, DAYTON ALBERT, college dean; b. Mankato, Minn., Sept. 5, 1943; s. Harland A. and Dorris V. (Williams) K.; m. Marilyn G. Jones, Dec. 16, 1965; children: H. Bradford, Roslynn. BSEd, Evangel Coll., Springfield, Mo., 1965; MEd, U. Mo., 1973, EdS, 1974, EdD, 1981. Cert. elem. sch. tchr., sch. supt., Mo.; ordained to ministry Assemblies of God Ch., 1976. Tchr. Springfield R-12 Sch., 1965-68; asst. dir. lab. sch. U. Mo., 1972-74; supt. Hi-Way R-III Sch., Mexico, Mo., 1974-76; minister of music and Christian edn. Pawnee Assembly, Ill., 1976-78; dir. Christian edn. The Stone Ch., Palos Heights, Ill., 1978-80; ch. adminstr. Oak Brook Christian Ctr., Ill., 1980-82; acad. dean Trinity Bible Coll., Ellendale, N.D., 1982-90, v.p. acad. affairs, 1990-92; nat. dir. Christian higher edn. Gen. Coun. of the Assemblies of God, Ellendale, 1992—. V.p. Ellendale Civic Assn., 1984-85; pres. Ellendale Pub. Sch. Bd., 1985-91; mem. accrediting evaluation teams Accrediting Assn. Bible Colls., 1984—, chairperson Pentecostal Textbooks Project Bd., 1995—. With USAF, 1968-72. Mem. Phi Mu Alpha Sinfonia, Phi Delta Kappa, Kappa Delta Pi. Republican. Avocations: golf, woodworking, biking. Home: 2123 E Camorene St Springfield MO 65803-4870 Office: Gen Coun of the Assemblies of God 1445 N Boonville Ave Springfield MO 65802-1894

KINGWELL, BRONWYN A., medical researcher; b. Melbourne, Victoria, Australia, Mar. 5, 1966; d. William J. and Judith A. (Smith) K.; m. Andrew N. Plant, July 26, 1996. BSc with honors, U. Melbourne, 1988, PhD, 1991. Rsch. officer Baker Med. Rsch. Inst., Melbourne, 1991, sr. rsch. officer, 1995—; hon. rsch. assoc. dept. medicine Monash U., Melbourne, 1994—, hon. lectr. dept. physiology, 1997—. Contbr. articles to profl. jours., chpts. to books. Recipient Young Tall Poppy award, 1999; named Young Achiever of Yr., Channel 10, Melbourne, 1992, Young Achiever Sci. and Tech., 1992; Nat. Health and Med. Rsch. Coun. rsch. fellow. Mem. Australia Soc. Med. Rsch. (rsch. week com., bd. dirs. 1999—), Internat. Soc. Heart Rsch., Internat. Soc. Hypertension. Avocations: weight training, running, singing, aerobics, Latin dancing. Office: Baker Med Rsch Inst, Commercial Rd, Prahran 3181, Australia

KINIGAKIS, PANAGIOTIS, research scientist, engineer, author; b. Chanea, Greece, July 11, 1949; s. John and Evangelia (Vozinakis) K.; m. Kalliopi Paleologos, July 31, 1977; children: Evangelia, Maria Anna. BS, Superior Agrl. Sch., Athens, Greece, 1971, MS, 1973; MS in Food Sci., Rutgers U., 1979. Packaging devel. specialist Am. Cyanamid Co., Clifton, N.J., 1979-81; sr. packaging engr. Warner Lambert Co., Morris Plains, N.J., 1981-83; tech. svcs. supr. M&M Mars Inc., Hackettstown, N.J., 1983-87; sr. tech. prin. Kraft Foods Inc., Glenview, Ill., 1987—; agrl. engr. Food Agrl. Orgn. div. of UN, Chanea, 1975-77. Patentee pkg. equipment and mfg. systems; contbr. articles to profl. jours. Advisor Greek Orthodox Youth Assn., Randolph, N.J., 1986, Hamilton, N.J., 1990. Mem. ASM, TAPPI, Internat. Materials Info. soc., Inst. Food Tech., Inst. Packaging Profls. (cert.), Soc. Plastics Engrs., N.Y. Acad. Scis. Greek Orthodox. Avocations: volleyball, soccer, tennis, scuba diving. Home: 1704 Freedom Ct Mount Prospect IL 60056-1979 Office: Kraft Foods Inc 801 Waukegan Rd Glenview IL 60025-4391

KININMONTH, PETER WYATT, company executive; b. Bebington, Cheshire, Eng., June 23, 1924; s. Alec Marshall and Helen Wyatt (Webster) K.; m. Priscilla Margaret Sturge, June 30, 1961; children: James, Alexander, Philippa, David. MA with honors, Brasenose Coll., Oxford, Eng., 1948. Dir. Thomas Stephens & Sons, Ltd., London, 1951-68; mng. dir. Keith Shipton & Kininmonth Ltd., London, 1968-72; chmn. bd. P.W. Kininmonth Ltd., London, 1972-82, 96—; dep. chmn. Lowndes Lambert Ltd., London, 1982-94; chmn. bd. P.K. Portraits Ltd., London, 1997—; bd. dirs. Fitzmilton (UK) Plc, Dublin, 1975—. High sheriff Greater London, 1979; chmn. Richmond Fellowship, London, 1990-94. Capt. Indian Army, 1942-46. Ch. of England. Avocations: music, gardening, golf. Home: The Stags Head, Salisbury SP5 5AA, England

KINJO, SEIKI, humanities educator; b. Naha, Okinawa, Japan, Apr. 29, 1933; s. Moriharu and Kamiko (Ashimine) K.; m. Yoneko Shiroma, Mar. 5, 1956; children: Aki, Iwao. BA, Wake Forest U., 1955; MA, U. Mich., 1961; postgrad., Mich. State U., 1961-62. Instr., asst. prof. U. of the Ryukyus, Naha, Okinawa, Japan, 1955-65; asst. prof., prof. Doshisha U., Kyoto, Japan, 1965-74; prof. Kobe Coll., Nishinomiya, Japan, 1974-98, chmn. dept. English, 1977-81, dean Sch. Letters, 1981-85, 89-93, dir. Coll. Libr., 1987-89, 93-95, dean Grad. Sch. Letters, 1989-91, 95-97; dir. coll. libr. Kobe Coll., Nishinomiya, 1997-98; prof. emeritus St. Andrew's U., Osaka, Japan, 1998—, dean Sch. Letters, 2000—; lectr. Kyoto (Japan) U., 1974-95; vis. scholar Wolfson Coll. Cambridge (Eng.) U., 1985-86. Author: Shakespeare's Tragedies, 1984, Shakespeare's Flora, 1990, Shakespeare's Flowers, 1996, English Literature Through Flowers, 1997: co-author: Introduction to English Literature, 1987, Shakespeare's Histories, 1994, Introduction to Shakespeare, 2000. Examiner English proficiency test, 1987—; mem. exec. com. Kyoto Internat. Sch., 1968-70. Named Garoia scholar, 1952-55, U.S. Govt. scholar, 1959-61. Mem. English Literary Soc. Japan (council 1990-93), Shakespeare Soc. Japan, Kansai Shakespeare Study Cir. (rep. 1981-83), Internat. Assn. of Univ. Profs. of English. Avocations: swimming, tennis, NOH. Home: 5-15-4 Sakasedai, Takarazuka 665, Japan Office: St Andrew's Univ, Manabino 1-1, Izumi Osaka 595-1198, Japan

KINKEL, KLAUS, German government official; b. Metzingen, Germany, Dec. 17, 1936; married; 4 children. Law student, U. Tübingen, U. Bonn, U. Cologne, Germany, 1956-60; Dr. jur., 1964. With dist. adminstr.'s office Fed. Office Civilian Protection Fed. Ministry of Interior, Balingen, Germany, 1965-70; priv. sec. Fed. Minister of Interior Genscher, head Min.'s office Fed. Min. of Interior, Germany, 1970-74; head polit. staff Fed. Fgn. Office, Germany, 1974-77, head policy planning staff, 1977-79; pres. Fed. Intelligence Svc., Germany, 1979-82; state sec. Fed. Ministry of Justice, Germany, 1982-91; fed. min. justice Germany, 1991-92, fed. min. fgn. affairs, 1992-98; dep. chancellor Fed. Republic Germany, 1993-98; fed. chmn. Free Dem. Party, Germany, 1993-95; mem. German Bundestag, 1994—; first dep. chmn., parliamentary group Fed. Dem. Party, Germany, 1998—. Mem. Free Democratic Party, 1991—, chmn. until 1995. Office: Office Fed Chancellor, Adenauerallee 141, 053113 Bonn 1, Germany

KINLOCH, ANTHONY JAMES, mechanical engineering educator, researcher; b. London, Oct. 7, 1946; s. Nathan and Hilda May (Stevens) K.; m. Gillian Patricia Birch, Sept. 6, 1969; children: Ian Anthony, Elizabeth Sarah, David Michael Robert. PhD, U. London, 1972, DSc in Engring., 1989. Higher scientific officer Ministry of Def., London, 1972-74, sr. scientific officer, 1974-78, prin. scientific officer, 1978-86; reader Imperial Coll., U. London, 1984-90, prof. adhesion, chair dept., dir. postgrad. rsch., 1990—. Author: Adhesion & Adhesives, 1987; editor: Durability of Structural Adhesives, 1983; contbr. articles to profl. jours. and conf. procs. (Thomas Hawksley Gold medal 1997). Recipient Disting. Rsch. award Adhesion Soc. Japan, 1994. Fellow Royal Acad. Engring., Inst. Materials (Griffith medal and prize 1996), Royal Soc. Chemistry, U.S. Adhesion Soc. (3M Outstanding Excellence in Rsch. award 1992). Avocations: opera, tennis. E-mail: a.kinloch@ic.ac.uk. Fax: 44 (0) 171 823 8845. Office: Imperial Coll Dept Mech Eng, Exhibition Rd, London SW7 2BX, England

KINNE, ROLF K.H., research scientist; b. Berlin, Sept. 27, 1941; s. Karl-Heinz E. and Louise (Paetschke) K.; m. Evamaria Saffran, Oct. 26, 1967; 1 child, Daniel. MD, Free U., Berlin, 1967; PhD, Johann W. Goethe U., Frankfurt, Germany, 1970; MD (hon.), U. Naples, Italy, 1997. Rsch. assoc. Max-Planck-Inst. Biophysics, Frankfurt, 1967-79; prof. Johann W. Goethe U., 1976, U. Dusseldorf, Germany, 1985; chmn., prof. Albert Einstein Coll. Medicine, Bronx, N.Y., 1980-83; dir. Max-Planck-Inst. Systemphysiologie, Dortmund, Germany, 1985-90, dir. dept. epithelial cell physiology, 1990—; founder, chmn. Membrane Transport Soc. N.Y., 1981-83; v.p. Mound Desert Island Biol. Lab., Salsbury Cove, 1992—. Recipient Robert Pitt Meml. Lectr. award Internat. Congress Physiol. Sci., Budapest, Hungary, 1980, Homer Smith award Am. Soc. Nephrology and N.Y. Heart Assn., 1998. Fellow N.Y. Acad. Scis.; mem. Assn. for Advancement of Biomed. Sci. in Dortmund (founder, chmn. 1987—). Office: Max-Planck-Inst Mol Physiol, Otto-Hahn-Str 11, 44227 Dortmund Germany

KINNEAR, JOHN KENYON, JR., architect; b. Bklyn., Aug. 9, 1948; s. John Kenyon and Helen (Knowlton) K.; m. Alice Taylor, Jan. 30, 1971 (div. July 1982); m. Donna Manheim, Nov. 27, 1982. BArch, Pratt Inst., 1972. Registered arch., N.Y., Conn.; cert. Nat. Coun. Archtl. Registration Bds. Prin. Janko Rasic Assocs. Architects, N.Y.C., 1972—; chmn. archtl. adv. com. Town of Ridgefield, Conn. Recipient Monsanto DOC Nat. Design award, 1993. Mem. AIA, Nat. Trust for Hist. Preservation, Nelson Soc., Soc. for Nautical Rsch., Am. Friends of the Georgian Group (v.p.), Sandanona Hare Hounds, Mashomack Preserve Club. Avocations: horseback riding, historic ship modeling. Home: 90 Cains Hill Rd Ridgefield CT 06877-4209 Office: Janko Rasic Assocs Archts 109 E 37th St New York NY 10016-3040

KINNEY, CAROL NAUS ROBERTS, real estate broker; b. Mpls., May 7, 1923; d. Edward Paul and Esther (Colwell) Naus; m. Thomas R. Roberts, May 2, 1942 (dec. Feb. 1968); children: Thomas Naus, Margaret Elizabeth, Shelley; m. Harry E. Kinney, Aug. 30, 1970 (div. April 1988). Student, Mt. Holyoke Coll., 1940-42; BA in Bacteriology magna cum laude, U. Minn., 1946. Mem. staff Los Alamos Scientific Lab., 1964-70; co-owner Harry E. Kinney Gen. Contractor, Albuquerque, 1977-81, 86; real estate broker Christopher Webster, Albuquerque, 1992-94, Kate Southard Real Estate, Albuquerque, 1994-98, Carol Kinney Real Estate, Albuquerque, 1998—. City Councillor Los Alamos, N.Mex., 1968-70; chair 100 Yr. Cmty. Outreach U. N.Mex., Albuquerque, 1986-89; chair bd. of ethics and campaign practices City of Albuquerque, 1990-94; bd. N.Mex. Gov.'s Mansion Found., 1988-92, 96—. Honored as Albuquerque Vol. Jr. League of Albuquerque, 1985; entered into Albuquerque Sr. Hall of Fame, 1989—; Albuquerque's First Lady, 1974-78, 81-85. Mem. The Nature Conservancy (trustee 1976-90, 92—), N.Mex. Symphony (trustee 1992—, exec. com. 1998—), Rio Grande Nature Ctr. (trustee 1984-86, 88—), Beta Sigma Phi (internat. hon. mem.), Phi Beta Kappa. Republican. Unitarian. Avocations: skiing, camping, contractor/foreman for building own home. E-mail: ckinney@albuquerquehomes.com. Fax: 505-343-9554. Home and Office: 2917 Calle Del Rio NW Albuquerque NM 87104-3143

KINNEY, PAUL WILLIAM, investment company executive; b. Denver, Nov. 3, 1952; s. Thomas Grayson and Margaret Jane Kinney; children: Lauren Michele, Hope Elizabeth. AB, Occidental Coll., L.A., 1975; MPA, U. Colo., Denver, 1978. 1st v.p. investments Dean Witter Reynolds Inc., Glendale, Calif., 1978-99; sr. v.p., fin. Morgan Stanley Dean Witter, Glendale, Calif., 1999—. Pres. bd. dirs. Glendale (Calif.) Symphony Orch. Assn., 1995—; bd. dirs. Glendale Cmty. Found., 1995—, cfo. Mem. Investment Mgmt. Cons. Assn., Pi Alpha Alpha. Office: Morgan Stanley Dean Witter 801 N Brand Blvd Ste 908 Glendale CA 91203-1243

KINNIMENT, DAVID JOHN, electrical engineer, educator; b. Stanmore, Middlesex, Eng., July 10, 1940; s. Herbert John and Iris Henriette (Vivaudou) K.; m. Anne Lupton, Aug. 11, 1962; children: Michelle, Sarah. BSc, Manchester (Eng.) U., 1962, MSc, 1964, PhD, 1968. head dept. elec. and electronic engring., Newcastle U., 1982-90, 95-97; dir. Edec Multimedia Ltd., Eng., 1996—. Lectr. Manchester U., 1964-72, sr. lectr., 1972-79; prof. Newcastle U., Newcastle upon Tyne, Eng., 1979—; head dept. elec. and electronic engring. Newcastle U., 1982-90, 95-97; dir. Edec Multimedia Ltd., Eng., 1996—. Contbr. articles to profl. jours. Mem. IEEE, Inst. Elec. Engring.. Avocations: walking, Scottish history. Home: Sike View Kirkwhelpington, Newcastle upon Tyne NE19 2SA, England Office: Engring U Newcastle, Merz Ct, Newcastle upon Tyne NE1 7RU, England

KINNISON, ROBERT WHEELOCK, retired accountant; b. Des Moines, Sept. 17, 1914; s. Virgil R. and Sopha J. (Jackson) K.; m. Randi Hjelle, Oct. 28, 1971; children: Paul F., Hazel Jo Lewis. BS in Acctg., U. Wyo., 1940. CPA, Wyo., Colo. Ptnr. 24 hour auto service, Laramie, Wyo., 1945-59; pvt. practice acctg. Laramie, Wyo., 1963-71, Las Vegas, Nev., 1972-74, Westminster, Colo., 1974-76; pvt. practice acctg. Ft. Collins, Colo., 1976-97, ret., 1997. Served with U.S. Army, 1941-45, PTO. Mem. Wyo. Soc. CPAs, Am. Legion (past comdr.), Laramie Soc. CPAs (pres. 1966), VFW, Laramie Optimist Club (pres. 1950), Sertoma Club. Home: PO Box 168 Fort Collins CO 80522-0168

KINNO, HITOSHI, mechanical engineer, educator; b. Tokushima, Japan, Mar. 10, 1917; s. Keihichi and Maki (Isoda) K.; m. Chikako Nii, Dec. 27, 1950 (dec. 1995); children: Hiroshi, Yukio. Grad., Tokushima Tech. Coll., 1939; DEng, Osaka (Japan) U., 1959. Design engr. Sumitomo Machine Co., Niihama, Japan, 1939-45; asst. prof. Tokushima Tech. Coll., 1945-51; asst. U. Tokushima, 1951-54, lectr., 1954-56, asst. prof., 1956-61, prof., 1961-82, prof. emeritus, 1982—; pres. Earth Sci. Lab. Corp., Tokushima, 1996—; dir. Yoko Civilization Inst., Tokyo, 1986-90. Author: Waterhammer Control in Centrifugal Pump Systems, 1958, On the Mechanisms of the First Breakup of Pangaea in Early Mesozoic, 1991, The Origin of Earthquake Caused by Plate Motion, 1996, Land Protect Systems Against Sea Level Rise, 1998. Named to 3d Imperial Order of Rising Sun Emperor of Japan, 1990. Mem. N.Y. Acad. Scis. Shinto. Avocations: fishing, photography. Home: Tomidabashi 8-1-1-1105, Tokushima shi 770-0937, Japan

KINNOCK, NEIL GORDON, former British government and political leader; b. Mar. 28, 1942; s. Gordon and Mary (Howells) K.; m. Glenys Elizabeth Parry, 1967; 2 children: Stephen, Rachel. B.A. in Indsl. Rels. and History, Univ. Coll., Cardiff, Wales. Tutor, organizer in indsl. and trade union studies Workers Ednl. Assn., 1966-70; v.p., admin. reform European Union; M.P. for Bedwellty, 1970-83, for Islwyn, 1983—; parliamentary pvt. sec. to sec. of state for employment, 1974-75; mem. nat. exec. com. Labor Party, 1978-92, parly com. Parliamentary Labor Party, 1979-92; leader Labor Party, leader of Opposition, 1983-92; chief Opposition spokesman on edn., 1979-83. Author: Making Our Way-Investing in Britain's Future, 1971; also articles and pamphlets; mem. editorial bd. Labor Rsch. Dept., 1974—. Mem. Welsh Hosp. Bd., 1969-71; bd. dirs. Fair Play for Children, 1979—, 7:84 Theatre Co. (Eng.) Ltd., 1979—. Mem. Socialist Ednl. Assn., Assn. Liberal Edn. (pres. 1980-82). Office: House of Commons, London SW1, England

KINNUNEN, ESKO SAKARI, neurologist, researcher; b. Kinnula, Finland, Oct. 17, 1949; s. Vihtori and Lempi (Piispanen) K.; m. Anne-Marie Wiklund, July 28, 1973; children: Peter, Tom, Johan. MD, Helsinki (Finland) U., 1977, specialist in neurology, 1982, Doctorate, 1984. Asst. physician dept. neurology U. Helsinki, 1979-82, sr. physician dept. neurology, 1982-85, asst. prof., 1990—; cons. neurologist Meltola Hosp., 1984-96; researcher Nat. Pub. Health Inst., Helsinki, 1985-86, Inst. Occupational Health, Helsinki, 1987-90; chief physician dept. neurology Hyvinkää, 1990—; pvt. practice, Helsinki, 1980—. Contbr. sci. articles to med. jours. Sgt. Finnish Army 1969-70. Recipient 15 awards for sci. works various donation founds., 1980-93, Hon. award Am. Acad. Neurology, 1989. Mem. Finnish Med. Assn., Finnish Neurol. Assn. Avocations: marathon races, hunting. Home: Frisinniityntie 33, 02240 Espoo Finland Office: Hyvinkää Hosp, Sairaalankatu 1, 05850 Hyvinkää Finland

KINNUNEN, SVEN, retired structural engineering educator; b. Tallinn, Estonia, Feb. 23, 1930; arrived in Sweden, 1944; s. Joonas and Helmi (Keller) K.; m. Kai Pürkop, Apr. 13, 1963; children: Hannes, Peeter. MSc in Civil Engrnig., Royal Inst. Tech., Stockholm, 1955, Lic. in Structural Mechanics & Engring., 1959, PhD in Structural Mechanics & Engring., 1963. Part-time asst. dept. structural mechanics and engring. Royal Inst. Tech., Stockholm, 1955-63; part-time structural engr. Nylanders Konstruktionsbyrå AB, Stockholm, 1955-63; chief structural engr. Nylander & Hernelind Konstruktionsbyrå AB, Stockholm, 1963-64; sr. lectr. structural mechanics and engring. Royal Inst. Tech., Stockholm, 1964-70, prof. structural mechanics and engring., 1971-96, prof. emeritus, 1996—, head dept. structural engring., 1979-80, 84, 1992-95, dean Sch. Civil Engring., 1984-87. Contbr. articles to profl. jours. Active Com. Euro-Internat. du Béton (CEB), 1965-98; head Swedish Nat. Delegation in CEB, 1991-98. Mem. Swedish Concrete Assn. (Gold medal 1998), Swedish Assn. Civil Engrs. Achievements include research on structural design of reinforced concrete structures, especially slabs supported on columns. Home: Mardvaegen 12, S-131 50 Saltsjoe-Duvnaes Sweden

KINOSHITA, AKITOSHI, medical oncologist, pulmonologist; b. Nagasaki, Japan, Aug. 5, 1959; s. Hisaaki and Jitsuko Kinoshita; m. Yukiko Fujikawa, Oct. 12, 1986; children: Yuko, Mayumi, Takaaki. MD, Nagasaki U., 1984, PhD, 1993. Staff, 2d dept. internal medicine Nagasaki U. Sch. Medicine, 1984-86, 88-92; chief dept. pulmonology Hokusho Ctrl. Hosp., Nagasaki, 1986-88, Nagasaki Mcpl. Citizens' Hosp., 1992-96, Nagasaki Chuo Nat. Hosp., Omura, Japan, 1996—. Reviewer Am. Cancer Soc. Mem. Internat. Assn. for Study of Lung Cancer, Japanese Cancer Assn., Asian Pacific Soc. Respirology, Japanese Respiratory Soc., Japan Soc. Clin. Oncology, Japanese Soc. Internal Medicine, Japan Soc. Bronchology, Japan Lung Cancer Soc. Home: 2-241-14 Kushima, Omura 856-0834, Japan Office: Nagasaki Chuo Nat Hosp, 2-1001-1 Kubara, Omura 856-0835, Japan

KINOSHITA, KYOICHI, aerospace researcher; b. Miki, Japan, May 5, 1948; s. Motoji and Asako Kinoshita; m. Yoshimi Hashimoto, Nov. 23, 1973; children: Atsushi, Takamori. BSc, Waseda U., Tokyo, 1971, MSc, 1973, DSc, 1985. Rsch. scientist NTT, Tokai, Japan, 1973-80; sr. rsch. scientist NTT, Tokyo, 1980-93, Atsugi, Japan, 1994—; invited scientist Nat. Space Devel. Agy. of Japan, Tsukuba, 1995—. Editor: Phase Transitions, 1989—, Jour. Japan Soc. Microgravity Application, 1995—. Recipient Merit of Edn. award Miki-City, Japan, 1998, Outstandinf Paper award Phys. Soc. Japan, 1998. Avocations: fishing, gardening. Home: 6-7-1 Sumiyoshi-cho, Hoya 202-0005, Japan Office: NTT Basic Rsch Labs, 3-1 Morinosato Wakamiya, Atsugi 243-0198, Japan

KINOSHITA, SHINJI, cardiologist, educator; b. Otaru, Hokkaido, Japan, Jan. 7, 1931; s. Sakuzo and Torayo (Takahashi) K.; m. Hitomi Sano, Oct. 2, 1962; children: Yorko, Makoto. MD, Hokkaido U., 1955; DMS, 1959. Intern City of Otaru Hosp., Japan, 1954-55; rsch. assoc. 2nd dept. medicine Sch. Medicine Hokkaido U., Sapporo, 1955-68; instr., 1968-76, assoc. prof., 1976-83, prof. Health Adminstrn. Ctr., 1983-94, dir., 1986-94, prof. emeritus, 1994—; prof. Hokkaido Women's U., 1997—. Inventor color-vectorcardiograph; contbr. articles to profl. jours. including Circulation, Am. Jour. Cardiology. Mem. Japanese Circulation Soc. (hon. Hokkaido br.), Japanese Soc. Elextrocardiology, AHA (reviewer 1978-81). Home: 4-Jo 3-Chome 3-27, Tonden, Kita-ku, Sapporo Hokkaido 002-0854, Japan Office: Hokkaido Women's U, Bunkyodai 23 Ebetsu, Hokkaido 069-8511, Japan

KINSELLA, BRIAN F., mechanical engineer, consultant; b. Dublin, Nov. 6, 1952; s. Francis A. and Anne M. Kinsella; m. Ann Brown, Feb. 14, 1986. Dip.Eng., Dublin Inst. Tech., 1974; MSc, Dublin U., 1976. Chartered engr., Ireland. Grad. engr. Electricity Supply Bd., Dublin, 1974-76; project engr. Ewbank Engring., Dublin, 1976-86; sr. engr. Ewbank Preece Oheocha, Dublin, 1986-93; prin. engr. Mott MacDonald Epo, Dublin, 1993—. Contbr. articles to profl. jours. Mem. Instn. of Mech. Engrs., Instn. of Engrs. of Ireland, N.Y. Acad. Scis. Roman Catholic. Avocations: cycling, swimming, Diy.

KINSELLA, THOMAS, poet; b. Dublin, Ireland, May 4, 1928; s. John Paul and Agnes (Casserly) K.; m. Eleanor Walsh, 1955, 3 children. With Irish Civil Service, 1946-65, asst. prin. officer Dept. Fin., 1960-65; artist in residence So. Ill. U., 1965-67, prof. English, 1967-70; prof. Temple U., Phila., 1970-90; dir. Dolmen Press Ltd., Cuala Press Ltd, Dublin; founder Peppercanister, Dublin, 1972. Author: Poems, 1956, Another September, 1958, Downstream, 1962, Nightwalker and Other Poems, 1966, Notes from the Land of the Dead, 1972, Butcher's Dozen, 1972, Finistere, 1972, New Poems, 1973, Selected Poems 1956-68, 1973, Song of the Night and Other Poems, 1978, The Messenger, 1978, Fifteen Dead, 1979, One and Other Poems, 1979; Songs of the Psyche, 1984; Her Vertical Smile, 1984; St. Catherine's Clock, 1987; Out of Ireland, 1987, Blood and Family, 1988, Poems From Center City, 1990, Personal Places, 1990, Madonna and Other Poems, 1991, Open Court, 1991, From Centre City, 1994, The Dual Tradition: an Essay on Poetry and Politics in Ireland, 1995, Collected Poems, 1996, The Pen Shop, 1997, The Familiar, 1999, Godhead, 1999; editor: Selected Poems of Austin Clarke, 1976; (with Sean O'Tuama) Poems of the Dispossessed 1600-1900, 1980; The New Oxford Book of Irish Verse (with translations), 1986; transl. (from Old Irish) The Tain, 1970. Recipient Guinness Poetry award, 1958, Irish Arts Council Triennial Book award, 1960, Denis Devlin Meml. award, 1966, 69, 88, 94; Guggenheim fellow, 1968-69, 71-72. Mem. Am. Acad. Arts and Scis., Irish Acad. Letters. Home: Killalane, Laragh County Wicklow, Ireland

KINSER, DONALD LEROY, materials science educator; b. Loudon, Tenn., Sept. 28, 1941; s. Fred D. and Annie (Watkins) K.; m. Barbara Lange, June 10, 1964; children: Elizabeth, Cynthia. BS, U. Fla., 1964, PhD, 1968. Asst. prof. materials sci. Vanderbilt U., Nashville, 1968-71, assoc. prof., 1971-76, prof., 1976—, chmn. applied engring. sci., 1996-98; cons. in field. Co-editor Jour. Noncrystalline Solids, 1988-98; contbr. articles to profl. publs.; patentee in field. Recipient sr. postdoc. award NATO, 1973, Cert. of Recognition, NASA, 1976, 80. Fellow Am. Ceramic Soc., Soc. Glass Tech.; mem. AAAS, ASME, NSPE, Internat. Soc. Optical Engring., Am. Soc. Engring. Edn., Nat. Inst. Ceramic Engrs., Materials Rsch. Soc., Sigma Xi, Sigma Tau. Home: 1306 Winchester Rd Brentwood TN 37027-7113 Office: Vanderbilt U 610 Olin Hall Nashville TN 37235

KINSER, KATHERINE ANNE, lawyer; b. Russellville, Ark., Apr. 25, 1954; d. Thomas Kinser and Nancy (Seminatore) Barber; m. Frank W. Sullivan III, Aug. 19, 1988. BA, U. Ark., Little Rock, 1979; JD, So. Meth. U., 1984. Bar: Tex. 1984, U.S. Supreme Ct. 1990; cert. family law specialist, Tex. Assoc. Michael F. Pezzulli, P.C., Dallas, 1984-86; pvt. practice, Dallas, 1986; ptnr. McCurley, Kinser, McCurley & Nelson, L.L.P., Dallas, 1986—; speaker in field. Contbr. articles to legal publs. Fellow Am. Acad. Matrimonial Lawyers; mem. ABA, State Bar Tex. (family law coun.), Tex. Acad. Family Law Specialists, Tarrant County Family Law Bar Assn., Dallas Bar Assn. (family law sect., sec. 1988-89, v.p. 1990-91, pres. 1991-92,

mock trial com. 1987—), Sports Lawyers Assn., Phi Alpha Delta. Avocation: scuba diving.

KINSEY, CHARLES JOHN, industrial auctioneer, consultant, cattle breeder, farmer; b. Regina, Saskatchew, Can., Aug. 4, 1922; came to U.S., 1929; s. Alfred Richardson and Lola Mae (Lagergren) K.; m. Shirley Elaine Grady, June 25, 1950; children: Rebecca Diane, David Allan, Jane Elizabeth, Thomas Charles. BS, U. Ill., 1951. Fieldman Am. Hampshire Swine Registry, Am. Hampshire Herdsman, Peoria, Ill., 1946-48; exec. sec. Park Ridge (Ill.) C. of C., 1953; indsl. auctioneer S.L. Winternitz & Co., Inc., Chgo., 1954-57; ptnr. Kinsey-Koploy Co., Detroit, 1957-65; pres., prin. Charles Kinsey & Co., Inc., Detroit, 1965—; pres. Mich. Auctioneers Assn., 1960-61; v.p. Mich. Angus Assn., 1963; cons. A-Line Mfg. Co., Centralia, Ill., 1982—. Author: The Lives and The Times of The Kinsey Brothers, Ernest and Alfred, 1997. Mem. First Presbyn. Ch. Choir, Farmington Hills, Mich., 1959—. Served U.S. Army, 1944-46, Persian Gulf Command, ETO. Recipient Am. Farmer Degree FFA Vocat. Agrl., Urbana, 1940, State PRes. Ill. Assn. Future Farmers Am., 1940-41, Thomas E. Wilson award Ill. 4H Club, Chgo., 1943, State Ill. 4H Livestock Champion, Nat. Hampshire Pig Club contest winner, 1939. Mem. U. Ill. Alumni Assn. (life), Sigma Phi Epsilon (life). Independent. Avocations: baritone soloist, creative writing, voice concerts. Home and Office: Charles Kinsey & Co Inc 40011 Jefferson Novi MI 48375-2026

KINSLOW, MARGIE ANN, volunteer worker; b. Salt Lake City, Dec. 7, 1931; d. Diamond and Sarah (Chipman) Wendelboe; m. James Ferol Kinslow, Apr. 6, 1954 (dec. July 1982). Student, U. Utah, 1949-53. Jr. vol. chmn. various hosps., Okla., Mont., Colo., 1967-87; pres. Ch. Woman's Orgn., Bartlesville, Okla., 1968; fin. advisor, jr. v.p., vol. chmn. Swedish Med. Ctr., Englewood, 1971-92; pres. Delta Gamma Alumnae, Denver, 1975-76; jr. vol. chair Colo. Assn. Hosp. Aux., Denver, 1977-82, 2d v.p., 1982-84; transp. chair, master class chmn. Rocky Mountain Regional Auditions, Met. Opera, Denver, 1986—. Office vol. Rep. Office, Billings, Mont., 1969-70, Colo. Senator, Denver, 1974-76; vol. various polit. candidates, Denver, 1974-90; various offices Newcomers, Okla., Mont. and Colo., 1967-75. Recipient Stellar award, 1979, Cable award, 1991. Mem. PEO, Gen. Fedn. of Women's Clubs (bd. dirs. 1994—, corr. sec. Western region), Colo. Gen. Fedn. of Women's Clubs (pres. 1994-96, various offices 1986-94), Denver Lyric Opera Guild, Cherry Creek Woman's Club (pres. 1985, Hoby corp. bd. 1997—), Littleton Rep. Women's Club. Episcopalian. Avocations: bridge, travel, people, the arts.

KINSMAN, OONAGH SUSAN, microbiologist; b. Calcutta, Jan. 22, 1954; arrived in Ireland, 1956, England, 1979; d. Harold Knill and Margaret Eileen (Ellis) K.; m. Adrian James Michael Stevenson; 1 child, Eileen. BA, Trinity Coll., Dublin, 1975, PhD, 1979. Guest scholar Biomed. Ctr., Uppsala, Sweden, 1978; postdoctoral fellow Inst. of Dermatology, London, 1979-82; rsch. microbiologist Glaxo R&D, Greenford, England, 1982-95; contracts/consultancy officer Glaxo Wellcome PLC, Stevenage, England, 1995—. Contbr. articles to profl. jours. and chpts. to books. Mem. Soc. for Gen. Microbiology. Avocations: tennis, travel, eating well. Office: Glaxo Wellcome PLC, Gunnels Wood Rd, Stevenage Herts SG1 2NY, England

KINSTLER, EVERETT RAYMOND, artist; b. N.Y.C., Aug. 5, 1926; s. Joseph E. and Essie K.; m. Lea C. Nation, June 23, 1958 (div. 1984); children: Katherine G., Dana C.; m. Peggy Chartier, 1996. Ed., Art Students League, N.Y.C., 1943-45; hon. doctorate, Rollins Coll., 1983. Started career as illustrator N.Y.C., 1943; began specializing in portraiture, 1955; instr. Art Students League, N.Y.C., 1969-74. Portraits include over 35 U.S. cabinet officers, ofcl. White House portrait former Pres. Gerald R. Ford, former Pres. Ronald Reagan, J. Edgar Hoover, Richard K. Mellon, Mrs. Irenee duPont, Jr., Kurt Waldheim, sec.-gen. UN, Casper Weinberger, sec. of def., William Casey, dir. CIA, Cyrus Vance, sec. of state, Astronaut Alan B. Shepard, Jr., William Bowen, pres. Princeton U., James Cagney, John D. Rockefeller III, Byron Nelson, Frank Cary, pres. IBM, Charles Scribner, Jr., John Wayne, John Kemeny, pres. Dartmouth Coll., William Simon, sec. Treasury, Elliot Richardson, ambassador to Gt. Britain, Tennessee Williams, John Connally, gov. of Tex., Charles Brown, CH., ATT, Russel Long, U.S. Senator, Morris Udall, mem. U.S. Congress, Katharine Hepburn, Gregory Peck, former Pres. Richard M. Nixon; Bartlett Gramatti, pres. Yale U., George P. Shultz, former U.S. Sec. of State, Paul Newman, Thomas Kean, former Gov. N.J., former Pres. George Bush, Arthur Ashe, Tony Bennett, Carol Burnett, Elizabeth Dole, Betty Ford, Lady Bird Johnson, William Webster, former dir. CIA, Harry Blackmun, U.S. Supreme Ct. Justice, former U.S. Sec. of State Warren Christopher, Placido Domingo, President Bill Clinton, Gene Hackman, also numerous others; represented in permanent collections, Butler Inst. Am. Art, Nat. Portrait Gallery, Washington, Nat. Acad. Design, Mus. City N.Y., Met. Mus. Art, N.Y.C., The Pentagon, Am. Embassy, Paris, Carnegie Mus., N.Y. Stock Exchange, Bklyn. Mus., White House, Smithsonian Instn., Retrospective Exhibition Boston U., Butler inst. Am. Art, Fairfield, Conn., 1999; numerous colls., univs., bus. firms; Author: Painting Portraits, 1971, Painting Faces, Figures, Landscapes, 1981. Recipient Artists' Fellowship Medal, 1986, Nat. Arts Club medal, 1993, Allied Artists medal, 1997, Copley medal Nat. Portrait Gallery, 1999. Mem. Allied Artists Am. (dir. 1958-60), Artists Fellowships, Inc. (pres. 1967-70), Am. Watercolor Soc., Pastel Soc. Am., Audubon Artists, NAD, Actor's Fund Am. (life), Lambs Club (life), Century Assn. Club (N.Y.C.), Lotos Club (N.Y.C.) (life), Nat. Arts Club (N.Y.C.), Dutch Treat Club (N.Y.C.), Players Club (life), Yale Club N.Y. (life). Office: care Nat Arts Club 15 Gramercy Park S New York NY 10003-1705

KINT, ARNE TONIS, industrial engineer, mechanical engineer; b. Tallinn, Harjumaa, Estonia, Nov. 2, 1932; came to U.S., 1957; s. Tõnis Kint and Salme (Redlich) K.; m. Saima Kärp, Aug. 30, 1964. BSME, Stockholm Tekniska Inst., 1954; BS in Indsl. Engring., Ga. Tech., 1960; MS in Indsl. Engring., U. Calif., 1963. Registered profl. indsl. engr., Calif.; cert. profl. materials handling and mgmt., Mich. Mech. engr. Philips Neon Co., Stockholm, 1954-57; student indsl. engr. Weirton (W. Va.) Steel Co., 1959; plant, foundry engr. H.C. Macaulay Foundry Co., Inc., Berkeley, Calif., 1960-67; indsl. engring. project leader Matson Navigation Co., San Francisco, 1967-69; area indsl. engr. Interpace Corp., Pitts., 1969-72; cons. indsl. engr. Oakland, Calif., 1972-73; work design, analysis supr. Truck Divsn. Internat. Harvester Co., Inc., San Leandro, Calif., 1973-75; sr. systems project engr. Engineered Sys. & Devel. Corp., Santa Clara and San Jose, Calif., 1975-89; cons. ind. engr. Applied Engring. and Design, Inc., San Jose, Calif., 1989-90; project engr. Jacobs Engring. Group, Martinez, Calif., 1990-92; cons. ind. engr. Indsl. Engring. USA, Oakland, Calif., 1992-98; cons. to pres. Fabricated Metals, Inc., San Leandro, Calif., 1998-99; project mgr. Mason West, Inc., San Francisco, Calif., 1999—. Bd. dirs. Estonian Info. Ctr., Stockholm, 1946-75; pres. Estonian League of Liberation, San Francisco, 1968-73. Decorated Gold Svc. medal Estonian Nat. Found., 1971. Mem. Estonian Soc. San Francisco (pres. 1962-63), Swedish Am. C. of C., Estonian Ski Club. Avocations: skiing, boating, hunting, travel, fishing. Home: 312 Alta Vista Ave Oakland CA 94610-1941

KINTZELE, JOHN ALFRED, lawyer; b. Denver, Aug. 16, 1936; s. Louis Richard and Adele H. Kintzele; children: John A., Marcia A., Elizabeth A.; m. Suzanne Hinsberger; stepchildren: William Karp III, Christopher Karp. BS in Bus., U. Colo., 1958, LLB, 1961. Bar: Colo. bar 1961. Assoc. James B. Radetsky, Denver, 1962-63; pvt. practice law Denver, 1963—; corp. officer, dir. Kintzele, Inc.; rep. 10th cir. U.S. Ct. of Claims Bar. Chmn. Colo. Lawyer Referral Service, 1978-83, Election commr., Denver, 1975-79, 83-86. Mem. ABA, Colo. Bar Assn., Denver Bar Assn., Am. Judicature Soc. Democrat. Roman Catholic. Home: 10604 E Powers Dr Englewood CO 80111-3957 Office: 1317 Delaware St Denver CO 80204-2704

KINZIE, JEANNIE JONES, radiation oncologist, nuclear medicine physician; b. Great Falls, Mont., Mar. 14, 1940; d. James Wayne and Lillian Alice (Young) Jones; m. Joseph Lee Kinzie, Mar. 26, 1965 (div. Sept. 1982); 1 child, Daniel Joseph; m. Johnson Wachira, Oct. 7, 1991. Student, Oreg. State U., 1960; BS, Mont. State U., 1961; MD, Washington U., 1965; MBA, U. Phoenix, 1997. Diplomate Am. Bd. Radiology; diplomate Am. Bd. Nuclear Medicine; cert. advanced master gardener Colo. State U., 1997. Intern. in surgery U. N.C., Chapel Hill, 1965-66; resident in therapeutic radiology Washington U., St. Louis, 1968-71, instr. in radiology, 1971-73; asst. prof. in radiology Med. Coll. of Wis., Milw., 1973-75; asst. prof. in radiology U. Chgo., 1975-78, assoc. prof. in radiology, 1978-80; assoc. prof. of radiation oncology Wayne State U., Detroit, 1980-85; prof. radiology U. Colo., Denver, 1985-95; dir. radiation oncology U. Hosp., Denver, 1985-91; fellow in nuclear medicine U. Colo., 1996-98, asst. clin. prof. nuclear medicine, 1998—; cons. Denver Vets. Hosp., Denver Gen. Hosp., Rose Med. Ctr., FDA Ctr. for Devices and Radiologic Health, Denver; sci. adv. bd. Cancer League Colo., 1985-88; examiner Am. Bd. Radiology, 1985-88; adv. physician Colo. Med. Found., 1988-98; chmn. faculty promotion com. U. Colo. Health Scis. Ctr., 1988-89. Assoc. editor Internat. Jour. Radiation Oncology Biology and Physics, 1985-95; contbr. articles to profl. jours.; chpts. to books. Mem. Faith Bible Chapel Ch. NIH grantee, 1973-75. Fellow Am. Coll. Radiology; mem. AMA, Colo. Med. Soc., Denver Med. Soc. (del. to Colo. Med. Soc. Ho. of Dels. 1989—), Colo. Radiol. Soc., Metabolic Bone Disease Soc. Colo., Soc. Nuclear Medicine, Rocky Mountain Oncology Soc. (bd. dirs. 1989-93, pres. 1991-93), Am. Soc. Therapeutic Radiologists, Am. Cancer Soc. (bd. dirs. Denver unit 1986-87), Wilderness Med. Soc., Xeriscape Colo. Republican. Avocations: stamp collecting, cross country skiing, gardening, rug latching, mountain climbing.

KINZIG, WOLFRAM ULRICH, Protestant theologian, church historian; b. Mannheim, Germany, Mar. 7, 1960; s. Werner Reinhard and Edelgard (Szalinski) K.; m. María del Carmen Rascón Chávez, Sept. 9, 1989; children: Adrian Jörg, Susanna Stefanie. Student, U. Heidelberg, Germany, 1978-85, U. Lausanne, Switzerland, 1981-82; postgrad., Christ Church, Oxford U., 1985-86, Trinity Coll., Cambridge U., 1986-87; D in Theology, Heidelberg U., Germany, 1988; Habil. in Hist. Theology, U. Heidelberg, Germany, 1991. First tchg. cert. in Latin and Evang. Theology, 1984, 1st theol. exam., Baden, Germany, 1985. Fellow Peterhouse, Cambridge, 1988-92, King's Coll., Cambridge, 1992-95; privatdozent U. Heidelberg, 1992-96; prof. church history U. Bonn, Germany, 1996—. Author: In Search of Asterius, 1990, Erbin Kirche, 1990, Novitas Christiana, 1994; co-author: Tauffragen und Bekenntnis, 1999. Fellow 21st Century Trust, London, 1989—. Recipient Studienstiftung des Deutschen Volkes, 1982-88, Heisenberg-Stipendium Deutsche Forschungsgemeinschaft, 1992-96. Evangelical Protestant. Avocations: music, English detective novels, art history. Home: Pestalozzistr 7H, D-53757 Sankt Augustin Germany Office: Evangelisch-Theol Seminar, Am Hof 1, D-53113 Bonn Germany

KIPKOECH, IAN MARTIN, procurement executive, director; b. Nairobi, Kenya, Apr. 25, 1964; s. William Kimutai and Mary Chepkirui (Smith) M.; m. Elizabeth Patricia Atkinson; children: Ziana Mary, William Kibet, Natasha Nalika. MA, Mass. Inst. Tech., 1989; MBA, Howard U., 1991. Adminstr. PanAm. World Airway, 1985-88; mng. dir. Nietrad, Plc., U.K., 1988-89, 99—, Geotrade Ltd., East Africa, 1989-92; exec. dir. internat. procurement and supply Kenya Logistical Support Svcs., East Africa, 1993—; dir. Chesumot Farm, Kenya; chmn. Lynx Mgmt. & Holdings, Kenya, Sesaat Properties, Kenya. dist. chmn. Kenya African Nat. Union, 1994; mem. City Coun., Kileleshwa, 1997. Mem. Rotary. Avocations: charities, hunting, sailing. E-mail: imk@nbnet.co.ke. Home: Gatunda Rd PO Box 21772, Nairobi Kenya Office: Kenya Logistical Support Svcs, Haile Secassie Ave PO Box 59324, Nairobi Kenya

KIPMAN, SIMON-DANIEL, psychiatrist, psychoanalyst; b. Paris, Mar. 30, 1936; s. Nathan and Anna (Langleben) K.; m. Marie-Annick Juhel, Oct. 11, 1969; children: Aurelien, Amélie, Lise, Hai Tu Truong. MD, Sch. Medicine, Paris, 1963; psychiatrist, Paris, 1968. Pres. GEPSY, 1970—; gen. sec. French Assn. Psychiatry, 1986-93, French Syndicate of Psychiatry, 1986-87; pres., founder French Fedn. Psychiatry, 1986—; pres. AFP-SPF, 1987—; mem. precaution and prevention com., Ministry of Environment, 1994—. Author: L'enfant et les sortileges de la maladie, 1984, La r'queur de l'intuition, 1990; editor: La sexualité oubliée des enfants, Une theorie pour l'avenir. Lt., Health Svcs., 1962-63, France. Fellow APA; mem. French Am. Soc. Psychiatry (hon. pres.), French Argentinian Soc. Psychiatry (hon. pres.), Geneva Initiative, Order des Medecins Francais (profl.), Ligue de Dairt de l'Homme. E-mail: s.d.kipman@wanadoo.fr. Office: 7 rue du Montparnasse, F-75006 Paris France

KIPP, GISELA MILLER, anthropology and history of education educator; b. Düsseldorf, Germany, Aug. 31; d. Gerhard and Ruth (Meierling) Schroeder; m. Martin Kipp; 1 child, Cornelia. PhD, U. Cologne, 1975. Sr. lectr. U. Fed. Armed Forces, Germany, 1976-92; from interim prof. to prof., chair U. Duesseldorf, Germany, 1996—. Author: Shaftesbury, 1975, Education and Biology, 1992, Education Third Reich, 1995. Office: Heinrich H U Duesseldorf, Universitaetsstrasse 1, Düsseldorf 40225, Germany

KIPP, JOHN THEODORE, lawyer, rancher; b. Guadalajara, Mex., Apr. 19, 1932; (parents Am. citizens); s. Eugene Harvey and Theresa (Greer) K.; 1 child, John Grant. BBA, U. Tex., 1954, JD, 1958. Bar: Tex. 1958, U.S. Dist. Ct. (no. dist.) Tex. 1962, U.S. Supreme Ct. 1964. Assoc. Gardere & Wynne, LLP and predecessor, Dallas, 1958-63, ptnr., 1964-98, of counsel, 1998—. Past chmn. Dallas County chpt. Am. Heart Assn.; trustee, treas. Dallas Hist. Soc. Lt. USN, 1954-56, Korea; mem. USNR (ret.). Mem. State Bar Tex. (chmn. corp. law com. 1973-75, bus. law sect. 1976-77), Dallas Bar Assn. Avocations: hunting, fishing, ranching, photography, golfing. Home: 3823 Hawthorne Ave Dallas TX 75219-2212 Office: Gardere & Wynne LLP 1601 Elm St Ste 3000 Dallas TX 75201-4761

KIPPER, BARBARA LEVY, corporate executive; b. Chgo., July 16, 1942; d. Charles and Ruth (Doctoroff) Levy; m. David A. Kipper, Sept. 9, 1974; children: Talia Rose, Tamar Judith. BA, U. Mich., 1964. Reporter Chgo. Sun-Times, 1964-67; photo editor Cosmopolitan Mag., N.Y.C., 1969-71; vice chmn. Chas Levy Co., Chgo., 1984-86, chmn., 1986—. Trustee Spertus Inst. Jewish Studies, Chgo. Hist. Soc., Golden Apple Ind., Joffrey Ballet of Chgo. Recipient Deborah award Com. Women's Equality, Am. Jewish Congress, 1992, Shap Shapiro Human Rels. award The Anti-Defamation League of B'nai B'rith, Personal PAC's Leadership award, 1996, Disting. Cmty. Leadership award, ADL, 1999; named Nat. Soc. Fund Raising Exec.'s Disting. Philanthropist, 1995. Mem. Com. of 200, Coun. on Founds., Chgo. Coun. on Fgn. Rels., Chgo. Network, Women's Issues Network, The Standard Club, Execs. Club of Chgo., Econ. Club of Chgo, Internat. Women's Forum. Jewish. Office: Chas Levy Co 1200 N North Branch St Chicago IL 60622-2449

KIPSHIDZE, NODAR NICOLAEVICH, medical educator; b. Tbilisi, Georgia, Oct. 12, 1923; s. Nicolas A. and Daria V. (Gabashvili) K.; m. Leli Cheishvili, June 9, 1949; children: Nickolas, Nina. MD, Med. U., Tbilisi, 1946; Candidate Med. Scis., Tbilisi, 1952; D Med. Scis., Moscow, 1962. Med. diplomate. Prof. Med. U., Tbilisi, 1952-54, 57-61; Inst. Cardiology, Moscow, 1954-57; dir. Inst. Therapy, Tbilisi, 1961-95, Inst. Exptl. and Clin. Therapy, Tbilisi, 1995—; prof. Med. U., Tbilisi, 1995—; academician Russian Sci. Acad., 1975, Georgian Sci. Acad., 1996; pres. Georgian Soc. Internal Medicine, 1980—, Georgian Assn. Atherosceosis, 1990—, Georgian Soc. Gerontology and Geriatrics, 1982, Georgian com. Internal Physicians Pvt. Nuclear Warm, 1984. Author: Myocardiac Infarction, 1967; Cardiomyopathy, 1988, Atlas of Echocardiography, 1987, Prolapse of Mitral Valve, 1985, Longliving People, 1980. Recipient USSR state awards, 1989, Georgian Rep. state awards, 1981, Russian Med. Acad. awards, 1987. Fellow Am. Coll. Phys. (hon.); mem. Soc. Internal Medicine of Georgian Rep. (pres. 1986—), Soc. of Atherosclerosis of Georgian Rep. (pres. 1993—). Orthodox Christian. Avocation: music. Home: 9 Andrapapidze St, 38009 Tbilisi Georgia Office: Inst Exptl and Clin Therapy, 4 Ljubljana St, 380059 Tbilisi Georgia

KIPTANUI, FRANKLYNN KIPN'ETICH, chemistry educator, consultant; b. Eldama Ravine, Kenya, Feb. 2, 1964; s. Laban Kibirir Sittoni and Dorcas Jeruto (Tallami) K.; m. Marylynn Jirry Maiyo, Dec. 12, 1990; children: Rossy, Mike, Valentine. Diploma, Aberdeen, London, 1982; Degree, Oxford U., 1986, M, 1992, D, 1994; M in Nuc. Chemistry, U. Moscow, 2000. Med. diplomate. Clin. officer Ministry of Health, Kenya, 1982-84, provincial med. officer, 1988-92, health inspector, 1992-93, dir. health svcs., 1992-96; prin. med. colls., Kenya, 1996—; dep. med. cons., Kenya, 1990-92; leader group work W.H.O., Lodwar, 1994; asst. chem. valuator; govt. chemistry advisor; dep. pres. nuc. chemistry, Africa. Author: Medicine and Medics, 1996; editor: Nation Newspaper; contbr. short stories to Whispers. Recipient Gold medal, 1999. Avocations: international golf, swimming, lawn tennis, table tennis, hockey. E-mail: fminterne@afols.com. Home: PO Box 750, Eldaman Ravine Kenya Office: PO Box 500, Nairobi Nairobi, Kenya

KIRAKOWSKI, JERZY ZDZISŁAW JOZEF, psychology educator; b. London, Sept. 22, 1949; s. Zdzislaw Józef and Maria Wanda (de Baumgarten) K.; m. Maire Domhnat McKeown, Nov. 24, 1982; children: Tadeusz, Aengus, Anna-Sophia. MA in Social Sci., Edinburgh U., 1973, PhD, 1977. Univ. demonstrator Edinburgh U., Scotland, 1975-77; coll. lectr. U. Coll. Cork, Ireland, 1977-99, statutory lectr., 1999—; tech. expert European Commn. DG XIII, Brussels, 1988—, project architect/MUSIC project, 1990-93, dep. project mgr. RESPECT project, 1996-97; dir. Human Factors Rsch. Group, 1985—; tech. mgr. SOL project, 1998-2000; mem. adv. com. UTEST, 1998—. Co-author: (with T. Ryan) Ballinspittle-Moving Statues and Faith, 1985, (with M. Corbett) Effective Methodology for the Study of Human-Computer Interaction, 1990; (with M. Porteous) Sumi Questionaire, 1992; author: Human-Computer Interaction from Voltage to Knowledge, 1988. Prin. viola Cork Symphony Orch., 1978-83. Mem. Psychol. Soc. of Ireland, Usability Profls. Assn. Avocations: music, hill walking, scuba diving, yoga, New Testament scholarship. Office: Human Factors Rsch Group, University Coll Cork, Cork Ireland

KIRALI, MEHMET KAAN, cardiovascular surgeon; b. Eskisehir, Turkey, Aug. 25, 1966; s. Ziya and Sherife (Umarusman) K.; m. Muge Turan, Sept. 19, 1989; 1 child. MD, Istanbul (Turkey) U., 1990. Cons. cardiac surgeon Kosuyolu Heart and Rsch. Hosp., Istanbul, 1997-98, rsch. asst. prof., 1998—. Home: Atakoy 4 Kisim, TO 91 Daire 13, 34750 Istanbul Turkey

KIRBY, BRIAN JOHN, physician, academic administrator, educator; b. Southend-on-Sea, Eng., Aug. 25, 1936; s. George and Lily Ann (Deighton) K.; m. Rachel Mary Pawson; children: Timothy Pawson, Juliet Clare. MB, Ch.B, U. Leeds, Eng., 1960, OBE, 1998. House appts. St. James's Univ. Hosp., Leeds, 1960-63; registrar in medicine Cen. Middlesex Hosp., London, 1963-65, rsch. fellow, 1965-67; instr. medicine Med. Coll. Va., Richmond, 1967-68; registrar in cardiology Royal Postgrad. Med. Sch., London, 1968-69; prof. medicine, acting dir. med. sch., cons. physician U. Edinburgh, Scotland, 1969-74; prof., dept. dir. med. sch., cons. physician U. Exeter (Eng.), Royal Devon and Exeter Hosp., 1974—; chmn. adv. bd. on the Registration of Homeopathic Products, S.W. Action on Smoking and Health, Exeter; mem. Com. on Safety of Medicines; mem. Safety Efficacy and Adverse Reactions Com., London; vice chmn. Com. on the Rev. of Medicine; chmn. Coronary Prevention Group, London. Contbr. articles to profl. jours. Recipient Queens Anniversary prize, 1999; rsch. grantee MRC, 1965-67, Brit. Heart Found., Northcott Devon Rsch. Found., Southwestern Regional Health Authority, 1987-90, Nat. Hosp. Trust, 1991—, Healthy Heart Rsch. Trust, 1990, others. Fellow Royal Soc. Arts, Royal Coll. Physicians London, Royal Coll. Physicians Edinburgh, Royal Soc. Medicine. Avocations: walking, skiing, sailing. Office: Postgrad Med Sch, Sch Postgrad Med/Hlth Scis, Barrack Rd, Exeter EX2 5DW, England

KIRBY, IAN JOHN, English educator; b. Ilford, Essex, Eng., Feb. 15, 1934; arrived in Switzerland, 1971; s. William George and Adelaide Bessie (Andrews) K.; m. Pamela Jean Wren, July 22, 1961; children: Neil, Catherine. BA, U. London, 1955, PhD, 1973. Postgrad. cert. edn., London, 1956. English master Fletton High Sch., Peterborough, Eng., 1956-57, Barking (Eng.) Abbey Sch., 1957-61; lectr. English, Uppsala (Sweden) U., 1961-67; prof. English, U. Iceland, Reykjavik, 1967-71, U. Lausanne, Switzerland, 1971—. Author: Biblical Quotation in Old Icelandic-Norwegian Literature, Vol. 1, 1976, Vol. 2, 1980, Bible Translation in Old Norse, 1986, and numerous articles. Mem. Internat. Assn. Univ. Profs. English (editor Bull. 1978-89, exec. com. 1983—, pres. 1986-89, sec.-gen. 95—), Viking Soc. for No. Rsch., English Assn. Mem. Ch. of England. Avocations: theatre, tennis, mountain walking, bridge. Office: U Lausanne, BFSH 2, 1015 Lausanne Switzerland

KIRBY, MICHAEL DONALD, judge; b. Sydney, Australia, Mar. 18, 1939; s. Donald and Jean Langmore (Knowles) K. BA, Sydney U., 1959, LLB, 1962, B of Econs., 1965, LLM, 1966, LLD (hon.), 1996; DLitt (hon.), U. Newcastle, 1987, Ulster U., 1998; LLD (hon.), Macquarie U., 1994, Sydney U., 1996, Nat. Law Sch. U., India, 1997, Nat. Law Sch. U., Buckingham, 2000. Pvt. practice Sydney, 1962-67; barrister NSW, 1967-74; mem. NSW Bar Coun., Sydney, 1974; dep. pres. Australian Conciliation and Arbitration Commn., Sydney, 1975-83; judge Fed. Ct. Australia, 1983-84; judge, pres. Ct. Appeal Supreme Ct. New South Wales, 1984-96; acting chief justice NSW, 1988, 90, 93, 95; justice High Ct. of Australia, Canberra, 1996—; adminstr., NSW, 1991; chmn. Australian Law Reform Commn., 1975-84, expert group on privacy and trans border data flows OECD, 1978-80; gov. Internat. Coun. on Computer Comm., Washington, 1984—; commr. Internat. Com. Jurists, Geneva, 1985—, exec. com., 1989-95, chmn. 1992-95, pres., 1995-98; dep. pres. Australian Conciliation and Arbitration Commn., 1974-83; mem. Adminstrv. Review Coun. of Australia, 1976-84; mem. Australian Nat. Commn. for UNESCO, 1980-84, hon. mem., 1996—; mem. adv. bd. Australian Ctr. for Media and Telecommunications Law and Policy, 1993—; mem. Permanent Tribunal of Peoples, 1992—; ind. chmn. Constl. Conf. in Malawi, 1994, numerous others; pres. Ct. Appeal, Solomon Islands, 1995-96. Author: Industrial Index to Australian Labor Law, 1978, 2d rev. edit., 1983, Reform the Law, 1983, The Judges, 1983, Through the World's Eye, 2000; co-editor: A Touch of Healing, 1986. Commr. Global Com. on AIDS, WHO, Geneva, 1989-91; mem. ILO Fact Finding and Conciliation Commn. to South Africa, 1991-92; pres. Nat. Book Coun. Australia, 1980-83; mem. Coun. Australian Opera, Friends of Mus. Applied Arts & Scis., Overseas Svc. Bur., Australian Assn. Edn. of Gifted and Talented Children; mem. coun. U. Newcastle, 1977-83, dep. chancellor, 1978-83, mem. adv. coun. Human Rights Ctr.; chancellor Macquarie U., Sydney, 1983-94; trustee AIDS Trust Australia, 1987-92; chmn. expert group on right of peoples UNESCO, 1989; spl. rep. of Sec.-Gen. of UN for Human Rights in Cambodia, 1993-96; mem. Internat. Jury for UNESCO Prize Teaching Human Rights, 1994-96; mem. Internat. Bioethics Com. UNESCO, 1996—; mem. ethics com. Human Genome Orgn., London, 1995—, mem. UN Jud. Group on Strengthening Jud. Integrity, Vienna, 2000—. Decorated Companion Order of Australia, Companion Order St. Michael and St. George; recipient Australian Human Rights medal Australian Human Rights and Equal Opportunity Commn., 1991, UNESCO prize for Human Rights Edn., 1998. Mem. Australian Acad. Forensic Scis. (pres. 1987-89), Commonwealth Sci. Indsl. Rsch. Orgn. (exec. com.), Acad. Forensic Sci. Office: High Ct Australia, Canberra 2600, Australia

KIRBY, WILLIAM, olympic athlete; b. Perth, Australia, Sept. 12, 1975. Mem. swim team Australia; winner 100 meter butterfly Australian Championship, 1993; winner silver in 200 meter butterfly Commonwealth Games, 1998; winner gold in 4x200 meter freestyle relay Pan Pacific Championship, 1999; fourth pl. in 200 meter freestyle Telstra Selection Trials, 2000, third pl. in 200 meter butterfly, 2000; winner gold in 4x200 meter freestyle Olympics, Sydney, Australia, 2000. Named World Record Holder in 4x200 meter freestyle relay. Office: Australian Swimming Inc, PO Box 940, Dickson ACT 2602, Australia*

KIRCHER, JOHN JOSEPH, law educator; b. Milw., July 26, 1938; s. Joseph John and Martha Marie (Jach) K.; m. Marcia Susan Adamkiewicz, Aug. 26, 1961; children: Joseph John, Mary Kathryn. BA, Marquette U., 1960, JD, 1963. Bar: Wis. 1963, U.S. Dist. Ct. (ea. dist.) Wis. 1963, U.S. Ct. Appeals (7th cir.) 1992. Sole practice Port Washington, Wis., 1963-66; with Def. Research Inst., Milw., 1966-80, research dir., 1972-80; with Marquette U., 1970—, prof. law, 1980—, assoc. dean acad. affairs, 1992-93; chmn. Wis. Jud. Council, 1981-83. Author: (with J.D. Ghiardi) Punitive Damages: Law and Practice, 1981, 2d edit (with C.M. Wiseman), 2000; editor Federation of Insurance and Corporate Counsel Quarterly; mem. editorial bd. Def. Law Jour.; contbr. articles to profl. jours. Recipient Teaching Excellence award Marquette U., 1986, Disting. Service award Def. Research Inst., 1980, Marquette Law Rev. Editors' award, 1988. Mem. ABA (Robert B. McKay Professor award 1993), Am. Law Inst., Wis. Bar Assn., Wis. Supreme Ct. Bd. of Bar Examiners (vice chair 1989-91, chair 1992), Am. Judicature Soc., Nat. Sports Law Inst. (adv. com. 1989—), Assn. Internationale de Droit des Assurances, Scribes. Roman Catholic. Office: PO Box 1881 Milwaukee WI 53201-1881

KIRCHER, LYNN FRANCIS, artist; b. Decatur, Ill., Oct. 18, 1947; s. Edward John Kircher and Betty Gene Kekeisen; m. Jane K., Dec. 14, 1980; children: Melisa, Khristopher, Jennifer. Diploma in fine and applied art, Colo. Inst. Art, Denver, 1970, AAS, 1997. Cert. Colo. State Bd. Cmty.

Colls., 1978-98. Educator Colo. Inst. Art, 1978-97; artist Kircher & Assocs., Denver, Jarasco, Colo., 1978—; egional ednl. cons. Houghton Mifflin, Colo. region, 1992—; faculty trainer Bel Ray Inst., Denver, 1998—. Sculptor numerous commissioned works. Chmn. bd. Art at the Stations, Inc., Denver, 1995-97; mem. visual arts selection com., Denver Sch. Arts, 1993-93; arts cons. Costilla County Econ. Devel. Coun., San Luis, Colo., 1989—; mem. profl. devel. com., Colo. Pvt. Sch. Ass.n, Denver, 1995. With USN, 1965-68. Decorated Bronze Star; named to Hall of Fame, Colo. Inst. Art, 1994. Mem. AIA (assoc.), Nat. Sculpture Soc. Roman Catholic. Avocations: fishing, racquetball, exploring. E-mail: kircher@amigo.net. Home and Studio: Kircher and Assocs PO Box 53 Jaroso CO 81138-0053

KIRCHGÄSSNER, GEBHARD, economist, educator; b. Konstanz, Germany, Apr. 15, 1948; s. Paul and Marianne (Stief) K.; m. Maria Verhaagh, Aug. 13, 1976; 1 child. Diploma, U. Konstanz, 1973, DrRerPol, 1976. Asst. U. Konstanz, Germany, 1976-77, Technol. U. Zurich, Switzerland, 1977-84; prof. econs. U. Osnabruck, Germany, 1984-92, U. St. Gallen, Switzerland, 1992—; dean dept. econs. U. St. Gallen, 1999—; dir. Swiss Inst. for Internat. Econs. and Applied Econ. Rsch., St. Gallen, 1992—.

KIRCHHOFF, VOLKER WALTER JOHANN HEINRICH, laboratory director; b. Berlin, Aug. 9, 1942; arrived in Brazil, 1951; s. Hermann D.F. and Lilly E.K.K. Kirchhoff; m. Maria Antonietta Copriva, Mar. 20, 1970; children: Denis, André. BSc, E.E. Mauá, São Paulo, 1969; MSc, INPE, São José dos Campos, Brazil, 1972; PhD, Pa. State U., 1975. Rsch. assoc. Inst. Nat. Pesquisas Espaciais, São José dos Campos, 1975-80, lab. head, 1985—, asst. dir., 1989-92, dep. dir., 1993—; Brazilian coord. Inst. Nat. Pesquisas Espaciais/NASA-SCAR-B, 1995; mem. Internat. Ozone Commn., Geneva, 1990-96, Internat. Assn. Meteorology Atmospheric Physics, 1990—. Author: Queimadas na Amazônia, 1992, Ozônio e Radiação UV-B, 1995; editor-in-chief SBGf, 1992-94. Named one of Brazil's Most Important Scientists, Super Interessante, 1996; recipient Group Achievement award NASA, 1994, Ozone Layer award Ministry Environment, Brasilia, 1997. Mem. AGU, COSPAR/Brazil. Home: Apt 101, Afonso César de Siqueira, 12245000 Sao Jose de Campos Brazil Office: INPE, CP 515, 12201970 Sao Jose dos Campos Brazil

KIRCHNER, EMIL JOSEPH, political science educator; b. Waldberg, Bavaria, Germany, Mar. 19, 1942; arrived in Eng., 1974; s. Emil and Anna (Soeder) K.; m. Joanna Bartlet, Dec. 13, 1975; children: Tristan, Stefan. Diploma in internat. trade, Akademie fur Welthandel, Frankfurt, 1965; BA in Econs., Case Western Res. U., 1969, MA in Polit. Sci., 1970, PhD in Politics and Internat. Politics, 1976. Tchg. asst. Case Western Res. U., 1971-72; temp. lectr. U. Essex, Colchester, 1974-77, lectr., 1977-90, sr. lectr., 1990-92, prof. European studies, 1992—, Jean Monnet chair in European polit. integration, 1997—; vis. prof. U. Conn., 1986-87, Charles U., Prague, 1997; cons. Inst. for Advanced Rsch. and Long-Range Planning, Paris, 1991-93, Metra Sofres, 1995, European Svcs. Devel., 1998. Author: Decision-Making in the European Community: The Council Presidency & European Integration, 1992; co-author: Recasting the European Order Security Architecutres and Economic Cooperation, 1997, The Politics of the New Europe, 1997, The Future of European Security, 1994, The Federal Republic of Germany and NATO, 40 Years After, 1992; exec. editor Jour. European Integration, 1997—; editor: Decentralization and Transition in the Visegrad: Poland, Hungary, the Czech Republic and Slovakia, 1999; co-editor: Com. Governance in the European Union, 2000. Gov. Colchester Royal Grammar Sch., 1993—. Jean Monnet fellow European U. Inst. (Italy), 1985-86. Mem. Assn. for the Study of German Politics, Univ. Assn. for Contemporary Studies. Avocations: walking, swimming, traveling. Office: U Essex Dept Govt, Wivenhoe Park Colchester, Essex CO4 3SQ, England

KIRCHNER, JAMES WILLIAM, retired electrical engineer; b. Cleve., Oct. 17, 1920; s. William Sebastian and Marcella Louise (Stuart) K.; m. Eda Christene Landfear, June 11, 1950 (dec. May 1977); children: Kathleen Ann Kirchner Duda, Susan Lynn Kirchner Buonpane. BS in Elec. Engring., Ohio U., 1950, MS, 1951. Registered profl. engr., Ohio. Instr. elec. engring. Ohio U., Athens, 1950-52; mgr. liaison engring. Lear Siegler Inc., Maple Heights, Ohio, 1952-64; coordinator engring. services Case Western Res. U., Cleve., 1964-72, gen. mgr. Med. Ctr. Co. (CWRU), 1972-91; ret., 1991; sec. of corp. Thermagon, Inc., Cleve., 1992. Mem. Portage County Republican Exec. Com., 1961-62; treas. PTA, Aurora, Ohio, 1963-65, v.p., 1965-66; mem. The Ch. in Aurora, 1956—. Served with USAAF, 1942-45, PTO. Mem. NSPE (life), IEEE (life), Ohio Soc. Profl. Engrs. (life), Cleve. Engring. Soc. (chmn. environ. com. 1976), Am. Soc. Engring. Edn. (life). Home: Reserves of Aurora 535 Treetop Ct Aurora OH 44202-7317

KIREZIS, NICK STAMATIOS, economist, researcher, consultant; b. Heraklion, Crete, Greece, Oct. 24, 1966; s. Stamatios Nick Kirezis and Maria Dimitrios (Mavrogianni) Kirezi; m. Evagelia Dimitrios Bliamti, Sept. 27, 1997. B, Econ. U., Athens, 1988, postgrad. Mktg. mgr. Halkiadakis SA, Heraklion, 1991-94, Creta Channel SA, Heraklion, 1994-95; mktg. and rsch. mgr. Diktis DE, Heraklion, 1995—; prof. mktg. TEI of Heraklion, 1990—. Author: Managing Supermarkets, 1994. Pres. ENOMAR, Heraklion, 1998—; active Econ. Chamber, Heraklion, 1992, Consumer Instn., Heraklion, 1996, ESOMAR, Brussels, 1998. Avocations: reading, fishing, chess, football, travelling. Home: 23 Kondylaki St, 71305 Heraklion Crete, Greece Address: Diktis OE, 2 Malikouti St, 71202 Hezaclion Crete, Greece

KIRIAKOPOULOS, KOSTAS MARIOS, civil engineer; b. Athens, Greece, Jan. 28, 1960; came to U.S., 1978; s. Marios K. and Rodo A. (Thermidou) K. BS, Iowa State U., 1982, MS, 1985. Registered profl. engr. Teaching asst. math. dept. Iowa State U., Ames, 1981-82, grad. teaching asst., 1982-85, rsch. asst. civil engring., 1984-85; staff engr., site inspector Woodward-Clyde Cons., Wayne, N.J., 1985-86; civil engr. Greek War Navy Pub. Works Dept., Athens, Greece, 1987-89; civil engr., constrn. mgr. Gen. Constrn. Co., Athens, Greece, 1989—; cons. in field. Recipient Grad. scholarship Iowa State U., 1984-85. Mem. ASCE, Am. Soc. Testing Materials, Tech. C. of Greece. Christian Orthodox. Avocations: tennis, fishing, billiards, yachting. Home: 78 Peloponnisou Str, Agia Paraskevi, 15341 Athens Greece Office: Gen Constrn Co, 30 Kapodistriou Ave, 15123 Athens Greece

KIRICK, DANIEL JOHN, agronomist; b. Port Jervis, N.Y., Nov. 8, 1953; s. Daniel and Mary Theresa Kirick; m. Jean Marie Guse, Sept. 27, 1986; children: Nicholas, John, Kristina, Kimberly. BA in Biology, History, U. Minn., Duluth, 1976; BS in Agronomy, U. Minn., St. Paul, 1977. Cert. profl. agronomist. Agronomist Delft (Minn.) Farm Chems., 1978, Skelly Fertilizer, Trimont, Minn., 1978-80, Mower County Svc. Co., Sargeant, Minn., 1980-86, Cenex Supply, Ellis, S.D., 1986-88, Rice (Minn.) Farm Supply, 1988-91, Kirick Agronomy Svcs., St. Cloud, Minn., 1992—. Mem. Comty. Edn. Devel. Adv. Coun., Sauk Rapids, Minn., 1990-94, Youth Devel. Bd., Sauk Rapids, 1990, Benton County Ext. Com., 1993-98, Ctrl. Minn. Forage Coun., 1994—. Mem. AAAS, Weed Sci. Soc. Am., Soil Sci. Soc. Am., Crop Sci. Soc. Am., Am. Soc. Agronomy. Roman Catholic. Home: PO Box 206 Rice MN 56367-0206 Office: Kirick Agronomy Svcs 9144 County Road 4 Saint Joseph MN 56374-9748

KIRIHATA, TOSHIAKI, computer engineer, researcher; b. Siga, Japan, Apr. 10, 1961. BS in Precision Engring., Shinshu U., Nagano, Japan, 1984, MS in Precision Engring., 1986. Rschr. IBM Japan Ltd., Tokyo, 1986-87, IBM Yasu Tech. Applications Lab., Japan, 1987-89; lead engr. IBM Yasu Tech. Applications Lab., 1989-91, IBM Microelectronics Divsn., Burlington, Vt., 1991-93, IBM, Hopewell Junction, N.Y., 1993-96; project leader IBM, Hopewell Junction, 1996-97; product design team leader IBM T.J. Watson Rsch. Ctr. IBM Rsch., Hopewell Junction, N.Y., 1997-99; product design mgr. IBM Microelectronics, Hopewell Junction, N.Y., 2000—. Mem. IEEE (sr.). Office: IBM 1580 Rte 52 Bldg 630 Hopewell Junction NY 12603

KIRIIKE, NOBUO, psychiatrist, educator; b. Osaka, Japan, June 4, 1946; s. Masanobu and Harue (Hiraoka) K.; m. Hiroko Watanabe, Apr. 26, 1976; children: Yoshiko, Yusuke, Yasuko, Atsuko. MD, Med. Sch. Osaka City U., 1971, postgrad., 1971-73, PhD, 1981. Residency Osaka City U. Med. Sch. Hosp., 1973-75; asst. Osaka City U. Med. Sch., 1975-77, 80-82, lectr., 1982-92, assoc. prof., 1992-99, prof., chmn., 1999—; with Kitano Hosp., Osaka, 1977-78; rsch. fellow dept. pharmacol. rsch. Nebraska State U., 1979-80; mem. psychiat. rev. bd. Osaka City Govt., 1993—. Contbr. articles to profl. jours. Fellow Japanese Soc. Psychiat. Diagnosis, Japanese Soc. Biol. Psychiatry; mem. Japanese Soc. Psychiat. Neurology, Internat. Soc. Neurochemistry; N.Y. Acad. Sci. Avocations: music, golf. Home: Sumiyoshi-ku, 1-10-19 Tezukayamanishi, Osaka 558-0052, Japan Office: Osaka City U Med Sch, 1-4-3 Asahi-cho Abeno-ku, Osaka 545-8585, Japan

KIRILA, CAROL ELIZABETH, osteopathic physician, internist; b. Mount Clemens, Mich., Oct. 28, 1952; d. Andrew William and Mary Margaret (Schmeltz) K. Diploma, Rsch. Med. Ctr. Sch. Nursing, Kansas City, Mo., 1974; BS in Biology, U. Mo., Kansas City, 1987; DO U. Health Scis., Coll. Osteo. Medicine, 1991. RN, Mo. Lab. asst. Lakeside Hosp., Kansas City, 1969-74, RN, inservice instr., 1976-87, part time staff nurse, relief supr., 1988-91; staff nurse Children's Mercy Hosp., Kansas City, 1974, U. Health Scis. Hosp., Kansas City, 1974-76, Rsch. Med. Ctr., Kansas City, 1976; part time staff nurse Kendallwood Pvt. Duty, 1988-91; intern Still Regional Med. Ctr., Jefferson City, Mo., 1991-92; resident internal medicine U. of Mo. Kansas City Sch. of Medicine, 1992-95; staff physician Internal Medicine Assn. St. Joseph, Mo., 1995-96, Permante Med. Group, Kansas City, Mo., 1996-98; mem. faculty U. of Health Scis., Coll. Osteo. Medicine, 1998—. Catechumenate sponsor St. James Ch., Kansas City, 1982; mem. Manheim Park Neighborhood Assn., Kansas City, 1982-91. Recipient cert. of recognition U. Health Scis. Coll. Osteo. Medicine, 1988-89, Outstanding Svc. and Achievement award U. Mo.-Kansas City, 1986, Pres.'s award Mo. Assn. Osteo. Physicians and Surgeons, 2000. Mem. Am. Osteo. Assn. Democrat. Episcopalian. Avocations: plants, reading, music, cooking, fitness. Home: 217 W 99th St Kansas City MO 64114-4170

KIRILLOV, IGOR RAFAILOVICH, engineering executive, researcher; b. Vologda, USSR, Mar. 6, 1940; s. Rafail M. Zinchin and Anna A. Kirillova; m. Tatyiana E. Bobrova, July 29, 1960; children: Natasha, Igor, Andrey. Student, Efremov Inst., Leningrad, USSR, 1970, DSc, 1984. Engr. Efremov Inst., 1963-66, sr. engr., 1966-70, sr. rschr., 1970-75; lab. head Efremov Inst., Leningrad-St. Petersburg, 1975—. Co-author: Calculation and Design of Liquid Metal MHD Machines, 1978 (Russian), Magnetohydrodynamics in Nuclear Energetics, 1987 (Russian); contbr. articles to profl. publs.; patentee in field. Recipient Bronze medal All-Union Indsl Exhbn., 1980, Silver medal, 1987. Mem. RF Acad. of Sci. (coun. on direct energy conversion 1995—), Internat. Hydromag Assn. (coun. mem. 1995-97). Avocations: skiing, hiking. Office: Efremov Inst, Sovetsky Prospect 1, 189631 Saint Petersburg Russia

KIRITSAKIS, APOSTOLOS PAUL, food products educator, researcher; b. Elos, Chanea, Crete, Greece, Apr. 23, 1944; s. Konstantinos and Helen (Zoyridakis) Kiritsakis; m. Eleftheria Karamesinis, Aug. 15, 1947; children: Kostas, Ioanna. Bachelor, Aristotel U., Thessaloniki, Greece, 1968; MS, Mich. State U., 1977, PhD, 1983; hon. diploma, U. WA, New Norcia, 1998; PhD, Assn. Tech. Edn. Inst., Thessaloniki, 1999. Rschr. Ministry of Agr., Chanea, Greece, 1972-74, 78-80; prof. Technol. Ednl. Inst., Thessaloniki, 1981—; chmn. dept. Technol. Edn. Inst., Thessaloniki, 1984-85; cons. Satuco, Tunis, Tynisia, 1998—, Olive Oil Cos., Greece, 1992—, Olive Oil Cos., Albania, 2000, Olive Cos., Melbourne, Australia, 2000. Author: Olive Oil (in Greek), 1988 (Award 1988), (in English), 1991, 2d edit., 1998, El Aceite de Oliva, 1992, (in Spanish); assoc. editor Jour. Am. Oil Chem. Soc., 2000—. Officer Artillery, 1969-71. Recipient Disting. Honor, Hellenic Club of Writers, Athens, 1998, Kissamos Club Athens, 1999. Mem. Club of Cretan Chestnut Festival (pres. 1983—), Am. Chemists Soc., Olive Acad. of Italy, Fulbrighters of Thessaloniki (pres. 1998—), Pancretan Assn. Macedonia. Orthodox. Avocations: traveling, organizing social meetings, folk dance, folklore. Home: 86 P Syndika St, 542-48 Thessaloniki Greece Office: Sch Food Tech and Nutrition, Dept Food Tech/Tech Edn Ins, 54101 Thessaloniki Greece

KIRIYENKO, SERGEI, former prime minister of Russia; b. Russia, July 27, 1962. Grad., Gorki Inst. Rwy. Transport, 1984. Sec. Komsomol, Gorki Krasnoye Sormovo Shipyard; pres. Garantiya Bank, Nizhniy Novgorod, Russia; head Norsi-Oil, Nizhniy Novgorod, 1996-97; 1st dep. min. fuel and energy Russian Fedn., 1997, min. fuel and energy, 1997, acting prime min., 1998; chmn. com. reps. Govt. Gzaprom, 1997; now leader Union Right Forces in Russia. *

KIRK, BRIAN DOUGLAS, sculptor, art educator; b. Washington, Mar. 16, 1953; s. Russell Daler and Lillian Kirk; m. Lisa Kirk, June 20, 1984 (div. Aug. 1994); children: Jesse Ryan, Jeremy Matthew; m. Cynthia Kirk, Aug. 4, 1994. Student, St. Mary Coll. of Md., 1972-74; BA in Fine Arts, George Washington U., 1976. Cert. tchr. art edn. K-12, Va. Program dir. Army Cmty. Svcs. Dept. of Def., Mons, Belgium, 1985-87; program supr. Loudoun County Dept. of Youth and Family Svcs., Leesburg, Va., 1987-93; art tchr. Broad Run H.S., Ashburn, Va., 1993—; welded sculpture instr. Art League, Alexandria, Va., 1997—; tchr./mentor Smithsonian Instn. Naturalist Ctr., Leesburg, 1996-98. One man shows include metal sculpture New Metal Works, 1998 (Art Club Washington award), Imerging Artist, 1997 (Arnold Porter award); photography exhibited Faces and Places of Asia, 1998, Writers Group-Poet Lore, 1998, 99. Mem. art adv. com. George Washington U., Ashburn, Va., 1998—. Fulbright Tchr. fellow Internat. Inst. of Edn., Tokyo, 1997, Weedon Asian Studies fellow U. Va., Beijing, 1998. Mem. Internat. Sculpture Ctr., Washington Sculptors Group. Avocations: fishing, canoeing, galleries and museums. Home and Office: 161 Bell Hollow Ln Bluemont VA 20135-4822

KIRK, CASSIUS LAMB, JR., lawyer, investor; b. Bozeman, Mont., June 8, 1929; s. Cassius Lamb and Gertrude Violet (McCarthy) K.; AB, Stanford U., 1951; JD, U. Calif., Berkeley, 1954. Bar: Calif. 1955. Assoc. firm Cooley, Godward, Castro, Huddleson & Tatum, San Francisco, 1956-60; staff counsel for bus. affairs Stanford U., 1960-78; chief bus. officer, staff counsel Menlo Sch. and Coll., Atherton, Calif., 1978-81; chmn. Eberli-Kirk Properties, Inc. (doing bus. as Just Closets), Menlo Park, 1981-94; mem. summer faculty Coll. Bus. Adminstrn. U. Calif., Santa Barbara, 1967-73; past mem. adv. bd. Allied Arts Guild, Menlo Park; past nat. vice chmn. Stanford U. Annual Fund; past v.p. Palo Alto C. of C. With U.S. Army, 1954-56. Mem. VFW, Stanford Faculty Club, Order of Coif, Phi Alpha Delta. Republican. Home and Office: 1330 University Dr Apt 52 Menlo Park CA 94025-4241

KIRK, DONALD, journalist; b. New Brunswick, N.J., May 7, 1938; s. Rudolf and Clara (Marburg) K.; m. Susanne Smith, May 31, 1965 (div.); m. Emiko Hayashi, Dec. 12, 1985 (div.); children: James Paul, John Winston. AB, Princeton U., 1959; MA, U. Chgo., 1965; postgrad. (Ford Found. fellow), Columbia U., 1964-65. Reporter Chgo. Sun-Times, 1960-61, N.Y. Post, 1961-64; free lance corr., writer, 1965—; Asia corr. Washington Star, 1967-70; Far East corr. Chgo. Tribune, 1971-74, N.Y. and UN corr., 1975-76; world editor, spl. corr. USA Today, 1982-90; vis. fellow Cornell U., Ithaca, N.Y., 1986-88; Fulbright rschr., Philippines, 1995-96. Author: Wider War: The Struggle for Cambodia, Thailand and Laos, 1971, Tell It To The Dead: Memories of a War, 1975, Korean Dynasty: Hyundai and Chung Ju Young, 1994, Tell It To The Dead: Stories of a War, 1996, Looted: The Philippines After the Bases, Business Guide to the Philippines, 1998, Korean Crisis: Unraveling of the Miracle in the IMF Era, 2000. Recipient Page One award Chgo. Newspaper Guild, 1960; citations Overseas Press Club, 1967, 72, 73, Best Asia article award 1974; George Polk Meml. award for fgn. reporting, 1975, Fulbright scholar, New Delhi, India, 1962-63; Edward R. Murrow fellow Coun. Fgn. Rels., N.Y.C., 1974-75. Mem. Am. Soc. Journalists and Authors, Soc. Profl. Journalists. Clubs: Nat. Press (Washington); Overseas Press (N.Y.C.); Fgn. Corrs. (Hong Kong); Internat. House of Japan. Home: 4343 Davenport St NW Washington DC 20016-4513

KIRK, JAMES ALLEN, mechanical engineering educator; b. Cleve., Nov. 3, 1944; s. Charles J. and Helen T. (Tulas) K.; m. Cynthia L. Ambler, Feb. 6, 1976; 1 child, Heather E. BSEE, Ohio U., 1967; MSME, MIT, 1969, PhD, 1972. Registered prof. engr., Md., Ohio. Rsch. engr. Ford Motor Co., Dearborn, Mich., 1966-67; rsch. assoc. MIT, Cambridge, Mass., 1968-72; asst. prof. mech. engring. U. Md., College Park, 1972-77, assoc. prof. mech. engring., 1977-86, prof. mech. engring., 1986-98, prof. emeritus mech. engring., 1998—; pres. Flywheel Sys., Inc., 1997-2000; pres. FARE, Inc., College Park, Md. 1988—; owner Kirk Cons. Co., College Park, Md., 1977-88. Author: Scientific Automobile Accident Reconstruction, 1992, Vehicle Dynamics and Tire Forces, 1993, Forensic Engineering, 1993; contbr. articles to profl. jours. Mem. ASME, ASM Internat., Am. Soc. Engring. Edn. (Dow Outstanding Young Faculty award 1977), Soc. Automotive Engring. (Ralph Teetor award 1975), Nat. Assn. Profl. Accident Reconstrn. Specialists, Soc. Mfg. Engrs. Achievements include designed magnetically suspended flywheel for NASA and emergency stopping system for U.S. capitol-house subway system. Home: 7210 Windsor Ln Hyattsville MD 20782-1045 Office: Fare Inc 4321 Hartwick Rd Ste 116 College Park MD 20740-3210

KIRK, JOHN MACGREGOR, lawyer; b. Flint, Mich., Mar. 9, 1938; s. R. Dean and Berenice E. (Mac Gregor) K.; m. Carol Lasko, June 8, 1971; children: John M. Jr., Caroline Dwyer. BA, Washington & Lee U., 1960, LLB, 1962; LLM in Taxation, NYU, 1967. Bar: Mich. 1962, U.S. Ct. Mil. Appeals 1966, U.S. Supreme Ct. 1966, U.S. Tax Ct. 1969, U.S. Dist. Ct. (ea. dist.) Mich. 1982, U.S. Ct. Appeals (6th cir.) 1983. Trial atty. tax divsn. U.S. Dept. Justice, Washington, 1967-72; assoc. Boyer & Briggs, Bloomfield Hills, Mich., 1972-74; ptnr. Butler, Long, Gust, Klein & Van Zile, Detroit, 1975-78; mem. Meyer, Kirk, Snyder & Lynch P.L.L.C., Bloomfield Hills, 1978—. Mem., past pres. Friends of Baldwin Pub. Libr., Birmingham, Mich., 1972—. Mem. ABA, State Bar Mich., Oakland County Bar Assn., Detroit Bar Assn., Birmingham Rotary, Walloon Yacht Club (treas., past commodore 1960—). Republican. Presbyterian. Home: 4350 Yale Ct Bloomfield Hills MI 48302-1669 Office: Meyer Kirk Snyder and Lynch PLLC 100 W Long Lake Rd Ste 100 Bloomfield Hills MI 48304-2773

KIRK, PAUL GRATTAN, JR., lawyer, administrator; b. Newton, Mass., Jan. 18, 1938; s. Paul Grattan and Josephine Elizabeth (O'Connell) K.; m. Gail Ellen Loudermilk, May 11, 1974. AB, Harvard Coll., 1960, LLB, 1964. Dir. ITT Corp., N.Y.C., 1989-98, Bradley Real Estate, Inc., Northbrook, Ill., 1990—, Rayonier Inc., Jacksonville, Fla., 1994—, Hartford (Conn.) Fin. Svcs. Group, 1994—, Hartford Life Ins. Co., Inc., 1994—; chmn., CEO Kirk and Assocs., Inc., Boston, 1990—; ptnr., of counsel Sullivan & Worcester, LLP, Boston, 1977-98. Trustee Stonehill Coll., 1984—, St. Sebastian's Sch., 1990—; treas. Dem. Party U.S., Washington, 1983-85, chmn., 1985-89; co-chmn. Commn. on Presdl. Debates, Washington, 1987—; chmn. John F. Kennedy Libr. Found., Boston, 1990—, Nat. Dem. Inst. for Internat. Affairs, Washington, 1992—; chmn. nominating com. Harvard Bd. Overseers, 1992-93, com. to visit dept. athletics, 1999—. Capt. U.S. Army, 1961-68. Recipient W. Averell Harriman Democracy award Nat. Dem. Inst. for International Affairs, 1988. Roman Catholic. Home: PO Box 1453 Marstons Mills MA 02648-5433 Office: Sullivan & Worcester LLP One Post Office Sq Boston MA 02109

KIRK, REA HELENE (REA HELENE GLAZER), special education educator; b. N.Y.C., Nov. 17, 1944; d. Benjamin and Lillian (Kellis) Glazer; 3 stepdaughters. BA, UCLA, 1966; MA, Ea. Mont. Coll., 1981; EdD, U. So. Calif., 1995. Life cert. spl. edn. tchr., Calif., Mont. Spl. edn. tchr. L.A., 1966-73; clin. sec. speech and lang. clinic Missoula, Mont., 1973-75; spl. edn. tchr. Missoula, Gt. Falls, Mont., 1975-82; br. mgr. YWCA of L.A., Beverly Hills, Calif., 1989-91; sch. adminstrn., ednl. coord. Adv. Schs. of Calif., 1991-94; dir. Woman's Resource Ctr., Gt. Falls, Mont., 1981-82, Battered Woman's Shelter, Rock Springs, Wyo., 1982-84; dir. Battered Woman's Program, Sweetwater County, Wyo., 1984-88, San Gabriel Valley, Calif., 1988; with Spl. Edn., Pasadena, 1994-96, prin., 1995; asst. prof. U. Wis., Platteville, 1996—; mem. Wyo. Commn. on Aging, Rock Springs; mem. Cmty. Action Bd. City of L.A. Pres., bd. dirs. battered woman's shelter, Gt. Falls; pres. Women's Resource Ctr., Gt. Falls, Religious Congregation, Rock Springs; founder, advisor Rape Action Line, Gt. Falls; founder Jewish religious svcs., Missoula; 4-H leader; hostess Friendship Force; Friendship Force ambassador, Wyo., Fed. Republic Germany, Italy; mem. YWCA Mont. and Wyo.; v.p. Coun. Devel. Disabilities, Wis.; bd. dirs. Coun. Children with Behavior Disorders, Wis., Family Advocates, Platteville; organizer Women's Readers Theater, Platteville, Wis.; advisor Pioneer Svc. Club, Platteville. Recipient Gladys Byron scholar U. So. Calif., 1993, Dept. Edn. scholar U. So. Calif., 1994, honors Missoula 4-H, Underkoffler Excellence in Tchg. award Faculty Senate, 2000; recognized as signigicant Wyo. woman as social justice reformer and peace activist Sweetwater County, Wyo.; nominated Wyo. Woman of the Yr., 1981, 82; honored by L.A. Mayor Bradley for Anti-Poverty work. Mem. Coun. for Exceptional Children (v.p. Gt. Falls 1981-82, bd. dirs., Professionally Recognized Spl. Educator 1998), Wis. Coun. Exceptional Children (bd. dirs., pres. S.W. region), Wis. Divsn. Mentally Retarded/Developmenally Disabled), Wis. Assn. Children with Behavior Disorders, Assn. for Children with Learning Disabilities (Named Outstanding Mem. 1982), Phi Delta Kappa, Delta Kappa Gamma, Kappa Delta Pi (co-counselor 2000), Pi Lamda Theta.

KIRKALDY-WILLIS, IAIN DUNBAR, social sciences educator; b. Nairobi, Kenya, Dec. 7, 1942; arrived in Can., 1960; s. William Hay and Peggy (Chapman) K.-W.; m. Mary Heather Elizabeth Dodds, Febr. 15, 1977 (div.); children: Christopher, Kimberley, Wenona, Anna Laara. BA, U. We. Ont., London, 1964; MA, U. B.C., Vancouver, 1966. Tchr. Ramakrishna Mission Ashram, Calcutta, India, 1966-68; in-svc. tng. program dir. Missionary Bros. of Charity, Calcutta, 1969; gardener Viittakivi Internat. Ctr., Hauho, Finland, 1971-74; maintenance person Saltings Open Ctr., Fordingbridge, England, 1975-76; social forestry field worker, rschr. Almora, Kumaon Hills, India, 1976-78; machine operator, floor mgr. Permanagh Wood Products, Derrygonnelly, No. Ireland, 1978-79; gardener Sylvia Koti Home-Sch. for Mentally Handicapped Kids, Lahti, Finland, 1979-80; mem. environ. healing pilot project Manali, Kulu Dist., India, 1980-81; homesteader and tchr. Kansalais Opisto, Hauho, 1982-84; tchr. Vittakivi Internat. Ctr., Hauho, 1984-88; homesteader, human identity rschr., Canary Island La Palma, 1989. Home and Office: Lista De Correos, 38730 Mazo Spain

KIRKBRIDE, MAX VERLYN, retired career officer; b. Ravenwood, Mo., May 15, 1916; s. John Wesley and Grace Elnora (Ross) K.; m. Martha Charlene Beedle, Apr. 20, 1946 (dec. July, 1979); 1 child, Max Verlyn Jr. BS, N.W. Mo. State U., 1940; grad., Command and Gen. Staff Coll., Ft. Leavenworth, Kans., 1946, Armed Forces Staff Coll., Norfolk, Va., 1955, U.S. Army War Coll., Carlisle Barracks, Pa., 1960. Commd. 2d lt. U.S. Army, 1940, advanced through grades to col., 1955, ret., 1971; dir. clerical sch., Armored Force Sch., Ft. Knox, Ky., 1940-43; dep. G1 and G1 (pers.) Hdqs XX Corps U.S. Army ETO, 1943-46; advisor; U.S. Mil. Mission to Iran, Teheran, 1948-50; battalion and regimental cmmdr. 1st cavalry divsn. U.S. Army, Korea, Japan, 1953-55; chief of staff No. Area Command, Frankfurt, Germany, 1960-63; dir. Standards & Systems Office, Pentagon Washington, D.C., 1963-66; dep. J5 and J5 (long range plans) U.S. Mil. Assistance Command, Saigon, Vietnam, 1966-67; prof. mil. sci. U. Calif., Davis, 1967-71; prof. mil. sci. U. Iowa, Iowa City, 1956-59; v.p. Rancho Bernardo Sr. Svcs., San Diego, Calif., 1974—; sec., bd. dirs. Oaks No. Mgmt. Corp. 2, San Diego, 1988—. Co-author (text book) Military Correspondence, 1940; supr. (reference book) Military Personnel, 1965. V.p. Rancho Bernardo Newcomers Club, San Diego, 1973, pres. Rancho Bernardo Newcomers Alumni, Inc. 1975; dir. tax counseling for the elderly, San Diego, 1976-92. Decorated Army Commendation medal, 1943, Bronze Star medal, 1945, U.S. Army, Legion of Merit, 1966, 67, 71; recipient U. Calif. medal, 1971. Republican. Home: 12751 Gateway Park Rd Poway CA 92064-2072

KIRKEBO, ARNE, physiology educator, scientist; b. Bergen, Norway, Mar. 23, 1934; s. Bjarne Gerhard and Klara (Gundersen) K.; m. Ågot Birkhaug, Nov. 25, 1966; children: Jon Birkhaug, Camilla Birkhaug. CandReal, U. Bergen, 1963, PhD, 1981. Asst. prof. U. Bergen, 1964-71, assoc. prof., 1971-92, prof. physiology, 1993—, head dept. physiology, 1984-85, 94-98. Sgt., Norwegian Army, 1953-54. Mem. Scandinavian Assn. Physiology. Avocations: wildlife, biology. Office: U Bergen Dept Physiology, Arstadvei 19, 5009 Bergen Norway

KIRKER, KELLEY VANCE, computer executive; b. Clark AFB, Philippines, Sept. 17, 1959; s. Thomas Duncan Kirkner and Carolyn Dawn Cooper-Kirkner; m. Jennifer Ann Kus, Apr. 3, 1982 (div. Sept. 1996); children: Ashley, Amy, Jason; m. Kara Lynn Anderson, June 12, 1997; 1 stepchild: Kristin. BS in Computer Sci., Trinity U., San Antonio, Tex., 1981. Programmer Texaco, Inc., Houston, 1982-83, programmer analyst, 1983-85; sr. programmer Texaco, Inc., 1985-86; v.p. programming M.L.S.I., Inc., 1987-89, v.p. prodn., 1989-94; pres./COO IT/IS, Inc., 1994-99, CEO/pres., 1999—; dir., COO Internet Law Libr., 2000—, Houston, Nat. Law Libr. Avocations: golf, softball. Office: IT/IS Inc 4301 Windfern Rd Houston TX 77041-8915

KIRKGAARD, VALERIE ANNE, talk radio host, writer, producer, consultant; b. Merced, Calif., Aug. 18, 1940; d. Basil Stuart and Audrey (Thompson) Coghlan; m. Alonzo Bryson Kirkgaard, Oct. 6, 1962 (div. Aug. 1983); children: Jennifer Alexandra, John Erik. AA, Santa Monica City Coll., 1961; BA, UCLA, 1968; M of Counseling, Goddard Coll., L.A., 1982; M. of Enlightenment, Sci. of Mind Ch., San Diego, 1992; Doctorate, Harrington U., 1999. Bd. dirs., care organizer Norwalk State Hosp., L.A., 1976-78; liaison to bd. dirs. Gay and Lesbian Cmty. Svcs. Ctr., 1976-99; therapist in pvt. practice Kirkgaard & Assocs, Pasadena, Pacific Palisades, Santa Monica, Calif., 1975—; ear coning educator, mfr., 1992—; prodr., host radio and TV Waking Up In America, 1987-99; radio host/prodr. Wake Up America, 1987-92; radio prodr. Terry Cole Whittaker; radio prodr./host Open Forum, Waking Up In America, others; spkr. in field. Author: Breakfast At Bob's, 1982, Take Two Breaths and Call Me in the Morning, 1988; environ. editor United Fitness Mag., 1992; columnist Hollywood Times, 1976, Century City News, 1990-92, others; prodr., host talk radio mag. Waking Up in America.inventor; author numerous articles; numerous appearances and interviews. Olympic Torch relayer Olympic Com., Santa Fe Springs, Calif., 1984. Mem. Calif. Assn. Marriage Family and Child Counselors, Women's Mus. of Art, Los Angeles County Mus. Art, World Vision, World Affairs Coun., The Hunger Project, Cousteau Soc., Mus. of Tolerance, Greater L.A. Press Club, Scriptwriters Network, Pacific Palisades C. of C., Roar Found. Avocations: polo, horseback riding, hiking, racquetball, reading, gardening. Office: Kirkgaard & Assocs 869 Via De La Paz Ste F Pacific Palisades CA 90272-5202

KIRKHAM, JAMES ALVIN, manufacturing executive; b. Sumner County, Tenn., June 18, 1935; s. Shirley Barnes and Ouida Redempta (Bursby) K.; m. Shirley Ann Clouse, Sept. 3, 1954; children: Denise Anne, James Alvin II, Hughe Allan. Welder Ind. Wire Co., 1952-54; driver Arthur Lowe Cigar & Candy Co., 1954-56; time study Insley Mfg. Co., 1957; salesman Am. Chicle Co., 1958-59; mgr. Ace Battery, Inc., Indpls., 1967—; v.p. L P Industries, Inc., Indpls., 1977—; pres. Rubber Recycling Corp., 1989—; ptnr. TKT Leasing, Indpls., 1978—, LDJ Leasing, Indpls., 1979—, Vets. Interstate Plan, Inc. Sec. Johnson County Pk. Bd.; bd. dirs. English Ave. Boys Club, State 4-H Horse and Pony Orgn.; pres. bd. dirs. Ind. Horse Coun. Found., Inc.; pres. PTO, Clark Twp. Sch. Dist.; v.p. Johnson County 4-H Fairboard; active Boy Scouts Am.; chmn. fundraising equestrian events 10th Pan Am. Games; treas. Ind. Horse Coun. Inc. Recipient Golden Boy award Indpls. Boys Club Alumni Assn., 1970; named Outstanding Show Mgr., Ind. State Fair, 1971; named to Ind. Horseman Hall of Fame, 1998. Mem. Am. Horse Show Assn., Ind. Saddle Horse Assn., Ind. Motor Truck Assn., Indpls. Motor Truck Assn., U.S. C. of C., Indpls. C. of C., Masons, Shriners, Moose Lodge, Ind. Pony Exhibitors Club, Am. Hackney Club, Ind. Pony of Am. Club, Ind. Shetland Pony Breeders Club. Home: 1213 N Matthews Rd Greenwood IN 46143-8343 Office: 2166 Bluff Rd Indianapolis IN 46225-1983

KIRKHAM, M. B., plant physiologist, educator; b. Cedar Rapids, Iowa; d. Don and Mary Elizabeth (Erwin) K. BA with honors, Wellesley Coll.; MS, U. Wis., PhD. Cert. profl. agronomist. Plant physiologist U.S. EPA, Cin., 1973-74; asst. prof. U. Mass., Amherst, 1974-76, Okla. State U., Stillwater, 1976-80; from assoc. prof. to prof. Kans. State U., Manhattan, 1980—; guest lectr. Inst. Water Conservancy and Hydroelectric Power Rsch., Inst. Farm Irrigation Rsch., China, 1985, Inst. Exptl. Agronomy, Italy, 1989, Agrl. U. Wageningen, Inst. for Soil Fertility, Haren, The Netherlands, 1991, Massey U., New Zealand, 1991, Lincoln U., New Zealand, 1998, Environ. and Risk Mgmt. Group HortResearch, 1998, Palmerston North, New Zealand, 1998; William A. Albrecht seminar spkr. U. Mo., 1994; vis. scholar Biol. Labs., Harvard U., 1990; vis. scientist environ. physics sect. dept. sci and indsl. rsch., Palmerston North, New Zealand, 1991, The Horticulture and Food Rsch. Inst. New Zealand, Ltd., Crown Rsch. Inst., Palmerston North, 1998, Landcare Rsch., Lincoln, New Zealand, 1998; participant Internat. Grassland Congress, New Zealand, 13th Internat. Soil Tillage Rsch. Orgn. Conf., Aalborg, Denmark; spkr. Internat. Conf. Vadose Zone Hydrology, Davis, Calif., 1995, 4th Congress European Soc. for Agronomy, Veldhoven, The Netherlands, 1996, Internat. Workshop Characterization and Measurement of Hydraulic Properties of Unsaturated Soil, Riverside, Calif., 1997, Internat. Symposium on Plant Growth and Environ., Seoul, 1993, 15th Internat. Congress of Soil Sci., Acapulco, 1994, 16th Internat. Conf., Montpellier, France, 1998; invited paper Internat. Grasslands Congress, New Zealand; invited keynote spkr. 5th Internat. Conf. on Biogeochemistry Trace Elements, Vienna, Austria, 1999, 2d Internat. Conf. on Contaminants in Soil Environ. in Australasia-Pacific Region, New Delhi, 1999; ; peer rev. panel mem. USDA/Nat. Rsch. Initiative, Washington, 1994. Cons. editor Plant and Soil Jour., 1979—; mem. editl. bd. BioCycle, 1978-82, Field Crops Rsch. Jour., 1983-91, Soil Sci., 1997—, Jour. Crop Prodn., 1998—; mem. editl. adv. bd. Trends in Agrl. Scis.-Agronomy, 1992—; contbr. more than 180 articles and papers to sci. jours. Recipient Best Reviewer award Water Resources Engring. divsn. Jour. Irrigation and Drainage Engring., ASCE, 1996; NSF postdoctoral fellow U. Wis., 1971-73, NDEA fellow, E.I. du Pont de Nemours and Co. summer faculty fellow, 1976, grantee NSF, USDA, Office Water Rsch. and Tech., U.S. Dept. Energy, Dept. Sci. and Indsl. Rsch., New Zealand; Kans. State U. faculty devel. grantee, New Delhi, 1999, Phi Kappa Phi scholar award Kansas State Univ., 2000. Fellow AAAS, Am. Soc. Agronomy (editorial bd. 1985-90), Soil Sci. Soc. Am. (travel grantee to internat. congress Japan 1990), Royal Meteorol. Soc., Crop Sci. Soc. Am. (editorial bd. 1980-84); mem. Am. Soc. Plant Physiology (editorial bd. 1982-87), Am. Soc. Horticultural Sci., Internat. Soil Tillage Rsch. Organ., Internat. Soil Sci. Soc. (elected 1st vice chmn. commn. soil physics 1994-98), Bot. Soc. Am., Am. Meteorol. Soc., Société Française de Physiologie Végétale, Japanese Soc. Plant Physiology, Scandinavian Soc. Plant Physiology, N.Y. Acad. Sci., Soc. for Exptl. Biology (London), Growth Regulator Soc. Am., Water Environment Fedn., Phi Kappa Phi, Gamma Sigma Delta, Sigma Xi (sec. Kans. State U. chpt. 1997-99). Home: 1420 Mccain Ln Apt 244 Manhattan KS 66502-4680 Office: Kans State U Dept Agronomy Throckmorton Hall Manhattan KS 66505-5501

KIRKINEN, HEIKKI, retired history educator; b. Liperi, North Kare, Finland, Sept. 22, 1927; s. Sulo Agapus and Anna (Hirvonen) K.; m. Maire Mirjam Rehvonen, June 20, 1953; 1 child, Teo Johannes. PhD, U. Helsinki, 1961. Lectr. history Finnish Orthodox Sem. Finland, Helsinki, 1953-59, U. Jyväskylä, 1960-62; rchr. Acad. Finland, Helsinki, 1962-66; assoc. prof. Sorbonne, U. Paris, Paris, 1966-70; prof. history U. Joensuu, 1970-90, rector, 1971-81, prof., dir. Inst. History, 1981-90; assoc. prof. Sorbonne Nouvelle U., France, 1984-85; assoc. dir. studies Ecole Pratique des Hautes Etudes, Paris, 1988-89; now rschr., writer. Author: Les Origines de la Conception Moderne de L'homme-Machine, 1960, Karelia Between East and West, I. Russian Karelia in the Renaissance (1478-1617), 1970, Karelia on the Battlefield, Karelia Between East and West, II, 1976, Europas Födelse, Bonniers Varldshistoria 7, 1984, Byzantine Tradition and Finland, 1987, Structures and Forces in History, 1987, The Roots of the Kalevala Tradition in North Karelia, 1988, Europe of Regions and Finland, 1991; co-author: History of the Karelian People, 1994, (with H. Sihvo) The Kalevala, An Epic of Finland and All Mankind, 1985, Provincial Government-New Level of Democracy, 1996; editor-in-chief: History of Russia and the Soviet Union, 1986, 2nd rev. edit. 2000; editor: Problems of Rural Development in Finland and in France, 1982; (with Jean Perrot) Le Monde Kalévaléen en France et en Finlande Avec un Regard sur la Tradition Populaire et L'épopée Brétonnes, 1987, Europe of Provincies and Finland, 1991, History of the Karelian People (with H. Shivo and P. Nevalainen) 1994, Provincial Government - New Level of Democracy, 1996; editor: Protection and Development of Our Intangible Heritage, 1999. Decorated comdr. Order of White Rose (Finland), comdr. Ordre Palmes Académiques, officer Order Nat. Mérite (France). Mem. European Acad. Scis., Arts and Letters, History Soc., Kalevala Soc. (hon.), Finnish Lit. Soc., Acad. Scis. Finland. Finnish Orthodox. Avocations: music, fishing. Home: Roskildenkatu 4D7, 80140 Joensuu Finland Office: U Joensuu, PO Box 111, 80101 Joensuu Finland

KIRKITSOS, PHILIP, air quality analyst, environmental consultant; b. Athens, Greece, Sept. 2, 1961; s. Diogenis and Nafsika K.; m. Catherine Pelekassi Kirkitsos, Dec. 26, 1991; 1 child, Alexander. BS in Physics, Aristotle U. Thessaloniki, Greece, 1983; MS in Meteorology, U. Athens, Greece, 1986; diploma in environ. studies, U. Aegean, Greece, 1987, PhD in Air Pollution (with honors), 1992; postgrad. diploma in distance edn., Open U. Greece, 1999. Environ. rschr. U. Aegean, Lesvos, Greece, 1986-95; tchr. Greece, 1991—, Pub. and Pvt. Insts., Greece, 1991—; cons. in field. Co-author: (chpt.) 1990, Waste Reduction Management: A Strategy for the Present and the Future, 1995; contbr. articles to profl. jours. Active Sea Turtle Protection Soc. Greece, Athens, 1984—, Mediterranean S.O.S. Network, Athens, 1990—; project mgr. Ecological Recycling Soc., Athens, 1990—, dir., 1995—; cons. organizing com. 2004 Olympic Games, Athens, 2000—. Named Spl. postgrad student U. Aegean, Lesvos, Greece, 1986-92. Home: 18B Themistokleous str, 15122 Amaroussion Greece Office: 3 Mamai Str, 10440 Athens Greece

KIRKLAND, JUDY JOYLENE, computer specialist; b. Great Falls, Mont., June 16, 1952; d. Howard Harold and Marvelle Ann (Plummer) Scoones; m. Paul M. Kirkland, May 22, 1976 (div. Feb. 1982); 1 child, William Howard. Cert in Acctg. Data Processing, Helena (Mont.) Vo-Tech Ctr., 1975; BS in Home Econs., Mont. State U., 1986. Adminstrv. asst. State of Mont., Helena, 1979-82; work/study sec. Mont. State U., Bozeman, 1982-86; title ins. clk. Am. Title, Billings, Mont., 1986-87; legal sec. Corner Pockets of Am., Billings, 1987-89; word processing operator Mont. State U., Bozeman, 1989-92; temporary sec. Tenera, Idaho Falls, Idaho, 1992-94, Express Svcs./INEL, Idaho Falls, 1995-96; adminstrv./sales asst. TCI Media Svcs., Idaho Falls, 1996-97; customer svc. rep. fin. Idaho Innovation Ctr., Idaho Falls, 1997—, quickbooks profl. advisor, 1998—; sec., dir. Musicians West Inc., Pocatello, Idaho, 1994—; computer trainer Computer Tng. Wheels, Idaho Falls, 1992-93; adminstrv. asst. Summer Music Festival, Pocatello, 1994-95. Graphic artist posters, brochures, programs Musicians West, 1st Presbyn. Ch., Idaho Falls Symphony Chorale, Mark Neiwirth, Brian Wilhour, 1992—. Crisis line counselor Bozeman Help Ctr., 1985-86; team mem. Life Tng. various locations, 1988-93; music vol. 1st Presbyn. Ch., Idaho Falls, 1996-97; adult CPR/1st aid cert. ARC, Idaho Falls, 1996—. Mem. Idaho Falls Symphony Chorale, Westminster Choir, Tau Pi Phi, Alpha Psi Omega. Avocation: piano, music theory, yoga, spirituality, reading. Home: PO Box 52094 Idaho Falls ID 83405-2094 Office: Idaho Innovation Ctr 2300 N Yellowstone Hwy Idaho Falls ID 83401-1662

KIRKOS, JOHN, orthopedic surgeon, educator; b. Alexandroupolis, Greece, Oct. 30, 1950; s. Margaritis and Veatriki (Arvanitidou) K.; m. Helen Panagiotopoulou, Nov. 26, 1977; children: Margaritis, Artemis. MD, Aristotle U., 1975, PhD, 1985. Cert. in orthopaedic surgery, Greece. Resident Kilkis (Greece) Gen. Hosp., 1979-82, registrar, 1982-87, sr. registrar, 1987-89; lectr. Med. Sch., Aristotle U., Thessaloniki, Greece, 1989-94, asst. prof., 1994—; clin. observer Royal Orthopaedic Hosp., Birmingham, Eng., 1991; vis. prof. SUNY, Buffalo, 1996, Med. U. S.C., Charleston, 1997. Contbr. articles to profl. jours. Capt. M.C., Greek Army, 1975-77. Am. Orthopaedic Assn. travelling fellow, 1997. Mem. Orthopaedic and Traumatology Assn. Macedonia and Thrace (pres. 1999—), Hellenic Assn. Orthopaedic Surgery and Traumatology. Greek Orthodox. Avocations: photography, fishing. Home: 138 Al Papanastasiou St, GR-54249 Thessaloniki Greece Office: G Gennimatas Gen Hosp, Ethnikis Aminis 41, GR-54635 Thessaloniki Greece

KIRKOW, PETER BORIS, economist, political scientist; b. Jena, Thuringia, Germany, June 19, 1966; s. Wassil and Gertrud (Sdunkowski) K. Diploma, Free U., Berlin, 1991; M in Social Sci., U. Birmingham, England, 1992, PhD in Polit. Economy, 1995. interpretor Russian and Bulgarian. Rsch. fellow U. Birmingham, 1995-98; sr. economist, analyst Ctrl., Eastern Europe ICE Securities, London, 1998—; cons. Gesellschaft für Technische Zusammenarbeit, Germany, 1995, Orgn. Econ. Cooperation and Devel., British Petroleum, 1997. Contbr. articles to profl. jours. Avocations: theatre, classical music, soccer. Office: ICE Securities Ltd, 119 Cannon St Sherborne Ho, London EC4N 5AT, England

KIRKPATRICK, ANNE SAUNDERS, systems analyst; b. Birmingham, Mich., July 4, 1938; d. Stanley Rathbun and Esther (Casteel) Saunders; children: Elizabeth, Martha, Robert, Sarah. Student, Wellesley Coll., 1956-57, Laval U., Quebec City, Can., 1958, U. Ariz., 1958-59; BA in Philosophy, U. Mich., 1961. Systems engr. IBM, Chgo., 1962-64; sr. analyst Commonwealth Edison Co., Chgo., 1981-97. Treas. Taproot Reps., DuPage County, Ill., 1977-80; pres. Hinsdale (Ill.) Women's Rep. Club, 1978-81. Club: Wellesley of Chgo. (bd. dirs. 1972-73). Home: 222 E Chestnut St Unit 8B Chicago IL 60611-2376

KIRKPATRICK, JEANE DUANE JORDAN, political scientist, government official; b. Duncan, Okla.; d. Welcher F. and Leona (Kile) Jordan; m. Evron M. Kirkpatrick; children: Douglas Jordan, John Evron, Stuart Alan. AA, Stephens Coll.; AB, Barnard Coll.; MA, Columbia U., PhD; postgrad. (French govt. fellow), Inst. Polit. Sci., U. Paris; LHD (hon.), Georgetown U., U. Pitts., U. Charleston, Hebrew U., Colo. Sch. Mines, St. John's U., Universidad Francisco Marroquin, Guatemala, Coll. of William and Mary, U. Mich., Syracuse U.; hon. degree, Loyola U., U. Rochester, Chgo. Asst. prof. polit. sci. Trinity Coll., 1962-67; assoc. prof. polit. sci. Georgetown U., Washington, 1967-73, prof., 1973—, Leavey prof., 1978—; sr. fellow Am. Enterprise Inst. for Pub. Policy Rsch., 1977—; mem. cabinet U.S. permanent rep. to UN, 1981-85; mem. Def. Policy Rev. Bd. (DPB), 1985-93; chair Commn. on Fail Safe and Risk Reduction (FARR), 1990-92; mem. Pres.'s Fgn. Intelligence and Adv. Bd. (PFIAD), 1985-89. Author: Elections USA, 1956, Perspectives, 1962, The Strategy of Deception, 1963, Mass Behavior in Battle and Captivity, 1968, Leader and Vanguard in Mass Society; The Peronist Movement in Argentina, 1971, Political Woman, 1974, The New Presidential Elite, 1976, Dismantling the Parties: Reflections on Party Reform and Party Decomposition, 1978, The Reagan Phenomenon, 1983, Dictatorships and Double Standards, 1982, Legitimacy and Force (2 vols.), 1988, The Withering Away of the Totalitarian State, 1990; syndicated columnist, 1985-97; contbr. articles to profl. jours.; editor, contbr. various pubs. Trustee Helen Dwight Reid Ednl. Found., 1972—, pres., 1990—. Recipient Disting. Alumna award Stephens Coll., 1978, B'nai B'rith Humanitarian award, 1982, Award of the Commonwealth Fund, 1983, Gold medal VFW, 1984, French Prix Politique, 1984, Dept. Def. Disting. Pub. Svc. medal, 1985, Bronze Palm, 1992, Disting. Svc. medal Mayor of N.Y.C., 1985, Presdl. Medal of Freedom, 1985, Jamestown Freedom award, 1990, Centennial medal Nat. Soc. DAR, 1991, Disting. Svc. award USO, 1994, Laureate of the Lincoln Acad. of Ill., Medallion of Lincoln, 1996, Jerusalem 3000 award, 1996, Casey medal of hon., 1998, Tomas Garrigue Masaryk Order, 1998. Mem. Internat. Polit. Sci. Assn. (exec. coun.), Am. Polit. Sci. Assn. (Hubert Humphrey award 1988), So. Polit. Sci. Assn. Office: Am Enterprise Inst 1150 17th St NW Washington DC 20036-4603

KIRKWOOD, JOHN ROBERT, neuroradiologist; b. Albany, N.Y., Mar. 19, 1941; s. John Kinloch and Rita Arline (Schwick) K.; m. Norma Starr Miller, June 17, 1967 (dec. Mar. 1973); 1 child, Timothy; m. Gale Arcuni Duncan, Aug. 3, 1974; children: James Duncan, Christopher, Allison. BA in Psychology magna cum laude, Yale U., 1963, MD, 1967. Diplomate Am. Bd. Med. Examiners; diplomate in diagnostic radiology and neuroradiology Am. Bd. Radiology. Intern Children's Hosp. Med. Ctr., Boston, 1967-68; resident in diagnostic radiology U. Calif. Med. Ctr., San Francisco, 1968-71; fellow, instr. neuroradiology Brigham Hosp., Boston, 1971-72; chief neuroradiology Walter Reed Army Med. Ctr., Washington, 1972-73; asst. prof. radiology George Washington U. Hosp., Washington, 1973-74; from asst. prof. to assoc. prof. radiology Tufts U. Sch. Medicine, Boston, 1974—; vice chmn. dept. radiology, Baystate Med. Ctr., Springfield, Mass., 1987-95, chmn. dept., 1997—, pres., 1997—; pres. Radiology and Imaging, Inc., Springfield, 1995-97, chmn., 2000—. Author: Essentials of Neuroimaging, 1990, 2d edit., 1995; contbr. rsch. articles to profl. jours. Major U.S. Army, 1972-73. Fellow Am. Coll. Radiology; mem. AMA, Am. Soc. Neuroradiology, Mass. Radiology Soc. (sec. 1995, v.p. 1998, pres.-elect 1999, pres. 2000—). Avocations: sailing, skiing, golf, art, music. Office: Dept Radiology Baystate Med Ctr 758 Chestnut St Springfield MA 01199-0001

KIROVSKAYA, IRINA ALEXEEVNA, chemistry educator, researcher; b. Talmenka, Altai, Russia, Feb. 10, 1938; d. Alexei Filippovitch and Anis'ya Evdokimovna (Sergeeva) Svintsov; m. Alexander Grigor'evitch Kirovskiy, July 25, 1959; children: Andrei Alexandrovitch Kirovskiy, Tatiana Alexandrovna Kirovskaya. Grad., State U., Tomsk, 1960, postgrad., 1963-64, D of Chem. Scis., 1988. Lectr., leader, holder chair State U., Tomsk, 1971-79; holder chair Tech. U., Omsk, 1980—, holder chair phys. chemistry sect. of rectors inst. soviet, 1982-87, prof., 1990—; cons. Inst. Chem. Problems of Microelectronics, Moscow, 1991—; Tomsk Electric Bull Factory; Sci Rsch. Inst. of Semiconductor Device, Tomsk, 1971—; Automatica Plant, Omsk; Omsk Sci. Rsch. Inst. of Device Construction, 1980—; mem. of Doctoral Dissertations Soviet, Tomsk, 1971—, Omsk, 1980—; chair of Dissertations Soviet, Omsk, 1998—. Author: Surface Properties of Diamond-Like Semiconductors, 1984, 1988, Absorption Processes, 1995, and others; 18 learning books; contbr. 350 articles to profl. jours.: Kinetics and Catalysis', Inorganic Materials, Physical Chemistry, Talanta, etc. Named Meritorious Sci. and Engring. worker, Pres. of Russia, 1994; Soros Prof., 1998; named one of leading women of the city Mayor of Omsk, 1995. Mem. Acad. Natural Sci. (chair regional divsn. 1997—), Internat. Acad. for Univ. Edn. Ecology and Nature using Petrov's Acad. of Sci. and Arts.; N.V. Acad. Scis., other, 1996—, D.I. Mendeleev All-Union Chemistry Soc. Knowledge (honored mem. Govt. 1984-88). Achievements include patents in gas detectors, catalysts, surface treatment. Avocations: planting flowers, swimming, reading, sewing, activities with grandson. Home: Ordzhonikidze 13 Kv 180, Omsk 644099, Russia Office: Omsk State Tech U, St Mira 11, Omsk 644050, Russia

KIRSCH, DONALD, financial consultant, writer; b. N.Y.C., Oct. 9, 1931; s. William and Eva (Wasserman) K.; m. Dorothy Ann Tejw, June 6, 1959; children: Mark Adam, Karen Rebecca Hoffman, Jonathan Bradford. BS, NYU, 1952. Editorial staffer Wall Street Jour., N.Y.C., 1952-53; writer AP, N.Y.C., 1954-55; pres. Wall Street Cons., N.Y.C., 1955—; chmn. Wall St. Group, Calif., Inc., Los Angeles, 1963—; chmn., pres. The Wall Street Group, Inc., N.Y.C., 1959—; adj. assoc. prof. NYU Grad. Sch. Arts and Sci., 1974-79; founding chmn. Typesetting Products, Inc., Talleres Graficos de Interamericanos, Inc., San Juan, P.R., 1962-80; chmn. Eurofinancing Ltd., 1968; bd. dirs. Co*star Entertainment Inc., MedNet Inc. (chmn. strategic planning com.), Medi-Mail Inc., Dialscan Systems, Audiofidelity Enterprises Inc., Interstate Nat. Dealers Svcs., Inc. Author: FInancial and Economic Journalism: Analysis Interpretation and Reporting, 1978 (Librarians Assn. award 1978), Investor Relations for the Over-the-Counter or Newly Public Company, (with others) The Handbook of Investor Relations; contbr. numerous articles to profl. jours. Trustee Nat. Symphony Orch. of the John F. Kennedy Ctr. for Performing Arts, treas. bd. trustees, 1996-98; trustee Big Bros.; mem. bd. mgrs. Episcopal Social Svcs., N.Y. Mem. N.Y. Soc. Security Analysts, Met. Pres'. Orgn., Young Pres. Orgn. (chmn. met. chpt. 1976-77), Chief Execs. Orgn., Am. Assocs. Royal Acad. Trust (mem. nat. coun.), Econs. Club N.Y., Friar's Club, The Metropolitan (N.Y.C.), Masons. Office: The Wall St Group Inc 32 E 57th St New York NY 10022-2513

KIRSCH, LAURENCE STEPHEN, lawyer; b. Washington, July 20, 1957; s. Ben and Bertha (Gomberg) K.; m. Celia Goldman, Aug. 19, 1979; children: Rachel Miriam, Max David. BAS, MS, U. Pa., 1979; JD, Harvard U., 1982. Bar: D.C. 1982, U.S. Ct. Appeals (3d cir.) 1983, (5th cir.) 1997, U.S. Dist. Ct. D.C. 1985, U.S. Ct. Appeals (D.C. cir.) 1985, U.S. Supreme Ct. 1987; registered environ. assessor, Calif. 1988. Law clk. to presiding judge Pa. Dist. Ct., Phila., 1982-83; vis. asst. prof. law U. Bridgeport (Conn.) Law Sch., 1983-84; assoc. Cadwalader, Wickersham & Taft, Washington, 1984-90, ptnr., 1991—; chmn. steering coms. Superfund. Editor-in-chief Indoor Pollution Law Report, 1987-91; mng. editor Harvard Environ. Law Rev., 1981-82; contbr. articles to profl. jours. Mem. ABA, Fed. Bar Assn., AAAS, Air Pollution Control Assn. (indoor air quality com.), Environ. Law Inst., Nat. Inst. Bldg. Scis. (indoor air quality com.), Am. Soc. Testing and Measurement (indoor air quality com.), Phi Beta Kappa. Home: 7212 Longwood Dr Bethesda MD 20817-2122 Office: Cadwalader Wickersham & Taft Ste 700 1333 New Hampshire Ave NW Washington DC 20036-1511

KIRSCH, LYNN, lawyer; b. New Orleans, Oct. 31, 1964; d. Henry C. and Therese M. ((Guenther) K. BS in Bus. Mgmt., Fla. State U., Panama City, 1992; JD, U. Ariz., 1995. Bar: Nev. 1995, U.S. Dist. Ct. Nev. 1995, U.S. Ct. Fed. Claims 1997, U.S. Ct. Appeals (9th cir.) 1998, U.S. Supreme Ct. 1999. Law clk. U.S. Atty.'s Office, Phoenix, 1993, Slutes, Sakrison, Evan, Grant & Pelander, Tucson, 1993-94, Lionel, Sawyer & Collins, Las Vegas, 1994; judicial extern Fed. Dist. Ct., Tucson, 1994; rsch. asst. U. Ariz., Tucson, 1994-95; law clk. Jacob & Fishbein, Tucson, 1994-95; assoc. Goold, Patterson, DeVore & Rondau, Las Vegas, 1995-97, Curran & Parry, Las Vegas, 1997-99, Bernhard & Leslie, Las Vegas, 1999—; mem. Justice of the Peace pro-tempore panel, Las Vegas Twp., County of Clark; alt. mcpl. ct. judge City of Las Vegas, 1999-2000. Article editor U. Ariz. Law Rev., 1994-95. Mem. Jr. League of Las Vegas, 1998—, league atty., 2000-2001; mem. State of Nev. Commn. on Postsecondary Edn., 1998—, Social Register of Las Vegas, House of Blues Found. Adv. Bd. Recipient Cert. Appreciation, U.S. Atty.'s Office, Phoenix, 1993, AmJur award Lawyers Coop. Publ., Tucson, 1993. Mem. ABA (litigation sect., young lawyers divsn., assoc. editor The Affiliate 1999-2000), ATLA, State Bar Nev. (chair young lawyers sect. 1999-2000, so. Nev. disciplinary bd., fee dispute arbitration com.), Clark County Bar Assn. (trial by peers com., cmty. svc. com.), Nev. Trial Lawyers Assn., So. Nev. Assn. Women Attys. Avocations: horseback riding, hiking, skydiving. Office: Bernhard & Leslie 3980 Howard Hughes Pkwy Ste 550 Las Vegas NV 89109-5905

KIRSCH, PEER, chemist, researcher; b. Herford, Germany, May 9, 1965; s. Peter Gerhard and Gerhild Marie Frieda (Rick) K.; m. Annette Gisela Schulz, Jan. 4, 1989; 1 child, Alexander David. Diplom-Chemiker, U. Heidelberg, Germany, 1990, Dr.rer.nat., 1993. Postdoctoral fellow U. Heidelberg, 1993, Riken Inst., Wako-shi, Saitama, Japan, 1994-95; head of lab. Merck KGaA, Darmstadt, Germany, 1995—. Contbr. articles to profl. jours.; patentee in field of liquid crystals. Recipient Grad. award fonds der Chemischen Industrie, Germany, 1993; Sci. and Tech. Agy. fellow, 1993, Feodor Lynen fellow Alexander von Humboldt Found., 1993. Mem. German Soc. Chemistry, Japanese Liquid Crystal Soc., Am. Chem. Soc. (fluorine divsn.). Avocations: chamber music (cello), history, Japanese literature. Office: Merck KGaA Liquid Crystals, Frankfurter Str 250, 64293 Darmstadt Germany

KIRSCH, URI, civil engineer, educator; b. Haifa, Israel, Dec. 22, 1938; s. Moshe and Ester (Karabchevski) K.; m. Aira Chorin, Aug. 16, 1962; children: Joab, Yael. BSc, Technion, Haifa, 1964, MSc, 1967, DSc, 1970. Cert. civil engring. Fulbright rsch. scholar UCLA, 1970-71; vis. prof. Case Western Res. U., Cleve., 1975-76, Carnegie Mellon U., Pitts., 1982-83; prof. Technion, Haifa, 1984—, Sigmund Sommer chair in structural engring., 1986, head divsn. structures, 1986-91, dep. to sr. v.p., 1995-96, sr. v.p., 1997—; vis. prof. Va. Tech., Blacksburg, 1988-89, U. Pitts., 1995; Carnegie fellow, vis. prof. Hriot-Watt U., Edinburgh, Scotland, 1989; Humboldt awardee, vis. prof. Essen (Germany) U., 1995, U. Pitts., 1995, U. Mich., 1999-2000; bd. dirs. Azorim Co., Tel Aviv. Author: Optimum Structural Design, 1981, Structural Optimization, 1993. Mem. Internat. Soc. for Structural and Multidisciplinary Optimization (v.p. 1995—). Avocations: music, hiking. Office: Technion, Dept Civil Engring, 32000 Haifa Israel

KIRSCHENBAUM, LISA L., portfolio manager, financial advisor; b. N.Y.C., May 7, 1971; d. J. Michael and Paulenne Lydia (Roeske) K. BA, Brandeis U., 1994. Lic. portfolio mgr. Pres., CEO Financier's Internat. Inc., Mendham, N.J., 1992-95; account exec. T.R. Winston, Inc., Bedminster, N.J., 1994-95; Quantum Portfolio Mgr., Fin. Advisor Prudential Securities, N.Y.C., 1995-97; fin. cons. Chase Investment Svcs. Corp., N.Y.C., 1997-99; v.p., sr. fin. exec. CitiGold Pvt. Banking Group, N.Y.C., 1999—. Mem. Women's Rep. Com. Somerset County, 1994—. Mem. Internat. Platform Assn., N.Y. Health and Racquet Club, Mendham Raquet Club. Republican. Avocations: skiing, chess, deep sea fishing, boating, tennis. Home: 80 Chapin Rd Bernardsville NJ 07924-1102 Office: CitiGold Fin Ctr 666 5th Ave Frnt 5 New York NY 10103-0001

KIRSCHKE, HEIDRUN, biochemist, educator; b. Kiel, Germany, Oct. 9, 1933; d. Werner and Herta (Preiser) Ribbeck; m. Siegfried Kirschke, Mar. 29, 1956; children: Gert, Ria, Andrea. Diploma in chemistry, Martin-Luther U., Halle-Wittenberg, Germany, 1960, Dr.rer.nat., 1966, habilitation, 1974. Sci. asst. faculty medicine Inst. Physiol. Chemistry Martin-Luther U. Halle-Wittenberg, 1961-80, head proteolysis rsch. group, 1980-95, prof. biochemistry, 1990—. Author: (with others) Methoden zur Aktivitätsbestimmung von Proteinasen, 1984, Lysosomal Cysteine Proteases, 2nd edit., 1998; editor: (with others) Proteinases in Mammalian Tissues and Cells, 1982, Proteolysis in Cell Functions, 1997; contbr. articles to profl. jours. Mem. Internat. Com. on Proteolysis (hon.), Gesellschaft für Biochemie und Molekularbiologie, Adv. Panel on Peptidase Nomenclature. Home: Jean-

Paul-Strasse 2, D-14558 Bergholz-Rehbrücke Germany Office: Martin Luther U Halle-Wittenberg, Hollystrasse 1, D-06097 Halle Germany

KIRSCHNER, KENNETH HAROLD, lawyer; b. Bklyn., Dec. 1, 1953; s. Samuel and Stella K.; m. Andrea Chase, Feb. 8, 1997. BS, Cornell U., 1975; JD, NYU, 1978, LLM, 1981. Bar: N.Y. 1979, U.S. Ct. Appeals (2d, 5th and D.C. cirs.), 1979, U.S. Dist. Ct. (so. and ea. dists.) N.Y., 1979, U.S. Supreme Ct. 1982. Assoc. Kelley Drye & Warren, N.Y.C., 1978-82; assoc. Breed Abbott & Morgan, N.Y.C., 1982-86, ptnr., 1986-93; ptnr. Kelley Drye & Warren LLP, N.Y.C., 1993—; adj. asst. prof. mgmt. NYU, 1988—. Contbr. articles to profl. jours. Office: Kelley Drye & Warren 101 Park Ave Fl 30 New York NY 10178-0062

KIRSCHNER, ROD, secondary education educator; b. St. Joseph, Mo., May 1, 1949; s. Jasper Jordan and Betty June (Newman) K.; m. Lelia Jane Huff, July 25, 1981; children: Bryce, Matthew, Rodney II. BA, Coll. of Emporia, 1972; MS, Northwest Mo. State U., 1977. Cert. secondary tchr., Ohio, Mo., Ky., Kans. Dir. high sch. rels. So. Ohio Coll., Cin.; asst. basketball coach St. Mary of Plains Coll., Dodge City, Kans.; tchr., Am. history, head basketball coach Dodge City Sr. High Sch.; tchr., basketball/soccer coach Summit County Day Boys Middle Sch., Cin.; tchr., dept. chair history and social studies, head basketball coach Beechwood High Sch., Ft. Mitchell, Ky., 1990-94; head basketball coach Horton H.S., 1994—; phys. edn. tchr. Everest Mid. Sch., Horton, M.S., 1995—; head track coach Horton H.S., 1997-99; conducted basketball camps in Antwerp, Ronse, Belgium, 1999, 2000. Contbr. to 40 Winning Strategies by 40 Winning Coaches. Mem. ASCD, NEA, AAHPERD, Nat. Assn. Basketball Coaches, Nat. Fedn. Interscholastic Coaches Assn., Kans. Coaches Assn., Kans. Edn. Assn., Kans. Assn. Health, Phys. Edn., Recreation, and Dance, Kans. Basketball Coaches Assn., KC, Lions Internat. (past pres.). Office: 1120 1st Ave E Horton KS 66439-1811

KIRSCHT, JUDITH MARY, English educator; b. Chgo., Sept. 21, 1933; d. Allan Titsworth and Loise Gardner Keynon; m. John Patrick Kirscht, Sept. 19, 1953 (div. Mar. 1974); children: Miriam Louise, Paula Clarice (dec.). BA, U. Chgo., 1953; MA, U. Mich., 1974, MFA, 1985. Lectr. U. Mich., Ann Arbor, 1979-86; lectr. English, U. Calif., Santa Barbara, 1986-98, acting dir. writing program, 1998—; part-time instr. Washtenaw C.C., Ann Arbor, 1976-79, Henry Ford C.C., Dearborn, Mich., 1977-79, Ea. Mich. U., Ypsilanti, 1978-79. Mem. Nat. Coun. Tchrs. English. E-mail: jkirscht@humanities.ucsb.edu. Home: 7043 Scripps Crescent St Goleta CA 93117-2953 Office: U Calif Writing Program Santa Barbara CA 93117

KIRSH, HERBERT, state legislator; b. N.Y.C., May 17, 1929; s. Issadore and Yetta K.; m. Sue Kirsch; children: Mike, Kevin, Bruce, Larry. BA with honors, Duke U., 1949. With Kirsh's Dept. Store, Clover, S.C., 1949-95; mayor pro tem Clover, S.C., 1971-75, mayor, 1975-79; mem. S.C. Ho. of Reps., 1979—; vice chmn. Edn. Improvement Act select com., mem. several coms.; chmn. bd. Clover Cmty. Bank; owner antique bus., 1995—. Scoutmaster Troop 2347 Boy Scouts Am.; past pres. Clover C. of C.; tchr. Sunday Sch. With USNR, 3 yrs. Named Clover Man of Yr., 1976, S.C. Legislator of Yr. S.C. County Govts., 1994, S.C. Firemen's Assn., 1994, Legislator of Yr. S.C. Recreation and Park Assn., 1989; recipient Disting. Svc. award S.C. Mcpl. Assn., 1985, Legis. award S.C. Commn. on Alcohol and Drug Abuse, 1985, Leadership award S.C. State Office Adult Edn., 1987, Svc. award Carolina Men's Apparel Club, 1992, S.C. Assn. Taxpayers, 1993, Svc. and Leadership award Carolina and Va. Fashion Exhibitors Inc., 1989. Mem. Clover Jaycees (charter), Clover Optimists (charter), Clover Rotary (charter), Mason, Shriners, Lions (nat. del.). Office: SC Ho of Reps PO Box 31 Clover SC 29710-0031

KIRSHBAUM, JON ALAN, information systems consultant, retired educational administrator; b. L.A., Nov. 5, 1942; s. George Alexander and Mary Elizabeth (Ball) K.; m. Anne Nofrey, Aug. 11, 1961 (div.); 1 child, Warren Ashley (dec.); m. Linda Louise Carl, Dec. 15, 1976; stepchildren: Gary Nicholas, Grant Adam. BS in Comprehensive Mktg., No. Ill. U., 1965, MBA in Fin., 1971, postgrad., 1988-93; MDiv, McCormick Theol. Seminary, Chgo., 1980. Cert. chief sch. bus. ofcl. IRD sales/DPD br. office adminstr. IBM Corp., Chgo., 1965-67; systems analyst/sr. assoc. planner IBM Corp., Endicott, N.Y., 1967-71; seminary asst. Lincoln Park Presbyn. Ch., Chgo., 1972-73; team/project leader Chgo. Pub. Schs., 1974-89, data base adminstr., 1989-92, supr. desktop pub., 1992-94, core team mem., Time re-engring. project, 1994-95; project leader Info. Technologies, Chgo., 1995-96; prin. cons. Keane, Inc., Lisle, Ill., 1996-99; sr. tech. analyst Mantiss Info. Corp. an Extant, Inc. Co., Chgo., 2000—; freelance travel writer, 1998—. Mng. editor: Today's Traveler Mag., Chgo., 1991-92, exec. editor/v.p. mktg., 1992-97. Mem. DuPage Art League, DuPage County (Ill.) Geneal. Soc. (bd. dirs. 1986-89, pres. 1989-90), DuPage County Hist. Soc., Glen Ellyn (Ill.) Hist. Soc., Morton Arboretum, Salem (Ohio) Hist. Soc., Project Mgmt. Inst. (midwest chpt.), Soc. Profl. Journalists, Chgo. Headline Club, N.Am. Travel Journalists Assn. (regional v.p. 1993-94), East West News Bur. Internat., Vernon County (Mo.) Hist. Soc., U.S. Lighthouse Soc. (New Dungeness chpt.), The Nature Conservancy (Ariz. chpt.), Rainshadow Natural Sci. Found., The Wheaton History Ctr., Field Mus. Natural History, Nat. Trust Historic Preservation. Presbyterian. Avocations: fishing, genealogy, photography, travel. Office: Extant Inc Chicago IL 60601

KIRSHENBAUM, RICHARD IRVING, public health physician; b. Bklyn., Aug. 19, 1933; s. Joseph and Anne (Hantman) K.; m. Jean Shicher, Aug. 17, 1957; children: Miriam, Susan, Rachel. AB, Temple U., 1955; DO, Phila. Coll. Osteo. Medicine, 1959; MPH, Columbia U., 1971. Diplomate Am. Bd. Preventive Medicine. Resident intern Met. Hosp., Phila., 1959-60; pvt. practice medicine Bklyn., 1960-70; resident in pub. health N.Y.C. Dept. Health, 1970-73, pub. health physician, 1973-81, regional health dir. for Queens County, 1977-80, chief epidemiologist for Manhattan Borough, 1980-81; pub. health physician N.Y. State Dept. Health, N.Y.C., 1981-98; retired, 1998. Contbr. articles to profl. jours. Lt. col. Med. Corps N.Y. Army NG, 1981-91, USAR, 1991-93. Recipient Physician's Recognition award AMA 1973, 76, 79, 82, 85, 88, 90, 93, 96, 98. Fellow Am. Coll. Preventive Medicine. Home: 313 Whitman Dr Brooklyn NY 11234-6935

KIRSNER, ROBERT SCOTT, dermatologist; b. Bklyn., Oct. 25, 1962; s. Bernard and Joan (Schneider) K.; m. Catherine Froelich, Apr. 13, 1991; children: William, Emily, Matthew. Student, So. Ill. U., 1980-81; BA in Chemistry, Tex. A&M U., 1984; MD, U. Miami, 1988, postgrad., 1996—. Diplomate Am. Bd. Dermatology, Nat. Bd. Med. Examiners, Am. Acad. Wound Mgmt. (accreditation adv. bd. 1997—, bd. dirs. 1997—). Intern in internal medicine U. Miami, Jackson Meml. Hosp., 1988-89, resident in internal medicine, 1989-90, fellow in wound healing, 1990-92, resident in dermatology, 1992-94, chief resident, 1994-95; instr. dept. dermatology U. Miami, 1995, asst. prof., 1995—; vis. prof. U. South Fla., 1995, Panama Canal Commn., 1996, St. Louis U., 1998; asst. chief inpatient svcs. Cedars Med. Ctr., Miami, 1995—, cons., 1995-98, co-dir. wound cure ctr., 1997-98, dir., 1998—; physician Jackson Meml. Med. Ctr., 1995—, VA Med. Ctr., Miami, 1995—; internat. com. Dermatology Therapy Internat., 1996—; dir. wound healing preceptorship Ortho-McNeil Pharm., 1997—; lectr., presenter in field. Author: (chpt.) Conn's Current Therapy, 1999; co-author: The Miami Review for the Certifying examination of the American Board of Dermatology, 1996, 97, 98, (chpt.) Cutaneous Medicine in Surgery, 1995; editor CME supplement-Wounds, 1998—, Current Topics in Wound Healing, 1999—; co-clin. editor Ostomy/Wound Mgmt., 1997-99, cons. editor, 1999—; mem. editl. bd. Ctrs. Wound Healing Excellence, 1997—; reviewer Archives Dermatology, 1993—, Am. Jour. Managed Care, 1995—, Jour. Am. Acad. Dermatology, 1996—, Advances Wound Care, 1997—, Am. Jour. Medicine, 1998—, So. Med. Jour., 1998—, Am. Family Physician, 1999—, Jour. Am. Med. Woman's Assn., 1999—; contbr. over 110 articles to profl. jours. Recipient Young Investigator award UpJohn Corp., 1991; NIH fellow, 1985. Fellow Am. Acad. Dermatology (quality care com. 1995—, cost-effectiveness task force 1996—); mem. AMA, Internat. DermatoEpidemiology Assn., Med. Dermatology Soc. (health policy com. 1999—), Assn. Advancement Wound Care (founding, bd. dirs. 1995—, treas. 1998—), Soc. Investigative Dermatology, La Soc. Chilena Dermatologia Venereologia, Wound Healing Soc., European Soc. Tissue Repair, Residency Curriculum Exch. Group, Miami Dermatol. Soc. Office: U Miami 1444 NW 9th Ave Miami FL 33136-1406

KIRSTA, YURI BOGDANOVICH, research scientist, educator; b. Ashkhabad, USSR, Aug. 22, 1951; s. Bogdan Tarasovich and Regina Stefanovna (Dobrzhanskaya) K.; m. Al'mira Makhmudovna Galeeva, Aug. 16, 1978 (div. Feb. 1986); children: Vlada, Bogdan; m. Nina Leonidovna Myasoedova, July 4, 1986; 1 child, Dmitri. Physicist, Novosibirsk (Russia) State U., 1975; Molecular Biologist, Moscow State U., 1976; Candidate Scis. in Biology, Ashkhabad, Russia, 1983; DSc in Biology, Inst. Water & Environ. Probs., Barnaul, Russia, 1994. Cert. ecology, applied math., physics, molecular biology. Investigator All-Union Inst. Molecular Biology, Novosibirsk, 1975-78; jr. and sr. rschr. Desert Inst., Ashkhabad, 1978-87; leading and prin. rschr. Inst. Water and Environ. Problems, Barnaul, 1987—, sr. rschr., 1995—; prof. Altai State U., Barnaul, 1993—, Altai State Poly. U., Barnaul, 1997-98. Author: Modeling of Desert Ecosystems, 1986. Recipient prize in sci. and tech. area Komsomol Orgn. USSR, Moscow, 1984. Avocation: studying of the Russian Veda tradition. Office: Inst Water & Environ Prob, 105 Papanintsev St, 656099 Barnaul Russia

KIRSTEIN, PETER THOMAS, engineering educator; b. Berlin, June 20, 1933; s. Walter and Eleanor Stephanie (Jacobsohn) K.; m. Gwendolen Margaret White; children: Sara Lynn, Claire Fiona. BA, Cambridge U., 1954; MSc, Stanford U., 1955, PhD, 1958; DSc, London U., 1970. Rsch. assoc. Stanford U., 1957-58, lectr., 1958; staff mem. CERN, Switzerland, 1959-63; scientific rep. GE, Switzerland, 1963-67; reader U. London, 1967-70; prof. U. Coll. London, 1970—, head dept. computer sci., 1980-95, dir. rsch., 1995—; cons. in field. Author: Space Charge Flow, 1967; contbr. articles to profl. jours. Fellow Brit. Computer Soc., Elec. Engring., Inst. Physics, Royal Acad. Engrs. Home: 31 Bancroft Ave, London N2 OAR, England Office: Univ Coll London, Gower St, London WCIE 6BT, England

KIRTLEY, JANE ELIZABETH, law educator; b. Indpls., Nov. 7, 1953; d. William Raymond and Faye Marie (Price) K.; m. Stephen Jon Cribari, May 8, 1985. BS in Journalism, Northwestern U., 1975, MS in Journalism, 1976; JD, Vanderbilt U., 1979. Bar: N.Y. 1980, D.C. 1982, Va. 1995, U.S. Dist. Ct. (we. dist.) N.Y. 1980, U.S. Dist. Ct. D.C. 1982, U.S. Ct. Claims 1982, U.S. Ct. Appeals (4th cir.) 1982, U.S. Ct. Appeals (D.C. cir.) 1985, U.S. Ct. Appeals (10th cir.) 1996, U.S. Ct. Appeals (5th cir.) 1997, U.S. Ct. Appeals (6th cir.) 1998, U.S. Ct. Appeals (6th and 11th cir.) 1998, U.S. Supreme Ct. 1985. Assoc. Nixon, Hargrave, Devans & Doyle, Rochester, N.Y., 1979-81, Washington, 1981-84; exec. dir. Reporters Com. for Freedom of Press, Arlington, Va., 1985-99; Silha prof. media ethics & law U. Minn. Sch. Journalism & Mass Comm., Mpls., 1999—; dir. Silha Ctr. for Study of Media Ethics and Law, Mpls., 2000—; mem. adj. faculty Am. U. Sch. Comm., 1988-98. Exec. articles editor Vanderbilt U. Jour. Transnat. Law, 1978-79; editor: The News Media and the Law, 1985—, The First Amendment Handbook, 1987, 4th edit., 1995, Agents of Discovery, 1991, 93, 95, Pressing Issues, 1998-99; columnist NEPA Bull., 1988-99, Virginia's Press, 1991-99, Am. Journalism Rev., 1995—, W.Va.'s Press, 1997-99, Tenn. Press, 1997-99; mem. editl. bd. Govt. Info. Quar., Comm. Law and Policy. Bd. dirs. Freedom Forum 1st Amendment Ctr., Nashville, Sigma Delta Chi Found., Indpls. Mem. ABA, N.Y. State Bar Assn., D.C. Bar Assn., Va. State Bar Assn., Sigma Delta Chi. Home: 3645 46th Ave S Minneapolis MN 55406-2937 Office: 111 Murphy Hall Dr 206 Church St SE Minneapolis MN 55455-0488

KIRVASSILIS, GEORGE V., anesthesiologist; b. Thessaloniki, Greece, Aug. 23, 1960; s. Vassilis and Toula K.; m. Peli Galiti, Jan. 31, 1988; children: Vassilis, Nikolas, Dimitri, Andrew. MD with honors, Aristotele U., Thessaloniki, 1984. Diplomate Am. Bd. Anesthesiology. Rsch. fellow cardiac anesthesia Washington U., St. Louis, 1988-89; resident in internal medicine St. Luke's Hosp., St. Louis, 1989-90; resident in anesthesiology Washington U., St. Louis, 1990-92, chief resident in anesthesiology, 1992-93, staff cardiac anesthesiologist, 1993-95; fellow pediat. and cardiac anesthesia Boston Childrens Hosp./Harvard Med. Sch., 1995-96; pediat. cardiac anesthesiologist Onasis Hosp., Athens, Greece, 1996—. With Greek Air Force, 1985-87. Mem. Am. Soc. Cardiovascular Anesthesiologists, Internat. Anesthesia Rsch. Soc., Greek Soc. Anesthesiologists.

KIRWAN, KATHARYN GRACE (MRS. GERALD BOURKE KIRWAN, JR.), retail executive; b. Monroe, Wash., Dec. 1, 1913; d. Walter Samuel and Bertha Ella (Shrum) Camp; m. Gerald Bourke Kirwan Jr., Jan. 13, 1945. Student, U. Puget Sound, 1933-34; BA, BS, Tex. Woman's U., 1937; postgrad., U. Wash., 1941. Libr. Brady (Tex.) Sr. High Sch., 1937-38, McCamey (Tex.) Sr. High Sch., 1938-43; mgr. Milady's Frock Shop, Monroe, 1946-62, owner, mgr., 1962-93. Meml. chmn. Monroe chpt. Am. Cancer Soc., 1961-93; mem. Snohomish County Police Svcs. Action Coun., 1971; mem. Monroe Pub. Libr. Bd., 1950-65, pres. bd., 1964-65; mem. Monroe City Coun., 1969-73; mayor City of Monroe, 1974-81; commr. Snohomish County Hosp. dist. 1, 1970-90, chmn. bd. commrs., 1980-90; mem. East Snohomish County Health Planning Com., 1979-81; mem. Snohomish County Law and Justice Planning Com., 1974-78, Snohomish County Econ. Devel. Coun., 1975-81, Snohomish County Pub. Utility Dist. Citizens Adv. Task Force, 1983; sr. warden Ch. of Our Saviour, Monroe, 1976-77, 89, sr. warden, 1976-77, 89-90; mem. Monroe Breast Cancer Screening Project community planning group Fred Hutchinson Cancer Rsch. Ctrs., 1991-93. With USNR, 1943-46. Recipient Malstrom award for Hist. Homes and Bldgs. of Monroe, 2000, award of project excellence Washington Mus. Assn., 2000. Mem. AAUW, U.S. Naval Inst., Ret. Officers Assn., Naval Res. Assn., Bus. and Profl. Women's Club (2d v.p. 1980-82, pres. 1983-84), Washington Gens., Snohomish County Pharm. Aux., C. of C. (pres. 1972), Valley Gen. Hosp. Guild (pres. 1994, 95, 96), Valley Gen. Hosp. Found. (sec. 1993-97). Episcopalian. Home: 538 S Blakely St Monroe WA 98272-2402

KIRWIN, ANDREW DEAN, protective services official; b. Albuquerque, Apr. 22, 1964; s. Robert Francis Kirwin and Barbara Jane Cooper; m. Wendy Ann Tomas, Aug. 27, 1988 (div. Dec. 1993); m. Deborah Ellen West, Feb. 14, 1996; 1 child, Daniel Alexander. BS magna cum laude, U. Colo., Denver, 1999. Cert. paramedic, Colo.; cert. fire officer I, Colo., cert. pub. safety diver, dive rescue specialist Dive Rescue Internat. Firefighter Castlewood Fire Dept., Englewood, Colo., 1987-90; paramedic Castlewood Fire Dept., Englewood, 1990-96, lt., 1996—; chair Metro Dive Team, Denver, 1994-99; comdr. Castlewood Dive Rescue Team, Englewood, 1994—; cons. Neighborhood Planning, 1998. Vol. 9 Health Fair, Denver, 1983-90; coll. organizer Perot for Pres. (Colo.), Denver, 1992; active Greater Park Hill Cmty., Inc., Denver, 1995— (co-chair edn. com.); rschr. Norton for Senate Campaign, Denver, 1996; grant reviewer Undergraduate Rsch. Opportunities Program U. Colo. Denver, 1998. Undergrad. Rsch. Opportunities Program grantee, U. Colo., Denver, 1997. Mem. Internat. Assn. Firefighters (sec. 1989—), Internat. Assn. Dive Rescue Specialists, Human Factors and Ergonomics Soc., Divers Alert Network, Soc. for Applied Anthropology, High Plains Soc. for Applied Anthropology, Golden Key Nat. Honor Soc. Avocations: sailing, SCUBA, photography. E-mail: akirwin@uswest.net. Home: 355 Elm St Denver CO 80220-5740 Office: Castlewood Fire Dept 7900 E Berry Pl Englewood CO 80111-2319

KIRYUKHIN, ALEXEY VLADIMIROVICH, hydrogeologist; b. St. Petersburg, Russia, Nov. 22, 1956; s. Vladimir Andreevich and Ludmila Vasilievna (Pluzhnikova) K.; m. Nina Ivanovna Borodich, Oct. 2, 1958; children: Tanya, Peter. PhD in Hydrogeology, Mining Inst., St. Petersburg, 1984; DSc in Hydrogeology, Inst. Earth Crust Russia Acad., Irkutsk, 1993. Engr. Inst. Volcanology, Petropavlovsk-Kamchatsky, Russia, 1979-81, jr. scientist to sr. scientist, 1981-90, sr. scientist, 1990—, chief geothermal and geochemistry dept., 1995, dep. dir., 1996; vis. scientist Lawrence Berkeley (Calif.) Nat. Lab., 1991, 98, Geol. Survey Japan, Tsukuba, 1994, 96; prof. math. modeling Kamchatka State Tech. U., Petropavlovsk-Kamchatsky, 1992-2000; cons. West Japan Engring. Cons., Fukuoka, Japan, 1996; vis. scientist Lawrence Berkeley Nat. Lab., 1998. Co-author: Heat Transfer Models of Hydrothermal Systems of Kamchatka, 1987, High Temperature Hydrothermal Reservoirs, 1991; contbr. articles to profl. jours. Grantee USSR Acad. Scis., 1989, Internat. Atomic Energy Agency, 1996, Russian Funds Basic Studies, 1997. Mem. Geothermal Assn. (hon. assoc. mem.). Avocations: mountain and cross county skiing, climbing volcanoes, swimming hot springs, jogging. Home: Karbysheva 10/1-9, 683006 Petropavlovsk Kamchatsky Russia Office: Inst Volcanology, Piip 9, 683006 Petropavlovsk Kamchatsky Russia

KIRYUKHIN, YURI BORISOVICH, physics researcher; b. Kazan, Russian, Sept. 14, 1945; s. Yrgeleevich Bronislav Ludvigovich and Maria Petrovna Kiryukhina; m. Tatyana Petrovna Karelina, June 5, 1975; 1 child, Titova Maria. Grad., Perm State U., Russia, 1972. Engr. factory, Podolsk, Russia, 1972-74, sr. engr., 1974-76; rschr. Br. of Atomic Energy Inst., Troitsk, Russia, 1976-85; sr. rschr. Br. of Atomic Energy Inst., Troitsk, 1985-87, head of group of excimer lasers, 1987-91; head of group of excimer lasers Innovation and Fision Rsch. Troitsk Inst., 1991-2000. Patentee in field; contbr. articles to profl. jours. Sr. sgt. Soviet Union Army, 1964-67. Recipient honors Soviet Union Govt., Chernobil, 1986, medal Pres. of Russia, Chernobil, 1996. Avocations: sports, tennis. Office: Innovation/Fision Rsch Inst, Oktabrskaya Str, Troitsk 142092, Moscow

KIRZHNER, FELIX MICHAEL, mining engineer; b. Beresi, Moldova, May 16, 1949; arrived in Israel, 1991; s. Michael Alex and Riva Moisey (Gafter) K.; m. Elean Ilya Izgur, July 23, 1976; 1 child, Rudolf. MSc, Mining Inst., Moscow, 1966, PhD, 1977, DSc, 1985. Sr. scientist, head lab. Mining Inst., Yakutsk, Russia, 1976-90; sr. rschr. Technion, Haifa, Israel, 1990—. Author: Mining Methods for Faulted Seams, 1986, Effectiveness of Hydraulics in Supporting Permafrost, 1988; contbr. articles to profl. jours. Mem. Internat. Soc. Rock Mechs., Israel Assn. Scientists-Immigrants. Avocation: travel. Office: Technion, Haifa 32000, Israel

KISAK, PAUL FRANCIS, engineering company executive; b. Pitts., July 15, 1956; s. Paul F. and Catherine M. (Svaranovic) K.; married. BSE in Nuclear Engring., Engring. Physics and Engring. Sci., U. Mich., 1982; MBA, Ea. Mich. U., 1984; postgrad., U. Va., 1986, George Washington U., 1985-87, UCLA, Naval Postgrad. Sch., Argonne Nat. Lab., Los Alamos Nat. Lab., Sandia Nat. lab., Lawrence Livermore Nat. Lab. Lic. realtor, contractor. Intelligence officer, engr. CIA, Langley, Va., 1983-86; engr., diplomat U.S. Dept. of State, Washington, 1986-87; engr., program mgr. Space Applications Corp., Vienna, Va., 1987-88; founder, pres. KKI, Inc., Middletown, Va., 1986—; sr. scientist, program mgr. Info. Tech. & Application Corp., Reston, 1987-89; cons. devel. PFK Enterprises, Washington, 1986—; pub., editor, author, mem. mgmt. adv. group CIA; mem. working group Strategic Def. Initiative, 1986—; ind. pub., editor, writer. Holder software copyrights and trademarks. Caseworker U.S. Senator John Glenn, Columbus, Ohio, 1979; trustee League of Student Orgns.; charter mem. Coloquy Mega Found.; del. Loudoun County Rep. Nat. Party, 1988—. Ea. Mich. U. scholar, Ohio State U. scholar; recipient Presdl. Sports awards, George P. Schultz U.S. Dept. State Tribute of Appreciation award, Cold War cert.; named to NRA Legion of Honor. Mem. AIAA, ASME, Internat. Soc. Profl. Engrs., Am. Phys. Soc., Am. Math. Soc., Am. Nuc. Soc., Am. Astronautical Soc., Am. Mgmt. Soc., Assn. MBA Execs., Am. Fedn. Ret. Intelligence Officers, Bioengring. Soc., Mensa, Intertel, Texnikoi, Camelopard Socs., Colloquy, Thinkers Internat., Naval Intelligence Profls., Marine Corp. League Det.# 890, ISPE, Beta Gamma Sigma, Pi Mu Epsilon. Avocations: flying, reading, sports, movies, woodworking.

KISELEV, PETER ANDREEVICH, biochemist, educator; b. Witebsk, Belarus, Russia, Jan. 2, 1948; s. Andrei Ustinovich and Maria Iosiphovna (Moskaleva) K.; m. Svetlana Nikolaevna Kovalenko, Apr. 27, 1974; children: Leonid, Ekaterina, Victor. Deg. in chemistry, Martin-Luth. U., Halle, Germany, 1972; PhD, Inst. Bioorganic Chemistry, Minsk, Russia, 1976; D in Chem. Sci., Inst. Bioorganic Chemistry, Moscow, 1990. Rschr. Inst. Bioorganic Chemistry, Minsk, 1975-80, head rsch. dept., 1980—; prof. Internat. Sakharov Inst. Radioecology, Minsk, 1994—. Contbr. articles to profl. jours. Grantee German Rsch. Found., 1987, 95. Mem. Belarus Soc. Photobiol. Biophysics, Belarus Soc. Biochemistry. Avocations: chess, tennis. Home: Karbysheva Str 9-203, 220119 Minsk Belarus Office: Inst Bioorganic Chemistry Acad Scis, Zhodinskaya Str 5/2, 220141 Minsk Belarus

KISELIEV, VLADIMIR VALERIEVICH, physicist, researcher; b. Barancha, Russia, Feb. 23, 1951; s. Valery Alekseevich and Alexandra Vasilievna (Sosnina) K.; m. Galina Alekseevna Spiridonova, Nov. 19, 1977; children: Dmitry, Evgeny, Mark. Grad., Urals State U., Sverdlovsk, Russia, 1973, postgrad. in theoretical physics, 1976, PhD, 1984; DSc in Physics and Math., Inst. Metal Physics/Russian, Acad. of Scis., 1999. Jr. rsch. scientist Inst. Metal Physics, Sverdlovsk, 1976-86, rsch. scientist, 1986-91; sr. rsch. scientist Inst. Metal Physics, Ekaterinburg, Russia, 1991-2000, leading rsch. scientist, 2000—. Contbr. over 50 articles to profl. jours. and conf. procs. Avocations: travel, mountain walking. Office: Inst Metal Physics, Kovalevskaya 18, 620219 Ekaterinburg Russia

KISELIK, PAUL HOWARD, manufacturing company executive; b. Newark, Nov. 29, 1937; s. Jerome W. and Rose (Ramo) K.; m. Teri Nimaroff, Sept 6, 1959; children: Daniel, Jonathan. BS in Indsl. Engring., Lehigh U., 1960; MS in Mgmt. Engring., N.J. Inst. Tech., 1965. Registered profl. engr., N.J., Pa. V.p. Nimrow Carton Co., Elizabeth, N.J., 1961-71; pres. Sebro Packaging Corp., South Hackensack, N.J., 1971—; pres. Rayart Folding Box Co., South Hackensack, 1971—, Lane Graphics, South Hackensack, 1984—; sr. ptnr. Green St. Assn., South Hackensack, 1979—. Author: Equity Financing of a Small Business, 1965. Lt. U.S. Army, 1960-61. Mem. TAPPI, Newtonian Soc., Morristown-Beard Sch. Alumni Assn. (v.p. 1979-81), Asa Packer Soc., Tau Beta Pi, Alpha Pi Mu. Avocation: raising dogs.

KISELIS, ALGIRDAS ANTANAS, economist, researcher; b. Rokiskis, Lithuania, Mar. 6, 1939; s. Antanas and Adele (Grikienyte) K.; m. Rima Galvelyte Kiseliene, Oct. 22, 1983; children: Jonas, Antanas. PhD in Econ., Vilnius U., Lithuania, 1973. Lectr. Vilnius (Lithuania) U. Faculty Econ., 1970-72; sr. lectr. Vilnius U., 1972-79, assoc. prof., 1979—; founder, dir. Sci. and Ency. Pub. Inst., Vilnius, 1996—; economical cons. Indsl. Enterprises, Lithuania, 1985-95, 96; vice chmn. of Observer Coun., Investment Joint Stock Co., Lithuania, 1992-94; mem. State Commn. fro Commemoration of Millenium of the First Mentioning of Lithuania Name; mem. parliament Lithuanian Lang. Commn. of the Coordination Coun. of the Lithuanian Seimas; econs. cons. ARD Assocs. in Rural Devel. Inc., Burlington. Contbr. over 55 pubs. to profl. jours. Chmn. Coun. Musical Children Sch. "Azuoliukas", Vilnius, 1995—. Roman Catholic. Avocations: classic music, swimming, amateur gardener. E-Mail: algirdas.kiselis@ef.vu.lt Fax: 3702 36-61-27. Home: Kalvariju 182-30, LT-2042 Vilnius Lithuania Office: Vilnius U Dept Econs, Sauletekio 9, LT-2040 Vilnius Lithuania

KISER, JOY MARIAN, librarian, writer, historian; b. Akron, Ohio, Jan. 29, 1947; m. James R. Kiser, Jan. 27, 1968 (div. Oct. 1978); children: Heather Joy, Adam James. BA in Art History/English/Photography, U. Akron, 1988; MA in Art History, Case Western Res. U., 1990; MLS, Kent State U., 1994. Med. libr. Wooster Cmty. Hosp., Wooster, Ohio, 1992-95; asst. libr. Cleve. Mus. Natural History, 1995-98, head libr., 1998—. Contbr. articles to profl. jours. Mem. Ohio Preservation Coun., Soc. for the History of Natural History (London), Spl. Librs. Assn. (natural history caucus). Avocations: gardening, carpentry, dressage riding, photography, writing. E-mail: joyful@mail.bright.net. Home: 15307 Clinton Rd Doylestown OH 44230-9781 Office: Cleve Mus Natural History 1 Wade Oval Dr Cleveland OH 44106-1767

KISER, NAGIKO SATO, retired librarian; b. Taipei, Republic of China, Aug. 7, 1923; came to U.S., 1950; d. Takeichi and Kinue (Sōma) Sato; m. Virgil Kiser, Dec. 4, 1979 (dec. Mar. 1981). Secondary teaching credential, Tsuda Coll., Tokyo, 1945; BA in Journalism, Trinity U., 1953; BFA, Ohio State U., 1956, MA in Art History, 1959; MLS, cert. in library media, SUNY, Albany, 1974. Cert. community coll. librarian, Calif., cert. jr. coll. tchr., Calif., cert. secondary edn. tchr., Calif., cert. tchr. library media specialist and art, N.Y. Pub. rels. reporter The Mainichi Newspapers, Osaka, Japan, 1945-50; contract interpreter U.S. Dept. State, Washington, 1956-58, 66-67; resource specialist Richmond (Calif.) Unified Sch. Dist., 1968-69; editing supr. CTB/McGraw-Hill, Monterey, Calif., 1969-71; multimedia specialist Monterey Peninsula Unified Sch. Dist., 1975-77; librarian Nishimachi Internat. Sch., Tokyo, 1979-80, Sacramento City Unified Sch. Dist., 1977-79, 81-85; sr. librarian Camarillo (Calif.) State Hosp. and Devel. Ctr., 1985-93. Editor: Short Form Test of Academic Aptitude, 1970, Prescriptive Mathematics Inventory, 1970, Tests of Basic Experience, 1970. Mem. Calif. State Supt.'s Regional Coun. on Asian Pacific Affairs, Sacramento, 1984-91. Library Media Specialist Tng. Program scholar U.S. Office Edn., 1974. Fellow Internat. Biog. Assn. (life); mem. ALA, Am. Biog. Inst.

(life, dep. gov. 1988—), Libr. Congress (nat. mem.), Calif. Libr. Assn., Med. Libr. Assn., Asunaro Shogai Kyoiku Kondankai (Lifetime Edn. Promoting Assn., Japan), The Mus. Soc., Internat. House of Japan, Matsuyama Sacramento Sister City Corp., Japanese Am. Citizens League, Japanese Am. Nat. Mus., Japanese Am. Cultural and Cmty. Ctr., Ikenobo Ikebana Soc. Am., L.A. Hototogisu Haiku Assn., Ventura County Archeol. Soc., Internat. Platform Assn., Internat. Soc. Poets, AAUW, Ventura County Chpt. Mem. Christian Science Ch. Avocations: flower arranging, ballroom dance, classical music.

KISH, ELISSA ANNE, educational administrator, consultant; b. Bklyn., Sept. 29, 1934; d. Robert Joseph and Yolanda Filomina (Romano) Lucadamo; m. Joseph Laurence Kish Jr., Oct. 16, 1955; children: Grace Edna Kish, Joseph Robert, Frances Caroline Kish Burrell. BA, CUNY, 1956; EdM, Rutgers U., 1965. Elem. tchr. N.Y. City Pub. Schs., Bklyn., 1956-57, U.S. Army Dependent Schs., Hanau, West Germany, 1958, Piscataway (N.J.) Pub. Schs., 1961-62, New Brunswick (N.J.) Pub. Schs., 1965, 71-76; vice prin. Hopatcong (N.J.) Pub. Schs., 1977-78; asst. supt. Dunellen (N.J.) Pub. Schs., 1978-80; supr. K-12 instrn. Elmwood Park (N.J.) Pub. Schs., 1980-90; interim high sch. adminstr. Dunellen Pub. Schs., 1991-92; adminstr. ctrl. office Elmwood Park Pub. Schs., 1992-96; cons. Newark Pub. Schs., 1976-77; evaluator Middle States Assn., Navesink, N.J., 1988; cons. State U. N.Y., Garden City, 1992, Mt. Vernon Pub. Schs., N.Y., 1992; mem. fine arts & humanities coun. Town of Wareham, Mass., 1996—. Author: Nutrition Program For Schools, 1979; contbng. author: Curriculum & Values: An Inquiry, 1976. Mem. strategic planning team Town of Elmwood Park, 1993-95; officer, mem. Westfield Coll. Women's Club, Westfield, N.J., 1969-92; founder, 1st pres. Vocational Adv. Coun., Elmwood Park, 1980-90; trustee Christopher Montessori Acad., Westfield, 1968-72. Recipient numerous grants for rsch. and curriculum devel., 1979—. Mem. ASCD, NEA, Elmwood Park Prins. and Suprs. Assn. (pres. 1989-90), Elmwood Park Adminstrs. Assn. (pres. 1986-89), Nat. Geographic Soc., Smithsonian Assocs., Kappa Delta Pi, Alpha Epsilon Phi. Avocations: theatre, opera. Home and office: 1309 San Miguel Ln Fort Myers FL 33903-1541

KISH, JOSEPH LAURENCE, JR., management consultant; b. July 13, 1933; s. Joseph Lawrence and Grace Veronica (Skippin) K.; m. Elissa Anne Lucadamo, Oct. 16, 1955; children: Grade Edna, Joseph Robert, Frances Caroline Kish Burrell. BA in Econs., Bklyn. Coll., 1955; postgrad., NYU, 1955-56. Mgmt. analyst N.Y. State Dept. Welfare, Albany, 1956-59; sys. analyst Lockheed Electronics Co., Plainfield, N.J., 1959-61; corp. mgr. Olin Mathieson Chem. Corp., N.Y.C., 1961-66; pres. Iron Mountain, Inc., N.Y.C., 1966-67; v.p. Fenvessy Assocs., N.Y.C., 1976-81; pres. Acumen, Inc., Raritan, N.J., 1981-83; v.p. Fenvessy & Schwab, Inc., N.Y.C., 1983-86; exec. v.p. Data Port Mgmt. Corp., N.Y.C., 1986—; professorial lectr. Am. U.; adj. prof. NYU, Columbia U., SUNY-Nassau; comml. arbitrator Am. Arbitration Assn. Author: Paperwork in Transition, 1965, Microfilm in Business, 1966, Business Forms Design and Administration, 1972, Micrographics, 1980, Greater Efficiency in the Small Office, 1982, Word Processing in the Transitional Office, 1983, Office Management Problem Solver, 1986; contbr. numerous articles on bus. mgmt. to tech. jours. Bd. mgrs. Ships-A-Shore Condominium Assn., Cape Cod, Mass., 1981—. With inf. AUS, 1956-58. Recipient Grillo Best Bus. Book Yr. award Adminstrv. Mgmt. Soc., 1980-81. Mem. Am. Mgmt. Assn. (Silver medallion), Assn. Mgmt. Cons., Nat. Micrographics Assn., Inst. Mgmt. Cons., Assn. Records Mgrs. and Adminstrs., Am. Legion, German-Am. Social Club (Cape Coral, Fla.), N.Y. Athletic Club, Royal Palm Yacht Club, Elks, KC. Home: 1309 San Miguel Ln Fort Myers FL 33903-1541 Office: DataPort Mgmt Corp World Trade Ctr New York NY 10048

KISH, JULES GENE, retired mechanical engineer; b. Bridgeport, Conn., Aug. 10, 1933; s. Jules and Mary K.; m. Sandra Joyce Kish, Dec. 1, 1990. BSME, Bridgeport U., 1960; MSME, Yale U., 1965. Chief transmission design Sikorsky Aircraft, Stratford, Conn., 1962-99. Patentee overrunning clutch spring, actuated and overrunning spring clutch assemblies, elastomeric load sharing device, elastomeric torsional isolator, gear tooth topological modification, fail-safe drive system, self-scavenging hybrid lubrication system, helicopter powertrain system, others; contbr. papers to mags. and profl. confs.; author specialized reports for military use. Corp. U.S. Army, 1954-56, Korea. Recipient Cert. of Recognition NASA, 1990; named Engr. of Yr. Fairfield U., Conn., 1993. Mem. Am. Helicopter Soc. Avocations: wood carving, oil painting, antique toys. E-mail: juleskish@aol.com. Home: 21 Waterview Lndg Milford CT 06460-5366

KISHEK, RAMI ALFRED, scientist; b. Palestine, Mar. 14, 1973; came to U.S., 1989; s. Alfred Jiries and Lillian Q. Kishek; m. Xueying Ni. BSE in Elec. Engring., U. Mich., 1993, MSE in Nuclear Engring., 1995, PhD in Nuclear Engring., 1997. Staff scientist FM Techs., Fairfax, Va., 1996; tchg. asst. U. Mich., Ann Arbor, 1996, rsch. asst., 1993-97; rsch. assoc. U. Md., College Park, 1997-99, asst. rsch. scientist, asst. project mgr. electron ring, 1999—. Referee in field; contbr. over 30 articles to profl. jours. Mem. IEEE, Am. Phys. Soc. Achievements include a comprehensive theory on multipactor discharge as well as studies of intense charged-particle beams and heavy ion fusion; discovered space charge waves in charged particle beams, simulation studies revealed mechanism for equipartitioning and resonance. Office: Inst for Plasma Rsch/UMCP Energy Rsch Bldg 223 College Park MD 20742-0001

KISHI, KAZUSHI, ceramist, researcher; b. Matsuyama, Ehime, Japan, Aug. 15, 1954; s. Eiji and Miyoko (Hino) K.; m. Naoko Mitsumune, Nov. 25, 1989; children: Eiko, Shunsuke. B, Ehime U., Matsuyama, Japan, 1979; D, Kyushu U., Fukuoka, Japan, 1990. Inspector of fertilizer Ministry of Agr., Forestry and Fisheries, Nagoya, Japan, 1979-80; rschr. Kyushu Nat. Indsl. Rsch. Inst., Tosu, Japan, 1980-89; sr. rschr. Kyushu Nat. Indsl. Rsch. Inst., Tosu, 1989—; assoc. prof. Saga (Japan) U., 1995-97. Contbr. articles to profl. jours. Avocation: reading historical novels. Office: Kyushu Nat Indsl Rsch Inst, Shukumachi, Tosu 841-0052, Japan

KISHI, KOICHIRO, medical educator, researcher; b. Tokyo, Apr. 6, 1940; s. Kimpei and Sonoko (Kaneko) K.; m. Toshiko Dezawa, Oct. 10, 1971; children: Yuichiro, Junya, Hiroaki. MD, Gunma U., 1965, PhD, 1970. Rsch. asst. Gunma U., Maebashi, Japan, 1970-73, lectr., 1973-74; prof. Sch. Medicine Gunma U., Maebashi, 1995—; asst. prof. Nat. Rsch. Inst. Police Sci., Tokyo, 1974-84; prof. medicine Fukui Med. Sch., 1984-95, Gunma U., Maebashi, Japan, 1995—. Editor: Forensic Serology, 1990; author: Isozymes, 1990; contbr. articles to profl. jours. Grantee Japan Brain Found., 1985-87, Meiji Life Found. of Health and Welfare, 1986, Rsch. Found. for Traffic Preventive Medicine, 1991, Uehara Meml. Life Sci. Found., 1992, Sagawa Traffic & Social Found., 1992-93, Sasakawa Health Sci. Found., 1993. Mem. Medico-Legal Soc. Japan (exec. 1975—, dir. 1994—), Japanese Soc. Human Genetics (exec. 1990-93, v.p. 1990), Internat. Assn. Human Biologists (v.p. 1990), Assn. Forensic Surgeons (advisor 1986), Assn. Forensic Surgeon Dentists (advisor 1987), Med. Assn. Kitakanto (exec. 1988), Japan Soc. DNA Polymorth Rsch. (pres. 1997—). Office: Gunma U Sch Medicine Dept Legal Medicine, Showa-machi 3-39-22, Maebashi 371, Japan

KISHI, KYOICHI, nutrition educator; b. Osaka, Japan, Aug. 13, 1941. MB, Kyoto Prefectural U. Medicine, 1941; MD, Tokushima (Japan) U., 1979. Instr. Tokushima U., 1967-79, lectr., 1979-80, assoc. prof., 1980-84, prof., 1984—; dir. dept. nutrition Tokushima U., 1995-97. Editor Jour. Nutritional Sci. and Vitaminology. Mem. domestic com. Japan Internat. Coop. Agy., Tokyo, 1987-97. Mem. Japan Soc. Nutrition and Food Sci. (bd. dirs. 1994-98, Young Scientist award 1981, Achievement award 1993). Office: Sch Medicine Tokushima U, 3-Kuramotocho, Tokushima 770-8503, Japan

KISHI, MASAHICHI, communication engineering educator; b. Iwakura, Aichi, Japan, Oct. 5, 1946; s. Goroh and Kaneko (Furuhashi) K.; m. Masami Tanaka, May 3, 1976. Bachelor's degree, Keio U., Tokyo, 1969, Master's degree, 1971, Doctorate, 1974. Cert. engr. Engr. Nippon Telegraph and Telephone Corp. (NTT) Musashino Elec. Comm. Lab., Tokyo, 1974-81; staff engr. NTT Yokosuka Elec. Comm. Lab., 1981-87; prof. Aichi Inst. Tech., Toyota, Aichi, Japan, 1987; cons. Nippon Telegraph and Telephone Corp., Yokosuka Elec. Comm. Lab., Japan, 1988-90, Minato Electronics, Yokohama, Japan, 1989-96, Fujitsu, Tokyo, 1990-96, Hitachi, Tokyo, 1997—, Denso, Aichi, 1998—. Contbr. articles to sci. procs. E-mail: kishi@res.aitech.ac.jp. Home: 66-1 Miyawaki, Nagakute Aichi 480-1100, Japan Office: Aichi Inst Tech, Yachigusa, 470-0356 Yagusa Toyota 470 0356, Japan

KISHI, SATORU, bank executive. CEO Bank of Tokyo-Mitsubishi, chmn. Office: Bank of Tokyo-Mitsubishi, 2-7-1 Marunouchi Chiyoda-ku, Tokyo 100-8388, Japan*

KISHIDA, AKIHIRO, surgeon; b. Takashima, Japan, Feb. 2, 1953; s. Takatoshi and Chikako K.; m. Sachiko Miyake, Oct. 14, 1979; children: Soya, Lena, Yuya. MD, Hokkaido U., 1978; D in Med. Sci., Shiga U. Med. Sci., 1997. Diplomate Am. Bd. Surgery. Surg. resident St. Luke's Internat. Hosp., Tokyo, 1978-83, St. Joseph Mercy Hosp., Pontiac, Mich., 1983-88; asst. prof. Shiga U. Med. Sci., Japan, 1988-90; fellow Pitts. U., 1990-92; asst. prof. Shiga U. Med. Sci., 1993-97, Hokkaido U., Sapporo, Japan, 1997-2000; dir. surg. and emergency Chiba-Nishi Gen. Hosp., Japan, 2000—. Author: Surgery Today, 1997. Home: 3-21-9-201 Tokiwadaira, Matsudo-city Japan

KISHIDA, YUTAKA, physician, researcher; b. Kyoto City, Japan, Feb. 19, 1949; s. Hideo and Shinako (Suma) K.; m. Taeko Kageishi, Apr. 29, 1978; children: Masashi, Yuki, Maki. MD, Nara Prefectural Med. Coll., Kashihara, Japan, 1974; PhD, Osaka U., 1982. Diplomate Japanese Bds. Internal Medicine, Gastroenterology, Hepatology, Oriental Medicine, Gastroenterol. Endoscopy, Occpl. Environ. Medicine. Rsch. trainee Osaka U. Med. Sch., 1974-77; med. staff Osaka U.Med. Sch., 1976-82; med. staff internal medicine Osaka Prefectural Hosp., 1974-76, chief med. staff internal medicine, 1982-83; head med. staff in internal medicine Shin-Senri Hosp., Suita, Japan, 1983-85; subhead of internal medicine Osaka Rousai Hosp., Sakai, Japan, 1985-92, acting head of gastroenterology, 1992—; head gastroent. endoscopy Osaka Kousei Nennkin Hosp., 1992-94; med. dir. Japan Tobacco Inc./Ctr. Preventive Medicine, Osaka, 1994—; dir. Uemachidai Liver Conf. Group, Osaka, 1993—; lectr. Senri Nursing Sch., Suita, 1983-85, Osaka Rousai Hosp. Nursing Sch., 1985-92; assoc. staff in internal medicine Osaka Kousei Nennkin Hosp., 1994—; cons. Unitika Co. Ltd. Med. Inst., 1983—. Contbr. articles to profl. jours. Mem. AAAS, Japan Soc. Internal Medicine, Japan Soc. Gastroenterology, Japan Soc. Hepatology, Japan Soc. Gastroenterol. Endoscopy, Japan Soc. Biochemistry, Japan Soc. Ultrasonics in Medicine, Japanese Cancer Assn., Japan Soc. Occupational Health, N.Y. Acad. Scis. Buddhist. Avocations: skiing, mountaineering, walking, art, reading. Home: 14-5 Izumigaoka, 617-0846 Nagaokakyo City Kyoto, Japan Office: Japan Tobacco Inc Ctr Preventive Medicine, 2-5-41 Namba-Naka Naniwa-ku, 556-0011 Osaka City, Japan

KISHIKAWA, TOSHIAKI, radiochemistry educator; b. Fukui, Japan, Feb. 3, 1939; s. Masamichi and Fumi (Ikegami) K.; m. Atsuko Ishihara, Sept. 23, 1970; children: Yasuhiro, Mari, Yosuke. B Engring., Kumamoto (Japan) U., 1965, M Engring., 1967; DSc, Tohuku U., Sendai, Japan, 1973. Lic. radiation safety supr. 1st category, Japan. Rsch. assoc. dept. indsl. chemistry Kumamoto U., 1967-74, lectr. Kurokami Radioisotope Lab., 1974-84, assoc. prof., 1984—, assoc. prof. Grad. Sch. Sci. and Tech., 1988—; lectr. Yatsushiro (Japan) Nat. Tech. Coll., 1974-77; hon. rsch. fellow Radiation Ctr., U. Birmingham, Eng., 1986-87; mem. cons. com. Kyushu Energy Forum, Econ. Fedn. Kyushu-Yamaguchi (The Kyu-Kei-Ren), Fukuoka, Japan, 1989—; mem. tech. com. Rsch. Ctr. for Nuclear Sci. and Tech., U. Tokyo, 1995—; chmn. organizing com. Asia-Pacific Symposium on Radiochemistry, Kumamoto, 1997; mem. internat. tech. adv. com. 2d Internat. Conf. on Isotopes, Sydney, Australia, 1997; assoc. editor Jour. Radioanalytical and Nuclear Chemistry, 1997—; organizer, chmn. steering com. 41st Symposium on Radiochemistry, Japan, 1997; guest editor-in-chief of Jour. Radioanalytical and Nuclear Chemistry, Asia-Pacific Symposium on Radiochemistry, 1997-99; mem. establishing com. Japan Soc. Nuclear and Radiochem. Scis., 1998-99. Author: Fundamentals of Radiochemistry, 1994; contbr. articles to sci. jours., including Jour. Nuclear Sci. and Tech., Nuclear Instruments and Methods in Physics Rsch.; guest editor-in-chief Jour. Radioanalytic and Nuclear Chemistry procs. Asia-Pacific Symposium on Radiochemistry, 1997-99; co-author (with Akito Arima): Powers of the 21st Century: A Race between Education and Catastrophe. Mem. com. 3d Kumamoto Scout Group, 1985—. Fellow Sakkokai Found., 1970. Mem. Chem. Soc. Japan, Atomic Energy Soc. Japan (bd. dirs. Kyushu br. 1993-95, 96—), Japan Radioisotope Assn. (bd. dirs. Kyushu br. 1995-98, mem. steering com. Heisei 10th Ann. Conf. Radiation Safety Suprs. 1998), Japan Soc. Nuclear and Radiochem. Scis. (mem. establishing com. 1998-99, bd. dirs. 1999—)(. Home: 13-26 Kokai-honmachi, Kumamoto 860-0851, Japan Office: Kumamoto U Faculty Engring, 39-1 Kurokami 2-Chome, Kumamoto 860-8555, Japan

KISHIMOTO, HIROSHI, research institute executive; b. Osaka, Japan, Nov. 26, 1941; s. Mitsuji and Toyoko (Kamae) K.; m. Kyoko Goto, Oct. 31, 1971; children: Akira, Noriko, Kei. B in Engring., Osaka U., 1964, M in Engring., 1966, D in Engring., 1974. Researcher Ctrl. Rsch. Inst. Mitsubishi Elec., Itami, Japan, 1966-69; asst. Osaka U., 1969-75, assoc. prof., 1976; researcher Japan Atomic Energy Rsch. Inst., Tokai-mura, 1976-93; dir. Japan Atomic Energy Rsch. Inst., Naka-machi, 1993-97; exec. dir. Japan Atomic Energy Rsch. Inst., Tokyo, 1997—. Contbr. articles to profl. jours. Mem. Japan Soc. Plasma Sci. and Nuclear Fusion (v.p. 1997-99), Phys. Soc. Japan, Inst. Elec. Engrs. Japan, Fusion Coun., Internat. Thermonuclear Exptl. Reactor (mgr. adv. com. 1997-98, co-chair spl. working group 1998-99), Athletic Soc. Japan (climbing instr. 1973—). Office: Japan Atomic Energy Rsch In, 2-2-2 Uchisaiwai-Cho, 100-0011 Chiyoda-Ku Tokyo 100-0011, Japan

KISHITA, KAZUTAKA, adhesive company executive, chemist; b. Yamakawa, Japan, Dec. 25, 1946; came to U.S., 1966; s. Eihiro and Hisako Kishita; m. Ryoko Kishita, June 26, 1972 (dec. Dec. 1981); children: Kirt, Takumi; m. Keiko Judy Kishita, Oct. 11, 1982. AA, Harbor Coll., 1970; BA, Calif. State U., Dominguez Hills, 1972. Rsch. leader Asahi Chem. Co. Ltd., Hachioji, Japan, 1973-74; chemist Three Bond Co., Ltd., Hachioji, 1974-75; prodn. mgr. Three Bond Co., Ltd., L.A., 1975-81; chief engr. Three Bond Co. Ltd., Fukuoka, Japan, 1981-83; exec. v.p. Three Bond of Am., Torrance, Calif., 1983-97; pres. Three Bond Mfg., Torrance, Calif., 1997-98; v.p. Three Bond Internat., Torrance, 1999—. Patentee in field. Bd. dirs. Little Co. of Mary Hosp. Found., Torrance, 1998—. Mem. Soc. of Advanced Material Process Engring., Japanese Ednl. Resource Ctr. (pres. 1996—, Appreciation award 1997, 98, 99), Torrance Area C. of C., Calif. C. of C., Japan Bus. Assn. (bd. dirs. 1982-88). Avocations: golf, volunteer work, music, gardening. Office: Three Bond Internat 20815 Higgins Ct Torrance CA 90501-1830

KISLETSOV, ALEXANDER VASILEVICH, automatic systems company executive, educator; b. Khabarovsk Territory, USSR, Jan. 21, 1945; s. Vasiliy Ivanovich and Vera Stepanovna (Burjachenko) K.; m. Natalia Kojemiakuna, Jan. 30, 1968 (div. Oct. 1990); children: Olga, Tatiana; m. Svetlana Anatolena Suhareva, Dec. 4, 1993; 1 child, Anastasia. Grad. engr.-physicist, Engr.-Phys. Inst., Moscow, 1968; Candidate Phys. and Math. Sci., Physics Inst., Moscow, 1973; DEng, Air Force Acad., Moscow, 1988. Cert. engr., USSR. Chief engr. Sci. Rsc. Inst., Moscow, 1971-73, head rsch. group, 1973-81; gen. dir. Automatic Sys. Corp., Samara, Russia, 1981—; asst. prof. Aviation Inst., Kuibyshev, USSR, 1985-90; prof., dir. chair Aerospace U., Samara, 1990—; dir. chair Med. U., Samara, 1991—; participant VIII Internat. Conf. on Accelerators, CERN, Geneva, 1971, 3d Internat. Conf. on Trends in Quantum Electronics, Bucharest, Romania, 1988, Internat. Conf. on Laser Methods for Biol. and Environ. Application, Heraklion, Crete, Greece, 1996. Author: Selected Papers on Novel Laser Methods in Medicine and Biology, 1999; contbr. articles to sci. jours., including Jour. Tech. Physics, Atomic Energy, Plasma Physics, Kvantovaya Elektron, Laser Physics. Town dep. Soviet of People's Deps., Kuibyshev, 1984-89, dist. dep., Samara, 1989-93. Recipient gold medal State Prize of USSR, 1986, Lenin Prize of USSR, 1990; awards for inventions include silver medal, Big Memory medal, gold medals. Mem. Engrs. Acad., Internat. Engrs. Acad., N.Y. Acad. Scis. Achievements include patents for device for laser mirror alignment, aircraft landing system, laser beacon, gas-flow laser with locked contour, device for laser therapy. method of treatment for destructive lung Tb, nitrogen laser and medical laser mounting. Avocations: water and mountain skiing. Fax: (846-2) 586-155. Office: Automatic Sys Corp, Smyshlyaevskoe Sh 1A, 443109 Samara Russia

KISLIAKOV, DIMITAR SAVOV, civil engineering educator; b. Sofia, Bulgaria, Dec. 23, 1960; s. Sava Dimitriev and Todorka Georgieva (Kurukyuvlieva) K.; m. Teodora Ivanova Kalaydjieva, June 17, 1989; 1 child, Sava. M in Engring., U. Arch., Civil Engr., Geodesy, Sofia, 1986, PhD, 1990. Cert. civil engring. Tchg. asst. U. Arch., Civil Engring., Geodesy, Sofia, 1990-96, sr. lectr., 1996—; design engr. Energoproekt, Sofia, 1986-87. Contbr. articles to profl. jours. Fellow Conf. German Acad. Scis.; mem. Gesellschaft für Angewandte Mathematik und Mechanik, European Mechanics Soc. Avocations: Tai Chi Chuan, mountain trekking. Office: U Arch Civil Engr & Geodesy, 1 Chr Smirnenski Blvd, 1421 Sofia Bulgaria

KISLIAKOV, SAVA DIMITRIEV, engineering educator; b. Plovdiv, Bulgaria, Sept. 16, 1934; s. Dimitry Nikolaev and Christina Prodromova (Orlova) K.; m. Todorka Gueorguieva Kouroukyuvlieva, Apr. 24, 1958; children: Dimitar, Albena. MEng, U. Architecture Civil Engring. and Geodesy, Sofia, Bulgaria, 1958, PhD, 1963; DSc, U. Architecture Civil Engring, Sofia, Bulgaria, 1976. Tchg. asst. U. Architecture, Civil Engring. and Geodesy, 1958-66, assoc. prof., 1966-80, prof., 1980—, vice rector, 1991-94; structural engr. Chimproekt, Sofia, 1959-62; sr. rsch. assoc. Nauchen Institut Gradoustroistvo i Architectura, Sofia, 1969-72; UNESCO fellow Imperial Coll., London, 1971; rsch. fellow MIT, Cambridge, 1973; vis. prof. Tech. U., Braunschweig, Germany, 1974-75, Berg U., Wuppertal, Germany, 1982, 89-90. Contbr. articles to profl. jours. Mem. Am. Math. Soc., Gesellschaft Deutscher Naturforscher und Arzte, Gesellschaft fur Angewandte Mathematik und Mechanik. Avocations: chess, philosophy, languages, sports, music. Home: Komplex Mladost 1, 1784 Sofia Bulgaria Office: U Arch Civ Eng and Geodesy, Blvd Chr Smirnenski 1, 1421 Sofia Bulgaria

KISLIK, VLADIMIR SAMUEL, chemist, researcher, consultant; b. Kislovodsk, USSR, Feb. 1, 1935; arrived in Israel, 1989; s. Samyel Joseph and Bronia Isaac (Gorbach) K.; m. Evgenia Israel Barass, Jan. 28, 1967 (div. 1973); 1 child, Max; m. Bella Frants Gulko, May 16, 1984. MSc, Inst. Rare Metals, Moscow, 1958; PhD, Inst. Radioactive Metals, Moscow, 1965; Prof., Hebrew U. Jerusalem, 1998. Engr., rschr. nuclear industry, Ural, USSR, 1958-66; head R&D dept. Isotope Inst., Kiev, USSR, 1966-68; head R&D group Acad. of Sci., Kiev, 1968-73; rschr. R&D Co., Jerusalem, Israel, 1989-91; rschr., assoc. prof. Hebrew U., Jerusalem, 1991—; lectr. Phys.-Engring. Inst., Ural, 1961-64; cons. Plutonium Prodn. Plant, Ural, 1962-66; lectr. Metall. Coll., Kiev, 1972-73; cons. Missiles enterprises, Moscow, 1970-73; lectr. at confs. Author: Plutonium Chemistry and Production Technology, 1962 (prize); contbr. moe than 60 articles to profl. jours. Activist, Underground Jewish Movement, Kiev, 1974-81, Moscow, 1985-89; prisoner of Zion, Gulag Prison Camp, Ukraine, 1981-84. Recipient prize for new technology Ministry of Nuclear Industry, Moscow, 1964, 66, Ministry of Chem. Industry, Kiev, 1968, prize for new materials Missiles Industry, Moscow, 1972. Mem. AAAS, N.Y. Acad. Scis. Home: Dolev, DN Modiim, 71935 Dolev Israel Office: Jewish U Jerusalem, Campus Givat Ram, 91904 Jerusalem Israel

KISLYAKOV, ANATOLI IOSIFOVITCH, physicist; b. St. Petersburg, Russia, Jan. 14, 1935; s. Iosif Luk'yanovitch and Lidiya Pavlovna Markelova; m. Svetlana Stanislavovna Matulevskaya, July 4, 1959; children: Elena, Tat'yana. PhD, St. Petersburg Tech. U., Russia, 1958; D of Physics % Math., Ioffe Phys. Tech. Inst., Russia, 1983. Jr. rschr. Ioffe Inst., Russia, 1958-77, sr. rschr., 1977-86, leading rschr., 1986-95, prin. rschr., 1995—. Co-author: (with L.I. Krupnik) Active Particle Beam Diagnostics of Hot Plasma, 1981, (with A.V. Khudoleev, S.S. Kozlovskij & M.P. Petrov) High Energy Neutral Pratticle Analyzer, 1997. Avocation: yachting. Office: AF Ioffe Phys Tech Inst, Polytechnitcheskaya str 26, 194021 Saint Petersburg Russia

KISNER, JACOB, poet, editor, publisher; b. Chelsea, Mass., Apr. 30, 1926; s. Louis and Sarah (Kotel) K.; m. Gladys Selma Feinstein, May 29, 1947; 1 daughter, Lesley Kisner Cafarelli. Student, Calvin Coolidge Coll., 1945-46, Burdett Coll., 1943-45, Harvard Univ. Extension, 1944-48, Mass. State Univ. Extension, 1944-50, Cambridge Ctr. for Adult Edn., 1946-51. With Boston American advt. dept., 1943; Sunday dept. writer Boston Globe, 1943-45; local news editor Jewish Advocate, Boston, 1945-46; founder, editor, pub. Dorchester (Mass.) Herald, 1946-47; copywriter Harold Cabot & Co. Advt. Agy., Boston, 1948; trade reporter Fairchild News Svc., Boston, 1948-49; with Boston Pub. Libr. Cataloguing Dept., 1949; sr. proof-reader Rec. and Statis. Corp., Boston, 1950-54; participant NBC Comedy Writers Devel. Project, 1956; editor Crossroads, Toronto, Ont., Can., 1964-67; Am. editor View, Can., 1967—; rsch. dir. N.Y. bur. Moneytree Publs., N.Y.C., 1972—; stamp and autograph dealer, 1973-82; owner, operator Penthouse F Stamps, 1982—; discoverer Lord and Taylor find of Finnish postal hist.; free-lance writer, 1943—. Author: (plays) First Came Paula, 1954, Speak of the Devil, 1955, The Monkey's Tail, 1956; (TV plays): The Late Mr. Honeywell, 1957, A World Apart, 1957; (poetry) I Am Hephaestus, 1966; numerous pub. articles, revs., rsch. on stamps and postal hist.; contbr. poetry to various lit. jours. and anthologies. Saxophonist, leader big band Jack Kenton, 1943-46; philatelic journalist; discussion moderator Great Books Found., Boston, 1948-51; judge of poetry contests, Rochester, N.Y., also N.Y. Poetry Forum, 1969—; sec. Am.-European Friendship Assn., 1948-51; chmn. Nat. Poetry Day Com., 1970; N.Y. State dir. and N.Y.C. chmn. World Poetry Day Com., 1971—; v.p., bd. dirs., incorporator N.Y. Poetry Forum, 1973-75; founder postmaster Park Ave Local Post, 1978—. Recipient Spl. Commendation for poem on death of Martin Luther King, Jr., So. Christian Leadership Conf., 1968, Internat. Who's Who in Poetry award, London, 1969, World Peace award Ky. State Poetry Soc., 1970, Gold Medal award Internat. Poets' Shrine, Hollywood, 1971, Radio award for Poetry of Superior Broadcast Quality, Sta. WEFG-FM, Winchester, Va., 1970, Spl. Citation award Poetry Pageant, 1970, Writer's Digest award, 1971. Mem. Am. Newspaper Guild, Acad. Am. Poets (founder), Wilson MacDonald Poetry Soc. Can. (exec. com. 1967-77, v.p. 1977—), Am. Philatelic Soc., Trans-Miss. Philatelic Soc., Soc. Philatelic Ams., Soc. Israel Philatelists, Am. Revenue Assn., Confederate Stamp Alliance, United Postal Stationery Soc., Scandinavian Collectors Club, Perfins Club, Am. Philatelic Rsch. Libr., Scandinavian Philatelic Libr. So. Calif., N.Mex. Philatelic Assn., Finnish Study Group, Scandinavian Philatelic Found. Address: Penthouse F 254 Park Ave S Ph F New York NY 10010-7208

KISNER, WENDELL HOWARD, JR., plastic surgeon; b. L.A., Dec. 5, 1939; s. Wendell Howard Sr. and Jennie Junkin Kisner; m. Jane Johnsey, June 26, 1957; children: Wendell, Aaron, Meg, Walter. BS, Tulane U., 1961, MD, 1965. Diplomate Am. Bd. Plastic and Reconstructive Surgery. Intern in surgery U. Kans. Med. Ctr., 1965-66; resident in gen. surgery LDS Hosp., Salt Lake City, 1966-67, Ochsner Clinic, New Orleans, 1969-71; resident in plastic surgery U. Miss., 1971-72; chief resident in plastic surgery U. Tenn., 1972-73; pvt. practice Salem, Oreg., 1973-75, Baton Rouge, 1975—; rsch. fellowship microvascular surgery Ochsner Clinic, 1970; instr. surgery U. Miss., 1971-72, U. Tenn., 1972-73; clin. instr. surgery U. Oreg., 1973-75; clin. asst. prof. plastic surgery dept. surgery La. State U. Med. Sch., 1975—; lectr. in field. Contbr. articles to profl. jours., poetry to anthologies. Meet physician, head NCAA Track and Field Championship, Baton Rouge, 1982, 87; charter mem., bd. mem. Baton Rouge Opera, 1983; bd. mem. Baton Rouge Symphony, 1998—. Capt. USAF, 1967-69. Mem. Am. Assn. Hand Surgery, Am. Coll. Surgeons, Am. Soc. Plastic and Reconstructive Surgeons (sports medicine com., mktg. com., panel mem. sports injuries 1986), Southeastern Soc. Plastic and Reconstructive Surgeons (chmn. pub. rels. com., historian 1990-91, trustee 1992-94, asst. sec. 1994-96, v.p. 1996-97, pres.-elect 1997-98, pres. 1998-99), Baton Rouge Surg. Soc. (pres. 1989), Costa Rica Plastic Surgery Soc. (corr.), La. Soc. Plastic Surgery, La. State Med. Soc., East Baton Rouge Parish Med. Soc., Surg. Assn. La., Undersea and Hyperbaric Med. Soc., Am. Coll. Hyperbaric Medicine, Am. Soc. Aesthetic Plastic Surgery, U.S. Olympic Sports Medicine Soc., Mardi Gras Krewe of Bacchus. Avocations: hunting, fishing, golfing, camping, herpetology. E-mail: trotman@earthlink.net. Office: 7777 Hennessy Blvd Ste 8002 Baton Rouge LA 70808-4368

KISO, YOSHIAKI, biochemistry educator; b. Onomichi, Hiroshima, Japan, Dec. 10, 1945; s. Akiharu and Michiko (Nishii) K.; m. Michiko Okamoto, May 6, 1973; children: Aiko, Takaaki. BS, Kyoto (Japan) U., 1968, MS, 1970, PhD, 1973. Rsch. fellow Japan Soc. for the Promotion of Sci., Kyoto, 1973-74; rsch. assoc. Kyoto U., 1974-75, U. Pitts., 1975-77; assoc.prof. U. Tokushima, Japan, 1977-83; prof. Kyoto Pharm. U., 1983—, dean Grad.

Sch. Pharm. Sci., 2000—; vis. lectr. Kyoto U., 1986-87, Kobe (Japan) U., 1990-91; vis. rsch. Nat. Inst. Agrobiol. Resources, 1996-97; ad hoc mem. sci. coun. Japanese Ministry Edn., 1994-96, 98—; mem. internat. adv. bd. Archiv der Pharmazie-Pharm. and Medicinal Chemistry, 1995—; dir. Ctr. for Frontier Rsch. Med. Sci., 1999—. Author: Chemistry of Biomolecule, 1989, Molecular Design, 1990; editor: Peptide Chemistry 1985, 1986; mem. editl. bd. Pharm. Soc. Japan, 1986-88, 92-97, Jour. Peptide Rsch., 1997—. Recipient award Naito Found., Tokyo, 1982, Japan Pharm. Rsch. Found., 1985; grantee Takeda Found., Osaka, Japan, 1989, Fugaku Found., Tokyo, 1990. Mem. Am. Chem. Soc., Pharm. Soc. Japan, Am. Peptide Soc., Japanese Chem. Soc., Japanese Biochem. Soc., Japanese Pharmacological Soc., Japan Endocrine Soc., Japan Peptide Soc. (treas. 1990-94), Soc. Synthetic Organic Chemistry (bd. dirs. 1997-98), Pharm. Soc. Japan (Kinki br. bd. dirs. 1997—). Home: 15-26 Inaba-cho, Ibaraki City 567-0827, Japan Office: Kyoto Pharm U, Yamashina Ku, Kyoto 607-8412, Japan

KISPAL, GYULA, biochemist, researcher; b. Mohacs, Hungary, Mar. 13, 1957; s. Gyula and Iren (Pakozdi) K.; m. Judit Takacs, Oct. 31, 1981; children: Gabriella, Julianna. MD, U. Med. Sch. Pecs (Hungary), 1981, PhD, 1989, Habilitation, 1995. Rsch. fellow U. Med. Sch. Pecs (Hungary), 1986-89, assoc. researcher, 1989, asst. prof., 1989-95, assoc. prof., 1995—. Contbr. articles to profl. jours. Home: Garai 34, 7624 Pécs Hungary Office: Inst Biochemistry, U Med Sch Szigeti 12, 7624 Pécs Hungary

KISS, EVA, chemist; b. Budapest, Mar. 7, 1955; d. Istvan Gordon and Crescencia (Zelenak) K.; m. Miklös Idei, May 24, 1980; children: Daniel, Marton. MS, Eotvos U., 1978, univ. dr., 1982; PhD, Hungarian Acad. Sci., 1992. Assoc. prof. Eotvos U., Budapest, 1978-82, 2000—, rsch. assoc., 1983-94, sr. rsch. assoc., 1995—. Contbr. articles to profl. jours.; editor: Procs. Conf. on Colloid Chemistry, 1986. Mem. Hungarian Chem. Soc. (sec. divsn. colloid chemistry 1985-90), Hungarian Acad. Sci. (colloid chemistry com. 1990—), Internat. Assn. Colloid Interface Sci., European Colloid Interface Sci. Office: Eotvos U Dept Colloid Chemistry, PO Box 32, 1518 Budapest 112, Hungary

KISS, FERENC, science educator, researcher; b. Debrecen, Hungary, July 22, 1958; s. Károly and Károlyne Ilona (Jaczina) K.; m. Agnes Bènyei, Aug. 24, 1982 (div. 1994); children: Gergely, Eszter; m. Judit Vallner, Aug. 15, 1996; 1 child, Levente. Maths. Tcrh., György Bessenyei Coll., Nyiregyhaza, Hungary, 1982; Chemist, Lajos Kossuth U., Debrecen, 1986, PhD, 1989. Researcher György Bessenyei Coll., Nyiregyhaza, Hungary, 1982-84; asst. prof. György Bessenyei Coll., Nyiregyhaza, 1984-89, head dept., 1993, assoc. prof., 1992-94; researcher U. Calif., Berkeley, 1989-91; prof. U. Wolverhampton (Eng.), 1994, U. Henry Poincarè, Nancy, France, 1997-98. Co-author: Environmental Chemistry, 1994, Sustainable Development at Local Governments, 1998, Education for Sustainable Development, 1999; co-author, editor: (CD ROM) Introduction to Environmental Science, 1998. Mem. Found. Clean Air, Nyiregyhaza, 1996, Found. for the Environment, Nyiregyhaza, 1995. Recipient award for the Environ. Edn. Ministry of Environment, 1999; named One of Ten Outstanding Young People Jr. Chamber Hungary, 1996. Mem. Hungarian Acad. Scis. (Pro Scientia award 1991), Biochem. Soc. Avocations: photography. Office: György Bessenyei Coll, Sostoi ut 31/B, 4401 Nyiregyhaza Hungary

KISS, PETER, pediatrician, geneticist; b. Budapest, Hungary, Mar. 13, 1928; s. Imre and Laura (Singer) K.; m. Judit Kovacs. MD, Szeged (Hungary) Coll., 1953; PhD, Hungarian Acad., 1987. Asst. lectr. Biochem. Inst. U., Szeged, 1952-56; pediat. City Hosp., Budapest, 1956-69, sr. house officer, 1969-72, head pediat. dept., 1972-93; head genetic svc. Bethesda Pediatric Hosp., Budapest, 1982-94; chief cons. Tng. Sch. Tchrs. Handicapped Children, 1982—. Editor Pediat. Quar. Med. Jour. Bokay award Hungarian Pediat. Assn., 1972, 86. Mem. Hungarian Accreditation Com. (counsellor 1993). Avocations: bridge, opera. Home: Diosarok 26/B, H-1125 Budapest Hungary

KISS, SANDOR ANDRAS, agro-biochemist, researcher; b. Oroshaza, Hungary, Sept. 9, 1925; s. Andras and Etelka (Fazekas) K.; m. Sandorne Erzsebet Tarr, July 21, 1951 (dec. Aug. 1973); 1 child, Beata Andrea; m. Erzsebet Toth, May 9, 1975. Grad. in Chemistry, U. Scis., Szeged, Hungary, 1951; Doctor, Agrl. U., Gödöllö, Hungary, 1970; Candidate of Sci., Acad. Scis., Budapest, Hungary, 1974; PhD, Agrl. U., Gödöllö, 1995. Prof.'s asst. Chem. U., Veszprem, Hungary, 1951-55; head rsch. group Chem. Works, Kazincbarcika, Hungary, 1955-87; prof. Agrl. Acad., Putnok, Hungary, 1972-84; cons. Rsch. Inst. Irrigation, Szarvas, Hungary, 1982-90, U. Scis., Szeged, 1992—. Author: Analytical Methods of Nitrogen Industry, 1964, Fertilization and Biology of Magnesium, 1983; co-author: Magnesium in Biological System, 1995, Biochemical Role of Magnesium, 1996; mem. editl. bd. Magnesium Rsch., 1995—, Bioletyn Magnezologiczny, 2000—. Lt. Hungarian Mil., 1956. Mem. Hungarian Magnesium Soc. (pres. 1989—), Biomineral Soc. (hon.), Internat. Magnesium Soc. (hon.). Avocations: photography, turistical. Home: Fö fasor 73A/2, H-6726 Szeged Hungary Office: Hungarian Magnesium Soc, Fö utca 68, H-1027 Budapest Hungary

KISSA, ERIK, retired chemist, consultant; b. Apr. 7, 1923; came to U.S., 1951, naturalized, 1956; s. Mats and Selma (Jakobson) K.; m. Selma Alide Tamm, Sept. 6, 1952; children: Erik Harold, Karl Martin. MS, Tech. U., Karlsruhe, Germany, 1951; PhD, U. Del., 1956. Rsch. chemist E. I. du Pont de Nemours & Co. Inc., Wilmington, Del., 1951-67, sr. rsch. chemist, 1967-74, rsch. assoc. Jackson Lab., 1974-86, sr. rsch. assoc., 1986-90, rsch. fellow, 1990-93; ret., 1994; cons., 1994—; UN tech. expert, India, 1978, 79, China, 1982, Korea, 1986-88. Author: Fluorinated Surfactants, 1993, Dispersions, 1999, Fluorinated Surfactants and Repellents, 2000; editor: Detergency Theory and Technology, 1987; contbr. articles, chpts. on surface chemistry, textile chemistry, and analytical chemistry to profl. publs.; U.S. and internat. patentee in field. Recipient Soap and Detergent Assn. award, 1991. Fellow Am. Inst. Chemists; mem. Am. Oil Chem. Soc., Am. Chem. Soc., Internat. Assn. Colloid and Interface Scientists, Fiber Soc., Du Pont Country Club, Del. Camera Club. Lutheran. Home and Office: 1436 Fresno Rd Wilmington DE 19803-5122

KISSA, KARL MARTIN, electrical engineer; b. Wilmington, Del., June 5, 1961; s. Erik and Selma (Tamm) K. BS, Duke U., 1982; MEE, U. Del., 1986, PhD, 1989. Tech. staff C.S. Draper Lab., Cambridge, Mass., 1989-94; photonic device engr. United Techs. Photonics, Bloomfield, Conn., 1994-95; sr. optical engr. JDS Uniphase, Bloomfield, 1995—. Vol. Harvard Sq. Meals Program, Cambridge, Mass., 1991-94. Mem. IEEE, Phi Beta Kappa, Tau Beta Pi, Eta Kappa Nu. Episcopalian. Home: 9 Rebecca Ln Simsbury CT 06070-1424 Office: JDS Uniphase 45 Griffin Rd S Bloomfield CT 06002-1353

KISSANE, SHARON FLORENCE, writer, consultant, educator; b. Chgo., July 2, 1940; d. Bruno William and Agnes Evelyn (Payne) Mrotek; m. James Quin Kissane, July 2, 1966 (dec. June 1989); children: Laura Janine Ehrke, Elaine Marie Kissane. BA, De Paul U., 1962; MA, Northwestern U., 1963; PhD, Loyola U., 1970. Cert. tchr., Ill. Tchr. Notre Dame H.S., Chgo., 1959-61, Our Lady of Solace Sch., Chgo., 1961-62; tech. writer, editor Commerce Clearing House, Chgo., 1962-63; tchr. U. Ill., Chgo., 1963-66; mgr. Amalgamated Ins. Co., Chgo., 1966-68; writer Herald Newspapers, Des Plaines, Ill., 1968-69; assoc. dir. Montague Coll. Psycho-Ednl. Clinic, Chgo., 1970-72; dir. Learning Ctr., libr. Stevenson Elem. Sch., Des Plaines, 1972-73; dir. Park Ridge (Ill.) Reading Ctr., 1973-78; pres. Kissane Comms. Ltd., Barrington, Ill., 1979—; learning disabilities specialist Montessori Sch., Lake Forest, Ill. Author: What is Child Abuse?, 1993, Gang Awareness, 1995; co-author: Polish Biographical Dictionary, 1992, Career Success for People With Physical Disabilities, 1996, Autobiography of Mousie Garner, Vaudeville Stooge; contbr. articles to profl. jours. and encyclopedia of advt. Bd. dirs. Barrington (Ill.) Children's Choir, 1984-85, LA FEP Student Exch. Program, Barrington, 1983-84, Barrington Area United Way, Operation Smile Internat., Chgo.; mem. task force Dist. # 220, Barrington, 1983-86; founding mem. Barrington Area Arts Coun., 1980, Park Ridge Hist. Soc., 1972; mem. curriculum com. Barrington H.S., 1981-84; elections judge South Barrington Precinct, 1989—. Recipient Dale Carnegie Speech scholarship Jr. Achievement, 1958; named Hon. Citizen of Korea, 1965; recipient La Cittá del Sole, Italy; honored as local author, Ill. Assn. Conv., 1999. Mem. Nat. Assn. Women Bus. Owners (bd. dirs. 1982-83), Internat. Platform Assn., MIT Forum, Ill. Libr. Assn. (Conn. chpt.), Barrington Profl. Women, Midwest Soc. Profl. Cons., Northwestern U. Entertainment Alliance, Phi Delta Kappa, Kappa Gamma Pi. Republican. Avocations: painting, post-card art, music, sports. Office: Kissane Comms Ltd 15 Turning Shore Dr South Barrington IL 60010-9597

KISSEL, WILLIAM THORN, JR., sculptor; b. Feb. 6, 1920; s. William Thorn and Frances A. (Dallett) K.; m. Barbara Eldred Case, June 17, 1943 (dec. June 1978); children: William Thorn III (dec.), Michael C. Grad., Choate Sch., 1939; BA, Harvard U., 1944; postgrad., Pa. Acad. Fine Arts, 1951-53; grad., Barnes Found., 1953, Rinehart Grad. Sch. Sculpture, Balt., 1958; BFA (hon.), Md. Inst. Coll. Art, 1996. T. Exhibited sculpture Lever House, N.Y.C., N.A.D., N.Y.C., Balt. Sculptor's Exhibit, York, Pa., Beverly, Mass., Gloucester, Woodmere Gallery, Germantown, Pa.; represented in pvt. collections, U.S.; executed large granite meml., Montclair, N.J.; also many animal sculpture studies and commns. Pilot, lt. (j.g.) USNR, 1943-45. Recipient Mass. Sculptor's award Regional Exhibit, 1958, Speyer award NAD, 1966, 68, Am. Artists Profl. League award, 1966; fellow Pa. Acad. Fine Arts, 1951-53. Fellow Am. Artists Profl. League, Nat. Sculpture Soc. Republican. Episcopalian. Home: 223 Greenspring Valley Rd Owings Mills MD 21117-4118

KISSELEV, VADIM DMITRIEVICH, physicist; b. Dalni, Primorski, Russia, May 8, 1958; s. Dmitri Feoktistovich Kiselev and Aleksandra Vasilievna Kibenko Kiseleva; m. Margarita Nikolaevna Lilko, Oct. 17, 1981; children: Vadim, Vassili. BA, Sch. # 23, Vladivostok, Russia, 1975, diploma in elec. engring., 1980, PhD in Physics and Math., 1991. Rschr. Pacific Oceanological Inst., Vladivostok, 1980-82, jr. scientist, 1982-93; asst. gen. dir. Pacific Devel. Ltd., Vladivostok, 1992-94; sr. scientist Pacific Oceanological Inst., Vladivostok, 1993—; gen. dir. Duet Ltd., Vladivostok, 1994—. Contbr. articles to profl. jours. Grantee Soros Found., 1993. Avocation: swimming. E-mail: kisselevvadim@hotmail.com. Office: Pacific Oceanological Inst, 43 Baltiiskaya St, 690041 Vladivostok Russia

KISSINGER, HENRY ALFRED, former secretary of state, international consulting company executive; b. Fuerth, Germany, May 27, 1923; came to U.S., 1938, naturalized, 1943; s. Louis and Paula (Stern) K.; m. Ann Fleischer, Feb. 6, 1949 (div. 1964); children: Elizabeth, David; m. Nancy Maginnes, Mar. 30, 1974. A.B. summa cum laude, Harvard U., 1950, M.A., 1952, Ph.D., 1954. Exec. dir. Harvard Internat. Seminar, 1951-69; mem. faculty dept. govt., Ctr. for Internat. Affairs Harvard U., 1954-69; dir. def. studies program Harvard Internat. Seminar, 1958-69, assoc. prof. govt., 1959-62, prof., 1962-69; faculty Ctr. Internat. Affairs, Harvard U., 1960-69; asst. to Pres. for Nat. Security Affairs, 1969-75; Sec. of State, 1973-77; founder, chmn. Kissinger Assocs., Inc., N.Y.C.; chmn. Nat. Bipartisan Commn. on Ctrl. Am., 1983-84; mem. internat. adv. com. Chase Bank; study dir. nuclear weapons and fgn. policy Coun. Fgn. Rels, 1955-56; dir. spl. studies project Rockefeller Bros. Fund, Inc., 1956-58; cons. Ops. Rsch. Office, 1950-61; cons. to dir. Psychol. Strategy Bd., 1952; cons. Ops. Coordinating Bd., 1955, Weapons Systems Evaluation Group, 1959-60, Dept. State, 1965-69; trustee Ctr. Strategic and Internat. Studies; hon. chmn. World Cup USA, 1994; bd. dirs. ContiGroup Cos., Inc., Freeport McMoran Copper & Gold, Inc., FirstMark Holding, The TCW Group, Inc.; adv. bd. dirs. Am. Express Co., Forstman Little & Co. Author: Nuclear Weapons and Foreign Policy, 1957, A World Restored: Castlereagh, Metternich and the Restoration of Peace, 1812-22, 1957, The Necessity for Choice: Prospects of American Foreign Policy, 1961, The Troubled Partnership: A Reappraisal of the Atlantic Alliance, 1965, White House Years, 1979, For the Record, 1981, Years of Upheaval, 1982, Observations: Selected Speeches and Essays, 1984, Diplomacy, 1994, Years of Renewal, 1999; Editor: Problems of National Strategy: A Book of Readings, 1965, Confluence, An Internat. Forum, 1951-58; contbr. to profl. jours. Internat. adv. coun. Chase Manhattan, Am. Internat. Group; trustee Ctr. Strategic and Internat. Studies; exec. com. Trilateral Commn; chair Eisenhower Exch. Fellowship; chancellor Coll. William & Mary; bd. dirs. Internat. Rescue com. Served with AUS, 1943-46. Recipient citation Overseas Press Club, 1958, Woodrow Wilson prize for best book fields of govt., politics, internat. affairs, 1958, Disting. Pub. Svc. award Am. Inst. Pub. Svc., 1973, Nobel Peace prize, 1973, Presdl. Medal of Freedom, 1977, Medal of Liberty, 1986; named Hon. Knight Comdr. of St. Michael and St. George, 1995; Guggenheim fellow, 1965-66. Mem. Am. Polit. Sci. Assn., Council Fgn. Relations, Am. Acad. Arts and Scis., Phi Beta Kappa. Clubs: Metropolitan (Washington); Century, River Club, Brook Club (N.Y.C.), Bohemian (San Francisco).

KISSLING, FRED RALPH, JR., publishing executive, insurance agency executive; b. N.Y.C., Feb. 10, 1930; s. Fred Ralph and Sarah Elizabeth (FitzGerald) K.; m. Mary Jane Gallaher (dec. 1999); children: Sarah FitzGerald, Jayne Kirkpatrick. BA, Vanderbilt U., 1952, MA, 1958. Spl. agt. Northwestern Mut. Life Ins. Co., Nashville, 1953-58; gen. agt. Northwestern Mut. Life Ins. Co., Lexington, Ky., 1962-80, New Eng. Mut. Life Ins. Co., 1981-87; mgr. life dept. Bennett & Edwards, Kingsport, Tenn., 1958-62; pres. Employee Benefit Cons., Inc., Lexington, 1961—; owner Lexington House, Inc., 1966—, Kennington Assocs., 1967—; prin. Kissling Orgn., 1980—, pub. Leader's mag., 1967—, editor, 1996—; owner, editor Fin. and Estate Planners Quar., 1993—; owner and pub. Fin. Svcs. Advisor, 1993—, Fraternal Monitor, 1999—; owner, pub., editor Probe Pub. Inc., 1997—; pub. Estate Rsch. Inst. Inc. Author: Sell and Grow Rich, 1966; editor: Questionnaire in Pension Planning, 1970, Questionnaire in Estate Planning, 1971. Adv. bd. Salvation Army, Lexington, 1971—, chmn., 1988-91; gen. chmn. United Way of Blue Grass, 1975, bd. dirs., 1975-78, 80-83; trustee, chmn. bd. Lexington Children's Theatre, 1979-81, pres., 1981-83. Mem. Am. Soc. CLU's (chpt. pres. 1969-70, 80-81, regional v.p. 1971-73), Ky. Gen. Agts. and Mgrs. Assn. (pres. 1965-66), Million Dollar Round Table (life mem., v.p., program chmn. 1976), Assn. for Advanced Underwriting (bd. dirs. 1976-84, pres. 1982-83), Am. Soc. Pension Actuaries (bd. dirs. 1971-78, pres. 1989-90), U. Akron Sales Insts. (adv. dir. 1996—), Am. Philatelic Soc., Sigma Chi, Lexington Club, Iroquois Hunt Club, Lafayette Club, Spindletop Hall, Masons, Shriners, Jefferson Club. Office: 98 Dennis Dr Lexington KY 40503-2915

KIST, EDWARD, insurance executive; b. 1944. With Nationale-Nederlanden, 1969—; various gen. mgmt. positions NN Gen., NN Life and NN Internat., 1977-86; pres. NN-US Corp., 1986, chmn., 1991; mem. exec. bd. ING Group, 1993—, vice chmn., 1999—, chmn., exec. bd., 2000—. Office: ING Group NV, Strawinskylaan 2631, 1077 Amsterdam The Netherlands*

KISTEMAKER, JACOB, retired physicist, educator; b. Kolhorn, N.H., The Netherlands, Apr. 23, 1917; s. Gradus and Elisabeth (Blaauboer) K.; m. Jacoba Catherina Keizer; children: Renée, Emilie, Willem. MSc, U. Leiden, The Netherlands, 1940, D Physics and Math., 1945; D Physics (hon.), Marie Curie U., Lublin, Poland, 1978; D Tech. Physics (hon.), Tech. U., Liège, Belgium, 1979; D Tech. Physics, U. Lisbon, Portugal, 1984. Asst. Kamerlingh Onnes lab. U. Leiden, 1939-46; rsch. physicist Fundamenteel Onderzoek Materie Found., Amsterdam, The Netherlands, 1947-53; dir. lab. for atomic physics Fundamenteel Onderzoek Matorie Found., Amsterdam, 1953-82; prof. physics Leiden U., Haarlem, The Netherlands, 1955-84; advisor Inst. Atomic and Molecular Physics Fundamenteel Onderzoek Materie Found., Amsterdam, 1982-87; conservator Teylers Mus., Haarlem, 1955-82; mem. Euratom Fusion Group, 1957-82; cons. Lab. Soil Dynamics, Delft, The Netherlands, 1983-90; rsch. coord. Netherlands Ultra Centrifuge Project, 1955-62; past bd. mem. Space rsch. Group The Netherlands, Inst. Isotope Geology, Amsterdam, Found. Parapsychol. Rsch., The Netherlands; co-founder Dutch Vacuum Soc., Found. Young Rschrs.; advisor Ministry Edn. and Scis., 1983-87; mem. Dutch Steering Com. Energy Rsch., 1974-76. Author: (with Sun Xiaochun) Chinese Sky During the Han, 1997, (with J. Bigeleisen and A.O.C. Nier) Proceedings Internat. Symposium on Isotope Separation, 1958; mem. editl. bd. Zeitschr Naturforsch, Radiation Rsch., Jour. Chem. Physics; contbr. over 200 articles to profl. jours. Recipient Krupp-Energy award, 1977. Fellow Am. Inst. Physics; mem. Royal Dutch Acad. Scis., Acad. Royal Brussels (assoc.), Russian Acad. Sci. (fgn. mem.). Home: Jan Steenlaan 27, Flat C2, 3723 BT Bilthoven The Netherlands Office: FOM Inst Amolf, Kruislaan 407, PO Box 41883, 1009 DB Amsterdam The Netherlands

KISTLER, GONZAGUE SERGE, medical company executive, microbiologist, researcher; b. Zûrich, Switzerland, Mar. 8, 1932; s. August and Claire (Calgari) K.; m. Verena Ursula Rohr. Diploma, Photography Sch. Arts/Professions, Zürich, 1952; baccalaureate, Bern, 1956; diploma Medicine, U. Zürich, 1962. Rsch. fellow dept. neurology Univ. Hosp., Zürich, 1961-62; rsch. fellow dept. anatomy Univ., Zürich, 1963-66, sr. rsch. asst. dept. anatomy, 1967-68, head cell biol. divsn. dept. anatomy, 1977-79, prof. emeritus Med. Faculty, 1993; chief med. officer dept. pub. health City of Zürich, 1980-83; chief med. officer Ministry of Health State of Zürich, 1983-93. Contbr. over 90 articles to scientific publications. Mem. Swiss Soc. Oncology (sec. 1977-79, pres. 1979-85). Home: Im Waidli 4, CH-8142 Zürich Uitikon-Waldegg, Switzerland

KISUKE, IIDA, mechanical engineering educator; b. Tokyo, Nov. 10, 1927; Iida Bunnojo Komatsu and Iida Kiyoko; m. Yoko Kimura, Mar. 17, 1969; 3 children. B, Tokyo U., D. Lectr. Meiji U., Tokyo, 1956-60, asst. prof., 1960-65, prof., 1965—. Author: Principle of Metal Machining, Studies on Shot Peening, 1995. Mem. Japan Soc. Mech. Engring., Japan Soc. Precision Engring., Soc. Shot Peening Tech. Japan. Avocations: mountain climbing, travel, skiing, movies, hand working. Home: 2-4-11 Nakamachi Machida, Tokyo 194-0021, Japan Office: Soc Shot Peening Tech Japan, Higashimita Toma, Kawasaki 214-8571, Japan

KITA, EISUKE, computer scientist, educator; b. Ise, Japan, Mar. 8, 1964; d. Hisashi and Takako (Sakaoka) K.; m. Kiyoko Yamamoto, Nov. 6, 1995; 1 child, Yasutada (dec. 1998). M, Mie U., Tsu, Japan, 1988; D, Nagoya (Japan) U., 1991. Cert engr. Tchg. asst. Nagoya U., 1991-94, asst. prof., 1994-99, assoc. prof., 1999—. Author: Numerical Analysis Schemes for Partial Differential Equation, 1998, Numerical Analysis and Its Applications, Linear Algebra by Computer, An Introduction to Trefftz Method. Office: Nagoya U, Chikusa Ku Furo Cho, Nagoya 464-8601, Japan

KITA, TAKASHI, physicist, researcher; b. Yamatotakada, Nara, Japan, Feb. 5, 1963; s. Yakichi and Emiko (Wada) Kanata; m. Kiyomi, May 9, 1993; 2 children. BSc, Kwansei Gakuin U., Nishinomiya, Japan, 1985, MA in Sci., 1987; PhD in Engring., Osaka U., Toyonaka, Japan, 1991. Tech. asst. Osaka U., Toyonaka, 1989-90; rsch. assoc. Kobe (Japan) U., 1990-2000, assoc. prof., 2000—. Author: Properties of Lithium Niobate, 1989; contbr. articles to profl. jours. Recipient incentive rsch. award Hyogo Sci. and Tech., 1994, Japan Material Rsch. Soc. award, 1995; grantee Mazda Found., 1996. Mem. Japan Soc. Applied Physics, Physical Soc. Japan. Avocations: computer networking. Office: Kobe U, 1 1 Rokkodai, Kobe 657-8501, Japan

KITABATAKE, YOSHIFUSA, environmental policy educator; b. Komatsu, Ishikawa, Japan, Oct. 1, 1944; s. Naonobu and Sumiko (Ogawa) K.; m. Noriko Imamori, May 25, 1975; two children. BA, Hitotsubashi U., Kunitachi, Japan, 1968, M in Commerce, 1970; PhD, Cornell U., 1974. Rschr. Nat. Inst. for Environ. Studies, Tsukuba, Japan, 1974-86; assoc. prof. U. Tsukuba, Japan, 1986-92; prof. Kyoto (Japan) U., 1992—; chief-priest Komatsu (Japan) Tenmangu Shrine, 1998—. Shinto. Home: 2 Tenjin-machi Komatsu, Ishikawa 923-0025, Japan Office: Kyoto U Grad Sch Human Environ Studies, Sakyo-ku, Kyoto 606-8501, Japan

KITADA, SHINICHI, biochemist; b. Osaka, Japan, Dec. 9, 1948; came to U.S., 1975; s. Koichi and Asako Kitada. MD, Kyoto U., 1973; MS in Biol. Chemistry, UCLA, 1977, PhD, 1979. Intern Kyoto U. Hosp., Japan, 1973-74; resident physician Chest Disease Research Inst., 1974-75; rsch. scholar lab. nuclear medicine and radiation biology UCLA, 1979-87, rsch. scholar Jules Stein Eye Inst., 1988-91; rsch. biochemist La Jolla (Calif.) Cancer Rsch. Found., 1992—. Author papers in field. Japan Soc. Promotion Sci. fellow 1975-76. Mem. Am. Oil Chemists Soc., N.Y. Acad. Scis., Sigma Xi. Home: 920 Kline St Ste 301 La Jolla CA 92037-4320 Office: The Burnham Inst 10901 N Torrey Pines Rd La Jolla CA 92037-1062

KITAGAKI, MUNEHARU, academic administrator; b. Kasumi, Hyogo-ken, Japan, Sept. 24, 1929; s. Kiyohisa and Tei (Aoyama) K.; m. Keiko Matsubara, May 8, 1960; children: Kanna Kitagaki Okuda, Manabu. BA, Doshisha U., Kyoto, Japan, 1952, MA, 1954, DLitt, 1981; BPhil, U. St. Andrews, Scotland, 1957; LHD, Northwestern Coll., Orange City, Iowa, 1997. From tchg. asst. to prof. English Doshisha U., Kyoto, 1954-90, prof. emeritus, 1990—; pres. Keiwa Coll., Shibata, Japan, 1991—; trustee Kobe Coll., Nishinomiya, Japan, 1979-99. Author: Principles and Problems of Translation in 17th Century England, 1981, Joseph Neesima and Amherst College, 1993 (Toyoda Minoru prize 1994). Bd. trustees, chmn. Japan-U.S. Cultural Found. of Doshisha, Japan, 1997—. Folger Shakespeare Libr. fellow, Washington, 1969, Harvard-Yenching Inst. fellow, Cambridge, Mass., 1969-70. Mem. Rotary (pres. Shibata chpt. 1996-97). Mem. United Ch. of Christ. Office: Keiwa Coll, Shibata-shi, Niigata-ken 957-8585, Japan

KITAGAWA, AUDREY EMIKO, lawyer, retired; b. Mar. 31, 1951; d. Yonoichi and Yoshiko (Nagaishi) K. BA cum laude, U. So. Calif., 1973; JD, Boston Coll., 1976. Bar: Hawaii 1977, U.S. Dist. Ct. Hawaii 1977. Assoc. Rice, Lee & Wong, Honolulu, 1977-80; pvt. practice Honolulu, 1980-96; head Sri Ramakrishna Spiritual Family, 1992—. Mem. Hist. Hawaii Found., 1984. Mem. ABA, Hawaii Bar Assn., Honolulu Club. Republican. Office: 927 Pensacola St Honolulu HI 96814-2242

KITAGAWA, HIROYUKI, geochemist, researcher; b. Hikone, Shiga, Japan, July 6, 1963; s. Shizuo and Masako (Okamoto) K.; m. Makiko Yamakawa, June 18, 1992; children: Yuri, Emi. BS, Shizuoka (Japan) U., 1986, MS, 1988; DS, Nagoya (Japan) U., 1991, DSc (hon.), 1997. Rsch. assoc. Internat. Rsch. Ctr. for Japanese Studies, Kyoto, 1991—; assoc. prof. Nagoya U., 1999—; vis. rschr. Ctr. for Isotope Rsch., Groningen, The Netherlands, 1995-96; inventor in field. Contbr. articles to profl. jours. Fax: 81 52 789 3436. Office: Nagoya U Inst Hydro-Atmos Sci, Furo-cho, Chikusa-ku Nagoya 464-8601, Japan

KITAGAWA, KAZUO, physician, strokologist; b. Osaka, Japan, Dec. 25, 1958; s. Mitsuharu and Setsuko (Kadota) K.; m. Mika Nakamura, Sept. 30, 1990; children: Yuka, Lisa. MD, Osaka (Japan) U. Med. Sch., 1983, PhD, 1990. Clin. fellow Osaka U. Med. Sch., 1983-84, rsch. fellow, 1986-90; clin. fellow Nat. Osaka-Minami Hosp., 1984-86; postdoctoral rsch. scientist Coll. Physicians & Surgeons Columbia U., N.Y.C., 1990-93, Brookdale Ctr. for Molecular Biology, Mount Sinai Med. Ctr., 1993, Osaka (Japan) U. Med. Sch., 1993-97; asst. prof. First Dept. Medicine Osaka U. Med. Sch., 1997—. Recipient Kusano award Japan Heart Found. and Japanese Soc. of Stroke, 1991, Award Encouraging Rsch., Japan Heart Found., 1996. Office: Osaka U Grad Sch Medicine, 2-2 Yamadaoka Dept Med & Therapeutics, Suita 565-0871, Japan

KITAGAWA, TEIZO, molecular biology educator; b. Kyoto, Japan, Sept. 7, 1940; s. Teijirou and Kazuko (Ueno) K.; m. Masako Kondou, Apr. 21, 1967; children: Hirochika, Yuki. BE, Osaka (Japan) U., 1963, MS, 1965, PhD, 1969. Postdoctoral fellow U. Minn, Mpls., 1971-73; rsch. assoc. Inst. for Protein Rsch. Osaka U., 1966-80, assoc. prof. Med. Sch., 1980-83; prof. Inst. for Molecular Sci., Okazaki, Japan, 1983—, Grad. Univ. for Advanced Study, Tokyo, 1988—; adj. prof. Tokyo Inst. Tech., 1985-86; chmn. dept. Inst. Molecular Sci., Okazaki, Japan, 1987-94. Author: Introduction to Raman Spectroscopy, 1998; editl. bd. Jour. Phys. Chem., 1994-97, Chem. Physics, 1994—. Mem. IUPAC (assoc.), Japanese Chem. Soc. (Sci. award 1989), Japanese Spectroscopic Soc. (Sci. award 1996), Japanese Biophys. Soc. Office: Okazaki Nat Rsch Inst, Myodaiji, Okazaki 444-8585, Japan

KITAHARA, SHIZUO, allergist; b. Tokyo, Nov. 20, 1922; s. Buntaro and Tamiko K.; m. Yoko Kitahara, April 19, 1931; 1 child, Taeko. MD, Tokyo U., 1945. Intern and resident Tokyo U. Hosp., 1946-56; chief allergist Doai Meml. Hosp., Tokyo, 1956-69; CEO Allergy Clinic, Tokyo, 1969—. Author: Anti-Allergics, 1970, Manual of Allergic Diseases, 1975, Treatment of Bronchial Asthma, 1985, Cure for Asthmatic Patients, 1994. Fellow Japan Allergy Soc.; mem. Am. Coll. Allergists, Am. Acad. Allergists, N.Y. Acad. Sci. Avocation: music. E-mail: shiz@blue.b-city.net. Home: 32-20 Minami-Ogikubo 4, Suginami-ku, Tokyo 167, Japan Office: Allergy Clinic, 11-18 Kita-Otsuka 1, Tokyo 170, Japan

KITAJIMA, YOSHITOSHI, printing company executive; b. Tokyo, Aug. 25, 1933; s. Orie and Toshiko Kitajima; m. Kiyoko Sumitomo; children: Yoshinari, Motoharu, Naoko. B Econs., Keio U., Tokyo, 1958. With Fuji Bank Ltd., 1958—; with Dia Nippon Printing Co., Ltd., Tokyo, 1963—, dir., 1967—, exec. v.p., 1975-79, pres., CEO, chmn. bd., 1979—; pres. Hokkaido

Coca-Cola Bottling Co., Ltd. Mem. Fedn. Econ. Orgns., Tokyo Am., Tokyo Rotary. Office: Dai Nippon Printing Co Ltd, 1-1 Ichigaya-Kagacho 1-chome, Shinjuku-ku Tokyo 162-8001, Japan

KITAKOJI, TAKAHIKO, orthopaedist, researcher; b. Kyoto, Japan, Feb. 19, 1961; s. Hironaka and Kiyoo (Yamaguchi) K.; m. Emi Katayama, Nov. 2, 1986; children: Natsumi, Marino. M Med., Nagoya (Japan) U., 1986, MD, PhD, 1999. Resident Fukuroi (Japan) Mcpl. Hosp., 1986-87, orthopedist, 1987-91; chief orthopedics Aichi Prefectural Hosp. & Rehab. Ctr. for Disabled Children, Okazaki, Japan, 1991-93; dir. Izu Rehab. and Welfare Ctr. for Children with Disabilities, Tagata-gun, Japan, 1993; orthopedist Nagoya U., 1994-98, asst. prof., 1998—. Office: Nagoya U Sch Medicine, 65 Tsurumai-cho Showa-ku, Nagoya 466-8550, Japan

KITAMOTO, YUTAKA, microbiologist, educator; b. Kyoto, Japan, June 12, 1940; s. Yojiro and Yoshi Kitamoto; m. Sachiko Itoh, Jan. 19, 1974; children: Fumie, Kazuhiko. B in Agr., Kyoto Inst. Tech., 1965; M in Agr., Kyoto U., 1967, D in Agr., 1970. Rschr. Kyoto U., 1970-71; rsch. assoc. Tottori U., 1971-75, lectr., 1975-79, assoc. prof., 1979-88, prof., 1988—, councilor, 1995; hon. scientist RDA, Korea, 1998—; vis. prof. U. Sask., Saskatoon, Can., 1973-74; mem. exec. com. for founding of Oita Mushroom Rsch. Inst., 1987-88. Author: Genetics and Breeding of Edibile Mushrooms, 1993; inventor prodn. of novel white Enokitake mushroom comml. strain by breeding. Mem. Soc. for Mushroom Tech. of Japan (pres. 1991-92, editor-in-chief 1993—), Mycol. Soc. Japan (v.p. 1995-96, pres. 1997-99), Japan Soc. for Biosci., Biotech., and Agrochemistry. Avocations: fishing, audio, horticulture. Home: Kumoyama 137-18, Tottori 680, Japan Office: Tottori U, Koyama-cho Minami 4-101, Tottori 680-0945, Japan

KITAMURA, AKIHIDE, surgeon; b. Osaka, Japan, June 13, 1949; s. Katsuko Koga, Oct. 23, 1976; children: Yukihiro, Aya, Hitoshi. MD, Osaka Med. Coll., 1975, PhD in Med. Sci., 1983. Resident in surgery Toranomon Hosp., Tokyo, 1975-77; asst. prof. dept. biochemistry Shimane Med. U., Izumo, 1977-83; chief surgeon Osaka Med. Coll., 1983-88; v.p. Ootori Icho Hosp., Sakai, 1988-91; surg. staff Minamiosaka Gen. Hosp., Osaka, 1991-97, dir. dept. surgery, 1997—. Author: ADP-ribosylation Reactions, 1982; contbr. articles to profl. jours. Grantee, Ministry of Edn., Sci. and Culture, Tokyo, 1981-86, Okinaka Meml. Inst. of Adult Disease, Tokyo, 1983-86, Osaka Anti-Cancer Assn., 1984-85. Mem. Japanese Soc. Surgery (med. specialist), Japanese Soc. Gastrointestinal Surgery, Japanese Soc. Biochemistry, Japanese Soc. Gastrointestinal Endoscopy (qualified endoscopist), Japan Soc. Coloproctology (med. specialist). Avocations: photography, music, tennis, golf, travel. E-mail: akihide@doc-net.or.jp. Fax: 06 6685 5208. Office: Minamiosaka Gen Hosp, 1-18-18 Higashikagaya, Suminoe Osaka 559-0012, Japan

KITAMURA, HIRONORI, anatomist, educator; b. Fukuyama, Japan, Dec. 18, 1920; s. Yukichi and Masa (Mitsunari) K.; m. Mitsuko Yasuda, Dec. 25, 1948; children: Akihide, Emi. DDS, Tokyo Med. Dental U., 1942, D in Med. Sci., 1960; BA in Psychology, Nippon Mgmt. U., 1972; PhD, Union U., 1984. Pvt. practice Fukuyama, Japan, 1946-55; asst. prof. Tokyo Med. and Dental U., 1956-61; rsch. assoc. dental sch. U. Wash., Seattle, 1961-63; rsch. assoc. cleft palate rsch. ctr. U. Pitts., 1963-65; prof. anatomy Kanagawa Dental Coll., Yokosuka, Japan, 1965-88, prof. emeritus, 1988—; oral anatomy educator Sch. Dental Hygienists, Hiratsuka, Japan, 1987-97. Author: Atlas of Developmental Anatomy of Face, 1966, Embryology of Mouth and Related Structures, 1989; author, editor: Color Atlas of Human Oral Histology, 1992, Oral Embryology and Pathohistology, 1998, Dental Malformations and Pathohistology, 1998, Human Soul and Body: One Spirti with Four-souls, 1999. Mem. Japanese Assn. Anatomists (councillor 1956—), Japanese Assn. Oral Biologists (councillor 1965—). Home: Minami-ku Nagata Higashi, 3-8-5 #406, Yokohama 232-0072, Japan

KITAMURA, JUNICHI, medical educator; b. Tano, Miyazaki, Japan, Jan. 18, 1952; s. Fujiharu and Hinako Kitamura. MD, Shimane (Japan) Med. Sch., 1982, PhD, 1993. Intern U.S. Naval Hosp., Yokosuka, Japan, 1983-84; resident Nat. Inst. Neurology and Psychiatry, Tokyo, 1984-89; chief medicine Nat. Inst. Ment. Hand, Saitama, Japan, 1989-91; rsch. fellow Nat. Inst. Neurology and Psychiatry, Tokyo, 1987-91; asst. prof. Saitama Med. Sch., 1991-93; lectr. Nippon Med. Sch., Kanagawa, Japan, 1993-97; assoc. prof. Nippon Med. Sch. Chiba-Hokusoh Hosp., Chiba, Japan, 1998—; head rehab. ctr. Nippon Med. Sch. Chiba-Hokusoh Hosp., Chiba, Japan, 1998—. Contbr. articles to med. jours. Sasagawa grantee Sasagawa Found., 1994. Mem. Japanese Neurol. Soc., Japanese Rehab. Med. Soc., Japanese EEG and EMG Soc., N.Y. Acad. Sci. Buddhist. Avocations: fishing, swimming. E-mail: kita-j@nms.ac.jp. Home: 2-402 464-14 Seto, Inba Chiba 270-1613, Japan Office: Nippon Med Sch, 1715 Kamagari Inba, Inba Chiba 270-1694, Japan

KITAMURA, TOSHINORI, psychiatrist; b. Yokohama, Kanagawa, Japan, Oct. 16, 1947; s. Masanori and Kikuko (Matsumoto) K.; m. Fusako Oami, Mar. 17, 1973. MD, Keio Gijuku U. Sch. Medicine, Tokyo, 1972. Psychiatrist Inst. Psychiatry, Tokyo, 1973-76; hon. rsch. fellow U. Birmingham, U.K., 1976-80; clin. instr. Keio Gijuku U., Tokyo, 1980-83, lectr., 1983; chief sect. mental health for elderly NIMH, Ichikawa, Japan, 1983-91; dir. dept. sociocultural environ. rsch. NIMH, Ichikawa, 1991—; vis. lectr. Keio Gijuku U., 1986—; head Group for Research Assessment in Psychiatry, Tokyo, 1981—; mem. com. Med. Selection Japanese Astronauts, 1987-88, 95-96, com. Psychiatric Diagnostic Criteria Japan, 1987-89, com. Guideline for Psychiatric Treatment, 1987-88. Editor-in-chief Archives of Psychiat. Diagnostics and Clin. Evaluation, Tokyo, 1989-91; editor Brit. Jour. Psychiatry, 1994-97, Internat. Jour. Behavioral Medicine, 1994-97, Internat. Jour. Offender Therapy Comparative Criminology, 1998—, Arch. Women's Mental Health, 1998—; contbr. articles to profl. jours. including Brit. Jour. Psychiatry, Psychol. Medicine, Jour. Affective Disorder, others. Fellow Royal Coll. Psychiatrists, Brit. Coun. Japan Assn., Japanese Assn. Psychiatry and Neurology (coun. 1991-94). Home: 8-12-4-305 Akasaka, Minato-ku, Tokyo 107, Japan Office: NIMH, 1-7-3 Konodai Ichikawa, Chiba 272, Japan

KITANO, KAZUAKI, microbiologist, researcher; b. Kawachinagano, Osaka, Japan, May 5, 1939; s. Jiichi and Chiyo (Nishibata) K.; m. Naoko Miyoshi, Oct. 10, 1967; children: Yoko, Seiko, Yuko, Mutsuko. BA, Osaka U., 1962, PhD, 1977. Rsch. scientist Takeda Chem. Industries, Ltd., Takasago, Hyogo, Japan, 1962-71; rsch. assoc. Takeda Chem. Industries, Ltd., Osaka, 1972-77, rsch. head, 1980-86, sr. rsch. head, 1987-91, dir. discovery rsch. labs. II, 1992-95, dir. rsch. on rsch. pharm. discovery rsch. divsn., 1995-96, leader human genomics project pharm. discovery rsch. divsn., 1995-97; rsch. assoc. Rockefeller U., N.Y.C., 1978, asst. prof., 1979; chmn. biotech. com. Japan Pharm. Mfrs. Assn., Tokyo, 1988-92, rsch. mgr., Japan Scis. and Tech. Co., 1997—. Author: (books) Practical Methods in Monoclonal Antibody, 1987, Animal Cell Bioreactors, 1991; contbr. articles to Jour. of Takeda Rsch. Labs., Progress in Indsl. Microbiology. Mem. Am. Soc. Microbiology, Japan Soc. Biosci., Biotech. and Agrochemistry, Soc. of Fermentation and Bioengring. (Saito prize 1975), Japanese Assn. Animal Cell Tech. (councillor). Achievements include discovery of single beta-lactam antibiotic of bacterial origin; establishment of a novel fermentation process for L-glutamate from acetate, novel screening system for beta-lactam antibiotics, effective production process for interferons by using recombinant E. coli, effective serum-free media for mammalian cells. Home: 120 Hatohara, Kawachinagano 586-0055, Japan Office: Japan Scis Tech Corp, 1-4-2 Shinsenri-higashimachi, Senri Life Sci Ctr 11 F Toyonaka 565-0082, Japan

KITANO, KIYOMITSU, oceanographer; b. Sendai, Japan, Mar. 21, 1926; s. Rokuro and Hisako (Segawa) K.; m. Seiko Sugawara, Nov. 20, 1961; children: Shinichi, Michiko. BA, Meterol. Coll., Kashiwa, Japan, 1947; MA, Tohoku U., Sendai, 1952; postgrad., U. Wash., 1959-60; DSc, Tokyo U., 1962. Asst. Kakioka (Japan) Geomagnetic Obs., 1947-49; oceanographer Tohoku (Japan) Regional Fish Rsch. Lab., 1952-57, Hokkaido(Japan) Regional Fish Rsch. Lab., 1957-64; chief 1st oceanog. lab. Regional Fish Rsch. Lab., 1964-86; prin. Kitano Ocean Cons., Sendai, 1986—; vis. rschr. U. Sydney, N.S.W., Australia, 1981; vis. scholar Woodshole Oceanog. Lab., 1980; Prime Min. Office vis. rschr. survey of satellite oceanography, Europe, Can., U.S., 1977. Author: Oceanography—The Past, 1980, Ocean Science—Their History and Relation to Man, 1990; contbr. articles to sci. jours. Mem. com. on oceanography North Pacific Fisheries Commn., 1958-59. Rockefeller Found. scholar, 1959-60; Australia Japan Found. fellow, 1981; grantee for attendance to 1st Oceanog. Congress at UN, 1959. Mem. Am. Geophys. Union, Am. Meteorol. Soc., Oceanog. Soc. Japan. Avocation: music. Home: 1-13-11-1104, Hachihonmatsu, Sendai 982, Japan Office: Kitano Ocean Cons, Hachihonmatsu 1-13-11-1104, Sendai 982, Japan

KITANO, TAKESHI, film director, actor; b. Tokyo, Jan. 18, 1948. Appeared in films Merry Christmas, Mr. Lawrence, 1983, Yasha, 1985, Komikku zasshi nanka iranai!, 1986, Sono otoko, kyobo ni tsuki, 1989, 3-4x jugatsu, 1990, Sonatine, 1993, Kyoso tanjo, 1993, Minna Yatteruka, 1994, Johnny Mnemonic, 1995, Gonin, 1995, Hana-bi, 1997, Tokyo Eyes, 1998, Kikujiro no natsu, 1999; dir. (films) Sono otoko, kyobo ni tsuka, 1989, 3-4x jugatsu, 1990, Ano natsu, ichiban shizukana umi, 1992; writer, dir., editor (films) Sonatine, 1993, Minna Yatteruka, 1994, Kids Return, 1996, Hana-bi, 1997; writer, editor (films) Ano natsu, ichiban shizukana umi, 1992; editor (films) Kyoso tanjo, 1993; actor, Gohatto, 1999, l'imprevisible, 1999, Brother, 2000. Office: Toredo Akasaka Bldg, 5-4-14 Akasaka 6th Fl, Minato-ku Tokyo, Japan*

KITAZAWA, YOSHIAKI, medical educator; b. Tokyo, Apr. 1, 1937; s. Katsuro and Suzu (Miyakoshi) K.; m. Mariko Ishikawa, Mar. 4, 1991. MD, Chiba U., Japan, 1961, PhD, 1967. Diplomate Japanese Bd. Ophthalmology. Instr. ophthalmology, asst. prof. Chiba U., Japan, 1967-76; assoc. prof. ophthalmology U. Tokyo, 1976-84; prof. ophthalmology, chmn. dept. Gifu U., Japan, 1985-2000, prof. emeritus, 2000—. Author: Clinical Glaucoma, 1985, The Atlas of Gonioscopy, 1995. Recipient Alcon award Alcon Rsch. Inst., 1994. Mem. Internat. Glaucoma Soc. (pres. 1994-98, sec. 1990-94), Internat. Perimetric Soc. (v.p. 1994—), Asia-Oceanic Glaucoma Soc. (pres. 1996—), Assn. Rsch. for Vision and Ophthalmology, Japanese Glaucoma Soc. (pres. 1998—), Am. Acad. Ophthalmology. Avocations: classical music, golf. Fax: 3-37221168. Home: 4-37-19 Den-en-Chofu Ota-ku, Tokyo 145-0071, Japan Office: Akasaka Kitazawa Eye Clinic, 5-5-13 Akasaka Shuzan Bldg, Minato-ku Tokyo 107-0052, Japan

KITBUNCHU, MICHAEL MICHAI CARDINAL, archbishop of Bangkok; b. Samphran, Thailand, Jan. 24, 1929. Ordained priest Roman Catholic Ch., 1959. Rector minor sem. Bangkok, 1965-72; consecrated archbishop of Bangkok, 1973, elevated to Sacred Coll. of Cardinals (1st cardinal from Thailand), 1983; titular ch. St. Laurence in Panisperna. Mem. Congregation for Evangelization of Peoples, Congregatio de Cultu Divino et Disciplina Sacramentorum, Praefectura Rerum Oeconomicarum Sanctae Sedis. Address: Cath Mission Bangkok, 51 Oriental Ave, Bangrak Bangkok 10500, Thailand*

KITCHEL, KAREN EMMA, artist; b. Battle Creek, Mich., May 19, 1957; d. Paul K. and Doris Jean Kitchel; m. Gary Michael Keene, Aug. 25, 1979. BA, Kalamazoo Coll., 1979; MFA, Claremont Grad. Sch., 1982. Critic, essayist New Art Examiner, Chgo., 1993-99. One-person shows include Barnsdall Pk, Hollywood, Calif., 1991, Couturier Gallery, L.A., 1992, Holter Mus. Art, Helena, Mont., 1997, Palm Springs (Calif.) Desert Mus., 2000; exhibited in group shows The Woman's Bldg., L.A., 1985, Riverside Art Mus., 1988, Laguna Art Mus., Laguna Beach, Calif., 1989, Ctr. for Visual Arts, Denver, 2000, Ucross Found., Wyo., 2000, Loveland (Colo.) Mus., 2000; represented in permanent collections Palm Springs Desert Mus., Denver Art Mus., Basil H. Alkazzi Found., N.Y.C., Hilton Hotels, Inc., Las Vegas, Nev.; mem. edit. bd. Eye Level mag., 1998-00. Chmn. Ctrl.-Terry Neighborhood Task Force, Billings, Mont., 1993=94 media liaison Clean Air Coalition, Billings, 1994, 95; mem. strategic planning com. Mont. Art Coun., Helena, Mont., 1994-95; mem. Cmty. Devel. Bd., Billings, 1996-97. Recipient Sheldon Bergh award Basil Alkazzi Found., N.Y.C., 1999; residency grantee Calif. Arts Coun., 1987-90; artist fellow Mont. Arts Coun., 1993. Mem. Coll. Art Assn. (panelist 1982—). Avocations: cross-country bicycling in U.S. and Europe. E-mail: kitchel@earthlink.net.

KITCHENS, JOYCE ELLEN, lawyer, assistant county guardian; b. Jesup, Ga., Oct. 8, 1948; d. Arthur Ellis and Ray Lucille (Burton) K.; m. Larry Keith Brumfield, Aug. 23, 1969 (div. July 1973); m. Jerry Baxter Barnes; stepchildren: Craig Randall Barnes, Suzanne Cynthia Barnes. BA in English Lit., Purdue U., 1970, MA in English Lit., 1972; JD, Emory U., 1982. Bar: Ga. 1982, U.S. Dist. Ct. (no. dist.) Ga. 1982, U.S. Dist. Ct. (mid. dist.) Ga. 1992, U.S. Ct. Appeals (11th cir.) 1982, U.S. Ct. Mil. Appeals 1996, U.S. Tax Ct. 1995, U.S. Ct. Appeals, 1999. Staff atty. Dept. Vet. Affairs, Atlanta, 1982-89, asst. dist. counsel, 1989-91; pvt. practice Atlanta, 1991—; cons. Fedn. Hwy. Adminstrn., Atlanta, 1993—; adj. faculty Emory U. Sch. Law. Mem. Fed. Bar Assn. (pres. Atlanta chpt. 1991-92, 11th cir. officer 1992-98, dep. sec. 1998-99, sec. 1999-00), Ansley Kiwanis (past pres. 1992-93, Disting. Svc. award 1991). Democrat. Presbyterian. Avocations: reading, travel, adventure. Office: PO Box 53278 Atlanta GA 30355-1278

KITCHIN, ALAN W.N., lawyer; b. Northampton, Eng.; s. Norman Tyson and Shirley (Boyd) K. BA, MA, Cambridge U., 1975. Admitted as a solicitor, Supreme Ct. of Eng. and Wales; admitted as a Gaikokuho Jimu Bengoshi, Japanese Ministry of Justice, 1991. Ptnr. Ashurst Morris Crisp, London, 1986; ptnr. in charge Tokyo office Ashurst Morris Crisp, 1991—; head Asian practice Asia for Ashurst, Tokyo, 1998—; chmn. infrastructure and privatisation com. LawAsia. Co-author International Trade for the Nonspecialist. Sr. Coll. scholar Cambridge U., 1974, Tapp scholar, 1975. Mem. Walton Heath Golf Club, Luffenham Heath Golf Club, Tokyo Lawn Tennis Club. Office: 8th Fl Kioicho Bldg, 3-12 Kioicho Chiyoda-ku, Tokyo 102-0094, Japan

KITCHIN, ROSEMARIE ATKIN, automotive executive; b. Springfield, Ill., June 6, 1939; d. Bernard and L. Lucille (McCarty) Atkin; m. Dec. 11, 1960 (div. 1974); children: Kraig Thomas, Kevin Thomas. BSJ, Northwestern U., 1961. Dir. pub. rels. Chrysler Corp., Highland Park, Mich., 1976-79; v.p. Martin Fromm, Kansas City, Mo., 1979-84; editor Chilton Co., Radnor, Pa., 1984-90; internal cons. Radiator Specialty Co., Charlotte, N.C., 1990-92; dir. comm. Top Source, Inc., N.Y.C., 1992-93; owner Kitchin's Ink, Charlotte, N.C., 1993—; dir. comm. Motor & Equipment Mfr., Research Triangle Park, N.C., 1995—; dir. ABS Edn. Alliance, Research Triangle Park, 1995—; exec. sec. Automotive Pub. Rels. Coun., Research Triangle Park, 1995—. Sec.-treas. Durham Conv. Bur., 1998—; treas. Inter Neighborhood Coun., Durham, 1996-98. Recipient Automotive Replacement Edn. award Northwood U., 1984. E-mail: rkitchin@mema.org and rkitchin@aol.com. Office: Motor & Equipment Mfrs 10 Laboratory Dr Research Triangle Park NC 27709

KITCHING, ALAN, typographic artist, educator; b. Darlington, Durham, Eng., Dec. 29, 1940; s. Walter and Katheleen (Davies) K.; m. Rita Haylett, Dec. 22, 1962; children: Robert Caslon, John Blake. Student, Darlington Tech. Coll., Durham, Eng., 1960. Apprentice compositor J.W. Brown & Son, Durham, Eng., 1955-61; designer Burrells, Wisbech, Cambridge, Eng., 1962-63; tech. asst. Watford Coll. Tech., Eng., 1963-68; free-lance graphic designer Eng., 1971-76; dir. Omnific Studios, London, 1976-88; prin. The Typography Workshop, London, 1988—; sr. tutor typography RCA, 1989—. Author: Typography Manual, 1970; contbr. letterpress graphics, typography to Eye mag., 1994. Recipient Royal Designer for Industry award Royal Soc. Arts, London, 1994. Mem. Alliance Graphique Internat., Chelsea Arts Club. Avocation: playing accordian. Office: The Typography Workshop, 19 Cleaver St, London SE11 4DP, England

KITE, THOMAS O., JR., professional golfer; b. Austin, Tex., Dec. 9, 1949; m. Christy Kite; 3 children. Student, U. Tex. Profl. golfer PGA, 1972-2000, PGA Srs., 2000—; mem. Ryder Cup Team, 1979,81,83,85,87,89,93., Capt., 1997. Named PGA Rookie of Yr., 1973, PGA Player of Yr., 1989; winner Air New Zealand Open, 1974, European Open (Eur), 1980, Oki Pro-Am (Spain), 1996; winner numerous golf tournaments including Bicentennial, 1976, B.C. Open, 1978, Inverrary Open, 1981, Bay Hill Open, 1982, Tournament Players Championship, 1985, 89, 91, Western Open, 1986, Kemper Open, 1987, Nestle Invitational, 1989, Nabisco Championship, 1989, Atlanta Classic, 1992, U.S. Open, 1992, L.A. Open, 1993, The Countrywide Tradition, 2000; recipient Vardon trophy, 1981, 82,. Achievements include being the PGA leading money winner, 1981, 89.

KITELEY, BRIAN ALAN, English literature educator, writer; b. Mpls., Minn., Sept. 26, 1956; s. Murray James and Jean (Vettel) K.; m. Cynthia Coburn, Aug. 27, 1991. BA, Carleton Coll., 1978; MA, CCNY, 1985. Lectr. Am. U. Cairo, 1987-89; asst. prof. Ohio U., Athens, 1992-94, U. Denver, 1994—. Author: Still Life with Insects, 1989, I Know Many Songs, But I Cannot Sing, 1996. Recipient Nat. Endowment Arts, 1991, Guggenheim Fellowship, 1992, Whiting Found. Writers award, 1996. Office: U Denver English Dept Pioneer Hall Denver CO 80208

KITMAN, MARVIN, journalist; b. Pitts., Nov. 24, 1929; s. Myer and Rose (Kaufman) K.; m. Carol Sibushnick, Oct. 28, 1951; children: Jamie Lincoln, Suzy, Andrea Jordana. BA, CCNY, 1953. Columnist Armstrong Daily, N.Y.C., 1956-63; media critic Newsday Newspaper, Melville, N.Y., 1969—; cons. Al Capp Enterprises, N.Y.C., 1961-63; staff writer Saturday Evening Post, N.Y.C., 1965-66; news mng. editor, founding mem. Monocle Mag., N.Y.C., 19 63-69, TV critic New Leader mag., N.Y.C., 1969-89; TV critic 10 O'clock News WNEW-TV, N.Y.C., 1980-87. Author: The Number One Best Seller, 1966, The Marvin Kitman TV Show: Encyclopedia Televisiona, 1972, You Can't Judge a Book By Its Cover, 1970, The Coward's Almanac, or The Yellow Pages, 1975, I am a VCR, 1989, The Making of the Prefident, 1789, 1989; co-author: George Washington's Expense Account, 1970; (under pseudonymn William Randolph Hirsch) The Red Chinese Air Force Diet, Exercise and Sex Manual, 1967. Avocations: watching TV, riding trains, writing movie scripts. Office: Newsday 235 Pinelawn Rd Melville NY 11747-4226

KITO, SHOZO, medical educator; b. Nagoya, Japan, Jan. 29; s. Chiyojyu and Tane (Goshima) K. MD, Tokyo U., 1951, PhD, 1959. Lic. physician, Japan. Instr. Sch. Medicine Tokyo U., 1967-71; asst. prof. Tokyo Women's Med. Coll., 1971-73; prof. Sch. Medicine Hiroshima (Japan) U., 1973-90, prof. emeritus, 1995—; prof. U. of the Air, 1990-97, Hyogo (Japan) U., 1998—. Author, editor: Neurotransmitter Receptors: Mechanisms of Action and Regulation, 1984, Neuroreceptors and Signal Transduction, 1988, Amyloid and Amyloidosis, 1988, Neuroreceptor and Mechanisms in the Brain, 1991. Mem. Japanese Soc. Internal Medicine, Soc. for Neurosci., Internat. Sco. Neurosci. (emeritus). Avocations: theater, writing book reviews, tennis. Home: 3-3-1-603 Higashi-Nobusue, Himeji Hyogo 670-0965, Japan Office: Hyogo U Rsch Inst, 2301 Shinzaike Hiraokacho, Kakogawa Hyogo 675-0101, Japan

KITOH, AKIO, meteorologist, researcher; b. Osaka, Japan, Apr. 1, 1953; s. Atsuko Sadano, Oct. 10, 1978; children: Ai, Yu. BS, Kyoto U., 1975, MSc, 1977, DSc, 1991. Rschr. Meteorol. Rsch. Inst., Tsukuba, 1980-87, sr. rschr., 1987-94, head lab., 1994—; affil. prof. U. Tsukuba, 1995—. Contbr. articles to profl. jours. including Jour. Meteorol. Soc. Japan, Jour. Climate, Climate Dynamics. Mem. Meteorol. Soc. Japan (award 1993), Am. Meteorol. Soc. Home: Ninomiya 1-14-46, Tsukuba Ibaraki 305-0051, Japan Office: Meteorol Rsch Inst, Nagamine 1-1, Tsukuba Ibaraki 305-0052, Japan

KITOVA, SNEJANA MILANOVA, chemist; b. Sofia, Bulgaria, May 30, 1950; d. Milan Ivanov and Penka Radeva (Petrowska) K.; m. Simeon Slavov Nikolov, Aug. 1, 1987; 1 child, Cyril. Diploma in Chemistry, State U. Sofia, Bulgaria, 1973; PhD, Bulgarian Acad. Scis., 1980. Chemist Inst. Phys. Chemistry, Sofia, 1973-74; rsch. assoc. Cen. Lab. of Photoprocesses/Bulgarian Acad. Scis., 1981—; supr. scientific projects Ministry of Edn. and Scis., 1993-2000, Bulgarian Acad. of Scis., 1993-2000. Patentee in field; contbr. numerous articles to profl. jours. Mem. N.Y. Acad. Scis., Bulgarian Union Scientists. Avocations: computers, skiing, swimming. Office: Cen Lab Photoprocesses, Acad G Bonchev Bl 109, 1113 Sofia Bulgaria

KITROMILIDES, PASCHALIS MICHAEL, political scientist, educator; b. Nicosia, Cyprus, Nov. 5, 1949; s. Michael Ioannis and Magda (Paschalides) K.; m. Mary G. Constantoudaki, May 3, 1978; 1 child, Michael Emmanuel. BA, Wesleyan U., 1972; MA, Harvard U., 1975, PhD in Polit. Sci., 1979. Lectr. govt. Harvard U., Cambridge, Mass., 1978-79; rsch. assoc. Ctr. European Studies Harvard U., Cambridge, 1976-79, postdoctoral fellow, 1979-80; lectr. polit. sci. U. Athens, 1980-83, prof. polit. sci., 1983—; vis. prof. politics Brandeis U., 1987; dir. Centre d'Etudes d'Asie Mineure, Athens, 1980—; vis. fellow Clare Hall Cambridge, 1989-90, St. Anthony's Coll., Oxford, 1993, St. Cross Coll. Oxford, 1997; dir. Inst. for Neohellenic Rsch., Nat. Rsch. Found., Greece. Author: Social Contract Theories, 1984, Iossipos Moisiodax, 1985, Utilitarian Liberalism, 1986, Modern Political Thinkers, 1989, 92, 98, 99, The French Revolution and Southeastern Europe, 1990, The Enlightenment as Social Criticism, 1992, Enlightenment, Nationalism, Orthodoxy, 1994, Modern Political Theory, 1996, 2000, Modern Greek Enlightenment, 1996, 99; editor, co-author: Small States in the Modern World, 1979, Culture and Society in Contemporary Europe, 1981; editor Bull. of Ctr. for Asia Minor Studies, 1980-2000; assoc. editor Jour. Modern Greek Studies, 1985-90; translator: Second Treatise of Government (John Locke), 1990; compiler: World Bibliographical Seris, vol. 28: Cyprus, 1982, rev. edit., 1995. Fulbright scholar, 1969, 85; Sheldon traveling fellow Harvard U., 1975, Krupp fellow Harvard Ctr. European Studies, 1977. Mem. Am. Polit. Sci. Assn., Hellenic Polit. Sci. Assn. (sec.-gen. 1980-84), Hellenic Polit. Sci. Assn. (pres. 1988-92), Phi Beta Kappa. Greek Orthodox. Home: Markou Drakou 40, Athens 11 476, Greece Office: U Athens Dept Polit Sci, Omirou 19, Athens 106 72 Greece

KITSOS, PETROS, banker; b. Thessaloniki, Greece, Aug. 13, 1965; came to U.S., 1990; s. George and Melpomeni (Yiannakou) K. BA, Hamilton Coll., Clinton, N.Y., 1988; postgrad., Aristotle U., Thessaloniki, 1989; MBA, Harvard U., 1992. Civil aviation editor Tech. Eds., S.A., Athens, 1983-84; with Nat. Bank of Greece, Thessaloniki, 1984-90, v.p., 1990; assoc. Salomon Bros. Inc., N.Y.C., 1991-93, v.p., 1993-99, mng. dir., 1999—; sr. ptnr. KPG Cons., Inc., Thessaloniki, 1988-91. Contbr. articles to profl. jours. Mem. Hellenic Econ. Assn., Greek Econ. Chamber, Phi Beta Kappa. Greek Orthodox. Home: 3 Mak Aminis St, 546 31 Thessaloniki Greece

KITT, EUGENE CLARK, organization administrator; b. N.Y.C., Aug. 11, 1950; s. William and Jessie (Felder) K. BS in Edn., CCNY, 1975; MS in Urban Edn., Fordham U., 1977; MS in Non-Profit Mgmt., New Sch. Social Rsch., 1991; LHD, Ea. North Theol. Inst., 1997. Guidance counselor Madison Sq. Boys & Girls Club, 1973-78; exec. dir. Co-op City's Youth Activities Com., 1978-80; assoc. dir. Upward, Inc., N.Y.C., 1980-87, exec. dir., 1987—, cons., 1996—. Author: Profiles of Excellence - Achieving Excellence in the Non-Profit Sector, 1991, Poetry to Live By, 1999. Named Community Leader of Yr. Salem Bapt. Ch., 1990, Proclamation N.Y. State Senate, 1996; named to Internat. Poetry Hall of Fame, 1998. Mem. Am. Mgmt. Assn. Democrat. Baptist. Avocations: fishing, photography. Home: 682 Doblin St Elmont NY 11003-4123 Office: Upward Inc 216 E 120th St New York NY 10035-3001

KITT, OLGA, artist; b. N.Y.C., July 29, 1929; d. Elias and Mary (Opiela) K.; m. Nicholas Rawluk, Aug. 6, 1955 (div. 1960); 1 child, Wade. BA, Queens Coll., 1951; MA, State U. Iowa, 1952; studied with Meyer Schapiro, N.Y.C., 1954; studied with Hans Hofmann, N.Y.C., Provincetown, 1954-55; postgrad., Inst. Fine Arts, NYU, 1955, NYU, 1960-62; studied with Robert Beverly Hale, N.Y.C., 1979. Gallery asst. Chappellier Gallery, N.Y.C., 1952-53; asst. to Walter Pach N.Y., 1953-56; teaching asst. CCNY, 1953-58; tchr. art N.Y., 1962-80. One-person shows include CCNY, 1957, Manhattan Coll., Riverdale, N.Y., 1980, Blackout Gallery, N.Y.C., 1997; exhibited in group shows at Whitney Mus., N.Y.C., 1954, Bronx County Hist. Soc., 1978, Mus. Modern Art, N.Y.C., 1978, Art Students League, N.Y.C., 1979, Bronx Mus. Arts, 1979; represented in permanent collections including Bronx Arts Ensemble, Riverdale Press, Riverdale YM-YWHA, U. Iowa, Iowa City, Fordham U., Fordham Prep. Sch., Hostos Coll., N.Y.C., Harris Sch. of Art, Tenn.; represented in pvt. collections. Home: 5610 Netherland Ave Bronx NY 10471-1703 Studio: 495 S Broadway Yonkers NY 10705-3221

KITTEL, AGNES, cell biologist; b. Békéscsaba, Hungary, Aug. 25, 1956; d. Frigyes and Irén (Vukmanovits) K.; m. Imre Zsolt Sziman; children: György, Petra, Imre Kristóf. MS in Chemistry, Eötvös Lóránd U., Budapest, Hungary, 1981, D in Biochemistry, 1988, PhD in Biology, 1996. Rsch. coworker Inst. Chemistry and Biochemistry Semmelweis Med. Sch., Budapest, 1981-83; rschr. Inst. Exptl. Medicine Hungarian Acad. Scis., Budapest, 1988-89, 92-95, sr. mem., 1996—; prin. investigator Hungarian-Flemish Sci. and Tech. Coop. project, 1998—. Unido-Internat. Ctr. for Genetic Engring. and Biotech. fellow, Milan, 1995; Eötvös Hungarian State fellow U. Calif-San Diego, La Jolla, 1995-96, Soros fellow Harvard Med. Sch., Boston, 1998,

fellow Rehovot Weizmann Inst., 2000. Mem. European Neurosci. Assn., Fedn. European Neurosci. Socs., European Molecular Biology Orgn., European Soc. Neurochemistry, Internat. Soc. Neurochemistry (assoc.), Internat. Brain Rsch. Orgn. Avocations: music, literature, history, swimming, biking. Office: Inst Exptl Medicine, Szigony U 43, H 1083 Budapest Hungary

KITTIKHOUN, ALOUNKEO, ambassador. Permanent rep. Lao People's Dem. Republic Un, N.Y.C., 1993—. Office: Permanent Mission of Lao UN 317 E 51st St New York NY 10022-6702

KITTL, PABLO ALFREDO, materials scientist, researcher; b. Buenos Aires, Nov. 18, 1934; arrived in Chile, 1965; s. Erwin Franz and Georgina Amalia (Duclout) K. Tech. cons., Nat. U. de Cuyo, San Juan, Argentina, 1953; lic. in physics, U. San Luis, Argentina, 1964, U. Chile, Santiago, 1980. Prof. spl. physics U. San Luis, 1963-64; rschr. IDIEM U. Chile, 1965-80, chief electron microscopy lab, Materials Dept., 1980-95, prof. physics, 1980—; vis. prof. UCLA, 1973, Fed. U. São Carlos, Brazil, 1978. Author: Scientific and Technological Development, particularly in the Case of Chile, 1995; contbr. over 185 articles to profl. scientific jours. (hon. mention L.Am. Jour. Metallurgy and Materials, 1987). Fellow Am. Acad. Mechanics; mem. Chilean Acad. Scis. (corr.), Scientific Soc. Argentina. Avocations: restoring and collecting antiques, books, pictures, etc. Home: Torrealba 85 & Catedral 5871, Viña del Mar Santiago, Chile Office: U Chile Dept Mech Engring, Beaucheff 850 Cas 2777 C 21, Santiago Chile

KITTLITZ, RUDOLF GOTTLIEB, JR., chemical engineer; b. Waco, Tex., Apr. 19, 1935; s. Rudolf Gottlieb and Lena Hulda (Landgraf) K.; children: Lenell, Theresa, Liesel, Rolf. BSChemE, U. Miss., 1957; postgrad., U. Ala., 1998—. Registered profl. engr., Calif. Engr., polychems. research E.I. du Pont de Nemours & Co., Wilmington, Del., 1957-60; engr., textile fibers dept. E.I. du Pont de Nemours & Co., Seaford, Del., 1960-62; sr. engr., textile fibers dept. E.I. du Pont de Nemours & Co., Seaford, 1962-67, Chattanooga, 1967-68; sr. research engr. E.I. du Pont de Nemours & Co., 1968-83; sr. research engr. textile fibers E.I. du Pont de Nemours & Co., Seaford, 1983-87, research assoc. textile fibers, 1987-92, sr. rsch. assoc. fibers, 1992-94; sr. rsch. assoc. fibers Chattanooga, 1995—; lectr. in field.; adj. prof. U. Tenn.-Chattanooga, 1980-82; Citizen Amb. Program del. to Russia, 1991. Co-author: Quality Assurance for the Chemical and Process Industries--A Manual of Good Practices, 1987, 2d edit. 1999, ANSI/ASQC Q90/ISO 9000: Guidelines for Use by the Chemical and Process Industries, 1992, Specifications for the Chemical and Process Industries--A Manual for Development and Use, 1996. Vice chmn. Community Action Com., Seaford, 1966; mem. ISO/TC 69, 1996—. Fellow Am. Soc. for Quality (cert. quality and reliability engr., chmn. Chattanooga sect. 1975-76, councilor region 11 chem. divsn. 1975-80, chmn. Del. sect. 1984-85, exec. regional dir. 1987-91, dir.-at-large 1991-93, parliamentarian 1993-99, 2000—, W.G. Hunter award 1989); mem. AAAS, Am. Statis. Assn. Democrat. Baptist. Home: Condo 307 1000 Reads Lake Rd Chattanooga TN 37415-2057 Office: DuPont Nylon 4501 N Access Rd Chattanooga TN 37415-3899

KITTRELL, MARIE BECKNER, retired educator; b. Winchester, Ky., Oct. 25, 1905; d. Lucien and Marie Daviess (Warren) Beckner; m. James Bingham Kittrell, June 23, 1928 (dec.); children: James Bingham Jr., Marie Beckner Kitrell Lynn, Lucien Cartwright (dec.), Lucy Hunter Kittrell Combs. BA, U. Ky., 1926. Social editor Winchester newspaper, 1925, 26, 27; senate clerk revisions law com. Washington, 1927-28; sch. tchr.; sec. to supt. schs., editor sch. newspaper Ludlow, Ky., 1927; writer, producer, hostess TV show, 1957-71; hostess mgr. Thomas Hunt Morgan House, Lexington, 1967-69. Freelance writer. Pres. Jr. League Lexington, 1936-40, Young Women's Rep. Club; originator, pres. Jr. League Horse Show, Lexington, 1937-41; nat. adv. com. mem. women's fair N.Y. World's Fair, 1939; mem. Bd. Child Guidance Svc., Bd. Manchester Cmty. Ctr., Lexington, adv. bd. Ky. Hist. Markers Program, Fayette County Com. Ky. Civil War Centennial Commn.; chair program arrangements Lexington & Fayette County Sesqui-Centennial Ky. Statehood, 1942. Named May Queen Ct. Mem. League Am. Pen Women, Monday Club, Ky. Hist. Soc., U. Ky. Alumni Assn., Filson Club (life), Colonial Dames Am. (past pres., registrar), Delta Delta Delta. Presbyterian. Avocations: piano, stampl collecting, ballroom dancing.

KITTRIE, NICHOLAS N(ORBERT NEHEMIAH), law educator, international consultant, writer; b. en route Bilgoraj, Poland, Mar. 26, 1930; (parents Brit. citizens); came to U.S., 1944; s. S.K. Kronenbergh and Perla F. (Ver Standig) K.; m. Sara Yudovic de Burak, June 1, 1962; children: Orde Felicien, Norda Nicole, Zachary McNair. Student, U. Cairo, 1946, U. London, 1947; LLB, U. Kans., 1950, MA, 1951; postgrad., U. Chgo., 1954-55; LLM, Georgetown U., 1963, SJD, 1968. Bar: Kans. 1953, D.C. 1958, U.S. Supreme Ct. Rsch. asst. U. London, 1947; instr. Western civilization dept. U. Kans., 1948-50; legal analyst Kans. Govt. Rsch. Ctr., 1951-54; asst. to dir. legis. svc. ABA, 1955-56, project dir., 1956-58; rsch. assoc. Yale Law Sch., 1958; legal asst. to U.S. Senator Wiley, 1959; counsel to U.S. Senator Estes Kefauver, antitrust and monopoly subcom. U.S. Senate, 1959-62; ptnr. DeGrazia & Kittrie, Washington, 1962-67; prof. criminal and comparative law Washington Coll. Law, Am. U., 1963—, dir. Inst. for Advanced Studies in Justice, 1970-78, dean, 1977-79, Mooers scholar and prof. law, 1983—, prof., 1994—; univ. prof. Am. U., Washington, 1994—; dir. Inst. Law and Policy, 1980—; lectr. U. Ottawa, summer 1966; vis. lectr. Salzburg Law Sch., summers 1999—; rsch. scholar Univs. Warsaw and Berlin, summers 1967, 68; rsch. assoc. Ctr. Studies Criminal Justice U. Chgo., 1967-68; dir. Law and Policy Inst., Jerusalem, summers 1970-76, Inst. Law and Mass Media, 1978—; chmn. Eleanor Roosevelt Inst. for Justice and Peace, 1989—; vis. fellow Inst. Advanced Legal Rsch. U. London, 1973-74, Nat. Inst. Justice U.S. Dept. Justice, 1979-80; vis. prof. London Sch. Econs., 1974; cons. Pres.'s Commn. Marijuana and Drug Abuse, 1972, v.p.'s commn. to combat terrorism, 1985; permanent rep. of AIDP to UN Social and Econs. Coun., 1975—; mem. task force on role of psychology in criminal justice Am. Psychol. Assn., 1975-76; dir. 1st Washington Devel. Corp., Bank of Chios, Athens, Greece; dir., gen. counsel Liberty House Investments; v.p. Nickal Corp.; chmn. KVK Communications Ltd. Author: International Legal Responsibility for Colonial People, 1951, Survey of Adminstration of Criminal Justice, 1956, (with others) The Mentally Disabled and the Law, 1959, The Right to be Different: Deviance and Enforced Law, 1971, The Comparative Law of Israel and the Middle East, 1971, The Real Estate Settlement Process and Its Cost, 1972, Crescent and Star: Arab-Israeli Perspectives on the Middle East Conflict, 1972, The Juvenile Drug Offender, 1972, Medicine, Law and Public Policy, 1975, Sanctions, Sentencing and Corrections, 1981, The Tree of Liberty: Rebellion and Political Crime in America, 1986, 2d edit., 1998, The Uncertain Future: Gorbachev's Eastern Bloc, 1988, The War Against Authority: From the Crisis of Legitimacy to a New Social Contract, 1995, Rebels With a Cause: The Minds and Morality of Political Offenders, 2000; chmn. editorial bd. Jour. Criminology, 1973-75, Justice mag., 1973-75; mem. editorial bd. Law and Human Behavior, 1976-80; mem. editorial adv. bd. The Washington Times; mem. exec. bd. Paragon House Pubs.; sr. cons. U.S. News and World Report Books; contbr. articles to profl. jours. Chmn. UN Alliance of NGOs on Crime Prevention and Criminal Justice, 1998—, sci. com. U. Messina, Italy; mem. senate Am. U., 1964-72. Served with Brit. Middle East Command, 1944-45. Raymond fellow U. Chgo., 1954-55; rsch. fellow Yale Law Sch., 1955; sr. fellow NEH, 1973-74. Mem. ABA, AAAS (mem. coun. 1972—), Am. Soc. Criminology (pres. 1975), Internat. Assn. Penal Law (v.p. Am. sect., sec.-gen. 1975-80), Internat. Assn. Comparative Pub. Law (bd. dirs. 1976—), Am. Soc. Pub. Adminstrn., Am. Judicature Soc., Am. Soc. Internat. Law, Internat. Inst. Space Law, Inter-Am. Bar Assn., Kans. Bar Assn., D.C. Bar Assn., Rose Haven Yacht Club (bd. dirs., Cosmos Club, Phi Delta Phi (Sam Green award 1989), Pi Sigma Alpha. Fax: 202-387-3629. Home: 6908 Ayr Ln Bethesda MD 20817-4902 also: 42427 Cochran Mill Rd Leesburg VA 20175-4617 Office: Am U Sch Law 4801 Massachusetts Ave NW Ste 354 Washington DC 20016

KITTSON, MANN, metal and plastic manufacturing company executive; b. Hong Kong, July 13, 1919; children—Phebe, Julia, Susanna, Samson, Amy. M.S., Loughborough U., 1985. Mgr. Chung Mei Metal and Plastic Factory, Ltd., Hong Kong, 1963—. Active Boy Scout Assn. Hong Kong, 1963—. Avocations: music; violin. Home: Flat A 24/F Block 4, Nan Fung Sun Chuen/39 Greig, Quarry Bay Hong Kong Office: Chung Mei Metal & Plastic, Chung Mei Bldg, Kowloon Hong Kong

KITUA, ANDREW YONA, epidemiologist, medical researcher; b. Kilimanjaro, Tanzania, Sept. 18, 1949; s. Yona Andrea and Nasemba Mose (Mmbuji) K.; m. Marguerite Charles Marie, Dec. 6, 1980; children: Nasemba Rita, Navoneiwa Judith, Anthony Yona. MD, Milan State U., 1979; Diploma Reconstructive Microsurgery, Brescia (Italy) U., 1979; MSc, U. London, 1989; PhD in Clin. Epidemiology, Basel (Switzerland) U., 1996. Physician Tanzanian Ministry Health, Dar es Salaam, 1979-82; physician Seychelles Ministry Health, Victoria, 1983-85, dir. epidemiology and rsch., 1985-92; dir. Ifakara (Tanzania) Health Devel. and Rsch. Ctr., 1992-97; dir. gen. Nat. Inst. for Med. Rsch., Dar es Salaam, 1998—; mem. Nat. Focal Point Essential Nat. Health Rsch., Tanzania; mem. Coun. of Global Forum for Health Rsch., 1999—; mem. steering com. Coun. on Health Rsch. for Devel.; sec. Health Rsch. Users Trust Fund, Dar es Salaam, 1998—, Nat. Health Rsch. Forum, Dar es Salaam, 1999—. Contbr. articles to med. jours., including Social and Preventive Medicine, Lancet, Tropical Medicine and Internat. Health, African Jour. Health Scis. Mem. steering com. for malaria vaccines WHO, Geneva, 1995-97. Grantee Tanzanian Health Rsch. Tng. Fund, WHO, 1999. Mem. African Malaria Soc. (pres. East Africa br. 1999—), Royal Soc. Tropical Medicine and Health, Internat. Epidemiol. Assn., Coun. Global Forum for Health Rsch. Avocations: fine art, swimming. Fax: 255 51 130660/131864. E-mail: akitua@twiga.com. Office: Nat Inst for Med Rsch, Ocean Rd, PO Box 9653, Dar es Salaam Tanzania

KITUOMBA See ODAGA, ASENATH BOLE

KITYK, IVAN VASYL, physicist; b. Lvov, Ukraine, Nov. 22, 1957; s. Vasyl Ivan and Stefania Michael (Rizniak) K.; m. Irena Skomorovska, Feb. 13, 1961; 1 child, Mary. Degree in physics, Lvov U., 1979. Laser designer Polaron, Lvov, 1979-82; scientific rschr. Lvov and Moscow U., 1986-93; prof. U. Czestochowa, 1994—; prof. physics Internat. Lab. Low Temperature and High Magnetic Field, Wroclaw, Poland, 1996—; cons. Angers du Main (France) U., 1995—, Moltech GmbH, Berlin, 1993—, Inst. Superhard Water, Kiev, Ukraine, 1994—, Tech. U., Petersburg, Russia, 1992-95. Author: Electronic Structure and Optics of Non-Linear Crystals, 1996, Optical Properties of Sodicene Glasses, 1996, Nonlinear Optics of Solids, 1996, Optoelektronic of Superconductors, 1996; contbr. articles to profl. jours. Local chief RUCN, Lvov, 1990-92. Grantee Sorosprise award, 1993. Mem. N.Y. Acad. Scis., Shevchenko Sci. Soc., Nat. Geog. Soc. Roman Catholic. Avocations: football, music. E-mail: i.kityk@wsp.czest.pl. Office: Inst Physics Internat Lab, High Magnetic Field Low Tem, Wroclaw Poland

KITZES, WILLIAM FREDRIC, lawyer, safety analyst, consultant; b. Bklyn., Nov. 24, 1950; s. David Louis and Rhoda Rachel (Feldman) K; m. Sandra Shimasaki, Apr. 7, 1979: children: Justin, Dana. BA, U. Wis., 1972; JD, Am. U., 1975. Bar: D.C. 1977. Legal advisor on product recalls U.S. Consumer Products Safety Commn., Washington, 1975-77, program mgr., 1977-80, regulatory counsel, 1980-81; v.p., gen. mgr. Inst. for Safety Analysis, Rockville, Md., 1981-83; prin. Consumer Safety Assocs., Potomac, Md., Boca Raton, Fla., 1983—; cons. Toro Co., Bloomington, Minn., 1987, Vendo Co., Fresno, Calif., 1987, Nat. Assn. Attys. Gens., Washington, 1987, Arctic Cat, Inc., thief River Falls, Minn., 1995—, Global Furniture, Toronto, Ont., 1997, Product Safety Online, Boca Raton, 1997—. Counsel Friends of Charlie Gilchrist, Montgomery County, Md., 1983; chmn. Fla. Consumers Coun., 1995—. Recipient silver medal for meritorious svc. U.S. Consumer Products Safety Commn., 1976. Mem. Am. Soc. Safety Engrs., Human Factors Soc., System Safety Soc., Nat. Safety Coun., Internat. Consumer Product Health and Safety Orgn. Home and Office: Consumer Safety Assocs 4501 NW 25th Way Boca Raton FL 33434-2506

KITZINGER, UWE, college president; b. Nuremberg, Germany, Apr. 12, 1928; m. Sheila Helena Elizabeth Webster, Oct. 4, 1952; children: Celia, Tessa, Nell, Polly, Jenny. BA, 1951, MA, 1953, MLitt, 1956, 80; LLD (hon.), Buena Vista, 1986. Sec. econ. sect. Coun. of Europe, Strasbourg, 1951-58; lectr. U. Saar, 1954-56; fellow Nuffield Coll., Oxford (Eng.) U., 1956—; investment bursar, Nuffield Coll., 1961-76; vis. prof. U. West Indies, 1964-65, Harvard U., Cambridge, Mass., 1969-70, U. Paris, 1970-73; advisor to v.p. ext. rels., EEC, Brussels, 1973-75; dean INSEAD, Fontainbleau, 1976-80; dir. Oxford Ctr. Mgmt. Studies, 1980-84; pres. Templeton Coll., Oxford, 1984-91; co-founder Lentils for Dubrovnik, 1991; vis. scholar Harvard U., 1993—; sr. rsch. fellow Atlantic coun. U.K., 1993—; founding chmn. Com. Atlantic Studies, 1969-71, Maj. Projects Assn., 1981-87; founding pres. Internat. Assn. Macro-Engring. Socs., 1987-92, 96-99, chmn., 1999—; pres. Fedn. Brit. des Alliances Françaises, 1998—; mem. Brit. Acad. Com. Ency. Br it., 1969-99; mem. coun. Oxfam, 1981-85; adv. bd. Pace U., N.Y.C., 1981-92, Berlin Sci. Ctr., 1983-92; internat. bd. dirs. Inst. Transition Democracy, Zagreb, 1997—; mem. internat. adv. bd. Conflict Mgmt. Group, Cambridge, Mass., 1997—, Asian Disaster Preparedness Ctr., Bangkok, 2000—. Founding editor Jour. Common Market Studies, 1962—; author: German Electoral Politics, 1960, The Challenge of the Common Market, 1961, The Second Try, 1968, Diplomacy and Persuasion, 1973, Europe's Wider Horizons, 1975; (with D.E. Butler) The 1975 Referendum, 1976, 96; co-editor: Macro-Engineering and the Earth, 1998. Mem. Royal Inst. Internat. Affairs (coun. 1973-85), Order of the British Empire (comdr. 1980), Order of the Morning Star, Croatia, 1997, Royal Thames Yacht Club, United Oxford and Cambridge U. Club. Office: 519 Lowell House Cambridge MA 02138-7566 Home: La Riviere, 11100 Bages France

KITZMAN, JERRY MATSON, pharmaceutical executive; b. Elkhorn, Wis., Dec. 11, 1947; s. Walter Eugene and Florence Leona (Knilans) K.; m. Renate Ulrike Bernold, Dec. 29, 1981; 1 child, Daniela Helen. BA, Northwestern U., 1970; MA, UCLA, 1978, postgrad., 1979. Tchg. asst., assoc., fellow UCLA, 1978-79; tchr. Latin Marlborough Sch., L.A., 1981-82; supr., planner Schein Pharms., Phoenix, 1983—. Contbr. article to profl. jour. Lt. j.g. USN, 1970-74. Fulbright fellow, 1980-81; recipient award for excellent damage control USS Cook USN. Mem. AAAS, N.Y. Acad. Scis., Planetary Soc. Republican. Baptist. Avocations: astronomy, fossil and rock collecting, stamp collecting, national parks. Home: 4665 W Desert Crest Dr Glendale AZ 85301-4116 Office: Schein Pharm 620 N 51st Ave Phoenix AZ 85043-2702

KIVELA, SIRKKA-LIISA, general practice medical educator; b. Temmes, Finland, Jan. 14, 1947. MD, Oulu U., 1971; PhD, Tampere U., 1983. Gen. practitioner Posio Health Ctr., Finland, 1971-72, chief med. officer, 1972-80; sr. lectr. Tampere U., Finland, 1980-88; from asst. prof. pub. health to prof. gen. practice Oulu U., 1988-2000; prof. gen practice Turku U., 2000—. Avocations: sports, poetry. Fax: 358-2-3338439. Home: Sairashuoneekatu 14a11, 20100 Turku Finland Office: Dept Gen Practice, Turku U Lemminkaisenkatu 1, 20520 Turku Finland

KIVERNITAKIS-SINANIS, NICHOLAS, civil engineer; b. Heraklion, Crete, Greece, Dec. 26, 1951; s. John Kivernitakis and Anna Sinani; m. Maria Michelaki, Apr. 19, 1982; children: Anthony, Anna. Diploma in engring., U. Per Stranieri, Perugia, Italy, 1986; laurea in engring., U. Degli Studi, Ancona, Italy, 1994. Collaborator dept. engring. U. Ancona, 1982-88; adminstrv. staff IESL/Forth, Heraklion, Greece, 1989-95; adminstrv. staff dept. physics U. Crete, Heraklion, 1996—. Author: La Gelivita Degli Aggregati Lapidei, 1994, Teaching The Italian Language, 1995, Ode A Candia, 1997, 2d edit., 1998. Erasmus scholar European Union, Ancona, 1993. Mem. Tech. Ch. Greece. With Greek Army, 1980-82. Avocations: philatelia, music, translating Italian and English into Greek and Viceveria. Office: Dept Physics U Crete, U Crete Dept Physics, PO Box 2208, 71003 Heraklion Crete, Greece

KIVIKARI, URPO KALEVI, international economics educator; b. Turku, Finland, Oct. 1, 1939; s. Niilo and Lahja (Halme) K.; m. Ildikó Zerinváry, Oct. 30, 1976. D of Polit. Sci., U. Turku, 1972. Sch. tchr. Primary sch., Turku, 1960-63; lectr. econs. Turku U., 1964-73, assoc. prof., 1974-87; prof. internat. econs. Turku Sch. of Econs., 1987—; pres. univ. senate U. Turku, 1977-82; pres. Union of Univ. Profs., 1989-92; dir. Inst. Turku Sch. of Econs., 1987—; mem. numerous bd. dirs. Author: The Legacy of the Hansa, 1996, Foreign Trade Liberalization in the Process of Economic Transformation in Russia, 1997; editor: Transition Economies of the East, 1993. Hon. Consul of Hungary, Turku/S.W. Finland, 1989—; v.p. Werner Hacklin Found., Pori, Finland, 1990—. Mem. Finnish-Russian Soc. (regional pres. 1995—), Finnish-Hungarian Soc. (v.p. 1989-97), Finnish Econ. Assn. Lutheran. Avocations: tennis, nature, social questions. Home: Linnankatu 8 A 15, 20100 Turku Finland Office: Turku Sch Econs, Rehtorinpellonkatu 5, 20500 Turku Finland

KIVIKAS, TÖIVELEMB, physicist, executive; b. Tallinn, Estonia, July 14, 1937; arrived in Sweden, 1944; s. Albert and Anna (Varik) K.; m. Tiiu, Dec. 31, 1965; children: Mart, Triinu, Malle. Ph lic, U. Lund, Sweden, 1964, PhD, 1971; postgrad., CERN, Geneva, 1964-67, INSEAD, Fontainebleau, France, 1980. Lectr. U. Lund, 1958-72, asst. prof., 1973-74; devel. mgr. Alfa-Laval AB, Lund, 1974-76; devel. mgr. AGA AB, Stockholm, 1976-78, bus. area mgr., 1978-81; v.p. Esab AB, Göteborg, Sweden, 1981-84; pres. Innocap AB, Stockholm, 1985-87; sr. mgmt. cons. PA Cons. Group, Stockholm and Cambridge, Eng., 1987-88; gen. mgr. nuclear div. Studsvik, Nyköping, Sweden, 1988-89; pres., CEO Studsvik AB, Nyköping, 1990-97; bd. dirs., pres. Estinvest AB, Stockholm, 1997—; bd. dirs. Atle Teknik AB, Stockholm, Zander & Ingeström AB, Stockholm; chmn. The Swedberg Nat. Lab., U. Uppsala, Sweden, 1994-2000; hon. mem. U. Tartu, Estonia. Author: (textbook) University Physics, 1971; patentee heat exchangers; contbr. articles to profl. jours. Mem. Swedish Phys. Soc. (bd. dirs. 1982), Royal Acad. Sci. (bd. dirs. Swedish nat. com. physics sect. 1982), European Phys. Soc., Royal Swedish Acad. Engring. Scis. (bdep. chmn. bd. dirs. bus. execs. coun. 1996), Sweden-Estonia C. of C. (chmn.), Masons. Avocations: sailing, golf, tennis. Home: Wirsens Väg 10 B, 182 63 Djursholm Sweden Office: Estinvest AB, Kungsgatan 30, 111 35 Stockholm Sweden

KIVIKOSKI, ASKO ILMARI, obstetrician , gynecologist; b. Helsinki, Finland, Aug. 3, 1932; came to U.S., 1984; MD, U. Turku, Finland, 1958, DSc, 1967. Diplomate Am. Bd. Ob-gyn. Intern U. Turku, 1962, resident in ob/gyn., 1962-65, asst. prof., 1966-76; resident in surgery City Hosp., Turku, 1965-66; researcher Washington U., St. Louis, 1971-72; fellow in perinatology Mt. Sinai Hosp., N.Y.C., 1978-79; head dept. ob/gyn. Ctrl. hosp., Lahti, Finland, 1976-84; staff Barnes Hosp., St. Louis, 1984-87, 97—; chief gynecol. svcs. St. Louis Regional Med. Ctr., 1987-97; asst. prof. Washington U., St. Louis, 1984-92, assoc. prof., 1992—. Author articles on anatomy, obstetrics and perinatology. Mem. Am. Coll. Ob-Gyn., Am. Inst. Ultrasound in Medicine, N.Y. Acad. Sci. Office: Washington Univ Sch Medicine Dept Ob/gyn 4911 Barnes-Jewish Hosp Plz Saint Louis MO 63110-1036

KIVIOJA, AARNE, orthopaedic surgeon, educator; b. Helsinki, Finland, Mar. 17, 1953; s. Olli and Helja (Anttila) K.; m. Tuula Rantalainen, 1977; children: Leena, Tuomo, Antero, Elina, Tapio. M.Sci. (Tech), Helsinki Polytech., 1978; DSc, U. Helsinki, 1990. Surgeon Univ. Ctrl. Hosp., Helsinki, 1980-88; rsch. fellow, sr. lectr. Helsinki U., 1989; surgeon-in-chief Finnish Nat. Med. Bd., 1990; cons. orthopaedic surgeon Univ. Ctrl. Hosp., Helsinki, 1991—. Mem. Nat. Orthopedic Assn. (treas. 1989-93), Finnish Intensive Care Assn. (sec. 1992-94), Internat. Soc. Limb Saving Surgery. Avocations: skiing, hiking. Office: Helsinki U Ctrl Hosp, Topeliuksenkatu 5, 00260 Helsinki Finland

KIVRIKOGLU, HUSEYIN, NATO official, military officer; b. Bozüyük, Turkey, 1934; m. Olcay Kivrikoglu; 1 child. Grad., Army Acad. Turkey, 1955. Commd. arty. officer Armed Forces of Turkey, 1955, advanced through grades to gen., 1993, early assignments include platoon and battery comdr., 1955-65, staff officer 9th Infantry Divsn. Command, 1967-70, planning officer, Chief of Ops. Allied Forces So. Europe, 1970-72; instr. Army Coll. Armed Forces of Turkey, Ankara, 1972-73; def. rsch. br. chief, Dir. of Gen. Plans and Policy Armed Forces of Turkey; comdr. Cadet Regiment at Army Acad. Armed Forces of Turkey, Ankara, 1978-80; chief ops. ctr., SHAPE Armed Forces of Turkey, Mons, Belgium, 1980-83; comdr. 3rd and 11th bragades Armed Forces of Turkey, 1983-84, chief of personnel Turkish Gen. Staff Hdqrs., 1984-90, comdr. 5th corps, then undersec. Ministry of Def., 1990-93, comdr. NATO Allied Land Forces Southeastern Europe, 1993-96, comdr. 1st Army Istanbul, 1996-97, comdr. Land Forces, 1997-98; chief of Gen. Staff, Turkish Armed Forces, 1998—. Decorated Sv. Medal of Turkish Armed Forces, U.S. Order of Merit, Pakistan Order of Distinction, others. Office: Gen Staff, Genelkurmay Baskanligi, 06100 Ankara Turkey also: NATO Hdqrs, Blvd Leopold III, 1110 Brussels Belgium*

KIVULS, JURIS, plastic surgeon; b. N.Y.C., July 18, 1952; s. Arvids and Alma Kivuls; m. Sarma Kreismanis, Oct. 20, 1984; children: Andris, Aleks, Kristine. BS in Chemistry, CUNY, 1973; MD, U. Pa., 1977. Diplomate Am. Bd. Plastic Surgery. Intern Hosp. U. Pa., 1977-78, resident in gen. surgery, 1978-83, resident in plastic surgery, 1983-85; plastic surgeon Kaiser Permanente, Bellflower, Calif., 1985—. Soccer coach, referee Am. Youth Soccer Orgn., 1995—. Fellow ACS; mem. AMA, Am. Soc. Plastic Surgeons, Am. Soc. Aesthetic Plastic Surgery, Liploplasty Soc. (bd. dirs. 1996-2000, chair rsch. com. 1994-2000), Am. Cleft Palate Assn., Calif. Soc. Plastic Surgeons. Avocations: skiing, volleyball, running, sailing. Office: Kaiser Permanente Dept Plastic Surgery 9400 Rosecrans Ave Bellflower CA 90706-2200

KIWANUKA, SEMAKULA MATHIAS MULUMBA, United Nations ambassador; b. 1939; m. Mary Regina Kiwanuka; 6 children. BA, Makerere U., 1962; PhD in History, London U., 1965; Postgrad. Diploma, Oxford U., 1978. Amb. and permanent rep. Republic of Uganda, N.Y.C., 1996—; exec. dir. Mgmt. and Tng. Inst., Dean Sch. of Postgrad. Studies, Makerere; counterpart chief tech. adv. UN Development Prog.; cons. UN Environment Prog.; dir. studies Univ. Calabar, Nigeria; prof. history, vis. scholar U. Cambridge. Mem. Royal Coun. Kingdom Buganda. Office: UN 336 E 45th St New York NY 10017-3400 also: PO Box 384, Kampala Uganda

KIYANITZA, LUBOV DENISOVNA, library director; b. Kiev, Ukraine, May 30, 1943; d. Denis Vasilievich and Maria Ivanovna (Shepelenko) K.; m. William Konstantinovitch Kuindzhy, dec. 12, 1995; children: Violetta, Sviatoslav. Grad. commodity expert, Book-Trade Coll., 1971; library bibliographer, State Krupskaya Inst. of Culture, 1980. Instr. periodical press dissemination City Press Agy., Uman, 1967-71; libr. supr. Chem. Engring. Coll. Libr., Novochercassk, 1971-78; sector supr. Libr. of Novocherkassk, 1978-83; dep. dir. for rsch. work Politechnical Inst., Novochercassk, 1983-86; dir. libr. South-Russia State Tech. U., 1986—; supr. methodic ctr. univ. librs. Rostov region, 1994; supr., participant practical sci. seminars, 1990—; lectr. Libr. Politechnical Inst., 1979-83. Mem. Nat. Libr. Trade Union (Medal of Honour 1985), North Caucasus Assn. Univ. Librs. Avocations: history of arts, philately, travel. Home: 7-3 Galina Petrova str, 346409 Novocherkassk Russia Office: Libr State Tech Univ, Prosveschenia str, 346400 Novocherkassk Rostov, Russia

KIYINGI, AGGREY, cardiologist, consultant, research scientist; b. Kyadondo, Buganda, Uganda, Oct. 25, 1953; arrived in Australia, 1981; s. Azaliya Kiyingi and Peresika Norah (Nakirijja) Sebowa; m. Robinah Erina Kayaga Kasirye, Sept. 3, 1977; children: Samallie Nakagulire, Kibuka Simbwa, Kirabo Sebowa, Sanyu Nakiyingi. MB CHB, Makerere (Uganda) U., 1977; FRACP, U. Sydney, Australia, 1989. Medical diplomate. Intern Mulago Hosp., Kampala, Uganda, 1977-78; postgrad. medicine Butabika & Mulago Hosps., Kampala, Uganda, 1978-80; sr. med. officer Mutomo and Kaloleni Hosps., Kenya, 1981; registrar medicine Westmead Hosp., Sydney, 1982-85; sr. registrar medicine Hornsby Hosp., Sydney, 1986; sr. registar cardiology Concord Hosp., Sydney, 1987-89; cons. cardiologist St. John of God Hosp., Richmond, NSW, Australia, 1989—, Holroyd Hosp., Guildford, NSW, Australia, 1990—, Merrylands & Penrith, Australia, 1989—, Warringah Mall Med. Ctr., 1990—; hon. sr. lectr. Makerere Med. Sch., Kampala, 1990—, Cardio Scan Holter Svcs., New Castle, Australia, 1990—, Kampala Heart Centre, Uganda, 1995—; bd. dirs. Dehezi Pty Ltd., NSW, Australia. Author: Intensive Care, 1979; contbr. articles to profl. jours. Bd. dirs. KSO, Sydney, 1988—; prin. sponsor Buziga Women's Assn., Kampala, 1993—; sponsor Buziga Tech. Coll., Kampala, 1993—; condr. Buddo Nightingales, Uganda, 1976-80; activist environ. preservation, Uganda, 1992—. Fellow Royal Australian Coll. Physicians. Am. Coll. Angiology, ; mem. AAAS, ARBS (dep. gov.), Australia and New Zealand Cardiac Soc., N.Y. Acad. Scis., Am. Heart Assn. (Clin. Coun. Cardiology), Internat. Fedn. Cardiology. Mem. Christian Ch. Avocations: singing (tenor), conducting, piano and organ playing, tennis, internat. travel. Office: Ste 10 258 Merrylands Rd, Merrylands NSW 2160, Australia

KIYONO, KEN, international relations educator; b. Miyazaki-shi, Japan, Apr. 9, 1931; m. Kimiko Yamato; children: Ayako, Akira. BA, U. Idaho,

1963, MA, 1965. Lectr. Kyoritsu U., Kitakyushu-Shi, Japan, 1966-68; assoc. prof. Nagasaki U., Nagasaki-Shi, Japan, 1968-82; prof. Kumamoto Gakuen U., Kumamoto-shi, Japan, 1982—; dean econ. faculty Kumamoto Gakuen U., Kumamoto-shi, 1996-97; dir. Inst. Fgn. Affairs, Kumamoto, 1984-85; chmn. Internat. Exch. Com., Kumamoto, 1986-89. Bd. trustees Kamamoto YMCA, 1992-98; monitor Kyushu Fin. Bur., Kumamoto, 1992-98. Mem. Japan Assn. Internat. Rels. (trustee 1975—), Japan-Brazil Assn. (bd. trustees 1985—), Montana Club (trustee 1989—), Test of English for Internat. Comm. (Kumamoto rep. 1992—), Kumamoto Students' (Daiquku) Karate U. (chmn. 1986—). Avocations: mountain climbing, fast walking, music appreciation. Office: Kumamoto Gakuen U, 5-1 Chome, 862-0871 Kumamoto-shi Japan

KIZAWA, MAKOTO, information sciences educator; b. Kiryu-shi, Gumma-ken, Japan, Apr. 18, 1925; s. Shusaku and Tei (Sakata) K.; m. Yukiko Nishi, Jan. 21, 1951; children: Tadashi, Satoru. B of Engring., U. Tokyo, 1948, D of Engring., 1969. Rschr. Electrotech. Lab., Tokyo, 1948-70; prof. Osaka U., Toyonaka, Japan, 1970-80; prof. U. Libr. and Info. Sci., Tsukuba, Japan, 1980-83, v.p., 1983-87; prof. Kanagawa Inst. Tech., Atsugi, Japan, 1988-96; prof. emeritus U. Libr. and Info. Sci., 1991—; mem. ICSU/CODATA Task Group on Computer Use, Frankfurt, Germany and Paris, 1967-76, sec. Task Group on Accessibility and Dissemination of Data, 1972-80, mem. nominating com., Paris, 1986-98; chmn. Japanese Nat. Com. for ISO/IEC JTC1/SC17, Tokyo, 1972-98. Author: Digital Magnetic Recording (in Japanese), 1979, A Treatize of Data in Science and Technology (in Japanese), 1983; co-editor: Dictionary of Terms in Computer Technology (in Japanese), 1973. Recipient Niwa prize Japan Info. Ctr. Sci. and Tech., 1969, Standardization award Ministry of Internat. Trade and Industry, Tokyo, 1989. Mem. Inst. Elec. Engrs. Japan (Electrotechnical award 1951), Inst. Electronics, Info. and Comm. Engrs., Info. Processing Soc. Japan. Home: 3-13-6 Hachimanyama, Setagaya-ku, Tokyo 156-0056, Japan

KIZIL, MURAT, chemistry educator, researcher; b. Derik, Turkey, Jan. 1, 1966; s. Halil Ibrahim and Nuriye Kizil; m. Göksel Uysan; 1 child, Dilan Tuba. BSc (hon.), U. Dicle, Turkey, 1989, MSc, 1991; PhD, U. Nottingham, Eng., 1996. Asst. prof. U. Dicle, 1996—. Contbr. articles to profl. jours. Mem. Chem. Soc. Eng. Muslim. Avocations: reading, socialising, cinema, jogging. Office: U Dicle Faculty of Sci, Dept Chemistry, 21280 Diyarbakir Turkey

KIZILGUN, HAKAN, international trade company executive; b. Bergama, Turkey, July 28, 1965; s. Tuncay and Sevim (Asar) K. DS, U. Utrecht, The Netherlands. Translator, interpreter Tolkencentrum, Eindhoven, Holland, 1989-96; Turkologist, rschr. pvt. practice, Eindhoven, Holland, 1991—; internat. trader, marketeer and project mgr. Kizilgun Worldwide Trade, Eindhoven, Holland, 1995—; fin. cons. Inst. Co., Eindhoven, 1995-96; cons. Work and Trade, 1996-97. Editor Mag. Mozaik, 1996—; chief editor TV, Radio Omroep Eindhoven, 1995-97; contbr. articles to profl. jours. Mem. Com. Dems. '66, Eindhoven, 1994-95, mem. adv. coun., 1994-95; treas. FNV-Youth Union, Eindhoven, 1993-94; 2d treas. Abvakabo Unio, Eindhoven, 1993-94. With Turkish Arty., 1995. Mem. Com. Dems. '66, Eindhoven, 1994-95, mem. advice coun., 1994-95; treas. FNV-Youth Union, Eindhoven, 1992-94; 2d treas. Abvakabo Unio, Eindhoven, 1993-94. With Turkish Artelery, 1995. Mem. Acad. Soc. Eindhoven, Found. Turkistan (treas., coord. culture & sci.). Moslim. Avocations: reading, travel, walking, collecting stamps and coins, politics. Home and office: St Lambertusstr 32, 5615 PH Eindhoven The Netherlands

KIZUKA, HARUO, journalism educator; b. Tokyo, Japan, Mar. 26, 1936; s. Yasuyoshi and Sumiko Kizuka; m. Chieko Miyamoto, June 8, 1962; children: Keiko, Harutake. BA, U. Calif., Berkeley, 1961. News commentator NHK, Tokyo, 1961-71; lectr. Sci. U. Tokyo, 1971-73, assoc. prof., 1974-77, prof., 1978—. Author: An Introduction to Journalism English, 1980, A Vocabulary Aid to Reading Newspapers, 1982, A Dictionary of Verb-Noun Collocations, 1987, Common Mistakes in Current English Usage, 1997. Mem. Japan Assn. for Current English Studies. Avocations: playing tennis, watching baseball, traveling. Home: 1-37-73 Irima-cho Chofu-shi, Tokyo 182-0004, Japan Office: Sci U Tokyo, 103 Kagurazaka Shinjuku-ku, Tokyo 162-8601, Japan

KIZUKA, MASATAKA, English educator; b. Tokyo, June 12, 1964; s. Sadao and Takeko (Yamamoto) K.; m. Keiko Shimura, June 12, 1991; 1 child, Yasutaka. BA, U. Waseda, 1987; MA, U. Essex, 1990; MEd, U. Tokyo, 1991. Sr. lectr. Mejiro Gakuen Women's Coll., Tokyo, 1991-94, Tokyo Woman's Christian U., 1994—. Mem. Japan Assn. Lang. Tchg. (publicity chair 1994-98), Japan Assn. Tchg., Internat. Assn. Tchg. English as Fgn. Lng. Avocations: playing baseball, tennis. Home: 3-34-12 Buzo, 336-0025 Urawa Saitama, Japan Office: Tokyo Woman's Christian U, 2-6-1 Zempukuji, Suginami-ku Tokyo 167-8585, Japan

KJAER, ANDREAS, physician, researcher; b. Copenhagen, Apr. 12, 1963; s. Henry J.H. and Charlotte M. (Berger) K.; m. Anne-Mette Lebech, June 15, 1991; children: Anna Sophie, Amalie Christine. MD, U. Copenhagen, 1989, PhD, 1994, DrMedSci, 1996; Diploma in Econs., Copenhagen Bus. Sch., 1994, MBA, 1997. Lic. physician, Denmark; cert. ECFMG; lic. specialist in clin. physiology and nuclei medicine, 2000. Physician Copenhagen Univ. Hosp., 1990-91; rsch. fellow dept. med. physiology U. Copenhagen, 1991-95, assoc. prof., 1994, physician, 1994—; vis. rsch. fellow Salk Inst., La Jolla, Calif., 1988, 91, Emory U., Atlanta, 1993. Contbr. numerous articles on neuroendocrinology to profl. jours. Capt. Royal Danish Navy, 1985, 89-90. Honeywell Futurist Competition scholar, 1985. Mem. Danish Endocrine Soc. (bd. dirs.), Endocrine Soc. U.S. Home: Marielystvej 11, DK-2000 Frederiksberg Denmark Office: U Copenhagen/Med Physiology, Blegdamsvej 3 Bldg 12.3, DK-2200 Copenhagen Denmark

KJAER, NIELS, theologian, scholar; b. Aarhus, Denmark, Apr. 27, 1949; s. Torvald and Ruth Hedvig (Meyer) K.; m. Elisabeth Oellgaard, Aug. 10, 1973 (div. July 24, 1989); children: Mette, Annemari. MDiv, U. Aarhus, Denmark, 1975. Ordained to ministry Luth. Ch., 1975. Perpetual curate Luth. Ch. Utterslev, Copenhagen, 1975-77; vicar Luth. Ch. Lyö, Faaborg, Denmark, 1978-99; scholar, 1999—; cons. Projekt-Teatret, Odense, Denmark, 1990—. Author: Sören Kierkegaard Og Emily Dickinson, 1989, Emily Dickinson, 1997; contbr. articles to profl. jours. Named Hon. Officer, Dickinson-Higginson Press, 1986. Mem. Emily Dickinson Internat. Soc. (charter, dir. Emily Dickinson ctr. 1990—), Emily Dickinson Soc. Japan (hon.). Avocation: travel (North America, Europe, North Africa, Middle East, Far East). Home: Snogebaeksvej 36B, 8210 Århus V, Denmark

KJAERGAARD, THORKILD, museum director, historian, administrator; b. Nørre Felding, Jutland, Denmark, Mar. 15, 1945; s. Aage and Ingrid (Nielsen) K.; m. Anne Horner, Jan. 8, 1975 (dec. Mar. 1975); 1 child, Andreas; m. Gerd Malling, May 26, 1978. Diploma in European Studies, Coll. d'Europe, Bruges, Belgium, 1969; grad., Copenhagen U., 1976, PhD, 1991. From rschr. to assoc. prof. Copenhagen U., 1975-82; rschr. European U. Inst., Florence, Italy, 1983-86; curator Frederiksborg Castle Mus. Nat. History, Hillerød, Denmark, 1989-98; adminstr. The Found. Cultural Bridge 2000, 1998; dir. Castle Mus., Sønderborg, Denmark, 1999—; vis. assoc. prof. history Kans. U., 1987. Author: Le Danemark et la Révolution Française, 1989, The Danish Revolution, 1500-1800: An Ecohistorical Interpretation, 1994; contbr. articles to profl. jours. Mem. The Futures Coun. (The Copenhagen Inst. for Futures Studies). Recipient scholarship Carlsberg Found., 1987. Mem. Danish Soc. Agrarian History, Assn. Castles and Museums Around the Baltic Sea (pres. 1991-94). Home: Egebjergvej 2A, 6430 Nordborg Denmark Office: Sønderborg Castle Mus, 6400 Sønderborg Denmark

KJAER-HANSEN, KAI, editor; b. Copenhagen, Apr. 29, 1945; s. Herman Peter and Else (Kjaer) Hansen; m. Kirsten Lilli Møller, Mar. 9, 1968; children: Barbara, Niklas, Mikal. MDiv, U. Copenhagen, 1972; DD, U. Lund, Sweden, 1982. Lectr. Free Faculty Theology, Aarhus, Denmark, 1973-76, 78-85; pastor Danish Israel Mission, Jerusalem, 1976-78; bible translator Danish Bible Soc., Copenhagen, 1986-92; editor Danish Israel Mission, Christiansfeld, Denmark, 1987—, Lausanne Consultation on Jewish Evangelism, Aarhus, 1990—, United Christian Coun. in Israel/Mishkan, Jerusalem, 1995—; chmn. Lausanne Com. for World Evangelization, Denmark, 1982-92; cons. Danish Israel Mission, 1987—, chmn., 1997—; internat. coord. Lausanne Consultation on Jewish Evangelism, 1991—; Bishop candidate The Evang. Luth. Ch., Denmark, 1996. Author: Joseph Rabinowitz and the Messianic Movement, Danish edit., 1988, Study Edition of Matthew, 1994, Study Edition The Acts of the Apostles, 1995, Joseph Rabinowitz and the Messianic Movement, English edit., 1995, Jewish Identity and Faith in Jesus, 1996; editor The Death of Messiah, 1994. Evangelic Lutheran. Avocations: badminton, soccer. Home and Office: Ellebaekvej 5, 8520 Lystrup Denmark

KJELLGREN, OLLE R.H., oncologist, educator; b. Arvika, Sweden, Jan. 23, 1920; s. Erik G.H. and Elsa L. (Lundgren) K.; m. Kerstin L.U. Ortegren; m. Erik, Inga, Aina, Mia. MD, Karolinska Inst., Stockholm, 1946; PHD, U. Gothenburg, Sweden, 1958. Resident in surgery, ob-gyn, resident in gen. oncology and gynecol. oncology; prof. gynecol. oncology U. Umeå, Sweden, 1969—, sr. cons. dept. gynecol. oncology, 1962-84; vis. prof. dept. ob-gyn. Kenyatta Nat. Hosp., Nairobi, Kenya 1974, dept. gynecology Roswell Park Meml. Inst., Buffalo, 1960. Contbr. over 120 articles to profl. publs.; author 2 textbooks on oncology and gynecology, co-author 5 textbooks. Named Knight Order of Nordic Star of Sweden, 1974. Fellow Internat. Acad. Cytology (hon.), Swedish Acad. Cytology (hon.); mem. Lions (Melvin Jones fellow 1991), Odd Fellows. Avocations: backpacking, mountain climbing. Home: Slöjdgatan 1, S-90325 Umeå Sweden Office: Univ Hosp, Dept Gyn Oncology, S-90185 Umeå Sweden

KJELLGREN, PER, mechanical engineer; b. Stockholm, Sweden, Dec. 17, 1969; s. Bengo and Marianne (Hogstrom) K. MS in Applied Mechanics, Royal Inst. Tech., Stockholm, Sweden, 1991, Lic. Engring. Aeronautics, 1998. Engr. ABB Atom, Sweden, 1991; vis. sci. U. Tokyo, 1991-95; software scientist AZE AB, Sweden, 1995-96; rsch. asst. Royal Inst. Tech., Sweden, 1996-98; vis. scientist U. Az., Tucson, 1998—. Contbr. articles to profl. jours. Recipient scholarship U. Tokyo, 1991-95. Office: U. Az. Dept Aerospace PO Box 210119 Tucson AZ 85721-0119

KJELLSTRÖM, GREGOR LOUIS, retired engineering executive; b. Stockholm, Dec. 10, 1932; m. Barbro Margareta Andersson, Mar. 25, 1961. BS in Math. and Physics, U. Stockholm, 1958. Amanuens Royal Bd. Water Power, Stockholm, 1958-60; engr. Turbin AB de Laval, Ljungström, Sweden, 1960-63; specialist in analysis and statis. optimization Ericsson Telecom AB, Stockholm, 1963-93; ret., 1993. Contbr. articles to profl. jours. Avocations: Darwinian evolution, choral singing, classical music, gardening, Internet. E-mail: gregor.kjellstrom@telia.com. Home: Hagvägen 29A, 141 70 Huddinge Sweden

KJOK, SOLVEIG, artist, art historian, linguist; b. Lillehammer, Norway, Mar. 16, 1968; d. Erik and Ingunn (Haugsrud) K. BA in French Lit., U. Vienna, Austria, 1991; M in French Lit., U. Paris, 1992; MA in Romance Lang. and Lit., U. Cin., 1993, MA in Art History, 1996; MFA in Painting, Parsons Sch. Design, N.Y.C., 1998. Graphic designer Agence Karen, Paris, 1988; tchg. asst. art history U. Cin., 1995-96, dir. ind. studies of Norwegian lang./culture, 1993-96; resident Larroque Artists' Colony, Urt, France, 1997-98; tchg. asst. painting Parsons Sch. Design, N.Y.C., 1997-98; lectr. in field. Contbr. articles to profl. jours.; translator: French/Norwegian, Paris, 1988; Spanish/Norwegian translator/interpretor Medellin, Bogota, Colombia, 1993; translator English, German novels, articles, short stories into Norwegian, various pub. houses, 1985—; one-woman shows include Brodie Gallery, Cin., 1996, Kreditkassen, Bagn, Norway, 1987; exhibited in group shows at Gjensidigegården, Fagernes, Norway, 1985, Valdrestunet, Bagn, 1987, Art et Dessin, Paris, 1988, Mus. of U. Medellin, 1993, KZF Gallery, Cin., 1994, 840 Gallery, Cin., 1995, 96, Machina dell'Arte, Cin., 1996, Schoharie County Arts Coun., 1996, Gallery Alexy, Phila., 1996, Glenn Eure's Ghost Fleet Gallery, Nags Head, N.C., 1996, Amos Joseph Fine Art, Santa Fe, 1996, N.J. Ctr. Visual Arts, 1997, Pleiades Gallery, N.Y.C., 1997, Viridian Artists, Inc., 1997, Akademie der bildenden Künste Munich, 1997, A.I.R. Gallery, N.Y.C., 1997, Artists' Space, N.Y.C., 1997, Brenda Taylor Gallery, N.Y.C., 1998, Cmty. Cultural Ctr., Phila., 1998, Manefisken Galleri, Oslo, 1998, Valdres Kunstforening's Gallery, Norway, 1998, PS 122 Gallery, N.Y.C., 1998, Cameron/Weiland Gallery, N.Y.C., 1998, Galeri Steen, Oslo, Norway, 1999, others; works in pvt. and pub. collections. Mem. Cin. Artists Group Effort, 1994—. Recipient Alpha Kappa Alpha Grad. Merit award; grantee Ga. Rotary Student Program, 1989, Lise & Arnfinn Heje's Legacy, Oslo, 1990, Thom Wilhelmsen's award, Oslo, 1991, Knut Hamsun's Legacy, Oslo, 1992, Olav and Lizzie Juvkam's legacy, 1990-94, Einar Storsveen's Legacy, 1992-94; Cin. Women's Club scholar, 1995, U. Cin. scholar, 1993-96, Parsons scholar, 1997-98; AAUW fellow, 1997-98; Joahn Jorgen Brochs Legat. grant, 1998, Rsch. grant Astrup-Fearnley, Oslo, 1996, Thesis Rsch. grant Astrup-Fearnley Found., Oslo, 1996, Artist grant Norwegian Ministry Culture, 1998; recipient Edwin Gould Found. award Nat. Arts Club, N.Y.C., 1998, Excellence in Drawing award Internat. Icarus Exhbn., 1998, Spl. Gallery prize Contemporary Realism III Exhibit, Phila., 1998, others. Mem. Internat. Assn. Univ. Women, Coll. Art Assn., Norwegian Soc. Young Artists, Norwegian Visual Artists, Drawing Assn. Norway. Avocation: long distance running. Home: 44 Eagle St Brooklyn NY 11222-1013

KJØNSTAD, ASBJØRN, law educator; b. Frol, Norway, Feb. 6, 1943; s. Arne Kristan and Nelly (Stavern) K.; m. Lise-Lena Stubberød, 1971; children: Hilde, Sunila; m. Ayala Orkan, 1995. Degree, U. Oslo, 1970, Doctorate, 1978; JD (hon.), U. Lund, Sweden, 1996. Legal advisor Nat. Ins. Adminstrn., 1970-72; rsch. fellow U. Oslo, 1972-78, prof. pvt. law, 1978-84, head Inst. Pvt. Law, 1983-84, prof. social law, 1985—, dean faculty of law, 1986-88; mem. bd. Nat. Coun. Tobacco and Health, 1972-93, 97—; chair Royal Commn. on Social Security Law, 1982-90, 91-95, 99—; v.p. European Inst. Social Security, 1993-97; mem. Region Com. I for Med. Ethics, 1985-95; mem. bd. U. Oslo, 1986-88, 99—; vis. scholar Boston U. Law Sch., 1995-96; guest prof. Leuven U., 1997. Author: Social Security and Compensation for Personal Injuries, 1977, The Industrial Injuries Insurance, 1979, Medical Law, 1987, Norwegian Social Law, 1987, A Simplified National Insurance Act, 1990, Introduction to Social Security Law, 1998, The National Insurance Disablement Pension, 1992, Health Priority and Patient's Rights, 1992, Social Services and the Rule of Law, 2000, Constitutional Protection of Social Security Benefits, 1994, Aspects of Health Law, 1994, Welfare Law, 1997, Law, Power and Poverty, 1997, Social Security Act, 1998, Welfare Law II—Social Services, 1999, European Social Security Law, 1999, Tort Liability for the Norwegian Tobacco Industry, 2000; editor European Social Security Law, 1999; contbr. articles to profl. jours.; editor Norwegian Law Jour., 1991—. Mem. Norwegian Acad. Sci. Avocations: outdoor exercise and activities, skiing, jogging, marathon running. Fax: 47-22-13-80-75. E-mail: asbjorn.kjonstad@jus.uio.no. Address: U Oslo, Lillevannsveien 37, 0788 Oslo 0162, Norway

KJURKCHIEVA, DIANA PETROVA, astronomer, educator; b. Michurin, Burgas, Bulgaria, Aug. 22, 1952; d. Peter Donchev Stoev and Yanka Belcheva Staneva; m. Pencho Zhechev Kjurkchiev, Apr. 8, 1973; 1 child, Yulian Penchev. MA, Sofia (Bulgaria) U., 1976, PhD, 1985. Asst. prof. Shoumen (Bulgaria) U., 1977-92, assoc. prof., 1992—, dean faculty of physics, 1993-94, 98-99, vice-rector, 2000—; coord. Ctrl. European Exch. Program U. Studies, 1995—. Contbr. articles to profl. jours. Grantee NSF, 1993. Mem. Internat. Astron. Union (grantee 1994, 95), European Astron. Union. Avocations: dancing. Home: 53 Aprilsko Vastanie, 9700 Shumen Bulgaria Office: Shumen U K Preslavski, Dept Physics, 9700 Shumen Bulgaria

KJUS, LASSE, Olympic athlete; b. Oslo, Norway, Jan. 14, 1971. Winner gold medal men's combined alpine skiing XVII Winter Olympic Games, Lillehammer, Norway, 1994; winner silver medal men's combined alpine skiing XVIV Winter Olympic Games, Nagano, Japan, 1998. Office: Norwegian Olympic Committee and Confederation of Sports, Idrettens Hus Hauger Skolevei 1, 1351 Rud Norway*

KLAAR, HANS-JOACHIM, metallurgical engineer; b. Breslau, Germany, May 22, 1935; s. Alfred Heinrich and Paula (Buttgereit) K.; m. Dec. 23, 1970; children: Andreas, Christiane. Diploma in metallurgy engring., Aachen (Germany) Tech. U., 1968, D in Engring., 1975. From sci. asst. to sr. adminstr. Aachen Tech. U., 1969-76, adminstrn., 1976-78, sr. adminstr., 1978-98, acad. dir., 1998-2000, 2000—; vis. prof. Dalian U. Tech., China, 1995—, Poly. U. Bucharest, Romania, 1997—; scientific com. Nat. Nuclear Energy Agy of Indonesia, 2000—. Fin. head Protestant Ch., Aachen, 1979; chmn. VDEh, Düsseldorf, Germany, 1990, Social Orgn. Housing Work Advice Registrated Assn., Aachen, 1992. Mem. DEM, DGE. Mem. German Soc. for Electron Microscopy, Soc. German Metallurgists. Home: Kirchrather Str 27, D-52074 Aachen Germany Office: GFE of Aachen Tech U, Ahornstr 55, D-52056 Aachen Germany

KLACZAK, ADAM ZBIGNIEW, technical manager; b. Cracow, Poland, Feb. 16, 1928; s. Antoni and Władystawa (Jeziorowska) K.; m. Maria Chrzanowska, June 27, 1954 (dec. July 1987); 1 child, Zbigniew (dec. Apr. 1992). Diploma in engring., U. Tech., Cracow, 1951, D in Tech. Scis., 1970. Cert. engring. Designer Designing Dept., Cracow, 1951-67, chief checking staff, 1970-78, cons., 1981-89; acad. tchr. U. Tech., Cracow, 1967-70; mem. supervision staff Polservice, Libya, 1978-81; tech. mgr. Tech. Office, Cracow, 1989—. Contbr. articles to profl. jours. Recipient Gold award City of Cracow, 1987. Avocations: traveling, swimming, collecting postage stamps. Home: Odrzanska 10/12, 30-408 Cracow Poland Office: Kontech Lab Tech, pl Sikorskiego 13, 31-115 Cracow Poland

KLADNIG, WOLFGANG FRIEDRICH, chemist, educator; b. Vienna, Austria, July 24, 1944; s. Friedrich Otto and Hermine Maria (Preisinger) K.; m. Ingrid Rauchmann, June 9, 1984; 1 child, Viktoria Katherine. Diploma in engring., Tech. U. Vienna, 1970, PhD, 1972; DSc (hon.), U. Malta, 1993. Asst. prof. Tech. U. Vienna, 1970-74; vis. scientist Imperial Coll., London, 1973; scientist dept. phys. chemistry IVIC, Caracas, Venezuela, 1974-77; indsl. cons. BASF, Caracas, 1977; fellow, assoc. scientist dept. chem. engring. Worcester (Mass.) Poly. Inst., 1977-79; project mgr., engr. chem. plants Voest Alpine AG, Linz, Austria, 1979-81; project mgr. product planning Voest Alpine AG, Linz, 1981-84; mgr. R&D, materials scis., siderurgical divsn. Voest Alpine AG, 1984-87; ceramics devel. engr. Ruthner Rsch. Ctr., Vienna, 1987-91; divisional mgr. product and devel. Jos. Heiser Gmbh, Kienberg, Austria, 1991-98; sr. project mgr. Worthington-Heiser Cylinders Gmbh, Kienberg, 1998-2000; head chem. labs. Neumayer Gmbh, Leobersdorf, Austria, 2000—; lectr. U. Linz, 1987-95; presenter in field. Contbr. articles to profl. jours.; patentee in field. Mem. Verein Osterr Chemiker, Austrian Soc. Chem. Industry, Gesellschaft Deutscher Chemiker, Dechema, Catalysis Soc., Am. Chem. Soc., N.Y. Acad. Scis., Austrian Venezuelan Soc., Sigma Xi. Roman Catholic. Home: 106/10/4 Krottenbachstr, 1190 Vienna Austria

KLAER, KARL-HEINZ, government official; b. Bildstock, Saarland, Germany, Jan. 16, 1947; s. Heinz and Lilo (Hartmann) K.; m. Renate Schmidt, Nov. 28, 1975; children: Erik, Tatjana. PhD in History, U. Bonn, Germany, 1979. Editor, translator, expert Luchterhand, Neuwied, Germany, 1972-75; editor Neue Gesellschaft, Bonn, 1976-79; tchr., rschr. U. Kassel, Germany, 1980-83; chief cabinet, speechwriter for Chmn. Willy Brandt Sozialdemokratische Partei Deutschlands, Bonn, 1983-87, polit. dir., 1987-91; state sec., chief of staff Rhineland Palatinate State Govt., Mainz, Germany, 1991-94; state sec., plenipotentiary fed. and European affairs Rhineland Palatinate State Govt., Bonn, 1994—; bd. dirs. Zweites Deutsches Fernsehen/German TV II, Mainz. Author: Breakdown of II. International, 1981; author, editor: Encyclopedia of Socialism, 1986; editor: The Electorate of the Extreme Right, 1989. Sgt. German Air Force, 1967-68. Mem. Com. of Regions (European Union). Mem. Social Dem. Party. Lutheran. Office: State Govt Rhineland, Heussallee 18-24, 53113 Bonn Germany

KLAIBER, KLAUS-PETER, NATO official. BS, Tübingen U.; PhD in Law, Mainz U.; postdoctoral, Univ. Inst. Internat. Studies, Geneva. Third sec. German Embassy, Kinshasa, Zaire, 1971; dep. head trainee dept. Ministry of Fgn. Affairs, Germany; first sec. polit. affairs German Embassy, Washington; dep. head of mission German Embassy, Nairobi, Kenya; dep. head European polit. co-operation German Fgn. Ministry; dep. dir. Office of Minister of Fgn. Affairs, 1985-87; minister-counsellor polit. affairs German Embassy, London, 1988-91; dep. polit. dir. Fgn. Office, head security policy subdivsn. German Fgn. Ministry, 1992-95, head policy planning divsn., 1995-97; asst. sec. gen. for polit. affairs NATO, 1997—; meeting chmn. Sr. Polit. Advisers of Allied Delegations; dir. polit. affairs divsn. internat. staff, NATO. Office: NATO Hdqrs, Blvd Leopold III, 1110 Brussels Belgium*

KLAIC, ALEKSANDAR, electrical engineer; b. Vinkovci, Croatia, Feb. 8, 1964; s. Petar and Ivana-Olga (Oprešnik) K.; m. Djurdja Zigmundovac, July 13, 1996; 1 child, Luka. BSEE, Sch. Elec. Engring./Computing, Zagreb, 1990, MSEE, 1997. Rsch. asst. Marine Rsch. and Spl. Techs., Zagreb, 1990-91, rsch. engr., 1991-93, project engr., 1993-95; project engr. Ministry of the Interior, Zagreb, 1995-97, head tech. dept., 1997—; tchg. fellow H.S. for Civil Engring., Zagreb, 1993-95, Graphic Arts Faculty, Zagreb, 1992-96; cons. Sitel Profl. Electronics, Zagreb, 1993-94, Radaring, Zagreb, 1995-96. Contbr. articles to sci. and profl. jours. Mem. Croatian Assn. for Robotics, Croatian Soc. Comm., Computing, Electronics, Measurement and Automation. Roman Catholic. Avocations: music, guitar, tennis, computers. Home: Ljutomerska 2C, 10040 Zagreb Croatia Office: Ministry of the Interior, Ulica Grada Vukovara 33, 10000 Zagreb Croatia

KLAIDMAN, STEPHEN DAVID, writer; b. N.Y.C., May 28, 1938; s. Moe Klaidman and Pauline Hinerfeld; m. Kitty Cecile Ehrenreich, Dec. 27, 1959; children: Elyse Susanne, Daniel Marc. Student, CCNY, 1955-59. Copy editor N.Y. Times, N.Y.C., 1962-69; dep. fgn. editor The Washington Post, 1970-75, reporter, 1976-77; news editor, chief editl. writer Internat. Herald Tribune, Paris, 1977-82; sr. rsch. fellow Kennedy Inst. Ethics, Georgetown U., Washington, 1982—; cons. Dept. of Def., Washington, 1982-83, Dept. of Edn., Washington, 1998-99; counselor Adv. Com. on Human Radiation Experiments, Washington, 1995-97. Author: The Virtuous Journalist, 1987, Health in the Headlines, 1991, Saving the Heart, 2000. Recipient 1st prize Woodrow Wilson Internat. Ctr. for Scholars, Media Studies Competition, 1991, Lowell Mellett award Pa. State U., 1992; grantee NEH, Washington, 1985. Avocations: reading, listening to music, basketball, tennis. E-mail: sklaid@aol.com.

KLAIN, DAVID RICHARD, naval officer; b. Caracas, Venezuela, June 21, 1967; s. Richard Morris and Carol (Piccoli) K.; m. Kimberly Kay Evans, Dec. 15, 1990; 1 child, Douglas. BS in Polit. Sci., U.S. Naval Acad., 1989; MA in Internat. Affairs, Cath. U. Am., 1997. Main propulsion asst. USS THACH Yokosuka, Japan, 1989-91, officer combat info. ctr. USS THACH, 1991-92; anti-submarine warfare officer USS VELLA GULF Norfolk, Va., 1993-95; policy and joint doctrine officer Office of Chief Naval Ops. USN, Washington, 1995-96, adminstrv. asst. to dir. divsn. strategy and policy office chief naval ops., 1996-97; weapons officer USS THE SULLIVANS Mayport, Fla., 1997-99; combat sys. officer USS THE SULLIVANS USN, Mayport, Fla., 1999—; rep. com. terminology to NATO Dept. Def. USN, Washington, 1995-96. Contbr. articles to profl. jours. Mem. U.S. Naval Inst. (Author of Yr. group award 1998), Surface Navy Assn. Avocations: sailing, flying, travel, golf. E-mail: dklain@sullivans.navy.mil. Home: 1609 Teal Way Woodbridge VA 22191-3730 Office: Uss The Sullivans Ddg 68 FPO AA 34093-1287

KLAINMAN, ELIEZER ISAAK, health facility administrator, cardiologist, researcher, consultant; b. Nathanya, Israel, Apr. 12, 1951; s. Shelomoh Gershon and Hanna Beracha (Kriger) K.; m. Yaffa Friedman, Aug. 18, 1975; children: Hanna, Efrat, Michal. MD, Tel Aviv U., 1978, cert. in cardiology, 1986. Specialist in cardiology Beilinson Med Ctr., Petach-Tiqua, 1979-86, specialist in basic sci. in nuclear cardiology, 1985-86; founder, dir. Maccabi Cardiac Inst., Raanana, 1987-94; dir., coord. Body and Mind Series, Raanana, 1993-94; founder, dir. Mishmar Hayarden Cardiac and Rehab. Inst., Givatayim, 1994—; head Cardiac and Rehab. Inst., Lev-Amit MC, Holon, 2000—; lectr. Judaism Jewish Philosophy, Raaana Cmty., 1990-98; head lectr. Tesler Nursing Sch., 1988-98; lectr. basic med. scis. Sackler Med. Sch., Tel Aviv U., 1989-2000, Maynei-Hayeshua Hosp. Nursing Sch., 1999—; prin. investigator clin. trials Cardiac and Rehab. Inst., Givatayim, 1997-98; prof. med. scis. cardiology Ben-Gurion U., 1998—; prof. med. care mgmt. Israeli br. New Eng. U., 2000—. Contbr. articles to profl. jours. of Cardiology, Cardiac Rehab. and Exercise Physiology including Internat. Jour. Cardiology, Clin. Cardiology, Jour. Electrocardiology, European Heart Jour., among others. head cmty., founder Youth Synagogue, 1969-72; vol., lectr. Rotary Club, Givatayim, Israel, 1995-98. Recipient Excellence in Profl. Medicine award Kupat Cholim, Dan Dist., Cardiac Inst., 1997, hon. cert. Rotary Club, 1996. Mem. AAAS, Israel Cardiology Soc., N.Y. Acad. Scis., European Heart Soc., Israel Soc. Hypertension, Planetary Soc., Israel

Sport Medicine Soc. Avocations: Jewish philosophy, body and mind, cantor music, classical music, physics and philosophy of science. Home: 13 Opsterland St, 43350 Raanana Israel Office: Mishmar Hayadren Card Rehab Inst, 18 Mishmar Hayarden St, 53588 Givataim Israel

KLAITS, ROBERT S., real estate executive; b. Phila., June 17, 1944; s. Albert and Esther Klaits; m. Barbara L. Klaits. Student, Temple U. V.p. Fremar Corp., Margate, N.J.; CEO, Island Structures, Inc., Margate. Republican. Jewish. Home and Office: Island Structures Inc 7 Seaside Ct Margate City NJ 08402-1669

KLAMANN, JOERG-DIETER, chemist; b. Berlin, May 3, 1958; s. Dieter Paul and Elfriede Marie (Schonewald) K.; m. Kay Linda Greenfield, Dec. 19, 1992. MS, Hamburg U., Germany, 1984; PhD, Rheinische Friedrich-Wilhelms U., Bonn, Germany, 1988. Mgr. rsch. & devel. plastic additives Henkel KGaA, Dusseldorf, Germany, 1990-96, tech. dir. plastic additives, 1996-99; tech. dir. plastic technol. Cognis, Dusseldorf, Germany, 1999—. Contbr. articles to profl. jours. Study Found. German People grantee, Hamburg, 1982-84, Assn. German Chem. Soc. grantee, 1985-88; postdoctoral rsch. fellow Nat. U., Canberra Australia, 1988-89; recipient Fulbright award, 1981-82. Mem. German Chem. Soc. VCI Plastic Additive Coun., European Stabilizer Prodrs. Assn., European Chem. Industry Coun. Office: COGNIS GmbH, Werk Neynaber Chemie, 27608 Loxstedt Germany

KLAN, PETR, control scientist; b. Prague, Feb. 24, 1957; s. Josef and Nadezda (Soukupova) K.; m. Vera Lukavska, May 31, 1981 (div. 1983); 1 child, Jiri; m. Alena Hradilova, Apr. 5, 1988; children: Simon, Matej. Engr., Tech. U., Prague, 1981; Mgr., Charles U., Prague, 1994; PhD, Acad. of Scis., Prague, 1993. Scientist Acad. of Scis., Prague, 1981—; lectr. U. Pardubice, 1993. Inventor in field. 2d lt. Czech Army, 1981-82. Avocation: showing films. Office: Inst Computer Sci, POD Vodarenskov 2, 182 07 Prague 8 Czech Republic

KLAPAN, IVICA, otorhinolaryngologist, consultant; b. Metkovic, Croatia, Nov. 16, 1959; p. Luka and Lenka Klapan; m. Nives Milicic, Oct. 1, 1988; children: Kim, Lea. MD, U. Zagreb, Croatia, 1983; MMS, U. Zagreb, 1986, PhD, 1990. Physician Pub. Hosp., Ploce, Croatia, 1983-86; ENT resident ENT Dept. Salata, Zagreb, 1986-90, otorhinolaryngologist, 1990—; asst. prof. Sch. Medicine U. Zagreb, 1992; cons. Medicus 2000, Polyclinic, Zagreb, 1998; cons. Polyclinic for Med. Diagnostics, Nemetova, Zagreb, 1997-98. Author, founder: 3D-Computer Assisted Surgery, 1987 (Ekspertiza's laureate 1987). Recipient Travel award European Assn. for Cancer Rsch., Liverpool, 1991, 93; Found. scholar Garnett Passe and Rodney Williams Found., Sydney, 1987; fellow U. Pitts., 1989. Mem. Internat. Soc. for Computer Aided Surgery, N.Y. Acad. Sci. Avocations: tennis, karate, diving. E-mail: kim@sirius.phy.hr. Fax: 385-1-425-629. Home: Ilica 173, 10000 Zagreb Croatia Office: ENT Dept, Salata 4, 10000 Zagreb Croatia

KLAPPER, BYRON D., financial company executive; b. N.Y.C., May 2, 1938; s. Irving and Lottie K.; m. Karin I. Klapper, June 28, 1964; children: Kimberly, Lonn-Eric. BS in Journalism, U. Kans., 1964; cert. Wharton Sch., U. Pa., 1974. Reporter Topeka (Kans.) Daily Capitol, 1963, U.P.I., Kansas City, Mo.; editor Am. Cyanamid Co., Wayne, N.J., 1964-67; media rels. staff Bethlehem Steel Corp., N.Y.C., 1968; speech writer Burlington Ind., Inc., N.Y.C., 1969; reporter Wall St. Jour., N.Y.C., 1970-80; sr. v.p. Std. and Poors Corp., N.Y.C., 1980-90; mng. dir. Fitch Investors Svc., N.Y.C., 1990-98, Am. Capital Access, Inc., 1998—; columnist skiing Morritown Daily Record, 1988—, Editor-in-chief, SnoSports., Internet Ski Mag.; bd. dirs. Powell Techs., Inc., Visions West, Inc. Contbg. editor Barron's N.Y.C., 1967-69; pub. S&P's Creditweek, 1981—; publ. Creditweek Internat., 1983, Mcpl. Bond Book, 1984, S&P's Creditwire, 1986. Recipient Nat. Journalism award, William Randolph Hearst Found., 1960, 62, New Products award, McGraw Hill, 1986. Mem. Ea. Ski Writers Assn. (dir. 1985-91), Govt. Fin. Officers Assn., Pub. Securities Assn., Bond Market Assn., Downtown Athletic Club, Fgn. Corres. Club Japan (hon.), N.Am. Ski Journalists Assn. (dir. 1998—). Avocations: writing, photography, skiing, computers, triathlon. Home: 37 Tara Ln Montville NJ 07045-9699

KLAPPER, HELMUT KARL, biologist, researcher; b. Rutenau, Germany, June 2, 1932; s. Josef and Eva Maria Therese (Lausch) K.; m. Maria Charlotte Hobein, Mar. 3, 1956; children: Kornelia, Michael, Oliver. MSc in Biology, U. Leipzig, Germany, 1956, Dr. rer. nat., 1962; Habilitation, Tech. U., Dresden, Germany, 1978. Hydrobiologist Water Control Agy., Magdeburg, Germany, 1956-70; scientist Office R & D, Halle, Germany, 1971-74, Inst. Water Mgmt., Berlin, 1975-86, Water Control Agy., Magdeburg, Germany, 1987-90; head dept. Inst. Inland Water Rsch., Magdeburg, 1991-97, sr. scientist, 1997—; rsch. coun. Group Water, Berlin, 1966-80; scientific coun. Ecol. Rsch., Halle, 1986-90, Environ. Protection, Acad. Sci., Berlin, 1987-90, Min. Environ. Protection, Saxonia-Anhalt, 1992-94; hon. prof. U. Halle, Germany, 1992—. Author: Control of Eutrophication in Inland Waters, 1991; contbr. over 200 articles to profl. publs.; patentee in field. Recipient Excellent Water Mgr. decoration Min. Environ. Protection Berlin, 1980, First prize Chamber Tech. Berlin, 1988. Mem. Soc. Internat. Limnologorum, Freshwater Biol. Assn., German Soc. Water Protection. Avocations: sport diving, travelling, photography, writing. E-mail: klapper@gm.ufz.de. Home: Schrotebogen 10, D39126 Magdeburg Germany Office: Ctr Environ Rsch, Brückstrasse 3 a, D39114 Magdeburg Germany

KLAR, DANIELA, biologist; b. Pirmasens, Germany, Sept. 22, 1956; d. Walter and Helma (Seibert) K. Degree, U. Kaiserslautern, Germany, 1983; PhD, German Cancer Rsch. Ctr., Heidelberg, 1988. Scientific asst. A. Hettich Zentrifugen, Tuttlingen, Germany, 1989—. Avocations: ballet, piano, foreign languages. Home: Bischofszeller Str 31/1, D-78532 Tuttlingen Germany Office: A Hettich Zentrifugen GmbH, Gartenstr 100, D-78532 Tuttlingen Germany

KLARESKOG, LARS GÖRAN, rheumatologist, educator; b. Nässjö, Sweden, May 18, 1945; s. Jngue and Ruth Klareskog. MD, Uppsala U., Sweden, 1974, PhD, 1978. Rsch. scientist Uppsala U., 1979-82, assoc. prof., 1982-83, clin. fellow, 1983-90, prof., chmn. clin. immunology, 1990-93; prof., chmn. dept. rheumatology Karolinska Inst., 1993—; chmn., dir. dept. medicine Karolinska, 1993-99. Contbr. articles to profl. jours. Mem. Karolinska Inst. (Nobel assembly 1995—, Nobel com. 1995-98). Office: Dept Rheumatology, Karolinska Hosp, S-17176 Stockholm Sweden

KLARFELD, JONATHAN MICHAEL, journalism educator; b. Springfield, Mass., Dec. 11, 1937; m. Patricia Holland, Sept. 7, 1974; children: Victoria, Alexander. AB, Colgate U., 1960. Reporter, editor Holyoke (Mass.) Transcript-Telegram, 1962-65, UPI, Springfield, Boston, 1965-66, Boston Globe, 1966-68; press sec. Boston Parks/Redevel. Auth., 1968-70; reporter, writer Boston Record-Am., 1970-72; mgr. pub. info. Mass. Blue Cross, 1972-74; assoc. professor journalism Boston U., 1975—, dir. print journalism, 1979-96, dir. print and online journalism program, 1996—; editl. cons. Lawyers Weekly Pubs., Boston, Lansing, Mich., Richmond, Va., Providence, 1983-92; press analyst Oxbow Corp., West Palm Beach, Fla., 1984-96; news media critic/columnist Boston Herald, 1994, 95; cons. in libel and invasion of privacy cases. Contbr. articles to numerous newspapers, periodicals. Mem. New England Gilbert & Sullivan Soc., Sorcerers Rugby Club (pres. 1974-80), Newton Squash and Tennis Club (bd. govs. 1999—), New Eng. Gilbert and Sullivan Soc., Delta Kappa Epsilon. Unitarian. Avocations: squash, tennis, Gilbert and Sullivan. Office: Boston U Sch Journalism Boston MA 02215

KLAS, ERI, conductor; b. Tallinn, Estonia, June 7, 1939. Student, Tallinn State Conservatory, Leningrad State Conservatory; Dr. (hon.), Estonian Acad. of Music, 1994. Asst. condr. Boris Khaikin Bolshoi Theatre, Moscow, 1960-72; condr. Orch. Estonian Radio, 1864-70; condr. Nat. Opera Theatre Estonia, 1965—, music dir., 1975-95; laureate conductor, 1996—; music dir. Royal Opera, Stockholm, 1985-89; chief condr. Arhus Symphony Orch., Denmark, 1996—, Netherland Radio Symphony Orch., 1996; condr. Nobel Prize Ceremonial Concert, Stockholm, 1989; prin. guest conductor Finnish Nat. Opera, 1990—; chief conductor Aarhus Symphony Orch., Denmark, 1991-96; prof. Sibelius Acad. Helsinki, 1994—. Condr. numerous operas, operettas, mus., ballets; condr. symphony orchs. in 25 countries. Chmn. bd. Estonia Nat. Cultural Found., 1991—. Decorated Order of Nordsternier, Sweden. *

KLASEK, ANTONIN, chemistry educator; b. Olomouc, Czech Republic, Feb. 12, 1941; s. Antonin and Ruzena (Hruba) K.; m. Helena Becickova, Apr. 8, 1962 (div. 1975); children: Helena, Jarmila; m. Marie Korycankova, Aug. 25, 1976; 1 child, Jiri. Grad., Tech. Sch. Chemistry, Prerov, Czech Republic, 1959; diploma in engring., Prague Inst. Chem. Tech., 1965, DR, 1969; DSc, Tech. U. Brno, Czech Republic, 1988. Rsch. asst. med. faculty Palacky U., Olomouc, Czech Republic, 1965-75, sr. lectr., 1975-76; assoc. prof. faculty of tech. Tech. U., Zlin, Czech Republic, 1976-89, prof. faculty of tech. dept. environ. chemistry and tech., 1989—; expert regional law court, Brno, 1974—; mem. scientific bd. faculty of tech. Tech. U., Zlin, 1976—, dean, 1985-89, head dept. rubber and plastics, 1986-89, vice dean, 1997—. Author: (with J. Simonikova) Chemistry, 1977, Practice on Chemistry, 1997; Biopolymers, 1980; (with J. Kupec) Practice on Biopolymers, 1983; co-author: General and Inorganic Chemistry, 1975; author: (with others) Recent Developments in the Chemistry of Natural Carbon Compounds, 1975, Handbook of Applied Polymer Processing Technology, 1996; contbr. numerous articles to profl. jours. Mem. Czech Chem. Soc., Macromolecular Divsn. Czech Chem. Soc. (vice chmn. 1993—), N.Y. Acad. Scis. Avocations: music, gardening, skiing. E-mail: klasek@zlin.vutbr.cz. Home: Nad Vyvozem 4851, CZ-76005 Zlin Czech Republic Office: Tech U Faculty Tech, Dept Envir Chem NAM.TGM 275, 76272 Zlin Czech Republic

KLASINC, LEO, chemist, educator; b. Zagreb, Croatia, May 20, 1937; s. Viktor and Anita (Tavcar) K.; m. Darka Jerkovic, Apr. 2, 1961; children: Natasa, Anton-Jan. BSc in Chemistry, U. Zagreb, 1960, PhD, 1963. Asst. R. Boskovic Inst., Zagreb, 1961-66, asst. prof., 1968-74, assoc. prof., 1974-76, prof., rsch. adviser, 1976—; rsch. assoc. Nuclear Rsch. Ctr., Karlsruhe, Germany, 1966-68, guest scientist, 1972-84; vis. prof. La. State U., Baton Rouge, 1984—; titular mem. Internat. Union Pure Applied Chemistry. Contbr. over 250 articles to profl. jours. Recipient Ruder Boskovic award Republic of Croatia, 1988, Acad. award Croatian Acad. Scis. and Arts, 1996. Mem. Am. Phys. Soc., Am. Chem. Soc., Croatian Chem. Soc., Internat. Soc. Quantum Biology, Croatian Acad. Scis. and Arts (assoc.). Avocations: water sports, reading, music, bridge. Home: Šubićeva 18, HR-10000 Zagreb Croatia Office: Ruder Bosković, Bijenička 54, HR-10002 Zagreb Croatia

KLAT, SAMIR RAMEZ, engineering company executive, consultant; b. Alexandria, Egypt, Dec. 19, 1937; s. Ramez Zahi and Marie (Bassili) K.; div. 1994; children: Anthony Ramez, Michael Zahi, Fiona; m. Helen Eriksson. BSc in Engring., Imperial Coll. Sci. and Tech., London, 1960; A, City and Guild Inst. London, London, 1960; PhD, Imperial Coll. Sci. and Tech., London, 1965, D.I.C. (diploma of Imperial Coll.), 1965. Chartered mech. engr., chartered fuel technologist, chartered engr. Rschr. English Elec., U.K., 1961-65; cons. D.B. Drake & Ptnrs., U.K., 1961-65; engring. advisor Lumsden/Sargent Racing, U.K., 1962-65; chmn. Soc. Fonciere Tripoli, Lebanon, 1966-91; dir. Drap D'Or, Lebanon, 1965-68; lectr. Am. U. Beirut, Lebanon, 1968-72; indsl. advisor Lebanese Govt., 1968-72; sr. engr. Arab Fund for Social and Econ. Devel., Kuwait, 1973-75; mgr. project dept. Indsl. Bank Kuwait, 1975-79; mem. op. bd. Alghanim Group, Kuwait, 1979-82; v.p. corp. devel. Alghanim Industries, Kuwait, 1978-82; CEO Al-Ahlia Investment Co., Kuwait, 1982-84; dir. Klat Assocs., Eng., 1984-86; mng. dir. Indsl. Diamond Engring AB, Ltd., Lemland, Finland; guest spkr. several internat. confs. Author: Combustion Mechanisms in Dual-Fuel Engines, 1965; contbr. numerous articles to tech. and profl. publs.; patentee in fields of fuel injection, combustion mechanisms, and rotary percussive drilling. Lebanese Govt. rep., several internat. confs., 1968-77; mem. Lebanese Govt. Commn. Oil Affairs and Negotiations, Lebanon and Saudi Arabia, 1968-72. Fellow Inst. Mech. Engrs. (U.K.), City and Guilds of London Inst., Royal Soc. Arts. Christian Orthodox. Avocations: sailing, photography, reading, research. Fax: 358-18-35430. Office: Indsl Diamond Engring AB, Herro 11, FIN22610 Lemland Åland, Finland

KLAUBER, JAMES SHULER, financial consultant, state legislator; b. Greenwood, S.C., Nov. 5, 1966; s. William Adolph and Betty Jane Klauber; m. Karen Elizabeth Hughston, May 23, 1992 (div. Nov. 1999); 1 child, Elizabeth Grace. BA, The Citadel, 1989; JD, U. S.C., 1993. Bar: S.C. 1993. Ptnr. Klauber & Long, Greenwood, 1994-98; fin. cons. IJL Wachovia, Greenwood, 1998—; Bar: S.C. 1993. Mem. Greenwood City Coun., 1990-92; legislator S.C. Ho. of Reps., Greenwood, 1992—. Maj. S.C. Army N.G., 1984—. Recipient Housing Achievement award S.C. Housing Authority, 1997; named Disting. Citizen of Yr., S.C. Assn. Housing Authority Exec. Dirs., 1995. Mem. Sons Confederate Veterans, Rotary (Paul Harris fellow). Republican. Methodist. Avocations: scuba diving, travel, history. E-mail: klauher@emeraldis.com. Office: IJL Wachovia 340 Main St Ste C Greenwood SC 29646-2773

KLAUBER, JULIE B., library director. BA, Bklyn. Coll., 1971; MS in Libr. Svc., Columbia U., 1972. N.Y. state pub. librs. profl. cert. Student aide humanities reference divsn. Bklyn. Coll. Libr., 1968-71; bibliographic asst. Columbia U. Butler Libr., N.Y.C., 1971-72; reference libr. Great Neck (N.Y.) Libr., 1972-73, head adult svcs., 1973-76, asst. to the dir., 1976-80; reading for the handicapped divsn. chief Suffolk Coop. Libr. Sys., Bellport, N.Y., 1984-86; adminstr. for outreach svcs. Suffolk Coop. Libr. Sys., Bellport, 1986—. Author: AIDS Information Resources for People with Disabilities: A Handbook for Information Providers in Libraries, AIDS Organizations, and Disability Organizations, 1993, When the Print Is Too Small: Resources and Services for Older Adults with Visual Impairments in Suffolk County, 1991; co-author: (with A. Klauber) Inclusion & Parent Advocacy: A Resource Guide, 1996; chief rschr., editl. assoc. The Independent Scholar's Handbook, 1982; disability editor Library Outreach Reporter, 1989-91; editor monthly column Media: Review on Books and Audio, 1991-93; mng. editor Disability Resources Monthly, 1993—; contbr. articles to profl. jours. mem. Great Neck Peninsula Bicentennial Planning Com., 1975-76; mem. adult edn. adv. com. Great Neck Pub. Schs., 1976-79, exec. com., 1978-79; mem. cmty. sch. adv. bd., Town of Huntington, 1983-87, mem. citizens adv. coun. on the handicapped, 1985-87; adv. bd. mem. Help for the Visually Handicapped, 1987—; mem. ad-hoc com. County Exec.'s Task Force on Abuse of the Disabled, 1991-92; mem. task force com. Suffolk County Exec.'s Task Force on Family Violence, 1992-93; bd. dirs., hon. mem. Self-Initiated Living Options, 1998—. Recipient Cmty. Svc. award Town of Huntington, 1984-87, Outstanding Vol. award Am. Diabetes Assn., 1992; named Media Rep. of the Yr., N.Y. State Developmental Disabilities Resource Coun., 1997, Outstanding Individual of Yr., Self-Initiated Living Options, Inc., 1997. Mem. ALA (adv. mem. subcom. for the revision of stds. and guidelines of svc. of the Libr. of Congress Network of Librs. for the Blind and Physicalled Handicapped Assn. Specialized and Coop. Libr. Agys. divsn. 1993-95, Nat. Orgn. on Disability award 1999), N.Y. Libr. Assn. (vice chairperson roundtable on libr. svcs. for spl. populations 1988-89, chairperson, 1989-90), Suffolk County Libr. Assn., Phi Beta Kappa. Avocations: reading, writing, web designing. E-mail: jklauber@disabilityresources.org. Home: 4 Glatter Ln South Setauket NY 11720

KLAUCK, HANS-JOSEF, theology educator; b. Hermeskeil, Germany, June 4, 1946; s. Franz-Rudolf and Anna-Maria (Maier) K. Diploma in Theology, U. Bonn, Germany, 1972; ThD, U. Munich, 1978, D of Edn., 1981. Asst. prof. U. Munich, 1975-81; prof. U. Bonn, 1981-82, U. Wurzburg, Germany, 1982-97, U. Munich, 1997—; acad. dean Theol. Faculty, Wurzburg, 1995-97. Author: Herrenmahl und Hellenistischer Kult, 1982, The Religious Context of Early Christianity, 2000; editor Biblische Zeitschrift jour, 1991—; contbr. over 80 articles to profl. jours. Mem. Soc. New Testament Studies. Roman Catholic. Avocations: music, literature. Office: Univ Munich, Geschwister-Scholl-Platz 1, D-80539 Munich Germany

KLAUDER, JOHN RIDER, physics educator; b. Reading, Pa., Jan. 24, 1932; s. David Streeper and Jean (Rider) K.; m. Robertha Howell, Sept. 11, 1953 (div. 1980); children: Karol Jean, Katherine Jane, Kim Ann, John Christopher; m. Agnes Nadasdi, July 26, 1980; 1 child, Jennifer Ann. BS, U. Calif., Berkeley, 1953; MS, Stevens Inst. Tech., 1956; PhD, Princeton U., 1959. Mem. tech. staff, then dept. head AT&T Bell Labs., Murray Hill, N.J., 1953-88; prof. depts. math. and physics U. Fla., Gainesville, 1988—; cons. Los Alamos (N.Mex.) Nat. Lab., 1978-89. Author: Beyond Conventional Quantization, 1999; co-author: Fundamentals of Quantum Optics, 1968, Coherent States, 1985; editor Jour. Math. Phys., 1979-86. Fellow AAAS, Am. Phys. Soc.; mem. Internat. Assn. Math. and Physics (pres. 1988-91), Internat. Union Pure and Applied Physics (assoc. sec. gen. 1984-90). Office: U Fla Dept Math/Physics Gainesville FL 32611

KLAUER, KARL CHRISTOPH, psychology educator; b. Bad Kreuznach, Germany, Oct. 30, 1961; s. Karl Josef and Elisabeth (Stehle) K. Diploma in psychology, Hamburg U., 1985, PhD in Psychology, 1988. Asst. lectr. Hamburg U., 1985-88; asst. prof. Free U., Berlin, 1988-94; prof. Heidelberg (Germany) U., 1994-96, Bonn (Germany) U., 1996. Asst. editor: Diagnostica, 1996—, British Jour. of Math. and Statis. Psychology, 1996—, Psychometrika, 1992—; editor Zeitschrift fuer Exptl. Psychologie, 1997—; contbr. articles to profl. jours. Recipient Award for Disting. Contbn. European Assn. for Psychol. Assessment, 1995, Award for Outstanding Rsch. Internat. Fedn. of Classification Socs., 1993; Heisenberg scholarship German Rsch. Soc., 1993. Mem. Germany Psychol. Soc. (sec. gen. 1994-96, Heinz-Heckhausen Jungwissenschaftlerpreis 1990), German Psychology Orgn. (planning com. 1994-96, bd. dirs.). Roman Catholic. Home: Zur Kleinbahn 10, 53844 Troisdorf Germany Office: Psychologisches Inst, U Bonn Roemerstrasse 164, 53117 Bonn Germany

KLAUS, SIDNEY NATHAN, dermatologist; b. Detroit, June 29, 1931; arrived in Israel, 1987; s. Morris Joshua and Mae (Schwartz) K.; m. Anne Isabel Shivas, Mar. 18, 1989; children: Jeffrey, Peter. BA, U. Mich., 1953, MD, 1957; MA (hon.), Yale U., 1974. Diplomate Am. Bd. Dermatology. Asst. prof. Yale U. Med. Sch., New Haven, 1964-69, assoc. prof., 1969-74, prof., 1974-87; Phillip Frost prof., chmn. dept. dermatology Hebrew U. Med. Sch., Jerusalem, Israel, 1987-99; prof. Dartmouth Med. Sch., 1999—; Dozor vis. prof. Ben Gurion U., Beersheba, Israel, 1979; mem. med. and grant adv. bd. Skin Cancer Found., N.Y.C., 1983-86; cons. Teva Pharm. Industry, Petah Tikva, Israel, 1991-98. Editor (books) Biologic Basis of Pigmentation, 1979, Pathophysiology of Melanocytes, 1979, Biologic Molecular and Clinical Aspects of Pigmentation, 1984, Global Dermatology, 1994. Lt. USN, 1959-61. Mem. Internat. Soc. Dermatology (v.p. 1991-94), Am. Acad. Dermatology (chmn. Va. task force 1984-87), Assn. of Profs. of Dermatology (chmn. grad. edn. com. 1979-82), Am. Fedn. for Clin. Rsch. (chmn. dermatology sect. 1971), Internat. Pigment Cell Soc. (pres. 1985-88). Achievements include demonstration of process of pigment transfer in mammalian skin, analysis of skin color science during 17th and 18th Centuries. Office: Dartmouth-Hitchcock Med Ctr 1 Medical Center Dr Lebanon NH 03756-0002

KLAUS, VACLAV, Czech government official; b. Prague, June 19, 1941; s. Václav and Marie K.; m. Livia Klausová, 1968; 2 children. Diploma, Prague Sch. Econs., 1963; attended, Cornell U.; numerous hon. degrees including, U. Ariz., 1997, U. Dallas, 1999; hon. degree, Jacksonville U., 1995, U. Buckingham, U.K., 1996, U. Passau, Germany, 1996, U. Toronto, 1997, Tech. U. Ostrava, Czech Republic, 1997, DePaul U., 1999. Rschr. Inst. Econs. Czechoslovak Acad. Scis., 1970; various pos. Czechoslovak State Bank, 1971-86; head dept. macroeconomic policy, Inst. Forecasting Acad. Scis., 1987—; chair Civic Forum Movement, 1990-91; min. finance Czech Rep., 1989-92; chair Civic Dem. Party, 1991—; dep. prime minister, 1991-92; prime minister Czech Rep., 1992-97; chair state defense coun., 1993-97; prof. fin. Prague Sch. of Econs.; pres. Chamber of Deputies/Czech Parliament, 1998—; hon. prof. Rochester Inst. Tech., 1991, Suffolk U., 1991, U. Fr. Marroquín, 1993, U. Gadalajara, 1993, Prague Sch. Econs., 1994, Belgrano U., 1994, Tufts U., 1994, U. Law, Econs., Sci. Aix-Marseille, 1994. Author: A Road to Market Economy, 1991, Tomorrow's Challenge, 1991, Economic Theory and Economic Reform, 1991, Signale aus dem Herzen Europas, 1991, I Do Not Like Catastrophic Scenarios, 1991, Why Am I a Conservative?, 1992, The First on the Right Side, 1992, Dismantling Socialism: A Road to Market Economy II, 1993, The Year-How Much is it in the History of the Country?, 1993, The Czech Way, 1994, Rebirth of a Country: Five Years After, 1994, Economic Theory and Reality of Transformation Processes, 1995, Between the Past and the Future, 1996, Renaissance: The Rebirth of Liberty in the Heart of Europe, 1997, The Defence of Forgotten Ideas, 1997, Close to the Edge, 1997, Thus Spoke Václav Klaus, 1998, Why I am not a Social Democrat, 1998, The Country Without Governing, 1999, The Way Out of the Trap, 1999, From the Opposition Treaty to the Tolerance Patent, 2000; contbr. articles to jours. Co-founder Czechoslovak Civic Forum Movement, chmn. 1990—; co-founder Divic Dem. Party, chmn. 1991—. Recipient Freedom award, 1990, Schumpeter prize, 1991, Walter M. Courtis prize, 1992, Max Schmiedheiny Freedom prize, 1992, Peutinger prize, 1993, Ludwig Erhard prize, 1993, Hermann Lindrath prize, 1993, Konrad Adenauer prize, 1993, Club of Europe award, 1994, Fondation du Forum Universale Crans Montana award, 1994, Transatlantic Leadership award European Inst., Washington, 1995, James Madison Internat. prize Madison Inst., Jacksonville, 1995, Goldwater medal for Econ. Freedom, Phoenix, 1997, others. Mem. Mont Pelerin Soc. Avocations: tennis, skiing. Office: Parliament, Snemovni 4, 11826 Prague 1, Czech Republic

KLAUSA, VYTAUTAS, biochemist, researcher; b. Koj, Krasnojarsk Region, USSR, June 12, 1956; s. Jonas Klausa and Zita (Puodžiunaite) Klausiene. Degree, Vilnius (Lithuania) U., 1979; PhD, Inst. Biochemistry, Vilnius, 1992. Engr.-chemist Inst. Biochemistry, Vilnius, 1979-82, rsch. asst., 1982-94, rsch. assoc., 1994—; lectr. Vilnius U., 1992—, Vilnius Pedagogical Inst., 1995-97. Contbr. articles to profl. jours. Grantee Internat. Sci. Found., 1993. Mem. Lithuanian Soc. Geneticists and Breeders. Avocations: paleontology, collecting butterflies, amateur astronomy and photography. Home: Buivydiškiu 15-73, 2010 Vilnius Lithuania Office: Inst Biochemistry, Mokslininku 12, 2600 Vilnius Lithuania

KLAUSMEYER, DAVID MICHAEL, scientific instruments manufacturing company executive; b. Indpls., Aug. 29, 1934; s. David M. and V. Jane (Donnellan) K.; m. Julie Ann Johnson, Oct. 29, 1955; children: Kathleen M., Kevin M., Gregory J. BSS, Georgetown U., 1955. Asst. to pres. White Cons. Ind., Cleve., 1957; auditor Ernst & Ernst, Cleve., 1957-59; pres. Photopipe, Inc., Cleve., 1960-63; v.p. McGregor & Werner Internat., Inc., Washington, 1964-70; internat. cons. Stratford of Tex., Houston, 1971-72; pres. FLR Corp., Houston, 1972-74, Southwest Cons., Houston, 1981-86, Imaging Products, Houston, 1987-90; pres. Nanodyanmics, Inc., N.Y.C., 1988—, also bd. dirs.; pres. Corp. Devel., Houston, 1974-81; ptnr. Klausmeyer & Assoc., Houston, 1970—; dir. U.S. investment banking G.H. Securities, Grand Cayman Island, 1995—; bd. dirs. S.W. Venture Reification, Houston, TWK Techs., Charlotte, N.C.; pres. Arsenal Stallions, Inc., 1997—; mng. ptnr. Millcreek Farms, 1992—. Bd. dirs. Catholic Endowment Found. Galveston-Houston, 1999—. With USCG, 1955-57. Republican. Roman Catholic. Home: 288 Litchfield Ln Houston TX 77024-6035 Office: Nanodynamics Inc 10878 Westheimer Rd # 178 Houston TX 77042-3202

KLAUSS, KENNETH KARL, composer, educator; b. Parkston, S.D., Apr. 8, 1923; s. Christian and Paulina (Engel) K. MusB in Composition, U. So. Calif., 1946. Tchr. composition and piano L.A., 1946-50; composer Lester Horton Theater, L.A., 1949-50; tchr. music San Francisco, 1950-61; composer, educator L.A., 1961—; lectr. in music for dance Idyllwild (Calif.) Sch. Music and Arts, 1967-74; lectr. in music history So. Calif. Inst. Architecture, Santa Monica, 1970-76; composer in residence Perry/Mansfield Camp, Steamboat Springs, Colo., 1966; guest performer, composer, lectr. Libr. Congress, Am. U., Washington, 1996. Composer: (opera) Fall of the House of Usher, 1952; author, composer: (poetry/music orchestration) Story of the World Volumes I to VIII, 1952-86, 86-96. Founder, patron Klauss/James Archive and Art Mus., Parkston, 1995—. Recipient hon. mention opera competition Ohio U., Athens, 1954. Democrat. Avocations: history, poetry. Home: 440 Wren Dr Los Angeles CA 90065-5040

KLAVINS, MARIS, chemist, educator; b. Riga, Latvia, Mar. 12, 1956; s. Karl Klamanis and Zenta Klavina; m. Inta Stackober, Aug. 16, 1986; children: Laura, Linards. Dipl. chemist, U. Latvia, 1979, D of Chemistry, 1992; cand. chemist, Moscow U., 1985. Rschr. Inst. Applied Biochemistry, Olaine, Latvia, 1984-89; head lab. Inst. Biology, Salaspils, Latvia, 1989-92; docent U. Latvia, Riga, 1992-94, prof., 1995—; pres. Latvian Soc. Biometeorology, Riga, 1995—; expert Latvian Coun. Sci., Riga, 1996—. Author: Aquatic Humic Substances, 1992, Environmental Chemistry; patentee in field; contbr. articles to profl. jours. Mem. Man and Biosphere, Internat. Soc. Humic Substances (nat. coord., conf. award 1992). Avocations: gardening, stamp collecting. Office: Univ Latvia, Raina Blvd 19, LV 1586 Riga Latvia

KLEAR, JULIE ANN, artist, educator; b. Frankfurt, Germany, Nov. 26, 1970; d. John Michael and Gloria Jean K. BFA, Art Acad. Cin., 1993; MFA, Bowling Green State U., 1999. Artist in residence Art. Acad. Cin., 1992-93, asst. Art for Kids program, 1990-93; art dir., arts educator Hoff Barthelson Music Sch., Scarsdale, N.Y., 1993-96; arts educator K-8 Blessed Sacrament Sch., Toledo, 1994-95; artist in residence LEAP (Learning through Extended Art Program), N.Y.C., 1995-96; head educator, asst. dir. Harrison St. Sch., N.Y.C., 1996-97; instr. drawing, design Bowling Green (Ohio) State U., 1997-99; instr. workshops for children and teenagers Mus. Fine Arts, Boston, 1999—. Exhbns. include Muse Gallery, 1998, Main Line Art Ctr., 1998, Toledo Mus. Art, Muscarelle Mus. Art, others. Vol. food preparation and distbn. St. John's Ch., Cin., 1992-93; vol. after sch. reading program Grace Cmty. Ctr., Toledo, 1988-89. Avocations: traveling, reading, cooking, swimming. Home: 38 Speridakis Ter Cambridge MA 02139-4017 Office: Mus Fine Arts 465 Huntington Ave Boston MA 02115-5597

KLEBANOWSKI, ADAM SYLWESTER, electrical engineer, educator, consultant; b. Warsaw, Poland, Jan. 23, 1940; arrived in Australia, 1982; s. Jerzy and Eugenia (Janczak) K.; m. Barbara Teofila Jasinska, Dec. 30, 1964; 1 child, Pawel. MSc in Elec. Engring., Tech. U. Warsaw, 1963, PhD in Tech. Scis., 1973. Lectr. Tech. U. Warsaw, 1963, asst. prof., 1963-78; asst. prof., head of elec. engring. dept. Libyan Higher Inst. Mech. and Elec. Engring., Hoon, 1981; design engr. State Electric Commn. Victoria, Melbourne, Australia, 1982-89, protection engr., 1990-91; protection sys. engr. PowerNet Victoria, Melbourne, 1992—; sr. protection engr., internat. cons. SECV Internat., Melbourne, Australia and S.E. Asia, 1992—; cons. pvt. practice, 1995—; part-time lectr. Swinburne U. Tech., Monash U., Melbourne U., Melbourne, 1985-98, Victoria U. Tech., Melbourne, 1989—; lectr. Elec. Supply Assn. Australia, 1991—; presenter papers in field. Author: Problems on Power System Protection, 1972, 73; co-author: Power System Protection, 1994, 95, 96, 97, 98. Active Solidarity, Warsaw, 1981-82. Mem. IEEE Power Engring. Soc., N.Y. Acad. Scis., Polish Tech. and Profl. Assn. Australia. Home: 15 Pippin Ave, Glen Waverly Melbourne VIC 3150, Australia Office: Power Net Victoria, 890 Wellington Rd, Rowville VIC 3178, Australia

KLEBBA, RAYMOND ALLEN, property manager; b. Chgo., Apr. 16, 1934; s. Raymond Aloysius and Marie Cecelia (Tobin) K.; m. Barbara Ann Gurbal, Oct. 7, 1961; children: Anne, Daniel, Mary, Theresa. Student, Loyola U., Chgo., 1954-56; cert. property mgr., Inst. Real Estate Mgmt., 1970. Corr., rep. Western R.R. Assn., Chgo., 1956-61; pres. Midland Warehouse, Chgo., 1961-68; v.p., gen. mgr. Strobeck, Reiss Sch. Mgmt. Co., Chgo., 1968-70, real estate mgr. and broker, 1970-83; v.p., dir. Mid-Am. Nat. Bank, Chgo., 1983-90; br. mgr. Bank of Highwood/Deerfield, Ill., 1990-94; v.p. sales First Colonial Mortgage Corp., Chgo., 1994-95; bus. mgr. St. Matthias Parish, Chgo., 1995-98. Mem. Chgo. Bd. Realtors (vice chmn. comml. and indsl. asing property mgmt. coun.), Inst. Real Estate Mgmt. (life, chmn. chpt. of yr. com. 1975-76), Rotary, Moose, K.C. Avocations: bowling, golf, gardening, treasure hunting, fishing (Chicagoland individual casting champion 1999). Home: 4933 N Leavitt St Chicago IL 60625-1308

KLECKNER, ROBERT GEORGE, JR., lawyer; b. Reading, Pa., Mar. 14, 1932; s. Robert George and Elizabeth (Endlich) K.; m. Carol Espie, June 15, 1955; children: Anthony Savage, Susan Duffield. BA, Yale U., 1954; LLB, U. Pa., 1959. Bar: Pa. 1960, N.Y. 1964. Pvt. practice Reading, 1960-63; assoc. Sullivan & Cromwell, N.Y.C., 1963-70; house counsel Goldman, Sachs & Co., N.Y.C., 1970-78; cons. N.Y.C., 1978-80; house counsel Johnson & Higgins, N.Y.C., 1980-97; sr. atty. legal dept. Marsh & McLennan Cos., Inc., N.Y.C., 1997; ret., 1997. 1st lt. USAR, 1955-57, Korea. Mem. ABA, Assn. Bar City N.Y., Berks County (Pa.) Bar Assn., Union Club, Univ. Club, Phi Beta Kappa. Republican. Lutheran. Home: 80 East End Ave New York NY 10028-8004

KLECKNER, WILLARD RICHARDS, electrical engineer, consultant, educator; b. Plainfield, N.J., Sept. 29, 1937; s. Willard Ralph and Gladys Alta (Richards) K.; m. Linda Re Kleckner; 1 child, Tamara Lee. BSEE, Pa. State U., 1959, BSBA, 1959, MBA, 1976; LLB, La Salle U., 1965; PhD in Bus. Adminstrn. and Engring., Calif. Western U., 1980. Cons. engr. Kleckner Enterprises, Whitehall, Pa., 1961-65, Hazleton, Pa., 1975-78; labor rels. mgr. Eaton Corp., Phila., 1965-73; dir. labor rels. Beverage Mgmt. Corp., Columbus, Ohio, 1973-75; dir. adminstrn. Penn-Dixie Industries, Inc., Nazareth, Pa., 1978-81; v.p. adminstrn. Merrick Corp., Roseland, N.J., 1981-83; dir. engring., rsch. devel. AquaScis. Internat., Inc., Lincoln Park, N.J., 1988-90; cons. elec., environ. safety and R&D engr. Kleckner Assocs., Hibernia, 1990-93; prin., indsl. hygienist, safety engr., environ. engr. Kleckner Enterprises, Inc., Long Valley, N.J., 1993-95, Oxford Environ., Inc., Pine Brook, N.J., 1994-95, Kleckner Enterprises, Inc., Lecanto, Fla., 1995—; lectr. on indsl. rels. and safety, 1975—; lectr. on low frequency electromagnetic field radiation; cons. Country Oaks Inn, Lecanto, Fla., 1995—. Contbr. articles to profl. jours. Instr., lectr. on safety and environ., 1977—, on internal and external electronic security equipment, 1975—, on water tech., 1988. With USN, 1955-61. Mem. IEEE (sr.), APA, Am. Arbitration Assn., Am. Soc. Safety Engrs., Am. Paramedic Assn., Assn. Locksmiths Am., Am. Indsl. Hygiene Assn., Nat. Registry of Environ. Profls., NASA, Pa. State U. Alumni Assn. Republican. Presbyterian. Office: Kleckner Enterprises Inc PO Box 189 Lecanto FL 34460-0189

KLEE, ANDREAS PETER, gynecologist; b. Wiesbaden, Germany, June 8, 1960; s. Hermann Karl and Ingeborg (Ebeling) K.; m. Andrea Renate Kopsch Klee, May 1991; children: Tristan, Franziska, Niklas. Degree in Biology, U. Mainz, Germany, 1986; PhD in Biology, U. Bochum, Germany, 1990; MD, U. Wurzburg, Germany, 1993. Collaborator Hoechst Pharmacy, Wiesbaden, Germany, 1983-93; asst. sr. physician City Hosp., Wiesbaden, Germany, 1992-99, leading head physician, 2000—. Mem. German Soc. Gynecology and Obstetrics. Fax: 0611-260522. Home: Rheintal 42, 65199 Wiesbaden Germany

KLEESCHULTE, DAVID GENE, manufacturing executive; b. St. Charles, Mo., Dec. 27, 1942; s. Virgil Kleeschulte and Pearl Bochorst; m. Sharon Amelia Bush, Aug. 11, 1973; children: David, Daniel, Dawn, Douglas, Amber. BBus, Ramapo Coll., 1983. Chief engr., wheel prodn. Abex Corp., Calera, Ala., 1974-81; chief engr., mech. prodn. Abex Corp., Mahwah, N.J., 1981-84, v.p. engring., 1984-88; v.p. mfg. ABC Rail Corp., Calera, Ala., 1988-94; v.p., internat. ABC Rail Corp., Chgo., 1994-96; pres. China investment corp. ABC-NACO, Inc., Birmingham, Ala., 1996—; vice-chmn., dir. Datong ABC Castings Co., Ltd., China, 1991—; adv. bd. Internat. Wheelsets Congress, 1988—. Mem. Riverchase Country Club, the Club, ASTM, Am. Mgmt. Assn., Mid-Am. Com. Avocation: golf. E-mail: Kleeschulted@abc-naco.com. Office: ABC-NACO Inc 100 Riverpoint Corp Ctr Birmingham AL 35243

KLEIMAN, BERNARD, lawyer; b. Chgo., Jan. 26, 1928; s. Isadore and Pearl (Wikoff) K.; m. Gloria Baime, Nov. 15, 1986; children—Leslie, David. B.S., Purdue U., 1951; J.D., Northwestern U., 1954. Bar: Ill. 1954. Practice law in assn. with Abraham W. Brussell, 1957-60; dist. counsel United Steel Workers Am., 1960-65, spl. counsel, 1997—, gen. counsel, 1965-97; ptnr. Kleiman, Cornfield & Feldman, Chgo., 1960-75; prin. B. Kleiman (P.C.), 1976-77, Kleiman, Whitney, Wolfe & Elfenbaum, P.C., 1978-99; Mem. collective bargaining coms. for nat. labor negotiations in basic steel, aluminum, tire and can mfg. industries. Contbr. articles to legal jours. Served with U.S. Army, 1946-48. Mem. ABA, Allegheny County Bar Assn.

KLEIN, ARNOLD WILLIAM, dermatologist; b. Mt. Clemens, Mich., Feb. 27, 1945; s. David Klein; m. Malvina Kraemer. BA, U. Pa., 1967, MD, 1971. Intern Cedars-Sinai Med. Ctr., Los Angeles, 1971-72; resident in dermatology Hosp. U. Pa., Phila., 1972-73, U. Calif., Los Angeles, 1973-75; pvt. practice dermatology Beverly Hills, Calif., 1975—; clin. prof. dermatology/medicine U. Calif. Ctr. for Health Scis; mem. med. staff Cedars-Sinai Med. Ctr.; asst. clin. prof. dermatology Stanford U., 1982-89; asst. clin. prof. to clin. prof. dermatology/medicine, UCLA; mem. Calif. State Adv. Com. on Malpractice, 1983-89; med. adv. bd. Skin Cancer Found., Lupus Found. Am., Botox adv. bd., Allergan; presenter seminars in field. Assoc. editor Jour. Dermatologic Surgery and Oncology; reviewer Jour. Sexually Transmitted Diseases, Jour. Am. Acad. Dermatology; mem. editorial bd. Men's Fitness mag., Shape mag., Archives of Dermatology; contbr. numerous articles to med. jours. Founder R. Tarlow/Dr. Arnold Klein Fund for Breast Cancer Treatment. Mem. AMA, Calif. Med. Assn., Am. Soc. Dermatologic Surgery, Internat. Soc. Dermatologic Surgery, Am. Assn. Cosmetic Surgeons, Assn. Sci. Advisors, Los Angeles Med. Assn., Am. Coll. Chemosurgery, Met. Dermatology Soc., Am. Acad. Dermatology, Dermatology Found., Scleroderma Found., Internat. Psoriasis Rsch. Inst., Lupus Found., Discovery Fund for Eye Rsch. (dir.), Hereditary Disease Found. (dir.), Jennifer Jones Simon Found. (trustee), Am. Venereal Disease Assn., Soc. Cosmetic Chemists, AFTRA, Los Angeles Mus. Contemporary Art (founder), Dance Gallery Los Angeles (founder), Am. Found. AIDS Research (founder, dir.), Children's Mus. L.A. (founder), Friars Club, Phi Beta Kappa, Sigma Tau Sigma, Delphos. Office: 435 N Roxbury Dr Ste 204 Beverly Hills CA 90210-5004

KLEIN, CALVIN RICHARD, fashion designer; b. N.Y.C., Nov. 19, 1942; s. Leo and Flore (Stern) K.; m. Jayne Centre, Apr. 26, 1964 (div. 1974); 1 dau., Marci; m. Kelly Rector, Sept. 1986. A.A., Fashion Inst. Tech., 1962. Pres., designer Calvin Klein, N.Y.C., 1969—; critic Parsons Sch. Design; critic, cons. Fashion Inst. Tech., dir., 1975—. Recipient Coty award, 1973, 74, 75, Woolmark award for Career Achievement, 1987; named Outstanding Am. talent in women's fashion design Coun. Fashion Designers of Am., 1981, 83, 87; Womenswear/Menswear Designer of the Year, Coun. Fashion Designers of Am., 1993. Mem. Council Fashion Designers, Mus. Modern Art, Met. Mus. Art, Whitney Mus., Guggenheim Mus. Office: Calvin Klein Inc 205 W 39th St Fl 17 New York NY 10018-3102

KLEIN, CHRISTOPHER CARNAHAN, economist; b. Anniston, Ala., July 5, 1953; s. Wallace Carnahan and Frances Luvona (Meaders) K.; m. Vicki Lynn Brown, May 7, 1983; children: Hannah Marie Brown, Colin Christopher Brown. BA in Econs., U. Ala., 1976; PhD in Econs., U. N.C., 1980. Economist FTC, Washington, 1980-86; economist Tenn. Pub. Svc. Commn., Nashville, 1986-93, rsch. dir., 1993-94, dir. utility rate div., 1994-95; chief utility rate divsn. Tenn. Regulatory Authority, Nashville, 1995-97, chief econ. analysis divsn., 1997—; mem. adj. faculty Mid. Tenn. State U., Murfreesboro, 1990-94; adj. assoc. prof. Vanderbilt U., 1998—; mem. Fed.-State Joint Bd. Staff, 1994-96; mem. rsch. adv. com. Nat. Regulatory Rsch. Inst., Columbus, Ohio, 1990-95, chmn., 1993-95; mem. staff subcom. on gas Nat. Assn. Regulatory Utility Commrs., 1990-94. Contbr. articles to profl. jurs. Recipient cert. of commendation FTC, 1985. Mem. Am. Econ. Assn., So. Econ. Assn., Indsl. Orgn. Soc., Transp. and Pub. Utilities Group, Alpha Pi Mu. Avocations: writing poetry, tube hi-fi, photography. Office: Tenn Regulatory Authority 460 James Robertson Pkwy Nashville TN 37243-9021

KLEIN, DEBORAH RAE, health facility administrator; b. Detroit, Mar. 29, 1951; d. Chester Anthony and E. Jacquelyn (Hollenbeck) Simpson; m. Robert Joseph Klein, Apr. 15, 1977; 1 child, Jeffrey. BS in Nursing, Mich. State U., 1974; MS in Health Adminstrn., U. Houston, 1984. Grad. nurse St. Mary's Hosp., Livonia, Mich., 1974; RN U.S. Army, Ft. Polk, La., 1974-78; DON Byrd Meml. Hosp., Leesville, La., 1978-79, Alvin (Tex.) Cmty. Hosp., 1979-83; adminstrn. resident Katy (Tex.) Med. Ctr., 1983-84, DON, 1984-85, COO, DON, 1985-90; v.p. Doctors' Hosp., Tulsa, 1990-97; dir. ops. improvement Okla. divsn. Columbia HCA, 1997-98; v.p., COO SouthCrest Hosp., Tulsa, Okla., 1998-2000; v.p. clin. integration Hillcrest HealthCare Sys., Tulsa, 2000—; cons. in field; diplomat Am. Coll. Healthcare Execs.; adj. faculty Bartlesville Wesleyan Coll., 1999—. Sec., treas. Sam Houston coun. Boy Scouts Am., 1984-88. Capt. U.S. Army, 1972-78. Republican. Roman Catholic. Avocation: reading. Home: 8823 E 62d Ct Tulsa OK 74133-1307 Office: Hillcrest HealthCare Sys 110 W 7th St Ste 2730 Tulsa OK 74119

KLEIN, DIDIER, environmental educator; b. Chalezeule, France, May 9, 1960; s. Bernard and Arlette (Gavet) K.; children: Sebastien, Jean Baptiste. M of Chemics, U. Franche Comte, 1983, PhD in Physics and Chemistry, 1990. Prof. U. of Franche Comte, Montbeliard, 1991—; team leader materials characterization and radioactivity measurement, 1992—; cons. French Radioprotection Soc., 1996—, French Assn. for Normalisation, Paris. Town councillor Taillecourt Coun., 1995—. Mem. French Soc. of Radioprotection (cons.), French Nuclear Soc. (cons., Prize 1988). Fax: 33-384573286. E-mail: didier.klein@utbm.fr. Home: 11 Rue des Paquerettes, 25400 Taillecourt France Office: LERMPS, UTBD, Sevenans, 90010 Belfort Cedex France

KLEIN, ECKART, law educator; b. Oppeln, Upper Silesia, Apr. 6, 1943; s. Rudolf and Sonja (Stromeyer) K.; m. Ulrike Scherenberg, Apr. 11, 1969; children: Philipp, Oliver, Anne Désirée. Student, Univ. Heidelberg, 1968, Land Baden Württemberg, 1971; law doctorate, Univ. Heidelberg, 1973. Asst Univ. Heidelberg, 1972-74; law clerk Fed. Constitutional Ct., Karlsruhe, 1974-76; rsch. fellow Max Planck Inst., Heidelberg, 1976-81; prof. law Univ. Mainz, 1981-94; prof. law Univ. Potsdam, 1994—, dir. Human Rights Ctr.; judge higher adminstrv. Ct., Rhineland Palatinat, 1984-94, Brandenburg, 1995—; judge Constitutional Ct., Bremen, 1995—. Author: Treaties Providing for Objective Territorial Regimes, 1980; co-author: Constitutional Procedure Law, 1991; editor: The Institution of a Commissioner of Human Rights, 1995; editor and co-author: Commentary on the Treaty Establishing The European Communities, 1997. Active UN Human Rights Com., 1995—. With Air Force, 1962-63. Mem. Am. Soc. Internat. Law, Internat. Law Assn., Rotary. Avocation: reading. Home: Heideweg 45, D 14482 Potsdam Germany Office: Univ Potsdam, August Bebel Str 89, D 14482 Potsdam Germany

KLEIN, ELAINE CHARLOTTE, educational administrator; b. Herreid, S.D., June 14, 1939; d. Herman F. and Minnie (Weigum) K.; 1 child, Erika Katherine. BA, U. Puget Sound, 1961; MA, U. Wash., 1964; Cert. Adminstr., Seattle U., 1976; postgrad., Western Wash. U., 1986. Cert. secondary sch. adminstr., Wash., K-12 tchr., Wash. Tchr. Edmonds Sch. Dist., Lynnwood, Wash., 1961-77; asst. prin. Meadowdale Jr. H.S., Lynnwood, Wash., 1977-80; asst. prin. Mountlake Terrace (Wash.) H.S., 1981-93, prin., 1993-97; exec. dir. cmty. svcs. Frederick County Pub. Schs., Frederick, Md., 1997—; adj. faculty Heritage Inst., Antioch U., Seattle Pacific U., Western Wash. U.; instr. Mt. St. Mary's Coll., Emmitsburg, Md.; cons. Am. Coll. Testing Passport Portfolio, Iowa City, 1995-97; workshop presenter. Author: (chpt.) ACT Manual for Administrators, 1997; grant writer. Pres. Pacific N.W. region Internat. Tng. in Comm., Alaska, B.C., Wash., 1993-94. Recipient Award for Excellence in Edn. award Wash. State Legislature, 1997; named Wash. State Prin. of Yr., 1997, Adminstr. of Yr. Maryland Assn. Edn. Office Personnel, 1999, Friend Edn. Mt. St. Mary's Coll., 1999. Mem. ASCD, Am. Assn. Sch. Adminstrs., Nat. Assn. Secondary Sch. Prins. and Affiliates, Rotary (Mountlake Terrace pres. 1996-97). Methodist. Avocations: public speaking, reading, traveling, advocating for public schools. Office: Frederick County Pub Schs 115 E Church St Frederick MD 21701-5403

KLEIN, GEORGE, research scientist; b. Budapest, Hungary, July 28, 1925; s. Henrik and Ilona (Engel) K.; m. Eva Klein, Nov. 8, 1947. MD, Karolinska Inst., Stockholm, 1951; DSc (hon.), U. Chgo., 1966; MD (hon.), U. Debrecen, 1988; PhD (hon.), Hebrew U., Jerusalem, 1989, Tel Aviv U., 1994. Instr. histology Budapest U., 1945, instr. pathology, 1946; rsch. fellow Karolinska Inst., 1947-49, asst. prof. cell rsch., 1951-57, prof. tumor biology, 1957-93, head dept. tumor biology, 1957-93, rsch. group leader Microbiology and Tumor Biology Ctr., 1993—; guest investigator Inst. Cancer Rsch., Phila., 1950; vis. prof. Stanford U., 1961; Fogarty scholar NIH, 1972; vis. prof. Hebrew U., Hadassah Med. Sch., 1973-89, Dunham lectr. Harvard U., 1966; Clowes Meml. lectr. Am. Assn. Cancer Rsch., 1967; Lennander lectr. Swedish Med. Assn., 1967; Harvey lectr., 1973; mem. sci. adv. coun. Swedish Med. Bd., Cancer Rsch. Inst. N.Y.C.; mem. sci. coun. Ludwig Inst., N.Y. Author: The Atheist and the Holy City, 1990, Pieta, 1992, Live Now, 1997, Istallet for Hemland, 1984, Ateisten och den Heliga Staden, 1987, Pieta, 1989, (with Per Ahlmark) Motstandet, 1991, Utvagen, 1992, (with Lars Gyllensten) Hack i hal pa Minerva, 1993, Den Sjunde Djavulen, 1995, Korpous Blick, 1998; contbr. more than 1,200 articles to profl. jours; editor: Advances in Cancer Rsch., 1972—, Advances in Virol Oncology, 1980-92. Recipient (with Eva Klein) Bertha Goldblatt Teplitz award, 1960, prize Danish Pathol. Soc., 1967, Rabbi Shai Shacknai prize in tumor immunology, 1972, Bertner award, 1973, award Am. Cancer Soc., 1973, prix Griffuel, 1974, Harvey prize, 1977, Bjorken prize, 1978, Sloan prize Gen. Motors Cancer Rsch. Found., 1979, award Santa Chiara Acad., Italy, 1979, (with Eva Klein) Erik Fernstrom prize, 1983, anniversary prize Swedish Med. Assn., 1983, Letterstedt prize Royal Swedish Acad. Sci., 1989, Dobloug prize Swedish Acad. Lit., 1990, Lisl and Leo Eitinger's prize Oslo U., 1990. Mem. Royal Swedish Acad. Scis., U.S. NAS (fgn. assoc.), Acad. Europa, Acad. Cancer Immunology, Am. Philos. Soc. (fgn.), Hungarian Acad. Scis. (hon.), Am. Assn. Immunologists (hon.), French Soc. Immunology (hon.), AAAS (hon. fgn.), Am. Assn. Cancer Rsch. (hon.). Office: Karolinska Inst Microbiol & Tumor Biology Ctr, Box 280, S-17177 Stockholm Sweden

KLEIN, GILLIAN, publisher, editor, humanities educator; b. Johannesburg, South Africa, May 13, 1939; arrived in Eng., 1961; d. Harry and Enid (Ash) Falkow; children: Graeme, Leanne. BA with honors, U. Witwatersrand, Johannesburg, 1958; PhD, London U., 1997. Fellow Royal Soc. Arts, London, 1993. Libr. Inner London Edn. Authority, 1967-81, advisor, 1981-90; lectr. U. Warwick, Eng., 1989-94; editl. dir. Trentham Books Ltd., Stoke-on-Trent, Eng., 1986—; lectr./trainer Trentham Consultants, Eng., 1994—; lectr. U. Middlesex, 1993-94, 96-97. Founder, editor (profl. jour.) Multicultural Teaching, 1982—; author children's and profl. books, including: Reading into Racism, 1985, School Libraries for Cultural Awareness, 1985, Education Towards Race Equality, 1993; (with J. Eggleston) Achieving Publication in Education, 1997. Trustee Anne Frank Ednl. Trust U.K., London, 1994—. Avocations: travel, architecture and art, books, theatre. Office: Trentham Books Westview Ho, 734 London Rd, Stoke-on-Trent ST4 5NP, England

KLEIN, HANS, theology educator, priest; b. Sibiu, Romania, Nov. 9, 1940; s. Albert and Maria (Walcher) K.; m. Heide Schneider, June 29, 1963; children: Heide, Marianne, Johannes, Peter. Lic., Inst. Theology, Cluj-Sibiu, Romania, 1962, Doctorate, 1972. Ordained priest Evangelical Luth. Ch., 1963. Priest Evangelical Luth. Ch., Lugoj, Romania, 1963-66, Crit, Romania, 1966-72; asst. prof. Old Testament Inst. Theology, Cluj-Sibiu, 1972-82, prof. N.T., 1982—; 1st priest Evangelical Luth. Ch., Sibiu, 1993-98, bishop-vicar, 1994-98; dean Inst. Theology, 1998—. Author: Barmherzigkeit, 1987, Leben neu entdecken Biblische Theologie, 1991, Bewahrung im Glauben, 1996. Pres. Forum for German Minority in Sibiu, 1990-92, Forum for German Minority in Transilvania, 1992-95. Mem. Studiorum N.T. Soc., Wissenschaftliche Gesellschaft für Theologie. Office: Inst Teologic, Gen Magheru Nr 4, 2400 Sibiu Romania

KLEIN, IRMA MOLLIGAN, career development educator, consultant; b. New Orleans, Jan. 5, 1929; d. Harry Joseph and Gesina Francis (Bauer) Molligan; m. John Vincent Chelena (dec. 1978); 1 child, Joseph William; m. Chris George Klein, Aug. 14, 1965; 1 step-son, Arnold Conrad Klein. BS in Bus., Augustine Coll.; postgrad., Mktg. Inst., Chgo., Loyola U., Chgo., Realtors Inst., Baton Rouge. Mgr. Stan Weber & Assocs., Metairie, La., 1971-75; tng. dir. Stan Weber & Assocs., Metairie, 1975-81; cons. Coldwell Banker Comml. Co., New Orleans, 1981; dir. career devel. Coldwell Banker Residential Co., New Orleans, 1982-85; pres. Irma Klein Career Devel., Inc., 1994-95, Klein Enterprises, Inc., 1994—; instr. U. New Orleans, Bonnabel H.S., Realtors Inst., La. Real Estate Commn. Author: Career Development, 1982; Training Manual, 1978, Obtaining Listings, 1986, Participative Marketing, 1986, Marketing & Servicing Listings, 1987, Designing Training Curriculum, 1987, Participative Management. Active Friends of Longue Vue Gardens, La. Hist. Assn. Meml. Hall Found. Mem. La. Realtors Assn. (bd. dirs. 1973-74, grad. Realtors Inst. 1976), Jefferson Bd. Realtors (v.p. 1984), Edn. and Resources (cert., pres. La. chpt.), Rsch. Club of New Orleans (pres. 1984-85), Realtors Nat. Mktg. Inst. (amb. Tex. and La. 1985—, Outstanding Achievement award 1985, cert. broker 1980, residential specialist 1977), Nat. Assn. Realtors (nat. conv. spkr. 1986), CRB (pres. La. chpt. 1982-83, chmn. edn.), CRS (pres. La. chpt. 1988-90), Am. Dental Assts. Assn., La. Dental Assts. Assn. (pres. 1964), Les Quarante Ecolieres (pres. 1994-96), Antique Study Group, Confederate Lit. (New Orleans) (pres.), Rsch. Club (New Orleans), Metairie Woman's Club (sec. 1997-99, pres.-elect 1999, pres. 2000-01), Odyssey Ho. La. Republican. Roman Catholic. Avocation: antiques.

KLEIN, JEAN E., university dean, business management educator; b. Limoges, France, Sept. 30, 1940; s. Pierre and Jeanne (Blum) K. M.Law, Pantheon-Sorbonne, France, 1963; HEC Degree, HEC Sch. of Mgmt., France, 1963; PhD in Econs. with hons., Pantheon-Sorbonne, France, 1969. Asst. U. Pantheon-Sorbonne, Paris, 1963-66; postdoctoral fellow MIT, Cambridge, Mass., 1970; assoc. prof. HEC Sch. Mgmt., Paris, 1966-74, prof., 1975—, dean, 1975-80, 89—; prof. mgmt. Conservatoire National des Arts et Metiers, Paris, 1989—; cons. O.E.C.D., Paris, 1967—; adminstr. Soc. Brun, Paris, 1978—, Sofica Sofinergie (PARIBAS), Paris, 1988—, ofcr. Acad. Palms, French Govt., 1997. Author: International Financial Management, 1974, L'Economie mondiale, 1985, Le Dollar, 1993, International Financial Strategy and Management, 1995, Multinational Financial Management, 1996; author/actor film: A Planet Without Boundaries, 1986. Cons. Foundation nationale for mgmt. (FNEGE), Paris, 1982—, Bulgarian Govt., Sofia, 1990. Fulbright fellow, 1967; decorated officer of the Acad. Palms, French Govt., knight of the Merit Order, French Govt. Fellow Racing Club of France. Avocations: bridge, golf. Home: 38 rue Saint-Sulpice, 75006 Paris France Office: HEC Group, 1 rue de la Libération, 78000 Jouy en Josas France

KLEIN, JERRY EMANUEL, insurance and financial planning executive; b. Cin., Apr. 4, 1933; s. Milton H. and Ida S. (Dunsker) K.; m. Arlene Ruth Rosen, July 3, 1957 (dec. Nov. 1974); children: Marjorie, Bradley, Amy; m. Nancy Cohen Hahn, Aug. 7, 1982. BMech. Engring., Cornell U., 1956; MBA, Ohio State U., 1959. CLU, ChFC. Fin. engring. Avco Electronics, Cin., 1959-61; spl. agt. Northwestern Mut. Life of Milw., Cin., 1961—. Vice chmn. Am. Jewish Com., 1978; pres. Social Health Assn., 1964-66, Jewish Vocat. Svc., 1978-80, Cancer Family Care, 1981-83; chmn. fin. com. Jewish Fedn., 1981-83, treas., mem. exec. com., 1981-84; bd. dirs. Children Psychiat. Ctr., 1973-86, Jewish Family Svc., 1984-94, Jewish Vocat. Svc., 1964-92, Cin. Jewish Fedn., 1972-92, Halom House, 1992, treas., 1998—; chmn. HILB Scholarship Com., 1985—; bd. dirs. Radio Reading Svc., 1997; bd. dirs. Cin. Assn. Blind, 1999—. 1st lt. USAF, 1956-58. Recipient Kate S. Mack award Jewish Fedn., 1975, Human Rels. award NCCJ, 1992. Mem. Million Dollar Round Table (life), Nat. Assn. Life Underwriters, Estate Planning Coun. Cin., Assn. CLUs. Jewish. Office: Northwestern Mut Fin Network Rookwood Tower 2d Fl 3805 Edwards Rd Cincinnati OH 45209

KLEIN, JO ANN MARTUCCI, corporate communications specialist; b. Mt. Vernon, N.Y., Mar. 4, 1947; d. Joseph Anthony and Ann Gloria Isabell (Paparatto) Martucci; m. Henry Alexander Klein, Oct. 22, 1972. Student in Math., Columbia U., 1965-67; AA, Fairleigh Dickinson U., 1984, BS, 1986. Cert. tchr., spl. edn., N.Y. Exec. asst. Gordon W. White Inc., N.Y.C., 1965-66; asst. editor Columbia U., N.Y.C., 1966-69, mgr. data processing/classified documentation, 1969-72, directing editor, 1966-75; asst. security officer Riverside Research Inst., N.Y.C., 1972-75; internal cons. Consolidated Edison, N.Y.C., 1975-95, security officer, 1995—, dir.-editor Info. Tech. Express newsletter, 1989-95; cons. and lectr. in field. Contbr. articles to profl. jours. Chair major gifts program Juvenile Diabetes Found., N.J. and N.Y. chpt., 1972-95; chair publicity and fundraising Am. Diabetes Assn., N.J., 1985-95; v.p. Juvenile Diabetes Found., 1994—. Author: The New Math, 1966. Mem. NAFE, Office Products Exchange Network Inc. (founder 1981, pres. 1984-87, chair 1988-96, dir.-editor OPEN newsletter 1984-95), Am. Mgmt. Assn., Assn. Info. Systems Profls., Assn. Women in Computing, Cons. Interface, Am. Soc. Indsl. Security, Women of Accomplishment Assn. Avocations: golf, swimming, interior decorating, photography, handicrafts.

KLEIN, JOSEPHINE F.H., psychotherapist, writer; b. Oct. 17, 1926. BA in French with honors, U. London, 1948; BA in Sociology with honors, London Sch. Econs., 1949; PhD, U. Birmingham, Eng., 1952. Author: The Study of Groups, 1956, Working with Groups, 1961, Samples of English Cultures, 1965, Our Need for Others and Its Roots in Infancy, 1987, Doubts and Certainties in the Practice of Psychotherapy, 1995. Fellow London Ctr. Psychotherapy; mem. Brit. Assn. Psychotherapists.

KLEIN, LAWRENCE ROBERT, economist, educator; b. Omaha, Sept. 14, 1920; s. Leo Byron and Blanche (Monheit) K.; m. Sonia Adelson, Feb. 15, 1947; children: Hannah, Rebecca, Rachel, Jonathan. B.A., U. Calif.-Berkeley, 1942; Ph.D., MIT, 1944; M.A., Lincoln Coll., Oxford U., 1957; LL.D. (hon.), U. Mich., 1977, Dickinson Coll., 1981; Sc.D. (hon.), Widener Coll., 1977, Elizabethtown Coll., 1981, Ball State U., 1982, Technion, 1982,

U. Nebr., 1983; Dr. honoris causa, U. Vienna, 1977; Dr.Ed., Villanova U., 1978; Dr. (h.c.), Bonn U., 1974, Free U. Brussels, 1979, U. Paris, 1979, U. Madrid, 1980; DSc, Nat. Central Univ. Taiwan, 1985; DHC, So. Helsinki Sch. Econs., 1986; Dr. Humane Letters, Bark Coll., 1986, Balhent Univ., 1989, St. Norbert Coll., 1989; DHC, Univ. Lodz, 1990; D. Litt, Univ. Glasgow, 1991; DSc, Rutgers Univ., 1992; PhD H.C., Burdlan Univ., 1994; D. honors H.C., Carleton Univ., 1997; DHC, Univ. Pircenes, 1999, Acad. Economic Studies, 1999. Faculty U. Chgo., 1944-47; research assoc. Nat. Bur. Econ. Research, 1948-50; faculty U. Mich., 1949-54; research assoc. Survey Research Center, 1949-54, Oxford Inst. Stats., 1954-58; faculty U. Pa., Phila., 1958—, prof., 1958—, Univ. prof., 1964—, Benjamin Franklin prof., 1968—; now prof. econs. and emeritus U. Pa.; vis. prof. Osaka U., Japan, 1960, U. Colo., 1962, CUNY, 1962-63, 82, Hebrew U., 1964, Princeton U., 1966, Stanford U., summer 1968, U. Copenhagen, 1974; Ford vis. prof. U. Calif. at Berkeley, 1968, Inst. for Advanced Studies, Vienna, 1970, 74; hon. prof. Shanghai Tiao Tong Univ., 1984; honorary prof. Nanbai Univ., 1993, Shanghai Acad. Soc. Sci., 1994; dir. W.P. Carey & Co., 1984—; adv. State Information Ctr., Beijing, 1992—; cons. Canadian Govt., 1947, UNCTAD, 1966, 67, 75, 77, 80, McMillan Co., 1965-74, E.I. du Pont de Nemours, 1966-68, State of N.Y., 1969, AT&T, 1969, Fed. Res. Bd., 1973, UNIDO, 1973-75, Congl. Budget Office, 1977—, Council Econ. Advisers, 1977-80; chmn. bd. trustees Wharton Econometric Forecasting Assocs., Inc., 1969-80, chmn. profl. bd., 1980—; trustee Maurice Falk Inst. for Econ. Research, Israel, 1969-75; adv. council Inst. Advanced Studies, Vienna, 1977—; chmn. econ. adv. com. Gov. of Pa., 1976-78; mem. com. on prices Fed. Res. Bd., 1968-70; prin. investigator econometric model project Brookings Instn., 1963-72, Project LINK, 1968—; sr. adviser Brookings Panel on Econ. Activity, 1970—; mem. adv. com. Inst. Internat. Econs., 1983, honorary mem. Chinese Bd. Soc. Scis., 1997, Romanian Acad. 1999—; coordinator Jimmy Carter's Econ. Task Force, 1976; mem. adv. bd. Strategic Studies Center, Stanford Research Inst., 1974-76, corresponding fellow of the British Acad., 1991—. Author: The Keynesian Revolution, 1947, Textbook of Econometrics, 1953, An Econometric Model of the United States, 1929-1952, 1955, Wharton Econometric Forecasting Model, 1967, Essay on the Theory of Economic Prediction, 1968, An Introduction to Econometric Forecasting and Forecasting Models, 1980; Author-editor: Brookings Quar. Econometric Model of U.S.; Ecometric Model Performance, 1976, Lectures in Econometrics, 1983; Editor: Internat. Econ. Rev, 1959-65; asso. editor, 1965—; Editorial bd.: Empirical Econs, 1976—. Recipient William F. Butler award N.Y. Assn. Bus. Economists, 1975; Golden Slipper Club award, 1977; Pres.'s medal U. Pa., 1980; Alfred Nobel Meml. prize in econs., 1980. Fellow Econometric Soc. (past pres.), Am. Acad. Arts and Scis., Nat. Assn. Bus. Economists; mem. Am. Philos. Soc., Nat. Acad. Scis., Social Sci. Rsch. Coun. (fellow 1945-46, 47-48, com. econ. stability, dir. 1971-76), Am. Econ. Assn. (John Bates Clark medalist 1959, exec. com. 1966-68, pres. 1977), Eastern Econ. Assn. (pres. 1974-76). Office: U Pa Mc Neil Bldg Rm 335 3718 Locust Walk Philadelphia PA 19104-6209

KLEIN, LEO, plastic surgeon; b. Olomouc, Moravia, Czech Republic, Apr. 18, 1952; s. Leo Klein and Jarmila (Kominkova) Kleinova; m. Vaclava Fukova, Mar. 12, 1977; children: Grazina, Martina. MD, Charles U. Hradec Kralove, Czech Republic, 1976; PhD in Surgery, Charles U., Prague, 1994; Assoc. Prof. in Surgery, Purkinje Mil. Med. Acad., 1998. Lic. gen. surgeon, plastic and reconstructive surgeon. Mil. physician Mil. Brigade, Hranice, Czech Republic, 1977-80; gen. surgeon Mil. Hosp., Olomouc, Czech Republic, 1980-84; deputy chief dept. of plastic surgery and burns unit Charles U. Tchg. Hosp., Hradec Kralove, 1990-94, head of dept. plastic surgery and burns unit, 1995-98; dept. chief of treatment divsn. Med. Corps HQ Gen. Staff, Prague, 1999; ACE med. advisor NATO-Supreme Hdqrs. Allied Powers Europe (SHAPE), Mons, Belgium, 1999—. Co-author: (book) Extensive Burns Trauma, 1999, Disaster Medicine, 1999; contbr. articles to profl. jours. Maj.-gen. Army Med. Corps, Prague, 1999—. Recipient medal of svc. to country Min. of Def., 1982, 87. Mem. Internat. Soc. for Burn Injuries, World Assn. Disaster and Emergency Medicine, European Assn. Tissue Banks. Avocations: langs., photography, dogs, sports. Office: Log Divsn, Med Br NATO-SHAPE, B-7010 Mons Belgium

KLEIN, MARTIN I., lawyer; b. N.Y.C., Nov. 12, 1947; m. Diane Levbarg. BA, Lehigh U., 1969; JD, Am. U., 1972. Bar: N.Y. 1973, Fla. 1978, Calif. 1981, D.C. 1981; solicitor Supreme Ct. Eng., 1996—. Mem. profl. staff U.S. Senate Com. on Labor and Pub. Welfare, 1969-72; legis. aide U.S. Senator Jacob K. Javits, 1969-72; ptnr., head creditors' rights dept. Dreyer & Traub, N.Y.C., 1980-93; ptnr., head dept. bankruptcy Shea & Gould, N.Y.C., 1993—; pvt. practice Martin I. Klein, P.C., 1995—; lectr. Am. Law Inst.-ABA Com. on Continuing Profl. Edn., 1975—, The Practising Law Inst., 1975—, Mathematica, 1981—; adj. assoc. prof. law Benjamin Cardozo Sch. Law, Yeshiva U., 1980—; lectr. Columbia U. Sch. Law, 1980—; mem. med. malpractice mediation panel appellate div. Supreme Ct. State N.Y. 1980—; trustee, treas., pres. Cen. Synagogue, N.Y.C., 1986—; arbitrator, N.Y.C. Small Claims Ct. Contbr. articles on fin. real estate and comml. law to profl. jours. Del. Shite House Conf. on Youth, 1971. Mem. ABA, N.Y. State Bar Assn., Fla. Bar Assn., Calif. Bar Assn., D.C. Bar Assn., N.Y. County Lawyers Assn. (mem. com. on bankruptcy), Am. Arbitration Assn. (mem. comml. panel). Address: 9 W 57th St Ste 4160 New York NY 10019-2701 Office: 205 Worth Ave Palm Beach FL 33480-4606

KLEIN, MELVYN NORMAN, lawyer, investment executive; b. Chgo., Dec. 27, 1941; s. Harry H. and Bertha M. (Gleicher) K.; m. Annette Lorraine Grossman, Mar. 13, 1976; children: Jacqueline Anne, Jenna Katherine. Student, London (Eng.) Sch. Econs. and Polit. Sci., 1962; BA in Econs. with highest honors, Colgate U., 1963; JD, Columbia U., 1966; postgrad., Johns Hopkins Sch. Advanced Internati. Studies, 1966-67; LHD (hon.), Tex. A&M U., Corpus Christi, 1997. Bar: D.C. 1968, Tex. 1980. Legis. asst. Rep. Sidney Yates, Washington, 1966; assoc. McKinsey & Co., Washington, 1967-68; sr. v.p. Donaldson, Lufkin and Jenrette, Inc., N.Y.C., 1969-77; counsel Brownstein, Zeidman & Schomer, Washington, 1978-93; pvt. practice, Corpus Christi, 1979—; spl. counsel United Techs. Corp., 1985; bd. dirs. Anixter Internat., Bayou Steel Corp., Sante Fe Energy Resources, Cockrell Oil Corp., Hanover Compressor Corp., ACTV, Inc.; sr. investment adv. Sprout Capital Group III, 1977-87; gen. ptnr. GKH Ptnrs., L.P., 1987—; adj. prof. bus. Tex. A&M., Corpus Christi; mem. adv. com. internat. econ. policy, U.S. Sec. State, 1999. Guest columnist Corpus Christi Caller-Times newspaper, 1980—. Staff mem. V.P. Hubert Humphrey Presdl. Campaign, 1968; chmn. Corpus Christi Bus. Devel. Comm., 1979-86; chmn. bd. govs. Art Mus. South Tex.; bd. dirs. S. Tex. Ednl. Broadcasting System, 1984-86; mem. exec. com. Pres.'s Pvt. Sector Study of Cost Control in Fed. Govt.; mem. internat. bd. advisors Columbia U. Sch. Internat. Affairs. Mem. ABA, World Pres.'s Orgn., Horatio Alger Assn. Disting. Ams., Am. Bus. Conf. (founding mem., chmn. capital formation and tax policy com. 1980-86), D.C. Bar Assn., State Bar Tex., Philos. Soc. Tex., Corpus Christi Yacht Club, Corpus Christi Country Club, River Oaks Country Club (Houston), Corpus Christi Town Club, Std. Club (Chgo.), Rotary. Home: 210 Jackson Pl Corpus Christi TX 78411-1216 Office: GKH Ptnrs 200 W Madison St Ste 3800 Chicago IL 60606-3414

KLEIN, MICHAEL ELIHU, physician; b. N.Y.C., Apr. 6, 1946; s. Leo and Edith (Rigrod) K.; m. Elizabeth Angela McGehee, Oct. 8, 1988; children: Michael, Debra, Daniel. BA, Wesleyan U., Middletown, Conn., 1967; MD, Yale U., 1972, MPH, 1972. Diplomate in internal medicine and hematology Am. Bd. Internal Medicine. Asst. dir. hematology U. Md., Balt., 1979-83; sr. investigator U. Md. Cancer Ctr., Balt., 1979-83; pvt. practice specializing in hematology/oncology Cowley Assocs., Camp Hill, Pa., 1983-97, Ctrl. Pa. Hematology & Oncology, Lemoyne, 1997—; cons. in hematology and oncology Polyclinic Hosp., Harrisburg, Pa., 1983—, Holy Spirit Hosp., Camp Hill, 1983—. Author: Political Dynamics National Health Insurance in New York, 1972; contbr. articles to profl. jours., chpts. to books. Founder, bd. dirs. Number Nine, New Haven, 1971. Comdr. lt. USPHS, 1974-77. Mem. AMA, Am. Soc. Clin. Research, Am. Soc. Clin. Oncology, Am. Soc. Hematology, Am. Legion, Balt. Blood Club (pres. 1979-83). Avocations: stamp collecting, baseball, reading. Office: Ctrl Pa Hematology & Oncology 50 N 12th St Ste 100 Lemoyne PA 17043-1440

KLEIN, MICHAEL ROGER, lawyer, business executive; b. N.Y.C., Apr. 10, 1942; s. Jesse and Stephanie (Siegel) K.; m. Diane Atkinson, July 4, 1967 (div. June 1974); m. Joan Ilona Fabry, Feb. 19, 1977; children: Nicholas Jesse, Alexander Fabry. BBA, U. Miami, Coral Gables, Fla., 1963, JD, 1966; LLM, Harvard U., 1967. Bar: Fla. 1966, D.C., 1969, U.S. Dist. Ct. (D.C. cir.) 1970, U.S. Supreme Ct., 1970. Asst. prof. law La. State U., Baton Rouge, 1967-69; assoc. Wilmer, Cutler & Pickering, Washington, 1969-74, ptnr., 1974—; pres. Zenith Gallery, Inc., Washington, 1978—; chmn. LePavillon of D.C., Washington, 1983-89, CoStar Group Inc., Bethesda, Md., 1988—; bd. dirs. Perini Corp., SRA Internat. Inc., PreceptMortgage.com, LLC. Author: Eminent Domain, 1969; contbr. articles to profl. jours. Trustee Ctr. for Law in the Pub. Interest, L.A., 1975-91, Am. Himalayan Found., 1996—; chmn. bd. trustees Advocates for Pub. Interest, Washington, 1986-89; dir. Support Ctr. of D.C., Inc., 1991-95. Mem. Am. Law Inst. Jewish. Office: Wilmer Cutler & Pickering 2445 M St NW Ste 500 Washington DC 20037-1487

KLEIN, PETER MARTIN, lawyer, retired transportation company executive; b. N.Y.C., June 2, 1934; s. Saul and Esther (Goldstein) K.; m. Ellen Judith Matlick, June 18, 1961; children: Amy Lynn, Steven Ezra. AB, Columbia U., 1956, JD, 1962. Bar: N.Y. 1962, D.C. 1964, U.S. Supreme Ct. 1966. Asst. proctor Columbia U., 1959-62; asst. counsel Mil. Sea Transp. Svc., Office Gen. Counsel, Dept. Navy, Washington, 1962-65; trial atty. civil div. U.S. Dept. Justice, N.Y.C., 1966-69; gen. atty. Sea-Land Svc., Inc., Menlo Park, N.J., 1969-76, v.p., gen. counsel, sec., 1976-79; v.p., gen. counsel, sec. Sea-Land Industries, Inc., Menlo Park, 1979-84; assoc. gen. counsel R.J. Reynolds Industries, Inc., Winston-Salem, N.C., 1978-84; sr. v.p., gen. counsel, sec. Sea-Land Svc., Inc. (formerly Sea-Land Corp.), Charlotte, N.C., 1984-94, sr. v.p.-law, sec., 1994-95, ret., 1996—; mem. adv. com. on pvt. internat. law Dept. State, 1974-95; mem. U.S. delegation UN Conf. of Trade and Devel., UN Commn. on Internat. Trade Law, 1975-76, trade regulation adv. bd. Bur. Nat. Affairs, 1986-88; alt. mem. N.Am. coun. London Ct. of Internat. Arbitration, 1988-95. Trustee Jewish Edn. Assn. Met. N.J., 1973-76; trustee Temple B'nai Abraham of Essex County, N.J., 1973—, v.p., 1976-81, pres. 1981-83; mem. Essex County Dems. Com., 1986-88; mem. Livingston Twp. Planning Bd., 1996—, vice chmn. 1997-99, chmn., 2000—. With USN, 1956-59, Antarctica. Mem. ABA, FBA, Am. Maritime Assn. (bd. dirs., chmn. coms. on law and legis. 1974-78), Am. Polar Soc., Navy League U.S. (life), U.S. Naval Inst. (life), N.Y. State Bar Assn., D.C. Bar Assn., Internat. Bar Assn., Maritime Law Assn. Home: 22 Sandalwood Dr Livingston NJ 07039-1409

KLEIN, PHILIPP HILLEL, electronic materials consultant; b. N.Y.C., Sept. 14, 1926; s. Raphael and Lillian Rae (Wald) K.; m. Charlotte Feuerstein, June 21, 1953; children: Joshua David, Daniel William, Jonathan Henry. BS in Chemistry, Syracuse U., 1948, MS in Phys. Chemistry, 1951, PhD in Phys. Chemistry, 1953. Rsch. assoc. Knolls Atomic Power Lab., Schenectady, N.Y., 1952-56; phys. chemist GE Electronics Lab., Syracuse, N.Y., 1956-61; mem. rsch. staff Sperry Rand Rsch. Ctr., Sudbury, Mass., 1961-66; rsch. chemist NASA Electronics Rsch. Ctr., Cambridge, Mass., 1966-70; sect. head U.S. Naval Rsch. Lab., Washington, 1970-87, rsch. cons., 1987-90; prin. Philipp Klein Cons., Washington, 1990—. Assoc. editor Materials Letters, 1985-89; editor Advanced Energy Conversion, 1962; contbr. articles to profl. jours. With USNR 1945-46. Fellow Am. Inst. Chemists; mem. IEEE (life, chmn. com. on solid state devices 1962-63), Am. Ceramic Soc. (electronics com. 1968-70), Am. Assn. for Crystal Growth (program chmn. 1985-87), Am. Phys. Soc., Sigma Xi. Achievements include patents on the purification of fluorides, preparation of laser hosts, and deposition of silicon carbide shapes. Office: Philipp Klein Cons 2017 Hillyer Pl NW Washington DC 20009-1005

KLEIN, RICHARD J.T., environmental scientist; b. Diemen, The Netherlands, Oct. 5, 1969; arrived in Germany, 1999.; s. Louis H.T. Klein and Rose A.M.L. Kuijpers; m. Ruth I.T. Sijpestein, May 30, 1997. MSc in Earth Scis., Vrije U., Amsterdam, 1992; MSc Environ. Scis., U. East Anglia, Norwich, U.K., 1996; PhD in Geography, Christian Albrechts U., Kiel, Germany, 2001. Asst. campaigner Greenpeace, Amsterdam, 1992; rsch. assoc. Inst. for Environ. Studies, Vrije U., Amsterdam, 1992-98; sci. officer Coastal Zone Mgmt. Ctr., The Hague, 1993-95; sr. rsch. assoc. Potsdam Inst. for Climate Impact Rsch., 1999—; cons. UNEP, Nairobi, Kenya, 1995-97; (coordinating) lead author IPCC, Geneva, 1994—. Contbr. articles to profl. jours. Brit. Coun. scholar, 1995; recipient award CIWEM, 1997. Avocations: contemporary art, design and architecture, cycling, trekking. Office: Potsdam Inst Climate Im Rsc, Telegrafenberg C4, 14473 Potsdam Germany

KLEIN, ROSALYN FINKELSTEIN, social worker; b. N.Y.C., Dec. 4, 1946; d. Philip and Hilda (Myers) Finkelstein; m. Edward R. Klein, June 14, 1970; children: Brian, Dana, Jennifer. BA, Hunter Coll., 1970; MA, NYU, 1973; MSW, Fordham U., 1983. Lic. clin. social worker, Conn.; diplomate Am. Bd. Examiners Clin. Social Work; cert. clin. supr. Acad. Cert. Social Workers; cert. speech and lang. pathologist. Speech pathologist N.Y.C. Bd. Edn., Bklyn., 1970-74, Princeton (N.J.) Med. Ctr., 1974-76; clin. supr. So. Conn. State U., New Haven, 1977; speech pathologist Easter Seal Rehab., Meriden, Conn., 1977-79; social worker Greenwich (Conn.) Dept. Social Svc., 1983—; social worker Milford (Conn.) Mental Health Ctr., 1985-86, Jewish Family Svc., Greenwich, 1995-98; field instr. Fordham U., 1987—, Stamford (Conn.) Psychiatry and Geriat., 1998—; mem. future planning com., operating com., mem. supervisory com., conflict mediation com. Greenwich Dept. Social Svcs., 1995—. Mem. Hadassah, Orange, 1976-94, Dem. Town Com., Greenwich, 1996-97; treas. Sisterhood/Synagogue, Orange, 1984-86. Recipient Award of Excellence, Town of Greenwich, 1999. Mem. Conn. Soc. Clin. Social Workers. Avocations: walking, traveling, reading, theater.

KLEIN, SHIRLEY SNYDERMAN, retail executive; b. Balt., Oct. 23, 1929; d. Julius Herman and Fannie (Dannenberg) Snyderman; m. Ralph Lincoln Klein, Jan. 4, 1953; children: Andrew P., Michael J., Howard S. BA, Towson State Tchr.'s Coll., 1951. Office staff accts. receivable, jr. controller Klein's Tower Plz., Inc., Forest Hill, Md., 1952-60, jr. buyer, 1960-70, v.p., buyer children's, ladies, linens, 1970—; treas. Mortgage Svc. Co., Inc., 1956-64; bd. dirs. Upper Chesapeake Health Sys., chair found., 1993—; v.p. Klein's Supermarkets, 1979—; v.p. Colgate Investments, 1970—. Pres. Hadassah Harford County, 1966-68; v.; adv. bd. John Carroll Sch., Md. Diocese, 1967, bd. mem., 1970; chmn. Retinitis Pigmentosa Found., Harford County, Md., 1971; bd. dirs. Harfard Opera Theatre Guild, 1976-79; treas. Harford County Commn. for Women, 1977-82; v.p. Jewish Nat. Fund., Balt., 1990-95; vice chair Israel Bonds Balt., 1980-97. Mem. LWV. Home: 109 W Jarrettsville Rd Forest Hill MD 21050-1319

KLEIN, STEPHEN THOMAS, performing arts executive; b. Cleve., Mar. 9, 1947; s. Howard B. and Lilly (Gatchell) K.; m. Mary Ussery, Nov. 19, 1972; children—William Howard, Sarah Katherine. B.F.A., Boston U., 1970. Orch. Mgr. Cleve. Orch., 1978-82; exec. dir. Denver Symphony Orch., Colo., 1982-85, Nat. Symphony Orch., Washington, 1985-94; mng. dir. Pitts. Pub. Theater, 1994—.

KLEIN, STEVEN DOUGLAS, financial planner, securities broker; b. Bklyn., Aug. 16, 1952; s. Arthur and Muriel Joan (Senft) K.; children: Jason Adam, Samantha Royce. BA, SUNY, New Paltz, 1973; cert. fin. planning, Adelphi U., 1980. CFP; registered fin. planner; registered investment advisor. Dir. sales J&B Mgmt. Co., Ft. Lee, N.J., 1976-92; pres. Ameriprop, Inc., Melville, N.Y., 1989—, Jasam Fin. Planning, Inc., Melville, N.Y., 1991—. Mem. Network Allied Profls., Inc. (dir. 1991—), Assn. Profl. Fin. Cons., Internat. Assn. Fin. Planning, Inst. Cert. Fin. Planners, SUNY at New Paltz Alumni Assn. (bd. dirs. 1997—). Avocations: golf, travel. Office: Jasam Fin Planning Inc 445 Broadhollow Rd Ste 128 Melville NY 11747-3601

KLEIN, TIBERIU ALADAR, truck company executive; b. Brasov, Romania, Mar. 30, 1950; s. Aladar E. and Reghina A. (Smil) K.; m. Cameluta-Silvia Ioana Tomescu, Aug. 30, 1973; 1 child, Liviu. B, Dr. Mesota Coll., Brasov, 1969; diploma in engring., Transilvania U., Brasov, 1974; cert. in R&D mgmt., Inst. Mgmt. & Informatics, Bucharest, Romania, 1994; profl. cert. in mgmt., Open U. Bus. Sch., Brasov, 2000. Supr. truck assembly line design dept. Roman SA, Brasov, 1974-85, head truck assembly line design dept., 1987-91, head tech. dept., 1991-97, mgr. R&D dept., 1997-99, mgr. truck divsn., 1999—; head. tech. assistance assembly line Heavy Truck Factory, Qingdao, China, 1986; coord. truck design, coord. investment policy Roman SA, Brasov, 1997—. Merit scholar Transylvania U., 1970-74. Mem. Soc. Automotive Engring., Romanian Soc. Automotive Engring. Jewish. Achievements include inventor Roman Truck Delivery in Twin Units Package System, Compact Systems for Trucks CKD Sets Package. Avocations: history, traveling, athletics. Home: Str. Paraului 4/E9/B/5, 2200 Brasov Romania Office: Roman SA, Str. Poienelor 5, 2200 Brasov Romania

KLEIN, WOLFGANG, academic administrator; b. Spiesen, Germany, Feb. 3, 1946; s. Alois and Anne (Mieger) K. PhD, U. Saarbrücken, Germany, 1970. Assoc. prof. U. Heidelberg, Germany, 1972-76; prof. U. Frankfurt, Germany, 1976-80; dir., sci. mem. Max-Planck Inst. for Psycholinguistics, Nijmegen, The Netherlands, 1980—. Author: Zweitspracherwerb, 1984, Utterance Structure, 1993, Time in Language, 1994, (with R. Dietrich & C. Noyau) The Acquisition of Temporality in a Second Language, 1995. Mem. Berlin-Brandenburgische Akad. Wissenschaften, Berlin, 1994. Recipient Leibniz prize Deutsche Forschungsgemeinschaft, 1995. Office: Max Planck Inst Psycholing, Wundtlaan 1, 6525 XD Nijmegen The Netherlands

KLEINBERG, JUDITH G., lawyer, children's advocate; b. Hartford, Conn., Jan. 28, 1946; d. Burleigh B. and Ruth (Leven) Greenberg; m. James Paul Kleinberg, Aug. 30, 1970; children: Alexander, Lauren. BA cum laude, U. Mich., 1968; JD, U. Calif., Berkeley, 1971. Atty. pvt. practice, San Francisco, 1971-74; legal affairs reporter comml. and pub. TV, San Francisco, 1974-76; prof. law Mills Coll., Oakland, Calif., 1977-84; chief of staff The Global Fund for Women, Los Altos, Calif., 1987-88; pub. interest atty., non-profit corp. law/orgn. specialist alternative dispute resolution Palo Alto, Calif., 1988-94; exec. dir. Kids in Common: A Children & Families Collaborative, San Jose, Calif., 1994—; chair Am. Promise, Silicon Valley, 1997—; arbitrator/mediator, legal adv. for abortion rights, women and children's rights and environ. groups, Santa Clara County and Calif., 1980—; speaker in field; chair Am.'s Promise - Silicon Valley. Mem. bd. editors Calif. Law Rev., 1969-71. Mem. steering com. lawyers coun. No. Calif. sect. ACLU, bd. dirs., 1990-92; founder, chairperson No. Calif. Friends of Pediat. AIDS Found.; past pres. Com. for Green Foothills; mem. legis. and steering coms. Calif. Coalition for Childhood Immunization, 1995-98; mem. Calif. Children's Advs. Roundtable, 1995—; bd. dirs. Palo Alto SAFE, Support Network for Battered Women, 1990-92, Palo Alto Coun. PTAs, Leadership Midpeninsula, 1994-96, Silicon Valley Coun. of Nonprofits; pres. Palo Alto Stanford divsn. Am. Heart Assn., 1994-95; v.p. Assn. for Sr. Day Health, 1994-95; founder Safer Summer Project; pres., legal counsel Calif. Abortion and Reproductive Rights Action League, 1980-86; mem. Palo Alto City Coun., 2000—. Recipient Calif. Pks. and Recreation Soc. Merit award, 1995, World of People award Girl Scouts Am., Santa Clara County, 1996. Mem. Nat. Assn. Child Advocates, Calif. Women Lawyers (v.p. 1986-88).

KLEINE, MICHAEL WERNER, physician; b. Halle, Germany, June 28, 1950; s. Werner J. and Annelise B. (Helbig) K. Abitur, Schloss Ising, Germany, 1971; MD, Ludwig Maximalians U., Munich, 1977. Cert. allergist, phlebologist, sports medicine. Pvt. practice Planegg, Germany, 1985—; physician German Nat. Icehockey Team, 1982-88; lectr. in field. Contbr. numerous med. papers to profl. publs. Mem. Internat. Fedn. Sports Medicine, N.Y. Acad. Sci. Avocations: golf, traveling. Office: Med Practice, Egenhofenstr 18, 82152 Planegg Germany

KLEINE, TILMANN OTTO, neurochemist, educator; b. Heidelberg, Germany, Nov. 4, 1936; s. Hogo Otto and Lydia Ernestine (Bauer) K.; m. Barbara Dorothea Spiess, Feb. 2, 1973; children: Arne, Riklef. MD, U. Heidelberg, 1963; PhD, U. Hamburg, Eppendorf, Germany, 1968. Asst. pharmacol. inst. U. Heidelberg, 1964-65; asst., lectr. physiol. chem. inst. U. Hamburg (Germany), 1965-70; chief clin. chem. labs. Ctr. Nervous Diseases U. Marburg (Germany), 1970—, prof. neurochemistry, 1973—, chief dept. neurochemistry, 1980—. Author, editor: Neue Methoden für die Liquordiagnostik, 1980; co-author: Labor und Diagnose, 1984, Lehrbuch der Klinischen Chemie & Pathobiochemie, 1987, 89, 95; contbr. 630 articles to profl. jours. Mem. German Soc. Clin. Chemistry (clin. chemist 1972—), German Soc. Lab. Medicine (specialist for lab. medicine 1974—), N.Y. Acad. Scis., German Soc. Chemistry, Academia Brasileira de Neurologia. Home: Am Grassenberg 24, D-35037 Marburg Germany Office: Med Zentrum Nervenheikunde, Rudolf-Bultmann Strasse 8, D-35033 Marburg Germany

KLEINEN, GUENTER, music educator; b. Cologne, Germany, Jan. 10, 1941; s. Joseph and Berta (Kamper) G.; children: Thomas Christopher, Katharina, Johanna Maria. Ing. grad., Robert Schumann Konservatorium, Dusseldorf, 1963; Dr. phil., U. Hamburg, 1967. Asst. Hochschule Braunschweig, 1968-74; akad. rat Hochschule Westfalen-Lippe, Munster, 1974-77; prof. music edn. and systematic musicology U. Bremen, 1977—; vorsitz Arbeitskreis Musikpaedagogische Forschung, 1981-86, Vorsitz Deutsche Gesellschaft fur Musikpsychologie, 1984-94. Author: Experimentelle Studien zum Musikalischen Ausdruck, 1968, Zur Psychologie musikalischen Verhaltens, 1974, Massenmusik, 1984, Die psychologische Wirkkiclkeit der Musik, 1994, Musik und Kind, 2000. Office: Universitaet Bremen FB9, Postfach 330 440, D-28334 Bremen Germany

KLEINER, HILDA FENG-KAI LIN, pediatrician, pathologist; b. Hong Kong, Dec. 13, 1927; d. Ding-Choy Lin and Kam-Man So; m. Paul Kleiner, Jan. 19, 1957; children: Carolyn, Franklin. MD, Nat. Med. Coll. of Shanghai, China, 1949. Resident Montreal (Can.) Children's Med. Ctr., 1952-54; sr. resident, fellow Children's Hosp. Phila., 1954-56; chief resident Meml. Hosp. Cancer/Sloan-Kettering Inst., N.Y.C., 1956-57; instr. in pediats. Bellevue Hosp./NYU Med. Ctr., N.Y.C., 1957; pediatrician, lab. dir. Children's Med. Ctr., Quezon City, The Philippines, 1960-90; pvt. practice pediats., 1970—; assoc. prof., head dept. microbiology U. East Ramon Magsay Say Meml. Med. Ctr., Manila, 1973-93; sect. head microbiology United Dr.'s Med. Ctr., Quezon City, 1992—; med. cons. DuPont Pharms., 1976-86; med. dir. Synthélabo Labs. Paris, Philippine br., 1986-96, Sonix Pharms., Manila, 1997—. Contbr. articles to profl. jours. Fellow Philippine Pediatric Soc., Philippine Soc. Pathologists (treas. 1995, diplomate); mem. Philippine Med. Women's Assn. (bd. dirs. 1999—, pres. San Juan chpt.). Avocations: tap dancing, ballroom dancing, gardening. Home: 961 Stanford St, Wack Wack Village, 1550 Mandaluyong The Philippines

KLEINERT, ANNEMARIE ELISABETH, historian; b. Geseke, Germany, Feb. 1, 1947; d. Ferdinand and Hedwig (Bargenda) Ludwig; m. Hagen M. Kleinert; 1 child, Michael. PhD, U. Berlin, Germany, 1976. Asst. U. Berlin, Germany, 1975, U. Hannover, Germany, 1976-81; rschr. U. Berlin, 1985, 87; vis. lectr. U. Calif., San Diego, 1986. Author: Die Frühen Modejournale in Frankreich, 1980, Portrait of an Artist, 1982, Freie Universitat Berlin, 1987, Le Journal des Dames, 2000; contbr. articles to profl. jours. Roman Catholic. Avocations: languages, writing. Home: Liebensteinstr 6, 14195 Berlin Germany

KLEINERT, MATTHIAS, diversified company executive. Bd. dirs. DaimlerChrysler AG, Stuttgart, Germany. Office: DaimlerChrysler AG, D-70546 Stuttgart Germany

KLEINMAN, YOSEF, internist; b. Krakov, Poland, Feb. 12, 1948; s. Chaim and Zipora (Geminder) K.; m. Pnina Neugroshl, Mar. 24, 1950; children: Esti, Naomi, Avivit, Ricki. MD, Hebrew U., Jerusalem, 1973. Intern Hadassa U. Med. Hosp., 1973, resident, 1977-82; internist Hadassah U. Hosp., Jerusalem, 1977-79; instr. Hadassah Med. Sch. of Hebrew U., Jerusalem, 1979-82, lectr., 1982-85; dir. metabolic diseases and nutritional svc. Bikur-Cholim Hosp., Jerusalem, 1987—, dir. wound ctr. clinic, 1989—, dir. emergency lab., 1992-97, dir. emergency rm., 1994-95, chmn. Internal Medicine Sect., 1997—; vis. assoc. prof. Washington U. Med. Ctr., St. Louis, 1985-87. Contbr. articles to profl. jours. Maj. Israel Def. Forces, 1973-77. Recipient A. Felix prize for outstanding rsch. in atherosclerosis, Hebrew U.-Hadassah Med. Sch., 1983. Mem. Am. Diabetes Assn., Am. Hosp. Assn. (arteriosclerosis coun. 1992—). Home: 49/31 Arzei Habira St, 97356 Jerusalem Israel Office: Bikur-Cholim Hosp, Dept Internal Med 5 Strauss St, 91004 Jerusalem Israel

KLEINPOPPEN, HANS JOHANN WILLI, physics educator, researcher; b. Duisburg, Germany, Sept. 30, 1928; s. Gerhard and Emmi (Maass) K. Diploma in physics, U. Giessen, Germany, 1955; D in Physics, U. Tübingen, Germany, 1961, Habilitation, 1967. Privatdozent U. Tübingen, 1967—; prof. experimental physics U. Stirling, Scotland, 1968-96, prof. emeritus, 1996—; vis. assoc. prof. Columbia U., N.Y.C., 1968; vis. fellow U. Colo., Boulder, 1968; vis. prof. U. Bielefeld, Germany, 1978-97; vis. scientist

Fritz-Haber Inst. of Max-Planck Gesellschaft, Berlin, 1988—; chmn. several nat. and internat. confs., workshops, and summer schs. in atomic, optical, and molecular physics, Germany, Eng., Scotland, Italy, 1968, 74, 78, 80-82, 84, 87, 93, 94, 95. Co-editor of 13 books on atomic and molecular physics and a monograph series (with P. G. Burke C.B.E. Belfast) on physics of atoms and molecules. Recipient the Leverhulme Trust Emeritus fellowship, 1998-2000; participant Hans Kleinpoppen Symposium on Complete Scattering Experiments, Lucca, Italy, 1998. Fellow Am. Phys. Soc., Royal Astronomical Soc., Inst. Physics London, Royal Soc. of Edinburgh, Royal Soc. Arts, N.Y. Acad. Scis. Home: Orber Str 12, 14193 Berlin Germany Office: Fritz-Haber Inst, Berlin 1495 Stirling U, 14195 Stirling Scotland

KLEINROK, ZDZISLAW, pharmacologist; b. Kozlow, Poland, Oct. 4, 1928; s. Jan and Maria (Mroz) K.; m. Maria Janoszka, July 2, 1953; 1 child, Janusz. Physician, Silesian Med. Sch., 1953, MD, 1960, PhD, 1966. Asst. lectr. Silesian Med. Sch., Zabrze, Poland, 1949-66, asst. prof., 1966-67; asst. prof. Med. U. Sch., Lublin, Poland, 1967-74, assoc. prof., 1974-82, prof., 1982—; dean med. faculty Med. U. Sch., 1972-74, rector, 1984-90, 96-99; dr. h.c. U. Tartu, Estonia, Med. Sch. Katowice, Poland, Open Internat. U. for Complementary Medicine, Munich. Author: Pharmacometry, 1982, Handbook of Pharmacology, 1987; contbr. 438 articles to sci. pubs. Mem. Internat. Soc. Biochem. Pharmacology, European Behavioral Pharmacology Soc., Polish Pharm. Soc. (pres. 1974-76), Polish Acad. Scis. (spec. com. physiological scis. 1980—, mem. com. exptl. therapy 1984—). Avocations: history, bridge. Home: Usmiechu 21, PL20-534 Lublin Poland Office: Med U Sch Dept Pharmacology, Jaczewski 8, PL20-090 Lublin Poland

KLEINSMITH, LEWIS JOEL, cell biologist, educator; b. Detroit, Apr. 13, 1942; s. Ralph Louis and Sylvia (Raphael) K.; m. Cynthia Weinstein, June 14, 1964; children: Alyssa Jan, Francesca Lynn. B.S., U. Mich., 1964; Ph.D., Rockefeller U., 1968. Asst. prof. dept. zoology U. Mich., Ann Arbor, 1968-71; assoc. prof. U. Mich., 1971-74, prof. biology, 1975—, Arthur F. Thurnau prof., 1988; Vis. prof. biochemistry U. Fla. Med. Sch., Gainesville, 1974-75. Author: The World of the Cell, 4th edit., 2000, Principles of Cell and Molecular Biology, 2d edit., 1995; editor: Chromosomal Proteins and Their Role in the Regulation of Gene Expression, 1975; contbr. chpts. to books, articles to profl. jours.; developer of ednl. computer software. Recipient Henry Russel award, 1971; Distinguished Service award U. Mich., 1971; Higher Edn. Software award EDUCOM, 1988; Guggenheim fellow, 1974-75. Fellow AAAS; mem. Am. Soc. Biol. Chemists, Am. Soc. for Cell Biology, Am. Inst. Biol. Scientists, Phi Beta Kappa, Sigma Xi. Home: 2642 Essex Rd Ann Arbor MI 48104-6554

KLEINT, CHRISTIAN, physicist, researcher; b. Löbaû, Saxony, Germany, Apr. 3, 1926; s. Walter and Gertrûd (Kleinig) K.; m. Margit Förster, Dec. 13, 1952; children: Christoph, Friedemann. Diploma in Physics, U. Leipzig (Germany), 1954, Dr. rer. nat., 1961, Dr. rer. nat. habil., 1968. Tchr. Oberschûle, Löbaû, Germany, 1946-49; asst. U. Leipzig (Germany), 1955-61, mem. scientific staff, 1961-69, sr. asst., 1969-70, sr. lectr., 1970-90, prof., 1992—; mem. Physkalische Gesellschaftder DDR, Germany, 1955-91; group rep. Vereinigung für Kristallographie, 1975-91; mem. various coms. on solid state, vacuum physics, Berlin, 1976-89. Co-editor: Werner Heisenberg in Leipzig 1927-1942, 1993; contbr. numerous articles to profl. jours. Pvt. Antiaircraft Forces, 1944-45, prisoner of war, 1945-46, France. Recipient Gold Medal U. Wroclaw, Poland, 1981. Mem. Deutsche Physikalische Gesellschaft, Deutsche Gesellschaft Kristallographie. Avocations: history of Leipzig, physics. Home: Am Weiher 5, D-04451 Borsdorf Saxony, Germany Office: U Leipzig Fak Physik Geowissenschaften, Linnéstr 5, D-04103 Leipzig Germany

KLEINWÄCHTER, VLADIMIR, retired biophysicist, researcher; b. Brno, Czechoslovakia, Apr. 24, 1933; s. Antonin and Arnoŝtka (Krulová) K.; m. Hana Reisová, Dec. 1, 1956; children: Martin, Petra. RNDr, Masaryk U., Brno, 1956; CSc, Czechoslovak Acad. Sci., Brno, 1960. Rechr. Inst. Biophysics Czechoslovak Acad. Sci., 1956-99, dep. dir. Inst. Biophysics, 1999-97, acting dir. Inst. Biophysics, 1997; assoc. prof. faculty natural sci. Masaryk U., Brno, 1992—; ret., 1999; chmn. nat. com. IUPAB, Czech Republic, 1990-99. Author: Basic Staining of Cell Nuclei, 1981. Chmn. Czech Ilco, Brno, 1993—. Recipient Joint award Czechoslovak Acad. Sci. and Acad. Sci. of German Dem. Republic, 1984. Mem. Czechoslovakia Biol. Soc. (chmn. biophys. sect. 1990—), European Ostomy Assn. (mem. coord. com. 1995-98, v.p. 1998—). Mem. Czechoslovak Hussite Ch. Avocations: music, skiing, hiking. Home: Smidkova 5a, 61600 Brno Czech Republic

KLEITMAN, NAOMI, neuroscientist; b. Lafayette, Ind., Dec. 23, 1955; d. David and Judith (Goodstein) K. BS, U. Calif., Davis, 1977; MA, U. Ill., 1980, PhD, 1985. Postdoctoral fellow Washington U., St. Louis, 1985-88, rsch. assoc., 1988-89; rsch. asst. prof. U. Miami, 1989-93; adj. asst. prof. U. Miami, 1993-97, adj. assoc. prof., 1997—; dir. edn. The Miami Project to Cure Paralysis, Miami, 1993—. Editor/co-editor: The Miami Project newsletter; contbr. articles to profl. jours. Treas. Kendall Trace Homeowner's Assn., Miami, 1991-95; mem. adv. coun. Brain and Spinal Cord Injury Project, Tampa, Fla., 1995—. Recipient Calif. Gov.'s scholarship 1973, NSF fellowship, 1978-81, others. Mem. AAAS, Soc. for Neurosci., Sigma Xi, Phi Kappa Phi. Office: Miami Project/Cure Paralysi 1600 NW 10th Ave # R48 Miami FL 33136-1015

KLEKOWSKI, ROMUALD ZDZISŁAW, ecologist, researcher; b. Pinsk, Poland, Jan. 1, 1924; s. Aleksander Romuald Klekowski and Janina (Frost) K.; m. Zuzanna Stromenger, 1948 (div. 1961); m. Krystyna Ramlau, Sept. 19, 1961; children: Michał, Marta. MS, U. Łódź, Poland, 1950; D of Natural Scis., Polish Acad. Scis., Warsaw, 1960, D Habilitatus, 1966. From asst. to adj. prof. U. Łódź, 1945-52; head dept. experimental hydrobiology Inst. Experimental Biology, Polish Acad. Scis., Warsaw, 1952-75, dep. dir., 1970-73; dir. Inst. Ecology, Polish Acad. Scis., Warsaw, 1973-82, head of dept. ecol. bioenergetics, 1975-90; dep. sec. biol. divsn. Polish Acad. Scis., Warsaw, 1970-73, 84-86, sec. biol. divsn., 1987-95, prof. Internat. Ctr. Ecology; lectr. in field. Contbr. numerous articles to profl. jours. Recipient Medal of Victory and Freedom, 1947, Companion of the Order Polonia Restituta, 1971, Commander of the Order Polonia Restituta, 1977, Commander of the Order Polonia Restituta with Star, 1986, Entire achievement award Prime Minister, 1997. Mem. Polish Acad. Scis., Belarus Acad. Scis. Home: Jaktorowksa Str 2/50, 01-202 Warsaw Poland Office: Int Ctr Ecol Polish Acd Sci, 05-092 Lomianki Dziekanow Lesny, Poland

KLEMMER, KONRAD GERHARDT, zoologist; b. Frankfurt, Germany, Nov. 25, 1930; s. Georg and Helene (Köhler) K.; m. Sigrid Rohlack, 1962, children: Reinhard, Helmut. PhD, Goethe U., Frankfurt, 1957. Asst. curator Senckenberg Rsch. Inst., Frankfurt, Germany, 1956, curator, 1963; head Senckenberg Sch. for Tng. Tech. Assts., Frankfurt, Germany, 1966; chmn. pub. rels. Senckenberg Natural History Mus. and Rsch. Inst., Frankfurt, Germany, 1987-95; pres. Deutsche Ges fuer Herpetologie und Terrarienkunde, Frankfurt, Germany, 1969-82; chmn. CITES Coun., 1977-92. Editor and author: Grzimek's Animal Encyclopedia, 1971. Office: Senckenberg Mus, Senckenberganlage 25, D-60325 Frankfurt Germany

KLEMPERER, PAUL DAVID, economics educator, consultant, researcher; b. Aug. 15, 1956; s. Hugh G. and Ruth M.M. (Jordan) K.; m. Margaret Meyer, 1989; children: David, Katherine, William. BA in Engring. with 1st class honors with distinction, Cambridge U., 1978; MBA, Stanford U., 1982, PhD in Econs., 1986. Sr. mgmt. cons. Arthur Andersen & Co., 1978-80; Harkness fellow Commonwealth Fund, 1980-82; John Thomson fellow, tutor St. Catherine's Coll. Oxford (Eng.) U., 1985-95, lectr. ops. rsch. and math. econs., 1985-90, reader econs., 1990-95, Edgeworth prof. econs., 1995—, fellow Nuffield Coll., 1995—; vis. prof. MIT, 1987, U. Calif.-Berkeley, 1991, 93, Stanford U., 1991, 93, Yale U., 1994, Princeton U., 1998; cons. to U.S. FTC, U.K. Dept. of Trade and Industry, OFT., NAO, pvt. firms. Editor: RAND Jour. Econ., 1993-99; assoc. editor, editl. bd. Rev. Econ. Studies, 1989-97, Jour. Indsl. Econs., 1989-96, Oxford Econ. Papers, 1986—, Internat. Jour. Indsl. Orgn., 1993—, European Econ. Rev., 1997—, Economic Policy, 1998-99, Rev. of Econ. Design, 1997—, Economic Jour., 2000—; pub.: , The Economic Theoryf Auctns, 2000; contbr. articles to econs. jours. Fellow Econometric Soc., Brit. Acad. E-mail: paul.klemperer@economics.ox.ac.uk. Office: Nuffield Coll, Oxford OX1 1NF, England

KLEN, RUDOLF, medical researcher; b. Praha, Czech Republic, July 2, 1915; s. Leo and Selma (Hellerová) Klein; m. Vera Kulŝtejnová, Aug. 26, 1948 (dec. Feb., 1970); children: Hana, Lenka. MD, Charles U., Prague, 1946; D of Pub. Health, Govt. Bohemia, 1947. Asst. Med. Sch., Hradec Kralove, Czech Republic, 1946-50; head regional health dept. Hradec Kralove, 1951-52; founder, head tissue bank Tchg. Hosp., Hradec Kralove, 1952-82, rschr., 1983-88, 91—; prof. Charles U., Hradec Kralove, 1992—; v.p. C-1 commn. Internat. Inst. Regrigeration, Paris, 1975-87; cons. Internat. Atomic Energy Agy., Vienna, 1986; pres. Czechoslovak Assn. Low-Temperature Biology, 1975-90. Author: (book) Biological Principles of Tissue Banking, 1957, 3d revised edit., 1982; co-author: Chromosome Aberrations Atlas, 1983, Terminology of Cryobiology, 1978; patentee: disinfection of abiotic tissue grafts, 1964, alternative source of human albumin, 1978. Lt. Czechoslovak Army, 1947. Fellow Czechoslovak Biol. Soc. (Hon. Mem. Brno 1987), European Assn. Tissue Banks; mem. Indian Cryogenic Coun. (hon. 1987), European Assn. Tissue Banks (1st hon. mem. 1992). Jewish. Avocations: fine arts. Home: Ŝtefánikova 387, 500 11 Hradec Králové Czech Republic Office: Fakultni Nemocnice, Sokolská 48, 500 05 Hradec Králové Czech Republic

KLENER, VLADISLAV, radiation protection researcher, consultant; b. Bratislava, Slovakia, Jan. 15, 1927; s. Eduard and Frantiska (Novakova) K.; m. Blanka Bickova; children: Thomas, John. MD, Charles U., Prague, Czech Republic, 1951, PhD, 1956, diploma in internal medicine, 1969. Registrar, jr. cons. Nat. Hosp., Strakonice, Czech Republic, 1952-59; chief sr. cons. Nat. Hosp., Lnare, Czech Republic, 1959-60; rschr. Inst. Indsl. Hygiene and Occupl. Diseases, Prague, 1961-68; dir. Ctr. Radiation Hygiene, Prague, 1968-82, 91-96; prof. Charles U. Med. Faculty Hygiene, Prague, 1982-91; advisor State Office Nuclear Safety, Prague, 1996—. Author: Radiation Hygiene, 1987 (award Czech Literal Found. 1988); mem. editl. bd. Occupl. Medicine; contbr. articles and revs. to med. jours., including Health Physics Jour. Fellow IAEA, Japan, 1965. Mem. Internat. Radiation Protection Assn. (Outstanding Svc. award 1992), Czech Med. Soc. (hon., Pro Meritis medal 1977), Christian Acad. Roman Catholic. Office: State Office Nuclear Safety, Senovazne Nam 9, CZ-11000 Prague 1, Czech Republic

KLENIN, VITALY JOSEPHOVICH, physicist, educator; b. Orenburg, USSR, Aug. 9, 1936; s. Joseph Ivanovich and Vera Konstantinovna (Alyoshina) K.; m. Olga Vasilievna Fomichyova, Oct. 2, 1959. BSc, Leningrad (USSR) State U., 1959; PhD, Saratov (USSR) State U., 1968, DSc, 1992. Engr., rschr. Lab. Phys. and Chem. of Polymers Saratov State U., 1959-68, sr. rschr., 1968-76; head newly organized lab. disperse polymeric systems Saratov State U., 1976-85, assoc. prof., chair phys. and chem. of polymers and colloids, 1976-92, prof., chair tech. chemistry, 1992-95, prof., head of newly organized chair of polymers, 1995—; mem. acad. bd. chemistry dept. Saratov State U., 1996—, mem. dissertation acad. bd., 1997—; mem. panel on high-molecular compounds Russian Acad. Scis., 1998—. Author: Thermodynamics of Systems Containing Flexible-Chain Polymers, 1995, 99; co-author: Characteristic Functions of Light Scattering from Disperse Systems, 1977; contbr. articles to profl. jours. Grantee Russian Found. Basic Rsch., 1995, 97-99; scholar Outstanding Scientists Russia Found., 1994-96. Avocations: painting, gardening, market-gardening. Home: 18a Radishcheva St Apt 38, 410028 Saratov Russia Office: Saratov State U Chem Dept, 83 Astrakhanskaya St, 410026 Saratov Russia

KLENK, HANS-PETER, biochemist, researcher; b. Schwaebisch Hall, Germany, Apr. 21, 1956; s. Otto and Else (Baumann) K.; m. Gudrun Luettgens, Apr. 21, 1988 (div. 1990); m. Renate Lorenz, Dec. 27, 1999. MS, Eberhard-Karls U., Tuebingen, Germany, 1984; PhD, Ludwig-Maximilians U., Munich, 1994. Collaborative investigator Max-Planck Inst. for Biochemistry, Martinsried, Germany, 1991-94; postdoctoral rschr. Dalhousie U., Halifax, N.S., Can., 1994-96; mem. faculty TIGR, Rockville, Md., 1996-97; lab. dir. Goettingen (Germany) Genomics Lab., 1997-98; v.p. Epidauros AG, Bernried, Germany, 1998—. Contbr. articles to profl. jours. Mem. Germany Soc. for Applied and Gen. Microbiology, Internat. Fedn. Classification Socs., Internat. Soc. Molecular Evolution., German Soc. for Biochemistry and Molecular Biology, Am. Soc. for Microbiology. Avocations: chess, tennis. Home: Poeckinger Fussweg 7a, D-82340 Feldafing Germany Office: Epidauros Biotechnologie AG, Am Neuland 1, D-82347 Bernried Germany

KLEPINGER, JOHN WILLIAM, trailer manufacturing company executive; b. Lafayette, Ind., Feb. 7, 1945; s. John Franklin and R. Wanda (North) K.; m. Mary Patricia Duffy, May 1, 1976; 1 child, Nicholas Patrick. BS, Ball State U., 1967, MA, 1968. Sales engr. CTS Corp., Elkhart, Ind., 1969-70; exec. v.p. Woodlawn Products Corp., Elkhart, 1970-78; v.p. Period Ind., Henderson, Ky., 1976-78, Sotebeer Constrn. Co., Inc., Elkhart, 1978-81; gen. mgr. Wells Industries Inc., Ogden, Utah, 1981—; gen. mgr. Wells Cargo, Inc., Phoenix, 1995—, western regional mgr., 1999—; regional dir. Zion's First Nat. Bank, Ogden, 19865. Bd. dirs. St. Benedict's Hosp., Ogden, 1986-94, chmn., 1987-94; bd. dirs. Weber County Indsl. Devel. Corp., Nat. Job Tng. Partnership Inc., 1986-89; mem. Weber-Morgan Pvt. Industry Coun., 1983-96, Utah Job Tng. Coordinating Coun., 1988-96, chmn. 1993-94. Named Ogden Bus. Man of Yr., Weber County Sch. Dist., 1984. Mem. Nat. Assn. Trailer Mfrs. (bd. dirs., vice chmn. 1994-95, chmn. 1995-97, sec., treas. 1998-99), Weber County Prodn. Mgrs. Assn. (pres. 1984-85, 92-93), Nat. Assn. Pvt. Industry Couns. (bd. dirs. 1986-96, pres. 1988-92), Nat. Alliance Bus. (bd. dirs. 1987-90), Ogden Area C. of C. (bd. dirs. 1986-96, treas. 1986-89), Phoenix C. of C., Exch. Club (bd. dirs. Ogden 1984-86). Roman Catholic. Avocations: finance, community service, leadership, sports, travel. Office: Wells Cargo Inc 6902 W Hadley St Phoenix AZ 85043-4300

KLEPP, KURT OTTO, chemistry educator; b. Bad Aussee, Styria, Austria, Sept. 13, 1944; s. Ferdinand Franz-Joseph and Auguste Anselma (Kretz) K.; m. Viktoria Agnes Goetz, May 10, 1973; 1 child, Sandra. PhD in Chemistry, U. Vienna, Austria, 1971, Habilitation in Inorganic Chemistry, 1987. Asst. U. Vienna, 1972-77; maître asst. U. Geneva, Switzerland, 1977-81; guest rschr. Rheinisch-Westfaelische Technische Hochschule, Germany, 1981-85; asst. prof. Kepler U., Linz, Austria, 1986, assoc. prof., 1987—. Contbr. 140 articles to sci. jours. Mem. German Chem. Soc. Avocations: classical music, photography, Byzantine art and history. E-mail: kurt.klepp@jk.uni-linz.ac.at. Office: Dept Inorganic Chemistry, 69 Altenbergerstrasse, A-4040 Linz Austria

KLEPPER, ROBERT KENNETH, writer, silent film historian, journalist; b. Springfield, Mo., Nov. 11, 1966; s. Kenneth Herbert and Altha Ann (Shumate) K. Reference asst. Pensacola (Fla.) Pub. Libr., 1983-84; office worker Pensacola Tax Collector Office, 1984-85; purchasing agt. asst. Gen. Oceanics, Miami, 1992-93; historian, writer various publs., 1993-99; reviewer books and videos relating to silent era The Silents Majority Internet Website, 1996; reviewer videos Classic Images and Films of the Golden Age, 1996—; dist. historian Future Bus. Leaders Am., 1983-84, pres., 1984-85, mem. Fla. Future Bus. Leaders Am. State Exec. Coun. Author: Silent Films on Video, 1996, Silent Films 1877-96, 1999; co-prodr. (video) Nurse Marjorie (1920), 1997, (video) The Ghost of Rosy Taylor (1918), 1998, Hail the Woman (1921); wrote 1998 introduction Little Mary Sunshine (1916); contbr. articles to jours. Vol. Body Positive, People with AIDS Coalition, Miami, Fla., 1992-93; vol. receptionist Escambia AIDS Svcs., Pensacola, 1994-95; mem. Silent Film Soc., Atlanta, 1994-95; sec. ACLU N.W. Fla, 1988; vol. worker Lois Benson for Congress, Pensacola, 1995. Named Outstanding Dist. Pres., Fla. state chpt. FBLA, 1985, Internat. Man of Yr. 1998-99. Mem. Friends of Marion Davies Fan Club, Libr. Congress (nat. mem. 1999), Am. Film Inst. Republican. Avocations: watching silent films, collecting movie memorabilia, drug and alcohol rehab counseling, AIDS counseling. Home: PO Box 878 Clarkston GA 30021-0878

KLEPSCH, EGON ALFRED, German government official; b. Bodenbach, Elbe, Germany, Jan. 30, 1930; s. Egon and Hermine (Hölzl) K.; m. Anita Wegehaupt, Apr. 15, 1952; children: Andreas, Carola, Wolfram, Marion, Gisela, Christoph. PhD (hon.), U. Austral de Chile, 1992, U. Buenos Aires, 1993; LLD (hon.), U. Sunderland, 1993. Mem. Christian Dem. Union, 1951—; fed. chmn. Young Christian Dems., 1963-69; chmn. EU Young Christian Dems., 1964-70; v.p. European People's Party, 1977-92, mem. bur., 1992—; mem. Bundestag, 1965-80, chmn. dep. policy working party of CDU/CSU group, 1969-72, 76-80; mem. parliamentary assemblies Coun. of Europe, Western European Union, 1969-80; mem. European Parliament, 1973-94, chmn., 1977-82, 84-92, v.p., 1982-84, pres., 1992-94; mem. bur. Christian Dem. Union, 1977—; chmn. Europa-Union Deutschland, 1989—; vice chmn. German coun. European Movement, 1990—. Decorated grande ufficiale Dell'Ordine al Merito (Italy), grand officier de l'Ordre Grand-Ducal de la Couronne de Chene (Luxembourg), gran cruz de la Orden de Mayo (Argentina), gran cruz Orden al Merito (Chile), grand cross Legion of Phoenix (Greece), Grosskreuz des Verdienstorden der Bundesrepublik Deutschland (Germany), Verleihung des Companion of Honour der hochsten Stufe des maltesischen Verdienstordens, Verleihung des Heiligen Kreuzes der Apostel Paulus und Titus durch die Heilige Synode der Kirche von Kreta, grand cross Order of Merit (Hungary), grand-croix de L'Ordre de la Couronne (Belgium), commander de la legion d'honneur de la rep. francaise, 1994, Louise-Weiss-Preis, 1992, Grosses goldenes Ehrenzeichen am Bande für Verdienste um die Republik Österreich, 1995. Mem. Inst. Internat. Pub. Law and Internat. Rels. (hon.). Avocation: chess. Home: Pastor-Busenbender Str 14, D-56072 Koblenz Germany Office: c/o European Parliament, 97-113 Rue Belliard, 1040 Brussels Belgium*

KLESOV, VLADIMIR ALEKSEYEVICH, mechanical engineer, researcher; b. Makeyevka, Ukraine, Oct. 12, 1953; s. Aleksey Mironovich and Nina (Andreyevna) K.; m. Tatyana Nikolayevna Braslavets, Oct. 30, 1976; children: Yana, Vitaliy. BS, Civil Engirng. Inst., Mekeyevka, Ukraine, 1982, State U., Donetsk, Ukraine, 1992; MTech, Inst. of Machines and Systems, Kharkov, Ukraine, 1987. Machinist Power Sta., Mekeyevka, 1972-73; electrician Kirov Metall. Plant, Mekeyevka, 1976; chief project engr. Specialized Bd. Ukraine/Coke Chemistry Repair, Mekeyevka, 1982-84; chief mechanic, rescue unit Mine, Mekeyevka, 1984-89; chief mechanic Coop. Soc. Signal, Mekeyevka, 1989-90; dir. joint stock co. Engr., Mekeyevka, 1991—; mem. sci. coun. Regional Adminstrn., Donetsk, 1998—. Contbr. articles to profl. jours. SErved with Russian Navy, 1973-76, Kuril Islands. Mem. N.Y. Acad. Scis. Christian Orthodox. Avocations: classical music, literature.

KLESSINGER, MARTIN, educator; b. Berlin, Sept. 14, 1934; s. Johann and Ruth (Osburg) K.; m. Heidi Ussling; children: Sabine, Stephan. Diplom.chemiker, U. Freiburg, Germany, 1960; Dr.rer.nat., U. Gottingen, Germany, 1961. Lectr. U. Freiburg, Germany, 1970-71; prof., dir. organic chem. dept. U. Munster, Germany, 1971—. Author: Elektronenstruktur Organizscher Molekule, 1982. Avocation: viola. Home: Gorlitzerstr 108, D-48157 Munster Germany

KLESTIL, THOMAS, president of Austria; b. Vienna, Austria, Nov. 4, 1932; children—Ursula, Thomas, Stefan; m. Margot Klestil-Löffler. Doctorate, U. Econs., Vienna, 1957. Staff Office for Econ. Coordination in Fed. Chancellory, Vienna, 1957-59; mem. Austrian del. to OECD, Paris, 1959-62; with Fed. Ministry Fgn. Affairs, 1962-92; consul gen. of Austria Fed. Ministry Fgn. Affairs, Los Angeles, 1969-74; dir. office internat. orgns. Fed. Ministry Fgn. Affairs, Vienna, 1974-78; permanent rep. of Austria to UN Fed. Ministry Fgn. Affairs, N.Y.C., 1978-82; ambassador to U.S. Fed. Ministry Fgn. Affairs, Washington, 1982-87; sec. gen. Fed. Ministry Fgn. Affairs, 1987-92; pres. Austria, 1992—. Office: Office of the Fed Pres, Hofburg, A-1010 Vienna Austria

KLETT, ALFRED HERMANN, physicist, business executive; b. Messkirch, Germany, June 11, 1953; s. Georg and Rosa (Restle) K.; m. Regine Peschina, Dec. 27, 1990; children: Kazim, Lara, Sophie. Physics diploma, U. Freiburg, Germany, 1981, D of Natural Sci., 1987. Rsch. fellow U. Freiburg, 1981-87, postdoctoral fellow, 1987-91; head detector divsn. EG&G Berthold, Bad Wildbad, Germany, 1991-96, bus. element mgr., 1997—; mem. Paul Scherrer Inst. Villigen, Switzerland, 1981-87, European Orgn. for Nuclear Rsch., Geneva, 1987-91, Ctr. d'Etudés Nucléaire, Saclay, 1988-91. Contbr. numerous articles to profl. jours.; patentee radiation detectors. Mem. IEEE, German-Swiss Radiation Protection Assn. Office: EG&G Berthold, Calmbacher Strasse 22, 75323 Bad Wildbad Germany

KLETZ, TREVOR ASHER, chemical engineer, author; b. Darlington, Durham, U.K., Oct. 23, 1922; s. William and Frances (Amshewitz) K.; m. Denise Valerie Winroope, Oct. 28, 1958 (dec. 1980); children: Anthony Michael, Nigel Howard. BSc in Chemistry, Liverpool U., 1944; DSc in Chem. Engring., Loughborough U., 1986. Chartered chemist, chartered engr. Rsch. chemist Imperial Chem. Industries, Billingham, Eng., 1946-51, various prodn. positions, 1952-67; safety advisor Imperial Chem. Industries, Wilton, Eng., 1968-82; adj. prof. Loughborough U., 1978-82, rsch. fellow, 1982-86, sr. vis. rsch. fellow, 1986—; self-employed process safety cons. Cheadle, Eng., 1986—. Author: Critical Aspects of Safety and Loss Prevention, 1990, An Engineer's View of Human Error, 3d edit., 2000, Hazop and Hazan - Identifying and Assessing Chemical Industry Hazards, 4th edit., 1999, Lessons from Disaster - How Organizations have no Memory and Accidents Recur, 1993, What Went Wrong? - Case Histories of Process Plant Disasters, 4th edit., 1998, Learning from Accidents, 2d edit., 1994, Computer Control and Human Error (with others), 1995, Dispelling Chemical Engineering Myths, 3d edit., 1996, Process Plants: A Handbook for Inherently Safer Design, 2nd edit., 1998, By Accident, 2000; contbr. numerous articles to profl. jours. Decorated officer Order Brit. Empire, 1997; recipient Award for Personal Achievement in Chem. Engring., Chem. Engring. mag., 1990. Fellow Instn. of Chem. Engrs. (Coun. medal 1986, Ned Franklin medal 1993, Brennan medal 1995), AIChE (Bill Doyle award 1985), Royal Acad. Engring., Royal Soc. Chemistry. Jewish. Avocations: reading, walking, railways. E-mail: T.Kletz@Lboro.ac.ak. Home: 64 Twining Brook Rd, Cheadle Hulme SK8 5RJ, England

KLEVANSKI, IOSSIF, aerospace engineer; b. Moscow, Jan. 3, 1959; arrived in Germany, 1992; s. Issaak and Khana (Groubnik) K.; m. Elena Chifrina, Aug. 21, 1982; 1 child, Maja. MS in Engring., Moscow Aviation Inst., 1981. Engr. Sci. and Rsch. Inst., Moscow, 1981-82; engr. Tupolev Design Bur., Moscow, 1982-87, head stability and controlability group, 1987-90; chief specialist Flight Safety Commn., Moscow, 1990-92; aircraft engr., programmer Nayak Aircraft Svc. GmbH, Cologne, Germany, 1994-99; rschr. German Aerospace Ctr., Cologne, 1999—; chief of calculation group Commn. for Flight Accident Investigation, Moscow, 1990-92. Contbr. articles to profl. jours.; patentee in field. Avocation: chess. Home: Hans-Schulten-Str 8, D-51109 Cologne Germany Office: German Aerospace Ctr, Porz-Wahnheide Linder Hoehe, D-51147 Cologne Germany

KLEVEN, MARK S., research scientist; b. Roseau, Minn., May 18, 1953; s. Howard Albert and Shirley Ruth (Kling) K. BA with honors, BS in Psychology, Biology-Math., Bemidji State U., 1977; MA in Physiol. Psychology, Marquette U., 1979; PhD in Pharmacology, U. Minn., 1986; postdoctoral student, U. Chgo., 1986. Rsch. asst. dept. psychology Marquette U., 1977-79; USPHS predoctoral fellow dept. pharmacology U. Minn., 1979-85; NIMH postdoctoral fellow dept. psychiatry Pritzker sch. medicine U. Chgo., 1986-87, rsch. assoc. dept. pharm. and physiol. scis. Pritzker sch. medicine, 1987-89, rsch. assoc., asst. prof., 1989-92; head behavioral pharmacology, neurobiology II Pierre Fabre Medicament, 1992—; spl. rev. cons. population rsch. com. Nat. Inst. Child Health and Human Devel., 1990, 91. Author: (with others) Serotonin: from Cell Biology to Pharmacology and Therapeutics, 1990, The Neurobiology of Drug and Alcohol Addiction, 1992; ad hoc referee Biol. Psychiatry, Brain Rsch., European Jour. Pharmacology, others; contbr. articles to profl. jours. Mem. Am. Soc. Pharmacology and Exptl. Therapeutics, European Behavioral Pharmacology Soc., European Coll. Neuropsychopharmacology, Internat. Study Group Investigating Drugs as Reinforcers, Soc. Neuroscience, Soc. Stimulus Properties Drugs, Alpha Phi Sigma, Psi Chi, Alpha Sigma Nu. Avocations: mountain biking, squash, tennis. Home: 99 ave du Sidobre, Castres Tarn, France Office: Pierre Fabre Rsch Inst, 17 ave Jean Moulin, 81106 Castres Tarn, France

KLEVIT, ALAN BARRE, fine art dealer, publishing executive, motivational speaker, writer; b. Balt., June 25, 1935; s. Robert and Minnie (Goodman) K.; m. Marilyn Rosenthal, Nov. 26, 1955; children: Mindy Faith, Lawrence Michael, Richard Steven. BS in Econs., Georgetown U., 1956, MA in Econs., 1960; MA in Pub. Adminstrn. and Urban Affairs, Am. U., 1970. Asst. mgr. AS Beck Shoe Co., Washington, 1956-57; stat., economist Commerce Dept., Washington, 1957-60; securities analyst, rsch. dir. T.J. McDonald & Co., Washington, 1960-62; mgmt. analyst, div. chief Fed. Aviation Adminstrn., Washington, 1962-73; CEO Art Fair, Inc., Silver Spring, Md., 1974-90; founder, dir. Klevit Fine Art, Internat., Silver Spring and

Malibu, Calif., 1987—; founder, exec. officer Robert Klevit Found. for Humanitarianism, Silver Spring and Malibu, Calif., 1987—; dir. Stardust Pub., Malibu, 1990—; co-founder, dir. Charity Editions, Silver Spring and Malibu, 1987; mem. faculty Mgmt. by Objectives Fed. Exec. Sch., Charlottesville, Va., 1969-71; motivational speaker, Malibu, 1988—. Author: Three Days in Sedona, 1990, How to Make Your Dreams Come True, 1991, Follow the Rainbow, 1991, (book and audiocassette) Pass the Pickles, Please and Other Stories, 1995; (video) Journey Within, 1993; host radio show: Today's Art World with Alan Klevit, 1983-84, (TV Show) Off the Beaten Path with Alan Klevit, 1992—; contbr. articles to mags. and newspapers including regular contbns. to Malibu Mag.; writer, prodr., featured performer tv commls., 1994—. Bd. dirs. Summer Opera, Washington, 1987—, Marine & Mountain Wildlife Rescue, Malibu, 1991—; mem. Hammer Mus., LA County Mus. Mem. Inst. for Econometric Rsch., World Wildlife Fedn., Inst. for Noetic Scis., Planetary Soc., Malibu C. of C., Masons. Avocations: charity art auctioneer, theater, classical music, travel, karate. Office: Stardust Pub PO Box 6356 Malibu CA 90264-6356

KLEZL, ZDENEK, orthopedic surgeon; b. Prague, Oct. 20, 1956; s. Zdenek Klezl and Helena (Lomicka) Klezlova; m. Radka Kostnerova; children: Zdenek, Katerina. MD, Charles U., 1983, PhD, 1996. Diplomate Bd. Orthopedics and Bd. Traumatology. Resident in gen. surgery NNF-Praha, 1984-85; resident in orthopedics Ortho-univ. Hosp., Praha, 1985-88; head sub-dept. ICU Ortho-univ. Hosp., Prague, 1988-91; fellow dept. orthopedics U. Louisville, Ky., 1991-92; head subdept. ortho sta. Univ. Hosp., Prague, 1992-95; dep. head Ortho-trauma dept. Ctrl. Mil. Hosp., Prague, 1995—; head postgrad. tng. program Mil. Med. Acad., Hradec Kralovo, Czech Republic, 1997—; head pvt. orth clinic Prague, 1994—. Contbr. articles to profl. jours., chpts. to books. Mem. Czech Spine Soc., Czech Soc. for Orthopedics and Taumatology, Czech Med. Chamber, German soc. for Orthopedics and Traumatology, World Ortho Soc. Roman Catholic. Avocations: tennis, sailing, windsurfing, travel. Home: Nad Kralovskou Oborou 41, 170-00 Praha 7 Czech Republic Office: Ctrl Mil Hosp Dept Orthoped, U Vojenske nemocnice 1200, 169-02 Praha 6 Czech Republic

KLIKA, ZDENĚK, geochemistry educator, researcher; b. Ostrava, Czech Republic, Feb. 10, 1943; s. Bohumil and Cecilie (Nováková) K.; m. Christiana Broschová, June 24, 1967; children: Michaela, Martin. MSc, Technical U. Chemistry, Prague, Czech Republic, 1966; PhD, VŠB Tech. U., Ostrava, Czech Republic, 1982. Cert. geochemist. Rschr. Plant-Dusíkárny, Ostrava, Czech Republic, 1966-69; head dept. analytical chemistry and material testing VŠB Tech. U., Ostrava, Czech Republic, 1969-85, reader, 1985-90, assoc. prof. geochemistry, 1990-99; prof. geochemistry VŠB Tech. U., Ostrava, 1999—; cons. Ostrava-Karviná Mines, Ostrava, 1980-89, Most Coal Soc., Most, 1992-94. Contbr. articles to profl. jours. 1st lt. Czech Army, 1967-68. Mem. N.Y. Acad. Sci. Avocations: skiing, tennis. Home: M. Majerové 1702, 70800 Ostrava-Poruba Czech Republic Office: VSB-TUO Dept Anal Material Testing, 17 listopadu, 70833 Ostrava-Poruba Czech Republic

KLIM, MICHAEL, Olympic athlete; b. Gdynia, Poland, Aug. 13, 1977. Recipient Gold medal 4 x 100-meter freestyle, 4 x 200-meter freestyle Sydney Olympics, 2000, 7 medals (4 gold) World Championships, 1998, 100-meter freestyle, 100-meter butterfly Pan Pacific Championships, 1999; anchor 4 x 200-meter freestyle team; set world record in 100 fly, 1999. Office: Australian Swimming Inc, PO Box 940, Dickson ACT 2602, Australia*

KLÍMA, MICHAL, political scientist; b. Prague, July 1, 1959. PhDr, Charles U., Prague, 1985; PhD in Polit. Sci., Taras Schevchenko Kiev U., 1994; MA in Govt., U. Manchester, Eng., 1992. Assoc. prof. U. Econs., Prague, 1985—. Office: U Econs Dept Polit Sci, nam W Churchilla 4, 130 67 Prague Czech Republic

KLIMA, ROGER RADIM, physiatrist; b. Prague, Czechoslovakia; came to U.S., 1982, naturalized, 1988; s. Josef and Radka Klima. BA, Zatlanka Coll., Prague, 1971; MD, Charles U., Prague, 1978. Diplomate Am. Bd. Phys. Medicine and Rehab., Am. Bd. Electrodiagnostic Medicine. Resident in surgery Charles U., 1978-79, resident in orthopedic surgery, 1979-81; fellow, clin. clk. Beverly Hills Med. Ctr. and Cedars-Sinai Med. Ctr., L.A., 1984-86; resident in surgery U. Medicine and Dentistry-N.J. Med. Sch., Newark, 1986-87; resident in phys. medicine and rehab. U. Medicine and Dentistry-N.J. Med. Sch./Kessler Inst., Newark and West Orange, 1987-90; mem. phys. medicine and rehab. faculty Stanford (Calif.) U. and affiliated hosps., 1990—; dir. phys. medicine and rehab. outpatient svcs. Palo Alto (Calif.) VA Health Care Sys., 1992—, also co-dir. comprehensive pain mgmt.; clin. instr. in phys. medicine and rehab. U. Medicine and Dentistry-N.J.Med. Sch., 1989-90; clin. instr. in phys. medicine and rehab. Stanford U. Sch. Medicine, 1990-96, asst. prof., 1996—. Contbr. articles to profl. jours. Recipient first ann. Thompson Humanitarian award Stanford U. Phys. Medicine and Rehab., 1994, 97, 2000. Mem. Am. Acad. Phys. Medicine and Rehab. (liaison resident physician coun. 1989-90), Assn. Acad. Physiatrists, Am. Assn. Electrodiagnostic Medicine. Office: Stanford U Med Ctr Divsn Phys Medicine and Rehab Rm NC 104 Stanford CA 94305

KLIMAS, ANTANAS ALGIRDAS, hydrogeologist, educator; b. Kaunas, Lithuania, Aug. 22, 1939; s. Jonas Klimas and Ieva (Kurtinaityte) Klimiene; m. Irena Anastazija Galinyte, Apr. 7, 1962; children: Gytis, Jurgita. Diploma in geology, Vilnius (Lithuania) U., 1962, D of Natural Scis., 1975. Hydrogeologist Vilnius Hydrogeol. Expedition, 1962-69, head of divsn., 1969-87; chief hydrogeologist Artva Hydrogeol. Co., Vilnius, 1987-95, Vilnius Hydrogeology Ltd., 1995—. Co-author: Geology of Lithuania, 1994. Recipient Bronze medal Exhbn. Nat. Econ. Achievements, Moscow, 1978, 84, Silver medal, 1990. Mem. Internat. Assn. Hydrogeologists, Am. Inst. Hydrology, Nat. Com. Lithuanian Geologists (sec. gen. 1994—), Geol. Soc. Lithuania (vice chmn. 1994-96). Home: Architektu 6-8, 2043 Vilnius Lithuania Office: Vilnius Hydrogeology Ltd, Basanaviciaus 37-1, 2009 Vilnius Lithuania

KLIMBACHER, WOLFGANG, literary historian; b. Villach, Austria, Sept. 6, 1960; s. Walter and Hildegard (Moser) K. Magister Philosophiae, U. Klagenfurt/Carinthia, Austria, 1986, PhD, 1993. Roofer/shingler Villach, Austria, 1980; tchr. h.s. Klagenfurt, 1988-91, pvt. tutor, 1991-92; asst. U. Klagenfurt, 1992-93, 93—, lectr., 1993; mem. exec. bd. Soc. Mnemosyne, Klagenfurt, 1992. Co-author: Expressionism in Austria, Literature and Arts, 1994, Literature and Nation, 1995. Capt. mountain inf. Austrian Army, 1981-87. Recipient Sports Badge Bronze Dept. Tng., Sports and Arts, 1987, Mil. Svc. medal Austrian Army, 1981, 91, 93, Mil. Svc. Cross 3rd Class, 1990. Fellow Pro Scientia, 1991-93; mem. Hölderlin-Gesellschaft. Democrat. Roman Catholic. Avocations: mountain tourng, running, jogging, swimming, biking. Home: Neubaugasse 28/1, A-9500 Villach Austria Office: U Inst German Lang and Lit, Univ Str 65-67, A-9022 Klagenfurt Austria

KLIMCHOUK, ALEXANDER, research speleologist, consultant; b. Aug. 29, 1956; s. Boris Klimchouk and Tamara (Melnichouk) Boldyreva; m. Natalia Yablokova, Feb. 28, 1975; children: Oleg, Aleksey. MSc in Geomorphology, Kiev (Ukraine) State U., 1983; PhD in Hydrogeology, Nat. Acad. Scis., Kiev, 1998. Technician, engr. Inst. Geol. Sci., Kiev, 1973-79, sr. engr., 1979-84, head divsn., 1984-90, scientist, 1990—; v.p. Nat. Assn. Soviet Speleologists Coun. Hydrogeology and Engrng. Geol., Russian Acad. Scis., 1985-91; dir. Kiev Karst & Speleological Ctr., 1990-93; mem. adv. bd. Internat. Jour. Speleology, 1995—; pres. Com. Karst Hydrogeology and Speleogenesis. Author: Structural Prerequisites of Speleogenesis in Gypsum, 1995; editor: Speleogenesis: Evolution of Karst Aquifers, 1998, Gypsum Karst of the World, 1996; contbr. over 140 articles to sci. jours. Soldier Soviet Army, 1977-79. Named hon. citizen Ala., S.D., 1990. Mem. Ukrainian Speleological Assn. (pres. 1992-97, hon. pres. 1998), Nat. Speleological Soc. (hon.), Internat. Union Speleology (adv. sec., bur. mem. 1991—. Avocation: caving. Home: Kibalchicha str 7A kv 59, 02183 Kiev Ukraine Office: Inst Geol Sci, PO Box 136, 01030 Kiev Ukraine

KLIMCZUK, STEPHEN JOHN, business executive, foundation director; b. North Hollywood, Calif., Jan. 14, 1963; s. Leon and Wanda (Kotowicz) K.; m. Iris C.B. Massion, Sept. 6, 1991; children: Caroline, Julia, Christina, Isabella (dec.). BA in Econs., UCLA, 1983; MBA, Harvard U., 1987. Assoc. cons. Bain & Co., Palo Alto, Calif., 1983-84; fin. analyst John Nuveen & Co. Inc., San Francisco, 1984-85; assoc. Goldman, Sachs & Co., N.Y.C., 1987-88; mgr. Nat. Review Inc., N.Y.C., 1988-89; dir., mem. bd. World Economic Forum, Geneva, 1989-95; dir. global bus. policy coun. A.T. Kearney, Inc., Alexandria, Va., 1996—; mng. dir. World Link Publs. S.A., Geneva, 1991-92. Freeman, City of London, 1998. Recipient Cavaliere, S.M.O. Constantiniano di San Giorgio, 1987; named officer Most Venerable Order of St. John, 1994; invested Knight of Malta, 1996. Fellow Royal Soc. Arts (London), Salzburg Seminar; mem. Harvard Club of N.Y.C. Roman Catholic. Avocations: travel, history, visual arts, mountain walking. Office: 333 John Carlyle St Alexandria VA 22314-5745

KLIMEK, JOSEPH JOHN, physician, educator; b. Wilkes-Barre, Pa., Sept. 14, 1946; s. Joseph John and Frances Carol (Pavloski) K.; m. Jane Marie Stout, June 26, 1971 (div.); 1 child, Adam. AB cum laude, Princeton U., 1968; MD, Pa. State U., 1972. Diplomate Am. Bd. Internal Medicine, Am. Bd. Infectious Diseases. Intern, resident in internal medicine Hartford (Conn.) U., then fellow in infectious disease, 1972-76, chief epidemiology, 1976-87, dir. subsplty. medicine, 1985-87, assoc. dir. medicine, 1987-90, assoc. dir. dept. medicine and chmn. AIDS program, 1987-90, dir. dept. medicine, 1990—, chmn. AIDS task force, 1985-90, assoc. chmn. dept. medicine, 1995—; asst. prof. medicine U. Conn., Farmington, 1977-84, assoc. prof., 1984-90, prof., 1990—; assoc. chmn. dept. medicine U. Conn. Sch. Medicine, 1995—; Conn. mem. numerous faculties pharm. industry; co-founder, co-dir. Hartford Office Paranormal Exploration (HOPE), 1998—. Sr. assoc. editor Am. Jour. Infection Control, 1980-95; med. editor Asepsis, The Infection Control Forum; also mem. numerous editl. bds. in field; contbr. articles to med. jours. Recipient Disting. Alumnus award, 1978, ARC award, 1986. Fellow ACP, Infectious Disease Soc. Am.; mem. APHA, AAAS, Am. Profls. in Infection Control, Am. Soc. Microbiology, Am. Fedn. Clin. Rsch., Soc. Hosp. Epidemiologists Am., Am. Venereal Disease Assn., Am. Med. Writers Assn. Achievements include integrated internal medicine residency of Hartford Hospital with University of Connecticut School of Medicine; developed hospital community linkage network for AIDS care in Greater Hartford; introduced primary care medicine practice model to all ambulatory services; expanded care to indigent with two bilingual satellite practices; developed hospital cardiac services product line. Home: 10 Mathers Xing Simsbury CT 06070-2478 Office: Hartford Hosp 80 Seymour St Hartford CT 06115-2701

KLIMEK, MAREK, obstetrician and gynecologist; b. Cracow, Poland, Oct. 8, 1964; s. Rudolf and Ewa (Kownacka) K.; m. Małgorzata Patrzyk, Mar. 15, 1986; 1 child, Patrycja. MD with distinction, Jagiellonian U., Cracow, 1989, PhD, 1992. Asst. ob/gyn. chair Jagiellonian U., Cracow, 1989-95, sr. asst., 1995-98, head of grant of com. of sci. investigation, 1995-98, assoc. prof., 1998—; dir. Fertility Clinic, Cracow, 1995—. Contbr. articles to profl. jours. Com. of Sci. Investigations grantee, 1995. Mem. European Assn. Gynecologists and Obstetricians, N.Y. Acad. Scis., European Soc. for Gynaecol. Endoscopy. Roman Catholic. Avocations: skiing, tennis, swimming. Home: Szlak 3/5, 31-161 Cracow Poland Office: Jagiellonian Univ, Kopernika 23, 31-501 Cracow Poland

KLIMEK, RUDOLF, obstetrics and gynecology educator; b. Cracow, Poland, Dec. 12, 1932; s. Sylwester and Józefa Klimek; m. Ewa Kownacka, Apr. 21, 1961; 1 child, Marek. MD, Med. Faculty Jagiellonian U., Kraków, 1955, PhD, 1961; ordinary prof. of med., 1980; PhD habil., Jagiellonian U., 1964. Cert. obstetrician and gynecologist, neuroendocrinologist. Clin. investigator Jagiellonian U. Sch. Medicine, 1957-65, head cen. endocrine lab., 1965-69; U. chair/head dept. endocrinology and fertility ob-gyn. chairs Jagiellonian U., Kraków, 1969—, dean Sch. Nursing, 1975-81; cons. in gynecol. endocrinology; mem. sci. bd. Polish Ministry Health and Social Welfare, 1981-86; sci. bd., exec. bd. FIGO, 1982-94; exec. bd. EAGO, 1986-91; bd. UPIGO, 1993—, UMES, 1993—; expert advisory panel FIGO, 1997—. Author, co-author, editor of over 450 publications including 39 books. Recipient Bachelor's Cross Polonia Restituta, 1975, 1st Grade Edn. award Polish Health and Social Welfare Ministry, 1976, 77, Gold medal City of Cracow, 1978, medal World Polonia, 1987, International Man of the Year IBC, Cambridge, 1997-98. Fellow Royal Soc. Medicine, World Assn. Perinatal Medicine, World Lit. Acad. (life), Internat. Acad. Human Reprodn., Internat. Acad. Geocancerology and Environ., Internat. Soc. Magnetic Resonance in Medicine; mem. Polish Gynecol. Soc. (hon., pres.), Russian German Hungarian, Israeli, Czech and Slovak Ob/Gyn Soc. (hon.), Polish Med. Soc. Magnetic Resonance (hon.), Internat. Soc. Endocrinology, French Endocrine Soc., Am. Fertility Soc., Polish Gynecologists' World Club (pres. 1988), N.Y. Acad. Scis., Internat. Soc. Prenatal and Perinatal Psychology and Medicine (pres. 1991). Avocation: highlanders' folklore. Home: Sebastiana 10/3, 31-049 Cracow Poland Office: Jagiellonian U Ob-Gyn Dept, Kopernika 23, 31-501 Cracow Poland

KLIMENKO, ALEXANDRE VICTOROVICH, physicist, researcher, educator; b. Moscow, USSR, Oct. 19, 1947; s. Victor Ivanovich and Tamara Romanovna (Trembatch) K.; m. Ekaterina Andreevna Fedorova, Sept. 7, 1974; 1 child, Victor. Diploma in engring., Moscow Energy Inst., 1971, PhD, 1975, DSc, 1990. Sr. rschr. Moscow Energy Inst., 1971-82, assoc. prof., vice rector rsch. dep., 1982-85, head rsch. divsn., 1985-90, vice rector on rsch., prof., 1990—; vis. scholar Oxford (Eng.) U., 1980; dep. head Russian Nat. Com. on Heat Transfer, 1993. Author: Monodispersion of Substance: Principles and Application, 1991, Energy, Nature, and Climate, 19979; editor: Handbook of Thermal Engineering, 1999; contbr. articles to profl. jours. Recipient 1st prize Rschr. of Yr. award Ministry for Higher Edn., 1985, 88, State award of Russia, Russian Govt., 1993. Mem. Russian Acad. Sci. Avocations: sports, travel. Home: AP 155 H1, 1812 Year St, 121170 Moscow Russia Office: Moscow Energy Inst, 14 Krasnokazarmennaya St, 111250 Moscow Russia

KLIMENKO, VLADIMIR, physics educator, earth/social science researcher; b. Moscow, Russia, Nov. 26, 1949; s. Victor and Tamara (Trembatch) K.; m. Irene Zenkova, July 31, 1996; 1 child, Anastassia. Diploma in engring., Moscow Energy Inst., 1972, PhD, 1975, DSc, 1985. Rsch. fellow Moscow Energy Inst. and Russian Acad. Scis., Moscow, 1972-88; prof. physics Russian Acad. Scis., Moscow, 1988-91, head global energy problems lab., 1989—; vis. scholar Oxford (Eng.) U., 1977-78, Helsinki Tech. U., Espoo, Finland, 1988-89; Alexander von Humboldt scholar Westphalian Wilhelms U., Munster, Germany, 1991-93, 96, Rhine Friedrich-Wilhelms U., Bonn, 1998; mem. heat transfer coun. USSR Acad. Sci., Moscow, 1986-91; heat transfer lab. dir. Moscow Energy Inst., 1988-92; dep. dir. Mining and Indsl. Co., Moscow, 1996-98; rep. Wolfson Coll., Oxford U., 1991—. Author: Boiling Cryogenic Liquids, 1995, Energy, Nature, and Climate, 1997; contbr. numerous articles to profl. jours. including Solar Physics, Acta Orientalia, Geophys. Rsch. Letters, and Meteorology and Hydrology. Mem. Internat. Acad. Refrigeration, Russian Acad. Refrigeration, Alexander von Humboldt Club, Internat. Acad. Scis., Russian Geog. Soc. Avocations: traveling, swimming, tennis. Home: 4 Mozhaiski Val Apt 40, 121151 Moscow Russia Office: Moscow Energy Inst, 14 Krasnokazarmennaya St, 111250 Moscow Russia

KLIMENKO, VLADIMIR YURIEVICH, physicist; b. Enakievo, USSR, Mar. 25, 1949; s. Yuri Petrovich Klimenko and Evgeniya Ivanovna Kompaniets; m. Zinaida Prokhorovna Korobtseva, Sept. 1, 1987. MSc, Moscow State U., 1971; PhD, Russian Acad. Sci., Moscow, 1981. Jr. rschr. Inst. Chem. Physics Russian Acad. Sci., Chernogolovka, 1972-85, sr. rschr. Inst. Chem. Physics, 1985-95, dir. High Pressure Ctr. Inst. Chem. Physics, 1990—; rsch. fellow U. Pierre and Marie Curie, Paris, 1993-95, U. St. Andrews, Eng., 1998—. Chmn. subcouncil Ministry Sci., Moscow, 1989-95, lider nat. program, 1992-93. Mem. Am. Phys. Soc. Home: 12-5, Central St, 142432 Chernogolovka Russia Office: Inst Chem Physics, 4, Kosygin St, 117334 Moscow Russia

KLIMLEY, NANCY LEE, volunteer, civic leader; b. Chgo.; d. William Peter and Flora (Sutherland) Enzweiler; m. Francis Joseph Klimley; children: Lisa, Brooks. BA, St. Mary's Coll., Notre Dame, Inc., 1951. Asst. fashion coord., dir. Carson Pirie Scott, Chgo.; asst. social dir. Lake Shore Club, Chgo., editor mag.; Chmn. women's divsn. Chgo. Heart Assn., 1958—, pres. women's coun., 3 times. Bd. dirs. Chgo. Boys and Girls Club, 1970—, Brookfield Zoo, 1982—, Libr. of Internat. Rels., 1980-92, Northwestern U. Settlement, 1962-78, Great Lakes Hosp. League, 1962, Boy Scouts Am., 1965, Aides to the Handicapped, 1965, ARC, Mus. of Scis.; bd. dirs. Children's Home and Aid Soc., 3-time pres. woman's bd., sponsor parent bd. 1962—; bd. dirs. Fashion Group, treas., 1958; bd. dirs. Am. Opera Soc., 1962-76, Ill. Opera Guild, 1962-76, Artists Adv. Coun., 1970-80, Republican Women Vols., 1958; bd. dirs., mem. exec. com. USO, 1980—, benefit chmn. 5 years, founder, pres. woman's adv. bd.; founding mem., benefit chmn. Joffrey Ballet; chmn., hon. chmn. The Consular Ball. Recipient Golden Heart award, Heart of Yr. award Am. Heart Assn., Fund Raising award Children's Home and Aid Soc., Golden Eagle award USO, others. Mem. Chgo. Hist. Soc., Guild of the Chgo. Hist. Soc., Antiquarians of the Art Inst. (life), Woman's Athletic Club (bd. dirs.), Saddle and Cycle Club. Republican. Roman Catholic. Avocations: antiques, collecting and reading books, world of fashion as an art form, interior decorating. Home: 3240 N Lake Shore Dr Chicago IL 60657-3954

KLIMOV, ALEXANDER IVANOVICH, virologist; b. Moscow, Mar. 25, 1943; s. Ivan Yakovlevich and Nina Timopheevna (Babkina) K.; m. Marina Lyubomirovna Khristova, Dec. 26, 1969; children: Petr Alexandrovich, Tatyana Alexandrovna. M in physics, Moscow State Univ., 1968; PhD, Rsch. Inst. Viral Preparatios, Moscow, 1975, D in virology, 1986. Rsch. asst. dept. biophysics Moscow State Univ., Moscow, 1968-71; jr., sr. rschr. Rsch. Inst. Viral Preparations, Moscow, 1971-86, head lab. of genetics of RNA Viruses, 1986-91, dir. world health orgn. Ctr. on Influenza, 1986-96; vis. scientist influenza br. divsn. viral & rickettsial dise Ctr. for Disease Control and Prevention, Atlanta, 1991-97, chief strain surveillance sect., 1997—; adv. Com. for Vaqccine and Sera Min. Public Health, Moscow, 1989-91, adv. Problem Commn. Influenza and Acute Respiratory Diseases, Moscow, 1987-91. Contbr. articles to profl. jours; inventor in field. Recipient Academician Tymakov's award Acad. of Medical Scis. USSR, 1988. Office: Influenza Br Ctr for Disease Control Mailstop G 16 1600 Clifton Rd NE Atlanta GA 30329-4018

KLIMOVIČ, MICHAL, pediatrician, anesthesiologist, internist; b. Czech Republic, Oct. 3, 1962; s. Frantisek and Vera (Galuska) K.; m. Zuzana Jakubik, Sept. 24, 1960; children: Adam, Natalie, Simon. MD, U. Masaryk, 1988. Med. Diplomate 1988. Resident Children's Hosp., Brno, Czech Republic, 1988-92; asst. chief pici Children's Hosp., 1995-96, chief picu, 1997. Co-author: Grant: ECMO Program, 1994, Grant: HFOV-Ventilation, 1995. Office: Childrens Hosp Mendel, Brno 662 63, Czech Republic

KLIMOWICZ, TADEUSZ, philologist; b. Berezovka, Belarus, May 2, 1950; s. Eugeniusz and Leokadia (Antonowicz) K.; m. Danuta Janina Stawecka, Mar. 26, 1975; children: Bartosz Pawel, Marta Aleksandra. MA, U. Wrocław, Poland, 1973. Asst. U. Wrocław, 1973-78, assoc. prof., 1978-87, asst. prof., 1987-92, prof., 1992-94, full prof., 1994—. Author: The Motives of Creation of Valerij Brjusov, 1988 (Prize of Minister 1989), Searching, Obsessed and Demented, 1992, Citizens of Arcadia, 1993, A Guide to Modern Russian Literature and its Environs, 1996 (Prize of Minister 1997). Home: Litewska 26/22, 51-354 Wrocław Poland Office: U Wrocław, Pocztowa 9, 53-313 Wrocław Poland

KLINE, DAVID ADAM, lawyer, educator, writer; b. Keota, Okla., Sept. 27, 1923; s. David Adam and Lucy Leila (Wood) K.; m. Ruthela Deal, Aug. 25, 1947; children: Steven, Timothy, Ruthanna. JD, Okla. U., 1950. Bar: Okla. 1949. Law clk., spl. master U.S. Dist. Ct. Okla., 1952-61; 1st asst. U.S. atty. We. Dist. Okla., 1961-69; judge We. Dist. Okla. U.S. Bankruptcy Ct., Oklahoma City, 1969-82; sr. shareholder Kline & Kline, Oklahoma City, 1983—; pres. Nat. Conf. Bankruptcy Judges 1977-78; mem. arbitration panel program U.S. Dist. Ct. (we. dist.) Okla., 1985— mem. faculty Fed. Jud. Ctr., Washington, Nat. Seminar Bankruptcy Judges, 1971-86; adj. prof. law Oklahoma City U., 1980-84; cons. Norton Bankruptcy Law and Practice, 1986, Callaghan & Co.; bd. dirs. Consumer Credit Counseling Svc. Ctr., Okla., chmn., 1992. Author: A Little Book (A New Thing in the Earth), 1993, A Little Book II (The Blood of the Lion), 1995, A little Book III (The Revelation), 1997, A Little Book IV (A Still Small Voice), 1998; digest editor Am. Bankruptcy Law jour., 1974-77; contbg. author Cowans Bankruptcy Law and Practice, 1983, interim and 1986 edits.; contg. co-writer Briefcase, 1988-2000. Fellow Am. Coll. Bankruptcy. Office: Kline & Kline 720 NE 63rd St Oklahoma City OK 73105-6405

KLINE, JAMES EDWARD, lawyer; b. Fremont, Ohio, Aug. 3, 1941; s. Walter J. and Sophia Kline; m. Mary Ann Bruening, Aug. 29, 1964; children: Laura Anne Kline, Matthew Thomas, Jennifer Sue. BS in Social Sci., John Carroll U., 1963; JD, Ohio State U., 1966; postgrad., Stanford U., 1991. Bar: Ohio, 1966, N.C., 1989, U.S. Tax. Ct., 1983. Assoc. Eastman, Stichter, Smith & Bergman, Toledo, 1966-70; ptnr. Eastman, Stichter, Smith & Bergman (name now Eastman & Smith), Toledo, 1970-84, Shumaker, Loop & Kendrick, Toledo, 1984-88; v.p., gen. counsel Aeroquip-Vickers, Inc. (formerly Trinova Corp.), Toledo, 1989-99; exec. v.p. Cavista Corp., 2000—; pres., CEO Cavalear Corp., Sylvania, Ohio, 2000—; corp. sec. Sheller-Globe Corp., 1977-84; adj. prof. U. Toledo Coll. Law, 1988-94; bd. dirs. Plastic Techs., Inc. Author: (with Robert Seaver) Ohio Corporation Law, 1988. Trustee Kidney Found. of Northwestern Ohio, Inc., 1972-81, pres., 1979-80; bd. dirs. Toledo Botanical Garden (formerly Crosby Gardens), 1974-80, pres., 1977-79; bd. dirs. Toledo Zool. Soc., 1983-96, pres., 1991-93; bd. dirs. Toledo Area Regional Transit Authority, 1984-90, pres., 1987-88; bd. dirs. Home Away From Home, Inc (Ronald McDonald House NW Ohio), 1983-88; trustee Toledo Symphony Orch., 1981—, St. John's H.S., 1988-91, Ohio Found. Ind. Colls., 1991-2000; trustee Lourdes Coll., 1988-96, chmn., 1994-96. Fellow Ohio Bar Found.; mem. ABA, Nat. Assn. Corp. Dirs., Ohio Bar Assn. (corp. law com. 1977—, chmn. 1983-86), Toledo Bar Assn., Mfrs. Alliance (chair Law Coun. II 1997-99), Toledo Area C. of C. (trustee 1994—, chmn. 2000—), Inverness Club, Toledo Club (trustee 1990-97), Stone Oak Country Club, Ottawa Skeet Club, Answer Club. Roman Catholic. Home: 216 Treetop Pl Holland OH 43528-8451 Office: Cauista Corp 6444 Monroe St Sylvania OH 43560-1430

KLINE, MARY FRANCES, graphic artist, sales executive; b. Balt., Mar. 13, 1961; d. Robert Joseph and Catherie Marie (O'Brien) Hagen; m. Michael Richard Kline, Oct. 19, 1985; 1 child, John Patrick. BFA, Kutztown State U., 1983. Graphic designer Mark Trece, Inc., Balt., 1983-84, Eichhorn Printing Co., Balt., 1984-85, Bruning Paint Co., Balt., 1985-86; mgr. arts and graphics Crown Cen. Petroleum Corp., Balt., 1986-91; acct. exec. Moneypenny Graphics, Inc., 1991-93; account exec. Harvey & Daus., Inc., Hunt Valley, Md., 1993-96; sales Fidelity Color, Inc., Lancaster, Pa., 1996-98, London Litho, Inc., Balt., 1998—. Mem. Am. Mktg. Assn. (bd. dirs. Balt. chpt.). Republican. Roman Catholic. Avocations: sports, travel. Home: 1382 North Bend Rd Jarrettsville MD 21084-1338 Office: London Litho Inc 11110 Pepper Rd Hunt Valley MD 21031-1203

KLINE, SIDNEY DELONG, JR., lawyer; b. West Reading, Pa., Mar. 25, 1932; s. Sidney D. and Leona Clarice (Barkalow) K.; m. Barbara Phyllis James, Dec. 31, 1955; children: Allison S. McCanney, Leslie S. Davidson, Lisa P. Gallen. BA, Dickinson Coll., 1954, LLD, 1998; JD with honors, The Dickinson Law Sch., 1956, LLD, 1994. Bar: Pa. 1956, U.S. Dist. Ct. (ea. dist.) Pa. 1961, U.S. Supreme Ct. 1967. Assoc. Stevens & Lee, Reading, Pa., 1958-62, ptnr., shareholder, 1963-97, pres., 1977-93, chmn., 1993-97, counsel, 1998—; bd. dirs. Reading Eagle Co. Pres., United Way of Berks County, Reading, 1972-74, campaign chmn., 1986; bd. dirs. Reading Ctr. City Devel. Fund, 1976-98, pres., 1992-97; trustee Dickinson Sch. Law, 1978—, sec., 1988—; trustee Dickinson Coll., 1979—, chmn., 1990-98; bd. dirs. Greater Berks Devel. Fund, 1998—. Served with U.S. Army, 1956-58. Recipient Doran award United Way Berks County, 1978, Richard J. Caron Cmty. Svc. award Caron Found., 1993, Thun Cmty. Svc. award, 1995. Fellow Am. Coll. Trust and Estate Coun., Nat. Soc. Fund Raising Execs. (Outstanding Vol. Fund Raiser Greater Northeastern Pa. chpt. 1992), Pa. Bar Assn., Berks County Bar Assn., Berkshire Country Club (Reading), Moselem Springs Golf Club (Fleetwood, Pa.), The Club at Pelican Bay (Naples, Fla.). Republican. Lutheran. Office: PO Box 679 111 N 6th St Reading PA 19603-0679

KLINE, STEPHEN THOMAS, communications executive; b. Des Moines, Feb. 2, 1950; s. Richard Charles and Elizabeth Mae (Feltenstein) K.; m. Susan Jane Lee, Aug. 26, 1972 (dec. Jul. 1982); m. Jean Ann Veenis-Kline, Sept. 01, 1985; children: Kaci Christine, Karyn Elizabeth, Sasha Noelle. BA, Luther Coll., 1986. Asst. news editor Omaha World Herald, Omaha, Nebr., 1973-80, sports editor, 1980-81; newsman The Associated

Press, Omaha, Nebr., 1981-83; dir. media rels. Creighton Univ., Omaha, Nebr., 1984-90; state broadcast editor The Associated Press, Omaha, Nebr., 1990-96; dir. pub. rels. Creighton Univ., Omaha, Nebr., 1996—. Author: (video) A More Perfect Union, 1987; contbr. articles to profl. jours. Bd. dirs. Downtown Omaha, Inc., 1998—. Recipient Journalist of Yr. award Sigma Delta Chi, 1995. E-mail: skline@creighton.edu. Office: Creighton Univ 2500 California Plz Omaha NE 68178-0001

KLING, PHRADIE (PHRADIE KLING GOLD), small business owner; b. N.Y.C., July 2, 1933; d. Samuel A. and Mary Leah (Cohen) K.; m. Lee M. Gold, Sept. 5, 1955 (div. 1976); children: Judith Eileen, Laura Susan, Stephen Samuel, James David. BA, Cornell U., 1955; MA in Human Genetics, Sarah Lawrence Coll., 1971. Genetic counselor assoc. Coll. Medicine and Dentistry N.J., Newark, 1970-73; assoc. genetic counselor Sarah Lawrence Coll., Bronxville, N.Y., 1970-73; genetic counselor N.Y. Fertility Rsch. Found., N.Y.C., 1971-73; staff assoc., genetic counselor depts. pediatrics, ob-gyn and neurology Columbia U. Coll. Physicians and Surgeons, N.Y.C., 1973-78; asst. in genetics St. Luke's Hosp. Ctr., N.Y.C., 1977-79; health program assoc. Conn. Dept. Health Svcs., Hartford, 1978-84; edn. cons. Conn. Traumatic Brain Injury Assn., Rocky Hill, 1984-85; office mgr. Anderson Turf Irrigation Inc., Plainville, Conn., 1986-92; owner, mgr. KlingWorks, contract adminstrn., Avon, Conn., 1992—; speaker, instr. on health and health ethics issues, Conn., N.Y., N.J., 1971-85; dir. confs. on genetics and traumatic brain injury, 1980-85; project dir. ednl. field testing Biol. Scis. Curriculum Study, 1981-83; scientist AAAS Sci.-by-Mail, 1991-2000. Mem. Farmington River Watershed Assn., Simsbury, Conn., 1988—; docent Sci. Mus. Conn., West Hartford, 1989-90. Recipient citation for dedicated svc. Conn. Safety Belt Coalition, 1985. Mem. Am. Human Genetics Soc., Bus. and Profl. Microcomputer Users Group (bd. dirs.), Conn. Assn. for Jungian Psychology (bd. dirs.), Am. Mensa (chpt. coord. gifted children 1985—). Avocations: computer genealogy, canoeing, swimming, music. Home and Office: 33 Hunter Rd Avon CT 06001-3618

KLINGBIEL, PAUL HERMAN, information science consultant; b. Watertown, Wis., Nov. 3, 1919; s. Herman Carl and Elsa Helen (Zilisch) K.; m. Mildred Louise Wells, Nov. 30, 1968; stepchildren: Alice J. Blessley, Jo Ann Grayson. PhB, U. Chgo., 1948, BS, 1950; MA, Am. U., 1966. Abstractor Armed Svcs. Tech. Info. Agy., Dept. Def., Washington, 1953-58; editor Tech. Abstract Bull., 1958-60; dir. Office of Lexicography, 1960-66; phys. sci. adminstr., linguistics rsch. Def. Documentation Ctr., 1966-79; sr. cons. Aspen Systems Corp., 1979-81; systems analyst PRC Data Svcs. Co., Linthicum Heights, Md., 1981-82; lectr. Am. U., Washington, 1966-69; cons. divsn. med. scis. Nat. Acad. Scis., 1969-70. Contbr. articles to profl. jours. With AUS, 1943-46. Recipient Meritorious Civilian Svc. award, 1974, Disting. Career award, 1979. Fellow AAAS; mem. Assn. Computational Linguistics, N.Y. Acad. Scis. Lutheran. Achievements include research in the field of computational linguistics.

KLINGENBERG, CHRISTIAN FRIEDRICH, scientific research educator; b. Hamburg, Germany, Dec. 26, 1955; s. Wilhelm and Christine K.; m. Dietlind B. Reichle, June, 1989; children: Esther, Sophia. PhD, NYU, 1984; habilitation, Heidelberg (Germany) U., 1993. Asst. prof. Heidelberg (Germany) U., 1986-95; prof. Wurzburg (Germany) U., 1995—. Contbr. articles to profl. jours. Avocations: singing in a profl. choir, listening to classical music, astronomy. Home: 3-4 Pleikartsforsterhof, 69124 Heidelberg Germany Office: Wurzburg U Dept Math, Am Hubland, 97074 Würzburg Germany

KLINGENBERG, CLAUS ANDREAS, pediatrician; b. Oslo, Norway, Feb. 25, 1967; s. Rolf Georg and Cecilie (Landmark) K.; m. Anne-Grete Sandaune, Mar. 18, 1999. MD, U. Ulm, Germany, 1993. Intern, 1992-94; mil. physician Norwegian Air Force, 1994-95; resident in pediat. Univ. Hosp. Tromsø, Norway, 1995—. Lt. Norwegian Air Force, 1994-95. Mem. Assn. Norwegian Physicians. Office: Univ Hosp, Dept Pediat, N-9038 Tromsø Norway

KLINGENHAGEN, DECLAN FRED, retired engineer, consultant; b. San Diego, May 21, 1926; s. Fred John Klingenhagen and Alice May Ryan; m. Ann Constance Williams, May 31, 1952; children: Ann Marie, Alice Jean, Fred John II, David Declan, Valerie Joan. BSEE, Cath. U. Am., 1950. Profl. engr. N.J., N.Y., Ill., Ala., Pa. S.C. Engr. various cos., 1951-54; from engr. to dept. chief Western Elec. Co., N.Y.C., 1954-74, sr. engr., 1977-81; dist. mgr. Bell Sys. Ctr., Lisle, Ill., 1974-77; mem. rev. bd. OSHA, Columbia, S.C., 1992-99; pvt. practice cons. Columbia, 1981—.

KLINGENSTEIN, WERNER, physicist; b. Goeppingen, Germany, Oct. 1, 1949; s. Wilhelm and Elisabeth (Nill) K.; m. Marlies Maczey, Apr. 14, 1978; 1 child, Annemarie. Diplomate, U. Stuttgart, Germany, 1976, PhD, 1980. Rschr. U. Stuttgart, 1976-80; with Siemens AG, Munich, 1980-90, Siemens SCI, Burlington, Vt., 1990-92; mgr. R&D Siemens AG, Munich, 1993-99; tech. strategies Infineon Techs. AG, 1999—. Inventor in field. Mem. IEEE, Deutsche Physikalische Gesellschaft. Home: Latschenweg 1, D-85551 Kirchheim Germany Office: Infineon AG, St Martinstrasse 53, D-81541 Munich Germany

KLINGER, DOUGLAS EVAN, money management executive; b. Phila., Dec. 22, 1964; s. Norman Ashton and Sondra Ann Klinger; m. Jennifer Ann Dobrota, Apr. 11, 1992. BA in Econs. and Finance, Trinity Coll., Hartford, Conn., 1986. Mem. instnl. brokerage Kidder Peabody and Co. Inc., Hartford, 1984-86; credit analyst Provident Nat. Bank, Phila., 1986-87, relationship mgr. PNC Fin. Corp., 1987-88; dir. corp. markets PNC Instnl. Mgmt. Corp., Wilmington, Del., 1988-90; v.p., dir. corp. markets mgmt. Provident Instnl. Mgmt. Corp., Lehman/Provident IFG, Wilmington, Del., 1990-92; mng. dir. PNC Bank Investment Mgmt. & Rsch., Phila., 1993-98; dir. mktg. PNC Funds, Phila., 1993-98; pres. Cigna Health Svcs., Hartford, Conn., 1998—. Mentor Free Enterprise Fellowships Program. Mem. Trinity Club Phila., Skytop Club, St. A Club of Phila., Pa. Horticultural Soc., U.S. Treasury Mgmt. Assn. Avocations: sailing, fishing, skiing, gardening, reading. Home: 2 Grant Estate Rd West Simsbury CT 06092-2100 Office: Cigna Corp 900 Cottage Grove Rd Hartford CT 06152-0001

KLINGER, MICHAEL ISRAEL, physicist; b. Baltsi, USSR, Nov. 10, 1930; arrived in Israel, 1994; s. Israel and Sara K.; m. Irina Ashkinazi, Nov. 12, 1959; 1 child, Pavel. PhD, Inst. Physics, Kiev, USSR, 1954; DSc, Inst. Metal Physics, Sverdlovsk, USSR, 1964. Assoc. prof. U. Chernovits, USSR, 1954-56; from rschr. to prin. scientist Ioffe Phys.-Tech. Inst., Leningrad, USSR, 1956-91, prof., 1991—; prof. U. Bar Ilan, Tel Aviv, Israel, 1994—. Author: Quantum Theory of Electron Transport in Semiconductors, 1976, Problems of Transport Theory in Semiconductors, 1979, Atomic Quantum Diffusion in Solids, 1983, Glassy Disordered Systems, 1988. Fellow Trinity Coll., Cambridge (Eng.) U., 1994—. Fellow Russian Phys. Soc.; mem. Israel Phys. Soc. Office: Bar Ilan Univ, Ramat Gan, 52900 Tel Aviv Israel

KLINGER, WOLFGANG GOTTFRIED, pharmacologist, toxicologist; b. Stadtroda, Germany, July 3, 1933; s. Heinrich Paul and Frieda Carla (Kaiser) K.; m. Helga Erna Schneider Klinger, Mar. 1, 1958; children: Matthias, Barbara. MD, Med. Faculty U. Jena, 1957; specialist in Pharmacology, 1963, MD, 1966; MD, 1970. Sr. rsch. and teaching asst. Med. Faculty U. Jena, Germany, 1963-66; lectr. for Pharmacology and Toxicology, 1966-69, full prof. of Pharmacology, 1969-73, full prof. of Pharmacology and Toxicology, 1973—, dir. Inst. Pharmacology Toxicology, 1973-98; dean Med. Faculty U. Jena, Germany, 1974-81, 90-93. Author: Unwanted Side Effects, 5 edits., 1969-89; contbr. papers, review articles and monographs to profl. jours. Avocations: piano, flute, horses, travel. Home: Am Pfaffenstieg 3, D-07743 Jena Germany Office: Inst Pharm Toxicology, Nonnenplan 4, D-07743 Jena Germany

KLINK, KURT, chemist; b. Tubingen, Germany, Oct. 12, 1954; s. Hans and Kirsten (Eiken) K.; m. Eve Vogt, July 15, 1983; children: Ingmar, Arne. D in Natural Scis., Tech. U., Clausthal, 1984. Product mgr. Perstorp Analytical GmbH, Rodgau, Germany, 1985-86; head chemistry dept. Gebr. Heyl GmbH & Co., Hildesheim, Germany, 1986-90; lab. mgr. Riedel-de Haen AG, Seelze, Germany, 1990-94; mng. dir. KKC Dr. Klink GmbH, Neuenberg, Germany, 1995—. Contbr. articles to profl. jours. Mem. German Chem. Assn., Am. Chem. Soc. Home: Neumarker Str 23, 4 Rue d'Ensisheim, F-68740 Rumersheim-le-Haut France Office: Riedel-de Haen AG, Wimsorfer Str 40, Abt TV (QK), D-3016 Seelze Germany

KLINK, ROBERT MICHAEL, consulting engineer, management consultant, financial consultant, property developer; b. Hamilton, Ind., Sept. 5, 1939; s. Robert Eli and Marie Ann Klink; m. Jessie Joyce Plummer, Sept. 10, 1960 (dec. Feb. 1966); children: Kevin Mark, Kent Michael, Kelly Martin, Kris Montgomery, Jeffrey Arthur. Student, Tri State Coll., Angola, Ind., 1957; degree in Hwy. Engring., Purdue U., 1959; cert. in grad. sch. mgmt., Harvard U., 1976. Cert. behavorial cons. Hwy. engr. Ind. State Hwy. Commn., Ft. Wayne, 1959-65; staff engr. Cities Svc. Oil Co., Inc., South Bend, Ind., 1965-66; client svcs. mgr., asst. to v.p. Clyde E. Williams & Assocs., South Bend, 1966-72; pres. Alpha Devel. Corp., South Bend, 1970-72; sr. v.p., CFO Snell Environ. Group, Inc., Lansing, Mich., 1972-77; pres. Klink Devel. Co., Dayton, Ohio, 1972-91; pres., chmn. Solar GeoThermo Energy Systems, Inc., Dayton, 1982—; pres., mng. ptnr. Klink Enterprises Co., Dayton, 1977—; pres., chmn. bd. Design Enterprise, Ltd., Dayton, 1977-91; chmn., pres. Cons. Info. Agy., Chattanooga, 1991—; bd. dirs. Pono Kai Resort, Kapaa, Kauai, Hawaii, Imperial Hawaii, Honolulu; cons. World Bank/USAID, Dacca, Bangladesh, Country of Brazil, Rio de Janeiro; cons. engr., mgmt. cons., project developer, cons. to govtl. agys. and Fortune 500 cos.; lectr., spkr. in field. Patentee Solar and Geo Thermo Energy System; co-author: Water Handling Handbook, 1977. Trustee Centerville (Ohio) Cmty. Ch., 1982-88, Okemos (Mich.) Cmty. Ch., 1972-77; mem. The Presdl. Roundtable, Washington, 1989—, Rep. Senatorial Inner Circle, Washington, 1985—, Nat. Rep. Congrl. Com., 1986—, The Presidents Assn.; tchr. Woodland Park Bapt. Ch., Chattanooga; mem. Woodland Park Bapt. Ch. Chattanooga, 1998—; mem. Downtown Kiwanas Club Chattanooga. Recipient Outstanding Citizen award Am. Legion, Butler, Ind., 1953, Resolution of Appreciation Centerville City Coun., 1978, Resolution of Appreciation Greene County, 1989; named Hon. Citizen of Tenn., Nashville, 1989. Mem. Am. Water Works Assn. (life), Nat. Water Pollution Control Fedn., Profl. Svcs. Mgmt. Assn. (com. chair), Soc. for Mktg. Profl. Svcs. (com. chair), Ind. Hoosier Assocs., Ohio Early Birds. Christian and Missionary Alliance. Avocations: gardening, landscaping, woodworking, classic automobiles, golf.

KLINKENBERG, JEAN-MARIE, humanities educator, researcher, consultant; b. Verviers, Liege, Belgium, Oct. 8, 1944; s. Louis and Marie (Gerard) K.; children: Hugo, Marie, Fanny-Sun. Lic. in arts, State U. Liege, 1967, D in Arts, 1971. Asst. State U. Liege, 1967-79, prof., 1979—; vis. prof. at various univs., Montreal, Aachen, Urbino, Jyvaskyla, Oviedo, Sao Paulo, Mexico, Brussels, Leuven, Tel Aviv, among others; cons. Labor (Pub.), Brussels, 1984—, Larousse (Pub.), Paris, 1986—. Author: Rhetorique Generale, 1982, Style et Archaisme dans La Legende d'Ulenspiegel de Charles De Coster, 1973, Rhetorique de la Poesie: Lecture Lineaire, Lecture Tabulaire, 1977, Collages, 1978, A Semiotic Landscape, 1979, Rhetoriques, Semiotiques, 1979, La Litterature Francaise de Belgique, 1980, Langages et Collectivites: Le Cas du Quebec, 1981, (with Lise Gauvin) Trajectoires: Litterature et Institutions au Quebec et en Belgique Francophone, 1985, Charles De Coster, 1985, Raymond Queneau, Andre Blavier: Lettres Croisees, 1949-76, 1988, Le Sens Rhetorique, Essais de Semantique Litteraires, 1990, Ecrivain Cherche Lecteur, L'ecrivain Francophone et ses publics, 1991, Traite du Signe Visuel, Pour une Rhetorique de L'Image, 1992, Espace Nord l'Anthologie, 1994, Des Langues Romanes, Introduction aux Etudes Linguistique Romane, 1994, Sept Lecons de Semiotique et de Rhetorique, 1996, (with Daniel Blampain, Andre Goosse, and Marc Wilmet) Une Langue, Une Communaute, Le Francais en Belgique, 1997, Precis de semiotique generale, 2000; contbr. over 400 articles in 15 langs. to profl. jours. Pres. Coun. French Lang., Brussels, 1993-99, Commn. for Pub., Brussels, 1984. Decorated Francaise Found., 1996; decorated Ordre des Francophones d'Amerique (Que., Can.), Ordre de Leopold II (Belgium), Ordre de la Couronne (Belgium), Ordre des Arts et Lettres (France); grantee Francaise Found., 1996. Mem. Internat. Assn. for Visual Semiotics (v.p. 1992). Avocations: trekking, gliding, reading, painting, swimming. Home: Fond Pirette 125, B-4000 Liege Belgium Office: State U Liege, 3 Place Cockerill, B-4000 Liege Belgium

KLIPPERT, RICHARD HOBDELL, JR., engineering executive; b. Oakland, Calif., Jan. 25, 1940; s. Richard Hobdell and Carol Ione (Knight) K.; m. Penelope Ann Barker, Sept. 5, 1979; children: David, Deborah, Candice, Kristina. BS in Bus., Oreg. State U., 1962; postgrad. in polit. sci., U. Calif., Berkeley, 1968-69; postgrad. in polit. sci. and mgmt., George Washington U., 1972-73; grad., Naval War Coll., 1973. Commd. ensign USN, 1962, advanced through grades to comdr., 1971, ret., 1982, expert Antisubmarine Warfare; mem. Combat Search and Rescue, Southeast Asia, 1964-67; exec. officer H.S. Squadron, 1974; mem. Flag Staff, 1974-79; chief engr. Light Airborne Multipurpose Sys. MK-III, Washington, 1979-82; sr. engr., mgr. IBM, 1982-83, engring. mgr., 1983-84, mgr. HH-60 sys. engring., 1984-85, mgr. V-22 engring., 1985-88, program mgr. Document Mgmt. Sys. Integration, 1988—, dir. publ. solutions, 1990—; program mgr. USDA SCOAP/ASCS Programs, 1992; program mgr. SAIC, Sacramento, 1997—, dir. Syss. Integration Solutions divsn.; capture mgr. WARSIM Program, 1994; loaned exec. Boulder County United Way, 1993; dir. USDA FSA programs Unisys Fed. Sys., 1995-97; acct. exec. FDA. Author: The Moon Book, 1971; contbr. papers to tech. lit. Decorated Silver Star, Navy Commendation; recipient Outstanding Achievement and golden Circle awards IBM, 1986, Cert. Program Mgr., 1993. Mem. Soc. Naval Engrs., Assn. Image and Info. Mgmt., Soc. Automotive Engrs., Naval inst., Sigma Chi. Republican. Avocations: golf, tennis, photography, bridge. Office: SAIC 3800 Watt Ave Sacramento CA 95821-2670

KLIŠKIĆ, MAJA, chemical engineering educator, researcher; b. Split, Croatia, Oct. 16, 1953; d. Vladimir and Neva (Brkljačić) Miletić; m. Lorenco Kliškić, Oct. 4, 1980; children: Nevena, Danica. BSc in Chem. Tech., Faculty of Tech., Split, 1980, MSc in Chem. Engring., 1991, PhD in Chem. Engring., 1994. Asst. of electrochemistry Faculty of Tech., Split, 1983-94; asst. prof. dept. electrochem. and material protection Faculty of Chem. Tech., Split, 1994—. Contbr. articles to profl. jours. Mem. Croatian Chem. Soc., Croatian Soc. Chem. Engring., N.Y. Acad. Scis. Roman Catholic. Home: Starčevićeva 24, 21000 Split Croatia Office: Faculty of Chem Tech, Teslina 10/V, 21000 Split Croatia

KLISSURSKI, DIMITAR GEORGIEV, chemistry educator, researcher; b. Glogene, Lovech, Bulgaria, Dec. 16, 1933; s. Georgi Dikov and Rada (Ivanova) K.; m. Dikova Rumiana Petkova, Apr. 17, 1966; 1 child, Radosveta. BSc, Tech. U. Sofia, Bulgaria, 1956, MSc, 1957; Ph D, Bulgarian Acad. Scis., Sofia, 1968, DSc, 1981. Rsch. officer Inst. Gen. and Inorganic Chemistry, Sofia, Bulgaria, 1959-70; assoc. prof. Inst. Gen. and Inorganic Chemistry, Sofia, 1970-83, prof., 1983—; dep. dir. Inst. of Gen. and Inorganic Chemistry, Sofia, 1972-93,; dir. rsch. lab., 1975—. Author: (books) Sulphuric Acid, 1968, Heterogeneous Catalysis, 1971.; contbr. numerous articles to internat. profl. jours.; mem. editl. bd. Jour. Materials Chemistry and Physics, 1978-92. Mem. Coun. Internat. Congress on Catalysis, 1992, Internat. Mechanochem. Assn., 1990. Decorated Kiril I Metodi order, Bulgarian Govt., Sofia, 1972; named to a Disting. Svc. Order, Bulgarian Acad. Scis., 1978; recipient N.S. Kurnakov medal Russian Acad. Scis., 1985. Mem. Bulgarian Chem. Soc., Bulgarian Club of Catalysis, Bulgarian Mechanochem. Soc. (pres. 1988—). Avocations: fishing, tourism. Office: Bulgarian Acad Scis, Inst Gen & Inorganic Chem, 1113 Sofia Bulgaria

KLISZCZ, JOANNA ELIZABETH, psychologist; b. Walbrzych, Poland, Apr. 23, 1956; d. Seweryn Rozen and Jozefa Dudzinska; m. Andrzej Kliszcz, Dec. 24, 1988; 1 child. MA, Theol. Acad. of Warsaw, 1979; PhD in Psychology, U. Gdansk, Poland, 1993. Asst. Mental Clinic, Gdansk, 1982-88; asst. Dept. of Family Medicine, Med. U. of Gdansk, Gdansk, 1987, tutor, 1995—. Co-author: Manual on Communication Between Doctor and Patient, 1993, 2d edit., 1999; contbr. articles to profl. publs. Mem. med. edn. com. Polish Acad. Scis., 1993-95. Mem. Assn. of Med. Edn. in Europe, N.Y. Acad. Scis. Avocations: books, traveling, natural films. E-mail: jks@box43.gnet.pl. Home: Oskara Kolberga 17/1, 81-881 Sopot Poland Office: Med U Gdansk Dept Fam Med, ul Debinki 2, 80-211 Gdansk Poland

KLITZING, KLAUS VON, research facility administrator, physicist; b. Schroda, June 28, 1943; s. Bogislav and Anny (Ulbrich) von K.; m. Renate Falkenberg, May 27, 1971; children: Andreas, Christine, Thomas. Diploma, Tech. U. Braunschweig, 1969; Ph.D., U. Wuerzburg, 1972; Habilitation, 1978. Faculty mem. Tech. U., Munich, 1980-84; dir. Max Planck Institut KFK, Stuttgart, Fed. Republic Germany, 1985—. Recipient Nobel prize in physics Royal Swedish Acad. Sci., 1985. Office: Max Planck Inst Feskörperforschung, Heisenbergstr 1, D-70569 Stuttgart Germany

KLITZING, LEBRECHT VON, medical physicist; b. Neuweisstritz, Poland, Apr. 1, 1939; s. Bogislav von and Anny (Ulbrich) K.; m. Lisa Hille, May 5, 1966 (div. 1989); children: Regine, Peter; m. Gaby Tessmann, May 11, 1990; children: Esther, Marie-Therese. Diploma and Drs. Degree, Tech. U. Braunschweig, Germany, 1966. Asst. Tech. U. Braunschweig, 1966-67, Max-Planck Inst., Wilhelmshaven, Germany, 1967-69, Gesellschaft fuer Molekularbiol. Forschung, Braunschweig, 1969-70, U. Bonn, Germany, 1970-75; head dept. clin. rsch. Med. U. Luebeck, Germany, 1975—. Contbr. some 95 articles to profl. jours.; presenter in field. Home: Lohstrasse 170A, D-23617 Stockelsdorf Germany Office: Med U, Ratzeburger Allee 160, D-23538 Lübeck Germany

KLITZMAN, ROBERT LLOYD, physician, author; b. N.Y.C., July 1, 1958; s. Joseph Arthur and Joan Marilyn (Kahn) K. AB, Princeton U., 1980; MD, Yale U., 1985. Diplomate Am. Bd. Psychiatry and Neurology. Rsch. asst. Nat. Inst. Health, Bethesda, Md., 1980-81; researcher Papua New Guinea Inst. Med. Rsch., 1980-81; intern The N.Y. Hosp. Cornell U. Med. Ctr., N.Y.C., 1985-86, resident, 1986-89; fellow Columbia Presbyn. Med. Ctr., N.Y.C., 1989-96, asst. prof. clin. psychiatry, 1996—, asst. prof. sch. pub. health, 2000—. Author: A Year-long Night, 1989, In a House of Dreams and Glass, 1995, Being Positive: The Lives of Men and Women with HIV, 1997, The Trembling Mountain, 1998; contbr. articles to profl. jours., chpts. to books. Recipient Keese prize Yale U., 1985; Robert Wood Johnson Found. clin. scholar U. Pa., 1991-93; DuPont fellow, 1982, Burroughs-Wellcome fellow Am. Psychiat. Assn., 1987, MacDowell Colony fellow, 1991, Aaron Diamond Found. fellow, 1993-96, Merck Co. Found. fellow Corp. of Yaddo, 1994; Picker-Commonwealth scholar, 1996-98, vis. scholar Russell Sage Found., 1999-2000; NIMH Career Devel. awardee, 1996-99. Mem. PEN, Am. Psychiat. Assn. (mem. N.Y. County dist. br. com. on AIDS 1989—, commn. on AIDS 1988-89, steering com. of AIDS edn. project 1987-88).

KLOCHKOVA, VALENTINA, astrophysicist; b. Zhuravskoe, Russia, Apr. 1, 1947; d. Georij Ivanovich and Raisa Efimovna (Stepantsova) Rysukhina; m. Sergei Nikolaevich Klochkov, June 27, 1970 (div.); m. Vladimir Eugenjevich Panchuk; 1 child, Nonna. DSc, Spl. Astrophys. Observatory, 1992. Rschr. Spl. Astrophys. Observatory, Cherkessian Republic, 1970-91, scientist, 1992-96, head of lab., 1996—. E-mail: valenta@sao.ru. Home: Building 2 app 28, 369167 Nizhnij Arkhyz Russia Office: Spl Astrophys Observatory, 357147 Nizhnij Arkhyz Russia

KLOCHKOVA, YANA, olympic athlete; b. Simferopol, Ukraine. Mem. swim team Ukraine; winner silver in 400 meter medley World Championship, 1998; winner gold in 200 meter individual medley Olympics, Sydney, Australia, 2000, winner gold in 400 meter individual medley, 2000. Office: Ukrainian Swimming Fedn, Esplanadna str 42, Kiev-23 252023, Ukraine*

KLOCKNER, CONSTANTIN, orthopaedic surgeon; b. Frankfurt, Germany, Jan. 16, 1964; s. Hermann and Sigried (Krug) K. MD, J.W. Goethe U., Frankfurt, 1992. Physician German Scoliosis Ctr., Bad Wildungen, 1993-94; physician Traumatology, Frankfurt, 1994-95, Fulda, 1995-96; orthopaedic surgeon Free U., Berlin, 1996—. Recipient fellowship COTREL, 1999. Office: Orthopaedic U Clin Free U, Clayallee 229, D-14195 Berlin Germany

KLOEHN, RALPH ANTHONY, plastic surgeon; b. Milw., Dec. 18, 1932; s. Ralph Charles and Virginia Mary (Kosak) K.; m. Mary Theresa Landers, Nov. 4, 1961; Children: Colleen, Gregory, Kristine, Patricia, Timothy, Philip, Michelle. BS, Marquette U., 1954, MD, 1958. Diplomate Am. Bd. Plastic Surgery. Rotating intern Charity Hosp. La., New Orleans, 1958-59; gen. surgery resident Marquette U. Hosps., Milw., 1961-65; resident in plastic and maxillofacial surgery U. Tex. Med. Br., Galveston, 1965-68; fellowship in plastic and reconstructive surgery African Med. Rsch. Found., Nairobi, Kenya, 1968-69; pvt. practice medicine specializing in plastic surgery Milw., 1969—; med. cons. McGhan Med. Corp., Santa Barbara, Calif., Mentor/Sonique Surg. Sys., Santa Barbara. Contbr. articles to profl. jours. Lt. USNR, 1959-61. Fellow ACS, Internat. Coll. Surgeons; mem. AMA, Am. Soc. Aesthetic Plastic Surgery, Am. Soc. Plastic Surgery, Am. Soc. Maxillofacial Surgeons, Can. Soc. Aesthetic for (Cosmetic) Plastic Surgery. Republican. Roman Catholic. Avocations: photography, sports fishing, watercolor painting. Home: N14 W 30082 High Ridge Rd # 5 Pewaukee WI 53072 Office: Affiliated Cosmetic and Plastic Surgeons 2323 N Mayfair Rd Ste 503 Milwaukee WI 53226-1507

KLOEPPER, DAVID ALAN, management consultant; b. Colby, Kans., Dec. 8, 1945; s. Robert Mayer and Justine (Peterson) K.; m. Evelyn Maria Gritzbach, June 27, 1969. BS in Metallurgy, MIT. Process devel. engr. Grumman Aerospace, Bethpage, N.Y., 1968-72; mgr. svc. engring. Hilti, Inc., Stamford, Conn., 1972-79; nat. sales mgr. F & S Cen. Mfg., Bklyn., 1979-82; v.p. ops. and adminstrn. Imperial Bolt & Mfg. Co., South Plainfield, N.J., 1982-85; nat. sales mgr. Indsl. Bolt & Nut, Irvington, N.J., 1985-86, T.A. & D.A. Troy, Fairfield, N.J., 1986-87; project mgr. Don Aux Assocs., Hasbrouck Heights, N.J., 1987—, practice leader, 1992—. Pres. Van Vorst Park Neighborhood Assn., Jersey City, 1981-82. Republican. Avocations: movies, classical music. Home: 308 Varick St Jersey City NJ 07302-3404 Office: Don Aux Assocs 777 Terrace Ave Hasbrouck Heights NJ 07604-3110

KLOESS, LAWRENCE HERMAN, JR., lawyer; b. Mamaroneck, N.Y., Jan. 30, 1927; s. Lawrence H. and Harriette Adelia (Holly) K.; m. Eugenia Ann Underwood, Nov. 10, 1931; children: Lawrence H. III, Price Mentzel, Branch Donelson, David Holly. AB, U. Ala., 1954, JD, 1956; grad., Air Command & Staff Coll., 1974, Air War Coll., 1976; grad. Indsl. Coll. of the Armed Forces, Nat. Def. U., 1977. Bar: Ala. 1956, U.S. dist. Ct. (no. dist.) Ala. 1956, U.S. Ct. Appeals (5th cir.) 1957, U.S. Ct. Mil. Appeals 1971, U.S. Supreme Ct. 1971, U.S. Ct. Appeals (11th cir.) 1981. Sole practice Birmingham, Ala., 1956-60, 62-66; corp. counsel Bankers Fire and Marine Ins. Co., 1961-62; dist. counsel for Ala. Office Dist. Counsel U.S. Dept. Vets. Affairs, Montgomery, 1966-95. Contbr. articles on law to profl. jours. Vice chmn. Salvation Army adv. bd., 1981, mem. bd., 1978-81; mem. nat. conf. bar pres.'s ABA, 1981—; mem. adminstrn. bd. Frazer Meml. United Meth. Ch., 1987-90, 92—; mem. adv. coun. Ret. and Sr. Vol. Program, Montgomery, 1997—; mem. Montgomery Symphony League, 2000—. Col. Judge Adv. Gen. USAFR, 1954-86, ret. Bd. dirs., sec. Air Force Judge Adv. Gen. Sch. Found., 1996—. Decorated Legion of Merit, Meritorious Svc. medal with oak leaf cluster, USAF Commendation medal; named Outstanding Judge Advocate USAFR, 1977, 79. Mem. ABA (nat. conf. bar. pres. 1981—), Ala. State Bar Assn. (chmn. editl. adv. bd. Ala. Lawyer 1975-79, editl. bd. 1970-82, character and fitness com., chmn. law day com. 1973, chmn. citizen edn. com. 1974, CLE adv. com. 1983), Ala. Law Found. (trustee), Montgomery County Bar Assn. (chmn. law day com. 1972, chmn. state bar liaison com. 1975, chmn. bd. dirs. 1977, bd. dirs. 1979, chmn. and editor Montgomery County Bar Jour., ABA Merit award 1979-80, v.p. 1980, pres. 1981), Fed. Bar Assn. (pres. Montgomery Fed. Bar Assn. 1973), Citizens Conf. on Ala. Ct. (exec. com., sponsor of new jud. article to state constn. 1973), Citizens Conf. on Criminal and Juvenile Justice (mem. staff 1974), Farrah Law Soc., REs. Officers Assn. of U.S. (chpt. pres. 1978, state pres. 1982), Air Force Ret. Judge Adv. Assn., Ret. Officers Assn. (life), Air War Coll. Alumni Assn. (life), Sigma Delta Kappa (pres. U. Ala. chpt.), Theta Chi (Outstanding Alumni award 1976), Montgomery Capital Rotary Club (pres. 1979, Paul Harris fellow), Montgomery Rotary Club (v.p. 1996, pres. 1998), Maxwell-Gunter Officers (Montgomery), Capital City Club, Montgomery Country Club, Blue Gray Cols. Assn., Mystic Soc. (Krewe of phantom host), Hon. Order Ky. Cols., Svc. Corps. of Ret. Execs. Assn. (bd. dirs. 1996—), Ala. Soc. for Cripple Children and Adults (bd. dirs. 1999—), English Speaking Union (bd. dirs. 1997—). Republican. Home: 7157 Pinecrest Dr Montgomery AL 36117-7413

KLOEWER, JUTTA MARINA, materials scientist; b. Minden, Germany, July 17, 1955; m. Martin K.E. Voigt, Dec. 5, 1997. Diploma in engring., U.

Hannover, 1982; PhD, U. Aachen, 1989. Jr. scientist Max-Planck-Inst fur Eisenforschung, Dusseldorf, Germany, 1986-89; head high temperature lab. Krupp VDM, Germany, 1989-98, mgr. application engring. and process devel., 1989—. Coord. Amnesty Internat., London, 1997—. Mem. German Soc. Materials (bd. cons.), Am. Soc. Materials. Office: Krupp VDM, Kleffstasse 23, 58762 Altena Germany

KLOHS, MURLE WILLIAM, chemist, consultant; b. Aberdeen, S.D., Dec. 24, 1920; s. William Henry and Lowell (Lewis) K.; m. Dolores Catherine Borm, June 16, 1946; children: Wendy C., Linda L. Student Westmar Coll., 1938-40; BSc, U. Notre Dame, 1947. Jr. chemist Harrower Lab., Glendale, Calif., 1947, Rexall Drug Co., L.A., 1947-49; sr. chemist Riker Labs., Inc., L.A., 1949-57, dir. medicinal chemistry, Northridge, Calif., 1957-69, mgr. chem. rsch. dept., 1969-72, mgr. pharm. devel. dept., 1972-73, mgr. tech. liaison and comml. devel., 1973-82; cons. chemist, 1982—. Contbr. articles to profl. jours. Served to lt. USNR, 1943-46. Riker fellow Harvard U., 1950. Mem. Am. Chem. Soc., Am. Pharm. Assn., Adventures Club (L.A.). Home and Office: Lake Wildwood 19831 Echo Blue Dr Penn Valley CA 95946-9414

KLOKOČNÍK, JAROSLAV, geodesist, astronomer; b. Prague, Czech Republic, Aug. 2, 1948; s. Jaroslav and Božena (Šturcová) K.; m. Eva Pelikánová, 1982; children: Michal, Zuzana. Diploma in engring., geodesy, Czech. Tech. U., Prague, 1971; PhD, Acad. Scis., Prague, 1980, DSc, 1996. Rschr. worker Astron Inst. Czech Acad. Sci., Ondřejov, Czech Republic, 1981—; rsch. worker Deutsche Geodät. Forschunginst, Munich, 1988, 90; rsch. worker, cons. Helwan Inst. for Astron., Cairo, 1987, 90, 92, 94, 98; assoc. prof. Hamburg U., 1990, 91, 92, 94, Czech Tech. U., Prague, 1994—; rsch. worker Max-Planck Inst. for Meteorology, 1990-94, Nat. Ocean and Atmospheric Adminstn., Silver Spring, 1990—, NASA Goddard Space Flight Ctr., Greenbelt, 1994—, Geodet. Rsch. Inst., Potsdam, 1999—. Author of 4 textbooks; contbr. articles to profl. jours. Mem. COSPAR, Internat. Assn. Geodesy, Am. Geophys. Union, Internat. Astronomy Union, European Geophys. Soc. Avocations: hiking, cross-country skiing, mountain biking, photography, jazz and classical music. Office: Astron Inst Czech Acad Sci, Fričova 1, CZ-25165 Ondřejov Czech Republic

KLOOS, PETER, anthropology educator; b. Haarlem, The Netherlands, June 21, 1936; s. Janpiet and Maria Wilhelmina (Moolenaar) K.; m. Joke Therese Schryvers, May 2, 1992; children: Esther, Bart, Jonatan, David. MA, U. Amsterdam, 1962, PhD, 1971. From lectr. to sr. lectr. U. Amsterdam, 1969-74; chargé de Cours Free U. Brussels, 1968-71; asst. prof. U. Leiden, The Netherlands, 1974-88; prof. dept. anthropology Free U. Amsterdam, 1988—. Author: The Maroni River Caribs, 1971. Mem. Netherlands Anthropology Assn. Home: Heivlinder 11, 2317 JS Leiden The Netherlands Office: U Amsterdam Dept Anthropol, De Boelalaan 1081C, 1081 HV Amsterdam The Netherlands

KLOOSTERMAN, ROBERT CHRISTIAN, researcher; b. Hague, Netherlands, Sept. 26; s. Harry Hubertus and Betsy Johanna (Delfos) K.; m. Joanne Pauline Van der Leun. PhD in Econ. History, Leiden (Netherlands) U., 1985. Jr. rschr. Leiden U., 1979-85; postdoctoral rschr. U. Amsterdam, 1987-93; sr. rschr. U. Utrecht, Netherlands, 1993-97, sr. rschr., head sect. infrastructure, transport and space, 1997—; seconded to Dutch Sci. Coun. for Govt. Policies, The Hague; ind. mem. com. on ethnic entrepreneurship in the Netherlands, Social-Econ. Coun.; co-coord. internat. rsch. network on immigrant entrepreneurship European Union. Contbr. articles to profl. jours. Royal Dutch Acad. Sci. rsch. fellow, 1987. Mem. Dutch Labour Party. Home: Lorentzkade 47, 2313 GD Leiden Netherlands

KLOPF, GORDON JOHN, educational consultant, former college dean; b. Milw., Jan. 10, 1917; s. Milton and Lillian (Spiegler) K. BS, U. Wis., 1939, MA, 1941, PhD, 1950; postgrad., U. Mich.; LHD (hon.), Bank St. Coll. of Edn., 1998. Tchr., counselor pub. schs. Burlington, Wis., 1939-41; counselor men's activities, instr. speech Wayne U., 1942-47; coord. student activities summer insts. for sch. counselors U. Wis., Madison, 1947-51; prof. tng. personnel, guidance workers serving with AUS, U.S. Dept. State, Am. Council on Edn. project Tokyo U., Kyoto U., Kyushu U., Japan, 1951-52; dean students coll. for tchrs. SUNY, 1952-59; ednl. specialist in guidance Dept. State, Japan, 1954; assoc. prof. edn., dept. guidance, student personnel adminstrn. Tchrs. Coll., Columbia U., N.Y.C., 1960-64; asst. to pres., chmn. guidance programs Bank Street Coll. Edn., N.Y.C., 1964-69, dean of faculties, provost, 1965-80, dean emeritus, 1980-85, dean Ctr. for Leadership devel., dir. Sch. and Gen. Ledership and Supervision Program, disting. specialist in ednl. leadership, 1980-85; pres. Gordon J. Klopf, ednl. cons., N.Y.C., 1983—; vis. prof. Tchrs. Coll. Columbia U., 1959-60; continuing edn. cons. Fall River (Mass.) Pub. Schs., 1979-89, Kennesaw State Coll., 1985-94; cons. U.S. Office Edn., Washington, 1964-81, P.R. Dept. Instrn., 1965—, Mendoza Found., Ministry of Edn., Venezuela, 1971-80; clin. prof. gerontology, Southampton campus L.I. U.; mem. U.S. Planning Com. and UN World chairperson for Internat. Yr. of Older Persons, 1999, chair 1998—. Author: Student Leadership and Government, 1949, rev., 1955; Planning Student Activities in the High School, 1950; College Student Government, 1960, Teacher Education In a Social Context, 1967, Perspectives On Learning, 1967, New Careers in the American School, 1968, New Careers and Roles in Education, 1968, Teams for Learning, 1969; The Principal and Staff Development in the School, 1976; co-author: The School as Locus of Advocacy for All Children, 1987; author-editor: Education Before Five, 1977; co-author: Mentoring, 1982, The School Principal and Special Education, 1982; co-author numerous other works in field. editor: Operational Studies in Guidance, 1962, Orientation, 1963, Encounter and Dialogue, 1963, Student Personnel Work in the Future, 1966, Jour. Research and Devel. in Edn., Vol. 5, No. 3, 1972; editor, chmn. The Role and Preparation of the Counselor in the Secondary School, 1963; adv. editor Brit. Young Children's Ency., 16 vols., 1970; chair UN-NGO Com. on Internat. Yr. of the Older Person, 1999. Past chmn. adv. coun. U.S. Student Assn.; nat. chmn. Project Follow Through, 1967-68; trustee U.S. Com. for UNICEF, 1971-81, chmn. edn. com., 1975-80, chairperson bd. Action for Children, chmn. non-govt. orgn. edn. working group, 1988—, chairperson DPI-Non Govt. Orgn., exec. com. UN, 1990-96, co-chairperson UNICEF Forum on Children in Ctrl. Am., 1993-94; trustee Bklyn. Children's Mus., 1980-89; bd. dirs. Daytop Inc., 1973—; trustee Hampton Day Sch., 1975-94, pres. 1984-86, chmn. evaluation com., 1995; mem. coun. The Hayground Sch., Bridgehampton, N.Y.; mem. edn. Parish Art Mus., Southampton; v.p., program chmn. Elem. Sch. Ctr., N.Y., pres. 1985-87, v.p., 1987-90, bd. dirs.; pres., bd. dirs. chairperson Morningside Heights Housing Corp. Program; program chair, bd. dirs. Morningside Heights Retirement and Health Svcs., chmn. UN-NGO, 1999, UNICEF working NGO group in edn, yr. older person UN, 1999, UNICEF world confs. on children, N.Y. Brown U. scholar, 1995-97. Mem. N.Y. State Deans Assn. (research chmn., past v.p.), Am. Personnel and Guidance Assn., Western N.Y. Personnel and Guidance Assn. (past pres.), AAUP, Am. Coll. Personnel Assn., Buffalo World Hospitality Assn. (past chmn.). Home: 70 La Salle St Apt 4B New York NY 10027-4705 also: Jason's Ln PO Box 1208 East Hampton NY 11937-0996

KLOPFENSTEIN, REX CARTER, electrical engineer; b. Pittsfield, Mass., Mar. 3, 1938; s. Glenn A. and Jasimine V. (Carter) K.; m. Linda Gilgore, Oct. 6, 1962; children: Mark W., Eric G. BSEE, U. Conn., 1959; MEE, Syracuse U., 1963. Engr. GE, Syracuse, N.Y., 1959-63; lab. mgr. Melpar Divsn. E Sys., Falls Church, Va., 1963-70; mgr. hardware engring. Logicon Inc., Fairfax, Va., 1977-78; software and test mgr. Acuity Sys. Inc., Reston, Va., 1978-81; engring. mgr. AMF Electronic Rsch. Lab., Sterling, Va., 1981-82; tech. staff The MITRE Corp., McLean, Va., 1970-77, lead engr., 1982-96; lead engr. Mitretek Sys., Inc., McLean, Va., 1996—; sec. tech. com. X3K5 Am. Nat. Standards Inst., Washington, 1992-94. Co-author: Microcomputer Design and Application, 1977; contbr. articles to profl. jours. Mem. Rep. Nat. Com., chmn. honor roll, 1997. Named Engr. of Yr., D.C. Coun. Engring. and Archtl. Socs., 2000. Fellow Washington Acad. Scis. (bd. mgrs. 1996-98, pres.-elect 1998, pres. 1999-2000); mem. IEEE (No. Va. sect. sec. 1991-92, vice-chmn., treas. 1992-93, chmn. 1993-94, nat. area coun. vice-chmn. 1994-95, chmn. 1995-96, assoc. editor, editor 1998-99, web site mgr. 1997—), Assn. for Computing Machinery, Tau Beta Pi, Chi Phi. Avocation: photography. Home: 4224 Worcester Dr Fairfax VA 22032-1140 Office: Mitretek Systems Inc 7525 Colshire Dr Ste 600 Mc Lean VA 22102-7400

KLÖPFFER, WALTER, chemist, educator; b. Graz, Austria, June 6, 1938; arrived in Germany, 1964; s. Otto and Josefine (Lammer) K.; m. Hedwig Gerlinde, Dec. 16, 1964; 1 child, Astrid Eva. PhD, U. Graz, 1964; prof., U. Mainz, 1975. From rschr. to rsch. leader Battelle Inst., Frankfurt, Germany, 1964-91; rsch. leader Soc. for Environ. Cons. and Analysis Ltd., Dreieich, Germany, 1992—; prof. U. Mainz, 1975—; expert OECD Chem. Group, Paris, 1978-82; mem. steering com. on life cycle assessment SETAC Europe, 1992-93; cons. Life Cycle Assessment. Author: Polymer Spectroscopy, 1984, Verteilung u. Abbau v. Umwelt Chemikalien, 1996; editor in chief Internat. Jour. LCA, LCA-Documents; contbr. articles to profl. jours. Mem. Ges. Oesterr. Chemiker, Ges. Deutsch. Chemiker, Am. Chem. Soc., Bunsenges. Phys. Chem., European Photochemistry Assn., Soc. Environ. Toxicology and Chemistry, N.Y. Acad. Scis. Roman Catholic. Achievements include discovery of excitons in polymers; development of testing and evaluation methods for environmental chemicals, life cycle assessment. Home: Am Dachsberg 56E, D-60435 Frankfurt Germany Office: CAU GmbH, Daimlerstr 23, D-63303 Dreieich Germany

KLOPMAN, GILLES, chemistry educator; b. Brussels, Belgium, Feb. 24, 1933; came to U.S., 1965; s. Alge and Brana (Brendel) Klopman; m. Malvina Pantiel, Sept. 5, 1957. BA, Athenee d'Ixelles (Belgium), 1952; lic. chemistry, U. Brussels, 1956; D.Chemistry, 1960. Rsch. scientist Cyanamid European Rsch. Inst., Geneva, Switzerland, 1960-67; postdoctoral fellow U. Tex., 1964-65; assoc. prof. Case Western Res. U., Cleve., 1967-69, prof. chemistry, 1969—, chmn. dept., 1981-86, interim dean sci. and math., 1986-88, C.F. Mabery prof. of rsch., chmn. dept., 1988-95; v.p. Biofor, Ltd., PA, 1986-95; pres. Discovery Software Inc., 1991-93, Multicase, Inc., 1995—. Recipient Kahlbaum prize Swiss Chem. Soc., 1971; grantee NSF, NIH, EPA, PRF, ONR. Mem. Am. Chem. Soc. (Morley medal 1993), Brit. Chem. Soc. Belgium Chem. Soc. (Stas Spring medal 1960), Swiss Chem. Soc., AAUP, Sigma Xi. Author: All Valence Electrons SCF Calculations, 1970; Chemical Reactivity and Reaction Paths, 1974; contbr. articles to profl. jours. Home: 22 Hyde Park Cleveland OH 44122-7536 Office: Case Western Res U 10900 Euclid Ave Cleveland OH 44106-1712

KLÖPPEL, GÜNTER KARL PAUL, pathology educator, hospital administrator; b. Darmstadt, Hessen, Germany, Apr. 22, 1943; s. Kurt and Elsbeth (Krönke) K.; m. Rita Häge, May 2, 1970; children: Ulrike, Renate, Cordelia. Grad. in medicine, U. Hamburg, Fed. Republic of Germany, 1967, MD, 1970, DrHabil, 1976. Resident in pathology Inst. Pathology, U. Hamburg, 1970-75, specialist, 1975, lectr., 1976-81, prof., 1981-87; prof., head dept. pathology Acad. Hosp. Jette Free U. Brussels, 1987-95; head dept. pathology U. Kiel, Germany, 1995—. Editor, author: Pancreatic Pathology, 1984, Atlas of Exocrine Pancreatic Tumors, 1991; co-author: Diabetic Pancreas, 1985, Functional Endocrine Pathology, 1991, The Pancreas, 1993, Histopathology of Endocrine Tumors, 1993, Acute Pancreatitis, 1994, Radiology of the Pancreas, 1994, WHO Classification of Tumors of the Exocrine Pancreas, 1996, Textbook of Diabetes, 1997, AFIP Fascicle on Tumors of the Pancreas, 1997; mem. editl. bd. Ultrastructural Pathology, Jour. Pathology, Histopathology, Endocrine Pathology, Pancreas; mng. editor Virchows Archiv. Recipient Martini prize U. Hamburg, 1972, 81, Voss prize Werner Otto Stiftung, 1982, Ferdinand Bertram prize German Diabetes Soc., 1983, Konjetzny prize Hamburger Krebsgesellschaft, 1983, Bard Urology award, 1987, Nizze prize German Soc. Urology, 1986, prize Hoechst Aktiengesellschaft Found., Graz, 1987. Mem. German Soc. Pathology, German Diabetes Soc., European Assn. Study Diabetes, European Pancreatic Club, Soc. Histochemistry, Am. Pancreatic Assn., Internat. Acad. Pathology, Pathology Soc. Gt. Britain and Ireland, Belgian Soc. Gastroenterology (hon.), Spanish Soc. Pathology (hon.). Avocations: music, literature, history, sports. Office: U Kiel U Hosp Dept Pathology, Michaelisstrasse 11, D-24105 Kiel Germany

KLOPPER, WILLEM MAARTEN, chemistry educator, researcher; b. Oppendoes, The Netherlands, Apr. 18, 1961; s. Maarten and Annigje (Bot) K.; m. Sonja Sommer, May 6, 1995; children: Tanja Sophia, Sven Morten. Diploma in Chemistry, Ruhr U., Bochum, Germany, 1985, D of Natural Scis., 1989; pvt. docent, Swiss Fed. Inst. Tech., Zurich, Switzerland, 1998. Rsch. assoc. Ruhr U., 1984-90; postdoctoral rsch. fellow U. Minn., Mpls., 1991; rsch. assoc. Ruhr U., 1992-93; sr. rschr. Swiss Ctr. Sci. Computing (Swiss Fed. Inst. Tech.), Zurich, 1993-96; lectr. U. Oslo, Norway, 1996-98, U. Utrecht, The Netherlands, 1999—. Author: (chpt.) Encyclopedia of Computational Chemistry. Recipient fellowship German Sci. Found., Germany, 1991-92, fellowship Swiss Sci. Found., Switzerland, 1993-94, rsch. grant Swiss Fed. Inst. Tech., Zurich, 1994-96; fellowship Royal Netherlands Acad. Arts and Scis., 1999—, Hans G.A. Hellmann prize Arbeitsgemeinschaft Theoretische Chemie, Germany, 1999, ann. award Internat. Acad. Quantum Molecular Scis., 1999. Mem. Royal Netherlands Chemical Soc. Address: Beverakker 70, NL3994EM Houten The Netherlands

KLOSTERMAN, RICHARD EARLE, city planning and geography educator, researcher; b. Brookings, S.D., Apr. 2, 1947; s. Earle Wayne and Ann Carolyn (Moore) K.; m. Kathryn Joan Brown, Dec. 27, 1975; children: Michelle, Kimberly. BSCE, Purdue U., 1969; PhD in City and Regional Planning, Cornell U., 1976. Asst. prof. Fla. State U., Tallahassee, 1975-82; assoc. prof. U. Akron, 1983-91, prof., 1992—; vis. scholar MIT, Cambridge, Mass., 1990, Rutgers U., New Brunswick, N.J., 1998; vis. prof. U. Ill., Champaign, 1993; vis. fellow U. Hong Kong, 1994. Author: Community Analysis & Planning, 1990; co-editor: Spreadsheet Models for Urban and Regional Analysis, 1993, Planning Support Systems, 2000; software developer: What If? Planning Support System, 1998. Avocations: tennis, skiing, hiking. Office: U Akron Buchtell Ave Akron OH 44325-0001

KLOT, JENNIFER, children's fund administrator; b. Montclair, N.J., July 30, 1964; d. David N. and Ruth (Kane) K. BA, Rutgers U., 1986; M in Regional Planning, Cornell U., 1988. E.L.F.E. cert. Asst. African-Am. Inst.ance Program, N.Y.C., 1984-85; founder, idr. Youth Global Alliance Program, New Brunswick, N.J., 1984-86; cons. Internat. Women's Tribune Ctr., N.Y.C., 1987; field researcher The Black Sash and Planact, Johannesburg, South Africa, 1988-89; project dir. Talking Music of Africa, Johannesburg, 1989-90; regional rep. Ashoka: Innovators for the Pub., Johannesburg, 1990-93; acting exec. dir. Fund for Edn. in South Africa, N.Y.C., 1993-94; cons. Devel. Fund for Women (UNIFEM) UN, N.Y.C., 1993-94, program mgr. study on impact of armed conflict on children, 1994-97; policy adv. UNICEF, N.Y.C., 1994—; vis. scholar U. Witwatersrand, Johannesburg; field researcher U. Nairobi (Kenya), 1985; presenter in field. Contbr. articles to profl. jours., chpts. to books; lead alto sax African Jazz Pioneers, 1990-92. Named Amb. of Goodwill Rotary, 1989. Home: 277 Avenue C Apt 5B New York NY 10009-2538 Office: UNICEF 3 UN Plz New York NY 10017

KLOTE, JAMES DENVER, financial consultant; b. Detroit, June 9, 1964; s. James Denver Klote Sr. and Gloria Ann DeVos; m. Mary McNerney, Apr. 12, 1999. BA, Capital U., 1987. Divsn. dir. United Way, Columbus, Ohio, 1987-90; sr. cons. Ward Dreshman & Reinhardt Inc., Worthington, Ohio, 1990-97, pres., 1997-98; pres. James D. Klote & Assocs. Inc., Bethesda, Md., 1998—; cons. Va. State Golf Assn., Richmond, 1997-98. Vol. Ark. Republican Party, Little Rock, 1994-96; candidate U.S. Ho. of Reps., 1996. Mem. Nat. Soc. Fundraising Execs. Republican. Episcopalian. Avocations: investing, golf. Home: 8015 Quarry Ridge Way Bethesda MD 20817-6950 Office: James D Klote & Assocs Inc 6905 Rockledge Dr Ste 600 Bethesda MD 20817-1878

KLOTSVOG, FELIX NAUMOVICH, economist, science administrator; b. Klintsy, Brjansk, USSR, Aug. 5, 1934; s. Naum Fedorovich K. and Rosa Lvovna Serebrennikova; m. Tamara Konstantinovna Popova, Sept. 3, 1960; children: Galina Golubeva, Helen. Student, Fin. and Econ. Inst., Leningrad, USSR, 1955; D of Economical Sci., Inst. Econs. State Planning Commn., Moscow, 1987, Prof., 1990. Chmn. Regional Planning Com., Kasly, Cheljabinsk Region, USSR, 1955-57; scientific rsch. worker Inst. Econs. State Planning Com. USSR, 1960-65, head dept. Inst. Econs., 1965-91; had lab. Inst. Econ. Forecasting Russian Acad. Scis., 1991—; prof., lectr. Inst. Nat. Economy, 1968-78, Moscow Inst. Biotech., 1985-93, Moscow State U., 1993-95. Contbr. articles to profl. jours. Recipient State Prize of USSR for the development of analysis and planning methods of interbrantions proportions, 1968. Mem. All Russian Soc. Russian Scientists of Socialist Orientation (co-chmn. 1993—). Avocations: music, tourism. Home: Mosrentgen 25-21, 142771 Moscow Russia Office: Inst Econ Forecasting, Nahimovsky Prospect 47, 117418 Moscow Russia

KLOTT, DAVID LEE, lawyer; b. Vicksburg, Miss., Dec. 10, 1941; s. Isadore and Dorothy (Lipson) K.; m. Maren J. Randrup, May 25, 1975. BBA summa cum laude, Northwestern U., 1963; JD cum laude, Harvard U., 1966. Bar: Calif. 1966, U.S. Ct. Claims. 1968, U.S. Supreme Ct. 1971, U.S. Tax Ct. 1973, U.S. Ct. Appeals (Fed. cir.) 1982. Ptnr. Pillsbury, Madison & Sutro, San Francisco, 1966—; tax adv. group to sub-chpt. C J and K, Am. Law Inst.; tchr. Calif. Continuing Edn. of Bar, Practising Law Inst., Hastings Law Sch., San Francisco; bd. dirs., counsel Marin Wine and Food Soc.; exec. v.p., sec. Global Ctr. Inc., 2000—; vice-chmn. HL Ventures, LLC, 2000—. Commentator Calif. Nonprofit Corp. Law; bd. dirs. Joan Shorenstein Barone Found. for Harvard, The Phyllis J. Shorenstein Fund for the Asian Art Mus. San Francisco; counsel Drum Found. Mem. ABA (tax exempt fin. com.), Calif. State Bar Assn. (tax sect.), San Francisco Bar Assn., Am.-Korean Taekwondo Friendship Assn. (1st dan-black belt), Harvard Club, Northwestern Club, Olympic Club, City Club San Francisco (founding mem.), Bay Club (charter mem.), Harbor Point Racquet and Beach Club, Internat. Wine and Food Soc. (vice-chmn., bd. dirs., exec. com., bd. govs. Ams.), Beta Gamma Sigma, Beta Alpha Psi (pres. local chpt.). Office: Pillsbury Madison & Sutro 50 Fremont St # 964 San Francisco CA 94105-2230

KLOTZ, UTA, editor-in-chief; b. Warburg, Germany, July 7, 1960; d. Josef and Josefine (Meyer) K. MA, U. Münster, Germany, 1987. Asst. Taschen Verlag, Cologne, Germany, 1988-89, Ritterbach Verlag, Frechen, Germany, 1990-91; gallery owner, 1998—. Editor-in-chief: Kunsthandwerk Design, Neues Glas/New Glass jours., 1991—; contbr. articles to profl. jours. Mem. Deutscher Jour. Avocations: travel, sailing. Home: Brabanter Str 19, 50674 Cologne Germany Office: Uta Klotz, Brüsseler Str. 31, 50674 Cologne Germany

KLOTZ, WENDY LYNNETT, analytical chemist; b. Lebanon, Pa., June 15, 1966; d. William Lewis and Helen Irene (Schrader) Unger; m. Brian Lee Klotz, Sept. 29, 1990. BS, Delaware Valley Coll., Doylestown, Pa., 1988; postgrad., LaSalle U., Phila., 1989-92, Villanova U., 1992—. Cert. chemist. Chemist Rohm and Haas Co., Bristol, Pa., 1987-89; scientist Rohm and Haas Co., Spring House, Pa., 1989—. Active advertising The Hunger Project, Bucks County, Pa., 1986. Mem. AAAS, Am. Inst. Chemists (Outstanding Senior award 1988), Am. Chem. Soc. (Analytical Chemistry Undergraduate award 1987), Sigma Xi. Office: Rohm and Haas Co PO Box 904 727 Norristown Rd Spring House PA 19477-0904

KLÖTZER, WALTER T., prosthetic dentistry educator; b. Neuss, Germany, Feb. 13, 1932. DMD, U. Munchen, Germany, 1959, MD, 1968; habilitation, U. Tubingen, Germany, 1972. Rsch. assoc. U. Munchen, 1955-67; head rsch. assoc. U. Zurich, Switzerland, 1967-69; fellow U. Conn., 1969-70; assoc. prof. U. Tubingen, 1971-76; prof., head prosthodontic dept. U. Marburg Dental Sch., Germany, 1976-97; cons. Fedn. Dentaire Internat., 1972-88; chmn. working group biologic testing of dental materials, German Orgn. for Standardization, 1973-88. Contbr. articles to profl. jours., books. Internat. Assn. Dental Rsch. fellow, 1969; grantee Studienstiftung Deutsches Volk, 1964, JADR Sr. Dental Scientists Exch. Program, 1969. Mem. Deutsche Gesellschaft fur Zahn-Mund und Kieferheilkunde, Deutsche Gesellschaft fur Zahnarztliche Prothetik und Werkstoffkunde, ADA, Chgo. Dental Soc., Internat. Coll. Prosthodontists, Internat. Assn. Dental Rsch., European Prosthodontic Assn., others. Address: Zürichbergstrasse 203, CH-8044 Zürich Switzerland

KLOTZKIN, CHARLES EDWARD, secondary school educator; b. N.Y.C., Oct. 5, 1938; s. Benjamin and Emma (Brown) Klotsky; m. Helene Susan Zuckerman, Apr. 12, 1987; 1 child, Beverly Elaine. BS, CCNY, 1961. Soils engr. N.J. Hwy. Dept., Trenton, 1963-64; tchr. N.Y.C. Bd. Edn., 1964-95; coverage coord. DeWitt Clinton H.S., Bronx, 1991-95. Del. United Fedn. Tchrs., James Monroe Sch., 1976-80, founder, dir. unit CAP, 1971-74. Democrat. Jewish. Avocations: photography, travel, rock and mineral collecting, Citroëns.

KLUG, AARON, molecular biologist; b. Aug. 11, 1926; s. Lazar and Bella (Silin) K.; m. Liebe Bobrow, 1948; 2 children. B.Sc., U. Witwatersrand; M.Sc., U. Cape Town; PhD, DSc, Cambridge U.; DSc (hon.), U. Chgo., 1978, Columbia U., 1978; D (hon.), U. Strasbourg, 1978; DSc (hon.), Stockholm U., 1980, U. Witwatersrand, 1984, Hebrew U., Jerusalem, 1984, Hull U., 1985, U. St. Andrews, 1987, U. Western Ont., 1991, Warwick U., 1994, Capetwon U., 1997; D Litt, Cambridge U., 1998, Stirling U., 1978. Jr. lectr., 1947-48; rsch. student Cavendish Lab. Cambridge (Eng.) U., 1949-52; Rouse-Ball rsch. student Trinity Coll., 1949-52; Colloid Sci. dept., 1953; Nuffield rsch. fellow Birkbeck Coll., London, 1954-57, dir. virus structure rsch. group, 1958-61; mem. staff Med. Rsch. Coun. Lab. Molecular Biology, Cambridge U., 1962—, joint head div. structural studies, 1978-86, dir., 1986-96; Leeuwenhoek lectr. Royal Soc., 1973; Dunham lectr. Harvard U. Med. Sch., 1975; Harvey lectr., N.Y.C., 1979, Lane lectr. Stanford U., 1983; Silliman lectr. Yale U., 1985; Cetus lectr. Berkeley U., 1986; Pauli lectr., Zürich, 1986; Nishina Meml. lectr., Tokyo, 1986; J. T. Baker lectr. Cornell U., 1987; Jean Weigle lectr., Geneva, 1989, Steenbock lectr. U. Wis., Madison, 1989; Innovators in Biochem. lectr. U. Va., Richmond, 1990; Calbiochem. lectr. U. Calif., San Diego, 1991. Contbr. articles to sci. jours. Recipient Heineken prize Royal Netherlands Acad. Sci., 1979, Louisa Gross Horwitz prize Columbia U., 1981, Nobel prize in chemistry, 1982, Gold medal of Merit, U. cape Town, 1983, Copley medal Royal Soc., 1985, Harden medal Biochem. Soc., 1985; Knight, 1988, Order of Merit, 1995. Fellow Royal Soc. (pres. 1995—), Peterhouse (Cambridge hon.), Royal Coll. Physn, (hon., Baly medal 1987), Royal Coll. Pathologists (hon.), Trinity Coll. (Cambridge, hon.), Birkbeck Coll. (London, hon.); mem. Am. Acad. Arts and Scis. (fgn. hon.), French Acad. Scis. (fgn. assoc.), Max-Planck-Gesellschaft (fgn. assoc.), NAS (fgn. assoc.), Am. Philos. Soc. (fgn. mem.). Office: Med Rsch Coun Lab Molecular, Biology, Hills Rd, Cambridge CB2 2QH, England*

KLUGE, HOLGER, retired bank executive; b. Hamburg, Germany, Mar. 11, 1942; married; 2 children. BComm with honors, Sir George Williams Univ., Montreal, 1971; MBA with honors, Sophia U., Tokyo, 1977. Mem. branch ops. staff Can. Imperial Bank of Commerce, Montreal, 1959-81, v.p. Asia Pacific ops., 1981-84, sr. v.p. internat. ops., 1984-86, exec. v.p. support svcs. Corp. Bank, 1986-88, exec. v.p. Eastern Can., Europe, Mid. East, Africa and Latin Am. Corp. Bank, 1988-90, exec. v.p. internat., 1990, pres. Personal and Comml. Bank (formerly Individual Bank), 1990-99, bd. dirs., 1992-99, dir. corp. coun. on youth in the economy, ret., 1999; ind. dir. 724 Solutions Inc.; bd. dirs. Husky Oil Ltd.; chmn., dir. Can. Imperial Bank of Commerce West Indies Holdings Ltd., CEF Holdings, Ltd., TAL Investment Counsel, Ltd. Bd. dirs., chmn. bd. Can. Youth Bus. Found. Mem. Can. Banking Assn. (vice chmn.). Office: 4101 Yonge St Ste 702, Toronto, ON Canada M2P 1N6*

KLUGE, LEN H., director, actor, theater educator; b. Lakeview, Mich., Oct. 28, 1945; s. Leonhard H. and Edna Alvena (Paris) K. Diploma, Am. Acad. Dramatic Arts, 1967; student, Actors Studio, N.Y.C., 1968-69; BFA, Cen. Mich. U., 1977, MA in Counseling, 1978. Actor various mediums, N.Y., Calif., 1967-75; therapist Ionia County Mental Health Dept., Mich., 1978-79; exec. dir. Nat. Coun. on Alcoholism, Lansing, Mich., 1979-81; artistic dir. Spotlight Theatre, Grand Ledge, Mich., 1982—; prof. theater Spring Arbor Coll., 1993-95; dir. The Actors Workshop and Ensemble Acting Co., Lansing, 1986—. Appeared in: (soap opera) Another World, 1968-69, (off-Broadway play) Man with the Flower in His Mouth, 1969, (film) Rennaisance Man, 1994, spl. performance as Clarence Darrow for Do the Right Thing program, Punta Gorda, Fla., 1996, 97, 98; performed for Boarshead Pub. Theatre, 1997-99. Mem. Ctr. for the Arts, Lansing; bd. dirs. Child Abuse Prevention Svcs., 1993—; spl. Recipient Obie award, 1969, Thespie X award Lansing State Jour., 1982, 84, 86-90, Decade of Excellence award for body of work, 1993, Barney award Okemos Barn Theatre, Lansing, 1984, Riverwalk Theater, 91, 95, 96, 99, Star X award Spotlight Theatre, 1984-97. Lutheran. Avocations: baseball, writing, teaching, lecturing, travel, cigars. Home: 1937 Byrnes Rd Lansing MI 48906-3402

KLUGER, JEFFREY, cardiologist, health facility administrator; b. Bronx, N.Y., Aug. 3, 1945; m. Virginia Kluger; children: Alexander, Scott. AB, Columbia Coll., 1967; MD, N.Y. Med. Coll., 1971. Diplomate Nat. Bd. Med. Examiners, Am. Bd. Internal Medicine, Am. Bd. Cardiovascular Disease, Am. Bd. Clinical Electrophysiology. Intern Beth Israel Hosp., N.Y.C., 1971-72, jr. and sr. resident in medicine, 1972-74, chief med. resident, 1974-75; fellow in medicine Cornell U. Med. Coll., N.Y.C., 1975-77; physician-in-charge cardiology clinic N.Y. Hosp., N.Y.C., 1977-80; from clinical asst. to assoc. staff dept. medicine Hartford (Conn.) Hosp., 1980-93, sr. staff, 1993—; med. dir. emergency paramedic svc. N.Y. Hosp., N.Y.C., 1977-80, dir. coronary ICU, chmn. cardiac ICU com., 1978-80; assoc. dir. cardiology Hartford Hosp., 1980-96, com. mem., 1981—, program dir. cardiology tng. program, 1981-93, dir. cardiac arrhythmia svc., 1981—, dir. cardiac ICU, co-dir. arrhythmia/cardiovascular pharmacy rsch. group, 1982—, dir. cardiac arrhythmia unit, 1997—; courtesy staff dept. medicine John Dempsey Hosp., 1992—, St. Francis Med. Ctr., 1994—, New Britain Gen. Hosp., 1996—; asst. prof. medicine Cornell U. Med. Coll., N.Y.C., 1977-80, U. Conn. Sch. Medicine, Farmington, 1980-89, assoc. prof. medicine, 1989—; asst. clinical prof. U. Conn. Sch. Pharmacy, Farmington, 1985-88, clin. prof., Storrs, 1988—. Chmn. edn. com. N.Y.C. Emergency Coun., 1978-80. Cardiology fellow, 1997. Fellow Am. Coll. Cardiology, Am. Coll. Clinical Pharmacology; mem. AAAS, AMA, Am. Heart Assn., Am. Soc. for Clinical Pharmacology & Therapeutics, Am. Soc. Internal Medicine, N.Am. Soc. Pacing & Electrophysiology, Internat. Soc. for Holter & Noninvasive Electrocardiology. Home: 17 Mountain Terrace Rd West Hartford CT 06107-1531 Office: Hartford Hosp 80 Seymour St Hartford CT 06102-8000

KLUGMANN, EUGENIUSZ, physicist, researcher; b. Starogard, Poland, Nov. 22, 1933; s. Jan and Gertruda (Falenska) K.; m. Teresa Galazka, Apr. 20, 1958; children: Ewa, Michal. MS in Physics, Poznan (Poland) U., 1955, PhD in Physics, 1966. Asst. Dept. Physics Gdansk (Poland) U., 1957-66; sr. technologist Tech. U., Gdansk, Poland, 1966-69, asst. prof., 1969-2000; vis. reader U. Nigeria, Nsukka, 1977-79; vis. prof. U. Sheffield, Eng., 1982, 83, 85, Elec. Engring. Inst. St. Petersburg, Russia, 1976. Author: Electrodynamics, 1964; co-author: Solid-State Physics, 1972, Semiconductor Devices, 1996, Alternative Sources of Energy, Photovoltaic Power Engineering, 1999. Recipient British Coun. award, Eng., 1983, Royal Soc. award, 1985; grantee Rsch. Com., Warsaw, Poland, 1995, 96. Fellow Polish Phys. Soc.; mem. N.Y. Acad. Scis. Home: Gryglewskiego 21, 80-301 Gdańsk Poland Office: Technical Univ Gdansk, Narutowicza 11/12, 80-952 Gdańsk Poland

KLUIVERT, PATRICK, professional soccer player; b. Amsterdam, Holland, July 1, 1976. Forward Ajax Amsterdam Football Club, 1994-97; winner European Cup, 1995; forward AC Milan, Italy, 1997-98, Holland Nat. Team; striker FC Barcelona, 1998. Office: FC Barcelona c/o Nou Camp, Avda Aristides Maillol s/n, 08028 Milan Spain*

KLUNZINGER, THOMAS EDWARD, writer, actor, director, township treasurer; b. Ann Arbor, Mich., Sept. 11, 1944; s. Willard Reuben and Katherine Eileen (McCurdy) K. BA in Advt. cum laude, Mich. State U., 1966. Copywriter Campbell-Ewald Advt. Co., Detroit, 1966-70; travel cons. Moorman's Travel Svc., Detroit, 1973-74; media dir. Taylor for Congress Campaign, East Lansing, Mich., 1974; comms. specialist House Republican Staff, Lansing, Mich., 1975-80; trustee Meridian Twp., Ingham County, Mich., 1980-84; vice chmn. Econ. Devel. Corp., 1982-84; compliance officer The Eyde Co., Lansing, 1985-88; legis. aide MIch. Ho. of Reps., Lansing, 1988-90; comm. officer MIch. Capital Healthcare, 1994-96; Mem. Ingham County Rep. Com., 1976—, sec., 1986-88, 91-92, 96, Mich. Rep. State Com., 1981-85, 6th Dist. Rep. Com. sec., 1989-93; mem. Ingham County Bd. Canvassers, 1993-96; treas. Meridian Twp., 1996—; bd. dirs. Capital Area Transp. Authority. Author: Chester!, 1981, Heavy Lady, 1983, Double Standards, 1985, A Villa in Unadilla, 1985, Losing It, 1987, The Wizards of Kyshtym/Deine Kleine Beine, 1988, Lounge Lizards/Managing Gran, 1989, Like A Brother, 1989, Loose Dogs Will Bite, 1990, Beloved Friend, 1990, To Be Announced, 1991, Okemos Passing, 1992, Song of the Whale, 1993, Mimsy Borogroves and the Tooth Fairy, 1993, What About the Hungarian?, 1995, The Passion of Richard II, 1996, The Hunchback of Notre Dame, 1997, Out at Home, 1998, The Real Boy's Pirate Show, 1998, As I Was Saying..., 1999, Breakfast in Berlin, 1999, Folles, 2000, Blond Ambition, 2000, Rock the Cradle, 2000. Pres. Riverwalk Theatre, 1990-92, sec., 1993-95. Mem. Dramatists Guild, Am. Numis. Assn., Mich. Numis. Soc. (sec. 1991-96, editor 1993—). Address: PO Box 585 Okemos MI 48805-0585

KLUTH, FREDERICK JOHN, computer consultant, artist; b. Charleston, W.Va., Nov. 13, 1942; s. Fred Carl and Edna Adrienne (Overbeke) K.; m. Martha Starrow Schaffer, Sept. 5, 1964; 1 child, Thomas William. BA, Johns Hopkins U., 1964; MA in Edn., U. Akron, 1987. Computer cons. FJ Kluth Co., Kent, Ohio, 1997—. Artist of drawings and prints, various internat. exhbns., 1993-99; contbr. articles to profl. jours.; author web site: http://apk.net/nfjk. Mem. tech. adv. coun. Summit County (Ohio) Solid Waste Policy Com., 1989-92; resource mem. infrastructure com. Akron Reg. Devel. Bd., 1991-92. Fellow Ohio Acad. Sci. (coord. 1993-99); mem. Ohio Math. and Sci. Coalition, Interex. Unitarian-Universalist. Avocation: tennis. Office: FJ Kluth Co 1060 Deleone Dr Kent OH 44240-2026

KLUTZOW, FRIEDRICH WILHELM, neuropathologist; b. Bandoeng, Preanger, Dutch East Indies, Aug. 6, 1923; came to U.S., 1953; s. Rudolph F.W. and Pauline (Van Thiel) K.; m. Apr. 2, 1954; children: Judith A., Michael J.; m. Merlene Hutto Byars, Dec. 10, 1999. MD, U. Utrecht, Netherlands, 1951. Diplomate Am. Bd. Neuropathology and Anatomic Pathology. Chief of staff Cmty. Meml. Hosp., Oconto Falls, Wis., 1965-68; pathology resident U. Wis., Madison, 1968-71, Armed Forces Inst. Pathology, Washington, 1971-72; neuropathologist VA Hosp., Mpls., 1972-75; dir. pathology dept. VA Hosp., Brockton, Mass., 1975-83, Wichita, Kans., 1983-87; chief of staff VA Hosp., Bath, N.Y., 1987-90; neuropathologist VA Hosp., Bay Pines, Fla., 1991—; clin. assoc. prof. pathology U. Rochester (N.Y.) Sch. Medicine, U. South Fla., Tampa; cons. in neuropathology, Minn. Bd. Med. Practice, 1999—; invited spkr. 24th Internat. Congress on Arts & Comm. seminar on medicine Oxford (Eng.) U., 1997, 26th Internat. Congress, Lisbon, Portugal, 1999. Prin. author: Neuropathology Manual: The Practical Approach, 1996; contbr. articles to profl. jours. Col. USAR, 1979-85. Recipient Outstanding Career award VA, 1990; Paul Harris fellow Rotary Internat., Bath, 1990. Fellow Coll. Am. Pathologists; mem. Am. Assn. Neuropathologists. Republican. Achievements include research of the persistent vegetative state and the practical approach to lesions in neuropathological diagnoses. Home: PO Box 2505 West Columbia SC 29171-2505

KLYACHKO, BORIS, computer consulting executive; b. Novosibirsk, Russia, Jan. 8, 1960; arrived in Australia, 1990; s. Saul and Eugenia (Ioffe) K.; m. Ilona Volpert (div.); 1 child, Yetta; m. Anna Tcherniak, Oct. 25, 1998. BSc with honors, Novosibirsk Inst. Elec. Engrs., Novosibirsk, 1982, MSc, 1986. Electronics engr. Novosibirsk Inst. Elec. Engrs., 1982-90; analyst/programmer, cons. Nat. Mut. Life Ins., Melbourne, Victoria, Australia, 1990-94; cons., mng. dir. QBF Computer Svcs., Melbourne, 1994—. Contbr. articles to profl. publs. Home: 103 Clarence St, Victoria Caulfield South 3162, Australia

KLYM, KENDALL, journalist, dancer, educator, choreographer; b. Hartford, Conn., Feb. 9, 1964; s. Nicholas and Lillian (Ostrowski) K. BA magna cum laude, Baylor U., 1994. Classical ballet dancer Kansas City (Mo.) Ballet, 1984-86; soloist ballet dancer Chgo. City Ballet, 1986-87; classical ballet dancer Dallas Ballet, 1987-88; pantomime dancer Tivoli Pantomine Theatre, Copenhagen, Denmark, 1988; prin. dancer State Ballet of Mo., Kansas City, 1988-89; ballet dancer Louisville Ballet, 1990-91; editl. intern Seeds Mag., Waco, Tex., 1992; assoc. editor Adventure West Mag., Incline Village, Nev., 1993; editor The Baylor Corral, Waco, 1993-94; city coun. reporter, feature writer Neighbors publ. of The Fresno (Calif.) Bee; staff reporter Carmel (Calif.) Pine Cone/Monterey Times; copy editor, page designer North County Times, Oceanside, Escondido, Calif.; dancer, choreographer, tchr. Tapestry Dance Co., Austin, Tex.; pub. rels. cons. Seeds Mag., Waco; freelance writer Presbyn. Today mag.; guest ballet tchr. Danse Sedona (Ariz.), Dance Inc., Phoenix, Tucson Regional Ballet, Sierra Vista (Ariz.) Ballet, 1997; choreographer, mktg. dir. Ballet Fantasque, Monterey, Calif., 1997; ballet tchr. Austin Musical Theatre Performing Arts Acad. Editor: The Asian Cultural Review, 1993, The Baylor Corral, 1993-94; freelance dance reviewer The Fresno Bee, Presbyterians Today mag.; freelance arts reviewer, features and travel writer Austin Am.-Statesman; contbr. articles to profl. jours. Group organizer Highland Presbyn. Ch., Louisville, 1990-92, Ctrl. Presbyn. Ch., Waco, 1992-94, fellowship group 1992-94; participant Habitat for Humanity, Waco, 1992. Recipient Fresno-Madera Area Agy. on Aging award for media coverage of sr. issues, 1995. Mem. Alpha Chi. Avocations: spelunking, hangliding, canoeing, camping. Home: 708 Patterson Ave Austin TX 78703-4724

KLYUEV, VLADIMIR VLADIMIROVITCH, control systems scientist; b. Moscow, Russia, Jan. 2, 1937; s. Vladimir Matveevitch and Anna Danilovna K.; m. Larisa Mikhailovna Degtereva, July 23, 1960; children: Serguei, Zakhar. Degree in engring., Moscow State Tech. U., 1960, MSc in Engring., 1964, DSc, 1973. Engr., sci. worker Moscow State Tech. U., 1960-64, sr. sci. worker, head lab., head dept. Inst. Introscopy, 1964-70, dir. Inst. Introscopy, 1970—; gen. dir. Moscow Sci. Indsl. Assn. Spectrum, 1976—; chmn. ISO/TC 135 Non-Destructive Testing, Geneva, 1980-92; mem. presidium Znanie, 1978—, Highest Certifying Com. Russia, 1989—. Author: Test Equipment, 1982, Equipment for NDT of Materials, 1986, Technical Means for Diagnostics, 1989, X-Ray Engineering, 1992, Practice of Radiographic Testing, 1998; mem. editorial bd. Defectoscopia, 1970—, European Jour. Non-Destructive Testing, 1990—; editor-in-chief Testing Diagnostics jour., 1998. Recipient Prize of Coun. of Mins. of USSR, 1983, State Prize of Russian Fedn. in field of sci. and tech., 1997; decorated Order of the Labour Red Banner, 1971, Order of the Labour Red Banner, 1976, Order of Friendship of Peoples, 1981. Mem. Russian Acad. Scis. (corr.), Academia Europaea, Russian Soc. for Non-Destructive Testing and Tech. Diagnostics (pres. 1990—), Internat. Com. for Non-Destructive Testing, European Com. for Non-Destructive Testing, Sci. Coun. on Automated Systems Diagnostics, European Fedn. for Non-Destructive Testing (bd. dirs. 1998—); contbr. over 150 articles to profl. jours. Achievements include 75 Russian patents in field. Avocation: hockey. Fax: (095) 246-88-88; e-mail: spektr@co.ru. Office: Moscow Sci Indsl Assn Spectrum, 35 St Usacheva, 119048 Moscow Russia

KLYUSOV, ANATOLY ALEXANDROVICH, chemistry researcher; b. Jenisejsk, Russia, July 2, 1940; s. Alexander Maximovich and Ludmila Nikiforovna (Pjankova) K.; m. Lubov Nicolaevna Gribanova, Aug. 15, 1975; children: Vsevolod, Igor. Degree in engring., Tech. Inst., St. Petersburg, 1963; DPhil, Mendeleev Chem. & Tech. Inst., Moscow, 1973; PhD, Mendeleev Chem. & Tech. Inst., 1993. Master Cement Plant, St. Petersburg, 1963-64; head of lab. Indsl. Inst., Tumen, 1964-68, Oil & Gas Geol. Inst., Tumen, 1968-75, Sci. and Rsch. Inst. Gas Industry, Tumen, 1975-94; head of chair, prof. Acad. Arch. and Civil Engring., Tumen, 1994-95; chief rschr. All-Russian Sci.-Rsch. Inst. Natural Gases and Gas Techs., Moscow, 1995—. Author: Cement and Concrete Research, 1994; contbr. articles to profl. jours.; patentee in field. Recipient award Honored Inventor of Russia, Presidium of the Supreme Soviet of USSR, 1987, Russian State Prize winner, 1989. Fellow Royal Soc. Chemistry (U.K.); mem. Internat. Informatization Acad. (pres. regional divsn. 1994—), Presidium of ther Regional Soc. Inventors, Presidium of the Regional Chemistry Soc., N.Y. Acad. Scis. Orthodox. Avocations: dogbreeding, forest walking. Home: Brateevskaya str 16-6, kv 343, 115408 Moscow Russia Office: VNIIGAZ Pos Razvilka, Leninsky Dist, 142717 Moscow region Russia

KNAPIKOWSKI, RALF, chemist, waste water engineer; b. Merseburg, Germany, Nov. 6, 1965; s. Hans-Dieter and Ulrike (Staffe) K. Diploma in Chemistry, Tech. H. Merseburg, U. Leipzig, 1992; Dr., U. Leipzig, 1996; diploma in Pedagogics, U. Dresden, 1999. Sci. collaborator U. Leipzig, 1992-96; adv. engr. Appl. Physics, 1996—; prof. water tech. Coll. Constrn., U. Leipzig, 1997—. Contbr. articles to sci. jours. Avocation, chorus in honor of people's battle Leipzig. Home: Landwehrstrasse 50, 04435 Schkenditz Germany

KNAPP, ALBERT BRUCE, gastroenterologist; b. N.Y.C., Aug. 9, 1955; s. Russell Sage and Bettina (Liebowitz) K.; m. Alice Anne Cohen, Sept. 7, 1986. BA, Columbia U., 1975, MD, 1979. Intern, resident Albert Einstein Med. Ctr., N.Y.C., 1979-82; fellow in gastroenterology Brigham & Women's Hosp. and Harvard Med. Sch., Boston, 1982-85; assoc. attending Lenox Hill Hosp., N.Y.C., 1985—, St. Vincent's Hosp., N.Y.C., 1985—; asst. prof. NYU Med. Sch., N.Y.C., 1990—. Author textbook in field, 1982; contbr. numerous articles to profl. jours. Trustee N.Y. Police Found., N.Y.C., 1991—. NIH rsch. grantee, 1982. Fellow ACP (jour. reviewer Annals of Internal Medicine 1985—); mem. Am. Gastroenterol. Assn. (jour. reviewer Gastroenterology 1985—), Am. Assn. Gastrointestinal Endoscopy, Am. Assn. for Study of Liver Disease (Rsch. award 1984). Office: 21 E 79th St New York NY 10021-0125

KNAPP, CHARLES WILLIAM, environmental health scientist; b. Harvey, Ill., Feb. 15, 1972; s. Ralph William and Charlene Fay Knapp; m. Mara Lynn Rewyer, Oct. 13, 1995; 1 child, Naomi-Brooke. BS in Bus., U. Kans., 1994, MS, 1999. Tchg. asst. civil engring./math. dept. U. Kans., Lawrence, 1994-99, rsch. asst. civil engring., 1996—. Fire fighter Sarcoxie Fire, Jefferson County, Kans., 1998—; mem. environ. com. Lake Dabinawa, Jefferson County, 1999. Ross McKinney Environ. Engring. fellow U. Kans., 1998, Spahr-McNown fellow U. Kans., 1998—. Mem. Golden Key, Phi Kappa Phi. Avocations: naui scuba diving, American Tae Kwon Do, mountain biking competitions.

KNAPP, ÈVA, literary historian; b. Marcali, Hungary, May 26, 1956; István and Istvánné (Kollár) K.; m. Gábor Tüskés, Dec. 3, 1980; 1 child, Anna. PhD, Loránd Eötvös U., 1984; postgrad., Hungarian Acad. Sci., 1991. Asst. libr. U. Libr., Budapest, 1979-80, libr., 1980-87, libr. dept. manuscripts, 1987-91, acting head of dept., 1991-93, head dept., 1993—. Author: (in Hungarian) Books of Miracles about Shrines in Hungary for the Baroque Period, 1985, Valuable Historical Maps, 1989, Catalogue of Manuscripts of the University Library Budapest, 2000; co-author: (in Hungarian) Baroque Popular Graphics About Places of Pilgrimage in Hungary, 1987; (in German) Popular Piety in Hungary: Studies in Comparative Literature and Cultural History, 1996; (in English) The Soprou Collection of Jesuit Stage Designs, 1999; contbr. articles to profl. jours. Herzog August Bibliothek fellow, 1997. Mem. Hungarian Soc. for Literary Studies. Avocation: gardening. Office: Univ Libr, Ferenciek tere 6, H-1053 Budapest Hungary

KNAPP, GARY ALAN, minister, psychotherapist; b. Jackson, Miss., Feb. 2, 1951; s. George Shellie and Ivy Mae (Warren) K. BA, Miss. Coll., 1977, M in Community Counseling, 1983; MDiv, New Orleans Bapt. Theol. Seminary, 1979. Lic. profl. counselor, Miss., Mental health counselor, Fla.; cert. mental health counselor, Wash.; nat. cert. counselor. Pastor Knoxo Bapt. Ch., Tylertown, Miss., 1978-80; sr. min. Griffith Meml. Bapt. Ch., Jackson, 1980-87; psychotherapist, pres. Clin. Counseling Assocs., Jackson, 1983-87; chief counseling svcs. Family Svc. Ctr., Cecil Field, Fla., 1987-90; sr. couselor Family Svc. Ctr., Yokosuka, Japan, 1990-91; dep. dir. Family Svc. Ctr., Atsugi, Japan, 1991—, dir., 1991—; psychotherapist Assocs. for Evaluation & Therpay, Jacksonville, Fla., 1989. Mem. AACD, Mil. Educators and Counselors Assn., Am. Assn. Profl. Hypnotherapists, Hinds-Madison Bapt. Assn. (vice-moderator 1986-87, named Internat. Man of Yr. 1992). Lodge: Lions (pres. Jackson chpt. 1982-83). Avocations: fishing, music.

KNAPP, GEORGE ROBERT, investment executive, business advisor, lawyer; b. Bethlehem, Pa., Oct. 8, 1947; s. Donald Albert and Adelaide Marie (Shogren) K.; children: Katherine, Laura, Sarah; m. Susan Jane Rutter. BA, Colgate U., 1969; JD, Harvard U., 1972. Bar: Pa. 1973, U.S. Dist. Ct. (we. dist.) Pa. 1973. Assoc. Kirkpatrick & Lockhart, Pitts., 1972-78, ptnr., 1978-96; pres. Stonewood Capital Mgmt., Pitts., 1996—; pres., bd. dirs. Tippins Industries, Pitts., 1996—; bd. dirs. On Target Commn., Inc., Pitts., TMC Investment Co. (Del.), Newbold Corp. (Va.), Emglo Products, Inc., Johnstown, Pa. Hon. consul Kingdom of Denmark, 1995—. Mem. Duquesne Club (Pitts.), Valleybrook Country Club (Pitts.). Republican. Presbyterian. Avocations: travel, music, athletics. Office: Tippins Industries Inc 1090 Freeport Rd Pittsburgh PA 15238-3102

KNAPP, KLAUS HERBERT, electronics engineer, science journalist; b. Berlin, June 17, 1934; s. Herbert F. and Margarete Ch. (Heuwinkel) K.; m. Gisela A. Theus, July 1, 1943; Gabriele, Christian, Constanze; m. Marlene J. Rosendorfer. Dipl.ing., Tech. U., 1958. R&D engr. Siemens, Munich, 1958-65, asst. to R&D head, 1965-68, head tech. press dept., 1969-79, sr. dir. R&D, 1987-89, sr. dir. semiconductors, 1990-96; editor-in-chief Funkschau Mag., Munich, 1980-86; chmn. bd. of curators Eduard Rhein Found., Hamburg, Germany, 1988-99; v.p. Union Internat. de la Presse Electronique, Bern, 1986-88; sci. lectr. Political High Sch., Munich, 1969-73; sci. journalist, 1996—. Contbr. over 700 articles to profl. publs. Jury mem. Law Ct., Munich, 1968-72. Mem. IEEE (sr.), Union Internat. de la Presse Electronique (life). Achievements include 8 patents. Home: Aindorferstr 128b, 80689 Munich Germany

KNAPP, MILDRED FLORENCE, retired social worker; b. Detroit, Apr. 15, 1932; d. Edwin Frederick and Florence Josephine (Antaya) K. BBA, U. Mich., 1954, MA in Cmty. and Adult Edn., 1964, MSW, 1967. Dist. dir. Girl Scouts Met. Detroit, 1954-63; planning asst. Coun. Social Agys. Flint and Genessee County, 1965; sch. social worker Detroit Pub. Schs., 1967-98; field instr. grad. social workers. Mem. alumnae bd. govs. U. Mich., 1972-75, scholarship chmn., 1969-70 76-80, chair spl. com. women's athletics, 1972-75, class agt. fund raising Sch. Bus. Adminstrn., 1978-79; mem. Founders Soc. Detroit Inst. Art, 1969—, Friends Children's Mus. Detroit, 1978—, Women's Assn., Detroit Symphony Orch., 1982-89, MIch. Humane Soc., 1991—; vol. Coun. Detroit Symphony Orch., 1990—; trustee, fin. chmn. Children's Mus. Recipient Appreciation cert.; Mott Found. fellow, 1964; HEW grantee, 1966. Mem. NASW, Acad. Cert. Social Workers, Nat. Cmty. Edn. Assn. (charter), Sch. Social Work Assn. Am. (charter), Outdoor Edn. and Camping Coun. (charter), Mich. Sch. Social Workers Assn. (pres. 1980-81), Detroit Sch. Social Workers Assn. (past pres.), Detroit Assn. U. Mich. Women (pres. 1980-82), Detroit Fedn. Tchrs., Madame Alexander Doll Club. Methodist. Home: 702 Lakepointe St Grosse Pointe MI 48230-1706

KNAPP, PEGGY DURDA, international company administrator; b. Mpls., Jan. 2, 1944; d. Joseph and Dolores Catherine Durda; m. Bobby Lee Knapp, Apr. 16, 1966 (div. Feb. 1973); 1 child, Noelle Catherine. Attended, U. Minn., Mpls., 1961-64, Christian Life Sch. Theology, 1996—. Stewardess Northwest Airlines, Mpls., 1964-66; sales mgr. LDS, Dallas; aeration ind. internat. dir. Chaska, Minn. Divsn.; mem. bd. dirs. Joseph Durda Found., Mpls. Contbr. articles to profl. jours. Vol. Minn. AIDS Project, Mpls., 1993-95, Parkland Hosp., Dallas, 1986-88; Christian Ch. counselor, 1998—; vol. pre-sch. spl. needs children, 1997—; lic. min., treas. bd. dirs. Heart's Cry Internat. Ministry, 1999. Mem. Nat. Assn. Golf Supts., Nat. Golf Found., Assn. Women Execs. Republican. Avocations: reading, painting, crafts, floral design. Office: Aeration Industries Inc 4100 Peavey Rd Chaska MN 55318-2386

KNAPP, TILLMANN WILHELM, engineering company executive; b. Wiesbaden, Germany, Feb. 28, 1941; s. Wilhelm and Norgard (Melzer) K.; m. Elke Walther, Mar. 24, 1970; 1 son, Helge. MS in Engring., Wiesbaden Tech. Sch., 1961. Tech. asst. Beer Maschinenbau, Wiesbaden, 1961-69; tech. mgr. Kindler U. Schiermeier, Munich, 1969-70, Beckman Instruments, Munich, 1970-72; mgr. R & D Ratisch Instrument, Munich, 1972-73; mng. dir. J.U.M. Engring., Munich, 1973-85; pres. J.U.M. Engring., 1985—; pres. J.U.M. N.Am., Inc., 1994; v.p. J.U.M. Engring. Lone Star Group, Inc., 1997. Mem. Instrument Soc. Am., Air and Waste Mgmt. Assn., Soc. Automotive Engrs. Home: Korbinianstrasse 20, 80807 Munich Germany Office: JUM Engring GmbH, Gauss Strasse 6, 85757 Karlsfeld Germany

KNAUFF, HANS GEORG, physician, educator; b. July 8, 1927; arrived in Can., 1984; s. Friedrich and Sophie (Sauer) K.; m. Sigrid W. Keppner, Aug. 28, 1956; children: Ursula V. Wrangel, Barbara K. Student, U. Erlangen, 1947-49, U. Freiburg, 1949, U. Basel, 1949-51, U. Heidelberg, 1951-52; MD, U. Heidelberg, 1953. Asst. pharmacology dept. Heidelberg U., 1953; with pharmacology dept. Univ. Coll., London, 1953, Royal Coll. Surgeons, London, 1954; with Pathol. Inst., Heidelberg U., 1955, Med. Clinic, U. Munich, 1955-63; privat dozent for internal medicine Munich and Marburg, 1967-83; prof. U. Marburg, 1967-83; prof. internal medicine, Marburg. Contbr. articles to sci. jours. Lutheran. Mem. German Soc. for Internal Medicine. E-mail: 1steinweg@home.co. Home: 2155 Westhill Wynd, West Vancouver, BC Canada V7S 2Z3

KNAUTH, PHILIPPE CARL, chemistry, educator; b. Mannheim, Germany, May 24, 1960; s. Heinz Wilhelm and Colette Jeanne (Roche) K. Diploma chemistry, U. Saarbrücken, Germany, 1984, PhD, 1987; habil., U. Aix-Marseille, 1996. Sci. asst. U. Saarbrücken, 1983-87; postdoctoral fellow CNRS, Marseille, 1987-89; R&D engr. Bayer Co., Uerdingen, Germany, 1989-90; rsch. scientist CNRS/U. Marseille, 1990-99; prof. U. Provence, 1999—; vis. scientist MIT, Boston, 1997-98. Patentee in field. Grantee German Govt., Bonn, 1987-89, NATO, 1997-98. Mem. Deutsche Bunsen-Gesellschaft, Soc. Française de Chimie, Internat. Soc. Solid State Ionics, Materials Rsch. Soc. Roman Catholic. Avocations: music, arts, literature. Home: 87 Blvd Tellène, 13007 Marseille France Office: U Provence, Centre St Charles Case 26, 13331 Marseille Cedex 3, France

KNEBEL, CONSTANCE, potter, ceramist; b. Nov. 2, 1934. Student, Northeastern U., 1953-54, Boston Sch. Art, 1954-55. Asst. to editor Esquire Mag., N.Y.C., 1961-70; photographer Time, Inc., N.Y.C., 1971-83; freelance potter, ceramicist Honolulu, 1983-97, Canaan, N.Y., 1997—. E-mail: cknebel@taconic.net. Home: 271 Tunnel Hill Rd Canaan NY 12029-2706

KNEBEL, SVEN E., artist, painter, sculptor, writer; b. Zurich, Switzerland, Jan. 25, 1927; s. Otto and Martha Knebel; m. Dorrit Knebel-Honegger, Feb. 2, 1952; children: Kerstin, Allen, Iver, Dinah. Grad., Acad. Art, Zurich, Sculptor Sch. Zurich. Prof. Art Sch. Zurich. Editor, author book poetry; editor Spektrum, 1958-94. Mem. Internat. Unesco, GSMBA. Home: in Hofli Regensberg, CH 8158 Zurich Switzerland Studio: Napfgasse 4, CH-8001 Zurich Switzerland

KNECHT, BEN HARROLD, surgeon; b. Rapid City, S.D., May 3, 1938; m. Jane Bowles, Aug. 27, 1961; children: John, Janelle. BA, U. S.D., 1960; MD, U. Iowa, 1964; cert. total quality mgmt., U. Wash., 1998. Diplomate Am. Bd. Surgery. Intern Los Angeles County Gen. Hosp., 1964-65; resident in surgery U. Iowa Sch. Medicine, Iowa City, 1968-72; surgeon Wenatchee (Wash.) Valley Clinic, 1972—; med. dir. Cascade Hosp. and Surgery Ctr., 1997—; chmn. med. informatics Wen Valley Clinic, 1995—, chmn. gen.-vasc. surg. dept., 1996—; dir. emergency rm. Ctrl. Wash. Hosp., Wenatchee, 1972-79, chmn. libr., 1976-86, chief surgery, 1983-86; chmn. claims rev. panel Wash. State Med. Assn., Seattle, 1979-82, prof. liability com. risk mgmt., 1985-90; clin. prof. surgery U. Wash.; mem. adv. risk mgmt. com. Wash. State Physicians Ins. Subscribers, 1990-98, regional adv. com. Nat. Libr. Medicine, 1991-93. Fundraiser Cen. Wash. Hosp. Found., 1987; del. Gov.'s Conf. on Librs., 1991; bd. dirs. United Way, 1974-77; mem. founding bd. Cascade Unitarian Fellowship, 1986-88; mem. ad hoc com. on tchg./learning Wenatchee H.S., 1999—; post leader Med. Explorers, 1973-76. Lt. comdr. USN, 1965-68, Vietnam. Mem. AMA (alt. del. 1985-87, del. 1988-98, surg. caucus exec. com. 1991-94), ACS (bd. dirs. Wash. chpt. 1981-84), Am. Coll. Physician Execs., Am. Soc. Quality, North Pacific Surg. Assn., Wash. State Med. Assn. (trustee 1979-98), Chelan-Douglas County Med. Soc., Am. Soc. Gen. Surgery (founding bd. 1994—, bd. dir.1992—), Rotary (chmn. youth com. 1976-78), Alpha Tau Omega. Avocations: snow and water skiing, reading, hiking, computing. Office: Wenatchee Valley Clinic 820 N Chelan Ave Wenatchee WA 98801-2028

KNEGTEL, RONALD MARCEL ALPHONS, research scientist; b. Utrecht, The Netherlands, May 17, 1968; arrived in the U.K., 1999; s. Marcel Knegtel and Maria Smit; m. Frauke Gerrigje Florence Lockefeer, Oct. 19, 1995. BSc in Chemistry cum laude, Utrecht U., 1987, MSc in Chemistry cum laude, 1990, PhD in Chemistry cum laude, 1994. Rschr. protein crystallography dept. Groningen (The Netherlands) U., 1994-95; rschr. dept. pharm. chemistry U. Calif., San Francisco, 1995-96; rsch. scientist N.V. Organon, Oss, The Netherlands, 1996-99; investigator Vertex Pharms. (Europe) Ltd., Abingdon, U.K., 1999—. Contbr. chpts. to books and articles to profl. jours. Recipient prize for sci. and tech. Dutch State Mines, The Netherlands, 1992; NWO Talent fellow Dutch Orgn. for Sci. Rsch., The Netherlands, 1995. Mem. Royal Dutch Chemistry Soc., N.Y. Acad. Scis., Greenpeace. Avocations: music, science. Fax: 44 0 1235 820

440. E-mail: rknegtel@vpharm.com. Office: Vertex Pharm (Europe) Ltd, 88 Milton Pk, Abingdon OX14 4RY, United Kingdom

KNELLER, ALISTER, former chief justice of Gibraltar; b. Nov. 11, 1927; s. Arthur and Hester (Farr) Kneller. MA, Cambridge U., 1954, LLM, 1995. Resident magistrate Kenya, 1955-62, sen. dep. registrar, 1962-64, sen. state counsel, 1964-65, registrar of High Ct., 1965-69, Puisne judge, 1969-82, judge ct. appeal, 1982-86; chief justice Gibraltar, 1986-95. Knight Bachelor New Year's Honours List, 1995. Mem. Gray's Inn (hon. bencher 1995), United Oxford and Cambridge U. Club. Avocations: music, reading. Home: East View, Brookside Runcton, Chichester PO20 6PX, England

KNEPPER, RONALD ALAN, sculptor, educator; b. Ft. Wayne, Ind., May 9, 1955; s. Robert Lester and Janet Vera (Dressler) K.; m. Melissa Waters, Sept. 8, 1972 (div. Sept. 1977); children: Jennifer Lynn Knepper Tyson, Angelique Mae; m. Carol Brentegani Ferreira Dos Santos, Mar. 30, 1985; 1 child, Francesca Brentegani. BFA, Ind. U., 1982; MA, N.Mex. State U., 1985; MFA, Mills Coll., 1987. Vis. artist Biola U., La Mirada, Calif., 1986, Kent Inst. Art and Design, Canterbury, Eng., 1989, Hacettepe U., Ankara, Turkey, 1990; guest lectr. Bilkent U., Ankara, Turkey, 1989-90; adj. prof. Ind.-Purdue U., Ft. Wayne, 1992; dir. Kouros Gallery, N.Y.C., 1994-95; instr. Parsons Sch. Design, N.Y.C., 1995—; mem. gallery adv. bd. Mills Coll, Oakland, Calif., 1985-87; freshman advisor Bilkent U., 1989-90; edn. co-chair Names Project AIDS Quilt, Ft. Wayne, 1994. Group exbhns. include Ft. Wayne Mus. Art, 1993, South Bend (Ind.) Regional Mus. Art, 1993, Indpls. Mus. Art, 1994, Artists Space Gallery, 1994, Kouros Gallery, 1995, 96; represented in permanent collections Trinity English Luth. Ch., Concordia Luth. Seminary Libr., N.Mex. State U. Art Gallery, Zion Luth. Ch., Artworks Gallery, Palo Alto Group Women Collectors, Mills Coll. Art Gallery, Urart Sanat Galerisi, Siyah/Beyaz Sculpture Garden, GAllery Nev Sculpture Garden, Bilkent U., Haceteppe U. Art instr. Blaising Social Svcs., New Haven, Ind., 1993. With USN, 1972-73. Recipient grant Pollock-Krasner, 1992-92, fellowship Arts United Greater Ft. Wayne, 1992-93, residency Sculpture Space, Inc., 1994. Mem. Internat. Sculpture Ctr. Democrat. Lutheran. Avocations: photography, travel, music. Home: 186 Pinehurst Ave Apt 5A New York NY 10033-1730

KNERLY, STEPHEN JOHN, JR., lawyer; b. Lakewood, Ohio, Dec. 15, 1949; s. Stephen John Sr. and Mary Louise (Johnson) K.; m. Catherine Arion de Bravura; 1 child, Alexandra M. C. AB summa cum laude, Bowdoin Coll., 1972; AM, Fletcher Sch. Law & Diplomacy, 1973; JD, Case Western Res. U., 1976. Bar: Ohio 1976. Law clk. Stephen J. Knerly and Assocs., Cleve., 1973-74; law clk. Hahn, Loeser, Freedheim, Dean et al, Cleve., 1975-76, assoc., 1976-83; ptnr. Hahn, Loeser & Parks, Cleve., 1984—; CEO, mng. ptnr. Hahn, Loeser & Parks, LLP, Cleve., 1993—. James Bowdoin scholar Bowdoin Coll., 1972. Mem. Phi Beta Kappa. Home: 10390 Mitchells Mill Rd Chardon OH 44024-8613 Office: Hahn Loeser & Parks LLP 3300 BP Tower 200 Public Sq Ste 3300 Cleveland OH 44114-2303

KNEZ, MARTIN, geologist; b. Ljubljana, Slovenia, July 25, 1964. Diploma, U. Ljubljana, 1989; MS, 1992, PhD, 1996. Rschr. Karst Rsch. Inst. Sci. Rsch. Ctr. Slovenian Acad. Scis. and Arts, Postojna, 1989—. Contbr. numerous articles to profl. jours. Achievements include stratigraphic and lithopetrologic research of upper cretaceous and paleogene beds on karst terrains, research of selective corrosion and erosion of carbonate rocks and speleogenetic research of karst caves as part of underground karst aquifer. Fax: 386 05 700 1999. E-mail: knez@zrc-sazu.si. Office: Karst Rsch Inst ZRC SAZU, PO Box 59, SI-6230 Postojna Slovenia

KNIERIEM, BEULAH WHITE, retired educator, clergyman; b. Appomattox, Va., Oct. 31, 1930; d. George Harrison and Virgie Ade (Kestner) White; m. Robert William Knieriem, July 11, 1953; children: Shawn, Roxanne, Roberta. AA, Mars Hill (N.C.) Coll., 1950; BA, Lynchburg (Va.) Coll., 1952; student, Baldwin-Wallace Coll., 1964-69, Ashland Sem., 1992-93. Lic. elem. tchr., Ohio; lic. to ministry, 1995. Tchr. Bd. Edn., Cleve., 1966-79; lifetime Stephen min. United Ch. of Christ, Cleve., 1990—; interim min., 1997—; min. nursing homes, Cleve., 1990—; chaplain Ky. Cols., 1990—. Democrat. Avocation: running. Home: 7324 Grant Blvd Cleveland OH 44130-5351

KNIEST, FRANS M., biologist; b. Venlo, The Netherlands, Mar. 24, 1957; s. Henk J. and Yvon (Simais) K.; m. Bernadette Cambeen, Sept. 21, 1985; children: Stèphanie, Svenka. Doctor, Cath. U., 1981, PhD, 1990. Scientific rschr. Academic Hosp., Utrecht, 1982-88; asst. dir. Indoor Med. Biology Rsch. Ctr., Mainz, Germany, 1988-92; head rsch. dept. Allergopharma, Reinbek, Germany, 1992—. Patentee fine dust collector. Avocations: painting, butterflies, mites.

KNIEWALD, JASNA, toxicologist, educator, scientist; b. Zagreb, Croatia, June 24, 1938; d. Radivoj and Jelena (Operman) Novak; m. Zlatko Kniewald, July 14, 1962; children: Ines, Hrvoje. BSc, Tech. U. Zagreb, 1962, PhD, 1965. Rsch. assoc. Inst. Physical Chem., Zagreb, Croatia, 1962-75; sr. rsch. assoc. Technol. Faculty U. Zagreb, 1976-86; from rsch. advisor to prof., head toxicology lab. Faculty Food Sci. & Biotech. U. Zagreb, 1987—. Co-author: Food and Development, 1987, Technology and Development, 1989, Food Technology and Biotechnology, 1990; author: (textbooks) Methods in Scientific Work, 1993, Toxicology-Practice, 1997; contbr. articles to profl. jours. Mem. European Soc. Toxicology, European Sci. Found., Croatian Acad. Tech. Scis. Avocations: skiing, swimming. Home: Rakovčeva 6, 10000 Zagreb Croatia Office: U Zagreb, Pierotti Str 6, 10000 Zagreb Croatia

KNIGHT, ALICE DOROTHY TIRRELL, state legislator; b. Manchester, N.H., July 14, 1903; d. Nathan Arthur and Clara (Stiles) Tirrell; m. Norman Knight, Nov. 15, 1952. B.A., U. N.H., 1925, postgrad., 1933; postgrad. Boston U., 1941-42. Tchr. Newton Falls (N.Y.) High Sch., 1925-26; prin. Oswegatchie (N.Y.) Union Sch., 1926-27, Bartlett Sch., Goffstown, N.H., 1932-35; home lighting specialist Pub. Svc. Co. N.H., Manchester, 1935-39; tchr. merchandising Mt. Ida Jr. Coll., Newton Centre, Mass., 1939-45; home svc. dir. Boyd Corp., Portland, Maine, 1945-47; dist. home economist Frigidaire Sales Corp., Boston, 1948-64; mem. N.H. Ho. of Reps., 1967-74, 76-78, 80-90; rep to N.H. Gen. Ct., 1967-91; mem. joint legis. com. on elderly affairs, 1983-87; pres. Greater Manchester Community Concert Assn., 1985-87; co-chmn. Goffstown Bicentennial Com. of the Constn., 1986—. Mem. budget com. Town of Goffstown, 1966-72; mem. Gov.'s Adv. Com. Alcoholism, 1972-73, 74-78, Statewide Health Coordinating Coun., 1977-78, N.H. Hist. Soc.; past pres. bd. dirs. Hillsborough County North Cancer Soc.; bd. dirs. N.H. Cancer Soc. Recipient award N.H. Program on Alcohol and Drug Abuse, 1971, 75, Gov.'s Recognition award Hillsborough County, 1986, Pub. Svc.award Union Pomona Grange, 1987. Mem. Nat. Home Fashions League (pres. 1957-58), Nat. Order State Legislators, Vis. Nurses Assn. (bd. dirs. Greater Manchester chpt. 1981-87), N.H. Coun. World Affairs, Nat. Grange (life), DAR (regent 1974-76), Nat. Order Women Legislators (treas. 1968-71), Manchester Bus. and Profl. Women (pres. 1972-74), Nat. Soc. New Eng. Women, Order Eastern Star (life), Soroptomist (life, Boston), Goffstown Unity Club, Goffstown Garden Club (pres. 1976-78), Goffstown Shirley Club (pres. 1977-78), Goffstown Hist. Soc. (life). Republican.

KNIGHT, COLIN, computer educator, consultant; b. Kent, Eng.; s. Joseph and Edith (Brooks) K.; m. Diana Carole Grundy; children: Peter, Steven, John. BSc, Chelsea Coll., London, 1965, MSc, 1967. Chartered engr.; chartered mathematician. Sr. lectr. Poly. of South Bank, London, 1967-78; sr. cons. Infotech, Maidenhead, Eng., 1978-80; tng. mgr. SEMA, London, 1982-86; tng. dir. Midsummer Computing, 1987-90; bursar King Edward VI Sch., Louth, Eng., 1991-97; cons. info. tech. Thames Water, Reading, Eng., 1980-92; sr. lectr. Grimsby Coll., 1997—. Fellow Inst. Pers.; mem. Nat. Bursars Assn. (treas. 1994-97), Brit. Computer Soc., Inst. Math. Avocations: gardening, sheep breeding, boating. Office: Grimsby Coll, Nuns Corner, Grimsby DN34 5BQ, England

KNIGHT, DEREK JOHN, regulatory affairs professional; b. Oakham, Rutland, England, Jan. 21, 1959; s. Keith Windsor and Dorothy Mary (Featherstone) K.; m. Ruth Elizabeth Harrison; children: Leora, Gareth. BA in Chemistry, Oxford U., England, 1981, PhD in Chemistry, 1983, MA (hon.), 1984. Process support chemist Boots Co. PLC, Nottingham, England, 1984-86, product registration officer, 1986-99; head registration svcs. Safepharm Labs. LTD., Derby, England, 1989—; spl. dir. Safepharm Labs. LTD., 2000—. Contbr. chpts. to books. Fellow Royal Soc. Chemistry (co. rep. 1996—), Brit. Inst. Regulatory Affairs; mem. Brit. Assn. for Advancement of Sci. Avocations: psychology, interpersonal skills. Office: Safepharm Labs LTD, PO Box 45, Derby DE1 2BT, England

KNIGHT, DORIS RATHBUN, retired government and history educator; b. N.Y.C., Feb. 22, 1936; d. Roger E. and Armenia (Bertoli) Rathbun; m. Paul R. Knight, Apr. 19, 1958; 1 child, Roger. BA, U. Mass., 1957, MA, 1962, postgrad., 1962-63, 72-73. Editl. asst. Merriam-Webster Unabridged Dictionary, 3d edit., Springfield, Mass., 1958-60; prof., chair social sci. divsn. Holyoke (Mass.) C.C., 1963-94. Guest columnist Jour.-Tribune, Biddeford, Maine, 1994-97. Mem., chair planning bd. Northampton, Mass., 1977-82; mem. planning bds. Southampton, Mass., 1983-92, Kennebunkport, Maine, 1995-99, vice chmn., 1998-99, zoning bd. appeals, 1999—, chair, 2000—; vice chair Dem. Town Com., Southampton, 1990-94; vice chair R.S.V.P. So. Maine Adv. Coun., 1998-99, chair, 1999-2000. Mem. Newcomers Club (pres. 1997-98). Avocations: reading, writing, travel, local history research.

KNIGHT, EDWIN WALTER, occupational physician; b. Perth, Australia, Nov. 1, 1934; s. Walter Albert and Amelia Julia (Knapp) K.; m. Maureen Ann Malone, Feb. 7, 1959; children: Gillian Marina, Simon John, Deirdre Helen, Roger Michael (dec.), Sophie Louise, Richard Francis. MB, BS, U. Adelaide, Australia, 1957. Jr. resident med. officer Footscray & Dist. Hosp., Melbourne, Australia, 1958; sr. resident med. officer Footscray & Dist. Hosp., Melbourne, 1960; gen. practice Melbourne, 1961-72; med. cons. The Herald and Weekly Times, Melbourne, 1972—; med. cons. David Syme & Co., Melbourne, 1973-96, Nissan Motor Mfg. Co., Melbourne, 1977-85, Nat. Safety Coun. Victoria, Melbourne, 1979-84; staff health physician Alfred Hosp., Melbourne, 1996—; hon. sr. lectr. dept. epidemiology and preventive medicine Monash U., Melbourne, 1987—; mem. bd. mgmt. Inter Ch. Trade and Industry Mission, 1975-85, chmn., 1982-83; chmn. Australia and New Zealand Soc. Occup. Medicine-Victorian/Tasmanian Br., 1983-85; mem. regional com. Victoria Faculty Occupl. Medicine, 1993—, chmn., 1995. Author: Dollar Doctor, 1974, Childrens Doctor, 1977, revised edit., 1992, Emotional Illness, 1979, Emergency Doctor, 1983, Family Doctor, 1986, Living With Stress, 1987, The Family Medical Diary, 1991; co-author: Square Pegs Square Holes, 1981, Look Good Feel Great, 1987; med. columnist The Weekly Times, 1972-96, Australasian Post, 1973-92, The Sun News Pictorial, 1975-90, The Australian Womens Weekly, 1978, New Idea, 1979-82. Fellow Royal Australian Coll. Gen. Practitioners, Australasian Coll. Occupl. Medicine, Australasian Faculty Occupl. Medicine; mem. Australian and New Zealand Soc. Occupl. Medicine, Victorian Racing Club, Melbourne Cricket Club, Kooyong Lawn Tennis Club. Avocations: running, reading, bridge. Home: 9 Ranfurlie Cres Glen Iris, Melbourne VIC 3146, Australia Office: Herald & Weekly Times, 40 City Rd Southbank, Melbourne VIC 3006, Australia

KNIGHT, JAMES ATWOOD, consulting executive; b. Providence, Apr. 26, 1954; s. Richard Brayton and Louise (Atwood) K.; m. Cynthia Forbes Olney, June 11, 1983; children: Hilary Atwood, James Atwood Jr., Remington Forbes, William Olney, Elsie Lawson. BS, Boston U., 1975; MBA, Dartmouth Coll., 1984. Sr. assoc. Strategic Decisions Group, Menlo Park, Calif., 1984-88; mgr. Apple Computer, Cupertino, Calif., 1988-90; with Holt, Chgo., 1990, Boston Cons. Group, Chgo., 1991-95; v.p. SCA Consulting L.L.C., Chgo., 1995-97, mng. ptnr., 1997—. Author: Value Based Management, 1997; contbr. chpt. to book. Avocations: skiing, squash. Home: 606 Tiverton Rd Lake Forest IL 60045-1655 Office: SCA Consulting LLC 200 W Madison St Ste 1900 Chicago IL 60606-3471

KNIGHT, KEITH DESMOND ST. AUBYN, Jamaican government official; b. Brompton, Jamaica, May 24, 1941; m. Pauline Knight; 2 children. Student, Howard U., U. Pitts. Bar: Jamaica 1973. M.P., 1989—; min. nat. security and justice Govt. of Jamaica, Kingston, 1989—; spokesman nat. security People's Nat. Party, 1984-89, chmn. security force com., 1993, mem. exec. coun. Mem. exec. and nat. exec. coun. People's Nat. Party, also chmn. Security Force Commn. Mem. Jamaica Nat. Assn. (founder, past pres.). Office: Min Nat Security Box 472, 12 Ocean Blvd Kingston Mall, Kingston 10, Jamaica*

KNIGHT, LILA CUCKSEE, executive secretary, poet; b. Chattanooga, Apr. 11, 1931; d. William Henry and Anna Leona (Bonine) Cucksee; children: David, Jonathan, Paul, Joel Knight, Sheryl Knight Carlock. Diploma in Sectl. Sci., Edmondson Jr. Coll., 1983; diploma, Life Underwriters Tng. Coun., Chattanooga, 1986. life ins. lic. Modern Woodmen Sch., 1983. Preneed sales woman Lakewood Memory Gardens, Rossville, Ga., 1983, Tenn./Ga. Meml. Park, Rossville, 1983; dist. rep. Modern Woodmen of Am., Rossville, 1983-84; ins. agent United Ins. Co. Am., Chattanooga, 1984-86; area sales mgr. World Book/Child Craft, Chattanooga, 1986; sr. clerk Gwinnett Mental Health/Mental Retardation/Sub. Abuse Ctr., Lawrenceville, Ga., 1986-89; spl. edn. sch. bus driver Gwinnett County Sch. Sys., 1990-97; pres. Knight Innovations, Inc. Author of numerous poems; inventor in med. field (U.S. Patent issued for the "Recovery Shield"). Mem. Lakeview Home-Sch. Orgn., Fort Oglethorpe, Ga., 1955-86. Mem. Internat. Soc. Poetry, Boys Town, Sr. Friends Club. Republican. Baptist. Avocations: poetry, hiking, swimming, singing.

KNIGHT, ROBERT EDWARD, banker; b. Alliance, Nebr., Nov. 27, 1941; s. Edward McKean and Ruth (McDuffee) K.; m. Eva Sophia Youngstom, Aug. 12, 1966. BA, Yale U., 1963; MA, Harvard U., 1965, PhD, 1968. Asst. prof. U.S. Naval Acad., Annapolis, Md., 1966-68; lectr. U. Md., 1967-68; fin. economist Fed. Res. Bank of Kansas City (Mo.), 1968-70, rsch. officer, economist, 1971-76, asst. v.p., sec., 1977, v.p., sec., 1978-79; pres. Alliance (Nebr.) Nat. Bank, 1979-94, also chmn., 1983-94; pres. Robert Knight Assocs., banking and econ. cons., Cheyenne, 1979—; chmn. Eldred Found., 1985—; vis. prof., chair banking and fin. East Tenn. State U., Johnson City, 1988; mem. faculty Stonier Grad. Sch. Banking, 1972—, Colo. Grad. Sch. Banking, 1975-82, Am. Inst. Banking, U. Mo., Kansas City, 1971-79, Prochnow Grad. Sch. Banking, U. Wis., 1980-84; mem. extended learning faculty Park Coll., 1996—; mem. Coun. for Excellence for Bur. Bus. Rsch. U. Nebr., Lincoln, 1991-94, mem. Grad. Sch. Arts and Scis. Coun., Harvard, 1994—; chmn. Taxable Mcpl. Bondholders Protective Com., 1991-94. Contbr. articles to profl. jours. Bd. dirs. People of Faith (Royal Oaks) Found., 1999—, Stonier Grad. Sch. Banking, 1979-82, Nebr. Com. for Humanities, 1986-90; trustee Knox Presbyn. Ch., Overland Park, Kans., 1965-69; bd. regents Nat. Comml. Lending Sch., 1980-83; mem. Downtown Improvement Com., Alliance, 1981-94; trustee U. Nebr. Found., 1982-94; mem. fin. com. United Meth. Ch. Alliance, 1982-85, trustee, 1990-93; mem. Box Butte County Indsl. Devel. Bd., 1987-94. Woodrow Wilson fellow, 1963-64. Mem. Am. Econ. Assn., Am. Fin. Assn., So. Econ. Assn., Nebr. Bankers Assn. (com. state legis. 1980-81, com. comml. loans and investments 1986-87), Am. Inst. Banking (state com. for Nebr. 1980-83), Am. Bankers Assn. (econ. adv. com. 1980-83, cmty. bank leadership coun.), Western Econ. Assn., Econometric Soc., Rotary, Masons. Home and Office: 429 W 5th Ave Cheyenne WY 82001-1249

KNIGHT, ROBERT MILTON, journalist, educator; b. Tacoma, Dec. 2, 1940; s. Lawrence Leslie Knight and Marian Delphine (Humphrey) Gordy, (stepmother) Margaret Irene (Michael) K.; m. Susan Jan Guthrie, July 3, 1965; children: Kelly Leslie, Leigh April. BS in Journalism, U. Colo., 1967; MA in Integrated Profl. Studies, De Paul U., 1996. Statehouse reporter The New Mexican, Santa Fe, 1968-70; gen. newsman Sta. KOB-TV and Radio, Albuquerque, 1970-71; statehouse corr. Sta. KOAT-TV, Albuquerque, 1971-73; freelance journalism Chgo., 1973-74; product mgr. Deltak, Inc., Schiller Park, Ill., 1974-76; mgr. corp. comm. Advanced Sys., Inc., Elk Grove Village, Ill., 1976-79; account exec. Hill & Knowlton, Inc., Chgo., 1979-81; freelance writer Knight, Writer, Chgo., 1981-94; sr. editor City News Bur. of Chgo., 1994-98; mem. adv. bd. PC/Expo Chgo., 1989-90; lectr. Northwestern U., 1984-98; lectr. journalism and English, Gettysburg Coll., 1998—. Author: A Journalistic Approach to Good Writing: The Craft of Clarity, 1998; contbr. articles to newspapers and mags. With USN, 1959-61. Mem. Soc. Profl. Journalists (bd. dirs. Chgo. Headline Club chpt. 1992—, regional conf. chairperson 1993, chpt. pres. 1994-95), Ind. Writers Chgo. (bd. dirs. 1983-85, program chairperson 1991-93). Home: 1225 Beecherstown Rd Biglerville PA 17307-9511

KNIGHT, SANDRA NORTON, civil engineer; b. Chattanooga, Mar. 2, 1962; d. Johnny Lee Norton and Wanda Dean (Pledger) Weaver. Student, Chattanooga State Tech. C.C., 1980-82; BSCE, U. Tenn., 1986; postgrad., Fla. State U., 1990. Registered profl. engr., Tenn. Traffic engr. technician City of Knoxville; project mgr. Fla. Dept. Transp., Tallahassee, 1987-93, Cook & Spencer Cons., Chattanooga, 1993-96; engr. design mgr. City of Chattanooga, 1996; county engr. Bradley County, Cleveland, Tenn., 1996—. Bldg. inspector Town of Decatur, Tenn., 1996-99, alderman, 1995-99. Mem. ASCE (sec.-treas. 1994-95, v.p. 1995-96, pres. 1996-97, v.p. Tenn. sect. 1998-99, pres.-elect Tenn. sect. 1999—, pres. Tenn. sect. 1999-2000, Young Engr. of Yr. 1991, 96, 97), TSPE (sec. Chattanooga chpt. 1998-99, v.p. 1999-2000, profl. engr. in govt. Tenn. sect. 2000). Republican. Baptist. Avocations: Siberian huskies, reading. Office: Bradley County Engr PO Box 1167 Cleveland TN 37364-1167

KNIGHT, STELLA CATHERINE, medical researcher; b. Birmingham, U.K., Dec. 30, 1942; d. Leslie Rowland Vincent and Hilda Kathleen (Young) K. BSc, U. Birmingham, 1964, PhD, 1967; diploma in history of art, U. London, 1984. Rsch. fellow U. Birmingham, 1967-71; internat. rsch. fellow NIH, Bethesda, Md., 1969-70; scientist Clin. Rsch. Ctr., Harrow, U.K., 1971-89; spl. appt. Med. Rsch. Coun., London, 1989—; prof. immunopathology Imperial Coll. Sch. Medicine U. London, 1994—; bd. dirs. Vintec Labs., Watford, U.K.; dir. preclin. rsch. Northwick Park Inst. for Med. Rsch., Harrow, 1994—. Author: (with others) Clinical Aspects of Immunology, 1994; contbr. articles to profl. jours. Recipient Strategic Rsch. award ICI Plc, 1991, Acad. Ptnr. for Smart awards Dept. of Trade and Industry U.K., 1988, 92. Fellow Inst. of Biology; mem. Med. Rsch. Club (treas. 1989-92), British Soc. for Immunology. Home: 11 Nightingale Rd, Bushey WD23 3NJ, England Office: Antigen Presentation GroupImperial Coll Sch Med, Northwick Park Hosp, Harrow HA1 3UJ, England

KNIGHT, COUNT VON VLORE, BARON DE NARES See VON EFANS-TARAFDAR, QUENTIN

KNIGHT-JONES, PHYLLIS KATHLEEN, marine biologist, consultant; b. London, Mar. 24, 1933; d. Arthur John and Phyllis Mildred (Yeates) Fisher; m. Elis Wyn Knight-Jones, Jul. 26, 1969; 1 child, Gaynor. MSc, Swansea, Wales, 1977, PhD, 1980. Puppeteer Europe, N. Africa, India, 1951-64; rsch. tech. Glaxo, Stoke Poges, Eng., 1964-69; rsch. assoc. Univ. Wales, Swansea, 1970-83; fellowship Australia, 1983; rsch. fellow Univ. Wales, 1984—; hon. rsch. fellow Nat. Mus. Wales, Cardiff, 1984—; cons. in tubeworm taxonomy, 1972—. Contbr. articles to profl. jours. Fellow Linnean Soc.; mem. Inst. Biology, Marine Biological Assn., Systematics Assn. Avocation: watercolor painting. Home: Bryngwyn Llanrhidian, SA31EE Swansea Wales United Kingdom Office: Univ Wales Sch Biol Sci, SA2 8PP Swansea Wales United Kingdom

KNIGHTS, KATHLEEN MARY, biochemical pharmacologist; b. Adelaide, Australia, July 23, 1951; d. Harold Stanley and Dulcie Joan (Smith) Holzberger; m. John Oliver Miners, Apr. 4, 1987. BSc with honors, N.E.L.P., London, 1978; PhD, Flinders U. South Australia, Adelaide, 1985. Nat. Health and Med. Rsch. Coun. rsch. officer Flinders U. South Australia, 1984-86, rsch. fellow, 1987, lectr., 1989-93, sr. lectr., 1994-99, assoc. prof., 1999—; lectr. SACAE, Adelaide, 1987-88; grant referee Nat. Health and Med. Rsch. Coun. Australia; jour. referee Biochem. Pharmacology, Chirality, Life Scis., Molecular Pharmacology. Contbr. over 35 articles to sci. jours. Rsch. grantee Nat. Health and Med. Rsch. Coun. Australia, 1990-95, 97-99, Arthritis Found. Australia, 1987-88, 90, 93, Ramaciotti Found., 1990. Mem. Australian Soc. Clin. and Exptl. Pharmacology and Toxicology (councillor 1997—, treas. 1998—), Internat. Union Pharmacology, Internat. Soc. for Study of Xenobiotics. Avocations: swimming, fencing, kendo. Office: Flinders U South Australia, Dept Clin Pharmacology, Adelaide SA 5042, Australia

KNIPPING, DETLEF, art historian; b. Hamm, Germany, May 1, 1963. Curator Bayerisches Landesamt für Denkmalpflege, München, Germany, 1995—. Contbr. articles to profl. jours. Home: Kopernikusstrasse 2, 81679 München Germany Office: Bayerisches Landesamt, Hofgraben 4, 80539 Munich Germany

KNISEL, WERNER, physician; b. Saulgau, Bad-Wuertt, Germany, Apr. 18, 1953; s. Karl and Anneliese (Angele) K. MD, U. Tuebingen, Bad-Wuertt, 1979. Specialist in internal medicine, endocrinology, diabetes. Clin. scientist dept. internal medicine Univ. Hosp., Tuebingen, 1980-90; med. dir. Reha-Klinik Kandertal, Malsburg-Marzell, 1990—. Contbr. articles to publs. in field. Mem. European Assn. for the Study of Diabetes, other scientific orgns. Roman Catholic. Office: Reha-Klinik Kandertal, Malsburg-Marzell D-79429, Germany

KNOBBE, LOUIS JOSEPH, lawyer; b. Carroll, Iowa, Apr. 6, 1932; s. Louis C. and Elsie M. (Praeger) K.; m. Jeanette M. Sganga, Apr. 3, 1954; children: Louis, Michael, Nancy, John, Catherine. BSEE, Iowa State U., 1953; JD, Loyola U., L.A., 1959. Bar: Calif. 1960, U.S. Supreme Ct. 1963; U.S. Patent and Trademark Office. Tech. staff Bell Telephone Labs., 1953-54; patent engr. GE, Washington, 1955-56, N.Am. Aviation, Downey, Calif., 1956-59; patent lawyer Beckman Instruments, Fullerton, Calif., 1959-62; co-founder, ptnr. Knobbe, Martens, Olson & Bear, Newport Beach, Calif., 1962—; lectr. Am. Intellectual Property Law Assn., Computer Law Assn., Inc., L.A. Intellectual Property Law Assn., San Diego Bar Assn., Orange County Patent Law Assn.; adj. prof. Sch. Law U. San Diego, 1987—. Co-author: Attorney's Guide to Trade Secrets, 1972, 2d edit., 1996, How to Handle Basic Patent, 1992; contbg. author: Using Intellectual Property Rights to Protect Domestic Markets, 1986; contbr. articles to profl. jours. Bd. dirs. Orange County (Calif.) Performing Arts Ctr., 1975-83, Orange County chpt. Assn. Corp. Growth; past pres. Philaharmonic Soc. Orange County; bd. mem., past v.p. Opera Pacific, Orange County. Fellow Inst. Advancement Engring.; mem. ABA, IEEE (past chmn. Orange County sect., Centennial medal 1984), Am. Intellectual Property Law Assn., Am. Arbitration Soc. (mem. panel neutrals), State Bar Calif., Orange County Bar Assn. (mem. civil mediation panel), Orange County Patent Law Assn., San Diego Patent Law Assn., Licensing Execs. Soc., Santa Ana North Rotary, First Friday Friars, Pacific Club, Balboa Yacht Club, Phi Kappa Phi, Tau Beta Pi, Eta Kappa Nu. Avocations: boating, still and video photography, travel and exploration in Lake Powell, Death Valley, deserts of Arizona and Baja, California. Office: 620 Newport Center Dr Fl 16 Newport Beach CA 92660-6420

KNOBLOCH, CHARLES SARON, lawyer; b. Wayne, Mich., May 11, 1959; s. Faustyn Edwin and Ameaila Caroline (Marquardt) K. BS in Applied Geophysics with honors, Mich. Tech. U., 1980; JD, U. Houston, 1991; Coll. of William and Mary, Madrid, 1990; Diploma in Internat. Law, U. San Diego, Russia, 1991. Bar: Tex. 1992; cert. patent atty. U.S. Patent & Trademark Office, 1994, Coll. of State Bar of Tex., 1994-96. Pvt. practice Houston, 1992—; with DuPont/Conoco, Houston/Jakarta, 1980—; finalist, Outstanding Young Texans, Jaycees, 1993, adv. bd. Tex. Accts. and Lawyers for the Arts, 1997; bd. dirs. Houston Intranet, Inc., 1995; pres. Omni-law.com, 1993—. Chair M.D. Anderson Cancer Ctr. Network, Houston, 1997; nominated attendee John Ben Shepperd Pub. Leadership Forum, Austin, Tex., 1995. Recipient Engrg. Excellence award DuPont, Imaging Tech. award, 1996. Mem. Houston Intellectual Property Law Assn., Indonesian Petroleum Assn. (data mgmt. com., ad hoc legal com. 1999), Amer. Bar Assn. (corp. law com.), Am. Assn. of Petroleum Geologists (co-chair data mgmt. Bali 2000). Office: DuPont Conoco Jakarta Pouch PO Box 4569 Houston TX 77210-4569

KNOBLOCH, HANS-JOERG, German literature educator; b. Gablonz/Neisse, Germany, Mar. 16, 1942; arrived in S.Africa, 1983; s. Alfred A.S. and Hildegard E. (Seidel) K.; m. Christine M. Horzinek, Oct. 28, 1966 (div. 1992); children: Katja, Janina. PhD, U. Heidelberg, 1972; Asst. Prof., Rand Afrikaans U., S. Africa, 1988, Prof., 1989. Lectr. Fachhochschule Karlsruhe, Germany, 1972-82; lectr. Rand Afrikaans U., Johannesburg, S. Africa, 1983—, head German dept., 1988—; freelance writer, 1973—; mem. senate

Coll. of Edn., Windhoek, Namibia, 1987-92, Rand Afrikaans U., 1989—; guest prof. U. Augsburg, Germany, 1990; convener/organizer Biannual Mtg. of Scholars of Germanic Studies at Rand Afrikaans U., 1990—. Author: (book) Das Ende des Expressionismus: Von der Tragödie zur Komödie, 1975; editor and co-author: (books) Schiller heute, 1996, Deutschsprachige Gegenwartsliteratur, 1997, Hundert Jahre Brecht-Brechts Jahrhundert?, 1998. Bertolt Brecht guest professorship, U. Augsburg, 1995. Mem. Internat. Assn. Germanic Studies, Internat. Brecht Soc., Assn. for Germanic Studies in So. Africa. Roman Catholic. Avocation: tennis. Office: Rand Afrikaans Univ, PO Box 524, ZA-2006 Auckland Park South Africa

KNOCH, TOBIAS AURELIUS, physicist, researcher; b. Mannheim, Germany, May 19, 1971; s. Wolfgang Franz and Waltraut (List) K. BSc. in Math. and Physics, U. Heidelberg, Germany, 1994, MSc, 1997. Rschr. 3D Human Genome Study Group German Cancer Rsch. Ctr., Heidelberg, 1996—. Author: The Three-Dimensional Organization of a Self Replicating Nano Fabrication Site: The Human Cell Nucleus, 1997. Scholar Ministry of Edn., State of Baden-Württemberg, Stuttgart, Germany, 1989, 90, 91, German Nat. Scholarship Found., Bonn., German Acad. Exch. Office, Bonn, 1996; recipient travel award Molecular Graphics and Modelling Soc., 1998, Poster prize, DKFZ, 2000. Mem. AAAS, Bund für Umwelt und Naturschutz Deutschland. Avocations: philosophy, arts, travel expeditions. Office: German Cancer Rsch Ctr, Im Neuenheimer Feld 280, 69120 Heidelberg Germany

KNÖCHLEIN, GERMAR, physicist; b. Mainz, Germany, Aug. 19, 1969; s. Erwin and Magdalena Maria (Kirch) K. Diploma, U. Mainz, Mainz, 1994; PhD, U. Mainz, 1997. Rschr. U. Mainz, 1994-97; vis. rschr. U. Mass., Amherst, 1995-96, TRIUMF, Vancouver, B.C., 1997—; risk analyst risk supervision unit Landesbank Rheinland-Pfalz, Mainz; lectr. U. Applied Scis., Wiesbaden. Contbr. articles to profl. jours. Airman 2nd class German Air Force, 1988-89. Scholar Deutscher Akademischer Austauschdienst. Fellow German Nat. Scholarship Found.; mem. German Amateur Radio Club, German Phys. Soc. Office: Landesbank Rheinland-Pfalz, Grosse Bleiche 54-56, D-55098 Mainz Germany

KNOELL, DIETER RUDOLF, medical educator; b. Landau, Germany, Jan. 2, 1951; s. Theodor Karl Eugen and Ninni (Daeuwel) K. MA, Freie U., Berlin, 1977; PhD, U. Koblenz-Land, 1991. Prof. Hochschule fur Kunst und Design, Halle, Germany, 1995—. Author: Die Gesunden u.d. Normale, 1972, Zur Lage der Nation, 1978, Aesthetik Zwischen Krit, Theorie U. Positivismus, 1986, Kritik der deutschen Wendekoepfe, 1992, Zur gesellschaftlichen Stellung der Kunst, 1995. Mem. N.Y. Acad. Scis. Home: Advokatenweg 13, 06114 Halle Germany Office: Hochschule f Kunst Design, Seebener Str 1, 06116 Halle Germany

KNOLL, JOACHIM, education educator, consultant; b. Freystadt, Germany, Nov. 23, 1932. PhD summa cum laude, U. Erlangen, Germany, 1956. Asst. U. Erlangen, 1956-57; spl. corr. SWF Radio, 1957-59; asst. prof. U. Hamburg, 1959-60; assoc. prof. P.H. Bonn, 1961-64; prof. U. Bochum, 1964-98, prof. emeritus, 1998—; mem. UNESCO Commn., Germany, 1985—; mem. gov. bd. Internat. Congress of Univ. Adult Edn., Can., 1975-85. Editor Internat. Year Book of Adult Edn., 1969-98; co-editor Zeitschrift für Religions und Geistegeschichte, 1987—, Bildung und Erziehung, 1978—. Mem. Assn. History of Ideas (gov. bd. dirs. 1964—), N.Y. Acad. Scis. Home: Breitestr 159, G-22767 Hamburg Germany

KNÖPPEL, HANS-ARMIN, librarian; b. Flensburg, Germany, Sept. 13, 1941. PhD, U. Kiel, Germany, 1969. Acquisition libr. Univ. Libr., Wuerzburg, Germany, 1972-91; chief libr. Univ. Libr., Greifswald, Germany, 1991—. Lutheran. Office: Greifswald Univ Bibliothek, Rubenowstr 4, D-17487 Greifswald Germany

KNOPS-GERRITS, PETER-PAUL HENDRIK, chemical engineer; b. Hasselt, Limburg, Belgium, Jan. 5, 1969; s. Françis Xavier and Monica (Koninckx) K.-G.; m. Anne Debrabandere; 1 child, Julie Knops-Gerrits. Degree in chem. engring., Katholieke U., Leuven, Belgium, 1992, PhD in chem. Engring., 1997; postgrad., Hong Kong U., 1994, Hokkaido U., Sapporo, JaEan, 1997. NASA intern in life scis. Cornell U., Ithaca, N.Y., 1992; postdoctoral fellow div. chem. and chem. engring. & Beckman Calif. Inst. Tech., Pasadena, 1997-99; lectr. in field. Contbr. numerous articles to internat. jours., chpts. to books. Mem. N.Y. Acad. Sci., Fonds Voor Wetenschappelijk Onderzoek, Belgian Am. Ednl. Found. (hon.), Belgian Nat. Sci. Found. Avocations: skiing, scuba diving, literature.

KNOT, KLAAS HENDERIKUS WILLEM, economist, researcher; b. Bedum, The Netherlands, Apr. 14, 1967; s. Piet H. and Janny G. (Dijkstra) K. MD, U. Groningen, The Netherlands, 1991, PhD, 1995. Rschr. U. Groningen, 1991-95; economist De Nederlandsche Bank, Amsterdam, 1995-98, div. chief, 1999—; economist IMF, Washington, 1998-99; divsn. chief Nederlanasche Bank, 1999—; vis. asst. prof. U. Utrecht, The Netherlands; vis. rschr. U. Groningen, 1995-98. Author: Fiscal Policy and Interest Rates in the European Union, 1996; contbr. articles to profl. jours. Mem. European Econ. Assn., Am. Econ. Assn. Office: De Nederlandsche Bank ANB Supervision, PO Box 98, 1000 AB Amsterdam The Netherlands

KNOTEK, PETR, psychologist; b. Litomysl, Czech Republic, Dec. 23, 1940; s. Alois and Anna (Bockova) K.; divorced; 1 child, Ivan. BSc in Pedagogy, Charles U., 1964, BSc in Psychology, 1969, MSc in Psychology, 1970; PhD, Acad. Scis. Prague, Czech Republic, 1982. Rschr. Rsch. Inst. Psychiatry, Prague, 1973-78; head rsch. lab. Univ. Hosp., Prague, 1978-83; head dept. mental hygiene Rsch. Inst. Psychiatry, 1983-86; head pain study dept. Inst. Physiology, Prague, 1988-92, Stapro, Pardubice, Czech Republic, 1992-95; psychologist Univ. Hosp., Prague, 1995—; cons. psychologist Intercosmos Internat., 1989-90; cons., lectr. in field. Editor, co-author: Pain-Psychosocial Problems, 1994; contbr. articles to profl. jours. Mem. Internat. Brain Rsch. Orgn., N.Y. Acad. Scis., Internat. Assn. Study of Pain, Stress and Anxiety Rsch. Soc. Avocations: music, sports, philosophy, mathematics, gardening. Home: Pod kastany 21, 160 00 Prague 6 Czech Republic

KNOTTENBELT, JOHN DUNCAN, emergency physician; b. Ft. Beaufort, South Africa, June 21, 1944; s. Alfred Priestley and Margaret Elaine (Carr) K.; m. Christine Marie Fairley, Dec. 31, 1966; children: Richard George., William John, John Alfred. BSc, U. Cape Town, 1984; MBChB, U. Birmingham, 1968. Med. supt., cons. surgeon Gwelo Hosp., Zimbabwe, 1977-79; cons. surgeon Harare Hosp., Zimbabwe, 1979-81; trauma registrar Groote Schuur Hosp., Cape Town, South Africa, 1981-83; sr. trauma specialist Groote Schuur Hosp., Cape Town, 1983-90; head dept., assoc. prof. trauma surgery Univ. Cape Town, 1990-94; accident & emergency cons. Northwick Park Hosp., Harrow, UK, 1995—; head trauma unit Univ. Cape Town Groote Schuur Hosp., 1987-94. Author, editor: Trauma Handbook, 1992, 3d edit., 1998; contbr. articles to profl. jours. Fellow Royal Coll. Surgeons (England), Royal Coll. Surgeons (Edinburgh), Royal Coll. Physicians, Faculty Accident and Emergency Medicine. Avocations: bridge, chess, computing. Home: 1 Oakley Grange, Harrow, Middlesex HA1 3JU, England Office: Northwick Park Hosp Accident & Emergency Dept, Watford Rd, HA1 3UJ Harrow England

KNOTTNERUS, PAUL, statistician; b. Hillegom, The Netherlands, June 28, 1948; s. Simon Leonard and Hendrika Christina (Kuipéri) K. MBA in Econometrics, U. Amsterdam, The Netherlands, 1973, PhD in Econs., 1989. Cons. Dutch Telecom, The Hague, The Netherlands, 1976-78, mgr. dept. econometrics, 1978-89, mgr. unit consultancy, 1989-95; mgr. R&D Stats. Bur., Voorburg, The Netherlands, 1995—. Author: (book) Linear Models with Correlated Disturbances, 1991; contbr. articles to profl. jours. Mem. Econometric Soc., Vereniging voor Statistiek, Royal Netherlands Economic Assn., Wiskundig Genootschap. Home: Haarlemmerstraat 143, 1013 EN Amsterdam The Netherlands Office: CBS, Prinses BeatrixLaan 428, 2273 XZ Voorburg The Netherlands

KNOTTS, GLENN R(ICHARD), foundation administrator; b. East Chicago, Ind., May 16, 1934; s. V. Raymond and Opal Ione (Alexander) K. B.S., Purdue U., 1956, M.S., 1960, Ph.D., 1968; M.S., Ind. U., 1964; Dr. Med. Sci. (hon.), Union Coll., 1975; Sc.D. (hon.), Ricker Coll., 1975. Mem. profl. staff Bapt. Meml. Hosp., San Antonio, 1957-60; instr. chemistry San Antonio Coll., 1958-60; adminstrv. asst. AMA, Chgo., 1960-61, research assoc., 1961-62, dir. advt. eval., div. sci. activities, 1963-69; exec. dir. Am. Sch. Health Assn., Kent, Ohio, 1969-72; vis. disting. prof. health sci. Kent State U., 1969-72, prof., mem. grad. faculty dept. allied health scis., 1972-75, coordinator grad. studies and research, 1975; editor-in-chief, prof. med. journalism U. Tex. M.D. Anderson Cancer Ctr., Houston, 1975-85, head dept. med. info. and publs., 1975-79, dir. div. ednl. resources, 1979-85; dir. devel. U. Tex. Health Sci. Ctr. at Houston, 1985-88; prof. U. Tex. Grad. Sch. Biomed. Scis., 1983—; adj. prof. dept. journalism Coll. Communications U. Tex.-Austin, 1984—; exec. dir. Hermann Eye Fund, Houston, 1989—; vis. prof. health edn. Madison Coll., Va., summer 1965, Union Coll., Ky., summers 1965, 66, 69; vis. prof. health edn. Utah State U., summer 1965; vis. lectr. Ind. U., 1965-66; vis. lectr. pharmacology Purdue U., 1968-69; vis. prof. Pahlavi U. Med. Sch., Iran, summer 1970; adj. prof. allied health scis. Kent State U., 1975—; prof. dept. biomed. communications U. Tex. Sch. Allied Health Scis., Houston, 1976—; prof. dept. behavioral scis. U. Tex. Sch. Pub. Health, 1977—; cons. health scis. communications, 1969—; pres. Health Scis. Inst., 1973—; mem. exec. com. Internat. Union Sch. and Univ. Health and Medicine, Paris, 1969-72. Co-author various texts and filmstrips on health sci.; contbr. numerous articles to profl. jours.; cons. editor: Clin. Pediatrics, 1971—; contbg. editor: Annals of Allergy, 1972—; exec. editor: Cancer Bull., 1976-85; mem. numerous editorial bds. Bd. dirs. Med. Arts Pub. Found., Houston, 1977-80, Art League of Houston, 1986-88, Delia Stewart Dance Co., Houston, 1988-90; mem. adv. bd. World Meetings Inc., 1971-80, bd. trustees Mus. Art Am. West, 1987-89; trustee Houston Mus. Natural Sci., 1987-89. Served with U.S. Army, 1956-58. Recipient Gold medal French-Am. Allergy Soc., 1973; named Disting. Alumnus Purdue U., 1999. Fellow Am. Pub. Health Assn., Am. Sch. Health Assn. (mem. exec. com. 1968-72, editor Jour. Sch. Health 1975-76, Disting. Service award 1973), Am. Inst. Chemists, Royal Soc. Health; mem. Internat. Union Health Edn., AAHPER, Am. Acad. Pharm. Scis., Am. Med. Writers Assn., Am. Pharm. Assn., AAUP, Am. Chem. Soc., AAAS, AMA, Purdue U. Alumni Assn., Ind. U. Alumni Assn., Union Coll. Alumni Assn., Ricker Coll. Alumni Assn., Sigma Xi, Rho Chi, Sigma Delta Chi, Eta Sigma Gamma, Phi Delta Kappa, Kappa Psi. Republican. Presbyterian. Clubs: Marines Meml. (San Francisco); Univ. Faculty; Doctors (Houston), Pelican (Galveston, Tex.); Headliners (Austin), Internat. (Chgo.). Lodge: Rotary. Home: PO Box 20787 Houston TX 77225-0787 Office: Hermann Eye Fund 6411 Fannin St Houston TX 77030-1501

KNOTTS, ROBERT LEE, insurance executive; b. Thornton, W.Va., Jan. 14, 1942; s. James Bailey and Lena Louise (Jacobs) K.; m. Dottie Lue Watts, Aug. 20, 1967; children: Brice Alan, Lance Eric, Chandra Marie. ChFC, CLU. Sales, truck driver Wholesale Grocery, Grafton, W.Va., 1960-67; lineman, crew leader Monongahelia Power Co., Grafton, 1967-78; agt., registered rep. N.Y. Life Ins., N.Y. Life Ins. & Annuity Corp., Charleston, W.Va., 1978—, NYLIFE Securities Corp., Charleston, 1978—; sec. bd. dirs. Grafton Homes, Inc., 1990-97. V.P. Taylor County Econ. Devel. Authority, Grafton, 1985-87; pres. Taylor Devel. Group, Inc., Grafton, 1987—. With USMC, 1960-64. V.p. Taylor County Econ Devel. Authority, Grafton, 1985-87, pres. Taylor Devel. Group, Inc., 1987—; treas. Taylor County Dem. Exec. Com., 1990-98. With USMC, 1960-64. Mem. Nat. Assn. Life Underwriters, Fairmont Assn. Life Underwriters, North Ctrl. W.Va. Chartered Fin. Cons., N. Ctrl. W.Va. Estate Planning Coun., Grafton Rotary (pres. 1979-81, 95-96, pres. edn. endowment 1991-96). Methodist. Office: NY Life Ins Co PO Box 599 Grafton WV 26354-0599

KNOWLES, RICHARD ALAN JOHN, English language educator; b. Southbridge, Mass., May 17, 1935; s. Clarence Fay and Mildred Elizabeth (Branniff) K.; m. Jane Marie Boyle, Sept. 1, 1958; children: Jonathan Edwards, Katherine Mary. BA magna cum laude, Tufts U., 1956; MA, U. Pa., 1958, PhD, 1963. Physics asst. Tufts U., Medford, Mass., 1954-56; asst. instr. English U. Pa., Phila., 1956-60; from asst. prof. to prof. U. Wis., Madison, 1962-90, Dickson-Bascom prof. humanities, 1990—; vis. lectr. U. Pa., 1967, George Washington U., Am. U., 1969, Cath. U., Washington, 1985; manuscript reader various univs., 1965—; cons. Am. Players Theater, Spring Green, Wis., 1980-83; poetry judge Brittingham Poetry Prize, Madison, 1986—, NEH referee, panelist, Washington, 1988—. Author: (with others) Shakespeare Variorum Handbook, 1971; editor: (with others) English Renaissance Drama, 1978; editor: New Variorum As You Like It, 1977; co-editor New Variorum Shakespeare, 1978—; mem. editl. bd. Shakespeare Notes, 1996—. Officer, producer Madison Savoyards, Wis., 1978—; pres. Friends U. Wis. Librs., Madison, 1982-84. Folger Libr. fellow, Washington, 1968, Guggenheim fellow, N.Y., 1976-77; NEH fellow 1983-87; Rsch. fellow Humanities Rsch. Inst., Madison, 1990. Mem. MLA, Shakespeare Assn. Am., Internat. Assn. Univ. Profs. English, Assn. Lit. Critics and Scholars, Nakoma Country Club. Democrat. Avocations: theater, chamber music, opera, gardening, carpentry. Home: 2226 Commonwealth Ave Madison WI 53705-5302 Office: U Wis Dept English 600 N Park St Madison WI 53706-1403

KNOWLES, RICHARD NORRIS, chemist; b. Wilmington, Del., Aug. 8, 1935; s. Francis and Dorothy Edith L.; m. Alice Keith Pfohl, Aug. 30, 1957 (div. May 1987); children: Elizabeth Nelson, Dorothy Lawrence, Cynthia Norris; m. Claire Elaine Frerichs, Dec. 31, 1988; stepdaughter, Christine J. Stoelling. BS, Oberlin Coll., 1957; PhD, U. Rochester, 1961. With DuPont Co., Wilmington, Del., 1960-96; asst. works mgr. Chambers Works, N.J., 1980-83; mgr. Niagara Falls (N.Y.) Plant, 1983, Belle (W.Va.) Plant, 1987-95; dir. cmty. awareness emergency response & industry outreach Wilmington, 1995-96; work with Chem. Mfrs. Assn. in Responsible Care; assoc. Dalmau Network; prin. Richard M. Knowles & Assocs.; advisor to mayor Niagara Falls, N.Y., 1999—. Contbr. articles to profl. jours.; patentee (40) in field; featured in The New Pioneers, 1998, The Soul at Work, 1999. Elder Westminster Presbyn. Ch.; bd. dirs. Nat. Inst. Chem. Studies, Berkana Inst. Recipient Chem. Emergency Planning and Preparedness Ptnr. award EPA, 1995, 96. Mem. Am. Chem. Soc., Assn. Quality and Patricipation, Audubon Soc., Nature Conservancy (DuPont Agrl. Products Crystal award 1991), Almost Heaven Hammered Dulcimer Soc. Achievements include 40 patents in field. Office: 6989 Rebecca Dr Niagara Falls NY 14304-3050

KNOWLSON, JAMES REX, education educator, writer; b. Ripley, Derbyshire, Eng., Aug. 6, 1933; s. Francis Frederick and Elizabeth Mary (Platt) K.; m. Elizabeth Selby Coxon, Aug. 2, 1958; children: Gregory Michael, Richard Paul, Laura Elizabeth. BA with honors, Reading U., U.K., 1956, Diploma in Edn., 1959; PhD, Reading U., 1964. Asst. master Ashville coll., Harrogate, U.K., 1959-60; asst. lectr. in French Glasgow U., U.K., 1960-63, lectr. in French, 1963-69; lectr. in French Reading U., 1969-75, sr. lectr., reader in French, 1975-81, prof. of French studies, 1981-94, part-time prof. French studies, 1994-98, prof. emeritus, 1998—; Leverhulme rsch. fellow U.K., 1975-76; dir. Beckett Internat. Found., 1988-94, founder, advisor, 1994—. Founding editor: Jour. of Beckett Studies, 1976-80; author: (books) Light and Darkness in the Theatre of Samuel Beckett, 1972, Universal Language Schemes in England and France 1600-1800, 1975, Damned to Fame: The Life of Samuel Beckett, 1996 (George Freedley Meml. award); co-author: Frescoes of the Skull: The Later Prose and Drama of Samuel Beckett, 1979. Mem. Beckett Soc. (pres. 1997-99), Soc. of Authors. Avocations: badminton, cricket, theatre. Office: Dept French Studies, Reading U/White Knights, RG6 2AE Reading Berkshire, England

KNOWLTON, LESLIE BROOKS, journalist; b. Orange, N.J., July 18, 1952; d. Bruce Douglas and Elizabeth (Snow) Knowlton; m. Charles Gottlieb Herzog, Dec. 27, 1979 (div. 1992); 1 child, Siri Whitney Herzog. BA, U. Conn., 1977; MA, Calif. State U., Long beach, 1983; postgrad., City Coll., 19985. Dir. rsch. Grubb & Ellis Co., Newport Beach, Calif., 1985-87; reporter Orange County Businessweek, Irvine, Calif., 1987-89; reporter/desk asst. L.A. Times, Costa Mesa, Calif., 1989-90; free lance journalist L.A. Times, Psychiat. Times, Fitness Mag., other publs., N.Y.C., 1989—. U. Conn. Faculty scholar, 1976, Univ. scholar, 1976. Mem. Am. Soc. Journalists and Authors, Author's Guild, Nat. Writers Union, N.Y. Newswomen's Club, Deer Isle Yacht Club, Phi Kappa Phi, Psi Chi. Avocations: fiction, boating, hiking. Summer address: 339 W 87th St Apt 1 New York NY 10024-2639

KNOWLTON, WILLIAM ALLEN, political and military consultant, educator; b. Weston, Mass., June 19, 1920; s. Frank Warren and Isabelle (Riese) K.; m. Marjorie Adams Downey, Nov. 27, 1943; children: William Allen, Davis Downey, Timothy Riese, Hollister Knowlton Petraeus. BS, U.S. Mil. Acad., 1943; MA, Columbia U., 1957; grad., Nat. War Coll., 1960; LLD (hon.), Akron U., 1972. Commd. 2d lt. U.S. Army, 1943, advanced through grades to gen., 1976; with 7th Armored Div., World War II, Army Gen. Staff, 1947-49, SHAPE, France, 1951-54; assoc. prof. social scis. U.S. Mil. Acad., 1955-58, supt., 1970-74; bn. comdr. 3d Armored Cav. Regt., 1958-59; mil. attache Tunisia, 1961-63; brig. comdr. Ft. Knox, Ky., 1963-64; with Office Chief Staff U.S. Army, 1964-65; mil. asst. to spl. asst. to sec. and dept. sec. def. Office Sec. Def., 1965-66; sec. Joint Staff, dir. pacification support, dep. asst. chief staff for civil ops. revolutionary devel. support U.S. Mil. Assistance Command, Vietnam, 1966-67; asst. div. comdr. 9th Inf. Div., Vietnam, 1968; sec. gen. staff Office Chief Staff U.S. Army, 1968-70; chief staff hdqrs. U.S. European Command, Stuttgart, W.Ger., 1974-76; comdr. Allied Land Forces Southeast Europe, Izmir, Turkey, 1976-77; U.S. rep. NATO Mil. Com., Brussels, 1977-80; ret., 1980; cons. on internat. affairs and strategic intelligence R & D Assocs., Marina del Rey, Calif.; sr. assoc. Burdeshaw Assocs. Ltd., 1981-91; dir. Aeronca Inc., 1982-86, Chubb Corp., Fed. Ins. Co., Vigilant Ins. Co., Chubb Life Am., 1983-93; sr. fellow CAPSTONE course Nat. Def. U., 1984-95, sr. fellow emeritus CAPSTONE course, 1995—; sr. rsch. fellow Inst. Advanced Technology U. Tex., Austin, 1998—; lectr. Am. U., 1995—. Contbr.: Ency. Americana and nat. mags. Trustee Davis and Elkins Coll., 1982-90. Decorated Def. D.S.M., Army D.S.M., Silver Star with 2 oak leaf clusters, Legion of Merit with oak leaf cluster, D.F.C., Bronze Star with V device, Air medal with 9 oak leaf clusters, Army Commendation medal with oak leaf cluster, knight comdr. cross Order Merit W. Ger., officer Legion of Honor France, Vietnamese Nat. Order and Gallantry Cross with palm; recipient George Washington honor medal Freedoms Found., Valley Forge, 1957, 58, Lemnitzer award, 1994; named Hon. Col. Regiment, 40th armor Berlin. Mem. Am. Mil. Inst., 7th Armored Divsn. Assn. (hon. pres.), Coun. Fgn. Rels., Soc. Mayflower Descs., Washington Inst. Fgn. Affairs (v.p. 1998), S.R., Soc. Colonial Wars, Univ. Club (N.Y.C.), Army and Navy Club (Washington), Phi Kappa Phi. Home: 4520 4th Rd N Arlington VA 22203-2343

KNOX, GEORGE, art historian; b. London, Jan. 1, 1922; s. Inman and Hilda (Ball) K.; m. Ursula Leacock, 1945; m. Patricia Isaacs, 1964; children: Benedict, Sarah, Matthew, Martha, Erasmus, Emma. BA, London U./Courtauld Inst. Art, 1950, MA, 1954, PhD, 1969; DLitt, U. Victoria, 1996. Lectr. Slade Sch. Fine Art, Univ. Coll., London, 1950-52, U. Durham, Eng., 1952-58; sr. lectr. Portsmouth Coll. Art, 1963-69; asst. prof. Queen's U., 1969-70; prof. dept. fine arts U. B.C., 1970-87; prof. emeritus U. B.C., Vancouver, Can., 1987—; mem. Inst. Advanced Studies, Princeton, 1980-81; mem. Can. Com. for History of Art, 1980-92, pres., 1985-92; mem. Internat. Com. History of Art, 1985—; v.p. Can. Soc. for 18th Century Studies, 1985-86. Author numerous exhbn. catalogs, monographs, articles and revs.

KNUDSEN, AAGE, gynecological oncologist; b. Manna, Jutland, Denmark, July 11, 1958; s. Evald and Ellen (Thomsen) K.; m. Charlotte Overgaard; children: Mikkel, Mathias. MD, U. Aarhus, Denmark, 1984, PhD, 1994. Resident Hjørring (Denmark) Hosp., 1984-88; resident Aalborg (Denmark) Hosp., 1988-90, fellow, 1990-92; attending physician Univ. Hosp. of Aarhus, 1992-96, cons., 1996-97; cons. U. Hosp. Aalborg, 1997—; adj. instr. East Carolina U., N.C., 1994; rsch. asst. Brown U., Providence, 1994. Home: Poppelvej 24, DK 9000 Ålborg Denmark Office: U Hosp Aalborg, Dept Ob-Gyn, DK-9000 Ålborg Denmark

KNUDSEN, BJARNE FREDBERG, medical consulting company executive; b. Copenhagen, Denmark, Mar. 31, 1944; s. Aage Fredberg and Tove (Christiansen) K.; m. Lis Hjorth Christensen, Mar. 31, 1965 (div. Dec. 1991); children: Hans-Christian, Rasmus; m. Connie Selmann. Singer Danish Broadcasting, Copenhagen, 1963-72; info. chief R. Bunngaard & Co., Naerum, Denmark, 1969-72; clin. trials mgr. Miles Scandinavia, Birkerod, Denmark, 1972-76; pres. Alk-Abello Allergologisk Lab., Copenhagen, Denmark, 1976-80; scientific dir. Bayer Kemi Nordic Countries, 1980-83, Bayer Kemi Europe, 1983-84; dir. clin. and regulatory affairs Meadox Med., Inc. Europe, 1984-86; pres. Endelave Med. Nordic Med. Cons., Denmark, 1986—; CEO Scanphyt APS., pres. bot. ops., 1999—; mem. Ctr. Danish Plantmedicine; bd. dirs. European Herb Growers Assn. Avocations: singing, house reconstruction. Office: EMPAS, Birkevej 87, DK-5672 Brondby Denmark also: Internat Sci Park, Forskerparken 10, DK-5230 Odense M Denmark

KNUDSEN, IB, food agency toxicologist; b. Asminderod, Denmark, May 24, 1940; s. Jens Carl and Anna (Wernersson) K.; m. Bodil Bygum Nielsen, Aug. 27, 1966. DVM, Royal Vet. and Agrl. U., Copenhagen, 1966, Cert. Vet. Microbiology/Hygiene, 1967. Asst. prof. Royal Vet. and Agrl. U., 1968-70; rsch. Inst. of Toxicology Nat. Food Agy. of Denmark, Copenhagen, 1970-73, sr. scientist Inst. Toxicology, 1973-80, dep. dir. Inst. Toxicology, 1980-87, exec. dir. Inst. Toxicology, 1987—; mem. scientific com. for Food of the European Union, 1989-92, vice chmn., 1992-97, chmn., 1997—; expert FAO-WHO, Rome, Geneva, 1990, 92, 96, 97, WHO, Geneva, 1993, 94; mem. sci. steering com. European Union, 1997—. Editor: (book) Genetic Toxicology of the Diet, 1986. Mem. European Environ. Mutagen Soc., European Soc. Toxicology, Nordic Environ. Mutagen Soc. (chmn. 1986-90). Office: Inst Food Safety & Toxicology Danish Vet & Food Adminstrn, 19 Morkhoj Bygade, DK-2860 Søborg Denmark

KNUDSEN, JOHN ROLAND, retired mathematics educator, consultant; b. Bklyn., July 12, 1916; s. Johan Sevrin and Ingeborg (Roland) K.; m. Ruth Ida Strube, June 7, 1942; children: John Karl, Thomas Paul. BS cum laude, NYU, 1937, PhD, 1951; postgrad., Johns Hopkins U., 1937-39. Teaching fellow Johns Hopkins U., Balt., 1937-39; asst. prof. math. NYU, N.Y.C., 1939-57, assoc. prof. math., 1957-72, prof. math., 1972; tech. staff mem. AT&T Bell Labs, Holmdel, N.J., 1972-83; ret., 1983; cons. AT&T Bell Labs, Murray Hill, N.J., 1957-64, Holmdel, N.J., 1968-72, 83-87; vis. prof. Bangalore (India) Univ., 1968. Co-author: Real Variables, 1969. Mem. Math. Assn. Am., Am. Math. Soc., Phi Beta Kappa. Home: 10105 Jupiter Hills Dr Austin TX 78747-1322

KNUDSEN, LAURA GEORGIA, linguist; b. Kenosha, Wis., Sept. 21, 1969; d. Richard Dennis and Georgia Elizabeth (Perrin) Wright; m. Martin Christian Knudsen, Aug. 20, 1994. BA in Linguistics, Ind. U., 1991, MA in Linguistics, 1996. Linguist Ind. U., Bloomington, 1987—, tchr. ESL, Ctr. for English Lang. Tng., 1995—; tchr. ESL Aichi U., Toyohashi, Japan, 1998; presenter in field;. Contbr. articles to profl. jours. Fulbright scholar IIE, Budapest, 1996-97; FLAS fellow U.S. Dept. Edn., Ind. U., 1993-94, GANN fellow, 1991-92. Mem. Linguistic Soc. Am., Ind. U. Linguistic Club (sec. 1996, pres. 1998), INTESOL. Avocation: aikido. Office: c/o GE Wright RR 1 Box 148 Fort Branch IN 47648-9714

KNUDSEN, OLAV FAGELUND, international politics educator; b. Stockholm, July 31, 1943; s. Arne and Riborg Marie Krog (Fagelund) Kn.; children: Camilla, Lena, Dag. MA, U. Denver, 1969, PhD in Internat. Studies, 1972. Asst. prof. polit. sci. U. Oslo, 1971-74, assoc. prof., 1974-84, prof., 1985-90; dir. rsch. Norwegian Inst. Internat. Affairs, Oslo, 1988-90, sr. rschr., 1996-98; dean Faculty of Social Scis. U. Oslo, 1981-84; dir., CEO Norwegian Inst. Internat. Affairs, Oslo, 1990-95; chmn. dept. polit. sci. U. Oslo, 1978-80; head rsch. Södertörns Högskola U. Coll., Stockholm, 1998-2000, prof. polit. sci., 2000—; cons. Parliamentary Assembly of Coun. of Europe, Strasbourg, France, 1974-75; head of inquiry Nordic Coun. Ministers, Oslo, 1976-80; editor-in-chief Internasjonal Politikk, Oslo, 1990-92. Author: Politics of International Shipping, 1973, Anarchy and Community, 1994, Multinational Corporations, 1980; contbr. articles to profl. jours. Woodrow Wilson dissertation fellow, 1969; Norwegian Rsch. coun. grantee, 1974, 84, 91; vis. scholar European Consortium for Polit. Rsch., 1978, U. Ky., 1984-86, Nihon U., 1991. Mem. Internat. Studies Assn., Internat. Inst. Strategic Studies, Norwegian Assn. for Internat. Studies (chmn. 1990-92), Nordic Internat. Studies Assn. (pres. 1993-96), European Consortium for Polit. Rsch. (chmn. steering com. of the standing group on internat. rels. 1998—). Avocations: sailing, music. Office: U Coll Södertöns Högskola, Box 4101, S-14104 Huddinge Sweden

KNUDSEN, RAYMOND BARNETT, clergyman, association executive, author; b. Denver, Nov. 11, 1919; s. Franklin Ole and Julia (Nielsen) K.; m. Edna Mae Nielsen, Jan. 26, 1940 (dec. Mar. 1992); children: Raymond Barnett, Silas John, Mark Allen, Ann Delight Knudsen Semotan; m. Virginia

Harris Foster, Apr. 23, 1994. Student, Coll. Emporia, 1937-38, Wheaton Coll., 1938-39; BA, U. Denver, 1941; ThM, McCormick Theol. Sem., 1948; postgrad., U. Chgo., 1948; DD, Burton Coll., 1955, LLD, 1964; ThD, Miami Bible Inst., 1987. Ordained to ministry Presbyn. Ch., 1948. Co-founder Knudsen Printing Co., Denver, 1928; pastor 1st Presbyn. Ch., Akron, Colo., 1937-39, 8th Ave. Presbyn. Ch., Denver, 1939-40; dir. Martin M. Post Larger Parish, Logansport, Ind., 1941-44; asst. Faith Presbyn. Ch., Chgo., 1945; pastor 1st Presbyn. Ch., Warsaw, Ill., 1946-52, 5th Presbyn. Ch., Springfield, Ill., 1952-63; sr. pastor Webb Horton Meml. Presbyn. Ch., Middletown, N.Y., 1963-70; exec. dir. for donor support Nat. Coun. Chs. of Christ in U.S.A., 1970-71, asst. gen. sec., 1971-77; pres. Nat. Consultation on Fin. Devel., 1977-85, chmn., 1985-88, chmn. emeritus, 1988—; chmn. bd. dirs. Eleemysonary Publ. Co., Marlboro, N.J., 1995—; lectr. philosophy Orange County (N.Y.) C.C., 1964-70, Lectures Internat., 1994—, Norwegian Am. Cruise Line, 1996—; chaplain Moore McCormick Cruise Line, 1965, Holland Am. Lines, 1994—, Celebrity Cruise Line, 1995—, Crown Princess Cruise Line, 1996—; instr. Drew U. Sch. Theology, 1978-86, Perkins Sch. Theology So. Meth. U., 1986—; chmn. broadcasting press Synod of Ill., Presbyn. Ch., 1954-60, mem. gen. council, 1954-62; chmn. founding com. Ill. Presbyn. Home, Springfield, 1954; pres. Middletown Council Chs., 1967-69; chmn. Fifty Million Dollar Fund, Hudson River Presbytery, 1964-70; pres. Webb Horton Presbyn. Assocs.; v.p. Inst. Activation Research.; cons. Episc. Diocese of Pitts., 1977-85, Orthodox Ch. in Am., 1978-88, Christian Meth. Episc. Ch., 1983-88, Hawaii conf. United Ch. of Christ, 1983-86, Asbury Hills Camp, 1983-86; cons. Fla. Council of Chs., 1986—, Pitts. Experiment, 1987-88, Jesus Fellowship, Inc., 1987-93, 1st Bapt. Ch., Washington, 1987-90, Cornstone Consultation, 1990—, Higher Dimensions, Tulsa, 1990, David M. Wright M.D. Found., Richmond, Va., 1991, Alfalit, Inc., Miami, Fla., 1991, Abundant Life, Richmond, 1991; chaplain Ann Norton Sculpture Gardens, Inc., 1993—. Author: The Trinity, 1936, New Models for Financing the Local Church, 1974, 2d edit., 1985, New Models for Creative Giving, 1976, 2d edit., 1985, Models for Ministry, 1976, Developing Dynamic Stewardship, 1977, The Workbook, 1977, New Models for Church Administration, 1979, Steward Enlistment and Commitment, 1986, Let Your Money Do the Talking, 1987, From "Commitment?" to "Commitment!", 1987, Wiltshire Village Cookbook, 1993, 20 Seconds, 1995, The Word and Words Made Fresh Vols. I & II, 1999; mem. rev. bd. Antenna, 1963-90; contbr. religious columns to publs.; syndicated newspaper column The Counselor. Mem. Middletown Narcotics Guidance Coun., 1969-70; pres. bd. dirs. Occupations, Inc., 1964-69, treas., 1969-71, pres. emeritus, 1976—; bd. dirs. Aid to Retarded Children N.Y., 1963-66, United Presbyn. Student Found., 1962-70, Presbyn. Sr. Svcs., N.Y.C., 1981-85, Presbyn. Panel, 1981-87, Christian Collegiate Schs., Richmond, 1991; mem. exec. bd. Orange County chpt. Aid to Retarded Children; trustee Orange County Workshop for Disabled, 1963, Homemaker Svc. Orange County; pres. bd. trustees Camp Townsend, 1964-70; active Pres. Clin. Nat. Steering Com., 1995—; mem. Palm Beach County Unmet Needs Com., 1999—. Recipient Author citation N.J. Inst. Tech., 1980, Cert. for Outstanding Ministry, Wheaton Coll., 1991; Dr. Raymond B. and Edna M. Knudsen ann. lectureship established in honor, 1992; Edna Mae Knudsen Meml. Fund established to fin. Knudsen Libr. and Needy Students at McCormick Theol. Sem., 1992; Dr. Raymond B., Edna M. Knudsen and Virginia F. Librs. established 1st Presbyn. Ch., West Palm Beach, Fla., 1990 and Palms West Presbyn. Ch., Loxahatchee, Fla. Mem. Nat. Temperance League (hon. v.p. chmn. nominating com. 1961-62), Alcohol Edn. Found. (bd. dirs.), Counselor Assn. Inc. (pres. 1954-82, chmn. bd. dirs. Ill. Soc. 1955-88, chmn. emeritus 1988—), Greenview Shores Civic Assn. (founder, pres. Fla. Soc. 1990-92), Lectures Internat., Masons, Rotary (chmn. internat. contacts). Home and Office: 1457 Brampton Cove Wellington FL 33414-8962

KNUDSEN, THOR ANDERSEN, surgeon; b. Breum, Denmark, July 10, 1947; s. Harald and Jenny (Andersen) K.; m. Gitte Islev, Oct. 22, 1988; children: Dine, Jan, Markus, Mette. MD, U. Copenhagen, 1978. Specialist in surgery U. Sweden, Ostersund, 1986—, U. Denmark, Copenhagen, 1986—; specialist in endoscopic examinations and treatment, laparoscopic operations and laser surgery speciality of the prostate. Avocations: cross country skiing, marathon running. Home: Olgavej 50, 7800 Skive Denmark

KNUDSEN, VIVI BRUHN, lawyer; b. Copenhagen, June 2, 1957; d. Hans Mathias and Helene Inger Margrethe (Bruhn) Hansen; m. Knud Aage Knudsen, Dec. 18, 1982; 1 child, Brian. Degree in law, U. Copenhagen, 1987. Lab. tech. Dumex A/S (rsch. & devel. divsn.), Copenhagen, 1980-85; ptnr. Lett, Vilstrup & Ptnrs., Copenhagen, 1985—. Mem. Danish Soc. Environ. Law, Soc. Danish Engrs. (environ. sect.), Danish Bar Assn. (environ. law sect.). Office: Lett Vilstrup & Ptnrs, Bredgade 3, DK-1260 Copenhagen Denmark

KNUDSON, RUTHANN, environmental consultant; b. Milw., Oct. 24, 1941; d. Sidney Olaus and Clara Ruth (Tappe) K. BA magna cum laude, U. Minn., 1963, MA, 1966; PhD, Wash. State U., 1973; postgrad., U. Idaho, 1988. Seasonal ranger Nat. Park Svc., Bandelier Nat. Monument, N.Mex., 1963; instr. U. No. Colo., Greeley, 1966-68; asst. rsch. prof. U. Idaho, Moscow, 1974-79, assoc. rsch. prof., 1979-81; dir. cultural resource svcs. Woodward Clude Cons., San Francisco, 1981-86, v.p., shareholder, 1985-88; archaeologists Nat. Park Svc., Washington, 1990-96; supr. Agate Fossil Beds Nat. Monument, 1996—; prin. Knudson Assoc. (formerly Paleo-Designs), 1974—; vis. asst. prof. Wright State U., Dayton, Ohio, 1974; cons. Am. Folklife Ctr., Washington, 1981-83, NRC, Washington, 1982, 83; resource cons. Calif. Heritage Task Force, 1983-94, Office Tech. Assessment, Washington, 1986; Woodward lectr., 1985; mem. Nebr. Panhandle Tourism Coalition, 1996—. Author: Cambria Village Ceramics, 1967; Organizational Variability in Late Paleo-Indian Assemblages, 1983, Contemporary Cultural Resource Mamangement, 1986; co-editor: The Public Trust and the First Americans, 1995, The 10,000 year old Lubbuck Artifact Assemblage, 1998, Using Cultural Resources to Enhance Ecosystem Management, 1999, Using the Past to Shape National Park Service Policy for Wildlife, 1999, Cultural Resource Management in Context, 2000. Bd. dirs. Preservation Action, Washington, 1980-85, 89-90, Californians for Preservation Action, 1981-82; sec.-treas. Idaho NOW, 1977-78; co-chmn. Nebr. Panhandel Tourism Coalition, 2000—. Recipient Preservation award Nat. Conf. State Historic Preservation Officers, 1981, Conservation award Am. Soc. Conservation Archaelogy, 1981. Mem. Soc. Applied Anthropoligy, Am. Anthropol. Assn. (Margaret Mead award 1983), Soc. Am. Archaeology (exec. bd. 1979-81, exec. com. 1983-85, legis. coord. 1979-82, chmn. com. pub. archaeology 1980-82, 84-85), Women's Coun. Energy & Environ. (bd. dirs. 1994-96), Soc. Vert. Paleontology, Geol. Soc. of Am., Phi Beta Kappa. E-mail: paleoknute@aol.com. Home: 343 River Rd Harrison NE 69346-2734 Office: Agate Fossil Beds Nat Monument 301 River Rd Harrison NE 69346-2734

KNUDSON, THOMAS CLIFFORD, oil company executive; b. Harlingen, Tex., Apr. 24, 1946; s. Angus Julius Knudson and Lois Elaine Hart; m. Candace Clare K., May 31, 1980; children: Christopher Michael, Clare Cooper, Suzanne Rainey. BS in Aerospace Engring., U.S. Naval Acad., 1967, MS in Aerospace Engring., 1968. Commd. ensign USN, 1967, advanced through grades to lt. comdr., 1974, ret., 1974; fighter pilot, 1967-74; various positions Conoco, various cities, 1975-87; gen mgr. refined products N.Am. Conoco, Houston, 1987-89; mng. dir. DuPont-Conoco Nordic Conoco, Stockholm, 1989-92; gen. mgr. exploration prodn. bus. devel. Conoco, Houston, 1993-94, v.p. natural gas, 1994-97; chmn. exploration prodn. Europe Conoco, London, 1997—; founding chmn. BCSD—North Sea Region, London, 1998—, BCSD—Gulf of Mex., Austin, Tex., 1993-97; vice chmn. Internat. Oil & Gas Prodn. Assn., London, 1997—; dir. Applied Sustainability, Austin, 1998—. Dir. Covenant Ho. Tex., Houston, 1994-97; sr. warden Ch. St. John the Divine, Houston, 1995. Mem. Order of St. Lazarus (comdr.). Episcopalian. Office: Conoco Expl Prodn Europe, 116 Park St, London W1Y 4NN, England

KNUEPFER, ROBERT CLAUDE, JR., lawyer; b. Oak Park, Ill., Feb. 23, 1952; s. Robert Claude Sr. and Suzanne (White) K.; m. Nancy Jo Bauderer, Aug. 20, 1977; children: Robert Claude III, Jennifer Jo, Lauren Elizabeth, Joseph James. BA, Denison U., 1974; JD and M in Mgmt., Northwestern U., 1978. Bar: Ill. 1978, U.S. Dist. Ct. (no. dist.) Ill. 1978, U.S. Ct. Appeals (7th cir.) 1980, U.S. Dist. Ct. (no. dist.) Ill. 1983, U.S. Supreme Ct. 1989. Law clk. to hon. judge William J. Bauer U.S. Ct. Appeals (7th cir.), Chgo., 1978-80; asst. U.S. atty. criminal divsn. Office of U.S. Atty., Chgo., 1980-83; assoc. Baker & McKenzie, Chgo., 1983-87, ptnr., 1987-92; mng. ptnr. Baker & McKenzie, Budapest, Hungary, 1992-95; ptnr. Baker & McKenzie, Chgo., 1995—; pres. Am. C. of C., Budapest, 1994-95; chmn., bd. dirs. Nat. Svc. League, Budapest, 1994-95; bd. dirs. Leadershape, Inc., 1986—; adj. prof. Northwestern U., 1997—. Active Chgo. Coun. on Fgn. Rels., 1984—, Hinsdale (Ill.) Plan Commn., 1990-92; chmn. Glen Ellyn (Ill.) Zoning Bd. Appeals, 1983, Hinsdale Village Caucus; chmn. bd. ATO Nat. Frat., Champaign, Ill., 1986-92, nat. pres., 1990-92; chmn. ATO Found., Indpls., 1995—; bd. dirs. Met. Family Svcs. Assn. DuPage County, 1986—, pres., 1997—; mem. exec. bd. Des Plaines Valley Coun. Boy Scouts Am., 1998—. Mem. ABA, Fed. Bar Assn., Ill. Bar Assn. (corp. and securities sect. coun. 1990, 1996—), Chgo. Bar Assn., DuPage County Bar Assn., Legal Club Chgo., Law Club Chgo., Execs. Club Chgo., Chicagoland C. of C. (bd. dirs. 1995—), Rotary Club (founding pres. Budapest City 1995), Econ. Club Chgo., Phi Beta Kappa, Omicron Delta Epsilon, Omicron Delta Kappa. Office: Baker & McKenzie 130 E Randolph St Ste 3500 Chicago IL 60601-6314 also: Baker & McKenzie, Andrassy ut 125, H-1062 Budapest Hungary

KNÜPPEL, PETER CHRISTIAN, research chemist; b. Schwelm, Germany, Dec. 14, 1958; s. Peter Hanns and Christa (Liesendahl) K.; m. Cornelia Pleuser, Mar. 21, 1981; children: Daniel, Johannes, Rahel, Debby. Diploma in chemistry, U. Wuppertal, Germany, 1986, D Natural Scis., 1988. Sci. coworker U. Wuppertal, 1986-88; postdoctoral fellow U. Tex., Austin, 1988-89; rsch. chemist Bayer AG, Leverkusen, Germany, 1989-93, project mgr. crop protection, 1994-97; wit strategic planning divsn. Bayer AG, Emeryville, Calif., 1998-99; head bus. segment Nucleic Acid Detection Bayer Diagnostics, 1999—. Contbr. articles to sci. jours. Grantee Deutsche Forschungsgemeinschaft, 1988. Mem. Am. Chem. Soc., German Chem. Soc. Home: 10 Tiptoe Ln Burlingame CA 94010-6243 Office: Bayer Corp 4560 Horton St Emeryville CA 94608-2916

KNUSSMANN, RAINER, human biology educator; b. Mainz, Germany, Apr. 15, 1936; s. Jakob and Maria Theresia (Schneider) K.; m. Renate Reuschling, Dec. 30, 1960; children: Elke Knussmann-Hartig. DrRerNat, U. Mainz, 1960, Habil., 1965. Sci. asst. U. Mainz, 1962-65, lectr., 1965-69; head dept. U. Düsseldorf, Germany, 1969-72; mng. dir. Inst. Human Biology, U. Hamburg, Germany, 1972-98, dean faculty of biology, 1979-80; mng. dir. emeritus U. Hamburg, 1998—. Author: Humerus, Ulna und Radius der Simiae, 1967, Vergleichende Biologie des Menschen, 1980, 96; editor: (handbook) Anthropologie, 1988, 92; editor sci. jour. Homo, 1990—. Mem. Gesellschaft für Anthropologie (founder), European Anthrop. Assn. (founder), Joachim Jungius Gesellschaft, Gesellschaft für Anthropologie und Humangenetik (pres. 1975-79). Office: Inst fur Humanbiologie, Allende-Platz 2, 20146 Hamburg Germany

KNUTSON, RONALD DALE, economist, educator, academic administrator; b. Montevideo, Minn., July 12, 1940; s. Claus and Alice (Peterson) K.; m. Sharron DeGree, Sept. 16, 1961; children: Scott, Ryan, Nicole. BS, U. Minn., 1962, PhD, 1967; MS, Pa. State U., 1963. Prof. Purdue U., 1967-73; staff economist Agrl. Mktg. Svc., USDA, Washington, 1971-73; adminstr. Farmer Coop. Svc., 1973-75; prof. dept. agrl. econs. Tex. A&M U., 1975—, dir. Agrl. Food Policy Ctr., 1989—; econ. cons. Kraft, Borden Inc., Sun-Diamond, Am. Bankers Assn., Milk Industry Found., GAO, U.S. Dept. Justice, Am. Farm Bur. Fedn., White House Food and Nutrition Study, NAS, U.S. Congress, Nat. Commn. on Productivity Exec. Office Pres.; project leader Rural Devel. Policy; chmn. milk pricing adv. com. U.S. Dept. Agr.; mem. Pres. Reagan's Transition Task Force for Agr., 1980-81; mem. agrl. policy adv. com. Sec. Agr. and Trade Rep., 1980-87. Author: (with J.B. Penn and B.L. Flinchbaugh) Agricultural and Food Policy, 4th edit., 1997. Bd. dirs. Farm Found. Recipient Lifetime Achievement award So. Agrl. Econs. Assn., 1995, Faculty Disting. Achievement award in Ext., 1984, Former Students of Tex. A&M U., Faculty Disting. Achievement award in Tchg., 1998 Assn. Former Students of Tex. A&M U., Regents Prof. Svc. award The Tex. A&M U. Sys., 1999; Rsch. grantee Govt. of Trinidad and Tobago, 1999—. Mem. Am. Agrl. Econs. Assn. (bd. dirs. 1999—), So. Agrl. Econ. Assn. Home: 1011 Rose Cir College Station TX 77840-2327 Office: Tex A&M U Agrl Food Policy Ctr College Station TX 77843-0001

KNUTSON, THOMAS JOEL, communication educator, consultant; b. La Crosse, Wis.; s. Thomas and Ruth Evelyn (Veir) K. BA, U. Wis., River Falls, 1965; PhD, Ind. U., 1970. Instr. U. Conn., Storrs, 1969-70; asst. prof. San Jose (Calif.) State U., 1970-74; vis. prof. U. Wash., Seattle, 1974-75; asst. prof. W.Va. U., Morgantown, 1975-78; prof. dept. comm. studies Calif. State U., Sacramento, 1979—; vis. prof. Ill. State U., Normal, 1972-73, ABAC Assumption U., Bangkok, 1993-96, Bangkok U., 1994—; founding prof. 1st Global C.C., Nongkhai, Thailand, 1995—; mem. adv. bd. Ednl. Records Evaluation Svc., Sacramento, 1996—; mem. Calif. Bd. Behavioral Sci. Examiners, Sacramento, 1991-95; hon. prof. Western Ill. U., Macomb, 1988, Ministry Edn. Russian Fedn., Moscow, 1996. Co-author: Decision Making in Small Groups: The Search for Alternatives, 1980; contbr. articles to profl. jours. Bd. dirs. World Affairs Coun., Sacramento, 1995—; mem. Calif. Commn. on Peace Officer Stds. and Tng., Sacramento, 1997—. Fulbright scholar, Seoul, 1992, Kaluga, Russia, 1996. Mem. Internat. Comm. Assn. (chmn. com. ann. confs. 1975-78), Internat. Assn. for Intercultural Comm. Studies, Fulbright Assn. (Fulbright award selection com. 1996-99), Phi Beta Delta (pres. 1994-97). Republican. Avocations: writing, tennis, dog training, gardening. Fax: 916-278-7216. E-mail: tjkcom@saclink.csus.edu. Home: 1311 Vanderbilt Way Sacramento CA 95825-6630 Office: Calif State U Dept Comm Studies Sacramento CA 95819-6070

KNUTSSON, ANDERS, retired judge. Chmn. Supreme Court of Sweden, Stockholm; ret. Office: Högsta Domstolen, Box 2066, S-103 12 Stockholm Sweden*

KNYAZEV, DMITRII ANATOLIEVICH, chemistry educator; b. Moscow, Mar. 1, 1932; s. Anatolii Anatolievich Knyazev and Anna Konstantinovna Tyapkova; m. Aleksandra Grigorievna Kumantseva, Feb. 15, 1955; 1 child, Vadim Dmitrievich. MS in Phys. Chemistry and Engring., Mendeleev Inst. Chem. & Tech., Moscow, 1955, PhD in Chem. Sci., 1961, D in Chem. Scis., 1972. Head betatron lab. Mendeleev Moscow Inst. Chemistry and Tech., 1955-58, engr., 1958-60, jr. rschr., then sr. rschr., 1960-72, sr. lectr., 1972-73, prof., 1973-74; chmn., prof. dept. inorganic and analytical chemistry Timiryazev Agrl. Acad., Mosocw, 1974-97, prof., 1997—; chmn. sect. analytical chemistry of agr., Russian Acad. Scis. Analytical Chemistry Coun., Moscow, 1976-97; chmn. sect. agrl. instns. of higher edn., Sci. coun. on chemistry, State Com. on Higher Edn. of Russia, 1983—; chmn. organizing com. All Union Conf. on Analytical Chemistry in Agr., Moscow, 1988-91. Author: Inorganic Chemistry, 1990; contbr. articles to profl. jours. Grantee Internat. Soros Found., 1993, 95; named hon. scientist, Russian Fedn., Moscow, 1997. Mem. N.Y. Acad. Sci. Avocations: fiction and science fiction, hiking. Office: Timiryazev Agrl Acad, 49 Timiryazevskaya Ulitsa, 127550 Moscow Russia

KNYAZEV, SERGEY P., biologist; b. Moscow, Feb. 18, 1956; s. Pavel P. and Ljubov M. (Archipova) K.; 1 child, Marina. MS, Voronezh State U., USSR, 1978; PhD, Inst Cytology and Genetics USSR Acad. Scis., Novosibirsk, USSR, 1983. Researcher Inst. Cytology and Genetics, Novosibirsk, USSR, 1981-87; assoc. prof. Novosibirsk State Agrarian U., 1987—. Co-author: Genetics and Morphology of Hyrbrid Pigs, 1992, Genetics and Morphology of Wild Boar, 1985, Genetics of the Dog, 1999; contbr. articles to profl. jours. Fellow Internat. Soc. Animal Genetics; mem. N.Y. Acad. Scis. Home: Leningradskaya 37, 630008 Novosibirsk Russia Office: Novosibirsk Agrarian U, 630039 Novosibirsk Russia

KNYCHA, JOSEF, journalist; b. Summerside, P.E.I., Can., Apr. 19, 1953; s. Michael Stanley and Marjorie Mary (Gallant) K. Student pub. schs., Auburn, N.S., Can. Reporter Halifax Herald Ltd., N.S., 1971-81; editor The Mirror, Cameron Publs., Kentville, N.S., 1981-82, editor The Register, 1982-84; bus./markets/automotive editor Star-Phoenix, Saskatoon, Sask., Can., 1984-89, asst. news editor, 1990-96; exec. editor World of Wheels Pub. Inc., Toronto, Can., 1996—; editor Cross Country Publs., Brandon Man., 1989-90. Southam fellow U. Toronto. Mem. Automobile Journalists Assn. Can. (past pres.). Office: World of Wheels Pub Inc, 1200 Markham Rd Ste 300, Scarborough, ON Canada M1H 3C3

KNYIHÁR, ELIZABETH, neurologist; b. Békéscsaba, Hungary, Jan. 30, 1940; d. János and Erzsébet (Szolár) K.; m. Bertalan Bert Csillik, Apr. 30, 1972; children: Anita, Andrea. MD, U. Med. Sch., Szeged, Hungary, 1964; PhD, Acad. Sci., Budapest, Hungary, 1978, DSc, 1990; Dr.med.habil., Albert Szent-Györgyi U., Szeged, 1999. Intern Szeged U. Med. Sch., 1963-64, resident in neurology, 1980-84; asst. dept. anatomy Albert Szent-Györgyi U. Med. Sch., 1964-71; rsch. assoc. dept. anatomy U. Med. Sch., Szeged, 1971-90; assoc. prof. neuropathology Harvard U. Med. Sch., Boston, 1977-78; sci. advisor dept. anatomy Albert Szent-Györgyi U. Med. Sch., 1991-93, sci. advisor dept. clin. neurology, 1993—; leader Electron Microscope Lab., Albert Szent-Györgyi U. Med. Sch., 1968-93; rsch. cons. sect. neurobiology Yale U. Med. Sch., 1992-95; Széchenyi professorship dept. clin. neurology Albert Szent-Györgyi U. Med. Sch., 1999—. Co-author: The Protean Gate, 1986 (Niveau prize 1987), Outlines of Human Anatomy, 1999; contbr. articles to profl. jours.; co-inventor Iontophoresis of vinca alcaloids to alleviate intractable pain. Recipient Disting. Educator award Hungarian Ministry Health, 1989. Mem. Internat. Brain Rsch. Orgn., Hungarian Anat. Soc., Anatomische Gesellschaft. Lutheran. Avocations: tennis, classical music. Home: 24 Pillich Kalman utca, H-6726 Szeged Hungary Office: Albert Szent Gyorgyi U, Semmelweis St 6, H-6701 Szeged Hungary

KO, DAE SIK, electrical engineer, educator; b. Kanghwa, Korea, Apr. 24, 1959; s. Soonhak Ko and Bongrae Jeun; m. Jumza Yang, Sept. 19, 1987; children: Youlim, Soyoung. BS, Kyunghee U., Seoul, Korea, 1982; MS, Kyunghee U., 1987, PhD, 1991. Engr. Digital Co., Seoul, 1984-85; asst. prof. Mokwon U., Taejon, Korea, 1991-95; assoc. prof. Mokwon U., Taejon, 1995—, dir. Libr. and Computer Ctr., 1997—; chmn. dept. elec. engring. Mokwon U., Taejon, 1991-93, chmn. grad. sch., 1996—. Author: Electrical and Electronic Engineering Experiment, 1994; contbr. articles to profl. jours. With Korean Army, 1982-84. Kyunghee U. fellow, 1988, U. Calif. Santa Barbara fellow, 1995-96. Mem. IEEE, Acoustical Soc. Korea (Disting. Rsch. award 1996), Korea Inst. Telematics Electronics (Disting. Paper award 1996). Home: 108-902 Kyoungsung Keunmaul Apt, Galma-Dong Taejon 302 171, Korea Office: Dept Elec Engring Mokwon U, 24 Mokdong Chungku, Taejon 301 729, Korea

KO, HYEONGSEOK, engineering educator; b. Chonju City, Republic of Korea, Aug. 14, 1962; s. Eusup Ko and Jungbae (Park) K.; m. Eunjoo Lee, Dec. 28, 1989; 1 child, Juhong. BS, Seoul Nat. U., 1985, MS, 1987; PhD, U. Pa., 1994. Vis. asst. prof. U. Iowa, Iowa City, 1994-95; asst. prof. Seoul Nat. U., 1996—. Contbr. articles to profl. jours. Govtl. fellowship Korean Govt., 1989-91; grant Korea Creative Rsch. Initiatives, 1997— . Mem. ACM. Roman Catholic. Avocations: tennis, playing violin and guitar, playing bridge. Office: Seoul Nat U, Sch Elec Engring, Seoul 151-742, Republic of Korea

KO, JAEJUNG, chemical educator; b. Puan, Korea, July 21, 1950; s. Kwangsol Ko and Aesun Park; m. Youngnam Kim, June 30, 1979; 1 child, Eric.; BSc, Seoul Nat. U., 1975, MS, 1979; PhD, Brown U., 1984. Postdoctoral fellow Ind. U., Bloomington, 1983-85, Houston U., 1988-89; prof. Korea Nat. U. Edn., Chungju, 1985-95, Korea U., Chochiwon, 1995—. Contbr. articles to profl. jours. With Korean Army, 1975-76. Mem. Am. Chem. Soc., Korea Chem. Soc. Avocations: hiking, music listening, volleyball. Home: Kyusu Apt Ka-dong 303, Kangraemyun Woltanri, Chungwonkun Korea Office: Korea U, Dept Chemistry, Chochiwon 339-700, Korea

KO, JAN MING, civil engineering educator; b. Macau, China, Jan. 10, 1943; s. To and Pui Yin (Lau) K.; m. Moon Shan Liu, Aug. 1, 1972; children: Ling Tung, Pui Fung. BSCE with honors, U. Hong Kong, 1966, PhD in Structural Engring., 1969. Lectr. in civil engring. Hong Kong Bapt. Coll., 1969-71, lectr., assoc. head civil engring. dept., 1971-77, sr. lectr., assoc. head civil engring. dept., 1977-79; lectr. civil and structural engring. dept. Hong Kong Poly., 1979-82, sr. lectr. civil and structural engring. dept., 1982-87, prin. lectr., 1987-92, head civil and structural engring. dept., 1992—, prof., chair civil and structural engring. dept., 1995—, assoc. v.p. and dean faculty constrn. and land use, 2000; advisor to dept. constrn. Vocat. Tng. Coun., Hong Kong, 1992—; mem. adv. com. on structural discipline Hong Kong Instn. Engrs., 1993—; mem. engring. panel Hong Kong Rsch. Grants Coun., 1995—; mem. Appeal Tribunal (Bldgs.) Panel, 1999—. Editor-in-chief Advances in Structural Engring., 1997—. Mem. organizing and planning panel Beijing-Hong Kong Acad. Exch. Ctr., 1985—; mem. course rev. panel Hong Kong Coun. for Acad. Accreditation, 1993. Fellow ASCE, Hong Kong Assn. for Advancement of Sci. and Tech. Ltd. (mem. coun. 1994—, sr. v.p. 1998-2000), Hong Kong Instn. Engrs. (chmn. edn. and exam. com. 1996-2000), Instn. Structural Engrs.; mem. Hong Kong Instn. Sci. (founding mem.), Hong Kong Soc. Theoretical and Applied Mechanics (pres.). Avocations: travel, reading. Office: Hong Kong Poly U, Yuk Choi Rd, Hong Kong Hong Kong

KO, JEA-SEUNG, dentist, educator; b. Kwangju-City, Korea, Jan. 23, 1942; s. Kwang-Hoo and Byung-Heui (Kim) K.; m. Hai-Young Cha, June 1, 1969; children: Soo-Jin, Hong-Suk. DDS, Seoul (Korea) Nat. U., 1967, MSD, 1969, PhD, 1974. Instr., asst. prof., then assoc. prof. Seoul Nat. U., 1975-86, prof., 1986—, asst. dean Coll. Dentistry, 1989-91, assoc. dean Coll. Dentistry, 1991-93, dean Coll. Dentistry, 1998—, dir. Dental Rsch. Inst., 1997-99; vis. asst. prof. UCLA, 1979-80, vis. prof., 1994-95; vis. assoc. prof. U. Mich., Ann Arbor, 1984-85; vis. scientist Harvard Med. Sch., Boston, 1994-95. Capt. Korean Dental Corps, 1967-70. Mem. Internat. Assn. for Dental Rsch. (v.p. Korean divsn. 1998—), Am. Soc. for Bone and Mineral Rsch., Korean Assn. Oral Anatomy (pres. 1994-99).

KO, JONGSUN, electrical engineering educator; b. Iksan, Republic of Korea, Mar. 20, 1960; s. Kilrok Ko and Yangkeun Yoo; m. Young Mee Baek, May 10, 1986; children: Jieun, Jimin. BS, Seoul Nat. U., Republic of Korea, 1984; MS, Korea Advanced Inst. Sci./Tec., Taejon, Republic of Korea, 1989; PhD, KAIST, Taejon, Republic of Korea, 1994; postdoctoral, U. Tenn., 1999-2000. Sr. rschr. Samsung, Suwon, Republic of Korea, 1983-96; prof. Wonkwang U., Iksan, Republic of Korea, 1996—. Contbr. articles to profl. jours. Mem. IEEE, Korean Inst. Elec. Engring. Avocations: travel, skiing, tennis, swimming, movies. Home: 301-106 Jeil 2 Cha, 763, 768-1 Youngdeung-dong, Iksan-SI Jeonbuk 570-160, Republic of Korea Office: Wonkwang U, 344-2 Sinyoung-Dong, Jeonbuk Iksan 570-749, Republic of Korea

KO, KOWAN YOUNG, physics educator, researcher; b. Che-ju, South Korea, Sept. 13, 1961; s. Chang Reung and Kyung Suk (Moon) K.; m. Ok Sun An, Apr. 7, 1989; 2 children. BSc, Ulsan (Korea) Inst. Tech., 1986, MSc, 1988, PhD, 1990. Tchr. asst. Ulsan (Korea) U., 1988-90, part time lectr., 1989-90; full time lectr. Ulsan (Korea) Coll., 1991-93, prof., 1993-97, 1998—, head Open Edn. Industry Complex Ctr., 1999—, head Bus. Incubator Ctr., 1999—; hon. rschr. Salford (Eng.) U., 1995—; head metal mold design Ulsan (Korea) Coll., 1996-97; head of Open Edn. Industry Complex Ctr., Ulsan Sci. Coll., 1999—. Author: Plastic Deformation, Machine Materials Engineering, Machine Materials and Its Applications, 1999. Home: 102 dong No 1204, Lucky Apt Hwangsung-dong, 780-130 Kyung-ju, Kyungsang South Korea Office: Ulsan Coll, San-29 Muge-dong Nam-gu, 680-749 Ulsan South Korea

KO, MYOUNG-SAM, control engineering educator; b. Hamhung, Korea, Jan. 1, 1930; s. Chi-Young and Sun-hee (Kim) K.; m. Won-nam Lo, Apr. 13, 1962; 1 child, Woo-Sung. BS, Seoul (Korea) Nat. U., 1955, MS, 1960, PhD, 1972. Instr. to prof. control engring. Coll. Engring. Seoul Nat. U., 1962—, chmn. elec. engring. dept., 1976-78, chmn. control engring. dept., 1979-92; prof. emeritus control engr. Seoul Nat U., 1993—; pres. Korean Inst. Elec. Engrs., Seoul, 1987-88, Korean Assn. Automatic Control,Seoul, 1989-90; dir. Automation & System Rsch. Inst., Seoul, 1988-92; vis. prof. dept. elec. engring. The U. Tokyo, 1993; vis. prof. scholar Stanford U., 1995; mem. Presdl. Coun. on Sci. and Tech., 1985-99. Contbr. articles to profl. jours. Cpl. Republic of Korea Army, 1955-57, Korea. Recipient Order of Nat. Svc. Merit Pres. Republic of Korea, 1989. Fellow Japanese Soc. Instrumentation and Control Engrs. (internat. award 1991), Korean Inst. Elec. Engrs. (paper award 1973); life mem. IEEE (centenary award 1984). Achievements include development of industrial robot controller, automatic monitoring system for textile industry and FMS pilot plant at the inst. Home: Bangwi-dong Songpa-ku, Olympic Apt 310-503, Seoul 138-150, Korea Office: Seoul Nat U Auto and Sys Rsch Inst, 56-1 Shinlim-dong Kwanak-ku, Seoul 151-742, Republic of Korea

KO, NORMAN WAH MAN, mechanical engineering educator; b. Wuchow, China, Feb. 14, 1938; m. Wendy Wai Ching Wong, Sept. 3, 1965. BS in Engring., U. Hong Kong, 1963, DSc, 1995; PhD, U. Southampton, Eng., 1969. Chartered engr. Lectr. mech. engring. dept. U. Hong Kong, 1969-79, from sr. lectr. to reader mech. engring. dept., 1976-87, prof. mech. engring. dept., 1987—; sculptor, painter Hong Kong, 1979—. Editor procs. in field; contbr. rsch. papers to internat. jours.; patentee in field. Recipient Urban Coun. Fine Arts award in sculpture, 1983. Fellow Hong Kong Instn. Engrs., Inst. of Mech. Engrs., Inst. of Acoustics (founder Hong Kong br.), Royal Soc. Arts; mem. ASME. Office: U Hong Kong Mech Engring, Pokfulam Rd, Hong Kong Hong Kong

KO, PING-KEUNG, dean, engineering educator. Dean sch. engring. Hong Kong U. Sci. & Tech. Office: Hong Kong U Sci & Tech, Clear Water Bay, Kowloon Hong Kong*

KO, TAE JO, mechanical engineering educator; b. Jinhae, Republic of Korea, Feb. 1, 1961; s. Duk Yong Ko and Jeong Sun Yoo; m. So Mi Shin, Oct. 23, 1988; children: Joon Ha, Joon Young. BS, Busan (Republic of Korea) U., 1983, MS, 1985; PhD, Pohang U. Sci. Tech., Republic of Korea, 1994. Rsch. mgr. Daewoo Heavy Industries Co., Ltd., Changwom, Republic of Korea, 1985-94; prof. mech. engring. Yeungnam U., Gyoungsan, Republic of Korea, 1994—. Mem. ASPE. Avocation: golf. Office: Yeungnam U Dept Mech Engrng, Daedong 214-1, Gyoungsan Kyoungbuk 712-749, Republic of Korea

KOBA, HENRI, ambassador to UN; b. Aug. 30, 1936; m. Juliette Koba; 9 children. Student, La Sorbonne, Paris; diploma, l'Ecole de Journalisme (OCORA), Paris. Amb. to Congo Ctrl. African Republic, N.Y.C., 1980; amb. to Egypt and Sudan Ctrl. African Republic, Washington, 1988; permanent rep. to UN Ctrl. African Republic, amb. to U.S. Office: Embassy Central African Republic 1618 22nd St NW Washington DC 20008-1920*

KOBAK, ALFRED JULIAN, JR., obstetrician, gynecologist; b. Chgo., Feb. 10, 1935; s. Alfred J. and Rose B. (Baron) K.; m. Sue B. Stein, May 3, 1959; children: William, Steven, Jane, Deborah. BS, U. Ill., 1957, MD, 1959. Diplomate Am. Bd. Ob-Gyn. Intern Michael Reese Hosp., Chgo., 1959-60; resident Cook County Hosp., 1960-62, 64-65; practice medicine specializing in ob-gyn. Valparaiso, Ind., 1965—; mem. med. staff Porter Meml. Hosp., Valparaiso, 1965—, pres., 1981-82; asst. clin. prof. ob-gyn Ind. U.; clin. instr. ob-gyn Rush Med. Sch., Chgo.; pres. Ob-Gyn Assocs., Valparaiso, 1970—. Contbr. articles to med. jours. Bd. dirs. Northwest Ind. Jewish Fedn., 1970-84, Porter County Bd. Health, 1991—, pres., 1997. Served to capt. USAF, 1962-64. Fellow ACS, Internat. Coll. Surgeons, Am. Coll. Ob-Gyn.; mem. AMA, Am. Soc. for Reproductive Medicine, Ind. Med. Assn., Ctrl. Assn. Obstetricians and Gynecologists, Porter County Med. Soc. (pres. 1979, 86), Chgo. Gynecol. Soc. (v.p. 1998-99), Sand Creek Club. Republican. Office: 1101 Glendale Blvd Valparaiso IN 46383-3724

KOBANOV, NIKOLAI ILLARIONOVICH, research scientist; b. Pochinok, Smolensk, USSR, Jan. 10, 1942; s. Illarion Ilyich Kobanov and Feokla Fedorovna; m. Galina Ivanovna Eremeeva, July 8, 1969; 1 child, Olga. Student, Irkutsk State U., 1964-69; PhD, Major Astron. Obs., Leningrad, Russia, 1980; DSc, Inst. Solar-Terrestrial Physics, Irkutsk, 1994. Worker Tulun, Irkutsk, 1958-59; radio-operator Bratsk, Irkutsk, 1959-60, Irkutsk, 1960-61; engr. Inst. Solar-Terrestrial Physics, Irkutsk, 1969-81, sr. scientist, 1981-95, leader scientist, 1995—. Contbr. articles to profl. jours. With Russian Infantry, 1961-64. Recipient Hon. medal All-Union Soc. Inventors, Moscow, 1986. Mem. European Astron. Soc., Astron. Soc. Achievements include 22 patents in field. Avocation: horticulture. E-mail: kobanov@iszf.irk.ru. Office: Inst Solar Terrestrial Phys, Lermontov 126, 664033 Irkutsk Russia

KOBASKO, NIKOLAI IVANOVICH, thermal science scientist; b. Chornivka, Ukraine, Dec. 6, 1934; s. Ivan Petrovich and Mariya Vasilievna (Semeniuk) K.; m. Irina Igorevna Bronzova (div. 1979); 1 child, Alexander Nikolaevich Bronzov. Physicist, tchr. physics, Chernovtsy State U., 1959; PhD, Acad. Scis. of Ukraine, Kiev, 1969. Physics tchr. h.s. Letychev, Ukraine, 1959-60; engr. Machine Constrn. Plant, Kiev, 1960-62; rschr., head of lab., head of rsch. group Thermophysics Inst. of NAS, Kiev, 1999—; chmn. organizing com. for 10 sci. seminars and confs., 1979-91; cons. Project of Intensive Steel Quenching Methods, Cattering, Ohio, 1997-99; co-founder IQ Techs., Inc., U.S.A., 1999—; organizer, pres. Intensive Techs. Ltd., Kiev, 2000—. Author: (book) Steel Quenching in Liquid Media Under Pressure, 1980; co-author: (handbook) Theory and Technology of Quenching, 1992; patentee in field. Recipient Best Inventor's Cert., Acad. Scis. Ukraine. Mem. Am. Soc. Materials (mem. quenching and cooling com. 1994—, Heat Treating Soc. certs. of appreciation 1994-99), Internat. Fedn. Heat Treatment and Surface Engring. (mem. tech. com. sci. and technol. aspects of quenching 1979—). E-mail: nikolai@nik3.kiev.ua., nikobasko@email.msn.com. Home: 81 Vernadskogo Str Apt 120, 252142 Kiev Ukraine Office: Engring Thermophysics Inst, 2a Zhelyabova Str, 252057 Kiev Ukraine

KOBAYASHI, ATSUSHI, internet industry executive; b. Tokyo, Aug. 22, 1958; s. Takashi and Yoshiko Kobayashi; m. Rumiko Kido, Apr. 28, 1985; children: Ai, Ren. BA, Sophia U., Tokyo, 1984; MPA, Harvard U., 1991. Mgr. Nissho Iwai Corp., Tokyo, 1984-93; dir., gen. mgr. Datatec Corp., Tokyo, 1993-94; mgr. The Kansai Electric Power Co. Inc., Osaka, Japan, 1994-98; prin. Korn/Ferry Internat., Tokyo, 1999; gen. mgr. SpeedNet Inc., Tokyo, 1999—, Softbank Networks, Inc., Tokyo, 1999—; dir., gen. mgr. Xtage Inc., Tokyo, 2000—; dir. IP Revolution Inc., Tokyo, 2000—, Internet Brains Office Inc., Tokyo, 2000—. Author: Business in English, 1987; translator: The Making of a Japanese Prime Minister, 1994. Home: E-708 4-1 Honmokuhara, Naka-ku Yokohama 231-0821, Japan Office: 22F Ark Mori Bldg 1-12-32, Akasaka Minato-ku, Nihonbashi Chuo-ku Tokyo 107-6022, Japan

KOBAYASHI, FUMINORI, physician; b. Toyohashi, Aichi, Japan, June 26, 1955; s. Isao and Yoshiko (Oba) K.; m. Wakaba Ito, May 23, 1981; 4 children. Student, Hamamatru U. Sch. Medicine, 1981; MD, Kyoto (Japan) U., 1993. Resident Kyoto U. Faculty of Medicine, 1981-83, asst., 1992-94; staff Hyogo Prefectural Amagasaki (Japan) Hosp., 1983-86, head physician, 1994—; staff Kyoto Posts and Telecomms. Hosp., 1986-90; subhead physician Kobe (Japan) City Gen. Hosp., 1990-92. Avocations: tennis, Igo. Office: Hyogo Prefectural Amagasaki Hosp, 1-1-1 Higashidaimotu-cho, Amagasaki 660-0828, Japan

KOBAYASHI, HIDEAKI, diplomat; b. Nagano, Japan, Dec. 19, 1945; s. Itsuji and Setsuko Kobayashi; m. Toshiko Sugiyama, June 27, 1971; children: Yosuke, Kota, Ryuhei, Maya. BA, Tokyo U., 1968. 1st sec. Embassy of Japan, London, 1978-80, Mexico City, 1980-83; dep. dir. legal affairs divsn. Fgn. Ministry, Tokyo, 1983-84, dir. ind. s.e. divsn., 1984-86, dir. regional policy divsn., 1986-88, dep. dir. gen. consular divsn., 1993-95; counselor Embassy of Japan, Canberra, Australia, 1988-90; min. Embassy of Japan, Warsaw, Poland, 1990-93; dep. sec. gen. Fair Trade Commn., Tokyo, 1995-97; min. plenipotentiary Embassy of Japan, Washington, 1997-99; amb. extraordinary and plenipotetiary Permanent Mission of Japan to the UN. Mem. Cosmos Club. Office: Permanent Mission of Japan to the UN #230 866 United Nations Plz Rm 230 New York NY 10017-1822

KOBAYASHI, KOHROH, electronics company executive; b. Nagano, Japan, Oct. 1944; s. Tsuneo and Fumie K.; m. Kazuyo Kimura, Oct. 11, 1970; children: Yukifumi, Miki. PhD, Tokyo Inst. Tech., 1977. Cert. electronics engring. Gen. mgr. Opto-Electrics Rsch. Labs., NEC Corp., Kawasaki, Japan, 1992-97, Fundamental Rsch. Labs., NEC Corp., Tsukuba, Japan, 1997-99; v.p. NEC Corp., Kawasaki, 1999—. Author: Optoelectric Integrated Devices, 1999; co-author: Optoelectronic Technology and Lightwave Communication Systems, 1980. Recipient Ookouchi Meml. Tech. award, Tokyo, 1987, Achievment award Inst. Electronics, Info. and Comm. Engrs., Tokyo, 1989, Paper award Japan Soc. Applied Physics, Tokyo, 1997. Fellow IEEE. Fax: 81-44-856-2049. E-mail: kobayashi@da.jp.nec.com. Office: NEC Corp, 4-1-1 Miyazaki Miaymae-ku, Kanagawa Kawasaki 216-8555, Japan

KOBAYASHI, MAKIO, pathology educator; b. Oyama City, Japan; s. Magonosin and Michi K.; m. Yoshiko Chihara, Apr. 20, 1975. MD, Nihon U., Tokyo, 1970, DMedSci, 1974. Rsch. assoc. Nihon U. Sch. Medicine, 1974-79, asst. prof., 1979-80; rsch. assoc. Wesely C. Bowers Lab. of Pharmacology and Exptl. Pathology, Boston, 1980-82; assoc. prof. Yamanashi Med. Coll., Japan, 1982-90; prof. Tokyo Women's Med. U., 1990—; instr. Dokkyo Med. Coll., Koshigaya Hosp., Saitama, Japan, 1991—. Fellow Japanese Pathol. Soc. (coun. 1977); mem. Japanese Assn. Neuropathologists (coun. 1992). Office: Tokyo Womens Med Coll, 8-1 Kawadacho Shinjuku-ku, Tokyo 162-8666, Japan

KOBAYASHI, MASAMI, chemist, educator; b. Komoro, Nagano, Japan, May 18, 1959; s. Masatoshi and Tamiko (Kojima) K.; m. Akiko Morisaki, Feb. 4, 1995; 1 child, Mayumi. B in Engring., U. Tokyo, 1984, M in Engring., 1986, DEng, 1989. Postdoctoral fellow U. Tokyo, 1989-90, asst., 1991-95; tech. ofcl. U. Tsukuba, Japan, 1990-91, lectr., 1995-98, assoc. prof., 1998—. Contbr. articles to sci. jours. (Bot. Soc. prize 1994, Plant Cell Physiol. prize 1998). Avocations: tennis, skiing, skating, reading, listening to music. Home: Hakusan 2-9-12-301, Chiba Abiko 270-1154, Japan Office: Inst Materials Sci, U Tsukuba Tennoudai 1-1-1, Tsukuba Ibaraki 305-8573, Japan

KOBAYASHI, MASAYOSHI, chemical reaction engineering educator; b. Hakodate, Hokkaido, Japan, Sept. 27, 1938; s. Itsurou Kobayashi and Kimi Chujoh; children: Sawako, Toshinari. B, Hokkaido U. Edn., Hakodate, 1961; D Engring., Hokkaido U., Sapporo, Japan, 1975. Tchr. sci. Kohnan Jr. High Sch., Muroran, Japan, 1961-62; rsch. assoc. faculty engring. Hokkaido U., Sapparo, 1962-78; postdoctoral fellow Northwestern U., Evanston, Ill., 1977-78; assoc. prof. Kitami (Hokkaido) Inst. Tech., 1978-79, prof. chem. reaction engring., 1979—; dir. Soc. Small Bus. Group, Kitami, 1985—; engring. adviser Govt. Hokkaido, 1991—. Author: Catalysis Reviews, 1974, Unsteady State Processes in Catalysis, 1990. Chmn. Activation of food cos. in Hokkaido, Govt. of Hokkaido, Sapporo, 1988—; mem. Application of Advanced Tech. in Hokkaido, Govt. Hokkaido, Sapporo, 1991—; chmn. Technoplaza in Okhotsk, Abashiri, Hokkaido, 1991—, Okhotsk Info. Assn., Abashiri, 1996—. Avocations: painting, listening to music. E-mail: koba@betta.chem.kitami-it.ac.jp; kmasa@f2.dion.ne.jp. Office: Kitami Inst Tech, 165 Koencho Hokkaido, Kitami 090, Japan also: Advanced Tech Inst Co, 132-28 Toryo-cho, Kitami 090-0061, Japan

KOBAYASHI, NAOKI, microelectronics engineer, researcher; b. Nagano, Japan, Sept. 22, 1952; m. Tomoko Takebuchi, Apr. 25, 1987; 1 child, Midori. BS, Tohoku U., Japan, 1976, MS, 1978. Rschr. Fujitsu, Japan, 1982-91; sr. rschr. Dai Nippon Printing, Kamifukuoka, Japan, 1991—. Mem. IEEE, Inst. Electronics, Info. and Comm. Engrs. (Encouragement award 1984). Office: Dai Nippon Printing Co Ltd, 1-1-1 Ichigaya-Kagacho, Shinjuku-ku, Tokyo 162-8001, Japan

KOBAYASHI, NORITAKE, business educator; b. Tokyo, Feb. 23, 1932; s. Daijyo and Makiko (Tadokoro) K.; m. Mieko Mary Margaret Nishino, May 21, 1960; children: Norikazu, Sumiko, Kumiko. AB cum laude, Harvard U., 1953, postgrad., 1953-54; LLB, Keio U., Japan, 1954, PhD, 1973. Lectr. Keio U., Tokyo, 1956-62; assoc. prof. Keio U., Yokohama, Japan, 1962-73, prof. Grad. Sch. Bus. Adminstrn., 1973-96, dir. sch. bus., 1980-83, dean Grad. Sch. Bus. Adminstrn., 1987-91; Mitsubishi chair, prof. Keio U., Tokyo, 1991-96, prof. emeritus, 1996—; dean Coll. of Cross-Cultural Comm. and Bus. Shukutoku U., Saitama, Japan, 1996-2000, dean The Grad. Sch. Internat. Bus. and Culture, 2000—; vis. prof. Ind. U., Bloomington, 1968, Asian Inst. Mgmt., Philippines, 1970, Internat. Mgmt. Inst., Geneva, 1974; bd. dirs. Mazda Motor Corp., 1980-96, Bosch Japan K.K. 1992—, Fuji Xerox Co., Ltd., 1999—. Author: Joint Venture in Japan, 1967, The World of Japanese Business, 1969, International Business, 1972, Japanese Multinational Enterprises, 1980, Management, A Global Perspective, 1997. Trustee emeritus Brown U.; mem. adv. bd. Carnegie Bosch Found. Recipient Mgmt. Sci. Pub. Prize Nihon Keiei Kyokai, 1981. Fellow Acad. Internat. Bus.; Workshop to Study Motivational Enterprises (pres.); mem. Comparative Law Assn. Japan, Mgmt. Assn. Japan, Am. Acad. Polit. and Social Sci., Japan-Am. Soc., Keio U. Alumni Assn., Tokyo-Am. Club, Harvard Club, Tokyo Club. Home: 9-13 Shirokane 4-chome, Minato-ku, Tokyo 108-0072, Japan Office: Shukutoku U, 1150-1 Fujikubo Miyoshi, Irumagun 354-8510, Japan

KOBAYASHI, SEIEI, English literature educator; b. Maebashi, Gunma, Japan, Nov. 22, 1941; s. Mokuhei and Shizuko (Yamada) K.; m. Chieko Ohto, Apr. 4, 1970; children: Shigehisa, Naoki. BA, U. Tokyo, 1965, MA, 1969. Lectr. Kyoritsu Women's Jr. Coll., Tokyo, 1970-74, asst. prof., 1974-80; asst. prof. Hosei U., Tokyo, 1980-81, prof., 1981-93; prof. English lit. Chuo U., Tokyo, 1994—. Author: An Essay on Shakespeare's History Plays, 1981; contbg. author: The Discourse of Vision-The Meeting Point of Popular Culture and Art (ed. Y. Midzunoe), 1994, Essays on World Modern Drama (ed. M. Osada), 1996, Celtic Illusion (ed. Y. Midzunoe), 1998, A Dictionary of English and American Drama, 1999; co-editor: Kadokawa—Scott Foresman English-Japanese Dictionary, 1992; co-translator: Joseph Zsuffa, Béla Balázs The Man and Artist, 2000. Mem. English Lit. Soc. Japan, Shakespeare Soc. Japan, Renaissance Inst. Avocations: music, photography. Office: Chuo U Faculty Sci & Tech, 1-13-27 Kasuga, Bunkyo 112-0003, Japan

KOBAYASHI, SHOICHI, think tank executive, economist; b. Annaka City, Gunma, Japan, Jan. 6, 1944; s. Ichiro and Ichi (Kimura) K.; m. Mayumi Kobayashi, Mar. 12, 1951; children: Goki, Masaki. Student, Norwalk (Conn.) C.C., 1968; BA, U. Hawaii, 1970, MA, 1972, PhD, 1975. Intern UN Commn. for Trade and Devel., 1972; asst. prof. U. Hawaii, Honolulu, 1974-78; sr. economist Engring. Cons. Firms Assn., Tokyo, 1977-80, chief economist, 1986-90, vice chmn., 1900-97; dep. project mgr. Japan Consortium Cons. Firms, Iraq, 1981-86; chmn. Japan Devel. Inst., Tokyo; deputy chmn. consultative com. common fund commodities UN Commn. for Trade and Devel., The Netherlands, 1998—; councillor Multilateral Investment Guarantee Agy., Washington, 2000—. Mgr. Myammer Youth Scholarship Assn., Tokyo, 1998—. Mem. Japan Devel. Assn., Internat. Soc. Devel., Phi Kappa Phi. Home: 2-4-8 Tsujdo Taiheidai, Kanagawa Fujisawa 250-0044, Japan Office: Japan Devel Inst Yaesu, Nagaoka Bldg 2-8-4 Shinkawa, Tokyo Chuo-Ku 104-0033, Japan

KOBAYASHI, SUSUMU, supercomputer company executive; b. Kumamoto, Japan, Apr. 3, 1939; s. Senkichiro and Michiko Kobayashi. BS, Tokyo Inst. Tech., 1963. Programmer Osaka (Japan) Gas Co., Ltd., 1963-65, C. Itoh Computing Services Co., Ltd., Tokyo, 1965-67; applications analyst, systems engr. Control Data Far East, Inc., Tokyo, 1967-75; asst. gen. mgr. systems dept. JMA Systems, Inc., Tokyo, 1975-79; dir. Nuclear Data Corp., Tokyo, 1979-89, Yokogawa Supertek Corp., Tokyo, 1989-90; tech. advisor sales div. Yokogawa Cray ELS Ltd., Tokyo, 1990-92; tech. advisor Cray Rsch. Japan Ltd., Tokyo, 1990-96; advisor The Tsukuba Press Ltd., Tsukuba-shi, Japan, 1996-97; pres. Tera Computer Japan (now called Cray Japan, Inc.), Tokyo, 1997-2000, 2000—. Translator, editor: Fortran 4 (D.D. McCracken), 1968, Lisp 1.5 Primer (C. Weissman), 1970, A Few Good Men from Univac, (D.E. Lundstrom), 1992, The Official Computer Widow's (and Widower's) Handbook (by Experts on Computer Widow/Widowerhood), 1992, Future Computer Opportunities (Jack Dunning), 1993, Enabling Technologies for Petaflops Computing (T. Sterling, P. Messina, P.H. Smith), 1997, The Supermen, (Charles J. Murray), 1998; contbr. articles to electronics mags. Mem. AIAA, Assn. Computing Machinery, IEEE, Inc., Japan Math. Soc., Japan Info. Processing Soc., Am. Assn. for Artificial Intelligence, Astron. Soc. of Pacific. Avocations: motoring, audio/visual. Fax: 81 3-5623-0908. E-mail: skob@cray.com. Home: 85-2-206 Migawa 2-chome, Mito Ibaraki 310-0912, Japan Office: Cray Japan Inc Nihonbashi Bl 3F, 41-12 Nihonbashi Hakozaki-cho, Chuo-ku Tokyo 103-0015, Japan

KOBAYASHI, TOSHIRO, materials science educator; b. Sapporo, Hokkaido, Japan, May 20, 1939; s. Koichi and Tomoe (Yoshizumi) K.; m. Fumiko Fukuda, May 1, 1969; children: Chiharu, Toshiya. B in Engring., Hokkaido U., Sapporo, 1962, D in Engring., 1972. Registered profl. engr., Japan. Researcher Fuji Electric Corp. R&D Ltd., Yokosuka, Kanagawa, Japan, 1962-73; assoc. prof. Nagoya (Aichi, Japan) U., 1973-82; prof. Toyohashi (Aichi, Japan) U. Tech., 1982—, chmn. materials sys. engr., 1990—; chmn. advanced engring. materials com. JSPS, 1993—, chmn. prodn. systems engring., 1999—. Inventor high resistivity al alloy, tekko-zairyo-Kogaku, CAI impact testing system; contbr. numerous articles to profl. jours. Recipient Japan Invention award Japan Invention Soc., 1981, Nishiyama Meml. prize Japan Inst. Iron & Steel, 1989, Mishima prize, 1997; recipient Iidaka prize Japan Foundrymen's Soc., 1993. Fellow ASM; mem. ASTM, Minerals, Metals and Materials Soc., Inst. of Materials. Avocations: classical music, golf. Home: 21-16 Kodare Ogasaki-cho, Toyohashi 441-8066, Japan Office: Toyohashi U Tech, 1-1 Hibarigaoka Tempakucho, Toyohashi 441-8580, Japan

KOBDISH, GEORGE CHARLES, lawyer; b. Casper, Wyo., June 30, 1950; s. Richard Matthew and Jo Earl (Uttz) K.; m. Mary Ellen Griffith, Jan. 24, 1969; children: George Charles, Jr., Kelly Rebecca, Kimberlee Nelle. BBA with honors, U. Tex., 1971, JD, 1974. Bar: Tex. 1974, U.S. Dist. Ct. (no. dist.) Tex. 1975. Asst. atty. gen. State of Tex., Austin, 1974-76; assoc. McCall, Parkhurst & Horton LLP, Dallas, 1976-80, ptnr., 1981—. Bd. dirs. North Dallas Shared Ministries, 1993-2000, pres. 1996-98; bd. dirs. Notre Dame of Dallas Schs., Inc., 2000—; lay gen. chairperson Cath. Cmty. Appeal, 2000—. Mem. Am. Coll. Bond Counsel, Nat. Assn. Bond Lawyers, Tex. Bar Assn., Dallas Bar Assn., Royal Oaks Country Club, Tower Club, Dallas Friday Group, Serra Club of Dallas (bd. dirs., pres. 1998-99), Phi Delta Theta. Roman Catholic. Home: 7147 Araglin Ct Dallas TX 75230-2097 Office: McCall Parkhurst & Horton LLP 717 N Harwood St Ste 900 Dallas TX 75201-6586

KOBE, LAN, medical physicist; b. Semarang, Indonesia; naturalized; d. O.G. and L.N. (The) Kobe. BS in Physics, IKIP U., Bandung, Indonesia, 1964; MS in Physics, IKIP U., 1967; MS in Med. Physics and Biophysics, U. Calif.-Berkeley, 1975. Physics instr. Sch. Engring. Tarumanegara U., Jakarta, Indonesia, 1968-72; rsch. fellow dept. radiation oncology U. Calif.-San Francisco, 1975-77; clin. physicist in residence dept. radiation oncology UCLA, 1977-78, asst. hosp. radiation physicist, 1978-80, hosp. radiation physicist, 1980—; instr. radiation oncology physics to resident physicians and med. physics grad. students. Contbr. sci. papers to profl. publs. Newhouse grantee U. Calif.-Berkeley, 1974-75, grantee dean grad. divsn. U. Calif.-Berkeley, 1975; recipient Pres. Work Study award U. Calif., Berkeley, 1974-75, Outstanding Svc. award, 1986, devel. Achievement award, 1988, Ptnrs. in Excellence award UCLA, 1996. Mem. Am. Soc. for Therapeutic Radiology and Oncology, Am. Assn. Physicists in Medicine (nat. and So. Calif. chpts.), Am. Bd. Radiology (cert.), Am. Assn. Individual Investors (life). Office: UCLA Dept Radiation Oncology Los Angeles CA 90095-0001

KOBELEV, NIKOLAI PAVLOVICH, physicist; b. Bogovarovo, Russia, Nov. 28, 1948; s. Pavel Efimovich and Mariya Andreevna (Skryabina) K.; m. Svetlana Ivanovna Salienko, June 9, 1973; children: Nikita, Dmitrii. Physicist, engr., Moscow Phys. Tech. Inst., 1972; cand. phys. and math. scis., Inst. Solid State Physics, 1980. Probationer, engr., scientist Inst. Solid State Physics Russian Acad. Sci., Chernogolovka, Moscow, Russia, 1972-90; sr. scientist Inst. Solid State Physics Russian Acad. Sci., Chernogolovka, 1990—. Contbr. several articles to profl. jours. Avocation: gardening. Home: Tsentralnaya str 10A 59, 142432 Chernogolovka Moscow Russia Office: Inst Solid State Physics, Russian Acad Scis, 142432 Chernogolovka Moscow Russia

KOBER, ARLETTA REFSHAUGE (MRS. KAY L. KOBER), educational administrator; b. Cedar Falls, Iowa, Oct. 31, 1919; d. Edward and Mary (Jensen) Refshauge; BA, State Coll. Iowa, 1940; MA, U. No. Iowa; m. Kay Leonard Kober, Feb. 14, 1944; children: Kay Mary, Karilyn Eve. Tchr. high schs., Soldier, Iowa, 1940-41, Montezuma, Iowa, 1941-43, Waterloo, Iowa, 1943-50, 65-67, co-ordinator Office Edn. Waterloo Cmty. Schs., Waterloo, Iowa, 1967-84; head dept. co-op. career edn. West H.S., Waterloo, 1974-84. Mem. Waterloo Sch. Health Council; nominating com. YWCA, Waterloo; Black Hawk County chmn. Tb Christmas Seals; ward chmn. ARC, Waterloo; co-chmn. Citizen's Com. for Sch. Bond Issue; pres. Waterloo PTA Council, Waterloo Vis. Nursing Assn., 1956-62, 82—; pres. Kingsley Sch. PTA, 1959-60; v.p. Waterloo Women's Club, 1962-63, pres., 1963-64, trustee bd. clubhouse dirs., 1957-58; mem. Gen. Fedn. Women's Clubs, Nat. Congress Parents and Tchrs.; Presbyterial world svc. chmn. Presbyn. Women's Assn.; bd. dirs. Black Hawk County Republican Women, 1952-53, United Svcs. Black Hawk County, Broadway Theatre League, St. Francis Hosp. Found.; deacon Westminster Presbyn. Ch., 1995-98; del. Iowa Rep. Conventions, 1996, 98. Mem. AAUW (v.p. Cedar Falls 1946-47), NEA, Internat. Platform Assn., LWV (dir. Waterloo 1951-52), Black Hawk County Hist. Soc. (charter), Delta Pi Epsilon (v.p. 1966-67), Delta Kappa Gamma. Club: Town (dir.) (Waterloo), P.E.O. Home: 3436 Augusta Cir Waterloo IA 50701-4608 Office: 503 W 4th St Waterloo IA 50701-1554

KOBER, GISBERT HERBERT, cardiologist, clinician; b. Ziegenhals, Germany, Aug. 30, 1939; s. Kurt B. and Hildegard E. (Mucha) K.; m. Ingeborg Geier, Apr. 5, 1965; children: Andreas, Henning, Philipp. Med. student, J.W. Goethe U., Frankfurt, Germany, 1959-62, U. Vienna, Austria, 1962-63, U. Marburg, Germany, 1963-64; MD, J.W. Goethe U., 1965, specialist in internal medicine, 1973, specialist in cardiology, 1974, habilitation, 1974. Med. asst. Univ. Hosp., Giessen, 1965-67; rsch. fellow in medicine Berlin U. Physiology, 1967-68; trainee in internal medicine Univ. Hosp., Frankfurt, 1968-73, trainee in cardiology, 1973-74, prof. internal medicine and cardiology, 1977-91; chief Clinic Nordrhein, Bad Nauheim, Germany, 1991—. Author: Die Koronare Herzerkrankung, 1976, Koronarangiographie, 1980; editor, author: Nitrate und Nitrattoleranz in der Behandlung der KHK, 1983, Nitrates IV, 1983. Recipient Kurt Adam award Soc. Med. Edn., Berlin, 1981, Nitrolingual award Pohl-Boscamp, Hohenlockstedt, 1981. Fellow Am. Heart Assn., European Soc. Cardiology; mem. German Cardiology Assn. (chief working group cardiomyopathy 1982-86, chief working group coronary interventions 1986-90, Arthur Weber award 1991), Rotary. Avocations: biking, hiking, tennis, classical music. Office: Clinic Nordrhein, Ernst Ludwig Ring 2, D-61231 Bad Nauheim Hessen, Germany

KOBETZ, RICHARD WILLIAM, criminologist, consultant; b. Chgo., Oct. 23, 1933; s. Nestor Joseph and Mary (Zurek) K.; m. Eleanore Marian Sever, Oct. 8, 1960; children: Kevin, Kimberly and Candice (twins). AA, Chgo. City Jr. Coll., 1959; student, Ill. Tchrs. Coll., 1964-66; MS in Pub. Adminstrn., Ill. Inst. Tech., 1968; D of Pub. Adminstrn., Nova U., 1978. Diplomate Am. Bd. Forensic Examiners; cert. personal protection specialist. Police officer Winnetka (Ill.) Police Dept., 1954-55; from police officer to sgt. to lt. Chgo. Police Dept., 1955-68; asst. dir. Internat. Assn. Chiefs of Police, Washington, 1968-79; exec. dir., trainer, cons. Exec. Protection Inst., Berryville, Va., 1979—; dir., trainer, cons. North Mountain Pines Tng. Ctr., Winchester, Va., 1979—; security cons. numerous U.S. corps., 1979—; active various security and enforcement agys., 1979—. Author: The Police Role and Juvenile Delinquency, 1971, Juvenile Justice Administration, 1973, Target Terrorism: Providing Protective Services, 1979, Providing Executive Protection, 1990, Vol. II, 1994; contbr. articles to profl. jours., chpts. to books. Acad. Security Educators and Trainers disting. fellow, 1987. Mem. Acad. Security Educators and Trainers (pres., v.p. 1982—), Internat. Assn. Chiefs of Police (Achievement award 1979), Am. Soc. Indsl. Security, Am. Soc. Criminology, Am. Soc. for Pub. Adminstrn. Republican. Roman Catholic. Club: Nine Lives Assocs. (Berryville) (exec. sec. 1978—). Avocations: shooting, hiking, travel. Home and Office: Highlander Lodge Journey's End 276 Journeys End Ln Bluemont VA 20135-1862

KOBIELAK, SYLWESTER JOZEF, civil engineer, structural engineer, researcher; b. Zasutowo, Poznań, Poland, Dec. 31, 1937; s. Stanisław and Maria (Strzelczyk) K.; m. Barbara Irena Waliszko, May 19, 1964; children: Piotr, Wojciech, Anna, Jan. MSc, Wrocław (Poland) Tech. U., 1963, PhD, 1973, D of Habilitation, 1992. Registered profl. engr. (the expert lic.) in the field of bldg. engring. Technician Wrocław (Poland) Indsl. Co., 1955-58; design sr. asst. Wrocław (Poland) Bldg. Co., 1958-63; sr. designer Copper Mine Co., Wrocław, Poland, 1964-67; from asst. lectr. to lectr. Wrocław Tech. U., Poland, 1967-92, assoc. prof., 1992—; prof. Mil. Engring. Coll., Wrocław, Poland, 1995—; expert Assn. of Polish Civil Engrs., Wrocław, Poland, 1977—; prof. U. Mosul, Dept. Architecture, Iraq, 1989; vis. scholar Northwestern U., Dept. Civil Engring., Evanston, Ill., 1985, vis. scholar Bldg. Engring. Inst., Novosibirsk, Russia, 1975; vice-chmn., editor conf. procs. internat. conf. Challenges to Civil and Mech. Engring. in 2000 and Beyond, Wrocław Tech. Univ., Poland, 1997. Author: Devices and Methodology of Particulate Solids Pressure Measurements in Bin, 1990,

Application of Pressure Cells in Civil Engineering, 1991; editor: (conf. procs.) Reinforced and Post-Tensioned Concrete Silos and Tanks, 1992; mem. editorial bd. of mil. jour. Opinions and Experiences, 1995; co-patentee in field. Sec. Bldg. and Mech. Engrng. Com. of the Polish Acad. Sci., Wrocław Branch, Poland, 1993—. Recipient Gold Cross of Merit award Coun. of State, Poland, 1983, Zenczykowski award Assn. Polish Civil Engrs., Warsaw, 1993. Mem. ASCE, Lehigh Univ. Coun. on Tall Bldgs. and Urban Habitat, 1991, Polish Acad. Sci. (concrete sect.), Seismic and Paraseismic Engring. Polish Group, Scis. of Polish Assn. Civil Engrs. and Technicians. Roman Catholic. Avocations: swimming, jogging, mountain tourism. Home: 47 Wyścigowa St, 53-011 Wroclaw Silesia, Poland Office: Wrocław Tech U, 27 Wybrzeze Wyspianskiego, 50-370 Wroclaw Silesia, Poland

KOBLET, HANS RUDOLF, retired virologist; b. Burgdorf, Berne, Switzerland, Aug. 21, 1928; s. Rudolf and Melly (Leder) K.; m. Katharina Dür, July 6, 1956; children: Hans-Beat, Andreas. Med. degree, U. Berne, 1954, MD, 1959. Doctoral fellow, postdoctoral fellow U. Berne, Switzerland, 1955-58; rsch. fellow Tufts U., Boston, 1958-61, U. Geneva, 1966-68; asst. rschr. U. Zurich, 1968-74; prof. biochemistry U. Berne, 1974-93; ret., 1993; vis. prof. U. Nagasaki, Japan, 1987. Author: Physikalische Begriffe in der Klinischen Biochemie, 1964, 65, 71; editor: Physiology and Pathophysiology of Plasma Protein Metabolism, 1964; contbr. chpts. in books Advances in Virus Research, 1990, Arthropod Cell Culture Systems, 1994. Col. Swiss Army, 1978-93. Grantee Swiss Nat. Sci. Found., 1961-93; recipient Rsch. award Soc. Internal Medicine, 1964. Mem. Swiss Soc. Microbiology and Molecular Biology, Am. Soc. Virology, Soc. in vitro Biology, Soc. Virology, AIDS Aufklärung Schweiz (exec. com.), Japanese Swiss Soc., N.Y. Acad. Scis. Freisinnig-demokratische. Avocations: chess, literature, Japanese culture. Home: Pestalozzistrasse 15, CH-3400 Burgdorf Switzerland

KOBLIHA, JAROSLAV, tree breeder, educator; b. Prerov, Czechoslovakia, Jan. 27, 1956; s. Jaroslav and Miloslava (Brzobohata) K.; m. Magdalena Ludwig, Mar. 23, 1985; children: Hana, Jan. Degree in engring., U. Agr., Brno, Czechoslovakia, 1980, PhD, 1986; prof., Czech U. Agr., Prague, 1995. Sci. asst. U. Agr., Brno, 1980-85, sci. rschr., 1986-90; sr. lectr. Czech U. Agr., Prague, 1991-95, prof., 1995—. Author: Tree Breeding, 1988 (Rectors prize 1988), Population Genetics and Genetic Conservation of Forest Trees, 1995; contbr. articles to profl. jours. including Forestry. Mem. N.Y. Acad. Scis., Czech Acad. Agrl. Scis., several rsch. groups and working parties. Avocations: hunting, gardening. Home: Dvouletky 958, 281 63 Kostelec nad Cernymilesy Czech Republic Office: Czech U Agr Prague, Faculty Forestry, 165 21 Kostelec nad Cernymi lesy Czech Republic also: Tree Breeding Station, Truba, 28163 Kostelec nad Cernymi lesy, Czech Republic

KOBREN, STEVEN MARK, internist; b. Syracuse, 1959. MD, SUNY Downstate, N.Y., 1983. Diplomate Am. Bd. Internal Medicine. Internist LI Jewish Hosp., New Hyde Park, N.Y., 1983-84, res., 1984-86, chief res. internal medicine, 1988-89, fellowship cardiology, 1986-88; cur. hosp. appt. North Shore U. Hosp., St. Francis Hosp. Mem. NYSIM, Am. Coll. Cardio., Am. Coll. Physicians. Office: 488 Gt Neck Rd Ste 300 Great Neck NY 11021

KOBRIN, VLADIMIR ISAAKOVICH, physiology educator, researcher; b. Haldensleben, Magdeburg, Germany, July 2, 1947; s. Isaak Volphovich and Valentina Pavlovna (Volkova) K.; m. Ludmila Michailovna Boldysheva, Aug. 5, 1971; children: Pavel, Alexander. MD, PhD, 2d Med. Inst., Moscow, 1972. Asst. 2d Med. Inst., Moscow, 1975-85, dozent, 1985-89, prof., 1989—; head dept. physiology State Jewish Acad., Moscow, 1992—, vice rector, 1993—. Co-author: Handbook of Human Physiology, 1997; contbr. over 150 articles to profl. jours. including Jour. Physiology, Jour. Cardiology, among others. Grantee Rsch. Coun. Norway, 1996, Russian Sci. Found., 1997. Mem. N.Y. Acad. Scis., Nat. Geog. Soc. E-mail: vikobrin@intu-net.ru. Avocation: amateur radio. Home: PO Box 14, 143002 Odintzovo 2, Russia Office: Russian Med U, Ostrovityanova 1, 117869 Moscow Russia

KOBRYN, ALEXANDER EUGENIJOVYCH, theoretical and applied physics researcher; b. Lviv, Ukraine, Aug. 6, 1970; s. Eugene Volodymyrovych and Valentyna Leonidivna (Cherevata) K. Grad., Lviv State U., 1992; PhD in Physics, Inst. Condensed Matter Physics, Lviv, 1997. Engr., class II, class I Inst. Condensed Matter Physics, 1992-95, leading engr., 1995-97, jr. rsch. fellow, 1997-98, rsch. fellow, 1999-2000; rsch. assoc. Inst. Physics U. Tsukuba, Ibaraki, Japan, 2000—; electronic prodn. mgr. Condensed Matter Physics Jour., Lviv, 1993-98; jr. rsch. fellow object Shelter, Chernobyl, Ukraine, 1995-98; head dept. info. Western Ukrainian Sci. Ctr., Lviv, 1997-98. Contbr. articles to profl. jours. Recipient grant Soros Found., 1994. Avocation: travelling. Home: 44 Chervona Kalyna Av ap 80, UA79070 Lviv Ukraine Office: Inst Physics, U Tsukuba, UA290011 Ibaraki 305 8571, Japan

KOBYLANSKI, PAWEL M., architect; b. Poznan, Poland, Jan. 27, 1958; s. Mieczyseaw F. and Maria (Baranska) K.; m. Anna T. Burian, June 7, 1980; children: Marta, Sonia, Olga. MArch, Poznan Tech. U., 1981. Jr. designer Miastopeozeky, Poznan, 1981-85, sr. designer, 1986-88; site engr. Kombinant Budowlany, Poznan, 1985-86; pres. Architect, Ltd., Poznan, 1988—, Archtl. Investment Agy., Inc., Poznan, 1990—, Internat. Devel. Cons., Poznan, 1997—; pres. Assn. of Pub. Architects, SARP, Poznan, 1987-99; lectr. Poznan Tech. U., 1995—. Contbr. articles to profl. jours. Bd. dirs. Poznan Assn. of Home Builders, Warsaw, 1976—. Avocations: music, tourism, skiing, reading. Office: Pentagram Ltd, Kochanowskiego 18 8, 60846 Poznan Poland

KOBZA, DENNIS JEROME, architect; b. Ullysses, Nebr., Sept. 30, 1933; s. Jerry Frank and Agnes Elizabeth (Lavicky) K.; B.S., Healds Archtl. Engring., 1959; m. Doris Mae Riemann, Dec. 26, 1953; children—Dennis Jerome, Diana Jill, David John. Draftsman, designer B.L. Schroder, Palo Alto, Calif., 1959-60; sr. draftsman, designer Ned Abrams, Architect, Sunnyvale, Calif., 1960-61, Kenneth Elvin, Architect, Los Altos, Calif., 1961-62; partner B.L. Schroder, Architect, Palo Alto, 1962-66; pvt. practice architecture, Mountain View, Calif., 1966—. Served with USAF, 1952-56. Recipient Solar PAL award, Palo Alto, 1983, Mountain View Mayoral award, 1979. Mem. C. of C. (dir. 1977-79, Archtl. Excellence award Hayward chpt. 1985, Outstanding Indsl. Devel. award Sacramento chpt., 1980), AIA (chpt. dir. 1973), Constrn. Specifications Inst. (dir. 1967-68), Am. Inst. Plant Engrs., Nat. Fedn. Ind. Bus. Orgn. Club: Rotary (dir. 1978-79, pres. 1986-87). Home: 3840 May Ct Palo Alto CA 94303-4545 Office: 2083 Old Middlefield Way Mountain View CA 94043-2465

KOČÁRNIK, IVAN, insurance company executive; b. Třebonín, Kutná, Czech Republic, Nov. 29, 1944; married; 3 children. Student, Prague Inst. Econs. Rschr. Inst. Fin. and Credit System; dir. rsch. dept. fed. ministry fin. Govt. Czechoslovakia, 1985-89, dep. min. fin., 1990-91; vice premier, min. fin. Govt. Czech Republic, Prague, 1992-97; chmn. bd. Česká pojišťovna, 1997-2000, chmn. bd. suprs., 2000—; chair Cou. Econ. and Social Agreement, 1992-97; gov. World Bank, 1992—. Mem. Civil Democratic Party. Office: Czech Ins Co, Na Pankráci 121, 140 00 Prague 4, Czech Republic

KOCH, ANDREAS, hotel manager; b. Berlin, Apr. 19, 1955; s. Max Klaus and Ilona Sigrid (Pannenberg) K. Student hotel bus., Brillat-Savarin Secondary Sch., Berlin, 1974-75. Comml. trainee Bristol Hotel Kempinski, Berlin, 1974-75, 1976-77, asst. income audit, 1975-76; asst. sales mgr. Hotel Schweizerhof Berlin, 1976-77, asst. gen. mgr., 1978-79; gen. mgr. Berlin Excelsior Hotel, 1979-85; mem. bd. Atlas Hotel AG, Berlin-Sasbachwalden, 1985-86; gen. mgr. Holiday Inn Cologne-Bonn Airport, Cologne, Fed. Republic Germany, 1986-87, Hotel Ambassador Berlin, 1987-88; president's rep. Neptune Computer GmbH, Wimsheim-Stuttgart, Fed. Republic Germany, 1989-90; dir. rms div. Heathrow Penta Hotel, London, 1990, Cable Beach Club, Broome, Western Australia, 1990-94; gen. mgr. Swiss-Grand Hotel Bondo Beach, Sydney, 1994-95, Hotel Grand Chancellor, Christchurch, New Zealand, 1995-96, Sedona Hotels Inernat., Sinapore, 1996-98, Seashells Resort, Broome, 1999—; owner, mgr. Akonsult, Berlin, 1983-88; owner Uonsul Air Svc., Berlin and Alice Springs, 1985—; hon. judge Indsl. Tribunal, Berlin, 1985-89; apprentice examiner Berlin C. of C., 1981—. Mem. Hotel Sales and Mktg. Assn., Skal Amical du Tourisme (bd. dirs. 1982), Businessmen's Club Berlin, Gymnasium Steglitz Old Boys Club. Avocations: flying, trotting races, swimming, travel. Home: 32 Teban Gardens Rd #06-356, Singapore 600032, Singapore Office: Seashells Resort Broome, PO 5198, 6726 Broome Australia

KOCH, BARBARA LOUISE, foreign service family nurse; b. Harrisburg, Pa., July 16, 1946; d. Robert A. and Miriam Irene (Shaffer) K.; m. Magdy El Shereiy, April 8, 1988. Diploma in nursing, Washington Hosp. Ctr. Nursing, 1970; cert., U. N.D., Grand Forks, 1991. RN N.Y., cert. P.A., Gerontological NP, ANCC, physician asst., Family Nurse Practitioner. Staff nurse Wash. Hosp. Ctr., 1970-71; grant student U. Rochester (N.Y.), 1971-72; pvt. practice with gen. surgeon and family practitioner Victor M. Breen, M.D., Roy Robinson, M.D., Dansville, Wayland, N.Y., 1972-78; foreign svc. U.S. Dept. State, Wahington, D.C., 1978—, sr. fgn. svc. appt., 1999—. Democrat. Episcopalian. Home and Office: Am Embassy Kiev C/O Dept State Washington DC 20521-5850

KOCH, EBERHARD GEORG JOHANN, shipping executive, ship owner; b. Deichsende, Fed. Republic Germany, Mar. 18, 1951; s. Siegmund August and Elly Anna (Riehl) K.; m. Renate, Dec. 28, 1987; 1 child, Nicole Madeleine. Diploma in Nautical Scis., Nautical High Sch., Bremen, Federal Republic of Germany, 1974, Diplom-Nautiker. Second mate German Shell Tankers, Hamburg, 1974-75; second mate, chief mate U.K.-Tankschiff, Hamburg, 1976-77; mgr., transport Veba Oel AG Gelsenkirchen-Buer/Veba Poseidon Schiffahrt GmbH, Hamburg, 1977-84; mng. dir. Krohn Shipping Group, Vienna, 1984—; ptnr. Oesterreichischer Lloyd Ship Mgmt. Gesmbh, Vienna and Norderstedt, Germany, also Cypres and Malta, 1991—, E. Koch Schiff Gesmbh, Vienna, 1991—, Oesterreichischer Lloyd SeereedereiGesmbH. Mem. Austrian Assn. Shipowners (sec. 1984—). Avocations: travel, motorboat-sport. Home: Egenbuttelweg 58b, 22880 Wedel Germany Office: Oesterreichischer Lloyd Ship Mgmt Gesmbh Bornbarch, Bus Park Nord, D 22848 Norderstedt Hamburg, Germany

KOCH, EDWARD RICHARD, lawyer, accountant; b. Teaneck, N.J., Mar. 25, 1953; s. Edward J. and Adelaide M. K.; m. Cora Susan Koch, Apr. 12, 1997, one child: Edward Peter. BS in Econs. magna cum laude, U. Pa., 1975; JD, U. Va., 1980; LLM in Taxation, NYU, 1986. Bar: N.J. 1980, U.S. Dist. Ct. N.J. 1980, U.S. Tax Ct. 1981, U.S. Ct. Claims 1981. Staff acct. Touche Ross & Co. (now Deloitte & Touche), Newark, 1975-77; assoc. Winne, Banta & Rizzi, Hackensack, N.J., 1980-82; tax atty. Allied Corp. (now Honeywell Internat. Inc.), Morristown, 1982-87; asst. v.p. ChemBank (now Chase Manhattan), N.Y.C., 1987-90; tax mgr. Paul Scherer & Co. LLP, N.Y.C., 1990-97, ptnr., 1998—. Vice chmn. law and legis. com. U.S.A. Track and Field, Indpls., 1985-89—, chmn., 1989—, chmn. ins. com., 1984-88, bd. dirs., 1989—; pres. N.J. Athletics Congress, Red Bank, 1986-90; mem. Jury of Appeals, 1988, U.S. Olympic Men's Marathon Trials, Holy Family Sch. Edn. Coun., 1992-96; Olympic Track and Field ofcl., 1996. Mem. AICPA, N.J. Soc. CPAs, Am. Assn. Attys.-CPAs, N.J. State Bar Assn., N.J. Striders Track Club (chmn. 1981-96). Republican. Roman Catholic. Avocations: running, track and field. Home: 130 Grant St Haworth NJ 07641-1951 Office: Paul Scherer & Co 335 Madison Ave Fl 9 New York NY 10017-4605

KOCH, GÜNTER RUDOLF, computer scientist; b. Freiburg, Germany, Aug. 4, 1947; s. Wilhelm R. and Elisabeth Ch. (Blessing) K.; m. Gabi Unger, May 17, 1974; children: Julia, Benjamin. BEE, U. Karlsruhe, 1972, M in Computer Sci., 1975. Mgr. Teledata GmbH, Freiburg, 1974-75; sr. asst. U. Karlsruhe, 1975-81; tech. dir. Protec GmbH, Karlsruhe, Germany, 1977-79; mng. dir. 2i Indsl. Informatics, Freiburg, 1982-93, 2i Consult, 1993, European Software Inst., Zamudio, Spain, 1993-96; dir. Synlogic AG, Basel, Switzerland, 1997; chief cons. Sun Microsystems, Geneva, 1997; mng. dir. Austrian Rsch. Ctrs., 1998—; cons. Commn. European Communities, Brussels, 1984—; vis. prof. Tech. U., Graz, Austria, 1991-93, prof. Danube U., Krems, 1998—; chmn. tech. com. European Purdue Workshop, Brussels, 1977-79; bd. dirs. ARSENAL Rsch., Ltd., Vienna. Author: Introduction to Computer Science, 1978, Microprocessor Programming, 1981; contbr. articles to profl. jours. Mem. steering bd. Mgmt. Circle Friedrich Ebert Stiftung, Bonn, 1990-97; bd. dirs. YACEE Internat., Freiburg, 1990-93; active Tech. Politics Circle, Stuttgart, Germany, 1990-93. Mem. IEEE Computer Soc. (adv. bd. 1991—), Verein Deutscher Ingenieure, Gesellschaft für Mess-und Regelungstechnik, ACM, Austrian Rsch. Assn. (v.p.). Avocations: writing, theatre. Fax: 43-2254-780-2010. E-mail: guenter.koch@arcs.ac.at. Office: Austrian Rsch Ctrs, A-2444 Seibersdorf Austria

KOCH, HEINRICH PAUL, educator; b. Pressburg, Slovakia, June 16, 1931; arrived in Austria, 1945; s. Joseph and Paula Koch; m. Ingeborg Berger; children: Andreas, Christian. MPharm, U. Vienna, Austria, 1955, PhD, 1960; PhD, 1998. Rsch. asst. U. Vienna, Austria, 1955—; prof. pharm. chemistry U. Vienna, 1967—; postdoctoral U. London, Eng., 1964; dir. R&D Madaus Co., Cologne, Germany, 1971-73; lectr. U. Bonn., Germany, 1971-73; adj. prof. biopharmaceutics U. Cin. (Ohio) Coll. Pharmacy, 1979—. Author of 10 books; mem. of 6 editorial bds.; contbr. over 400 articles to profl. jours.; patentee in field. Recipient Ernst Scheurich award Sci. Soc., Germany, 1986, Harry Auterhoff award Sci. Soc., Germany, 1986, Ilse Richter award Sci. Soc., Germany, 1993. Avocations: history, geography, traveling, science philosophy. Office: Univ Vienna, Althan St 14, A-1090 Vienna Austria

KOCH, HERBERT, chemist; b. Baden, Switzerland, July 20, 1942; s. Albert Koch and Maria Burkart; m. Maria Mai. Diploma in chemistry, U. Zurich, Switzerland, 1970, D Chemistry, 1975. Asst. lectr. U. Zurich, Switzerland, 1975-76, U. Lausanne, Switzerland, 1976-77; pharmacology lab. dir. U. Bern, Switzerland, 1977-81; lab. dir. Swiss Vet. Office, Bern, 1981—. Contbr. articles to profl. jours. Mem. SAC, Codex Alimentarius Rome. Avocations: jogging, riding bicycle. Office: Swiss Veterinary Office, Schwarzenburgstr 161, CH-3003 Bern Switzerland

KOCH, JØRN ERLAND, geneticist, researcher; b. Sønder Ørslev, Idestrup, Denmark, Nov. 25, 1957; s. Knud Anker and Anna Else (Rasmussen) K.; m. Helle Merete Svensson, Dec. 31, 1994; children: Henriette, Rebekka, Rakel. MD, U. Aarhus, Denmark, 1986, PhD, 1997. Genetics rschr. Inst. Human Genetics U. Aarhus, 1983-92; cancer geneticist dept. cytogenetics Danish Cancer Soc., 1993—; cons. molecular staging Boehringer Mannheim, Hybaid, 1992—; tchr. genetics and histology, 1987-92; ofcl. examiner genetics Danish Univs., 1990—. Inventor Prins Technique; co-inventor rolling circle amplification. Bd. dirs. Aarhus U. Ctr. for Leukemia and Lymphoma Rsch., 1999—. Pvt. Danish Army, 1977-78, Vordingborg. Grantee John and Birthe Meyer Found., 1998. Mem. Danish Hematological Soc., Danish Soc. for Med. Genetics. Home: Vittenve 124, DK8382 Hinnerup Denmark Office: Danish Cancer Soc Cytogenet, Tage Hansens Gade 2, DK8000 Århus Denmark

KOCH, MAGALY, geologist, researcher; b. Büderich, Germany, Mar. 2, 1959; d. Franz D. and Floralba (Mejia) K. MSc in Geology, U. Cologne, Germany, 1986; Diploma in Hydrology, Poly. U. Catalonia, Barcelona, Spain, 1987; PhD in Geology, Boston U., 1993. Rsch. assoc. Ctr. for Remote Sensing, Boston U., 1993-96, rsch. asst. prof., 1998—; rsch. fellow Earth Scis. Inst. "Jaume Almera", CSIC, Barcelona, 1996-98; vis. scientist geography dept. U. Nottingham, Eng., 1996, geology dept. Autonomous U. Madrid, 2000; cons. UNDP-UNESCO Geo Devel. Project for Capacity Bldg. Egyptian Geological Survey & Mining Authority and Nat. Authority for Remote Sensing and Space Scis., Cairo, 1999. Contbr. articles to profl. jours. TMR Marie Curie Rsch. grantee Commn. of European Communities, 1995, Brit. Coun. Spl. Visit grantee, 1996. Mem. Remote Sensing Soc. U.K., Marie Cure Fellowship Assn., European Commn., Am. Soc. for Photogrammetry and Remote Sensing. Avocations: film, travel, art. Office: Boston U Ctr Remote Sensing 725 Commonwealth Ave Boston MA 02215-1401

KOCH, MICHAEL GERHARD, epidemiologist; b. Prenzlau, Germany, Aug. 21, 1941; s. Gerhard Walter and Hildegard Helene (Hirschberg) K.; m. Lisbeth Andersson, June 7, 2000; children: Ivar Nathan, Jessica Yeal, Viveca Miriam, Angelica Dalia. MD, U. Kiel, 1966. Physician various hosps., Sweden, 1967-71; state physician Karlsborg, Sweden, 1972-80, head health dist., 1981-90; regimental physician Karlsborg, 1991—; epidemiologist, Bavaria, 1988-89, Switzerland, Germany, China, 1989—. Mem. Swedish Carnegie Inst. (Bejerot award 1989). Avocations: animal rights/health, protection of nature, prevention of drug abuse. Office: K3/HSA, S-546 81 Karlsborg Sweden

KOCH, OLAF MANFRED, hematologist, educator; b. Nordenham, Germany, Dec. 21, 1956; s. Manfred Bruno and Hannelore (Schreiner) K.; m. Chun-Kyung Lee; children: Mia Lee and Insa Lee. MD, U. Cologne, Germany, 1982; PhD, U. Munster, Germany, 1994. Fellow in hematology U. Munster, Germany, 1984-88; attdg. physician U. Bonn, 1988-91; vis. scientist Meml. Sloan-Kettering Cancer Ctr., N.Y.C., 1991-92; attdg. physician U. Munster, 1992-96; head dept. hematology/oncology Paracelsus-Klinik Osnabrück, Germany, 1996—; lectr. in hematology U. Munster, Germany, 1994—. Contbr. numerous articles to profl. jours. Mem. Greenpeace, Hamburg, Germany, 1995. Mem. Am. Soc. Clin. Oncology, Am. Soc. for Cancer Rsch., Am. Soc. Hematology, N.Y. Acad. Sci. Avocations: meditation, modern art, foreign countries. Office: Paracelsus Klinik, Am Natruper Holz 69, 49076 Osnabrück Germany

KOCH, RAINER PHILIPP, museum director; b. Leipzig, Germany, Dec. 8, 1944; s. Philipp and Anne Marie (Wunderlich) K.; m. Benita von Lerche, Nov. 9, 1966; children: Saika, Annika. Staatsexamen, U. Giessen, Germany, 1971; PhD, U. Berlin, 1974; Habilitation, U. Frankfurt, Germany, 1982. Wissenschaftlicher asst. U. Berlin, 1972-75; wissenschaftlicher asst. U. Frankfurt, 1975-82, privat dozent, 1983, prof. history, 1994—; mus. dir. Historischees Mus., Frankfurt, 1983—. Lt. German Arty., 1964-66. Mem. Lions. Office: Historisches Museum Frankfurt, Saalgasse 19, D-60275 Frankfurt am Main 1, Germany

KOCH, ROBERT, art educator; b. N.Y.C., Apr. 7, 1918; s. Millard Fillmore and Ella (Heidelberg) K.; m. Gladys Leah Rooff, Aug. 5, 1942; children: B'rak Elana Asher, Mitchell David. AB, Harvard U., 1939; MA, NYU, 1953; PhD, Yale U., 1957. Asst. instr. Queen's Coll., N.Y.C., 1951-53; grad. asst. Yale U., New Haven, 1953-56; asst. prof. So. Conn. State U., New Haven, 1956-59; lectr. U. Calif., Berkeley, 1960-61; assoc. prof. So. Conn. State U., New Haven, 1959-66, prof., 1966-79, prof. emeritus, 1979—. Author: Louis C. Tiffany, Rebel in Glass, 1964, Louis C. Tiffany's Glass, Bronzes, Lamps, 1971, Louis C. Tiffany's Art Glass, 1977; contbr. articles to profl. jours. Pres. Temple Shalom of Norwalk, Conn., 1966-69; hon. trustee Mark Twain Meml. 1st Lt. U.S. Army, 1942-45. Recipient Faculty Scholar award So. Conn. State U., 1973-74. Mem. Coll. Art Assn., AAUP. Democrat. Jewish. Avocations: collecting books, antiques. Home: 143 Hoyt St Apt 7G Stamford CT 06905-5746

KOCHANUJAN, ANAND, information technologist; b. Aden, Yemen, Feb. 11, 1961; s. Naduvil Vadakute and Jayanthi Kochanujan; m. Sabita Varma, Oct. 27, 1987; 1 child, Sharmishta. BSc with honors, U. Bombay, 1981, BSc in Tech., 1984. Trainee programmer/analyst Ramac Cons., Bombay, 1983-85; programmer/analyst Prudential Mgmt. Svcs., Bombay, 1985; sys. engr. Blue Star Ltd., Bombay, 1985-89; sr. sys. analyst Data Processing Ltd., Gaborone, Botswana, 1989-94; mgr. info. tech. Pricewater House Coopers, Gaborone, 1995—; cons. Govt. Computer Bur., Gaborone, 1995-99. Mem. IEEE, Assn. for Computing U.K., Chartered Inst. Mgmt. Accts. U.K. (student mem.). Office: Pricewater House Coopers, Debswana House PO Box 294, Gaborone Botswana

KOCHAR, KANWAL PREET, physiologist, educator; b. Jalandhar, Punjab, India, Jan. 7, 1960; d. Jaswani Singh Kohli and Amrit Kaur Sodhi; m. Gurinder Singh Kochhar, Aug. 21, 1983; 2 children. MBBS with honors, Rohtak Med. Coll., India, 1982; MD, All India Med. Scis., New Delhi, 1988, PhD, 1998. Med. diplomate. Asst. rsch. officer All India Inst. Med. Scis., 1983, jr. resident, 1984, jr. demonstrator, 1985-88, sr. demonstrator, 1988-93, asst. prof., 1993-98, assoc. prof., 1998—; chief investigator Ethics and Attitudes to Medicine, 1993—. Author: Journey on Health Track, 1996; editor: Going About Research, 1999; assoc. editor Annals of Nat. Acad. Med. Sci., 1995—. Jt. sec. Indian Drs. for Peace and Devel., 1997—; mem. Hindi Sci. Coun., 1996. Mem. All India Bioethics Assn. (v.p. 1998—), Med. Rsch. Soc. U.K., Internat. Bioethics Network, N.Y. Acad. Scis. Sikh. Avocations: classical Indian music, reading, crosswords puzzles, interior design, English literature. Home: F-115 Ansari Nagar, New Delhi 110029, India Office: Dept Physiology, All India Inst Med Scis, New Delhi 110029, India

KOCHAR, MAHENDR SINGH, physician, educator, administrator, scientist, writer, consultant; b. Jabalpur, India, Nov. 30, 1943; came to U.S., 1967, naturalized, 1978; s. Harnam Singh and Chanan Kaur (Khaturia) K.; m. Arvind Kaur, 1968; children: Baltej (Baj), Ajay (Jay). MB, BS, All India Inst. Med. Scis., New Delhi, 1965; MSc, Med. Coll. Wis., 1972; MBA, U. Wis., Milw., 1987. Diplomate Am. Bd. Internal Medicine, Nephrology and Geriatrics, Am. Bd. Family Practice, Am. Bd. Mgmt., Am. Bd. Clin. Pharmacology. Intern All India Inst. Med. Scis. Hosp., New Delhi, 1966-67, Passaic N.J. Gen. Hosp., 1967-68; resident in medicine Allegheny Gen. Hosp., Pitts., 1968-70; fellow in clin. pharmacology Milw. VA Med. Ctr., 1970-71, attending physician, 1973; fellow in nephrology and hypertension Milw. County Gen. Hosp., 1971-73, attending physician, 1973-95; attending physician St. Michael Hosp., Milw., 1974—, dir. hemodialysis unit, 1975-80; clin. asst. prof. medicine and pharmacology and toxicology Med. Coll. Wis., Milw., 1973-75, asst. prof., 1975-78, assoc. prof., 1978-84, prof., 1984—, assoc. dean continuing med. edn., 1985-86, assoc. dean grad. med. edn., 1987-99, sr. assoc. dean acad. affairs, 1994-95; sr. assoc. dean grad. med. edn. Med. Coll. Wis., 1999—; attending physician St. Joseph's Hosp., Milw., 1975—; chmn. medicine Northpoint Med. Group, Milw., 1974-75; dir. Milw. Blood Pressure Program, 1975-78; dir. Hypertension Clinic, Milwaukee County Downtown Med. and Health Services, 1975-79; chief hypertension. VA Med. Center, Milw., 1978-2000, assoc. chief staff for edn., 1979-2000; exec. dir. Med. Coll. Wis. Affiliated Hosps. Inc., Milw., 1987—. Author: Hypertension Control, 1978, 2nd rev. edit., 1985; editor: Textbook of General Medicine, 1983, Concise Textbook of Medicine, 2d edit., 1990, 3d edit., 1998. Recipient Grad. of Last Decade award U. Wis., Milw., 1998. Fellow ACP/Am. Soc. Internal Medicine (pres., gov. Wis. chpt. 1994-98, mem. bd. regents 1997—, chmn. bd. govs. 1998-99, Laureate award 2000), Am. Coll. Cardiology (gov. Am. Coll. Cardiology dept. vets. affair, 1999-2000), Am. Acad. Family Physicians, Royal Coll. Physicians Can., Am. Coll. Clin. Pharmacology, Am. Heart Assn. (high blood pressure coun.), Royal Coll. Physicians (London), Am. Coll. Physician Execs.; mem. AMA (alt. del.), Am. Assn. Physicians from India (pres. Wis. chpt. 1995-97), Am. Fedn. Med. Rsch., Milw. Acad. Medicine (pres. 1996-97, trustee 1997—, pres.'s award 1998), Milw. County Med. Soc. (bd. dirs. 2000—), Milw. Internist Club, Wis. State Med. Soc. (alt. del. ho. dels. AMA), Mensa, Highlander Elite Tennis Club, Univ. Club Milw. E-mail: kochar@mcw.edu. Home: 18630 Le Chateau Dr Brookfield WI 53045-4924 Office: Med Coll Wis 8701 Watertown Plank Rd Milwaukee WI 53226

KOCHARYAN, ROBERT, president; b. Stepanakert, Armenia, Aug. 31, 1954; married; three children. Grad., Yerevan Polytech. Inst., 1982. Engr., electrotechnician Karabakh Silk Prodn. Factory, Stepanakert, Armenian, 1981-87; sec. factory CP Cttee, 1987-89; dep. Armenian Supreme Coun., 1990-91; co-founder Karabakh Movement, 1988—; elected Supreme Coun. Nagorny-Karabakh Repub. in Azerbaijan, 1989-94, pres., 1994-96; chair State Cttee of Defense and leader of Repub., 1992-94; prime min. Republic of Armenia, 1997-98, pres., 1998—. With Soviet Army, 1972-74. Office: Office of the President, ul Marshal Baghramiam 26, Yerevan 375095, Armenia

KOCHER, JUANITA FAY, retired auditor; b. Falmouth, Ky., Aug. 9, 1933; d. William Birgest and Lula (Gillespie) Vickroy; m. Donald Edward Kocher, Nov. 18, 1953. Grad. high sch., Bright, Ind. Cert. internal auditor and compliance officer. Bookkeeper Mchts. Bank and Trust Co., West Harrison, Ind., 1952-56, teller, asst. cashier, 1962-87, br. mgr., 1979-87, internal auditor, 1987-96, ret., 1996; bookkeeper Progressive Bank, New Orleans, 1956-58; with proof dept. 1st Nat. Bank, Cin., Ohio, 1958-59; teller 1st Nat. Bank, Harrison, Ohio, 1959-62; bookkeeper Donald E. Kocher Constrn., Harrison, 1981—. Mem. Am. Bankers Assn., Ind. Bankers Assn. Home: 11277 Biddinger Rd Harrison OH 45030

KOCHER, KLAUS KARL, strategy consultant; b. Basel, Switzerland, Aug. 3, 1941; s. Walter and Maria (Joos) K.; m. Silvia Hollenstein, Feb. 10, 1977; children: Thomas, Urs. DSc in Math., Swiss Fed. Tech. Inst., Zürich, Switzerland, 1970. Pres. Internat. Student Travel Conf., Zürich, 1970-78; sr.

cons. McKinsey & Co., Zürich, 1971-74; dir. Rank Xerox, Zürich, 1974-78; pres. Kocher & Gaide, Zürich, 1978—. Home and Office: Frohburgstr 128, 8057 Zurich Switzerland

KOCHER, MARGARET, technical writer; b. Salem, Mass., Feb. 6, 1921; d. J. Willard and Margaret (Mason) Helburn; m. Eric Kocher, Apr. 26, 1947; children: Eric Glenn, Terry, Christopher, Debra Margaret Mildred. BA cum laude, Harvard U., 1941; MA, Am. U., 1969. Lic. comml. pilot, instrument and instr. rating, FAA. Casting aide, stage mgr. The Theatre Guild, N.Y.C., 1941-42; sales pilot Republic Aviation, Farmingdale, N.Y., 1945; analyst, writer, crash injury rsch. Cornell Med. Ctr., N.Y.C., 1946-47; tech. and chief editor Vitro Engring., Washington, 1956-59; rschr., writer Ctr. for Applied LInguistics, Washington, 1967-69; instr. linguistics Queens Coll., N.Y.C., 1970-72, Adelphi U., Garden City, N.Y., 1970-72; exec. sec. project 208 N.Y.C. Dept. Environ. Protection, 1976-80; writer N.Y. Inst. Tech., Old Westbury, 1981-82; pub. participation specialist Helen Neuhaus Assocs., N.Y.C., 1980-83; prin. Kocher Assocs., N.Y.C., 1982—. Author: Guide to Kuala Lumpur, 1955, Energy Information Guidance Manual, 1982, The World of Waste, 1988; co-author: Human Resources Directory, 1981. Chair bldg. and grounds com. Alley Pond Environ. Ctr., 1993-95; mem. nominating com. Citywide Recycling Adv. Bd., N.Y.C., 1991-93; bd. dirs. Alley Pond Environ. Ctr., N.Y., 1991—. Pilot, USAF, 1943-44. Recipient Cert. of Appreciation U.S. EPA, 1979, Earthling award for Lifetime Achievement, The City Club of N.Y., 1993. Mem. LWV (chair environ. com. N.Y.C. chpt. 1982-93, bd. dirs. Tri-State met. region 1986-98), Transp. Alternatives, Environ. Def. Fund, Nat. Resources Def. Coun., Nat. Wildlife Fedn., Nature Conservancy, Sierra Club. Avocations: bicycling, hiking, swimming, knitting, crossword puzzles.

KOCHHAR, ASHOK KUMAR, engineering educator; b. Amritsar, India, Jan. 31, 1949; arrived in U.K., 1966; s. Sansar Chand and Satya (Vohra) K.; m. Rupa Mehta, Apr. 18, 1987. BSc in Engring., U. London, 1970; PhD, U. Bradford, 1975. Engring. apprentice Rolls Royce, Derby, U.K., 1966-70; rschr. U. Bradford, U.K., 1971-76, lectr., reader, prof., 1976-92; Lucas prof. mfg. systems, engring. and head mfg. divsn. U. Manchester Inst. of Sci. and Tech., U.K., 1992-97, head of dept. mech. engring., 1997-98; prof. mfg. sys. engring. and mgmt., head sch. engring. and applied sci. Aston U., 1999—; cons. ITT, U.K., 1976-82, Thorn-EMT, U.K., 1982-84, Robinson Nugent, Swizerland, 1984-85, Lucas Industries, U.K., 1986-96, British Aerospace U.K., 1996—; numerous others; mem. organizing coms. numerous internat. confs. in mfg. Author: (books) Development of Computer Based Production Systems, 1979, Micro-Processors and their Manufacturing Applications, 1983; editor 30th Internat. MATADOR Conf., 1993, 31st, 1995, 32d, 1997; contbr. numerous articles to profl. jours.; mem. editl. bd. Jour. of Engring. Mfg., Integrated Mfg. Systems, Internat. Jour. of Advanced Mfg. Tech., Internat. Jour. of Mfg. Systems Design, editor: Proceedings of the 30th-32nd Internat MATADOR Conf., 1993-97. Mem. Ct. of U. Cranfield. Recipient U.K. Govt. of Trade and Industry prize Nat. Mfg. Intelligence Competition. Fellow Instn. of Mech. Engrs. (Joseph Whitworth prize, Donald Julius Groen prize, A.M. Strickland prize), Instn. of Elec. Engrs., Royal Acad. Engring.; mem. Internat. Fedn. of Info. Processing Group on Computer Aided Prodn. Mgmt., Coun. of Instn. of Elec. Engrs. Avocations: reading, current affairs, music. Office: Sch Engring and Applied Sci, Aston U, Aston Triangle Birmingham B4 7ET, England

KOCHHAR, GURMOHAN SINGH, engineering educator; b. Ferozepur, Punjab, India, July 4, 1949; arrived in Trinidad and Tobago, 1979; s. Labh Singh and Harcharan Kaur Kochhar; m. Jaishree Kulkarni, Jan. 12, 1977; children: Amrita, Arti, Amrik. BE, U. Baroda, India, 1970; MS, U. Wis., Madison, 1972; PhD, U. West Indies, St. Augustine, Trinidad, 1976. Registered profl. engr., Trinidad & Tobago Bd. Engrg. Design engr. V.H. Middleton Engring., Calgary, Alta., Can., 1977-78, Stevenson, Raines & Ptnrs., Calgary, 1978-79; from lectr. to sr. lectr. mech. engring. U. West Indies, 1989-96, prof. mech. engring., 1989-96, 1996—, dep. dean faculty engring., 1990-94, dean faculty engring., 1994-2000, advisor to vice chancellor and campus prin., 2000—; grad. asst. mech. engring. U. West Indies, St. Augustine, 1972-76; design engr. V.H. Middleton Engring., Calgary, Can., 1977-78. Editor: Preventive Maintenance, 1989, conf. procs. Regional Conf. on Maintenance Engring., 1989, Conf. Procs. Rational Use of Energy, 1991; co-author: Infrastructure for Development—A Policy Agenda for the Caribbean, 1996. V.P. West Indies Group U. Tchrs., St. Augustine, 1982-87. Grantee Orgn. Am. States Washington, 1989, U. West Indies, 1990. Mem. ASME, ASHRAE, Assn. Profl. Engrs. Trinidad and Tobago. Office: U West Indies, Faculty Engring, Saint Augustine Trinidad and Tobago

KOCHTA, RUTH MARTHA, art gallery owner; b. N.Y.C., Jan. 5, 1924; d. Harry Joseph and Anna (Braun) Evers; m. Albert Emil Kochta, Nov. 7, 1948; children: Alan, Carol. Student, CUNY, Queens, 1965-68, Art Students League, 1970-75. Artist Queens, N.Y. and Lenox, Mass., 1965—; dir. Imperial Gallery, N.Y.C., 1981; owner, dir. Clark Whitney Gallery, Lenox, 1983-2000. Work exhibited at Nat. Acad., N.Y.C. 1969, Audubon Artists, N.Y.C. 1971, Heckscher Mus., Huntington, N.Y., 1972, Elizabet Ney Mus., Austin, Tex., 1972, Wadsworth Atheneum, Hartford, Conn., 1975, Philathea Mus., Ont., Can., 1976, New Britain (Conn.) Mus., 1978, Guild Gallery, N.Y.C. 1979, other exhibits. Recipient over 50 awards in various competitions. Home and Office: Devonshire Estates 329 Pittsfield Rd Lenox MA 01240-2306

KOCIECKI, ROBERT EUGENE, business executive; b. Chgo., June 12, 1966; s. Eugene and Diana Kociecki; m. Lisa Marie Stuckmann, June 27, 1992. BS, DePaul U., Chgo., 1988. Store ops. Venture Stores, Inc., Chgo., 1981-94; v.p. Office Depot Eastern Europe, Warsaw, Poland, 1994-98, sr. v.p. internat. ops., 1998—; bd. dirs. Office Depot Poland, Office Depot Hungary. Mem. Bus. Ctr. Club (Poland). Avocations: auto restoration, music. E-mail: rkociecki@officedepot.com.pl. Office: Office Depot, ul Towarwa 22, Warsaw Poland 00-893

KOCKA, FRANK EDWARD, microbiologist; b. Chgo., May 28, 1938; s. Francis James and Lucille Ella (Beck) K. BS in Biology, Ill. Inst. Tech., 1961, MS in Microbiology, 1966; PhD in Microbiology, Kans. State U., 1969. Rsch. assoc., lectr. Purdue U., West Lafayette, Ind., 1969-71; sr. microbiologist Searle Diagnostic, Columbus, Ohio, 1971-73; dir. rsch. Wilson Diagnostic, Glenwood, Ill., 1973; asst. prof., assoc. dir. clin. microbiology U. Chgo., 1973-76; assoc. prof. pathology and microbiology Chgo. Med. Sch., North Chicago, Ill., 1976-94, prof., 1995—; chief microbiology North Chicago VA Hosp., 1976-82; chmn. microbiology Cook County Hosp., Chgo., 1983-97; chief infectious disease lab. Ill. Dept. Pub. Health, Chgo., 1997-99, dir. Chgo. lab., 2000—. Fellow Am. Acad. Microbiology, Acad. Clin. Lab. Scientists and Physicians; mem. Am. Soc. Microbiology (mem. com. 1989-94), Ill. Soc. Microbiology (pres. 1977-78), South Ctrl. Assn. Clin. Microbiology (chair com.), Sigma Xi. Lutheran. Achievements include patent for inhibition of antibacterial action of blood. Avocation: orchid culture. E-mail: fkocka@idph.state.il.us. Home: 3200 N Lake Shore Dr Apt 1008 Chicago IL 60657-3931 Office: Infectious Disease Lab 2121 W Taylor St Chicago IL 60612-7260

KOČKA, JAN VILÉM, physicist; b. Mladá Boleslav, Czechoslovakia, Jan. 19, 1946; s. Vilém V. and Jana A. (Vokálová) K.; m. Sylva Vodrážková, May 8, 1970; children: Viktor, Tomáš. D Natural Scis., Charles U., Prague, Czechoslovakia, 1969; PhD, Acad. Scis., Prague, 1975; DrSc, Charles U., Prague, Czechoslovakia, 1990. Rsch. worker Inst. Solid State Physics, Acad. Scis., Prague, 1974-77; postdoctoral fellow Cavendish Lab. U. Cambridge, 1977-78; rsch. worker Inst. Physics, Acad. Scis., Prague, 1978—, head dept., 1990—; vis. prof. Institut für Physikalische Elektronik, U. Stuttgart, 1990, Tokyo Inst. Tech., 1993; mem. steering com. Internat. Conf. on Amorphous Semiconductors, 1991—; mem. adv. bd. Charles U., Prague, 1991—. With Czechoslovakia mil., 1969-70. Mem. Union of Czechoslovak Physicists and Mathematicians, Solidus Sporting Club. Office: Inst Physics, Cukrovarnická 10, 162 00 Prague 6, Czech Republic

KOCOUREK, JAN FRANTISEK, biochemistry educator, research scientist; b. Prostejov, Moravia, Czech Republic, Jan. 10, 1926; s. Jan and Amalie Rosalie (Knappova) K.; m. Nadia Marie Fialova, July 11, 1956; children: Jan, Martina. PhMr., Charles U., Prague, 1949, RNDr., 1952, CSc, 1966. Instr. dept. pharm. chemistry Charles U., 1950-52, instr. dept. biochemistry, 1952-55, asst. prof., 1955-66, assoc. prof., 1966-91, prof., 1991—; vis. scientist ARC Blood Rsch. lab., Washington, 1967-69; vis. prof. dept. biochemistry, U. Calif., Berkeley, 1969; head Lab. for Prodn. and Control of Lectin Preparations, Faculty of Sci., Charles U., Prague, 1983—. Co-author: The Monosaccharides, 1963, Methods in Enzymology, Vol. XXXIV, 1974, Methods in Carbohydrate Chemistry Vol. VII, 1976, The Lectins: Properties, Functions, and Applications in Biology and Medicine, 1986; author or co-author about 100 scientific papers in field. Mem. Federal Assembly of Czech and Slovak Federal Repu., Chamber of Nations, Prague, 1992; sec. Com. of Defense and Security of the Federal Assembly of Czech and Slovak Federal Republic, Prague, 1992. Mem. The Czech Soc. for Biochemistry and Molecular Biology, The Biochem. Soc. (London), Internat. Lectin Soc. Mem. Civic Dem. Party. Avocations: study of langs. and history, tourism. Home: Hrusicka 2515 Sporilov II, PO Box # 20, CZ-14101 Prague 4, Czech Republic Office: Lab Prodn Control Lectin Pr, Charles U Albertov 2030, CZ-12840 Prague 2, Czech Republic

KOCOWSKA, BARBARA, publishing house executive, translator; b. Tarnów, Poland, Sept. 3, 1955; d. Adam and Antonina (Fischer) K. BA, Wroclaw U., 1979. Rsch. asst. Wroclaw U., 1979-82; archive researcher History Monuments Preservation Office, Wroclaw, 1982-83; copy editor Ossolineum Pub. House, Wroclaw, 1983-84, fgn. rights officer, 1984-91, dep. editor in chief, 1991-92, mng. dir., 1992-93; exec. sec. Dolnoslaskie Pub. House, Wroclaw, 1993-97; head book dept. Polish Romer Cartographical Pub. House Ltd., Wroclaw, 1997-2000; project mgr. Dolnoslaskie Pub. House, Wroclaw, 2000—. Book translator some 30 titles. Avocations: sailing, skiing, travel. E-mail: kocowska@wd.wroc.pl. Fax: 71-3288954. Office: Wydawnictwo Dolnoslaskie, Straznicza 1-3, 50-206 Wrocław Poland

KOCSIS, ZOLTAN, pianist, composer, conductor; b. Budapest, May 30, 1952; s. Otto and Maria (Matyas) K. Ed., Budapest Music Acad. Asst. prof. Music Acad. Budapest, 1976-79, prof., 1979—; producer archive sect. Hungaroton Rec. Co.; co-founder, artistic dir. Budapest Festival Orch., 1983-97; chief condr., artistic dir. Hungarian Nat. Philharm. Orch. Performed throughout Europe, U.S., Mex., Can., Japan, Australia, Far East; toured with numerous major orchs.; numerous world premieres and 1st perfromances in Hungary; appeared at Festival Estival, Paris, 1977, Edinburgh Festival, 1978, Salzburg Festival, Luzern Festival; author numerous publs.; arrangements for piano and 2 pianos; recs. Huntaroton and PHILIPS. Recipient 1st prize Beethoven Piano Competition, Hungaroton Radio and TV, 1970, Liszt prize, 1973, Kossuth prize, 1978, Edison prize, Gramophone prize. Office: Mélykút, u 4, H-1116 Budapest Hungary

KOCUM, ESRA, biologist, educator; b. Antalya, Turkey, Apr. 1, 1969; d. Hasan and Zeliha (Bozdemir) K. BSc, Marmara U., Istanbul, Turkey, 1991; PhD, U. Essex, Colchester, U.K., 1998. Lectr. Canakkale 18 Mart U., Turkey, 1998—. Mem. Am. Soc. Limnology and Oceanography. Office: 18 Mart U Fen-Edebiyat, Fakultesi Biyoloji Bolumu, 17100 Canakkale Turkey

KOCYIGIT, HIKMET, rheumatologist; b. Denizli, Turkey, Mar. 20, 1956; s. Ilhan Ziya and Aynur Kocyigit; m. Funda Uluoz, Dec. 10, 1983; 1 child, Aykut. Med. diploma, Ege U., Izmir, Turkey, 1981; specialization phys. medicine and rehab., Ege U., 1985. Cons. Erzincan (Turkey) Mil. Hosp., 1985-87, Usak (Turkey) State Hosp., 1987-94; chief intern Izmir Ataturk Tng. Hosp., 1994—. Contbr. articles to med. jours. Grantee Sci. and Tech. Rsch. Coun. Turkey, 1999. Mem. Turkish Soc. Phys. Medicine and Rehab., Turkish Soc. Rehab. Medicine, Turkish Soc. Osteoporosis, N.Y. Acad. Scis. Avocations: listening to classical music, playing tennis, photography, skiing. Fax: 90 232 4616586. E-mail: drhikmet@hotmail.com. Home: 1408 Sokak # 2/4, 35220 Alsancak Izmir, Turkey Office: Izmir Ataturk Egitim Hastanesi, Fizik Tedavi ve Reh Klinigi Basin Sitesi, 35350 Izmir Turkey

KOCZY, LASZLO TAMAS, electrical engineering educator, computer science educator, researcher, bibliographer; b. Budapest, Hungary, Mar. 18, 1952; s. Laszlo R. and Zsuzsanna I. (Nagy) K.; m. Anna Judit Petrasovits, July 10, 1975; children: Laszlo A., Judit R., Agnes B. MSEE, Tech. U. Budapest, 1975, M in R&D in Control Engring., 1976, D in Tech., 1977, Candidate Engring. Sci., 1989, Dr. habil., 1998; DSc, Hungarian Acad. Sci., 1998. Demonstrator dept. process control Tech. U., Budapest, 1974-76, rsch. fellow dept. comm. electronics, 1976, asst. prof. elec. engring., 1976-81, sr. asst. prof., 1982-90, jr. prof., 1991-99, prof., 1999—, course dir., grad. study programs faculty elec. engring., 1986-92; dep. dir. Internat. Edn. Ctr. Tech. U., Budapest, 1992—; chair and prof. Fuzzy Theory Tokyo Inst. Tech., 1993-94; cons. devel. projects BHG Telecom., Budapest, 1977-84, Rsch. Inst. Telecom., Budapest, 1982-87; cons. grad. edn. Hungarian Post, Videoton SEL Co., Budapest, 1982-91; cons. Lab. for Internat. Fuzzy Engring., Yohohama, Japan, 1993-94; vis. prof. Dalian, China, 1990, Pohang, Korea, 1992, Linz, Austria, 1997, 97, Trento, Italy, 1995, 96, Sydney, Australia, 1997, 98, 99, Perth, Australia, 2000. Author: Software in Switching, 1983, Bibliography of the Hungarian Heraldry and Geneology, 1984; contbr. numerous articles including on fuzzy sets and switching, to profl. jours., also articles on bibliography of Hungarian heraldic and geneal. lit. Mem. Am. Math. Soc., Assn. Modeling and Simulation in Enterprises, Internat. Fuzzy Sys. Assn. (v.p.), BUSEFAL Group (corr.), Polish Math. Soc., Sci. Soc. Telecom., Soc. Heraldry and Genealogy (pres. sect.), Soc. Holy Crown, The Sovereign Mil. Order of Malta. Greek Catholic. Mem. Christian Dem. Party. Avocations: collecting old books, yachting. Home: Kassai U 10, H-2040 Budaors-Kamaraerdo Hungary Office: Tech U Budapest, Dept Communication, Stoczek u 2, H-1111 Budapest Hungary

KODA, KAZUO, management educator; b. Tokyo, July 28, 1930; s. Itsuro and Suzuko Koda; m. Hiroko Nakamura, May 7, 1960; children: Tatsuo, Kyoko. BA, Keio U., Tokyo, 1954; exch. visitor, UCLA, 1962-63. Full-time lectr. Inst. Bus. Adminstrn. & Mgmt., Tokyo, 1961-63, asst. prof., 1964-67, prof., 1968-78; prof. Sanno Coll.-The Sanno Inst. of Mgmt., Tokyo, 1979-91; prof. grad. sch. Sanno Coll., Tokyo, 1992—; chief mgmt., rsch. & consulting divsn. Inst. Bus. Adminstrn. & Mgmt., Tokyo, 1969-72; bd. dirs. Sanno Inst. Mgmt., 1970-94; mem. adv. bd. Orgn. Devel. Inst., Chesterland, Ohio, 1980-86. Author: Changing for Improvement of Managment Organization, 1965, Theory and Practice of Organization Development, 1969, Concept and Practices of Organizing Business Structures, 1977, Management by Objectives, 1989. Com. mem. Ministry of Internat. Trade and Industry, Japanese Govt., Tokyo, 1973-75, Ministry of Home Affairs, 1974-78, 84-90, 93-94. Recipient Accomplishment in Coll. Edn. award Ministry of Edn.-Japanese Govt., 1990. Mem. Japanese Orgnl. Soc., Japan Soc. Mgmt. Diagnosis, Japan Soc. for Mgmt. Info. Avocations: walking, 8 mm video camera. Home: 1-26-12 Aobadai Aoba-ku, Yokohama Kanagawa 227, Japan Office: Sanno Coll Inst Mgmt Sch Mgmt and Informatics, 6-39-15 Todoroki, Tokyo Setagaya 158, Japan

KODAKA, KUNIO, plastics company executive; b. Toyko, Apr. 4, 1932; s. Shintaro and Hana (Tonegawa) K.; m. Masako Kodaka, Oct. 10, 1959; children: Akiko, Ichiro. BS, Waseda U., Tokyo, 1955. V.p. gen. mgr. Achilles KCI Corp., N.Y.C., 1963-71; gen. mgr. internat. ops. Kohokoku Chem. Ind. Corp., Tokyo, 1971-77, bd. mem., 1973-77; pres., chief exec. officer HOP Industries Corp., Garfield, N.J., 1977-97; treas., dir. Have our Plastics Corp., Mississauga, Ont., Can., 1985-97; dir. Tashin Shoji Co., Ltd., Osaka, Japan, 1981-97; pres., CEO Tamerica Products, Inc., Ontario, Calif., 1994—; chmn. Abante Corp., Berkeley, Calif., 1996—. Mem. Haworth Country Club. Home: 10800 Beechwood Dr Rancho Cucamonga CA 91737-2430 Office: HOP Industries Corp 174 Passaic St Garfield NJ 07026-1355 also: Tamerica Products Inc 1560 S Archibald Ave Ontario CA 91761-7629 also: Abante Corp 2607 7th St Berkeley CA 94710-2571

KODAKI, NOBUO, retired medical educator, researcher; b. Yokota, Japan, Sept. 14, 1921; s. Akio and Otaru (Suzuki) Fujiwara; m. Naoko Kodaki, Nov. 30, 1952; 2 children. MA, Kyoto U., Japan, 1949; D of Med. Sci., Tottori U., Yonago, Japan, 1966. Govt. official Nat. Pers. Auth., Tokyo, 1949-50; instr. Shimane U., Matsue, Japan, 1950-66, prof., 1966-77; prof. Shimane Med. Univ., Izumo, Japan, 1977-87, prof. emeritus, 1987. Editor Shimane Univ. Ednl. Sci. Decorated 3d Rank Rising Sun medal Emperor Tokyo, 1996. Fellow Mental Health Assn. Shimane (dir. 1966-77). Church of England. Avocations: writing poems and novels, traveling. Home: 789 Saikamachi, 690-0056 Matsue Japan

KODALI, NAGESWARARAO, human factors engineer, researcher; b. Vijayawada, India, Aug. 15, 1960; came to U.S., 1984; s. Pattabhi Ramayya and Sarogini (Koduru) K.; m. Indrani Bhattacharya, Dec. 26, 1991; children: Sanand, Sreeja, Sreeja. B in Tech., J.N.T. U., Karinada, India, 1982; MDes, IIT, Bombay, 1984; MS, Tufts U., 1988, PhD, 1994. Rsch. intern Honeywell, Mpls., 1991-92; prin. software devel. engr. Unisys, Bluebell, Pa., 1994-96; sr. human factors engr. Kohl Group, Middleton, N.J., 1996-97; sr. tech. staff AT&T Labs., Middletown, 1997—. Author (with others): Applications of Fuzzy Sets Methodologies in Industrial Engineer, 1989, Computer-Aided Ergonomics, 1990. Mem. Human Factors and Ergonomics Soc., Assn. Computing Machinery. Office: AT&T Labs Middletown NJ 07748

KODAMA, FUMIO, science educator; b. Kobe, Hyohgo, Japan, July 11, 1941; s. Isamu and Shigeko (Tsuda) K.; m. Minako Akiyama; children: Miki, Eri, Tomohisa, Kodama. BS in Mech. Engring., U. Tokyo, 1964, MS in Mech. Engring., 1967, PhD in Engring., 1974. Prof. U. Saitama, Urawa, Japan, 1973-93; prof. strategy industry creation U. Tokyo, Rsch. Ctr. Advanced Econ. Engring., 1994—; dir.-in-rsch. Nat. Inst. Sci. and Tech. Policy, Tokyo, 1988-91; vis. prof. Harvard U., Cambridge, Mass., 1991-92, Stanford (Calif.) U., 1992-93, dist. assocs. Asia/Pacific Rsch. Ctr., 1992—; advisor Japan Soc. for the Promotion Machine Industry, Tokyo, 1992—, EU-Japan Ctr. for Indsl. Devel., Tokyo, 1995—; adj. prof. Nat. Ctr. for Sci. and Info. Sys., Tokyo, 1995-98. Author: Haiteku-no-Gijyutu-Paradaimu, 1991 (Sakuzo Yoshino prize 1991), Emerging Patterns of Innovation, 1995; editor Rsch. Policy, Sussex, Eng., 1994—. Recipient Mins. award for rsch. excellence Sci. and Tech. Agy., Tokyo, 1991. Mem. IEEE (engring. mgmt. sect.), Japan Soc. for Sci. and Policy Rsch. Mgmt. (bd. mem. 1986—), Engring. Acad. Japan. Avocations: golf, reading, sight-seeing. E-mail: kodama@fklab.rcast.u-tokyo.ac.jp. Home: Kamiochiai 1-9-1-802, Yono Saitama 338-0001, Japan Office: Rsch Ctr Univ Tokyo, Komaba 4-6-1, Tokyo 153-8904, Japan

KODAMA, HIROKO, pediatrician, educator; b. Manchuria, China, Jan. 18, 1946; d. Takuji and Shizue (Kubota) Okada; m. Masaaki Kodama, Dec. 16, 1976; three children. MD, Osaka (Japan) U., 1970. Med. diplomate. Asst. prof. Jichi Med. Sch., Kawachi-gun, Japan, 1981-87; asst. prof. Teikyo U., Tokyo, 1988-89, assoc. prof., 1990—. Contbr. articles to profl. jours. Mem. Soc. for the Study of Inborn Error of Metabolism, Japanese Soc. for Inherited Metabolic Diseases (councilor 1994—), Japanese Soc. Pediat. Neurology (councilor 1995—), Japan Soc. for Biomed. Rsch. on Trace Elements (councilor 1995—), Soc. Study Wison's Disease (councilor 1997—). Office: Teikyo U Sch Medicine, 11-1 Kaga-2 Itabashi-ku, Tokyo 173-8605, Japan

KODAMA, JUNZO, physician, researcher; b. Kobe-shi, Hyogo-ken, Japan, Aug. 10, 1927; s. Kanjiro Matsui and Fumie (Tanikawa) K.; m. Akiko Takagi, Oct. 14, 1956; children: Hiroko, Mineo, Takayuki. Degree, Med. Sch. Osaka, Japan, Osaka U., 1960; MD, Julius Maximilians U., Würzburg, Germany, 1963. Asst. Julius Maximilians U., 1963-67; head physician Kokuritsu-Osaka Byoin, 1967-83; head of dept. clin. lab. Nat. Ctr. Cardiovascular Disease, Suita, Japan, 1983-90; med. dir. Inst. Med. Care and Health Maintenance Sanyo Electronics Group, Moriguchi, Japan, 1990-96. Inventor in field. Recipient award Seijinhyo Kenkyu Shinko Zaidan, Osaka, 1972; grantee Ministry Edn. and Culture, Tokyo, 1973, Ministry of Welfare, Tokyo, 1975. Mem. Japanese Soc. Internal Medicine, Internat. Soc. Hematology. Buddhist. Avocations: carpentry, model railways. Home: 1380 Shiniotsubo Mikage, Kobe 658-0056, Japan Office: 214 Furente Nishikan, Ikeda-cho 9-7, Nishinomiya 662-0911, Japan

KODAMA, TOHRU, biotechnology educator; b. Ohtsu, Shiga, Japan, Oct. 6, 1935; s. Minoru and Teruko (Mihara) K.; m. Hiroko Noma, Oct. 1, 1963; children: Takeshi, Rumiko. BS, U. Tokyo, 1959, D of Agr., 1971. Cert. applied microbiology. From asst. prof. to prof. U. Tokyo, Japan, 1960-96; prof. emeritus U. Tokyo, 1996—; prof. Shinshu U., Nagano, Japan, 1996—; mem. Sci. Coun. of Japan, 1997-2000. Editor Applied Microbiology Biotechnology, 1988-91, Jour. Fermentation Bioengring., 1991-97, Jour. Gen. Applied Microbiology, 1993-95. Mem. Am. Soc. Microbiology, Japan Soc. Biosci. Biotech. Agrochemistry (dir. 1976-80, 87-91, coun. 1992—), Soc. Ferment. Bioeng. Japan (dir. 1991-97, pres. 1995-97, coun. 1998—, Boeing award 1994, Sr. Scientist award 1996). Avocations: listening to classical music, driving. Home: 3-29-3 Komaimachi, Komae-shi Tokyo 201-0016, Japan Office: Shinshu U Faculty Textile, 3-15-1 Tokida, Ueda Nagano 386-8567, Japan

KODAVANTI, MALLIKHARJUNA SWAMY, physicist, researcher; b. Dharmavaram, India, Aug. 3, 1946; s. Malli Babu and Anna Purna K.; m. Adi Lakshmi Guntu Boina, June 16, 1970; children: Arjun, Gita Rajya Lakshmi. BS, Govt. Arts Coll., Rajahmundry, India, 1964; MS in Tech., Jeypore Vikram Deo Coll. Sci. Tech., Waltair, India, 1967; PhD in Applied Physics, Andhra U., Waltair, India, 1976. Scientist Regional Rsch. Lab., CSIR, Bhubaneswar, India, 1971-92; dep. dir. Regional Rsch. Lab., CSIR, Bhubaneswar, 1992—. Patentee in field; contbr. over 90 articles to profl. jours. Coun. Scientific Indsl. Rsch. fellow Andhra U., 1967-71, German Acad. Exch. Svc. fellow, 1977-78; recipient Cert. of Merit, Nat. Rsch. Devel. Corp., 1977, Invention award, 1987, First prize Shri Hari Om Ashram Prerit, 1989. Fellow Acoustical Soc. India; mem. Asian Physics Soc, Indian Inst. Chem. Engrs., Indian Inst. Min. Engrs., Indian Inst. Metals. Avocations: music, volleyball, trivia. Home: # 509 RRL Colony, Bhubaneswar 751013, India Office: Regional Rsch Lab, Bhubaneswar 751013, India

KODERA, KOUJI AUGUSTINE, marketing professional; b. N.Y.C., Feb. 19, 1967; s. Junichi and Hisako (Hanaoka) K.; m. Motoko Tsubota, May 18, 1995. B in Law, Keio U., Japan, 1990. With mktg. Europe Mitsubishi Electric Corp., Japan, 1990-97; bus. devel. mgr. Mitsubishi Electric Europe, France, 1997-98, mktg. mgr., 1998-99; sales and mktg. mgr. Mitsubishi Electric France, 1999—. Avocations: skiing, golf.

KODNER, MARTIN, art dealer, consultant; b. St. Louis, Nov. 25, 1934; s. Charles and Sofia K.; m. Penny Ann Worth. BS, St. Louis Coll. Pharmacy, 1956. Pres., dir. Kodner Gallery, St. Louis, 1974—; bd. dirs. Centerre Bank Ladue, St. Louis; mem. adv. bd. Boatmans Bank, Ladue, Mo.; expert cons. on Am. artists Oscar E. Berninghaus, Charles (Carl) Wimar. Contbr. articles to profl. jours. Mem. Jefferson Soc., Mo. Hist. Soc., St. Louis City Art Mus., Appraiser's Assn. Am., St. Louis Club, Lotos Club (N.Y.). Office: Kodner Gallery 9918 Clayton Rd Saint Louis MO 63124-1102

KODRATA, MONTI, marketing professional; b. Surabaya, Indonesia, Nov. 16, 1937; s. Budi and Suryani Kodrata; m. Sonya Susilowati Setiadi, Feb. 12, 1966; children: Raphael, Maximus, Mario. D of Econs., U. Airlangga, Surabaya, Indonesia, 1966. Mktg. sales mgr. Berlina, Jakarta, Indonesia, 1972-78; sales mgr. Kalbe Farma, Jakarta, Indonesia, 1978-80; mng. dir. Trapa, Singapore, 1980-85; dir. ops. Enseval, Jakarta, 1985-90, Interdelta/Kodak, Jakarta, 1990-94; group mktg. mgr. Catursentosa Adiprana, Jakarta, 1995-96; bus. devel. mgr. Caturkarda Depo Bangunan, Jakarta, 1997—; sr. lectr. Cath. U., Jakarta, 1972-80, 94—; lectr. U. Airlangga, Surabaya, 1967-70. Contbr. articles to mags. Mem. Singapore Inst. Mgmt. Roman Catholic. Avocations: photography, sport, jazz, electronics. Office: Caturkarda Depo Bangunan, Tarum Barat 46, Jakarta 13440, Indonesia

KODYM, MILOSLAV, psychologist, researcher; b. Sobeslav, Czechoslovakia, Aug. 1, 1930; s. Ruzena Kodymova; m. Miroslava Lintnerova, Sept. 8, 1951; children: Miloslava, Roman, Tereza. PhD, U. Prague, 1967, CSc, 1971. Tchr. Pedagogic Sch., Ceske Budejovice, Czechoslovakia, 1953-59; mem. faculty Faculty Pedagogy, Ceske Budejovice, 1959-79; sci. worker, dir. Inst. Psychology, Prague, Czechoslovakia, 1979-91; sci. worker, dep. dir. Inst. Edn. Fed. Ministry Interior, 1991-93; chief editor Czechoslovak Psychology, Czechoslovak Acad. Scis., 1979-91; pres. sci. bd. pedagogy and psychology, 1982-91; chief psychology dept. Faculty Pedagogy, Prague, 1985-91; dep. dir. Inst. Transport, Prague, 1993-95; sci. worker Police Acad., 1995—. Author: Problem Solving and Performance, 1972, Selection of Talents, 1978, On the Theory of Abilities, 1987; author, editor: Psychological Aspects of Personality Development, 1987. Recipient silver medal Czechoslovk Acad. Scis., 1980, state honors for excellent work, 1985, laureat Internat. Prize for Excellent Results in Social Scis., Acads. Scis. Moscow-Prague, 1985. Mem. (corresponding) Extranjero de la Soc. Cubana de la Salud, Czechoslovak Psychol. Assn. (com. 1982—). Avocations: sports, music. Home: Machuldova 596/21, 142 00 Prague 4, Czech Republic

KOECHER, OTTO MICHAEL, electrical engineer; b. St. Poelten, Austria, June 21, 1948; s. Julius and Katharina (Wittmann) K.; m. Maria Johanna Fuhs, Sept. 4, 1976; children: Rainer, Andrea. Grad. in Elect. Engring., Hohere Tech. Bundeslehranstalt, St. Poelten, 1967. Technician Elin Union, Vienna, Austria, 1967-69, Brown Boveri & Cie, Baden, Switzerland, 1969-76, Hartmann & Braun, Vienna, 1976-77; sr. engr. Elin Union, Vienna, 1977-85; area sales mgr. Asea Brown Boveri-Kent, Vienna, 1985-87; tchr. Hoehere Tech. Bundeslehrahstalt, 1987-89; owner Tech. Buro for Automation, St. Poelten, 1989—. Office: Tech Buro for Automation, Hermann Richter Gasse 4, A-3100 Sankt Poelten Austria

KOEHL, CAMILLE JOAN, accountant; b. Chgo., Nov. 9, 1943; d. Alfonse James and Genevieve V. (Riche) Daurio; children: David A., Laura L., Robert M., Karen M. BS in Acctg., De Paul U., 1976; postgrad., Roosevelt U., 1987—. CPA, Ill.; CFP. Treas. Meritex Corp., Carpentersville, Ill., 1966-68; contr. Di Com Corp., Glenview, Ill., 1968-72; v.p., treas. Ridge Road Co., Northbrook, Ill., 1982-87, Decker Gardens, Inc., Northbrook, 1979-87, S&L Engring. Co., Northbrook, 1972-87; ptnr. HJS Constrn. Co., Barrington Hills, Ill., 1979—; pres. Lé Tan Ltd., Palatine, Ill., 1984—, CJK Enterprises Ltd., Lakemoor, Ill., 1985—; owner Camille J. Koehl & Assoc., Lakemoor, 1978—; pres. Koehl Constrn. and Devel. Corp., Lakemoor, 1990—, Pressing Matters Ltd., McHenry, Ill., 1990—. Mem. Internat. Bd. Cert. Fin. Planners, Ill. CPAs. Avocations: golf, reading. Home and Office: 2020 W Il Route 120 # A Mchenry IL 60050-1101

KOEHLER, CAROL JEAN, nurse; b. Berlin, Wis., Apr. 26, 1943; d. Raymond H. Wendt and Lorna M.L. Kobiske; m. Ronald F. Koehler, Aug. 5, 1967; children: Catherine, Susan, Daniel, Angela, Ada, Aaron. Diploma, Inst. Children's Lit., 1987; grad. cert. nursing asst., Fox Valley Tech. Coll., 1991. LPN, Wis. Owner Bus. Builders, Manawa, Wis., 1974—; caregiver Waupaca (Wis.) County, 1984-90; news reporter Manawa Advocate and Appleton (Wis.) Post-Crescent, 1987-93; nursing asst. Manawa Nursing Ctr., 1991-93; staff nurse Wis. Vets. Home, King, 1993-94, St. Joseph's Residence, New London, Wis., 1994-96; agy. nurse STAT Temporary Svcs., Appleton, 1996—; back fitness instr. Nat. Safety Coun., King, Wis., 1994. Host mother Am. Intercultural Student Exchange and Youth for Understanding, Manawa, 1982-86; foster mother, 1988-91. Republican. Lutheran. Avocations: German language, travel, walking, photography, baking. Home: PO Box 178 Manawa WI 54949-0178

KOEHLER, J. MICHAEL, chemist, researcher; b. Halle, Germany, Jan. 19, 1956; s. Helmut and Brigitte (Asperger) K.; m. Gabriele Neubert, Feb. 4, 1956; children: Johannes, Antonie, Valentin, Albrecht. Dipl.chemist, Friedrich-Schiller U., Jena, 1981, Dr.rer.nat. habil., 1992; Dr.rer.nat., Acad. Sci. of GDR, Berlin, 1986. Aspirant Friedrich-Schiller U., Jena, 1981-82; sci. co-worker Phys.-Tech. Inst., Jena, 1982-85, project leader, 1986-90; rsch. scholar Max-Planck Soc., Dortmund, Germany, 1991; head dept. Inst. Phys. High Tech., Jena, 1992—. Author: Ätzverfahren für die Mikrotechnik, 1998, Etching in Microsystem Technology, 1999; co-editor: Microsystem Technology: A Powerful Tool for Biomolecular Studies, 1999, Umweltdiagnostik mit Mikrosystemen, 1999; contbr. numerous articles to profl. jours.; patentee microsys. tech., biomed. chip devices. Recipient Sci. award Tech. U. Cottbus, 1997. Mem. Electrochem. Soc., Gesellschaft Deutscher Chemiker. Roman Catholic. Avocations: jazz, local prehistory, legends. Office: Inst Physikalische Hochtech, Winzerlaerstr 10, 07745 Jena Germany

KOEHN, WILLIAM JAMES, lawyer; b. Winterset, Iowa, Mar. 24, 1936; s. Cyril Otto and Ilene L. (Doop) K.; m. Francia C. Leeper, Sept. 6, 1958; children: Cynthia Rae, William Fredric, James Anthony. BA, U. Iowa, 1963, JD cum laude, 1963. Bar: Iowa 1963, U. S. Ct. Appeals (8th cir.) 1971, U.S. Ct. Appeals (10th cir.) 1972, U.S. Ct. Appeals (2d cir.) 1972, U.S. Ct. Appeals (5th cir.) 1977, U.S. Supreme Ct. 1971. Mem. Davis, Brown, Koehn, Shors & Roberts, P.C., Des Moines, 1963—; prof., lectr. in U.S., Can., Europe. Bd. editors Iowa Law Rev., 1961-63; contbr. articles to profl. jours. C0-founder Big Bros.-Sisters of Greater Des Moines, 1969, pres., 1976-77; chmn. Des Moines Friendship Commmn., 1970-71; bd. dirs. Greater Des Moines YMCA, 1983-90; co-chmn. Des Moines Bicentennial Commn., 1975-76; chmn. Environ. and Pub. Works Commn.; mem. adv. com. civil justice reform act, 1990; chmn. worldwide dispute resolution com., Lex Mundi, 1989-94, bd. dirs., 1992-96. Lt. USNR, 1958-61. Mem. ABA (environ. litigation sub-com., construction com., internat. lit. environ. commn.), Iowa Bar Assn. (environ. coun. 1989-92, 1999-2000, litigation com. 1992-95, proflism. com. 1994-2000), Polk County Bar Assn., Iowa Trial Lawyers Assn., Order of Coif. Republican. Home: 9 Meadow Ln Cumming IA 50061-1015 Office: Fin Ctr 666 Walnut St Des Moines IA 50309-3904

KOELLEN, OTTMAR, aerospace engineer, educator; b. Kratzenburg, Rheinland, Germany, May 16, 1951; s. Hermann and Maria (Link) K.; m. Buarien Puangthong, Sept. 22, 1983; children: Linda, Karin, Sarah. Dipl., RWTH Aachen, 1978, D of Engring., 1987. Asst. prof. RWTH Aachen, Germany, 1978-85; engr. space propulsion DASA, Germany, 1985—; lectr. Hochschule Bremen, Germany, 1992-97. Contbr. articles to profl. jours. Mem. AIAA, Planetary Soc. Office: Astrium, RI Huenefeldstr 1-5, 28199 Bremen Germany

KOELLER, ROBERT MARION, lawyer; b. Quincy, Ill., Apr. 8, 1940; s. Marion Alfred and Ruth (Main) K.; m. Marlene Meyer, June 1962; children—Kristin, Katherine, Robert. A.B., MacMurray Coll., 1962; LL.B., Vanderbilt U., 1965. Bar: Ind. 1968. Asst. gen. csl. Nat. Homes Acceptance Corp., Lafayette, Ind., 1967-70; gen. csl., sec. Herff Jones Co., Indpls., 1970-74; ptnr. Warren, Snider, Koeller & Warren, Indpls., 1974-76; sole practice, Indpls., 1976—; mem. Coons, Maddox & Koeller, Indpls., 1993-96, Maddox, Koeller Hargett & Caruso, 1996—; dir. various cos. Mem. ABA, Ind. Bar Assn., Indpls. Bar Assn. Republican. Methodist. Office: Ste 190 7351 Shadeland Station Way Indianapolis IN 46256-3924

KOELLING, THOMAS WINSOR, lawyer; b. Jefferson City, Mo., Oct. 10, 1951; s. Oscar Alvin and Helen Louise (Shields) K.;m. Rebecca Ann Nentwig, Nov. 24, 1973; children: Zachary Thomas, Mathew Garret. BS in Criminal Justice Adminstrn., Ctrl. Mo. State U., Warrenburg, 1978; JD, U. Mo., 1981. Bar: Mo. 1981, Colo. 1982, U.S. Dist. Ct. (we. dist.) Mo. 1981, U.S. Dist. Ct. Colo. 1981, U.S. Ct. Appeals (8th cir.) 1982, U.S. Ct. Appeals (10th cir.) 1981, U.S. Supreme Ct. 1992. Assoc. Tinsley, Frantz et al, Lakewood, Colo., 1981-82, Rex Johnson Law Office, Colorado Springs, Colo., 1982-85; ptnr. Koelling & Crawford, P.C., Kansas City, Mo., 1985—; legal advisor Kansas City Ski Club, 1987, Competitors Assn., Kansas City, 1995—; adj. prof. dept. criminal justice and legal studies Mo. Western State Coll., St. Joseph, Mo., 1998—. With USAF, 1972-76. Mem. ABA, Am. Coll. Legal Medicine, Am. Soc. Law, Medicine Ethics, Am. Trial Lawyers Assn., Mo. Assn. Trial Lawyers, Clay County Bar Assn. Roman Catholic. Avocations: snow skiing, fly fishing, backpacking. Home: 9617 N Campbell St Kansas City MO 64155-2056 Office: Koelling & Crawford PC 5950 N Oak Trfy Ste 202 Kansas City MO 64118-5164

KOELZ, ANNE MARIE, nephrologist; b. Burgdorf, Switzerland, Apr. 12, 1942; d. Dora Ida (Knoepfel) K. MD, U. Basel (Switzerland), 1968. Rsch. fellow Royal Victoria Infirmary, Newcastle, Eng., 1974; lectr. in medicine Trinity Coll., Dublin, Ireland, 1975-76; head dept. (ad interim) Kantonsspital, Liestal, Switzerland, 1986; head of dept. Bezirksspital, Dornach, Switzerland, 1987—. Contbr. articles to profl. jours. Grantee Lichtenstein Stiftung, Basel, 1974. Mem. Zonta, Rotary. Home: Wallstrasse 13, 4051 Basel Switzerland Office: Bezirksspital, Spitalweg, 4143 Dornach Switzerland

KOENEN, LUDWIG, classical studies educator; b. Cologne, Germany, Apr. 5, 1931; came to U.S., 1975; s. Klaus Eugen and Elisabeth (Piel) K.; m. Margarete Ursula Christine Bolder, Aug. 8, 1955; children: Klaus, Margarete, Heinrich, Marcus. Dr. Phil., U. Cologne, 1957; postgrad., U. London and Oxford, 1959-60; Dr. habil., U. Cologne, 1968. From asst. prof., curator to head curator, assoc. prof. U. Cologne, Germany, 1956-75; prof. U. Mich., Ann Arbor, 1975-89, chair dept. classical studies, 1985-94, H.C. Youtie prof. papyrology, 1989-95, H.C. Youtie Disting. Univ. prof. papyrology, 1995-2000; dir. project Publication of the Petrapapyri Am. Ctr. Oriental Rsch. NEH, 1995—. Co-author: Didymos der Blinde, Kommentar zu Hiob III, 1968, IV, 1985, Der Kölner Mani Codex, 1988; author: (monograph) Eine Agonistische Inschrift aus Ägypten, 1976; co-editor: Zeitschrift für Papyrologie und Epigraphik, 1967—, Papyrologische Texte und Abhandlungen, 1968—, Beiträge zur Klassischen Philologie 1987-90, Beiträge zur Altertumskunde, 1990—, American Studies in Papyrology, 1977-87, Archiv für Religionsgeschichte, 1999—; chmn. editorial bd.: Monograph Series of Am. Philol. Assn., 1986-87; contbr. articles jours. Recipient fellowship Nat. Endowment for the Humanities, 1981-82. Fellow Brit. Acad. (corr.); mem. Am. Philos. Soc., Am. Acad. Arts and Scis., Am. Philol. Assn. (v.p. 1989-92, 94, pres. 1993), Am. Soc. Papyrologists (v.p. 1978-80, pres. 1981-85), Internat. Assn. Papyrologists (internat. com.), Ctr. for Hellenic Studies (sr. fellow 1985-90), German Archeol. Inst. (corr. mem., pres. 1995—), Beirat, Institut für Neutestamentliche Textforschung (Münster), Nordrhein-Westfälische Akademie der Wissenstr (corr.). Home: 1312 Culver Rd Ann Arbor MI 48103-2959 Office: Univ Mich 2016 Angell Hall Ann Arbor MI 48109

KOENIG, GOTTFRIED MICHAEL, composer; b. Magdeburg, Germany, Oct. 5, 1926; arrived in The Netherlands, 1964; s. Johannes and Elfriede (Eiselt) K.; m. Ruth Dolores Cardew, Oct. 13, 1960; children: Susanna, Tristram. Grad., Music Acad., Detmold, Germany, 1950, Music Acad., Cologne, Germany, 1954, U. Bonn, Germany, 1964. Asst. electronic music studio Sta. WDR Radio, Cologne, 1954-64; lectr. Music Acad., Cologne, 1962-64; artistic dir. Inst. of Sonology Utrecht (The Netherlands) U., 1964-86. Author: Ästhetische Praxis, 1991-99; composer various instrumental and electronic music. Recipient Incentive award Fed. State of North-Rhine Westphalia, Düsseldorf, Germany, 1961, Matthijs Vermeulen prize City of Amsterdam, 1987, Christoph and Stephan Kaske Music prize, Munich, 1999. Mem. Internat. Confedn. Electroacoustic Music (hon.), German Assn. Electronic Music (hon. life). Avocation: computer graphics.

KOENIG, JUERGEN, nutrition scientist; b. Geislingen an der Steige, Germany, Aug. 9, 1963; s. Siegfried and Ingrid Steiner. MSc in Nutrition, U. Giessen, Germany, 1988, PhD in Natural Scis., 1990. Sci. asst. Inst. Nutrition U. Giessen, 1988-90; univ. asst. Inst. Nutritional Scis. U. Vienna, Austria, 1990—. Fax: 43131336773. E-mail: juergen.koenig@univie.ac.at. Home: Theresiengasse 32/31, A-1180 Vienna Austria Office: Inst Nutrition Sci U Vienna, Althanstr 14, A-1000 Vienna Austria

KOENIG, LOUIS WILLIAM, political science educator, author; b. Poughkeepsie, N.Y., May 28, 1916; s. Casper and Pauline (Graf) K.; m. Eleanor Margaret White, July 30, 1945; 1 child, Juliana. BA, Columbia U., 1938, MA, 1940, PhD, 1944; LHD (hon.), Bard Coll., 1960. Adminstrv. addt. Nat Resources Planning Bd., Washington, 1941; legis. analyst U.S. Bur. Budget, Washington, 1941-42; procedures analyst Office Price Adminstrn., Washington, 1943-44, assoc. adminstrv. history project, 1944-46; instr., asst. prof. Bard Coll., Annandale-on-Hudson, N.Y., 1944-50; assoc. prof., prof. polit. sci. NYU, N.Y.C., 1950-86, adj. prof., 1986—; mem. fgn. affairs task force Hoover Commn., Washington, 1948-49; intelligence analyst Dept. State, Washington, 1950; staff assoc., cons. Fund for Advancement Edn., Ford Found., N.Y.C., 1954-55; lectr. exec. seminars CSC, King's Point, N.Y., Oak Ridge, Tenn., U. Va., Charlottesville, 1964—; lectr. Nat. War U., Washington, 1966—, Air War Coll., 1965—; vis. prof. Columbia U., N.Y.C., 1965, 78, CUNY, 1968, C.W. Post Ct., L.I. U., Brookville, N.Y., 1986—; instr. non-fiction writing Bread Loaf Writers' Conf., Middlebury Coll., 1960; cons. program in polit. theory and constl. law Rockefeller Found., N.Y.C., 1962-63; cons. N.Y.C. Charter Revisin Commn., 1987-88; dir. seminar for coll. tchrs. NEH, Washington and N.Y.C., 1976, 77, 79, 81; dir. seminar on polit. parties, Robert A. Taft Inst., N.Y.C., 1982; commentator on presdl. inauguration, author and performer NBC-TV, 1969. Author: The Presidency and the Crisis: From the Invasion of Poland to Pearl Harbor, 1944, The Truman Administration, 1956, repub. 1979, The Presidency Today, 1956, The Invisible Presidency, 1960, The Chief Executive, 1964, 6th edit., 1996, Congress and the President, 1965, Bryan, A Political Biography of William Jennings Bryan, 1971, paperback edit. 1975, Toward a Democracy, 1973, An Introduction to Public Policy, 1986; co-author: Congress, the Presidency, and the Taiwan Relations Act, 1985; chmn. bd. editors Presdl. Studies Quar., 1972-94. Chmn. concerned Christian for social responsibility Cmty. Ch., Garden City, N.Y., 1968-74, chmn. bd. missions, 1976-80. Gilder fellow Columbia U., 1940. Mem. ASPA, Am. Polit. Sci. Assn., Phi Beta Kappa. Avocations: gardening, stamp collecting, travel. Home: 135 Chestnut St Garden City NY 11530-6424

KOENIG, MARIE HARRIET KING, public relations director, fund raising executive; b. New Orleans, Feb. 19, 1919; d. Harold Paul and Sadie Louise (Bole) King; m. Walter William Koenig, June 24, 1956; children: Margaret Marie, Susan Patricia. Major in Voice, La. State U., 1937-39; Pre-law, Loyola U., 1942-43; BS in History, U. LaVerne, 1986. Adminstrv. asst. to atty. gen. State of La., New Orleans, 1940-44; contract writer MGM Studios, Culver City, Calif., 1944-46; asst. sec., treas. Found. for Ind., L.A., 1950-56, Found. for Social Rsch., L.A., 1950-56; dir. communications Incentive Rsch. Corp., L.A., 1969-78; rsch. supr., devel. dept. Calif. Inst. Technology, Pasadena, Calif., 1969; dir. funding devel. Rep. Party of L.A. County, South Pasadena, 1989-92. Author: Does the National Council of Churches Speak for You?, 1978; delivered lecture series on U.S. fgn. policy. Named Hon. Citizen Colonial Williamsburg Found., 1987; active Nat. Trust for Historic Preservation, 1986, Friends of the Huntington Libr., 1986, Town Hall of L.A., 1986—, Pasadena City Women's Club, 1982-84; past mem. Coun. Women's Clubs; charter mem. Nat. Mus. of Women in Arts; bd. mem. Pasadena Opera Guild; contbg. mem. L.A. World Affairs Coun., 1990, L.A. County Mus. Art, 1999; past pres., pub. chmn., Pasadena Rep. Women Federated; charter mem. Freedoms Found. at Valley Forge L.A. County Chpt., Autry Mus. Western Heritage, 1986, Women of L.A.; pres. Greater L.A. Women's Coun., Navy League of the U.S. Recipient Pres.'s award So. Calif. Motion Picture Coun., 1996, Cert. Recognition Calif. State Assembly, 1989, 95, Recognition of Excellence, Achievement and Commitment U.S. Ho. Reps., 1989, Cert. Merit Rep. Presdl. Task Force, 1986, Cert. Appreciation U.S. Def. Com., 1984, Hon. Freedom Fighter award U.S. Def. Com., 1985, Cert. Appreciation Am. Conservative Union, 1983, Cert. Commendation Rep. Cen. Com. L.A. County, 1972, Cert. Appreciation Eisenhower-Nixon So. Calif. Com., 1952; named Disting. Citizen of Yr. L.A. Area Coun. Boy Scouts Am. Mem. Women in Communications, Greater L.A. Press Club, World War II Meml. (charter). Republican. Avocations: reading, music, opera. Home: 205 Madeline Dr Pasadena CA 91105-3311

KOENIG, ROBERT AUGUST, clergyman, educator; b. Red Wing, Minn., July 14, 1933; s. William C. and Florence E. (Tebbe) K.; m. Pauline Louise Olson, June 21, 1962. BS cum laude, U. Wis., Superior, 1955; MA in Ednl. Adminstrn., U. Minn., 1965, PhD, 1973; MDiv magna cum laude, San Francisco Theol. Sem., 1969; postgrad. (John Hay fellow), Bennington Coll., summer, 1965. Ordained to ministry Presbyn. Ch., 1970. Supr. music Florence (Wis.) H.S., 1955-56; dir. instrumental music Chetek (Wis.) Pub. Schs., 1958-62; tchr. instrumental music and humanities Palo Alto (Calif.) Sr. H.S., 1962-65; asst. to min. St. John's Presbyn. Ch., San Francisco, 1964-65; min. Sawyer County (Wis.) larger parish, 1969-74; tchr. gen. music Jordan Jr. H.S., Palo Alto, 1966-69; instr. Coll. Edn. U. Minn., 1969-71; adminstv. asst. to pres. Lakewood State C.C., White Bear Lake, Minn., 1971-72; asst. to exec. dir. Minn. Higher Edn. Coord. Bd., St. Paul, 1972, coord. commn. and pers. svcs., 1972-74; instr. Inver Hills C.C., Inver Grove Heights, Minn., 1974; min. First Presbyn. Ch. of Chippewa Falls (Wis.), 1974-85; sr. pastor Grove Presbyn. Ch., Danville, Pa., 1985-88, First Presbyn. Ch., South St. Paul, Minn., 1988-98; mem. study com. Presbytery of Chippewa, 1973-74, mem. min. rels. com., 1974-77; adj. asst. prof. ednl. adminstrn. U. Minn., Mpls., 1976-77; mem. faculty U. Wis. Ext., Eau Claire, 1977, chmn. 3d Ann. Bibl. Seminar, 1977, mem. faculty Communiversity, 1977-85; mem. internat. coord. com. ch. mission Synod of Lakes and Prairies, 1978-79; mem. ministerial rels. com. Presbytery of No. Waters, 1977-82, chmn. ministerial rels. com., 1981-82, moderator, 1983; chmn. Synod Designation Pastor Plan Cabinet, 1982-84; chmn. Presbytery Coun., 1982-84; chairperson Christian edn. com. Presbytery of Northumberland, 1987-88, mem. Presbytery coun., 1987-88; mem. Christian edn. com. Synod of the Trinity, 1987-88, mem. com. on ministry Presbytery of the Twin Cities Area, 1999—, Danville-Riverside Area Ministerial Assn., 1985-88, pres., 1987-88; mem. South St. Paul Ministerial Assn., 1988-98, pres., 1989-90. Contbr. articles to profl. jours. Bd. dirs. North Ctrl. Career Devel. Ctr., Mpls., 1978-84, chmn. fin. com., 1979-84, bd. dirs. devel. found., 1983-85; pres. Chippewa Valley Ecumenical Housing Assn., 1984-85; mem. alumni bd. U. Minn., 1999—; bd. dirs. Coll. Edn. and Human Devel. Alumni Soc. U. Minn., 1999—. With U.S. Army, 1956-58, Korea. Mem. Masons (grand chaplain Wis. chpt. 1977-80, 83-85), Elks (Danville chpt.). Home: 6045 Bowman Ave E Inver Grove Heights MN 55076-1502

KOENIG, ROBERT EMIL, clergyman; b. St. Louis, Aug. 31, 1919; s. Hermann Emil and Martha Ida (Baur) K.; m. Norma Caroline Evans, July 18, 1943; children: Elsa Koenig Weber, Robert, Richard, Martha Koenig Stone, Thea Koenig Burton, Laura Koenig Godinez. BS, U. Chgo., 1941; BD, Chgo. Theol. Sem., 1945; PhD, U. Chgo., 1953; DD, Elmhurst Coll., 1987. Pastor St. John's Evang. & Reformed Ch., Hinsdale, Ill., 1943-46; from instr. to assoc. prof. religion Elmhurst (Ill.) Coll., 1946-54; dir. curriculum Bd. Christian Edn., Phila., 1954-61; editor-in-chief United Ch. Bd. for Homeland Ministries, Phila., 1961-84; interim pastor St. Paul's United Ch. Christ, Fort Washington, Pa., 1985-87, Bethany United Ch. Christ, Phila., First United Ch. of Christ, Quakertown, Pa., St. Vincent United Ch. of Christ, Phoenixville, Pa., Collenbrook United Ch., Brownback's United Ch. of Christ, Spring City, Boehm's United Ch. of Christ, 1988-89; adj. prof. Christian edn. Lancaster (Pa.) Theol. Sem., 1988-89; cons., dir. Koenig Ch. Edn. Cons., Inc., Havertown, Pa., 1988—; adj. instr. Defiance Coll., 1995-2000. Mng. editor PRISM Mag., 1990—. Pres. Ardmore (Pa.) Jr. High Home and Sch. Assn., 1962-63; mem. Penn Wynne (Pa.) Libr. Bd., 1985-89; pres. Univ. Glee Club of Phila., 1987-88; mem. ElderNet, Lower Merion, Pa., 1986—, pres., 1988-89, treas., 1994-96. Democrat. Avocations: singing, playing violin, hiking. Home and Office: 566 Haverford Rd Havertown PA 19083-2642

KOENIG, YVAN HENRI, Egyptologist, researcher; b. Grenoble, Isere, France, Sept. 17, 1947; s. Raoul Michel and Marie Jeanne (Cocat) K.; m. Viviane Gabrielle Stern, July 9, 1971; children: Raphael, David. Maitrise d'Histoire, U. Sorbonne, Paris, 1969, doctorat, 1976; habilitation, U. Lille III, France, 1993. Asst. Institute d'Art, Paris, 1969-70; lecteur U. Liege, Belgium, 1972-76; pensionnaire French Inst. Oriental Archaeology, Le Caire, Egypt, 1976-80; chargé de recherche Nat. Ctr. Sci. Rsch., Paris, 1981-99; chargé de conférences Ecole Pratique des Hautes Etudes, Paris, 1981-99; chargé de Cours Cath. Inst. Paris/Faculty of Theology and Religious Scis., Paris, 1998-99; chargé de mission Louvre, Paris, 1971-72; missions CNRS, Egypt: Louxor, 1987, 88, 94, 95, 96, IFAO, 1982, 93, 97, 99; com. mem. SFE, Paris, 1994-99. Author: Catalogue des étiquettes hiératiques, 1979-80, Le Papyrus Boulaq 6, 1981, Magie et Magiciens de l'Egypte Ancienne, 1994, Les Ostraca hiératiques de la BNUS, 1998. Mem. French Soc. Egyptology (com. mem. 1994). Orthodox. Avocations: theology, modern greek, philosophy. Home: 66 rue Danjou, 92100 Boulogne France Office: Musiée du Louvre, Dep Antiquites Egyptiennes, 75058 Paris France

KOENIGSTEIN, GEORG FRIEDRICH, artist, educator; b. Vienna, Austria, July 30, 1937; s. Leopold and Friederike (Dü) K.; m. Christine Vesely, May 7, 1965; children: Martin, Christian. MA, Acad. Fine Arts, Vienna, 1961. Tchr. High Sch., Vienna, 1961-71; prof. Coll. Edn., Vienna, 1971—; scientific and artistic bd. Theodor-Körner-Found., 1984—. Author: Architecture and Environmental Design, 1983; editor Klosterneuburg, 1987—. Recipient Silver Füger medal Acad. Fine Arts, 1958, Golden Füger medal, 1960, Order of Merit in Gold Republic of Austria, 1998. Roman Catholic. Avocations: Tai ji, Qi Gong. Home and Office: Anzengrubergasse 50, A 3400 Klosterneuburg Austria

KOEPF, WERNER KARL, computer company executive; b. Erdweis, Austria, Jan. 8, 1942; came to Fed. Republic Germany, 1961; s. Rudolf and Marie (Loew) K.; m. Ludmila Kravtschuk, Nov. 23, 1990; children (by previous marriage): Maximilian, Johanna, Christiane, Angelika, Anastasia. BS in Elec. Engring., St. Poelten, 1961; Diplom Volkswirt, U. Munich, 1966. Sales mgr. German dist. Texas Instruments Corp., Freising, Fed. Republic Germany, 1967-68; ops. mgr. Europe Texas Instruments Corp., Geneva, 1968-70, Slough, Eng., 1970-71; gen. mgr. cen. Europe dist. Texas Instruments Corp., Munich, 1971-76, v.p. distbg. Europe, 1976-82, v.p. mktg. Europe, 1982-85, v.p. internat. systems div., 1985-87, v.p. sc. group, 1987-89; CEO European Silicon Structures, Luxembourg, 1989-93; v.p., mng. dir. gen. bus. group Compaq Computer Corp., Munich, 1993-99; v.p., gen. mgr. Europe, Mid. East, Africa Compaq Computer Emea BV, Munich, 1999—; pres. Tex. Instruments Internat. Trade Corp., Dallas, 1982-84; chmn. ES2 S.A., 1990—; bd. dirs. Eucad Ltd. U.K., chmn. US2, 1991-93. Recipient award for excellency in studies Ministry of Edn., Vienna, Austria, 1961. Roman Catholic. Office: Compaq Computer EMEA GmbH, Sueskindstrasse 4, D-81929 Munich Germany

KOEPKE, WULF, museum director; b. Duesseldorf, Germany, Dec. 26, 1952. PhD, U. Berlin, 1984. Cert. anthropologist. Mem. Rotary.

KOEPPEL, MARY SUE, communications educator, editor; b. Phlox, Wis., Dec. 12, 1939; d. Alphonse and Emma Petronella (Marx) K.; m. Robert B. Gentry, May 31, 1980. BA, Alverno Coll., 1962; MA, Loyola U., Chgo., 1968; postgrad., U. Wis., St. Louis U., U. N.H., U. Calif., U. North Fla., U. Minn. Tchr. St. Joseph H.S., Milw., 1962-68, Pius XI H.S., Milw., 1968-72; instr., head dept. comms., dir. learning ctr. Waukesha County Tech. Inst., Pewaukee, Wis., 1972-80; pres., exec. bd. West Suburban Coun. Tchg. Profession, 1976-80; adv. Waukesha chpt. Parents Without Partners, 1975-80; cons. Learning Ctrs., 1976—, also coll. and univ. faculties; instr. comms. Fla. C.C., Jacksonville, 1980—; instr. Inst. for Tchrs. of Writing, Westbrook Coll., Portland, Maine, summers 1980-84, instr. nat. master tchr. seminar, summers 1982—, TV interviewer, 1989—; instr. Nat. Inst. for Tchrs. of Writing, Greenfield, Mass., 1987-94. Editor-in-chief Kalliope Jour. Women's Literature and Art, 1988—, Lollipops, Lizards and Literature, 1994; editor Instructional Network Notes, 1982-85; author: Writing Resources for Conferencing and Collaboration, 1989, Writing Strategies Plus Collaboration, 1997, 3d edit., 2000, Write Your Life-The Memory Catcher, 1998; contbr. articles to profl. jours.; co-founder Letters Coun., 1996; interviewer (TV) Worth Quoting, 1994—, Author to Author, 1994—; contbg. editor State Street Rev., 1992—. Mem. Sherman Park Cmty. Ctr., 1975-80; co-founder, bd. dirs. Instructional Network for Coll. Faculty, 1981-85. Recipient Red Schoolhouse award for tchg. excellence Assn. Fla. C.C.'s, 1983; grantee NDEA, 1968, Art Ventures grantee, 1992, Tchg. and Learning Ctr. grantee, 1999; scholar Fla. Humanities Coun., 1999. Mem. Nat. Coun. Tchrs. of English, Am. Pen Women. Office: Kalliope 3939 Roosevelt Blvd Jacksonville FL 32205-8945

KOEZE, PETER, physicist; b. Breda, The Netherlands, July 11, 1942; s. Johannes Georg and Laura (Voorhagen) K. MS in Phys. Engring., Tech. U., Delft, The Netherlands, 1965; PhD in Physics, State U., Utrecht, The Netherlands, 1968, BS in Psychology, 1980. Rschr. Found. F.O.M., Utrecht, The Netherlands, 1965-68; geophysicist Shell Co., London, 1968-70, Brunei Shell Co., Seria, 1970-71; cons. Ctr. Indsl. Devel., Rotterdam, The Netherlands, 1972, Found. F.O.M., 1973-74; advisor to governing bd. The Netherlands Bank, Amsterdam, 1974—; bd. dirs. Tech. Found., Utrecht, 1989-98; com. chmn. Banknote Printers' Conf., Europe, 1991-96. Author: Catalogue of Dutch Bank Notes, 1999; contbr. articles to profl. jours.; patentee in field. Mem. Netherlands Photonics Soc. (chmn. 1978-84), Netherlands Phys. Soc. (com. mem. 1974—), Royal Inst. Engrs., European Physics Soc. Avocations: calligraphy, typography, design, stock picking, reading. Home: Nieuwegracht 39 B, 3512 LD Utrecht The Netherlands Office: The Netherlands Bank, Westeinde 1, 1017 ZN Amsterdam The Netherlands

KOFF, HOWARD MICHAEL, lawyer; b. Bklyn., July 25, 1941; s. Arthur and Blanche Koff; m. Linda Sue Bright, Sept. 10, 1966; 1 son, Michael Arthur Bright. BS, NYU, 1962; JD, Bklyn. Law Sch., 1965; LLM in Taxation, Georgetown U., 1968. Bar: N.Y. 1965, D.C. 1966, U.S. Supreme Ct. 1969, U.S. Ct. Appeals (2d, 3d, 4th, 5th, 7th, 9th and D.C. cirs.), U.S. Dist. Ct. (no. dist.) N.Y. 1981. Appellate atty. tax divsn. U.S. Dept. Justice, Washington, 1965-69; tax supr. Chrysler Corp., Detroit, 1969-70; chief tax counsel Conn. Gen. Life Ins. Co., Hartford, Conn., 1970-77, Rohm & Haus Co., Phila., 1977-78; ptnr. Dibble, Koff, Lane, Stern and Stern, Rochester, N.Y., 1978-81; pres. Howard M. Koff, P.C., Albany, N.Y., 1981—; lectr. tax matters. Editor-in-chief Bklyn. Law Rev., 1964-65; charter mem. editl. adv. bd. Jour. Real Estate Taxation; contbr. articles to legal jours. Chmn. pub. adv. coun. N.Y. State Ethics Commn. Recipient Founders Day award NYU, 1962, Lawyers Coop. award for gen. excellence Lawyers Coop. Pub. Co., 1965. Mem. ABA (past chmn. subcom. on partnerships tax sect.), FBA (past pres. Hartford County chpt.), Albany County Bar Assn., Estate Planning Coun. Ea. N.Y., Albany Area C. of C., Rotary, Colonie Guilderland

N.Y. Club. Republican. Home: 205 W Bentwood Ct Albany NY 12203-4905 Office: 600 Broadway Albany NY 12207-2205

KOFF, SHIRLEY IRENE, writer; b. Oakland, Calif., Aug. 31, 1948; d. Lawrence Ray and Stella Pauline (Durham) Butler; m. Robert Allen Koff, June 12, 1971; children: Jennifer, Katherine. BA, Calif. State U., 1971, MA, 1972. Adj. prof. Pellissippi State U., Knoxville, 1989-93; asst. mgr. Adolfo II, Pigeon Forge, Tenn., 1994-98; poet, writer; tchr. adult religious edn. classes and seminars; expert info. provider internet resource AskAnything.com. Tchr., lay min., bd. dirs. First Assembly of God Ch., Sevierville, 1996-99; core group leader, founding mem. Wellspring Congregation, United Meth. Ch., 1999—. Mem. AAUW, Mensa. Democrat. Avocations: writing, speaking, teaching. Home: 1214 Amber Ln Sevierville TN 37862-6101

KOFFLER, STEPHEN ALEXANDER, investment banker; b. Providence, R.I., Sept. 22, 1942; s. Irving I. and Jessie Lillian (Seltzer) K.; m. Enid Freya Mellion, June 15, 1963; children: Samara Rachel, Debra Lyn. BMetE, Rensselaer Poly. Inst., 1964, MS, 1967, PhD, 1968. Security analyst Auerbach Pollak & Richardson, N.Y.C., 1968-70; asst. v.p. investment banking A.G. Becker, Inc., N.Y.C., 1970-72; v.p., treas. Mattel, Inc., Hawthorne, Calif., 1972-74; sr. v.p., chief fin. officer Audio Magnetics, Inc., Gardena, Calif., 1974-75; cons. Koffler & Co., L.A., 1975-81; mng. dir. Becker Paribas, Inc., L.A., 1981-84, Merrill Lynch, L.A., 1984-91; exec. v.p., dir. investment banking dvsn. Sutro and Co., Inc., L.A., 1991-94; mng. dir. Smith Barney Inc., L.A., 1994-96; pres. Koffler & Company, L.A., 1996—. Bd. dirs. L.A. Music Ctr. Opera, 1989-96. Mem. Am. Soc. for Metals, Nat. Assn. Securities Dealers Inc. (mem. corp. fin. com. 1994-95), Riviera Tennis Club, Regency Club, Teton Pines Country Club, Brentwood Country Club. Avocations: tennis, golf, hiking, opera. Office: Koffler & Co 11755 Wilshire Blvd Ste 2370 Los Angeles CA 90025-1569

KOFMEHL, KENNETH THEODORE, political science educator; b. Spokane, Wash., Jan. 31, 1920; s. Theodore August and Gladys (MacKenzie) K.; m. Jerrie Lorraine McGhee, May 22, 1985. BA in Polit. Sci., U. Idaho, 1941; MA in Polit. Sci., Columbia U., 1949, PhD in Polit. Sci., 1956. Vis. instr. U. Kans., Lawrence, 1955-56, vis. asst. prof., 1956-57; asst. prof. Purdue U., Lafayette, Ind., 1957-62; assoc. prof. Purdue U., Lafayette, 1962-67, prof. Polit. Sci., 1967-90, prof. emeritus, 1990—; cons. subcom. on Constitution, U.S. Senate Judiciary com., Washington, 1966-80, com. on Sci. and Pub. Policy, NAS, Washington, 1964, select com. on Coms., U.S. House Reps., Washington, 1973. Author: Professional Staffs of Congress, 1962, 2d rev. edit., 1969, 3rd rev. edit., 1977; contbr. articles to profl. jours. Panelist congl. debate Tippecanoe County Sta. WASK-AM, Lafayette, 1976; moderator LWV and Ind. Commn. on Humanities discussion group on Mondale-Dole debate, West Lafayette, 1976. Capt. U.S. Army, 1942-46, PTO. Decorated Bronze Star medal with two oak leaf clusters, 1945; recipient undergrad. tchg. award Std. Oil Found., 1969; named Outstanding Alumnus U. Idaho, 1991. Mem. Phi Eta Sigma, Phi Beta Kappa, Blue Key, Omicron Delta Kappa, Pi Sigma Alpha, Phi Gamma Delta. Democrat. Presbyterian. Avocations: birdwatching, swimming, hiking, bicycling, reading. Home: 400 N River Rd Apt 1129 Lafayette IN 47906-3136

KOGA, MASARU, engineer; b. Fukuoka, Japan, May 29, 1970; s. Katsuhiro and Keiko Koga. BEng, Hiroshima (Japan) U., 1993; MEng, Kyushu U., Fukuoka, 1995; DEng, Kyushu U., 1997. Rschr. Hitachi (Japan) Ltd., 1997—. Recipient SICE award, 1996. Office: Hitachi Ltd, Omika 7-chome, Hitachi 319-1292, Japan

KOGA, SHINJI, physicist, educator; b. Fukuoka, Japan, Sept. 24, 1953; s. Hakune and Kazuko (Shimomura) K. BS, Kyushu U., Fukuoka, Japan, 1977; MS, Kyoto (Japan) U., 1979, PhD, 1983. Rsch. assoc. Osaka (Japan) Kyoiku, 1983-94, asst. prof., 1994—. Contbr. articles to profl. jours. Mem. IEEE, AAAS, Phys. Soc. Japan, N.Y. Acad. Scis. Avocation: table tennis. Office: Osaka Kyoiku U Dept Physics, Asahi ga oka 4-698-1, Kashiwara Osaka 582-8582, Japan

KOGA, TATSUZO, aerospace engineer, educator; b. Taipei, Taiwan, Apr. 14, 1935; s. Iwazo and Yoshi (Matsumura) Koga; m. Tamiko Hamano, May 21, 1977; children: Jun, Kei. B in Engring., U. Tokyo, 1961; PhD, Stanford U., 1968. Rsch. assoc. Stanford (Calif.) U., 1968; prin. scientist Nat. Aerospace Lab., Tokyo, 1974-78; head Thermo-Structural Lab. Nat. Aerospace Lab., Tokyo, 1978-80; prof. U. Tsukuba, Japan, 1980—, dean coll. engring., 1988-90, provost, 1993-94, v.p., 1994-99; dir. Tsukuba Gigabit Lab., Japan, 1999—; tech. advisor Nat. Personnel Authority, Tokyo, 1973-74; mem. Com. Indsl. Standards, 1975-80. Contbr. articles to profl. jours. and chpts. to books. Mem. AIAA, Japan Soc. Mech. Engrs. (award 1980), Japan Soc. Aero. Space Sci., Sigma Xi. Achievements include research in buckling criterion for pressurized spherical shells, effects of boundary conditions on vibrations and buckling of cyclindrical shells, bending and torsional rigidities of orthotropic laminates, isometric membrane valv, advanced telecommunications networking technologies and applications. Home: 3-19-2 Yakushidai, Moriya 302-0105, Japan Office: Tsukuba Gigabit Lab, 2-5-5 Azumadai, Tsukuba 305-0031, Japan

KOGA, TOSHIHIKO, dental educator; b. Fukuoka, Japan, June 22, 1948; s. Moto and Tsugie (Koga) K.; m. Keiko Ito, Apr. 7, 1974; children: Saori, Takae, Takahide. DDS, Kyushu U., 1973, PhD, 1979. Asst. prof. Kyushu U., Fukuoka, Japan, 1973-79; prof. Kyushu U., 1992—; assoc. prof. Kagoshima (Japan) U., 1980-83; chief Nat. Insts. Health, Tokyo, 1982-87, dir., 1987-93; dir. U. Dental Hosp., Kyushu U., Japan, 1999—; cons. Ministry Health and Welfare, Tokyo, 1989, Ministry of Edn., Tokyo, 1989-90, Japan Dental Assn., 1992-94. Author: Methods in Gene Technology, 1994, Periodontal Disease: Pathogens and Host Immune Response, 1991, Molecular Microbiology Immunology of S. mutans, 1986; editor: Japanese Jour. Med. Sci. Biology, 1990-93. Recipient Kuroya prize for encouragement of rsch. Japanese Soc. for Bacteriology, 1986, Naito prize Naito Found., 1993. Mem. Am. Soc. for Microbiology, Internat. Assn. Dental Rsch. Avocations: reading, baseball. Home: Minoshima 4-1-1-1410, Hakata-ku Fukuoka 810-0017, Japan Office: Kyushu U Sch Dentistry, 3-1-1 Maidashi Higashi-ku, Fukuoka 812-8582, Japan

KOGAN, BORIS ISAEVICH, engineering educator; b. Konotop, Sumskaya, Ukraine, July 4, 1937; s. Isai Benzionovich and Nekhama Mendelevna (Dvorkina) K.; m. Lilia Alexandrovna Rybak, Aug. 1, 1961; children: Igor, Elena. Degree, Textile Inst., Ivanovo, Russia, 1960. Process engr., sr. foreman Engring. Works, Penza, Russia, 1960-63; sr. engr. GIPROMach Inst., Penza, 1963-64; sr. engr. dept. process planning, chief engr. VNIPTIM Inst., Kemerovo, Russia, 1964-97; prof., chair tech. engring. Kuzbass State Tech. U., Kemerovo, 1997—. Author: Quality Technological Providing in Mining Tools and Machine-Building Production, 1996, Progressive Technology of Mining Machine-Building, 2000; contbr. over 200 articles to profl. jours.; patentee in field. Recipient USSR Inventor award, 1974, Bronze medal, 1978, VDNKh medal, 1977, Disting. Work medal Kemerovo Regional Soviet of Working People's Deps. on behalf of Presidium of Supreme Soviet of the USSR, Kemerovo, 1987. Avocations: swimming, travel. Home: Apt 46, 103 Krasnoarmeiskaya St, 650027 Kemerovo Russia Office: Kuzbass State Tech U, 28 Vesennyaya St, 650026 Kemerovo Russia

KOGAN, GERALD, psychotherapist; b. Phila., Mar. 22, 1931; s. Charles and Rose (Eisenberg) K.; m. Jutta Wittenberg, Nov. 20, 1954 (div. 1967); children: Steven, Lynn; m. Wiltrud Krauss, May 11, 1983. BA, San Francisco State U., 1959, MA, 1961; PhD, U. Calif., Berkeley, 1973. Cert. clin. psychologist; cert. clin. psychotherapist; cert. marriage & family therapist. Pscyhologist, lectr. Diablo Valley Coll., Concord, Calif., 1961-78; pvt. practice Berkeley, Calif., 1964-78; lectr. U. Calif., Berkeley, 1964-76; staff psychologist Inst. Social & Personal Rels., Berkeley, 1964-77; tng. therapist Pacific Inst. Clin. Tng. Edn. & Consortion, Berkeley, 1970-82; therpist, instr. Gestalt Inst. San Francisco, 1970-83; gestalt therapist trainer, tng. co-dir. Gestalt Edn. Network Internat., Frankfurt, Germany, 1981—; lectr. Boston U., Germany, 1985-90; pvt. practice Frankfurt, 1981—. Author: God in a Red Machine, 1969, A Handbook of Gestalt Therapy, 1978, Your Body Works, 1981; contbr. articles to books and profl. jours. With U.S. Naval Air Svc., 1948-52. Mem. APA, German Psychol. Assn., German Psychotherapy Assn., German Assn. Gestalt Therapy (co-founder), Internat. Coun. Psychologists, Assn. Advancement Gestalt Therapy, Internat. Gestalt Therapy Assn. Avocations: dog raising, film, painting, poetry, travel. Home: Melem str 10, 60322 Frankfurt Germany Office: Gestalt Edn Network Inter, Oberweg 5, 60318 Frankfurt Germany

KOGAN, VICTOR ALEXANDROVICH, chemist; b. Rostov-on-Don, Russia, Aug. 9, 1936; s. Alexander Borisovich and Lyubov Shmuelevna (Solodukho) K.; m. Maiya Eugenevna Povetkina, Nov. 21, 1959; children: Kogan Irina Victorovna, Boris Victorovich. Diploma in chemistry, Rostov State U., 1959, PhD in Chemistry, 1964, DSc in Chemistry, 1975. From asst. prof. to prof. Rostov State U., 1962-78, prof., 1978-83, head, phys. colloid chemistry, 1983—; v.p. Nat. Conf. Chemistry Inorganic Coord. Compounds Unaquaous Media, 1975, 85, 87; Soros prof. Internat. Sci. Found., N.Y.C., Moscow, 1994—. Co-author: Dipole Moments in Chemistry of the Complex Compounds, 1976, Complexes of Transition Metals with Hydrazones: Physical-Chemical Properties and Structure, 1991; mem. editl. bd. Russian Jour. Coord. Chemistry, 1995—; contbr. articles to profl. jours. Recipient State prize, 1989; named honored scientist of Russia, 1998; grantee Internat. Assn. Promotion Cooperation Scientists Ind. States Former Soviet Union, 1995—, Russian Found. Fundamental Rsch., 1995—. Avocations: music, traveling, photography. E-mail: kogan@chimfak.rnd.runnet.ru. Office: Rostov State U, Zorge St 7, 344090 Rostov-on-Don Russia

KOGAN, VICTOR MIRONOVICH, chemist, researcher; b. Moscow, June 17, 1953; s. Miron Israelievich Kogan and Malvina Yakovlevna Lyachovitskaya; m. Elena Yurjevna Protopopova, June 25, 1975 (div. Oct. 1982); 1 child, Ilya; m. Irina Victorovna Tarakanova, Dec. 30, 1983. Degree in Chem. Engring., Moscow Inst. Oil & Gas, 1976; PhD in Chemistry, USSR Acad. Scis., Moscow, 1989. Cert. chem. engring. Jr. rsch. worker All-Union Inst. Desinfection and Sterilization, Moscow, 1976-78; jr. rsch. worker N.D. Zelinsky Inst. Organic Chemistry, Moscow, 1979-89, rsch. worker, 1989-91, mgr. rsch. group, 1991—; vis. prof. U. des Scis. et Technologies de Lille, Villeneuve d'Ascq, France, 1992; vis. rschr. SK Corp., Ulsan and Taejon, South Korea, 1997-2000. Contbr. articles to profl. jours. Avocations: history, classical music, mountaineering. E-mail: vmk@ioc.ac.ru. Fax: (7 095) 1355328. Office: ND Zelinsky Inst Organic, 47 Leninsky Prospect, 117913 Moscow Russia

KOGAN, VLADIMIR ALEXANDROVICH, physicist; b. Rostov-on-Don, Russia, Feb. 18, 1959; s. Alexander T. and Irina I. (Budagova) K.; m. Olga S. Sokolova, July 9, 1983; children: Anna, Daniel. BA in Physics, State U., Rostov-on-Don, 1981, PhD in Physics, 1988. Engr. Rostov State U., 1981-84, rsch. scientist, 1985-88, sr. rsch. scientist, 1989-93; project leader Philips Analytical, Netherlands, 1994-96, sr. developer, 1997—. Contbr. articles to profl. jours. Mem. Soc. Photo-Optical Instrumentation Engrs. Avocations: books, travel, music. Office: Philips Analytical, Lelyweg 1, 7602EA Almelo The Netherlands

KOGANEZAWA, HIROKI, plant pathologist; b. Kita-aiki, Nagano, Japan, Feb. 1, 1944; s. Zentaro and Naka Koganezawa; m. Yasuko Hiramoto, Apr. 27, 1975; children: Maki, Yuki. B of Agr., U. Tokyo, 1968, M of Agr., 1970, D of Agr., 1973. Rschr. Nat. Fruit Tree Rsch. Sta., Morioka, Iwate, 1973-89; plant pathologist Internat. Rice Rsch. Inst., Los Baqos, The Philippines, 1989-94; head Shikoku Nat. Agrl. Experiment Sta., Zentsuji, Kagawa, 1994-2000; assoc. dir. Chugoku Nat. Agrl. Experiment Station, Fukuyama, Hiroshima, Japan, 2000—; affiliated asst. prof. U. of The Philippines, Los Baqos, 1991-94. Editor: (book) Plant Virus Disease Control, 1998. Mem. Phytopathol. Soc. Japan, Assn. for Plant Protection of Shikoku (dep. pres. 1996—), Am. Phytopathol. Soc. Fax: 81-849-24-7893. E-mail: hkogane@cjk.affrc.go.jp. Office: Chugoku Nat Agrl Exper Sta, Nishifukatsu, Fukuyama, Hiroshima 721-8514, Japan

KOGIKU, KIICHIRO, economics educator; b. Okayama, Japan, July 30, 1927. BS, U. Denver, 1954; MA, U. Wis., 1957, PhD, 1959. Asst. prof. econs. Western Mich. U., Kalamazoo, 1959-62; asst. prof., assoc. prof., then prof. U. Calif., Riverside, 1962-86; prof. Aoyama Gakuin U., Tokyo, 1986—. Author: Introduction to Macroeconomic Models, 1968, Microeconomic Models, 1971; author, editor: Resource Allocation Models, 1990. Brookings Rsch. prof. Brookings Instn., Washington, 1965; Fulbright Rsch. prof. Fulbright Commn., Washington, 1978. Mem. Am. Econ. Assn., Econometric Soc., Western Econ. Assn. Internat. Office: Aoyama Gakuin U Int Pol Ecn, 4-4-25 Shibuya Shibuya-ku, Tokyo 150-8366, Japan

KOGURE, GOHEI, advertising executive; b. Gunma, Japan, Sept. 19, 1924; s. Goro and Hiro (Shinagawa) K.; m. Noriko Shigehara, Apr. 30, 1951; children: Mariko, Kei. BA in Econs., U. Tokyo, 1948. Exec. dir. Dentsu Inc., Tokyo, 1971-73, mng. dir., 1973-79, sr. mng. dir., 1979-85, pres., CEO, 1985-93, former chmn., now co. adviser. Mem. Japan Advt. Agys. Assn. (chmn.). Office: Dentsu Inc, 1-11 Tsukiji, Chuo-ku Tokyo 104-8426, Japan also: Japan Advt Agys Assn, 8-12 Ginza 4-chome, Chuo-ku, Tokyo 104-0061, Japan*

KOGUT, KENNETH JOSEPH, consulting engineer; b. Chgo., Dec. 3, 1947; s. Joseph Henry and Estelle Theresa (Swiercz) K.; m. Darlene Agnes Jedlicka, June 15, 1974. Student, Lewis Coll., 1966-68; BME, U. Detroit, 1971, ME, 1972, postgrad., 1972—. Registered profl. engr., Ill.; cert. energy mgr. Mech. engr. Fluor Pioneer Inc., Chgo., 1972-73, cons. engr., 1973-75; project mgr. Engring. Corp. Am., Chgo., 1976-77; sr. cons. pub. utilities DeLoitte, Haskins & Sells, Chgo., 1977-79; individual practice as energy and mgmt. cons., 1979—. Author: Energy Management for the Community Bank. Alfred P. Sloan fellow, 1971-73; reciepient award Pres.'s Program for Energy Efficiency, Corp. Energy Mgmt. award, 1981, Regional Energy Profl. Devel. award, 1984, Regional Energy Engr. of Yr. award, 1987, Ill. Energy award, 1988, Illiana Energy Mgmt. Exec. of Yr. award Assn. Energy Engrs., 1992, 96, Disting. Svc. award Assn. Energy Engrs., 1999, Excellence in Engring. award Am. Soc. Heating Refrigeration and Air-Conditioning Engrs. Ill. chpt., 1994. Mem. Am. Nuclear Soc., Nat., Ill. socs. profl. engrs., Assn. Energy Engrs. (pres. Chgo. chpt. 1985, pres Ill. chpt. 1990-93, regional v.p. 1993-95, dir. chpt. devel., 1996, internat. pres-elect 1997, internat. pres. 1998), Environ. Engrs. and Mgrs. Inst., Demand-Side Mgmt. Soc., Exec. Hosp. Engrs. Soc. Ill., Energy Svcs. Mktg. Soc., Blue Key, Tau Beta Pi, Pi Tau Sigma, Polish Nat. Alliance. Address: 5232 170th Pl Oak Forest IL 60452-4450

KOH, JAI KYOUNG, dermatologist, educator; b. Seoul, Republic of Korea, Mar. 21, 1936; came to U.S., 1965; s. Byoung Kook Koh and Dong Ju Kim; m. Young Ja Ryu, Oct. 21, 1962; children: Han Jong, Hee Jung, Sang Won. Pre-med. cert., Seoul Nat. U., 1956, MD, 1960, MS, 1962; postgrad., U. Minn., 1966-69. Diplomate Am. Bd. Dermatology, Am. Bd. Dermatopathology, Korean Bd. Dermatology. Rotating intern Seoul Nat. U. Hosp., 1960-61, resident in dermatology, 1961-62; rotating intern Mt. Sinai Hosp., Mpls., 1965-66; resident in dermatology U. Minn. Hosp., Mpls., 1966-69; asst. prof. dermatology Howard U. Coll. Medicine, Washington, 1969-72; assoc. prof. dermatology U. Nebr. Coll. Medicine, Omaha, 1972-91, Creighton U. Sch. Medicine, Omaha, 1975-91; section chief of dermatology, staff cons. Omaha VA Med. Ctr., 1972-91; assoc. prof. pathology Creighton U., U. Nebr., 1984-89; prof. dermatology Asan Med. Ctr., Seoul, 1989—, chmn. dept. dermatology, 1989-98. Author, editor textbooks; contbr. numerous articles to profl. dermatology jours. Capt., med. officer Republic of Korean Army, 1962-65. Fellow Am. Acad. Dermatology; mem. Korean Dermatol. Assn., Korean Soc. Investigative Dermatology (pres. 1999—). Presbyterian. Avocations: hiking, golf, skiing, tennis, swimming. Home: 300-301 Ihchon-Dong Yong, San Gu Sam Ick Apt 2-408, Seoul 140-031, Republic of Korea Office: Asan Med Ctr Dept Dermatol, 338-1 Pungnapdong Songpagu, Seoul 138-736, Republic of Korea

KOH, JOHN TZE-TZUN, chemist, educator; b. St. Louis, Apr. 3, 1967. BSc, West Chester (Pa.) U., 1989; MS, Columbia U., 1990, PhD, 1994. Postdoctoral fellow U. Calif., Berkeley, 1994-96; prof. chemistry U. Del., Newark, 1996—. Contbr. articles to Jour. Am. Chem. Soc., Carbohydrate Rsch., Biochemistry. Am. Cancer Soc. fellow, 1994; Columbia U. awardee, 1994. Mem. AAAS, Am. Chem. Soc. Avocations: photography, bicycling. E-mail: johnkoh@udel.edu. Office: U Del Dept Chemistry Newark DE 19716

KOH, SEOK JOO, researcher; b. Kim-Je, Jun-Buk, Republic of Korea. BS, Korean Advanced Inst. Sci. and Tech., Taejon, 1992, MS, 1994, PhD, 1998. Sr. rschr. ETRI, Taejon, 1998—. Fax: 03082-42-861-5404. E-mail: sjkoh@pec.etri.re.kr. Office: ETRI, Kajung-Dong Yusung-Gu, Taejon 305-350, Republic of Korea

KOH, SEOK-KEUN, materials scientist, researcher; b. Seoul, Republic of Korea, May 3, 1958; s. Youn-Kyu K. and Sang-Hyun Yoon; m. Mi-Hwa Joo, Apr. 16, 1983; children: Jae-Young, Jeong-Eun. BS, Yonsei, Seoul, Republic of Korea, 1981; MS, Yonsei, 1983, Rutgers U., 1987; PhD, Rutgers U., 1989. Head of sect. Ion Beam Engring Exp., Kyoto, Japan, 1989-91; sr. scientist Korea Inst. Sci. and Tech., Seoul, Republic of Korea, 1991-97; prin. scientist Korea Inst. Sci. and Tech., Seoul, 1997—; CEO P&I Co., 2000—; cons. Samyang Co., Seoul, 1996-97, LG Electronics, Seoul, 1997-98. Contbr. articles to profl. jours.; inventor. Mem. Korean Vacuum Soc. (mem. com. 1995-97), Korean Phys. Soc. (mem. com. 1997-98), Am. Phys. Soc., Materials Rsch. Soc. Avocations: tennis, golf, skiing. Home: Hanstr Apt 101-203 Cheongryong, DongdaemoonGu, 130-011 Seoul Republic of Korea Office: KIST Thinfilm Tech Rsch Ctr, PO Box 131 Cheongryang, 130-650 Seoul Republic of Korea

KOH, YONGBOK, surgeon, educator; b. Seoul, Korea, Feb. 2, 1941; s. Sung Dae Koh and Sang Soon Joo; m. Yeong Nam Kim, Oct. 4, 1969; children: Won Jun, Won Hae, In Jun. MD, Cath. U. Seoul, 1966, PhD, 1974. Lic. medicine, Korea, surgeon, Korea. Intern, resident St. Mary's Hosp., Cath. U., Seoul, 1966-71, instr. surgery, 1974-76; surgeon NYU Med. Ctr., 1977-79; prof. surgery St. Mary's Hosp., Cath. U., Seoul, 1980—; vis. prof. U. Iowa Hosps. and Clinics, Iowa City, 1996; chmn. bd. dirs. Korean Vascular Surgery Soc. Co-author: Modern Surgery, 1994. Lt. comdr. Korean Navy, 1971-74. Fellow ACS, Internat. Coll. Surgeons, Am. Coll. Angiology; mem. Transplantation Soc. (chmn. sci. program 1990—). Roman Catholic. Office: Kang Nam St Marys Hosp, 505 Banpo Dong Seochoku, 137-040 Seoul Republic of Korea

KOHÁK, ERAZIM VÁCLAV, philosophy educator, writer; b. Praha, Czechoslovakia, May 21, 1933; s. Miloslav and Zdislava (Procházková) K.; m. Frances Macpherson, June 2, 1955 (div. Apr. 1977); children: Mary, Susan, Katherine; m. Sheree Dukes Conrad, 1981 (div. 1988); m. Dorothy Gray Mills, Aug. 24, 1991. BA, Colgate U., 1954; postgrad., Yale Div. Sch., 1954-55; MA, Yale U., 1957, PhD, 1958. Asst. prof. Gustavus Adolphus Coll., St. Peter, Minn., 1958-60; asst. prof. philosophy Boston U., 1960-70, assoc. prof., 1970-77, prof., 1977-95, dir. grad. studies dept. philosophy, 1970-82, 85-90, chair dept. philosophy, 1982-85, prof. emeritus, 1995—; prof. ordinarius Charles U., Prague, 1991-2000, prof. emeritus, 2000—; vis. prof. Bowling Green (Ohio) State U., 1970; sr. fellow Inst. für die Wissenschaften vom Menschen, Vienna, 1985. Author: Idea and Experience, 1976, The Embers and the Stars, 1982, Jan Patočka: His Thought and Writings, 1989, Člověk, dobro a zlo, 1993, Zelená svatozář, 1998, The Green Halo, 1999, Hesla mladych svištu, 2000. Trustee Somerville (Mass.) Pub. Librs., 1976-80, Bass Park, Sharon, N.H., 1982-90. Recipient Gt. Gold medal Charles U., 1994, Colloquium in his honor Ctr. for Philosophy of Sci., Boston, 1995; Danforth fellow, 1954, Medal of Merit, Czech republic, 1998. Democrat/Social Democrat. Episcopalian/Czech Brethren Ch. Avocations: writing, hiking, carpentry. Home: Babákova 2200, 148 00 Praha Czech Republic

KOHALMI, MAUREEN EVELYN, small business owner, manager; b. Taumarunui, New Zealand, Apr. 27, 1953; d. Dennis and Blanche (Nash) Maginnity; m. John Ernest Kohalmi; children: Kylie McLeod, Shannon Stubbs, Paige Kohalmi. Cert. in advanced mktg. Product mgr. Trimex P/L, Sydney, Australia, 1983-85, Juvena Cos, Sydney, 1985-87; mktg. mgr. Bausch-Lomb, Sydney, 1987-91; mktg. dir. Eventive, Sydney, 1991; mng. dir. Ideas on Deck P/L, Sydney, 1991—; pres. Sunglass Assn. Australia, 1988-91. Hon. pub. rels. cons. Liberal Party, City of Sydney, 1994; pres. Parents and Friends Assn., Marist sisters Coll. Woolwich, 1994-96; founder Boronic Calisthenics, 1997. Recipient Nat. Small Bus. award, Australian Nat. Tng. Authority, 1995. Avocations: family, reading, walking, calisthenics. Office: Ideas on Deck P/L Unit 18, 5 Parsons St City West, Balmain Rozelle NSW 2039, Australia

KOHAN, BETSY BURNS, lawyer; b. La Mesa, Calif., Jan. 24, 1949; d. William Richard and Winifred Marion Burns; m. Dennis Lynn Kohan, Mar. 8, 1986; children: Toni Kick, Bart, Elyse, David Karowsky. BA, Stanford U., 1971; JD, U. Colo., 1974. Bar: Colo. 1974, Calif. 1985. Ptnr. Karowsky, Witwer & Oldenburg, Greeley, Colo., 1974-82; pvt. practice, Greeley, 1983-84; v.p., assoc. gen. counsel Sun Savs., San Diego, 1985-86; v.p., asst. gen. counsel Imperial Savs. & Loan Assn., San Diego, 1986-88, Am. Real Estate Group, Irvine, Calif., 1988-90, Columbia Savs. & Loan Assn., Irvine, 1990-91; staff atty. FDIC, Irvine, 1991-94; prof. Anhui Inst. Fin. and Trade, Bengbu, China, 1994, Guangzhou (China) Inst. Fgn. Trade, 1995; sr. counsel Nissan Motor Acceptance Corp., Torrance, Calif., 1996—; mem. Commn. on Legal and Jud. Edn., Colo. Supreme Ct., Denver, 1983-84. Contbr. articles to legal publs. Chmn. Colo. Commn. on Women, Denver, 1978-80; vice chmn. bd. trustees U. No. Colo., 1980-84. Named Outstanding Coloradoan, Colo. Jaycees, 1980, Outstanding Young Lawyer, Colo. Bar Assn., 1979. Mem. L.A. Bar Assn. (comml. law com. 1997—). Home: 525 E Seaside Way Unit 204 Long Beach CA 90802-8001 Office: Nissan Motor Acceptance Corp 990 W 190th St Fl 8 Torrance CA 90502-1046

KOHAN, DENNIS LYNN, international trade educator, consultant; b. Kankakee, Ill., Nov. 22, 1945; s. Leon Stanley and Nellie (Foster) K.; m. Julianne Johnson, Feb. 14, 1976 (dec. Sept. 1985); children: Toni, Bart, Elyse; m. Betsy Burns, Mar. 8, 1986; 1 child, David. BA, Ill. Wesleyan U., 1967; MPA, Gov.'s State U., 1975; postgrad., John. Marshall Law Sch., 1971-74. Police officer Kankakee County, 1967-75; loan counselor, security officer Kankakee Fed. Savs. & Loan, Kankakee, 1975-76; mgr. Bank Western, Denver, 1976-85; mgr. real estate lending dept. Cen. Savs., San Diego, 1985-87; maj. loan work-out officer Imperial Savs., San Diego, 1987-88; cons. Equity Assurance Holding Corp., Newport Beach, Calif., 1987-88; compliance officer Am. Real Estate Group and New West Fed. Savs. and Loan, Irvine, Calif., 1988-90; co-founder Consortium-Real Estate Asset Cons., Costa Mesa, Calif., 1990-91; investigator, criminal coord. Resolution Trust Corp., Newport Beach, Calif., 1991-94; instr. for Internat. Trade Anhui Inst. Fin. and Trade, Bengbu, People's Republic of China, 1994-95; instr. Guangzhou Inst. Fgn. Trade, People's Republic of China, 1995—; owner Kohan Internat. Bus. Forensics, 1995—; investigator Office Inspector Gen. L.A. Unified Sch. Dist., 2000—; instr. U. No. Colo. Coll. Bus., Greeley, 1981-85; chmn. bd. North Colo. Med. Ctr., Greeley, 1983-85; pres. bd. Normedco, Greeley, 1984-85; part-time prof. bus. pub. adminstrn. So. Calif. Internat. Coll., 1998—. Vol. cons., chmn. ARC, Colo., 1979-85; campaign mgr. Donley Senatorial campaign, Colo., 1982, Kinkade City Coun. campaign, Colo., 1983; chmn. Weld County Housing Authority, 1981. Staff sgt. U.S. Army, 1969-71, Vietnam. Mem. Nat. Assn. Realtors, Shriners, Kiwanis.

KOHARA, HIROSHI, maketing educator; b. Tokyo, Jan. 2, 1946; s. Etsuko and Ishiwata, May 5, 1974. MBA, Takushoku U., Tokyo, 1971, PhD, 1998. Instr. Takushoku U., 1974-79, assoc. prof., 1979-87, prof., 1987—. Author: The History of Marketing in Japan, 1994 (Japan Bus. Book award 1995), The History of Marketing in America, 1991, The Principles of Marketing, 1999. Home: 2-26 Miharu-Cho, Yokosuka 238-0014, Japan Office: Takushoku U, 3-4-14 Kohinata Bunkyo, Tokyo 112-8585, Japan

KOHL, DANIELE MARGUERITE, immunologist, vaccinologist; b. Luxembourg, Oct. 11, 1951; d. Justin and Barbara (Thommes) K. Diploma in Biol. Scis. and Zoology, U. Louvain, Belgium, 1975, diploma in immunology. Rsch. fellow I.R.E., Belgium, 1976; head lab. immunology Immuno S.A., Vienna, Austria, 1976-78; new product mgr. SmithKline Beecham Biologicals, s.a., Rixensart, Belgium, 1978-86; product mgr. SmithKline Beecham Biols. s.a., Rixensart, Belgium, 1986-96, worldwide mgr. vaccine tng., 1986—; cons. vaccinology WHO; tutor Ministry of Health, assoc. dir. worldwide vaccine tng. and edn., 1996—. Exhibited photography and paintings, 1990, 92, 94, 95, 96, 97, 98, 99, 2000. Recipient Internat. Photography award, 1991, 95, 96. Mem. Soroptimists, ABC/D-click, Belgian Royal Assn. of Profl. Artists. Avocations: photography, painting, languages, walking, horse riding. Home: 45 rue Rosier Bois, B-1330 Rixensart Belgium Office: SmithKline Beecham Biols, 89 Rue de l'Institut, B-1330 Rixensart Belgium

KOHL, HELMUT, former chancellor of Germany; b. Ludwigshafen, Germany, Apr. 3, 1930; s. Hans and Cäcilie (Schnur) K.; m. Hannelore Renner, 1960; children: Walter, Peter. Student law, polit. sci. and history, U. Frankfurt; PhD, U. Heidelberg, 1958; DPhil. Staff mem. trade assn., 1958; mem. Landtag Rheinland-Pfalz, 1959; chmn. Chistian Dem. Union party Landtag group, 1963; minister pres. Rheinland Pfalz, 1969-76; vice chmn. Christian Dem. Union party Germany, 1969, chmn., 1973-98; chmn., leader of opposition in Deutsche Bundestag CDU/CSU Parliamentary Party, 1976-82; chancellor of Fed. Republic Germany Bonn, 1982-91, chancellor of reunited Germany, 1991-98. Author: Hausputz hinter den Fassaden, 1971, Zwischen Ideologie und Pragmatismus, 1973, Bundestagsreden, 1978, Der neue Realismus, 1980, Die CDU. Porträt einer Volkspartei, 1981, Der Weg zur Wende, 1983, Deutschlands zukunft in Europa, 1990, Bilanzen und Perspeektiven Regierungspolitik 1989-91, 1992, Ich wollte Deutschlands Einheit, dargestellt von Kai Diekmann und Ralf Georg Reuth, 1996, Bilanzen und Perspeektiven, Auf dem Weg ins 21 Jahrhundert, Regierungspolitik 1992-96, 1997. Decorated grand cross 1st class Order of Merit Fed. Republic Germany, Order of Merit of Rhineland-Palatinate, numerous other foreign decorations. Office: Deutscher Bundestag, Unter den Linden 71, 10117 Berlin Germany

KOHL, KATHLEEN ALLISON BARNHART, lawyer; b. Ft. Leavenworth, Kans., Jan. 11, 1955; d. Robert William and Margaret Ann (Snowden) Barnhart. BS, Memphis State U., 1978; JD, Loyola U., New Orleans, 1982. Bar: La. 1982, U.S. Dist. Ct. (ea. dist.) La. 1982, U.S. Dist. Ct. (no. dist.) Tex. 1985, U.S. Ct. Appeals (5th cir.) 1986, U.S. Ct. Appeals (11th cir.) 1988, U.S. Supreme Ct. 1994. Assoc. Garrity & Webb, Harahan, La., 1982; revenue officer IRS, Dallas, 1984; sr. trial atty. EEOC, Dallas, 1984-86; sr. criminal enforcement counsel U.S. EPA, Dallas, 1986-91, chief water enforcement sect., office regional counsel, 1991-92; dep. dir. criminal enforcement counsel divsn. U.S. EPA, Washington, 1992-93, dir. criminal enforcement counsel divsn., 1993-94; sr. criminal enforcement counsel U.S. EPA, Dallas, 1994—; spl. asst. U.S. atty. U.S. Atty.'s Office, Montgomery, Ala., 1988-89; vis. instr. Fed. Law Enforcement Tng. Ctr., Glynco, Ga., 1987—; adj. prof. environ. crimes seminar Cornell U. Law Sch., spring 1993, environ. law Sch. Law Tex. Wesleyan U., fall 1998; instr. EPA Nat. Acad., 1997—. Vol. instr. New Orleans Police Acad., 1981. Mem. La. Bar Assn. Office: EPA 1445 Ross Ave Ste 1200 Dallas TX 75202-2733

KOHLA, BAYOUMI HASSAN, petrochemical company executive, consultant; b. Alexandria, Egypt, Sept. 25, 1953; s. Hassam Ali Kohla and Hiat (Mohamed) Badr; m. Aza Mohamed Labib, July 2, 1987; children: Aya, Alaa, Hassam. BSc of Spl. Chemistry, Faculty of Sci., Alexandria, 1976. Lab. chemist Trinco, Alexandria, 1978-80; safety inspector Alexandria Petrochem. Co., 1980-86, safety sect. head, 1986-88; fire fighting supt. Egyptian Petrochem. Co., Alexandria, 1988-89; safety engr. ADNOC, Abu Dhabi, 1989-93; safety inspection and study mgr. Egyptian Petrochem. Co., Alexandria, 1993—; safety gen. mgr., 1999—; cons. Elhylen project, Alexandria, 1994-96, Poly Ethylen project, Alexandria, 1995-96. Author: Modern Understanding of Safety, 1994. Mem. Magazin Hydrocarbon Processing, Union Alexandria Sporting Club, Smouha Club, Shlalet Club. Avocations: traveling, care of animals. Home: 5 Dr Moustafa Tabala Str, Alexandria Egypt Office: Egyptian Petrochem Co, 36 KM Desert Rd, Alexandria Amiria, Egypt

KOHLBERGER, PETRA, physician, researcher, educator; b. Vienna, Austria, Aug. 17, 1969. MD, U. Vienna, 1993. Prof. dept. ob/gyn U. Vienna, 1993—. Office: Dept Ob/Gyn Univ of Vienna, Waehringer Guertel 18, A-1090 Vienna Austria

KOHLEGGER, KARL, judge. Presiding judge Supreme Ct., Vaduz, Liechtenstein. Office: Oberster Gerichtshof, Office of Presiding Judge, FL-9490 Vaduz Liechtenstein*

KOHLER, ADRIAN PETER, puppeteer, designer; b. Port Elizabeth, South Africa, Dec. 20, 1951; s. Harold and Thelma K.; m. Basil John Richard Jones, 1971. BA in Fine Art, U. Cape Town, 1974. Lectr. U. Botswana, 1978-80; dir. Handspring Puppet Co., South Africa, 1981—. Performed works include Starbrites, 1991 (Vita award, 1990, 91), Woyzeck on the Highveld, 1991 (prodn. of yr. 1992, 93), Faustus in Africa, 1995 (prodn. of yr. 1995, 96), Spider's Place, 1995 (Artes award, 1996), UBU & The Truth Commission, 1997, Il Riturno D'Ullise, 1998, The Chimp Project, 2000. Grantee U.S. Info. Svc., 1991. Avocation: stone carving. Home: 15A Clairvaux Rd, Kalk Bay 7975, South Africa Office: Handspring Puppet Co, 1 Magnet St, Johannesburg 2094, South Africa

KÖHLER, CHRISTER SVEN-OVE, pharmaceuticals executive; b. Linköping, Sweden, Oct. 24, 1947; s. Sven Wilhelm and Birgitta Runa (Johansson) K.; m. Lena Elisabeth Haglund, Dec. 24, 1982; children: Victor, Leo. PhD, U. Bergen, Norway, 1982. Lab. chief Astra, Södertalje, Sweden, 1982-88; prof. U. Bergen, 1984; sr. dir. Astra, Södertalje, Sweden, 1988-91; v.p. Roche, Basel, Switzerland, 1992-97; sr. v.p. Astra, Sweden, 1997-99; global v.p. Astrazeneca, Sodertalje, Sweden, 1999—. Avocations: sailing, vine.

KÖHLER, EKKEHART, cardiologist; b. Leipzig, Sachsen, Germany, Sept. 7, 1941. MD, U. Lübeck, Germany, 1968. Asst. in pharmacology U. Düsseldorf, Germany, 1969-75, asst. in internal medicine and cardiology, 1975-82; med. dir. clinic for cardiology and angiology Salzetalklinik, Bad Salzflen, Germany, 1982-98; med. dir. dept. invasive cardiology Meiningen (Germany) Hosp., 1998—. Author: Klinische Echokardiographie, 5th edit., 2000, Ein- und Zweidimensionale Echokardiographie mit Dopplertechnik, 6th edit., 1996; (CD-ROM) Videoatlas Klinische Echokardiographie, 1997; editor: Akutmedizinische und Rehabilitative Behandlung Herzkranker, 1996. Office: Meiningen Hosp, Bergstr 3, 98617 Meiningen Germany

KOHLER, FRED CHRISTOPHER, tax specialist; b. Cleve., Oct. 21, 1946; s. Fred Russell and Ruth Mary (Harris) K. BS (Austin scholar), Northwestern U., 1968; MBA (Faville fellow), Stanford U., 1970. Sr. analyst adminstrv. svcs. dissn. Arthur Andersen & Co., San Francisco, 1970-75; fin. systems analyst, sr. cost acct. Hewlett Packard Co., Palo Alto, Calif., 1975-77, internat. mktg. systems adminstr., 1977-80, sr. planning and reporting analyst corp. hdqrs., 1980-86, fin. planning and reporting mgr., 1986-90, tax mgr., 1990-92; sr. tax mgr. Hewlett Packard Co., 1992—. Mem. World Affairs Coun. No. Calif., Commonwealth Club, Churchill Club, Northwestern U. Alumni Club No. Calif., Stanford U. Alumni Assn., Beta Gamma Sigma. Home: 1736 Oak Creek Dr Apt 211 Palo Alto CA 94304-2112 Office: 3000 Hanover St Palo Alto CA 94304-1112

KÖHLER, HORST, finance company executive; b. Skierbieszów, Poland, Feb. 22, 1943; m. Eva KÖhler; two children. D in Econs. and Polit. Scis., U. Tübingen, Germany, 1976. Various positions German Ministries Econs. and Fin., 1976-89; German dep. min. fin., 1990-93; German dep. gov. World Bank, 1990-93; pres. German Savings Bank Assn., 1993-98, European Bank for Reconstruction and Devel., 1998-2000; mng. dir., chmn. exec. bd. Internat. Monetary Fund, 2000—; rep. fed. chancellor preparation Group Seven Econ. Summits, Houston, 1990, Munich, 1992, Tokyo, 1993. Fax: 202-623-4661. Office: Internat Monetary Fund 700 19th St NW Washington DC 20431-0001

KOHLER, LENNART INGEMAR, pediatrician, educator; b. Halmstad, Sweden, July 23, 1933; s. David A. and Ester T. (Andersson) K.; m. Eva-Mari Johansson, 1957 (div. 1983); children: Marie, Sven, Annika; m. Birgitta A. Rhodin, 1989. MD, U. Lund, Sweden, 1962, PhD, 1973; PhD (hon.), Athens Sch. Pub. Health, 1993. Pediatrician Univ. Hosp., Lund, 1962-78; head county Child Health Svcs., 1969-78; assoc. prof. social pediatrics U. Lund, 1973-78; prof. social and preventive medicine Nordic Sch. Pub. Health, Göteborg, 1978-86, prof. social pediatrics, 1987-98, dean, 1978-95; sci. adviser Swedish Nat. Bd. Health and Welfare; mem. sci. bd. Ctr. for Cmty. and Social Pediatric Rsch., U. Warwick, Eng.; mem. sci. bd. Pub. Health U. Bielefeld, U. Düsseldorf, Germany, Valencia Sch. Pub. Health; temporary adviser to WHO in pub. health and child health. Mem. editorial bd. World Paediatrics and Child Care, European Jour. Pub. Health, Internat. Jour. Health Scis., Childhood; contbr. numerous articles to sci. and profl. jours. Recipient Great prize Allmanna Barn-huset, Sweden, 1996, Nordic Pub. Health prize, 1997, ASPHER's European Stampar Medal Pub. Health, 1998. Mem. Swedish Pediatric Assn. (sci. sec. 1973-75), European Soc. Social Pediatrics (sec. gen. 1977-87, v.p. 1987—), Assn. Schs. in Pub. Health in European Region (pres. 1987-89, bd. dirs. 1985-97), Nordic Assn. Care of Sick Children (pres. 1980-85), Internat. Pediatric Assn. (adv. expert panel on social pediatrics). Home: Blamusslegatan 2, S-42679 V Frolunda Sweden Office: Nordic Sch Pub Health, PO Box 12133, S-40242 Göteborg Sweden

KÖHLER, PIOTR SEBASTIAN, botany historian; b. Cracow, Poland, June 21, 1962; s. Marian and Danuta (Mucha) K. MSc with distinction, Jagiellonian U., 1987, DS, 1993. Tech. asst. Jagiellonian U., Cracow, Poland, 1985-89, asst., 1989-94, adj., 1994—. Author: Zielnik Józefa Jundzitta Herbarium of Józef Jundzitta, 1995; contbr. articles to profl. jours. Fellow Polish Bot. Soc. (sec. sect. history of botany 1992—), Com. on History of Biology at Polish Acad. Sci., N.Y. Acad. Scis. Avocation: history and theory of music. Office: Hortus Botanicus U, Kopernika 27, 31-501 Cracow Poland

KÖHLER, RODOLFO, financial executive; b. Buenos Aires, July 27, 1938; s. Federico and Hjordis Maria (Skaring) K.; married, Apr. 11, 1975; children: Patricio, Solange, Alejandro, Javier. Grad. in Banking, U. Católica, Buenos Aires, 1982. Clk. Lloyds Bank, Buenos Aires, 1954-60; bus. mgr. Bank of Am., Buenos Aires, 1960-81; adminstrv. mgr. Mfrs. Hanover T.C., Buenos Aires, 1981-82; internat. officer Banco de Galicia y Buenos Aires, 1982-88; br. mgr. Deutsche Bank, Buenos Aires, 1988-91; adminstrv. and fin. mgr. Nelson Hurst Argentina, Buenos Aires, 1991-92; ins. broker AXA Equity and Law, Isle of Man, U.K., 1992-98, Old Mut. Internat., Guernsey, U.K., 1998—, Scottish Life Internat., Isle of Man, 1998—, Hansard Internat., Isle of Man, 1998—, Colonial Life/Swiss Life, Bermuda, 1999—, C.N.A. Internat. Life, Cayman Islands, 1999—, Premier Life, Luxembourg, 1999—. Mem. San Isidro Golf Club (share holder). Roman Catholic. Avocations: stamps, reading, cinema, football, swimming. Home: Ravelo 872 Boulogne, 1609 Buenos Aires Argentina

KÖHLER, THEODOR WOLFRAM, philosophy educator; b. Frankenstein, Silesia, Germany, Nov. 6, 1936; arrived in Austria, 1978; s. Adolf and Clara (Gurski) K. PhD, Pontif. Athenaeum S. Anselmo, Rome, 1969. Asst. prof. Pontifical Athenaeum San Anselmo, Rome, 1970-74, extraordinary prof., 1974-78; prof. U. Salzburg, Austria, 1978—, dean faculty of theology, 1985-87, pres., 1989-91. Mem. Internat. Soc. for Study of Medieval Philosophy. Roman Catholic. Avocation: hunting. Office: U Salzburg, Franziskanergasse 1, A-5020 Salzburg Austria

KOHLHAUSSEN, MARTIN, banker; b. Marburg/Lahn, Hessen, Germany, Nov. 6, 1935; married; 3 children. Law degree, U. Frankfurt-am-Main, Freiburg, Germany, 1965; Dr.h.c., U. Chemnitz, 1998. Br. mgr. various banks, Frankfurt, Hanau, Germany, 1965-76, Tokyo, N.Y.C., 1976-81; bd. dirs. Commerzbank AG, Frankfurt-am-Main, 1982—, chmn. bd. dirs., 1991—, now chmn., mng. dir. corp. comm. and econ. rsch. strategy and controlling. Office: Commerzbank AG, Kaiserplatz, D-60261 Frankfurt Germany*

KOHLI, ALKA, government official; b. New Delhi, Dec. 27, 1947; d. Ayodhya Nath and Mitter (Mehra) Seth; 1 child, Pooja. BA in English with honors, Lady Shri Ram Coll., 1967. Info. asst. Tourist Office Govt. of India, New Delhi, 1971-83; mgr. Tourist Office Govt. of India, Milan, 1989-94; dir. Tourist Office Govt. of India, London, 1998—; asst. dir. Ministry of Tourism, New Delhi, 1983-93, dir., 1994-98. Avocations: sports, music, reading, traveling. Office: India Tourist Office, 7 Cork St, London W1X 2LN, England

KOHLI, ANIL, medical educator, researcher; b. New Delhi, Oct. 6, 1962; s. Harish Chander and Sarla (Anand) K.; m. Vatsla Virmani, Feb. 15, 1994; children: Avikal, Avikrit. MBBS, U. Coll. Med. Scis., New Delhi, 1985, MD, 1992. Resident U. Coll. Med. Scis., 1989-92, sr. demonstrator, 1992-94, lectr., 1994-96, sr. lectr., 1996-98, reader, 1998—. Contbr. articles to profl. jours; asst. editor Jour. Forensic Medicine and Toxicology, 1995-97; assoc. editor Jour. Forensic Medicine Toxicology, 1997—. Avocations: chess, cricket. Home: B-5/196 Safdarjung Enclave, New Delhi 110029, India Office: Univ Coll Med Scis, New Delhi 110095, India

KOHLI, HARINDER S., mechanical engineer, CEO; b. Apr. 11, 1945. BSc, Punjab (India) U., 1966; MBA, Harvard U., 1972. Mktg. exec. Union Carbide India, New Delhi, 1967-70; dir. The World Bank, Washington, 1986-93, sr. adv., 1994-98; pres., CEO Centennial Group, Inc., Washington, 1998—. Home: 6516 Deidre Ter Mc Lean VA 22101-1605

KOHLI, RAJESH, marketing medical consultant; b. Madras, India, Feb. 23, 1957; s. Sudarshan and Parkash K.; m. Rachna Kohli, Oct. 3, 1982; children: Ridhima, Meera. M in Comm., Loyola Coll., Madras, 1978; DEM, Davars Coll., Madras, 1979. AMIBM, Inst. Bus. Mgmt., India, 1978. Pvt. practice India, 1978—; owner Med. Equipment Supply, Bangalore, 1993—. Recipient Rashtriya Ekta award; named Eminent Citizen of India. Avocations: reading, travel, badminton, cinema. Home: Near Koramangala Club, No 86 17th D Main 6th Blk, Koramang Bangalore 560 095, India Office: Med Equipment Supply Co, S 918 Manipal Ctr S Blk 47, DickenRd Bangalore 560 042, India

KOHLI, ULRICH ARNOLD, lawyer; b. Schwarzenburg, Switzerland, Dec. 31, 1947; s. Werner and Cecile Kohli; m. Verena Hostettler; m. Stefanie, Markus, Thomas. PhD in law, U. Bern, 1969. Journalist Berner Zeitung, Bern, 1971; legal advisor Chem. Bank, N.Y.C., 1972-73; legal counsel Bank Julius Baer, Zurich, 1974-79; owner Law Firm of Kohli & Ptnr., Zurich, 1979—; pres. Kohli Comm. Inc., N.Y.C., 1997—. Author: (as James Douglas) (novels) Brennpunkt Philadelphia, 1994, Goldauge, 1996, Zero Philadelphia, 1997, Der Sintfluter, 1998, Atemlos nach Casablanca, 2000; film producer Mindbender, 1996; co-author movie scripts. Justice of Zurich Tax Ct., 1987-93; pres. Dem. Party of Zollikon-Zurich, 1975-79. Col. Tanks, 1987-95. Mem. Swiss Rifle Assn. (shooting medals), Swiss Ski Fedn. (instr.), Swiss Officer Assn., Swiss Bar Assn. Avocations: golfing, skiing, shooting, yachting. E-mail: ulikohli@aol.com. Home: Im Hausacher 10, 8706 Feldmeilen Switzerland Office: Kohli & Ptnrs, 10 General Willestrasse, 8027 Zurich Switzerland

KOHN, HAROLD ELIAS, lawyer; b. Phila., Apr. 5, 1914; s. Joseph C. and Mayme (Rumm) K.; m. Edith Anderson, Dec. 30, 1946; children: Amy, Ellen, Joseph Carl. AB, U. Pa., 1934, LLB, 1937; LLD (hon.), Temple U., 1990. Bar: Pa. 1938, D.C. 1972. Pres. Kohn, Swift & Graf, P.C., Phila.; spl. counsel transit matters City of Phila., 1952-53, 56-62; counsel to gov. State of Pa., 1972; mem. bd. Southeastern Pa. Transp. Authority, 1972-77; mem. Pa. Jud. Inquiry and Rev. Bd., 1973-77; mem. Pa. Supreme Ct. Continuing Legal Edn. Bd., 1992-97; bd. consultors Villanova U. Law Sch. Trustee Temple U., U. of Arts; bd. dirs. Wilma Theatre, Moss Rehab. Hosp., Phila. Geriatric Ctr.; treas., bd. dirs. Kohn Found.; pres., bd. dirs. Arronson Found., Lavine Found.; past bd. dirs. Phila. Psychiat. Ctr.; trustee, mem. exec. com. Phila. Fedn. Jewish Agys.; past mem. exec. com. United Jewish Appeal; past v.p., bd. dirs. Phila. chpt. ACLU. Mem. ABA, Pa. Bar Assn., Phila. Bar Assn., D.C. Bar Assn., Internat. Acad. Trial Lawyers, Jud. Conf. 3d Cir., Am. Law Inst., Order of Coif, Phi Beta Kappa. *Died June 14, 1999.*

KOHN, WALTER, educator, physicist; b. Vienna, Austria, Mar. 9, 1923; m. Mara Schiff; children: J. Marilyn , Ingrid E. Kohn Katz, E. Rosalind. BA, U. Toronto, Ont., Can., 1945, MA, 1946, LLD (hon.), 1967; PhD in Physics, Harvard U., 1948; DSc (hon.), U. Paris, 1980; PhD (hon.), Brandeis U., 1981, Hebrew U. Jerusalem, 1981; DSc (hon.), Queens U., Kingston, Can., 1986, Fed. Inst. of Tech., Zurich, 1994, U. Wuerzburg, 1995, Tech. U. Vienna, 1996; PhD (hon.), Weizmann Inst., Israel, 1997. Indsl. physicist Sutton Horsley Co., Can., 1941-43; geophysicist Koulomzine, Que., Can., 1944-46; instr. physics Harvard U., Cambridge, Mass., 1948-50; asst. prof. physics Carnegie Mellon U., Pitts., 1950-60, assoc. prof. physics, 1953-57; prof. physics U. Calif., San Diego, 1960-79, chmn. dept. physics, 1961-63; dir. Inst. for Theoretical Physics, U. Calif., Santa Barbara, 1979-84; prof. dept. physics U. Calif., Santa Barbara, 1984-91, prof. of physics emeritus, rsch. prof. of physics, 1991—; rsch. physicist Ctr. for Quantized Electronic Structures, U. Calif., Santa Barbara, 1991—; vis. scholar U. Pa., U. Mich., U. Wash., U. Paris, U. Copenhagen, U. Jerusalem, Imperial Coll., London, ETH, Zurich, Switzerland; cons. Gen. Atomic, 1960-72, Westinghouse Rsch. Lab., 1953-57, Bell Telephone Labs., 1953-66, IBM, 1978; mem. or chmn. rev. coms. Brookhaven Nat. Labs., Argonne Nat. Labs., Oak Ridge Nat. Labs., Ames Lab., Tel Aviv U. (physics dept.), Brown U., Harvard U., U. Mich., Simon Frazer U., Tulane U., Reactor Divsn. NIST, Gaithersburg, Md.; chmn. S.D. divsn. Acad. Senate, 1968-69; dir. NSF Inst. Theoretical Physics, U. Calif. Santa Barbara, 1979-84; mem. senate rev. com. U. Calif. Management Nat. Labs., 1986-89; adv. bd. Statewide Inst. Global Conflict and Cooperation, 1982-92; mem. bd. govs. Weizmann Inst. of Sci., 1997—. Contbr. over 200 sci. articles and revs. to profl. jours. With inf., Can. Army, 1944-45. Recipient Buckley prize, 1960, Davisson-Germer prize, 1977, Nat. Medal of Sci., 1988, Feenberg medal, 1991, Niels Bohr/UNESCO Gold Medal, 1998, Nobel prize in chemistry, 1998; Lehman fellow Harvard U., 1946-46, fellow Nat. Rsch. Coun., 1950-51, sr. fellow NSF, 1958, Guggenheim fellow, 1963, sr. postdoctoral fellow NSF, 1967. Fellow AAAS, Am. Phys. Soc. (counselor-at-large 1968-72), Am. Acad. Arts and Scis.; mem. NAS, Internat. Acad. Quantum Molecular Scis., Am. Philos. Soc. Achievements include research on electron theory of solids and solid surfaces. Office: U Calif Dept Physics Santa Barbara CA 93106

KOHNERT, DIRK, institute administrator, editor; b. Melle, Germany, Mar. 18, 1946. MA in Econs., U. Kiel, Germany, 1972, PhD, 1981. Lectr. U. Bielefeld, Germany, 1982-84; coord. regional planning dept. Ministry of Planning, Bissau, Guinea-Bissau, 1985-86; sr. devel. expert GTZ, Cotonou, Benin, 1987-90; dep. dir. Inst. African Affairs, Hamburg, Germany, 1991—; cons. Ministry Fgn. Affairs, Ministry for Cooperation, Non Govtl. Orgns., Bonn, 1991—. Editor: Afrika Spectrum; author, editor numerous books; contbr. numerous articles to profl. jours., on econ., social and cultural devel., planning, and evaluation. Mem. Soc. for Internat. Devel. Office: Inst African Affairs, Neuer Jungfernstieg 21, D-20354 Hamburg Germany

KOHNO, ISAO, internist; b. Yamanashi, Japan, Oct. 13, 1964; s. Kimio and Mitsuyo (Okumara) K. MD, Yamanashi Med. U., 1993, Phd. Resident in internal medicine Yamanashi Med. U., 1993-95, asst. prof., 1995—. Contbr. articles to med. jours. Fellow Japanese Soc. Internal Medicine, Japanese Circulation Soc., Japanese Coll. Cardiology. Office: Yamanashi Med U Dp Int Med2, 1110 Shimokato, Tamaho, Nakakoma Yamanashi 409-3898, Japan

KOHOUT, JAROSLAV, sociologist, psychologist, researcher; b. Klatovy, Czech Republic, May 19, 1927; s. Frank and Frank (Veselakova) K.; m. Nadja Vybiralova, June 23, 1953; children: Jaroslav, Petra. PhD, High Sch. Pol. & Social Scis., 1953; attended, Charles U., Prague, 1966; D Social Scis., Czechoslovak Acad. Scis., 1978. Tchr. econs. Min. Fgn. Trade, 1950-52; prof. sociology and psychology Prague Sch. Econs., 1952-91, head dept. sociology and psychology, 1963-71, dean faculty mgmt., 1971-86; dep. sec. Sci. Czechoslovak Acad. Scis., 1986-91. Contbr. numerous articles to profl. jours. Com. mem. Czechoslovak Komitet Sci. Mgmt., 1975-90; pres. Czechoslovak Sociol. Assn., 1984-88. Recipient Gold medal Czechoslovak Acad. Scis., 1987. Avocations: writing, violin, guitar, bag pipes. Office: Sch Econs-Dept Psychology, Nam W Churchilla 4, 130 00 Prague 3, Czech Republic

KOHRI, KENJIRO, urologist, educator; b. Osaka, Japan, Jan. 13, 1949; s. Sadayuki and Chikako Kohri; m. Yoko Aono. MD, Osaka (Japan) U., 1973, PhD, 1979. Med. diplomate. Prof. urology Nagoya (Japan) City U., 1993—. Recipient Sakaguchi prize Japanese Urol. Assn., 1980, Inada prize Acta Urologica, 1986, Chunichi Culture prize, 1999. Avocation: golf. Office: 1 Kawasumi, Mizuho-ku, Nagoya, Aichi Japan

KOHRING, GERT WIELAND, microbiologist; b. Bielefeld, N. Rhine, Germany, Aug. 3, 1954; s. Gustav Adolf and Anneliese Grete (Kieselbach) K.; m. Susanne Pape, Aug. 11, 1989; 1 child, Malte. BS, U. Bielefeld, Germany, 1978; Diploma in Biology, U. Goettingen, Germany, 1981, Dr.rer.nat., 1984. Rsch. assoc. U. Goettingen, 1984-86, U. Ga., Athens, 1986-88; acad. counsellor U. Saarbruecken, Germany, 1988—. Co-author: (books) Methods in Microbiology 20, 1988, Environmental Biotechnology, 1988; contbr. articles to profl. jours. Mem. Am. Soc. Microbiology, German Soc. Microbiology, Dechema. Avocations: history, art, travel, tennis, soccer. Office: U Saarbruecken Applied Microbiology, Im Stadtwald PO Box 151150, D-66041 Saarbruecken Germany

KOHRING, VICTOR H., state legislator; b. Waukegan, Ill., Aug. 2, 1958; s. Heinz H. and Dolores E. Kohring. AAS in Bus. Adminstrn., Matanuska-Susitna C.C., Palmer, Alaska, 1985; BA in Mgmt. Sci., Alaska Pacific U., 1987, MBA, 1989. State legislator Ho. of Reps., Dist. 26 Wasilla and Peters Creek/Chugiak, AK, 1994, re-elected 1996, 98—; mem. ho. fin. com. Ho. of Reps., 1994, 96, 98—; chmn. house budge subcoms. for dept. edn., 1995-96, adminstrn., 1995-96, environ. conservation, 1997-98, cmty. and regional affairs, 1997-98, commerce and econ. devel., 1997-98, law, 1999—, natural resources, 1999—; constn. exec., 1978—; real estate developer, 1978-82. Bd. dirs. Alaska Housing Fin. Corp., Anchorage, 1991-94; vice chmn., mem. Iditarod Trail Com.; mem. Matanuska-Susitna Borough Econ. Devel. Commn., 1993-94; mem. Wasilla Planning and Utilities Commn., 1991-94; chmn., mem. Alaska del. Rep. Nat. Conv., Dallas, 1984, dist. del. rep., 1984, 86, 90, 92; treas. Rep. Party Alaska, Mat-Su, 1990, fin. chmn., 1990-91. Mem. NRA, Christian Businessman's Assn., Greater Wasilla C. of C., Chugiak-Eagle River C. of C., Anthony J. Dimond H.S. Alumni Assn., Pioneers of Alaska. Republican. Home: PO Box 870515 Wasilla AK 99687-0515 Office: Alaska Ho of Reps State Capitol Bldg Juneau AK 99801

KOHSHI, KIYOTAKA, neurosurgeon, researcher; b. Ozu machi, Kumamoto, Japan, June 9, 1958; s. Torai and Shizue (Sakata) K.; m. Katsuko Narahara, March 21, 1986; 2 children. MD, U. Occupl. & Environ. Health, Japan, 1984. Resident U. Hosp., Kitakyushu, Japan, 1984-86; neurosurgeon Kyushu Rosai Hosp., Kitakyushu, Japan, 1986-87; lectr. U. Occupl. & Environ. Health, Japan, 1988—; cons. Kyoei Kasai Co., Tokyo, 1995—, Daido Hoxan Inc., Tokyo, 1996—. Editor: Japanese Jour. Hyperbaric Medicine, 1996. Avocations: walking, swimming. Office: U Occupl/Environ Health, 1-1 Iseigaoka Yahatanishiku, kitakyushu 807-8555, Japan

KOHT, HARALD SVERDRUP, political scientist, educator; b. N.Y.C., June 18, 1943; arrived in Norway, 1946; s. Paul Gruda and Grete (Sverdrup) K. MA, Oslo U., 1971; PhD, Am. U. Washington, 1994. Cons. Road Directorate, 1973-75, City of Oslo, 1975-77, Norwegian Radium Hosp., 1977-81; asst. prof. Oslo Univ. Coll., 1981-89, assoc. prof., 1989—; vis. prof. U. Latvia, 2000—. Contbr. articles to profl. jours. Chair Norwegian Neighborhood Assn., 1997-99. Mem. Norwegian Polit. Sci. Assn. (chair 1975-77). Home: Kapellveien 43B, N-0487 Oslo Norway Office: Oslo Coll, Pilestredet 52, N-0167 Oslo Norway

KOHUT, JOHN WALTER, corporate executive; b. N.Y.C., Nov. 13, 1946; s. Walter and Stelle (Dudar) K.; m. Linda Susan Ram, Jan. 3, 1987; 1 child, Katherine Grace. BBA in Fin. and Econs., U. Miami, Coral Gables, Fla., 1969. Mgmt. trainee Bankers Trust Co., N.Y.C., 1969-73, asst. treas. in comml. banking, 1973-76, asst. v.p. spl. loans, 1976-79; v.p. European Energy Bankers Trust Co., London, 1979-82, v.p. Global Aerospace, 1982-85; mng. dir. Pvt. Equity B.T. Securities Corp., N.Y., 1985-90; pres., chief exec. officer W. Atlee Burpee Co., Warminster, Pa., 1990-91, Ramko Venture Mgmt., Inc., N.Y.C., 1991—; bd. dirs. U.S. Automotive Mfg., Inc., Richmond, Va., chmn., prin. fin. officer, 1997-2000; v.p. Pyramid Investors, N.Y.C., 1988-90. Bd. dirs. 309 E. 49th St. C.A., N.Y.C., 1985-91; elected committeeman Rep. County, Somerset, N.J., 1976-79; mem. adv. com. on comml. aspects of space NASA, 1984-87; bd. adv. St. Bartholomew Community Preschool, N.Y.C., 1992-97. Mem. AIAA (bd. dirs. 1987-91), Turnaround Mgmt. Assn., Am. Bankruptcy Inst., Tau Kappa Epsilon. Roman Catholic. Home: 45 E 89th St Apt 21B New York NY 10128-1256 Office: Ramko Venture Mgmt Inc 711 5th Ave New York NY 10022-3111

KOIDA, MASAO, pharmacology educator, researcher; b. Osaka, Japan, Sept. 20, 1936; s. Teru and Masami (Seki) K.; m. Mitsuru Okamoto, Mar. 24, 1967. BA, Sch. Pharmacy, Osaka, Japan, 1959; MS, Faculty Pharm. Sci., Osaka, Japan, 1961, PhD, 1966. Assoc. prof. Showa Sch. Pharmacy, Tokyo, 1967-69; asst. prof. Mt. Sinai Sch. Medicine, N.Y.C., 1969-70; assoc.

prof. Nagasaki (Japan) U., 1970-84, U. Ill., Chgo., 1974-76; prof. Setsunan U., Hirakata, Japan, 1984—. Contbr. articles to profl. jours. Mem. Japanese Soc. Pharmacology, Japanese Soc. Biochemistry. Avocations: baseball, golf, Mahjong. E-mail: koida@pharm.setsunan.ac.jp. Home: Hoshida-Nishi 5-18 2-501, Katano 576-0015, Japan Office: Setsunan U, Nagaotogecho 45-1, Hirakata 573-0101, Japan

KOIDE, MORIHIKO, electronics company executive; b. Tokyo, Sept. 9, 1935; s. Shogo and Shizuko K.; m. Tomoko Aono, 1961. BSc, Waseda U., 1960. With Hitachi Ltd., Yokohama, Japan, 1960—; dir., gen. mgr. Hitachi Sales Corp. Can., after 1974; gen. mgr. Hitachi Consumer Products Am., after 1979, exec. v.p., 1982-86; pres. Hitachi Consumer Products de Mex., 1986—. Mem. IEEE, Am. Mgmt. Assn., Japanese Inst. TV Engrng. Home: 4-23-9 Kanahodo Asao, Kanagawa 215-0006, Japan Office: Sekonic Co Ltd, 7-24-14 Oizumi Gakuen-Cho, Tokyo 178, Japan also: Diamond Office Mgmt Co Ltd, 1-39-5 Dai 2 Mori Bldg, Morino Machiola City, Tokyo 194-0022, Japan

KOIKE, SATOSHI, mathematician; b. Kobe, Japan, June 30, 1952; s. Akira and Shizuko (Murakami) K. BS, Osaka U., Toyonaka, Japan, 1976; MS, Chiba (Japan) U., 1978; DSc, Kyoto (Japan) U., 1981. Rsch. fellow JSPS, Japan, 1981-82; asst. Hyogo U. Tchr. Edn., Yashiro, Japan, 1982-85, assoc. prof., 1985—. Author: Pitman Research Notes in mathematics, 1998; contbr. articles to profl. jours. Mem. Math. Soc. Japan. Avocation: bicycling. Home: 2-355 Nakajiyugaoka Shijimi, Miki Hyogo 673-0552, Japan Office: Hyogo U Tchr Edn, 942-1 Shimokume, Yashiro 673-1415, Japan

KOINUMA, HIDEOMI, materials chemistry educator; b. Tokyo, Oct. 26, 1941; s. Kiju and Miyako (Sasago) K.; m. Reiko Ueda, Nov. 3, 1968; children: Miyuki, Makiko, Yuji. BS, Tokyo U., 1965, MS, 1967, PhD, 1970. Postdoctoral rsch. assoc. U. Kans., Lawrence, 1970-72; rsch. assoc. Tokyo U., 1972-79, asst. prof., 1979-81, assoc. prof., 1981-87; prof. materials chemistry Tokyo Inst. Tech., 1987—, dir. ceramics rsch. ctr., 1994-96; guest rschr. Nat. Inst. of Rsch. for Inorganic Materials, 1998—. Author: Amorphous Materials, 1985, Ceramic Superconductors, 1987; editor: (symposium procs.) Chemical Aspects of High-Tc Superconductors, 1989; patentee in Japan and U.S. Mem. Material Rsch. Soc., Chem. Soc. Japan (prize 1997), Soc. Polymer Sci. Japan, Japanese Soc. Applied Physics, Ceramic Soc. Japan (prize 1998), Pakistan Soc. Semicondr. Sci. and Tech. (hon.), Am. Phys. Soc., Materials Rsch. Soc. India (hon.). Avocations: outdoor sports, bathing in hot springs. Home: 3-47-8 Ogikubo, Suginami-ku 167, Japan Office: Tokyo Inst Tech, 4259 Nagatsuta, Yokohama 226, Japan

KOIRALA, GIRIJA PRASAD, government official of Nepal. Prime min., min. of def., fin., fgn. affairs, health, and Royal Palace affairs Nepal, Katmandu, 1992—, min. women, children and social welfare, min. labor and transport mgmt., min. gen. adminstrn. Address: Office of Prime Min, Ctrl Secretar Singha Durbar, Katmandu Nepal*

KOIVU, SAKU, hockey player; b. Turku, Finland, Nov. 23, 1974. Forward Montreal (Que.) Canadiens, 1995-96. Recipient ice hockey Bronze medal Olympic Games, Nagano, Japan, 1998. Avocation: golf. Office: Montreal Canadiens, 1260 rue de la GauchetiereW, Montreal, PQ Canada H3B 5E8*

KOIVUKANGAS, EINO OLAVI, scientific research director; b. Halsua, Finland, Nov. 12, 1941; s. Einar Olavi and Vieno Rakel (Karvonen) K.; m. Pirjo Tuulikki Haverinen, Aug. 21, 1966; children: Siru Susanna, Sari Hannele. MA in History, U. Turku, Finland, 1967, PhD in History, 1986; PhD in Demography, Australian Nat. U., Canberra, 1972. Asst. rschr. dept. gen. history U. Turku, 1972, 74; rschr. Finnish Acad. Sci., 1973; dir. Inst. Migration, Turku, 1974—; local dir. Cultural Found. Finland, 1986-98; docent U. Turku, 1991—. Author: Scandinavian Immigration and Settlement in Australia Before World War II, 1974, Finnish Migration to Australia After World War II, 1975, Sea, Gold and Sugarcane, 1986, Delaware 350; coauthor: (with Simo Toivonen) A Bibliography on Finnish Emigration and Internal Migration, 1978, (with John Martin) The Scandinavians in Australia, 1986, From the Midnight Sun to the Long White Cloud; Finns in New Zealand, 1996; editor-in-chief: Finns in Africa, Australia, New Zealand and Latin America, History of Finnish Emigration, 1998; editor 10 books; editor-in-chief Jour. Siirtolaisuus-Migration, 1974—, Sportveteran, 1998—; contbr. articles to profl. jours. Pres. League Finnish Australian Socs. Helsinki, 1984—; v.p. Finland Soc., 1991-97; auditor City of Turku, 1977-92, chmn., 1977-89; bd. dirs. U. Village Found., Turku, 1978-83, vice chmn., 1984-89, chmn., 1990, mem. coun., 1978—, chmn., 1991-94; mem. Cultural Bd. of City of Turku, 1993-96. 2d lt. inf. Finnish Army, 1960-61. Decorated knight 1st class Order of Finnish Lion; Order of Australia; Australia U. champion hammerthrowing and discus, 1971, Finnish veteran champion in hammer, 1994, 96, 97, 98, 99, Scandinavian champion, 1995, 3d in weight pentathlon world championships in South Africa, 1997. Mem. Turku Paasikivi Soc. (chair 1996—), Assn. European Migration Instns. (pres. 1993-94), Finnish Vet. Athletic Assn. (bd. dirs. 2000—), Coun. European Turku, also other sci. socs., Rotary (pres. 1995-96, Paul Harris award). Lutheran. Avocations: athletics. E-mail: olakoi@utu.fi. Office: Inst Migration, Piispankatu 3, 20500 Turku Finland

KOIVUSAARI, PASI MATTI, management consultant; b. Sysmä, Finland, Dec. 17, 1953; s. Eero and Siiri (Moisiomäki) K.; m. Anneli Raili Korpela; children: Jaakko, Katariina. Grad., Comml. Coll., Helsinki, Finland, 1976; BSc in Econs., U. Uppsala, Sweden, 1978. Edp coord. Hankkija, Helsinki, Finland, 1978-81, logistics mgr., 1981-82; cons. JL-Consultants, Helsinki, Finland, 1982-88, Boyden Internat., Helsinki, Finland, 1988—; sr. ptnr. Boyden World Corp., Helsinki, Finland, 1989—. Mem. The Finnish Mgmt. Consultants (bd. dirs. 1990-92). Office: Oy Boyden Internat, Eteläranta 4 B 10, FIN00130 Helsinki Finland

KOIZUMI, HIDEAKI, research scientist, educator; b. Tokyo, Oct. 5, 1946; s. Hidenobu and Taeko (Tsukura) K.; m. Keiko Watanabe, June 25, 1977; children: Hanae, Eiichiro. BSc, U. Tokyo, 1971, PhD, 1976, DSc, 1976. Guest worker Nat. Bur. Stds. U.S. Dept. Commerce, Washington, 1976; rsch. physicist Lawrence Berkeley Lab. U. Calif., Berkeley, 1977-78; sr. engr. Instrument divsn. Hitachi Ltd., Tokyo, 1983-91, chief rsch. scientist Ctrl. Rsch. Lab., 1992-98; gen mgr. Advanced Rsch. Lab., 1999—; prof. Rsch. Inst. Electronic Sci. Hakkaido U., Sapporo, Japan, 1995-97, Grad. Sch. of Arts and Scis., U. Tokyo, Japan, 1998—; spkr. in field. Inventor in field; contbr. articles to profl. jours. and Ency. Analytical Sci., 1995. Exec. com. mem. Centennial Radium Discovery, Tokyo, 1996-99. Recipient sci. and tech. min.'s prize Ministry Internat. Trade and Industry, 1976, 83, Ohkochi Meml. prize in Tech. Ohkochi Meml. Found., 1977, 2000. Mem. Chem. Soc. Japan (trustee), Soc. Computer-aided Surgery (bd. dirs.), Japan Soc. Analytical Chemistry (trustee, Soc. prize 1976). Buddhism. Avocations: music, art, martial arts (Iai-do). Office: Hitachi Ltd Adv Rsch Lab, Hatoyama, Saitama 350-0395, Japan

KOIZUMI, HITOSHI, chemist; b. Yokohama, Japan, Apr. 19, 1957; s. Isamu and Haruno (Hosaka) K.; m. Nobuko Sanuki Koizumi, Nov. 6, 1988. BS, Tokyo Inst. Tech., 1980, MS, 1982, DSc, 1988. JSPS fellow Tokyo Inst. Technology, 1984; instr. faculty of engring. Hokkaido U., Sapporo, Japan, 1984-97; assoc. prof. Hokkaido U., Sapporo, 1997—; guest scientist Hahn-Meitner Inst., Berlin, Germany, 1990-91. Contbr. articles to profl. jours. Office: Grad Sch Engring, Hokkaido University, Sapporo 060-8628, Japan

KOIZUMI, MASATOSHI, linguist; b. Sendai, Japan, June 10, 1964; s. Toshiharu and Shizuka (Sato) K. BA, Internat. Christian U., Tokyo, 1988; MA, Ohio State U., 1991; PhD, MIT, 1995. Asst. prof. Tohoku Gakuin U., Sendai, Japan, 1995-96, assoc. prof., 1996-00; assoc. prof. Tohoku U., Sendai, Japan, 2000—. Author: Phrase Structure in Minimalist Syntax, 2000; editor: Formal Approaches to Japanese Linguistics 1, 1994, Formal Approaches to Japanese Linguistics 2, 1996. Mem. AAAS, Linguistics Soc. Am., Linguistics Soc. Japan. Avocations: mountain climbing, tennis. Office: Tohoku U, Kawauchi Aoba-ku, Sendai 980-8576, Japan

KOJ, ALEKSANDER, biochemistry educator, researcher; b. Gana, Poland, Feb. 26, 1935; s. Franciszek and Zofia (Stachowiak) K.; m. Anna Marchlewska; 1 child, Justina. MD, Kraków U., 1957; DSc, Jagiellonian U., Kraków, 1968; PhD (hon.), Cleve. State U., 1990, U. Hartford, 1995, SUNY, Buffalo, 1998. Asst. Med. Acad., Kraków, 1957-68; assoc. prof. Jagiellonian U., 1969-76, prof., 1976—, dir. Inst. of Molecular Biology, 1977-81, prorector, 1984-87, rector, 1987-90, 1993-99. Co-author, co-editor: The Acute Phase Response to Injury and Infection, 1985. Rsch. grantee Nat. Sci. Found., Kraków, 1975, Nat. Inst. of Health, Kraków, 1980; recipient Ont. Heart Found. award, Hamilton, 1983, Polish Sci. Found. award, 1996, Jurzykowski Found. award, 1998. Mem. Biochem. Soc. U.K., Polish Biochem. Soc. (chmn. Kraków br. 1972-75), Polish Acad. Scis., Acad. Scis. & Lettres (Kraków). Roman Catholic. Avocations: music, touring. Home: 13 Mickiewicza Ave, 31-120 Cracow Poland Office: Jagiellonian U, 3 Mickiewicza Ave, 31-120 Cracow Poland

KOJAC, JEFFREY STANLEY, military officer; b. L.A., Nov. 30, 1967. BA, St. John's Coll., Annapolis, Md., 1989; cert., Amphibious Warfare Sch., 1992, Marine Aviation Tactics Sch., 1997, MIT, 1998. Commd. 2d lt. USMC, 1989, advanced through grades to maj., 1999; instr. Marine Corps Comm.-Electronics Sch., 1993-96; comdr. Tactical Air Ops. Ctr., 1997-99; staff writer Commandant of the Marine Corps, 1999. Contbr. articles, revs. to U.S. Naval Inst. Procs., Mil. Rev., Airpower Jour., Parameters, Talon, Marine Corps Gazette, Naval War Coll. Rev., Joint Force Quar. Participant Pacific Coun. on Internat. Policy, L.A., 1995-96. Recipient Navy Commendation medal, USMC, 1996, 99, Navy Achievement medal, 1998. Mem. U.S. Naval Inst., Marine Corps Assn., Soc. for Mil. History.

KOJEVNIKOV, ALEXEI BORISOVICH, historian, educator; b. Moscow, USSR, Aug. 25, 1961; s. Boris Ivanovich and Natalia Nikolaevna (Mel'nikova) K.; m. Olga Viktorovna Schipacheva, 1982 (div. 1986); children: Kojevnikov, Dmitri Alexeevich. MS, Moscow State U., 1984; PhD, Inst. History Sci. Tech., Moscow, 1989. Jr. rsch. assoc. Inst. History Sci. Tech., Moscow, 1985-91; asst. prof. Moscow State U., Russia, 1991-92; Humboldt fellow Max-Planck Inst. Physics, Munich, 1991-93; fellow Ind. U., Bloomington, 1994-95; assoc. historian Am. Inst. Physics, College Park, Md., 1997—; rsch. assoc. Inst. History Sci. Tech., Moscow, 1991—. Author: Rockefeller Philanthropies and Soviet Science, 1993; editor: Paul Dirac and Physics of the 20th Century, 1990; contbr. articles to profl. jours. Mem. Am. Assn. Advancement Slavic Studies, History Sci. Soc. Avocations: hiking. Home: 625 Hauser Blvd Apt 306 Los Angeles CA 90036-3746 Office: Am Inst Physics Physics Ellipse College Park MD 20740

KOJEVNIKOV, BORIS OLEG, lawyer, foreign legal consultant; b. Rome, Oct. 16, 1950; came to U.S., 1977; s. Oleg Vladimir and Oxana (Artem) K.; m. Irina Maxim Baranova, Aug. 8, 1974; children: Oxana, Oleg. Law Degre, Inst. Fgn. Rels., Moscow, 1972, Cand Legal Scis., 1984. Legal adviser USSR Ministry Fgn. Trade, Moscow, 1972-77, Amtorg Trading Corp., N.Y.C., 1977-82, Comecon, Moscow, 1982-84; dir. legal dept. Chamber Commerce and Industry, Moscow, 1984-91; v.p. Prosystem GmbH, Vienna, 1991-96; v.p., mem. Golubov & Tiagai, N.Y.C., 1996—; arbitrator Internat. Comml. Arbitration ct., Moscow, 1984—, Internat. Arbitration Ctr., Vienna, 1989-94. Author 4 books; contbr. more than 20 articles to U.S., Russian and German periodicals. Fellow Chartered Inst. of Arbitrators; mem. Assn. Bar City N.Y., U.S.-USSR Trade and Econ. Coun. Inc. (USSR co-chmn. legal com. 1989-91), Canada-USSR Bus. Coun. (USSR co-chmn. legal com. 1989-91), Internat. Chamber of Commerce (USSR coord. ICC-USSR joint task force, 1989-90). Avocations: tennis, squash. Home: 7 Summit St Englewd Clfs NJ 07632-1443 Office: Golubov & Tiagai PLLC 475 5th Ave Rm 1112 New York NY 10017-6220

KOJIĆ-PRODIĆ, BISERKA, chemist; b. Aug. 29, 1938; married, Apr. 19, 1968; 1 child, Kristina. Degree in sci., U. Zagreb, Croatia, 1960. Technician dept. structural and inorganic chemistry U. Uppsala, Sweden, 1960-61, postdoctoral rsch. assoc. chemistry, 1972; rsch. asst. Ruder Bošović Inst., Zagreb, 1961-68, rsch. assoc., 1968-76, sr. rsch. assoc., 1976-81, sr. scientist dept. material scis., head of X-ray lab., 1981-97; sr. scientist dept. phys. chemistry Lab. for Chem. and Biocrystallography, Zagreb, 1991-94, head, 1997—; mem. faculty natural scis. Ruder Bošović Inst., Zagreb; head nat. Affiliated Ctr. Cambridge Crystallographic Data Ctr., 1987—; coord., prin. investigator European com. EU, 1991-94; vis. scientist U. Utrecht, The Netherlands, 1983-84, Synchrotron Sta. DESY, Hamburg, 1988; vis. scientist Med. Found. Buffalo, 1976-77, Tex. Christian U., Ft. Worth, 1976-77. Contbr. sci. articles to internat. jours. Recipient Nat. Sci. award Nat. Sci. Adv. Bd., Zagreb, 1971, award Nat. Acad. Sci. and Art, 1997. Mem. Internat. Union Crystallography Commn. on Chem. Crystallography. Office: Rudjer Bošković Inst, Bijenička 54 POB 1016, 41001 Zagreb Croatia

KOJIMA, AKINORI, public health counselor, pathologist; b. Yao, Osaka, Japan, Nov. 2, 1943; s. Takaji and Kazuko Taguchi K.; m. Yukiko Tanaka, Nov. 2, 1973; children: Tomoko, Reishi. MD, Kyoto U., 1968, D.Med.Sci., 1977. Rschr. Aichi Cancer Ctr. Rsch. Inst., Nagoya, Japan, 1971-77, sr. rschr., 1977-90; dir. Environ. Health Dept. Nagoya City Pub. Health Rsch. Inst., 1990-93; dir. Nagoya City Moriyama Health Ctr., 1993-94; counselor pub. health Pub. Health Bur., City of Nagoya, 1994-97; dir. Nagoya City Pub. Health Rsch. Inst., 1997—; vis. investigator Jackson Lab., Bar Harbor, 1978-80. Recipient Eleanor-Roosevelt fellowship UICC, 1978. Achievements include the establishment of exptl. models of organ-specific autoimmune diseases in mice. Office: Nagoya City Pub Health Rsch Inst, 1-11 Hagiyama-cho Mizuho-ku, 467-8615 Nagoya Aichi, Japan

KOJIMA, HIROSHI, hematologist, educator; b. Osaka, Japan, Dec. 18, 1958; s. Takashi and Kaoru (Hiro) K.; m. Hisako Hoshino, June 15, 1987; children: Mariko, Yuriko. MD, U. Tsukuba, Japan, 1984, PhD, 1990. Rsch. fellow Blood Ctr. Southea. Wis., 1992-94; asst. prof. hematology U. Tsukuba, 1990—. Contbr. articles to med. jours. Mem. Am. Soc. Hematology, Japanese Soc. Hematology, Japanese Soc. Internal Medicine. Office: Univ Tsukuba Div Hematology, Inst Clin Medicine, Ibaraki Tsukuba 305-8575, Japan

KOJIMA, KAZUO, chemist, materials scientist, researcher; b. Togakushi Village, Nagano, Japan, May 18, 1953; s. Morizoh and Machiko Kojima; m. Tomoko Yotsuji, Nov. 1, 1980; children: Aoi, Moeru. BS, Ritsumeikan U., Kyoto, Japan, 1977; MS, Kyoto U., 1979, DS in Inorganic Chemistry, 1988. Rsch. assoc. Ritsumeikan U., 1979-91; assoc. prof. chemistry Ritsumeikan U., Kusatsu, Japan, 1991-99; prof. chemistry Ritsumeikan U., Kusatsu, 1999—; part-time lectr. Kyoto U., 1996-99. Contbr. articles to profl. jours. Mem. Chem. Soc. Japan, Phys. Soc. Japan, Soc. Glass Tech. Office: Ritsumeikan U Dept Chem, 1-1-1 Noji-higashi, Kusatsu, Shiga 525-8577, Japan

KOJIMA, MASAKAZU, electrical and mechanical engineer; b. Kanasawashi, Japan, July 24, 1944; s. Norimasa and Suzuko (Nakayama) K.; m. Yukiko Wakimoto, May 5, 1974; children: Yumi, Yun. B of Engring., Kanazawa U., 1967, M of Engring., 1969; D, Tohoku U., 1975. D. Instr. Kanazawa (Japan) U., 1969-72; mgr. rsch. and devel. Nakamura-Tome Machine Tools, Kanazawa, 1972-73; assoc. prof. Tohoku U., Sendai, Japan, 1973-87; dir. Sanyo Denki Co., Tokyo, 1987-95; cons. M & Y Co., 1995-98; dir. R&D Wittenstein GmbH & Co. KG, Igeisheim, Germany, 1999—; guest prof. Skinsyuu U., Nagano, Japan, 1993-94; rschr. German univ., industry, 1974-75, 78-80. Buddhist. Home: Nishi-Ochiai 4-23-14, Shinjyuku Tokyo 161, Japan

KOJIMA, SEIJI, physicist, educator; b. Tokyo, Apr. 22, 1951; s. Shoji and Akiko (Nishi) K.; m. Toshiko Iiyama, Nov. 1984; 1 child, Takahiko. BS, U. Tokyo, 1974, DSc, 1979. Rsch. assoc. U. Tsukuba, 1980-81, asst. prof., 1981-94, assoc. prof., 1994—; sec. Optical Soc. Japan, 1986-88, Japan Soc. Cakorimeery and Thermal Analysis, 1999—; mem. program com. Symposium on Ultrasonic Electronics, 1993—, World Conf. on Ultrasonics, 1996—, Japan-Russia Symposium on Ferroelectrics, 1997-98. Editor Jour. Spectroscopy Soc. Japan, 1988-93, Jour. of the Phys. Soc. of Japan, 1998—; contbr. articles to profl. jours. Foster parent Foster Plan Soc., 1991—. Grantee Murata Sci. Found., 1990, Asahi Glass Found., 1991, Nippon Sheet Glass Found., 1994, Japan Securities Scholarship Found., 1996, Ogasawara Sci. Found., 1997, Applied Materials Found., 1998. Mem. Phys. Soc. of Japan, Japan Soc. of Applied Physics, Chem. Soc. of Japan, Laser Soc. Japan. Buddhist. Avocation: travel. Home: 11-3 Migimomi Tsuchiura, Ibaraki 300-0837, Japan Office: Materials Sci U Tsukuba, Tsukuba, Ibaraki 305-8573, Japan

KOJIMA, TAKUJI, chemist, researcher; b. Tokyo, Mar. 18, 1956; s. Shoji and Akiko (Nishi) K.; m. Miyako Okita, Apr. 21, 1983; children: Kei, Midori, Nodoka, Kaoru. B in Engring., Waseda U., Tokyo, 1979; D in Engring., U. Tokyo, 1994. Rschr. Japan Atomic Energy Rsch. Inst., Takasaki, 1979-93, sr. rschr., 1994-98, prin. rschr., 1999—. Contbr. articles to profl. jours. Mem. ASTM, Japan Soc. Applied Physics, Atomic Energy Soc. Japan. Buddhist. Avocations: chess, flower gardening. Home: 6-10 Ukechi, Takasaki Gunma 370-0067, Japan Office: Japan Atomic Energy Rsch Inst, 1233 Watanuki, Takasaki Gunma 370-1292, Japan

KOJIMA, TOSHIHARU, poet, educator; b. Gifu, Japan, Apr. 27, 1934; s. Kazuo and Fumi (Fujita) K.; m. Miyoko Kimura, June 12, 1977; children: Jun, Kawori. B in Lit., Waseda U., 1957; M in Lit., Grad. Sch. of Waseda, 1960. Instr. Tokyo Kasey Gakuin U., 1965—, asst. prof., 1974-80, prof., 1981—; part-time lectr. Waseda U., Tokyo, 1971—. Author: The Noble Demon, 1976, (poems) The Songs of Winds, 1988; transl. Poems (Jean Genet), 1967, Paulina 1880 (P.J. Jouve), 1973, Baphomet (P. Klossowsky), 1985, A Skylark in Assisi (poems), 1998, The Little Prince for Grown-up Persons, 2000. Mem. Japanese Soc. of French Lang. and Lit., The Collegium Mediterranitarum, The Writers' Assn. Home: 1-15-8 Jindaiji Kita, Chofu Tokyo 182-0011, Japan Office: 2600 Aihara Machida, Tokyo 194-0002, Japan

KOJIRI, TOSHIHARU, civil engineering educator; b. Kyoto, Japan, Apr. 7, 1948; s. Riichi and Sada (Hattori) K.; m. Junko Yasuda; children: Tomoko, Yoko. B of Engring., Kyoto (Japan) U., 1972, M of Engring., 1974, DEng, 1981. Rsch. asst. Kyoto (Japan) U., 1974-81, assoc. prof., 1981-85; assoc. prof. Gifu (Japan) U., 1985-92, prof., 1992-97; prof. Kyoto (Japan) U., 1997—; vis. assoc. prof. U. Waterloo, Can., 1987-88. Editor: (book) Applications of Artificial Intelligence in Water Resources Management, Applications of Fuzzy Theory and Pattern Recognition into Hydrological Events, 1992, Water Internat., 1998—. Mem. Japan Soc. Civil Engring. (sec. 1995), Japan Fuzzy Soc. (com. mem. 1989-97, Japan Soc. Hydrology and Water Resources (bd. mem. 1999—), Internat. Assn. of Hydrol. Sci., Internat. Water Resources Assn. (bd. mem.), Internat. Assn. Hydraulic Rsch. (com. mem. 1996—), Sci. Coun. Japan (mem. expert of water resources 1998—). Avocations: tennis, drive, gardening, music (jazz). Office: Water Resources Rsch Ctr, Kyoto U Gokasyo, Uji 611-0011, Japan

KOK, FRANS JOHAN, investment banker; b. Zaandam, Netherlands, May 14, 1943; came to U.S., 1963; s. Cornelis and Aaf K.; m. Mary M. Shirley, Dec. 23, 1971. BA in Econ., Occidental Coll., L.A., 1967; MA in Econs., Calif. State U., L.A., 1969; MBA, Insead, Fontainebleau, France, 1971, Harvard U., 1972. Assoc. Booz, Allen & Hamilton, Washington, 1974-78; chief economist EPA, Washington, 1978-80; CFO, co-founder Long Lake Energy Corp., N.Y.C., 1980-83; mng. dir. Ferris, Baker-Watts, Inc., Balt., 1983-89, 1st Nat. Bank Md., Balt., 1989-94; chmn., CEO, Johan Hekelaar, Inc., Chevy Chase, Md., 1994—; bd. dirs. MaxPitch Media, Inc., Fairfax, Va. Home: PO Box 1256 Purcellville VA 20134-1256

KOK, WILLEM, prime minister of The Netherlands; b. Bergambacht, The Netherlands, Sept. 29, 1938; married; 3 children. Student, Nijenrode Bus. Sch. Asst. internat. officer constrn. sect. Netherlands Fedn. Trade Unions, 1961-65, econ. officer, then sec. sect., 1965-69, sec. of Fedn., then vice chmn., 1969-73, chmn., 1973-75; chmn. Fedn. Netherlands Trade Unions, 1975-79, European Trade Union Confedn., 1979-82, Labor Party, 1986-89; vice chmn. Socialist Internat., 1989; dep. prime min., min. fin. Govt. of The Netherlands, The Hague, 1989-94, prime min., min. gen. affairs, 1994—; former vice chmn. Socio-Econ. Coun.; former employees' chmn. Joint Indsl. Labor Coun.; former vice chmn. bank couns. Nederlandsche Bank; vis. lectr. Inst. for Social Studies. With Netherlands Army. Office: Office of Prime Minister, Binnenhof 20, PO Box 20001, 2513 AA The Hague The Netherlands*

KOKAWA, HIROYUKI, engineering educator; b. Tsu City, Mie, Japan, Jan. 28, 1952; s. Toshio and Chieko (Noda) K.; m. Taeko Sakuma, Mar. 9, 1980; children: Kazuho, Mitsuha. B of Engring., Tohoku U., Sendai, Japan, 1974, M of Engring., 1976, PhD in Engring., 1979. Rsch. instr. Tohoku U., Sendai, 1979-84, assoc. prof., 1984-95, prof., 1995—; vis. scientist U. Toronto, Can., 1989-90. Tech. advisor Miyagi Prefectural Govt., Japan, 1994—. Recipient Silver medal Honda Meml. Found., 1981, Acad. Achievement prize Japan Inst. Materials, 1995. Mem. Am. Welding Soc. (Prof. Masubuchi award 1992), Japan Welding Soc. (mem. council bd. 1995—), Minerals, Metals, Materials Soc. Avocations: tennis, swimming, hiking, classical music, traveling. Home: 3-20-25 Kaigamori, Aoba-ku Sendai 981-0942, Japan Office: Grad Sch Engring, Aoba-yama 02 Tohoku Univ, 980-8579 Sendai Miyagi Japan

KOKHANOVSKY, ALEXANDER A., physicist; b. Ivenez, Belarus, June 4, 1961; s. Anatolii A. and Nadezda V. (Kovrova) K.; m. Marina L. Bulash, Jan. 30, 1982; children: Andrew, Maria. MS, Belarussian U., Minsk, Belarus, 1983; PhD, Inst. Phys., Minsk, Belarus, 1991. Rschr. Inst. Physics, Minsk, Belarus, 1983—, NASDA, Tokyo, 1996-97, Tech. U., Clausthal, Germany, 1997-98, Imperial Coll., London, 1999-2000. Author: Light Scattering Media Optics, 1999; contbr. articles to profl. jours. Sci. Tech. Agy. Japan fellow, Tokyo, 1996, Alexander von Humboldt fellow, Bonn, 1997, EPSRC fellow, London, 1999. Mem. IEEE, Am. Geophys. Union, European Geophys. Union, Belarussian Phys. Soc. Avocations: swimming, sauna, reading, chess, travel.

KOKITA, TOSHIO, food and pharmaceutical company executive; b. Shinagawa, Tokyo, Japan, Nov. 10, 1949; s. Masao and Ai (Handa) K.; m. Sachiko Kawahara, Apr. 29, 1975; children: Takashi, Ayako. BSc, Nihon U., Tokyo, 1972. Diplomate in agr. With R&D dept. S.S. Pharm. Co., Ltd., Tokyo, 1972-90; bd. dirs., v.p. Nutrichem Diat Pharma GmbH, Roth, Germany, 1990—. Contbr. articles to Jour. Pharmacology and Therapeutics, Jour. Nara Med. Assn., Gekkan Keidanren. Avocations: reading, tennis, opera, cooking. Home: Klosterfeldstr 2, 91180 Heideck Germany Office: Nutrichem Diat Pharma GmbH, Am Espan 1-3, 91154 Roth Germany

KOKKAS, VASSILIOS, composer; b. Athens, Greece, Sept. 30, 1965; arrived in Germany, 1990; s. Christos B. and Astrid (Nehrig) K. Grad. in Fugue, Contemporary Conservatory, Athens, 1990; grad. in Composition, Berlin Sch. Arts, Germany, 1996. Artistic dir. Ensemble Mosaik for Contemporary Music Berlin Sch. Arts, 1997—; artist-in-residence Kultur Fonds Found., 2000. Composer Circular Music for Orch., Agapi Ston Kremno (City Plans of Thessaloniki), 1996-99, Cultural Capital of Europe, 1997, Bravo Juliett-Les Anges Sont Blancs, 1998, 4 Time Space Studies, 1999, Sounding Spaces, 1999; creator internat. performances of instrumental and electroacoustic works, sound installations, computer and film music, 1990—, Tchg. music and Architecture at Berlin Sch. of Arts, 1998—. Berlin Acad. Arts scholar, 1998. Mem. Soc. Musical Performing Rights and Mech. Reprodn. Rights, Internat. Computer Music Assn., Greak Soc. Aesthetics, Berliner Soc. Contemporary Music (internat. sect.). Avocations: languages, philosophy. Home and Office: Manteuffelstr.68, 10999 Berlin Germany

KOKKINAKIS, GEORGE, electrical engineering educator; b. Chios, Greece, Mar. 17, 1937; s. Constantine and Artemis Kokkinakis; m. Maria D. Los, Sept. 7, 1968; children: Artemis, Costas. Diploma in Elec. Engring., Tech. U., Munich, 1961, Dr. in Engring., 1966, Diploma in Engring. Econs., 1967. Engr. Ministry of Coord., Athens, Greece, 1968-70; prof. elec. engring. U. Patras, Greece, 1970—, dean engring. faculty, 1975-76, head elec. engring. dept., 1989-91; dir. Wire Comm. Lab., Patras, 1970—. Author: Telephony, 1978, Electrotechnology, 1979, Telecommunication Systems, 1988; contbr. over 200 articles to profl. jours. Lt. Tech. Corps, Greek Army, 1962-64. Mem. IEEE (sr.), VDE, Tech. Chamber of Greece, SEFI, Hellenic Ops. Rsch. Soc. Greek Orthodox. Office: Univ of Patras, Rion, 26500 Achaia Patras Greece

KOKOSZKA, ANDRZEJ WLODZIMIERZ, psychiatrist, psychotherapist, psychologist; b. Oswiecim, Poland, May 9, 1957; s. Wlodzimierz and Maria (Bisaga) K.; m. Bogna Ewa Opolska, Oct. 4, 1981; children: Agata, Jakub. MD, Copernicus Sch. Medicine, Krakow, Poland, 1981; MA in Psychology, Jagiellonian U., 1984; PhD, Copernicus Sch. Medicine, 1991. From asst. to lectr. Collegium Medicum Jagiellonian U., Krakow, 1982-95;

psychotherapeutic tng. Inst. of Group Analysis, Heidelberg, Germany; assoc. prof. Med. U. Warsaw, Poland, 1996-99, prof., 1999—, head II dept. psychiatry, 2000—. Author: An Introduction to Psychotherapy, 1990, To Understand in Order to Cure and Support: Psychotherapy According to Kepinski, 1996 (Award 1997), An Integrating Model of Mental States: A Neojacksonian-psychodynamic Approach, 1997; contbr. articles to profl. jours. on consciousness and psychotherapy. Mem. Polish Psychiat. Assn. (psychotherapy sect.), N.Y. Acad. Scis. Avocations: skiing, sailing. Office: Med U Warsaw II/Dept Psyc, ul Nowowiejska 27, 00-665 Warsaw Poland

KOKOT, FRANCISZEK JÓZEF, nephrology educator; b. Olesno, Silesia, Poland, Nov. 24, 1929; s. Franciszek and Franciszka (Kostka) K.; m. Malgorzata Skrzypczyk, Dec. 26, 1955; children: Stefan, Klaudiusz, Jan, Tomasz. Physician diploma summa cum laude, Silesian Sch. Medicine, Katowice, Poland, 1953, MD, 1957; Dr. h.c. (hon.), Med. Acad. Wroclaw, 1990, Med. Acad. Katowice, 1993, Pomeranian Med. Acad., Szczecin, 1995, U. Kosice, Slovakia, 1997, Med. Acad. Lublin, 1997, Med. Acad. Warsaw, 1999, Jagielloman U., Cracow, 2000. Technician dept. chemistry Silesian Sch. Medicine, Katowice, 1949-50, asst. and sr. asst. dept. pharmacology, 1950-57, asst. prof. dept. internal medicine, 1957-62, assoc. prof. dept. internal medicine, 1962-69, extraordinary prof. dept. internal medicine, 1969-74, extraordinary prof. dept. nephrology, 1974-82, ordinary prof. dept. nephrology, 1982—; rsch. fellow Clinique Therapeutique, Geneva, 1958-59; WHO fellow Middlesex Hosp., London, 1970. Mem. European Dialysis and Transplant Assn., Polish Acad. Scis., Polish Acad. Arts and Scis.; hon. mem. Bulgarian Soc. Nephrology, German Soc. Nephrology, Yugoslavian Soc. Nephrology, Hungarian Soc. Nephrology, Macedonian Soc. Nephrology, Italian Soc. Nephrology, Czechoslovakia Soc. Nephrology, Romanian Soc. Nephrology. Roman Catholic. Home: Al Korfantego, 40-004 Katowice Poland Office: Silesian Sch Medicine, Francuska 20 Dept Nephrol, 40-027 Katowice Poland

KOKUBO, HIDEYUKI, editor, parapsychologist; b. Toyohashi, Aichi-ken, Japan, Oct. 23, 1958; s. Sachio and Humiko (Yamashita) K. BSc, Nagoya (Japan) U., 1981. Mem. editorial staff Sanseido Co., Ltd., Tokyo, 1981-96; guest rsch. assoc. Nat. Inst. Radiol. Scis., Chiba-shi, Japan, 1996—; lectr. Tokai Women's Jr. Coll., 1996-2000, Meiji U., 1998—; presenter in field. Mem. editorial staff: Shousetu-Kagaku, 1990; editl. mgr. Jour. Soc. Life Info. Sci.; editor Japanese Jour. Parapsychology. Mem. Nat. League for Support of Sch. Textbook Screening Suit, Tokyo, 1981. Mem. Japanese Soc. Parapsychology (chmn. summer seminar 1989, chmn. conv. 1991, bd. dirs. 1991—), Parapsychol. Assn., Japan Inst. Hypnosis, Parapsychology Rsch. Room (chmn. 1991—). Avocations: UFO research, Igo. Office: Bio-Emission Lab Nat Inst Radiol Scis, Anagawa 4-9-1, Inaga Chiba 263-8555, Japan

KOKUBO, HIROYASU, pharmacist, researcher; b. Nagoya, Japan, Nov. 6, 1958; s. Yukimasa and Ikuko (Hasegawa) K.; m. Miyuki Kobayashi, Mar. 19, 1988; 3 children. BS in Pharmacy, Shizuoka Coll. Pharmacy, 1982, MS in Organic Chemistry, 1984, PhD in Pharm. Tech., 1998. Rschr. Shin-Etsu Chem. Co., Niigata, 1988-95, sr. rschr., 1995—. Contbr. articles to profl. jours. including Chem. Pharm. Bull. Patentee in field. Mem. Std. Formation Rsch. Assn. (com. 1988—). Avocation: ship model. Home: 8-5 Sanae, Joetsu Niigata 942-0031, Japan Office: Shin-Etsu Chem Co Ltd, 28-1 Nishifukushima, Niigata 942-0031, Japan

KOKUINA, ELENA, immunologist, educator; b. Moscow, June 30, 1955; arrived in Cuba, 1966; d. Victor Lapshuk and Sofia Kokuina; 1 child, Daniel. MD, Inst. Med. Scis. Havana, Cuba, 1980; immunologist 1st degree, Pub. Health Ministry, Havana, 1983, immunologist 2d degree, 1990. Immunologist Inst. Hematology and Immunology, Havana, 1980-83; head Immunology Lab., Hermanos Ameijeiras Hosp., Havana, 1983—; instr. immunology Inst. Med. Scis. Havana, 1990—. Contbr. articles to med. jours. Mem. Cuban Immunology Soc. Avocations: swimming, reading, playing with her son. Home: 7A 6606, Playa, Havana 13, Cuba Office: HCQ Hnos Ameijeiras, San Lazaro 701, Havana 10300, Cuba

KOLA, ISMAIL, genetics educator; b. Johannesburg, South Africa, Jan. 30, 1957; s. Sarah Kola. BSc, U. South Africa, 1981; BPharm cum laude, Rhodes U., 1982; PhD, U. Cape Town, 1985. Rsch. fellow Centre for Early Human Devel. Monash U., Clayton, 1985-97, sr. rsch. fellow, 1987-93, reader in mol. genetics and devel. biology Inst. Reprodn., 1994-97, assoc. dir., 1994—, prof. human mol. genetics, 1997-2000; vice pres. rsch., global head genomics Pharmacia & Upjohn, Kalamazoo, Mich., 2000—; cons., mem. genomics adv. bd. SmithKline Beecham Pharms., Phila., 1994-97. Contbr. articles to profl. jours. Sec. South Africa ANC, Melbourne, Australia group, 1986-90; pres. Black Students Soc., Johannesburg, 1975-77; del. mem. South Africa Students Com., Johannesburg, 1975-77; patron Opera Australia, Melbourne, 1998. Recipient Bronte Stewart prize for the Most Meritorius PhD, U. Cape Town, 1985, Westpac/amgen award Australian Soc. for Med. Rsch., 1995, Silver Jubilee Rsch. prize Monash U., 1996. Office: Pharmacia & Upjohn 301 Henrietta St Kalamazoo MI 49007-4940

KOLACHEV, BORIS ALEXANDEROVICH, metallurgist, educator, researcher; b. Kimri, Russia, Apr. 4, 1928; s. Alexander Petrovich and Maria Yakovlevna (Rumjanzeva) K.; m. Galina Vasiljevna Sinizina, Dec. 29, 1952; children: Svetlana, Julia. Degree in engring., Moscow Inst. Aircraft Tech., 1952, MS, 1955, DSc in Phys. Metallurgy, 1967. Asst. Moscow Inst. Aircraft Tech. (now Russian State Technol. U.), 1955-58, sr. lectr., 1959-68, prof., 1968-90, honored prof., 1990—; expert high cert. com. Govt. USSR, Moscow, 1975-92; dep. chief com. phys. metallurgy High Edn. Ministry, USSR, 1972-90. Author: Hydrogen in Titanium, 1962, Hydrogen Embrittlement of Non-ferrous Metals, 1966, Physical Metallurgy of Titanium, 1974, Hydrogen Embrittlement of Metals, 1986, others; contbr. articles to profl. jours. Mem. N.Y. Acad. Sci. Home: Pobeda Prospekt 14-64, 142800 Stoopino Russia Office: Russian State Technol U, Pristanzionnaja St 27, 142800 Stoopino Russia

KOLACZ, JACEK TOMASZ, research scientist; b. Sosnowiec, Poland, Jan. 27, 1964; s. Jan and Barbara (Kruszec) K.; m. Joanna Nowak, June 15, 1989; children: Piotr, Julia. MSc in Mining and Metallurgy, U. Krakow, 1989; PhD, U. Tech., 1995. Sci. asst. Trondheim U. of Tech., Norway, 1990-95; rsch. scientist SINTEF Rsch. Orgn., Norway, 1995—. Contbr. articles to profl. jours.; patentee in field. Achievements include research in mineral processing, process control and instrumentation. Avocations: electronics, photography, piano. Office: Sintef, Forskningv 1, Oslo 0314, Norway

KOLAK, CZESLAWA, language professional, educator; b. Poland, June 20, 1948; d. Stefan Kardas and Aniela Fido; m. James Edward Kolak, Dec. 27, 1975; children: Anna, Marynia. BA in Polish Philosophy, Coll. Edn., Cracow, Poland, 1973; MA in Slavic Lang. & Lit., U. Ill., Chgo., 1976; MA in Sch. Adminstrn. & Supervision, Roosevelt U., 1996; postgrad., U. Chgo. Instr. lang. Northeastern U., Chgo., 1978-86, 99—, Loyola U., Chgo., 1987-94. Polish Club advisor Foreman H.S., Chgo., 1985—, coord. Close Ups Program New Ams., 1996. Recipient Commn. Nat. Edn. medal Nat. mInistry Edn. Poland, 1998; Nat. Fgn. Lang. Resoucre Ctr. grantee U. Hawaii, 1993. Mem. AAUW, TESOL, Polist Inst. Arts and Scis., Legion Young Polish Women, Nat. Assn. Bilingual Edn., Ill. Fgn. Langs. Assn., Esperanto Soc. Avocations: traveling, reading, religious and folk art. Office: Foreman HS 3235 N Le Claire Ave Chicago IL 60641

KOLÁŘ, IVAN, mathematics educator; b. Brno, Czech Republic, May 22, 1936; s. Josef and Eva (Hálová) K.; m. Jitka Sedláková; children: Martin, Eva. Grad. in math., Masaryk U., Brno, 1959, PhD, 1969; MS, Tech. U., Brno, 1966; DSc, Czech Acad. Scis., Prague, 1976. Asst. prof. Tech. U., Brno, 1959-69; rschr. Czech Acad. Scis., 1969-91; prof. Masaryk U., 1991—. Author: Introduction into Thom's Catastrophe Theory, 1988; co-author: Structured Bundles, Pitagora Editrice, 1991, Natural Operations in Differential Geometry, 1993, The Mathematical Legacy of Eduard Čech, 1993. Mem. Union Czech Mathematicians, Am. Math. Soc. Home: Kamenacky 43, 63600 Brno Czech Republic Office: Masaryk U, Janackovo nam 2A, 66295 Brno Czech Republic

KOLÁŘ, JAROMÍR JAN, radiologist; b. Ostrava, Czechoslovakia, July 30, 1926; s. František and Františka (Sywalová) K.; m. Olga Srbová, Dec. 15, 1962. MD, Charles U., Praha, Czechoslovakia, 1950, DMS, 1965. Intern Municipal Hosp. Usti nad Labem (Czech Republic), 1950-55; resident Radiol. Clin., Prague, 1951-58; radiodiagnostic dept radiological clin Charles U., Prague, 1955-76; from lectr. to assoc. prof. radiology Radiol. Clin. Praha, 1964-76; prof. radiology, head Clinic for Diagnostic Radiology Med. Sch. Praha, 1980—; vis. prof. Radiol. Clin., Nijmegen, Holland, 1968-69. Author: The Physical Agents and Bone, 1965 (Best Publ. award 1966), Whole-Body Skeletal Response in Local Bone Disease, 1981 (Czech Acad. Sci. award), Röntgendiagnostik Arbeitsbedingter Skelettleiden, 1981 (Czech. Med. Assn. award 1982); co-author: Encyclopaedia of Medical Radiology, 1977; Editor Czech. Radiology, 1980—. Recipient Boris Rajewski medal European Assn. Radiology, Austria, 1993. Mem. Czech. Radiol. Soc. (gen. sec. 1969—), Internat. Skeletal Soc., Internat. Radiol. Soc. Fax: 420-2-6608-3390. Home: Přesličková 5, 106 00 Praha 10, Czech Republic Office: Clin Diagnostic Radiology, Budínova 2, 180 81 Prague Czech Republic

KOLARZ, GERNOT, medical administrator, physician, researcher; b. Vienna, Austria, June 22, 1942; s. Herbert J. and Margit E. (Auer) K.; m. Anna Julcher, Apr. 8, 1969; 1 child, Barbara. MD, U. Vienna, 1966. Specialist internal medicine, rheumatology, nuclear medicine. Physician Elisabeth-Spital, Vienna, 1966; physician 2d Med. Clin. U., Vienna, 1966-72, asst. prof., 1972-73, assoc. prof., cons. rheumatology, 1973; rsch. fellow Meml. Mcpl., Taplow, U.K., 1973; med. dir. Rheuma-Sonderkrankenanstalt, Baden, Austria, 1978—. Co-editor Z. Rheumatologie, 19945; contbr. articles to profl. jours. Recipient Georg Grabner prize Faculty Medicine U. Vienna, 1993. Mem. Austrian Soc. Rheumatology (hon.; bd. dirs. 1975-94, pres. 1995-96, v.p. 1996-98), German Soc. Rheumatology, Inst. Rheumatology (sec. 19965). Avocations: photography, cycling, swimming. Office: Rheuma Sonderkrankenanstalt, A Malchergasse 1, A2500 Baden Austria

KOLAT, PAVEL, nuclear and thermal engineering executive; b. Ostrava, Czech Republic, July 21, 1943; s. Bronislav and Magda (Cerna) K.; m. Jarmila Sevcikova, Dec. 7, 1972; children: Boris, Libor. Diploma in engring., Tech. U., Ostrava, Czech Republic, 1967, PhD, 1975, DSc, 1991. Asst. prof. Tech. U., Ostrava, 1968-84, assoc. prof., 1984-93, head dept. power engring., 1991, prof. nuclear engring., 1993—; mgr. Acad. Sport Club, Ostrava, 1994; Czech del. program com. for energy European Commn., Brussels. Author: Heat and Mass Transfer, 1986; co-author: Power Machines and Air Conditioning Equipments, 1992. Capt. Czech Mil. Airforce, 1967-68. Named Hon. Citizen City of Knoxville, Tenn., 1997. Mem. Energy and Heat Assn. Democrat. Unitarian. Avocations: flight sports, mountaineering, traveling, painting. Home: Tesinska 1161, 739 34 Senov Czech Republic Office: Tech U Ostrava, 17 Listopadu Ave, 708 33 Ostrava-Poruba Czech Republic

KOLB, CHARLES CHESTER, humanities administrator; b. Erie, Pa., Sept. 4, 1940; s. John Christian and Edna Lucille (Church) K.; m. Joy Bilharz, June 3, 1972 (div. Mar. 1991); 1 child, Nancy Gwenyth; m. P. Jean Drew, July 20, 1991; 1 child, Catherine Claire Fraley. BA in History, Pa. State U., 1962, PhD in Archaeology and Anthropology, 1979. Instr. anthropology Pa. State U., University Park, 1966-69, Bryn Mawr (Pa.) Coll., 1969-73; from instr. to asst. prof. anthropology Pa. State U., Erie, 1973-84; dir. rsch. and grants Mercyhurst Coll., Erie, 1984-89, asst. dir. Hammermill Libr., 1989; humanities adminstr. program officer divsn. state programs NEH, Washington, 1989-91, program officer divsn. preservation and access, 1991-96, sr. program officer, 1997—; manuscript reviewer Holt, Rinehart and Winston, Inc., 1977-89, Prentice-Hall, Inc., 1979-85, William C. Brown, Pubs., 1982-85, U. Tex. Press, 1988—, U. Utah Press, 1991—, U. Press of Fla., 1994—, AltaMira Press/Sage, 1995—, U. Pa. Mus. Applied Sci. Ctr. Archaeology, 1996—, Dover Pub., 1996—; grant proposal reviewer NEH, 1981-89, NSF, 1982—, Wenner-Gren Found. for Anthropol. Rsch., 1987-89; co-founder, ann. symposium co-organizer Ceramic Studies Interest Group, 1986—. Author: Marine Shell Trade and Classic Teotihuacan, 1987; editor: A Pot for All Reasons, 1988, Ceramic Ecology, 1988, 89, 97; contbr. articles to profl. jours., chpts. to books; book and film reviewer Sci. Books and Films, 1977—; manuscript reviewer Am. Antiquity, 1978—, Current Anthropology, 1979—, Ancient Mesoamerica, 1990—, Ethnohistory, 1995—, Jour. Material Culture, 1995—, Hist. Archaeology, 1995—, L.Am. Antiquity, 1995—, H-NET Revs., 1996—, Jour. Archaeol. Sci., 1998—, H-NET Revs., 1996—; abstractor Ceramic Abstracts, 1990-96, Art and Archaeology Technical Abstracts, 1996—; regional editor La Tinaja: Newsletter of Archaeol. Ceramics, 1991—; N.Am. corr. Old Potter's Almanack, 1992—; reviewer CHOICE, 1992—, ScienceNETLinks, 1999—; contbr. Encyclopedia of Asia, 2000. Mem. Commonwealth Pa., Gov.'s Conf. on Librs. and Info. Systems, 1989. Mem. Am. Ceramic Soc., Am. Chem. Soc., Am. Ethnological Soc., Am. Soc. Ethnohistory, Archaeol. Inst. Am., Assn. Field Archaeology, Coun. Mus. Anthropology, Materials Rsch. Soc., Prehist. Ceramic Rsch. Group, Soc. Am. Archaeology, Soc. Archaeol. Scis. (life, assoc. editor for archaeol. ceramics Bull. 1997—), Soc. Hist. Archaeology, Soc. Am. Archivists, Register Profl. Archaeologists, U.S. Naval Inst. (life), Soc. for Pa. Archaeology, N.Y. State Archaeol. Assn., Paleopathology Assn., Pearl Harbor History Assocs. (life), Naval Hist. Found., Sigma Xi, Alpha Kappa Delta, Phi Kappa Phi, Pi Gamma Mu. Achievements include rsch. in tech. and cultural interpretations of archaeol. ceramics by using physiochem. analyses and petrographic microscopy, ceramics from Afghanistan, Ctrl. Asia, Mexico, Guatemala, East Africa, Great Lakes Basin. Home: 1005 Pruitt Ct SW Vienna VA 22180-6429 Office: NEH Divsn Preservation & Access 1100 Pennsylvania Ave NW Washington DC 20004-2501

KOLB, DEREK ANDREW, information systems specialist; b. Rochester, N.Y., July 14, 1964. BS in MIS, St. John Fisher Coll., 1986. Cert. netware engr.-intranetware; cert. network expert-CNX, Microsoft cert. profl. systems engr.; CISCO cert. network assoc.; CISCO cert. design assoc.; project mgmt. cert. program Project Mgmt. Ctr. of Excellence. Customer engr. JWP/Eastman Kodak, Rochester, 1990-92; PC specialist Prudential Bank, Atlanta, 1992-93; dir. info. tech. Zoo Atlanta, 1993—. Mem. IEEE, IEEE Computer Soc., Network Profl. Assn., Nat. Computer Security Assn, Project Mgmt. Inst. Home: 2575 Delk Rd SE Apt 1440D Marietta GA 30067-6526 Office: Zoo Atlanta 800 Cherokee Ave SE Atlanta GA 30315-1440

KOLB, ERICH FRIEDRICH, veterinary biochemist; b. Seibelsdorf, Bavaria, Germany, Apr. 7, 1927; s. Georg and Hedwig (Götz) K.; m. Helga Markert, Mar. 21, 1962; 1 child, Hans-Joachim. DVM, U. Munich, 1952, D.rer.nat., 1953; DVM habil., U. Leipzig, 1956; D.h.c., U. Bucarest, 1991. Asst. vet. U. Leipzig (Germany), 1954-56, lectr., 1956-57, asst. prof., 1957-61, prof. vet. biochemistry, 1961-92, prof. emeritus, 1992—; provisional dir. Inst. for Vet. Physiol. Chem. U. Leipzig, 1956-57, dir., 1957-92, dean vet. faculty, 1957-59, dep. dean, 1961-65. Author: Of the Life and the Behavior of Domestic Animals, 8th edit., 1987, Biochemistry and Pathobiochemistry of Domestic Animals, 2d edit., 1982; co-author: Physiological Chemistry, 8th edit., 1990; editor: Physiology of Domestic Animals, 4th edit., 1989; collaborator Rev. Jour. for Agrl. Scis., 1961-91; contbr. over 580 articles to profl. jours. With Germany Army, 1944-45. Mem. Sci. Soc. Vet. Medicine, Soc. of the Friends of the Vet. Med. Faculty of Leipzig. Lutheran. Avocations: music, natural sciences, popular publications on vitamins, nutrition and tumor research. Home: Maulwurfweg 2, D-04329 Leipzig Germany

KOLB, JOHN CARL, family therapist, minister; b. Bay City, Mich., Apr. 6, 1943; s. Carl Henry Edwin and Renate Marie (Krieger) K.; m. Malinda Marie Hartman, June 5, 1966 (div.); children: Rebecca Marie, Debra Renee, Charles, Walter; m. Charlene Gail Lieder Waterman, July 25, 1998; stepchildren: Kristi Michele, Scott Ryan, David John Waterman. BA, Concordia Sr. Coll., 1964; MDiv, Concordia Sem., St. Louis, 1968; MST, Christian Theol. Sem., Indpls., 1972; postgrad., McCormick Theol. Sem., 1975-76. Ordained to ministry Luth. Ch., 1968. Pastor Emanuel Luth. Ch., Arcadia, Ind., 1968-72; pres. Hamilton County (Ind.) Mental Health Assn., 1971-72; pastoral resident Luth. Gen. Hosp., Park Ridge, Ill., 1972-73; mental health therapist Northwestern Meml. Hosp. and Northwestern Inst. Psychiatry, Chgo., 1973-76; pastoral care fellow, chaplain Evanston (Ill.) Hosp., 1974-75, social worker, group therapist, asst. team leader Refocus Program, 1976-78; family therapist Luth. Child and Family Svcs., Indpls., 1978-98; pvt. practice marriage and family therapist, 1998-99; chaplain Regency Pl., Greenfield, 1998-99; pastor Grace Luth. Ch., Dyer, Ind., 1999—; pastor Hosanna Luth. Ch., Oaklandon, Ind., 1980-88; vis. prof. Concordia Theol. Sem., Ft. Wayne, 1984-86; pastoral advisor Ind., Ky Dist. Luth. Laymen's League; chmn. Ind. Dist. of LCMS Pastors and Wives Retreat Com.; pres. Trinity Luth. Parent Tchr. League, 1982-84; bus. and religion instr. Concordia U. Wis., Indpls., 1993-99; Ind. Dist. reconciler, 1993—. Contbr. articles to religious publs. Garret Theol. Sem. fellow, 1974-75. Mem. Am. Assn. Pastoral Counselors (pastoral affiliate), Am. Assn. Marriage and Family Therapists (clin.). E-mail: jck@gateway.net. Home: 8307 Sheffield Ave Dyer IN 46311-2752 Office: 8303 Sheffield Ave Dyer IN 46311-2752

KOLB, JOHN CONNER, financial markets executive; b. Dallas, Apr. 29, 1965; s. Nathaniel Key and Catherine Lou (Conner) K.; 1 child, Jane Catherine. BS in Econs., So. Meth. U., 1988. Spl. projects coord. Cystic Fibrosis Found., Bethesda, Md., 1988-90; head trader, securities lending Baring Securities, N.Y.C., 1990-93; regional head (Ams.) equity fin. Paribas Corp., N.Y.C., 1993-95; global head equity fin. Banque Paribas, London, 1995-98; head U.K., Europe Equity Fin. Commerzbank, London, 1998—; bd. mem. Equity Borrowers Working Com., London Investment Banking Assn., 1996-97. Com. mem. Cystic Fibrosis Found., 1990-95; mem. Oaklawn Tex. Found., Dallas, 1987—. Mem. Phi Theta Kappa. Avocations: skiing, jogging, tennis, motorcycling. Home: 14 Holland Park Rd, London W14 8LZ, England Office: Commerz Bank AG, 60 Gracechurch St, London EC3V 0HR, England

KOLB, LAWRENCE COLEMAN, psychiatrist; b. Balt., June 16, 1911; s. Lawrence and Lillian Hess (Coleman) K.; m. Madeleine Currie, July 3, 1937; children: Pamela Currie Leadbitter, Mary Clark Estes, Richard Jennings. BA, Trinity Coll., Dublin U., Ireland, 1932; MD, Johns Hopkins U., 1934; DSc (hon.), Albany Med. Coll., 1993, Columbia U., 1999. Diplomate: Am. Bd. Psychiatry and Neurology (dir. 1960-68, pres. 1968). Intern medicine, surgery Strong Meml. Hosp., Rochester, N.Y., 1934-36; fellow neurology Johns Hopkins U., 1936-38, instr., 1939-40; Markle fellow neurology Nat. Hosp. Queens Sq., Eng., 1938-39; psychiatrist Milw. Sanitorium, 1941; dir. research projects NIMH, also pvt. practice psychiatry, 1946-49; research assoc. Washington Sch. Psychiatry, 1946-49; cons. Mayo Clinic; also assoc. prof. psychiatry U. Minn., 1949-54; dir. N.Y. State Psychiat. Inst.; prof., chmn. dept. psychiatry Columbia U., 1954-75, prof. emeritus, 1975—, Lawrence C. Kolb prof. psychiatry Coll. Physicians and Surgeons, 1977; prof. Albany Med. Coll., 1978; dir. psychiat. service Presbyn. Hosp., N.Y.C., 1954-75; commr. N.Y. State Dept. Mental Hygiene, 1975-78; Disting. physician in psychiatry U.S. VA, 1978-88; pres. med. bd. Presbyn. Hosp., N.Y.C., 1962-64, trustee, 1971-73, hon. trustee, 1974—; prof. psychiatry Albany Med. Coll., 1978—; cons. nat. adv. council USPHS, HEW; mem. panel med. scis. to asst. sec. of def., 1954-60; mem. career investigator com. NIMH, 1956-60, chmn., 1962, mem. bd. sci. counsellors, 1959-62, chmn., 1962; mem. spl. adv. com. to commr. hosps., N.Y.C., 1961; mem. Salmon Com. Mental Hygiene; adv. bd. P.R. Inst. Psychiatry, 1972—. Author: (with O.R. Langworthy and L.G. Lewis) Physiology of Micturition, 1940, The Painful Phantom, 1954, Modern Clinical Psychiatry, 10th edit, 1982, (with L. Ruizin) The First Psychiatric Institute, 1993. Bd. dirs. Founds. Fund for Research in Psychiatry, 1959-61; bd. dirs., pres., chmn. bd. Research Found. for Mental Hygiene, 1960-76; trustee Austin Riggs Center, pres. 1983-85; trustee Silver Hill Found., 1967-74. Recipient Henry Wisner Meml. award, 1962; Oscar K. Diamond award, 1971; Joan Plehn award for human service Mental Health Assn. N.Y. and Bronx Counties, 1972; Richard H. Hutchings award N.Y. State Hosps. Alumni Assn., 1975; Dedication of Lawrence C. Kolb Research Lab. N.Y. State Psychiat. Inst., 1983, Paul H. Hoch Disting. Svc. award Office Mental Health, N.Y. State, 1990, Pioneer award Internat. Soc. Traumatic Stress, 1991. Fellow Am. Psychiat. Assn. (pres. 1968, Disting. Service award 1983), Am. Acad. Neurology, N.Y. Acad. Sci.; mem. Am. Coll. Psychiatry (Bowis award 1977), Am. Neurol. Assn., Am. Psychoanalytic Assn., Assn. Research Nervous and Mental Diseases (pres. 1969), Johns Hopkins Soc. Scholars, Sigma Xi, Alpha Omega Alpha. Clubs: Century Assn. (N.Y.C.), University (N.Y.C.); Vidonia Practioners. Home: PO Box 31187 Sea Island GA 31561-1187

KOLBASOV, BORIS NIKOLAYEVICH, nuclear engineer-physicist; b. Moscow, Nov. 7, 1929; s. Nikolaj Vasil'evich and Olga Flegontovna (Dobrotina) K.; m. Sophiya Alexandrovna Zhmayeva, Aug. 25, 1952; children: Yelena, Dmitrij, Anna. Engr.-physicist, Inst. of Mechanics, 1953; jr. scientist, Kurchatov Inst., 1963. Scientist Kurchatov Inst., Moscow, 1956-61, sr. engr., 1961-69, sr. scientist, 1974-76, 87—, divsn. dep. head, acting lab. head, 1976-87; sr. officer Internat. Atomic Energy Agy., Vienna, Austria, 1969-74; chmn. bd. coordinating for fusion reactor safety, Moscow, 1994—. Co-author: International Tokamak Reactor, 1979-88, International Thermonuclear Experimental Reactor Plant Systems, 1991; dep. editor-in-chief Problems of Atomic Science and Engineering: Series Thermonuclear Fusion, 1978—. Sec. Communist Party sect. orgn., Kurchatov Inst., 1965-66, Communist Party Inst. com. mem. 1979-91. Recipient medals Pres. of the Supreme Soviet of the USSR, 1970, 1985, medal Pres. Russian Fedn., 1997. Home: Rogov St 18-1-177, 123098 Moscow Russia Office: Kurchatov Inst, 1 Kurchatov Square, 123182 Moscow Russia

KOLBASOV, GRIGORY ALEXANDROVICH, zoologist, researcher; b. Moscow, July 17, 1967; s. Alexander Matveevich Kolbasov and Tatiana Vladimirovna Petrova; m. Svetlana Yurievna Nikiforova, Jan. 23, 1988 (div. Feb. 1995); 1 child, Vladimir; m. Natalia Alexandrovna Soprunova, Mar. 16, 1995; children: Matvei, Elizaveta. Grad., Moscow State U., 1989, PhD, 1992. Scientist staff Moscow State U., 1992—. Contbr. articles to profl. jours. Scholar Soros Fund, Moscow, 1992-93; grantee Russian Found. for Fundamental Sci., Moscow, 1997-98, 99—, Lerner-Gray Fund for Marine Rsch., N.Y., 1999. Avocations: sea diving, motoboard driving. Home: Ryazanskiy prospect 91 4 60, 109542 Moscow Russia Office: Dept Invertebrate Zoology, Moscow State U Biol Faculty, 119899 Moscow Russia

KOLBE, HARTMUT REINHOLD, agronomist, researcher; b. Woltrup-Wehbergen, Germany, Apr. 17, 1951; s. Reinhold and Rosalie (Hauck) K. Grad. agrl. engr., Engring. Coll. Agr., Osnabrück, Germany, 1976; grad. engr. agr., Georg-August U., Göttingen, Germany, 1980, D in Agrl. Sci., 1990. Jr. rschr. Inst. Agrl. Chemistry, U. Göttingen, 1980-91; sr. rschr. dept. soil culture and crop prodn. Saxony State Inst. for Agr., Leipzig, Germany, 1992—; vis. rschr. dept. physiology and plant nutrition Inst. for Potato Rsch. and Prodn., Brasov, Romania, 1980, 81, 82, 84; dir. rsch. working group on organic agr., dept. soil culture and crop prodn., Saxony State Inst. for Agr., Leipzig, 1992—; invited expert on the relation between agr. and environment Chinese Ministry of Agr./Chinese Acad. Agrl. Sci., Beijing, 1993, 95, 98, 99. Author: Potato Fertilization under Different Ecological Conditions, 1990, Weather Influences on Potato Yield and Composition, 1994, Potato Nutrition and Tuber Quality, 1995, Land Use and Water Protection, 2000; co-author: Plant Nutrition-Physiology and Applications, 1990, Ware Potatoes: Production, Quality, Storage, Marketing, 1997, Practical Estimates for Realizing an Environmental Sound Soil Cultivation, 1997; contbr. articles to profl. jours. Active Social Peace Svc., Hannover, Germany, 1971-73. Mem. AAAS, European Assn. for Potato Rsch., Internat. Fedn. Organic Agr. Movements, German Agrl. Assn. Office: Fachbereich Bodenkultur und, Pflanzenbau Gustav-Kuehn 8, D-04159 Leipzig Germany

KÖLBEL, FRANTIŠEK PAVEL, physician, researcher; b. Praha, Czech Republic, July 13, 1933; s. František Karel and Anna (Filipová) K.; m. Věra Pazourková, July 1, 1961; children: František, Věra. MD, Charles U., Praha, 1957, ScD, 1989. Staff doctor Mcpl. Hosp., Čáslav, Czechoslovakia, 1957-58; staff doctor 3rd med. dept. Faculty Medicine, Charles Univ., Praha, 1958-64, asst. prof., 1964-86, assoc. prof., 1986-90; assoc. prof., chief dept. medicine 2nd Faculty Medicine, Charles U., 1990-92, prof., chief dept. medicine, 1992—, chief dept. medicine, 1990-99. Author: Cardiac Hypertrophy, 1967; co-author: Stress, 1984, Endogenous Digitalis-Like Substance, 1988 (State award), Trends of Contemporary Cardiology, 1995, 2nd edit., 1999. Fellow Am. Coll. Cardiology; mem. Czech Soc. of Cardiology (vice chmn. 1991-93, treas. 1993-95), Assn. of Czech Physicians (chmn. 1994—), Czech Soc. of Cardiology (hon. 1993), Czech Soc. of Internal Medicine (hon. 1993), Assn. of Czech Physicians (chmn. 1994), Czech Soc. of Internal Medicine. Roman Catholic. Avocations: tennis, bicycle, hunting. Office: Dept Med 2d Fac Med, Charles U V uvalu 84, 150 18 Praha 5, Czech Republic

KOLCZYNSKI, CHARLOTTE ANN, music librarian; b. Buffalo, N.Y., Oct. 8, 1952; d. Henry Walter and Elizabeth Kolczynski; m. Arthur Joseph Ness, Dec. 29, 1982. BS in Music Edn., Rosary Hill Coll., 1974; MM in Music History, SUNY, Potsdam, 1978; MLS, SUNY, Buffalo, 1987. Music libr. SUNY, Buffalo, 1985-87; reference libr. music dept. Boston Pub. Libr.,

1987—; music book reviewer Choice: Current Revs. for Acad. Librs., Middletown, Conn., 1985—. Mem. Am. Musicol. Soc., Music Libr. Assn. Office: Boston Pub Libr 700 Boylston St Boston MA 02116-2813

KOLDAEVA, MARINA VIKTOROVNA, physicist; b. Tambov, Russia, June 2, 1969; d. Viktor and Valentina (Salukaeva) Cutarin; m. Vladimir Koldaev, Apr. 27, 1991; 1 child, Maria. Grad., Moscow Inst. Physics & Tech., 1992. Engrng. physicist Engrng. Centrum Plasmadynamics, Moscow, 1992-95; jr. scientific rschr. Inst. Crystallography, Moscow, 1999—. Avocation: painting. Office: Inst Crystallography, Leninsky pr 59, 117333 Moscow Russia

KOLDAU, LINDA MARIA, music journalist; b. Munich, Oct. 28, 1971; d. Martin Johann and Adelheid Elisabeth (Lindner) K. MA, Mainz (Germany) U., 1996. lector MGG edition, Kassel, Germany, 1994—; music journalist Frankfurter Allgemeine Zeitung, Frankrut, 1992—; author: Südfunk 2, Baden, 1995—. Rsch. grant Centro tedesco in Venezia, 1998. Mem. Gesellschaft für Musikforschung, Soc. for 17th Century Music, Am. Musicol. Soc. Mem. Free Reformed Ch. Home: Spessartstr 2, 64342 Seeheim Germany

KOLE, JULIUS S., lawyer; b. Chgo., July 27, 1953; s. Jack H. and Ruth (Rakowsky) K.; m. Dorie Elrod, June 27, 1976; children: Ryan, Frederick, Abby. BS in Fin., U. Ill., Chgo., 1975; JD, John Marshall Law Sch., 1978. Bar: Ill. 1978. Asst. pub. defender Cook County Pub. Defender, Chgo., 1978-80; prin. Law Offices of Julius S. Kole, Buffalo Grove, Ill., 1980—. Fellow Ill. State Bar Assn., Lake County Bar Assn. Jewish. Avocations: sports, reading, motorcycling. Office: 750 W Lake Cook Rd Ste 135 Buffalo Grove IL 60089-2075

KOLEK, VÍTĚZSLAV, internist, oncologist, pneumologist; b. Olomouc, Moravia, Czech Republic, Sept. 7, 1953; s. Vítězslav and Ludmila (Štáblová) K.; m. Pavla Stonawská, Mar. 8, 1980; children: Zuzana, Martin. MD, U. Palacky, Olomouc, 1977, PhD, 1982. Cert. in internal medicine, oncology and pneumology. Resident internal dept. U. Hosp. Olomouc, 1977-81, lectr. pulmonary dept., 1981-91, prof. internal medicine, 1997—, head bronchology dept., 1984—, sec. pulmonary dept., 1983—; cons. regional hosps. in Moravia; chmn. Czech Bronchological Com., Prague, 1994-96, chmn. 1996—; project leader Grant Z 333-3 Ministry of Health, Prague, 1991-95. Author books on pulmonary diseases; contbr. articles to profl. jours. Co-chmn. regional com. Union Czech Med. Drs., 1995—. Fellow CCP; mem. Am. Coll. Chest Physicians, European Respiratory Soc., World Assn. Sarcoidosis and Other Granulomatous Disorders, Czech Pneumophtiseological Soc. (mem. exec. com. 1994—), Internat. Union Tuberculosis and Lung Disease. Roman Catholic. Avocations: sports (tennis, skiing), classical painting, opera. Home: Kischova 3, 779 00 Olomouc Moravia, Czech Republic Office: U Hosp Pulmonary Dept, Olomouc IP Pavlova 6, 775 20 Olomouc Moravia, Czech Republic

KOLESAR, TIBOR PAUL, physician, researcher; b. Budapest, Hungary, Aug. 18, 1935; arrived in Sweden, 1957; s. Paul and Judit (Martincsek) K.; m. Anna Maria Margareta Larsen, Jan. 3, 1959; children: Lena, Per. Student, Swedish Vet. Coll., Stockholm, 1957-58; MD, U. Lund, Sweden, 1967. Med. officer Lidkoping, Sweden, 1971-76, resident internal medicine, 1971-76; chief Dept. Medicine, Koping, Sweden, 1976-95; chief med. supt. Koping, Sweden, 1982-91; cons. physician Koping, 1996—. Mem. Internal Med. Soc., Med. Soc. Vastmanland, Med. Chief Soc. Stockholm, Med. Soc. Stockholm, Rotary Club Scheele, Koping. Avocations: sailing, painting, mountaineering. E-mail: tibor.kolesar@koping.mail.telia.com. Home: Mullgatan 18, 73130 Koping Sweden

KOLESKE, JOSEPH VICTOR, chemical engineer, consultant; b. Stratford, Wis., Jan. 23, 1930; s. Joseph John and Mary Helen (Jilek) K.; m. Mary Anne Casey, Nov. 3, 1951; children: Robert Casey, Krista Koleske Killmeier. BS in Chem. Engrng., U. Wis., 1958; MS, Inst. Paper Chemistry, Appleton, Wis., 1960, PhD, 1963. Corp. rsch. fellow Union Carbide Corp., South Charleston, W.Va., 1963-88; sr. cons. Consolidated Rsch. Inc., Kingsford, Mich., 1988—; short course lectr. radiation chemistry, N.D. State U., 1996—. Author: Free Radical Radiation Curing, 1997, Alkylene Oxides and Their Polymers, 1990, Poly Ethylene Oxide, 1976, Poly Vinyl Chloride, 1969, Cationic Radiation Curing, 1991, others; editor: ASTM Paint and Coating Testing Manual, 1995; mem. editl. rev. bd. Jour. Coatings Tech., 1979—; contbg. editor Paint & Coatings Industry mag., 2000—; contbr. chpts. to books and more than 100 articles to profl. jours.; patentee in fields of chemistry, polymer blends, and coatings. With USAF, 1950-54. Recipient Interstab Award, U. So. Miss., 1981, Award for Sci. Achievement, Am. Chem. Soc., 1978. Mem. ASTM (Charles Dudley award, 2000), Radtech Internat., Fedn. Socs. for Coating Techs., Serra of Charleston. Roman Catholic. Avocations: philately, writing, reading. Home and Office: 1513 Brentwood Rd Charleston WV 25314-2307

KOLESNICHENKO, ANATOLY FEDOROVICH, research scientist; b. Kiev, USSR, June 12, 1937; came to U.S., 1998; s. Fedor Kolesnichenko and Irina Fedotovna Samofalova; m. Inna Veniaminovna Borysova, 1959; children: Ekaterina, Anastasija. MSc, Kiev Poly. U., 1960; Candidate of Sci., Ukrainian Acad. Sci., Kiev, 1969; PhD, Russian Acad. Sci., Moscow, 1984, prof., 1990. Engr. bldg. power sta. Kiev, 1960-63; sci., head of lab. Ukrainian Acad. Scis., 1963-96, prof., 1990; head sci. divsn., dir. Ukrainian-Can. Sci. Union Net Shape Cast (Ukraine) Ltd., 1992-97; sci. rschr. process R&D, Inland Steel Co. (subs. Inland Steel Industries, Inc.), East Chicago, Ind., 1998—. Author 4 books; contbr. over 225 articles to sci. jours.; inventor in field; editor Jour. Magnetohydrodynamics, 1990—. Fax: 219-399-6562. E-mail: afkole@inland.com. Home: 17 Lockerbie Dr Valparaiso IN 46385-9287 Office: ISPAT Inland Inc Rsch Labs 3001 E Columbus Dr East Chicago IN 46312-2939

KOLESNICHENKO, YAROSLAV IVANOVYCH, physicist, researcher; b. Pyatigorsk, Russia, Feb. 2, 1943; s. Ivan Vasyljovych and Maria Andriivna (Balko) K.; m. Lidia Semenivna Ponomarenko, July 24, 1968; children: Bohdan, Oleh. Student, Dnipropetrovsk State U., Ukraine, 1964-69; M of Physics and Math., Ukrainian Acad. Scis., Kiev, 1969; D of Physics and Math., I.V. Kurchatov Inst. Atomic Energy, Moscow, 1978. Engr., jr. rschr. Inst. Physics Ukrainian Acad. Scis., Kiev, 1965-70, sci. rschr. Inst. Nuc. Rsch., 1970-82, head divsn. fusion theory, 1982—; prof., 1989; mem. sci. coun. controlled fusion and plasma processes Ministry of Sci. and Tech. of Ukraine, Kiev, 1991—. Mem. editl. bd. Nuc. Fusion-IAEA, 1976-84. Grantee Internat. Sci. Found., 1994-95, CRDF-Ukrainian Govt., 1997-99, 2000-2001. Mem. Ukrainian Phys. Soc. (co-head Inst. br. 1991-96). Fax: 380-44-2651368. E-mail: ftd@nucresi.freenet.kiev.ua. Office: Inst Nuc Rsch UAS, Prospect Nauky 47, 03680 Kiev Ukraine

KOLESNICHENKO, YURIY ALEKSEEVICH, physicist; b. Kharkov, Ukraine, Jan. 6, 1953; s. Aleksey Nikiforovich and Mariya Davidovna (Berlina) K.; m. Tamara Kirillovna Moshkalo, Feb. 2, 1974; 1 child, Aleksey Yu. MS, Kharkov State U., 1975; PhD, Inst. Low Temperature Physics, Kharkov, 1980, DSc, 1991. Jr. rschr. Inst Low Temperature Physics, Kharkov, 1975-85, sr. rschr., 1985-92, prin. rschr., 1992—; sr. reader Inst. Radioelectronics, Kharkov, 1981-84; prof. Kharkov State U., 1991-96. Inventor in field. Recipient 1st prize Ukraine YCL Ctrl. Com. and Sci. Tech. Soc., 1984. Mem. Ukrainian Phys. Soc. Home: 19 Danilevsky, 310058 Kharkov Ukraine Office: Inst Low Temperature Physic, & Engrng, Lenin Ave 47, 310164 Kharkov Ukraine

KOLESNIKOV, IVAN MICHAILOVICH, chemistry educator, consultant; b. Korotcha, Belgorad, Russia, July 1, 1929; s. Michail Samoilovitch and Olga Ivanovna (Kudrina) K.; m. Olga Sergeevna Mushenko; 1 child, Sergei Ivanovitch. MSc, State Gubkin Acad. Oil & Gas, Moscow, 1954, PhD, 1959, DSc, 1964. Mem. tech. coun. Russian Oil Ministry, 1972-74; mem. chem. sci. coun. VNIINP, 1988-90; prof. State Gubkin Acad. Oil & Gas, 1970—, mem. chem. sci. coun., 1974—, dir. kinetics and catalysis lab., 1971—; cons. Petrochem. Min., Moscow, 1971-74; cons. A.O. Mag., Moscow, 1993—, Aviation firm Sukhoi, 1993—. Author: Heterogenous Catalysts for Petrochemical Processes, 1991, Thermodynamic of Physico-Chemical Processes, 1994, Optimierung der prozesse der Katalyse und Katsyn, 1996; contbr. over 600 articles to profl. jours. including Jour. Structural Chemistry, Jour. Phys. Chem. Kinet and Cat. Chmn. Electoral Commn., 1983-84. Recipient Best Textbook award Burgas Polytech. Inst., Bulgaria, 1991. Mem. N.Y. Acad. Scis. Avocations: reading, coin collecting. Achievements include formulated general quanto-chemical principle, theory of cat. by polyhedra, thermodyn of spontaneous and nonspontaneous process. Home: Khahovka 16-1-25, 113461 Moscow Russia Office: State Gubkin Acad Oil & Gas, Leninsky Prospect 65, 117296 Moscow Russia

KOLESOV, SERGEY MIKHAILOVITCH, merchant marine officer, shipping consultant; b. Kiev, Ukraine, Dec. 11, 1971; s. Mikhail Semenovitch and ludmila Alexandrovna (Zapolskikh) K.; m. Elena Valerievna Kaliazina, Feb. 3, 1993. Ed, Voice of Prophecy Bible Sch., Watford, Eng., 1993-94; student, Petrozavodsk River Sch., Russia, 1986-90, World English Inst., 1996-98. Cert. marine capt., radar observer, radio telephone operator. With Mcht. Marine, 1990—; 3rd officer, then 2nd officer White Sea & Onega Shipping Co., Petrozavodsk, Russia, 1990-94; 2nd officer Square Ltd., Piraeus, Greece, 1994-95, Aquarian Shell Marine, Athens, Greece, 1995-97; chief officer Aquarian Shell Marine, 1998, Empros Lines Shipping Mgmt., Piraeus, Greece, 1999—; receiving-filing agt. Rost Shiping Co., Kiev and St. Petersburg, Russia, 1994—; authorized by Internat. Registries, Reston, Va.; offshore cons. Biqwell, Kiev, 1995-97; charge d'affairs, Hutt River Principality, Australia, 1995—; monitor Brit. Broadcasting Corp., 1994-99, Deutsche Welle, Cologne, Germany, 1994—, Radio Korea Internat., 1995. Organizer Granma Club, 1994. Mem. Radio Praha Club Prague (DX diploma), RBSWC-WW (D. Herner Meml. award 1992), Amnesty Internat., Radio Budapest Short Wave Club (monitor), WWCR Short Wave Club, Radio Prague Monitoring Club, Radio Slovakin Internat. DX Club, Radio Bucharest Short Wave Club. Russian Orthodox. Avocations: short-wave radios, travel. Office: Rost Shipping Co, PO Box 174, 03150 Kiev Ukraine

KOLETTIS, THEOFILOS, cardiologist; b. Athens, Greece, Mar. 15, 1961; s. Miltiades and Agatha Kolettis; m. Rebecca Mardula, Oct. 9, 1994 (div. Apr. 1999). MD, Athens U., 1984, PhD, 1991. Cert. in medicine, cardiology. Sr. house officer Naval Hosp. Salamis, Athens, 1985-86; med. officer Naval Helicopter Base, Marathon, Greece, 1986-87; gen. practitioner Lesvos, Greece, 1987-88; registrar Royal Infirmary Edinburgh, Scotland, 1988-90, Athens Gen. Hosp., 1990-91; clin. rsch. assoc. Ea. Heart Inst./U. Newark, N.J., 1991-93; attending physician Onassis Cardiac Surgery Ctr., Athens, 1993—. Author: (book chpt.) Implantable Cardioverter Defibrillator, 1994; contbr. articles to profl. jours. Mem. Am. Heart Assn., N.Am. Soc. for Pacing and Electrophysiology. Avocations: karate, swimming. Fax: 011-301-9493373. E-mail: elbee@forthnet.gr. Office: Onassis Cardiac Ctr, 356 Syngrou Ave, Athens Kallithea 176 74, Greece

KOLEV, DIMITER NIKOLOV, biochemistry educator; b. Sofia, Bulgaria, June 8, 1933; s. Nikola Stoykov and Maria Dimitrova (Kojuharova) K.; m. Maria Ivanova Markovska, Oct. 27, 1956 (dec. June 1985); 1 child, Spas Dimitrov. Degree in pharmacy, Med. Acad., Sofia, 1956; degree in chemistry, U. Sofia, 1965; PhD in Biochemistry, Acad. Agrl. Scis., Sofia, 1974. Pharmacist Sofia, 1956-60; sci. worker Sci. Rsch. Inst. of Chemistry and Pharmacy, Sofia, 1960-66; sci. worker Inst. Biochemistry Bulgarian Acad. Scis., Sofia, 1966-69; assoc. prof. Acad. Agrl. Scis., Sofia, 1969-78; prof. Lab. for Food Conservation, Sofia, 1978-79; prof. Faculty of Biology U. Sofia "St. Kliment Ohridski", 1979—; head dept. biochemistry Faculty of Biology, Sofia, 1991-2000. Author: Enzymes, 1970, 2d edit., 1976, Hormones, 1972, Enzymology, 1988; co-author: (with M. Koleva) Polysaccharides, 1985. Scholar Alexander von Humboldt Found., 1970-71, 89-90. Mem. Union of Scientists in Bulgaria. Avocations: history, sports, music, pictorial and plastic arts. E-mail: dkolev@biofac.unisofia.lg. Home: 111 Knjaz Boris I Str, BG-1000 Sofia Bulgaria Office: U Sofia Stq Kliment Ohridski, 8 Dragan Tzankov Blvd, BG-1421 Sofia Bulgaria

KOLEV, VASIL, electrical engineer; b. Tchirpan, Bulgaria, Nov. 22, 1949; m. Emilia Vasileva, July 19, 1970; children: Stanislava, Alexandra. MSEE, Tech. U. Sofia, 1972; PhD, Bulgarian Acad. Scis., 1982. From scientific fellow to assoc. prof. Inst. Physiology Bulgarian Acad. Sci., Sofia, 1974—. Mem. Internat. Brain Rsch. Orgn., Soc. Psychophysiol. Rsch. Avocations: photography, computers, astronomy, aviation. E-mail: kolev@iph.bio.bas.bg. Office: Inst Physiology, Acad G Bonchev str bl 23, Sofia 1113, Bulgaria

KOLEY, ALOK RANJAN, physiology educator; b. Calcutta, India, Jan. 3, 1951; s. Chittaranjan and Debjani (Manna) K.; m. Pampa Sarbadhikary, Feb. 18, 1980; 1 child, Soham. BSc, U. Calcutta, 1970, MSc, 1973, PhD, 1988. Lectr. City Coll., Calcutta; lectr. A.M. Coll., Calcutta, reader, 1992-94, 95—; postdoctoral rsch. assoc. Kans. U. Med. Ctr., Kansas City, 1990-92, U. Nebr. Med. Ctr., Omaha, 1994-95. Patentee microtome section antitangler, foamy shaving cream applicator; contbr. articles to profl. publs. Rsch. grantee Univ. Grants Commn., 1976, 84. Mem. Soc. Exptl. Biology and Medicine, Physiol. Soc. India (life). Avocations: drawing, music, reading, research, travel. Office: AM Coll Dept Physiology, 102/1 Raja Rammohan Sarani, Calcutta 700009, India

KOLH, PHILIPPE HENRY, cardiothoracic and vascular surgeon, researcher; b. Liege, Belgium, May 9, 1964; s. Xavier Martin and Genevieve Jeanne (Courtois) K. BS, U. Liege, 1985, MD summa cum laude, valedictorian, 1989. Bd. cert. gen. surgery, Belgium; cert. specialist in cardiothoracic surgery; cert. specialist in vascular surgery. Resident in gen. surgery U. Hosp. of Liege, 1989-93, asst. prof. surgery, 1995—; fellow in heart and pulmonary transplantation Yale U., New Haven, 1993-94; fellow in cardiac surgery Mass. Gen. Hosp.-Harvard U., Boston, 1994-95. Fellow Internat. Soc. Cardiothoracic Surgeons, Royal Belgian Surg. Soc.; mem. AMA, Internat. Union Angiology (prize 2000), Belgian Soc. Cardiothoracic Surgery, Internat. Soc. for Heart and Lung Transplantation, European Assn. Cardiothoracic Surgery, European Soc. Cardiovasc. Surgery (First Cardiac Poster prize 1998), Belgian Soc. Transplantation, Cardiovascular Sys. Dynamics Soc., Mass. Med. Soc., Belgian Soc. Cardiology, Belgian Soc. for Fundamental and Clinical Physiology and Pharmacology, Belgian Soc. Vascular Surgery, Soc. Thoracic Surgeons, Am. Heart Assn. (basic cardiovasc. scis. and cardiothoracic vascular surgery couns.). Avocations: swimming, tennis, hiking. Fax: (32) 42213158. E-mail: philippe.kolh@chu.ulg.ac.be. Home: 2/7B30 Quai Van Hoegaerden, 4000 Liège Belgium Office: Chu Liege, B 35 Sart Tilman, 4000 Liège Belgium

KOLKER, CHRISTOPHER TRENT, physician; b. Reno, Nev., July 7, 1969; s. Ronald Gene and Marjorie Ann Kolker; m. Bharathi Srini, Jan. 30, 1993 (div. 1998); 1 child, Sephra Alice. BA, Rhodes Coll., 1991; MD, U. Okla., 1996. Diplomate Am. Bd. Family Medicine. Resident St. Anthony's Hosp., Oklahoma City, 1996-99, mem. faculty, 1999—; pvt. practice Oklahoma City, 1999—. Fellow Omicron Delta Kappa, Phi Beta Kappa; mem. Lions. Democrat. Episcopalian. Avocations: chess, bicycling, tennis. Home: 113 Sunup Dr Clinton OK 73601-2904

KOLKIN, IAKOV GRIGOREVICH, surgeon, medical educator; b. Orsk, Orenburg, USSR, Mar. 26, 1942; s. Grigoriy Iakovlevich and Evgenia Davidovna Kolkin; m. Tatyana Petrovna Permakova, July 31, 1976; 1 child, Victoria Lakovlevna. Grad., Donetsk State Med. Inst., Ukraine, 1965; specialization in thoracic surgery, Advanced Tng. Inst. of Drs., Kiev, Ukraine, 1967; advanced studies in clin. surgery, 1st Moscow Med. Inst., 1989. Cert. Ukraine-Am. Joint Tng. and Consultation Dept. Thoracic surgeon Dist. Clin. Hosp., Donetsk, 1965-71, head of thoracic dept., 1972-87; asst. dept. faculty surgery Donetsk State Med. Inst., 1987, assoc. prof. dept. faculty surgery, 1988-91, clin. prof. dept. faculty surgery, 1991—; Author: (monographs) Clinical, Diagnostic and Surgical Treatment of Relaxation Diaphragm, 1971, Pathogenesis, Diagnosis and Treatment of Hiatal Hernias, 1981, (book) Hiatal Hernias, 1996; patentee in field; contbr. articles to profl. jours. Capt. Ukrainian Med. Svc., 1978. Recipient Excellent Health Dept. award Health Min. of USSR, 1978. Mem. Directorate Soc. Surgeons of Ukraine, N.Y. Acad. Scis. Office: Donetsk State Med U, Illicha 16, Donetsk 83098, Ukraine

KOLLA, PETER, forensic scientist, consultant; b. Puettlingen, Saarland, Germany, Jan. 17, 1960. Diploma in chemistry, U. Saarbrücken, Germany, 1985, D Natural Scis., 1988. Cert. forensic expert. Sci. asst. U. Saarbrücken, 1984-86; rsch. scientist Max Planck Inst., Mülheim, Germany, 1986-88; forensic scientist Fed. Criminal Dept., Wiesbaden, Germany, 1989—; mem. Internat. Explosives Technical Commn. Internat. Civil Aviation Org., Montreal, 1999—. Contbr. articles to sci. jours., including Jour. Forensis Scis., Advanced in Analysis and Detection of Explosives, Analytical Chemistry. Avocation: soccer. Office: Bundeskriminalamt, Thaerstrasse 10, 65173 Wiesbaden Germany

KOLLENZ, GERT, chemist, educator; b. Graz, Austria, Apr. 13, 1940; s. Ernst and Maria (Grogger) K.; m. Gerhild Nagele, Dec. 28, 1968; children: Katrin, Florian. PhD in Chemistry, U. Graz, 1967. Univ. asst. U. Graz, 1967-72; rsch. fellow Ciba-Geigy AG, Basel, Switzerland, 1972; dozent U. Graz, 1972-82, prof. chemistry, 1982—; rschr. in organic chemistry; vis. prof. Ain Shams U., Cairo, 1990, U. Queensland, Brisbane, Australia, 1993. Author more than 120 articles on chemistry and sci. Recipient Rsch. award of Styria, 1975. Mem. Internat. Isotope Soc., Internat. Soc. Heterocyclic Chemistry, N.Y. Acad. Sci. Roman Catholic. Avocations: classical music, tennis, skiing, sailing. Home: Am Mariagruener Wald 2, A-8043 Graz Austria Office: U Graz, Heinrichstrasse 28, A-8010 Graz Austria

KOLLER, ARNOLD, former Swiss government official; b. Appenzell, Switzerland, Aug. 29, 1933; m. Erica Brander, Sept. 23, 1972; 2 children. B in Econs., U. St. Gallen, 1957; LLB, U. Fribourg, 1959, PhD in Law, 1966. Pres. Supreme Ct. Kanton Appenzell Innerrhoden, Switzerland, 1973-86; prof. Swiss, European comml. and econ. law U. St. Gallen, Switzerland, 1972-86; minister def. Swiss Govt., 1987-89, chief dept. justice and police, 1989-99; pres. Swiss Confedn., 1990, 97. Mem. Swiss parliament Nat. Council, 1971-86; pres. Christian Dem. group in Swiss parliament, 1980-84, nat. council Swiss parliament, 1984-85. Served to lt. col. Avocations: skiing, tennis.

KOLLER, LASZLO GYULA, electronic engineering educator, researcher; b. Budapest, Hungary, Apr. 27, 1943; s. Gyula and Terezia (Habetler) K.; m. Marianna Satori, Apr. 26, 1974; children: Boglarka, Balazs. TechDr, Tech. U. Budapest, 1980, PhD, 1994; CandTechStudies, Hungarian Acad. Scis., Budapest, 1994. Tech. adminstr. Co. for Power Plant Investment, Budapest, 1967-69; tech. supr. Co. for Food Indsl. Design, Budapest, 1969-70; sr. lectr. Nat. Pedagogic Inst., Budapest, 1971-72; tech. supr. Co. for Comml. Investment, Budapest, 1972-74; assoc. prof. Tech. U. Budapest, 1974—. Contbr. articles to profl. jours.; holder Hungarian and German patents. Sec. bd. trustees Found. for Human Electrotechics, 1995—. Recipient Gold degree of the eminent inventor prize Hungarian Patent Office and Hungarian Indsl. Ministry, 1988, Praise of Min. award Ministry of Edn., Budapest, 1989; Ministry of Edn. grantee, 1998—. Mem. Hungarian Electrotech. Assn., Hungarian Chamber of Engrs., Hungarian Corp. Standards. Roman Catholic. Avocations: inventing, opera, driving, athletics. Home: Dutka A'kos u 91/A, 1029 Budapest Hungary Office: Tech U Budapest/Elec Engrg, EgryJ u 18, Budapest Hungary 1111

KOLLER, SHIRLEY LEAVITT, sculptor; b. Youngstown, Ohio, Apr. 6, 1921; d. Benjamin Harrison and Rose (Cohen) Leavitt; m. Herbert Richard Koller Mar. 7, 1943 (wid. June 1988); children: Donald Lee, Susan Koller Van Horne, Laura Frances. Diploma, Cleve. Inst. of Art, 1942; BS, Western Res. U., Cleve., 1942; MFA, The Am. U., 1972. Lectr. No. Va. C.C., Alexandria, Va., 1977-92; curator of art AAAS, 1997—; lectr. to sr. citizens Jewish Cmty. Ctr. of Greater Washington, Rockville, md., 1990, 95, Washington Hebrew Congregation, Washington, 1995; appearance on Peter Jennings/ABC World News Tonight, 1991, Arlington Cable, 1990, Voice of Am. Radio, 1992; adj. faculty Md. Coll. of Art & Design, 1991-93; vis. artist Fairfax County Pub. Schs., 1982-85; visual art specialist, Fillmore Arts Ctr., Washington, 1977-81. Artist: (3-D wall installation) The Joy of Transportation, 1989-93 (comm. 1989); writer: (newsletter) Eye Wash, 1990-92; curator art exhbit installations, 1989—, including Tri-State Ednl. Assn. exhibits, Washington; one-person shows include Watkins Gallery, Am. U., 1972, Gate House Gallery, Washington, 1994, Mansion Art Gallery, Rockville, 1993, Friedholm Fine Arts Gallery, Asheville, N.C., 1991, O Street Studios, Washington, 1990, AAAS/Atrium Gallery, Washington, 1989-90, others; exhibited in group shows at Gallery 10, Washington, 1998, Tri-State Sculptors Ednl. Assn., Washington, 1997, Associated Artists of Winston-Salem, N.C., 1996, 99, Tri-State Sculptors Conf. Exhbn., U. S.C., Spartenburg, 1996, ARTS 901 E Street, Washington, 1996, AAAS Exhibit, Washington, 1995-96, Newhouse Ctr. for Contemporary Art, S.I., N.Y., 1995-96, Mill River Gallery, Ellicott City, Md., 1999, Tysons Galleria II, Vienna, Va., 1999, Washington Sculptors Group, 1998, 99, Coastal Carolina U., Myrtle Beach, 1999, Washington Sculptors Group, 1999, 2000, Grounds for Sculpture, 2000, others; work collected at Ballston Metro Sta., Arlington, Va., First Am. Bank, Va. Commonwealth U., U. Md., AAAS/Washington, Akin Group, Law Offices, Washington, IBM Rsch. Hdqtrs., Durham, N.C., Internat. Sculpture Ctr., Hamilton N.J., Tri State Sculptors Edn. Assn., U. N.C., Brevard, others. Recipient Editor's Choice award Internat. Libr. Photography, 1998. Mem. Tri-State Sculptors Ednl. Assn. (life mem. 1994), Washington Sculptors Group. Democrat. Jewish. Avocations: travel, lecturing, gourmet cooking. Home: 2700 Virginia Ave NW Washington DC 20037-1908

KOLLER-ANDORF, IDA, professional society executive, editor; b. Vienna, Austria, Apr. 13, 1930; d. Franz Joseph and Theresia (Kuntner) Koller; m. Richard Othmar Andorf, May 18, 1963 (div. 1972); m. Jaro Srutek, Aug. 19, 1977. Student, pub. schs., Vienna. Cert. auditor-cons. Sec., dist. mgr. Kellner & Kunz K.G., Vienna, 1949-66; mgr. Eirich-Edit., 1966-67; vice dir., mgr. ea. office Swedish Graengesberg-Concern, 1967-69; auditor, tax cons. Dr. Ernst Winkler, Vienna, 1969-73; mgr. Ernst Schubert & Co. K.G., Austrian Culture Ctr., Vienna, 1974-84; pres. Friedrich Hebbel Soc., Vienna, 1980-2000; mgr. Kunst und Sprache; participant various seminars. Editor, founder Hebbel-Mensch und Dichter im Werk, vol. 1-7, 1985-2000; mgr. organizer performance Hebbel in Wie: 1845-1863, Gmunden: 1845-1855; founder, guide Dist. Mus. VIII, Vienna; author: Die Welt als Zuchthaus, 2000; contbr. articles on painting, sculpture and artists to profl. jours. Founder Action com. for Promotion Culture and Arts. Mem. Gustinus-Ambrosi Soc. (co-founder, gen. sec. 1975), Interessengemeinschaft österreichischer Autoren, Verband wissenschaftlichen Gesellschaften Östrreichs, Goethe Soc., Grillparzer Soc., Wildgans Soc., Hebbel Soc. (Wesselburen, Germany), Kammerhofmuseum of the City-Hall (Gmunden, Austria), also other sci., human rights, animal rights and ecol. orgns. Roman Catholic. Avocations: culture, arts, philosophy, history, archaeology. Home: Frauengasse 14, A-1170 Vienna Austria Office: Friedrich Hebbel Gesellsch, PO Box 69, A-1082 Vienna Austria

KOLLIAS, COSTAS THEMISTOKLEOUS, psychiatrist; b. Pireaus, Greece, June 30, 1963; s. Themistokles Costas and Eleftheria Athianosiou (Konstadelou) K.; m. Aleandra Ioustinianou Mavroyianni, Jan. 15, 1994; 1 child, Eleftheria Maria. Degree med. sci., Athens U., 1988; degree cognitive behavioral psychother., Inst. of Cognitive Behavior, 1997; cert. in English, U. Cambridge, 1982; Sup III, Inst. Français d'Athènes, 1982; degree as psychiatrist, Eginition Hosp., Athens, 1998. Rural doctor Kacanzas Trizinias, 1992-93; resident Eginition U. Hosp., Athens, 1993-98; psychiatrist Inst. Mental Health Care, Athens U., 1998; pvt. practice in psychiatry Athens, 1998—; psychiatrist Eginition U. Hosp., 2000—; chmn. European Forum for All Psychiat. Trainees, 1996-97, rep. UEMS meeting in Austria, 1997; lectr. in field. Contbr. articles to profl. jours. Navy Petty officer USN, 1990-92. Scholarship U. Athens, 1999. Mem. Hellenic Assn. of Psychiat. Trainees (chmn. 1996-98), Assn. European Psychiat., European Soc. of Behavioral and Cognitive Psychotherapy, Hellenic Psychiat. Assn., Hellenic Assn. of Behavioral and Cognitive Psychotherapy. Orthodox Christian. Home: 4 Freattidos Ave, 18537 Piraeus Greece Office: 161-163 Praxitelous St, 18533 Piraeus Greece

KOLLINS, MICHAEL JEROME, automotive engineer, historian, writer; b. St. Clairsville, Ohio, Mar. 20, 1912; s. Michael Arthur and Mary Ann (Peck) K.; student Coll. City Detroit, 1928-32; m. Julia Dolores Advent, Jan. 16, 1934; children: Michael Lewis, Richard, Laura. Chief sect. svc. engrng. and tech. data Studebaker-Packard Corp., Detroit, 1945-55; mgr. tech. svcs. Chrysler Corp., Detroit, 1955-64, mgr. warranty adminstrn., 1964-68, mgr. Highland Park Svc. ctr., 1968-75; pres. Kollins Design & Engring., Detroit, 1975—. Contbr. articles to publs. Trustee Nat. Automotive Hist. Collection, 1982—; bd. dirs. Capuchin Charity Guild, 1983—; active Birmingham (Mich.) Chorale, Meadowbrook (Mich.) Festival Chorus; nat. advisor Motorsports Hall of Fame, 1988—. With USN, 1942-45. Mem. U.S. Auto Club (vice-chmn. tech. com. 1971-82, dir. cert. com. 1983—), Am. Automobile Assn. (contest bd.), Soc. Automotive Engrs., Soc. Automotive

Historians, Engring. Soc. Detroit (industry ambassador 1972—). Designer racing cars, 1932-39, sports cars, spl. luxury vehicles, 1951—, automotive performance and safety devices, 1946—. Home: 821 Highwood Dr Bloomfield Hills MI 48304-3024 Office: Kollins Design & Engring PO Box 214 Bloomfield Hills MI 48303-0214

KOLLMAN, NILS PETER, sales executive, engineering executive; b. Stockholm, May 21, 1966; s. Paul Rudolf and Dagmar Bibbi (Hultgren) K. Student, Uppsala (Sweden) U., 1986; MBA in Marketing, Stockholm Sch. Econs., 1991. Ministry advisor Ministry Fgn. Affairs, Stockholm, 1992-93; metals trader Axel Johnson AB, Stockholm, 1993, Comtrade AB, Stockholm, 1994-97; area sales mgr. Arla OST, Vaxjo, Sweden, 1997-98; export mgr. OLW Shacks AB, Stockholm, 1998; sales mgr. Autofill AB, Stockholm, 1999—; translator various cos., Stockholm, 1990-94; tchr., interpreter Stockholm Sch. Econs., 1992; fencing instr. Söders Theatre, Stockholm, 1982. Treas. Royal Sch. Tech., Stockholm, 1988-89; authorized rep. Stockholm U., 1988-89. 2nd lt. The Interpreter Sch., 1985-86. Avocations: fencing, tae-kwon-do, travel, trekking. Office: Autofill Products AB, Agavagen 1, 18184 Stockholm Sweden

KOLLMANN, FRANZ GUSTAV, engineering educator; b. Füssen, Germany, Aug. 15, 1934; s. Franz Friedrich and Otti Kollman; m. Barbara Hederich, May 31, 1964; children: Marcella, Katharina. Diploma in engring., Tech. Hochschule Munich, 1956, D in Engring.; D in Engring. (hon.), Tech. U. Chemnitz, Germany, 1994. Rsch. engr. BMW, Munich, 1960-66; tech. mgr. KraussúMaffei A.G., Munich, 1966-73, v.p., 1974-75; prof. Tech. U. Braunschweig, Germany, 1976-82, Tech. U. Darmstadt, Germany, 1982-2000. Author: Welle-Nabe-Verbindungen, 1983, Maschinenakustik, 1999. Mem. Rotary. Avocations: classical music, poetry, skiing, mountaineering. Office: Tech U Darmstadt, Magdelenenstr. 4, Darmstadt D-64293, Germany

KOLLTVEIT, BÅRD JOHANNES, museum director; b. Odda, Norway, Apr. 27, 1942; s. Olav and Magnhild (Holmboe) K.; m. Kari Aspang; children: Thyra, Olav. MA, Bergen U., 1969. Lectr. Askøy (Norway) Grammar Sch., 1969; curator Norwegian Maritime Mus., Oslo, 1970-82, head curator, 1982-84, mus. dir., 1985—; pres. Internat. Congress of Maritime Museums, 1987-93. Author numerous books on Norwegian domestic and overseas shipping history. Recipient Cavalier (Portuguese) Order of Infante dom Henrique, 1981, Cavalier (Dutch) Oranje-Nassau Order, 1986. Avocations: painting, photography, travel. Office: Norsk Sjofartsmuseum, Bygdoynesveien 37, N-0286 Oslo N-0286, Norway

KOLMAN, ADA, scientist, educator; b. Moscow, Nov. 26, 1939; arrived in Sweden, 1975; d. Ernest Kolman and Jekaterina Koncevaja; m. Frantisek Janouch, Feb. 14, 1963; children: Katerina Janouch, Erik Janouch. MSc, Lomonosov State U., Moscow, 1961; PhD, Stockholm U., 1981. Rsch. asst. Inst. Antibiotics, Moscow, 1961-63, Inst. Epidemiology, Prague, Czechoslovakia, 1963-64, Inst. Microbiology, Prague, 1966-73; rsch. asst. Stockholm U., 1975-81, rsch. scientist, 1981-84, assoc. prof., 1984—. Contbr. articles to profl. jours. Mem. European Environ. Mutagen Soc., Swedish Soc. for Radiobiology, Nordic Environ. Mutagen Soc., Scandinavian Soc. Cell Toxicology (bd. mem. 1998—), Swedish Fund for Rsch. Without Animal Experiments (bd. mem. 1995—). Avocation: translating scientific and belles-lettres from Czech to Russian language. Office: Dept Molecular Genome Rsch Stockholm Univ, SE-10691 Stockholm Sweden

KOLMANN, CHARLES FOSTER, communications executive; b. Phila., Nov. 17, 1948; s. Charles A. and Virginia (Jones) K.; m. Marcia Ann Siwula, June 25, 1977; 1 child, Matthew Arthur. BA, LaSalle U., 1970. Cert. in secondary edn. English tchr. Downingtown (Pa.) Sch. Dist., 1970-73; theatre/communications tchr. Tredyffrin-Easttown Sch. Dist., Berwyn, Pa., 1973-75; English tchr. Phila. Sch. Dist., 1975-84; with CBS, Inc., 1970—; from asst. dir. broadcast div. to staff announcer, promotion writer, prodr. broadcast div. Sta. WCAU-TV, Phila., 1970-87; dir. promotion Sta. KTVI-TV (Times-Mirror Broadcasting), St. Louis, 1987-90; promotion mgr. Sta. WCIX-TV, Miami, Fla., 1990-94; dir. comm. Sta. WWJ-TV, Detroit, 1994-97; dir. advt. and promotion Sta. WBBM-TV, Chgo., 1997—. Campaign mgr. Childs for State Senate, Phila., 1980; active vestry St. Paul's Ch., Aramingo, Phila., 1970-87. Recipient TV edn. grant U.S. govt., 1976, 80. Mem. Promax Internat., Nat. Acad. TV Arts & Scis. Republican. Episcopalian. Avocations: model railroading, marine tropical aquaria. Office: WBBM TV 630 N Mcclurg Ct Chicago IL 60611-4495

KOLMANOVSKII, VLADIMIR BORISOVICH, mathematics and electronics educator; b. Volgograd, Russia, Feb. 6, 1942; s. Boris Livovich Kolmanovskii and Nina Michailovna Sadkova; m. Tatjana Livovna Maizenberg, July 20, 1971; children: Ilya, Olga. PhD, Moscow State U., 1966, candidate of sci., 1969; DSc, Acad. Sci. of USSR, 1979. Rschr. Acad. of Sci. of USSR, 1969-86; prof. Moscow Inst. Electronics and Math., 1986—; sr. rschr. Space Rsch. Inst. Russian Acad. of Sci., 1994—. Author 10 monographs; contbr. over 150 articles to jours. in field; mem. editl. bd. Automatic and Remote Control, Dynamic Systems and Applications, Stochastic Analysis and Application, Jour. Inequalities and Applications. Mem. Moscow Math. Soc. (chmn. inst. sect.), Am. Math. Soc., Russian Acad. Nonlinear Scis., Russian Acad. Navigation Scis. Avocations: foreign languages, music, travel. Home: Novospasskii 3-1-20, 109172 Moscow Russia Office: B Vuzovskii 3/12, 109018 Moscow Russia

KOLMEN, SAMUEL NORMAN, consultant; b. Brownsville, Tex., Mar. 20, 1930; s. Joseph and Cyla (Gerson) K.; m. Barbara Kass, June 13, 1954; children: Benita Kolmen Solomon, Jeannette Kolmen Rosato. BA, U. Tex., Austin, 1954; PhD in Physiology, U. Tex. Med. Br., Galveston, 1957. James W. McLaughlin fellow in infection and immunology U. Tex. Med. Br., Galveston, 1955-57; Jeane B. Kempner postdoctoral fellow in medicine, London, 1957-58; asst. prof., assoc. prof., prof. U. Tex. Med. Br., Galveston, 1958-75; prof. physiology, chmn. dept. Coll. Sci. and Engring., Sch. Medicine Wright State U., Dayton, Ohio, 1975-84, prof., asst. dean Sch. Medicine, 1980-84; asst. to pres. in rsch. Wright State U., Dayton, 1979-84; prof., assoc. dean, co-founder liaison com. for computing Hahnemann U. Sch. Medicine, Phila., 1984-89; dir. med. edn. and rsch. Mercy Hosp. Pitts., 1989-94; pres. Kolmen & Assocs., 1994—; rsch. coord. Shriners Burns Inst., Galveston, 1970-75; cons. Nat. Bd. Med. Examiners, Phila., 1989. Contbr. over 35 articles to sci. jours. Pres. Congregation Beth Jacob, Galveston, 1970-72; bd. dirs. Jewish Assn. South Dayton, 1976-83; mem. sci. rev. coun. Miami Valley chpt. and Ohio Regional coun. Am. Heart Assn., 1981-83; vol. cons. Allegheny Policy Coun., 1994—, Coalition on Math. and Sci. (K-12), 1994-96; vol. Career and Passport Commn., 1994—, Operation Safety Net, 1994-96. Recipient Disting. Alumnus award U. Tex. Med. Br., 1981. Democrat. Achievements include development of technique for chronic lymphatic studies; research on erythocyte adsorption of fibrinolytic agents, vitamin K influence on fibrinogen metabolism, septicemia in burned animals by intestinal portal of entry, fibrinogen metabolic turnover and delivery. Office: Kolmen & Assocs 256 Sweet Gum Rd Pittsburgh PA 15238-1348

KOLMES, STEVEN ALBERT, biologist, educator; b. Poughkeepsie, N.Y., Sept. 17, 1954; s. Isaac and Beatrice (Stoller) K.; m. Linda Ann Fergusson, June 20, 1987; children: Sara Kjellaug, Elijah John. BS in Zoology, Ohio U., 1976; MS, U. Wis., 1978, PhD, 1984. Lectr. U. Wis., Madison, 1983-84; asst. prof. biology Hobart & William Smith Colls., Geneva, N.Y., 1984-89, chmn. biology dept., 1988-90, assoc. prof., 1989-94, prof., environ. studies coord., 1994-95; Molter chair sci., environ. studies dir., prof. biology U. Portland, Oreg., 1995—; vis. scientist Univ. Coll., Cardiff, Wales, 1987, Simon Fraser U., Burnaby, B.C., 1985, 86; biology coord. Simcalc Project, Dartmouth, Mass., 1994-95, mem. adv. bd., 1993-95; mentor Oreg. Collaborative Excellence in Preparation of Tchrs., 1995-99; mem. Willameter River and Lower Columbia River Salmonid Tech. Recovery Team, 2000—. Issue editor Coun. on Undergrad. Rsch. Quar., 1996-98; contbr. articles to profl. jours. Mem. vestry St. Peter's Ch., Geneva, 1992-95. Fulbright rsch. scholar, 1991; grantee USDA, 1993-95, NSF, 1996-98. Mem. AAAS, Animal Behavior Soc. (mem. membership com. 1993-96), Entomol. Soc. Am., Fulbright Assn. (life). Democrat. Episcopalian. Achievements include research in inactive constituents of pesticide formulations, honeybee colonies containing behaviorally distinct patrilines. Office: Univ Portland Dept Biology 5000 N Willamette Blvd Portland OR 97203-5743

KOLMIN, KENNETH GUY, lawyer; b. N.Y.C., Oct. 22, 1951; s. Frank William and Edith Kolmin; m. Suzan L. Frumm, Sept. 3, 1978; children—Stephen Todd, Jennifer Dana, Robert Scott. BS summa cum laude, SUNY-Albany, 1973; MS, Syracuse U., 1975, JD cum laude, 1975. Bar: Ill. 1976, U.S. Dist. Ct. (7th dist.) Ill. 1976, U.S. Tax Ct. 1980, U.S. Supreme Ct. 1985; CPA, Ill. Tax cons. Arthur Young and Co., Chgo., 1976-79; atty. Shefsky Saitlin & Froelich, Chgo., 1979-81; ptnr. Rooks Pitts & Poust, Chgo., 1981-84, Schwartz & Freeman, 1984-96, Sonnenschein, Nath & Rosenthal, Chgo., 1996—. Contbr. articles to profl. jours. Mem. ABA, AICPA, Ill. Bar Assn., Ill. Soc. CPAs. Home: 975 Eastwood Rd Glencoe IL 60022-1122 Office: Sonnenschein Nath & Rosenthal 8000 Sears Tower Chicago IL 60606

KOLMODIN-HEDMAN, BIRGITTA CHRISTINE, medical educator; b. Lindesberg, Sweden, Aug. 13, 1937; m. E. Hedman (dec. 1985); 1 child, Per-Oscar. MD, Karolinska Inst., Stockholm, 1974. Specialist in occupl. medicine, prof. occupl. medicine Nat. Inst. Occupl. Health, Umea, Sweden, 1981-90; staff divsn. occupl. medicine Huddinge U. Hosp., Karolinska Inst., Stockholm, 1990—. Pres. Swedish Br. Zonta Internat., 1988-90. Office: Karolinska Inst Dept PH, Norrbacka Level 3, 17176 Stockholm Plan 3, Sweden

KOLMOGOROV, VADIM LEONIDOVICH, mechanical engineer, educator; b. Berezniky, Russia, Feb. 16, 1931; s. Leonid and Zoya (Netsvetayeva) K.; m. Elsa Titova, June 22, 1955; children: Mikhail, Sergey. Grad., Tech. U. Ekaterinburg, 1953, PhD, 1958, DSc, 1965, DSc (hon.), 1997. Postgrad. rschr. Tech. U. Ekaterinburg, Russia, 1953-56; head rsch. lab. Plant Pervouralsk, Russia, 1956-60; from br. head to dept. chair Tech. U. Ekaterinburg, 1960-86; dep. dir. Inst. Engring. Sci., Ekaterinburg, 1986—. Mem. Russian Acad. Sci. (corresponding). Home: Ap 1 11 Gotvald St, 620034 Ekaterinburg Russia

KOLOBOV, ALEXANDER V., research scientist; b. Armavir, Krasnodar, USSR, Apr. 10, 1955; arrived in Japan, 1994; s. Vladimir A. and Marina M. (Gumenyuk) K.; m. Veronica A. Makarova, Oct. 6, 1989; 1 child, Ilariya. MSc, Electrotech. Inst., Leningrad, Russia, 1979; PhD, Ioffe Phys.-Tech. Inst., Leningrad, Russia, 1984, DSc, 1991. Cert. in engring. Rschr. Ioffe Phys.-Tech. Inst., Leningrad, 1979-94; sr. rschr. Joint Rsch. Ctr. for Atom Tech. Nat. Inst. for Advanced Interdisciplinary Rsch., Tsukuba, Japan, 1994—; sr. vis. fellow Cambridge (Eng.) U., 1988-89; rschr. Ecole Supérieure de Physique et de Chimie Industrielles, Paris, 1991-92; prof. Katholieke U. Leuven, Belgium, 1993; mem. sci. bd. Jour. Optoelectronics and Advanced Materials, Romania. Co-author: Electronic Properties of Amorphous Chalcogenides, 1996; contbr. over 130 articles to sci. jours. Recipient Kapitza, Royal Soc. London, 1993. Avocations: hiking, linguistics. Office: JRCAT-NAIR, 1-1-4 Higashi, Tsukuba Ibaraki, Japan

KOLOCZEK, HENRYK JAN, biochemist, researcher; b. Piasek, Silesia, Poland, May 13, 1953; s. Antoni Franciszek and Anna Klara (Jastrzemska) K.; m. Ada Gross, Oct. 29, 1988; 1 child, Henryk Jr. MSc, Jagiellonian U., Cracow, Poland, 1978, PhD, 1985. Asst. Med. Acad., Katowice, Poland, 1978-80; postdoctoral staff U. Pa. Sch. Medicine, Phila., 1985-87; asst. prof. Jagiellonian U., Cracow, 1987-95; head biochem. dept. U. Agr., Cracow, 1995—; vis. prof. Nagoya (Japan) U., 1993-94. Author: Biochemistry with Elementary Biophysics, 1997. Recipient award Min. of Edn., Polish Ministry of Edn., 1988. Home: ul Sliska 16, 30-516 Cracow Poland Office: Univ Agr, al 29 Listopada 54, 31-425 Cracow Poland

KOLODKO, GRZEGORZ W., Polish government official, educator, researcher; b. Tczew, Poland, Jan. 28, 1949; m. Alicja Kolodko; children: Julia, Gabriela. BA, SGPiS, Warsaw, 1972, PhD, 1976. Prof., 1984; mng. dir. Rsch. Inst. Fin., Warsaw, 1989-94; cons. IMF, Washington, 1991-92, 99-2000; dep. prime min. economy Warsaw, Poland, 1994-97, min. fin., 1994-97; cons., vis. prof. various fgn. univs. Author: Strategy for Poland, 1994, From Shock to Therapy: The Political Economy of Postsocialist Transformation, 2000; contbr. numerous articles in field. Recipient Ministry Nat. Edn. award, Polish Acad. Scis. award, 1980-95; Fulbright scholar U. Ill., 1985-86. E-mail: grze@troi.cc.rochester.edu. Office: Warsaw Sch Econs, al Hiepodleglosci 162, 00-950 Warsaw Poland

KOLODNY, STEPHEN ARTHUR, lawyer; b. Monticello, N.Y., 1940. BA in Bus. Adminstrn., Boston U., 1963, JD, 1965. Bar: Calif. 1966, U.S. Dist. Ct. (cen. dist.) Calif. 1966; cert. family law specialist. Sole practice L.A., 1966-95; with Kolodny & Anteau, L.A., 1995—; lectr. on family law subjects; adj. prof. U. Houston, ABA Trial Advocacy Inst., 1990—, co-chair, 1998—. Co-author: Divorce Practice Handbook, 1994; author: Evidence ABA Advocate, 1996. Mem. ABA (family law sect., author ABA Advocate), Am. Acad. Matrimonial Lawyers (past pres. So. Calif. chpt., bd. govs.), Am. Coll. Family Trial lawyers (founding dir.), Internat. Acad. Matrimonial Lawyers (bd. govs., past pres. USA chpt.), Calif. State Bar Assn. (cert. family law specialist 1980—, lectr. State Bar panel, CEB programs, mem. family law sect., article author), Los Angeles County Bar Assn. (lectr., mem. and past chmn. family law sect.), Beverly Hills Bar Assn. (lectr., mem. family law sect.). Fax: 310-271-3918. E-mail: kolodny@kolodny-anteau.com.

KOLODNY, YEHOSHUA, geologist; b. Pinsk, Belarus, Sept. 28, 1936; arrived in Israel, 1948; s. Nechemia and Rachel (Pliskin) K.; m. Amira Tova Pnini, May 15, 1960; children: Noam, Uri, Tamar-Rachel. MSc, Hebrew U., Jerusalem, 1965; PhD, UCLA, 1969. Rsch. fellow Calif. Inst. Tech., Pasadena, 1973-74; assoc. prof. Hebrew U., Jerusalem, 1975, chmn. studies, 1976-78, prof. geology, 1980, 85—; prof. Stanford (Calif.) U., 1991-92; dean scis. Hebrew U., 1999—; vis. prof. UCLA, 1978-79, 85, U. L. Pasteur, Strasbourg, France, 1985; chmn. dept. geology Hebrew U., Jerusalem, 1980-82; chmn. Inst. Earth Sci., Jerusalem, 1990-91, 93-96; rsch. fellow Yale U., 1998-99. Editor Israel Jour. Earth Sci., 1992—, Chem. Geology, 1983—. Councilor Geochem. Soc., 1981-84; pres. Geol. Soc., Israel, 1975-76. Lt. Israel mil., 1955-58. Recipient P. Grader award Geol. Soc. Israel, 1971, R. Freund award, 1991; Geochem. fellow Geochem Soc./European Assn. Geochem., 1999. Home: 20 Hovevei Zion Str, 92226 Jerusalem Israel Office: Inst Earth Sci, Hebrew Univ, 91904 Jerusalem Israel

KOLODZIEJ, ANDRZEJ STANISŁAW, chemical engineering researcher; b. Chorzow, Poland, Dec. 17, 1957; s. Zdzisław and Teresa (Stryczek) K.; m. Gabriela Kimla, Nov. 7, 1990; 1 child, Katarzyna. MS in Engring., Silesian Tech. U., Gliwice, Poland, 1981; PhD Polish Acad. Scis., Inst. Chem. Engring., Gliwice, 1989. Rschr. Polish Acad. Scis. Inst. Chem. Engring., Gliwice, 1981—. Co-author: Technical Encyclopaedie: Chemistry, 1986; contbr. articles to profl. jours. Polish govt. grantee, 1990, 97; European Union grantee, 2000. Roman Catholic. Avocations: house and garden activities, dogs, mountain climbing, history books. E-mail: ask@iich.gliwice.pl. Office: Polish Acad Scis Inst Chem, Engring Baltycka 5, 44-100 Gliwice Poland

KOŁODZIEJ, JÓZEF, agrometeorologist, researcher; b. Lisów, Krosno, Poland, Nov. 28, 1935; s. Jakub and Helena Wanda (Wójcik) K.; m. Anna Wiktoria Pasieczna, Apr. 2, 1963; children: Jerzy Lech, Małgorzata Barbara. MS, U. Agr., Lublin, Poland, 1961; D, U. Agr., 1968, PhD, 1973. Asst. U. Agr., 1963-68, lectr., 1968-74, asst. prof., 1974-82, assoc. prof., 1982-93, prof., 1993—, head dept. agrometeorology, 1975—; vice dean agr. faculty, U. Agr., 1978-84. Co-author: Atlas of Unconvenient Meteorological Incidences for Agricultural Production in Poland, 1990, Plant Cultivation, 1977, 3d rev. edit., 1982, Atlas of Soil Moisture in Poland, 1996. Decorated Order Polonia Restituta; recipient fin. award, 1974, medal Min. Edn., 1980. Mem. European Soc. Agronomy, Polish Geophys. Soc., Polish Geog. Soc., Internat. Soc. Biometeorology. Avocations: theater, cinema, tourism, hunting. Home: Rayskiego 4/24, 20 060 Lublin Poland Office: U Agriculture Dept Agrometeorology, Akademicka 15, 20 950 Lublin Poland

KOLOMIYSKY, ARKADIY NAUMOVICH, physicist, researcher, educator; b. Potsdam, Germany, July 26, 1947; arrived in Russia, 1950; s. Naum Veniaminovich Kolomiysky and Shuamis Zimelevna Lin. MS/Engr. in Physics, Moscow Inst. Physics & Tech., 1971; PhD in Physics and Math., I.V. Kurchatov Atomic Energy Inst., Moscow, 1981. Rsch. engr. I.V. Kurchatov Atomic Energy Inst., Moscow, 1971-73; rsch. scientist Br. I.V. Kurchatov Atomic Energy Inst., Troitsk, Moscow, Russia, 1973-83; group leader Br. I.V. Kurchatov Atomic Energy Inst., Troitsk/Moscow, 1983-87; sr. scientist Br. I.V. Kurchatov Atomic Energy Inst., Troitsk, 1987-90; lead scientist Troitsk Inst. Innovation and Fusion Rsch., Troitsk, 1990—; assoc. prof. Moscow Inst. Physics and Tech., 1978—. Contbr. articles to profl. jours. Avocations: literature, theatre, travels. E-mail: akolom@triniti.ru. Fax: 7 095 334-5056. Office: Troitsk Inst Innovation, Pushkovyh str, 142092 Troitsk Moscow reg Moscow, Russia

KOLOMOETS, NIKOLAY VASILIEVICH, research scientist; b. USSR, Dec. 7, 1930; s. Vasiliy Dorofeevich and Marija Lukjanovna K.; m. Ljudmila Aleksandrovna Bagaeva, July 7, 1955 (wid. May 1982); 1 child, Marija Nikolaevna Leonova; m. Margarita Vasilievna Pavlova, Mar. 15, 1986; 1 child, Elena Valerievna Petukhova. Cand. of Phys./Math. Scis., Phys.-Tech. Inst., Leningrad, 1961; D Tech. Scis., Inst. of Sources of Current, Moscow, 1968; Prof., Moscow Phys./Tech. Inst., 1970. Major rschr. Inst. of Semiconductors, Leningrad, 1954-63; dir. divsn. Enterprise NPO KVANT, Moscow, 1963-90; dir. Sci. Ctr. Inst. New Technology, Moscow, 1990-93; invited rschr. Korea Inst. Sci. and Tech., Seoul, 1993—; cons. sci. Ctr., Inst. of New Technology, Moscow, 1993—; chmn. Thermoelectric Divsn. of Energy Conversion Cmty., Acad. of Sci. of USSR, 1972-90; mem. qualifying Scientific Soviet, Moscow State U., 1985—, mem. Soviet: Narrow-zone Semiconductors, 1975-85; mem. qualifying sci. Soviet Phys. Tech. Inst., Moscow, 1975-88. Author: (book) Film Thermoelements.Phusiks and Application, 1985; editor: (book) Engineering Method Calculation of Thermoelectric Generators, 1990; contbr. numerous articles to profl. jours. and publs.; patentee in field of thermoelectric semiconductors materials. Recipient sci. medals USSR Govt., 1970, 73, Vietnam govt., 1985. Avocations: sports, mountain skiing. E-mail: nkolomoets@mail.u. Office: Korea Inst Sci/Tech, Cheongryang/PO Box 131, 130-650 Seoul South Korea

KOLOMYTKIN, OLEG, biophysicist, consultant; b. Kaunas, Lithuania, USSR, July 20, 1947; came to US, 1995; s. Vladimir and Evdokiya (Nekhaeva) K.; m. Irina Chernikova, Mar. 30, 1977; children: Rotislav, Dmitry, Igor. BS, Moscow Phys.-Tech. Inst., 1972; PhD, Russian Acad. Scis., Pushchino, Moscow region, 1978; D Phys. and Math. Scis., Russian Acad. Scis., 1990. Physicist, engr. Rsch. scientist Inst. Biophysics, Pushchino, Moscow, USSR, 1972-78; sr. rsch. scientist Russian Acad. Scis., 1978-89, dir. lab. radiation biophysics Inst. Cell Biophysics, 1989-97; rsch. scientist La. State U. Health Sci. Ctr., Shreveport, La., 1995—; mem. elected scientific coun. Inst. Cell Biophysics, Pushchino, Moscow region, 1991-96; mem. organizing com. Internat. Symposium Va. Commonwealth U., Richmond, Va., 1991, 94. Contbr. articles to profl. jours., chpts. to books. Grantee Internat. Sci. Found., 1993, 94, 95. Mem. European Bioelectromagnetics Assn., Bioelectromagnetics Soc. Achievements include visualization of ionic channels by a scanning tunneling microscope; finding response of brain receptor systems to microwave energy exposure, finding switches of electrophysiological states of the cells by Interleukin-1. Avocations: sports. E-mail: okolom@lsuhsc.edu. Home: 1331 Woodrow St Shreveport LA 71103-4247

KOLOMYTZ, ERLAND GEORGIEVICH, ecologist, science administrator; b. Muslyumovo, Russia, Jan. 27, 1936; s. Georgiy Dmitriyevich and Taisiya Georgievna (Dmitriyeva) K.; m. Natalia Anatolyevna Surova, Aug. 17, 1979; 1 child, Yana. MSc, Moscow State U., 1960, D in Geography, 1976; PhD, Geographical Inst., Moscow, 1964. Jr., then sr. rschr. Inst. Geography of Siberia and Far East, Irkutsk, Russia, 1960-71; sr. rschr. Pacific Ocean Inst. Geography, Vladivostok, Russia, 1971-76, head lab., 1984-86; head lab. High Mountain Geographical Inst., Nalchik, Russia, 1976-84; chair Pedagogical Inst., Nizhny Novgorod, Russia, 1986-90, prof., 1990-96; head lab. Inst. Ecology of Volga River Basin, Togliatty, Russia, 1990—; tchr. Far East U., Vladivostok, 1974-76; prof. Kabarda Balkaria U., Nalchik, 1980-82, Pushchino (Russia) U., 1997—. Author: Snow Cover of Mountain Taiga Landscapes of the Northern Over Baikal Region, 1966, Snow Structure and Landscape Indication, 1976, Methods of Crystallomorphological Analysis of Snow Structure, 1977, Polymorphism of Landscape Zonal Systems, 1998. Grantee, Russian Found. for Fundamental Rsch., 1994, 96, 98. Home: D-1, 272, 142290 Pushchino Moscow, Russia Office: Inst Ecol Volga Riv Basia, Komzin St, 10, 445003 Togliatty Samara, Russia

KOLOSOV, VALERY NIKOLAEVICH, physicist; b. Vosvyshenka, USSR, Mar. 22, 1953; s. Nikolai and Paula (Shutova) K.; m. Tatiana Nikolaevna Kruchkova, Apr. 29, 1977 (dec. Nov. 1989); children: Svetlana, Sergei. Grad. in physics, Moscow State U., 1979; PhD, Kharkov Phys.-Tech. Inst., Ukraine, 1990. Turner Engring. Works, Petropavlovsk, USSR, 1970-71; probationer Inst. Chemistry & Technology Rare Elements Russian Acad. Sci, Apatity, Russia, 1979-80; from sr. lab. asst. to sr. rschr. Inst. Chemistry & Technology Rare Elements Russian Acad. Sci., Apatity, 1980—; tutor Inst. Econs. & Mgmt. St. Petersburg State Acad. Econs., Russia, 1998—. Author: Electrolytical Superconducting Materials, 1996, Refractory Metals in Molten Salts, 1998, Advances in Molten Salts, 1999; contbr. articles to profl. jours. Sr. sgt. Soviet Army, 1971-73. Mem. N.Y. Acad. Scis. Office: Kola Sci Ctr Inst Chemistry, Fersman Str 26a, 184200 Apatity Murmansk, Russia

KOLOSOVSKY, ERNEST DMITRIEVICH, dermatologist; b. Osipovichi, Bielorussia, Aug. 25, 1939; s. Dmitri Ivanovich Kolosovsky and Maria Matveevna Sneguireva; m. Inna Olegovna Klepatskaya, Aug. 2, 1986; 1 child, Nadezhda. MD, Med. Acad. Post Diploma Edn., St. Petersburg, 1986. Diplomate Russian Bd. Dermatovenereology. Intern dept. dermatology Med. Skill Improvement Inst., Minsk, USSR, 1965; practical dermatologist Dermatology Clinic, Mogilev, USSR, 1966-70; rschr. Med. Acad. I. Mechikov, St. Petersburg, Russia, 1971-73; cons. in dermatology and pediatrics Outpatient Clinic, St. Petersburg, 1980—; rsch. group leader Ctrl. Lab. Med. Acad. Post Diploma Edn., St. Petersburg, 1995—. Contbr. numerous articles to profl. jours.; 7 patents in field. Mem. Med. Trade Union; participant homeopathic symposia and congresses. Lt. medicine Soviet Armed Forces, 1962-64. Recipient Cert. of Good Work, Moscow Com. of Komsomol, 1979, Vet. of Labor medal, 1989. Mem. Soc. Dermatologists St. Petersburg. Avocations: skiing, skating. Home: 102-5-135 Toreza Prospect, 194017 Saint Petersburg Russia Office: Med Acad Post Diploma Edn, 41 Kirochnaya St, Saint Petersburg Russia

KOLOZYN-KRAJEWSKA, DANUTA MARIA, food technologist, educator; b. Warsaw, Poland, Sept. 10, 1954; d. Jerzy and Stanislawa Elzbieta (Wawrzela) Kolozyn; m. Karol Jan Krajewski, May 14, 1977; children: Urszula, Helena. BSc, MSc, Warsaw Agrl. U., 1978, PhD, 1983, qualification for asst. prof., 1999. Asst. acad. tchr. Warsaw Agrl. U., 1982-83, asst. prof., rschr., 1983—; cons. Swed Farm, Sweden, 1995-97. Author: Food Commodities, 1985, 89, 97, 98, 99, Commodity Science, 1999, (with T. Sikora) HACCP-Concept and System of Food Safety Assurance, 1999; patentee in field of dairy spread technology, 1990. Mem. Polish Food Technologists Soc. (pres. Warsaw br. 1995—), Nat. Tech. Orgn., Polish Commodity Soc. (mem. revision commn. 1995—), N.Y. Acad. Scis. (Silver Cross of Merit 1999). Roman Catholic. Avocations: poetry, swimming, travel. Home: Pawlaczyka 1/47, 02 791 Warsaw Poland Office: Warsaw Agrl U Human Nutritn, Nowoursynowska 166, 02 787 Warsaw Poland

KOLSKY, STEPHEN DEREK, humanities educator; b. London; arrived in Australia, 1982; s. Muriel (Comar) K.; m. Helen May Hassard, Oct. 2, 1993; 1 child, Daniel. BA with honors, U. Hull, Eng., 1977; PhD, U. London, 1981. Lectr. U. Liverpool, Eng., 1980-82; lectr. U. Melbourne, Australia, 1982-89, sr. lectr., 1989—; vis. rsch. fellow Royal Holloway, U. London, 1997. Author: Mario Equicola, The Real Courtier, 1991; co-editor Spunti e Ricerche, 1985-92; author numerous articles on The Italian Renaissance. Villa I Tatti fellow Harvard U., Florence, Italy, 1992-93; grantee Australian Rsch. Coun., 1996, 98, 99, 2000. Mem. Renaissance Soc. Am., Soc. for Italian Studies of Gt. Britain and Ireland. Avocations: walking, classical music, opera, cinema. Office: U Melbourne, Dept French & Italian Studies, Parkville 3052, Australia

KOLSTAD, JENS, food microbiologist; b. Trondheim, Norway, Oct. 30, 1954; s. Birger Johan and Berit Marie (Johansen) K.; m. Greta Wigdahl, Mar. 3, 1984; children: Maria Wigdahl Kolstad, Ricard Wigdahl Kolstad. Baccalaureat Francais, Lycee Corneille, Rouen, France, 1974; CandMag, U. Oslo, 1978, CandReal, 1982; DrScientiarum, Agrl. U. Norway, 1989. Brit. Coun. scholar Nat. Inst. for Rsch. in Dairying, Eng., 1982-83; rsch. asst. Agrl. U. Norway, 1985-88; rsch. scientist Norwegian Coll. Vet.

Medicine, 1988-90; mgr. food microbiology/aseptic sys. Elopak A/S, Norway, 1990—. Contbr. articles to profl. jours. Served with Army Med. Svc., 1984, Norwegian Def. Rsch. Establishment, 1984. Mem. Soc. for Applied Microbiology. Avocations: hiking, music. Home: Honsveien 119, 1384 Asker Norway Office: Elopak A/S, Elopak Corp Offices, Postbox 124, N-3431 Spikkesed Norway

KOLTA, SHERIF ZAHER, banker; b. Cairo, Egypt, Nov. 4, 1955; s. Zaher and Soad Shafik (Andrawis) K.; 1 child, Mariam. BA in Econs., Am. U. Cairo, 1978. Head of credit Nat. Bank of Abu Dhabi, Cairo, 1978-89; head of credit studies Riyadh (Saudi Arabia) Bank, 1989-92, 93-96; mgr. loan quality control Egyptian Am. Bank, Cairo, 1992-93, 96—; sr. mgr. corp. banking Am. Express Bank HO, Cairo, 1997—. Active Egyptian-Am. Friendship Assn., 1978—, Am. Cultural Ctr., 1978—. Recipient scholarship Am. U. Cairo, 1976-78. Mem. Econs. Soc. (cert.), Am. U. Alumni Assn., Gezira Sporting Club. Avocations: tennis, golf, squash, music, political readings. Home: 13 Mansour Mohamed St, Zamalek Cairo Egypt Office: Am Express Bank HO, 4 Syria St, Mohandessin Cairo Egypt

KOLTAI, TAMAS, industrial engineering educator; b. Budapest, Hungary, Nov. 7, 1958; s. Imre and Kornelia (Grün) K. M in Mech. Engring., Tech. U. Budapest, 1983; PhD in Indsl. Engring., Hungarian Acad. Scis., 1986. Asst. prof. Tech. U. Budapest, 1986-89, assoc. prof., 1990—; adj. prof. Internat. Mgmt. Ctr., Budapest, 1990—; vis. scholar U. Mich., Ann Arbor, 1989-90; vis. prof. U. Seville, Spain, 1990-92, adj. prof., 1994-96. Editor Periodica Polytechnica, Budapest, 1995—; co-editor Harvard Business-manager; contbr. chpt. to book, articles to profl. jours. Recipient Best Paper award 9th European Meeting on Cybernetics and Sys. Rsch., 1988. Mem. Prodn. and Ops. Mgmt. Soc., European Ops. Mgmt. Assn., Sci. Assn. Machine Industry. Avocations: history, classical music, tennis. Office: Tech U Budapest Dept Indst Mgmt, Muegyetem Rkp 9 T bld, 1521 Budapest Hungary

KOLTOVER, VITALI K., biophysicist; b. Orekhovo-Zuyevo, Russia, May 15, 1944; s. Kiva Moses and Kapitolina Yakovlevna (Nefedjeva) K.; m. Larisa Tofovna Kasumova, Mar. 6, 1970; 1 child, Ilya. MS in Physics, Kiev State U., 1966; PhD in Physics and Math., Inst. of Chem. Physics, Moscow, 1971, DSc in Biophysics, 1988; Diploma (hon.), Russian Acad. Scis., 1999. Rsch. fellow Inst. Plant Physiology, Kiev, Ukraine, 1966-68; predoctoral fellow Inst. Chem. Physics, Moscow, 1969-71; jr. scientist Inst. Chem. Physics, Chernogolovka, Russia, 1972-85; sr. scientist Inst. Chem. Physics, Chernogolovka, 1985-91, head bioreliability group, 1992—; vis. scientist Vet. U., Vienna, 1991-92; dep.-chmn. Com. on Reliability of Biol. Systems, USSR Acad. Scis., 1979-92; expert cons. Russian Found. Basic Rsch., Moscow; vis. prof. U. Calif. Berkeley, 1989, U. Pa., Phila., 1990. Co-author: Reliability and Aging of Biological Systems, 1987; author: Theory of Reliability, Superoxide Radicals and Aging, 1983; contbr. articles to profl. jours. Mem. Internat. Union of Radioecology, Am. Acad. of Anti-Aging Medicine, N.Y. Acad. Scis. Jewish. Avocations: collecting gramophone records, world and Russian history, cats. Office: Inst of Chem Physics, Russian Acad of Scis, Chernogolovka 142432, Russia

KOLTSOV, ALEXANDER BORISOVICH, petrologist, educator; b. Leningrad, Russia, Mar. 9, 1952; s. Boris Ivanovich and Natalya Georgievna (Larionova) K. Degree, Leningrad State U., 1974, PhD, 1978; DSc, St. Petersburg State U., 1997. Engr. Leningrad State U., 1978-79, jr. scientist, 1980-82, vice-dir., 1983-87; sr. scientist St. Petersburg State U., 1988-96, lectr. dept. petrology, 1996-99, prof., 1999—, head lab., 1997—; program mgr. deep-drilling project, Muruntau, Russia, 1986-91. Author: Gold-silver Metasomatites in Black Schists, 1987, Geological Setting, Petrological and Geochemical Peculiarities of Gold-Ore Metasomatites in Black Schists, 1995, Metasomatic Processes on Gold Deposits in Metaterrigenious Rocks, 2000; also papers. Mem. Russian Minerol. Soc. Avocation: travel. E-mail: olga@os2489.spb.edu. Office: St Petersburg State U, Universitetskaya nab 7/9, 199034 Saint Petersburg Russia

KOLTSOV, ANATOLY IVANOVICH, chemistry and spectroscopy researcher, editor; b. Leningrad, Russia, June 4, 1935; s. Ivan Alexeevich and Alexandra Stepanovna (Sapunova) K.; m. Svetlana Vasilievna Mahortych, Jan. 20, 1967; 1 child, Andrey. PhD, Russian Acad. Scis., Leningrad, 1966; D of Chemistry, U. Leningrad, 1978. Jr. rschr. Inst. Macromolecular Compounds Russian Acad. Scis., Leningrad, 1959-71, sr. rschr., 1971-76, head of group, 1977-79, head of lab., 1979—, prof., 1983—; invited lectr. U. Leningrad, 1972-73; lectr. poly. inst., Leningrad, 1970-85. Author: Nuclear Magnetic Resonance in Organic Chemistry, 1968, NMR Spectroscopy in Organic Chemistry, 1983; contbr. articles, editor jours. in field. Grantee Russian Found. Basic Rsch., 1993-96, Internat. Sci. Found., 1994, 95. Mem. Assn. Theoretical Organic Chemistry (St. Petersburg rep.), Mendeleev Chem. Soc. (co-chmn. regular seminar 1971—). Avocations: geographical literature, swimming, skiing, mountaineering. Home: Prospect Thoreza 35-1-152, 194223 St Petersburg Russia Office: IMC RAS, Bolshoi Prospect 31, 199004 St Petersburg Russia

KOLTUNIEWICZ, ANDRZEJ BENEDYKT, chemical engineering educator, researcher; b. Wrocław, Poland, Mar. 11, 1951; s. Romuald Koltuniewicz and Irena Mazurek; m. Magdalena Olipra, Sept. 7, 1974; children: Rafal, Bartosz. MSc, Tech. U. Wroclaw, 1974, DSc, 1978, prof., 1996. Cert. in chem. engring. Instr. Chem. Engring. Inst. Tech. U. Wroclaw, 1974-78, asst. prof., 1978-96, assoc. prof. dept. chemistry, 1996—; designer of membrane processes. Author: (book) The Yield of Pressure Driven Membrane Processes in the Light of Surface Renewal Theory, 1996; sci. sec. Chem. and Process Engring. Jour., 1980-97; contbr. articles to profl. jours. Grantee Ministry of Edn., 1992, 96; fellow Royal Chem. Soc., 1995. Mem. Desalination Soc., European Membrane Soc. Avocations: water sports, traveling, bridge, dogs. Fax: 48-71-320-2919. E-mail: akolt@i-ic.pwr.wroc.pl. Home: ul Litewska 68/1, 51-354PL Wrocław Poland Office: Tech U Wrocław, ul Norwida 4/6, 50-373PL Wrocław Poland

KOM, AMBROISE, literature educator; b. Yogam, Cameroon, Dec. 15, 1946; s. Defomamotcha and Marguerite Wayou; m. Dorothée Njuidje; children: Nouepeyiô, Messà, Ghainsom. Lic in letters, U. Yaounde (Cameroon), 1970, diploma higher studies, 1971; D 3d cycle, U. Pau (France), 1975; D Letters, U. Sorbonne, Paris, 1981. Instr. Brown U., Providence, 1972-75, asst. prof., 1975; asst. prof. Dalhousie U., Halifax, N.S., Can., 1975-77; asst. prof., researcher U. Sherbrooke (Que., Can.), 1978-82; assoc. prof. U. Rabat (Morocco), 1982-84; assoc. prof. lit. U. Yaounde, 1984-88, prof., 1988-97; prof. Coll. of the Holy Cross, Worcester, Mass., 1997—. Author: Le Harlem de Chester Himes, 1978, Dictionnaire des Oeuvres Littéraires Négro-Africaines de Langue Française, 1983, George Lamming et le destin des Caraïbes, 1986, Le Cas Chester Himes, 1990, Education et democratie en Afrique, 1996, Dictionnaire des oeuvres litteraires de langue francaise en Afrique au sud du Sahara, vol. 2, 1996, La Malediction francophone, 2000, Francophonie et dialogue des cultures, 2000. Home: 17 Merlin Ct Worcester MA 01602-1363 Office: Coll of the Holy Cross, Dept Modern Lang/Lit, Box 89A, Worcester Cameroon

KOMADA, NORIKAZU, materials science researcher, chemist; b. Tokyo, Mar. 15, 1952; s. Noriyuki and Chisato (Ohta) K.; m. Kyoko Hasegawa, Nov. 15, 1976; children: Naoko, Shinichi, Akiko. B Engring., U. Tokyo, 1975; MS, U. Mich., 1984, PhD, 1986. First class supr. radiation protection; supr. nuclear fuel handling. Researcher Mitsubishi Materials Corp., Omiya-shi, Japan, 1975-83, sr. researcher, 1989-92, mgr., 1992-99; sr. researcher Tokyo Elec. Power Co., 1986-89; asst. gen. mgr. corp. R & D divsn. Mitsubishi Materials Corp., Tokyo, 1999—. Contbr. articles to profl. jours. Home: 4-13-10 Aoge, Kuki-shi 346-0011, Japan Office: Mitsubishi Materials Corp, 1-5-1 Otemachi Chiyoda-ku, 330-8508 Tokyo 100-8117, Japan

KOMAI, HIROYOSHI, cardiovascular surgeon; b. Kusatsu, Japan, Feb. 1, 1961; s. Norihiko and Setsuko (Yamada) K.; m. Masami Saito, Nov. 24, 1996. MD, Wakayama (Japan) Med. Coll., 1985, PhD, 1995. Bd. cert. mem. Japanese Assns. Surgery and Thoracic Surgery. Trainee Wakayama Med. Coll., 1985-87; resident Nat. Cardiovasc. Ctr., Suita, Japan, 1987-90; rsch. fellow Inst. Child Health, London, 1991-92; hon. sr. registrar Hosps. for Sick Children, London, 1992-93; staff surgeon Wakayama Med. Coll., 1994-99, lectr., 1999—. Author: Cardiopulmonary Bypass in Neonates, Infants and Children, 1994. Avocations: travel, skiing. Home: 3-10 Tanakamachi #404, Wakayama 640-8329, Japan Office: Wakayama Medical College, 811-1 Kimiidera, Wakayama 641-0012, Japan

KOMAKI, HISATOKI, academic administrator; b. Kyoto, Japan, Aug. 29, 1926; s. Saneshige and Kiyoko Komaki; m. Yoriko Komaki. PhD in Agrl. Chemistry, Kyoto U., 1959. Prof. Mukogawa U., 1962-80; hon. prof. Univ. Transnat., Paris, 1980-89; hon. pres. Internat. Earth Environ. U., Otsu, Japan, 1989—. Author: Selected Works of Professor Dr. Hisatoki Komaki - Four Steps to Absolute Peace, 9 vols. Recipient nomination Nobel prize for Physiology and Medicine, 1975, Medal of Honour with Dark Blue Ribbon, Japanese Govt., Red Cross of Japan; Paul Harris fellow Rotary Internat. Mem. Japan Soc. for Biosci., Japan Acad. Sci., Japan Soc. Nutrition and Food Sci. Address: 12 Donokamicho, Matsugasaki Sakyo, Kyoto 606-0917, Japan

KOMAKI, JUNJI, psychologist; b. Ise-shi, Japan, Feb. 25, 1936; s. Kenzo and Shizuko (Nishiura) K.; m. Masako Kitajima, Jan. 26, 1975. BA, Kyoto U., 1958, MA, 1960, LLD, 1965. Instr. Nagoya Inst. Tech., 1963-69; assoc. prof. Kanazawa U., 1970-79, prof., 1980—; councillor Kanazawa U., 1988-94; dean Kanazawa U. Faculty of Letters, 1994-97. Author: Introduction to Data Analysis, 1995, Mind and Instrument, 1995, The Japanese Psychological Research, 1996. Mem. Hokuriku Psychol. Assn. (pres. 1996-97). Avocations: skiing, swimming, reading, music, travel. Home: Kitayasue 1 13 31, Kanazawa 920-0022, Japan Office: Kanazawa U, Kakuma machi, Kanazawa 920-1192, Japan

KOMANDUR, SRIDHAR, communications network designer, researcher; b. Hyderabad, India, Jan. 30, 1969; came to U.S., 1990; s. Ramanujam and Vasantha Komandur; m. Kanaka Komandur, 1995. MSc in Computer Sci., Birla Inst. Tech. & Sci., Pilani, India, 1990; MS in Computer Sci., U. Ctrl. Fla., 1992; PhD in Computer Sci., U. Pitts., 1999. Prin. software engr. Lucent Techs., Westford, Mass., 1998—. Treas. computer sci. dept. U. Pitts., 1993-97. Mem. Comm. Soc. of IEEE. Avocations: reading investment news, skiing, hiking, reading network industry related news. Office: Lucent Techs 1 Robbins Rd Westford MA 01886-4128

KOMANSKY, DAVID H., financial services executive; b. 1939. Grad., U. Miami, 1965. Comptr. Colonial Press, Miami, Fla., 1966-68; with Merrill Lynch & Co., N.Y.C., 1968—, exec. v.p., 1990-92, dir., 1991—, exec. v.p. debt markets, 1992-93, exec. v.p. debt and equity markets, 1993-95, pres., COO, 1995-96; CEO Merrill Lynch & Co., 1996; chmn., CEO Merrill Lynch & Co., Inc., 1997—. Office: Merrill Lynch & Company World Financial Center North Tower 250 Vesey St Fl 4 New York NY 10080-0002

KOMAR, VICTOR GRIGORJEVICH, engineering educator, researcher; b. Sysran, Russia, Sept. 29, 1913; s. Gregory Jakovlevich and Olga Ephremovna (Kouleshova) K.; m. Marina Anatoljevna Borisova (dec. July, 1935); 1 child, Vsevolod; m. Lorena Valerianovna De Pascual, Feb. 25, 1989. Diploma in Elec. Engring., All-Union Indsl. Inst., Moscow, 1937; PhD, Highest Attestation Com., Moscow, 1950. Engr. Moscow Transfer Works, Moscow, 1930-37; rschr. Cinema Rsch. Inst., Moscow, 1937-42, Cinema & Photo Rsch. Inst. (NIKFI), Moscow, 1942-50; dir., deputy dir. NIKFI, Moscow, 1950-81, head of 3-D Cinematography Laboratory, 1964-86, head of Cine-Holography Laboratory, 1986—; lectr. Leningrad Cine-engr. Inst., Samarkand, 1942-44; asst. prof. Moscow Energy Inst., 1944-51, prof., 1951-63. Patentee in field. Deputy of Frunze Dist. Moscow, 1969-71; mem. Communist Party of USSR, Moscow, 1942-91. Recipient Honored Science Worker award Supreme Soviet of Russia, Moscow, 1968, Award of the State Com. of Russia on Cinematography, 1999, Cinematography award Pres. Russia. Mem. SMPTE (Outstanding Contribution to Motion Picture Tech. award, 1972, fellow 1977), British Kinematograph, Sound and TV Soc. (hon. fellow 1973—), Cinematographer Union of Russia (Work for Cinematography award, 1998), Fedn. Nationale des Cinemas Francais (Cinematography award), Internat. Info. Acad. (academician 1995). Home: Leningradsky prospect453243, 125167 Moscow Russia Office: Cine & Photo Inst, Leningradsky prospect 47, 125167 Moscow Russia

KOMAREK, DAVID, pediatrician; b. Hradec Kralovi, Czechoslovakia, Apr. 27, 1970; s. Lummr and Lenka Komarkova; m. Monika Faitlova, Dec. 7, 1991; children: Ondra, Luka. MD, Charles U., Praha, Czechoslavakia, 1994. Registar Dept. Pediat. Tchg. Hosp., Hradec Kralovi, 1994—; registar Pediatric Immunology Clinic Charles U., Hradec Kralovi, 1994—, lectr., 1997—; cons. Ctr. Health Praha; sci. mgr. Pediatric Immunology Ctr., Charles U., Hradec Kralovi. Contbr. articles to profl. jours. Mem. European Soc. Primary Immunodeficiencies, Internat. Soc. Infectious Diseases (corr.). Fax: 420-49-5832030. Office: Charles U Sch Medicine, Teaching Hosp Dept Pediat, CZ-50005 Hradec Kralovi Czechoslovakia

KOMÁREK, MIROSLAV, linguist, educator; b. Lazniky, Czech Republic, Apr. 20, 1924; s. Augustin and Ludmila (Suchna) K.; m. Květoslava Kacálek, Dec. 27, 1949; children: Alena, Jan. MA, Palacky U., Olomouc, Czech Republic, 1949; PhD, Czechoslovak Acad. Scis., 1959; DSc, Charles U., 1981. Asst. prof. slavic philology Palacky U., Olomouc, 1949-62, assoc. prof., 1962-89, prof., 1989—, dir. Slavic Dept., 1967-74, dir. Inst. of Slavic Studies, 1989-95; vice-chmn. Grammatical Com. of Internat. Com. of Slavists, 1984-97; mem. evaluating com. Czech Acad. Scis., 1994—. Author: Czech Historical Grammar-Phonology, 1958, Contributions to Czech Morphology, 1978, Outline of the Czech Morphological Development, 1974; contbr. articles to profl. jours. Mem. Societas Linguistica Europaea, Internat. Soc. Phonetic Scis., Cir. Linguistique de Prague.

KOMAROMI, JOZSEF, mechanical engineer; b. Sept. 4, 1941; s. György and Maria (Faa) K.; m. Margit Varga, June 20, 1964; children: Jozsef Andras. Dipl. Mech. Engr., Tech. U., Budapest, 1964; Dipl. Economist, U. Economy, Budapest, 1976, D in Econs., 1990. Ship machinist Hungarian Shipping Line, Budapest, 1964-65, designer, 1964-70; designer Hungarian Shipyards and Crane Factory, Budapest, 1970-78; sales exec. Szim Machine Tool Works, Budapest, 1978-79; tech. and sci. adv. Freight Transport Orgn., Addis Ababa, Ethiopia, 1979-81; head sales dept. Szim Machine Tool Works, Budapest, 1981-88; tech. and econ. advisor Hungarocamion, Budapest, 1988-97; internat. press exec. FUTTA'R Kft, 1997—; tech. advisor Ministry of Machine Industry, 1973-77; expert of justice Mcpl. Ct. Budapest, 1976—; lectr. in field; supr. car repair shop, Tengiz, Kazakhstan, Tengizchevroil, 1997. Author two books; contbr. articles in profl. jours. Fellow Hungarian Soc. Mech. Engrs. Avocations: photography, model building, languages (German, French, Russian, etc.). Office: FUTTA'R Kft51, Margo Tivadar u 220, H 1181 Budapest H-1442, Hungary

KOMAROMY, PETER, chemical engineer, researcher; b. Veszprem, Hungary, Nov. 24, 1963; s. Lajos and Lenke (Börzsönyi) K.; m. Ildiko Bor, Jan. 22, 1994; 1 child, Luca. BS, U. Veszprem, Hungary, 1985, MS, 1987, D of univ., 1993. Cert. chem. engr. Jr. mem. Rsch. Inst. Chem. Engring., Veszprem, 1987-93, rsch. worker, 1993—; mem. Workgroup Indsl. Biotech., Acad. Com. Veszprem, 1992—. Contbr. articles to profl. jours; patentee in field. Calvinist. Avocations: electronics, gardening, car repair, cycling, skiing. Home: Kengyel u. 30/A, H-8200 Veszprem Hungary Office: Rsch Inst Chemical Engring, Egyetem 2, H-8200 Veszprem Hungary

KOMAROV, SERGEY VICTOROVICH, chemist, researcher; b. Sverdlovsk, Mar. 27, 1958; s. Victor Tikhonovich and Nina Dmitrievna Komarov; m. Nataliya Yurievna Popandopulo Komarov, May 26, 1979 (div. Dec. 1996); 1 child, Olga; m. Yuko Kaneko, June 1, 1997; 1 child, Roman. Master's degree, Moscow Steel and Alloys Inst., 1981, PhD, 1985. Cert. in engring. Asst. prof. Moscow Steel and Alloys Inst., Moscow, 1984-89, 91-93; rschr. Nagoya (Japan) U., 1989-91, asst. prof., 1993-98, assoc. prof., 1998—. Fax: 81 052 789 3225. E-mail: komar@numse.nagoya-u.ac.jp. Home: A-122 Nirabari Kuroishi, 2845-256 Tempaku-cho, Nagoya Aichi 468-0021, Japan Office: Nagoya U Sch Engring, Furo-cho Chikusa-ku, Nagoya Aichi 464-8603, Japan

KOMAROV, VLADISLAV MIKHAILOVICH, biophysicist, educator; b. Kolpashevo, Tomsk, Russia, Aug. 23, 1945; s. Leonid Aleksandrovich Medvedev and Mariya Porphirjevna (Komarova) Medvedeva; m. Galina Nikitichna Peretyat'ko, Oct. 6, 1967; children: Ludmila, Mikhail. MS in Physics, Tomsk State U., 1967; PhD in Physics and Maths., L. Ya. Karpov Phys. Chem. Inst., Moscow, 1978. Student phys. fac. Tomsk State U., 1962-67; postgrad. L. Ya. Karpov Phys. Chem. Inst., Moscow, 1968-71; rsch. asst. Inst. Biol. Phys. Acad. Scis., Pushchino, Russia, 1971-90; rsch. scientist, 1990-91; scientist Inst. Cell Biophys. Acad. Scis., 1991-97, lead scientist, 1997—; reader Pushchino State U., 1995-97; dep. dir. Inst. Cell Biophys. Acad. Sci., Pushchino, 1997—. Contbr. articles to profl. jours. Recipient award Russian Fund Fundamental Rsch., 1999—. Office: Inst Cell Biophys, Acad Scis, 142292 Pushchino Moscow, Russia

KOMAROVA, EMILIA NICOLAEVNA, biologist, researcher; b. Borisoglebsk, Russia, Oct. 5, 1940; d. Nicolai Vasiljevich and Klavdia Vasiljevna (Matveeva) K.; m. Stanislav Petrovich Kalugin; 1 child, Levasheva Irina Anatolievna. Bachelor's degree, Moscow U., 1969. Jr. rschr. Inst. Plant Physiology, Russian Acad. Scis., Moscow, 1979-80, rschr., 1980—. Contbr. numerous papers to sci. jours. Mem. Soc. Russian Plant Physiologists, Fed. European Soc. Plant Physiologists. Avocations: travel, poetry, analysis of Visockii art. Office: Russian Acad Scis, Botanisheskaya 35, 127276 Moscow Russia

KOMATINA, DEJAN M., hydraulics educator, civil engineer; b. Belgrade, Yugoslavia, Dec. 14, 1964; s. Miomir M. and Zorica S. (Popovic) K. BS in Civil Engring., U. Belgrade, 1989, MS in Civil Engring., 1993, PhD in Civil Engring., 1999. Asst. prof. Faculty of Civil Engring., U. Belgrade, 1989—; rschr. Inst. Nuc. Scis., Belgrade, 1995-96; mem. com. on large dams, Belgrade, 1997. Author: River Renaturalization, 1992, Free-surface Flow of Solid-liquid Mixtures, 1997 (Andrejevic Found. award 1997); contbr. articles to sci. jours. Mem. Yugoslav Soc. Hydraulic Rsch., Yugoslav Soc. Mechanics, Internat. Assn. Hydraulic Rsch. Avocations: football, tennis, chess. Fax: 381-11-3370-223. E-mail: dkomat@grf.bg.ac.yu. Office: Fac Civil Engring, Bulevar revolucije 73, 11000 Belgrade Serbia, Yugoslavia

KOMATSU, CHOSEI, music director, conductor; b. Japan, Mar. 1, 1958; s. Chosho and Kiyoko (Yamada) K.; m. Christine Walters, July 31, 1990. BA, Tokyo U., 1982; DMA in Orch. Conducting, Eastman Sch. Music, 1989. Exxon/Arts Endowment condr. Buffalo Philharm. Orch., 1986-88; assoc. condr. Balt. Symphony Orch., 1988-92; music dir. Kitchener-Waterloo Symphony Orch., 1993-99; prin. condr. Japan Shinsei Symphony Orch., 2000—; music dir. Takefu Internat. Music Festival, Japan, 1994-97; music dir. Can. Chamber Ensemble, 1993-99; guest appearances with Tokyo Philharm., Japan Philharm., Bolshoi Theater, Saltzburg Festival, Moscow Radio Symphony, others. Office: 19 Stonegate Dr, Kitchener, ON Canada N2A 2Y7

KOMATSU, EISUKE, linguistics and French literature educator; b. Nagoya, Aichi Pre., Japan, Sept. 20, 1940; s. Hitoshi and Shizue (Ogawa) K.; m. Mieko Hirose, Dec. 23, 1977; 1 child, Miwa. Bachelor's degree, Keio U., Tokyo, 1964, MA in French Lit., 1968, Doctorate, 1971; postgrad., Paris U., 1973-76. Prof. linguistics and French lit. Gakushuin U., Tokyo, 1980—; guest rschr. Harvard U., 1986-87. Author: Ferdinand de Saussure, 1993, Saussure's First Course of Lectures on General Linguistics, 1990, 2d Course, 1997, 3d Course, 1993. Mem. French Lit. Soc. Japan, Am. Soc. Semiotics. Home: 187-59 Shimoyasumatsu, Tokorozawa 359-0024, Japan Office: Gakushuin U, 1-5-1- Mejiro, Toshima-ku, Tokyo 171-8588, Japan

KOMATSU, KENJI, economics educator; b. Komoro, Japan, Jan. 3, 1935; s. Hisao and Chiyoko (Tamura) K.; m. Akiko Kobayashi, Nov. 12, 1960; children: Masayoshi, Nobuyoshi. B in Econs., Waseda U., Tokyo, 1958, M in Econs., 1960; D of Econs., Waseda U., 1985. Rschr. Inst. World Economy, Tokyo, 1963-66, sr. rschr., 1966-68; lectr. Chiba U., Chiba City, 1968-71, asst. prof., 1971-83, prof. econs., 1983-99, prof. emeritus, 1999—, dean faculty of law and econs., 1993-95; prof. internat. polit. sci. and econs. Nihon U. Grad. Sch. Social and Cultural Studies, Saitama, Japan, 1999—; vis. prof. Waseda U., Tokyo, 1969-93; vis. scholar UCLA, 1976-77; rsch. assoc. Harvard U., Cambridge, Mass., 1977. Author: Inflation in Our Time, 1980, Japanese Economy, 1982; co-author: Economic Policy, 1981, The American Economy, 1985. Mem. Japan Assn. Econ. Policy (bd. dirs.), Assn. Monetary Econs., Assn. Internat. Econs., Mont Pelerin Soc. Avocations: go-game, music, art, swimming, skiing. Home: 1-6-50-403 Akabanedai, Kita-ku, Tokyo 115-0053, Japan Office: Nihon U GSSC, 4-25 Nakatomi-minami, Saitama Tokorozawa 359-0003, Japan

KOMATSU, KOICHI, chemistry educator; b. Kyoto, Japan, May 24, 1942; s. Shoichi and Tazuko (Dohi) K.; m. Yoko Hori, July 15, 1973; children: Kenichi, Yoji. B in Engring., Kyoto U., 1966, M in Engring., 1968, PhD, 1971. Postdoctoral rsch. fellow U. Wis., Madison, 1975-76; instr. chemistry Kyoto U., 1971-75, 76-84, lectr., 1984-89, assoc. prof., 1989-95, prof. organic chemistry, 1995—; Assoc. editor Chemistry Letters, Jour. Chem. Soc. Japan, 1992-95, Jour. Synthetic Chemistry, 1995—, Methods of Organic Chemistry, supplement vol. E17 Cyclopropenylium Salts; patentee in field (2). Contbr. numerous articles to acad. jours.; patentee in field (2). Richardson scholar Davidson Coll., N.C., 1963; grantee Nishida Meml. Fund for Fundamental Organic Chemistry, Nishida Found., Tokyo, 1993, Yamada Sci. Found., Osaka, Japan, 1994; acad. grantee Inamori Found., Kyoto, 1995, Ciba-Geigy Found., Takarazuka, 1996. Fellow Royal Soc. Chemistry; mem. Chem. Soc. Japan (mem. exec. com. 1990-92), Am. Chem. Soc. (organic chemistry divsn.). Avocations: playing piano and guitar, skiing, sailing. Office: Kyoto U, Inst Chem Rsch, Uji Kyoto 611-0011, Japan

KOMATSU, TAMIKUNI, chemical engineer, researcher; b. Kure, Hiroshima, Japan, May 9, 1948; s. Yuso and Yaeka Komatsu; m. Akiko Matsumoto, Mar. 11, 1979; 1 child, Shunnpei. BS, Hiroshima U., 1972, MS, 1974, DEng, 1993. Rsch. staff Rayon Factory Asahi Chem. Industry, Nobeoka, 1975-76; sr. rsch. staff Product Rsch. Ctr. Asahi Chem. Industry, Fuji, 1976-82, sr. rschr. Tech. Rsch. Ctr., 1982-91, mgr. Analytical Rsch. Ctr., 1991-92; assoc. dir., 1993—; rschr. Advanced Chem. Processing Tech. Assn., Tokyo, 1991—. Contbr. articles to profl. jours. including Polymer, Jour. Materials Sci., Jour. Polymer Sci., Macromolecules, Jour. Materials Chemistry, Jour. of the Chem. Soc. Recipient Tech. Authentication award Doboku Kenkyu Ctr. Found., 1991, article prize Nippon Kogyo Syuppan, 1991. Mem. Am. Chem. Soc., Soc. Polymer Sci. Japan, Carbon Soc. Japan, Japan Inst. Metals, N.Y. Acad. Scis., Planetary Soc. Avocations: swimming, art appreciation, movie appreciation, reading, traveling. Home: Ninomiya Dai-ni Apt 1-201, Ninomiya 4-13-1 Tsukuba-shi, Ibaraki 305, Japan Office: Nat Inst Material Chem Rsch, Higashi 1-1 Tsukuba-shi, Ibaraki 305, Japan

KOMENDA, STANISLAV, statistician, biometrician, consultant; b. Louka, Czech Republic, May 7, 1936; s. Karel and Ružena (Plechl) K.; m. Eva Hokr, July 5, 1959; children: Novak Sylvia, Malik Eva, Duben Marketa. Grad., Charles U., Prague, Czech Republic, 1959, Rerum Naturalium Doctor, 1973; Scientist Candidatium, Charles U., 1979, DSc, 1991. Asst. prof. Palacky U., Olomouc, Czech Republic, 1959-78, rsch. fellow, 1978-90, assoc. prof., 1990-93, prof., 1993—; head Biometric Inst. faculty medicine Palacky U., 1988—, head dept. politology faculty philosophy, 1993-95. Author: Proportion of Body Dimensions in Children and Youth, 1978, Random Analysis in Educational Theory and Practice, 1981 (Rector's prize 1982), Halftime of Forgetting, 1998, Thoughts 9, 1998, Reflexions and Aphorisms, 1999, Creation and Testing of the Tests, 1995; chief editor (in Czech) Pacemaker jour., 1988-90. Vice chmn. Masaryk Soc., Olomouc, 1990—; mem. Cmty. Czech Writers, Prague, 1993—. With Czech Nat. Army, 1959-60. Recipient Dr. A. Hrdlička medal Czech Anthropol. Soc., 1995. Mem. N.Y. Acad. Scis., Internat. Soc. Engring. Edn., Med. Soc. J.E. Purkyně (prize 1972, 74, 83), Czech Stats. Soc. Roman Catholic. E-mail: komendas@risc.upol.cz. Home: 9 Neredinska St, 77900 Olomouc Czech Republic Office: Palacky Univ Fac Medicine, 3 Hnevotinska St, 77515 Olomouc Czech Republic

KOMILOV, ABDULAZIZ, Uzbek government official; b. Yangiyul, Uzbekistan, Nov. 16, 1947. PhD History Fgn. Policy Internat. Rels., Acad. of Min. of Fgn. Affairs of USSR, 1978. Diplomate Amb. Extraordinary and Plenipotentiary Sch., 1966; diplomatic svc., 1972—; attaché Embassy of USSR, Lebanon, 1973-76; rsch. fellow Inst. Oriental Studies USSR Acad. Scis., 1978-80, sr. officer Inst. World Econ. and Internat. Affairs, 1988-91; second sec. Embassy of USSR, Syria, 1980-84; officer Middle East dept. Ministry of Fgn. affairs, USSR, 1984-88; counsellor Embassy of Uzbekistan, Russian Fedn., 1991-92; dep. chmn. Nat. Security Svc., Uzbekistan, 1992-94; first dep. min. fgn. affairs Govt. of Uzbekistan, Tashkent, 1994, min. fgn.

affairs, 1994—. Office fax: 998 71 139-15-17. Office: Ministry of Fgn Affairs, 9 Uzbekistan St, 700029 Tashkent Uzbekistan

KOMIYAMA, HIROSHI, chemical engineer, educator; b. Tokyo, Japan, Dec. 15, 1944. BS, U. Tokyo, 1967, MEng, 1969, PhD, 1972. Asst. U. Tokyo, 1972-77; postdoctoral fellow U. Calif., Davis, 1973-74; lectr. U. Tokyo, 1977-81, assoc. prof., 1981-88, prof., 1988-2000, dean sch. engring., 2000—. Author: Rate Processes, 1990, The Responce to the Global Environmental Problems, 1995, Reaction Engineering, 1995, Introduction to Thermodynamics, 1996, Technology for Global Sustainability, 1999. Recipient Best Paper of Yr. award Soc. Chem. Engrs. Japan, 1979, Best Rsch. of Yr. award Soc. Chem. Engrs. Japan, 1992. Home: 5-4-4 Daita Setagaya-ku, Tokyo 155-0033, Japan Office: Univ Tokyo Faculty Engring, 7-3-1 Hongo Bunkyo-ku, Tokyo 113-8656, Japan

KOMLOS, PETER, violinist; b. Budapest, Hungary, Oct. 25, 1935; s. Laszlo and Franciska (Graf) K.; m. Edit Feher, 1960; 2 sons; m. Zsuzsanna Arki, 1984; 1 son. Educated, Budapest Music Acad. founded Komlos String Quartet, 1957; 1st violinist Budapest Opera Orchestra, 1960; leader Bartok String Quartet, 1963; extensive concert tours to USSR, Scandinavia, Italy, Austria, W.Ger., Czechoslovakia, 1958-64, to U.S., Can., N.Z., Australia, 1970, Japan, Spain, Portugal, 1971; Far East, U.S., Europe, 1973; recordings include Beethoven's string quartets for Hungaroton, Budapest; Bartok's string quartets for Erato, Paris, all Bartok's Quartets, 1991-92, Different Haydn Quartets, Canyon Classic-Japan, Mendelssohn-Schonberg Pieces, Hunghroton, 1992. Recipient 1st prize Internat. String Quartet Competition, Liè ge, 1964, Liszt prize, 1965, Gramopone Record prize of Germany, 1969, Kossuth prize, 1970, second Kossuth prize, 1997, UNESCO Music Coun. placque, 1981; named Eminent Artist, 1980.

KOMM, KERMIT MATTHEW, software engineer; b. LaGrange, Ill., Apr. 9, 1964; s. Charles Paul and Dorothy Anna Jean (Groves) K. BS in Elec. Engring., UCLA, 1986. Dir. ops. Leviathan Devel., L.A., 1986-90; software engr. FortuNet, Las Vegas, Nev., 1991; v.p. software engring. Future Techs., Las Vegas, 1991-95; v.p. engring. Innovation Mgmt. Group, Las Vegas, 1995—. Author: (software) My-T-Mouse, 1993, Joystick-to-Mouse, 1995, My-T-Soft AT, 1998, The Magnifier, 1998. Avocations: travel, driving, hiking. Office: Innovation Mgmt Group Inc 4425 E Sahara Ave Ste 9 Las Vegas NV 89104-6357

KOMMEDAHL, THOR, plant pathology educator; b. Mpls., Apr. 1, 1920; s. Thorbjorn and Martha (Blegen) K.; m. Faye Lillian Jensen, June 2, 1924; children: Kris Alan, Siri Lynn, Lori Anne. B.S., U. Minn., 1945, M.S., 1947, Ph.D., 1951. Instr. U. Minn., St. Paul, 1946-51, asst. prof. plant pathology, 1953-57, assoc. prof., 1957-63, prof., 1963-90, prof. emeritus, 1990—; asst. prof. plant pathology Ohio Agrl. Research and Devel. Ctr., Wooster, 1951-53, Ohio State U., Columbus, 1951-53; prof. Univ. Coll., U. Minn., St. Paul, 1990—; cons. botanist and taxonomist Minn. Dept. Agr., 1954-60, Sci. Mus. Minn., 1990—; 7th A.W. Dimock lectr. Cornell U., 1979; external assessor U. Pertanian Malaysia, 1994-97. Author: Pesky Plants, 1989; co-author: Scientific Style and Format, 1994; editor Minn. Fulbright newsletter, 1993—, Procs. IX Internat. Congress Plant Protection, 2 vols., 1981, Corn Disease newsletter, 1970-76; assoc. editor The Boghopper, 1996—; cons. editor McGraw Hill Ency. Sci. and Tech., 1972-78; editor-in-chief Phytopathology, 1964-67; sr. editor: Challenging Problems in Plant Health, 1982, Plant Disease Reporter, 1979; contbr. articles to profl. jours. Bd. mem. Park Bugle, 1998—. Recipient Elvin Charles Stakman award, 1990, Award of Merit, Gamma Sigma Delta, 1994; Guggenheim fellow, 1961, Fulbright scholar, 1968. Fellow AAAS, Am. Phytopathol. Soc. (councilor 1958-60, pres. 1971, publs. coord. 1978-84, Disting. Svc. award 1984, 93, sci. adv. 1984—, mem. adv. bd. office internat. programs 1987-93, editor Focus 1981—); mem. Am. Inst. Biol. Scis., Bot. Soc. Am., Coun. Sci. Editors, Internat. Soc. Plant Pathology (councilor 1971-78, sec.-gen. and treas. 1983-88, treas. 1988-93, editor newsletter 1983-93), Mycol. Soc. Am., Minn. Acad. Sci., N.Y. Acad. Scis., Weed Sci. Soc. Am. (award of excellence 1968), Fulbright Assn. (Minn. chpt., editor newsletter 1995—). Baptist. Home: 1666 Coffman St Apt 322 Saint Paul MN 55108-1340 Office: U Minn 495 Borlaug Hall 1991 Upper Buford Cir Saint Paul MN 55108-0010

KOMMONEN, BERTEL WILHELM, veterinarian, researcher; b. Joutseno, Karelia, Finland, Dec. 7, 1947; s. Harry Robert and Lisa (Tainio) K.; m. Signe Christine Ek, June 17, 1978; children: Johan Erik, Robert Michael. DVM, Coll. Vet. Medicine, Vienna, Austria, 1975, Coll. Vet. Medicine, Helsinki, Finland, 1977; PhD, Coll. Vet. Medicine, Helsinki, Finland, 1988. Cert. vet. medicine, Finland, 1977. Asst. prof. surgery Coll. Vet. Medicine, Helsinki, 1984-90, acting prof. surgery, 1990-91, acting. assoc. prof. diagnostic radiology, 1992-93, acting prof. surgery, 1993-95, asst. prof. surgery, 1995—; rschr. dept. ophthalmology Coll. Medicine, U. Ark. Med. Sci., Little Rock, 1991-92; rschr. dept. ophthalmology U. Helsinki, 1988; adj. assoc. prof. ophthalmology Coll. Medicine, U. Fla., Gainesville, 1988-89. Contbr. articles to profl. jours. 2d lt. Finnish mil., 1967-68. Recipient rsch. funding Sigrid Juselius Found., Helsinki, 1991, 92, Coll. Vet. Medicine, Helsinki, 1993-96. Mem. Assn. Rsch. in Vision and Ophthalmology, Internat. Soc. Clin. Electrophysiology of Vision, Finnish Vet. Assn. Lutheran.l. Avocations: jogging, outdoor activities, model aeroplanes. Office: U Helsinki Faculty Vet Medicine, PO Box 57, 00014 Helsinki Finland

KOMOLOWSKI, LONGIN, federal official; b. Czaplinek, Jan. 5, 1948; married; 2 children. Grad., Szczecin Poly. Min. Labor and Social Policy, 1997—; dep. prime min. Solidarity Election Action. Address: Aleje Ujazdowskie 1/3, 00-583 Warsaw Poland Office: Min Labor Social Policy, ul Nowogrodzka 1/3, 00-513 Warsaw Poland*

KOMORI, TERUHISA, psychiatrist, researcher; b. Suzuka, Mie, Japan, July 3, 1954; s. Kenji and Chieko (Kiba) K.; m. Eri Oda, Apr. 24, 1983; children: Shuya, Koki. MD, Mie U. Sch. Medicine, Tsu, Japan, 1989. Lectr. Mie U. Sch. Medicine, Tsu, 1993—. Contbr. articles to profl. jours. Mem. Japanese Soc. Psychiatry and Neurology, World Fedn. Socs. of Biol. Psychiatry, Internat. Soc. Neuroimmunomodulation. Buddhist. Avocations: travel, reading, gardening, appreciation of art, studying history. Office: Dept Psychiatry Mie U, 2-174 Edobashi, Tsu 514-8507, Japan

KOMOROSKI, RICHARD ANDREW, medical sciences educator, spectroscopy researcher; b. St. Louis, Feb. 4, 1947; s. Andrew Henry and Frances Mae (Esterman) K.; m. Eva Maria Marczewski, May 12, 1979; children: Elizabeth Anne, Christopher Mark, Laura Catherine. BS, St. Louis U., 1969; PhD, Ind. U., 1973. Chemist Mo. Analytical Labs., St. Louis, 1969; postdoctoral fellow Fla. State U., Tallahassee, 1973-76; sr. rsch. chemist Diamond Shamrock Corp., Painesville, Ohio, 1976-79; rsch. assoc. BF Goodrich Co., Brecksville, Ohio, 1979-85; prof. depts. radiology, pathology, psychiatry, biochemistry U. Ark. for Med. Scis., Little Rock, 1986—; cons. ARCO Oil and Gas Co., Plano, Tex., 1988-90; grant reviewer Petroleum Rsch. Fund, Ark. Sci. and Tech. Authority, NSF, NIH. Editor: High Resolution NMR Spectroscopy of Synthetic Polymers in Bulk, 1986; contbr. over 100 articles to sci. publs.; referee numerous sci. jours. Tutor Bldg. Bright Futures program Christ the King Parish, Little Rock, 1988-92; mem. Parents' Club Bd. Mt. Notre Dame H.S., Cin. Advanced study travel grantee NATO, Pisa, Italy, 1972; rsch. grantee Whitaker Found., 1987, State of Ark., 1987, 95, USAF, 1989, NIH, 1993, 98. Mem. AAAS, Internat. Soc. Magnetic Resonance in Medicine, Ampere Soc., European Soc. Magnetic Resonance in Medicine and Biology, Am. Chem. Soc. (alt. coun. Cleve. sect. 1984-86, chair pub. affairs 1982-84), Soc. Biol. Psychiatry. Achievements include research in nuclear magnetic resonance applications to in vivo biochemistry, materials and polymers, and nuclear magnetic resonance applications in detection of psychoactive drugs, and in psychiatry. Office: NMR Lab 151K/NLR VA Med Ctr 2200 Fort Roots Dr North Little Rock AR 72114-1709

KOMOROWSKI, BRONISLAW, minister of defense; b. Oborniki, Poland, June 4, 1952; married; 5 children. Grad., U. Warsaw. Jr. editor Slowo Powszechne newspaper, 1977-80; with Pub. Opinion Rsch. Ctr. Solidarity Ind. Trade Union, Mazovia, 1980-81; tchr. at seminary Niepokalanow, 1981-89; cabinet dir. Office of Coun. of Mins., 1989-90; civilian vice min. nat. def. Poland, 1990-93; chmn. Sejm Nat. Def. Commn.; min. nat. def. Poland, 2000—; activist Workers Def. Com., Movement for Defense of Civic Rights; chmn. Sejm Nat. Def. Commn. representing Solidarity Electoral Action. Pub., editor Historical and Literary Library, ABC. Active in ind. democratic opposition during Polish People's Rep.; organizer patriotic rallies, Warsaw; interned during martial law in camps at Bialoleka and Jawor; scouting instr., co-founder Polish Cmty. Party.; chmn. Maritime and River League, Polish Libs. Assistance Fund. Office: Ministry Nat Def, ul Klonowa 1, 00-909 Warsaw Poland*

KOMOROWSKI, STANISLAW MAURICE, finance educator, consultant; b. Paris, May 19, 1917; arrived in Poland, 1922; s. Jerzy and Henryka (Marconi) K.; m. Janina Elisabeth Blauth, Apr. 29, 1941; children: Maria, Anna, Jerzy. MS, Mining Acad., Krakow, Poland, 1948; PhD, U. Warsaw, Poland, 1968. Engr. Trzyniec (Poland) Steelworks, 1939; steel foundry mgr. Lilpop, Rauloevenstein Nasszana S.A., Warsaw, Poland, 1939-44; gen. mgr. Pafanag Rolling Stock, Wroclaw, Poland, 1945-48, FSO Automobile Factory, Warszawa, 1948-49; expert Prozamet Consulting Orgn., Warszawa, 1949-60, Cekop Fgn. Trade Orgn., Warszawa, 1960-64; dir. rsch. and planning UN Econ. Com. to Africa, Addis-Araba, Ethiopia, 1965-72; cons. State Planning Commn., Warsawa, 1972-78; prof. U. Warsawa, 1978-93; cons. Warsawa, 1993—. Contbr. articles to profl. jours. With Polish Underground Army, 1940-48. Mem. Assn. Polish Mech. Engrs., Assn. Sci. Orgn. and Mgmt. Avocation: hunting. Home: Olimpijska 37, 02636 Warszawa Poland

KOMPANICHENKO, VLADIMIR NICOLAJEVICH, research scientist, educator, researcher; b. Yalta, Crimea, USSR, Oct. 28, 1952; s. Nicolai Firsovich and Lidija Rodionovna (Busygina) K.; m. Alla Leonidovna Voronina, Mar. 19, 1999; children: Alla, Philipp. Degree in engring., U. Rostov, 1974; D degree, Far East Geology Rsch. Inst., Vladivostok, Russia, 1983. Engr. Far East Mineral Resources Rsch. Inst., Khabarovsk, 1974-79, rschr., 1979-83, sr. rschr., 1983-93; sr. rschr. Complex Analysis of Regional Problems Inst., Birobidzhan, 1993—; tchr. State Med. U., Khabarovsk, 1994-95, U. Transp., 1995—; chmn. Future Generation Problems Rsch. Ctr., Khabarovsk, 1995—. Author: Evolution Magmatic and Oremagmatic Systems, 1984, Origin of Biosphere in the Bowels of the Earth, 1991, Self-Organization of Individual-The Way to Flourishing of Humankind, 1994, Hydrothermal Origin of Life in Earth Depth, 1996; contbr. articles to profl. jours. Mem. Internat. Soc. for Origin of Life, N.Y. Acad. Scis., Internat. Sociol. Assn. Avocations: literature, art, music, tourism, sports. Office: Future Generations Ctr FGC, 31 Gerasimov St, 680021 Khabarovsk Russia

KOMPATSCHER, PETER, plastic surgeon, consultant; b. Bozen, Italy, May 20, 1951; arrived in Austria, 1980; s. Johann Kompatscher and Elisabeth Franzelin; m. Brigitte Maria Weilander, Aug. 24, 1990; 1 child, Arno. MD, U. Innsbruck, Austria, 1977. Registered med. doctor. Resident traumatology Fed. State Hosp., Bozen, 1977-78; resident gen. surgery U. Hosp., Ulm, Germany, 1978-79; resident gen. surgery U. Hosp., Innsbruck, 1979-83, resident plastic surgery, 1983-87; cons. plastic surgeon Fed. State Hosp., Feldkirch, Austria, 1988—; nat. del. for Austria, Med. Specialities in the European Union, Brussels, 1995—. Contbr. articles to profl. jours.; nat. editor Internat. Video Jour. Plastic Surgery. With Italian Mil., 1977-78. Recipient Aeska award Austrian Dematol. Soc., 1989, Durig Böhler awards Fed. State Vorarlberg, Austria, 1992, 95. Mem. Nat. Soc. Plastic, Aesthetic and Reconstructive Surgery (gen. sec. 1993-97, v.p. 1997-99, pres. 1999—), Italian Soc. Plastic Surgery, Internat. Soc. Aesthetic Plastic Surgery, Internat. Burn Soc., Nat. Soc. Hand Surgery, German Soc. Microsurgery, Rotary Club. Roman Catholic. Avocations: motorcycling, skiing, reading. Home: IM Buchholz 14, 6820 Frastanz Austria Office: Dept Plastic Surgery, Landeskrankenhaus Feldkirch, 6800 Feldkirch Austria

KOMPRDA, TOMÁŠ, nutritionist, educator; b. Jihlava, Czech Republic, Nov. 27, 1954; s. Jiří Komprda and Dagmar Kothbauerová; m. Jana Králová, Dec. 29, 1979; 1 child, Zuzana. MS, Chem. U., Pardubice, Czech Republic, 1979; PhD, Agrl. U., Brno, Czech Republic, 1989; DVM, Vets. U., Brno, 1994. Rschr. Vets. Rsch. Inst., Brno, 1980-83, Plant Breeding Inst., Troubsko, Czech Republic, 1983-89; rschr. Agrl. U., Brno, 1989-95, asst. prof., 1995—. Contbr. articles to profl. jours. Capt. chem. corps Czech Army, 1979-80. Rsch. grantee Grant Agy. Czech Republic, 1993, 97, 99. Mem. Czech Soc. Nutrition. Avocations: basketball, karate, history, hiking. E-mail: komprda@mendelu.cz. Home: Vaňkovo, Náměstí 6, 60200 Brno Czech Republic Office: Mendel U Agr and Forestry, Zemědělská 1, 61300 Brno Czech Republic

KÖMÜRCÜGIL, HASAN, engineering educator; b. Kilitkaya, G. Magusa, Cyprus, Feb. 22, 1965; s. Hasim Ali and Havva (Ismail) K.; m. Icten Erbilen, June 12, 1993; 1 child, Icim. B Engring., Eastern Mediteranean U., G. Magusa, 1989, M Engring., 1991, PhD, 1998. Rsch. asst. Eastern Mediterranean U., G. Magusa, 1989-91, 93-98, asst. prof. engring., 1998—. Mem. IEEE, IEEE/PES, IEEE/IES. Avocations: playing football, swimming, listening to music, hunting. Home: 4 Etap Sosyal Konutlar, Venus Sokak, G Magusa Mersin10, Turkey Office: Eastern Mediterranean U, Computer Engring Dept, G Magusa Mersin10, Turkey

KÖMÜRLÜOGLU, MEHMET MUSTAFA, machine tool trader; b. Sivas, Turkey, Oct. 12, 1956; s. Mehmet Suzi and Nevin (Okatan) K.; m. Sadan Guler, May 18, 1983; children: Mehmet Ali, Sena. BSME, Bogaziçi U., Istanbul, Turkey, 1981. Sales mgr. Burla Makina, Istanbul, 1983-86; editor Makina & Metal, Istanbul, 1988—; owner Mustek Takim Tezgahlari Ltd., Istanbul, 1997—. 2d lt. Turkish Land Forces, 1981-83. Mem. Soc. of Manufacturing Engrs., Am. Welding Soc., Machine Tool Businessman's Assn. of Turkey (vice chmn. 1994-96, chmn. 1996-98). Home: Ataturk C Eston, B Blok D 26, 81080 Istanbul Turkey

KONAKOV, NIKOLAI DMITRIJEVICH, ethnologist, educator; b. Drezden, Germany, Dec. 2, 1946; s. Dmitrij and Natalja (Ostanina) K.; m. Antonina Kiseljova, July 12, 1975; 1 child. DSc, Inst. Ethnography, 1979. From postgrad. to dir. dept. ethnology & folklore Komi Sci. Ctr., Syktyvkar, Russia, 1975—. Author: Komi Hunter and Fishermen, 1983, Ethnoareal Groups of Komi, 1991, Traditional Outlook of Komi, 1996; contbr. articles to profl. jours. Office: Komi Sci Ctr Ethnology, 26 Kommunisticheskaya Str, 167610 Syktyvkar Komi, Russia

KONAN, LAMBERT KOUASSI, Ivory Coast minister agriculture, animal resources; b. Tubalo, Mankono, Ivory Coast, Mar. 27, 1930; m.; 7 children. Degree, Ecole Nat. Profl., Nantes, France, 1952; postgrad. studies, Indsl. Elec. Sch., Paris, 1953-55. Inspector gen. Elec. Energy of Ivory Coast, Abidjan, 1959-67, dep. mng. dir., 1967-69, mng. dir., 1969-90; chief of staff Ministry of Agr., Abidjan, 1970-76; pres. Motoagri divsn. Sodesucre Co., Abidjan, 1970-76; 5 Cofruitel, Abidjan, 1982-85; minister agriculture and animal resources Govt. Ivory Coast, Abidjan, 1990—. Mem. exec. com. Dem. Party of Côte d'Ivoire-African Democratic Rally, 1965-70, 1980—, polit. bur., 1970-80. Office: Min Agr Ani Res Rue Lecoeur, Immeuble Caisse Stabilisat, BP V-82 Abidjan Ivory Coast also: 2424 Massachusetts Ave NW Washington DC 20008*

KONARE, ALPHA OUMAR, Malian government official; b. Kayes, 1946; m. Adam Ba.; 4 children. Attended Ecole Nat. Supérieure, U. Warsaw, Poland. Tchr. Dir. Inst. Human Scis., Bamako, 1974; tchr. historic and ethnographic divsn. Min. Culture, 1975-78; min. youth, Sports and Culture, 1978-80; rsch. fellow Inst. Supérieure de Formation et de Recherche Appliquée, Bamako, 1980-89, Jamana, 1983, Les Echos, Grin Grin, 1989; pres. Mali, 1992—. Author: Le Concept du Pouvoir en Afrique, Bibliographie Archéologique du Mali, (with Adam Ba) Les Grandes Dates du Mali, Sikasso Tata, Les Constitutions du Mali, Les Partis Politiques au Mali. Office: Office of Pres, BP 1463, Bamako Mali*

KONDAPI, VISWANATH, electrical engineer; b. Gurazala, India, Nov. 16, 1938; s. Kondayya and Venkata (Subbamma) K.; m. Nalini, June 14, 1967; children: Harita, Yoshita. M in tech., Osmania Univ., Hyderabad, India, 1983. Jr. elec. engr. Andhra Pradesh State Elec. Bd., Hyderabad, India, 1961, chief elec. engr., 1995. Fellow Inst. of Engrs. India; mem. Inst. Elec. and Electronics Engrs. Inc., (sr.), Inst. Plant Engrs. India (life), Indian Soc. Tech. Edn. India (life), Ctrl. Bd. Irrigation and Power India (life), Computer Soc. India (life). Avocations: music, gardening, photography, contract bridge. Home: A 106 Matrusri Apts, 500029 Hyderabad India Office: Andhra Pradesh State Elec Bd, 500049 Hyderabad India

KONDAS, NICHOLAS FRANK, shipping company executive; b. Eger, Hungary, Sept. 26, 1929; came to U.S., 1957.; s. Miklos and Ilona (Racz) K.; m. Elfriede O. Strauss; children: Walter, Nicolette. MS in Econs., Karl Marx U., Budapest, Hungary, 1952. Mgr. Szovosz Cent., Budapest, Hungary, 1952-56; assembler S. Goldberg Inc., Hackensack, N.J., 1957-67; supr. Alfred Industries, Richfield Park, N.J., 1967-68; mgr. C.R. Bard, New Providence, N.J., 1968-69; v.p. Seatrain Lines Inc., N.Y.C., 1969-81; gen. mgr. Harper Robinson Co., San Francisco, 1981-82; v.p. Farrell Lines Inc., N.Y.C., 1982—; pres. Dionic Resources Inc., 1994—; v.p. Transp. Sys. Internat., Washington, 1980—, Pacific Enterprises Inc., 1992—; pres. Dionic Resources Inc., 1994—. Served to lt. Hungary Army Res., 1952-56. Mem. Nat. Def. Transp. Assn., 1982—. Avocation: photography. Office: Farrell Lines Inc 1 Whitehall St Fl 12 New York NY 10004-2185

KONDO, KATSUHIKO, botanist; b. Nagoya, Japan, May 5, 1944; s. Tokuyoshi and Suzue (Sakai) K.; m. Kazuko Morita, Aug. 18, 1974; children: Yucca, Masahiko. BA, Tokyo U. Agriculture, Tokyo, 1968; MA, U. N.C., Chapel Hill, 1971; D of Philosophy, U. N.C., 1975. Lecturer U. Md., College Park, 1976; rsch. assoc. Hiroshima (Japan) U., 1976-79, asst. prof., 1979-82, assoc. prof., 1982-89; prof. Hiroshima U., Higashi-Hiroshima, 1989—, dir. lab. plant chromsome and gene stock, 1989—; hon. prof. Inst. Botany Chinese Acad. Scis., 1991. Editl. adv. bd. Caryologia; contbr. articles to profl. jours. Trustee Agrl. Gene Bank Hiroshima, Hiroshima City Pk. Assn. Recipient William Chamber Coker fellow U. N.C., 1974. Fellow Linnean Soc. London; mem. Genetic Soc. Japan (councilor), Bot. Soc. Japan (councilor), Soc. Chromosome Rsch. (councilor, editor 1993—, bd. dirs. 1994—), Hiroshima Biotech. Assn. (trustee), Japan Mendel Soc. (councilor). Avocations: fishing, wildlife games. Home: 2-10-1 Nishi, Misuzu-ga-oka Saeki-ku, Hiroshima 731-5114, Japan Office: Hiroshima U, 1-4-3 Kagamiyama, Higashi-Hiroshima 739-8526, Japan

KONDO, KAZUHIRO, educator, researcher; b. Yachiyo, Chiba, Japan, Sept. 2, 1959; s. Teruo and Masae (Kobayashi) K.; m. Yukari Okumura, Jan. 14, 1995. B in Engring., Waseda U., Tokyo, 1982, M in Engring., 1984; PhD, Waseda Univ., 1998. Rschr. Hitachi, Kokubunji, Japan, 1984-92, Texas Instruments, Tsukuba, Japan, 1992-96, Tex. Instruments, Inc., 1996-98; assoc. prof. Yamagata U., 1999—. Organizing mem. Ski Assn. of Kokubunji, 1990-92. Mem. IEEE, Inst. Electronics, Info. and Comm. Engrs. of Japan, Acoustical Soc. Japan. Avocations: skiing, jogging, reading novels, watching movies. Office: Yamagata Univ Fac Engrg, 4-3-16 Jonan, Yonezawa, Yamagata 992-8510, Japan

KONDO, KEN-ICHI, educator; b. Takamatsu, Japan, Feb. 23, 1948; s. Yoshinobu and Umeno (Tsutui) K.; m. Mitsuko Sato, May 3, 1970 (div. Mar. 1982); 1 child, Sayaka. BS, Tokyo Inst. Tech., 1971, MS, 1973, PhD, 1976. Rsch. assoc. Titech, Tokyo, 1976-80, 81-82, assoc. prof., 1982-94, prof., 1994—; vis. assoc. Calif. Tech. U., Pasadena, 1980-81; vis. rschr. Nat. Inst. Rsch. Inorganic Materials, Tsukuba, Japan, 1984-98; exec. New Diamond Forum, Tokyo, 1993-95, Japan Soc. high Pressure Sci. & Tech., Kyoto, 1995—, AIRAPT, 1999—. Avocations: skiing, sailing, cooking. Office: Materials & Structures Lab, 4259 Midori, Yokohama 226-8503, Japan

KONDO, MICHIO, research scientist; b. Nara, Japan, May 14, 1957; s. Tomoji and Itoshi (Kawabata) K.; m. Hiroko Takabatake, June 9, 1991; children: Junnichiro, Kenjiro. BS, Kyoto U., 1980; MS, Osaka U., 1982, PhD, 1988. Rsch. assoc. Tokyo U., 1988-94; sr. rschr. Electrotech. Lab., Tsukuba, Japan, 1994—; dep. leader Thin Film Silicon Superlab., Tsukuba, 1997—.

KONDRASHOVA, MARGARITA SERGEYEVNA, retail commercial manager; b. Moscow, Nov. 2, 1957; d. Sergei Alexandrovich Kondrashov and Rosa Vassilievna Roshina; m. Sergei Ivanovich Kuznetsov, Aug. 29, 1981; children: Varvara, Vassily. Economist for internat. trade, Moscow State Inst. Inter. Rel., 1979, Portuguese mil. interpreter, 1979. Cert. economist for fgn. trade. Tchr. Portuguese lang. and economy of Portugal Moscow State Inst. for Internat. Rels., 1979-88; adminstrn. mgr. BP Moscow Rep. Office, 1991-94; HR & adminstrv. mgr. BP Trading Ltd., Moscow, 1994-97, adminstrn. mgr., bus. security rep., 1997-99; retail product mgr. BP Amoco, Oil Bus. Unit, Moscow, 1999-2000, retail comml. mgr., 2000—; Portuguese interpreter Cen. Com. of Communist Party of the Soviet Unit, Moscow, 1980-87; mem. admission commn. Moscow State Inst. for Internat. Rels., 1982-84; mem. human resources discussion group Maj. Oil Cos. in Russia, 1994-99. Author: Manual for University Students, Part 1, 1988, Part 2, 1989; editor: (book) This Is BP, 1995. Capt. res. Mil. Interpreting, 1974-79. Avocations: horse riding, home interior design, writing poetry, leisure with family. Fax: 7 095 7378999. E-mail: kondram@bp.com. Office: BP Amoco Russia, Paveletskaya Sq 2 bld 1, Moscow 113054, Russia

KONDRATJEV, ALEKSEI ALEKSANDROVICH, chemist, educator; b. Durtuly, D. Sharan, Russia, May 18, 1930; s. Aleksandr Semionovich and Maria Tikhonovna (Ignatjeva) K.; m. Tatiana Ilinichna Fioktistova, May 28, 1956; children: Piotr, Juri, Elena. Kandidat Tech. Sci., Moscow U. of Chem. Engring., 1963; PhD in tech. sci., Ufa (Russia) Oil Inst., 1974. Asst. lectr. Ufa Oil Inst., 1953-60, sr. lectr., 1960-64, dotsent head of dept., 1964-71, sr. rschr., 1971-73, prof., head dept., 1974-88, prof., 1988-96, posttrad. students cons., 1964-95, head doctoral sch., 1994—. Author: Light From Simbirsk, 1998; contbr. over 170 articles to profl. jours.; patentee (over 75) in field. mem. Communist Party, Russia, 1953-91, leader UFA Chuvash Culture Club, 1986-89; chmn. Chuvash Culture Soc. of Bashkortostan, 1989-98; mem. com. Forum Chuvash of Bashkortostan, 1999—. Honour Scientist of Bashkortostan, 1993, Honor Cultural Worker of Chuvashia, 1995, Honour Medal of Labor, WWII, Govt. Russia; recipient Lenin Jubilee medal Govt. Russia, 1970, Deed of Honour, Supreme Soviet, 1968, 78, others. Mem. Local Lore Club Ufa, Bashkortostan Engring. Acad. Avocations: science, local lore. Home: Apt 311, 48 - 50 Let SSR Str, Ufa Bashkort, Russia Office: Ufa State Oil Tech Univ, 1 Kosmonavtov, 450062 Ufa Bashkort, Russia

KONDRATYEV, BORIS PETROVICH, astronomer, educator; b. Verkhni Ufalei, Russia, Jan. 11, 1950; s. Pyotr Alexandrovich and Ekaterina Nikolaevna (Gekovich) K.; m. Svetlana Leonidovna Pantiukhina, Aug. 20, 1983; children: Ivan, Ekaterina; m. Tamara Nikolaevna Ivashchuk, Mar. 15, 1972. Grad., State U., Kazan, Russia, 1975, PhD, 1982, DCs, 1990. Educator Mech. Inst., Izhevsk, 1975-77; sci. worker Astrophys. Inst., Alma-Ata, 1982-85; head of chair Pedagogical Inst., Glazov, 1985-90; head of chair, prof. Udmurt State U., Izhevsk, 1991—. Author: The Dynamics of Ellipsoidal Gravitation Figures, 1989; co-author: The Solution of the Paradox of Schredinger's Cat, 1994; contbr. articles to profl. jours. Grantee Russian Ministry Edn., 1992—. Mem. N.Y. Acad. Scis. Avocations: chess, violin, history. E-mail: kond@uni.udm.ru. Office: Udmurt State U, Universitetskaya 1, 426034 Izhevsk Udmurtia, Russia

KONERMANN, MARTIN, physician, researcher; b. Münster, Nordrhein-Westfalen, Germany, Jan. 21, 1956; s. Clemens Heinrich and Ursula (Springer) K.; m. Gabriele Angelika Lange, Aug. 24, 1978; 1 child, Philipp. Med. diploma, Westfälische Wilhelms U., Münster, Germany, 1980, MD, 1983. Med. asst. Marienhospital, Marl, Germany, 1982, Franz-Hosp., Dülmen, Germany, 1983-84, Herz-Jesu-Krankenhaus, Münster, Germany, 1984-87; med. asst. Ruhruniversität, Bochum, Germany, 1987-92, med. superior, 1993-96; med. dir. Marienkrankenhaus, Kassel, Germany, 1996—; asst. med. educator Ruhruniversität, Bochum, 1989-92, med. tchr., 1993—; clin. dir. Marienkrankenhaus, Kassel, Germany, 1996, hosp. dir., 1999—. Author, editor: Sleep Related Breathing Disorders of Children and Adults, 1994; author: Sleep Related Disorders, 1997; contbr. over 100 articles to profl. publs. Capt. Bundeswehr, 1981-82, Germany. Recipient Indsl. award Bristol-Myers Squibb, 1993, Boehringer Mannheim, Germany, 1994. Mem. Lions Club Internat., Marburger Bund, Deutsche Gesellschaft für Schlafforschung und Schlafmedizin, Bund Deutscher Internisten. Roman Catholic. Avocations: art exhibitions, skiing, running, fishing, sponsoring art. Home: Vor der Prinzenquelle 22, 34130 Kassel Hessen, Germany Office: Marienkrankenhaus, Marburger Str 85, 34127 Kassel Hessen, Germany

KONEZNY, LORETTE M. SOBOL, publishing executive; b. N.Y.C., Sept. 5, 1948; d. Jack and Florence (Silver) Sobol; m. Gerald Walter Konezny, June 4, 1972 (div. 1988); 1 child, Scott David. BS, U. Bridgeport, 1971; postgrad., Adelphi U., 1972-73, Parsons Sch. Design, 1977. Instr. Middle

Sch., Malverne, N.Y., 1971-72; pvt. instr. art L.I., 1972-76; instr. art, adult art edn. programs Rockville Centre, Oceanside and Lawrence, N.Y., 1976-79; pres. website pennotes.com Pen Notes, Inc., Freeport, N.Y., 1979—; art cons. Rockville Centre High Sch., 1976-77. Exhibited in group shows Adelphi U., 1973, Hewlett East Rockway Temple, 1976, Moscow Internat. Book Fair, 1987; represented in permanent collection Yeshiva U., L.A.; bus. cons. Baldwin C. of C., 1986; author, pub.: Learning to Tell Time, 1982, revised, Learning Time, 1995, Learning to Print, 1984, Learn Handwriting, 1986, revised, 1992, Learn to Write Numbers, 1987, rev. edit., 1997, Get in Shape to Write, 1998; patentee in field; pub. Aprendiendo A Escribir Las Letras, 1989; exhibited at Moscow Internat. Book Fair, 1987. Mem. L.I. Networking Entrepreneurs (founding pres. 1984-85), Soc. Scribes. Office: Pen Notes Inc 61 Bennington Ave Freeport NY 11520-3913

KONG, CHEONG CHOONG, airline executive; married; 3 children. BS, U. Adelaide, Australia, 1964; MS, Australian Nat. U., 195, PhD, 1967. Mng. dir., CEO Singapore Airlines Ltd.; bd. dirs. Singapore Airlines, Singapore Airport Terminal Svcs. Pte. Ltd., SIA Engring. Co. Pte. Ltd. Mem. USáSIN Bus. Coun.; mem. adv. coun. Australia-Asia Inst. Mem. Singapore Internat. Found. (gov. 1991—). Office: Airline House 9D, 25 Airline Rd, Singapore 819829, Singapore*

KONG, FAN AO, chemistry researcher; b. Wuhan, Hubei, China, June 9, 1936; s. Da Cong K. and Jue Jun Yang; m. Qing Lai Xu; children: Donna, Xiang. BS, Peking U., 1958. Rsch. asst. Chinese U. Sci. and Tech., Hefei, 1958-77, lectr., 1978-80, assoc. prof., 1983-87, prof., 1987—; vis. scholar U. So. Calif., L.A., 1980-82; researcher Inst. Chemistry Chinese Acad. Scis., Beijing, 1989—. Contbr. articles to profl. jours. Office: Inst Chemistry, 2nd N 1st St, 100080 Beijing China

KONG, JACKSON, civil and structural engineer, researcher; b. Hong Kong, Jan. 19, 1965; arrived in Canada, 1986; s. Kar Chun Kong and Lan Tung Chu; m. Sara Kam Bik Chan, May 6, 1995; 1 child, Felisse Wing Fay Kong. BS, U. London, 1986; M Applied Sci., U. Waterloo, Can., 1988; M Engring., U. Toronto, 1990; PhD, U. Hong Kong, 1994. Structural engr. Stone & Webster Engring., Toronto, 1986-87; tchg. asst. U. Waterloo, Can., 1987-88; tchg. asst. U. Hong Kong, 1990-94, asst. prof., 1994-95; rsch. scholar U. Toronto, 1995-96; structural engr. Robert Benaim Assocs., Hong Kong, 1999—; invited spkr. internat. confs.; guest lectr. dept. civil engring. U. Hong Kong, 2000—. Contbr. articles to profl. jours., chpt. to book. Vol. Queen Mary Hosp., Hong Kong, 1995-96. Croucher Found. fellow, Eng., 1995. Avocations: martial arts, astronomy. Office: U Hong Kong, Dept Civil Engring, Hong Kong China

KONG, KENNETH SEHKIANG, software testing engineer; b. K. Terengganu, Terengganu, Malysia, Nov. 6, 1969; came to U.S., 1995; s. Seng Fook and Chiewsia (Ong) K. BSBA in Computer Info. Systems, Hawaii Pacific U., 1997, MBA in Fin., 1998. Asst. EDP adminstr. Schering Plough (m) Sdn Bhd, Kuala Lumpur, Malaysia, 1991; programmer, software support Syntex Computer (m) Sdn Bhd, Petaling Jaya, Malaysia, 1992; asst. sales mgr. Adlycom Sdn Bhd, Petaling Jaya, 1992-93; svc. mktg. exec. Unifloor (m) Sdn Bhd, Petaling Jaya, 1994; computer technician ISLE Computer Consulting, Honolulu, Hawaii, 1996-99; computer profl. Volt Svcs. Group, Redmond, Wash., 1999—. Mem. Hawaiian Island Investment Group, Delta Mu Delta, Epsilon Delta Pi. Home: 13711 NE 10th Pl # A3208 Bellevue WA 98005-2819 Office: Volt Svcs Group 8471 154th Ave NE Redmond WA 98052-3863

KONG, LILY, executive; b. Singapore, Feb. 8, 1963; d. Chin K. and Su Moy Tok; m. Twe Jeat Lee, Feb. 21, 1990; children: Yi, Shi. BA in Econs. & English, Nat. U. Singapore, 1985. Dir. Orchard Sch. Arts & Commerce, Singapore, 1986—, Singapore Comml. Sch., 1986—, Kinderkids Kids Playhouse, 1996—, Le Galleria Hotel, 1997—. Avocations: reading, writing. Office: 05-09 United House, 20 Kramot Ln, Singapore 228 773, Singapore

KONG, LING XUE, scientific researcher, consultant; b. Xiantao, Hubei, China, May 24, 1963; arrived in Australia, 1992; s. Xiang Han Kong and Pu Xiang Yuan; m. Mary Fenghua She, Sept. 5, 1989; 1 child, Chen Charlie. BS, China Textile U., Shanghai, 1983, MS, 1988; PhD, U. NSW, Sydney, Australia, 1997. Asst. lectr. Hubei Inst. Sci. and Tech., Wuhan, Hubei, China, 1983-85; lectr. Hubei Inst. Sci. and Tech., Wuhan, 1990-92; mech. engr., ops. mgr. Guangzhou Sanhe Textile Co. Ltd., Guangdong, China, 1988-90; rsch. fellow Deakin U., Geelong, Victoria, Australia, 1997—; vis. scholar Nat. Taiwan U., Australian Acad. Sci. and Nat. Sci. Coun., Taipei, 1999. Contbr. articles to profl. jours. Achievements include development of novel metal forming technique; new characterising method for thin film coating; streamline of manufacturing of fasteners. Avocations: soccer, swimming, reading. E-mail: lKong@deakin.edu.au. Fax: 61 3 5227 2167. Office: Deakin U Sch Engring & Tech, Pigdons Rd, Geelong VIC 3217, Australia

KONG, MEI YING, science educator; b. Shanghai, China, Feb. 14, 1934; d. Jin Zhuang Kong and Da Ying Zhou; m. Hai Ren Yu, Feb. 7, 1961; children: Hui, Jin. Grad., Sichuan U., Chengdu, China, 1956. Asst. prof. dept. physics Sichuan U., Chengda, 1956-60, lectr. dept. physics, 1960-63; lectr. Inst. Semiconductors, Chinese Acad. Sci., Beijing, 1964-84, assoc. prof., 1985-88, prof., 1989—, head molecular beam epitaxy group, 1974-90, dir. microstructure materials, 1986-92; dep. dir. acad. com. Inst. Semiconductors, Chinese Acad. Scis., Beijing, 1991-96, Lab. for Semiconductor Materials, Beijing, 1991-95. Contbr. articles to profl. jours. Recipient spl. allowance for Significant Contbns., Chinese Govt., 1991; recipient 2nd prize for brilliant exploits in developing sci. and tech. in Sci., Kwang-Hua Sci. and Tech. Found., 1994. Fellow Chinese Acad. Sci. (sci. and tech. com. of materials 1990—), Nat. Key Lab. for Superlattic and Microstructures (acad. com. 1989—); mem. Chinese Materials Rsch. Soc. (councilor 1991-99). Avocations: reading, dancing, listening to music, walking, traveling. Home: PO Box 912, Beijing 100083, China Office: Inst Semiconductors, Xiao Zhuang Haidian Dist, Beijing 100083, China

KONG, TAK-KWAN, geriatrician, consultant; b. Hong Kong, China, July 3, 1956; s. Wing-ki and Chan-foung (Tsing) K.; m. Sau-ying Lau Kong, Mar. 8, 1987; children: Ming-yan, Ming-chi. MBBS, U. Hong Kong, 1980. Med. officer psychiatry Castle Peak Hosp., Hong Kong, 1982; med. officer geriatrics Princess Margaret Hosp., Hong Kong, 1983-89; commonwealth med. fellow U. Hosp. South Manchester, U.K., 1988-89; sr. med. officer Princess Margaret Hosp., Hong Kong, 1989-92, cons. geriatrician, 1992—, cons. in charge, 1995—; bd. mem. Specialty Bd. Geriatric Medicine, Edn. and Accreditation Com., Hong Kong Coll. Physicians, 1996—; hon. clin. assoc. prof. The U. Hong Kong, 1995—; profl. adv. Cmty. Rehab. Network, The Hong Kong Soc. for Rehab., 1996—. Editor-in-chief Jour. Hong Kong Geriatrics Soc., 1993-98; contbr. articles to profl. jours. Fellow Royal Coll. Physicians (Edinburgh, Glasgow, London), Hong Kong Acad. Medicine; mem. Hong Kong Geriatrics Soc., British Geriatrics Soc., Royal Coll. Physicians U.K. Avocations: computers, music. Office: Princess Margaret Hosp, Princess Margaret Hosp Rd, Hong Kong China

KONG, XIANG YAN, science educator, researcher; b. Hefei, Anhui, China, Mar. 13, 1932; s. Fan Chang and Zhi Cong (Wu) K.; m. Yuan Lin Li, May 1, 1962; children: Hang, Fang. Bachelor, Peking (China) U., 1956. Practice rsch. fellow Acad. Sci. China, Beijing, 1956-62; designer Acad. Astronautic Tech. China, Beijing, 1962-75; assoc. prof. U. Sci. and Tech. China, Hefei, 1981-86, prof., 1986—. Author: Gas Dynamics, Advanced Mechanics of Fluids in Porous Media; designer sounding rockets; software developer; contbr. articles to profl. jours. Fellow Com. Aerodynamics China; mem. Soc. Theoretical and Applied Mechanics China. Avocations: music, theatre, literature. Home: Jinzhai Rd 96, 230026 Hefei China Office: USTC Dept Modern Mechanics, Huangshan Rd, 230027 Hefei China

KONG, XIANGLI (CHARLIE) (XIANGLI KONG), mechanical and control engineer, educator; b. Chifeng, China, Mar. 11, 1953; came to U.S., 1989; s. Fanxin Kong and Yuzhen Yan; m. Xiuxian Han, Jan. 28, 1978; children: Ling Xin, Brian Lingyu. B of Engring., Shenyang (China) Poly. U., 1978; MSc, Xian (China) Jiaotong U., 1981, PhD, 1985. Lectr. Xian Jiaotong U., 1983-86, assoc. prof., 1986-89; engring. dir. Hill Equipment Corp., Whittier, Calif., 1990-92; pres., CEO MS-Tech Corp., La Mirada, Calif., 1992—; vis. assoc. prof. UCLA, 1988-90, tchr. computer-controlled machines course, 1993—, team leader, key contbr. advanced PC-CNC sys. Contbr. articles to profl. jours. Named Outstanding Young Scientist, Chinese Sci. & Tech. Assn., 1987, Outstanding Young Educator, Fok Yingtong Found., 1988; recipient more than 10 rsch. achievement awards. Office: MS-Tech Corp 14770 Firestone Blvd Ste 208 La Mirada CA 90638-5944

KONG AH MUN, SIMON, engineering lecturer, researcher; b. Singapore, Aug. 30, 1953; s. Kong Seow Yit and Tang Mooi; m. Lim Siew Mee, Nov. 24, 1985; 1 child, Kong Xieheng. Diploma in Chem. Process Tech., Singapore Poly., 1977; postgrad. Plastics and Rubber Inst., South Bank U., London, 1980; MS in Polymer Sci. and Engring., U. Ulster, No. Ireland, 1993. Assoc. engr. Philips Singapore, 1977-79; quality mgr. Ngai Mee Packaging, Singapore, 1981-87; lectr. Singapore Polytechnic, 1987—; assoc. engr. Philips Singapore, 1997—; cons. JPL Singapore Pte Ltd., 1999, Ngai Mee Packaghing Singapore Pte Ltd., 1989. Contbr. articles to profl. jours. Assn. Overseas Tech. scholar, Japan, 1982; Commonwealth Head of Govt. REgional Meeting scholar, 1983; UN scholar, Bombay, 1991, others. Mem. ASME, Soc. Plastics Engrs. (sr.), Am. Chem. Soc., Inst. of Materials (U.K.). E-mail: amkong@sp.edu.sg. Office: Singapore Polytechnic, 500 Dover Rd, Singapore 139651, Singapore

KONG-HI YOUN (VICTORINUS), archbishop; b. Jinnampo, Dem. People's Rep. Korea, Nov. 8, 1924; s. Sang (Peter) Youn and Sang-Sook (Victoria) Choi. Student, St. Willibrod's Major Sem., Dok-Won, Dem. People's Republic Korea, 1944-49; ThM, Urban Coll., Rome, 1957; ThD, Gregorian U., Rome, 1960; DLitt, Sogang U., Seoul, Republic of Korea, 1985. Ordained priest Roman Cath. Ch., 1950. Asst. priest Cathedral Myong-dong, Seoul, 1950; chaplain U.N. POW Camp, Pusan, Republic of Korea, 1951-52; v.p. Cath. Libr., Pusan, 1952-54; tchr. Holy Ghost Mid. and High Sch., Seoul, 1954-56; bishop and ordinary Diocese of Suwon, Republic of Korea, 1963-73; adminstr. Archdiocese of Seoul, 1967-68; archbishop and ordinary Archdiocese of Kwangju, Republic of Korea, 1973—; rep. found. Kwangju Cath. Coll., 1974—; chmn. Episc. Conf. Korea, Seoul, 1975-81; Episc. moderator Justice and Peace Com., Seoul, 1975-88; rep. Episc. com. Bicentennial Cath. Ch. Korea, 1980-84. Author: Radio Message, 1963. Active movement to protect human rights Kwangju Uprising Meml. Com. Home and Office: Archbishop's House, 5-32 Im-dong, Puk Kwangju 500-010, Republic of Korea

KONGOR AROP, GEORGE, federal official. 2d v.p. Govt. of Sudan. Office: Office of Pres, The Palace, Khartoum Sudan*

KONIG, BERNARD, university rector. Rector U. Cologne, Germany. Office: U Cologne, Albertus-Magnus-Platz, D-50931 Cologne Germany*

KONIG, FRANZ CARDINAL, cardinal, archbishop emeritus of Vienna; b. Rabenstein, Austria, Aug. 3, 1905; D.D.; Ph.D.; hon. degrees univs. Vienna, Innsbruck, Salzburg, Zagreb, Am. univs. Ordained priest Roman Catholic Ch., 1933; prof. high sch.; lectr. U. Vienna, 1946-48, extraordinary prof., from 1948; titular bishop, Livias, 1952, bishop coadjutor, St. Poelten, 1952; archbishop of Vienna, 1956-85; cardinal, 1958; titular ch. St. Eusebius; pres. Secretariat for Non-Believers, 1965-80, Pax Christi Internat., 1985-90; archbishop emeritus of Vienna. Mem. Am. Acad. Arts and Scis. Author: Christus und die Religionen der Erde, 1951, Religionswissenschaftliches Woerterbuch, 1956, Zarathustras Jenseitsvorstellungen und das Alte Testament, 1964, Die Stunde der Welt 1971, Der Aufbruch zum Geist, 1972, Das Zeichen Gottes, 1973, Der Mensch ist fuer die Zukunft angelegt, 1975, Kirche und Welt, 1978, Glaube ist Freiheit, 1981, Der Glaube der Menschen, 1985, Der Weg der Kirche, 1986, Lexikon der Religionen, 1987, König/Ehrlich, Juden und Christen haben eine Zukunft, 1988, Jetzt die Wahrheit leben, 1991, in slowenischer Sprache, 1992. Address: Wollzeile 2, A-1010 Vienna Austria*

KÖNIG, GERHARD, editor; b. Berlin, May 21, 1939; s. Gerhard and Lena (Müller) K.; m. Monika Ballweg, Apr. 18, 1976; children: Markus, Marina. Diploma, U. Berlin, 1967. Asst. U. Berlin, 1967-68; pub. editor Ernst Klett Pub., Stuttgart, Germany, 1968-72; lectr. Zentrum f. Didaktik, Karlsruhe, Germany, 1972-78; mng. editor Fachinformationszentrum, Karlsruhe, 1978—; lectr. Pedagogical Inst., Karlsruhe, 1985—. Author: Begriffsworterbuch Mathematik; contbr. articles to profl. jours. Head KTV, 1980-94. Avocations: sports, reading, publishing, photography, cooking. Home: Lauenburger str 45, 76139 Karlsruhe Germany Office: Fachinformationszentrum, Zentralblatt fuer Didaktik, 76344 Eggenstein Germany

KÖNIG, HEINZ JOHANNES ERDMANN, mathematics educator; b. Stettin, Germany, May 16, 1929; s. Josef and Meta (Bognitz) K.; m. Helga, Oct. 2, 1954, (wid. Feb. 1979); m. Karin Grewin, Nov. 21, 1980; 1 child, Daniel. Doctoral degree, U. Kiel, Fed. Republic Germany, 1952; Habilitation, U. Würzburg, Fed. Republic Germany, 1956; doctoral degree (hon.), U. Karlsruhe, Fed. Republic Germany, 1979. Dozent Tech. U. Aachen, Fed. Republic Germany, 1957-60, assoc. prof., 1960-62; prof. U. Köln, Fed. Republic Germany, 1962-65; prof. U. Saarbrücken, Fed. Republic Germany, 1965-94, prof. emeritus, 1994—; vis. prof. Calif. Inst. Tech., Pasadena, 1967-68, vis. fellow, 1982-83; vis. prof. U. Washington, Seattle, 1970, U. Witwatersrand, Johannesburg, South Africa, 1992; vis. scholar, U. Tex., Austin, 1978; vis. fellow Australian Nat. U., Canberra, 1988-89. Author: (with K. Barbey) Abstract Analytic Function Theory, 1977, Analysis I, 1984, (with M.M. Neumann) Mathematische Wirtschaftstheorie, 1986, (with R. Raeder) Theory of Distributions, 1995, Measure and Integration, 1997; contbr. numerous articles to profl. jours. Founding pres. Assn. Friends Hebrew U. in the Saar State, 1977—. Decorated officier Ordre Grand Ducal Couronne de Chêne (Luxembourg). Mem. Royal Soc. Sci. (Liège, Belgium) (corr.), German Math. Soc., Am. Math. Soc., French Math. Soc., European Math. Soc., Soc. Math., Econs. and Ops. Rsch. (founding pres. 1977-81). Home: Auf Gierspel 36, D-66132 Saarbrücken Germany Office: U Saarland, D-66041 Saarbrücken Germany

KÖNIG, HELMUT, microbiologist, researcher. Degree in Biology and Chemistry, U. Heidelberg, 1976. With U. Munich, 1976-80, U. Regensburg, 1980-87; prof. U. Ulm, Germany, 1987-96, U. Mainz, Germany, 1996—. Achievements include contributions to the knowledge of structure and biosynthesis of cell walls of archaebacteria; systematics and physiology of symbiotic flora of wood feeding insects. Office: Univ Mainz, 55099 Mainz Germany

KÖNIG, ROLF, immunologist, educator; b. Saarbrücken, Saarland, Germany, July 4, 1953; came to the U.S., 1987—; s. Kurt Lothar König and Inge Kneip; m. Rita Müggler; children: Michael Christopher, Jessica Anita. MS, U. Bern, Switzerland, 1980, PhD, 1984. Rsch. assoc. U. Mass., Amherst, 1985, U. Bern, 1985-87; vis. fellow NIH, Bethesda, Md., 1987-91; vis. assoc. NIH/Nat. Inst. Allergy and Infectious Diseases, Bethesda, 1991-93; asst. prof. U. Tex., Galveston, 1993-99; assoc. prof. U. Tex. Med. Br., Galveston, 1999—. Assoc. editor Jour. Immunology, 1999—; contbr. articles to profl. jours. Mem. AAAS, N.Y. Acad. Sci., AAI. E-mail: rokonig@utmb.edu. Fax: 409-747-6869. Office: U Tex Med Br 301 University Blvd Galveston TX 77555-5302

KONIGSBERG, ALLEN STEWART See ALLEN, WOODY

KONIGSBERG, ROBERT LEE, electrical engineer; b. N.Y.C., May 23, 1921; s. Max and Rose (Saper) K.; m. Helen Mae Aronson, June 11, 1950; children: Richard L., Jane F. BEE, Cooper Union, 1942; MAdE, NYU, 1948; MSE, Johns Hopkins U., 1954. Test/standardization engr. Western Electric Co., Kearny, N.J., 1942-46, product engr. filter dept., 1946-47; electronics engr. telemetering group Fairchild Engine & Aircraft Corp., Farmingdale, N.Y., 1947; electronic engr. radar component design DeMornay Budd Co., Bronx, N.Y., 1948; electronics engr. telemetering instrumentation Glenn L. Martin Co., Balt., 1948-51; rsch. assoc. radiation lab. Johns Hopkins U., Balt., 1951-56, prin. profl. staff engr. Applied Physics Lab., Laurel, Md., 1956-88, ret., 1988; part time cons., 1989—; part-time instr. engring. Johns Hopkins U., 1965-71. Contbr. articles to profl. jours. Recipient Group Achievement award to MAGSAT Project Team NASA, 1979, Group Achievement award to AMPTE Project Team NASA, 1985. Mem. IEEE, Sigma Xi, Tau Beta Pi. Democrat. Jewish. Avocations: amateur radio; tennis. Home: 2218 Ridgemont Dr Finksburg MD 21048-1717

KONIJN, JOSEPH, physicist; b. Berlin, Oct. 23, 1931; s. S. Konijn and E.J. de Winter; m. Wilhelmina de Kramer; children: Josepha Marion, Eric Simon Hendrik, Gunnar Arne. Degree, Delft U. Tech., The Netherlands, 1956, PhD, 1958. Physicist AB Atomenergi, Nyköping, Sweden, 1960-63, Inst. Kernfysisch Onderzoek/NIKHEF, Amsterdam, The Netherlands, 1963-96; prof. physics U. Colo., Boulder, 1968-69; sci. asst. European Lab. Particle Physics, Geneva, 1977. 1st lt. Dutch Air Force, 1958-60. Mem. Dutch Phys. Soc. (treas. 1993—), Am. Phys. Soc., European Phys. Soc., N.Y. Acad. Scis., European Phys. Soc. Home: Valeriaanstraat 99, 3765 EL Soest The Netherlands Office: NIKHEF, PO Box 41882, NL1009DB Amsterdam The Netherlands

KONING, J., banker; b. Oldemarkt, The Netherlands, Jan. 5, 1943. Grad. in econs., U. Amsterdam, The Netherlands, 1969. With study dept. Nederlandsche Bank NV, Amsterdam, from 1969, alt. chief study dept., until 1980, chief study dept., 1980-87, asst. dep. dir., 1983-87, dep. dir., 1987-92, exec. dir. to governing bd., 1992—. Office: De Meder;amdscje Baml NV, Westeinde 1 PO Box 98, 1000 AB Amsterdam The Netherlands*

KONIOR, JEANNETTE MARY, elementary school educator; b. Bronx, N.Y., Jan. 7, 1947; d. Stephen Louis and Frieda Anna (Schmautz) Sirko.; m. Richard Henry Drago, Nov. 13, 1971 (div. Mar., 1989); 1 child, Christina Angelina; m. John Anthony Konior, Feb. 20, 1993; stepchildren: John Adalbert, Joseph Anthony. AA in Social Sci., Orange County C.C., Middletown, N.Y., 1983; BS in Elementary Edn., SUNY, New Paltz, 1985, MS in Elementary Edn., Secondary English, 1993. Cert. tchr. elementary, secondary English, N.Y. Sec. M.W. Kellogg Co., N.Y.C., 1964-69; legal sec. Kaye, Scholar et al., N.Y.C., 1969-72; records coord. Orange & Rockland Utilities, Pearl River, N.Y., 1975-76; personal sec. Hercules, Inc., Middletown, 1976-82; substitute tchr. various dists., Orange County, N.Y., 1986-87; tchr. Archdiocese of N.Y. Most Precious Blood Sch., Walden, N.Y., 1987—; student tchr. advisor Most Precious Blood Sch., 1992—, editor-in-chief Yearbook, 1988—, dir. Christmas Play, 1987, coord. various classroom plays, 1987-99. Vol. religious edn. tchr. St. Matthew's Ch., Bklyn., 1969-70, Mt. Carmel Ch., Middletown, 1973-83, St. Mary's Ch., Montgomery, N.Y., 1992-93, St. John's Ch., Woodstock, N.Y., 1994—; chmn. membership com. Village on Green 1 Homeowners' Assn., Middletown, 1980-81, v.p., sec., 1981-82, pres., 1982-84; mem. Parents without Ptnrs., 1990-91. Avocations: dressmaking, swimming, boating, walking, reading, writing. Office: Most Precious Blood Sch 180 Ulster Ave Walden NY 12586-1095

KONISHI, EIJI, virologist, vaccinologist, researcher; b. Kobe, Japan, Dec. 2, 1951; s. Tomoshichi and Hisae (Nishikawa) K.; m. Hatsuko Taura, May 14, 1978; children: Tomohide, Akihide, Kazuhide, Yukihide. BSc, Kobe U., 1974, MSc, 1976, PhD, 1980. Rsch. affiliate Kobe U., 1980-96, assoc. prof., 1996—; rsch. scientist Yale U., New Haven, 1990-92, lectr., 1993-96. WHO grantee, Switzerland, 1996. Mem. Japanese Soc. for Vaccinology, Japanese Soc. for Virology. Office: Kobe U Sch Medicine, 7-10-2 Tomogaoka Sumaku, Kobe 654-0142, Japan

KONISHI, IKUO, gynecologist, researcher; b. Uchinomicho, Kagawa, Japan, Jan. 8, 1952; s. Keiji Kondo and Miyoko Konishi; m. Yumiko Shimizu, June 4, 1978; children: Atsuo, Aiko. MD, Kyoto U., Japan, 1976, PhD, 1988. Resident in ob.-gyn. Kyoto U. Hosp., 1976-78, Kurashiki Ctrl. Hosp., Okayama, Japan, 1978-81; rsch. fellow in ob-gyn. U. Ark. for Med. Sci., Little Rock, 1992; asst. prof. ob-gyn. Kyoto U., 1986-92, assoc. prof., 1993-98; prof., chmn. ob-gyn. Shinshu U., Matsumoto, 1999—. Author: Ultrastructure of Smooth Muscle, 1990; contbr. articles to profl. jours. Mem. Japan Soc. Ob-gyn. (councilor 1993—), Internat. Soc. Gynecol. Pathologists, Internat. Gynecologic Cancer Soc., Internat. Soc. for Preventive Oncology, Am. Soc. for Reproductive Medicine, N.Y. Acad. Scis. Office: Dept Ob-Gyn Shinshu U Sch Med, Asahi 3-1-1, Matsumoto 390-8621, Japan

KONISHI, YOSHIHIRO, electronic engineer, educator; b. Nara-shi, Japan, Sept. 24, 1928; d. Biryo and Yaeko (Yamamoto) K.; m. Yoriko Nakagawa, May 1, 1956; three children. BS, Kyoto U., 1950, D in Engring. Chief rschr. NHK Broadcasting Co., Tokyo, 1951-83; v.p. Uniden Co., Tokyo, 1983-93; prof. Tokyo Poly. Inst., Atsugi, Japan, 1993-99; vis. prof. Osaka U., Japan, 1973-83. Author: Microwave Electronic Technology, 1997; editor: Microwave Integrated Circuit, 1991; patentee in field. Recipient medal with purple ribbon Japanese Emperor, 1982, Carrier award IEEE Microwave Theory and Techniques Soc. Fellow IEEE; mem. Inst. Electronics Engring. Japan, Inst. TV Japan. Buddhist. Avocations: golf, swimming, cinema. Office: K Lab Corp, 1-29-4 Kamitsuruma, Kanagawa 228-0802, Japan

KONKEL, HARRY WAGNER, civic volunteer, retired career officer; b. Jackson, Wyo., July 11, 1935; s. Maurice and Beatrice Helen (Nelle) Wagner; m. Susan Donnell Konkel, June 3, 1960; children: James Donnell Konkel, Susan Konkel. Student, U. Wyo., 1953; BS, U.S. Naval Acad., 1958; BS in Elec. Engring., Naval Postgrad. Sch., 1965; MA, Naval War Coll., 1974. Commd. ensign USN, 1958, advanced through ranks to capt., 1979, ret., 1985, elecs. material officer, weapons officer USS Trathen, 1959-63, engr. officer USS Richard E. Byrd, 1965-67; asst. fleet elecs. maintenance officer US Atlantic Fleet USN, Norfolk, Va., 1967-70; exec. officer USS Keppler USN, 1970-71, commdr. USS Laffey, 1971-72, commdr. USS DAmato, 1972-73, engr. officer USS America, 1978-79, head availabilities sect., maintenance policy and progamming branch Ships Maintencance and Modernization Divsn. Office Chief of Naval Opers., 1979-81, commdr. USS Yellowstone, 1982-84; dir. electronic and spl. warfare divsn. Naval Electronic Systems Command, 1974-77; head surface ship fleet modernization program design mgmt. divisn. Naval Sea Systems Command, 1984; dep. dir. ship maintenance and modernization divsn., head ships maintenance and modernization branch Office of Chief of Naval Ops., 1984-85. Bd. trustees Gunston Sch., Centreville, Md., 1981-91, Gould Acad., Bethel, Me., 1987-93, Osher Libr. Assocs., 1993—; bd. dirs. Humane Soc. Hancock County, Findlay, Ohio, 1986-87; nat. dir. Navy League US, 1989-97, Portland Mus. Art, fellow 1993-96, trustee, 1996—; pres. Osher Libr. Assocs., Osher Map Libr., 1995-98, USNA Blue and Gold, 1994—. Decorated Legion of Merit, Meritorious Svc. medal with one gold star, Navy Commendation Medal with two gold stars. Mem. Am. Soc. Naval Engrs., Am. Inst. Conservation of Historic and Artistic Works, Am. Philatelic Soc., Am. Numismatic Assn., Am. Orchid Soc., U. Wyo. Alumni Assn., US Naval Acad. Alumni Assn., Naval Postgrad. Sch. Alumni Assn., Naval War Coll. Aluni Assn., US Naval Inst., Navy League US, Retired Officers Assn., Surface Navy Assn. (lifetime plankowner mem.), USS Damato Assn., USS Laffey Assn., USS Trathen Assn., USS Keppler Assn., USS Am. Assn., Army-Navy Country Club, Bohemian Club, Portland Country Club. Republican. Episcopalian. Avocations: golf, stamp and coin collecting. Home: 71 Carroll St Portland ME 04102-3522

KONNO, KOICHI, English language educator; b. Fukushima, Japan, Mar. 14, 1928; s. Yoshimi and Chiyo Konno; m. Tokiko Hirano, Jan. 1955; children: Kazuo, Takashi. BA, Waseda U., Tokyo, 1959, MA, 1966. Asst. tchr. Tsuruoka (Yamagata, Japan) Mcpl. 1st Mid. Sch., 1948-54; tchr. Kokushikan High Sch., Tokyo, 1959-62; lectr. Kokushikan U., Tokyo, 1962-66, asst. prof., 1966-67; lectr. English, Waseda U., 1969-73, asst. prof., 1973-78, prof., 1978-98; lectr. Tokyo U. Econs., 1972-74, Chuo U., Tokyo, 1973-75, Atomi Jr. Coll., Tokyo, 1987-91. Contbg. author: Dictionary of Modern English and American Literature Appreciation, 1976, Dictionary of English and American Literature, 1978, From Joyce to Joyce, 1982. Mem. James Joyce Soc. Japan, English Lit. Soc. Japan, Japan Soc. Comparative Lit., English Lit. Soc. Waseda U. (pres. 1992-98). Avocations: cycling, horticultue, swimming, painting. Home: 8-19-15 Sunagawa-cho, Tachikawa-shi Tokyo 190, Japan Office: Waseda U, 1-24-1 Toyama-cho Shinjuku, Tokyo 160, Japan

KONNOV, IGOR' VASIL'YEVICH, mathematics educator, researcher; b. Lutsk, Ukraine, Feb. 8, 1958; s. Vasiliy Fedorovich and Asya Borisovna Konnov; m. Victoria Nikolaevna Ustyugova, Mar. 20, 1992. First-class diploma, Kazan (USSR) U., 1980, Candidate of Sci. (hon.), 1987, DS in Physics and Math., 1998. Asst. Kazan U., 1980-88, assoc. prof., 1988-98, prof., 1998—. Author: Methods of Nondifferential Optimization, 1993, Methods for Solving Finite-Dimensional Variational Inequalities, 1998.

Mem. Math. Programming Soc., Kazan Math. Soc., Working Group on Generalized Convexity. Avocation: history. E-mail: ikonnov@ksu.ru. Office: Kazan Univ, ul Kremlevskaya 18, 420008 Kazan Russia

KONO, TAKESHI, dermatologist; b. Osaka, Japan, Aug. 30, 1954; s. Hiroshi and Osumi (Teranishi) K. MD, Osaka City U., 1980, PhD, 1984. Intern Osaka City U., 1980-82; resident, 1982-84; staff dept. dermatology Osaka (Japan) City U. Med. Sch., 1984-89, lectr., 1986-92, asst. prof., 1984—; rsch. fellow divsn. dermatology U. Toronto, Can., 1992-94; cons. Osaka Gen. Hosp. of West Japan Railway Co., Osaka, 1996—; chmn. staff union Osaka City U. Med. Sch., 1996. Contbr. articles to profl. jours. Recipient Osaka City Mayor award Osaka City Office, 1990; E.C. Stevens fellowship U. Toronto, 1993. Mem. Japan Soc. of Investigative Dermatology (councilor 1994—), Japanese Dermatol. Assn., N.Y. Acad. Scis. Avocations: history, music, hiking, travel. Office: Dept Derm Osaka City U Med, 1-4-3 Asahimachi Abeno-ku, Osaka 545-8585, Japan

KONO, YOHEI, Japanese government official; b. Jan. 15, 1937. Grad. dept. poli sci., econ., Waseda U., 1959; post grad., Stanford U. Mem. from Kanagawa Ho. Reps., Japan; parliamentary vice-min. edn. Govt. of Japan; dir.-gen. Sci. and Tech. Agy.; chief cabinet sec. Govt. of Japan, 1992-93; chair rsch. com. fgn. affairs Liberal Dem. Party, 1990-92, pres., 1993-95; cofounder New Liberal Club, 1976-86; fgn. min. Japan, 1994-95, dep. prime min., 1994-96; min. of foreign affairs Govt. of Japan, Tokyo, 1999S; mem. Miyazawa faction Liberal Dem. Party, 1994-96. Office: Ministry of Foreign Affairs, 2-2-1 Kasumigaseki, Chiyoda-ku Tokyo 100-8919, Japan*

KONOFAOS, NIKOLAOS ELEFTHERIOU, educator; b. Corfu, Greece, Apr. 11, 1965; s. Eleftherios N. and Maria D. (Grammenou) K.; m. Olga G. Skamnelou, July 5, 1997. BS in Physics, U. Ioannina, Greece, 1987; PhD, Bradford, England, 1993. Dir. internat. liaison U. Ioannina, Greece, 1996-98, rschr., 1997-99; sr. educator TEI Epirus, Arta, Greece, 1999—; instr. State Inst. Profl. Edn., Ioannina, 1997—. Contbr. articles to profl. jours. Lt. Greek Army, 1993-95. Mem. IEEE, Inst. Physics, Materials Rsch. Soc. Avocations: travel, football, music, cinema. Home: Sakellariou 1-3, GR-45333 Ioannina Greece

KONOLA, CLAUDETTE JUNE, finance company executive, financial analyst; b. Deadwood, S.D., Sept. 2, 1948; d. Donald John Konola and Rose Marie Larive-Konola. BSc, Univ. Colo., 1981. Mgmt. trainee Am. Nat. Bank, Denver, 1974-80; training coord. loan analysis United Bank Denver, 1980-81; asst. v.p. Canadian Commercial Bank, Denver, 1981-83, First Interstate Bank of Denver, 1983-88; v.p. Ctrl. Bank Denver, 1988-93; revolving loan fund adminstr. Mesa county Western Colo. Bus. Devel. Corp., Grand Junction, Colo., 1994-96; southwest regional dir. Cmty. Reinvestment Fund, Inc., Mpls., 1996—. Pres. Downtown Denver Bus. and Profl. Women, Denver, 1985-87; treas. Women's Bean Project, Denver, 1991-93; sec., treas. Riverside Task Force, Grand Junction, 1995-98; co-founder Colo. Women's Hall of Fame, 1986. Democrat. E-mail: claudette@crfusa.com. Office: Cmty Reinvestment Fund PO Box 552 Clifton CO 81520-0552

KONONOVA, OLGA NICKOLAEVNA, chemist; b. Voronezh, USSR, July 18, 1946; d. Nickolay and Lubov (Averianova) Kryssin; m. Yuri Kononov, Aug. 18, 1972; children: Vera, Alexander. Diploma in chemistry, Voronezh (USSR) State U., 1970; D of Natural Scis., Martin Luther U., Halle-Wittenberg, Germany, 1973; PhD in Chem. Scis., Krasnoyarsk (USSR) State U., 1974. Jr. rschr. Voronezh State U., 1970-71; asst. Krasnoyarsk State U., 1974-75, sr. asst., 1975-79, rschr., lectr., 1982—; rsch. scientist Martin Luther U., 1980-81; dep. dean chem. dept. Krasnoyarsk State U., 1993—. Contbr. articles to profl. jours. Russian Univ.'s grantee Ministry of Edn., 1997. Mem. Russian Chem. Soc. Avocation: reading novels, knitting, sewing, playing computer games. Office: Krasnoyarsk State U, Svobodny Pr 79, 660062 Krasnoyarsk Russia

KONONOVICH, ALEXANDER LVOVICH, ecologist; b. Moscow, Aug. 3, 1936; s. Lev Petrovich Kononovich and Dora Iljinichna Lejpunskaja; m. Alina Alexandrovna Dobrjakova; children: Marija, Mihail. Magister, MIFI, Moscow, 1962; PhD, Inst. Biophysics, Moscow, 1973. Engr. Inst. Atom Energy, Moscow, 1962-67; sci. worker Inst. Biophysics, Moscow, 1967-76; head lab. Inst. Nuclear Power Sci., Moscow, 1976-96, head scientist, 1996—; lectr. Moscow State U., 1994-97. Author: The Ecology Basis of the Water Environment Radio Protection, 1998; contbr. articles to profl. jours. Recipient medal for nat. economy achievement, 1984, Hon. Diploma for work for liquidation of Chernoble consequences, 1986. Mem. Internat. Union of Radioecology, Europe Nuclear Soc., Ukraine Nuclear Soc. Home: Batajsky 53 Fl 107, 109144 Moscow Russia Office: Inst Applied Ecology, Pjatnickaja 44 Bldg 3, 109017 Moscow Russia

KONONSKI, ALEX IVANOVICH, chemistry educator, researcher; b. Skvyra, Kiev, Ukraine, Jan. 6, 1929; s. Ivan Ivanovich and Natlia Seminivna (Mateyenko) K.; m. Maria Iosypivna Lozinska, Apr. 3, 1955; children: Oksana, Sergey. Degree in vet. sci., Agrl. Inst., Bila Tserkva, Ukraine, 1953, MS, 1961, DSc, 1970. Vet. Bila Tserka, 1953-57; aspirant Agrl. Inst., Bila Tserka, 1957-60, asst., 1960-70, head chair, 1970—, dean, 1970-86. Author: Histochemistry, 1976 (Exhbn. Achievements People's Exch. 1980), Biochemistry of Animals, 1980, 3d edit., 1992 (Edn. Com. 3d prize 1989), Physical and Colloid Chemistry, 1986 (State Com. Edn. award 1988), Organic Chemistry, 1994; chief editor Inst. New Bull., 1975-81. Chmn. Sci., Bila Tserkva, 1975-95. Capt. Soviet Army, Ukraine. Recipient Cert. of Hon., Supreme Soviet, Ukraine, Hon. Worker of H.S., Ukraine. Mem. Ukrainian Acad. Scis. and Nat. Progress, N.Y. Acad. Scis. Avocations: memoirs, winter swimming, gardening. Office: Agrl Inst, 4 Ploshoha Voli, Bila Tserkva Kiev, Ukraine

KONOPELCHENKO, BORIS GEORGIEVICH, mathematics educator; b. Avchala, USSR, Feb. 27, 1948; arrived in Italy, 1993; s. Georgii Emelyanovich and Maria Alekseevna (Vetchinkina) K.; m. Valentina Dmitrievna Shuravko, Aug. 10, 1984; children: Natalia, Igor. Diploma, U. Novosibirsk, USSR, 1971; Candidate of Sci., USSR, 1973, DSc, 1986. Postgrad. student Inst. Nuclear Physics, USSR, 1971-73; jr. rschr. Inst. Nuclear Physics, 1973-75, sr. rschr., 1975-86, leading rschr., 1986-93; prof. Lecce U., Italy, 1993—. Author: Nonlinear Integrable Equation, 1987, Introduction to Multidimensional Integrable Equations, 1992, Solitons, in Multidimensions, 1993; contbr. over 100 rsch. papers to profl. jours. Mem. Am. Math. Soc., N.Y. Acad. Scis. Avocation: music. Office: Univ Lecce Dipartimento Fisica, Via Arnesano, 73100 Lecce Italy

KONOPINSKI, VIRGIL JAMES, industrial hygienist; b. Toledo, Ohio, July 11, 1935; s. Mack and Mary Veronica (Jankowski) K.; m. Joan Mary Wielinski, June 27, 1964; children: Ann Marie, Carol Sue, Peter JAmes. BSChemE, U. Toledo, 1956; MSChemE, Pratt Inst., 1960; MBA, Bowling Green State U., 1971. Registered profl. engr., Ohio, Ind., Calif.; cert. indsl. hygienist; cert. safety profl. Assoc. engr. Owens Illinois, Toledo, 1956, 60; real estate developer Grand Rapids, Ohio, 1961; chem. engr. USPHS, Cin., 1961-64; sr. environ. engr. Vistron Corp., Lima, Ohio, 1964-67; environ. specialist, asst. to dir. environ. control Owens Corning Fiberglas, Toledo, 1967-72; gen. mgr. Midwest Environ. Mgmt., Maumee, Ohio, 1972-73; staff specialist, indl. hygienist Williams Bros. Waste Control, Tulsa, Okla., 1973-75; dir. divsn. indsl. hygiene and radiol. health Ind. State Bd. Health, Indpls., 1975-87; exec. v.p. ACT of Ind., Indpls., 1987-89; sr. cons. Occusafe, Indpls., 1990-91; regional safety engr., human resources analyst/safety U.S. Postal Svc., Indpls., 1991—; bd. dir. IOSHA indsl. hygiene, 1975-83; cons. indoor air, radon, occupational health, Zionsville, 1987-91, Cary, 1991—; lectr. Contbr. articles to profl. jours. With USNR, 1956-59. Mem. Am. Indsl. Hygiene Assn., Am. Conf. Govt. Indsl. Hygienists, Am. Soc. Safety Engrs., Naval Res. Assn., Ret. Officers Assn. Republican. Roman Catholic. Home: 14 Fairfield Ln Cary IL 60013-1946 Office: 4th Flr 244 Knollwood Dr Fl 4 Bloomingdale IL 60108-2208

KONOSU, SHINJI, mechanical engineering educator; b. Niigata, Japan, Dec. 30, 1946; s. Jiro and Harumi (Jinushi) K.; m. Sawako Sekino, Feb. 20, 1982; children: Risako, Masaki. BS in Engring., Tohoku U., 1970, MS in Engring., 1972, D in Engring., 1975. Asst. dept. mech. engring. Tohoku U., Sendai, Japan, 1975-76, asst. prof., 1976-77; rschr. JGC Corp., Yokohama, Japan, 1977-89, prin. engr., 1989-91; assoc. prof. dept. mech. engring. Ibaraki U., Hitachi, Japan, 1991-2000, prof. dept. mech. engring., 2000—. Coauthor: Encyclopedia of Advanced Material Applications, 1989; contbr. articles to profl. jours. Mem. Japan Soc. Promotion of Sci., Japan. Soc. Mech. Engring., Soc. Materials Sci. Japan. Avocation: horticulture. Home: 3326-5 Koya, Hitachinaka Ibaraki 312 0002, Japan Office: Ibaraki U Faculty Engring, 12-1 Nakanarusawa 4 chome, Hitachi 316-8511, Japan

KONOVALOVA, LIUDMILA VASILIEVNA, philosopher, educator; b. Moscow, Russia, Sept. 10, 1937; s. Vasiliy Sergeyevich and Nina Petrovna (Boyeva) K.; m. Vladimir Nikolayevich Gavrilov, May 5, 1964; children: Vera, Ekaterina. M in Philosophy, Moscow State U., 1959; PhD, Inst Philiosophy-Russian Acad., Moscow, 1963; D in Philisophy, Inst Philiosophy-Russian Acad., 1985. Assoc. rschr. Inst. Philiosophy/Russian Acad. Sci., Moscow, 1963-69; sr. rschr. Inst. Philiosophy/Russian Acad. Sci., 1969-85; lectr. Moscow Inst. Fin. and Statistics, 1969-85; prof. State Theater Inst., Moscow, 1985-99; chief rschr. Inst. Philiosophy, Moscow, 1985—. Mem. Russian Philiosophical. E-mail: katya belaya@usa.net. Home: d 36/kv58 Malaya Filevskaya, Moscow 121433, Russia Office: Russian Acad Sci, 14 Volkhonka St, Moscow Russia

KONRAD, HELMUT, history educator; b. Wolfsberg, Carinthia, Austria, Jan. 29, 1948; s. Lorenz and Irmgard (Waich) K.; m. Alida Mirella Konrad-Hueller, July 17, 1978; children: Clemens David, Irene Julia Anita. PhD, U. Vienna, 1973; U. Dozent, U. Linz, Austria, 1981, Univ. Prof., 1983; Full Prof., U. Graz, Austria, 1984; PhD, U. Skhodra, Albania, 1996. Asst. prof. U. Linz, 1972-81, assoc. prof., 1981-84; prof. U. Graz, 1994—; vis. prof. U. Cornell, Ithaca, N.Y., 1990-91; dean faculty of humanities, U. Graz, 1987-89, rector, 1993—. 1997 Author six books, 1978-96; editor 27 books, 1978-96; contbr. several hundred articles to profl. jours. and publs. Social Democrat. Avocations: cooking, lit., fine arts. Office: Univ Graz, Univeritatsplatz 3, A-8010 Graz Austria

KONRAD, JAROSLAV, veterinarian; b. Lutova, Czech Republic, Jan. 13, 1926; s. Jan and Marie (Senkyrova) K.; m. Ludmila Linduskova, Sept. 7, 1950; children: Jaroslav, Jan. DVM, Vet. U., Brno, Czech Republic, 1950, PhD, 1961, DSc, 1969. Asst. prof. Vet. U., 1950-54, prof. internal medicine, 1966-93; prof. internal medicine Vet. U., Vienna, 1994, Brno, 1995—; vet. intern Vet. Hosp., Ces. Budejovice, Czech Republic, 1954-62; prof. vet. disciplines Agrl. Coll., Ces. Budejovice, 1960-66; prof. Fur Animal Breeding, Agrl. U., Brno, 1995—; dir. Regional Vet. Hosp., Ces. Budejovice, 1960-62; dept. head Agrl. Coll., 1962-66; head internal clinic Vet. U., 1966-90; rector U. Vet. and Pharm. Scis., Brno, 1990-94. Co-author: Internal Diseases of Domestic Animals, 1972, Internal Diseases of Horse and Small Animal, 1984, Internal Diseases of Domestic Animals (German), 1985, Breeding of Fur Animals, 1996; author: Fur Animal Diseases, 1989; editor: Acta Veterinaria, 1990-94. Recipient Mussemeier medal Humboldt U., 1993. Mem. Czech Acad. Agrl. Scis. (chmn. various coms., Silber medal 1991, Gold medal 1996), Sci. Coun. U. South Bohemia, Czech Breeder Union (mem. ctrl. coun., chmn. vet. com.). Roman Catholic. Avocations: tourism, literature, music. Office: U Vet and Pharm Scis, Palackeho 1-3, 612 42 Brno Czech Republic

KONSCHAK, KLAUS, physicist, radiation protection consultant; b. Königs Wusterhausen, Germany, Jan. 10, 1945; s. Heinz and Ilse (Gaul) Albrecht; m. Rosemarie Leidhold, Oct. 15, 1982; children: Thomas, Alexander. Dipl-Physicist, Tech. U. Dresden, Germany, 1968; DrRerNat, Tech. U. Dresden, 1973; Prof., Engring. Coll., Zittau, Germany, 1992. Cert. radiation protection officer. Sci. fellow Tech. U. Dresden, 1968-73, Rsch. Inst. of Polygraphics, Dresden, 1973-77; docent, prof., head of rsch. reactor Engring. Coll., Zittau, 1977-93; sci. fellow IFU e.v. Inst., Lauchhammer, Germany, 1993-94, Gamma-Svc. GmbH, Radeberg, Germany, 1995—. Contbr. articles to profl. jours. Avocation: photography. Home: Hauptstr 87a, D-01616 Strehla Germany

KONSIN, PEET, physicist, researcher; b. Tartu, Estonia, May 15, 1939; s. Johannes and Leida (Paukson) K.; m. Viive Punt, July 5, 1964. Cert., State U. Tartu, 1963, Cand. Sci., 1970, ScD, 1978. Sr. lectr. Poly. Inst. Tallinn, Estonia, 1963; rsch. assoc. Inst. Physics and Astronomy, Tartu, 1968-74, sr. rsch. assoc., 1974-86, leading rsch. assoc., 1986—. Contbr. over 175 articles to profl. jours. Chmn. Trade Union of Inst. of Physics, Tartu, 1978-80. Sr. lt. Soviet Army, 1964-65. Mem. Estonian Phys. Soc., Estonian Soc. Scientists. Avocations: history of physics, chess, music, gardening, sports. Home: Eha 34-1, 51003 Tartu Estonia Office: U Tartu Inst of Physics, Riia 142, 51014 Tartu Estonia

KONSTANTINOS, TEPETES, surgeon, consultant; b. Athens, Greece, Feb. 11, 1960; s. Nikolaos and Spyridoula (Karvelis) T.; m. Maria Kouris, Sept. 26, 1998; 1 child, Nikolas Jason. MD, Sch. Medicine, Patras, Greece, 1983; DSc, Sch. Medicine, 1990. Resident U. Hosp., Patras, Greece, 1983-89; cons. surgeon U. Hosp., 1990—; visiting asst. prof. U. Hosp., Pitt., 1991-93; assoc. specialist U. Hosp., Liverpool, United Kingdom, 1996-97. Sec. gen. Patras Med. Coun., 1987-89. Mem. European Soc. Surgical Oncology, European Digestive Surgery. Avocations: swimming, basketball, reading old newspapers. Home: 1 Pente Pigadion St, 26441 Patras Greece Office: U Hosp Patras, Rion, 26500 Patras Greece

KONSTANTINOV, TZVETAN KRUMOV, musician, concert pianist, educator; came to U.S., 1979; s. Krum Christov and Maria Apostolov (Veselkov) K.; m. Lee-Ann Larson, Mar. 7, 1980; children: Alexander, Christian. MusM, Bulgarian State Conservatoire, Sofia, Bulgaria, 1974; postgrad., Hochschule Fur Musik, Vienna, Austria, 1979. Prof. Bulgarian State Conservatoire, Sofia, 1974-77, Levine Sch. Music, Washington, 1984-89, George Washington U., Washington, 1989—; bd. dirs. Met. Chorus. Am. debut at Meany Hall, Seattle, 1980; performer TV documentary including Music To Promote Democracy, 1990, Spotlight, 1988, Capital Concerts, 1989, Voice of Am., TV broadcast performance, 1999; performances at Carnegie Hall and Kennedy Ctr. Organizer extensive tours throughout Europe and U.S. Recipient Diploma for Highest Achievements Fifth All-Bulgarian Competition, 1969, Laureate Second Nat. Competition, 1970. Mem. AAUP, Am. Liszt Soc., Am. Assn. for Promoting Bulgarian Culture, Am. Beethoven Soc., Friday Morning Music Club. Avocations: arts, hiking, languages, golfing, jogging. Home: PO Box 554 Mc Lean VA 22101-0554 Office: George Washington U Dept Music Washington DC 20052-0001

KONSTAS, EPAMINONDAS, shipping executive; b. Athens, Mar. 1, 1933; s. Fokion and Gurli (Kyhlberger) K.; divorced; 1 child, Nausikaa. Diploma, City of London Coll., Ecole Superieure de Commerce, Lausanne, Switzerland. Lines mgr. Soc. Gestion Evge, La Tour de Peilz, Switzerland, 1950-65; gen. mgr. Emilio Huart S.A., Cadiz, Spain, 1965-67; dir. Cie Maritime Charguers Reunis, Paris, 1968-71; mng. dir. Johnson Line, Burssels, 1971-73; dir. internat. affairs Aucona S.A., Madird, 1973-75; mng. dir. Hellas Ferries S.A., Piraeus, Greece, 1976-81, Hellas Shipping Agys. Co. Ltd., Piraeus, 1982—; pres. ALMO Internat.; cons. UNCTAD, Geneva, 1980—. Author: Eating Out in Athens, 1990. Mem. Internat. Maritime Club Madrid (founder, pres. 1972-75). Avocations: skiing, skin-diving, windsurfing, reading history. Home: Alkyonis 32, Paleon Falirn Athens 17561, Greece Office: Hellas Shipping Agys Co Ltd, Aklyonis 32, Paleon Falirn Athens 17561, Greece

KONSTEN, JOOP, surgeon; b. Heerlen, Limburg, The Netherlands, Apr. 7, 1963; s. Pierre K. and Marlies Van Velsen. MD, U. Maastricht, The Netherlands, 1988, PhD, 1993. Surg. rsch. fellow U. Hosp., Maastricht, The Netherlands, 1990-93, surg. resident Venlo Hosp., 1993-97; surgeon Univ. Hosp. Rotterdam, Dylzigt, 2000—. Capt. Med. Svcs., 1988-90. Mem. Dutch Assn. Surgery (resident 1993-97), Gastro-Intestinal Surg., Trauma, for Med. Specialists. Office: U Hosp Rotterdam, Dept Surgery PO Box 2040, 3000 CA Rotterdam The Netherlands

KONSUL, KHALIL ANTON, petroleum engineer, researcher; b. Madaba, Jordan, Dec. 23, 1937; s. Anton Salem and Hanne Khalil (Sawalha) K.; m. Hanan Abdullah Farah, Jan. 20, 1984. Diploma in Engring., Tech. U., Clausthal, Germany, 1972. Petroleum engr. Iraqi Petroleum Co., Khanquin, 1975-78; rschr. Petroleum Inst., Clausthal, 1978-80; salesman Smith Co., Celle, Germany, 1981; petroleum engr. Natural Resources Authority/Jordan, Amman, 1982-99; organizer Founding Conf., Arab Astron. Union, 1998; organizing com. Conf. on Arab-Islamic Tech. in Amman, 1996, 98. Chief editor Space and Astronomy, 1998—; contbr. articles to profl. jours. Mem. Jordanian Astron. Soc. (founder, v.p. 1987-91, pres. 1991-98), Jordanian Soc. History Sci. (co-founder, mgmt. com. 1989-98), Madaba Cultural and Art Club (co-founder), Planetary Soc., Internat. Meteor Orgn., Royal Astron. Soc. Can., Internat. Occultation Assn., Arab Union for Astronomy and Space Scis. (co-founder, pres. 1998—). Office: AUASS, PO Box 141568, 11814 Amman 11814, Jordan

KONTANI, HIROSHI, physicist; b. Nagoya, Japan, July 30, 1968; s. Masaaki and Sachiko K. PhD in Physics, Kyoto U., 1996. Assoc. rschr. ISSP, U. Tokyo, 1995—.

KONTAXAKIS, GEORGE, biomedical engineer, electrical engineer; b. Athens, Greece, July 5, 1967; s. Nikolaos and Aggeliki (Antoniadou) K. Diploma in elec. and electronic engring., Nat. Tech. U. Athens, 1990; MS in Biomed. Engring., Rutgers U., 1992, PhD in Biomed. Engring., 1996. Tchg. asst. Grad. Sch. Rutgers U., New Brunswick, N.J., 1992-95; math. tutor Equal Opportunity Fund Dougglass Coll., New Brunswick, N.J., 1992-95; German acad. exch. postdoctoral fellow U. Frankfurt, Germany, 1996; guest scientist fellow German Cancer Rsch. Ctr. Med. PET Group Biol. Imaging, Heidelberg, 1996-99; rsch. engr. dept. cognitive computing and med. imaging Fraunhofer Inst. Computer Graphics, Darmstadt, Germany, 1999-2000; sr. rschr. med. imaging group Tech. U. Madrid, 2000—; rsch. assoc. Biomed. Engring. Lab., Nat. U. Athens, 1996—; vis. rsch. assoc. divsn. particle physics U. Athens, 1996—; vis. rsch. assoc. dept. stats. Maquarie U., Sydney, Australia, 1999. Contbr. articles to profl. jours. FCC lic. operator Voice of Greece show Rutgers U. Radio Sta., New Brunswick, 1992-96; mem. Hellenic Sailing Sch., Athens, 1987. Grantee State Fellowships Found. Greece, 1985, 86, 88, 89, Sigma Xi, 1994; Marion Johnson fellow Rutgers U., 1990-92, 95; recipient Michael G. Mulinos Postgrad. Essay award Hellenic Med. Soc. N.Y., 1995. Mem. IEEE, Sigma Xi. Avocations: skiing, sailing, traveling, classical guitar. E-mail: g.kontaxakis@ieee.org. Home: Pl. Luca de Tena 4, 2A, 28045 Madrid Spain

KONTOROVICH, ALEXEY EMILIEVICH, geologist; b. Kharkov, Ukraine, Jan. 28, 1934; s. Emil Ilich Kontorovich and Valentina Fedorovna Sarianaki; m. Ekaterina Alexandrovna Tikhonova, Sept. 11, 1957. Grad., Tomsk State U., 1956; Cand. Geol. Mineral. Scis., Novosib. State U., 1964, D Geol.-Mineral. Sci., 1969; Prof., Siberian Rsch. Inst. Geol.-Geophysics and Mineral. Resources, 1971. Asst. State U., Tomsk, 1956-57; physics tchr., 1957-58; sr. engr., sr. scientist, head of lab., head dept. Siberian Rsch. Inst. of Geology, Geophysics and Mineral Resources, Novosibirsk, 1958-87; dep. dir. Siberian Rsch. Inst., Geol., Geophysic and Mineral Resources, Novosibirsk, 1987-89; dep. dir. gen. United Inst. Geol., Geophysics and Mineralogy Siberian Br. Russian Acad. Scis., Novosibirsk, 1989—, dir. Inst. Petroleum Geol., 1997—; head dept. Novosib. State U., 1990—, Siberian Br. of Russian Acad. of Scis., 1988—. Assoc. dep. editor: Russian Geology and Geophysics Jour.; mem. editl. bd. Oil and Gas Geology Jour., Geology, Geophysics and Devel. of Oil and Gas Fields Jour. Decorated Order of the Red Banner of Labour, 1981; recipient medals for devel. of mineral resources and oil-gas complex in West Siberia, 1987, State prize Russian Fedn., 1994, Gubkin prize Russian Acad. of Scis., 1974, others. Mem. Acad. of Scis. Trade Union, Russian Acad. Scis. Office: Inst Petroleum Geology 3, Acad Koptyug Ave 3, 630090 Novosibirsk Russia

KONTOROVITCH, VALERI YAKOVLEVICH, communication educator; b. Scerdlovsk, Russia, July 29, 1941; arrived in Mex., 1993; s. Jakob E. and Lia F. (Mazover) K.; m. Alla G. Yakovleva, June 24, 1964 (div. 1976); 1 child, Marina; m. Zinaida A. Lovtchikova, Mar. 2, 1983. MS, Bonch-Bruevish Inst. Telecomm., Leningrad, Russia, 1964, PhD, 1968, DS, 1986. Engr. Rsch. Inst., Leningrad, Russia, 1964-65; jr. rsch. assoc. Bonch-Bruevich Inst. Telecomm., Leningrad, Russia, 1967-70, sr. rsch. assoc., 1970-76, head rsch. lab., 1976-88, prof., 1988-92; head dept. State U. Telecomm. (formerly Bonch-Bruevich Inst. Telecomm.), St. Petersburg, Russia, 1992-94, prof., 1994—; prof. Cinvestav-IPN, Mex., 1993—. Inventor in field. Mem. IEEE (sr.), AAAS, N.Y. Acad. Scis., Acad. Mexicana de Cienciac. Avocations: classic music, travel, classic literature. Office: Cinvestav-IPN, Av IPN #2508, 07000 Mexico City DF, Mexico

KONTOŠIĆ, IVICA, occupational health physician, medical educator; b. Rijeka, Croatia, Dec. 24, 1958; s. Josip and Katica (Samaržija) K.; m. Ruža Mužic, Aug. 17, 1991; children: Dario, Ivana. MD, Rijeka U., 1982, MSc, 1989, PhD, 1997. Gen. practitioner Health Ctr. Rijeka, 1986-91, specialist in occupl. health, 1992-99; asst. Sch. Medicine Rijeka U., 1993-97, sr. asst., 1997—; specialist in occupl. health Croatian Inst. Occupl. Health, 1999—. Author: Occupational Health, 1996; contbr. articles to profl. jours.; mem. editl. bd., mem. adv. bd. Medicina, 1998. Mem. Croatian Med. Assn. (letter of thanks 1993, diploma for 125th anniversary 1998), Croatian Soc. Occupl. Medicine (acknowledgment 1996), Croatian Soc. Maritime, Diving and Hyperbaric Medicine (2d v.p. 1996). Office: Croatian Inst Occupl Health, Riva 16, 51000 Rijeka Croatia

KONTOYANNIS, CHRISTOS GEORGE, chemistry educator, researcher; b. Athens, Greece, Oct. 18, 1961; q; s. George C. and Maria J. (Panagopoulos) K.; m. Argiroula C. Alexandropoulos, May 25, 1991; children: Maria-Christine, George. BSc, U. Patras (Greece), 1983; MSc, Georgetown U., 1985, PhD, 1988. Researcher ICE/HT-Forth, Patras, 1990-92; faculty dept. pharmacy U. Patras, Patras, 1992—. Author: (in Greek) Experiments in Instrumental Analysis, 1993; contbr. articles to profl. jours. Georgetown U. rsch. fellow, 1983-88; European Sci. Found. grantee, 1994. Mem. Assn. Greek Chemists, Electrochem. Soc., Georgetown U. Hellenic Club (pres. 1987-88). Home: Egeou 11, GR 26441 Patras Greece Office: U Campus, U Patras Dept Pharmacy, GR 26500 Patras Rion, Greece

KONTRA, MIKLÓS, linguist, educator; b. Budapest, Hungary, Oct. 12, 1950; s. György and Ilona (Kozma) K.; m. Edit Hegybíró, July 25, 1975; children: Mark and Veronica (twins). MA in English and Russian, Kossuth Lajos U., Debrecen, Hungary, 1974; PhD in Linguistics, Eotvos Lorand U., Budapest, 1977. Assoc. instr. English Jozsef A. Univ., Szeged, Hungary, 1974-77, asst. prof., 1977-78; Hungarian lector Ind. U., Bloomington, 1978-81; asst. prof. English Kossuth L. Univ., Debrecen, Hungary, 1981-85; researcher Linguistics Inst., Hungarian Acad. Scis., Budapest, 1985-92; assoc. prof. József A. Univ., Szeged, 1991-99, prof., 1999—. Author: A nyelvek kozotti kolcsonzes, 1981; editor: Ferenc Fabricius-Kovacs Bibliography, 1984; contbr. numerous articles on linguistics to edn. jours. Fulbright scholar Ind. U., 1992-93; ACLS fellow Mich. State U., 1995-96. Mem. Linguistic Soc. Hungary, Linguistic Assn. Can. and U.S., Am. Dialect Soc. Office: Linguistics Inst Hungarian Acad Scis, PO Box 701/518 H-1399, H-1250 Budapest Hungary

KONTUSH, ANATOL, biophysicist, researcher; b. Odessa, former USSR, Oct. 26, 1960; arrived in Germany, 1992.; s. Sergei Kontush and Svetlana Shchekatolina; m. Natalia Kasperovich, June 10, 1989; children: Konstantin, Mikhail. PhD in Biochemistry, Inst. Food Industry, Odessa, 1989; PhD in Biophysics, U. Hamburg, Germany, 1996. Rsch. scientist Inst. Food Industry, 1989, sr. rsch. scientist, 1989—; rsch. scientist U. Hamburg, 1992—. Author: Mechanisms of Pesticide Action, 1991, Moscow-Odessa, 1992, Odessa Globe, 1997; contbr. articles to profl. jours. Named Champion of Intellectual Club, Soviet TV, Moscow, 1987. Mem. Internat. Soc. Free Radical Rsch., 1993—, World-Wide Odessa Club. Office: U Hamburg Biochem Lab, Martinistr 52, 20246 Hamburg Germany

KONUK, HALUK, electrical engineer, researcher; b. Kutahya, Turkey, Apr. 4, 1965; came to U.S., 1987; s. Ali Konuk and Vacide Beder. BS, Bogazici U., Istanbul, Turkey, 1986; MS, Case Western Res. U., 1989; PhD, U. Calif., Santa Cruz, 1996. Switch software engr. NETAS, Istanbul, 1986-87; CAD software engr. CLSI, Rockville, Md., 1989-91; VLSI test technologist Hewlett-Packard, Palo Alto, Calif., 1995—. Contbr. articles to profl. publs.; patentee in field.

KONVITZ, JOSEF WOLF, history educator, international civil servant; b. N.Y.C., July 27, 1946; s. Milton Ridvas and Mary (Traub) K.; m. Isa Naomi Schwartzberg, June 15, 1969; children: Eli Raphael, Ezra Daniel. BA with honors, Cornell U., 1967; MA, Princeton U., 1971, PhD, 1973. Asst. prof.

history Mich. State U., East Lansing, 1973-78, assoc. prof., 1978-85, prof., 1985-95; prin. adminstr. Urban Affairs Div./OECD, Paris, 1992-96, head of divsn., 1996-99, head divsn. territorial policies and prospects, 1999—; dir. assoc. studies Ecole des hautes etudes en sciences sociales, Paris, 1989; mem. bd. experts Port and City Project, Plan-Constrn.-Architecture, French Ministry Equipment, 1990-95; vis. prof. U. of the West of Eng., 1998—. Author: Cities and the Sea, 1978, The Urban Millennium, 1985, Cartography in France 1660-1848, 1987 (Nebenzahl prize 1985); editor: What Americans Should Know, 1986; mem. bd. editors Jour. Urban History, 1991—; contbr. numerous articles to profl. jours. Grantee Am. Council Learned Socs., 1982, NEH, 1984; fellow NEH, 1979, Am. Philos. Soc., 1984, Woodrow Wilson Internat. Ctr. for Scholars, 1987. Mem. Am. Hist. Assn., Soc. French Hist. Studies, Soc. History Tech., Soc. History Sci., Urban History Assn. (bd. dirs. 1989-93). Jewish. Avocations: gastronomy, decorative arts. Office: OCDE Terr Devel Svcs, 2 rue Andre Pascal, 75775 Paris CEDEX 16, France

KÓNYA, JÓZSEF, clinical microbiologist, researcher; b. Debrecen, Hungary, Oct. 8, 1964; s. Jozsef Zoltan Konya and Klara Magdolna Timon; m. Eva Dienes, Feb. 7, 1987; children: Tamas, Szabolcs. MD, U. Med. Sch. Debrecen, 1989, PhD, 1998. Intern and resident Dept. Microbiology, U. Med. Sch., Debrecen, Hungary, 1989-93; asst. lectr. U. Med. Sch. Debrecen, Debrecen, Hungary, 1993-98; asst. prof. U. Debrecen Med. Sch., 1999—; vis. scientist Karolinska Inst., Stockholm, 1994-96, 99. Mem. Hungarian Soc. Microbiology. Avocations: mountain hiking, biking. Office: U Debrecen Med Sch, Dept Microbiology Box 17, H 4012 Debrecen Hungary

KÓNYA, JÓZSEF ZOLTÁN, chemistry educator; b. Debrecen, Hungary, Feb. 11, 1937; s. József and Julianna (B. Kiss) K.; m. Klára Timon, Jan. 20, 1962; children: József, Klára. Degree chemistry, Kossuth U., 1959, PhD, 1964. Rschr. Agricultural Quality Controlling Inst., Debrecen, 1959-60; jr. rsch. fellow Kossuth U., Debrecen, 1960-64, rsch. fellow, 1964-82, assoc. prof., 1982—. Contbr. numerous articles to profl. publs. Pres. local corrosion com., 1982—. Recipient Gold medal Hungarian Fire Dept., 1985. Mem. Hungarian Acad. of Scis. (radioanalytical com. 1985—), ISE. Calvinist. Office: Kossuth U, Egyetem ter 1, H-4010 Debrecen Hungary

KOO, CHRISTINE, solicitor; b. Shanghai, China, Oct. 30, 1951; d. Sai Choi Cheung and Kam Far Wong; m. Yuk Chan Koo; children: Mary, Sally. LLB with hons., U. Hong Kong, 1978, PCH, 1979; MCI Arb, Royal Melbourne Inst. Tech., Australia, 1986-87; postgrad., Beijing U., 1993-95. Solicitor Supreme Ct. Hong Kong, 1981, Supreme Ct. Eng., 1984; barrister, solicitor Supreme Ct. Victoria, Australia, 1985; fellow Life Mgmt. Ins. Assn. (FLMI). Articled clk., trainee solicitor, asst. solicitor Messrs. Johnson, Stokes & Master, Hong Kong, 1979-83; solicitor Registrar Gen. Dept. Land Office, Hong Kong, 1983-85, acting sr. solicitor, 1985-86; solicitor class I Melbourne & Met. Bd. Works, Hong Kong, 1986-87, solicitor class II, 1987-88; gen. counsel legal dept. Nat. Mutual Ins. Australia and Nat. Mutual Asia, Melbourne and Hong Kong, 1988-95; gen. mgr. Nat. Mutual Trustees Ltd. Nat. Mutual Ins. Australia and Nat. Mutual Asia, Hong Kong, 1988-95; prin. ptnr. Christine M. Koo & Co., Hong Kong, 1995—; mem. guidelines com. Mandatory Provident Fund Schemes Authority, Hong Kong, 1999—; ind. dir. Bank Comm. Trustee Ltd., Hong Kong, 1999—, Bank of East Asia (Trustees) Ltd., Hong Kong, 1999—, China Life Trustees Ltd., Hong Kong, 1999—, The Tai Ping Trustees (H.K.) Ltd., Hong Kong, 1999—. Dir. St. Stephen's Ch. Coll., 1999—. Fellow Hong Kong Inst. Dirs. Ltd.; mem. Law Soc. Hong Kong (comml. law com. 1997—, mainland legal affairs com.), Actuarial Soc. Hong Kong (hon. legal advisor 1996—), Hong Kong Gen. Ins. Agts. Assn. (hon. legal advisor 1997—), Hong Kong Fedn. Insurers (ind. mem. legal working com. 1990—), Chinese Life Assurance Assn. Hong Kong (hon. legal advisor 1995—), Australian Chinese Assn. Hong Kong Ltd. (sec. 1996—), Hong Kong Retirement Scheme Assn. (exec. com. 1997—), Hong Kong Fedn. Women Profls., Hans Andersen Club (hon. legal advisor 1996—). Avocations: child-abuse concern group, youth problem group. Office: Rm 32D Lippo Ctr Ctr Twr I, Queensway, Hong Kong China

KOO, JA-HYUN, biochemist, educator; b. Seoul, Mar. 27, 1947; s. Kook-Hwae and Yang-Hee (Kim) K.; m. Bok-Sil Kim, Nov. 10, 1974; children: Bang-Bon, Jun-Bon. BS, Korea U., Seoul, 1969, MS, 1971; PhD, Yonsei U., Seoul, 1981. Lectr. Coll. Medicine Hanyang U., Seoul, 1976-80, from asst. prof. to assoc. prof. Coll. Medicine, 1980-88; rsch. fellow NIH, Bethesda, Md., 1983-85; prof. Coll. Medicine Konkuk U., Choong-Ju, Korea, 1988—, dir. Med. Rsch. Inst., 1990-93, dean Coll. Medicine, 1993-95, prof., chmn. dept. biochemistry Coll. Medicine, 1988—. Author: Current Topics in Cellular Regulations, 1982, Enzyme Dynamics and Regulation, 1988. Fogarty Internat. fellow, 1983. Mem. AAAS, Korean Soc. Med. Biochemistry and Molecular Biology (bd. trustees 1988—, v.p., editor-in-chief jour. 1999), Biochem. Soc. of Republic of Korea (bd. trustees 1981—, pres. regional Choong-Chung chpt.), N.Y. Acad. Scis. Fax: 82-441-851-3944. E-mail: jhkoo@kku.edu. Office: Konkuk U Dept Biochemistry, # 322 Danwol-dong, Choong-Ju 380-701, South Korea

KOO, LEE HAUW, business executive; b. Surabaya, Indonesia, Feb. 2, 1959; arrived in The Netherlands, 1968; s. Tiong Ing and Hwie Kien (Tan) K.; m. Marina Johanna Leyendekkers; children: George Nicolaas Daming, Elise Johanna Meiling. MS in Medicine, U. Amsterdam, 1983, MD, 1985, MPA, 1987; MBA, Henley Mgmt. Coll., 1991. Intern U. Hosp., Amsterdam, 1983-85; product mgr. Smith-Kline Beecham, Amstelveen, The Netherlands, 1985-87, group product mgr., 1987-88; dep.publisher VNU Publ. Corp., Amsterdam, 1988-90, publisher, 1990-91; mktg., sales dir. Europe Avery Dennison Corp., Hazerswoude, The Netherlands, 1991-95, gen. mgr. Europe, 1995-97; area gen. mgr. Asia Pacific Akzo Nobel Decorative Coatings, Singapore, 1997-98; v.p., gen. mgr. Europe and Asia Pacific Avery Dennison Corp., Hazerswoude, The Netherlands, 1998—. Office: Avery Dennison, PO Box 118, 2394 ZG Hazerswoude The Netherlands address: Dykstraat 28, 2371 Vg Roelofarendsveen The Netherlands

KOO, SHOU-ENG, economics educator; b. Yenchen, Jiangsu, China, Jan. 13, 1911; came to U.S., 1945.; s. Yun Peng Koo and Sze Chih; m. Chi-Hung Hu, Aug. 9, 1966 (div. Oct. 1979); children: Boping Gu, Zhong-ping Gu, Wei-ping Gu; m. Ailin Dong, Mar. 22, 1989. BA, Nat. Ctrl. U., Nanjing, China, 1931; MA, Columbia U., 1946, PhD, 1961. Asst. prof. John Carroll U., Cleve., 1961-66; vis. assoc. prof. U. Ga., Athens, 1966-67; assoc. prof. Ind. U., Indpls., 1967-74, prof., 1974-87, prof. emeritus, 1987—; vis. prof. Taiwan U., Taipei, 1973-74, Nanjing U., 1980-81, Nankai U., Tianjian, China, 1983, Fudan U., Shanghai, China, 1985-86, U. Fin. and Econ., Shanghai, 1987-88; spl. lectr. Beijing U., 1999. Author: An Input-Output Study for Metropolitan Indianapolis, 1973, Foreign Investment and Industrialization in Taiwan, 1976, Tariff and the Development of the Cotton Industry in China: 1842-1937, 1982, China Opens to the Outside World, 1988. Mem. C.A. Nat. Ctrl. U. Alumni Assn. (pres. 1996—), N.Am. Inst. Internat. Comm. (v.p. 1992—), The 1990 Inst. Avocations: tennis, cruise tour, walking.

KOO, SUN HOE, medical educator; b. Taejon, South Korea, Oct. 27, 1956; parents Wan Seo Koo and Eun Seung Chae; m. Kyo Chan Ahan, Jan. 17, 1982; 1 child, So Young Ahan. MB, Chunanam Nat. U., Taejon, 1981, M of Medicine, 1985, MD, 1989. Cert. specialist in clin. pathology. From instr. to asst. prof. to assoc. prof. Chunanam Nat. Univ. Hosp., Taejon, 1985-96, prof., 1997—, also bd. dirs. Contbr. rsch. papers to profl. jours. Recipient award Korea Sci. Found., 1995-98. Mem. Korean Assn. Clin. Pathology (bd. dirs. 1998-2000), Korean Med. Genetics Assn., Korean Assn. Hematologists. Avocation: golf. Fax: 82-42-257-5365. E-mail: shkoo@cnuh.co.kr. Office: Chunaman Univ Hosp, Daesadong 640, Taejon 301-040, South Korea

KOOIJ, ARIE VAN DER, religious studies educator; b. Nieuwe-Tonge, The Netherlands, Mar. 8, 1945; s. Arie van der Kooij and Annigje Roest; m. Elizabeth Maria van der Neut, June 17, 1971; children: Mirjam, Tanja. M, U. Utrecht, The Netherlands, 1969, D, 1978. Lectr. U. Utrecht, 1970-89; prof. U. Leiden, The Netherlands, 1989—; dean faculty of theology U. Leiden, 1992-94. Author: Die alten Textzeugen des Jesajabuches, 1981, The Oracle of Tyre, 1998; co-author: Rapport van de Verkenningscommissie Godgeleerdheid, 2 vols., 1989; co-editor: (with P.B. Dirksen) Abraham Kuenen: His Major Contributions, 1993, The Peshitta as a Translation, 1995, (with K. van der Toorn) Canonization and Decanonization, 1998; editor Vetus Testamentum jour., 1997—; contbr. articles to jours. in field. Mem., sec. assessment com. Ministry of Edn., 1987-89. Mem. Dutch Reformed Ch. Office: Faculty of Theology LeidenU, PO Box 9515, 2300 RA Leiden The Netherlands

KOOIJMAN, ARTHUR, linguist, translator; b. Heerlen, Limburg, Netherlands, Dec. 11, 1955; s. Cor and Nel (Van Scheppingen) K. BA in Philosophy, U. Utrecht, Netherlands, 1985, MA in Linguistics with distinction, 1986. Head translation dept. Aldus Europe, Edinburgh, 1988-93; freelance translator, 1993—. Translator: Rupert Brooke: 1914, 1998, De Experimentele Roman, 1998; contbr. articles to profl. jours. Home: Saharadreef 3, 3564 CV Utrecht Netherlands

KOOIJMANS, PIETER HENDRIK, judge International Court of Justice; b. Heemstede, The Netherlands, July 6, 1933; m. A. Kooijmans-Verhage; 4 children. Degree, Free U., Amsterdam, The Netherlands, 1964. Mem. Faculty of Law Free U. of Amsterdam, 1960-65, prof. European law and pub. internat. law, 1965-73; state sec. for fgn. affairs Govt. of The Netherlands, 1973-77; prof. pub. internat. law U. Leiden, The Netherlands, 1978-92, 95-97; minister of fgn. affairs Govt. of The Netherlands, 1993-94; judge Internat. Ct. of Justice, The Hague, The Netherlands, 1997—. Author textbooks in field; contbr. articles to profl. jours. Head Netherlands del. to UN Commn. on Human Rights, 1982-85, 92, chair commn., 1984-85, spl. reporter on questions relevant to torture, 1985-92; mem. various UN and Orgn. on Security and Coop. in Europe missions to former Yugoslavia, 1991-92. Office: care Internat Ct of Justice, Peace Palace, 2517 KJ The Hague The Netherlands

KOOIMA, LINDA KAY, neonatal and pediatrics nurse; b. Rock Valley, Iowa, Aug. 26, 1948; d. Thomas and Frances Mae (Harmelink) K.; m. Orlando Sabas Arroyo, Apr. 12, 1976; children: Annie Josephine, Solomon Jordan. Dipl. nursing, Northwestern U., 1969; BA in Spanish, S.D. State U., 1989. RN, Ill., S.D., Ariz., Calif., Fla. Critical care nurse Children's Meml. Hosp., Chgo., 1969-70; nurse neonatal ICU, Moffitt Hosp. U. Calif., San Francisco, 1970-76; clinic nurse S.D. State U., Brookings, 1985-88; mother and baby nurse Santa Barbara (Calif.) Cottage Hosp., 1988-89; neonatal nurse Santa Ana (Calif.) Hosp. and Med. Ctr., 1990, Hoag Presbyn. Meml. Hosp., Newport Beach, Calif., 1991; pediatric camp nurse Camp Gulliver, Coral Gables, Fla., 1993-95; utilization rev. nurse Initial Health Care, Miami, 1995-98; travel nurse mother/baby Star-Med Co., 1998-2000. Mem. Assn. Camp Nurses. Republican. Avocation: scuba diving. Home: 13890 SW 100th Ln Miami FL 33186-6869

KOOK, ABRAHAM IZHAK, neuroimmunologist; b. Haifa, Israel, Aug. 29, 1937; s. Nahum and Hanah (Frank) K.; m. Aya Ben-Yaakov, Feb. 1960 (div. Oct. 1983); three children. MSc, Cornell U., 1965; PhD, McGill U., 1970. Sr. scientist Weizmann Inst. Sci., Rehovot, Israel, 1972-80; assoc. prof. Technion Faculty Medicine, Haifa, 1980-81; dir. labs. Wolfson Hosp., Holon, 1981-84; assoc. prof. Tulane U. Med. Ctr., New Orleans, 1984-87; vis. prof. NIH, Bethesda, Md., 1987-88; dir. rsch. wing Rebecca Sieff Med. Ctr., Safed, Israel, 1989—. Fellow Israel Biochem. Assn., Israel Immunol. Soc., N.Y. Acad. Scis.

KOOLMAN, OLINDO, Aruban government official. Gov. gen. Aruba. Office: Plaza Henny Eman 3, Oranjestad Aruba*

KOOLURIS DOBBS, LINDA KIA, artist; b. Orange, N.J., Jan. 28, 1949; m. Kildare Dobbs, May 7, 1981. AA, Pine Manor Coll., 1968; student, Sorbonne, 1968-69; BFA with honors, Sch. Visual Arts, 1972. Several coll. tchg. positions, 1975-94. Exhibited works at Gallery Sheila Roth, Toronto, Bronxville Art and Frame Gallery, Atrium Gallery, Chubb group of Ins. Cos., Warren, N.J., Vancouver Art Gallery, Newbury Fine Arts, Boston and Edgartown, Mass., Art Gallery of Hamilton, Toronto Watercolour Soc., Vancouver Maritime Mus., Visual Arts Burnaby, B.C., Sutton Gallery, Toronto; works in more than 130 in Can., 50 abroad collections in Can., including AT&T, Artform (Norway), Glaxo Wellcome Inc., Inland Pacific Enterprises, Temple Scott & Assocs., Uniglobe, Advance Travel, AGF Mgmt. Ltd., Toronto Stock Exch., Ont. Govt. Art Collection, Parliament Bldg., Queen's Park, Pine Manor Coll. (U.S.), Mt. Sinai Hosp., Merrill Lynch, Scotia McLeod, Probyn & Co.; numerous portrait commns.; subject of articles. Recipient Ann. Art Purchase prize Pine Manor Coll., 1968, 2d prize Fin. Post Ann. Reports awards, 1981. Mem. Toronto Watercolour Soc. (Hon. Mention, Ann. Fall Show 1991). Address: 330 Spadina Rd Ste 1005, Toronto, ON Canada M5R 2V9

KOOMEN, CORNELIS JAN, telecommunications, micro and consumer electronics executive; b. Zaandam, The Netherlands, Sept. 25, 1947; s. C.J. and G. (Dykman) K.; m. Jantiena Catharina de Jong; children: Casper Jan, Jeroen. MS, Tech. U., Delft, The Netherlands, 1972, PhD, 1982. Rschr. RVO/TNO, The Hague, The Netherlands, 1973-74, Philips Rsch. Labs., Eindhoven, 1974-83; system engr. Philips Telecommunications and Data Systems, Hilversum, The Netherlands, 1983-84; software coord. Philips Electronics, Eindhoven, 1984-86; mgr. Philips Rsch. Labs., Eindhoven, 1987-89; IC exec., tech. mgr., dir. Philips Telecom. and Data Systems, Hilversum, 1989-90; dir. Philips Comm. Systems, Hilversum, 1990-91; dir., v.p. Philips Semiconductors, Eindhoven, 1991-94, exec. v.p., 1995-98; chmn. Philips Semiconductors, N.Am., 1996-98; pres. and CEO digital video group Philips Consumer Electronics, Palo Alto, Calif., 1997-2000; chmn. Securealink, Campbell, Calif., 2000—; prof. Tech. U., Eindhoven, The Netherlands, 1984—; module dir. Found. Toptech Studies, Delft, 1987-92. Author: The Design of Communicating Systems; editor Internat. Fedn. of Info. Processing Computer Hardware Description Langs. conf. proc., 1985-87; patentee in field; contbr. articles to profl. jours. Chmn. Cultural Com., Waalre, The Netherlands, 1977-81. Named Prof. Bahlerprice, Royal Inst. Engrs., 1986. Mem. IFIP WG 10.2, Soc. for Gen. Edn. (chmn. 1985-88). Avocations: aguarel painting, sailing, tennis. Home: 15415 Via Caballero Monte Sereno CA 95030-2101 Office: Securealink 1999 S Bascom Ave Ste 700 Campbell CA 95008-2216

KOONCE, JOHN PETER, investment company executive; b. Coronado, Calif., Jan. 8, 1932; s. Allen Clark and Elizabeth (Webb) K.; m. Marilyn Rose Campbell, Sept. 21, 1952; children: Stephen Allen, William Clark, Peter Marshall. BS, U.S. Naval Acad., 1954; postgrad., U. So. Calif., 1957, U. Alaska, 1961, U. Ill., 1968-69; MS in Ops. Rsch., Fla. Inst. Tech., 1970; postgrad., Claremont Grad. Sch., 1970. Indsl. engr. Aluminum Co. Am., Lafayette, Ind., 1954-56; electronic rsch. engr. Autonetics Divsn. N.Am. Aviation, Downey, Calif., 1956-57; sys. field engr. Remington Rand Univac, Fayetteville, N.C., 1957-59; project engr. RCA Svc. Co., Cheyenne, Wyo., 1959-60; project supr. RCA Svc. Co., Clear, Alaska, 1960-62, Yorkshire, Eng., 1962-64; re-entry signature analyst RCA Svc. Co., Patrick AFB, Fla., 1964-66; mem. tech. staff TRW Sys. Group, Washington, 1966-68; mgr. ops. rsch. sys. analysis Magnavox Co., Urbana, Ill., 1968-69; tech. advisor EDP, to USAF, Aeroject Electro Sys. Co., Azusa, Calif., Woomera, Australia, 1969-72; investment exec. Shearson Hammill, L.A., 1972-74, Reynolds Securities, L.A., 1974-75; v.p. investments Shearson Hayden Stone, Glendale, 1975-77; v.p. accounts Paine, Webber, Jackson & Curtis, Inc., L.A., 1977-82; pres. Argo Fin. Corp., Santa Monica, Calif., 1982-83, Fin. Packaging Corp., Flintridge, Calif., 1983—; fin. lectr. Princess Line Cruise Ships; tchr. investments Citrus Coll., Azusa, Calif., Claremont (Calif.) Evening Sch.; host, commentator Sta. KWHY-TV, L.A., (weekly) West of Wall Street, 1986-87. Contbr. articles to bus. jours. V.p. Claremont Rep. Club, 1973, pres., 1974; chmn. Verdugo Hosp. Assos., 1979. Recipient Merit cert. RCA, 1966. Mem. Nat. Assn. Security Dealers, Santa Maria Valley C. of C., Navy League U.S., Naval Acad. Alumni Assn., La Can. Flintridge Tournament Roses Assn. (patron), Masons (32d degree, master 1987, pres. dist. officers assn.), Shriners, Kiwanis (pres. La Canada 1995-96), Marbella Golf and Country Club (founding). Home: 415 Foxenwood Dr Santa Maria CA 93455-4228 Office: 15233 Ventura Blvd Ste 404 Sherman Oaks CA 91403-2218

KOONG, LIN LOONG, accountant; b. Seremban, Malaysia, Nov. 12, 1964; m. Boon Gaik Neoh. Cert., Chartered Inst. Mgmt., Eng., 1990, Malaysia Inst. Acountancy, 1994, Malaysia Inst. Taxation, 1995. Lic. auditor, Malaysia. Co. sec. Insan Mgmt., Kuala Lumpur, Malaysia, 1990; tax mgr. Lew Pow Onn & Co. Pub. Accts., Kuala Lumpur, 1991-95; audit mgr. S.C. Internat. Pub. Acct., Kuala Lumpur, 1995; sr. mgr. Nat. Mgmt. Sdn BHD, Kuala Lumpur, 1996; prin. cons. Nat. Bus. Sdn BHD, Kuala Lumpur, 1997; auditor L.L. Koong and Co., Kuala Lumpur, 1999—; fin. cons. Kuala Lumpur Mut. Fund, Berhad, Malaysia, 1995. Spkr. on fin. planning and taxation. Hon. auditor Malaysia Stone Lovers Soc., Malaysia Pilot Assn., Malaysia Cleaning Industry Assn. Mem. Chartered Inst. Mgmt. Accts., Inst. Taxation, Internal Auditors. Avocations: traveling, reading. Office: Ste 9-5 Lelev 9, WISMA UOA II, Jalan Pinang 50450, Malaysia

KOOPMAN, PETER ANTHONY, developmental biologist, researcher; b. Geelong, Australia, Dec. 3, 1959; s. Cornelis and Anna (Bos) K. BS (hon.), U. Melbourne, Australia, 1981; BA, 1985, PhD, 1986. Postdoctoral fellow Med. Rsch. Coun., London, 1986-88; staff scientist, 1988-91; sr. rsch. fellow The U. Queensland, Australia, 1992-96; prin., 1997—; co-instr., 1995-96, instr. 1997-98, Cold Spring Harbor Mouse Embryology Course, program leader in develop. biology, Ctr. for Molecular and Cellular Biology, U. Queensland, Brisbane, Australia, 1994—. Author of over 50 reviews and research papers in international jours.; patentee in field. Recipient AMP-ASMR Biomedical Rsch. award Australian Soc. Med. Rsch., Brisbane, 1992, Australian Rsch. fellowship, 1992, sr. rsch. fellowship, 1997, Australian Rsch. Coun., Julian Wells medallist, 1998. Mem. Australian and N.Z. Soc. for Cell and Developmental Biology. Achievements include joint discoverer of the Y-chromosomal sex determining gene SRY, the campomelic displasia disease gene Sox9, the male-specific transplantation antigen gene UTY.

KÖÖRNA, ARNO, economist, educator; b. Tallinn, Estonia, Feb. 2, 1926; s. Artur and Anna-Helena (Schultz) K.; m. Eha Lind, Dec. 28, 1946; children: Silvia, Vello. PhD, Tartu U., Estonia, 1955; academician, Estonian Acad. Scis., Tallinn, 1973, PhD in Econs., 1970. Prof. Tartu U., 1972-75; sec. gen. Estonian Acad. Scis., 1973-82, v.p., 1982-91, pres., 1991-94, ex-pres., 1995. Author: Economic Motivation of Quality, 1978, Science in Estonia, 1993, Estonian Science in Transition, 1994; contbr. articles to profl. jours. Mem. Estonian Parliament, Tallinn, 1985-90; chmn. Estonian Sci. Coun., Estonia, 1992-94. Mem. Internat. Assn. IUS Primi Vini (mem. standing com.), World Futures Socs. Fedn., Russian Acad. Humanities, Ctrl. European Acad. Sci. and Art (hon.). Home: Kapi 9-22, 10136 Tallinn Estonia Office: Estonian Acad Scis, Kohtu 6, 10130 Tallinn Estonia

KOPÁCSI, SÁNDOR, electrical engineer; b. Budapest, Hungary, Aug. 16, 1965; s. Sándor and Mária (Klimes) K.; m. Krisztina Janzsó, Aug. 28, 1993; children: Anna., Peter. Degree in elec. engring., Tech. U. Budapest, 1990, specialized degree in engring., 1993, PhD, 1996; degree in engring. econs., U. Economical Scis., Budapest, 1996; MBA, Tech. U., Budapest, 2000. Cert. in control and measurement techniques. Sr. rschr. Computer and Automation Inst., Budapest, 1990—; mng. dir. CIM-EXP Cons. Ltd., Budapest, 1996—; vis. rschr. KIST, Seoul, Republic of Korea, 1991, Tech. U. Chemnitz, Germany, 1996, 97, 99; tech. advisor pub. office Hungarian News Agy., 1993. Contbr. articles to sci. publs. With Hungarian mil., 1984-85. Mem. Hungarian Sci. Soc. Automation and Measurement, Assn. for Logic Programming. Avocations: photography, video techniques. Office: Computer and Automation Ins, Kende Utca 13-17, 1111 Budapest Hungary

KOPAL, VLADIMÍR, law educator; b. Jaroměř, Czechoslovakia, Aug. 14, 1928; s. Vladimír and Anna (Brožová) K.; m. Vlasta Zobínová, Apr. 20, 1961. JD, Charles U., Prague, Czechoslovakia, 1951; PhD in Law, Czechoslovak Acad. Scis., Prague, 1963, DS, 1982. Rsch. fellow Inst. of Law Czechoslovak Acad. Scis., 1954-74, chief dept. internat. law, 1975-80; docent Charles U., Prague, 1969, prof. internat. law, 1989-93; prin. officer outer space affairs divsn. UN, N.Y.C., 1981-88, chief outer space affairs divsn., 1983-88; prof. law U. Pilsen, Czech Republic, 1997—; gen. counsel Internat. Astronaut. Fedn., Paris, 1967—; dir. Internat. Inst. Space Law, Paris, 1961—; conciliator, arbitrator UN Conv. on the Law of the Sea, 1996—; chmn. legal subcom. Com. on Peaceful Uses of Outer Space UN, 1999—; participant/officer specialized internat. confs., including UN Conf. on Exploration and Peaceful Uses of Outer Space. Author: The Question of Revising the UN Charter, 1957, The Problem of UN Armed Forces, 1961, Problems of the New Codification of the Law of the Sea, 1983, also over 250 papers in field. With Czech armed forces, 1951-53. Recipient prize Czechoslovak Acad. Scis., 1955, gold medal, 1989; prize Internat. Astronautical Fedn., 1988, golden Hermann-Oberth medal, 1992. Fellow AIAA; mem. Internat. Acad. Astronautics (sect. social scis. 1961—, legal counsel 1967—), French Nat. Acad. Air and Space (fgn. assoc.), Deutsche Gesellschaft Luft und Raumfahrt (hon.), French Soc. for Internat. Law, Internat. Coun. Environ. Law, Euro-Asian Acad. Scis., also others. Home: Vidlicová 2200, 160 00 Prague 6 Dejvice, Czech Republic Office: U Pilsen Faculty Law, Americká 42, 306 14 Plzeň Czech Republic

KOPATSIS, ANTHONY, surgeon; b. Queens, N.Y., Oct. 15, 1965; s. Paul and Dorothy Sklavos Kopatsis; m. Kelly Marie Greening, Jan. 30, 1993; 1 child, Katherine Kopatisis. BS, L.I. U., 1987; MD, Wayne State U., 1992. BCLS, ACLS, ATLS. Intern surgery S.I. U. Hosp., 1992-93, resident, chief resident, 1993-97; traums/surg. critical care fellowship Lincoln Med. and Mental Health Ctr., South Bronx, N.Y., 1997-98; instr. surgery SUNY Health Sci. Ctr., Bklyn., 1999—; asst. dir. trauma and surg. critical care, 1999—. Fellow ACS (assoc.); mem. AMA, Soc. of Critical Care Medicine, Med. Soc. of the State of N.Y., N.Y. Roadrunners Club, New York Triathlon Club. Avocations: snowboarding, jogging, painting. Home: 1320 York Ave Apt 35F New York NY 10021-4831

KOPEC, JOHN WILLIAM, research scientist; b. Chgo., Nov. 5, 1936; s. John Frank and Marie Eva (Wreshnig) K.; m. Jean Elois Prather, Dec. 28, 1958 (div. June 1977); children: Brian More, Vaune Estra. AA, Chgo. City Coll., 1974; student, Ill. Inst. Tech., Chgo., 1974-80. Systems analyst Motorola, Chgo., 1959-61; asst. exptl. engr. Ill. Inst. Tech. Rsch. Inst., Chgo., 1961-68, extpl. engr., 1968-74; lisison engr. Ill. Inst. Tech. Rsch. Inst., Chgo. and Geneva, Ill., 1974-81; supr. Riverbank Acoustical Labs., Ill. Inst. Tech. Rsch. inst., Chgo. and Geneva, Ill., 1986-94, lab. mgr., 1994—; ret. Riverbank Acoustical Labs., Ill. Inst. Tech. Rsch. inst., Chgo. and Geneva, 1998. Author: The Sabines at Riverbank, 1997; contbr. articles to Jour. Acoustical Soc. Am.; paper reviewer, contbr. articles Internat. Noise Control Engrs. With USAF, 1955-59. Fellow Acoustical Soc. Am. (chmn. archives and history 1992-94, sec. tech. com. 1991-94, mus. curator 1985-98); mem. ASTM (chmn. awards com., sec. E 33.01 1980-98 , appreciation award 1994), N.Y. Acad. Scis., Soc. Automotive Engrs. (task group, paper reviewer), Can. Acoustical Soc. Achievements include one of first smokeless fires for firefighters of U.S. Navy and U.S. Air Force; one of first to discover ionization of turbulent flow in a hypersonic wind tunnel; discovered Wallace Clement Sabine files previously thought destroyed; developed one of first rapid transit speech noise floor map, also an industrial colored noise floor map. Home: 5206 S Lotus Ave Chicago IL 60638-1632

KOPEC, KAREL EMIL, horticulture educator; b. Ostrava, Czech Republic, Mar. 9, 1929; s. Emil and Helena (Tomisová) K.; m. Božena Lauermannová, Aug. 4, 1932; children; Vladimír, Helena. Diploma, U. Agr., Brno, Czech Republic, 1952, CSc, 1960; DrSc, U. Agr., Nitra, Slovak Republic, 1990. Tchr. U. Agr., Brno, 1952-72, prof. horticulture, 1990-95, prof. emeritus, 1995—; rschr. Rsch. Inst. Vegetable and Hurbanovo, 1972-90; projector of tech. Sempra, Brno, 1983-85. Author: Storage of Horticultural Crops, 1977, Care of Harvested Horticultural Products, 1992, Total Quality Control of Horticultural Products, 1997, Tables of Nutritive Values of Fruits and Vegetables, 1998, Sensory Analysis of Fruits and Vegetables; contbr. articles to profl. jours. Recipient Silver medal Acad. Agr. Sci., Czech Republic,

1989. Mem. Internat. Soc. Hort. Sci., Czech Acad. Agr. Sci. Avocations: literature, theatre. Home: Nádražní 20, CZ 69144 Lednice Na Moravě Czech Republic

KOPECZI, BELA, educator; b. Nagyenyed, Romania, Sept. 16, 1921; arrived in Hungary, 1940; s. Arpad and Anna (Tomai) K.; m. Edit Bölcskei. Prof. U. Eötvös, Budapest. Minister Culture and Edn., Budapest, 1982-88. Office: Hungarológiai Tanács, Orszagos Szechenyi Konyvtar, H-1827 Budapest Hungary

KOPELEV, YURIY, retired physicist, educator; b. Odessa, Ukraine, Dec. 31, 1931; arrived in Germany, 1995; s. Fridel and Sarra (Kozman) K.; m. Zoya Zuza, Nov. 5, 1954; 1 child, Igor. Physicist magna cum laude, U. Odessa, 1952; Cand. Sci. (Physics), U. Rostov, 1966; Dr. (Tech.), ENIMS, Moscow, 1986. Tchr. physics Tech. Coll., Isaevo, Ukraine, 1952-54; lab. asst., Pedagogical Inst., Odessa, 1954-59; rsch. worker Technol. Inst., Odessa, 1959-66, reader, 1966-87, prof., head dept., 1987-93; prof. mechanics U. Opole, Poland, 1993-95. Co-author: Norms of Cutting Conditions, 1979, Select Poems of Half a Century, 1998; contbr. articles to profl. jours. Mem. GAMM. Avocation: poetry. Home: Heilmeyersteige 55, 89075 Ulm Germany

KOPELMAN, LEONARD, lawyer; b. Cambridge, Mass., Aug. 2, 1940; s. Irving and Frances Estelle (Robbins) K.; m. Carol Hunsberger. B.A. cum laude, Harvard U., 1962, J.D., 1965. Bar: Mass. 1966. Assoc. Warner & Stackpole, Boston, 1965-73; sr. ptnr. Kopelman and Paige, Boston, 1974—; lectr. Harvard U., 1965—; permanent master Mass. Superior Ct., 1971—; hon. consul gen. of, Finland, Mass., 1975—; U.S. del. Soc. for Internat. Devel.; Chmn. Mass. Jud. Selection Com. for the Fed. Judiciary, 1971—; chief counsel AAUP. Trustee Cathedral of the Pines, 1972; pres. Hillel Found. of Cambridge, Inc., 1973—; trustee Faulkner Hosp., 1974—, Parker Hill Med. Ctr., 1976—; dir. gen. Consular Corps Coll. NEH grantee, 1975. Mem. ABA (exec. coun. 1969—), Mass. Bar Assn. (chmn. mcpl. law sect.), Am. Judges Assn., Mass. C. of C. (pres. 1974-77), Harvard Faculty Club, Algonquin Club (pres.), Harvard Club, Union Club, Hasty Pudding Club, St. Botolph Club. Home: 33 Yarmouth Rd Chestnut Hill MA 02467-2815 Office: Kopelman and Paige 31 St James Ave Boston MA 02116-4101

KOPERA, HANS, pharmacologist; b. Köflach, Styria, Austria, June 9, 1924; s. Karl and Maria (Huber) K.; m. Ilse Kein; children: Hansjörg, Sabine, Gert Friedrich. MD, U. Graz, Austria, 1951. Rschr. dept. pharmacology U. Graz, 1951-55, from lectr. to prof. dept. pharmacology, 1967-89; clin. trainee U. Hosp., Graz, 1955-58; head clin. rsch. N.V. Organon, Oss, The Netherlands, 1959-66; ret.; mem. steering com. Internat. Study Group Steroid Hormones, Rome, 1986-94; trustee Internat. Health Found., Geneva, 1975-94. Editor-in-chief periodical Maturitas, 1989-94; editor: Empfängnisverhütung mit Steroiden, 1988, Anabolic-Andorgenic Steroids, 1993; co-author: Oral Contraceptives and Lipoproteins, 1982; author: Hormonelle Therapie für die Frau, 1991; contbr. over 180 articles to profl. publs. Brit. Coun. scholar Oxford (Eng.) U., 1954. Mem. N.Y. Acad. Scis., Soc. Ob-Gyn. Buenos Aires (hon.), Internat. Study Group Steroid Hormones (hon.). Office: Dept Clin and Exptl Pharm, Universitätsplatz 4, A-8010 Graz Styria, Austria

KOPF, DAVID, history educator; b. Paterson, N.J., Mar. 12, 1930; s. Morris Kopf and Ida Fishman; m. Mary Alice Green, June 6, 1954 (div. 1975); children: Sarah Ellis, Walter Seymour. BA, NYU, 1951, MA, 1956; PhD, U. Chgo., 1964. Asst. prof. history U. Mo., Columbia, 1964-67; assoc. prof. history U. Minn., Mpls., 1967-73, prof. history, 1973—; sr. fellow Am. Inst. Indian Studies, Calcutta, 1969-71, Thai Univs., Asia Found., 1986; vis. prof. Inst. Bangla Desh Studies, Rajshahi U., 1975; lectr. tour Australian Univs., 1982; del. to internat. seminar commemorating Bicentenary of Asiatic Soc. Bengal, Calcutta, 1984; chmn. ann. conf. Bengal studies, U. Mo., 1966; guest lectr. Thai Univs., 1986; del. Jawa. Nehru Centenary, London, 1989, First Ancient World History Conf., Tianjin, China, 1993. Author: British Orientalism and the Bengal Renaissance, 1969 (Berkeley award 1969); co-author: A Comparative History of Civilizations in Asia, 2 vols., 1977, The Brahmo Samaj and the Shaping of Modern Indian Mind, 1979, Holocaust and Strategic Bombing, 1995, Scratches on Kali's Mind, 1995; editor: Bengal: Regional Identity, 1969; bd. editors Jour. World History, 1989. Fgn. area tng. fellow Ford Found., India, 1960-61; rsch. fellow Ford Found., Bangladesh, 1975-76, Guggenheim Found., India, Nepal, Sri Lanka, 1979-80; recipient Watumull prize Am. Hist. Assn., 1969. Mem. Assn. Asian Studies (south Asia editor of newsletter, 1965-68), Am. Inst. Indian Studies (trustee 1972-75), Internat. Soc. Comparative Studies of Civilizations (exec. coun. 1980-86, 1st v.p. 1992). Office: Dept History Univ Minnesota 752 Social Science Bldg Minneapolis MN 55455

KOPLIKU, ARDJAN, corrosion and materials engineer; b. Shkodër, Albania, July 13, 1958; arrived in Italy, 1985; s. Bahri and Kadrije (Dobi) K.; m. Narvin Karalliu, Aug. 29, 1966; children: Elira, Robert. Degree in Physics, U. Tirana, Albania, 1983; PhD in Materials Engring., Politecnico di Milan, 1989. Asst. prof. U. Tirana, 1983-85; rschr. Politecnico di Milan, 1985-86, 90-91; corrosion and materials specialist AGIP divsn. ENI S.p.A., San Donato Milanese, Italy, 1991—. Contbr. articles to profl. jours. Lt. Albanian Mil., 1983. Mem. Soc. Petroleum Engrs., Nat. Assn. Corrosion Engrs. Avocations: photography, reading, tourism. Home: Piazza Santa Barbara 3/A, 20097 San Donato Milanese, Italy Office: AGIP SpA, Via Emilia 1, 20097 San Donato Milanese, Italy

KOPNOV, VITALY ANATOLIEVICH, mechanical engineering educator; b. Ekaterinburg, Russia, Nov. 1, 1959; s. Anatoly Trofimovich and Olga Petrovna (Tihonova) K.; m. Elena Dmitrievna Goloviznina, Dec. 14, 1980; children: Dimitri, Alexander. MD, Urals State U., Ekaterinburg, 1981; PhD, Chelyabinsk State Poly. U., Russia, 1990. Registered mech. engr. Rschr. Reliability Engring. Ctr., Ekaterinburg, 1981-91; sr. lectr. Urals State Forest Engring. Acad., Ekaterinburg, 1992-99; head Quality of Life Inst., Ekaterinburg, 2000—; cons. Intensonic Ltd., Ekaterinburg, 1993-95, Region Hosp. No. 1, Ekaterinburg, 1985-97. Avocation: water tourism. Home: Strelochnikov 33/2-33, PO Box 64, 620107 Ekaterinburg Russia Office: Quality of Life Inst, Quality of Life Inst, Sibirski trackt 37, 620032 Ekaterinburg Russia

KOPPEL, ILMAR ALEKSANDER, chemistry educator; b. Võru, Estonia, Jan. 16, 1940; s. Aleksander and Alide (Poder) K.; m. Juta Asenbush, June 28, 1967; 1 child, Ivar. MSc, Tartu (Estonia) U., 1963, PhD, 1968; DSc, Inst. Chem. Physics, Moscow, 1986. Sr. rschr. Tartu U., 1967-75, head lab. of chem. kinetics and catalysis, 1975-87, prof. chemistry, chair dept. analytical chemistry, 1987-92, prof., dir. Inst. Chem. Physics, 1992—, prof., head Ctr. Strategic Competence, 1996-98. Co-author 5 monographs; contbr. articles to profl. jours. Recipient various grants and awards in field. Fellow Royal Soc. Chemistry (U.K.); mem. AAAS, Am. Chem. Soc., Internat. Sci. Found. (com. mem. 1993—), Estonian Sci. Found. (chair expert com. 1997—), Estonian Acad. Scis. Office: Tartu Univ, 18 Ülikooli St, EE50090 Tartu Estonia

KOPPELMAN, LEE EDWARD, regional planner, educator; b. N.Y.C., May 19, 1927; s. Max and Madelyn Judith (Eisenberg) K.; m. Constance E. Lowinger, June 18, 1948; children: Leslie, Claudia, Laurel, Keith. BEE, CCNY, 1950; MS, Pratt Inst., 1964; D in Pub. Adminstrn., NYU, 1970; LLD, L.I. U., 1978; DHL, Dowling U., 1991. Cert. landscape architect, N.Y.; cert. profl. planner, N.J. Cons. on site planning and landscape architecture, 1950-60; dir. planning Suffolk County Planning Dept., 1960-88; exec. dir. L.I. Regional Planning Bd., 1965—; leading prof. polit. sci., dir. ctr. regional policy studies SUNY, Stony Brook, 1967—; adj. prof. environ. scis. Syracuse U., 1976-83; cons. U.S. Dept. Housing and Urban Devel., 1972-78, UN on Land Use and Coastal Zone Planning; mem. Coastal Zone Mgmt. Adv. Com., 1973-75, Nassau/Suffolk Comprehensive Health Planning Council, Melville, N.Y., 1973-76, Nat. Shoreline Erosion Adv. Panel, 1974-81; exec. dir. tax relief on L.I. Bi-County State Commn., 1991-92; adv. coun. Schs. of Art, Architecture and Planning Cornell Univ., 1995—. Co-author: Planning Design Criteria, 1968 (3rd edit. 1981), Housing: Planning and Design, 1974, A Methodology to Achieve the Integration of Coastal Zone Science and Regional Planning, 1974, The Urban Sea: Long Island Sound, 1976, Site Planning Criteria, 1978, Long Island Comprehensive Waste Treatment Management Plan, Vols. 1 and 2, 1979, Time Saver Standards for Site Planning, 1982, Long Island Segment of the Nationwide Urban Runoff Program, 1982, Financing Government on Long Island, 1992, The Long Island Comprehensive Special Groundwater Protection Area Plan, 1992, Airport Joint Use Feasibility Study: Calverton Airport, 1993, Financing Government on Long Island, working paper, vols. 1, 2, and 3, 1993, Groundwater and Land Use Planning Experience from North America, 1996. Recipient cert. of tribute Temp. State Commn. on Water Resources Planning, 1964, career achievement med. Engring. and Archtl. Alumni CCNY, 1977, Disting Alumnus award NYU, 1985, medal of honor L.I. Assn., 1987, Lone Eagle award Pub. Rels. Soc. Am., 1987, Disting. Leadership award nat. honors program Am. Planning Assn., 1989; named Citizen of Yr. L.I. chpt. Nat. Soc. Profl. Engrs., 1983. Mem. Am. Inst. Architects (hon.), Am. Inst. Planners, N.Y. State County Planners Assn. (pres. 1967-68), Internat. Fedn. Planning and Housing, Assn. Architecture and Engrins., Sigma Xi. Home: 2 Dune Ct East Setauket NY 11733-1527 Office: SUNY Ctr Regional Policy Studies Stony Brook NY 11794-0001

KÖPPEN, THOMAS MATTHIAS, museum adminstrator, researcher; b. Berlin, May 24, 1961; s. Wilhelm and Linda (Sperling) K. Magister Artium, TU, Berlin, 1987. Trainee Deutsches Tech. Mus., Berlin, 1987-89; freelance, 1989-92; dir. Mus. Axle, Wheel and Carriage, Wiehl, Germany, 1993—. Editor: Achse Rad und Wagen, 1995—. Fellow Gesellschaft Technikgeschichte. Home: Haupstr 47, D-51674 Wiehl Germany Office: BPW Bergische Achsen KG, Ohlerhammer 1, D-51674 Wiehl Germany

KOPPENBRINK, WALTER EDWIN, III, internist; b. Kansas City, Mo., July 18, 1950; s. Walter Edwin Jr. and Elizabeth (Wieman) K.; m. Joan Waisanen, May 27, 1972; children: Kristin Renée, Kimberly Diane. BA, U. Mo., 1972; MD, Washington U., St. Louis, 1976. Diplomate Am. Bd. Internal Medicine. Res., fellow Maricopa County Hosp., Phoenix, 1976-80; critical care physician John C. Lincoln Hosp., Phoenix, 1980-83; pvt. practice North Valley Med. Assocs., Phoenix, 1983-97; cons. physician Mayo Clinic, Scottsdale, Ariz., 1997-2000; med. dir. Bryans Ctr., Phoenix, 1988-90, Subacute unit, 1990-98, Hospice of Ariz., 1995-00; adj. prof. Ariz. State U., Phoenix, 1994-95. Bd. Dirs. Phoenix Youth at Risk, 1990-97, Phoenix Theatre, 1994-99, Ariz. Crohn's & Colitis Found., Phoenix, 1993-94, med. adv. bd., 1998-00. Named Vol. of Yr., Phoenix Youth at Risk, 1997, Top Doc, Phoenix Mag., 1997. Mem. Am. Med. Dirs. Assn., Ariz. Med. Assn., Phoenix Gastroenterology Soc. Presbyterian. Avocations: scuba, skiing, sailing, travel, oenology. Office: Mayo Clinic Regional Practice 9327 N 3d St Phoenix AZ 85020

KOPPER, GERD G., communication expert, consultant; b. Berlin, Germany, June 7, 1941. MA, Ind. U., 1965; DrPhil, Free U. Berlin, 1967. Japanese Lang. diploma. Cons. OECD, Paris, 1968-71; head R&D Bertelsmann, Guetersloh, Germany, 1970-71; fgn. corr. Tokyo, 1972-76; policy cons. Bonn, Germany, 1976-78; prof. U. Dortmund, Germany, 1978—, dir. Brost Inst., 1991—; chmn. WKB, Dusseldorf, Germany, 1983-89, fmK, Dortmund, 1988—; rsch. cons. LfR, Dusseldorf, 1988-91; expert mem. KEF, Mayence, Germany, 1988-96, v.p., 1994-96. Author: Massenmedien, 1982, Medien-u. Kommunikationspolitik, 1992; co-author: Medien-Prozess, 1991; editor: Innovation in Journalism Training, 1993. V.p. EJTA, Utrecht, 1991-92, pres., 1992-93. Office: U Dortmund, D-44221 Dortmund Germany

KOPRIVA, IVICA, engineering educator; b. Pakrac, Slavonia, Croatia, Aug. 28, 1962; s. Autun and Stefanija (Surtan) K. BSEE, Mil. Tech. Faculty, Zagreb, Croatia, 1982; MSEE, Faculty Elec. Engring., Zagreb, Croatia, 1987, DSEE, 1990, PhD in Elec. Engring., 1998. Devel. engr. Radio Industry Zagreb, 1987-91; DSP Dengu egnr. G.D. Electronics, Vanabar, Croatia, 1992-94; scientific cons. Mil. Tech. Coll., Zagreb, 1994-98; head def. dept. Inst. Def. Studies R&D, Zagreb, 1997—. Contbr. articles to profl. jours. Mem. IEEE, USA. Avocations: hiking, farming, reading. Home: Domagojeva 12, 10000 Zagreb Croatia Office: Inst Def Studies SSD, Dijelieva 46, 1000 Zagreb Croatia

KOPROSKI, ALEXANDER ROBERT, real estate executive; b. Stamford, Conn., Apr. 6, 1934; s. Alexander J. and Gladys J. (Kryger) K.; m. Patricia A. Velliquette; children: Lisa, Susan, Gregory, Beth. Student, U. Conn., 1952-54; BS in Mktg. and Fin., Tri-State U., Angola, Ind., 1959. Lic. real estate broker, Conn., N.Y. Commnl. and indsl. broker S.H. Silberman, Inc., Stamford, 1960-73; owner, CEO, comml. and indsl. broker Al Koproski Realty, Stamford, 1973—; mem. Coastal Mgmt. Adv. Com. Past pres. Holy Name Home and Sch. Assn.; past chmn. Poles for Ford Com., Kosciuszko Park Meml. Com., Southea. Conn. Pulaski Meml. Com., Hartford; past mem. Stamford Bicentennial Commn., Resource Recovery Task Force, Polish Am. Affairs Coun., Mayor's South End Adv. Com., Stamford C.E.T.A. Manpower Program; mem. Stamford Hist. Soc.; mem. South End Revitalization Com., Stamford, 1996—; past chmn. lay adv. bd., past chmn. 75th ann. yr. book Holy Name of Jesus Cath. Ch.; past bd. dirs. Polish Am. Congress Conn., Polish Am. Cen. Com. Stamford; bd. dirs. Polish Slavic Info. Ctr., Stamford, 1975—, Am. Ctr. Polish Culture, Washington, 1990—, reelected treas., fund raiser; mem. Polish studies adv. com. Ctrl. Conn. State U., 1994; chmn. Little League, Dialdowo, Poland, nat. dir. Polish Nat. Youth Baseball Found., 1997; elected lay adv. bd. Holy Name of Jesus Ch., Stamford; grand marshal N.Y.C. Pulaski Parade, 2000. With U.S. Army, 1955-57. Named Citizen of Yr., Polish Am. World, N.Y.C., 1978, Layman of Yr., Stamford Kiwanis Club, 1979; recipient Krzyżem Kawalerskim Orderu Zasługi Rzeczypospolitej Polskiej medal Govt. of Poland, 1994, Ellis Island Medal of Honor, 1998; honoree Stamford Old Timers, 2000. Mem. Stamford Bd. Realtors, Am. Coun. Polish Cultural Clubs (nat. fundraising chmn. Washington project), Kosciuszko Found. (co-chmn. nat. coun.), Polish Am. Cultural Soc. (historian, Citizen of Yr. 1975), Am. Assn. Mil. Order of Malta, Exch. Club, Holy Name Athletic Club (pres., CEO, Citizen of Yr. 1982, past pres.), Polish Am. Bus. and Profl. Club (past pres.), Oceanview Beach and Tennis Club (past treas.). Republican. Roman Catholic. Avocations: swimming, fundraising, travel. Home: 222 Ocean Dr E Stamford CT 06902-8134 Office: Polish Slavic Info Ctr PO Box 631 Stamford CT 06904-0631

KOPROWSKA, IRENA, cytopathologist, cancer researcher; b. Warsaw, Poland, May 12, 1917; came to U.S., 1944; d. Henryk and Eugenia Grasberg; m. Hilary Koprowski, July 14, 1938; children: Claude, Christopher. BA, Popielewska/Roszkowska, Warsaw, 1934; MD, Warsaw U., 1939. Cert. Am. Bd. Pathology, Internat. Bd. Cytology. Intern in medicine Villejuif Lunatic Asylum, Seine, France, 1940; asst. pathologist Rio de Janeiro City Hosp., Miguel Couto, Brazil, 1942-44; rsch. fellow dept. pathology Cornell U. Med. Coll., N.Y.C., 1945-46, rsch. asst. dept. pharmacology, 1949-50, rsch. fellow dept. of anatomy, 1949-54; rsch. fellow applied immunology Pub. Health Rsch. Inst. of The City of N.Y., 1946-47; asst. pathologist N.Y. Infirmary for Women and Children, N.Y.C., 1947-49; asst. prof. dept. pathology SUNY Downstate Med. Ctr., Bklyn., 1954-57; assoc. prof. pathology, dir. cytology lab./Sch. Cytotech. Hahnemann Med. Coll., Phila., 1957-64, prof. pathology dir. cytology lab., sch. cytotechnology, 1964-70; prof. pathology, dir. cytology lab. Temple U. Sch. Med., Phila., 1970-87, prof. emerita, 1987—; cons. WHO, Switzerland, Egypt, Iran, Latin Am., India, 1960-85, Armed Forces Inst. Pathology, Air Force Cytology Rescreen Project, 1979-80. Author: Woman Wanders Through Life and Science, 1997; contbr. articles on cancer rsch. to profl. and sci. jours. Named Woman Physician of Yr., Polish Am. Med. Assn., 1977; grantee USPHS-Nat. Cancer Insts., 1954-75, rsch. grantee Bender Co., Vienna, Austria, 1983-89. Fellow Am. Soc. Clin. Pathologists (emeritus), Coll. Am. Pathologists (emeritus), Coll. Physicians of Phila., Internat. Acad. Cytology (hon.), Internat. Acad. Pathology (emeritus); mem. Am. Assn. for Cancer Rsch. Inc. (emeritus), Am. Assn. Pathologists Inc. (emeritus), Am. Med. Women's Assn., Am. Soc. Cytology (life, Papanicolaou award 1985), Am. Soc. Exptl. Pathology, Argentinian Soc. Cytology (hon.), Path. Soc. Phila. Avocations: reading, writing. Home: 334 Fairhill Rd Wynnewood PA 19096-1804

KOPROWSKI, KENNETH MITCHELL, communications executive, educator; b. Green Bay, Wis., May 28, 1949; s. Mitchell Frank and Lorraine Alice (Krysiak) K.; 1 child, Jacob; m. Pamela Ann Cardinale, June 10, 1978; 1 child, Lauren Aimee; stepchildren: Anthony J. Romeo, Joseph S. Romeo. BA in English Lit., U. Ill., Chgo., 1971; MA in Creative Writing, Syracuse U., 1974. Editor United Parcel Svc., Greenwich, Conn., 1974-77; mgr. publs. Internat. Paper Co., N.Y.C., 1977-79; editor Texaco, Inc., Harrison, N.Y., 1979-81; mgr. pub. rels. Pepsi Cola Co., Inc., Purchase, N.Y., 1981-82; mgr. corp. comm. Am. Can Co., Greenwich, 1982-85, dir. corp. comm., 1985-88; mng. dir. corp. comm. Primerica Corp., 1988-90; nat. dir. comm. Price Waterhouse U.S., 1990-92; mng. dir. River Comm., Inc., Irvington, N.Y., 1993-97; v.p. comm. GE Capital Structured Fin. Group, 1997—; advisor mktg. and comm. Pvt. Industry Coun. So. Conn., 1984-89; adj. asst. prof. comm. NYU Mgmt. Inst., 1993—; adj. prof. Pace/Cornell program, White Plains, N.Y., 1984. Pres. bd. dirs. Domus Found., Inc., Stamford, Conn., 1985-92, sec., mem. exec. com., 1992-97, mem. adv. bds., 1997—. Rsch. fellow dept. English, Syracuse U., 1971-72, tchg. fellow, 1972-74. Mem. Poets and Writers, Pub. Rels. Soc. Am. (Found. fellow 1981). Office: GE Capital Structured Fin Group 120 Long Ridge Rd Stamford CT 06927-0001

KOPUZ, KASIM, educator, consultant; b. Rize, Turkey, Feb. 1, 1965; s. Necmettin and Sadiye K.; m. Zumrut, Aug. 25, 1998. MA in History, Binghamton (N.Y.) U., 1999. Imam Islamic Org. So. Tier, Binghamton, 1993—; cons. in field. Active Broome County Counsil of Ch., Binghamton, 1999. Home: 158 Hawley St Apt 9 Binghamton NY 13901-4037 Office: Islamic Org So Tier 37-39 Caroll St Binghamton NY 13901

KOPYTKO, EDWIN EDWARD, nursing administrator; b. Chgo., 1953; s. Kazimierz and Anna Kopytko; m. Therese Kuras, 1984; children: Alexander, Katherine. BA, Loyola U., 1974; diploma, Augustana Hosp. Sch. Nursing, 1980; MS, Rush U., 1983. Mental health worker Barclay Hosp., Chgo., 1977-78; staff nurse Rush-Presbyn.-St. Luke's Hosp., Chgo., 1980-83, asst. unit leader, 1983-88, unit leader, 1988-98, unit dir., 1998—; parish counselor St. Agnes/St. Kieran Roman Cath. Ch., Chicago Hts., Ill., 1992-97. Contbr. articles to profl. jours. Grantee Sigma Theta Tau and Chgo. Cmty. Trust Fund, 1985-86. Mem. Ill. Nurses Assn. (dist. 20 bd. dirs. 1996—, membership chair 1996-98, sec. 1997—), St. Agnes Holy Name Soc. (rec. sec., bd. dirs. 1992—). Avocations: fishing, books on tape. E-mail: kopytko@rush.edu. Office: Rush-Presbyn-St Lukes Med Ctr 1653 W Congress Pkwy Chicago IL 60612-3833

KORABIOWSKA, MONIKA, physician; b. Cracow, Poland, Nov. 13, 1966; d. Jerzy Garbacz and Irena Korabiowska. Physician, Jagiellonian U., Cracow, 1992, MD, 1994. Scholar European Comm Program Tempus/U. Goettingen, 1992-94; scholar Alexander Von Humboldt Found. U. Goettingen, 1995-97. Contbr. articles to profl. jours. and publs. Grantee European Community Tempus, Brussels, 1992, 93, Alexander Von Humboldt Found., Bonn, 1995, 96. Roman Catholic. Avocations: horseback riding, travel, music of Mozart. Office: Dept Pathology, U Göttingen Robert Koch St, 37075 Göttingen Germany

KORAĆ, ŽELIMIR, surgeon; b. Srem Mitrovica, Yugoslavia, Sept. 13, 1957; s. Stanko and Tatjana (Maslov) K.; m. Nataša Šimić, June 8, 1991; 1 child, Filip. Doctor, Med. U., Zagreb, Croatia, 1981, surgeon, 1991, postgrad., 1991-92, MSc, 1995; DSc in Trauma surgery, Cornell U., Salzburg, Austria, 1999. Med. trainee U. Trauma Ctr., Zagreb, 1981-83; doctor Emergency Med. Ctr., Karlovac, 1983-85, B Surgery Med. Ctr., D. Resa, Croatia, 1986; specialization in surgery U. Hosp. Merkur, Zagreb, 1987-91; surgeon, cons. for surgery Gen. Hosp. Karlovac, 1991—. Co-author: Fractures and Dislocations, 1998; contbr. articles to profl. jours. Recipient praise Croatian Med. Assn., Karlovac, 1997. Mem. Croatian Assn. Surgeons, Croatian Assn. Trauma Surgeons, Croatian Assn. Orthopaedic and Trauma Surgeons. Avocations: diving, spear fishing. Home: Kurelčeva 1c, 47000 Karlovac Croatia Office: Opća Bolnica Karlovac, A Štampara 3, 47000 Karlovac Croatia

KORAKITIS, ROMYLOS A., astrophysicist; b. Piraeus, Greece, Feb. 10, 1953; s. Antonios N. and Rosa N. (Remanda) K.; m. Christina P. Kouveliotis, Apr. 26, 1982; 1 child, Orestis. Diplome in Physics, U. Athens, Greece, 1975; MS in Astronomy, U. Sussex, Eng., 1977, PhD in Astrophysics, 1979. Sci. officer Royal Greenwich Obs (Eng.), 1979; lectr. Nat. Tech. U., Athens, Greece, 1982-90, asst. prof., 1991—; prof. Mil. Geog. Svc., Athens, 1986-89; exec. sec. Nat. Space Com., Athens, 1994. Postgrad. studies grantee State Scholarship Found., 1976-79. Fellow Royal Astron. Soc.; mem. Internat. Astron. Union, European Astron. Soc., Greek Phys. Soc., N.Y. Acad. Scis., Greek. Sci. Soc. Lasers (founding mem.), Greek Astro. Soc. (founding mem.), Nat. Astronomy Com. Avocations: computers, music. Home: 39 Gen Rogakou St, GR-15125 Marousi Greece Office: Nat Tech U Dept Topography, 9 Heroon Polytechniou St, GR-15780 Zografos Greece

KORANDA, PAVEL, nuclear medicine physician, educator; b. Olomouc, Moravia, Czech Republic, Aug. 22, 1957; s. Pavel and Vlasta (Krejčí) K.; m. Helena Titzová, Dec. 19, 1986; children: Eliška, Tomáš. MD, Palacky U., Olomouc, 1982, PhD, 1999. Physician U. Hosp., Olomouc, 1982-89; sr. lectr. Palacky U., Olomouc, 1990—. Mem. European Assn. Nuclear Medicine, German Soc. Nuclear Medicine, Czech Soc. Nuclear Medicine. Home: Werichova 23, 779 00 Olomouc Czech Republic Office: U Hosp Dept Nuc Medicine, I P Pavlova 6, 775 20 Olomouc Czech Republic

KORÁNYI, PÁL, cell and molecular biologist; b. Ártánd, Hungary, June 13, 1955; s. János and Jánosnè (Bartus) K.; m. Erika Bartus, May 28, 1983; children: Erika, Dávid. Cert. isotope technician, Tech. U., Budapest, Hungary, 1977; diploma in biology, Eötvös Lóránd U., Budapest, 1978, D Natural Scis., 1983, PhD, 1995. Rsch. biologist Agrl. Combine, Bábolna, Hungary, 1978-79; head lab. Agrl. Coop., Solymár, Hungary, 1979-86; head dept. Nat. Inst. for Agrl. Quality Control, Budapest, 1986—; advisor Nat. Tech. Libr., Budapest, 1980-91; outside collaborator Eötvös Lóránd U., 1988—. Author, editor, translator various sci. books and jour. articles in field. Travel grantee OFMB, Soros Found.; rsch. grantee OTKA, OMFB, Hungarian Acad. Sci., DAAD, EC Phare, USDA, UNIDO, European Molecular Biology Orgn. Mem. Hungarian Biol. Soc., Internat. Seed Testing Assn. (mem. com. 1989—). Avocations: travel, gardening, collecting minerals. Home: To u 2, H-2049 Diosd Hungary Office: Nat Inst Agrl Quality Ctrl, Keleti K u 24, H-1024 Budapest Hungary

KORAUA, BAORO LAXTON, financial services company executive; b. Phoenix Islands, Republic of Kiribati, Oct. 26, 1959; arrived in Solomon Islands, 1963; s. Paul Beaumont Laxton and Kura Koraua; m. Nusetta Serita Bunga, Dec. 21, 1980 (div. Oct. 1995); children: Alex Laxton, Mareta Laxton, Pauline Laxton; m. Grace Miriam Laxton Gegeyo; children: Romney Laxton, Paul Laxton, Toby Laxton. Diploma in fin., Solomon Islands Coll. Higher Edn., Solomon Islands, 1986; B of Bus., U. New England, Australia, 1989; postgrad., U. Ctrl. Queensland, Australia, 1994. CPA, Solomon Islands. Audit trainee Solomon Islands Govt., 1980-84; internal auditor Solair Ltd., Solomon Islands, 1984-86; from. sr. lectr. to prin. lectr. SICHE, Solomon Islands, 1987-93; fin. contr. Solomon Airlines, Honiara, Solomon Islands, 1993-95, mgr. fin., 1995—. Mem. Inst. Solomon Islands Accts. (pres. 1994-98), Australian Soc. CPAs. Avocations: volleyball, rugby, fishing. Office: Solomon Airlines, PO Box 23, Honiara Solomon Islands

KORB, JAN, molecular biologist, researcher; b. Trutnov, Czech Republic, July 30, 1937; s. Jan Korb and Marie (Jirousková) K.; m. Lubica Gonzurová, Sept. 20, 1985; 1 child, Jan. MSc, U. Chem. Engring., Prague, Czech Republic, 1961; PhD, Inst. Organic Chemistry and Biochemistry, Prague, 1966; DSc in Molecular Genetics, Czech Acad. Sci., Prague, 1990. Assoc. rsch. specialist Kuwait Inst. for Sci. Rsch., 1982-84; sci. worker Inst. Organic Chemistry and Biochemistry, Czech Acad. Scis., 1967-75, sr. scientist Inst. Molecular Genetics, 1976-81, head dept. micromorphology of biopolymers, 1985—, dep. dir. Inst., 1999—; Lect. summer schs. and workshops in electron microscopy, Prague, 1976=88; lectr. biochemistry and electron microscopy Charles U., Prague, 1986-92. Contbr. over 60 articles on retrovirology and electron microscopy to internat. sci. jours. Mem. Czechoslovak Acad. Scis. (biochemistry award 1967, 74), Czechslovak Soc. for Electron Microscopy, Czech Soc. for Biochemistry and Molecular Biology, European Assn. for Cancer Rsch. Roman Catholic. Avocations: photography, music, travel. Home: Kurkova 1208/10, 182 00 Prague 8, Czech Republic

KORBER, HANS-JOACHIM, consumer products executive. CEO Metro Holding AG, Dusseldorf, Germany. Office: Metro AG, Ivo-Beucker Str 43, 40237 Dusseldorf Germany*

KORBITZ, BERNARD CARL, retired oncologist, hematologist, educator, consultant; b. Lewistown, Mont., Feb. 18, 1935; s. Fredrick William and Rose Eleanore (Ackmann) K.; m. Constance Kay Bolz, June 22, 1957; children: Paul Bernard, Guy Karl. B.S. in Med. Sci., U. Wis.-Madison, 1957, M.D., 1960, M.S. in Oncology, 1962; LL.B., LaSalle U., 1972. Asst. prof. medicine and clin. oncology, U. Wis. Med. Sch., Madison, 1967-71; dir. medicine Presbyn. Med. Ctr., Denver, 1971-73; practice medicine specializing in oncology, hematology, Madison, 1973-76; med. oncologist, hematologist Radiologic Ctr. Meth. Hosp., Omaha, 1976-82; practice medicine specializing in oncology, hematology, Omaha, 1982-95, ret., 1995; sci. advisor Citizen's Environ. Com., Denver, 1972-73; mem. Meth. Hosp., Omaha, 1977—; dir. Bernard C. Korbitz, P.C., Omaha, 1983-96; bd. dirs., pres. B.C. Korbitz P.C., ret., 1996. Contbr. articles to profl. jours. Webelos leader Denver area Council, Mid. Am. Council of Nebr. Boy Scouts Am.; bd. elders King of Kings Luth. Ch., Omaha, 1979-80; bd. elders St. Mark Luth. Ch., Omaha, 1993-98; mem. People to People Del. Cancer Update to People's Republic China, 1986, Eastern Europe and USSR, 1987; mem. U.S. Senatorial Club, 1984, Republican Presdl. Task Force, 1984. Served to capt. USAF, 1962-64. Named Medford (Wis.) H.S. Athletic Hall of Fame, 1997. Fellow ACP, Royal Soc. Health; mem. Am. Soc. Clin. Oncology, Am. Soc. Internal Medicine, AMA, Nebr. Med. Assn., Omaha Med. Society, Omaha Clin. Soc., Phi Eta Sigma, Phi Beta Kappa, Phi Kappa Phi, Alpha Omega Alpha. Avocations: photography, fishing, travel. Home: 9024 Leavenworth St Omaha NE 68114-5150

KORDAS, GEORGE, physicist, researcher; b. Nikea, Attikis, Greece, June 11, 1949; s. Konstantine and Aikaterini Tzelalidou K.; 1 child, Aikaterini. Diploma in Physics, U. Erlangen, 1974, D. of Engring., 1979. Cert. engr. Assoc. prof. U. Ill., Urbana, 1986-90; rsch. asst. to assoc. prof. Vanderbilt U., Nashville, Tenn., 1982-86; scientist Nat. Ctr. for Scientific Rsch. Demokritos, Athens, 1990—; cons. Greek glass and ceramic industry, Athens, 1990—. Contbr. articles to profl. jours. Recipient fellowship Konrad Adenauer Found., Bonn, 1975, others. Avocations: photography, swimming, travel, painting. Office: NCSR Demokritos, Aghia Paraskevi Attikis 153 10, Greece

KORDAS, MICHEL M., export consultant, business and marketing educator; b. LaBassée, France, Sept. 20, 1948; came to U.S., 1975; s. Michel M. Kordas Sr. and Yvette Wasteels-Kordas; m. Suzanne Baker-Kordas, May 19, 1974; children: Marianne, Alexandre, Camille. BA in Liberal Arts and Mgmt., Concordia U., Mequon, Wis., 1995, M in Internat. Bus., 1998. V.p. Kordas Internat., Inc., West Bend, Wis., 1981-98; pres. Global Bus. Rsch. Corp., West Bend, 1998—. Avocations: poetry, arts, music, teaching. E-mail: kordasm@earthlink.net. Office: handtech.com/global 8878 Orchard Valley Rd West Bend WI 53090-9032

KORDE, UMESH ARVIND, ocean engineer, researcher, educator; b. Nagpur, India, June 13, 1960; s. Arvind Yeshwant and Sunanda Arvind K.; m. Toyomi Tanaka, Sept. 1, 1988. BTech with honors, Indian Inst. Tech., Kharagpur, 1982; MEng, U. Tokyo, 1988; PhD, U. Notre Dame, 1993. Sr. sci. officer Indian Inst. Tech., Madras, 1982-85, sr. project officer, 1989-90; Monbusho rsch. fellow Inst. Indsl. Sci.-U. Tokyo, 1986-88; rsch. asst. U. Notre Dame, 1990-93; asst. prof. mech. engring. Christian Bros. U., Memphis, 1993-96; sci. and tech. fellow Japan Marine Sci. and Tech. Ctr., Yokosuka, 1997-99, prin. investigator, 1997-99; asst. prof., chair dept. Ind. Inst. Tech., Ft. Wayne, 1999—. Contbr. articles to sci. jours. Rsch. grantee Japan Sci. and Tech. Agy/NSF, 1997, NSF, 1995; British Coun. fellow, U. Edinburgh, 1983. Mem. Soc. Mfg. Engrs. (cert. mfg. technologist), Am. Geophys. Union, Soc. Naval Architects and Marine Engrs., Soc. Mfg. Engrs. Avocations: classical music, reading, meditation. Office: Ind Inst Tech Dept Mech Engring 1600 E Washington Blvd Fort Wayne IN 46803-1228

KORDES, HAGEN, education researcher, author; b. Luebeck, Germany, Feb. 11, 1942; s. Hubert and Aenne (Schnittker) K.; m. Margret Guenther (div. 1978); m. Padmini Darmalengam, July 6, 1983; children: Khamini-Lise, Kamalla-Lily, Kanita-Lilo. Diploma in philosophy, Philosophische Hochschule, Frankfurt, Fed. Republic Germany, 1963; diploma in social scis., U. Sorbonne, Paris, 1967; PhD in Philosophy, Westfälische U., Münster, Fed. Republic Germany, 1974. Prof. philosophy Lycée Condorcet, Paris, 1964-67; action researcher Community Devel., People's Republic of Benin, 1967-69; evaluator Ministry Edn., Düsseldorf, Fed. Republic Germany, 1971-78; prof. ednl. scis. Westfalische U., 1978—; animation evaluator German Svc. for Devel., People's Republic Benin, 1974-80, World Peace Svc., Ivory Coast, 1976—; edn. evaluator German Soc. for Tech. Coop., People's Republic Benin, 1980-82. Author, editor and/or co-editor over 25 books in German, French, English and Tamil, including: The Go Between, 1990, Processing Experiences of Estrangement, 1992, The Go Beyond, 1992, To accompany one another in estrangement, 1994, The sorting out-experiment, 1994, Developmental Task and course of human shaping, 1996, Case work and the course of human shaping, 1997, Interculturation and Exclusion. Social Work in the Global World, 1998; contbr. over 100 articles to profl. jours. Founder, bd. dirs. Citizen's Initiative for Refugee Asylum, Fed. Republic Germany; German counterpart Third World Network, Penang, Malaysia. Mem. German Soc. for Ednl. Scis. Home: Brochterbecker Strasse 7, D-4542 Tecklenburg Germany Office: Georgskommende 33, D-4400 Münster Germany

KORDESCH, KARL VICTOR, education educator; b. Vienna, Austria, Mar. 18, 1922; arrived in U.S., 1953; s. Viktor and Katherina (Mayr) K.; m. Erna Maria Boehm, June 22, 1946; children: Johanna, Albert, Catharina, Martin. PhD, U. Vienna, Austria, 1948, D of Tech., 1990. Asst. U. Vienna, 1948-53; rsch. scientist U.S. Signal Corps., Long Branch, N.J., 1953-55; corp. rsch. fellow Union Carbide Corp., Parma, Ohio, 1955-77; prof. Tech. U. Graz, Austria, 1977-92; prof. emeritus U. Graz, Austria, 1992—; dir. Inst. for Inorganic Tech., Graz, 1977-92; pres. Kordesch and Assoc., Inc., Richmond Hill, Ontario, Can., 1990—; cons. in field. Author: Batteries, vol. 1: Manganese Dioxide, 1979, vol. 2: Lead Acid Batteries and Electric Vehicles, 1977, Brennstoffbatterien, 1985; over 80 patents in field. Recipient Wilhelm Exner medaille Engring. Soc. Austria, 1968, State prize for Energy Related Rsch., Austria, 1981, Erwin Schroedinger prize Austrian Acad. Sci., 1990, Frank M. Booth award Internat. Power Sources Symposium Com., 1991, Golden badge of Honor, Govt. of Syria, 1992. Mem. Austrian Chem. Soc. (Auer v. Welsbach medal 1992), German Chem. Soc., Am. Chem. Soc. (Outstanding Chemist award 1964), Electrochem. Soc. (Vittoria De Nora Gold medal 1986), Internat. Soc. Electrochem. (sec. gen. and v.p. 1981-89). Home: Carneri Gasse 18, A-8010 Graz Austria also: 13 Circle Dr The Plains OH 45780 Office: Kordesch and Assoc, 30 Pollard St, Richmond Hill, ON Canada L4B 1C3

KORDIĆ, SNJEŽANA, linguist, educator, researcher; b. Osijek, Slavonia, Croatia, Oct. 29, 1964; arrived in Germany, 1993; d. Slavko and Anka (Bogdan) K.; m. Atila Rusić, Oct. 3, 1992. B Serbo-Croatian Lang./South-Slavic Lit., Joseph George Strossmayer U., Osijek, 1988; postgrad. std. linguistics, U. Zagreb, 1992, D.Sc. philol., 1993. Tchr. Secondary Sch., Sisak, Croatia, 1988-90; asst. prof. modern Serbo-Croatian lang. Joseph George Strossmayer U., Osijek, Croatia, 1990-91; asst. prof., lectr. U. Zagreb, Croatia, 1991-95; lectr. Serbo-Croatian lang., sci. contbr. Ruhr U., Bochum, Germany, 1993-98; assoc. prof. Slavic langs. Westfälische Wilhelms U., Münster, Germany, 1998—. Author: Relativna rečenica, 1995, 2d German edit., Der Relativsatz im Serbokroatischen, 1999, Serbo-Croatian, 1997, Kroatisch-Serbisch: Ein Lehrbuch für Fortgeschrittene mit Grammatik, 1997; contbr. Linguistic Bibliography Permanent Internat. Com. Linguists; contbr. articles to profl. jours. Grantee Com. for Internat. Coop. Dubrovnik, 1990, 91, Com. for Internat. Coop. Bratislava, 1993, German Assn. Rschrs., Belgrade, 1996, 98, Osijek, 1999. Fellow Croatian Applied Linguistica Soc., Croatian Soc. Philology, German Assn. Researchers. Avocations: astronomy, microscopy, photography. Office: WWU Bispinghof 3-A, Slavisch-Baltisches Seminar, D-48143 Münster Germany

KORDONS, ULDIS, lawyer; b. Riga, Latvia, July 9, 1941; came to U.S., 1949; s. Evalds and Zenta Alide (Apenits) K.; m. Virginia Lee Knowles, July 16, 1966. AB, Princeton U., 1963; JD, Georgetown U., 1970. Bar: N.Y. 1970, Ohio 1978, Ind. 1989. Assoc. Whitman, Breed, Abbott & Morgan, N.Y.C., 1970-77, Anderson, Mori & Rabinowitz, Tokyo, 1973-75; counsel Armco Inc., Parsippany, N.J., 1977-84; v.p., gen. counsel, sec. Sybron Corp., Saddle Brook, N.J., 1984-88, Hillenbrand Industries Inc., Batesville, Ind., 1989-92; pres. Plover Enterprises, Cin., 1992-95, Kordons & Co., LPA, Cin., 1996—. Lt. USN, 1963-67. Mem. N.Y. Bar Assn., Ohio Bar Assn., Ind. Bar Assn.

KORDYUM, ELIZABETH LVOVNA, botanist; b. Kiev, Ukraine, Nov. 3, 1932; d. Lev. A. Gordon and Helena D. Visiulina; m. Vitaly A. Kordyum, Nov. 6, 1954; children: Alexander, Maria. BS, Kiev State U., 1955, PhD, 1960; ScD, Botanical Inst., St. Petersburg, Russia, 1968, prof., 1986. Jr. scientist Botanical Garden, Kiev, 1955-59; jr. scientist Inst. Botany, Kiev, 1959-64, sr. scientist, 1964-75, head dept., 1975—. Author: Cytoembryology of Umbelliferae, 1967, Evolutionary Cytoembryology of Angiosperms, 1978 (N.G. Kholodny prize Nat. Acad. Sci. Ukraine 1979), Microorganisms in Space Flight, 1983 (State prize Ukraine 1984), Biology of Plant Cells in Microgravity and Under Clinorotation, 1997. Recipient Gold medal, 2 Silver medals, 3 Bronze medals Exhbn. Achievements Nat. Economy, Moscow, 1978-89; named Hon. Scientist Ukraine, 1984; grantee Internat. Sci. Found., 1994, 98. Mem. Internat. Acad. Astronautics (mem. com.), Commn. Life Sci., Internat. Soc. Gravitational Physiology. Avocations: travelling, music, reading, conversation. Home: Artema Str 53 f 33, 04053 Kiev Ukraine Office: Inst Botany NAS Ukraine, Tereschenkovskaya 2, 01004 Kiev Ukraine

KOREC, JACEK, corporation executive; b. Warsaw, Poland, Aug. 27, 1951; s. Anatol and Natalia (Galazka) K.; m. Alicja Lawnicka, Nov. 27, 1971; 1 child, Bartosz. MS, Tech. U., Warsaw, 1974, DSc, 1978. Sci. asst. Inst. Tech. Elec. Materials, Warsaw, 1974-81; Alexander von Humboldt fellow Rheinisch Westfalische Tech. Hochschule, Aachen, Germany, 1981-83; asst. Rheinish Westfalische Tech. Hochschule, Aachen, Germany, 1983-86; rschr. Allgemeine Elec. Ges. Rsch. Inst., Frankfurt, Germany, 1986-88; sr. mgr. Daimler-Benz AG Rsch. Inst., Frankfurt, 1988-96; prin. scientist Siliconix, Santa Clara, Calif., 1991-96; mem. adv. bd. Power Semiconductor Rsch. Ctr., N.C. State U., Raleigh, 1991-96; mem. program com. Internat. Conf., Internat. Symposium Power Semiconductor Devices, 1993, 96, 97, publicity chmn., 1997. Contbr. articles to profl. jours.; patentee in field. Avocations: guitar, fishing, sailing.

KOREC, JAN CHRYZOSTOM CARDINAL, bishop; b. Bosany, Slovakia, Jan. 22, 1924. Ordained priest Roman Cath. Ch., 1950. Consecrated bishop, 1951, workman, 1969-89; rector Theol. Sem. St. Cyril and Method, Bratislava, 1989-90; bishop of Nitra, 1990—, elevated to the Sacred Coll. of Cardinals, 1991, with titular ch. of Sts. Fabian and Venanzian. Author: About Competence in Science, On Beginning and Developing a Life, About Origin of Man, Jesus from Near and Distance, Church's Christ and Ours, To the Marriage and Family, The Sentencies about Human Being, To the History with Regard, Over Old Testament, Jesus of the Gospel, Christ's Priest, Salvation in Christ, The Struggle of the Church Over the Gospel According to St. Luke, Year Over the Gospel, Church in the Centre of the Problems, Church in Development, Mother of Jesus, About Priest's Mission, others; contbr. articles to profl. jours. Religious prisoner, Czechoslovakia, 1960-68. Office: Biskupsky Urad, Post Schranka 46A, 950 50 Nitra-Hrad Slovakia*

KORENBLIT, IKHIEL YAKOV, physicist; b. Dumbrovin, Moldova, Aug. 23, 1933; s. Yakov and Hana (Elman) K.; m. Lena Rabinovich, June 24, 1961 (dec. 1975); m. Irina Khienkin, Feb. 27, 1988. M in Physics, U. Chernovtsy, 1955; PhD, Phys.-Tech. Inst., Leningrad; DSc, Leningrad Nuclear Physics Inst. Tchr. h.s. Kamenetsk, Bielorussia, 1955-56; lectr. Textile Inst., Leningrad, 1961-62; from jr. rschr. to rschr. Joffe Phys.-Tech. Inst., Leningrad, 1962-83; from rschr. to sr. rschr. Leningrad Nuclear Phys. Inst., Gatchina, Russia, 1972-91; rsch. assoc. prof. Sch. Physics & Astronomy, Tel-Aviv, 1991—. Author: Spin Glasses, 1984; contbr. articles to profl. jours. Home: 3/1 Yanush Kortzak, 42495 Netanya Israel Office: Tel Aviv U, Sch Phys & Astronomy, 69978 Tel Aviv Israel

KORENEV, ALEXANDER NICOLAEVICH, psychiatrist, researcher; b. Lubertsy, Moscow, USSR, Mar. 4, 1963; s. Nicolaj Nicolaevich and Svetlana Konstantinovna (Bachtijarova) K.; m. Elena Vladimirovna Neftakova, May 7, 1986 (div. May 1996); 1 child, Alexej Alexandrovich Korenev. MD, Moscow Med. Inst., 1986; D of Psychiatry, Acad. Med. Sci., Moscow, 1988, candidate of Med. Scis., 1995. Lic. Psychiatrist. Psychiatrist Acad. Med. Sci., Moscow, 1988-90, rschr., 1990-96, sr. rschr., 1996—; psychiatric cons. Ctrl. Residental Clinic, Moscow, 1988-89. Contbr. to profl. jours. Moscow Congress fellow Korenev, 1992, X-World Congress Psychiatry fellow, Madrid, 1996. Mem. World Psychiatric Assn., Nat. Soc. Moscow, New York Acad. Scis. Russian Orthodox. Achievements include highest physician category awarded by Acad. Med. Sci., Moscow, 1997. Avocation: volleyball. Home: Ak Vargi 20-98, 117133 Moscow Russia Office: Inst Clin Psychiatry Ment Health Res Ctr, Kaschirskoe Sh 34, 115522 Moscow Russia

KORENEV, SERGEY ALEXANDROVICH, physicist; b. Sretensk, Russia, May 27, 1951; s. Anna K.; m. Valentina Perelevskay, Apr. 24, 1951; children: Anton, Ivan. MS, Tech. U. Moscow, 1976; PhD, Joint Inst. Nuclear Rsch., Dubna, Russia, 1987, DSc, 1995. From scientist to prin. scientist Joint Inst. Nuclear Rsch., 1976-98; prof. physics N.J. Inst. Technology, Newark, 1996-98; mgr. radiation physics STERIS Corp., Libertyville, Ill., 1998—. Mem. Am. Phys. Soc. Office: 2500 Commerce Dr Libertyville IL 60048-2494

KORENKOV, MICHAEL, surgeon; b. Moscow, July 29, 1962; arrived in Germany, 1992; s. Igor and Tatjana (Leschinskaja) K.; m. Marina Pak, Oct. 28, 1983; children: Leonid, Michael. MD, 1st Med. Inst., Moscow, 1985; PhD, Ctrl. Inst. for Med. Edn., Moscow, 1990. Surg. ho. officer Ctrl. Inst. for Med. Edn., Moscow, 1985-87; surg. resident Botkin Hosp., Moscow, 1987-90; staff surgeon dept. surgery Ctrl. Inst., Moscow, 1990-92. Contbr. articles to profl. jours., chpts. to books. Mem. European Assn. Endoscopic Surgery, German Surg. Soc. Avocations: literature, travel. Home: Von-Wesselrode Weg 47, 51149 Overath Germany Office: Dept Surgery 2 U Cologne, Ostmerheimer St 200, 51109 Cologne Germany

KOREVAAR, JACOB, retired mathematics educator; b. Lange Ruige Weide, The Netherlands, Jan. 25, 1923; came to U.S., 1949, naturalized, 1959; s. Nijs Korevaar and Cornelia A. Wepster; m. Johanna E. Ladestein, Aug. 1950 (div. 1970); 5 children; m. Pia R. Pfluger, Aug. 1971; 3 children. Student, U. Leiden and Utrecht, 1940-49; PhD in Maths., U. Leiden, 1949; hon. doctorate, U. Gothenburg, Sweden, 1978. Prof. maths. Tech. U., Delft, The Netherlands, 1951-53; prof. maths. U. Wis., Madison, 1953-64, chmn. applied maths. and engring. physics, 1956-61; prof. maths. U. Calif., San Diego, 1964-74, chmn. dept. maths., 1971-73; prof. maths. U. Amsterdam, 1974-93, dir. Math. Inst., 1980-83; tchg. asst. Tech. U., Delft, 1943-46; sci. worker Math. Ctr., Amsterdam, 1947-49; vis. lectr., prof. Purdue U., 1949-51, U. Mich., 1950, Stanford U., 1961-62, Claremont Grad. Sch., 1969-70, U. Oreg., 1970, Imperial Coll., London, 1970-71, Tech. U., Eindhoven, 1971, Calif. Inst. Tech., 1988, Bar Ilan U., Israel, 1992; lectr. in field; mem. vis. com. for Maths. in Belgium, 1995-96. Coordg. editor: Indagationes Mathematicae, 1984-98; contbr. articles to profl. jours. Fellow AAAS; mem. Am. Math. Soc. (chmn. summer rsch. inst. La Jolla, 1966), Math. Assn. Am. (Lester R. Ford prize 1987, Chauvenet prize 1989), Royal Netherlands Acad. Scis. (corr. mem. 1959-74, chmn. maths. section 1994-96), Netherlands Math. Soc. (hon., chmn. 1982-84). Avocations: hiking, study of foreign languages, listening to classical music. E-mail: korevaar@wins.uva.nl. Home: Mecklenburglaan 25, 1404 BE Bussum The Netherlands Office: Math Inst U Amsterdam, Plantage Muidergracht 24, 1018 TV Amsterdam The Netherlands

KORFF, Y. A., grand rabbi; b. Boston, Aug. 30, 1949; s. Nathan and Helen (Pfeffer) K.; children: Kimberlee A., Yaakov Yisroel, Dovid Yehoshua, Mordechai, Boruch. BJE, Hebrew Coll., 1968; BA, Columbia U., 1969; DD, Rabbinical Acad., 1971; JD, Bklyn. Law Sch., 1972; MA in Internat. Rels., Fletcher Sch. Law and Diplomacy, Tufts U.-Harvard U., 1973, MA in Law and Diplomacy, 1975; PhD in Internat. Law, Tufts U.-Harvard U., 1976; grad. resident Divinity Sch., Harvard U., 1975; LLM, Boston U., 1980. Bar: Mass. 1974, U.S. Dist. Ct. Mass. 1975, U.S. Tax Ct. 1976, U.S. Ct. Appeals (1st cir.) 1976, U.S. Supreme Ct. 1978, D.C. 1980, U.S. Ct. Internat. Trade, 1981. Ptnr. Hill, Livingstone & Assocs. and Interprise Internat., Inc., Boston, 1974-81, Lewenberg & Korff, Boston, 1974-94; rabbi Beth Sholom, Hull, Mass., 1969-71, Charles River Pk. Synagogue, Boston, 1971-74, Beth Sholom, Providence, 1974-75, Temple Aliyah, Needham, Mass., 1975-83, Congregation B'nai Jacob, Newton, Mass., 1983—; Zvhil-Mezbuz Rebbe Zvhil-Mezbuz Beis Medrash, Boston and Newton, Mass., 1993—; spl. cons. to dist. atty. Norfolk County, Mass., 1975-85; spl. asst. to atty. gen. Commonwealth of Mass., Boston, 1977-85; judge Rabbinical Ct. Justice, Boston, 1975—; hon. consul Austria, dir. Austrian Consulate, Boston, 1987—; sr. v.p., bd. dirs. Viacom, Inc., N.Y.C., 1987-94, Viacom Internat., N.Y.C., 1987-94; pres. Nat. Amusements Inc., Dedham, 1988-94, pres., mng. dir. Nat. Amusements (UK) Ltd., Dedham, 1987-94; bd. dirs. Coun. on Religion and Law, Boston, 1978-84; bd. dirs., mem. exec. com. Nat. Assn. Theatre Owners, 1988-94. Owner, pub. The Jewish Advocate, The Jewish Times, Guide to Jewish Boston and New England, Boston, 1990—. Mem. Friends of Fletcher Sch. Law and Diplomacy, Boston, 1974-94, Boston Consumers Coun., 1975-80; trustee Dana Farber Cancer Inst., Boston, 1990-95; bd. visitors Hebrew Coll. Boston, 1990—; Jewish chaplain City of Boston, 1974—. Mem. Am. Arbitration Assn., Harvard U. Club (Boston). Office: 15 School St Boston MA 02108-4307

KORFIATIS, CON, air transport executive; b. Sydney, NSW, Australia, Sept. 5, 1964; s. Anastasios and Stamata (Maragos) K.; m. Suzana Djilas, Dec. 7, 1991 (div. Feb. 1999); 1 child, Michael Amerose. B in Econs., Monash U., Melbourne, Australia, 1986. Sr. mgr. Ernst & Young, Melbourne, 1986-93; corp. acctg. mgr. Ansett Australia Airlines, Melbourne, 1993-94, internat. strategic planning mgr., 1994-95, comml. dir., 1995-97; gen. mgr. Indonesia Ansett Australia Airlines, Jakarta, 1997-99; mgr. mktg. projects Singapore Airlines, 1999—. Hon. treas. Kildonan Child and Family Svcs., Melbourne, 1995-97. Mem. Inst. Chartered Accts. in Australia (assoc.). Avocations: golf, tennis, reading, theatre.

KORGE, PAAVO, cell physiologist; b. Tartu, Estonia, Sept. 6, 1943; came to U.S., 1989; s. Kuno and Elsa (Ruus) K.; m. Sirje Kipper, Dec. 26, 1964; children: Indrek, Kristjan. PhD in Physiology, Tartu U., 1969, DSc in Physiology, 1974. From jr. scientist to assoc. prof. Tartu U., 1967-76, prof., 1978-89; asst. prof. Washington State U., Pullman, 1989-92, prof., 1992—; vis. scientist Copenhagen U., 1976-78; sci. bd. dirs. Tartu U., 1976-89; chmn. all union conf. on hormonal regulation phys. activity, 1973, 77, 82, 87. Author: Molecular Mechanism of Glucocorticoid Action, 1981, Hormons and Physical Fitness, 1983, Glucocorticoids in the Regulation of Heart Function and Metabolism, 1984; contbr. articles to profl. jours. Grantee USSR Sports Com., 1978-82, Inst. Aviation, Leningrad, USSR, 1983-88; USSR Ministry Higher Edn. scholar, 1976; recipient Young Scientist award Estonian Govt., 1978. Mem. N.Y. Acad. Scis. Avocations: basketball, tennis. Home: 1751 S Bentley Ave Apt 4 Los Angeles CA 90025-4300 Office: UCLA Sch Medicine Cardiovascular Rsch Labs MRL Bldg R3-645 675 Cir Dr So Los Angeles CA 90024-1760

KORHONEN, KALLE-HEIKKI, soil mechanics educator; b. Salo, Finland, Aug. 13, 1926; s. Kalle and Sulo Rauha (Karppi) K.; m. Meeri Ahvalo, June 26, 1949; children: KAlle Tapani, Heikki Juhani. Engr., Tech. Inst., Tampere, Finland, 1950; Civil Engr., Helsinki (Finland) U. Tech., 1955, D Tech., 1962. Prof. State Inst. Tech. Rsch., Finland, 1965-74; prof. soil mechanics Oulu (Finland) U., 1974-79, Helsinki U. Tech., 1979-92; cons. engr. in lawsuits between builders and constructive cos., Finland, 1964-90; chmn. Finland-Soviet sci. working group Found. in Difficult Circumstances, 1971-88; chmn. exec. organizing com. 8th European Conf. on Soil Mechanics and Found. Engring., Helsinki, 1983. Author: On Failure of Draining Channels By Sliding and the Methods Employed for Their Prevention, 1962, Foundation of Small Houses, 1966, Consolidation of Weak Soils, 1977; contbr. articles to profl. jours. and books. 2d lt. Finnish mil., 1944, 61. Mem. Geotech. Soc. Finland, Finnish Skeptics Soc. Conservative. Avocations: philosophy of science, literature, sporting. Home: Tuomaantie 10, 02180 Espoo Finland Office: Helsinki U Tech, 02150 Espoo Finland

KORILI, SOPHIA, chemical engineer; b. Athens, Greece, Dec. 4, 1961; d. Adrianos and Eugenia (Gapkiadou) K.; m. George P. Sakellaropoulos, Jan. 7, 1990. Diploma, Aristotle U., Thessaloniki, Greece, 1985, PhD, 1994. Registered profl. engr. Rsch. engr. Aristotle U., 1985-88, rsch. and teaching asst., 1988-94; rsch. assoc. U. Catholique de Louvain, Louvain-La-Neuve, Belgium, 1994-95; rschr. Aristotle U., 1995—; rschr. Chem. Process Engring. Rsch., Inst., Thessaloniki, 1989—; asst. prof. U. Publica Navarra, Pamplona, Spain, 1998—. Co-author: Use of Solid Fuels for Power Generation, 1994; co-contbr. articles to profl. jours. European Union fellow and grantee, Belgium, 1994-95. Mem. Am. Inst. Chem. Engrs., Greek Tech. Chamber, Hellenic Catalysis Soc., Marie Curie Fellowship Assn. Office: Aristotle U, PO Box 1520, 54006 Thessaloniki Greece

KORINEK, KARL, law educator, judge; b. Vienna, Austria, Dec. 7, 1940; s. Franz and Viktoria (Schuschu) K.; m. Gertraud Haller, Aug. 31, 1965; children: Elisabeth, Stephan. JD, U. Vienna, 1963. Legal cons. Austrian Fed. C. of C., Vienna, 1964-73; asst. prof. law U. Salzburg (Austria), 1970; prof. ordinary law U. Graz (Austria), 1973-76; prof. ordinary U. Econs. and Bus. Adminstrn., Vienna, 1976-94; judge Austrian Constl. Ct., Vienna, 1978-98; v.p. Austrian Constnl. Ct., Vienna, 1999—; prof. ordinary pub. law U. Vienna, 1994—; v.p. Austrian Constnl. Standards Inst.; v.p. 1st Austrian Bank. Contbr. over 10 books and 200 articles on Austrian constl. and adminstrv. law tolegal jours. Decorated Grosses Goldenes Ehrenzeichen Austria, Grosses Silbern Ehrenzeichen (Vienna), Order of Knighthood (Malta), Grosses Goldenes Ehrenreidieu (Syria), Grosses Verdienstreuz mit Stern Germany ; recipient various sci. awards. Mem. Austrian Acad. Sci., European Acad. Sci. et Artium, Austrian Cath. Acad. Mem. Conservative Party. Roman Catholic. Office: U Vienna Faculty Law, Schottenbastei 10, A-1010 Vienna Austria

KOŘÍSTEK, VLADIMÍR JOSEPH, retired surgeon; b. Zábludov, Czech Republic, May 14, 1927; s. František and Božena (Pešová) K.; m. Jana Matlová, Sept. 29, 1961; 2 children. MD, Masaryk U., Brno, Czech Republic, 1951. Resident in surgery Hosp. Svitavy, Brno, 1953-59; from asst. prof. to prof. surgery Masaryk U., Brno, 1959-92, retired, 1992; cons. in field. Author: Experimental Liver Transplantation, 1975, Cardiovaskuar Diseases, 1987; contbr. articles to profl. jours. Baylor U. fellow, 1965-66; recipient State prize Czech Republic, 1985, 87. Mem. Acad. Scis., Czech Med. Assn., Czech Surg. Soc., Internat. Soc. Cardiovasc. Surgery, Transplantation Soc. Roman Catholic. Avocation: hunting. Home: Jugoslávská 67, 613 00 Brno Czech Republic

KORKHOV, VADIM, physicist, researcher; b. Patireche, Russia, Feb. 1, 1948; arrived in Latvia, 1955; s. Pavel and Olga (Turchina) K.; m. Galina Afanaseva Korkhova, Nov. 6, 1969; children: Sergei, Alexander. Degree in Physics, Latvian U., Riga, USSR, 1971; degree in Engring. Sci., Inst. Polymer Mechanics, Riga, USSR, 1989, PhD in Engring., 1992. Engr. Inst. Microdevices, Riga, Latvia, 1971-72; lt. USSR Army, Riga, Latvia, 1972-74; engr. Inst. Polymer Mechanics, Riga, Latvia, 1974-80, jr. rschr., 1980-85, sr. rschr., 1985-92, rschr. assoc., 1992—. Patentee: USSR, 1990; contbr. scientific papers to profl. jours. Home: Auduma St 33-16, LV-1024 Riga Latvia Office: Inst Polymer Mechanics, Aizkraukles St, LV-1006 Riga Latvia

KORKMAZ, CENGIZ, mechanical engineer, executive; b. Ankara, Turkey, Jan. 8, 1959; s. Namik Kemal and Vecihe (Cilingiroglu) K. BS, Bosphorus U., Istanbul, Turkey, 1981. Cons. engr. EnergoProjekt, Adana, Turkey, 1981-82; site engr. Kut-En J.V., Medinah, Saudi Arabia, 1982-83; ammunition specialist M.N.D., Ankara, 1983-85; sales mgr. Akdag Co., Istanbul, 1985-86; br. mgr. Palmet Co., Ankara, 1986-89; owner Turkish Import Co., Ankara, 1989—; rep. ICEM Srl Barbiano, Italy, 1987—, Astra Holdings Corp., 1989-94, Kleerkast, N.Y.C., 1987—; gen. coord. Ideal A.S., Ankara, 1990—, Rotuba, 1996—, ITSA, 1997—. Lt. Turkish Min. Def., 1983-85. Mem. Sports Internat. Clubs, Bosphorus U. Alumni, Ankara Tennis Club, Ankara C. of Trade. Avocations: tennis, skiing, computers, art. Office: Titco, Pk 226 Kavaklidere, 06693 Ankara Turkey

KORLIAKOV, ALEKSANDR V., university president; b. Chernushka, Perm, Russia, Mar. 23, 1950; s. Vyacheslav I. and Vera V. (Plehanova) K.; m. Tatiana B. Abrashina; children: Aleksandr, Eugene, Irina, Vera. PhD, World Distributed U., Moscow, 1997, Grand PhD, 1998; DSc, Internat. Informatization Acad, Moscow, 1998. Comml. mgr. Veteran Co., St. Peter-

sburg, Russia, 1992-94; dir. gen. Admiral's Meml. Fund, St. Petersburg, 1995-96; academician sec. Acad. Informatization, St. Petersburg, 1997-98; v.p. St. Petersburg U. Transnat. Bus., 1998—; pres. World Distributed U., St. Petersburg, 1999—; cons. Baltic Informatization Acad., St. Petersburg, 1995-96, Perm Informatization Acad., 1996-97, Westert-Vral Informatization Acad., 1997-99. Author: Technogenesis and Humanity Survival, 1998, Principles Training for PhD, 1998, Geophysical Guaranteeing Underwater Navigation, 1999; editor: Ecology. Nuclear Energy. Utilization of Nuclear Submarines, 1999. Mem. presidium Submarine Vets. Coun., St. Petersburg, 1992—; asst. dep. State Duma, Moscow, 1999. Comdr. Soviet Navy, 1968-91. Mem. Internat. Informatization Acad. (prize in honor of acad. E. Evreinov and medal 1998, prize in honor of the acad. Yu. Khariton and medal 1999), N.Y. Acad. Scis., St. Petersburg Union of Scientists. Christian Orthodox. Avocation: travel. Home: 2/14 Baltiska St Apt 49, 198095 St Petersburg Russia Office: World Distributed U, 69 Krasno Putilovska St, 198152 St Petersburg Russia

KORMANEC, JAN, molecular biologist; b. Zilina, Slovakia, Dec. 19, 1959; s. Daniel and Emilia (Plosticova) K.; m. Katarina Duranova, June 30, 1984; children: Zuzana, Matej, Dominika. DSc, Commenius U., 1984; PhD, Slovak Acad. Scis., Bratislava, 1980. Guest investigator Max-Planck-Inst Exptl. Medicine, Gottingen, Germany, 1988-89; head dept. Inst. Molecular Biology Slovak Acad. Scis., 1990—; guest investigator Max-Planck Inst. Molecular Physiology, 1995-96. Roman Catholic. Avocations: tennis, basketball. Office: Inst Molecular Biology Slovak Acad Scis, Dubravska 21, 842 51 Bratislava Slovakia

KORMAS, KONSTANTINOS ARISTOMENIS, biologist, researcher; b. Kavala, Greece, Nov. 24, 1969; s. Aristomenis Konstantinos and Maria Anastasios (Kapsoyeoryi) K. BSc in Biology, U. Athens, Greece, 1994, PhD, 1998. Rschr. U. Athens, 1992—. Christian Orthodox. Office: Dept Zoology Marine Biology, U Athens, 15784 Panepistimiopolis Greece

KORNAROS, STYLIANOS EVANGELOS, surgeon, researcher, consultant; b. Tinos, Cyclades, Greece, June 8, 1953; s. Evangelos Nikolaos and Maroula Constantinos (Darmi) K.; m. Zoi Constantinos Daniil, June 29, 1981; 1 child, Evangelos. MD, Athens U., 1977; PhD, U. Athens, 1988; diploma In-Depth Studies for Surg. Scis., U. R. Descartes Med. Cochin, Paris, 1993. Resident in trauma and gen. surgery Bons Secours Hosp., Metz, France, 1977-78; resident gen. and vascular surgery Brabois U. Hosp., Nancy, France, 1978-79; resident digestive surgery Bellevue U. Hosp., St. Etienne, France, 1979-80; resident vascular and gen. surgery U. Montpellier, France, 1980-82; cons. surgeon Sotiria Tchg. Hosp., Athens, Greece, 1983-87, Tzanio Tchg. Hosp., Piraeus, Greece, 1987—; rschr. Inst. Exptl. Surgery, Nancy, 1978; cons. surgeon Rangeuil U. Hosp., Toulouse, France, 1990-91; rschr. Inst. Biol. Rsch., Athens, 1991-92. Author: The Surgery of the Subclavian Artery, 1984, Colon Cancer Carcinogenesis, 1994; poetry: Corpus Poeticum; inventor in field. Mem. France Surg. Assn., France Soc. Digestive Surgery, N.Y. Acad. Scis. Avocations: philosophy, physics, mathematics. Fax: 00301-2289141. Home: Tertseti 4, 11141 Athens Greece Office: Tzanio Hosp 3rd Surg Dept, Afentouli 1, 18536 Piraeus Greece

KORNATH, ANDREAS JOSEF, chemistry educator, researcher; b. Pszczolki, Poland, May 6, 1965; arrived in Germany, 1975; s. Gregor and Helene (Leschka) K. Diploma, U. Dortmund, Germany, 1990, PhD, 1993. Postdoctoral rschr. U. Ala., 1994; asst. prof. U. Dortmund, 1995—; rsch. visitor U. So. Calif., L.A., 1999. Contbr. articles to sci. jours.; inventor in field. Recipient awards Westfaelische-Abhaltsche Sprengstoff Aktiengesellschaft, 1989, Grad. Fond Nordrhein-Westfalen, 1991, Rudolf Chaudoire award, 1998. Roman Catholic. Home: Holtbruegge 43, D 44265 Dortmund Germany Office: U Dortmund, Otta Hahn Str 6, D 44227 Dortmund Germany

KORNBECK, KLAUS JACOB, scholar, journalist; b. Roskilde, Denmark, Aug. 16, 1968; arrived in Luxembourg, 1981; s. Jack and Line Wett (Frederiksen) K.; m. Malgorzata Laskowska, 2000. Cert. in European studies, U. Trier, Germany, 1995; BSc, Open U., U.K., 1996; MA, U. Trier, 1997. Robert Schuman scholar European Parliament, Luxembourg, 1997; tchr. English and German Ctr. Langues Luxembourg, 1998-99; ofcl. translator coun. of EU Secretariat Gen., Brussels, 1999—; adminstr. Assn. Rayonnement des Langues Européenes, Neuilly-sur-Seine, France, 1992-95, v.p., 1995-98; mem. adv. bd. African Students' Assn. of Trier, 1992-95; vis. scholar sci. and tech. options assessment unit European Parliament, 1995. Editor: (anthology of essays) Sprachpolitik und Interkulturalität, 1996; contbr. articles to profl. jours. including Social Work in Europe, European Jour. Social Work, Vocat. Tng., Profl. Social Work, Social Work Edn., others. Student officer for fgn. students U. Trier, 1991-92, mem. students' parliament, 1992-94, mem. univ. assembly, 1995. Mem. Kathol. Deutsch Burschenschaft Moselfranken (sr.). Avocations: collecting beer labels, travel. E-mail: jacob.kornbeck@consilium.eu.int. Home: Av du Maelbeek 9 Bte 27, B-1000 Brussels Belgium Office: Sec Gen Con JL 1070 FK 14, Rue de la Loi 175, B-1048 Brussels Belgium

KORNBERG, ARTHUR, biochemist; b. N.Y.C., N.Y., Mar. 3, 1918; s. Joseph and Lena (Katz) K.; m. Sylvy R. Levy, Nov. 21, 1943 (dec. 1986); children: Roger, Thomas Bill, Kenneth Andrew; m. Charlene Walsh Levering, 1988 (dec. 1995). BS, CCNY, 1937, LLD (hon.), 1960; MD, U. Rochester, 1941, DSc (hon.), 1962; DSc (hon.), U. Pa., U. Notre Dame, 1965, Washington U., 1968, Princeton U., 1970, Colby Coll., 1970; LHD (hon.), Yeshiva U., 1963; MD honoris causa, U. Barcelona, Spain, 1970. Intern in medicine Strong Meml. Hosp., Rochester, N.Y., 1941-42; commd. officer USPHS, 1942, advanced through grades to med. dir., 1951; mem. staff NIH, Bethesda, Md., 1942-52, nutrition sect., div. physiology, 1942-45; chief sect. enzymes and metabolism Nat. Inst. Arthritis and Metabolic Diseases, 1947-52; guest research worker depts. chemistry and pharmacology coll. medicine NYU, 1946; dept. biol. chemistry med. sch. Washington U., 1947; dept. plant biochemistry U. Calif., 1951; prof., head dept. microbiology, med. sch. Washington U., St. Louis, 1953-59; prof. biochemistry Stanford U. Sch. Medicine, 1959—, chmn. dept., 1959-69, prof. emeritus dept. biochemistry, 1988—; Mem. sci. adv. bd. Mass. Gen. Hosp., 1964-67; bd. govs. Weizmann Inst., Israel. Author: For the Love of Enzymes, 1989; contbr. sci. articles to profl. jours. Served lt. (j.g.), med. officer USCGR, 1942. Recipient Paul-Lewis award in enzyme chemistry, 1951; co-recipient of Nobel prize in medicine, 1959; recipient Max Berg award prolonging human life, 1968, Sci. Achievement award AMA, 1968, Lucy Wortham James award James Ewing Soc., 1968, Borden award Am. Assn. Med. Colls., 1968, Nat. medal of sci., 1979. Gairdner Foundation International Awards, 1995. Mem. Am. Soc. Biol. Chemists (pres. 1965), Am. Chem. Soc., Harvey Soc., Am. Acad. Arts and Scis., Royal Soc., Nat. Acad. Scis. (mem. council 1963-66), Am. Philos. Soc., Phi Beta Kappa, Sigma Xi, Alpha Omega Alpha. Office: Stanford U Sch of Med Dept Biochemistry Beckman Ctr Rm B400 Stanford CA 94305-5307

KORNBERG, SIR HANS LEO, biochemist; b. Herford, Germany, Jan. 14, 1928; s. Max and Margarete (Silberbach) K.; m. Monica Mary King, Oct. 6, 1956 (dec. June 1989); children: Julia Margaret, Rachel Elizabeth, Jonathan Paul, Simon Alexander; m. Donna Haber, July 28, 1991. B.Sc., U. Sheffield, 1949, Ph.D., 1953, D.Sc. (hon.), 1979; M.A., Oxford U., 1958, D.Sc., 1961; Sc.D. (hon.), U. Cin., 1974; Sc.D., Cambridge U., 1975; D.Sc. (hon.), Warwick U., 1975, Leicester U., 1979, Bath U., 1980, Strathclyde U., 1985, South Bank U., 1994, Leeds U., 1995, La Trobe U., 1997; D.U. (hon.), Essex U., 1979; M.D. (hon.), Leipzig U., 1984; LLD (hon.) Dundee U., 1999. John Stokes research fellow U. Sheffield, 1951-53; Commonwealth Fund fellow Yale U., U. Calif., Berkeley, Pub. Health Research Inst., N.Y., 1953-55; mem. sci. staff M.R.C. cell metabolism rsch. unit, Oxford, 1955-60; prof. biochemistry U. Leicester, 1960-75; Sir William Dunn prof. biochemistry Cambridge (Eng.) U., 1975-95, fellow Christ's Coll., 1975—, Master, 1982-95; lectr. Worcester Coll., Oxford, 1958-60; Leeuwenhoek lectr. Royal Soc., 1972; Weizmann Meml. lectr., Rehovot, 1975; mem. Sci. Rsch. Coun., 1967-72, chmn. sci. bd., 1969-72; mem. U.G.C. Biol. Sci. Com., 1967-76; U.K. rep. NATO-ASI Panel, 1970-76, chmn., 1974-75; chmn. Royal Commn. on Environ. Pollution, 1976-81; mem. Agrl. Rsch. Coun., 1981-84; mem. Priorities Bd. for Rsch. and Devel. in Agr., 1984-90; chmn. adv. com. on Genetic Modification, 1986-95. Mng. trustee Nuffield Found., 1972-93; gov. Hebrew U. Jerusalem, 1976-97, hon. gov., 1997—; sci. gov. Weizmann Inst. Sci., Rehovot, Israel, 1981-90, emeritus gov., 1990—; trustee Marine Biol. Lab., Woods Hole, Mass., 1982-87, 88-93, Wellcome Trust, 1990-92; gov. Wellcome Trust Ltd., 1992-95; bd. dir. U.K. Nirex Ltd., 1986-95; pres. Biochem. Soc. U.K., 1990-95, Assn. Sci. Edn., 1991-92; Internat. Union of Biochemistry and Molecular Biology, 1991-94. Recipient Colworth medal Biochem. Soc., 1963, Otto Warburg medal German Biochem. Soc., 1973; created knight bachelor, 1978; hon. fellow Worcester Coll., Oxford, 1981, Brasenose Coll., Oxford, 1982, Wolfson Coll., Cambridge, 1990. Fellow Royal Soc. (council 1975-77), Inst. Biology (v.p. 1970-72), Royal Soc. Arts, Royal Coll Physicians (London) (hon.), Am. Acad. Microbiology; hon. mem. Am. Soc. Biochemistry and Molecular Biology, Am. Acad. Arts & Scis. (fgn. assoc.), German Soc. Biol. Chemists, Japanese Biochem. Soc.; mem. NAS (fgn. assoc.), Am. Philos. Soc., German Acad. Scis. (Leopoldina), Italian Nat. Acad. Sci. (Lincei), Phi Beta Kappa. Author: (with Hans Krebs) Energy Transformations in Living Matter, 1957; contbr. articles to profl. jours. Office: The University Professors Boston U 745 Commonwealth Ave Boston MA 02215-1401

KORNBLUM, JOHN CHRISTIAN, ambassador; b. Detroit, Feb. 6, 1943; s. Samuel Christian and Ethelyn (Tonkin) K.; m. Helen Sen, Sept. 10, 1987; children: Alexander Christian, Stephen John. BA, Mich. State U., 1964; postgrad., Georgetown U., 1967-69. Officer-in-charge Berlin and Ea. affairs Bonn, 1970-73; mem. policy planning staff Dept. State, 1973-75, officer-in-charge European regional polit. affairs, 1977-79; polit. advisor U.S. Mission, Berlin, 1979-81; dir. Office Ctrl. European Affairs Dept. State, 1981; U.S. minister and dep. commandant Berlin, 1985; dep. U.S. rep. to North Atlantic Treaty Orgn. Brussels, 1987; amb., U.S. rep. to Conf. on Security and Coop. in Europe, 1991, asst. sec. state European and Canadian affairs, 1996, amb. to Fed. Rep. Germany, 1997—; mem. U.S. Del. to Quadripartite Negotiations, Berlin, 1970-72; coord. Belgrade meeting of CSCE, 1977; chmn. U.S. Del. to Helsinki Follow-up Meeting of CSCE, 1992; head U.S. Del. to Conf. on Security and Coop. in Europe, Vienna, Austria, 1992; sr. dep. asst. sec. state European Affairs, 1994. Decorated Knight's Cross, Fed. Republic of Germany, 1991, Order Merit Rep. Austria, 1994; recipient Disting. Alumni award Mich. State U., 1999; named Hon. Citizen Sarajevo, 1997, Hon. Knight, Aachen (Germany) Carnival Assn., 1999. Methodist. Avocations: music, sports, gardening, traveling. Office: Am Embassy Psc 120 Box 1001 APO AE 09265-1001

KORNBLUTH, RALPH ROSS, physician; b. Montreal, Que., Can., Apr. 18, 1938; came to U.S., 1965; s. Max and Sarah (Tieger) K.; m. Anita DuBow, Apr. 2, 1966; children: Deborah Rochelle Berger, Ira David, Michael Ari. BS, McGill U., 1962, MD, 1964. Diplomate Nat. Bd. Med. Examiners. Rotating intern Jewish Gen. Hosp., Montreal, 1964-65; cons. Douglas Hosp., Verdun, Can., 1965; resident psychiatrist Michael Reese Hosp., Chgo., 1965-68; cons. Ill. State Hosp. System, Chgo., 1968; staff psychiatrist Portsmouth (Va.) Psychiat. Ctr., 1970-71; attending physician Fairfax (Va.) Hosp., 1971-74; pvt. practice Fairfax, 1971—; supr. of psychologists, Fairfax, 1971—. Mem. com. B'nai Israel Congregation, Rockville, Md., 1978—; vice chmn. med. div. United Jewish Appeal, Washington, 1980. Lt. comdr. USN, 1968-71. Recipient Physician's Recognition award AMA, 1979—, Resident's award Ill. Psychiatry Soc., 1968, Rsch. award 1st place Psychosomatic and Psychiat. Inst., 1968. Mem. Am. Physicians Fellowship, Fairfax County Med. Soc. (credentials com. 1987—, mental health com. 1992, physicians affairs com. 1994—, profl. affairs com. 1995—), Am. Psychiat. Assn. (internat. affairs com. 1991—, pvt. practice com. 1991—), Washington Psychiat. Soc. Jewish. Avocations: breeding tropical fish, swimming, sports, collecting art, reading. Home: 9812 Woodford Rd Potomac MD 20854-5034 Office: 8303 Arlington Blvd Ste 207 Fairfax VA 22031-2903

KORNELIUS, WILLIE LOUIS, textile executive; b. Terempa, Indonesia, Sept. 1, 1965; s. Irianto and Usna K.; m. Sandra Novia Jonathan, Dec. 3, 1994; 1 child, Priscilla Gloria Louis. BS, Singapore, 1989, MBA, 1992; PhD, U. Idaho, 1996. Pub. asst. Singapore, 1986-90; mktg. mgr. EDI, Singapore, 1989-92; gen. mgr. Textile, Indonesia, 1990-95, dir., 1995—. Avocations: golf, tennis, reading. Home: Jl Budi Sari VII No 3 A, Bandung 40141, Indonesia Office: Pristex Sukses Nandiri, jl Budi Sari VII No 12B, Bandung 40141, Indonesia

KORNELL, RONALD FRANK, economist; b. Chgo., June 4, 1935; s. Benedyct John and Esther Klimek-Wiorski; m. Patty Wilson, Oct. 17, 1963 (dec.); 1 child, E. Michael; m. Alyne Vidal, Jan. 5, 1977; 1 child, Nathalie. BA Econs./Internat. Affairs, U. Ill., 1957, MA Econs., 1958; Ops. Rsch., U. Mich., 1966; postgrad., Am. U., 1969-71. Internat. banking officer Bank of Am., San Francisco, 1962; project fin. officer Export-Import Bank, Washington, 1962-65; economist/planner Litton Industries, L.A., Athens, 1965-69; dir. internat. fin. Northrop-Page Comms., Vienna, Va., 1971-77; economist/aid coord. O.E.C.D., Paris, 1977-79; dir. E. Africa Louis Berger S.A., Paris, 1979-80; v.p. East and Southern Africa Louis Berger Internat., Inc., Washington, Nairobi, Kenya, 1980-85; group v.p. Asia-Pacific ops. Louis Berger Internat., Inc., Bangkok, 1985—. Mem. Am. Soc. Civil Engring., Am. Econ. Assn., Road Engring. Assn. Asia and Australasia, Am. C. of C. in Thailand, Transp. Rsch. Bd.. Home: Jaspal Apt 7A, 34 Soi 23 Sukumvit Rd, Bangkok 10110, Thailand Office: Louis Berger Internat Inc, 104 Surawongs Rd, Bangkok 10500, Thailand

KORNET, ENE, obstetrician; b. Tartu, Estonia, Nov. 23, 1938; d. Rein and Maria (Kovamees) Soovik; m. Eugen Kornet, Sept. 14, 1960; 1 child, Toomas. Univ. diploma in medicine, Tartu U.; postgrad., Tartu (Estonia) U., 1967-69, PhD in Medicine, 1975. Cert. obstetrician. Gynecologist Pelgulinna Women's Hosp., Tallinn, Estonia, 1963-66; head dept. Valga (Estonia) Hosp., 1970-96; chief gynecologist Valga County, 1970-96; pres. Valgamaa Med. Assn., 1990-94. Contbr. articles to profl. jours. Local pres. Estonian Nat. Movement of Independency, Valga County, 1989-96. Mem. Estonia Soc. Gynecologists, Estonian Med. Assn. (bd. mem. 1990-94). Mem. Pro Patria Union. Lutheran. Avocation: chess. Home: AASA 16, 68205 Valga Estonia Office: Valga Hosp, PEETRI 2, 68205 Valga Estonia

KORNEVA, ELENA ANDREEVNA, immunophysiologist, pathophysiology educator; b. Kzyl-Orda, KazSSR, USSR, Dec. 5, 1929; d. Andry Nocolaevich Kornev and Antonina Andreevna Kozlova; m. Stanislav Iosifovich Klenin (div. 1972); 1 child, Irin Klenina. MD, 1st Med. Inst, Leningrad, USSR, 1953, PhD, 1958. Rsch. asst. Inst. Exptl. Medicine, Leningrad, USSR, 1956-65, sr. rschr., 1965-69, head sci. organizing dept., 1969-75, head lab. neuroimmunology, 1975—, head dept. gen. pathology and pathophysiology, 1982—; prof. pathophysiology St. Petersburg (Russia) State U. Sch. Medicine, St. Petersburg, Russia, 1997—; chair of All USSR Commn. on Physiol. Mechanisms of Host Resistance, 1982-90; mem. State Highest Attestation Commn., 1985-90. Author: Evolution of Reflex Regulation of Cardiac Activity, 1965 (in Russian), Neurohumoral maintenance of immune homeostasis, 1978, The regulation of defence functions of the body, 1982, Homrones and Immune Systems, 1986, others; editor: Handbook of Immunophysiology, 1993; contbr. articles to profl. jours; patentee Nat. Govt. Com. for Discoveries, Patents, 1970; mem. editl. bd. Brain, Behavior and Immunity, U.S., 1986-98, Internat. Jour. Neuroimmunomodulation, 1993—. Dep. of Regional Govt., bd. dirs., 1972-78. Mem. Internat. Soc. NeuroImmunoModulation (co-founder, bd. dirs., Presdl. citation 1990), Fund of Psychoneuroimmunology (hon. dir.), Internat. Rsch. Soc. Psychoneuroimmunology (co-founder, bd. dirs. 1993-95), Internat. Soc. Immunorehab. (hon.), N.Y. Acad. Scis., Internat. Soc. Neuroscis., Immunological Soc. (pres. St. Petersburg br. 1985—), Nat. Sci. Soc. for Neuroimmunology, NeuroImmunomodulation (pres. 1992—), Internat. Soc. Pathophysiology, Acad. Med. Sci. USSR (corr. 1986—), Russian Acad. Med. Sci. (academician 1996—, chmn. neuroimmunophysiology problem com. of sci. coun. of exptl. and applied physiology, 1990—), Japanese Soc. Pathophysiology (hon.). Democrat. Avocations: painting, hunting forest mushrooms. Fax: (812) 234-94-93. E-mail: korneva@vk5270.spb.edu. Office: Inst Exptl Medicine RAMS, Acad Pavlov's St 12, 197376 St Petersburg Russia

KORNFELD, ROBERT JONATHAN, playwright, photographer; b. Newtonville, Mass., Mar. 3, 1919; s. Lewis Felix and Lillian (Seiferth) K.; m. Celia Seiferth Kornfeld, Aug. 23, 1945; 1 child: Robert J. Jr. AB, Harvard Coll., 1941. Script writer Sta. XEQ, Mexico City, 1938-39; editor Fed. Writers Project, New Orleans, 1941-42; reporter The Examiner, San Francisco, 1942-43; copy writer Conner Co., San Francisco, 1944, Albert Frank Agy., N.Y.C., 1945-47, Agrl. Adv. & Rsch., N.Y.C., 1947-50, Knox Kornfeld & Smith, N.Y.C., 1950-60; writer Robert Kornfeld Assoc., N.Y.C., 1961-78; playwright Robert Kornfeld Assoc., 1979—. Author Landmarks of the Bronx, 1990, (plays) The Art of Love, 1988 (Brio award), 616 Royal Street, 1994, Matisse, 1995, The Hanged Man, 1996, Acting Out, 1996, Queen of Carnival, 1997, Father New Orleans, 1997, Hot Wind from the South, 1998, The Celestials, 1998, Retrospective, 1999, Passage in Purgatory, 2000, The Celestials, 2000; photograph The Mask, 2000. Chmn. Riverdale Hist. Dist., 1975—, Toscanini Collection, 1984-87, Landmarks Task Force, 1975-99; bd. dirs. Hist. Dist. Coun., 1978—, Riverdale Nighborhood House, 1968-90. Pvt. U.S. Army, 1939-40. Recipient proclamation of thanks N.Y. City Coun. for Toscanini Collection, 1984, Preservation award Met. Hist. Structures Assn., 1989, award for establishing Riverdale Hist. Dist. N.Y. City Coun., State Assembly, Riverdale Neighborhood House, 1990, Bronx Landmarks Guardian award Bronx Borough pres., 1995. Mem. Dramatists Guild, N.Y. Theatre League, P.E.N. (freedom to write com.), Harvard Club (N.Y.C.), Riverdale Yacht Club, Nat. Arts Club (co-chair lit. com.). Home: 5286 Sycamore Ave Bronx NY 10471-2838

KORNHERR, ANDREAS, chemist, researcher; b. Vienna, Austria, Jan. 23, 1972; s. Erich and Margarete (Polleres) K. MSc, U. Vienna, 1997, Dr, 2000. Asst. U. Vienna, 1997—. Contbr. articles to profl. jours. Recipient Diploma Thesis award Austrian Chem. Soc., Vienna, 1998. Roman Catholic. Avocation: underwater photography. Home: Hellwagstr 14/8/16, A-1200 Vienna Austria Office: Inst Phys Chemistry, Währingerstr 42, A-1090 Vienna Austria

KORNICKER, LOUIS SAMPSON, museum curator; b. N.Y.C., May 23, 1919; s. Howard and Lena (Cohen) K.; m. Beatrice Nyman; children: Lance, Steven, William. BS, U. Ala., 1941; BSChemE, 1942; MA, Columbia U., 1954; PhD, 1957. Tech. group supr. Hercules Powder Co., Chattanooga, Tenn., 1942-45; sr. process engr., pilot plant supt. Cities Svc. Refining Co., Lake Charles, La., 1945-48; sec., treas. Uncle Sam Chem. Co., N.Y.C., 1948-57; asst. dir. Inst. Marine Sci. U. Tex., Port Aransas, 1957-60; geologist Office Naval Rsch., Chgo., 1960-61; prof. oceanography Tex. A&M U., College Station, 1961-64; curator dept. invertebrate zoology Smithsonian Inst., Washington; adj. prof. biology George Washington U., 1968—. Author: Antarctic Ostracoda (Myodocopina), 1975, Research: Revision, Distribution, Ecology and Ontogeny of the Ostracode Subfamily Cyclasteropinae, 1981, Antrctic and Subantarctic Myodocipina (Ostracoda), 1993; assoc. editor: Biology and Paleobiology of Ostracoda, 1975; mem. editl. bd. Palaeogeography, Palaeoclimatology and Palaeocology, 1960-87; mem. bd. assoc. editors Antarctic Research Series Am. Geophys. Union, 1978-90. Mem. Soc. Systematic Zoology, Crustacean Soc., Sigma Xi. Office: Smithsonian Instn Nat Mus Natural History Washington DC 20560-0001

KORNMANN, MICHEL EDMOND, materials engineer; b. Paris, 1945. Engr. degree, Sch. of Mines, 1967, DSc, 1970. Rsch. engr. CNRS, 1967-71; rsch. engr., group leader Battelle, Geneva, 1971-95; mgr. M3D, Geneva, 1995-99; tech. mgr. Ctr. Technique des tuiles et briques, France, 1999—. Author 12 patents; contbr. articles to profl. jours. Office: CTTB, 200 av Gal de Gaulle, F-92140 Clamart Switzerland

KORNS, LEOTA ELSIE, writer, mountain land developer, insurance broker; b. Canton, Okla., Jan. 19, 1916; d. James Abraham and Ida Agnes (Engel) Klopfenstine; m. Richard Francis Korns, July 1, 1943 (wid. Dec. 17, 1988); 1 child, Michael Francis. BS, Pitts. State U. of Kans., 1966. Sec. various firms, Kans. City, Mo., 1937-45; cons. Electrolux Corp., St. Paul, 1946-49; sec. health, safety and waste IAEA, Vienna, Austria, 1959-60; tchr. Montezuma-Cortez H.S., Cortez, Colo., 1966-67; ins. agent Korns Ins. Agy., Durango, Colo., 1968—; owner, pres. Korns Investments, Inc., Durango, Colo., 1970—; bd. dirs. LaPlata County Landowners Assn., Durango, 1981-87; authored and instr. women's history course, U. N.Mex., Albuquerque, Ft. Lewis Coll., Durango, and Mesa (Ariz.) C.C., 1970-75; also spkr. in field. Author: (novel) Yesterday Should Have Been Over, 1965; (play) Angry Young Men, 1957; writer numerous short stories including The Combine, 1960. Convenor, mem. NOW, Durango, 1970—; precinct capt. La Plata County Rep. Party, 1981—. Mem. Unity Sch. Christianity, Trimble Hot Springs. Avocations: mountain walking, swimming, piano, cross-country skiing. Home: 556 2d Ave Durango CO 81301-5604

KOROBEINIK, YURI FYODOROVITCH, mathematics educator, science researcher; b. Rostov on Don, USSR, July 18, 1930; s. Fyodor Nikolaevitch and Anastasia Efremovna (Veremenko) K.; m. Nina Vladimirovna Zavyalova, Apr. 21, 1962; 1 child, Michail. Diploma in math., Rostov State U., 1952, degree in Math., 1955, DSc in Math., 1965. Asst. prof. math. analysis Rostov State U., 1955-66, prof. math., 1967—, dep. rector, 1967-70, head of lab. of complex analysis Sci. Rsch. Inst. Mechanics, 1974-86, head of chair math. analysis, 1976—, head of theoretical dept. Sci. Rsch. Inst. Mechanics, 1986-92, prof. emeritus, 1998—. Author: Shift Operators on Number Sets, 1983, Stone-Weierstrass Theorem, 1992; mem. editorial bd. Communications of the North-Caucasus Sci. Centre Jour., 1971—; contbr. numerous articles to profl. jours. Named Hon. Scientists of Russia Pres. Russian Republic, 1991. Mem. Am. Math. Soc., Rostov Math. Soc. (chmn. 1985-99). Avocations: skiing, reading fiction in Russian and English. Home: Apt 85 Krepostnoj pereulok No87, Rostov on Don Russia Office: Rostov State U, Zorge 5, Rostov on Don Russia

KOROBEINIKOVA, LARISA ALEKSANDROVNA, philosopher, educator; b. Tomsk, Siberia, Russia, Sept. 12, 1958; d. Aleksandr Feopenovich and Elizabeta Stepanovna (Bajanova) K. Diplom, Toms State U., 1980, B Philos. Sci., 1989; PhD, St. Petersburg State U., Russia, 1994. Asst. chair philosophy Tomsk Politechnic Inst., 1985-86, asst. dept. philosophy, 1989-92, sr. rsch. worker dept. philosophy, 1992-94, docent dept. culturology, 1994-96, prof. philos. sci. dept. culturology, 1996—; cons. adminstrn., Tomsk, 1997—. Author: Modern Culture: Alternatives of Progress, 1994, Culturology of XX Century: Alternative Conception of Cultural Progress, 1995, Metamorphoses of Modern Culture, 1997, Culturology: Evolution of Spheres of Modern Culture, 1997. Pub. lectr. Knowledge Soc., Tomsk, 1986—; pub. journalist Krasnoe znamja newspaper, Tomsk, 1985—; leader Edn. in Siberia Soc., Tomsk, 1997—. Russian Humanitarian Sci. Found. grantee, 1997, Ministry of Edn. grantee, 1996—. Mem. Philosophy Soc. Avocations: drawing, skiing, swimming. Home: Nachimova 15-81, 634034 Tomsk Russia Office: Tomsk State U, Lenina 36, 634050 Tomsk Siberia

KOROBOV, ALEXANDER ISAAKOVICH, chemist; b. Kharkov, USSR, July 27, 1957; s. Isaak Evseevich and Mariya Samoilovna (Dondysh) K. Diploma, Kharkov U., USSR, 1979, PhD in Phys. Chemistry, 1987. Rsch. fellow Kharkov Inst. Civil Engring., Ukraine, 1979-88, sr. rsch. fellow, 1988-90; sr. rsch. fellow Kharkov U., Ukraine, 1990-99; leading rsch. fellow Kharkov U., 1999—; interpreter Pharm. Com., Kharkov, 1995—; educator Thames Valley U., London, Kharkov br., 1994-97. Contbr. articles to profl. jours. Mem. N.Y. Acad. Sci. Avocation: swimming. Office: Kharkov Univ, PO Box 10313, 310023 Kharkov Ukraine

KOROL, ANATOLIY MYKOLA, physicist, educator; b. Kiev, Ukraine, July 24, 1946; s. Mykola Stepan and Paraskovia Maxim (Sushchenko) K.; m. Galina Mykola Kotova,Aug. 29, 1985; 1 child, Olyana. PhD in Physics, Kiev U., 1976, D in Phys.-Math. Scis., 1999. Rschr. Kiev U., 1970-79; assoc. prof. Inst. Food and Industry, Kiev, 1979-91, leading rschr., 1991-99, prof., 1999—. Contbr. articles to profl. jours. Grantee G. Soros Found., 1996-97. Mem. Am. Phys. Soc. Avocations: bridge, basketball. Home: Kurskaya 12B Flat 75, 252049 Kiev Ukraine Office: Inst for Food and Industry, Volodimirska 68, 252033 Kiev Ukraine

KOROLENKO, PAVEL VASIL'EVICH, physicist; b. Dolgoprudny, Russia, Mar. 3, 1945; s. Vasilii Ivanovich and Anastasia Safonivna (Litovchenko) K.; m. Svetlana Vitalievna Korolenko, Aug. 4, 1973; 1 child, Anton Pavlovich. Diploma, Moscow Sate U., 1972, DSc, 1994. Asst. Moscow State U., 1970-77, assoc. prof., 1977-97; prof. Moscow State U., ž, 1998—; lectr. in field; cons. Moscow State U., 1970—. Author: Optics of Coheret Radiation, 1989, 98, Interaction of Radiation with Matter, 1992; contbr. more than 130 articles to profl. jours. Mem. Communist Party of The Soviet Union, 1970-90, Communist Party of Russian Fedn., 1991—. Grantee Russian Found. for Basic Rsch., 1995-97, 1997-98, Russian Min. of Edn. of Russian Fedn., 1998-00. Avocation: sports. E-mail address:

korolenko@optics.npi.msu.su. Fax: (095) 939-1717. Office: Moscow State U, Vorob'evy gory, 119899 Moscow Russia

KOROLKOV, DIMITRI VASILJEVICH, chemist, educator; b. St. Petersburg, Russia, Oct. 17, 1937; s. Vasili and Olga (Andreeva) K.; m. Tatjana Korableva, June 14, 1951; 1 child, Elena. MS, St. Petersburg State U., 1960, PhD, 1964, DSc, 1979. From asst. to prof. St. Petersburg State U., 1964—. Author: Bases of Inorganic Chemistry, 1982, Principle of Periodicity, 1992, Clusters and Superstructures, 1995, Electronic Structure and Properties of Non-Transition Element Compounds, 1996. Mem. Russian Acad. Natural Scis., Internat. High Edn. Acad. Scis., Russian Chem. Soc. Office: St Petersburg State U, Universitetsky ave 2, 198904 Saint Petersburg Russia

KOROM, MICHAEL, historian, educator; b. Magyarcsanád, Csongrád, Hungary, July 1, 1928; s. Michael Korom and Margith (Bakai) K.; m. Etelka Kiss, Feb. 15, 1932; children: Michael, Zsuzsanna. Student, L. Eötvös U., Budapest, Hungary, 1948-52, PhD, 1960; candidate in hist. scis., Lomonosov U., Moscow, 1957; D of Hist. Scis., Acad. Sci. Hungary, Budapest, 1976. Sci. researcher Inst. Workers Movement, Budapest, 1952-60; chief chair, docent A. József U., Szeged, Hungary, 1960-67; dir. gen. New Cen. Hungarian Archives, Budapest, 1975-79; prof. L. Kossuth U., Debrecen, Hungary, 1979-83; prof. history L. Eötvös U., 1978—; prof., chief researcher Inst. Polit. Scis., Budapest, 1983—. Author: (with others) A magyarországi munkásmozgalom, 1939-45, 1959, A fasizmus bukása Magyarországon, 1961 (Hungarian Acad. Scis. award 1963), A Kommunista Párt harca a munkásosztály vezette antifasiszta parasztegység megteremtéséért a második világháboru idöszakában, 1964, (with others) Makó, az elsö felszabadult magyar város, 1974, A Hitler-ellenes nemzeti kormány megteremtésének fökérdései Magyarországon, 1975, (with others) A magyar népi demokrácia története, 1944-62, 1978, Magyarország Ideiglenes Nemzeti Kormánya és a fegyverszünet, 1944-45, 1981, Népi demokráciánk születése, 1981, (with others) Magyarorszag felszabadulásának megindulása, 1982, A népi bizottságok és a közigazgatás Magyarországon, 1944-49, 1984, (with others) Isztorijá Vengerszkoj Národnoj Demokrátyi, 1944-75, 1984, A magyar népi demokrácia elsö évei, 1986, A magyar fegyverszünet 1945, 1987, A személyi kultusz néhány kérdése és az európai népi demokráciak, 1987, (with others) Tanulmányok Erdély történetéböl, 1988. Chmn. ednl. history bd. Ministry Edn., Budapest, 1965. Mem. Assn. Hungarian Historians (sec. 1964-72). Mem. Hungarian Socialist Worker Party. Home: Torokvesz ut 95-97/c/49, 1025 Budapest Hungary

KOROMA, ABDUL G., judge of international court of justice. Student, Kings Coll., U. London, Kiev State U. Bar: Lincoln's Inn, High Ct. Sierra Leone. Joined Govt. of Sierra Leone, 1964, various positions, 1964-69; with Ministry External Affairs, 1969; del. UN Gen. Assembly; dep. permanent rep. to UN Govt. of Sierra Leone, 1978-81, permanent rep. to UN, 1981-85, former amb. to EEC, former permanent rep. to UNESCO, amb. to Ethiopia and Orgn. African Unity, 1988; high commr. in Zambia and Tanzania, 1988; judge Internat. Ct. of Justice, The Hague, 1994—; mem. Internat. Law Com., chair 43d session; mem. dels. to 3d UN Conf. on Law and the Sea, UN Conf. on Succession of States in Respect to Treaties, UN Commn. on Internat. Trade Law, Spl. Com. on the Rev. of UN Charter and on Strengthening Role of Orgn. Com. on Peaceful Uses of Outer Space; vice chair UN Charter Com., 1978; chmn. UN Spl. Com. of 24, UN 6th Com.; lectr. numerous univs.; mem. internat. planning coun. Internat. Ocean Inst. Contbr. articles to profl. jours. Pres. Henry Dunant Ctr., Geneva. Decorated insignia Comdr. of Rokel. Mem. Am. Soc. Internat. Law, Lincoln's Inn (hon. bencher). Office: Internat Ct of Justice, Peace Palace Carnegieplein, 2517 KJ The Hague The Netherlands

KOROMA, JAMES SANPHA, banker, economist; b. Yonibana, Sierra Leone, May 15, 1946; m. Anne Konima, June 24, 1972; children: Pawusu, Siddique, Abu. BA in Econs., U. Durham, Freetown, 1969; MA in Fin., Syracuse U., 1971; MSc in Devel. Adminstrn., U. Birmingham (Eng.), 1974. Trainee Western Electric Co., Allentown, Pa., 1969; sr. rsch. fellow Leiden (The Netherlands) U., 1971-72; sr. asst. sec. Ministry Internal Affairs, Freetown, 1974-75; sr. asst. sec. Ministry Fin., Freetown, 1975-77, dep. sec., 1977-82, dept. fin. sec., permanent sec., 1982-85; permanent sec. Ministry Devel. and Econ. Planning, Freetown, 1985-86; mng. dir. Nat. Devel. Bank Ltd., Freetown, 1986-90; chief tech. adv. Dept. Econ. and Social Devel. U.N., Lagos, Nigeria, 1991-93; founder, mng. dir. Union Trust Bank Ltd, Freetown, Sierra Leone, 1995—; gov. Bank of Sierra Leone, 1998—; cons. World Bank, Washington, 1985-86, founder Union Finance and Investment Ltd., 1994—. Fellow Inst. Dirs. (Eng.), Freetown Golf Club; mem. Royhal Inst. Dirs. Home: Bullion Lodge, Hill Station, Freetown Sierra Leone Office: Bank of Sierra Leone, PO Box 30 Siaka Stevens St, Freetown Sierra Leone

KORONAKIS, DEMETRIOS EYSTATHIOS, biologist, astrologer; b. Athens, Attikis, Greece, Dec. 26, 1955; s. Eystathios Demetrios and Despina Basilios (Tgagala) K.; m. Martha Nikolaos Stathaki, Feb. 11, 1990; 1 child, Eystathios. BSc, Athens (Greece) U., 1980; MPH, Athens Sch. of Hygiene, 1985. Biologist Water Co., Athens, Greece, 1983-90; sr. biologist Water Co., Athens, 1991—; dir. Kronos Lab, Athens, 1983-85, Urania Lab, Athens, 1986-91; rsch. dir. Astrologianova, Athens, 1992-95, Urania Lab, Athens, 1996—. Author: (books) Tales of Medical Astrology, 1991, Medical Astrology, 1993, 360 Medical Degrees, 1996; (software) Personal Astrogeography, 1995. Mem. Internat. Environmetrics Soc., Nat. Biologist Union, Am. Fedn. Astrologers (rsch. mem.), Astrological Assn., N.Y. Acad. Scis. Avocations: radio amateur, collecting antique radios. Home: Joaninon 63, 15234 Xalandri Attikis, Greece Office: Urania Lab, POB 25003, 10026 Athens Attikis, Greece

KOROTAEV, SERGUEI MARATOVICH, physicist; b. Ekaterinburg, Russia, Feb. 18, 1950; s. Marat Fedorovich and Gertruda Fedorovna (Sviridova) K.; m. Tatyana Grigoryevna Podovuzhnaya, July 7, 1972; children: Andrey, Victoria, Constantin. Engr., oceanologist, Hydrometeorol. Inst., 1972; PhD, Inst. Terr. Magn., 1979; D of Physics and Math., Inst. Physics of Earth, 1993. Rschr. Inst. Terr. Magn. Ion. Rad. Wave Prop., Troitsk, Russia, 1974-92; leading rschr. Geoelectromagnetic Rsch. Inst., Troitsk, 1992-94, head lab, 1994—; expert State Com. Sci. and Tech., Moscow, 1983-87. Co-author: Time Variations Account in Marine Magnetic Survey, 1984, From Relation to Substational Time, 1994, One the Way to Understanding Time Phenomenon, 1996. Mem. Party of Dem. Choice of Russia, dep. chmn. local br., Troitsk, 1994—. Lt. USSR Aviation, 1972-74. Grantee Internat. Sci. Found., 1992, Russian Basic Rsch. Found., 1993, 96. Mem. Am. Geophys. Union, N.Y. Acad. Sci. Avocation: photography. Home: Microregion V-41-92, 142092 Troitsk Moscow, Russia Office: Geoelectromagnetic Rsch, PO Box 30, 142092 Troitsk Moscow, Russia

KOROTCHENKOV, OLEG A., physicist; b. Kiev, Ukraine, June 27, 1958; s. Alexander and Alise K.; m. Olena V. Fedorchenko, Aug. 16, 1985; 1 child, Julia. Univ. diploma, Kiev Univ., 1980, cand. of scis., 1986, D of scis., 1999. Teaching asst. Kiev Univ., Kiev, 1980-82; researcher Kiev Univ., 1985-86, asst. prof., 1986-93, assoc. prof., 1993—. Contbr. articles to profl. jours. Recipient fellowship The Swedish Inst., Stockholm, 1994, JSPS, Tokyo, 1995. Mem. Ukrainian Physical Soc., Physical Soc. Japan. E-mail: olegk@mail.univ.kiev.ua. Home: Zakrevskogo St, Kiev 02217, Ukraine Office: Kiev Univ, Glushkova Ave, Kiev 03680, Ukraine

KOROTEEV, ANATOLY SAZONOVICH, physicist; b. Moscow, July 22, 1936. Degree in engring., Moscow Aviation Inst., 1959; DS, Keldysh Rsch. Ctr., Moscow, 1971. Dir., physicist Keldysh Rsch Ctr, Moscow, 1988—; dept. head Phys. and Tech. Inst., Moscow. Author: Low-Pressure Plasma Generator, 1966, Applied Dynamics of Heat Plasma, 1975, Electric Arc Plasmotrons, 1980, Plasmotrons: Design, Parameters, Calculation, 1993; contbr. over 200 articles to profl. publs. Recipient USSR State prize, 1982, Order for Svc. to Fatherland in 4th Degree, 1996. Mem. Russian Acad. of Sci. (academician), Russian Space Agy. (bd. dirs. 1992), Internat. Acad. Astronautics. Avocations: history, skiing. Office: Keldysh Rsch Ctr 8, Onezhskaya, 125438 Moscow Russia

KOROTKICH, VICTOR VASILIEVICH, mathematician; b. Novokuznetsk, USSR, Oct. 16, 1954; s. Vasiliy Iosifovich and Larisa (Plotnikova) K.; m. Galina Horkina, Feb. 12, 1977; children: Grigori, Maria. MS, Moscow Phys. Tech. Inst., 1978; PhD, USSR Acad. Scis., 1986. From rschr. to sr. rschr. Russian Acad. Scis., Moscow, 1982-95; from rschr. to sr. lectr. Ctrl. Queensland U., Rockhampton, Mackay, Australia, 1995—; cons. ABC, Wageningen, The Netherlands, 1992, Oil and Gas Inst., Moscow, 1990-92, Inst. U.S.A. and Can. Studies, Moscow, 1990. Author: Recent Advances in Global Optimization, 1992, Recent Advances in Multicriteria Analyses, 1995, Fuzzy Systems Design, 1998, A Mathematical Structure for Emergent Computation, 1999; editor: Elsevier's Dictionary of Biometry, 1994, With Fuzzy Logic in the New Millennium, 2000. Avocations: reading, music, walking, hockey. Office: Ctrl QLD U, Planlands 4740, Mackay QLD, Australia

KOROTKIN, FRED, writer, philatelist; b. Duluth, Minn., Oct. 25, 1917; s. Morris and Ethel (Billert) K. B.A., U. Minn., 1949. Writer-instr. Palmer Writers Sch., Mpls., 1961-66; editor Finance & Commerce, and Daily Market Record, Mpls., 1966-67; stamp editor Mpls. Star, 1970-74, White Bear Press, 1976, Minn. Suburban Newspapers, Inc., 1983-85, The EnterpriSe, 1988-89, Post Publs. Weekend, 1989-91; Mem. philatelic adv. panel Am. Revolution Bicentennial Commn., 1971-74, Am. Revolution Bicentennial Adminstrn., 1974, philatelic advisor, 1974-76; regional rep. Interphil '76, 1974-76, USO, AARP, So. Poverty Law Ctr./Klanwatch Project. Contbr. revs., articles to popular mags., newspapers. Pres. North High Alumni Assn., Mpls., 1946-47; mem. nat. adv. bd. The Generation After; assoc. Simon Wiesenthal Ctr. for Holocaust Studies; mem. St. Louis Park Centennial Commn., 1985-86; charter mem. U.S. Holocaust Meml. Mus., U.S. World War II Meml.; founding mem. F.D.R. Meml. Recipient Disting. Topical Philatelist Hall of Fame award and invited to sign Disting. Topical Philatelist scroll of honor, 1962, Silver medal for Keeping Posted column in Mpls. Star Am. Philatelic Soc.-Chgo. Philatelic Soc. Conv., 1974, Silver award for Keeping Posted column in Post Publs. Weekend, sponsored by Coun. Philatelic Orgns., 1989, True Grit award Grit Mag., 1997, 98. Mem. Am. Topical Assn. (founding pres. chpt. 1957-61, nat. pres. 1968-70, 70-72, dir., nat. adv. com.), Internat. Philatelic Press Club (gov.), Internat. Assn. Philatelic Journalists, Am. Philatelic Soc. (speakers' bur. 1977—, writers unit), New Zealand Stamp Collector's Club Inc. (hon., anonymously donated annual Fred Korotkin Cup for best thematic entry 1966—), Christchurch Philatelic Soc., Inc., Royal Philatelic Soc. New Zealand, Collectors Club N.Y., Manuscript Soc., Statue of Liberty-Ellis Island Found. Inc. (charter), Nat. Com. To Preserve Social Security, Am. United for Separation of Ch. and State, Holocaust Survivors Assn. USA (nat. adv. bd.), Keren Or, Inc., Jerusalem Instn. for the Blind, Internat. Platform Assn., People for the Am. Way, DAV (life; comdr. Mpls. chpt. No 1, 1986), Paralyzed Vets. Am. (hon.). Home: Apt 512 4925 Minnetonka Blvd Minneapolis MN 55416-2271 also: PO Box 11053 Minneapolis MN 55411-0053

KOROTKOV, ALEXANDER, electrical engineering scientist, educator; b. St. Petersburg, Russia, Sept. 9, 1961; s. Stanislav and Valentina (Vysotskaya) K.; m. Marie Gagarin, Jan. 25, 1986; 1 child, Varvara. Diploma in engring., Tech. U., St. Petersburg, 1984, PhD, 1991, DSc, 2000. Cert. in engring., rsch., edn. Rschr. Tech. U., St. Petersburg, 1984-91, lectr., 1992-93, sr. lectr., 1994-95, assoc. prof., 1996—; vis. scientist U. Erlangen, Germany, 1995, Fraunhofer Inst., Erlangen, 1997-99. Author: (book) Microelectronic Analog Filters, 1999; co-author: (textbook) Computer Aided Design, 1998; contbr. papers to profl. jours. DAAD fellow, 1995; Volkswagen-Stiftung grantee, 1997-99. Mem. IEEE (sr.), N.Y. Acad. Scis. Office: St Petersburg Tech U, Polytechnic St 29, 195251 Saint Petersburg Russia

KOROTKOV, ALEXANDER N., physicist, educator, researcher; b. Voronezh, Russia, Dec. 12, 1963; came to U.S., 1993; s. Nikolai Efimovich and Nelli Il'inichna Korotkov; m. Galina A. Korotkova, Oct. 23, 1982 (div. Dec. 1996); 1 child, Mariya; m. Julija Auzane, Aug. 2, 1997. MS in Physics, Moscow State U., 1986, PhD in Physics, 1991. Engr., scientist, sr. scientist Moscow State U., 1986-93, sr. scientist, 1996-98; postdoctoral rschr. SUNY, Stony Brook, 1993-96, rsch. scientist, rsch. asst. prof., 1998—. Contbr. articles to profl. jours. Mem. Am. Phys. Soc. Office: SUNY Dept Physics Stony Brook NY 11794-0001

KOROTKOV, EUGENE VADIMOVITCH, bioengineer, researcher, educator; b. Moscow, July 31, 1951; s. Vadim Fedorovitch and Ekatreina Ivanovna (Yakovleva) K.; m. Maria Aleksandrovna Shalnova, Aug. 14, 1975; 2 children. MSc, Moscow Phys. Engring. Inst., 1974, postgrad., 1974-76; PhD, Inst. Biophysics, Pushino, Russia, 1981; DSc, Inst. Chem. Physics, Moscow, 1993. Jr. rsch. worker Inst. Chem. Physics, 1979-84, sr. rsch. worker, 1994—; prof. Moscow Phys. Engring. Inst., 1994—; leading scientist Ctr. Bioengring., Russian Acad. Scis., Moscow, 1995—, mem. sci. com., 1997—; vis. fellow Lancashire U., Preston, Eng., 1996-99; pres. B.N. Elzin Stipendia, 1996—. Author: Proceedings of Pacific Symposium on Biocomputing, 1997; contbr. articles to sci. jours. Grantee Royal Soc., London, 1996, 97, Russian Found. Fundamental Investigation grantee INTAS Russian Min. Scis., 1997-99. Office: Russ Acad Scis Ctr Bioeng, 60-tya Oktgabrya Prosp 7/1, 117312 Moscow Russia

KOROTKOVA, MARIA ALEXANDROVNA, computer scientist, educator; b. Moscow, Feb. 7, 1953; d. Alexander Vsevolodovich and Nina Michaelovna (Dergachova) Shalnov; m. Eugene Vadimovitch Korotkov, Aug. 14, 1975; children: Ekaterina, Alexander. BS, Moscow Phys. Engring. Inst., 1974, MS, 1976, postgrad., 1979; PhD, Sci. Inst. Computer Tech., Moscow, 1988. Engr. Moscow Phys. Engring. Inst., 1979-88, rsch. worker, 1988-91, assoc. prof., 1991—, vice head dept., 1996—. Russian Fund Fundamental Investigation grantee, 1995-96, 98-2000. Office: Moscow Phys Engring Inst, Kashirskoe shosse 31, 115409 Moscow Russia

KORPYS, KONRAD KAROL, industrial designer, educator; b. Olszyna, Poznan, Poland, Sept. 25, 1921; s. Ludwik and Zuzanna (Knabe) K.; m. Irena Wanda Buszko, May 1, 1954; 1 child, Joanna. MSc in Engring., Politechnic, Gliwice, Poland, 1949. Designer Miastoprojekt, Katowice, Poland, 1950-55; mgr. design dept. Miastoprojekt, Katowice, 1955-61; mgr. design dept. Energoprojekt, Katowice, 1961-70, main designer, 1970-88, sr. designer, 1988—; lectr. Politechnik, Katowice, 1955-82; PZITB expert Polish Engring. Union, Katowice, 1958—. Contbr. articles to profl. jours.; inventor in field; designer copula on cathedral in Katowice, 1969. Recipient Gold Mark of Distinction Polish Engring. Union, 1971, Energetics Ministry of Poland, 1982. Fellow Sci. Union of PZITB. Solidarity. Roman Catholic. Avocations: philosophy, history, gardening. Home: 14 Stowikow St, 40 534 Katowice Poland Office: Energoprojekt, 15 Jesionowa St, Katowice Poland

KORSHAK, YVONNE, art historian; b. Chgo., May 30, 1936; d. Donald Korshak and Irma B. Jaffe; m. Robert J. Ruben; 1 child, Karin. BA cum laude, Radcliffe Coll., Cambridge, Mass., 1958; MA, U. Calif. Berkeley, 1966; PhD, U. Calif., 1973. Asst. prof. U. Md., College Park, 1972-74, Fordham U., N.Y.C., 1974-75; from asst. prof. to prof. Adelphi U., Garden City, N.Y., 1975—, chairperson Dept. Art and Art History, 1978-81, dir. honors program, dir. mus. studies, 1979—; project dir. seminar on the modern condition NEH, 1990. Author: Frontal Faces in Attic Vase Painting, 1987, co-editor: Selections from Permanent Collection, 1983. Recipient Pres.'s award for excellence in teaching, 1990. Mem. Coll. Art Assn. Am., Archaeological Inst. Am., Long Island Art Historians Assn., American Soc. for Eighteenth Century Studies, American Philological Assn. Office: Adelphi U Dept Art And Art History Garden City NY 11530

KORSHUNOV, ANDREY, neuropathologist; b. Moscow, Jan. 6, 1961; s. Gennadyi and Luidmila K.; m. Tatyana Drojjova, Oct. 11, 1986. MD, Semachko Inst., Moscow, 1984; MSc, N.N. Burdenko Inst., Moscow, 1987, D in Med. Scis., 1993. Resident in neuropathology N.N. Burdenko Inst., 1984-87, rsch. asst., 1987-90, sr. rschr., 1990-95, chief neuropathology dept., 1995—. Author: Atlas of Tumors of the Central Nervous System, 1998; contbr. articles to profl. jours. Mem. Russian Assn. Pathologists, Assn. Clin. Pathologists, Can. Assn. Neuropathologists. Avocation: dogs. Home: Volgogradsky pros 155-1-86, 109378 Moscow Russia Office: NN Burdenko Inst, Fadeeva 5, 125047 Moscow Russia

KORSHUNOV, MICHAEL ANATOLIEVICH, physicist, researcher; b. Leningrad, USSR, Sept. 6, 1952; s. Anatoly Vasilievich and Valentina Vasilievna (Rezvova) K.; m. Nina Dmitrievna Putinceva, Mar. 25, 1975; 1 child, Maxim. Grad., State U. Krasnoyarsk (USSR), 1975; postgrad., Inst. Physics, Krasnoyarsk, 1988; Degree of candidate Phys. and Math. Sci., Inst. Physics, Krasnoyarsk, Russia, 1990. Lab. asst. Inst. Physics, Krasnoyarsk, USSR, 1975-76; sr. engr. Inst. Physics, Krasnoyarsk, 1976-85; researcher Inst. Physics, Krasnoyarsk, Russia, 1988-97; scientist Inst. Physics, Krasnoyarsk, 1997—. Contbr. articles to profl. jours. Avocations: painting, archaeology, fencins. Fax: (3912) 43-89-23. Home: Marx st the house 88 apt 42, 660049 Krasnoyarsk Russia Office: LV Kirenskii Inst Physics, Academcamp, 660036 Krasnoyarsk Russia

KORSTEN, PETER J. S., consulting company executive; b. Veghel, The Netherlands, Aug. 31, 1960; s. Henri G.L. and Petronella M.E. (Verhaegen) K.; m. Marian H.I. Van Herk; 1 child, Christiaan. BBA, Nijenrode, The Netherlands, 1982; MBA (Dean's List), Imede/IMD, Lausanne, Switzerland, 1989. Bus. analyst Gilde Venture Fund, Utrecht, The Netherlands, 1984-86; product mgr. Mattel Inc., Amsterdam, Brussels, 1986-88; mgr. The Boston Cons. Group, Amsterdam, 1990-97; ptnr. PricewaterhouseCoopers, Amsterdam, 1998—; leader corp. and ops. strategy Europe, Middle East, Africa PricewaterhouseCoopers; bd. dirs. Forum Humanum, The Netherlands, 1982-86. 1st lt. The Netherlands Army, 1983-88 (recipient Royal Medal, 1999). Recipient Mktg. Excellence award NCD, Netherlands, 1982. Mem. Orde van Organisatie-adviseurs, Vereniging voor Strategische Beleidsvorming, Nederlands Inst. voor Mktg., Voorgezette Co. van Verre, Internat. Inst. for Mgmt. Devel. Office: Price Waterhouse Coopers, Archimedeslaan 21, Utrecht The Netherlands

KORSUNOV, ANATOLY RUVIMOVICH, radiophysics educator; b. Omsk, Russian, July 27, 1942; arrived in Ukraine, 1950; m. Tamara Bondarenko, June 4, 1977. M, Tech. U., Kharkov, Ukraine, 1968. Engr. Kharkov Designer, Kharkov, Ukraine, 1968-70; rschr. Radiophysics Inst., Kharkov, Ukraine, 1970-73, scientific worker, 1973-77; sr. rsch. worker Ukraine Engr. Pedagog Acad., Kharkov, 1977-98, educator, 1997—, vice dean, 1995—. Contbr. articles to profl. jours. Home: Korchaginec B13-365, 310178 Kharkov Ukraine Office: Ukraine Engr & Pedagog Acad, Univezsitetskay 16, 310003 Kharkov Ukraine

KORTE, BERNHARD HERMANN, mathematician, researcher; b. Bottrop, Germany, Nov. 3, 1938; s. Bernhard F. and Agnes (Schmidt) K.; m. Sabeth Tensholter, Aug. 1, 1966; 1 child, Dagmar. PhD in Math., U. Bonn, 1968, Habilitation, 1970; PhD (hon.) U. Rome, 1987. Rsch. assoc. U. Bonn, Fed. Republic Germany, 1965-70, dir. Institut fur Gellschafts und Wirtschftswisseschaften, 1972—; prof. U. Regensburg, Fed. Republic Germany, 1971, U. Bielefeld, Fed. Republic Germany, 1971; prof. Ops. Rsch. U Bonn., 1972—, dir. Inst. Ops. Rsch., 1972—, dep. univ. coun., vice rector, 1980-88, dean, 1984-87; disting. sr. fellow RUTCOR Rutgers U., New Brunswick, N.J., 1985—, dir. rsch. Inst. Discrete Math., 1987—; hon. prof. applied math. Acad. Sinica, Beijing, 1988—, U. Ponteficia Cath. Rio de Janeiro, 1988—. Recipient Grand Officier Cross of the Order of Merit of the Italian Republic, Order of Merit of Northrhine-Westphalia, 1986; Prix Alexandre de Humboldt of the French Min. Rsch., 1990, State Prize Northrhine-Westphalia, 1996. Contbr. numerous articles to sci. jours. Fellow Inst. Combinatorics and Its Applications; mem. Rhenisch Westfalian Acad. Scis., German Acad. Leopoldina, Am. Math. Soc., Ops. Rsch. Soc. Am., Math. Programming Soc., Deutsche Mathematiker Vereinigung, N.Y. Acad. Scis. Home: Im Erlengrund 26, 53347 Impekoven Bonn Germany Office: Rsch Inst Discrete Math, Lennéstrasse 2, 53113 Bonn Germany

KORTEN, DAVID C., writer, think-tank executive; b. Longview, Wash., July 30, 1937; s. Theodore Frederick Korten and Margaret Rebecca Heltzel; m. Frances Fisher, June 21, 1962; children: Diana, Alicia. AB in Psychology, Stanford U., 1959, MBA, 1961, PhD, 1968. Asst. dean, Fulbright asst. prof., Coll. Bus. Adminstrn. Haile Sellassie I U., Addis Ababa, Ethiopia, 1963-66; program mgr., asst. behavioral and social scis. Office of Sec. of Def., Washington, 1969-70; vis. assoc. prof. Ctrl. Am. Inst. Bus. Adminstrn., Managua, Nicaragua, 1970-73, Harvard U. Grad. Sch. Bus., Cambridge, Mass., 1970-75; inst. assoc. Harvard Inst. Internat. Devel., Cambridge, Mass., 1975-77; lectr. population studies Harvard Sch. Pub. Health, Cambridge, Mass., 1976-78; coord. Mgmt. Insts. Working, Manila, The Philippines, 1977-83; vis. prof. Asian Inst. Mgmt., Manila, The Philippines, 1977-85; project specialist Ford Found., Manila, The Philippines, 1978-81; Asia regional advisor on devel. mgmt. (Manila and Jakarta) Agy. Internat. Devel., Washington, 1981-88; v.p. for Asia Inst. Devel. Rsch., Boston, 1988-89; founder, pres. People-Centered Devel. Forum, Bainbridge Island, Wash., 1990—; co-founder, bd. chair The Positive Futures Network, Bainbridge Island, 1996—; bd. mem. Context Inst., Bainbridge Island, 1994-96. Author: The Post-Corporate World: Life After Capitalism, 1999, Globalizing Civil Society, 1998, When Corporations Rule the World, 1995 (Tomorrow's 10 Best award 1998, pub. in 11 langs.), Getting to the 21st Century: Voluntary Action and the Global Agenda, 1990, Planned Change in a Traditional Society: Psychological Problems of Modernization in Ethiopia, 1972; co-author: Casebook for Family Planning Management, 1977; Editor: Community Management: Asian Experience and Perspectives, 1986, People-Centered Development: Contributions Toward Theory and Planning Frameworks, Bureaucracy and the Poor: Closing the Gap, 1981; contbr. numerous articles to profl. jours. and mags.; mem. editl. adv. bd. Devel., 1998—, Environment and Urbanization, 1993—, World Bus. Acad. Perspectives, 1997-99; mem. editl. adv. bd. Kumarian Press, Inc., 1991—. Mem. Citizen's Com. for Nader/LaDuke, 1997-99; chair ACLU of North West Fla., 1968. Capt. USAF, 1968-70.

KORTH, PENNE PERCY, ambassador; b. Hattiesburg, Miss., Nov. 3, 1942; m. Fritz-Alan Korth, Dec. 15, 1965 (div. 1997); children: Fritz-Alan Jr., Maria Korth Chieffalo, James Frederick. Sr. Washington assoc., client liaison and rep. trust and estate div. Sotheby's, 1986-89; amb. to Mauritius, Port Louis, 1989-92; pres. Firestone and Korth Ltd., Washington, 1993-97; commr. U.S. Adv. Commn. Pub. Diplomacy, 1997—; bd. dirs. Chevy Chase Bank; rep. Sotheby's Internat., 1997—. Bd. dirs. Meridian Internat. Ctr., Coun. of Am. Ambs., Van Cliburn Found., Marjorie Merriweather Post Found., Washington, 1995—; co-chmn. Am. Bicentennial Presdl. Inauguration, 1988-89. Mem. Assn. for Diplomatic Studies and Tng. (bd. dirs. 1996—), Sulgrave Club. Home: 2540 Massachusetts Ave NW Washington DC 20008-2832 Office: Chevy Chase Bank Pvt Banking 8401 Connecticut Ave Ste 2 Chevy Chase MD 20815-5889

KORTHALS, ALBERT HENDRIK (BENK), Netherlands government official; b. Voorschoten, The Netherlands, Oct. 5, 1944. Degree in Law, U. Leiden, The Netherlands, 1973. Pvt. law practice Rotterdam, The Netherlands, 1974-98; min. justice; mem. Lower Ho. of the States Gen., 1982-98; mem. coun. People's Party for Freedom and Democracy, chmn. umbrella com.; bd. dirs. Inst. for Housing and Urban Devel. Studies; chmn. Assn. for Legal Aid to Conscripts. With Royal Netherlands Navy. Fax: 31-70-370 79 37. Office: Ministry of Justice, PO Box 20301, 2500 EH The Hague The Netherlands*

KORTING, HANS CHRISTIAN, dermatology educator; b. Tübingen, Germany, Mar. 21, 1952; s. Günter Waldemar and Johanna Herta (Kühnert) K.; m. Monika Hildegard Schäfer, Apr. 25, 1980; children: Sabine Denise, Christina Maria. MD, Johannes Gutenberg U., Mainz, Germany, 1977; PhD, Ludwig Maximilians U., Munich, 1985. Resident dept. internal medicine Bundeswehrzentralkrankenhaus, Koblenz, Germany, 1977-78; resident dept. bacteriology and microbiology Wehr Med. Inst., Koblenz, 1978-79; resident dermatol. clinic Ludwig Maximilians U., 1979-85, sr. lectr., 1986-92, prof., 1992—, sec. gen. XIV Fortbildungswoche, 1994. Co-author: Sexuell Übertragbare Erkrankungen, 1990, Dermatotherapie, 1995, Ultraschall in der Dermatologie, 1999; co-editor: Liposome Dermatics, 1992, Topical Glucocorticoids with Increased Benefit/Risk Ratio, 1993, Diagnostische Verfahren in der Dermatologie, 1997, The Benefit/Risk Ratio, 1999. Recipient Paul Schürmann prize German Soc. for Def. Medicine and Def. Pharm., 1980, Paul Gerson Unna prize German Dermatol. Soc., 1990, Forschungs=Förderungs prize German Speaking Mycology Soc., 1994, Yves Rocher prize, Comite Scientifique de la Fondation, 1995. Mem. German Sexually Transmitted Diseases Soc. (sec. gen. 1998—), Gesellschaft Dermopharmazie (co-chmn. 1995—), Deutschsprachige Mykologiesche Gesellschaft (chmn. 1999—), German Dermatol. Soc. (chmn. com. on therapy 1998—, com. on quality assurance 1999—). Roman Catholic. Home: Ignaz Günther Weg 4, D-85764 Oberschleissheim Bavaria, Germany also: Im Dol 54, D-14195 Berlin Berlin, Germany Office: Ludwig Maximilians U Derm, Frauenlobstrasse 9-11, D-80337 Munich Germany

KORTLANDT, FREDERIK HERMAN HENRI, Slavic languages and comparative linguistics educator; b. Utrecht, The Netherlands, June 19, 1946. BA, U. Amsterdam, 1967, MA, 1969, PhD, 1972. Asst. prof. U. Amsterdam, 1969-72; prof. Slavic langs. U. Leiden, The Netherlands, 1972—, prof. descriptive and comparative linguistics, 1985—. Author: Modelling the Phoneme, 1972, Slavic Accentuation, 1975; contbr. numerous articles to linguistic jours. Spinoza prize laureate, 1997. Mem. Royal Dutch Acad. Home: Cobetstraat 24, NL-2313 KC Leiden The Netherlands Office: U Leiden Faculty Letters, PO Box 9515, NL-2300 RA Leiden The Netherlands

KORTMANN, WALTER, economics educator, researcher; b. Holzwickede, Germany, Feb. 26, 1958. Diploma in elec. engring., U. Dortmund, Germany, 1976; diploma in econs., U. Dortmund, 1986, PhD, 1994. Rsch. asst. U. Dortmund, 1986-89; chief economist Pub. Utility Corp., Dortmund, 1989-95; rsch. dir. Inst. Econs. and Sys. Rsch., Dortmund, 1990—. Author: Diffusion, Markentwicklung und Wettbewerb, 1995, Mikroökonomik, 1997, 2d edit., 1999, Reale Ausseuwirtschaftslehre, 1998. Mem. Am. Econ. Assn., Gesellschaft für Wirtschafts- und Sozialwissenschaften. Home: PO Box 1221, D-59435 Holzwickede Germany

KÖRTZINGER, ARNE, marine chemist, researcher, chemical oceanographer; b. Bremen, Germany, June 14, 1963; s. Wilfried and Karin (Lilie) K.; m. Andrea Menke, Mar. 18, 1988. Pre-diploma in chemistry, U. Hannover, Germany, 1986; diploma in chemistry, U. Kiel, Germany, 1991, PhD, 1995. Postgrad. rschr. Inst. Marine Rsch., U. Kiel, 1991-95, postdoctoral rschr., 1995-99; vis. scholar U. Wash. Sch. Oceanography, Seattle, 1999-2000. Contbr. articles to sci. jours. Author travel guides, 1988, 91. Avocation: travel. E-mail: akoertzinger@ifm.uni-kiel.de. Fax: 49-431-565876. Office: U Kiel Inst Marine Rsch, Düsternbrooker Weg 20, Kiel 24105, Germany

KORUN, MATJAŽ ALEŠ, physicist, researcher; b. Ljubljana, Slovenia, Nov. 13, 1947; s. Saša and Marija (Kladnik) K.; m. Marija Lelija Hladky, Dec. 19, 1972; children: Matic, Maja. BSc, U. Ljubljana, 1972, MSc, 1976, PhD, 1982. Postgrad. asst. J. Stefan Inst., Ljubljana, 1973-82, applied rschr., 1982-92, postdoc. assoc., 1992-95, rschr., 1995-99, sr. rschr., 1999—; del. Internat. Com. Radionuclid Metrology, 1993. Mem. Internat. Radiation Physics Soc., Internat. Union Radioecology, N.Y. Acad. Scis. Roman Catholic. Achievements include calibration of gamma-ray spectrometers with point sources and calculation of detection probabilites for volume samples, calculation of self-attenuation factors and coincidence summing corrections for volume samples of arbitrary shape, measurements and calculation of total efficiencies, measurements of the average path lengths of photons in samples of arbitrary shape, calculation of the depth distribution of radionuclei in the soil from in-situ measured gamma-ray spectra. Office: Jožef Stefan Inst, Jamova 39, 1000 Ljubljana Slovenia

KORUNIČ, DAVID JOHN, financial executive, consultant; b. Christchurch, New Zealand, Nov. 27, 1965; s. Milan Desmond and Janice Marion (Roscoe) K.; m. Vacentia Ratna Dewi Bunawan, Dec. 1, 1990. dir. PT Asuransi Allianz Life, Jakarta, Indonesia, 1997—, MBA Life, Kuala Lumpur, Malaysia, 1998—; sr. dir. First Life Ins., Seoul, Republic of Korea, 1999—. Mem. New Zealand Soc. Accts., Hong Kong Soc. Accts. Avocations: rugby, squash, movies, cars, cooking. Office: First Life Ins, 1303-35 Seocho 4-Dong, Seoul 197-074, Republic of Korea

KORYAKIN, YURI IVANOVICH, nuclear power economics educator; b. Moscow, June 14, 1924; s. Ivan Nikitovich and Helena Grigoryevna (Klimova) K.; m. Rimma Filippovna Korobeinikova, Feb. 7, 1952; 1 child, Michael. Engr., physicist, Moscow Engring. Phys. Inst., 1953, D of Econ. Scis., 1970. Engr. R&D Inst. of Power Engring., Moscow, 1953-58, sr. engr., 1958-60, head of dept., 1961-90, head scientist, 1990—; lectr. Moscow Energetical Inst., Moscow, 1966-70, Moscow Tech. U., 1966-71. Author: Economes of Nuclear Power, 1969, Siting Energy Facilities, 1983, Economic Losses Caused by The Chernobyl Accident, 1990, Energetics and Russian Geopolotics, 1997; editl. bd. Atomic Energy, 1956—; contbr. articles to profl. jours. Sgt. maj. The Soviet Army, 1941-47. Mem. N.Y. Acad. Scis. Office: R&D Inst Power Engring, Gen PO Box 788, 101000 Moscow Russia

KORZENIOWSKI, KRZYSZTOF (KRIS KORZENIOWSKI), electrical engineer, educator, consultant; b. Lodz, Poland, Dec. 3, 1935; arrived in Papua New Guinea, 1985; s. Mieczyslaw Jan and Marianna Genowefa (Lewandowska) K.; m. Miroslawa Halina Rajf, June 6, 1970; children: Michael, Maciej. MSc, Lodz (Poland) U. Tech., 1960, PhD, 1975. Cert. elec. engr., Poland; registered engr., Papua New Guinea. Prodn. engr. M-3 Power Transformer Plant, Lodz, 1959-61; instrument lab. mgr. Film Studios, Lodz, 1961-63; project engr. Elektromontaz Indsl. Electrification, Lodz, 1963-67; dep. mgr. export Elester Control & Switch Gear Co., Lodz, 1968-69; sr. rsch. fellow Lodz U. Tech., 1970-81; prin. lectr. UNESCO project, Kwara State Coll. Tech., Ilorin, Nigeria, 1981-84; assoc. prof. Papua New Guinea U. Tech., Lae, 1985-98; cons. process control Unitech Devel. & Cons., Lae, 1990—; cons. electric rwys. Papua New Guinea Govt., Lae, 1993—, Nat. Capital Dist., Port Moresby, Papua New Guinea, 1996—. Contbr. articles to profl. jours. Recipient Silver Jubilee award Papua New Guinea U. Tech., Lae, 1992. Fellow Soc. Profl. Engrs. Papua New Guinea; mem. IEEE (sr.), World Conf. Transport Rsch., Soc. Instrument and Control Engrs. Japan., PNG Electric Rail Engring. Group. Roman Catholic. Avocations: yoga, Alpine skiing, history of 20th century. Home and Office: PNG Electric Rail Engring, Szermiercza 7, 94-048 Lodz Poland

KORZH, RUSLAN A., management consultant; b. Zaporozhye, Ukraine, Jan. 1, 1967; m. Valentina, Nov. 3, 1990; 1 child, Vladislav. Diploma in internat. econs., Kiev State U., 1990; M in Mgmt., Northwestern U., 1994. From comml. exec. to mktg. mgr. Antonov Design Bur., Kiev, Ukraine, 1990-93; assoc. A.T. Kearney, Chgo., 1994-96; from mgr. to prin. A.T. Kearney, Moscow, 1996—. Author: Basics of Accounting, 1992. Sr. sgt. strategic nuclear forces Ukraine, 1985-87. Mem. Am. C. of C. in Russia. Avocations: photography, video, scuba diving, car racing, hiking. Office: AT Kearney, 52/4 Kosmodamianskaya Nab, Riverside Towers Moscow, Russia 113054

KOS, SANJA, public relations officer; b. Zagreb, Croatia, Nov. 24, 1964; d. Vojislav and Vlasta (Krznarić) Smiljanić; m. Igor Kos, Sept. 25, 1993; 1 child, Borna. LLB, U. Zagreb, 1988. Journalist Nat. Vjesnik Daily Newspaper, Zagreb, 1988-90, asst. editor bus. sect., 1990-91, editor bus. sect., mem. editl. bd., 1991-92, editor fin. supplement, 1996-97; pub. rels. officer Zagrebácka Banka, Zagreb, 1997—. Active Croatian Coun. of the European Movement, Zagreb, 1990-92. Mem. Croatian Journalists Assn. Office: Zagrebácka Banka, Paromlinska 2, 10 000 Zagreb Croatia

KOS, ZORKO, civil engineer, educator; b. Šumber, Istra, Croatia, Feb. 2, 1930; s. Dinko and Antica (Radovic) K.; m. Marica Trpčic, Dec. 3, 1960; children: Edo, Mirjana. Diploma in Civil Engring., U. Zagreb, Croatia, 1956, PhD, 1979. Cert. civil engr. Mgr. Istra Water Authority, Labin, Croatia, 1956-61; cons. Libyan Ministry Agr., Tripoli, 1962-65; mgr. Gen. Water Resources Co., Rijeka, Croatia, 1966-76; prof. civil engring. U. Rijeka, 1976—, dean faculty civil engring., 1977-81, 91-95; advisor irrigation FAO, Rome, 1973-98. Author: Irrigation and Drainage, 4 vols., 1984-91; editor, main author: Irrigation and Drainage, 11 vols., 1981-98; contbr. articles to profl. jours. Recipient chartered disting. mem. Yugoslav Soc. Civil Engrs., Belgrade, 1983, 84, state award for sci. Govt. Croatia, Zagreb, 1993, life achievement award Rijeka Authority, 2000. Mem. Internat. Water Resources Assn. (rep. for Croatia 1975), Croatian Acad. Tech. Scis., Croatian Soc. Irrigation and Drainage (pres. 1981-85). Avocations: gardening, skiing. Home: Carmen Sylva 7, 51410 Opatija Croatia Office: Gradjevinski Fakultet, Viktora Cara Emina 5, 51000 Rijeka Croatia

KOSACHEVSKAYA, ELENA ALEKSANDROVNA, science administrator; b. Ussuriysk, Russia, June 21, 1930; d. Alexandr Efimovich and Natalia Pavlovna (Stecenko) Bobko; m. Leonid Yakovlevich Kosachevskiy, Jan. 5, 1951; children: Ludmila, Larisa. PhD, Odessa State U., 1977. Prof. Donetsk State U., Ukraine, 1977-82; vice-chmn. Nat. Com. Soviet Mathematicians, Moscow, 1982-88; vice-chmn. Far East Dept. Russian Acad. Scis., Moscow, 1988—. Author: Projective Geometry, 1971, Differential Geometry, 1975, Tensor Analysis, 1977; contbr. articles to profl. jours. Mem. European Acad. Arts Scis. and Humanities, European Mechanics Soc., German Soc. Applied Math. and Mechanics, Russian Engring. Acad. Fax: 938-18-31. Home: Stroiteley, 117311 Moscow Russia Office: Russian Acad Scis, Leninsky prospect 32A, Moscow Russia

KOSAKAI, AKIRA, research company executive; b. Nagoya, Japan, Dec. 3, 1940; children: Katsura, Tamaki, Megumi. B of Liberal Arts, Tokyo U. Fgn. Affairs, 1964. Dir. Distbn. Info. Ctr. Co. Ltd., Tokyo, 1969-79; pres., CEO KMS Inc., Tokyo, 1980—. Editor: (periodical) Overseas Mktg. Index. Avocation: running in marathons. Home and office: Shoei-Haitsu No 302, 1-1096-7 Ogawa-Cho, Kodaira-Shi Tokyo 187-0032, Japan

KOSAKOVSKYY, ANATOLIY LUKIANOVICH, otolaryngologist; b. Netreba, Rovensky, Ukraine, Oct. 8, 1952; s. Luka Denisovich and Raisa Ivanivna (Maslovska) K.; m. Nadia Vasilivna Kosakovska, May 22, 1976; 1 child, Ilona Anatoliivna. Degree, Chernivetsky Med. Inst., Ukraine, 1973, MD, 1975; Candidate of Sci., Kyiv State Inst., Ukraine, 1985, DSc, 1994; postgrad, Kyiv State Inst. Adv. Med. Tng., Ukraine, 1982-85. Intern Rovensky Region Hosp., Rovno, Ukraine, 1975-76; otolaryngologist Volodymyretsky (Ukraine) Dist. Hosp., 1976-80; clin. resident Kyiv (Ukraine) State Inst. Advanced Med. Tng. Physicians, 1980-82, asst. prof., 1985-96, prof., 1997—; head otolaryngology dept. Volodymyretsky (Ukraine) Dist. Hosp., 1976-80; head Bd. Young Scientists Kyiv (Ukraine) State Inst., 1984-85; head. dept. overseas devel. and internat. econ. rels. Kyiv Med. Acad. Postgrad. Edn., 1994-98, mem. trade union com., 1995—, mem. rectorate, 1995—, mem. sci. coun., 1997, prof. dept. pediat. otolaryngology, 1997, prorector internat. rels., 1998—; mem. jour. editl. bd. "Ukrainsky Medychny Chasopys," "Family Practice." Author: Neurosensor and Hearing Disorder, 1989, Etiology, Clinical Picture, Diagnosis, Treatment and Prophylaxis of Chronic Cicatricial Laryngotracheal Stenosis in Children, 1998; inventor: A. Kosakovskyy's device for suturing, 1988, Sprayer device, 1991; contbr. articles to profl. jours; contbr. over 150 scientific papers and 165 inventions and rationalizations. Named Honored Inventor of Ukraine Supreme Soviet of Ukraine, 1990, Honors Inventor and Rationalizer Bd. Invention and Rationalization Orgn. of Ukraine, 1991, Best Young Rationalizer of the City of Kyiv, 1984. Mem. N.Y. Acad. Scis., Kyiv Sci. Soc. Otolaryngology, Internat Biog. Ctr. Adv. Coun., Internat. Pers. Acad., European Sci. Soc. Otolaryngology, Internat. Sci. Soc. Otolaryngology, Am. Biog. Inst. (mem. rsch. bd. advisors). Avocations: inventions, modeling, billiards, fishing, hunting. Fax: (00380-44) 456-90-27. Home: PO Box 70, 03179 Kyiv Ukraine Office: Kyiv Med Acad Postgrad Edn, 9 Dorogozhitska St, 04112 Kyiv Ukraine

KOSANOVIC, CLEO, chemist, researcher; b. Limassol, Cyprus, Dec. 28, 1957; d. Demetrios and Katerina (Christodoulou) K.; m. Danko Dane Kosanovic, Mar. 6, 1982; children: Roman, Sara. Diploma in Chem. Engring., Faculty of Tech., Zagreb, Croatia, 1981, MS, 1986; PhD, U. Zagreb, Croatia, 1994, Greek lang. interpreter, 1994. Asst. Chromos-Kutrilin, Zagreb, Croatia, 1982-84, scientific asst., 1984-86, sr. scientific asst., 1986-92; scientific asst. Boskovic Inst., Zagreb, Croatia, 1992-94, sr. scientific asst., 1994-99, asst. prof., 1999—. Inventor: Scale Inhibitor (gold medallion), 1990, Corrosion Inhibitor (silver medallion), 1991. Mem. Croatian Acad. Sci. and Art., Internat. Zeolite Assn., Nat. Geographic Soc., Croatian Chem. Soc. Avocations: bicycling, volleyball, walking, reading. E-mail address: cleo@rudjer.irb.hr. Fax: 385 1 4680084. Home: B Magovca 99, 10000 Zagreb Croatia Office: Rudjer Boskovic Inst, Bijenicka 54, 10001 Zagreb Croatia

KOSAR, GULDEREN, public relations consultant; b. Kyrklareli, Turkey, Aug. 8, 1954; s. Hikmet and Melahat (Sirma) K. Student, Ataturk U. Media dir., account exec. Rota Advt. Agy. Ltd., Istanbul, Turkey, 1982-83; advt. and pub. rels. dir. Cumhuriyet Daily Newspaper, Istanbul, 1983-87; advt. dir. Veb Dailies Group, Istanbul, 1987-90; advt. pub. rels. coord. Asil Nadir Press Group, Istanbul, 1990-91; shareholder Metropol Comm. Ltd., Istanbul, 1991-92; founder, ptnr., CEO Capital Pub. Rels. Ltd., Istanbul, 1992-96; founder, CEO Pronto Pub. Rels. Ltd., Istanbul, 1996—. Author: Public Relations in Turkey, Case Studies in Public Relations. Mem. Tüsaid, ATC, Kader. Mem. Internat. Pub. Rels. Assn., Internat. Advt. Assn., Turkish Pub. Rels. Assn. Fax: 90-212-274 91 49. Office: Pronto Pub Rels & Cons Ltd, Koresehitleri Cad Deniz is Hani, No 50 Istanbul 80300, Turkey

KOSAROV, DIMITER, neurophysiologist; b. Sofia, Bulgaria, Apr. 12, 1928; s. Stephan Tanev and Stanka Dimitrova (Docheva) K.; m. Magdalina Radoslavova Naumova, July 10, 1958; children: Stephan, Radoslav. MD, Med. Faculty, Sofia, 1965; D in Med. Scis., Bulgarian Acad. Scis., 1985. Neurologist Balneologic Device, Varshetz, Bulgaria, 1965-66; assoc. rschr. Inst. Physiology Bulgarian Acad. Scis., Sofia, 1967-81; assoc. rschr. Inst. Biophysics Bulgarian Acad. Scis., Sofia, 1982-90, prof., 1991-94. Editor: Motor Control, 1973, Motor Units in Human Skeletal Muscles, 1983. Fellow Bulgarian Soc. EEG and EMG (sec. 1970-80), Bulgarian Soc. Physiology (sec. 1981-83). Mem. Orthodox Ch. Avocations: philately, wood carving. Home: 2 Kiril Vidinski St, 1421 Sofia Bulgaria Office: Bulgarian Acad Scis, Inst Biophysics, 1421 Sofia Bulgaria

KOSÁRY, DOMOKOS, historian; b. Selmecbánya, Hungary, July 31, 1913; s. János and Lola (Réz) K.; m. Klára Huszti, Dec. 15, 1937 (widowed 1978). Degree, U. Budapest, Hungary, PhD, 1936; postgrad., Sorbonne U., Paris, 1936-37, Inst. Hist. Rsch., London, 1938-39. Prof. Eötvös Coll. U. Budapest, 1937-50; dir. inst. history Teleki Inst., 1945-49; archivist; scientific researcher, scientific counsellor Inst. History Hungarian Acad. Scis., Budapest; corresponding mem. Hungarian Acad. Scis., Budapest, 1982, ordinary mem., 1985, pres., 1990-96; pres. Nat. Com. Hungarian Historians, Budapest, 1985-90; founder, editor-in-chief Revue d'Histoire Comparée, Budapest, 1943-48; prof. U. Budapest, 1946-49. Author: Introduction to the Sources and Literature of Hungarian History, vols. 1-3, 1951-58, book on Artur Görgey, 1936, new enlarged edit., 1994, on Lajos Kossuth, 1946, studies on history of Hungary's international relations from the Middle Ages up to the 20th century; editor (with others) History of City of Budapest, vols. II-III, History of Hungarian Press, vols. I-II, 1979-85, Culture in 18th Century Hungary, 1980; contbr. articles to numerous profl. publs. Pres. Revolutionary Coun. Historians, 1956. Recipient Laureate of Hungarian State prize, 1988, Grand Cross award Hungarian Republic, 1993, Széchenyi Grand prize of Hungarian Republic, 1995; named Officer of Ordre des Palmes Académiques de la République Française, 1988, Officer of Légion d'honneur, France, 1996. Mem. Acad. Europaea (London), Acad. Europeénne (Paris), Brit. Acad., Croatian Acad. Arts and Scis., Romanian Acad. Scis. Address: Hungarian Acad Scis, Inst of History, H-1014 Budapest Uri u 53, Hungary

KOSASIH, EDDI NIKO, internist, educator; b. Bangil, East Java, Indonesia, Oct. 9, 1929; s. Poen Khwat and Mariakasih Kho; m. Lenni Maria Tjoa; children: Cecilia, Agus Susanto, Sabina Susie. MD, Mcpl. U., Amsterdam, Holland, 1957; Cert. in Clin. Pathology, U. Indonesia, Jakarta, 1961; Cert. in Internal Medicine, U. North Sumatra, Indonesia; Cert. in Immunology, U. Singapore, 1972. Student asst. RIV Lab., Amsterdam, The Netherlands, 1955; lectr. Med. Faculty U. Indonesia, Jakarta, 1957-65; sr. lectr. Med. Faculty U. North Sumatra, Medan, 1965-83, prof. Med. Faculty, 1984—; founder, chmn. Clin. Pathology, U. North Sumatra, 1971-78, chmn. postgrad. studies in clin. pathology, 1978-96; mem. bd. studies in Clin. Pathology, Consortium Health Scis., 1983—; physician embassies of Australia, Can., New Zealand, and U.S. Author: (book) Pemeriksaan Laboratorium Klinik, 1984, Capita Selecta Hematologi Klinik, 1982, Pemanfaatan komputer untuk pelayanan Kesehatan, 1987. Avocations: communication, internet. Office: Clinic & Lab, 5-c Jalan Thamrin, Medan 20234, Indonesia

KOSASKY, HAROLD JACK, fertility researcher; b. Winnipeg, Man., Can., Oct. 19, 1927; s. Jack and Lillian (Resnick) K.; m. Shirley Anne Johnston, Sept. 3, 1955; children: Julia, Leah, Robert. BA, U. Manitoba, Can., 1948; MD, U. Manitoba, 1953. Diplomate Am. Bd. Ob-gyn.; lic. Coll Physicians and Surgeons Can., Med. Coun. Can., Ky. State Bd. Health, Idaho State Bd. Health, Mass. Bd. Registration in Medicine. Intern Deer Lodge VA and Grace Hosps., Winnipeg, Man., Can., 1952-53; resident in gen. surgery Col. Belcher Hosp., Calgary, Alta., Can., 1953-54; resident in psychiatry Warren (Pa.) State Hosp., 1955-56; jr. asst. resident, asst. resident, sr. resident in ob-gyn. Chgo. Lying-In Hosp., 1956-59; exch. fellow in ob-gyn. Newcastle Gen. Hosp., U. Durham, Eng., 1959-60; asst. and assoc. prof. U. Louisville Sch. Med., 1961-65; asst. and assoc. in ob-gyn. various hosps., Boston, 1966-81; gynecologist and obstetrician Boston Hosp. for Women, 1965-81; gynecologist Brigham & Women's Hosp., Boston, 1981—; instr. ob-gyn. Harvard U., 1965—; cons. Ovutime, Boston, 1972—; pres. Saltime Co., 1994, chmn. 1999; asst. vis. surgeon Boston City Hosp., 1967-69; mem. Ky. Govs. Task Force on Mental Retardation, 1964-65, Com. on Malignancy, chmn., 1963-65. Contbr. numerous articles to profl. jours.; co-inventor Ovutime; inventor Saltime Ovulation group of instruments. Fellow ACS, Royal Coll. Surgeons of Can. (cert.), Royal Soc. Health, Boston Obstetric Soc. (emeritus); mem. AAAS, Gen. Med. Coun. Gt. Britain (lic.), Royal Coll. Obstetricans and Gynecologists, Assn. Prof. Ob-gyn., Louisville Obstet. and Gynecol. Soc. (sec., treas. 1962-65), Louisville Med. Forum (v.p.). Episcopalian. Club: Harvard. Office: 25 Boylston St Chestnut Hill MA 02467-1715

KOSA SOMOGYI, ISTVAN, chemist; b. Szekesfehervar, Hungary, Feb. 10, 1930; s. Istvan and Erzsebet (Hoffmann) K.S.; m. Lidia Pavlovna Katchalova, Apr. 10, 1956; 1 child, Gyorgy. Diploma, U. Veszprem, 1954; PhD, Inst. Tech., Leningrad, 1958; DSc, Hungarian Acad. Sci., 1972. Chartered chem. engr. Jr. rsch. chemist Rsch. Inst. for Aluminum, Hungary, 1954; post-grad. fellow Inst. Tech., Leningrad, 1955-58; rsch. chemist Ctrl. Rsch. Inst. for Physics, Budapest, 1958-72, dept. head, 1972-86, sci. cons., 1986-88; sci. cons. Kossuth Lajos U., Debrecen, Hungary, 1990—; post-doctoral Internat. Atomic Energy Agy. fellow U. Leeds, England, 1962-63. Co-author: Amorphous Semiconductors, 1977; editor: Proceeding of International Conference on Amorphous Semiconductors, 1982, Procs. 8th Internat. Conf. on Non-Crystalline Semiconductors, 1986; contbr. articles to profl. jours. Mem. Soc. Hungarian Chemists, Com. Atomic and Molecular Physics Hungarian Acad. Scis. Avocations: playing recorders, gardening, drawing. Home: Apostol utca 25, H-1025 Budapest Hungary

KOSCIELAK, JERZY, scientist, science administrator; b. Lodz, Poland, Sept. 6, 1930; s. Jozef and Regina (Pokrzywa) K.; m. Anna Kitaszewska, 1969 (div. 1974); 1 child, Katarzyna. MB, Med. Acad., Warsaw, Poland, 1953, MD, 1960, DrSci, 1966. Asst. dept. physiol. chemistry Med. Acad., Warsaw, 1950-51; asst. and sr. asst. dept. biochemistry Inst. of Hematology, Warsaw, 1951-67; rsch. fellow Harvard Coll., Cambridge, 1964-65; head immunochem. lab. Inst. of Hematology, Warsaw, 1968-69, head dept. biochemistry, 1969—; sci. sec. Inst. of Hematology, Warsaw, 1969-97, dir., rsch. 1997—, prof., 1973—. Editor-in-chief Acta Haematologica Polonica jour., 1976-85; contbr. articles to profl. jours. Mem. Polish Biochem. Soc. (chmn. Warsaw divsn. 1967-69), Forum of Carbohydrates Coming of Age (FCCA), Polish Acad. Sci., N.Y. Acad. Scis., Internat. Glycoconjugate Orgn. (Polish rep. 1988—, pres. 1993-95), Found. for Glycobioloby Glyco XII (founder, pres. 1993—). Avocation: history. Office: Inst of Hematology, Chocimska 5, 00957 Warsaw Poland

KOSEL, ARNOLD ISRAILEVICH, physician, neurosurgeon; b. Saratov, Russia, Nov. 9, 1940; m. Olga Naumovna; children: Inna Arnoldovna, Alexander Arnoldovich. Degree in medicine, Saratov Med. Inst., 1965, B in Neurosurgery, 1968; M in Neurosurgery, Gorkiy Med. Inst., 1980; DSc, Internat. Acad. Arts & Scis., Moscow, 1997. Postgrad. physician in neurosurgery Saratov Inst. Traumatology and Orthopedy, 1967-69; neurosurgeon Saratov Regional Hosp., 1969-70; head dept. neurosurgery Chelyabinsk Hosp. Tube-Rolling Works, 1970-80; head neurosurg. svc. Mcpl. Clin. Hosp. Emergency Svc., Chelyabinsk, 1980-90, head Laser Surgery Lab., 1990-95; dir. Cheylabinsk State Inst. Laser Surgery, 1996—. Author: Pathophysiology of Cardiovascular Reactions for Anesthesia and Alteration of Body Position of Patients with Spinal Cord Pathology, 1994; inventor Kosel's method of trigeminal neuralgia treatment, Kosel's method of pituitary adenoma treatment, and Kosel's method of drug dependence treatment. Named Hon. Physician Ministry Health Russian Fedn., 1995; named Man of Yr. Chelyabinsk Mcpl. Adminstrn., 1996. Mem. Acad. Laser Scis. Russian Fedn., Med. and Tech. Acad. Russian Fedn., Acad. Med. Scis. Russian Fedn. (corr.). E-mail: cgih@cgilh.chel.su. Office: Chelyabinsk State Inst, Pobedy 287, 454021 Chelyabinsk Russia

KOSENKO, LARISA VICTOROVNA, biochemist, microbiologist, researcher; b. Dnepropetrovsk, Ukraine, USSR, May 31, 1938; d. Victor Yephimovich and Zinaida Abramovna (Kruchakova) K.; m. Oleg Alexandrovich Kishko, Nov. 1, 1966; children: Tatyana, Pavel. Degree in biology and biochemistry, T.G. Shevchenko State U., Kiev, Ukraine, 1961; PhD, Ukrainian Acad. Scis., Kiev, Ukraine, 1969, DSc, 1995. Jr. rsch. worker Rentgeno-Radiol. and Oncol. Inst., Kiev, 1961-62; engr. Zabolotny Inst. Microbiology and Virology Ukrainian Acad. Scis., Kiev, 1962-67, jr. rsch. worker, 1967-79, sr. rsch. worker, 1979-96, prin. rsch. worker, 1996—. Co-author: (with I. Y. Zakharova) The Methods of Investigation of Microbial Polysaccharides, 1982; contbr. articles to profl. jours. G. Soros grantee Internat. Sci. Found., 1993; recipient D.K. Zabolotny award of Ukrainian Acad. Scis., 1988. Mem. Ukrainian Biochem. Soc., Ukrainian Microbiol. Soc., NY Acad. Scis. Avocation: reading about animals and nature. Home: Stelmaha 3 Apt 56, 03040 Kiev Ukraine Office: DK Zabolotny Inst Microbiol, Zabolotny Str 154, 03143 Kiev Ukraine

KOSHIBE, HEIHACHIRO, agricultural company executive; b. Tokyo, June 4, 1926; s. Moyozo Arai and Koh Koshibe; m. Masako Nakayama, Dec. 26, 1954. BA, Tokyo Agrl. U., 1926. Mng. dir. Mikado Seeds, Chiba, Japan, 1926-56, pres., 1956-93; CEO Mikado Group, Chiba, 1993—; chmn. Chiba Overseas Trade Coop, Chiba; mem. exec. com. ASSINSEL, Nyon, Switzerland. Author: Horticulture and Agricultural Seeds. Chmn. Election Control Commn., Chiba, Policemen's Friendship Assn., chiba. Decorated Nat. Order #5A, Emperor of Japan, 1997, recipient Yellow medal, 1986. Mem. Japan Seed Trade Assn. (exec. v.p.), Internat. Seed Fedn. (hon. life), Rotary (chpt. gov. 1993-94). Avocation: reading. Home: 7-6-28 Makuhari Hongo, Hanamigawa, Chiba City 262-0033, Japan Office: Chuo-ku, 1203 Hoshikuki, Chiba City 260-0808, Japan

KOSHIJIMA, TETSUO, chemistry educator, consultant; b. Kanazawa, Ishikawa, Japan, Sept. 24, 1926; s. Taichiro and Yukiko (Ohta) K.; m. Ranko Shimomura, Nov. 29, 1954; children: Masaki, Kyoko. Rsch. assoc. Wood Rsch. Inst. Kyoto (Japan) U., 1952-62, prof. Wood Rsch. Inst., 1975-90; prof. emeritus, 1990—; chief researcher biopolymer Nat. Inst. Indsl. Rsch. and Tech., Osaka, Japan, 1962-75; prof. Faculty of Agr. Kinki U., Osaka, 1990-97; cons. Japan Chem. Engring. and Machinery Co., 1997—. Author: You Can Make Science from Wood, 1988; editor, author: Cellulose Resources, 1990, Microwave-Heating Technology Collection, 1992; inventor, patent benzylated lignocellulosic substance and producing method, 1997. Fellow Internat. Acad. Wood Sci.; mem. Japanese Soc. Carbohydrate Rsch., Japan Wood Rsch. Soc., Japan TAPPI. Home: 8 Takabecho Shugakuin, Sakyo-ku Kyoto 606-8022, Japan Office: Japan Chem Engr and Mach, 6-23 4-Kashima Yodogawa-ku, Osaka 532-0031, Japan

KOSHIMIZU, TOSHIO, system integrater executive; b. Yokohama, Japan, Mar. 21, 1930; s. Toshioki and Ikuko (Nomura) K.; m. Hiroko Aoki, Aug. 8, 1932. BA, Tokyo U. Commerce, 1953. Acctg. staff Mitsubishi Corp., Japan, 1953-66; gen. mgr. corp. planning Mitsubishi Corp., 1977-87, statutory auditor, 1987-89; asst. to pres. Mitsubishi Internat. Corp., 1966-77; exec. v.p., chief fin. officer IX Corp., Japan, 1989-96, sr. exec. v.p., chief fin. officer, 1996-2000; exec. v.p., CFO Active Work Corp., Japan, 2000—; pres., CEO, Advance and Technology, Inc., Japan, 1996-2000. Mem. Josuikai/Tokyo. Office: 4-9-25 Shibaura Minato-ku, Tokyo 108, Japan

KOSHIYAMA, MASAFUMI, gynecologist; b. Ueno City, Mie, Japan, May 9, 1960; s. Moritoshi and Kiyoe Koshiyama; m. Shigeyo Yamazaki, Nov. 23, 1988; children: Erina, Hiroki. Yamanashi (Japan) Med. U., 1986; MD, DMS, Kyoto (Japan) U., 1997. Designated physician for eugenic protection law, Japan Med. Assn. Resident Kyoto U., 1986-87, staff physician, 1991-94; staff physician Nagahama (Japan) Nisseki Hosp., 1987-90, Toyooka (Japan) Hosp., 1990-91, Tenri (Japan) Hosp., 1995-2000, Osaka Nat. (Japan) Hosp., 2000—. Contbr. articles to med. jours. Mem. N.Y. Acad. Scis., Japan Soc. Ob-gyn. (qualifying physician in ob-gyn.), Japan Soc. for Cancer Therapy, Japanese Cancer Assn. Avocation: driving. Office: Dept Ob-gyn Osaka Nat Hosp, 2-1-14 Hoenzaka Chuoku, Osaka 540-0006, Japan

KOSHKIN, VLADIMIR MOISEEVICH, physicist, educator; b. Kharkov, Ukraine, Nov. 20, 1936; s. Moisey Lvovich and Dora Markovna (Gorfunkel) K.; m. Nina Yakovlevna Fogel, June 14, 1959 (div. 1985); 1 child, Il'ya; m. Olga Vladimirovna Sayapina, Jan. 25, 1992; 1 child, Mikhail. MSc, State U., Kharkov, 1959, DSc, 1972; PhD, Inst. Low Temp. Acad. Scis., Kharkov, 1964. Engr. Plant Toploautomat, Kharkov, 1959-60; sr. rschr. Inst. Basic Chemistry, Kharkov, 1960-65; prof. Inst. for Single Crystals Acad. Scis. Ukraine, 1981—; head dept. Inst. Single Crystals Acad. Scis. Ukraine, Kharkov, 1965-82; head dept. Polytechnic U., Kharkov, 1982—; vis. prof. Nat. U., Australia, 1995, Polytechnic U., Mex., 1996, Internat. Ctr. Theoretical Physics, Italy. Author: (with Y. Dmitriev) Chemistry and Physics of Compounds with Loose Crystal Structure, 1994; (poetry) Pronouns, 1996, To Stay in September, 1999; contbr. over 200 articles to profl. jours. Recipient diploma of discovery USSR, 1982, Gold prize USSR Exhbn., 1983, Honor diploma Ukraine Exhbn., 1983. Mem. Internat. Acad. Informatization, USSR Phys. Soc. (bd. dirs. 1989-91), Ukraine Phys. Soc. (bd. dirs. 1990-92), Materials Rsch. Soc., Assn. on Empirical Aesthetics, Assn. Authors of Discoveries, N.Y. Acad. Scis. Avocations: writing poetry, social journalism, mountain and river tourism, table tennis. Fax: 0572-478273. E-mail: koshkin@kpi.kharkov.ua. Home: 1 Gaceva St Apt 174, 310108 Kharkov Ukraine Office: Polytechnic U, 21 Frunze St, 310002 Kharkov Ukraine

KOSHY, VETTITHARA CHERIAN, chemistry educator, technical director and formulator; b. Kumbanad, Kerala, India, Jan. 5, 1952; came to U.S., 1984; s. Vettithara and Mariamma Cherian; m. Valsamma Koshy, Jan. 31, 1983; children: Rincy Mary, John Cherian. BSc in Chemistry, Kerala U., India, 1973; MSc in Chemistry, Ravishankar U., India, 1975, PhD in Chemistry, 1983; MS in Econ. Aspects of Chemistry, U. Detroit, 1992. Rsch. fellow chemistry Ravishankar U., Raipur, 1976-81; lectr., head dept. chemistry J.M. Patel Coll., 1981-83; lectr. dept. chemistry D.B. Sci. Coll., Gondia (India) Edn. Soc., India, 1983-84; group leader and evening supr. in R & D Widger Chem. Corp., Warren, Mich., 1984-87; mgr. automotive divsn., R & D Croda Caourep Corp., Westland, Mich., 1987-89; dir. R & D, quality control and mfg. Autotek, inc., Farmington Hills, Mich., 1989-94; pres. Koshy Speciality Products, Inc., Bloomfield Hills, Mich., 1994—; engr. Dale Packaging Inc., Livonia, Mich., 1994-95; sr. chemist Novamax Techs. (U.S.) Inc., Warren, 1995-96; tech. mgr. Henkel Corp. Novamax Techs., 1996-98; sr. rsch. scientist Henkel Surface Techs., Madison Heights, 1998—. Contbr. articles to Jour. Chem. Engring., Croatica Chemica Acta, Indian Acad. Scis., Nat. Acad. Scis. Sci. Letters, among others. Pres. sci. assn. J.M. Patel Coll., Bhandara, India, 1981-82; pres. chem. soc. Ravishankar U., Raipur, 1977-78, pres. rsch. scholars assn., 1979-81. Recipient numerous grants. Mem. Am. Chem. Soc., Am. Inst. Chemists, Soc. Automotive Engrs. (assoc.), Fedn. Kerala Assns. N.Am. (region 7 v.p. 1998-2000). Achievements include development of a formula for a universal sealer for automotive application. Home: 7030 White Pine Dr Bloomfield Hills MI 48301-3715 Office: Henkel Surface Techs 32100 Stephenson Hwy Madison Heights MI 48071-5514

KOSINSKI, LESZEK ANTONI, geography educator; b. Warsaw, June 13, 1929; came to Can., 1968, naturalized, 1974; s. Jakub and Emilia (Opacka) K.; m. Maria Leokadia Bodakiewicz, Apr. 2, 1951. MA in Econs., Ctrl. Sch. Planning & Stats., 1951; MA in History, U. Warsaw, 1954; PhD, Polish Acad. Scis., 1958, Docent, 1983. Jr. rschr. Inst. Town Planning and Arch., Warsaw, 1950-54; sr. rschr. Inst. Geography, Polish Acad. Scis., 1954-68; prof. geography U. Alta., Edmonton, Can., 1969-94; sec.-gen. Internat. Social Sci. Coun., Paris, 1994—; sec.-gen., treas. Internat. Geography Union, 1984-92. Author numerous books including The Population of Europe: A Geographical Perspective, 1970, (with W. Zelinsky) Emergency Evacuation of Cities, 1991; editor: (with R.M. Prothero) People on the Move: Studies on Internal Migration, 1975, (with J.I. Clarke and M. Khogali) Population and Development Projects in Africa, 1985, Ecological Disorder in Amazonia, 1992, Issues in Global Change Research: Problems, Data and Programmes, 1996, (with V. Hoffman-Martinot) Quels Partenariats Pour la ville? Approches Internationales, 1999; contbr. articles to profl. jours. Served with Polish Underground, 1943-44. Mem. Can. Population Soc. (pres. 1984-86), Can. Assn. Slavists, Internat. Union for Sci. Study of Population, Assn. Population Geographers of India, Can. Assn. Geographers (Award for Svc. to the Profession of Geography 1994), Société, Géographie Paris (hon.), Polish Geog. Soc. (hon.), Russian Geog. Soc. (hon.). Avocations: travel, photography, skiing. Office: ISSC, Maison de l'UNESCO, 1, rue Miollis, 75732 Paris Cedex 15, France

KOSINSKY, ANATOLIY VASILIEVICH, engineering educator; b. Krasnodar, Russia, Feb. 12, 1930; s. Vasily Sergeevich and Evdokiya Dmitriyevna (Gusyeva) K.; m. Valentina Afanasievna Troshkina, Jan. 20, 1961. Degree in electromech. engring., Moscow Energy Inst., 1952; PhD, Radio Inst., Moscow, 1960; D Tech. Scis., Moscow Inst. Electronics/Math., 1986. Engr. M.V. Lomonosov State U., Moscow, 1952-54; engr. Radio Inst., Moscow, 1955-57, head rsch. group, 1958-61, head lab. control, 1961-63; assoc. prof. Moscow Inst. Electronics and Math., 1963-86, prof., 1986—, mem. acad. coun. PhD and DSc, 1976—, mem. state coun. entring. cert., 1963—; chmn. Electoral Dist., Moscow, 1978, vice chmn., 1982; cons. in field. Author: (with M.A. Babikov) Details and Equipment of Automation, 1975, (with V.R. Matveevsky and A.A. Kholomonov) Analogous-digital Converters of Moves, 1991; contbr. over 200 articles to profl. jours.; 40 patents in field. Mem. Trade Union H.S., Russia, 1947—, Russian Soc. Red Cross, 1947—. 2d lt. Soviet Army, 1970. Recipient Splendid Worker medal USSR, 1970, Vet. of Work medal USSR, 1986, 850 Yrs. of Moscow medal, 1997, prize USSR Nat. Economy Fair, 1983. Mem. N.Y. Acad. Scis., Sci.-Tech. Soc., Russian Soc. Znanie. Avocations: travel, reading, theater, fishing. Home: Lomonosovsky Prospekt, D 14 KV 116, 117296 Moscow Russia Office: Moscow State Inst Elec/Math, ul B Tryokhsvyatitelskiy, 109928 Moscow Russia

KOSITCHEV, ANATOLY, philosophy educator; b. Moscow, July 1, 1914; m. Maria Ivanovna Orlova; 1 child, Svetlana. MA, State Pedagogical Inst., Moscow, 1940; PhD in Philosophy, Moscow State U., 1950. Assoc. prof. dept. philosophy Moscow State U., 1951-71, prof., 1971—, chmn. dept., 1971-93. Decorated Order of Patriotic War, Order of Red Banner of Labor (USSR); recipient 16 medals. Mem. Philos. Soc. Russia (mem. prsidium 1970-90). Home: Vorob'evy Gory, High Bldg, Sector K Apt 136, 119899 Moscow Russia Office: Moscow State U Fac Philos, Vorob'evy Gory, 119899 Moscow Russia

KOSKENVUO, KIMMO, public health physician; b. Kangaslampi, Finland, May 22, 1936; s. Kaarlo Armas and Inkeri Helena (Lähde) K.; m. Marja-Leena Josephine Linblad, Oct. 10, 1965; children: Inka, Helena. Lic. medicine, Helsinki (Finland) U., 1962, MD, 1974. Cert. specialist in pub. health and adminstrn. Nat. Bd. Health, Finland. Served to lt. gen. Finnish Def. Forces; physician various mil. and civil orgns., 1963-69; chief Med. Bur. Def. Staff, Helsinki, 1970-72, 74-76; acting prof. pub. health U. Turku, Finland, 1973; chief med. sect. Def. Staff, Helsinki, 1976-78; docent in mil. healthcare Helsinki U., 1977; surgeon gen. Finnish Def. Forces, 1978-96; mem. ctrl. bd. Finnish Red Cross, Helsinki, 1978-95; mem. sci. def. coun. Ministry of Def., Helsinki, 1979—; chmn. sect. disaster medicine Nat. Adv. Bd. Health, FInland, 1978-96, adv. expert on pub. health, 1981-93; chmn. 1st aid com. ctrl. bd. Finnish Red Cross, 1978-95; hon. mem. Internat. Com. Mil. Medicine, 1984. Editor-in-chief: (textbooks) Field Surgery and Medicine, 1994, Military Health and Medical Care, 1996, Prevention of Diseases, 1998, Medical Law, 2000. Named to Order Sl1.K of Finnish Zion, 1982. Mem. Finnish Med. Assn. (Pohjola award 1991), Swedish Royal Acad. War Scis., Finnish Med. Officers (hon.).

KOSKI, PIRKKO KAARINA, theater educator; b. Jyvaskyla, Finland, Dec. 22, 1941; d. Juho and Elina (Jokinen) Hautamaa; m. Heikki Koski, Aug. 31, 1962; children: Kimmo, Marja. Degree, U. Tampere, 1963, M in Social Scis., 1964, MA, 1980; PhD, U. Helsinki, 1992. Freelance dir. Finland, 1964-79; dir., mng. dir. Ctrl. Union Finnish Theatre Orgn., Helsinki, 1979-81; mus. dir. The Theatre Mus., Helsinki, 1981-89; from assoc. prof. to prof. U. Helsinki, 1989—; theatre reviewer Demari newspaper, Finland, 1978-94, Kanava jour., Finland, 1997—. Author: Folk Theatre Vol. I, 1986, Vol. II, 1987, Theatre Director and Time, 1992; editor: The World Is Changing: The National Theatre of Finland, 1999; contbr. articles to profl. jours. Office: U Helsinki, Fabianinkatu 33 BB Box 3, 00014 Helsinki Finland

KOSKINEN-OLSSON, TARJA, company executive; b. Tampere, Finland, Jan. 4, 1950; m. Henry Olsson, July 9, 1994; children: Riku, Mari. Degree in econs. in bus. adminstrn., Tampere U., 1972. Asst. dir. Finnish Composers' Internat. Copyright Bur., Finland, 1972-86; asst. dir. Kopiosto, Finland, 1986, CEO, 1987—; bd. dirs. Anti-Piracy Ctr., 1979—, Audiovisual Eureka, 1992—; coord. projects VERDI, INDECS; frequent lectr. in world intellectual property. Mem. Finnish Copyright Soc. (bd. dirs. 1989—), Finnish Copyright Inst. (bd. dirs. 1989—), Internat. Fedn. Reprodn. Rights Orgns. (vice chmn. 1992-93, chmn. 1993-99). Office: Kopiosto, Hietaniemenk 2, 00100 Helsinki Finland

KOSMAS, ELIAS, information systems specialist; b. Alexandria, Egypt, July 22, 1960; s. George and Helen Isabel (Nemtsa)K.; m. Helen Vagena Kosmas, Apr. 29, 1987; 1 child, George. BS in Math., Okla. State U., Stillwater, 1981; BS in Computing and Info. Scis., 1982; MS in Bus. Sys. Analysis & Design, The City U., London, 1984. Teaching and rsch. asst. dept. math. Okla. State U., Stillwater, Okla., 1979-81, teaching and rsch. asst. dept. computers, 1981; I.T. instr. Xini Computer Inst., Athens, Greece, 1982; sys. analyst Axon Computrs, Athens, Greece, 1983; programming tutor The City U., London, 1984; sys. analyst Greek Air Force, Athens, Greece, 1985-86, Procter & Gamble, Athens, Greece, 1986; info. sys. mgr. Toyota Hellas S.A., Athens, Greece, 1986-96; info. tech. dir. Incharge Holdings Hellas S.A., Athens, 1997-99, retail ops. dir., 2000—; bd. dirs. Greek Inst. for Info. Tech., Athens. Author: The Small Business Manager's Guide to the Evaluation and Selection of a Computer System, 1984, Mathematical Analysis of Inflation, 1980, A Simplified Approach to Understand the Notion of the Universal and Deterministic Turing Machine, 1981. Mem. Greek Mgmt. Assn., Greek Computer Soc., Assn. for Computing Machinery, Math. Hon. Soc. Avocations: tennis, fencing, philosophy. Office: Toyota Hellas SA, 168 Kifisou Ave, 12242 Egaleo Greece

KOSMAS, EPAMINONDAS N., chest physician, researcher; b. Athens, May 28, 1958; s. Nickolaos and Georgia (Berbili) K.; m. Alkistis Konstantatos, July 29, 1984; 1 child, Nickolaos. MD, U. Athens, 1983, PhD, 1997. Resident Chest Diseases Hosp., Athens, 1984-89; clin. rsch. fellow McGill U., Montreal, 1991-92; attending physician A. Fleming Hosp., Athens, 1989—, dir. sleep lab., 1996—; cons. exercise lab., U. Athens, 1997—, U. Thessalia, 1998—; cons. exercise and rehab., Cardiol. Ctr., Athens, 1998—. Contbr. articles to profl. jours. Fellow ACCP; mem. Am. Thoracic Soc., European Respiratory Soc. Avocations: computers and multimedia, tennis, basketball, hiking. Office: A Fleming Hosp Respiratory, Divsn Pigis Ave & Zaimi Str, 15127 Melissia Greece

KOSMULSKI, MAREK, chemistry researcher, educator; b. Lublin, Poland, July 30, 1956; s. Zdzislaw and Teresa (Zólkowska) K.; m. Izabela Mazur, Mar. 26, 1980; children: Michal, Pawel. MSc, Maria Curie Sklodowskiej U., Lublin, 1979, PhD, 1984, DSc, 1995. Tchg. asst. Maria Curie Sklodowska U., 1979-84, rsch. assoc., 1984-88; rsch. assoc. Clarkson U., Potsdam, N.Y., 1989-91, Polish Acad. Scis., Cracow, 1988-97; prof., head dept. electrochemistry Tech. U. Lublin, 1997—; guest scientist Åbo Acad., Finland, 1995, 98, N.C. State U., 1999; Alexander von Humboldt fellow, Forschungszentrum Karlsruhe, Germany, 1995-97, Forschungszentrum Rossendorf, Germany, 2000. Author: Rozgrywka pojedynczego koloru, 1990; contbr. articles to sci. jours., Ency. Brydza. Recipient scientific award Ministry Edn., Warsaw, Poland, 1990. Mem. Polish Chem. Soc. Roman Catholic. Avocations: collecting cheese labels, bridge.

KOSOWSKI, STANISLAW WINCENTY, physicist; b. Zarki, Poland, July 27, 1940; s. Wincenty and Bronislawa (Banas) K.; m. Hanna Borkowska, 1970 (div. 1980); children: Anna, Wojciech, Paulina, August. M of Physics, Jagiellonian U., Cracow, Poland, 1963; D of Tech. Scis., Polish Acad. Scis., Warsaw, Poland, 1968; D of Tech. Scis. habil., Polish Acad. Scis., 1973. Adj. faculty Inst. Fundamental Tech. Rsch. Polish Acad. Scis., Warsaw, 1968-74, docent, 1975-85; postdoctoral fellow Meml. U. Newfoundland, St. John's, Can., 1975-76, asst. prof., 1976-77; writer, 1985—. Author, editor: Joyful Creation of Balcerowicz, 1991, Wałesa Casus, 1998, Presidential Elections '95, 1998; contbr. articles to profl. jours. Avocations: writing poetry, music, economics, jogging, swimming. Home: Pereca 2 m 1214, 00-849 Warsaw Poland

KOSPARTOV, STEFAN DIMITROV, English educator; b. Sofia, Bulgaria, Aug. 27, 1949; s. Dimiter Nikolov and Maria Stefanova (Jambazova) K.; m. Lubka Nikolova Bacheva, Nov. 19, 1981; children: Maria Stefanova. MEd, Sofia U., 1973, PhD, 1986; MA, Nat. Acad. Theater and Film, Sofia, 1982; cert. of attendance, Coll. Europe, Brugge, Belgium, 1998. Cert. English lang. and lit., film dramaturgy. Asst. dir. Nat. Feature Film Studio, Sofia, 1976-82; lectr. English State Libr. Inst., Sofia, 1982-87, Inst. for Fgn. Students, Sofia, 1987-88; sr. lectr. English Med. Acad., Sofia, 1988-91, Nat. Acad. Theater & Film, Sofia, 1991—; cons. Free Trade Union Inst., Sofia, 1992-94; exec. dir. Bulgarian Inst. Analysis and Rsch., 1995—; head Phare program dept. Ministry of Justice, 1997-98, dir. gen. internat. programs, 1998—. Author: (screenplays) Preventive Detention, 1982, Shakespeare and the Rest, 1986; translator (screenplay) Cries and Whispers, 1980, (novel) House of Cards, 1997. Mem. exec. bd. Conservative Party, Bulgaria, 1990—; fgn. affairs sec. assn. Promyana, Sofia, 1997—; mem. planning com. Activities for the Devel. and Consolidation Dem. Stability, Coun. of Europe, 1998—. Named Internat. Visitor, USIA, 1994. Mem. Union Bulgarian Filmmakers. Bulgarian Orthodox. Avocations: bridge, mountaineering. Home: Blvd Vassil Levsky 4, 1124 Sofia Bulgaria Office: Nat Acad Theater & Film, Rakovsky St 108-A, 1000 Sofia Bulgaria

KOSS, PETER, research management consultant; b. Vienna, Mar. 21, 1932; s. Paul and Hilde (Fiedler) K.; m. Elsa Vedra, May 26, 1956; children: Michael, Christoph, Stephan. PhD in Physics, U. Vienna, 1958, univ. dozent venia legendi, 1967, univ. prof., 1981. Rsch. asst. U. Vienna, 1955-58; rsch. fellow MIT, Cambridge, 1959; with Atomics Internat., Canoga Park, Calif., 1959; head dept. metallurgy Austrian Rsch. Ctr., Seibersdorf, Vienna, 1963-81, tech. sci. mng. dir., 1981-96; cons. in field. Recipient Decoration of Honor for Merit in Silver (Austria), 1969, Cross of Honor for Sci. and Arts, 1975. Mem. Austrian Phys. Soc., Chem. Phys. Soc. E-mail: peter.koss@aon.at.

KOSSARIK, IGOR AFANASJEVICH, corporate executive; b. Moscow, June 8, 1934; s. Afanasij Kossarik and Maria Goncharova; m. Elena Vitaljevnal Kossarik, Jan. 1, 1977; 1 child, Anatoli. Diploma Philology/Economy, Moscow State U., 1957; Diploma Economy and Transport, State Acad. for Internat., Trade, 1967; Hon. Diploma Economy/Trade, U. Internat. Studiorum, Superiorum Pro Deo/St. Paul's Chapel/Columbia U. Apprenticeship Sovfacht, Moscow, 1958-62; vice gen. dir. Soyuzvneshtrans, Moscow, 1963-79; gen. dir. Asotra, Wien, Austria, 1979-83, Soyuztransit, Moscow, 1983-86; vice gen. dir. Ministry, Moscow, 1986-90; pres. Italsotra, Turin, Italy, 1990—; chmn. bd. Concern Sojuzvneshtrans, Moscow; prof. State Inst. for Fgn. Rels. in Moscow, 1969-88; mem. Fiata Working Group Rd. Transport of the Surface Transport Inst. in Zurich. Contbr. articles to profl. jours. Mem. Port of Turin Internat. Propeller Club. Avocations: art, music, sports, travel. Fax: (095) 913 63 62. Office: Concern Sojuzvneshtrans, 17 Gogolevski Blvd, 121019 Moscow Russia

KOSSMANN, STEFAN ANTONI, medical educator, researcher; b. Rybnik, Upper Silesia, Poland, July 22, 1933; s. Jan and Maria (Adamczyk) K.; m. Alina Maria Piotrowska, June 25, 1965; 1 child, Marek. Physician's Diploma, Silesian Med. U., Katowice, Poland, 1957, MD, 1964, PhD, 1976, Prof., 1984. Med. diplomate. Asst. Silesian Med. U., Katowice, 1957-76, asst. prof., 1976-84, assoc. prof., 1984-95, prof., 1995—, head Coll. Postgrad. Edn., 1993—. Contbr. 135 articles to profl. jours. Chmn. Regional Ethics Com. Scientific Rsch., Katowice, 1993—. Lt. Army Sanatorium, 1965-67. Decorated Polonia Restituta Cross State Coun. Rep. of Poland, 1986. Mem. Polish Soc. Allergology, N.Y. Acad. Scis. Roman Catholic. Avocations: classical music, tourism. Office: Clinic Internal Diseases, ul Medykow 14, 40-752 Katowice Poland

KOSTADINOV, DIMITAR TEMELKOV, medical educator; b. Sofia, Bulgaria, Aug. 14, 1956; s. Temelko Dimitrov and Nevena Stanimirova (Ladjova) K.; m. Galina Ivanova; children: Ivaylo, Momtchil. Grad., Higher Inst. Med. Acad., Sofia, 1982; pneumology, Higher Med. Sch., Sofia, 1989; degree in otorhinolaryngology, U. Medicine, Sofia, 1994, MD, 1993. Med. diplomate. Physician Clinic of Pulmonary Disease, Haskovo, Bulgaria, 1982-84; asst. Inst. Pulmonary Disease, Sofia, 1985-88, asst. prof. bronchology dept., 1989—. Author: Laser Application in Clinical Practice, 1988, PDT and Biomedical Lasers, 1992. Mem. Balkan Union Oncology, European Soc. Photobiology, Internat. Photodynamic Assn. Office: Inst Pulmonary Diseases, D Nestorov Str 19, 1431 Sofia Bulgaria

KOSTECKI, JERZY LUCJAN, physicist, researcher; b. Aleksandrów Kujawski, Poland, May 15, 1949; s. Wladyslaw and Lucyna (Koltunska) K.; m. Barbara Wojtowicz, Mar. 11, 1973; 1 child, Marcin. MS in Physics, Mil. U. of Tech., Warsaw, 1974, PhD in Physics, 1990. Asst. Inst. of Plasma Physics and Laser Microfusion, Warsaw, 1974-75, sr. asst., 1975-88, main specialist, 1988-92; main specialist Mil. U. of Tech., Warsaw, 1992-94, asst. prof., 1994—; Contbr. articles profl. jours. including: Laser and Particle Beams, SPIE Proceedings, Jour. Tech. Physics. Mem. Polish Fishing Assn. Avocations: fishing, camping, computers. Address: Żolkiewskiego 54, 04-305 Warsaw Poland Home: Zolkiewskiego 54, 04-305 Warsaw Poland Office: Mil Univ Tech, Mil Univ Tech, Kaliskiego 2, 00-908 Warsaw Poland

KOSTECKI, MARTIN PAUL, industrial engineer; b. St. Louis, Feb. 21, 1944; s. William Valentina and Anna Bernadette (Smugala) K.; m. Mary Jacqueline Davis, Aug. 29, 1970; children: Christina, Daniel, Timothy. Cert. Indsl. Mgmt., Washington U., St. Louis, 1970, BS in Indsl. Mgmt., 1971; MS in Indsl. Adminstrn., Purdue U., 1972. Mgr. indsl. engirng. Wagner Electric Co., St. Louis, 1972-73; dir. indsl. engring. Combustion Engring., St. Louis, 1974-79; v.p. ops. Colt Industries, Inc., St. Louis, 1980-81; dir. engring. Food Ctr. Stores, St. Louis, 1981-82; sr. dir. ops. svcs. ConAgra, Inc., Omaha, Nebr., 1982—; advisor Trend Mfg., Chesterfield, Mo., 1978-82; cons. Futura Coatings, Florissant, Mo., 1980-84. Author: (manuals) Regression Used in Production Standards, 1977, Forecasting Grocery Checkout Activity, 1981; editor: (manual) G.E. Regrssion Analysis Model, 1974. Corp. USMC, 1961-64. Mem. Am. Legion, Oddfellows Club (sec. 1970), Olympia Soccer Club (pres. 1991). Roman Catholic. Avocations: coaching soccer, mentoring youth, fitness. Home: 1217 N 123rd St Omaha NE 68154-1415 Office: ConAgra Inc Five ConAgra Dr Omaha NE 68102

KOSTECKI, WOJCIECH, political scientist, researcher; b. Warsaw, Poland, Feb. 14, 1956; s. Izabella Kaczmarek, Sept. 26, 1981; 1 child, Weronika. MA, Warsaw U., 1978, PhD in Polit. Sci., 1984. Lectr. Warsaw U., 1978-84; head peach rsch. group Polish Inst. for Internat. Affairs, Warsaw, 1988-92; sr. rsch. fellow Inst. for Polit. Studies, Warsaw, 1993-97; head conflict rsch. unit Nat. Def. Acad., Warsaw, 1995-97; prof. Warsaw Sch. Econs., 1998—; dir. Conflict Prevention Inst., Kielce, 1998—; guest scholar Copenhagen Peace Rsch. Inst., 1993-94. Author: Foreign Policy, 1988 (award Polish Inst. Internat. Affairs 1989), Contemporary Peace Research, 1990, Europe After the Cold War, 1996. Global Security Fellows Initiative U. Cambridge, 1997-98. Mem. Internat. Peace Rsch. Assn. (convenor Ea. Europe Commn. 1990—), European Peace Rsch. Assn. (bd. dirs. 1993—), Toda Inst. for Global Policy Studies (internat. adv. bd. 1996—). Avocations: literature, sports, family life. Office: Inst for Polit Studies, 21 Swietokrzyska St, Kielce Poland

KOSTERE, KIM MARTIN, psychologist, consultant; b. Detroit, Jan. 22, 1954; d. Walter Thomas and Shirley Marian (Goebel) K. BA, Mercy Coll., 1977; MA, Ctr. Humanistic Studies, Detroit, 1983; PsyS, Ctr. Humanistic Studies, 1986; PhD, Union Inst., Cin., 1989. Therapist Metro T.A.G., Livonia, Mich., 1978-81, Highland Waterford Ctr., Waterford, Mich., 1981-83; psychologist, v.p. substance abuse svcs. Square Lake Counseling Ctr., Bloomfield Hills, Mich., 1983-90; psychologist, co-dir. Counseling Ctr., P. C., Bloomfield Hills, Mich., 1991-99; cons., 1999—; co-founder, dir. Ont. (Can.) NLP Inst., 1979-80; adj. faculty in psychology Edison C.C., Naples, Fla., 1999—, Capella U., Mpls. Author: A Brief Account of the Center for Humanistic Studies, 1987; co-author: Get the Results You Want, 1987, Maps, Models and the Structure of Reality, 1989, Utilizing the Metaphor: An Ericksonian/NLP Approach, 1992. Democrat. Roman Catholic.

KOSTERIN, SERGEY ALEKSEEVICH, biochemist, researcher; b. Kiev, Ukraine, Aug. 25, 1950; s. Aleksey Grigorievich and Tamara Alekseevna (Andreeva) K.; m. Antonina Vasilievna Bova, Sept. 9, 1952; children: Aleksey, Aleksandr. M. Biology, U. Kiev, 1973; PhD, Biochem. Inst., Kiev, 1976, ScD, 1988. Rsch. scientist Biochem. Inst., Kiev, 1977-80, sr. scientist, 1980-86, head dept., 1987—, vice-dir., 1998—; prof. Kiev-Mogilian Academia, 1986—; vis. prof. McMaster U., Hamilton, Ont., Can., 1990, McMaster U., Hamilton, 1992, The Univ., Halveston, 1992, Liverpool, Eng., 1995, 97. Co-author: The Biochemical Kinetics, 1976, Intracellular Ca 2+ Regulation in Muscles, 1987, Control of Uterine Contractility, 1994; author: Ca 2+ Transport in Smooth Muscles, 1990 (Palladin award Ukranian Acad. Scis. 1992). Recipient awards Internat. Sci. Found., Kiev, Ukraine, 1995, Ministry Sci., Kiev, 1997-98. Mem. Ukrainian Biochem. Soc. Avocations: history of science, classic music, classic literature. Fax: 044 229-63-65. Office: A V Palladin Inst Biochem, 9 Leontovich Str, 252030 Kiev Ukraine

KOSTIC, MILIVOJE, mechanical engineering educator, engineer; b. Bioska, Serbia, Yugoslavia, Mar. 20, 1952; came to U.S., 1986; s. Milos and Vida (Panic) K.; m. Dragica Manic, May 4, 1980; children: Milosh, Marko. BSc, U. Belgrade, Yugoslavia, 1975, MS, 1978; PhD, U. Ill., Chgo., 1984. Registered profl. engr., Ill. Rschr. The Vinca-Belgrade Inst., 1976-78; asst. U. Belgrade, 1978-81; asst. U. Ill., Chgo., 1982-84, rsch. assoc., 1986-88; chief rschr. Cooper & Aluminum Rolling Mills, Sevojno, Yugoslavia, 1985-86; asst. prof. mech. engring. No. Ill. U., DeKalb, 1988-92, assoc. prof., 1992—. Contbr. articles to profl. jours.; reviewer of books, papers and articles. Recipient prize Belgrade U., 1975, C. of C. prize, 1978, Belgrade October prize City of Belgrade, 1978, Yugoslav Nat. award for excellence in h.s. math., 1970; Fulbright grantee, 1981. Mem. ASME, ASEE, Soc. Rheology. Office: No Ill U Engring Bldg Rm 208 Dekalb IL 60115

KOSTIC, PETAR JOVAN, physicist; b. Zemun, Serbia, Nov. 20, 1953; s. Jovan Petar and Mira Branko (Sever) K. BS in Elec. Engring., Physics, U. Belgrade, 1980, MS in Elec. Materials, 1985, PhD, 1988. Rschr., asst. scientist Serbian Acad. Sci., Belgrade, 1981-87; vis. scientist Argonne (Ill.) Nat. Lab., 1987-88; asst. scientist U. Belgrade, 1988-91; vis. scientist, asst. scientist Argonne Nat. Lab., 1991-96; vis. rschr. U. Calif., Santa Cruz, 1997—. Mem. Am. Physics Soc., Materials Rsch. Soc. E-mail: petar@physics.ucsc.edu. Office: U Calif Dept Physics Santa Cruz CA 95064

KOSTIKOV, RAFAEL RAVILOVICH, chemistry educator, researcher; b. Leningrad, USSR, May 31, 1938; s. Ravil Sungatovich Bekmukhametov and Olga Dmitrievna Kostikova; m. Elena Ivanovna Modorova, Apr. 16, 1961; children: Tatiana, Alexei. MSc, Leningrad U., USSR, 1960, PhD, 1967, DSc (hon.), 1980. Cert. chemist. Asst. Leningrad U., USSR, 1962-70, asst. prof., 1970-82; prof. organic chemistry Leningrad U. (name now St. Petersburg State U.), Russia, 1982-85, 89—; chief phys. organic dept. Leningrad U., USSR, 1985-89; invited lectr. Leipzig U., Germany, 1972, Hamburg U., Germany, 1982, 93, 97, Kaiserslautern U., Germany, 1982, Bochum U., Germany, 1983, Bielefeld U., Germany, 1982, 93, 95, Le Mans U., France, 1992, Goettingen U., Germany, 1995, Clausthal U., Germany, 1996, Renne U., France, 1997; vis. prof. chemistry U. Paris, 1997. Author: (with B.V. Ioffe, V.V. Razin) Physical Methods of Determination of Structure of Organic Compounds, 1976, 2d rev. edit. 1984, (with V.Ya. Bespalov) Principles of Theoretical Organic Chemistry, 1982, (with A.P. Molchanov, H. Hopt) Topics in Current Chemistry, 1990, (with A.F. Khlebnikov, M.S. Norikov) Advances in Heterocyclic Chemistry, 1996; mem. editorial bd. Russian Jour. Organic Chemistry, 1989-92, 96—, Modern Problems in Organic Chemistry, 1990—; contbr. over 200 articles to profl. jours. Named Soros prof., J. Soros Internat. Sci. Found., 1994-96; grantee DAAD, Germany, 1996. Mem. Russian Chem. Soc., Russian Acad. Natural Scis. (corr.). Home: Novolitovskaya ul, 194100 Saint Petersburg Russia

KOSTINA, MARINA NIKOLAEVNA, biologist, scientist; b. Moscow, Apr. 17, 1938; d. Nikolay Viktorovich Stepakov and Anna Kuzminichna (Litvinova) S.; m. Nikolay Nikolaevich Kostin, Dec. 31, 1968 (div. Apr. 1978); children: Nikolay Nikolaevich, Ekaterina Nikolaevna. D of Biol. Scis., Russian Inst. Plant Protection, 1993. Libr. asst. USSR State Lenin Libr., Moscow, 1955-58; sr. lab. asst. Mendeleev Chemist-Technol. Inst., Moscow, 1960-62; med. epidemiologist Moscow Disinfection Sta., 1962-65; jr. scientist Sci. Rsch. Inst. for Disinfection and Sterilization, Ministry Pub.

Health, Moscow, 1968-70, sr. scientist, 1970-89; head of lab. biol. insecticides Sci. Rsch. Inst. for Disinfectology, Ministry Pub. Health, 1989—; cons. dept. animal health protection Bayer Ag, Moscow, 1994-99; cons. Ministry Pub. Health Russian Fedn., 1995—. Contbr. numerous articles to profl. jours.; patentee in field. Head trade union med. workers Moscow Disinfection Sta., 1962-65, head cultural sect. trade union, Scientific Rsch. Inst. for Disinfectology, 1965-71. Recipient Medal Vet. of Labor, Supreme Soviet USSR, 1988, Medal Pres. of Russian Fedn., 1997. Mem. Royal Entomol. Soc., Internat. Union for the Study of Social Insects (Russian langs. sect.), Ministry of Agrl. of Russian Fedn. (state commn. on chem. means for plant protection 1989—). Avocation: poetry, tourism. Home: Chertanovskaya Str 39 Bd 2, Apr 135, 113519 Moscow Russia Office: Sci Rsch Inst Disinfect, Nauchny Proyezd 18, 117246 Moscow Russia

KOSTISHKO, BORIS MICHAILOVICH, physicist; b. Saransk, Mordoviya, Russia, Dec. 9, 1965; s. Michail Efremovich and Valentina Borisovna (Kostishko; m. Alla Evgen'evna Kuznetsova, June 16, 1988; children: Boris, Irina. PhD, Moscow State U., 1992. Asst. Moscow State U., 1992-94; docent in physics Ulianovsk (Russia) State U., 1994—, vice dean dept. physics, 1996-2000. Contbr. articles to profl. jours. Grantee Minvuz, 1998, U. Russia, 1998, RFBR, 1999. Home: Avtozavodskay, 432008 Ulyanovsk Russia Office: Ulyanovsk State Univ, L Tolstogo 42, 432 700 Ulyanovsk Russia

KOSTKA, ELMER BOHUMIL, secondary school educator; b. Chgo., Nov. 16, 1922; s. Vincent and Anastasia (Flemer) K.; m. Mildred Musil, June 26, 1954. BS, U. Ill., 1949, MS, 1950. Tchr. indsl. edn. Chgo. Bd. Edn., 1950-88; chmn. tech. dept. Steinmetz H.S., Chgo., 1959-68, editor yrbook., 1964-68. Sgt. U.S. Army Air Corps, 1942-45. Mem. Am. Legion. Avocations: collecting books, coins and stamps. Home: 16154 Pine Dr Tinley Park IL 60477-6311

KOSTKA, RONALD WAYNE, marketing consultant; b. Chgo., Sept. 13, 1931; s. James V. and Marie (Zvolanek) K.; m. Madonna Lou Miller, June 8, 1957 (div. Dec. 1980); children: Paul, Daniel, Jane; m. Irene Mary Harnett, Sept. 14, 1991. BS in journalism, U. Ill., Urbana, 1957. Reporter Champaign News Gazette, Champaign, Ill., 1956-57; copy editor Mpls. Tribune, Mpls., 1957-58; pub. rels. mgr. 3M Co., St. Paul, Minn., 1958-92; cons. mktg. Pub. Rel., Minnetonka, Minn., 1992—. Contbr. articles to profl. jours. Firearms safety instr. State of Minn., Minnetonka, 1967-77. Staff Sgt. USAF, 1951-55, Korea. Decorated Air medal (4 OLC), Purple Heart, Hwarang (Republic of Korea). Mem. DAV, Nat. Muzzle Loading Rifle Assn., NRA, Soc. of Profl. Jours. (cert 1957), Minnetonka Game & Fish Club. Avocations: canoeing, hunting, competitive skeet shooting. Home: 1004 Sunset Dr S Minnetonka MN 55305-1164

KÖSTLER, HERMANN, librarian; b. Wien, Austria, Mar. 21, 1943. Lic.Phil., U. Gregoriana, Rome; Dr.Phil., U. Innsbruck, Austria. Librarian Hochschule für Philosophie, Munich, 1972-74, State's Librs. Eichstätt, Dillingen, Neuburg, Germany, 1974-77, Bayerische Staatsbibliothek, Munich, 1977-81, Generaldirektion, Munich, 1981-83; librarian, dir. Zentralbibliothek, Zürich, 1983—. Office: Zentralbibliothek Zurich, Zähringerplatz 6, CH-8025 Zurich Switzerland

KOSTNER, GERT M., biochemist, educator; b. Vienna, Austria, Nov. 9, 1940; s. Maximilian and Erna Kostner; m. Nahid Asgari, Dec. 23, 1963; children: Karam, Bernd, Frank, Tino. PhD, U. Graz, Austria, 1966. Asst. prof. Med. Rsch. Found., U. Okla., 1969-70; asst. prof. physiol. chemistry U. Graz, 1966-83, pvt. dozent med. biochemistry, 1973, full prof. biochemistry/med. biochemistry, 1983—. Mem. editorial bd. European Jour. Clin. Investigation, 1993, Clin. Chimica Acta, 1990, Atherosclerosis, 1985. E-mail: gerhard.kostner@kfunigraz.ac.at. Home: Gustav Hofer Weg 5, A-8044 Graz Austria Office: Inst Med Biochemistry, Harrachgasse 21, A-8010 Graz Austria

KOSTORZ, GERNOT, physics educator; b. Kattowitz, Germany, Mar. 9, 1941; arrived in Switzerland, 1980; s. Helmut and Johanna (Bänsch) K.; m. Dorothea Rogge, Apr. 29, 1966; children: Anja, Claudia. Diploma in physics, U. Göttingen, Fed. Republic Germany, 1965, D. in Natural Scis., 1968. Postdoctoral appointee Argonne (Ill.) Nat. Lab., 1968-69, rsch. assoc., 1969-71; rsch. physicist Inst. Laue-Langevin, Grenoble, France, 1971-78; lectr. U. Grenoble, 1974-78; sr. scientist Max-Planck-Inst. für Metallforschung, Stuttgart, Fed. Republic Germany, 1978-80; prof. physics Swiss Fed. Inst. Tech., Zürich, Switzerland, 1980—; head Inst. Applied Physics, Swiss Fed. Inst. Tech., Zürich, 1984—, chmn. materials dept., 1984-86, physics dept., 1996-98. Eschbach vis. scholar Northwestern U., Evanston, Ill., 1995; vis. prof. Charles U., Prague, 1996. editor: Neutron Scattering, 1979, High-Tech Ceramics, 1989, Jour. Applied Crystallography, 1999—; co-editor Jour. Applied Crystallography, 1980-89; editor Materials Sci. and Engring. A, 1984—; mem. editl. bd. Zeitschrift für Metallkunde, 1984—; contbr. numerous articles to profl. jours. Mem. Deutsche Gesellschaft für Metallkunde (bd. dirs. 1986-89), Fedn. European Materials Socs. (v.p. 1990, 91, pres. 1992, 93), Inst. Materials, Am. Phys. Soc., Materials Rsch. Soc., European Materials Rsch. Soc. (exec. com. 1989-91), Metals Sci. Soc. Czech Rep. (hon.). Avocation: classical music. Office: Angewandte Physik, ETH Zurich, CH 8093 Zürich Switzerland

KOSTOV, IVAN, government official. Prime min. Govt. of Bulgaria, 1997—. Office: Office of Prime Min, 1 Dondoukov Blvd, 1000 Sofia Bulgaria*

KOSTRZEWSKI, JAN KAROL, epidemiologist, researcher; b. Cracow, Poland, Dec. 2, 1915; s. Jan Michal and Maria (Sulikowska) K.; m. Ewa Maria Sobolewska, Sept. 3, 1948; children: Anna, Magdalena, Piotr, Maria. Diploma, Med. Faculty Warsaw U., 1945; M.D., Jagiellonian U. Med. Faculty, Cracow, 1948; M.P.H., Harvard, 1958; Doctor Honoris Causa (hon.) Mil. Med. Acad., Poland, 1979, Med. Acad., Lublin, Poland, 1985. Medical diplomate. Asst. in vaccine prodn. Nat. Inst. Hygiene, Warsaw, 1942-51, head dept. epidemiology, 1951-61; vice-minister, chief sanitary insp. Ministry of Health, Warsaw, 1962-67, minister health and social welfare, 1968-72; sec. med. sect. Polish Acad. Scis., Warsaw, 1972-79, v.p., 1980-83, pres., 1984-89; prof. epidemiology Warsaw Med. Acad., 1954-58; mem. panel of experts WHO, Geneva, 1960—; v.p. World Health Assembly, Boston, 1969-70, mem. exec. bd., Geneva, 1973-76, chmn., 1975-76; vice-chmn. internat. commn. global eradication smallpox, WHO, Geneva, 1978-79, chmn. expanded programme immunization, global adv. group, 1978-85; chmn. internat. comm. eradication smallpox in India, Nepal, Bhutan, 1977, Ethiopia, 1979; chmn. research strengthening group Spl. Programme for Rsch. and Tng. in Tropical Diseases, 1982-86; chmn. tech. adv. group Diarrhoeal Disease Control Programme, 1985-88; Heath Clark lectr. London Sch. Hygiene and Tropical Med., 1986, 87. Author: Health of Polish People Morbidity and Mortality, 1977; (editor and co-author) three books on communicable diseases in Poland; (co-author and co-editor) Epidemiology: A Guide to Teaching Methods, 1973; (chief editor) Jour. Epidemiological Rev., 1953-88, Polish Science, 1986-89; also numerous sci. papers. Mem., vice chmn. Patriotic movement for nat. rebirth, Warsaw, 1983-89; M.P., 1985-89. Lt. Polish resistance Army, 1944-45, Polish Army, 1948-49. Fellow Indian Nat. Sci. Acad.; mem. Polish Epidemiol. Assn. (mem. exec. com. 1957-88, pres. 1988-91), Acad. Med. Scis. (USSR), Academie Nationale de Medecine Paris (corres.), Internat. Epidemiol. Assn. (council mem. 1977-84, pres. 1977-81), Internat. Ctr. for Diarrhoeal Diseases Rsch. (trustee Bangladesh 1979-85, chmn. 1983-84), Societas Medica Polonorum (hon.), Assn. Microbiologists Epidemiologists USSR (hon.), Polish Epidemiol. Assn. (hon.). Roman Catholic. Avocations: sports; photography. Home: Al Roz 10m6, 00556 Warsaw Poland Office: Polska Akademia Nauk, 00-901 Warsaw Poland

KOSTYUK, INNA FEDOROVNA, medical educator, department chair, consultant; b. Kharkov, Ukraine, July 13, 1937; d. Fedor Alexeevich and Maria Mychailovna Sytanovsky; m. Vladimir Petrovich Kostyuk, Dec. 31, 1957; 1 child, Veronica Vladimirovna Hoffmann. Degree in occupl. pathology, 1st Med. Inst., Moscow, 1972; degree in pedagogy, Med. Inst. Leningrad, 1980. Ordinator Hosp. # 27, Kharkov, 1960-63; postgrad. rschr. dept. hosp. therapy Med. Inst., Kharkov, 1963-66, jr. mem. tchg. staff dept. hosp. therapy, 1966-69, asst. prof. dept. hosp. therapy, 1969-77; prof., chair dept. internal and occupl. diseases Kharkov State Med. U., 1977—; sci. cons. Kharkov State Med. U., 1969—, sci. supr., 1978—. Author: Occupational Diseases, 1998. Mem. Ukraine Ecol. Acad. Scis., Internat. Soc. Cardiology (sec. epidemiology and prevention), N.Y. Acad. Scis. Avocations: skiing, Russian poetry. Home: Culture St 12 Apt 32, 61058 Kharkov Ukraine Office: Med U, Lenin Prospect 4, 61022 Kharkov Ukraine

KOSTYUKOVA, OLGA IVANOVNA, mathematician, researcher; b. Minsk, Belarus, Jan. 28, 1954; d. Ivan Gerasimovich and Lidiya Dmitrievna (Levdikova) K.; m. Dudin Alexander Nikolaevich, Sept. 24, 1977; children: Anastasiya, Sergey. Student, Byelorussian State U., Minsk, Belarus, 1971-76, post-grad., 1976-79, candidate of physics and math., 1980; D in physics and math., Inst. Math. and Mechanics, Ural br. of Acad. Scis. of Russia, Sverdlovsk, Russia, 1991. Jr. rsch. fellow Inst. Math., Minsk, 1980-84, sr. rsch. fellow, 1984-92, leading rsch. fellow, 1992—; assoc. prof. Byelorussian U., Minsk, 1987-91, prof., 1991—. Author: Constructive Methods of Optimization Part III, 1986, Part IV, 1987, Part V, 1999; contbr. articles to profl. jours. Home: Voronyanskii Str 3-1-209, Minsk 220039, Belarus Office: Inst Math, Surganov Str 11, Minsk 220072, Belarus

KOSUGE, SADAO, marine scientist, consultant; b. Tokyo, Apr. 27, 1933; s. Eijirou and Chica Kosuge; m. Fumiyo Kanetsugu; 1 child, Hiroshi. BSc, Tokyo U. Edn., 1957, DSc, 1966. Asst. curator Nat. Sci. Mus., Tokyo, 1957-73; dir. The Coral Mus., Kochi Prefecture, Japan, 1973-84, Inst. Malacology, Tokyo, 1975—, Lab. for Biol. Econ. and Tech. Rsch. for Organic Jewelry, Tokyo, 1992—; lectr. Okayama (Japan) U., 1996-97; sci. cons. The Coral Mus., Kochi, Japan, 1985—, Sea and Shell Mus., Iwate, Japan, 1995—, Sea Treasure Mus., Okinawa, Japan, 1996—. Office: Inst Malacology Tokyo, 6-36 Midoricho 3 chome, Tanashi 188-0002, Japan

KOSYK, WOLODYMIR, history educator; b. Zaluzany, Drohobych, Ukraine, USSR, Nov. 26, 1924; s. Mykola and Maria (Dibuch) K.; m. Tatiana Netchyporuk, Aug. 18, 1956 (dec. July 1971). D, Ukrainian Free U., Munich, Germany, 1975, Sorbonne U., Paris, 1979. Editor-in-chief L'Est Européen, Paris, 1962-99; lectr. Ukrainian Free U., Munich, 1976-84, prof., 1984-99; prof. Nat. U. Ivan Franko, Lviv, Ukraine, 1995—; lectr. Inst. Nat. Langues et Civilisations Orientales, 1984-89. Author: Concentration Camps in USSR, 1962, La Politique de la France à l'égard de l'Ukraine 1917/18, 1981, The Third Reich and Ukraine, 1993, Ukraine in German Documents, 1999. Pres. Union of Ukrainians in France, Paris, 1962-99. Decorated chevalier l'Ordre des Arts et des Lettres French Govt., 1998. Office: W Kosyk, PB 51-06, 75261 Paris Cedex 06, France

KOSZELA, ZBIGNIEW, nuclear engineer, researcher; b. Pulawy, Poland, June 2, 1953; arrived in Sweden, 1990.; s. Jozef and Jadwiga (Molenda) K.; m. Anna Fedyszak, Jan. 24, 1976; children: Przemyslaw, Andrzej, Adam. MS, Warsaw (Poland) U. Tech., 1978, PhD, 1984. Rsch. worker Inst. Nuclear Rsch., Swierk, Poland, 1981-88; head of numerical laboratory Ctrl. Laboratory Radiol. Protection, Warsaw, 1988-90; rsch. engr. ABB Atom AB, Västerås, Sweden, 1990—. Contbr. articles to profl. publs. Home: Herrgärdsgatan 3, 72216 Västerås Sweden Office: ABB Atom AB, Mimer Stora Gatan 3, 72163 Västerås Sweden

KOSZINOWSKI, ULRICH HELMUT, virologist, educator; b. Loetzen, Germany, Aug. 2, 1944; m. Elke Renate Ossig, Sept. 15; children: Michael Arndt, Judith Sophie, Julia Alice. MD, Georg-August U., Göttingen, 1969, Habilitation Med. Microbiol. & Hygiene, 1975. Asst. scientist Georg-August U., 1971-76; vis. scientist London U., 1976-77; scientist German Cancer Rsch. Ctr., Heidelberg, Germany, 1978-80; dir. Fed. Rsch. Ctr. for Animal Virus Diseases, Tübingen, Germany, 1980-87; prof., chmn. virology dept. U. Ulm, Germany, 1987-93, U. Heidelberg, 1993-96; prof. U. Munich, 1996—. Contbr. articles to Jour. Virology, Cell, Nature, Jour. Exptl. Medicine, Proceedings Nat. Acad. Sci. Mem. Am. Soc. Microbiology, Brit. Soc. for Immunology, Gesellschaft für Virologie. Achievements include research in antiviral immune control, biology of herpesvirus infection, immune evasion of herpesviruses, cloning of herpes virus genomes as infectious bacterial plasmids. Home: Klementinenstr 14, D 80805 Munich Germany Office: Max von Pettenkofer Inst, Pettenkoferstr 9a, D 80336 Munich Germany

KOSZTOLANYI, CHARLES CORNEILLE, retired research engineer; b. Budapest, Hungary, Oct. 10, 1926; arrived in France, 1957; s. Károly and Amanda (Ribarcz) K.; m. Suzanne Veillat, July 11, 1959; children: Anne-Marie, Marie-Claire. Degree in chem. engr., Tech. U., Budapest, 1949; D of Engring., U. Nancy, France, 1964, DSc, 1971. Cert. engr. Engr. Hungarian Nat. Rlwy. Corp., Budapest, 1949-57; rsch. engr. Ctr. Radiogeol. Rsch., Nancy, 1959-80, Ctr. for Rsch. Geol. Uranium, Vandoeuvre, France, 1980-88; prof. chemistry Geol. H.S., Nancy, 1972-88; head of geochronol. lab. Ctr. Radiogeol. Rsch., 1965-71, head chem. dept., 1971-80; head Raman Microprobe Lab., Ctr. for Rsch. Geol. Uranium, 1980-88. Author: 35 sci. publs.; Emlékezéseim, 1993; D'un côté à l'autre du Rideau de Fer, Pensee Universelle Paris 1997; A Gondviselés utján, Lakitelek, 1998. Treas. Nancy-Metz Acad. sect. CFTC Trade Union, 1983—. Mem. Hungarian Acad. Scis. (hon.), Hungarian Assn. Cleve., Lorrainese French-Hungarian Assn. (pres. 1978—). Avocations: French and Hungarian literature, history, stamp collecting.

KOSZTOLÁNYI, GYÖRGY, geneticist, educator; b. Szekszárd, Hungary, Mar. 10, 1942; s. György and Sára (Mirth) K.; m. Zsuzsanna Cselényi, Oct. 17, 1969; children: Rita, Szabolcs. MD, Med. U. Pecs, Hungary, 1966; PhD, Med. U. Pecs, 1993; DSc, Hungarian Acad. Scis., 1989. Cert. specialist in pediat. and human genetics. Asst. pathologist Pecs County Hosp., 1966-71; asst. prof. dept. pediat. U. Pecs, 1971-93, prof. genetics, 1994—. Home: Alkotmany 32, H-7624 Pecs Hungary Office: Univ Med Sch Dept Med Genet, Jozsef A u 7, H-7623 Pecs Hungary

KOTAB, PETR, lawyer, educator; b. Prague, Bohemia, Czechoslovakia, June 1, 1963; s. Vladimir and Eva (Kadarova) K. LLM, Charles U., 1985, JD, 1986, postgrad., 1986-89. Bar: Czech Republic. Comml. lawyer Prague, 1990-91; coun. Altheimer & Gray, Prague, 1991-95, ptnr., 1995—; lectr. Charles U. Law Sch., Prague, 1985—, Ctrl. European U., Prague, 1992-93, U. Econs., Prague, 1992-99; chmn. supervisory bd. Creditanstalt Czech Investment Fund, Prague, 1991-96; mem. supervisory bd. Komercni Banka, Prague, 1997-98; mem. Commn. Fin. Law Legis. Coun., Prague, 1991-92; mem. Privatization Commn. Ministry Industry, Prague, 1990-93; appellate commn. Czech Securities Commn., Prague, 1998—. Co-author: Foreign Investment in Central and Eastern Europe, 1993, (textbook) Introduction to Financial Science and Financial Law, vol. 1, 1994, vol. 2, 1995, Financial Law, 1995, 2d edit., 1999, Doing Business in the Czech Republic, 1999. Mem. Czech Advocacy Chamber, Internat. Bar. Assn., Internat. Fiscal Assn. Avocations: music, numismatics, modern technology, literature. Office: Altheimer & Gray, Platnerska 4, 110 00 Prague 1, Czech Republic

KOTAITE, ASSAD, United Nations agency administrator; b. Nov. 6, 1924; s. Adib Kotaite and Kamle Abousamra; m. Monique Ayoub, 1983. Degree, French U., Beirut, U. Paris, Acad. Internat. Law, The Hague. Head legal and internat affairs, dir. civil aviation Lebanon, 1953-56; Lebanese rep. Coun. of Internat. Civil Aviation Orgn., 1956-70, sec. gen., 1970-76, pres., 1976—; pres. Internat. Ct. Aviation and Space Arbitration, Paris, 1995—. Office: Internat Civil Aviation Orgn, 999 University St Ste 12.20, Montreal, PQ Canada H3C 5H7

KOTAL, PETR, biochemist, researcher; b. Tabor, Czech Republic, Mar. 11, 1957; s. Vaclav and Ludmila (Hulkova) K.; m. Monika Kalatova, Jan. 31, 1991; children: Veronika, Tereza, Jakub. Diploma in clin. biochemistry, Charles U., Prague, Czech Republic, 1982, PhD, 1986, DSc, 1996. Rschr. Charles U., 1981-90, head clin. lab., 1990-92; mgr. R & D, Procter and Gamble, Prague, 1992-97, Procter & Gamble Europe, Germany, 1997-99; regulatory mgr. for Ctrl. and Ea. Europe Procter & Gamble Europe, Prague, 1999—; postdoctoral rschr. Leuven (Belgium) U., 1988-89; prin. scientist, mem. med. faculty Charles U., 1990—. Co-author (textbook chpt.) Management of Liver Disorders, 1993; contbr. numerous articles to profl. jours.; patentee in field (Czech & Slovak Gastroenterology award, 1998). Subchmn. Deregulation Com. Prime Min., Prague, 1996-97. Mem. Biochem. Soc., Hepatol. Soc., Czech Soap and Detergent Industry Assn. (bd. dirs.), Sports Club (chmn. 1996—). Avocations: cross country skiing, wildwater canoeing, orienteering run, family. Home: NA Borovem 8, 14200 Prague Czech Republic

KOTANKO, PETER, physician, researcher; b. Braunau, Upper Austria, Austria, May 16, 1957; s. Alfred and Elfriede (Krisai) K.; m. Ulrike Türke, July 22, 1988; children: Julia, Magdalena. MD, U. Innsbruck (Austria), 1982; diploma in nephrology, U. London, 1996. Physiology rschr. U. Innsbruck (Austria), 1982-87, registrar dept. medicine, 1987-89; cons. Hosp. Barmherzige Brüder, Graz, Austria, 1989—; lectr. in internal medicine U. Innsbruck, Austria. Contbr. articles to profl. jours. Recipient Young Researcher award Ministry of Sci., Vienna, 1979, Otto Loewi award Austrian Hypertension Soc., 1994, David Kerr award Royal Postgrad. Med. Sch., London, 1996. Mem. Am. Diabetes Assn., N.Y. Acad. Scis. Roman Catholic. Avocations: scuba diving, theatre, travel. E-mail: kotanko1@eunet.et. Office: Krankenhaus Barnherzige Brüder, Marschallgasse 12, A-8020 Graz Austria

KOTARBIŃSKI, JACEK, marketing consultant; b. Ciechanów, Mazowsze, Poland, Sept. 25, 1967; parents Zygmunt Bogdan Myczewski and Danuta Urszula Zgliczyñska; married; children: Dominika, Maciej. Diploma betriebrsiwirt, Kepler U., Linz, Austria, 1992; M of Mktg. Adminstrn., Westerham Acad., Munich, Germany, 1996. Mktg. cons. Micon Mktg. Cons., Gdynia, Poland, 1991—. Mem. Assn. Econ. Cons. Fax: 48 58 621 76 18. E-mail: micon@itnet.pl. Office: Micon Mktg Cons, Pomorska 48, 81-314 Gdynia Pomorze, Poland

KOTARSKI, JAN, obstetrician-gynecologist, educator; b. Lublin, Poland, Apr. 26, 1949; s. Czesław and Jadwiga (Ossowska) K.; m. Anna Izabela Plochow, Sept. 28, 1973; children: Małgorzata, Maria. Degree in medicine, U. Med. Sch., Lublin, 1972, MD, 1979, Habilitation, 1990. Intern U. Med. Sch., Lublin, 1972-73, asst., 1972-79, cons., 1979-99, prof., 1999—. Co-author: Klimakterium, 1996 (award Min. of Health 1997), Prostaglandins in Obstetrics and Gynecology, 1998 (award Min. of Health 1999); author: Endometriosis, 1997 (award Min. of Health 1998). Mem. com. Solidarity Trade Union, 1980—. Recipient award Polish Ministry of Health, 1996, Rsch. Achievement award, 1997, Pub. award, 1999. Mem. Polish Gynecol. Soc., N.Y. Acad. Scis., World Endometriosis Soc. Roman Catholic. Avocations: tennis, hunting. E-mail: kotarski@eskulap.am.lublin.pl. Office: I Dept Gynecol Surgery, ul Staszica 16, 20-082 Lublin Poland

KOTERA, NOBUO, electronic engineering educator; b. Osaka, Japan, Dec. 26, 1938; s. Yoshinobu and Asako (Hatta) K.; m. Kaoru Arichi, Apr. 20, 1968. BA, Kyoto U., 1963, MA, 1965; PhD, Osaka U., 1971. Rsch. assoc. Cen. Rsch. Lab. Hitachi Ltd., Kokubunji City, Tokyo, 1965-68, researcher, 1968-79, sr. researcher, 1979-89; prof. Kyushu Inst. Tech., Iizuka City, Fukuoka, Japan, 1989—. RCA scholar, 1962; recipient IR100 award, 1975. Avocation: travel. Office: Kyushu Inst Tech, Kawazu 680-4, Iizuka Fukuoka 820, Japan

KOTHARI, JHANWAR LAL, gemstone trading company executive; b. Bikaner, Rajasthan, India, Sept. 3, 1947; s. Lal Chand and Mohini Devi (Sethia) K.; m. Leela Devi Minny, May 6, 1971; children: Manisha, Neal. BA, Rajasthan U., Jaipur, India, 1968; postgrad., Gemological Inst., L.A., 1970. V.p. Gemeralds Inc., San Francisco, 1970-82; mng. dir. Kothari & Co. Ltd., Bangkok, Thailand, 1982—; v.p. Manifold Returns, Inc., L.A., 1989—; bd. dirs. Kothari (Hong Kong) Co. Ltd., Southwealth Pte. Ltd., Singapore, Republic of Singapore, Kothari & Co. (Taiwan) Ltd. Pres. Sri Jain Coll., Rajasthan U., Bikaner, India, 1968. Mem. U.S. C. of C., Gemology Inst. Am. Alumni Assn. Jain. Avocations: reading, table tennis, travel. Office: Kothari and Co (Thailand), 297 Surawongse Rd # 701, Bangkok 10500, Thailand

KOTHARI, RAJIV DINESH, chemical engineer, researcher; b. Kuala Lumpur, Malaysia, Nov. 30, 1975; s. Dinesh Kumar and Sudha Dinesh (Malani) K. B.Eng with honors, U. Sheffield (Eng.), 1996. Human resources exec. Capital Edge Pvt. Ltd., Kuala Lumpur, 1993-94; lectr. Taylor's Coll., Kuala Lumpur, 1997-98; dir. Millennium Pvt. Merchants Ltd., Kuala Lumpur, 1998—; engr. Dept. Chem. Engring., Sheffield, Eng., 1996—; tech. cons. Setiavilla Resources Pvt. Ltd., Kuala Lumpur, 1999—. Contbr. articles to profl. jours. Mem. Inst. Chem. Engrs. (grantee 1998), SPIE, Inst. of Physics. Avocations: hockey, travel, squash, politics. Office: Dept Chem Engring, Newcastle St, Sheffield S1 3JD South Yorkshire, England

KOTHARI, SHANKER LAL, botany educator, researcher; b. Chandras, India, Dec. 28, 1954; s. Sukh Lal and Tammu Devi (Bohra) K.; m. Pramila Devi Pokharana, June 22, 1978; children: Priyanka, Aditi. BSc, U. Udaipur, 1974, MSc, 1976; PhD, U. Rajasthan, 1984. Asst. prof. Govt. Coll., Rajasthan, 1976-79; asst. prof. U. Rajasthan, Jaipur, India, 1979-89, assoc. prof. dept. botany, 1989-95, 96—; prof., head dept. botany MDS U., Ajmer, India, 1995-96; Fulbright scholar U. Ill., 1983-84; Commonwealth acad. staff fellow, Nottingham, Eng., 1989-90, Rockefeller Biotech. career fellow, 1991-96. Mem. editl. bd IBS; contbr. more than 85 articles to profl. jours. Recipient Prof. Hiralal Chakravarty award ISCA, 1993, Nahar award Rajasthani Welfare Assn., 1996, Citizens award Jaipur Nagar Nigam, 1997. Fellow Nat. Acad. Scis. India, Indian Bot. Soc. Avocation: reading. Home: 12 Kalyan Colony, D-Block, Malviya Nagar, Jaipur India Office: U Rajasthan, Dept Botany, Jaipur India

KOTHARI, SWATANTRA SINGH, economist; b. Calcutta, India, 1930; s. Shiva Singh and Ratan Kunwar K.; m. Rajkumari Lodha, 1951; 4 daughters. Chartered Taxation Advisor, Chartered Inst. Taxation, London, 1952; PhD in Econs., North Bengal U., Siliguri, India, 1998. Chartered acct. Sr. ptnr. S.S. Kothari & Co., Calcutta, 1953—; chmn., dir. Kothari Mgmt. & Indsl. Consultants Ltd., Calcutta; dir., mem. mgmt. com. Bank of India, Bombay, 1989-95; dir. Jayshree Tea & Industries Ltd., Calcutta, Nicco-Uco Alliance Credit Ltd., Calcutta; trustee, mem. exec. com. Internat. Inst. Devel. Studies, 1980; exec. pres. Ctr. for Econs. & Taxation Studies, Calcutta, 1976—. Author New Economic Strategies for Growth in Developing Countries, 1992, also articles in field. Mem. Parliament (Lok Sabha), New Delhi, 1967-70 (mem. Pub. Undertakings Com., Cons. Com. Ministry of Fin., Com. for West Bengal). Recipient Medal of Honor Am. Biog. Inst., 1988, Samaj Ratna Rajasthan Vidyapeeth, 1980. Fellow Inst. Chartered Accts. of India (mem. coun.), Inst. Mgmt. (London), Royal Economic Soc. (London); mem. Indian C. of C., Calcutta Club. Hindu. Avocation: writing dramas. Office: S S Kothari & Co, 21 Old Court House St, 700 001 Calcutta India

KOTIL, ROSTISLAV, defense attache; b. Ceske, Velenice, Czech Republic, Mar. 28, 1949; s. Vaclav and Blazena (Matuskova) Kotil; m. Dagmar Sindlerova, Mar. 10, 1973; children: Richard, Valerie, Rostislav. Grad., Mil. Acad. Commd. lt. Czech. Rep. Armed Forces, 1971, advanced through grades to maj. gen., 1994, platoon comdr. to co. comdr., 1971-74, tank bat. comdr., operational staff officer 1st tank divsn., chief of staff 3rd mechanized regiment in Louny, 1979-81, regiment comdr., 1981-87, dep. divsn. comdr. 19th mechanized divsn. in Plzen, chief of staff mechanized divsn., 1990-91; strategic planning dir. CSFR Fed. Ministry of Def., Prague, 1991-92, divsn. comdr. 4th motorized divsn. in Havlickuv Brod, 1993-96, first dep. of the chief of ACR gen. staff, 1996-98; def. attaché of the Czech Rep. Washington, 1998—; chief mil. liaison officer UNPROFOR, Zagreb, Croatia, 1993; sector South comdr. UNPROFOR/UNCRO, Croatia, 1994-95. Recipient Medal in Svc. for Peace UN, 1994, Meritious Svc. medal Can. Govt., 1995. Avocations: photography, sports. Office: Embassy of the Czech Republic 3900 Spring of Freedom St Washington DC 20008

KOTIN, MIKHAIL LVOVICH, linguistics educator; b. Moscow, Mar. 13, 1959; s. Lev Yakovlevich and Viktoriya Yevgenyevna (Akinchevich) K.; m. Tatyana Innokentyyavna Barkovskaya, Oct. 3, 1981; 1 child, Andrey. Diploma in German, Humboldt U., Berlin, 1982; PhD, Lomonosov U., Moscow, 1989; Doctor Habil., Humboldt U., Berlin, 1995. Asst. prof. Coll. of Grafic Arts, Moscow, 1982-85; rschr. Lomonosov U., Moscow, 1985-88, sr. lectr., 1988-91; assoc. prof. State U. of Pedagogy, Moscow, 1991-93, prof., 1996—; rsch. fellow Humboldt U., Berlin, 1993-94, 98; Editor: Das Wort, Moscow, and Bonn, Germany. Author: (book) Genus verbi in German, 1998; contbr. articles to profl. jours. Sgt. Russian Army, 1982-84. Recipient prize Humboldt U. Berlin, 1983, rsch. fellowship Alexander Humboldt Found., Bonn, 1993-94. Mem. Internat. Assn. of Germanic Studies, Russian Club of the Fellows of the Alexander Humboldt Found., Societas Linguistica Europeae. Mem. Russian Orthodox Ch. Avocations:

lit., philosophy, theology, classical music. Home: Nagatinskaya nabereznaya, 18-152, RU115533 Moscow Russia Office: State Univ of Pedagogy, Prospekt Vernadskogo 88, RU117218 Moscow Russia

KOTKIN, DAVID See COPPERFIELD, DAVID

KOTLARCHUK, IHOR O. E., lawyer; b. Ukraine, July 31, 1943; came to U.S., 1946, naturalized, 1957; s. Emil and Lidia N. (Maceluch) K. BS in Fin., Fordham U., 1965, JD, 1968; LLM, Georgetown U., 1974, MA in Govt., 1982. Bar: N.Y. 1969, D.C. 1972, U.S. Ct. Mil. Appeals, U.S. Tax Ct., U.S. Supreme Ct. Sr. trial atty. criminal sect. tax divsn. U.S. Dept. Justice, Washington, 1973-78, civil sect. tax divsn., 1978-80, fraud sect. criminal divsn., 1980-84, internal security sect. criminal divsn., 1984-97; retired, 1999. Pres. Ukranian Assn. Washington, 2000—. With U.S. Army, 1969-73, Vietnam; judge advocate gen., 1996; ret. col. USAR. Decorated Bronze star, Legion of Merit. Mem. ABA, N.Y. State Bar, D.C. Bar Assn., Res. Officers Assn., Phi Alpha Delta. Ukrainian Catholic. Address: 205 S Lee St Alexandria VA 22314-3307

KOTLER, RONALD LEE, physician, educator; b. Pitts., June 10, 1956; s. Milton and Marion (Oppenheimer) K.; m. Jane Ellyn Cobin, Feb. 20, 1982; children: Jennifer, Rachel, Drew. BA, Emory U., 1978; MD, U. Pa., 1982. Diplomate Am. Bd. Internal Medicine, Am. Bd. Pulmonary Disease, Am. Bd. Critical Care Medicine, Am. Bd. Sleep Medicine. Intern Pa. Hosp., Phila., 1982-83, resident, 1983-85; fellow pulmonary disease Hosp. U. Pa. Phila., 1985-87; clin. assoc. in medicine U. Pa. Sch. Medicine, Phila., 1987-88, clin. asst. prof., 1988-95, 97—; clin. asst. prof. Thomas Jefferson U., Phila., 1994—; co-dir. hosp. sleep lab. Pa. Hosp., Phila., 1991—. Contbr. articles to profl. jours. Lectr. City Phila. Dept. Health, Phila., 1988, 89, Pa. Hosp., 1995. Fellow ACP, Am. Coll. Chest Physicians; mem. Am. Thoracic Soc., Phi Beta Kappa, Omicron Delta Kapp, Alpha Omega Alpha. Avocation: tennis. Office: Casey Lugano Kotler Assocs 700 Spruce St Ste 500 Philadelphia PA 19106-4027

KOTLYAR, VICTOR VICTOROVICH, computer-optics researcher; b. Orenburg, Russia, Jan. 15, 1957; s. Victor Ivanovich and Alisa Victorovna (Lebedeva) K.; m. Margarita Innocentyevna Shanina, July 15, 1978; children: Maria, Ekaterine. MS in Physics, Samara (Russia) State U., 1979; Candidate in Physics and Math., State U., Saratov, Russia, 1988; D in Physics and Math., Inst. Unique Instrumentation, Moscow, 1992. Jr. rschr. Lebedev Phys. Inst., Samara, 1981-87, sr. rschr., 1987-88, 1988-89, head of group, 1989-91; head lab. Image Processing Sys. Inst., Samara, 1991—; lectr. Samara State Aerospace U., 1988-93, assoc. prof., 1993-95, prof., 1995—; acad. sec. Image Processing Sys. Inst., Samara, 1988—. Co-author: Iterative Methods for DOE Computation, 1997, Methods of Computer Optics, 2000; contbr. articles to profl. jours. Grantee Soros Found., Moscow, 1993, Russian Found. for Basic Rsch., Moscow, 1997; recipient Gov.'s Regional prize Adminstrn. of the Samara Region, 1998; hon. diploma Russian Acad. Sci., 1999. Mem. Internat. Soc. for Optical Engring., Internat. Assn. on Pattern Recognition. Avocations: tourism, car travelling. Home: Apt 145, 1 Molodyezhnaya St, 443115 Samara Russia Office: 151 Molodoguardeiskaya St, 443001 Samara Russia

KOTOLUP, JAMES ALEXANDER, finance company executive, accountant; b. Alliance, Ohio, Jan. 7, 1971; s. Nick and Linda K. (McIlvain) K. Assoc. Degree, Stark Tech. Coll., 1991. CFO Mobile Cons., Inc., Alliance, 1991—; tax acct. Jak Enterprise, Alliance, 1993—. Mem. Nat. Soc. Pub. Accts. Avocations: stock market, auto racing, wood working. Office: Mobile Cons Inc 111 Glamorgan St Alliance OH 44601-2944

KOTONSKI, WLODZIMIERZ, composer; b. Warsaw, Aug. 23, 1925; s. Stansilaw and Marianna Krysiak; m. Jadwiga Chlebowska, 1951; 1 child, Piotr. MMus, Warsaw State Higher Sch. Music. With Exptl. Music Studio Polish Radio and Elec. Music Studio of Westdeutscher, Cologne, 1966-67; asso. prof. composition, ord. prof., head elec. music studio F. Chopin Acad. Music, Warsaw, 1993-95, ret., 1995; chief music dir. Polish Radio and TV, 1974-76; vis. prof. composition, Stockholm, 1971, Buffalo, N.Y. 1978, Jerusalem, 1990; lectr. on composition, U.S.A., 1982, Republic of Korea, 1994-95. Compositions include orch. and chamber music, elect. and tape music and instrumental theatre; author: Goralski and Zbojnickim, 1956, Percussion Instruments in the Modern Orchestra, 1967, Electronic Music, 1989, Lexicon of Modern Percussion, 1999. Music advisor Chmn.'s Com. for Radio and TV, 1977-79. Recipient Minister of Culture and Art prize 2d class, 1973, 1st class, 1989, prize of Pres. Polish Radio and TV Com. 1st class, 1979, Gold Cross of Merit, Officer's Cross Order Polonia Restituta. Mem. Polish Composer's Union (dep. chmn. 1965-71), Polish Sect. Internat. Soc. Contemporary Music (chmn. 1983-89).

KOTOULAS, OTHON BASIL, physician, educator; b. Athens, Greece, July 18, 1932; s. Basil J. and Helen A. (Evangelides) K.; m. Angela S. Sideris, Jan. 22, 1961; children: Basil, Sofocles. MD, Athens U., 1957; PhD, McGill U., Montreal, 1970. Resident in internal medicine Athens Mcpl. Hosp., 1958-60; resident in internal medicine dept. clin. therapeutics Athens U., 1960-63; rsch. fellow, resident in pathology Washington U., St. Louis, 1963-67; fellow, sr. resident in pathology McGill U., Montreal, 1967-70; asst. in electron microscopy dept. clin. therapeutics Athens U., 1970-73, from registrar to assoc. prof. dept. histology and embryology, 1973-77; prof., chmn. dept. anatomy, histology and embryology U. Ioannina, Greece, 1977-99, emeritus prof., 2000—, dean Med. Sch., 1979-80; mem. com. biomed. rsch. Nat. Health Sys., Athens, 1984-87, bd. accreditation of titles (Dikatsa), 1984-87. Editor: Histology, 1986, 94, 97; acting editor Iatriki, 1975-77; contbr. articles to profl. jours. Candidate nat. parliament Pasok Party, Ioannina, 1989-93, vice sec. party Ioannina, 1990-92. Lt. Greek Air Force, 1958-60. Mem. Soc. Pathology and Pathologic Anatomy, Assn. Med. Studies, Assn. Des Anatomistes (France), N.Y. Acad. Scis. Greek Orthodox. Avocation: chess. Home: 15 Thiseos St, Kastri, 14671 Athens Greece Office: U Ioannina Med Sch, Dept Anatomy, Histology and Embryology, 45110 Ioannina Greece

KOTRLA, MIROSLAV, physicist; b. Pribram, Czech Republic, Dec. 28, 1957; s. Miroslav and Gizela (Danisovska) K.; m. Jindřiška Röschová, Mar. 31, 1982; children: Jakub, Jan. RNDr, Charles U., 1982, PhD, 1988. Rsch. worker Inst. of Physics/ČSAV, Prague, 1982-89, 91, 1993—; postdoctoral fellow Internat. Sch. for Advanced Studies, Trieste, Italy, 1990, U. Genova, Italy, 1992; referee Phys. Rev. jour., Jour. Physics, 1997—; external tchr. Faculty of Maths. and Physics, Prague, 1994—. Contbr. articles to profl. jours. Rsch. grantee Acad. Sci. of Czech Republic, Prague, 1993-94, 95-97, Dept. Edn. Czech Republic, 1999—. Mem. Union of Czechoslovak Mathematicians and Physicists (phys. sci. sect.). Avocations: yoga, philately, strategic games. Office: Inst of Physics/Acad Sci, of Czech Rep/Na Slovance 2, CZ 18221 Prague 8 Czech Republic

KOTSCHY, PETER, dentist; b. Vienna, May 11, 1939; s. Emmerich and Frida (Thürmer) K.; m. Christine Rischer, Sept. 28, 1968 (div. Nov. 1996); children: Andrea, Ines, Klaus; m. Martina Kainhofer, June 2, 1997. MD, U. Vienna, 1966, DDM, D of Oral Surgery, 1968. Dentist in pvt. practice, Vienna, 1968—; lector U. Vienna, 1988-96; v.p. Postgrad. Dental Inst. Austria, Vienna, 1976-82. Author: Medizinisches Jahrbuch, 1988, 95; contbr. articles to Internat. Jour. Periodontics and Restorative Dentistry, Austrian Jour. Stomatology, others. Founder Prophylaxis project Vienna Kindergarden, 1978, Austria Prophylaxis Programme, 1980. Mem. Austrian Soc. Periodontology (pres. 1991—), Vienna Drs. Assn. (officer 1968—), Austrian Dental Fedn. (bd. dirs. 1966—), Austrian Dental Soc. (bd. dirs. 1978—, v.p. 1990—, Sci. award 1992), Internat. Coll. Dentists (pres. European sect. 1996-97, bd. dirs. 1986—). Avocations: golf, skiing, music, theatre. Office: Lindengasse 41/15, A-1070 Vienna Austria

KOTSERIDIS, YORGOS, food chemist, consultant; b. Thessaloniki, Greece, Aug. 25, 1969; s. Stelios Kotseridis and Martha Soi. Diploma in agrl. engring., Aristotelium U., Thessaloniki, 1992; M in Enology, Faculty Pharmacy, Montpellier, France, 1994; PhD in Enology & Viticulture with honors, Faculty Enology, Bordeaux, France, 1999. Cert. in food tech. Wine analyst Tantalis SA, Thessaloniki, 1991-92; enologist JP Moueix ETS, Bordeaux, 1995, Chateau Calon Segur SA, Bordeaux, 1996; chem. analyst Martin Vialatte/Enological Products, Montepellier, 1999, Imeca-Delatofolla, Montpellier, 1999; head food tech. dept. Erevnon Ltd./R&D, Thessaloniki, 1999—; cons. Hatzimichalis SA, Athens, Greece, 1995-96, Erevnon Ltd. State scholar, 1994-95, 96-99. Avocations: basketball, music. Fax: 003031902132. Office: Erevnon Ltd, Poliviou 81-83, GR-54351 Thessaloniki Greece

KOTSOS, VASILIOS ANDREAS, physicist, researcher; b. Atalanti, Fthiotidos, Greece, Jan. 17, 1956; s. Andreas Kotsos and Pagona Kotsou (Nikolaou) A. BS in Physics, U. Athens, Greece, 1980, MS in Electronic Physics, 1984; PhD in Clusters Physics, U. Thessaloniki, Greece, 1996. Physicist Higher Sch., Atalanti, 1980-81; electronic physicist Tech. Inst., Lamia, Greece, 1987-96; rschr. U. Thessaloniki, 1990—. Author: Hilbert Spaces and Its Applications, 1990. With Greek Army, 1984-86. Recipient Pened award Ministry of Tech., Greece, 1991-94. Mem. Greek Phys. Soc., Am. Phys. Soc. Achievements include research in theoretical and experimental investigation on electronic structure, magic numbers, spectra, discontinuities on spectra, effective potentials, radii and others on atomic clusters and especially on metal clusters. Office: Tech Ednl Instn, 3d Km ONR Lamia-Athens, 35200 Lamia Greece

KOTTA, ANANDA MOHAN, engineering educator; b. Yanam, India, Jan. 25, 1943; s. Venkata Raju and Kamalavathi Kotta; m. Rama Lakshmi Tabjulla, Mar. 11, 1974; children: Lathika, Sahithi. BSc, Andhra (India) U., 1963, B in Engring., 1966; M in Tech., Jawaharal Nehru Tech. U., Kakinada, India, 1980. Assoc. lectr., dir. tech. edn. Andhra Pradesh, India, 1969-75; lectr. Coll. Engring. Jawaharal Nehru Tech. U., Kakinada, India, 1975-83, asst. prof., 1983-97, prof., 1997—; head dept. electronics and comm. engring. Jawaharal Nehru Tech. U., Kakinada, 1999—; pres. tchrs. assn.; student advisor; placement and tng. advisor; cons. engr. various cos. Program officer Nat. Svc. Scheme, 1980-82; active various local civic activities, 1991-94. Fellow Instn. Electronics and Telecom. Engrs.; mem. Indian Soc. Tech. Edn., Instn. Engrs. Hindu. Avocation: social service. Home: 67-11-3A Lalbahadur Nagar, Kakinada 533003, India Office: Coll Engring, Jawaharal Nehru Tech U, Kakinada 533003, India

KOTTAPALLI, SESHAGIRIRAO, biochemical educator; b. Baruva, India, Feb. 7, 1962; s. Narasayya and Nirmaladevi (Badiya) K.; m. Sylaza Gollamandala; children: Narassayya Vamsi, Bhagyarekha. MS, Nagarjuna U., India, 1985; M in Philosophy, U. Hyderabad, India, 1986; PhD, U. Hyderabad, 1992. Lectr. U. Hyderabad, India, 1990—. Inventor in field. Recipient Sci. and Tech. fellowship, JST, Japan, 1996-98. Mem. Soc. Biological Chemists, The Orchid Soc. India. Home: B-21 Faculty Qts, 500 046 Hyderabad India Office: Dept Plant Scis, U Hyderabad, 500 046 Hyderabad India

KOTTAYIL, SANTOSH GEORGE, pharmaceutical development executive; b. Manalady, Kerala, India, Apr. 18, 1963; came to U.S., 1987; s. Thuruthel Varkey and Graceamma (Joseph) Mani; m. Anita George, Dec. 30, 1993. BSc, U. Poona, Pune, India, 1983, MSc, 1985; PhD, U. Ky., 1993. Rsch. intern DuPont Merck, Wilmington, Del., 1991; sr. scientist Oramed, Mundelein, Ill., 1992; sr. scientist in pharm. devel. Unimed Pharms. Inc., Buffalo Grove, Ill., 1993-95, mgr. pharm. devel., 1995-98, assoc. dir., 1998-99, dir., 1999—; mem. selection com. for dean Coll. Arts and Scis., U. Ky., Lexington, 1991. Mem. Am. Chem. Soc. Achievements include synthesis and evaluation of novel and improved chemical entities for the treatment of pain. Avocations: hiking, cycling. Home: 8068 Rfd Long Grove IL 60047-4814 Office: Unimed Pharms Inc 2150 E Lake Cook Rd Buffalo Grove IL 60089-1862

KOTTER, LUDWIG, food scientist; b. Augsburg, Germany, Mar. 21, 1920; s. Dominikus and Kreszentia (Ertle) K.; m. Elisabeth Fischer (dec. Feb. 1965); children: Johanna, Thomas, Florentine; m. Helga Lennartz, Aug. 3, 1984. PhD, U. Munich, Federal Republic of Germany, 1951; PhD (hon.), U. Utrecht, The Netherlands, 1971. Prof., head dept. hygiene and tech. of food U. Munich, 1960-89, dean Sch. Vet. Medicine, 1963-65, rector magnificus, 1965-67; prof. Tech. U. Munich, 1972-88; pres. Soc. Nutrition Biology, Germany, 1964-79; mem. Commn. for Comprehensive Reform of Food Law, German Food and Health Adminstrn., 1964-70; presidium Fed. German Food Law Commn., 1964-88; exec. officer Bavarian Commn. Rectors, 1965-67; presiding bd. Commn. of Rectors of West German Univs., 1966-68; mem. Fed. German Health Coun., 1967-85; mem. WHO Expert Adv. Panel of World Soc. for Protection of Animals, 1982-88. Contbr. articles to profl. jours. Mem. bd. Carl-Friedrich-Siemens Found., 1969-83; mem. City Coun., City of Munich, 1978-84. With German Navy, 1940-45. Recipient Golden medal Swabian Trades, 1966, Bavarian Order of Merit, State of Bavaria, 1968, Officer's Cross of Order of Merit of Fed. Republic Germany, 1984. Fellow Italian Soc. Vet. Sci.; mem. Austrian Soc. Nutrition Rsch., German Animal Soc. Avocations: cooking, visiting theater and concert performances, study of philosophy.

KOTTIRSCH, GEORG, chemist, researcher; b. Erding, Germany, Nov. 10, 1958; s. Georg and Erika (Kaiser) K.; m. Simone Elble, May 12, 1995; 1 child, Florian. Diploma in Chemistry, U. Munich, 1985, PhD, 1988. Postdoctoral Stanford U., Palo Alto, Calif., 1988-89; rsch. scientist Sandoz-Pharma, Basel, Switzerland, 1989-93, project leader, 1993-95, group leader, 1995-96; head chemistry, arthritis Novartis-Pharma, Basel, Switzerland, 1996-99; dir. drug devel. arthritis and bone metabolism Novartis Pharms., East Hanover, NJ, 1999—. Contbr. articles to profl. jours. Mem. AAAS, German Chem. Soc., Swiss Chem. Soc., Am. Chem. Soc. Avocations: badminton, rock climbing, mountain biking, photography, entomology. Home: 18 Windsor Pl Madison NJ 07940-1162 Office: Novartis Pharm 59 Rte 10 East Hanover NJ 07936

KOTTIS, GEORGE CHRISTOPHER, economist, educator; b. Filiates, Greece, Nov. 7, 1933; s. Christopher A. and Euthalia (Konti) K.; m. Athena Petraki, Apr. 23, 1966. BA in Econs., Athens Sch. Econs. and Bus., 1958; MSc in Econs., London Sch. Econs., 1964; PhD in Econs., Wayne State U., 1970. Exec. Hermes en Grece, Athens, 1958-61; economist Doxiadis Assocs. Internat., Athens, 1964-65; spl. advisor Ministry of Industry, Athens, 1965-66; instr. Wayne State U., Detroit, 1968-69; asst. prof. U. Calgary, Can., 1969-71; assoc. prof. York U., Toronto, Can., 1971-74; prof. econs. Athens U. Econs. and Bus. Sci., 1974—, vice-rector, acting rector, 1988-89, chmn. dept. bus. adminstrn., 1993-98; economist World Bank, Washington, 1972-74; sec. gen. Ministry of Nat. Economy, Athens, 1989-90; bd. dirs. Bank of Piraeus, Athens, 1991, Ergo Investment, Athens, 1976—, Found. for Resettlement of Greeks from Albania, Athens, 1991—. Author: Economics of Environmental Protection, 1975, Microeconomics of Location, 1976, Introduction to Economics: Basic Concepts and Microeconomics, 1978, Introduction to Economics: Macroeconomics, 1979, Industrial Decentralization and Regional Development, 1980, Selected Economic Issues, 1981, Liberalizing Foreign Trade, The Case of Greece, 1989, Microeconomics: Theory and Applications, 1989, Introduction to Modern Microeconomics, 1989, Introduction to Modern Macroeconomics, 1991, Guide For the Study of Economics, 1991, Ecology and Economics, 1994, Contemporary Economic Issues, 1995, Economics for All, 1996, The Extraterrestrial and Ohr Education, 1997, Modern Microeconomics, 2000, Modern Macroeconomics, 2000, Exercises and Solutions of Political Economy, 2000; also several rsch. monographs; contbr. over 40 articles to acad. jours. and pubs.; participation in numerous TV and radio programs. Lt. Greek Army, 1956-58. Grantee Fulbright Found., 1966, Mendelson, 1967, Resources for Future, 1969; scholarship Greek Scholarship Found., 1961-64; recipient Disting. Alumnus award Econs. Inst. (U.S.), 1985, award Soc. Greek Lit. Writers, 1995. Fellow Soc. of Friends of People; mem. Athens Club, Hellenic Econ. Assn. (pres. 1989-91), Am. Econ. Assn. Orthodox Christian. Avocations: painting, yoga, study of Eastern philosophies. Home: 14 Loukianou St, 10675 Athens Greece Office: Athens U Econs and Bus Scis, 76 Patission St, 10434 Athens Greece

KOTTLER, RAYMOND GEORGE MICHAEL, economist, researcher; b. Washington, Dec. 11, 1966. Diplomas, Goethe Inst., Staufen, Fed. Republic Germany, 1986, Tech. U. Dresden, German Dem. Republic, 1988, U. Vienna, Austria, 1988; BA in Econs., German, Rutgers U., 1989. Mgmt. trainee Met. Life Ins. Co., N.Y.C., 1989-90; environ. info. systems coord. Johnson & Johnson, New Brunswick, N.J., 1990-92; asst. economist Fed. Res. Bank N.Y., 1993-96; fin. analyst, client svcs. coord. Fed. Res. Bank of N.Y. - Rsch. and Market Analysis Group, 1996—. Mem. Rutgers First Aid Squad, 1985-89, crew chief, ambulance driver, 1987-89; cons. Literacy Vols. Am.-N.J., East Brunswick, N.J., 1991-93; mem. pres.'s com. on edn. for civic leadership/cmty. svc. Citizen Edn. and Cmty. Svc. project, Rutgers U., 1988-91, co-chair pres.'s mng./promoting diversity com. task force Com. to advance Our Common Purposes, Rutgers U., 1990-91; co-chair cmty. svc. com. Rutgers Alumni Assn., 1991-94; mem. Rep. Presdl. Task Force, Rep. Senatorial Com., Rep. Presdl. Roundtable; nominee Rep. Senatorial Com. Inner Circle. Scholar Fed. Republic Germany Acad. Exch. Program, 1986, German Dem. Republic Fgn. Ministry, 1988, Austrian Ministry Sci. and Rsch., 1988, Merrill Lynch Disting. scholar, 1985-89, Garden State Disting. scholar, 1985-89; honoree Rep. Wall of Honor, Washington, 1993; recipient Ronald Reagan Eternal Flame of Freedom award, 1994, Legion of Merit medal, Legion of Honor. Mem. Rutgers Alumni Assn. (bd. dirs. 1988—, reunion chair 1989—, Rutgers Loyal Sons/Loyal Daus. award 1999, Rutgers Class of 1931 award 1999), Cap and Skull Soc., Phi Sigma Iota, Delta Phi Alpha, Omicron Delta Epsilon. Republican. Roman Catholic. Avocations: camping, swimming, boating, outdoor activities, gardening.

KOTTLOWSKI, FRANK EDWARD, geologist; b. Indpls., Apr. 11, 1921; s. Frank Charles and Adella (Markworth) K.; m. Florence Jean Chriscoe, Sept. 15, 1945; children: Karen, Janet, Diane. Student, Butler U., 1939-42; AB, Ind. U., 1947, MA, 1949, PhD, 1951. Party chief Ind. Geology Survey, Bloomington, summers 1948-50; fellow Ind. U., 1947-51, instr. geology, 1950; adj. prof. N.Mex. Inst. Mining and Tech., Socorro, 1970-95; econ. geologist N.Mex. Bur. Mines and Mineral Resources, 1951-66, asst. dir., 1966-68, 70-74, acting dir., 1968-70, dir., 1974-91, state geologist, 1989-91, dir. emeritus, state geologist emeritus, 1991—; geologic cons. Sandia Corp., 1966-72. Contbr. articles on mineral resources, stratigraphy and areal geology to tech. jours. Mem. Planning Commn. Socorro, 1960-68, 71-78, chmn., 86-90; mem. N.Mex. Energy Resources Bd.; chmn. N.Mex. Coal Surface Mining Commn.; sec. Socorro County Democratic Party, 1964-68. Served to 1st lt. USAAF, 1942-45. Decorated D.F.C., Air medal; recipient Richard Owen Disting. Alumni award in Govt. and Industry, U. Ind., 1987. Fellow AAAS, Geol. Soc. Am. (councilor 1979-82, mem. exec. com. 1981-82, Disting. Svc. award coal geology divsn., Cady Coal Geology award 1996); mem. AIME, Am. Assn. Petroleum Geologists (hon.; dist. rep. 1965-68, editor 1971-75, pres. energy minerals divsn. 1987-88, hon. mem. energy minerals divsn. 2000, Disting. Svc. award), Assn. Am. State Geologists (pres. 1985-86), Soc. Econ. Geologists, Am. Inst. Profl. Geologists (Pub. Svc. award 1986), Am. Commn. Statigraphic Nomenclature (past sec., chmn.), Cosmos Club, Rotary Internat. (Paul Harris fellow), Sigma Xi. Home: 703 Sunset St Socorro NM 87801-4657 Office: NMex Bur Mines NMex Tech 801 Leroy Pl Socorro NM 87801-4681

KOTTOW, MIGUEL HUGO, ophthalmologist, educator; b. Tel-Aviv, Oct. 6, 1939; arrived in Chile, 1947.; s. Ernest J. Kottow and Herta K. Lang; m. Helga E. Keim; children: Daniel, Andrea. MD, U. Chile, 1964; Dr. Medicine, U. Bonn, Germany, 1976; MA in Sociology, U. Hagen, Germany, 1991. Lic. physician, Chile, Germany, U.S. Physician Nat. Health Svc., Chile, 1964-74; with San Juan de Dios, Santiago, Chile; pvt. practice Santiago, 1967-72, 83-86, 88—; physician Prisch Clinic, Germany, 1978-83; prof. ophthalmology U. Chile, Santiago, 1990—; prof. Faculty of Philosophy, Santiago, 1996—; dir. bioethics U. Chile, 1993-95; cons. bioethics WHO/PAHO, Argentina. Author: Anterior Segment Fluorescein Angiography, 1978, Introduction to Bioethics, 1995; contbr. articles to profl. jours. Mem. Chilean Med. Assn. (ethics dept. 1996—), Chilean Soc. Ophthalmology. Office: Guardia Vieja 339, Santiago Chile

KOTWAL, PRAKASH, orthopaedic surgeon; b. Jalgaon, India, May 5, 1951; parents P. D. and Usha Kotwal; m. Arundhati Kotwal, Feb. 23, 1981. MB BChir, Mahatma Gandhi Meml. Med. Coll, Indore, India, 1973, MS, 1977. From asst. prof. to assoc. prof. to additional prof. All India Inst. Med. Scis., New Delhi, 1980-98, prof., 1998—; officer-in-charge emergency svcs. All India Inst. Med. Scis., 1997-99. Author: (book) Essentials of Orthopaedics and Applied Physiotherapy, 1998. Fellow Internat. Med. Sci. Acad.; mem. Assn. Spine Surgeons India (sec., co-sec.), Indian Orthopaedic Assn. (life). Avocations: reading, photography. Home: 412 Asiad Village, New Delhi 110 049, India Office: All India Inst Med Scis, New Delhi 110029, India

KOTYK, ARNOST, biochemistry educator; b. Melnik, Czechoslovakia, July 11, 1930; s. Arnost and Julie (Nitkova) K.; m. Helena Kotorova, June 10, 1965; children: Marketa, Lucie, Jiri. Student, U. Calif., Berkeley, 1948-50; MSc, Charles U., Prague, Czechoslovakia, 1954; PhD, Czechoslovak Acad. Sci., Prague, 1957; ScD, Czechoslovak Acad. Sci., 1978; student, U. Calif., Berkeley, Y. Jr. rsch. scientist Inst. Microbiology Czechoslovak Acad. Sci., Prague, 1957-62, rsch. scientist, 1962-67, sr. rsch. scientist, 1967-84, 85—; assoc. prof. 17 November U., Prague, 1964; lectr. J.E. Purkyne U., Brno, Czechoslovakia, 1980-86; prof. Charles U., Prague, 1989; pres. standing com. on molecular and cell biology UNESCO, 1988-90; prof. Masaryk U., Brno, 1992. Author: Cell Membrane Transport, 1970, 2d edit., 1975, Membrane Transport, 1977, Biophysical Chemistry of Membrane Functions, 1988, Intracellular pH and Its Measurement, 1989. Recipient State prize Pres. of Republic of Czechoslovakia, 1978. Mem. Internat. Union Biochemistry and Molecular Biology (mem. exec. com. 1988-97, chmn. nomenclature com. 1996—), Internat. Coun. Sci. Unions (mem. gen. com. 1991-97). Avocations: singing, choir conducting. Office: Inst of Physiology CSAV, Videnska 1083, Prague 142 20, Czech Republic

KOTYNEK, GEORGE ROY, mechanical engineer, educator, marketing executive; b. Lake Forest, Ill., Apr. 18, 1938; s. Anton Joseph and Zdenka K.; m. Virginia Jean Hyde, Sept. 4, 1965 (div. 1973); children: John Anton, Joseph George. BSME, Ill. Inst. Tech., 1960. Registered profl. engr., Ill. Efficiency engr. Commonwealth Edison Co., Chgo., 1959-63; instr. physics Glenbard East High Sch., Lombard, Ill., 1963-67; systems engr. Sargent and Lundy, Chgo., 1967-77; prin. engr. Fluor Corp., Chgo., 1977-85; mgr. fossil tech. Stearns Catalytic World Corp., Oak Brook, Ill., 1985-86; mgr. mktg. Volund USA Ltd., New Providence, N.J., 1986-94; tech. cons. VECTRA Techs., Inc., Lincolnshire, Ill., 1994-96; sr. tech. cons. Duke Engring. & Svcs., Inc., Bannockburn, Ill., 1996—; mem. hazardous materials adv. com. Waubonsee C.C., Sugar Grove, Ill., 1992—. Contbr. articles to profl. publs. Mem. People to People Internat. Conventional and Nuclear Power Engring. Delegation to People's Republic of China, 1987. Mem. ASME (newsletter editor 1980-82, vice chmn. membership 1982-83, vice chmn. programs 1983-84). Achievements include design of 2,700-MW electric generating station for cyclic service. Office: Duke Engring & Svcs Inc 215 Shuman Blvd Ste 172 Naperville IL 60563-2580

KOTZEV, DIMITER LUBOMIROV, chemist, researcher; b. Sofia, Bulgaria, Oct. 22, 1950; arrived in the U.K., 1990; s. Lubomir Ivanov and Anna Mihailova (Kesyakova) K.; m. Vega Petrova Dilyanova, Jan. 20, 1974; children: Anna D., Lubov D. BSc in Chem. Engring., Higher Inst. Chem. Tech., Sofia, 1972, PhD in Chem. Scis., 1980. Chemist Higher Inst. Chem. Tech., Sofia, 1972-74; rsch. scientist Sci. Indsl. Ctr. for Specialty Polymers, Sofia, 1975-80, sect. leader, 1981-86, sci. sec., sect. leader, 1986-90; R&D mgr. Chemence Ltd., Corby, U.K., 1990-99; new tech. and rsch. mgr., performance polymers Ciba Splty. Chems., Duxford, Cambridge, Eng., 2000—. Inventor in field; contbr. articles to profl. jours. Grantee European Commn., 1990, 93. Avocation: travel. Home: 21 Carron Close, Corby Northants NN17 2LB, United Kingdom Office: R&D Adhesives and Tooling, Ciba Splty Chems, Duxford Cambridge CB2 4QA, England

KOUAME, NGUESSAN, sociology educator, researcher, consultant; b. Port-Bouët, Abidjan, Côte d'Ivoire, May 27, 1949; s. Kouame Kouakou and Adjoua Nguessan; m. Rose Kouabla Anet, Dec. 25, 1983; children: Olga, Rachel, Ghislaine, Nathalie, Clement, Emmanuel. BA, Abidjan U., Côte d'Ivoire, 1974, MA, 1975, PhD, 1979. Cert. sociologist. Prof. Youth and Sports Nat. Inst., Abidjan, Côte d'Ivoire, 1979-81; assoc. prof. U. Abidjan, Côte d'Ivoire, 1980-83, prof., 1983—; prof. Bouaké Agrl. Inst., Côte d'Ivoire, 1981-88, Nat. Inst. of Soc. Tng., Abidjan, Côte d'Ivoire, 1982-95, Nat. Inst. Tng. Health Sector Personnel, Abidjan, Côte d'Ivoire, 1999—; acting dir. Urban and Archtl. Rsch. Ctr., Côte d'Ivoire, 1978; cons. Bandama Valley Authority, Côte d'Ivoire, 1979-80, Ministry Agrl., Côte d'Ivoire, 1995; dir. Inst. Ethno-Sociology, Côte d'Ivoire, 1984-91; invited prof. U. Catholique de Louvain, Belgium, 1985-86. Author: Haruba (Baoulé rural housing), 1978, Urban Violence in Africa, 1994; contbr. articles to profl. jours. Sec. gen.

Ivorian Consumers League, Abidjan, Côte d'Ivoire, 1990—; nat. sec. Social and Dem. Movement, Abidjan, 1990-94; treas. Racines, Abidjan, 1995—; mem steering and fin. com. of program in support of decentralized cultural initiatives of European Union in Ivory Coast, 1998-99. Scholar Crossroads Africa, U.S., 1976, Environnement and Devel. in Africa, Morocco, 1978, Goethe Inst., Germany, 1984. Mem. N.Y. Acad. Scis., Social Scis. Interdisciplinary Group in Ivory Coast (founder 1992), Ivory Coast Nat. Fedn. Consumers Assn. (sec. gen. 1998—), Nat. Geographic Soc. Roman Catholic. Avocations: photography, music, soccer. Office: Inst D'Ethno-Sociologie, U Cocody Abidjan, Abidjan 22BP 535, Côte d'Ivoire

KOUASSI, GEORGES YAO, refining company financial company; b. Grand Bassam South, Ivory Coast, Mar. 25, 1955; s. Konan Kouassi and Diby Comoin; m. Diele Elise, May 26, 1990; children: Marie Laura Affoue Jessica, Georges-William Denis. BSc, Cath. Faculty of U. onns, Belgium, 1983. Fin. officer Ivory Coast Refining Soc., Abidjan, 1984-89, human resources adminstr., 1989-95, fin. mgr., 1995—. Mem. Dem. Party of Ivory Coast. Mem. Dehima. Avocations: soccer, tennis, basketball. Office: Soc Ivoirienne de Raffinage, Route de Vridi, 01 BP 1269, Abidjan South, Côte d'Ivoire

KOUDELKA, LADISLAV, chemistry educator; b. Protivanov, Czechoslovakia, Aug. 3, 1942; s. Karel and Vincencie (Trundová) K.; m. Valerie Lozáková, Nov. 27, 1943; children: Katerina, Veronika. MS, Inst. Chem. Tech., Pardubice, Czechoslovakia, 1964, PhD, 1977; DSc, Charles U., Prague, Czechoslovakia, 1991. Asst. prof. Inst. Chem. Tech., 1967-90; assoc. prof. faculty chem. tech. U. Pardubice, 1990—, vice rector, 1991-94. Bd. dirs. Town Coun., Pardubice, 1994-98; chmn. Chamber Choir of Pardubice, 1993—. Mem. Czech Soc. Indsl. Chemistry (presidium mem. 1993—), U. Pardubice Club (pres. 1995—). Mem. Freedom Union. Avocations: choral singing, cross-country skiing, tennis. Home: Okrajová 294, 53009 Pardubice Czech Republic Office: Univ Pardubice, Nam cs legii 565, 53210 Pardubice Czech Republic

KOUFA, KALLIOPI KONSTANTINOU, international law educator; b. Thessaloniki, Greece, Mar. 6, 1936; d. Konstantine I. Koufas and Anna J. Frankel. Lic. in polit. sci., diploma, Grad. Inst. Internat. Studies, Geneva, 1960; LLB with distinction, Aristotle U., Thessaloniki, 1966, LLM in Pub. Law with honors, 1968, PhD in Pub. Internat. Law with honors, 1974. Asst. prof. pub. internat. law and diplomatic history Aristotle U. Thessaloniki Law Sch., 1970-75, lectr., sr. lectr. pub. internat. and European law, 1976-82, prof. with tenure pub. internat. law and internat. orgn., 1984—, dir. dept. internat. studies, 1987-93, 96, dir. Inst. Internat. Law and Internat. Rels. Thessaloniki, 1993—, dir. Inst. for Balkan Studies, 1990-92, mem. governing bd., 1992—, pres., 1997—; participating scholar European Sci. Found., Strasbourg, France, 1986-90; nat. coord. Erasmus Law Program with 10 European univs. network, Thessaloniki, 1989—; Greek del., legal adviser to Greek dels. to 3d and 6t coms. UN Gen. Assembly and UN Commn. on Human Rights, N.Y.C., Geneva, 1990—, various meetings on human dimension Conf. on Security and Coop. in Europe, 1990-91, Greek del. to World Conf. on Human Rights, Vienna, Austria, 1993—; alt. UN Subcommn. on Prevention of Discrimination and Protection of Minorities, Geneva, 1994—; spl. rapporteur of UN Subcomm. on Prevention of Discrimination and Protection of Minorities on Terrorism and Human Rights, 1997; mem. UN subcom. working group on contemporary forms of slavery, 1999. Author: Universalism and Regionalism in International Society, 1975, Act of State in International Relations, Vol. I, 1981, Vol. II, 1983, Introduction to the Organization of International Society, 1987; editor, co-editor Hellenic Rev. Internat. Rels., 1978—, Balkan Studies, 1990-92, Thesaurus Acroasium, 1993—; contbr. articles to Hellenic Rev. Internat. Rels., Thesaurus Acroasium, Armenopoulos, To Syntagma. Mem. Interdisciplinary Commn. for Peace Edn., Inst. Edn. for Peace, Thessaloniki, 1994—. Mem. Thessaloniki Bar Assn., Am. Soc. Internat. Law, AAA (intergroup higher edn.), Assn. Attenders and Lectrs. Inst. Internat. Law and Internat. Rels. Thessaloniki (founder, sec.-gen. 1977-82), Greek Soc. Internat. Law and Internat. Rels., Alumni Assn. Grad. Inst. Internat. Studies Geneva, Internat. Law Assn. (v.p. Greek br.). Greek Orthodox. Avocations: water sports, theatre arts, architecture, painting. Home: 2 Aristotelous St, 546 23 Thessaloniki Greece Office: Inst Internat Law-Rels, Inst Internat Law and Rels, Leof Megalou Alexandrou 15, 546 40 Thessaloniki Greece

KOUGH, ROBERT HAMILTON, retired clinical hematologist, consultant; b. Harrisburg, Pa., Feb. 19, 1921; s. Harry Milton and Olive Jane (Smith) K.; m. Nancy Jane Trunnell, June 18, 1943; 1 child, Elizabeth Trunnell Beiler. BS, Pa. State U., 1942; MD, U. Pa., 1945. Diplomate Am. Bd. Internal Medicine, Am. Bd. Hematology. Intern Hosp. of U. Pa., Phila., 1945-46; med. resident, Am. Cancer Soc. fellow in hematology Hosp. U. Pa., Phila., 1955-58; from asst. instr. to assoc. in pharmacology U. Pa. Med. Sch., Phila., 1949-52; mem. med. staff Carlisle (Pa.) Hosp., 1952-55; assoc. in hematology Geisinger Med. Ctr., Danville, Pa., 1958-65; head hematology Geisinger Med. Ctr., 1965-74, dir. dept. hematology and oncology, depts. medicine, 1974-86, sr. cons. in hematology and oncology, 1986-91; mem. various coms. Geisinger Med. Ctr., 1959-91; affiliate Leukemia Group B Cancer Control Program, Cornell U., N.Y.C., 1974-78, Eastern Cooperative Oncology Group, Fox Chase, Pa., 1977-86, Mayo Clinic, 1986-87, North Ctrl. Cancer Treatment Group, Mayo Clinic, 1986-91; clin. prof. medicine Pa. State U., Hershey, 1975-87. Prin. author: Anemias Case Studies, 1981; contbr. articles to profl. jours. Active Mid Atlantic Oncology Program, 1984-86; corp. mem. Pa. Blue Shield, Camp Hill, 1972-87, mem. dental affairs com., 1977-79, med. affairs com., 1973-79, med. rev. com. 1980-86, corp. bd. nominating com., 1982-85, mem. profl. adv. coun., alt., 1985-86; bd. dirs. Capital Blue Cross, Harrisburg, Pa., 1969-93, hon. dir., 1993; cons. drug-related patient needs Dept. Health, Edn. and Welfare, NIH, Rockville, Md., 1971, med. surg. task force Dept. Health Commonwealth of Pa., Harrisburg, 1981; Pa. Liaison Coun. for Internal Medicine, 1980-87. Lt. (j.g.) M.C., USN, 1946-49. Recipient awards Pa. State chpt. Alpha Epsilon Delta, Phi Sigma Phi. Fellow ACP (life mem., regional planning com. 1964, program com. 1978, 79, 82, gen. chmn. 1981, book reviewer Annals of Internal Medicine 1964-74, manuscript reviewer Socioecons. 1981); mem. AAAS, AMA, Am. Cancer Soc. (chmn. profl. rels. com. Montour county unit 1959-64, Crusade award 1963), Am. Group Practice Assn. (editl. adv. com. Group Practice 1966-73), Am. Med. Writers Assn. (ad hoc com. on awards 1959), Am. Soc. Clin. Oncology, Am. Soc. Internal Medicine (ho. of dels. 1980-85, reference com. D 1980, meetings com. 1978-83, survey com. 1976, manpower pool 3d party payors 1980), Assn. Cmty. Cancer Ctrs. (Washington) (instl. rep. 1978), Am. Soc. Hematology, Pa. Med. Soc. (med. svcs. com. 1964-72, profl. liability commn. 1979-85, malpractice ins. task force 1966-71, Dept. Pub. Assistance com. 1966, profl. liability appeal com. 1986, pub. policy com. 1984, internal medicine adv. com. 1980-84, contbg. editor Pa. Medicine 1970-84), Pa. Soc. Internal Medicine (med. svcs. com. 1973-80, chmn. 1975-79, membership com. 1980-86, chmn. 1980-86, legis. com. 1981-83, peer rev. com. 1980-86, program chmn. 1978-79, chmn. nominating com. 1980, pres. 1979-80), Pa. Soc. Hematology and Oncology (organizing com. 1964-81, exec. com. 1982-95, pres. 1986-87), Montour County Med. Soc. (chmn. com. on comprehensive health planning 1970, censor, pres.-elect 1971-72, pres. 1972-73), Phila. Hematology Soc., Phi Eta Sigma, Phi Kappa Phi, Phi Beta Kappa, Alpha Omega Alpha. Republican. Lutheran. Achievements include pioneering rsch. with others in human vols. on the ctrl. control of respiration, cerebral blood flow and oxygen toxicity at 1 atm and 3.5 atm O2 partial press; author of 1st authenticated report of an unprovoked attack, with a bite, by a rabid insectivorous bat, alerting public to the insectivorous bat as a significant reservoir of rabies in spite of rarity of an obvious bite and in spite of fact that the method of transmission from bat to man and animals is not obvious; rsch. on recognition of membrane abnormalities of erythrocytes in myeloproliferative disorders by Merocyanine 540.

KOUIKOGLOU, VASSILIS STAVROS, electrical engineer, educator; b. Nafplion, Greece, Apr. 28, 1961; s. Stavros Vassilis and Sofia Nikos (Tsagaraki) K.; m. Vassiliki Fotios Paggeiou, Jan. 4, 1997. Degree, Nat. Tech. U. Athens, 1985; PhD, Tech. U. Crete, Greece, 1989. Vis. asst. prof. Tech. U. Crete, 1991-95, asst. prof., 1995-2000, assoc. prof., 2000—. Contbr. articles to profl. jours. Mem. IEEE, Tech. Chamber of Greece, Sigma Xi. Office: Tech U Crete, Univ Campus, 73100 Chania Greece

KOUKOLÍK, FRANTIŠEK, pathologist; b. Prague, Nov. 22, 1941; s. František and Blažena (Zimmermannová) K.; m. Hana Čábelová, Nov. 21, 1962; children: Jan, Tomáš. MD, Charles U., 1965. Resident dept. pathology Charles U., Prague, 1965-69; from resident dept. surgery to chief dept. pathology City Hosp., České Budějovice, Czechoslovakia, 1970-93; with dept. pathology Thomayer's U. Hosp., Prague, 1983—. Author: Brain and Its Mind, 1995, Sloth and Universe, 1995, Goslings and St. Augustine, 1994 (Book of Yr. 1995), Adam and Eve, 1997, On Diseases and Peoples, 1998, Machiavellian Intelligence, 1999, Human Brain: Funcional Systems, Norm and Disorders, 2000; co-author: Different Child, 1994, The Revolt, 1996, Ants and Universe, 1997, Brain and Its Relation to Human Behavior, 1997, (with P. Koubsky) Chimp and Universe, 1998, (with P. Koubsky) Owl and Universe, 1999, (with R. Jirák) Alzheimer's Disease and Other Dementias, 1998, (with R. Jirák) Diagnosis and Therapy of Dementia Syndrome, 1998 ; writer TV series Brain and Its Mind, 1993, 94, Britannica broadcasts, 1995, Personalities personally, 1995, When Soul Squabbled With Body, 1997; contbr. articles to sci. jours. Mem. Internat. PEN Club, N.Y. Acad. Scis. Home: Filipova 2016, 148 00 Prague Czech Republic Office: Thomayer's Univ Hosp, Videnska 800, 140 59 Prague Czech Republic

KOUKOULOMMATIS, PANAGIOTIS N., health care products company executive; b. Athens, Greece, July 25, 1968; s. Nikolaos P. and Pinglopi H. (Zaharaki) K. MSc in Biochemistry, U. Bucharest, Romania, 1991, PhD in Enzimology, 1998. Diplomate biochemistry. Biocchemist 251 G.A.F. Hosp., Athens, 1991-93; with sales dept. Bayer, Athens, 1993-94; product mgr. Biometric S.A., Athens, 1994-97; pvt. cons. diagnostic products, Athens, 1997—. Christian Orthodox. Avocations: reading, sailing, travel, basketball, photography. Home: 25 Evritanias, 11523 Athens Greece

KOULIEV, ELDAR, ambassador; b. Baku, Azerbaijan, Aug. 29, 1939; s. Gulam and Mirvary Kouliev; m. Irina Kouliev; children: Dilara, Mourad. Arabic philology, Baku State U., 1963; with, Soviet Fgn. Min. Dipl Acad, 1976-78. Fgn. min. Azerbaijan Soviet Republic, 1965; vice-consul UN, Aswan, Egypt, 1969; Soviet consul Aswan, 1971; first sec. Soviet Embassy, Egypt, 1973; consul Soviet Consulate Gen., Istanbul, Turkey, 1978-83; min., counsellor Embassy, Yemen, 1988-90; permanent rep. to Azerbaijan, UN, N.Y.C., 1994—; sr. counsellor Fgn. Ministry Russian Fedn., 1992-94. Office: Permanent Mission of the Republic of Azerbaijan 866 United Nations Plz Rm 560 New York NY 10017-1822

KOULOURIANOS, DIMITRI THEODORE, economist; b. Koroni, Greece, Dec. 4, 1930; s. Theodore and Paraskevi (Tsakonas) K.; m. Roula Varvoutsis, Sept. 2, 1966; children: Theodore, Athina. BBA, Athens (Greece) Econ. U., 1953; MA in Econs., U. Calif., Berkeley, 1964, PhD in Econs., 1967. Economist Bank of Greece, Athens, 1957-67, World Bank, Washington, 1968-81; min. of fin. Greek Govt., Athens, 1982-83; amb. OECD, Paris, 1986-90; bd. dirs. European Bank for Reconstrn. and Devel., London, 1991-93; cons. Athens, 1993-98; mem. European Parliament, 1999—. Pvt. Greek Army, 1953-55. Home and Office: 8 Andrea Ghini St, 15233 Halandri Athens, Greece

KOULOUVARI, PANAGIOTA, graphic art technologist, research scientist; b. Athens, Greece, Nov. 23, 1971; d. Vasilios and Maria (Tsikaloudaki) K. First degree, Technol. Ednl. Instn., Athens, 1994; MPhil, U. Stirling, Scotland, 1997. Rsch. scientist dept. media tech. and graphic arts Royal Inst. Tech., Stockholm, 1998—; participant confs. in field. Pub., editor, author, printer, bookbinder: Printer's Notebook, 1997; contbr. to conf. procs. Scholar State Scholarships Found., Greece, 1996-00. Orthodox. Office: Royal Inst Tech, Drottning Kristinas vag 47S, 100 44 Stockholm Sweden

KOUMANAKOS, DEMETRE, information systems specialist; b. Athens, Nov. 16, 1962; s. Andreas and Sophia (Skliri) K.; m. Anna Vrettou, May 16, 1993; 1 child, Andreas. AA, U. Laverne, Calif., BS. Mng. dir. Telecomp, Athens, 1989-92; with computer network/comm. support dept. Intracom SA, Athens, 1990-92, computer network developer/constrn. supr., 1992-95, project coord., 1995-99; info. sys. mgr. Androulidakis Media Group, Athens, 1999—; European Union project devel. programming cons., Athens, 1995-99. Active Greenpeace, Athens, 1996, Flying Drs., Athens, 1995. With Greek Army, 1989-90. Mem. IEEE Computer Soc., Assn. for Computing Machinery. Avocations: amateur radio sv1ens, photography, electronics, auto mechanics. Home: Ermou 8 Ekali, 14565 Athens Greece Office: Androulidakis Media Group, 10 Davaki Str, 11526 Athens Greece

KOUMBOULIS, FOTIS NICHOLAS, system engineer, researcher, educator; b. Athens, July 30, 1964; s. Nicholas F. and Helen A. (Mandalos) K. MSc in Elec. Engring., Nat. Tech. U. Athens, 1987, PhD in Control Systems, 1991. Teaching asst. Nat. Tech. U. of Athens, 1987-91; assoc. rschr. Nat. Rsch. Ctr. Demokritos, Athens, 1988-92; system engr./rschr. Nat. Def. Rsch. Ctr., Athens, 1992-95; cons. U. Thessaly, 1995—. Contbr. articles to profl. jours. Recipient Mother Premium award Inst. of Elec. Engrs., U.K., 1994. Mem. IEEE, Soc. Indsl. and Applied Math., Tech. Chamber Greece, N.Y. Acad. Scis. Avocations: number theory, chess, swimming, painting, music. Home: 53 Aftokratoros Irakliou St, Maroussi Athens, Greece 15122 Office: U Thessaly/Dept Mech & Indust Eng, 38334 Pedion Areos, Volog Greece

KOUOMEGNI, AUGUSTIN KONTCHOU, minister of communications of Cameroon; b. Nkongsamba, Mifi, 1945; married; 6 children. BA in Law, Yaoundé (Cameroon) U., 1969; PhD in Polit. Sci., Paris U.; M in Polit Sci., France, 1981. Prof. pub. law, polit. Sci. Yaoundé U., 1974—; min. info., culture Govt. of Cameroon, 1990-92, min. comm., 1992—, sr. min. in charge of external rels., 1997—. Office: Ministry External Rels, BP 18, Yaoundé Cameroon*

KOURI, GUSTAVO PEDRO, virologist; b. Havana, Cuba, Jan. 11, 1936; s. Pedro and Mercedes (Flores) K.; m. Lidia Cardella (div. 1979); children: Lilliam, Vivian, Gustavo; m. Maria G. Guzman, Nov. 25, 1980; 1 child, Pedro. MD, Havana U., 1962; PhD, Nat. Ctr. Sci. Rsch., Havana, 1973; ScD, Charles U., Prague, Czechoslovakia, 1990. Chief virology dept. Nat. Ctr. for Sci. Rsch., Havana, 1965-70, dep. dir., 1965-70; vice-dean med. faculty Havana U., 1970-73, vice rector, 1973-76; nat. dir. for sci. Ministry of Higher Edn., Havana, 1976-78; dir. gen. Tropical Medicine Inst. "Pedro Kouri", Havana, 1979—; dir. WHO Collaborating Ctr. for Biol. Vector Control, Havana, 1990—; temp. advisor Pan Am. and WHO to present; lectr. in field; cons. in field. Contbr. numerous articles to profl. jours. Grantee TDR, 1979, 81, 82, 83, 84, 85, 86, IDRC, 1983, 86, French Govt., 1989; recipient Carlos Finlay Nat. Order and medal Cuban State Coun., 1990, Silver medal Charles U., 1988, Cesar Uribe medal NIH, Colombia, 1991, Hero of the Republic of Cuba, 1996. Fellow Third World Acad. Scis.; mem. AAAS, N.Y. Acad. Sci., Cuban Acad. Sci. (mem. de merito, v.p. 1996), Real Academia de Medicina y Cirujia de Galicia, Royal Soc. Tropical Medicine Hygiene, Latin Am. Fedn. Tropical Medicine (pres. 1993-97), Cuban Soc. Microbiology and Parasitology (pres. 1980), Latin Am. Fedn. Parasitology (pres. 1995-97). Achievements include research on Dengue Hemorrhagic Fever. Office: Inst Medicina Tropical, Autopista Novia del Mediod, Havana Cuba

KOUROS, PANTELIS, government official; b. Nicosia, Dec. 10, 1932; m. Ourania Tsakiri; children: Kyriakos, Maria. Student in bus. admin. and pub. rels., Greece, Cyprus. Founding mem. Pancyprian Unified Fighting Front; membership dir., dep. gen. sec. Pancyprian Nat. Youth Orgn.; dir. ops. then comdr. Cyprus Civil Def.; presdl. liaison Ctrl. Intelligence Svc. Cyprus; dir. polit. affairs Dem. Rally Party; dep. min. to pres. Rep. of Cyprus. Office: Presidential Palace, Nicosia Cyprus*

KOURSE, SAUL BERNARD, retired engineering associate; b. Carbondale, Pa., Jan. 26, 1925; s. Moses and Dinah (Cohen) K.; m. Linda Eichner, June 1966 (dec. Oct. 1987). Student, NYU, 1941-43; BS in Elec. Tech., N.Y. Inst. Tech., N.Y.C., 1965. Teletype operator U.S. Dept. Agr., N.Y.C., 1955-58; engring. assoc. AT&T/Western Elec. Co., Newark, 1966-69; teletype operator Engring. Corp. Office Equipment, Miami, Fla., 1975-76. With U.S. Army, 1943-46. Dem. nat. committeeman, 1993—. Life mem. DAV, VFW, Jewish War Vets.; mem. World Jewish Congress. Avocations: basketball, tennis, watching football, baseball, chess, pool. Home: 1300 Sycamore Ln Rm D271 Lake City FL 32025-6266

KOURY, AGNES LILLIAN, real estate property manager; b. Denver, Oct. 16, 1935; d. John Joseph and Lucy Maria (Plomteaux) K.; m. William L. May, July 21, 1958 (div. 1961); 1 child, Tia Leslie Koury. BSBA, U. Denver, 1958; protocol cert., Southeastern U., 1964; paralegal cert., Georgetown U., 1978; MA, Marymount U., 1991. Registered profl. realtor, Va. Com. sec. N.Mex. Ho. of Reps., Santa Fe, 1959; contracts sec. Atomic Energy Commn., Albuquerque, 1959-63; ptnr. legal sec. Sughrue, Rothwell, Washington, 1963-65; legal asst. McClure & Trotter, Washington, 1965-67; case worker U.S. Ho. of Reps., Washington, 1968; adminstrv., rsch. asst. Harvard U., Washington, 1969-73; asst. mgr. Koury's Real Estate, Sant Fe, 1974-85; owner, mgr. various realty properties, Santa Fe and Arlington, 1985—. Pres. Yorktown Condominium, Arlington, 1972-74, bd. dirs.; treas. Birches Homeowners Assn., Arlington, 1987-90; chmn., vol. spkrs. bur. Hospice of No. Va., Arlington, 1993—, mem. spkrs. bur., 1985—, mem. 20th anniversary com., 1996-97, chmn. Tree of Lights event, 1999; bd. dirs. Arlington Symphony Assn., 1990-99, chmn. music scholarship competition for no. Va. high sch. students, 1994-2000, chmn. muisic scholarship competition for Washington met. area, 2000—. Mem. Delta Sigma Epsilon, Phi Gamma Nu (Outstanding Mem. 1958). Roman Catholic. Avocations: travel, writing, poetry, playing piano, picture puzzles. Home and Office: 4741 23rd St N Arlington VA 22207-3408

KOUSHKI, PARVIZ AMIR, civil engineer, educator; b. Sabzevar, Iran, Apr. 28, 1943; s. Asadollah and Showkatagha (Arabshahi) K.; m. Alison Marie Larkin, Aug. 22, 1972; children: Jasmine Khaatoon, Amir Kazimir. BSCE, MS, U. Azerbijon, 1965; proficiency diploma, NYU, 1968; MS in Traffic, U. Mass., 1970; PhD, U. Wis., 1974. Advisor to mayor Tehran, 1975; asst. prof. Poly. U., Tehran, 1976-78; mng. dir. Bur. Traffic Safety, Tehran, 1978-79; asst. prof. Clarkson U., Potsdam, N.Y., 1979-82; assoc. prof. King Saud U., Riyadh, Saudi Arabia, 1982-90, U. Alaska, Fairbanks, 1990-92; prof. Kuwait U., 1992—; bd. dirs. RAHAB Cons., Tehran; co-dir. Ctr. for Urban Studies Tehran Poly. U., 1976-78; cons. World Bank, Washington, 1992—; mem. Nat. Safety Orgn., Kuwait, 1994—. Lt. Iranian Army, 1965-66. Mem. ASCE, Persian Soc. Engrs., Transp. Rsch. Bd., N.Y. Acad. Scis., Amnesty Internat., Worldwatch Inst., Vol. in Tech. Assistance. Avocations: mountain climbing, marathon running, tennis, music, calligraphy. Home: Dezasheeb Ave Yasaman # 55, Tehran Iran Office: Kuwait U, PO Box 5969 Safat, Kuwait 13060, Kuwait

KOUTEK, BOHUMIR, chemist, researcher; b. Ceske Budejovice, Czech Republic, Oct. 12, 1939; s. Jindrich Koutek and Marie Rasochova Koutkova; m. Jana Trpkova Pacesova, June 12, 1965 (div. 1971); 1 child, Tomas; m. Brigita Lichenvnikova, Apr. 9, 1974; 1 child, Veronika. MS, Inst. Chem. Tech., Prague, Czech Republic, 1961; PhD, Czechoslovak Acad. Sci., Prague, 1966. Postdoctoral rsch. assoc. Inst. Organic Chemistry & Biochem. Czechoslovak Acad. Sci., 1968-72, rschr., 1973-81, sr. rschr., 1982—, head dept. natural products, 1994—; deputy dir. Inst. Scientific Affairs, 1998—; vis. scientist Royal Inst. Tech., Stockholm, 1982, SUNY, Stony Brook, 1993; inventor in field. Contbr. articles to profl. jours. Maj. Czech Army, 1963-63. Postdoctoral fellow Swedish Forest Product Inst., Stockholm, 1968-69; U.S. Agy. Internat. Devel. grantee, Washington, 1991-95, Grant Agy. Czech Republic grantee, Prague, 1993, 95, 97. Mem. Czech Chem. Soc., N.Y. Acad. Scis. Avocations: books, country music, table tennis. Office: Inst Organic Chemistry, Flemingovo nam 2, 6 Prague 16610, Czech Republic

KOUTKOVA, ALICE SEMYENOVNA, English language educator, researcher; b. Taganrog, Russia, Apr. 7, 1931; d. Semyen Konstantinovich and Yevdokiya Borisovna (Lyagoushina) Dyemin; m. Alexandr Andreyevich Koutkov, July 16, 1950 (div. 1974); 1 child, Vladimir Alexandrovich Koutkov (dec. 1978); m. Grigory Vasiliyevich Moryev, Nov. 3, 1978 (dec. 1997). Student, Aircraft Coll., Taganrog, Russia, 1948-51, Pedagogical Inst., Rostov-Don, Russia, 1954-59; PhD, State Tech. U., Novocherkassk, Russia, 1975, asst. prof., 1979, prof., 1989. Cert. aircraft designer. Designer Taganrog Aircraft Plant, 1951-54; English lang. educator Radio Inst., Taganrog, 1959-60; English lang. educator State Tech. U., Novocherkassk, 1960-84, head English and French dept., 1984—; mem. sci./methods in fgn. langs. coun., State Edn. Com., Russia, 1994. Author (in English): Computers and Programming, 1969, Man-Computer-Future, 1987, 2d edit., 1995, Computer-Aided Design, 1988, 2d edit., 2000, In the World of Personal Computers, 1997, Business Correspondence, 1998, Robotic Acronyms, 1998, Virtual Reality, 1999, American English, 1999, internet in Planet's Life, 2000; contbr. numerous articles to profl. jours. and conf. procs.; corr. various newspapers, 1978—. Decorated State Edn. Com., Moscow, 1989, 90, 96, Gold Star award Cambridge, 2000. Mem. TESOL, N.Y. Acad. Scis., Moscow Assn. Applied Linguistics, Russian Acad. Scis. and Art. Democrat. Russian Orthodox. Avocations: computers, informatics, painting, music, embroidering. E-mail: koutkova@srstu.novoch.ru. Home: B Khmelnitskiy 151 kv 16, 346428 Novocherkassk Russia Office: South Russia State Tech U, Prosveshcheniya, 132, 346428 Novocherkassk Russia

KOUTROUBINAS, STILIANOS P., engineering design company executive; b. Drosopigi, Ioannina, Greece, June 11, 1965; s. Petros S. and Vasiliki N. (Simou) K.; m. Dimitra C. Nikolaou, July 9, 1994; 1 child, Christine. BS, U. Patros, Patra, Greece, 1989, PhD, 1999. Rschr. U. Patras, 1989-94; sr. engr. DCT Hellas, Patras, 1996-98; mng. dir. ATMEL Hellas, Patras, 1999—. Served with Greek Army, 1994-96. Mem. IEEE, Tech. Chamber of Greece. Greek Orthodox. Avocations: travel, sports. Office: ATMEL Hellas SA, Patras Sci Pk- Stadiou St, 26500 Rio Greece

KOUTROULIS, ARIS GEORGE, artist, educator; b. Athens, Greece, May 14, 1938; came to U.S., 1953; s. George Aris and Julia (Eftimiades) K.; m. Mary Ann Schmid, 1964 (div. 1973); m. Jill Warren, July 4, 1982; 1 child, Georgina. BFA, La. State U., 1961; Master Printer, Tamarind Lithography Workshop, L.A., 1964; MFA, Cranbrook Acad. Art, Bloomfield Hills, Mich., 1966. Chmn. bd. Willis Gallery, Detroit, 1970-71; pres. Common Ground of the Arts, Detroit, 1969-72; guest artist Ox-Bow Summer Sch. Art, Saugatuck, Mich., 1973; co-dir. Ox-Bow Summer Sch. Art, Saugatuck, 1975; assoc. prof. art Wayne State U., 1966-75; head painting dept. Ctr. Creative Studies, Detroit, 1975-81; prof., chmn. Fine Arts Dept. Ctr. Creative Studies, 1981—. exhibited one-man shows Hanamura Gallery, Detroit, 1966, Montgomery Mus. Fine Arts, Ala., 1966, Va. Poly. Inst., 1968, Baton Rouge Gallery, 1968, Wayne State U., 1969, Mich. Council for Arts, 1969, Gertrude Kasle Gallery, Detroit, 1970, Detroit Artists Market, 1973, Klein-Vogel Gallery, Detroit, 1974, Detroit Inst. Arts, 1976, Gloria Cortella Gallery, N.Y.C., 1977, Gallery Renaissance, Detroit, 1980, Haber-Theodore Gallery, N.Y.C., 1980, OK Harris Gallery, N.Y.C., 1980, 81, 82, 83, 85, 87, 90, 92, 98, Mich. Traveling Exhbn., 1981, Cantor/Cemberg Gallery, Birmingham, Mich., 1982, 88, Dubins Gallery, L.A., 1984, Nimbus Gallery, Dallas, 1986, Argo Gallery, Athens, Greece, 1988, Argo Gallery, Cypres, 1991, 94, OK Harris Works of Art, Birmingham, Mich., 1991, Art Gallery Registry Resort, Naples, Fla., 1992, Bell Gallery, B'haui, 1995, Ctr. Gallery, Detroit, 1996; exhibited group shows Decorative Arts Ctr., N.Y.C., 1973, Detroit Inst. Arts, 1974, Bykert Gallery, N.Y.C., 1974, Bklyn. Mus., 1977, Brooks Meml. Art Gallery, Memphis, 1977, La. State U. Gallery, 1978, Tyler Sch. Art, Temple U., 1978, Mus. Fine Arts, Springfield, Mass., 1978, Van Doren Gallery, San Francisco, 1978, Consulate Gen. Greece, N.Y.C., 1978, Landmark Gallery, N.Y.C., 1978, Cranbrook Mus. Art, Bloomfield Hills, Mich., 1979, Detroit Inst. Arts, 1980, Mus. Fine Arts Tampa, 1987, 51st nat. mid-yr. exhbn. Butler Inst. Am. Art, Youngstown, Ohio, 1987, Flint Mus. of Art. Mich., 1989, Japan Expo, Tokyo, 1989, Ctr. Gallery Ctr. Creative Studies, Detroit, 1989, 95, 97; represented in pub. collections including Mus. Modern Art, Nat. Gallery Art, Detroit Inst. Arts, L.A. County Mus. Art, Cranbrook Mus. Art, Detroit Engring. Soc., Detroit Pub. Libr., U. Mich. Art Mus., Anglo-Am. Mus., Amon Carter Mus. Western Art, Ft. Worth, UCLA Grunwald Graphic Arts Found., Ball State U. Art Mus., Vores Mus., Athens, The Goulandis Mus. Modern Art, Andros, Greece; represented in corp. collections; commd. Standard Oil Corp., San Ramon, Calif., Arbor Drugs, Inc., Bracewell/Patterson, Washington, Mich. Found. for Arts, Detroit Engring. Soc., Art for Detroit, City of Detroit, WDIV-TV4, Detroit, Tampa Mus. Collection, Criterion Ctr., N.Y.C., Masco Corp., Taylor, Mich. Address: PO Box 307 Denver NY 12421-0307

KOUTSELINIS, ANTONIOS, forensic medicine and toxicology educator; b. Volos, Greece, Nov. 17, 1935; s. Stephanos and Evangelia Koutselinis; m. Hellen Kaneli. MD, U. Athens (Greece), 1959, PhD, 1960, specialist in microbiology, 1964, specialist forensic medicine toxicology, 1984. Assoc.

prof. forensic medicine and toxicology U. Athens, 1980, prof., chmn. dept. forensic medicine, 1981—, dean med. sch., 1995—, vice rector, 2000—. Author: Toxicology, 1967, Narcotics, 1973, Cosmetics, 1984, Forensic Medicine, 1989, Toxicology, 1998, Bioethics, 2000; contbr. articles to profl. jours. Mem. Nat. Drug Orgn. (pres. 1989-94). Orthodox. Avocations: photography, video. Office: Med Sch of Athens, 75 M Asias St, 115 27 Athens Greece

KOUTSKY, JAROSLAV, materials science engineer, educator, researcher; b. Rokycany, W. Bohemia, Czech Republic, June 18, 1929; s. Josef and Alzbeta (Storkova) K.; m. Dagmar Ruzickova, Aug. 6, 1955; 1 child, Stepan. Diploma in engring., Tech. U., Ostrava, 1952, PhD, 1959, DSc, 1964. Lectr. Tech. U., Ostrava, 1952-56; mgr. Ctrl. Rsch. Inst., Skoda, 1956-69; apptd. univ. prof. Tch. Coll., Cairo, 1967, head chair, 1969-72; head divsn. Tch. Coll., Plzen, 1972-78, Nuclear Rsch. Inst., Prague, 1978-89; head dept. West Bohemian U., Plzen, 1989—; cons. Ministry of Industry and Trade, Prague, 1995—. Author: Material Defects of Tools, 1969, Fractures of Steel Parts, 1976 (Editor's prize 1976), Alloy Steels for Power Engineering, 1981 (Nat. prize 1981), Radiation Damage of Structural Materials, 1994. Recipient F. Krizik gold medal Czechoslovakia Acad. Sci., 1989. Mem. Czech Soc. Metal Sci. (com. mem. 1966—), N.Y. Acad. Sci., Polish Soc. Materials. Avocation: tennis. Home: Rabynska 750, 14200 Praha 4, Czech Republic Office: U West Bohemia, Univerzitni 22, 30614 Plzen Czech Republic

KOUTSODIMOU, AGLAIA, researcher; b. Athens, Greece, May 20, 1963; d. Elias and Efthalia (Samara) K. BS in Chemistry, U. Athens, Greece, 1986, PhD in Chemistry, 1993. Rsch. asst. U. Athens, Greece, 1986-87; lectr. Peripheral Gen. Hosp., Athens, Greece, 1994-96; assoc. prof. Tech. Inst. Athens, 1996-99; assoc. rschr. NCSR Demokritos, Athens, 1996—. Contbr. articles to profl. jours. Mem. Assn. Greek Chemists, Greek Biophys. & Biochem. Soc., Hellenic Soc. Thermal Analysis. Greek Orthodox. Avocations: painting, swimming. Home: B Logothetidi 19, 115 24 Athens Greece Office: NCSR Demokritos, 153 10 Athens Greece

KOUTSOGIORGAS-COUCHELL, STEVEN, plastic surgeon; b. Karyai, Laconia, Greece, Apr. 29, 1948; s. Harry George and Maria Niok (Kaperonis) K.; m. Livia George Tsakogiannis, Feb. 25, 1993; children: Maria, Katerina. BS in Biology, Wofford Coll., Spartanburg, S.C., 1973; MS in Biochemistry, So. Meth. U., 1974; MD, U. Tex./U. Athens, 1979. Diplomate Am. Bd. Surgery, Am. Bd. Plastic Surgery. Resident in gen. surgery Columbia U./Meml. Sloan Kettering Cancer Ctr., N.Y.C., 1979-84; fellow plastic surgery, asst. prof. Tulane U., New Orleans, 1984-86; pvt. practice specializing in plastic surgery Athens Med. Ctr., 1987—. Mem. Greek Soc. of Rec. Microsurgery (treas. 1993—). Greek Orthodox. Avocations: vine growing, wine making. Home: Spartis 15, Kifisia Athens Greece Office: 46 Voukourestiou str, 10673 Athens Greece

KOUTSOYIANNIS, DEMETRIS, civil engineer; b. Mesounta, Greece, Apr. 27, 1955; s. Nicolaos and Aglaia (Papakosta) K.; Irene Karakosti, Jan. 4, 1979 (div. Dec. 1982); m. Anna Patrikiou, May 20, 1987; 1 child, Quetzal-Aggelos. Diploma in Civil Engring., Nat. Tech. U., Athens, 1978; D of Engring., Nat. Tech. U., Athens, Greece, 1988. Faculty mem. Polytechniki Engring. Co., Athens, Greece, 1979-81, Meter Cons. Co., Athens, Greece, 1981-83; rsch. asst. Nat. Tech. U., Athens, Greece, 1981-90, lectr., 1990-95, asst. prof., 1995—; cons. engr., Athens, 1983—; project coord. Hydroscope, Athens, 1992-94. Author: Design of Sewer Networks, 1993, Statistical Hydrology, 1996; co-author Engineering Hydrology, 1997; contbr. articles to profl. jours. Seaman Hellenic Navy, 1984-86. Achievements include hydrologic design of ten major dams in Greece; inspiration and leadership of the Hydroscope project; research in stochastic disaggretation models in operational hydrology and rainfall modeling. Office: Nat Tech U, HEroon Polytechniou 5, GR-15780 Athens Greece

KOUVOPOULOU, MARILDA GAY, public relations executive; b. Lethbridge, Canada, Feb. 4, 1965; d. Yiannis and Niki (Golfinopoulos) K. Bsc in Mktg. Mgmt., Am. Coll. Greece, 1987; MA in Pub. Rels., European Univ., Athens, 1997, MBA, 1998. From sec. to creative mgr. to sec. to client svcs. mgr. BOLD/O&M Advt. Agy., Athens, 1987-89; sec. tp gen. mgr. Effective Mgmt. Internat. Ltd., Athens, 1989-90; sec. tp gen. mgr. SCOPLIFE SA, Athens, 1990-92, from asst. mktg. mgr. to mktg. mgr., 1992—. Avocations: music, arts & crafts, travel, puzzles. Office: SCOPLIFE SA Life Ins, 64 Kifissias Ave, 151 25 Maroussi Athens, Greece

KOUYATÉ, LANSANA, economist, international official, diplomat. Formerly economist, spl. rep. of UN Sec.-Gen. to Somalia and Rwanda; former exec. sec., now sec.-gen. Econ. Cmty. of West African States, Abuja, Nigeria, 1997—. Office: ECOWAS, Secretariat Bldg, Asokoro Abuja Nigeria*

KOUZAEV, GUENNADI ALEXEEVICH, electronics and mathematics educator; b. Pokhivistnevo, Russia, Feb. 7, 1958; s. Aleksey Egorovich and Tatayna Yakovlevna (Molostova) K.; m. Nadezhda Georgievna Gaidar, Feb. 11, 1984. MS, Electrotech. Inst. Telecomms., Kuibshev, Russia, 1980; PhD, Inst. Radio Engrg./Electronics, USSR Acad. Sci., Moscow, 1986; DrSci, Moscow State Inst. Electronics, 1998. Rschr. Russian Inst. Space Instrument Design, Moscow, 1984-89; sr. rschr. Moscow State Inst. Electronics and Math., 1989-92, predoctoral rschr., 1992-95, assoc. prof., 1995-98; prof. Moscow State Inst. Electronics, 1998—; part-time project head, dept. head Advanced Tech. Inst./Russia Acad. Natural Scis., 1994-97; organizer, chair internat. tech. confs. Mem. editl. bd. Jour. Wave Process Physics and Radiotech. Sys., Samara, 1998—; vice-editor Internat. Jour. Ecology in the 21st Century, 2000—; contbr. articles to profl. jours.; patentee in field. Recipient USSR Govt. prize for young scientists, 1990, Russian Govt. prize in field of sci. and engring., 1997. Mem. Am. Assn. Inventors and Authors, Assn. Med. Physicists of Russia, Trans Black Sea Regiona Sci. Union of Applied Electromagnetism, A.S. Popov Soc. for Radio Engring., Electronics and Telecomms., Russian Soc. Inventors. Avocations: fishing, reading. Home: apt 33 dom 3 ul Titova, Pos Lesnoy, Puskhino dist, Moscow 141291, Russia Office: Moscow State Inst Elec/Math, 3/12 Bol Trekhsvaytitelsky, Moscow 109028, Russia

KOUZES, RICHARD THOMAS, physicist, educator; b. Arlington, Va., July 8, 1947; s. Thomas and Thelma Virginia (Loss) K.; m. Janice Mary Costantino, Feb. 28, 1970; children: Ross, Emily. BS, Mich. State U., 1969; MS, Princeton U., 1972, PhD, 1974. Sr. rsch. physicist Princeton (N.J.) U., 1976-91; sr. scientist Pacific N.W. Nat. Lab., Richland, Wash., 1991-95; prof. W.Va. U., Morgantown, 1995-2000; sr. staff scientist Pacific N.W. Nat. Lab., Richland, Wash., 2000—. Author: Astrophysics Simulations, 1995; editor: Neural Network Applications in Energy, Environment & Health, 1996. Mem. IEEE (sr.), Am. Phys. Soc., Sigma Xi. Home: 1005 Country Ct Richland WA 99352-9500

KOVAČ, MAJA, physiologist, researcher; b. Ljubljana, Slovenia, Sept. 16, 1949; d. Mirko Kovač and Milica Kacin. BS, U. Ljubljana, 1974, MSc, 1978, PhD, 1987. Asst. plant physiology U. Ljubljana, 1982-90, asst. prof. plant physiology, 1990-95, assoc. prof., 1995—. Contbr. articles to profl. jours. Recipient Nat. Sci. award Fund B. Kidrič, 1989. Mem. Fed. European Soc. Plant Physiology, Slovenian Soc. Plant Physiology. Home: Dalmatinova 11, 1000 Ljubljana Slovenia Office: Nat Inst Biology, Večna pot 111, 1000 Ljubljana Slovenia

KOVAČ, MIROSLAV, agriculturist, consultant; b. Pakrac, Croatia, Oct. 4, 1967; s. Tihomir and Ljubica (Karaula) K.; m. Vesna Marinić, Apr. 29, 1995; 1 child, Lovro. B in Agronomy, U. Zagreb, Croatia, 1992; postgrad. biotech. fac., Inst. of Nutrition, Univ, Lublana, Sloveniya, 2000. Head horse dept. Croatian Livestock Selection Ctr., Zagreb, 1993-95; adminstr. State Farm of Dairy Cows, Pula, Croatia, 1995-97; head br. office Croatian Agrl. Ext. Inst., Pazin, 1997-98; advisor Croatian Agrl. Ext. Inst., Požega, 1998—; chmn. organizing com. Internat. Horse Breeding Symposium, Rovin, Croatia, 1995-96. Author: Croatian Posavac-Indigenous Horse of Croatia, 1994, Balanced Ratio for the Dairy Cows (brochure), 1999, editor: Monography of Istriah Cattle, 1999; contbr. articles to profl. jours. Recipient Economy Promotion award County of Sisak, Croatia, 1995. Mem. Posavina Horse Breeding Assn. (founder, sec. gen. 1993-96), Istrian Cattle Breeders Assn. (sec. gen. 1996-98), The Trakehner Horse Breeders Assn. (sec. gen. 1997-99). Roman Catholic. Avocations: basketball, house painting, hairdressing, bicycling. E-mail: miroslav.kovac@po.tel.hr. Home: Dr V Maček 10-4, HR-34000 Požega Croatia Office: Croatian Agrl Ext Inst, ul Grada Vukovara 78, HR-10000 Zagreb Croatia

KOVACEVIC, RADOVAN, mechanical engineering educator; b. Niksic, Yugoslavia, July 17, 1947; came to U.S., 1987; s. Bozo and Zagorka (Vujicic) K.; m. Ljiljana Sokic, Dec. 10, 1972; children: Ivana, Jelena. BS, U. Belgrade, Yugoslavia, 1969, MS, 1972; PhD, U. Titograd, Yugoslavia, 1978. From asst. prof. to prof. U. Titograd, Titograd, 1975-86; assoc. prof. Syracuse (N.Y.) U., 1987-90; assoc. prof. U. Ky., Lexington, 1991-95, prof., 1995-97; Herman Brown chair prof. So. Meth. U., Dallas, 1997—; cons. prof. Harbin (China) Inst. Tech., 1994. Co-author: Principles of Abrasive Waterjet Technology, 1998; contbr. over 140 articles to profl. jours. Achievements include patents for high-pressure waterjet-assisted cooling/lubrication system in machining, method of monitoring and control for the 3D shape of weld pool based on vision system, new control of gas metal arc welding. Office: So Meth U 1500 International Pkwy # 100 Richardson TX 75081-2325

KOVACEVICH, RICHARD M., banker. BA, Stanford U., 1965, MBA, 1967. Exec. v.p. Kenner div. Gen. Mills, Inc., Mpls., 1967-72; prin. Venture Capital, 1972-75; v.p. consumer services Norwest Corp., Mpls., from 1975, then sr. v.p. N.Y.C. banking group, then exec. v.p., mgr. N.Y.C. bank div., then exec. v.p.. mem. policy com., vice-chmn., chief operating officer banking group, from 1986, now pres., chief oper. officer, vice chmn., also dir., chmn., CEO, 1996—, now chmn., CEO; pres., CEO Wells Frargo & Co. (merged with Norwest Corp.), San Francisco, 1999—. Office: Wells Fargo & Co MSC-A0101121 420 Montgomery St San Francisco CA 94104-1205

KOVACH, ANDREW LOUIS, administrative executive; b. Greensboro, Pa., Feb. 4, 1948; s. Andrew and Pauline (Nassar) K.; m. Cindy Juliani, Nov. 28, 1970; 1 child: Courtney. BS in Indsl. Engineering, W.Va. U., 1969. Engr. DuPont, Martinville, Va., 1970-73; supt. engr. Allied Corp., Syracuse, N.Y., 1973-75; mgr. employee rels. Allied Corp., Morristown, N.J., 1976-80, mgr. orgnl. devel., 1980; dir. human resources Allied Corp., N.Y.C., 1981-82, dir. comml. devel., 1983-87; ptnr. Thomas Andrew Assoc., Morristown, N.J., 1987—; sr. v.p. human resources, info. systems Morristown Meml. Hosp., 1988-96; v.p. human resources and shared svcs. Atlantic Health Sys., Florham Park, N.J., 1996—; chmn. bd. Morristown Meml. Physician Hosp. Orgn. Mem. ethics com. Morris Twp.; co-compliance officer Atlantic Health Sys. Mem. Morristown Club (bd. dirs.), Park Ave. Club. Presbyterian. Office: Atlantic Health System 325 Columbia Tpke Ste 202 Florham Park NJ 07932-1213

KOVACH, JOSEPH WILLIAM, management consultant, psychologist, educator; b. Hammond, Ind., Oct. 4, 1946; s. William Charles and Florence (Miotke) K. BA in Speech, St. Joseph Coll., Whiting, Ind., 1969; MA in Psychology, Roosevelt U., 1974; PhD, Ill. Inst. Tech., 1981; PhD in Clin. Psychology, Chgo. Sch. Profl. Psychology, 1986. Diplomate Am. Bd. Psychological Specialties of Am. Coll. Forensic Examiners; lic. sch. psychologist, Ill., Ind., Mo.; cert. marriage & family therapist, Ind. Asst. corp. merchandising mgr. Kroch's & Brentano's, Chgo., 1965-70; regional ops. mgr. Interstate Dept. Stores, Inc., Highland, Ind., 1971-73; prof., chmn. psychology, dir. grad. studies workplace psych. Calumet Coll. St. Joseph, Whiting, Ind., 1984—; dir. Ednl. Rsch. Exch., Calumet City, Ill., 1988—; pres. Joseph W. Kovach and Assocs., Ltd., Calumet City, 1969—; dir. Buzan Centre Ltd. of Chgo., 1992—; sr. cons. Calumet City Youth Svc. Bur., 1973-75; supr. Loyola U. Med. Ctr., Maywood, Ill., 1980-83, Northwestern Meml. Hosp., 1973-83, rsch. assoc., 1979-81; pre-doctoral intern Chgo. Read Mental Health Ctr., 1983-84, asst. program dir., 1988-89; sch. psychologist intern Sch. Dist. 163, Park Forest, Ill., 1986; grad. asst. Roosevelt U., Chgo., 1970-71; rsch. assoc. Northwestern U. Med. Sch., 1974-76, Loyola U. Med. Ctr., Maywood, 1976-78; adj. mem. faculty Thornton C.C. (name now South Suburban Coll.), South Holland, Ill., 1976, 97-98, Purdue U. Calumet, Hammond, Ind., 1976-89; presenter Internat. Conf. of The Role of Social Science in the Devel. of Education, Business and Government Entering the 21st Century, Kaunas, (Lith.), 1998, 24th Internat. Congress on Arts and Comm., Oxford, Eng.; co-organizer USA Memory Championships; organizer Midwest Memory Championships. Columnist: Bus. in Rev./The Times, Munster, Ind., Executive Excellence and Personal Excellence, Provo, Utah., Talking to the Boss, Skokie, Ill. Bd. dirs. Milton H. Erickson Inst. No. Ill.; co-founder, bd. dirs. Internat. Acad. for Study of Virtual Reality; trustee Calumet Coll. St. Joseph; chaplain Sheriff's Dept., Lake County, Ind. Mem. APA, Midwest Psychol. Assn., Ill. Sch. Psychologists Assn. Office: PO Box 113 Calumet City IL 60409-0113

KOVACH, RONALD, footwear manufacturing executive; b. N.Y.C., Dec. 22, 1946; s. Edward Joseph and Louise Christine (Ragno) K.; m. Linda Cathrine Clark, May 5, 1969; children: Meredith Alexa, Matthew Alexander. BA with honors, U. Calif., Riverside, 1968, MA, 1970; postgrad., UCLA, 1970-74. Asst. v.p. Big 5 Sporting Goods, El Segundo, Calif., 1972-91; dir., founder Eagle Claw Saltwater Fishing Schs., Huntington Beach, Calif., 1989—; ind. cons. to sporting goods industry Huntington Beach, 1992—; bd. dirs. Penn Fishing U.; lectr., condr. seminars, Huntington Beach, 1985—; frellance photojournalis, Huntington Beach, 1985—; co-owner FX (fishing expeditions outdoor apparel); bd. dirs. Advt. Maj. Footwear Co.; cons. in field; host Fishing Expdns. on Outdoor Channel. Author: Bass Fishing in California: Secrets of the Western Pros, 1985, Trout Fishing in California: Secrets of the Top Western Anglers, 1987, Saltwater Fishing in California: Secrets of the Pacific Experts, 1989, Serious Bass Fishing: Winning Secrets of Advanced Bass Anglers, 1994, The Serious Pacific Angler: Advanced Secrets of The Eagle Claw Fishing School, 1994; host: Fishing Expeditions Sta. XTRA-sports Radio, L.A.; host: Fishing Expdns. TV; co-host: World of Big Game Fishing Show ESPN-TV; contbr. numerous articles to various publs. Organizer Proposition 132, Calif. anti-gill net initiative, 1990. Calif. State scholar U. Calif., 1970; rsch. NIMH fellow UCLA, 1972. Mem. Internat. Game Fish Assn., Nat. Resource Def. Coun., Calif. Trout, Bass Anglers Sportsman Soc., Outdoor Writers Assn. Am., Outdoor Writers Calif., United Anglers, Pacific Offshore Rsch. Found., Scripps Inst. Oceanography. Avocations: fishing, travel, racquetball. Home: 17911 Portside Cir Huntington Beach CA 92649-4931 Office: 7351 Heil Ave Ste D Huntington Beach CA 92647-4534

KOVACHEV, LJUBOMIR STEFANOV, surgery educator; b. Dimitrovgrad, Haskovo, Bulgaria, Nov. 26, 1942; s. Stefan Lazarov and Stefanka Yankova (Lambeva) K.; m. Anelia Ljubomirova Panteleeva, Feb. 7, 1981; 1 child, Stefan Ljubomirov. MD, Higher Inst. Medicine, Sofia, Bulgaria, 1972; PhD, Higher Med. Medicine, Pleven, Bulgaria, 1985. Registrar in surgery City Hosp., Dulovo, Bulgaria, 1972-75, Dist. Hosp., Pernik, Bulgaria, 1975; asst. prof. surgery Higher Med. Inst., 1976-85, assoc. prof., 1986—, head dept., 1987—, dean, 1987-93. Contbr. articles to med. jours., including Internat. Surgery, Surgery Today-Japan Jour. Surgery, Lancet, Zentralblat für Chirurgie, Surg. Radiol. Anatomy, Brit. Jour. Surgery, European Jour. Surgery. Fellow Internat. Coll. Surgeons; mem. Eurosurgery. Orthodox. Avocations: sports, history, geography. Home: Entr D Apt 2, George Kochev St 39, 5800 Pleven Lovec, Bulgaria Office: Higher Med Inst, Kl Ohridsky St 1, 5800 Pleven Lovec, Bulgaria

KOVACIC, TONKA, chemical engineering educator, researcher; b. Split, Croatia, May 30, 1940; d. Kajo and Zorka (Trumbic) Feric; m. Andelko Kovacic, Nov. 27, 1965 (dec.); children: Ana, Šime. BS, U. Zagreb, 1964, MS, 1973, PhD, 1978. Asst. prof. U. Split Faculty of Tech., Split, 1979-87, U. Zagreb Faculty of Civil Engring., Split, 1975-87; prof. U. Split Faculty of Tech., Split, 1987—, vice dean, 1995-99; chief dept. petrochemistry and polymers, Faculty of Tech., Split, 1983-91, 98—. Contbr. articles to profl. jours. Mem. Croatian Chem. Soc. for Dalmacia (pres. 1993-95), Croatian Chem. Soc., Soc. Plastics and Rubber Engrs. (grantee 1987). Roman Catholic. Home: D Simunovica 19, 21000 Split Croatia Office: U Split Faculty Chem Tech, Teslina 10, Split Croatia

KOVACIC, WILLIAM EVAN, law educator; b. Poughkeepsie, N.Y., Oct. 1, 1952; s. Evan Carl and Frances Katherine (Crow) K.; m. Kathryn Marie Fenton, May 18, 1985. AB with honors, Princeton U., 1974; JD, Columbia U., 1978. Bar: N.Y. 1979. Law clk. to sr. dist. judge U.S. Dist. Ct. Md., Balt., 1978-79; atty. planning office bur. competition FTC, Washington, 1979-82, atty. advisor to commr., 1983; assoc. Bryan, Cave, McPheeters & McRoberts, Washington, 1983-86; prof. George Mason U. Sch. Law, Arlington, Va., 1986-99, George Washington U. Law Sch., Washington, 1999—; cons. in field; mem. U.S. Senate Judiciary Subcom. on Antitrust and Monopoly, Washington, 1975-76. Contbr. legal articles to profl. jours. Assoc. Father Ford Found. Columbia U. Cath. Campus Ministry, N.Y.C. 1985—. Harlan Fiske Stone fellow Columbia U., 1976-78. Mem. ABA (antitrust law and pub. contract law sects.), Fed. Bar Assn. Roman Catholic. Avocations: hiking, camping, photography. Office: George Washington U Law Sch 720 20th St NW Washington DC 20052-0001

KOVÁČIK, VLADIMÍR, chemistry researcher; b. Turzovka, Slovakia, Jan. 28, 1938; s. Ludovít and Štefánia (Šimková) K.; m. Mária Gurínová, Dec. 10, 1969; children: Roman, Oliver, Nadežda. Engr., Tech. U., Bratislava, Slovakia, 1962; MSc, Slovak Acad. Scis., Bratislava, Slovakia, 1967, DSc, 1989. Doktorant Inst. Chemistry, Slovak Acad. Scis., 1963-67, sci. worker, 1967-89, leading scientist, 1989—. Contbr. over 110 articles to profl. jours., 1965—. Lt. Slovakian Mil., 1962-63. Recipient Štúr award in natural scis., Bratislava, 1988. Mem. Arbeitsgemeinschaft Massenspektrometrie, Am. Soc. Mass Spectrometry. Home: Budatinska, 85106 Bratislava Slovakia Office: Inst Chemistry SASc, Dúbravská, 84238 Bratislava Slovakia

KOVACS, AGNES, olympic athlete; b. Budapest, Hungary, July 13, 1981. Mem. swim team Hungary; winner bronze in 200 meter breaststroke Olympics, Atlanta, 1996; winner gold in 200 meter breaststroke Olympics, Sydney, Australia, 2000; winner double gold European Championship, 1997; winner 200 meter breaststroke World Championship, 1998, winner 100 meter breastroke and 200 meter breaststroke, 1999. Named Sportswoman of Yr. in Hungary, 1997. Office: Hungarian Swimming Assn, Arpad Fejedelem utja 8, Budapest Hungary*

KOVACS, AIMEE, conference speaker, minister; b. Laredo, Tex.; d. Arturo and Hilaria; m. James Kovacs; six stepchildren and 1 son. BS, U. Tex.; M in Bibl. Counseling, Friends Internat. Christian U., D in Ministry in Dance, PhD. Cert. tchr. Tex. and N.J.; cert. min. Eagles House, N.Y. Mktg. staff Abbington Assocs., N.J.; tchr. N.J. Sch. Sys.; min. The Eagle House, N.Y.C.; pres. Kingdom Glory, Inc., West Long Branch, N.J.; pres. World Wide Dominion Dancers, N.J.; mem. mktg. staff Abbington Assocs., N.J.; host TV program on Nigeria, NTV. Author: Dancing Into The Anointing, 1996; choreographer (dance concert) World of Dance, 1967, (play) Monmouth Players; writer, dir. (play) Comedy of Teachers, 1975; prodr. (video) World of Dance, 1998; host, sponsor (TV program) Victory is a Choice, Nigeria. Team mother West Long Branch (N.J.) Sports, 1984-87; art appreciation vol. West Long Branch Elem., 1987; class mother Rumson Country Day Sch., 1988; choreographer UN, N.Y., 1993; mothers club Christian Bros. Acad., Lincroft, 1995-96; vol. Children of the World Found., 1998. Named Sweetheart, Pan Am. Student Forum, Tex., 1962, Ms. Sail Boat Race, Atlantic Highlands Yacht Club, 1976, Mrs. West Long Branch, Mrs. N.J. Internat. Pageant, 1996, Mrs. Colts Neck, Mrs. N.J. Internat. Pageant, 1997, Mrs. Monmouth County, Mrs. N.J. Internat. Pageant, 1998; Martin High Choir scholar, Laredo, Tex., 1962. Mem. Battle Ground Country Club, Elisha House, B. Hinn Ptnrs. Republican. Avocations: golf, sailing, skiing, dancing, gardening. Home and Office: Kingdom Glory Inc PO Box 40 West Long Branch NJ 07764-0040

KOVACS, ALAN L., lawyer; b. N.Y.C., May 21, 1947; s. Edward J. and Hilda Kovacs; m. Caryn R. Bronstein, Aug. 5, 1972; children: Erica, Michele. BA, Amherst Coll., 1969; JD, Columbia U., 1972; LLM, Boston U., 1980. Bar: N.Y. 1993, Mass. 1995. Asst. dist. atty. N.Y.C. Dist. Attys. Office, 1972-75; assoc. Gadsby & Hannah, Boston, 1976-78; asst. atty. gen., chief antitrust divsn. Atty. Gens. Office, Boston, 1978-85; counsel Ferriter, Scobbo, Caruso, Boston, 1985-97; founder Law Office of Alan L. Kovacs, Boston, 1997—; chmn. Antitrust Task Force Nat. Assn. of Attys. Gen., 1983-85; commr. payment adv. commn. Mass. Hosp., Boston, 1995-97. Dir. Newton (Mass.) Girls Soccer League, 1985—; mem. Newton Dem. Com., 1986—; class agent Amherst (Mass.) Coll. Alumni Fund, 1994—. Mem. ABA, MBA, Boston Bar Assn. Home: 257 Dedham St Newton MA 02461-2044 Office: 1 Boston Pl Ste 3620 Boston MA 02108-4401

KOVACS, ALESSANDRO LEONE, physics educator; b. Bologna, Italy, Nov. 17, 1936; m. Madeleine Studer, Jan. 11, 1968; children: Stefano, Daniela. Degree in Physics, U. Bologna, 1960; PhD in Statis. Thermodynamics, Free U., Brussels, 1962. Rschr. Columbia U., N.Y.C., 1962-63; encharged prof. U. Naples, Italy, 1963-65, U. Bologna, 1966-72; full prof. U. Rome, 1973—; coord. theoretical group Nat. Inst. Condensed Matter. Home: Via Giacinta Pezzana 109, 00197 Rome Italy Office: U La Sapienza Biomed Scis, PA Moro 5, 00185 Rome Italy

KOVACS, FLORA, financial executive, economist; b. Budapest, Hungary, Jan. 4, 1972; d. Arpad and Arpadné (Hevesy) K. B Econ. Sci., Coll. Fin. and Acctg., Hungary, 1995; MBA, U. Budapest, 1998. Credit mgr. in fin. Budapest Marriott Hotel, 1995-96; asst. fin. contr. Motorola Ltd., Budapest, 1996-97; contr. M-RTL TV, Budapest, 1997-99; fin. dir. UPS Hungary Ltd., Budapest, 1999—. Mem. Hungarian MBA Assn. Home: Birtok U 14, 1147 Budapest Germany Office: UPS Hungary Ltd, Kozma u 4, 1108 Budapest Hungary

KOVACS, FRANCISCO MANUEL, physician, researcher, educator; b. Palma de Mallorca, Baleares, Spain, Jan. 30, 1964; s. Rene and Maria Juana (Reus) Kovacs. Grad. in medicine and surgery, U. Barcelona, Spain, 1983, D in Medicine and Surgery, 1986. Pres. Fundación Kovacs, Palma de Mallorca, Spain, 1989—; mgr. sci. dept. Fundación Kovacs, Palma de Mallorca, 1989—; prof. U. Medicina, Barcelona, 1988—; mem. experts bd. for evaluation of neurorreflexotherapy Ministry Edn. and Sci., Ministry Health, Madrid, 1989—; Spanish rep. Cost B4 Project, Brussels, 1994-98, Spanish rep. Cost B13 Project, Brussels, 1998—. Contbr. articles to profl. jours. Hon. consul of Hungary in Balearic Islands, Spain, 1993—. Lt. doctor Spanish Air Force, 1983. Avocations: pianist, judo, marksman, acrobatic pilot, parachutist. E-mail: kovacs@kovacs.org. Office: Fundación Kovacs, Paseo Mallorca 36 3o 1a, 07012 Palma de Mallorca Baleares, Spain

KOVÁCS, GEORGE LASZLO, computer engineering educator, researcher; b. Budapest, Hungary, Oct. 30, 1943; s. Paul K. and Éva A. (keresztes) K.; m. Noémi E. Faragó, Mar. 15, 1986; children: Zoltán, Enikö, Márton. Diploma, Tech. U. Budapest, 1966; postgrad., U. Colo., 1972-73; D in Tech., Tech. U. Budapest, 1976, PhD, 1978; DSc, Hungary Acad. Scis., Budapest, 1997. Rsch. assoc. Computer and Automation Rsch. Inst., Budapest, 1966-79, head of CAD, 1979-87, head of CAD rsch. dept., 1987-91, head of CIM Rsch. Lab., 1991—; prof. Tech. U., 1995; vis. rschr. Dubna, Russia, 1977-79, BMW, Munich, 1983; vis. prof. IIE, Cuernavaca, Mex., 1986-87, U. Trento, Italy, 1994, 97. Recipient Excellent Innovator/Inventor award, Budapest, 1991. Mem. IEEE (sr.), Ea. European Map/Top Insterest Group (dep. pres. 1993—), IFAC, IFIP. Avocations: sports, music, rock and mineral collecting, arts. Home: Verecke 116/1, 1025 Budapest Hungary Office: Computer & Automation Inst, Kende u 1377, 1111 Budapest Hungary

KOVÁCS, GÉZA, economics educator; b. Böhönye, Somogy, Hungary, Apr. 22, 1928; s. József and Anna (Pio) K.; m. Etelka Joó, Feb. 10, 1951; 1 child, Etelka. Master's degree, Hungarian U. Econs., Budapest, 1952; Univ. Dr., Karl Marx U. Econs., Budapest, 1958; DSc, Hungarian Acad. Scis., Budapest, 1967. Registered economist. From asst. prof. to assoc. prof. U. Econs., Budapest, 1952-68; dep. dean econs. faculty Karl Marx U. Econs., Budapest, 1962-65, dean econs. faculty, 1965-68; prof. Budapest U. Econs., 1968—; head of dept. nat. planning Karl Marx U. Econs., Budapest, 1967-71, head of sect. futures rsch. nat. planning dept., 1968-89; cons. Nat. Planning Office, Budapest, 1957-72; pres. Hungarian Acad. of Scis. Futures Rsch. Com., Budapest, 1974-86; pres. Coun. for Mut. Econ. Aid Task Force Com. on Prognostics, Budapest-Moscow/Hun-Su, 1984-87; founder rsch. seminar futurology Karl Marx U. Econs., 1968; mem. Hungarian Acad. of Scis. Regional and Interdisciplinary Com., 1992—; mem. Budapest U. of Econ. Scis. Faculty Econs. Prof.'s Body, pres., 1992—. Author: Long-Range Perspectives and Planning, 1970, Critical Turning Points in the Future, 1975, Long-term Tendencies of Development, 1985, Modernisation and Social Security, 1995. Recipient Golden Order of Labor award Hungarian Govt.,

1982, award of Albert Szentgyörgyi, Hungarian Govt., 1995. Office: Budapest U Econ Scis, Fövám tér 8, 1093 Budapest Hungary

KOVACS, GYOERGY, physician, educator; b. Budapest, Hungary, May 29, 1953; s. Laszlo Kovacs and Klara Takacsi-Nagy; m. Natalie; 1 child, Timea. MD, Szeged (Hungary) Med. Sch., 1977; univ. prof. in radiotherapy, U. Med. Sch. Kiel, Germany, 1992. Bd. cert. in Hungarian and German radiotherapy. Resident Mcpl. Ctr. Radiation Oncology, Budapest, 1978-81, asst. prof., 1981-87, head of dept., 1987-89; fellow Hungarian Acad. Scis. Robert-Roessle Inst., Berlin-Buch, Germany, 1984-87; fellow Alexander von Humboldt Found., Munster, Germany, 1989-91; univ. prof., dept. chmn. radiation therapy U. Med. Sch. Kiel, 1991—, head Interdisciplinary Brachytherapy Ctr., dep., 1999—. Contbr. sci. papers to profl. jours. Mem. German Soc. Radiation Therapy (founding mem., head brachytherapy working group 1997—), German Soc. Radiation Oncology (head working group of brachytherapy 1997—), European Soc. for Radiation Oncology (coun. mem. group of brachytherapy 1996—, Best Poster award 1991), Am. Assn. Radiation Oncologists (bd. cert.), Am. Soc. Radiation Oncology, Hungarian Soc. Radiation Oncology. Avocations: horse riding, photography, books. Office: Klinik Strahlentherapie, Arnold Heller Str 9, D-24105 Kiel Germany

KOVÁCS, IMRE, surface chemist, researcher; b. Baja, Hungary, Mar. 11, 1960; d. Imre and Imrené (Katalin Rentz) K. Chemist, Jozsef Attila Tudomang Egyetem, Univ., 1984; Dr. of Univ., JATE, Szeged, Hungary, 1990; Cand. of Scis., Hungarian Acad. Scis., Budapest, Hungary, 1995. Fellow Hungarian Acad. Scis., Szeged, 1984-87, asst. rschr., 1987-90, rschr., 1990—. Contbr. articles to profl. jours. including Surface Sci., Jour. Phys. Chem., Catalysis Letters. Mem. Union of Hungarian Chemists. Office: MTA IKI Dept Surface Sci and Catalysis, PO Box 77, H-1525 Budapest Hungary

KOVACS, ISTVAN, civil engineer; b. Labatlan, Hungary, Apr. 25, 1953; s. Ferenc and Gizella (Hodi) K.; m. Eva Varosi, July 16, 1977; children: Szilard, Adrienn. Civil Engr., Budapest Tech. U., 1977, Specialized Engr., 1981; Diploma in Mgmt. Studies, Buckinghamshire Coll., 1999. Foreman Capital Waterworks, Budapest, 1977-80; tech inspector, supr. Reg. Waterworks, Vac, Hungary, 1980-84, head prodn. dept., 1984-89, dir. entity, 1989-93; sales dir. IMI Épületgepesz Ltd., Budapest, 1993-97; gen. mgr., mng. dir. IBP Hungary Ltd., Budapest, 1997—; cons. Hungarian Hydrology Soc., 1978-90; expert Hungarian Std. Inst., Budapest, 1981-82. Fellow Open Bus. Sch.-Szamalk, Japan Internat. Coop. Assn.; mem. Soc. Bldg. and Architect. Avocations: sporting events, exhibitions, tours. Home: Somogyi u 52, 2600 Vac Hungary Office: IBP Hungaria KFT, Köérberki U 36, 1112 Budapest Hungary

KOVÁCS, LÁSZLÓ, physics educator, researcher; b. Nagykanizsa, Hungary, Jan. 27, 1942; s. József and Józsefné (Guerra) K.; m. Gyöngyi Burján, July 24, 1965 (April 1997); 1 child, László; m. Katalin Kovács, Nov. 25, 1999. MS, Eötvös Loránd U., Budapest, Hungary, 1965; PhD, Kossuth Lajos U., Debrecen, Hungary, 1973. Tchr. Landler Jenö H.S., Nagykanizsa, Hungary, 1965-83, Berzsenyi Dániel Coll., Szombathely, Hungary, 1983—; vice prin. Landler H.S., Nagykanizsa, 1968-73; head dept. physics Berzsenyi Coll., Szombathely, 1983-991; rsch. assoc. Nat. Pedagogy Inst., Budapest, 1974-77; inspector of physics County Zala, Hungary, 1978-80, County Vas, Hungary, 1991-93; vis. scholar Hungarian Acad. Scis., London, 1976, Giessen, 1992, Washington, 1993, München, 1998, 99; expert for various TV stations, 1998—. Author: Kisérletek a szilárdtestfizika köréböl, 1981, Mikola Sándor, 1995; editor: Studia Physica Savariensia, 1995—. Recipient medal Ministry of Culture, Budapest, 1974, award, 1991. Mem. Eötvös Soc. (exec. com. 1970-89, chmn. tchrs. 1980-84, Mikola Sándor prize 1973, v.p. 1999—, Eötvös medal 1999), European Phys. Soc. (exec. com. history of sci. divsn. 1992—, Volta medal 1999). Avocations: hiking, piano playing. E-mail: klaci@fs2.bdtf.hu. Home: Màrtirok tere 5/c, 9700 Szombathely Hungary Office: Berzsenyi Daniel Coll, Karolyi Gaspar ter 4, 9700 Szombathely Hungary

KOVACSICS, JÓZSEF, statistics educator; b. Vasszentmihály, Hungary, Sept. 30, 1919; s. István Kovacsics and Anna Nika; m. Mária Antónia Petrován, Dec. 28, 1943 (dec. 1965); children: József, Mary, Lorèna, Cecilia, Róbert; m. Katalin Anna Nagy, Nov. 25, 1967; 1 child, A'gnes. LLD, U. Eötvös, Loránd, Budapest, 1946; candidature, Budapest Acad. Scis., 1957, academician doctor, 1972. Statistician Ctrl. Statis. Office, Budapest, 1945-53, dir. libr., 1954-59; head dept. stats. U. Pécs, Hungary, 1957-59; head dept. stats. U. Eötvös, Loránd, 1959-89, prof. stats. and info., 1965-89, prof. emeritus, 1995—; editor Ctrl. Statis. Office Budapest Rev. of Hist. Demographie, 1978; population expert UN, N.Y.C., 1981; cons. Ctr. Statis. Office, Budapest, 1985. Author, editor: Sources of Historical Statistics, 1957, Statistics, 3rd edit., 1979, Legal Informatics, 1980; contbr. articles to profl. publs. Pres. Commn. for Legal Informatics Hungary, 1992—. Ensign Hungarian Air Def., 1942-44. Mem. Internat. Statis. Inst., Internat. Union for Sci. Study of Population, Acad. Scis. (com. for demography), Laureatus Academiae. Home: Haraszt-u 22, 1118 Budapest Hungary Office: Univ Eötvös Loránd, Egyetem-tér 1-3, 1364 Budapest Hungary

KOVAL, ADOLF GRIGORIEVICH, research scientist, laboratory director; b. Pavlovsk, Russia, Aug. 7, 1932; s. Grigoriy Alekseevich and Evdokiya Alekseevna (Danilchenko) K.; m. Valentina Mihajlovna Palehina; 1 child, Vladislav. Degree in physics, Ural State U., Sverdlovsk, USSR, 1952, Kharkov (USSR) State U., 1972; D Phys. Sci., Kharkov (USSR) State U., 1989, Kharkov (USSR) State U., 1989. Rschr. Kharkov Phys. Tech. Inst., 1955-72; head rsch. lab. ion processes Kharkov State U., 1955—; lectr. Kharkov Agrl. Inst., 1963-66. Contbr. articles to profl. jours. Mem. Russian Acad. Sci. (mem. Coun. Phys. Electronics), Ukraine Nat. Acad. Sci. (mem. Coun. Physics Status Solidy).

KOVAL, IVAN VASILIVICH, chemist, educator; b. Podgorodneye, Ukraine, Jan. 2, 1942; s. Vasiliy Iosifovich and Irina Kirilovna (Obora) K.; m. Ludmila Egorovna Zibulja, Aug. 18, 1969; 1 child Andrey Ivanovich. Degree in Science, Inst. Chemical Technology, Dniepropetrovsk, Ukraine, 1970; D in Chemistry, Inst. Organic Chemistry, Kiev, 1987. Lab. asst. Dniepropetrovsk, 1960-62; student Chem-Tech. Inst., Dniepropetrovsk, 1962-67, post graduate student, 1967-70, asst., 1970-71, instr., 1971-88; prof. head dept. Chem. Tech. Inst., Dniepropetrovsk, 1989—. Contbr. articles to sci. jours. Avocations: tourism, fishing. Home: S. Kovalevsky St. 77/137, 320120 Dnepropetrovsk Ukraine Office: Ukrainian State Chem-Tech, Gagarina Ave 8, 320005 Dnipropetrovsk Ukriane

KOVALCHENKO, MIKHAYLO SAVICH, materials engineer, educator; b. Vinnitsa, Ukraine, Mar. 2, 1934; s. Sava Tymofiyovich and Varvara Yevmenivna (Tupchiyenko) K.; m. Vira Semenivna Sinelnikova, July 19, 1933; 1 child, Andriy. Degree in engring., Kyiv (Ukraine) Poly. Inst., 1956; PhD, Acad. Scis. Ukraine, Kyiv, 1962; D in Tech. Sci., Higher Cert. Commn. of USSR, Moscow, 1974, prof., 1976. Engr. Inst. Metal Ceramics and Spl. Alloys (now Inst. for Problems of Materials Scis.), NAS Ukraine, Kyiv, 1956-58, jr. rsch. fellow, then sr. rsch. fellow, 1959-67, head dept., 1967—; educator Kiev Poly. Inst., 1958-68, prof., 1988-96; expert Higher Cert. Commn. of USSR, Moscow, 1982-91, Higher Cert. Commn. of Ukraine, Kiev, 1993-96. Author: Theoretical Principles of Hot Treatment of Porous Materials by Pressure, 1980, (with G.V. Samsonov) Hot Pressing, 1962, (with V.V. Ogorodnikov, Y.I. Rogovoi, A.G. Krainii) Radiation Damage of Regractory Compounds, 1979; contbr. articles to Powder Metallurgy and Metals Ceramics, 1961-2000, Strength of Mateirals, 1998, 2000. Recipient prize for Sci. and Tech., Coun. Ministries of USSR, Moscow, 1986, 89, State prize for Sci. and Tech., Ukraine, 1994; named The Merited Sci. and Engring. Worker of the Ukraine, 1998. Office: IN Frantsevich Inst, NAS, 3 Krzhizhanovsky St, Prob M, 03142 Kyiv 142, Ukraine

KOVALENKO, ANDRIY FEDOROVYCH, physicist, educator; b. Lviv, Ukraine, June 9, 1963; s. Fedir Vasyliovych and Liudmyla Semenivna (Soshyna) K.; m. Irina Nikolayevna Sultanova, Feb. 27, 1988. MSc in Physics, Lviv State U., 1985, PhD in Physics and Math., 1993. Engr. Inst. Theoretical Physics, Kiev, Ukraine, 1985-87; sci. rschr. Inst. Condensed Matter Physics, Lviv, 1990-95, sr. sci. rschr., 1996—; postdoctoral Inst. Chemistry, Nat. Autonomous U. Mexico, Mexico City, 1995-96; vis. prof. Inst. Molecular Sci., Okazaki, Japan, 1997-98, fellow, 1998-99, asst. prof., 2000—; computer adminstr., cons. Inst. Condensed Matter Physics, Lviv, 1990-95. Contbr. articles to profl. jours. Grantee Internat. Sci. Found., 1993, 94. Mem. Ukrainian Phys. Soc. Avocations: swimming, internet, chess, football. E-mail: andriy@ims.ac.jp. Home: Panas Myrnyi Str 9 Apt 2, 290026 Lviv Ukraine Office: Inst Molecular Sci, Myodaiji, Okazaki 444 Aichi 444-8585, Japan

KOVALENKO, ARTEM VITALIEVICH, physicist; b. Kiev, Ukraine, Nov. 10, 1966; s. Vitaly Petrovich and Maya Ivanovna (Kas'yan) K.; m. Anna Alexandrovna Apostolova, May 7, 1992 (div., 1994); 1 child, Anastasiya. MS, Kiev Taras Schevchenko U., Ukraine, 1990; PhD, Inst. Physics, Kiev, Ukraine, 2000. Engr. Kiev Taras Shevchenko U., Kiev, Ukraine, 1990-92, Inst. Physics, Kiev, 1992-97; rschr. Inst. Physics, Kiev, Ukraine, 1997-99. Contbr. articles to profl. jours. Mem. Ukrainian Physical Soc. Home: 2 240 Kharkovskoye Shosse, 253160 Kiev Ukraine Office: Inst Physics, 46 Prospekt Nauki, 252022 Kiev Ukraine

KOVALENKO, VLADIMIR SERGEEVICH, education educator; b. Kiev, June 20, 1941; s. Sergey Nicolaevich Kovalenko and Galina Dmitrievna Bobrovskaya; m. Nina Vladimirovna Melnichenko, June 26, 1965; children: Nataly, Oksana. M in Engring., Polytechnical Inst., Kiev, Ukraine, 1963; PhD in Engring., Polytechnical Inst., Kiev, 1968; DS, Polytechnical Inst., Tula, Russia, 1980. Engr. Indsl. Plant, Kiev, 1962-63; asst. prof. Polytech. Inst., Kiev, 1963-69, 1969-81, prof., dept. head, 1981—, dean, engring. faculty, 1981—; head rsch. lab. Polytech. Inst., 1968-93; dir. Laser Technology Rsch. Inst., Kiev, 1993—; Disting. vis. prof. Ohio State U., Columbus, 1993; expert of UNDP, Acad. of Sci., China, 1992; UN expert from Ukraine, 52 UN Gen. Assembly, 1997; vis. prof. Okayama U., Japan, 1999. Author 20 books in field, including: Application of Optical Quantum Generators in Technology, 1967, Material Machining With Pulsed Laser Radiation, 1977 (KPI award 1985), Electrophysical and Electrochemical Methods of Material Machining, 1975, Laser Technology, 1989, others. Vice-chmn. Laser Assocs. of CIS, Moscow, 1985-92; vice-chmn. commn. Ministry of Edn., Kiev, 1990—; chmn. coun. State Highest Qualification Commn. of Ukraine, Kiev, 1992-97. Recipient State prize of Ukraine, 1982, Golden medal State Exhbn., Moscow, 1988, USSR Coun. of Mins. prize, 1990; named hon. scientist of Ukraine, 1993; decorated Order for Merits, 1997. Mem. IEEE, Internat. Instn. for Prodn. Engring. Rsch., Optical Soc. of Ukraine (coun. mem. 1991), Laser Inst. of Am., Acad. of Engring. Sch. of Ukraine. Avocations: reading, gardening, jogging, swimming, music. Office: Nat Tech Univ of Ukraine, 37 Prospect Peremohy, 252056 Kiev Ukraine

KOVALERCHUK, BORIS, mathematician, computer scientist, educator; b. Tashkent, Russia, Aug. 9, 1949. MS in Maths., Novosibirsk U., 1971; PhD, Soviet Acad. Scis., 1977. Lectr. Tashkent U., 1980s-mid 1990s; vis. prof. SUNY, Binghamton, 1994-95, La. State U., Baton Rouge, 1995-96; assoc. prof. Ctrl. Wash. U., Ellensburg, 1996—. Author: Data Mining in Finance, 2000. Mem. N.Y. Acad. Scis., Internat. Fuzzy Sys. Assn., Soc. Computer Applications in Radiology. Office: Central Wash U 400 8th Ave Ellensburg WA 98926

KOVALEVSKY, ALEXANDER ALBERTOVICH, mathematician; b. Yasinovataya, Donetsk, Ukraine, Aug. 29, 1957; s. Albert Petrovich and Olga Alexandrovna (Bondarenko) K.; m. Irina Faustovna Rusanova, July 3, 1976; children: Oleg, Marina. Candidate of Sci., Inst. Applied Math. and Mech., Donetsk, 1985, DS, 1995. Engr. Inst. Applied Math. and Mechanics, Nat. Acad. Scis. Ukraine, 1983-85, jr. sci. rschr., 1985-91, sci. rschr., 1991-92, sr. sci. rschr., 1992-97, leading sci. rschr., 1997—; vis. prof. U. Degli Studi Roma La Sapienza, 1995, U. Ferrara, Italy, 1995, U. Catania, Italy, 1995-2000, U. Pierre et Marie Curie, Paris, 1998; reviewer Math. Revs. of Am. Math. Soc., 1995—, Zentralblatt Math of European Math. Soc., 2000—. Contbr. over 60 articles to sci. publs. Rsch. fellow Italian Nat. Coun. Rsch., Rome, 1999. Avocations: basketball, volleyball, poetry. Office: Inst Applied Math and Mech, Rosa Luxemburg St 74, 83114 Donetsk Ukraine

KOVALEVSKY, JEAN, astronomer; b. Neuilly dur Seine, France, May 18, 1929; s. Jean and Hélène (Pavloff) K.; m. Jeannine Reige, May 18, 1956; children: Jean-Paul, Madeleine, Pierre. Licence ès Sci., Ecole Normale Supérieure, Paris, 1952; Agrégation de Mathématiques, Ecole Normale Supérieure, 1954, Dr.S., 1959. Rsch. asst. Paris Obs., 1955-60, Yale U. Obs., 1957-58; chief rsch. and computing svc. Bur. des Longitures, Paris, 1960-71; dir. Groupe de Recherchews de Géodésie Spitiale, Paris, then Grasse, France, 1971-79, Centre d'Etudes de Recherches Géodynamiques et Astronomiques, Grasse, 1974-82, 88-92; pres. bur. Nat. Métrologie, 1995—; sec. Com. Internat. des Poids et Mesures, 1991-96, pres., 1997—; lectr. Paris U., 1960-73. Author: Introduction to Celestial Mechanics, 1967; (with J.J. Levallois) Traité de Géodesie, 1970, Modern Astrometry, 1995; editor: L'Astronomie, 1964-70; contbr. articles to profl. jours. Served with French Navy, 1952-53, 56. Decorated Légion d'honneur, comdr. Ordre Nat. du Merite. Mem. Internat. Acad. Astronautics, French Acad. Scis., Academia Europaea, Academia delle Scienze di Torino, Internat. Astron. Union, Internat. Com. Space Rsch. (chmn. working group 1965-74), Internat. Assn. Geodesy, Société Astronomique de France (pres. 1970-73), French Nat. Com. Astronomy (chmn. 1973-76, 89-92). Home: La Padovane 8 Rue Saint Michel, 06130 Grasse France Office: Cerga Ave Copernic, 06130 Grasse France

KOVALEVYCH, VOLODYMYR MYCHAILOVYCH, geologist; b. Ivano-Frankivsk, Ukraine, Jan. 5, 1941; s. Mychailo Ivanovych and Olimpia Ivanivna (Kalynovych) K.; m. Iryna Makarivna Derzijanz, July 16, 1939; 1 child, Jurij. Engr., geologist, U. Lviv, 1962, PhD, 1976; DS, Inst. Geol. Scis., 1990. Engr., geologist Kiev (Ukraine) Geology, 1962-66, Inst. Geology and Geochemistry Combustible Min, Lviv, Ukraine, 1966-97; main scientist Inst. Geology and Geochemistry Combustible Min, Lviv, 1997—; chmn. state exam. commn. on geochemistry U. Lviv, 1996-98. Author: Physico-Chemical Conditions of Formation of Salt in Stebnyk Potash Deposit, 1978, Halogenesis and Chemical Evolution of the Ocean in Phanerozoic, 1990; contbr. articles to profl. jours. Grantee Austrian Inst. for Ea. and S.E. Europe, 1997, Internat. Sci. Found., 1994-96. Greek Catholic. Home: Turgeneva 48/9, 290015 Lviv Ukraine Office: Inst Geology & Geochemistry, Naukova 3A, 79053 Lviv Ukraine

KOVALYOV, SERGEY BORISOVICH, bank executive; b. Rel'tovo, Moscow, Russia, Aug. 22; s. Boris Andreevich and Nadezhda Anatolievna (Yakovlev) K.; m. Maria Petrovna Vladykina, Mar. 3, 1979; children: Darya, Peter. Grad., Moscow Inst. Fin., 1979. Economist, sr. econs. Techsnabexport, Moscow, 1979-87, attaché, 1987-88; attaché, 3rd sec. USSR/Russian Embassy, Stockholm, 1989-92; mgr. Tokobank, Moscow, 1992, gen. mgr., 1992-93, dep. mng. dir., 1993-94, mng. dir., 1994-95, mng. dir., bd. dirs., 1995-98; mng. dir. Artobank, Moscow, 1998—. Recipeint Medal in Memory of 250 Anniversary of Moscow, Pres. of Russia, 1997. Avocations: traveling, reading, historical books. Office: Autobank, 41 Lesnaya St, 101514 Moscow Russia

KOVANDA, JAN, engineering educator; b. Praha, Czech Republic, Feb. 6, 1956; s. Vladimír and Libuše (Janíčková) K. Degree in engring., Tech. U., Praha, 1980, PhD (hon.), 1988. Rschr. Motor Car Rsch. Inst., Praha, 1980-93; assoc. prof. Tech. U., Praha, 1994—. Inventor road obstacle for speed limitation; author reports, conf. pros., lecture notes in field; author: Motor Vehicle Design, 1995-97. Grantee Czech Grant Agy., 1996-98. Mem. Czech Acad. Sci. Avocations: history, art, cycling, skiing. Office: Czech Tech U K 221, Technická 4, 166 07 Praha 6, Czech Republic

KOVANDA, KAREL, Czech Republic government official; b. Gilsland, England, Oct. 5, 1944; married; 3 children. Degree in agr., Prague Sch. Agr., 1969; PhD in Polit. Sci., MIT, 1975; MBA, Pepperdine U., 1985. Tchr. various colls. Calif.; cons. Radio Beijing, 1977-79; mgr. various U.S. pvt.-sector cos., 1980-90; with Ministry Fgn. Affairs, Czechoslovakia, with adminstrv. dept., 1991-92; head Euroatlantic dept. Ministry Fgn. Affairs, Czech Republic, 1993; permanent rep. of Czech Republic UN, N.Y.C., 1993-97; dep. fgn. min. Govt. of Czech Republic, Prague, 1997-98; head Czech delegation to NATO and Western European Union, 1998—; rep. of Czech Republic. UN Security Coun., N.Y.C., 1994-95; v.p. UN Econ. and Social Coun., 1996; pres. UN Econ. and Social Coun., 1997. Office: Czech Del to NATO, NATO Hdqrs, 1110 Brussels Belgium

KOVÁR, MARTIN MARIA, mathematician, researcher, educator; b. Brno, Moravia, Czechoslovakia, Nov. 5, 1966; s. Milan and Milena (Prachařová) K. PhD, Masaryk's U., Brno, 1994. Cert. in topology and geometry. Asst. prof. Masaryk's U., Brno, 1990-92, Tech. U. Brno, 1992—. Contbr. articles to profl. jours. Mem. N.Y. Acad. Scis. Roman Catholic. Office: Tech U Brno, Dept Math, Technicka 8, 61669 Brno Czech Republic

KÖVÁRI, ISTVÁN J., electrical engineer, retired technical advisor; b. Kisvarda, Hungary, Aug. 21, 1940; s. Janos and Janosne (Terebessy) K.; m. Marianne Labady, May 10, 1972; children: Zsigmond, Mihaly. BScEE, Tech. U., Budapest, Hungary, 1963, MScEE, 1965. Cert. elec. engr. From sci. co-worker to sci. worker Ctrl. Rsch. Inst. for Physics (later CRIP), Budapest, 1963-78; rsch. group leader CRIP, Budapest, Hungary, 1969-78; sr. sci. worker CRIP, Budapest, 1978-84, rsch. dept. leader, 1978-84, expert com. leader, 1983-84; tech. advisor Videoton Devel. Inst., Budapest, 1984-90, project mgr., 1986-90. Developer: Application of Data Recording Peripherals, (Conf. on Computer Techniques, 1971, Inst. prize, 1975, others), Magnetic Tape Recorder (Year Book of CRIP, 1981-82, Gold medal named Eminent inventor, 1981); contbr. numerous articles to profl. jours. Russian, Hungarian and English; inventor in field. Recipient Eminent Schoolboy prize, Cultural Minister, Kisvarda, 1958, Work prize Presdl. Coun. of Hungary, Budapest, 1975, Janossy prize, 1983, CRIP,. Mem. Computer Soc. of John von Neumann (sr. mem.). Avocations: radio receiver techniques, automobile electronics, excursions. Home and Office: Tavadat BT (Teledata Ltd), Bela Kiraly U 4/A, H-1125 Budapest Hungary

KOVARSKI, ALEXANDER L., scientist, educator; b. Moscow, July 2, 1944; s. Lev B. Pevzner and Berta M. Kovarskaya; m. Galina G. Lipatova, Oct. 11, 1967; 1 child, Maxim A. Grad., Mendeleev Chem. Tech. U., Russia, 1966, candidate sci., 1972; DSc in Polymer Chemistry, 1989. Sr. rschr. Semenov Inst. Chem. Physics, Moscow, 1969-95; head rsch. group Emanuel Inst. Biochem. Physics Russian Acad. Scis., Moscow, 1995—; prof. High Chem. Coll. Mendeleev Chem. Tech. U. Russia, Moscow, 1997—. Author: Spin Labels and Probes in Physical Chemistry of Polymer, 1986, Molecular Dynamics Of Additives in Polymers, 1997, Spectroscopy of Electron Spin Resonans, 1998; editor, co-author: High Pressure Chemistry and Physics of Polymers, 1994. Mem. Acad. Creative Endeavors. Avocations: painting, ancient history. Home: Goncharnaya St, 109172 Moscow Russia Office: Emanuel Inst Biochem Physic, Kosygin St, 117977 Moscow Russia

KOVARSKII, VLADIMIR LVOVICH, physicist, researcher, educator; b. Zaporozhye, USSR, Feb. 18, 1958; s. Lev Zelikovich and Sophia Isaakovna (Bryskina) D.; m. Lyudmila Zinovyevna Shapiro, Aug. 18, 1986; children: Anna, Daniel, Peter. Diploma in physics, MS, Don. State Univ., Donetsk, 1979; PhD, Don. Phys & Tech Inst, Donetsk, 1986. Jr. rsch. fellow Don Phys. & Tech. Inst., Donetsk, 1986-87, rsch. fellow, 1987—. Contbr. articles to profl. jours. With Soviet Army, 1979-81. Home: Schorsa str 69-22, 340114 Donetsk Ukraine Office: Donetsk Phys & Tech Inst, R Luxemburgh Str 72, 340114 Donetsk Ukraine

KOVÁSZNAI, VIKTÓRIA LUKÁCS, art historian, museologist, researcher; b. Budapest, Hungary, Apr. 16, 1942; d. József Kovásznai and Etel Zakar; m. Lajos Lukács, Feb. 4, 1961; 1 child, András. PhD, Eötvös Loránd U., Budapest, 1978. Art historian Hungarian Nat. Gallery, Budapest, 1967—, dir. medal cabinet, 1981. Author: (books) Czinder, 1980, The Medallic Art of József Reményi, 1980, Miklos Borsos, 1989, Laszlo Szlavics, Jr., 1997, Chapters from the History of Hungarian Medallic Art, 1999; organizer: (exhbn.) Miklós Borsos, 1970. Recipient Award for Culture Minister of Culture, Budapest, 1986, Modern Hungarian medals I, 1993, Rethy Laxzlo prize, 1997. Fellow Fedn. Internat. de la Medaille; mem. Hungarian Numismatic Soc. (v.p.). Office: Hungarian Nat Gallery, Pf 31, H-1250 Budapest Hungary

KOVATIS, PAUL EVAN, orthopedic surgeon, researcher, consultant; b. Cedar Grove, N.J., Apr. 17, 1963; s. Pericles Peter and Elizabeth Jane K. BS in Biology summa cum laude, Upsala Coll., East Orange, N.J., 1985; MD, U. Medicine and Dentistry N.J., 1989. Intern U. Medicine and Dentistry N.J., 1989-90, resident in orthopaedic surgery, 1990-95; fellow Hosp. Spl. Surgery, N.Y., 1996-97; attending orthopaedic surgeon Hackensack (N.J.) U., 1996—; clin. cons. Capezio Balletmakers, Inc., N.J., N.Y., EBI Med. Sys. Inc., N.J., 1998—, Zimmer Orthopaedics, N.J., 1999—. Contbr. articles to profl. jours. Mem. nat. nominating com. Outstanding Young Women Am., 1998—. Mem. Am. Orthopaedic Foot and Ankle Soc., Am. Assn. Foot and Ankle Surgeons, Am.Hellenic Progressive Edn. Assn. (v.p. 1997—), Phi Beta Kappa. Greek Orthodox. Avocations: baseball, physical fitness, theatre, travel. Home: 300 Prospect Ave Hackensack NJ 07601-7712 Office: Orthopedic Spine and Sports Medicine 2 Forest Ave Paramus NJ 07652-5214

KÖVES, PAL, statistician; b. Hodmezovasarhely, Hungary, June 28, 1925; s. Janos and Maria (Muller) K.; m. Edit Terstyanszky, Mar. 24, 1956; 1 child, Jozsef. MS, U. Econ. Scis., Budapest, 1951, Dr. Univ., 1958; PhD, Hungarian Acad. Scis., Budapest, 1963, DSc, 1978. Lectr. U. Econ. Scis., 1951-54, sr. lectr., 1954-63, assoc. prof., 1963-75, full prof., 1975-91, prof. emeritus, 1995—. Author: (books) Index Numbers/Statisztikai indexek, 1956, Index Theory and Economic Reality, 1983; co-author: (book) General Statistics/Altalanos statisztika 1960, 1981. Recipient award for Outstanding Rsch. and Ednl. Activity, Hungarian Min. of Culture and Edn., 1994; index number formula E Koves S named for in his honor Internat Comparison Program, UN Statis. Office, 1975. Mem. Internat. Statis. Inst., Hungarian Statis. Assn.

KÖVESDI, ISTVAN, physicist, researcher; b. Budapest, Hungary, July 4, 1952; s. Istvan and Margit (Szijj) K.; m. Eva A'goston (div. 1997); 1 child, Petra. Grad. cum laude, U. Budapest, 1978, D summa cum laude, 1981. Diplomate physics and organic chemistry. Rschr. ELTE U., Budapest, 1978-89; sr. rschr. EGIS Ltd., Budapest, 1989—. Author: ZX Spectrum Service Book, 1983, NMR Spectroscopy, 1984, Numeric Analysis of Electronic Circuits, 1992 (Author of Yr. 1992), Physics Workbook for Osborne Physical Encyclopedia, 1998. Lt. Hungarian mil., 1971. Avocations: home cinema, computer programming, sailing, tennis. Office: EGIS Pharms Ltd, PO Box 100, Budapest Hungary

KOVLER, KONSTANTIN, civil engineer, educator; b. Moscow, June 12, 1957; arrived in Israel, 1990; s. Leonid and Rosa (Eidus) K.; m. Nona Pinsky, Dec. 8, 1979; two children. MSc, State U. Civil Engring., Moscow, 1978, DSc, 1986. Engr. rsch. fellow State U. Civil Engring., Moscow, 1978-85; sr. rsch. fellow Budnikov Rsch. Inst. Bldg. Materials & Structures, Kraskovo, Russia, 1986-88; docent State Open U., Moscow, 1989-90; rschr. Technion, Haifa, Israel, 1990-96, sr. lectr., 1996—. Mem. Am. Concrete Inst., Internat. Union Testing & Rsch. Labs., Internat. Assn. Fracture Mechs. Home: Ha-Shita 4, 36800 Nesher Israel

KOVNER, KATHLEEN JANE, civic worker, portrait artist; b. Cambridge, Mass., Nov. 25, 1919; d. David Leo and Kathleen Elizabeth (Lalley) Lane; m. Benjamin Kovner, June 20, 1938; children: Kathleen Barbara (dec.), Michael Anthony, Peter Christopher. Student, Art Students League, N.Y.C., 1937-40. Owner, CEO Helen Bennett Ltd., Stamford, Conn., 1948-59; cons. Bride's Mag., N.Y.C., 1967-70; co-chair membership com. Women's Nat. Rep. Club, N.Y.C., 1980-81, chmn. membership com., 1981-87, v.p., 1986-87, also bd. dirs.; ltd. ptnr. 519 8th Ave Corp., N.Y.C., 18-19th St. Corp., N.Y.C., Kaufman Arcade Bldg., N.Y.C., 19th St. Assn., N.Y.C., dir. Nelson Tower Assoc., N.Y.C., 1998. Portrait artist in oils, with various portraits in pvt. collections. Fundraiser St. Ignatius Loyola, N.Y.C., 1960-61, Jeanine Pirro-Campaign for Dist. Atty., Westchester County, N.Y., 1993, 97. Republican. Roman Catholic.

KOWAL, REBEKAH JANE, English language educator; b. Norfolk, Va., Aug. 24, 1966; d. Ira Joseph and Sheila (Slawsby) K.; m. David Scott Bullwinkle, Aug. 8, 1998. BA, Columbia U., 1988; PhD, NYU, 2000. Grad. tchg. asst. NYU, N.Y.C., 1992-98, lectr., 1995; asst. prof. of English, Mellon postdoc. fellow Haverford (Pa.) Coll., 1999—. Regional fellow U. Pa. Humanities Forum, 2000—. Mem. Am. Studies Assn., Soc. of Dance History Scholars, Coll. Art Assn., Am. Hist. Assn. Avocations: modern dance, ballet, yoga, hiking, biking, swimming.

KOWALCZUK, ZDZISLAW, electronic engineer, educator; b. Gdansk, Poland, Oct. 22, 1953; s. Kazimierz and Filomena (Kobus) K.; m. Maria Regina Rompczyk, Mar. 2, 1954; children: Anita, Monika. MS, Tech. U. Gdansk, 1978, PhD, 1986; DSc, Silesian Tech. U., 1993. Asst. inst. computer sci. Tech. U. Gdansk, 1978-80, sr. asst., 1980-86, asst. prof., 1986-91, asst. prof. dept. automatic control, 1992-93, prof., 1994—; rschr. U. Oulu, Finland, 1985; vis. fellow rsch. sch. Australian Nat. U., Canberra, 1987; vis. assoc. prof. elect. and computer engring. George Mason U., Fairfax, Va., 1990-91; lectr., Gdansk, 1991-94. Contbr. articles to profl. jours. Active Solidarity, Gdansk, 1980—. 2d lt. Polish Air Force, 1979. Recipient Rsch. Excellence award Polish Nat. Edn. Ministry, 1990; grantee Kosciuszko Found., 1990, GM, 1991, Polish Nat. Rsch. Com., 1993-99, Polish Nat. Sci. Found. awd., Tech. Scis., 1999. Mem. IEEE. Roman Catholic. Avocations: football, sailing, tennis, music. Home: Wzg Bernadowo 163, 81-583 Gdynia Poland Office: Tech U Gdansk, Narutowicza 11/12, 80-952 Gdańsk Poland

KOWALCZYK, JAN, nutritionist, biochemist, researcher; b. Bondyrz, Zamosc, Poland, May 31, 1931; s. Stanisław and Bronisława (Węclaw) K.; m. Henryka Radzikowska, June 25, 1957 (div. 1982); 1 child, Tomasz. MSc in Chemistry, U. M.C.S., Lublin, Poland, 1955; PhD in Animal Nutrition, Polish Acad. Scis., Jablonna, 1971; ScD in Animal Nutrition, Agrl. U., Warsaw, 1992, named prof. agrl. sci., 1995. Tchr. secondary sch., Lublin, Poland, 1950-55; jr. sci. worker U. M.C.S., Lublin, 1955-61; sr. sci. worker Polish Acad. Scis., Jabłonna, Poland, 1961-92; head lab. Polish Acad. Scis., Jabłonna, 1961-90, asst. prof., 1992-95, prof., 1995—; head dept. animal physiology and nutrition Polish Acad. Scis., Jabłona, 1994—; asst. prof. Wash. State U., Pullman, 1978-79; cons. Inst. Animal Scis., Havana, Cub, 1968-70;. Editor-in-chief: Jour. Animal and Feed Scis.; mem. editl. bd. Egyptian Jour. Nutritional Sci., 1996—, Archives of Animal Nutrition, 1997—, Acta Fytotechn. Et 20 Tech., 1997—, Animal Biology, 1997—; contbr. 150 articles to profl. jours. Mem. Polish Alpine Climbing Club (gen. sec. 1961-75), German Physiol. Soc. Roman Catholic. Avocations; tourism, mountain climbing, sailing, diving. Office: Inst Animal Physiology Polish Acad Scis, Instytucka 3, 05-110 Jabłonna Poland

KOWALCZYK, JERZY STEFAN, chemist, educator; b. Siedlce, Poland, Oct. 20, 1923; s. Aleksander and Stefania (Bujnik) K.; m. Doris Maria Wisniewska, Mar. 29, 1943; children: Wojciech, Piotr. MS, Tech. U. Gdańsk, Poland, 1950, DS, 1962. Asst. Tech. U. Gdańsk, 1950-62, adj., 1962-68, prof. asst., 1968-75, prof. chemistry, 1975-94, head chromat. rsch. group, 1970-94; ret., 1995; expert Polish Port. Orgn., Gdańsk, 1960-89; lectr. in field. Contbr. over 130 articles to profl. publs.; patentee apparatus for chromatography. Recipient award for sci. activity Ministry of Edn., 1975, 80, 89, award for edn. activity Ministry of Edn., 1978, 84. Mem. Polish Chem. Soc. Home: Burzyńskiego 12K/24, 80-462 Gdańsk Poland Office: Tech U Gdańsk, Narutowicza 11/12, 80-952 Gdańsk Poland

KOWALCZYK, MACIEJ STANISLAW, obstetrician, gynecologist, sexologist; b. Cracow, Poland, June 8, 1956; s. Bogumil Wieslaw and Teresa Maria (Matowska) K.; 1 child, Maciej Stanislaw Jr. MD, Med. Acad., Cracow, 1984; postgrad., Polish Acad. Sci., Cracow, 1984, Inst. Gyn.-Ob, Cracow, 1988-91, Instn. Sexology and Pathology Interhuman Bonds, Warsaw, 1990-93. Intern Narutowicz Hosp., Cracow, 1984-85; gen. practice medicine ambulatory Cracow-Srödmiescie, 1984-85; gen. practice ambulatory medicine First Aid Svc., 1985-87; asst. obstetrician and gynecologist Szpital Polozniczy, Cracow, 1986—; asst. in ob-gyn Maternity Amb. for Sch. Tchrs., Cracow, 1987-92; tchr. Cathedral Normal Anatomy, Med. Acad., Krakow, 1984-86; prof. Med. Coll. for Midwives, 1991; mem. commn. in Social Ins. Instn., Cracow, 1986-88. Contbr. articles to profl. jours. Recipient Organon Poster award, Yokohama, Japan, 1995. Mem. AAAS, Polish Gynecol. Soc., Polish Andrological Soc. (initiator), Polish Sexological Soc., Polish Radiol. Soc. (ultrasound sect.), Am. Soc. Colposcopy and Cervical Pathology, N.Y. Acad. Sci., Internat. Soc. Ultrasound in Ob-Gyn., Am. Inst. Ultrasound in Medicine, Polish Sonographic Soc., European Soc. Contraception, European Menopause Soc., European Soc. Human Reproduction and Embryology, European Tourist Club. Roman Catholic. Avocation: numismatics. Home: Odrowaža 22/7, 30-009 Cracow Poland Office: Szpital Polozniczo-Ginekologiczny, ul Siemiradzkiego 1, 31-137 Cracow Poland

KOWALEWICZ, ANDRZEJ, engineering educator, researcher; b. Warsaw, Poland, Feb. 6, 1932; s. Wincenty and Helena (Zbrozyna) K.; m. Teresa Wanda Karzewska, Apr. 19, 1985; 1 child, Krzysztof. MA, Warsaw U. Tech., 1956, PhD, 1963, DrHabil, 1970. Rschr. Inst. Aviation, Warsaw, 1956-66, asst. prof., 1966-78, prof., 1990—; prof. Tech. U. of Radom, Poland, 1978—; expert UN Indsl. Devel. Orgn., Bucharest, Romania, 1981, Dehra-Dun, India, 1983; vice rector Tech. U. of Radom, 1987-90, dir. inst., 1997—. Author: Combustion Systems of High Speed Piston I.C. Engines, 1980 (award Minister of Edn. 1980), Mixture Formation and Combustion, 1984 (award Minister of Edn. 1984), Selected Problems of Internal Combustion Engines, 1996, Supercharging of Internal Combustion Automotive Engines, 1998 (award Min. of Edn. 1998), Fundamentals of Combustion Processes, 2000; editor: The Archive of Automotive Engineering, 1996; contbr. over 75 articles to sci. jours. Decorated Bachelor's Cross of Order of Revival of Poland, Pres. of Nat. Bd., 1985; recipient Com. of Nat. Edn. medal Minister of Edn., 1979, Silver award Main Tech. Orgn., 1980. Mem. Polish Sci. Soc. of Automotive Engring. (charter, bd. dirs.), Polish Inst. of Combustion (bd. dirs.), Polish Acad. Sci., Soc. Polish Mech. Engrs. (cert. expert in internal combustion engines 1980). Roman Catholic. Avocation: tourism. Home: Mickiewicza 34/36 apt 56, 01-616 Warsaw Poland Office: Tech U Radom, Al Chrobrego 45, 26-600 Radom Poland

KOWALEWSKI, TOMASZ ALEKSANDER, physicist; b. Lodz, Poland, Sept. 25, 1947; s. Zdzislaw and Salomea (Kozielewska) K.; m. Teresa Rycerz, July 17, 1969; children: Ingrid, Oskar. MSc, Warsaw U., 1969; PhD, Polish Acad. Scis., 1982. From rsch. asst. to sr. rsch. assoc. Polish Acad. Scis., Warsaw, 1969-86; sr. rsch. assoc. Max-Planck-Inst, Gottingen, Germany, 1985-88, Georg August U., Gottingen, 1988-93; assoc. prof. Polish Acad. Scis., 1995—; vis. scholar Stanford (Calif.) U., 1982; vis. fellow New South Wales U., Australia, 1993, Technion U., Israel, 1995-96. Vice dir. CDN Underground Press, Warsaw, 1982-85. Home: Akermanska 7/13, PL02-760 Warsaw Poland Office: IPPT Pan Polish Acad Scis, Swietokrzyska 21, PL00-049 Warsaw Poland

KOWALEWSKI, ZBIGNIEW LUDWIK, mechanical engineer; b. Warsaw, July 24, 1957; s. Kazimierz Władysław and Jadwiga Helena (Kobyłecka) K. MSc, Warsaw U. Tech., 1981; PhD, Inst. Fundamental Technol.Rsch, Warsaw, 1988, DSc, 1997. Asst. Warsaw U. Tech., 1981-82; sr. asst. Inst. Fundamental Technol. Rsch., Warsaw, 1985-88, asst. prof., 1988-97, assoc. prof., 1997—. Brit. Coun. fellow U. Manchester, Eng., 1992-93; Deutsche Forschungsgemeinschaft grantee, U. Kassel, Germany, 1995, Brit. Coun., Imperial Coll. in London, U. Swansea grantee, 1996. Mem. European Mechanics Soc. Fax: 826-98-15. Office: Inst Fundamental Tech Rsch, Swietokrzyska 21, 00-049 Warsaw Poland

KOWALSKA, IRINA, endocrinologist; b. Białstok, Poland, Oct. 3, 1962; d. Włodzimierz and Tatiana (Karp uk) Krawczuk; m. Andrzej Tomasz Kowalski, Aug. 30, 1991; children: Jan, Małgorzata. MD, Med. U. Białystok, 1987; PhD, 1990; First degree in internal medicine, U. Hosp. Białystok, 1990; Second degree in internal medicine, Med. Ctr. Postgrad. Tng., 1994, Degree in Endocrinology, 1999. Med. diplomate. Resident U. Hosp. Białystok, 1987-88, dr. dept. endocrinology, 1989—; acad. tchr. dept. physiology Med. Acad., Białystok, 1987-89. Contbr. articles to profl. jours. Recipient award Polish Ministry Health, 1992. Mem. Polish Soc. Endocrinology (award 1999), Polish Soc. Diabetes, European Assn. Study Diabetes. Avocations: sports, internet, languages. Office: Dept Endocrinology, MC Skłodowskiej 24A, 15-276 Białystok Poland

KOWALSKA, TERESA, chemistry educator; b. Gliwice, Poland, July 19, 1946; d. Władysław and Zuzanna (Hanin) K. MSc in Chemistry, High Pedagogical Sch., Katowice, Poland, 1968; PhD in Chemistry, Silesian U., Katowice, 1972; DSc in Chemistry, Maria Curie-Sklodowska U., Lublin, Poland, 1988; Professorial Title, Adam Mickiewicz U., Poznan, Poland, 1999. Cert. chemist. Lectr. Silesian U., Katowice, 1972-73, sr. lectr., 1973-90, asst. prof., 1990-91, assoc. prof. chemistry, 1991-2000, prof. chemistry, 2000—. Editor Chromatographica Acta; contbr. articles to profl. jours. Recipient Bronze Cross of Merit, Pres. Polish Republic, Warsaw, 1979, Golden Cross of Merit, 1993. Mem. Polish Chem. Soc. (sec. Katowice br. 1973-74, vice-head Katowice br. 1985-87). Roman Catholic. Avocations: travel, reading poetry, reading world belletristic. Home: Cieszyńska 5, 41-500 Chorzów PL, Poland Office: Inst Chem, Silesian U, 9 Szkolna St, 40-006 Katowice Poland

KOWALSKI, LUIZ PAULO, head and neck surgeon, educator; b. Curitiba, Brazil, Aug. 16, 1956; s. Paulo and Ibra da Luz Kowalski; m. Ivonete Sanches Giacometti, June 13, 1992; children: Carolina Giacometti Kowalski and Giuliana Giacometti Kowalski. MD, U. Fed. Paraná, Curitiba, 1979; MS, Escola Paulista de Medicina, São Paulo, Brazil, 1986, PhD, 1989, prof. oncology, 1996. Med. resident Fundação Antonio Prudente, São Paulo, 1980-83; dir. head and neck surgery A. C. Camargo Hosp., São Paulo, 1990—; attending surgeon Hosp. Heliópolis, São Paulo, 1984-90; chief epidemiology unit Fundação Oncocentro de São Paulo, 1990; pres. head and neck dept. Paulista Med. Assn., São Paulo, 1994-95. Editor Acta Oncológica Brasilian, 1993—; contbr. articles to profl. jours. Recipient grants for study. Mem. Am. Head and Neck Soc., Brasilian Soc. Head and Neck Surgery. Fax: 55-11-3272-5098. E-mail: lp kowalski@mol.com.br. Office: Fundação Antonio Prudente, R Prof Antonio Prudente 211, 01509-010 São Paulo Brazil

KOWALSKI, THADDEUS LAWRENCE, judge; b. Chgo., Aug. 10, 1931; s. Anton Kowalski and Victoria Gruszka; m. Patricia Anne Geraghty, Oct. 4, 1968; children: David Mark, Neil Patrick. AB, U. Ill., 1953; JD, Northwestern U., Chgo., 1958. Atty. Jaroszewski & Kowalski, Chgo., 1958-63, Ill. Atty. Gen.'s Office, Chgo., 1963-64; trial atty. Cook County Pub. Defender, Chgo., 1964-68, dist. chief 1st mcpl., 1969-80; assoc. judge Cir. Ct. of Cook County, Chgo., 1980—. Author: Public Defenders Handbook, 1979. Bd. dirs. Nat. Polish Am. Jewish Am. Coun., Washington, 1985—; chmn. adv. bd. Felician-Montay Coll., Chgo., 1975-80; commr. Ill. Commn. on Human Rels., Chgo. and Springfield, Ill., 1974-80; pres. Polish Am. Congress, Chgo., 1974-78. 1st lt. U.S. Army, 1953-55. Recipient Creative Sentencing award N.W. Neighborhood Fedn., Chgo., 1993, appreciation award Gang Free/You and Me, Chgo., 1994, Street Intervention Program award YMCA, Chgo., 1996, cert. of appreciation Ravenswood Cmty. Coun., Chgo., 1998. Mem. Ill. Judges Assn. Avocations: sports cars, travel, flying. Home: 1917 N Cleveland Ave Chicago IL 60614-5215 Office: Cir Ct of Cook County Br 23 5555 W Grand Ave Chicago IL 60639-2909

KOWOL, GERHARD HELMUT, mathematician, educator; b. Vienna, Austria, May 28, 1947; s. Johannes Alfred and Elfriede Maria (Rudloff) K.; m. Christine Maria Stengl, July 8, 1971; children: Alexandra, Christian. PhD, U. Vienna, 1971, Habilitation in Math., 1978. Asst. prof. U. Vienna, 1971-80, 81-84; vis. prof. Monash (Australia) U., 1980-81; asst. Acad. for Human Scis., Dornach, Switzerland, 1984-86; univ. prof. U. Vienna, 1988—. Author: Algebra I, 1982, Algebra II, 1984, Equations, 1990, Prime Numbers, 1995; contbr. articles to profl. jours. Mem. Anthroposophical Soc. Office: U Vienna Inst Math, Strudlhofgasse 4, A 1090 Vienna Austria

KOYAMA, HIROMI MARIA, banker; b. Hyogo ken, Japan, Mar. 21, 1937; d. Hajime and Miiko (Yamamoto) Ichikawa; children: Akira, Kohei. BA, U. Sacred Heart, Tokyo, 1960. Cert. high sch. English tchr. Asst. to adminstr. Permanent Mission to UN, N.Y.C., 1960-63; tchr. Mrs. Hajime Yasuda English Sch., Tokyo, 1964-67; advisor Dexia Banque Internat. a Lusembourg SA, Tokyo, 1986—; resident rep. Banque Internat. a Lusembourg SA, Tokyo, 1991—; auditor Internat. Asset Mgmt. Japan KK, Tokyo, 1988-90; dir. Dexiam Japan, Tokyo, 2000—; part-time advisor English lang. Mitsubishi Paper Co. Ltd., Tokyo, 1965-67; bd. dirs. Belgo-Luxembourg C. of C., Japan, 1995—. Coord. scholarship com. Coll. Women's Assn., Japan, Tokyo, 1980-85. Mem. Japan-Swiss Soc., Nadeshiko Kai (Tokyo), Jingu Rotary Club. Roman Catholic. Avocations: music, piano. Home: 2-8-4 Kakinokizaka Meguro, Tokyo 152-0022, Japan Office: Banque Internat a Luxembourg SA, 12F Fukoku Life Bldg 2-2-2 Uchsaiwaicho, Chiyoda-ku Tokyo 100-0011, Japan

KOYAMA, MITSUTO, psychologist; b. Okayama, Japan, Mar. 10, 1952; s. Takeo and Yukie Koyama; m. Eriko Kawamura, May 3, 1979; children: Asako, Tamiko, Ryota, Kenta. BA, Hirosaki U., 1977; MA, Osaka U. Edn., 1979; PhD, Hokkaido U., 1991. Clin. psychologist Sasson Hosp., Otaru, 1980-85; assoc. prof. psychology Sapporo Gakuin U., Ebetsu, 1985-93, prof. psychology, 1993—; rehab. psychologist Tomakomai-Higashi Hosp., 1985—; bd. dirs. Hokkaido Cert. Bd. for Clin. Psychologists; supr. Hokkaido Marriage and Family Counseling Ctr., Sapporo. Author: Counseling and Adjustment after Cerebrovascular Accident, 1985, The Meaning of Illness, 1989, Therapeutic Settings in Psychotherapy of the Patient with Organic Brain Disorders: The Development of Insight into Disease as a Moment of Psychological Healing, 1992; editor: Aphasia: Voice of Patients, 1995. Rsch. grant Sapporo Gakuin U., 1993. Mem. APA, ACA, Assn. of Japanese Clin. Psychology (bd. dirs.). Avocations: fishing, tennis. Office: Sapporo Gakuin U, 11 Bunkyodai, Ebetsu 069-8555, Japan

KOYAMBA, ALPHONSE, bank executive. Sec. of state for fin., industry and commerce Govt. of Ctrl. African Republic, 1972, min. of fin., 1974-75, 3d dep. prime min., 1976, 1st dep. prime min., 1976-78; gov. Internat. Monetary Fund, 1979-80; dir. Ctrl. African States Bank, Banqui, Central African Republic, 1982—. Office: Banque Etats l'Afrique Centrale, PO Box 851, BP 851 Bangui Central African Republic*

KOYANO, KEIICHIROU, gas company executive; b. Tokyo, Jan. 21, 1953; s. Takaji and Michiyo (Shimizu) K. Student, Nihon U., Tokyo, 1973-77. V.p. Fuji Tubame Co. Ltd., Shizuoka, Japan, 1983—. Home: Ryogaecho 1-4-1, Shizuoka Japan Office: Tubame Co Ltd, Gofukucho 1-4-5, Shizuoka Japan

KOZA, CHRISTIAN KLAUS, computer company executive; b. Vienna, Austria, Apr. 15, 1963; s. Franz and Franziska (Schmid) K.; m. Eva Maria Koza, Oct. 25, 1988; children: Konstanze Cornelia, Clemens Alexander, Gregor Marian. M in Engring., Tech. U., Vienna, 1986, PhD, 1989. Asst. Tech. U., Vienna, Austria, 1986-89; project mgr. Softlab Ges. m.b. H, Vienna, 1989-91; head of fault-tolerant computing group, rsch. engr. Alcatel Austria Rsch. Centre, Vienna, 1991-94, mgr. fault tolerance, 1994-96; mgr. nat. and internat. payment systems Eisle Bank, 1996—. Mem. IEEE Computer Soc. (program com. 1994, indsl. chair real-time symposium 1995), Assn. Computer MAchinery. Avocation: radio controlled aerobatic. Home: Tannengasse 5/17, A-1150 Vienna Austria Office: Alcatel Austria AG, Geiselberg str 21-25, A-1110 Vienna Austria

KOZACZKA, EUGENIUSZ TADEUSZ, acoustics educator; b. Ćwików, Cracow, Poland, July 22, 1942; s. Kazimierz and Julia (Los) K.; m. Henryka Grazyna Soroko, July 20, 1969; children: Slawomir, Marcin. MS, Mil. Tech. U., Warsaw, 1971, DSc, 1980; PhD, Polish Acad. Scis., Gdansk, 1976. Commd. officer Polish Navy, 1971; advanced through grades to capt., 1987; asst. prof. Naval Acad., Gdynia, Poland, 1977-81; assoc. prof. Naval Acad., Gdynia, 1981-90, prof., 1990-97; prof. Tech. U., Koszalin, Poland, 1997; ret., 1997; mem. sci. coun, Facutly Electronics and Telecomm. Tech.-Agrl. Acad., Bydgoszcz, Poland, 1997—. Author: Investigation of Underwater Disturbances Produced by Ship's Propeller, 1978, Introduction to the Theory of Non-Lincar Hydroacoustics, 1987, Nonlinear Properties of Water, 1996; editor: Proceedings of the Internat. Symposium of Hydroacoustics and Ultrasonics, 1997. Decorated Batchelor Cross of Polonia Restituta Pres. Polish Republic, 1991; recipient award Commander-In-Chief Polish Navy, 1981, Ministerial award Min. of Edn., 1989. Mem. Polish Acoustical Soc., Polish Acad. Scis. (mem. com. on acoustics 1981—, scientific coun. Inst. Oceanology 1990—, pres. hydroacoustic sect. com. acoustics 1994—), European Acoustic Assn. Avocations: mountain tourism, sailing, skiing, cross-country skiing. Home: Saperów 16, 84-230 Rumia Gdansk, Poland Office: Naval Acad, Smidowicza 71, 81-919 Gdynia Gdansk, Poland

KOZAI, TOYOKI, horticulture educator, researcher; b. Tokyo, Sept. 25, 1943; s. Yoshishige and Miyo (Tanaka) K.; m. Michiko Hirano, Aug. 17, 1969; children: Yoshitake, Yuri, Yoshiharu. BSc, Chiba U., Matsudo, Japan, 1967; MSc, U. Tokyo, 1969, PhD, 1972. Cert. environ. engr. in agr. Rsch. asst. Osaka Prefecture U., Sakai, Japan, 1973-77; assoc. prof. horticulture Chiba U., 1977-90, prof., 1990—, dean, 1999—. Editor, author: High Technology in Protected Cultivation, 1988, Transplant Production Systems, 1992, Automation and Environmental Control in Plant Tissue Culture, 1995, Plant Production in Closed Ecosystems, 1996; mem. editl. bd. Hort. Revs., 1996-97, Plant Cell, Tissue and Organ Culture, 1998—. Mem. Japanese Soc. Environ. Control in Biology (v.p., acad. prize 1992), Japanese Soc. High Tech. in Agr. (pres., acad. prize 1991), Soc. Agrl. Meteorology Japan (dir., acad. prize 1982), Internat. Soc. for Hort. Sci. (editl. adv. mem. 1991—), Japanese Acad. Agrl. Scis. (acad. prize 1997). Avocations: martial arts, gardening, table tennis, walking. Office: Chiba U Faculty Horticult, 648 Matsudo, Matsudo Chiba 271-8510, Japan

KOZAK, JAN TOMAS, geophysicist, researcher; b. Prague, Czechoslovakia, Apr. 28, 1938; s. Jan and Ema (Vavrinova) K.; m. Anna Duskova, June 13, 1963; children: Cyril, Elisabeth, Adela. RerNatDr, Charles U., Prague, 1963; PhD, Czech Acad. Sci., 1970. Rschr. Standards Office, Prague, 1963-65; rschr. Acad. Sci., Prague, 1965-70, sr. rschr., 1970-79, leading rschr., 1979—, dept. head, 1992-93. Author: Historical Earthquake in Europe, 1991, PRAG 1562, 1995; co-author: Terremoti in Italia, 1992; author numerous articles on history of arts, hist. cartography, lab. and obs. geophysics. Officer, Civic Movement, Prague, 1990-91. Recipient The Czech-Polish Cooperatioin award, 1988; Fulbright grantee, U.S., 1994-95. Mem. Am. Geophys. Union, N.Y. Acad. Sci. Avocations: history, history of arts, historical town iconography. Home: Kubelikova 7, 13000 Prague 3, Czech Republic Office: Inst Rock Structure/Mechs, V Holesovickach 41, 18209 Prague 8, Czech Republic

KOZÁK, JÁNOS, agriculture educator, researcher; b. Kenderes, Szolnok, Hungary, Dec. 20, 1945; s. István and Istvánné (Szalmási) K.; m. Jánosné Barna, Mar. 18, 1972; children: János, Aniko, Iván, István, Eszter. Technicist, Agrl. Tech. Sch., Karcag, Hungary, 1964; agrl. engr., U. Agrl. Scis., Gödöllö, Hungary, 1968, profl. agrl. engr., 1975, DSc, 1979; cand. Econs., Hungarian Acad. Scis., 1988. Asst. analyst Coop Farm, Törökszentmiklós, Hungary, 1969-70; leading animal breeder Lenin Coop Farm, Kunhegyes, Hungary, 1970-78; rschr. U. Agrl. Scis., Gödöllö, Hungary, 1978-90; dir. goose-breeding rsch. sta. U. Agrl. Scis., Gödöllö, 1989-99, assoc. prof. dept. pig and poultry breeding, 1990-99, vice dir. Inst. Animal Breeding, 1997—, prof. dept. pig and poultry breeding, 1999—; leader complex rsch. on devel. of goose breeding R&D Ministry Agr., Budapest, Hungary, 1989-95; mem with consultative rights Tech. Comm. Internat. Down and Feather Bur., Aschaffenburg, Germany, 1994—. Author (dissertation) Vertical Relations and Possibilities for the Improvement of Interest in Goose Production, 1987; (book) Micellaneous Poultry Breeding, 1996, Evaluation of the Environmental Conditions for Fowl-Keeping with Consideration of European Union Requirements, 1999, Poultry Industry in Hungary: Evaluation the Harmonisation of Regulations with European Union, 1999; assoc. editor A Baromfi The Poultry Jour., Budapest, Hungary; contbr. articles to profl. jours. Recipient Excellence award Ministry of Agr. and Food, Hungary, 1989. Mem. World Poultry Sci. Assn., World Rabbit Sci. Assn., Internat. Assn. Agrl. Economists, Hungarian Goose Assn. (com. mem.). Roman Catholic. Avocation: philately. Home: Egyetem tér 11/A, 2100 Gödöllö Pest, Hungary Office: U Agrl Sci, Páter Károly u 1, 2103 Gödöllö Pest, Hungary

KOZAWA, OSAMU, pharmacology educator; b. Kasugai, Aichi, Japan, Aug. 11, 1957; s. Hiroshi and Souko (Hasegawa) K.; m. Sachi Fujimura, May 15, 1988; children: Kei, Aya, Fumi. MD, Gifu (Japan) U., 1982; PhD, Nagoya (Japan) U., 1989; postgrad., Kobe (Japan) U., 1985-87. Intern Chukyo Hosp., Nagoya, 1982-84; resident Takayama Kumiai Hosp., 1984-85; physician Nagoya U. Hosp., 1989-90; sr. rschr. Inst. Devel. Rsch. Aichi Prefectuary Colony, Kasugai, 1990-95; postdoctoral fellow Ludwig Inst. Cancer Rsch., Uppsala, Sweden, 1994-95; assoc. prof. medicine Gifu U., 1995—. Contbr. articles to profl. jours. Mem. Am. Physiol. Soc., Japanese Endocrinol. Soc. (councilor), Japanese Biochem. Soc., Japanese Cancer Soc. Home: 3-47 Shinogi, Kasugai, Aichi 486-0851, Japan Office: Gifu Univ Sch Med, Tsukasa 40, Gifu 500-8705, Japan

KOZBERG, RONALD PAUL, health and human services administrator; b. N.Y.C., Apr. 8, 1951; s. Raymond and Muriel (Tolmas) K.; m. Donna Lynn Walters, June 8, 1974; 1 child, Mariel Gailey. BA, Queens Coll., 1973; M of Rehab. Counseling, U. Fla., 1974; M of Pub. Health, Columbia U., 1986. Cert. rehab. counselor. Program dir. South Beach Psychiat. Ctr., S.I., N.Y., 1974-76; dir. rehab. svcs. Bklyn. Developmental Ctr., 1976-85; dir. stds. and compliance Bronx Developmental Svcs., 1985-91; pres. Expert Strategies, Inc., Warren, N.J., 1991—; technology com. chairperson Union County Edn. Coun., Westfield, N.J., 1993—. Author: The Do's and Dont's of Interviewing, 1992. Recipient Dean's Coun. award Dean of Health Related Professions, 1974. Mem. Nat. Rehab. Adminstrs. Assn. (N.E. regional bd. mem. 1982), Nat. Rehab. Counselors Assn. (N.Y. state sec., treas. 1981-82), Nat. Rehab. Assn. (pres., Spl. Citation 1974), Am. Pub. Health Assn. Avocations: golf, tennis, photography. Home: 45 Dug Way Watchung NJ 07069-6011 Office: Expert Strategies Inc PO Box 4264 Warren NJ 07059-0264

KOZBERG, STEVEN FREED, psychologist; b. Mpls., Apr. 30, 1953; s. Martin L. and Lois (Bix) K. BA, Macalester Coll., 1975; MA, U. Minn., Duluth, 1978; PhD, U. Wis., 1981. Lic. psychologist, Minn. Rsch. asst. dept. counseling and guidance U. Wis., Madison, 1978-79, tchg. asst., 1980-81; rsch. asst. Guidance Inst. for Talented Students, 1979-80; counseling psychologist, asst. prof. psychology Carleton Coll., Northfield, Minn., 1981-88; counseling psychologist, lectr. psychology Carleton Coll., Nrthfield, Minn., 1988-92; counseling psychologist, sr. lectr. psychology Carleton Coll., Northfield, Minn., 1992-95, sr. lectr. psychology, 1995—; pvt. practice, Mpls., 1995—; clin. asst. prof. psychiatry dept. psychiatry U. Minn., 1999—; staff psychologist divsn. child and adolescent psychiatry, dept. psychiatry U. Minn., Mpls., 1997-99. Mem. APA, Am. Psychol. Soc., Minn. Psychol. Assn., Midwestern Psychol. Assn., Phi Kappa Phi. Home: 9901 Saint Johns Rd Minnetonka MN 55305-4640 Office: Lake Pointe Corporate Ctr 3100 W Lake St Ste 465 Minneapolis MN 55416-4500

KOZBIAL, RICHARD JAMES, retired elementary education educator; b. Toledo, Nov. 11, 1933; s. Phillip and Bernice Bronislawa (Durka) K.; m. Jane Ardys Verny, July 8, 1961 (dec. Nov. 1983); children: Ardys Jane, Beth Lynne. EdB, U. Toledo, 1957, EdM, 1976. Tchr. Toledo Pub. Schs., 1956-58, 1962-84, Van Dyke Sch. Dist., Warren, Mich., 1958-62; intern tchr. cons. Toledo Pub. Schs., 1984-87, cons., 1987-93; supr. student tchrs., course facilitator U. Toledo, 1987-97, vis. prof., 1997-99, mem. faculty, 1997-99; ESL tchr. Szeged, Hungary, 1993-95; supr. alt. plan U. Toledo, 1993-99, instr. integrated social studies/lang. arts/reading block, 1996-99, ret., 1999; mem. textbook selection coms. Toledo Pub. Schs.; instr. student tchr. tng. programs Toledo U., 1962-84; instr. student tchr. tng. Bowling Green State U., 1962-84, Mich. State U., 1958-59; organizer Multi-Cultural Awareness Workshop Toledo Elem. Tchrs. Internat. Inst., 1986-90; organizer Outdoor Edn. Program; participant Multi Unit Edn. Plan; mem. U. Toledo Internat. Edn. Com., 1997-98. Author Spelling Curriculum Guide Toledo Pub. Schs., 1968; prodr. (TV programs) WGTE Famous Ams. Born in Feb., Israel. Up with People Host Family, Ohio Arab Affairs Coun., 1989—, YCMA, ISS, USIA Host Family, 1986—; mem. Planned Parenthood N.W. Ohio, Toledo Mus. Modern Art, Nat. Trust Historic Preservation, 1988—; vestry mem. Trinity Episc. Ch., 1984-87, sesquicentennial com., chmn. music; baritone soloist Canterbury Choir; bereavement vol. Hospice N.W. Ohio, Nat. Hospice Assn.; exec. bd. Toledo/Poznan Alliance (Dozynki com. chmn. 1990, 95, 2000); mem. Bedford Polish Culture Club, 1989-99; sponsor, coord. host families Zulu Choir, Durham, South Africa, Poznan (Poland) Nightengales. Named Outstanding Your Educator, Toledo C. of C., 1965-66; Jennings Founder scholar, 1979-80; recipient Miss Peach award Toledo Blade, 1963, Award of Excellence, 1983, Internat. Inst. Hall of Fame Disting. Svc. award, 1994, Letter of Commendation, Gov. of Ohio, 1994. Mem. Am. Fedn. Tchrs., Ohio Fedn. Tchrs., Toledo Fedn. Tchrs. (life), Internat. Inst. Inc. (life, chmn. edn. com., bd. dirs. 1985-91, pres. 1988-89), Assn. Two Toledos (bd. dirs., 1st v.p. 1990-91), U. Toledo Alumni Assn. (life), U. Mich. Alumni Assn., Am. Assn. Ret. Persons, Lucas County Ret. Tchrs. (life), Mid. East Affairs Coun. (bd. dirs.), Ellis Island Found., Smithsonian Assocs., Nat. Coun. Sr. Citizens, Toledo Sister Cities Internat. (bd. dirs., chmn. entertainment Masked Bash 1996, com. English lang. camp for students from Poland 1995, 96, chmn. host families), Am. Ctr. Polish Culture, Inc.,

Greenpeace, Phi Delta Kappa, Kappa Delta Pi (various offices including corr. sec., treas., v.p., pres., Point of Excellence award 1992). Democrat. Avocations: gardening, travel, reading, stained glass, calligraphy, phys. fitness, folk dancing. Home: 3823 Grantley Rd Toledo OH 43613-4218

KOZEL, ANA, astronomical artist; b. Buenos Aires, 1937; m. A. Trossero; children: Alejandro, Andrea. Exhibited paintings Nat. Air and Space Mus., Mus. of Ams., O.A.S., Washington, 1985, 1st Art Exhbn. Earth Orbit EUROMIR, 95. Mem. Internat. Assn. Astron. Arts, Planetary Soc. Avocation: photography.

KOZHEMYAKIN, GENNADIY NICKOLAEVICH, technologist, researcher; b. Lugansk, Ukraine, Feb. 24, 1950; s. Nickolay Tikhonovich and Nadezhda Ivanovna Kozhemyakina; m. Nataliya Yrevna Sereda, Apr. 26, 1970 (div. June 1990); children: Oleg, Maksim; m. Marina Nickolaevna Lesnichaya, Jan. 18, 1991. Degree in Engring., Ea. Ukrainian State U., Lugansk, 1972; D in Engring., Moscow Inst. Steel & Alloy, 1982. Electronics engr. Ea. Ukrainian State U., Lugansk, 1972-78, assoc. prof., 1981-92, prof., 1995—; head Sci. Prodn. Co. Loter, Lugansk, 1992-95; postgrad. staff A.A. Baikov Inst. Metallurgy Acad. Scis., Moscow, 1978-81; cons. sci. rsch., Lugansk, 1982-97; bd. dirs. Technopark Ltd., Lugansk. Patentee in field; contbr. articles to profl. jours. Mem. Am. Inst. Ultrasound in Medicine, N.Y. Acad. Sci. Avocation: fishing. Home: Subscriber Box 214, 348050 Lugansk Ukraine Office: Ea Ukrainian State Univ, Block Molodezhniy 20A, 348034 Lugansk Ukraine

KOZHEVNIKOV, VLADIMIR MIKHAILOVICH, geophysicist, physicist; b. Chita, Russia, Mar. 3, 1947; s. Mikhail Vladimirovich and Lidiya Andreevna (Shakhova) K.; m. Liudmila Georgievna Skoknina, Aug. 21, 1974; children: Maria, Mikhail. Grad., Irkutsk (Russia) U., 1970; Candidate Physics & Math., U. Moscow, 1994. Lic. physicist. Technician Inst. of Earth's Crust, Irkutsk, 1969-71, engr., 1971-75, sr. engr., 1975-77, rschr., 1977-95, sr. rschr., 1995—. Author: An Area of Anomalous Mantle Beneath the Baikal Rift, 1979; contbr. articles to profl. jours. Avocations: fishing, chess. Home: 273c Lermontov Str Apt 28, 664033 Irkutsk Russia Office: Inst Earths Crust, 128 Lermontov Str, 664033 Irkutsk Russia

KOZHEVNIKOV, YURI PAVLOVICZ, botanist; b. Volkhov, Leningrad, Russia, July 22, 1942; s. Pavel Alexeevicz Kozhevnikov and Vera Pavlovna (Makkaveeva) Shevczuk; m. Irina Anatoljevna Zadorozhnjuk, 1974 (div. 1976); m. Masako Hamaguchi, June 6, 1984; 1 child, Akiko Hamaguchi. Student, Leningrad State U., 1965-70, candidate of sci., 1978; DSc, U. St. Petersburg, 1998. Joiner, fireman, 1958-61, prisoner, 1961-64, mill worker, 1965; aspirant Bot. Inst., St. Petersburg, 1970-74, jr. sci. worker, 1977-90, sr. sci. worker, 1990-99, chief sci. worker, 1999—; jr. sci. worker Inst. Biol. Problems, Magadan, 1974-77. Author: Geography of Vegetation on Chukotka, 1989, Geosystems Aspects of Chukotkan Vegetation, 1989, Vegetation of Northern Asia in Historical Perspective, 1996, Matrjena, Matrjenicz and Others, 1999. Grantee Internat. Sci. Fund, 1995. Mem. N.Y. Acad. Scis. Avocations: violin, bicycling, reading, birds, painting. Home: Prof Popova 1 4, 197022 St Petersburg Russia Office: Bot Inst Russian Acad Sci, Prof Popova 2, 197022 St Petersburg Russia

KOZHNEVIKOV, ARKADII ALEXEYEVICH, physicist, educator; b. Topky, Russia, Apr. 25, 1952; s. Alexey K. and Olga Yushkevich; m. Natalya Morozova, Dec. 29, 1977; 1 child, Anna. MS, Novosibirsk State U., 1974, PhD, 1977. From jr. rsch. scientist to rsch. scientist Inst. Automation & Electrical Measurements, Novosibirsk, Russia, 1977-87; from rsch. scientist to sr. rsch. scientist Lab. Theoretical Physics Inst. Maths., Novosibirsk, 1987—; from asst. prof. to assoc. prof. Novosibirsk State U., 1978—. Office: Sobolev Inst Maths, acad Koptyug prospect 4, 630090 Novosibirsk Russia

KOZHUHAROV, CHRISTOPHOR, physicist; b. Plovdiv, Bulgaria, Jan. 7, 1946; arrived in Fed. Republic Germany, 1970.; s. Vassil and Nadejda (Aceva) Kojouharov; m. Molly Sue Affleck, Aug. 5, 1983. Mgr inz., Politechnika Slaska, Gliwice, Poland, 1969; Dr. rer. nat., Technische U., Munich, 1974. With Technische U., Munich, 1974-78, GSI, Darmstadt, Germany, 1979—. Office: Planckstr. 1, 64291 Darmstadt Germany

KOZICH, VALERY PAVLOVICH, physicist; b. Vitebsk, Belarus, Jan. 22, 1954; s. Pavel Nikiphorovich and Tatyana Danilovna (Rekutz) K.; m. Nadejda Nikolaevna Popova, July 13, 1978; children: Elena, Pavel. MSc in Physics, Moscow State U., 1977; PhD in Physics and Math., Inst. Physics, Minsk, Belarus, 1983. Probation rsch. assoc. Inst. Physics, Minsk, 1977-78, jr. rsch. assoc., 1978-85, sr. rsch. assoc., 1985-98, leading rsch. assoc., 1998—. Contbr. articles to profl. jours. Recipient All-Union Komsomol award, Moscow, 1984. Achievements include inventions in solid-state and dye lasers; research and development in transient spectroscopy using incoherent light and dual-beam z-scan technique for studying light induced changes in the refractive index. Home: Yakubova St 66-3-256, 220095 Minsk Belarus Office: Inst of Physics, Skaryna Ave 70, Minsk Belarus

KOZIEJ, STANISLAW, director defense ministry; b. Glinnik, Poland, July 8, 1943; s. Antoni and Zofia (Rojek) K.; m. Stanislawa Chrzescijanska Dec. 25, 1967; children: Anna, Andrzej. Doctor, Gen. Staff Acad., Warsaw, 1977, Doctor Habilitowany, 1986. Co. comdr. Polish Army, Walcz, 1965-70; specialist Gen. Staff Polish Army, Warsaw, 1977-81; head of staff dept. Military Dist., Wroclaw, 1987-88; prof. Nat. Defense Acad., Warsaw, 1988-95; dept. dep. dir. Nat. Security Office, Warsaw, 1995-99; dept. dir. Ministry of Def., Warsaw, 1994-99. Author: Theory of War Art, 1993, Combat Raids, 1987, Efficiency of Defense, 1988; contbr. some 400 articles to profl. jours. Brigadier Gen., Army, 1993. Avocations: chess, fencing, books. Office: Ministry of Defense, Krolewska 1, 00-909 Warsaw Poland

KOZIOŁ, MICHAEL JOHN, biochemist, researcher; b. Southington, Conn., July 12, 1951; s. Stanley Michael and Janina Mary (Piela) K. BA in Chemistry Biology summa cum laude, St. Michael's Coll., Winooski, Vt., 1973; PhD, U. Oxford, Eng., 1980. Air pollution researcher Botany Sch. U. Oxford, Eng., 1980-85; head sci. support labs. Latinreco, S.A. (Nestle R&D Co.), Quito, Ecuador, 1985-98; prof., head dept. food engring. U. San Franciso de Quito, 1999—; mem. botanical sci. delegation to China, People to People, 1988, to USSR, 1990, Spokane, Wash.; invited lectr. U. San Francisco de Quito, 1990—. Author: ABC de la Nutrición; editor: Gaseous Air Pollutants and Plant Metabolism. Recipient Rhodes scholarship Oxford, Eng., 1973, Conservation fellowship U.S. Nat. Wildlife Fedn., Am. Petroleum Inst., Oxford, 1976, EPA Cephalosporin Rsch. fellowship, Oxford U., 1983. Mem. N.Y. Acad. Scis., Am. Chem. Soc., Assn. Official Analytical Chemists, Inst. Biology. Achievements include rsch. in plant stress metabolism, especially in response to atmospheric pollutants; nutritional evaluation and reintroduction of native lost crops; ethnobotany and the identification of naturally ocurring antimicrobial, antitox. Office: Nestle R&D Ctr-Quito Colegio Ciencias, Univ San Francisco de Quito, Casilla 1712841, Ecuador

KOZLOSKI, LILLIAN TERESE D., history of aerospace technology educator; b. Pitts., Sept. 11, 1934; d. Andrew and Juliana (Yevchak) Dzmura; m. Joseph Kozloski, May 22, 1956; children: Lisa, Cynthia, Charles, Christopher, Dolores Anne. AS, Mt. Aloysius Coll., 1954; BIS, George Mason U., 1981. Mus. technician Smithsonian Air & Space Instn., Washington, 1981-85, mus. specialist, 1985-95, ret., 1995; lectr. U.S. Space Gear Enterprises, Spotsylvania, Va., 1996—; cons. Smithsonian Instn., Washington, 1996, N.Y. Times, 1996; lectr. on living and working in space. Author: U.S. Space Gear History of Space Suit Technology, 1994; contbr. articles to profl. publs. Mem. AAUW, Am. Assn. Mus., N.Y. Acad. Scis., Soc. for History of Tech. Roman Catholic. Achievements include categorization and study of Nat. Air and Space Mus. collection of space suits; collected and organized space suit into loan collections and preservation and study collection. Home: 5035 Ridge Rd Spotsylvania VA 22553-6334

KOZLOV, EUGENE S., home video company executive; b. Sverdlovsk, Russia, Apr. 11, 1964; s. Stanislav G. and Victoria K. (Chernyshova) K.; m. Alla V. Ozerova, May 31, 1986; children: Alexei, Eugene. Grad., Sverdlovsk Tchrs. Tng. Inst., Russia, 1986. Tchr. English Sverdlovsk, 1988-89; mgr. overseas Uralchimmash, Ekaterinburg, Russia, 1989-91; head of overseas Uralniichermet, Ekaterinburg, 1991-92, TESO, Ekaterinburg, 1992-93; v.p. EA Internat., Ekaterinburg, 1993-94; sr. v.p. EA Home Video, Ekaterinburg, 1995—. Contbr. articles to profl. jours. Avocations: music, sports, travel, movies. Home: 22/5 Bolshakov St-35, 620100 Ekaterinburg Russia Office: EA Home Video, 45 Chaikovski St, 620142 Ekaterinburg Russia

KOZLOV, LEONID YAKOWLEVICH, institute administrator; b. Novokuznezk, Kemerovo, Russia, Dec. 13, 1935; s. Yakov Abramovich and Nadezhda Nikolaevna (Kalmykova) K.; m. Nina Semenovna Vinogradova, March 12, 1966; 1 child, Lindner Natalya. Diploma in Engring., Moscow Steel and Alloys Inst., 1958, PhD in Tech., 1965, DSc, 1983. Mgr. foundry shop Iron Foundry, Elez, Russia, 1958-59, tech. dir., 1959-60; rschr. Moscow Steel and Alloys Inst., 1960-63, asst., sr. tchr., 1963-66, dozent, prof., 1966-88, head foundry dept., 1988—, dean engring. faculty, 1972-78, dean ferrous metals faculty, 1978-93; guest prof. Indian Inst. Tech., Kharagpur, India, 1970-72. Co-author: Laboratory Experiments in Foundry Practice, 1971, 2d edit., 1990, Foundry Production, 1971, 2d edit., 1987. Recipient badge U. ME, Moscow, 1977, Labour Red Banner Order Govt. Moscow, 1980; named honored scientist Pres. Russia, Moscow, 1996. Mem. Internat. Com. Foundry Tech. Assns. (exec. 1991—, pres. 1996), Sci. and Processing Cast Iron Assn. (internat. orgn. com., permanent acting Internat. Symposium). Avocations: football, fishing. Fax: 7-95-9541252. Home: Leninsky prosp 18-9, 117071 Moscow Russia Office: Moscow State Inst Steel &, Alloys, Leninsky pr 4, 117936 Moscow Russia

KOZLOV, MIKHAIL VASILIEVICH, entomologist, researcher; b. St. Petersburg, Russia, Aug. 31, 1962; s. Vasily Ivanovich and Mira Arsenievna (Maslova) K.; m. Elena Zvereva, Nov. 29, 1989; children: Vitaly, Danil. MSc, Leningrad State U., 1984; PhD, Novosibirsk Biol. Inst., 1986. Rsch. asst., rschr., head rsch. group All Union Plant Protection Inst., Leningrad, 1984-91; rsch. asst., rschr., sr. rschr. U. Turku, Finland, 1991—. Author: Human Impact on Populations of Terrestial Insects, 1990; co-author: Gall-forming Insects of the European Part of the U.S.S.R., 1991; editor: Aerial Pollution in Kola Peninsula: Proc. Internat. Workshop, 1993; contbr. over 90 articles to profl. jours., chpts. to books. Mem. Russian Entomol. Soc., Finnish Lepidopterological Soc., European Lepidopterological Soc. Avocation: numismatics. Office: Univ of Turku, Sect Ecology, FIN20014 Turku Finland

KOZLOV, SERGEI VASYLIEVICH, polymer chemist; b. Saratov, Russia, Feb. 7, 1937; s. Vasylii Sergeevich Koslov and Fanni Iosifovna Berger; m. Nataliya Efimovna Golberg, Oct. 8, 1966; 1 child. Grad., Inst. Fine Chem. Tech., Moscow, 1960; PhD in Chemistry, Phys.-Tech. Inst., Moscow, 1972. Jr. rsch. worker Karpov Inst. Phys. Chemistry, Moscow, 1960-64, Inst. Chem. Physics, Moscow, 1964-82; sr. rsch. worker Inst. Chem.-Photog. Industry, Moscow, 1982-91, Karpov Inst. Phys. Chemistry, 1991—; chemistry educator Sch., Moscow, 1995-97. Author: Redistribution of Silver Centers after Chemical Sensibilization and at Development, 1985; contbr. articles to profl. jours. Recipient medal Presidium of Supreme Soviet of USSR, 1989. Mem. Trade Union.

KOZLOV, YURI PAVLOVICH, ecologist, educator; b. Kiev, Ukraine, May 15, 1935; s. Pavel Vasilyevich Kozlov and Tamara Pavlovna Shutko; m. Tamara Michailovna Dmitrieva, Oct. 6, 1957; children: Elena, Anastasya. MSc, Moscow State U., 1958, PhD, 1962, DSc in Biology, 1969. Rschr. Moscow State U., 1961-71, head lab., 1971-77; rector Irkutsk (USSR) State U., 1977-89; dean, prof. Russian U. People's Friendship, Moscow, 1990—, head chair sys. ecology, 1992—. Author: Free Radical Oxidation in Biological Membranes, 1972, Free Radicals in Biological Systems, 1973, Molecular Mechanisms of Damage of Calcium Transport in Muscle, 1983; contbr. over 300 articles to profl. jours. V.p. Way of Life XXI Century Movement, Moscow, 1993—. Recipient State prize USSR Coun. Mins., 1983; named Hon. Scientist Russian Fedn., 1985; Soros Scientific fellow, 1997. Mem. Acad. Social Ecology (pres. 1993—), Assn. Unity Ecology (pres. 1994—), Russian Acad. Ecology (v.p. 1994—), Baikal Club (v.p. 1994—). Avocations: cars, hunting, angling, gardening. Fax 095 952 89 01. E-mail: kozlov@mail.rudn.yssi.ru. Home: 15-1 Garibaldi St Apt 92, 117335 Moscow Russia Office: Faculty Ecology, 8/5 Podolskoye St, 113093 Moscow Russia

KOZLOVA, ARIADNA STANISLAVOVNA, physicist, educator; b. Pavlovo-Posad, Russia, May 28, 1957; d. Stanislav Georgievich Kozlov and Ariadna Vladimirovna Leonova. Student, Orekhovo Zuevo Pedagogical Inst., 1974-78, 81-83, Moscow Aviation Inst., 1984-88; PhD, High Temperature Inst. Acad. Scis., Moscow, 1991; postgrad., Moscow State Tech. U., 1993-96. Tchr. physics Adelino, Ryazan, Russia, 1978-79; sr. technician elec. br. All Union Oil Refining Rsch. Inst., Electrogorsk, 1979-80; tchr. physics and math. Electrogorsk, 1980-81; tutor dept. physics Orekhovo-Zuevo Pedagogical Inst., 1981-83; engr. dept. physics Moscow State Tech. U., 1983-84, corr., 1984-88, rsch. worker dept. physics, 1987-93, 96—; educator dept. math. Orekhovo-Zuevo Pedagogical Inst., 1981-83; educator dept. physics MAI, Moscow, 1984-92, educator dept. electronical devices, 1995-96. Contbr. articles to books and jours. Chmn. Komsomol Lenin Young Communist League of the Faculty, MAI, 1983-85, vice-chmn. trade union, 1991-97. Mem. Russian Pushkin Soc., Nat. Geog. Soc., N.Y. Acad. Scis. Avocations: theatre, music, basketball. Office: Moscow Aviation Inst, Volokolamskoye shosse 4, 125871 Moscow Russia

KOZLOVSKI, VITALI VASIL'EVICH, physicist, educator; b. St. Petersburg, Russia, Feb. 9, 1953; s. Vasili Jakovlevich and Evdokija Fedorovna (Alimpieva) K.; m. Olga Jakovlevna Ivanovskaya, Jan. 27, 1974 (div. 1983); 1 child, Serguei; m. Irina Alexandrovna Rumjanzeva, July 28, 1984; 1 child, Svetlana. Degree in engring. and physics, State Tech. U., St. Petersburg, 1976, PhD, 1983, DSc in Physics, 1996. Engr. Rsch. Inst., St. Petersburg, 1976-83, rschr., 1983-89; sr. rschr. Rsch. Inst. Giricond, St. Petersburg, 1989-93; assoc. prof. State Tech. U., St. Petersburg, 1994-96, prof. physics, 1997—. Contbr. articles to profl. jours. Avocations: philately, photography, fishing, skiing. Office: State Tech U Exptl Physics, Polytechnicheskaya 29, 195251 Saint Petersburg Russia

KOZLOWSKI, THOMAS JOSEPH, JR., lawyer, trust company executive; b. Norristown, Pa., July 29, 1950; s. Thomas Joseph Sr. and Mary Elisa (Alvarez) K.; m. Michelle Mary Chanpagne, Jan. 9, 1971; children: Brian Christopher, Scott Michael, Mark Daniel. BSBA in Acctg., Georgetown U., 1971, JD, 1979; MBS, George Washington U., 1975. Bar: D.C. 1979, Va. 1980; CPA Va. Sr. acct. Touche Ross & Co., Washington, 1972-75; dir. internal audit Pentagon Fed. Credit Union, Arlington, Va., 1975-77; supr. acct. Snyder, Newrath & Co., Washington, 1977-79; v.p., sec. Owens & Co., Inc., Arlington, 1979-86; sr. v.p. fin. Realty Investment Co., Inc., Silver Spring, Md., 1986-89; sr. v.p., treas. The Selzer Group, Inc., N.Y.C., 1989-93; pres. The Collector's Gallery of Va. Inc., Alexandria, 1992-96; exec. v.p., dir. family office group Merrill Lynch Trust Co., Princeton, N.J., 1993—; bd. dirs. Owens & Co., Alexandria, Va. Editor Jour. Law & Policy in Internat. Bus., 1976-79. Arbiter Fairfax County (Va.) Consumer Protection Commn., 1977-95; treas. Commonweal Found., Inc., Silver Spring, 1986-89; bd. dirs. Resdl. Youth Svcs., Inc., Alexandria, 1981-89, treas., 1982-84, v.p., 1984-85; treas. Coplex Found., N.Y.C., 1989-93; mem. planned giving adv. coun. Pa. State U., 2000—. Fellow D.C. Inst. CPAs; mem. ABA, AICPAs, D.C. Bar Assn., Va. State Bar Assn., Inst. Mgmt. Acctg. (cert. mgmt. acctg., cert. disting. performance 1975). Democrat. Roman Catholic. Avocations: reading, photography. Office: Merrill Lynch Trust Co 800 Scudders Mill Rd Plainsboro NJ 08536-1606

KOŹMIŃSKI, CZESŁAW, agrometeorologist, consultant; b. Czarnocin, Kielce, Poland, Sept. 28, 1932; s. Jan and Maria (Wójcik) K.; m. Zofia Krzak, June 26, 1960; children: Urszula, Barbara, Kamila. PhD, U. Wrocław (Poland), 1962; DSc, U. Agr., Szczecin, Poland, 1968. Asst. U. Agr., 1955-61, adj., 1961-68, asst. prof., 1968-75, prof., 1975—, dep. dean, 1968-72, head agrometeorology dept., 1970, prorector, 1972-76, asst. mgr. Inst. Soil Sci., 1973-78; mem. Agrophysics Com., Lublin, 1995—. Author: (with others) The Soil Temperature in Poland 1979-89, 1990, others; patentee in field; contbr. over 250 articles to profl. jours. Active Peoples Provincial Coun., Szczecin, 1978-86. Mem. Szczecin Scientist Soc. (sec. 1983-86), European Soc. Agronomy. Avocations: tourism, World War II history. Office: Univ Agr, Papieża Pawła VI, 71-434 Szczecin Poland

KOŹMIŃSKI, JERZY, ambassador; m. Irena Koźmińska; 1 child, Kinga. Grad., Ctrl. Sch. Planning and Statistic, Warsaw. With Ctrl. Sch. Inst. Fgn. Trade Econs., Warsaw; dir. gen. Office of Coun. of Mins. Govt. of Poland, 1989, under sec. of state in Prime Min.'s Office, 1991-93; first dep. min., sec. of state Polish Ministry of Fgn. Affairs, 1994; amb. to U.S. Govt. of Poland, Washington, 1994-2000; chmn. Polish-Am. Freedom Found. Founding mem. Found. for Econ. Edn., Warsaw, 1992. Office: Polish Am Freedom Found ste 1902 375Park Ave New York NY 10152*

KOZOL, JONATHAN, writer; b. Boston, Sept. 5, 1936; s. Harry Leo and Ruth (Massell) K. BA, Harvard U., 1958; Rhodes scholar, Magdalen Coll., Oxford U., 1958-59. Tchr. Boston pub. schs., 1964-65, Newton pub. schs., 1966-68; dir., trustee Store-front Learning Center, 1968-74; vis. lectr. Yale U., 1969, numerous univs., 1971-97; prof. edn. Trinity Coll., 1980; cons. U.S. Office Edn., 1965-66; inst. Ctr. for Intercultural Documentation, Cuernavaca, Mex., 1969, 70, 74. Author: Death At An Early Age, 1967 (Nat. Book award, 1968), Free Schools, 1972, The Night Is Dark and I Am Far From Home, 1975, Children of the Revolution, 1978, Prisoners of Silence, 1980, On Being A Teacher, 1981, People of the Book, 1982, Alternative Schools, 1983, Illiterate America, 1985, Rachel and Her Children, 1988 (Robert F. Kennedy Book award, 1989), Savage Inequalities, 1991 (New Eng. Book award, 1992, Amazing Grace, 1995 (Anisfield-Wolf Book award, 1996), Ordinary Resurrections, 2000; corr.: Los Angeles Times, USA Today, 1982-83; contbr. to N.Y. Times Book Rev., 1968-85; reporter-at-large The New Yorker mag., 1988. Trustee New Sch. for Children, Roxbury, Mass.; bd. dirs. Nat. Literacy Coalition, 1980-83. Recipient Olympia Thousand Dollar award, 1962, Lannan Literary award, 1994; Saxton fellow in creative writing Harper & Row, 1964; Guggenheim fellow, 1970, 84; Field Found. fellow, 1972; Ford Found. fellow, 1974; Rockefeller Found. fellow, 1978, fellow in humanities, 1983. Mem. P.E.N., Nat. Coalition for the Homeless, Fellowship of Reconciliation. Address: PO Box 145 Byfield MA 01922-0145

KOZU, TOSHIAKI, electrical engineering executive; b. Kyoto, Japan, Jan. 30, 1952; s. Yasuhisa and Reiko (Tanaka) K.; m. Keiko Ogawa, Nov. 23, 1979; children: Masaaki, Yukiko, Misako. BEE, Kyoto U., 1975, MEE, 1977, DEE, 1992. Rsch. ofcl. Comm. Rsch. Lab., Tokyo, 1977-82, sr. rsch. ofcl., 1986-91, chief microwave remote sensing sect., 1995-98; acting sect. chief Telecomm. Satellite Corp., Tokyo, 1983-85; asst. sr. engr. Nat. Space Devel. Agy., Tokyo, 1992-94; prof. Shimane U., 1999—; vis. scientist NASA Goddard Space Flight Ctr., Greenbelt, Md., 1987-89; vis. engr. Nat. Space Devel. Agy., Tokyo, 1995-98. Co-author: Spaceborne Weather Radar, 1990; contbr. articles to profl. jours. Mem. organizing staff environment seminar City of Koganei, Tokyo, 1996. Mem. IEEE, Remote Sensing Soc. Japan, Inst. Elec. Info. Comm. Engrs. Avocations: Japanese flute playing, jogging, tennis. Office: Shimane U Fac Sci & Engr, 1060 Nishi-kawatsu, Matsue 690-8504, Japan

KOZUBOWSKI, TOMASZ J., mathematics and statistics educator, researcher; b. Warsaw, Poland, June 26, 1962; came to U.S., 1986; s. Jan A. Malgorzata Kozubowski; m. Agnieszka R. Riau, Sept. 14, 1982 (div. June 1986); 1 child, Kamil J.; m. Anna K. Panorska, Nov. 12, 1993; 1 child, Joseph A. Grad., U. Warsaw, 1986; MS, U. Tex., El Paso, 1988; PhD, U. Calif., Santa Barbara, 1992. Asst. prof. U. Tenn., Chattanooga, 1992-98, asoc. prof., 1998—; vis. assoc. prof. U. Calif., Santa Barbara, 1999-2000; referee Am. Jour. Math. and Mgmt. Scis., Annals of Probability, Statistics and Decisions, Math. Revs., Zentralblatt für Mathematik; textbook reviewer M.H. DeGroot; presenter in field. cons. Chattanooga Orthopaedic Group Found. for Rsch., 1997, Blue Cross Blue Shield Tenn., Chattanooga, 1997-2000. Co-author: The Laplace Distribution Revisited: New Applications, 2000; contbr. more than 25 articles to profl. jours. including European Jour. Ops. Rsch., Statistics and Probability Letters, Statistics and Desicions, Jour. Multivariate Analysis, Extremes, among others. Fellow U. Tenn. Fond., 1994, 97, faculty rsch. grantee, 1995, 98; Ctr. Excellence for Computer Applications Rsch. grantee, 1997, 98. Mem. Am. Math. Soc., Am. Statis. Assn., Bachelier Fin. Soc., Bernoulli Soc. for Math. Statistics and Probability, Inst. Math. Statistics, Actuarial Faculty Forum. Avocations: hiking, chess, photography. Office: Univ Nev Dept Math Reno NV 89557-0001

KOZUCHOWSKI, KRZYSZTOF, climatologist; b. Zakopane, Poland, Mar. 16, 1945; s. Wilhelm and Janina (Chomentowska) K.; m. Anna Slomczynska, Mar. 30, 1972; 1 child. M, U. Lodz, 1968, DSc, 1973. From asst. to prof. U. Lodz, Poland, 1968—. Author: Greenhouse Effect, 1995, Atmosphere, Climate, Ecoclimate, 1998; contbr. articles to profl. jours. Home: Kusocinskiego 92/39, 94-054 Łódź Poland

KOZULIN, ALEX, psychology educator, researcher; b. Moscow, June 30, 1949; came to U.S., 1979; s. Michael Kozulin and Olga Chetverikova; m. Galina Mengeritsky; 1 child, Henrik. MD, Inst. Medicine, Moscow, 1972; PhD, Psychol. Inst., Moscow, 1978. Rsch. fellow, lectr. Inst. Advanced Med. Studies, Moscow, 1972-75; rsch. assoc. Psychol. Inst., Moscow, 1975-79; rsch. assoc. Ctr. for Philosophy and History of Sci. Boston U., 1980-82, asst. prof. Dept. Psychology and Divsn. Psychiatry, 1984-90; sr. lectr. Ben-Gurion U., Beer-Sheva, Israel, 1982-84; rsch. dir. Internat. Ctr. for Enhancement of Learning Potential, Jerusalem, 1990—; vis. scholar Harvard U. Russian Rsch. Ctr., Cambridge, Mass., 1989; vis. assoc. prof. Bar Ilan U. Sch. Edn., Ramat Gan, Israel, 1992; vis. prof. U. Witwatersrand, Johannesburg, South Africa, 1996. Author: Psychology in Utopia: Toward a Social History of Soviet Psychology, 1984, Vygotsky's Psychology: A Biography of Ideas, 1990, Psychological Tools: A Sociocultural Approach to Education, 1998; editor: Thought and Language, 1986, The Ontogeny of Cognitive Modifiability: Applied Aspects of Mediated Learning Experience and Instrumental Enrichment, 1997. Mem. Am. Psychol. Soc., European Assn. Rsch. in Learning and Instrn., Internat. Soc. for History of the Behavioral Scis. E-mail: akozulin@compuserve.com. Office: ICELP, 47 Narkis St PO Box 7755, Jerusalem 91077, Israel

KPODO, VICTOR KWAKU AGBEMAVA, mechanical engineer, educator, consultant; b. Anlo-Afiadenyigba, Volta, Ghana, Apr. 1, 1942; s. Alfred Agbemava and Vinolia Ameyo (Hiame) K.; m. Heartwill Atsufi Semey, Mar. 16, 1974; children: Aseye, Tegbee, Makafui, Ewenam, Dzifa. Diploma in Engring., U. Sci. & Tech., Kumasi, Ghana, 1964, BSc in Engring., 1967; MSME, U. Minn., 1970; PhD in Mech. Engring., U. Salford, U.K., 1979. Mech. maint. engr. Volta River Authority, Akosombo, Ghana, 1967-73; lectr. U. Sci. and Tech., Kumasi, Ghana, 1973-96, 98—; log and maint. mgr. World Vision Internat., Accra, Ghana, 1988-89; dean divsn. applied arts and tech. edn., head Kumasi campus Univ. Coll. of Edn. of Winneba, 1996-98; chmn., exec. dir. Nayra Engring. Ltd., Kumasi, 1986—; engring. svc. cons. U. Sci. & Tech., 1980—; prin. ptnr. Sovak Engring. Cons., Kumasi, 1982—. Mem. synod com. Evang. Presbyn. Ch. of Ghana, 1991—, mem. synod com. exec., 1996-99, pres. Bible study and prayer fellowship, 1988-92. Mem. Ghana Instn. of Engrs. (v.p. 1991-93, Ashanti br. chmn. 1993-97), Emprestec Bus. Forum (Kumasi chpt. v.p. 1991-94). Office: Nayra Engring Ltd, University PO Box 85, Kumasi UPO85GH, Ghana

KPOTSTRA, ROLAND YAO, diplomat. Rep. to UN Govt. of Togo, 1996—. Office: Permanent Mission of Togo to UN 112 E 40th St New York NY 10016-1724*

KRA, PAULINE SKORNICKI, French language educator; b. Lodz, Poland, July 30, 1934; came to U.S., 1950, naturalized, 1955; d. Edward and Nathalie Skornicki; m. Leo Dietrich Kra, Mar. 10, 1955; children: David Theodore, Andrew Jason. Student, Radcliffe Coll., 1951-53; BA, Barnard Coll., 1955; MA, Columbia U., 1963, PhD, 1968; MA, Queens Coll., 1990. Lectr. Queens Coll., CUNY, 1964-65; asst. prof. French, Yeshiva U., N.Y.C., 1968-74, assoc. prof., 1974-82, prof., 1982-99, prof. emerita, 1999—; programmer/ analyst dept. med. informatics Columbia U., N.Y.C., 1998—. Author: Religion in Montesquieu's Lettres persanes, 1970; contbr. articles to profl. jours. Mem. MLA, Am. Assn. Tchrs. French, Am. Soc. 18th Century Studies, Société Française d'étude du XVIII Siècle, Soc. Montesquieu, Assn. for Computers and Humanities, Assn. for Lit. and Linguistic Computing, Phi Beta Kappa. Home: 10914 Ascan Ave Forest Hills NY 11375-5370

KRAAIJENHAGEN, JACOB HENDRIK, plastic surgeon; b. The Hague, The Netherlands, June 15, 1942; s. Hendrik and Corona (de la Chambre) K.; m. Jacintha Steger (div.); children: Aernout Hendrik, Rutger Christoffel, Willem Friso; ptnr. Marianne Köhn Von Jaski. BS, 1960; MD, U. Leiden, 1968; degree in plastic surgery, U. Utrecht, 1976. Intern Odstock Hosp.,

Salisbury, Eng., 1973-74; resident Acad. Hosp., Utrecht, 1974-76; cons. plastic surgeon Diaconessenhuis, Utrecht, The Netherlands, 1976-93, Eemland Ziekenhuis, Amersfoort, The Netherlands, 1976-93; cons. aesthetic surgery Acad. Hosp., Utrecht, 1980-90; cons. plastic surgery Molendael, Baarn, The Netherlands, 1989—, Jan Van Goyen Kliniek, Kliniek, 1992—, Med. Centrum Amsterdam, Ziekenhuis Hoge Beuken, Antwerp, Belgium, 1993—; pres. D.S.A.P.C., 1984-97; cons. U. Groningen. Res. major Dutch Army, 1968-70. Mem. Arti et Amicitiae, Dutch Soc. for Aesthetic Plastic Surgery (pres. 1984—), Internat. Soc. Aesthetic Plastic Surgery (Holland, nat. sec. 1988—), Acad. for Aesthetic Plastic Surgery (dir. 1994), Dutch Soc. Aesthetic Plastic Surgery (hon.), De Kring De Amstel Club. Avocation: visual arts. Home: Groenburgwal 16, 1011 HV Amsterdam The Netherlands Office: Beukenlaan 4/32, 2020 Antwerp Belgium

KRAATZ, KAY SNIDER, systems analyst; b. Rochester, N.Y., Jan. 7, 1945; d. Allan Goodwill and Elizabeth (Henry) Snider; m. Stephen L. Kraatz, Apr. 29, 1967; children: Robert Allan, Stephen Jeffrey. BA, Miami U., Oxford, Ohio, 1967; MA, Mich. State U., 1974; AAS, Cayuga C.C., Auburn, N.Y., 1987. Programmer Seven Lakes Girl Scout Coun., Geneva, N.Y., 1984; sr. programmer analyst MONY Fin. Svc., Syracuse, N.Y., 1984-92, Am. Gen., Syracuse, N.Y., 1992-95, First Fed., Rochester, 1995-97; sr. bus. analyst Intertek Testing Svcs., Cortland, N.Y., 1997—. Pres., v.p. programs Skaneateles (N.Y.) Area Br. AAUW, 1981—; state coord. Nat. Women's Hall of Fame, Seneca Falls, N.Y., 2000; mem., docent Friends of Burnet Park Zoo, 1983—. Named to Nat. Women's Hall of Fame, 2000. Fellow Life Mgmt. Inst.; mem. Am. Assn. Univ. Women (N.Y. state pres. 1998-2000). Avocations: hiking, canoeing. E-mail: kraatz@dreamscape.com. Home: PO Box 458 Skaneateles NY 13152-0458 Office: 3393 US Rt 11 Cortland NY 13045

KRABBE, NIELS, musicologist, music educator, music librarian; b. Copenhagen, Oct. 3, 1941; s. Otto and Anna Margrethe (Christiansen) K.; m. Anna Marie Berggreen Petersen, Dec. 3, 1966; children: Signe, Ida, Søren. BA, Copenhagen U., 1963, MA, 1969. Lectr. Copenhagen U., 1970, head music dept., 1984-96, prof. music, 1974-96; head music dept. Royal Libr. Copenhagen, 1996—. Author books; editor in chief Carl Nielsen's Works, 1997—; contbr. articles to profl. jours. Home: Stolpevej 16, 2605 Brondby Denmark Office: Royal Libr Copenhagen, PB 2149, 1016 Copenhagen Denmark

KRAB-JOHANSEN, ANDERS BJORN, correspondent; b. Christianshaab, Denmark, Dec. 29, 1966; s. Bjorn Herbert and Anne Bjorn (Jensen) K.; m. Mette Olesen, June 22, 1991; children: Emma, Agnes. MS in Journalism, Columbia U., 1994; MA in Polit. Sci., U. Copenhagen, Denmark, 1995. Program host Denmark's Radio, Copenhagen, 1990-93; journalist Dagbladet Borsen, Copenhagen, 1995-96, fgn. corr., 1997—; commentator BBC, England, 1997—. Author: The Fourth Criterion, 1995. With Danish Royal Guards, 1986-87. Home: Ave Brugmann 506, B-1180 Brussels Belgium Office: Dagbladet Borsen, Rue Belliard 19, B-1040 Brussels Belgium

KRACKE, JUDY SUTTON, sculptor; b. Amarillo, Tex., Jan. 18, 1940; d. W.M. and Zuma Vance Sutton; children: Kristen, Kurtis. AA, Christian Coll., 1960; BS, U. Tex., 1962; MA, West Tex. A&M U., 1985, MFA, 1986. Tchr. Spring Br. Ind. Sch. Dist., Houston, 1962-66, Tex. Children's Hosp., Houston, 1964-66, Galveston (Tex.) Sch. Dist., 1974-75; tchr. dept. psychiatry Baylor Coll. Medicine, Houston, 1964-66; tchr. Amarillo Mus. Art, 1977-79, Amarillo Coll., 1978-91; part-time instr. West Tex. A&M U., 1984—; dir. One Sun, One Earth, One Peace, 1992—, Tritotems, Scottsdale C.C., 1994, Passages, Scottsdale C.C., 1994; vis. artist Ea. N.Mex. U., Clovis, 1989, Midwestern State U., Wichita Falls, Tex., 1990, Tex. Christian U., Ft. Worth, 1990, Calif. State U., Bakersfield, 1992, Nat. U. Cordoba, 1992-93; subject various interviews. One woman shows include Brookhaven Coll., Dallas, 1990, White Chapel, Tempe (Ariz.) Art Ctr., 1991, Spirit Mount, Calif. State U., Bakersfield, 1992, Jaime Conci Art Gallery, Cordoba, Argentina, 1993, Mildura (Australia) Arts Centre, 1995, Mildura Project Sculpture, 1995, Swan Hill (Australia) Regional Mus., 1996, Rogue Art Gallery, Victoria, Canada, 1996, No. Gallery WTAMU, Canyon, Tex., 1999, d/f/d/s Gallery, Kansas City, Mo., 1999; exhibited in group show at Dallas Mus. of Art, 1991, Nelson Park, Abilene, 1993, Presbyn. Home for Children, Amarillo, 1993, Radford (Va.) U., 1994, Scottsdale (Ariz.) C.C., 1994, Art Mus. of Ams., Washington, 1997, Cedarhurst Sculpture Pk., Mt. Vernon, Ill., 1997, Guadalupe Fine Art, Santa Fe, 1998, numerous others; pub. sculptures Stratford (Tex.) Gate, Stone Soup, Amarillo, Tex., Breaking New Ground, Irving (Tex.) Arts Ctr.; sculptures commd. by various orgns. Pres. Galveston Fine Art Assn., 1973-74. Recipient Purchase award Shreveport Art Guild, Barnwell Mus., 1974, Design award 7 Who Care Award, KVII, Amarillo, 1985, 2d place award Amarillo Gateway Design, 1991, Achievement award AAUW, 1994, Woman of Distinction award Soroptimist Internat. of Amarillo, 1996; grantee Amarillo C. of C., 1993, Tex. Commn. on Arts, 1991, Abilene (Tex.) Cultural Affairs Coun., 1991-92, Short List Rolex award for enterprise, 1998. Office: 4019 Montague Dr Amarillo TX 79109-5018

KRACKE, ROBERT RUSSELL, lawyer; b. Decatur, Ga., Feb. 27, 1938; s. Roy Rachford and Virginia Carolyn (Minter) K.; m. Barbara Anne Pilgrim, Dec. 18, 1965; children: Shannon Ruth, Robert Russell, Rebecca Anne, Susan Lynn. Student, Birmingham So. Coll.; BA, Samford U., 1962; JD, Cumberland Sch. Law, 1965. Bar: Ala. 1965, U.S. Tax Ct. 1971, U.S. Supreme Ct. 1971. Individual practice law Birmingham, Ala., 1965—; pres. Kracke, Thompson & Ellis, 1980—. Editor, Birmingham Bar Bull, 1974—; bd. editors Ala. Lawyer, 1980-86; contbr. articles to profl. jours. Deacon Ind. Presbyn. Ch., Birmingham, 1973-76, elder, 1999—, pres. adult choir, 1968-99, chief adminstrv. officer, 1970-99, pres., treas. Nov. Orgn. Recital Series, 1999—, Housing Agy. Retarded Citizens; pres. Ala. chpt. Nat. Voluntary Health Agys.; mem. exec. com. legal counsel Birmingham Opera Theatre, 1983-95; bd. dirs. Ala. Assn. Retarded Citizens, Jefferson County Assn. Retarded Citizens, 1983-91, pres.-elect, 1994-96, pres. 1996-98, past pres., 1998-2000; coord. com. mem. Nat. Conv. of the ARC of U.S., 1999—; bd. dirs., founding pres. Birmingham chpt. Juvenile Diabetes Found., bd. dirs. The ARC of Ala., 1996-98, Found. of ARC, 1998—. With USNR, 1955-61. Mem. Birmingham (exec. com., chmn. law libr., law day 1976, history and archives com.), Ala. Bar Assn., ABA (award merit law day 1976), Am. Judicature Soc., Ala. Hist. Assn., So. Hist. Assn., The Club, Phi Alpha Delta (pres. chpt. 1964-65), Rotary (pres. Shades Valley club 1988-89, Paul Harris fellow, sec. dist. 6860 1990-91, dist. coord. comm., bd. dir., sec. ednl. found.), Sigma Alpha Epsilon. Home: 4410 Briar Glen Dr Birmingham AL 35243-1743 Office: Kracke Thompson & Ellis Lakeview Sch Bldg 808 29th St S Birmingham AL 35205-1004

KRADIN, RICHARD LAWRENCE, physician, researcher; b. N.Y.C., Jan. 12, 1950; s. George and Betty Kradin; m. Linda Sherlock, Aug. 22, 1978 (div. Oct. 1, 1993); children: Rachel, Sarah, Robert, Michael. BA, NYU, 1971, MS, 1972; MD, Thomas Jefferson U., 1976. Diplomate Am. Bd. Internal Medicine, Am. Bd. Pathology. Tchg. asst. NYU, N.Y.C., 1972—; staff dept. pathology, staff pulmonary unit Mass. Gen. Hosp., Boston, 1983—, mem. Ctr. for Psychiat. Studies, 1997—; dir. Mind-Body Inst., Beth Israel Deaconess, Boston, 1999—; cons. NIH, Bethesda, Md., 1986—; cons. in asbestos disease, 1986—. Author, editor: Immunopathology of Lung, 1996. Recipient rsch. grant NIH, 1982—, rsch. grant Coun. On. Tobacco Rsch., 1984-86, Cancer Rsch. grant Upjohn Co., 1985. Avocations: musician (studio guitarist), Antiquarian book collector. E-mail: rkradin@partners.org.

KRAEHN, GERTRAUD MARIA, dermatologist, molecular biology researcher; b. Munich, Mar. 17, 1964; d. Joseph and Irmengard Anna (Bloechl) K.; m. Uwe Seuftleben. Approbation, Ludwig-Maximilians U., Munich, 1993, MD, 1993. Bd. cert. dermatologist. Rschr. in physiol. chemistry U. Würzburg, Germany, 1991-93; resident, rschr. in dermatology Ludwig-Maximilians U., 1993-97; cons., researcher in dermatology and dermato-oncology U. Ulm, Germany, 1997—; ptnr. investigator Melanoma Lab., dept. dermatology, Ludwig-Maximilians U., 1997; prin. investigator Lab. for Molecular Biology and Genetics, dept. dermatology, U. Ulm, 1997—. Contbr. articles to profl. jours. Mem. Health Politics workshop, Munich and Ulm, 1987—. Mem. Soc. Operative and Oncologic Dermatology, European Soc. Pigment Cell Rsch., German Cancer Soc. Roman Catholic. Avocations: art, painting, sailing. Fax: 0049-731-602-3448. Home: Herrenkellergasse 10, 89073 Ulm Germany Office: U Ulm Dept Dermatology, Oberer Eselsberg 40, D-89081 Ulm Germany

KRAEMER, PHILIPP, manufacturing company executive, inventor; b. Hahn, Germany, Jan. 17, 1931; s. George Heinrich and Anna Erna K.; m. Rosemarie Sandner, June 2, 1956; children: Lynda, Irene, Sandra. Student vocat. sch., Darmstadt, Germany. Tool and die maker, 1956-61; tool maker Quality Tool & Massey Ferguson, 1961-64; founder Kraemer Tool & Mfg. Co. Ltd., Brampton, Ont., Can., 1964, pres., gen. mgr. Mem. Pollution Control Assn., Can. Mfg. Assn. Lutheran. Patentee oil-sand separator, 8 other patents; co-inventor Sound Perfection, Spadafora violine bow-guide. Home: 34 Kendleton Dr, Rexdale, ON Canada M9V 1V4 Office: Devon Rd, Brampton, ON Canada L6T 5A4

KRAEMER, ROBERT R., health educator, researcher; b. Fayetteville, Ariz., Sept. 9, 1952; s. William S. and Louise Russert Kraemer; m. Ginger R. Kraemer, June 22, 1980; children: Ryan, Bradley, Kyle. Student, Hendrix Coll., 1970-72; BA in Zoology, U. Ark., Fayetteville, 1975, MEd in Phys. Edn., 1980, EdD in Exercise Physiology, 1985. Secondary sch. tchr. Bentonville (Ark.) Jr. H.S., 1976-82; rsch. asst. human performance lab. U. Ark., 1982-85; asst. prof. exercise physiology, lab. dir. dept. phys. edn. West Tex. State U., Canyon, 1985-87; asst. prof. exercise physiology, exercise lab. coord. Kans. State U., 1987-91; assoc. prof. exercise physiology, exercise lab. coord. Southeastern La. U., Hammond, 1991-96, prof. exercise physiology, exercise lab. coord., 1996—; presenter in field. Contbr. articles to profl. jours. Grantee West Tex. State U., 1985-86, Killgore Rsch. Ctr., Canyon, 1986, Kans. State U., 1987, 88, 89, 91, Kans. Alliance Health, Phys. Edn., Recreation and Dance, 1988, Southeastern La. U., 1992, 94, 96, 97, 99. Fellow AAHPERD, Am. Coll. Sports Medicine (regional chpt. rep. Ctrl. States chpt. 1991); mem. Am. Physiol. Soc., Endocrine Soc, Phi Delta Kappa. Democrat. Fax: (504) 549-5119. E-mail: rkraemer@selu.edu. Home: 211 Woodbridge Blvd Hammond LA 70402-0001 Office: Southeastern La U Dept Kinesiology Slu 10845 Hammond LA 70402-0001

KRAFFT, FRITZ ADOLF, science and pharmacy educator; b. Hamburg, Germany, July 10, 1935; s. Carl and Frida (Hamann) K.; m. Astrid Wagner, Dec. 23, 1969; 1 child, Birte; children by previous marriage, Angela, Andreas. Student, U. Hamburg, Germany, 1955-62, PhD, 1962, habilitation, 1968. Scholar Studienstiftung des Deutschen Volkes, 1959-62; Wissenschaftlicher asst. Inst. for Geschichte der Naturwissenschaften, U. Hamburg, Germany, 1962-68; privatdozent Inst. for Geschichte der Naturwissenschaften, U. Hamburg, 1968, Wissenschaftlicher Oberassistent, 1968-70; prof. history of sci. Johannes Gutenberg U. Mainz, Germany, 1970-88; prof. history of pharmacy Philipp U., Marburg, Germany, 1988-2000; dean faculty pharmacy Philipp U., 1993-94; Exec. bd. German Assn. for Geschichte der Medizin, Naturwissenschaft und Technik, 1964-67; exec. bd. Assn. for Wissenschaftgeschichte, 1974—, pres., 1977-83; mem. Nat. Com. Fed. Republic of Germany in the Internat. Union History and Philosophy of Sci., Divsn. History Sci., 1977-93, 98—, pres. 1981-89; exec. bd. Fachgruppe Geschichte der Pharmazie of German Pharm. Assn., others. Author: Vergleichende Untersuchungen zu Homer und Hesiod, 1963, Dynamische und Statische Betrachtungsweise in der antiken Mechanik, 1970, Grosse Naturwissenschaftler, Biograph. Lexikon, 1970, 2d rev. edit. 1986, Otto von Guericke, 1978, Im Schatten der Sensation: Leben und Wirken von F. Strassmann, 1981, Lise Meitner, 1988, Otto Hahn und die Kernchemie, 1991, Die Bunsen-Briefe der UB Marburg, 1996; others; co-author books; founder, editor Berichte zur Wissenschaftsgeschichte, 1978—; editor Quellen und Studien znr Geschichte der Pharmazie, 1992—, Natur Wisenschaft-Theologie, 1999—; contbr. articles to profl. jours. Mem. Fachbereichsrat Math./Pharmacy and Versammlung/Konvent of Univ. Mainz/Marburg, Acad. Internat. Hist. Sci. (corr. 1971, effective 1981), Deutsche Akad. der Naturforscher Leopoldina, others. Office: Philipps Univ, 10 Roter Graben, 35032 Marburg Germany

KRAFT, ALEXANDER V.G., lawyer; b. Berlin, July 3, 1972; s. Volker G. and Regine K. JD, Free U. Berlin, 1996; LLM, U. San Diego, 1998. Bar: N.Y. Rsch. asst. U. San Diego, 1997-98; mgmt. trainee, European regional mgr. Sotheby's Internat. Realty, N.Y.C., Munich, 1998—. Mem. N.Y. State Bar Assn. Avocation: golf. Home: Harthauser Strasse 5, 81545 Munich Germany Office: Sotheby's Internat Realty, Odeonsplatz 16, Munich Germany 80539

KRAFT, CARL DAVID, lawyer; b. Elgin, Ill., July 28, 1952; s. Howard David and Edna Leota Kraft; m. Joan Marie Kaps Evans, May 24, 1975 (div. Jan. 1981); m. Kathleen Susan Webb, Nov. 19, 1983; children: Matthew A., Andrew W. BA, No. Ill. U., 1974; JD, Washington U., St. Louis, 1977. BAr: Mo. 1977, U.S. Dist. Ct. (ea. dist.) Mo., U.S. Ct. Appeals (8th cir.), U.S. Supreme Ct.; cert. civl trial lawyer. Atty. Richard Edwards Law Office, Clayton, Mo., 1977-78, Evans & Dixon, St. Louis, 1978-85; ptnr. Kraft & Harfst, St. Louis, 1985—. Bd. dirs., pres. Luth. Ministries Assn., St. Louis, 1988-95; evaluator, judge, coach H.S. Mock Trial, St. Louis, 1983—; sec. Glendale (Mo.) Luth. Ch. Coun., 1996—. Recipient Vol. Lawyer Svc. award Legal Svcs. Eastern Mo., 1984. Mem. ATLA, Mo. Bar Assn., Mo. Assn. Def. Lawyers. Home: 7642 Westmoreland Ave Saint Louis MO 63105-3807 Office: Kraft & Harfst 12901 N 40 Dr Saint Louis MO 63141-8634

KRAFT, DONALD EUGENE, architecture and engineering company executive; b. Rochester, N.Y., Aug. 10, 1929; s. Nicholas Raymond and Rosella Theresa (Miller) K.; m. Rosemarie Ursula Kraus, April 17, 1965; children: Eva Maria, Christian Martin, Donald Alexander Nicholas. Student, U. Rochester, 1948-51; BS in Engring., Bus. Adminstrn., Econs., Empire State Coll., 1977. Registered profl. engr., N.Y. Engr. stds. dept. Kodak Park, 1950-52; sales rep. C.A. Brewer, Inc., 1952-56; civil and san. engr. design Lozier Engrs. and Morrison & Morrison, 1956-61; v.p. gen. mgr. Profl. Chem. Corp. Dental Equipment, 1962-65; project engr. new product devel. Caldwell Mfg. Co., Inc., 1965-71; applications engr. Schlegel Corp., 1971-72; pres. Don Kraft Co., Penfield, N.Y., 1973—; sales engr., project mgr. turnkey automated prodn. equipment Alliance Tool Corp., 1978-81; gen. ptnr. Arens Assoc. Architecture and Engring. Svcs., Penfield, N.Y., 1986—; cons. in field. Patentee in hydraulics, pneumatics, dental equipment, automotive, window hardware and weather seals. With USN, 1947-48, USNR, 1947, 48-49, 54-58. Mem. Rochester C. of C., Civic Music Assn., Meml. Art Gallery, Rochester Yacht Club. Republican. Roman Catholic. Achievements include trisected an angle using only a straight edge and a compass, solving a 2400 year old problem, and working on gravity machine research and development and up-to-date formulas. Home and Office: 1930 Harris Rd Penfield NY 14526-1822

KRAFT, KENNETH HOUSTON, JR., insurance agency executive; b. Chgo., Apr. 2, 1934; s. Kenneth Houston and Elizabeth (Preston) K.; m. Ruth Neely, Aug. 11, 1956 (div. Sept. 1979); children: Katherine Elizabeth, Carolyn Ruth, Kenneth Houston III; m. Kathleen Hartung, Mar. 16, 1985. BS in Fin., Purdue U., 1956. Pres., chmn. bd. Kraft Ins. Agy., Inc., Winter Park, Fla., 1960—, KHK Fin. Corp., Winter Park, 1974—; chmn. bd. Echo Pub. Co., Sulfur Springs, Tex., 1970—; sr. mem. bd. dirs., mem. exec., fin., comml. loan, audit and examining coms. Barnett Bank Cen. Fla., Orlando, 1965-98; founding dirs. Goodings Groceries of Fla., Altamonte Springs, Fla., Schwartz Electro-Optics, Orlando, Internat. Laser Sys., Orlando, KHK Fin. Corp., Carson City, Nev., Princeton Fin. Corp., Orlando, Falcon Aviation, Orlando, TV-9 Inc., ABC affiliate, Orlando, First Ctrl. Corp., Orlando, Inglewood Daily News, Inglewood Citizen Co., L.A. Bd. dirs. Winter Park C. of C., 1965-70, Orange County chpt. ARC, Orlando, 1963-65, Orange County chpt. United Way, Winter Park, 1970-72, Winter Park YMCA, 1972-75, citrus grower Kraft Groves, 1966—; mem. Fla. Citrus Mut., Lakeland, 1966—, Com. of 100 of Orange County, Inc., Orlando, 1983—; bd. trustees Winter Park Meml. Hosp., 1969-88, also exec. com., compensation com., chmn. long range planning com.; chmn. Winter Park Cmty. Trust Fund, 1981-92; mem. grievance com. 9th Jud. Cir., 1987-90; active Boy Scouts Am., Rollins Coll. Fiat Lux Soc., Corp. Coun., Crummer Grad. Sch. Bus., Winter Park, Fla.; mem. selection com. COMPUSA Fla. Citrus Bowl, 1999. Lt. (j.g.) USNR, 1956-58. Named Outstanding Young Man of Winter Park, Winter Park Jaycees, 1970. Mem. Ctrl. Fla. Assn. Ins. Agts. (pres. 1963-64), Fla. Assn. Ins. Agts., Nat. Assn. Ins. Agts., So. Grand Bank Owners Assn., U.S. Naval Inst., U.S. Navy League, Purdue U. Alumni Assn. (pres. coun., dirs. cir. Krannert Grad. Sch. Mgmt., Deans Club Sch. Sci.), Gold Club Purdue Musical Orgn., All-Am. John Purdue Club, Country Club of Orlando (pres. 1994-95), U. Club, Citrus Club, Captiva Island Yacht Club, Useppa Island Club, Masons, Rotary (bd. dirs. Winter Park Club 1968-74), Sigma Chi, Delta Delta. Republican. Presbyterian. Home: 231 Chelton Cir Winter Park FL 32789-6004 also: 1765 Venus Dr Sanibel FL 33957-3427 Office: Kraft Ins Agy Inc PO Box 1443 Winter Park FL 32790-1443

KRAFT, PÅL, medical educator, researcher; b. Oslo, Norway, Feb. 19, 1959; s. Tore and Astrid (Skarpnord) K.; m. Solveigh Marie Breivik, Mar. 30, 1985; children: Brage, Magnus, Sunniva. MA in Sociology, U. Oslo, 1985, D in Dental Surgery, 1986; Bus. Candidate, Norwegian Sch. Mgmt., Oslo, 1989; PhD, U. Bergen (Norway), 1991. Sr. rsch. officer Norwegian Health Screening Svcs., Oslo, 1986-87; project leader Nat. Inst. Pub. Health, Oslo, 1987-89, doctoral fellow, 1989-91, rsch. dir., 1992-95; researcher WHO, Geneva, 1991-92; prof. U. Bergen, 1995—; pres. bd. Norwegian Tobacco Coun., Oslo, 1994-96; dir. Rsch. Ctr. Health Promotion, Bergen, 1996-98; adj. prof. Norwegian Sch. Mgmt., Oslo, 1995-97, Hedmark Coll., Rena, Norway, 1994—. Contbr. articles to profl. jours. Mem. European Assn. Exptl. Social Psychology, European Health Psychology Soc., Soc. Personality and Social Psychology. Avocations: reading, running, tracking, music.

KRAFT, SCOTT COREY, correspondent; b. Kansas City, Mo., Mar. 31, 1955; s. Marvin Emanuel and Patricia (Kirk) K.; m. Elizabeth Brown, May 1, 1982; children: Kate, Kevin. BS, Kans. State U., 1977. Staff writer AP, Jefferson City, Mo., 1976-77, Kansas City, 1977-79; corr. AP, Wichita, Kans., 1979-80; nat. writer AP, N.Y.C., 1980-84; nat. corr. L.A. Times, Chgo., 1984-86; bur. chief L.A. Times, Nairobi, Kenya, 1986-88, Johannesburg, South Africa, 1988-93, Paris, 1993-96; dep. fgn. editor L.A. Times, 1996-97, nat. editor, 1997—. Recipient Disting. Reporting in a Specialized Field award Soc. of the Silurians, 1982, Peter Lisagor award Headline Club Chgo., 1985, Feature Writing finalist Pulitzer Prize Bd., 1985, Sigma Delta Chi award, 1993. Office: LA Times Nat Editor Times Mirror Square Los Angeles CA 90053

KRAFT, ULRICH RALF, marketing executive; b. Essen, Germany, Feb. 23, 1961; s. Wolfgang and Lieselotte (Specht) K.; m. Alice Theisel, May 31, 1985; 1 child, Jasmin. Dipl.Ing., Tech. U., Berlin, 1985, Dr.Ing., 1988. Rsch. assoc. Tech. U. Berlin, 1985-89; project mgr. Daimler-Chrysler Aerospace, Munich, 1989-95; dept. head projects DASA/DSS, Munich, 1995-97, mktg. mgr., 1997—. Contbr. articles to profl. jours. Recipient Carl-Ramsauer Rsch. award, AEG, 1989. Mem. IEEE (Mit/AP German sect. bd. dirs. 1997—). Avocations: astrophysics, history, guitar. Office: Dornier Satellitensysteme, PO Box 801169, 81663 Munich Germany

KRAFT, VAHUR, bank executive; b. Tartu, Estonia, Mar. 11, 1961; married; 1 child. Degree in Fin. and Credit, Tartu U., 1984. Br. head Estonian Savings Bank, 1984-90; vice chmn. bd. Estonian Social Bank, 1990-91; v.p. Bank of Estonia, Tallinn, 1991-95, pres., 1995—; vice gov. IMF, Estonia, 1992-95, gov., 1995—. Fax: 372 6 680 836. Office: Eesti Pank, Estonia Ave 13, 15095 Tallinn Estonia

KRAFTSON, RAYMOND HARRY, business executive; b. Delaware County, Pa., June 20, 1940; s. Harry A. and Elisabeth (Hallstrom) k.; m. Marguerite Knewstub; children: Donald W., Marguerite O., Audrey E., Michele S. BA, U. Pa., 1962; JD, Coll. of William and Mary, 1967. Trial atty. SEC, Washington, 1967-68; counsel Ringe, Peet & Mason, Phila., 1968-70, Monsanto Co., St. Louis, 1970-71; sr. v.p., gen. counsel Life of Pa. Fin. Corp., Phila., 1972-78; sr. staff counsel INA Corp., Phila., 1978-80; v.p., gen. counsel, dir. Safeguard Scientifics, Inc., Wayne, Pa., 1980-90; pres. Ailes Communications Inc., N.Y.C., 1990-91, The J.D. Group, Ltd., Villanova, Pa., 1991-95; pres. and CEO PulseGroup Inc., Bryn Mawr, Pa., 1995-99; sr. v.p. Asset Mgmt. Svcs., LLC, N.Y.C., 1999—; bd. dirs. Hoffman Surgical Equipment Co., Conshohocken, Pa. Mng. editor William and Mary Law Rev., 1966-67. Pres. Gladwyne Montessori Sch., 1986-88; v.p., trustee The Baldwin Sch., Bryn Mawr, 1987-91; vestry mem. St. David's Ch., 1988-94, The Am. Missionary Fellowship, 1992—; bd. chmn. Urban Equity Ptnrs., 1996—; bd. mem. Wooden Boat Factory, 1998—. Mem. Nat. Assn. Corp. Dirs., Merion Cricket Club (Haverford), The Racquet Club (Phila.), Phila. Club. Republican. Episcopalian. Avocations: antique and classic boats and cars. E-mail: rhk@pulse-group.com. Office: Ariane Ptnrs LLC 444 Madison Ave Fl 25 New York NY 10022-6903

KRAG, EINAR, medical officer; b. Esbjerg, Denmark, Mar. 30, 1937; s. Jørgen and Erna Beate (Bugge) K.; m. Gertrud Sørensen, Sept. 10, 1960; children: Vibeke, Ulrik. MD, U. Aarhus, Denmark, 1962; DMSc, U. Aarhus, 1967. Specialist cert. in internal medicine and gastroenterology. Resident, rsch. fellow U. Hosps., Aarhus, 1962-72; vis. rsch. fellow Mayo Clinic, Rochester, Minn., 1972-73; sr. resident U. Hosps., Copenhagen, 1973-76, chmn. gastroenterology Hvidovre U. Hosp., Copenhagen, 1977-95; med. dir. Bispebjerg U. Hosp., Copenhagen, 1995-96; chief med. officer, dir. gen. Nat. Bd. Health, Copenhagen, 1996—; cons. physician The Mcpl. Life Ins. Co., Copenhagen, 1978-96, The Pub. No Fault Ins. Co., Copenhagen, 1992-96; pres. Danish Gastroenterol. Soc., 1980-81; spkr. in field. Author: The Pseudo-ucler Syndrome, 1967; editor-in-chief Jour. Danish Med. Assn., 1991-96; contbr. articles to profl. jours. Lt. Med Corps Royal Danish Army, 1965-66. Decorated knight Her Majesty the Queen of Denmark, 1997. Mem. Danish Med. Assn. Avocations: history, architecture, opera, traveling. Office: Nat Bd Health, PO Box 2020, DK-1012 Copenhagen Denmark

KRAGNES, EARL NEWTON, retired minister; b. Pitts., Sept. 13, 1921; s. Alfred Martin Kragnes and Margaret Lohr; m. Anna C. Kragnes, Nov. 4, 1943; children: Kathy, Janice, Cheryl, Philip. BA, Johnson Bible Coll., 1944; MA, Phillips Theol. Sem., 1946, B Divinity, 1948. Ordained Christian Ch. (Disciples of Christ), 1942. Pastor N.E. Christian Ch., Oklahoma City, 1948-49; assoc. min. Crown Heights Christian Ch., Oklahoma City, 1949-53; field rep. Nat. Coun. Chs. N.Y.C., Oklahoma City, 1953-56; dir. religious edn. Mo. Coun. Chs., Jefferson City, 1957-59; exec. dir. Okla. Coun. Chs., Oklahoma City, 1959-74; dir. mgr. interreligious liaison office AARP, Washington, 1974-93; ret.; bd. dirs. Nat. Interfaith Coalition on Aging, Washington, 1974-93. Contbr. chpt. to book. Cons. adv. bd. inst. Lifelong Learning, Montgomery Coll., Rockville, Md., 1997—. Recipient Spiritual Well-being of Elderly award Nat. Coun. on Aging, Inc., 1993. Avocations: volunteer work, recording for the blind and dyslexic. Home: 407 Russell Ave Apt 601 Gaithersburg MD 20877-2856

KRAHMER, DONALD LEROY, JR., lawyer; b. Hillsboro, Oreg., Nov. 11, 1957; s. Donald L. and Joan Elizabeth (Karns) K.; m. Suzanne M. Blanchard, Aug. 16, 1986; children: Hillary, Zachary. BS, Willamette U., 1981, MM, 1987, JD, 1987. Bar: Oreg. 1988. Fin. analyst U.S. Bancorp, Portland, 1977-87; intern U.S. Senator Mark Hatfield, 1978; legis. aide State Sen. Jeannette Hamby, Hillsboro, Oreg., 1981-83, State Rep. Delna Jones, Beaverton, Oreg., 1983; bus. analyst Pacificorp, Portland, 1987; mgr. mergers/acquisitions Pacificorp Fin. Svcs., Portland, 1988-89; dir. Pacificorp Fin. Svcs., 1990; CEO, pres. Atkinson Group, Portland, 1991—; ptnr. Black Helterline, Portland, 1991—; bd. dirs., sec. Marathon Fin. Assocs., Portland, 1989; bd. dirs. Self-Enhancement, Inc.; chmn. Willamette Forum; bd. dirs. Oreg. Entrepreneur Forum, 1993-2000, editor, 1993, chmn. adv. bd., 1995, chmn. bd., 1998; founder co-chmn. Oreg. Emerging Bus. Initiative, 1997—; bd. dirs. Concordia Univ. Found., 1995-97. Treas. Com. to Re-Elect Jeannette Hamby, 1986; bd. dirs. fin. com./devel. com. Am. Diabetes Assn., Portland, 1990-96; founder Needle Bros., 1994; chmn. Atkinson Grad. Sch. Devel. Com., Salem, 1989-92; Bd. Vis. Coll. Law, Willamette U., 1997—; mem. adv. bd. Ctr. for Law and Entrepreneurship, U. Oreg. Sch. Law, 1997—; founder Conf. of Entrepreneurship, Salem, 1984, chmn. Entrepreneurship Breakfast Forum, Portland, 1993; chmn., founder Oreg. Conf. on Entrepreneurship and Awards Dinner, 1994-99, sr. v.p., 1999—; mem. exec. com., bd. dirs. Cascade Pacific Coun. Boy Scouts Am., 1998—, chmn. cmty. fund. dir., 1997, chmn. Scoutrageous, 2000; vice chmn. Govs. Coun. on Small Bus., State of Oreg.; mem. Govs. Econ. Devel. Joint Bds. Working Group, 1999—. Recipient Pub.'s award Oreg. Bus. Mag., 1987, Founders award Willamette U., 1987, award Scripps Found., 1980, Bus. Jour. 40 Under 40 award, 1996, Oreg. State Bar Pres.'s award, 1999. Mem. ABA, Oreg. Bar Assn. (chmn. exec. com., fin. instns. com. sec., exec. com., bus. law sect., chmn. 1999, sec. 1998), Multnomah County Bar Assn., Washington County Bar Assn., Assn. for Corp. Growth, Oreg. Biosci. Assn., Portland Soc. Fin. Analysts, Japan-Am. Soc. Oreg., Assn. Investment Mgmt. and

Rsch., City Club, Software Assn. of Oreg., Oreg. Biotech. Assn., Multnomah Athletic Club, Arlington Club. Republican. Lutheran. Home: 16230 SW Copper Creek Dr Portland OR 97224-6500 Office: Black Helterline 1200 Union Bank Calif Tower 707 SW Washington St Ste 1200 Portland OR 97205-3289

KRAJČA, JAROMIL MILOSLAV, hydrochemist, researcher, expert witness; b. Jihlava, Czech Republic, Feb. 20, 1932; s. Josef Rudolf and Ludmila Marie (Hrnčiříková) K.; m. Milada Bínová, Apr. 20, 1956 (div. 1989); 1 child, Milada; m. Zdeňka Emilie Malašková, May 25, 1990 (dec. Dec. 1998); children: Zdeněk, Dana; m Eva Mastná, May 20, 2000; children: Eva, Jana. Grad., Secondary Chemistry Sch., Brno, Czech Republic, 1952. Rschr. Rsch. Inst. Petroleum, Brno, 1955-65; head hydrotech. dept. Rsch. Inst. Geol. Engring., Brno, 1965-77, rschr., 1978-89, head divsn. water monitoring, 1990-91; owner, dir. JAK Ltd, Brno, 1992—. Author: Gases in Ground-Waters (in Czech), 1977, (in Russian), 1980; co-author, editor: Natural Water Sampling (in Czech), 1983, (in English), 1989; co-author: Fluid Sampling for Geothermal Prospecting, 1992; contbr. over 250 articles to profl. jours.; 30 patents in field. Active Ecol. Com., Brno, 1990-95. Recipient State award, Praha, 1968. Mem. Sci.-Tech. Soc., Czech Assn. Hydrogeologists, Czech Geol. Soc. Avocation: classical music. Home: Vaculikova st No 11, 63800 Brno 38 Czech Republic Office: JAK Ltd, PO Box 17, 63817 Brno 38 Czech Republic

KRAJČOVIČ, RUDOLF, linguistics educator; b. Trakovice, Slovakia, July 22, 1927; s. Rudolf and Mária (Michalová) K.; children: Dana, Peter. MA, Comenius U., Bratislava, Slovakia, 1953, CSc, 1959, PhD, 1984. Asst. lectr. Comenius U., 1950-53, asst. prof., 1953-64, assoc. prof., 1964-86, prof., 1986—; lectr. State Lomonosov's U., Moscow, 1970-71, 75-76, 81—, Internat. Congress Slavists, Sofia 1963, Warsaw 1973, Kiev 1983, Internat. Congress Onomastic Scis., Cracow 1981. Author: Slovak and Other Slavic Languages, 1974, A Historical Phonology of the Slovak Language, Heidelberg, 1975, History's Evidence Slovak, 1977, 1980 (Bratislava Book of Yr. 1983), The Development of the Slovak Language and Dialectology, 1988; contbr. articles to profl. jours. Recipient Stur's award Mus., Modra, Slovakia, 1986, Silver Medal award Comenius U., 1987, Medal award Safarik's U., 1995, medal Min. of Culture, Slovakia, 1997, prize Prof. L. Novak's Matica Slovakia, Martin, 2000. Mem. Assn. Slovak Linguists (dep. chmn. 1967-70), Czechoslovak Com. Onomastics, Slovak Com. Onomastics (bd. dirs.), Internat. Com. Slavic Onomastics, Internat. Com. Onomastic Scis., Soc. Linguistica Europae.

KRAJEWSKI, WOJCIECH MICHAL, electrical engineer, researcher; b. Warsaw, Poland, Sept. 29, 1953; s. Stefan and Janina (Jackowska) K. MSc, Warsaw Tech. U., 1977, PhD cum laude, 1984. Rsch. fellow Warsaw Tech. U., 1977-81; rsch. scientist Inst. Elec. Engring., Warsaw, 1981-84, asst. prof., 1984—; cons. rsch. projects Warsaw Tech. U., 1986-89, Ministry of Environ. Protection, Natural Resources and Forestry, Poland, 1991-94; vis. prof. Rensselaer Poly. Inst., Troy, N.Y., 1991. Co-author: (chpt.) Electromagnetic Fields in Electrical Engineering, 1988; editl. bd. Electrosoft, Southampton, U.K., 1986-91; contbr. articles to profl. jours. Mem. Trade Union Solidarity, Warsaw, 1980—. Mem. Assn. Polish Electriciants. Roman Catholic. Avocations: music, economy. Home: Miedzynarodowa 40m47, 03-922 Warsaw Poland Office: Inst Elec Engring, Pozaryskiego 28, 04-703 Warsaw Poland

KRAJICEK, RICHARD, tennis player; b. Rotterdam, The Netherlands, Dec. 6, 1971. Profl. tennis player, 1989—. Recipient 17 single titles and 3 double titles. Avocations: golf, basketball. Office: ATP Tour Internat Hdqr 201 Atp Tour Blvd Ponte Vedra Beach FL 32082*

KRAJICKOVA, DAGMAR, neurologist, educator; b. Stare Mesto, Czech Republic, Nov. 15, 1948; d. Josef and Drahomira (Ringlova) Tyl; m. Zdenek Krajicek, July 15, 1972; children: Katerina, Iveta. MD, Charles U., 1973, PhD, Charles U., 1992. Resident dept. neurology U. Hosp. Czech Republic, Sumperk, 1973-76; resident dept. neurology U. Hosp. Czech Republic, Hradec Králové, Czech Republic, 1976-84, sr. resident dept. neurology, 1984-97, sr. lectr., 1997—; head stroke unit dept. neurology U. Hosp., Hradec Králové, 1992—. Contbr. (textbooks) Cerebral and Spinal Cord Vascular Diseases, 1997, Cerebrospinal Fluid, 1997; contbr. numerous articles to profl. jours. Mem. Neurol. Soc. Czech Republic. Avocations: literature, painting, music, sculpture. Office: Dept Neurology, U Hosp Nezvalova, 500 05 Hradec Králové Czech Republic

KRAJNÍK, EDUARD, mathematics educator, researcher; b. Prague, Czechoslovakia, Nov. 19, 1942; s. Eduard and Jarmila (Škrábková) K.; m. Ludmila Dudová, Apr. 19, 1980; children: Martina, Markéta. Student, Charles U., Prague, Czechoslovakia, 1962-67, D in Nat. Scis., 1988; PhD, Czech Tech. U., Prague, Czechoslovakia, 1987. Asst. prof. Czech Tech. U., Prague, 1970-92, assoc. prof., 1992—; cons. Rsch. Inst. Engring. Edn., Prague, 1978-79; vis scholar Jr. Lyceum, Malta, 1980-82; vis. prof. Seattle C.C., 1990-91. Author: (with others) Signal Processing III: Theory and Applications, 1986, Signal Processing VI: Theory and Applications, 1992, Mathematical Theory of Networks and Systems, 1998. Mem. IEEE, Soc. Czech Mathematicians and Physicists. Roman Catholic. Avocations: photography, hiking. Home: Přesličková 11, 106 00 Prague 10, Czech Republic Office: Czech Tech U, Technická 2, 166 27 Prague 6, Czech Republic

KRAKAU, TORSTEN CARL-ERIK, ophthalmology educator; b. Helsingborg, Sweden, July 27, 1921; s. Erik Viktor and Svanhild Frideborg (Schlyter) K.; m Marie-Louise von Leithner, Apr. 4, 1953. MD, U. Lund, 1948, PhD. 1953. Prof. exptl. ophthalmology U. Lund, 1966-86; prof. emeritus U. Lund, Malmoe, 1986. Recipient Alcon Rsch. Inst., Ft. Worth, 1990. Mem. Royal Physiographic Soc., Dansk Oftalmolog Selsklab, Soc. Francaise Ophthalmology. Home: Bengt Lidforss v 1, 22465 Lund Sweden Office: Univ Eye Clinic, L Mas, 20502 Malmö Sweden

KRAKER, DEBORAH SCHOVANEC, special education educator; b. Enid, Okla., May 28, 1960; d. Charles Raymond and Marcella Ruth (Mack) Schovanec; m. Kevin Mark Kraker, July 10, 1987. BS, U. Ctrl. Okla., 1982; postgrad., Okla. State U., Stillwater, 1995—. Cert. tchr. spl. edn., learning disability/mentally handicapped. Customer svc. mgr. Skaggs, Oklahoma City, 1982-92; tchr. spl. edn. Edmond (Okla.) Pub. Schs., 1993—; tchr. Francis Tuttle Vocat. Tech. Ctr., Oklahoma City, 1993, 94, 95, mem. adv. bd., 1993-96. Mem. adv. bd. Francis Tuttle Vocat. Tech. Ctr., 1993—. Mem. NEA, Okla. Edn. Assn. (del. nat. assembly 1996), Edmond Assn. Classroom Tchrs. (v.p. 1997-98), Coun. for Exceptional Children, Assn. Classroom Mems. (exec. bd.), Okla. Commn. Tchr. Preparation (mem. portfolio rev. team, mem. accreditation rev. team, mem. program accreditation), Learning Disabilities Assn., Kappa Delta Pi. Republican. Roman Catholic. Avocations: reading, sewing, cooking, collecting antiques. Home: 2721 Berkshire Way Oklahoma City OK 73120-2704

KRAKOFF, KENNETH B., dentist, consultant; b. Columbus, Ohio, Apr. 13, 1925; s. Morris Joseph and Frieda (Cohen) K.; m. Corinne Bette Goldman, July 4, 1948; children: David M., Steven P. DDS, Ohio State U., 1949. Resident VA, L.A., 1949-50; pvt. practice, Toledo, 1950-51, 53—; chief dental svc. Toledo Hosp., 1971-91; chmn. dentistry Med. Coll. Ohio, Toledo, 1975-79; pres. Depcon, Toledo, 1987—; dental cons. Owens Ill., Inc., Toledo, 1987-91; sec. Oral Health Assocs., Inc., Toledo, 1989—; mem. dean's adv. com. Ohio State U. Coll. Dentistry, Columbus, 1977-82; ProMedica, Toledo, 1997-. Contbr. articles to orifh, hiyrs,. Mem. dental adv. bd. Regional Med. Planning, Toledo, 1969-83; pres.. bd. dirs. Health Planning Assn., Toledo, 1969-85; bd. dirs., v.p. Lucas County unit Am. Cancer Soc., Toledo, 1983-95; pres. N.W. Ohio Health Planning, Inc., Toledo, 1994-99; trustee Med. Mission Svcs. Found., Toledo, 1999-00. With U.S. Army Air Force, 1943-46, USAF, 1951-53. Recipient Outstanding Svc. cert. Assn. for Retared Children, Toledo, 1965, Disting. Svc. award Health Planning Assn., 1972, 73, 76, 81, 85; Pace Setter award Am. Cancer Soc., 1988, Life Saver award, 1993; Golden Buckeye award Ohio State U. Coll. Dentistry, 1999. Mem. ADA (del. 1973-76), Am. Assn. Hosp. Dentists, Pierre Fauchard Acad. (medal 1993), Am. Soc. Dentistry for Children (pres. Ohio unit 1972-75, 81-82), Ohio Dental Assn. (com. chmn., del. 1969-77), Toldeo Dental Soc. (pres. 1969-70), Toledo Soc. Dentistry for Children (pres. 1965-66), Toledo C. of C. (health sys. study com. 1993-96). Avocations:

photography, golf, tennis, skiing. E-mail: kkrakoff@aol.com. Office: 2910 W Central Ave Toledo OH 43606-3026

KRAKOVER, SHAUL, philosophy educator, researcher; b. Bratislava, Slovakia, Oct. 17, 1947; s. Naftali Tsvi and Rivka (Schwarc) K.; m. Mazal Gabay, July 8, 1945; children: Yossi, Ohad, Ariel, Naftli. BA in Geography and Econs., Ben-Gurion U. of the Neger, Beer-Sheva, Israel, 1972; MA in Urban Geography, Hebrew U., Jerusalem, 1978; PhD in Urban Geography, U. Md., 1982. Univ. prof. dept. geography Ben-Gurion U. of the Negev, Beer-Sheva, 1982—; city and regional planner Enviroplan, Beer-Sheva, 1988-95. Co-author: (atlas) Atlas of the Negev, 1986; co-author: Industrial Geography of Israel, 1993. Postdoctoral fellowship The Ohio State U., 1987. Jewish. Avocation: lecturing. Office: Dept Geography, Ben-Gurion U of the Negev, 86105 Beer-Sheva Israel

KRAKOWIAK, LEO, lawyer; b. Belem, Pa., Feb. 5, 1948; s. Icek and Nair Arensur (Abensur) K.; m. Marlene Golombek, Jan. 15, 1972; children: Ricardo, Silvia Krakowtak Rosenthal, Claudia. JD, U. Sao Paulo, 1971. Ptnr. Advocacia Krakowiak, Sao Paulo, 1971-2000. Contbr. articles to profl. jours. Coun. Albert Einstein Hosp., 1999-2000; former bd. govs. Tel Aviv U. Office: Advocacia Krakowiak S/C, Av Brasil 525, 01431000 Sao Paulo Brazil

KRAKOWSKI, LESZEK BRONISLAW, veterinarian, researcher, educator; b. Widawa, Poland, Dec. 13, 1960; s. Henryk Leszek and Alina (Adamczyk) K.; m. Jadwiga Teresa Bożek, Sept. 18, 1982 (div. Apr. 1986); 1 child, Karolina Maria. Izabela Cetnar, Oct. 24, 1992; 1 child, Magdalena Nina. DVM, U. Agr. Lublin, Poland, 1990. Assist. prof. U. Agr. Lublin, 1989-97, adj. prof., 1997-99. Mem. Polish Soc. Vet. Scis., Polish Hunting Club. Avocations: hunting, pop music, painting. Home: Królowej Jadwigi 6/28, 20-282 Lublin Poland Office: U Agr, Dept Animal Reprod, Głęboka 30, 20-612 Lublin Poland

KRALJ, METKA, biology and science educator, researcher; b. Ljubljana, Slovenia, Apr. 30, 1956; d. Dušan and Breda (Medvešek) K. Grad. in Biology, U. Ljubljana, 1979; MS, Internat. Sch. Hydraulics and Environ. Engring., Delft, The Netherlands, 1985, U. Ljubljana, 1991; PhD, U. Ljubljana, 1998. Rschr. Inst. Biology, Ljubljana, 1982-86; tchg. asst. faculty medicine U. Ljubljana, 1986-95, tchg. asst. faculty edn., 1995-99, assoc. prof. faculty edn., 1999—. Co-author primary sch. sci. textbooks; contbr. articles to profl. jours. Recipient Rsch. award U. Ljubljana, 1980. Avocation: translation of popular science texts to Slovene language. Home: Celovska 134, 1000 Ljubljana Slovenia Office: Faculty Edn, Kardeljeva ploscad 16, 1000 Ljubljana Slovenia

KRALL, YUNG N., health facility administrator; b. Can Tho, S. Vietnam, May 24, 1946; d. Quang Minh Dang and Pham Thi Tran; m. John James Krall, Aug. 3, 1968; 1 child, Lance David. B. Phan Thanh Gian, Can Tho, 1965. Agt., cons. Dept. Justice CIA/FBI, Hawaii, 1975-80, Washington, 1975-80, London, 1975-80; sr. epidemiologist Ga. Pub. Health, Atlanta, 1984-96; dir. multinat. rels. Emory Northlaken Med. Ctr., Tucker, Ga., 1996—; mem. adv. bd. Victim Witness Assistance Program, Atlanta, 1993-95. Author: A Thousand Tears Falling, 1995. Active alumni Leadership Atlanta, 1993—; vol. Ga. Severe Wealth Response, 1998—; mem. Atlanta Regional Commn., 1994—. Recipient Americanism medal DAR, 1998, Cmty. Svc. award DeKalb County Bd. Health, 1997, 98, 99, Cmty. Svc. award DeKalb County, 1999. Mem. Vietnam Vets. Am. (life). Avocations: deep sea fishing, gardening, public speaking, writing. E-mail: keyseat@msn.com. Address: PO Box 33391 Decatur GA 30033-0391

KRAMARENKO, ALEXANDER VICTOROVICH, medical equipment company executive, psychiatrist; b. Kharkov, Ukraine, Nov. 7, 1957; s. Victor Eugen'yevich and Nadezhda Sergeyevna (Shlyk) K.; m. Lesya Miroslavovna Melnik, Feb. 17, 1989; 1 child, Yury Alexandrovich. MD, Med. Inst., Kharkov, Ukraine, 1980. Resident Rsch. Inst. Neurology and Psychiatry, Kharkov, 1980-81; physician Regional Psychiat. Clinic, Kharkov, 1980-81, head dept., 1981-82; head med. svc. regiment Garrison Med. Hosp., Rovno, Ukraine, 1982-84; with Dist. Mil. Hosp., Kiev, Ukraine, 1985; sci. rschr. Aviation Inst., Kharkov, 1984-90; head rsch. lab. of computer diagnostical systems DX-Systems Ltd., Ctrl. Clin. Hosp., Kharkov, 1990—. Contbr. articles on electroencephalography to profl. jours. Lt. Med. Svc Ukraine mil., 1982-84. Avocations: DX-CB radio communication, design of amateur radio communication devices, analog-pulses devices, tourism. Home: 57 Ryleyev St Apt 8, 310014 Kharkov Ukraine Office: DX-Systems, Ctrl Clin Hosp, 5 Balakirev Bystreet, 310018 Kharkov Ukraine

KRAMER, AARON R., radio news director; b. Neenah, Wis., Oct. 19, 1969; s. Richard Kramer and Jody Zahn. BS in Pub. Adminstrn., U. Wis. Stevens Point, 1997, BS in Polit. Sci., 1997. News dir., co-gen. mgr. WRPN-AM, Ripon, Wis. Mem. Ripon Tiger Booster Club. Republican. Lutheran. Avocations: investments, travel, gardening, sports. E-mail: akramer@itol.com. Home: 609 Harvey St Ripon WI 54971-9557 Office: WRPN-AM Radio 112 Watson St Ripon WI 54971-1327

KRAMER, ALLAN FRANKLIN, II, researcher, botanical garden official; b. N.Y.C., Dec. 10, 1950; s. Walter Frederick and Dorothea (Russell-Hurley) K. AB, Coll. of Holy Cross, 1972; MS, Pratt Inst., 1979. Sr. document analyst Aspen Systems Corp., N.Y.C., 1979-81, team leader analyst, 1981-83, mgr. rsch. staff, 1983-86; sr. editor Bus. Guides, Inc. div., sr. rsch. mgr. Lebhar-Friedman, Inc., N.Y.C., 1987-91; conservator Bklyn. Botanic Garden, 1991—, trustee, 1995-97. Mem. exec. com. Bklyn. Bot. Garden Aux., 1991—, v.p. 1993-95, pres. 1995-97, dir., 1997—; mem. pres.'s coun. Coll. Holy Cross, class chmn.; dir. Park Slope Geriatric Ctr, dir. Vol. Svcs. Opportunity Project, Brooklyn Conservatory of Music, chmn. devel. com., mem. exec. bd.; mem. Prospect Park Coun. The Woodlands Coun., New Leadership Coun., United Hosp. Fund; trustee Bklyn. Bot. Garden 1995-97; dir. Park Slope Vol. Ambulance Corps., Park Slope Neighborhood Family Ctr., CAMBA. Fellow Bklyn. Mus., Roebling Soc., Bklyn. Hist. Soc.; mem. Soc. Scholarly Pub., Am. Soc. Info. Sci., Spl. Librs. Assn., Am. Assn. Bot. Gardens and Arboreta, New Eng. Soc. in City of Bklyn. (v.p., dir.), Hundred Yr. Assn. N.Y., Royal Oak Found., Friendly Sons of St. Patrick (chmn.), Soc. Old Bklyn. (life), Battle of Bklyn. Conservancy (dir.), Assn. St. George the Martyr (Knight), Greek Order of St. Dennis of Zante (Knight), Montauk Club (pres.), Mcpl. Club Bklyn., Bklyn. C. of C., Surf Club of Quogue, English Speaking Union, Beta Phi Mu (life). Avocations: sailing, travel, antiquing. Home: 35 Prospect Park W Brooklyn NY 11215-2370 Office: Bklyn Botanic Garden 1000 Washington Ave Brooklyn NY 11225-1008

KRAMER, AXEL, hygiene and environmental physician; b. Gotha, Thuringia, Germany, Jan. 4, 1946; s. Helmut and Gabriele (Strübing) K.; m. Birute Kazlauskaite, Sept. 6, 1973 (div. 1997); children: Nikolaus, Sebastian. MD, U. Greifswald, Germany, 1972. Intern, then resident E. Moritz Arndt U., Greifswald, 1972-90, prof., 1990—, dir. Inst. Hygiene and Environ. Medicine, 1990—, vice dean med. faculty, 1994-98; cons. German Inst. Standardization, Berlin, 1994—, Commn. of Disinfection, German Assn. Hygiene Microbiology, 1991—; mem. Robert Koch Commn. Infection Control, Berlin, 1996—. Mem. editl. bd. Jour. Hygiene and Medicine, 2bl. Hyg. Umweltmed., Dtsch. Fachzeitshr. Wundbehandlung, Ocular Infection and Hygiene; editor: Handbook of Antiseptic, 8 vols., 1979-87, (series of books) Microbial Environment and Antimicrobial Measures, 1977—, Hosp. Hygiene, Mgmt. and Quality Assurance, 2000, booklets on biol. importance of thiocyanate, 1984, 87, 90; contbr. chpts. to books, more than 300 articles to profl. jours.; 57 patents in field. Recipient Prize of Ernst Moritz Arndt U., Greifswald, 1971, 88, Prize of Max v. Pettenkofer, Assn. of Hygiene, Berlin, 1979, Prize of Carl Flügge, Assn. Gen. and Communal Hygiene of Germany, Halle, 1987. Mem. Austrian Assn. Hygien Microbiol. Preventive Medicine, German Assn. Hosp. Hygiene (mem. sect. hosp. hygiene 1992-94), Internat. Soc. Eye Rsch., Assn. Hygiene and Environ. Medicine, Internat. Environ. Medicine. Evangelic Ch. Avocations: literature, writing, music, fine arts, photography. Home: Georg-Engel St 20, Greifswald 17489, Germany Office: Inst Hygiene and Environ Me, Hain St 26, Greifswald 17487, Germany

KRAMER, BENJAMIN ROBERT, sheriff's deputy, accident reconstructionist; b. Middletown, Ohio, Feb. 21, 1962; s. Benjamin Rudyard and

Bonita Sue (McClanahan) K.; m. Donna May Kramer, May 15, 1995; children: Joshua, Thomas. AS in Law Enforcement, Clin State Coll., 1998. Cert. Ohio Peace Officer Tng. Coun. Police officer Carlisle (Ohio) Police Dept., 1989-93; dep. sheriff Butler County Sheriff's Office, Hamilton, Ohio, 1994—. Author Vincenza Community Security Plan, 1986. Active Rep. Nat. Com., Washington, 1993, Ohio Rep. Party. Served with U.S. Army, 1980-88, Italy. Decorated Army Commendation medal (2). Mem. Buckeye State Sheriff's Assn. (assoc.), Fraternal Order of Police, Am. Legion, Masons, Scottish Rite, Eagles, Shriners. Pentecostal. Avocation: judo. Office: Butler County Sheriff's Ofc 123 Court St Hamilton OH 45011-2825

KRAMER, CHAIM MENACHEM (JESSE MICHAEL KRAMER), publisher, author, editor; b. Bklyn., Aug. 6, 1945; arrived in Israel, 1975; s. Harold Kramer and Lucy Sterman Kramer; m. Gita Rosenfeld, Apr. 6, 1965; children: Rachel, Aaron, Raphael, Miriam, Zivia, Zvi. DD, Breslov Rabbinical Coll., Jerusalem, Israel, 1964. Guidance counselor Jerusalem Acad. Jewish Studies, Jerusalem, 1976-78; dir. Breslov Yeshiva, Jerusalem, 1979-85; founder, dir. Breslov Rsch. Inst., Jerusalem, 1979—. Author: Annotated Likutey Moharan, vols. 1-7, 10-11, 1988—, Crossing the Narrow Bridge, 1989, Through Fire and Water, 1992, Mashiach: Who? What? Why? How? Where? and When?, 1994, Treasury of Unearned Gifts, 1996, Anatomy of the Soul, 1998. Jewish. Avocations: chess, swimming. Office: Breslov Rsch Inst, 8 Avinadav St PO Box 5370, 91053 Jerusalem Israel

KRAMER, EDWARD GEORGE, lawyer; b. Cleve., July 15, 1950; s. Archibald Charles and Katherine Faith (Porter) K.; m. Roberta Darwin, June 15, 1974. BS in Edn., Kent State U., 1972; JD, Case Western Res. U., 1975. Bar: Ohio 1975, U.S. Dist. Ct. (no. dist.) Ohio 1975, U.S. Ct. Appeals (6th cir.) 1980, U.S. Supreme Ct. 1980. Assoc. dir. The Cuyahoga Plan of Ohio, Cleve., 1975-76; exec. dir. The Housing Advs., Inc., Cleve., 1979—; sr. ptnr. Kramer & Assocs., LPA, Cleve., 1981—; spl. counsel atty. gen. State of Ohio, Columbus, 1983-95; pres. Atty. Svcs., Inc., 1987—, ASI Info. Sys.; dir. Housing Law Clinic, 1989-95; dir. Fair Housing Law Clinic, 1995—; adj. lectr. Cleve. State U., 1991-94, adj. prof., 1994—; alt. consumer rep., FTC, Washington, 1976-77; cons. HUD, Washington, 1978-80, joint select com. sch. desegregation, Ohio Gen. Assembly, Columbus, 1979; mem. visitors com., Case Western Res. U. Sch. Law, Cleve., 1977-83; mem., chmn. Ford Motor Consumer Appeals Bd., 1989-93; bd. advisors Brownstone Pub. Author: How to Settle Small Claims: A Guide to The Use of Small Claims Courts, 1973, (with others) A Guide to Regional Housing Opportunities, 1979, (with Buchanan) Mobile Home Living: A Guide to Consumers' Rights, 1979; contbr. articles to legal jours. Chmn. Ohio Protection and Advocacy System for Developmentally Disabled, Columbus, 1978-80; trustee Muscle Disease Soc., Cleve., 1979-81; sec. Cuyahoga County Housing and Econ. Devel. com., Cleve., 1983—; mem. Cleve. Mayor's Com. on Employment of Handicapped, 1978-79; mem. fair housing adv. bd. John Marshall Law Sch. Named Disting. Recent Grad. Case Western Reserve U. Law Alumni Assn., 1985; Roscoe Pound fellow. Mem. ABA (sect. on urban state & local govt. law, com. on housing and urban devel., forum on constrn. industry), ACLU (litigation com.), Cleve. Bar Assn. (trustee 1995-98; mem. com. on homeless, chmn. law sch. liaison), Nat. Employment Lawyers Assn., Assn. Trial Lawyers Am. (employment rights sect., 2d vice chair, newsletter editor, 1st vice chair, chair-elect), Assn. Am. Law Schs. (com. on clin. legal edn.), Planetary Soc., Boat Club Nautica, Palm Beach Club (London), Old River Yacht Club, Cleve. Grays, Masons, Tyrian (worshipful master), Order of Eastern Star (James A Garfield chpt.). Democrat. Mem. United Ch. Christ. Avocations: softball, scuba diving, collecting coins and stamps, chess, reading. Office: Kramer & Assocs LPA 3214 Prospect Ave E Cleveland OH 44115-2614

KRAMER, FRANK RAYMOND, classicist, educator; b. Baraboo, Wis., Jan. 2, 1908; s. Chris Edward and Mabel (Shaw) K.; m. Hetty Louise Eising, Dec. 20, 1935; children: Bryce Allen, Anita Louise (Mrs. James Cyril Shew). B. Humanities, U. Wis., 1929, M.A. in Greek and Latin, 1931, Ph.D., 1936. Mem. faculty Heidelberg Coll., Tiffin, Ohio, 1938-78; prof. classics Heidelberg Coll., 1944-78; asso. in residence U. Wis., 1948-49, 51-52; vis. prof. Ohio State U., summer 1962, prof. classics, 1978-79; research Am. Sch. Classical Studies, Athens, 1965. Author: Voices in the Valley, Mythmaking and Folk Belief in the Shaping of the Middle West, 1964; also articles; contbr. American National Biography. Grantee Wis. Com. Study Am. Civilization, 1948-49, 51-52; Grantee Social Sci. Research Council, 1951. Mem. Am. Philol. Assn., Classical Assn. Middle West and South, Ohio Classical Conf. (pres. 1948-49), Phi Alpha Theta, Eta Sigma Phi. Democrat. Mem. United Ch. Christ. Home: 192 Saint Francis Ave Apt 24 Tiffin OH 44883-4413

KRAMER, GORDON, mechanical engineer; b. Bklyn., Aug. 1937; s. Joseph and Etta (Grossberg) K.; m. Ruth Ellen Harter, Mar. 5, 1967 (div. June 1986); children: Samuel Maurice, Leah Marie; m. Eve Burstein, Dec. 17, 1988. BS, Cooper Union, 1959; MS, Calif. Inst. Tech., 1960. With Hughes Aircraft Co., Malibu, Calif., 1959-63; sr. scientist Avco Corp., Norman, Okla., 1963-64; asst. divsn. head Batelle Meml. Inst., Columbus, Ohio, 1964-67; sr. scientist Aeroject Electrosystems, Azusa, Calif., 1967-75; chief engr. Beckman Instrument Co., Fullerton, Calif., 1975-82; prin. scientist McDonnell Douglas Microelectronics Co., 1982-83, Kramer and Assocs., 1983-85; program mgr. Hughes Aircraft Co., 1985-96, ret., 1996; personal fin. advisor Am. Express, 1999—; cons. Korea Inst. Tech. NSF fellow, 1959-60. Mem. IEEE. Democrat. Jewish. Home: 153 Lake Shore Dr Rancho Mirage CA 92270-4055

KRAMER, HORST EMIL ADOLF, physical chemist; b. Friedrichshafen, Baden-Württemberg, Germany, Apr. 20, 1936; s. Max and Maria Magdalena (Kaufmann) K.; m. Ingeborg Maria Giesen, July 30, 1964; 1 child, Boris W.W. Diploma chemistry, U. Stuttgart, Baden-Wuerttemberg, 1961, D in Natural Scis., 1964, Habilitation, 1970. Rsch. asst. Inst. Phys. Chemistry U. Stuttgart, 1966-70, lectr., 1970-74; prof. phys. chemistry Inst. Phys. Chemistry, Stuttgart, 1974—; dean faculty chemistry U. Stuttgart, 1988-90, Assoc. editor Photochemistry and Photobiology, 1978-80; mem. editorial bd. Photobiochemistry and Photobiophysics, 1983-86; contbr. articles to profl. jours., chpts. to books. Mem. Gesellschaft Deutscher Chemiker, Fachgruppe Photochemie der Gesellschaft Deutscher Chemiker. Avocations: history, tennis, sailing, model railway. Home: Falkenweg 8, D-71126 Gaeufelden Germany Office: U Stuttgart Inst Phys Chemistry, Pfaffenwaldring 55, D-70569 Stuttgart Germany

KRAMER, KAREN SUE, mind-body psychologist; b. L.A., Sept. 6, 1942; d. Frank Pacheco Kramer and Velma Eileen (Devlin) Moore; m. Stewart A. Sterling, Dec. 30, 1965 (div. 1974); 1 child, Scott Kramer Sterling. BA, U. Calif., Berkeley, 1964; MA, U.S. Internat. U., 1976; PhD, Profl. Sch. Psychology, 1980. Psychometrist U. Calif. Counseling Ctr., Berkeley, 1966-67; social worker Alameda County Welfare Dept., Oakland, Calif., 1967-69; vol. coord. San. Diego County Probation Dept., 1971-73; officer San Diego County Probation Dept., 1973-76; counselor and coord. clin. and outreach programs Western Inst., San Diego, 1976-77; program coord. and counselor Women's Resource Ctr., Oceanside, Calif., 1977-78; pvt. practice psychology San Diego, 1978-81; planner/analyst San Diego County Dept. Health Svcs., 1979-81; pvt. psychology Nat. U., San Diego, 1979-81; social svcs. program cons. Calif. Dept. Social Svcs., Emeryville, 1981-83; affirmative action officer State Compensation Ins. Fund, San Francisco, 1983-87; cmty. psychologist Calif. Dept. Mental Health, 1987-89; pvt. practice psychology Berkeley, 1990—; personal analyst State Comp. Ins. Fund, 1989-91; regional property mgr. State Compensation Ins. Fund, San Francisco, 1991-95; prof. Nat. U. San Diego, 1979-81; pres. North County Coun. Social Concerns, Vista, Calif., 1977-78; advisor USMC Camp Pendleton Human Svcs., 1977-79; mem. adv. bd. Alameda County Mental Health, Chinatown Resources Devel. Ctr., San Francisco, 1984-87, 2000—, San Francisco Rehab., 1984-87; bd. dirs. Network Cons. Svcs., Napa, Calif.; founder Qi Gong in China-Ednl. Svcs., 1994; asst. dir. Qigong for Children, Am. Found. Traditional Chinese Medicine; cons. Am. Found. Traditional Chinese Medicine, 1999, Success Strategies programs for Health, Sports, Tests, Life; prof. Psychology, Am. Coll. TCM, 1999; pub. chmn. Intuition Network Conf., 1997; advisor Calif.-Hawaii Inst., 1998—; apptd. Alameda County Mental Health Bd., 2000. Editl. advisor (website) Alternative Medicine, 1998. Mem. Alameda County Mental Health Bd., 2000—. mem. Calif. Peer Counselors Assn. (adv. bd. 1987-90), Calif. Prevention Network (bd. dirs. 1989-93, editl. advisor jour. 1992-93). E-mail: karen kramer@compuserve.com.

KRAMER, DAME LEONIE JUDITH, university administrator; b. Melbourne, Victoria, Australia, Oct. 1, 1924; d. Alfred L. and Gertrude Gibson; m. Harold Kramer, 1952 (dec.); children: Jocelyn, Hilary. Student, Presbyn. Ladies Coll., Melbourne, 1930-41; BA, U. Melbourne, 1945; PhD, Oxford (Eng.) U., 1953; MA, U. Sydney, 1989; DLitt (hon.), Tasmania U., 1977, Queensland U., 1991, New South Wales U., 1992; LLD (hon.), U. Melbourne, 1983, Australian Nat. U., 1984. Tutor, lectr. U. Melbourne, 1945-49; tutor, postgrad. stud. St. Hugh's Coll., Oxford, 1949-52; lectr. Canberra Univ. Coll., 1954-56; lectr., sr. lectr., then assoc. prof. U. New South Wales, Australia, 1958-68; prof. Australian lit. U. Sydney, Australia, 1968-89; prof. emeritus U. Sydney, 1989—; mem. univs. council U. Sydney, Australia, 1968-89, dep. chancellor, 1989-91, chancellor, 1991—; vis. prof. Harvard U., Cambridge, Mass., 1981-82; chair Australian Broadcasting Commn., 1982-83; bd. dirs. Australia and New Zealand Banking Group Ltd., 1983-94, Western Mining Corp., 1984-96, Quadrant Mag. Co. Ltd., 1986-99. Author: (as L.J. Gibson) Henry Handel Richardson and Some of Her Sources, 1954, (as Leonie Kramer) A Companion to Australia Felix, 1962, Myself When Laura: Fact and Fiction in Henry Handel Richardson's School Career, 1966, Henry Handel Richardson, 1967, (with Robert D. Eagleson) Language and Literature: A Synthesis, 1976, (with Robert D. Eagleson) A Guide to Language and Literature, 1977, A.D. Hope, 1979; contbr. Six Australian Writers, 1971; editor: Coast to Coast, 1965, Selected Stories, 1971, Oxford History of Australian Literature, 1981, (with Adrian Mitchell) The Oxford Anthology of Australian Literature, 1985, My Country: Australian Poetry and Short Stories - two hundred years, 1985, James McAuley, 1988, Collected Poems of David Campbell, 1989, Collected Poems of James McAuley, 1995; editorial advisor: Quadrant mag., Poetry Australia mag., Australian Literary Studies jour.; mem. adv. bd. World Book Ency., 1989-99; mem. internat. adv. bd. Ency. Britannica, 1991-98. Chmn. bd. dirs. Nat. Inst. Dramatic Art, 1987-91, dep. chmn. bd. dirs. 1991-95; bd. dirs. St. Vincent's Hosp., Sydney, 1988-93; commr. Electricity Commn. New South Wales, 1988-95; mem. coun. Nat. Roads and Motorists' Assn., 1984-95, Queen Elizabeth II Trust, 1989—; chmn. Operation Rainbow Australia Ltd., 1996—. Recipient Britannica Inaugural award, 1986; sr. fellow Inst. Pub. Affairs, 1988-96; hon. fellow St. Hugh's Coll., 1994. Fellow Australian Acad. Humanities, Australian Coll. Edn., Australia-Britain Soc. (nat. pres. 1984-93), Inst. Pub. Affairs (sr.); mem. Asia Soc., Australian Inst. Co. Dirs. (New South Wales coun. 1992—). Avocations: gardening, music. Home: 12 Vaucluse Rd, Vaucluse 2030 NSW, Australia

KRAMER, LOUIS DEYONG, dentist; b. London, July 13, 1926; s. Hyman Jack and Priscilla Sarah (Deyong) K.; m. Anita Ross, Jan. 9, 1951; children: Judith, David Ross. B.Dental Surgery, U. Liverpool, England, 1950; Lic. Dental Surgery, Royal Coll. Surgeons, England, 1951. Registered dentist, U.K. House officer United Liverpool Hosps., 1950-51; sch. dental officer Liverpool Health, 1953-58; sr. hosp. dental officer United Liverpool Hosps., 1958-64; part-time lectr. U. Liverpool, 1964-88; dean Postgrad. Dental Edn., U. Liverpool, Mersey Region, 1985-92; dental advisor to RHA-Mersey, NHS, Liverpool, 1985-92. Co-author: An Enquiry into Dental Education. Chair Southport Dist. Local Dental Com., Southport; vice chair Regional Liaison com. of Local Dental Com.; elected mem. Gen. Den. Coun. Eng., 1984—; chair Southport Hebrew Edn. Bd., 1960. Capt. Royal Army Dental Corps, 1951-53. Recipient Full Blue award U. Liverpool Athletics Union, 1949. Fellow Royal Soc. of Medicine; mem. Royal Coll. Surgeons Eng. (gen. dental surgery 1979), Brit. Psychol. Soc. (lay mem., chair discipline com. 1999—), Brit. Dental Assn. (hon. life), Brit. Soc. for Restorative Dentistry (hon. life, pres. 1991-92), Liverpool and Dist. Odontol. Soc. (pres. 1980-81), West Lancs. West Cheshire and North Wales Br. of Brit. Dental Assn. (pres. 1973-74). Jewish. Avocations: skiing, walking, silversmithing. Home: 33 Court Rd, Southport PR9 9ET, England

KRAMER, MARTIN SETH, humanities educator, researcher; b. Washington, Sept. 9, 1954; s. Alvin and Anita Joan (Seidel) K.; m. Sandra Adine Jacobs, Aug. 26, 1978; children: Anat Jean, Keren Yael, Adam Benjamin. BA, Princeton U., 1975, MA, 1978. Rsch. assoc. Moshe Dayan Ctr. Mid. Ea. and African Studies Tel Aviv U., 1981—; vis. prof. Cornell U., Ithaca, N.Y., 1984, U. Chgo., 1991-92; vis. prof. social sci. Georgetown U., Washington, 1994-95. Author: Islam Assembled: The Advent of the Muslim Congresses, 1986, Arab Awakening and Islamic Revival: The Politics of Ideas in the Middle East, 1996; editor: (book) Shiism, Resistance and Revolution, 1987, The Islamism Debate, 1997, The Jewish Discovery of Islam, 1999; mem. editl. bd. Mid. East Quarterly, Phila., 1993—. Grantee Harry Guggenheim Found., 1988-90; fellow Am. Rsch. Ctr. Cairo, 1979, Woodrow Wilson Internat. Ctr. for Scholars, 1989-90, 2000. Jewish. Fax: 972-3-6415802. E-mail: kramerm@ccsg.tau.ac.il. Home: 70/3 Rambam St, 43602 Raanana Israel Office: Moshe Dayan Ctr Mid Ea Stud, Gilman Bldg, 69978 Ramat Aviv Israel

KRAMER, MATTHEW HENRY, legal philosopher, law educator; b. Boston, June 9, 1959; s. Alton Marshall and Alma Eunice (Bixon) K. BA, Cornell U., 1981; JD, Harvard U., 1985; PhD, Cambridge U., 1989. Rsch. fellow Darwin Coll., Cambridge, Eng., 1989-91; vis. fellow Inst. Rsch. in Humanities, Madison, Wis., 1991-94; lectr. law faculty Cambridge U., 1994-99, reader, 1999—; fellow, dir. studies in law Churchill Coll., Cambridge, 1994—. Author: Hobbes and the Paradoxes of Political Origins, 1997, John Locke and the Origins of Private Property, 1997 (MacCormick prize 1998), In the Realm of Legal and Moral Philosophy, 1998, A Debate Over Rights, 1998, In Defense of Legal Positivism, 1999. Recipient rsch. scholarship Trinity Coll., Cambridge, 1985-88, rsch. leave award Brit. Acad., London, 1997. Mem. U.K. Assn. Legal and Social Philosophy (v.p. 1998-2000), Soc. Pub. Tchrs. Law, Mind Assn. Avocations: Bible commentary, Shakespearean drama, long-distance running. Home: Churchill Coll, Cambridge CB3 ODS, England Office: Faculty Law, 10 West Rd, Cambridge CB2 1RH, England

KRAMER, NORMA DOMENICA ANDREA, artist; m. Vernon V. Kramer, 1966. Student, Traphagen, 1946-47, Pratt Inst., N.Y.C., 1948-50, CCNY, 1951-52, Art Students League, 1979-87, Nat. Acad. Design, N.Y.C., 1988-89. In mdse. mgmt. and sales Henri Bendel, Mainbocher, Macy's, N.Y.C., 1946-50; publs. mgr. Met. Mus. of Art, N.Y.C., 1951-58; editl. asst., exhbn. asst., registrar Am. Fedn. Arts., N.Y.C., 1958-65; asst. to Harold Rosenberg, poet, art critic, bull. editor, campaigns mgr., dir. rsch. The Advt. Coun., N.Y.C., 1965-89. One-man shows include 3 Arts Club Homeland, Balt., 1998, Pearl Gallery, Balt., 1999; exhibited in group shows at Nat. Inst. Architects, 1949, Met. Mus. Art, 1957, Epiphany Ch., N.J., 1983, Am. Watercolor Soc., 1984, Nat. Acad. Design, 1988, Cork Gallery, Lincoln Ctr., 1986, Nat. Arts Club, 1987, Pearl Gallery, 1996—, Old Forge Art Ctr., 1985, Art Dirs. Club, 1989, Hubbard Telescope Space Ctr., John/Hopkins, 1999; represented in permanent collections. Recipient award Traphagen, 1947, 1st prize Pratt Inst., 1950, concours prizes, purchase award Art Students League, 1984-87, Award of Excellence for solo watercolor exhbt., 2d Ave. Fair., N.Y.C., 1980, 2d Prize award Rose Soc. Md., 1998. Mem. Three Arts Club of Homeland, Art Students League (life), Am. Watercolor Soc. (assoc.), Balt. Watercolor Soc. (assoc.). Gallery Rep: The Pearl Gallery 815 W 36th St Baltimore MD 21211-2508

KRAMER, PAUL R., lawyer; b. Balt., June 6, 1936; s. Phillip and Lee (Labovitz) K.; m. Janet Amitin, Sept. 1, 1957; children: Jayne, Susan, Nancy. BA, Am. U., 1959, JD, 1961. Bar: Md. 1961, D.C. 1962, U.S. Supreme Ct. 1965, U.S. Ct. Appeals (6th cir.) 1992, U.S. Dist. Ct. 1963, U.S. Ct. Appeals (4th cir.) 1964, U.S. Ct. Appeals (9th cir.) 1996. Staff atty., dep. dir. Legal Aid Agy. Fed. Pub. Defender's Office, Washington, 1962-63; asst. U.S. atty. Dist. Md., 1963-69; dep. U.S. atty. Md. Balt., 1969-83; exec. bd. Balt. area coun. Boy Scouts Am., 1970-83, adv. counsel to exec. bd., 1983—; instr. U. Md. Sch. Law, 1975-80; assoc. prof. law Villa Julie Coll., 1976-80; assoc. professorial lectr. George Washington U., 1979; instr. Nat. Coll. Dist. Attys., 1979; permanent mem. 4th cir. fed. jud. conf. Mem. ABA, Fed. Bar Assn. (pres. Md. chpt. 1973-74, nat. dep. sec. 1981-82, nat. sec. 1982-83, nat. cir. v.p. 1973-81, 86-87, cir. officer 4th cir. 1992-93, v.p. 4th cir. 1996—, chmn. nat. cir. v.p. 1978-80, nat. coun. 1973—, jud. selection com. 1971-79, 88—, faculty Fed Practice Inst. 1981-86, strategic long range planning com. 1995-96), Md. Bar Assn. (subcom. litig. dist. ct. 1990—), Balt. Bar Assn. (jud. selection com. 1992—, chair judiciary sub-com. on policy 1993-94, chair criminal law com. 1994-95, grievance commn. Md. 1993—, drug ct. com. 1994-95, dist. ct. com. 1990—), Nat. Assn. Criminal Trial Attys., Md. Trial Lawyers Assn., Md. Criminal Def. Atty.'s Assn., U.S. Atty. Alumni Assn., Masons (past master). Office: 231 Saint Paul Pl Baltimore MD 21202-2028

KRAMER, WILLIAM DAVID, lawyer; b. Anniston, Ala., Feb. 2, 1944; s. John Robert and Janice Marian (Dye) K.; m. Johanna Scalzi, Dec. 1, 1973; children: Elizabeth Annemarie, David MacLaren. Student, Case Western Res. U., 1959-60; AB in Govt. with honors magna cum laude, Oberlin Coll., 1965; JD, M in Pub. Adminstrn., Harvard U., 1969. Bar: Mass. 1969, D.C. 1973, U.S. Ct. Appeals (D.C. cir.) 1974, U.S. Dist. Ct. D.C. 1976, U.S. Ct. Appeals (10th cir.) 1978, U.S. Ct. Internat. Trade 1983, U.S. Ct. Appeals (fed. cir.) 1983. Assoc. dir. Gov.'s Com. on Law Enforcement and Adminstrn. Criminal Justice, Boston, 1969-71, dep. dir., 1971-73; assoc. Squire, Sanders & Dempsey, Washington, 1973-79, ptnr., 1979-92; ptnr. Baker Botts LLP, Washington, 1992-2000; mem. Verner, Liipfert, Bernhard, McPherson and Hand, Chartered, Washington, 2000—; mem. internat. law sect. D.C. Bar. chmn. bd. dirs. Children's Chorus of Washington, 1995-97, mem. adv. bd., 1997—. Mem. Phi Beta Kappa. Fax: 202-371-6279. Office: Verner Lipfert Bernhard McPherson & Hand Chartered 901 15th St NW Washington DC 20005-2327 also: Verner Liipfert Bernhart etc 901 15th St NW Ste 700 Washington DC 20005-2327

KRAMER, WORTH ALAN (LANCE KRAMER), industrial products company executive; b. Cleve., Sept. 9, 1941; s. Worth Hollis and Alice Farnhum (Hogue) Funk; m. Laura Ann Root, May 25, 1974; children: Courtney, Andrew. BA, Hillsdale Coll., 1966; MBA, So. Ill. U., 1972. Accts. receivable mgr. Monsanto Co., St. Louis, 1972-74; contr. Interface Tech., St. Louis, 1974, exec. v.p., 1974-75, pres., 1975-79; v.p. fin. and adminstrn. Smith-Scharff, St. Louis, 1979-82; sec., treas. Watlow Electric Mfg. Co., St. Louis, 1982—, v.p. fin. and adminstrn., 1988—, v.p. fin. and adminstrn. Office of the Chmn., 1991-96, v.p., sec., chief people officer, 1996-99, strategic ops. dir., 2000—; small bus. adv. com. Regional Commerce and Growth Assn., St. Louis, 1977-82; adv. bd. Nations Bank, 1993-97, St. Louis Leadership Inst., 1996—. Trustee Oak Springs Lane Improvement Assn., St. Louis, 1990—; vestry mem. St. Timothy Episcopal Ch., St. Louis, 1985-87, 98—, sr. warden, 1986; bd. dirs. St. Louis Hearing and Speech Ctrs., 1987-89, Am. Assn. Indsl. Mgmt., 1975-80; active fin. com. Episcopal Diocese of Mo., 1989-92, conv. del., 1990-91. Decorated Purple Heart, Bronze Star with Navy Air medal; named Spl. Honoree Beta Gamma Sigma, 1992. Mem. Fin. Exec. Inst., Internat. Execs. Roundtable, Chief Execs. Roundtable (chmn. 1979-80), Fin. Exec. Roundtable (chmn. 1983-84), Greenbriar Hills Country Club (St. Louis), Alpha Tau Omega. Republican. Avocations: tennis, scuba diving. Home: 2536 Oak Springs Ln Saint Louis MO 63131-1114 Office: Watlow Electric Mfg Co 12001 Lackland Rd Saint Louis MO 63146-4039

KRAMM, DEBORAH ANN, data processing executive; b. Pasadena, June 24, 1949; d. Donald F. and Mary (Roach) Coonan; m. Kenneth R. Kramm, Dec. 20, 1969; children: Deidre Lyn, Jonathan Russel. BA, U. Calif., Irvine, 1971; MS, Mich. Tech. U., 1981. Math. asst. NASA-Jet Propulstion Lab., Pasadena, 1967-70; libr. asst. U. Calif. Irving Libr., 1967-71; rsch. assoc. animal behavior lab. Mich. Tech. U., Houghton, 1971-80; programmer, analyst Shell Oil Co., Houston, 1981-85; corp. auditor EDP, 1985-87; team leader SLA, 1988-90, supr. resource planning adminstrn., 1990-91, adminstrv. coord. product devel. ctr.-design ctr., 1991-93, bus. analyst sr. systems analyst, 1993-96, engagement mgr., 1996-97, mgr. engagement svcs., 1998-99, mgr. sales and contract support, 1999—; chmn. bd. MMARK, Houston, 1983-85. Contbr. articles to profl. jours.; designer (program application software) Shell Point-of-Sale Terminal, 1982-85. Treas. KFHS Orch., 1986-88; co-leader Boy Scouts Am., Houston, 1981-83. AAUW scholar, 1980, Calif. State scholar, 1967-71. Mem. NAFE, AAUW (pres. br. 1975-81), Shell Data Processors Club, Houston Bus. Forum (pres. bd. dirs.). Home: 5814 Pinewilde Dr Houston TX 77066-2324 Office: Shell Svc Internat 1500 Old Spanish Trl Houston TX 77054-1818

KRAMM, DEBORAH LUCILLE, lawyer; b. Milw.; d. Hartzell McDonald and Alice Lucille (Johnson) K.; m. Gary Baiz, June 18, 1988. Student, Trinity Coll., Deerfield, Ill., 1971-73; BS, Bradley U., 1974; JD, New Eng. Sch. of Law, 1977; postgrad., Georgetown U., 1978. Bar: N.Y. 1982, Ill. 1980, Mass. 1978. Trademark atty. U.S. Trademark Office, Washington, 1977-78; assoc. Hume, Clement, Willian, Brinks & Olds, Chgo., 1978-81; atty. Avon Products, Inc., N.Y.C., 1981-84; atty. Tiffany & Co., N.Y.C., 1981-84, v.p., sec., 1984-85; counsel Am. Brands, Inc., Old Greenwich, Conn., 1986-95; of counsel Piper Marbury Rudnick & Wolfe, Chgo., 1996-2000; ptnr. Holland & Knight, Washington, 2000—. N.Y. bd. dirs. Nat. Found. for Advancement for Arts, 1987-91; chmn. Martha Graham Guild, 1988—; trustee Martha Graham Ctr. for Contemporary Dance, Inc., N.Y.C., 1989—. Curt Tiege scholar, 1973. Mem. U.S. Trademark Assn. (bd. dirs. 1984-87), Cosmetic, Toiletry and Fragrance Assn. (chmn. trademark com. 1984). Office: Holland & Knight 2100 Pennsylvania Ave NW Washington DC 20037

KRAMM, EDWARD, engineering educator, researcher; b. Moscow, July 2, 1936; s. Alexander and Maria (Oborskaya) K.; m. Irine Shorikova. MSc, Inst. Chem. Engring., Moscow, 1960, PhD, 1968; DSc, Inst. Applied Biotech., Moscow, 1993. Engr., chief design Plant Chem. Devices, Moscow, 1964-65; sr. lectr., prof. U. Engring. Ecology, Moscow, 1969-94; prof. Tech U. Czenstochowa, Poland, 1994-97, U. Engring. & Ecology, Moscow, 1997—; sci. sec. Ministry Microbiol. Industry, Moscow, 1973-85. Contbr. articles to profl. jours.; inventor in field. Mem. N.Y. Acad. Sci. Avocation: history of architecture. Home: Apt 31, 1 Linejny proezd, 127238 Moscow Russia Office: U Engring and Ecology, Staraya Basmannaya 21/4, 107884 Moscow Russia

KRAMVIS, ANDREAS CONSTANTINOS, electronics company executive; b. Nicosia, Cyprus, June 14, 1952; came to U.S. 1984; s. Constantinos Andreas and Electra (Nicolaou) K.; m. Shirley Anne Newcombe, July 16, 1977; children: Christopher, Nicholas, Catherine. BA, MA, Cambridge U., Eng., 1974; MBA, Manchester Bus. Sch., Eng., 1976. Subsidiary dir., gen. mgr., internat. fin. acct. Cadbury-Schweppes PLC, London, 1976-82; subsidiary pres. Combined Technologies Corp., London and Princeton, 1982-87; v.p. mktg. Ademco USA divsn. of Pittway Corp., Syosset, N.Y., 1987—; pres. Ademco Internat. divsn. of Pittway Corp., Syosset, N.Y., 1989—; dir. numerous Ademco Subsidiaries. Avocations: tennis, chess, reading, classical music. Home: 66 Randolph Dr Dix Hills NY 11746-5500 Office: Ademco Mfg Ademco Internat 180 Michael Dr Syosset NY 11791-5381

KRANEPOOL, HARRY ANTHONY, science educator; b. Bklyn., July 26, 1941; s. Harry M. and Marie R. (Sorrentino) K. BS, St. Francis Coll., Bklyn., 1962; MSED, Bklyn. Coll., 1972; MA in Edn., CCNY, 1977. Cert. sci., math., biology and chemistry tchr., N.Y., N.J., Pa. Sci. chmn. Bishop Loughlin Meml. H.S., Bklyn., 1968—. Author: Chemistry, A Modern Approach, 1977-87, rev. edits., 1992, 96. Recipient BQ Stanys Svc. award, 1999. Fellow Sci. Assn. Tchrs. N.Y.; mem. LIUNA-AFL-CIO (pres. LFA 1261), N.Y. State Coun. of Ednl. Assns. (pres. 1989-93), NSTA (dir. Region II 1990-92), Stanys (pres. 1987-89, Svc. award 1985), Sci. Coun. N.Y.C. (pres. 1998-2000), N.Y. State Sci. Olympiad (treas. 1995—). Democrat. Roman Catholic. E-mail: lfahak@aol.com. Home: 31-31 138th St Apt 4D Flushing NY 11354-2625 Office: Lay Faculty Assn Local 1261 13825A 31st Dr Flushing NY 11354-2664

KRANJC, ANDREJ ALEKSEJ, geographer, researcher; b. Ljubljana, Slovenia, Nov. 5, 1943; s. Franc and Ida (Dejak) K.; m. Marija Alenka-Maja Ravbar, Jan. 11, 1969; 1 child, Kristof. Diploma, U. Ljubljana, 1971, Magisterium, 1977, DSc, 1986. Diplomate geography and archaeology. Sci. co-worker Karst Rsch. Inst., Postojna, Slovenia, 1987-91, sci. counselor, 1995—, head, 1988-95; assoc. mem. Slovene Acad. Scis. & Arts, Ljubljana, 1995, asst. prof. phys. geography, 1996—. Author: Recent Fluvial Cave Sediments, 1989, Dolenjski Kraski Svet, 1990; editor Acta Carsologica, 1993—, Slovene Classical Karst, 1997, KRAS, 1999. Recipient Silver Star Nat. award Yugoslav Nat. Assembly, 1988, Bronze awward Yugoslav Tech. Assn., 1984, French Palme Academique, 1998, Min. Sci. Rsch. award. Mem. Internat. Quarternary Assn., Karst Commn. Internat. Geog. Union, Assn. Tracer Hydrology (organizing sec. 7th Symposium on Water Tracing 1993-97), Speleohistory Commn. Internat. Speleol. Union. Avocation: speleology (caving). E-mail: kranjc@zrc-sazu.si. Home: Rožna c 6, SI-6230 Postojna Slovenia Office: Karst Rsch Inst, Titov Trg 2, SI-6230 Postojna Slovenia

KRANOTH, PERETZ, public servant; b. Subotica, Yugoslavia, Apr. 10, 1937; arrived in Israel, 1949; s. Julio and Rose (Ungar) Kornshtein; m. Yora Berca Kranoth; Nov. 30, 1965; children: Nati, Uri. BA, Hebrew U., Jerusalem, 1963, MA, 1975. Test coord. Civil Svc. Commn., Jerusalem, Israel, 1965-69, Min. Labour, Jerusalem, Israel, 1970-75; head of testing dept. Min. Labour and Social Affairs, Jerusalem, Israel, 1975—; mem. testing com. for Dental Technicians, Min. Health, Jerusalem, 1991. Author: Yearly Flyer of Testing Dept. Activities, 1975—. Lt. Israel Def. Forces, 1955-58. Mem. Israel Psychol. Assn., Israel Nat. Union of Grads. in Social Scis. and Humanities, Israel Assn. Grads. in the Social Sci. and Humanities, Israeli Bridge Assn., Israeli Tchrs. Union. Avocations: bridge, swimming. Office: Min Labour and Soc Affairs, PO Box 905, 91008 Jerusalem Israel

KRANYIK, ELIZABETH ANN, secondary education educator; b. Bridgeport, Conn., Nov. 15, 1957; d. Andrew Ladislaus and Marion Irene (Slater) K.; m. Charles Edward Porzelt III, Nov. 28, 1992; children: Charles Edward Porzelt IV, Marial Elizabeth Porzelt. BS summa cum laude, Western Conn. State U., 1979; MA, Fairfield U., 1989. Cert. h.s. tchr., gen. sci. endorsement, Conn. Tchr., program coordinator Fairfield (Conn.) Elem. Summer Sch., 1973-85; tchr. St. Maurice Sch., Stamford, Conn., 1980-82, Our Lady of Lourdes Sch., Melbourne, Fla., 1982-85, St. Pius X Sch., Fairfield, 1985-87, Bridgeport Pub. Schs., 1988-93, Bridgeport Regional Vocat. Aquaculture Sch., 1993—; freelance tutor; cons., tchr. Mill River Wetlands Prog., Fairfield, 1985-87, honors tchr., 1991; cons. Ocean Classroom, Bridgeport, Conn., 1989-90, NASA Newest Scholar, 1991, Sound Educators Assn., 1992—. Vol., tour guide H.M.S. Rose Found., Bridgeport, 1985—. Mem. Nat. Sci. Tchrs. Assn., Alliance Francais (Merit award 1979), Sound Educators Assn., Southeastern New Eng. Marine Educators, Phi Delta Kappa. Congregationalist. Avocations: nature study, reading, swimming, carpentry. Home: 129 Jockey Hollow Rd Monroe CT 06468-1270

KRAPAC, LADISLAV LADO, physician; b. Orebić, Dalmatia, Croatia, June 27, 1947; s. Dragutin and Rajna (Bujas) K.; m. Dunja Machiedo, Dec. 13, 1975; children: Marin, Josip, Ivor. MD, Med. Faculty, U Zagreb, 1971, MSc, 1976; PhD, U. Zagreb, 1986; phys. medicine and rehab. specialist, Zagreb, 1981. Jr. rschr. Inst. Med. Rsch., Zagreb, 1972-76; occupl. medicine staff Health Clin. Medvescak, Zagreb, 1976-78; head ctrl. disability Inst. Med. Rsch., Zagreb, 1978-88, sr. rsch. asst., 1988-96; head dept. U. Hosp. Dubrava, Zagreb, 1996—. Mem. editl. bd. Reumatizam, 1986—; contbr. chpt. to book and articles to profl. jours. Mem. adv. bd. Liječnicki Vjesnik, Zagreb, 1982-88; coun. mem. Fiz Med. Rehab., Zagreb, 1983—, editor in chief, 1999; mem. City Coun., 1993-99. Mem. Croatian Soc. Rheumatology (supr. bd. 1986), Croatian Cath. Med. Soc. (mem. presidency 1992-98), Croatian League Against Rheumatish (mem. presidency 1990). Mem. Croatian Social Liberal Party. Roman Catholic. Avocations: music, history of art, recreative activities, prevention of chronic diseases. Home: Medvešćak 26, 10000 Zagreb Croatia Office: Univ Hosp, Dubrava Av G Suska 6, 10000 Zagreb Croatia

KRASIKOV, NIKOLAI NIKOLAYEVICH, physics educator, researcher; b. Kovrov, Russia, Sept. 13, 1938; s. Nikolai Ivanovich and Zoya Mikhailovna (Vershinina) K.; m. Tatiana Sergeyevna Zhelokhovtseva, Oct. 14, 1973 (dec. July 1997); children: Olga, Polina. Diploma in engring., Mining Inst., St. Petersburg, Russia, 1961; Cand Sci, Technol. Inst. St. Petersburg, 1970, DSc, 1983. Chief geophysicist geol. expdn., Irkutsk, Russia, 1961-65; scientist Mendeleyev Metrological Inst., St. Petersburg, 1965-67; assoc. prof. physics Poly. Inst., Novopolostk, Belarus, USSR, 1971-75, U. Ivanovo, USSR, 1976-80, Naval Acad., St. Petersburg, 1980-86; prof., chief dep. Technol. Inst., Kovrov, 1986—; cons. chem. factory Nvopolotsk, 1971-75, environ. svc., Kovrov, 1986—. Contbr. articles to profl. jours. including Trans. USSR Acad. Scis., Biophysics, Progress in Biophysics and Molecular Biology; patentee for methods of fluid electroactivation. Grantee Ministry Edn., 1994-95, Internat. Soros Sci. Edn. Program, 1995-97. Mem. Ecol. Soc., Znaniye Soc. (chief Kovrov unit 1991-93), Electrotech. Acad., Ecol. Acad., N.Y. Acad. Scis. Orthodox. Avocations: history, arts, swimming. Home: Nogina per 5-46, 601901 Kovrov Russia Office: Kovrov Technol Inst, Mayakovsky St 19, 601910 Kovrov Russia

KRASIKOV, YURII VLADIMIROVITCH, psychologist, educator; b. Ordzonikidze, Russia, Nov. 16, 1946; s. Dick-Vladimir Vladimirovitch Krasikov and Irina Pavlovna Sokolova; m. Polina Aleksandrovna Reshetnikova, Feb. 5, 1967; 1 child, Nicholas. PhD, USSR Acad. Sci., Moscow, 1980; DSc, Moscow State U., 1991. Redactor Ir Pub. House, Ordzonikidze, 1968-70; engr. Labor Control Quality Prodn., Ordzonikidze, 1970; redactor TV Studio, Ordzonikidze, 1971-76, 83-85, corr., 1979-80; asst. North-Ossetian State U., Ordzonikidze, 1980-83, 85-86, 1988-94, rschr., 1986-88, prof., 1994-99; head, psych. chair, 1999—. Mem. APA, Internat. Coun. Psychologist (area chair for Russian Fedn.). Avocations: mountaineering, traveling. E-mail: krasikov@nosu.ru or indep@nosu.ru. Home: Apt 3 Pozharsky St 14, 362021 Vladikavkaz Russia Office: North Ossetian State U, Vatutina 40, 362025 Vladikavkaz Russia

KRASILNIKOV, NIKOLAY NIKOLAEVICH, communications educator, researcher; b. Irkutsk, Russia, Jan. 22, 1927; s. Nikolay Nikolaevich and Anna Safonovna (Tolochko) K.; m. Galina Ivanovna Marnosova, May 4, 1953 (div. Aug. 1980); 1 child, Nikolay Nikolaevich; m. Olga Ivanovna Posohova, Jan. 3, 1981. MS, Leningrad Inst. Aviation Instrument Making, 1952; DSc, Acad. Comm., Leningrad, 1964. Engr. Inst. Television, Leningrad, 1950-54; asst. prof. Leningrad Inst. Aviation Instrument Making, 1954-57, head dept., 1957-94; prof. Sate Univ. Aerospace Instrumentation, St. Petersburg, 1994—; cons. I.P. Pavlov Inst. Physiology, Russian Acad. Scis., St. Petersburg, 1994—. Author: Statistical Theory of Image Transfer, 1976, Theory of Image Transfer and Perception, 1986, Spatial Vision, 1999; contbr. articles to profl. jours. including Jour. Optical Tech. and Internat. Jour. Imaging Sys. and Tech. Fellow Sci. and Tech. Soc. of Radio Engring., Electronics and Comms., 1951; recipient medal for Leningrad Def. Supreme Soviet of USSR, 1944. Fellow Russian Acad. Scis. House; mem. N.Y. Acad. Scis. Avocations: classical music, history, tourism, creation of electronic manual. Office: State U. Aerospace Instru, 67 Bolshaia Morskaia, 190000 Saint Petersburg Russia

KRASNER, DANIEL WALTER, lawyer; b. N.Y.C., Mar. 18, 1941; s. Nathan and Rose Krasner; m. Ruth Pollack, Dec. 20, 1964; children: Jonathan, Lisa, Noah, Rebecca. BA, Yeshiva Coll., 1962; LLB, Yale U., 1965. Bar: N.Y. 1966, U.S. Dist. Ct. (so. dist.) N.Y. 1967, U.S. Supreme Ct. 1978. Assoc. Pomerantz Levy Houdek & Block, N.Y.C., 1965-76; sr. ptnr. Wolf Haldenstein Adler Freeman & Herz, N.Y.C., 1977—. Vice chmn. Westchester Day Sch., Mamaroneck, N.Y., 1979-86; v.p., trustee Bd. Jewish Edn., N.Y.C., 1981—. Democrat. Avocations: tennis, golf, sailing. Office: Wolf Haldenstein Adler Freeman & Herz 270 Madison Ave New York NY 10016-0601

KRASNOPEVTSEV, EUGENE ALEXANDROVICH, education educator; b. Tomsk, Siberia, Russia, Sept. 6, 1944; s. Alexander Theodorovich Telegin and Nina Benjaminovna Krasnopevtseva; m. Galina Borisovna Frolova, Sept. 5, 1968; children: Spartak, Svetlana. BS, State U., Novosibirsk, 1967, MS, 1969; PhD, Tech. U., 1994. Instr. State Pedagogical U., Novosibirsk, Siberia, Russia, 1969-79; asst. prof. State Pedagogical U., Novosibirsk, 1979-95, assoc. prof., 1995—; assoc. prof. Novosibirsk State Tech. U., Novosibirsk, 1999—. Editl. bd.: History of Physics, 1997, Panoramic Interferometry, 1999; inventor in field. Mem. Russian Gentry Assembly. Avocation: statis. rsch. of homeric hexameter. Home: Vilyuskaya 24/86, 630126 Novosibirsk/Siberia Russia Office: State Pedagogical Univ, Vilyuskaya 28, 630126 Novosibirsk/Siberia Russia

KRASNOVA, NATALYA IVANOVNA, geologist; b. St. Petersburg, Russia, Feb. 18, 1941; d. Ivan Ivanovich and Olga Ivanovna (Nikiforova) K.; m. Anatoliy Liginov, Nov. 13, 1979. PhD, St. Petersburg U., Russia, 1973. Lab. asst. St. Petersburg U., Russia, 1963-83, sr. scientist, 1984—. Co-author: Genesis of Mineral Individuals and Aggregates, 1995. Mem. All Russian Mineral Soc., St. Petersburg Soc. Naturalists. Avocations: travel, videos. E-mail: ikrasn@comset.net. Home: Varvarinskaya 6a, 194 356 St Petersburg Russia Office: St Petersburg U Dept Minera, Univ Emb 7/9, 199 034 St Petersburg Russia

KRASNOW, JEFFREY HARRY, lawyer; b. San Francisco, Oct. 7, 1946; s. Clement K. and Winifred (Spandorfer) K.; m. Rita Jane Moore, Mar. 23, 1969; children: Mark Samuel, Daniel Edward. BA, Old Dominion U., 1969; JD, U. Va., 1972. Bar: Va. 1972, W.Va. 1990, U.S. Dist. Ct. (ea. and we. dists.) Va., U.S. Ct. Appeals (4th, 5th and 6th cirs.), U.S. Supreme Ct. Diplomate Ct. Practice Inst.; cert. civil trial specialist. Assoc. Frank N. Perkinson Jr. Esq., Roanoke, Va., 1972-74; ptnr. Perkinson, Krasnow and Perkinson, Roanoke, 1974-77; pvt. practice Roanoke, 1977-82; sr. ptnr. Jeffrey H. Krasnow Esq., Roanoke, 1982-86, Jeffrey H. Krasnow & Assocs., Roanoke, 1987-95; Jeffrey H. Krasnow & Assocs. P.C., Roanoke, 1995—. Mem. ABA, Assn. Trial Lawyers Am. (sustaining), Va. Trial Lawyers Assn. (sustaining, bd. govs. 1995-99), Va. State Bar (lawyer advt. and solicitation com. 1992-96), Roanoke Bar Assn., Nat. Bd. Trial Advocacy (cert. specialist civil trial advocacy). Fax: 540-982-7680. E-mail: krasnow@aol.com. Office: PO Box 120 Roanoke VA 24002-0120

KRASNY, SERGEY ANATOLYEVICH, surgeon, urologist; b. Minsk, Belarus, Sept. 23, 1966; s. Anatoly Matveevitch and Svetlana Dmitrievna (Tararaka) K.; m. Larisa Mikhailovna Beregovtzova, Aug. 5, 1988; children: Vladislav, Anastasia. Diploma with honors, Minsk State Med. Inst., 1989. Intern Minsk State Med. Inst., 1989-90; urologist Minsk Children Diagnostic Ctr., 1990-92; jr. expert Rsch. Inst. Oncology, Minsk, 1992-96, sr. expert, 1996-97, leading expert, 1997—, prof., 1996—; expert med. programs Belorussian TV, Minsk, 1995—; cons. regional oncological dispensers Health Ministry, Minsk, 1996—. Author: Treatment of Renal Cancer Patients with Local and Regional Spread of the Process, 1995; contbr. articles to profl. publs. Mem. Belarussian Urologists Orgn., Internat. Acad. Info. Techs. (corr.), N.Y. Acad. Scis. Avocations: literature, music, sports, travel, gardening. Office: Rsch Inst Oncology, Lesnoy-2, 223052 Minsk Belarus

KRASOWSKY, ARNOLD JANOVICH, mechanical engineering researcher, educator; b. Zaporozhye, Ukraine, July 27, 1933; s. Jan Vikentievich and Ekaterina Evdokimovna (Yukhimenko) K.; m. Ludmila Anatolievna Bedritskaya; children: Andrey, Aliona. Diploma in engring., Kiev (Ukraine) Poly. Inst., 1956; PhD, Kiev Inst. Material Sci., 1964, DSc in Physics and Math., 1973. Cert. in Engring. and Fracture Mechanics. Engr. Kolomna (Russia) Engring. Plant, 1956-60; scientist Inst. Material Sci., Kiev, 1964-66; sr. scientist Inst. for Problems of Strength, Nat. Acad. Scis., Kiev, 1966-68, dept. head, 1968—; prof., lectr. Kiev Poly. Inst., 1971-88; cons. Nuc. Power Plant, Zaporozhye, Ukraine, 1995—. Author: Brittleness of Metals at Low Temperatures, (in Russian) 1980; co-author: Strength of Materials at Extreme Conditions, vols. 1-2, (in Russian) 1980 (USSR State award in sci. 1982), Resistance of Materials to Deformation and Fracture vols. 1-2 (in Russian), 1993-94 (Ukrainian State award in Sci. 1997); contbr. articles to profl. jours. Mem. Nat. Acad. Scis. Ukraine (elected corr.), Am. Soc. Metals Internat. Avocations: chess, literature, music, travel. Home: Sapernoye Pole str 26A, ap 55, 01042 Kiev Ukraine Office: Inst Problems Strength NAS, Timiryazevskaya str 2, 01014 Kiev Ukraine

KRASSA, KATHY BOLTREK, molecular biologist; b. N.Y.C., Dec. 6, 1946; d. Henry and Gloria Beatrice (Poliakoff) Boltrek; m. Robert Frederick Taylor Krassa; children: Josh Boltrek, Vicky Krassa. BS, Cornell U., 1968; postgrad., L.I. U., 1973-74; PhD, U. Colo., 1987. Lab. tech. U. Colo., Boulder, 1968-70; teaching asst. C.W. Post Coll., L.I. U., Glen Cove, N.Y., 1973-74; rsch. assoc. Nassau County Med. Ctr., East Meadow, N.Y., 1975-79; teaching asst. U. Colo., Boulder, 1980-81, rsch. asst., 1981-87, postdoctoral rschr., 1988-91; CEO Molecular Jeanetics, Boulder, 1991—. Author: Structure and Function of the Single-Stranded DNA Binding Protein of the Bacteriophage T4, 1987; contbr. articles to profl. jours. NIH grantee, 1974, 82, Am. Cancer Soc. rsch. grantee, 1988, 89. Avocations: tap dancing, reading, doll collecting, designing clothing.

KRASTEVA, YONKA KROUMOVA, English and Russian language educator; b. Veliko Turnovo, Bulgaria, Nov. 26, 1949; d. Kroum Krastev and Dimitra Mincheva (Stoyanova) Nedev; divorced; 1 child, Maria Mitreva. MA, U. Sofia, Bulgaria, 1972; PhD, Inst. for Lit., Sofia, 1988. Tchr. English English Lang. Sch., Rousse, Bulgaria, 1972-74; coord. Am. studies U. Veliko Turnovo, 1974—; head of dept. U. Veliko Turnovo, 1987-88, 92-95, coord. tempus project, 1994-97. Author: The West and the American Dream, 1996; contbr. article to jours. in field. Grantee Fulbright Found., 1984, 89, rsch. grantee Am. Coun. Learned Socs., 1994, John F. Kennedy Inst., Berlin, 1992, 97. Mem. MLA, European Assn. Am. Studies, European Soc. Study English. Avocations: hiking, travel, skiing' e-mail: archer@mbox.digsys.bg. Home: 25E T Tarnovski, 5003 Veliko Turnovo Bulgaria Office: U Veliko Turnovo, 2 T Tarnovski, 5000 Veliko Turnovo Bulgaria

KRASTS, GUNTARS, Latvian parliament official; b. Riga, Latvia, 1957; married; 3 children. Degree in Econs., U. Latvia, 1982. Rsch. assoc. Latvian State Rsch. Inst. of Rural Econs., 1983-91; chmn. bd. RANG ltd. liability corp., 1991-95; min. econs. Govt. of Latvia, Riga, 1995-97, prime minister, 1997-98; vice prime minister for Euroepan Union affairs Republic of Latvia, Riga, 1998-99, chmn. parliament fgn. affairs com., 1998—. Contbr. articles to profl. jours. Mem. For Fatherland and Freedom. Avocations: swimming, skiing, tourism. Office: Parliament of Latvia, Feraba Iela 10/12, LV-1811 Riga Latvia

KRASUSKI, ALFRED, physician, researcher; b. Poland, May 28, 1947; s. Mieczysław and Kazimiera Weronika (Kardynalski) K. BS, Med. U. Gdańsk, Poland, 1970, MD, 1980. Med. diplomate. Intern dept. surgery Med. U. Gdańsk, 1971; resident dept. internal medicine Med. U. Gdansk, 1971, resident dept. ob-gyn., 1972; asst. Med. U. Gdańsk, 1970-80, adj., 1980—. Mem. Solidarity Trade Union, Gdańsk, 1980—. Grantee Med. U. Gdańsk, 1991, 97. Mem. Polish Microbiol. Soc., N.Y. Acad. Scis. Roman Catholic. Avocation: mountaineering. Home: Kombatantów A 1 M 12, PL80-464 Gdańsk Poland Office: Med U Gdańsk Dept Micro, Studzienki 38, PL80-227 Gdańsk Poland

KRASZEWSKI, ADAM, reseaarch chemist; b. Kobylec, Poland, Nov. 26, 1947; s. Seweryn and Wanda (Filut) K.; m. Maria Miroslawa Mindykowska, Apr. 12, 1975; children: Igor, Malorzata, Jan. MSc, A. Mickiewicz U., Poznan, Poland, 1972; PhD, Inst. Organic Chemistry, Warsaw, Poland, 1977; asst. prof., Inst. Biochem. Physics, Warsaw, Poland, 1985; full prof., Polish Acad. Sci., 1998. Postdoctoral City of Hope, Duarte, 1977-78; adj. tutor Inst. Bioorganic Chemistry, Poznan, 1978-85, assoc. prof. chemistry, 1985-98, full prof. chemistry, 1998—; head of lab., Inst. Bioorganic Chemistry, 1983-88, 88—, vice dir., 1987-91. Contbr. articles to profl. jours.; inventor in field. Mem. N.Y. Acad. Scis., Polish Chem. Assn., Polish Biochem. Assn. Mem. Solidarity. Avocations: skiing, sailing, tennis, gardening. Office: Inst Bioorganic Chemistry, Noskowskiego 12/14, 61-704 Poznan Poland

KRASZEWSKI, ANDRZEJ WOJCIECH, electrical engineer, researcher; b. Poznan, Poland, Apr. 22, 1933; arrived in Can., 1980.; s. Tadeusz Jozef and Waleria Barbara (Pietrzyk) K.; m. Janina Wiktoria Okula, June 24, 1956 (dec. Jan. 1998); children: Marcin Jan, Andrzej Maria (dec. Aug. 1991). BSEE, Tech. U., Warsaw, Poland, 1954, MSEE, 1958; DSc in Tech. Sci., Polish Acad. Scis., Warsaw, 1973. Rsch. engr. Indsl. Inst. for Telecoms., Warsaw, 1953-58; sr. rsch. engr. Lamina Works, Iwiczna, Poland, 1958-60; asst. prof. dept. electronics Tech. U., 1960-62; microwave labs. mgr. UNIPAN Scientific Instruments, Warsaw, 1963-72; co-founder, mgr. microwaves WILMER Instruments, Warsaw, 1972-80; assoc. prof. dept. electrical engring. U. Manitoba, Winnipeg, Manitoba, Can., 1976-77; vis. prof. dept. electrical engring. U. Ottawa, Ontario, Can., 1980-86; rsch. electronics engr., Agrl. Rsch. Svc. U.S. Dept. Agriculture, Athens, Ga., 1987—. Author: Microwave Switching Circuits, 1966, Microwave Gas Discharge Devices, 1967; editor: Microwave Aquametry, 1996, Microwave Sensors Update, 2000; contbr. chpts. to books, over 250 articles to profl. jours. Recipient Gold medal Internat. Fair, Leipzig, Germany, 1964, 65, 77, IR-100 award Indsl. Rsch. Inst., Chgo., 1976, Sci. award Ministry Sci. and Tech., Warsaw, 1977, Sci. State prize, Warsaw, 1980; Rsch. in Engring. grantee Natural Sci. and Engring. Rsch. Coun., Ottawa, 1985, Rsch. grantee Binat. Agrl. R&D, Washington, 1989. Fellow IEEE (editorial bd. 1992—), Assn. for Microwave Power in Europe for Rsch. and Edn., Internat. Microwave Power Inst. (editorial bd. 1975-84), Material Rsch. Soc., N.Y. Acad. Scis., Sigma Xi. Roman Catholic. Achievements include 20 patents on moisture content determination using microwave parameter measurements; pioneer works in microwave aquametry, experimental RF&MW dosimetry, permittivity of tissues in-vivo, DNA solutions, applications of microwave techniques for measurement of nonelectrical quantities; research in plant structure and composition using electromagnetic waves, multi-parameter microwave measurements for density-independent moisture content determination, microwave switching circuits, microwave gas discharge devices. Office: USDA Russell Rsch Ctr 950 College Station Rd Athens GA 30605-2720

KRASZNAHORKAY, ATTILA JÁNOS, experimental nuclear physics researcher; b. Bakonszeg, Hungary, Jan. 1, 1954; s. János Krasznahorkay and Ilona Pelbárt; m. Mária Kripkó, Dec. 23, 1978; children: Ilona, Attila. MSc, Lajos Kossuth U., Debrecen, Hungary, 1978, PhD, 1982; Candidate in Phys. Sci., Hungarian Acad. Sci., Budapest, 1990. Rsch. fellow Inst. Nuc. Rsch., Hungarian Acad. Sci., Debrecen, 1978-80, rsch. worker, 1980-89, head nuc. spectroscopy dept., 1994—; postdoctoral staff Kernfysisch Versneller Inst., Groningen, The Netherlands, 1990-91; vis. rsch. scholar Osaka (Japan) U., 1998-99; mem. nuc. physics bd. Hungarian Acad. Scis., Budapest, 1994—. Editor Heavy Ion Physics, Procs. of the Internat. Symposium on Exotic Nuc. Shapes, 1998; contbr. articles to profl. jours. Mem. Roland Eötvös Phys. Soc. (sec. nuc. physics sect. 1997—, Pál Selényi prize 1995). Fax: 36-52-416181. E-mail: kraszna@atomki.hu. Home: Kanális ut 143, Debrecen Hungary Office: Inst Nuc Rsch Hung Acad Sci, Bem tér 18/c, H-4001 Debrecen Hungary

KRATHEN, DAVID HOWARD, lawyer; b. Phila., Nov. 17, 1946; s. Morris S. and Lillian E. Krathen; m. Francine Ellen Krathen, Oct. 21, 1973; children: Richard, Stefanie, Michael. BBA, U. Miami, 1969, JD, 1972. Bar: Fla. 1972, D.C. 1972, U.S. Supreme Ct. 1976, N.Y. 1984, Colo. 1989. Atty. advisor ICC, Washington, 1972-73; asst. pub. defender 17th Jud. Cir., Ft. Lauderdale, Fla., 1973-74; ptnr. Krathen, Rastatter, Stark & Tarlowe, Ft. Lauderdale, 1978-84; pvt. practice Law Offices David Krathen, P.A., Ft. Lauderdale, 1984—; mem. Fla. Bar Grievance Com. 17 C, 1982-85, 1988-91, vice chmn., 1985, 89-90, chmn. 1990-91; mem. Jud. Adminstrn., Selection and Tenure Com., 1982-85, 4th Dist. Ct. of Appeal Jud. Nominating Commn., 1983-87, chmn. 1986-87; mem. jud. nominating commn. 17th Jud. Cir., 1991-95, chmn., 1994-95; apptd. by Fla. Gov. to State Ethics Commn., 1995-99. Mem. ATLA, Acad. Fla. Trial Lawyers (diplomate), Broward County Bar Assn. (bd. dirs. 1988-89), Broward Med. Assn. (com. joint med. legal 1997—), Broward County Trial Lawyers Assn. (bd. dirs. 1983-84, sec. 1984-85, v.p,. 1985-86, pres. 1987-88), Fla. Bar (bd. cert. civil trial lawyer 1984—), Nat. Bd. Trial Advocacy (bd. cert. civil trial advocate 1986—), Am. Bd. Trial Advocacy (advocate 1989—, sec. Ft. Lauderdale chpt. 1991-92, pres.-elect 1993-95, pres. 1995-96). Office: 888 E Las Olas Blvd Ste 200 Fort Lauderdale FL 33301-2239

KRATKA, JIRINA ELIZABETH, plant pathologist, researcher; b. Mladá Boleslav, Czech Republic, Oct. 4, 1938; d. Jan and Maria (Ponec) Lanz; m. Jaroslav Kratky. Magister, Charles U., Prag, Czech Republic, 1960, Rerum Naturalis D, 1975; PhD, Acad. Sci., Prag, 1974; DSc, Agrl. U., Brno, Czech Republic, 1991. Dep. head dept. mycology Rsch. Inst. Crop Prodn., Prag, 1989-92, head dept., 1993—, cons., 1980—, cons. divsn. plant medicine, 1990—; cons. Chem. U. Agrl. U., Prag, 1993—; cons. Palacky U., Olomouc, Czech Republic, 1993—. Contbr. articles to profl. jours. Mem. Fedn. European Socs. Plant Pathology, Acad. Sci. Agr., Mycol. Soc. Roman Catholic. Avocations: history of world, classical music, skiing, travel. Home: Spolupráce 2, 140 00 Prague Czech Republic Office: RICP, Drnovská 507, 161 06 Pragus Czech Republic

KRATKA-SCHNEIDER, DOROTHY MARYJOHANNA, psychotherapist; b. New Britain, Conn., Apr. 29, 1934; d. Josef Matthew and Mari Catherine (Stifil) Kratka; m. Warren Andrew Schneider, Apr. 26, 1975. BS in Nursing, Columbia U., 1960; MSW, Fordham U., 1969; EdD in Counseling Psychology, U. San Francisco, 1983. RN, Conn.; bd. cert. diplomate in clin. social work. Instr. pub. health nursing U. Conn., Storrs, 1963-64; participant Voter Registration Drive, Greenwood, Miss., 1965; pub. health nurse Jesuit Med. Mission Bd., Tanzania, East Africa, 1965-67; chief psychiat. social worker Knickerbocker Hosp., N.Y.C., 1969-74; coordinator social services Rockefeller U. Hosp., N.Y.C., 1974-77; asst. prof. Calif. State U., Sacramento, 1985-88, assoc. prof., 1985-88; counseling psychologist VA, San Francisco, 1987-89; psychologist, social worker Dept. Transp., 1989-93; pvt. practice Corte Madera, Calif., 1993—; bd. dirs. Nat. Assn. Soc. Work Referral Service, San Francisco, 1984-86. Bd. dirs. Health Systems Adv. Com., San Francisco, 1978, Cmty. Mental Health, Marin County, Calif., 1998—; mem. Cath. Charities Bd. for Aging, San Francisco, 1985, bd. dirs., 1983-85; apptd. to Marin County Cmty. Mental Health Bd., 1998—; apptd. to Marin County Grand Jury, Superior Ct., 1999—. NIMH grantee, 1967-69. Mem. APA, Internat. Assn. Profl. Counselors and Psychotherapists (diplomate psychotherapy), NASW (diplomate in clin. social work), Register for Clin. Social Workers of NASW, Amnesty Internat., Kappa Delta Pi. Democrat. Roman Catholic. Avocations: hiking, watercolors, flying, swimming. Office: Diablo Med Plz Ste 200 Novato CA 94947

KRATZ, HOWARD RUSSEL, physicist, researcher; b. Mattoon, Wis., Nov. 2, 1916; s. Samuel H. and Clara A. (Jones) K.; m. Mary K. Bunsa, June 2, 1942; children: Marilyn Kratz Locker, William H. BA, Ripon Coll., 1938; PhD, U. Wis., 1942. Tchg. asst. U. Wis., Madison, 1938-41; rsch. asst. Princeton (N.J.) U., 1941-42; mem. staff Metall. Lab., U. Chgo., 1942-44; mem. staff Los Alamos (N.M.) Sci. Lab., 1944-46, GE Rsch. Lab., Schnectady, N.Y., 1946-59, Gen. Atomic, San Diego, 1959-72; sr. scientist Sys., Sci., and Software, San Diego, 1972-79; ret., 1979—. Contbr. articles to Phys. Revue, Rev. Sci. Instruments, Jour. Optical Soc. Am., Jour. Am. Instrument Soc. Recipient 1972 best paper award Am. Instrument Soc., 1973. Mem. Am. Phys. Soc., Sigma Xi. Democrat. Unitarian. Home: 102 Spanish Oak Ln Hendersonville NC 28791-2906

KRATZSCH, KONRAD ADOLF RICHARD, librarian; b. Plauen-Unterlosa, Germany, Apr. 10, 1931; s. Victor and Helene (Rosenmüller) K.; m. Vera Werner, May 21, 1955; 1 child, Bettina. PhD, U. Jena, 1968. Libr. Pub. Libr. Erfurt, Germany, 1952-55; scientist Ctrl. Inst. Pub. Librs., Berlin, 1955-60; libr. Ctrl. Libr. Pedagogics, Berlin, 1961-63, Herzogin Anna Amalia Libr., Weimar, Germany, 1963-95. Author; Register der Goethe-Jahrbücher 1880-1968, 1970, Gebetbuch der Margarete von Rodemachern, 1973, 78, Achim von Arnim, 1980, Alte Handschriften aus der Zentralbibliothek der deutschen Klassik, 1980, Wiegendrucke der Zentralbibliothek der deutschen Klassik, 1981, Illuminierte Holzschnitte der Luther-Bibel von 1534, 1982, Alte Globen aus den Beständen der Nationalen Forschungs-und Gedenkstätten der klassischen deutschen Literatur, 1984, Verzeichnis der Luther-Drucke 1517-1546 aus den Beständen der Zentralbibliothek der deutschen Klassik, 1986, Die Benutzungsordnung der Weimarer Bibliothek von 1798 (Facs), 1990, Kostbarkeiten aus den Beständen der Herzogin Anna Amalia Bibliothek, 1993; editor: Achim von Arnim. Erzählungen, 1968, 84, Almanach dramatischer Spiele (Facs.), 1972, Das Weimarer Liederbuch (Facs.), 1976, Biblia pauperum/Apokalypse (Facs.), 1977, R. M. Rilke. Briefwechsel mit Rolf Freih. von Ungern-Sternberg, 1980, Jahrbuch der Weltbegebenheiten (Facs), 1984, Hartmann Schedel Weltchronik (Facs.), 1990, Historische Bestände der Herzogin Anna Amalia Bibliothek, 1992; co-editor: Luther. Biblia (Facs.), 1983. Home: Rainer Maria Rilke Str 5, 99425 Weimar Germany

KRAU, EDGAR, psychologist, researcher, educator; b. Stanislau, Poland, Apr. 9, 1929; arrived in Israel, 1977; s. Adolf and Ella (Lam) K.; m. Mary Epure, Dec. 27, 1958; 1 child, Nicole. MA, U. Cluj, Romania, 1951, PhD, 1964. Lic. Psychologist, Israel. Chief rsch. fellow Inst. Pedagogical Scis., Cluj, Romania, 1961-63; with U. Cluj, Romania, 1963-77; head psychology dept. Acad. Romanian Republic, Cluj, 1968-77; prof. U. Haifa, Israel, 1977-81; prof. Tel-Aviv U., Israel, 1981-97, prof. emeritus, 1997—; prof. Thames Valley U., Haifa, Israel, 1997—; mem. Internat. Test Commn., 1971-73; chmn. Internat. Colloquium on Human Resources Devel., Jerusalem, 1984; mem. sci. com. XXI Internat. Congress of Applied Psychology, 1986; editor-in-chief (jour. of labor studies) Man and Work, 1987—. Author: The Contradictory Immigrant Problem, 1991, Social and Economic Management in the Competitive Society, 1998, (with P. Goguelin) Projet Professionnel - Projet de Vie, 1992, The Realization of Life Aspirations Through Vocational Careers, 1997; co-author: Treatise on Industrial Psychology, 1967 (Romanian Acad. Vasile Conta award 1972); co-author, editor: Self-realization, Success and Adjustment, 1989; author Jour. Vocational Behavior, 1981-89 (hon. mention award 1986). Recipient diploma of high ctr. for logic and comparative scis. award, Bologna, Italy, 1972, Homagial Biography-Bibliography, Revue Européenne de Psychologie Appliquée, 1993. Mem. APA (affiliate), Israeli Psychol. Assn. (instr. 1979—), N.Y. Acad. Scis. Home: 2 Hess St, 33398 Haifa Israel

KRAUS, CHRISTINA SHUTTLEWORTH, classics educator; b. Hartford, Conn., May 25, 1958; d. Guenther Martin Kraus and Barbara Elizabeth Shuttleworth; m. Peter Morgan, 1996; 1 child, Eleanor Maud. BA, Princeton U., 1980; PhD, Harvard U., 1988. Asst. prof. NYU, N.Y.C., 1988-94; lectr. Univ. Coll. London, 1994-97; Munro fellow in classical langs. and lit. Oriel Coll., Oxford (Eng.) U., 1997—, Consol. Univ. Fund lectr., 1997—; mem. bd. mgmt. Classical Jours. Bd., 1998—. Author: Livy Ab Vrbe Condita VI, 1994; editor: The Limits of Historiography, 1999. Vis. scholar Leverhulme Found., Durham, Eng., 1992-93. Mem. Am. Philol. Assn., Classical Assn. Eng. and Wales (coun. 1997-2000), Roman Soc. (coun. 1995-98). Office: Oxford U Oriel Coll, Oriel Sq, Oxford OX1 4EW, England

KRAUS, JIŘI, linguist, researcher; b. Praha, Czech Republic, May 25, 1935; s. Miroslav and Marie (Pickartová) K.; m. Věra Klimová, Apr. 25, 1974; children: Alena, Petr. Grad., Charles U., Prague, 1958, PhD, 1968; CSc, Acad. Scis., Prague, 1967, DSc, 1990. Postdoctoral fellow Czech Lang. Inst., Prague, 1963-67, rsch. fellow, 1967-90, vice dir., 1990-94, dir., 1994—; prof. Charles U., Prague, 1995—. Author: Rhetoric in the History of Language Communication, 1981, Rhetoric and European Culture, 1998; editor, author: Akademicky slovnik cizich slov I, II, 1995 (Czech Translators prize 1996), 4th edit., 2000; chief editor Naše řeč, 1990—. Grantee Agy. Czech Republic. Home: Vysočanská 234, 19000 Prague Czech Republic Office: Czech Lang Inst, Letenská 4, 11851 Praha 1, Czech Republic

KRAUS, OTTO HEINRICH, zoology educator; b. Frankfurt, Germany, May 17, 1930; s. Otto Hermann and Helene (Lehmann) K.; m. Margarete Richter, Dec. 23, 1957; 1 child, Beate. Dr. phil. nat., U. Frankfurt, Germany, 1955, pvt. dozent, 1965; full prof. zoology, U. Hamburg, Germany, 1969. Sci. asst. Forschungs-Inst. Senckenberg, Frankfurt, 1955-60, curator, 1960-69; dir. Zoology Inst. and Mus., U. Hamburg, 1969—, prof. emeritus, 1995—; mem. Internat. Commn. Zoological Nomenclature, London, 1963—, pres., 1989-95. Contbr. over 150 rsch. articles to sci. pubs. Mem. Acad. Scis. N. Germany (pres. 1978-82, 96—). Home: Rotbuchenstieg 15, D 22297 Hamburg Germany Office: U Hamburg Inst Zoology, ML King Platz 3, D 20146 Hamburg Germany

KRAUS, PETER ANDREW, obstetrician-gynecologist, educator; b. Budapest, Hungary, June 5, 1942; Arrived in Australia, 1948; s. Imre and Clara (Elfer) K.; m. Heather Edith Eddington, Nov. 29, 1965; children: Ian, Philip, Michael. MB, BS, U. Sydney, Australia, 1967. Cert. specialist ob-gyn., Australia. Intern Launceston (Australia) Gen. Hosp., 1967; resident med. officer Albury (Australia) Base Hosp., 1968, Women's Hosp., Sydney, 1969; sr. ho. officer Princess Margaret Hosp., Swindon, Wilts, U.K., 1969-70; registrar Princess Alexandra Hosp., Harlow, Essex, U.K., 1971-72; pvt. med. practice Albury/Wodonga, Australia, 1972-77, Windsor, NSW, Australia, 1977-96; specialist ob-gyn., clin. sr. lectr. Townsville (Australia) Health Svc. Dist./U. Queensland, 1996—. Parish councillor, ch. warden St. Matthew's Anglican Ch., Albury, 1974-77; parish councillor St. Matthew's Anglican Ch., Windsor, 1985-89; active Rotary Club Windsor, 1984-95, pres., 1989-90. Wing comdr. Royal Australian Air Force Res., 1979—. Fellow Royal Coll. Ob-gyn. (Eng.), Royal Australia New Zealand Coll. Ob-gyn.; mem. Nat. Assn. Specialist Ob-gyn. (com. mem. 1998—), Australasian Menopause Soc. (com. mem. 1999—). Avocations: flying, radio control model aircraft, photography, sailing. E-mail: pkraus@medeserv.com.au and krausp@health.qld.gov.au. Fax: 61 7 47 752734. Home: 1 Cylad Ct, Annandale QLD 4814, Australia Office: Kirwan Hosp for Women, PO Box 187, Thuringowa Central QLD 4817, Australia

KRAUSE, MARIA WICHURA, physiotherapist; b. East London, Cape, South Africa, May 10, 1941; d. Stephanus Benjamine and Maria Sybella (Wichura) De Klerk; m. John Brebner Krause; children: Otto, Marguerite, René. Diploma in physiotherapy, Pretoria Sch. Physiotherapy, South Africa, 1961; tersiary edn. diploma, U. the Orange Free State, South Africa, 1982, MSc, 1989. Dept. head U. the Orange Free State, Bloemfontein, South Africa, 1988—. Active Stds. Generating Body, South Africa, 1999. Mem. HPCSA. Office: Univ Van Die OVS, PO Box 339, 9300 Bloemfontein South Africa

KRAUSE, PETER JAMES, pediatrician, researcher, educator; b. Denver, Mar. 17, 1945; s. Peter and Frances (Coles) K.; m. Carol Ann Blawie, May 24, 1975; children: Rebecca Ann, Peter John Paul, Kathleen Helen. BA with honors in Biology, Williams Coll., 1967; MD, Tufts U., 1971. Diplomate Am. Acad. Pediatrics. Intern in pediatrics Yale-New Haven Hosp., 1971-72, resident in pediatrics, 1972-73; resident in pediatrics Stanford U. Med. Ctr., Palo Alto, Calif., 1973-74; rsch. fellow pediatric infectious diseases UCLA Sch. Medicine, 1976-79; chief, pediatric infectious diseases Hartford (Conn.) Hosp., 1979-96; attending physician, dir. pediatric AIDS program Conn. Children's Med. Ctr., Hartford, 1996-98; chief, pediatric infectious diseases Conn. Children's Med. Ctr., 1998—; asst. prof. pediatrics Sch. Medicine. U. Conn., Farmington, 1979-84, assoc. prof., 1985-91, prof., 1991—; speaker to profl. groups. Author: (with others) Textbook of Pediatric Infectious Diseases, 1987, 4th edit., 1998, Pediatrics. The National Medical Series for Independent Study, 1987, 91, 95, 98, Conn's Current Therapy, 1991, Current Pediatric Therapy, 1992, Nelson Textbook of Pediatrics, 2000; mem. editl. bd. Jour. Clin. Microbiology, 1991-99; contbr. over 100 articles to scholarly and profl. jours. Maj. U.S. Army, 1974-76. Recipient nat. rsch. svc. award NIH, 1977-79. Fellow Am. Acad. Pediatrics, Pediatric Infectious Diseases Soc., Infectious Diseases Soc. Am.; mem. AAAS, Am. Soc. Microbiology, Am. Fedn. Clin. Rsch. (sr.), Soc. Pediatric Rsch. (sr.), Assn. Clin. Scientists, Infectious Diseases Soc. Conn., N.Y. Acad. Scis., Sigma Xi. Office: Conn Children's Med Ctr 282 Washington St Hartford CT 06106-3322

KRAUSE, THOMAS EVANS, record promotion and radio consultant; b. Mpls., Dec. 17, 1951; s. Donald Bernhard and Betty Ann (Nokleby) K.; m. Barbara Ann Kaufman, Aug. 17, 1974 (div. Apr. 1978); m. Nicole Michelle Purkerson, Aug. 13, 1988; children: Andrew Todd Evans, Allison Michelle. Student, Augsburg Coll., 1969-73; BA, Hastings Coll., 1975. Lic. 3d class with broadcast endorsement FCC. Air personality Sta. KHAS Radio, Hastings, Nebr., 1974-75; air personality, news dir. Sta. KWSL Radio, Sioux City, Iowa, 1975-76; asst. program dir. Sta. KISD Radio, Sioux Falls, S.D., 1976-78; music dir. Sta. KVOX Radio, Fargo, N.D., 1978; program dir. Sta. KPRQ Radio, Salt Lake City, 1978-79; air personality Sta. KIOA Radio, Des Moines, 1980; program dir., ops. mgr. Sta. KKSS Radio, Sioux Falls, 1981-83; program dir. Stas. KIYS/KBBK Radio, Boise, Idaho, 1983-87; program dir., ops. mgr. Sta. WSRZ AM/FM Radio, Sarasota, Fla., 1988-90; owner, cons. Tom Evans Mktg., Seattle, 1990—; editor., pub. Northwest Log, Seattle, 1991-96; mgr. neverMAN, 1994—; co-founder Sta. KCMR Radio, Augsburg Coll., Mpls., 1973; TV show coord./host Z-106 Hottraxx, Sarasota, 1988-90; air personality/guest disc jockey various radio stas., Pacific N.W., 1990—; host Am. Music Report. Sta. KIX-106 Radio, Canberra, Australia, 1992; instr. Sta. KGRG-FM and KENU-AM, Green River Coll., Auburn, Wash., 1994—. Contbr. articles to various trade publs., mags. Bd. judges Loyola U. Marconi Awards, Chgo., 1992-93; bd. dirs. Habitat for Humanity, Snohomish County, Wash., 1992-96, Martin Luther King Day Celebration, Sarasota County, Fla., 1989-90, Shoreline/So. County YMCA, 1992-95; dist. coord. Carter for Pres., Nebr. 1st Dist., 1975-76; hon. chair March of Dimes Walk Am., Sioux Falls, 1977; head coach Seattle Beavers Baseball Club, 1999—; media vol., MC or spokesperson M.S. Soc., MDA, Am. Diabetes Assn., Human Soc., others. Mem. Free Methodist Ch. Avocations: sports, films, science fiction, photography, travel. Office: Tom Evans Mktg 16426 65th Ave W Lynnwood WA 98037-2710

KRAUSEN, ANTHONY SHARNIK, surgeon; b. Phila., Feb. 22, 1944; s. B.M. and Kay S. (Sharnik) K.; m. Susan Elizabeth Park, Sept. 6, 1970; children: Park, Allison. Student, Germantown Acad., 1949-61; BA, Princeton U., 1965; MD, U. Mich., 1969. Intern Presbyn. Med. Ctr.,

Denver, 1969-70; resident St. Joseph Hosp., Denver, 1970-71, Barnes Hosp., St. Louis, 1972-76; with Milw. Med. Clinic, 1976—, head dept. facial plastic surgery, 1984—; mem. staffs Columbia, St. Michael, St. Mary Hosp., Oankee. Pres. Contemporary Art Soc., Milw. Art Mus., 1983; bd. dirs. Friends of Art. Served with U.S. Army Nat. Guard, 1970-76. Fellow ACS, Am. Acad. Cosmetic Surgery, Am. Acad. Facial Plastic and Reconstructive Surgery, Am. Acad. Otalaryngology; mem. Nat. Neurofibramatosis Soc. (med. advisor Wis. chpt. 1985-92), Wis. Otolaryngological Soc. Clubs: Ivy (Princeton, N.J.), Town Club (Milw.). Office: 3003 W Good Hope Rd Milwaukee WI 53209-2042

KRAUSER, ROBERT STANLEY, health care executive; b. N.Y.C., Aug. 24, 1937; s. Benjamin and Eva (Ferester) K.; m. Mary Kay Edwards, June 12, 1977 (dec. May 1999); children: Robert Edwards, Kathryn Edwards. BA, U. Vt., 1958; MS, Columbia U., 1959. Rschr., portfolio analyst Merrill, Lynch, Pierce et al, N.Y.C., 1961-63; dir. spl. situations rschr. Orvis Bros., N.Y.C., 1964-66; dir. rsch. Amott, Baker, N.Y.C., 1966-69; v.p. rsch. counsel Bruns, Nordemann & Rea, N.Y.C., 1970-75; v.p. rsch. assoc. Rosenkrantz, Ehrenkrantz, N.Y.C., 1976-77; investment banker Herzfeld & Stern, Stamford, Conn., 1978-82; chmn., pres. Viral Response Sys., Inc., Greenwich, Conn., 1983—. Patentee in field. With U.S. Army, 1959, res. Recipient Certificate of Recognition Eli Whitney Mus., 1987. Mem. Nat. Assn. Chain Drug Stores, Am. Mensa (Philanthropic award 1987), Inventors Assn. Conn. (Inventor of Yr. 1988), U.S. Tennis Assn. (ranked 1995), The Wimbledon Soc., Landmark Club, East Hampton Tennis Club (mixed doubles champ 1972), Armonk Tennis Club, Grand Slam Tennis Club (singles champ 1977, 78). Republican. Avocations: tennis, skiing, swimming, travel, medical reading. Home: 444 Taconic Rd Greenwich CT 06831-2850 Office: Viral Response Sys Inc 34 E Putnam Ave Ste 105 Greenwich CT 06830-5435

KRAUSS, HENRY FREDERICK, JR., optometrist; b. Sewickley, Pa., Apr. 10, 1952; s. Henry Frederick and Mirella Anna (Guerrieri) K.; m. Sally Winston Miller, July5, 1975; children: Molly Anne, Henry Neil, Malinda Paige, Michael Winston. BS, Centre Coll., Ky., 1976; OD, U. Houston, 1980. Optometrist, owner Eye Care Assocs., Richardson, Tex., 1980—; v.p. ProComp Systems Inc., Albuquerque, 1983-86; ptnr. K-W Distbrs., Dallas, 1983-86, Summit Seminars, Richardson, 1985—; owner, operator Profl. Enhancement Strategies, 1997—. Bd. dirs. Found. for Edn. and Rsch. in Vision, 1988-89, S.W. Vision Svc. Plan, 1982-84. Fellow Am. Acad. Optometry; mem. Am. Optometric Assn., Tex. Optometric Assn. (Young Optometrist of Yr. award 1985), North Tex. Optometric Assn. (pres. 1983-84), Am. Pub. Health Assn. (vision care sect.). Republican. Mem. LDS Ch. Avocations: golf, tennis, photography, horsemanship, sailing. Office: Eye Care Assocs 660 W Campbell Rd Richardson TX 75080-3301

KRAUSS, JOHN LANDERS, public policy, urban affairs consultant, mediator; b. Orange, N.J., Oct. 20, 1948; s. George Howard Jr. and Shirley (Landers) K.; m. M. Elizabeth Wood, May 23, 1976 (div. Sept. 1988); m. Eleanor C. Werbe, June 29, 1991. BA with honors in Polit. Sci., Colo. Coll., 1971; JD, Ind. U., Indpls., 1976. Bar: Ind. 1976, U.S. Dist. Ct. (so. dist.) Ind. 1976, U.S. Ct. Appeals (7th cir.) 1979, U.S. Supreme Ct. 1986, D.C. 1999; cert. mediator. Spl. asst. to gov. Office of Gov. of Ind., Indpls., 1971-72; dep. dir. Greater Indpls. Progress Com. Inc., Indpls., 1972-73, exec. dir., 1973-81; dir. dept. met. devel. City of Indpls., 1981-82, dep. mayor, 1982-91; sr. fellow Ind. U. Ctr. for Urban Policy and Environment, Indpls., 1991—; exec. dir. Gov.'s Gambling Impact Study Commn., 1998-99; mediator Ind. Dept. Edn., 1998—, U.S. Postal Svc., 1998—; mediator and fact finder Ind. Edn. Employment Rels. Bd., 1991—; exec. dir. Ind. Adv. Commn. on Intergovtl. Rels., 1995—; assoc. Kettering Found., Dayton, Ohio, 1997—; mem. state adv. bd. Ind. Small Bus. Devel. Ctrs.; chmn. Charles L. Whistler Award Com.; bd. dirs. Nyhart Co., Inc.; cons. U.S. Govt. projects in Ukraine, Morocco, Russia, Estonia, Turkey and South Africa; external mediator The World Bank, 2000—; adj. assoc. prof. law Ind. U. Sch. Law, Indpls., 2000—. Trustee Indpls. Mus. Art, Ptnrs. for Livable Comtys., Washington; bd. dirs. Indpls. Project, Inc., Ind. Swiss Found., Ind. Convention and Vis. Assn.; past mem. exec. com., bd. dirs. Eiteljorg Mus. Am. Indian and Western Art; past mem. exec. com. Pan Am. Games Organizing Com., 1987; past vice chmn. Greater Indpls. Progress Com., Inc.; past mem. exec. com. Indpls. Econ. Devel. Corp., Commn. for Downtown, Inc.; founding dir. and v.p. Ind. Sports Corp. Ford Found. Venture grantee for ind. rsch. Mem. AIA (past bd. dirs. Indpls. chpt.), Soc. Individuals in Dispute Resolution, Am. Soc. Pub. Adminstrn. (pres. Ind. chpt. 1992-94, bd. dirs. Ind. chpt.), Am. Arbitration Assn. (comml. panel mediators and arbitrators 1998—), Contemporary Club Indpls., Dramatic Club, Sagamore of the Wabash, State of Ind., Pi Gamma Mu. Office: Ind U Ctr Urban Policy/ Envn 342 N Senate Ave Indianapolis IN 46204-2630

KRAUSS, LEO, urologist, educator; b. N.Y.C., Nov. 5, 1928; s. Moe and Marie (Shapiro) K.; m. Harriet Powell, Dec. 4, 1955; children: Robert, Jennifer. BA summa cum laude, Syracuse U., 1948; MD, NYU, 1953. Diplomate Am. Bd. of Urology. Attending urologist N. Shore U. Hosp., Plainview, N.Y., 1963—, Manhasset, N.Y., 1987—; chief of urology Syosset (N.Y.) Comty. Hosp., 1963-78; urologist pvt. practice, Plainview, 1963—; consulting urologist USAF, Plattsburgh, N.Y., 1961-63, VA Hosp., Tupper Lake, N.Y., 1961-63; asst. prof. urology SUNY, Stony Brook, 1976—. Contbr. articles and abstracts to profl. jours. Bd. dirs. Long Island Cancer Coun., Huntington, N.Y., 1977-79. Capt. USAF, 1954-56, Korea. Named Attending Urologist of Yr., Nassau County Med. Ctr., E. Meadow, N.Y., 1981. Fellow Am. Coll. Surgeons; mem. AMA, N.Y. State Urolog. Soc., Am. Assn. Clin. Urologists, Am. Fedn. for Clin. Rsch., Am. Urolog. Assn., Phi Beta Kappa, Alpha Omega Alpha. Avocations: tennis, travel, reading. Home: 33 Orchard Dr Woodbury NY 11797-2827 Office: Leo Krauss MD PC 875 Old Country Rd Plainview NY 11803-4942

KRAUSZ, PETER THOMAS, artist, gallery director, educator; b. Brasov, Romania, Aug. 19, 1946; s. Tibor Thomas and Judith Noemi (Mozes) K.; m. Irina Kozak, Sept. 14, 1971; 1 child, Anne-Nathalie. Ed., Fine Arts Acad., Bucharest, Romania, 1964-69. Exhbn. dir. The Saidye Bronfman Ctr., 1980-91; prof. dept. history of art U. Montreal, 1991—; lectr. Concordia U., Montreal, 1980-91. Exhbns. include Marlborough/Godard Gallery, Montreal, 1976, Forum/76, Montreal Mus. Fine Arts, 1976, Mira Godard Gallery, Toronto, 1979, 97, 99, Waddington Gallery, Montreal, 1979, Optica Gallery, Montreal, 1985, Galerie Articule Montreal, 1986, Galerie J. Yahouda Meir, Montreal, 1988, 89, Galerie Dresdnere, Toronto, 1988, 89, 90, 93, 94, 95, Robert McLaughlin Gallery, Oshawa, 1989, Mus. Que., 1990, Galerie Lallouz, Montreal, 1992, Concordia U. and Leo Kamen Gallery, Toronto, 1996, 97, Galerie de Bellefeuille, Montreal, 1997, Musee d'art de Joliette, 1999; organizer, curator numerous exhbns.; author: Drawing--A Canadian Survey 1977-1982, 1983, Ten Aspects--Recent Concerns in Canadian Drawing, 1984. Can. Coun. grantee, 1975, 77, 79, 84, 86, 92, 98. Ministry of Cultural Affairs grantee, 1983, 88, 89, 92, 93, 98. Office: PO Box 6128 Sta A, Montreal, PQ Canada H3C 3J7

KRAUT, JOANNE LENORA, computer programmer, analyst; b. Watertown, Wis., Oct. 29, 1949; d. Gilbert Arthur and Dorothy Ann (Gebel) K. BA in Russian, U. Wis., 1971, MS in Computer Sci., 1973. Computer programmer U. Wis. Sch. Bus., Madison, 1969-72, Milw. Ins. Co., 1973-74; tech. coord. Wis. Dept. Justice, Madison, 1974-83; tech. svcs. supr. CRC Telecomm. (formerly Benchmark Criminal Justice Systems), New Berlin, Wis., 1983-89; sr. programmer/analyst Info. Comm. Corp., Pub. Safety Software, Inc., 1989-91; advanced systems engr. EDS, 1991-93; tech. specialist Time Ins., Milw., 1993-96; staff analyst Exacta Corp., Brookfield, Wis., 1996-98; prin. engr. Johnson Controls, Inc., 1998—. Mem. Lakewood Gardens Assn. (dir. 1981-83), Dundee Terrs. Condominium Assn. (officer 1983-99), Hartland Police & Fire Commn. (1998-99). Mem. AAUW, Phi Beta Kappa. Home: 37836 Division St Oconomowoc WI 53066-8910 Office: Johnson Controls Inc 507 E Michigan St Milwaukee WI 53202-5211

KRAUT, JOEL ARTHUR, ophthalmologist; b. Jersey City, July 21, 1937; s. Alan and Lillian Betty (Kravitz) K.; m. Cathy Jane Kleven, June 30, 1963 (div. 1998); children: David Terence, Amy Melissa. AB cum laude, Princeton U., 1958; MD, Columbia U., 1962. Diplomate Am. Bd. Ophthalmology. Intern Boston U. Med. Ctr., 1962-63; resident in ophthalmology NYU-Bellevue Med. Ctr., N.Y.C., 1963-66; chief ophthalmology USAF Hosp., Tachikawa, Japan, 1966-68; pvt. practice specializing in ophthalmology Brookline, Mass., 1968—; asst. prof. Ophthalmology Harvard Med. Sch., 1996—; clin. assoc., clin. instr. ophthalmology Harvard U. Med. Sch.; clin. instr. ophthalmology Tufts U. Sch. Medicine, 1968-91, clin. assoc. prof. ophthalmology, 1991—, assoc. surgeon ophthalmology, 1981-91, surgeon in ophthalmology, 1991—; dir. Low Vision Ctr., Mass. Eye & Ear Infirmary, 1968—, med. dir. Rehab. Ctr., bd. surgeons, 1993—, pres. eye staff, 1994-96, pres. med. staff, 1995-96, bd. dirs.; mem. med. staff Beth Israel Deaconess Med. Ctr., 1991—; bd. dirs. physiol. optics dept. ophthalmology Tufts-New Eng. Med. Ctr., 1968-73; cons. U.S. 5th Air Force, Japan, 1966-68; ophthalmology adv. com. Tufts U. Health Plan; spl. gift com. Princeton U. Contbr. chpts. to textbooks, articles to med. and profl. jours. Chmn. United Way campaign, 1973; bd. dirs. Boston Aid to Blind, 1987-95 (Man of Vision award 1996); mem. adv. bd. Mass. Commn. for Blind, 1988-94 (Disting. Svc. award 1994). Recipient Disting. Svc. award Mass. Commn. for Blind, 1994, Disting. Svc. award Mass. Eye and Ear Infirmary, 1997; Cane scholar, 1954-58, St. John-Princeton scholar, 1958-62; U. Calif. Rsch. fellow, 1960. Fellow ACS; mem. Royal Soc. Medicine, Am. Acad. Ophthalmology (state councillor 1998—, mem. low vision rehab. com. 1995—, honor award 1991), New Eng. Ophthal. Soc. (mem. com. nomination 1997—), Mass. Ophthal. Soc., Nat. Assn. Visually Handicapped (adv. b. 1991—), Soc. Geriatric Ophthalmology, Intraocular Lens Soc., New Eng. Implant Soc. (sec. 1979-81, pres. 1981-83), Mass. Med. Soc. Greater Boston, Med. Soc., Mass. Soc. Eye Physicians and Surgeons (exec. bd. 1988—, recorder 1991-94, treas. 1995-96, pres.-elect 1996, pres. 1996-1998.), Hazel Hotchkiss Wightman Tennis Club, du Bailliage de la Chaine des Rotissurs, Princeton U. Club (spl. gifts com. 1992-93, 96-98), Phi Beta Kappa, Sigma Xi. Office: 16 Webster St Brookline MA 02446-4938

KRAUT, WILLIAM, financial executive; b. Dec. 1, 1944; B.S. in Acctg., St. Peter's Coll., 1966; M.B.A. in Fin., Fairleigh Dickinson U., 1974; m. Marcia Fruchter; children: Brian Justin, Matthew Scott. C.P.A., N.J., N.Y.; diplomate Am. Bd. Forensic Acctg. With Peat, Marwick, Mitchell and Co. Newark, 1966-73, sr. mgr., 1973-77; CFO Appollo Technologies, Inc. Whippany, N.J., 1978-79, Amper, Politziner & Mattia, Iselin, N.J., 1980—, ptnr.-in-charge quality assurance and profl. standards, 1982—, ptnr.-in-charge acctg. and auditing dept., 1985-90. Bd. dirs. Congregation Anshe Emeth, South River, N.J., 1983-84, Hebrew Sch., 1982-85; officer B'nai B'rith Men, 1983-84; officer Old Bridge Jaycees, 1972-73. C.P.A., N.J., N.Y. Mem. Am. Inst. C.P.A.s, N.J. Soc. C.P.A.s (state mgmt. adv. services com., state ethics com., peer rev. exec. com. 1990-96), Fin. Execs. Inst., Delta Sigma Pi (life mem.; co-founder Zeta Eta chpt.); diplomate Info. Sys. Audit and Control Assn. Lodges: Masons, Shriners. Office: Amper Politziner & Mattia 2015 Lincoln Hwy Edison NJ 08817-3377

KRAUTER, STEFAN CHRISTOF WERNER, electrical engineer; b. Goeppingen, Fed. Republic Germany, Apr. 5, 1963; s. Werner and Charlotte (Rau) K. Student, Max Planck Soc. Plasma Physics, 1984; Dipl.-Ing., Tech. U. Munich, Fed. Republic Germany, 1988; PhD, Tech. U. Berlin, 1993; postgrad., Prof. M. Green U., NSW, Australia, 1994. Postgrad. tchr., rsch. Inst. Elec. Machines, Tech. U. Berlin, 1989—; fellow, advisor, tchr. project-orientated edn. bd. Tech. U. Berlin, 1989-91, 1994-95; prof. Fed. U. Rio de Janeiro-COPPE-EE, 1998—, founder photovoltaic Lab.; founder Intstruct News Svcs., Solarserver, SolarInfo, SolarSci., Rio Solar Ltd., 2000; chairing com. Internat. Solar Ctr., Berlin, 1992—; trustee symposia in field, 1991-95; lectr. Fed. Univ. Rio de Janeiro, 1994-97, Tech. Univ. Berlin; co-founder Solon AG for PV-systems, Berlin, 1996; head of rsch. and devel. dept. Solon AG, 1996—. Author procs. in field, 1990—. Berlin solar prize, 1995. Mem. Internat. Solar Energy Soc., German Soc. for Solar Energy, Eurosolar. Achievements include research on optical and thermal optimization of photovoltaic modules, influence of skylight polarization on reflection, incidence angles of diffuse light, optical interaction of module encapsulation layers, partly structured surfaces, optical dispersion, spectral mismatch, measurement of free convective heat transfer coefficient, thermal simulation, cooling strategies, systems optimization, solar home systems, photovoltaic pumping systems, building integration, reduction of carbon-dioxide emissions, life-cycle analysis of energy systems. E-mail: krauter@coe.ufrj.br. Office: UFRJ-COPPE-EE PV-Labs, Caixa Postal 68504, 21945970 Rio de Janeiro Brazil also: Tech U Berlin, Sec EM4 Einsteinufer 11, D-10587 Berlin Germany

KRÄUTLER, BERNHARD, chemistry educator; b. Dornbirn, Austria, Nov. 2, 1946; s. Alfons H. and Margarete (Ganser) K.; m. Rita Doll, Oct. 26, 1973; children: Raphael, Vincent, Nike. Diploma in chemistry, Eidgenoessische Tech. Hochs., Zurich, 1970; Dr.sc.nat., Eidgenoessische Tech. Hochs., 1977. Guest prof. U. Ill., 1985; dozent Eidgenoessische Technische Hochschule, 1986-91; prof., chair organic chemistry U. Innsbruck, Austria, 1991—. Author/editor: Vitamine II, 1989, B12 and B12 Proteins, 1998. Mem. Am. Chem. Soc., Swiss Chem. Soc. (Werner prize 1987), Gesellschaft Deutscher Chemiker, Gesellschaft Österr. Chemiker (pres. 1999—), Austrian Acad. Scis. (corr., Ernst-Späth prize 1996). Office: U Innsbruck, Innrain 52a, A-6020 Innsbruck Austria

KRAVCHENKO, ELEONORA ALEKSANDROVNA, chemist, researcher; b. Moscow, Oct. 30, 1939; d. Aleksandr Aleksandrovich and Valentina Andreevna (Mikhireva) K.; m. Aleksandr Leonidovich Kotkin, Sept. 1, 1963; 1 child, Irina Aleksandrovna. Diploma in physics, Moscow State U., 1964; PhD in Gen. and Inorganic Chemistry, Acad. Scis. USSR, Moscow, 1973. Tchr. sci. Tarkwa (Ghana) Sch. Mines, 1964-65; jr. rsch. scientist Inst. Gen. and Inorganic Chemistry, Acad. Scis. USSR, 1965-80, sr. rschr., head Nuc. Quadrupole Resonance group, 1980—; mem. Internat. Com. on Nuclear Quadrupole Interactions, 1994-97. Author: (with Yu. Buslaev and L. Kolditz) Nuclear Quadrupole Resonance in Inorganic Chemistry, 1987; contbr. articles to sci. jours., including Jour. Molecular Chemistry, Coordination Chemistry Revs., Zeitschrift für Naturforschung. Grantee Russian Found. for Basic Rsch., 1993-94, 96-98, Japan Soc. for Promotion Sci., 1997. Avocations: travel, swimming, skiing, theatre. Office: RAS Inst Gen-Inorganic Chem, Leninskii Prospect 31, 117907 Moscow Russia

KRAVCHENKO, SVETLANA VLADIMIROVNA, child neurologist, researcher; b. Dnepropetrovsk, Ukraine, Feb. 15, 1965; d. Vladimir Illich and Raisa Yakovlevna (Livshits) Agafina; m. Albert Vladimirovitch Kravchenko, Oct. 3, 1987; 1 child, Anastasia. MD, Dnepropetrovsk Med. Inst., 1988, Candidate Med. Scis., 1991, DMS, 1997. Resident Dnepropetrovsk Med. Inst., 1988-90; neurologist Child Hosp. N5, Dnepropetrovsk, 1990-94, chief child neurology dept., 1994—. Patentee in field. Home: Gagarin Av 15 24, 320005 Dnepropetrovsk Ukraine Office: Child Hosp N5, Fuchik St 5, 320044 Dnepropetrovsk Ukraine

KRAVCHENKO, VLADISLAV, mathematician; b. Odessa, USSR, Feb. 15, 1968; arrived in Mex., 1994.; s. Viktor and Viktoriya (Cherkasskaya) K.; m. Kira Hmelnitskaya, July 22, 1989; 1 child, Kiril. MS in Math., State U. Odessa, 1991; PhD in Math., State U. Rostov, Russia, 1994. Rsch. asst. Oceanic Hydrophys. Inst., Ukraine, 1992-94; prof. Nat. Poly. Inst., Mexico City, 1995—; vis. prof. Centro Investigación y de Estudios Avanzados del I.P.N., Mex., 1994-95. Co-author: (with M. Shapiro) Integral Representations for Spatial Models of Mathematical Physics, 1996; author: Elementos del anélisis moderno y teoría electromagnética, 1996. Mem. Am. Math. Soc. Avocation: champion of open chess championship of Mexico. Office: ESIME-Zacatenco del IPN Det, Edificio 1 2do piso, 07738 Mexico City Mexico

KRAVCHUK, NICHOLAY PETROVICH, physicist, researcher; b. Tver, Russia, Dec. 2, 1950; s. Peter Ignatovich and Aleksandra Ivanovna (Tabolina) K.; m. Tatjana Lvovna Stankeyeva, May 6, 1974; children: Vladislav, Jana. BS, Moscow Engring. Physics Inst., 1974; cand. sci. physico-math., Joint Inst. Nuclear Rsch., 1991. Engr. Joint Inst. Nuclear Rsch., Dubna, Russia, 1974-80; rschr. Joint Inst. Nuclear Rsch., Dubna, 1980—. Contbr. articles to profl. jours. Recipient Silver medal Nat. Econ. Achievement USSR, 1986, Medal Pres. Russia, 1997. Avocations: decorative art, photography, skiing, swimming. Home: Blokhintseva 10-16, 141980 Dubna Moscow, Russia Office: Joint Inst Nuclear Rsch, Jolio Curie 6, 141980 Dubna Moscow, Russia

KRAVCHUK, ROBERT SACHA, management educator, financial consultant; b. Stamford, Conn., July 4, 1955; s. Sacha and Estelle Helen (Wachowski) K.; m. Natalie Marie Kuzma, June 24, 1978; children: Elisabeth Aasta, Timothy Robert. BA, BS cum laude, U. Conn., 1977; MPA, U. Hartford, 1979; MBA, Columbia U., 1980; MA, Syracuse U., 1987, PhD, 1989. Cert. internal auditor, mgmt. acct., group ins. underwriter Conn. Gen. Life Ins. Co., Hartford, 1977-79; sr. control analyst CIGNA Corp., Hartford, 1981-82, cash flow product mgr., 1982-83; assoc. Booz, Allen & Hamilton, N.Y.C., 1984-86; instr. Le Moyne Coll., 1988-89; asst. prof. pub. adminstrn. U. Hartford, 1990-93; undersec. office policy & mgmt. State of Conn., Hartford, 1991-93; resident budget advisor Govt. of Ukraine, 1993-94; fin. advisor Fedn. Bosnia-Hercegovina, Sarajevo, 1995-96; asst. prof. polit. sci. U. Conn., 1994-98; assoc. prof. sch. pub. & environ. affairs Ind. U., Bloomington, 1998—; adj. prof. William Paterson Coll., Wayne, N.J., 1980; adj. instr. Le Moyne Coll., Syracuse, N.Y., 1986-88, U. Hartford, 1989-90. Co-author: Politics and Society in Ukraine, 1999. Mem. State Senate Reps. Office, Hartford Conn., 1989-90. Doctoral fellow Maxwell Sch. Citizenship and Pub. Affairs, Syracuse U., 1986-89. Fellow Life Mgmt. Inst.; mem. Am. Soc. pub. Adminstrn., Am. Polit. Sci. Assn., Govt. Fin. Officers Assn., K. of C. Roman Catholic. Home: 3809 Laura Way Bloomington IN 47401-8827 Office: Ind U Sch Pub & Environ Affairs SPEA 410-D Bloomington IN 47405-1701

KRAVEC, CYNTHIA VALLEN, microbiologist; b. Newark, Sept. 8, 1951; d. William George and Elizabeth Irene (VanAllen) K. BS, Syracuse (N.Y.) U., 1974; MS, Seton Hall U., S. Orange, N.J., 1980; MBA, Monmouth Coll., W. Long Branch, N.J., 1986. Registered microbiologist. Sr. technician GIBCO/Invenex, Millburn, N.J., 1974-79; rsch. scientist Wampole Labs. div. Carter-Wallace Inc., East Windsor, N.J., 1979-90; scientist Roche Diagnostic Systems subsidiary Hoffmann-LaRoche, Inc., Nutley, N.J., 1990-98, Schering-Plough, Kenilworth, N.J., 1998—. Contbr. articles to profl. jours. Mem. Am. Soc. Microbiology, Tissue Culture Assn., Soc. of Indsl. Microbiology. Home: 1006 Coolidge St Westfield NJ 07090-1215 Office: Schering-Plough Rsch Inst 2015 Galloping Hill Rd Kenilworth NJ 07033-1300

KRAVTSOV, ANDREY VLADIMIROVICH, physicist, researcher; b. Leningrad, Russia, Mar. 27, 1939; s. Vladimir Alexandrovich Kravtsov and Natalia Nikolaevna Kholina; m. Inessa Ivanovna Rousetskaya, Dec. 29, 1962 (div. Apr. 1984); children: Alexander, Peter; m. Larissa Nikolaevna Osnovskaya, Feb. 25, 1989. Grad., Leningrad State U., 1961; PhD, Leningrad Nuclear Phys. Inst, Leningrad, 1971. Jr. rschr. St. Petersburg (Russia) Nuc. Physics Inst., 1961-71, rschr., 1971-90, sr. rschr., 1990—. Home: VO 7 Liniya, 199004 St Petersburg Russia Office: St Petersburg Nuc Physics, 188350 Gatchina Russia

KRAVTSOV, VLADIMIR EUGENYEVICH, physicist; b. Corky, USSR, Oct. 17, 1952; s. Eugeny Andreevich and Lyudmila Vladimirovna (Khlebnikova) K.; m. Larissa Nikolaevna Laushkina, Sept. 20, 1977; children: Maria, Ilia. MS, Moscow Inst. Physics Tech., 1976, PhD, 1979; Dr.rer.nat.habil., Ruprecht-Karl U., Heidelberg, Germany, 1993. Scientific staff UNESCO Intrnat., Ctr. Theoretical Physics, Trieste, Italy, 1998—; vis. scientist Inernat. Ctr. Theoretical Physics, Trieste, 1993-95. Contbr. articles to profl. jours. Sr. rsch. fellow Inst. Spectroscopy Russian Acad. Sci., 1979-95, Humboldt fellow, 1989-91, rsch. fellow U. Heidelberg, 1991-93, sr. rsch. fellow Landan Inst. Theoretical Physics, Moscow, 1995—. Office: Internat Ctr Theoret Physic, 11 Strada Costiera, 34100 Trieste Italy

KRAW, GEORGE MARTIN, lawyer, essayist; b. Oakland, Calif., June 17, 1949; s. George and Pauline Dorothy (Herceg) K.; m. Sarah Lee Kenyon, Sept. 3, 1983. BA, U. Calif., Santa Cruz, 1971; student, Lenin Inst., Moscow, 1971; MA, U. Calif., Berkeley, 1974, JD, 1976. Bar: Calif. 1976, U.S. Dist. Ct. (no. dist.) Calif. 1976, U.S. Supreme Ct. 1980, D.C. 1992. Pvt. practice, 1976—; ptnr. Kraw & Kraw, San Jose, 1988—; Mem. ABA, Nat. Assn. Health Lawyers, Inter-Am. Bar Assn., Union Internationale des Avocats. Office: Kraw & Kraw 333 W San Carlos St Ste 1050 San Jose CA 95110-2735

KRAWCZYK, JULIE ANN, mechanical engineer; b. Pitts., Dec. 28, 1970; d. Richard John and JoAnn K. BS in Mech. Engring., U. Pitts., 1993, MS in Mech. Engring. Design engr. Nat. Draeger Inc., Pitts., 1993-95; mech. engr. Westinghouse Air Brake Co., Pitts., 1995-97; equipment engr. SONY Electronics, Inc., Mt. Pleasant, Pa., 1997—. Inventor extend life brake cylinder, compressor inlet value.

KRAYZELBURG, LENNY, Olympic athlete; b. Odessa, Ukraine, Sept. 28, 1975; s. Oleg and Yelena Krayzelburg. Student, UCLA. Recipient Gold medal 100-meter backstroke, 200-meter backstroke, 4 x 100-meter medley (team) Sydney Olympics, 2000, Summer Nats. Phillips Performance award, 1997-99, Gold medal 100-meter backstroke, Silver medal 200-meter backstroke U.S. Open Championships, San Antonio, 1999, Gold medal 100-meter backstroke, Silver medal 200-meter backstroke Janet Evans Invitational, L.A., 2000; named USA Swimming Swimmer of Yr.; broke 3 world records 50-meter backstroke, 100-meter backstroke, 200-meter backstroke Pan Pacific Championships, 1999. Avocations: reading history books, working with computers, basketball, L.A. Lakers. Office: USA Swimming 1 Olympic Plz Colorado Springs CO 80909-5746*

KRČMÉRY, VLADIMIR, JR., medical educator, university dean; b. Bratislava, Slovak Republic, July 23, 1960; s. Vladimir Sen and Helena (Kettner)K; m. Theresea von Brezánjy; children: Michael Maria, Monica Maria, Lucia Theresia. MD, U. Bratislava, Slovak Republic, 1985, PhD, 1990, DSc, 1994. Asst. rschr. U. Bratislava (Slovak Republic) Sch. Medicine, 1985-90; asst. prof. in medicine U. Bratislava Postgrad. Med. Sch., 1990-92; assoc. prof. in medicine and oncology U. Trnava, Slovak Republic, 1992-96; prof. medicine Sch. Pub. Health U. Trnava and Košice, Trnava, 1996—; assoc. dir. S. Postgrad Med. Sch., Bratislava, 1990, dir., 1991-93; vice dean Sch. of Pub. Health, U. Trnava, 1993-94, dean, 1994—. Author: (book) Current Pharmacotherapy, 1994; editor Antiinfective Drugs, Chemotherapy, 1994—. Recipient Infectious Disease award European Soc. Clin. Microbiology, Munich/Taufkirchen, 1990, Immunocompromised Host Soc. award, Boulder, Colo., 1992. Mem. European Soc. Biomodulation and Chemotherapy (v.p. 1994-96, Young Investigator's award 1988), Internat. Soc. Infectious Diseases (coun. mem. 1995-2000), Internat. Soc. Chemotherapy (coun. mem. 1995-98). Roman Catholic. Home: Smetanova 16, 81103 Bratislava Slovakia Office: U Trnava Dean's Office, Hornopotocna 23, 91734 Trnava Slovakia

KREBS, EDWIN GERHARD, biochemistry educator; b. Lansing, Iowa, June 6, 1918; s. William Carl and Louise Helena (Stegeman) K.; m. Virginia Frech, Mar. 10, 1945; children: Sally, Robert, Martha. AB in Chemistry, U. Ill., 1940; MD, Washington U., St. Louis, 1943, DSc (hon.), 1995; DSc honoris causa, U. Geneva, 1979; hon. degree, Med. Coll. Ohio, 1993; DSc (hon.), U. Ind., 1993, U. Ill., 1995; D honoris causa, U. Nat. De Cuyo, 1993. Intern, asst. resident Barnes Hosp., St. Louis, 1944-45; rsch. fellow biol. chemistry Wash. U., St. Louis, 1946-48; prof., chmn. dept. biol. chemistry Sch. Medicine U. Calif., Davis, 1968-76; from asst. prof. to prof. biochemistry U. Wash., Seattle, 1948-66, prof., chmn. dept. pharmacology, 1977-83, prof. biochemistry and pharmacology, 1984-91; investigator, sr. investigator Howard Hughes Med. Inst., Seattle, 1983-90, sr. investigator emeritus, 1991—; mem. Phys. Chemistry Study Sect. NIH, 1963-68, Biochemistry Test Com. Nat. Bd. Med. Examiners, 1968-71, rsch. com. Am. Heart Assn., 1970-74, bd. sci. counselors Nat. Inst. Arthritis, Metabolism and Digestive Diseases, NIH, 1979-84, Internat. Bd. Rev., Alberta Heritage Found. for Med. Rsch., 1986, external adv. com. Weis Ctr. for Rsch., 1987-91; mem. subgroup interconvertible enzymes IUB Spl. Interest Group Metabolic Regulation; internat. adv. bd. Advances in Second Messenger Phosphoprotein Rsch.; external adv. com. Cell Therapeutics Inc., Seattle; adv. bd. Kinetek, Vancouver, B.C. Mem. editorial bd. Jour. Biol. Chemistry, 1965-70; mem. editorial adv. bd. Biochemistry, 1971-76; mem. editorial and adv. bd. Molecular Pharmacology, 1972-77; assoc. editor Jour. Biol. Chemistry, 1971-93; mem. internat. adv. bd. Advances in Cyclic Nucleotide Rsch., 1972—; editorial advisor Molecular and Cellular Biochemistry, 1987—. Recipient Nobel Prize in Medicine or Physiology, 1992, Gairdner Found. award, Toronto, 1978, J.J. Berzelius lectureship, Karolinska Institutet, 1982, George W. Thorn award for sci. excellence, 1983, Sir Frederick Hopkins Meml. lectureship, London, 1984, Rsch. Achievement award Am. Heart Assn., Anaheim, Calif., 1987, 3M Life Scis. award FASEB, New Orleans, 1989, Albert Lasker Basic Med. Rsch. award, 1989, CIBA-GEIGY-

Drew award Drew U., 1991, Steven C. Beering award, Ind. U., 1991, Welch award in chemistry Welch Found., 1991, Louisa Gross Horwitz award Columbia U., 1989, Alumni Achievement award Coll. Liberal Arts and Scis. U. Ill., 1992, Kaul Found. award for excellence, 1996; John Simon Guggenheim fellow, 1959, 66. Mem. NAS, Am. Soc. Biol. Chemists (pres. 1986, ednl. affairs com. 1965-68, councillor 1975-78), Am. Acad. Arts and Scis., Am. Soc. Pharmacology and Exptl. Therapeutics. Achievements include lifelong study of the protein phosphorylation process. Office: U Wash J-681F Health Sci Bldg PO Box 357370 Seattle WA 98195-7370

KREBS, LEO FRANCIS, lawyer; b. Botkins, Ohio, June 9, 1937; s. Eugene L. and Velma L. K.; m. Paula Anne Calvert, Nov. 4, 1961; children: Matthew, Mark, Thomas, Peter. BA, U. Dayton, 1959; JD, Georgetown U., 1965. Bar: Ohio 1966, U.S. Dist. Ct. (so. dist.) Ohio 1966, U.S. Ct. Appeals (6th cir.) 1974, U.S. Supreme Ct. 1975. Legal dep. Montgomery Probate Ct., 1966-68; assoc. Bieser, Greer & Landis, Dayton, Ohio, 1968-74, ptnr., 1974—. Assoc. editor Georgetown Law Rev., 1964-65. Chmn. fin. com. Holy Angels, 1986-98, former chmn., bd. dirs. parish coun.; former bd. dirs. Cath. Social Svcs. Dayton, 1987-90; former mem. Oakwood YMCA Baseball Commn.; coach YMCA baseball. 1st lt. U.S. Army, 1959-62. Fellow Am. Coll. Trial Lawyers, Ohio State Bar Found.; mem. ABA, Ohio State Bar Assn., Ohio Assn. Trial Attys., Dayton Bar Assn., Phi Delta Phi. Avocations: hiking, tennis. Office: Bieser Greer & Landis 6 N Main St Ste 400 Dayton OH 45402-1914

KREBS, PIERRE, philosopher, humanities educator; b. Alger, France, Dec. 20, 1946; s. Hugo and Jeanne (Legrand) K.; divorced; children: Ingrid, Finn. Diploma in law, U. Montpellier, France, 1967; diploma, Higher Sch. Journalism, Paris, 1970, Sch. Higher Social Studies, Paris, 1971; M of Letters, Polit. Sci., History, U. Kassel, Germany, 1982; DEA in French Lit. & Civilization, U. Paris, 1986; PhD, U. Paris-Val de Marne, 1992. Prof. various insts., Germany; lectr. various philosophical and metapolitical theories. Author: From Further the Words, 1978, Writer, Demons and Words: Geometry of the Mystery, 1980, The European Rebirth: A Call for Self-Recognition, 1981, Valéry and Wagner Face to Face: the Measure of Proximity, 1992, The Thule-Seminar: The Spirit of the Future Today in the Dawn of Ethnos, 1994, The New Party of the Spirit: the Thule-Seminar Introduces Itself, 1995, The Struggle for Being: Ethnic Suicide in the Multi-Racial Society of the Judeo-Christian Civilization of the West, or the Ethnocultural Rebirth of Europe in the Organic Democracy of Indo-European Character, 1997, Strategy of the Cultural Revolution, 1997; author, editor: (anthology) The Indestructible Inheritance—Alternatives to the Principle of Equality, I, 1980, The Courage of Identity—Alternatives to the Principle of Equality, 1988; dir. mag. Elemente der Metapolitik; contbr. numerous articles to profl. publs. Avocations: sculpture, parachuting. Office: Thule Seminar eV, Postfach 41 03 47, 34065 Kassel Germany

KREBS, ROCKNE, artist; b. Kansas City, Mo., Dec. 24, 1938; s. Arthur Sanford and Lorine (Fisher) Krebs; m. Nizette Brennan, Oct. 30, 1991; children: Heather, Rockne Brennan, Nizette Cameron. BFA, U. Kans., 1961. Exhbns. include Gallery of Modern Art, Washington, 1968, Corcoran Gallery Art, Washington, 1969, U.S. Pavilion Expo 70, Osaka, Japan, 1970, Art Inst. Chgo., 1970, L.A. County Mus., 1970, New Orleans Mus., 1971, Phila. Mus. Art, 1973, Omni-Internat. Complex, Atlanta, 1973-76, Walker Art Ctr., Mpls., 1974, Art Prk, Lewiston, N.Y., 1975, U.S. Bicentennial Exop Sci. and Tech. Kennedy Space Ctr., Cape Canaveral, Fla., 1976, Balt. Inner Harbor, 1977, Fort Worth Art Mus., 1978, Disneyland Hotel, Anaheim, Calif., 1979, The Mall, Washington, 1980, Cin. Contemporary Art Ctr., 1985, Meml. Art Gallery, Rochester, N.Y., 1987, U. Rochester (N.Y.), 1987, Okla. Art Ctr., 1988; executed laser and neon artwork Urban Scale-Pine Ave. and City of Long Beach, Calif., 1992, laser artwork Pegasus Cloud Projection at Downtown Plz., City of Sacramento, 1993, neon, laser, fiber optic and search lights artwork Red River Bridge, Shreveport, La., 1993-95, animated laser projection Olympics CNN Ctr., Atlanta, 1996. Pioneer use of lasers in art. Rschr, author: The Laserman Letters to Myself, 1996-99. Patentee in field. Lt. USN, 1961-64. E-mail: ripelight@msn.com. Office: PO Box 292 194 Old Mill Ln Burgess VA 22432

KREBS, RYAN ARNOLD, lawyer, physician; b. Cedar Rapids, Iowa, Dec. 22, 1952; s. Donald William and June Maxine (Arnold) K.; m. Kyndal LaCele Gibbins, Aug. 1, 1993; 1 child, Kimberly Suzanne. BS, Stanford U., 1975; MD, Southwestern Med. Sch., 1979; JD, U. Tex., 1994. Bar: Tex. 1994. Internship, residency in internal medicine Univ. Mich., 1979-82; owner Law Offices Ryan Krebs, MD, JD, 1982—. Mem. ATLA, ABA, Tex. Trial Lawyer Assn., Coll. of State Bar Tex. Democrat. Methodist. Avocations: reading, fly fishing. Fax: 512-494-0420. E-mail: rkrebs@raykrebsmdjd.com. Home: 12410 Beartrap Ln Austin TX 78729-7377 Office: 500 W 13th St Austin TX 78701-1827

KREEK, MARY JEANNE, physician; b. Washington; d. Louis Francis and Esperance (Agee) K; m. Robert A. Schaefer, Jan. 24, 1970; children: Robert A., Esperance Anne. D honoris causa, Uppsala U., Sweden, 2000. Med. rschr. NIH, Bethesda, Md., 1957-62; intern, resident Cornell N.Y. Hosp. Med. Ctr., N.Y.C., 1962-65, fellow, 1965-67; instr. medicine Cornell Med. Coll., 1966-67; acad. medicine specializing in internal medicine, endocrinology, gastroenterology, clin. pharmacology N.Y.C., 1966—; mem. staff N.Y.-Presbyn. Hosp-Weill Sch. Medicine of Cornell U., 1968-77, clin. asst. prof., asst. attending physician, now assoc. attending physician, adj. assoc. prof.; ast. prof. Rockefeller U., 1967-72, sr. rsch. assoc., physician, 1972-83, assoc. prof., physician, 1983-94, prof., sr. physician, head of lab., 1994—; head Int. Lab. on Biology of Addictive Diseases, 1975-94, head of lab., 1994—; sr. physician Rockefeller U. Hosp., 1994—; adj. prof. Beijing Med. U., 1996—; mem. gene medicine study sect. NIH, 1973-77; co-chmn. John E. Fogarty (NIH) Internat. Conf. Hepatotoxicity Due to Drugs and Chems., 1977, charter mem. peer rev. oversight group, 1996—; vis. prof. Pahlavi U., Shiraz, Iran, summer 1977; spl. adv. Nat. Inst. Drug Abuse, 1976-86, mem. Nat. Adv. Coun., 1991-95; mem. NIH Peer Rev. Oversight Group, 1996-2000; prin. investigator Rsch. Ctr. Biol. Basis Addictive Diseases, 1987—; mem. gastroenterology adv. com. FDA, 1975-79, 92-96, NIH Gen. Clin. NIH Gen. Rsch. Ctr. Study Sect., 1979-83, chmn., 1982-83; mem. exec. com. Coll. Problems Drug Dependence, 1982-87, 89-94, chmn. exec. com., 1985-87, chair sci. program com., 1991-96; fellow CPDD, 1992—; dir. NIH-NIDA Rsch. Ctr., 1987—. Recipient Borden Rsch. award, 1962, Career Scientist award Health Rsch. Coun. City N.Y., 1974-75, Dole/Nyswander award, Rsch. Scientist award NIH Gen. Clin. sect., 1978—, Mentor of Mentors award Am. Soc. Addiction Medicine, 1995, Assn. for Med. Edn. and Rsch. in Substance Abuse-Betty Ford award for outstanding rsch., 1996, R. Brinkley Smithers Disting. Scholar award Am. Soc. Addiction Medicine, 1999, Nathan B. Eddy award, Lifetime Rsch. award Coll. on Problems of Drug Dependence, 1999. Fellow ACP, Am. Coll. Neuropsychopharmacology, Am. Fedn. for Clin. Rsch.; mem. Shakespeare Soc. of Wellesley, Am. Gastroent. Assn., N.Y. Gastroent. Assn. (pres. 1987), Endocrine Soc., Am. Assn. Study Liver Diseases, Internat. Assn. Study Liver, Internat. Narcotic Rsch. Conf. Group (exec. com. 1993-97), Rsch. Soc. on Alcoholism, Soc. on Neurosci., Phi Beta Kappa, Sigma Xi. Home: 1175 York Ave New York NY 10021-7169 Office: Rockefeller U New York NY 10021

KREHL, PETER OTTO KLAUS, electrical engineer; b. Berlin-Charlottenburg, Germany, Aug. 29, 1940; s. Erich Gottlieb and Hildegard Martha (Gunkel) K. Diploma, Tech. U. Berlin, 1966, PhD in Elec. Engring., 1969. Free-lance collaborator, patent atty. Berlin/London, 1965-72; instr. Tech. U. Berlin, 1967-72; vis. scientist Stanford Rsch. Inst., Menlo Park, Calif., 1972-74; cons. rschr. Old Dominion U., Norfolk, Va., 1987; staff scientist Ernst-Mach-Inst. der Fraunhofer-Gesellschaft, Freiburg, Germany, 1974—; cons. Naval Postgrad. Sch. Monterey, Calif., 1973-74; dir. Pulstec Instrumente GmbH, Freiburg, 1980-83; lectr. Tech. Coll., Offenburg, Germany, 1988-91; cons. U. Ulm, Germany, 1995-98. Contbr. chpt. to book, articles to profl. jours.; inventor in field. Recipient Fulbright scholarship German Fulbright Commn., Bad Godesberg, 1972-74, medal Tech. U. Berlin, 1966. Mem. British Assn. High-Speed Photography. Avocations: riding, driving, literature, history of natural sciences. Home: Im Lehle 34, 79331 Nimburg Baden, Germany Office: Ernst-Mach-Institut, Inst Kurzzzeitdynamik, 79104 Freiburg Baden, Germany

KREIG, ANDREW THOMAS, trade association executive; b. Chgo., Feb. 28, 1949; s. Albert Arthur and Margaret Theresa (Baltzell) K. AB, Cornell U., 1970; MSL, Yale U., 1983; JD, U. Chgo., 1990. Bar: D.C. 1991, Mass. 1991, Ill. 1991. Writer, editor Hartford (Conn.) Courant, 1970-84; media dir. Conn. House Spkr., Hartford, 1984; freelance author, journalist, lectr. Hartford and Chgo., 1985-89; law clk. U.S. Dist. Judge Mark L. Wolf, Boston, 1990-91; assoc. Latham & Watkins, Washington, 1991-93; v.p., comms. dir. Wireless Comms. Assn. Internat., Inc., Washington, 1993-96, v.p., gen. counsel, 1996, pres., 1997—; ethics com. Soc. Profl. Journalists, 1987-90. Author: Spiked: How Chain Management, 1987, 2d edit., 1988; editor Spectrum, 1994—; bd. editors Pvt. & Wireless Cable, 1994—, Wireless Internat., 1996—; contbr. articles to profl. jours. V.p. Residences Market Square, Washington, 1993-98; co-chair Fixed Wirless Com. Coalition, 2000—. Ford Found. fellow Yale Law Sch., New Haven, 1982-83. Mem. Fed. Com. Bar Assn. (legis. com.). Home: PH8 701 Pennsylvania Ave NW Washington DC 20004-2608 Office: Wireless Comms Assn Ste 810 1140 Connecticut Ave NW Washington DC 20036-4010

KREINER, ANDRÉS JUAN, physicist, researcher; b. Buenos Aires, Sept. 14, 1950; s. Ervin and Ingeborg Rosemarie (Genrich) K.; m. Ana María Llois, Feb. 21, 1975; children: Javier Alejandro, Victoria Carolina. M., U. Buenos Aires, 1973; PhD in Physics, U. Munich, 1978. Researcher Argentine Atomic Energy Commn., Buenos Aires, 1974—; vis. scientist Brookhaven Nat. Lab., Upton, N.Y., 1980-81, rsch. assoc., 1985; invited full prof. U. Paris XI, 1987; rsch. dir. Nuclear Rsch. Ctr., Strasbourg, France, 1988; vis. scientist Joint Inst. for Heavy Ions Rsch. ORNL, Oak Ridge, Tenn., 1990; invited full prof. U. Paris XI, 1991; fellow Argentine Rsch. Coun., Buenos Aires, 1983—; assoc. prof. U. Buenos Aires, 1984-93, full prof., 1993—; dir. Sch. Sci. and Tech. Nat. U. San Martin, 1995—; cons. Argentine Rsch. Coun., Buenos Aires, 1984, coord. phys. adv. com., 1989; chmn. phys. dept. Argentine Atomic Energy Commn., Buenos Aires, 1989—. Contbr. numerous articles to profl. jours. Fellow Humboldt Found., 1987; rsch. grantee Antorchas Found., Argentine, 1990; recipient 1st prize in physics Coca Cola Found., 1982, Spl. Mention Noriega-Morales Prize OAS, 1986, 1st prize in exptl. physics NAS, 1995; Honor diploma In Sci. and Tech. Konex Found., 1993. Mem. Am. Phys. Soc., Argentine Phys. Assn., N.Y. Acad. Scis. Home: Del Kaiser 2230, 1682 Martín Coronado Argentina Office: Comision Nacional Energia, Atomica Av Libertador 8250, 1429 Buenos Aires Argentina

KREINER, ARMIN, theology educator; b. Friedrichshafen, Germany, June 4, 1954; s. Wenzel and Luise (Schindele) K.; m. Heidemarie Müller, July 31, 1981. MA, U. Munich, 1981, PhD, 1985, postgrad., 1991. Asst. instr. U. Munich, 1981-91, lectr., 1991-94; prof. theology U. Mainz, Germany, 1995—. Author: The End of Truth?, 1992, God and Evil, 1994, God in Suffering, 1997; co-author: (TV series) Suffering, 1994; editor: Religious Experience and Reflexion, 1993; co-editor: (series) Studies in Fundamental Theology and Philosophy of Religion, 1997—; also articles. Mem. Brit. Soc. for Philosophy of Religion. Roman Catholic. Office: U Mainz, Saarstrasse, D-55099 Mainz Germany

KREISER, FRANK DAVID, real estate executive; b. Sept. 20, 1930; s. Harry D. and Olive W. (Quist) K.; m. Patricia Williams, Aug. 23, 1973; children: Sally, Frank David, Susan, Paul, Mark, Patti, Richard. Student, U. Minn., 1950-51. Cert. residential broker. Real estate executive, 1960—; founder, owner Frank Kreiser Real Estate, Inc., Mpls., 1966-89, pres., 1979—; owner F. & P.K. Properties, 1973—; membership chmn. RELO, 1987-88; br. mgr. Merrill Lynch Realty, 1989-90, br. mgr., v.p. Burnet Realty, 1990-97; broker Coldwell Banker, 1998—; ptnr., founder B & K Properties Co., Mpls., 1976-96; chmn. bd., founder Transfer Location Corp., Atlanta, 1979-84 . With U.S. Army, 1948-50, Korea. Mem. Nat. Assn. Realtors, Mpls. Bd. Realtors (dir. 1972), Minn. Assn. Realtors, Realtors Nat. Mktg. Inst., Minn. Multi Housing Assn., Edina C. of C., 50th France Bus. Assn. (pres. 2000—), Edina Country Club. Lutheran. Address: 5036 France Ave S Minneapolis MN 55410-2033

KREIZINGER, LOREEN L, lawyer, nurse; b. Syracuse, N.Y., Apr. 16, 1959; d. David F. and Blanche L. (Heaney) Mosher; m. Kenneth R. Kreizinger, Aug. 30, 1985; 1 child, Katelyn Rose. Grad. in nursing, Crouse-Irving Meml. Hosp., Syracuse, 1981; BS in Bus. with honors, Nova U., 1987, JD, 1990. Bar: Fla. 1990; RN, N.Y., Fla. Nurse ICU and infants neonatal unit, Syracuse, Ft. Lauderdale, Fla. 1979-86; med. malpractice cons. Krupnick, Campbell et al, Ft.Lauderdale, 1986-90, assoc., 1990-92, of counsel, 1992—; pvt. practice, Ft.Lauderdale, 1992—; instr. adult intensive care Crouse-Irving Meml. Hosp. 1981-82; adj. prof. Nova U., Ft. Lauderdale, 1994—; summer instr. legal aspects of nursing Fla. Bd. Nursing, 1990-92; guest spkr. TV talk show Med. Malpractice, 1991. Sec., bd. dirs. Shepherd Care Ministries, Hollywood, Fla., 1993, 94; mem. choir 1st Bapt. Ch. Ft. Lauderdale, 1994—. Mem. ABA (law and medicine com. 1990—), FBA, ATLA (spl. L-Trytophen com. 1991-94), Fla. Bar Assn., Fla. Assn. Women Lawyers, Fla. Acad. Trial Lawyers, Broward County Women Lawyers Assn., Broward County Trial Lawyers Assn., Phi Alpha Delta. Republican. Avocations: sailing, snow skiing, rollerblading. Office: 515 E Las Olas Blvd Ste 1150 Fort Lauderdale FL 33301-2281

KREJCI, ALEŠ, physicist, travel industry consultant; b. Brno, Czech Republic, Nov. 28, 1957; s. František A. and Věra (Nováková) K.; m. Hana Hrdlickova, Nov. 27, 1997; 1 child, Jana. MSc, Charles U., Prague, Czech Republic, 1981, RNDr., 1982; PhD, Czechoslovak Acad. Scis., Prague, 1988. Postdoctoral fellow Inst. Plasma Physics, Prague, 1984-87, rschr., 1988-90, project leader, 1991-96; dep. Czech Rep. Internat. Ctr. for Dense Magnetised Plasma UNESCO, 1992-96; dir. pub. relation agy. World Trend, Prague, 1996—; dep. Czech Rep. Internat. Ctr. for Dense Magnetised Plasma, UNESCO, 1992-96; internat. mgr. MADI Travel Fairs, Prague, 1995—. Author: Across the USA with Empty Pocket, 1991; editor Tourism Courier, 1996—, Czech Travel News, 1998—, www.travel-fairs.com, 2000—; contbr. over 65 articles to profl. jours. Recipient Sci. Project award Acad. Scis. of Czech Republic, 1991; grantee Czech Republic, 1994. Mem. Czech Phys. Soc. (sec. 1993-96), Fedn. Int. Journalistes et Écrivains du Tourisme (bd. of Czech Republic), Pacific Asia Travel Assn. (Czech/Slovak chpt., chmn. 1999—). Avocations: travel, Buddhist art, photography, public lectures, journalism. Home and Office: World Trend, Na Hřebenkách 65, CZ-15000 Prague 5, Czech Republic

KREJCI, LUDEK, mechanical engineer; b. Zeretice, Czech Republic, Mar. 13, 1930; s. Josef and Marie (Junek) K.; m. Ruzena Doubek, July 30, 1965. MA, Czech Tech. U., 1953; PhD, Czech Acad. Scis., 1961. Rsch. asst. Inst. Thermomechanics Acad. Sci. of Czech Republic, Prague, 1953-57, SKODA Turbine Divsn., Pilsen, Czech Republic, 1958-59; rsch. scientist Inst. Thermomechanics Acad. Sci. of Czech Republic, 1960-68, sr. rsch. scientist, 1968-88, prin. rsch. scientist, 1989-92, cons., 1993—; cons. Czech Tech. U., 1958—, Heat and Mass Transfer Inst. Acad. Sci. Belarus, Minsk, 1965-78, SKODA Rsch. Inst., 1960—; vis. scientist U. Minn. Dept. Mech. Engring., Mpls., 1992. Author: Heat Transfer Processes in the Plasma Torch, 1974; contbr. articles to profl. jours. Mem. cultural com. Civic Forum Coord. Ctr., Prague, 1989-91; bd. dirs. Coll. Encouragement Independent Sci. and Cultural Activities, Prague, 1989—; mem. Czech Soc. Arts and Scis., Washington and Prague, 1992—. Fellow Czech Soc. Mechanics; mem. N.Y. Acad. Scis., Czech Soc. History of Sci. & Tech., Rotary. Roman Catholic. Avocations: sci. and tech. history, art history, gardening, travel, hiking. Home: Lipova 388, CZ-50732 Kopidlno Czech Republic Office: Inst Thermomechanics, Dolejskova 5, 18200 Prague Czech Republic

KREJS, FRANZ REINHARD, venture capital executive; b. Waidhofen, Austria, Sept. 26, 1941; s. Philip and Margarita (Wobora) K. divorced; 1 child, Christiane. Diploma, Tech. U. Vienna, Austria, 1967; MS, U. Pa., 1969, PhD, 1972. Rsch. assoc. U. Wash., Seattle, 1972-74, U. Pa., Phila., 1975-78; project mgr. WARC, Phila., 1978-80, Innova, Vienna, 1980-82, Fgg, Vienna, 1982-83; Techno Venture Mgmt., Munich, Germany, 1983-85; pres. Horizonte Venture Mgmt., Vienna and Ljubljana, Sarajevo, 1985—; cons. Unido, Vienna, 1982-83. Contbr. articles to profl. jours. Fellow Haney Found, 1970-72, U. Pa., 1969-70. Mem. Am. Phys. Soc., N.Y. Acad. Sci., Licensing Exec. Soc. Home: Lustkandlgasse 12/12, A-1090 Vienna Austria Office: Horizonte Venture Mgmt, Bauernmarkt 6, A-1010 Vienna Austria

KREJSEK, JAN, immunologist, allergist, educator; b. Nove Mesto na Morave, Czech Republic, Dec. 2, 1958; s. Jan and Anezka (Chrastova) K.; m. Vera Novotna, July 17, 1982; children: Vera, Jan, Silvie. MSc, Purkyne's U. Sci., Brno, Czech Republic, 1982; PhD, Charles U., Prague, Czech Republic, 1993. Bd. cert. microbiology and immunology. Rsch. worker Dist. Occupational Medicine Sta., Hradec Kralove, Czech Republic, 1982-85; lectr. Charles U. Sch. Medicine, Hradec Kralove, 1986-96, asst. prof. immunology, 1996—; sr. cons. Inst. Clin. Immunology, Hradec Kralove, 1991. Contbr. articles to profl. jours. Home: Pod Haltyrem 125, 50009 Hradec Kralove Czech Republic Office: Charles U Sch Medicine, Inst Clin Immunol & Allergy, 50005 Hradec Kralove Czech Republic

KREKEL, HENK-GUUS, management consulting company executive; b. Rotterdam, The Netherlands, May 8, 1949; s. Henk and Annemarie (Stöve) K.; m. Ria Vos, Aug. 20, 1976; children: Angelina, Nicole, Annefleur. D in Bus. Econs., Erasmus U., Rotterdam, The Netherlands, 1975, chartered acct., 1980. Ptnr. Peat Marwick Nederland, The Hague, 1976-87; dir. KPMG Holding, Amsterdam and Utrecht, The Netherlands, 1987—; dir. pers. and tng. KPMG, 1992-95, mem. internat. human resources com., 1992-96, chmn. industry group, 1994-96, mem. world class fin. group, 1996—. Mem. bd. supervisory dirs. Drechtsteden Ziekenhuis, Dordrecht, 1991-97. Capt. Dutch Army, 1975-96. Mem. Dutch Inst. Chartered Accts. (registered acct.), Nivra Amsterdam, Kiwanis. Avocations: soccer, tennis, golf, running, biking. Home: Volkerak 8, 3332 VE Zwyndrecht The Netherlands Office: KPMG Consulting NV, Vijzelmolenlaan 4, 3447 GX Woerden The Netherlands

KRELL, ANDREAS, physicist, ceramics engineering researcher; b. Dresden, Saxony, Germany, Feb. 9, 1952; s. Karl-Heinz and Margarethe (Mueldner) K.; m. Elisabeth Porzel, 1981; children: Katherina, Christiane. Diploma in physics, Dresden (Germany) U., 1974; PhD, Acad. Scis., Berlin, 1982, Habilitation, 1987. Rschr. Acad. Scis., Dresden, 1974-84, head rsch. group, 1984-90; head oxide ceramics rsch. group Inst. Ceramic Technologies and Materials Rsch., Dresden, 1990-92; head rsch. group, head dept. materials Fraunhofer-IKTS, Dresden, 1992—; tenor in Dresden Philharm. Chamber Choir. Contbr. more than 85 articles on microstructural tailoring and testing of submicron ceramics to profl. jours. including Am. Ceramics Soc., Materials Sci. Engring., Jour. Materials Sci., Wear, among others; patentee in nanotechnology and processing for mfg. ceramic tools, implants, chem. devices, filters, armor, transparent high-strength parts, coatings. Recipient Fraunhofer award Fraunhofer Soc., 1996. Mem. German Ceramic Soc., Am. Ceramic Soc., European Structural Integrity Soc. Lutheran. Fax: 49 351 2553 600. E-mail: krell@ikts.fgh.de. Office: Fraunhofer-Inst Ceram Tech, Winterbergstrasse 28, D-01277 Dresden Germany

KRELL, FRANK-THORSTEN, zoologist, researcher; b. Stuttgart, Germany, Aug. 17, 1966; s. Karlheinz Friedrich and Pia (Müller) K. Diploma in biology, Tübingen (Germany) U., 1992, Dr.rer.nat., 1996. Sci. employee U. Würzburg, Germany, 1995-98; guest scientist Alexander Koenig Rsch. Inst., Bonn, Germany, 1999—; rsch. entomologist Natural History Mus., London, 2000—; guest scientist Humboldt U., Berlin, 1998—. Co-author: Die Käfer Mitteleuropas, vol. 13, 1992, vol. 15, 1998, L3, 1996, L4, 1997; contbr. articles to profl. jours. Mem. Entomological Soc. Am., Soc. Systematic Biologists, Deutsche Zoologische Gesellschaft. Home: 9 Pleasance Rd, D-53347 Orpington BR5 3AR, England Office: Natural History Mus, Dept Entomology Cromwell Rd, D-53113 London SW7 5BD, England

KREMENTZ, JILL, photographer, author; b. N.Y.C., Feb. 19, 1940; d. Walter and Virginia (Hyde) K.; m. Kurt Vonnegut, Jr., Nov. 1979; 1 child, Lily. Student, Drew U., 1958-59; attended Art Students League. With Harper's Bazaar mag., 1959-60, Glamour mag., 1960-61; pub. relations staff Indian Industries Fair, New Delhi, 1961; reporter Show mag., 1962-64; staff photographer N.Y. Herald Tribune, 1964-65, staff photographer Vietnam, 1965-66; assoc. editor Status-Diplomat mag., 1966-67; contbg. editor N.Y. mag., 1967-68; corr. Time-Life Inc., 1969-70; contbg. photographer People mag., 1974—. Contbr. photography numerous U.S. and fgn. periodicals.; one-woman photography shows Madison (Wis.) Art Center, 1973, U. Mass., Boston, 1974, Nikon Gallery, 1974, Del. Art Mus., Wilmington, 1975, Newark Mus., 1991; Staley-Wise Gallery, 1996, The Margaret Mitchell House, Atlanta, 1990; represented in permanent collections Mus. Modern Art, Library of Congress; photographer: The Face of South Vietnam (text by Dean Brelis), 1968, Words and Their Masters (text by Israel Shenker), 1974; photographer, author: Sweet Pea: A Black Girl Growing Up in the Rural South (foreword by Margaret Mead), 1969, A Very Young Dancer, 1976, A Very Young Rider, 1977, A Very Young Gymnast, 1978, A Very Young Circus Flyer, 1979, A Very Young Skater, 1979, The Writer's Image, 1980, How It Feels When a Parent Dies, 1981, How It Feels to be Adopted, 1982, How It Feels When Parents Divorce, 1984, The Fun of Cooking, 1985, Lily Goes to the Playground, 1986, Jack Goes to the Beach, 1986, Katherine Goes to Nursery School, 1986, Jamie Goes on an Airplane, 1986, Tanya Goes to the Dentist, 1986, Benjy Goes to a Restaurant, 1986, Holly's Farm Animals, 1986, Zachary Goes to the Zoo, 1986, A Visit to Washington, D.C., 1987, How It Feels to Fight For Your Life, 1989, A Very Young Skier, 1990, A Very Young Musician, 1990, A Very Young Gardener, 1990, A Very Young Actress, 1991, How It Feels to Live With a Physical Disability, 1992, The Writer's Desk, 1996, The Jewish Writer, 1998. Recipient Nonfiction award Washington Post/Children's Book Guild, 1984, ACCH Joan Fassler Meml. Book award, 1990, Equality, Dignity, Independence award Nat. Easter Seals, 1992. Mem. PEN. Address: care Alfred A Knopf Inc 201 E 50th St New York NY 10022-7703

KREMER, CARLOS, chemist; b. Montevideo, Uruguay, Mar. 27, 1961; s. Leopoldo Rodolfo and Lila (Antunez) K.; m. Maria Teresa Hermida, Dec. 18, 1986; children: Christian, Erik. BS, Faculty Chemistry, Montevideo, Uruguay, 1984, MS, 1986, PhD, 1996. Teaching asst. U. Uruguay, 1984-90, prof. inorganic chemistry, 1990—. Contbr. articles to profl. jours. Fellow TWAS, IAEA; mem. N.Y. Acad. Scis. Achievements include development of technetium, rhenium and samarium complexes for radiopharmaceuticals. Home: Rivera 2272/801, 11200 Montevideo Uruguay Office: Faculty Chemistry, Faculty of Chemistry, G Flores 2124 CC 1157, Montevideo Uruguay

KREMER, JEANNETTE MARGUERITE, information science consultant, retired educator; b. Belo Horizonte, Brazil, July 6, 1946; d. François Joseph and Marguerite (Melchior) K. Bachelor's degree, Fed. U. Minas Gerais, Belo Horizonte, 1968; diploma 3d degree, U. Nancy, France, 1967; MS, U. Ill., 1977, PhD, 1980. Cert. in libr. and info. sci. Libr. Fed. U. Minas Gerais, Belo Horizonte, 1968-69, prof., 1980-95, rschr., cons., 1995—; libr. Usinas Siderurgicas Minas Gerais, Belo Horizonte, 1969-76; vice-dir. libr. sch. Fed. U. Minas Gerais, Belo Horizonte, 1990-94; cons. Coordenação de Aperfeiçoamento de Pessoal de Nível Superior-Capes, Brasília, Brazil, 1981-98, Conselho Nacional do Desenvolvimento Científico e Tecnológico-CNPq, Brasília, 1987-2000. Editor: Revista da Escola Biblioteconomia da Fed. U. Minas Gerais, 1988-91; contbr. articles to profl. jours. Recipient Cert. of Appreciation, Kiwanis Club of Champaign, 1979, Berner-Nash award for outstanding doctoral dissertation. Mem. Sociedade Brasileira Para o Progresso da Ciência, Beta Phi Mu, Phi Kappa Phi. Roman Catholic. Avocations: traveling, photography. Home: Rua Eduardo Porto 572, Cidade Jardim, 30380060 Belo Horizonte Brazil

KREMER, KURT, research scientist, administrator; b. Kapellensüng, Germany, June 17, 1956; m. Claudia Kurtenbach; 4 children. Diploma in physics, U. Cologne, Germany, 1980; PhD in Physics, U. Mainz, Germany, 1983. Cert. in theoretical physics of soft matter, computer simulations. Fellow Exxon Corp., Annandale, N.J., 1984-85; asst. prof. U. Mainz, 1986-88; sr. staff scientist FZ, Jülich, Germany, 1988-95; dir. Max-Planck-Inst. for Polymer Rsch., Mainz, 1995—; Whitby lectr. U. Akron, 1999; G.T. Piercy Disting. Prof., U. Minn., 1991. Contbr. chpts. to books, articles to profl. jours. Mem. German Phys. Soc. (Walter-Schottky prize 1992), Deutscher Hochschulverband. Office: Max-Planck-Inst Polymer Res, PO Box 3148, 55021 Mainz Germany

KREMER-HAYON, LYA, education educator, researcher; b. Bucharest, Romania, June 24, 1932; d. Joshua and Naomi (Brayer) Yaron; m. Eytan Kremen, Aug. 12, 1954 (div. 1980); m. Jacob Hayon, Jan. 31, 1981; children:

Eldad, Nadav. Grad., State Coll., Haifa, Israel, 1954; BSc, U. Minn., Mpls., 1961; MA, U. Tel-Aviv, 1972; PhD, Jerusalem U., 1997. Student tchr. supr. Tchrs. Coll., Haifa, 1952-58, lectr., vice prin., 1959-71; lectr. U. Haifa, 1972—, head tchr. edn. dept., 1978-83, head edn. dept., 1986-89, head Ctr. Ednl. Adminstrn., 1990—; cons. Ministry of Edn., Jerusalem, 1980-85. Editor Megamoth, Jour. Ednl. Adminstrn. Recipient Israeli prize for tchr. edn. Ministry of Edn., 1970. Avocations: music, bridge.

KREMERY, VLADIMIR CYRILLUS, oncologist, educator; b. Bratislava, Slovakia, July 23, 1960; s. Vladimir and Helena (Kettner) Krcmery; m. Theresia Maria Von Brezanyi, Nov. 10, 1986; children: Michael, Monica, Lucy, Veronica. MD, Comenius U., Bratislava, 1985, PhD, 1991; DSc, Comenius U., 1993; FRCP, Royal Coll. Physicians, Edinbourgh, 1999. Bd. exam in medicine oncology, infectious diseases. Asst. prof. Commen U. Bratislava, 1993; vis. prof. U. Scranton, Pa., 1995; prof. U. Kosice, Slovaka, 1996, Masar U. Brno, Czech Republic, 1997. Author: (book) Manual of Autonomical Therapy, 1993, 2d 1999. Lt. Slovak Med. Corps. Recipient Young investigators award, Gr. Satta Meml. award, U. Verona, Italy, 1997. Fellow Infectious Diseases Soc. Am., Royal Soc. Health, Royal Coll. Physicians. Roman Catholic. Office: U Tvnava Sch Pub Health, 91743 Tvnava Slovika

KREMIN, DAVID KEITH, lawyer; b. Chgo.; s. Aaron and Rose (Doane) K. BS, U. Ill., 1977; JD with highest honors, ITT, 1983. Bar: Ill. 1983, U.S. Dist. Ct. (no. dist.) Ill. 1983. Assoc. Lenard, Ring & Assocs., Chgo., Rosenfeld, Rotenberg, et al., Chgo.; ptnr. David K. Kremin & Assocs., P.C., Chgo.; judge advocate Belmont Yacht Club, Chgo.; arbitrator Ill. Cir. Ct., Chgo.; instr. Roosevelt U. Bd. dirs. Old Town Chamber. Mem. ATLA, Ill. Trial Lawyers Assn., Internat. Bar Assn., Nat. Lawyers Assn., Ill. Bar Assn., Chgo. Bar Assn., Decalogue Soc. Fax: 312 456-9900. Office: David K Kremin & Assocs 77 W Washington St Ste 1720 Chicago IL 60602-2903

KREMPEL, ROGER ERNEST, public works management consultant; b. Oct. 8, 1926; s. Henry and Clara Krempel; m. Shirley Ann Gray, June 16, 1948, children: John, Sara, Peter. Student, Ripon Coll., 1944, Stanford U., 1945; BCE, U. Wis., Madison, 1950. Registered profl. engr., Wis., Colo.; registered land surveyor, Wis. Asst. city engr. Manitowoc, Wis., 1950-51; city engr. dir. pub. works Janesville, Wis., 1951-75; dir. water utilities, pub. works Ft. Collins, Colo., 1975-84; dir. natural resources, streets and stormwater utilities Ft. Collins, 1984-88; faculty affiliate Internat. Sch. for Water Resources Colo. State U.; pub. works mgmt. cons., 1988—; lectr. various univ., coll., nat. confs. and seminars. Contbr. numerous articles to profl. publs. Past pres. bd. Janesville YMCA. With U.S. Army, 1944-46. Recipient numerous tech. and profl. awards, Disting. Svc. citation U. Wis. Coll. Engring., 1989, Outstanding Leadership and Cmty. Devel. award Janesville C. of C., 1972. Fellow ASCE (life, Gov. Civil Engr. award 1984, Wis. Outstanding Civil Engring. Achievement award 1970); mem. NSPE, ASCE (Mgmt. award 1990), Am. Water Works Assn. (life), Am. Pub. Works Assn. (life mem., past pres. Colo. and Wis. chpts., past mem. rsch. found., Man of Yr. 1971, Nichols award 1984, Swearingen award 1988), Pub. Works Hist. Soc. (pres. 1993-95), Wis. Soc. Profl. Engrs. (past pres.), Am. Acad. Environ. Engrs. (diplomate 1982-91), Colo. Engrs. Coun. (pres. 1990-91, honor award 1989).

KRENEK, MARY LOUISE, political science researcher, educator; b. Wharton, Tex., Dec. 8, 1951; d. George P. Jr. and Vlasta (Zahn) Krenek. AA, Wharton County Jr. Coll., 1972; BA, Tex. A&I U., Corpus Christi, 1974; MA, St. Mary's U., San Antonio, 1992; Czech lang. cert., Charles U., Prague, Czech Republic, 1994. Cert. secondary and elem. tchr., Tex. Polygraph examiner San Antonio, 1979-81; ind. contractor market, polit. and social rsch. San Antonio and Houston, 1982—; substitute tchr., tchr. San Antonio Ind. Sch. Dist., 1981-82, Houston Ind. Sch. Dist., 1991-98; instr. govt. Wharton County Jr. Coll., 1997-99; assoc. J.C. Penney Co., Inc., 1994-2000; with Am. Acad. Excellence, Houston, 2000. Del. Tex. Dem. Conv., 1971-72. 1st lt. U.S. Army, 1975-78, lt. col. USAR, 1978—. Mem. CESAT, Houston Czech Cultural Ctr., Nat. Assn. of Self-Employed, Res. Officers Assn. (sec.-treas. Alamo chpt., jr. v.p. Dept. Tex., sec. Greater Houston chpt., ROTC coord.), Wharton County Hist. Mus. Assn. (assoc.), Am. Polit. Sci. Assn., Women in Mil. Svc. for Am. Meml. Found. (charter), St. Mary's U. Alumni Assn., Am. Legion, Pi Sigma Alpha. Roman Catholic. Avocations: reading, writing, travel. Home: 10502 Fountain Lake Dr Stafford TX 77477-3711 also: PO Box 310 Egypt TX 77436-0310

KREPPNER, KURT, research scientist; b. Kitzingen, Bavaria, Germany, Mar. 8, 1938; s. Philipp and Edith (Loschky) K.; m. Angelika Maria Cosack, Sept. 8, 1964; children: Jascha, Janoscha, Jana. Diploma, U. Hamburg, Germany, 1963; PhD, U. Darmstadt, Germany, 1969. Asst. prof. Tech. U., Berlin, 1964-66, U. Darmstadt, Germany, 1966-68; rsch. scientist Max Planck Inst., Berlin, 1968-75, sr. rsch. scientist, 1975—; cons. NDR, Hamburg, 1974-95, Mich. State U., East Lansing, 1993-95, Family Inst., Vehlefanz, Germany, 1998—. Author: Problems of Measuring in Social Sciences, 1975; editor: Family Systems, 1989. Mem. Soc. Rsch. Child Devel., Soc. Rsch. Adolescence, Internat. Soc. for Study Behavioral Devel. Avocation: music. Home: Veronikasteig 2, D-14163 Berlin Germany Office: Max Planck Inst, Lentzeallee 94, D-14195 Berlin Germany

KREPS, JUANITA MORRIS, economics educator, former government official; b. Lynch, Ky., Jan. 11, 1921; d. Elmer M. and Cenia (Blair) Morris; m. Clifton H. Kreps, Jr., Aug. 11, 1944; children: Sarah, Laura, Clifton. AB, Berea Coll., 1942; MA, Duke U., 1944; PhD, 1948; LLD (hon.), Bryant Coll., 1972, U. N.C. at Chapel Hill, 1973, Tulane U., Colgate U., 1980, Trinity Coll., 1981, U. Rochester, Grove City Coll., 1984, Davidson Coll., 1990, Lenoir-Rhyne Coll., 1991, U. Notre Dame, 1992, Duke U., 1993; LittD (hon.), Cornell Coll., 1973, Western Md. Coll., 1982; LHD (hon.), Denison U., 1973, U. Ky., Queens Coll., St. Lawrence U., 1975, Wheaton Coll., 1976, Claremont Grad. Sch., Berea Coll., 1979. Instr. econs. Denison U., 1945-46, asst. prof., 1948-50; mem. faculty Duke U., 1955-77, assoc. prof., 1962-68, prof. econs., 1968-77, James B. Duke prof., 1972-77, James B. Duke prof. emerita, 1979—, asst. provost, 1969-72, v.p., 1973-77, v.p. emerita, 1979—; sec. U.S. Dept. Commerce, 1977-79; mem. adv. com. Congl. Commn. for the Future of Worker Mgmt. Rels., Secs. of Commerce and Labor, 1993-94. Author: (with C.E. Ferguson) Principles of Economics, 2d rev. edit, 1965, Lifetime Allocation of Work and Income, 1971, Sex in the Marketplace: American Women at Work, 1971, Women and the American Economy, 1976; co-author: (with Richard Perlman and Gerald Somers) Contemporary Labor Economics, 1973; Editor: Employment, Income and Retirement Problems of the Aged, 1963, Technology, Manpower and Retirement Policy, 1966, Sex, Age and Work, 1975. Bd. dirs. Am. Coun. on Germany, Rsch. Triangle Found., Ednl. Testing Svc., 1972-77; mem. Nat. Manpower Policy Task Force; trustee Berea Coll., 1972-78, 80-98, Duke Endowment, 1979—, Nat. Humanities Ctr., 1983-86, U. N.C., Wilmington, 1993—, HumRRO, 1980-83, Coun. Fgn. Rels., 1983-89, Kenan Inst. Pvt. Enterprise of U. N.C., Chapel Hill, 1995—; pres. bd. overseers Tchrs. Ins. and Annuity Assn., 1992-96; bd. dirs. TIAA, 1968-72, 85-96, Coll. Retirement Equities Fund, 1972-77. Named to Presl. Commn. on Nat. Agenda for the 80's, 1979; recipient N.C. Pub. Svc. award, 1976, Stephen Wise award, 1978, Woman of Yr. award Ladies Home Jour., 1978, Duke U. Alumni award, 1983, Haskins award Coll. Bus. and Pub. Adminstrn., NYU, 1984, First Corp. Governance award Nat. Assn. Corp. Dirs., 1987, Dir.'s Choice Leadership award Nat. Women's Econ. Alliance Found., 1987, Disting. Meritorious Svc. medal Duke U. Alumni, 1987. Fellow Gerontol. Soc. (v.p. 1971-72), Am. Acad. Arts and Scis.; mem. AAUP, AAUW (Achievement award 1981), Am. Econ. Assn. (v.p. 1983-84), So. Econ. Assn. (pres. 1975-76), Indsl. Rels. Rsch. Assn. (exec. com.). Office: Duke U 115 E Duke Bldg Durham NC 27708-0768

KRESINA, THOMAS FRANCIS, immunologist, educator, administrator; b. Balt., June 18, 1954; s. Thomas Francis and Bertha (Miller) K.; m. Marilee Keim, June 10, 1979 (div. 1991); children: Rachel Ann, Jennifer Lynn, Rebecca Marie; m. Laura Cheever June 12, 1993. BS, Cath. U. Am., 1975; PhD, U. Ala., Birmingham, 1979; MA, Brown U., 1987. Postdoctoral fellow Brandeis U., Waltham, Mass., 1980-82; asst. prof. Case Western Res. U., Cleve., 1982-87; assoc. prof. dept. medicine Brown U., Providence, R.I., 1987-93; dir. Liver, Biliary and Pancreas Disease programs, AIDS program Nat. Inst. Diabetes and Digestive and Kidney Diseases, NIH, Bethesda, Md., 1993-99; chief biomed. rsch. and AIDS coord. Nat. Inst. Alcohol Abuse and Alcoholism, NIH, Bethesda, Md., 1999—; mem. spl. study sect. NIH, Washington, 1989, 91, 92. Editor: Monoclonal Antibodies, Cytokine and Arthritis, 1991, Immune Modulation, 1997, Gene Therapy, 2000; contbr. chpts. to books, articles to jours. Asst. troop leader R.I. unit Girl Scouts U.S., 1989-91; sci. adviser George Peters Elem. Sch., Cranston, R.I., 1990-91; mem. bd. dirs. PTO, Cranston, 1989-93. Grantee NIH, 1983-93, various pvt. founds. Mem. Am. Assn. Pathologists, Am. Assn. Immunologists, N.Y. Acad. Sci., Sigma Xi. Achievements include discovery of idiotypie immune network in schistosomiasis, cytokine antagonists in experimental arthritis, anti-idiotypie antibody vaccine in schistosomiasis, human monoclonal antibodies in schistosomiasis and cryptosporidium. Office: NIAA NIH 6000 Executive Blvd Rm 402 Bethesda MD 20892-0001

KRESL, PETER KARL, economist, educator; b. Oak Park, Ill., Oct. 2, 1938; s. Orville Joseph and Lillian Gunhild Kresl; m. Lois Suard, May 8, 1993; 1 child, Nils Erik. BA, Roosevelt U., Chgo., 1964; MA, No. Ill. U., 1965; PhD, U. Tex., 1970. Faculty Bucknell U., Lewisburg, Pa., prof. econs. and internat. relations. Author: Urban Economy and Regional Trade Liberalization, 1992. With USAF, 1958-62. Recipient Donner medal Assn. for Can. Studies in the U.S. Home: 107 Stadium Blvd Lewisburg PA 17837-9508 Office: Bucknell Univ Dept Economics Lewisburg PA 17837

KRESSE, WILLIAM JOSEPH, lawyer, educator, accountant; b. Evergreen Park, Ill., June 12, 1958; s. Robert Alvin and Ellenmary M. (Mulhall) K. BBA, U. Notre Dame, 1980; JD, U. Ill., 1985, MS, 1996, postgrad., 1997—. Bar. Ill. 1985, U.S. Dist. Ct. (no. dist.) Ill. 1985, U.S. Tax Ct. 1987, U.S. Ct. Appeals (7th cir.) 1989, U.S. Supreme Ct. 1989, U.S. Ct. Mil. Appeals 1990, U.S. Ct. Claims 1993. Acct. Deloitte, Haskins & Sells, Chgo., 1980-82; assoc. Hinshaw, Culbertson, Moelmann, Hoban & Fuller, Chgo., 1985-87; law clk. to sr. judge U.S. Dist. Ct. (no. dist.) Ill., Chgo., 1987-90; assoc. Ross & Hardies, Chgo., 1990, Gleason, McGuire & Shreffler, Chgo., 1991-92; pvt. practice, Chgo., 1992—; corp. sec. Micro Records Co., Evergreen Park, Ill., 1987—, pres. 1995—; arbitrator arbitration program Cook County (Ill.) Cir. Ct., 1990—; mem. faculty St. Xavier U. Sch. Mgmt., Chgo., 1992-96, asst. prof., 1996—; lectr. U. Ill. Chgo., 1999—; election ctrl. atty. Chgo. Bd. Election Commrs. Author: (with others) Chicago Lawyer's Court Handbook, 1989, 92. Bd. dirs. St. John Fisher Sch. Bd., Chgo., 1988-94, pres., 1993-94; field adv. Met. Tribunal, Archdiocese of Chgo., 1994—; bd. dirs. Hist. Soc. U.S. Dist. Ct. for No. Dist. Ill., 1997—. Mem. ABA, FBA, AICPA, Chgo. Bar Assn. (co-chmn. young lawyer sect. bench/bar rels. com. 1988-89, bd. dirs. young lawyer sect. 1989-91, treas. young lawyer sect. 1991-93), Ill. Bar Assn., 7th Cir. Bar Assn., Hist. Soc. U.S. Dist. Ct. for No. Dist. Ill. (bd. dirs. 1997—), Ill. CPA Soc., Midwest Bus. Adminstrn. Acad., Nat. Lawyers Assn., KC, Elks, Delta Theta Phi. Roman Catholic. Avocations: current events, trivia, politics. Office: 10221 S California Ave Chicago IL 60655-1623 also: St Xavier U 3700 W 103rd St Chicago IL 60655-3105

KRESSEL, NEIL JEFFREY, psychologist; b. Newark, N.J., Aug. 28, 1957; s. Morris Israel and Betty (Weiss) K.; m. Dorit Fuchs, Aug. 11, 1991; children: Samuel Warren K., Hannah Ya'el K. BA, MA, Brandeis U., 1978; MA, Harvard U., 1981, PhD, 1983. Sophomore tutor Harvard U., Cambridge, 1979-83; asst. prof. William Paterson U., Wayne, N.J., 1984-93, chmn. dept. psychology, 1992-95, assoc. prof., 1993-99, prof., 1999—; fellow Inst. of Rational Emotive Therapy, N.Y.C., 1993-94; adj. assoc. prof. mgmt. Stevens Inst. Tech., Hoboken, N.J., 1989-94; adj. asst. prof. NYU, 1990-91; manuscript cons. Political Psychology, N.Y.C., 1990-91; social, clin. and indsl. psychology, N.Y.C., 1983-91, Leonia, N.J., 1991-94, Wayne, 1994—. Editor: Political Psychology, 1993; author: Mass Hate: The Global Rise of Genocide and Terror, 1996; contbr. articles to profl. jours. Mem. Internat. Soc. Polit. Psychology, Zionist Orgn. Am., Am. Psychology Law Soc., Nat. Assn. of Scholars. Jewish. Office: William Paterson U Dept Psychology Wayne NJ 07470

KRESSIN, NANCY RUTH, research health psychologist; b. Cheverly, Md., Aug. 3, 1959; d. Robert H. and Ruth (Parker) Kressin; m. John Joseph Derbort, Sept. 8, 1990; 1 child, Jordan Robert Grant Kressin Derbort. BSPH, U. N.C., 1980; MA, Syracuse U., 1987, PhD, 1992. Rsch. assoc., interviewer supr. SUPPORT study/Beth Israel Hosp., Boston, 1988-89; conf. and grants adminstr. Henry A. Murray Rsch. Ctr., Radcliffe Coll., Cambridge, Mass., 1989-92; rsch. health scientist VA Normative Aging Study, Boston, 1992-96; rsch. health psychologist, asst. prof. Ctr. for Health Quality, Outcomes and Econ. Rsch., Boston, 1996—, Boston U. Sch. Pub. Health; grant reviewer NIH, Bethesda, Md., 1994-99. Manuscript reviewer Med. Care, 1998—; contbr. articles to profl. jours. Mem. com. Roslindale (Mass.) Village Main St., 1995; mem. Roslindale Recycling Com., 1995. Grantee Nat. Inst. Dental Rsch./NIH, 1994, 95, Am. Heart Assn., 1999, VA, 1998. Mem. APA (health psychology divsn. 1995—), Internat. Assn. Dental Rsch. (Hatton awards com. 1999-2000). Fax: 781 687-3106. Office: VA Ctr for Health Quality Outcomes and Econ Rsch 200 Springs Rd # 152 Bedford MA 01730-1114

KRESTINSKI, IOVRI A., publishing executive; b. Moscow, Mar. 3, 1972; s. Alexander I. Karpukhin and Ida G. (Shabaeva) Smirnova; m. Fatima A. Algebraistova, 1992; children: Arina, Ioann, Seraphima. Actor Odessa (Ukraine) Pictures, 1989-91; chief adminstr. Sch. Dramatical Art Theatre, Moscow, 1991-92; exec. dir. TriKita Corp., Moscow, 1992-94; gen. dir., pub. Pharm. Newsletter Bionika Pub. Co., Moscow, 1994—. Mem. AAAS, Russian Assn. Pharm. Mktg. (chmn. bd. dirs. 1999). Home: 8-2-131 Sumskaya St, 113208 Moscow Russia Office: Bionika Pub Corp, PO Box N1, 117420 Moscow Russia

KRETTLI, ANTONIANA URSINE, parasitologist, educator; b. Virgem da Lapa, Brazil, Oct. 23, 1943; divorced; 1 child, Aline Ursine Krettli. BS in Pharmacy Chemistry, Fed. U. Minas Gerais, Brazil, 1965, MS in Parasitology, 1971, ScD in Parasitology, 1978, MD, 1998; postdoctoral studies, Pasteur Inst., 1980, NYU, 1986. Asst. prof. parasitology Fed. U. Minas Gerais, 1967-78, assoc. prof., 1978, prof., 1981—; predoctoral fellow NYU Med. Sch., N.Y.C., 1972-74, rschr. dept. med. and molecular parasitology, 1986; head malaria lab. Centro de Pesquisas Rene Rachou, 1974—; mem. WHO joint rsch. project Dept. Immunoparasitology Pasteur Inst., 1980; vis. scientist NIH, Bethesda, Md., 1990-91; WHO cons. Nat. U. Honduras, 1991; WHO temporary advisor TDR Com., 1993-96; referee various sci. jours., 1987—; spkr. in field. Contbr. numerous articles to profl. jours. Mem. Brazilian Acad. Sci. Home: Apt 301 Grajau, Rua Frederico Nogueira 14, 30430640 Belo Horizonte MG, Brazil Office: Centro Pesquisas R Rachou, Av Augusto Lima 1715 B Pret, 30190002 Belo Horizonte MG, Brazil

KREUTER, KONRAD FRANZ, software engineer; b. Nuremberg, Germany, Mar. 20, 1939; s. Kurt E. and Eva Friedel Kreuter; m. Gerit D. Mayer, 1966; children: Fei Silke, May Frauke. Diploma, U. Mainz, Fed. Republic Germany, 1965, Dr rer. nat., 1968. With Siemens AG, Karlsruhe, Fed. Republic Germany, 1969-72; software engr. ESG, Munich, 1972-76; asst. prof. computer sci. FHT Mannheim, 1976-77; sr. cons. Sesa Deutschland GmbH, Frankfurt, Fed. Republic Germany, 1977-81; software engr. BBC Brown Boveri & Cie AG, Mannheim, Germany, 1981-88, ABB Asea Brown Boveri ACE/EL, Mannheim, 1988-95; sr. cons. Software Gesellschaft Leutershausen, Hirschberg, Germany, 1995-99, Telelogic GmbH, Bielefeld, Germany, 1999—. Co-designer (programming language) PEARL. Mem. Landeselternbeirat Baden Württemberg, 1990-93. Recipient Ehrennadel honor Land Baden-Württemberg, 1990. Mem. N.Y. Acad. Scis., GI Gesellschaft für Informatik, Assn. Computer Machinery. Achievements include patents on electrical switchgear interlocking. Home: Leutershausen Schlehdornweg 2, D-69493 Hirschberg Germany

KREUTNER, SHIMSHON JACOB, cultural organization administrator; b. Leipzig, Germany, Nov. 10, 1916; arrived in Palestine, 1935; s. Israel and Fanny (Bratspis) K.; m. Ruth Zinner, Mar. 31, 1936; children: Hanna, Ruhama. Dir. World Zionist Orgn., Jerusalem, 1948-61; dir. gen. United Israel Appeal, Jerusalem, 1962-79; chmn. World Jewish Bible Ctr., Jerusalem, 1980—. Author: (historical novels) Yearning for Jerusalem, (in Hebrew) 1954 (lit. award), Sehnsucht nach Jerusalem, (in German) 1988, (history) Home and Key, (Hebrew) 1996 (lit. award), Die Ehrlichs, (in German) 1996. Hon. mem., bd. govs. Hebrew U. Jerusalem. Office: World Jewish Bible Ctr, PO Box 7024, 94144 Jerusalem Israel

KREUTZBERG, GEORG W., neuroscientist; b. Ahrweiler, Germany, Sept. 2, 1932; s. Josef H.A. and Hanni (Niessen) K.; m. Karin Franken; children: Achim, Jan. MD, U. Freiburg, 1961; Docent in Neuropathology, U. Tech., Munich, 1971; D (hon.), Med. U. Szeged, Hungary, 1991. Intern U. Hosp., Freiburg, 1957-58, Bonn, 1959; postdoctoral fellow Neuropathology Inst., Bonn, 1960; research assoc. Max Planck Inst., Munich, 1961-64; sect. chief Max Planck Inst., 1968-77, mem., head dept. neuromorphology, 1977-2000, chmn. bd. dirs. for psychiatry, 1985-95; research fellow dept. psychology MIT, Cambridge, 1964-65; guest scientist Rockefeller U., N.Y.C., 1967; prof. Med. Sch., U. Tech. Munich, 1977—; mem. Otto Loewi Ctr., Hebrew U., Jerusalem, 1986—. Author/editor 15 books in neurosci.; mem. editl. bd. 15 internat. jours. in neurosci.; contbr. numerous articles to profl. jours. Recipient Rudolf F. Weiss prize, German Soc. Phy-Pharmacology, 1987, K.J. Zuelch prize, 1991, GSF prize, 1992. Mem. Internat. Soc. Neuropathology (v.p. 1986-90, pres. 94-97), German Cell Biology Soc. (pres. 1981-85), Internat. Brain Research Orgn. (councillor 1976-84), German Neurosci. Soc. (pres. 1999—). Office: Max Planck Inst Neurobiology, Am Klopferspitz 18A, 82152 Planegg Martinsried, Germany

KREUZER, SIEGFRIED G., utilities executive; b. Seugast, Germany, May 3, 1958; s. Erich and Resi (Neubauer) K.; m. Christa A. Weiss, June 14, 1986; children: Lucas, Julian. MS, IHK, Germany, 1982. Electronics tchr. TA-AG, 1982-88; product mgr. CIMM, Inc., 1988-90; sales mgr. EMTRON, 1990-93; key account mgr. CPI, 1993-96; mng. dir. Artesyn Tech., Amberg, Germany, 1996—; mem. supervisory bd. Artesyn Austria, Amberg, Germany, 1999—; dir. OEM sales Europe, Artesyn Techs. Europe, Amberg, Germany, 2000—. Mem. Am. C. of C. Avocations: golfing, skiing, family activities. Home: Von Kleist Str 2, 92224 Amberg Germany Office: Artesyn Tech, Ziegelgasse 8, 92224 Amberg Germany

KREVANS, JULIUS RICHARD, university administrator, physician; b. N.Y.C., May 1, 1924; s. Sol and Anita (Makovetsky) K.; m. Patricia N. Abrams, May 28, 1950; children: Nita, Julius R., Rachel, Sarah, Nora Kate. B.S. Arts and Scis, N.Y. U., 1943, M.D., 1946. Diplomate: Am. Bd. Internal Med. Intern, then resident Johns Hopkins Med. Sch. Hosp., mem. faculty, until 1970, dean acad. affairs, 1969-70; physician in chief Balt. City Hosp., 1963-69; prof. medicine U. Calif., San Francisco, 1970—, dean Sch. Medicine, 1971-82, chancellor, 1982-93, chancellor emeritus, 1993—. Contbr. articles on hematology, internal med. profl. jours. Served with M.C. AUS, 1948-50. Mem. A.C.P., Assn. Am. Physicians. Office: U Calif San Francisco Sch Medicine San Francisco CA 94143-0001

KRICHAK, SIMON OSCAR (SHIMON KRICHAK), meteorologist, researcher; b. Moscow, Russia, July 31, 1944; arrived in Israel, 1990; s. Oscar Gregory and Rachel Solomon (Getnikova) K.; m. Valentina Alexey Novikova, Apr. 27, 1967 (div. Aug. 1981); 1 child, Anna Alexey Novikova; m. Galina Michael Safro, Feb. 6, 1982; 1 child, Alexandra (dec.). MSc, Hydrometeorol. Inst., Leningrad, Russia, 1966; PhD, Hydrometcentre of USSR, Moscow, 1972. Technician High Mountain Geophys. Obs., Nalchik, USSR, 1963; technician Hydrometcentre of USSR, Moscow, 1966, jr. rschr., 1966-72, sr. rschr., 1973-89; sr. rschr. Israel Meteorol. Svc., Bet Dagan, Israel, 1990-93; sr. rsch. assoc. Tel Aviv U., 1994—; Author weather prediction model for Israel; contbr. articles to profl. jours. Mem. Israel Meteorol. Orgn., Israel Assn. Immigrant Scientists. Avocations: travel, literature, music. Home: Elkabez 15/23, 75776 Rishon Le Ziyyon Israel Office: Tel Aviv U Campus, Dept Geophysics, 69978 Tel Aviv Israel

KRIEBEL, RICARDO, dentist; b. San Jose, Costa Rica, Apr. 12, 1920; s. Ricardo and Enriqueta (Rodriguez) K.; m. Julieta Coronado, Jan. 29, 1949; children: Ricardo, Irene, Ilse, Anna, Marlene. DDS, Northwestern U., 1942. Practice dentistry San Jose, 1942—. Fellow Internat. Coll. Dentists; mem. ADA (hon.), Colegio de Cirujanos Dentistas Costa Rica, Acad. Operative Dentistry, Acad. of Dentistry Internat., Pierre Fauchard Acad. (Cert. of Merit 1981), Chgo. Dental Soc., Century Club, Country Club of Costa Rica, Union Club, Omicron Kappa Upsilon. Roman Catholic. Home: PO Box 10308, San Jose 1000 Costa Rica

KRIEG, ARTHUR M., pharmaceutical company officer, educator; b. Cleve., Aug. 17, 1957; s. Arthur Frederick Krieg and Monsita Alcaide; m. Deborah Lanners Krieg, Oct. 11, 1985; children: Alexandra, Elizabeth, Peter. BS in Biology, Haverford Coll., 1979; MD, Washington U., St. Louis, Mo., 1983. Cert. in internal medicine and rheumatology. Resident in internal medicine U. Minn., Mpls., 1983-86; med. staff fellow NIH, Bethesda, Md., 1986-91; prof. U. Iowa, Iowa City, 1991—; chief sci. officer Coley Pharm. Group, Wellesley, Mass., 1997—; med. adv. bd. Kid Needs, 1998—. Mem. editl. bd. Lupus News, 1990—; adv. editor Arthritis and Rheumatism, 1996—; editor Antisense and NUcleic Acid Drug Development; contbr. articles to profl. jours.; patentee in field. Recipient Scholar award Pfizer, 1993; grantee Am. Soc. Clin. Investigation, Henry Kunkel Investigation award Am. Coll. Rheumatology, 1998. Mem. Alpha Omega Alpha. Avocations: hiking, camping, skiing. E-mail: arthur-krieg@uiowa.edu. Office: U Iowa 540 EMRB Iowa City IA 52246

KRIEG, DOROTHY LINDEN, soprano, performing artist, educator; b. Moline, Ill.; d. Carl Victor Lundin and Maybelle Eugenia (Bohman) Linden; m. Eugene D. Krieg, Nov. 24, 1949; m. John C. Ludke, Feb. 1, 1996. Studied piano, voice, pvt. instrs., from 1932; student, Am. Conservatory, 1938-44; studied, opera and oratorio with numerous Maestri. Tchr. Midwestern Conservatory, Chgo., 1947-49; pvt. practice teaching singing Chgo., 1952-94, L.A., 1994—; past treas. Nat. Assn. Tchrs. Singing Chgo. Began singing career in vaudeville at age 4; later appeared with Midwest Opera Co.; artist Moments of Opera show, Colosimo's and on TV; appearances in Chgo. area include supper clubs Singer's Rendevous, Caruso's, Singing Sorinis, Pucci's, Black Forest in Three Lakes, Wis., Northernaire Showboat in Three Lakes, Wis., ballrooms Drake Hotel, Conrad Hilton Hotel, Blackstone Hotel, others, polit. convs., USO shows; concert artist Chgo. Symphony Orch., from 1950's appearing at Orch. Hall, on tour and on TV with condrs. Fritz Reiner, Rafael Kubelic, George Schick, others; soprano soloist ann. performances Messiah, Marshall Field Choral Soc., 27 yrs., Bryn Mawr Community Ch., Chgo., 17 yrs., Chgo. Temple, 10 yrs., other chs. and temples throughout Chgo.; soloist major oratorio socs. including Swedish Choral Club, Apollo Club, Rockefeller Chapel Choir, Collegium Musicum, St. Louis Bach Soc., Cornell Coll., Calvin Coll., Testor Chorus, Rockford, Ill.; soloist U.S. premieres Vivaldi's Gloria and Handel's Psalm 112, Orch. Hall with Chgo. Symphony; female soloist Chgo. Swedish Glee Club, Chgo. Swedish Male Chorus, Schwaebisher Saengerbund, Chgo. Master Bakers Chorus, Combined German Male Choruses at Civic Opera Ho., others; tchr. voice prodn., phrasing, stage deportment, coach opera, oratorio, English, French and Italian lit., German lieder. 1st pl. winner West Side div. Chicagoland Music Festival Contest, 1939; named Western Springs Music Club scholar. Mem. Seal Watch (Can., Magdalen Islands), Greenpeace, Internat. Fund Animal Welfare, Internat. Soc. Animal Rights, People for Ethical Treatment of Animals, Whale Adoption Project. Avocations: cats, gemology, stereo and video recording, Swedish culture. Address: 15459 Celtic St Mission Hills CA 91345-1303

KRIEGER, ROBERT LEE, JR., human resource/management consultant, educator, writer, travel/meeting planner, political analyst, internet marketing consultant; b. Louisville, Nov. 13, 1946; s. Robert Lee and June Elise (Waters) K. BBA, U. Memphis, 1968, MBA, 1969. Cert. pers. cons., travel planner, mgmt. cons. Adminstrv. asst. to mayor City of Memphis, 1969-72; dir. devel. programs U. Memphis, 1972-74; pvt. cons. practice, Memphis, 1974-76; exec. v.p. Randall Howard & Assocs., Memphis, 1976-95; pres. KR Internat. Inc., Memphis, 1995—; mem. faculty U. Memphis Coll. Bus., 1984—; worldwide travel cons. and meeting planner, 1962—; keynote spkr. numerous profl. groups. Trustee, life mem. Rep. Presdl. Task Force, Washington, 1980—; mem. Rep. Nat. Adc. Com., Washington, 1972—, Rep. Regional Steering Com.; mem. U.S. Olympic Soc., Boulder, Colo., 1968—. Recipient U.S. Treasury award U.S. Dept. Treasury, 1971, Nat. Presdl. Medal of Merit, Rep. Presdl. Task Force, 1984, Rep. Legion of Merit, President's award Memphis Cotton Carnival Assn., 1968-85. Mem. Data Processing Mgmt. Assn., Am. Mgmt. Assn., Soc. Profl. Jouranlists, Anm. Film Guild, Met. Opera Guild, U.S. Navy League, Nat. Wildlife Fedn., U. Memphis Alumni Assn., Mensa, Alpha Delta Sigma. Episcopalian. Avocations: writing, bowling, movies, photography, travel. Home: 2948 Dalebrook St Memphis TN 38127-8316

KRIEGLSTEIN, JOSEF, medical educator; b. Pechgruen, Germany, Mar. 10, 1938; m. Marlene; children: Kerstin, Heike, Roland. PhD, U. Erlangen-Nuernberg, Germany, 1965; MD, U. Erlangen-Nuernberg, 1967; habil. in Pharmacology and Toxicology, U. Mainz, Germany, 1970. Lectr. U. Mainz, 1970-72, assoc. prof., 1972-73, sci. councillor, prof., 1973-74; prof. pharmacology and toxicology U. Marburg, Germany, 1974—, mng. dir. Inst. Pharmacology and Toxicology, 1975—, dean faculty Pharmacy, 1976-77, 86-87, 97-98. Named Internat. Hon. Citizen Cit of New Orleans, 1999. E-mail: kriegist@mailer.uni-marburg.de. Office: Inst Pharmacology & Toxicol, Ketzerbach 63, D 35032 Marburg Hessen Germany

KRIER, BRIAN PAUL, family practice physician; b. Milw., Oct. 11, 1961; s. Paul William and Bette Lou K.; m. Frances Smith, Oct. 8, 1986; children: Arhtur Solomon, Sarah Elizabeth, Natalia Eve. MD, U. Tex. Health Sci. Ctr., 1986; MA in Gerontology, Northeast La. U., 1998. Resident in family practice La. State U./E.A. Conway Hosp., Monroe, 1986-89; capt., then major USAF, Italy, Germany, 1989-94; assoc. prof. family medicine La. State U./E.A. Conway Hosp., 1994—. Fellow Am. Acad. Family Physicians; mem. La. State Med. Soc., Christian Med. & Dental Soc., Ouachita Parish Med. Soc., Am. Geriatric Soc., Soc. Tchrs. Family Medicine. Avocations: horseback riding, tennis, golf.

KRIER, FERNANDE GERMAINE, linguist, educator, researcher; b. Chauffailles, France, May 31, 1940; d. Pierre and Anne (Koehl) K. Grad., U. Saarland, Saarbrücken, Germany, 1969; DEA, U. Paris, 1972, D in Linguistics, 1975, LHD, 1983. Lectr. linguistics U. Paris, 1973-76; asst. prof. Romance langs. U. Kiel, Germany, 1976-85; vis. prof. Romance langs. U. Trier, Germany, 1985-86; prof. Germanic langs. U. Rennes II Haute Bretagne, 1986—. Author: Maltese in Contact with Italian. A Phonological, Grammatical and Semantic Study, 1976, The Border Area of Franco-Provençal and Swiss-German in Valais, 1985; contbr. articles to profl. jours. Mem. Assn. Former Trainees European Union, Soc. Internat. Linguistique Fonctionnelle, Soc. Linguistica Europaea, Soc. de Linguistique de Paris, Internat. Soc. for Dialectology and Geolinguistics. Avocations: hiking, golfing, body-building, cross country skiing. Office: U Rennes II Haute Bretagne, 6 Ave Gaston Berger, 35043 Rennes France

KRIFKA, MANFRED, linguist, educator; b. Dachau, Germany, Apr. 24, 1956; came to U.S., 1990; s. Jakob and Anna Krifka; m. Zuzana Krifka Dobes, July 19, 1991; 1 child, Lydia. MA, U. Munich, 1981, PhD, 1990. Rschr. U. Konstanz, Germany, 1983-84; lectr. U. Munich, 1984-86, U. Tübingen, 1986-89; asst. prof. U. Tex., Austin, 1990-93, assoc. prof., 1993-2000, prof., 2000—; Guest scientist IBM Germany, Heidelberg, 1994, 95, Max Planck Inst., Nijmegen, Germany, 1998. Author: Nominal Referenz, 1989, Focus in Grammar, 2000; editor jour. Linguistics and Philosophy; contbr. articles on semantics and syntax to profl. publs. Fellow Ctr. for Advanced Study, Stanford, Calif., 1995, Inst. Advanced Studies, Jerusalem, 1997. Mem. Linguistic Soc. Am. (mem. nominating com. 1998—), Deutsche Gesellschaft Sprachwissenschaft. Avocation: hiking. E-mail: krifka@mail.utexas.edu. Office: Univ Tex Dept Linguistics Austin TX 78712-1196

KRIGER, MARK PHILLIP, management education educator, consultant, writer; b. Boston, May 22, 1946; s. William and Sadee (Schlar) K.; m. Lucy Jane Miller, June 25, 1977; 1 child, Joshua Francis. BA, U. Mass., 1968; MA in Computer Sci., U. Calif., Berkeley, 1970; MS in Philosophy, MIT, 1975; DBA in Mgmt., Harvard U., 1983. Rsch. assoc. Harvard U., Cambridge, Mass., 1973-76; pvt. practice cons. Winchester, Mass., 1976-78; lectr. Northeastern U., Boston, 1980-82, asst. prof., 1982-88, assoc. prof., 1988; assoc. prof. SUNY, Albany, 1988-95; prof. Norwegian Sch. Mgmt., 1995—; cons. in field. Co-author: The Hidden Side of Leadership, 1986; author chpts. in books; ad hoc reviewer Adminstrv. Sci. Quar., Strategic Mgmt. Jour., and others; contbr. articles to profl. jours. including Acad. Mgmt. Jour., Columbia Jour. World Bus., Jour. Mgmt. Inquiry, Jour. Mgmt. Studies, Jour. Orgnl. Change Mgmt., Mgmt. Internat. Rev., Sloan Mgmt. Rev., Strategic Mgmt. Jour. Assoc. commr. Town Conservation Commn., Winchester, 1985-87. NDEA fellow MIT, 1968-69, U. Calif.-Berkeley fellow, 1969-70, Harvard U. Bus. Sch. fellow, 1981-82; recipient Beckhard award MIT, 1988. Mem. Nat. Acad. Mgmt. (internat. mgmt. div. 1986, Best Paper award), Strategic Mgmt. Soc., Eastern Acad. Mgmt. (membership chair N.Y. State chpt. 1989-90, track chair 1990-91), MIT Club Norway (dir. 1995—), Harvard Bus. Sch. Club Ea. N.Y. (dir. 1992-95). E-mail: mark.kriger@bi.no. Office: Norwegian Sch Mgmt, PO Box 580, N-1301 Sandvika Norway

KRIKORIAN, VAN Z., lawyer; b. Framingham, Mass., Feb. 7, 1960; s. George O. and Agnes A. (Kalousdian) K.; m. Priscilla A. Dodakian, June 1, 1985; children: Ani, Sarah, Lena, George. BA in Internat. Affairs, George Washington U., 1981; JD, Georgetown U., 1984. Bar: Vt. 1985, D.C. 1986, U.S. Tax Ct. 1987, N.Y. 1994, U.S. Ct. Internat. Trade 1996. Law clk. Hon. Jerome Niedermeier U.S. Dist. Ct., Burlington, Vt., 1984-85; assoc. Gravel & Shea, Burlington, Vt., 1985-88; dir. govt. and legal affairs Armenian Assembly Am., Washington, 1988-92; counsellor, dep. rep. to UN Rep. of Armenia, N.Y.C., 1992; counsel Patterson, Belknap, Webb & Tyler, LLP, N.Y.C., 1993-98; ptnr. Vedder, Price, Kaufman & Kammhol, 1998—; adj. prof. comml. law St. Michael's Coll., Winooski, Vt., 1987-88. Contbr. more than 20 articles to profl. jours. Ofcl. U.S. del. to Moscow Conf. on Security and Cooperation in Europe, 1991; vice chair fin. com. Dole for Pres., Washington, 1995. Mem. ABA, Assn. of the Bar of the City of N.Y., D.C. Bar Assn., Vt. Bar Assn., U.S.-Armenian Bus. Coun. (chmn. 1996—), Armenian Assembly Am. (trustee, chmn. bd. dirs. 1998—). Office: Vedder Price Kaufman & Kammholz 805 3rd Ave New York NY 10022-7513

KRIMBAS, COSTAS B., evolutionary genetics educator; b. Athens, Greece, Sept. 12, 1932; s. Basilios D. and Aristea B. (Issyhaki) K.; m. Micheline Grobety, 1954 (div. 1970); 1 child, Alexandra; m. Helene Georgopoulou, June 15, 1970. Cert. in genetics, Sorbonne U., Paris, 1955; PhD, Athens U., 1956. Lic. in biology, Lausanne. Prof. evol. biology U. Paris VI, 1979-80; prof. genetics Agrl. U. Athens, 1961-93, rector, 1974-75, 82; prof. history and philosophy of biology U. Athens, 1993-2000; vis. prof. Harvard U., Cambridge, Mass., 1970; S.C. Garvin vis. endowed prof. Va. Tech. and State U., Blacksburg, 1994. Author: Darvinika, 1986, Thrausmata Katoptrou, 1993, Ekteinontas ton Darvinismo, 1998, Yannis Sarejannis Ke i ennoia tis asthenias, 1999; editor: Drosophila Invrsion Polymorphism, 1992, Evolutionary Genetics, 2000, Thinking about Evolution, 2000. Office: U Athens, 37 J Kennedy Str, 16121 Athens Greece

KRING, CHARLES UDELL, retired civil engineer; b. Belle Rive, Ill., Aug. 31, 1910; s. Charles Harvey and Carolyn (Schoenmetzler) K.; m. Marguerite F. Kay, Aug. 25, 1945 (dec. Dec. 1999); children: Mary, Judith, Gary. BSCE, U. Ill., 1932, MSCE, 1939, PhD in Civil Engring., 1948. Registered profl. engr., Calif. Field engr. San Francisco-Oakland Bay Bridge, 1934-35; engr. Golden Gate Bridge, 1936-37; supt. Ben Hur Constrn. Co., St. Louis and Indpls., 1937-38; bridge engr. Parsons, Brinkerhoff, Hall & Macdonald, N.Y., 1941-42; chief structural engr. Bermuda Architect-Engrs., 1942-43; cons. engr. Charles U. Kring Assocs., San Jose, Calif., 1946—; pres. Kring Constrn. Co., Inc., San Jose, 1948—; owner, mgr. Foxworthy Shopping Ctr., San Jose, Calif., 1956-84, Olympia Plaza Shopping Ctr., Seaside, Calif., 1966-77; owner Kaydell Angus Farm, Los Gatos, Calif., 1959-96; lectr. Air U. Maxwell Field. Author: Selection of Weapons and Estimation of Force Requirements for Aerial Bombardment, 1947. Col. USAF, 1943-45, World War II. Decorated Medal of Freedom. Mem. ASCE, Commonwealth Club, San Jose Country Club, Tau Beta Pi. Republican. Avocations: photography, golf, skiing. Home: 7336 Via Laguna San Jose CA 95135-1332 Office: Kring Constrn Co Inc 1035 Minnesota Ave San Jose CA 95125-2431

KRINSKY, FREDDA S., clinical chemist, consultant; b. Bklyn., May 17, 1952; d. Sam and Priscilla Krinsky. BS in Med. Biology, L.I. U., 1975, MS in Med. Biology, 1979; MBA in Corp. Fin., Adelphi U., 1987. Med. technologist Johns Hopkins Hosp., Balt., 1975-78; clin. chemist SmithKline Clin. Labs., Lake Success, N.Y., 1980-83; lab. adminstr. Cen. Gen. Hosp., Plainview, N.Y., 1983-86; cons. Strategies & Techs., Plainview, N.Y., 1987-96; corp. tech. staff Grumman Corp., Bethpage, N.Y., 1988-91, legal and patent staff liaison, 1990-91; adminstrv. ops. staff ROLM, Jericho, N.Y., 1991-92; cons. Chase Manhattan, N.Y.C., 1993-96; CEO Krinsky & Co. LLC, Highlands Ranch, Colo., 1998—; clin. adj. instr. Sch. of Med. Biology, L.I. U., Greenvale, N.Y., 1983-86; coord. continuing lab. medicine-edn., Johns Hopkins Hosp., Balt., 1976-78. Grantee HEW, 1978-79. Mem. AAAS, Internet C. of C., Rockies Venture Club, Internat. Leadership Coun., Forum of Women Entrepreneurs, Women in Tech. Achievements include development of a database system for tracking intellectual properties, method for facilitating the technology transfer of the inventions within the appropriate strategic business unit for exploitation both internally and externally. E-mail: krinskycompany@uswest.net. Home and Office: 10073 Charissglen Ln Highlands Ranch CO 80126-5526

KRINTAS, THEODORE, finance company executive; b. Athens, Oct. 3, 1966; s. Nickolaos and Tzeny (Theodorides) K. MBA, Athens U. Econs. & Bus., 1990. Analyst Alpha Trust S.A., Athens, 1992-93, investments officer, 1993-94, gen. mgr., 1995-98; investment com. mem. Orion Internat. Investment Fund S.A., Athens, 1994-98; exec. dir. Marfin Investment Svcs. S.A., 1998—; dir. Orion Internat. Investment Fund, 1995-98, Alpha Data S.A., Athens, 1995-98; lectr. fin. U. Hertfodshire, 1997—. Contbr. articles and rsch. papers to profl. jours. V.p. A.U.E. MBA's Assn., Greece, 1995. with Greek Navy, 1991-93. State Scholar Found. scholar, 1988, Erasmus U. scholar, Birmingham, 1990; recipient State Scholar Found. Performance award, 1986. Mem. Chartered Inst. Mktg. Greek Chamber of Econs., Market Technicians Assn. Greek Orthodox. Avocations: music, sailing, photography. Home: 8 Ikaron St, 175 63 Athens Greece Office: Marfin Investment Svcs SA, 44 Kifissias Ave, 151 25 Athens Greece

KRIPA, BUJAR, electronic engineer, researcher; b. Tirana, Albania, June 23, 1956; arrived in Italy, 1991; s. Skender and Lumturi (Mahmuda) K.; m. Iris Kongoli, July 13, 1986; children: Inid, Endi. BSc in Elec. Engring., Tirana (Albania) Polytech. U., 1981; cert informatic specialist, Honeywell Bull, Paris, 1984, 88; postgrad. studies, Informatic, Applied Math Inst., 1988-91; D in Elec. Engring., U. Tor Vergata, Rome, 1996. Electronic engr. Albanian Radio/TV Sta., Tirana, Albania, 1981-84; sci. rschr. informatic and applied math. Inst. Albanian Acad. Sci., Tirana, Albania, 1984-91; electronic engr., rschr., automation specialist Groupe Schneider/Merlin Gerin Vanossi Sud S.P.A., Rieti, Italy, 1991—; mem. cons. and adv. bd. Informatic Network of Albania, Tirana, 1984-91; adj. pro U. Tirana, 1984-91; cons. Elettronica Reatina, Rieti, Italy, 1993-94; automation educator State's Inst. E.Vanoni, Rieti-Italy, 1998-99. Officer Albanian Artillery, 1980. Mem. IEEE. Achievements include programation of PLC April PB400 as a supervisory system of 11 machines, The Realisation of Automated Systems for High Cadences Microwelding (copper, silver, termoplastic), Realisation of PC-based High-speed Data Acquisition Systems. Home: Viale Maraini No 15, Interno 7, 02100 Rieti Italy Office: Groupe Schneider Vanossi Sud SPA, E Greco No 9, 02010 Rieti Italy

KRIPKE, SAUL AARON, philosophy educator, researcher; b. Bay Shore, N.Y., Nov. 13, 1940; s. Myer Samuel and Dorothy E. Kripke. BA, Harvard U., 1962; DHL (hon.), U. Nebr., 1977, Johns Hopkins U., 1997, U. Haifa, Israel, 1998. Fellow Harvard U., Cambridge, Mass., 1963-66; lectr. Harvard U., Cambridge, 1966-68; from lectr. to asst. prof. Princeton (N.J.) U., 1965-66, McCath prof. philosophy, 1978-98; assoc. prof. Rockefeller U., N.Y.C., 1968-72, prof., 1972-76; vis. prof. The Hebrew U., 1998—. Mem. editl. bd. Jour. Symbolic Logic, Jour. Philos. Logic, Jour. Applied Logics; author: Naning and Necessity, 1980, Wittgenstein on Rules, 1982; contbr. articles to profl. jours. Grantee NEH, 1998, NSF. Fellow Am. Acad. Art and Scis., Brit. Acad.; mem. Assn. for Symbolic Logic (exec. com. 1997-99).

KRIPLANI, ALKA, medical educator; b. Raipur, India, Aug. 25, 1955; d. Ram Saran Das and Shakuntala Devi Malhotra; m. Ajay Kumar Kriplani, May 18, 1981; children: Divya, Isha. MB BChir, PT JLN Med. Coll., Raipur, 1977, MD, 1981. Sr. resident Lady Hardinge Med. Coll., New Delhi, 1982-85; pool officer Maulana Azad Med. Coll., New Delhi, 1986-88; asst. prof. All India Inst. Med. Scis., New Delhi, 1988-91, assoc. prof., 1991-96; addit. prof., 1996-98; prof. All India Inst. Med. Scis., New Delhi, 1998—; undergrad./postgrad. examiner various univs., Delhi, Rajasthan, Himachal Pradesh; chief guide, co-guide postgrad. theses in ob-gyn.; mem. selection com. various orgns.; presenter in field; organizer nat. confs. and programs for postgrads. in field of ob-gyn. Editor-in-chief: Asian Jour. Ob-Gyn. Practice, 1996; contbr. numerous sci. papers to profl. jours., chpts. to books. Recipient Best Paper Presentation awards and prizes for best sci. publs. in field of ob-gyn. Fellow Indian Coll. Obstetricians and Gynecologists; mem. Nat. Acad. Med. Scis. India, Fedn. Ob-Gyn. Soc. India (life), Fedn. Internat. Soc. Gynecologists and Obstetricians (life), Nat. Assn. Voluntary Sterilization and Family Planning Assn. India (life), Indian Assn. Gynecol. Endoscopists (life), Indian Soc. Perinatology and Reproductive Biology. Avocations: reading, writing articles. Home: E-35 Ansari Nagar, 110029 New Delhi India Office: All India Inst Med Scis, Ansari Nagar, 110029 New Delhi India

KRISCHAK, GERT DIETER, orthopedic surgeon; b. Ulm, Germany, Jan. 21, 1971; s. Gert Joachim and Renate (Perlick) K. MD, U. Ulm, Germany, 1997. Rsch. fellow dept. orthoped. rsch. and biomechs. U. Ulm, 1992-97, rsch. asst. dept. orthop. rsch. and biomechs., 1997-98, med. asst. dept. orthop. surgery, 1998—. Contbr. articles to profl. jours. Capt. German Med. Corps, 1998-99. Mem. German Assn. Traumatology, German Assn. Biomechs. Avocations: water and winter sports, archeology. Home: Krausstr 17, D-89077 Ulm Germany Office: U Ulm Dept Orthop Surgery, Steinhövelstr 9, D-89070 Ulm Germany

KRISHAN, BAL, business educator; b. Shimla, India, May 16, 1954; s. Ram and Kailash Parkash; m. Manjui Bali, Dec. 2, 1978; children: Siddhant, Sidharth. BCom, Govt. Coll., Chandigarh, India, 1973; MBA, HPU, Shimla, India, 1975, MPhil, 1977, PhD. Lectr. HPU, Shimla, 1975, reader, 1989, prof., 1992; coord. UCG, Delhi, 1995-97; coord. HPU, Simla, 1996-99, project dir., 1995, dean, 1993-95. Avocations: astrology and yoga. Office: Himachal Pradesh Univ, Summer Hill, 171005 Shimla India

KRISHAN, KUMAR, retired information scientist; b. Dera Ghazi Khan, Pakistan, Dec. 5, 1933; arrived in India, 1947; S. Anand Swarup and Hardevi (Dewan) Gosain; m. Brij Bala Jerath, Aug. 30, 1938; children: Anita, Sanjay, Seema. MA, Panjab (India) U., 1958; MLS, U. Delhi, India, 1960. Lectr. Inst. Libr. Sci., U. Delhi, 1961-64; lectr. U. Delhi, 1964-73, reader, 1974-84, head dept. libr. and info. sci., 1982-85, 91-93, 97-98, prof., 1984-98; dep. libr. Panjab U. Libr., 1973-74. Editor Library Herald, 1985—; contbr. articles to profl. jours. Mem. Indian Libr. Assn. (pres. 1988-90, Diamond Jubilee award 1994), Indian Assn. Tchrs. Libr. and Info. Sci. (pres. 1985-89, Motiwale Best Tchr. award 1994). Hindu. Home: K 14 Rajouri Garden, New Delhi 110027, India

KRISHNA, AKHOURI PRAMOD, geologist; b. Chatra, Bihar, India, June 7, 1962; s. Akhouri Gopi and Ravi Bala (Dayal) K.; m. Sabita Chhetri, Nov. 21, 1993; 1 child, Harshita. ISc, St. Xavier's Coll., Ranchi, India, 1978, BSc with honors, 1980; MTech. in Applied Geology, U. Roorkee, India, 1984. Scientist exec. grade 2 NCB, New Delhi, 1985-93; rsch. scientist B G.B. Pant Inst. Himalayan Environ. and Devel., Gangtok, Sikkim, India, 1993-97; rsch. scientist C G.B. Pant Inst. Himalayan Environ. and Devel., Gangtok, India, 1998—. Editor: Perspectives of Mountain Risk Engineering in the Himalayan Region, 1997; contbr. articles to sci. jours., procs., books. Cadet, Nat. Cadet Corps, Patna, India, 1971-73. Mem. IEEE, GRSS, Indian Soc. Remote Sensing (life), Sikkim Sci. Soc. (life), Mountain Forum (U.S.), Nat. Inst. of Ecology and Indian Soc. of Ecol. Econs. Avocations: travel, music, singing, dancing, photography. Home: 187/C Ashoknagar, Ranchi, Bihar Ranchi 834002, India Office: GB Pant Inst Himalayan Envi, P O Tadong, Sikkim Unit, Sikkim Gangtok 737102, India

KRISHNA, GOPAL, scientist, pharmacokineticist; b. Kanpur, India; came to U.S., 1990; s. Hari V. and Urmila Dhariyal; m. Shalini Dumka. BS, Jadavpur U., Calcutta, India, 1990; PhD, Va. Commonwealth U., 1996. Tchg. asst. Va. Commonwealth U., Richmond, Va., 1990-92, rsch. asst., 1992-96; sr. scientist Schering-Plough, Kenilworth, N.J., 1996-98, assoc. prin. scientist, 1999—; sec. grad. student orgn. Va. Commonwealth U., Richmond, 1994; mem. rsch. com. PharmD candidate. Co-author: Pharmacokinetic/Pharmacodynamic Analysis, 1996; editor Pharmacokinetics/Biopharmaceutics Web Page; author papers in field; reviewer manuscripts in field. Mem. AAAS, Am. Assn. Pharm. Scientists (Outstanding Paper award 1996), Am. Chem. Soc., N.Y. Acad. Sci., Rho Chi. Achievements include rsch. interests in gastrointestinal absorption and metabolism of drugs in humans; in vitro model to predict oral absorption and metabolism in humans; pharmacokinetic and pharmacodynamic data analysis and modeling; cytochrome P450's; intestinal intubation or regional absorption studies in humans; gamma-scientigraphy studies; in vitro-in vivo correlations; deconvolution to assess rate of absorption; phase I, II, and bioequivalence studies; use of culture cell model, Caco-2, and ussing chamber to study drug transport; p-glycoprotein mediated durg efflux; high-througout absorption screening methods; mathematical modeling and simulation of pharmacokinetic data; oral drug absorption, population pharmacokinetic data analysis using NONMEM. Home: 58 Timber Ridge Rd N Brunswick NJ 08902-5515 Office: Schering Plough Rsch Inst K15-3700 2015 Galloping Hill Rd Kenilworth NJ 07033-1300

KRISHNA, SIMILE SRINIVASAN, entomologist, educator; b. Thanjavur, Tamil Nadu, India, Sept. 14, 1932; s. Simile Krishna Iyer Srinivasan and Sundaram Iyer Saraswathi; m. Shyamala Viswanathan, Feb. 1, 1960; children: Suvasini, Priya. BSc, Alagappa Coll., Karaikudi, India, 1952; MSc, Balwant Rajput Coll., Agra, India, 1955; PhD, Delhi (India) U., 1960. From lectr. to prof. Gorakhpur U., 1963-91, prof., 1991-93; prof. emeritus scientist Coun. Sci. and Indsl. Rsch., Delhi, 1993-96; prof., scientist entomology rsch. inst. Loyola Coll., Chennai, India, 1996—. Editor jour. Hexapoda; mem. editl. bd. Jour. Advanced Zoology, Phytophaga, Shashpa; contbr. over 125 articles to profl. jours. Grantee Univ. Grants Commn., Delhi, 1974-80, 83-86, Indian Nat. Sci. Acad., Delhi, 1978-82. Avocations: cricket, classical music, reading. Home: 48/47 Sai Darshan Apt IV Fl, II Main Rd Kasturbanagar, Adyar Chennai 600 020, India

KRISHNA, TANAY, electrical communications engineer, designer, researcher; b. Patna, Bihar, India, Sept. 28, 1966; s. Binoy and Annapurna (Virnave) K.; m. Smita Verma, June 21, 1995; 1 child. BS, Ranchi (India) U., 1987; M in Engring., Indian Inst. Sci., 1991. Rsch. engr. C-DOT, New Delhi, 1991-95, sr. rsch. engr., group leader, 1995—; reviewer IEEE Very Large Scale Integration Design, 1993-96. Inventor: two patents pending for satellite communications, 1994. Mem. SRC C-DOT, New Delhi, 1994. Recipient Gate Inst. scholarship Indian Inst. Scis., Bangalore, 1987-91; winner of FPGA Design Contest, IEEE, Bombay, India, 1993. Mem. IEEE, Computer Soc. of IEEE (sr.), VLSI Soc. India. Avocations: cricket, reading, travel. Office: C-DOT, 39 Main Pusa Rd, New Delhi 11005, India

KRISHNAMOHAN, NANDIGANA, physicist, researcher; b. Visakhapatnam, Andhra Pradesh, India, Oct. 20, 1952; m. Nandigana Lakshmi, Feb. 15, 1979; children: Venkata Raghavendra Santosh Kumar, Venkata Raghavendra Vishal. BSc, A.M.A.L. Coll., Anakapalli, India, 1971; MSc in Tech., Andhra U., Waltair, India, 1974; MS in Mech. Engring., Indian Inst. Tech., Madras, 1982, PhD, 1989. Jr. rsch. fellow Indian Inst. Tech., Kanpur, 1975-76; jr. rsch. fellow Indian Inst. Tech., Madras, 1976-77, sr. tech. asst., 1977-85, tech. officer, 1985-93, tech. officer s.g., 1993—; guest rschr. U. Malaya, Kuala Lumpur, Malaysia, 1985; vis. scientist U. Oldenburg, Germany, 1991, Lulea U. Tech., Sweden, 1993, 95, 99. Contbr. articles to profl. jours.; inventor in field. INSA-DFG Exch. of Scientists fellow, Bonn, Germany, 1991. Mem. Optical Soc. India (sec. Madras chpt.), Nat. Symposium of Optics (sec. 1994). Avocations: chess, cricket, tennis. Office: Indian Inst Tech Dept Physics, Applied Optics Lab, 600036 Madras India

KRISHNA MOHAN, THAMATTOOR RAMAN, physicist, researcher; b. Kozhikode, Kerala, India, May 8, 1956; s. Thamatoor Pushpakom Raman Nambisan and Thamatoor Pushpakom Devaki Nambisan. BSc, Malabar Christian Coll., Kozhikode, 1976; MSc, Jawaharlal Nehru U., New Delhi, 1978, MPhil, 1982; PhD, Jawaharlal Nehru U., 1988. Rsch. assoc. Jawaharlal Nehru U., New Delhi, 1988-90; fellow CSIR Ctr. Math. Modelling and Computer Simulation, Bangalore, India, 1990-91; scientist C CSIR Ctr. Math. Modelling and Computer Simulation, Bangalore, 1991-95; scientist E1, asst. dir. Ctr. Math. Modelling and Computer Simulation, Bangalore, 1995—; convenor Coun. for Scientific and Indsl. Rsch. Tech. Adv. Bd. Phys., Earth and Marine Scis. Tech., India, 1995-98, convenor, mem. expert com. for establishment of seismic network in Karnataka, Bangalore, 1994-95. Contbr. articles to profl. jours. Mem. adv. bd. Inst. for Cultural Rsch. and Action, Bangalore, 1995—; mem. Indiranagar Sangeeth Sabha, Bangalore, 1995—, People's Union for Civil Liberties, Karnataka, 1995-96. Mem. Indian Complex Systems Soc. (life), Indian Soc. for Math. Modelling and Computer Simulation. Avocations: Hindustani classical music, reading, yoga, furniture design. Office: C-MMACS, NAL Belur Campus, Bangalore 560037, India

KRISHNAMOORTHY, SAVITHA, dental surgeon, educator; b. Ernakulam, India, Jan. 6, 1971; d. Krishnamoorthy Neelakantan and Vally (Venkataraman) K.; m. Venkateshwaran Ramachandran, July 1, 1998. B of Dental Surgery, Coll. Dental Surgery, Manipal, India, 1993, M Dental Surgery, 1997. Asst. prof. Yenepoya Dental Coll., Mangalore, India, 1997—; clin. instr. Yenepoya Dental Hosp., Mangalore, 1997—. Recipient Prithvi Rawal award The Internat. Coll. Dentists, 1993, Gold medals (2) Coll. Dental Surgery, 1993. Fellow Acad. Gen. Edn.; mem. Assn. Oral and Maxillofacial Surgeons, Indian Dental Assn. (Dr. S.R. Prabhu prize 1993). Avocations: gardening, music, cooking, jogging, reading. Home: 52 Stoney Point Ct Germantown MD 20876-5567

KRISHNAMURTHI, M., research scientist; b. Rarawai, Ba, Fiji, Aug. 21, 1937; s. Munian and Buuvanammal Krishnamurthi; m. Sarada Krishnan, Dec. 13, 1959; children: Siva, Murali, Sai, Sakthi. BSc with honors, Annanialai U., India, 1959, MA, 1960; PhD, U. South Pacific, 1993. Chemist CSR Australia, Lautoka, Fiji, 1960-61, tech. field officer, 1961-665, plant breeder, 1965-73; dir. sugarcane rsch. FSC Ltd., Lautoka, Fiji, 1974-90; FAO cons. UN, Colombo, Sri Lanka, 1990-93; advisor, cons. R&D E.I.D. Parry, Chenna, India, 1993—; v.p. Mitr Phol Sugar Corp., Bangkok, 1996—. Contbr. articles to profl. jours. Gen. mgr. schs. Tisi Sangani, Fiji, 1983-89, v.p., 1976-83; mem. coun. U. South Pacific, Suva, Fiji, 1968-73; chmn. bd. govs. Govt. H.S., Lautoka, 1975-86. Mem. SABRAO (sec. 1968-97), ISSCT (v.p. South Pacific chpt. 1977-90). Hindu. Avocation: Indian indigenous medicine. Home: No 20 Brouder Pl, Hill Park, Manurewa Manukar, New Zealand Office: Mitr Phol Cane & Sugar R&D, 99 Moo 10 Khoksa AT, 36110 Phukeo, Chaiyaphum Thailand

KRISHNAMURTHY, MAYURAM RAJAGOPALAIYER, electrical engineer, educator; b. Mayuram, India, Dec. 15, 1928; s. Lakshminarayanan and Rukmani (Subramanian) Rajagopala; m. Santha Narayanaswamy, July 11, 1956; children: Sivaraman, Sridharan. B of Engring. with honors, Madras (India) U., 1951; M of Tech., Indian Inst. Tech., 1956, PhD, 1963. Jr. engr. Tamil Nadu Electricity Bd., Madras, 1951-54; assoc. lectr. Indian Inst. Tech., Kharagpur, 1954-58, lectr., 1958-63, asst. prof., 1963-68; prof., head elec. engring. dept. Regional Engring. Coll., Tiruchy, India, 1969-87, dean rsch., 1987-89; ret., 1989; cons. Bharat Heavy Electricals Ltd., Tiruchy, 1970-89, Lucas-TVS Ltd., Madras, 1985. Contbr. over 50 articles to profl. jours.; 5 patents in field of single winding dual purpose motors. Recipient Invention award Nat. Rsch. Devel. Corp., Delhi, India, 1970, 74, Project award Dir. Tech. Edn., Madras, 1989, Emeritus fellowship Univ. Grants Commn., Delhi, 1989. Fellow IEEE (sr., Ousanding Counselor award 1982, Centennial medal 1984, Cert. for outstanding contbn. 1987, Appreciation Cert. 1994, life), Instn. Engrs. India (life). Hindu. Avocations: astrology, cooking, music, student leadership training, creative activities. Office: TNHB Hig Block No 4/5th Flat, New Beach Rd/Tiruvalluvar/Nagar, Tiruvanmiyur Madras 600 041, India

KRISHNAMURTHY, VIKRAM, electronics engineer, educator; b. Calcutta, India, Nov. 12, 1966; arrived in Australia, 1989; s. Edayathu and Bani (Sen) K.; m. Sharmila Sharma, Nov. 22, 1997. B of Engring. with honors I, U. Auckland, New Zealand, 1988; PhD, Australian Nat. U., Canberra, 1992. Registered elec. and electronic engr. Sr. rsch. engr. CRC for Robust and Adaptive Sys., Canberra, 1992-94; assoc. prof., dep. head dept. elec. and electronic engring. U. Melbourne, Australia, 1998-99, prof., 2000—. Contbr. numerous articles and papers to profl. jours. and confs.; holder 2 internat. patents. Recipient Outstanding Young Investigator medal Australian Telecomm. and electronic Rsch. Bd., 1996; Queen Elizabeth II fellow Australian Nat. U., 1994; rsch. grantee Australian Rsch. Coun. Mem. IEEE (sr.), Soc. Indsl. and Applied Math., Nat. Geographic Soc. Avoca-

tions: cricket, table tennis. Office: U Melbourne, Dept Elec Engring, Parkville VIC 3052, Australia

KRISHNAMURTHY, VISWANATHAN, chemical engineer; b. Kamalapuram, Madras, India, May 12, 1947; s. Krisnamoorthy and Jayalakshmi K.; m. Usha Raman, Nov. 12, 1978; children: V. Deepa, V. Divya. BS, St. Xaviers Coll., Tirunelveli, India, 1966; B Technology, IIT, Madras, India, 1969. Engr. Indian Space Rsch. Orgn., Trivandrum, 1969-77; sect. head Indian Space Rsch. Orgn., Sriharikota, 1977-84, mgr., 1984-94, dep. gen. mgr., 1994-97, gen. mgr., 1997—; mem. expert panel for accreditation of testing NDT Labs in India/Dept. Sci. and Technology. Recipient Nat. Independence Day award Nat. Rsch. and Devel. Corp., New Delhi, 1996., UN Gold Medal award World Intellectual Property Orgn., 1997. Fellow Indian Soc. for Non-Destructive Testing (Nat. NDT award 1993, gen. sec. internat. com. on NDT 1992-96), Neutron Radiography Working Group of India (chmn. 1994—), Bur. of Indian Stds. (chmn. radiographic com. 1991—), Astronaut. Soc. India (life), Acoustic Emission Working Group of India, Nat. Non-Destructive Testing (mem. cert. bd.), others. Achievements include devel. of spl. NDT techniques and methodologies for the qualification of various componetns and sub-systems that go into launch vehicles and satellites. Avocations: Carnatic music, travel, playing cricket. Home: 367 PHC-I, Sriharikota AP 524 124, India Office: Solid Propellant Space Booster Plnt, Indian Space Rsch Orgn, 524 124 Sriharikota Andhra Pradesh, India

KRISHNAN, AVINASH BALKRISHNAN, oil company executive, software engineer; b. Indore, Madhya Pra, India, Apr. 29, 1958; s. Balkrishnan Chandukutty and Sharda Kunnapu Pallikandy K.; m. Sheela Avinash Dixit, Aug. 25, 1985; children: Charag K., Medha K. B.Engring., GSITS, Indore, India, 1979; Higher Diploma in Software Engring., APTECH, Doha, Qatar, 1997. Chartered engr. Engr. Hindustan Petroleum, Cochin, India, 1979-82; sr. engr. Hindustan Petroleum, Bombay, 1982-84; asst. mgr. Hindustan Petroleum, Indore, 1984-86; mgr. Hindustan Petroleum, Nagpur, 1986-87, National Gas, Muscat, Oman, 1987; engr. Nat. Oil Dist. Co., Mesaieed, Qatar, 1991—; cons. in LPG, Internet and software. Mem. Rotract Internat., Indore, 1977-79, Young Giant Internat., Indore, 1979. Recipient Cert. of Excellence, Aptech, Doha, 1997. Fellow Instn. Engrs. (India); mem. ASTM, ASME, Inst. Petroleum (Eng.), Am. Nat. Stds. Inst., Nat. Fire Protection Assn., Nat. Assn. Corrosion Engrs., Internet Soc. Internat., Assn. Energy Engrs. (sr.). Avocations: computer software/LPG equipment design and development. E-mail: abalkrishnan@hotmail.com. Home: 65 Narayan Baug, Indore 452004, India Office: National Oil Distbn Co, PO Box 50033, Mesaieed Qatar

KRISHNAN, KRISHNASWAMY RANGA RAMA, psychiatry educator; b. Madras, Tamilnadu, India, Apr. 22, 1956; came to U.S., 1981; s. N. Krishnaswamy and Sulochana Krishnaswamy Reddy; m. Sripriya Chitamoor, May 21, 1987; children: Vaishnavi, Prahlad. PUC, Loyola Coll., Madras, India, 1973; MBBS, U. Madras, India, 1978. Chief resident Duke Med. Ctr., Durham, 1981-83, asst. prof., 1984-89, assoc. prof., 1990-95, prof., 1995—, chmn. psychiatry, 1998—. Office: Duke U Med Ctr PO Box 3950 Durham NC 27710-0001

KRISHNAN, PALANIAPPA, agricultural engineering educator; b. Kanadukathan, Tamil Nadu, India, Apr. 25, 1953; came to U.S., 1974; s. Lakshmanan and Umayal (Thenappan) K.; m. Chitra Palaniappa Palaniappan, June 18, 1980; 1 child, Prashanth. BTech with honors, Indian Inst. Tech., Kharagpur, 1975; MS, U. Hawaii, 1976; PhD, U. Ill., 1979. Rsch. assoc. U. Ill., Urbana, 1979-80; rsch. assoc. Oreg. State U., Corvallis, 1980-83, asst. prof., 1983-85; asst. prof. agrl. engring. U. Del., Newark, 1985-91, assoc. prof., 1991—, dir. ops. rsch. program, 1996—; cons. Am. Agrotech Lab., Sacaton, Ariz., 1983-86, Rodale Rsch. Ctr., Kutztown, Pa., 1986—, Christiana Care, Newark, Del., 1998—; faculty advisor Indian Students Assn., Newark, 1988-92; chmn. career guidance com., 1990—, sect. found. liaison leader, 1992—. Assoc. editor: Food Process Engineering Institute, 1994-99; contbr. articles to nat. and internat. jours.; patentee in field. Hunter fellow U. Ill., Urbana, 1977-78; rsch. grantee Oreg. State U., Corvallis, 1981; teaching grantee U. Del., Newark, 1987; recipient Excellence in Advising award U. Del., 1997. Mem. INFORMS, ASQ, Am. Soc. Engring. Edn., Am. Soc. Agrl. Engrs. (sec., vice-chmn., chmn. agrl. pest control and fertilizer application com. 1988-92), Newark Lions (lion tamer 1989, bd. dirs. 1990-92, 94—, pres. 1991-92, 99—). Home: 45 Bristol Ln Newark DE 19711-2998

KRISHNAN, RAJESH, chemical engineer; b. Madras, Tnadu, India, Oct. 9, 1972; came to U.S., 1994; s. Krishnan and Mangalam Krishnan. B Tech in Chem Engring., Banaras Hindu U., India, 1994; MSChemE, U. N.Mex., 1996. Sensor engr. VIA Med. Corp., San Diego, 1996-1997; R&D engr. TheraSense Inc., Alameda, Calif., 1997—. Author: Analytical Letters, 1995, Electroanalysis, 1996, Biosensors and Bioelectronics, 1996. Mem. Planetary Soc., Am. Chem. Soc. Avocations: music, painting, reading. Office: Therasense Inc 1360 S Loop Rd Alameda CA 94502-7000

KRISHNAN, SUMATHY, educator; b. Vellore, India, June 11, 1966; s. C. K. and P. Jeya; m. Sivakesava Sakhamuri, Dec. 10, 1995; 1 child, Sakhamuri Shalni. B of Engring., Tamil Nadu Agrl. U., Coinbatore, India, 1988, M of Engring., 1990; PhD, India Inst. Tech., Madras, 1995. Asst. prof. U. Hong Kong, 1996—; vis. lectr. Anna U., Madras, India, 1995; coord. energy systems U. Hong Kong, 1997-98. Contbr. articles to profl. jours. Recipient Gold medal Tamilnadu State Inst. Engring., 1989, 90; postdoctoral rsch. fellow Korea Inst. Energy Rsch., Taijon, 1995-96; Nat. Merit scholar, India, 1983-88; rsch. grantee Hong Kong U., 1996, 97, 98, 99. Mem. Internat. Assn. Solar Energy Edn. (corp. mem.), Internat. Solar Energy Soc. (life, chartered engr.), Inst. Energy (corp. mem.). Avocations: recreational activities, music. Home: Flat 7 14/F Block A, Wah Ming Ctr No 421, Hong Kong Hong Kong Office: U Hong Kong Dept Mech Engr, Pokfulan Rd, Hong Kong Hong Kong

KRISHNARAO, RAGHAVARAPU VENKATA, ceramics engineer, scientist; b. Gampalagudem, India, Apr. 19, 1959; s. Raghavarapu Pardhasaradhi and Lingamarla Venkataravamma; m. Tavvala Sudhalatha, Feb. 15, 1995; 1 child, Deepak. Diploma in metallurg. engring., Govt. Poly. U., Vijayawada, India, 1979; AMIIM, Indian Inst. of Metals, Calcutta, 1984; MTech, Indian Inst. of Tech., Kharagpur, 1990, PhD, 1992. Supr. M/S Galada Continuous Castings Ltd., Hyderabad, India, 1980-83; tech. asst. Nat. Aeronaut. Lab., Bangalore, India, 1983-88; rsch. fellow Nat. Metallurg. Lab., Jamshedpur, India, 1992; dep. project mgr. Nonferrous Materials Tech. Devel. Ctr., Hyderabad, 1992-94; scientist Def. Metallurg. Rsch. Lab., Hyderabad, 1994—. Contbr. articles to sci. and profl. jours.; patentee in field. Mem. Indian Ceramic Soc. (life), Indian Inst. of Ceramics (life). Avocations: music, TV, social gathering, travel. Office: Def Metallurg Rsch Lab, Kanchanbagh, Hyderabad 500058, India

KRISHNASWAMY, K.S., astrophysicist; b. Bangalore, India, Apr. 23, 1938; s. K. Subbarao and D. (Kalyanamma) K.; m. Shyamala Krishnaswamy; children: Suresh, Sujata. BSc in Physics with honors, Delhi U., 1957, MSc in Physics, 1959; PhD in Astronomy, U. Calif., Berkeley, 1965. Rsch. assoc. Calif. Tech. Inst., 1965, U. Chgo., 1965-66; sr. rsch. assoc. Rice U., Houston, 1969-70, NAS-NRC-NASA, 1966-69, 73-75, 1986-88; sr. prof. Tata Inst. Fundamental Rsch., Bombay, India, 1992—; vis. scientist Internat. Ctr. for Theoretical Physics, Trieste, Italy, 1995; sr. vis. fellow SERC, Eng., 1980-81. Author: Physics of Comets, 1986, rev. edit., 1997; editor: Astrophysics: A Modern Perspective, 1996. Recipient Dr. Vikram Sarabhai Rsch. award Phys. Rsch. Lab., 1979. Fellow Indian Acad. Scis.; mem. Internat. Astron. Union. Home: 301 Satyendra TIFR Housing, Colony Homi Bhabha Rd, Bombay 400 005, India Office: Tata Inst Fund Rsch Astroph, Homibhabha Rd, Mumbai 400005, India

KRISSEL, SUSAN HINKLE, transportation company executive; b. Miami, Nov. 21, 1947; d. Jack Boyd and Carolyn (Frates) Hinkle; m. Richard Krissel, Mar. 19, 1972; children: John Boyd, Carolyn Frates. BA, U. Miami, 1970, MEd, 1977. Grad. admissions counselor Fla. Internat. U., Miami, 1971-74, budget coord. external degree program, 1974-78, transcript officer, 1978-82; owner, dir. Southeastern Consolidated Industries, Inc., 1982—. Bd. dirs. Jr. League Miami, 1985-86, Beaux Arts, U. Miami, Coral Gables, 1980-84, Parents Assn. Trinity Episcopal Sch., Miami, 1988-91; pres. Woman's Cancer Assn., U. Miami, 1980-81, Palmer Trinity Parents Assn., 1992-93; trustee Palmer Trinity Sch., 1992-93; mem. Young Patronesses of the Opera, bd. govs., 1999—. Mem. The Flamingo Forum, Jr. League Miami, Beaux Arts. Episcopalian. Avocations: reading, boating, travel, needlepoint, golf. Home: 8750 SW 63rd Ct Miami FL 33143-8069

KRISTAL-BONEH, ESTELA LILIANA, epidemiologist, physiologist; b. Buenos Aires, Nov. 4, 1960; arrived in Israel, 1978.; d. Ernesto Kristal and Raquel Yudowsky; m. Hanoch Boneh; 1 child, Yaniv Boneh. BSc in Biology, Ben Gurion U., Israel, 1983, MSc in Biology with distinction, 1985, PhD in Physiology, 1989. Lab. tech. Ben-Gurion U., 1981-83, rsch. asst., tchg. asst., instr., 1983-89; sr. rschr. Occupl. Health Inst. Raanana, 1990-2000; lectr. occupl. medicine Tel-Aviv U., 1995—; presenter in field. Contbr. articles to profl. jours. Active Israelis Def. Force, 1979-80. Grantee Pub. Com. for Prevention and Rsch. in Occupl. Health, Ministry of Labor, Israel, 1991-93, 93-96, 94-96, 94-97, 96, 97, 97-98. Mem. Internat. Commn. on Occupl. Health (com. in cardiovasc. health), Internat. Soc. for Ambulatory Monitoring, Israel Soc. for Epidemiology, Israel Soc. for Physiology and Pharmacology, Israeli Soc. Hypertension. Home: 15/1 Rothschild St, Kfar Saba Israel

KŘISTEK, VLADIMIR, civil engineer, educator; b. Prague, Czech Republic, Oct. 15, 1938; s. František and Antonie (Dušková) K.; m. Vladimira Blechová, June 7, 1966; 1 child, Markéta. MSc, Tech. U. Prague, 1962, PhD, 1967, DSc, 1977. Asst. prof., assoc. prof., sr. rsch. prof. Tech. U. Prague, 1962-87, prof., head dept., 1987—; ptnr. Kristek, Trcka Ltd., Prague, 1991—; coun. mem. Acad. Engring. of the Czech Republic. Contbr. articles to profl. jours. Recipient State prize Govt. Czech Republic, 1977, 88, Acad. Scis., 1982, 89. Mem. Reunion Internat. Labs. (sr.), Fedn. Internat. Precontrainte. Home: Sadova 8, 161 00 Prague 6 Ruzyne, Czech Republic Office: Faculty Civil Engring, Thakurova 7, 166 29 Prague 6, Czech Republic

KRISTENSEN, ANDERS BUCH, diplomat; b. Egvad, Denmark, July 14, 1938; s. Kristian Buch and Erna (Plauborg) K.; m. Grethe Paulsen, June 16, 1967; children: Marina, Christel, Kirza. BA, Copenhagen Sch. Econs., 1968; MA, Danish Agrl. U., 1965, PhD, 1969. Head divsn. Danish Slaughterhouses, Denmark, 1967-72; dir. Steff-Houlberg, Denmark, 1972-77; polit. advisor Govt. of Denmark, 1977-85; dir. Superfos, 1986-89; head divsn. Ministry of Agr., 1990-95; min. councellor Ministry of Fgn. Affairs, 1995—. Office: Rue DArlon 73, 1040 Brussels Belgium

KRISTENSEN, PAUL EJNAR, mechanical engineer, venture capital principal; b. Randers, Denmark, June 1, 1943; s. Ejnar Laurits and Esther Gerda (Christensen) K.; m. Leonie Renate Braendli, July 29, 1968. BSME, Danmarks Ingenioerakademi, Copenhagen, 1968. Registered profl. engr. Project engr. Swiss Fed. Inst. Reactor Rsch., Wuerenlingen; project mgr. CERN, Geneva, 1972-78; prin. Conceptec, Le Muids, Vaud, Switzerland, 1978-83; exec. dir. ERG Ltd., Perth, Western Australia, 1983-86; dir. Kinetic Ltd., Dunsborough, Western Australia, 1989-92; chmn., owner Capital Techs. Pty. Ltd., Perth, Western Australia, 1986—; dir. Dynamic Digital Depth, Inc. (formerly Xenotech Inc.), Calgary, Alberta, Canada, 1994—; bd. dirs. Structural Monitoring Sys. Ltd., Ad Venture Capital; exec. chmn. United Venture Mgrs. Pty Ltd. Mem. coun. Ctrl. Met. Coll. Tech. and Further Edn. & Advanced Mfg. Tech. Ctr., 1998—. Mem. Australian Instn. Engrs., Rotary Club of Perth. Fax: 618-9386-5122. E-mail: capt.pk@p085.aone.net.au. Home: 16 Kings Park Ave Crawley, Crawley WA 6009, Australia Office: Capital Techs Pty Ltd, 152-158 St Georges Ter 18th, Perth 6000, Australia

KRISTENSEN, PREBEN SANDER, economics educator; b. Aarhus, Denmark, June 4, 1944; s. Hugo and Edith (Pedersen) K.; m. Sonja Theilmann, Oct. 20, 1988; children: Lise Marie, Louise. MSc in Bus. Econs., Aarhus Bus. Sch., 1972. Asst. prof. Cophenhagen Bus. Sch., Denmark, 1972-74; asst. prof. Aalborg U., Denmark, 1975-76, assoc. prof., 1977-89, reader, 1992, dir. bus. studies, 1994-99; sr. rschr. Ministry of Agrl., Denmark, 1990-91. Contbr. articles to profl. jours. Home: Vandverksvej 22, 9000 Ålborg Denmark Office: Aalborg Univ, Fibigerstraede 4, Ålborg 9220, Denmark

KRISTENSEN, REINHARDT MOEBJERG, invertebrate zoology educator; b. Brande, Denmark, Dec. 6, 1948; s. Richard Moebjerg and Anna (Sørensen) K.; m. Gerda Jensen, June 24, 1972; children: Nadja, David. BSc, U. Aarhus, 1971; MSc, U. Copenhagen, 1976, PhD, 1979. Scientific leader Arctic Sta., Godharn, Greenland, 1976-79; postdoctoral fellow Smithsonian Inst., Washington, 1982-83; asst. prof. Inst. of Cell Biology and Anatomy, Copenhagen, 1983-88; curator Zool. Mus., Copenhagen, 1988-96; prof. U. Copenhagen, 1996—; zool. dir. Arctic Sta., 1986—; MAB-No. Sci. Network, Copenhagen, 1988-94; head invetebrate dept. Zool. Mus., Copenhagen, 1992-94; vis. prof. Queensland (Australia) Mus., 1995-96. Editor Zool. Anzeiger, 1995—; contbr. articles to profl. jours. Steering com. Danish Polar Ctr., 1991-95; scientific coordinating group Internat. Arctic Polynya Program, 1993-96. Recipient Award for Arctic and High Mountain Biology Rsch., 1981, Award Smithsonian Instn., 1983; ARBS grantee, 1995-96. Mem. Danish Natural History Soc. (pres., chmn. 1998-2000), Am. Microscopical Soc., Ornithological Soc. Social Democrat. Avocations: bird watching, archaeology, traveling/tracking. Home: Tjoernen 101, DK-2990 Nivaa Denmark Office: Zool Mus U Copenhagen, Universitetsparken 15, DK-2100 Copenhagen Denmark

KRISTIANSEN, KARI HELENE, librarian; b. Drammen, Buskerud, Norway, June 15, 1964; d. Kjell Arnulf and Torhild (Dolplass) K.; m. Annar Engell; children: Henrik, Helene. Libr., Norwegian Info. & Libr. Sch., Oslo, 1992; mgmt., Norwegian Info. & Libr. Sch., 1993. Coord. Total Norge A/S, Oslo, 1992—; editor Nord Ild, Oslo, 1995-96; bd. mem. Norwegian Forum Petroleum Info., Oslo, 1997-98. Editor Information Power, 1995. Office: Total Norge A/S, Haakow VII Gate 1, 0131 Oslo Norway

KRISTIANSEN, ROALD ERNST, religion educator, researcher; b. Narvik, Norway, Oct. 1, 1953. Cand. mag., Oslo U., 1976, Cand. theol., 1979; PhD, Emory U., Atlanta, 1987. Ordained United Meth. Ch., 1983. Lectr. Meth. Theol. Sem., Bergen, Norway, 1980-83, 86-91; assoc. rschr. NCC Ctr., Kyoto, Japan, 1985-86; assoc. prof. Finnmark Coll., Alta, Norway, 1991-97, U. Tromsø, Norway, 1997—; dir. Inter-Ch. Ctr. for Barents Region, Alta, 1995-96. Author: Creation and Emptiness, 1987, Ecotheology, 1993, Religion i Kontekst, 1996, Religion and Education in the Barents Region, 1996; editor Teologisk Forum, 1986-91. Fellow Japan Found., 1985-86; grnatee Sasakawa Found., 1994, Norwegian Rsch. Coun. Mem. European Soc. for Study of Sci. and Theology, Am. Acad. Religion, Lomonosov Found. Home: Tussygveien 18B, 9013 Tromsø Norway Office: U Tromsø, Dept Religion, 9037 Tromsø Norway

KRISTIN, KAREN, artist; b. L.A., Aug. 27, 1943; d. Earle Barnard and Ann Maxine (Taylor) Immel; m. Richard Edward Amend, Aug. 21, 1976 (div. Aug. 1981); m. Gary Marchal Lloyd, Oct. 1, 1985 (div. Sept.1989). Student, Art Ctr. Coll. Design, 1961, Valley Jr. Coll., 1962, Pierce Jr. Coll., 1967, 68, UCLA, 1969, 70. Lectr. UCLA Ext. Program, 1973-76; scenic artist Hollywood, Calif., 1978-83; ptnr., designer, lead painter Sky Art Scenic Art Svcs., Hollywood, Calif., 1983-88; owner, pres., lead painter, designer Sky Art Karen Kristin, Inc., Englewood, Colo., 1989—; spkr., lectr. in field. Co-author (under Karen Kristin Amend): Handwriting Analysis: The Complete Basic Book, 1980, Achieving Compatibility with Handwriting-Analysis, vol. I, Understanding Your Emotional Relationships, 1992, vol. II, Exploring Your Sexual Relationships, 1992; prin. murals include The Cirque Du Soleil Theater, Las Vegas, 1993, N.Mex. Mus. Natural History, 1989, 90, Forum Shops at Caesars, Las Vegas, 1992, 97, Kansas City Station Hotel and Casino, Kansas City, Mo., 1996, Sunset Station Hotel and Casino, Las Vegas, 1997, Venetian Hotel and Casino, Las Vegas, 1998; sky art backdrops for numerous movies, commls., and TV. Mem. Am. Assn. Handwriting Analysts (spkr. 1991—), Am. Handwriting Analysis Found. (sprk. 1991—), Human Graphics Ctr., Graphex Internat. and Gold NIBS, Universal Soc. of Integral Why (mentor 1994—). Democrat. Avocations: photography, reading, traveling, camping, fishing. Office: Sky Art Karen Kristin Inc 3051 S Broadway Englewood CO 80110-1528

KRISTJANSDOTTIR, INGILEIF STEINUNN, molecular biologist; b. Reykjavik, Iceland, Sept. 28, 1955; d. Jon Kristjan and Elin (Oskarsdottir) Ingolfsson; m. Thorsteinn Baldursson, Sept. 12, 1976 (div. Nov. 1984); 1 child, Kristin Thyri; m. Didrik Soemundsson, Aug. 9, 1997; 1 child, Solveig Margret. BS in Biology, U. Iceland, 1980; MS in Plant Breeding, Swedish Agrl. Univ., 1984; Agr.Dr. of Plant Breeding, Swedish Agrl. U., 1991. Researcher plant breeding Swedish Agrl. Univ., Uppsala, 1985-92, 93-94, project position, 1992-93; researcher environ. stress Iceland Forest Rsch. Sta., Mosfellsbae, 1994-96; rschr. environ. sci. Iceland Hort. Coll., Hveragerdi, 1996—. Contbr. articles to profl. jours. Mem. Icelandic Soc. Natural Scientists, Swedish Acad. Soc. Univ. Tchrs., N.Y. Acad. Scis. Democrat. Achievements include development of a method to make it possible to distinguish genotypes that can keep high biomass yield productivity when the temperature decreases, method that can be used on gourd/aboural plants as well as on potatoes where it was developed. Office: Iceland Hort Coll, IS-810 Hveragerdi Iceland

KRISTJANSSON, HALLDOR VIDALIN, advertising and marketing professional; b. Reykjavik, Iceland, May 26, 1946; s. Kristjan Eiriksson and Sigrun Sigurdadottir; m. Gudlaug Gunnarsdottir; children: Solveig, Jon, Gunnar. BA, U. Iceland, 1996, MA, 1999. Pers. mgr. Alafoss, Iceland, 1977-80; exec. v.p. Alafoss, N.Y., 1981-86; mktg. mgr. Icelandic Nat. Broadcasting, Reykjavik, 1987—. Mem. bd. dirs. Icelandic Dem. Party, 1997. Mem. Soc. Sociology Iceland (treas. 1999). Avocations: media, politics, sports, tourism. Office: Icelandic Nat Broadcasting, Efstaleiti 1, 150 Reykjavik Iceland

KRISTMANNSSON, THORSTEINN, airline pilot; b. Reykjavik, Iceland, Feb. 25, 1963; s. Kristmann Eidsson and Kristin Thorsteinsdottir; m. Hanna Lara Steinsson, Sept. 1, 1990; children: Haukur, Kristmann. Grad. in social scis., Hamrahlid Coll., Reykjavik, 1985; grad., Icelandic Flight Acad., 1987. Parts mgr. Eagle Air Domestic Inc., Reykjavik, 1988-90; pilot Islandsflug Inc, Reykjavik, 1990-95; stud. jur. dept. law U. Iceland, 1992-95; pilot Icelandair Inc., Reykjavik, 1995—; translator for Icelandic State TV, RUV, 1993—. Home: Brautarland 3, 108 Reykjavik Iceland

KRISTMUNDSDOTTIR, SIGRIDUR DUNA, anthropology educator; b. Reykjavik, Iceland, Aug. 13, 1952; d. Kristmundur Eli Jonsson and Sigridur Juliusdottir; m. Hjalmar Helgi Ragnarsson, Aug. 18, 1977 (div. 1988); 1 child, Ragnar; m. Fridrik Klemens Sophusson, Aug. 4, 1990; 1 child, Sigridur Fransiska. BS, LSE, Eng., 1975; MA, U. Rochester, 1980, PhD, 1990. Part-time lectr. anthropology U. Iceland, 1980-84; mem. Parliament, Women's Party, 1983-87; prof. anthropology U. Iceland, 1990—; mem. Parliamentary Coun. of Faroe Islands, Greenland and Iceland, 1985-87; mem. Constn. Com. of Republic of Iceland, 1985-92; chmn. The Icelandic Lit. Prize, 1991; mem. expert com. on social sci. rsch. of environ. policy issues Nordic Environ. Rsch. Program, 1991—; chmn. pub. rels. com. U. Iceland, 1991-93; mem. consultative com. on women UNESCO, 1994-97; bd. dirs. Inst. for Gender Studies, U. Iceland. Mem. editl. bd. Nordic Jour. Women's Studies, 1991-95; contbr. articles to profl. jours. Dir. Conf. Women an dDemocracy Turn of th eNew Millenium, Reykjavik, 1999. Recipient fellowship The Icelandic Sci. Found., Nordic Africa Inst., Women's Studies Fund, U. Iceland, Susan B. Anthoy Fellowship in Women's Studies, U. Rochester, U. Iceland Rsch. Fund. Mem. Royal Anthrop. Inst., European Assn. Social Anthropologists, Order of Falcon. Home: Bjarkargata 10, 101 Reykjavik Iceland Office: Univ Iceland, Dept Social Scis, 15-101 Reykjavik Iceland

KRISTMUNDSDÓTTIR, THÓRDÍS, pharmacy educator; b. Reykjavík, Iceland, Nov. 13, 1948; s. Kristmundur and Ástdis (Gisladóttir) Jakobsson; m. Eirikur Örn Arnarson, Dec. 12, 1971; children: Hildur, Kristin Björk. Exam. Pharm., U. Iceland, Reykjavík, 1971; MSc, U. Manchester, Eng., 1974, PhD, 1976. Cert. in pharmaceutics, 1977. Rsch. fellow dept. pharmacy U. Manchester, 1977-79; rschr. dept. pharmacy U. Iceland, Reykjavík, 1979-86, prof., 1986—, head dept. pharmacy, 1993—; vice chmn. biomed. sci. sect. Icelandic Coun. of Sci., 1987-94; vice chmn. Cancer Soc. Sci. Coun., Iceland, 1990-91, chmn., 1991-92; governing bd. Nordic Rsch. Courses, 1990-91, Nordic Acad. for Advanced Study, 1991-96. Editor The Icelandic Pharm. Jour., 1980-84; contbr.: (book) Polymeric Delivery Systems, 1993; contbr. articles to profl. jours. I.C.I. Rsch. grantee, Eng., 1974-76, U. Iceland Rsch. Fund./Icelandic Coun. Sic. Rsch. grantee, 1981—; NATO Sci. scholar, 1974. Mem. Icelandic Acad. Sci., Internat. Pharm. Fedn., N.Y. Acad. Sci., Nordic Assn. Pharmacy Edn. (gov. bd. 1997—). Home: Hrolfsskalavor 12, 170 Seltjanarnes Iceland Office: Univ of Iceland, Dept Pharmacy, Hagi Hofsvallagata 53, 107 Reykjavik Iceland

KRISTOF, LADIS KRIS DONABED, political scientist, writer; b. Cernauti, Romania, Nov. 26, 1918; came to U.S., 1952, naturalized, 1957; s. Witold and Maria (Zawadzki) Krzysztofowicz; m. Jane McWilliams, Dec. 29, 1956; 1 son, Nicholas. Student, U. Poznan, Poland, 1937-39; BA, Reed Coll., Portland, Oreg., 1955; MA, U. Chgo., 1956, PhD, 1969. Regional exec. dir. Sovromlemn, Romania, 1948; sales mgr. Centre du Livre Suisse, Paris, France, 1951-52; lectr. U. Chgo., 1958-59; assoc. dir. Inter-Univ. Project History Menshevism, N.Y.C., 1959-62; mem. faculty dept. polit. sci. Temple U., 1962-64; research fellow Hoover Instn., Stanford U., 1964-67; faculty polit. sci. U. Santa Clara, 1967-68; asso. Studies Communist System, Stanford, 1968-69; mem. faculty polit. sci. U. Waterloo, Ont., Can., 1969-71; prof. polit. sci. Portland (Oreg.) State U., 1971-89, prof. emeritus, 1990—; vis. prof. U. Wroclaw, Poland, 1990, U. Iasi, Romania, 1991, U. Punjab, India, 1992. Author: The Nature of Frontiers and Boundaries, 1959, The Origins and Evolution of Geopolitics, 1960, The Russian Image of Russia, 1967, The Geopolitical Contours of the Post-Cold War World, 1992; also articles in Romania; co-author, co-editor: Revolution and Politics in Russia, 1972. Active Internat. YMCA Center, Paris, 1950-52, NAACP, Chgo., 1957-59, Amnesty Internat., Portland, 1975—. Served with Corps Engrs. Romanian Army, 1940-43. Fulbright scholar Romania, 1971, 84. Mem. Am. Polit. Sci. Assn., Assn. Am. Geographers, Am. Assn. for Advancement of Slavic Studies, Internat. Polit. Sci. Assn., Western Slavic Assn. (pres. 1988-90), Am.-Romanian Acad. Arts and Scis. (v.p. 1995—). Home: 23050 NW Roosevelt Dr Yamhill OR 97148-8336 Office: Portland State Univ Dept Polit Sci Portland OR 97207

KRISTOFFEL, NIKOLAI, physics educator, researcher; b. Rakvere, Virumaa, Estonia, Mar. 5, 1932; s. Nikolai and Klaudia (Tamm) K.; m. Lilian Jaek, Nov. 21, 1964 (dec. 1990); children: Katrin, Jaanus. Diploma in physics cum laude, Tartu (Estonia) State U., 1955, PhD in Phys. and Math. Scis., 1959; DSc in Phys. and Math. Scis., Leningrad (Russia) State U., 1967. Rsch. fellow Inst. Physics and Astronomy Estonian Acad. Scis., Tartu, 1958-60, sr. rsch. fellow, 1960-75, lab. head Inst. Physics, 1976-97, prof. emeritus, sr. rsch. fellow, 1998—; various positions Tartu State U., 1958-74; prof. theoretical physics Tartu U., 1974-97; mem. couns. on solid state theory and ferroelectrics and dielectrics USSR Acad. Scis., Moscow, 1970-90; mem. various sci. couns., Tartu. Author: (monograph) Theory of Small Radius Impurity Centers in Ionic Crystals, 1974; contbr. over 300 articles on solid state theory to sci. jours. Mem. Tartu City Coun., 1969-75. Recipient State prize in sci. of Estonia, Tallinn, 1965, 85. Mem. Estonian Phys. Soc. (founding, Annual prize 2000), European Acad. Scis. and Arts. Orthodox. Avocations: chess (international master in correspondence chess), stamps, fishing, bridge. Home: Aardla 140-3, EE-50145 Tartu Estonia Office: Inst Physics, Riia 142, EE-51014 Tartu Estonia

KRISTOL, DANIEL MARVIN, lawyer; b. July 7, 1936; s. Abraham Louis and Pearl Cecile (Oltman) K.; m. Katherine Fairfax Chinn, Nov. 4, 1968; children: Sarah Douglas, Susan Fairfax. BA, U. Pa., 1958, LLB, 1961. Bar: Del. 1961, U.S. Dist. Ct. Del. 1962. Assoc., ptnr. Killoran & VanBrunt, Wilmington, Del., 1961-76; dir. Prickett, Jones, Elliott & Kristol, Wilmington, 1976-99; ptnr. predecessor Prickett, Ward Burt & Sanders, Wilmington, 1976-99; dir. Richards, Layton & Finger, Wilmington, 1999—; pub. defender Ct. Common Pleas, Wilmington, 1966-69; asst. solicitor City of Wilmington, 1970-73; spl. counsel Div. Housing State of Del., 1972-87, gen. counsel Del. State Housing Authority, 1973-99. With USAR, 1964-67. Mem. ABA, Del. State Bar Assn. (chmn. real and personal property com. 1974-78, chmn. world peace through law com. 1980-81), Am. Coll. Real Estate Lawyers, Wilmington Country Club, Greenville Country Club, Mill Reef Club (Antigua, W.I.), Wilmington Club. Republican. Jewish. Office: PO Box 551 Wilmington DE 19899-0551

KRISTO NAGY, ISTVÁN IMRE, editor-in-chief, art and literature critic; b. Sándorfalva, Hungary, June 16, 1921; s. István Imre Kristo Nagy and Katalin Sára Kenéz; m. Márta Irma Koncz, Jan. 7, 1959; children: Judit, István Jr. Diploma in chemistry, U. Szeged, Hungary, 1944; diploma in esthetics, U. Budapest, Hungary, 1964. Cert. pharmacist. Journalist Budapest, 1936-97, editor, 1941-97; editor-in-chief Magveto Pub. House, Budapest, 1959-89; lectr. Jozsef Attila Free U., Budapest, 1960-99. Author: Democracy, 1946, Faulkner, 1966, Book of Wisdoms, 1982, Edvard Munch, 1983, History of World Literature, 1993. Minsterial refergent Min. Nat. Def., Budapest, 1942-44; dir. ind. youth orgn., Budapest, 1942-48; active YMCA, 1939-48, Boy Scouts, 1939-48; mem. nat. coun. People's Patriotic Front, Hungary, 1974-89; v.p. Coun. Social Interest, Budapest, 1993-98; mem. presidency Pen Club, Budapest, 1991-97. Recipient Hungarian Culture medal, Cultural Min. Hungary, Gold and Silver Hon. Medal Works, People's Patriotic Front, Hon. Cross Republic Hungary, Pres. Hungary, 1996. Avocations: collecting art, traveling. Home: Teréz Krt 18 III 2, 1066 Budapest Hungary

KRITZ, MARY MONICA, educator, demographer; b. Madison, Wis., May 5, 1939; d. Reuben T. and Aurelia (Schoenmann) K.; m. Douglas T. Gurak, June 15, 1970. BA, U. Wis., 1961, MS, 1970, PhD, 1972. Asst. prof. Purdue U., West Lafayette, Ind., 1972-74; assoc. dir. population scis. Rockefeller Found., N.Y.C., 1974-89; assoc. prof. Cornell U., Ithaca, N.Y., 1990—; mem. adv. bd. Ctr. for Migration Studies, N.Y.C., 1990—; cons. MacArthur Found., Chgo., 1999. Editor: International Migration Systems: A Global Approach, 1992; contbr. articles on women's status in Nigeria and internat. migration to profl. jours. Mem. adaptation panel global change Nat. Acad. of Scis., 1989-91; mem. staff select com. on population Ho. of Reps., Washington, 1978. Grantee Rockefeller Found., 1990-94, Family Health Internat., 1994-95, Rockefeller Archive Ctr., 1998-99. Mem. Population Assn. Am. (chair internat. affairs com. 1993-95, mem. coun. 1989-92), Am. Sociol. Assn. (sect. on internat. migration), Internat. Union for Sci. Study of Population (nomination com., chair internat. immigration com. 1986-90), Union for African Population Studies, Gamma Sigma Delta. Avocations: genealogy, physical fitness, gardening. E-mail: mmk5@cornell.edu. Home: 14 Rosina Dr Ithaca NY 14850-9766 Office: Population and Devel Program Cornell U 221 Warren Ithaca NY 14853

KRITZ, REUVEN RUDOLF, humanities educator, writer; b. Vienna, Austria, Nov. 11, 1928; arrived in Israel, 1938; s. Leo Arieh and Valerie (Grund) K.; m. Ila Reifer, Feb. 17, 1953; children: Netta, Michael, Ori, Guy, Nir. Tchr.'s cert., Seminar Hakibbutzim, 1950; BA, Hebrew U., 1963, MA, 1966, PhD, 1971. Sr. lectr. Tel Aviv (Israel) U., 1973-94; prof. Hochschule fur Judische Studien, Heidelberg, Germany, 1994—; vis. prof. UCLA., 1970-71, Hebrew Coll., Brookline, Mass., 1971, 81, U. Tex., 1976, Hochschule fur Judische Studien, Heidelberg, 1986, 91. Author: Fresh Morning, 1955, Barash prize, 1957, Little Sister, 1960, Azure Years, 1960, Alon and Irit, 1961, Sins of Youth, 1962, A Waving Kerchief, 1963, Students, 1964, Cancer at Night, 1966, Rabban Shimeon and the Odyssey, 1967, How to Analyze a Story, 1968, Lights, 1970, On Rahel's Poetry, 1970, What's Strange in Strange Stories, 1975, Patterns of Narrative, 1976, Fiction of the Struggle for Independence Era, 1978, 120 Mini-Essays, 1983, Introduction to Hebrew Poetry, 1984, Problems of Criticism—A Personal View, 1989, Miscellany, 1990, under pen name Ricky Keller: Concerto for Jarring Boy and Orchestra, 1975, This Knocking, 1977, They Simply Float, 1979, Down Sunset Boulevard, 1981, Uzzai, 1983, Not Finished, Not Come, 1993, Hoffmann's Tales in Tel Aviv, 1997, Motorbike and Viper, 1999; co-author: (with Ori Kritz), 3 vols., The Kibbutz Tales, 1997. With Israeli Army, 1948, 56, 67, 73. Avocations: literature, gardening. Fax: 00-972-3-6412459. Home: 13 Berliner, 69057 Tel Aviv Israel

KRITZAS, CHARALAMBOS, archaeologist; b. Heraklion, Crete, Greece, Apr. 6, 1944; s. Byron and Helen (Gigourtsoglou) K. Diploma in History and Archaeology, U. Athens, 1967; postgrad., Ecole Normale Supérieure, Paris, 1981-83; DEA, U. Paris I, 1982; Elève Titulaire, Ecole Pratique Hautes Etudes, Paris, 1983. Curator of antiquities of the Argolid and Corinthia Greek Archaeol. Svc., Nauplia, 1970-77; curator of antiquities of Athens Greek Archaeol. Svc., 1983-87, ephor of antiquities of Heraklion, 1987-93; dir. Epigraphical Mus. Greek Archaeol. Svc., Athens, 1994—; dir. Dept. of Archaeol. Sites Greek Ministry of Culture, Athens, 1977-81. Contbr. over 40 articles to profl. jours. Mem. Archaeol. Soc. Athens, Hellenic Inst. Marine Archaeology (co-founder), German Archaeol. Inst. (corr.), Internat. Assn. Greek and Latin Epigraphy (com. mem.), Assn. Greek Studies in France, Soc. Cretan Hist. Studies (mem. mng. com. 1987-93). Orthodox. Office: Epigraphical Mus, 1 Tossitsa St, Athens 10682, Greece

KRIVAN, VLASTIMIL, mathematician; b. Strakonice, Czechoslovakia, Aug. 15, 1958; s. Vlastimil and Libuse (Pechlatova) K.; m. Sarka Novackova, Aug. 15, 1987; children: Marketa, Karolina. DSc, Charles U., 1982. Research Inst. Entomology, Ceske Budejovice, Czech Republic, 1983-96, head dept. theoretical biology, 1996—. Mem. Am. Math. Soc., European Soc. for Math. and Theoretical Biology (bd. dirs.). Home: Hodejovicka 338, 370 08 Stare Hodejovice Czech Republic Office: Inst Entomology, Branisovska 31, 370 05 Ceske Budejovice Czech Republic

KRIVENKO, PAVEL VASILJEVICH, university administrator, scientist; b. Nikolaevskaya Oblast, Ukraine, Sept. 15, 1938; s. Vasilyi Maximovich and Lubov Lukjanovna (Yakovenko) K.; m. Lilia Egorovna Tkachova, Nov. 4, 1963; 1 child, Andrei. Diploma in engring., Dnepropetrovsk Civil Engring. Inst., 1961; PhD in Engring., Kiev Civil Engring. Inst., 1971; DSc in Engring., Kiev Polytech. Inst., 1986. Sr. master Bldg. Adminstrn., Kiev, 1961-66; sr. scientist Civil Engring. Inst. (now Kiev Nat. U. Constrn. & Architecture), 1969-71, head of lab., 1971-87, head of dept., 1988—, vice rector, 1988—; dir. scientific rsch. Inst. for Binders and Materials, Kiev, 1991—; head tech. com. for standardization, Kiev, 1994—, head certification body for products, 1995—. Author: Special Slag Alkaline Cements, 1992; co-author: Durability of Slag Alkaline Concrete, 1993. Recipient State prize Sci. and Engring., 1999. Fellow Acad. for Constrn. of Ukraine; mem. Assn. Reconfiss (pres. 1991—), Acad. of Engring. Scis. of Ukraine (academician 1991—), Am. Soc. of Civil Engrs. E-mail: sribm@mail.kar.net. Office: Kiev Nat U Constrn/Arch, Vozdukhoflotsky Prospect 31, 03037 Kiev Ukraine

KRIVENTSOV, VICTOR, hotel executive, lawyer; b. Moscow, Dec. 7, 1969; s. Vladislav and Galina (Muradova) K.; m. Nadejda Chtcheglova, Dec. 4, 1994 (div. Dec. 1996); m. Elena Karina, Jan. 25, 1998. BS, Moscow State Law Acad., 1992; diploma, Internat. Bus. Sch., Moscow, 1992, Wade World Trade Sch., U.K., 1996, Paralegal Sch., Scranton, Pa., 1996. Inspector Atty. Gen.'s Office, Moscow, 1987-88; office mgr. Dist. Atty.'s Office, Moscow, 1988-89, interrogation officer, 1990-92; pres. Kriventsov & Kalougine Law Firm, Moscow, 1992-94, K & K Bus. Group Internat., Pattaya, Thailand, 1994-96; dir. sales Ea. Europe Royal Cliff Beach Resort, Pattaya, 1996—; cons. Internat. Assn. Young Journalists, Moscow, 1992-94, Russian Soc. for Rsch. in Earth Mysteries, Moscow, 1992-94, Russian Grain Stock Exch., Moscow, 1993-94; spkr. in field. Co-author: (book) I Am Defending Against Criminal, 1989, (catalogue series) Elite of Russian Business, 1992-94; editor: Thailand Guidebook (by Ilev-Tour), 1996. Recipient prize Atty. Gen. of Moscow, 1990, 91. Mem. Notary Public Assn., Chaopraya River Club, Russian Cmty. (chmn. 1996—). Avocations: collecting plastic cards, snooker. Fax: (66-38) 250141. Home and Office: Royal Cliff Beach Resort, 353 M.12 Pratumnak Rd, Pattaya Chonburi 20260, Thailand

KRIVOLAPCHUK, VLADIMIR VASILYEVICH, physicist, researcher; b. Alma-Ata, Kazakhstan, USSR, Oct. 4, 1946; s. Vasiliy Kuzmich and Tamara Alexandrovna (Dovgyallo) K.; m. Natalya Dmitrievna Klimovets, Apr. 8, 1972; 1 child, Yuri Vladimirovich. Physicist, Leningrad (USSR) State U., 1976; PhD in Physics and Maths., A.F. Ioffe Phys. Tech. Inst., 1985. Practical researcher A.F. Ioffe Phys. Tech. Inst., Leningrad, 1976-78, jr. researcher, 1978-89, sr. researcher, 1989—. Avocations: aviation, training dogs. Office: AF Ioffe Phys Tech Inst, Politekhnischeskaya 26, 194021 Saint Petersburg Russia

KRIVOSHIK, ANDREW PETER, engineer, physician; b. Elizabeth, N.J., Feb. 20, 1968; s. Peter Enoch and Elizabeth Elsie Krivoshik; m. Susan Elise Lyon, Aug. 10, 1991; children: Amy, David. BSE with honors, Princeton (N.J.) U., 1990; MD-PhD, U. Ill., 1999. Registered profl. engr., Ill., Minn. Tech. cons. KEA Inc., Elizabeth, N.J., 1983-90; technician IBM TJ Watson, Yorktown Heights, N.Y., 1988, 89; Univ. fellow U. Ill., Urbana, 1990-91, 98-99, Nat. Inst. on Drug Abuse fellow, 1993-98; resident physician Mayo Clinic, Rochester, Minn., 1999—; elec. item writer Nat. Coun. of Examiners for Engring. and Surveying, 1996—. Contbr. articles to profl. jours. Recipient rsch. svc. award USPHS, 1993-98; USPHS fellow NIH, 1991-93. Mem. NSPE, IEEE, Biophys. Soc., Cum Laude Soc., Tau Beta Pi. Office: Mayo Clinic 200 1st St SW Rochester MN 55905-0002

KRIVTSUN, IGOR VITALJEVICH, physicist, researcher; b. Konstantinovka, Donetsk, Ukraine, Oct. 21, 1954; s. Vitaly Grigorjevich Krivtsun and Rimma Vassiljevna Bondarenko; m. Olga Ivanovna Polyanskaya, Jan. 31, 1976 (div. Apr. 1982); 1 child, Olga; m. Elena Yakovlevna Bossenko, July 9, 1982; 1 child, Ekaterina. BS, Kiev (Ukraine) State U., 1976; PhD, Inst. Theoretical Physics, Kiev. Cert. in theoretical and math. physics. Jr. fellow E.O. Paton Electric Welding Inst., Kiev, 1976-84, fellow, 1984-87, sr. fellow, 1987—; head theoretical group of dept. of gas discharge physics and plasma devices E.O. Paton Electric Welding Inst., Kiev, 1990—; lectr. plasma theory course Moscow Physics and Tech. Inst., Kiev, 1990-94. Author: (book) Welding and Surfacing Review, 1995, (software) Computer Aided Simulation of Plasma Spraying Process, 1998; patentee in field. Mem. Communist Party of Soviet Union, Kiev, 1988-91. Grantee Internat. Assn., 1994, 95. Avocations: touring, music. Fax: 38 044 268 0486. E-mail: ivk@modul.kiev.ua. Office: E O Paton Elec Welding Inst, 11 Bozhenko St, Kiev 03680, Ukraine

KRIVULIN, NIKOLAI KIMOVICH, mathematician, educator; b. Ulyanovsk, Russia, Nov. 29, 1958; s. Kim Petrovich and Julia Aleksandrovna (Hordikainen) K.; m. Svetlana A. Pavlova, Feb. 7, 1992. MS in Math., St. Petersburg U., 1983, PhD of Math., 1990. Software engr., asst. prof. St. Petersburg (Russia) U., 1983-85, 87-91, postdoctoral rsch. fellow, 1992-94; assoc. prof. St. Petersburg (Russia) State U., 1994—, deputy dean faculty of math. and mechanics, 1998-99, head dept. info. mgmt., 1999—; vis. prof. math. Mcpl. Coll. Practical Psychology, St. Petersburg, 1992-93. Author: (with others) Elements of the Queueing Theory, 1998; contbr. articles to profl. jours. Grantee Internat. Sci. Found., 1995, Russian Found. Fundamental Rsch., 1996-98, 2000—, Russian Found. Humanities Rsch., 1997, 98, 2000—, Eurasia Found., 1999-2000. Mem. St. Petersburg Math. Soc., Am. Math. Soc., N.Y. Acad. Scis. Office: Saint Petersburg Univ, Bibliotechnaya Sq 2, 198904 Saint Petersburg Russia

KŘIVY, IVAN, mathematics educator, researcher; b. Vsetin, Czech Republic, May 22, 1940; s. Bohuslav and Vlasta (Tlustošová) K.; m. Eva Švandová, July 5, 1964; children: Ivana, Marcel. Degree in Engr. Tech. Physics, Czech Tech. U., Prague, 1962; PhD, Charles' U., Prague, 1974, MS, 1975, assoc. prof., 1988. Cert. nuclear physics engring., solid state physics, applied math. Head of structure analysis Nuclear Rsch. Inst., Czech Republic, 1962-75; vice-dir. Data Processing Ctr., Holešov, Czech Republic, 1975-77; vice-dean Pedagogical Faculty, Ostrava, Czech Republic, 1977-91; head of math. dept. U. Ostrava, 1991-97, dean faculty of sci., 1997—; reviewer Am. Chem. Soc., Columbus, 1967-80, Springer Verlag, Berlin, 1986-96; mem. sci. bd. Tech. U., Ostrava, 1991-93. Author: Modelling in Population Biology and Ecology, 1991; patentee in field; contbr. articles to profl. jours. Recipient hon. diploma Am. Chem. Soc., 1979; grantee TEMPUS Office Brussels, Portsmouth, U.K. Polytechnic, 1991, TEMPUS Office, U. Cordoba, Spain, 1996. Mem. Am. Math. Soc. (reviewer 1992-96), Soc. for Computer Simulation, 1993, Soc. for Indsl. and Applied Math., 1996. Avocations: history of plastic arts and painting, recreational sports, gardening. Home: Sokolská 57, 701 00 Ostrava Czech Republic Office: U Ostrava, 30 dubna 22, 701 03 Ostrava Czech Republic

KRIZ, DARIO, biochemist; b. Malmö, Skåne, Sweden, Sept. 4, 1965; s. Daniel and Amalia K. Degree in electronic engring., Nordic Tech. Inst., Stockholm, 1981; MSc, Lund (Sweden) U., 1988, student in pre-clin. medicine, 1992, PhD in Pure and Applied Biochemistry, 1994; degree, U. Cambridge, Eng., 1993. Rschr. pathology dept. Malmö (Sweden) Hosp., 1984-85; technician Bioinvent Inc., Lund, 1986; CEO Chemel Inc., Lund, 1990-97; head European Inst. Sci., Lund, 1997—; tech. asst. analytical chemistry Lund U., 1990, rschr., 1996-97, head Chemel Rsch. Inst., Lund, 1994-97, rschr. Lund Med. Laser Ctr., 1994-97, vis. prof. U. Regensburg, Germany, 1997—, head European Inst. Sci., 1998—; mem. editl. bds. various profl. jours., 1998—. Patentee in field; contbr. over 20 articles to profl. jours. Recipient Berzelius award Swedish Chem. Soc., 1983, Finalist award 16th European Philips Contest, 1984, award Swedish Rsch. Coun. for Engring. Scis., 1995, 96; grantee Affarsstrategerna and European Cmty., 1997. Mem. Internat. Soc. Electrochemistry, N.Y. Acad. Scis., Am. Chem. Soc. Avocations: sports, reading. Home: Bosjökloster Bomhaset, 243 95 Höör Sweden Office: European Inst Sci, IDEON, 223 70 Lund Sweden

KRIZAN, BOZIDAR, educator; b. Zagreb, Croatia, Dec. 6, 1946; s. Zdenko and Jarmila (Prochazkova) K.; m. Jadranka Juranic, May 9, 1970; children: Vedran, Zlatan. BSME, U. Zagreb, Rijeka, Croatia, 1971; MSME, U. Zagreb, Croatia, 1981; DS in Mech. Engring., U. Rijeka, 1990. Engr. Shipyard V. Lenac, Rijeka, Croatia, 1971-74; asst. Faculty Engring., Rijeka, Croatia, 1974-90, asst. prof., 1990-96, assoc. prof., 1996-2000; full prof. Faculty Engring., Rijeka, 2000—; head dept. Faculty Engring., 1992-98, vice dean, 1998—; lectr. Faculty Maritime Studies, Rijeka, 1993-96. Author: Fundamentals of the Calculation and Design of Machine Elements, 1998; editor: 4th Symposium Design, 1996. Mem. Croatian Soc. Machine Elements & Design, Croatian Deutscher Akademischer Austauschdienst Club. Avocations: music, travel, skiing. Home: Zagrebacka 13, 51000 Rijeka Croatia Office: Faculty Engring, Vukovarska 58, 51000 Rijeka Croatia

KRIZAN, KELLY JOE, physician, leather craftsman; b. Winner, S.D., Jan. 16, 1951; s. Miles Woodrow and Sadie Mae (DeSmet) K.; m. Susan Barker, Aug. 21, 1971 (div. Aug. 1983); children: Jennifer Rebecca, Nicholas Miles; m. Cynthia Lydia Obras, Aug. 6, 1983. BS, S.D. State U., 1973; BS in Medicine, U. S.D., 1976; MD, Tufts U., 1978. Diplomate Am. Bd. Family Practice. Commd., Am. Bd. Radiology. (first active duty capt. U.S. Air Force, 1978, advanced through grades to lt. col., 1984. Intern USAF Med. Ctr., Scott AFB, Ill., 1978-79, resident, 1979-81; staff physicain USAF Hosp., Hill AFB, Utah, 1981-83; chief emergency svcs., chief family practice USAF Hosp., Hill AFB, Utah, Incirlik AB, Turkey, 1983-84, chmn. dept. family practice, 1985-86; resident radiology U. Wash., 1986-90, clin. asst. prof., 1990—; chmn. dept. radiology 13th AF Med. Ctr., Clark AB, Philippines, 1990-91, St. Mary's Health Care Ctr., Pierre, S.D., 1993—, chmn. radiology, 1993—, chief of staff, 1997, St. Mary's Healthcare Ctr. . Artist leather goods, winner various awards. U.S. Presdl. scholar, 1969. Fellow Am. Acad. Family Physicians; mem. Am. Coll. Radiology, Am. Roentgen Ray Soc., Radiological Soc. N.Am., Phi Kappa Phi. Roman Catholic.

KRLÍN, LADISLAV, physicist, researcher; b. Prague, Czech Republic, June 19, 1932; s. Vojtěch and Marie (Čekalová) K.; m. Eva Pavlásková, June 10, 1961; children: Jan, Tomáš. Diploma in electrotech. engring., Czech Tech. U., Prague, 1956; PhD, Acad. Sci., Prague, 1964, DSc, 1991. Rschr. Czech. Acad. Sci., Prague, 1956-69, 71-90, U. Fribourg (Switzerland), 1969-70; vis. prof. U. Innsbruck (Austria), 1990-91; top rschr. Inst. Plasma Physics Czech Acad. Sci., Prague, 1991—; lectr. faculty of math. physics Charles U., Prague, 1991—, mem. br. coun., 1992—; mem. br. coun. Grant Agy., Acad. Sci., Prague, 1995-98; mem. preparatory sci. com. Ctr. of Nonlinear Studies, Polish Acad. Sci., Warsaw, 1995. Co-author: Waves and Instabilities in Plasmas, 1994, Deterministic Chaos and Mathematical Methods of Turbulence, 1996; mem. editorial bd. UNIVERSUM, 1992—; contbr. articles and revs. to profl. jours. Mem. Christian Acad. of Czech Rep., 1992—. Recipient prize Czech Literary Fund, 1998; grantee Czech Acad. Sci., 1992, 2000, Czech Rep., 1995. Mem. European Phys. Soc., Czech Phys. Soc. (com. mem. 1974-93), Czech Acad. Sci. (medal 1999). Roman Catholic. Avocations: classical music, history, science-religion relations. Office: Inst Plasma Physics POB 17, Acad Sci Za Slovankou 3, 182 21 Prague 8 Czech Republic

KRMPOTICH, FRANK ZVONKO, fiberglass company executive, consultant; b. Zagreb, Croatia, Feb. 17, 1948; came to U.S., 1983; s. Franjo and Anica (Pavlich) K.; m. Jana Snjezana Fabjanovich, May 25, 1973; children: Kris, Tomi. BSME, U. Zagreb, 1978; Degree in Arctic Engring. (hon.), U. Anchorage, 1985. Design engr. Fiberglass Fabricator, Zagreb, 1976-79; sr. design engr. Mech. Engring. Inst., Zagreb, 1979-84; prin. engr. Alaska Engring., Anchorage, 1984-87; sr. design engr. Test Co., Anchorage, 1987-89, Ershigs, Bellingham, Wash., 1989-90, Chemetics Internat., Vancouver, B.C., Can., 1991-93; sr. design cons. engr. Fiberglass Cons. Engring., Bellingham, 1990-91, CEO, 1994—; cons. engr., Bellingham, 1990—. Patentee FRP Equipment Design, 1994. Pres. Croatian Bus. Assn., Zagreb-Seattle, 1991. Mem. ASME, NSPE, Nat. Assn. Corrosion Engrs., Soc. Plastic Industry. Republican. Roman Catholic. Avocations: tennis, hockey, soccer. Home: 3111 Crestline Dr Bellingham WA 98226-4206

KRMPOTIC-NEMANIC, JELENA, anatomist, otorhinolaryngologist, medical educator; b. Srem. Mitrovica, Vojvodina, Yugoslavia, Mar. 15, 1921; d. Matija and Marija (Krnjević) Krmpotić; m. Nenad Bohaček, 1950 (div. 1952); m. Georg Nemanic, Apr. 30, 1966. MD, U. Zagreb, Croatia, 1944, Habil., 1948. Resident, anatomy dept. U. Zagreb, 1944-49, reader in anatomy, 1949-53, extraordinary prof., 1953-63, dir. dept. anatomy, 1961-80, ordinary prof., 1963-92, ret., 1991; hon. prof. U. Munich, Germany, 1981. Co-author: Tunnel Syndromes, 1991, 2d edit., 1996; contbr. articles to med. jours. Recipient Austrian Cross of Honor for Sci. and Arts. Mem. Austrian Otorhinolaryngology Soc. (hon.), Coll. Otorhinolaryngology Amicitiae Sacrum, Croatian Acad. Scis. and Arts (ordinary). Roman Catholic. Avocation: foreign languages. Home: Vinkovićeva 3, 11000 Zagreb Croatia Office: U Zagreb Dept Anatomy, Šalata 11, 11000 Zagreb Croatia

KROB, JOSEF, philosophy educator; b. Ž'där nad Sdzavou, Czech Republic, Dec. 9, 1956; s. Miroslav and Josefa (Pennertová) K.; m. Věra Brabcová, Jan. 20, 1979; children: Josef, Veronika. BA, Masaryk U., Brno, Czech Republic, 1981, PhDr., 1984, PhD, 1992; PhD, Free U. Brussels, 1992, Maison Scis. de l'Homme, Paris, 1995, 2000. Asst. prof. philosophy Masaryk U., Brno, Czech Republic, 1984-97, assoc. prof., 1997—. Co-author: Introduction in Ontology, 1994, Three Studies of French Philosophy, 1997; co-editor, co-author: The End of Ontology?, 1993, About French Philosophy, 1999, Seeking of Time, Space, Sense, 1999; co-editor: Czech Philosophy in the 20th Century, 1995; contbr. articles to profl. jours. Avocation: computers. Home: Oblá 79, 634 00 Brno Czech Republic Office: Faculty of Arts Masaryk U, A Nováka 1, 66088 Brno Czech Republic

KROEGER, SUSAN JEAN, accountant; b. Glenridge, N.J., July 3, 1961; d. John Alfred and Patricia Ann (ferrante) Kroeger; m. George Clarence Merrill, June 18, 1983; children: C.J., B.J., G.J., P.J. BA, William Paterson Coll., 1986. CPA, N.J., ins. broker; lic. real estate sales person, N.J. Clk. Crum & Foster, Parsippany, N.J., 1980-86; internal auditor Crum & Foster, Parsippany, 1986-87; sr. acct. Ernst & Young & Co., Iselin, N.J., 1987-89; pvt. practice Parsippany, 1989—; real estate sales assoc. ERA, Gallo & DeCroce, 1993—. Exec. bd. dirs. PTA, Rockaway Meadow; mgr., Par Troy West Little League; treas. Cubscout Pack 215; coach Parsippany Soccer Club. Mem. AICPA, N.J. Soc. CPAs, North Ctrl. Jersey Real Estate Assn., Garden State Multiple Listing Svc. Republican. Roman Catholic. Avocations: camping, golfing.

KROEGER, UWE, actor; b. Kamen-Methler, Germany, Dec. 4, 1964; s. Hermann Walter and Elisa Beth (Ernst) K. Student, Sch of Arts, Berlin, Germany, 1986-88. Actor. Appeared in (theatre) Godspell, 1986, The Fat Pig, 1987-88, Rocky Horror Show, Starlight Express, 1988-89, Les Miserables, 1989-90, Jesus Christ Superstar, 1990Starmania, 1991-92, Elisabeth, 1992-94, 96-97, Miss Saigon, 1994-95, Sunset Boulevard, 1995-97, Beauty and the Beast, 1997, Cabaret, 1998-99, It's Showtime, 1999, Mozart!, 1999, numerous TV shows and recordings. Avocations: sports, travel, theatre. Office: Gianzlichter Agy, Trattnerhof 2, 1010 Vienna Austria

KROELL, WALTER, aerospace executive. Chmn. German Aerospace Ctr., Cologne. Office: German Aerospace Ctr, Linder Hoehe, 51147 Cologne Germany

KROELLER, EDGAR HARTMUT, retired economist; b. Wuerzburg, Bavaria, Germany, Nov. 17, 1926; arrived in France, 1962; s. Lorenz and Friederike (Martini) K.; m. Anneliese Mitternacht, Aug. 27, 1948. Student, U. Mich., 1949-50; dipl. volkswirt, U. Munich, 1953, dr. oec. publ., 1955. Dir. agrl. census UN Food and Agrl. Orgn., Libya, 1956-62; head econ. and environment divsn. OECD, Paris, 1962-91, cons., 1992-94. Author: The American Labor Market, 1956; contbr. articles to profl. jours.

KROEMER, HERBERT, electrical engineering educator; b. Weimar, Ger., Germany, Aug. 25, 1928. Diplom-Physiker, Gottingen U., Ger., 1951, Dr. rer. nat., 1952; Doctorate (hon.), Tech. U. Aachen (Ger.), 1985, U. Lund, 1998. Prof. elec., computer engring. U. Calif., Santa Barbara; Faculty Rsch Lecturer U. Calif, 1985—; Donald W. Whittier Chair in Electrical Engineering U. Calif., 1986—. J.J. Ebers Award of the Electron Devices Group of the IEEE, 1973, Heinrich Welker Medal of the Internat. Symposium on GaAs and related compounds, 1982, Nat. Lecturer, IEEE Electron Devices Soc., 1983, Jack Morton Award of the IEEE, 1986, Alexander von Humboldt Rsch. Award, 1994, Nat. Acad. of Engineering, 1997, Nobel Prize, 2000. mem. NAE, IEEE (J.J. Ebers award 1973, Jack Morton award 1986), Am. Phys. Soc. Office: U Calif Elec-Computer Engring Dept Santa Barbara CA 93106

KROES, NEELIE, academic administrator; b. Rotterdam, The Netherlands, July 19, 1941. MS in Econs., Erasmus U., Rotterdam, The Netherlands. Asst. prof. econs. Erasmus U., 1965-71; mem. Parliament Rotterdam, The Netherlands, 1971-77; sec. state Transport & Pub. Works, Rotterdam, The Netherlands, 1977-81, mem. cabinet, 1982-89; advisor European Transp. Commr., Brussels, Belgium, 1989-91; pres. Nijenrode U., The Netherlands, 1991-2000; mem. competitiveness adv. group to the comm. European Commn., 1997—. Office: Nyenrode U, Straatweg 25, 3621 BG Breukelen The Netherlands

KROGER, JANE ELIZABETH, psychology educator; b. Berkeley, Calif., Oct. 17, 1947; arrived in Norway, 1996; d. Roscoe R. and Gloria G. (Hager) K. BA, U. Calif., Davis, 1969, MSc, 1971; diploma in sociology, U. Stockholm, 1970; PhD, Fla. State U., 1977. Lectr. Massey U., Palmerston, New Zealand, 1972-75; sr. lectr. Victoria U., Wellington, New Zealand, 1977-92; reader Victoria U., Wellington, 1992-95; prof. U. Tromsø, Norway, 1996—. Author: Identity in Adolescence, 2nd edit., 1996, Identity Development: Adolescence Through Adulthood, 2000; editor: Discussions on Ego Identity, 1993; mem. editl. bd. Jour. Adolescence, Internat. Jour. Behavioral Devel. Grantee Roy MacKenzie Found., New Zealand, 1992. Mem. Internat. Soc. for the Study Behavioral Devel., Soc. for Rsch. on Identity Formation, Soc. for Rsch. on Adolescence, Soc. for Rsch. on Child Devel.

KROGH, THOMAS EDVARD, curator, geochronologist; b. Peterborough, Ont., Can., Jan. 12, 1936; s. Johan Edvard and Marjorie Ruth (Byers) K.; m. Kathleen Myers, Sept. 9, 1961; children: Erik, Kari, Sara, Jason. BSc, Queen's U., 1959, MSc, 1961, DSc (hon.), 1991; PhD, MIT, 1964. Staff scientist Carnegie Instn., Washington, 1964-75; curator Royal Ont. Mus., Toronto, 1975—; prof. geology U. Toronto, 1976—. Recipient Past Pres. medal Mineral. Assn. Can., 1994, J.T. Wilson medal Can. Geophys. Union, 1991. Fellow Am. Geophys. Union, Geochem. Soc., Geol. Assn. Can. (Logan medal), Norwegian Acad. Sci., Royal Soc. Can. Avocations: gardening, cooking. Fax: 416-586-5814. Home: 6348 Second Line RR #4, Tottenham, ON Canada L0G 1WO Office: 100 Queen's Park, Toronto, ON Canada M5S 2C6

KROGH, TORBEN, journalist; b. Copenhagen, Denmark, Aug. 26, 1943; s. Erik and Lilli (Hasle) K.; m. Leila Moller, Aug. 19, 1966; two children. MA, Danish Sch. Journalism, Aarhus, 1965. Editor-in-chief Information, Copenhagen, 1969-72, 84-87, Socialistisk Dagblad, Copenhagen, 1974-81, Udenrigs, Copenhagen, 1993—; cons. in field; chair Danish Sch. Journalism, 1990—, Danish Inst. Journalism Tng., 1990—; exec. bd. UNESCO, 1991-95, pres. gen. conf., 1995-97; chmn. Danish Nat. Commn. for UNESCO. Author: Viggo Horup, 1984, History of the Danish Labour Movement, 1982, Gert Petersen, 1987; author, editor: Danish Media Policy, 1996, Farewell to the Parties, 1998. Mem. Danish Fgn. Policy Assn. Home: Osterled 5, 2100 Copenhagen Denmark

KROGH-JESPERSEN, MARY-BETH, academic administrator; b. Schenectady, N.J., Aug. 10, 1949; d. George Henry and Barbara V. (Norton)

Baillie; m. Karsten Krogh-Jespersen, Dec. 20, 1975; children: Erik, Sheila Ann, Michelle Grace. BA in Chemistry, Northeastern U., 1972; MBA, Pace U., 1990; PhD in Chemistry, NYU, 1976. Lectr. in chemistry Rutgers U., New Brunswick, N.J., 1979-81; prof. Pace U., N.Y.C., 1981-92, chair dept. chemistry, 1990-92; dean coll. of sci. Rochester (N.Y.) Inst. Tech., 1992-95; vice provost Rowan Coll., Glassboro, N.J., 1995-96; assoc. v.p. for acad. affairs Richard Stockton Coll., Pomona, N.J., 1996-2000; campus exec. office Pa. State U.-Worthington, Scranton, 2000—. Contbr. articles to profl. jours. Mem. Am. Chem. Soc., Am. Phys. Soc. Roman Catholic. Office: Pa State U - Worthington 120 Ridgeview Dr Dunmore PA 18512-1602

KROGNESS, PAMELA, special education administrator; b. Hastings, Nebr., Apr. 15, 1952; d. Clinton J. and Doris Marie Sahling; m. Daniel Patrick Gillen, June 5, 1983 (div. May 1985); m. Stephen Velie Krogness, July 6, 1976. BA, Hastings Coll., 1974; MS, U. Nebr., 1978; postgrad., U. NEbr., 1972-73. Cert. tchr. elem. edn., learning disabilities, behavioral disorders, adminstr. Tchr. Omaha Pub. Schs., 1974-83, tchr., cons., 1985-95; tchr. Spl. Sch. Dist., St. Louis, 1983-84, Lincoln (Nebr.) Pub. Schs., 1984-85; asst. elem. adminstr. Cobb County Schs., Marietta, Ga., 1995-97, spl. edn. supr., 1997-99, spl. edn. asst. dir., 1999—; mem. adv. bd. Cobb County Spl. Edn., Marietta; coord. Ptnrs. in Edn., Cobb County-Mt. Bethel Elem. Sch., Marietta; cons. in field. Deacon Ctrl. Presbyn. Ch., Omaha, 1992-95, summer Bible sch. tchr., 1993-95; charity dr. coord. Peachtree Presbyn. Ch., Atlanta, 1999; presch. Sunday sch. tchr. Peachtree Presbyn. Ch., Atlanta, 1995-97. Grantee Elks Club, 1993-95; recipient award Women's Guild/U. Nebr. Med. Ctr., 1993. Mem. Coun. for Exceptional Children (treas. local chpt. 2000—), Coun. Adminstrs. Spl. Edn., Woodhill Country, Phi Delta Kappa. Avocations: travel, reading, bicycling, walking, art fairs. Office: Cobb County Schs 514 Glover St SE Marietta GA 30060-2706

KROGSTIE, JOHN, information systems researcher; b. Oslo, Norway, May 23, 1967; s. Per Asbjorn and Bjorg (Thingstad) K.; m. Birgit Rognebakke, Sept. 9, 1995; children: Øystein, Håvard. MSc, Norwegian Inst. Tech., Trondheim, Norway, 1991, PhD, 1995. Mgr. Andersen Consulting, Norway, 1991-2000; sr. rsch. scientist SINTEF, Oslo, 2000—; lectr. Norwegian Inst. Tech., 1996-98, adj. assoc. prof. 1998—; reviewer ESPRIT project European Cmty., Brussels, 1996-97; conf. program coord. IFIP, 1995; mem. program coms. numerous internat. confs. Editor: Proceedings of the IFIP 8.1 WC on Information Systems Development for Decentralized Organizations, 1995; contbr. articles to sci. pubs. including Jour. Software Maintenance, Jour. Automated Software Engring., Info. and Software Tech. Requirements Engring. Jour., others. Malaysia coord. Amnesty Internat., Norway, 1995-96. Mem. IEEE, ACM. Avocations: sports, reading, music. Home: Kjonejordet 6, N1352 Kolsas Akershus, Norway Office: SINTEF, Forskningsvn 1, Oslo Norway

KROH, JERZY, retired science educator; b. Warsaw, Aug. 28, 1924; s. Wladyslaw and Zofia (Rezler) K.; m. Aleksandra Czech, 1963; 1 child, Jan. MSc in Chemistry, Tech. U. Lodz, Poland, 1947, PhD in Chemistry, 1950; MSc in Physics, U. Lodz, 1950; PhD in Chemistry, U. Leeds, England, 1960; DSc (hon.), Strathclyde U., Scotland, 1983, Leeds U., England, 1987, Pavia U., Italy, 1989, Tech. U. Lodz, 1995. Asst. U. Lodz, 1947-50; tutor Tech. U. Lodz, 1950-62, assoc. prof., 1963-68, full prof., 1968—, dean food chemistry dept., 1962-66, rector, 1981-88; dir. Inst. Applied Radiation Chemistry, Lodz, 1970-94; pres. Radiation Rsch. Found.; mem. Miller Trust Radiation Rsch. Contbr. articles to profl. jours.; regional editor: Radiation Physics and Chemistry, Jour. Radioanalytical and Nuclear Chemistry. Dep. mayor Lodz for Edn. and Sci., 1996-98. Recipient Silver and Golden Star Japanese Order Sacred Treasure, 1989. Fellow Royal Soc. Edinburgh (hon.); mem. Polish Acad. Scis., Internat. Assn. Radiation Rsch., Polish Assn. Radiation Rsch. Avocations: tourism, foreign travels. Home: Zeromskiego 10 c/2, 90-710 Lodz Poland Office: Inst Applied Radiation Chem, Wroblewskiego 15, 93-590 Lodz Poland

KROHN, KENNETH ALBERT, radiology educator; b. Stevens Point, Wis., June 19, 1945; s. Albert William and Erma Belle (Cornwell) K.; 1 child, Galen. BA in Chemistry, Andrews U., 1966; PhD in Chemistry, U. Calif., 1971. Acting assoc. prof. U. Wash., Seattle, 1981-84, assoc. prof. radiology, 1984-86, prof. radiology and radiation oncology, 1986—, adj. prof. chemistry, 1986—; guest scientist Donner Lab. Lawrence Berkeley (Calif.) Lab., 1980-81; radiochemist, VA Med. Ctr., Seattle, 1982—; affiliate investigator Fred Hutchinson Cancer Rsch. Ctr., 1997—. Contbr. articles to profl. jours.; patentee in field. NDEA fellow; recipient Aebersold award, 1996. Fellow AAAS; mem. Am. Assn. for Cancer Rsch., Am. Chem. Soc., Radiation Rsch. Soc., Soc. Nuclear Medicine, Acad. Coun., Sigma Xi. Home: 550 NE Lakeridge Dr Belfair WA 98528-8720 Office: U Washington Imaging Rsch Lab PO Box 356004 Seattle WA 98195-6004

KROKHIN, OLEG NICOLAEVITSH, physicist, researcher, educator; b. Moscow, Mar. 14, 1932; s. Nicolay Gerasimovitsh and Alexandra Andreevna (Vdovenko) K.; m. Nina Feodos'evna Martisheva, July 5, 1954; children: Natalya Olegovna Krokhina. Grad., Moscow State U., 1955; DSc, P.N. Lebedev Physical Inst., Moscow, 1962, D in Physics, Math., 1967. Physicist, engr. Cheliabinsk (Russia)-70, 1956-59; from scientist to sr. scientist P.N. Lebedev Physical Inst., 1959-65, divsn. head, 1965-73, 78-86, vice dir., 1973-78, prin. scientist, 1986-90, lab. head, 1990-94, dir., 1994—; assoc. prof. Moscow Physical Engring. Inst., 1964-68, prof., 1968—. Contbr. more than 200 articles to sci. jours. Recipient Lenin prize in physics Govt. USSR, 1964, State prize in physics Govt. USSR, 1982. Mem. Russian Acad. Scis., Russian Com.(supreme cert. com. 1980). Avocations: skiing, swimming, manual work. Office: PN Lebedev Physical Inst, Leninsky Prospect 53, 117924 Moscow Russia

KROKIDAS, DIMITRIOS ELIAS, electrical engineer, sales executive; b. Athens, Greece, Apr. 26, 1966; s. Elias Dimitrios and Ann Evangelos (Sofras) K. Diploma, Inst. Français D'Athenes, Athens, 1984; diploma in Elec. Engring., Democritus U. of Thrace, Xanthi, Greece, 1990; MSc in Elec. Sys. Design, Cranfield (Eng.) U., 1993. Registered profl. engr., Greece. Gen. mgr. Hellenic Tech. Enterprises, Piraeus, Greece, 1992—; sales exec. Tenora Engring. Ltd., Athens, 1994—. Active Conservative Party Orgn. Scis., Athens, 1990, Dem. Engrs. Movement, Athens, 1990, Hellenic Maritime Mus., 1990. Served Hellenic Air Force, 1990-91. Mem. IEEE, Hellenic Assn. Elec. and Mech. Engrs., Hellenic Ornithol. Soc., N.Y. Acad. Scis., Tech. Chamber of Greece. Christian Orthodox. Avocations: aviation, aircraft modelling, book collecting, music, records. Home: 72a Delfon St, GR-165 61 Glyfada Greece Office: Hellenic Tech Enterprises, 136 Karaiskou St, GR-185 36 Piraeus Greece

KROL, JOHN A., retired diversified chemicals executive; b. Gilbertsville, Mass., Oct. 16, 1936; m. Janet Ruth Valley, Sept. 12, 1938; children: Cynthia, Deborah. BS, MS in chemistry, Tufts U., 1958, MS in Phys. Chemistry, 1959. With textile fibers sect. of DuPont Chestnut Run Rsch. Lab., Wilmington, Del., 1963-65; mktg. rep. Centre Road Office, Wilmington, Del., 1965-66, supr. indsl. tech. mktg., 1966-69; mktg. mgr. N.Y.C., 1969-70; mktg. mgr. industrial fibers Akron, Ohio, 1970-72; regional mktg. mgr. Textile Fibers, Wynnewood, Pa., 1972-73; product mgr. Dacron, Wilmington, Del., 1973-75; mfg. supt. Dacron, Old Hickory, Tenn., 1975-77; asst. plant mgr. mfg. DuPont, Old Hickory, Tenn., 1975-78; mktg. dir. DuPont Carpet Fibers and FIberfill divsn., Wilmington, 1978-80, dir., 1980-83; v.p. fibers DuPont DeNemours & Co., Wilmington, 1983-86, v.p. agrl. products dept., 1986-87; group v.p. agrl. products, 1987-90; sr. v.p. fibers DuPont DeNemours & Co., Wilmington, 1990-91, vice chmn., 199297, dir., CEO/pres., 1995-98; chmn. DuPont DeNemours & Co., 1997-98; bd. dirs. Mead Corp., JP Morgan, Milliken Co., Armstrong World Industries; trustees Tufts Univ., Univ. Del., Hegley Mus.; corp. liaison bd. Am. Chemical Soc.; adv. bd. Teijen Corp., Bechtel Corp. Pres. Consortium for Grad. Degrees for Ministries. Served to lt. USN, 1959-63. Mem. Natl. Agrl. Chems. Assn. (bd. dirs. 1987—), Radley Run Country Club (West Chester, Pa.), Wilmington Country Club (bd. dirs.), Bonita Bay Country Club (Naples, Fla.), Olde Fla. Country Club. Republican. Roman Catholic. Avocations: golf, skiing, squash, tennis. Office: DuPont 1007 N Market St Fl 2 Wilmington DE 19801-1229

KROL-DOBROV, CHAREL B., European studies and Dutch language educator; b. The Hague, The Netherlands, Dec. 9, 1960; s. Carel and Bastiana (Moleveld) K.; m. Natalya Andreyevna Dobrova-Krol, Apr. 1999. DSc in History, Leiden U., 1986, LLM, 1985, PhD, 1987; LLD, U. Maastricht, 1994. Lectr. U. Amsterdam, The Netherlands, 1988; rsch. asst. U. Maastricht, The Netherlands, 1989-94; prof. Odessa State U., Ukraine, 1995—; mng. dir. Tempus/Tacis project Odessa in Europe—Europe in Odessa, 1998. Author: If Only the King Knew...! Of Authority and Knowledge, Inviolability and Infallibility, and their Histories, 1994. Mem. Acad. Engrs. Ukraine (acad. councillor 2000—). E-mail: charel@krol.odessa.ua. Office: Odessa State U, Ul Dvoryanskaya 2, 65026 Odessa Ukraine

KROLL, SOL, lawyer; b. Russia, Aug. 10, 1918; m. Ruth Saslow; children: Gerald, Judy, Elise, Elliott. LLB, St. John's U., 1942. Bar: N.Y. 1942, U.S. Supreme Ct. 1956. Former U.S. counsel to Assn. Francaise des Socs. D'Assurances Transports; former mem. com. of interfraud task force N.Y. Ins. Dept. Contbr. articles on Am. ins. law to various ins. mags. Mem. ABA, Fed. Bar Assn., N.Y. State Bar Assn., Internat. Assn. Ins. Counsel, Industry Adv. Com. on Ins.; bd. govs. Internatl. Ins. Soc. Home: 600 Cantitoe St Bedford NY 10506-1107 Office: 110 E 59th St New York NY 10022-1304

KROMBHOLZ, HEINZ, psychologist; b. Biebesheim, Germany, May 15, 1948; s. Rudolf and Luise (Ernst) K.; m. Ingrid Maria Mader, Dec. 22, 1998; children: Martin R.A., Lisa M.F.B. Diploma in Psychology, U. Giessen, Germany, 1974; PhD, Free U., Berlin, 1987. Rsch. scientist U. Giessen, Germany, 1975-79, State Inst. Early Childhood Edn. and Rsch., Munich, Germany, 1981—. Author: (books) Sports Achievement and Cognitive Achievement in Elementary School, 1988, The Family in Western Germany, 1991; also articles in profl. jours. Office: State Inst Early Child Edn, & Rsch Prinzregentenstr 24, D-80538 Munich Germany

KROMKA, JAMES THOMAS MICHAEL, designer, illustrator; b. Phoenix, Mar. 10, 1954; m. Linda Mae, Oct. 12, 1985. Student, Pasadena Coll. Design, 1972-74. Staff artist Riverside County Libr. System, 1969-72; circulation promotional artist Press Enterprise, Riverside, Calif., 1970-71; artist Lily div. Owens-Ill., Riverside, 1972-73; owner, mgr. Slinky Ink Graphics, Walnut Creek, Calif., 1974-76; co-designer, co-owner, constrn., mgr. Aesop's Restaurant, Riverside, 1976-78; owner, mgr. Bouhouze Custom Paint, Edgemont, Calif., 1978-79; graphic designer, dir. Robertshaw Controls, Corona, Calif., 1979-82; art dir., illustrator, prodn. artist Tobi's Graphics, Inc., El Monte, Calif., 1982-83; graphic designer, tech. illustrator Graphic Art Svcs., Chino, Calif., 1983-85, D. Sign Design Kustoms, 1985-98; tchr. animation MTI Coll., 1998-99; art dir., illustrator Interactive Illusion Inc., Costa Mesa, Calif., 1999—. Home: 2556 Reservoir Dr Norco CA 92860-2327

KROMMER, KAROLY FERENC, obstetrics-gynecology educator; b. Pecs, Hungary, Mar. 7, 1938; s. Karoly and Ilona (Apathy) K.; m. Piroska Derenyi, May 10, 1969; children: Judit, Agnes, Lucia, Kinga. MD, U. Med. Sch., Pecs, 1962, PhD, 1992. Resident dept. ob-gyn. U. Med. Sch., Pecs, 1962-64, instr. dept. ob-gyn., 1965-66, splst. in ob-gyn. dept. ob-gyn., 1967-69, splst. radiotherapy dept. ob-gyn., 1970-75, asst. prof. dept. ob-gyn., 1976-92, assoc. prof., 1993-97, prof. dept. ob-gyn., 1998, specialist in med. oncology dept. ob-gyn., 1998, head divsn. oncology dept. ob-gyn., 1976—; supr., advisor oncologists Region S.W. Hungary, Pecs, 1993—. Fellow Internat. Union Against Cancer; mem. European Assn. Gynecologists and Obstetricians, European Soc. Therapeutic Radiology and Oncology, European Soc. Med. Oncology, N.Y. Acad. Sci. Roman Catholic. Avocations: music, tourism. Office: Pote, Noi Klinika, Edesanyak 17, Pecs H-7624, Hungary

KRONE, ANDREAS GEORG, neurosurgeon, educator; b. Tubingen, Germany, Mar. 20, 1954; s. Heinrich-Adolf and Elisabeth (Büchner) K.; m. Verena Schubert; children: Manuel, Lukas. Grad., U. Würzburg, 1980, MD, 1980, Habil, 1990. Cert. neurosurgeon. Prof. neurosurgery U. Würzburg, 1997. Co-author: Die Chirurgie, 1999, Neurologische Intensivtherapie, 1999; contbr. articles to profl. jours. Wilhelm Tönnis grantee DGNC, 1990. Mem. German Neurosurg. Assn. Roman Catholic. Avocations: piano, sports, family. Home: Lärchenweg 12, D-97084 Würzburg Germany Office: Univ Neurosurg Clinic, J Schneider-Str 11, D-97080 Würzburg Germany

KRONE, JULIE, jockey; b. Benton Harbor, Mich., July 24, 1963; d. Don and Judy Krone. Profl. jockey Tampa Bay (Fla.) Downs, others, 1981—; first female jockey to win a Triple Crown race; first woman to win 5 races in a day at Saratoga, N.Y.; leading woman jockey in U.S., 1986-88; leading woman jockey money won, 1986—; winningest female jockey in history with nearly 3,400 victories. Author: (with Nancy Ann Richardson) Riding for My Life, 1995. Winner of 19 Grade I races including $77 Million in purses; races won include Cornhusker Handicap, AK-Star Ben Racetrack, Omaha, 1988, Flower Bowl Handicap, Belmont Park, 1988, Modesty Stakes, Arlington Park, Ill., 1989, Budweiser Md. Classic, Pimlico, 1989, Belmont Stakes, Elmont, N.Y., 1993, The Molson Million, Toronto, Can., 1995, The Meadowlands Cup, East Rutherford, N.J., 1995, The Ill. Derby, Chgo., 1995, N.J. Derby, Cherry Hill, 1992, 94, 95; first rode in Ky. Derby, 1991; recipient Comeback award Am. Sportscasters Assn., 1994, ESPY Award winner female athlete of yr., 1993. Address: Jockeys Guild Inc PO Box 250 Lexington KY 40588-0250

KRONE, NORMAN BERNARD, commercial real estate developer, lawyer; b. Memphis, Sept. 13, 1938; s. Irving and Eva (Sauer) K.; m. Norma Lee Moon; children: John, Christine, David. LLB, Stetson U., 1964. Bar: Fla. 1964, Ohio 1987, U.S. Dist. Ct. (mid. dist.) Fla. 1965, U.S. Ct. Appeals (7th cir.) 1968. Atty. Lifsey & Johnston, Tampa, Fla., 1964-65; pvt. practice Tampa, Fla., 1965-66; property mgmt. atty. Ford Motor Co., Dearborn, Mich., 1966-67; audit mgr. Montgomery Ward & Co., Chgo., 1967-68, corp. real estate mgr., 1968-75; exec. v.p. Momtgomery Ward Properties Corp., Chgo., 1970-75; from v.p. to sr. v.p. Walgreen Co., Deerfield, Ill., 1975-85; pres., CEO The Hausman Cos., Cleve., 1987—; sr. exec. v.p. Henry S. Miller, Grubb & Ellis Comml./Retail Svcs.; trustee Internat. Coun. Shopping Ctrs., N.Y.C., 1976-79; dir. Myers Industries, Lincoln, Ill., 1976-83; mem. adv. bd. Commerce Exch. Bank, Beachwood, Ohio, 1997—; instr. Intercoun. Shopping Ctrs.-Inst. Profl. Devel.; dean U. Shopping Ctrs.-Internat. Coun. Shopping Ctrs., mem. cert. governance com., cert. leasing specialist, mem. ednl. adv. com., mem. small ctr. com., chmn. retail adv. com., 1975-76; spkr. conventions and confs. Author, editor: The Lease and Its Language, 1996; contbr. articles to mags. Acting judge City of Tampa, 1964-66; bd. dirs. Met. Housing and Planning Coun., Chgo., 1977-80, New City YMCA, 1976-78; mem. sch. bd. Palisades Cmty. Sch. Dist., 1968-69; mem. strategic planning com. Met. Chgo. YMCA, 1976-77; 1st pres. Cleve. Pops Orch.; mem., bd. dirs. Walgreen Hist. Found., 1984-87; co-founder, pres., mem. exec. com. Realty Resources (a network of comml. brokerage firms), 1987—. Named Entrepreneur of Yr. Operation Breadbasket, 1977. Mem. Cleve. Bar Assn. (spkr.), Real Estate Inst., Beachwood C. of C. (pres. 1996, exec. com. 1992—), Acacia Country Club (bd. dirs. 1997-99, chmn. planning com. 1998-99, sec. 1998). Avocations: flying, woodworking, golf. E-mail: nkrone@hausmancos.com. Home: 8650 Hunting Hill Dr Mentor OH 44060-7858 Office: The Hausman Cos 2101 Richmond Rd Beachwood OH 44122-1390

KRONHAUSEN, PHYLLIS C., psychologist, consultant; b. Minn., Jan. 26, 1929; d. Eberhard W. Kronhausen. BBA cum laude, U. Minn., 1947; EdD, Columbia U., 1958. Diplomate Am. Acad. Psychotherapists; cert. psychologist, Calif. Asst. consul U.S. Consulate, Bombay, 1947-52; pvt. practice psychologist, 1958—. Co-author: Erotic Art, vols. I, 1967, vol. II, 1970, Formula for Life, 1989, 2d edit., 1999. Grantee NIH, 1956. Home: Apartado 203, Alajuela Erica Ctrl Costa Rica

KROON, LUUK, NATO official, military officer; b. Ridderkerk, The Netherlands, Dec. 1942; m. Annie Kroon. Joined Royal Netherlands Navy, 1961, advanced through grades to adm., 1998, various positions, primarily on naval vessels, 1961-1972; with Office of Directorate Material, Ministry of Def. Royal Netherlands Navy, The Hague, 1972-75; comdg. officer minehunter HNLMS Staphorst Royal Netherlands Navy, 1976-77; staff officer minewarfare, Naval Hdqrs. Royal Netherlands Navy, The Hague, 1978-81; comdg. officer HNLMS Jaguar Royal Netherlands Navy, 1981-82, comdr. S-class frigate HNLMS Callenburgh, 1982-84; naval staff planner, Office of Chief of Def. Royal Netherlands Navy, The Hague, 1984-89, dep. chief of Naval Staff, Office of Plans, 1989-92, comdr. Netherlands Task Group, 1992-93; adm. Netherlands fleet, comdr. maritime forces Royal Netherlands Navy, 1993-95, comdr.-in-chief, 1995-98, chief of Netherlands Def. Staff, 1998—. Office: The Netherlands Def Staff, Plein 4 PO Box 20701, 2500 The Hague The Netherlands also: NATO Hdqrs, Blvd Leopold III, 1110 Brussels Belgium*

KROPIWNICKI, JERZY JANUSZ, federal official; b. Czestochowa, July 5, 1945; married; 1 child. MA in Econs., Ctr. Sch. Planning and Stats., Warsaw, Poland, 1968; PhD, Lodz U., 1973. Asst. prof. Lodz U., 1968—; co-founder Christian Nat. Union, 1989, mem. exec. bd., 1989-93, 98—, v.p., 1991-93, 2000—, head social and econ. policy com., 1994—, mem. nat. coun., 1995-98; min. Labor and Social Policy, 1991-92; min., head ctrl. planning office, 1992-93; min., head Govt. Ctr. Strategic Studies, 1997—, min. regional devel. and constrn., 2000—; prof. BWSH U. Wis., Madison, 1977-78, 90-91; prof. WSzEH, Skierniewice, 1995—; chmn. bd. dirs., organizer Agy. for Regional Devel., Lodz, 1991-92. Co-founder, mem. NSZZ Solidarnosc and Anti-Community Opposition, 1980—, regional mgmt. mem., 1980-90, v.p. regional mgmt., 1981-90, nat. exec. bd., 1981-90, polit. prisoner, 1981-84, underground activity, 1984-89. Solidarity Election Action. Office: Govt Ctr Strategic Studies, ul Wspolna 4, Warsaw Poland

KROPMAN, DANIEL JOSIF, physicist; b. Tartu, Estonia, Apr. 17, 1931; s. Josif Leib and Zilja Aabram (Shapiro) K.; m. Helju Eevald Sepp, Jan. 20, 1973; children: Mark, Ruth. Grad., U. Tartu, 1960; PhD, Inst. Semiconductors, Kiev, Ukraine, 1978. Engr. Tondi Electronics, Tallinn, Estonia, 1960-68, head of lab., 1969-80, head rsch. group, 1980-92; lectr. Estonian Maritime Acad., Tallinn, 1993—. Contbr. articles to profl. jours. Avocations: surface and interface science, defects engineering. Home: Kuldnoka Str 15-64, EE 10619 Tallinn Estonia Office: Estonia Maritime Acad, Estonia Maritime Acad, Mustakivi 25, EE 13912 Tallinn Estonia

KROSKE, JOACHIM, broadcasting executive; b. Bad Lausic, Saxony, Germany, 1944. Degree in Bus. Econs., Doctorate, 1971. Various positions in fin., acctg. and info. processing Philips, 1972; past comml. mgr. Drägerwerke AG; past mng. dir. Bosch Co.; mem. bd. mgmt. Deutsche Telekom, 1990—. Office: Deutsche Telekom AG, Friedrich Evert Allee 140, Postfach 2000 Bonn 53105, Germany*

KROST, GERHARD, engineering educator; b. Essen, Germany, Aug. 24, 1953; s. Helmut and Ilse (Vidal) K.; m. Wiebke Katharina Massing, June 10, 1979; children: Karoline, Sebastian, Matthias. Diploma in engring., Tech. U., Darmstadt, Germany, 1978; Dr. in Engring., U. Erlangen, Germany, 1983; habiltation, U. Duisburg, Germany, 1992. Rsch. asst. U. Erlangen, 1978-85; acad. lectr. Gerhard-Mercator U., Duisburg, 1985-92, pvt. docent, 1992-98, prof., 1998—; guest prof. U. Krasnoyarsk, Russia, 1998; convenor working group CIGRE, paris, 1995—. Contbr. over 60 articles to profl. jours. With German armed forces, 1972-73. Mem. Conf. Internat. des Grands Reseaux Electriques, IEEE, Verein Deutscher Elektrotechniker. Avocations: cello, sailing. Home: Nachbarsweg 105, D-45481 Muelheim Germany Office: Gerhard-Mercator U., FB9-EAN Bismarckstr 81, D-47057 Duisburg Germany

KROT, ALEXANDER MIKHAILOVICH, cybernetics and radiophysics researcher, educator; b. Golshany, Oshmiany, Belarus, Sept. 5, 1960; s. Mikhail Stepanovich and Polina Adamovna (Kulagina) K; m. Polina Pavlovna Tkachova; 1 child, Alexandra (Alisa). Dipl., Belarusian State U., Minsk, 1982; postgrad., Inst. Eng. Cybernetics, Minsk, 1982-85, 88-91; PhD, Nat. Acad. Scis. Belarus, Minsk, 1985, ScD, 1991, prof. degree, 1997. From junior rsch. worker to leading rsch. worker Inst. Engring. Cybernetics, Minsk, Belarus, 1985-93, head rsch. lab., 1993—; prof. dept. radioengring. sys. Belarusian State U. Informatics and Radioelectronics, Minsk, 1993-97, prof. dept. radiophysics, Belarusian State U., 1996-98; mem. sci. and spl. couns. Nat. Acad. Scis. Belarus, Inst. Eng. Cybernetics, Belarusian State U.; mgr. sci. project B-95 Internat. Sci. and Tech. Ctr., 1997-2000. Author: Discrete Models of Dynamic Systems Based on Polynomial Algebra, 1990, (with E.B. Minervina) Fast Algorithms and Programs for Digital Spectral Processing of Signals and Images, 1995; mem. editl. bd. Achievement in Modern Radioelectronics, Electromagnetic Waves and Electronic Systems (Moscow), Nonlinear Phenomena in Complex Systems; editor procs. of IEC "Intelligent Systems" (Minsk); contbr. articles to profl. jours. Recipient Komsomol's awards Minsk, 1988, Belarus, 1990, A.S. Popov award Radioengring. Soc., 1991, award Nat. Acad. Sci. Belarus, 1993; grantee Internat. Sci. Found., 1993. Mem. Am. Math. Soc., Belarusian Assn., Assn. for Image Analysis and Recognition, Internat. Assn. for Pattern Recognition (sec. 1993-96), Internat. Soc. Optical Engring. (Russian br.), World Scientific and Engring. Soc., Hardware Description Langs. Application and Devel. Assn. (v.p. 1993—). Avocations: numismatics, gravitation theory. Home: 94 Rafiev Apt 87, 220098 Minsk Belarus Office: Nat Acad Sci Belarus, 6 Surganov, 220012 Minsk Belarus

KROTKIEWSKI, HUBERT MARCIN, chemist, researcher; b. Jelenia Gora, Poland, Oct. 3, 1950; s. Edward Brunon and Zofia (Ochman) K.; m. Bozena Morawska, Dec. 29, 1975; children: Marcin Michał, Joanna Maria. Chem. Engr., Poly. Sch., Wroclaw, Poland, 1973; PhD, Inst. Immunol./Exptl. Therapy, Wroclaw, 1982, Habilitation, 1994. Engr. Inst. Nuclear Rsch., Swierk, Poland, 1974-75; asst. Inst. Immunology & Exptl. Therapy, Wroclaw, 1975-82, adiunkt, 1982-95, assoc. prof., 1996—, dep. dir. sci. affairs, 1997-99. Editor Archivum Immunologiae et Therapiae Experimentalis, 1991—. Avocations: travel, housekeeping. Office: Inst Immunol/Exptl Therapy, R Weigla 12, 53-114 Wroclaw Poland

KROTO, HAROLD WALTER, chemistry researcher, educator; b. Oct. 7, 1939; s. Heinz and Edith K.; m. Margaret Henrietta Hunter, 1963; 2 children. Student, U. Sheffield, 1958-64. Postdoctoral fellow NRCC, 1964-66; rsch. scientist Bell Tel. Labs., N.J., 1966-67; lectr. U. Sussex, Brighton Sussex, Eng., 1968-77, reader, 1977-85, prof. chemistry, 1985-91, Royal Soc. Rsch. prof., 1991—; chmn. Vega Sci. Trust. Contbr. 280 articles to profl. jours. Created knight, 1996; recipient award Sunday Times Book Jacket Design Competition, 1964, Tilden lectr., 1981-82, Internat. New Materials prize Am. Phys. Soc., 1992, Italgas prize for innovation in chemistry, 1992, Longstaff medal Royal Soc. Chemistry, 1993, Hewlett Packard Europhysics prize, 1994, Science pour L'art prize Moet Hennessy Louis Vuitton, 1994; co-recipient Nobel prize in chemistry, 1996. Office: U Sussex, Sch Chem Phys & Environ Sci, Brighton Sussex BN1 9QJ, England

KROZER, VIKTOR, electrical engineering educator; b. St. Petersburg, Russia, Nov. 28, 1958; arrived in Israel, 1968; arrived in Germany, 1972; s. Szymon and Rachel (Takserman-) K.; m. Catharina Schmeer, Dec. 23, 1983; children: Alice, Joël. Diploma in engring., Tech. U. Darmstadt, Germany, 1984, PhD in Elec. Engring., 1991. Vis. scientist European Space Agy., Darmstadt, 1984-86; rsch. scientist Tech. Hochschule Darmstadt, 1986-91, sr. scientist, 1991-96; vis. scientist U. Rome II, 1995-96; prof. elec. engring. Tech. U. Chemnitz, Germany, 1996—; vis. prof. U. Polit., Madrid, 1998-99. Contbr. numerous articles and papers to scientific jours. Mem. IEEE, CDE. Office: Tech U Chemnitz, Reichenhainerstr 70, D-09126 Chemnitz Germany

KRŠIAK, MILOSLAV, pharmacologist, researcher; b. Bratislava, Slovakia, May 7, 1939; arrived in Czech Republic, 1947; s. Mikuláš and Ludmila (Baxantová) K.; m. Miloslava Slavíčková, June 25, 1963; children: Helena, Jan. MD, Charles U., Prague, Czechoslovakia, 1962, PhD, 1966, DSc, 1982. Asst. dept. pharmacology, faculty paediatrics Charles U., Prague, 1962-63, head pharmacology dept., 1991—; postdoctoral fellow dept. pharmacology U. Coll., London, 1967-69; rsch. scientist Inst. Pharmacology/Czechoslovak Acad. Sci., Prague, 1969-93; chmn. adverse drug reactions com. Ministry Health, Prague, 1988-96, presidium of rsch. coun. of ministry, 1994-98; chmn. com. for pharmacology Grant Agy. Ministry Health, Prague, 1994-99. Contbr. articles to profl. jours. Riker fellow Internat. Union Pharmacology, 1967; recipient J.E. Purkynje medal Czech Med. Soc., 1983. Mem. European Behavioral Pharmacol. Soc. (com. mem. 1986-92), Internat. Soc. for Rsch. on Aggression (coun. mem. 1991-98), Internat. Brain Rsch. Orgn., Czech Pharmacol. Soc. (hon. mem., chmn. 1998—), Soc. for Neurosci., Internat. Assn. Study of Pain. Avocations: human ethology, philosophy. Office: Charles Univ Dept Pharmacology, 3rd Med Faculty, 100 00 Prague Czech Republic

KRSUL, JOHN ALOYSIUS, JR., lawyer; b. Highland Park, Mich., Mar. 24, 1938; s. John A. and Ann M. (Sepich) K.; m. Justine Oliver, Sept. 12, 1958; children: Ann Lisa, Mary Justine. BA, Albion Coll., 1959; JD, U. Mich., 1963. Bar: Mich. 1963. Assoc. Dickinson Wright PLLP, 1963-71; ptnr. Dickinson Wright PLLP, Detroit, 1971-99, consulting ptnr., 2000—. Asst. editor: U. Mich. Law Rev, 1962-63. Recipient Disting. Alumnus award Albion Coll., 1984; Sloan scholar, 1958-59; Fulbright scholar, 1959-60; Ford. Found. grantee, 1964. Fellow Am. Bar Found. (life, chmn. Mich. chpt. 1988-89); mem. ABA (sect. gen. practice, chmn. 1989-90, exec. coun. 1984-91, ho. of dels. 1979—, chmn. standing com. on membership 1983-89, tort and ins. practice sect., exec. coun. 1991-94, chmn. fin. com. 1993-94, bd. govs. 1991-99, exec. com. 1993-94, 96-99, treas. 1996-99, editl. bd. ABA Jour. 1996-99), Am. Bar Retirement Assn. (bd. dirs. 1999—), Detroit Bar Assn. (dir. 1971-80, pres. 1979-80), Detroit Bar Assn. Found. (dir. 1971-84, pres. 1979-80), State Bar Mich. (commr. 1973-83, pres. 1982-83), Mich. State Bar Found. (trustee 1982-83, 85-99, chmn. fellows 1986-87), Fellows of Young Lawyers Am. Bar (bd. dirs. 1977-86, chmn. bd. 1984-86, pres. 1983-84), Am. Judicature Soc. (dir. 1971-79, exec. com. 1973-74), Nat. Conf. Bar Pres. (exec. coun. 1986-89), Am. Bar Endowment (bd. dirs. 1996-99), Am. Bar Ins. Cons. Inc. (bd. dirs. sec. 1988-95), Sixth Cir. Jud. Conf. (life), Orchard Lake Country Club, Detroit Club, Phi Beta Kappa, Omicron Delta Kappa, Phi Eta Sigma, Delta Tau Delta. Home: 7094 Huntington Dr Sawyer MI 49125-9319 Office: Dickinson Wright PLLC 500 Woodward Ave Ste 4000 Detroit MI 48226-3416

KRUCKENBERG, TERESA MAY, research engineer, consultant; b. New Orleans, Aug. 23, 1963; d. Harold Dean and Joanna Marie (Clutter) K.; m. Matthew Reymond McDonald, Mar. 23, 1998; 1 child: Emily Jane. B-SChemE, Okla. State U., 1985; MSME, San Diego State U., 1993. Composite structures rsch. and devel. engr. Hercules Aerospace, Salt Lake City, 1985-89; sr. rsch. engr. BF Goodrich Aerospace (Rohr), San Diego, 1989-94, CRC-ACS, Sydney, Australia, 1994—; cons. Wilson Composite Group, Folsom, Calif., 1998-99; cons. BF Goodrich Aerospace, San Diego, 1999. Author chpt. Resin Transfer Moulding for Aerospace Structures, 1998; editor Resin Transfer Moulding for Aerospace Structures, 1998. Mem. Soc. Mfg. Eng., Soc. for Advancement of Materials and Process Engring. (chmn. Australia chpt. 1996-97), Australian Composites Structures Soc. Avocations: scuba diving, hiking. Office: CRC-ACS, 361 Milperra Rd, NSW Bankstown 2200, Australia

KRUEGER, ALAN DOUGLAS, communications company executive; b. Little Rock, Dec. 24, 1937; s. Herbert C. and Estelle B. Krueger; m. Betty Burns, Apr. 4, 1975; children: (by previous marriage) Scott Alan, Dane Kieth, Kip Douglas, Bryan Lee. Student, U. Ill., 1956, Wright Coll., 1957-58. Project engr. Motorla, Inc., Chgo., 1956-64; service mgr., field tech. rep. Motorla, Inc., Indpls., 1964-67; pres. Comm. Maintenance, Inc., Indpls., 1967-68, Comm. Unltd., Inc., Indpls., 1968—. Recipient Friend of the Child award, 1995. Mem. Indpls. Zoologian Soc., Specialized Mobile Radio Wireless Operator Network. Methodist. Club: Elks. Home: 6242 N 575 E Franklin IN 46131-8759 Office: Comm Unltd Inc 4545 Southeastern Ave Indianapolis IN 46203-2307

KRUEGER, ARLIN JAMES, physicist; b. Oct. 22, 1933; s. Rudolph August and Mathilda E. (Pooch) K.; m. Susan J. Peacock, Dec. 28, 1978; children: Sandra, Timothy, Terry. BA, U. Minn., 1955, postgrad., 1956-58; postgrad., Colo. State U., 1976-78, PhD, 1984. Physicist Naval Weapons Ctr., China Lake, Calif., 1959-69; physicist-astrophysicist Goddard Space Flight Ctr., Greenbelt, Md., 1969-2000; W.H. Elkins prof. physics U. Md., Balt., 2000—; developer of rocket and satellite instruments: sensor sci. Nimbus-7 Total Ozone Mapping Spectrometer (TOMS), 1975-93, Rocoz Optical Rocket Ozonesonde, 1961-79, Volcanic Ash Mapper (VOLCAM), 1998; mem. com. ext. U.S. Std. Atmosphere; instrument scientist U.S.-USSR Meteor 3/TOMS mission, U.S. Earth Probe/TOMS mission; prin. investigator Japanese ADEOS/TOMS mission, NASA Earth Sys. Scis. Pathfinder, Volcanic Ash Monitor (VOLCAM) Satellite Program, NASA Airborne Antarctic Ozone Experiment/TOMS Real-Time Support, NASA Airborne Arctic Experiment/TOMS Real Time Support; co-investigator Earth Observing Sys. Volcanic Eruption Investigation, Rsch. on Antarctic Ozone Hole; adv. volcanic hazards panel Office Fed. Coord. of Meteorology; invited lectr. Nat. Inst. Polar Rsch., Tokyo, AT&T Bell Labs., U.S. Naval Acad., Goddard Space Flight Ctr. Colloquium, Gordon Rsch. Conf. on Volcano-Climate, Fermi Sch. Physics, Italy, Russian Acad. Scis., Moscow; Quaternary Rsch. lectr. U. Wash.; invited participant and spkr. sci. workshops and confs. Contbr. articles to profl. publs. Recipient NASA Exceptional Sci. Achievement medal; Goddard rsch. and study fellow Colo. State U., 1976-78. Mem. AAAS, Am. Meteorol. Soc., Internat. Assn. Meteorology and Atmospheric Physics (internat. ozone commn.), Am. Geophys. Union, Sigma Xi. Achievements include research on stratospheric ozone, remote sensing from satellites, volcanic eruptions, volcanic aviation hazards, atmosphere of Mars. Office: Goddard Space Flight Ctr Code # 916 Greenbelt MD 20771-0001

KRUEGER, BETTY JANE, telecommunications company executive; b. Indpls., Oct. 4, 1923; d. Forrest Glen and Hazel Luellen (Taylor) Burns; m. Alan Douglas Krueger, Apr. 4, 1975; 1 son by previous marriage--Michael J. Vornehm. Student, Butler U., 1948-49. Supr., instr. Ind. Bell Telephone Co., Indpls., 1941-54; supr. communications Jones & Laughlin Steel Co., Indpls., 1954-56, Ford Motor Co., Indpls., 1956-64, U.S. Govt., Camp Atterbury, Ind., 1964-66; dir. communications Meth. Hosp. of Ind., Indpls., 1966-79; pres., owner Rent-A-Radio, Inc. of Ind., Indpls., after 1979; sec.-treas. Communications Unltd., Inc. Former pres. Am. Legion Aux.; chmn. for Ind., Girls State U.S.A., 1972-77; probation officer vol., 1973-74; suicide prevention counselor, 1972-73; mem. Nat. Wildlife Fund. Recipient award for outstanding community service Ford Motor Co., 1961. Mem. Am. Soc. Hosp. Engring., Am. Hosp. Assn., Nat. Assn. Bus. and Ednl. Radio, Inc., Nat. Mus. Women in Arts, Internat. Teletypewriters for the Deaf, Assn. Public Safety Communications Officers, Inc., Am. Bus. Women. Methodist. Home: 6242 N 575 E Franklin IN 46131-8759 Office: 4545 Southeastern Ave Indianapolis IN 46203-2307

KRUEGER, BONNIE LEE, editor, writer; b. Chgo., Feb. 3, 1950; d. Harry Bernard and Lillian (Soyak) Krueger; m. James Lawrence Spurlock, Mar. 8, 1972. Student, Morraine Valley Coll., 1970. Adminstrv. asst. Carson Pirie Scott & Co., Chgo., 1969-72; traffic coord. Tatham Laird & Kudner, Chgo., 1973-74; traffic coord. J. Walter Thompson, Chgo., 1974-76, prodn. coord., 1976-78; editor-in-chief Assoc. Pubs., Chgo., 1978—, Sophisticate's Hairstyle Guide, 1978—, Sophisticate's Beauty Guide, 1978—, Complete Woman, 1981—; pub., editorial svcs. dir. Sophisticate's Black Hair Guide, 1983—, Sophisticate's Soap Star Styles, 1994-95. Mem. Statue of Liberty Restoration Com., N.Y.C., 1983; campaign worker Cook County State's Atty., Chgo., 1982; poll watcher Cook County Dem. Orgn., 1983; mem. Chgo. Architecture Found. Mem. Soc. Profl. Journalists, Am. Health and Beauty Aids Inst. (assoc. mem.), Lincoln Park Zool. Soc., Landmarks Preservation Coun. of Ill., Art Inst. Chgo., Chgo. Hist. Soc., Mus. Contemporary Art, Peta, Headline Club, Sigma Delta Chi. Lutheran. Office: Complete Woman 875 N Michigan Ave Chicago IL 60611-1803

KRUEGER, FRANZ RAINER, physicochemist; b. Frankfurt/O, Germany, Nov. 21, 1944; s. Franz and Hedwig (Pesch) K. Diploma in physics, U. Giessen, 1969; PhD, Tech. U. Darmstadt, Germany, 1974. Rsch. asst. Technische Hochschule, Darmstadt, Germany, 1970-78; hon. rsch. fellow Govt. of West Germany, 1979-83; cons. engr., rschr., Darmstadt, 1984—; cons. Max-Planck-Inst., Heidelberg and Munich, 1984—. Author: Physik and Evolution, 1984. Mem. Internat. Soc. Search for Origin of Life, German Phys. Soc., European Phys. Soc., Verein Deutsche Ingenieure. Avocations: science theory of evolution, prebiotic chemical evolution, origin of cognition and writing. Home and Office: Messeler Str 24, D-64291 Darmstadt Germany

KRUEGER, GERALD PETER, psychologist; b. Evanston, Ill., Apr. 3, 1944; s. Albert August and Pauline Mary (Didier) K.; m. Jessica Ann Prendergast, Aug. 26, 1967; children: Michael G., Deborah L., Kevin A. BA in Psychology, U. Dayton, 1966; MA in Exptl. and Engring. Psychology, Johns Hopkins U., 1975, PhD in Exptl. Psychology, 1977; grad., U.S. Army Command and Gen. Staff Coll., 1980, U.S. Army War Coll., 1988. Cert. profl. ergonomist Bd. Certification Profl. Ergonomics. Engring. psychology rschr. Bunker-Ramo Corp., Wright-Patterson AFB, Ohio, 1966-69; human factors rsch. psychologist U.S. Army Human Engring. Lab., Aberdeen, Md., 1969-71; R & D coord. Def. Advanced Rsch. Projects Agy., Saigon, Vietnam, 1971-72; mil. police ops. officer U.S. Army, Ft. Meade, Md., 1972; aviation psychologist Aeromed. Rsch. Lab. U.S. Army, Ft. Rucker, Ala., 1976-80; R & D programs staff officer U.A. Army Med. R & D Command, Ft. Detrick, Md., 1980-84; dep. chief dept. behavioral biology Walter Reed Army Inst. Rsch., Washington, 1984-88; dir. biomed. applications rsch. divsn. U.S. Army Aeromed. Rsch. Lab., Ft. Rucker, 1988-90; comdr., scientific tech. dir. U.S. Army Rsch. Inst. Environ. Medicine, Natick, Mass., 1990-94; ret. col. U.S. Army, 1994; v.p. ergonomics R & D svcs. Biomechanics Corp. Am., Melville, N.Y., 1994-95; prin. rsch. scientist, ergonomist Star Mountain, Inc., Alexandria, Va., 1995-98; pres. Krueger Ergonomics Cons., Inc., 1998—; prin. scientist, ergonomist Wexford Group Internat., Vienna, Va., 2000—; tchr. U.S. Armed Forces Inst., Saigon, 1971, Johns Hopkins U., 1974-75, U. So. Calif., 1977-80; adj. asst. prof. med.-clin. psychology Uniformed Svcs. U. Health Scis., Bethesda, Md., 1997—. Book review editor Ergonomics in Design Mag.; assoc. editor Mil. Psychology, 1991—; guest editor jours. in field; contbr. articles to profl. jours. Recipient Richard M. Griffith Meml. award So. Soc. Philosophy & Psychology, 1978, order of mil. med. merit for career contbns. army med. dept., 1992, numerous mil. awards, medals and skill proficiency badges, including Legion of Merit, 1994, Bronze Star U.S. Army, 1972, meritorious svc. medals with 2 oak leaf clusters. Fellow APA (pres. divsn. mil. psychology 1995-96, pres.-elect divsn. engring. psychologists); mem. Soc. for Indsl. Orgnl. Psychologists, Am. Indsl. Hygiene Assn., Am. Psychol. Soc., Assn. U.S. Army, Nat. Def. Indsl. Assn., Human Factors and Ergonomics Soc., Aerospace Med. Assn., Aerospace Human Factors Assn., Applied Ergonomics (Moscow), Soc. for Human Performance in Extreme Environments, Army War Coll. Alumni Assn., VFW, Am. Legion. Roman Catholic. Avocations: participating in running events, organizing community activities. Office: Krueger Ergonomics Consultants 4105 Komes Ct Alexandria VA 22306-1252

KRUEGER, GERHARD RICHARD FRANZ, pathologist; b. Berlin, Nov. 21, 1936; s. Richard F. H. and Irmgard E. M. (Dieke) K.; m. Maria-Barbara Philipp, June 2, 1960; children: Rolf, Claudia S., Elke. MD, Free U., Berlin, 1962; diploma, Soc. Med. Hosp. Gen. Mex. Diplomate Mex. Socs. Medicine & Pathology. Intern Free U. Berlin, Germany, 1962-64; pathologist Mcpl. Hosp. Spandau, Berlin, Germany, 1964-65; rsch. scientist Nat. Cancer Inst., Bethesda, Md., 1965-67; rsch. pathologist Nat. Cancer Inst., Bethesda, 1968-72; pathologist Free U., Berlin, 1967-68; prof. pathology, sect. head immunopathology lab. U. Cologne, Germany, 1972-91; prof. dept. pathology U. Cologne, vice-dean med. faculty, 1996, dean med. faculty, 1997—; prof. pathology and lab. medicine dept. U. Tex. Med. Sch., Houston, 1991-92; chmn. Internat. Inst. Immunopath., Inc., Houston, 1989—; vis. prof. dept. pathology lab. medicine U. Tex. Med. Sch., Houston, 1992—. Author: Immunopathology, 1986; co-author: Human Herpesvirus-6, 1992, Autoimmune Liver Diseases, 1999; contbr. articles to profl. jours. Med. examiner U. Cologne, State of Northrine-Westfalia, Germany, 1974-98; mem. hon. sci. com. Internat. Inst. Anticancer Rsch. Avocations: painting, photography, art. E-mail: grfkrueger@aol.com.

KRUEGER, JAMES A., lawyer; b. Sept. 21, 1943; s. A.A. and Margaret E. (Hurley) K.; m. Therese Eileen Connors, Aug. 2, 1968; 1 child, Colleen. BA cum laude, Gongaza U., 1965; JD, Georgetown U., 1968; LLM, NYU, 1972. Bar: Wash. 1969, U.S. Supreme Ct. 1972, U.S. Tax Ct. 1972, U.S. Dist. Ct. (we. dist.) Wash. 1980, U.S. Ct. Appeals (9th cir.) 1982. Mem. staff U.S. senator from Wash., 1967-68; assoc. Kane, Vandeberg & Hartinger, Tacoma, 1972-76; ptnr. Kane, Vandeberg, Hartinger & Walker, Tacoma, 1976-90; shareholder Vandeberg & Johnson PS, Tacoma, 1990—; spl. dist. counsel Wash. State Bar Assn., 1984-94; adj. prof. law, U. of Puget Sound, 1974-76. Co-author: Representing the Close Corporation, 1979, Partnership Agreements, 1981, Planning for the Small Business Enterprise, 1982, The Partnership Handbook, 1984. Chmn. bd. Cath. Cmty. Svcs. of Pierce and Kitsap Counties, 1983-84; bd. dirs. United Way of Pierce County, 1973-82, 99—. Capt. U.S. Army, 1968-72. Decorated Bronze star. Mem. ABA, Wash. State Bar Assn. (spl. dist. counsel), Tacoma-Pierce County Bar Assn. Roman Catholic. Office: 1201 Pacific Ave Ste 1900 Tacoma WA 98402-4315

KRUGER, BARBARA, audiologist, speech and language pathologist; b. Corpus Christi, Tex., Aug. 16, 1944. BA in Psychology cum laude, CUNY, 1967, MA in Speech Pathology, 1970, PhD in Audiology and Hearing Sci., 1975. Asst. prof. audiology, dir. hearing rsch. lab. Columbia U., N.Y.C., 1975-78; asst. prof. otolaryngology, dir. audiology and speech lang. pathology Albert Einstein Coll. Medicine, Montefiore Med. Ctr. Yeshiva U., Bronx, N.Y., 1978-87; cons. Kruger Assocs., Commack, N.Y., 1987—; dir. Audiology and Comm. Svcs., 1987—; founder, bd. dirs. The Hearing Care Group; adj. prof. Columbia U., 1979-82; chmn. earphone calibration Internat. Electrotech. Commn., Am. Nat. Standards Inst., workgroup hearing aids real-ear probe microphone measurement; cons. Albert Einstein Coll. of Medicine, Kennedy Ctr., 1987-90; apptd. N.Y. State Hearing Aid Dispensing Adv. Bd. in Dept. of State, 1999—; co-chair Open Data structure Hearing Related Data. Spencer Found. grantee, 1976-78, Am. Otological Soc. grantee, 1978-79, Rose M. Badgeley Residuary Charitable Trust grantee, 1981-84; recipient Program Project award NIH, 1984-86. Fellow Am. Speech-Lang. Hearing Assn., Am. Acad. Audiology; mem. L.I. Speech-Lang. Hearing Assn. Home and Office: 37 Somerset Dr Commack NY 11725-1636

KRUGER, GUSTAV OTTO, JR., oral surgeon, educator; b. N.Y.C., Sept. 28, 1916; s. Gustav Otto and Anna Charlotte (Mellquist) K.; m. Helyn E. Hollingsworth, Apr. 12, 1947; children: Deborah Ann (Mrs. M. Henry King III), Tristram Coffin, Abigail Hollingsworth Imus. BS, George Washington U., 1938, AM, 1939; DDS, Georgetown U., 1939, ScD (hon.), 1977. Diplomate Am. Bd. Oral and Maxillofacial Surgery (pres. 1964). Intern Johns Hopkins Hosp., 1939-40; fellow Mayo Found., 1940-42, 45-48; mem. faculty Georgetown U. Sch. Dentistry and Grad. Sch., 1948-87, prof. oral surgery, chmn. dept., 1948-87, prof. emeritus, 1987—, assoc. dean, 1966-82; chief dental dept. Georgetown U. Hosp., Washington, 1948-82; cons. VA hosps., Martinsburg, W.Va. and Washington, U.S. Naval Hosp., Bethesda, D.C. Gen. Hosp., Washington; cons. to Pres.'s physician, 1960-64; cons. Walter Reed Army Med. Ctr.; mem. cancer tng. com. Nat. Cancer Inst., USPHS, 1967-71, chmn., 1969-71. Author: Textbook of Oral and Maxillofacial Surgery, 1959, 6th edit., 1984; contbr. articles to profl. jours. Capt. Dental Corps AUS, 1942-45, CBI, PTO. Recipient Arnold K. Maislen award N.Y. U., 1970; Simon P. Hullihen award W.Va. Soc. Oral Surgeons and W.Va. Med. Ctr., 1980; named Man of Year Georgetown U. Alumni Assn., 1961, Disting. Svc. award, 1992. Fellow AAAS, Am. Coll. Dentists (chmn. D.C. sect. 1969-71), Internat. Coll. Dentists (chmn. D.C. sect. 1967-70); mem. ADA (chmn. oral surgery sect. 1961, mem. rev. commn. on advanced edn. in oral surgery 1965-71, chmn. commn. 1969-71), D.C. Dental Soc. (pres. 1960, Sterling V. Mead award 1989), Am. Assn. Oral and Maxillofacial Surgeons (program chmn. 1961, 79th Ann. Meeting dedication 1997), Middle Atlantic Soc. Oral and Maxillofacial Surgeons (pres. 1952), Am. Acad. Oral Pathology, Am. Acad. Oral and Maxillofacial Radiology, Internat. Assn. Dental Research, Am. Coll. Oral and Maxillofacial Surgeons (Harry Archer award 1992), Wash. Dental Study Club (pres. 1993), Kiwanis (co-chmn. orthop. com. 1971-86), Xi Psi Phi, Sigma Gamma Epsilon, Omicron Kappa Upsilon. Home: 6806 Bradgrove Cir Bethesda MD 20817-3001

KRUGER, JOSEPH, II, manufacturing company executive; b. Montreal, Que., Can., 1945; m. Susan Kruger; 2 children. BSc, Clarkson Coll., 1967, DSc (hon.), 1987. Chmn., CEO Kruger Inc., Montreal; bd. dirs. Bank of Can. Decorated chevalier Nat. Order of Que., Order of Can. Mem. Mt. Royal Club, Club St.-Denis, St. James's Club, Lyford Cay Club (Nassau, Bahamas). Office: Kruger Inc 3285 Bedford Rd, Montreal, PQ Canada H3S 1G5*

KRUGER, LOUIS MAX, economist, consultant; b. Norfolk, Va., Nov. 5, 1916; s. Joseph D. and Sadie (Saunders) K.; m. Shirley Linn Kruger, Dec. 28, 1946 (dec. Mar. 1998); children: Anne Kruger Grossman, Albert A. Student, Coll. William and Mary, 1936-39, Temple U., 1939-40, U.S. Army Coll. Armed Forces, 1954-56. Pres. Ultramar Agys. Co., N.Y.C., 1946—, L.M. Kruger Assoc., N.Y.C., 1950—; authority Econ. and Social Devel., Upper Amazon River Area, 1940—; mem. U.S. Civil Svcs. Commn., Washington, 1998; cons. Northwood Inst., Midland, Mish., 1964-67, Internat. Trade Devel., Bogota, Colombia, 1964, Sonneborn Inst. Israel Ind. Program, 1947-67, Gen. Coun. for Jews in Aviation in Palestine, 1956-58, L.Am. Devel. program, 1967. Fundraiser Jewish philanthropies, N.Y.C., 1959, State Israel Bonds, Washington, 1964. With U.S. Army Spl. Svcs., 1945-46. Mem. Masons. Democrat. Avocations: history of the Jews, science, government, finance and development. Home: 333 W 56th St Apt 7D New York NY 10019-3770

KRUGER, PIETER WILLEM BINGLE, transportation engineer; b. Venterstad, Cape, South Africa, Aug. 3, 1937; s. Nicolaas and Jacoba (Bingle) K.; m. Hester Hendrina Labuscagne, Dec. 10, 1960; children: Ester, Nicolaas, Gert. BSc in Civil Engring., U. Pretoria, South Africa, 1959; M in Engring., U. Calif., Berkeley, 1962, D in Engring., 1964. Reg. profl. engr., South Africa. Co-founder BKS Group (Pty.) Ltd., Pretoria, 1965—, exec. chmn., 1989—. Elder Reformed Ch., Pretoria, 1966—; vice chmn. Menlo Park School Bd., Pretoria, 1988-91; bd. mem. South African Rds. Bd., 1989-95; mem. Civil Engring. Found., pres., 1996—; mem. Civil Engring. Adv. Coun., 1996—; pres. South African Acad. Engring., 1996—; assoc. mem. Transp. Rsch. Bd. Fellow South African Inst. Civil Engrs. (pres. 1995, Pres.'s award 1988, Chmn's award 1993); mem. ASCE. E-mail: bingle@bks.co.za. Office: Hatfield Gardens D, Corner Arcadia and Grosvenor St, Hatfield 0083, South Africa

KRUGLYAK, SEMYON, geneticist, researcher; b. Leningrad, Russia, June 10, 1972; came to U.S., 1979; s. Abram and Etya K. BA cum laude, Cornell U., 1994, MS, 1997, PhD, 1998. Rsch. assoc. U. So. Calif., L.A., 1998—. Contbr. articles to profl. jours. Recipient Dept. Def. grad. fellowship, tchg. award Cornell U., 1996, 98. Mem. Phi Beta Kappa. Jewish. Avocations: tennis, volleyball, running, reading, chess. E-mail: sk27@cornell.edu. Office: U So Calif 293 Drb Los Angeles CA 90089-0001

KRUIMEL, JAN PAUL, civil servant, consultant, sculptor; b. Oudenryn, The Netherlands, Sept. 26, 1949; s. Philibert Francois and Jacoba Deliane (Rom Colthoff) K.; m. Neeltje Maria Van der Horst Kruimel, Sept. 17, 1976; children: Henriette, Anneli. BA, H.E.S. Bus. Sch., The Hague, The Netherlands, 1972; MA in Law, Ryksuniversiteit, Leyden, The Netherlands, 1977. Tax cons. KAFI, Arnhem, The Netherlands, 1976-80; deputy head tax dept. Min. Internal Affairs, The Hague, The Netherlands, 1980-84; head tax dept., 1984-86, head Fiscal and Adminstrv. Affairs Divsn., 1986-90, project mgr., 1990-95; sec. Chancery of the Netherlands Royal Orders of Knighthood, 1995—; sec. chpt. of Civil Orders of Knighthood, 1995—; cons. Cadaster Project Costa Rica, 1987-91; rep. for The Netherlands, Assessing Officer, Internat. Assn. Chgo., 1988-94. Editor, author: Belastingblad, 1982—, Vakstudie Lokale Belastingen, 1980—; author: Theorie en praktyk van de Gemeentelyke Onroerende-Zaakbelastingen, 1981—; sculptor: Medallic Art, Small Sculptures, 1980—; contbr. numerous books on taxation and local authorities. Recipient State award for Fiscal Scientific Publs., State Sec. of Fin., 1983, Global award Internat. Assn. Assessing Officers, Commendation medal Vol. Police, 1998; Named Officer Order Leopold II (Belgium), 2000. Mem. Soc. Numismatic Artists and Designers, Netherlands Assn. for Tax Law, De Witte Club, Rotary Club Scheveningen. Avocations: field hockey, cross country skiing. Home: Lange Voort 261-A, Oegstgeest NL2343CE, The Netherlands Office: Chancery of Royal Orders of Knighthood, Nassaulaan 18 PO Box 30436, The Hague NL2500GK, The Netherlands

KRUITHOF, BERNARDUS, historian, education; b. Pretoria, South Africa, Jan. 26, 1952; s. Pieter and Johanna Hendrieka Martina (Judels) K.; m. Clara Martha Van Der Wusten, Dec. 21, 1976; children: Maartje M., Toos A., Thomas P. D of History, U. Amsterdam (The Netherlands), 1976, DLitt, 1990. Asst. prof. U. Amsterdam, 1977—; sci. coord. Inst. for Rsch. in Social Scis., 1990—. Author: Sin and Virtue in Minister Land, 1990; editor: History of Education, 1982. Home: Meerkoetstraat 7, NL1452XS Ilpendam The Netherlands Office: U Amsterdam, Wibautstraat 4, NL1091GM Amsterdam The Netherlands

KRUITHOF, EGBERT K.D., biochemist, researcher; b. Pynacker, The Netherlands, Nov. 12, 1949; arrived in Switzerland, 1978; s. Oosten Kruithof and Henrika Snyders; m. Ten Bokkel Huinink, May 25, 1978; children: Remco, Sander. Degree in chem. engring., Delft U. Tech., The Netherlands, 1974; PhD, U. Lausanne, Switzerland, 1988. Biochemist Inst. Exptl. Gerontology, Ryswyk, The Netherlands, 1975-78, U. Lausanne Hosp., 1978-94; biochemist, head of rsch. U. Geneva Hosp., 1994—; head reference lab. European Concerted Action Studies, 1986-92; sec. gen. 6th Internat. Congress on Fibrinolysis, Lausanne, 1982. Contbr. numerous articles to med. jours., including Jour. Exptl. Medicine, Jour. Biol. Chemistry, others; mem. editl. bd. Thrombosis Haemostasis, 1988-96, Fibrinolysis and Proteolysis, 1988—. Recipient award French Soc. Biology, 1986, Swiss Soc. Hemotology, 1987. Mem. Internat. Soc. Fibrinolysis and Proteolysis (chmn. 2000—). Avocations: alpinism, Judo, Jiujitsu. Home: Chemin de la Verne 23, CH 1073 Savigny Switzerland Office: Univ Hosp, Div Angiolog Hemostasis, CH 1211 Geneva Switzerland

KRUKLINSKI, MICHAEL, chemicals executive; b. Celle, Germany, Nov. 1, 1965; s. Heins and Karin (Strasse) K.; m. Christy Murphy, Sept. 9, 1999; 1 child, Emily. MBA, Siemens, Celle, Germany, 1985. Sr. v.p. Siemens AG, Germany, 1985-96, First Am. Corp., Nashville, 1996—; prof. (hon.) Owen Bus. Sch.; dir. ColdWell Banker; cons. in field. Office: AmSouth 315 Deaderick St Nashville TN 37238-0002

KRULL, JEFFREY ROBERT, library director; b. North Tonawanda, N.Y., Aug. 29, 1948; s. Robert George and Ruth Otilie (Fels) K.; m. Alice Marie Hart, Apr. 12, 1969; children: Robert, Marla. BA, Williams Coll., Williamstown, Mass., 1970; MLS, SUNY, Buffalo, 1974. Cert. profl. libr., N.Y., Ohio, Ind. Traffic mgr. New England Tel. Co., Burlington, Vt., 1970-71; tchr. Harrisburg (Pa.) Acad., 1971-72; reference libr. Buffalo and Erie County Pub. Libr., 1973-76; head libr. Ohio U., Chillicothe, 1976-78; dir. Mansfield-Richland County Pub. Libr., Ohio, 1978-86, Allen County Pub. Libr., Ft. Wayne, Ind., 1986—; mem. exec. com. Ft. Wayne Area Libr. Svc. Authority, 1986-90, v.p., 1989; mem. exec. com. Ind. Coop. Libr. Svcs. Authority, 1992—, pres., 1994-95; mem. Online Computer Libr. Ctr. Pub. Libr. Adv. Coun., 1994-97; pres. Ft. Wayne Area INFONET, 1995—. Pres. Three Rivers Library Alliance, 1997—; trustee Ohionet, Columbus, 1984-86. Mem. ALA, Pub. Libr. Assn. (pres. met. librs. sect. 1990-91, statistical report adv. com.), Libr. Adminstrn. and Mgmt. Assn. (sec. libr. orgn. and mgmt. assn. 1996-97), Ohio Libr. Assn. (bd. dirs. 1985-86), Ind. Libr. Fedn. (vice chmn. legis. com. 1987—), Beta Phi Mu. Home: 3017 Oak Borough Run Fort Wayne IN 46804-7808 Offices: Allen County Pub Libr PO Box 2270 900 Webster St Fort Wayne IN 46801-2270

KRUMDIECK, SUSAN PRAN, mechanical engineer, educator; b. USAF Academy, Colo., June 14, 1963; d. Julius William and Leona Lou Ryter; m. Colin William Krumdieck, June 4, 1983; children: Kierra Elizabeth, Kyan William. BSME, Ariz. State U., 1986, MSME, 1989; PhDME, U. Colo., 1999. Rsch. asst. Nat. Renewable Evergy Lab., Wind Energy Rsch. Ctr., Golden, Colo., 1985, Ctr. for Energy Sys. Rsch., Tempe, Ariz., 1986-89; energy analyst Energy Simulation Specialists, Tempe, 1987-89; pres., dir. rsch. Boulder Materials Sys., 1999-2000; rsch. asst. U. Colo., Boulder, 1995-99, prof., 2000—; cons. proposal team Ctr. for High Temperature Materials and Sys., Boulder. Vol. area elem. schs. DAV scholar, 1981-85; grad. scholar Am. Power Prodrs. Assn., Tempe, 1989; 1st pl. scholar Air and Waste Mgmt. Assn., Boulder, 1995, 3rd pl. scholar, 1996; Achievement Rewards for Coll. Scholars Found. scholar, Denver, 1997. Mem. Soc. Automotive Engrs. (Doctoral Scholars award 1996-99). Methodist. Avocations: vocal performance, recreational sports. Fax: 303-492-3498. E-mail: krumdies@ucsu.colorado.edu. Office: Univ Colo PO Box 427 Boulder CO 80309-0427

KRUMGALZ, BORIS, chemistry educator, researcher; b. Kharkov, Ukraine, Russia, Sept. 24, 1937; arrived in Israel, 1976; s. Shaul and Nina (Vakhnenko) K.; m. Ludmila Malysheva, June 29, 1973; 1 child, Shaul. MSc in Chem. Processes with honors, Leningrad Tech. Inst., 1960, PhD in Chem. Sci., 1965. Sr. lectr., assoc. prof. Northwestern Polytech. Inst., Leningrad, 1966-73; prof. Inst. Oceanography, Haifa, Israel, 1980, sr. scientist, 1977—. Contbr. more than 200 articles to profl. jours. Mcpl.

counsellor Municipality of Nesher, Israel, 1988-93. Avocations: tennis, swimming, philately. Fax: 972-4-8511911. E-mail: boris@ocean.org.il. Home: Hairusim 26, 36843 Nesher Israel Office: Nat Inst Oceanography, Tel Shikmona PO Box 8030, 31080 Haifa Israel

KRUMMACHER, JOHANN-HENRICH KARL, minister, writer; b. Heidelberg, Badenia, Germany, Dec. 27, 1946; s. Daniel Moritz Adolf and Margarete Hedwig Emma (Gabbert) K.; m. Ingrid Elisabeth Weng, July 16, 1986; children: Marcus, Florian, Benjamin, Daniel, Jakob, Lukas. Abitur gymnasium, Heidelberg, 1966; student, U. Heidelberg, U. Tübingen, 1966-72. Ordained to ministry Luth. Ch., 1972. Curate Luth. Ch., Sigmaringen, Germany, 1972-75; pastor Luth. St. John's Ch., Kornwestheim, Germany, 1975-85; pastor, master philosophy Hegel Gymnasium, Stuttgart, Germany, 1986-92; pastor Luth. St. Georg's Ch., Zavelstein, Germany, 1992-96; exec. dir. Protestant Acad., Bad Boll, Germany, 1996—; editor, consultative theologian Radius Books, Stuttgart, 1986—; chief editor Das Plateau, Stuttgart, 1990—; mem. synod Luth. Ch. Wuerttemberg, Stuttgart, 1983-85; mem. ct. of doctrine Luth. Ch., Stuttgart, 1983-85; companion Radius Pub. Co., 1985—, supervisory bd., 1992—. Author numerous books and radio essays on ethics and culture. Initiator Shalom svcs. with ecumenical liturgy in Fed. Republic of Germany, 1977-85; pres. Soc. for Ch. and Art, Stuttgart, 1993; bd. dirs. Found. for Ch. and Art, Stuttgart, 1998; trustee Friends of the Hebrew U. Jerusalem, 1998. Mem. Lions. Home: Schulstrasse 30, D-75385 Bad Teinach Germany Office: Akademieweg 11, D-73087 Bad Boll Germany

KRUNGKRAI, JERAPAN, biochemist, educator; b. Ayudhaya, Thailand, June 8, 1958; s. Wing and Somjitr (Jirapinant) K.; m. Sudaratana Rochanakij, June 13, 1986; children: Jiraratana, Jakrapan. BS, Chiangmai (Thailand) U., 1979; MS, Mahidol U., Bangkok, 1981, PhD, 1986. Rsch. assoc. AFRIMS (US), Bangkok, 1986-87; lectr. Chulalongkorn U., Bangkok, 1987-91, asst. prof., 1991-92, assoc. prof., 1993—, chmn. dept. biochemistry, 1994-98; rsch. assoc. Rockefeller U., N.Y.C., 1988-90. Contbr. articles to profl. jours. including Biochem. Pharmacology, Biochemistry, Drugs of the Future, others. King of Thailand Biomed. Rsch. fellow Rockefeller U., 1988-90; WHO grantee, 1990—; Career Devel. grantee Nat. Sci. and Tech. Devel. Agy. Thailand, 1994-99. Mem. Sci. Soc. Thailand (Outstanding Young Scientist 1992), N.Y. Acad. Scis. Buddhist. Home: 80/132 Ramkhamhaeng 24, Bangkapi Bangkok 10240, Thailand Office: 1873 Rama IV Rd, Bangkok 10330, Thailand

KRUPATKIN, ALEXANDER ILYICH, clinical physiologist researcher, neurologist; b. Moscow, Feb. 17, 1961; s. Ilya Lvovich and Eva Naumovna (Roytberg) K. MD, Med. Inst., Tver, Russia, 1983, Dr.-Neurologist, 1984; Cons. in Psychotherapy, Med. Inst., Moscow, Russia, 1987; PhD, Ctrl. Inst. Traumatology, Moscow, Russia, 1989; DMSc, Moscow, 1999. Physician Regional Hosp., Tver, Russia, 1983-84; jr. rschr. Ctrl. Inst. Traumatology & Orthopaedics, Moscow, Russia, 1984-90, rschr., 1990-91, sr. rschr., 1991—. Author: (book) Polarographic method in traumatology & orthopaedics, 1986; contbr. articles to profl. jours. Mem. N.Y. Acad. Scis., Russian Assn. Functional Diagnosis. Avocations: collecting postage stamps, excercise. Home: Voljsky bulvar kvartal 95, korpus 3 kvartira 4, 109125 Moscow Russia Office: Ctrl Inst Traumatology & Orthopaedics, Ul Priorova 10, 125299 Moscow Russia

KRUPNIK, NAUM YAKOV, mathematician, educator, researcher; b. Kishinev, Moldova, Dec. 31, 1932; arrived in Israel, 1990; s. Yakov Mark and Brana Isaak (Oreshter) K.; m. Sofia Gersh Pohis, June 27, 1938; children: Mark, Ilya. MS, U. Kishinev, 1959; PhD, U. Leningrad, 1965; Doctoral, Math. Inst., Tbilisi, 1987. Sr. lectr. U. Kishinev, 1962-68, prof., 1968-89; full prof. Bar-Ilan U., Israel, 1990—; vice chair dept. Bar-Ilan U., 1997-98. Author: Banach Algebras with Symbol, 1987, (with I. Gohberg) One-Dimensional Linear SIE vol. 1, 1992, vol. 2, 1993; contbr. articles to profl. jours. Home: Ha-Narkiss 16/11, 75424 Rishon-Le-Ziyon Israel Office: Bar-Ilan Univ, 52900 Ramat-Gan Israel

KRUPNOV, ANDREI FEDOROVICH, physicist; b. Kirgiz-Miaki, Bashassr, Russia, Jan. 31, 1934; s. Fedor Andreevich and Nadezhda Mikhailovna (Saltykova) K.; m. Albina Dmitrievna Trusova, July 26, 1956; children: Fedor, Sergei. Degree in Physics, Gorky (Russia) State U., 1957, PhD, 1965; ScD, Lebedev Inst., Moscow, 1975. Jr. rschr. Radiophys. Rsch. Inst., Gorky, 1957-65, sr. rschr., 1965-77; head microwave spectroscopy lab., prof. Applied Physics Inst. Russian Acad. Scis., Gorky, 1977—; cons. prof. Inst. Electronic Measurements KVARZ, Nizhnii Novgorod, Russia, 1989—. Mem. editl. adv. bd. Jour. Molecular Spectroscopy, 1976—; co-author: Molecular Spectroscopy: Modern Research, 1976, Modern Aspects of Microwave Spectroscopy, 1979 ; contbr. articles to profl. jours. Recipient State Prize in Sci., Russia, 1980, Joint Prize of Russia and CSSR Acad. of Scis., 1982; Presdl. fellow Russian Acad. Scis., 1994-96, state fellow, 1997—. Home: 140 M Gorky St Apt 102, 603000 Nizhnii Novgorod Russia Office: Applied Physics Inst, 46 Uljanova St, 603600 Nizhnii Novgorod Russia

KRUPP, GUIDO, molecular biology educator, researcher; b. Kaiserslautern, Germany, July 19, 1952; s. Urban and Helene (Schaller) K. Dipl.chem., U. Muenchen, Germany, 1979; Dr.rer.nat., U. Wuerzburg, Germany, 1981; Dr.habil. in Microbiology, U. Kiel, Germany, 1990, Dr.habil. in Biochemistry, 1994. Akad.rat. U. Wuerzburg, 1981-83; postdoctoral staff Yale U., New Haven, 1983-87; hochschul doz. U. Kiel, 1987-90, priv.-doz., 1990—; cons. IntelliGene Ltd., Jerusalem, 1996-99, artus GmbH, Hamburg, 1999—. Assoc. editor (book series) Biotechnology Annual Review, 1994. Home: Wannseebogen 30A, D-24111 Kiel Germany Office: U Kiel Inst Hematopathol, Niemannsweg 11, D-24105 Kiel Germany

KRUSE, CHRIS G., pharmaceutical company administrator, educator; b. Amersfoort, The Netherlands, Aug. 3, 1952; s. Cornelis Kruse and Gerda Van de Kamp; m. Maria J.W. Van Wynen, Jan. 31, 1975; 3 children. MSc, U. Leiden, The Netherlands, 1974, PhD in Chemistry, 1978. Sci. asst. Leiden U., 1974-78; scientist Philips Forschungslabor, Aachen, Germany, 1978-80; group leader Duphar, Weesp, The Netherlands, 1981-87; sect. leader Solvay Duphar, Weesp, 1987-92; dept. leader Solvay Pharms., Weesp, 1992-95, rsch. program mgr., 1995—; asst. prof. U. Nymegen, The Netherlands, 1987-97; prof. U. Amsterdam, The Netherlands, 1997—. Editor Eur. Jour. Organic Chemistry; contbr. over 65 articles to profl. jours.; over 25 patents in field. Elder Dutch Reformed Ch., 1980—. Mem. Royal Netherlands Chem. Soc. (chmn. 1996—, chmn. sect. med. chem. 1996—), Dutch Forum Tech. and Sci., N.Y. Acad. Scis. Avocations: birding, sports, mountain hiking. E-mail: chris.kruse@solvay.com. Home: Randenbroekerweg 38, 3816 BJ Amersfoort The Netherlands Office: Solvay Pharms, CJ van Houtenlaan 36, 1381 CP Weesp The Netherlands

KRUSE, JOHN ALPHONSE, lawyer; b. Detroit, Sept. 11, 1926; s. Frank R. and Ann (Nestor) K.; m. Mary Louise Dalton, July 14, 1951; children: Gerard, Mary Louise, Terence, Kathleen, Joanne, Francis, John, Patrick. BS, U. Detroit, 1950, JD cum laude, 1952. Bar: Mich. bar 1952. Ptnr. Alexander, Buchanan & Conklin, Detroit, 1952-69, Harvey, Kruse, PC, Detroit, 1969—; Guest lectr. U. Mich., U. Detroit, Inst. Continuing Legal Edn.; city atty. Allen Park, Mich., 1954-59; twp. atty., Van Buren Twp., Mich., 1959-61. Co-founder Detroit and Mich. Cath. Radio. Past pres. Palmer Woods Assn.; mem. pres.'s cabinet U. Detroit; mem. product liability adv. coun. Providence Hosp.; bd. dirs. Providence Hosp. Found. Legatus; trustee Ave Maria Coll. Named one of 5 Outstanding Young Men in Mich., 1959, Outstanding Alumnus, U. Detroit Sch. Law, 1989, Humanitarian award Neuromuscular Inst. 1988. Mem. Detroit Bar Assn., State Bar Mich. (past chmn. negligence sect.), Assn. Def. Trial Counsel (bd. dirs. 1966-67), Am. Judicature Soc., Internat. Assn. Def. Counsel, Equestrian Order of the Holy Sepulchre, Cath. Campaign for Am. Roman Catholic. Club: Detroit Golf (past pres.). Home: 5569 Hunters Gate Dr Troy MI 48098-2342 Office: 1050 Wilshire Dr Ste 320 Troy MI 48084-1526

KRUSE, PETER DAVID, palaeontologist, geologist; b. Sydney, NSW, Australia, Nov. 18, 1953; s. Donald George and Alice May (Chatterton) K.; m. Peta Christine O'Malley, Aug. 23, 1986. BSc with honors, U. Sydney, 1976, PhD, 1981. Rsch. asst. dept. geology and geophysics U. Sydney, 1980-81, 83-84; geologist No. Territory Geol. Survey, Darwin, Australia, 1984—; corr. mem. Internat. Geol. Correlation Programme (IGCP) Subcomm. on Cambrian Stratigraphy, 1984—, voting mem., 1996—; convener Commonwealth Territories Stratigraphic Names Subcom., 1987-95, 2000—; contbr. IGCP Project 303, 1989-93, Project 366, 1994-97, Project 380, 1998-99. Author: (book) Cambrian Palaeontology of the Daly Basin, 1990, Cambrian Palaeontology of the Eastern Wiso and Western Georgina Basins, 1998; contbr. articles to profl. jours. Recipient Edgeworth David prize U. Sydney, 1974, Commonwealth Postgrad. Rsch. award, 1976-79, French Govt. Profl. and Tech. scholarship CNIES, Mus. Nat. d'Histoire Naturelle, Paris, 1982. Mem. Geol. Soc. Australia, Assn. Australasian Palaeontologists, Palaeontol. Assn. Avocations: theology, philately, touch football, French, Russian. Office: No Territory Geol Survey, PO Box 2901, Darwin 0801, Australia

KRUTH, JEAN-PIERRE, mechanical engineering educator, researcher; b. Knokke, Belgium, May 8, 1952; s. Marcel A. and Marie-Therese A. (Baudoin) K.; m. Myriam J.C.H. Van der Linden, Sept. 6, 1975; children: Xavier, Jean-François, Laurence, An-Pascale. BS in Engring., Cath. U., Leuven, Belgium, 1972, MS, 1975, PhD, 1979. Rsch. fellow Inst. Sci. Rsch. in Industry and Agr./Cath. U., Leuven, 1975-78; acad. asst. Cath. U., Leuven, 1978-79; univ. tech. expert Tech. Inst. Bandung, Indonesia, 1979-82; rsch. engr. Rsch. Ctr. Belgian Metalworking Industry, Heverlee, Belgium, 1983-87; CAD/CAM cons. Inst. for Sci. Rsch. in Industry and Agr./IRSIA, Heverlee, Belgium, 1983-87; full prof. Cath. U., Leuven, 1987—; founding bd. dir. Materialise, Metris Internat. Holding & Metris N.V., Heverlee, Belgium Soc. Mech. and Environ. Engring., Brussels; head PMA divsn. K.U. Leuven, 1993-95; bd. dirs. MIH Co.; pres. bd. Metris Co. Mem. editl. bd. numerous jours.; contbr. over 150 articles to books and profl. jours. Recipient Brite-Euram award European Union, Sevilla, Spain, 1992, Knight of Laser Tech. award Laser-Assisted Net-shape Engring., Erlangen, Germany, 1997. Fellow Soc. Mech. Engrs.; mem. Romanian Soc. Mech. Engrs. (hon.), Internat. Instn. Prodn. Engring. Rsch. (F.W. Taylor medal 1987), Royal Flemish Engring. Assn., Internat. Measuring Confedn. (Belgian del. 1993—). Roman Catholic. Avocations: tennis, swimming, water skiing, alpine skiing. Fax: 32-16-322987. Office: KU Leuven PMA, Celestijnenlaan 300B, B-3001 Heverlee Leuven Belgium

KRUTIKOV, VICTOR SERGEEVICH, physicist, mathematician, educator; b. Donetsk, Ukraine, Mar. 12, 1936; s. Sergey Matveevich and Angelina Ivanovna (Kovalevskaya) K.; m. Janna Pavlovna Vasilyeva, Oct. 29, 1956; children: Natalya Krutikova-Lopatnyova, Olga. Shipbuilder engr., Nikolaev Shipbuilding Inst., Ukraine, 1959, PhD, 1975; DSc in Physics and Math., Inst. Hydromechanics, Kiev, Ukraine, 1995. Cert. shipbuilder engr. Shipbuilder engr. Shipbuilding Orgn. Ocean, Nikolaev, 1959-71; jr. rsch. worker Nikolaev Shipbuilding Inst., 1971-75; leading sci. team Inst. Pulse Rsch. and Engring. Nat. Acad. Scis. Ukraine, Nikolaev, 1975-85, sr. sci. worker Inst. Pulse Rsch. and Engring., 1986-96, leading sci. worker Inst. Pulse Rsch. and Engring., 1996—, orgn. com. scientific sch. Inst. Pulse Rsch. and Engring., 1997; mem. sci. coun. Inst. Pulse Rsch. and Engring., Nat. Acad. Scis. Ukraine, 1995; mem. specialized sci. coun. Ukrainian State Maritime Tech. U., 1998. Author: (book) One-dimensional Problems in Continuum Mechanics with Moving Boundaires, 1985; contbr. articles to mags. Grantee Internat. Sci. Found. Mem. N.Y. Acad. Scis. Avocations: open-air recreation activity, orchard and vineyard trimming, traveling. E-mail: ipre@iipt.aip.mk.ua. Home: 301 Oktyabrsky Prospect # 2, Nikolaev 327050, Ukraine Office: Nat Acad Scis Ukraine, 43-a Oktyabrsky Prospect, Nikolaev 327018, Ukraine

KRUYF, GERRIT G. DE, theology educator; b. Gouda, The Netherlands, Aug. 1, 1952; s. Willem and Neeltje (Karsemeyer) de K.; m. Adriana J. de Heer, Aug. 29, 1975. PhD, State U. Utrecht, The Netherlands, 1981. Ch. minister Netherlands Reformed Ch., Rynsaterwoude, 1977-81, Rotterdam, 1981-88; researcher Netherlands Reformed Ch., Leiden, 1989-92; prof. Faculty of Theology, Brussels, 1985-88; prof. Christian ethics State U. Leiden, 1992—. Author: Heiden, Jood en Christen, 1981, Het Diepste Woord, 1984, Waakzaam en Nuchter, 1994, (De Savornin Lohmanprys 1996), Christelyke ethiek, 1999. Home: Stationsstraat 21 A, 2405BL Alphen aan den Ryn The Netherlands Office: Ryksuniversiteit Leiden, Postbus 9515, 2300 RA Leiden The Netherlands

KRYLOV, ANDREI ANATOLIEVICH, business executive; b. Moscow, Apr. 27, 1963; s. Anatoly and Ludmila K.; m. Natalia Smochina, Nov. 2, 1996. Grad., Moscow Aviation Inst., 1986. Adminstrv. asst. Ford Found., Moscow, 1992-94; head corp. svcs. Credit Suisse First Boston, Moscow, 1994-97; gen. svcs. mgr. Merrill Lynch, Moscow, 1998-99; head adminstrv. dept. Reemtsma, Moscow, 1999—. Office: Reemtsma, Degtiarny per 4 bldg 1, Moscow Russia 103009

KRYLOV, VICTOR VLADIMIROVICH, physical acoustics researcher, educator; b. Tambov, Russia, May 19, 1952; s. Vladimir and Julia Krylov; m. Elena Panfilova, Mar. 29, 1975; 1 child, Katya Krylova. MSc in Radiophysics, Power Engring. Inst., Moscow, 1975; PhD in Physics and Math., M.V. Lomonosov State U., Moscow, 1981, DSc, 1989. Rsch. scientist M.V. Lomonosov State U., 1980-88, sr. rsch. scientist, 1988-93; vis. fellow U. Edinburgh, 1990-91; prin. rsch. fellow Nottingham Trent U., 1993-94, prof. acoustics, head struct. mech. and acoustics rsch. grp., 1994—. Author: Introduction to Physical Acoustics, 1984, Surface Acoustic Waves in Inhomogeneous Media, 1991, 95, Basic Principles of Sound Radiation and Scattering, 1989, others; editor: Noise and Vibration from High Speed Trains, 2000; contbr. numerous articles to sci. jours. Recipient Highest Nat. Young Scientist award All-Union Commn., Moscow, 1984; grantee Royal Soc. Engring. and Phys. Scis. Rsch. Coun., U.K., European Commn. Fellow Inst. of Acoustics; mem. Acoustical Soc. Am., European Mech. Soc., Edinburgh Math. Soc. Avocations: music, poetry, history. Office: Nottingham Trent U Civ Eng, Burton St, Nottingham NG1 4BU, England

KRYMSKII, SERGEY BORISOVICH, philosophy educator; b. Artiomovsk, Donbass, Ukraine, June 2, 1930; s. Boris Sergievich and Sofia Mikhailovna (Vinarskaya) K.; m. Inna Emilianovna Komarovna, Nov. 27, 1955. Grad., Kyiv Taras Shevchenko U., Kiev, Ukraine, 1953; Candidate of Philosophy, Inst. Philosophy, Kiev, Ukraine, 1963. Tchr. lolic Secondary Sch. #95, Kiev, 1954-57; sr. lab. asst. Inst. Philosophy, Kiev, 1957-60, jr. rschr. logics and methodology sci. dept., 1960-64, sr. rschr. logics and methodology sci. dept., 1964-85, head methodology social rschrs. dept., 1985-90, sr. rschr. logics and methodology sci. dept., 1990—; prof. sociology dept. Internat. Solomon U., Kiev, 1994—; prof. philosophy dept. Kiev-Mogila Acad., 1996—. Author: The Genesis of Forms and Laws of Thinking, 1962, The Scientific Knowledge and Principles of Its Transformation, 1974, World Outlook Categories in the Modern Natural Science, 1983, The Epistemology of Culture, Roads and Cross-roads of Modern Civilization, 1998, Philosophy as the Way of Humanity and Hope, 2000. Recipient prize Presidium of the Ukrainian Nat. Acad. Scis., 1994; named Honored Worker of Sci. and Tech. of Ukraine, Pres. of Ukraine, 1996, Honored Edn. Activist, Ministry Edn. Ukraine, 1996. Mem. N.Y. Acad. Sci. Avocations: classical music, history and archeology of Kiev. Home: Apt 3, 22 Saksaganskaya, 01033 Kiev Ukraine Office: Inst Philosophy, 4 Triokhsviatytelskay, 01001 Kiev Ukraine

KRYMSKY, VICTOR GRIGORIEVICH, control systems researcher; b. Ufa, Republic of Bashkortostan, Nov. 16, 1951; s. Grigory Aronovich and Maria Markovna (Barats) K.; m. Tatiana Makhmutovna, Mar. 31, 1984; 1 child, Maria. Degree in engring., Ufa Aviation Inst., Russia, 1973, PhD, 1979; DS, Ufa State Aviation Tech. U., Russia, 1997. Engr. Ufa Aviation Inst., Russia, 1973-77, asst. prof., 1977-79, sr. lectr., 1979-81, assoc. prof., 1981-88; leading rschr. Ufa State Aviation Tech. U. (formerly Ufa Aviation Inst.), Russia, 1988-97, prof., 1997—; dir. Interclass Ctr. Edn. & Rsch., Ufa, 1995—. Co-author: (with Yu. Gusev & V. Efanov) Optimization of Electronic Control Units, 1982, Multi-level Control for Dynamic Plants, 1987; (with S. Kusimov, B. Iliasov and V. Vasiliev) Dynamic Systems Control under the Conditions of Uncertainty, 1998; (with S. Kusimov, A. Sultanov and V. Bagmanov) Simulation and Treatment of Images in the Optical Systems for Space Vision, 1999; (with S. Kusimov, B. Illiasov et al) The Problems of Creation and Development of Control and diagnostic Systems for Gas-Turbine Engines, 1999. Travel grantee Cultural Initiative Found., Moscow, 1991, rsch. grantee Russian Com. High Edn., Moscow, 1992, 94, 98, Linkage grantee NATO, 1998. Mem. Soc. Risk Analysis. Avocation: boating. Office: Ufa State Aviation Tech U, 12 K Marx St, 450000 Ufa Russia

KRYŃSKI, ANDRZEJ, humanities educator; b. Bielsk Podlaski, Poland, July 2, 1948; s. Wacław and Irena (Owczarek) K. MSc in Econ. Social Scis., U. Brussels; MA in Pastoral Theology, U. Louvain-La Neuv, Belgium; MA in Pedagogic Studies, Lublin (Poland) Cath. U., PhD. Tchr. Blind Children Inst., Laski, Poland, 1970-74; dir. Bd. dirs. Cath. Schs., Bertoua, Cameron, 1980-90, Ctr. European Langs., Czestochowa, Poland, 1991-92; rector U. Fgn. Langs. and Econs., Czestochowa, 1992—; cons. Ceran Lingua Internat., Spa, Belgium, 1992—, Orgn. for Intenrat. Coop. on Devel. Projects, Brussels, 1992—, Sabic Study and Cons. for Internat. Coop., Brussels, 1992—; project dir. Vlanderen-Europa 2002, Czestochowa, 1993-94, MBA European Programme, Czestochowa, 1995-96, CEI-Rome Edn. Ctr., Bertoua, 1999—, others; project cons. Vlaams Regering, Belgium, 1994-95, Leaders' Tng., Lvov, Ukraine, 1994-95. Contbr. numerous articles to profl. jours. Recipient Medal of Honour, City of St. Barthelemy d' Anjou, 1997, Medal, Ministry Nat. Edn., 1997, Distinction Citizen of Merit for devel. of Czestochowa region, 1998, Golden Cross of Merit for Republic of Poland, 1999, KWP Cross, 1999. Mem. Polish Assn. Lasalle (chmn. 1992—), Found. Ednl. Mgmt., Mgr. Found. Forum, Polish Soc. Econ. Legal and Ct. Translators, European Assn. Internat. Edn., European Found. Mgmt. Devel., Fedn. des Univs. Cath. Europeennes, Assn. Tchr. Edn. in Europe, MUCIA Global Edn. Group, UNIAPAC. Roman Catholic. Avocations: hiking, organ music, cycling. Fax: 048/34/324/96-62. E-mail: wsjoe@hermes.wsjoe.czest.pl. Home: ul Lompy 10, 432-200 Czestochowa Poland Office: Czestochowa U Fgn Langs, ul Pułaskiego 4/6, 42-400 Czestochowa Poland

KRYSIAK, EWA JANINA, librarian; b. Warsaw, Poland, Sept. 29, 1949; d. Waclaw and Janina Zofia (Rojek) K.; 1 child, Agnieszka Bankowska. MA, Warsaw U., 1981. Libr. Nat. Library, Warsaw, 1971-78, ref. libr., 1978-92, online, electronic libr., union catalog libr., 1992-98, exec. mgr., coord., 1998—; intern Libr. Congress, Washington, 1993-94. Mem. Polish Libr. Assn. (pres. 1993-97, pres. chpt. 1997—, Silver Pin 1991). Roman Catholic. Avocations: computers, reading, music, dogs, scents/perfume. E-mail: ekrysiak@bn.org.pl. Home: Nubijska 8/2, 03977 Warsaw Poland Office: Nat Libr, Al Niepodleglosci 213, 00973 Warsaw Poland

KRYUCHKOV, FELIX ADAMOVICH, chemist, researcher; b. Minsk, Byelorussia, May 18, 1936; s. Adam Yakovlevich and Bronya Borisovna (Sorkina) K.; m. Larisa Alexandrovna, Jan. 18, 1957; children: Edward Felixovich, Tsigvintseva Tatyana Felixovna. Engr. Chemist, Leningrad Tech. Inst., St. Petersburg, Russia, 1959; D Chem. Scis., Moscow Chem. Tech. Inst., 1965. Cert. sr. rsch. Highest Commn. on Cert. USSR, Moscow, 1969. Jr. rschr. Rsch. Inst. Synthetic Resins, Vladimir, Russia, 1959-62, sr. rschr., 1962-65, head lab., 1965-74, leading rschr., 1974-92; leading rschr. Polymersintez Sci.-Ind. Assn., Vladimir, 1992-97; chief specialist Izolan Co., Vladimir, 1997—. Contbr. articles to profl. jours. Recipient author's certs. Com. Inventors USSR Inventions Bull., Moscow, 1962-90, award Coun. Ministers, USSR, Moscow, 1982, 3 medals Head Com. of Exhbn. of Achievements Nat. Economy, Moscow, 1968, 76, 78, govt. medals for disting. pub. svcs. Rsch. Inst. Synthetic Resins, 1970, 71, 88; named Honored Chemist, Ministry Chem. Industry, Moscow, 1987. Mem. Inventor Soc. Soviet Union (honored inventor 1985), N.Y. Acad. Scis. Avocations: tourism, photography. Office: Izolan Co, PO Box 19, 600016 Vladimir Russia

KRZESIŃSKA, MARTA, physicist, researcher, educator; b. Kielce, Poland, July 15, 1949; d. Marceli and Maria (Dyk) Pieta; m. Andrzej Marian Krzesiński, Sept. 11, 1976; children: Adam, Jacek. MS in Physics, Silesian U., Katowice, Poland, 1972, PhD in Physics, 1983. Asst. Silesian Tech. U., Gliwice, 1972-73, sr. asst., 1976-84; asst. prof. Inst. Coal Chemistry/Polish Acad. Scis., Gliwice, 1984—. Contbr. articles to profl. jours. Bd. dirs., sec. inst. orgn. Solidarity Party, Gliwice, 1981—. Mem. Polish Acad. Scis. (mem. sci. sec. CPBP no. 01.16 program, sci. sec. sci. coun. inst. coal chemistry), European Acoustics Assn., Polish Acoustical Soc., Am. Chem. Soc. Roman Catholic. Avocations: travel, Chopin music, painting, bridge, dance. E-mail: marta@gepard.karboch.gliwice.pl. Home: Tarnogórska 114D, 44-100 Gliwice Poland Office: Inst Coal Chemistry, Sowińskiego 5, 44-121 Gliwice Poland

KRZTOŃ, JAN, design engineer, consultant; b. Rzeszow, Poland, Nov. 1, 1931; s. Ignacy and Anna (Płonka) K.; m. Dorota Rozalia Koj, Oct. 25, 1958; children: Bogusław, Arkadiusz. Engr., Poly. U., Wrocław, Poland, 1956; diploma, Poly. U., Gliwice, Poland, 1984. Designer Ctrl. Boiler Design Office, Tarnowskie Gory, Poland, 1956-71, tech. dir., 1971-77, dir., 1977-90; mgr. design Ahlstrom Fakop, Sosnowiec, Poland, 1993-95, Foster Wheeler Energy Fakop, Sosnowiec, 1995—; mem. cons. team Poly. U., Gliwice, 1994-98, Rsch. Inst., Warszawa, Poland, 1980-89, Lodz, Poland, 1972-85, Ministry, Warszawa, 1985-87. Recipient meritorious state energetic State Coun., 1987. Roman Catholic. Avocations: tourism, sports. Home: Stonecznikow, 42-606 Tarnowskie Gory Silesia, Poland Office: Foster Wheeler Energy Fakop, Staszica, 41-200 Sosnowiec Silesia, Poland

KRZYSZTOFIK, WOJCIECH JAN, electrical engineer, educator, consultant; b. Swidnica, Poland, Mar. 28, 1949; s. Franciszek and Marianna Rozalia (Pawlik) K.; m. Elżbieta Zagała, Apr. 21, 1973; children: Jowita, Paulina, Jarosław. MSEE, Tech. U. Wroclaw, Poland, 1974, PhD in Elec. Engring., 1983. Rsch. asst. Tech. U. Wroclaw, 1974-76, sr. rsch., tchg. asst., 1976-79, lectr. elec. engring., 1979-83, asst. prof., 1986—; vis. prof. Chalmers U. Tech., Gothenburg, Sweden, 1988; prof. elec. engring. Mosul (Iraq) U., 1988-90; asst. dir. Inst. Tele. and Acoustics, Tech. U. Wroclaw, 1985-88, asst. dean dept. elec. engring., 1991-95. Co-author: Electromagnetic Environments and Consequences, 1994; contbr. articles to mags. and profl. jours.; 5 patents in field. Recipient award Min. Higher Edn., Warsaw, 1987. Mem. IEEE, Assn. Polish Elec. Engrs. Poland, Polish Soc. Theoretical and Applied Electrotechnics. Democrat. Christian Catholic. Avocations: music, sailing, foreign travel, science. Home: Sepa-Szarzynskiego 72/5, 50-334 Wroclaw Poland Office: Wroclaw U Tech, Wybrzeze Wyspianskiego 27, 50-370 Wroclaw Poland

KRZYZANOWSKI, JERZY ROMAN, Polish literature educator; b. Lublin, Poland, Dec. 10, 1922; came to U.S., 1959; s. Julian and Emilia (Sobieszczanska) K.; m. Elzbieta Gabryela Kuraszkiewicz, Sept. 12, 1948; children: Kris, Justyn, Daniel. MA, U. Warsaw, Poland, 1959; PhD, U. Mich., 1965. Sr. editor State Sci. Pubs., Warsaw, 1951-59; lectr. U. Calif., Berkeley, 1959-60; instr. U. Mich., Ann Arbor, 1960-63; asst. prof. U. Colo., Boulder, 1963-64; assoc. prof. U. Kans., Lawrence, 1964-67; prof. Polish lit. Ohio State U., Columbus, 1967—. Author: Ernest Hemingway, 1963, Wladyslaw Stanislaw Reymont, 1972, Legenda Somosierry, 1987, U Szarugi, 1995, Atrodyte, 1999, and others. Bd. dirs. Polish Inst. Arts and Scis. in Am., N.Y.C., 1983-89. 2d lt. Polish Home Army, 1943-44. Grantee NEH, 1984, U.S. Dept. Edn., 1985. Home: 4546 Crompton Dr Columbus OH 43220-3053 Office: Ohio State U 232 Cunz H Columbus OH 43220-3053

KSANFOMALITY, LEONID VASILIEVICH, astronomer, researcher; b. Kerch, Crimea, Russia, Jan. 28, 1932; s. Ksanfomality Vasilii and Mickhailova; m. Irina Shoulgina; children: Natlia, Elen. Degree in engring., St. Petersburg Tech. U., 1956; PhD in Astrophysics, Tbilisi State U., 1963; DSc in Physics and Math., Space Rsch. Inst., Moscow, 1978. Chief of lab. Astrophys. Obs., Abastumany, Russia, 1958-67, Space Rsch. Inst., Russia, 1968—; lectr. Moscow Planetarium, 1970-79, Znaniye Soc., Moscow, 1970-90. Contbr. articles to profl. jours.; patentee in field. Recipient State award Supreme Soviet, USSR, 1975, 83, 84, 88, State award Russia, Disting. Scientist of the Russian Fedn., 1999. Mem. Internat. Astron. Union. Avocations: scientific electronic/optical instrumentation, tourism. E-mail: ksanf@iki.rssi.ru. Home: Apt 135, 98-10 Profsoyuznaya St, 117810 Moscow Russia Office: 84/32 Profsoyuznaya St, 117810 Moscow Russia

KU, YOUNG, chemical engineering educator, researcher; b. Taichung, Taiwan, Oct. 1, 1955; s. Chung-Liu Ku and Hwa-Ou Chou; m. Siao-Yu Wu, Jan. 20, 1983; children: Lin, Rong. BS, Tunghai U., Taichung, 1977; MS, U. Ky., 1982; PhD, Purdue U., 1986. Rschr. Nat. Bur. Stds., Taipei, Taiwan, 1979-80; assoc. prof. chem. engring. Nat. Taiwan Inst. Tech., Taipei, 1986-92; prof. Nat. Taiwan Inst. Tech., 1992—; cons. Environ. Protection Adminstrn., Taipei, 1988, Indsl. Devel. Bur., Taipei, 1988, Indsl. Tech. Rsch. Inst., Hsinchu, Taiwan, 1988. Contbr. articles to Indsl. Engring. Chem. Rsch., Jour. Chinese Environ. Engring., Water Rsch. Recipient outstanding

rsch. award Nat. Sci. Coun., Taipei, 1992, 93. Mem. AIChE, Chinese Inst. Environ. Engrs., Water Environ. Fedn. Home: 6F-2 No 6 Ln 68 Alley 41, Keelung Rd Sect 4, Taipei 106, Taiwan Office: Nat Taiwan U Sch Tech, 43 Keelung Rd Sect 43, Taipei 106, Taiwan

KUAH, AUDREY LENG LENG, travel company executive; b. Singapore, Aug. 1, 1970; d. Jimmy Lai Seng Kuah and Catharine Goh. BA, Nat. U. Singapore, 1992. Postgrad. diploma in mktg., Chartered Inst. Mktg. (U.K.). Sr. media planner J. Walter Thompson, Singapore, 1993-95; asst. mgr. mktg. United Overseas Bank, Singapore, 1995-96; regional mktg. comm. mgr. Sedona Hotels Internat., Yangon, Myanmar, 1996-98; bus. devel. mgr. (Asia) Insight Vacations Pte. Ltd., Singapore, 1998—. Mem. CIM U.K. Avocations: travel, reading, concerts, musicals, plays. Home: Blk 455 Sin Ming Ave, # 09-487, Singapore 570455, Singapore

KUBA, ATTILA, mathematician; b. Kecskemet, Hungary, May 30, 1953; s. Endre and Ilona (Molnar) K.; m. Anna Kozma, Feb. 1, 1975; children: Andras, Peter. MSc, Jozsef Attila Univ., 1987; PhD, 1997. Scientific worker, and assoc. prof. Jozsef Attila Univ., Szeged, Hungary, 1976—. Mem. Hungarian Humboldt Assn. Office: Arpad ter 2, H-6720 Szeged Hungary

KUBA, JOHN ALBERT, mortician; b. Cedar Rapids, Iowa, Apr. 14, 1940; S. Edward Rudolph and Josephine Marie (Barta-Letovsky) K. Student, Coe Coll., Cedar Rapids, 1958-59, Tex. A&I U., 1959-61, Washington U., St. Louis, 1961-62; grad., Wis. Inst. Mortuary Sci., 1963. Ptnr., owner E&J Homes Ltd., Kuba Funeral Homes, Cedar Rapids, 1963-94; pres., CEO Sisley Grove Cemetery, Cedar Rapids, 1966—, E&J, Inc., Cedar Rapids, 1966—; trustee Czech Nat Cemetery, Cedar Rapids, 1966-81, fin. sec., 1981-94; owner Velvet Feed Bag Restaurant, 1979-84, Czech Village Shirt, ETC Shop, 1991, founder. Author: Cooking in America, 1971. V.p. Linn County Hist. Mus. Assn., Cedar Rapids, 1966-69, Czech Fine Arts, 1970-75; fin. sec. Linn County Dem. Ctrl. Com., 1970-74; vol. San Antonio AIDS Found.; docent Inst. Texan Cutures, San Antonio Conservation Soc.; mem. Bexar County Czech Heritage Soc., Victoria County Czech Heritage Soc., Unity Found., S.A. Equal Right Polit. Caucus; sec. Minn.-Iowa dist. Civitan Internat. Spl. Olympics, South Bend, Reno-Tahoe, Mpls.-St. Paul. Recipient Outstanding Lt. Gov. Civitan Internat., 1989-90, Outstanding Community Svc. and Humanitarian award Modern Woodmen of Am., 1990. Mem. Czechoslovak Soc. Am. Franternal Life Assn. (pres. 1964-67, sec.-treas. 1971—, Fraternalist of Yr. 1991), Western Fraternal Life (sec. 1986-89), K.C. (past faithful navigator 4 degrees), 16th Ave Merchants Assn. (sec.), Minowa Dist. Civitan (gov. 1980-81, fellow 1991, dist. honor key 1991), Tex. Czech Heritage Soc., Victoria County Czech Heritage Soc., Bexar County Czech Heritage Soc., Lodge Jr. Am. Czech #388 (pres., sec., treas., sec.-treas., fin. sec.), Cath. Order of Foresters, K.C., Moose Lodge, Eagles, Elks, Cath. Workman, Cedar Rapids Sokol, Fedn. of Czech Groups, Czech Heritage Found., Linn County Hist. Soc., Czech Fine Arts, W.F.L.A., Alamo Bus. Coun. San Antonio, Assn. for the Mentally Disabled, Civitan Club. Roman Catholic. Avocations: archaeology, gourmet cooking, travel, gardening, mystery reading. Home: PO Box 716 Helotes TX 78023-0716

KUBA, MIROSLAV, neurophysiology educator, researcher; b. Vysoke-Myto, Czech Republic, Sept. 12, 1954; s. Miroslav and Marie (Řeháčková) K.; m. Zuzana Kratochvilova, July 14, 1979; Veronika, Martin, Karolina. MD, Charles U., Hradec Kralove, Czech Republic, 1979, PhD, 1984. Rschr. Faculty Medicine Charles U., 1979-83, tchr., 1983-94, assoc. prof., 1994—, vice-dean, 1994—, head electrophys. lab., 1987—, head dept. pathophysiology, 1999—; rsch. fellow Max-Planck Inst., Bad Nauheim, Germany, 1989-90. Rsch. grantee Commn. European Cmty., Brussels, 1994, James S. McDonnell Found., 1994, McDonnell Pew Found., Oxford, Eng., 1991. Mem. Internat. Soc. for Clin. Electrophysiology of Vision, Internat. Brain Rsch. Orgn. Roman Catholic. E-mail: kuba@lfhk.cuni.cz. Home: Sovova 1066, 50002 Hradec Králové Czech Republic Office: Charles U, Simkova 870, 50001 Hradec Kralove Czech Republic

KUBALL, HANS-GEORG MAX, physical chemistry educator and scientist; b. Freienwalde, Pommern, Germany, Nov. 25, 1931; s. Hans and Maria (Strassner) K.; m. Elisabeth Rammensee, Aug. 8, 1963 (div. Feb. 1989); children: Martin, Jürgen; m. Monika Bartels, June 13, 1997. Diploma in chemistry, U. Würzburg, Germany, 1959, D Natural Sci., 1963, Habilitation, 1968. Mem. faculty U. Würzburg, 1960-72; prof. phys. chemistry U. Kaiserslautern, Germany, 1973-2000, prof. emeritus, 2000—. Contbr. articles on exptl. and theoretical spectroscopy, chirality, and liquid crystal phases to profl. jours. Grantee Fonds Chem. Industry, 1972. Mem. German Chem. Soc., Bunsengesellschaft Phys. Chemistry, Internat. Liquid Crystal Soc. Lutheran. Avocations: chess, tennis, music. Home: Römerweg 4, 67705 Stelzenberg Germany Office: U Kaiserslautern, PF 3049, Erwin Schrödingerstr, 67653 Kaiserslautern Germany

KUBAN, VLASTIMIL, analytical chemist; b. Trojanovice, Moravia, Czech Republic, Aug. 27, 1944; s. Vlastimil and Anna (Stavarkova) K.; m. Zdenka Kasanova, Dec. 9, 1943; children: Petr, Pavel, Zdenek. RNDr, Purkyne U., Brno, Czech Republic, 1966, Purkyne U., Brno, Czech Republic, 1968; PhD, Purkyne U., Brno, Czech Republic, 1975; DSc, U. Pardubice, Czech Republic, 1993. Jr. rschr. Inst. Analytical Chemistry, Czechoslovak Acad. Scis., Brno, 1966-68; rsch. asst. chemistry Purkyne U., Brno, 1968-72, sr. rschr., 1972-92; asst. prof., dept. vice head Masaryk U., Brno, 1992-94, prof., 1994; prof. analytical chemistry, dept. head Mendel U., Brno, 1994—; vis. scientist Royal Inst. Tech., Stockholm, 1988, 89, 90, Tex. Tech. U., Lubbock, 1991-92, Nat. U. Yokohama, Japan, 1995. Contbr. articles to profl. jours. Mem. Czech Chem. Soc., Czech Spectroscopic Soc. Avocations: tourism, sports, gardening. Home: Vojanova 6, CZ 61500 Brno Czech Republic Office: Mendel U Agr & Forestry, Dept Chemistry & Biochem, Zemedelska 1, CZ 61300 Brno Czech Republic

KUBAT, MIROSLAV, computer science educator; b. Prague, Czechoslovakia, May 26, 1958; came to U.S., 1998; s. Josef Kubat and Daria Kubatova; m. Alice Minaříková, Nov. 21, 1981 (div. 1987); m. Vera Řeháková, Aug. 18, 1990; 1 child, Jaroslav. MSc, Brno (Czechoslovakia) Tech. U., 1982, PhD, 1990. Rschr. Tech. U. Graz, Austria, 1992-94; sr. rschr. U. Linz, Austria, 1994-95, U. Ottawa, Ont., Can., 1995-97; assoc. prof. U. La., Lafayette, 1998—. Co-editor: Machine Learning and Data Mining, 1998; contbr. articles to profl. jours. Office: U La Lafayette PO Box 44330 Lafayette LA 70504-0001

KUBÁT, RUDOLF, physician; b. Plzen, Czech Republic, Nov. 17, 1939; s. Rudolf Kubát and Ludmila (Vácová) Kubátová; m. Vera Roubícková, Dec. 27, 1961; children: Hořenovská, Hana, Ksírová Zdenka; m. Jaroslava Veverková, May 17, 1990. MD, Charles U., 1962, CSc, 1989. Asst. physician Hosp. Karlovy Vary, Czech Republic, 1962-78; head physician Hosp. Kadan, Czech Republic, 1978-90, 91-94, Hosp. Melník, Czech Republic. Inventor in field. Office: Hosp, Prazská 528, CZ 27690 Melník Czech Republic

KUBE, HAROLD DEMING, retired financial executive; b. Buffalo, Wyo., June 16, 1910; s. Carl Christen and Inez (Mather) K.; m. Shirley Smith; children: Robert Ford, Thomas Smith. BS, U. Nebr., 1932; MBA, Harvard U., 1934. Owner Beef Cattle Farm, Warrenton, Va., 1950—; co-owner Resources Devel. Assocs., 1965-80; dir. emeritus Jefferson Savs. and Loan Assn., Warrenton, 1980—, Greater Washington Investors, Inc., 1987—; bd. dirs. A & K Land and Cattle Corp., Warrenton. Co-author: Manufacturing Distribution in U.S., 1938. With USN, 1944-46. Mem. Am. Econ. Assn. Episcopalian. Avocation: golf. Home and Office: 6470 Beverleys Mill Rd Broad Run VA 20137-2101

KUBECZKA, KARL HEINZ, pharmacist, educator; b. Ostrara, Czechoslovakia, Mar. 31, 1935; s. Julius and Margit (Ritschel) K.; m. Brigitte Fechtig, Feb. 23, 1963 (dec. 1984); children: Uta, Boris; m. Christa Müller, Mar. 30, 1990. Degree in pharmacy, U. Karlsruhe, Germany, 1961, doctorate, 1967; habilitation, U. Hamburg, 5, 1972. Asst. prof. U. Hamburg, 1972-74, U. Wurzburg, 1969-72; prof., dept. head U. Hamburg, 1974-89, prof., 1974-89. Contbr. articles to profl. jours. Mem. Gesellschaft für Arzneipflanzenforschung, German Pharm. Soc., Gesellschaft deutscher Nat. Roman Catholic. Avocation: flute. Home: Wisplerstr 52, D 2000 Hamburg Fed Republic Germany Office: U Hamburg Dept Pharm Biology, Bundstr 43, D-20146 Hamburg 13 Fed Republic Germany

KUBELKA, WOLFGANG LEOPOLD, pharmacy educator; b. Vienna, Austria, Feb. 18, 1935; s. Otto and Rosa (Stefan) K.; m. Erika Englisch, Aug. 10, 1961 (dec. Mar. 28, 1986); children: Peter, Christina, Eva.; m. Claudia Linford, Nov. 4, 1987. M in Pharmacy, U. Vienna, 1959, PhD in Pharmacy, 1965. Asst. U. Vienna, 1958-73, docent pharmacognosy, 1973-77, ao. prof., 1977-83, prof., 1983; dir. Inst. Pharmacognosy U. Vienna, 1983—, dean faculty of natural scis., 1987-91, 99, vice dean faculty of natural scis., 1991-98; advisor jour. Pharmazie. Editor Scientia Pharmaceutica, 1985—; contbr. more than 110 articles to profl. jours. Mem. Austrian Pharm. Soc. (pres. 1984-87), Austrian Soc. for Phytotherapy (v.p. 1991—), Soc. for Medicinal Plant Rsch. (advisor 1978-98), Austrian Soc. for Ethnomedicine (pres. 1982-84, 90-92), Am. Soc. of Pharmacognosy, Soc. Econ. Botany and others. Roman Catholic. Avocations: classical music, mountaineering, skiing, photography. Home: Habichergasse 50, A-1160 Vienna Austria Office: Univ Vienna Inst Pharmacognosy, Althanstrasse 14, A-1090 Vienna Austria

KUBIACZYK, IRENEUSZ, mathematician; b. Sokolniki Wielkie, Poznań, Poland, Oct. 16, 1946; s. Marcin and Helena (Błaszyk) K.; m. Genowefa Irena Grabias, Sept. 6, 1947; children: Beata, Piotr. PhD, A. Mickiewicz U., Poznań, 1977, habilitation, 1987. Vice chmn. Math. Inst. A. Mickiewicz U., Poznań, 1987-91, head Postgrad. Sch. Math., 1991—; chmn. divsn. differential equations A. Mickiewicz U., 1991—, prof., 1992—; prof. Tech. U., Zielona Góra, 1994—, chmn. City Coun. of Sroda, 1998—; pres. Poznan divsn. of the Polish Math. Soc., 1997—. Contbr. articles to profl. jours. Recipient award Polish Ministry Edn. Mem. Am. Math. Soc., Polish Math. Soc. Avocations: sports, music.

KUBICA, BENEDYKT PIOTR, software engineer; b. Katowice, Silesia, Poland, Oct. 19, 1958; s. Leon and Aniela (Miczek) K.; m. Anna Kryj, Aug. 7, 1982; children: Marta, Agata. MS in Engring., Silesian Tech. U., Gliwice, Poland, 1982. Maintenance Polish Railway, Signalling & Telecomm., Tarnowskie Gorwy, Poland, 1982-84; design engr. Railway Design Office, Katowice, Poland, 1984-91; tech. fellowship for signalling engrs. Coras Iompair Eireann-Irish Rail, Dublin, Ireland, 1991-92; software engr. Westinghouse Signals, Ltd., Chippenham, Eng., 1992—. Recipient Best Computer Program '89 award Transport Engrs. Asssn.-Nat. Computer Club, 1989. Mem. IEEE, N.Y. Acad. Scis., Assn. for Computing Machinery. Office: Westinghouse Signals Ltd, Mainline Systems POB 79 Pew Hill, Chippenham SN15 1JD, England

KUBÍČEK, LADISLAV, physical metallurgy educator, scientist; b. Prague, Czech Republic, Mar. 26, 1930; s. Ladislav and Anna (Kousalová) K.; m. Irina Fedorová, Jan. 21, 1956 (dec. July 1990); 1 child, Irena; m. Zuzana Kupcová, Feb. 26, 1994; children: Vladimir, Pavel. Grad., Indsl. Coll. Machinery, Prague, 1948; diploma in engring., U. Non-Ferrous Metals, Moscow, 1953, PhD, 1959; DrS, Czechoslovak Acad. Sci., Prague, 1972. Asst. to mgr. Rsch. Inst. Metals, Panenske Břežany, Czech Republic, 1953-59, sci. officer, 1960-61, tech. dir., 1961-70, mng. dir., 1970-81; prof., dean chair Univ.-Chem. Tech., Prague, 1978-94; sci. sec. Czechoslovak Acad. Sci., 1981-84; vice-chmn. State Commn. Tech. & Investment Devel., Prague, 1984-90. Contbr. over 160 articles to profl. jours. Mem., chmn. com. industry Czech Nat. Coun. Czech Parliament, 1976-86. Recipient State award, 1989, Merit Gold Order Sci., 1983, Nat. award Czech Republic, 1976. Mem. IIASA (vice-chmn. steering coun. 1986-91, hon. scholar award 1990), Czechoslovak Soc. Doctrine Metals (chmn. 1970-74), Czech Commn. Sci. Graduation (chmn. 1977-84), Coun. Mutual Econ. Assistance (chmn. sci. coun. rsch. coordination 1973-86). Achievements include patent for metal alloy basedon iron-nickel-cobalt for glass filings, heat resistant NiCr alloy for high temperature applications and for direct solidification, method for manufacture of engine pistons. Office: Vysoka skola chemicko tech, Technická 5, 166 28 Prague Czech Republic

KUBÍČEK, PETR, physicist, researcher, consultant; b. Ostrava, Czech Republic, Nov. 13, 1942; s. Mikuláš Vojtěch and Božena (Šustková)K.; m. Jarmila Caletková, Dec. 11, 1971; children: Jarmila, Marcela, Petra. Dip. Ing. in tech. and nuclear physics, Czech Tech. U., Prague, Czech Republic, 1965; PhD in Exptl. Physics, Charles U., Prague, Czech Republic, 1972, DSc in Applied Physics, 1991; D Tech. Sci., Tech. U., Ostrava, 1993. Pedagogue, scientist Tech. U., Ostrava, 1965-80; scientist Czech Acad. Sci., Ostrava, 1980-84, Sci. Coal Inst., Ostrava, 1985-92; asst. prof. exptl. physics Czech. Tech. U., Prague, 1992, prof. applied physics nuc. faculty, 1995; asst. prof. applied math. U. Ostrava, 1994; pvt. sci. activity Ostrava, 1993—; sci. sec. com. for nuclear tech. Sci. Tech. Assn., Ostrava, 1978-90, mem. organizing com. sci. conf., 1976-82. Contbr. over 150 articles to sci. jours., and procs., including Jour. Electroanalytical Chemistry, Jour. Less Common Metals, Ann. Chemie, Czech Jour. Physics B., Chem. Papers, Czech Jour. Physics A, Nuclear Energy, Metallic Materials, others; numerous patents in field. Home: Na Ctvrti 14, 705 00 Ostrava-Hrabuvka Czech Republic

KUBICEK, VLADIMIR, andrologist; b. Jihlava, Czech Republic, June 6, 1963; s. Vladimir and Jana (Markova) K.; m. Vladimira Cizkova, Aug. 28, 1963; children: Jan, Katerina. MD, U. Carolina Pragensis, Czech Republic, 1987; PhD, Charles U., Czech Republic, 1999. Diploma in urology, 1st and 2d grade. Andrologist Andrology Care Ctr., Ceske Budejovice, Czech Republic, Ctr. Reproductive Medicine, Prague, Czech Republic; pvt. practice Andrology Clinic, Ceske Budejovice, Czech Republic. Author: Erektilni Dystunkce V Ambulanci, 1996, Muzska Infertilita a Erektilni D ysfunkce, 1996. Mem. Czech Urol. Soc. (chmn. andrology sect.). Roman Catholic. Avocations: music, painting. Office: Andrology Care Ctr, U Tri Lvu 4, 370 000 Ceske Budejovice Czech Republic

KUBIDA, WILLIAM JOSEPH, lawyer; b. Newark, Apr. 3, 1949; s. William and Catherine (Gilchrist) K.; m. Mary Jane Hamilton, Feb. 4, 1984; children: Sara Gilchrist, Kathleen Hamilton. BSEE, USAF Acad., 1971; JD, Wake Forest U., 1979. Bar: N.C. 1979, U.S. Patent Office 1979, Ind. 1980, U.S. Dist. Ct. (no. dist.) Ind. 1980, U.S. Dist. Ct. (so. dist.) Ind. 1980, U.S. Ct. Appeals (7th cir.) 1981, U.S. Dist. Ct. Ariz. 1982, U.S. Ct. Appeals (9th and fed. cirs.) 1982, Ariz. 1982, Colo. 1990, U.S. Dist. Ct. Colo. 1990, U.S. Ct. Appeals (10th cir.) 1990. Patent and trademark atty. Lundy and Assocs., Ft. Wayne, Ind., 1979-81; patent atty. Motorola, Inc., Phoenix, 1981-85; intellectual property counsel Nippon Motorola, Ltd., Tokyo, 1985-87; ptnr. Lisa & Kubida, Phoenix, 1987-89; engring. law counsel Digital Equipment Corp., Colorado Springs, Colo., 1989-92; of counsel Holland & Hart, Denver, Colorado Springs, 1992-93, ptnr., chmn. intellectual property practice group, 1993-99; ptnr., chmn. patient practice group Hogan & Hartson LLP, Colorado Springs, 1999—; bd. dirs. Colorado Springs Tech Incubator,. 1st lt. USAF, 1971-76. Mem. Am. Intellectual Property Law Assn. (computer software sect.), Japan Am. Soc. Colo. (bd. dirs.), Licensing Exec. Soc. (Pacific Rim subcom.), Country Club Colo., Mensa, Intertel, Phi Delta Phi. Republican. Presbyterian. Home: 4165 Regency Dr Colorado Springs CO 80906-4368

KUBIK, MAREK PIOTR, chemical engineer, educator, researcher; b. Samice, Poland, Oct. 19, 1947; s. Roman and Janina (Dabrowska) K.; m. Iwona Janina Żurakowska, Nov. 19, 1954; 1 child, Wojciech. Masters, Tech. U., Łodź, Poland, 1971, D of Chemistry, 1980. Rschr. Tech. U. Łodź, 1971-73, sr. rschr., 1973-80; adj. prof. Rsch. Inst. Pomology and Floriculture, Skierniewice, Poland, 1980—, head Lab. of Contamination and Pesticide Residue Analyses, 1999—. Author: Falling in Love With Bees, 1997, Ecological Girl and Another Short Stories, 1999, (chpt.) Plant Regulators, 1997; patentee in production of 1,3,5-triazacycloheptane-2-4-diones. V.p. Wild Life Preservation, Skierniewice, 1987—; pres. Dist. Commn. Nature Preservation, Skierniewice, 1993—. Avocation: bee keeping. Home: Mszczonowska 49/59, 96-100 Skierniewice Poland Office: Rsch Inst Pomology, Pomologiczna 18, 96-100 Skierniewice Poland

KUBIKOWSKI, TOMASZ, theater and performance educator; b. Wroclaw, Poland, Dec. 9, 1962; s. Zbigniew and Aldona (Huber) K.; m. Edyta Smyrska, Feb. 14, 1987. MA, State Coll. Theater Arts, Warsaw, Poland, 1985, U. Warsaw, 1990; PhD, Jagiellonian U., Krakow, Poland, 1992. Journalist Teatr Monthly, Warsaw, 1990-92; editor Dialog Monthly, Warsaw, 1992-95; scholar Alexander Zelwerowicz Theater Acad., Warsaw, 1994—, pro-rector, 1999—; vis. prof. U. Richmond, Va., 1994; dramaturge Ateneum Theater, Warsaw, 1996-99; selectioner Shakespeare Festival, Gdansk, Poland, 1998—; selecting bd. mem. Warsaw Theater Festival, 1996—; mem. internat. jury Svenska Teaterbiennalen, Malmoe, Sweden, 1995; bd. dirs. European League Insts. Arts, Amsterdam, The Netherlands, 1998—. Author: The Seven Beings of Theater, 1994, (drama) The Science of Colors, 1999; contbr. essays to jours. Mem. Internat. Theater Inst., Performance Studies Internat. Avocations: swimming, mountain hiking. Home: Ul Nowy Swiat 23/25 m 29B, 00-029 Warsaw Poland Office: Aleksander Zelwerowicz Acad, Ul Miodowa 22/24, 00-246 Warsaw Poland

KUBIN, MILAN, physician, researcher; b. Hradec Kralove, Czech Republic, Apr. 18, 1927; s. Antonin and Franciska (Svoboda) K.; m. Miloslava Rezac, July 26, 1951; children: Eva, Jan. MD, Charles U., Prague, Czech Republic, 1951, D Med. Scis., 1987. Rschr. in Tb, Nat. Inst. Pub. Health, Prague, 1951—, head of nat. reference lab., 1970-95. Co-author: The Mycobacteria--A Source, 1984, Infections Caused by Atypical Mycobacteria, 1975. Capt. Czechoslovak Army, 1952-54. Mem. Internat. Union Against Tb (sec. 1960-70), European Soc. Mycobacteriology (pres. 1991-92). Avocations: photography, poetry, skiing. Office: Nat Inst Pub Health, Srobarova 48, 10042 Prague Czech Republic

KUBINEK, ROMAN, medical educator; b. Olomouc, Czech Republic, June 5, 1957; s. Josef and Emilie K.; m. Dagmar Matuskova, July 27, 1979; children: Radim, Marketa. D in Natural Sci., U. Palacky, Olomouc, 1981, PhD in Applied Physics, 1990. Asst. prof. nature sci. faculty U. Palack, Olomouc, 1982-94, sr. lectr. med. faculty, 1994—. Author: Physics in Calculations, 1997, Experimental Method Biophysics-Scanning Electron Microscopy, 1998, Fast Course of Physics, 1999, Hospital--Guide for Patient, 2000. Mem. Czech Soc. Electron Microscope, Czech Spectroscopic Soc., Czech Soc. Physics and Math., Czech Photobiol. Soc. Roman Catholic. Avocations: music, playing violin, sports, traveling. E-mail: Kubin@tunw.upol.cz. Fax: 0042068/5632167. Home: Wanklova 3, 772 00 Olomouc Moravia, Czech Republic Office: U Palack Dept Biophysics, Hnevotinska 3, 775 15 Olomouc Moravia, Czech Republic

KUBLER, FRANK LAWRENCE, lawyer; b. Pensacola, Fla., July 4, 1957; s. Frank Martin and Esther Helen (Flora) K. AA, Miami-Dade Jr. Coll., 1978; BS in Mech. Engring., U. Miami, Coral Gables, Fla., 1981, BA in History, 1982, JD, 1986. Bar: Fla. 1986, U.S. Cir. Ct. (11th cir) 1988, U.S. Cir. Ct. (fed. cir.) 1989, U.S. Patent Office 1987. Assoc. Dominik, Stein, Saccocio, Reese, Colitz & Van der Wall, Miami Lakes, Fla., 1986-90; pres. Law Office of Frank L. Kubler, Miami Lakes, 1990—; cons. Oltman, Flynn & Kubler, Ft. Lauderdale, Fla., 1990-96, ptnr., 1996—. Mem. Inter-Am. Law Rev., 1985. Mem. Patent Law Assn. South Fla. (v.p. 1993-94, pres. 1994-95), Mensa, Rotary (dir. 1992-94, chmn. scholarship com. 1994-95), Tau Beta Pi. Office: 915 Middle River Dr Ste 415 Fort Lauderdale FL 33304-3561

KUBLI, LAURIE JEAN, social worker; b. Pitts., Apr. 19, 1963; d. Ludwig Walter Sr. and Doris Ann Kubli. BS, U. Pitts., 1985; MEd, Slippery Rock U., 1997. Editor sports Pitts. News, 1984-85; substitute tchr. various sch. dists. Pitts., 1985-88; tchr. Camden (N.J.) Sch. Dist., 1988-89; telephone operator Conquest Operator Svcs., Butler, Pa., 1994-95; caseworker Butler County Children and Youth Agy., 1995—; With U.S. Army, 1989-93. Cmty. rep. Head Start Policy Coun., Butler, 1998-00. Mem. AAUW. Democrat. Lutheran. Avocations: writing, playing volleyball. E-mail: tigerkub1@aol.com. Office: Butler County Children and Youth Agy 124 W Diamond St Butler PA 16001-5780

KUBLI, RUDOLF EDUARD, information technology executive; b. Zurich, Switzerland, Nov. 19, 1945; s. Hugo H. and Lea A. (Mueller) K.; m. Dorothee V. Weinmann, July 10, 1971; children: Nicole, Marcel. Diploma in Elec. Engring., Swiss Fed. Inst. Tech., Zurich, 1971, PhD, 1977; cert. Exec. Engring. Program, Stanford U., 1985. Rschr. Inst. Biomed. Engring. and Med. Computing S.F.I.T. and U. Hosp. Zurich, 1971-78; head tech. assessment Mettler Instrumente Ag, Greifensee, Switzerland, dep. head qualty assurance, 1978-84; head ctrl. rsch. and tech. transfer Mettler-Toledo AG, Greifensee, 1984-90; v.p. group IT architecture stds. UBS Union Bank Switzerland, Zurich, 1991-98; exec. v.p., chief tech. officer Atraxis Group (SAir Group), Zurich, 1998—; mem. bd. Elmes Staub Ag, 1990-92; bd. mem. GHF, Zurich, 1984—. Contbr. articles to profl. jours.; patentee in field. Recipient 2nd prize Comdex Internet, Frankfurt, 1997. Mem. IEEE, Stanford Alumni Assn. Avocations: jazz, philosophy. Home: Goldauerstrasse 29, CH-8006 Zurich Switzerland

KUBO, ATSUSHI, medical educator; b. Tokyo, Sept. 5, 1943; s. Kesami Kubo; m. Tomoe Kubo. MD, Keio U., Tokyo, 1968. Physician Keio U. Sch. Medicine, Tokyo, 1969-77, asst. prof., 1977-80, assoc. prof., 1980-93, prof., 1993—. Author: Scintigram Atlas, 1997, Nuclear Medicien Notebook, 1999. Recipient award Japanese Soc. Nuc. Medicine, 1978. Mem. Japanese Assn. Med. Scis. (mgr. 1996—), Japan Radiol. Soc. (trustee 1987—), Japanese Soc. Nuc. Medicine (dir. trustee 1995—). Avocations: golf, gardening, listening to music, driving, ice skating. Home: 4-14-1 Kamilkedai Ohta-ku, Tokyo 145-0064, Japan Office: Keio U Sch Medicine, 35 Shinanomachi Shinjuku-ku, Tokyo 160-8582, Japan

KUBO, GARY MICHAEL, advertising executive; b. Chgo., Aug. 15, 1952; s. Robert S. and Hideko (Nishimura) K.; m. Harriet Davenport, June 14, 1975; children: Michael J., R. Scott. BS, Ill. State U., 1974. Rsch. project dir. Foote, Cone & Belding Communications, Chgo., 1974-76, account rsch. supr., 1976-79, rsch. mgr., 1979-80; assoc. rsch. dir. Young & Rubicam, Chgo., 1980-83; ptnr., group rsch. dir. Tatham, Laird & Kudner Advt., Chgo., 1983-89; v.p., dir. strategic planning and rsch./Midwest, Bozell, Inc., Chgo., 1989-91; sr. v.p., dir. strategic planning and rsch./Midwest, 1991-93; sr. v.p. dir. strategic planning rsch. Ogilvy & Mather, Chgo., 1993-95; prin. The KUBO Group, Ltd., Chgo., 1995—. Bd. Dirs. Chgo. Coun. Urban Affairs, 1992—. Mem. Advt. Rsch. Found., Am. Mktg. Assn. (speaker 1983-84, exec. bd.). Avocations: racquet sports, running, music. Home: 2129 Scarlet Oak Ln Lisle IL 60532-2855

KUBO, JUNICHI, chemical engineer, chemist; b. Ako-shi, Hyogo-ken, Japan, May 12, 1937; s. Toshio and Fumiko (Kamegawa) K.; m. Michiko Yuuki, Nov. 25, 1964; children: Keiko, Tadakazu. Bachelor's, Kyoto (Japan) U., 1961, D in Organic Chemistry, 1992. Rschr. Ctr. Tech. Rsch. Labs., Nippon Oil Co. Ltd., Yokohama, 1962-74; supr. Nippon Petroleum Refinery Co., Tokyo, 1974-77, Nippon Petroleum Refinery Co., Muroran (Japan) Refinery, 1977-80; sr. rsch. assoc. Ctrl. Tech. Rsch. Lab., Nippon Oil Co. Ltd., Yokohama, 1980-93, sr. rsch. counselor, 1993-97; sr. counselor Ako Kasei Co., Ltd., 1997—. Author some 40 articles on new applications of hydrogen-donating hydrocarbons from petroleum. Mem. N.Y. Acad. Scis., Am. Chem. Soc., Japan Petroleum Inst. Avocations: tennis, golf, painting. Home: Nakasu 5-59 Kariya, Ako-shi Hyogo-ken 678-0233, Japan Office: Ako Kasei Co Ltd, Sakoshi 329 Ako-shi, Hyogo 678-0193, Japan

KUBO, KEN-ICHI, physicist, educator, researcher; b. Mizukami, Japan, May 18, 1936; s. Rin-nosuke and Tane (Ohyabu) K.; m. Kimie Amano, May 23, 1965; children: Takuro, Tatsuhiko. BS, Tokyo Sci. U., 1962; MS, Tokyo Inst. Tech., 1964, DSc, 1969. Rsch. asst. Inst. for Nuclear Study, U. Tokyo, 1967-74, Faculty of Sci., U. Tokyo, 1974-78; assoc. prof. Tokyo Met. U., 1978-85, prof. physics, 1985-2000, prof. emeritus, 2000—; pres. Tokyo Met Coll Aero. Engring., 2000—; rsch. fellow Max Planck Inst. for Nuclear Physics, Heidelberg, Germany, 1972-74; rsch. scientist Tex. A&M U., College Station, 1975-78; sr. vis. fellow Nuclear Physics Lab., Oxford, Eng., 1980; vis. fellow Oxford U., 1990. Contbr. articles to profl. jours. Sr. h.s. prin. Sr. H.S. Affil./Tokyo Met. U., 1991-92; dir. gen. edn. Tokyo Met. U., 1993-97, councilor, 1993-97. Mem. Japan Phys. Soc., Am. Phys. Soc. Fax: 03 3724 3619. Home: 2-7-7-803 Yakumo Meguro-ku, 152-0023 Tokyo Japan Office: Tokyo Met Coll Aero Engring, 8-52-1 Minami-senju, Arakawa-ku, Tokyo 116-0003, Japan

KUBODERA, KEN'ICHI, researcher engineer; b. Kanagawa, Japan, Aug. 10, 1947; s. Shun'ichi and Machie Kubodera; m. Mariko Sakaue, Apr. 23, 1974; children: Yuko, Hiroshi. BS, U. Tokyo, 1970, MS, 1972, PhD in Engring., 1983. Rsch. engr. NTT Elec. Comm. Labs., Tokyo, 1972-92; exec.

mgr. NTT, Tokyo, 1992-96; exec. rsch. scientist NTT, Atsugi, 1996-99; gen. mgr. New Tech. Rsch. Labs., Sumitomo Osaka Cement Co. Ltd., Chiba, Japan, 1999—; part-time lectr. U. Tokyo, 1989-92; regional bd. nonlinear optics Gordon R. Breach Sci. Pub. Inc., 1991—. Author: Evaluation of Third-Order-Nonlinear Optical Effect, Nonlinear Optics of Organics and Semiconductors, 1989; contbr. articles to profl. jours. and confs. Mem. IEEE (sr.), Inst. Electronics, Info. and Comm. Engrs., Japan Soc. Applied Physics (chief sec. divsn. crystal tec 96-98). Avocation: golf. Home: 3-14-102 Tsutsujino, Sayama-Shi, Saitama 350-1321, Japan Office: New Tech Rsch Labs, 585 Toyotomi, Funabashi Chiba 274-8601, Japan

KUBOTA, EIJI, legal researcher; b. Kumamoto City, Japan, Oct. 22, 1966. B of Law, Kyushu U., Fukuoka, Japan, 1989, M of Law, 1992. Rsch. assoc. U. Tsukuba, Japan, 1997—. Contbr. articles to profl. jours. Mem. Japanese Assn. Internat. Law. Office: U Tsukuba, 1-1-1 Tennodai, 305-8573 Tsukuba Japan

KUBOTA, KEIJIRO, telecommunications educator; b. Tokyo, July 29, 1925; s. Kinoshita Jinnosuke and Yu Kubota; m. Takako Watanabe, Apr. 23, 1957; 2 children. Bachelor, Tokyo U., 1948, Doctor, 1962. Dept. head of lab. NTT, Tokyo, 1963-66; prof. Seikei U., Tokyo, 1966-91, head engring. dept., 1975-78, lectr., 1991-99; pres. Inst. of Image Electronics Engring. of Japan, 1987-90. Inventor in field. Chmn. com. Comms. System of Post Telecomms. Ministry, Tokyo, 1976-83. Avocation: golf. Home: 3-4-7 Higashikaigan-Minami, Chigasaki-shi, Kanagawaken 253, Japan

KUBOTA, KIYOSHI, physician; b. Tokyo, Dec. 1, 1952; s. Sakae and Chie (Masuda) K.; m. Noriko Yamada, July 26, 1991; 1 child, Junko. MD, Hokkaido U., Sapporo, Japan, 1978. Lic. physician, Japan. Resident Hokkaido U., Sapporo, 1978-83; rsch. fellow Clin. Rsch. Inst. Nat. Med. Ctr., Tokyo, 1983-84; rotating intern Nat. Med. Ctr., Tokyo, 1984-86; rsch. asssoc. Clin. Rsch. Inst. Nat. Med. Ctr., Tokyo, 1986-89; rsch. fellow U. Calif., San Francisco, 1989-91; vis. colleague Drug Safety Rsch. Unit, Southampton, Eng., 1991-94, hon. rsch. fellow, 1994-96; assoc. prof. phamacoepidemiology U. Tokyo, 1996—. Contbr. articles to profl. jours. Grantee Yasuda Meml. Scholarship, Tokyo, 1989, The British Coun. Tokyo, 1991. Office: U Tokyo Dept Pharmacoepidem, 7-3-1 Hongo, Bunkyo-ku 113-8655, Japan

KUBOTA, SUSUMU, seismologist, researcher; b. Iwamizawa, Hokkaido, Japan, Aug. 27, 1937; s. Tokutaro and Metsu (Imahori) K.; m. Chizuko Ikezaki, Nov. 24, 1968; children: Eri, Katsura, Yuki. BS, Hokkaido U., Sapporo, 1960, MS, 1962, DSc, 1971. Head earthquake predicition divsn. Japan Meteorol. Agy., Tokyo, 1988-91; dir. Kakioka Magnetic Observatory, Ibaraki, Japan, 1991-92, Local Meteorol. Observatory, Kagoshima, Japan, 1992-94; dir. gen. Dist. Meteorol. Observatory, Sapporo, 1994-97; pres. Meteorol. Coll., Kashiwa, Japan, 1997-98; sr. rschr. Assn. Devel. Earthquake Prediction, Tokyo, 1998—. Author: 1989 San Francisco Bay Area (Loma Prieta) Earthquake, 1990. Avocations: Shogi, Go. Home: Matsudo 618-1-807, Chiba Matsudo 271-0092, Japan Office: Assn Devel EQ Prediction, Sarugaku-cho 1-5-18, Tokyo Chiyoda 101-0064, Japan

KUBOYAMA, TETSUO, hotel executive; b. Fukuoka, Japan, Mar. 17, 1948. BA in Law, Keic U., Tokyo, 1971; BS in Hotel Adminstrn., Cornell U., 1975. Exec. trainee Imperial Hotel, Tokyo, 1972-73; asst. dir. catering, internat. sales Waldorf=Astoria, N.Y.C., 1975-78; mgr. project planning Hotel New Otani, Tokyo, 1978-80, exec. asst. to exec. v.p., 1984-87; asst. to gen. mgr. Hotel New Otani, L.A., 1980-84; dir. sales Hotel New Otani, Osaka, Japan, 1987-89; asst. gen. mgr. Tokyo Bay Hilton, Urayasu, Japan, 1989-91; pres., CEO NHV Hotels Internat., Sasebo, Japan, 1991-97; pres., CEO, cons. Windsor Hotels Internat., Tokyo, 1997—. Author: The Modern Hotel Management Method, 1993; pub., editor-in-chief Huis Ten Bosch ERASMUS, 1992-96, The Windsor, 1997. Mem. Am. Club, Am. C. of C. Japan, British C. of C. Japan, Waldorf=Astoria Dist. Alumni Assn. Avocations: karate, golfing, skiing, reading. Office: Windsor Hotels Internat Co, 4-3-1 Toranomon, Minato-ku Tokyo 105-6015, Japan

KUBY, SELMA MILLER, artist, poet; b. Bklyn., Jan. 25, 1920; d. Edward and Celia (Tomashoff) Miller; m. Milton Kuby, June 1942; children: Stuart A., Beth E. Kuby Levinthal, Laurel M. Kuby Sclafani, Stevan C. (dec.). Diploma in Art, Washington Irving H.S., 1938; studied with Morris Kantor, Art Students League, N.Y., 1938-39, 40-42; studied with Boardman Robinson, Lawrence Barrett, Otis Dozier, Paul Parker, David Friedenthal, Colorado Springs Fine Arts Ctr., 1939-40; studied with Harry Sternberg, Will Barnet, Art Students League, 1940-42; studied sculpting with Alfred Van Loen, 1969. Tchg. monitor Bklyn. Acad. Music, 1941-42, Bklyn. Mus., 1941-42; ind. artist Bklyn., 1940-50, Massapequa, N.Y., 1950-56, Huntington Station, N.Y., 1956—; art lectr. Walt Whitman H.S., Huntington Station, N.Y., 1965; owner, tchr. Ind. Art Sch., Huntington Station, N.Y., 1965-67. Paintings included in Art As Book Series, 1972-98, Bach in Space Series, 1992, Cosmos Series, 1995-99; one-woman show Hofstra U. Club, Hempstead, N.Y., 1976; exhibited in group shows Washington Irving, 1937-38, Colorado Springs Fine Arts Ctr., 1939-40, Art Students League, 1939-41, L.I. Artists Exhbn., Huntington, N.Y., 1962, Coop. Gallery, Sea Cliff, N.Y., 1980-81; represented in numerous permanent collections. Recipient fellowship Carnegie Found., 1939, 40, scholarship Art Students League, 1940, 41, Woman of Achievement award, 1941.

KUCAN, MILAN, Slovenian government official; b. Križevci, Jan. 14, 1941. Grad., Ljubljana Faculty of Law. Pres. Slovenian Assembly, 1978, League of Communists of Yugoslavia, 1982-88, Ctrl. Com. ZK Slovenia, Republic of Slovenia, 1990—; pres. of state, 1992—. Office: Office of Pres, Erjavceva 17, 61000 Ljubljana Slovenia*

KUCERA, DANIEL WILLIAM, retired bishop; b. Chgo., May 7, 1923; s. Joseph F. and Lillian C. (Petrzelka) K. BA, St. Procopius Coll., 1945; MA, Catholic U. Am., 1950, PhD, 1954. Joined Order of St. Benedict, 1944, ordained priest Roman Cath. Ch., 1949. Registrar St. Procopius Coll. and Acad., Lisle, Ill., 1945-49, St. Procopius Coll., Lisle, 1954-56; acad. dean, head dept. edn. St. Procopius Coll., 1956-59, pres., 1959-65; abbot St. Procopius Abbey, Lisle, 1964-71; pres. Ill. Benedictine Coll. (formerly St. Procopius Coll.), Lisle, 1971-76; chmn. bd. trustees Ill. Benedictine Coll. (formerly St. Procopius Coll.), 1976-78; aux. bishop of Joliet, 1977-80; bishop of Salina Kans., 1980-83; archbishop of Dubuque Iowa, 1983-95; ret., 1995. Mem. KC (4 degree).

KUCERA, FRANTISEK, ice hockey player; b. Prague, Czech Republic, Feb. 3, 1968. Mem. Czech Nat. Ice Hockey Team; hockey player Chicago Blackhawks, 1990-94, Hartford Whalers, Conn., 1994-96, Vancouver Canucks, 1996-96, Philadelphia Flyers, 1996-97. Recipient Gold medal men's ice hockey, Olympic Games, Nagano, Japan, 1998. Avocation: hard rock music. Office: Czech Olympic Com, Benesovská 6, 10100 Prague 10, Czech Republic*

KUCERA, HENRY, linguistics educator; b. Trebarov, Czechoslovakia, Feb. 15, 1925; came to U.S., 1949, naturalized, 1953; s. Jindrich and Marie (Kral) K.; m. Jacqueline M. Fortin, Oct. 6, 1951; children: Thomas Henry, Edward James. MA, Charles U., Prague, Czechoslovakia, 1947, PhDr, 1991; PhD, Harvard U., 1952; MA ad eundem, Brown U., 1958; DSc (hon.), Bucknell U., 1984; PhilD (hon.), Masaryk U., Brno, Czechoslovakia, 1990. Asst. prof. fgn. langs. U. Fla., 1952-55; mem. faculty Brown U., 1955—, prof. Slavic langs. and linguistics, 1963—, prof. cognitive sci., 1981-90, Fred M. Seed prof. linguistics and cognitive scis., 1982—, chmn. dept. Slavic langs., 1965-68, head resident fellow of the Coll., 1956-66; mem. Ctr. for Cognitive Sci., 1977-85, exec. com., 1980-86; mem. Ctr. for Neural Studies, 1973-90, exec. com., 1977-90; dir. Inst. for Cognitive and Neural Research, 1981-88; fellow Russian Rsch. Ctr., Harvard U., 1952, 79-87, rsch. assoc. Slavic dept., 1977-79; rsch assoc. MIT, 1960-63; vis. prof. U. Mich., 1967, U. Calif. at Berkeley, 1969; vis. scholar U. Vienna, 1968-69; pres. Lang. Software Systems, Inc., 1982—. Author: The Phonology of Czech, 1961, (with W.N. Francis) Computational Analysis of Present-Day American English, 1967, (with G. Monroe) A Comparative Quantitative Phonology of Russian, Czech and German, 1968, Computers in Linguistics and in Literary Studies, 1975, (with K. Trnka) Time in Language, 1975, (with W.N. Francis) Frequency Analysis of English Usage, 1982; also linguistic and lit. articles.; Editor: American Contributions to the Sixth International Congress of Slavists, 1968. Bd. dirs. Internat. Inst. Providence, 1960-67; bd. adminstrn. Howard Found., 1977-95; mem. R.I. Com. for Humanities, 1986-90. Ford fellow, 1954-55; Howard Found. fellow, 1960-61; Guggenheim fellow, 1960-61; sr. fellow NEH, 1968-69; Am. Council Learned Socs. fellow, 1969-70. Hon. fellow Linguistic Soc. of Czech Acad. Scis.; mem. MLA, Linguistic Soc. Am., Czechoslovak Soc. Arts and Scis. in Am. (v.p. 1980-82), Prague Linguistic Circle (hon.), Phi Beta Kappa. Home: 107 Freedom Shores Rd Freedom NH 03836-5105

KUCERA, JAN, urologist, educator; b. Olomouc, Czech Republic, Nov. 7, 1918; s. Jan and Marie (Stodtova) K.; m. Marta Svejnarova, June 7, 1947; 1 child, Helena. MD, Masaryk U., Brno, Czechoslovakia, 1947; degree, Post-grad. Inst. Prague, Czechoslovakia, 1959; DSc, U. Brno, 1960. Univ. asst. Palacky U., Olomouc, 1948-55, assoc. prof. surgery, 1955-63, prof. urology, 1963, vice dean Med. Faculty, 1964-66; dir. dept. urology Univ. Hosp. Olomouc, 1964-85; cons. prof. Masaryk U., 1985-88, emeritus, 1988—; chief expert Ministry of Health, Prague, 1974-91. Author: Surgery of Hydronephrosis, 1960, Tumors of the Urinary Bladder, 1965, Surgery of Hydronephrosis and of the Ureterohydronephrosis, 1963, Surgical Replacement of the Bladder, others; contbr. articles to sci. jours. Mem. Czechoslovak Soc. Urology (chmn. 1962-64), Czechoslovak Med. Soc., Hungarian Urol. and Nephrol.Soc., Bulgarian Urol. Soc., Polish Urol. Soc., others. Avocations: music, graphic and plastic art, pictures, embellished gardens. Office: Univ Hosp, Dept Urology, I P Pavlova 6, 775 00 Olomouc Czech Republic

KUCEROVA, HELENA, psychiatrist; b. Olomouc, Czechoslovakia, Apr. 18, 1949; d. Jan and Marta (Svejnarova) Kucera. MD, Coll. Medicine, Olomouc, Czech Republic, 1974; diploma in Psychiatry level I, Prague, 1979, diploma in Psychiatry level II, 1983. Diplomate of Medicine, Psychiatry. Asst. lectr. Coll. Medicine, Hradec Kralove, Czech Republic, 1974-76; med. registrar Mental Tchg. Hosp., Hradec Kralove, 1976-83; jr. cons. Mental Hosp., Brno, 1983-86, Sternberk, 1986-90; outpatient psychiatriast cons. pvt. practice, Hranice na Morave, 1991—; Contbr. articles to profl. jours. Mem. N.Y. Acad. Scis., Czech Med. Chamber, Czech Psychiatric Soc. Avocations: music, painting, architecture, sports. Office: MUDr Kucerova Helena, Svatoplukova 10, 75301 Hranice Czech Republic

KUCHA, RYSZARD, history of education educator; b. Husów Village, Poland, May 4, 1942; s. Andrzej and Bronislawa (Abram) K.; m. Ewa Anna Wawrzycka, Mar. 20, 1976; 1 child, Ewa Magdalena. MA in Edn., Maria-Curie Skłodowska U., Lublin, Poland, 1967, PhD in Edn., 1975, habilitation, 1983. Tchr. Maria Curie-Skłodowska U., 1967-75, sr. lectr., 1975-82, asst. prof., 1983-90, assoc. prof., 1991-96, prof., 1997—, head history dept., 1984—, vice dean edn., 1984-87, 87-90, 1993-96, 96-99; dir. Inst. of Edn., MCS U.; assoc. prof. Higher Pedagogical U., Kielce, Poland, 1991-96; vis. prof. Coll. Edn., Sask., Can., 1991; prof. Pedagogical U. TWP, Warsaw, 1993—. Author: History of Elementary Schools in the Kingdom of Poland (1864-1914), 1982 (Rector's award 1983), Schools and Education in Lublin (1864-1915), 1995 (Rector's award 1996); editor-in-chief: Schools in the Twentieth Century, 1992 (grantee 1990-91); co-editor in chief: Polish and Swedish Schools in the 19th and 20th Centuries, 1995 (grantee 1994-95), Lublin Pedagogical Yearbook, 1993—. Grantee Kosciuszko Found., 1980-81, Umeå U., 1995. Mem. European Assn. Internat. Edn., European Univs. Continuing Edn. Network, Polish Pedagogical Assn. Roman Catholic. Avocations: painting, drawing, jogging. Home: Boleslawa Chrobrego 24/58, 20-611 Lublin Poland Office: Maria Curie-Sklodowska U, Narutowicza 12, 20-004 Lublin Poland

KUCHAR, ANDREAS K., ophthalmologist; b. Vienna, Austria, July 14, 1959; s. Josef and Emma (Pfalzer) K. MD, Univ. Vienna, 1988. Diplomate European Bd. Ophthaomology. Resident Eye Clinic, Vienna, 1992-97, fellow, 1997—. Contbr. articles to profl. jours. Del. UEMS, 1997-99, EBO, 1996-99. Mem. OOG, DOG. E-mail: andreas.kuchar@a1plus.at. Home: Ferrogasse 46/7, 1180 Vienna Austria Office: Univ Eye Clinic, Wahringer Guertel 18-20, 1090 Vienna Austria

KUCHARSKI, TOMASZ, engineering educator; b. Ketrzyn, Poland, Sept. 25, 1950; s. Stefan and Leokadia (Nacewicz) K.; m. Malgorzata Iwanowska Kucharska, Aug. 29, 1987; 1 child, Joanna Laura. Technician, Tech. Sch. Ketrzyn, Poland, 1969; MS in Engring., Tech. U. of Gdansk, Poland, 1974; PhD, 1979, DSc, 1993. Lectr. Tech. U. Gdansk, 1979-93; asst. prof., 1993-97, assoc. prof., 1997—; dir. rschr. project for State Comm. for Sci. Rsch. Warsaw, 1994-96, 1998—. Author: Transient State Analysis and Modelling of the Structures, 1992, 93, Computer Science for Calculation, 1996, Mechanical Engineering Computation, 2000; contbr. articles to profl. jours. Mem. Polish Soc. Theoret. and Applied Mechanics, N.Y. Acad. Scis. Avocations: musician, tourism, walking. Office: Technical University of Gdansk, G Narutowicza 11/12, 80-952 Gdańsk Poland

KUCHEL, PHILIP WILLIAM, biochemist, educator; b. Adelaide, South Australia, Sept. 19, 1946; s. Rex Harold and Nora (Warner) K.; m. Merilyn Kuchel, Feb. 13, 1971; children: Myfanwy, Johanna, Astrid, Rhiannon. B in Med. Sci., U. Adelaide, 1968, MBBS, 1971; PhD, Australian Nat. U., 1975. Resident Royal Adelaide Hosp., 1971; Nuffield dominions demonstrator dept. biochemistry U. Oxford, England, 1975-76, NH&MRC C.J. Martin fellow, 1976-77; sr. lectr. in med. biochemistry U. Newcastle, New South Wales, 1978-80; prof. biochemistry U. Sydney, New South Wales, 1980-99, McCaughey prof. biochemistry, 1999—. Co-author: Schaum's Outline of Theory and Problems of Biochemistry, 1988, 2 edit., 1997, Biochemistry Through Questions, 1992; mem. editl. bd. Biochem. Jour., 1997—, NMR in Biomedicine, 1988—; contbr. over 200 articles to profl. jours. Fellow Australian Acad. Sci.; mem. Australian Soc. Biophysics (pres. 1988-89), Australian Soc. Biochemistry and Molecular Biology (pres. 1994-96, Boehringer Mannheim medal 1983, Lemberg medal 1999), Biochem. Soc. United Kingdom, Sydney Clock Makers Soc. (pres. 1992, sec. 1991), Antiquarian Horological Soc. Avocations: horology. Home: 9 Radley Pl, Cherrybrook NSW, 2126, Australia Office: U Sydney, Dept Biochemistry, Sydney NSW 2006, Australia

KUCHER, ECKHARD, consulting company executive; b. Schonheide, Germany, Oct. 19, 1952; s. Kurt and Dorothea (Struck) K.; m. Andrea Becker, Mar. 6, 1980; children: Katharina, Carsten. Diplom-Kaufmann, U. Bielefeld, Germany, 1980, PhD, 1984; postgrad., U. Ga., Athens, 1979-80. Mng. dir. and co-founder UNIC Strategy and Mktg. Cons., Bonn, Germany, 1984—; vis. scholar U. Chgo., 1983. Author: Scannerdaten und Preissensitivität bei Konsumgütern, 1985; co-editor, author: Wettbewerbsstrategie im Pharmamarkt, 1989, Handbuch Pharma Management, 1994; contbr. articles to profl. jours. 1st lt. German Army, 1972-74. Grantee German Acad. Exch. Svc., 1979-80, Friedrich-Flick-Stiftung, 1983. Mem. Mgmt. and Mktg. Assn. U. Bielefeld (chmn. 1982-88), Mgmt. and Mktg. Assn. U. Mainz (chmn. 1988-94). Avocations: tennis, fishing, reading. Office: Simon Kucher & Ptnrs, Haydnstrasse 36, 53115 Bonn Germany also: Simon Kucher & Ptnrs One Cambridge Ctr Cambridge MA 02142

KUCHLE, MICHAEL, ophthalmologist; b. Munich, Aug. 15, 1957; s. Hans Joachim and Ingrid (Zeilinger) K.; m. Beate Lehmann, Aug. 14, 1992; children: Andreas, Isabelle, Christian. MD, U. Erlangen, 1985; cert. ophthalmologist, Landesarztekammer, 1990. Diplomee European Bd. Ophthalmology. Resident Univ. Eye Hosp., Erlangen, Germany, 1986-91; staff mem. Univ. Eye Hosp., Erlangen, 1991—; prof. ophthalmology U. Erlangen-Nurnberg, 1994—. Author: Ophthalmological Textbooks; contbr. chpts. in books and articles to profl. jours. Fellow Johns Hopkins U., 1993-94. Office: Univ Eye Hosp, Schwabachanlage 6, 91054 Erlangen Germany

KUCHMA, LEONID DANYLOVICH, Ukrainian government official; b. Chernyhiv Region, Ukraine, Aug. 9, 1938. Student, Dnipropetrivsk State U. Constructor Rsch. Prodn. Union Pivdennyi Mashinobudivnyi, 1960-75, sec. party com., 1975-82; dep. dir. gen. Yuzhny Mashinostroitelny Zavod, 1982-86, dir. gen., 1986-92; mem. ctrl. com. CP, Ukraine, 1981-91; people's dep. Ukraine, 1991-94, prime min., 1992-93; chair Ukrainian Union of Industrialists and Entrepreneurs, 1993-96; pres. of the Ukraine Kiev, 1994—. Mem. Enring. Acad. Ukraine. Office: Adminstrn of President, vul Bankivska 11, 252005 Kiev Ukraine*

KUCHNER, EUGENE FREDERICK, neurosurgeon, educator, neuroscientist; b. N.Y.C., 1945; s. Morton H. and Edna Estelle (Marks) K. m. Joan Ruth Freedman, Sept. 2, 1968; children: Marc Jason, Eric Benjamin. AB, Johns Hopkins U., 1967; MD, U. Chgo., 1971. Diplomate Am. Bd. Neurol. Surgery, Am. Bd. Med. Examiners. Resident in surgery Yale U. Sch. Medicine, New Haven, 1971-72; resident in neurosurgery Montreal (Que., Can.) Neurol. Inst., McGill U., 1972-76, spine fellow, 1976; neurosurgeon SUNY Sch. Medicine, Downstate, 1976-79, Stony Brook, 1979—; cons. neurosurgeon North Shore U Hosp./NYU Sch. Medicine, 1997—; mem. staff North Shore U. Hosp.-Cornell U. Med. Ctr., cons. surgeon; mem. staff Univ. Hosp., Stony Brook, Nassau County Med. Ctr., St. John's Hosp., Mt. Sinai-NYU Health Sys., 1997—. Contbr. articles to profl. publs.; specialist in microsurgery, magnetic resonance imaging, spinal trauma, pituitary surgery. Recipient K.G. McKenzie Meml. award Royal Coll. Physicians and Surgeons Can., 1976, Open Scholarship award Johns Hopkins U., yearly, 1963-66, Scholarship award U. Chgo., yearly, 1967-70; NSF fellow, MIT fellow, 1968, Blackman-Hoffman Found. fellow, 1969-70, USPHS fellow, 1969. Mem. ACS, AMA, Am. Assn. Neurol. Surgeons, Congress Neurol. Surgeons, N.Y. Acad. Scis., L.I. Neurosci. Acad., Suffolk Acad. Medicine, Montreal Neurol. Ins. Fellows Soc., N.Y. State Neurosurg. Soc., N.Y. State Med. Soc., N.Y. State Soc. Surgeons, Am. Coll. Med. Quality, Healthcare Info. and Mgmt. Sys. Soc., Am. Epilepsy Soc., Am. Soc. Law Medicine and Ethics. Office: Stony Brook Med Ctr PO Box 721 Stony Brook NY 11790-0721

KUCHUK-YATSENKO, SERGEI IVANOVICH, metallurgical and welding engineer, educator; b. Zhitomir City, Kiev, Ukraine, Aug. 2, 1930; s. Ivan Yakovlevich Kuchuk-Yatsenko and Alexandra Ivanovna Babich; m. Alisa Vasiljevna Kornilova, Oct. 28, 1957; 1 child, Victor. Grad., Poly. Inst., Kiev, 1953; PhD, 1960. Rsch. engr. E.O. Paton Electric Welding Inst., Kiev, 1953-59, scientist, 1960-68, head of lab., 1968-78; prof., 1972; head of divsn. E.O. Paton Electric Welding Inst., Kiev, 1978-85, dep. dir., 1985—. Over 300 patents in field; contbr. numerous articles to profl. jours. Recipient Lenin prize, 1965, State Prize Ukraine, 1976, Acad. Nat. Acad. Sci. Ukraine, 1976, State Prize USSR, 1986. Mem. Ukrainian Soc. (pres. 1992—), Am. Welding Soc., N.Y. Acad. Sci. Home: Stretenskaya Str 17 Apt 18, 252025 Kiev Ukraine Office: EO Paton Elec Welding Inst, 11 Bozhenko Str, 252650 Kiev Ukraine

KUCSMAN, ARPAD, chemistry educator; b. Budapest, Hungary, Oct. 27, 1927; s. Arpad and Etelka (Buchberger) K. MSc, Eotvos U., 1949, PhD, 1959; DSc, Hungarian Acad. Scis., 1971. From asst. prof. to prof. chemistry Eotvos U., Budapest, 1960—; head organic chem. dept. Eotvos U., 1970-93; editl. bd. mem. Jour. Molecular Structure, 1981-98. Avocations: tourism, photography, music, bridge. Home: Sztoczek utca 17/b, H-1111 Budapest Hungary Office: Eotvos U Dept Organic Chem, PO Box 32, H-1518 Budapest 112, Hungary

KUCZMA, MIECZYSLAW SYLWESTER, engineering educator, researcher; b. Koscian, Poland, Oct. 20, 1956; s. Edmund and Czeslawa (Drozdzynska) K.; m. Bozena Maria Kuras, Aug. 15, 1981; children: Katarzyna, Pawel, Gabriela. MSc with honors, Poznan Tech. U., 1981, Phd with honors, 1990; M in Math. with honors, Mickiewicz U., Poznan, 1986, Tex. U., Austin, 2000. Asst. Poznan Tech. U., 1981-91, asst. prof., 1991—; with Hanover U. Inst. for Applied Mathematics, 1995-96; English translator, cons. Polish Union Bldg. Engrs. and Technicians; with Hannover U. Inst. for Applied Maths., Germany, 1995-96. Author: The Unilateral Contact Problem of Beams & Plates on Viscoelastic Foundations, 1991 (Rectors of Poznan Tech. U. award 1991), Application of Variational Inequalities in the Mechanics of Plastic Flow and Mantensitic Phase Transformations, 1999; contbr. articles to profl. jours. including Computer Method Applications Mech. Engring., Internat. Jour. Engring. Sci., and Archives of Mechanics, among others. Sub. lt. Polish mil., 1982-83. Recipient team award Polish Ministry of Nat. Edn., 1990; fellow Hannover U. Deutscher Akademischer Austauschdienst, 1991, EC 93, Brunel U., 1993. Mem. Polish Assn. Theoretical and Applied Mechanics, Gesellschaft fur Angewandte Mathematik und Mechanik, London Math Soc., N.Y. Acad. Sci. Avocations: foreign languages and literature, philosophy, sports. Office: Poznan Tech U Inst Structural Engring, IKB Piotrowo 5, 60-695 Poznan Poland

KUDELKA, JAMES, choreographer, artistic director; b. Newmarket, Ont., Can.. Student, Nat. Ballet Sch., Toronto. Dancer Nat. Ballet of Can., Toronto, 1972-81, artist in residence, 1992-96; prin. dancer Les Grands Ballets Canadiens, Montreal, 1981-84; resident choreographer Les Grands Ballets Canadiens, 1984-90; works created for San Francisco and Joffrey Ballets, Am. Ballet Theatre, Birmingham Royal Ballet; artistic dir. Nat. Ballet Can., 1996—. Ballets choreographed include: (for Nat. Ballet of Can.) Sonata, 1973 (Jean A. Chalmers award for Choreography), A Party, 1976, Washington Square, 1977, The Rape of Lucrece, 1980, Playhouse, 1980, All Night Wonder, 1981, Pastorale, 1990, The Miraculous Mandarin, 1993, The Actress, 1994, Spring Awakening, 1994, The Nutcracker, 1995, The Four Seasons, 1997, Swan Lake, 1999; (for Les Grands Ballets Canadiens) Genesis, 1982, In Paradisum, 1983, Alliances, 1984, Le Sacre du Printemps, 1987, La Salle des Pas Perdus, 1988, Concerto Grosso, 1988; (for American Ballet Theatre) Cruel World, 1994, States of Grace, 1995; (for San Francisco Ballet) Dreams of Harmony, 1987, The End, 1992, Terra Firma, 1995, Some Women and Men, 1998; (for Birmingham Royal Ballet) Le Baiser de la fée; (for Toronto Dance Theatre) Fifteen Heterosexual Duets; (for Montreal Danse) Six Tableaus for the Sexually Challenged; other choreography includes Passage, 1981, Intimate Letter, 1981, Hedda, 1983, Court of Miracles, 1983, Musings, 1991. Office: The National Ballet of Canada, 470 Queens Quay W, Toronto, ON Canada M5V 3K4

KUDEYAROVA, AGNIYA YULIEVNA, soil scientist, researcher; b. Czerkassy, Ukraine, USSR, July 31, 1940; d. Yuliy Alekseevich and Aleftina Vasilievna (Shapovalova) Pastuchov; m. Valeriy Nickolaevich Kudeyarov, Oct. 22, 1961; children: Yelena, Yuliya. Grad., Timiryazev Agrl. Acad., Moscow, 1962; postgrad., Inst. Fertilizers and Insectofungicides, Moscow, 1966-69, Kandidat's degree in soil chemistry, 1971; D in Biology, Moscow State U., 1997. Asst., jr. rsch. worker Inst. Fertilizers and Insectofungicides, Moscow, 1962-65; jr. rsch. worker Inst. Agrochemistry and Soil Sci., Pushchino, USSR, 1970-75; sr. rsch. worker Inst. Agrochemistry and Soil Sci., Pushchino, 1976, rsch. group leader, 1977-82; supr. postgrad. studies Inst. Soil Sci. and Photosynthesis, Pushchino, 1982, rsch. group leader, cons., 1982-99; rsch. group leader, cons. Inst. Physico-Chem. and Biological Problems Soil Sci., Pushchino, Russia, 1999—. Author: Pedogeochemistry of Fertilizer Ortho and Polyphosphates, 1993, Phosphatogenic Transformation of Soils, 1995 (Grant Russian Fedn. Basic Rsch., 1995); contbr. articles to profl. jours.; rev. Pochvovedeniye, Agrochimiya jours., 1978—. Recipient Russian Fedn. Pres. award in sci., 1997-2000; grantee Internat. Sci. Found. (Soros), Russian Fedn. Basic Rsch., 1994, State Sci. Individual Grant, 2000—. Mem. Dokuchaev Soil Sci. Soc., Mendeleev Chem. Soc. Avocations: drawing, travel, sightseeing, needlework, reading. Office: Inst Phys Chem Biolog Problems, Soil Sci Institutskaya St 2, 142290 Pushchino Moscow, Russia

KUDINOV, VALENTIN IVANOVICH, oil and gas executive; b. Novo-Pavlovka, Russia, May 24, 1931; s. Ivan Vasilievich and Akulina Semionovna (Bulokhova) K.; m. Tamara Yakovlevna Bondarenko, July, 1954; 1 child, Elena. Grad., Indsl. Inst., Russia, 1954; Cand. Tech. Sci., Indsl. Inst., 1976, D Tech. Sci., 1988. Engr., sr. engr. of oil field Chapaevskneft of Assn. Kuibyshevneft, Russia, 1954-60, chief of oil field, chief engr. of oil field dept., 1960-63; chief engr. Assn. Orenburgneft, City of Orenburg, 1963-73; head of assn., gen. dir. of assn./joint stock co., pres. Assn. Udmurtneft/Open Joint Stock Co., Izhevsk, Russia, 1973-96; head of dept. for devel. of oil and gas fields Udmurt State U., Izhevsk, 1993—; bd. dirs. Joint Stock Co. Udmurtneft, Izhevsk, Udmurt Republic, Russia, chmn. bd. dirs. Contbr. articles to profl. jours.; patentee in field. Deputy of Supreme Coun. of the Udmurt Republic, 1975-80, 85-90, 91-95, Izhevsk; deputy State Coun. of the Udmurt Republic, 1999—, mem. Presidium of the State Coun., 1995-99. Decorated Badge of Hon., Presidium of Supreme Soviet of USSR, Moscow, 1996, Order of Red Banner of Labor, 1971, 77, medal for Labor Valor, 1970; recipient I.M. Gubkin prize Cen. Scientific and Tech. Soc., Moscow, 1979, gold and silver medals Exhbn. of Nat. Econ. Achievement of USSR, 1979, 89, prize of Govt. of Udmurt Republic, 1997, Govt. of Russian Fedn., Moscow, 1998, State prize of Russian Fedn., 1999, numerous others. Mem.

Russian Mining Acad., Acad. of Tehcnol. Sci. of Russian Fedn., Internat. Acad. Info., Internat. Acad. Resources, Russian Engring. Acad., UNESCO, others. Avocations: hunting, literature. Office: 182 Krasnoarmeiskaya St, 426057 Izhevsky/Udmurt Russia

KUDO, SHINICHI, molecular geneticist; b. Yubari-shi, Hokkaido, Japan, Aug. 29, 1956; s. Ichiro and Kesayo (Kobayashi) K.; m. Shizuko Chiba, Apr. 29, 1984; 1 child, Masaki. MD, Asahikawa Med. Coll., Hokkaido, 1982; PhD, Sapporo Med. Coll., Hokkaido, 1986. Postdoctoral fellow Showa U. Inst., St. Petersburg, Fla., 1986-87; postdoctoral fellow La Jolla (Calif.) Cancer Rsch. Found., 1987-90, rsch. assoc., 1990-95; staff scientist Hokkaido Inst. Pub. Health, Sapporo, Japan, 1995-98, chief virology sect., 1998—. Contbr. articles to profl. jours. Mem. Am. Soc. Biochemistry and Molecular Biology, Am. Soc. Cell Biology, Am. Assn. Cancer Rsch. Achievements include clarification of the genetic basis of the MNSs blood group system; discovery that glycophorin A and B genes derived from common ancestor gene and glycophorin B gene was rearranged through homologous recombination at Alu repeat sequences; discovered glycophorin E gene. Avocations: golf, driving, hiking. Home: Nishino 3-1 Nishi-ku, Sapporo 063, Japan

KUDRIN, ALEKSEY LEONIDOVICH, federal official. Min. of fin. Russian Fedn., Moscow. Office: Ministry of Fin, ul Ilyinka 9, Moscow 103097, Russia*

KUDRYASHOV, IGOR EVGENIEVICH, neurophysiologist; b. Kokand, Uzbekistan, USSR, Dec. 9, 1947; s. Evgeniy Vladimirovich Kudryashov and Maria Philipovna Sokolova; m. Irina Vladimirovna Andreeva, May 26, 1979; 1 child, Timophey. Diploma, Moscow State U., 1971. Lab. asst. Brain Inst., Moscow, 1971-73, rschr., 1973-81; sr. rschr. Lab. Neurobionic Moscow Inst. Radiotechnic, Electronic, and Automatic, Moscow, 1981-90; sr. rschr. Inst. Oceanology, Moscow, 1990-92, Inst. Higher Nerv. Act. and Neurophysiology, Moscow, 1992—. Contbr. articles to profl. jours. Recipient awards Internat. Sci. Found., 1995, Found. of Russian Acad. of Med. Sci., Moscow, 1995, Russian Found. of Basical Sci., 1995-97, Found. of Med. Ctr. Primavera Medica, 1995-97. Home: Obrucheva 9.24, 117421 Moscow Russia Office: Inst Higher Nerv Act, Butlerova 5a, 117485 Moscow Russia

KUDRYASHOV, NIKOLAI ALEKSEEVICH, engineer, physicist, mathematician; b. Tver, USSR, Sept. 19, 1945; s. Aleksei Aleksandrovich and Ekaterina Alekseevna (Matveeva) K.; m. Helen Vladimirovna Spiridonova, Dec. 22, 1959; 1 child, Aleksei. MS in Theoret. and Math. Physics, Moscow Engring. Physics Inst., 1974, PhD in Math., 1978, DSc, 1986. Tchr. sch., Tver region, USSR, 1967-68; asst. prof. Moscow Engring. Physics Inst., 1979-82, assoc. prof., 1982-84, prof. dept. maths., 1984-86, head dept. applied maths., 1986—, Soros prof., 1996, leading scientific researcher, 1987-98; sr. researcher Lab. of Math. Simulation, 1982-87. Author: (textbook) Self-Similar Problems of Gas Dynamics, 1984, (textbook) Painleve Property and Bäcklund Transformations in Mathematical Physics, 1989, (textbook) Analytical Methods in the Theory of Nonlinear Evolution Equations, 1993. Grantee Soros Ednl. Program, 1994, London Math. Soc., 1997; recipient USSR nat. prize in sci. and tech. USSR Coun. of Mins., 1982. Mem. Russian Acad. Nature Scis. (academician 2000). Avocations: art, books, trips. Home: apt 213, Borisovskii proerd h 8 b 2, 115563 Moscow Russia Office: Moscow Engring Physics Inst, 31 Kashirskoe Strase, 115 409 Moscow Russia

KUDRYASHOVA, IRINA VLADIMIROVNA, neurophysiologist, researcher; b. Moscow, Mar. 5, 1953; d. Vladimir Pedorovich and Anna Petrovna (Oleynic) Andreev; m. Igor Evgenyevich Kudryashov, May 26, 1979; 1 child, Kudryashov Timophey. Doctorate, Moscow State U., 1982. Lab. asst. Brain Inst., Moscow, 1973-82; rschr. Inst. Higher Nervous Activity, Moscow, 1982-92, sr. rschr., 1992—. Contbr. articles to profl. jours. Grantee Internat. Sci. Found., 1995, Found. Russian acad. Med. Sci., Moscow, 1995, Russian Found. Basical Sci., 1995-97, Found. Med. Ctr. Primavera Medica, 1995-97. Home: Obrucheva 9, 24, 117421 Moscow Russia Office: Inst Higher Nervous, Activity, Butlerova 5a, 117485 Moscow Russia

KUDRYAVTSEVA, IRINA, physicist, researcher; b. Tartu, Estonia, Feb. 14, 1966; d. Arkadi and Vera (Leif) Il'ina; m. Vyacheslav Kudryavtsev, Nov. 19, 1988; children: Tatyana, Olga. PhD, Tartu U., 1997. Cert. physics. Engr. Inst. of Physics, Tartu, 1988-97, rsch. assoc., 1997—. Avocations: sport, literature. Home: Anne 85-52, 50401 Tartu Estonia Office: Inst Physics, Riia 142, 51014 Tartu Estonia

KUDRYAVTSEVA, LUDMILLA, chemist, researcher; b. Narva, Estonia, June 7, 1925; d. Sergei and Lydia (Velman) K. PhD, U. Leningrad, USSR, 1965, DCh, 1985. Lectr. Pedagogic Inst., Tallinn, Estonia, 1954-59; leading scientist Inst. of Chemistry, Tallinn, 1962—. Co-author: (in Russian) Ternary Azeotropic Systems, 1972. Mem. N.Y. Acad. Sci., Estonian Chem. Soc. Home: Ehitayate tee 88-64, 12915 Tallinn Estonia Office: Inst of Chemistry, Tallinn Tech U Inst Chem, Akadeemia tee 15, 12617 Tallinn Estonia

KUDUMAKIS, PANOS, acoustical engineering researcher; b. Feres, Greece, Jan. 13, 1964; s. Evangelos and Eleni (Mourikaki) K. BS in Electronics, Tech. Ednl. Inst. Piraeus, Greece, 1985; BS in Computer Engring., Nat. Tech. U., Athens, 1990; MS in Digital Music Tech., U. Keele, Staffordshire, Eng., 1991; PhD in Digital Sound Processing Engring., U. London, 1996. Programmer Greek Telecomm. Orgn., Athens, 1983-84; tech. coll. lectr. Greek Ministry of Edn., Athens, 1986-88; rsch. assoc. King's Coll. U. London, 1992-98; staff scientist Ctrl. Rsch. Labs. Ltd. (assoc. EMI Group PLC), 1998—; cons. Defence Rsch. Agy., Malvern, Eng., 1997; vis. rsch. fellow King's Coll. U. London, 1998—; external rsch. cons. U. Telekom (Multimedia U.), Melaka, Malaysia. Contbr. articles to profl. jours.; programmer software. Recipient award Audio Engring. Soc., N.Y.C., 1994, 95; grantee EPSRC, London, 1996-98. Mem. IEEE (reviewer), Audio Engring. Soc., Composers' Desktop Project, Tech. Chamber of Greece, British Stds. Instn., Moving Pictures Experts Group, Intellectual Propert Mgmt. Protection, Secure Digital Music Initiative. E-mail: pkudumakis@crl.co.uk. Office: CRL, Dawley Rd, Hayes Middlesex UB3 1HH, England

KUDVA, PREMNATH S., industrialist; b. Hubli, Karnataka, India, May 23, 1963; s. Srinivas V. and Sharada S. Kudva; m. Suchitra P. Kamath, Oct. 28, 1993; 1 child, Sneha. B in Engring. in Indsl. and Prodn., Manipal (India) Inst. Tech., 1984; postgrad. diploma in mgmt., T A Pai Mgmt. Inst., Manipal, 1986. Purchase exec. Canara Workshops Ltd., Mangalore, India, 1986-88, asst. gen. mgr., 1988-90, gen. mgr., 1990-92, exec. dir., 1992—; dir. CPC India Ltd., Mangalore; registrar V S Kudva Acad., Mangalore. Dir. Kanara Chamber of Commerce and Industries, Mangalore, 1993-95; sec. Canara Found., Mangalore, 1994—; sec., treas. V S Kudva Found., Mangalore, 1995—; joint sec. Rotary Dist. 3180, Mangalore, 1995-96. Mem. Mangalore Mgmt. Assn. (life), Rotary Club Mangalore Cen. (charter pres. 1987-89). Avocations: philately, numismatics, book collecting. Fax: 91 824 211604. E-mail: premkudva@vsnl.com. Home: Vivekananda Rd, 575004 Mangalore India Office: Canara Workshops Ltd, V S Kudva Rd Maroli, 575005 Mangalore India

KUEBLBECK, CHRISTIAN, physicist; b. Rosenheim, Germany, Dec. 31, 1968; s. Friedrich and Hildegard Ponn K. Diploma, U. Wuerzburg, Germany, 1993; PhD, U. Erlangen, 1999. Asst. U. Wuerzburg, 1993-95; rsch. engr. Fraunhofer Inst. IIS-A/Erlangen, Germany, 1995-97; mgr. group intelligent systems dept. elec. sys. inst. Fraunhofer Co., Erlangen, Germany, 1999—. Avocations: free climbing, biking, concerts. Office: Fraunhofer Inst Integ Cirs, IIS-A/Am Weichselgarten 3, 91058 Erlangen Germany

KUEBLER, MARGARET PATRICIA, lawyer; b. Memphis, Sept. 21, 1956; d. Charles William Kuebler and Emilie Stanford Smythe. BA in English and Art History cum laude, Hollins Coll., 1975; cert. in corp. law, Adelphi U., 1978; ScD Sch. of Hygiene/Pub. Health, John Hopkins U., 1983; MPH, MBA, U. Ala., 1984; postgrad., U. Miss., 1987, 88; postgrad. Faculty of Laws, U. Coll., London, 1988; JD, Pace U., 1989. Bar: Tenn. 1997. Lawyer's asst. Legal Aid Soc., Staten Island, N.Y., 1975, Roanoke, Va., 1975; asst. to treas. Realty Assocs., Inc., Bklyn., 1975-78; legal asst. Davis Polk & Wardwell, N.Y.C., 1978-79; rsch. asst. U. Ala. Hosps., Birmingham, 1982; rsch. asst. divsn. gynecologic oncology Johns Hopkins Hosp., Balt., 1983; rsch. analyst II Bapt. Meml. Hosp., Memphis, 1985; lawyer's asst. Borod & Huggins, Attys., Memphis, 1985-86, Glankler Brown, PLLC, Memphis, 1986; executrix Estate of Charles W. Kuebler, 1986—; asst. to technical dir.and merchandising mgr. plastics divsn. Toray Industries (America), Inc., N.Y.C., 1976; paralegal Morgan Guarantee Trust Co.; rsch. asst. pharmacology com. WHO, London, 1988. Contbr. short story and two poems to mag. Mem. Hollins' Art Assn. and Orgn. Women; counselor S.I. Acad. Day Camp; vol. Edn. and Rsch. Mus. Modern Art, Dept. Birmingham Mus. Art, S.I. Hosp.; nurses aide Silver Lake Nursing Home. Acad. scholar Hollins Coll., 1972-75, Johns Hopkins U., 1982-83, Pace U., 1986-87. Mem. ABA, APHA, Am. Trial Lawyers Assn., Tenn. Bar Assn., N.Y. State Student Bar Assn., Shelby County Bar Assn., Nat. Health Lawyers Assn., Pace U. Sch. Law's Health Law Soc., Hollins' Lit. Soc., Nat. Honor Soc., Population Assn. Am., Student Liaison Com., Model UN Security Coun. Debate Team, Pi Delta Phi. Episcopalian. Home: PO Box 487 Batesville MS 38606-0487

KUEBLER, NORBERT ROLF, oral and maxillofacial surgeon; b. Stuttgart, Germany, Apr. 3, 1960; s. Rolf Eugen and Liselotte Emilie (Hoessle) K.; m. Melanie Mueller, June 24, 1995; children: Matthias Constantin, Amelie Nicole. MD, U. Mainz, Germany, 1986, DMD, 1988; PhD, U. Wuerzburg, Germany, 1995. Resident U. Wuerzburg, Germany, 1989-94, sr. physician, 1995—, assoc. prof., 1995—; dir. bone rsch. lab., U. Wuerzburg, 1990—, dir. bone bank, 1991—, assoc. prof., 1995—. Contbr. articles to profl. jours. DFG grantee, 1988—; rsch. fellow UCLA, 1988-89. Mem. Deutsche Gesellschaft fuer Zahn-, Mund- und Kieferheilkunde, Deutsche Gesellschaft fuer Mund-, Kieter- und Gesichtschirurgie, European Assn. for Cranio-Maxillo-Facial Surgery, Deutsche Gesellschaft fuer Plastische und Wiederherstellungschirurgie. Home: Auf der Schanz 62, Würzburg D-97076, Germany Office: U Wuerzburg, Pleicherwall 2, D-97070 Wuerzburg Germany

KUEHL, REINER WILHELM, electronics company executive; b. Wilster, Germany, Apr. 16, 1949; s. Wilhelm Georg and Gertrud (Kellermann) Kuehl; m. Regina Susanne Scholz, May 7, 1982; children: Eik-Kristina, Siemen. MS, U. Applied Sci., Luebeck, 1973. Phys. engr. diplomate. Engr. Beyschlag, Heide, Germany, 1974-80; project mgr. Beyschlag, Heide, 1981-91, exec. mgr. product and process devel., 1992-98; exec. mgr. tech. and quality customer svc. BC Components, Heide, 1998—; cons. Philips, Hamburg, 1988-98; environ. coord. Philips/Beyschlag, Heide, 1992-93; mem. program com. CARTS Europe, Crowsborough, U.K., 1999—. Contbr. articles to profl. jours. Mem. exec. com. Hist. Soc. Friedrichstadt, 1981-89; chmn. Working Cir. Care and Preservation of Monuments, Friedrichstadt, 1990-92. Recipient Ecol. Needle award Employers' Assn. of State of Schleswig-Holstein, 1990. Avocations: historical research, literature, art, rowing, rare books. Office: BC Components, Rungholtstr 8-10, D-25732 Heide Germany

KUEHNE, KELLI, professional golfer; b. Dallas, May 11, 1977. Student, U. Tex. Profl. golfer, 1998—; tied for 20th pl. First Union Betsy King Classic, 1998; participant 24 tournaments, 1998. Named 6th in standings Rolex Rookie of Yr., 1998; placed 1st Corning Classic. Avocations: fishing, hunting. Office: care LPGA 100 International Golf Dr Daytona Beach FL 32124-1082*

KÜEHNE, KLAUS-MICHAEL, freight forwarding and logistics executive; b. Hamburg, Germany, June 2, 1937; s. Alfred K. and Mercedes (Greef) K. Chmn., pres. Kühne & Nagel Internat. AG, Schindellegi, Switzerland, 1992—. Office: Kühne & Nagel AG, Postfach 52, CH-8423 Ebrach-Embraport Zurich, Switzerland*

KUEHNL, PETER, physician; b. Karlsbad, Germany, Nov. 13, 1944; s. Franz Josef and Elisabeth (Marsch) K.; m. Ursula Ostermann, Oct. 7, 1977. MD, U. Heidelberg, Germany, 1970; Specialist in Internal Medicine, U. Frankfurt/Main, Germany, 1976, PhD in Immunohematology, 1981. Cert. in internal medicine, transfusion medicine, immunohematology, transplantation immunology. Asst. in internal medicine Univ. Hosp., Frankfurt/Main, 1971-76; asst. in immunohematology Inst. Immunohematology, U. Frankfurt/Main, 1976-80; head dept. tissue typing Red Cross Blood Bank, Frankfurt/Main, 1980-87; dir. dept. transplantation immunology Univ. Hosp., Hamburg, Germany, 1988-89, dir. dept. transfusion medicine and transplantation immunology, 1988—, full prof., 1988—; mem. commn. on blood and blood components, commn. on transfusion guidelines, commn. on infusion and transfusion Fed. Ministry Health, 1978—; mem. coun. European Com. Automation and Quality Assurance in Blood Transfusion Svcs., 1993—; mem. commn. on bone marrow donation Fed. Min. Health, 1993-96. Author: Elektrofokussierung in der Forensischen Serologie, 1978; co-author: Blutgruppenkunde, 1982. Mem. Internat. Soc. Blood Transfusion (bd. dirs. 1990-95), German Soc. Blood Transfusion and Immunohematology (bd. dirs. 1987-94, pres. 1999-2000), Soc. Bone Marrow Donor Registries of German Blood Banks (pres. 1994-97), Fed. Min. Health (mem. Arbeitskreis Blut). Roman Catholic. Avocations: golf, sailing. Office: Univ Hosp Transfusion Med, Martinistr 52, D-20246 Hamburg Germany

KUEHNLE, KENTON LEE, lawyer; b. Chgo., Nov. 10, 1945; s. Robert Louis and Mary Caroline (Recktenwald) K.; m. Sherry L. Esposito, June 6, 1970; children: Robert, Amanda, Matthew. BA, Augustana Coll., 1967; JD, Duke U., 1970. Bar: Ohio 1970, U.S. Dist. Ct. (so. dist.) Ohio 1971. Assoc. Dunbar, Kienzle & Murphey, Columbus, Ohio, 1970-77; ptnr. Loveland, Callard & Clapham, Columbus, 1977-80, Scott, Walker & Kuehnle, Columbus, 1980-86, Thompson, Hine & Flory, Columbus, 1986—; mem., lectr. standard forms com. Columbus Bd. Realtors; instr. paralegal program Capital U. Law Sch. Co-author: (seminar book) Foreclosure Law, 1989-98, Title Insurance Endorsements, 1991-97, Commercial Leasing, 1994-97, Condominium Law, 1981-97, Use of Internet for Real Estate Lawyer, 1997; contbr. articles to profl. jours. Mem. Augustana Coll. Alumni Bd., Rock Island, Ill., 1986-89; trustee Madison Plains Scholarship Found., Madison County, Ohio, 1986—; elder First Presbyn. Ch., Grove City, Ohio, 1990-93; pres. Computer Users Group, Columbus, 1985-86. Mem. ABA (sect. real property, probate and trust law 1973—, com. on condominium and coop. housing 1977—), Columbus Bar Assn. (chmn. real property com. 1976-78, chmn. micro computer subcom. 1986-87, 92-94, lectr. for bar assn. seminars), Ohio State Bar Assn. (bd. govs. real property sect. 1979-82, 90—, chmn. 1997-99, editor state real property sect. newsletter 1995-99, chmn. subcom. to rev. condominium statute 1980-81, lectr. continuing legal edn. programs), Am. Coll. Real Estate Lawyers, Coun. Ethics in Econs., Honesty in Bus., Legal Profession Task Force, Joseph Fletcher Lawyers Conf. (ann. ethics conf., spkr. selection chair). Avocations: computer programming, baseball, theology. Home: 11325 Big Plain Circleville Rd Orient OH 43146-9301 Office: Thompson Hine & Flory 10 W Broad St Ste 700 Columbus OH 43215-3435

KUENZLE, ROBERT CREED, industrialist, architect; b. Manila, Philippines, May 7, 1931; s. Adolf Paul and Renee (Bodmer) K.; m. Donna MacQuarrie, Feb. 20, 1959; children: Karina, Anja. Architect, ETH, Zurich, 1957. Diverse positions archtl. offices, Rio de Janeiro, Zurich, and San Francisco, 1958-63; founding ptnr. BKG Architekten AG, Zurich, 1963—, pres., 1973—; pres., chief exec. officer Philinvest AG, Zurich and Manila, 1975-87; pres. Kaba Holding AG, Rumlang, 1978—; pres., chief exec. officer Industrieholding Cham AG, 1983—; pres. Abel Cons. AG, Kusnacht, 1991-92; bd. dirs. SFS Holding AG, Heerbrugg, Ch, 1994—, Bank Hofmann, Zurich, 1995—. Contbr. articles to profl. jours. Elected ofcl. bldg. dept., Herrliberg, 1982-90. Capt. Swiss Army. Mem. Grasshopper Club (bd. dirs. 1986—). Avocations: music, lit., history, mountaineering, rowing. Office: BKG Architekten AG, Munchsteig 10, 8008 Zurich Switzerland

KUERTEN, GUSTAVO, professional tennis player; b. Florianopolis, Brazil, Sept. 10, 1976. Profl. tennis player, 1995; lost to Am. Justin Gimelstob Wimbledon, 1997; winner over Roland Garros, 1997; winner French Open, 1997, 2000; winner semifinals du Maurier Open, 1997. Named No. 1 player from Brazil, 1996; recipient 9 single titles and 7 doubles titles. Office: ATP Tour Internat Hdqs 201 ATP Tour Blvd Ponte Vedra Beach FL 32082*

KUESTERS, HANNS JUERGEN R., historian, political scientist, educator; b. Krefeld, Germany, Dec. 30, 1952; s. Hermann Joseph and Ingeborg Elisabeth (Heinze) K.; m. Karin Elisabeth Elsner, Mar. 22, 1978; 1 child, Nadescha. Diploma in polit. sci., U. Hamburg, Germany, 1977; Dr., U. Cologne, Germany, 1982; Habilitation, U. Bonn, Germany, 2000. Editor Found. Chancellor Adenauer House, Bad Honnef, Germany, 1982-88; scientist, asst. prof. U. Cologne, 1984-87, U. Bonn, Germany, 1987-92; editor Fed. Archive Koblenz, Bonn, 1992-94; head editl. staff Fed. Archives, Bonn, 1994—; mem. sci. bd. Found. Jean Monnet pour l'Europe, Lausanne, Switzerland, 1985. Author: Die Gründung der Europäischen Wirschaftsgemeinschaft, 1982, Adenauer Teegespräche, 1950-61, 84-88, Dokumente zur Deutschlandpolitik, 1949-50, 96-97, Deutsche Einheit, 1998, Der Integrationsfrieden, 2000. Recipient award Deutsche Gesellschaft fur Politische Wissenschaft, 1996, Deutsche Gesellschaft für Auswärtige Politik, 1976. Home: Drachenfelsstrasse 39, 53604 Bad Honnef Germany Office: Bundesarchiv, Bundgrenzschutzstrasse 100, 53757 Sankt Augustin Germany

KUFELDT, GEORGE, biblical educator; b. Chgo., Nov. 4, 1923; s. Henry and Lydia (Dorn) K.; m. Kathryn Rider, July 24, 1943 (dec. July 1956); children: Anita Kay Kufeldt Shelton, Kristina Sue Kufeldt Schmidt; m. Claudena Eller, June 21, 1957 (dec. Sept. 1978); m. Lydia Borgardt, Aug. 12, 1980. AB, Anderson Coll., Ind., 1945, ThB, 1946, MDiv, 1953; PhD, Dropsie U., 1974. Ordained to ministry Ch. of God, 1948. Pastor Ch. of God, Homestead, Fla., 1948-50, Ch. of God, Cassopolis, Mich., 1954-57, Ch. of God, Lansdale, Pa., 1957-61; prof. O.T. and Hebrew, Anderson U., 1961-90, prof. emeritus O.T., 1990—. Contbr. to Wesleyan Bible Commentary, vol. II, 1968, Nelson's Expository Dictionary of the Old Testament, 1980, Educating for Service, 1984, The Genesis Debate, 1986, Listening to the Word of God, 1990, Zondervan One-Vol. Bible Commentary, 1991. Dropsie U. fellow, 1961, 63; Land of the Bible Workshop grantee NYU, 1966. Mem. Nat. Assn. Profs. of Hebrew, Am. Hellenic Ednl. Progressive Assn. (pres., Achievement award 1990), Am. Hist. Soc. Germans from Russia (life, bd. dirs. 1991-98). Home: 907 N Nursery Rd Anderson IN 46012-2721

KUFIDIS, DIMITRIS CHARILAOS, veterinary medicine educator; b. Thessaloniki, Macedonia, Greece, Nov. 1, 1944; s. Charilaos and Ypatia (Dellatolla) K.; m. Stella Xirotiri, Sept. 7, 1972; 1 child, Harris. BSc in Chemistry, Aristotle U., Thessaloniki, 1969, PhD in Vet. Medicine, 1981. Asst. Aristotle U., 1971-81, lectr. vet. medicine, 1982-87, asst. prof., 1987-97, assoc. prof., 1998—; reviewer Jour. Agrl. and Food Chemistry. Contbg. author: Food Analysis by HPLC, 1992; contbr. articles to sci. jours., including Jour. Agrl. and Food Chemistry, Jour. AOAC Internat. Mem. Am. Chem. Soc., Royal Soc. Chemistry (Gt. Britain) (assoc.), Nutrition Soc. (Gt. Britain), Chromatographic Soc. (Gt. Britain). Avocations: photography, computers, net surfing, listening to music. Home: 25th Martiou St 80, 54248 Thessaloniki Greece Office: Aristotle U Fac Vet Med, University Campus, 54006 Thessaloniki Greece

KÜFREVIOĞLU, Ö. IRFAN, biochemistry educator; b. Ağri, Centre, Turkey, Oct. 21, 1959; s. Tahir and Mediha (Uluğ) K.; . Songüler Dilek, July 7, 1985; children: Rabia Meryem, Büsra. BSc, Atatürk U., Erzurum, Turkey, 1980, PhD in Biochemistry, 1985. Tchg. asst. Atatürk U., 1981-88, asst. prof. biochemistry, 1988-89, assoc. prof., 1989-94, prof., 1994—, dir. Biotech. Applied and Rsch. Ctr., 1995—. Contbr. articles to sci. jours., including Pharm. Rsch., Chimica Acta Turcica, Bioorganic and Medicinal Chemistry, Preparative Biochemistry and Biotech., Turkish Jour. Chemistry, Turkish Jour. Med. Sci., Agrl. and Food Chemistry, Jour. Environ. Sci. and Health, Proc. NAS, Turkish Jour. Botany, Turkish Jour. Medicine and Pharmacology, Jour. Plant Physiology. Scholar TÜBITAK, 1976-80; fellow German Acad. Exch. Svc., 1985-87. Mem. Turkish Chem. Soc., Turkish Biochem. Soc. Avocations: Internet, travel. Home: Atatürk U, Loj 46/3, 25240 Erzurum Turkey Office: Atatürk U Fac Scis-Arts, Dept Chemistry, 25240 Erzurum Turkey

KUFS, WILLIAM ARNO, restaurant owner; b. Albany, N.Y., Aug. 21, 1938; s. Herman William and Charlene Florance K.; widower; 1 child, Jason Herman. Student, Auburn (N.Y.) C.C., 1956-58, Ithaca Coll., 1958-60. Polit. columnist, spkr., 1956—; sports promoter Cen. N.Y., 1957-75. Polit. activist, spkr. and writer; founder Amemdment X; dir. Conservative Party, N.Y. State, 1962. Avocations: politics, trivia, writing.

KUFTARO, AHMAD, religious leader. Grand mufti Islamic Faith, Damascus, Syria. Office: Office of Grand Mufti, Damascus Syrian Arab Republic

KUGIMIYA, TOSHIYASU, medical educator; b. Nagasaki, Japan, Apr. 3, 1933; s. Yoriyuki and Tsuyuko (Tasaki) K.; m. Etsuko Aso, May 13, 1963; children: Yoshiko Kugimiya Sunahara, Tomoko. MD, Kyushu U., Fukuoka, Japan, 1958; D in Med. Sci., Nagasaki (Japan) U., 1963. Med. cert. Japan, 1959; cert. Ednl. Coun. for Fgn. Med. Grads., Evanston, Ill., 1964. Asst. prof. Nagasaki (Japan) U., 1969-77, assoc. prof., 1977-85, prof., 1985-98, prof. emeritus, 1998—; chmn. dept. cardiovascular surgery Nagasaki (Japan) U. Hosp., 1985-98; dir. Nagasaki Rosai Hosp., 1998—. Contbr. Current Encyclopedia of Surgical Operations, 1980, New Encyclopedia of Pediatrics, 1981, New Encyclopedia of Surgical Science, 1990. Mem. Internat. Soc. Cardio-Thoracic Surgeons (councilor), Internat. Coll. Surgeons (Congress pres. Japanese sect. 1997). Home: 33-43 Motoomachi, Nagasaki 852-8112, Japan Office: Nagasaki Rosai Hosp, 2-12-5 Setogoe, Sasebo 857-0134, Japan

KUGLER, ANDREJ, nuclear physicist; b. Prague, Czech Republic, Jan. 11, 1953. Grad., Charles U., Prague, 1976; PhD, Joint Inst. for Nuclear Rsch., Dubna, Russia, 1989. Jr. scientist Lab. Nuclear Reactions, Joint Inst. for Nuclear Rsch., 1981-84, scientist, 1984-90; jr. scientist Nuclear Physics Inst., Acad. Scis. Czech Republic, Řež, 1977-81, sr. scientist, 1990—, dep. dir., 1990-98; rep. of Czech Republic to Alice CB, Geneva, 1994; rep. of Nuclear Physics Inst. to TAPS EB, 1995, to Hades EB, Darmstadt, Germany, 1995; mem. com. for Czech Republic with CERN, Prague, 1993; mem. grant agy. Charles U., 1995-99. Office: Acad Scis Czech Republic, Nuclear Physics Inst, 250 68 Řež Czech Republic

KÜGLER, CHRISTIAN FRANZ ALFRED, internist, researcher; b. Nürnberg, Germany, Feb. 18, 1961; s. Alfred and Anneliese Maria Margareta (Silberbauer) K.; m. Elisabeth Agnes Jaeger, June 16, 1992; children: Anna Helena, Clara Cosima, Isabella Lara. Student, Ludwig-Maximilians U., Munich, 1980-81; MD, Friedrich-Alexander U., Erlangen-Nürnberg, 1988; habilitation, U. Erlangen, 1997. Lic. physician, Germany. Physician 1st dept. internal medicine U. Erlangen, 1989-91, physician, chair internal medicine and gerontology, 1991-97; cons. dept. internal medicine and angiology U. Essen (Germany), 1998—. Contbr. articles to profl. jours. Recipient Sandoz AG award, 1980; Bavarian scholar of the highly gifted Bayer Staatsministerium für Unterricht und Kultus, 1980-88. Mem. Am. Geriatric Soc., Gerontol. Soc. Am., German Assn. Internal Medicine, German Assn. Aging Rsch., German Soc. Angiology. Roman Catholic. Avocations: philology (Old Greek, Latin), philosophy, chess, fencing, long-distance running. Office: U Essen Dept & Clin Internal Med/Angiol, Hufelandstr 55, Essen D-45122, Germany

KUGLER, JOACHIM, psychologist; b. Dusseldorf, Germany, Mar. 23, 1959; s. Josef Dehrendorf and Erna K.; m. Simone Kugler-Haase, Aug. 28, 1998; 1 child, Katharina. Diploma in psychology, Heinrich-Heine U., 1984, MD, 1989, PhD, 1990, Habilitation, 1996. Rsch. fellow Harvard U., Cambridge, Mass., 1984-85; postdoctoral fellow Heinrich-Heine U., Dusseldorf, Germany, 1987-89; asst. prof. Ruhr-University, Bochum, Germany, 1990-96; assoc. prof. Aachen U. Tech., Germany, 1996-99; prof. Dresden U. Tech., Germany, 1999—. Editor: Rheumatism-Pain-Emotion, 1994, Psychoneuroimmunology, 1995, 97, Health Psychology, 1997. Mem. German Soc. Psychology, German Soc. Med. Psychology, German Sci. Found. Avocations: badminton, classical guitar. Office: TU Dresden Dept Health Scis/Pub Health, Löscherstr 18, 01309 Dresden Germany

KUGLER, JOHANN EMIL, neuropsychiatrist; b. Vienna, Austria, June 1, 1923; arrived in Germany, 1956; s. Johann and Maria Elisabeth (Derschatta) K.; m. Editha Kastner, June 3, 1949 (dec. May 1987); children: Wolfgang, Helga, Johannes; m. Eva Hueber Kugler-Riedl, Feb. 16, 1988. MD, U. Vienna, 1949, asst. prof., U. Munich, 1962, prof. neurophysiology, 1969. Fellow Gen. Hosp., Vienna, 1949-52; resident Neurosurg. Hosp., Bad Ischl,

Austria, 1952-56; head neurophysiology dept. U. Munich, 1956-88; cons. Inst. Clin. Rsch., Munich, 1988-95; cons. emeritus Psychiat. Clinic U. Munich, 1996—; sec.-gen. Alpine EEG Meetings, Europe, 1959, 86; del. Internat. Fedn. EEG Socs., Paris, 1965-69, Med. Syndicate, Munich, 1982-83; pres. Internat. Pharm. EEG Soc., Munich, 1984-88. Author: Electroencephalography, 1961; editor Jour. EEG-EMG, 1970-96. Mem. German EEG Soc. (hon., sec. 1959-65, pres. 1965-67, del. 1967-90), Austrian EEG Soc. (hon.), Hungarian EEG Soc. (hon.), also others. Avocations: skiing, surfing, history of neurosciences. Home: AU 13, A-5311 Loibichl Salzburg, Austria

KUHARIĆ, FRANJO CARDINAL, archbishop of Zagreb; b. Pribic, Croatia, Apr. 15, 1919. Ordained priest Roman Cath. Ch., 1945; consecrated titular bishop of Meta and aux. bishop of Zagreb, Croatia, 1964-69; apostolic adminstr., 1969—, archbishop, 1970, archdiocese of Zagreb, 1970; elevated to Sacred Coll. of Cardinals, 1983; pres. Croatian Bishops Conf., 1993; titular ch., St. Jerome of Croats. Mem. Council for Pub. Affairs of Ch., Congregation Clergy. Address: Kaptol 31 PP 553, 10000 Zagreb Croatia*

KUHENS, BRIAN SCOTT, investment company executive, publishing company exexcutive; b. Lowell, Mass., June 20, 1966; s. Culver LaVerne and Joan Avon (Madden) K.; m. Donna Gayle Hennequin, Dec. 27, 1986; 1 child, Sage Hennequin. BA in Philosophy, U. S.C., 1990. Series 7, 63, 65 lic. Nat. Assn. Securities Dealers; registered investment advisor Securities and Exch. Commn., Iowa Securities Bur., Va. Commonwealth. Gen. mgr. Sound Advice, Inc., Columbia, S.C., 1987-90; v.p., owner Wordsprint, Inc., Galax, Wytheville, Va., 1991-95; stockbroker, fin. cons., intermediate trainer Wheat First Butcher Singer, Galax, 1995-98; prodn. editor, pub. The History Project, Inc., Galax, 1996—; registered investment advisor, Wadena, Iowa, Galax, Va., 1998—. Editor COGITO, 1986, (plays) Character in Time: The US Presidents, 1997—; asst. editor Mobile Illustrated, 1989-90. Chmn. bd. trustees Twin County Regional Hosp., Galax, 1995-98, dir. ex officio, 1997-98; trustee Illyria Twp., Fayette County, Iowa, 1999—. Recipient Mgmt. Plus/Silver award Nat. Assn. Printers and Lithographers, 1994, 95, Highest Ranking-First Place/Mgmt. Excellence award Print Image Internat., 1995. Mem. Rotary Internat. (Paul Harris fellow 1997, William E. Skelton Charter fellow 1997), Rotary Club Galax (dir., pres. 1993—, Presdl. citation for integrity, love and peace 1995-96), Rotary Internat. (asst. gov. dist. 7570 1996-98, Dist. Gov.'s citation for outstanding svc. 1997). Avocations: music, hiking, numismatics, electronics, poker. E-mail: Galax4Good@aol.com. Fax: 540-238-8177.

KUHL, PATRICIA K., science educator; b. Mitchell, S.D., Nov. 5, 1946; d. Joseph John and Susan Mary (Schaeffer) K.; m. Andrew N. Meltzoff, Sept. 28, 1985; 1 child, Katherine. BA, St. Cloud (Minn.) State U., 1967; MA, U. Minn., 1971, PhD, 1973. Postdoctoral research assoc. Cen. Inst. for Deaf, St. Louis, 1973-76; research assoc. U. Wash., Seattle, 1976-77, asst. prof., 1977-79, assoc. prof., 1979-82, prof. speech, language, hearing, 1982—, William P. and Ruth Gerberding univ. prof., 1997—, dept. chair, 1994—, dir. Ctr. for Mind, Brain and Learning, 2000—; gov. bd. Am. Inst. Physics, 1994-96; trustee Neurosci. Rsch. Found., 1994—; bd. dirs. Wash. Tech. Ctr., U. Wash., 1994-96; invited presenter White House Conf. on Early Learning and the Brain, 1997. Editor Jour. Neurosci., 1989-96. Recipient Women in Research citation Kennedy Council, 1978, Virginia Merrill Bloedel Scholar award, 1992-94. Fellow AAAS, Am. Psychol. Soc., Acoustical Soc. Am. (assoc. editor Jour. 1988-92, chair medals and awards, 1992-94, v.p. 1997, Silver medal 1997, pres. 1999—); mem. Am. Acad. Arts and Scis. Office: U Wash Dept Speech & Hearing Sciences 1417 NE 42nd St # 354875 Seattle WA 98105-6247

KUHL, WOLF PETER, biochemist, educator; b. Schweidnitz, Germany, Dec. 2, 1942; s. Gerhard and Margarete (Elsner) K.; m. Gudrun Fläschendräger, Dec. 28, 1968; 1 child, Toralf. Dr.rer.nat., U. Leipzig, Germany, 1971, Dr.sc.nat., 1989, Dr.rer.nat.habil., 1991. Rsch. asst. chem. dept. U. Leipzig, Germany, 1971-78, sr. asst. biosci. dept., 1978-93; prof. biochem. U. Tech., Dresden, Germany, 1993—. Contbr. articles to profl. jours.; patentee in field. Mem. German Chem. Soc., European Peptide Soc. Avocations: music, foreign languages, walking. Office: U Tech, D-01062 Dresden Germany

KUHLBUSCH, THOMAS A.J., chemist; b. Recklinghausen, Germany, Nov. 12, 1964; came to U.S., 1995; s. Johannes and Elisabeth (Menke) K.; m. Anke Uelzmann, May 14, 1996. Diploma, Westfalen Wilhelms U., 1990; PhD, Gutenberg U., 1994. Rschr. Max Planck Inst Airchemistry, Mainz, Germany, 1994-95, Nat. Rsch. Coun., U.S. EPA, Athens, 1995-97, U. Duisburg, Germany, 1997—. Regional representative Greenpeace, Mainz, 1990-94. Mem. Am. Geophys. Union, Am. Chem. Soc., German Aerosol Found. Avocations: music, playing piano, sports, reading. Home: Neudorfer Str 131, 47057 Duisburg Germany Office: Univ Duisburg, FB9/AMT, Bismarck Str. 81, 47057 Duisburg Germany

KUHLE, MATTHIAS, geography educator, researcher; b. Berlin, Apr. 20, 1948; s. Gustav and Herta Cäcilie (Piehl) K.; m. Sabine Joergens, Oct. 12, 1979; children: Wolfgang, Anneliese, Bernhard, Arthur. Degree, Free U., Berlin, 1972; DSc, U. Goettingen, Germany, 1975, habilitation, 1980. Assoc. prof. geography U. Göttingen, 1983-89, prof. geography and high mountain geomorphology, 1990—; leader sci. expeditions to High Asia, Himalayas, Tibet, Kara-Korum, Tienshan, Pamir, Kuenlun, Arctic, Alaska, Andes, 1973—. Author: Mountain Landscapes: Formation in Boulder, Rock and Ice, 1985 (Literary award German Alpine Club 1986), Glaciogeomorphology, 1991; contbr. more than 140 articles to profl. jours.; guest editor Geojour.: Tibet and High Asia, 1988, 91, 94, 97, 99. Grantee German Rsch. Soc., 1975-98, German Volkswagen Found., 1993-94, Max Planck Soc., 1981-89. Mem. Internat. Geog. Union, Internat. Quaternary Assn., Internat. Geol. Cooperation Project, Lions. Avocations: mountaineering, photography, literature. E-mail: mkhule@grodg.de. Home: Am Hirtenberg 6, D-37136 Waake Germany Office: Geog Inst U Goettingen, Goldschmidtstr 5, D-37077 Göttingen Germany

KUHLE, SHIRLEY JEAN, real estate appraiser; b. Sioux Falls, S.D., Jan. 14, 1936; d. Earl John and Palma Ruth (Knutson) Albertus: m. Donald Eugene Kuhle, June 4, 1954; children: Kim Jean, Kathy Joan, Kenneth John, Kris June. Grad., Realtors Inst., 1969-77; cert. in mgmt. devel., U. Nebr., 1984. Cert. resdl. specialist; ARC home nursing instr. cert. advanced nat. victim crisis team counseling. Co-owner, asst. mgr. Beltline Tractor Sales, Inc., Lincoln, Nebr., 1960-84; appraiser Nebr. Real Estate Commn., 1974—; broker, 1964—; nat. bd. dirs. Nat. Orgn. Victims Assistance, Washington, 1979-84, 99—; mem. Nebr. Crime Commn., 1980-87; adminstr. Victim/Witness Unit, Lincoln Police Dept., 1981-87; counselor Homicide Support Group, 1988—; trainer victim issues, 1988. Author articles and tng. manuals on victim assistance. Mem. Lincoln/Lancaster County Justice Coun., 1981; v.p. Willard Cmty. Ctr., 1982-83; cons. Nebr. Parents Anonymous, 1981, Region VII Rural Domestic Violence Ctr., 1981; pres. Nebr. Task Force Domestic Violence, 1979, 80, 81; pres. Capitol Beach Cmty. Assn., 1979; pres., co-founder Nebr. Coalition Victims of Crime, 1986; mem. Nat. and Cmty. Crisis Response Team, Mental Health Congress in New Zealand. Program grantee Fed. Govt., 1980, 81; recipient admiralship State of Nebr., 1975, Polly Albertus Hurley award, 1986, Liberty Bell award, 1986; Meritorious Svc. citation City of Lincoln, 1978, Diana award Epsilon Sigma Alpha Internat., 1997; named to Ky. Col. Gov. of Ky., 1989. Mem. Nat. Orgn. Victims Assistance (life, exec. bd., 1979-84, conf. del.), Am. Fend. Police, Police Officers Assn., Combined Orgn. of Police Svcs., Nat. Criminal Justice Assn. (charter), Nebr. Admirals Assn. (Lincoln Port comdr. 1989-90, chief of staff 1990-99), World Soc. Victimology, Big Red Nuclear Submarine Club (active various coms. 1995—, hon. comdr.). Roman Catholic. Democrat. Home: 5009 S Sweetbriar Dr Sioux Falls SD 57108-2805

KUHLEFELT, PER-ERIK, consulting and trading company executive; b. Helsinki, Finland, Dec. 20, 1945; s. Jarl and Aina Eleonora (Nyström) K.; m. Gunilla Birgitta Hindsberg, Feb. 13, 1970; children: Pernilla Birgitta Eleonora, Jarl Fredrik. Ensign, Finnish Seewar, Helsinki, 1966; grad. in mech. engring., Tech. H.S., Helsinki, 1971. Product sales mgr. OY Fiskars AB, Helsinki, 1971-73; prodn. mgr. Wuppermann GmbH, Leverkusen, Germany, 1973-76; asst. sales mgr. OY Fiskars AB, 1977-79; sales mgr. OY Ovako AB, Billnäs, Finland, 1979-90; mktg. mgr. Ovako Arvika (Sweden) AB, 1990-93, Ovako Stahl GmbH, Düsseldorf, Germany, 1993-94; cons. export mgr. Colaert Sarl, Steenbecave, France, 1998-99; pres. Magnum Cons., Arvika, 1994—. Active Order of St. John, 1987; bd. dirs. Assn. of the Nordic Countries, 1998. Lutheran. Avocations: boating, fishing, skiing, gardening, stamps. Fax: 46 570 10515. E-mail: magnum.consulting@telia.com. Office: Magnum Consulting, Cisterngatan 31, 671 31 Arvika Varmland Sweden

KUHLEN, RALF ROBERT, physician, researcher; b. Viersen, Germany, Feb. 15, 1965; s. Klaus and Margarette (Schippers) K.; m. Konstanze Schoeningh; children: Philip, Daniel. MD, Free U., Berlin, 1991. Anaesthesiologist U. Berlin, 1991-95, Humboldt U., Berlin, 1996-97, U. Roden, 1997—. Mem. European Soc. Intensive Care Medicine, Deutsche Gesellschaft für Anaesthesiologie ünd Intensivmedizin, Am. Thoracic Soc., European Respiratory Soc., Deutsdie Interdiscipline Veciuping Iateusivmedize. Office: Virchow U, U Aachen Dept Anesthes, Pauwelsstrasse 30, 52074 Aachen Germany

KUHLER, RENALDO GILLET, museum official, scientific illustrator; b. Teaneck, N.J., Nov. 21, 1931; s. Otto August and Simonne L. (Gillet) K.; 1 child, Anne Marie Cooper. BA, U. Colo., 1961. Curator of history, illustrator exhibit, miniature diorama preparator Ea. Wash. State Hist. Soc. Mus., Spokane, 1962-67; mus. illustrator N.C. State Mus. Natural History, Raleigh, 1969—; semi-ret., 1999; designer, executor of art work for sci. illustrations, awards, brochures, pamphlets and periodicals Dept. Agr. and Mus., N.C., 1972-74; designer 36 illustrations for Handbook of Reptiles and Amphibians of Florida, Part 1 (Ray E. Ashton), 1981; contbr. many illustrations Atlas of Freshwater Fishes of North America (David Lee), Endangered Threatened and Rare Fauna of N.C. (Ross, Rohde and Lindquist), Distribution Survey of N.C. Mammals (Lee, Funderburg and Clark); Endangered Threatened and Rare Fauna of N.C., part 1 (Mary K. Clark), Potential Effect of Oil Spills on Seabirds, etc. (Lee and Socci), Poisonous Snakes of N.C. (William M. Palmer), Reptiles of North Carolina (William M. Palmer and Alvin Braswell); gen. illustrator: American Firearms and the Changing Frontier (Waldo E. Rosebush); also contbr. to jours. and bulls.; currently working on skull illustrations for Mammals of North Carolina (Mary Kay Clark); calligrapher; creator wood handicrafts; violin maker, 1949. Mem. Nat. Trust Hist. Preservation, Nat. Smokers Alliance. Democrat. Avocations: experimenting with laminated paper and models of ships and trains, carburator fittings for smoking pipes, designer hiking and summer office suits. Home: Apt 3 510 Tilden St Raleigh NC 27605-1524 Office: NC State Mus Natural Scis 210 N Salisbury St Raleigh NC 27603-1358

KUHLMAN, ELMER LEONARD, material handling engineer; b. Platte Ctr., Neb., July 28, 1926; s. William and Louise (Hellbusch) K.; m. Ruth Ann Lofgren, Mar. 19, 1949; children: Richard, Robert, Daniel, Philip. BBA, U. Minn., 1951; extension student, U. Wis., 1971, '74, '82; student MHE, Georgia Tech., 1978. Indsl. engr. Montgomery Ward, St. Paul, 1951-55, Aero. Div. Honeywell, Mpls., 1955-56; office supr., prodn. engr. Aero. Div. Honeywell, 1956-57; prodn. engr. Ordinance Div. Honeywell, 1957-60; sr. engr. Honeywell Packaging and Handling Engring., 1960-68, supr. Packaging and Material Handling, 1968-85, engring. fellow, 1985-88; sr. engring. fellow, 1988-91. Presenter profl. seminars and confs. Mem. Packaging Curriculum Com., U. Wis., Stout, Menominee, 1964, Industry Adv. Com. Tech. Ctr., Eden Prarie, Minn. 1972-82; chmn. Mfg. Tech. Adv. Group Aerospace Inds. Assn., Washington, 1985-87. With U.S. Naval Air Corps, 1944-46. Recipient Disting. Colleague award, Aerospace Inds. Assn., Mfg. Com., 1989. Fellow Inst. Packaging Profls. (pres. Minn. chpt. 1962-69, nat. bd. mem. at large 1985-89); mem. Nat. Inst. Package Handling and Logistics Engrs., Am. Def. Preparedness Assn. (chmn. packaging, handling and transp. div. 1978-81, Bronze medallion 1981), Nat. SecurityIndsl. Assn. (chmn. packaging handling engring com. 1989-91), Inst. Indsl. Engrs. Avocations: golf, travel, bridge. Office: Am Wood Packaging Assn PO Box 110 Hwy 210 West Aitkin MN 56431

KUHLMANN, FRED MARK, lawyer, business executive; b. St. Louis, Apr. 9, 1948; s. Frederick Louis and Mildred (Southworth) K.; m. Barbara Jane Nierman, Dec. 30, 1970; children: F. Matthew, Sarah Ann. AB summa cum laude, Washington U., St. Louis, 1970; JD cum laude, Harvard U., 1973. Bar: Mo. 1973. Assoc. atty. Stolar, Heitzmann & Eder, St. Louis, 1973-75; tax counsel McDonnell Douglas Corp., St. Louis, 1975-82, corp. asst. sec., 1977-88, corp. counsel fin. matters, 1982-87, assoc. gen. counsel, 1984-87, staff v.p., 1985-87; exec. v.p. McDonnell Douglas Health Systems Co. div. McDonnell Douglas Corp., Hazelwood, Mo., 1987-88, pres., 1988-89; pres. McDonnell Douglas Systems Integration Co. div. McDonnell Douglas Corp., Hazelwood, Mo., 1989-91; v.p., gen. counsel, sec. McDonnell Douglas Corp., St. Louis, 1991-92, sr. v.p. adminstrn., gen. counsel, sec., 1992-95, sr. v.p., gen. counsel, 1995-97; of counsel Bryan Cave, St. Louis, 1997-98; pres. Sys. Svc. Enterprises, St. Louis, 1998—; bd. dirs. Republic Health Corp., Dallas, 1988-90; mem. governing bd. Luth. Med. Ctr., 1989-95, chmn., 1990-92. Bd. dirs. Luth. Charities Assn., 1982-91, sec. 1984-86, chmn. 1986-89; elder Lutheran Ch. of Resurrection, 1977-80; mem. Regents Coun. Concordia Sem., 1981-84; chmn. cub scout pack 459 Boy Scouts Am., 1984-86; bd. dirs. Luth. High Sch. Assn., 1978-84, 91-97, pres. 1992-97, long range planning com. 1990-92, chmn. alumni assn. 1981; chmn. north star dist. Boy Scouts Am., 1990-93; bd. dirs. Mcpl. Theatre Assn., St. Louis, 1991—; chmn. long range planning com. St. Paul's Luth. Ch., 1988-91, 98—, pres., 1996-97; bd. dirs., mem. exec. com. United Way of Greater St. Louis, 1994-97, chmn. Vanguard divsn., 1994-97; mem. amb. coun. Luth. Family and Children's Svcs. of St. Louis, 1998—; bd. dirs. Luth. Charities Found., 1998—; mem. adv. bd. Webster U. Bus. and Tech. Sch., 1999—. Recipient Disting. Leadership award Luth. Assn. for Higher Edn., 1981. Mem. ABA, Mo. Bar Assn., Bar Assn. Met. St. Louis, Bellerive Country Club, Phi Beta Kappa, Omicron Delta Kappa. Republican. Avocations: tennis, golf, racquetball. Home: 1711 Stone Rdg Trails Dr Saint Louis MO 63122-3546 Office: Sys Svc Enterprises 77 Westport Plz Ste 500 Saint Louis MO 63146-3126

KUHLMANN, HANS-WERNER, research protozoologist; b. Bottrop, Germany, Dec. 6, 1955; s. Johannes and Maria (Menzik) K.; m. Dorothea Siegert, Oct. 2, 1986; children: Christina, Johannes, Matthias. PhD, Westfälische Wilhelms-U., Münster, 1986; habilitation, Wilhelms U., Münster, 1993. Prof. Inst. für Allg. Zoologie und Genetik, Münster, 1999—. Contbr. over 35 articles and 7 invited revs. to profl. sci. jours., including Sci., Jour. Cell Sci., Jour. Exptl. Zoology, others. Avocation: travel. Office: Inst fü Allg Zoologie, und Genetik, Münster Germany

KUHN, ANNE NAOMI WICKER (MRS. HAROLD B. KUHN), foreign language educator; b. Lynchburg, Va.; d. George Barnett and Annie (Hicks) Wicker; m. Harold B. Kuhn. Diploma Malone Coll., 1933, Trinity Coll. Music, London, 1937; AB, John Fletcher Coll., 1939; MA, Boston U., 1942, postgrad., 1965-70; postgrad. (fellow) Harvard U., 1942-44, 66-68; hon. grad. Asbury Coll., 1978. Instr., Emmanuel Bible Coll., Birkenhead, Eng., 1936-37; asst. in history John Fletcher Coll., University Park, Iowa, 1938-39; librarian Harvard U., 1939-44; tchr. adult edn. program U.S. Armed Forces, Fuerstenfeldbruck Air Base, Germany, 1951-52; prof. Union Bibl. Sem., Yeotmal, India, 1957-58; lectr. Armenian Bible Inst., Beirut, Lebanon, 1958; prof. German, Asbury Coll., Wilmore, Ky., 1962—, co-dir. coll. study tour to East Germany and West Germany, 1976, 77, 78, co-dir. acad. tours, 1979, 80; dir. acad. tour, Russia, 1981, 85, Scandanavia, 1982, Indonesia, Singapore, 1983, Hong Kong and Thailand, 1983, 85, East Germany, West Germany, France and Austria, 1983, Russia and Finland, 1984, 85, 89, China, 1979, 84, 85, 89, Estonia, Latvia, 1985, 89, Poland, 1989, 91, 92, Portugal, Spain, France, Ireland, Scotland, Norway, England, 1987, The Balkans, Hungary, Czech Republic, Slovak Republic, Bulgaria, Romania and Turkey, 1992, alumni academic tour Malta, Sicily, Greece, Macedonia, 1995; tchr. Seoul Theol. Sem., fall 1978. Author: (pamphlet) The Impact of the Transition to Modern Education Upon Religious Education, 1950; The Influence of Paul Gerhardt upon Wesleyan Hymnody, 1960, Light to Dispel Fear, 1987; transl. German ch. records, poems, letters; contbr. articles to profl. jours. Del. Youth for Christ World Conf., 1948, 50, London Yearly Meeting of Friends, Edinburgh, Scotland, 1948, World Council Chs., Amsterdam, 1948, World Friends Conf., Oxford, Eng., 1952, World Methodist Conf., Oslo, Norway, 1961, Deutscher Kirchentag, Dortmund, Germany, 1963, German Lang. Congress, Bonn, W. Ger., 1974, Internat. Conf. Religion, Amsterdam, Netherlands, Poland, West Berlin, Fed. Republic Germany, 1986, Internat. Missionary Conf., Eng., 1987, Congress on the Bible II, Washington, 1987; participant Internat. Congress World Evangelization, Lausanne, Switzerland, 1974; del., speaker Internat. Conf. on Holocaust and Genocide, Oxford and London, 1988; speaker Founders Week Malone Coll., Ohio, 1989, Nat. Quaker Conf., Denver; mem. acad. tour Poland, 1988; vol. of various special assignments in Ctrl. and Eastern Europe. Recipient German Consular award, Boston, 1965, Thomas Mann award Boston U., 1967; named Ky. Col., 1978. Fellow Goethe-Institut for Germanisten, Munich, 1966-68, 70-71. Mem. AAUW, Am. Assn. Tchrs. German, NEA, Ky. Ednl. Assn., Lincoln Lit. Soc., Protestant Women of Chapel, Harvard Univ. Faculty Club (Cambridge, Mass.), Harvard Univ. Club Eastern and Ctrl. Ky. (Lexington), United Daughters of the Confederacy, Delta Phi Alpha (award 1963, 65). Mem. Soc. of Friends. Home: 406 Kenyon Ave Wilmore KY 40390-1033

KUHN, FERENC, ophthalmologist; b. Budapest, Nov. 23, 1952; s. Endre and Agota (Gergely) K.; m. Mary Balogh, Oct. 17, 1977; children: Sophia, Judy. MD, Med. U. of Pecs, 1977. V.p. U.S. Eye Injury Registry, Birmingham, 1989—; assoc. dir. rsch. Helen Keller Eye Rsch. Found., Birmingham, 1989—; assoc. prof. dept. ophthalmology U. Ala., Birmingham, 1997—; editor-in-chief Jour. of Eye Trauma, Birmingham, 1991—; editor Hungarian Jour. of Ophthalmology, Budapest, 1998—; rsch. dir. Retina Rsch. Found., Birmingham, 1992—; vis. prof. U. Pecs, Hungary, 1997—; cons. WHO, Geneva; advisor Hungarian Eye Injury Registry, Pecs, 1990—. Author: Standardization of the Language of Eye Trauma, 1997, The Ocular Trauma Score, 2000. Grantee Ctrs. for Disease Control and Prevention. Fellow Am. Acad. Ophthalmology (Merit award 1997); mem. Internat. Soc. of Ocular Trauma (bd. dirs. exec. com. Tel Aviv 1995—), Hungarian Ophthalmol. Soc. (bd. dirs. 1977—), PanAm. Trauma Soc. (founding mem.), Assn. for Advancement of Automotive Medicine. Avocations: soccer, tennis, travel. Office: Helen Keller Eye Rsch Found 1201 11th Ave S Ste 3000 Birmingham AL 35205-3410

KÜHN, HARTMUT, physician, biochemical researcher; b. Mühlhausen, Thüringen, Germany, Aug. 23, 1953; s. Wilhelm and Elisabeth (Skodnik) K.; div.; children: Marvin, Christopher, Sabrina. Diploma in medicine, Humboldt U., Berlin, 1980; MD, Humboldt U., 1981, DSc, 1986; postgrad., Vanderbilt U., 1986-87. Sr. scientist Humboldt U., 1987-90, UCSF, San Francisco, 1991, U. Tokushima, Japan, 1992; prof. Humboldt U., 1994; rsch. group leader Humboldt U., 1986-96; external cons. Syntex, Palo Alto, Calif., 1993-95; coord. concerted action Eur. Commn., Brussels, 1994-96, 98—. Contbr. articles to profl. jours. Served with German Dem. Rep. Mil., 1972-74. Recipient Virchow award Min. Health German Dem. Rep., 1983. Mem. Biochem. Soc. German Dem. Rep. (Lohmann award 1989), German Atherosclerosis Soc. E-mail: hartmut.kuehn@charite.de. Office: Inst Biochemistry, Hessische Str 3-4, D-10115 Berlin Germany

KUHN, HEINZ-WOLFGANG, biblical studies educator; b. Coburg, Germany, Mar. 2, 1934; s. Horst and Therese (Schubarth) K.; m. Ursula Mohr, Aug. 13, 1964; children: Berthold, Annegret, Verena. ThD, U. Heidelberg, Germany, 1963, Habilitation N.T., 1969. Mem. faculty U. Heidelberg, 1960-73, prof. N.T., 1973-79, prof. n.t., 1979-86; prof., chair N.T. U. Munich, Germany, 1986-99; dean Protestant faculty U. Munich, 1993-95; vis. faculty U. Bonn, Germany, 1978-79, U. Göttingen, Germany, 1979-80; instr. U. Saarbrücken, Germany, 1975-76, 81; mem. Ecumenical N.T. Transl. Com., 1971-81; co-dir. Bethsaida Excavations Project, 1991—. Author: Enderwartung u gegenw Heil, 1966, Ältere Samml i Mk-Evangel, 1971, Kreuzesstrafe in Aufstieg u Niedergang roem Welt, 1982; co-editor Studien zur Umwelt des N.T., 1978—; contbr. articles to profl. jours. Recipient Bonifatius medal Conf. German Cath. Bishops, 1978, Bundesverdienstkreuz am Bande of Germany, 1998. Mem. Studiorum Novi Testamenti Societas, Wissensch Gesellsch Theologie, Soc. Biblical Lit., Deutscher Verein Erforschung Palaestinas. Home: 3 MuxelstraBe, D-81479 Munich 71, Germany

KUHN, JAMES E., judge; b. Hammond, La., Oct. 31, 1946; s. Eton Percy and Mildred Louise (McDaniel) K.; m. Cheryl Aucoin, Dec. 27, 1969; children: James M., Jennifer L. BA, Southeastern La. U., 1968; JD, Loyola U. of South, 1973. Bar: La. 1973, Colo. 1995, U.S. Supreme Ct. 1978. Asst. dist. atty. 21st Jud. Dist., La., 1980-90; judge 21st Jud. Dist., Livingston, St. Helena, Tangipahoa, 1990-95, Ct. Appeals (1st cir.), Baton Rouge, 1995—; instr. history, govt. and criminal justice Southeastern La. U., Hammond, 1991—; past mem. appellate ct. performance and standards com. La. Supreme Ct.; lectr. in field. Founder For Our Youth; past bd. dirs. La. Coun. Child Abuse, past sec.-treas. Conf. of Ct. Appeal Judges for State of La. Recipient Am. Jurisprudence award Loyola Law Sch. Mem. ABA, La. State Bar Assn. (Professionalism and Quality of Life com.), 21st Jud. Bar Assn., Livingston Parish Bar Assn., Delta Theta Phi. Home: 253 W Oak St Ponchatoula LA 70454-3330

KUHN, MICHAEL HEINRICH, meteorology and geophysics educator; b. Marburg an der Lahn, Germany, July 8, 1943; s. Alwin Heinrich and Hedwig Clara (Friedrich) K.; m. Barbara Grassmayr; children: Maria, Susanne, Stefan, Theresa, Verena. PhD, U. Innsbruck, Austria, 1971; postdoctoral studies, U. Mich., 1963. Field asst. U. Wash., Seattle, 1964; rsch. asst. U. Melbourne, Australia, 1966-68, Arctic Inst. N. Am., Washington, 1969-70; asst. prof. U. Innsbruck, 1971-80, assoc. prof., 1980-88, full prof. meteorology and geophysics, 1988—; rsch. assoc. Ohio State U., Columbus, 1977-78. Editor Zeitschrift für Gletscherkunde und Glazialgeologie, 1974—, Theoretical and Applied Climatology, 1985—. With Austrain army, 1972. Mem. Internat. Assn. for Meteorology and Atmospheric Physics (sec. gen. 1987-95), Internat. Commn. for Snow and Ice (pres. 1991-95), Austrian Acad. Scis. (corr.), Bavarian Acad. Scis. Avocation: gardening. Office: Inst Meteorologie und Geophysic, Inst Meteorologie & Geophys, Innrain 52, A 6020 Innsbruck Austria

KUHNA, KURT PETER, water analysis laboratory administrator; b. Karlsruhe, Germany, Feb. 27, 1951; s. Werner Günter and Gertrud (Kastner) K. Vocat. edn. and tng., Kerschensteiner, Stuttgart, Germany, 1969. Various positions in water treatment, 1966—; chief lab. Hager & Elsässer, Stuttgart, Germany, 1988—. Holder Guinness world record of walking (12000 and 13360 km), 1996, 97; recipient Internat. Popular Sports Achievement award for 30000 km Distance award, 1996, and 1200 Event Participation award, 1998, 125 Event Participation award for 120 km Schömberg/Nordschwarzwald, 1997. E-mail: kurt.kuhna@dergemont.com. and info@kpkproject.de. Home: Brunnenstrasse 25, D-72401 Haigerloch-Bad Imnau Germany Office: Philipp Müller H & E, Ruppmannstrasse 22, D-70565 Stuttgart Germany

KÜHNE, GERT-EBERHARD, psychiatrist, educator; b. Breslau, Germany, July 25, 1936; s. Paul and Margarete (Nawroth) K.; m. Rosemarie Heid, June 4, 1975; 1 child, Katharina. MD, Martin Luther U., Halle-Wittenberg, Germany, 1960, PD, 1969, DMS, 1972. Assoc. prof. Martin Luther U., 1970-73; prof., dir. psychiat. clinic Med. Acad., Magdeburg, Germany, 1974-83, Hans Berger Clinic, Friedrich Schiller U., Jena, Germany, 1983-92; prof., head divsn. substance abuse Psychosomatic Clinic, Bad Blankenburg, 1993-97; prof., sen. psychiat. Psychosomatic Clinic, Bad Soden Ts, Germany, 1998—; pres.-elect Curatorium Psychiat. Danube Symposia, Linz, Austria, 1980-82; cons. WHO-Expert Adv. Panel of Mental Health, Geneva, 1981-97, joint project on diagnosis and classification alcohol, drug abuse, mental health adminstrn. WHO investigator group composit internat. diagnostic interview, Geneva, 1981-97; dir. State Project Rsch. Group Psychoneurol. Disorders, Magdeburg, 1981-83; mem. Curatorium Rudolf Steiner Acad., Weimar-Taubach, Germany, 1999—. Author: (with J.U. Grünes and G. Koselowski) The Structured Psychopathological Evaluation System, 1983 (State Rsch. award 1984); editor: (with H. Klepel and J. Molcan) Neurobiological Aspects in Psychiatry, 1984, (with R.J. Vovin) Psychopharmacotherapeutic Bases in Rehabilitation of Mental Disorders, 1989, (with H.D. Brenner and G. Huber) Cognitive Therapy in Schizophrenics, 1990. Recipient Karl Bonhoeffer medal Assn. Psychiatry and Neurology of Germany, 1986, Albert Schweitzer medal Austrian Assn. Albert Schweitzer, 1991. Mem. Psychiat. Assn. Purkyne (corr.), Internat. Brain Rsch. Orgn., German Assn. Psychiatry, Psychotherapy and Nerve Sci., St. Andrew Vol. Corps (hon.), Souvereign Order St. John Jerusalem (Knight of Honor 1992—). Evangelical Lutheran. Home: Hausbergstrasse 1, 07749 Jena

Germany Office: Psychosomatic Clinic, Spessartstrasse 20, 63619 Bad Orb/ Spessart Germany

KUHNEN, HANS-PETER, museum director, archaeologist; b. Goeppingen, Germany, Mar. 23, 1953; s. Edgar-Karl and Erna (Gervautz) K.; m. Sibylle Bauer, Dec. 30, 1987; children: Lea Hella Ernestine, Maia Salome. PhD in Archaeology, U. Munich, 1982. Asst. U. Bonn, Germany, 1982; curator Prähistorische Staatssammlung, Munich, 1982-87, Kurpfälzisches Mus., Heidelberg, Germany, 1987-90; chief curator Württemberg Landesmuseum, Stuttgart, Germany, 1990-94; dir. Rheinisches Landesmuseum, Trier, Germany, 1994—; lectr. U. Munich, 1986-87, U. Heidelberg, 1988-90, U. Stuttgart, 1993-94; counselor Gesellschaft für Nützliche Forschungen, 1995—; adminstrv. dir. Förderkreis Rheinisches Landesmuseum, 1996—; corr. mem. Deuisches Archaologisches Institut, 1998—. Author: Nordwest-Palästina in Hellenistisch-Römischer Zeit, 1986, Studien zur Chronologie des Karmel, 1989, Palästina in Griechisch-Römischer Zeit, 1990; editor, author Religio Romana, 1996; editor Trierer Zeitschrift, 1994—. Scholar Fr.-Ebert-Stiftung, Israel, 1977. Office: Rheinisches Landesmuseum, Weimarer Alee 1, D-54290 Trier Germany

KUHNS, LARRY J., horticulturist, educator. Prof. ornamental horticulture Pa. State U., University Park. Recipient Outstanding Extension educator award, 1992. Office: Penn State U Dept of Horticulture Tyson Bldg University Park PA 16802

KUHNT, DIETMAR, energy and utilities executive. Ceo RWE Group, Essen, Germany. Office: RWE Group, Opernplatz 1, Essen 45128, Germany*

KUIJPERS, ROGIER JOZEF, engineering executive; b. Helmond, The Netherlands, Mar. 10, 1962; s. Frans Kuijpers and Jo Fransen. BSc, Hogeschool Heerlen, The Netherlands, 1988; MTS, Sch. Fotografie Fotonica, The Hague, The Netherlands. Sales engr. Difa Measuring Sys., Breda, The Netherlands, 1988-90; cons. OPTEL, Nijmegen, The Netherlands, 1990-92; designer ASML, Veldhoven, The Netherlands, 1992-96, techsup specialist, 1996-99, mgr., 1999—. Editor Dutch Mag. Photonics, 1992-99. Field hockey referee judge KNHB, The Netherlands, 1992-98. Avocations: field hockey, literature, cross country skiing. Fax: 31402303674. Home: beatrixlaan 88, 5707LX Helmond The Netherlands Office: ASML, De Run 1110, 5503LA Veldhoven The Netherlands

KUINTZLE, AUDRY JANE, financial executive; b. Bridgeport, Conn., Feb. 1, 1964; d. Charles and Leslie Jane Kuintzle. BS, Sacred Heart U., Fairfield, Conn., 1987, MBA, 1991. Portfolio adminstrn. rep. GE Capital, Danbury, Conn., 1990-92, sr. automate documentation specialist, 1992-95, ops. analyst, 1995-96, mgr. audit and integration, 1996-98, mgr. audit, integration, securities and imaging, 1998—. Mem. Fin. Women Internat. Avocations: cooking, travel, gardening. Office: Gen Electric Capital 44 Old Ridgebury Rd Danbury CT 06810-5107

KUIPER, KOENRAAD, education educator; b. Hanover, Germany, Feb. 22, 1944; s. Koenraad and Sara Jacoba K.; m. Alison Clare Wylde, May 11, 1968; children: Gabrielle Sara, Miranda Clare, Sonya Frances Evelyn. BA, Victoria U. of Wellington, 1965, MA, 1966; PhD, Simon Fraser U., Vancouver, BC., 1972. Cert. tchr., New Zealand. Tchr. Riccarton H.S., Christchurch, New Zealand, 1968; tchg. asst. Simon Fraser U., Vancouver, 1969-72; tchr. Burnside H.S., Christchurch, New Zealand, 1973-74; lectr. U. Canterbury, Christchurch, New Zealand, 1975-79; sr. lectr. U. Canterbury, 1979-95, assoc. prof., 1996—, head dept. linguistics, 1993-99; assoc. prof. U. Canterbury, Christchurch, 1996—. Mem. editl. bd. Jour. of Sociolinguistics, 1995—, Jour. of New Zealand English, 1998—; author: (books) Mikrokosmos, 1990 (Runner up PEN for Best First Poetry Book 1991), Smooth Talkers, 1996; co-author: (book) An Introduction to English Language: Sound, Word and Sentence, 1996; editor: (book) New Zealand English, 2000. Mem. Linguistic Soc. of New Zealand (pres. 1981-82, 89-91). Fulbright Travel grantee U.S. Govt., Bard Coll., 1988, Fulbright Exch. fellowship U.S. Govt., Bethany Coll., 1993, NWO fellowship Netherlands Scientific Orgn., Utrecht U., 1995-96, China/New Zealand Travel award New Zealand Govt., Dalian U. Fgn. Langs., 1997. Mem. Linguistic Soc. Am., Royal Soc. New Zealand, New Zealand Soc. Authors. Avocations: tennis, gardening. Office: Univ Canterbury, Clyde Rd, Christchurch New Zealand

KUIPERS, SIMON KLAAS, university administrator; b. Sauwerd, Groningen, Netherlands, Sept. 27, 1943; s. Barthold Jan and Cybrich Eltje (Talens) K.; m. Jeannette Maaike Jurriens, June 20, 1969; children: Barthold Jan, Marie-Jeannette, Mathilde Anna. MA, U. Groningen, 1968, PhD, 1970. Asst. prof. of econs. U. Groningen, 1968-74, assoc. prof. econs., 1974-77, prof. econs., 1977-2000, rector magnificus, 1991-94, pres., 2000—; crown mem. Social-Econ. Coun., The Hague, 1979-96; mem. Bank Coun., Amsterdam, 1984-96, Royal Netherlands Acad. Sci., 1988—. Mng. editor De Economist, 1977-98; contbr. 75 articles to profl. jours.; co-author 14 books. Office: U Groningen, PO Box 72, 9700 AB Groningen The Netherlands

KUITUNEN, MARKKU TAPIO, biologist, consultant; b. Tyrväntö, Häme, Finland, Nov. 22, 1953; s. Paul Bernhard and Signe Irene (Taube) K.; m. Pirjo Irmeli Soini, Dec. 10, 1983; children: Juho-Pekka, Selja Elina, Milja Maaria. MSc, U. Jyväskylä, Finland, 1982, PhD, 1989. Rschr. Ministry Agr. and Forestry, Helsinki, Finland, 1980-82; asst. prof. U. Jyväskylä, 1982-88, assoc. prof., 1988, prof., 1989—; vis. prof. U. Minn., Duluth, 1996; cons. City of Helsinki, 1992, 97; rschr. Internat. Inst. Cultural Edn., Budapest, Hungary, 1982-85. Contbr. articles to profl. jours.; editor-in-chief Soc. Finnish Biologists Periodical Sci. Jour., 1982-85. Grantee Acad. of Finland, 1994, 96, 98. Mem. Brit. Ecol. Soc., Soc. for Conservation Biology, Internat. Assn. Landscape Ecology. Lutheran. Avocations: photography, birds on stamps, gardening. Office: U Jyväskylä, PO Box 35, FIN40351 Jyväskylä Finland

KUJAWIŃSKA, COURTNEY KRYSTYNA JOANNA, Shakespeare scholar; b. Łódź, Poland, Mar. 5, 1952; d. Bernard and Helena (Towalska) K. MA, U. Łódź, 1976, PhD, 1985, Habil., 1992. Tchg. asst. U. Łódź, 1976-85, asst. prof., 1985-92, assoc. prof., 1992—, chair dept. Brit. and Commonwealth Studies Ctr., 1993—; vis. scholar U. Tex., Austin, 1988-91, 94-95; assoc. prof. Higher Pedagogical Coll., 1994—; bibliographer for Poland for the World Shakespeare Bibliography, 1981—; tchg. cons. Am. Peace Corps in Poland, 1993; Inst. Internat. Studies coord. Erasmus/Socrates Cultural Network in Europe, Poland, 1998—; part-time assoc. prof. Warsaw U., 1998—; contractor, coord. Tempus-Jep (European Union project in internat. edn.), 1998; convenor internat. confs. Editor: Liberalism: Yesterday and Today, 1998, British Studies: Interdisciplinary Approach, 1997; author: (monographs): Kingdom at Stage: Shakespeare's English History Plays, 1997, Th'Interpretation of Time: The Drama of Shaespeare's Roman Plays, 1992; contbr. articles to profl. jours. Frie-town chair Scouting Orgn., 1972-78. Grantee Kosciuszko Found., 1988, Brit. Coun., 1981, others. Mem. Polish Shakespeare Assn., Am. Shakespeare Assn., European Soc. for Study of English, Łódź Learned Soc. Office: Brit/Commonwlth Studies Ctr, U Lodz, Pl Wolnosci 2, 91-415 Łódź Poland

KUJAWSKI, DANIEL, science educator; b. Bujenka, Poland, Feb. 23, 1948; came to U.S., 1996; s. Jan and Czeslawa Kujawska; m. Danuta Radziszewska, July 14, 1974; 1 child, Anna. MSc, Warsaw (Poland) Tech. U., 1973, DSc, 1992; PhD, Polish Acad. Scis., 1978. Lectr., sr. lectr. Warsaw Tech. U., 1975-89; lectr., sr. rsch. assoc. U. Alta., Edmonton, Can., 1989-96; assoc. prof. Western Mich. U., Kalamazoo, 1996—; co-chmn. low-cycle fatigue com. Polish Group Fracture, 1987-89. Author: (textbook) Fatigue Life of Metals, 1991, (book) Modeling of the Fatigue Life and Crack Propagation in Metals, 1991. Killam postdoctoral scholar U. Alta., Edmonton, 1983-85. Mem. ASME. Avocations: tennis, swimming, walking. Achievements include rsch./testing and modeling of mech. behavior of metals and composites, fatigue and fracture mechanics. Fax: (616) 387-3358. E-mail: daniel.kujawski@wmich.edu. Office: Western Mich U Mech and Aero Engring Kalamazoo MI 49008

KUJAWSKI, ELIZABETH SZANCER, art curator, consultant; b. N.Y.C., Feb. 7, 1951; d. Henryk and Irene (Zilz) Szancer; m. Nathan Kujawski, Mar. 25, 1973; children: Melissa, Stephanie. BA cum laude in Art History and Italian, Douglass Coll., 1972; MA in Art History, Queens Coll., 1975. Info. asst. Whitney Mus. Am. Art, N.Y.C., 1972-75; asst. curator Collection of Nelson A. Rockefeller, N.Y.C., 1975-79; asst. dir. SKT Galleries, Inc., N.Y.C., 1979-82; prin., art curator, cons. Elizabeth S. Kujawski-Curatorial Cons., N.Y.C., 1982—. Mem. Nat. Assn. Corp. Art Mgmt., Assn. Profl. Art Advisors (pres. 1998-2000), Art Table, Inc. Avocations: tennis, piano, travel. Office: 767 5th Ave Ste 4200 New York NY 10153-0023

KUJAWSKI, MARIO JULIO, artist, educator; b. Buenos Aires, Argentina, May 13, 1944; s. Richard and Irma Dorothea K. BA, Brown U., 1966; MA, Ohio State U., 1969. Instr. Dayton (OHio) Art Inst., 1969-71, U. Dayton, 1971-73, Wright State U., Dayton, 1973-75, Montgomery County, Dayton, 1975-81; asst. prof. Kent (Ohio) State U., 1984-91; lectr. Beck Ctr. Arts, Lakewood, Ohio, 1995—; artists adv. bd. New Orgn. Visual Arts, Cleve., 1993-99; workshop leader State of Ohio, Cleve., 1998—; cons. Living Arts Ctr., Dayton, 1974-75. Represented in collections of Dayton Mus. Art, State of Ohio, Chrysler Corp., Sherwin Williams, Mead Data Ctr., Chase Manhattan Bank. Judge Parma (Ohio) City Schs., 1999. Jewish. Avocations: swimming, painting, reading. Studio: 35 Severance Cir Cleveland OH 44118-1504

KUKAL, ZDENEK, geologist; b. Prague, Czech Republic, Nov. 29, 1932; s. Karel and Marie (Urbanova) K.; m. Drahoslava Blazkova, Apr. 10, 1963; 1 child, Zdenek. BSc, MSc, U. Prague, 1955, PhD, 1960, DSc, 1991. Geologist Czech Geol. Survey, Prague, 1955-67, sr. geologist, project engr., 1971-76, 80-90, rsch. dir., 1990-91, dir., 1992-98; assoc. prof. U. Baghdad, Iraq, 1967-70; prof. geology U. Kuwait, 1977-80, Charles U. Coll. Sci., Prague, 1980-94; chief geologist State Orgn. for Minerals, Baghdad, 1976-77; reader Commenium Acad. Sci., Prague, 1970-94; mem. R&D Coun., Govt. of Czech Rep., 1994—. Author: High-Percentage Limestones, 1957 (Lord Mayor of Prague award 1957), Geology of Recent Sediments, 1971, Atlantis, 1980 (Czechoslovak Lit. Found. award 1980), Natural Catastrophes, 1983 (Czechoslovak Lit. Found. award 1983), Atlantis in the Light of Modern Research, 1985, Principles of Oceanography, 1986, The Rate of Geological Processes, 1989. Roman Catholic. Avocations: music, sports. Office: Czech Geol Survey, Klarov 3, 11821 Prague Czech Republic

KUKAN, EDUARD, Slovakian government official; b. Trnovec nad Vahom, West Slovakia, Dec. 26, 1939; married; 2 children. Student, Moscow Inst. Internat. Rels., Charles U., Prague, Czechoslovakia. With Czechoslovakian Fgn. Svc., 1964, mem. Africa dept., 1964-68; with Czechoslovakian Embassy in Zambia, 1968-73; mem. Secretariat of Min. of Fgn. Affairs, 1973-77; min. counsellor Czechoslovakian Embassy in U.S.A., 1977-81; head Dept. of Sub-Saharan Africa, 1981-85; amb. to Ethiopia Govt. of Czechoslovakia, 1985-88, permanent rep. to U.N., 1990-93; min. of fgn. affairs Govt. of Slovakia, Bratislavia, 1994, mem. of Parliament, 1994—; chmn. Dem. Union of Slovakia, Bratislavia, 1997-98; dep. chmn. Slovak Dem. Coalition, 1998; minister of fgn. affairs Slovak Republic, 1998—; spl. envoy for Balkans UN Sec. Gen., 1999; permanent rep. of Slovakia to UN, 1993-94. Mem. Slovak Dem. Christian Union, 2000. Office: Min Fgn Affairs, Hlboka Cesta 2, 833 36 Bratislava Slovakia

KUKHTIN, VALERII VASIL'EVICH, physicist; b. L. Rossosh, Voronezh, Russia, Sept. 10, 1939; s. Vasilii Kuz'mich and Anna Pavlovna (Surova) K.; m. Lidiya Aleksandrovna Znosko-Borovskaya, July 15, 1961; children: Tanya, Natasha. BS, Engring.-Phys. Inst., Moscow, 1962; PhD, Inst. Math., Kiev, 1969. Engr. Inst. Mechanics, Kiev, 1962-64; sci. worker Inst. Theoretical Physics, Kiev, 1964-99, sci. sec., 1972-76. Contbr. more than 40 articles to profl. jours. Mem. Narodnyi Rukh, Kiev, 1989-92. Mem. Ukrainian Phys. Soc., Ukrainian Biophys. Soc. Avocations: music, football, chess. Home: 16 Sofievska Str Apt 33, 252001 Kiev Ukraine

KUKIELCZAK, BARBARA MARIOLA, research scientist; b. Rabka, Poland, Aug. 25, 1965; d. Jerzy and Jadwiga (Garbiec) K. MSc, Jagiellonian U., Krakow, Poland, 1989, postgrad., 1990-95, PhD, 1995. Rsch. asst. Jagiellonian U., Krakow, 1990; rsch. dept. specialist Cosmetic Factory Miraculum, Krakow, 1995-96; rsch. asst. Oncology Ctr., Krakow, 1997; vis. fellow Nat. Inst. Environ. Health Scis., Research Triangle Park, N.C., 1997—. Author: Current Topics of Biophysics, 1995, Klinika Oczna, 1995, Photochemistry and Photobiology, 1998, Melanoma Research, 1999. Mem. Am. Soc. Photobiology. Roman Catholic. Avocations: reading, playing the piano, tennis, cooking, hiking. Office: Nat Inst Environ Health Scis 111 Alexander Dr Research Triangle Park NC 27709

KUKLIN, RUDOLF NIKITICH, physical chemist, researcher; b. Kirov, Russia, Jan. 2, 1939; s. Nikita Fedorovich and Tatjana Vasiljevna (Slobodina) K.; m. Alla Georgievna Pechorova, Jan. 18, 1975; children: Vasilii, Lioubov. Grad., Fisico-tech. Inst., Moscow, 1966, candidat in scis., 1969. Rsch. scientist Kvant State Rsch. and Prodn. Assn., Moscow, 1966-94; educator in theoretical physics Krupskaya Pedagogicheskii Inst., Moscow, 1970-76; sr. rsch. scientist Russian Acad. Scis Frumkin Inst. Electrochemistry, Moscow, 1995—. Inventor: Radiation Transitions in Heated Nuclei, Jadernaya Fisica, 1967 Relay-race Transport of Iones through membranes (with others) Biofisica, 1971, Interaction between ions in Electrolytes, Elektrokhimiya, 1977, Energy of Solvated Electron, Cation. Anion Electrokhimiya, 1979, Compact part of electrical double layer of metal electrolyte interface, Elektrokhimiya, 1978, 96. Electronic Structure of Nickel Hydroxides, 1991, Potential of "Disjoining" Forces, 1997, Contribution of the Solvent Surface Polarisation ot Properties of the Metal-Electrolyte Interface, 1998, Resonance Nature of Instabilities at the Boundaries of the Region of Electrode Idial Polarisabily, 2000. Grantee: Soroc Found., Moscow, 1994. Avocations: automobiles, gardening. Home: Krasnyi Mayak St 8-2-483, 113519 Moscow Russia Office: Russian Acad Scis Inst Elec, Leninskii Prospekt 31, 117071 Moscow Russia

KUKSTAS-VINCENT, LUCY ANNA, scientific communications company executive; b. Selsley, U.K., Feb. 2, 1958; arrived in France, 1980; d. Jonas Vilhelmas and Lesley Rosemary (Hughes0 Kukstas; m. Florian Perier (div. 1992); children: Anna, Darry; m. Jean-Didier Vincent, June 19, 1993; 1 child, Felicity. BSc, Sheffield (Eng.) U., 1979; DEA, U. Bordeaux II, France, 1988, PhD, 1991. Rschr. CNRS, Paris, 1991-92; mktg. dir. Item-Labo, Paris, 1992-94; gen. dir. Lunik, Bordeaux, France, 1994—; cons. Servier Lab., Paris, 1998—. Author: La Forme et la Frime, 1998. Mem. Soc. Neurosci., N.Y. Acad. Scis. Office: BP 32, 33880 Cambes France

KUKURIN, GORAN, hospitality company executive, consultant; b. Rijeka, Croatia, May 10, 1968; s. Ivan and Biserka (Kranjcec) K.; m. Sanja Zovic, May 27, 1995; children: Toni, Luka. Diploma in elec. engring., computer sci., U. Elec. Engring., Zagreb, Croatia, 1992. CEO Konte d.o.o., Porec, Croatia, 1992-93, gen. mgr., 1993—. Avocation: golf. Office: Konte d o o, Zagrebacka 1, 52440 Porec Croatia

KULA, EMANUEL, forestry educator, researcher; b. Ústí, Bohemia, Czech Republic, Jan. 5, 1951; s. Emanuel and Markéta (Lejčková) K.; m. Hana Mlčochová, Nov. 15, 1975; children: Petr, Jan. Degree in Engring., Faculty Forestry, Brno, Czech Republic, 1974, PhD, 1979, assoc. prof., 1986. Forest mgr. Forest Enterprise, Dobříš, Czech Republic, 1974-75; tchr. Faculty Forestry, Brno, 1975-90; rschr. faculty forestry and wood tech. Mendel U. Agr. and Forestry, Brno, 1990—; tchr. faculty of the environment Jan Evangelista Purkyně, Ústí, Czech Republic, 1999—. Author 2 textbooks; editor Zoology and Entomology, 1984, Forest Protection and Phytopathology, 1985; contbr. articles to profl. jours. Recipient Gold medal Agrl. U., Nitra, Slovak Republic, 1987. Avocations: hunting, photography, poetry, traveling, gardening. Office: Faculty Forestry & Wood, Zemědělská 3, 613 00 Brno Czech Republic

KULA, ERHUN IBRAHIM, economist, educator, writer; b. Istanbul, Turkey, Jan. 4, 1945; arrived in U.K., 1972; s. Nuri and Turkan (Ergur) K.; m. Karen Williams, June 21, 1979; children: Adam, Suzan. BSc, Marmara U., Istanbul, 1969; MSc, U. Swansea, Wales, 1976; PhD, U. Leicester, Eng., 1980. Ins. assessor Guven PLC, Istanbul, 1969; lt. Turkish Armed Forces, 1969-71; ins. assessor Guven PLC, Istanbul, 1971-72; lectr. U. Swansea, Wales, 1980-82, New U. Ulster, Coleraine, Ireland, 1982-84; sr. lectr. U. Ulster, Belfast, Ireland, 1984—; vis. prof. U. N. Mex., 1992, U. Bosphorus, Istanbul, 1995; course dir. postgrad. studies in econs., U. Ulster, 1998—. Author: Economics of Natural Resources, Environment and Policies, 1994, Investment and Project Appraisal, 1995, Time Discounting and Future Generations, 1997, History of Environmental Economic Thought, 1998; contbr. numerous articles to sci. jours. Mem. European Assn. Agrl. Economists, Agrl. Economics Assn., N.Y. Acad. Scis. Avocations: cycling, hill walking, reading. Office: Univ Ulster, Shore Rd Newtown Abbey, Belfast BT37 0QB, Ireland

KULA, JAN MARCIN, historian; b. Warsaw, Poland, Mar. 24, 1943; s. Witold and Nina (Jablonska) K.; m. Malgorzata Mscislawa Ciszecka, Dec. 2, 1972; children: Grzegorz, Agnieszka. MA, U. Warsaw, 1965; PhD Inst. History, Polish Acad. Scis., Warsaw, 1968, Habil. Inst. History, 1976. Rschr. Inst. History, Polish Acad. Scis., Warsaw, 1968-90; prof. Warsaw U., 1990—. Author: The Black Slavery in Brazil During the Sugar Cycle, 1970, The 1933 Revolution at Cuba, 1978, History of Brazil, 1987, The National and the Revolutionary, 1991. Mem. Polish Pen Club. E-mail: Kula1943@Plearn.edu.pl. Home: Klaudyny 34/116, 01-684 Warsaw Poland Office: Univ of Warsaw Inst History, Krakowskie Przed 26/28, 00-927 Warsaw Poland

KULA, KATHERINE SUE, dentist; b. Dayton, Ohio, Oct. 5, 1945; d. James Adam and Adelaide Charlotte (Thaler) Miller; m. Theodore John Kula Jr., Aug. 2, 1969; children: Stacy Charlotte, Theodore John III. BS, U. Dayton, 1966, MS, 1972; DMD, U. Ky., 1977; MS, cert. in pediat. dentistry, U. Iowa, 1979; cert. in orthodontics, U. Md., 1992. Sci. tchr. Lexington (Ky.) Cath. High Sch., 1969-71, chmn. sci. dept., 1971-73; resident U. Iowa Dental Sch., Iowa City, 1977-79; asst. prof. U. Md. Dental Sch., Balt., 1979-84, assoc. prof., 1984-92; assoc. prof. depts. orthodontics and pediatric dentistry U. N.C. Dental Sch., Chapel Hill, 1992-97, adj. prof., 1998—; chair dept.orthodontics & dentofacial orthopedics U. Mo., Kansas City, 1998—; mem. staff U. N.C. Hosp., Chapel Hill, 1992-97, dental faculty practice, 1992-98; outside grant reviewer NIH-NIDR, Washington, 1993—; manuscript reviewer Pediatric Dentistry Jour., Chgo., 1982—. Contbr. articles to profl. jours. and chpts. to books. Bd. dirs. Bridges-Leadership for Women, Chapel Hill, 1995-96. Grantee NIH-Nat. Insts. Dental Rsch., 1994, Am. Assn. Dental Schs., 1997. Fellow Am. Coll. Dentists, Am. Acad. Pediatric Dentists, Am. Acad. Pediatric Dentists (1st Pl. award table clinic ednl. rsch. found. 1994, rsch. award 1980); mem. Md. Soc. Dentistry for Children (pres., sec.-treas. 1979-92), Am. Assn. Dental Rsch. (sec.-treas. Balt. sect. 1979-92, Am. Assn. Dental Schs. (sec., chair, councilor orthodontics sect. 1993-2000, 1st pl. ednl. award 2000), Am. Assn. Orthodontists, Nat. Insts. Dental Rsch. Avocations: youth baseball and basketball. Office: U Mo Dental Sch Dept Orthodontics & Dentofacial Orthopedics Kansas City MO 64108

KULBACHINSKII, VLADIMIR ANATOLIEVICH, physics educator; b. Rasskazovo, Tambov, Russia, Dec. 7, 1947; s. Anatolii Nikolaevich and Lidiya Aleksandrovna (Chernushova) K.; m. Marina Vladimirovna Novakovskaya, Jan. 19, 1976; children: Andrei, Sergei. Degree in Physics, Moscow State U., 1972, PhD, 1978, DSc, 1991. Aspirant Moscow State U., 1972-75, sr. scientist, 1972-85, asst. prof., 1985-87, dozent, 1987-91, prof., 1991—. Contbr. articles to profl. jours. Soros grantee, 1996, 97, 98. Mem. Material Rsch. Soc., Internat. Thermoelectric Soc. Avocations: English, bicycling, fishing, computers, traveling. Office: Low Temperature, Moscow State U Dept Physics, 119899 Moscow Russia

KULCSÁR, GYULA, biochemist, researcher; b. Nagykanizsa, Hungary, Nov. 18, 1951; s. György and Anna (Kiskörösi) K.; m. Magdolna Szemler, July 31, 1978; children: Gabriella, Péter István. MSc, József Attila U. Scis., Szeged, Hungary, 1979, PhD, U. Med. Sch. Pécs, Hungary, 1997. Cert. rsch. chemist. Rsch. asst. Rsch. Group Chemistry Hungarian Acad. Scis., Pécs, 1979-81; asst. lectr. Inst. Biochemistry, U. Med. Sch., Pécs, 1981-93, asst. prof., 1993—; advisor Immunal Ltd., Budapest, 1993—. Inventor cancer biotherapy, 1995, cancer biotherapy and radiopharms., 1997; patentee in field. Mem. Internat. Soc. for Preventive Oncology, Hungarian Biochem. Soc., Hungarian Biol. Soc., N.Y. Acad. Scis. Avocations: computers, classical music, reading, soccer. Office: Inst Biochem U Med Sch Pecs, Szigeti ut 12, H-7624 Pécs Hungary

KULCSÁR-GERGELY, JUDITH, pharmacology educator; b. Szeged, Hungary, Feb. 27, 1927; d. Miklós and Alice (Reitzer) G.; m. András Kulcsár, Sept. 19, 1954; children: Lajos, Julia. Mg. Pharmaciae, Szeged (Hungary) U., 1950, Dr. Pharmaciae, 1958; Spl. Pharmacol. Toxicol., Budapest (Hungary) U., 1973; PhD, Budapest Hungarian Sci. Acad., DSc, 1982. Asst. prof. Szeged (Hungary) U., 1950-54; asst. prof. Med. U. Debrecen (Hungary), 1954-62, sr. lectr., 1962-81, full prof. pharmacology, 1982—. Contbr. articles to profl. jours. Recipient prize Hungarian Gastroenterol. Soc., 1979, 1991, prevention and therapy of osteoporosis prize Pharmacy, 1989. Mem. Hungarian Pharm. Soc. (Than Károly prize 1972, Gyory István prize 1986, bd. dirs. 1988—, pres. Drug Rsch. Assn. 1992—, Millecentenarim award 1996), Hungarian Med. Acad., Internat. Found. Allergy and Immunology Soc., Internat. Soc. Endocrinology, N.Y. Acad. Sci. Home: Piac u 43, 4023 Debrecen Hungary Office: Med U Debrecen, Nagyerdei krt 98, 4032 Debrecen Hungary

KULEMIN, GENNADY PETROVICH, research scientist; b. Uljanovsk, Russia, June 5, 1937; s. Peter Dmitrievich and Evdokia Jakovlevna Kulemin; m. Tamara Nikolaevna Harchenko, Aug. 23, 1968; 1 child, Jury. Engr., Kharkov Polytechnic Inst., 1960; candidate sci., Kharkov Mil. U., 1971; DS (hon.), Kharkov Aviation Inst., 1987. Asst. Kharkov (Ukraine) Aviation Inst., 1960-66; rschr. Inst. Radiophysics Electronics NAS, Kharkov, 1966-96, leading rschr. Inst. Radiophysics Electronics, 1996—; prof. Kharkov Aviation Inst., 1992-96, Kharkov Mil. U., 1996—. Author: The Scattering of Millimeter Waves by the Earth's Surface For Grazing Angles, 1987, Sinelnikov's prize, 1993; contbr. articles to profl. jours. Mem. URSI Commn. F, Internat. Acad. Sci. of Applied Electronics. Home: Lenin Ave 31-6 Apt 35, 310086 Kharkov Ukraine Office: Inst Radiophysics & Electr, Oc Proskura St 12, 310085 Kharkov Ukraine

KULESZA, CHESTER STEPHEN (BUD KULESZA), finance executive; b. Elizabeth, N.J., Jan. 12, 1947; s. Chester S. and Mary Ellen (Sales) K.; m. Kathleen Marie Hickman, June 14, 1969; children: Kevin Michael, Marie Kathleen. AAS in Acctg., Middlesex County Coll., Edison, N.J., 1969; BS in Commerce, Rider U., 1973. Cert. mgmt. acct. Inst. Mgmt. Accts., cert. fin. mgmt. With fin./acctg. depts. Johnson & Johnson, New Brunswick, N.J., 1969-73; asst. contr. ITT Automotive Morton Frozen Foods, Charlottesville, Va., 1973-81; sr. fin. mgr. RJR Delmonte Frozen Foods, San Francisco, 1981-83; v.p., contr. ITT Automotive Bus. & Consumer Comm., Raleigh, N.C., 1983-86; CFO, contr. ITT Automotive Electromech. Components, Fountain Valley, Calif., 1986-90; sr. v.p. fin. ITT Automotive-Worldwide, Auburn Hills, Mich., 1990—; presenter XV World Congress of Accountancy, 1997. Author of book foreword: The Practice Analysis of Management Accounting, 1996; contbr. articles to profl. jours. Chmn. acctg. and fin. adv. bd. Oakland U., Rochester, Mich., 1994—; mem. bus. adv. curriculum com. Detroit Coll. of Bus., Dearborn, Mich., 1996—; mem. acctg. accreditation com. Internat. Assn. Mgmt. Edn., St. Louis, 1997; lay leader, mem. adminstrv. bd., fin. com. Howarth United Meth. Ch., Lake Orion, Mich., 1997. With U.S. Army, 1964-67. Honoree Beta Gamma Sigma, 1997. Mem. Inst. Mgmt. Accts. (nat. pres. 1999—, bd. dirs.), Fin. Execs. Inst. (chair acad. rels. com. Detroit chpt. 1995—), Beta Alpha Psi (hon.). Republican. Avocations: accounting education, wine tasting, gourmet cooking, travel, choir. Home: 10301 Rhett Butler Dr Austin TX 78739-1674 Office: ITT Automotive 3000 University Dr Auburn Hills MI 48326-2356

KULEZNEV, VALERY NIKOLAEVICH, chemistry educator; b. Nijnii Taguil, Russia, Apr. 13, 1933; s. Nikolai Adrianovich and Taissiya Pavlovna (Kozina) K.; m. Margarita Vassil'eva, July 4, 1959; children: Evguenii, Julia. Degree in chem. engring., Lomonssov Inst. Chem. Tech., Moscow, 1955, PhD, 1959, DSc, 1974. Cert. chem. engr., polymer chemistry and processing. Engr. Lomonossov Inst. Fine Chem. Tech., Moscow, 1959-60, sr. rschr., 1961-64, assoc. prof., 1964-65, prof. polymer chemistry and physics, 1975-78, head chair plastics processing and chemistry, 1978—; asst. prof. Ural State U., Sverdlovsk, 1960-61; dep. editor Kolloidnii Jour., Moscow, 1964-65; mem. editl. bd. Polymers and Polymer Composites, Eng., 1998—, Elastomers and Rubber, Moscow, 1988—, Plastics, Moscow, 1992—. Author: Polystyrene. Plastics and Chemistry of Synthesis and Processing, 1975, Polymer

Mixtures. Structure and Properties, 1980, The Chemistry and Physics of Polymers, 1990; editor, author: Fundamentals of Plastics Processing, 1995. Mem. Meml., Russia, 1995—. Recipient V.A. Karguin prize Acad. Sci. USSR, 1990; named Hon. Chemist and Technologist, Pres. of Russia, 1994, Hon. Chemist Chem. Industry USSR, Ministry of Chemistry, 1980. Mem. Moscow House of Scientists, N.Y. Acad. Scis. Orthodox. Avocations: mountain tourism, Beethoven and Tchaikovsky, detective novels. E-mail: kulezner@unesco.mitht.rssi.ru. Home: Block 4 Apt 37, Bolotnikovskaya St 40, 113209 Moscow Russia Office: Moscow State U Chem Tech, Vernadskii Prospekt 86, 117571 Moscow Russia

KULHARA, PARMANAND, psychiatry educator; b. Balauda Bazar, India, Oct. 2, 1946; s. Babu Lal and Leelawati (Garewal) K.; m. Madhu Sahukar, Nov. 25, 1978; children: Madhur, Ritu. MB BChir, Govt. Med. Coll., Jabalpur, India, 1968; MD in Psychiatry, PGIMER, Chandigarh, 1972. Resident psychiatry PGIMER, Chandigarh, 1970-72, additional prof., 1983-99; sr. ho. officer Guy's Hosp., London, 1973-74, registrar, 1974; sr. registrar Manchester (Eng.) Area Health Authority, 1974-77; cons. N.W. Regional Health Authority, Manchester, 1977-83; prof., 1999—. Editor Indian Jour. Social Psychiatry. Recipient Dr. Vidya Sagar award Indian Coun. Med. Rsch., New Delhi, 1989, Marfatia award Indian Psychiat. Soc., 1999, Poona Psychiatrists Soc. award Indian Psychiat. Soc., 1999. Fellow Royal Coll. Psychiatrists London, Acad. Med. Scis. India. Office: Dept Psychiatry, PGIMER Sector 12, Chandigarh 160 012, India

KULICZKOWSKI, KAZIMIERZ, hematologist, consultant; b. Bystrzyca, Poland, Sept. 28, 1947; s. Władysław Kuliczkowski and Janina Surowiak; m. Danuta Aleksandra Smaron, Dec. 21, 1972; children: Wiktor, Justyna. MD, Med. Sch., Poland, 1971, PhD, 1977. Diplomate in Hematology, Polish Bd. Internal Medicine. Asst. Med. Acad., Wrocław, 1971-78, adj. prof., 1978-92, assoc. prof., 1992—; prof. pathology H.S. of Sports, Wrocław, 1995-98, head dept. hematology, 1998—. Home: Chorwacka 56/13, 51-107 Wrocław Poland

KULIK, ILIA ALEXANDROVICH, figure skater; b. Moscow, May 23, 1977; s. Alexander and Nadyezhda K. Amature figure skater, 1984-99, profl. figure skater, 1999—; with Stars on Ice; mem. Russian Nat. Figure Skating Team, 1992—. Recipient Gold medal Olympic Games, Nagano, Japan, 1998. Avocations: dancing, music. Office: C/O Michael V Carlisle Carlisle & Co LLC 24 E 64th St New York NY 10021*

KULIK, LIAT, social science educator; b. Suceava-Burdujena, Romania, Sept. 11, 1954; d. Haim and Seina (Tigelnic) Kasapu; m. Yeudah Kulik; children: Hagit, Shlomi, Tali. BA, Bar-Ilan U., Ramat-Gan, Israel, 1976, PhD, 1992; MS, Israel Inst. Tech., Haifa, 1980. Rschr. in social sci. Israel Ministry of Labor, Tel Aviv, 1980-94; lectr. Askelon (Israel) Coll., 1994-98, Bar-Ilan U., 1986—. Rsch. grantee Nat. Insvc., Jerusalem, Israel Ministry of Labor, Jerusalem. Home: Hevron 12, Bnei-Brak Israel Office: Bar-Ilan U, Sch Social Work, 52900 Ramat Gan Israel

KULIKOV, MICHAEL NIKOLAEVICH, physics educator; b. Saratov, Russia, Aug. 23, 1935; s. Nikolay Nikolaevich and Olga Eugenyevna (Nechayeva) K.; m. Margarita Vasilyevna Praslova, Mar. 8, 1958; 1 child, Vladimir. Degree in physics cum laude, Saratov (Russia) State U., 1958, PhD in Physics and Math., 1967. Rschr. Inst. Mechanics and Physics, Saratov, 1958-70; assoc. prof. dept. gen. physics Saratov State U., 1970-95, prof., 1995—; sec. commn. physics and electronics Volga Regional Coordination Coun. Russian Acad. Scis., 1986-91. Contbr. articles to sci. publs. Avocations: Russian history. Home: Bolshaya Kazatchya, 59/65-131, 410600 Saratov Russia Office: Saratov State U Dp Gen Phys, Astrakhanskaya 83, 410071 Saratov Russia

KULING, JOSEPH MARIE, information technology company executive; b. The Hague, The Netherlands, Aug. 23, 1929; s. Petrus Johannes and Johanna Maria (de Groot) K.; m. Catharina Maria Ponsen, May 31, 1955; children: Diederick M.A., Jessica A.M., Colette M.C., Joseph M., Clemetine J.M., Marnix A.E. BSc in, Acad. for Arts-Architecture, The Hague, 1951; postgrad., Acad. for Arts-Architecture, Rotterdam, The Netherlands., 1953. Draftsman v. Eck Concrete Constrn., The Hague, 1951-54; draftsman, constructor Nedam, The Hague, 1954-59; freelance constructor and draftsman, The Hague, 1959-61; exec. Tech. Bur. Enterprise, Nijmegen, The Netherlands, 1961-68, N.V. Tech. Bur. Kuling, Oeffelt, The Netherlands, 1968—. Mem. Christian Democrat Party. Roman Catholic. Avocations: music, sailing, reading. Home and Office: Hapseweg 5A, 5441 PA Oeffelt N Br, The Netherlands

KULINSKY, VLADIMIR ILICH, biochemist, educator; b. Kharkov, USSR, Feb. 15, 1932; s. Ilya Naumovich and Eugene Alexeevna (Lubeshko) K.; m. Inna Lipovna Berger, Mar. 21, 1953 (div. 1982); children: Elena, Anatol; m.Larisa Stanislavovna, Feb. 10, 1984. Physician, Medical Inst., Kharkov, USSR, 1955, cand., 1961; DSc, USSR Acad. Medical Sci., Moscow, 1971; prof., Medical Inst., Krasnoyarsk, USSR, 1973. Asst. Inst. Physician Improvement, Kharkov, 1959-62, docent, 1962-71; prof. biochemistry Medical Inst., Krasnoyarsk, USSR, 1971-89, Medical Univ., Irkutsk, Russia, 1989—. Contbr. articles to profl. jours. Grantee Internat. Sci. Found., 1993, State Sci. Program, Moscow, 1994-99, Internat. Soros Sci. Edn. Program, 1994-97, Russian Found. Fund. Invest., 1997-2000, State Sci. Stipendiary, 1997-2000. Mem. N.Y. Acad. Sci., Acad. Nauk Higher Sch. Avocations: Russian poetry, church architecture, chess. E-mail: kulinsky@ppirkuts.ru. Home: PO Box 2556, 664047 Irkutsk Russia Office: Irkutsk State Med Univ, Krasnogo Vosstaniya Str 1, 664003 Irkutsk Russia

KULISH, VICTOR VASYLIOVYCH, physicist; b. Medyka, Poland, Apr. 19, 1946; arrived in USSR, 1947; s. Vasyl Onysimovych and Poline Abramovna (Kravetz) K.; m. Svitlana Dmytrivna Muromtzeva, Mar. 27, 1971; 1 child, Vladymyr Victorovych. BS, Lviv Coll. Radioelectronics, Ukraine, 1965, Moscow Energetical Inst., 1969; MS, Moscow Energetical Inst., 1972; PhD, Kyiv State U., Ukraine, 1978; DSc, Inst. Physics, Ukraine, 1986. Sr. engr. Istok, Moscow, 1972-77, Kyiv State U., 1977-80; head of dept. Simpheropol Bldg. Inst., Ukraine, 1980-88, Sumy (Ukraine) State U., 1988—; expert Govt. of Ukraine, 1993-97. Patentee in field of relativistic electrodynamics; contbr. articles to profl. jours. Mem. Acad. Higher Edn., Acad. Engring. Scis. Office: Sumy State U, 2 Rymski Korsakov, 244007 Sumy Ukraine

KULISIEWICZ, MACIEJ WACLAW, educator; b. Zdunska Wola, Łódź, Poland, May 23, 1946; s. Zdzislaw and Hanna (Michalska) K.; m. Jozefa Bober, Sept. 23, 1975; children: Damian, Magdalena. MSc, Wroclaw (Poland) U. Tech., 1969, PhD, 1975, DSc, 1986. Cert. engring. Asst. Wroclaw U. Tech., 1969-75, asst. prof. mechanics and mech. vibrations, 1975-86, assoc. prof., 1987-92, prof., 1993—. Author: Modeling and Identification Methodology of Dynamic Mechanical Systems, 1994; contbr. articles to profl. jours. Mem. Polish Assn. Theoretical and Applied Mechanics. Fax: 48-71-211235. E-mail: M.Kulisiewicz@immt.pwr.wroc.pl. Home: Szewczenki 28d, 51-351 Wrocław Poland Office: Wrocław U Tech, Wybrzeze Wyspianskiego 27, 50-370 Wrocław Poland

KULIY, TARAS, physicist, educator, researcher; b. Lviv, Ukraine, Aug. 6, 1965; s. Ilarion Volodymyr Yaroslav and Halyna Kuliy; m. Luyiza Kopchak, July 11, 1992; children: Volodymyr, Yaroslav. MSc in Physics with honors, Ivan Franko State U. of Lviv, 1989, PhD in Theoritical Physics, 1999. Tchr. physics Ivan Franko State U. of Lviv, 1989—, docent, 99—. Contbr. articles to profl. jours. Mem. Ukrainian Phys. Soc. E-mail: kuliy@ktf.franko.lviv.ua. Home: vul Kopernika 47-15, UA-79000 Lviv Ukraine Office: Ivan Franko Nat U Lviv, vul Drahomanova 12, UA-79005 Lviv Ukraine

KULJANIN, SPASOJE, international trading company executive; b. Konjic, Bih, Yugoslavia, May 24, 1948; came to U.S., 1984; s. Luka and Desa (Magazin) K.; m. Dusanka Zelenovic, Dec. 21, 1971; children: Zana, Goran. M in Internat. Fin.; B of Economy, U. Sarajevo, Bosnia, 1972, Master's, 1979; degree in law, U. Belgrade, Serbia, 1976. Cons. UNIS-Igman, Konjic, Bosnia, 1972-84, mgr., 1976-78, v.p., 1978-83; v.p. UNIS Internat. Corp., Chgo., 1984-88; dir. comml. bank UNIS, Sarajevo, 1988-91; exec. dir. UNIS Holding, Sarajevo, 1991-92; v.p. Suntomo Tech. Inc., Elk Grove, Ill., 1992—; mem. adv. bd. UNIS Holding, Sarajevo, 1988-92, Nat. Bank Bosnia, Sarajevo, 1990-92. Author: Foreigner's Investment, 1989. Mem. Parliament, Sarajevo, 1990-92. Avocations: soccer, basketball, reading. Home: 5014 Church St Apt 301 Skokie IL 60077-1252

KULKA, JIRI, psychologist; b. Ostrava, Czech Republic, Dec. 8, 1950; s. Oldrich and Zdenka (Haschkova) K.; m. Jarmila Indrychova, Aug. 25, 1973; children: Radmila, Katerina. Degree in psychology, Masaryk U., Brno, Czech Republic, 1975, degree in musicology, 1986, PhD, 1977. Asst. prof. psychology Masaryk U., Brno, Czech Republic, 1972-85, Janacek Acad. Music, Brno, Czech Republic, 1982-90; dir. ARCANA, Soc. Health, Beauty & Personal Growth, Brno, Czech Republic, 1990—, ArcaNova Ltd., Brno, Czech Republic, 1995—; prof. Brno Inst. Graphoanalysis, 1996—; mgr. ARCANA Pub., Brno, 1990-97; dir. Czech-German Inst. of Positive Psychotherapy, 1998—. Author: Psychology of Art, 1991, Leos Janacek Aesthetic Thinking, 1990, Graphology, 1991, Methods of Social Psychology, 1983. Sec. Soc. Leos Janacek, Brno, 1988. Mem. Czech-Moravian Psychol. Soc., Brno Inst. Graphoanalysis. E-mail: kulka@arcana.cz. Office: ArcaNova Ltd, Kounicova 23, 602 00 Brno Czech Republic

KULKARNI, ARUIND GANESH, physician, educator; b. Malegaon, India, June 5, 1968; s. Ganesh Gopal and Saraswati Ganesh K.; m. Sunanda Arvind Chipalunicar Kulkarni, July 4, 1973; 2 children. MBBS, Miras Med. Coll., India, 1966; MD, Postgrad. Inst., Chandigarh, India, 1971. Lectr. PGI MER, Chandigarh, India, 1972-82; sr. lectr. head ABG Univ., Zaria, Nigeria, 1982-86; prof. KIMS, Karad, India, 1987-99; prof., head M&M Med. Coll., Kamothe, India, 1999—. Author over 60 papers in various national and international jours. Fellow Internat. Soc. Haematology, Internat. Soc. Blood Transfusion, Indian Soc. Blood Transfusion, Indian. Soc. Med. and Paediatric, N.Y. Acad. Scis. Avocations: chess, tennis. Home phone: 7423406. Office phone: 022-7423029. Home: Mahan Daulat Flat 15 Sec 3E, Kalamboli India Office: M&M Med Coll, Junct NH4 & Sion Panwel Hwy, Kamote 410209, India

KULKARNI, ASHOK BALKRISHNA, electronics educator; b. Bijapur, Karnataka, India, Aug. 8, 1948; s. Balkrishna Dadarao and Sudha Balkrishna Kulkarni; m. Lalita Ashok Chandriki, June 24, 1973; children: Anup, Aparna. BSc, Agra (India) U., 1966; MSc, Karnataka U., Kurukshetra, India, 1969, PhD, 1979; DMM, Punjabi U., Patiala, India, 1984. Rsch. fellow CSIR and Dept. Atomic Energy, Bombay, India, 1970-72; lectr. in physics Meerut U., 1972-83; reader in physics Gulbarga (India) U., 1983-87, prof., chmn. applied electronics dept., 1987—; pres. U. Gymkhana, Gulbarga, 1985-86. Editor: Recent Advanced in Electronic Materials, Devices and Systems, 1999; mem. editl. bd. Asian Jour. Physics, 1995—; contbr. articles to profl. jours. Rsch. grantee govt. of India, 1989—. Fellow Inst. Electronics and Telecomm. Engrs., United Writers Assn.; mem. India Assn. for Crystal Growth, N.V. Ednl. Soc. (life), Indian Soc. Tech. Edn. (life), Indian Physics Assn. Avocations: bridge, singing, reading, collecting coins, excursions. Home: Ashirwad MIG 3, II Phase Adarshnagar, Gulbarga Karnataka 585 105, India Office: Gulbarga U, Dept Applied Electronics, Gulbarga Karnataka 585 106, India

KULKARNI, JAYANT RAMCHANDRA, physiatrist; b. Bombay, Dec. 3, 1953; arrived in Eng., 1982; s. Ramchandra Anant and Sita Ramchandra K.; m. Valerie Christine Shaw, May 25, 1985; 1 child, Anita. MB, BChir, U. Bombay, 1979, CM in Orthop. with honors, 1982. Tutor in orthop. U. Bombay, 1981-82; surg. rotation Nat. Health Svc., Eng., 1983-86; cons. Nat. Health Svc., Manchester, Eng., 1991—; sr. registrar Dept. Health, Leeds, Eng., 1987-90; cons. rehab. medicine U. South Manchester; hon. lectr. U. Salford, 1991—, U. Manchester, 1994—. Co-author: Prescribing Upper Limb Prosthesis, 1994; contbr. articles to profl. jours. Fellow Royal Coll. Surgeons, Royal Coll. Physicians; mem. British Soc. Rehab. Medicine, British Med. Assn., Rotary (pres. 1997-98). Avocations: tennis, glass engraving, dogs. Office: Univ South Manchester, Withington Hosp Nell Ln, Manchester M20 8LB, England

KULKARNI, KUMAR BALKRISHNA, pediatrician; b. Satara, India, Nov. 1, 1943; s. Balkrishna Vasudev and Kusum Balkrishna K.; m. Kamal Kumar Ketkar, Jan. 21, 1972; children: Parijat, Niranjan. MBBS, Seth G.S. Med. Coll., Bombay, 1968; diploma in child health, Coll. Physicians Surgeons, Bombay, 1971. Pediatrician Sanjivani Nursing Home for Children, Gwalior, India, 1973—; rschr. clin. pediatrics Sanjivani Nursing Home for Children, Gwalior, 1980—; hon. lectr. physiology Vasundhara Raje Homeopathic Coll., Gwalior, 1996; with Ednl. Coun. Fgn. Med. Grads., 1973; spkr. in field; presenter in field. Contbr. over 68 articles to profl. publ.; author of poetry. Mem. Environment Cell, Gwalior, 1990-91. Recipient Soviet Land Quiz prize, 1984, Essay Competition prize, 1985. Mem. Indian Acad. Pediat. (Gwalior br. sec. 1993-94, mem. scientific com. 1996), Indian Med. Assn. (Outstanding Person 1996), N.Y. Acad. Scis. Achievements include research in controlling water loss in acute pediatric diarrhoea. Avocations: literature, languages, debate, writing poetry, singing. Home: Swami Vivekanand Marg, 3 Bank Colony, Gwalior 474001, India Office: Swami Vivekanand Marg, Sanjivani Nursing Home, Gwalior 474001, India

KULKARNI, MADAN, literature educator; b. Nagpur, India, June 26, 1942; s. Pandurang Krishanaji and Shantabai Pandurang Kulkarni; m. Arati Madan Kulkarni, June 15, 1967; children: Nirzar, Nitin. BA, Nagpur U., 1962, MA in Marathi, 1965, MA in Polit. Sci., 1967, PhD in Marathi, 1982; LittD in Marathi, Binzani City Coll., 1994. Lectr. Binzani City Coll., 1965-96, reader, 1984-96; prof., head dept. Marathi Nagpur U., 1996—. Author: Marathi Pradeshik Kadambari, 1984, Sun Images in Dalit Poetry, 1992, Poetry of Muktibodha, 1992, Novels in Dalit Literature, 1993, Jogtini's of Godess Yallamma, 1994, Musical Terms in Marathi Poetry, 1995, Waghya-Murli of God Khandolra, 1996, Selected Work of P. L. Deshpande: An Appreciative Look, 2000; editor: Vasant-Vaibhav, 1993, Biography of Shrikrishna, 1994, Dhawale (poem) of Mahadamba, 1998, Bharud's of Saint Eknath, 1998. Home: Gazal, 04, Prashanta-Nagar, Nagpur 440015, India Office: Nagpur U, Univ Campus, Amravati Rd, Nagpur 440010, India

KULKARNI, MEGHAASHAM DATTATRAYA, veterinarian, educator, researcher; b. Chopada, India, June 1, 1952; s. Dattatraya Baliram and Mangala (Galapure) K.; m. Nrutyala Sharadchandra Deshpande, June 23, 1980; children: Anurag, Aditi. BSc, Nagpur U., 1973, BVSc and A.M., 1977; MVSc in Medicine, Punjabrao Krishi Vidyapeeth, Akola, India, 1979. Asst. prof. vet. sci. AICRP on cattle, Rahuri, 1980-86; scientist, prin. investigator on cattle ICAR, Rahuri, 1986-89, prin. vet. officer, 1989-97; assoc. prof. vet. sci. Coll. of Agr., Pune, 1997-98; assoc. prof., head dept. vet. medicine K.N.P. Coll. Vet. Sci., Shirval Dist., Satara, India, 1998—; cons. M.P.K.V., Rahuri, 1980—; vet. lectr., 1980—; mem. Maharashtra Vet. Coun., 1997—. Contbr. articles to profl. jours. including Indian Vet. Med. Jour., Indian Vet. Jour., Indian Jour. Animal Rsch. Recipient Bishu Sudhama Meml. award Indian Vet. Assn., 1998. Mem. N.Y. Acad. Scis. Avocations: watching television, music, walking, reading, writing. Home: Sharawati Flat M 7, Dahan U Kar Colony A, Kothrud Pune 29 Pune, India 411005 Office: KNP Coll Vet Sci, Dept Vet Medicine, Shirval Dist Satara 412801, India

KULKARNI, RAGHAVENDRA GOVINDARAO, electronics engineer; b. Badami, India, July 28, 1956; s. Govindarao Bhimrao and Prabhavathi Srinivasarao (Deshpande) K.; m. Manjari Galagali, Apr. 6, 1988; children: Aditya, Pushkarni. B of Electronics and Comm., Coll. Engring., Gulbarga, India, 1979; M Tech in Elec. Engring., Indian Inst. Tech., Madras, 1982; D in Electronics and Elec. Comm. Engring, Indian Inst. Tech., Kharagpur, India, 1998. Dep. engr. Bharat Electronics, Bangalore, India, 1982-86, sr. engr., 1986-90, dep. mgr., 1991-96, mgr., 1996—; hon. lectr. U. Vishweshwarayya Coll. Engring., Bangalore, 1985-87. Contbr. articles to profl. jours.; responsible for numerous devels. in surface acoustic wave devices, 2 patents pending. Mem. IMAPS-India, IEEE. Avocations: playing cricket, playing chess, swimming. Home: 351 7th Cross III Block, HMT Layout, Vidyaranya Pura, Bangalore 560097, India Office: HMC Divsn/Bharat Electrs, Jalahalli Post, Bangalore 560013, India

KULL, HANS, software company executive; b. Aarau, Switzerland, Feb. 7, 1950; s. Ernst and Ida Heidi (Richner) K. BS in Electronics, Polytech. Sch. Engring., Winterthur, Switzerland, 1972; MS in Math., Swiss Fed. Inst. Tech., Zurich, 1979, PhD, 1990. Engr. Brütsch Elektronik, Schaffhausen, Switzerland, 1972-73; scientist Contraves, Zürich, 1979-81; head dept. Bauer Kaba AG, Wetzikon, Switzerland, 1981-84; CEO Kull Info. & Co., Schaffhausen, Switzerland, 1984-99; lectr. Polytech. Sch. of Engring., Winterthur, 1991-94; dir. Informatic Techs. Pty Ltd., Mt. Dunneed, Victoria, Australia, 2000—. Mem. IEEE, Assn. Computing Machinery. Office: Informatic Techs Pty Ltd, 2 Kalkarra Cr, Mount Duneed Vic 3216, Australia

KULLANDER, SVEN GUNNAR, physicist, researcher; b. Karlstad, Sweden, Mar. 9, 1936; s. Carl Fredrik and Anna Maria (Svensson) K.; m. Eva Elisabeth Westrom, Dec. 23, 1961; children: Anna, Fredrik, Klas, Elisabeth. MSc, Stockholm Royal Inst. Tech., Sweden, 1961; PhD in Physics, Uppsala U., 1964, D Philosophy, 1971. Rsch. asst. Enrico Fermi Inst. Nuclear Studies, U. Chgo., 1961-63; rsch. engr. Gustaf Werner Inst. for Nuclear Chemistry, Uppsala U., 1964-65; vis. scientist machine synchrocyclotron divsn. CERN, Geneva, 1966, staff exptl. physics divsn., 1967-72; assoc. prof. high energy physics divsn. Uppsala U., 1973-78, prof. high energy physics divsn., dir., 1979—; dir. Gustaf Werner Inst., 1979-86; guest prof. Max Planck Inst. Nuclear Physics, Heidelberg, 1987, Rsch. Ctr. Nuclear Physics, Osaka U., 1986-92; coord. CERN SC, Geneva, 1968-69; rsch. program adv. com. Kernforschungsanlage, Julich, Germany, 1995—; bd. dirs. Swedish Space Physics Inst., Kiruna, Sweden, 1993-99, Natural Sci. Rsch. Coun., 1980-83; chmn. Math. Physics Comm., 1980-83; coun. mem. CERN, 1980-83, rsch. bd., 1982-84; head dept. radiation scis. Uppsala U., 1986-89, dean faculty math. and natural scis., 1989-93. Author: Mikrokosmos, 1984, Tjernobyl in Perspective, 1986, Out of Sight, 1994. Sgt. Infantry, Karlstad, 1956-57. Mem. Finnish Soc. Science & Letters, The Royal Swedish Acad. Scis., The Royal Acad. Arts & Scis. of Uppsala, The Royal Science Soc. Uppsala, Rotary Uppsala. Avocations: tennis, gardening, travel. Home: Ostra Agatan 53, S-753 22 Uppsala Sweden Office: Dept Radiation Scis, Uppsala U PO Box 535, S-751 21 Uppsala Sweden

KULLBERG, DUANE REUBEN, accounting firm executive; b. Red Wing, Minn., Oct. 6, 1932; s. Carl Reuben and Hazel Norma (Swanson) K.; m. Sina Nell Turner, Oct. 19, 1958 (dec. Sept. 1989); children: Malissa Ryan, Caroline Godellas; m. Susan Turley, Dec. 30, 1992; stepchildren: Betsy Lucas, Jane Holtzermann. BBA, U. Minn., 1954. With Andersen Worldwide, 1954-89, ptnr., 1967-89, mng. ptnr., Mpls., 1970-74, dep. mng. ptnr., Chgo., 1975-78, vice chmn. acctg. and audit practice worldwide, 1978-80, mng. ptnr., CEO, 1980-89, ret., 1989; bd. dirs. John Nuveen Co., Carlson Cos., Inc., Chgo. Bd. Options Exch. Life trustee Northwestern U., Art Inst. Chgo., U. Minn. Found., chmn. bd. trustees, 1993-95; chair, bd. dirs. Swedish Coun. Am., 1997-99. With U.S. Army, 1956-58. Decorated comdr. Royal Order of Polar Star (Sweden), 1989; recipient Legend in Leadership award Emory U., 1992, Regents award U. Minn., 1995, Outstanding Achievement award U. Minn., 1990. Mem. Chgo. Club, Comml. Club, Mpls. Club. Home: 179 E Lake Shore Dr Apt 1001 Chicago IL 60611-1306 also: 6444 N 79th St Scottsdale AZ 85250-7919

KULLBERG, GARY WALTER, advertising agency executive; b. White Plains, N.Y., Dec. 15, 1941; s. Walter George and Neva Virginia (Franz) K.; m. Audrey Ellen Greenwald, June 20, 1976; 1 child, Eric Alan. BS, U. R.I., 1963. Contr. WCD, Inc., N.Y.C., 1963-66; v.p., mgmt. supr. Ogilvy & Mather, N.Y.C., 1966-77; sr. v.p., account group head Wells, Rich, Greene, N.Y.C., 1977-83; CEO, CFO, co-founder Fredericks Kullberg Amato Pisacane, Inc., 1983-88; pres. Kullberg Amato Pisacane/ABP, Inc., 1987-89; pres., COO PanCom Internat. Corp., 1989-91; CEO PanCom Comm. Corp., 1991-93, Kullberg Cons. Group, N.Y.C., 1993—; guest spkr. univs. Mem. bd. advisors, chmn. mktg. and mktg. comm. com. Manhattan Salvation Army; mem. bus. adv. coun. U. R.I. Coll. Bus., vice-chmn., co-chair publicity com. Mem. West Point Soc. N.Y. (career adv. com.), Am. Numismatic Assn., N.Y. Athletic Club, Phi Gamma Delta. Home and Office: Kullberg Cons Group 171 Forge Rd North Kingstown RI 02852-1007

KULLENBERG, GUNNAR ERIK B., international civil servant, researcher, educator; b. Goteborg, Sweden, July 1, 1938; s. Borje E. and Anna-Lisa (Stendahl) K.; m. Kristina V. Hyllengren, Apr. 29, 1967; children: Mats P., Maria I. BSc, U. Goteborg, 1963, PhD, 1967; Lic. Sci., U. Copenhagen, Denmark, 1972, DSc, 1974. Rsch. asst. U. Goteborg, 1963-65; rsch. asst. U. Copenhagen, 1965-68, assoc. prof., 1968-77; prof. U. Goteborg, 1977-78, U. Copenhagen, 1979-90; sr. asst. sec. IOC/UNESCO, France, 1985-89; sec.-gen. IOC of UNESCO, France, 1989-95, asst. dir.-gen., 1995-98; exec. dir. Internat. Ocean Inst., 1998—; scientist Can. Ctr. Inland Waters, 1972. Author: Mixing in the Sea, 1974; editor: Marine Pollution, 1982, Waste Disposal Options, 1985. Chmn. UN-GESAMP, 1975-78, ICES-Marine pollution, Europe, 1978-80, ICES-Consultative, Europe, 1983-85. Ltd. comdr. Swedish Navy, 1958-63. Recipient Romer award Danish Acad., 1972; Fulbright scholar Bigelow Lab., Boothbay, Maine, 1982. Mem. Danish Acad. Tech. Sci., Russian Acad. Natural Scis. Home: Fossa 5020, S-45033 Grundsund Sweden Office: Internat Ocean Inst, PO Box 3, Gzira Malta

KULLMAN, ERIC PETER, surgeon; b. Stockholm, Jan. 18, 1952; s. Jan Erik and Maja Rut (Westerlund) K.; m. Maria Birgitta Johansson, Jan. 12, 1985; children: Elisabeth, Peter. MD, Karolinska Inst., Stockholm, 1981; Splty. Cert. in Surgery, Ctrl. Hosp., Eslilstuna, Sweden, 1988; PhD in Surgery, Linkoping, Sweden, 1993. Intern Ctrl. Hosp., Eskilstuna, 1981-83, resident in surgery, 1983-88, sr. resident in surgery, 1988-89; sr. resident dept. surgery Univ. Hosp., Linkoping, 1989-93, asst. prof. surgery, 1993-96, assoc. prof., 1996—. Contbr. papers and abstracts to internat. sci. jours. Grantee Swedish Soc. for Med. Rsch., 1992, Lions Rsch. Found., 1991, Smith, Klein & French, 1990, Glaxo Sweden AB, 1992, Swedish Surg. Soc., 1991, others. Mem. Swedish Med. Assn., Swedish Assn. Surgery, Scandinavian Surg. Soc., Swedish Soc. Gastroenterology, Swedish Soc. Laparascopic Surgery, Scandinavian Assn. Digestive Endoscopy, European Assn. for Endoscopic Surgery, Swedish Soc. Medicine, Internat. Soc. of Surgery, Soc. Surgery of the Alimentary Tract. Office: Univ Hosp, Surg Dept, S-58185 Linköping Sweden

KULLMANN, DETLEF, software company executive; b. Muenster, Germany, June 1, 1963; s. Ortwin Kullmann and Renate (Bracht) Hilger-Kullmann. Abitur, Hohenschwangau, Germany, 1983; BBA, U. Cologne, Germany, 1989; M of Liberal Arts, Harvard U., 1996. Instr. German Air Force, Budel, The Netherlands, 1983-85; rschr., writer Europe, U.S.A., 1989-93; trainee Commerzbank AG, Erfurt, Germany, 1997; financial adv. Aachener & Münchener, Cologne, Germany, 1998; sales mgr. ABIT AG, Meerbusch, Germany, 1998—. Author, editor: Dokumentation der Familienforschung C/Kul(l)man(n), 1993. Capt. German Air Force Reserves, Germany, France, 1986—. Studienstiftung des deutschen Volkes scholar 1989-91. Mem. Der Gelbe Kreis, Harvard Club Rhein-Ruhr. Avocations: travel, bridge, hunting, family research. Home: Rheingoldstrasse 19, 50354 Huerth Cologne Germany

KULLO, IFTIKHAR JAN, physician, researcher; b. Srinagar, India, Mar. 12, 1962; s. Ghulam Nabi and Ameena Kalloo; m. Salma Iftikhar, June 27, 1991; children: Aliya, Rehan. Degree, Coll. Sci., Srinagar, Kashmir, 1980; MBBS, Govt. Med. Sch., Srinagar, Kashmir, 1987. Bd. cert. in internal medicine and cardiovasc. medicine Am. Bd. Internal Medicine. Intern in internal medicine Nassau County Med. Ctr., East Meadow, N.Y., 1992; resident in internal medicine Mayo Clin. & Found., Rochester, N.Y., 1993-94, fellow in cardiovasc. medicine, 1995-99, sr. assoc. cons., 1999—; Mem. administrv. bd. Ketab, N.Y., 1997. Contbr. articles to sci. jours. Grantee NIH, 1992. Mem. AMA, Am. Coll. Cardiology, Am. Soc. Pharmacology and Experimental Therapeutics, Am. Soc. Gene Therapy, Soc. Vascular Biology and Medicine, Sigma Xi. Muslim. Avocations: cricket, central asian history. E-mail: kullo.iftikhar@mayo.edu. Home: 4023 Alberta Dr NE Rochester MN 55906-3937 Office: Mayo Clinic 200 1st St SW Rochester MN 55905-0002

KULOK, WILLIAM ALLAN, entrepreneur, venture capitalist; b. Mt. Vernon, N.Y., July 24, 1940; s. Sidney Alexander and Bertha (Lembeck) K.; m. Susan B. Glick, June 26, 1965; children: Jonathan, Brian, Stephanie. BS in Econs., U. Pa., 1962. CPA, N.Y. Acct. David Kulok Co., N.Y.C., 1962-67; asst. to pres. Syndicate Mags., N.Y.C., 1967-70; founder Kulok Capital Inc., N.Y.C., 1970, pres., 1970—; pres. N.Am. Corp. Games, Internat. Prodns., Inc.; mng. dir. World Trade Ctr., Palm Beach; bd. dir. Listcomp Corp., Mail Mgmt. Corp., Mag. Devel. Fund, Lazard Spl. Equities Fund, ASA Internat. Ltd., N.Y. Import/Export Ctr., Inc., Ctr. for Exec. Edn.,

Arts & Events, Inc.; lectr. Wharton Sch., U. Chgo., NYU. Pres. N.Y. Soc. Ethical Culture, 1978-80; vice chmn. bd. Ethical Culture Schs., 1979, chmn., 1982-86; pres. N.Am. Corp. Games. Mem. AICPA, Sleepy Hollow Country Club, Loxahatchee Club, Tryall Golf and Beach Club (Jamaica, W.I.). Home: 116 Echo Dr Jupiter FL 33458-7716

KULSHRESTHA, SANJAY, pediatric surgeon; b. Agra, India, Feb. 4, 1959; s. Shantiwaroop and Vimlavati K.; m. Meeta; 1 child, Shradda. MBBS, SN Med. Coll. Agra U., 1984, MS, 1988; MCh, Inst. Med. Scis., Varanasi, India, 1991. Resident SN Med. Coll., Agra, 1986-88; CMO Batra Hosp. & Rsch. Ctr., Delhi, India, 1988-91; chief pediat. surgeon Siddharth Hosp. & Rsch. Ctr., Agra, 1991-95; chief cons. pediat. surgeon, in charge NICU Sarkar Hosp. Women & Children, Agra, 1995—; prof., head divsn. pediats., pediat. surgery Indian Coll. Maternal & Child Health, Agra, 1998—. Pres. All-India Soc. Against Birth Defects in Children, 1995—. Fellow Indian Coll. Maternal & Child Health; mem. N.Y. Acad. Scis., Indian Assn. Pediat. Surgeon, Indian Acad. Pediats., Nat. Neonatology Forum, Pediat. Intensive Care Group India, Asian & Indian Soc. Pediat. Urology, Indian Med. Assn., Indian Medicos Orgn. Home: 1/188-C Delhi Gate Gulab, Rai Marg, Agra 282002, India

KULSTAD, GUY CHARLES, public works official; b. Feb. 28, 1930; s. John Marlyn and Anne Mildred (Boyd) Kulstad Ibison; m. Bonnie Jane Sherman, Aug. 28, 1955 (div. Aug. 1996); children: Anne Marie Kulstad Hurst, Mark, Alice Kulstad Krause. BS in Civil Engring., U. Calif., Berkeley, 1958. Registered profl. engr., Calif., Oreg., Wash., traffic engr., Calif., land surveyor, Oreg.; cert. c.c. instr., Calif. Engring. aid County Rd. Dept., L.A., 1951, asst. civil engr., 1953-58; dir. pub. wks. Benicia, Calif., 1958-59; dep. dir. pub. wks. Solano County, Calif., 1959-65; dir. pub. wks. Humboldt County, Calif., 1965-92; mgmt. cons., 1992—; gen. mgr. Humboldt Bay Wastewater Authority 1975, 82-89. Mem. Employer support of N.G. and Res. With AUS, 1951-53. Recipient Outstanding Svc. award North Bay chpt. Calif. Soc. Profl. Engrs., 1964, Boss of the Yr. award Arcata Jaycees, Recognition award Humboldt Toastmaster, Meritorious Leadership award, Surveyor award Calif. Land Surveyors Assn., Illmars Lagzdin award for engring. contbns., Guy C. Kulstad award Humboldt County Dept. Pub. Wks. Fellow ASCE; NSPE, mem. Nat. Soc. County Engrs., Calif. County Engrs., County Engrs. Assn. Calif., Commonwealth Club of Calif., Sons of Norway.

KULYK, KAREN GAY, visual artist; b. Toronto, July 19, 1950; d. Joseph and Natalie Melanie (Solowski) K. BFA with honors, York U., 1973. Founder, curator Seedlings Gallery, Toronto, 1973-75; established studios worldwide, 1975—; tchr. various instns. in Can., Thailand, and Bermuda. Solo exhbns. include Kitchener-Waterloo Art Gallery, 1994, Rodman Hall, St. Catharines, Ont., 1995, Masterworks Found. Gallery, Hamilton, Bermuda, 1997, Quaker Gallery, London, 1996—, Carnegie Gallery, Dundas, Ont., Can., 1996, Nancy Poole's Studio, Toronto, 1996-99, Gallery on the Bay, Hamilton, Ont., 1997—, Wallack Gallery, Ottawa, Can., 1999, Zwicker Gallery, Halifax, N.S., Can., 1999—, Nat. Gallery Thailand, Grey Coll. U. Durham, Eng., 2000; exhibited in group shows at Harbinger Gallery, Waterloo, Ont., Touchstone Gallery, Hong Kong, Marianne Friedland Gallery, Fla., Sotheby's, Toronto, Chgo. Internat. Art Exhbn., York U., U. Toronto, Offices of Gov. Gen. of Can., Carleton U. Art Gallery, numerous others; represented in collections at Kitchener-Waterloo Art Gallery, Wilfred Laurier U., Waterloo, Art Gallery of Hamilton, Carleton U., York U., Agnes Etherington Art Gallery, Nat. Gallery of Bermuda, Can. Trust, Dominion Trust, Shell Can., Thai Airways Internat., Can. Airlines Internat., others, pvt. collections; illustration: Orff, 27 Dragons and a Snarkel; subject of several newpaper articles. Recipient Grollo d'Oro, award Treviso Intenrat. Art Competition, 1983; grantee Sheila Hugh Mackay Found., 1996. Home and Office: 5270 Morris St, Halifax, NS Canada B3J 1B4

KUMA, HISAO, information systems educator; b. Shinjuku, Tokyo, Japan, Oct. 30, 1936; s. Haruo and Motoko (Ikuta) K.; m. Kyoko Murakami, Feb. 12, 1965; children: Kazue, Yuki. B of Engring., Chiba (Japan) U., 1960; D of Engring., Tokyo U., 1982. Chief rschr. System Devel. Lab., Hitachi, Japan, 1960-87; vis. prof. U. Alta., Edmonton, 1987-88; prof. Grad. Sch. Informatics Teikyo Heisei U., Chiba, 1987—; vis. prof. Chiba U., 1991—. Author: Telemedicine, 1983, New Technology for the Medical Management Computer Systems in the Doctor's Office, The Computer in the Doctor's Office, 1980; contbr. articles to profl. jours. Recipient Faculty Enrichment award Can. Govt., 1993. Home: 17-10 Ohkubo 2 chome, Shinjuku-ku Tokyo 169-0072, Japan Office: Teikyo Heisei Univ, 2289 Uruido, Ichihara 290-0193, Japan

KUMAGAI, NAOHIKO, retired trading company executive. Past pres., chmn. bd. Mitsui & Co., Ltd., Tokyo. Office: Mitsui & Co Ltd, 2-1 Otemachi 1-chome, Chiyoda-ku Tokyo 100-0004, Japan

KUMAGAI, TAKASHI, engineering company executive; b. Tokyo, May 20, 1931; s. Naoyuki and Yukino (Sumida) K.; m. Kiwako Takeuchi, Mar. 26, 1955; children: Yukihiro, Hideki. BS, Tokyo U., 1955. Engr. Mamiya Camera Co. Ltd., Tokyo, 1955-64; pres. Shinko Engring. Rsch. Co., 1963—; lectr. automation mechanism Kanagawa U., 1979—. Contbr. articles to profl. jours; patentee in field. Group leader Tech. Tour Groupes, 1969—. Mem. Japan Cons. Engrs. Assn. (dir. 1977-79), Japan Indsl. Robot Assn., Japan Soc. Precision Engring., Automation Promotion Assn. (v.p. 1975-96). Club: Tsumagoi Yamaha. Home: 4-22-2 Kinuta, Setagaya-ku, Tokyo 157-0073, Japan Office: Shinko Engring Rsch Co, 6-6-18 Kinuta Setagaya-Ku, Tokyo 157-0073, Japan

KUMAKAWA, MASASHI, oil company executive; b. Yotsukaido City, Chiba Pref, Japan, Jan. 15, 1933; s. Munenaga and Kau (Ueda) K.; m. Mitsuko Toki, Apr. 30, 1958; children: Ken, Hajime, Manabu. BS, Tohoku U., Sendai City, Japan, 1955. Lic. cons. engr., mine safety engr. Chem. analyst, rschr. Teiseki Telnite Co., Ltd., Sakata City, Japan, 1955-61; chief prodn. dept. Japan Petroleum Exploration Co. Ltd., Tokyo, 1961-71; mng. dir. Japan Oil Engring. Co., Ltd., Tokyo, 1971-91; rep. North Japan Oil Co., Ltd., Sakata City, 1991-98; dir. Akita Prefecture Natural Gas Transmission Co., Ltd., Akita City, Japan, 1991-97; cons. Petroliam Nasional Berhad (Petronas Bhd), Kuala Lumpur, Malaysia, 1978; chief, mem. coms. Ministry of Internat. Trade and Industry and related orgns., Tokyo. Co-author: Handbook of Petroleum Development, 1963; promoter, editor: Symposium of Offshore Oil Development, 1970, Symposium of Japan Petroleum Inst., 1988, 89, 90, 91. Mng. dir., area chief Midoridai area br. Funabashi City Bereaved Families Assn., 1990—. Mem. Japanese Assn. Petroleum Tech. (dir. 1986-91), Japan Petroleum Inst. (mgr. resources dept. 1988-91). Buddhism (Jodo sect.). Avocations: Mahjong, mountain hiking, travel. Home: 2-3-504 Midoridai 1 chome, Funabashi 274-0818, Japan Office: 1-2-3 504 Midoridai, Funabashi City 274-0818, Japan

KUMALO, DUMISANI SHADRACK, diplomat. Rep. from S.Africa UN, N.Y.C. Office: Permanent Mission of South Africa 333 E 38th St Fl 9 New York NY 10016-2772*

KUMANYIKA, SHIRIKI K., nutrition epidemiology researcher, educator; b. Balt., Mar. 16, 1945; m. Christiaan B. Morssink; children: Chenjerai, Annoesjka. BA, Syracuse U., 1965; MS in Social Work, Columbia U., 1969; PhD in Human Nutrition, Cornell U., 1978; MPH, Johns Hopkins U., 1984. Asst. prof. nutrition Cornell U., Ithaca, N.Y., 1977-84; from asst. prof. to assoc. prof. epidemiology Johns Hopkins U. Sch. Hygiene and Pub. Health, Balt., 1984-89, asst. prof. internat. health, 1984-89; assoc. prof. nutritional epidemiology Pa. State U., University Park, 1989-92, prof. epidemiology, 1993-96; assoc. dir. for epidemiology Pa. State U. Coll. Medicine, Hershey, 1992-96; prof. epidemiology, prof. human nutrition and dietetics U. Ill. at Chgo., 1996-99, head dept. human nutrition and dietetics, 1996-99; chief of svc. U. Ill. Hosp. Nutritional Svcs., 1996-99; prof. epidemiology U. Pa. Sch. Med., Phila., 1999—, assoc. dean health promotion and disease prevention, 1999—; adj. prof. epidemiology dept. health evaluation scis. Coll. Medicine, Pa. State U., Hershey, 1996-99; mem. adv. bd. Women's Health Alliance. Contbr. articles to profl. jours. Bd. dirs. Nat. Black Women's Health Project, 1994-99, Nat. Rural Ctr., 1978-82; active WHO. NIH grantee; recipient Bolton L. Corson medal Franklin Inst., 1997. Fellow Am. Coll. Epidemiology, Am. Coll. Nutrition; mem. AAUP, APHA, Am. Diabetes Assn., Am. Dietetic Assn., Am. Inst. Nutrition, Am. Soc. for Clin. Nutrition, Assn. Black Cardiologists, Internat. Soc. on Hypertension in Blacks, Nat. Med. Assn., N.Am. Assn. Study of Obesity, Soc. for Epidemiol. Rsch., Soc. for Nutrition Edn., Internat. Soc. and Fedn. Cardiology, others. Office: Ctr Clin Epidemiology and Biostats U Pa Sch Med 8th Fl Blockley Hall 423 Guardian Dr Philadelphia PA 19104-4209

KUMAR, ALOKE, marketing executive; b. Calcutta, Feb. 5, 1956; s. Nirmal Chandra and Karuna (Paul) K.; m. Alokananda Mukherjee, Jan. 5, 1966; children: Abhishek. B in Commerce with honors, St. Xavier's Coll., 1977; MBA, Indian Inst. Mgmt., 1980. Media exec. Rediffusion, Calcutta, 1978-80; advt. mgr. Ananda Bazar Patrika, Calcutta, 1981-84, advertisement mgr., 1984-88, dep. mktg. controller, 1989-94; CEO Ganapati Parks Ltd., Calcutta, 1994%; exec. dir. Arts, Culture & Heritage Calcutta, 2000—; media advisor Honrary Consulate of Israel, Calcutta, 1996—; vis. faculty Indian Inst. Mass Communication, New Delhi, 1984—; mem. bd. Devel. and Ednl. Communication Unit, New Delhi, 1990—. Contbr. articles to profl. jours. Founder mem. Pub.-People United for Better Living in Calcutta, 1985; active News-Nature Environment and Wildlife Soc., Calcutta, Intach (Indian Nat. Trust for Art and Cultural Heritage), New Delhi; exec. mem. Soc. for Preservation of Calcutta and Heritage. Mem. St. Xavier's Coll. Alumni Assn. (life), Tollygunge Club, Calcutta Rowing Club. Avocations: collecting antique materials, reading, classical music, literature, poetry. Home: Karuna GC-18 Sector III, Calcutta 700 091, India Office: Ganapati Parks Ltd, 89C Norkeldanga Main Rd, Calcutta 700054, India

KUMAR, ANANTH, government official; b. 1959. Grad., Karnataka U., India. Gen. sec. Karnataka BJP Students Orgn., India, 1982-85, Nat. BJP Students, India, 1985; mem. Lok Sabha, India, 1996—; min. Ministry Civil Aviation, India, 1998—; min. tourism and culture Govt. India, New Delhi. Office: Tourism and Culture, Parliament St, New Delhi 110 0101, India*

KUMAR, B. MOHAN, silvicuture and agroforestry educator; b. Sooranad, Kerala, India, Oct. 14, 1953; s. K. N. Bhaskaran Pillai and K. Saraswathy Amma; m. Sheenu S. Nair; children: S. Maneesha S. Mohan, Mahesh B. Mohan. BSc in Agr., Kerala Agrl. U., 1975, MSc in Agr., 1978; postgrad. diploma in seed tech., Indian Agrl. Rsch. Inst., New Delhi, 1980, PhD in Plant Nutrition, 1983; postdoctoral diploma, Utah State U., 1987; diploma in mgmt., Indira Gandhi Nat. Open U., New Delhi, 1996. Jr. asst. prof. Kerala Agrl. U., 1975-80, from asst. to assoc. prof., 1980-89, head silviculture and agroforestry, 1989—; cons. Agrl. Devel. Svcs., London; vis. scientist Utah State U., Logan, 1986-87; mem. Monopolies and Restrictive Trade Practices Commn. Mem. editl. bd. Forest Ecology and Mgmt.; contbr. numerous articles to nat. and internat. jours. Kerala Agrl. U. rsch. fellow, 1976-78, Indian Agrl. Rsch. Inst. sr. rsch. fellow, 1980-83, USAID vis. fellow, 1986-87. Mem. Indian Nat. Sci. Congress (life), Indian Soc. Tree Scientists (life), Assn. Rice Rsch. Workers (life), Indian Soc. Agroforestry (life). Fax: 91-487-370019. Home: # 48 Pushpavihar, 680751 Nadathara Kerala, India Office: Kerala Agrl U Coll Forestry, Vellanikkara, 680 656 Thrissur Kerala, India

KUMAR, B. PREETHAM, engineering educator, researcher; b. Chennai, Tamilnadu, India, Mar. 29, 1960; came to U.S., 1992; s. R. and Jamuma Balasubramaniam; m. Priyadarsini Kumar, June 27, 1991; 1 child, Veena. BEng, Coll. Engring. Guindy, Chennai, 1982, MEng, 1984; PhD in Engring., Indian Inst. Tech., Chennai, 1992. Cert. engr. Project assoc. Indian Inst. Tech., 1984-92; lectr., rschr. U. Calif., Davis, 1992—; asst. prof. Calif. State U., Sacramento, 1992—. Author: Encyclopedia of Electrical and Electronics Engineering, 1998; contbr. articles to IEEE Transactions on Antennas and Propagation, 1989—. Named Prof. of Yr., IEEE Sacramento br., 1999. Mem. IEEE. Avocations: poetry, travel, cricket, table tennis. E-mail: kumarp@ecs.csus.edu. Home: 1301 Orchard Park Cir Davis CA 95616-5147 Office: Calif State U 6000 J St Sacramento CA 95819-2605

KUMAR, BINOD, materials engineer, educator; b. Jamalpur, Bihar, India, Jan. 13, 1946; came to U.S., 1971; s. Rambaran and Ramsunder (Rai) Singh; m. Shyama Thakur, May 23, 1969; children: Vineet, Sunita. MS, Pa. State U., 1973, PhD, 1976. Glass technologist Seraikella Glass Works, Konnagar, India, 1968-71; rsch. engr. Anchor Hocking Corp., Lancaster, Ohio, 1976-79; sr. rsch. engr. U. Dayton, 1980—, prof., 1992; cons. Zimmer, Inc., Warsaw, Ind., 1987-90, Mead, Inc., Dayton, 1988, JAFE, Inc., Greenville, Ohio, 1987-90, Rotor Seal Dynamics, Calif., 1995—, Tex. Tech. Industries, Maine, 1999—. Trustee India Found., Dayton, 1991-95. Mem. Am. Ceramic Soc., Electrochem. Soc., Indian Ceramic Soc. (life). Achievements include 90 publs. and patents contributing to the fields of glass tech., solid state ionics, lithium rechargeable batteries and high temperature superconductivity; also mentoring grad. students. Office: U Dayton 300 College Park Ave Dayton OH 45469-0001

KUMAR, GOPENDRA, retired geologist; b. Lucknow, UP, India, Nov. 27, 1936; s. Shyam Narain and Parvati Devi Mathur; m. Manju Mathur Kumar, Nov. 30, 1964; children: Nidhi Mathur, Shilpi Mathur. BS, Lucknow U., 1956, MS, 1958. Sr. tech. asst. Oil and Natural Gas Commn., Dehradun, India, 1959-60; asst. geologist, jr. geologist Geol. Survey India, Calcutta, 1960-67, 68-72; jr. geologist Cement Corp. India, New Delhi, 1967-68, Mineral Exploration Corp., Nagpur, India, 1972-76; sr. geologist, dir. Geol. Survey India, Calcutta, 1976-94; ret., 1994. Author: Geology of Arunachal Pradesh, India, 1997; assoc. editor Geosci. Jour., 1995. Recipient Nat. Mineral award Govt. India, 1985-86. Fellow Geol. Soc. India, Palaeontol. Soc. India; mem. Palaeobotanical Soc. Hindu. Avocations: badminton, cricket. Home: 48 Pandariba Old Kanpur Rd, UP Lucknow 226 004, India

KUMAR, K. M. DRUVA, psychiatrist, consultant; b. Bhadravati, Karnataka, India, Jan. 1, 1942; s. Setty K. Manjunath and Nagarathnamma Kumar; m. Gayathri Vajram Setty, Dec. 23, 1969; children: Sheela Aprameya, Jyothsna Dattathreya. MB BChir, Mysore (India) Med. Coll., 1965. Diplomate Am. Bd. Psychiatry and Neurology. Resident Pontiac (Mich.) State Hosp., 1967-68; resident Wayne State U., Detroit, 1968-70, clin. instr. psychiatry, 1970-76; pvt. practice Detroit, 1972-76; psychiatrist Psychotherapeutic Clinic, Flint, Mich., 1975-76; pvt. practice as cons. psychiatrist Bangalore, India, 1977—; med. dir. Drug Abuse Unit, Detroit, 1975-76; asst. med. dir. Psychotherapeutic Clinic, Flint, 1975-76; clin. dir. Wayne State U., Detroit, 1974-75. Author: Manoviplava, 1997 (S.S. Jayanam award 1996-97). Recipient Cmty. Leaders of Am. award, 1972. Fellow Indian Psychiat. Soc. (Eminent Psychiatrist award Karnataka br. 1997-98, S.S. Jayaram award 1996-97, LGP Acher award 1995-96, pres. 1982-83, chmn. ann. conf. 1997), Rotary Club Bangalore (awards). Avocations: shuttle badminton, treadmill. Office: 1341 Residency Rd, 560025 Bangalore India

KUMAR, KAPLESH, materials scientist; b. Lucknow, India, Nov. 9, 1947; came to U.S., 1970; s. Shiam and Vidya (Devi) Sunder; m. Savinder Kaur, May 27, 1974; children: Priyadarshini, Ruchira. B.Tech., Indian Inst. Tech., 1969; MS, Stevens Inst. Tech., 1971; ScD, MIT, 1975; JD magna cum laude, New Eng. Sch. Law, 1997. Bar: Mass. 1998; registered patent atty. Mem. tech. staff Charles Stark Draper Lab., Inc., Cambridge, Mass., 1975-80, chief materials devel. sect., 1980-88, chief materials sci. and tech. sect., 1988-91, prin. mem. tech. staff, 1992—; vis. lectr. IIM-ASM Internat., 1989; chmn. workshop on superconductivity and its applications to nat. needs, 1991; session chmn. Structures, Dynamics & Materials Conf., AIAA, 1996, 97. Author: (with others) Plasma Spraying: Theory and Applications, 1993; patentee in materials processing; pub. Applied Physics Review monograph, 1988; contbr. articles to profl. jours. Recipient Patent award Charles Stark Draper Lab., Inc., 1982, Outstanding Performance award, 1994, Invention Disclosure award NASA, 1983. Mem. ASM Internat. (mem. internat. materials revs. com. 1991—), AIAA (mem. materials tech. com. 1991-98), MIT Sangam Club for India Affairs (pres. 1972-73), India Assn. Greater Boston, Inc. (pres. 1995-97), IIT Soc. New Eng. (v.p. 1993-95), Indian Am. Forum for Polit. Edn. (pres. New Eng. chpt. 1998—). Achievements include research in intellectual property law; permanent and soft magnetic materials; structural materials; micromechanical devices, inertial instruments; subspecialties include materials; ceramics.

KUMAR, KUDERU B., psychologist; b. Kuderu, India, May 20, 1954; s. Kuderu and Belakavadi (Puttanna) Balachandradharamurthy; m. Shobha Shobhavathi, May 2, 1985; 1 child, Moulya. MA, Bangalore U., 1977; MPhil, U. Nimhans, 1982; PhD, Mangalore U., 1994. Rsch. asst. Indian Coun. Med. Rsch., 1982-83; from lectr. to assoc. prof. Kasturba Med. Coll., Manipal, India, 1983—. Recipient Dr. T.M.A. Pai Rsch. Gold medal, 1992, 96, Disting. Alumni award, 1996. Mem. Indian Assn. Clin. Psychologists, South Kanara Uro-Nephrology Club. Hindu. Avocations: music, chess, golf, cricket. Office: Kasturba Med Coll & Hosp, A Deemed Univ, 576 119 Manipal India

KUMAR, NITISH, government official. Min. Ministry Agrl. & Coop., India, 1989-90; founder Samata Party, India, 1994; min. Ministry Railways, India, 1998—; min. agrl. Office: Ministry Railways, Dr Rajendra Prasad Rd, New Delhi 110 001, India*

KUMAR, PARVEEN JUNE, gastroenterologist educator; b. Lahore, India, June 1, 1942; d. Cyril Proshuno Fazal and Graze Nazira (Faiz) K.; m. David Graham Leaver; children: Rachel Nira, Susannah Kiran. BSc (hons.), U. London, 1963, MB, BS, 1966, MD, 1976. House officer St. Bartholomew's Hosp., Reading, Eng., 1966-68, rschr. registrar, 1968-69; house physician Hammersmith Hosp., Reading, Eng., 1970-85; sr. lectr., hon. cons. physician St. Bartholomews and Homerton Hosps., 1985-94; reader in gastroenterology U. London, 1994-99, prof. clin. med. edn., 1999—; tutor Royal Coll. Physicians, 1988-93; dir. postgrad. med. edn. Bartholomew and Homerton Hosps., then Royal Hosp. Trust, 1993-96; undergrad. sub-dean St. Bartholomew's and Royal London Sch. Medicine and Dentistry, censor Royal Coll. Physicians, 1996-98, dir. continuing profl. devel.; non exec. dir. Nat. Inst. Clin. Excellence; vice chmn. Medicines Commn., 1994—. Co-editor: Kumar and Clark Clinical Medicine, 1987, 4th edition, 1998, Gastrointestinal Radiology, 1981; series co-editor Clinical Medicine, 1995, Psychiatry, 1996; contbr. articles to profl. jours. Fellow Royal Coll. Physicians, Royal Coll. Physicians Edinburgh; mem. British Soc. Gastroenterology. Avocations: opera, skiing. Office: St Bartholomew Royal London, Sch Med/Dent Turner St, London E1 2AD, England

KUMAR, PRATAP, obstetrician/gynecologist; b. Madras, India, May 27, 1954; s. Narayan and Meera Achar; m. Vidya Pratap, Jan. 15, 1982; children: Deepali, deepika. MB, BChir, Kasturba Med. Coll., Manipal, India, 1976, DGO, 1979, MD, 1981. Lectr. Kasturba Med. Coll., 1981-82, asst. prof., 1982-84, reader, 1984-86, assoc. prof., 1986-90, prof., 1990—, head dept. ob-gyn., 1997—; cons. Kasturba Hosp., 1981—; Loma Linda postdoctoral fellow, 1982; ; cons. Manipal Assisted Reprodn. Ctr.; participant various internat. congresses. Editor 2 edits. Ultrasound in Ob-Gyn., 1995, 97. Recipient Young Gynecologist award Asian Assn. Gynecologists Bangkok, 1983, UICC award Internat. Union Cancer, U.K., 1984, Sr. Scientist award Nat. Ob-gyn. Fedn., 1996, best publ. award Fedn. Ob-Gyn. India, 1998; selected for Indo-Belgium Exch. Program to Brussels, Govt. of India, 1997; mem. adv. bd. Nat. Bd. Exams. and Insp. of Hosps. Fellow Internat. Coll. Surgeons, Internat. Coll. Ob-Gyns.; mem. Nat. Fedn. Ob-gyn. India (v.p. 1998-99), Imaging Scis. of Ob-gyn. India (nat. chmn. 1991-95), World Com. Ultrasound, Lions (pres. Manipal club 1998-99). Avocations: playing sitar. E-Mail: drpratapkumar@usa.net. Home: 16-132 Anantnagar II Stage, Karnataka, Manipal 576119, India Office: Kasturba Med Coll, Dept Ob-gyn, Karnatak Manipal 576119, India

KUMAR, RAJENDRA, electrical engineering educator; b. Amroha, India, Aug. 22, 1948; came to U.S., 1980; s. Satya Pal Agarwal and Kailash Vati Agarwal; m. Pushpa Agarwal, Feb. 16, 1971; children: Anshu, Shipra. BS in Math. and Sci., Meerut Coll., 1964; BEE, Indian Inst. Tech., Kanpur, 1969, MEE, 1977; PhD in Electrical Engring., U. New Castle, NSW, Australia, 1981. Mem. tech. staff Electronis and Radar Devel., Bangalore, India, 1969-72; rsch. engr. Indian Inst. Tech., Kanpur, 1972-77; asst. prof. Calif. State U., Fullerton, 1981-83, Brown U., Providence, 1980-81; prof. Calif. State U., Long Beach, 1983—; cons. Jet Propulsion Lab., Pasadena, Calif., 1984-91, Aerospace Corp., El Segundo, Calif., 1995—. Contbr. numerous articles to profl. jours.; patentee; efficient detection and signal parameter estimation with applications to high dynamic GPS receivers; multistage estimation of received carrier signal parameters under very high dynamic conditions of the receiver; fast frequency acquisition via adaptive least squares algorithms, Kalman filter ionospheric delay estimator, others. Recipient Best Paper award Internat. Telemetering Conf., Las Vegas, 1986, 10 New Technology awards NASA, Washington, 1987-91. Mem. IEEE (sr.), NEA, AAUP, Calif. Faculty Assn., Auto Club So. Calif. (Cerritos), Sigma Xi, Eta Kappa Nu, Tau Beta Pi (eminent mem.). Avocations: gardening, walking, hiking, reading. Home: 13910 Rose St Cerritos CA 90703-9043 Office: Calif State U 1250 N Bellflower Blvd Long Beach CA 90840-0001

KUMAR, RAJESH NARAYAN, pediatrician; b. Dehra Dun, India, Feb. 2, 1950; came to U.S., 1975; s. Brijlal and Subhadra (Gurwara) K.; m. Vinita Nath, June 24, 1979; children: Aditya, Abhishek. MBBS, Armed Forces Med. Coll., Poona, India, 1973. Diplomate Am. Bd. Pediatrics. Intern No. Railway Cen. Hosp., New Delhi, India, 1974, Ellis Hosp., Schenectady, N.Y., 1975-76; resident in pediatrics Luth. Gen. Hosp., Park Ridge, Ill., 1976-78; attending physician Guadalupe Med. Ctr., Carlsbad, N.Mex., 1978-89; pres. Carlsbad Children's Med. Ctr., 1978-89; pediatrician Kumars Children Medi Care, New Delhi, 1990—. Fellow Am. Acad. Pediatrics. Republican. Hindu. Avocations: traveling, stamps. Home: 3108 Post Oak Ct Winter Haven FL 33884-1238 Office: Kumars Children Medi Care, C 17 Panchsheel Enclave, 110017 New Delhi India

KUMAR, RAKESH, company executive, researcher; b. Agra, India, Oct. 20, 1960; s. Tilak and Vimla Singh; m. Seema Rakesh Singh, Feb. 21, 1985; children: Shivangi, Deepika. Mem. Indian Assn. Med. Micro., Indian Acad. Vaccin. Immunology. Avocations: reading newspaper, magazines, TV watching, cricket. Home: Armar Nagari Housing Soc, Row House 8, 441028 Hadapsar Puna India Office: Serum Inst India, 212/2 Hadapsar Pune, 411028 Pune India

KUMAR, SANJAY S., neuroscientist; b. Hyderabad, India, Aug. 30, 1964; s. Santh and Vijay Lakshmi Kumar; m. Amrita Kumar, July 18, 1994; 1 child, Sampath. B Engring., Andhra U., 1986; MS, Drexel U., 1989; PhD, U. Pa., 1997; postdoctoral rsch. fellow, Stanford U., 1998. Rsch. fellow Drexel U., Phila., 1987-90; predoctoral fellow U. Pa., Phila., 1992-97; rsch. fellow Stanford (Calif.) U., 1998—; coord. neurocomputing workshop Drexel U. Contbr. articles to profl. jours. Recipient rsch. fellowship award Am. Epilepsy Soc. and the Milken Family Found., 1998, 99, Elliot Stellar award for neurosci. rsch. Phila. chpt. Soc. for Neurosci., 1996. Mem. Epilepsy Soc. (jr. mem., Rsch. award 1998-99), Tau Beta Pi, Eta Kappa Nu. Avocations: tennis, cricket, music, books. Office: Stanford Univ Med Ctr Dept Neurol/Neurol Scis Stanford CA 94305-5122

KUMAR, SIVANAPPAN, solar energy educator; b. Coimbatore, Tamilnadu, India, May 3, 1960; arrived in Thailand, 1996; s. Ramampalayam Karuthiruman and Kannammal Sivanappan; m. Velumathi Venkatachalam, Oct. 26, 1990; 1 child, Nithin Senthur. B in Engring. with honors, U. Madras, India, 1982; M in Engring., Asian Inst. Tech., Bangkok, 1983-84; PhD, Inst. Nat. Poly., Toulouse, France, 1989. Reader Madurai (India) Kamaraj U., 1990-95; asst. prof. Asian Inst. Tech., Bangkok, 1995-96, assoc. prof., 1996—; cons. UN-Econ. and Social Commn. for Asia and the Pacific, Bangkok, 1999. Contbr. articles to profl. jours. Mem. ASHRAE (assoc.), Internat. Assn. Solar Energy Edn. (sec./treas. 1996—, editor newsletter 1997—), Internat. Solar Energy Soc., Instn. Engrs. (India).

KUMAR, SUBODH, metallurgist, educator; b. Kanpur, India, Dec. 2, 1962; s. Madan Gopal and Tara Devi Gupta; m. Sharmistha Chakravarty, Dec. 15, 1993; 1 child, Suchit. BTech, Indian Inst. Tech., Kanpur, 1983, MTech, 1986; PhD, Imperial Coll., London, 1993. Ops. officer India Oil Corp., 1986-90; scientist Austrian Acad. Scis., 1993-96; asst. prof. Indian Inst. Sci., Bangalore, 1997—. Contbr. articles to profl. jours. Mem. AAAS. Office: Dept Metallurgy, Indian Inst Sci, Bangalore Karnataka 560 012, India

KUMAR, VIJAY, mechanical engineer, educator; b. Patna, Bihar, India, Apr. 12, 1962; came to U.S., 1983; s. S.R. and Hema Ramakrishnan; m. Maneesha Altekar, Nov. 6, 1988; children: Priya, Sonia. B in Tech., Indian Inst. Tech., 1983; PhD, Ohio State U., 1987. Asst. prof. U. Pa., Phila., 1987-93, assoc. prof., 1993-98, prof., 1998—, dep. dean, 2000—. Author, assoc. editor IEEE Transactions, 1994—, ASME Transactions, 1997—; inventor in field. Achievements include new results in robot kinematics, motion plan-

ning and theoretical kinematics. Avocations: music, running, biking. Office: Univ Pa 220 S 33rd St Philadelphia PA 19104-6315

KUMAR, VIJAYA BHAGAVATULA, electrical engineering educator, consultant; b. Porumamilla, India, Aug. 15, 1953; came to U.S., 1977; s. Ramamurthy and Saradamba Bhagavatula; m. Latha Bhagavatula, July 1, 1982; children: Ramamurthy, Madhusudan, Chandrasekhar. B.Tech. in EE, IIT, Kanpur, India, 1975; M.Tech. in EE, IIT, 1977; PhD in EE, Carnegie Mellon U., 1980. Asst. prof. dept. elec. and computer engrng. Carnegie Mellon U., Pitts., 1982-87, assoc. prof., 1987-91, prof., 1991—, assoc. dept. head, 1994-96, thrust leader, optical recording, 1998—; cons. Raytheon Systems Ctr., Tucson, 1997—, U.S. Army MICOM, Huntsville, Ala., 1993-95, Mytec Tech. Inc., Toronto, Ont., Can., 1995-98, Baker & McKenzie, San Francisco, 1998-99. Co-author (sect.) Handbook of Brain, 1995, (chpt.) Biometric Encryption, 1999; contbr. over 250 articles to profl. engrng. jours. Sec. S.V. Temple, Pitts., 1994, bd. dirs., pres. exec. com., 1992; mem. tri-svc. ATR tech. armament plan for conventional weapons com., 1995. Fellow IEEE (sr. mem.), Internat. Soc. Optical Engrs., Optical Soc. Am.; mem. Internat. Neural Network Soc., Sigma Xi. Avocations: traveling, bridge, table tennis. E-mail: kumar@ece.cmu.edu. Office: Carnegie Mellon U Dept Electric & Computer E Pittsburgh PA 15213

KUMAR, VINAI, pathology educator; b. V. Paraupur, Sultanpur, India, June 24, 1939; arrived in Belgium, 1971; parents Mahadeo Prasad and Kaushilya Srivastava; m. Suman Bala Srivastava, Feb. 3, 1963; children: Smita, Ashish, Kavita. B.V.Sc. & A.H., Agra (India) U., 1961, M.V.Sc., 1967; DSc, State U., Ghent, Belgium, 1975. Sr. rsch. asst. India Vet. Rsch. Inst., Izatnagar, 1961-71; scientist Inst. Tropical Medicine, Antwerp, 1975-80, sr. scientist, 1981-84, prof., 1984—; vis. scientist Vet. U., Budapest, Hungary, 1980, U. Ga., Athens, 1982; vis. prof. U. Morogoro, Tanzania, 1983. Editor (periodicals) Jour. Vet. Parasitology, 1989—, Vet. Parasitology, 1984—, (book) Helminth Zoonoses, 1987, Trematode Infections and Diseases of Man and Animals, 1999. Mem. Belgian Soc. Parasitology (treas. 1974—), N.Y. Acad. Scis. Avocations: history, historical novels, classical music, jogging. Home: Belgielei 75A, B 2018 Antwerp Belgium Office: Inst Tropical Medicine, Nationalestraat 155, B 2000 Antwerp Belgium

KUMAR, VINAY, physicist, researcher; b. Banda, India, Jan. 7, 1963; s. Suraj Bali and Giriraj Srivastava; m. Shubha Rani, Feb. 17, 1990; 1 child, Shuvi. BSc, Bundelkhand U., Jhansi, India, 1981, MSc, 1983; PhD, Indian Inst. Tech., Kanpur, India, 1990; PDF, Inst. Plasma Rsch., Gandhinagar, India, 1991. Postdoctoral fellow Inst. for Plasma Rsch., Gandhinagar, India, 1990-91; scientist Inst. for Plasma Rsch., Gandhinagar, 1991—; vis. scientist Joint European Torus, Abingdon, Oxford, Eng., 1996-97. Boyscast fellow Dept. Sci. and Tech. India, 1996-97. Mem. Plasma Sci. Soc. India, Indian Physics Assn. (Ahmedabad chpt.). Avocations: photography, reading, music, traveling. Office: Inst for Plasma Rsch, BHAT, Gandhinagar 382428, India

KUMAR, V.S. CHANDIRA, export company executive; b. Tirupur, India, Apr. 4, 1973; s. T.V. Shanmugam and R. Ruckmani. Quality contr. Buying Office, Bombay, India, 1992-93; mng. dir. Export Garments, Tirupur, India, 1993—. Office: Sentinel Clothing Co, 10 MG Pudur 3d St, 641604 Tirupur India

KUMARASINGHE, GAMINI, microbiologist, consultant; b. Elpitiya, Sri Lanka, June 23, 1944; Arrived in Singapore.; s. Don Hendrick and Premawathie (Dissanayake) K.; m. Sepalika Hylinee Wijemanne, Sept. 2, 1971; 2 children. MBBS, U. Ceylon, Sri Lanka, 1968; D Pathology, Royal Coll. Phys. & Surgeons, 1979. Med. officer various hosps., Sri Lanka, 1969-73; sr. house officer in medicine Honey Lane Hosp., Essex, 1974; from registrar to sr. registrar in clin. microbiology Hosp. for Sick Children, London, 1977-83; cons. microbiologist King K. Hosp., Al Khari, Saudi Arabia, 1984-88, Nat. U. Hosp., Singapore, 1989—. Fellow Royal Coll. Pathology, 1993, 94. Fellow Royal Coll. Pathologists, RCPA. Buddhist. Avocations: tennis, jogging, music, travel. E-mail: GaminiK@nuh.com.sq. Office: Nat Univ Hosp Microbiology, Nat Univ Hosp Lab Medicine, Lower Kent Ridge Road, 119074 Singapore Singapore

KUMARATUNGA, CHANDRIKA BANDARANAIKE, Sri Lankan government official; b. Colombo, June 29, 1945. Prime min. Govt. of Sri Lanka, Colombo, 1994, min. ethnic affairs and nat. integration, min. finance, min. policy planning, 1994—, pres., min. defense, 1994—, min. of Buddha Sasana. Office: Office Min Def, 15/5 Baladaksha Mawatha, POB 572 Colombo Sri Lanka*

KUMASHIRO, MASAHARU, ergonomics educator; b. Minokamo, Gifu, Japan, Feb. 28, 1947; s. Chihiro and Kimi (Domon) K.; m. Sayoko Maruta, Apr. 1, 1973; 1 child, Arisa. B in Engring., Kanagawa U., Yokohama, Japan, 1970; PhD, Hokkaido U., Sapporo, Japan, 1982. Instr. Hokkaido Inst. Tech., Sapporo, 1970-74, lectr., 1974-77; instr. Hokkaido U., Sapporo, 1977-79; assoc. prof. U. Occupl. and Environ. Health, Kitakyushu, Japan, 1979-86; prof. U. Occupl. and Environ. Health, Kitakyushu, 1986—; cons. RICOH Co. Ltd., Yokohama, 1992-94; adv. assoc. Mitsubishi Rsch. Inst., Tokyo, 1994—. Editor: Towards Human Work, 1991; editor, co-author: The Paths to Productive Aging, 1995; inventor in field. Named Hon. Rsch. fellow Birmingham (Eng.) U., 1981-82. Fellow The Ergonomics Soc. (profl. ergonomist); mem. Japan Ergonomics Soc. (exec. mem. 1992—), Internat. Ergonomics Soc. (chair tech. group for safety and health 1993—), Pan Pacific Coun. Occupl. Ergonomics (pres. 1997—), Soc. Occupl. Safety, Health and Ergonomics (pres. 1996—). Avocation: fishing. Office: IIES UOEH Japan, 1-1 Iseigaoka Yahatanishi, Kitakyushu Fukuoka 807-8555, Japan

KUMATE RODRIGUEZ, JESUS, physician; b. Mazatlan, Sinaloa, Mex., Nov. 11, 1924; s. Efren Kumate and Josefina Rodriguez; m. Bertha Guerra Rovelo, Mar. 2, 1957. BSc, Escuela Preparatoria, Mazatlan, Mex., 1940; MD, Med. Militar, Mexico City, 1946; PhD, Escuela Nal. Cienc. Biol., Mexico City, 1963; DSc (hon.), U. de Nuevo Leon, Monterrey, Mex., 1990, U. de Sinaloa, Mex., 1995. Diplomate Bd. Infectious Diseases. Asst. prof. Escuela Med. Militar, Mexico City, 1949-54; physician Hosp. Infantil, Mexico City, 1953-80; assoc. prof. Facultad de Medicina, Mexico City, 1960-70, prof., 1970-80; lectr. Polytechnic Inst., Mexico City, 1974-80; investigator Instituto Mexicano Seguro Social, Mexico City, 1981—; dir. Hosp. Infantil, 1979-80; coord. Nat. Insts. Health, Mexico City, 1983-84; undersec. Health Svcs., Mexico City, 1985-88, sec., 1988-94. Author: Manual de Infectologia. Maj. Mex. Army, 1940-54. Recipient Legion of Honor, Govt. of France, 1978-88, Disting. Svcs. award Def. Sec. Mex., 1988, Oswaldo Robles award Govt. Guatemala, 1993, Sacred Treasure Band, Japan, 1997, Order of Merit, Italy, 1998. Roman Catholic. Home: Corot 15-801, 03720 Mexico City Mexico Office: Instituto Mexicano Seguro Social, Cuauhtemoc 330, 06725 Mexico City Mexico

KUMAZAWA, MAKOTO, economics educator; b. Yokkaichi, Japan, Sept. 21, 1938; s. Akira and Aiko (Michiie) K.; m. Shigeko Kurita, Mar. 21, 1962; children: Arata, Toru. M in Econs., Kyoto (Japan) U., 1963, D in Econs., 1969. Lectr. Konan U., Kobe, Japan, 1966-69; assoc. prof. Konan U., 1969-74, prof., 1974—; dean faculty of econs. Konan U., 1984-85. Author: Oligopoly and Labor Union, 1970, A State Within the State, 1976, Light and Darkness of the Japanese Management, 1989, Portraits of the Japanese Workplace, 1996, Meritocracy in the Japanese Companies, 1997. Home: 2-28-9 Gotenyama, Takarazuka-shi Hyogo ken 665-0841, Japan Office: Konan U Faculty Econs, 8-9-1 Okamoto Higashinada-ku, Kobe Hyogo-ken 658-8501, Japan

KUMBAROGLU, GÜRKAN SELÇUK, industrial engineer, researcher; b. Trabzon, Turkey, Mar. 29, 1969; s. Sabri and Gülay (Ata) K.; m. Didem Tamac, Oct. 30, 1995. BS, Gazi U., Ankara, Turkey, 1990; MS, Middle East Tech. U., Ankara, Turkey, 1995. Logistics asst. Geb. Sulzer AG, Zuchwil, Switzerland, 1990-92; rsch. and teaching asst. Middle East Tech. U., Ankara, 1993—. Editorial asst. Transactions on Operational Rsch., Turkey, 1995—; co-author: (book chpt.) Systems Modelling for Energy Policy, 1997; contbr. articles to profl. jours. Mem. Operational Rsch. Soc. Turkey. Avocations: skiing, swimming, paragliding, trekking. E-mail: gurkan@ie.metu.edu.tr. Office: Middle East Tech U, Dept Indsl Engring, 60531 Ankara Odtu, Turkey

KUMBETLIAN, A. GARABET, mechanical engineer, educator; b. Mar. 11, 1936. Student, U. Bucharest, 1954-59, PhD, 1976. Prof., head of gen. technics dept. Maritime U. of Constanta; speaker nat. and internat. confs. Author: The Standardization of Consumption of Energy at the Power Plant of Ovidiu, 1966, Strength of Materials, 1974, 6th revised edit., 1998, A Collection of Problems of the Strength of Materials Discipline, 1980, 2d edition, 1988, The Basis of Experimental Methods by the Use of the Strain Gauges Methods, 1982; contbr. articles to profl. jours. Mem. Romanian Assn. Exptl. Mechs. (head Constanta br. 1977—), Scientists Acad., Computer Aided Engring., Internat. Maritime Lectr's. Assn. Office: Maritime Univ Constanta, Electromech Faculty, Constanta Romania

KUMBHAKAR, PATHIK, physicist; b. Bankura, India, Dec. 14, 1973; s. Chakradhar and Bela Rani (Das) K. BS in Physics with honors, Burdwan U., India, 1993; MS in Physics, Burdwan U., 1995. Jr. rsch. fellow Burdwan U., India, 1996-98; sr. rsch. fellow Burdwan U., 1998-99; lectr. R.E. Coll., Durgapur, India, 1999—. Contbr. articles to profl. jours. Recipient scholarship Govt. W. Bengal, 1990-93, UGC Govt. India, 1993-95; fellowship UGC Govt. India, 1996—. Mem. Optical Soc. Am., Indian Laser Assn. Avocation: reading. E-mail: recdgppr@dte.vsnl.net.in. Home: Raipur, 722134 Raipur India Office: Physics Dept, College RE, Durgapur 713209, India

KUMMER, WOLFGANG, physicist; b. Krems, Austria, Oct. 15, 1935; s. Friedrich and Maria (Burkhart) K.; m. Eleonore Pokorny, July 12, 1960. Diploma in engrng., Vienna (Austria) U. Tech., 1958, Dr. techn. wiss., 1960. Dir. Inst. for High Energy Physics, Austrian Acad. Scis., Vienna, 1966-71; prof. Vienna U. Tech., 1968—, head Inst. for Theoretical Physics, 1995—; coun. mem., pres. European Orgn. for High Energy Physics, Geneva, to 1987. Co-author: Einfuehrung in die mathematischen Methoden der Theoretischen Physik, 1976; contbr. some 150 articles to profl. jours. Bd. mem. Austrian Sci. Found., Vienna, 1977-85, v.p., 1983-85; chmn. Austrian Orgn. Univ. Profs., Vienna, 1980-82. Recipient Culture award Fed. Country of Lower Austria, Vienna, 1971, Cardinal Innitzer award Cardinal Innitzer Found., Vienna, 1981. Mem. Austrian Acad. Scis. (Erwin Schroedinger prize 1988), European Phys. Soc. (chmn. high energy physics bd. 1997-99), Austrian Phys. Soc. Roman Catholic. Fax: 43-1-58801-13699. E-mail: wkummer@tph.tuwien.ac.at. Office: Inst Theor Phys Vienna U, Wiedner Hauptstrasse 8-10, A-1040 Vienna Austria

KUMOMI, HIDEYA, physicist, researcher; b. Tokyo, Jan. 20, 1962; s. Ikuya and Taeko (Shiota) K.; m. Chieko Wakatsuki, Nov. 16, 1991; 1 child, Lino. BS, Waseda U., Tokyo, 1984, MS, 1986, PhD in Physics, 1996. Rsch. physicist Canon Inc., Tokyo, 1986—. Contbr. articles to profl. jours. Mem. Materials Rsch. Soc., Phys. Soc. Japan, Japan Soc. Applied Physics. Home: 194-9-401 Ohguchi-Nakamachi, Kanagawa-ku Yokohama 221-0003, Japan Office: Canon Inc, 3-30-2 Shimomaruko, Ohta-ku Tokyo 146-8501, Japan

KUMPFERT, JOERG G., mechanical engineer, researcher; b. Dortmund, Germany, Nov. 26, 1962; s. Guenter and Gerda (Jordan) K.; m. Susanne Hamacher, Dec. 20, 1991; children: Nadine, Sandra. Diploma in engirng., Ruhr U., Bochum, Germany, 1989, D of Engring., 1994. Materials engr. DLR-German Aerospace Ctr., Cologne, 1989-92; vis. scientist Wright Patterson AFB, Dayton, Ohio, 1992-93; rep., group leader DLR-German Aerospace Ctr., Cologne, 1994-98, group leader, 1998—. Author: Microstructure Properties in TiAL Base Alloys, 1995; author, co-editor: Titanium & Titanium Alloys, 1996; contbr. articles to sci. and profl. jours. Mem. Minerals, Metals and Materials Soc., German Materials Soc., Assn. Engrs. Germany. Avocations: family, sailing, computers, travel, tennis. Office: German Aerospace Ctr, Linder Hoehe, 51147 Cologne Germany

KUMPULAINEN, EERO JUHA, radiotherapy administrator, consultant; b. Kiuruvesi, Savo, Finland, June 1, 1953; s. Heino and Laina (Komulainen) K.; m. Kirsti Irmeli Hakamaa; children: Henrika, Elina, Vesa. MD, Oulu U., 1977. Doctor Central Hosp., Jyvaskyla, Finland, 1981-83, U. Hosp., Kuopio, Finland, 1983—. Mem. European Soc. for Med. Oncology, Lions. Home: Laiduntie 6, FIN70780 Kuopio Finland

KUMTA, PRASHANT NAGESH, materials science educator, engineering educator, consultant; b. Madras, India, Aug. 17, 1960; arrived in U.S., 1984; s. Nagesh Shanker and Soomathee Nagesh (Marballi) K.; m. Ujwala Prashant Kamath, Dec. 20, 1994; 1 child, Tanay. BTech, Indian Inst. Tech., Bombay, 1984; MS, U. Ariz., 1987, PhD, 1990. Undergrad. rsch. asst. Indian Inst. Tech., Bombay, 1983-84; grad. work asst. Oreg. Grad. Ctr., Beaverton, 1984-85; grad. tchg. asst. U. Ariz., Tucson, 1985-87, grad. rsch. asst., 1987-88, grad. rsch. assoc., 1988-90; asst. prof. Carnegie Mellon U., Pitts., 1990-95, assoc. prof., 1995-99, prof., 1999—; prin. investigator Eveready Battery Co., Cleve., 1993—; cons. Changs Ascending, Taiwan, 2000—; prin. investigator Jet Propulsion Lab., Pasadena, Calif., 1997—, Pitts. Plate Glass (PPG) Industries, 1998-2000; cons. Timo Industry, Pitts., 1992-93; mem. summer rsch. faculty Air Force Office, Washington, 1993. Author, editor: Role of Ceramics in Advanced Electrochemical Systems, 1996, Covalent Ceramics: Science and Technology of Non-Oxides, 1996, Chemical Processing Aspects of Electronic Ceramics, 1998, Processing and Characterization of Electrochemical Materials and Devices, 2000; contbr. articles to profl. jours.; patentee in field. Recipient Rsch. initiation award NSF, Washington, 1993; grantee NSF, Air Force Office, Army Rsch. Office, Advanced Rsch. Projects Agy., Washington, 1993—, Office of Naval Rsch., Washington, 2000—. Mem. Am. Ceramic Soc., Materials Rsch. Soc., Electrochem. Soc. Achievements include pioneering development of thio-sol-gel and hydrazide sol-gel processes to synthesize transition and rare-earth chalcogenides and nitrides, ceramics, novel complexed precursor approaches to new non-oxide ceramics, mechanochemical synthesis of oxide and non-oxide ceramics and composites, patents pending related to development of novel cathode materials for primary batteries, novel processes to fabricate lithium-ion electrodes and new biomaterials for bone tissue engineering; patent for new class of stable cathodes for lithium-ion batteries. Avocations: tennis, music, reading. Office: Carnegie Mellon U 4305 Wean Hall 5000 Forbes Ave Pittsburgh PA 15213-3890

KUNCHEVA, LUDMILA ILIEVA, engineer, educator; b. Sofia, Bulgaria, Aug. 25, 1959; d. Ilia Ivanov and Svetla Radoslavova Tomov; m. Roumen Koumanov Kountchev, Apr. 11, 1981; children: Diana, Kamelia. MSc, Tech. U., Sofia, 1982, degree in engring. and math., 1983; PhD, Bulgarian Acad. Scis., 1987. Rsch. assoc. Bulgarian Acad. Scis., Sofia, 1987-96, sr. rsch. assoc., 1996-97; lectr. U. Wales, Bangor, 1997—. Contbr. articles to profl. jours. Grantee EUFIT '96, 1996; fellow U. West Fla., 1996-97, Royal Soc., 1995-96, European Cmtys. Commn., 1993. Home: 22 Bryn Llwyd, Caernarfon Rd, Bangor Gwynedd LL57 4SW, Wales Office: U Wales, Sch Informatics, Bangor Gwynedd LL57 1UT, Wales

KUNDERA, MILAN, writer, educator; b. Prague, Czechoslovakia, Apr. 1, 1929; s. Lidvik and Milada (Janosikova) K.; m. Věra Hrabánková, 1967. Student Film Faculty, Acad. Music & Dramatic Arts, Prague; D.h.c., U. Mich., 1983. Asst. prof. film Film Faculty Acad. Music and Dramatic Arts, 1958-69; prof. U. Rennes, France, 1975-80, Ecole des Hautes études en Scis. Sociales, Paris, 1980—. Author: Směšné lásky (pub. as Laughable Loves, 1974; Czech Writers' Pub. House prize 1969), Zert, 1967 (pub. as The Joke, 1969; Czech Writers' Union prize 1968), La Vie est ailleurs, 1973 (pub. as Life Is Elsewhere, 1974, Prix Medicis 1973), La Valse aux adieux, 1976 (pub. as The Farewell Party, 1973; Premio Letterario Mondello 1978), Le Livre du rure et de l'oubli, 1979 (pub. as The Book of Laughter and Forgetting, 1980), Jakub a pán, 1971 (pub. as Jacques et son maître, hommage Denis Diderot, Jacques and His Master, L'Insoutenable L'248géreté de l'être, 1984 (pub. as The Unbearable Lightness of Being, 1984; L.A. Times book prize for fiction 1984), L'Art du roman, 1986 (pub. as The Art of the Novel, 1987), L'Immortalité, 1990 (pub. as Immortality, 1991), Les Testaments Trahis, 1993, La Lenteur (The Slowness), 1995, Identity. A Novel, 1998. Recipient Commonwealth award disting. svc. in lit., 1981, Prix Europa for lit., 1982, Jerusalem prize, 1985, Académie Française Critics prize, 1987, Nell Sachs prize, 1987, Osterrichischeve state prize, 1987, Ind. award for fgn. fiction, 1991.

KUNDT, WOLFGANG HELMUT, astrophysics educator; b. Hamburg, Germany, June 3, 1931; s. Helmut Rudolf and Käte Susanne Thänert) K.; m. Ulrike Schümann, Aug. 8, 1966; children: Liane Angelika, Rasko Helmut. Diploma, U. Hamburg, 1955, PhD, 1959, Habilitation, 1965. Lectr. U. Kiel, Germany, 1965-66; sci. advisor, prof. U. Hamburg, 1967-77; C3 prof. U. Bonn, Germany, 1978—; prin. investigator Helios E11, 1969-83; vis. scientist CERN, Geneva, 1972; guest prof. U. Bielefeld, Germany, 1973-74, dept. physics U. Pitts., 1966-67; cons. European Space Rsch. Orgn., Paris, 1974-78; dir. Erice Sch., Sicily, 1985—. Editor over 5 books on solar system, astrophys. jets and their engines, neutron stars and their birth events, supernova remnants and their birth events; contbr. over 220 articles on theoretical physics, astrophysics, geophysics, biophysics and cosmology to sci. jours., chpts. to books; 79 alternatives to current thinking in Understanding Physics'. Avocations: tennis, running, sailing, arts. Office: Bonn U IFA, Auf dem Hügel 71, D-53121 Bonn Germany

KUNDU, ANJAN, physicist, researcher; b. Calcutta, India, Jan. 24, 1953; s. Agaman Chandra and Bhanumati K.; m. Liudmila Vilievna Korshunova, Feb. 7, 1978 (div. 1996); 1 child, Konkona. Diploma in journalism, Patrics Lumumba U., Moscow, 1975, diploma in tchg., 1977, interpreter's diploma, 1977, MS in Physics and Maths., 1977, PhD in Physics and Maths., 1981. Rsch. assoc. Joint Inst. Nuclear Rsch., Dubna, USSR, 1981-83; scientific pool officer Coun. Scientific and Indsl. Rsch. Jadavpur U., Calcutta, 1983—; lectr. in physics Birla Inst. Tech. and Sci., Pilani, India, 1983-85; prof. theoret. physics Saha Inst. Nuclear Physics, Calcutta, 1985—; vis. scientist Patrice Lumumba U., Moscow, 1987, Rome U. La Sapienza, 1986, 91-92, 94, Math./Informatik U. G.H. Kassel, Germany, 1993, Inst. Theoret. Physics U. Bonn, Germany, 1994, 96, Prague Tech. Inst., 1994, U. Genoa, Italy, 1994, U. N.C., Chapel Hill, 1997, U. Hanover, Germany, 1999, U. Rome, U. Lapth, 2000; mem. adv. com. dept. sci. and tech. project Ctr. Nonlinear Studies, India, 1996—; presenter, lectr. in field. Co-author: Introduction to Energy Conversion, 1984; translator: Straight Lines and Curves, 1980; contbr. numerous articles to internat. sci. jours. Recipient Theoretical Physics Seminar Cir. Lectureship award, 1990, 92, 2000. Mem. Indian Phys. Soc. (life). Avocations: writing science fiction and other stories, photography, painting. Office: Saha Inst Nuclear Physics, 1/AF Bidhannagar, Calcutta 700 064, India

KUNDU, BALARAM, engineering educator, researcher; b. Arambag, W. Bengal, India, Jan. 5, 1968; s. Kshudinarayan and Pushpa Rani (Mondal) K. Grad., Baradangal R.N. Instn., India, 1986; BS, A.K.P.C. Mahaviddhyalaya, India, 1988; B in Engring., Bengal Engring. Coll., Durgapur, India, 1993; M in Engring., Bengal Engring. Coll., Shibpur, India, 1995; PhD, Indian Inst. Tech., Kharagpur, India, 2000. Cert. engr. Lectr. Jalpaiguri (India) Govt. Engring. Coll., 1998—. Recipient award Instn. Engrs. India. Hindu. Avocations: reading books, listening to the radio, playing football, travel, gardening. Home: PO-Salepur Dist-Hooghly, Pin 712616 Salepur West Bengal, India Office: Jalpaiguri Govt Engring Coll, Pin 735102 Jalpaiguri West Bengal, India

KUNDU, SIVARAM, journalist; b. Chandannagar, India, May 19, 1926; s. Basanta Kumar and Saratsashi (Pal) K.; m. Annapurna Dey, Mar. 9, 1956; children: Rabiprakash, Rita and Joyprakash (twins), Mita. Student, Raja Pearymohan Coll., India, 1945; Grad. Cert. in Trade Union Journalism, Internat. Confedn. Unions, Brussels, 1970. Columnist Sevak, Chandannagar, 1945-46, editor, 1946-47; corr. Press Trust of India, Calcutta, 1947-50, Ananda Bazar Patrika, Calcutta, 1950-80, Hindusthan Standard, Calcutta, 1950-80; editor Nababharat, Chandannagar, 1952; corr. The Statesman, Calcutta, 1959-65; editor Action, Chandannagar, 1989-90; mng. editor Bartaman Bharat, Chandannagar, 1977-83, editor, 1983—. Editor: Handbook of Press Club of Hooghly, 1972. Mem. Indian Nat. Congress, Chandannagar Town, 1992-2000; mem. consultative com. Suburban Railway Users, Ea. Railway, 1998-99; judge Lok Adalat. Mem. All India Newspaper Editors Conf., All Indian Small and Medium Newspaper Fedn., Press Club of Hooghly (sec.), Hooghly Dist. Editors Assn. (sec.), Indian Nat. Trust of Art and Cultural Heritage (life), Prabartak Samgha (life), Chandannagar Telephone Subscribers Assn. (sec.), Chandannar Railway Passengers Assn. (sec.). Avocations: photography, gardening, watching performing arts, workers education and social service. Home: 34 Kundu Ghat Rd, 712136 Chandannagar India Office: Bartaman Bharat, 34 Kundu Ghat Rd, 712136 Chandannagar India

KUNDU-RAYCHAUDHURI, SMRITI KANA, biomedical scientist; b. India, 1959; came to U.S., 1989; d. Mrityunjoy and Uma K.; m. Siba P. Raychaudhuri; 3 children. MD, All India Inst. Med. Scis., New Delhi, 1987. Postdoctoral fellow Stanford (Calif.) U. Med. Ctr., 1989-92, rsch. assoc., 1992-94, sr. rsch. scientist, 1995—; mem. AIDS clin. trials unit NIH, Bethesda, Md., 1989—; mem. sci. rev. bd. FDA, 1995. Contbr. articles to profl. jours. Mem. Am. Assn. Immunologists, N.Y. Acad. Scis., Am. Soc. for Microbiologists. Avocations: reading, music.

KUNES, JOSEF, science educator, consultant, researcher; b. Nechanice, West Bohemia, Czech Republic, Jan. 19, 1930; s. Alois and Josefa (Marešková) Kunes; m. Marie Vojtasová, Dec. 17, 1955; children: Ilja, Oleg. MSc, Tech. U., Pilsen, 1953, PhD, 1964; DSc, Tech. U., Prague, 1991. Asst. lectr. Tech. U., Pilsen, 1953-56, lectr., 1956-66, asst. prof., 1966-76; leading sci. worker SKoda Rsch., 1976-91; prof. U. West Bohemn, Pilsen, 1992—, Tech. U., Prague, 1994—; head dept. automatisation Tech. U., 1969-70; sub-dean faculty mech. engring., 1969-70; head divsn. thermomechanics Rsch. Ctr. New Techs., 2000—. Co-author: Hybride Modeling of Thermal Processes, 1987, Fundamentals of Modeling, 1989; author: Modeling of Thermal Processes, 1989; contbr. numerous articles to profl. pubis. Recipient Prize for Czech Literal Fund Best Sci. Book of 1990, Prize Czech Found. for Sci., 1995, Regional Prize for Results in Foundry Thermomechanics Rsch., 1988. Mem. Soc. for Mechanics, Soc. for Cybernetics, Czech Tech. Soc. Avocations: theatre, music, philosophy, nature. Home: Karbinala Berana 11, 30125 Plzen Czech Republic Office: U West Bohemia Fac App Sci, Dept Physcis PO Box 314, Plzen 30614, Czech Republic

KUNEVA, MARIANA KUNCHEVA, scientist, integrated optics researcher; b. Sofia, Bulgaria, Aug. 7, 1955; d. Kyncho Danailov Kynev and Rossitsa Ganeva Belcheva; 1 child, Gorgorov Rossen Nikolaev. MA, U. Sofia, 1978; PhD, Bulgarian Acad. Sci., Sofia, 1997. Constructor Inst. of Spl. Optics, Sofia, 1978-88; physicist Inst. Solid State Physics, Bulgarian Acad. Sci., Sofia, 1988-90, rsch. assoc., 1990—. Contbr. articles to Jour. Applied Physics, Procs. of SPIE, Applied Physics A. Recipient Bronze medal for painting Ministry of Culture, 1979. Mem. Bulgarian Phys. Union, SPIE (Bulgarian sect.), Bulgarian Scientists Union. Avocations: painting, drawing, playing the piano. Home: Compl Mladost-1, Bl 80 EntrA Apt 6, 1797 Sofia Bulgaria Office: Inst Solid State Physics, 72 Tzarigradsko Chaussee Bd, 1784 Sofia Bulgaria

KUNG, ALICE HOW KUEN, high tech company executive; b. Kowloon, Hong Kong, Nov. 26, 1956; d. Yam Sang and Yuet Shoung (Lew) K. BA in with honors-distinction in Econs., Stanford U., 1978; MBA, Harvard U., 1983. CPA, Calif. Staff auditor audit div. Arthur Andersen & Co., San Francisco, 1978-79, sr. cons. cons. div., 1980-81; cons. strategy mgmt. group Arthur D. Little, Inc., San Francisco, 1982; mgr. customer mktg. Gould AMI Semicondrs., Santa Clara, Calif., 1983-84; product mgr. voice messaging products IBM/Rolm Systems, Santa Clara, 1985-86, market and bus. planning mgr. Far East and L.Am., 1987-89; internat. mktg. dir. Minx Software, Inc., San Jose, Calif., 1989-92; dir. for Asia and Pacific SuperMac Tech., Sunnyvale, Calif., 1992-93; mng. dir. Radius Hong Kong, 1994; mktg. dir. Apple Asia, 1995; mng. dir. Passport Group, Ltd., 1996—; owner Orient Express, Mountain View, Calif., 1986-90. Vol. Harvard Community Ptnrs., Oakland, Calif., 1993. Scholar Harvard U., 1981-83. Mem. Asian Am. Mfrs. Assn., Sources 91 (organizing com., officer 1992), Asian Bus. League, Internat. Bus. Club, Phi Beta Kappa. Democrat. Avocations: swimming, hiking, movies, travel.

KUNG, HAROLD HING-CHUEN, engineering educator; b. Hong Kong, Oct. 12, 1949; s. Shien C. and Kai Sau (Wong) K.; m. Mayfair Chu, June 12, 1971; children: Alexander, Benjamin. BS in chem. engring., U. Wis., 1971; PhD in chemistry, Northwestern U., 1974. Rsch. sci. ctrl. rsch. and devel. dept. E.I. duPont de Nemours & Co., Wilmington, Del., 1974-76; asst. prof. chem. engring. Northwestern U., 1976, asst. prof. chem. engring. and chemistry, 1977, assoc. prof., 1981, prof. chem. engring. and chemistry, 1985-97, chmn. chemical engring., 1986-92; dir. Ctr. for Catalysis and Surface Sci.,

1993-97; chmn. Gordon rsch. Conf. on Catalysis, 1995; tech. advisor UNIDO Mission, 1995; John McClanahan Henske Disting. lectr. Yale U., 1996; mem. com. to rev. PNGV program Nat. Rsch. Coun., 1996-99; Olaf Hongen vis. prof. U. Wis., Madison, 1999. Author: Transition Metal Oxides, Surface Chemistry and Catalysis, 1989, Catalyst Modificaton-Selective Oxidation Processes, 1991; editor: Methanol Production and Use, 1994, Applied Catalysis A = General, 1996—; patents include Photolysis of Water Using Rhodate Semiconductive Electrodes, and Oxidative Dehydrogenation of Alkanes to Unsaturated Hydrocarbons. Japanese Soc. for Promotion of Sci. fellow, 1996. Mem. AIChE, Am. Chem. Soc., Chgo. Catalysis Club (program chair 1992, pres. 1993, Herman Pines award 1999), N.Am. Catalysis Soc. (Paul H. Emmett award 1991, Robert L. Barwell lectr. 1999), Phi Lambda Epsilon. Office: Dept of Chem Engring Northwestern University 2145 Sheridan Rd Evanston IL 60208-0834

KUNG, PANG-JEN, materials scientist, electrical engineer; b. I-Lan, Taiwan, May 13, 1959; s. Ching-Yu and A-Se (Yu) K.; m. Tzyy-Yun Tzeng, May 18, 1986; children: Naihau, Naiwei. MSChemE, Nat. Tsing Hua U., 1983; MSEE, Auburn U., 1988; MMetE, Carnegie Mellon U., 1991, PhD in Materials Sci., 1993; MBA, U. Conn., 1998. Jr. engr. Tatung Co., Taipei, Taiwan, 1979-80; teaching asst. Nat. Tsing Hua U., Hsin-Chu, Taiwan, 1981-82, rsch. asst., 1982-83; assoc. scientist Indsl. Tech. Res. Inst., Hsin-Chu, 1985-86; tchg. and rsch. asst. Auburn (Ala.) U., 1986-89; rsch. asst. Carnegie Mellon U., Pitts., 1989-91; staff rsch. asst. Los Alamos (N.Mex.) Nat. Lab., 1991-92, rsch. fellow, 1993-94; sr. scientist Advanced Fuel Rsch., Inc., East Hartford, Conn., 1995-98; chmn. Pioneer Techs., Inc., West Hartford, Conn., 1996-99; cons. InfiMed, Inc., Liverpool, N.Y., 1998-2000; chmn. acad. affairs Tatung Inst. Tech., Taipei, 1979-80; tech. info. editor Indsl. Tech. Rsch. Inst., Hsin-Chu, 1985-86; translator tech. articles Super Tech. Books Co., Taipei, 1986. Author, editor: Unit Operations in Chemical Engineering, 1986; contbr. articles to profl. jours. 2nd lt. Chinese Air Force, 1983-85. Recipient Editor's Choice award Nat. Poetry Assn., 1989, 90; Am.-Chinese Engr. scholar Am.-Chinese Assn. Engrs., 1980; Liang Ji-Duan fellow Carnegie Mellon U., 1991. Mem. AAAS, IEEE, SPIE, ASM, Am. Soc. Quality, Materials Rsch. Soc., Am. Vacuum Soc. (Paper award 1992), Soc. Info. Display, Beta Gamma Sigma. Achievements include research in diamond thin films and high Tc superconductors, superconducting quantum interference devices and biomagnetic systems, surface characterization and microstructural analysis, ferroelectric devices, giant magnetoresistive sensors, high-speed microelectronics, epitaxial heterostructures, in-process monitors, pulsed laser deposition, thermal evaporation, sputtering, pyroelectric sensor arrays, gas sensors, plasma-enhanced chemical vapor deposition, x-ray imaging materials, digital radiography and fluoroscopy. Office: Pioneer Tech Inc PO Box 270682 Hartford CT 06127-0682

KUNG, SHAIN-DOW, molecular biologist, academic administrator; b. China, Mar. 14, 1935; came to U.S., 1971, naturalized, 1977; s. Chao-tzen and Chih (Zhu) K. Grad., Chung-Hsing U., Taiwan, China, 1958; PhD, U. Toronto, Can., 1968. m. Helen C.C. Kung, Sept. 5, 1964; children: Grace, David, Andrew. Rsch. fellow Hosp. for Sick Children, Toronto, 1968-70; biologist UCLA, 1971-74; asst. prof. biology U. Md., Baltimore County, 1974-77, prof., 1977-82, 1982-86, acting chmn. dept., 1982-84, assoc. dean arts and sci., 1985-86; prof. botany U. Md., College Park, 1986-93; acting dir. U. Md. Ctr. for Agrl. Biotech., 1986-88, dir., 1988-93; dean sch. sci. Hong Kong U. Sci. and Tech., 1991-92, v.p. for acad. affairs, 1992-98; hon. prof. Fudan U., 1986, Beijing Agrl. U., 1987; acting provost Md. Biotech. Inst., 1989-91. Author 4 books; editor 14 books; contbr. chpts. to books, articles to profl. jours. Recipient PHilip Morris award for disting. achievement in tobacco sci., 1979, Outstanding Alumni award, 1990, Outstanding Svc. award, 1990; named Disting. Scholar, Nat. Acad. Sci., 1981; Fulbright grantee, 1982-83, grantee NSF, NIH. Mem. AAAS, Am. Soc. Plant Physiologists. Office: Hong Kong U Sci and Tech, Clear Water Bay, Kowloon Hong Kong China

KUNG (GONG) PIN-MEI, IGNATIUS CARDINAL (IGNATIUS KUNG (GONG) CARDINAL PIN-MEI), bishop; b. P'ou-tong, Shanghai, China, Aug. 2, 1901. Ordained priest Roman Cath. Ch., 1930; ordained bishop of Soochow, 1949; ordained bishop of Shanghai Apostolic Adminstr. Soochow and Nanking, 1950—. Apostolic adminstr. Souchou and Nanking, 1950—; prisoner of conscience People's Republic of China, 1955-85; elevated to Sacred Coll. Cardinals, 1979; formally invested titular Ch. St. Sixtus, 1991—.

KUNHARDT, MARTIN GERALD, plant breeder, researcher; b. Marandellas, Rhodesia, Oct. 21, 1956; arrived in S. Africa, 1980; s. Christopher John and Hilaria Ruth (Tenison) K. Diploma in Horticulture, U. Durban, South Africa, 1989. Cons. Rank Xerox, Durban, 1981-83, Design Syndicate, Durban, 1984-87; plant breeder Wahroonga, S. Africa, 1990-99. Contbr. articles to profl. jours. Curator Natural Heritage Site, Wahroonga, 1990—. With Rhodesian Army, 1975-81. Mem. Aggs, Natrual Heritage Found. Anglican. Avocations: conservation, wildlife and plant photography. Home and Office: Wahroonga Box 144, Merrivale 3291, South Africa

KUNIHOLM, BRUCE ROBELLET, university administrator; b. Washington, Oct. 4, 1942; s. Bertel Eric and Berthe Eugenie (Robellet) K.; m. Elizabeth Fairbank, June 29, 1968 (div. July 1987); children: Jonathan, Erin. AB in English, Dartmouth Coll., 1964; MA in History, Duke U., 1972, MA in Pub. Policy Sci., 1976, PhD in History, 1976. Instr. English Robert Acad./Robert Coll., Istanbul, Turkey, 1964-67; Coun. Fgn. Rels./NEH fellow Dept. State, Washington, 1979, internat. rels. officer policy planning staff, 1979-80; from instr. to lectr. policy studies and history Duke U., Durham, N.C., 1975-77, asst. prof. pub. policy studies and history, 1977-78, 80-84, assoc. prof. pub. policy studies and history, 1984-87, prof. pub. policy studies and history, 1987—, chmn. dept. public policy studies, 1989-94, dir. Terry Sanford Inst. Pub. Policy, 1989-94; vis. prof. Internat. Rels. Koc U., Istanbul, Turkey, 1995-96; prof. pub. policy studies and history, 1996—; vice-provost for acad. and internat. affairs, Duke U., Durham, N.C., 1996—; dir. Ctr. for Internat. Studies, 1999—; guest scholar Woodrow Wilson Internat. Ctr. Scholars, 1982; cons. NEH, USMC, Dept. State, U.S. Army, United Tech. Corp.; invited lectr. numerous orgns., colls., univs., fgn. countries including U.S. Senate Fgn. Rels.Com., CIA, State Dept., Chase Manhattan Bank, Harvard U., Brown U., Dartmouth Coll., Yale U., Princeton U., France, Eng., Germany, Italy, Kuwait, Saudi Arabia, Sudan, Can., Turkey, also others. Author: Origins of the Cold War in the Near East, 1980 (Stuart L. Bernath prize 1981), The Persian Gulf and United States Policy, 1984, The Palestine Problem and United States Policy, 1986; contbr. articles to profl. jours.; contbr. chpts. books. Bd. dirs. Found. for Ednl. Exch. between Can. and U.S. Capt. USMC, 1967-71, Vietnam. Decorated Bronze Star with V device; recipient Disting. Teaching award Trinity Coll., Duke U., 1989; rsch. grantee Harry S. Truman Libr., 1984, Duke U. Rsch. Coun., 1985-86, Inst. Turkish Studies, 1986-87, travel grantee Ctr. Soviet and East European Studies, 1991; Fulbright sr. rsch. fellow, Turkey, 1986-87, Woodrow Wilson Internat. Ctr. Scholars fellow Smithsonian Instn., 1986-87, sr. fellow Nobel Inst., Oslo, 1994. Mem. Am. Hist. Assn., Fulbright Fellows, Coun. Fgn. Rels., Orgn. Am. Historians, Soc. Historians Am. Fgn. Rels., Middle East Inst., Middle East Studies Assn., Internat. Inst. Strategic Studies, Phi Beta Kappa. Democrat. Avocations: triathlons, bluegrass banjo, wine. Home: 1719 Tisdale St Durham NC 27705-5631 Office: Duke U Office of Provost PO Box 90006 Durham NC 27708-0006

KUNII, AKIRA, human science educator; b. Nagoya, Japan, Dec. 17, 1934; s. Shiroh and Mitsu (Kojima) K.; m. Shizuko Yoshino, Oct. 25, 1969; children: Mami, Takashi. MD, Nagoya U., 1959, PhD, 1965. Asst. Columbia U. Coll. Physicians and Surgeons, N.Y.C., 1962-65; lectr. Sch. Medicine Nagoya (Japan) U., 1970-73, asst. prof. Sch. Med. Tech., 1973-80, prof. Coll. Med. Tech., 1980—, dean Coll. Med. Tech., 1992—; prof. health scis. Aichi (Japan) Mizuho Coll, 1998—. Co-author: The Lymphoreticular Tumours in Africa, 1964, The Thymus: Experimental and Clinical Studies, 1966, Effects of Interferon on Cells, Viruses and the Immune System, 1975; contbr. articles to profl. jours. Mem. AAAS, N.Y. Acad. Scis., Am. Assn. Cancer Rsch. Home: 23 Yakushiyama Narumicho, Midori Nagoya 458-0846, Japan Office: Aichi Mizuho Coll, 86-1 Haiwa Hiratobashi-cho, Aichi Toyota 470-0394, Japan

KUNII, OSAMU, epidemiologist, educator; b. Otawara, Tochigi, Japan, Oct. 20, 1962; s. Chuji and Ayako (Usui) K.; m. Naoko Tanimura, Jan. 26, 1991; children: Koshu, Taiga. Diploma of ayurveda, Udupi (India) Ayurveda Coll., 1985; MD, Jichi Med. Sch., Tochigi, 1988; diploma of tropical medicine, U. Nagasaki, Japan, 1993; MPH, Harvard U., 1994; PhD, U. Tokyo, 1999. Staff Saiseikai Utsunomiya Hosp., Tochigi, 1990-91; dir. Kuriyama Kokuho Clinic, Tochigi, 1991-93; lectr. Jichi Med. Sch., Tochigi, 1994-95; med. officer Internat. Med. Ctr. Japan, Tokyo, 1995-2000; asst. prof. dept. internatl. cmty. health U. Tokyo, 2000—; councilor Japan Overseas Christian Med. Coop. Svc., Tokyo, 1996-97; vis. lectr. Juntendo U., Tokyo, 1996—, Tsukuba U., Ibaraki, Japan, 1995-96. Editor: (books) Medical Check Sheet in 15 Languages, 1992, Dental Check Sheet in 15 Languages, 1992; co-author: (book) Medical Insurance for All Foreigners, 1990. Recipient Fulbright award Japan U.S. Ednl. Commn., 1993-94; named Outstanding Young Person, Grand Prix, Jr. Chamber, 1996; rsch. fellow U. Tokyo. Mem. Japanese Soc. Internat. Health, N.Y. Acad. Scis. Avocations: listening to and playing music, yoga. Office: U Tokyo Dept Intl Cmty Hlth, 7-3-1 Hongo, Bonkyoku Tokyo 113-0033, Japan

KUNII, TOSIYASU LAURENCE, information science educator; b. Tokyo, Jan. 1, 1938; s. Fujitoshi and Hisako (Saito) K.; m. Hideko Shimizu, Nov. 8, 1970; 1 child, Michiaki. BS, U. Tokyo, 1962, MS, 1964, DSc, 1967. Assoc. prof. U. Tokyo, 1969-78, prof., 1978-93; pres., prof. U. Aizu, Japan, 1993-97; advisor Fukushima Prefecture, Govt. Japan, 1997-2000; prof. Hosei (Japan) U., 1998—; prof. emeritus U. Tokyo, 1998—; hon. vis. prof. U. Bradford, Eng., 1998—. Editor-in-chief: The Visual Computer, 1984-99; assoc. editor-in-chief: Visualization and Computer Animation, 1990—; assoc. editor: IEEE Computer Graphics and Applications, 1982—. Fellow IEEE (Taylor L. Booth Edn. award 1998), Info. Processing Soc. Japan. Achievements include patent for assemblability discriminating method and assembling sequence generating method. Home: 1-25-21-602 Hongo Bunkyo-ku, Tokyo 113-0033, Japan Office: Hosei U Computer/Info Scis, 3-7-2 Kajino-cho, Minato-ku Koganei City Tokyo 184-8584, Japan

KUNIMATSU, KAZUSHI, dentist, educator; b. Sasebo, Nagasaki, Japan, Aug. 28, 1953; s. Eiichi and Yukiko (Ohkubo) K.; m. Naomi Yoshikawa, Mar. 31, 1985; children: Arisa, Misaki. BA, Iwate Med. Coll., Morioka, Japan; PhD, Nagasaki U. Dental qualification; periodontal specialist qualification. Instr. Nagasaki U., 1984-92, asst. prof., 1992—. Contbr. articles to profl. jours. Mem. Internat. Assn. Dental Rsch., Japanese Soc. Conservative Dentistry (councilor 1992—), Japanese Soc. Periodontology (councilor 1992—). Avocations: reading, listening to classical music. Office: Nagasaki U Sch Dentistry, 1-7-1 Sakamoto, 852-8588 Nagasaki Japan

KUNIN, MADELEINE MAY, former ambassador to Switzerland, former governor; b. Zurich, Switzerland, Sept. 28, 1933; came to U.S., 1940, naturalized, 1947; d. Ferdinand and Renee (Bloch) May; children: Julia, Peter, Adam, Daniel. B.A., U. Mass., 1956; M.S., Columbia U., 1957; M.A., U. Vt., 1967; numerous hon. degrees. Newspaper reporter Burlington Free Press, Vt., 1957-58; guide Brussels World's Fair, Belgium, 1958; TV asst. producer Sta. WCAX-TV, Burlington, 1960-61; freelance writer, instr. English Trinity Coll., Burlington, 1969-70; mem. Vt. Ho. of Reps., 1973-78; lt. gov. State of Vt., Montpelier, 1979-82, gov., 1985-91; disting. vis. in Pub. Policy Bunting Inst., Cambridge, Mass., 1991-92, Dartmouth Coll., Hanover, N.H., 1992; dep. sec. edn. Dept. Education, Washington, D.C., 1993-96; U.S. amb. to Switzerland, 1996-99; now scholar in residence Middlebury Coll.; fellow Inst. Politics, Kennedy Sch. Govt., Harvard U., 1983; lectr. Middlebury Coll., St. Michael's Coll., 1984; disting. pub. policy visitor Rockefeller Ctr., Dartmouth Coll., 1992; pub. policy fellow Bunting Inst., Radcliffe Coll., Harvard U., 1991-92; Vt. Joint Fiscal Com., 1977-78; mem. exec. com. Nat. Conf. Lt. Govs., 1979-80; founder, pres. Inst. Sustainable Cmtys., Montpelier, Vt., 1991; mem. 3 person com. to recommend v.p. to Bill Clinton, co-chair nat. com. Women for Clinton, 1992; scholar-in-residence Middlebury (Vt.) Coll., 1999—. Author: Living a Political Life: A Memoir, 1994, The Big Green Book, 1976; contbr. articles to profl. jours., mags. and newspapers. Scholar in residence Middleburg Coll.; Named Outstanding State Legislator, Eagleton Inst. Politics, Rutgers U., 1975; Montgomery fellow Dartmouth Coll., 1991. Fellow Am. Acad. Arts & Scis.; mem. Nat. Gov.'s Assn. (mem. exec. com.), Nat. Govs.' Conf. (chair com. on energy and the environ.), New Eng. Gov.'s Conf. (chairperson). Democrat. E-mail: mkunin@middlebury.edu. Office: Middlebury College 107 Geonomics House Middlebury VT 05753

KUNINAKA, AKIRA, agricultural chemistry researcher; b. Tokyo, Jan. 16, 1928; s. Ryo and Misao (Wakimura) K.; m. Sumiko Tanaka, May 9, 1958; children: Setsuko Miyashita, Osamu Kuninaka, Hisako Saito. B of Agriculture, U. Tokyo, 1951, D of Agriculture, 1959. Researcher Yamasa Corp., Choshi-shi, Chiba-ken, Japan, 1953—, dir., 1978-86, mng. dir., 1986-95, hon. head labs., 1995—; guest prof. Tokyo U. of Agr., Tokyo, 1994-98, Chiba (Japan) U., 1995-96; pres. Japan Immuno-Monitoring Ctr., Inc., Tokyo, 1982-86; rsch. assoc. dept. biochemistry MIT, Cambridge, Mass., 1963-66; chmn. Japan sect. Inst. Food Technologists, 1991-92. Recipient Purple Ribbon medal Prime Minister, Tokyo, 1983, Imperial Invention prize Invention Soc., 1964. Mem. Agrl. Chem. Soc. Japan (v.p. 1989-91, agrl. chemistry prize 1960). Home: 2-15-21 Araoi-cho, Chibaken Choshi 288, Japan Office: Yamasa Corp, 2-10-1 Araoi-cho, Chibaken Choshi 288, Japan

KUNITAKE, TOYOKI, chemistry educator; b. Kurume, Fukuoka, Japan, Feb. 26, 1936; s. Toyokichi and Fujie Kunitake; m. Hiroko Kitagawa, June 24, 1964; 1 child, Motoko. B in Engring., Kyushu U., Fukuoka, Japan, 1958; M in Engring., Kyushu U., 1960; PhD, U. Pa., 1962. Assoc. prof. Kyushu U., Fukuoka, Japan, 1963-74, prof. chemistry, 1974-99, dean faculty engring., 1992-94; group dir. RIKEN, 1999—. Co-author: Specialty Polymers, 1983; editor: Artificial Cells, 1983. Mem. Chem. Soc. Japan, Am. Chem. Soc., Polymer Soc. Japan (soc. award 1978). Home: Sakuragaoka 1-19-3, Shime-machi 811-2201, Japan Office: RIKEN, Wako 351-0198, Japan

KUNIYA, NOBUAKI, psychology educator; b. Tokyo, July 15, 1928; s. Inokichi and Teruko (Kunyia) Uchiyama; m. Shizue Shimura, Oct. 18, 1953; children: Naomi, Mikaya. MA, Tokyo U., 1958, PhD, 1986. Cert. clin. psychologist Japanese Bd. Cert. Clin. Psychologists. Pvt. practice Kamakura-shi, 1970-89; prof. psychology Japan Women's U., Tokyo, 1990-96; prof. child clin. psychology Seitoku U., Matudo, 1997—. Mem. Internat. Acad. Family Psychology (nat. rep. Japan), Japanese Assn. Family Psychology (exec. com. 1990-98), N.Y. Acad. Sci. Lutheran. Home: Kajiwara 2-14-9, Kamakura-shi 247-0063, Japan Office: Seitoku U, 550 Iwase, Matsudo-shi 271-8555, Japan

KUNIYASU, KEITH KAZUMI, secondary education educator; b. Honolulu, Apr. 16, 1955; s. Hajime and Betty Mieko (Yamamoto) K. AA in Liberal Arts, U. Hawaii, Pearl City, 1978, AS in Graphic Arts, 1978; BS in Tech. Edn., Western Wash. U., 1982; MEd in Tech. Edn., Oreg. State U., 1987. Cert. vocat. adminstr. Instrumental music instr. Aiea (Hawaii) Intermediate Sch., 1978-88; spl. edn. instr. Highlands Intermediate Sch., Pearl City, 1983-84; visual comm. instr. Oak Harbor (Wash.) High Sch., 1982-83; photography instr. Olympic Coll., Bremerton, Wash., 1984-85; comm. techs. instr. North Kitsap High Sch., Poulsbo, Wash., 1984-93; instr. comm. techs. River Ridge High Sch., Lacey, Wash., 1993—; edn. rep. curriculum/competency validation com. Wash. State Supt. Pub. Instrn., Olympia, 1988-93; cons. Wash. SkillsUSA- Vocat. Indsl. Clubs Am., 1990—; mem. Nat. Skills-USA Vocat. Indsl. Clubs of Am. Leadership Handbook Revision Team, 1995; pvt. woodwind instr., 1974-94; counselor, woodwind specialist Maui (Hawaii) Intermediate Select Band Camps, 1975-80; advisor Leeward C.C. Graphic Arts Club, Pearl City, 1978-80; sch. accreditation teams for various high schs. throughout Wash., 1988—; writing com. leadership curriculum Wash. State Supt. Instrn. Edn., Olympia, 1993—. Author: (pamphlet series) Care of Single Reeds, 1983, (brochures) Addressing Technology Education, 1988-92, Communication Technologies, 1995, What Is Hawk Communications?, 1995, VisCom Student Study Guide, 1987, 2nd edit., 1990, 3rd edit., 1993, 4th edit., 1996, From Goods to Services, 1988, Technology Education Facility, 1988, Communication Technologies at North Kitsap High School, 1989, Visual Communications, 1990, Bob's Law's (Robert's Rules of Order), 1995, 2nd edit., 1997. Organizer, pres. Pacific Islanders Club at Western Wash. U., Bellingham, 1981-82; organizer, bd. dirs. Leeward Fine Arts Coun., Pearl City, 1981-94. Named Advisor of Yr. Wash. SkillsUSA-Vocat. Indsl. Clubs Am., 1993. Mem. NEA, Internat. Tech. Edn. Assn. (affiliate rep. 1990-94), Internat. Graphic Arts Educators Assn., Grapic Arts Tech. Found., Am. Vocat. Assn., Wash. Vocat. Assn., Wash. Tech. Edn. Assn., SkillsUSA-Vocat. Indsl. Clubs Am. (advisor, regional coord. 1990-93, 94-96, 99—). Avocations: travel, cooking, music, reading, working with young adults. Office: River Ridge H S 8929 Martin Way E Lacey WA 98516-5932

KUNKEL, GEORGIE BRIGHT, freelance writer, retired school counselor; b. Chehalis, Wash.; d. George Riley and Myrtia (McLaughlin) Bright; m. Norman C. Kunkel, Apr. 25, 1946; children: N. Joseph D.C., Stephen Gregory, Susan Ann, Kimberly Jane Waligorska. BA in Edn., Western Wash. U., 1944; MEd, U. Wash., 1968. Tchr. pub. schs., Vader, Centralia, Seattle, Wash., 1941-67; counselor Highline Pub. Schs., Seattle, 1967-82; pvt. cons., Seattle, 1970—; sch. counselor rep. State of Art Conf., Balt., 1980. Author: You're Damn Right I Wear Puple! Color Me Feminist, 2000; editor Women and Girls in Edn., 1972-75; columnist Highline Times, Burien, Wash.; contbr. articles to profl. jours. Organizer Women and Girls in Edn., Wash. State, 1971; pres. Wash. State NOW, 1973; organizer, pres. Holmes Harbor Homeowners Assn.; pres. West Seattle Dem. Women's Club. Named Woman of Yr. in Wash. State, Women's Fedn. for World Peace, 1998; grantee Women Adminstrs. Wash. State, 1971, Edn. Svc. Dist., Seattle, 1980; recipient Woman of Achievement award Past Pres. Assembly, 2000; winner essay contest and appeared on Oprah show. Mem. NEA (sec. pub. rels.), ACA (pres. state br. 1982-83), Am. Sch. Counseling Assn. (pres. state divsn. 1980-81), Seattle Counselors Assn. (organizer, past pres. office exec., Counselor of Yr. award 1990). Unitarian. Avocation: singing with Raging Grannies and Rolling Crones. Home and Office: 3409 SW Trenton St Seattle WA 98126-3743

KUNKEL, GÜNTHER W.H., writer, conservationist; b. Mittenwalde, Germany, Sept. 26, 1928; arrived in Spain, 1964; s. Willi Hermann and Liesbeth (Piesnack) K.; m. Mary Anne Charlewood Turner, June 25, 1960; 1 child, Thomas Austin. Grad., Handelsschule, Berlin, 1945; D of hon. causes, U. Nacional Centro Peru. Sci. asst. Valdivia, Chile, 1957-60; prof. botany Huancayo, Peru, 1960-61; dendrologist German Forestry Mission to Liberia, 1961-63; phytogeographic and taxonomic rschr., govt. botanist Canary Islands, 1964-77; floristic rschr. West Sahara, Ghana, Persian Gulf, 1978-91; desert rschr. Almeria, Spain, 1991-94; founder Jardin Botánico del Desierto, Murcia, Spain, 1991; sec. I Congress Internat. Flora Macaronesica. Author: Beobachtungen über Klima und Vegetation in Südchile, 1956, Meteorologisch-mikroklimatologische Beobachtungen in Valdivia, 1959, The Trees of Liberia, 1965, Helechos Cultivados, 1967, Arboles exóticos, 1969, Flora de Gran Canaria, 1974-79, The Vegetation of Hormoz, Qeshm and Neighbouring Islands, 1977, Inventario Floristico de la Laurisilva de la Gomera, 1977, Las Plantas Vasculares de Fuerteventura, 1977, Endemismos Canarios, 1977, Flowering Trees in Subtropical Gardens, 1978, La Vida Vegetal del Parque Nacional de Timanfaya, 1978, Die Kanarischen Inseln und ihre Pflanzenwelt, 1980, 87, 93, Arboles y Arbustos de las Islas Canarias, 1981, Malas Hierbas de Almería, 1983, Los Riscos de Famara (Lanzarote), 1983, Plants for Human Consumption, 1984, El Libro de las Malas Hierbas, 1987, Flórula del Desierto Almeriense, 1988, 93, La Geografia en la Nomenclatura botánica Hispano-Lusitana, 1988, Geography Through Botany, 1990, Supplement, 1996, 2000, Diccionario de Botánica, 1986, 91, Flora y Vegetación del Archipiélago Canario, 1992, Arboles Ornamentales de Almería, 1996, Hierbas infestantes de la Comarca de Los Velez, 1998, Jardinería en Zonas Aridas, 1998-2000, La Geografía en la Nomenclatura Botánica del Peru, 1999, Gärten und Gartnern in Trockentgebieten, 2000; also 400 small books and articles, over 400 book revs.; editor: Cuadernos de Botánica Canaria, 1967-77, Monographiae Biologicae Canarienses, 1970-75, Biogeography and Ecology in the Canary Islands, 1976, Taxonomic Aspects of African Economic Botany, 1970, others. Recipient Cert. of Merit, Comendador del Orden de Mérito Agrícola, Bundesverdienstkreuz. Fellow Linnean Soc., Instituto Estudios Almerienses, Instituto Estudios Canarios; mem. AAAS, Assn. pour l'Étude Taxonomique de la Flore d'Afrique Tropicale (sec. gen.), The Explorers Club, El Museo Canario, N.Y. Acad. Scis., others. Home: Apartado de Correos 79, E-04820 Velez-Rubio Almeria, Spain

KUNNEL, JOSEPH MATHEW, lawyer; b. Ernakulam, Kerala, India, May 3, 1963; came to U.S., 1991; s. Matthew and Annakutty Kunnel; m. Valsamma Thottumkal, Jan. 19, 1989; children: Nicole Ann, Jimmy M., Megan E. B.Com., U. Kerala, India, 1983; LLB, U. Gulberga, Karnataka, India, 1987; LLM, Widener U., Wilmington, Del., 1993. Bar: Pa. 1994. Pvt. practice Kerala, 1987-91; ptnr. Pasquarella & Kunnel, Phila., 1994—. Pres Malayalee Assn. of Phila., 1997—. Mem. ABA, Pa. Bar Assn. (exec. com. minority bar), Phila. Bar Assn., Am. Immigration Lawyers Assn., Dist. Bar Assn. Kerala (sec. 1988-90). Avocations: reading, writing, travel. Office: Pasquarella & Kunnel 1401 Walnut St Philadelphia PA 19102-3128

KUNO, NAOHIKO, perinatologist; b. Anjo, Aichi, Japan, Apr. 3, 1963; s. Yasuo and Aiko (Asaoka) K. MD, Nagoya (Japan) U., 1990; PhD, Nagoya (Japan) U., 1997. Resident Japanese Red Cross, Nagoya 1st Hosp., 1990-93, faculty ob-gyn., 1997—; Turkey earthquake health del. Japanese Red Cross, Ismit, Turkey, 1999, East Timon health del. Internat. com. Red Cross, Dili, East Timon, 2000. Contbr. articles to profl. jours. Avocations: flute, motorcycle, orchids.

KUNSTADTER, GERALDINE SAPOLSKY, foundation executive; b. Boston, Jan. 6, 1928; d. Harry Herman and Nettie Sapolsky; m. John W. Kunstadter, Apr. 23, 1949; children: John W., Lisa, Christopher, Elizabeth. Student, MIT, 1945-48. Draftsman U. Chgo. Cyclotron Project, 1948; engring. asst. Gen. Electric Corp., Lynn, Mass., 1948-49; pres. Capricorn Investments Corp., 1971—; chair, dir. A. Kunstadter Family Found., N.Y.C., 1966—; host family program dir. N.Y.C. Commn. for UN, 1971-86; pres. Nat. Inst. Social Scis., 1979-81. Bd. dirs. Bridge to Asia Found., Menninger Found., Nat. Com. on U.S.-China Rels., Atlantic Coun. of U.S., Internat. Devel. Enterprises, Inc., Ballets Tech. Found., N.Y.C., Ctr. U.S.-China Arts Exch., Inst. World Affairs; adv. coun. East Asian studies program MIT Sch. Arch.; mem. Peace Links Leadership Network, Overseas Devel. Coun., N.Y.-Beijing Friendship City Com.; internat. hospitality com. Nat. Coun. Women. Recipient Windham award, 1970, Silver medal Nat. Inst. Social Sci., 1981. Mem. Inst. Current World Affairs, Coun. on Fgn. Rels., Am. Women's Club, Hurlingham Club, Lansdowne Club (London).

KUNTJORO-JAKTI, DORODJATUN, diplomat; b. Banten, Indonesia, 1939; married; three children. Grad., U. Indonesia; MA in Fin. Adminstrn., U. Calif., Berkeley, PhD in Polit. Economy. Head macroecon. studies U. Indonesia, 1973-74, head econs. and devel. studies, from dep. dir. to dir. Rsch. Inst. Econs. and Mgmt., asst. to dean faculty econs., 1988-93, dean faculty econs., 1994-98; amb. to U.S. Govt. Indonesia, Washington, 1998—; mem. adv. bd. Sch. Internat. and Regional Studies, U. Calif., Berkeley; mem. regional security study program Inst. S.E. Asian Studies, Singapore, 1981—; mem. Japan-ASEAN Dialogue, Japan Ctr. for Internat. Exch., 1982—; mem. adv. bd. Found. Asian Mgmt. Devel., Japan, 1988—; mem. Inst. for Monetary and Fiscal Policy, Ministry Fin., Japan, 1991—; econ. expert Non-Aligned Movement, 1993-95; mem. team of experts Pacific Bus. Forum, APEC Econ. Leaders Meeting, Bogor, 1994, Osaka, Japan, 1995; mem. team of experts APEC Bus. Adv. Coun., APEC Econ. Leaders Meeting, Manila, 1996, Vancouver, 1997. Author of books; mem. regional editing bd. Jour. Contemporary S.E. Asian Studies; contbr. articles to profl. jours. Fax: 202-775-5365. Office: Embassy of Republic of Indonesia 2020 Massachusetts Ave NW Washington DC 20036-1012

KUNTORO, MANGKUSUBROTO, government official; b. 1932. Gen. dir. mining Dept. Mines & Energy, Jakarta, Indonesia, 1993-97; advisor Investment Coord. Bd.; min. Dept. Mines & Energy, 1998-2000; pres. & dir. Perusahaan Listrik Negara (PLN Electricity), Jakarta, Indonesia, 2000—. Office: PLN (Persero), Jl Trunojoyo Blok M I/135, Jakarta 12160, Indonesia*

KUNTZ, WILLIAM FRANCIS, II, lawyer, educator; b. N.Y.C., June 24, 1950; s. William Francis I and Margaret Evelyn (Brown) K.; m. Alice Beal, May 20, 1978; children: William Thaddeus, Katharine Lowell, Elizabeth Anne. AB, Harvard U., 1972, AM, 1974, JD, 1977, PhD, 1979. Bar: N.Y. 1978. Assoc. Shearman & Sterling, N.Y.C., 1978-86; mem. Milgrim, Thomajan & Lee, N.Y.C., 1986-94; ptnr. Seward & Kissel, N.Y.C., 1994—;

assoc. prof. Bklyn. Law Sch., 1987—. Author: Criminal Sentencing, 1988. Bd. dirs. MFY Legal Svcs., Inc., N.Y.C., 1984-90, Boys Brotherhood Republic, N.Y.C., 1986-90, Habitat for Humanity, N.Y.C., 1987-90; chmn. Resources for Children with Spl. Needs, N.Y.C., 1986-89; mem. N.Y. Civilian Complaint Rev. Bd., 1987—, chmn., 1994. Mem. ABA, N.Y. State Bar Assn., N.Y. County Lawyers Assn. (bd. dirs. 1991-96), Assn. of Bar of City of N.Y. (chmn. mcpl. affairs com. 1992-95, judiciary com.), Bklyn. Bar Assn. (judiciary com. 1995—), Met. Black Bar Assn. Democrat. Roman Catholic. Office: Seward & Kissel 1 Battery Park Plz Fl 21 New York NY 10004-1485

KUNZ, MILAN, chemical engineer; b. Brno, Czech Republic, Aug. 6, 1931; s. František and Antonie (Picbauerová) K.; m. Marie Maděrová, July 20, 1954; children: Dagmar, Michal. MS in Engring., Mil. Tech. Acad., 1955. Rschr. Ctr. of Army, 1955-69; lectr. Mil. Tech. Coll., Cairo, 1970-74; patent atty. Rsch. Inst. of Macromolecular Chemistry, Brno, 1975-90; patent cons. Kania, Sedlák, Smola, Brno, 1990—. Contbr. articles to profl. jours. including Scientometrics, Jour. Chem. Info. Computer Sci., Match, Jour. Mat. Chem., Coll. Czech. Chem. Comm.; co-author 30 patents. Mem. N.Y. Acad. Sci. Home: Jurkovičova 13, 63800 Brno Czech Republic

KUNZ, WERNER, chemist, educator, researcher; b. Krummennaab, Germany, Oct. 30, 1960; s. Rudolf and Marianne (Treml) K.; m. Eva Treutinger, Aug. 22, 1986; 1 child, Stephanie Isabelle. Diploma in Chemistry, U. Regensburg, Germany, 1985, D of Natural Scis., 1988. Postdoctoral fellow Lab. Electrochemistry U. Pierre et Marie Curie, Paris, 1988-91; phys. chemistry rschr. Ctr. d'Etudes Nucleaires Saclay, France, 1992-93; asst. prof. U. Tech. Compiegne, France, 1993, prof., 1993-97; full prof., head lab phys. chemistry U. Regensburg, Germany, 1997—, dir. Inst. Phys. and Theoretical Chemistry, 1997—; head Nat. Ctr. Sci. Rsch. Lab., Compiegne, 1996; guest prof. U. Louvain, La Neuve, Belgium, 1997; founder, dir. postgrad. programme in phys. chemistry Compiegne U., 1994-96. Co-author: Physical Chemistry of Electrolyte Solutions, 1998, (chpt.) Water and Ionic Hydration, 1995; co-editor Jour. Molecular Liquids, 1997—; contbr. over 50 articles to profl. jours.; patentee in field. Recipient grant German Student Found., 1982-88, award German Chem. Industry, 1988, Postdoctoral Rsch. grant NATO and European Cmty., 1989-91. Mem. German Chem. Soc., German Bunsen-Soc. Phys. Chemistry, European Acad. Sci. (corr. mem.). Fax: 49 941 943 4532. E-mail: Werner.Kunz@chemie.uni-regensburg.de. Office: U Regensburg, Inst Phys and Theor Chem, D-93040 Regensburg Germany

KUNZE, REINER ALEXANDER, writer, poet; b. Oelsnitz, Erzgebirge, Germany, Aug. 16, 1933; s. Ernst Richard and Martha Helene (Friedrich) K.; m. Ingeborg Weinhold, July 17, 1954 (div. 1960); 1 child, Ludwig; m. Elisabeth Mifka, July 8, 1967; 1 child, Marcela. Diploma in Journalism, U. Leipzig, Germany, 1955; PhD (hon.), Technische Univ., Dresden, Germany, 1993. Tchr. U. Leipzig, 1955-59; lectr. in poetry U. Munich, 1989, U. Würzburg, Germany, 1990. Author: Sensible Wege, 1969, Zimmerlautstärke, 1972, Die Wunderbaren Jahre, 1976, Auf Eigene Hoffnung, 1981, Eines Jeden Einziges Leben, 1986, Das Weisse Gedicht, 1989, Wohin der Schlaf Sich Schlafen Legt, 1991, Am Sonnenhang, 1993, Wo Freiheit Ist..., 1994, Steine und Lieder, 1996, Ein Tag auf dieser Erde, 1998, Christian Ferber Ehrengabe, 2000. Recipient Übersetzerpreis Tschechoslow Schriftstellerverband, 1968, Deutscher Jugendbuchpreis, 1971, Literaturpreis der Bayer Acad. der Schönen Künste, 1973, Mölle-Literaturpreis, 1973, Georg-Trakl Preis, 1977, Georg-Büchner-Preis, 1977, Geschwister-Scholl-Preis, 1981, Eichendorff-Literaturpreis, 1984, Grosses Verdienstkreuz der Bundesrepublik Deutschland, 1993, Weilheimer Literaturpreis, 1997, Europapreis für Poesie, Serbien, 1998, Friedrich-Hölderlin-Preis, 1999. Mem. Bayer Acad. der Schönen Künste, Deutsche Acad. für Sprache und Dichtung, Freie Acad. der Künste Mannheim, Sächs Acad. der Künste, Collegium Europaeum Jenense (hon.), Ungarischer Schriftstellerverband (hon.), Tschechisches Pen-Zentrum (hon.). Home: Am Sonnenhang 19, D-94130 Obernzell-Erlau Bayern, Germany

KUNZENDORF, HELMAR WILFRIED, geochemist; b. Reisicht, Schlesien, Germany, Oct. 13, 1938; came to Denmark, 1966; s. Alfred and Frieda (Pilz) K.; m. Karin Nanna Jellum, Dec. 20, 1967; children: Astrid, Ida. MS in Physics, RWTH, Aachen, Germany, 1966; PhD in Geochemistry, RWTH, 1972. Scientist Risø Nat. Lab., Roskilde, Denmark, 1966-84; project leader Risø Nat. Lab., Roskilde, 1984-89, sr. scientist, 1991—; mgr. lead-210 dating ctr., 1995. Author: Marine Minerals, 1987, The Manganese Nodule Belt, 1988, CRC Handbook Geophysical Exploration, 1992, Trends in Chemical Geology, 1994; editor: Marine Mineral Exploration, 1986; edit. bd. (jour.) Marine Georesources & Geotechnology, 1988—; contbr. more than 130 articles to profl. jours., books. Mem. N.Y. Acad. Scis., Internat. Marine Minerals Soc., Internat. Assn. of Cosmochemistry and Geochemistry, European Union of Geosciences, Danish Geol. Soc. Lutheran. Home: Kildevang 6 Herslev, DK 4000 Roskilde Denmark Office: Risø Nat Lab, PO Box 49, DK 4000 Roskilde Denmark

KUNZI, KLAUS FRIEDRICH, physics educator; b. Thun, Bern, Switzerland, Feb. 19, 1939; s. Werner E. and Margaretha B. (Hausermann) K.; children: Manuel, Andreas. Diploma, U. Bern, 1965, PhD, 1970. Rsch. assoc. U. Bern, 1966-71, dept. head, 1974-88; vis. scientist MIT, 1971-72, rsch. assoc., 1972-74; prof. physics U. Bremen, Germany, 1988—; mem. govt. adv. panels.; guest prof. Tech. U. Denmark, 1983; advisor various govt. agencies and internat. orgns. Contbr. over 200 articles to books, jours. and procs. Mem. various societies. Avocations: reading, sailing, hiking. E-mail: kunzi@uni-bremen.de. Office: U Bremen, PO Box 330440, D 28334 Bremen Bremen, Germany

KUNZMANN, KLAUS R., urban and regional planner, educator; b. Karlsruhe, Germany, Sept. 30, 1942; s. Theodor and Friedel (Forster) K. Diploma in architecture, Tech. U. Munich, 1967; DSc, Tech. U. Vienna, 1971; DLitt (hon.), U. Newcastle, 1996. Lectr. Inst. Spatial Planning U. Vienna, Austria, 1967-71; head, dir. Kocks KG Cons. Engring., Dusseldorf, Germany, 1971-74; from asoc. prof. to prof. European spatial planning U. Dortmund, Germany, 1974—; advisor OECD, UNDP, European Union; vis. prof. dept. city and regional planning U. Wales, Cardiff, 1998—; vis. prof. dept. urban studies and planning MIT, Cambridge, 1999; vis. prof. dept. urban and regional planning U. Pa. Grad. Sch. Fine Arts, Phila. Mem. Acad. Regional Rsch. and Spatial Planning. Office: U Dortmund, 44221 Dortmund Germany

KUO, CHUNG J., electrical engineering educator, research director; b. Tainan, Taiwan, Republic of China, Sept. 26, 1960; s. Ming Fu and Chao Yin (Chiao) K. BE in Power Mech. Engring., Nat. Tsing Hua U., Taiwan, 1982, ME in Power Mech. Engring., 1984; PhDEE, Mich. State U., 1990. Rsch. asst. Nat. Tsing Hua U., 1983-84; instr. Army Ordnance Sch., Taiwan, 1985-86; rsch. asst. Mich. State U., East Lansing, 1986-88, teaching asst., 1988-90; assoc. prof. elec. engring. Nat. Chung Cheng U., Chiayi, Taiwan, 1990-96; prof. Nat. Chung Cheng U., Chiayi, 1996—; dir. signal and media lab. Nat. Chung Cheng U., Chiayi, Taiwan, 1990—, coord. computer vision, graphics and image processing group, 1992—; coord. Opto-Electronics Group Nat. Chung Cheng U., Chiayi, 1993—; vis. scientist Opto-Electronics and System Lab., Indsl. Tech. Rsch. Inst., Taiwan, 1991; adj. assoc. prof. Nat. Cheng Kung U., Taiwan, 1991—; conf. presenter and speaker in field. Contbr. articles to profl. jours. Recipient best engring. paper award Computer Soc. Republic of China, 1991; elec. engring. fellow Mich. State U., 1989-90; rsch. awardee Nat. Sci. Coun., 1991-95; travel grantee Semicondr. Soc. India, 1992. Mem. IEEE (travel grantee 1990—), Optical Soc. of Am., Optical Engring. Soc. of Republic of China, Internat. Soc. for Optical Engring. (travel grantee 1992—), Chinese Image Processing and Pattern Recognition Soc., Phi Kappa Phi, Phi Beta Delta. Office: Nat Chung Cheng U, Dept Elec Engring, Chia-Yi 62107, Taiwan

KUO, JAN-TAI, water resources engineer; b. Kaohsiung, Taiwan, July 18, 1949; s. Ho-Li and Show-Luan (Chang) K.; m. Kuang-Hsiang Yang Kuo, July 16, 1978; children: Chi-Fen Kuo, Chi-Wen Kuo. BS, Nat. Taiwan U., Taipei, 1971; MEE, Manhattan Coll., 1976; PhD, Cornell U., Ithaca, N.Y., 1981. Registered water resources engr. Project engr. AWARE Corp., Nashville, 1979-81; sr. scientist Gen. Software Corp., Landover, Md., 1981-82; assoc. prof. Nat. Taiwan U., Taipei, 1982-87, prof., 1987—; com. mem. Regional planning com. Ministry of the Interior, Taiwan, 1995—; cons. River Protection Orgn. China times, Taiwan, 1995-99. Mem. editl. bd. Jour. Water Quality and Ecosys. Modeling. mem., bd. dirs. New Environ. Found., Taipei, Taiwan, 1994—. 2nd lt. Chinese Army in Taiwan, 1971-73. Recipient Excellence in the Grad. Environ Engring. Sylvester Murphy award Manhattan Coll., 1976, Rsch. Paper award Chinese Inst. Civil and Hydraulic Engring., 1987, Rsch. Paper award Chinese Inst. Environ. Engring., 1996, Rsch. Assistantship award Manhattan Coll., Bronx, N.Y., 1974-76, John McMullen Grad. Fellowship award Cornell U., Ithaca, N.Y., 1976-77. Mem. ASCE (chair probalistic approaches to water resources engring. com. 1998), Chinese Taiwan Div. Internat. Union of Geodesy and Geophysics, Internat. Assn. for Hydraulic Rsch. (chmn. com. probalistic methods hydraulics 1998—), Internat. Water Assn. Avocations: gardening, photography, travel. Home: No 7 Lane 2 Hua-Chen 2nd Rd, Hsin-Tien City Taiwan Office: Dept Civil Engring, Nat Taiwan Univ, Taipei 106, Taiwan

KUO, JOHN TSUNGFEN, geophysicist, educator, researcher; b. Hangchow, Chejiang, China, Apr. 1, 1922; came to U.S., 1949; naturalized, 1967; s. Lee Chen and Che Chen (Ping) K.; m. Marilyn Dunlap, Apr. 14, 1957; children: Ping Andrea, Sonya Sue, J. David. BS in Geology, Physics and Math., U. Redlands, 1952, ScD (hon.), 1978; MS in Geophysics, Cal. Inst. Tech., 1954; PhD in Geophysics, Stanford U., 1958. Asst. prof. San Jose (Calif.) St. Coll., 1957-60; rsch. assoc. Stanford U., 1958-60; rsch. scientist Columbia U., N.Y.C., 1960-64, assoc. prof., 1964-67, prof., 1967-83, Vinton prof., 1983-85, Ewing and Worzel prof., 1985-92, Ewing and Worzel prof. emeritus, 1992—; participant DEEPSCAN, 1963; dir. Aldridge Lab. Applied Geophysics, 1964-92, Lamont-Doherty's Underground Geophys. Obs., Ogdensburg, N.J., 1967-77, Columbia U., Project Migration, Inversion, Diffraction and Scattering, 1979-89; disting. sr. vis. scholar U. Cambridge, Eng., 1970-71; vis. prof. U. Tex., Austin, 1977-78, Cornell U., N.Y., 1978, 92-97, Tech. U. Clausthal, Fed. Rep. of Germany, 1987; adj. prof. Cornell U., 1992-98; Columbia U. del. People's Republic of China, 1979; tech. adv. 20th Dist. Congressman, 1983—; hon. prof, co-dir. integrated basin studies Chengdu Inst. Tech., People's Republic of China, 1986; hon. prof. Acad. Sinica, 1979—, China U. Geoscis., Beijing, 1992; hon. sr. rschr. Inst. Geophysics, China Seismological Bur., People's Republic of China, 1995—. Mem. editl. bd. Bollettino di Geofisica, Italy, 1985-89; contbr. over 120 articles to profl. jours. Danforth Tchg. fellow, 1957—, Sr. Postdoctoral fellow NSF, 1970; Rsch. grantee NSF, NASA, U.S. Geol. Survey, Office Naval Rsch., Air Force Office Sci. Rsch., Air Force Geophysics, U.S. Bur. Mines; recipient Alexander von Humboldt award for disting. U.S. sr. scientist, Fed. Republic Germany, 1986, Hon. Knight for Life award Knights Round Table Internat., 1993. Fellow Geol. Soc. Am., Royal Astron. Soc. U.K.; mem. Internat. Union Geodesy and Geophysics (fellow Assn. Geodesy, pres. permanent commn. for Earth tides 1979-87), Am. Geophys. Union (life, assoc. editor Geophysics Rev.), Soc. Exploration Geophysicists (rep.-at-large, com. mem., chmn. com.), Seismol. Soc. Am., Petroleum Exploration Soc. N.Y., Redlands Round Table (hon.), China Geophys. Soc. (fgn. corr.), Sigma Xi. Home: 11 Hoffman Ln Blauvelt NY 10913-1707 Office: Columbia U New York NY 10027

KUO, SOW-HSONG, medical educator; b. Keelung, Taiwan, Dec. 17, 1940; s. Chian-Hai and Mei Kuo; m. Chuen-Mei Hsu; children: Lu-Chen, Lu-Ting. MD, Nat. Taiwan U., Taipei, 1967. Cert. Internat. Bd. Cytopathology. From resident to chief resident Nat. Taiwan Univ. Hosp., Taipei, 1968-72, attending physician, 1972—; from lectr. to assoc. prof. Nat. Taiwan U., Taipei, 1974-86, prof., 1986—; chief sect. thoracic medicine Nat. Taiwan Univ. Hosp., Taiwan, 1998—. Pres. Prof. Kuo's Acad. Found., 1997. 2d lt. Taiwanese Res. Army, 1967-68. Fellow Internat. Acad. Cytology, Am. Coll. Chest Physicians (gov. 1996-99); mem. Taiwan Soc. Clin. Cytology (pres. 1994—). Avocations: hiking, table tennis. Fax: 02 23932056. E-mail: shkuo@ha.mc.ntu.edu.tw. Home: 10 Ln 185 Ching-shan S Rd, Sec 2, Taipei 106, Taiwan Office: Nat Taiwan Univ Hosp, 7 Chung-shan S Rd, Taipei 100, Taiwan

KUO, TEI-WEI, computer scientist, educator; b. Taipei, Taiwan, China, July 18, 1964; s. Cheng-I and Ching-Yun (Hsu) K.; m. I-Ju Chen, Aug. 4, 1988; children: Kevin, Martin. BSE, Nat. Taiwan U., 1986; MS in Computer Sci., U. Tex., 1990, PhD, 1994. Assoc. tech. staff Microelectronics and Computer Tech. Corp., Austin, Tex., 1990; assoc. prof. dept. computer sci. and info. engring. Nat. Chung Cheng U., Chiayi, Taiwan, 1994—, registrar, 1998—; chair real time embedded systems, SIG Inst. Info. & Computing Machinery, Taiwan, 1998-99; program com. mem. IEEE Real Time Sys. Symposium, San Francisco, 1997, internat. liason co-chair, Phoenix, 1999, pub. chair (Far East) IEEE Real-Time Tech. and Applications Symposium, Montreal, 1997, program com. and session chair, Boston, 1996; program com. mem., session chair Third Internat. Workshop on Real-Time Computing, Seoul, Korea, 1996. Editor Jour. Real-Time Sys., 1998—; contbr. articles to profl. jours. Rotary Internat. scholar, 1989-90. Mem. IEEE. Avocations: basketball, travel, music. Office: Nat Chung Cheng Univ, Dept Computer Sci/Info Engr, Chiayi 621, Taiwan

KUO, TSONG-TEH, biologist, botanist, educator; b. Tainan, Taiwan, Feb. 27, 1933; married; 2 children. BS in Plant Pathology, Taiwan Provincial Tchg. Coll., Taichung, 1957; MS in Plant Pathology, Nat. Taiwan U., Taipei, 1960; PhD in Plant Pathology, U. Calif., Davis, 1965. Rsch. fellow divsn. biology Calif. Inst. Tech., 1970-71; dep. dir. Inst. Botany, Academia Sinica, 1971-77; prof. dept. botany Nat. Taiwan U., 1977—; vis. prof. dept. biochem. and biophys. scis. Sch. Hygiene and Pub. Health, Johns Hopkins U., 1977; coun. mem. agr. experiment Taiwan Agr. Rsch. Inst., 1974-93; coun. mem. sugar rsch. Taiwan Sugar Rsch. Inst., 1973-96; mem. culture com. Nat. Culture Devel. Coun.; dir. Biology Rsch. Ctr., Nat. Sci. Coun., 1971-87, mem. adv. com. biology sci., 1982-95; mem. acad. com. Ministry of Edn.; acting dir. Inst. Molecular Biology, Academia Sinica, 1994-95, rsch. fellow, 1987—, rsch. fellow Inst. Botany, 1968-96, dir., 1971-77, dep. dir., 1968-71, assoc. rsch. fellow, 1965-68, rsch. asst., 1960-65; disting. rsch. fellow Academia Sinica, 1997. Editor Bot. Bull. Academia Sinica, 1971—, Biomed. Jour., 1994-98; contbr. numerous papers to profl. jours. Recipient Chung-San Acad. award, China, 1968, Tzeng Ss-Kang Meml. award for sci. achievement, 1983; China Found. fellow, 1992. Mem. AAAS, Academia Sinica (academician), Am. Phytopathology Soc., Chinese Soc. Cell and Molecular Biology, Chinese Soc. Toxicology, Chinese Soc. Plant Pathology, Chinese Soc. Plant Protection, Chinese Soc. Microbiology (pres. 1983-85), Chinese Soc. Botany (pres. 1975-76), Chinese Soc. Biology (Rsch. award 1979), Chinese Soc. Biochemistry (pres. 1978-79), N.Y. Acad. Scis., Sigma Xi.

KUO, WEN-SHIUH, engineering educator; b. Tainan, Taiwan, China, Jan. 7, 1962; s. Chao-Shih Kuo and Hsiu-Ying Wang; m. Lih-Shiuh Lai, June 15, 1991; children: Meng-Yu Jennifer, Chi-Ting Jeffery. BS, Nat. Taiwan U., Taipei, 1984, MS, 1986; PhD, Pa. State U., State Coll., 1993. Assoc. rschr. ITRI, Hsin-chu, Taiwan, 1988-89, rschr., 1994-96; assoc. prof. dept. safery, health and environ. engring. Nat. Lien-Ho Inst. Tech., Miao-Li, Taiwan, 1996—, dept. chmn., 1998—. Contbr. articles to sci. jours., including Chemosphere, Ozone Sci. and Engring., others. 2d lt. Taiwan Army, 1986-88. Mem. IAWQ, WEF. Office: 30-10 Yuan-Tung St, Lung-Ching, Taichung Taiwan

KUO, WEN-SHYONG, engineering educator; b. Taitung, Taiwan, Sept. 13, 1959; s. Hsin-Ko and Li-Erh (Li) K.; m. Chieu-Yeh Chen. BS, Nat. Chiao-Tung U., Taiwan, 1982; MS, Nat. Tsing-Hua U., Taiwan, 1984; PhD, U. Del., 1992. Assoc. prof. Feng-Chia U., Taiwan, 1992-98, prof. engring., 1998—. Contbr. articles to profl. jours. Mem. SAMPE Taiwan. Office: Feng Chia U, Dept Aeronautical Engring, 407 Taichung Taiwan

KUO, YAO-HAUR, biochemistry educator, medicinal chemist; b. Kao-Hsiung, Taiwan, Feb. 10, 1956; s. Terng-Fang and Bih-Yueh Lee K.; m. Li-Ming Yang, April 3, 1959; children: Jenny Kuo, Shing-Fu Kuo. BA, Chinese Culture U., Taipei, 1976-80; MA, Chinese Culture U., 1982-84, PhD, 1984-88. Vis. scholar U. N.C., Chapel Hill, 1987-89; postdoctoral U. N.C., 1988-89; assoc. prof. Chinese Culture U., Taipei, Taiwan, 1989-91; rsch. fellow Nat. Rsch. Inst. Chinese Med., Taipei, Taiwan, 1992—. Office: Nat Rsch Inst Chinese Med, 155-1 Sec 2 Li-Nong St, Shin-Dain Shih-Pai Taipei 11221, Taiwan

KUPCHYNSKY, JERRY MARKIAN, orchestra conductor, educator; b. Stryj, Ukraine, Sept. 12, 1928; came to U.S., 1946; s. Jaroslav and Cecilia Elizabeth (Jurkiv) K.; m. Jean Estelle Brown, June 29, 1957 (dec.); children: Melanie Jean, Stephanie Joy; m. Joan M. Rear, Sept. 13, 1997. B in Music Edn., Murray State U., 1951, MA in Edn., 1952; MEd, Rutgers U., 1961. Cert. tchr., supr., N.J. Tchr. music Pub. Schs., Shawneetown, Ill., 1954-57; tchr. music Pub. Schs., East Brunswick, N.J., 1957-68, supr. music, 1968-95; guest condr. youth orchs. various Eastern states, 1965—; founder, condr. Middlesex Youth Symphony Orch., 1961, Imperial Symphony Orch., 1979; founder, dir. Summer Conf. String Tchrs., 1964—; founder, chair East Brunswick Young Musicians Project, 1985—. Contbr. articles to profl. publs. Bd. dirs. East Brunswick Arts Commn., 1979, N.J. Teen Arts Festival, 1976, Alliance Arts Edn., 1977. With U.S. Army, 1952-54, Korea. Recipient N.J. Gov.'s award Arts Edn. for Disting. Leadership Music Edn., 1989, Cert. of Merit, N.J. Coun. on Arts, 1970; named to Order Ky. Cols., Commonwealth of Ky., 1978; selected for Wall of Hon., Brunswick Bd. Edn., 1998. Mem. N.J. String Tchrs. Assn. (Disting. Svc. award 1974, 78, 84, 89), Music Educators Nat. Conf., N.J. Music Educators Assn. (dir. Disting. Svc. award 1986), Am. String Tchrs. Assn. (nat. pres. 1976-78, Disting. Leadership award 1980), Nat. Sch. Orch. Assn. (nat. pres. 1984-86, Disting. Leadership award 1987, Merle J. Isaac Lifetime Achievement award 1994), N.J. Prins. and Suprs. Assn. Home: 38 Mason Ave East Brunswick NJ 08816-4837

KUPCINET, ESSEE SOLOMON, performing arts producer; b. Chgo., Dec. 7; d. Joseph David and Doris (Schoke) Solomon; m. Irv Kupcinet, Feb. 12, 1939; children: Karyn (dec.), Jerry S. PhB, Northwestern U., 1937. Asst. to dir. psychology dept. Michael Reese Hosp., Chgo., 1939-41; exec. producer eight Jefferson Award Shows; producer 1st Literary Arts Ball, Cultural Center, Chgo., 1979; talent coordinator Kup's Show, Chgo., 1964-84; producer for spl. events, 1978—. Prodn. chmn. Acad. Honors, 1984-87; chmn. bd. trustees Acad. Sch. Performing Arts, 1984-86, hon. lifetime chair, 1986—; prodn. chmn. Variety Club Telethon, 1984, 85; bd. dirs. Mus. Broadcasting Commn.; exec. com. Chgo. Tourism Coun., 1984-88; exec. bd. Internat. Theatre Festival, 1985-86; mem. sponsors com. Chgo. Pub. Libr., 1985-86; co-founder Chgo. Acad. Arts. Decorated Knight of Orange Nassau (The Netherlands); recipient Spl. award Jefferson Com., 1976; Cliff Dwellers award, 1975; Emmy award CBS, 1977, 79; Artisan award Acad. Theatre Arts and Friends, 1977; Prime Minister's medal for service to Israel, 1974; Woman of Yr. award Facets Multimedia, 1982, Mass Media award NCCJ, 1988, others; named (with Irv Kupcinet) Mr. and Mrs. Chgo., Greater North Michigan Ave. Assn., 1987, Chgo. Acad. for the Arts, 1988, Woman of Yr., Variety Club #26, 1988; honored by Mus. Brekest, Conn., 1989; honored (with Irv Kupcinet) 10th Anniversary Chgo. Acad. for Arts, 1992. Mem. NATAS (governing bd., program chmn. 1982-91, Govs. awards 1986, 91), Arts Club. Jewish.*

KUPER, ADAM JONATHAN, anthropologist, educator; b. Johannesburg, Transvaal, Republic of South Africa, Dec. 29, 1941; s. Simon Meyer and Gerty (Hesselson) K.; m. Jessica Sue Cohen, Dec. 16, 1966; children: Simon, Jeremy, Hannah. BA, U. Witwatersrand, Johannesburg, 1961; PhD, U. Cambridge, Eng., 1966; D (hons.), U. Gothenburg, Sweden, 1978. Lectr. in Social Anthropology Makerere U., Kampala, Uganda, 1967-70; lectr. in Anthropology U. Coll. U. London, 1970-76; prof. African Anthropology and Sociology U. Leiden, The Netherlands, 1976-85; prof. social anthropology, head human scis. dept. Brunel U., Middlesex, Eng., 1985—; mem. Inst. for Advanced Study, Princeton, N.J., 1994-95. Author: Kalahari Village Politics: An African Democracy, 1970, Anthropologists and Anthropology: The British School, 1922-72, 1973, 2d rev. ed. 1983, 3rd rev. ed. 1996, Changing Jamaica, 1976, Regionaal Vergelijkend Onderzoek in Afrika, 1977, Wives for Cattle: Bridewealth and Marriage in Southern Africa, 1982, South Africa and the Anthropologist, 1987, The Invention of Primitive Society: Transformations of an Illusion, 1988; editor: The Social Anthropology of Radcliffe-Brown, 1982, The Social Science Encyclopedia, 1985, 2nd edit., 1996, Current Anthropology, 1985-93, Conceptualizing Society, 1992, The Chosen Primate, 1994, Culture: The Anthropologist' Account, 1999, Among the Anthropologists, 1999; contbr. more than 90 articles to profl. jours. Fellow British Acad.; mem. Acad. Europe. Avocations: cricket. Home: 16 Muswell Rd, London N10 2BG, England

KUPERSMITH, JOEL, physician, medical school dean; b. Nov. 26, 1939; s. Charles Douglas and Sally K.; m. Judith Freidman, June 15, 1969; children: David, Rebecca, Adam. BS, Union Coll., Schenectady, 1960; MD, N.Y. Med. Coll., 1964. Prof., chief clin. pharmacology Mt. Sinai Sch. Medicine, N.Y.C., 1974-86; chief cardiology divsn. Beth Israel Med. Ctr., N.Y.C., 1985-86; prof., chief cardiology divsn. U. Louisville Sch. Medicine, East Lansing, 1986-91; V.V. Cooke prof. medicine U. Louisville Sch. Medicine, Lubbock, 1987-91; prof., chair medicine Mich. State U., East Lansing, 1991-97; dean Sch. Medicine, dean Sch. Biomed. Scis. Tex. Tech U. Sch. Medicine, Lubbock, 1997—, v.p. clin. affairs, 1997—; chief cardiac arrhythmia clinic, Mt. Sinai Med. Ctr., 1977-85; assoc. prof. pharmacology, Mt. Sinai Med. Ctr., 1979-84. Author: Clinical Manual of Electrophysiology, 1997, The Pharmacologic Management of Heart Disease, 1993. Recipient Affirmative Action award U. Louisville, 1988, Alumni Assn. Disting. Achievement award N.Y. Med. Coll. Med. Sch., Coun. Deans, 1992. Mem. Assn. Profs. Medicine (program com. 1994), Am. Heart Assn. (exec. com. Coun. on Clin. Cardiology 1991-94), Am. Soc. for Clin. Investigation (sr.). Office: Tex Tech U Sch Medicine 2B107 3601 4th St # 2b107 Lubbock TX 79430-0001

KUPPERMAN, LOUIS BRANDEIS, lawyer; b. Augusta, Ga., Dec. 16, 1946; s. Herbert Spencer and Mollie (Kleven) K.; children: David Evan, Robert Dennis; m. Eileen Spadafina, Oct. 24, 1992. BS, Fairleigh Dickinson U., 1972; JD, Bklyn. Law Sch., 1975. Bar: Pa. 1975, U.S. Dist. Ct. (ea. dist.) Pa. 1978, U.S. Ct. Appeals (3d cir.) 1978, U.S. Supreme Ct. 1982. Jud. law clk. to Judge Jacob Kalish Ct. of Common Pleas of Phila. County, 1975-76, jud. law clk. to Judge Eugene Gelfand, 1976-77; corp. counsel Health Corp. Am., Wayne, Pa., 1977-78; ptnr. Dilworth, Paxson, Kalish & Kauffman, Phila., 1978-86; mem. firm, chmn. real estate dept. Baskin Flaherty Elliott & Mannino, P.C., Phila., 1986-90; ptnr., vice chmn. environ. law dept. Obermayer, Rebmann, Maxwell & Hippel, Phila., 1990—; lectr. Pa. Bar Inst. Author: Real Estate Tax Assessment Appeals, 1987. Chancellor's del. to Phila. Fairleigh Dickinson U., 1983, 86. Recipient Disting. Alumnus award Fairleigh Dickinson U., 1983. Mem. ABA, Pa. Bar Assn., Phila. Bar Assn., (chmn. real estate litigation com. 1983-85), Pyramid Club of Phila. Home: 80 Delancy Ct Phoenixville PA 19460-5741 Office: Obermayer Rebmann Maxwell & Hippel 1 Penn Ctr 19th Fl 1617 John F Kennedy Blvd Philadelphia PA 19103-1821

KUPREEV, NIKOLAI IVANOVITCH, academic administrator, engineering educator; b. Moscow, Dec. 21, 1946; s. Uvan Andreevitch and Olga Vasilievna (Timofeeva) K. Diploma Engr., Moscow Inst. Chem. Engring., 1970; Cert., Moscow Sity, 1972; Diploma Engr., Moscow Inst. Electronic Engring., 1975; D in Engring., All Union Rsch. Design Inst., Moscow, 1985; degree (hon.), Ministry Edn. Russian Fedn., 1997. Cert. mech. engr., mathemat. engr. Engr. All Union Rsch., Design & Tech. Inst. Hydraulic Machine, Moscow, 1970-73; rsch. engr., 1975-77, active researcher, 1978-81, leading scientific researcher, 1981-93; coord. Europump and Russian Pump Mfrs. Russian Pump Mfrs.' Assn., Moscow, 1993-98; dir. postgrad. studies Gidromash Scientific & Prodn. Assn. Close Stock Co., Moscow, 1998—; working group mem. Europump, Brussels, 1996. Contbr. articles to profl. jours. Collaborating press-photography Dist. Komsomol Com., Moscow, 1974, Dept. Moscow Town Komsomol Com., 1981. Recipient All-Union prize for youth scientific pub. showing reativity State Coms. for Scientific and Technique, 1978, Cert. Exposition Attendance Exhibn. Nat. Econ. Achievement, 1978. Mem. N.Y. Acad. Scis., Trade Union. Avocations: photography, improving English, travel. Office: GIDROMASH ZAO NPO, Second Mytishinskay St 2, 129626 Moscow Russia

KUPRYJANCZYK, JOLANTA, pathologist, educator; b. Lodz, Poland, Jan. 25, 1954; d. Jan Kupryjanczyk and Danuta Slomkowska-Kupryjanczyk; 1 child, Agnieszka. MD, Warsaw (Poland) Med. Sch., 1978; bd. cert. pathology, Med. Ctr. Postgrad. Edn., Warsaw, 1982, PhD, 1987. From asst. to sr. asst. Med. Ctr. Postgrad. Edn., Warsaw, 1979-86; rsch. fellow, DAAD fellow Inst. Pathology U. Heidelberg, Germany, 1986-87; asst. prof. Warsaw Med. Sch., 1987-91; rsch. fellow, Fulbright fellow, Kosciuszko Found. fellow Mass. Gen. Hosp., Harvard Med. Sch., Boston, 1991-94; asst. prof. Maria Sklodowska Curie Meml. Cancer Ctr. and Inst., Warsaw, 1994-96, assoc. prof. chief molecular pathology lab., 1996—; cons. gynecol. pathology; referee Int. Jour. Cancer, Polish jours., 1994—; spkr. in field. Author: (book

chpt.) Oncogenes and Tumor Suppressor Genes in Endometrial Cancer, 1998; contbr. articles to profl. jours. Mem. Internat. Soc. Gynecol. Pathologists, Internat. Acad. Pathology (mem. Polish divsn. 1995—), Polish Acad. Sci. (mem. com. for cellular and molecular pathology 1996—). Roman Catholic. Avocations: music, traveling, hiking. Fax: (4822) 6449085. E-mail: jolantak@coi.waw.pl. Office: Maria Sklodowska Curie meml Cancer Ctr & Inst Warsaw, Roentgena 5, 02 781 Warsaw Poland

KURA, GENICHIRO, chemist, educator; b. Moji, Fukuoka, Japan, Nov. 26, 1945; s. Masahide (Moriyama) and Tane Kura; m. Shinobu Katafuchi, May 17, 1971; children: Ken-ichiro, Noriko, Tomohiko. BS, Kyushu U., Fukuoka, 1968, MS, 1971, DSc, 1974. Asst. prof. Kyushu U., Fukuoka, 1975-77; assoc. prof. Fukuoka U. Edn., 1977-89, prof., 1989—. Contbr. articles to profl. jours. Mem. Chem. Soc. Japan, Japan Soc. for Analytical Chemistry. Avocations: playing tennis, playing soft-base ball, watching professional baseball. Home: Matsuzaki 4-24-9 Higashi-ku, Fukuoka 813-0035, Japan Office: Fukuoka Univ Edn, Akama, Fukuoka Munakata 811-4192, Japan

KURABAYASHI, HITOSHI, hematologist, educator; b. Isesaki, Japan, Sept. 19, 1956. MD, Asahikawa Med. Coll., Japan, 1983; PhD, Gunma U., Maebashi, Japan, 1994. Asst. prof. Gunma U., 1993—. Author: Cancer Research, 1989, British Journal Hematology, 1991, Stroke, 1991, Blood, 1994, Am. Jour. of Hematology, 1997, Am. Jour. of Phys. Medicine and Rehab., 1998, European Jour. of Phys. Medicine and Rehab., 1998, Annals of Hematology, 1999. Fellow Japanese Soc. Clin. Hematologists, Japan Geriatrics Soc., Japanese Assn. Phys. Medicine Balneology and Climatology; mem. ACP, N.Y. Acad. Scis, Assn. of Acad. Psychiatrists, Japan Soc. Internal Medicine, Japanese Soc. Hematology, Japanese Assn. Rehab. Medicine. Office: Gunma U Hosp Kusatsu Br Hosp, 627-3 Kusatsu, Gunma 377-1711, Japan

KURAKOV, LEV PANTELEYMONOVICH, academic administrator; b. Chuvash Republic, Russia, Jan. 4, 1943; s. Panteleymon and Tatyana (Ivanova) K.; m. Albina Sharshganova, July 20, 1974; children: Vladimir, Alexander. Diploma, Kazan Inst. Fin. & Econs., Russia, 1966. Head acct. Savs. Bank, Chuvash Republic, 1961-66; from vice dean, head econs. dept. to pres., rector Chuvash State U., 1970—. Author: Orientations for Revival, 1995, Industry of Education, 1996; co-author: Market and Anti-Monopoly Economic Relations, 1996; editor: Actual Problems on Contemporary Economic Systems, 1996. Mem. Russian Fedn. Engring. Acad., Internat. Engring. Acad., Internat. Acad. Scis. Avocations: beekeeping, swimming, arts, literature. Office: Chuvash IN Ulyanov State U, 15 Moskovsky prospekt, 428015 Cheboksary Chuvash, Russia

KURAMITSU, RIE, biochemical engineering educator; b. Fukuoka, Japan, Nov. 27, 1950; d. Masaharu and Sadako Kuramitsu. B in Engring., Hiroshima (Japan) U., 1975; M in Engring., Osaka (Japan) U., 1978; D in Agr., Hiroshima (Japan) U., 1998. Tech. officer Osaka U., 1978-83; lectr. biochem. engring. Akashi Nat. (Japan) Coll. Tech., 1991-95, assoc. prof., 1995-98; prof., 1999—. Author: (with others) Food Flavor and Safety, 1993, Chemistry of Novel Foods, 1995, Advances in Food Science and Technology, Vol. VII, 1997. Sci. vol. Acad. Japanese Tech., Tokyo, 1995—. E-mail: kuramitu@akashi.ac.jp. Office: Akashi Nat Coll Tech, Uozumi Akashi, Hoyogo 674-8501, Japan

KURANE, RYUICHIRO, microbiologist; b. Yachiho, Japan, Apr. 18, 1945; s. Kanyu and Toyoji (Deura) K.; m. Hiromi Iwasaka, Oct., 1973; children: Akiko, Naoko, Takashi. BS, U. Tokyo, 1969, MS, 1971, PhD, 1974. From rschr. to sr. rschr. Fermentation Rsch. Insts., Chiba, Japan, 1974-88, head lab., 1988-93; prof. Tokyo U. Agrl. and Tech., 1990-93; dir. planning Nat. Inst. Biosci. and Human-Tech., Tsukuba, Japan, 1993-95, dir. applied microbiology dept., 1995—; prof. microbiology U. Chiba Indsl. Tech., 2000—; tech. advisor to gov. Fukushima, Japan, 1987—; co-chmn. environ. biotech. spl. com. Orgn. for Econ. Corp. and Devel., Paris, 1994—, co-chmn. spl. com. biotech. clean indsl. products and processes, 1995-98, co-chmn. spl. com. biotech. sustainable indsl. devel., 1998—. Author: Isolation of Microorganism, 1986, Bio New Material, 1987, Biodegradable Plastics, 1995, Bioconversion, 1993, Bioremediation, 1997; mem. editl. bd. Jour. Clean Products and Processes, 1998—. Recipient Commendation award Min. State for Sci. and Tech., Japan, 1984, Min. State for Sci. and Tech. award, 1985, 94; Ichimura Acad. award Prince Mikasanomiya, 1995, Can. Govt. Commitment award, 1999. Avocations: hobbies, tennis. Office: Nat Inst Biosci Human Tech, 1-1 Higashi, Tsukuba Ibaraki 305-8566, Japan

KURASHOV, EVGENIJ ALEXANDROVITCH, hydrobiologist, researcher; b. Astrakhan, Russia, Mar. 18, 1960; s. Alexander Alekseevitch and Elena Konstantinovna (Gorbunova) K.; m. Julia Viktorovna Krylova, June 26, 1993; children: Dasha, Anna. MS, St. Petersburg State U., Russia, 1982; PhD, Zool. Inst., St. Petersburg, 1989; D of Biol. Scis., Inst. Limnology, St. Petersburg, 1997. Rsch. asst. Inst. Limnology, St. Petersburg, 1979-84, rsch. assoc., 1984-91, sr. rsch. scientist, 1991—. Contbr. chpts. to books, articles to profl. jours. Rsch. grantee Scheme of Ctrl. European U., 1993-94, German Sci. Found., 1995, Russian Found. Fundamental Investigations, 1997, Presidium of Russian Acad. Scis., 1998. Mem. Russian Soc. Hydrobiology, St. Petersburg Soc. Naturalists, Internat. Assn. Meiobenthologists. Russian Orthodox. E-mail: kea@ek4118.spb.edn. Home: Apt 557, Butlerova Str 13th Fl, 195256 Saint Petersburg Russia Office: Inst Limnology, Sevastyanova str 9, 196105 Saint Petersburg Russia

KURATA, AYAO, political scientist, educator; b. Shinjyo-cho, Nara, Japan, Feb. 16, 1926; s. Mitsuzo and Masuno (Nishimura) K.; m. Masako Kurata, May 7, 1950; children: Shigeru, Hiroshi. LLB, Doshisha U., Japan, 1948; Grad., Kyoto U., Japan, 1953. Assoc. prof. Konan U., Kobe, Japan, 1953-64, prof., 1964-66; prof. Kobe Gakuin U., 1967-96, dean Faculty of Law, 1973-77, pres., 1986-92, honor prof., 1996—; pres. Kobe Gakuin Women's Coll., 1996—; advisor prof. Shanghai Jiao-Tong U., People's Republic of China, 1990—; honor prof. East China U. of Politics and Law, People's Republic of China, 1992—; lawyer, 1996—; chief dir. Kansai 6 Univ. Baseball League, Osaka, 1982-98, advisor, 1998—; bd. dirs. Japan Univ. Baseball Fedn., Tokyo, 1984-98. Author: Civil Law (General Provisions), 1975, Civil Law (Obligations), 1987; also articles. With inf., Japanese Army, 1945. Mem. Japan Assn. Pvt. Law (bd. dirs. 1981-95), Assn. Pvt. Univs. in Japan (bd. dirs. 1986-92), Rotary Club. Avocations: travel, appreciation of arts and crafts. Home: 1-13 Shinohara honmachi, 5-chome, Nada-ku, Kobe 657-0067, Japan Office: Kobe Gakuin Women's Coll, 27-1 Hayashiyama-cho, Nagata-ku Kobe 653-0861, Japan Office: Shinko Bldg 7th Flr, 8 Kaigan-dori Chuo-ku, Kobe 650-0024, Japan

KURAVSKY, LEV SEMENOVITCH, computer science researcher; b. Retchitsa, Gomel Rgn, USSR, Aug. 28, 1960; s. Semen Naumovitch and Valentina Nikolaevna (Terentieva) K.; m. Elena Alexandrovna Pavlovskaya, Feb. 26, 1965; 1 child, Michael. MS, Moscow Aviation Inst., 1984; DS, Flt. Rsch. Inst., Zhukovsky, 1992. Ranked Sr. Rsch. Fellow, Scientific Coun. of Flt. Rsch. Inst. Engr. Flt. Rsch. Inst., Zhukovsky, 1984-86, engr. programmer, 1987-91, sr. rsch. assoc., 1992-98; assoc. prof. Moscow City Inst. of Psychology and Edn., 1997—, dept. head, 1999—; rschr. Russian Aviation Co., Moscow, 1996—; mgr. Aviasalon Co., Zhukovsky, 1995-97. Contbr. articles to profl. jours. and scientific confs.; devel. of software for scientific rsch. Recipient medal for Best Scientific Student's Work, USSR High Edn. Ministry, Moscow, 1984; grantee Russian Humanitarian Scientific Fund, 1995-96, NATO Advanced Study Inst., 1998; grantee, Russian Found. for Basic Rsch., 1999-2000. Mem. East-European Acoustical Assn., Internat. Inst. of Acoustics and Vibration. Avocations: skiing, cross-country racing.

KURDYUMOV, VADIM, physicist, researcher; b. Moscow, Jan. 17, 1960; s. Rimma Kurdyumova; m. Elena Antropova, Nov. 14, 1981; children: Petr, Alexandr. MSc, Moscow U. Engring. and Physics, 1982; PhD, Russian Acad. Scis., Moscow, 1989. Rsch. scientist Inst. for Problems in Mechs., Russian Acad. Scis., Moscow, 1984-94; postdoctoral fellow U. Poly. Madrid, 1994-96, rsch. fellow, 1996—. Fax: 34-91-336-63-71. E-mail: vadim@tupi.dmt.upm.es. Home: c/Juan Pradillo 21 1 izq, 28039 Madrid Spain Office: U Poly Madrid ETSI Aero Dpt, Plaza Cardenal Cisneros 3, 28040 Madrid Spain

KUREICHIK, VICTOR MICHAILOVICH, electrical and computer engineer; b. Selistra, Bulgaria, Nov. 2, 1945; s. Michale and E. (Alexander) K.; m. Larisa Kureichik, Oct. 9, 1965; children: Vladimir, Natali. Elec. Engring., Radio-Engring. Inst., Taganrog, Russia, 1967, PhD, 1971, DSc, 1978. Elec. engr. Radio Engring. Inst., Taganrog, Russia, 1968-71; dept. head CAD Rsch. Inst., Taganrog, Russia, 1971-78; vis. scholar Coll. of Engring., Syracuse, 1978-79; dean of faculty Radio Engring. Inst., Taganrog, 1982-87, dept. head CAD, 1987-99, vice rector, 1999—. Contbr. over 300 articles to profl. jours.; author 10 books. Mem. IEEE (sr.), Russian CAD Assn. (pres. 1989-92), Internat. Acad. Info., N.Y. Acad. Sci., Russian Acad. Natural Sci. (corr., Silver medal 1995). Achievements include 30 patents. Home: 65 Sverdlov st ap 13, 347900 Taganrog Russia Office: Radio Engring U, 44 Nekrasovsky Ln, Taganrog GSP-7A, 347928, Russia

KUREK, NIKOLAI SERGEEVICH, psychologist, researcher; b. Pytalovo, Pskov, Russia, July 23, 1949; s. Sergei Mikhailovich and Anna Ivanovna K.; m. Larisa Vladimirovna Gelman, Jan. 24, 1976; 1 child, Inna Nikolaevna; m. Maria Grigorievna Kirillova, Sept. 25, 1987; children: Kirillova, Marina. BA in Psychology, Lomonosov Moscow State U., 1976, DSc, 2000. Diploma psychology. Jr. sci. collaborator Inst. Psychiatry AMS, Moscow, 1976-82, sr. sci. collaborator, 1983-87; sr. lectr. Pedagogical Coll., South-Sakhalinsk, Russia, 1987-88; sr. sci. collaborator Rsch. Ctr. Med. Biol. Problems Addiction, Moscow, 1988-93; leading sci. collaborator Inst. Narcology of Russian Fedn. Pub. Health Ministry, Moscow, 1993—. Author: Deficiency of Psychic Activity: Personality Passivity and Disorder, 1996, On the Causes and the Consequences of the Prohibition on Psychotechnique and Paedology in the Soviet Union, 1996. Grantee Rsch. Support Scheme, Prague, Czech Republic, 1995-97, Russian Humanities Scis. Found., Moscow, 1995-96. Mem. N.Y. Acad. Scis. Avocations: music, literature, history. Home: 12-1-211 Medynskaya Str., 113546 Moscow Russia Office: State Sci Ctr Narcology, 3 Malyi Mogiltsevskii Pereu, Moscow Russia

KURER, PETER ANTON JOSEPH, lawyer; b. Zürich, Switzerland, June 28, 1949; s. Vital A. and Elsie J. (Huber) K.; m. Susi Eppner, May 19, 1979; children: Christian, Stefanie, Tobias. Lic.iur., U. Zürich, 1974, Dr.iur., 1978; LLM, U. Chgo., 1976. Bar: Zürich, 1980. Assoc. Homburger Rechtsanwälte, Zürich, 1980-85, ptnr., 1985—; vice chmn. bd. Kraft Jacobs Suchard AG, Zürich, 1990—; bd. dirs. Unisys (Schweiz) AG, Thalwil, Switzerland, Rothschilds Continuation Holdings AG, Zug, Switzerland, Sihl, Zürich, Switzerland, Holderbank Fin. Glarus, Switzerland, Netstal-Maschinen AG, Nafels, Switzerland. Author: Repräsentation im Gesetzgebungsverfahren, 1979; co-author: Commentary on Articles 675-682 Swiss Code of Obligations, 1994, Switzerland Report in International Corporate Procedures, 1992—. Mem. ch. bd. Roman Cath. Ch., Herrliberg, 1994—. 1st lt. Swiss Army, 1970—. Mem. Internat. Bar Assn., Swiss Bar Assn., Zürich Bar Assn., Swiss Arbitration Assn., Swiss Lawyers Assn., Swiss Assn. for Internat. Law, Brit.-Swiss C. of C. (legal and tax chpt.). Avocations: sports, literature, music, movies. Office: Homburger Rechtsanwälte, Weinbergstrasse 56/58, 8035 Zurich Switzerland

KURESHE, AKHTAR ALI, lawyer; b. Lahore, Punjab, Pakistan, Nov. 15, 1963; s. Nosha Ali and Aqeela Nosha (Sabir) Qureshi; m. Khadija Asghar, Jan. 6, 1995; children: Dua Qureshi, Waleed Qureshi. BA, U. Punjab, Lahore, 1986, MA in Polit. Sci., 1990; LLB, Punjab Law Coll., Lahore, 1989. Assoc. M/S Iqbal Bhatti Law Assoc., Lahore, 1990-92; from jr. assoc. to assoc. M/S Ijaz Husain Batalvi Barrister, Lahore, 1992-97; mng. ptnr. Kureshe Law Assoc., Lahore, 1997—; legal adv. Provincial Assembley of the Punjab, Lahore, 1998—; prof. Punjab Law Coll., Lahore, 1999—; cons., legal adv. Kirgyzstan Embassy, Lahore, 1999—. Author: Manual of Insurance Law, 1998; editor: PSC, 1999. Pres. Assn. Ednl. Coun., Lahore, 1986-88; gen. sec. Social Welfare Soc., Lahore, 1987-89; active Human Rights Commn. Pakistan, Lahore, 1990, Lahore Gymkhana, Lahore, 1996. Recipient Cert., Supt. Police, Lahore, 1987, Am. Consulate, Lahore, 1991. Mem. ABA, Internat. Bar Assn., Lawasia, Lahore High Ct. Bar Assn. (mem. exec. com.), Commonwealth Lawyers Assn. London, Royal Commonwealth Soc. London. Muslim. Avocations: swimming, golf, billiards, travel. Office: Kureshi Law Assoc, 4 Turner Rd, 54000 Lahore Pakistan

KURFÜRST, PAVEL, organologist; b. Zlin, Czechoslovakia, June 6, 1940; s. Josef and Zdenka (Stejskalová) K.; m. Miroslava Krupková, Mar. 5, 1983; children: Pavla, Michal, Jana. Grad. Faculty Arts, U. Brno, 1976; candidate sci., Acad. Scis., Prague, Czechoslovakia, 1983. Technician Radiocommunications, Prague, 1959-73, Tech. U., Brno, 1973-76; dir. Ethnographic Mus., Brno, 1976-83; asst. dir. Inst. Folk Art, Strážnice, Czechoslovakia, 1983-87; rsch. worker med. faculty U. Brno, 1987-92, mem. phil. faculty, 1992—; cons. State Collection Mus. Instruments, Prague, 1979—, Slovak Collection Mus. Instruments, Bratislava, Czechoslovakia, 1978—. Author: Die letzte Entwicklungsphase der Streichlyra in Mitteleuropa, 1986, Brünner Instrumentenbauer des 14.-19. Jahrhunderts, 1980, Die Kurzhalsgeige, 1980, Ala und Harfe mit zwei Resonatoren. Unbekannte Instrumente der europäischen Stilmusik des 13. zis 15. Jahrhunderts, 1985, Die Bauernfiedel, 1996, Organologie, 1999; editor: Contributions to the Study of Traditional Musical Instruments in Museum, 1987, Ethnographica, 1976-85; contbr. articles to profl. jours. Mem. Galpin Soc. London. Avocation: violin making. Home: Uzbecká 12, 62500 Brno Czech Republic Office: Phil Faculty U Brno, A Novaka 1, 60 000 Brno Czech Republic

KURIAN, PIUS, nephrologist, educator; b. Arpookara, Kerala, India, May 9, 1959; s. Pylo and Mariamma Kurian; m. Sally Kurian, May 11, 1986; children: Michelle Maria, Matthew Paul, Catherine Tresa. BSc, Kuriakose (India) Elias Coll., 1979; MB, BChir, Kottayam (India) Med. Coll., India, 1986. Diplomate Am. Bd. Internal Medicine, Am. Bd. Nephrology, Am. Bd. Forensic Examiners; specialist clin. hypertension, Am. Soc. Hypertension. Resident in internal medicine Nassau County Med. Ctr., East Meadow, N.Y., 1988-91; fellow in nephrology Nassau County Med. Ctr., East Meadow, 1991-94; attending physician in nephrology Mercy Med. Ctr. and Cmty. Hosp., Springfield, Ohio, 1994—; asst. prof. dept. medicine Wright State U., Dayton, Ohio, 1998; chief divsn. internal medicine Mercy Med. Ctr., Springfield, Ohio, 1999, chmn., dir. dept. medicine Mercy Med. Ctr., Springfield, Ohio, 2000; mem. governing bd. Covenant Health Sys. Fellow ACP; mem. AAAS, AMA, Am. Soc. Hypertension (specialist in clin. hypertension), Am. Soc. Nephrology, Am. Coll. Physicians Execs., Internat. Soc. Nephrology, Renal Physicians Assn., N.Y. Acad. Scis, Am. Diabetes Assn., Nat. Kidney Found. Roman Catholic. Office: 247 S Burnett Rd Springfield OH 45505-2639

KURIBAYASHI, MOTOTAKA, computer company executive, engineer; b. Kameoka-shi, Japan, June 6, 1959; s. Jirou Nishida and Toshiko K.; m. Kayoko Kusakabe, Oct. 15, 1989; children: Junya, Mina. B, Kyoto U., Japan, 1983, M, 1985, PhD in Engring., 1999. Engr. Toshiba R&D Ctr., Kawasaki, Japan, 1985-93; specialist Toshiba Semiconductor Device Rsch. Ctr., Kawasaki, Japan, 1993-95, DA Devel. Dept. Semiconductor DA & Test Engring. Ctr.Toshiba, Kawasaki, Japan, 1995-99, Physical DA Group DA Devel. Dept. Micro/Custom LSI Divsn., Kawasaki, Japan, 1999—. Patentee in field; contbr. articles to profl. jours. Mem. IEEE, IEICE, IPSJ. Avocations: playing baseball, tennis, Japanese archery, camera. Home: Shimokodanaka 3-32-30 B-201, Nakahara Kawasaki 211-0041, Japan Office: Toshiba Corp Semicond Co, 580-1 Horikawa cho, Sauirai Kawasaki 210-8510, Japan Address: Toshiba Corp, Semicond DA & Test Engn Ctr, Kawasaki Kanagawa 210-8520, Japan

KURIBAYASHI, TOSHIRO, physician; b. Kurume, Fukuoka, Japan, Feb. 16, 1945; s. Tetsuji and Yaeko (Noda) K.; m. Chizuko Takakura, Apr. 10, 1976; children: Yuko, Yoshiko. BS, Kyoto U., 1967; MD, Kyoto Prefectural U. Medicine, 1976, PhD, 1987. Cert. in cardiology. Asst. prof. Kyoto Prefectural U. Medicine, 1986-90, assoc. prof., 1990-94, guest prof., 1994—; physician Red Cross Hosp., Kyoto, 1994-96; dir. Kuribayashi Clinic, Fukuoka, 1996—; guest rschr. NIH, Bethesda, Md., 1991-92. Co-author: Developmental Mechanism of Heart Disease, 1995; contbr. articles to Am. Jour. Physiology, Pediatric Rsch., Am. Jour. Cardiology, others. Japanese Govt. grantee, 1986, 90, 93. Mem. Japanese Circulation Soc., Japanese Soc. Interna. Medicine. Avocations: horticulture, bicycling. Home and Office: Ozasa 5-5-18 Chuo-Ku, Fukuoka 810, Japan

KURIHARA, NORIO, chemist; b. Kyoto, Japan, Feb. 16, 1933; s. Yoshio and Fumi (Watanabe) K.; m. Kiyoko Miyazaki, June 30, 1962; children: Tatsuo, Naoko, Takeo. BS, Kyoto U., 1956, MS, 1958, D of Agrl., 1961. Instr. dept. of agrl. chemistry Kyoto U., 1961-71, assoc. prof. radiostope rsch. ctr., 1971-81, prof. radiostope rsch. ctr., 1981-96, dir., 1991-96, prof. emeritus, 1996—; rsch. assoc. dept. biochemistry U. Wis., Madison, 1962-63. Recipient Young Scientist award in Agrl. Chemistry Agrl. Chem. Soc. of Japan, 1969. Mem. Pesticide Sci. Soc. of Japan (exec. com. 1983-97, inspector 1997—, Disting. Rsch. award 1982), Japan Radioisotope Assn. (advisor 1996—), Japan Soc. of U. Isotope and Radiation Facilities (pres. 1995—). Avocations: cycling, teaching elementary school. Office: Emeritus Club Pasteur Bldg, 103-5 Tanaka Monzen-cho #5F, Sakyo-ku Kyoto 606-8225, Japan

KURIHASHI, KATSUAKI, ophthalmologist, dacryologist; b. Muroran, Hokkaido, Japan, Dec. 23, 1944; s. Yoshio and Yone Kurihashi; m. Fumiko Ota, Apr. 11, 1971; children: Miyako, Daisuke. MD, Sapporo (Japan) Med. Coll., 1971. Dir. Kurihashi Eye Clinic, Hamamatsu, Japan, 1980—; temp. lectr. Hamamatsu U. Sch. Medicine, 1989—. Author: Dacryology, 1998; patentee apparatus for intubation of lacrimal drainage pathway, Nunchakustyle silicone tubing; contbr. articles to profl. jours., ency.; mem. editl. bd. European Soc. Dacriology, 1992—. Avocations: photography, films, walking. Office: Kurihashi Eye Clinic, 1366-1 Hatsuio-cho, Hamamatsu Shizuoka 433-8112, Japan

KURILKINA, SVETLANA NIKOLAEVNA, physics educator; b. Klintzy, USSR, Jan. 20, 1963; d. Nikolay Egorovich and Anna Artemovna (Shevtzova) K.; m. Alexander Anatol'evich Barahvostov, Aug. 21, 1987 (div. Sept. 1992); 1 child, Pavel Alexandrovich Barahvostov. Candidate of Physics, Inst. Physics, Minsk, Belarus, 1991. Asst. dept. physics Gomel (Belarus) State U., 1984-92, tchr., 1992-93, docent, 1993—, Soros docent, 1995-96; mem. coun. for def. of a thesis Gomel State U., 1995-2000. Contbr. articles to profl. jours. Grantee, Soros Found. Belarus, 1995, Internat. Soros Sci. Edn. Program, 1995-96, Found. for Basic Investigations Belarus, 1996-98. Mem. Acad. Metrology Belarus. Avocations: hiking, dancing, music, playing piano. Home: ul Timofeenko 22, 116, 246032 Gomel Belarus Office: Gomel State Univ, ul Sovetskaya 104, 246699 Gomel Belarus

KURILO, IVAN VASYLOVYCH, science educator; b. Village Topilnytsya, Staryi Sambir, Ukraine, July 24, 1942; s. Vasyl Yosypovych and Kateryna Fedorivna (Hasydzhak) K.; m. Yaroslava Petrivna Bodnar, Sept. 1965; 1 child, Halyna. PhD in Physics, State U. Lviv, Ukraine, 1979; DSc in Physics, Chernivtsi (Ukraine) U., 1992. Tchr. physics Sch. vil. Nove Misto, Lviv, 1964-69; jr. scientist Lviv State U., 1970-71; sr. scientist Lviv Poly. Inst., 1972-82, sr. tchr., 1983-89, assoc. prof., 1989-94, prof., 1994—; cons. State U. Lviv Poly., 1992—. Contbr. articles to profl. jours. Mem. Ukrainian Phys. Soc., N.Y. Acad. Scis. Office: State U Lviv Poly, Stepana Bandery St 12, 79646 Lviv 13, Ukraine

KURILOV, VLADIMIR IVANOVICH, academic administrator; b. Troitskoye, Russia, May 25, 1948; s. Ivan Nikolayevich and Sofya Pavlovna (Alekseyenko) K.; m. Leonora Aleksandrovna Belous, Dec. 19, 1970 (div. 1990); children: Lana Kurilova, Aleksandra Kurilova; m. Concordia Aleksandrovna Chabanyuk, July 18, 1991; 1 child, Tatyana Mazurova. Cand. sci., Leningrad State U., Russia, 1974; LLD, U. Md., 1993; D of Bus. Adminstrn., Kyonggi U., Korea, 1995. Instr. Far Eastern State U., Vladivostok, Russia, 1972-75, assoc. dean dept. law, 1975-78, assoc. prof. law, 1978-82, dean dept. law, 1982-90, pres., 1990—; mem. State com. for Higher Edn., Moscow, 1994—, Acad. Social Scis., Moscow, 1994—, Acad. Natural Scis, Moscow, 1995—, Peter the Great Acad. Arts & Scis., Russia, 1995—. Author: Attestation in National Economy, 1981, An Individual, Labor, Law, 1989, The Universities of Russia and International Cooperation, 1993, Morality and Law, 1994. Chmn. Far Ea. br. Russian Commn. UN Ednl., Sci., and Cultural Orgn., 1990—, rep. Asian br., Bangkok, Thailand, 1990—. Recipient Honorary award State Com. for Higher Edn., 1992, Ministry Edn., Korea, 1994; named Honorary Citizen, City of Taichung, China, 1992. Mem. Assn. Univ. Pres. (bd. dirs. 1992—), Internat. Assn. Univ. Pres. (exec. com. 1994—), Russian Assn. Univ. Pres. Avocations: fine arts, Western and Oriental painting, Oriental martial arts. Office: Far Eastern State Univ, Ul Sukhanova 8 Vladivostok, 690600 Primorskogo Kraya Russia*

KÜRIS, PRANAS, judge. Lawyer degree, Vilnius U., 1961; PhD in Law, Moscow State U., 1965, Dr. Habilitation in Law, 1973. Lectr. Faculty of Law U. Vilnius, Republic of Lithuania, 1961-63; post-grad. Faculty of Law Moscow State U., 1963-65; assoc. prof. Faculty of Law U. Vilnius, 1965-69, 71-73, prof. internat. law Faculty of Law, 1973-92, dean Faculty of Law, 1969-71, 73-77; judge European Ct. of Human Rights, 1994—; judge Supreme Ct. of Lithuania, 1994-98, chmn., 1994—; judge European Ct. Human Rights, 1998—; prof. internat. law U. Vilnius, 1974—; min. of justice Lithuanian S.S.R., 1977-90, Republic of Lithuania, 1990-91, state counsellor, 1991-92; mem. Del. of the Republic of Lithuania for Negotiations with the U.S.S.R., 1990-92; extraordinary and plenipotentiary amb. of the Republic of Lithuania to Belgium, Luxembourg and the Netherlands, 1992-94. Author: Problems of Responsibility in International Law, 1970, Problems in Theory of International Law, 1973, Violations in International Law and Responsibility of States, 1973, Responsibility of States and its Foundations in Modern International Law, 1973, Outlines of International Law, 1985; contbr. chpts. to books and articles to profl. jours. Scholar Dept. Internat. Law, Faculty of Law, Moscow State U., 1963-65, Institut des Hautes Etudes Internationales, U. Paris, 1967-68, The Hague Acad. of Internat. Law Rsch. Ctr., 1970. Mem. Acad. Sci. Lithuania. Office: c/o Conseil de l'Europe, F-67075 Strasbourg France

KURISAQILA, APENISA NEIORI, government executive, physician; b. Naduri, Nadroga, Fiji, Nov. 13, 1933; parents Meli Neiori and Merewairita Butani; m. Temalesi Bua Lagi Kurisaqila; chilfren: Olivia Solei Neinoca, Wilisoni Tila Lagi, Litia Hoqo Nai. DSM, Fiji Sch. Medicine, Suva, Fiji, 1958; DTCH, Sch. Tropical Medicine, Liverpool, England, 1974. Med. officer Fiji Govt. Health Svcs., Fiji, 1958-72; min. health Fiji. Govt., Fiji, 1972-92; speaker House of Reps., Fiji Parliament, Fiji, 1992—. Sports chmn. Fiji Rugby Union, 1994. Mem. Internat. Med. Parlimrntry Assn. Avocations: gardening, fishing. Office: House of Representatves, Govt Bldg PO Box 2352, Suva Fiji

KURISH, JAMES BRIAN, finance executive; b. Amherst, Ohio, May 18, 1955; s. Andrew Stefan and Betty Louise (Bryner) K.; m. Mary Lyn Valkenburg, Dec. 23, 1988. BA, The Coll. of Wooster, Ohio, 1977; MS, U. Ill., Champaign, 1980; PhD, 1983; MBA, Yale U., New Haven, 1989. Mktg. analyst J.M. Smucker Co., Orrville, Ohio, 1976; researcher Dept. Energy, Oak Ridge, Tenn., 1976-79; asst. prof. Econ. U. Hartford, West Hartford, Conn., 1981-84; dir. grad. studies, 1984-85; asst. dean, exec. dir. Paris, 1985-87; assoc. The First Boston Corp., Chgo., 1989-92; dir. Govt. Fin. Officers Assn., Chgo., 1992-94; pres. J.B. Kurish & Assocs., Chgo., 1994-95; exec. dir. Mcpl. Issuer Rsch. and Analysis Ctr., Chgo., 1995-99; dir. Ctr. Fin. Rsch. and Svcs., Chgo., 1999—. Author: Debt Issuance, 1993, Pricing Bonds in a Negotiated Sale, 1994; contbr. articles to profl. jours. Mem. Govt. Fin. Officers Assn., Am. Econ. Assn. Home: 10th Fl 2120 N Lincoln Park West Chicago IL 60614 Office: U Ill Coll Bus Adminstrn Dept Fin M/C 168 601 S Morgan St Chicago IL 60607-7100

KURITA, AKIKO, literary agency executive; b. Kawasaki, Kanagawa, Japan, Jan. 26, 1934; d. Toshimaru and Minoru (Watanabe) K. Grad. h.s., Kobe, Japan, 1952. With internat. mgmt. divsn. C. Itoh Co., Ltd., Osaka, Japan, 1952-58; stenographer sec. Henderson Trippe, Tokyo, 1959-60, Philipp Bros. Inc., Tokyo, 1960-62; exec. sec. Time Inc., Tokyo, 1963-70; with divsn. children's books/fgn. rights Japanese authors Japan UNI Agy., Tokyo, 1970-80; mng. dir. Kurita-Bando Lit. Agy., Tokyo, 1981-83, Japan Fgn.-Rights Ctr., Tokyo, 1984—; cons. editor Asian/Pacific Book Devel. UNESCO, 1992—. Author: (book and cassette tape) English Note-Taking in Audio Method, 1976, (book) My Treasure Box with Dreams, 1986; co-author: American Publishing Scene, 1972. Trustee Tokyo Children's Libr., 1994—. Recipient Chevalier de l'ordre des Arts et des Lettres Ministry of Culture, Paris, 1997. Mem. Assn. for 100 Japanese Books (exec. dir. 1992-98, dir. 1999—), Japan Soc. Publ. Studies (mem. com.), Japanese Board of Books for Young Readers. Avocations: mountain climbing, reading books,

swimming, Yoga. Office: Japan Fgn Rights Ctr, 2-27-18-804 Nakaochiai, Shinjuku Tokyo 161-0032, Japan

KURIYAMA, KINYA, pharmacology educator; b. Kyoto, Japan, July 11, 1932; s. Haruya and Kouko Kuriyama; m. Chieko Imamura, Dec. 8, 1958; children: Takuya, Nagato. MD, Kyoto Prefecture U. Medicine, 1957, PhD, 1963. Rsch. assoc. Johns Hopkins Sch. Medicine, Balt., 1963-64; sr. rsch. scientist City of Hope Med. Ctr., Duarte, Calif., 1964-67; assoc. prof. Loma Linda (Calif.) U. Sch. Medicine, 1967-69; from assoc. prof. to prof. SUNY, Bklyn., 1969-72; prof., chmn. Kyoto Prefecture U. Medicine, 1971-96, pres., 1994-2000; pres. Meiji U. Oriental Medicine, 2000—. Exec. editor: Neurochemistry Internat., 1983—; editor: Med. Pharmacology, 1985, Neurotransmitters, 1986, Neurotransmitter Receptors and Signal Trans., 1988. Recipient Med. award Japan Med. Assn., 1980, Miyata Meml. award Miyata Found., 1993, Uehara Rsch. award Uehara meml. Found., 1985; Naito rsch. grantee Naito Found., 1988, Disting. Cultural award, Kyoto Press, 1995. Mem. Japanese Pharmacol. Soc. (coun. mem. 1987-93), Japanese Neurochem. Soc. (coun. mem. 1989-93, pres. 1977-78), Sci. Coun. Japan (coun. mem. 1989-93), Japanese Neirosci. Soc. (coun. mem. 1989-93), Japanese Neurosci. Soc. (coun. mem. 1990-92), Japan Soc. Alcohol Studies (pres. 1986-90, 95), Internat. Soc. Biomed. Rsch. on Alcohol (v.p. 1990-94, pres. 1994—), Internat. Soc. Neurochemistry (pres. 1993—). Buddhist. Avocations: tennis, driving, classical music. Home: 69-1 Iwagakakiuchi-cho, Kita-ku Kyoto 603, Japan Office: Meiji U Oriental Medicine, Hiyoshi-cho Funai-quos, Kyoto 629-0392, Japan

KURKE, DAVID SAMUEL, management executive, industrial psychologist; b. Havre de Grace, Md., Apr. 22, 1955; s. Martin Ira Kurke and Joy Barbara (Edinger) Kurke Joseph; m. Kathleen Marie Tighe, Feb. 22, 1986. B.S. cum laude, Va. Poly. and State U., 1979; postgrad. in cognitive psychology U. Wash., 1986. Research scientist Allen Corp. Am., Alexandria, Va., 1979-82; prin. scientist/mgr. edn. and tng. tech. Pacer Systems, Inc., Arlington, Va., 1982-85; v.p. tech. ops. Tech. Corp. Am., Falls Church, Va., 1985-86; mgt. dept. research and info. systems Walker and Dunlop, Inc., Washington, 1987—. Mem. exec. bd. Arlington Area Young Republicans, 1980-82; mem. Republican Nat. Com., Washington, 1980—, mem. Presdl. inaugural com., 1980-81; scoutmaster Boy Scouts Am., Washington, 1978; sr. counselor peer counselor program Va. Poly. Inst. and State U., 1974-75, chmn. univ. advisors com., 1978, co-chmn. student-faculty com. on psychology dept. affairs, 1977-78. Recipient Presdl. Achievement award Rep. Nat. Com., 1982; named Outstanding Sr. of Year, Va. Poly. Inst. and State U., 1979. Mem. Am. Soc. Tng. and Devel., Human Factors Soc., Soc. for Applied Learning Tech., Human Factors Soc. Computer Tech. Group, Mensa, Psi Chi. Jewish. Avocations: bicycling; backpacking; restoring antique cars; renovating old homes. Home: 5703 9th Rd N Arlington VA 22205-1307 Office: Walker and Dunlop Inc 1156 15th St NW Washington DC 20005-1704

KURLANDSKY, RUTH JESSICA GOULD, educator, consultant; b. Chgo., Nov. 5, 1948; d. Joseph E. and Shirley (Goldman) Gould; m. Lawrence Edward Kurlandsky, May 24, 1970; children: Shana, Hillel, Mara. BA in Psychology, U. Mich., 1969, MA in Spl. Edn., 1971; PhD in Coll. and Univ. Adminstrn., Mich. State U., 1990. Cert. tchr., Mich. Dir. univ. rels. Grand Rapids C.C. Trustee Congregation Ahavas Israel, Grand Rapids, 1994-2000, Jewish Fedn. of Grand Rapids, 1998—; ednl. specialist Balt. City Pub. Schs., 1979-80; exec. dir. Md. Cmty. Coord. Child Care, 1977-79; ednl. specialist in the divsn. for spl. edn. on spl. svcs. info. sys. Md. State Dept. Edn., 1974-77. Mem. North Ctrl. Assn. Commn. on Instns. Higher Edn. (cons., evaluator 1991—), Torch Club. Avocations: reading, studying, Bible history, knitting, walking. Office: Grand Rapids CC 143 Bostwick Ave NE Grand Rapids MI 49503-3201

KURLAT, ISABEL ROSA, neonatologist; b. Buenos Aires, Jan. 27, 1950; d. Alberto and Frida (Weber) K.; m. Leonardo Miguel Zitzer; children: Diego, Alejandro, Carolina. MD, U. Buenos Aires, 1975. Attending physician U. Buenos Aires, 1982-88, resident in pediats., 1986, resident in neonatology, 1988, attending physician, 1993-94, chief neonatology, 1995—, mem. hosp. epidemiology com., 1981-82; attending physician Pediat. Hosp., Buenos Aires, 1988-93; vis. prof. U. Calif., San Francisco, 1992-93; chief neonatology Santa Ana Hosp., Buenos Aires, 1996-98. Contbr. articles to profl. jours., chpt. to book. Pres. Fundation para el Recien Nacido, Argentina, 1999. Mem. L.Am. Soc. Pediat. Rsch., Cuban Pediat. Soc. (hon.), Sociedad Artentina de Pediatria (Jaime Braverman award 1984). Avocation: piano. Office: Hosp Clin Jose San Martin, Cordoba 2351, 1120 Buenos Aires Argentina

KURNIK, WLODZIMIERZ, mechanical engineer, researcher; b. Gorakalwaria, Poland, Nov. 20, 1950; s. Jaroslaw and Zofia (Akimow) K.; m. Ewa Gizela Kosiarek, July 13, 1974; children: Jerzy, Andrzej. MSc, Warsaw (Poland) U. Tech., 1974, PhD in Mech. Engring., 1978, DSc, 1988. Head lab. Warsaw U. Tech., 1985-89, head divsn., assoc. prof. mech. engring., 1989-90, vice-dean, 1990-96, prof. mech. engring., 1993—, dean Faculty Automobiles & Heavy Machinery Engring., 1996-99, vice-rector, 1999—. Author: Theory of Vibrations—Selected Tasks, 1990 (Min. Edn. award 1990), Mechanics of Composite Elements, 1997, Divergent and Oscillatory Bifurcations, 1997 (in Polish), Damping of Vibrations, 1998; editor (jour.) Machine Dynamics Problems, 1980—; contbr. articles to profl. jours. Recipient rsch. grants. Ministry of Edn., Poland, 1991, Com. Scientific Rsch., 1992-95, 96. Mem. Gesellschaft für Angewandte Mathematik und Mechanik, Polish Soc. Theoretical and Applied Mechs., Polish Soc. Applied Electromagnetism. Avocations: travel, cycling. Office: Inst Machine Design Funds, Warsaw U Tech Narbutta 84, 02-524 Warsaw Poland

KUROCHKIN, VLADIMIR DANILOVICH, chemist, researcher; b. Kiev, Ukraine, Nov. 24, 1946; s. Danilo Jakovich Kurochkin and Hanna Jakivna Doroshenko; m. Larisa Phylyppovna Kravchenko, Aug. 20, 1972. Degree in engring., Kiev Poly. U., 1972; DSc in Chemistry, Inst. Material Sci. Problems, 1985. Engr. Inst. Material Sci. Problems, Kiev, 1972-85, rsch. worker, 1985-88, sr. rsch. worker, 1988—; lectr. Ctr. Sci. and Tech. Info., Kiev, 1985—. Contbr. articles to jours. in field. Mem. Mendeleev Soc. Avocations: piano, painting, mountain climbing. Home: Blvd Perova 26 Flat 24, 03126 Kiev Ukraine Office: Inst Material Sci Problems, Krzhizhanovsky 3, 252142 Kiev Ukraine

KUROCHKINA, NATALYA ALEXANDROVNA, biophysicist; b. Verkhny Ufaley, USSR, Dec. 6, 1957; came to U.S., 1991; d. Tatyana Ivanovna Lezhneva; m. Boris Konstantinovich Kurochkin; 1 child, Andrei Borisovich Kurochkin. MS in Computer Sci., Moscow Inst. Radio, 1984; PhD in Physics-Math., Russian Acad. Sci., Puschino, 1990. Leading engr. Inst. Protein Rsch. Russian Acad. Sci., Puschino, 1984-91; vis. fellow Nat. Cancer Inst./NIH, Bethesda, Md., 1991-96; rsch. scientist Applied Thermodynamics, Hunt Valley, Md., 1996-98; dir. Sch. Theoretical Modeling, Chevy Chase, Md., 1999—. Contbr. articles to profl. jours. Mem. AAAS, Biophysical Soc. Home: # 2401 N 5500 Friendship Blvd Apt 2401N Chevy Chase MD 20815-7218 Office: Sch Theoretical Modeling PO Box 15676 Chevy Chase MD 20825-5676

KURODA, MITSUTOSHI, mechanical engineering educator; b. Tokyo, Oct. 7, 1963; s. Toshiaki and Reiko (Koyamo) K.; m. Mika Kuroda, Jan. 21, 1966; 1 child, Sumique. BE, Musashi Inst. Tech., Tokyo, 1986, D Engring., 1992. Asst. prof. Ashikaga Inst. Tech., Japan, 1992-95, assoc. prof., 1995-99; assoc. prof. Yamagata U., Japan, 1999—. Contbr. articles to profl. jours. Mem. Japan Soc. Civil Engrs. (Tanaka prize 1992), Japan Soc. Mech. Engrs. Office: Dept Mech Systems Engrg Yamagata U, 4-3-16 Jonan, Yonezawa Yamagata 992-8510, Japan

KURODA, TOSHIRO, ceramic laboratory administrator; b. Nagoya, Japan, Feb. 14, 1926; s. Hide and Masa Kuroda; m. Yuriko Kuroda, Nov. 14, 1959; children: Mariko, Toshiya. BS, Kyoto (Japan) U., 1948. Researcher Narumi China Corp., Nagoya, 1948-65, mgr. of rsch., 1965-76, dir., 1974, dir. mktg., 1976-81, v.p. tech. ceramics div., 1981-84; exec. rsch. Narumi Tech. Lab., Nagoya, 1985-88, adviser, 1989—. Recipient Invention prize Japan Soc. for Invention, 1981. Home: 32 2 Chome Ichiokacho, Mizuhoku, Nagoya 467-0063, Japan Office: Narumi Tech Lab, Narumi-Cho Midoriku, Nagoya 458-0844, Japan

KUROI, KATSUMASA, surgical oncologist; b. Hiroshima, Japan, Dec. 27, 1956; s. Isao and Emiko (Yuto) K.; m. Tsutae Sayamoto, June 19, 1979; children: Miki, Shoko, Ryo. MD, Hiroshima U., 1983, PhD, 1987. Resident in surgery Hiroshima U., 1983-84, med. staff dept. surg. oncology, 1990, rsch. assoc. dept. surg. oncology, 1990-97; med. staff in surgery Futami Ctrl. Hosp., Miyoshi, Japan, 1987-90; assoc. dir. dept. surgery Sera (Japan) Ctrl. Hosp., 1997-98; dep. dir. dept. surgery Tokyo Met. Komagome Hosp., 1998—. Mem. Am. Soc. Clin. Oncology, Am. Assn. Cancer Rsch., Japanese Cancer Assn., Japan Soc. Clin. Oncology, Japan Soc. for Surgery, Japanese Breast Cancer Soc. E-mail: kurochan-k@komagome-hospital.bunkyo.tokyo.jp. Fax: 03-3824-1552. Home: 3-37-1-304 Narimasu, Itabashi-ku Tokyo 175-0094, Japan Office: Tokyo Met Komagome Hosp, 3-18-22 Honkomagome, Bunkyo-ku Tokyo 113-8677, Japan

KUROIWA, TORU, journalist, educator; b. Tokyo, Aug. 5, 1940; s. Kikuro and Taka (Kuwano) K.; m. Chizuko Hisamatsu, Sept. 12, 1965. Bachelor in Law and Politics, Tokyo U., 1964; postgrad. St. Antony's Coll., Oxford U., Eng., 1970-72. London corr. The Mainichi Newspapers, Japan, 1975-82, Washington corr., 1984-87, chief London bur., European editor, 1989-95, sr. staff writer, 1995-98; vis. sr. staff writer, prof. social sci. Toyo Eiwa U., Yokohama-shi, Japan, 1999—. Author: Spiritually Rich British, 1984, Fighting and Leadership, Mrs. Thatcher, 1988, Mysterious Countries of English, U.S. and U.K., 1989, British Royal Family, 1995, British Way of Life, 1997, British Leadership After World War II, 1998, The Decisive Britain, Emergence of a New Leader--Tony Blair, 1998. Mem. Japan Press Club. Avocations: tennis, skiing. Home: 5-22-23 Tsurumaki, Setagaya-ku Tokyo 154-0016, Japan Office: Toyo Eiwa U, 32 Miho-Cho, Midoriku Yokohama-shi 226-0015, Japan

KUROKAWA, YASUTAKA, neurosurgeon; b. Nayoro, Hokkaido, Japan, Jan. 23, 1958; 1 child, Takayuki. Diploma, Sapporo (Japan) Med. U., 1983, MD, 1983, PhD, 1987. Bd. cert. neurosurgeon. Instr. Sapporo Med. U., 1987, sr. instr., 1994-97; clin. fellow Sapporo City Gen. Hosp., 1988-89; neurosurgeon Kushiro (Japan) City Gen. Hosp., 1989-93; rsch. fellow U. Calgary, Can., 1993-94; chief in neurosurgery Shin Sapporo Neurosurg. Hosp., 1997-98; vice dir. Obihiro Neurosurg. Hosp., 1998-99; dir. Asahikawa (Japan) Neurosurg. Hosp., 1999—; organizer Sapporo Video Conf. on Neurosurgery, 1990—. Contbr. articles to profl. jours. Scholarship Japan Nat. Edn. Found., 1977-87. Mem. Japan Neurosurg. Soc., Japanese Soc. of Stroke, Japanese Congress of Neurol. Surgeons. Avocations: listening to Mozart, visiting art museum. Fax: 81 166 35 5386. Office: Asahikawa Neurosurg Hosp, 9-18, Asahikawa 078-8219, Japan

KUROKAWA, YOSHITERU, educator, playwright; b. Tokyo, Dec. 7, 1933; s. Kinji and Tsuru (Fukuda) K.; m. Yoko Kurokawa, Apr. 1, 1955; 1 child, Ko. B.A., U. Tokyo, 1955. Lectr. Hosei U., Tokyo, 1962-64, asst. prof., 1964-66, prof. Am. theater, 1966—; dir. Aristophanes Co. Tokyo, 1981—. Author: A Fool's Death and Other Plays, 1966; Alone in Russia, 1979; Satirical Short Plays, 1980; The Mountain Where We Used to Chase Hares and Other Plays, 1985, How to Make Friends with Chinese, 1992, I Quit Being A Woman! and Other Plays, 1996, China Plays, 1996. Address: 4-24-19 Wakabayashi, Setagaya, Tokyo 154-0023, Japan

KUROL, JÜRI, orthodontist; b. Tartu, Estonia, Sept. 23, 1942; arrived in Sweden, 1944; s. Martin and Aino (Rämmal) K.; m. Olu Margareta Anderson, Aug. 1967 (div. 1987); 1 child, Pontus; m. Kari Line Road. Licensed Dental Surgeon, U. Lund, 1966; MS, U. Göteborg, 1974, PhD, 1984. Orthodontist Inst. for Postgrad. Dental Edn., 1970-97; prof., chmn. dept. orthodontics Lund U., 1997—; internat. adv. panel and referee to profl. jours.; external examiner to various univs.; lectr. and rschr. in field. Contbr. articles to profl. jours. Mem. European Fedn. Orthodontic Specialist Assn. (pres. 1998—), Swedish Assn. Orthodontists (bd. dirs. 1980-82, v.p. 1982-87, pres. 1988—). Avocations: outdoors, music, books, sailing. Office: Carl Gustafs väg 34, SE-21421 Malmö Sweden

KUROLI, GÉZA, entomologist, educator; b. Szerecseny, Hungary, Oct. 8, 1936; s. Gyula and Gyuláné (Veisz, Margit) G.; m. Valéria Szitás, Aug. 22, 1962; children: Éva, Mónika. Agrl. engr., Agrl. Acad., Mosonmagyaróvár, Hungary, 1960; plant protectional engr., Agrl. Univ., Gödöllő, 1961; DSc, 1995. Leader of plant protection group Pápa State Farm, Pápa, Hungary, 1960-62; head of dept. plant protection U. West Hungary, Mosonmagyaróvár, 1972—, prodean, 1975-82, 94-97, prorector, 1982-85, dean, 1985-94; cons. Inst. for Consultancy and Training, 1994—; dir. Model Farm, Szombathely, Hungary, 1993—; v.p. Hungarian Acad. of Scis. Plant Protection Com., Budapest, 1996—, Hungarian Agrl. Soc. Plant Protection Com., 1990—. Author, editor: Protection of Cultivated Plants, 1997; contbr. articles to profl. jours.; mem. editorial bd. Növényvédelem, 1995—, Acta Agronomica Óváriensis, 1995—, Rsch. & Practice in Agrl. and Food Tech., 1994—. Mem. Internat. Lenau Com., Mosonmagyaróvár, Hungary, 1985-93. Named Outstanding Worker of Agrl. Min. of Agrl., 1966, 74, Development of Agrl. , 1986, 91; recipient Middle Cross of Decoration of Hungarian Republic award Hungarian Gov., 1993. Mem. Club of Plant Protectional Profls., Club of Afrl. Profls. Roman Catholic. Avocations: hunting, tourism. Office: Univ West Hungary Fac Agr, Vár 2, 9200 Mosonmagyaróvár Hungary

KUROSAWA, MITSURU, law educator; b. Osaka, Japan, Jan. 17, 1945; s. Hisao and Toyo (Nakakita) K.; m. Kuniko Furukawa, Oct. 11, 1972; children: Ryoko, Tomoko. LLM, Osaka U., 1971, PhD in Law, 1993. Lectr. Niigata U., 1976-77, assoc. prof., 1977-84, prof. law, 1984-91; prof. law Osaka U., 1991—. Author: International Disarmament Law, 1986 (Adachi Minerchiro award 1987), Nuclear Disarmament and International Law, 1982; editor/author: The Triangle of Pacific States, 1995 (Can. Prime Minister award 1995), Issues in disarmament: An Introduction, 1996. Home: 2-8-1 Minami-Tanabe, Higashi-Sumiyoshi-ku, Osaka 546-0033, Japan Office: Osaka U Sch int Pub Policy, 1-31 Machikaneyama-cho, Toyonaka-shi Osaka Japan

KUROSAWA, TSUTOMU MIKI, science educator; b. Sapporo, Japan, Oct. 1, 1948; s. Yasuji and Kau (Kamibayashi) K.; m. Yumiko Takaoka, June 20, 1981; children: Mimoe, Hayato, Miyabi, Kazuto. DVM, Hokkaido U., Sapporo, 1972, PhD, 1986; DVCS, Massey U., New Zealand, 1976, MPhil, 1978. Diplomate lab. animal medicine. Postgrad. rsch. student Hokkaido U., 1972-74; asst. prof. Teikyo U., Tokyo, 1979-86; assoc. prof. Osaka U. Med. Sch., Suita, Japan, 1986—. Co-editor (video series) Lab. Animal Scis., 1988; co-author: Veterinary Laboratory Animal Sciences, 1996; contbr. articles to profl. jours. Mem. Soc. Lab. Animal Environment (v.p. 1995—), Internat. Standardization Orgn., (ISO/TC194) (mem. tech. com. 1995—). Avocation: mountain skiing. Home: Tsukumodai 5-9-D39-103, Suita Osaka 565-0862, Japan Office: Osaka U Med Sch, 2-2 Yamadaoka, Suita Osaka 565-0871, Japan

KUROSAWA, YOH, bank executive; b. Tokyo, Dec. 2, 1926; m. Yasuko Kurosawa; 1 child, Mari. LLB, U. Tokyo, 1950. With The Indsl. Bank of Japan Ltd., Tokyo, 1950—; seconded to Deutsche Bank AG, Germany, 1961-62; chief rep. Frankfurt Rep. Office The Indsl. Bank of Japan Ltd., 1966-71; gen. mgr. internat. dept. The Indsl. Bank of Japan Ltd., Tokyo, 1975-76, dir., 1976-79, mng. dir., 1979-84, dep. pres., 1984-90, pres., 1990-96, chmn. bd. dirs., 1996—; chmn. Industriebank von Japan Deutschland A.G., Frankfurt, The Indsl. Bank of Japan, Switzerland Ltd., Zurich, Indsl. Bank of Japan Canada Ltd., Toronto, IBJ Internat. plc, London. Decorated comdr. Order of the Lion of Finland, 1985, Gross Verdienstkreuz des Verdienstordens der Bundesrepublik Deutschland, Germany, 1991, Grand Officer Order of Merit Grand-Duchy of Luxembourg, 1995, Orden de San Carlos Grado Gran Cruz, Republic of Columbia, 1997; named Banker of Yr., Asian Fin., 1991, Grobes Silbernes Ehrenzeichen mit dem Stern Für Verdienste um dieRepublickl üsterreich. Avocations: tennis, classical music, lit. E-mail G@3pleasl. Office: The Indsl Bank of Japan Ltd, 1-3-3 Marunouchi Chiyoda-ku, i Tokyo 100-8210, Japan*

KUROSHIMA, AKIHIRO, environmental physiology educator; b. Sapporo, Hokkaido, Japan, Sept. 14, 1935; s. Kenji and Ishi (Tanaka) K. ; m. Michiko Suzuki, Mar. 30, 1959; children: Kazue, Masahiro, Kiyomi. MD, Hokkaido U., Sapporo, 1960, PhD, 1967. Intern Hokkaido U. Hosp., 1960-61; assoc. prof. Hokkaido U. Edn., Asahikawa, 1967-71, prof., 1971-73; prof. dept. physiology Asahikawa Med. U. Sch. Medicine, 1973—, dir. libr., 2000—. Author: Environmental Physiology, 1st edit., 1981, 2d edit., 1993; editor Japanese Jour. Physiology, 1995—. Recipient med. prize Hokkaiod Med. Assn., 1988. Mem. Japanese Soc. Biometerology (bd. dirs. 1985—), Internat. Soc. for Adaptive Medicine (v.p. 1990—), Physiol. Soc. Japan (bd. dirs. 1996—), Japan Soc. for Adaptation Medicine (bd. dirs. 1996—), Hokkaido Med. Assn. (bd. dirs. 1973—). Avocations: running, medicine history. Home: 2-6, 2-3 Midorigaoka, Hokkaido Asahikawa 078 8302, Japan Office: Asahikawa U Sch Medicine, 1-1, East 2-1 Midorigaoka, Hokkaido Asahikawa 078 8510, Japan

KUROYANAGI, TETSUKO, actress, television personality; b. Tokyo, 1934. Student, Tomoe Sch., Tokyo, Tokyo Coll. Music. TV talk show host Tetsuko's Room Asahi Broadcasting Co., 1976—; regular guest quiz program Discover Wonders of the World; goodwill amb. UNICEF, 1984—; dir. Chihiro Iwasaki Art Mus. Picture Books, 1995—. Author: From New York with Love, 1972, Totto-Chan, The Little Girl at the Window, 1981 (pub. 31 countries), Totto-chan Children: A Goodwill Journey to the Children of the World, 1997. Home and Office: 2 Tanizawa Bldg 3-2-11, Nishi-azabu Minato-ku, Tokyo 106-0031, Japan

KURPASKA, SLAWOMIR, agricultural engineer, educator; b. Dabrowa, Tarnowska, Poland, Jan. 30, 1961; s. Tadeusz and Bozena (Borek) K.; m. Anna Bialy, Aug. 23, 1986; children: Damian, Karolina. MSc, Agrl. U., Cracow, Poland, 1986, PhD, 1993. Cert. engring. From lectr. to asst. prof. Agrl. Univ., Cracow, 1986—; cons. in field. Contbr. articles to profl. jours. Sgt. Poland Mil. Svc., 1986. Grantee Tempus, Torino, Italy, 1997. Mem. Polish Agrl. Engring. Assn., Polish Agrophysics Assn. Roman Catholic. Avocations: recreational activities, literature. Office: Agrl Univ, Balicka 104, 30-149 Cracow Poland

KURSOV, VALERI, mathematics educator; b. Minsk, Belarus, U.S.S.R., Mar. 17, 1954; s. Vladimir and Anna Kursov; children: Vitali, Yori. Degree in math., Univ. Minsk, 1976, PhD in Math. Sci., 1983. Collaborator Inst. Math., Minsk, 1976-90; prof. math. Univ. Minsk, 1990—. Contbr. articles to profl. jours. Home: Ave Partizanski 38-34, 220107 Minsk Belarus

KÜRSTEN, MARTIN OTTO CHRISTIAN, geologist; b. Suhl, Germany, Oct. 12, 1931; s. Otto and Cläre (Hoffmann) K.; m. Barbara Hauerwas, Dec. 28, 1957; children: Martin, Bettina, Bernd. Dr.rer.nat., U. Bonn, Germany, 1956; prof., U. Würzburg, Germany, 1979. Govt. geologist Geol. Survey, Hannover, Germany, 1958-73, divsn. chief, 1973-86, pres., 1986-96; advisor to EC Commn., Brussels, Ministry of Sci. and Tech., Bonn. Author: Geology of Iran, 1962, Geology of Danakil, 1972; author geol. map Tanzania, 1969. Mem. German Geol. Assn. Avocations: playing in string quartet, beekeeping. Office: Fed Inst Geosci & Natural Resources, Postfach 51 01 53, 30631 Hannover Germany

KURT, ADNAN, biomedical company executive, research engineer; b. Tokat, Turkey, Nov. 1; s. Ziyaettin and Sukran (Alpay) K. BSEE, Bogazici U., Istanbul, 1984, MS in Physics, 1987; postgrad., Med. Sch., Istanbul, 1988-92. Rsch. asst. Bogazici U., 1985-91; rsch. engr. TU Med. Sch., 1991-95; bd. mgr. Sigma Ltd., Istanbul, 1991-96; tech. and bd. mgr. Mitra A.S., Istanbul, 1996-99; CEO Teknofil Ltd., Istanbul, 1994—; instr. Koc U., Istanbul, 1999—. Mem. IEEE, EMO, LEOS. Avocations: music, origami, Aikido, photography, trekking. Home: Cengiz Topel cd Kutay 2 D5, 80815 Itiler, Istanbul Turkey Office: Kok U Dept Physics, Cayir Cad, 80860 Istanbul Turkey

KURTANJEK, ZELIMIR FRANK, food science educator, researcher; b. Zagreb, Croatia, Aug. 15, 1946; s. Franjo Fabijan and Božena Marija (Ožvald) K. Diploma in phys. engring., U. Zagreb, Croatia, 1971, MSc in Control engring., 1975; PhD in Chem. Engring., U. Houston, 1980. Asst. U. Zagreb, 1971-75, asst. prof., 1981-87, prof., 1987—. Editor CABEQ Jour., 1999—; rschr. in field. Mem. AIChE, Croatian Soc. Chem. Engrs. (chmn. 1998), Croatian Soc. Chem. Engring. (bd. dirs. 1987-92). Roman Catholic. Avocation: yachting. Home: Nad Lipom 18, 10 000 Zagreb Croatia Office: PBF, Pierottijera 6, 10 000 Zagreb Croatiz

KURTH, REINHARD H., virologist, educator; b. Dresden, Germany, Nov. 30, 1942. U. Caen, France, 1966, U. Erlangen, Nuremberg, Germany, 1968. Rsch. asst. Max Planck Inst. for Virus Rsch., Tübingen, 1969-71; rsch. assoc. virology Robert Koch Inst., Berlin, 1971-73; rsch. assoc., head rsch. working group Imperial Cancer Rsch. Fund Labs., London, 1974-75; head rsch. group Friedrich Miescher Lab., Max Planck Soc., Tübingen, 1975-80; habilitation, venia legendi for virology U. Tübingen, 1976; sci. dir., prof., head human virology Paul Ehrlich Inst., Frankfurt, 1980-86; pres., prof. virology Paul Ehrlich Inst., Langen/Frankfurt, 1986-99; hon. prof. virology Johann Wolfgang Goethe U., Frankfurt, 1983; head Robert-Koch Inst., Berlin, 1996—. Contbr. over 260 articles to profl. jours. Recipient Cancer Rsch. award Wilhelm Warner Found., 1976, award Elisabeth Homberger Found., 1983, Johann Lukas Schönlein award Germany Soc. for Hematology, 1986, Hoppe-Seyler award German Soc. for Lab. Medicine, 1987, Heinz Ansmann award U. Düsseldorf, 1989, award Kuthe de Mouson Found., 1991, San Marino prize in medicine, 1998; fellow Deutsche Forschungsgemeinschaft, 1974-75. Mem. German Soc. for Hygiene and Microbiology, Soc. for Virology, Soc. for Immunology, German Cancer Soc., German AIDS Soc. (charter), Robert Koch Found., Internat. Assn. for Biol. Standardization, Internat. AIDS Soc. (charter), Soc. Gen. Microbiology, Am. Soc. for Microbiology, AAAS, N.Y. Acad. Scis., Soc. for Health and Rsch., Berlin-Brandenburg Acad. Scis., Berlin Scientific Soc. Office: Paul-Ehrlich-Institut, Robert Koch Inst, Nordufer 20, D-13353 Berlin Germany

KURTZ, ALFRED BERNARD, radiologist; b. Albany, N.Y., May 1, 1944; s. Leonard David and Esther (Lederman) K.; m. Barbara Ellen, July 3, 1973; children: Dana, Liza, Amy. BA, NYU, 1966; MD, Stanford U., 1972. Diplomate Am. Bd. Radiology. Internal medicine intern Montefiore Hosp. and Med. Ctr., Bronx, N.Y., 1972-73, resident in internal medicine, 1973-74, resident in diagnostic radiology, 1974-77; fellow in ultrasound and body CT Jefferson Med. Coll., Thomas Jefferson Univ. Hosp., Phila., 1977-78, assoc. prof. ob/gyn, 1982-85; assoc. dir. Div. of U.S. and Radiol. Imaging, Phila., 1982-86, Body Computed Tomography, Thomas Jefferson U. Hosp., Phila., 1986-89, Div. Diagnostic U.S., Thomas Jefferson U. Hosp., Phila., 1986-89; prof. radiology Jefferson Med. Coll., Thomas Jefferson U. Hosp., Phila., 1983—, prof. ob/gyn., 1985—, vice chmn. dept. radiology, 1989—; fellowship ultrasound and body ct. Montefiore Hosp. and Med. Ctr., Bronx, N.Y., 1977-78; examiner oral bds. in ultrasound category Am. Bd. Radiology, 1985—; med. advisor Blue Shield of Pa., Phila., 1983—; mem. adv. com. Ctr. of Excellence in Biomed. Imaging, Phila., 1987—. Author: Ultrasound: The Requisites, 1995, Obstetrical Measurements in Ultrasound: A Reference Manual, 1988; editor: Atlas of Ultrasound Measurements, 1990; assoc. editor Radiology; contbr. articles to profl. jours. Grantee Nat. Cancer Inst., NIH, 1993-96. Fellow Am. Inst. Ultrasound in Medicine (bd. govs. 1990-92, sec. 1993-97, pres.-elect 1999—), Am. Coll. Radiology (chmn. com. on edn. and tng. of commn. 1987-93, commn. on ultrasound 1987-93), Soc. Radiologists in Ultrasound (pres. 1991-93), Coll. Physicians Phila. Achievements include advancement of the ability of ultrasound to establish an accurate fetal age; establishment of ultrasound patterns for analysis of diffuse liver disease; advancement of ultrasound in evaluation of obstetrical and gynecologic problems including by intravaginal scanning and cross sectional imaging evaluation for ovarian cancer. Home: 1050 Indian Creek Rd Wynnewood PA 19096-3407 Office: Thomas Jefferson U Hosp 111 S 11th St Philadelphia PA 19107-5084

KURTZ, PAUL, philosopher, educator, publisher; b. Newark, Dec. 21, 1925; s. Martin and Sara (Lasser) K.; m. Claudine C. Vial, Oct. 6, 1960; children: Valerie L., Patricia A., Jonathan, Anne. BA, NYU, 1948; MA, Columbia U., 1949, PhD, 1952. Instr. Queens Coll., 1950-52; instr. philosophy Trinity Coll., Hartford, Conn., 1952-55; asst. prof. Trinity Coll., 1955-58, assoc. prof., 1958-59; assoc. prof. Vassar Coll., Poughkeepsie, N.Y., 1960-61; vis. prof. New Sch. Social Rsch., N.Y.C., 1960-65; assoc. prof. Union Coll., Schenectady, 1961-64, prof., 1964-65; vis. prof. U. Besancon, France, 1965; prof. philosophy SUNY, Buffalo, 1965-91, prof. emeritus, 1992—; moderator TV series. Author: (with Rollo Handy) A Current Appraisal of the Behavioral Sciences, 1964, Decision and the Condition of Man, 1965, The Fullness of Life, 1974, Exuberance, 1977, In Defense of Secular Humanism, 1983, A Skeptics Handbook of Parapsychology, 1985, The Transcendental Tempta-

tion, 1986, Forbidden Fruit, 1988, Eupraxophy, 1989, Philosophical Essays in Pragmatic Naturalism, 1990, The New Skepticism, 1992, Toward a New Enlightenment, 1994, The Courage To Become, 1997, Humanist Manifesto 2000, 1999, Embracing the Power of Humanism, 2000, Skepticism and Humanism: The New Paradigm, 2000; editor: American Thought Before 1900, 1966, American Philosophy in the Twentieth Century, 1966, Sidney Hook and the Contemporary World, 1968, Moral Problems in Contemporary Society, 1969; co-editor: International Directory of Philosophy and Philosophers, 4th edit, 1978-81, Tolerance and Revolution, 1970, Language and Human Nature, 1971, A Catholic/Humanist Dialogue, 1972, The Humanist Alternative, 1973, Idea of a Modern University, 1974, The Philosophy of The Curriculum, 1975, The Ethics of Teaching and Scientific Research, 1977, University and State, 1978, Sidney Hook: Philosopher of Democracy and Humanism, 1983, Building A World Community, 1989, Challenges to the Enlightenment, 1994; mem. editorial bd.: The Humanist, 1964-78, editor, 1967-78; mem. editorial bd. Philosophers Index, 1969-85, Question, 1969-81; pres. Prometheus Books, 1970—; mem. editl. bd.: The Skeptical Inquirer, 1976—; editor-in-chief: Free Inquiry Mag., 1980—; pub. The Sci. Rev. of Alternative Medicine, 1997—. Chmn. Coun. for Secular Humanism, 1980—, Coun. on Internat. Studies and World Affairs, 1966-69; trustee Behavioral Rsch. Coun., Great Barrington, Mass.; bd. dirs. U.S. Bibliography of Philosophy, 1958-70, Univ. Ctrs. for Rational Alternatives, 1969-96; bd. dirs. Internat. Humanist and Ethical Union, 1968—, co-chmn., 1986-94; chmn. Com. for Sci. Investigation Claims of Paranormal, 1976—. With AUS, 1944-46. Behavioral Rsch. Coun. fellow, 1962-63, French Govt. fellow, 1965, John Dewey fellow, 1986-87; recipient Bertrand Russell Soc. award, 1988, Internat. Rationalist award, 2000. Fellow AAAS; mem. Acad. Humanism (Laureate, pres. 1995—, Internat. Humanist award 1999, Internat. Rationalists award 2000). E-mail: paulkurtz@aol.com. Office: Prometheus Books Inc 59 John Glenn Dr Amherst NY 14228-2197

KURTZER, DANIEL, ambassador; b. Elizabeth, N.J.. BA, Yeshiva U., 1971; MA, Columbia, Columbia; PhD, Columbia, 1976. Dean Yeshiva Coll., Yeshiva U., N.Y.C., until 1979; joined Fgn. Svc., Dept. State, Washington, 1976, from 1979, with Bur. Internat. Orgn. Affairs, from 1976; 2d sec. for polit. affairs Am. Embassy, Cairo, 1979-82; 1st sec. for polit. affairs Am. Embassy, Tel Aviv, 1982-86; dep. dir. for Egyptian affairs Dept. State, from 1986, speechwriter, mem. sec.'s policy planning staff, until 1989, dep. asst. sec. for Nr. Ea. Affairs, 1989-94, prin. dep. asst. sec. for intelligence and rsch., 1994-97, acting asst. sec., 1997; amb. to Egypt, Am. Embassy, Cairo, 1997—. Office: Am Embassy Cairo Unit 64900 APO AE 09839-4900

KURTZMAN, NEIL A., medical educator; b. Bklyn., June 18, 1936; s. Louis S. and Roselie (Yegla) K.; m. Sandra Sabatini, Feb. 14, 1976; children from previous marriage: Jonathan, Laura. BA with honors, Williams Coll., 1957; MD, N.Y. Med. Coll., 1961. Intern Robert Packer Hosp., Sayre, Pa., 1961-62; resident Ohio State U. Hosp., Columbus, 1962-63; asst. chief med. services Nobel Army Hosp., Ft. McClellan, Ala., 1963-64; med. resident William Beaumont Gen. Hosp., El Paso, Tex., 1964-65, chief med. resident, 1965-66; fellow in nephrology U. Tex. Southwestern Med. Sch., Dallas, 1966-68; chief renal div. Brooke Army Med. Ctr., Ft. Sam Houston, Tex., 1969-72; prof., chief nephrology sect. U. Ill. Coll. Medicine, Chgo., 1972-84; Arnett prof. medicine Tex. Tech U. Health Scis. Ctr., Lubbock, 1985—, chief nephrology divsn., 1985-94, chief of staff univ. med. ctr., 1990-92, chmn. dept. internal medicine, 1985-98, Univ. Disting. prof., 1999—, disting. prof., 1999—; mem. gen. medicine B study sect. Nat. Inst. Arthritis, Metabolic and Digestive Diseases, Bethesda, Md., 1978-83; mem. merit rev. bd. VA, Washington, 1979-82, chmn., 1981-82; mem. sci. adv. bd. Nat. Kidney Found., N.Y.C., 1981-92, chmn., 1988-90, v.p., 1990-92, pres., 1992-94; prin. investigator regulation urinary acidification NIH, Bethesda, 1978—. Author: Handbook of Urinalysis and Urinary Sediment, 1974, Pathophysiology of the Kidney, 1977; also more than 270 sci. papers, more than 600 sci. presentations; editor-in-chief Seminars in Nephrology, 1981—, Am. Jour. Kidney Diseases, 1997—; assoc. editor Am. Jour. Nephrology; mem. editorial bd. 7 sci. jours.; referee 16 sci. jours. Faculty advisor Alpha Omega Alpha, U. Ill., 1977-84, Tex. Tech U. Health Sci. Ctr., 1985—. Served to lt. col. U.S. Army, 1963-72. Decorated U.S. Army Meritorious Svc. award; recipient Pres.'s award Nat. Kidney Found., 1990, Outstanding Acad. Achievement award N.Y. Med. Coll., 1993, So. Soc. for Clin. Investigation's Founder's award, 1996, Tex. chpt. Am. Coll. Physicians Laureate award, 1996, David M. Hume award Nat. Kidney Found., 1999. Fellow AAAS; mem. Am. Physiol. Soc., Am. Soc. Clin. Investigation, Assn. Am. Physicians, Ctrl. Soc. Clin. Research, So. Soc. Clin. Investigation, Alpha Omega Alpha. Office: Tex Tech U Health Scis Ctr Sch Of Medicine Lubbock TX 79430-0001

KURTZMAN, RALPH HAROLD, retired biochemist, researcher, consultant; b. Mpls., Feb. 21, 1933; s. Ralph Harold, Sr. and Susie Marie (Elwell) K.; m. Nancy Virginia Leussler, Aug. 27, 1955; children: Steven Paul, Sue. BS, U. Minn., 1955; MS, U. Wis., 1958, PhD, 1959. Asst. prof. U. R.I., Kingston, 1959-62, U. Minn., Morris, 1962-65; biochemist U.S. Dept. Agriculture, Albany, Calif., 1965-97; ret., 1997; instr. U. Calif., Berkeley, 1981-82; cons. Bliss Valley Farms, Twin Falls, Idaho, 1983-84; pres. Santa Clara Valley Tex. Instrument PC Users' Group, 1991-92, editor, 1993-97; cons. in field. Editor Internat. Jour. Mushroom Scis., 1995—; editor, pub.: Solliday/Sallade Family of Bucks County, Pa., 1999; inventor mushroom substrate (compost) preparation, 1982, decaffeination of beverages, 1973; contbr. articles to profl. jours. Chmn. Berkeley YMCA Camp Program Com., 1971-72; official Amateur Athletic Union (swimming), San Francisco, 1973-80; treas. Calif. Native Plant Soc., 1970. Mem. Am. Mushroom Inst., Mycological Soc. Am. (organizer symposium mushroom cultivation in Am. tropics 1998), Mycological Soc. Japan, Sigma Xi. Avocations: computers, wood working, photography, clock making. Home and Office: 445 Vassar Ave Berkeley CA 94708-1215

KURUP, ASOK, physician; b. Kuching, Sarawak, Malaysia, Oct. 18, 1967; s. Ramachandra and Anasuya K.; m. Bindu Nambiar, Sept. 7, 1995; 1 child, Ashwin. MBBS, Nat. U., Singapore, 1992; NMed, Nat. U. Singapore, 1997. House officer Ministry Health, Singapore, 1992-93, med. officer, 1993-97, med. officer (splst.), 1997-98; infectious diseases registrar Singapore Gen. Hosp., 1998—. Contbr. articles to profl. jours. Mem. Royal Coll. Physicians Edinburgh, Soc. Infectious Diseases Singapore. Avocations: badminton, swimming, squash. Home: Serangoon Ave 2 #02-378, Block 321, Singapore 550321, Singapore Office: Singapore Gen Hosp, Outram Rd, Singapore 19608, Singapore

KURUSU, KOJI, physician, medical association executive; b. Ibaraki, Japan, July 4, 1967; s. Kazuo and Shizue Kurusu. MD, Nippon Med. Sch., Tokyo, 1992, PhD, 1999. Intern Nippon Med. Sch., 1992-93; intern Tokyo Med. and Dental U., 1993-94, resident, 1994-97; physician Nippon Med. Sch. Rehab. Ctr., Kawasaki, Japan, 1992-93; chief Nippon Med. Sch. Rehab. Ctr., Kawasaki, 1997-98; physician Tokyo Med. and Dental U., 1993-97; CEO Kojyu-kai, Tokyo, 1998—. Dep. dir. Com. of Regional Welfare Edogawa Ward, Tokyo, 1998. Office: Nippon Med Sch, Rehabilitation Ctr, Nakahara Ku Kanagawa 211-8533, Japan

KURUVILLA, KOLLANPARAMPIL, electrical engineer; b. Kodukulanji, Kerala, India, July 20, 1943; came to U.S., 1988; s. Thomas and Susanna (Idicula) K.; m. Elizabeth Kuruvilla, Oct. 23, 1967 (dec. Jan. 1971); 1 child, Susan, m. Santha Mathew, Feb. 12, 1972; children: Babita, Nandita, Oscar. BSc in Engring., Kerala U., 1965; PhD, Kennedy Western U., 1997; postgrad., Trinity Coll./Theol. Sem., Newburgh, Ind., 1998—. Lectr. in elec. engring. Mar. Athanasius Coll. Engring., Kerala, 1965-66; elec. engr., exec. engr. Kerala State Electricity Bd., Trivandrum, 1966-87; elec. engr. Zambia Electricity Supply Corp., Lusaka, 1972-75; chief power sta. Soiedade Hidroelectrico do Révue, Mininstry of Power, Chimoio, Mozambique, 1979-81; project engr., design engr. Southeastern Pa. Transp. Authority, Phila., 1989—. Author: In Nature's Lap, 1995, A Smell of Africa (Safe in his Arms), 1998; inventor in field of safety and security measures; patentee in field. Nat. assoc. Libr. of Congress. Named Citizen of Yr., Hutt River Province, Australia, 1994, 96. Mem. Instn. Engrs. India, World Affairs Coun. of Phila., Handi Ham Club, Astronomy Club USA. Avocations: reading, music, reading about nature, painting, amateur radio, writing. Home: 133A Dawn Dr Lansdale PA 19446-5251 Office: Southeastern Pa Transp Authority 1234 Market St Ste 13 Philadelphia PA 19107-3721

KURVONEN, TIMO LAURI, research scientist; b. Orimattila, Finland, Oct. 14, 1964; s. Lasse Allan and Saara Kaija (Keskinen) K.; m. Marjo Tuulia Seppanen, July 1, 1994; children: Sampo, Jenni. MS, Helsinki U. Tech., 1991; PhD, Helsinki U. Tech., Espoo, Finland, 1994. Rsch. asst. Helsinki U. Tech., Lab. Space Tech., Espoo, Finland, 1989-91, rsch. scientist, 1991-95, 97—; prof. space & aviation Rovaniemi Inst. Tech., Finland, 1997-2000; chief technologist Nat. Bd. Edn., Helsinki, Finland, 2000—. Contbr. articles to profl. jours. Rsch. grantee Commn. European Union, Italy, 1995-97; rsch. fellow Joint Rsch. Ctr. European Commn., Ispra, Italy, 1995-97; rsch. scholar Antti and Jenny Wihuri Fund, Finland, 1993, Emil Aaltonen Found., Finland, 1996, 97, Tech. Devel. Found., Finland, 1997, 98. Avocations: old automobiles, sailing, skiing, cross-country skiing. Fax: 358-9-7747 7715. E-mail: lauri.kurvonen@oph.fi. Office: Nat Bd Edn, Hakaniemenkatu 2 PO Box 380, FIN-00531 Helsinki Finland

KURYK, DAVID NEAL, lawyer; b. Balt., Aug. 24, 1947; s. Leon and Bernice G. (Fox) K.; m. Alice T. Lehman, July 8, 1971; children: Richard M., Robert M., Benjamin A. BA, U. Md., 1969; JD, U. Balt., 1972. Bar: Md. 1972, U.S. Dist. Ct. Md. 1973, U.S. Ct. Mil. Appeals 1973, D.C. 1974, U.S. Ct. Appeals (4th cir.) 1974, U.S. Supreme Ct. 1976, U.S. Ct. Appeals (Fed. cir.) 1982. Assoc. Harold Buchman, Esq., Balt., 1970-76; pvt. practice Balt., 1976—. Mem. editl. bd. Md. Bar Jour., 1973-76. Sgt. USAF, 1967-73. Mem. ABA (products gen. liability and consumer law com. 1976—, com. auto law 1977), Md. State Bar Assn., Bar Assn. Balt. City, ATLA, U. Balt. Alumni Assn., Zeta Beta Tau. Democrat. Jewish. E-mail: kuryk@home.com. Home: 11200 5 Springs Rd Lutherville MD 21093-3520 Office: Am Bldg 231 E Baltimore St Ste 702 Baltimore MD 21202-3446

KURYLOWICZ, ANDRZEJ, book publishing executive, editor-in-chief; b. Warsaw, Poland, Apr. 10, 1954; s. Jerzy and Hanna (Dabrowska) K.; children: Aleksandra, Agnieszka. MSEE, Warsaw (Poland) Tech. U., 1978, PhD, 1982. Asst. prof. Warsaw Tech. U., 1982-87, adj. prof., 1987-92; mng. dir., pub. Prima Pub., Warsaw, 1992-2000, Albatros Pub, Warsaw, 1994—; editor-in-chief Amber Pub., Warsaw, 1991-92. Contbr. articles to profl. jours. Mem. Polish Book Chamber. Roman Catholic. Avocations: swimming, skiing, jazz and rock music, computers. Office: Albatros Pub, Kazury 2/12, 00795 Warsaw Poland

KURYSZKO, JAN JOZEF, histologist; b. Lubrza Prudnicka, Poland, Sept. 4, 1947; s. Stanisław and Anna (Dudar) K.; m. Anna Irena Kozłowska, June 29, 1974; children: Patrycja, Konrad. Asst. dept. histology and embryology U. Agr., Wrocław, 1974-82, sr. lectr., 1982-96, prof., 1996—. Author: Microscopic Anatomy Deomestic Animals and Human, 1995; editor Archivum Veterinarium Polonicum, 1993-96, Polish Jour. Vet. Sci., 1997—, Zool. Polish, 1998—. Recipient award Min. Nat. Edn., 1995. Mem. Polish Histochem. Cytochem. Soc., Soc. Cutaneous Ultrastructure Rsch., Polish Soc. Vet. Sci., N.Y. Acad. Sci. Avocations: philosophy, logic, tennis. E-mail: histo@gen.ar.wroc.pl. Office: Dept Histology Embryology, Kozuchowska 5, 51631 Wroclaw Poland

KURZ, HEINZ DIETER, economics educator; b. Pfaffenhofen, Bavaria, Germany, Mar. 29, 1946; arrived in Austria, 1988.; PhD in Econs., U. Kiel, Germany, 1975. Asst. prof. U. Kiel, Germany, 1975-79; prof. U. Bremen, Germany, 1979-88, U. Graz, Austria, 1988—. Author: Capital, Distribution and Effective Demand, 1990; co-author: (with N. Salvadori) Theory of Production, 1995; mng. editor European Jour. History of Economic Thought, 1993—, Metroeconomica, 1998—. Recipient award Christian-Albrechts U., Kiel, 1975; named Theodor-Heuss-Prof. German Fgn. Office, 1990-91. Office: U Graz Dept Econs 4 OG, RESOWI-Center, A-8010 Graz Austria

KURZBAN, IRA JAY, lawyer; b. Bklyn., May 9, 1949; s. Benjamin and Irene (Weiss) K.; m. Magda Montiel Davis, Apr. 15, 1989; children: Kathryn Montiel Davis, Paula Lindsay Davis, Magda Marie Davis, Sadie Bethany Kurzban, Benjamin Kurzban. BA magna cum laude, Syracuse U., 1971; MA, U. Calif., Berkeley, 1973, JD, 1976; hon. fellow, U. Pa. Law Sch., 1987. Bar: Calif. 1976, Fla. 1976, U.S. Dist. Ct. (no. dist.) Calif., 1976, U.S. Dist. Ct. (so. dist.) Fla., 1976, U.S. Ct. Appeals (5th cir.) 1978, U.S. Ct. Appeals (11th cir.) 1981, U.S. Supreme Ct. 1980. Ptnr. Kurzban, Kurzban, Weinger & Tetzeli P.A., Miami, Fla., 1977—; Fla. counsel Nat. Energy Civil Liberties Com., 1979-98; gen. counsel Am. Immigration Lawyers Assn., 1992-93; adj. prof. immigration and nationality law U. Miami Sch. of Law, 1979—, Nova Southeastern Law Sch., 1982—; instr. polit. sci. U. Calif. Berkeley, 1973; mem. civil justice adv. com. U.S. Dist. Ct. (so. dist.) Fla., 1993-94; mem. certification com. in immigration and univ. law Fla. Bar, 1994-96; lectr. in field. Author: Kurzban's Immigration Law Sourcebook: A Comprehensive Outline and Reference Tool, 6th edit., 1998; contbr. articles to profl. jours. Founder Berkeley Law Found. Recipient Tobias Simon pro bono svc. award Fla. Supreme Ct., 1982, Trial Lawyer of Yr. award Trial Lawyers for Public Justice, Carol King award Nat. Lawyers Guild, 1996; Polit. Sci. Dept. fellow U. Calif., Berkeley, 1971, Kent fellow Danforth Found., 1974-77, Law and Society fellow U. Calif., Berkeley, 1975-76. Fellow Am. Immigration Law Found. (hon.); mem. Am. ABA (chair refugee legal assistance com. 1983-84, mem. immigration coord. com. 1991-93), Am. Immigration Lawyers Assn. (pres. so. Fla. chpt. 1980-81, nat. pres. 1987, Jack Wasserman award for excellence in federal litigation 1983, Human Rights award 1992), Am. Inns of Ct. Office: Kurzban Kurzban Weinger & Tetzeli PA 2650 SW 27th Ave Miami FL 33133-3003

KUSAKA, SHUNJI, physician; b. Tokushima, Japan, Sept. 11, 1961; s. Toshio and Tsuneko K.; m. Kanae Yamada; children: Takuya, Hiroki. MD, Osaka U., Japan, 1986, PhD, 1998. Resident Osaka U. Med. Sch., Japan, 1986-87; faculty Tane Meml. Eye Hosp., Osaka, 1991-92; asst. prof. Ehime U. Sch. Medicine, Japan, 1992-97, Osaka U. Med. Sch., 1997—. Author: A Guidebook for Ophthalmic Assistant, 1996; contbr. articles to profl. jours. Clin. fellow Nat. Osaka Hosp., 1987-91, rsch. fellow U. Mich., Ann Arbor, 1994-97. Mem. Am. Acad. Ophthalmology, Soc. Neurosci., Assn. Rsch. & Ophthalmology and Visual Sci. Office: Osaka U Med Sch, 2-2 Yamada-oka, Osaka 565-0871, Japan

KUSCHINSKY, WOLFGANG, physiologist; b. Prague, Czechoslovakia, Mar. 15, 1944; s. Gustav and Ingeborg (Stoehr) K.; m. Beate Bangerter, 1972; children: Niels, Anja. MD, U. Heidelberg, Germany, 1967. Rsch. fellow U. Munich, 1968-74, privatdozent, 1974-80, prof., 1980-82; rsch. fellow NIH, Bethesda, Md., 1979-80; prof. U. Bonn, Germany, 1982-89; prof., chmn. U. Heidelberg, 1989—. Recipient Hugo-Spatz award German Neurol. Soc., 1986, Willy-Pitzer award Willy-Pitzer Found., 1987. Mem. Rotary, German Physiol. Soc. (sec. 1991-94), Internat. Soc. Cerebral Blood Flow Metabolism (dir. 1985-89, 93-97), Gesellschaft Gesundheit und Forschung (chmn. 1996—). Avocations: classical music. Office: U Heidelberg Dept Physiol, Im Neuenheimer Feld 326, D-69120 Heidelberg Germany

KUSHALAPA, KODIRA ACHAPPA, forester, researcher, consultant; b. Madikeri, India, May 14, 1937; s. Kodira Achappa Bojamma; m. Kodira Kushalapa Prema, May 16, 1968; 1 child, Preet. BA, U. Madras, India, 1957; Cert. in Forestry, So. Forest Rangers Coll., Coimbatore, India, 1962; diploma in Forestry, Assoc. Indian Forests Coll., Dehradun, India, 1967; MSc in Forestry with honors, U. Edinburgh, U.K., 1972; PhD, U. Mysore, India, 1988. Asst. conservator forests Govt. Karnataka, India, 1965-67, dep. conservator forests, 1972-73, state silviculturist, 1973-79, conservator of forests, 1984-91; with Indian Forest Svc., 1968-95; chief conservator of forests Ministry of Environ. and Forestry, Govt. of India, Bhopal, India, 1991-95; dir. Indian Plywood Inst., Bangalore, 1995-97; forestry cons. Tata Consultancy Svcs., Pune, India; exec. dir. Treelands Devel. Svcs. (P) Ltd., Bangalore, 1997—; dir. Bamboo Soc. India, Bangalore, 1996-97; forestry cons. India Eco-Devel. Project, 1999—. Editor: "My Forest" Journal 1971-91. Mem., dir. Coorg Edn. Fund, Madikeri, India, 1965—. Recipient Curries award Curries Trust London, 1967, fellowship Commonwealth Univs. Assn., London, 1970-72, award Rotary Club, Mysore, India, 1991. Fellow Inst. Agrl. Technologists; mem. Karnataka Hockey Assn. Avocations: photography, games, forest tours, botanising, wildlife. Home: No 666 III Cross I Block, Ramakrishna Nagar, Mysore 570023, India

KUSHCH, NATALIYA DMITRIEVNA, chemist, researcher; b. Psebai, Russia, Jan. 4, 1950; d. Dmitrii Illarionovich and Nadezhda Terent'eona (Sazankova) Ermakov; m. Pavel Prokof'evich Kushch, Sept. 2, 1972; children: Dmitrii, Alexander. PhD, Inst. Chem. Tech., Dnepropetrovsk, USSR, 1979. Sr. asst. Inst. Chem. Physics Russian Acad. Scis., Chernogolovka, Russia, 1977-78, jr. rschr., 1978-87, rschr., 1987-90, sr. rschr., 1990—; Contbr. articles to profl. jours.; patentee in field. Avocation: fishing. Home: Tsentralnaya 2-36, 142432 Chernogolovka Russia Office: Inst of Problems, of Chemical Physics RAS, 142432 Chernogolovka Russia

KUSHIRO, IKUO, petrologist, researcher; b. Osaka, Japan, Mar. 30, 1934; s. Shuichiro and Yoshiko (Kawaguchi) K.; m. Kazue Hamamoto, July 22, 1962; 1 child, Tetsuo. BSc, U. Tokyo, 1957, MSc, 1959, PhD, 1962. Rsch. assoc. U. Tokyo, 1962-69, assoc. prof., 1969-71, prof., 1974-94; petrologist Carnegie Instn. Washington, 1971-74; prof. Inst. for Study of Earth's Interior, Misasa, Japan, 1994-99, dir., 1995-99; prof. emeritus U. Tokyo, 1995—; dean faculty of sci. U. Tokyo, 1990-93, v.p., 1993-94. Contbr. articles to profl. jours. Recipient Japan Acad. prize, 1982, Geol. Soc. Japan award, 1988, Roebling medal Mineralogical Soc. Am., 1999, Arthur Holmes medal, 1999. Fellow Am. Geophys. Union (Harry H. Hess medal), European Union of Geosci. (hon., Arthur Holmes medal); mem. Japan Acad., Nat. Acad. Scis. U.S. (fgn. assoc.), Geol. Soc. London (hon.). Home: 4-7-8-201 Hakusan, Bunkyo-ku Tokyo 112-0001, Japan

KUSHNER, BORIS ABRAHAM, education educator; b. Krasnouralsk, Russia, Dec. 10, 1941; came to U.S., 1989; s. Abraham Isaak and Sinaida Boris (Meerovich) K.; m. Marina Vitaly Kameneva, Feb. 5, 1966; children: Julia, Alexandr. M in Math., Moscow U., 1964, PhD in Math., 1967. Sr. researcher Computing Ctr./Acad. of Scis. of USSR, Moscow, 1968-89; asst. prof. U. Pitts., Johnstown, Pa., 1990-94, assoc. prof., 1994-96, prof., 1996—; vis. prof. Carnegie Mellon U., Pitts., 1989-90. Author: (monograph) Lectures on Constructive Math Analysis, 1984; author 2 books of poetry; contbr. more than 80 papers in field to nat. and Russian publs. Mem. Math. Assn. Am., Am. Math. Soc., Assn. Symbolic Logic. Home: 329 Theatre Dr Apt 2b24 Johnstown PA 15904-3277 Office: Dept Math Univ Pittsburgh Johnstown PA 15904

KUSHNER, JACK, retired physician executive; b. Montgomery, Ala., Dec. 5, 1939; s. Louis Harry and Rose (Feldman) K.; m. Annetta Esther Horwitz, June 21, 1964; children: Reyna, Eve. BA, Tulane, 1960; MD, U. Ala., 1964; MGA, U. Md., 1990. Diplomate Am. Bd. of Neurosurgery. Intern George Washington U. Hosp., Washington, 1964-65; resident in surgery U. Mich., Ann Arbor, 1965-66; resident in neurosurgery Bowman Gray Sch. Medicine Wake Forest U., Winston-Salem, N.C., 1968-72; pvt. practice neurosurgery, Annapolis, Md., 1972-95; pres., CEO, Futuristic Instruments, Annapolis, 1995-98; chmn., bd. dirs. Telehealth, 1999; ret., 2000, cons. in field; spkr. in field; bd. dirs. E-Global Telehealth, 1999—. Author: Preparing To Tack: When Physicians Change Careers, 1995; contbr. articles to profl. jours. With U.S Army, 1966-68, Vietnam. Decorated Bronze Star. Fellow Am. Coll. of Surgeons (emerging tech. and edn. com.), Internat. Coll. of Surgeons; mem. Am. Assoc. Neurol. Surgeons, Congress of Neurol. Surgeons, So. Neurosurgical Soc., Pan Pacific Neurosurgical. Avocations: golf, tennis, yacht racing. E-mail: kushner20@aol.com. Fax: (410) 757-9243. Home: Ferry Farms 2030 Homewood Rd Annapolis MD 21402-1005

KUSHNER, MICHAEL JAMES, neurologist, consultant; b. Hackensack, N.J., July 18, 1951; s. Samuel and Ruth Ellen (Paul) K.; m. Sarah Joan Warden, Aug. 14, 1976; children: Hunter Paul, Paul Macrae (dec.). BA in Physics, Yale U., 1973; MD, NYU, 1977. Diplomate Am. Bd. Psychiatry, Am. Bd. Neurology, Am. Bd. Med. Examiners; cert. Am. Bd. Electrodiagnostic Medicine, Am. Bd. Pain Medicine. Intern Parkland Meml. Hosp., U. Tex., Dallas, 1977-78; resident in neurology Neurol. Inst., Columbia-Presbyn. Med. Ctr., N.Y.C., 1978-81; rsch. assoc. U. Pa., Phila., 1981-83, asst. prof. neurology, 1983-90; attending physician Hosp. of U. Pa., Phila., 1983-90; with Wilson (N.C.) Neurology Ctr., 1992—; clin. asst. prof. East. Carolina U. Sch. Medicine, 1997—; dir. SPECT facility Hosp. of U. Pa., 1986-90, asst. dir. neurovascular lab., 1987-90; mem. sensory disorders and lang. study sect. NIH, Bethesda, Md., 1988-90; cons. Dupont Med. Products Div., Billerica, Mass., 1987—; staff neurologist Wilson (N.C.) Neurology Ctr.; legal medicine cons.; neurology physician advisor N.C. Blue Cross/Blue Shield; asst. prof. East Carolina U. Sch. Medicine; dir. Wilson Regional MRI Ctr. Contbr. numerous articles to profl. jours. Interviewer alumni schs. com. Yale U., Phila., 1984—. Fellow Am. Acad. Neurology, Am. Heart Assn. (stroke coun.); mem. AMA, Internat. Soc. for Blood Flow and Metabolism, N.C. Neurol. Soc. (pres. 1995-97), Yale of N.Y.C., Yale of Cen. N.C., Yale of N.C. Republican. Episcopalian. Avocations: oenology, travel, swimming, golf. Home: 1110 Salem St NW Wilson NC 27893-2137 Office: Wilson Neurology Ctr PO Box 3148 Wilson NC 27895-3148

KUSHNER, TODD ROGER, computer scientist, software engineer; b. Bethesda, Md., June 18, 1956; s. Harvey David and Rose Molly (Rehert) K.; m. Lea Louise Friedman, Nov. 11, 1990; children: Joshua Philip, Daniel Stuart. BS in Life Scis., MIT, 1976; MS in Computer Sci., U. Md., 1980, PhD in Computer Sci., 1982. Rsch. technician NIH, Bethesda, 1976-77; programmer Tech. Mgmt. Inc., Washington, 1977-78, GTE-Telenet, McLean, Va., 1978-79; grad. rsch. asst. U. Md., College Park, 1980-82, mem. rsch. staff, 1985-88; computer scientist SRI Internat., Menlo Park, Calif., 1982-83; sr. software engr. Vicom Sys. Inc., San Jose, Calif., 1983-85; sr. engr. Stanford Telecoms., Reston, Va., 1988-89; adv. programmer IBM Corp., Gaithersburg, Md., 1989-93; sr. scientist CTA Inc., Rockville, Md., 1993-96; mem. sr. software staff Lockheed Martin Fed. Systems, Denver, 1996-99; mem. tech. staff Lucent Techs., Denver, 1999—; adj. lectr. U. Santa Clara, Calif., 1983, U. Md., Gaithersburg, 1989-90, Johns Hopkins U., Gaithersburg, 1989-93; participant Software Process Interchange Network, McLean, Va., 1993—. Contbr. articles to profl. publs. Grad. fellow Air Force Office Sci. Rsch., 1980. Mem. IEEE Computer Soc., Assn. Computer Machinery. Democrat. Jewish. Avocations: swimming, racquetball, skiing, golf. Office: Lucent Techs 1999 Broadway Ste 1800 Denver CO 80202-5718

KUSIĆ, ZVONKO, nuclear medicine and oncology physician, educator; b. Zagreb, Croatia, June 14, 1946; s. Bariša and Filomena (Dundić) K.; m. Iva Brćić, Sept. 15, 1985. MD, Sch. Medicine Zagreb, 1975, MSc, 1984, PhD, 1985. Cert. specialist in radiotherapy Sch. Medicine Zagreb, 1995, nuclear medicine, 1979. Resident nuclear medicine Univ. Hosp. Sestre Milosrdnice, Zagreb, 1976-79; IAEA fellow Guy's Hosp., London, 1980-81; vis. prof. Cornell U., Mich. U., N.Y.C., Ann Arbor, 1981-82, U. Cin., 1984; chief thyroid divsn. Univ. Hosp. Sestre Milosrdnice, Zagreb, 1987—, dir., 1995—; prof. oncology dept., head dept. nuclear medicine and oncology. Sch. of Medicine Zagreb, 1992—; advisor Ministry of Health, Zagreb, 1993-95; dean Sch. Medicine Zagreb, 1998. Editor-in-chief Acta Clinica Croatica, 1995—; contbr. articles to profl. jours. Chmn. Commn. Endemic Goiter and Iodine Prophylaxis, Zagreb, 1992—. Recipient High Decoration for Sci. Pres. Republic Croatia, 1995. Mem. Croatian Acad. Scis. and Arts, Am. Thyroid Assn., Croatian Ligue Against Cancer. Roman Catholic. Avocations: philosophy, psychology, reading. Home: Nova Ves 9, 10 000 Zagreb Croatia Office: Univ Hosp Sestre Milosrdnice, Vinogradska 29, 10 000 Zagreb Croatia

KUSIN, VLADIMIR VICTOR, retired communications executive; b. Frydek-Mistek, Czech Republic, Dec. 2, 1929; s. Victor and Miloslava (Mackova) K.; m. Daniela Kvetuse Cihackova, Nov. 21, 1953; children: Victor Joseph, Daniela Magdalena Kühnl. PhD, Charles U., 1968. Lectr., manual worker, translator, journalist Czechoslovakia, 1953-68; rsch. fellow U. Lancaster, U.K., 1968-69, U. Glasgow, U.K., 1970-78; chief analyst Radio Free Europe-Radio Liberty, Munich, 1980-91, ret., 1991; mem. exec. com. internat. com. Soviet and East European Studies, Glasgow, 1975-78, editor ICSEES Newsletter, 1976-78, dir. info. ctr., 1975-78; lectr. in field. Author: The Intellectual Origins of the Prague Spring, 1971, Political Grouping in the Czechoslovak Reform Movement, 1972, From Dubcek to Charter 77, 1978; co-author: Czechoslovakia, 1968-69, 1975; editor: The Czechoslovak Reform Movement 1968, 1973, Translator (into Czech) Geoffrey Bocca, The Life and Death of Harry Oakes, 1965, Tom Stoppard, Rosencrantz and Guildenstern Are Dead, 1968; contbr. numerous articles to profl. publs. Rsch. grant Social Sci. Rsch. Coun., 1970-71, Margery and Huntly Sinclair Trust, 1974, Internat. scholarly coop. grant Volkswagen Found., 1976-78. Avocation: post-communist issues. Home: J Felixe 1688, CZ-74401 Frenstat P.R., Czech Republic

KUSKY, TIMOTHY M., geologist, educator; b. Glen Cove, N.Y., Sept. 21, 1961; s. Ronald A. and Kathleen M. Kusky; m. Carolyn J; children: Shoshana, Daniel. BS, MS, SUNY, Albany, 1985; MA, Johns Hopkins U., 1988, PhD, 1990. Rsch. scientist NASA, Goddard Space Flight Ctr., 1986-89, U. Calif., Santa Barbara, 1989-90; prof. U. Houston, 1990-92; geologist U.S. Geol. Survey, Anchorage, Alaska, 1991-95; prof. Boston U., 1995-2000; cons. St. Louis U., 2000—; cons. GeoExploration Sys., Newark, 1997—. Author: Ground Water in Egypt, 1998; contbr. articles to profl. jours. Grantee U.S. Geol. Survey, 1999, NSF, 1997, Oman Min. Water, Oman, 1999, Govt. Saudi Arabia, 1998. Fellow Geol. Soc. Africa; mem. Am. Geophys. Union, Geol. Soc. Am., Internat. Assn. Tectonic & Structural Geologists, Union Concerned Scientists. Avocations: running, hiking, family. e-mail: kusky@eas.slu.edu. Home: 7436 University Dr Saint Louis MO 63130 Office: Dept Earth Atmosphere Sci St Louis U Saint Louis MO 63103

KUSSUL, NATALIYA NIKOLAYEVNA, mathematician, computer scientist, consultant; b. Vorkuta, Russia, Nov. 10, 1965; d. Nikolai Vasil'yevich and Maria Ivanovna (Tcherniack) Dzhum; m.Michail Ernstovich Kussul, Aug. 31, 1985; 1 child, Olga; m. Andreij Yuriyevich Shelestov, Feb. 4, 1995. MSc, U. Kiev, Ukraine, 1987; PhD, Inst. Cybernetics, Kiev, 1991. Investigator Inst. Cybernetics, Kiev, 1987-89, jr. scientific rschr., 1989-93, scientific rschr., 1993-95, sr. rschr., 1995-96; sr. rschr. Space Rsch. Inst., Kiev, 1996—; prof. Poly. Inst., Kiev, 1997—; cons. Internat. Tng. Computer Ctr., Kiev, 1995-96; interpreter pub. co., Kiev, 1996-97; editor Computer Pub. Co., Kiev, 1996-97. Contbr. articles to profl. jours. Grantee U.S. Civilian Rsch. and Devel. Found., 1997; recipient Young Scientist award Pres. Ukraine, 1995-97. Mem. Gesellschaft fur Angewandte Mathematik und Mechanik, Internat. Fuzzy Sys. Assn. Avocations: travel, literature, music. Home: Uritskogo str 13 ap 16, 252035 Kiev Ukraine Office: Space Rsch Inst, pr Glushkova 40, 252650 Kiev Ukraine

KUSTER, BERNHARD, biochemist; b. Remscheid, Germany, Oct. 25, 1967; s. Hans Klaus and Gisela Maria (Nubel) K.; m. Jo-Anna Brucher, July 10, 1992; children: Marius Benhamin, Joy Helena. Dipl.Chem., U. Cologne, Germany, 1994; DPhil, U. Oxford, England, 1997. Rsch. assoc. prof. U. So. Denmark, Odense, 1999; sr. rsch. scientist Protana A/S, Odense, 2000—. Fellow German Acad. Exch. Svc., 1994, European Molecular Biology Orgn., 1997. Mem. German Soc. Mass Spectrometry (Mattauch-Herzog award 1998), Am. Soc. Mass Spectrometry, German Chem. Soc. Office: Protana A/S, Staermosegaardsvej 16, 5230 Odense Denmark

KUSUNOKI, MICHIKO, crystallographer, researcher; b. Shizuoka, Yuicho, Japan, Dec. 8, 1952; d. Akira and Kazuko (Yamanashi) Toyoshima; m. Takashi Kusunoki, Apr. 26, 1980; children: Hiroshi, Tsuyoshi. PhD, Tokyo Inst. Tech., 1980. Rschr. Rsch. Devel. Corp. Japan, Nagoya, 1983-86, Tsukuba, 1988-90; sr. rschr. Japan Fine Ceramics Ctr., Nagoya, 1991—. Contbr. articles to sci. jours., including Jour. Am. Cermacis Soc., Applied Physics Letters, Materials Trans., Philosophical Mag. Letters; inventor mfg. method of carbon nanotube film. Recipient article prize Japan Inst. Metals, 1985, tech. devel. prize, 1997; Ceramographic prize Ceramic Soc. Japan, 1994. Avocations: playing piano, calligraphy, skating, camping. Office: Japan Fine Ceramics Ctr, 2-4-1 Mutsuno, Atsuta-ku, Nagoya 456-8587, Japan

KUSY, MIROSLAV, philosopher, political scientist, educator; b. Bratislava, Slovak Republic, Dec. 1, 1931; s. Stefan and Zlatica (Vojtková) K.; m. Jolana Vargová, Jan. 31, 1971; children: Alexandra, Dagmar. MA, Charles U., Prague, Czech Republic, 1954; PhD, Comemius U., Bratislava, Slovakia, 1957. Mem. Fed. Parliament of CSFR, Prague, Czech Republic, 1989-90, Slovak Nat. Coun., Bratislava, Slovakia, 1990-92; chancellor Office of the Pres. of Republic, Bratislava, Slovakia, 1991-92; pres. Comemius U., Bratislava, Slovakia, 1990-91, Milan Simecka Found., Bratislava, Slovakia, 1992; chair dept. polit. sci. Comemius U., Bratislava, Slovakia, 1990; state sec. Ministry for Press Rels., Prague, 1989; chair UNESCO chair for Human Rights, Bratislava, 1992. Author: On the Waves of Radio Free Europe, 1990, Forbidden Papers, 1990 (Sci. Tatarka award 1990), Essays, 1991; co-author: European Experience with the Real-Socialism, 1984. Col. Czechoslovak Army. Recipient J.A. Comemius award Pres. of the CSFR, 1992, Commemorative award Pres. of Hungarian Republic, 1996, Pres. of Slovak Republic, 1996. Home: Slowackeho 21, 82104 Bratislava Slovak Republic Office: Comemius U, Safarikovo nám 2, 81801 Bratislava Slovak Republic

KUTBI, ZUHEIR M.J., journalist. Intermediate ednl. Faculty Diploma, 1981, Baccalaureate in Geography, 1987, M in Geography, 1994, D in Geography, 1998. Author of Whisper of Al-Uraif, part 1, 1978, part 2, 1979, Social Diseases, 1980, Makkah Al-Mukaramah. The Holy City, 1984, Rain Drainage int eh Holy Capital, 1987, The Stage and Society, 1988, Makkah Al-Mukaramah. The Distinguished Situation, 1988, Men from Makkah Al-Mukaramah, part 1, 1989, part 2, 1990, part 3, 1991, part 4, 1992, part 5, 1994, part 6, 1995, Volcano Explosion, 1989, Al-Atar: The Art Master, 1990, Political Scales, 1990, Climate in Islamic Heritage, 1990, Gulf and Fear of Domination and Death Extinction, 1990, Al-Figi: Hijaz Philosopher, 1991, Don't Read this Dialogue, 1991, Don't Read this Book, 1991, Minerals in Islamic Heritage, 1991, Who is Standing by the Gulf War, 1991, Digging with No Bottom, 1991, The Rats of Life, 1992, My Dialogues, 1993, Gulf War: Force Equation and Balancing Destroying, 1993, Essays of...Mad, 1993, Abul-Ila: Native and Truth Poet, 1993, Al-Malki: The Scientist of Hijaz, 1993, Abu-Shadi and the Saudi Art, 1994, Ahmed Jamal: The Man of Invocation and Thinking, 1994, Mohammad Umar Tuffique: The Big Mind, 1994, Dialogue Art, part 1, 2, 3, 1994, Wrong Conceptions: Must Be Corrected, 1994, Me and My Donkey, 1994, The Arabic Cultured and Sultan, 1994, Anger Vessels, 1994, Damn: To Your Posture Faiz Badr, 1994, Makkah Al-Mukaramah in my Heart, 1995, Al-Sabban: The Men Maker, 1995, Cultured Death, 1995, Al-Uraif: As a Journalist and His Style, 1996, Heads with No Minds, 1997, Saudi Women Mind, 1997, Petroleum Culture Criticize Study, 1998, Cultured Donkey Corpse, 2000; contbr. articles to profl. jours. Fellow Al-Adab Al-Hadath, Abollo Al-Jadidah, Am. Geographic Soc., Saudi Geographic Soc., Kuwaity Geographic Soc., Iraqi Geographic Soc. Address: PO Box 9068, Makkah Saudi Arabia

KUTEMEYER, PETER MARTIN, industrial engineering executive; b. Freiburg, W. Germany, Nov. 19, 1938; came to U.S., 1954, naturalized, 1956; s. Martin Henry and Gertrude Barbara (Buechel) K.; m. Fresquez, June 25, 1961 (div. Aug. 1986); children: Michael, Kristina. BME with distinction, Ariz. State U., 1968, MS in Engring. Mechanics, 1969; MBA, U. Utah, 1977. Enlisted USAF, 1958, commd. 2d. lt. 1967, advanced through grades to capt., 1970; aero. engr., 1969-71, systems devel. engr., 1971-74, tech. liaison officer to W. German Fed. Govt., 1974-78; ret., 1978; indsl. mgr. Mining Progress, Inc., Highland Mills, N.Y., 1978-79, prodn. mgr., 1979-81; gen. mgr. Bischoff Environ. Systems div. Intertech Inc., Highland Mills, 1981-89; pres. PMK Enterprises, Inc., Wilmington, Del., 1989—; v.p., gen. mgr. Westfalia Ind. Equ. Inc., 1989-92. Mem. ASME, AIAA. Home: 5225 Pooks Hill Rd Apt 1020S Bethesda MD 20814-6718 Office: PMK Enterprises Inc # 543 2207 Concord Pike Wilmington DE 19803-2908

KUTER, KAY E., writer, actor; b. L.A., Apr. 25, 1925; s. Leo E. and Evelyn Belle (Edler) K. Student, Pomona Coll., 1943, UCLA, 1944; BFA in Drama, Carnegie Inst. Tech., 1949. Radio actor NBC, 1944; actor, 1944—. Actor in 198 musicals, off-Broadway, stock, repertory, touring, and Shakespearean stage prodns.; 46 feature films; more than 400 TV shows most recently "The Hollywood Sign", "Arliss", including 7 yrs. as a series regular (Newt Kiley) in Green Acres and Petticoat Junction; voiceover actor for cartoon series Aladdin, The Little Mermaid, Prince Valiant, Biker Mice From Mars, Fantastic Four; in cartoon spls. Olympic Mascot Izzy, Annabelle's Wish, The Jungle Book: Mowgli's Story, The Little Mermaid II; in CD-ROMS The Beast Within, Ultima 9, Grim Fandango, The Curse of Monkey Island, Heretic II; in radio prodns. Getting Married, Treasure Island, Macbeth, Satanic Verses, Heartbreak House; author: Carmen Incarnate, 1946, Ships That Never Sailed, 1994, Hollywood Houdini, Picture Perfect World, 1995; voiceover spokesman Hershey's Kisses, 1989—; editor: The Jester, 1956-60, The Jester 35th Anniversary, 1960, 50th Anniversary, 1976; contbr. to Nat. Libr. Poetry anthologies, 1995, 96, 97, 99, 2000 (Editor's Choice award); dir. more than 50 stage prodns. including Steve Allen's The Wake. Bd. dirs. Family Svc. of L.A., 1950-70. Mem. SAG (bd. dirs. 1970-73), ADA, AEA, AFTRA, ACLU, NOW, NARAL, Internat. Platform Assn., Book Publicists of So. Calif., Nat. Soc. Hist. Preservation, Smithsonian, Carnegie Mellon U. Westcoast Drama Alumni Clan (founding mem., officer, bd. dirs. 1968-80), Ephebian Soc., Internat. Soc. Poets (disting. mem.), Albert C. May Soc., Acad. Am. Poets, Andrew Carnegie Soc., Pacific Pioneer Broadcasters, Carnegie Mellon U. Alumni Assn. (regional v.p. 1976-79, Svc. award 1979), Masquers Club (bd. dirs. 1953-75, rec. sec. 1956-70, corr. sec. 1957-69. v.p. 1971-75), Actors' Fund of Am. (life mem.), others. Democrat. Avocations: composing, set design, piano. Home: 6207 Satsuma Ave North Hollywood CA 91606-3819

KUTHER, TARA L., psychology educator; b. N.Y.C., Apr. 26, 1972; d. Philip John Kuther and Irene Lopez. BA, Western Conn. State U., 1993; MA, Fordham U., 1995, PhD, 1998. Adj. instr. Lehman Coll., Bronx, N.Y., 1996-98, Iona Coll., Bronx, 1996-98; adj. instr. Western Conn. State U., Danbury, 1996-98, asst. prof., 1998—; bd. dirs. Danbury Regional Commn. on Childcare Rights and Abuse, Danbury, 1998—. Contbr. articles to profl. jours. Putting Children First fellow Tchrs. Coll. Columbia U., 1995. Mem. APA, Assn. for Practical and Profl. Ethics, Soc. for Rsch. in Adolescence, Soc. for Rsch. into Child Devel. E-mail: kuthert@wcsu.edu. Office: Western Conn State U Dept Psychology 181 White St Danbury CT 06810-6826

KUTILEK, MIROSLAV, soil science educator; b. Trutnov, Czech Republic, Oct. 8, 1927; s. Bohuslav and Amálie (Hofmanová) K.; m. Xena Rádová, Jan. 28, 1955; children: Štěpán, Blanka. Engr., Czech Tech. U., Prague, 1951, PhD, 1956, DSc, 1966. Asst. prof. faculty civil engring. Czech Tech. U., Prague, 1956-62, assoc. prof. divsn. water resources, 1962-65, 68-73, prof., 1973-90, 92-93, dep. dean divsn. water resources, 1974-85; reader faculty agr. U. Khartoum, Sudan, 1965-68; prof. Bayreuth U., Fachbereich Geoökologie, Germany, 1990-92; vis. prof. Institut de Mécanique U., Grenoble, France, 1979-80, 85, 91, U. Calif., Davis, 1981-82, Technische U., Braunschweig, Germany, 1989; expert World Meteorol. Orgn., Geneva, 1968-70, Internat. Atomic Energy Agy. Vienna, 1981-86; convener numerous internat. confs. Author: Soil Science in Water Management (in Czech), 1966, 2d edit., 1978, Direct Methods of Soil Moisture Estimation for Water Balanace Purposes, 1971, Moisture of Porous Materials (in Czech), 1984; co-author: (with D.R. Nielsen) Soil Hydrology, 1994; editor-in-chief Soil Tech., 1991-96, Elsevier, 1996-97, Soil and Tillage Rsch., Elsevier, 1998—; mem. editl. bds. Transport in Porous Media, 1986-93, Catena, 1986-94, Modeling of Geo-Biosphere Processes, 1992-93, Jour. Plant Nutrition and Soil Sci., 1995-98, Internat. Agrophysics, 1996—; contbr. articles to profl. jours., chpts. to books on theory transport in porous media, infiltration, soil water balance, soil pollution. V.p. European Cultural Club, Prague, 1992-95. Recipient Mendel's award in biol. scis. Acad. Scis., Prague, 1987. Mem. Internat. Union Soil Sci. (hon.), Internat. Soil Sci. Soc. (pres. com. soil physics 1986-90). Avocations: writing novels and short stories, painting, sports. Home: Nad Pat'ankou 34, 160 00 Prague 6 Czech Republic

KUTILEK, STEPAN, pediatrician; b. Prague, Czech Republic, July 16, 1957; children: Lucy, Jane. MD, Charles U., Prague, 1983. Registrar dept. pediats. 1st Med. Faculty, Charles U., Prague, 1983-92, asst. prof. pediats. dept. pediats., 1992—, head of outpatient dept. dept. pediats., 1993-96; postdoctoral rsch. fellow Loma Linda U., Calif., 1996-97; head clin. rsch. dept. Leciva a.s., Prague, 1998—. Contbr. chpts. to textbooks: Paediatric Osteology, 1996, Paediatric Nutrition, 1996, Azalides in Clinical Practice, 2000; contbr. articles and abstracts to profl. jours.; mem. editl. bd. Osteol. Bull., 1996—. Mem. Czech Pediat. Soc. (award 1994), Czech Soc. for Metabolic Skeletal Diseases (award 1997), Am. Soc. for Bone and Mineral Rsch., European Calcified Tissue Soc. Avocations: touring, hiking, swimming. Fax: 420 2 6724 3044. E-mail: kutilek@leciva.cz. Office: Dept Pediats, Ke Karlovu 2, 128 08 Prague 2, Czech Republic

KUTKA, NICHOLAS, nuclear medicine physician; b. Czechoslovakia, Dec. 17, 1926; s. Vladimir and Agatha (Flenko) K.; m. Anna Cizmar, Aug. 14, 1965 (dec. Oct. 1996); children: Andrew, Gregory. MD, Comenius U., Bratislava, Czechoslovakia, 1951; PhD, Slovak Acad. Scis., Bratislava, 1962. Diplomate in internal medicine Postgrad. Edn. of Physicians; diplomate Am. Bd. Nuclear Medicine, Am. Bd. Disability Analysts. Asst. prof. inst. physiology Comenius U., Bratislava, 1951; intern, resident in internal medicine Mil. Hosp., Bratislava, 1952-55; chief dept. inst. endocrinology Slovak Acad. Scis., Bratislava, 1956-69; tech. asst. Internat. Atomic Engery Agy., Bogota, Colombia, 1969-70; resident in nuclear medicine Duke U., 1971-73; asst. prof. radiology Baylor Coll. Medicine, Houston, 1973-95, assoc. prof. radiology, 1995—; dir. nuclear medicine Ben Taub Gen. Hosp., Houston, 1978-81; chief nuclear medicine service VA Med. Ctr., Houston, 1982-96, staff physician, 1996—; mem. med. staff univ. affiliated hosps. Houston, faculty Sch. Nuclear Medicine Tech.; fellow Internat. Atomic Energy Agy., Rome, 1962-63. Contbr. numerous articles to profl. jours; mem. editorial bd. Endocrinologia Experimentalis. Served with Health Service Czechoslovak Army, 1952-54. Recipient prize in nuclear medicine J.E. Purkyne, 1965. Mem. Harris County Med. Soc., Tex. Med. Assn., Soc. Nuclear Medicine, Am. Coll. Nuclear Physicians. Address: 2002 Holcombe Blvd #115 PO Box 20183 Houston TX 77225-0183

KUTLAKHMEDOV, YURI ALEXEEVICH, radioecologist, radiobiologist, researcher, educator; b. Village Chemuzsha, Russia, Oct. 7, 1942; arrived in Ukraine, 1943; s. Alexey Kuchatovich and Praskovya Ivanovna (Philippova) K.; m. Tatyana Porfirievna Marchenko, May 30, 1970; 1 child, Vishnyakova Vlada Yurievna. Diploma, U. Kiev, Ukraine, 1967; PhD in Biol. Scis., Acad. Scis. Ukraine, 1973, DSc Biol. Scis., 1986. Probationer-rschr. Inst. Physiology and Plants Acad. Scis. Ukraine, 1967-70, jr. rsch. worker Inst. Physiology and Plants, 1973-86; chief lab. Radioecology Inst. Cell Biology and Genetic Engring. Nat. Acad. Scis. Ukraine, 1986—; chief chair radiobiology Kiev Nat. U., 1996—; chief lab. Inst. Radioecology Agrarian Acad. Scis. Ukraine, 1997—; mem. Soviet for Protection of Dr. Dissertation, Kiev, 1986—, Inst. European Safety and Conversion, Kiev, 1988—, Ukraine Nat. Com. Radiation Safety, Kiev, 1990—; academian Ecol. Acad. Ukraine, Kiev, 1990—. Fellow Internat. Union Radioecologists. E-mail: ecoetic@mail.kar.net. Home: Vidradny 28 80, 252126 Kiev Ukraine Office: Nat Acad Scis Ukraine, Zabolothnogo St 148, Kiev Ukraine

KUTLE, ANTE, environmentalist; b. Siroki Brijeg, Bosnia and Herzegowina, May 5, 1949; arrived in Croatia, 1965; s. Dragutin and Mila (marusic) K.; m. Marica Bradic; children: Domagoj, Dijana, Marija, Lucija, Marinko. MD, Med. U., Zagreb, Croatia, 1973; Licentiate in Epidemiology, Zagreb, MSc in Epidemiology. Gen. practitioner Koprivnica (Croatia) Gen. Hosp., 1973-74, First-Aid Clinic, Ivanec, Croatia, 1974-77; health advisor City Inst. for Health Ins., Zagreb, 1977-90; rep. Croatian Parliament, Zagreb, 1990-96; dir. State Directorate for Environment, Zagreb, 1996—; mem. Parliamentary Com. for Environ. Protection, 1990-92, Parliamentary Com. for Phys. Planning and Environ. Protection, 1992-95; pres. Nature Friends Movement, Zagreb, 1991—. Editor: Inherited Croatian Breeds, 1996, Ionizing Radiation in Everyday Life, 1997, Pedology in Environmental Proection, 1997, Edible Fruits of Forest Trees and Shrubs, 1997; pub.: Elements of Environmental Law, 1997. Hon. mem. local brs. Croatian Democratic Union, 1990. Res. officer Croatian Army, 1991—. Recipient Croatian Trefoil, Pres. of Republic of Croatia, 1991, badge of katarina Zrinska, 1991, badge of Ante Starcevic, 1991. Mem. Croatian-Norwegian Friendship Soc. (v.p.). Roman Catholic. Avocation: nature activities. Office: State Directorate Protection Nature and Environment, Ulica Grada Vukovara 78, 10000 Zagreb Croatia

KUTOSH, SUE, artist; b. Elizabeth, N.J., Dec. 25, 1947; d. Stephen and Irene (Ribecky) K. BFA, Carnegie-Mellon U., 1971; MA, Kent State U., 1973. One-woman shows include Keane Mason Gallery, N.Y.C., 1978, West Broadway Gallery, N.Y.C., 1981, Kristen Richards Gallery, N.Y.C., 1983, N.Y. Botanical Gallery, Bronx, 1992, Montserrat Gallery, N.Y.C., 1996, Pleiades Gallery, N.Y.C., 1997; art included in books: The Films of Jane Fonda, 1981, Hispanic Hollywood, 1990, The Lavender Screen, 1993, Hollywood Babble On, 1994, New Art International, 1998-2000. Recipient Daytime Emmy, 1993-94. Mem. United Scenic Artists, Local 829, Catharine Lorillard Wolfe Art Club, N.Y. Artists Equity, Nat. Assn. Women Artists. Avocation: photography. Home: 200 E 16th St Apt 2-d New York NY 10003-3708

KUTTA, ANDREAS, urologist; b. Hagen, Westfalen, Germany, Jan. 20, 1961. MD, U. Bochum, 1990. Med. diplomate. Asst. surgeon U. Witten/Herdecke, Germany, 1985-87; asst. physician U. Bochum/Herne, Germany, 1987-89, U. Bern, Switzerland, 1989, U. Bochum/Herne, Germany, 1990-92; asst. med. dir. dept. urology Krankenhaus der Barmherzigen Bruder, Trier, Germany, 1992—. Contbr. articles to profl. jours. Office: Krankenhaus der Barmherzigen Brüder, Bruder/Nordallee 1, D-54292 Trier Germany

KUTTAB, SIMON HANNA, chemistry educator, consultant; b. Jerusalem, Apr. 17, 1946; s. Hanna Costandi and Huda Stawry (Kary) K.; m. Eileen Simon Rizek, Sept. 9, 1978; children: Rania, Johnny, Rani. BSc, Am. U. of Beirut, 1968; PhD, U. Kans., 1974. Cert. pharmacist. Asst. rsch. chemist U. Calif., Davis, 1974-75; rsch. assoc. U. Calif., San Francisco, 1975-76; asst. prof. Northeastern U., Boston, 1976-81; vis. rsch. scientist Va. Tech., Blacksburg, 1992-93, vis. assoc. prof., 1997-98; assoc. prof. Birzeit (Palestine) U., 1981—; dep. dir. Ctr. for Environ. Scis. and Occupl. Health, Birzeit U., 1984-97, dean of sci., 1989-92, chmn. dept. chemistry, 1986-89. Mem. Internat. Soc. for Study of Xenobiotics, Am. Chem. Soc. Avocations: sports, music. Home: PO Box 19684, 91196 Jerusalem Israel Office: Birzeit U, PO Box 14, Birzeit Palestine

KUTTEN, SHAY, computer science/information systems educator; b. Afula, Israel; s. Aharon and Sonya K. BA, Technion III, Haifa, Israel, 1981, MSc, 1984, PhD, 1987. Postdoctoral fellow IBM Rsch., Hawthorne, N.J., 1987-89; project leader and mgr. IBM Rsch., Hawthorne, 1990-94, rsch. staff mem., 1989—; assoc. prof. Technion, Haifa, Israel, 1999—; mem. editl. bd. Baltzer Publs./ACM, Wireless Network Jour., 1995-97; program com. chair Distributed Computing Symposium, 1998. Area editor Baltzer Pub./ACM Mobile Network, 1997-99. E-mail: kutten@ie.technion.ac.il. Office: IBM TJ Watson Research Ctr PO Box 704 Yorktown Heights NY 10598-0704

KUTTNER, BERNARD A., lawyer, former judge; b. Berlin, Germany, Jan. 13, 1934; s. Frank B. and Vera (Knopfmacher) K.; children: Karen M., Robert D., Stacey M. Gilby. AB cum laude, Dartmouth Coll., 1955; postgrad., U. Va. Law Sch., 1956; JD, Seton Hall U., 1959; postgrad., NYU. Bar: N.J. 1960, U.S. Supreme Ct. 1964, U.S. Ct. Mil. Appeals 1967, N.Y. 1982, D.C. 1982; cert. civil trial lawyer, N.J. Assoc. Toner, Crowley, Woelper & Vanderbilt, 1959-62; sole practice Newark, 1962-75; corp. counsel Irvington, N.J., 1963-66; judge N.J. State Divsn. Tax Appeals, 1977-79; instr. civil litigation Montclair State Coll., 1979-82; del. Jud. Conf. N.J. Supreme Ct., 1974-81; vice chmn. Supreme Ct. N.J. Dist. Ethics Com., 1984-85, chmn., 1985-86. Contbr. articles to legal publs. Commr. Essex County (N.J.) Park Commn., 1973-79; appointed bd. on Trial Atty. Certification, N.J. Supreme Ct., 1986-90. Served to lt. comdr. USNR, 1964-74. Mem. ABA (co-editor trial techniques newsletter sect. on tort and ins. practice, chmn. trial techniques com. 1988-89, sect. on litigation), ATLA, Inst. for Ethical Behavior (pres. 1985—), D.C. Bar Assn., Irvington Bar Assn. (pres. 1968-70), Essex County Bar Assn. (chmn. 1973-75, trial and appellate litigation, judiciary com. 1972-75, treas. 1975-79, pres. 1980-81, products liability com. 1981—), Am. Counsel Assn. Jewish. Office: Kuttner Law Offices 24 Lackawanna Pl Millburn NJ 07041-1618

KUUSISTO, JOHANNA MARIA, cardiologist, scientist; b. Vaasa, Finland, Apr. 27, 1959; d. Isak and Saara Johanna (Pennanen) K.; m. Markku Heikki Sakari Laakso, May 11, 1996; 1 child, Annamaria Aleksandra. Licent of medicine, U. Kuopio, Finland, 1984, MD, 1996, docent of internal medicine, 1996. Asst. physician dept. medicine Kuopio U. Hosp., 1985-90, sr. physician dept. medicine, 1991-97, lectr. in medicine, 1996-98, cardiologist, 1998—; vis. scientist dept. medicine/divsn. cardiology U. Wash., Seattle, 1993-94. Contbr. articles to profl. jours. Mem. Am. Heart Assn., Finnish Cardiac Soc. Avocations: literature, architecture, music, sports. Office: Kuopio U Hosp, Dept Medicine PO 1777, 70211 Kuopio Finland

KUUSK, ANDRES, geophysicist, researcher, educator; b. Vändra, Pärnu, Estonia, Oct. 26, 1947; s. Elmar and Auli (Puusta) K.; divorced; children: Tanel, Silja, Joel. Grad., Tartu (Estonia) U., 1970, DSc in Geophysics, 1991; PhD in Physics, Main Geophys. Obs., St. Petersburg, Russia, 1979. Jr. rsch. assoc. Tartu Obs., 1972-86, sr. rsch. assoc., 1986—; lectr. Tartu U., 1991—; vis. scientist Goddard Space Flight Ctr., NASA, Greenbelt, Md., 1994-95, Nat. Inst. Agronomy Rsch., Grignon and Avignon, France, 1995, Inst. Geography, Beijing, 1996; participant internat. sci. meetings. Co-author 3 sci. monographs, 1972, 91, 92; mem. editl. bd. Agrl. and Forest Meteorology, Agronomie, Agr. and Environment; contbr. articles to internat. sci. jours. Office: Tartu Observatory, 61602 Tõravere Estonia

KÜVELER, GERD, physician, researcher, educator, publicist; b. Gummersbach, Nordrhein-Westfalen, Germany, Jan. 3, 1950; s. Arno and Martel (Schmidt) K.; m. Renate Ebbers, Aug. 19, 1974; children: Jan, Tim. Diploma, U. Göttingen, 1979, Dr.rer.nat., 1982. Asst. U. Göttingen, 1979-85; mgr. Authority for Informatics, Düsseldorf, 1985-89; prof. U. Applied Scis., Wiesbaden, 1989—; mem. konvent U. Applied Scis., Wiesbaden, 1990-94, pro-dean, 1994-98. Author: UNIX and Xenix for Beginners, 1989, Bien debuter UNIX. APPRENDRE ET COMPRENDRE, 1989, Gerd Küveler erzählt vom Sonnensystem, 1992, Vieweg Technic Tools Mathematik, 1995, Zukunft gestern. Wie man sich früher die Zukunft vorstellte, 1995 (with D. Schwoch) Arbeitsbuch Informatik, 1996, Informatik für Ingenieure, 1999; contbr. articles to profl. jours. Mem. Astronomical Soc. of Germany. Mem. Social Dem. Party. Avocation: history of science fiction literature. Home: Kastanienstrasse 16, D-61479 Glashuetten Germany Office: Fachhochschule Wiesbaden, Am BrÜckweg 26, D-65428 RÜesselsheim Hessen, Germany

KUWAHARA, MOTOKO GOTO, physicist, educator; b. Nagoya, Japan, Apr. 6, 1934; d. Masao (Yagi) and Taki (Harata) Kuwahara; m. Goto Kunio. BS, Nagoya U., 1957; MS, Osaka City U., Japan, 1960. Prof. Momoyamagakuin U., Osaka. Author: Science, Technology and American Higher Education, 1994, Reform in University, 1994, Reform of the Higher Education System and Science Education, 1999, Gender in Science and Technology, 1999. Mem. Women's Studies Assn. Japan, Phys. Soc. Japan, Soc. Japanese Women Scientists.

KUWAHARA, TOSHIYA, dentist, prosthodontist; b. Osaka, Japan, Mar. 1, 1960; s. Setsushi and Akiko (Kawamura) K.; m. Shigeyo Kojima, Apr. 30, 1993; children: Lisa, Riku. DDS, Osaka U., 1984, PhD, 1989. Bd. cert. prosthodontist. Jr. instr. Osaka U. Dental Sch., 1989-91, sr. instr., 1991-96; postdoctoral fellow in maxillofacial surgery SUNY, Buffalo, 1993-95; vis. rsch. prof. SUNY, Buffalo, 1993-95. Mem. Internat. Assn. Dental Rsch., Internat. Coll. Prosthodontists, Am. Soc. Temporomandibular Joint Surgeons. Avocations: scuba diving, skiing, golf. Home: 1-103-6 Bessho Hachioji, Tokyo 192-0363, Japan Office: Kuwahara Dental Clinic, 100-1 Takahata Hino, Tokyo 191-0031, Japan

KUWANA, MASATAKA, rheumatologist, researcher; b. Tokyo, May 16, 1963. MD, Keio U., Japan, 1988, PhD, 1993. Bd. cert. rheumatologist. Resident Keio U., Tokyo, 1988-90, fellow, 1990-93, instr., 1996—; fellow U. Pitts., 1993-96; cons. Scleroderma Rsch. Conf., Kanazawa, Japan, 1997—; councilor Japanese Soc. Connective Tissue Rsch., Tokyo, 1998—. Rsch. fellow Arthritis Found., 1994; sr. rheumatology scholar Am. Coll. Rheumatology, 1995. Office: Keio U Sch Medicine, 35 Shinahomachi Shinjuku-ku, Tokyo 160-8582, Japan

KUWATA, KAZUHIRO, chemist; b. Antone-yu, Antone, Korea, Mar. 2, 1942; arrived in Japan, 1945; s. Kazumi and Hisayo (Matsumoto) K. B in Engring., Hiroshima (Japan) U., 1965, M in Engring., 1967, D of Engring., 1983. Chemist Osaka (Japan) Prefectural Govt., 1967-68; chemist Environ. Pollution Control Ctr., Osaka, 1968-86, chemist exec. staff, 1986-93; exec. staff Air Pollution Ctrl. Divsn. Environ. Bur. Osaka Prefectural Govt., Osaka, 1993-95, sr. exec. staff, 1995-96; sr. exec. staff Environ. Pollution Control Ctr., Osaka, 1996—. Contbr. to Ency. Analytical Sci., also articles to profl. jours. Mem. Am. Chem. Soc., Air and Waste Mgmt. Assn., Air Pollution Control Assn. Japan, Analytical Chem. Soc. Japan, Chem. Soc. Japan, Acad. Press. Avocations: Japanese art swords and fine arts, go game, music, sports. Fax: 81-6-6972-7665. Home: 2-11-53-316, Tamagushimotomachi, Higashi Osaka 578-0933, Japan Office: Environ Pollution Cntrl Ctr, 1-3-62 Nakamichi, Higashinari-ku Osaka 537-0025, Japan

KUYER, ASTRID DESIRIE THERESIA MARIA, research scientist; b. Laren, The Netherlands, Jan. 9, 1964; d. Wilhelmus Gerardus Kuyer and

Theresia Jacoba Gijsbertha Calis; m. Stanley Rudolf Hunte; children: Zaya Tresa Hunte, Romy Thelma Hunte. D in Italian Lit. and Linguistics, Rijksuniversiteit van Utrecht, The Netherlands, 1989; D in Pub. Adminstrn., U. van Amsterdam, The Netherlands, 1989. Mktg. asst. Heineken Mktg. Svcs., Amsterdam, 1990-91; account planner Catchline Comm., Amsterdam, 1991-94; R&D dir. Media Exposure, Amsterdam, 1994—; mem. tech. com. European Media and Mktg. Survey, InterView/NSS, Amsterdam, London, 1997—; mem. tech. com. Decision Makers Survey, SUMMO, Amsterdam, 1997—. Author: Effectief Adverteren, 1996; co-author: (with R. Hielkema) Seniors: Wishes and Demands of an Unrecognized Target Group, 1995; contbr. articles to profl. jours. Avocations: fine arts, classical music. E-mail: akuyer@zonnet.nl. Fax: 020-3550001. Office: Media Exposure, Maassluisstraat 2, 1062 GD Amsterdam The Netherlands

KUYVENHOVEN, ARIE, economics educator; b. Naaldwijk, The Netherlands, May 24, 1942; s. Arie Kuyvenhoven and Cornelia Christina Vreugdenhil; m. Cora Homburg, Nov. 4, 1966; children: Wito, Romke. BA in Econometrics, Netherlands Sch. Econs., 1963, MA in Econs., 1966; PhD in Econs., Erasmus U., Rotterdam, 1978. Asst. prof. Netherlands Sch. Econs., Rotterdam, 1966-71; sr. lectr. U. Lagos, Nigeria, 1971-73; assoc. prof. Erasmus U., Rotterdam, 1974-87; head of dept. Netherlands Econs. Inst., Rotterdam, 1979-88, dir., 1988—; prof. dev. econs. Wageningen U., 1987—; dean social studies Wageningen Agrl. U., 1992-98, chmn. dept. econs. and mgmt., 1998-2000; program dir. Sustainable Land Use and Food Security, Wageningen Agrl. U., Costa Rica and Mali, 1992-97; West Africa and China, 1997—; project dir. Ministry of Industry, Indonesia, 1982-86; cons. in field. Editor: Globalisation of Labour Markets in EU and LDCc, 1997, Multilateralism and Regionalism in Post-Uruguay Era: What Role for the EU, 1999; editor, co-author: Eco-Regional Approaches for Sustainable Land Use and Food Production, 1995; co-author: Industrialisation and Trade in Indonesia, 1990; author: Planning with the Semi-Input-Output Method, 1978; contbr. articles to profl. jours.; vice-chmn. bd. Economisch Statistische Berichten, 1989—. Nat. adv. coun. Devel. Cooperation, 1988-97; co-chmn. Network EU-LDC, Min. Fgn. Affairs, Netherlands, 1994—; bd. dirs. NGO Bilance, The Netherlands, 1995-99, IFPRI, Washington, 1998—. Mem. Internat. Assn. Agrl. Econs., Royal Soc. Econs. Avocations: piano, lit., painting, tennis, jogging. Office: Wag U/Dept Social Scis/Dev Econs Gr, PO Box 8130, 6700 EW Wageningen The Netherlands

KUZBARI, RAFIC, plastic surgeon; b. Damascus, Syria, Jan. 1, 1963; arrived in Austria, 1976; s. Nabil and Salwa (Daoudi) K.; m. Rim Jouman-Agha, July 8, 1995; children: Kinda, Aya. MD, U. Vienna, 1988. Resident U. Hosp., Vienna, Austria, 1989-92; resident Wilhelminenspital, Vienna, Austria, 1992-95, cons. plastic surgeon, 1995—; asst. prof. U. Vienna, 1999—. Contbr. articles to profl. jours. Muslim. Office: Wilhelminenspital, Montlearstrasse 37, A-1160 Vienna Austria

KUZIAN, ROMAN OGANESOVICH, research scientist; b. Stavropol, Russia, Mar. 1, 1959; m. Helen Kuzian, June 23, 1984; 1 child, Vera. Univ. degree, Moscow Inst. Physics & Tech., Dolgoprudny, Russia, 1981; PhD, Inst. High Pressure Physics, Troitsk, Russia, 1990. Cert. engr.-physicist. Rsch. scientist Inst. for High Pressure Physics, Troitsk, 1981-91; sr. rsch. scientist Inst. for Materials Sci., Kiev, Ukraine, 1991—; guest scientist Theory of Complex and Correlated Electron Sys., Dresden, Germany, 1997, Dresden U. Tech., 1999. Contbr. articles to rsch. publs. Recipient Soros Found. award Am. Phys. Soc., 1993; NATO grantee, 1999. Russian Orthodox. Avocations: literature, touring. Office: Inst Materials Sci, Krzhizhanovskogo 3, Kiev Ukraine

KUZMENKO, ALEXANDER IVANOVICH, biochemistry researcher; b. Kiev, Ukraine, Dec. 29, 1966; s. Ivan Iosifovich and Irina Vasil'evna (Ivashura) K. Diploma in organic & oil chemistry, Kiev's Polytech Inst., Ukraine, 1989; PhD in Oil Chemistry, Inst. Bioorganic Chemistry, Kiev, 1993. Engr. Kiev's Polytech. Inst., Ukraine, 1989; rschr. A.V. Palladin Inst. Biochem., Ukrainian Nat. Acad. Scis., Kiev, 1993—. Contbr. articles to profl. jours. Travel grantee Internat. Sci. Found., 1995; Pres. Ukraine Young Scientist scholar, 1995, Internatl. fellowship, Tokyo Univ., 1998, Post Doctoral fellowship, Pittsburgh Univ., 1999-2000. Mem. Ukrainian Biochem. Soc., Am. Aging Assn., European Iron Club, N.Y. Acad. Scis., Soc. for Free Radical Rsch., 1997, Euro. Soc. for Photobiology, 1997. Fax: 380 44 229-63-65. E-mail: akuzm@hotmail.com. Office: A V Palladin Inst Biochem, 9 Leontovich St, 01601 Kiev Ukraine

KUZMICHEV, VADIM VALENTINOVICH, physicist; b. Kiev, Ukraine, Mar. 14, 1969; s. Valentin Evdokimovich and Marina Ivanovna (Koshelenko) K. MS with honors, Kiev U., 1991, PhD, 1999. Rschr. Bogolyubov Inst. Theoretical Physics, Kiev, 1994—. Contbr. articles to profl. jours. Roman Catholic. Office: Bogolyubov Inst Theor Phys, Metrolohichna 14-B, 03143 Kiev Ukraine

KUZMICS, HELMUT, sociologist, researcher; b. Graz, Austria, June 22, 1949; s. Karl and Hildegard (Respondek) K.; m. Roswitha Raggautz, Dec. 29, 1973 (div. Apr. 1986); children: Christoph, Adrian; m. Gesine Fromm, Sept. 29, 1990; children: Maria-Theresia, Sonja. Econ., Univ. Graz, Austria, 1972; diploma in sociology, Inst. of Advanced Studies, Vienna, Austria, 1972-74; D of Econs., Univ. Graz, 1978. Asst. prof. Univ. Graz, 1974-88, assoc. prof., 1988-94, prof., 1994—; vis. fellow Univ. Hanover, Germany, 1990; vis. scholar Univ. Cambridge, 1990-91. Author: Price of Civilization, 1989; co-editor: Corruption, 1985, Never Ending Process of Civilization, 1991, Transformations of The We Feeling, 1993. Mem. Germany Sociology Assn., Internat. Sociology Assn. Avocations: music, mountains. Home: Schöckelstrasse 54, A 8045 Graz Austria Office: Graz Univ Inst Sociology, UniversitätsstraBe 15, A 8010 Graz Austria

KUZMIN, ALEXEI, physicist; b. Riga, Latvia, Aug. 12, 1968; s. Yuri and Ludmila (Chuiko) K.; m. Natalija Kevaska, July 29, 1995; 1 child, Alexandra Kuzmina. MS, U. Latvia, 1990, PhD, 1992. Jr. rschr. Inst. Solid State Physics, Riga, 1990-93, rschr., 1993—. Recipient Baltic prize Acad. Europaea, London, 1996. Mem. European Synchrotron Radiation Soc., Internat. X-ray Absorption Fire Structure Soc., Nat. Geographics Soc. Office: Inst Solid State Physics, Kengaraga Street 8, LV-1063 Riga Latvia

KUZMINOV, VADIM VASILEVICH, physicist, researcher; b. Nikopol, USSR, July 29, 1952; s. Vasili Nikolaevich and Galina Vasilievna (Paporkova) K.; m. Silva Ivanova Kalcheva, July 16, 1991; 1 child, Augustina. PhD, Russian Rsch. Ctr. Kurchatov Inst., Moscow, 1981. Rsch. staff mem. Petersburg Nuclear Physics Inst., Gatchina, Russia, 1980—. Contbr. articles to profl. jours. Grantee Internat. Science Found., 1994. Avocation: tourism. Home: Pionerstroya 7/1, 25, 198206 St. Petersburg Russia Office: Petersburg Nuc Physics Inst, RAS, 188350 Gatchina Russia

KUZNETSOV, VALERY VLADIMIROVICH, chemist, educator; b. Rostov on Don, USSR, June 27, 1949; s. Vladimir Ivanovich and Majya Konstantinovna (Lazareva) K.; m. Svetlana Alexeevna Poltavez, Jan. 29, 1993; children: Margarita, Alexei. M Chemistry, Odessa (USSR) State U., 1971; PhD, Physico-Chem. Inst., Odessa, 1984. Sr. engr. A.V. Bogatsky Physico-Chem. Inst., Odessa, 1975-79; jr. sci. fellow A.V. Bogatsky Physico-Chem. Inst., Odessa, 1979-85, sci. fellow, 1985-96, sr. sci. fellow, 1996-99; sr. lectr. Ufa State Oil Tech. U., Russia, 1999—; cons. to chem. edn., 1975—. Author: (with A. Green) Chemistry of Cyclic Boronic Acid Esters, 1988; contbr. more than 110 articles to Russian and Ukrainian chem. jours.; patentee in field. Mem. coun. Small Acad. Scis., Odessa region, 1992—. Sr. lt. Air Def., 1971-72, Odessa. Internat. Sci. Found. grantee, 1993. Avocation: travel. E-mail: physchem@paco.odessa.ua. Office: Ufa State Oil Tech Univ, ul Kosmonavtov 1, 450062 Ufa Russia

KUZNETSOV, VITALY GERMANOVICH, sedimentology and geology educator; b. Baku, Azerbaijan, USSR, July 24, 1937; s. German Ivanovich and Bella Davidovna (Kalish) K.; . Sophia Julievna Sabsay, Dec. 3, 1966; children: Vera Vitalievna, Lubov Vitalievna. Engr., Geologist, Oil and Gas Inst., Moscow, 1959, PhD, 1965, DSc, 1980. Engr. Petroleum Propecting Co., Orenburg, Russia, 1959-62; rsch. worker Rsch. Inst. Natural Gas, Moscow, 1965-68; lectr. Rsch. Inst., Oil and Gas Inst., Moscow, 1968-75; asst. prof. Oil and Gas Inst., Moscow, 1975-82; prof. State Acad. Oil and Gas, Moscow, 1982—; expert Ministry Econs., Moscow, 1987-94, Highest Attestation Commn., Moscow, 1985-90. Author: Geology of Reefs and Their Oil-Bearing, 1978 (Moscow Soc. of Naturalists award 1982), Natural Reservoirs of Oil and Gas Carbonate Sediments, 1992; co-author: Lithology and Facies Analyse, 1981 (Moscow Soc. Oil and Gas award 1983); editor, co-author: Recent and Fossil Reefs, 1990. Mem. Acad. Natural Sci., Am. Assn. Petroleum Geologists. Home: 23-2-133 Ostrovitanova, 117437 Moscow Russia Office: State Acad Oil and Gas, 65 Leninsky Prospekt, 117917 Moscow Russia

KUZNETSOVA, KLAUDIA PROKOFJEVNA, librarian, library director; b. Letovochnoe, Kazakhstan, Russia, Apr. 15, 1948; d. Prokofii Pavlovitch Kuznetsov and Maria Georgievna (Yakovleva) Kuznetsova; m. Vladimir Borisovitch Rjabokon, Feb. 11, 1971; 1 child, Olga. Philologist degree, Ural State U., Sverdlovsk, 1971. Libr. Sci. Libr. USU, Sverdlovsk, 1970-73, chief libr., 1975-79, dep. dir., 1979-94, dir., 1994—. Contbr. articles to profl. jours. Mem. Assn. Russian Librs., UNESCO Network of Assoc Librs. Avocations: sewing, knitting, cat. Home: Lunacharskogo 225-88, 620100 Ekaterinburg Russia Office: Ural State U, pr Lenina, 620083 Ekaterinburg Russia

KUŹNICKI, LESZEK, biologist, cell biologist. Head lab cell motility Inst. Exptl. Biology. Mem. Polish Acad. Scis. (pres. 1993-98), Internat. Commn. Protozoology. Office: Polish Acad Scis Nencki Ins, Exptl Biology Pasteura 3, PL-02093 Warsaw Poland

KUZUBASOGLU, HUSEYIN, packaging company executive; b. Istanbul, Turkey, July 18, 1954; s. Abdullah Durgut and Didar (Yolal) K.; m. Susan Martin, Dec. 23, 1983; children: Kaan, Melisa, Eren. Degree in analytical chemistry, North Staffordshire Poly., 1979, postgrad., 1979-80. Asst. gen. mgr. Billur Plastics, Istanbul, 1981-85; export mgr. Degere Inc., Istanbul, 1985-87; dir. Ekol Ofset AS, Istanbul, 1987—. Home: 1st Cad Zambak Sok No 3/1, 34800 Istanbul Yesilkoy, Turkey Office: Ekol Ofset A S, Koy Alti Mevkii Yenibosna, 34530 Istanbul Turkey

KUZUKI, RYOTA, gas distribution company engineer; m. Tomomi Kuzuki. M of Engring., U. Tokyo, 1989. With Residential Gas Facilities Devel. Ctr. Tokyo Gas Co. Ltd., 1989-92, chief corp. planning dept., 1992-95; dep. mgr. internat. coordination dept. The Japan Gas Assn., Tokyo, 1995-99; mgr. corp. planning dept. Tokyo Gas Co., Ltd., 1999—; sec. Internat. Gas Union Study Group 9.4, 1997-99. Editor report. Office: Corp Planning Dept, Tokyo Gas Co, 1-5-20 Kaigan, Minato-ku, Tokyo 105-8527, Japan

KUZUMAKI, NOBORU, educator; b. Kushiro, Japan, Mar. 27, 1943; s. Itaru and Tamako (Miyashita) K.; m. Michiko Maeda, May 3, 1971; children: Osamu, Satoshi. B of Medicine, Hokkaido U., Sapporo, 1967, MD, 1968, D of Med. Sci., 1975. Rsch. asst. Hokkaido U., 1975-79, prof., 1981—; asst. prof. Hamamatsu Med. Coll., Japan, 1979-81. Editl. bd. Japanese Jour. of Cancer Rsch., Tokyo, 1992-95; contbr. articles to profl. jours. Recipient Assn. award Hokkaido Drs. Assn., 1994, Govs. award Hokkaido Prefecture, 1994; Cancer Rsch. grantee The Princess Takamatsu Fund, 1991, rsch. grantee Uehara Meml. Life Sci. Fund, 1989. Mem. Japanese Cancer Assn. (councilor 1986—), Sapporo Cancer Seminor (dir. 1997—), Am. Assn. for Cancer Rsch. Phila., N.Y. Acad. Scis., Japanese Molecular Biology Assn., Japanese Cell Biology Assn. Avocation: music listening. Home: Hackiken-10 Nishi 3-2-1, Sapporo 063-0850, Japan Office: Inst Genetic Medicine Hokkaido U, Kita-15 Nishi-7 Kita-Ku, Sapporo 060-0815, Japan

KUZYAKOV, YAKOV VICTOROVICH, soil scientist, consultant; b. Moscow, Aug. 27, 1963; s. Victor and Noemi (Vermus) K.; m. Irina Felixovna Kozlovskaya, Oct. 5, 1991; children: Maria, Alexander. Engr., U. Halle, Germany, 1986; PhD, Agrl. Acad. Moscow, 1989. Rschr., chief tracer lab. Agrl. Acad. Moscow, 1990-93; rschr. Humboldt Univ., Berlin, 1993-96; postdoctoral rsch. U. Hohenheim, Germany, 1997—; cons. Ministry Agr., Stuttgart, Germany, 1996—. Contbr. articles to profl. jours. Grantee Soros Found., 1992. Fellow German Rsch. Found.; mem. German Soil Scientist Soc., Russian Soil Scientist Soc. Avocation: kayaking. Home: Dmitrovskoye Hwy 37-7-55, 127550 Moscow Russia Office: Inst Soil Sci, Univ Hohenheim, D-70599 Stuttgart Germany

KUZYUKOV, ANATOLIY NIKOLAYEVICH, research scientist, educator; b. Odessa, Ukraine, Jan. 6, 1937; s. Hikolay Alexandrovich Kuzyukov and Anna Parfiryevna Rachinskaya; m. Alla Nikolayevna Girko, Feb. 7, 1957; children: Olga, Andrey. Degree in metall. engring., Mining Metall. Inst., Irkutsk, Russia, 1959; Candidate Tech. Scis., NIKKHIMMASH, Moscow, 1971; D Tech. Scis., Inst. Physics and Chemistry, Moscow, 1991. Operator Oil-Chem. Plant, Angarsk, Russia, 1959, engr., 1959-62; key engr. Sci. Rsch. Inst. of Chem. Machine Bldg., Severodonetsk, Ukraine, 1962-68, maj. sci. officer, 1968-77, mgr. lab., 1977—; prof. Severodonetsk Tech. Inst., Eastern Ukrainian State U., 1992—. Author: Inspection of Defence of Chemical Machinery from Corrosion, 1982; contbr. over 120 articles to profl. jours.; inventor in field. Maj. lt. Ukraine armed forces. Recipient Orden Mark of Honor, 1971. Mem. All-Union Assn Corrosionists, Assn. Ukrainian Corrosionists, N.Y. Acad. Scis. Avocations: mountain skiing, volleyball, chess, literature, collecting stamps and postcards. Home: 40,58 Donetskaya St, 93400 Severodonetsk Ukraine Office: Niikhimash, 59 Sovetskii Pr, 93400 Severodonetsk Ukraine

KVAAL, SIGRID INGEBORG, dental surgeon; b. Oslo, Norway, Oct. 1, 1951; d. Ornulf and Elisabeth Kvaal. B in Dental Surgery, Royal Dental Hosp., London, 1978; PhD, U. Oslo, Norway, 1995. Cert. dental surgeon; forensic med. expert on odontol. cases. House surgeon Eng., 1978-81; comty. dental officer Troms, Norway, 1981-82; pvt. practice Oslo, Norway, 1982—; rsch. asst. U. Oslo, Norway, 1988-95; clin. instr. U. Oslo, 1995-99, rsch. asst., 1999—. Mem. Norwegian Forensic Assn. (hon. treas.), Norwegian Dental Assn., Norwegian Forensic Odentology Assn. (chmn. 1997—). Avocations: gardening, classical music, needlework. Office: Dental Faculty Dept Oral Pathology, Dental Fac Dept Oral Surg, PO Box 1109, N-0317 Oslo Norway

KVAČEK, JIŘÍ, paleobotanist, museum curator, consultant; b. Prague, Czech Republic, Dec. 28, 1963; s. Zlatko and Hana (Koubová) K.; m. Helena Stará, June 21, 1990; children: Barbora, Karolína, Adam. RNDr, Charles U., Prague, 1987; CSc in Geology, Czech Republic Acad. Sci., 1998. Curator Nat. Mus., Prague, 1987—. Editor: Acta Musei Nationalis Pragae Ser. B, 1993; contbr. articles to sci. jours., including Rev. Palaeobotany and Palynology, Internat. Jour. Plant Sci., Palaeogeography, Palaeoclimatology, Palaeoecology. Mem. Czech Bot. Assn. Home: Litoměřická 31, 190 00 Prague 9, Czech Republic Office: Nat Mus, Václavské nám 68, 115 79 Prague Czech Republic

KVALHEIM, OLAV MARTIN, educator, industrial consultant; b. Bergen, Norway, Dec. 18, 1951; s. Olav and Hallfrid (Standnes) K.; m. Ane-Mette Storkson, Sept. 8, 1973; children: Mette-Maren, Marius. Dr. Philos., U. Bergen, 1987; hon. degree, Hunan U., Changsha, Republic of China, 1991. Rsch. asst. Norwegian Rsch. Coun. for Sci and Humanities, Bergen, 1978-80, rsch. fellow, 1987-88; system analyst Bergen, 1980-86; assoc. prof. U. Bergen, 1989-92, prof., 1993—; pres. Pattern Recognition Systems AS, 1997—. Editor: (book series) Data Handling in Science and Technology, 1988-91; editor Chemometrics & Intell. Lab. Sys., 1992—; co-editor, contbr. Application of Chemometrics to Research and Industry, 1996; contbr. 140 articles to profl. jours. Recipient prize for Excellent Rsch. The Nansen Found., 1988, The Norwegian Rsch. Coun., 1996. Mem. Norwegian Chem. Soc., Chemometrics Group (founder, leader 1989-91), Norwegian Chem. Soc. (hon. mem. chemometrics group 1994). Avocations: bridge, sport fishing, mountaineering. Office: U Bergen, Realfagbygget Allegt 41, N-5007 Bergen Norway

KVALSETH, TARALD ODDVAR, mechanical engineer, educator; b. Brunkeberg, Telemark, Norway, Nov. 7, 1938; married; 3 children. B.S., U. Durham, King's Coll., Eng., 1963; M.S., U. Calif.-Berkeley, 1966, Ph.D., 1971. Research asst. engring. expt. sta. U. Colo., Boulder, 1963-64, teaching asst. dept. mech. engring.; mech. engr. Williams & Lane Inc., Berkeley, 1964-65; research asst. dept. indsl. engring. and ops. research U. Calif.-Berkeley, 1965-71, research fellow, 1973; asst. prof. Sch. Indsl. and Systems Engring. Ga. Inst. Tech., Atlanta, 1971-74; sr. lectr. indsl. mgmt. div. Norwegian Inst. Tech. U. Trondheim, 1974-79, head indsl. mgmt. div., 1975-79; assoc. prof. dept. mech. engring. U. Minn., Mpls., 1979-82, prof., 1982—; guest worker NASA Ames Research Ctr., Calif., 1973; mem. organizing com. 1st Berkeley-Monterey Conf. Timespan, Pay and Discretionary Capacity, 1973; mem. steering com. Internat. Conf. Human Factors in Design and Op. Ships, Gothenburg, Sweden, 1977; mem. bd. Norwegian Ergonomics Com., 1977-80; gen. session chmn. Conf. Work Place Design and Work Environ. Problems, Trondheim, 1978. Author book chpts., articles, presentations, reports in field; editor text books; mem. editl. bd., reviewer for numerous profl. jours., patentee in field. Mem. IEEE, AAAS, Inst. Indsl. Engrs. (sr.), Human Factors and Ergonomics Soc. (pres. upper Midwest chpt.), Nordic Ergonomics Soc. (coun. 1977-80), Internat. Ergonomics Assn. (gen. coun. 1977-80, v.p. 1982-85), Ergonomics Soc., Psychonomic Soc., Am. Psychol. Soc., Am. Statis. Assn., Sigma Xi. Lutheran. Club: Campus (U. Minn.). Home: 108 Turnpike Rd Minneapolis MN 55416-1149 Office: U Minn Dept Mech Engring Minneapolis MN 55455

KVARSTEIN, BERNT, urological surgeon; b. Lierne, Norway, Aug. 21, 1930; s. Gunnvald and Gundrun (Berge) K.; m. Anne-Kari Henga, June 23, 1955 (dec. June 1986); children: Helene, Gunnvald, Bernt Kristian. MD, U. Oslo, 1959, PhD, 1971. Intern Lillehammer Fylkessykehus and Sel and Heidal dists., 1960-61; sci. asst. Inst. Path. Anatomy U. Oslo, 1962-63, rsch. fellow Inst. Thrombosis Rsch., 1965-69; resident and registrar dept. ob/gyn. Univ. Hosp., Oslo, 1964, 69-70, registrar dept. surgery, 1970-73, sr. registrar divsn. urology, 1975-78; registrar, sr. registrar dept. surgery Drammen Hosp., Norway, 1973-75; specialist in gen. surgery, 1976, in urology, 1978; surgeon-in-chief Home for Congl. Sisters, Oslo, 1978-79; asst. surgeon-in-chief dept. surgery Akershus Ctrl. Hosp., U. Oslo, 1979-82, head sect. urology, 1988-89; urologist-in-chief dept. urology Ulleval Hosp., U. Oslo, 1988-89; head sect. urology Akerstrüs Cen. Hosp., 1989—. Contbr. articles on endocrinology, cardiovascular surgery and urology to profl. jours. Recipient C.R. Bard award, 1982, Astra Meditec award, 1991. Mem. Norwegian Med. Assn., Norwegian Surg. Assn., Norwegian Assn. Patients with Urol. Diseases (initiator found.), Nordic Surg. Assn., Norwegian Assn. Urology (pres. 1986-89), Nordic Urol. Assn., Société Internationale d'Urologie, Internat. Continence Soc., European Assn. Urology, N.Y. Acad. Scis. Address: Lijordv 25, 1359 Eiksmarka Norway

KVASNICKA, FRANTISEK, food chemist, researcher; b. Prague, Czech Republic, Oct. 11, 1954; s. Frantisek and Ruzena (Pavlickova) K.; m. Alexandra Kautna, Nov. 30, 1953; children: Sarka, Sylva. Engr., Tech. U., Prague, 1978, PhD, 1984. Shift master Sugar Factory, Prague, 1978-80; asst. lectr. Inst. Chem. Tech., Prague, 1984-90, sr. lectr. in chemistry and technology of feedstuffs, 1990-95; quality assurance, quality control mgr. SPOFA Ltd., Prague, 1996-98; assoc. prof. Inst. Chem. Tech., Prague, 1998—; cons. Brit. Sugar, Norwich, Eng., 1991-94, ITP-Analytical, CC, Johannesburg, 1994—, Recman, Ostrava, Czech Republic, 1989—. Contbr. articles to profl. jours. Recipient Silver medal Czech Agrl. Acad., 1985. Mem. Internat. Com. for Union Methods in Sugar Analysis. Avocations: astronomy, astrophysics, cosmology. Home: Slikova 550/6, 16900 Prague 6, Czech Republic

KVASNIČKA, JAN, cardiologist, educator; b. Prague, Czech Republic, Nov. 19, 1959; s. Stanislav and Věra (Vinklerová) K.; m. Hana Janoušková, June 4, 1989; children: Jan, Karolina. Degree, Charles U., Prague, 1984, PhD, 1991; diploma in interventional cardiology, U. Paris, 1992. From house officer to sr. house officer 2d dept. medicine Charles U., 1984-87, clin. lectr. 2d dept. medicine, 1988-90, 93, asst. 2d dept. medicine, 1995—; clin. fellow svc. functional explorations U. Paris, 1991, asst. svc. functional explorations, 1991-92, 99. Mem. Czech Med. Assn., Czech Cardiol. Assn. Home: Na Petynce 154, 169 00 Prague Czech Republic Office: Charles U, U Nemocnice 2, 128 08 Prague 2, Czech Republic

KVERNDOKK, SNORRE, economist, educator; b. Trondheim, Norway, Dec. 24, 1962; s. Kåre and Aud (Fiane) K.; m. Hege Gudrun Eliassen, Aug. 18, 1990; 1 child, Guro Eliassen Kūerndokk. Cand. oecon, U. Oslo, 1988, DrPolit in Econs., 1994. Rsch. fellow SNF-Found. for Rsch. in Econs. and Bus. Adminstrn., Oslo, 1989-92; rschr. Stats. Norway, Oslo, 1992-98; sr. lectr. dept. econs. U. Oslo, 1997; rsch. economist Frisch Ctr. Econ. Rsch., Oslo, 1998—. Lead author Working Group III, Intergovtl. Panel Climate Change, Third Assessment Report, 1998—; contbr. articles to profl. jours. Vice cpl. Norwegian Mil., 1983. Recipient Award for outstanding paper Energy Jour., 1993. Avocations: music, history, sports, social life. Home: Selvbyggervn 90, 0591 Oslo Norway

KVETINA, JAROSLAV, pharmacologist; b. Racineves, Czech Republic, May 19, 1930; s. Jaroslav and Marie (Aimova) K.; m. Helena Mala, Apr. 15, 1960 (div. 1973); 1 child Libnarova Marketa; m. Miluse Simkova, Feb. 7, 1975; children: Petr, Jan. RND, Masaryk U., Brno, Czech Republic, 1953; PhD in Medicine, Charles U., Prague, Czech Republic, 1964, DSc, 1975; D (hon.), U. Brno, Czech Republic, 2000. Lectr. Med. Faculty, Hradec Kralove, Czech Republic, 1955-69; prof. Faculty Pharmacy, Hradec Kralove, Czech Republic, 1969-90; dir. Inst. Exptl. Biopharmaceutics, Hradec Kralove, Czech Republic, 1990—; head dept. pharm. Med. Faculty Charles U., 1968-71, Faculty Pharmacy, dean, 1969-90. Contbr. articles to profl. jours. Mem. Czech Acad. Sci. (v.p. 1980), Czech Med. Assn. (hon.), French Pharm. Assn. (hon.). Home: Velke namesti 16, 500 01 Hradec Kralove Czech Republic Office: Inst Exptl Biopharmaceutics, Heyrovskeho 1207, 500 03 Hradec Kralove Czech Republic

KVITKO, ARKADY, mathematician; b. Slavyanka, Hasansky, Russia, June 6, 1949; came to U.S., 1989; s. Nikolay Zilberg and Leonora K.; m. Rachel Kravchenko, Apr. 30, 1974; children: Marina, Max. BS in Math. and Physics, City Coll., Odessa, Ukraine, 1970; MS in Ops. Rsch., Odessa State U., Odessa, Ukraine, 1974; PhD in Ops. Rsch., State U., Minsk, Russia, 1982. From asst. prof. to adj. prof. Odessa State U. City Coll., 1975-89; from SAS programmer, analyst to sr. statistician Merrill Lynch, N.Y.C., 1990-97, sr. ops. rsch. analyst, 1997—; cons., presenter in field. Co-author: (with M. Zholdak) Probabiltiy Theory and Information Systems, 1989; contbr. articles to profl. jours. Polytech. U. grant, 1982-89. Avocations: chess, reading.

KVIZ, BORIS, radiocommunications educator; b. Zagreb, Croatia, Sept. 19, 1931; s. Emanuel and Otilija (Ceraj) K.; m. Jelva Goić, July 31, 1965. BSc, Electrotechnical Faculty, Zagreb, 1957, PhD, 1964. Rschr. Inst. for Electronics Telecom. and Automation, Zagreb, 1959; asst. Electrotechnical Faculty, Zagreb, 1959-64, asst. prof., 1964-71, assoc. prof., 1971-76, full prof., 1976—; cons. Inst. for Electronics Telecom. and Automation, Zagreb, 1968-72; v.p. Soc. for Flight-Traffic Safety, Zagreb, 1970-74. Author: Radiotelemetry, 1980; contbr. articles to profl. jours. Mem. IEEE, Optical Soc. Am., Croatian Acad. Tech. Scis. Roman Catholic. Avocations: classical music, painting, walking. Home: Pantovčak 105, HR-10000 Zagreb Croatia Office: Faculty Elec Engring & Comp, Unska 3, HR-10000 Zagreb Croatia

KWA, SOON BEE, physician; b. Singapore, Sept. 5, 1930; m. Lucy Leow Oct. 30, 1955; children: Chong Teck, Chong Jin. MBBS, U. Malaya, 1955. Med. dir. Blood Transfusion Svc., Singapore, 1962-72, Kandang Kerbau Hosp., Singapore, 1968-72, Singapore Gen. Hosp., 1972-84; permanent sec. Ministry Health, Singapore, 1984-96; dir. Med. Svcs. Singapore, 1984-96; emeritus cons. Singapore Gen. Hosp., 1996—; sr. cons. hematologist, 1971-84; chmn. Jurong Bird Park, Singapore, 1980—; chmn. Singapore Zool. Gardens, 1995—; bd. dirs. Keppel Land Ltd., Somerset Holdings Ltd., Pontiac Land Pte Ltd. Registrar Singapore Med. Coun., 1984-96, mem., 1997—; mem. mgmt. com. Singapore Turf Club, 1996—; mem. Singapore Tourism Bd., 1997-99. Col. Singapore Armed Forces, 1972-84. Recipient Pub. Adminstrn. Gold medal Singapore Govt., 1962, Meritorious Svc. medal Singapore Govt., 1992. Fellow Royal Coll. Physicians Edinburgh, Royal Coll. Physicians Glasgow. Avocations: nature, wildlife. Office: Singapore Gen Hosp, Outram Rd, Singapore 169608, Singapore

KWAAN, JACK HAU MING, retired physician; b. Hong Kong, Apr. 9, 1928; came to U.S., 1953; s. Y.K. and Rose W. Kwaan; m. Min K. Ho, Feb. 11, 1973; children: Mary, Peter, Rebecca, Nicholas. MD, U. Hong Kong, 1952. Diplomate Am. Bd. Radiology, Am. Bd. Surgery, Am. Bd. Thoracic

Surgery. Resident in radiology Roswell Park Meml. Inst., 1955-56; chief resident Peter Bent Brigham Hosp., 1956-57; rsch. fellow in radiology Harvard Med. Sch., Boston, 1956-57; sr. cancer rsch. radiol. therapist Roswell Park Meml. Inst., Buffalo, 1958-59; asst. prof. radiology U. Ky., Lexington, 1963-65; resident in surgery U. Calif., Irvine, 1965-68; rsch. fellow oncologic surgery M.D. Anderson Hosp., Houston, 1968-69; resident in thoracic U. Calif., Irvine, 1969-71, chief resident thoracic surgery, 1970, asst. prof. surgery, 1972-73; chief vascular surgery sect., co-dir. vascular surgery tng. program U. Calif. Irvine/Long Beach VA Med. Ctr., 1974-87; prof. surgery U. Calif., Irvine, 1983-87; sr. resident in thoracic surgery U. So. Calif./L.A. County Med. Ctr., 1971; staff thoracic cardiovasc. surgeon Long Beach VA Hosp., 1972-73; asst. chief dept. surgery Valley Med. Ctr., Fresno, Calif., 1973-74; prof. surgery U. Okla., Tulsa, 1987-93; ret., 1993; chief dept. surgery Valley Med. Ctr., Fresno, Calif., 1973-74; chief vascular surgery sect. Long Beach VA Med. Ctr., 1974-87; surgical cons. Kaiser Permanente Hosp. Contbr. articles to profl. jours. Fellow Am. Coll. Surgeons; mem. Brit. Med. Assn., Gen. Med. Coun. London (registrant), Assn. Mil. Surgeons of U.S. (life), Assn. VA Surgeons, Internat. Cardiovascular Soc. Home: PO Box 50183 Long Beach CA 90815-6183

KWAK, JU-WON, molecular biologist, researcher; b. Jeonju, Chonbuk, Republic of Korea, Mar. 25, 1957; s. Gap-Dong and Hyo-Soon (Choi) K.; m. Bog-Ho Kim, Dec. 11, 1982; children: Hyung-Kyung, Jeong-Kyung. BS, Seoul (Korea) Nat. U., 1979; MS, Korea Adv. Inst. Sci. & Tech., Taejon, 1982, PhD, 1988. Prin. rsch. scientist Korea Rsch. Inst. Biosci. and Biotechnology, Taejon, 1982—, dir. biochem. divsn., 2000—; rsch. assoc. U. N.C., Chapel Hill, 1983-84, post-doctoral fellow, 1989-91; invited lectr. Chungnam Nat. U., Taejon, 1994. Contbr. articles to profl. jours. Mem. AAAS, Internat. Atherosclerosis Soc., Korean Soc. Lipidology (v.p. 1997-99, Merck Sharp & Dohme Korea Sci. award 1995). Avocations: bowling, singing. Home: Hanbit Apt 131-303, Eoeun-Dong 99 Yuseong, Taejon 305-755, Republic of Korea Office: KRIBB Cardiovasc Rsch Group, Yuseong PO Box 115, Taejon 305-600, Republic of Korea

KWAKYE, JOHNSON KWAKU, chemistry educator; b. Akim Akokoaso, Ghana, Mar. 6, 1946; s. Robert Yaw and Afua (Serwaa) Gyening; m. Margaret Amma Aidoo, Aug. 31, 1974; children: Amma Serwaa, Kwaku Gyening, Akosua Kraa, Adwoa Oforiwaa. B of Pharmacy, U. Sci. and Tech., Kumasi, Ghana, 1973; MS, U. Strathclyde, Glasgow, Scotland, 1976; PhD, U. Bath, Eng., 1979. From tchg. asst. to lectr. U. Sci. and Tech., Kumasi, 1973-86, sr. lectr., 1986—; head dept. pharm. chemistry U. Sci. and Tech., Kumasi, 1984-85; chief examiner Kumasi Poly., 1983—; cons. pharm. analysis WHO, 1985—; quality control com. West African Pharm. Fedn., Lagos, Nigeria, 1987-91. Co-author: (with others) International Pharmacopoeia, 3d edit., 1994; contbr. articles to profl. jours. Chmn. schs. mgmt. bd. U. Sci. and Tech., 1991—. Commonwealth scholar Commonwealth Secretariat, London, 1974. Fellow West African Postgrad. Coll. Pharmacists; mem. Pharm. Soc. Ghana (br. vice-chmn. 1984-86). Avocations: evangelism, counseling, gardening. Office: Univ Sci and Tech, University PO Box 201, Kumasi Ghana

KWAN, ANNE SIU-KING, anesthesiologist; b. Hong Kong; d. Chung and Lan-Wai (Law) K.; m. Nai-Ki Mak; 1 child, Carmen. MB, BS, U. NSW, Australia, 1981; diploma in epidemiology and stats., Chinese U., Hong Kong, 1996; diploma in pain mgmt., Hong Kong Coll. Anesthesiologists, 1997, diploma in acupuncture, 1998, diploma in palliative medicine, 1999. Sr. registrar Woden Valley Hosp., Australia, 1991-94; cons. United Christian Hosp., Hong Kong, 1994-96, dir. pain medicine, 1994—, chief svc., 1996—; hon. assoc. prof. dept. anesthesia and intensive care Chinese U. Hong Kong, 1998—. Contbr. articles to profl. jours. Chmn. United Christian Hosp. Doctors' Assn. Hong Kong, 1996, treas., 1995. Conf. grantee Soc. Anaesthetists Hong Kong, 1996. Fellow Australian and New Zealand Coll. Anesthetists, Hong Kong Coll. Anesthesiologists (coun. mem. 1995—, editor newsletter), Hong Kong Acad. of Medicine. Office: United Christian Hosp, 130 Hip Wo St, Kwun Tong Hong Kong China

KWAN, BENJAMIN CHING KEE, ophthalmologist; b. Hong Kong, July 12, 1940; came to U.S., 1959; s. Shun Ming and Lurk Ming (Lai) K.; m. Catherine Ning, Aug. 29, 1964; children: Susan San, David Daiwai. MD, Wash. U., St. Louis, 1967. Diplomate Am. Bd. Ophthalmology. Ptnr. So. Calif. Permanente Med. Ctr., Harbor City, 1976—, chief of svc. ophthalmology, 1976-88; clin. prof. dept. ophthalmology UCLA, 1995—. Chmn. winter blossom ball Chinese Am. Debutante's Guild, 1993. Capt. U.S. Army, 1969-71. Recipient Svc. award Asian Am. Sr. Citizens Svc. Ctr., 1993, Proclamation award Calif. Sec. of State, 1993, Svc. award East L.A. Chinese Everspring Sr. Assn., 1994. Fellow Am. Acad. Ophthalmology; mem. Chinese Am. Ophthal. Soc. (pres. elect 1997-99, pres. 1999-00, Svc. award 1994), Chinese Physician's Soc. So. Calif. (bd. dirs., pres. 1983, Svc. award 1983, 89), Orgn. Chinese Ams. (pres. L.A. chpt. 1986-87). Roman Catholic. Avocations: ballroom dancing, singing, snow skiing. Home: 6327 Tarragon Rd Rancho Palos Verdes CA 90275-5834 Office: 1050 Pacific Coast Hwy Harbor City CA 90710-3509

KWAN, MICHELLE, professional figure skater; b. Torrance, Calif., July 7. Grad. H.S. Nat. spokesperson Children's Miracle Network, co-chair ProKids program. Recipient Skating Mag. Readers' Choice award for figure skater of the year, 1993-94, 95-96, Dial award, 1997; named 1996 Female Athlete of Yr., U.S. Olympic Com. Achievements include being the youngest World Champion in U.S. history; third youngest World Champion; victories include: World Junior Championships, 1994, 96, Hershey's Kisses Internat. Challenge, 1995, 96, 97, Skate Am., 1995, Skate Can., 1995, Nations cup, 1995, U.S. Postal Svc. Challenge, 1995, State Farm U.S. Championships, 1996, Champions Series Final, 1996, Japan Open, 1997, 99, Thrifty Car Rental Skate Am., 1997, 1997 Skate Can., 1997, U.S. Championships, 1998, 99, World Championships, 1998, 99, Goodwill Games, 1998, 1998 Ultimate Four, 1998, Grand Slam Figure Skating, 1998, U.S. Pro Classic, 1998, 1998 Keri Lotion Figure Skating Classic, 1998, 1998 Masters Figure Skating, World Profl. Championships, 1998, others. Avocations: swimming, bowling, riding four wheeler, biking. Office: USFSA 20 1st St Colorado Springs CO 80906-3624

KWAN, PING HONG GEORGE, consultant; b. Nam Hoi, Kwangtung, China, Mar. 10, 1929; m. Anna Kwan Wai, 1952. Student, Open Learning Inst. Hong Kong, 1990, 92, 96, U. Oreg., 1995; diploma, cert., Space U., Hong Kong, 1998; MA candidate, Victoria U., Melbourne, Australia, 1999; grad. cert., diploma in sport/rec. mgmt., 1998. Proprieter, prin., chief instr. Vigour Gymnasium, Hong Kong, 1954-68; proprietor, chief editor Sports News Svc., Hong Kong, 1956-62; security inspector China Light and Power Co., Hong Kong, 1963-80; chief security supt. Am. Internat. Assurance, Hong Kong, 1980-82; sr. bldg. supt., mgr. Johns Lang Wootten Mgmt. Svcs. Co., Ltd., Hong Kong, 1984-87; proprietor Kwan's Gyn, 1984-89; pvt. practice cons. Hong Kong, 1988—; Asian continental chairperson IWF Master Weightlifting Com., 1994—. Author: Health, Strength and Beauty, 1962. Signalman Her Majesty Svc. Royal Navy, Hong Kong, 1950-54. Mem. Internat. Profl. Security Assn., Hong Kong Amateur Weightlifting and Powerlifting Assn. Avocations: driving, weightlifting, bodybuilding, reading, traveling. Home: Flat A, 3/F Wai Sing Mansion, Taikoo Shing Hong Kong

KWAN, VINCENT PO CHUEN, business executive, solicitor; b. Hong Kong, July 24, 1959; s. Chun and Sheuong (Ho) K.; m. Nikki Lay Keng Tan, Nov. 22, 1993; 1 child, Corinna Kwan. B in Social Scis., U. Hong Kong, 1983, postgrad. cert. in law, 1988, LLM, 1992; LLB, U. London, 1986, MS, 1999. Solicitor Hong Kong, Eng., Wales, ACT Australia. Acctg. officer Hong Kong Govt., 1983-86, auditor, 1986-87; trainee solicitor Deacons, Hong Kong, 1988-90; solicitor Deacons Graham & James, Hong Kong, 1990-93; exec. dir. Chuang's Consortium Internat. Ltd., Hong Kong, 1993-96; gen. mgr. Sino Land Co. Ltd., Kowloon, Hong Kong, 1997—. Recipient Ho Fook prize U. Hong Kong, 1980-81; scholarship Citibank, 1981-82, 82-83. Mem. Hong Kong Soc. of Accts. (duty acct. 1990—), Law Soc. of Hong Kong (duty lawyer 1992—). Home: Flat 1E Phase I, Blessings Gd 95 Robinson Rd, Hong Kong China Office: Sino Land Co Ltd, 12/F Tsim Sha Tsui Ctr, Kowloon Hong Kong

KWAN, YUN, judge. Chief judge Republic of South Korea. Office: Supreme Ct, 37 Sosomun-dong, Chung-gu Seoul, South Korea*

KWAŚNIEWSKI, ALEKSANDER, president of Poland; b. Bialogard, Poland, Nov. 15, 1954; s. Zdzislaw and Aleksandra Kwaśniewski; m. Jolanta Konty, 1979; 1 child. Educated, Gdańsk U. Former leader youth movement including chair coun. Polish Socialist Students' Union, Gdańsk, head culture dept. gen. bd., 1979-80, mem. exec. com., chief coun., 1980-81; editor in chief student's weekly Itd, Warsaw, 1981-84, Sztandar Młodych, Warsaw, 1984-85; mem. Coun. of Ministers, Warsaw, 1985-89, head socio-polit. com., 1988-89; min. for Youth, 1985-87, chair com. for youth and physical culture, 1987-90; mem. Polish United Workers' Party, 1977-90; now chmn. Social Democracy of the Republic of Poland; leader Democratic Left Alliance Caucus; chair constnl. com. Nat. Assembly; Pres. of Poland, 1995—. Chair Polish Olympic Com., 1988-91. Office: Kancelaria Prezydente RP, ul Krakowskie Przedmeigcie 48/50, 00-071 Warsaw Poland

KWEK, KIAN TENG, economics educator; b. Kuala Lumpur, Malaysia, Feb. 16, 1964; parents Khing Thiang and Kim Fong (Chia) K. B in Econs., U. Malaya, Kuala Lumpur, 1987, M in Econs., 1991; PhD in Econs., Monash U., Australia, 1999. Audit trainee Ernst & Whinney, Kuala Lumpur, 1984; tutor faculty econs. and adminstrn. U. Malaya, 1987-91, rsch. asst., 1990-91, lectr. faculty econs. and adminstrn., 1991—, asst. lectr., 1996-99; rsch. mortgage officer Nat. Mortgage Corp. Malaysia, Kuala Lumpur, 1991; rschr., presenter in field. Contbr. articles to profl. publs.; prodn. editor Malaysian Jour. Econ. Studies 1992-95, editorial asst., 1988-91. Scholar Pub. Svc. Dept. Malaysia, 1984-87. Mem. Malaysian Econ. Assn. (conv. organizing com. 1989, 91, 93, life, exec. com. 1992-95, sec. editl. bd. Ekonomika 1992-95, hon. pub. sec. 1994-95, hon. asst. sec. 2000—), Econometric Soc., Malaysian Inst. Stats., Internat. Ctr. for Aquatic Resources. Avocations: reading, writing, paper-clay artwork, painting, Christian music. Home: K-6 Setapak Garden, 5th MI Jalan Gombak, Wilayah, Persekutuan Kuala Lumpur 53000, Malaysia Office: U Malaya Econs & Adminstrn Divns Applied Econs, Lembah Pantai, Kuala Lumpur 59100, Malaysia

KWELAGOBE, DANIEL K., government official; b. Molepolole, Sept. 1, 1943; married; 2 children. Student, Moeding Coll., 1963-65, Gaborone Secondary Sch., 1967-68. Mem. Parliament Govt. Botswana, 1969-73, min. commerce and industry, 1973-74, asst. min. broadcasting and info., 1974, min. commerce and industry, min. pub. and info. svcs., min. agr., 1986-90; dep. gen. sec. Botswana Dem. Party, 1970-75, sec. gen., 1975; min. agr. Govt. Botswana, min. works, transport and comm., 1994-99, min. local govt., lands and housing, 1999—, min. commerce and industry; chmn. OAU Com. of Experts on Am. Refugees. Fgn. honor Order of Leopard, Ziare. Office: Ministry Works Transport & Comm, Pvt Bag 004, Gaborone Botswana*

KWIAT, KEVIN ANTHONY, electrical engineer; b. Jan. 10, 1957. BS, Syracuse U., 1980, BA, 1988, MS, 1988, PhD, 1996. Electronics engr. Air Force Rsch. Lab. Info. Directorate, Rome, N.Y., 1983—; adj. prof. of math. and computer sci. Syracuse U., Utica, N.Y., 1988—; adj. prof. computer sci. SUNY Inst. Tech., Utica/Rome, 1999—. Recipient IEEE Region I award for achievements in multiprocessing and fault tolerance, 1999. Mem. IEEE (region 1 award for leadership). Achievements include patent for dynamically reconfigurable FPGA apparatus and method for multiprocessing and fault tolerance. Home: 7 Bermuda Rd Whitesboro NY 13492-2205

KWIATKOWSKI, STEFAN MICHAL, educationalist; b. Lisewo, Poland, Jan. 21, 1948; s. Michał and Władysława (Bonder) K.; m. Elżbieta Kujszczyk, Apr. 28, 1973; children: Michał, Stefan. MSc, Warsaw Tech. U., 1971, ScD, 1975. Head of pedagogical dept. Warsaw Tech. U., Poland, 1982-85; dep. dir. Inst. of Econ. and Social Scis., Warsaw, 1985-90; dep. dir. Inst. for Ednl. Rsch., Warsaw, 1991-93, dir., 1993—; cons. Internat. Labor Office, Warsaw, 1993; advisor Ministry of Nat. Edn., Poland, 1996—; mgmt. com. PHARE project Distance Edn., 1996—. Author: Computers in Education and School Management, 1994, Elements of Vocational Education Theory, 1994, Vocational Education in the Context of Market Economy, 1994, New Conditions of School Education, 1997, Education in Poland in the Process of Social Changes, 1999, Education for All, 1999. Recipient Scientific award Ministry of Edn., 1983. Mem. European Ednl. Rsch. Assn. (exec. bd. 1996—), European Union (exec. bd. SMART program 1996—). Avocation: classical music. Home: Rubinowa 57, 05-500 Piaseczno Poland Office: Inst for Endl Rsch, Górczewska 8, 01-180 Warsaw Poland

KWIK, KING HAN, naval architect, researcher; b. Purworejo, Indonesia, May 30, 1935; m. Ilse Tulaar, Sept. 20, 1960; children: Harry, Anne. M of Engrng., Tech. U. Aachen, Germany, 1960; D of Engrng., Tech. U. Hannover, Germany, 1969. Sci. ofcl. U. Hamburg, Germany, 1960-69, lectr., 1969—; expert marine traffic engrng. German Ministry of Transport, Hamburg, 1983-87. Contbr. chpts. to books, articles to profl. jours.

KWON, BYOUNG-MOG, research scientist, educator; b. Yongin, Kyuaggi, Korea, Feb. 2, 1956; s. Jong-sik and Il-ye (Choi) K.; m. Young Ae Kim, Mar. 26, 1983; children: Seung-Hyuk, Seung-Bin. BS, Korea U., 1979; MS, KAIST, Seoul, 1981; PhD, UCLA, 1988. Rschr. KRICT, Taejeon, 1981-84; postdoctoral fellow U. Calif., San Diego, 1988-89; staff scientist Caltech, Pasadena, 1989-92; prin. rschr. KRZBB, Taejon, 1992—. Inventor in field. Mem. Am. Chem. Soc., N.Y. Acad. Scis. Home: Hanwood Apt 109-1703, Taejeon 305, Korea Office: KRIBB, 52 uen-dong, Yoosung-ku, Taejeon 305-400, Korea

KWON, CHUL SOO, psychiatrist; b. Seoul, Korea, Sept. 10, 1948; m. Sung Hee Chung, Apr. 6, 1974; 1 child: Soon Jeong (Susan). MD, Seoul Nat. U., Korea, 1974. Diplomate Am. Bd. Psychiatry and Neurology. Intern Washington Hosp. Ctr., 1975-76, res. gen. surgery, 1976-77; res. psychiat. Johns Hopkins Hosp., Baltimore, Md., 1977-80; fellowship behavior sci. Johns Hopkins U., Baltimore, Md., 1977-80, asst. psyc., 1980-86; dir. partial hospitalization program North Charles Genl. Hosp., Baltimore, Md., 1981-88; med. dir. partial hospitalization program Homewood Hosp. Ctr., Baltimore, Md., 1988-91; med. dir. psychiat. partial hospitalization program Union Meml. Hosp., Baltimore, Md., 1991—; physician St. Joseph Med. Ctr., Towson, Md., 1991—, Church Hosp., Balt., 1991-99, Maryland Gen. Hosp., Balt., 1991-98, Taylor Manor, Ellicott City, Md., 1987-98; memt. mem. EHP Group Practice, 1993—; physician JL Kernan Hosp., Balt., 1995—, Sheppard-Enoch Pratt Hosp., 1998—; physician, subinvestigator Ctr. for Behavioral Health, 1999—; instr. psyc., Johns Hopkins U., 1986-96; physician, subinvestigator Ctr. for Behavioral Health, 1999—. Mem. AMA, Am. Neuropsychiat. Assn., Johns Hopkins Med. and Surg. Assn., Md. Psychiat. Soc., Am. Acad. Clin. Psychiatrists, Am. Soc. Clin. Psychopharmacology (cert.), Internat. Psychogeriatric Assn., Korean Am. Med. Assn. Fax: 410-313-9641; 410-554-6603. E-mail: cskwon@jhu.edu. Home: 2908 Chainita Ct Ellicott City MD 21042-7625 Office: Union Meml Hosp Dept Psychiat 201 E University Pkwy Baltimore MD 21218-2829

KWON, E HYOCK, science academy executive; b. Seoul, Korea, July 13, 1923. Grad., Seoul Nat. U. Coll. Medicine, Korea, 1947, Seoul Nat. U. Grad. Sch., Korea, 1951, Seoul Nat. U., 1956; MPH, U. Minn., 1956; PhD, Seoul Nat. U., 1960. Asst. prof., assoc. prof., prof. Seoul Nat. U., Korea, 1956-80, dean Coll. Medicine, 1970-76, dean Sch. Pub. Health, 1976-78; gen. dir. Seoul Nat. U. Hosp., Korea, 1979-80; pres. Seoul Nat. U., 1980-83; min. Ministry Edn., Korea, 1983-85; pres. Korea Nat. U. Edn., 1985-88; min. Ministry Health and Social Affairs, Korea, 1988, Ministry Environ., Korea, 1991-92; chmn. found. Sungkyunkwan U., Korea, 1996—; vis. prof. U. Calif., Sch. Pub. Health, Berkeley, 1969; chmn. Korea Green Cross Corp., 1989-91. Fellow World Acad. Art and Sci.; mem. Nat. Acad. Scis. Korea (pres. 1992-96, 2000—). Office: Nat Academy of Sciences, San-94 Panpodong, Seocho-gu Seoul Republic of Korea*

KWON, HOON, materials scientist, educator; b. Seoul, Aug. 23, 1954; s. Jae-Myung and Jong-Jin Kwon; m. Won-Young Lee, Apr. 24, 1982; children: Ki-Yoon, Soon-Woo. PhD, Korea Adv. Inst. Sci. & Tech., Seoul, 1983. Asst. prof. Kookmin U., Seoul, 1985-89, assoc. prof., 1989-94, prof., 1994—; cons. Korea Inst. Indsl. Tech. Evaluation and Planning, Korea Indsl. Complex; vis. prof. Korea Sci. and Engring. Found., U. Md., 1988. Contbr. papers to sci. jours. Rsch. grantee Korea Sci. and Engring. Found., 1990, 97, Brain Korea 21 grantee Ministry of Edn., 1999. Mem. Korean Inst. Metals and Materials (mem. editl. com. 1997—), Minerals, Metals and Materials Soc. Avocations: tennis, swimming. Fax: 82-2-910-4320. E-mail: hkwon@kmu.kookmin.ac.kr. Home: 2-1007 Daegyo Apt Yuidodong, Seoul 150-010, Korea Office: Kookmin U, 861-1 Jeongneung-Dong, Seoul 136-702, Korea

KWON, JOON TAEK, retired chemistry researcher; b. Kimpo, Kyunggi Do, Republic of Korea, Mar. 10, 1935; came to U.S., 1955; s. Young Tae and Byoung Soon (Kim) K.; m. Moon Ja You, Aug. 15, 1964; children: Howard Albert, Daphne Elsa. BS in Chemistry, U. Ill., 1957; MS in Chemistry, Cornell U., 1959, PhD in Chemistry, 1962; postdoctoral fellow, U. B.C., Vancouver, Can., 1962-64. Instr. II dept. chemistry U. B.C., 1964-65; assoc. rsch. chemist Chemcell Ltd., Edmonton, Alta., Can., 1965-66; rsch. chemist Celanese Corp., Summit, N.J., 1967-70; sr. rsch. chemist Lummus Co., Bloomfield, N.J., 1970-78; prin. rsch. chemist ABB Lummus Global Inc., Bloomfield, N.J., 1978-99. Co-author: Handbook of Chemical Production Process, 1986; contbr. articles to profl. jours. Disting. commr. and mem. Silver Beaver lodge Monmouth council 347 Boy Scouts Am., vigil mem. Order of the Arrow. Indsl. matching grantee Nat. Rsch. Coun., Ottawa, Can., 1966-67. Fellow Am. Inst. Chemists; mem. Royal Soc. Chemistry, Soc. Chem. Industry (N.Am. sect.), Am. Chem. Soc., Korean Chem. Soc. (life, rec. sec. N.Am. 1975-93), Korean Scientists and Engrs. in Am. (pres. N.J. chpt. 1976-77), Catalysis Soc. Met. N.Y.C., U. Ill. Alumni Assn. (life), Cornell U. Alumni Assn. Methodist. Achievements include patent for prodn. process for propylene oxide and 13 other patents in field of organometallic chemistry and process rsch. Home: 142 Derby Dr Freehold NJ 07728-2767

KWON, JUNG-HYE, psychology educator, consultant; b. Taegu, Korea, Mar. 17, 1955; d. Young-Gak Kwon and Nam-Soon Kim; m. Do-Kyoung Kim; children: Kim, Hye-Youn, Kim, Chee-Mann. BA, Seoul (Korea) Nat. U., 1977, MA, 1979; PhD, UCLA, 1990. Lic. psychologist. Intern Seoul Nat. U. Hosp., 1981-83, clin. prof., 1992-95; intern Pacific Clin., Pasadena, Calif., Korea, 1988-89; lectr. Seoul Nat. U., 1991-93; dir. Seoul Inst. Cognitive Therapy, 1993-95; assoc. prof. Korea U., Seoul, 1995—; chief dir. Seoul Inst. Cognitive Therapy, 1995—. Author: Social Phobia: A Cognitive-Behavioral Treatment Mannual, 1998; mem. editl. bd. Korean Jour. Clin. Psychology; contbr. articles to profl. jours. Mem. Korean Psychol. Assoc. (bd. dirs. divsn. clin. psychology 1995—), Am. Psychol. Assoc., Assoc. for Advancement of Behavior Therapy. Office: Korea U, 5-1 Anam-dong Sungbuk-Ku, Seoul 136-701, Korea

KWON, OH BYUNG, information systems researcher, educator; b. Seoul, Rep. of Korea, Aug. 4, 1965; s. Yung Kuk Kwon and Ok Ran Yoon; m. Hee Soo Rim, Mar. 21, 1998; 1 child, Hyuk Jin. BA, Seoul Nat. U., 1988; MS, Korea Advanced Inst. Sci. Tech., Taejon, 1990, PhD, 1995. Rschr. Korea Advanced Inst. Sci. and Tech., 1995-96; prof. Yanbian U. Sci. and Tech., Yanji, China, 1995-96, Handong U., Pohang, Rep. of Korea, 1996—. Contbr. articles to profl. jours. Mem. com. Commerce At Light Speed/Electronic Commerce, Rep. of Korea, 1998, Citizen's Coalition for Econ. Justice, Rep. of Korea, 1998. Mem. Korea Mgmt. Sci. Ops. Rsch. Soc., KASBA. Presbyterian. Avocations: climbing, baduk. Home: Daerim 1st 1510 Duhodong, Pukku Pohang 781-840, Republic of Korea Office: Handong U Sch Mgmt & Econ, Pukku, Pohang KyungBuk 791-940, Republic of Korea

KWON, YOUNG-SAM, mechanical engineer, researcher; b. Seoul, Korea, Apr. 26, 1967; s. Tae-Gaup Kwon and Ok-Soon Park; m. Yun-Hee Chang, Jan. 29, 1994; children: Oh-Hyuk, Oh-Hun. BS, Hanyang U., Seoul, 1989; MS, Pohang (Korea) U. Sci. & Tech., 1991, PhD, 1995. Cert. mech. engrng. Postdoctoral staff Pohang U. Sci. and Tech., 1995-96; sr. rschr. Agy. for Def. Devel., Taejon, Korea, 1996—. Contbr. articles to profl. jours. Mem. Korean Soc. Mech. Engrs. Office: Agy for Def Devel 1st R&D, Yuseong PO Box 35-5, Taejong 305-600, Korea

KWONG, ALVIN LIN-PIK, financial controller; b. Hong Kong, Oct. 28, 1955; s. Heung Ting and Lai Han (Wong) K.; m. Angelica Oi Ming Tang, Apr. 8, 1999. BS, Nat. Taiwan Normal U., 1980; MBA, San Francisco State U., 1991. CPA, CFM, Md., CMA, CISA, CDP, cert. internal auditor; cert. fin. mgmt.; cert. info. systems auditor. Sci. panel chmn., tchr. Christian Faith Coll., Hong Kong, 1980-86; staff acct. Blue Star (N.A.) Ltd., Calif., 1992-93, fin. analyst, 1993-95; staff technician KPMG Peat Marwick LLP, Calif., 1995-96; fin. contr. Satchi Group, Hong Kong, 1996-97, Man Lok Group, Hong Kong, 1998—. Mem. Inst. Mgmt. Accts., Info. Systems Audit and Control Assn., AICPAs, Hong Kong Soc. Accts. (assoc.). Avocations: martial arts, jogging, fishing. Office: 9/F Fo Tan Indsl Ctr, 26-28 Au Pui Wan St, Fo Tan Shatin NT Hong Kong Hong Kong Home: Flat G 18/F Block J, No 52 Tai Chung Kiu Rd, Shatin Hong Kong

KWONG, YOK-LAM, physician, hematologist; b. Hong Kong, Oct. 7, 1958; s. Tong and Ying-Ha (Tse) K. MB, BS, U. Hong Kong, 1983. Intern Queen Mary Hosp., Hong Kong, 1983-84; med. officer Hong Kong Govt., 1984-87; fellow Royal Marsden Hosp., U.K., 1987-89; pathologist Queen Mary Hosp., 1990-92; lectr. dept. medicine U. Hong Kong, 1993-97, prof., 1997—. Fellow Royal Coll. Physicians (Edinburgh); mem. Royal Coll. Physicians (U.K.), Royal Coll. Pathologists (U.K.), N.Y. Acad. Scis., Hong Kong Inst. Sci., Hong Kong Acad. Medicine, Assn. Clin. Cytogeneticists. Office: Queen Mary Hosp Dept Medicine, Pokfulam Rd, Hong Kong Hong Kong

KWUN, OH CHEUN, chemist, educator; b. Mashan, Korea, Dec. 23, 1931; s. Young Jung and Meung Jea (Kim) K.; m. Young Ja Kim, Nov. 14, 1960; children: Hee Jae, Yong Shik. BS in Chemistry, Kyung Pook Nat. U., Taegu, Korea, 1956, MS in Phys. Chemistry, 1958, PhD in Phys. Chemistry, 1968. Asst. prof. chemistry Keunkuk U., Seoul, 1959-61; prof. chemistry Hanyang U., Seoul, 1961-97, prof. emeritus, 1997—; guest prof. Karlsruhe (Germany) U., 1972-73, Frankfurt (Germany) U., 1973-74; rsch. prof. MIT, Cambridge, 1974; dean Coll. Natural Scis. Hanyang U., 1977-79, dir. Inst. Environ. Scis., 1979-86, dir. Ctrl. Libr., 1979-86; advisor Sci. and Tech. Cons. Corp. Korea, 1996. Author: University Chemistry, 1972, Physical Chemistry, 1983 (Paiknam Acad. prize 1985), Experimental Physical Chemistry, 1990, 9 others; translator: Quantum Chemistry, 1986, Physical Chemistry, 1998, 10 others. Dir. Korea Inst. Chem. Culture. Mem. AAAS, Am. Chem. Soc., Korean Chem. Soc. (v.p. 1995-96), N.Y. Acad. Scis., Humboldt Club Korea (pres. 1995-98), IBC (hon.), ABI (hon.). Home: 801-123 Sin Hyundae Apt, Apkujung Dong Kangnam-Ku, Seoul 135-110, Korea Office: Dept Chemistry Hanyang U 17, Haengdang-Dong Seongdong-ku, Seoul 133-791, Republic Korea

KYAW, HLA, systems analyst; b. Yangon, Myanmar, Mar. 1, 1967; s. U. Kyi and Aye Aye Mya. MB, BS, Inst. of Medicine, 1993; internat. diploma in computer studies, NCC, U.K., 1995, internat. higher diploma in computer studies, 1997; diploma in computer sci., U. Computer Studies, Yangon, 1998. House surgeon Def. Svcs. Gen. Hosp., Yangon, Myanmar, 1993-94; computer programmer ACE Data Systems, Yangon, 1995-96, systems analyst, 1996-97, rschr., 1996-97; rschr., web page designer, mem. staff KMD Computer Ctr., Yangon, 1997—; analyst programmer KMD Computer Ctr., 1998—. Home: 14-G YIT Campus, PO Box 727, Yangon Myanmar

KYBAL, ELBA GÓMEZ DEL REY, economist, non-profit organization executive; b. Santa Fe, Argentina, Apr. 1, 1915; came to U.S., 1942; d. J. Ignacio and Concepción (del Rey) Gómez; m. Milic Kybal, July 16, 1950 (dec. July 1977); children: Cynthia, Alexander. BA in Internat. Rels., U. Litoral, Rosario, Argentina, 1940; MA in Econs., Harvard U., 1945, PhD in Econs., 1946. Economist Fed. Res. Bank, N.Y.C., 1946-47; economist, polit. affairs officer UN, N.Y.C., 1947-56, sr. economist; head specialized conf. Orgn. Am. States, Washington, chief L.Am. econ. integration, dir. under secretariat for econ. and social affairs, 1956-80; cons. Argentine Govt., Buenos Aires, 1978. Contbr. articles to profl. jours. Advisor InterAm. com. of women OAS, Washington, 1960-80; vol. cons. Pan Am. Devel. Found., Washington, 1980-82; vol. Argentine, Ecuadorian and Peruvian Found., Washington, 1988-90; pres. Pan Am. Liaison Com. of Women's Orgns., 1995-99; pres. Pan Am. Roundtable, Washington, 1999—; founder CEDA, Washington, 1970; bd. dirs. Gala Hispanic Theatre, Washington, 1997—. Named Vol. of the Yr., Pan Am. Devel. Found., 1981, Bus. and Profl. Women's Club, 1984. Mem. Phi Beta Kappa. Roman Catholic. Avocation: travel. Home: 700 New Hampshire Ave NW Washington DC 20037-2406

KYEONG, MUN GEON, telecommunications researcher; b. Seoul, Nov. 20, 1955; s. Soon Ho and Jung Hee (Seo) K.; m. Soo Jin Kim, Dec. 6, 1986; children: Hyun Chul, Jee Ae. BS, Korea U., 1980, MS, 1985; PhD, Tex. A&M U., 1993. Ind. rschr. Ill. Inst. of Tech., Chgo., 1982-84; asst. mgr. Oriental Precision Co. Rsch. Ctr., Sungnam, Korea, 1985; mem. rsch. staff Electronics and Telecomms. Rsch. Inst., Taejon, Korea, 1985-86, sr. mem. rsch. staff, 1986-95, prin. mem. rsch. staff, 1995—, mgr. of project, 1995—. Editor Internat. Mobile Telecomms.-2000; patentee in field; contbr. papers on smart antennas and mobile telecomm. With Korean Mil. Army, 1976-79. Fellowship Jeong-Soo Scholarship Found., 1974-81, Yook-Young-Soo Meml. Found., 1982-84, ETRI, 1989-93. Mem. IEEE Comms. Soc., Korea Inst. of Telematics and Electronics, Korean Inst. of Comm. Scis. Home: #108-1404 Daerim Doore APT, Shinsong-Dong, Yusong-Gu 305-345, Korea Office: ETRI Radio & Broadcasting Tech Lab, 161 Kajong-Dong Yusong-Gu, Shinsong-Dong Taejon 305-350, Korea

KYHOS, M. GAITHER GALLEHER, private school educator; b. Durham, N.C., Sept. 17, 1955; d. Earl Potter Jr. and Martha Hungerford (Wheelwright) Galleher; m. Thomas Flynn Kyhos, Sept. 4, 1982; children: Jennifer Chalfant, Patrick Flynn, Justin Farleigh. BA in Polit. Sci. cum laude, St. Lawrence U., 1977. Layout and prodn. asst. Nat. Geographic Mag., Washington, 1977-80, illustrations rschr., 1980-82, sr. rschr., 1982-85, sr. rschr./writer, 1985-88, sr. rschr./compiler, 1988-94; asst. tchr., social studies-resource St. Patrick's Episcopal Day Sch., Washington, 1994-97, co-head tchr., 1997—; mem. internat. adv. bd. Sellinger Sch., Loyola Coll. in Md., Balt., 1992-96; presenter in field. Author map supplements for Nat. Geographic Mag. Bd. dirs. Lt. Joseph P. Kennedy Inst., Washington, 1993-95; Vice Presdl. advance person The White House, Washington, in Ivory Coast, 1991, in Estonia, 1992. Mem. Nat. Coun. for Social Studies, Spinal Cord Injury Network, Ednl. Alliance/Nat. Geog. Soc., So. Poverty Law Ctr. Avocations: travel, biking, yoga, reading, golf. Office: St Patrick's Episc Day Sch 4700 Whitehaven Pkwy NW Washington DC 20007-1554

KYI, AUNG SAN SUU, government official; b. Rangoon, Burma, June 19, 1945; d. Gen. Aung San and Daw Khin Kyi; widowed; children: Alexander, Kim. BA in Philosophy/Econs., Oxford U., 1967. Asst. sec., adv. com. on adminstrv. and budgetary questions UN Secretariat, N.Y., 1969-71; rsch. officer Min. of Fgn. Affairs, 1972; sec. gen. Nat. League for Democracy, Myanmar, 1988—; vis. scholar Ctr. for Southeast Asian Studies, Kyoto U., 1985-86; popular polit. leader 1980s-90s, addressing mass rallies in Rangoon; placed under house arrest 1988-95, Rangoon. Author polit. writings. Recipient Rafto Human Rights prize, 1990, Sakharov prize, 1990, Nobel Peace prize, 1991. Buddhist. Office: Nat League for Democracy, No 97/B W Shwegonedine Rd, Bahan Twp Rangoon*

KYIANOV-CHARSKY, SERGEY ALEKSEEVITCH, physicist, educator; b. St. Petersburg, Russia, Sept. 18, 1965; s. Aleksey Sergeevitch Kyianov-Charsky and Valentina Nicholaevna Lasareva. Degree in Physics, U. St. Petersburg, 1988, PhD, 1996. Tchr. Physics Sch., St. Petersburg, 1988-90; lectr. Forestry Acad., St. Petersburg, 1990—. Contbr. articles to profl. jours. Avocations: sports, music, video and audio technics. Home: Nalitchnaya 30 20, 199226 St Petersburg Russia Office: Forestry Acad, Institutskiy per 5, 194018 St Petersburg Russia

KYLE, WILLIAM JOHN, climatologist; b. Ballymoney, N. Ireland, May 26, 1947; s. David and Agnes (Johnston) K.; m. Alida Albertina Breukelman, Feb. 6, 1970; children: Christopher David, Jeremy Trevor, Jennifer Marianne, Emily Alexandra. BS with honors, U. Nottingham, 1969; MS, McMaster U., 1971, PhD, 1974. Grad. teaching asst. McMaster U., Hamilton, Canada, 1969-74; univ. rsch. fellow U. Nottingham, England, 1974-77; prof. U. Hong Kong, 1977—; chmn. internat. organizing com. 2d Internat. Conf. on East Asia and Western Pacific Meteorology and Climate, Hong Kong, 1991-92. Editor-in-chief Hong Kong Meteorol. Soc. Bull., 1991—; editor: Procs. 2d Internat. Conf. on East Asia and Western Pacific Meteorology and Climate, 1993; contbr. articles to profl. jours. Fellow Royal Meteorol. Soc., Hong Kong Meteorol. Soc. (chmn. 1991-95, vice-chmn. 1989-90, 1997—); mem. Internat. Geographical Union Commn. on Climatology (corr.). Avocations: philately, numismatics. Office: U Hong Kong Dept Geography, Pokfulam Rd, Hong Kong China

KYLIN, (JOHAN) HENRIK, environmental science researcher; b. Lund, Sweden, Sept. 21, 1959; s. Anders Olof and Elsa Bertina (Bengtsson) K.; m. Brit Gina Anne-Marie Johansson, Aug. 13, 1988; children: Hanna Linnea, Erik Harald. MSc in Analytical Chemistry, Stockholm U., 1985, PhD in Environ. Chemistry, 1994. Rsch. asst. in environ. chemistry Stockholm U., 1985-89, dir. studies in analytical chemistry, 1989-94; rsch. supr. environ. assessment Swedish U. Agrl. Sci., Uppsala, 1995-98, dep. sect. head, 1995, sr. scientist, 1998, docent environ. assessment, 1999; participant in sci. expeditions to South Pacific Islands, the Arctic, and Antarctic. Author: Airborne lipophilic pollutants in pine needles, 1994; author numerous sci. papers and tech. reports, popular articles and book revs.; several appearances radio and TV. Grantee Swedish Civil Engrs. Environ. Fund, 1996, Swedish Environ. Protection Agy., 1987-94, 99, Swedish Natural Sci. Rsch. Coun., 1996-99, Knuts & Alice Wallenberg Found., 1996, Craford Found., 1997, J. Gust Richert Found., 1993, MISTRA, 1999-00. Mem. Soc. Environ. and Toxicological Chemistry, Swedish Chem. Soc., Internat. Assn. Gt. Lakes Rsch. Avocations: natural history, music, history. Office: Swedish U Agrl Scis Dept Environ Assessment, PO Box 7050, S-75007 Uppsala Sweden

KYLLONEN ROSE, JULIE FRANCES, college program administrator; b. Columbia, Mo., Mar. 18, 1943; d. Toimi Enoch Kyllonen and Frances Aileen Thompson; m. Charles Lincoln Rose, Mar. 17, 1972 (div. 1974). AA in Liberal Arts, Stephens Coll., 1963; AB in Polit. Sci., U. Mo., Columbia, 1965; MS in Fgn. Svc., Georgetown U., 1968. Clk.-typist US Peace Corps, Washington, 1965-67; jr. profl. Fgn. Census Rsch. Br. of U.S. Census Bur., Washington, 1967-68; office mgr. Teknekron Inc., Washington, 1968; archivist Eisenhower Presdl. Libr. Nat. Archives, Washington and Abilene, Kans., 1968-72; dir. admissions ELS Lang. Ctr., Oakland, Calif., 1974-78; program coord. for Sponsored Students Iowa State U., Ames, 1978-88; dir. internat. student affairs Western Ill. U., Macomb, 1988—; cons. Macomb Area Indsl. Devel. Corp., 1989-98; presenter and spk. in field, in U.S. and internationally. Fulbright-Hays fellow U.S. Dept. of Edn., Egypt, 1988, Malone fellow Nat. Coun. U.S.-Arab Rels., Saudi Arabia, 1996; scholar Rotary Internat. Group Study Exch. program, Korea, 1994, scholar NAFSA, China, 1989. Mem. NAFSA: Assn. Internat. Educators (chmn. Mid.-East Spl. Interest Group, Region IV newsletter editor 1991-95, coord. Nigerian Student Concerns 180-85), Soc. for Intercultural Edn., Tng. and Rsch. Internat., Macomb Area C. of C., Altrusa Internat. (bd. dirs. 1993-95), Univ. Women's Club (2d v.p. 1994-96), Delta Kappa Gamma. Avocations: artwear designer, fiber artist, weaver, mysteries. E-mail: J-Rose@wiu.edu. Office: Western Ill U Office Internat Edn One Univ Cir Macomb IL 61455

KYNCL, JOHN JAROSLAV, pharmacologist; b. Prague, Czechoslovakia, Aug. 16, 1936; came to U.S. 1971; s. Jan Petr and Marie (Mikesova) K.; m. Mila Marie Tomaides, Mar. 4, 1961; children: Marketa Kyncl Leisure, John Anthony. PhD, Komensky U., Bratislava, 1963; ScC, Czech. Acad. Sci., 1967. Pharmacologist Rsch. Inst. for Biochemistry & Pharmacy, Prague, 1963-68; A. von. Humboldt fellow U. Heidelberg, Ger., 1968-71; rsch. fellow Cleveland Clinic Found., 1971-72; E. Volwiler rsch. fellow Abbott Labs., North Chicago, Ill., 1972—. Contbr. over 100 articles to profl. jours. Fellow Coun. for High Blood Pressure Rsch. Am. Heart Assn.; mem. Am. Hypertension Soc., Am. Endocrine Soc., Internat. Hypertension Soc. (Paris), FASEB. Achievements include over 20 patents including invention of terazosin (Hytrin) and terlipressin (Glypressin). Home: 800 Green Bay Rd Lake Bluff IL 60044-1829 Office: Abbott Labs Abbott Park Rd North Chicago IL 60064

KYNŠTETR, PETR, federal official; b. Ostrovec, Czech Republic, May 31, 1951; s. František and Zdeňka (Blížková) K.; m. Hana Strašilová, July 7, 1978; children: Veronika, Zuzana. MS in Econs., Sch. Econs., Prague, 1975; PhD, Czech Acad. Scis., Prague, 1978. Scientist Econs. Inst. Czech Acad. Scis., Prague, 1976-83; official office of the chamber of deps. Parliament of the Czech Republic, Prague, 1983-90, sec. gen. office of the chamber of deps., 1990—. Co-author: National-Economic Balance - Instrument of Analysis of Reproduction Process in Czechoslovakia, 1979. Mem. Czech Econs. Soc. Avocations: sports, reading non-fiction. Office: Parliament Czech Rep, 4 Snemovni, 118 26 Prague 1, Czech Republic

KYOMEN, HELEN H., psychiatrist; b. Long Beach, Calif., July 11, 1959; d. Keiso and Yoshie Kyomen. MD, U. So. Calif., 1986; MS, Harvard Sch. Pub. Health, 1993. Diplomate Am. Bd. Psychiatry. Rsch. fellow divsn. on aging Harvard Med. Sch., Boston, 1990-92; asst. psychiatrist McLean Hosp., Belmont, Mass., 1992-95, asst. attending psychiatrist, 1995—. Contbr. articles to profl. jours. John A. Hartford scholar Harvard Med. Sch., 1990-91, fellow in geriatric medicine/psychiatry, 1990-92, fellow in clin. effectiveness, 1991-93. Mem. AMA, Am. Psychiat. Assn., Am. Assn. Geriatric Psychiatry, Am. Geriatrics Soc. (postdoctoral fellow 1992-94; New Investigator award 1997, Pres. Poster award 1997), Assn. Rsch. in Nervous and Mental Disease, N.Y. Acad. Scis. Avocations: guitar, singing, painting, sketching, ballroom dancing. Office: McLean Hosp 115 Mill St Belmont MA 02478-1048

KYONG, SANG-HYON, educator; b. Seoul, Korea, July 24, 1937; s. Jai-Sung and Wol-Sung Kyong; m. Yo-Won Park, June 5, 1965; children: Yunmee, Yuntai. BS, U. R.I., 1961; PhD, MIT, 1966. Mem. tech. staff Bell Tel. Labs., Holmdel, N.J., 1966-75; dept. head, divsn. dir., v.p. Electronics and Telecom. Rsch. Inst., Daejon, Korea, 1975-82; pres. Electronics and Telecom. Rsch. Inst., Daejon, 1984-92; exec. v.p. Korea Telecom, Seoul, 1982-84; pres. Nat. Computerization Agy., Seoul, 1992-93; vice min. Ministry Comm., Seoul, 1993-94; min. Ministry Info. and Comm., Seoul, 1994-95; prof. Korea Advanced Inst. Sci. and Tech., Seoul, 1996—; chmn. bd. govs. Electronics and Telecom. Rsch. Inst., Daejon, 1998-99; mem. Presdl. Coun. on Sci. and Tech., Seoul, 1998-99. Contbr. articles to IEEE Transaction on Automatic Control, Bell Sys. Tech. Jour., Procs. Internat. Switching Symposium, ITU World Telecom. Forum. Mem. Presdl. Coun. on Peaceful Reunification, Seoul, 1998—; bd. dirs. Internet Corp. for Assigned Names and Numbers, 2000—. Pvt. Korean Army, 1958-59. Recipient Civilian Order of Merit Moran, Govt. of the Republic of Korea, Seoul, 1986, Sci. and Tech. prize Ho-Am. Found., Seoul, 1990, Pub. Svc. Order of Merit Chongjo, Govt. of the Republic of Korea, Seoul, 1996, Grand prize Korea Inst. Comm. Scis., Seoul, 1996. Mem. IEEE, Internat. Coun. for Computer Comm. (gov., v.p. chmn. Asian com. 1989-93), Korea Nat. Acad. Engring. (chmn. internat. activities com. 1995—), Korea Engrs. Club. E-mail: shkyong@kgsm.kaist.ac.kr. Fax: 82-342-705-3377. Home: Emae Chon Apt 602-1805, Bundang 463-060, Republic of Korea Office: Korea Advanced Inst Sci, Chongryangri Dongdaemun, Seoul 130-012, Republic of Korea

KYOTANI, YOSHIHIRO, railway executive; b. Fukuyama, Hiroshima, Japan, Jan. 24, 1926; s. Moichi and Yoshie Kyotani; m. Utako, May 12, 1949; children: Hisako, Shigeru, Yuko. BE, Kyoto (Japan) U., 1948. Engr. Japanese Nat. Rys., Kobe, 1948-59; asst. rolling stock dept. Japanese Nat. Rys., Tokyo, 1962-66; chief train operation operating divsn. Japanese Nat. Rys., Takasaki, 1966-68; dep. dir. dept. tech. devel. Japanese Nat. Rys., Tokyo, 1968-76, dir., 1976-83, advisor, 1983-87; pres. TECHNOVA, Tokyo, 1987-89, chmn., 1989-95; pres. ATTECH, Tokyo, 1995—; bd. dirs. Japan Hainan Pacific Petrochem. Group, Ltd.; asst. ry. adminstr. Ministry of Transport, Tokyo, 1959-61, advisor, 1970-81; instr. Kyoto U., 1975-78; advisor Sci. and Tech. Agy., Tokyo, 1980-92, Meitec Co., 1984-91, Otsuka Electronics Co., Ltd., 1985-93, Japan Cen. Ry. Co., 1988-97, Seattle Colls. East-Asia Network, 1999—; dir. Japan Ship and Ocean Found., 1987-99, Agro-Create 21 Found., 1999—; guest prof. Zhejiang U., 1997—. Author: Foundation Design of Machine, 1955; Ultra-High Speed Shinkansen, 1971, Linear Motor Car, 1990; contbr. articles to profl. jours. Councilor Gakushikai, 1993—. Recipient Achievement prize Japanese Nat. Rys., 1973, Minister's prize Sci. and Tech. Agy., 1981, Minister's prize Transp., 1989, Medal with purple ribbon, 1988, awards World Congress Superconductivity, 1990, award Washington Sci. Acad., 1991, Superconductivity award for Excellence, 1991, 3d Orders Sacred Treasure, 1998. Mem. Inst. Elec. Engrs. Japan, Cryogenic Assn. Japan (dir. 1972-88, councilor 1988—), Japan Macro-Engrs. Soc. (vice chmn. 1985-99), Ry. Mechatronics Assn. (dir. 1994—). Buddhist. Home: 3-16-2 409 Masago Mihama-ku, Chiba-shi 260-0011, Japan Office: AATECH Inc, 3rd Fl Kagawa Bldg 1-5-17 Yaesu, Chuo-ku Tokyo 103-0028, Japan

KYPR, JAROSLAV, biophysicist, molecular biologist, researcher; b. Brno, Czech Republic, Dec. 6, 1952; s. Jaroslav and Eva (Konečná) K. Student, Masaryk U., Brno, 1976; PhD, Acad. Scis., Brno, 1983. Postdoctoral fellow Czech Acad. Scis., Brno, 1978-83, head lab. Inst. Biophysics, 1989—; mem. sci. coun. Acad. Scis. Czech Republic, Brno, 1994—. Contbr. articles to profl. publs. Fogarty fellow NIH, 1993-95; rsch. grantee Grant Agy. Czech Republic. Avocations: science, hiking, sports, literature, history. Home: Ramešova 5, 61200 Brno Czech Republic Office: Inst Biophys Czech Acad Sci, Královopolská 135, CZ-61265 Brno Czech Republic

KYPRIANOU, SPYROS, government official; b. Limassol, Cyprus, Oct. 28, 1932; s. Achilleas and Maria (Araouzou) K.; m. Mimi Papatheoklitou, Apr. 25, 1935; children: Achilleas, Marcos. Student higher edn., econs. and commerce, City of London Coll., 1950-51; student, Gray's Inn, London, 1950-54, diploma in comparative law. Barrister; sec. to Archbishop Makarios, London, 1952-54; sec. Cyprus Ethnarchy, London, 1954-56, 57-59; rep. Cyprus Ethnarchy, N.Y.C., 1956-57; pres., House of Reps. Governmnet of Cyprus, Nicosia; minister of justice, 1960; minister of fgn. affairs, 1960-72; individual practice law, 1972-76; participant peace meetings and govtl. formation meetings, 1974-76; founder Democratic Party of Cyprus, 1976, now pres.; mem. Ho. of Reps., 1976—, pres., 1976-77, 96—; pres. Republic of Cyprus, 1977-88; participant Com. Ministers of Council of Europe, Strasburg and Paris, pres. Apr.-Dec. 1967; participant numerous internat. confs. Decorated grand cross Order George I Greece; grand cross Fed. Republic Germany; grand star Republic UAR; grand cross Order of Boyaca (Colombia); grand cross Order of Merit (Chile); Order St. Aekaterini Sinai (eccles.); Grand Silver Cross of Austria, Star of Socialist Republic of Romania; Highest medal of Syria; Order of White Lion 1st class (Czechoslovakia); Gt. Star of Friendship of Peoples (E. Ger.); Highest Hon. Distinction of Yugoslavia; Ojaswi Rajanya Nepal Order; Grand Cross of Holy Sepulchre; Order Stara Planina with ribbon (Bulgaria); Highest Honor of Hungary, 1981; Grand Cross Order of Savior (Greece), 1983; Highest Decoration of Cuba, 1987, Collar of Order of Isabel la Catolica, 1987. Avocations: literature, music, sports. Address: Anexartisias/Antistaseos 1, Engomi Nicosia Cyprus*

KYRIAKIDES, CONSTANTINOS HEROD, pharmacist, marketing professional; b. Nicosia, Cyprus, Aug. 17, 1931; s. Herodotus Constantinos and Persephoni Loizoidi (Christofides) K.; m. Thelma Michaeloudes, Feb. 5, 1965; 2 children. Degree in pharmacy, Nicosia, Cyprus, 1955; degree in podiagry, London, 1956; degree in optics, Cologne, Ger., 1958; degree in marketing, Cyprus, 1981, Eng., 1989. Pharmacist Nicosia, Cyprus, 1955-60; mr. dir. comml. enterprises family bus., 1960-63; optician London, 1963-64; dir. family orgn. Nicosia, 1965-74; dir. family assoc. bus. London, 1974-75; bd. dirs. various cos., Cyprus; mem. senate bd. edn. tertiary level colls., 1980—. Contbr. numerous articles to profl. jours. Fellow Brit. Dispensery Opticians, Contact Lens Practitioners (London); mem. Pharm. Soc., Cyprus Inst. Mktg., Brit. Contact Lens Assn. Avocations: classical music, chess, swimming. Office: 256 Ledra St PO Box 1931, Nicosia 1515, Cyprus

KYRIAKOU, THEODORE, media company executive; b. Athens, Feb. 10, 1974; s. Theodore and Anna (Tehlemtzi) K. BSBA cum laude, Georgetown U., 1995. Exec. v.p. Antenna TV, Greece, 1995-98, exec. v.p., COO, 1998—, also bd. dirs., mng. dir., 2000—. Recipient Troedo medal Georgetown U., 1995. Avocations: skiing, scuba diving. Office: Antenna TV, 10-12 Kifisias Ave, 151-25 Athens Greece

KYRTATAS, DIMITRIS, historian; b. Athens, Sept. 22, 1952; s. John and Dora (Lambropoulos) K.; m. Katia Malachtari, Jan. 3, 1985; children: Kleopatra, Theodora. First degree, U. Thessaloniki, 1976; postgrad., London Sch. of Econs., 1976-77; PhD, Brunel U., 1983. Postdoctoral rschr. King's Coll., U.K., 1983-84; rschr. Acad. of Athens, Greece, 1985-90; asst. prof. U. Crete, Greece, 1990-95, assoc. prof., 1995—. Author: The Social Structure of the Early Christian Communities, 1987; contbr. articles to profl. jours. Pvt. Greek Army, 1981-83. Recipient Award Am. Legion Sch., 1971. Mem. Inst. of Classical Studies. Home: Dimokratias 34, 74100 Rethymno Greece Office: U Crete, Dept History/Archaeology, 74100 Rethymno Greece

KYU, ISU See CHIU, YISHU

KYU-MOON, KIM, orthodontist; b. Mokpo City, Korea, Jan. 14, 1938; s. Won-Chun and Yang-Lim (Chang) Kim; m. Chae Kwang-Ja; children: Young Suck, Soo-Kyung, Myoung-Sun. DDS, Seoul Nat. U., 1963; MSD, S.N.U., 1965, PhD, 1971. Clin. prof. S.N.U., Seoul, 1971-88; prof. Kyung Hee U., Seoul, 1991-94; v.p. Acad. of AAFOT, 1991-94; pres. Acad. of Korean Oral Pathology, 1993-95; corp. supr. Korean Dental Assn., 1995-2000; pres. Internat. Coll. of Dentist, 1998—. Author: Dental Management, 1987, Dental Emergency, Vol. I, 1991, Vol. II, 1994, Illustration of Orthodontic Dictionary, 2000. Lt. Korean Navy, 1965-68. Fellow Internat. Coll. Dentists; mem. Korean Dental Assn., Korean Mgmt. and Info. Coun., Korean Ortho-Rsch. Inst., Internat. Tweed Orthodontic Found., Acad. of Korean Orthodontics. E-mail: qmoon@netsgo.com. Home: 218-2 Poidong Kangnam ku, Seoul Republic of Korea Office: 98 Inhyun dong 1 Ka, Chung Ku, Seoul 100-281, Republic of Korea

KYUNG, KYU HANG, food microbiology educator; b. Kimpo, Kyonggi, Republic of Korea, Dec. 1, 1949; s. Sock Hyon and Kang Hae (Lee) K.; m. Jae Pong Chi, Feb. 9, 1979; children: Angela, Ho-Youn, Ji-Youn. BA, Dongguk U., Seoul, 1976; MS, Mich. State U., 1978, PhD, 1983. Grad. fellow Mich. State U., East Lansing, 1981; asst. prof. microbiology Sejong U., Seoul, 1983-88, assoc. prof., 1988-94, prof., 1994—; vis. scientist N.C. State U., Raleigh, 1992-93. Editor: Korean Jour. Food Sci. and Tech., 1990. With Korean Navy, 1969-72. Recipient Outstanding Rsch. Achievement award, The Korean Federation of Sci. and Tech. Soc., 1999. Mem. Inst. Food Technologists (profl.), Am. Soc. for Microbiology. Achievements include identification of antimicrobial compounds in both fresh and heated cabbage; isolation of bacteria resistant to antibacterial activity of garlic. Avocation: hiking. Home: Karak-Dong, 1-1007 Samhwan Apt, Seoul Republic of Korea Office: Sejong U, Kwangjin-ku, Seoul Republic of Korea

LAABS, RAINER, archivist, art historian; b. Berlin, Oct. 1, 1955; s. Guenter Pieter and Brigitte (Schloesser) L.; m. Gabriele Elisabeth Carl, Oct.2, 1980; children: Katharina, Friederike, Ulrich. MA, Freie Univ., Berlin, 1984. Asst. Axel Springer Pub. Group, Berlin, 1984-87, head media archive, 1987—. Author: Nicht nur fuer den Tag—Four Centuries of Newspaper in Art, 1987, 90, Das Brandenburger Tor-Focus of German History, 1990; co-author: Checkpoint Charlie and the Berlin Wall, 1997. Decorated knight of justice Order of St. John. Mem. Berliner Bibliophilen Abend (chmn. 1997—), Deutsche Gesellschaft fuer Medaillenkunst (advisor 1994-98). Lutheran. Avocations: bibliophily, art medals, music. Home: Prinzregentenstr 92, 10717 Berlin Germany

LAANANEN, DAVID HORTON, mechanical engineer, educator; b. Winchester, Mass., Nov. 11, 1942; s. Joseph and Helen Katherine (Horton) L.; m. Mary Ellen Storck, Sept. 9, 1967 (div. 1981); children: Gregg David, Robin Kaye; m. Delores Ann Talbert, May 21, 1988. BS in Mech. Engring., Worcester Poly. Inst., 1964; MS, Northeastern U., 1965, PhD, 1968. Project engr. Dynamic Sci., Phoenix, 1972-74; asst. prof. Pa. State U., State College, 1974-78; mgr. R&D Simula Inc., Phoenix, 1978-83; assoc. prof. Ariz. State U., Tempe, 1983-97, prof., 1997—, dir. aerospace rsch. ctr., 1992-93, dir. Airworthiness Assurance Ctr. of Excellence, 1997—. Referee: Jour. Aircraft, Jour. Mech. Design; contbr. articles to Jour. Aircraft, Jour. Am. Helicopter Soc., Jour. Safety Rsch., Jour. Thermoplastic Composite Materials, Composites Sci. and Tech. Fellow AIAA (assoc.; design engring. tech. com.); mem. ASME, Am. Helicopter Soc., Sigma Xi, Sigma Gamma Tau, Pi Tau Sigma. Democrat. Achievements include research in aircraft crash survivability, composite structures. Office: Ariz State U Dept Mech Aerospace En Tempe AZ 85287

LÄÄNEMETS, URVE, educational analyst, researcher; b. Liiva, Saaremaa, Estonia, July 24, 1947; d. Leopold and Alla (Kommel) Kaljo; m. Ivo Läänemets, July 26, 1969; children: Kaia, Irja. BA, MA in English, Tartu U., Estonia, 1970; cert., In-Svc. Tchr. Tng. Inst., Estonia, 1974; BA, MA in German, Tartu U., Estonia, 1979; PhD, Acad. of Pedagogical Scis., Moscow, 1989; in-svc. training, U. London, 1994-95. Cert. speech therapist. Tchr. English Tallinn Secondary School no. 47, 1970-71; tchr. English and Russian Tornimäe Class Sch., 1971-73; tchr. English and German Orissaare Secondary Sch., 1973-80; specialist Estonian In-Svc. Tchr. Tng. Ctr., 1980-84; rsch. assoc. Estonian Inst. for Pedagogical Rsch., Tallinn, Estonia, 1984-89; dep. dir. Estonian Edn. Ctr., Tallinn, Estonia, 1989-93; asst. prof. didactics Tallinn Pedagogical U., 1993-96; lectr. U. London, 1994-95; head of group Estonian Lang. Strategy Project, 1996-97; tchr. English and German Tallinn Nômme Upper Secondary Sch., 1997—; councillor, curriculum cons. Dept. of Edn., Tallinn, 1998—; part-time tchr. English and German, Tallinn Sch. of Langs., 1980-86, Tallinn Conservatory, 1986-93; part-time speech therapist Orissaare Sch. for SEN children, 1973-77; chmn. Rep. commn. of teaching German, Tallinn, 1982-89; chmn. of commn. of teaching English, Tallinn, 1984—; mem. project group Coun. Graz, Austria, 1993-96; freelance cons. Estonia, 1994—; mem. Bd. Students Rsch. Soc., 1980-87; sr. rsch. assoc. Estonian Acad. of Scis., 1992-95; mem. project group 13B of Coun. of Europe, 1993-96. Author: (monography) Development of the Content and Curricula in Estonia, 1995; author, co-author 18 textbooks for English periodical Smile, 1991-94; contbr. articles to profl. jours. Mem., cons. Jaan Tonisson Inst. of Human Rights, Tallinn, 1995—; expert in ednl. policy, Tallinn, 1992—. Grantee Acad. of Scis., Tallinn, Estonia, 1992-95, Swedish Acad. of Scis., Uppsala, 1994. Mem. European Ednl. Rsch. Assn., Estonian Acad. Ednl. Soc., Alumni Assn. U. London. Avocations: traveling, gardening, history, classical music, handicrafts. Home: 37 Päikese St, 10912 Tallinn Estonia Office: Dept Edn, 10 Vabaduse väljak, 10146 Tallinn Estonia

LAARI, JOUNI SEPPO, career officer, researcher; b. Lappeenranta, Finland, Dec. 30, 1961; s. Jukka Seppo and Eine Sisko (Leino) L.; m. Tarja Paivikki Makkonen, June 13, 1992; children: Karoliina, Eveliina. Grad., Finnish Officer Cadet Sch., Helsinki, 1985, Inf. Fighting Sch., Tuusula, Finland, 1990, Finnish Mil. Acad., Helsinki, 1995. Commd. officer Finnish Army, 1985, advanced through grades to maj., 1995; officer cadet Officer Cadet Sch., Helsinki, 1982-85; field officer Armoured Brigade, Hameenlinna, Finland, 1985-89; bn. comdg. officer Inf. Fighting Sch., Tuusula, Finland, 1989-90; staff officer Armoured Brigade, Hameenlinna, Finland, 1990-93; gen. staff officer Mil. Acad., Helsinki, 1993-95; G3 Armoured Brigade, Hameenlinna, 1995-97; gen. staff officer Finnish Def. Staff, Helsinki, 1997—; project officer Finnish Helicopter Program, Helsinki, 1998—. Author: Air Mechanization, 1997; contbr. articles to profl. jours. Mem. Finnish Mil. Sci. Soc. (bd. dirs. 1999—), Helicopter Assn. Internat., Army Aviation Assn. Am. Avocations: political and military history, manoeuvre theory, bibliography, helicopters, strategy and operational art. Home: Jarrumiehentie 6, 13210 Hameenlinna 8, Finland Office: Army Aviation Divsn, PO Box 919, 00131 Helsinki Finland

LABAKI, SALIM E., scheduling and cost control engineer; b. Dahr El Sawan, El Metn, Lebanon, July 11, 1961; arrived in Saudi Arabia, 1993.; s. Emile S. Labaki and Layla Milan; m. Alia Haddad, Feb. 14, 1998. BSCE, George Washington U., 1984. Cert. in engring. Planning and design mgr. Lahoud Group, Baabdath, Lebanon, 1985-90; mgr. scheduling and cost control, Baan ERP team leader Nesma Alfadl Cont. Co., Ltd., Al Khobar, Saudi Arabia, 1991—; cons. Nesma Alfadl Cont. Co., Ltd., Al Khobar. E-mail: slabaki@nesma-alfadl.ac. Fax: 966 3 864 3121. Office: Nesma Alfadl Cont Co Ltd, Prince Majid St Box 1498, Al Khobar Saudi Arabia

LABANA, RAVINDER SINGH, physician, consultant; b. Nangli, Punjab, India, Nov. 11, 1956; s. Gurcharan Singh Multani and Swaran K. Kaur; m. Paramjit Kaur Pammi, Aug. 5, 1984; 1 child, Polka. BS, Dayanand Anglovedic, Jalandhar, India, 1976; MBBS, Med. Coll., Jammu, India, 1976; MD, Med. Coll. Amritsar, India, 1989. Med. Diplomate. I.c. Rural Hosp. Govt., Punjab, India, 1983-85, Primary Health Ctr. Hosp., Hoshiarpur, Punjab, 1985-97; med. officer Govt. Coll. Amritsar, Punjab, 1990; pvt. practice, 1990—. Recipient Gold Medal Eye Meml. Soc., 1982. Mem. N.Y. Acad Scis., Diabetic Soc. Am., Parkinson's Soc. London. Sikh. Avocations: reading, gardening. Home: 151 Sahib Zada Ajit Singh, Garden Colony, 144003 Jalandhar Punjab, India Office: near bus stand, Hoshiarpur India

LA BARRE, STEPHANE CHRISTIAN, research scientist; b. Kisantu, Madimba, Congo, Nov. 3, 1949; s. Claude Edmond La Barreand Yvonne Marie Richir; m. Héléna Versavel, Dec. 30, 1994. BSc, U. NSW, Sydney,

Australia, 1974; MSc, U. Auckland, New Zealand, 1979; PhD, James Cook U. North Queensland, Townsville, Australia, 1984. Cert. marine biologist and marine chemist. Rsch. scientist Ctr. Nat. Rsch. Sci., Noumea, New Caledonia, 1984-90; post-doctoral staff U. Calif., San Diego, 1991, Scripp's Instn. Oceanography, LaJolla, Calif., 1992; rsch. scientist Ctr. Nat. Rsch. Sci., Paris, 1993—. Contbr. articles to profl. jours. Avocations: classical guitar, scuba diving, trekking.

LABARTHE, NORMA VOLLMER, science educator; b. Rio de Janeiro, May 1, 1952; d. Ramon Gomes-Leite and Maria Helena (Vollmer) L. DVM, U. Fed. Fluminense, Niteroi, Brazil, 1976; MS, U. Federal do Rio Grande do Sul, Porto Alegre, Brazil, 1981; DSc, Fundacao Oswaldo Cruz., Rio de Janeiro, 1997. Cert. vet. dr. Asst. prof. U. Fed. Fluminense, Niteroi, 1978—; dir. Policlinica Veterinaria, Niteroi, 1998-99. Mem. Associacao Patronal de Clinicos Veterinarios (hon.), Anclivepa, Am. Heartworm Soc. Roman Catholic. Avocations: swimming, horseback riding, animal-human relationship, animal welfare. Office: U Fed Fluminense, 64 Vital Brazil St, 24230340 Niteroi Brazil

LABASTIDA OCHOA, FRANCISCO, government official; b. Los Mochis, Mexico, Aug. 14, 1942; married; 4 children. BA in Econs., UNAM, 1964; MA. Chief Office Transports, 1966-67, Dept. social Welfare, 1968-72; sub-dir. Pub. Investments, 1972-75; dir. gen. Fiscal Promotion, 1976-79; under-sec., sec. Dept. Fin. & Pub. Credir, 1979-82; sec. Dept. Energy, mines & Parastatal Industry, 1982-86; ambassador for Mex., Portugal, 1993-94; sec. Agrl., Livestock & Rural Affairs, 1998—, Dept. of the Interior; mem. & presidential candidate PRI party, Mexico City; prof., coord. projects, dir. gen. IEPES, 1975-76. Office: c/o Dulce Maria Sauri Riancho, Insurgentes Norte No 59 Bldg 2 fl 1, 06359 Mexico DF Mexico*

LABE, ROBERT BRIAN, lawyer; b. Detroit, Sept. 2, 1959; s. Benjamin Mitchell and Gloria Florence (Wright) L.; m. Mary Lou Budman, Nov. 12, 1989; two children: Bridget and Katherine. BA with high honors, Mich. State U., 1981; JD, Wayne State U., 1984; LLM, Boston U., 1985. Bar: Mich. 1984, U.S. Dist. Ct. Mich. 1985, U.S. Tax Ct. 1985. Assoc. Weingarden & Hauer, P.C., Bingham Farms, Mich., 1988-92, shareholder, 1992-94; prin. Robert B. Labe, P.C., Southfield, Mich., 1994—; adj. prof. taxation and estate planning Walsh Coll., Troy, Mich., 1990-92; lectr. and presenter in field. Author: Research Edge-Taxation Guide, 1994, Bus. Succession Planning, 1996, Family Limited Liability Cos. and Limited Partnerships, 1998; mem. publ. adv. bd. Inst. Continuing Legal Edn. U. Mich., 1993—; contbr. articles to profl. jours. Bd. dirs. Oakland Bar Adams Pratt Found. Avocations: tennis, spectator sports. Office: Robert B Labe P C 2000 Town Ctr Ste 1780 Southfield MI 48075-1254

LABENDZ, DANIEL, physicist; b. Unterseen, Switzerland, Oct. 16, 1969; arrived in Germany, 1972; s. Gerhard-Otto and Maria (Küpper) L. Diploma in physics, U. Göttingen, Germany, 1996, PhD, 1999. Physicist Inst. Geophysics, Göttingen, 1998—. With German mil., 1989-90. Mem. AGU. Home: Zimmermannstr 621004, 37075 Gottingen Germany Office: Inst Geophysics, Herzberger LaudstroBe 180, 37075 Gottingen Germany

LABENSKY, SARAH ROSS, culinary educator; b. Murray, Ky., Mar. 16, 1958; d. James Mason and Lucille Thomson Ross; m. Steven Jay Labensky, Oct. 14, 1983 (div. May 1995); m. Louis David Moline, Sept. 3, 1995. BS, Murray (Ky.) State U., 1980; JD, Vanderbilt U., 1983; cert., Scottsdale C.C., 1986. Atty. Hocker and Axford, Tempe, Ariz., 1983-85; cook/chef Phoenix, 1985-90; prof. Scottsdale C.C., 1990-98; dir. Miss. U. for Women Culinary Arts Inst., Columbus, 1998—; cons. Viking Culinary Arts Ctr., Greenwood, Miss., 1998—. Author: On Cooking, 1995, 2d edit., 1999 (IACP nominee 1995), Webster's N.W. Dictionary of Culinary Arts, 1997, 2d edit., 2000, Applied Math for Food Service, 1998. Mem. Am. Culinary Fedn., Internat. Assn. of Culinary Profls. (bd. dirs. 1999—, cert. culinary profl.). E-mail: slabensk@muw.edu. Office: Miss Univ for Women Box W-1639 Columbus MS 39701

LABENZ-HOUGH, MARLENE, dispute resolution professional; b. St. Edward, Nebr., May 25, 1954; d. Ralph Labenz and Lorene (Laudenklos); m. Jeff Hough, Mar. 5, 1983. Assocs., Platte Coll., 1974; BS in Social Work magna cum laude, U. Nebr., 1976; MA in Clin. Psychology, Trinity U., 1980. Adminstrv. asst., mgmt. analyst II City of San Antonio Dept. Human Resources and Svcs., 1980, adminstrv. asst. II, 1980-82, casework supr., 1982-89, program coord., 1989-90; asst. dir. Bexar County Dispute Resolution Ctr., San Antonio, 1990-92, dir., 1992—. Bd. dirs. KidShare, 1993-96, YWCA, 1990-93; mem. ADR sect. coun. State Bar Tex., 1996-99. Mem. Coll. Tex. Mediators, Tex. Assn. Mediators (chair conf. 1999, bd. dirs. 1999—), Acad. Family Mediators, Soc. Profls. in Dispute Resolution (co-chair S.W. region chpt. 1993; Profl. Dedication award 1994; co-chair nat. conf. 1995), Nat. Assn. Cmty. Mediation (founding dir.), Conflict Resolution and Peer Mediation Coun., Tex. Mediation Trainers' Roundtable, Tex. Dispute Resolution Ctrs. Dirs. Coun., Alamo Area Mediators Assn., Alpha Xi Delta. Home: 2518 Ashton Village Dr San Antonio TX 78248-2200

LABERRIGUE-FROLOW, JEANNE, physicist, researcher; b. Paris, June 4, 1925; d. Vladimiz and Anne (Gretchanovski) Frolow; m. André Pierre Laberrigue, July 29, 1947 (div. Feb. 1984); children: Anne, Nathalie. DSc in Physics, U. Paris, 1955. Stagian to dir. rsch. Ctr. Nat. de la Rsch. Sci., France, 1947-93; dir. rsch. emerik Ctr. Nat. de la Rsch. Sci.; cons. Commissauat a l'energie atonique, France, 1964-80. Author: LaPhysique des Particules Elementaires, 1990; contbr. articles to profl. jours. Home: 160 Eaux Vives, 91120 Palaiseau Essonne, France Office: LPNHE U P et M Curie, 4 pl Jussiau T 33 r d c, 75252 Paris France

LABES, GABRIELE MARINA, molecular biologist, researcher; b. Bielefeld, Germany, Feb. 19, 1960; d. Bruno Ernst and Elisabeth Elfriede (Schulz) L. Diploma, U. Bielefeld, Germany, 1987, PhD, 1993. Mem. sci. staff U. Bielefeld, 1987-92; rschr. John Innes Inst., Norwich, Eng., 1992; mem. sci. staff Ctr. Agr. and Land Use Sys., Muencheberg, Germany, 1993-96; asst. head. Ministry Environment, Nature Conservation and Nuclear Safety, Govt. of Germany, Bonn, 1998-00; mem. sci. staff Flad & Flad Innovation Mktg. Comm. GhbH, Eckental, Germany, 2000—; tchr. pvt. sch., Bielefeld, 1988; lectr. Buero für Umwelt-Paedagogik, Rostock, Germany, 1997; presenter Citizens Make Programme, 1992. Contbr. articles to profl. jours. including Plasmid, Nucleic Acid Rsch., Jour. Bacteriology, Environ. Microbiology, others. Fellow European Molecular Biology Orgn., 1992. Mem. Bundesverband Boden. Avocations: photography, music. Office: Flad & Flad Innovation Mktg, Comm GmbH, Postfach 1161, D-90538 Eckental Germany

LABOON, LAWRENCE JOSEPH, personnel consultant; b. St. Louis, Aug. 4, 1938; s. Joseph Warren and Ruth (Aab) LaB.; children: Lindsey Beth, Allison Ruth; m. Glynys M. Brown, Sept. 16, 1989; children: Lawrence Bradley, Meredith Ashley. BS magna cum laude, Tex. Wesleyan U., 1962. Cert. pers. cons., 1968. Operating mgr. Firestone Tire & Rubber Co., Akron, Ohio, 1962-66; pres., CEO, Met. Pers., Inc., Phila., 1966—, chmn., 2000—; pres. Metro Tech, Valley Forge, Pa., 1977—, Metro Temps, Valley Forge, 1978—, Transport Tng. Corp., Valley Forge, 1993—; dir. Alpha-Indian Rock Savs. and Loan Assn., chmn. compensation com., 1986-90; chmn. pvt. employment agy. adv. coun. Pa. Dept. Labor and Industry, 1973-82; guest lectr. Drexel U., 1976-91; human resources del. to USSR, Citizen Amb. Program, 1991. Mem. People to People Internat. Mission, Vietnam, Asia, 1993. With USAF, 1954-60. Mem. Nat. Employment Assn. (cert., state certification bd. chmn. 1969-71, bd. dirs. 1972-74, chmn. bd. regents 1973), Pa. Assn. Pers. Svcs. (pres. 1971-72, Blanchet Meml. award 1973), Nat. Assn. Pers. Cons., Am. Soc. Pers. Adminstrn., Mid-Atlantic Assn. Temporary Svcs. (pres. 1983-84), TEMPNET (bd. dirs. 1986-88), Nat. Assn. Profl. Employers, Exec. Riders Ltd. (pres. 1986-88), Glenhardie Condominium Assn. (non-resident exec. bd. 1989-91), Alpha Chi. Republican. Methodist. Home: 255 Country Ln Phoenixville PA 19460-1708 Office: 1260 Valley Forge Rd Valley Forge PA 19482-0641

LABORIE, JEAN-LOUIS, marketing executive; b. Pamiers, France, Nov. 8, 1938; s. Louis and Marie (Lasserre) L.; m. Christiane Appert, Sept. 12, 1963; children: Philippe, Sophie, Anne-Cecile, Lise, Juliette. Grad., Ecole Centrale de Paris, 1963. Exec., dir. svc. SEMA, France; dir. opn., mng. dir., bd. dirs. SOFRES, France, 1972-87; dir. mktg., bd. cons. Eurocom Group, France, 1987-90; pres., CEO The Media Partnership Rsch., Issy les Moulineaux, France, 1991-99; v.p. Optimum Media Direction, Paris, 1999—; chmn. instr. d'Etudes Publs., Paris, 1979-86; pres., bd. dirs. European Soc. for Opinion and Mktg. Rsch., Amsterdam, 1989-91. Bd. dirs. Found. Information/Amsterdam. Office: OMD Europe, 15 Rue Pasquier, 75008 Paris France

LABRECQUE, JOHN JOSEPH, scientist, researcher; b. Troy, N.Y., Dec. 1, 1948; arrived in Venezuela, 1975; s. Arthur Joseph and Mary Marget (Dujack) LaB.; m. Maria A. Diaz Aponte, Aug. 11, 1976; 1 child, Stephanie. BA, U. Conn., Storrs, 1969; MS, Rensselear Poly. Inst., Troy, N.Y., 1971, PhD, 1975. Scientist N.Y. Dept. Health, Albany, 1974-75; rsch. scientist Inst. Venezolano Investigaciones Cientificas, Caracas, Venezuela, 1975—; chemist Internat. Atomic Energy Agy., Viena, Austria, 1986-87; cons. expert sect. IAEA, Viena, 1984-89. Contbr. numerous articles to profl. jours. Conicit grantee, Caracas, 1977—. Mem. AAAS, Am. Chem. Soc., Assn. Geoscientists in Internat. Devel., Soc. Applied Spectroscopy, Assn. Venezolana Para Avance La Ciencia, N.Y. Acad. Scis., Monteclaro Country Club, Sigma Xi, Phi Lambda Upsilon. Roman Catholic. Avocations: football, tennis. Home: Qta Manoha Calle Mirador, San Antonio Altos 1204, Venezuela Office: IVIC, Apartado 21827, Caracas 1020A DF, Venezuela

LABRECQUE, THOMAS G., bank executive; b. Long Branch, N.J., Sept. 17, 1938; s. Theodore Joseph and Marjorie (Uprichard) L.; m. Sheila English Cardone, June 16, 1962; children: Thomas, Douglas, Karen, Barbara. BA, Villanova U., 1960; postgrad., Am. U., 1962-64, NYU, 1965; D (hon.), Villanova U., U. Charleston, Drexel U., Marymount Coll. Mem. special devel. program The Chase Manhattan Corp., N.Y.C., 1964-65; with corp. portfolio adv. group portfolio and investment banking dept. The Chase Manhattan Corp., 1965-66, asst. treas., 1966-67, second v.p., 1967-69, 1967-69, v.p. and mgr. correspondent bank portfolio advisory, 1969-70; assoc. sec. planning to corp. exec. office The Chase Manhattan Corp., N.Y.C., 1970-71, sr. v.p. bank portfolio group, 1971-74, exec. v.p. treasury dept. and treas., 1974-76, mem. mgmt. com., 1976-80; vice chmn., CEO The Chase Manhattan Corp. and The Chase Manhattan Bank, N.A., N.Y.C., 1980-81, responsible for comml. banking, retail banking, trust and fiduciary investment, ops. dept. and corp. systems functon, 1980-81, pres., COO, 1981-90, chmn., CEO, also bd. dirs., 1990-1996, also bd. dirs., 1990-1996; pres., COO, bd. dirs. The Chase Manhattan Corp., 1996-97, pres., COO, 1996-1999, also bd. dirs.; ret., 1999; bd. dirs. Pfizer, Inc., Delphi Automotive Sys.; chmn. internat. adv. coun. Chase Manhattan Corp., 1999—. Trustee Brookings Instn., Central Park Conservancy, N.Y.U., U. Notre Dame; bd. dirs. New Visions for Pub. Schs., Internat. Rescue Com.; bd. visitors Duke U. Fuqua Sch. Bus.; chmn. Annenberg Nat. Task Force for Sch. Dist. Reform; past pres. Internat. Monetary Conf., Bankers Roundtable; mem. Coun. Fgn. Rels., Trilateral Commn., Bus.-Higher Edn. Forum. Lt. USN. Mem. Bus. Coun., Bus. Roundtable. Office: Chase Manhattan Bank NA 270 Park Ave Fl 12 New York NY 10017-2036

LABRIOLA, NORBERTO LUIS, artist, designer; b. Buenos Aires, Oct. 2, 1937. Artist Cultural Ctr., Buenos Airesw, 1976—. Mem. Rosacrucian Order. Avocations: drums, jazz. Home: Belgrano 1954 10 A, 1954 Buenos Aires Argentina Office: Av San Pedrito 661, 1406 Buenos Aires Argentina

LABROW, CHRISTOPHER REGINALD, investment advisor; b. Cheam, Eng., May 2, 1940; s. Reginald Francis and Dorothy Grace (MacRory) L.; m. Margaret Yvonne Pallister-Lyon, 1963 (div. 1976); children: Simon Christopher, Nicholas James, Jane Emma Williams; m. Suzannah De Beauvoir Roberts, May 9, 1996. Various exec. positions London, 1958-71; CEO Sedgwick EBC Ltd., London, 1971-83, The Etherington Group, London, 1983-88; chmn., investment mgr. Labrow Internat. Group, Gibraltar, 1988—. Fellow Pensions Mgmt. Inst.; mem. Securities Inst. Avocations: golf, sailing. Office: Labrow Internat Group, Water Gardens 4 PO Box 688, Gibraltar Gibraltar

LABSVIRS, JANIS, economist, educator; b. Bilska, Latvia, Mar. 13, 1907; s. Karlis and Kristina L.; Mag.Oec., Latvian State U., 1930; MS, Butler U., 1956; PhD, Ind. U., 1959; Dr. hist. (hon.), Latvian Acad. Scis., 1994. Tchr., Latvia, 1930-36; dir. dept. edn. Fedn. Latvian Trade Unions, 1936-37; v.p. Kr. Baron's U., Extension, Riga, Latvia, 1938-40, also exec. v.p. Filma, Inc., 1939-40; with UNRRA and Internat. Refugee Orgn., Esslingen, Germany, 1945-50; asst. prof. econs. Ind. State U., Terre Haute, 1959-62, assoc. prof., 1963-68, prof., 1969-73, prof. emeritus, 1973—; head dept. pub. and social affairs Latvian Ministry for Social Affairs, 1938-40; dir. Sch. of Commerce and Gymnasium, Tukums, Latvia, 1941-44. Danforth grantee, 1961; Ind. State U. research grantee, 1966; Mem. Am. Latvian Assn., Am. Assn. Advancement Slavic Studies, Assn. Advancement Baltic Studies, Am. Econ. Assn., Royal Econ. Soc. Lutheran. Author: Local Government's Accounting and Management Practices, 1947, 2d edit. 1992; A Case Study in the Sovietization of the Baltic States: Collectivization of Latvian Agriculture 1944-1956, 1959, 2d & 3d edit., 1988, 4th edit. 1989; Atminas un Pardomas, 1984, reprinted in Latvia, 3d edit., 1993, Kurp Ejam ?, 1996, reprinted in Latvia, 1997; Karlis Ulmanis, 1987, reprinted in Latvia, 2d edit., 1991, Kam Drosme Ir, 1990, reprinted in Latvia, 5th edit., 1992; contbr. articles profl. jours. Recipient Triju Zvaigznu Ordenis highest civilan medal President of Latvia, 1995. Home: 2617 Bridgeview Way Apt 1A Indianapolis IN 46220-1438

LABUNKA, MIROSLAV, history educator; b. Kotiv, Ternopil, Ukraine, Mar. 23, 1927; s. Oleksa and Eudokia (Klachok) L.; m. Maria Rovenchuk, Aug. 2, 1952 (dec. Oct. 1996); children: Alex M., Irene E., Illya M. BA, Ukrainian Cath. Sem., 1950; postgrad., Ludwig Maximilian U., Munich, 1950-51; Lic. en Sci. Historique, U. Catholique de Louvain, Belgium, 1955; MS in Libr. Sci., Columbia U., 1958, PhD, 1978. Sec. interpreter Internat. Refugee Orgn., Germany, 1950; gen. libr. asst., profl. libr., 1956-65; instr. LaSalle U., Phila, 1965-68, asst. prof., 1968-76, assoc. prof., 1976-93; prof. history St. Clement the Pope Ukrainian Cath. U., Rome, 1976—; rector Ukrainian Free U., Munich, 1995-98. Author: Metropolitan Ilarion of Kiev (1050-1053), 1990, the Novgorodian Legend of the White Cowl, 1998; asst. editor: Proc. of the Internat. Congress Commemorating the Millennium of Christianity in Rus-Ukraine, 1990. Named Eminent Educator, Min. of Edn. Ukraine, 1997; decorated St. Gregory the Great Order, Pope John Paul II, 1997. Fellow Shevchenko Sci. Soc., Ukrainian Acad. Arts and Scis. Democrat. Byzantine-Ukrainian Catholic Rite. Home: 5130 N 15th St Philadelphia PA 19141-1623

LACAL, JUAN-CARLOS, biologist, biochemist, researcher; b. Madrid, Mar. 28, 1957; s. Manuel Lacal and Josefina Sanjuan; m. Paloma Rodriguez, Apr. 12, 1957; 1 child, Sofia. BS, U. Autonoma, Madrid, 1979, MS, 1979, PhD, 1982. European Molecular Biology Orgn. fellow, 1983-84; vis. fellow Nat. Cancer Inst., NIH, Bethesda, Md., 1985-86; vis. assoc. Nat. Cancer Inst., NIH, Bethesda, 1987-88; colaborador cientifico Consejo Superior de Investigaciones Cientificas, Madrid, 1987, investigador cientifico, 1988—. Contbr. articles to profl. jours. Mem. European Assn. Cancer Rsch. (exec. com. 1996—), Spanish Fedn. Cancer Socs. (exec. com. 1991-94, 97—), Spanish Assn. Cancer Rsch. (sec. 1991-94, pres.-elect 1995-96, pres. 1997—), Fedn. of European Cancer Socs. (mem. coun. 1997—),m Revista de Oncologia (sec.-gen. 1999—). Avocation: music. Office: Inst Invest Biomedicas, Arturo Duperier 4, 28029 Madrid Spain

LA CAVA, DONALD LEON, communications executive; b. Fair Lawn, N.J., July 11, 1928; s. Paul and Angela (Viviano) La C.; m. Mary A. Morrison (div. 1980); children: Anita, Mark, Brigid, Kevin, Christopher, Peter, David, Daniel. BA in English, UCLA, 1982. V.p. Batjac Prodns., Hollywood, Calif., 1956-69; pres. Markab Mgmt., Beverly Hills, Calif., 1969-73, Triton Prodns., Encino, Calif., 1973-86; v.p. Jet Charter Am., Inc., 1986-97; mng. dir. No. Global Fin. & Investment, Reno, Nev., 1997-98; v.p. Internat. Jet Airways, 1986—, LaCava Aviation, 1996—. Served to lt. USNR, 1951-63, Korea. Mem. Dirs. Guild Am. Avocation: aviation. Home: 16936 Burbank Blvd Apt 127 Encino CA 91316-1814

LACAVE, ANGEL JIMENEZ, oncologist, educator; b. Alcanadre, La Rioja, Spain, May 7, 1946; s. Angel Jimenez and Rosalia Lacave; m. Maria Dolores Fonseca, Oct. 2, 1976; children: Paula, Manuel, Cristina. MD, U. Zaragoza, Spain, 1969; PhD, U. Pamplona, Spain, 1989. Intern Hosp. Gen. Asturias, Oviedo, Spain, 1969-70, resident, 1971-74, asst. doctor, 1974-78, head sect., 1978-82, head med. oncology dept., 1982—; asst. prof. U. Oviedo, 1994—; pvt. practice Oviedo, 1993—. Contbr. articles to profl. jours. Pres. Found. for Devel. of Oncology, 1994. Mem. European Orgn. for Rsch. and Treatment of Cancer, Am. Soc. Clin. Oncology, European Soc. Med. Oncology. Roman Catholic. Office: Hosp Gen Asturias Med Oncol, Julián Claveria S/N, 33006 Oviedo Asturias, Spain

LA CELLE, PAUL LOUIS, biophysics educator; b. Syracuse, N.Y., July 4, 1929; s. George Clarke and Marguerite Ellen (Waggoner) La C. A.B., Houghton Coll., 1951; M.D., U. Rochester, 1959. Resident U. Rochester Med. Center-Strong Meml. Hosp., 1960-62; asst. prof. medicine U. Rochester, 1967-70, asso. prof., 1970-74, prof., 1974—, chmn. dept. biophysics, 1977-96; sr. assoc. dean for acad. affairs and rsch. Sch. Medicine and Dentistry, U. Rochester, 1993-2000, interim sr. assoc. dean for grad. studies, 2000—; cons. to govt. Mem. Gates-Chili Sch. Bd., Rochester, 1964-72; trustee Houghton Coll., 1976-95. Served to lt. USNR, 1952-55. NIH spl. fellow, 1965-66; recipient von Humboldt Sr. Scientist award, 1982-83. Mem. Biophys. Soc., Microcirculation Soc., Biomedical Engring. Soc., Alpha Omega Alpha. Achievements include research in biophysics of blood cells, physiology of microcirculation. Office: U Rochester Sch Medicine and Dentistry PO Box 316 601 Elmwood Ave Rochester NY 14642*

LACEY, AARON MICHAEL, actor, director, screenwriter, executive producer; b. Washington, May 26, 1969. Advanced cert., Nat. Conservatory Drama Arts, 1993. CEO AML Productions, Washington, 1987—. Appearances include: (tv series) In Our Lives, 1987-94, (tv primetime spls.) Running Out of Time, 1989, Fatal Mix, 1990, (films) Major League II, 1993, Twelve Monkeys, 1995, Shadow Conspiracy, 1996; assoc. prodr., story writer, screenwriter, Edge, 1997; exec. prodr., story writer, screen writer, dir. Sync, 2000; screen plays include: (tv) (In Our Lives) Gangs, 1993, (films) Crimson Road, 1989, Cumulus Nine, 1990, Mind Walker, 1991. Supporter Anti Defamation League, People for Ethical Treatment of Animals, MADD, Wash. Regional Alcohol Program. Recipient Capital Region Emmy awards NATAS, 1991. Mem. Screen Actors Guild, Actors Equity Assn., Am. Fedn. TV Radio Artists. Avocation: karate (first-degree black belt).

LACEY, HENRY BERNARD, lawyer; b. Aurora, Colo., Nov. 30, 1963; s. Leonard Joseph and Colleen Trece (Ryan) L. BS, Ariz. State U., 1988, JD, 1991. Bar: Ariz. 1991, Oreg. 1996; U.S. Dist. Ct. Ariz. 1991, U.S. Ct. Appeals (9th cir.) 1992, U.S. Dist. Ct. Oreg. 1999. Jud. law clk. to Hon. Cecil F. Poole U.S. Ct. Appeals 9th Cir., San Francisco, 1991-92; assoc. Kimball & Curry, P.C., Phoenix, 1992-93; atty. Law Office of Henry B. Lacey, Phoenix, Portland, Oreg., Flagstaff, Ariz., 1993-94, 96-99; Flagstaff, Ariz., 1999—; vis. fellow Natural Resources Law Inst. Northwestern Sch. Law, Lewis and Clark Coll., Portland, Oreg., 1994-95; counsel/environ. group adv. bd. dirs. Coalition to Reform the Ctrl. Ariz. Project, Phoenix, 1993; vol. lawyer Land and Water Fund of the Rockies, Boulder, Colo., 1993—; vol. lawyer Portland Audubon Soc., 1996-99; bd. dirs. Brite, Inc., Phoenix, Mountain Air Cmty. Radio, Flagstaff. Gen. counsel Maricopa County, Ariz. Dem. Party, 1992-94. Mem. Order of Coif, Phi Delta Phi. Roman Catholic. Avocations: hiking, bicycling, reading, photography. Office: 120 N San Francisco St Flagstaff AZ 86001

LACEY, LAURA J., lawyer, educator; b. Deer Lodge, Mont., Mar. 5, 1947; d. Monte Lee Dittman and Violet Olga Lundby; m. Timothy Joseph Lacey, Sept. 21, 1968 (dec. Dec. 1990); children: Aaron, Shana, Marlena, Jonathan, Brian. BSN, Mont. State U., 1970; MSN, U. Calif., Sacramento, 1972; JD, Villanova U., 1996. Cert. inpatient obstetrical nursing NCC. Clin. instr. Mont. State U., Billings, 1979-84, asst. prof., 1985—; lectr. San Jose (Calif.) State U., 1972-77; pvt. practice lawyer Billings, 1997—. Home: 5538 Billy Casper Dr Billings MT 59106-1029 Office: 2880 Grand Ave Billings MT 59102-6525

LACH, ALMA ELIZABETH, food and cooking writer, consultant; b. Petersburg, Ill.; d. John H. and Clara E. Satorius; m. Donald F. Lach; 1 child, Sandra Judith. Diplome de Cordon Bleu, Paris, 1956. Feature writer Children's Activities mag., 1954-55; creator, performer childrens cooking TV show Let's Cook, 1955; food editor Chgo. Daily Sun-Times, 1957-65; hostess weekly food program on CBS, 1962-66; pres. Alma Lach Kitchens, Inc., Chgo., 1966—; performer TV show Over Easy, PBS, 1977-78; dir. Alma Lach Cooking Sch., Chgo.; lectr. U. Chgo. Downtown Coll., Gourmet Inst., U. Md., 1963, Modesto (Calif.) Coll., 1978, U. Chgo., 1981; resident master Shoreland Hall, U. Chgo., 1978-81; food cons. Food Bus. Mag., 1964-66, Chgo.'s New Pump Room, Lettuce Entertain You, Bitter End Resort, Brit. V.I., Midway Airlines, Flying Food Fare, Inc., Berghoff Restaurant, Hans' Bavarian Lodge, Unocal '76, Univ. Club Chgo. Author: A Child's First Cookbook, 1950, The Campbell Kids at Home, 1953, Let's Cook, 1956, Candlelight Cookbook, 1959, Cooking a la Cordon Bleu, 1970, Alma's Almanac, 1972, Hows and Whys of French Cooking, 1974, reprint, 1998; contbr. to World Book Yearbook, 1961-75, Grolier Soc. Yearbook, 1962; columnist Modern Packaging, 1967-68, Travel & Camera, 1969, Venture, 1970, Chicago mag., 1978, Bon Appetit, 1980, Tribune Syndicate, 1982; inventor: Curly-Dog Cutting Bd., 1995, Alma's Walker Tray, 1996. Recipient Pillsbury award, 1958, Grocery Mfrs. Am. Trophy award, 1959, certificate of Honor, 1961, Chevalier du Tastevin, 1962, Commanderie de l'Ordre des Anysetiers du Roy, 1963, Confrerie de la Chaine des Rotisseurs, 1964, Les Dames D'Escoffier, 1982, Culinary Historians of Chgo., 1993. Mem. Am. Assn. Food Editors (chmn. 1959), Tavern Club, Quadrangle Club (Chgo.). Fax: 773-363-2875. E-mail: alma@almalach.com. Home and Office: 5750 S Kenwood Ave Chicago IL 60637-1744

LACHANCE, PAUL ALBERT, food science educator, clergyman; b. St. Johnsbury, Vt., June 5, 1933; s. Raymond John and Lucienne (Landry) L.; m. Therese Cecile Cote; children: Michael P., Peter A., M.-Andre, Susan A. BS, St. Michael's Coll., 1955; postgrad., U. Vt., 1955-57; PhD, U. Ottawa, 1960; cert. in pastoral counseling, N.Y. Theol. Sem., 1981; DSc (hon.), St. Michael's Coll., 1982. Ordained deacon Roman Cath. Ch., 1977. Assigned to St. Paul's Ch. Princeton, N.J.; aerospace biologist Aeromed. Research Labs., Wright-Patterson AFB, Ohio, 1960-63; lectr. dept. biology U. Dayton, Ohio, 1963; flight food and nutrition coordinator NASA Manned Spacecraft Center, Houston, 1963-67; assoc. prof. dept. food sci. Rutgers U., New Brunswick, N.J., 1967-72, dir. Sch. Feeding effectiveness research project, 1969-72, prof., 1972—, faculty rep. to bd. trustees, 1988-90, dir. grad. program food sci., 1988-91, chmn. food sci. dept., 1991-97, chmn. univ. senate, 1990-93; faculty rep. to bd. govs. Rutgers U., New Brunswick, 1990-94, exec. dir. The Nutraceuticals Inst., 1997—; cons. Nutritional Aspects of Food Processing, Nutraceuticals; mem. nutrition adv. com. Whitehall-Robins/Centrum Consumer Divsn., 1989—; mem. sci. adv. bd. Roche chem. divsn. Hoffmann La Roche Co., 1976-88; mem. nutrition policy com. Beatrice Foods Co., 1979-86; trustee religious ministries com. Princeton Med. Ctr.; bd. dirs. J.R. Short Milling Co., 1990—. Mem. editl. adv. bd., Sch. Food Svc. Rsch. Rev., 1977-82, Jour. Am. Coll. Nutrition, 1986—, Jour. Med. Consultation, 1985—, Jour. Medicinal Foods, 1998—, Nutrition Reports Internat., 1963-83, Profl. Nutritionist, 1977-80; contbr. articles to profl. jours. Served to capt. USAF, 1960-63. Recipient Endel Karmas award for excellence in teaching food sci., 1988, WilliamCruess award for excellence in teaching Inst. Food Technologists, 1991. Fellow Inst. Food Technologists, Am. Coll. Nutrition, Am. Soc. Nutritional Sci.; mem. Am. Assn. Cereal Chemists, AAAS, N.Y. Inst. Food Technologists (chmn. 1977-78), Am. Soc. Clin. Nutrition, N.Y. Acad. Sci., Am. Dietetic Assn., Soc. Nutrition Edn., Am. Public Health Assn., Nat. Assn. Cath. Chaplains, Sociedad Latino Americano de Nutricion, Sigma Xi, Delta Epsilon Sigma. Home: 34 Taylor Rd Princeton NJ 08540-9521 Office: Rutgers U Food Sci 65 Dudley Rd New Brunswick NJ 08901-8520

LACHIEWICZ, PAUL FRANCIS, orthopedist, surgeon, educator; b. N.Y.C., July 16, 1951; s. Frank and Helen L.; m. Ava Maria Staler, June 24, 1977; children: Jayne, Anne, Mark, John, Mary Claire. BS, Manhattan Coll., 1973; MD, Cornell Univ., 1977. Intern, then resident U. Minn. Hosps., 1977-79; resident in orthopaedics Hosp. For Spl. Surgery, N.Y.C., 1979-82; prof. orthopaedics U. N.C., Chapel Hill, 1983—. Recipient Phillip D. Wilson award Hosp. for Special Surgery, N.Y.C., 1983. Fellow Am. Acad. Orthopaedic Surgeons; mem. Hip Soc., Knee Soc., So. Orthopaedic Assn. Avocations: running, skiing. Office: U NC CB 7055 Dept Orthopaedics Chapel Hill NC 27599-0001

LACHMANN, FRANK MICHAEL, psychologist, psychoanalyst; b. Breslau, Silesia, Germany, Dec. 9, 1929; came to U.S., 1938; s. Hans and Käte (Landsberg) L.; m. Annette Schamroth, July 15, 1962; children: Suzanne, Peter. BA, NYU, 1951; PhD, Northwestern U., 1955. Diplomate Am. Bd. Examiners in Profl. Psychology; cert. psychologist, N.Y., Mass. Pvt. practice psychoanalysis and psychotherapy N.Y.C., 1964—; mem. founding faculty Inst. for Psychoanalytic Study of Subjectivity, N.Y.C. Co-author: Psychoanalysis of Developmental Arrests, 1980, Self and Motivational Systems, 1994, The Clinical Exchange, 1996. Mem. Internat. Coun. for Psychoanalytic Self Psychology. Avocations: bicycling, skiing. Office: 393 West End Ave New York NY 10024-6138

LACHOWER, RAM, business executive; b. Tel-Aviv, Mar. 9, 1944; s. Yishayahu Lachower. BSc, Technion, Haifa, Israel, 1966, MA, 1969. Gen. mgr. Benco, Israel, 1966-67; divsn. mgr. IAI/MBT, Israel, 1968-71, IAI/ELTA, Israel, 1971-72; head of R&D Telrad, Israel, 1973-75; pres. RN Electronics, Israel, 1975-83; CEO Militram, Israel, 1983—; dir. Paz Oil, Israel, 1986—. Col. Res., 1962-95. Fellow IEEE; mem. VME Org (pres. 1987-95). Jewish. Office: Militram, PO Box 13324, Tel Aviv Israel

LACIĆ, MIODRAG, nuclear medicine physician; b. Brčko, Posavina, July 8, 1962; s. Mijo and Manda L.; m. Blaženka Lujić, Aug. 1, 1987; children: Mihovil, Jakov, Mislav. MD, U. Zagreb, Croatia, 1988; MS, U. Zagreb, 1993; PhD, 1998. Med. diplomate. Intern U. Hosp. "Jordanovac", Zagreb, 1989-90; resident U. Hosp. Sestre Milosrdnice, Zagreb, 1990-92; resident in nuclear medicine U. Hosp. Sestre Milosrdnice, Zagreb, 1992-96, nuclear medicine cons. dept. nuclear medicine and oncology, 1996—. Author: Clinical Nuclear Medicine, 1999; contbr. articles to profl. jour. Fellow I.A.E.A. (London, Berlin, Ljubljana, Co-operation project 1994, rsch. contract 1997), W.F.N.M.B./E.A.N.M., I.B.U.S., European Assn. Nuclear Medicine (award 1995); mem. Croatian Assn. Nuclear Medicine, Croatian Assn. Ultrasound in Medicine. Avocations: music, tennis. Office: Sestre Milosrdnice Dept Oncology & Nuclear Medicine, Vinogradska str 29, HR-10000 Zagreb Croatia

LĀCIS, ARIS, health facility administrator, cardiac surgeon; b. Jelgava, Latvia, Aug. 1, 1936; s. Teodor and Zelma (Gedrovics) L.; m. Aija Ozolina, Sept. 8, 1958; children: Aigars, Andis. MD, Riga (Latvia) Med. Inst., 1961. Resident gen. surgery Jelgava (Latvia) Gen. Hosp., 1961-62; resident thoracic surgery P. Stradine Clin. Hosp., Riga, Latvia, 1962-64; surgeon The Latvian Ctr. Pulmonary Surgery, Riga, 1964-69; asst. prof., chief surgeon Clinic Gen. and Cardiovascular Surgery, Riga Med. Inst., Riga, 1969-94; prof., head Latvian State Cardiology Ctr. Children, Riga, 1994—; head Clinic for Children's Cardiology, Latvian Med. Acad., Riga; spl. editl. cons. Latvian Med. Acad., Riga, 1990—; dep. dirs. gen. JBC, 1997—. Contbr. articles to med. jours., chpts. to books; author two monographs. Recipient Bronze medal in Sci. Soviet Union Ctrl. Exhibn. for Scientific Achievement, 1977, Commemorative medal Man of the Yr. Am. Psychol. Inst., 1995. Mem. The World Med. Assn. (assoc.), European Soc. Cardiology, Riga Hansa Rotary Club (pres. 1998-99), Internat. Soc. Cardiovascular Surgery, Assn. for European Paediatric Cardiology (nat. del.). Lutheran. Avocation: swimming. Fax: 371-2-565227. Home: Raumas str 45/3-108, LV 1084 Riga Latvia Office: Cardiology Ctr for Children, Tuglas str 20, LV 1038 Riga Latvia

LACITY, MARY CECELIA, information systems educator; b. Atlantic City, N.J., May 27, 1963; d. Paul V. and Joan B. L.; 1 child, Michael Christopher. BS in Bus., Pa. State U., 1985; PhD in Bus., U. Houston, 1992. Sys. analyst Exxon, Houston, 1985-87; cons. Tech. Ptrs., Houston, 1991; rsch. fellow Oxford (Eng.) U., 1994; asst. prof. info. sys. U. Mo., St. Louis, 1992-98, assoc. prof., 1998—. Author: IS Outsourcing, 1993, Beyond IS Bandwagon, 1995, Global IT Outsourcing, 2000; editor, author: Strategic I.S. Sourcing, 1997. Expert witness Congressional Com. to Restructure IRS, Washington, 1997. Recipient Rsch. award IBM, Brussels, 1994, Best Case Study Paper award European Conf. of IS, Copenhagen, 1999, Best Rsch. Paper, Athens, 1995, Rsch. award U. Mo., St. Louis, 1998. Mem. Internat. Conf. of IS (conf. chair 1998-99). E-mail: mary.lacity@umsl.edu. Office: Univ Missouri St Louis 8001 Natural Bridge Rd Saint Louis MO 63121-4499

LACK, LARRY HENRY, small business owner; b. Richland, Wash., Aug. 27, 1952; s. Eugene Herman and Myrtle (Wellman) L.; m. Patricia Ann Henry, Aug. 19, 1978; children: Vicki Marie, Rachel Ann. Enlisted USAF, 1970, disabled vet., 1978; aircraft mechanic Ill., S.C., Okla. AFBs., 1970-78; inventor, prin. Lack Industries, Inc., Shreveport, La., 1979-85, Phoenix, 1985—; CEO Stellar Internat., Phoenix, 1991-99; cons. U.S. Air Force, Altus AFB, 1978-80, Cates & Phillips Patent Attys., Phoenix, 1985—; pres. La. Innovators Tech., Shreveport, 1981-82; lectr. Glendale Community Coll. 1987-88; guest lectr. Ariz. State U., 1989-90; authored legislation to regulate invention promotion cos. in Ariz., 1989. Patentee in field. Mem. Internat. Platform Assn. Republican. Achievements include invention of Anasazi submersible, downhole positive displacement pump, the SunFlow solar pump, the Pegasus wind-driven pump, the scuba HeadLight, others. Avocations: scuba diving, parachuting, hunting, rock climbing, flying. Fax: 602-265-2307. Home: PO Box 7632 Phoenix AZ 85011-7632 Office: 6332 W Oraibi Dr Glendale AZ 85308-5200

LACK, LEON COLBURN, psychology educator; b. Kalamazoo, July 24, 1942; arrived in Australia, 1965; s. Arthur R. and Arlene E. (Woten) L.; m. Edith A. Fleming, Dec. 20, 1965 (div. 1975); 1 child, Jonathan; m. Margie R. Ripper; 1 child, Molly Kendall. AB, Stanford U., 1965; PhD, U. Adelaide, Australia, 1972. Registered psychologist. Tutor in psychology U. Adelaide, 1965-70; sr. tutor in psychology Flinders U., Adelaide, 1971-72, lectr. in psychology, 1973-75; sr. lectr. in psychology, 1976-96, assoc. prof. psychology, 1996—; cons. psychologist sleep unit Repatriation Hosp., Daw Park, Australia, 1992—. Author: Selective Attention and the Control of Binocular Rivalry, 1978, (book chpt.) Behavioral Medicine: International Perspectives, 1992; contbr. articles to profl. jours. Com. mem. Campaign for Peace in Vietnam, Adelaide, 1968-70, Adelaide Girls Choir, 1996-98; com. chair Flinders Child Care Ctr., Adelaide, 1973-75. Sleep Rsch. grantee Nat. Health and Med. Rsch. Coun., 1983-85, 95-97, 99-2001; grantee Australian Rsch. Coun., 1998—. Mem. Australasian Sleep Assn. (pres. 1992-94). Avocations: long-distance running, swimming.

LACK, PATRICIA ANN, drilling and pumping company executive, consultant; b. Phoenix, Oct. 15, 1946; d.J.V. and Vivian Margaret Henry; m. Ronald Lee Jackson, Mar. 6, 1964 (div. May 1969); 1 child, Vicki Marie Snyder; m. Larry Henry Lack, Aug. 19, 1978. Student, Glendale (Ariz.) C.C., 1985-86. Enlisted USAF, 1973, advanced through grades to E-6, 1984; equipment mgr. Supply Squadron, Eglin AFB, Fla., 1973-74; supr. inventory mgmt. 3d Supply Squadron, Clark Air Base, The Philippines, 1974-77; chief supply sr. advisor 443d Supply Squadron, Altus AFB, Okla., 1977-79; instr., br. chief curriculum devel. SAC Non-Commd. Officers Acad., Barksdale AFB, La., 1979-84; resigned, 1984; pres. Lack Industries, Inc., Phoenix, 1984-90; chmn. bd. Stellar Innovations, LLC, Phoenix, 1996—; freelance cons. and trainer, Phoenix, 1984-90; sexual discrimination recognition, protection, prevention trainer Glendale C.C. and to cos., Phoenix, 1984-90; cons. on career motivation enhancement to bus., Phoenix, 1984-95; counselor sexual assault recovery workshops, Phoenix, 1993—. Author: (novel) Willowman, 1993. Pub. spkr. to various women's groups and bus., Phoenix, 1990—. Mem. DAV (life), NRA (life), NRA Inst. for Legis. Action (life, honor roll 1995), Women Entrepreneurs Ariz. Republican. Avocations: flying, scuba diving, sport shooting, reading, camping. Fax: 602-376-9967. Office: Stellar Innovations LLC PO Box 7632 Phoenix AZ 85011-7632

LACKI, ALLAN VINCENT, industrial engineer; b. Kearny, N.J., Apr. 6, 1953; s. John Theodore and Jenny (Biondo) L.; m. Joan Terese Blake, Apr. 15, 1978; children: Karen Marie, Brian Cameron. BS in Indsl. Engring., N.J. Inst. Tech., 1975, MS in Mgmt. Engring., 1982. Indsl. engring. intern St. Luke's Hosp. Ctr., N.Y.C., 1974; sales engring. assoc. Faber Assoc., Clifton, N.J., 1975; plant indsl. engr. trainee Am. Can Co., Union, N.J., 1975; staff indsl. engr. Am. Can Co., Greenwich, Conn., 1976; methods engring. supr. Jersey Cen. Power, Morristown, N.J., 1976-81; ops. analyst sr. III GPU Energy, Parsippany, N.J., 1982-93; transp. engring. supr. GPU Energy, Morristown, 1994-96; power contracts specialist GPU Energy, Reading, Pa., 1997—; cons. in field. Contbr. articles to profl. jours. Event organizer Mine Hill (N.J.) Day Com., 1987-88. Mem. Inst. Indsl. Engrs. (chpt. v.p. 1999—), Soc. Automotive Engrs., Corvair Soc. Am., N.J. Assn. Corvair Enthusiasts (sec. 1988-96), Lehigh Valley Corvair Club, Lincoln Highway Heritage Corridor Assn., Phi Eta Sigma, Tau Beta Pi, Alpha Pi Mu (pres. local chpt. 1974-75). Achievements include development of power purchase contracts, management information systems and construction equipment. Avocations: antique auto restoration, writing, camping, web-site design. Home: 102 Atlantic Ave Sinking Spg PA 19608-9343 Office: GPU Energy Rt 183 & Van Reed Rd Reading PA 19605

LACKMANN, GERD-MICHAEL, pediatrician; b. Essen, Germany, Dec. 11, 1961; s. Fritz and Irmgard (Talkenberger) L. Degree, U. Regensburg, Germany, 1983; MD, Philipps U., Marburg, Germany, 1988. Cons., rschr. Städt Klinikum Fulda, Germany, 1994-97, Children's Hosp.-Heinrich-Heine U., Düsseldorf, Germany, 1998—. Contbr. articles to profl. jours.; inventor in neuropediat. Mem. Children's Health Orgn., Fulda, 1993—. Maj. German Army, 1988-94. Mem. German Assn. Pediat., German Assn. Neonatology, Oxygen Soc. Avocations: tennis, body building, literature, modern art. Fax: 0049-211-811-8757. Home: Schwohenend 33, 41352 Korschenbroich Germany Office: Childrens Hosp H-Heine Univ, Moorenstr 5, 40255 Düsseldorf Germany

LACROIX, FREDERIC, automotive service company executive; b. Bordeaux, France, July 27, 1966; arrived in Spain, 1995; s. Bernard and Nicole (Mur) L.; m. Maria Jose Michavila, July 17, 1997; 1 child, Ines. G-rad., Superieur de Gestion, Paris, 1989. Asst. audit Amperex, Paris, 1990; fin. analyst Midas France, Paris, 1991-93; asst. contr. Midas Europe, Paris, 1993-94; contr. Midas Spain, Madrid, 1994-96; gen. mgr. fin. Midas South of Europe, Madrid, 1996-98; contr. Europe Midas Europe, Madrid, 1999—. Avocations: golf, sailing, wine. Home: Avda De Europa 28-P4-3D, 28224 Pozuelo Madrid Spain Office: Midas C/Almazara, C/Almazara 2, 28760 Tres Cantos Spain

LACROIX, ROGER LOUIS, civil engineer, executive; b. Briançon, France, Feb. 24, 1928; s. Albert P. and Heloise (Thomassin) L.; m. Pascale Arlette Angelini, June 16, 1951; children: Denis, Martine. Student, Poly. Sch., Paris, 1949, Nat. Sch. of Bridges and Roads, Paris, 1951. Civil engr. Pub. Works Dept., Paris, 1951-56; tech. mgr. Total Distribution Co., Paris, 1956-60, Soc. Gen. D'Entreprises, Paris, 1960-76; chmn. SFP Structures, Paris, 1974-81; freelance consulting engr. Paris, 1981—; chmn. PPC, Chalon, France, 1988-99. Contbr. articles to profl. jours., text books. Decorated Officier de la Legion d'Honneur, France, Officier du Merite Nat., France, Chevalier des Palmes Academiques, France. Mem. Nat. Acad. Engring. (assoc. fgn. mem.), Royal Acad. Engring. (fgn. mem.), Fedn. Internat. de la Precontrainte (hon. pres.), Association Française pour la Constrn. (hon. pres.). Avocation: bridge. E-mail: lacroixr@compuserve.com. Home: 65 rue du Javelot, 75645 Paris cedex 13, France Office: 1 bis rue de Petit-Clamart, 78140 Velizy France

LA CROIX, SUMNER JONATHAN, economics educator; b. Hartford, Conn., Dec. 28, 1954; s. Harold F. and Miriam La C. BA in Math., Polit. and Social Thought, U. Va., 1976; MA in Econs., U. Wash., 1979, PhD in Econs., 1981. Asst. prof. econs. U. Hawaii, Honolulu, 1981-86, assoc. prof., 1986-90, prof., 1990—; sr. fellow East-West Ctr., Honolulu, 1993-96; vis. scholar dept. econs. U. Calif., Berkeley, 1995; Alena Wells Hirschorn vis. prof., Barnard Coll. dept. econs. Columbia U., N.Y.C., 1998-2000; assoc. faculty Ctr. for Chinese Studies, U. Hawaii, Honolulu, 1996—; co-chair econ. history seminar Columbia U., 1999-2000; mem. exec com. faculty senate U. Hawaii, Honolulu, 1997-98. Co-editor: Emerging Pattern of Investment in China, 1995, Japan's New Economy, 2000; contbr. articles to econ. jours. Ford Found. prof. Fudan U., Shanghai, 1990; recipient Puhlick award Life Found., Honolulu, 1990. Mem. Am. Econs. Assn., Econ. History Assn., Cliometrics Soc. Avocations: weightlifting, running, swimming, reading history. E-mail: sjla@gte.net. Office: U Hawaii Social Scie Bldg 542 2424 Maule Way Honolulu HI 96822

LACY, GREGORY LAWRENCE, protective services official; b. Long Beach, Calif., June 12, 1949; s. George Lawrence and Pauline L. (Smith) L.; m. Cheryl Ann Carey, Apr. 16, 1987 (div. May 1990); children: Megan Lee, Tess Jordan; adopted children: Randy J., Jennie A.; m. Suphan Wongruan, June 4, 1991 (div. May 1999). AS in Forestry, Bottineau (N.D.) Sch. Forestry, 1967; cert. law enforcement, N.D. Police Acad., Bismarck, 1967; AS in Engring., N.D. State Sch. Sci., 1972. Cert. EMT, emergency trauma tech., law enforcement, N.D., Alaska. Law enforcement officer Langdon (N.D.) Police Dept., 1972-77; law enforcement officer, tng. officer Smith Securty - Spl. Divsn., Anchorage, 1977-80; security officer, field tng. officer AHTNA-Am. Guard & Alert Security Co., Anchorage, 1980—; tng. officer Langdon Police Dept., 1973-77. Active Campaign for Sheriff Re-election, Cavalier County, Langdon, 1973-77; pub. fire arms tng. Langdon Police Dept., 1973-77. Mem. NRA (life), Air Couriers Assn., Gold Prospectors Assn. (life). Baptist. Avocations: hunting, fishing, photography, hiking, computers. Home: 3705 Arctic Blvd # 622 Anchorage AK 99503-5774 Office: Doyon Universal Svcs 701 W 8th Ave Ste 500 Anchorage AK 99501-3468

LACY, JOHN RUSSELL, state government administrator; b. Trenton, N.J., June 12, 1938; s. J(ohn) Russell and Mary Grey (Snedeker) L.; m. Joanne Ida Fitzpatrick, Apr. 20, 1963; 1 child, Shannon Rae. BA, Rutgers U., 1961. Pers. technician N.J. Dept. Civil Svc., Trenton, 1962-63; pub. info. dir. Internat. hdqrs. Babe Ruth Baseball, Trenton, 1963-68; comms. mgr. Univac Divsn.-Sperry Rand Corp., Blue Bell, Pa., 1968-69; dir. membership rels. N.J. Taxpayers Assn., Trenton, 1969-71; exec. asst. to state treas. N.J. Dept. Treasury, Trenton, 1971-73; exec. v.p. N.J. Retail Mechts. Assn., Trenton, 1973; owenr Lacy Comms., Hamilton, N.J., 1973—; pub. Mercer Messenger, Hamilton, 1983-88; dep. dir. N.J. State Lottery Commn., Trenton, 1988-90; dir. spl. projects/alumni affairs Mercer County C.C., Trenton, 1990-99; dir. N.J. Human Resource Devel. Inst., Trenton, 1999—. Mem. Hamilton Twp. Coun., Hamilton, 1976-99; pres. Hamilton YMCA, 1974-75; chmn. Hamilton Twp. Econ. Devel. Commn., 1973-75; pres. Mercer County League Municipalities, Hamilton, 1995-99; bd. dirs. Project Freedom, Inc. Named Humanitarian of Yr., Animals in Distress, Inc., 1990, Outstanding Chpt. Pres. in Mercer County, N.J. Jaycees, 1971. Mem. Hamilton Twp. Optimist Club (charter mem.), Ancient Order of Hibernians, VFW (hon.), DAV (life), Tau Kappa Epsilon. Republican. Methodist. Avocations: team sports, historical fiction and biographies, restoring antique furniture. Home: 9 Compton Way Hamilton NJ 08690-3920 Office: NJ Human Resource Devel Inst 200 Woolverton St Trenton NJ 08610

LACY, TERRY GOODWIN, retired educator, translator, editor, author; b. Balt., May 25, 1926; d. Robert and Dorothy H. (Goodwin) L.; m. C. Vernon cole, July 29, 1948 (div. 1975); children: Marjorie Allen, Robert Spaulding, David Morrell. BA, Smith Coll., 1948; MS, Colo. State U., 1968, PhD, 1972. Pvt. instr. flute Ft. Collins, Colo., 1951-61; instr. tech. journalism Colo. State U., Ft. Collins, 1972-73, asst. prof., 1973-74; instr. English U. Iceland, Reykjavik, 1975-98; ret., 1998; instr. extension U. Md., Iceland, 1976-77, banking sch., Reykjavik, 1981-83, Comml. Coll., Reykjavik, 1983-86; Fulbright-Hays sr. lectr., Reykjavik, 1973. Author: English-Icelandic Dictionary of Business Terms, 1982, 2nd edit., 1990, Grammar Exercises in Business English, 1986, Icelandic-English Dictionary of Business Terms, 1989, Music Dictionary, 1992, English Business Letters, 1994, Ring of Seasons: Iceland - Its Culture and History, 1998; translator, editor, 1975-98; contbr. articles to profl. jours. Chmn. pulpit com. Foothills Unitarian Ch., Ft. Collins, 1969-70, vice chmn., 1970; Dem. committeewoman, 1972-74; alto Filharmonia chorus, Reykjavik, 1973-94, Senorita Chorus, 1998—; pres. Ft. Collins Bird Club Audubon Soc., Ft. Collins. Ethnic Studies grantee Ford Found., 1970-72. Mem. Nordic Assn. Am. Studies (editorial bd. 1976-98, chmn. nominating com. 1989-92), Internat. Assn. Tchrs. English as a Fgn. Lang., Phi Beta Kappa, Phi Kappa Phi. Democrat. Unitarian.

LACZKÓ, TIBOR, English and Hungarian linguistics educator; b. Sátoraljaújhely, Hungary, Mar. 19, 1959; s. Sándor and Vilma (Csuha) L.; m. Edit (Rácz) Laczkó, Aug., 29, 1981; children: Péter, Gábor. BA in Edn., Kossuth U., Debrecen, Hungary, 1983; EdD, Kossuth U., 1987; PhD, Hungarian Acad. Scis., Budapest, Hungary, 1994. Jr. lectr. Kossuth U., Debrecen, Hungary, 1983-88; sr. lectr. Kossuth U., 1988-95, assoc. prof., chair, Dept. Eng. Linguistics, 1995-98, dep. dean Faculty Arts, 1995-98. Co-author: Hungarolingua 1, 1991, Hungarolingua 2, 1993, Hungarolingua 3, 1999; author: The Syntax of Hungarian Noun Phrases: A Lexical-Functional Approach, 1995. Recipient rsch. grant Soros Found., Stanford U., 1991, Mellon Found., Edinburgh U., 1996, Fulbright, Stanford U., 1998. Avocations: tennis, skiing, hiking, reading, music. Office: U Debrecen Dept Eng Ling, Egyetem Tér 1, H4010 Debrecen Hungary

LACZKOVICS, ISTVAN, sales executive; b. Tatabanya, Hungary, Nov. 14, 1966; s. Istvan and Maria (Gröber) L.; m. Tatjana Sergeeva, Aug. 17, 1989; 1 child, Katalin. MBA, Moscow Univ. Coop., 1990, Budapest Coll. Commerce, 1993; DBA, Trinity U. Internat. sales exec. Hokev, Budapest, Hungary, 1993; sales rep. Unilever, Budapest, 1993-95; internat. forwarding mgr. AVT, Budapest, 1995; internat. sales mgr. Olympos, Budapest, 1996; pres. TJO Inc., Jackson, Wyo., 1996—; sales, mktg. dir. Grabo KFT, Gyor, Hungary, 2000. Mem. Internat. Bodyguard Security Svc. Assn., Internat. Jaguar and Daimler Club, Nat. Geog. Soc., Amcham, Hungary. Home and Office: Igmandi 26, 1112 Budapest Hungary

LADANY, SHAUL PAUL, educator; b. Belgrade, Yugoslavia, Apr. 2, 1936; arrived in Israel, 1948; s. Dionis and Sofia (Kassowitz) L.; m. Shoshana Ahlfeld, Nov. 6, 1960; 1 child, Danit. BSc, Israel Inst. Tech., Haifa, 1960, MSc, 1961; PhD, Columbia U., 1968. Gen. mgr. Atzmon Sewing Machine Co., Sefad, Israel, 1964-65; supv. engr. Israeli Parliament, Jerusalem, 1962-64; lectr. Tel-Aviv U., Israel, 1968-74; prof. Ben-Gurion U. of Negev, Beer Sheva, Israel, 1975—; vis. prof. CUNY, N.Y.C., 1973-75, Ga. Inst. Tech., Atlanta, 1979-81, 85-86; chair Ben-Gurion U., 1989—, dept. chmn., 1976-78, chmn. univ. entrepreneurship ctr., 1992—. Editor: Hebrew-English Dictionary of Statistical Terminology, 1970, Management Science in Sports, 1976, The Walk to the Olympics, 1996; inventor in field. Lt. Israeli Mil., 1954-56, 67, 73. Mem. Israeli Indsl. Engrs. Soc., Survivors of Bergen-Belsen Concentration Camp, The Inst. Mgmt. Scis. Jewish. Avocation: race walking. Office: Ben-Gurion U, PO Box 653, 84105 Beer Sheva Israel

LADAR, JERROLD MORTON, lawyer; b. San Francisco, Aug. 2, 1933. AB, U. Wash., 1956; LLB, U. Calif., Berkeley, 1960. Bar: Calif. 1961, U.S. Supreme Ct. 1967. Law clk. to judge U.S. Dist. Ct. (no. dist.) Calif., 1960-61; asst. U.S. atty. San Francisco, 1961-70; chief criminal div., 1968-70; mem. firm MacInnis & Donner, San Francisco, 1970-72; prof. criminal law and procedure U. San Francisco Law Sch., 1962-83; pvt. practice San Francisco., 1970—; ptnr. Ladar & Ladar, San Francisco, 1994—; lectr. Hastings Coll. Law, Civil and Criminal Advocacy Programs, 1985—; chair pvt. defender panel U.S. Dist. Ct. (no. dist.) Calif., 1980-90; ct. apptd. chair stats. and tech. subcom. Fed. Civil Justice Reform Act Com. (no. dist.) Calif., 1990-95; ct. apptd. mem. Fed. Ct. Civil Local Rules Revision Com. (no. dist.) Calif., 1994—; ct. apptd. chmn. Criminal Local Rules Revision Com. (no. dist.) Calif., 1991—; mem. continuing edn. of bar criminal law adv. com. U. Calif., Berkeley, 1978-83, 89—; panelist, mem. nat. planning com. ABA Nat. Ann. White Collar Crime Inst., 1996—; ct. apptd. mem. Local Disciplinary Rule Draft com., 1998-99. Author: (with others) Selected Trial Motions, Grand Jury Practice, Asset Forfeiture, California Criminal Law and Procedure Practice, 5th edit., 2000, Direct Examination-Tips and Techniques, 1982, Collateral Effects of Federal Convictions, 1997, Insult Added to Injury: The Fallout From Tax Conviction, 1997, A Day At The Grand Jury, 2000. Trustee Tamalpais Union High Sch. Dist., 1968-77, chmn. bd., 1973-74; mem. adv. com. Nat. PTA Assn., 1972-78; apptd. mem. criminal justice act com. U.S. Ct. Appeals (9th cir). Fellow Am. Bd. Criminal Lawyers; mem. ABA, San Francisco Bar Assn. (editor in Re 1974-76), State Bar Calif. (pro-tem disciplinary referee 1976-78, vice chmn. pub. interest and edn. com. criminal law sect., mem. exec. com. criminal law sect. 1980-87, editor Criminal Law Sect. News 1981-87, chmn. exec. com. 1983-84), Am. Inns. of Ct. (exec. com. 1994-97), Fed. Bar Assn. (panelist), Nat. Sentencing Inst. (contbr.). Office: 507 Polk St Ste 310 San Francisco CA 94102-3339

LADD, ERIC JUSTIN, mental health services professional; b. Wooster, Ohio, Oct. 13, 1956; s. Paul Frederick Ladd and Janice Miriam Heineking. BBA, Ohio U., 1979. Sr. market analyst Grumman Ohio Corp., Columbus, 1979-88; telesales rep. Carlton Cards divsn. Am. Greetings, Cleve., 1988-90; pub. rels., investigator City of Cleve. Office Consumer Affairs, 1990-91; cons. State of Ohio Rehab. Svcs. Commn., Columbus, 1991-92; pres., CEO ROOMS, Inc., Columbus, 1992-98; exec. dir., CEO Ptnrs. Active Living Through Socialization Inc., Columbus, 1998—; chmn. Columbus consumer adv. coun. Bur. Vocat. Rehab. Author: A Matter of Principal, 2000; co-prodr. pub. svc. announcements Office Consumer Affairs, 1990-91 (Nat. PSA award 1991); editor BRIDGE Builders Communicator, 1998—. Commr. Ohio Dept. Mental Health.; bd.d irs. HOPE Hotline, Columbus, 1984-88, Ohio Advs. Mental Health, 1997—; co-chmn. Call for Action, Cleve., 1988-91; mem. Mayor's Com. People Disabilities, Columbus, 1999—. Recipient Cmty. Svc. award Columbus Dispatch, 1988, Vol. Achievement award City of Cleve., 1990; named Outstanding Vol. Cmty. Reentry, 1990. Mem. Consumer Operated Svcs. Ohio, Franklin County Mental Health Assn. (rep. coalition healthy cmtys. 1998—, Norman Guitry award 1999), Columbus Consumer Adv. Coun. (chmn. 1997—, Consumer Achievement award 2000). Avocation: playing instruments. Fax: 614-291-9079. Office: Ptnrs Active Living Through Socialization Inc 162 W 5th Ave Columbus OH 43201-3272

LADD, JEFFREY RAYMOND, lawyer; b. Mpls., Apr. 10, 1941; s. Jasper Raymond and Florence Marguerite (DeMarce) L.; m. Kathleen Anne Crosby, Aug. 24, 1963; children: Jeffrey Raymond, John Henry, Mark Jasper, Matthew Crosby. Student, U. Vienna, Austria; BA, Loras Coll.; postgrad., U. Denver; JD, Ill. Inst. Tech. Bar: Ill. 1973, U.S. Dist. Ct. 1973. V.p. mktg. Ladd Enterprises, Des Plaines, Ill., 1963-66; v.p. mktg. and fin. Ladd Enterprises, Crystal Lake, Ill., 1966-70; ptnr. Ross & Hardies, Chgo., 1973-81, Boodell, Sears, et al., 1981-86, Bell, Boyd & Lloyd, Chgo., 1986—; spl. asst. atty. gen. for condemnation State of Ill., 1977-82. Named Chgo. City Club's 1995 Citizen of Yr. Mem. ABA, Chgo. Bar Assn., Nat. Assn. Bond Lawyers, Ill. Assn. Hosp. Attys., Am. Acad. Hosp. Attys., Crystal Lake Jaycees (Disting. Svc. award), Crystal Lake C. of C. (past pres.), Econ. Club, Legal Club, Union League Club, Bull Valley Golf Club, Woodstock Country Club, Alpha Lambda. Roman Catholic. Avocations: golf, hunting, fishing, tennis, skiing. Office: Bell Boyd & Lloyd 3 First National Pla 70 W Madison St Ste 3300 Chicago IL 60602-4284

LADER, PHILIP, government official, diplomat, business executive, university president; b. Jackson Heights, N.Y., Mar. 17, 1946. BA, Duke U., 1966; MA, U. Mich., 1967, Oxford U., England, 1968; JD, Harvard U., 1972; DHL (hon.), U. S.C.; LLD (hon.), Limestone Coll.; LHD (hon.), Youngstown State U.; LLD (hon.), Lander U.; D. Ent (hon.), Columbia Coll.; D.B.S. (hon.), Mich. Tech. U.; DHL (hon.), Winthrop U. Bar: Fla. 1972, D.C. 1973, S.C. 1979. Assoc. Sullivan & Cromwell, N.Y.C., 1972; law clk. to U.S. cir. judge, 1973; pres. Sea Pines Co., Hilton Head Island, 1979-83, Winthrop U., Rock Hill, S.C., 1983-85; exec. v.p. Sir James Goldsmith's US Holding Co., 1986-88; pres./mng. dir. 1st Southern Corp., Hilton Head Island, 1989-91, 97; pres. Bus. Execs. for Nat. Security, Washington, 1991; pres., vice chmn. Bond U., Gold Coast, Australia, 1991-93; adminstr. SBA, Washington, 1994-97; mem. President's Cabinet, Washington, 1994-97; U.S. amb. to Ct. of St. James, 1997—; dep. dir. for mgmt. Office Mgmt. and Budget Exec. Office Pres., 1993; dep. chief of staff White House, asst. to Pres., 1993-94; chmn. Pres.'s Coun. on Integrity and Efficiency, 1993, chmn. Pres.'s Mgmt. Coun.; chmn. policy com. Nat. Performance Rev., 1993. Candidate for gov. of S.C., 1986; chmn. bd. visitors Duke U. Sanford Inst. Pub. Policy; bd. dirs. ARC, 1996-97; founder Renaissance Inst. Hon. fellow Pembroke Coll., Oxford U. Mem. Coun. Fgn. Rels., Mid. Temple, Chief Execs. Orgn., D.C. Met. Club, World Pres.'s Orgn., Soc. Internat. Bus. Fellows, Phi Beta Kappa. Episcopalian. Office: Am Embassy, 24 Grosvenor Sq, London W1A 1AE, England

LADIGES, PAULINE YVONNE, botanist; b. Eng., Jan. 19, 1948; arrived in Australia, 1952; d. Henry and Hannah (Vizard) Bennett; m. Ian Mervyn, Jan. 17, 1969 (div.); m. Gareth Jon Nelson, Oct. 26, 1991. Diploma in edn., U. Melbourne, 1971, MSc, 1972, PhD, 1976. Lectr. U. Melbourne, 1975-81, sr. lectr., 1982-87, assoc. dean students, 1983-87, reader, 1987-91, dep. head Sch. of Botany, 1991-92, prof., head Sch. of Botany, 1992—; bd. dirs. Royal Botanic Gardens, Melbourne, dep. chmn.; dir. Yarra Valley Water, Melbourne, 1998—; hon. rsch. assoc. N.Y. Bot. Gardens, 1992—. Co-author: Biology One, 1990 (Best Textbook 1990), Biology Two, 1991; co-

editor, author: Biology, 1994 (Best Textbook 1994); contbr. articles to profl. jours. Avocations: collecting antiques, botanical arts. E-mail: paulingl@unimelb.edu.au. Office: U Melbourne, Sch Botany, Melbourne VIC 3010, Australia

LADIMEJI, OLADAPO A., accountant; b. Kaduna, Nigeria, Feb. 2, 1951; arrived in England, 1956; s. Adepoju Adisa and Yetunde (Olaseni) L.; m. Elizabeth Toyin David, Aug. 28, 1982; 1 child, Sunmade. MA, Cambridge (England) U., 1974; MBA, INSEAD, France, 1984. Editl. com. Transition, Ghana, 1972-75, Race & Class, England, 1974-76; acct. trainee Edward Moore & Sons, London, 1979-82; tax sr. Deloitte Haskins & Sells, London, 1982-83; ptnr. Chantrey Vellacott, London, 1996—; trustee SCAR, London, 1993-94, Napata Fund, London, 1995. Contbr. articles to profl. jours. Centenary scholar Brighton Coll. Fellow Royal Soc. Encouragement of Arts and Industry; mem. Artistotelean Soc. Jewish. Avocations: music, literature, art. Home: Flat 5 10a Airlie Gardens, London W8 7AL, England Office: Chantrey Vellacott, 10/12 Russell Sq, London WC1 5LF, England

LADISCH, MICHAEL R., biochemical engineering educator; b. Upper Darby, Pa., Jan. 15, 1950; s. Rolf Karl and Brigitte M. (Gareis) L.; m. Christine Schmitz, July 26, 1975; children: Sarah, Mark. BSChemE, Drexel U., Phila., 1973; MSChemE, Purdue U., 1974, PhDChemE, 1977. Rsch. engr. Lab. Renewable Resources Engring. and dept. chem. engring. Purdue U., West Lafayette, Ind., 1977-78, asst. prof. food and agrl. engring., 1978-81, assoc. prof., 1981-85, prof., 1985—. Contbr. articles to profl. publs. Patentee in field. Chmn. com. on bioprocess engring. Nat. Rsch. Coun., 1991—. Recipient U.S. Presdl. Young Investigator award NSF, 1984. Fellow Am. Inst. Med. and Biol. Engrs.; mem. U.S. Nat. Acad. Engring., Am. Chem. Soc. (librarian 1982-84, chmn.-elect., 1985—, program chmn. 1985-86, past chmn. 1986—, coord. long range program 1990—, Van Lanen award BIOT div., 1990, W.H. Peterson award microbial div. 1977, Agrl. Rsch. award from Purdue U., 1985), Am. Inst. Chem. Engring., Am. Soc. Agrl. Engrs., N.Y. Acad. Sci. Office: Purdue U LORRE West Lafayette IN 47907

LADJEVARDI, HAMID, fund manager; b. Tehran, Iran, June 11, 1948; came to U.S., 1948; s. Ahmad and Banoo (Barzin) L.; children: Adella, Lilly. BA in Econs., BA in Polit. Sci., U. Calif., Berkeley, 1971; MBA, Harvard U., 1973. Dep. mng. dir. Behshahr Indsl. Group, Tehran, 1974-79; vice-chmn., fin. dir. Akam Group of Cos., Tehran, 1975-79; investment mgr., v.p. Morgan Stanley & Co., N.Y.C., 1980-92; mgr. Baltic Fund 1 LLC, N.Y., 1994—, Baltic Mgmt. LLC, N.Y., 1994; instr. Fairleigh Dickinson U., Rutherford, N.J., 1984; mem. supervising coun. Ober Haus Real Estate, Estonia, Alexela Oil, Estonia, Lindeks, Latvia, Kinnisvara Ekspress, Estonia; chmn. Baltic Fund Hotels, Vilnius, 1996—. Vice-chmn. U.S. Baltic Found. Mem. Fgn. Policy Assn., Carnegie Coun. on Ethics and Internat. Affairs, U.S. Senatorial Club, Harvard Club, Nat. Arts Club. Home: 11 Gramercy Park S Apt 3 New York NY 10003-1753 Office: Baltic Fund 1LP 15 E 26th St Ste 1809 New York NY 10010-1505

LADMER, WILLIAM EDWARD, food product engineering executive; b. N.Y.C., Jan. 21, 1942; s. Alfred Harold and Lucille (Peyser) L.; children: Lisa Beth, David. BSME magna cum laude, U. Ctrl. Ariz., 1966, MSIE, 1969. Registered profl. engr.; cert. plant engr. Engr. mgr. Boeing Corp., Seattle, 1966-72; pres. Ladmer Engring., San Diego, 1972-80, Allentown, Pa., 1982-90; engr. mgr. Sohio Petroleum, San Francisco, 1980-82; plant engr. mfg. Kraft Foods, Champaign, Ill., 1990-93; corp. engring. group mgr. McKee Foods, Collegedale, Tenn., 1993-97, E2M, Atlanta, 1997-98; plant engring. mgr. Pontiac Foods, Columbia, S.C., 1998—. Author: Design Build-What Can You-What Should You Expect, 1996, Project Engineering-Food Plants, 1991, Food Plant Sanitation, 1984. Firefighter Tri Cmty. Vol. Fire Dept., Collegedale, 1993-97. With U.S. Army, 1961-63. Mem. Inst. of Indsl. Engrs. (sr. mem.), Inst. of Plant Engrs. (sr. mem.), Soc. of Mfg. Engrs. (sr. mem.). Achievements include 2 patents on the method of 2 sided welding, application of leaded glass on substrate. Home: 30 Rosewalk Ln Elgin SC 29045-9407 Office: Pontiac Foods Pontiac SC 29223

LADO, FRANCISCO LUIS, internist, medical educator; b. La Coruña, Spain, Jan. 26, 1957; s. Francisco and María L. PhD in Medicine and Surgery, U. Santiago Compostela, 1997. Resident Univ. Hosp. Santiago, 1982-85, cons., 1999—, lectr., 1997—; cons. Hosp. de Monforte, Spain, 1986-91; mem. editl. bd. Spanish med. jour. Hipertensión Clínica, 1994—. Contbr. articles to profl. jours. Bd. dirs. Galician Soc. Internal Medicine, 1994-97. Mem. Spanish Soc. Internal Medicine. Avocations: chess, reading, water sports. Office: U Hosp Santiago, Dept Internal Medicine, 15706 Santiago Spain

LADOPOULOS, EVANGELOS GEORGE, civil engineer, mechanical engineer; b. Patras, Greece, 1962; s. George Evangelos and Aikaterini Athanasios (Sarmas) L. MSc in Civil Engring., Nat. Tech. U. Athens, Greece, 1984, MSc in Mech. Engring., 1987, DSc in Engring., 1990; DSc (hon.), N.Y. Acad. Scis., 1996, AAAS, 1997. Rschr. pvt. co. deal R&D program European Union, Athens, 1990—; educator Nat. Tech. U. Athens, 1990—. Contbr. articles to profl. jours. Cert. civil engr.; cert. mech.-elec. engr. Mem. Assn. Civil Engrs. Greece (rschr. 1994—), Assn. Mech.-Elec. Engrs. Greece (rschr. 1994—), N.Y. Acad. Scis. Avocations: swimming, football, basketball. Fax: 30-1-3644480. E-mail: eladopoulos@yahoo.com. Office: Interpaper Rsch Orgn, 56 Anagnostopoulou Str, 106 72 Athens Greece

LADURON, PIERRE, pharmacologist, neurobiologist; b. Namur, Belgium, Feb. 20, 1936; married; 4 children. Grad., U. Notre-Dame de la Paix Nemur, 1955; MD, U. Louvain, 1961, PhD in Pharmacology, 1969. Rsch. asst. U. Louvain, 1961-63; fellow Fonds Nat. de la Recherche Scientifique, 1962-63; rsch. asst. U. Ghent, 1964-68; head dept. pharmacology R.I.T. Genval, 1968-69; head dept. biochem. pharmacology Janssen Pharmaceutica, Beerse, Belgium, 1969-87; dir. rsch. in biology Rhone-Poulenc Santé, Vitry-sur Seine, France, 1987-92; assoc. prof. pharmacology U. Nancy, France, 1993-94; rsch. fellow Erasme U. Brussels, Belgium, 1995—; invited prof. Sch. Pharmacy U. Louvain, 1991—. Contbr. more than 320 articles to profl. jours. including Nature, PNAS, Jour. Neurosci., Molecular Pharmacology, Jour. Biol. Chemistry, Biochem. Pharmacology, European Jour. Pharmacology, others. Recipient travel scholarship Belgian Office Edn. and Culture, 1965, prize Assubel, 1978, Smith-Kline, 1986, van Gijsel prize, 1991. Office: Free U Brussels/Lab Rech, 808 Route Lennik, 1070 Brussels Belgium

LADVANSZKY, JANOS, electrical engineer; b. Budapest, Aug. 18, 1955; s. Janos Ladvanszky and Judit Gorog. Grad., Tech. U. Budapest, 1978; MSc, Hungarian Acad. Sci., 1988; DSc, Tech. U. Budapest, 1990. Rschr. in circuit theory and microwave circuit design Rsch. Inst. Telecomms., Budapest, 1978; scientific advisor Innovation Co. for Telecomms. Avocations: ham radio, sailing. Home: Vroci u 3, H-2013 Pomaz Hungary Office: Innovation Co Telecomms, Ungvar u 64-66, H-1142 Budapest Hungary

LADYGIN, VLADIMIR GEORGIEVICH, biologist, geneticist, researcher; b. Rasshevatskaya, Stavropol, Russia, Dec. 20, 1941; s. Georgii Vasil'evich and Elena Vasil'evna (Chernyshova) L.; m. Margarita Vasil'evna Antoninova, Jan. 23, 1969 (div. Nov. 1982); children: Antoninov Vladimir, Antoninov Dmitry; m. Olga Nikolaevna Golota, Mar. 11, 1983; 1 child, Maxim. Student, Moscow U., 1960-65; Cand., Inst. Biophysics, Pushchino, Moscow, 1970; D, Inst. of Photosynthesis, Pushchino, Moscow, 1993. Jr. rschr. Inst. of Biophysics, Puschino, 1965-79; sr. rschr. Inst. Photosynthesis, Puschino, 1979-93; head lab. Inst. Basic Biol. Problems, Puschino, 1993—; mem. acad. coun. Inst. Basic Biol. Problems, 1994—. Head trade union Inst. of Photosynthesis, 1981-88. Individual Soros grantee, 1993; Russian Acad. grantee, 1996, 99; Govt. of Russia scholar, 1994, 97. Mem. Plant Physiology Soc., Genetics Soc. Avocation: horticulture. Home: Microregion AB 9 flat 82, 142290 Pushchino Russia Office: Inst Basic Biol Problems, Institute St 2, 142290 Pushchino Russia

LAENG, MAURO FEDERICO, education educator; b. Rome, Feb. 15, 1926; s. Walther Gualtiero and Giuseppina (Carugo) L.; m. Graziella Ballanti; children: Enrico, Bruno. Laurea filosofia, U. Cattolica Milan, 1950; PhD, U. Statale Rome, 1963. Tchr. philosophy Classical Lyceum, 1950-57; tchr. Pedagogy Normal Sch., 1957-63; prof. comparative edn. U. Rome, 1963-66, prof. edn., 1967-96; emeritus prof. III U. Rome, 1996—. Author: Problemi di Struttura d Pedagogia, 1960, L'Educ Nella Civilta Tecnologica, 1969, 2d edit., 1984, Educazione Alla Liberta, 1980, 2d edit., 1985, 3d edit., 1990, Pedagogia Sperimentale, 1992, 2d edit., 1993; editor: Enciclopedia Pedagogica, 6 vols., 1990-94. Mem. AAAS, Ateneo di Sci. Lettere, N.Y. Acad. Scis. Home: via Lungomare Trieste 24, 64026 Roseto Abruzzi, Italy Office: III Univ Rome, V Castro Pretorio 20, 00185 Rome Italy

LAËNS, JEAN, internist, endocrinologist; b. Aureilhan, France, Aug. 19, 1946; s. Andre and Andreè (Pèrè) Laëns; m. Genevieve Lacombe, Jan. 22, 1971; children: Marie-Pierre, Elizabeth, Yannick. D in Medicine, U. Toulouse, France. Admissible to fellowship of internal medicine, Paris, 1977. Internist, specialist in endocrinology/metabolism Hosp., Toulouse, 1970-74, chief of clinic, 1974-77; chief of svc. Hosp., Tarbes, France, 1977—; expert pres la cour d'appel de Pau, France, 1989. Author numerous publs. in field. Recipient Golden medal Soc. Medicine, Toulouse, 1973, Faculty of Medicine, Toulouse, 1974. Mem. Assn. de Langue Française pour l'etude du Diabete et des Maladies Metaboliques, N.Y. Acad. Scis. Roman Catholic. Avocations: antique cars. Home: Impasse du Pic du Midi 7, 65690 Barbazan-Debat France Office: Hosp in Tarbes, BP 1330, 65013 Tarbes France

LAERUM, OLE DIDRIK, pathologist, surgical pathology consultant; b. Baerum, Norway, Apr. 23, 1940; s. Birger and Goro (Lynne) L. MD, U. Oslo, 1965, PhD, 1969; MD (hon.), Carol Davila Med. U., Bucharest, Romania, 1995. Diplomate in medicine and pathology, Norway. Rsch. fellow Inst. Pathology, U. Oslo, 1966-68, resident in pathology, 1970-71, sr. lectr., 1973-74; rector, pres. U. Bergen, Norway, 1990-95, prof. pathology, 1974—; vis. scientist Max-Planck-Institut, Tübingen, Germany, 1971-73, IARC, Lyon, France, 1996, U. Wash., Seattle, 1997; chmn. bd. The Rsch. Coun. of Norway, Oslo, 1992-94. Author or editor 21 books in Norwegian and English on sci. and cultural topics; author some 330 articles. Lt. Royal Norwegian Navy, 1968. Decorated comdr. Falcon Order (Iceland); comdr. St. Olaf Order (Norway); recipient Anders Jahre prize for Nordic Med. Rsch., U. Oslo, 1978, Norwegian Rsch. Coun. award for popular sci. authorship, Oslo, 1988. Fellow Norwegian Acad. Sci., Royal Norwegian Soc. for Scis. Avocations: Norwegian heritage and history, music (trumpet). Home: Gullfjordungsvegen 1, N-5700 Voss Norway Office: U Bergen Dept Pathology, The Gade Inst Haukeland Hosp, N-5021 Bergen Norway

LAFARGA, JUAN B., psychologist, psychotherapist; b. La Piedad, Mex., Mar. 31, 1930; s. Juan and Fannie (Corona) LaF. BA in Philosophy, Inst. Libre Philosophy, Mexico City, 1953, BA in Theology, 1960; MA in Psychology, Loyola U., Chgo., 1964, PhD, 1967. Lic. psychologist, Mex. Prof. dept. psychology U. Iberoamericana, Mexico City, 1967-95, founder, prof. dept. human devel., 1968-95, prof. emeritus, 1995, founder, prof. dept. psychotherapy, 1969-79, founder, prof. dept. edn., 1973-74, founder, prof. dept. rural devel., 1975-78; psychology dept. dir. U. Iberoamericana, Mexico City, 1981-89, acad. v.p., 1996, pres., 1996-98. Editor, author: Human Poetential Developement, vol. 1, 1979, vol. 2, 1981, vol. 3, 1982, vol. 4, 1984; founder, editor Tchg. & Rsch. in Psychology, 1975-84 (CNEIP award 1993), Mexican Jour. Psychology, 1985-89 (SMP Nat. award 1986), Prometeo, 1992-95. Recipient Jaime Castiello award U. Iberoamericana, 1994. Mem. Am. Psychol. Assn., Mexican Psychol. Assn., Nat. Coun. for Tchg. Psychology (sec. gen. 1992-96). Roman Catholic. Avocations: classical music, tennis, mountain climbing. Home: Margaritas 143, 05330 Mexico City Mexico Office: U Iberoamericana, Ave Jalisco 180-1, 11870 Mexico City Mexico

LAFAVE, RICHARD, engineer, consultant; b. Detroit, June 6, 1944; s. Arthur Victor and Marie Anne (Regan) L.; m. Carole Anne Mutch, June 26, 1971; children: Laura, David, Daniel. B in Welding Engring., Ohio State U., 1968, MBA, 1974. Registered profl. engr., Ohio, Pa. Indsl. engr. Jeffrey Mining Machinery Co., Columbus, Ohio, 1968-73; sr. research engr. Westinghouse Electric Co., Pitts., 1974-76; sr. cons. engr. Elliott Co., Jeannette, Pa., 1976—; tech. advisor Gateway Sch. Dist., 1987. Editor Pitts. Profl. Engr., 1992-95; co-inventor welding consumable, 1977; inventor welding method, 1999. Lay advisor Westmoreland County Community Coll., Youngwood, Pa.; mem. Pitts. Symphony Soc., 1987-89, Carnegie Inst., Pitts., 1987-89; parent advisor Gateway Sch. Dist., Monroeville, Pa., 1981. Recipient Highest Honors award Ohio Soc. Profl. Engrs., Columbus, 1968, 73, Arc Welding award J.F. Lincoln Found., Cleve., 1979, A.F. Davis Silver medal, 1995, Minnotte-Cable Svc. award, 2000. Mem. Am. Welding Soc. (tech. coms. 1979-99), Am. Council Internat. Inst. Welding, Nat. Soc. Profl. Engrs., Pa. Soc. Profl. Engrs., Chi Phi (Sparks medal 1968). Democrat. Roman Catholic. Office: Elliott Co N 4th St Jeannette PA 15644-1473

LAFF, JAY ELLIS, health facility acquisition executive, entrepreneur; b. Yonkers, N.Y., Dec. 9, 1942; s. Jesse M. and Charlotte (Greenstein) L.; m. Linda F. Glass, Dec. 26, 1965; children: Joshua F., Hillary J. BSBA, Bryant Coll., 1964; MBA in Hosp. Adminstrn., Wagner Coll., 1969. Cert. nursing home adminstr. Asst. adminstr. Albert Einstein Hosp., Bronx, N.Y., 1966-69; adminstr. French Hosp., N.Y.C., 1969-74; exec. dir. Freeport (N.Y.) Hosp., 1974-75; dir. bur. of long term care Pa. Dept. Health, Harrisburg, 1975-79; pres. Med. Ctr. for Aging, Inc., Doylestown, Pa., 1979-82, Med. Mgmt. Group, Inc., Doylestown, 1982-90; ptnr. Sencit Health Facility Acquisition Group, Harrisburg, 1986-95; dir. managed care PennMed Consultants, Inc., Allentown, Pa., 1995—; adminstr. Praxis Alzheimer's Facility, Easton, Pa., 1996-97; regional dir. Tendercare Inc., Sault St. Marie, Mich., 1997-2000; v.p. ops. Tandem Health Care, Inc., Ohio; mem. nursing home Pa. State Bd. Examiners, Harrisburg, 1975-79. Mem. citizen adv. panel Doylestown Intelligencer, 1991. Fellow Am. Coll. Health Care Adminstrs. (bd. dirs. Pa. chpt. 1990—, cert. com. 1989—, advancement and cert. com. 1989—). Avocations: reading, politics.

LAFFERRERIE, ANNIE MICHELE, ergonomic researcher, consultant; b. Radolfzell, Bade, Allemagne, Feb. 25, 1947; d. Michel André and Colette Marguerite (Renault) L.; m. Annie Michele Colette Vidal-Madjar, Nov. 23, 1968 (div. Dec. 1986); children: Boris, Maxime, Jérémie. D in Psychology, U. Paris, 1973, grad. in Ergonomics, 1987. Engr. Thomson-Sintra, Paris, 1969-73, CEGOS, Paris, 1973-75; maître de conférences Conservatoire Nat. Arts et Métiers, Paris, 1975—; rschr., prof., cons. Conservative Nat. des Arts et Métiers, Paris, 1975—. Organizer Médecins Du Monde, Paris, 1989. Mem. French Ergonomics Soc., French Psychology Soc., Syndicate Ergonomics Profls. Avocations: sports, exhibitions, concerts. Home: 34 Rue Du Monthuchet, 91160 Saulx Les Chartreux France

LAFFIE, DAVID, secondary school principal, molecular biologist; b. Houston, Tex., Feb. 3, 1944; arrived in China, 1987; s. Walter Goode and Helen Marie (Norris) Appleby; m. Norma Helen Rapone, June 1975 (div. May 1988); m. Samantha Solee, Aug. 6, 1988. BS, Drexel Univ., 1967; PhD, Univ. Pa., 1971. Group leader clin. products devel. Life Techs., Inc., Gaithersburg, Md., 1985-86; computer specialist U.S. Peace Corps, Washington, 1987-88; tchr. Sch. of the Nations, Macau, 1988-89; asst. prof. Univ. Macau, Macau, 1989-91, assoc. prof., 1991-94; prin. Canadian Coll. Macau, Macau, 1995—. Contbr. numerous articles to profl. jours. Mem. Local Spiritual Assembly of the Bahai's of Coloane, Macau, 1988—. Recipient Spl. Recognition award U.S. Peace Corps, 1988. Mem. Joseph Campbell Found., Phi Lambda Upsilon. Avocations: archery, study of history, astronomy and spritual development. Home: PO Box 9, Coloane Macau China Office: Can Coll Macau Edf Seng Vo, 2F/A 405 Av da Amizade, Macau China

LAFFINEUR, GÉRARD, bank executive; b. Rome, Dec. 18, 1961; s. Pierre and Maria-Laura (Petracchini) L.; m. Beatriz Oltra Pinto-Coelho; 1 child, Flavia. Engr., ENSIA, Paris, 1987; MBA, ESSEC, Paris, 1988. Asst. mgr. econ. and fin. studies dept. Crédit Lyonnais, Paris, 1988; agy. mgr. Société Générale, Paris, 1988-90, asst. mgr. fgn. trade fin. dept., 1990-91; with Fimat Internat., Société Générale Group, Paris, 1991-92; gen. mgr., mng. dir. Fimat Futuros España, Madrid, 1992-95, Fimat Internat. Banque, Sucursal en España, Madrid, 1995—; South European supr. Fimat Internat. Banque, Sucursal en España, Spain, Italy, Portugal, 1995—; mktg. mgr. SGFAM, Latin Amer., South Europe, 1996; head global banking and securities svcs. SG Milan, Italy, 1997. Mem. Cercle du Bois de Boulogne (Pigeon-Shooting Club, Paris), Royal Fedn. Fencing Madrid. Avocations: tennis, horseback riding, skiing, fencing, golf. Office: SG Milan, Via Olona 2, 20123 Milan Italy

LAFIELD, KAREN WOODROW, science educator, demographer; b. Fairfield, Ill., Oct. 14, 1950; d. Raymond and Margaret Ann (Simpson) Woodrow; m. William E. Mason, June 13, 1970 (div. July 1976); m. William L. Lafield, July 16, 1991. BA, U. Ill., Chgo., 1972; MA, U. Tenn., 1976; PhD, U. Ill., 1984. Demographic statistician U.S. Census Bur., Suitland, Md., 1983-92; adj. rsch. assoc. Ctr. for Social and Demographic Analysis SUNY, Albany, 1993-96; sr. rsch. analyst U.S. Commn. on Immigration Reform, Washington, 1994-95; rsch. scientist U. Tex., Austin, 1995-96; asst. prof. Miss. State U., Starkville, 1996-99, assoc. prof., 1999—; cons. NIH, Washington, 1994-99; cons.-rschr. Mex.-U.S. Binat. Migration Study, 1995-97; expert U.S. Immigration and Naturalization Svc., Washington, 1999—. Contbr. chpts. to books Migration Between Mexico and United States, 1998, Illegal Immigration: A Reference Handbook, 1999; mem. editl. bd. Population Rsch. and Policy Rev., Columbia, S.C., 1999—; contbr. articles to profl. jours. Rsch. grantee Nat. Insts. of Child Health and Human Devel., 1998-01. Mem. AAUS, Am. Sociol. Assn., Population Assn. Am., Am. Statis. Assn. (program com. 2000-01), So. Demographic Assn., N.Y. Acad. Scis. E-mail: woodrow lafield@soc.msstate.edu. Office: Miss State U 200 Bowen Hall Hardy Rd Mississippi State MS 39762

LAFINHAN, VICTOR OLATUNDE, marketing executive; b. Lagos, Nigeria, Aug. 1, 1954; s. John Bamidele and Dorcas Subuola (Aiyegbayo) L.; m. Rachel Bosede Olajide, Jan. 20, 1996; 1 child, Victoria. Diploma in bus. studies ctr. for bus. studies, Greenwich Coll., London, 1977, higher diploma in bus. mgmt. ctr. mktg./mgmt. studies, 1980; diploma Inst. Mgmt. Specialists, Greenwich Coll., Warwickshire, Eng., 1980. H.S. tchr. Nat. Youth Svc. Corps, Abeokuta, Nigeria, 1980-81; mktg. rep. Nigerian Explosives and Plastics Co., Lagos, Nigeria, 1982-85; mgr. Victor Lafinhan Enterprise, Ibadan, Nigeria, 1986-88; banking officer Nat. Bank, Iwo, Nigeria, 1989-92; CEO, pres. Victor Lafinhan Enterprise, Ibadan, 1993—; pres. Trent Tech. Co., Tbadan, 1999—. Publicity officer Nigerian Students, London, 1977-79; organizing officer Youth Corps, Abeokuta, 1980; ward mem. People's Dem. Party, Ibadan, 1999. Mem. Assn. Bus. Execs. London (assoc.), Inst. Mgmt. Specialists U.K., Nigerian Mktg. Assn. (assoc.), Nigerian Inst. Mgmt. (assoc.), Nigerian Inst. Mktg. Baptist. Avocations: reading, soccer, current affairs, music, traveling. Home: 8 Awogboro Crescent, Bodija Ibadan Nigeria also: UI Post Office, Box 19446, Ibadan Nigeria

LAFLEY, ALAN G., cosmetic company executive; b. Keene, N.H., June 13, 1947. AB, Hamilton Coll., 1969; MBA, Harvard Bus. Sch., 1977. Brand asst. Joy Procter & Gamble, 1977-78, sales tng. Denver Sales Dist., 1978-80, asst. brand mgr. Tide, 1978-80, brand mgr. Dawn & Ivory Snow, 1980-81, brand mgr. spl. assignment and Ivory Snow, 1981-82, brand mgr. Cheer, 1982-83, assoc. advt. mgr. PS&D Divsn. to advt. mgr., 1983-86, 86-88, gen. mgr. laundry products PS&D Divsn., 1988-91, v.p. laundry and cleaning products, 1991-92, group v.p., pres. laundry and cleaning products, 1992-94, group v.p., pres. Far East Divsn., 1994-95, exec. v.p., pres. Asia Divsn., 1995-98, exec. v.p., pres. N.Am. Divsn., 1998-99, pres. Global Beauty Care and North Am., 1999-2000; pres. & CEO Proctor & Gamble, 2000—. Trustee Hamilton Coll., Cin. Playhouse in the Park, Cin. Symphony Orchestra, Cin. Inst. of Fine Arts, The Seven Hills Sch.; past mem. Am. C. of C. in Japan, adv. coun. Schulich Sch. of Bus., York U., Toronto. With USN, 1970-75. Mem. Hamilton Club of So. Ohio, Harvard Club of Cin., Met. Club, Commonwealth Club of Cin. Office: The Proctor & Gamble Co 1 Procter And Gamble Plz Cincinnati OH 45202-3315*

LAFON, CYRIL, physicist, researcher; b. St. Yrieix la Perche, France, May 18, 1974; s. Roger and Danièle (Maud) L. MSc, U. Claude Bernard, Lyon, France, 1996, PhD, 1999. Rschr. INSERM Unit 281, Lyon, 1996-2000; rschr. Applied Physics Lab. U. Wash., Seattle, 2000—. Patentee in field. Referee French Fedn. Rugby. Winner Nat. Young Referee Contest for rugby, 1997, young rschr. contest City of Lyon, 2000. Mem. French Soc. Biomed. Engring. Achievements include patent for interstitial probe for hyperthermia applications. Avocations: rugby, guitar. Office: U Wash Applied Physics Lab 1013 NE 40th St Seattle WA 98105-6606

LA FOND, CHARLES FRANCIS, language school executive; b. St. Cloud, Minn., Sept. 15, 1957; s. Edward Marcus and Laura Jane (Van Evera) La F.; m. Elisabeth Maria Rammel, Aug. 21, 1982; 1 child, Stefanie. BA, St. John's U., Collegeville, Minn., 1978; MIM, Thunderbird Sch. Mgmt., Glendale, Ariz., 1980. Mgmt. trainee Berlitz Sch. Langs., Vienna, 1981-82, dir., 1982-84; owner, dir. Bus. Lang. Ctr., Vienna, 1984—; owner, dir. Buzan Ctr. Austria, Vienna, 1991—; trainer for presentation skills HPS Vienna, 1998—. Author: The Am-Pro Golf Caddie, 2000; editor newsletter Trattnerhof Tratsch, 1987—. Mem. Toastmasters Internat. (all offices, club pres. Vienna 1993-94, area gov. Europe 1993-95, 3d place Officers Contest 1994, 1st Pl. Officer's Contest 1995), Thunderbird Club (chpt. leader Austria 1984—). Avocations: skiing, public speaking, mind mapping, computers. Office: Bus Lang Ctr, Trattnerhof 2, Vienna A-1010, Austria

LAFONTE, ARNAUD ISMAEL, electrical engineer, company executive; b. Muriae, Brazil, Oct. 5, 1938; s. Emilio Lafonte Fernandes and Sebastiana Campos Lafonte; m. Terezinha Braga De Abreu, Oct. 5, 1967; children: Claudia, Delaine. Degree, Colegio Sao Paulo, Brazil, 1953, Colegio Juruena, Rio de Janeiro, 1956; degree in engring., Nacional Engenharia, Rio de Janeiro, 1963. Chief engr. distbn. CHESF, Rio de Janeiro, 1967-69, chief engr. power plants, 1969-70, asst. engr., 1970-75; adv. engr. Eletrobrás, Rio de Janeiro, 1975-96; advisor Ministry Mines and Energy, Brasilia, 1975-90; cons. Berenhauser, Rio de Janeiro, 1965-74; internat. coord. CIER, Montevideo, Uruguay, 1990-92; sci. cons. F&M 94 and F&M 97 SEE, France, 1993-98; cons. engr. Ecotec, Rio de Janeiro, 1997—; Author, editor articles, reports in field. Sgt. Brazilian Army, 1957-58. Recipient medal Agy. for Cooperation Sci. and Econ., 1987. Mem. AAAS, N.Y. Acad. Scis., Soc. Electriciens and Electroniciens, Soc. Bras. Math, Engrs. Club. Roman Catholic. Avocations: soccer, fishing, boating, jazz, collecting books. Home: Rua Marechal, Mascarenhas Morais 143 Apt 301, 22030040 Rio de Janeiro Brazil Office: Eletrobras, Av Pres Vargas 409 17th, Rio de Janeiro Brazil

LAFORCE, WILLIAM LEONARD, JR., photojournalist, columnist; b. Albemarle County, Va., Aug. 24, 1940; s. William Leonard and Florence Alberta (Sandridge) LaF.; m. Dorothy Lee Kesler, June 8, 1963 (div. 1987); children: William Perry, Glenn Edward. Student, U. Va., 1958-60; B.S., Johns Hopkins U., 1967, M.Liberal Arts, 1972. Dir. photography Balt. Sun papers, 1962-74; chief photographer, graphics editor and editl. page columnist N.J. edit. N.Y. Daily News, 1974-79; photojournalist N.Y. staff N.Y. Daily News, N.Y.C., 1979-94; contbg. photographer N.Y. Times, AP, 1994—; scholastic journalism faculty Columbia U., 1971-75; advisor Montclair U. Student Newspaper, 1980-84; lectr. to various news and photography orgns. Judge Miss Delmarva Pageant, 1969-74; planning com. Balt. City Fair, 1971; pres. Rumsey Island Residents Assn., Joppa, Md., 1969-72, Rumsey House Restoration Found., 1968-70, Mountain Lakes (N.J.) Fire Dept., 1977-79; Democratic committeeman, Mountain Lakes, 1976-78; chmn. Wildwood Sch. Bd., 1976-77; mgr. Mountain Lakes Little League, 1981, 85-86; bd. dirs. Joppatowne Civic Assn., 1969-71, vice chmn. citizens nominating com., 1977-81; mem. Pedestrian Safety Com., 1976-80; bd. dirs. Mountain Lakes Hist. Soc., 1987—, Am. Police Hall of Fame, 1987—; Morris County Disability Commn., 1995-97. Recipient Best Fire Photo in U.S. award Internat. Assn. Firefighters, 1967, Disting. Community Service award Jaycees, 1971, 1st Pl. Annapolis Fine Arts Festival, 1971, award for disting. community service Rumsey Island Residents Assn., 1972; Best Photo of Preakness Race award City of Balt., 1972, Page One award for best news photo in N.Y.C. Newspaper Guild, 1983, One Man Exhibition, Overseas Press Club, 1983; Best News Photo award N.Y. Press Club, 1984; 1st place Spot News award N.J. Press Assn., 1985, 91, Best PIX Story award N.Y.C. Police, 1986, 1st place Gen. News award N.J. Press Assn., 1991, nominated for Pulitzer award, 1984, 91. Mem. Nat. Press Photographers Assn. (dir. Mid-Atlantic region 1977-81, Pres.'s citation 1980, Bootstrap Leadership award 1981, chair nat. portfolio critique 1981-86, Williams award for 40 Years Contbn. to Photojournalism as a Profession 2000), Photographic Adminstrs. N.Y. (bd. dirs. 1986—, v.p. 1988-95), N.Y. Press Photographers Club, N.J. Press Photographers, N.Y. Press Club. Achievements include being the 1st to photograph in N.J. cts. since Lindbergh trial, 1978. Home and Office: PO Box 31 Mountain Lakes NJ 07046-0031

LAFRAMBOISE, JOAN CAROL, middle school educator; b. Bklyn., June 23, 1934; d. Anthony Peter and Nellie Eva (Zaleski) Ruggles; m. Albert

George Laframboise, Aug. 5, 1961; children: Laura J., Brian A. BS in Edn., Springfield (Mass.) Coll., 1956. Cert. tchr. social sci., and mid. sch.; cert. tchr. support specialist; cert. tchr. gifted. Tchr. Meml. Jr. H.S., Wilbraham, Mass., 1956-61, Midland Park (N.J.) Jr./Sr. H.S., 1961-63, Luke Garrett Middle Sch., Austell, Ga., 1983-93; tchr. lang. arts Pine Mountain Middle Sch., Kennesaw, Ga., 1993—. Coun. pres. Knights of Lithuania, Westfield, Mass., 1973-75, Holyoke, Mass., 1975-76, New Eng. dist. pres., 1976-77; mem. Wistariahurst Mus. Assocs., Holyoke, 1975-77. Jr. League mini-grantee, 1991. Mem. ASCD, NEA, Ga. Assn. Educators, Cobb County Assn. Educators, Nat. Coun. Tchrs. English, Nat. Coun. Social Studies. Home: 2891 Dara Dr Marietta GA 30066-4009

LAFRENZ, JÜRGEN HANS ROBERT, geography educator; b. Hamburg, Germany, May 1, 1938; s. Hans Emil and Anna Frieda (Patz) L. D in Geography, U. Hamburg, 1975, habilitation, venia legendi, 1985. Rsch. fellow U. Hamburg, 1965-76, 78-85, prof., 1985—, dir. Inst. für Geographie, 1992—; sci. coord. Deutscher Städteatlas Inst. Comparative History of Towns, U. Münster, Germany, 1976-78; project mgr. rsch. of water supply and disposal in S.W.-Nigeria, German Rsch. Assn. and Fed. Ministry of Sci. and Rsch., Bonn, 1998—. Editor: Deutscher Städteatlas, 1998—; contbr. numerous articles, monographs to profl. jours., presented many papers at sci. meetings and confs. Mem. Geographische Gesellschaft in Hamburg, Arbeitskreis für Historische Kartographie, Deutsche Gesellschaft für Kartographie (sect. Geschichte der Kartographie, Arbeitskreis für Genetische Siedlungsforschung, Inst. Planning History Soc., Soc. Am. City and Regional Planning History, European Assn. of Deans, Docomomo, Assn. Internat. Villes et Ports, Assn. European Soc. Planning, Internat. Assn. People-Environment Studies, Patriotische Gesellschaft von 1765 (Hamburg). Lutheran. Home: Opitzstrasse 10, D-22301 Hamburg Germany Office: Univ Hamburg Inst Geographie, Bundesstrasse 55, D-20146 Hamburg Germany

LAGANÀ, ANTONIO, chemical kinetics educator; b. Como, Italy, Nov. 4, 1944; s. Vincenzo and Giuseppa (Vinci) L.; m. Giovanna Lepri, June 23, 1945; 1 child, Leonardo. Laurea in Chemistry, U. Perugia (Italy), 1969. Tchr. physics and math. Istituto Magistrale A. Pieralli, Gubbio, Italy, 1971-75; lab. demonstrator U. Perugia (Italy), 1972-75; rsch. contractor U. Perugia, 1975-77; rsch. asst. U. Manchester (Eng.), 1977-78; lectr. chem. kinetics U. Perugia, 1979-85, prof., 1985—, prof. gen. and inorganic chemistry, 1994—; collaborator Los Alamos (N.Mex.) Nat. Lab., 1987-94, Centro Nazionale Universitario Calcolo Elettronico, Pisa, Italy, 1988-95; NATO fellow Calif. Tech., Pasadena, 1982; vis. prof. U. Cambridge, 1985; dir. Univ. Computer Ctr. Contbr. more than 180 articles to profl. jours. Cpl. Italian mil., 1970-71. Fellow Royal Soc. Chemistry; mem. Soc. Chimica Italiana, Assn. Italy Fisica, Assn. Italy Calcolo Automatico (rep. at Co-Operation in Sci. and Tech. Rsch. field (EC)), Computational Chemistry Group Italy (pres.). Avocation: economics. Office: Dept Chemistry U Perugia, Via Elce di Sotto 8, I-06123 Perugia Italy

LÅGAS, PENTTI ALVAR GUNNAR, psychiatrist; b. Vasa, Finland, Apr. 18, 1941; s. Karl Gunnar and Aino Bertta (Kinnari) L.; m. Ritva Riitta Pennanen, June 21, 1984; 1 child, Bengt. Med. candidate, Helsinki (Finland) U., 1965, MD, 1969, specialist in psychiatry, 1983. Cert. psychiatrist. Dept. physician Roparnäs Hosp., Vasa, 1973-82, sr. psychiatrist, 1983-93; specializing in psychiatry Helsinki (Finland) U., 1982-83; sr. psychiatrist Vasa (Finland) Ctrl. Hosp., 1993—; pvt. practice psychiatry, Vasa, 1975—; lectr. nurses schs., Vasa, 1983-95. Contbr. articles to profl. jours. Mem. Duodecim, Finnish Med. Assn. Helsinki, N.Y. Acad. Scis. Avocations: Spain, traveling. Home: Rantakatu 13 C 51, 65100 Vaasa Finland Office: Vaasa Ctrl Hosp Psychiatric, Sarjakatu 2, 65320 Vaasa Finland

LAGASSE, BRUCE KENNETH, structural engineer; b. Bklyn., Feb. 1, 1940; s. Joseph F. Lagasse and Dora S. Gould. BSME, U. Calif., Berkeley, 1964. Structures engr. Rockwell Internat., Canoga Park, Calif., 1964-69; mem. tech. staff Hughes Aircraft Co., Los Angeles, 1969-70; scientist/engr. Hughes Aircraft Co. (now Raytheon Sys. Co.), El Segundo, Calif., 1972-97; sr. engr. Litton Ship Systems, Los Angeles, 1971-72; prin. mech. engr. Raytheon Systems Co., El Segundo, 1997—; lectr., tech. edn. class coord. Hughes Aircraft Co., El Segundo, 1980-97; cons. in field, Van Nuys, Calif., 1979—. Libertarian state chmn., L.A., 1977-79, nat. committeeman, Washington, 1979-81; chair Libertarian Judicial Com. (state and national), 1996—. Mem. ASME. Avocations: reading, jogging, hiking, symphonic music, photography. Home: 7247 Balboa Blvd Van Nuys CA 91406-2702

LAGASSE, CHARLES-ETIENNE, Belgian government official, law educator; b. Brussels, July 30, 1948; s. André LaGasse and Genevieve Aubert; m. Cecile La Haye; children: Nicolas, Denis. D in Law, Cath. U. Louvain, Belgium, 1970, agrégé for tchg. at univ. level, 1980; cert. in Russian lang., Brussels Inst. Russian Lang., 1976. Rschr. Nat. Fund for Scientific Rsch., Belgium, 1970-75; mem. Commn. Française de la Culture de L'Agglomeration, Brussels, 1975-82; dir. cabinet Sec. State for Culture, Belgium, 1977-80; dir. adminstrn. Gen. Commissariat Internat. Rels. of French Cmty. of Belgium, 1983—; prof. pub. law Inst. Supeerieur Formation Sociale et Communication, Brussels, 1976—, Cath. Inst. Higher Comml. Studies, 1978; prof. Inst. Higher Studies Social Comm., Brussels, 1999; mem. C.A., Palais Beaux Arts, Brussels, 1996; v.p. Télé-Brussels, 1999. Author: L'Entreprise Soviétique et le Marché, 1979 (J.J. Merlot prize 1980), La Contre-Reforme de L'État, 1st edit., 1982, 2d edit., 1984, Les Institutions Politiques de la Belgique, 1st edit., 1988, 2d edit., 1990, Les Nouvelles Institutions Politique de la Belgique et de l'Europe, 1993, 2d edit., 1999; co-author (with Bernard Remiche): Une Constitution Inachevée, 1973. Mem. mcpl. coun. Ixelles, Brussels, 1970-89; dep. mem. Belgian Parliament, 1981-85. Conscientious objector svc., 1972-74, Brussels. Mem. Front Démocratique de Francophones. Avocations: aerobics, theatrical improvisation, piano. Home: Rue de la Vanne 37, 1000 Brussels Belgium Office: CGRI, 2 pl Sainetelette, 1080 Brussels Belgium

LAGDAMEO, MIKO A., Internet business development professional; b. Manila, Apr. 10, 1969; came to U.S., 1969; d. Mario S. and Marina A. Lagdameo. BA, Conn. Coll., 1991; MBA, Harvard U., 1997. Media planner D'Arcy Masius Benton & Bowles, N.Y.C., 1991; analyst Salomon Bros., N.Y.C., 1992-94, Salomon Bros. Internat., London, 1994-95; assoc. Montgomery Securities, San Francisco, 1997-99; sr. dir. bus. devel. Brodia.com, San Francisco, 1999—. Mem. Phi Beta Kappa. Avocations: traveling, art, horseback riding, rafting.

LAGE, CRISTINA, communications executive; b. Buenos Aires, Nov. 13, 1954; d. Ib Lage and Else (Olsen) H.; m. Poul Ingemann, 1978. BSc in Econs., Copenhagen Bus. Sch., 1977, MSc in Econs., 1980. Asst. v.p. Privatbanken, Copenhagen, 1982-85, v.p., 1985-87; sr. v.p., group treas. Internat. Svc. Systems, Copenhagen, 1987-92; fin. dir. Copenhagen Cultural Capital, 1992-94; group fin. dir. ISS Scandinavia, Copenhagen, 1994-96; dir. Louisiana Mus. of Modern Art, Humlebaek, Denmark, 1996-2000; CEO TV2/Danmark, Odense, 2000—. Office: TV2/Danmark, Rugaardsvej 25, DK 5100 Odense C, Denmark

LAGERBERG, DAGMAR ANNA-GRETA, child health researcher; b. Stockholm, July 25, 1941; d. Joen Carlsson and Valborg Clara Agnes (Holtermann) L. BA, U. Uppsala, Sweden, 1963, PhD in Sociology, 1975. Rsch. asst. dept. social medicine U. Uppsala, 1964-73, rschr. Cen. Unit Child Health, Univ. Hosp., dept. pediats., 1976—; assoc. prof. U. Uppsala, 1983; mem. sci. coun. Nat. Bd. Health and Welfare, Stockholm, 1984—; mem. program com. for social svc. stats. Nat. Cen. Bur. Stats., Stockholm, 1991-94; mem. consultative bd. Nat. Children's Ombudsman, Stockholm, 1996—; expert Govt. Commn. on Child Abuse and Neglect, 1999. Author: Child Abuse and Neglect--A Dilemma to the Child Health Services?, 1998; translator: (from Latin to Swedish) Spinoza: Ethics, 1989, (from French to Swedish) Montesquieu: The Spirit of Laws, 1990; referee Acta Paediatrica, 1995; contbr. articles and revs. to profl. jours. Decorated Knight Chevalier of Palmes Académiques, Pres. of France, 1992. Mem. Swedish Writers' Union. Lutheran. Avocations: literary activities, theology. Home: Vaksalagatan 42 B, S-753 31 Uppsala Sweden Office: Univ Children's Hosp, Dept Pediats, S-751 85 Uppsala Sweden

LAGERBLADE, MARY HELEN, relocation director; b. Moline, Ill., Aug. 15, 1942; d. Felix Joseph Rogenski and Stella Agnes Borowski; m. Roy Earl Lagerblade, May 30, 1969; children: Bridgit Janssen, Ross Joseph. BA, Western Ill. U., 1964. Tchr. Colona (Ill.) Sch., 1965-69; lic. realtor Boeye Realtors, Rock Island, Ill., 1991-95; relocation dir. Mel Foster Co., Davenport, Iowa, 1995—; mem. Relocation Dirs. Coun., 1996—; accredited real estate educator Nat. Assn. Realtors, Iowa, Ill., 1997—. Bd. dirs. Mississippi Valley Girl Scouts, Rock Island, 1997—; trustee Robert Young Mental Health Ctr., Moline, 1998—. Named Relocation Broker of Yr., Reliance Relocation Network, 1994, Relocation Broker of Yr., RELO-The Network, 1998. Mem. Ill. Quad City C. of C. (bd. dirs. 1998—), Rotary Club Rock Island (v.p. 1998—). Avocation: travel. E-mail: mlagerblade@melfoster.net. Office: Mel Foster Co Inc 3249 E 35th Street Ct Davenport IA 52807-2501

LAGERCRANTZ, JACOB HANS GUSTAV, physician; b. Stockholm, June 18, 1968; s. Richard and Birgitta (Rosén) L.; m. Svetlana Bajalica, June 17, 1995; children: Karolina, Marcus, Alexander. MD, Karolinska Inst., Stockholm, 1993; PhD, Karolinska Inst., 1996. Intern Karolinska Hosp., Stockholm, 1996—. Mem. Swedish House Nobility. Office: Dept Med Divsn Clin Pharm, Karolinska Hosp, 17176 Stockholm Sweden

LAGERSPETZ, KARI YRJÖ HENRIK, biologist, educator; b. Helsinki, Finland, Sept. 6, 1931; s. Yrjö and Lyyli (Levänen) L.; m. Kirsti Maria Johanne Ahlman, June 19, 1954; children: Eerik, Juhani, Olli, Mikko. Mag.Phil., U. Helsinki, 1954; Lic.Phil., U. Turku, Finland, 1958, PhD, 1960. Asst. U. Turku, 1954-64, lectr., 1960-64, prof., 1964-94, prof. emeritus, 1994—; rsch. prof. Acad. of Finland, 1976-79; vis. prof. Rockefeller U., N.Y., 1977. Author: Teleological Explanations and Terms in Biology, 1959, (in Finnish), The Animal and the Machine, 1966, From Chance to Control, 1983; co-author: (in Finnish) How to Write a Scientific Article, 1991; contbr. articles to profl. jours. Named Knight 1st Class Order of White Rose of Finland, 1986. Fellow Finnish Acad. Scis.; mem. Finnish Physiol. Soc. (chmn. 1982-90). Avocations: philosophy, summer home at Finnish seaside. Home: Vähä Hämeenk 7C, FIN20500 Turku Finland Office: U Turku, Dept Biology, FIN20014 Turku Finland

LAGEY, CLAUDE LEON R.S., pediatrician, orthopedist, surgeon; b. Elsene, Brussels, June 24, 1943; s. Henri Lagey and Simone Chauveheid; m. Jacqueline Caenberghs, Sept. 15, 1967 (div. 1990); children: Katrien, Tessa, Filip. Degree with great distinction, Koninlyk Atheneum, Hasselt, Belgium, 1961, Free U. Brussels, 1967; MD, Free U. Brussels, 1971. Cert. European Bd. Pediat. Surgery. Asst. Brugman U. Hosp., Brussels, 1971-82; pediatric orthopedic surgeon, 1982-95; head dept. pediat. orthop. Children's Hosp., Antwerp, Belgium, 1994—; head scientist U. Hosp., Utrecht, The Netherlands, 1980-82; cons. Stichting A.Kinsberger, Antwerp, 1985—, Iona Inst., Antwerp, 1989—, Merlyn Inst., Antwerp, 1990—; docent pediat. orthop. Hogesch., Antwerp, 1989—. Grantee NFWGO, 1980-81, Stichting Girard de Mielet van Coehoorn, 1981, 82. Mem. Belgian Soc. Surgery, Belgian Assn. Pediat. Surgery, Rotary. Avocations: hunting, forest mushrooms, nature, fishing, sheep farming. Office: Pediat Orthop, Prinses Jos Charlot Ln 18, 2600 Berchem Antwerp Belgium

LAGHI, PIO, archbishop; b. Province Forli, Italy, May 21, 1922; s. Anthony and Laura (Conti) L. STD, Pontifical Lateran U., Rome, 1947, JCD, 1950. Ordained priest Roman Cath. Ch., 1946, cardinal, 1991. Archbishop, 1969; entered diplomatic svc. Holy See, 1952; sec. Apostolic Nunciature, Nicaragua, 1952-54; sec. U.S. Apostolic Delegation, 1954-61, India, 1954-61; counselor Secretariate of State, Vatican City, Italy, 1964-69; apostolic del. to Jerusalem, 1969; apostolic pro-nuncio Cyprus, 1969-74; apostolic visitator Greece, 1972; apostolic nuncio Argentina, 1974-80; apostolic del. to U.S. Washington, 1980-84, apostolic pro-nuncio to U.S., 1984-90; permanent observer OAS, 1980-90; prefect Vatican's Congregation for Cath. Edn., Vatican City, Rome, 1990—; elevated to cardinal Roman Cath. Ch., 1991; now deacon St. Maria Ausiliatrice, Via Tuscolana. *

LAGNEBORG, RUNE GUNNAR, research institute executive, material scientist; b. Stockholm, Feb. 23, 1935; s. Gunnar Ernst and Alice (Olsson) L.; m. Inga Stina Lundblad; children: Johan, Anna. Diploma in Engring., Royal Inst. Tech., Stockholm, 1960, Lic. in Tech., 1963, D in Tech., 1967; MS, MIT, 1964. Rschr., sect. head Sandvik AB, Sandviken, Sweden, 1960-66; group leader Swedish AEC, Stockholm, 1966-69; prof. Royal Inst. Tech., 1969-74; mng. dir. Swedish Inst. for Metals Rsch., Stockholm, 1974-98; cons. materials sci. engr., 1998—. Contbr. 130 articles to profl. jours. Recipient Réaumur medal French Soc. Metallurgy, 1982, Rinman gold medal Jernkontoret, Stockholm, 1996. Mem. Swedish Acad. Engring. Scis., Swedish Soc. Materials Tech. (hon.). Home: Mjolnartorpsvagen 28, S-18266 Djursholm Sweden Office: Swedish Inst Metals Rsch, Drottning Kristinas vag 48, S-11428 Stockholm Sweden

LAGO, SANTIAGO, chemistry educator; b. Madrid, Mar. 2, 1952. PhD, U. Complutense, Madrid, 1979. Cert. chemistry. Asst. prof. U. Complutense, Madrid, 1974-81, assoc. prof., 1982-97; full prof. U. Corunna, Spain, 1997-98, U. Pablo de Olavide, Seville, Spain, 1998—; advisor Indsl. R&D Adv. Com., European Union, Brussels, 1992-94; dep. sec. gen. R&D Nat. Plan, Madrid, 1993-96. Vice-chmn. Orgn. for Econ. Cooperation and Devel. Megascience Forum, Paris, 1994-96. Humboldt fellow Humboldt Found., Bochum, Germany, 1981-82. Mem. AAAS, Royal Soc. Chemistry (thermodynamics group). Fax: 34-95-4349238. E-mail: slagara@dex.upo.es. Office: Fac Scis U Pablo Olavide, 41013 Seville Spain

LAGROSEN, STEFAN OLOF, marketing educator; b. Gothenburg, Sweden, Aug. 30, 1960; s. Gudmar Sievert and Ulla-Britt Mona (Larsson) Grosshög; m. Yvonne Eivor Hansson, May 30, 1995; children: Edvin, Emelie, Oscar. BSc, U. Sundsvall, 1984; MBA, U. Stockholm, 1993, PhD, 1997. Chmn. TM Stockholm, 1989-90; dir. MIU Acad., Norberg, Sweden, 1991-92; rschr. Muncipality of Täby, Stockholm, 1993-95, U. Stockholm, 1995-97; lectr. U. Gävle (Sweden)/Sandviken, 1997-98, U. Växjö, 1998—; cons. Lagrosen Quality Devel., Stockholm, 1988—. Author: Quality Management in Schools, 1997. Capt. Swedish Infantry, 1979-81, 86-89. Avocations: meditation, running, skiing. Home: Klövervägen 7, SE360 14 Väckelsång Sweden Office: U Växjö, SE 35195 Växjö Sweden

LAGUNAS, ROSARIO, biochemist; b. Navalcarnero, Madrid, Spain, May 14, 1935; d. Telesforo Lagunas and Rufina Gil; m. José Antonio Pestaña, Jan. 20, 1962; 3 children. BS, Complutense U., Madrid, 1958, PhD, 1963. Asst. researcher Inst. Investigaciones Biomedicas (CSIC), Madrid, 1966-71, researcher, 1971-91, rsch. prof., 1991—; treas. Spanish Soc. Biochemistry, 1981-82, sec., 1982-86. Mem. Acad. of Pharmacy, Spanish Soc. Biochemistry. Home: Romero Robledo 11 1oE, 28008 Madrid Spain Office: Inst Invest Biomed CSIC, Arturo Duperier 4, 28029 Madrid Spain

LAGUNEZ-OTERO, JAIME, researcher, scientist; b. Mexico City, Jan. 14, 1960; s. Mario Lagunez and Concepcion Otero-Rodriguez. BSc, UNAM, Mexico City, 1983; MSc, Weizmann Inst. Sci., Rehovot, Israel, 1986, PhD, 1992. Cert. in biomed. rsch. Rschr. UNAM, Mexico City, 1992—; mem. Supercomputing Com., Mexico City, 1996, 97, 98; mem., advisor Grad. Program on Biomed. Rsch., Mexico City, 1996-97. Contbr. articles to profl. publs.; spkr. in field. Goodwill amb. Rotary Club, Morelos, Mex. Fellow USA-Binat. Found., 1995. Mem. Nat. Sys. of Rschrs. of Mex. (Level I award 1996). Fax: 616-2203. E-mail: lagunez@servidor.unam.mx. Office: UNAM, Inst of Chemistry, Mexico City 04530, Mexico

LAHALIH, SHAWQUI M., engineer; b. Hebron, West Bank, Apr. 5, 1945; s. Mohammad Abdul-Hameed and Sarah A. (Sbaih) L.; m. Sahar Hassan Quisi, Aug. 13, 1977; children: Lisa, Amal, Ahmad, Mohammad. BS, Ill. Inst. Tech., 1969, MS, 1971, PhD, 1978. Rsch. engr. Am. Can Co., Batavia, Ill., 1974-75; rsch. scientist Union Carbide, Toxedo, N.Y., 1975-78; tech. advisor Am. Hosp. Supply, Calif., 1978-80; dep. mgr. KISR, Kuwait, Kuwait, 1980-90; sr. expert GOIC, Doha, Qatar, 1992-93; sr. rsch. engr. King Fahd U/RI, Dhahran, Saudi Arabia, 1994—; cons. in field; tech. advisor Pharmaseal, Glendale, U.S.A., 1978-80. Contbr. numerous articles to profl. publs.; 16 patents in product and process devel. Tchg. and rsch. asst. Ill. Inst. Tech., Chgo., 1969-74; rsch. grantee NSF/Kuwait Found. for Advancement Scis., 1971, 82, 85, Saudi Arabia Basic Ind. Corp., Riyadh, Saudi Arabia, 1996. Mem. AIChE, Soc. Rheology, Sigma Xi. Muslim. Avocations: basketball, running, softball, travel, sightseeing. Address: King Fahd U Rsch Inst, PO Box 1127, Dhahran 31261, Saudi Arabia

LAHAM, LUTFI, patriarchal vicar; b. Darayya, Syria, Dec. 15, 1933; arrived in Jerusalem, 1974; s. Zaki Elias and Martha Mikail (Kreit) L. PhD in Theology, Pontifical Oriental Inst., 1961. Rector, prof. theology St. Saviour Major Sem., Lebanon, 1961-64; prof. theology Kasliq U., Lebanon, 1966-69; founder, dir. Ctr. for Religious Culture and Apostolic Guidance, Lebanon, 1969-74; patriarchal vicar Greek Cath. Ch., Jerusalem, 1974—; founder, chmn., bd. dirs. Al-Liqa-Ctr. for Religious and Heritage Studies, Bethlehem, 1982—; founder DAR Al-Inaya Orthanage and Tech. Sch., Lebanon, 1966; founder, bd. dirs. St. Cyril Ctr-Adult Religious Edn., Jerusalem, 1975—. Author: The Voice of the Shepherd, Oriental Ecumenical Conference, Introduction to Oriental Liturgy and Symbols, Liturgical Book of the Melkite Church, The Melkite Church at the Second Vatican Council, History of the Church in the Holy Land, The Melkite Church, Anthologion of the Greek Catholic Church (4 vols.). Office: Greek Cath Patriarchate, PO Box 14130 Jaffa Gate, Jerusalem 91141, Jerusalem

LAHEY, RICHARD THOMAS, JR., education educator; b. St. Petersburg, Fla., Feb. 20, 1939; s. Richard Thomas and Ruth (Morris) L.; m. Eleanor Reinshagen, Dec. 23, 1961; children: Stephen, Patrick, Kathleen. BS in Marine Engring., U.S. Merchant Marine Acad., 1961; MS in Mech. Engring., Rensselaer Poly. Inst., 1964; ME in Engring. Mechanics, Columbia U., 1966; PhD in Mech. Engring., Stanford U., 1971. 3rd asst. engr. Cities Svc. Co., S.S. Fort Hoskins, 1961; engr. Knolls Atomic Power Lab., 1961-64; prin. devel. engr. GE, 1966-71, mgr. heat transfer mechanisms, 1971-72, mgr. core devel., 1972-73, mgr. core & safety devel., 1973-75; faculty Rensselaer Poly. Inst., Troy, N.Y., 1975—; Edward E. Hood Jr. prof. engring. Rensselaer Poly. Inst., 1989—; dean engring. Rensselaer Poly. Inst., 1994-98; dir. Ctr. for Multiphase Rsch., 1991-94; prof. Dept. Environ. & Energy Engring., 1995—, Dept. Chem. Engring., 1987—; chmn. Dept. Nuclear Engring. & Sci., 1975-87; vis. sr. faculty mem. Oxford U., U. Pisa (Italy), Imperial Coll. (U.K.), U. Cuyo (Argentina) and Claude Bernard U. (France). Contbr. more than 300 articles to profl. jours. Recipient Fulbright-Hayes fellowship, 1983-84, Alexander von Humboldt Sr. Scientist fellowship, 1994-95. Fellow ASME (chmn. Nucleonics Heat Transfer com. 1978-81, ECPD Coun. 1976-79), Am. Nuclear Soc. (bd. dirs. 1979-82, exec. com. 1980-82, chmn. Thermal-Hydraulics Divsn. 1979-82, chmn. Northeastern N.Y. sect. 1978-79, mem. ABET accreditation com. 1984-94, meritorious svc. award 1983); mem. NAE, Russian Acad. Sci., Am. Inst. Chem. Engrs. (chmn. Energy Transport Rsch. Field com. 1987-91), Am. Soc. Engring. Edn. (chmn. Nuclear Engring. Divsn. 1986-87). Avocation: enology. E-mail: laheyr@rpi.edu. Office: Rensselaer Poly Inst Troy NY 12180-3590

LAHMANN, ROBERT OSCAR, artist, retired; b. Port Washington, Wis., July 4, 1923; s. Oscar Otto and Edna Mildred Lahmann; m. Lorraine Loretta Lahmann, Apr. 14, 1956; children: Robert Charles, Ellen Jeyne Lahmann Christensen, Peter William, Emily Arlene Lahmann Boysa. Grad. in Art, Layton Sch. Art, Milw., 1950; student in Portrait Painting, Acad. Fine Arts, Chgo., 1956-57; studied with Guitano Busalacchi, Milw., 1957-65. Tchr. art, 1962-64; tchr. art Delafield, Wis., Pewaukee Wis.; pvt. tchr., 1962-64. Exhibited in group shows U. Wis., 1947 (1st prize), Layton Sch. Art, 1948-49, Bay Shore Exhibit, 1952, Bresslers Gallery Exhibit, 1960, Ramsburg Gallery, Oconomowoc, Wis., 1960, Watertown Open Show, 1961, Maple Dale Sch. Exhibit, 1977, Sentinal Art Show, 1979-80, North Lake Art Show, 1979-80, County Fair, 1979, 80, 81 (prize winner 1979, 80, 81), West Bend Gallery, 1981, 15th Ann. Arts Festival, 1981-82, Paine Gallery, 1998; sculptor Milw. County Zoo, 1960; artist stain glass, 1962; represented in permanent collections Landmark Gallery, Marquett U., City of Port Washington, St. John's Ch., Milw. Electric Tool Corp.; paintings donated to Friends of Channel 10-36. Recipient Andrew Clark award Wis. Regional Art Show Assn., 1979, Award of Excellence League of Artists, 1979, 80, 99, Best of Show award League of Artists, 1980, Purchase award Waukesha County Ct., 1981-85, Aaron Bohrod award Wis. Regional Art Show Assn., 1984-87. Mem. Wis. Regional Artist Assn., League Milw. Artists, West Bend Friends of Art.

LAHOTI, RAJENDRA K., surgeon, urologist; b. Vidisha, India, Sept. 26, 1945; s. Madan Mohan and Kamla Devi (Malpani) L.; m. Usha Rathi, Feb. 17, 1972; children: Ashish, Anupam. B Medicine B Surgery, U. Indore, India, 1968, MS in Gen. Surgery, 1972. Diplomate Am. Bd. Surgery, Can. Bd. Surgery. Cons. SICM Hosp., Indore, 1978—, Choithram Hosp., Indore, 1982—; dir. Medicare Hosp., Indore, 1990—, Indore Kidney Ctr., 1998—. Author: Establishment and Management of Small Hospitals and Nursing Homes, 1994. Fellow Royal Coll. Surgeons Can.; mem. Am. Coll. Surgeons, West Zone Urol. Soc. India. Avocations: badminton, visiting. Home: Vinod 9/1 S Tukoganj, Indore MP 452001, India Office: Medicare Ctr, 4/5 Old Palasia, Indore MP 452001, India

LAHOUD, EMILE, president of Lebanon; b. Baabdat, Lebanon, Jan. 12, 1936; m. Andree Amadouni, 1967; 3 children. Student, Mil. Coll., Lebanon, 1956; grad., Naval Engring. Coll., UK, 1959; postgrad., Naval Engring. Acad., UK, 1986. With Lebanese Army, 1959-98, advanced through grades to brig. gen., 1985; comdr.-in-chief Lebanese Armed Forces, 1989; pres. Republic of Lebanon, 1998—. Avocations: swimming, scuba diving, fishing. Office: Office of the Pres, Presdl Palace, Beirut Lebanon

LAHTI, MARKKU SAKARI, research scientist; b. Evijärvi, Finland, Feb. 15, 1968; s. Paavo Ilmari and Raija Sinikka L. MS, U. Oulu (Finland), 1993. Rsch. asst. U. Oulu, 1992-93, researcher, 1994-95, 97—, asst., 1996-97. Contbr. articles to profl. jours. Mem. Internat. Microelectronics and Packaging Soc. (Nordic). Avocations: skiing, golf. Home: Matilaisentie 1 B 4, Oulu 90570, Finland Office: 9004 Univ Oulu, Linnanmaa POB 4500, Oulu 90571, Finland

LAHVIS, SYLVIA LEISTYNA, art historian, educator, curator; b. Ilion, N.Y., Dec. 6, 1936; d. Arthur Leistyna and Margareta Maresch; m. W. Frederick Lahvis, Nov. 12, 1960; children: Garet Paul, Matthew Arthur. BA, U. Rochester, 1958; MA, Oberlin Coll., 1972; PhD, U. Del., 1990. Curatorial asst. Yale U. Art Gallery, New Haven; curator New Milford (Conn.) Hist. Soc., 1975-78; co-curator Univ. Gallery U. Del., Newark, 1985; curatorial dir. The Sewell C. Biggs Mus. Am. Art, Dover, Del., 1993-95; lectr. edn. dept. Albright-Knox Art Gallery, Buffalo; lectr. art history Wykeham Rise Sch., Washington, Conn.; instr. Canterbury Sch., New Milford; adj. prof. U. Del., 1986-87, Rutgers U., Camden, 1988, 91-92, dept. art history U. Del., 1989, Coll. Human Resources, 1988-89, adj. prof. dept. art history, 1989—, Master of Arts in Liberal Studies program, 1992—, U. Del; curator Index of Am. Sculpture, 1982-86, symposium com., 1985; vis. asst. prof. Washington U., Chestertown, Md., 1989, Del. Coll. Art and Design, 1997—; presenter in field. Contbr. articles to art jours. Interpace and Clevepak Corp. fellow U. Del.; Henry Luce Found. grantee. Mem. Coll. Art Assn., Assn. Am. Mus., Soc. Archtl. Historians, Decorative Arts Soc., Nat. Trust for Hist. Preservation, Archives of Am. Art, Phi Kappa Phi, Phi Beta Kappa. Democrat. Mem. Unitarian Ch. Avocations: singing, designing. Home: 2309 W 18th St Wilmington DE 19806-1203

LAI, BRENDAN, martial arts professional; b. Nov. 15, 1942. PhD, Eurotech. Rsch. U., 1990. Pvt. practice instr. martial arts San Francisco, 1968—. Inducted into Hall of Fame, Black Belt Mag., L.A., 1984, Hall of Fame, Inside Kung-Fu Mag., L.A., 1990; named Ky. Col., Commonwealth of Ky., 1985. Mem. U.S. Nat. Karate Assn. (hon. 10th degree black belt), United Kung Fu Fedn. N.Am. (v.p. 1993), Shandong Liu-Her Tang Lang Assn. (China, hon. chmn. 1991), Shandong Yantai Internat. Praying Mantis Assn. (China, hon. chmn. 1991), Internat. No. Praying Mantis Fedn. (chmn. 1993). Office: 2075 Mission St San Francisco CA 94110-1217

LAI, ERIC PONG SHING, family physician, educator; b. Kowloon, Hong Kong, May 20, 1946; s. Man Hoi and Lai Ming (Chiu) L.; m. Mimi Maria Mak Lai, Sept. 11, 1972; children: Gordon, Jennifer. BSc, Acadia U., Wolfville, Nova Scotia, 1971; MB, B CH, LRCS, LLMRCP, U. Ireland, Dublin, 1977; DFM, Chinese U. Hong Kong, 1989. Med. diplomate, Ireland, UK, Hong Kong. Rsch. fellow Med. Sch. McGill U., Montreal, Can., 1971; resident in medicine Chesterton Hosp. Cambridge (Eng.) U., 1977; resident New Addenbrooke Hosp., Cambridge, 1978; resident in gynecology Princess Margaret Hosp., Kowloon, Hong Kong, 1979-81; pvt. practice family physician Hong Kong, 1981-99; bd. dirs. First Med. Mgmt. Ltd., Calgary, Alta., Can., 1989; found. dir. Chinese Recreation Assn., Calgary; lectr. Hong Kong U., 1986-92, Chinese U. Hong Kong, 1986-92; facilitator

Hong Kong Coll. Gen. Practitioners, 1986-92; internat. dir. World Orgn. Health Promotion, 1993-2000; cons. G-Way Holdings Internat. Inc., 1993-2000; internat. med. dir. G-Way Health Centre, Can., 1995-2000. Mem. Hong Kong Dem. Found., 1990-92, Hong Kong Bd. Edn. Coll. Gen. Practitioners, 1986-92, chmn., 1991-92, com. chmn. refresher course, 1991-92; vice chmn. found. Kidney Ctr. Precious Blood Hosp., 1991; adviser S.E. Asia Rsch. Inst., 1992; mem. Pub. Edn. Com., 1993-95; med. cons. World Orgn. Health Promotion, Can., 1993-99. Named Henry Burton De Wolfe scholar to McGill U., 1971. Mem. Internat. Lions Club (v.p. Mt. Cameron chpt. 1986-90, pres. 1990-91, zone chmn. Internat. Club 1991-92, Melvin Jones fellow 1991-99). Democrat. Avocations: reading, meditation, writing poetry, walking, boxing.

LAI, FENG CHYUAN, mechanical engineering educator; b. Taipei, Taiwan, Aug. 6, 1956; came to the U.S., 1983; s. Chin-Mao and Matsuko (Suzuki) L.; m. Hongshing Cheng, July 26, 1986; children: Cathy B., Anthony C. BS, Nat. Tsinghua U., Hsinchu, Taiwan, 1978; Ms, U. Del., 1985, PhD, 1988. Asst. engr. Energy Rsch. Lab., Hsinchu, 1980-82; rsch. assoc. Colo. State U., Fort Collins, 1986-92; asst. prof. U. Okla., Norman, 1992-98, assoc. prof., 1998—. Contbr. articles to Internat. Jour. Heat & Mass Transfer, Jour. Heat Transfer, Jour. Thermophysics & Heat Transfer. Recipient New Investigators award Okla. Ctr. for the Advancement Sci. and Tech., Oklahoma City, 1995. Mem. AIAA (sr.), ASME, IEEE, ASHRAE. Office: AME Univ Okla 865 Asp Ave Norman OK 73019-1050

LAI, HONG-SHIEE, medical educator; b. Chang-Hwa, Taiwan, July 9, 1953; s. Heng-Shang and Yi-Hsia (Lee) L.; m. Ya-Chin Yang, June 18, 1983; children: Shou-Lun, Li-An. MD, Nat. Tawian U., Taipei, 1978, PhD, 1991. Resident Vet. Gen. Hosp., Taipei, Taiwan, 1978-79; resident Nat. Taiwan U. Hosp., Taipei, 1979-84, vis. staff, 1986-93, vice-chmn. surg. dept., 1996-99; assoc. prof. Nat. Taiwan U. Coll. Medicine, 1993-99, prof., 1999—; chief pediat. surg. divsn. Nat. Taiwan U. Hosp., 1995-99; chmn. diet dept. Nat. Taiwan U. Coll. Medicine; vis. staff King Fahad Hofuf Hosp., Saudi Arabia, 1984-86, Nat. Tawian U. Hosp., 1986-93. Editor: Farseeing Medical Dictionary, 1996; mem. editl. bd. Internat. Med. Jour. Nutrition, 1994. Fellow organ transplant team U. Pitts., 1987-88. Mem. Chinese Assn. Parenteral & Enteral Nutrition (sec. gen. 1993-97), Pacific Assn. Pediat. Surgeons. Avocations: piano, tennis, table tennis. Office: Nat Taiwan U Hosp, 7 Chung-Shan South Rd, Taipei 100, Taiwan

LAI, JOHN CHRISTOPHER, minister, educator, consultant; b. London, Ont., Can., May 25, 1953; s. Luigi Salvatore Lai and Betty Jean (Arthur) Norwich; m. Sandra Kay Huber, Mar. 14, 1981; 1 child, Christopher John. Cert. of completion, Calvary Pastor's Sch., Santa Ana, Calif., 1978; BA in Behavioral Sci. summa cum laude, Nat. U., San Diego, 1989; MA, Fielding Inst., Santa Barbara, Calif., 1993, postgrad., 1999—. Ordained to ministry Calvary Chapel Ch., 1978. Sr. pastor Calvary Chapel, Escondido, Calif., 1978-82; pres. VCF, Inc., San Marcos, Calif., 1982-90; prin. J.C. Assocs., 1987—; adj. instr. Horizon Sch. Evangelism, San Diego, 1979-81, U. Redlands, Calif., 1993—; adj. prof. Cathedral Bible Coll., Escondido, 1990; v.p. human resources Med. Analysis Systems, Camarillo, Calif., 1999—. Composer/lyricist songs including All of Me, 1982, I Receive You, 1982; co-composer/lyricist Glorious, 1988. Mem. ASCAP, ASTD, Am. Sociol. Assn., Am. Mgmt. Assn., O.D. Network, Soc. Sci. Study Religion, Religion Rsch. Assn., Soc. Human Resources Mgmt., Soc. Orgnl. Learning. Address: 5394 Quailridge Dr Camarillo CA 93012-4114

LAI, JOSHUA P.L., information technology manager; b. Hong Kong, Nov. 13, 1958; s. Wing Kin and Suk Chun (Wan) L.; m. Karen K.L. Chu, July 20, 1986; 1 child, Daniel. BS with hons., U. B.C., Vancouver, 1982; MBA, U. Strathclyde, U.K., 1994. Chartered engr. Info. tech. mgr. Hong Kong Bank, 1983—. Mem. IEEE, Brit. Computer Soc., Hong Kong Computer Soc. Office: II/F HSBC Centre Tower 3, 1 Sham Mong Rd, Kowloon, Hong Kong China

LAI, LOI LEI, engineering educator, scientist; b. Hong Kong, Feb. 7, 1956; arrived in Eng., 1978; s. Kang Nam and Tung Lan (Lam) L.; m. Li Rong Li, Feb. 13, 1989; children: Qi Ling, Chun Sing, Qi Hong. BS with honors, U. Aston, Birmingham, Eng., 1980, PhD, 1984. Chartered engr., Eng. Sr. lectr. Staffordshire U., Eng., 1984-88; dir. energy systems group City U., London, 1989—; hon. prof. North China Electric Power U., Beijing, 1994—; Royal Acad. Engring. Indsl. fellow GEC Engring. Rsch. Ctr., Eng., 1986-87; advisor Lucas Aerospace, Eng., 1992; cons. Marks & Spencer, Eng., 1993, BICC Group, Eng., 1994; rsch. prof. Tokyo Met. U., 1995. Author: Loi Lei Lai, Intelligent System Applications in Power Engineering-Evolutionary Programming and Neural Networks, 1998, The Dictionary of Contemporary Celebrities of Worldwide Chinese, Asian Pacific International Culture, 1999; contbr. articles to profl. jours. Sr. tech. advisor to Ministry of Power, UN, Beijing, 1996. Recipient High Quality Essay award Internat. Desalination Assn., 1995, Cert. of Honor, Asian Pacific Comm. Co. Ltd. Internat. Ctr., 1999. Mem. IEEE (sr.; recipient Third Millennium medal 2000), Instn. Elec. Engrs. (corp.), Instn. Elec. Engrs. U.K. (prize 1980). Avocations: cooking, playing chess, gardening. Home: 187 The Heights, Northolt UB5 4BU, England Office: City Univ Energy Systems, St John St, London EC1V 0HB, England

LAI, RICKY K. M., banker; b. Hong Kong, China, Sept. 4, 1971; s. Yung Hing Lai and Yok Lan Lau. Higher diploma English for Profl. Comm., City Poly. of Hong Kong, 1994; MBA, Lancaster (Eng.) U., 1996. Pro-mgr. mktg. Chase Manhattan Bank, Hong Kong, 1994-95; relationship mgr. corp. and instnl. banking Std. Chartered Bank, Hong Kong, 1996-99; cons. BICC Plc, Lancashire, Eng., 1995. Charter mem., 3d v.p. Leo Club Silverstrand, Hong Kong, 1995. Shell Outward Bound scholar City Poly. Hong Kong, 1993. Mem. Robert Morris Assoc. (assoc.), Royal Hong Kong Yacht Club. Avocations: sailing, fountain pen collecting, trekking, photography. Fax: 852 2641 5464. E-mail: lairick@hotmail.com. Office: Std Chartered Bank, 38 Kwun Tong Rd, Hong Kong China

LAI, RUAY-SHENG, physician, educator; b. Chia-I, Taiwan, Nov. 10, 1957; s. Lih-Yong Lai and Tzyy-Yuh Hwang; m. Pei-Ching Lee, 1989. MB, Taipei (Taiwan) Med. Coll., 1984. Med. diplomate. Vis. staff Vet. Gen. Hosp.-Kaohsiung, 1993—; lectr. Nat. Yang-Ming U., Taipei, 1997—; asst. prof. Foo-Yin Inst. Tech., Kaohsiung, Taiwan, 1998—. Contbr. articles to profl. jours. Fellow Am. Coll. Chest Physicians; mem. Soc. Internat. Medicine Taiwan, Soc. Pulmonary and Critical Care Medicine. Avocations: tennis, classical music. Office: Vet Gen Hosp-Kaohsiung, 386 Ta-Chung 1st Rd, Kaohsiung 813, Taiwan

LAI, SHIH-KUNG, urban planning educator; b. Tao Yuen Shen, Taiwan, Nov. 15, 1957; s. Kuo-Hao and Tsai-Yuan (Huang) L.; m. Chiung-Ku Lee, Nov. 15, 1993. BSE, Nat. Cheng Kung U., Tainan, Taiwan, 1979; MA in City and Regional Planning, Ohio State U., 1985; PhD, U. Ill., 1990. Tchg. subject: Planning Methods and Decision Theory. Vis. assoc. prof. Nat. Taipei (Taiwan) U., 1990-91, assoc. prof. planning methods, decision theory, complex spatial sys., 1992-97, prof., dir. Ctr. for Land Mgmt. and Tech., 1997—. Contbr. articles to profl. jours. Mem. Am. Planning Assn., Chinese Planning Assn. (acad. com. mem. 1990—), Inst. for Ops. Rsch. and Mgmt. Scis. Avocation: swimming. Office: Nat Taipei U, 67 Sec 3 Min Sheng E Rd, Taipei Taiwan

LAI, YEONG-KANG, science educator; b. Taipei, Taiwan, July 13, 1966. BS, Tamkang U., Taipei, 1988; MS, Nat. Taiwan U., 1990, PhD, 1997. Rschr. Academia Sinica, Taipei, Taiwan, 1992-93; asst. prof. Chang Gung U., Taoyuan, Taiwan, 1997-98, Dong Hwa U., Hualien, Taiwan, 1998—. Contbr. articles to profl. jours. Lt. army, Kaohsiung, Taiwan, 1990-92. Mem. Phi Tau Phi. Office: Nat Dong-Hwa U, 1 Sec 2 Da Hsueh Rd, 974 Shou-Feng Hualien Taiwan

LAI, YEONG-LIN, electronic engineering educator, scientist; b. Taipei, Taiwan, July 24, 1963. BSEE, Feng Chia U., Taichung, Taiwan, 1985; MS in Electronics, Nat. Chiao Tung U., Hsinchu, Taiwan, 1992, PhD in Electronics, 1997. Scientist Chung Shan Inst. Sci. & Technology, Taoyuan, Taiwan, 1985-89; sr. engr. Macronix, Inc., Hsinchu, Taiwan, 1992-93; from instr. to asst. prof. dept. electronic engring. Ming Hsin Inst. Technology, Hsinchu, 1994-98; asst. prof. dept. electronic engring. Chang Gung U., Taoyuan, 1998, Feng Chia U., Taichung, Taiwan, 1998—; cons. Hexawave, Inc., Hsinchu, Taiwan, 1993-97.

LAI, YOUNG-JOU, industrial engineer; b. Changhou, Taiwan, July 30, 1960; s. Ching-Yen and Ching (Chang) Lai; m. Jochun Wu, July 7, 1990; children: Sunny Yen-Wen, Tony Yen-An. BBA in Indsl. Mgmt. Sci., Nat. Cheng-Kang U., 1983; MS in Indsl. Engring., Kans. State U., 1989, PhD in Ops. Rsch., 1991. Asst. prof. Kans. State U., Manhattan, 1991-96; ops. rsch. analyst HCL Internat., Inc., Manhattan, 1992-96; ops. rsch. specialist Phillips Petroleum Co., Bartlesville, Okla., 1996—; adj. prof. Kansas State U., 1996—; spkr. in field. Author: Fuzzy Mathematical Programming, 1992, Fuzzy Multiple Objective Decision Making, 1994; contbr. articles to profl. jours. including Computers and Ops. Rsch., European Jour. of Operational Rsch., Fuzzy Sets and Systems, IIE Transaction, Internat. Jour. of Prodn. Rsch., Jour. of the Operational Rsch. Soc., Quality and Reliability Engring., others. Recipient 1997 Annual Wingman award of Refinery, Mktg., Transp., Phillips Petroleum Co. Mem. Inst. for Ops. Rsch. and Mgmt. Sci., Internat. Fuzzy Systems Assn., Prodn. and Ops. Mgmt. Soc., Phi Kappa Phi. Avocations: golfing, fishing, running, reading. Home: 2318 Windsor Way Bartlesville OK 74006-7549 Office: Phillips Petroleum Co 15b4 Phillips Bldg Bartlesville OK 74004-0001

LAI, ZHONG-FANG, medical educator; b. Ganzhou, Jiangxi, China, June 26, 1957; arrived in Japan, 1992; s. Muhan and Zhefei (Zeng) L.; m. Yu-Zhen Chen, June 15, 1984; 1 child, Mikako. M in Med. Scis., Chinese Acad. Chinese Medicine, Beijing, 1987; MD, Jiangxi Med. Sch., Nanchang, 1982; PhD, Kumamoto (Japan) U. Sch. Med., 1996. Resident in medicine Ganzhou Gen. Hosp., Jiangxi, 1982-84; physiology lectr. Cardiovasc. Inst., Fu Wai Hosp Chinese Acad. Medicine, Beijing, 1987-90; asst. prof. pharmacology Sch. Medicine Kumamoto (Japan) U., 1992—. Mem. Internat. Soc. for Heart Rsch., Physiology Soc. China, Chinese Med. Assn., Japan Pharmacology Assn. E-mail: lai-z@gpo.kumamoto-u.ac.jp. Office: Kumamoto U Sch Med, 2-2-1 Honjo, Kumamoto 860-0811, Japan

LAIKANOK, PRAMOAT, military officer; b. Sattahip, Cholburi, Thailand, Jan. 14, 1957; s. Sa-Nga and Prang (Sirmsomboon) L.; m. Surang Kurchim, Aug. 17, 1986; children: Mokkara, Rattasat, Peeranat. Cert. air traffic control, Air Tech. Sch., Bangkok, Thailand, 1976; cert. air traffic control operator, Air Traffic Sch., Miss., 1983, 87, Air Traffic Sch., Victoria, Australia, 1990; student, Sch. Toshiba Corp., Kawasaki, Japan, 1992; diploma in art, Rajabhat Inst., Suratthani, Thailand, 1996, BEd, 1999. Cert. aero. info. svc. officer, Thailand, 1982. Radar operator wing 4 Air Traffic Control Br., Nakhonsawan, Thailand, 1976-79; air traffic control operator wing 46 Air Traffic Control Br., Pitsanuloke, Thailand, 1979-80; radar operator wing 4 Takhli AFB, Nakhonsawan, Thailand, 1980-84; chief air traffic control tower Directorate Air Ops., Bangkok, 1984-85; chief radar unit wint 7 Air Traffic Control Br., Suratthani, 1985-86; navigation sect. instr. Directorate Edn. and Tng., Bangkok, 1986-88; dep. chief air traffic control br. RTAF, Bangkok, 1992-95, chief, 1995—, English instr., liaison, 1996—. Patentee in field. Pub. rels. officer Rajabhat Inst., Suratthani, 1994-96, chmn. English major students, 1997—. Mem. Air Force Club (vice chmn. wing 7 1998-99, chmn. sports 1991). Buddhist. Avocations: reading, teaching English, research, writing, sports. Home: Saimai, Saimai Bangkok 10220, Thailand Office: Air Traffic Control Br, Wing 7 Asia 41, Phunphin Suratthani 84130, Thailand

LAINCZ, BETSY ANN, nurse; b. Phila., Feb. 7, 1949; d. Harry Ellsworth and Betty Mary (Minton) Henderson; m. Douglas Dardaris, 1968 (div. 1975); children: Amy, Christopher; m. Fred J. Laincz, Jan. 12, 1982; children: Joshua, Emily, Michael. Student, Bucks County C.C., Newtown, 1969-87, Temple U., Phila., 1973, Upper Bucks Sch. of Nursing, Perkasie, 1983, Internat. Sch. of Shiatsu, Doylestown, 1995-96. Lic. nurse, Pa. Staff nurse, mental health technician Doylestown (Penn.) Hosp., 1983-85, data abstractor med. records, 1988-89; nurse, coun., asst. mgr. NutriSystem, Warrington, Pa., 1985-88; nurse Independence Court, Quakerstown, Pa., 1991; health svcs. supr. Bucks County Assn. Retarded Citizens, Quakerstown, 1992-95; nurse Penn Found. Drug and Alcohol Recovery Ctr., 1996-2000; owner, founder, operator Willow Agy., Perkasie, Pa., 1996—; supports and standards com. Bucks County Assn. Retarded Citizens, 1995; nurse recruiter, staffing specialist Healthskil, Willow Grove, Pa., 2000—. Editor (newsletter) Serendipity, 1996-98. Mem. United Friends Sch., co-chair fundraising, 1989-97, nominating com., 1995—, ann. auction com. 1990-97, devel. com, 1991-92, 98—; active Individual's Person Centered Planning Team, 1994—, Inst. of Noetic Scis., 1993—. Mem. Buck Womens Investment Club (v.p. 1995), The Smithsonian Instn., Libr. of Congress Assn., Nat. Assn. of Investers Corp., Co-op Am., Sierra Club. Republican. Mem. United Ch. Christ. Avocations: reading, writing, art, antiques. Home: 532 W Market St Perkasie PA 18944-1419

LAINE, ALE MATTI JUHANI, neuropsychologist, researcher, educator; b. Elimäki, Finland, Oct. 7, 1955; s. Ale Armas and Aira Kyllikki (Pukkila) L.; m. Merja Kaarina Kulmala; children: Aini, Milja. MA, U. Turku, Finland, 1980, PhD, 1990. Legitimated psychologist. Assoc. lectr. dept. psychology U. Turku, 1980—, clin. neuropsychologist Ctrl. Hosp., 1984—, docent neuropsychology, 1992—; rsch. asst. Aphasia Rsch. Ctr., Boston VA Med. Ctr., 1981-82; mem. exec. com. Ctr. for Cognitive Neurosci., U. Turku, 1990—; rschr. Acad. Finland, 1991-94, 95—; mem. Nat. Bd. for Specialization Tng. in Clin. Neuropsychology, 1996-98; chair nat. bd. Specialization Tng. In Psychology, 1999-00. Mem. editl. bd. Aphasiology, 1993—; co-editor (spl. issues) Nordic Jour. Linguistics, 1993, Aphasiology, 1996, 98; contbr. articles to profl. jours. Mem. European Fedn. Neurol. Socs. (mem. speech and lang. disorders scientist panel 1995—), European Soc. for Cognitive Psychology, Acad. Aphasia. Avocations: music, writing, sailing. Office: Dept Neurology 720, Univ Turku, FIN20520 Turku Finland

LAINE, ANTHONY WESLEY, avionics engineer; b. Hempstead, L.I., July 17, 1945; s. Sheldon Wesley Laine and Sarah Martha Goldberg/Laine; m. Donna Jean Spratley, Mar. 23, 1983. BSEE, MIT, 1971; PhD in Elec. Engring./Nuclear, Century U., 1985. Author: (book) Injuries, Trauma and Death Due to Nuclear War, 1987; co-author books on space and electromagnetics; contbr. numerous papers to sci. jours.; painter portraits including Prime Min. Golda Meir, Moshe Dayan, Pres. Ronald Reagan, Martin Luther King, Hank Aaron (portrait used for U.S. postage stamp), others; patentee in field. Nominated mem. Rep. Chmn.'s Adv. Bd., 1994; nominated rep. State of Ariz., 1995 Inaugural of Newly Elected Persons to Ho. of Reps. and U.S. Senate, 1995; nominated sr. leadership counsel Chmn.'s Adv. Bd., 1995; nominated State of Ariz. Del. to 1994 Mid-Term Conv., 1994. Recipient Cert. Recognition for extraordinary patriotism Pres. George Bush, 1992, award for exceptional leadership and dedication, 1992, Eisenhower award for spl. trust and confidence Pres. Reagan, Bush, and Ford, 1995; nominated for Nobel Prize for Physics, 1984. Mem. Rep. Pres.'s Club (nominated). Republican. Avocations: painting. Home: 29 Vanmark Way Saint Louis MO 63144-2437

LAINE, KATIE MYERS, communications consultant, executive coach; b. Bluffton, Ohio, Oct. 2, 1947; d. George Emerson and Eleanore (Keeney) Myers; m. Donald Edward Laine (div. Feb. 1990); 1 child, Brett Edward. BS in Edn., S.W. Tex. State U., 1970. Dir. vols. Austin (Tex.) Ctr. for Attitudinal Healing, 1983-86; talk show host Austin Cablevision, 1986-89; community rels. officer Laguna Gloria Art Mus., Austin, 1989-90; spl. events mgr. Ann Richards for Gov. Campaign, Austin, 1990—. Profl. TV talk show host Katie Laine and Friends. Mem. Mayor's Adv. Coun., Austin, 1989—, Austin Women's Polit. Caucus, 1989—, Emily's List, 1989—; vol. Mayor Lee Cooke Campaign, 1988, Ann Richards Campaign for Gov., 1989; tchr. Divorce Recovery Clinic; co-chair tng. team Coun. Cmty. Reconcilliation, 1999. Mem. NOW, Women in Communications, Nat. Assn. for Corp. Speaker Activities, Paramount Producers. Avocations: speaking, TV prodn., reading, dancing. Home: 8703 United Kingdom Dr Austin TX 78748-6400

LAINE, TAPIO PEKKA JUHANI, psychiatrist, researcher; b. Savonlinna, Finland, Dec. 1, 1961; s. Veikko Vihtori and Siina (Jortikka) L.; m. Anna Leena Leinonen; 1 child, Risto. MD, Oulu (Finland) U., 1987, degree in Psychiatry, 1998, degree in Family Therapy, 1999. Gen. practitioner City of Oulu, Finland, 1987-93; asst. physician Oulu (Finland) U. Hosp., 1993-98, sr. psychiatrist, 1998—; sec. EFNS Scientific Panel of Alcoholic Effects in Central and Peripheral Nervous System, 1999. Contbr. articles to profl. jours. Bass shouter Mieskuoro Huutajat, Oulu, Finland, 1987-98. Avocation: addiction medicine, dopamine transporter, alcohol. Phone: 358-40-5144163. E-mail address: plaine@sun3.oulu.fi. Home: Nokelantie 47 A 8, FIN90150 Oulu Finland Office: Oulu U Hospital, Peltolantie 5, FIN90220 Oulu Finland

LAING, EDWARD ARTHUR, government official, judge; b. Belize City, Belize, Feb. 27, 1942; d. Edward Arthur and Marjorie Eunice (Dunn) L.; m. Margery Victoria Fairweather, Apr. 5, 1969; children: Obi, Nyasha. B.A., Cambridge U., 1964, LL.M., 1966; LL.M., Columbia U., 1968. Bar: Eng. 1966, Ill. 1969, Belize 1970, Barbados 1972, D.C. 1985. Assoc. Baker & McKenzie, Chgo. and N.Y.C., 1968-69; sr. lectr. U. West Indies, Barbados and Jamaica, 1970-75; asst. prof. Notre Dame U., Ind., 1974-76; assoc. prof. U. Md., Balt., 1976-81; prof. Howard U., Washington, 1980-85; amb. to U.S. and Can., Govt. of Belize, Washington, 1985-90; prof. N.Y. Law Sch., 1990-93; elected judge Internat. Tribunal for the Law of the Sea, Hamburg, 1996—; permanent rep. of Belize to UN, 1993-97; magistrate, crown counsel Belize Govt., 1966-67; faculty adviser Internat. Trade Law Jour., Balt., 1976-81; participant numerous Summit Confs. and exec. bd. UN Devel. Program; internat. adjudicator trade and bus. law, law of the sea; cons. to UN agys. on internat. devel. and governance, consolidation of democracy and human rights, legal edn. Author: Introduction to Caribbean Law, 1973; contbr. articles to profl. jours. Ind. advisor Belize C. of C., 1981; founder and 1st pres. New York Belizean Com., NYC, 1999, Consortium for Belizean Devel., Washington, 1985. Recipient scholarship Govt. of Belize, 1961-66; Fulbright Travel grantee, 1967; Ford Found. Research grantee, 1972, World Intellectual Property Orgn. Acad. grantee, 1997. Mem. Am. Soc. Internat. Law. Avocations: outdoors camping; canoeing. Office: Internat Tribunal for the Law of the Sea, Wexstrasse 4, 20355 Hamburg Germany

LAING, MALCOLM BRIAN, geologist, consultant; b. Apr. 4, 1955; s. Alexander Duncan and Joan (Dawson) L.; m. Vicki Lynne; children: Megan Jenè, Brian Duncan. BS in Geology, Tex. Christian U., 1978. Geologist Electro-Seise, Inc., Ft. Worth, 1978-79, Exploration Logging Co., Houston, 1979-80, Thomas-Powell Royalty Co., Ft. Worth, 1980-82, Lentex Petroleum Inc., Abilene, Tex., 1982-84; cons., 1984-90, Tex. Dept. Health, 1990-92, Tex. Water Commn., 1992-93, Tex. Natural Resource Conservation Commn., 1993—; world wide cons. on WWII German aircraft. Co-author: FW-190D Walk Around, FW 190A/F Walkaround. Dir. Caprock chpt.; bd. dirs. Tex. Air Mus., 1995—. Mem. Am. Assn. Petroleum Geologists, Panhandle Squadron CAF (past leader), Phantom Squadron (past leader), West Tex. Wing CAF (past fin. officer, past CAF check pilot, past ops. officer). Republican. Methodist. Office: 4630 50th St Ste 600 Lubbock TX 79414-3520

LAING, NIGEL GEORGE, medical researcher; b. Edinburgh, Scotland, June 3, 1954; arrived in Australia, 1981; s. William and Elizabeth Catherine (Clark) L.; m. Susan Carol Fyfe, Apr. 22, 1982; children: James, Peter. BSc with honors, Edinburgh U., 1976, PhD, 1979. Rsch. asst. U.K. MRC, Edinburgh, 1976-79; European fellow Royal Soc., Oslo, 1980; sr. rsch officer Australian Nat. Health and Med. Rsch. Coun., Perth, 1981-86, 89-90; rsch. officer Telethon Found., Durham, N.C. and Perth, 1987-88; sr. rsch. fellow Australian Neuromuscular Rsch. Inst., Perth, 1991-96, Australian Nat. Health and Med. Rsch. Coun., Perth, 1997—; adj. sr. lectr. U. Western Australia, Perth, 1997—; adj. assoc. prof. Murdoch U., Perth, 1997—. Contbr. articles to profl. jours., chpts. to books. Paul Harris fellow Rotary Internat. Mem. World Muscle Soc. (mem. exec. bd. 1997-99), Neuromuscular Disorders (edit. bd. 1999—), Human Genetics Soc. Australia. Avocation: fishing. Office: Australian Neuro Rsch Inst, QEII Med Ctr, Nedlands 6009, Australia

LAING, ROBERT SCOTT, lawyer; b. Chgo., Aug. 7, 1952; s. Robert Bruce and Mary Edith (Lindsay) L. BA magna cum laude, Fla. Technol. U., 1973; JD, U. Fla., 1976. Bar: Fla. 1977, U.S. Dist. Ct. (so. dist.) Fla. 1978. Asst. pub. defender Pub. Defender's Office, Bartow, Fla., 1975-76, Vero Beach, Fla., 1976; asst. states atty. State's Atty.'s Office, West Palm Beach, Fla., 1976-77; pvt. practice West Palm Beach, 1977—. Contbr. numerous articles to profl. jours. Bd. dirs. Gainesville Cultural Commn., Fla., 1974-75; Fla. Dem. committeeman, Lakeland, 1976; mem. City Utilities Bd., Vero Beach, Fla., 1976. Mem. Assn. Trial Lawyers Am., Fla. Bar Assn. (chmn. gen. practice sect. 1980-81, chmn. fed. practice com. criminal law sect. 1982-83), ABA (vice chmn. criminal practice com. 1983-85, gen. practice sect., chmn. 1985-86), Acad. Fla. Trial Lawyers, Palm Beach County Bar Assn. (mem. cir. ct. criminal adv. com. charter), Palm Beach County Criminal Def. Lawyers Assn., Am. Judicature Soc., West Palm Beach Eagles (charter chpt. v.p. 1988-89), Phi Delta Kappa (nat. parliamentarian 1981-82, 83-84, nat. long range planning com. 1983-85, pres./caliph 1992-93), Moose (life mem., life legionnaire 1976—), Elks (treas. 1987-88, chaplain 1994-95). Office: Laing Law Bldg 2072 S Military Trl West Palm Beach FL 33415-6419

LAINSON, RALPH, parasitologist, researcher; b. Upper Beeding, Sussex, Eng., Feb. 21, 1927; s. Charles Harry and Anne (Denyer) L.; m. Ann Patricia Russell, 1956 (div. 1976); children: Karen Susan, Amanda Jane, Stephen Paul; m. Zéa Constante Lins, Apr. 12, 1989. BSc, London U., 1951, PhD, 1955, DSc, 1964; D (hon.), U. Fed. Pará, Brazil, 1982. Lectr. London Sch. Hygiene and Tropical Medicine, 1955-59, rsch. worker, 1962-65; officer-in-charge Dermal Leishmaniasis Unit, Cayo Dist., Belize, 1959-62; dir. The Wellcome Tropical Unit, Belém, Brazil, 1965-92; rsch. worker, cons. leishmaniasis Inst. Evandro Chagas Fundação Nat. de Saude, Belém, 1992—. Contbr. over 350 articles to profl. jours. Mem. steering com. WHO, Geneva, 1977-83. Named to Order of Brit. Empire, 1996; recipient Chalmers medal and Manson medal Royal Soc. Tropical Medicine and Hygiene, 1971, 83. Fellow Royal Soc. of London; mem. 3d World Acad. Scis. (assoc.), London Sch. Hygiene and Tropical Medicine (hon.), Royal Soc. Tropical Medicine and Hygiene, Brit. Soc. Parasitology (hon.), Soc. Protozoologists (hon.). Anglican. Avocations: philately, music, lepidoptera, fishing. Office: Inst Evandro Chagas, Ave Almirante Barroso 492, 66090-000 Belém Para Brazil

LAISSY, JEAN PIERRE, health facility administrator, radiologist; b. Neuilly-sur-Seine, France, May 10, 1953; s. Michel and Denise (Alleaume) L.; m. Elizabeth Gabrielle Ironde, Jan. 27, 1975; children: Thomas, Matthieu. MD, U. Paris VII, 1982; PhD, U. Paris V, 1993; Habilite a Diriger des Recherches, 1993. Intern Hosp. de Paris, 1978-82, asst. chef de clinique, 1982-86; praticien hospitalier Paris, 1987—; prof. radiology, 1997—; assoc. dir. radiology dept. Hosp. Bichat, Paris, 1991—; assoc. rschr. U. Paris VII, 1994—. Co-author several med. books, 1986—; co-author and co-editor: (med. book) Imaging Advances, 1995; contbr. articles to profl. jours. Capt. Med. Support to French Army, 1978-79. Mem. Radiol. Soc. N.Am., French Radiol. Soc. Office: Hop Bichat, 46 Rue Henri Huchard, 75018 Paris France

LAJOIE, JEAN-LOUIS PHILIPPE, law educator; b. Lyon, France, Dec. 1, 1946; s. Philippe Louis Joseph and Jeanne Louise Rome L.; m. Nicole Perrier, Oct. 9, 1977 (div. 1990); 1 child, Guillaume Philippe Paul; m. Monique Bouchard, 1990. Degree, U. Lyon, 1969, ML, 1970, diploma, 1971, LLD, 1983. Jurist Algeria, 1977-83; prof. constitutional law U. Lyon, 1983—, v.p., 1993-94; prof. Inst. Regional Adminstrn., Lyon, 1990-95; mem. specialist commn. U. Law Lille II, 1995-98, Toulouse 1, 1998—, Paris X, 1998—; v.p. univ. mgmt. com. Lyon U., 1993-94, dir. dept. carrieres juridiques, 1994—, mem. bd. faculty of law, 1994; vis. prof. U. Phnompenh, Cambodia, 1995—; mem. bd. Ecole Nat. Svcs. Veterinaires, 1995-98. Author: Methode de Science Juridique L'Hermes, 1986; contbr. articles to profl. jours. Mem. Assn. Nat. des Docteurs en Droit, Soc. Francaise de Finances Publiques, Assn. des Membres de L'ordre des Palmes Academiques. Avocations: skiing, bibliophilism. Home: 10 Rue Duquesne, 69006 Lyon France Office: IUT Lyon 3, 4 Cours Albert Thomas, 69372 Lyon Cedex08, France

LAJTHA, GEORGE, editor-in-chief; b. Budapest, Hungary, Mar. 10, 1930; s. George and Ilona (Fuhrer) L.;m. Judit Brebovszky; 1 child, Gabor. Elec. engr., Tech. Univ. Budapest, 1952, D habil. tech. sci., 1977, PhD (hon.), 1964. Rschr. Post Office Rsch. Inst., Budapest, 1952-63; sci. dir. PORI, Budapest, 1964-86; editor-in-chief Hungarian Telecomm. Jour., Budapest, 1986—; mem. Nat. Com. for Tech. Devel., 1990-95, owner Bekesy, Eotvos, Puskas and Szechenyi. Author: Planning and Theory of Telecommunication

Network, 1971, Optical Communication Systems and Their Components, 1978. Mem. Telecomm. Engrs. Soc. (presidium body), Acad. Sci. (chmn. telecomm. com. 1993-2000). Calvinist. Avocation: sports. Home: Budafoki ut 10/A, 1111 Budapest Hungary Office: Hungarian Telecomm Co, 1541 Budapest Hungary

LAKATOS, SUSAN CAROL, investment banker, artist; b. N.Y., 1960. BA, Georgetown U., 1981; MBA, Columbia U., 1989. CFA. Economist Washington Analysis Corp., 1980-84; v.p., economist Kidder, Peabody & Co., Inc., N.Y.C., 1984-89, investment strategist, 1989-92; pres. Ananda Advisors, 1992-2000; dir. rsch. Veronis Suhler, N.Y.C., 2000—; bd. dirs., chair com. on prices, Bus. Rsch. Adv. Coun., Washington, 1983-92. One person shows include Stables Art Ctr., Taos, 1996-98, Bareiss Gallery, Taos, 1998. Mem. fin. com. Columbia Bus. Sch. Mem. Assn. Investment Mgmt. and Rsch., N.Y. Soc. Securities Analysts, Fin. Womens Assn. N.Y. Office: 350 Park Ave New York NY 10022-6022

LAKDAWALA, SHARAD R., psychiatrist; b. Broach, India, Oct. 7, 1949; came to U.S., 1977; s. Ramprasad D. and Kailasben Lakdawala; m. Bhavna B. Khatri, Jan. 2, 1978; children: Viraj, Ravi. BJ, Med. Coll., Ahmedabad, India, 1972. Diplomate Am. Bd. Psychiatry and Neurology, Am. Bd. Geriat. Psychiatry. Intern Civil Hosp., Ahmedabad, 1972-73; resident in psychiatry B.J. Med. Coll. and Civil Hosp., Ahmedabad, 1974-75; med. officer in-charge psychiat. unit Kasama (Zambia) Gen. Hosp., 1975-77; rotating intern NYU Med. Ctr., 1977-78, Bellevue Hosp., 1977-78; resident CUNY/Mt. Sinai Svcs., 1978-81; pvt. practice, 1981—; dir. mental health svcs. Tampa Gen. Hosp., 1988-93, chmn. dept. psychiatry, 1990-93; med. dir., svc. dir. adult psychiatry Charter Hosp. Tampa Bay; sys. med. dir. Charter Behavioral Health Sys. Tampa Bay; chmn. dept. psychiatry Tampa Gen. Hosp.; past pres. med. staff Charter Hosp. Tampa Bay, svc. dir. adult psychiatry; mem. St. Joseph's Hosp.; systems med. dir. Charter Behavioral Health Sys. Tampa Bay; assoc. divisional med. dir. Charter Behavioral Health Sys., 1998—; cons. in field. Fellow Am. Psychiat. Assn., Fla. Psychiat. Soc., Tampa Psychiat. Assn. (v.p. 1989-90, pres. 1990-91), Am. Assn. Psychiatrists India (pres-elect Fla. chpt.). Office: 2908 W Waters Ave # 101 Tampa FL 33614-1855 also: 505 Eichenfeld Dr # 106 Brandon FL 33511-5956

LAKE, RUTH ANN, company executive; b. Marietta, Ohio, Sept. 24, 1953; arrived in Italy; d. Wiilis Wayne and Ellen Garmen (Turner) L.; m. Antoine S. Jabbour; 1 child, Lily Catherine. BA in Internat. Rels., U. de las Ams., Puebla, Mex., 1975; MPA, Am. U., Wash., 1980, MS in Bus. Comms., 1982. Program mgr. Internat. Programs Am. U., Wash., 1979-82; sr. cons. Galgano & Assocs., Milan, 1984-89; cons., project mgr. SINNEA, Bologna, Italy, 1989-91; ptnr., cons. Focus Cons. Internat., Milan, 1991—. Mem. Am. Soc. Tng. & Dent., Internat. Soc. for Intercultural Edn., Tng. & Rsch., Profl. Women's Assn. Milan. Democrat. Avocations: snorkeling, skiing, photography. E-mail: lakejabb@pmp.it. Home: via Europa 5, 20068 Peschiera Borromeo Italy

LAKE-BRUSE, KRISTY DEAN, pharmacologist, toxicologist, researcher, educator; b. Riverside, Calif., Dec. 22, 1958. BS in Biology, U. Mo., 1982; MS in Biology, Southwest Mo. State U., 1986; PhD in Pharmacology, Toxicology, Va. Commonwealth U., 1996. Vet. asst. Emergency Vet. Clinic, Overland Park, Kans., 1981-83; vet. asst., office mgr. Stanley (Kans.) Vet. Clinic, 1982-83; vet. asst. Sunset Animal Clinic, Suisun City, Calif., 1987, Berkeley (Calif.) Dog and Cat Hosp., 1987-88, Alameda County Emergency Animal Hosp., San Leandro, Calif., 1988-89; tchg. asst. Clover Hill High Sch., Richmond, Va., 1996; postdoctoral fellow Univ. Iowa, Iowa City, 1997—; rschr. U. Calif., Davis, 1987, Syntex, Palo Alto, Calif., 1988-92, Scios Nova, Inc., Mountain View, Calif., 1992-93; vis. prof. U. Iowa, 1999, Kirkwood Cmty. Coll., Cedar Rapids, Iowa, 1999. Contbr. articles to profl. jours. Mentor Thomas Jefferson High Sch., Richmond, Va., 1994-95, 95-96; sci. fair judge West Valley Elem. Sch., Cupertino, Calif., 1990, 91, 92, 93, Santa Clara Valley Sci. and Engring. Fair, San Jose, Calif., 1991, 92, Greater Metro Richmond (Va.) Sci. Fair, 1995, 96, Va. Jr. Acad. Sci., 1994, 95, 96. Recipient Young Investigator's award Am. Heart Assn., Incline Village, Nev., 1998, Caroline tumSuden/Frances A. Hellebrandt Profl. Opportunity award Am. Physiological Soc., San Francisco, 1998. Avocations: softball, scuba diving. E-mail: kristy-bruse@uiowa.edu. Fax: 319-353-5350. Home: 2269 235th St Williamsburg IA 52361-9623 Office: Dept Internal Medicine Univ Iowa 2000 ML Iowa City IA 52242

LAKHANPAL, BALBIR, sales executive; b. Chandigarh, India, Mar. 11, 1955; s. Narsingh Das and Asha (Sharma) L.; m. Rekha Raina, July 8, 1982; 1 child, Niranjan Das. BSChemE, Panjab U., Chandigarh, India, 1978. Registered profl. engr., India, U.K., U.S. Engr. Caltex Petroleum-Bapco, Bahrain, 1978-81, sr. engr., 1981-82, process specialist, 1982-91; mgr. tech. Grace Davidson, Worms, Germany, 1991-96, tech. mktg. mgr., 1996-97, dir. sales and tech. sales, 1997—. Contbr. articles to profl. jours. Co. rep. India Relief, Bahrain, 1990. Mem. AIChE, IChE (U.K.), IIChE (India). Avocations: golf, bridge, palmistery.

LAKHANPAL, SHARAD, physician; b. Lucknow, India, Oct. 15, 1951; came to U.S., 1980; s. Rajendra Nath and Indra (Kalia) L.; m. Rashmi Sharma, Nov. 17, 1980; children: Akshai, Shuchi, Virad. Student, Colvin Coll., Lucknow, 1969; MB, BS, K.G. Med. Coll., Lucknow, 1974, Dr.med., 1977. Diplomate Am. Bd. Internal Medicine, Am. Bd. Rheumatology. Rotating intern Ghandi Meml. and Assocs. Hosps., King George's Med. Coll., 1974, resident in medicine, 1975-78; sr. house officer in internal medicine Sunderland Hosp., Hemlington Hosp., Poole Hosp., Eng., 1979-80; resident in internal medicine Meml. Hosp., U. Mass. Med. Sch., Worcester, 1980-82; fellow Mayo Clin., Rochester, Minn., 1983-86; attending physician St. Paul Med. Ctr., Dallas, 1987—; asst. prof. medicine Southwestern Med. Sch., Dallas, 1989-96, assoc. prof. medicine, 1996—; instr. Southwestern Med. Sch., Dallas, 1987-89; referee to numerous med. jours. Sr. editor Jour. Biol. and Chem. Rsch., 1987—; mem. editl. bd. Jour. Indian Rheumatism Assn., 1999—; contbr. chpt. to book and articles to profl. jours. Bd. dirs. North Tex. chpt. Arthritis Found., 1992-98; trustee DFW Hindu Temple, Dallas, 1994-99; bd. dirs. United Way of Met. Dallas, 1995-97, mem. exec com., 1995-96. Recipient Platinum Jubilee Gold medal King Georges Med. Coll., 1986; Am. Rheumatism Assn. fellow, 1984, 85, scholar, 1986; Philips Hench scholar, 1986. Fellow ACP, Am. Rheumatism Assn. (founding), Am. Coll. Rheumatology; mem. Indian Rheumatism Assn. (editl. bd.), Arthritis Found. (sci. com. and chmn. profl. edn. com. North Tex. chpt., also bd. dirs. 1992-98), Lupus Found. Am. (med. adv. bd.), Tex. Med. Assn., Dallas County Med. Soc., Tex. Indo-Am. Physicians Soc. (pres. 1994-95), King George Med. Coll. Alumni Assn. in Am. (sec.-treas. 1988-89, v.p. 1991-92, pres. 1993-94), Dallas-Ft. Worth Rheumatology Club (organizing sec.), Am. Assn. Physicians of Indian Origin (sec. 2000—). Hindu. Avocations: running, travel, tennis. Office: Rheumatology Assocs 5939 Harry Hines Blvd Ste 400 Dallas TX 75235-5360

LAKHTAKIA, MERCEDES NOEMI, meteorologist; b. Buenos Aires, Jan. 8, 1958; came to U.S., 1982; Degree in meteorol. sci., U. Buenos Aires, 1981; MS, Pa. State U., 1985, PhD in Meteorology, 1991. Rsch. asst. Argentinean Navy Weather Svc., Buenos Aires, 1979-82; part-time asst. prof. meteorology U. Buenos Aires, 1981-82; grad. rsch. asst. U. Utah, Salt Lake City, 1982-83; grad. rsch. asst. Pa. State U., State College, 1984-91, rsch. assoc., 1991-99. Contbr. articles to sci. publs. World Meteorol. Orgn. fellow NOAA, 1983, grantee climate and global change, 1995-97; USAF Office Sci. Rsch. grantee, 1995-98. Mem. Am. Meteorol. Soc., Am. Geophys. Union. Avocations: cross-stitch, jigsaw puzzles, internet surfing, gardening. E-mail: m lakhtakia@yahoo.com. Home: 1811 Red Lion Dr State College PA 16801-3012

LAKIN, L. THOMAS, lawyer; b. May 21, 1940; children: Brad, Kyra Lakin St. Peters, Kris, Karey. BS, So. Ill. U.; JD, U. Louisville. mentor So. Ill. U., mem. past pres. orgn.; mem. bd. dirs., treas. exec. com. So. Ill. U. Edwardsville Found., mem. major gifts com.; mem. St. Anthony's Hosp. Adv. Bd., bd. dirs., mem. exec. and fin. coms.; mem. exec. bd. Lewis & Clark Found. Bd.,; active Alton Men's Garden Club, United Way Circle Giving Club, Greater St. Louis Labor Coun., Madison County Arts Coun., Madison County Urban League, St. Louis Symphony Bd., Mel Price Locks and Dam Visitors Ctr.; bd. dirs. KETC Channel 9; exec. com. Riverbend Growth Assn.; mem. Dem. Nat. Com., precinct committeeman Wood River Twp.; exec. bd. Madison County Ctrl. Dem. Com.; past chmn. Down STate Fin. for the Ill. Dem. Party; alt. del. Dem. Nat. Conv., 1976, del., 1988, others. Mem. ATLA (pres. young lawyers sect. 1973, vice chmn. young lawyers sect. 1973), Ill. Trial Lawyers Assn., Ill. State Bar Assn., Madison County Bar Assn., Wood River Bar Assn., Worker's Compensation Lawyers Assn., Lawyer's Pilots Bar Assn., So. Ill. U. Alumni Assn., Wood River Moose Lodge, Masons. Office: The Lakin Law Firm PC 250 Old St Louis Rd Wood River IL

LAKOSI, LÁSZLÓ, physicist, researcher; b. Badacsonytomaj, Veszprem, Hungary, June 28, 1934; s. László and Ilona (Mágel) L.; m. Éva Gelencsér, June 2, 1962; children: Alexandra, András. Physicist, R. Eötvös U., Budapest, Hungary, 1957, PhD, 1973; Candidate Phys. Sci., Hungarian Acad. Sci., Budapest, 1973, DSc in Physics, 1997. Cert. physicist. Rsch. assoc. Ctrl. Lab. Measurement Rsch., Budapest, 1958-64; rsch. engr. Gamma Works, Budapest, 1964-66, 73-79; rsch. assoc. Inst. Isotopes, Budapest, 1966-73, sr. scientist, 1979-88, head dept., 1988—. Contbr. articles to profl. jours. Fellow R. Eötvös Phys. Soc. Avocations: history, literature, philosophy. Home: Keleti K u 13/b II.12, H-1024 Budapest Hungary Office: Hungarian Acad Sci, Konkoly-Thege M ut 29/33, H-1121 Budapest Hungary

LAKOV, DIMITAR VASILEV, computer company executive, researcher; b. Sofia, Bulgaria, Nov. 10, 1945; s. Vassil Tzanov and Nadezhda Dimitrova (Popdimitrova) L.; m. Margarita Rajkova Saralieva Lakova, Nov. 21, 1971; 1 child, Kalin Dimitrov. MEE, Tech. U., Sofia, Bulgaria, 1966-70; MS, 1972; PhD, Inst. Cybernetics, 1978. Cert. elec. engring. Sr. rschr. Isomatic Lab., Sofia, Bulgaria, 1986-88; head dept. Inst. Indsl Cybernetics and Robotics, Acad. Scis., Sofia, Bulgaria, 1988-90; mng. dir. Robot and Control Sys. Rsch. Ctr. Bulgarian Acad. Scis., Sofia, Bulgaria, 1990-94, prof., 1994; rsch. dir. Inst. Computer and Comm. Sys. Bulgarian Acad. Scis., Sofia, Bulgaria, 1994—; proprietor Goldenbay Ltd., U.K., 1998. Author: Performance, 1980; inventor: Synchronisation in Serial Communication, Data Retention Device; editor: Fuzzy Based Expert Systems, 1994, 96; contbr. 80 publs. to profl. jours. Exec. Bulgarian Union of Informatics and Automatics, Sofia, Bulgaria, 1987—. Fellow Internat. Fuzzy Sys. Assn.; mem. Internat. Assn. for Advanced Modeling and Simulation, Soc. Internat. de Gestio I Economia Fuzzy Av. Torre Blanca. Avocations: alpinism, scuba diving, painting, music. Home: Geo Milev 44, 1111 Sofia Bulgaria Office: Inst Computer and Comm, Systems, Acad G Bonchev Bl 2, 1113 Sofia Bulgaria

LAKOV, KRASSIMIR IVANOV, economist; b. Sofia, Bulgaria, June 26, 1951; s. Ivan Lazarov and Christina Petrova (Liseva) L.; m. Nelly Petrova Petrounova, Aug. 5, 1973; children: Ivailo, Petia. BSc, Econ. U., 1974; PhD, Bulgarian Acad. Scis., 1985. Rschr. Inst. of Econs., Bulgarian Acad. of Scis., 1976-82, sr. rschr., 1985-90; chief of cabinet of the dep. prime min. Coun. of Ministers, 1990—; sr. econ. advisor Prime Min. of Bulgraia, 1991-92; bur. chief Radio Free Europe/Radio Liberty Inc., Sofia, 1994-95; analyst, editor, broadcaster Radio Free Europe, Prague, Czech Republic, 1995—; assoc. prof. Tech. U., Sofia, 1987-90; moderator, editor Bulgarian Nat. TV, Sofia, 1986-93; vice chmn., control bd. Nat. Elec. Co., Bulgaria, 1991—. Coauthor: Efficiency and Economic Growth, 1984 (Award 1985); contbr. articles to profl. publs. Bd. chmn. Environ. Mgmt. Tng. Ctr., Sofia, 1992-97. Recipient Nat. award Best TV Econ. and Polit. Journalism, 1993. Mem. Union of Czech Journalists. Home: U Dejvickeho Rybnicku 31, 160 00 Prague Czech Republic Office: Radio Free Europe/Liberty, Vinohradska 1, 1100 00 Prague Czech Republic

LAKRITZ, ESTHER, retired English language educator; b. Milw., Apr. 11, 1928; d. Alexander Himmelman and Mildred Hoffman; children: Simeon, Naomi, David. BS in Secondary Edn., Milw. State Tchrs. Coll., 1949; MLS, U. Wis., 1976. Author: (children's book) Randy Visits Doctor, 1962, (workbook) Developing Library Skills, 1989, (romantic suspense) To Track a Copycat, 1995, (mystery) Battlelines, 1999. Avocation: freelance writing. Home: 17460 Plaza Otonal San Diego CA 92128-1830

LAKRITZ, JEFFREY, veterinary educator; b. Hanford, Calif., Oct. 17, 1959; s. Simon and Mary Elizabeth L.; m. Antoinette Elisa Marsh, oct. 1, 1994. BS, U. Calif., Davis, 1981, DVM, 1987, PhD, 1996. Diplomate Am. Coll. Vet. Internal Medicine. Postgrad. rschr. U. Calif., Davis, 1996-98; asst. prof. U. Mo., Columbia, 1998—; vet. cons. Robert L. Young, Ft. Lauderdale, Fla., 1990—. Contbg. author: 5 Minute Veterinary Consult, 1999, Current Veterinary Therapy, 1996. Mem. AAAS, Am. Vet. Med. Assn., Mo. Vet. Med. Assn., Am. Soc. Microbiology, Am. Coll. Vet. Internal Medicine, Am. Assn. Equine Practitioners. Office: Univ Mo-Columbia 379 E Campus Dr Columbia MO 65211-0001

LAKSHMANAN, CHITTUR CHANDRASEKHARAN, chemical engineer; b. Madurai, Tamil Nadu, India, July 19, 1954; s. Chittur Sivaramakrishnan Chandrasekharan and Chandrasekharapuram Lakshmanan Meenakshi; m. Jayalakshmi Venkataraman, Oct. 24, 1996; 1 child, Karthik C. B.Tech, Coimbatore Inst. Tech., 1976; PhD, Indian Inst. Sci., 1981. Sr. rsch. fellow Monash U., Melbourne, Australia, 1981-84, vice chancellors rsch. fellow, 1984-86; rsch. engr. BHP, Melbourne, Australia, 1986-88, sr. engr., 1988-95; dep. gen. mgr. Reliance Industries, Mumbai, India, 1995; specialist chem. engr. India Tobacco Co. Ltd., Bangalore, 1995-99; dir.-tech. General Electric India Tech. Ctr., Bangalore, 1999—. Mem. AIChE, Soc. Petroleum Engrs., Indian Inst. Chem. Engrs. E-mail: lakshmanan.chittur@geind.ge.com. Fax: 91-80-841 0704.

LAKSHMI, RAMAN, engineer, researcher; b. Madras, Tamil Nadu, India, Dec. 6, 1956; d. Raju and Vasanthi (Rajagopalachari) Varadarajan; m. Alwar Raman, Nov. 1, 1979. BTech, Coll. Tech., Hyderabad, India, 1979. Engr. Scale B Solid Propellant Space Booster Plant/Shar Centre/ISRO, Sriharikota, 1983-86, engr. Scale C, 1986-89, engr.-in-charge, 1989-94, dep. mgr., 1994—; cosn. space generation task group Dept. Space Indian Space Rsch. Orgn. Hdqtrs., Bangalore, India, 1999. Author: Propellant and Explosives Technology, 1998; contbr. articles to profl. jours. including Def. Sci. Jour., High Energy Materials Soc. India, Jour. Polymer Composites. Recipient Extraordinary Merit Scholarship A.P. State Edn. Bd., 1972-79. Mem. Space Women's Assn. (gen. sec. 1994, 98). Hindu. Avocations: music, painting, wood carving, reading. Office: Shar Ctr ISRO, Solid Prop Space Booster Pl, Sriharikota, Nellore 524124, India

LAKSHMINARASAIAH, MANDALAPU, economics educator, researcher; b. Kurnool, India, Feb. 2; parents M. Narasaiah and M. (Koduri) Pullama; m. M. Rama Devi Bhimaneni; children: M. Sreekanth, M. Meenakshi. Degree, Sri Venkateswara U., Titupati, India, 1977; MA, Indore U., India, 1979; PhD, Sri Krishnadevaraya U., Anantapur, India, 1986. Asst. prof. econs. Sri Krishnadevaraya U., Anantapur, 1985-93, assoc. prof. econs., 1993-98, prof. econs., 1998—; participant rsch. inst., Ahmedabad, India, 1983, Ctr. Econ. and Social Studies, Hyderabad, India, 1989, Jawaharlal Nehru U., New Delhi, 1991, European symposium, Istanbul, Turkey, 1995. Contbr. articles to profl. jours. Pres. Rayalaseema Devel. Trust, Anantapur, 1996. Mem. Andhra Pradesh Econ. Assn. (joint sec.), Indian Econ. Assn. (joint sec.), Indian Soc. Agro Labor Econs. Mem. Indian Nat. Congress. Hindu. Avocations: yogasanas, freelance writing, photography. Home: 11-444F Aravindanagar, Anantapur 515 001, India Office: Sri Krishnadevaraya U, Dept Econs, Anantapur 515 003, India

LAKSHMINARAYANA, KARRI, microbiology educator, researcher; b. Vuyyuru, India, Nov. 30, 1941; s. Karri Adinarayana and Karri Narasaratnamma Vericherla; m. Patnala Katyayani, May 17, 1973; children: Bhanupriya, Anuradha, Jyotsna. BSc, Andhra U., Waltair, India, 1960; MSc in Biochemistry, M.S. U., Baroda, India, 1963, PhD in Microbiology, 1969; diploma in microbiology and biotech., U. Osaka and U. Tokyo, 1977. Asst. lectr. M.S. U., 1964-69, lectr., 1969; asst. microbiolobist CCS Haryana Agrl. U., Hisar, India, 1969-74, microbial physiologist, 1975-85, sr. microbial physiologist, 1985-86, prof. microbiology, 1985—, head dept., 1986-89. Contbr. over 60 articles and revs. to sci. jours. and popular publs. Recipient award Nat. Productivity Coun., Govt. of India, 1985; Japan Soc. for Promotion Sci. fellow U. Tokyo, 1993-94; grantee Indian Coun. Agrl. Rsch., 1999, Nat. Agrl. Technology Project. Mem. Assn. Microbiologists India (pres. Hisar chpt. 1985, R.M. Sharma award 1989, 91, 83), Assn. Food Sci. and Tech. (pres. 1998-99), N.Y. Acad. Scis. Hindu. Avocations: reading, playing chess. Office: CCS Haryana Agrl U, Dept Microbiology, Hisar 125 004, India

LAKSHMINARAYANAN, PANAPPAKKAM ARUMUGAM, engineer; b. Madras, Tamilnadu, India, Apr. 26, 1949; s. Panappakkam Anguchettiar Arumugam; m. Panappakkam Lakshminarayanan Loganayagi, Sept. 14, 1979; 1 child, Leela. B Tech., Indian Inst. Technology, Madras, 1971, MS, 1974, PhD, 1979. Diploma in Radio Engring. and Air Conditioning, Brit. Insts., Bombay. Rsch. assoc. Loughborough U. of Tech., Eng., 1978-82; sr. gen. mgr. rsch. and engring. Kirloskar Oil Engines, Ltd., Pune, India, 1983-95, exec. rsch. and engring., 1995-96, sr. gen. mgr., 1996—; exec. bd. Indian Combustion Inst., madras, 1996—. Contbr. articles to profl. jours. Recipient 1st prize for Best Paper, Indian Combustion Inst., 1993, Nat. Merit scholarship 1965-69, IIT Merit scholarship 1966-71; named Automobile Engr. of Yr., Inst. Automobile Engrs., Madras, 1994. Mem. Soc. Automobile Engrs. (Arch Colwell award 1984—), N.Y. Acad. Scis., Combustion Inst. of India (exec. bd. 1993—). Hindu. Avocations: chess, reading, meeting friends, visiting temples. Office: Kirloskar Oil Engines Ltd, L Kirloskar Rd, 411003 Pune India

LAKSONO, AGUNG, government official; b. 1949. Min. Ministry State, Youth & Sports, Jakarta, Indonesia, 1998-99; chmn. 2000 Nat. Games (PON); mem. for Southeast Sulawesi People's Consultative Assembly (MPR), Jakarta, Indonesia, 1999—. dep. chmn., Golkar, chmn. Golkar, 2000—. Office: DDP Golongan Karya, Jl Anggrek Nellymurni, Slipi Jakarta Barat 11480, Indonesia*

LAKTIONOV, EVGUENI VIKTOROVICH, chemist, researcher; b. Krasnodar, Russia, Nov. 30, 1967; s. Viktor Afanasievich and Alexandra Gavrilovna (Kaldina) L.; m. Olga Valerievna Sereda, Sept. 14, 1991; 1 child, Mikhail. MSc, U. Kuban, Krasnodar, 1992, postgrad.; postgrad., U. Montpellier, France; PhD for Chemistry, Univ. of Montpellier, 1998. Cert. electrodialysis rsch. and engring. Lab. asst. U. Kuban, Krasnodar, 1985-92, engr., 1992-93; probationer U. Twente, The Netherlands, 1995, U. Montpellier, 1996-98. Contbr. articles to profl. jours.; patentee in field. Pvt. soldier Railway Troops, 1986-88. Grantee Found. of Soros, 1995, 96, Adminstrn. Krasnodar Region, 1995-96. Orthodox. Avocations: tennis, jogging, badges collecting. E-mail: evgueni@caramail.com. Home: 3/1 Suvorova St, 350027 Krasnodar Russia Office: Kuban State Univ, 149 Stavropolskaya St, 350040 Krasnodar Russia Mailing: 201 Dzerzhinskogo str., ap. 95, 350005 Krasnodar Russia

LAL, AVTAR, pharmacologist, medical educator, researcher; b. Amritsar, Punjab, India, Sept. 27, 1960; s. Manohar and Kanta (Rani) L.; m. Jyoti Verma, Nov. 3, 1989; children: Alisha, Karan. M.B.B.S., Med. Coll. Amitsar, India, 1984, MD, 1988; DM, Post Grad. Inst. Med. Edn. and Rsch., Chandigarh, India, 1991. Jr. resident Med. Coll. Amritsar, 1987-88; sr. resident Post Grad. Inst. Med. Edn. and Rsch., Chandigarh, 1989-91; lectr. Mahatma Gandhi Inst. Med. Scis. Sewagram, Wardha, India, 1991-92, Jawahar Lal Nehru Med. Coll., Aligarh, India, 1992-93; lectr. U. Coll. Med. Scis. and Guru Teg Bahadur Hosp., Delhi, 1993-95, sr. lectr., 1995-97, reader, 1997—; mem. drug formulary Nat. Capital Territory, Delhi, 1995-97; mem. drug auditing Guru Teg Bahadur Hosp., 1995-96; mem. faculty med. scis. U. Delhi. Referee Indian Jour. Pharmacology, Indian Jour. Physiology and Pharmacology, Indian Jour. Pediat.; contbr. chpts. to books and articles to profl. jours. Mem. Indian Pharmacology Soc., Indian Soc. Clin. Pharmacol. Therapeut., Indian Med. Assn., Indian Acad. Neuroscis., Assn. Physiologists and Pharmacologists India, Indian Soc. Hypertension, Indian Med. Assn., N.Y. Acad. Scis., Acad. Med. Specialists, Delhi Soc. for Promotion of Rational Use of Drugs. Avocations: reading, music, television, computers, yoga. Home: 80 Gagan Vihar, Delhi 110 051, India Office: UCMS and GTB Hospital, Dilshad Garden, Delhi 110 095, India

LAL, HARBANS, biochemist, educator; b. Talwandi bhai, Ferozpur, India, July 20, 1947; s. Nanak Chand and Durga (Garg) A.; m. Veena Agrawal, Apr. 25, 1974; children: Ashish, Anubha. MSc in Biochemistry, Uttar Pradesh Agrl. U., Pant Nagar, India, 1969; PhD in Biochemistry, Banaras Hindu U., Varanasi, India, 1975; Fellow D. (hon.), Trevor Francis Internat. Acad. Ophthal., Brussels, 1989. Lectr. Med. Coll., Rohtak, India, 1976-81, reader, 1981-88, assoc. prof., 1988—; vis. asst. prof. La. State U. Med. Ctr., New Orleans, 1985, U. Vienna, Austria; guest spkr. Internat. Congress on Animo Acids, 1993. Author: Biochemistry for Dental Students, 1997, 2d rev. edit., 2000; contbr. articles to profl. jours; contbr. chapts. to books. Recipient WHO fellow award, 1983. Fellow Assn. Clin. Biochemists India; mem. Nutrition Soc. India (Young Scientist award 1984, convenor Rohtak chpt. 1995-98), Assn. of Clin. Biochemists of India (life, v.p. 1995). Avocations: reading, touring and sight-seeing, scientific writing. E-mail: harbansh@ndb.vsnl.net.in. Home: 15/8 FM Medical Enclave, Rohtak 124001, India Office: Pt BD Sharma Postgrad Inst Med Sc, Biochem Dept, Rohtak 124001, India

LAL, VINOD BEHARI, hematologist; b. Aligarh, India, Feb. 20, 1917; s. Shri Awadh Behari Lal and Shrimati Krishna Dulari; m. Kumari Sushil; children: Manju Talekar, Bharat B., P. B., Divya B., Madhu Malik. Degree in medicine, Agra Med. Coll., 1940, U. Lausanne, Switzerland, 1956; diploma blood transfusion/blood banking, U. Paris, 1957, DSc in Medicine, 1959; degree in hematology, U. Vienna, Austria, 1966; PhD in Cancer Genetics, U. Bernadean, 1980. Chmn., chief dr. Blood Bank Orgn., New Delhi, 1949—. Editor-in-chief: Blood Therapy Jour. Internat., 1968—. Provider free consultations to patients, free distbn. of medicine; organizer various social, cultural, and charitable events locally. Recipient Indira Gandhi award, 1992, Hind Rattan award, 1993, Sr. Citizen award Nat. Inst. Primary Health Care, 1996. Mem. Indian Assn. Blood Banks (nat. pres. 1961, chief editor Rakt Vani 1997, Cert. Participation VIIth nat. conv. 1996), Inst. Hematology (trustee chmn. 1961), N.Y. Acad. Scis. Avocations: music, reading, social activity. Fax: 091 11 2247189. Office: Inst Hematology, 36 Vijay Block Laxmi Nagar, Delhi 92, India

LALA, SUKH DEV, chemist; b. Chakwal, India, June 17, 1924; s. Hari Chand and Maya Wanti (Johar) L.; m. Shashi Prabha Dhawan, Dec. 7, 1951; children: Indu, Purnima, Deepak. BSc, Panjab U., 1944, MSc, 1945; PhD, Indian Inst. Sci., Bangalore, 1950, DSc, 1960. Rsch. assoc., lectr. Indian Inst. Sci., 1948-59; head divsn. organic chemistry Nat. Chem. Lab., Pune, India, 1960-74; rsch. dir. Malti-Chem Rsch Ctr., Nandesari, India, 1974-88; rsch. prof. Indian Inst. Technology, New Delhi, 1988-93; vis. prof. Dr. B. R. Ambedkar Ctr. Biomed. Rsch. U. Delhi, 1993—; nat. com. on sci. and technology Govt. India, 1977-80; vis. prof. chemistry U. Ga., Athens, 1969, U. Okla., Norman, 1970-71. Fellow Indian Nat. Sci. Acad., Indian Acad. Scis., 3d World Acad. Scis., Gujarat Sci. Acad.; mem. Indian Chem. Soc. (pres. 1978-79). Hindu. Avocations: gardening, painting, Indian classical music. Home: C-600 New Friends Colony, New Delhi 110065, India

LALE, CISSY STEWART (LLOYD LALE), freelance writer; b. Port Arthur, Tex., Jan. 15, 1924; d. Lloyd M. and May (Cowart) Stewart; m. Max Sims Lale, Oct. 9, 1983. BJ, U. Tex., 1945. Reporter Record-News, Wichita Falls, Tex., 1945, News-Messenger, Marshall, Tex., 1945-47; editor Times-Rev., Cleburne, Tex., 1947-49; women's editor, columnist Star-Telegram, Ft. Worth, 1949-87; freelance writer Children's Promise mag., Health-Scope mag., Ft. Worth, 1987-89. Author: Sweetie Ladd's Historic Fort Worth, 1999. Bd. dirs. Trinity Terr. Retirement Community, 1991-94. Recipient Ballard Heritage award North Tex. Hist. Soc.; Cissy Stewart Day proclaimed by Ft. Worth City Coun., 1987, portrayed in outdoor mural City of Ft. Worth, 1987. Mem. Women in Comm., Inc (nat. pres. 1968-71), Tex. State Hist. Assn. (pres. 1996-97), East Tex. Hist. Assn. (pres. 1994), Tex. Heritage, Inc. (bd. dirs. Ft. Worth chpt. 1990), Womans Club Ft. Worth, Ft. Worth Garden Club (v.p. 1995-96). Episcopalian. Home: # 101 3900 White Settlement Rd Fort Worth TX 76107-7822

LA LIBERTE, ANN GILLIS, graphic artist, consultant, designer, educator; b. St. Paul, Nov. 10, 1942; d. Edward Robert and Frances Caroline (Sullivan) Gillis; m. Paul Henry La Liberte, Aug. 22, 1964; children: Paul E., Elizabeth La Liberte Collins, Stephen A., Helen C., Peter N., Marc H. Student, Am U., 1963-64, Cardinal Stritch Coll., Milw., 1960-63; BA, Coll. St. Catherine, St. Paul, 1985. Artist, owner Ann La Liberte Papers and Posters, Minnetonka, Minn., 1968-71, A.L. Graphic Design and Drawings, Minnetonka, Minn., 1987—; artist-in-residence Tara Tonka Studio, Minnetonka, 1988—; artist Arts in Schs., Minn., 1985—; pvt. art tchr., dir. creativity and problem solving seminars, 1991—. Liturgical design cons. Midwest, 1977—; paintings, drawings, photography and sculpture exhibited

Mpls. and St. Paul area, 1983—; sculpture Life Exhibit, Paul VI Inst. for the Arts, Washington, 1988, on tour Vt., Ohio, Mo., Ill., Wis., 1988. Del. Minn. Ind. Reps., 1969, vice chmn. Minnetonka, 1970; promotional artist Soc. for Preservation Human Dignity, Palatine, Ill., 1973, Minn. Citizens Concerned for Life, 1980-88, Secular Franciscans, St. Paul, 1985; deanery rep. pastoral coun. Archdiocese of St. Paul and Mpls., 1978-82; chmn. devel. task force out-reach program Resurrection Ch., Mpls., 1980-81, cons. artist, 1983—; dir. liturg. design Ch. of Immaculate Heart of Mary, Minnetonka, 1989—; liturgical art and environ. cons. Mem. Nat. Assn. Liturgical Mins., Mpls. Inst. of Arts, Nat. Mus. Women in Arts (charter), Walker Art Ctr., Minnetonka Ctr. for Arts, Coll. of St. Catherine Alumna Assn., Artists for Life Nat. Slide Registry, Delta Phi Delta. Roman Catholic. Avocations: art history, swimming, hiking, travel, sculpture. Home: 13418 Excelsior Blvd Minnetonka MN 55345-4910

LALIOTIS, KONSTANDINOS, Greek government official; b. Dolina, Arcadia, Greece, 1951. Student Sch. Dentistry, U. Athens. Journalist, editor Agonistis mag., 1975-77; publ., mgr. Exormisi newspaper, 1977-85; dep. min. youth and sports Govt. of Greece, 1982-85, dep. min. press, govt. rep., 1985-86, MP, 1992—, min. environ., phys. planning, pub. works, 1993—. Founding mem. ctrl. com. PASOK, 1974—, mem. exec. bur. CC, 1976-85, 87—. Mem. Panhellenic Socialist Movement (PASOK). Office: Min Environ Phys Planning & Pub Works, Odos Amaliados 17, 115 23 Athens Greece*

LALITHAMBA, BHASKARAM YAGNESHWAR, literature educator; b. Mysore, Karnataka, India, Mar. 18, 1944; parents Yagneshwar Bhaskaram Somayaji and Bhaskaram Yagneshwar Gowramma. MA, U. Mysore. Lectr. Collegiate Edn., Karnataka, 1974-79, reader, 1979-91; prof., head Devi Ahilya U., Indore, 1992—, dean, 1995-97, 98—. Transl.: Vac'anōdyāna, 1986, others; contbr. poetry to anthologies. Treas. Jana Prakāshan, Bangalore, 1979-80; v.p. Mānini, Bangalore, 1980, Mahila Cherana, Indore, 1994; advisor Bharatiya Anawād Porishad, New Delhi, 1986—. Recipient Sahikya Sauhārd Samman award U.P. Hindi Sanshā, 1990, Bihas Rastabhasha Parishad, 1996, Dwivāgish Samman award Bharatiya Anuvad Parishad, 1994. Mem. Comparative Lit. Soc. (e.c. mem. 1999-00), Asiayi Sahikya Acad. (advisor 1997—), Bharatiya Anuvād Parishad (advisor 1986-00). Avocations: writing, critical analysis, table tennis. Home: Khandra Rd, Indore 452001, India Office: Devi Ahilya U, RNT Marg, Indore 452001, India

LALL, AMAR RAJ, economist; b. Amritsar, Punjab, India, Mar. 21, 1928; s. Inder Mohan and Daropadi (Chawla) L.; m. Kamla Saigal, Sept. 5, 1957; children: Anuradha, Anil, Chander. M in Econs., Govt. Coll., Lahore, Pakistan, 1948; BS in Econs., London Sch. Econs., 1951. Barrister, Eng. Legal advocate Delhi, 1953—; bd. dirs. Porritts & Spencer (Asia) Ltd., Faridabad, India; ptnr. Remfry & Son, Calcutta, 1973-83, Lall, Lahiri & Salhotra, New Delhi, 1983—; pres. Inst. of Intellectual Property, Rsch. and Practice, New Delhi, 1995—. Mem. Panchsheel Club (pres. 1994-96), Delhi High Ct. Bar Assn., Supreme Ct. of India Bar Assn. Avocations: walking, swimming, photography. Office: Lall Lahiri & Salhotra, N-128 Panchsheel Park, 110017 New Delhi India

LALL, SHYAM BALA, pharmacologist, toxicologist; b. Peshawar, India, Dec. 14, 1943; s. Davender and Indira (Rajpal) N.; m. Jagdish Chandra, Sept. 8, 1969. MBBS, Lady Hardinge Med. Coll., New Delhi, India, 1966; MD in Pharmacology, Postgrad. Inst. Med. Edn., 1971, Diploma in Ob-Gyn., 1980. Tutor Rohtak (India) Med. Coll., 1972-76, lectr., 1976-81; lectr. Delhi (India) U., 1981-83; asst. prof. All India Inst. Med. Scis., New Delhi, 1986-89, assoc. prof., 1989—, additional prof.; participant Internat. Programme on Chem. Safety/WHO, 1992—. Author: Management of Pesticide Poisoning, 1997, Management of Plant Poisoning, 1997, Management of Common Indian Snake and Insect Bites, 1997, Antidotes in Poisoning, 1997; editor: Essentials of Clinical Toxicology; contbr. articles to profl. jours. Recipient Proud Citizens award Delhi Govt., 1997. Fellow Acad. Med. Scis. Avocations: social service, painting. Home: F-152 Mansarover Garden, New Delhi 110015, India Office: All India Inst Med Scis, 110029 New Delhi India

LALLA, JOGENDER KISHINCHAND, pharmacy educator; b. Karachi, India, Dec. 1, 1939; s. Hiranand and Jaswanti Kishinchand (Java) L.; m. Dipika Jogender lalla, Oct. 31, 1976; 1 child, Shimona. Diploma in pharmacy, Mumbai U., 1960, B in Pharmacy, 1964, PhD in Tech., 1972. Retail pharmacist Popular Med. Stores, Chembur, Mumbai, 1951-75; assoc. lectr. dept. chem. tech. Mumbai U., 1965-67; prof., asst. dean Coll. Pharmacy, Ulhasnagar, India, 1971-75; dean Prin. K.M. Kundnani Coll. Pharmacy, Worli, Mumbai, 1975—; convenor sci. svcs. com. indian Pharm. Congress, Bombay, 1992-95; exec. joint sec. Hyderabad (Sind.) Nat. Collegiate Bd., Mumbai, 1994—; v.p. Ind. Pharm. Assn.; cons. Blue Cross labs. Ltd., 1992-99, Ion Exch. India Ltd., Bombay, 1992—, Lasor Labs. Ltd., Pune, Albert David Ltd.; bd. dirs. Vasundhra Rasayans Ltd., Chemo Pharma Lab. Ltd., Emcure Labs, Pune. Contbr. articles to profl. jours. Mem. Indian Pharm. Assn. (hon. gen. sec. 1992-98, v.p. 1998-2000). Avocation: music philately. Home: Prin Quarters KMK Coll Pharmacy, Plot 47 Dr RG Thadani Marg, Mumbai 400 018, India Office: KM Kundnani Coll Pharmacy, Plot No 47 RG Thadani, Mumbai 400 018, India

LALLI, MARY SCHWEITZER, writer, artist; b. Newark, Ohio, June 24, 1925; d. Clemence Sylvester and Ethel Ann (Deem) Schilling; m. Francis Edward Schweitzer, Aug. 23, 1947 (div. Oct. 1974); children: Dale Francis, Darrell Charles, David Edward; m. Joseph G. Lalli, June 21, 1975. BA, Denison U., 1947. Lic. tchr. English. Tchr. English, Ctrl. Jr. High, Newark, 1947-48; profl. artist Nat. Forum Profl. Artists, Phila., 1968-75; dir. art shows, Phila., 1968—; writer antique doll jour. Writer Doll Castle News, Doll Times, Doll Reader, Antique Doll World, Doll Collector's Price Guide, Doll World, 1983—; photojournalist Doll Times; columnist Doll Designs; exhibited in show at Rotunda, Harrisburg, Pa., 1999. Recipient 125 art awards including Phila. Plastic Club, 1972, 73, 78, award of honor Inst. Pub. Edn., Drexel Hill, Pa., 1980. Mem. Nat. League Am. Pen Women (1st v.p. 1985-89), DaVinci Art Alliance (sec.), Plastic Club (pres., v.p.), Chester County Art Assn. Avocations: attending art shows, doll shows, classical music concerts, doing research.

LALLO, LARRY JONATHON, community developer; b. Akron, Ohio, Aug. 2, 1953; s. Laddie Lallo and Vera Simpson; m. Susan Lallo; 1 child, Jason. BA, Akron U., 1980. Cert. econ. developer. Regional planner Allen County Planning, Lima, Ohio, 1980-82; devel. officer Akron Housing Authority, 1983-89; exec. dir. Barberton (Ohio) Cmty. Devel., 1990—; cons. Renkert Devel., Canton, Ohio, 1990-93; trsutee roads and bridges Willowdale Latie Club, North Canton, Ohio, 1996-98. Rsch. analyst: An Atlas of India, 1976. Constrn. team leader Mercy Teams, Nicaragua, 1998; mem. missions bd. High Mill Ch., North Canton, 1999. Master USCG. Named Outstanding Bus. Leader of Yr., South Summit C. of C., 2000. Mem. Am. Econ. Devel. Coun., Ohio Devel. Assn., Downtown Barberton Inc. (bd. dirs. 1998). E-mail: llallo@cs.com. Office: Barberton Cmty Devel Corp 104 3rd St NW Barberton OH 44203-8223

LALOUM, MAURICE CLAUDE, physics educator, researcher; b. Constantine, Algeria, Aug. 4, 1944; s. Gustave Hay and Jeanne Denise (Hazan) L. Degree in engring., Ecole Polytechnique, Paris, 1966; D in Exptl. Physics and Theoretical Sci., U. Orsay, 1974, DSc, 1974. Mil. engr. Ecole Polytechnique Coll. de France, 1966-67; sci. rschr. in particle physics CNRS, Paris, 1967-69, Coll. de France, Paris, 1969—. Contbr. more than 40 articles to profl. jours. including Physics Letters, Nuclear Physics, among others. Engr. French Mil., 1964-67. Home: 126 ave Emile-Zola, 75015 Paris France Office: Coll de France, 11 place Marcelin-Berthelot, 75231 Paris France

LALUMIÈRE, CATHERINE, diplomat; b. Rennes, Ille-et-Vilaine, Aug. 3, 1935; m. Pierre Lalumière, Apr. 4, 1960. Diploma in advanced studies in polit. sci., D in Pub. Law. Asst. lectr. U. Bordeaux, Bordeaux Inst. Polit. Studies, 1960; lectr. U. Paris I, Panthéon-Sorbonne, 1971; joined Socialist Party, 1973, leader regional list for the gen. election, 1986, nat. officer civil svc., 1975; state sec. civil svc. Pierre Mauroy's 1st Govt.; min. Ministry Consumer Affairs; state sec. European affairs Ministry of External Rels., 1984, mem. parliament 3rd Gironde, 1987; sec. gen. Coun. Europe, 1989—; mem. European Parliament, Brussels, Belgium, 1999—. Office: Parlement Europeen, 288 Bd St Germain, F-75007 Paris France*

LALWANI, MAHESH, economist, educator, researcher; b. New Delhi, India, Aug. 28, 1951; s. Gural and Lakshmi Lalwani; m. Shobha Akali/Rohra, Oct. 30, 1988; 2 children. BA with honors, HansRaj Coll., Delhi, 1970; MA, Delhi Sch. Econs., 1972, PhD, 1987. Lectr. Delhi U., 1972-88, reader, 1988-91; prof. econs. North Eastern Hill U., Shillong, INdia, 1991—; cons. Indian Social Inst., New Delhi, 1990-91, Inst. of Econ. Growth, New Del. Contbr. articles to profl. jours. UGC Teacher's fellow Delhi Sch. Econs., 1985. Mem. Indian Econometric Soc. (life), Indian Soc. Agrl. Econs. (life), Agri Econs. Rsch. Assn. (life). Hindu. Avocation: playing Indian classical music instrument Tabla. Office: North Eastern Hill U, Nongthymmai, 793014 Shillong India

LAM, ANDREW, financial advisor; b. Hong Kong, China; came to U.S., 1991; s. Joseph and Margaret Lam. BS, Stockton State Coll., Pomona, Calif., 1982; BSEE, U. Dayton, 1984; MBA, NYU, 1991. Elec. engr. Tex. Instruments, Lubbock, 1985-88; fin. cons. Merrill Lynch, Beverly Hills, 1988-89; broker Morgan Stanley, N.Y.C., 1991-94; asst. v.p. CS First Boston, Hong Kong, 1994-95; v.p. Lehman Bros., Hong Kong, 1995-97; 1st v.p. Prudential Bache, Hong Kong, 1997—. Avocations: golf, soccer, computers. Office: Prudential Bache Securities, 3 Garden Rd 40th Fl, Hong Kong China

LAM, ANTHONY CHI K., financial executive; b. Hong Kong, May 9, 1954; came to U.S., 1975; s. Joseph C.S. and Margaret B.W. (Kong) L.; m. Sabrina S.K. Lam; children: Jennifer Karman, Kimberly. BA, Stockton State Coll., 1977; MBA, Columbia U., 1983. Registered structural engr., Hong Kong. Sales engr. Getz Bros. Inc., Hong Kong, 1974-75; sales rep. Honeywell Inc., Pa., 1977-79; proprietor Bamboo Cottage, N.J., 1979-81; assoc. Merrill Lynch, N.Y.C., 1983-84, account exec., 1984-85, asst. v.p., 1985-87, v.p., 1987-90, dir., 1990-95; head fixed income Asia dept. Credit Suisse First Boston, 1995-99; regional head of sales all fin. markets in Asian and Japan ING Barings MD, Hong Kong, 1999—. Office: 39/F One Internat Fin Ctr, Central Hong Kong

LAM, CHING-WAN, physician, educator; b. Hong Kong, Oct. 6, 1967; s. Yuk-Ip Choy. B in Medicine and Surgery, Chinese U. Hong Kong, 1991. Intern Prince Wales Hosp., Hong Kong, 1991-92; med. officer Princess Margaret Hosp., Hong Kong, 1992-94; lectr. to asst. prof. Chinese U. Hong Kong, 1994-99, assoc. prof., 1999—; expertise Industry Dept., Hong Kong, 1999. Editor Hong Kong Soc. Clin. Chemistry, 1998—, external reviewer, U.S.A., 1999; contbr. articles to profl. jours. Recipient Clin. Chemists Recognition award Am. Assn. Clin. Chemistry, 1996; fellow Croucher Found., 1999. Fellow Royal Coll. Pathologists Australasia, Hong Kong Coll. Pathologists (edn. com. 1998—), Hong Kong Acad. Medicine; mem. Australasian Assn. Clin. Biochemists (Gold Medalist 1994), Hong Kong Soc. Clin. Chemistry (sci. com. 1999—). Avocations: recreational math. Office: Chinses U Hong Kong, 1/F Prince Wales Hosp, Shatin NT Hong Kong

LAM, CHUNG-YAU, engineering educator, researcher; b. Hong Kong, Aug. 4, 1955; arrived in Singapore, 1984; s. Chun-Fat and Shui-Mui (Wong) L.; m. Yuen-Yee Tse, Dec. 18, 1984; children: Yin-Cheung, Yin-To, Yin-Kiu. BS in Engring., U. London, 1979, PhD, 1983. Chartered mech. engr. Tutor U. London, 1979-83; lectr. Nanyang Tech. Inst., Singapore, 1984-88, sr. lectr., 1989-98, assoc. prof., 1999—; vis. scholar Hong Kong U. Sci. and Tech., 1994. Author: Applied Numerical Methods for Partial Differential Equations, 1994; editor Internat. Jour. Engring. Edn., 1995—; contbr. articles to profl. jours. Recipient Draper's Rsch. grant U. London, 1979, Applied Rsch. grant Nanyang Tech. U., 1989, 93. Mem. AIAA (sr.), Instn. Mech. Engrs. Avocations: stamp collection, music, jogging. Office: Nanyang Tech U Sch Mech, Prodn Engring Nanyang Ave, Singapore 639798, Singapore

LAM, GEOFFREY CHRISTOPHER, ophthalmologist; b. Wakefield, Yorkshire, Eng., July 30, 1956; arrived in Australia, 1977; s. Paul and Betty (Lee) L.; m. Blandine Sau-Shan Chan, Feb. 16, 1980; 1 child, Jonathan. MBBS, U. Western Australia, 1983. Intern Royal Perth (Australia) Hosp., 1983, jr. resident med. officer, 1984, sr. resident med. officer, 1985; resident med. officer Princess Margaret Hosp., Perth, 1986, cons., 1991—; registrar ophthalmology Perth Tchg. Hosp., 1987-90, chief resident ophthalmology, 1990. Mem. editl. bd. Australian New Zealand Jour. Ophthalmology; contbr. articles to profl. jours. Channel 7 Telethon Overseas fellow, 1991, UCLA fellow, 1991, Wilmer Eye Inst. fellow Johns Hopkins U., 1992. Fellow Royal Australian Coll. Ophthalmologists; mem. Australian Med. Assn., Am. Acad. Ophthalmology, Am. Assn. Pediat. Ophthalmology. Methodist. Avocations: golfing, computers. Office: 30 Churchill Ave, Subiaco 6008, Australia

LAM, KA SE, civil and structural engineering educator, researcher; b. Hong Kong, July 26, 1958; s. Hok Ming and Hung Chu (Chan) L.; m. Yuk Yee Tam, Nov. 22, 1990; children: Hiu Tung, Hiu Chak. BS in Engring., U. Hong Kong, 1980, MPhil, 1984, PhD, 1992. Safety insp. U. Hong Kong, 1985-87, asst. safety engr., 1987-88, asst. safety officer, 1988-92; asst. prof. Hong Kong Poly. U., 1992—. Mem. Hong Kong Meteorol. Soc. (com. 1997—), Am. Geophys. Union, Hong Kong Inst. Engrs. (assoc.). Roman Catholic. Avocations: contract bridge, swimming, soccer, badminton, reading. Home: 4G Block 17, South Horizons, Ap Lei Chau Hong Kong Office: Hong Kong Poly Univ, Civil Structural Engring, Hung Hom Hong Kong

LAM, KAREN SIU-LING, endocrinologist, educator, consultant; b. Swatow, Kwan Tung, China, Sept. 21, 1951; arrived in Hong Kong, 1956; d. Chak Ping and Shuet Bun (Wong) L.; m. Selwyn Kai-Mng So, Sept. 9, 1989; children: Victoria So, Benjamin So. MBBS with honors, U. Hong Kong, 1976, MD, 1990. Diplomate Hong Kong med. coun., 1977, Gen. med. coun. (Eng.), 1977. Med. officer Med. and Health Dept., Hong Kong, 1977-83; lectr. U. Hong Kong, 1983-89, sr. lectr., 1989-91, reader, 1981-97, prof. medicine, 1997—; vis. prof. Sun Yat Sen U. Med. Scis., Guangzhola, China, 1994-96; chmn. specialty bd. on endocrinology Hong Kong Coll. of Physicians, 1994—, regional coll. advisor, 1994—; chmn. working party on diabetes care Hong Kong Hosp. Authority, 1994-97; pres. Diabetes Hong Kong, 1997-2000. Contbr. more than 100 articles to profl. jours., chpts. to books including the Oxford Textbook of Medicine 2nd edit. Recipient Brit. Commonwealth fellowship Brit. Med. Coun., London, 1981-82, Fogarty Internat. fellowship, NIH, Bethesda, Md., 1986-87. Fellow Royal Coll. of Physicians (Edinburgh) Royal Coll. of Physicians (London), Hong Kong Acad. Medicine, Royal Australasian Coll. Physicians; mem. Hong Kong Soc. for Study of Endocrinology, Metabolism and Reproduction (sec. 1980-90, chmn. diabetes divsn. 1990-92, pres. 1992-94), Am. Endocrine Soc., Am. Diabetes Assn. Roman Catholic. Achievements include: founder patients' Mutual Aid Diabetes Soc., Hong Kong, Diabetes Hong Kong, Diabetes Ctr. Queen Mary Hosp. (first in Hong Kong). Avocations: singing, cooking, swimming, mountaineering, reading.

LAM, KUN KIN, bank executive; b. Singapore, Apr. 19, 1963; m. Yoke Leng Kan, Nov. 11, 1989. B in Accountancy, Nat. U. Singapore, 1986. CFA. Divsn. mgr. shorts term assets and currency Govt. of Singapore Investment Ltd., Singapore, 1987-95; treas. head, regional currency and derivatives Citibank N.A., Singapore, 1995-97, regional head Asia Pacific, 1998, region EM trading head Asia Pacific, 1999—. Recipient govt. scholarship Singapore Govt., 1981-87. Mem. Nat. U. Singapore Alumni Assn., Forex Assn. Singapore, ISFA, AIMR, Temasek Club. Avocations: golf, travel, reading, art. Office: Citibank NA, 5 Shenton Way # 01-01 UIC, 068808 Singapore Singapore

LAM, KWOK-HUNG GUY, lawyer; b. Canton, China, July 25, 1954; s. Pak Cheung and Sui Ping (Lee) L.; m. Yuen Fang To; children: Alexander, Benjamin. BSc in Mech. Engring., U. Toronto, 1977; LLB, Queen's U., Ont., Can., 1980; LLM, Columbia U., 1981. Sole practice Hong Kong, 1993—; chmn. Pacrim Internat. Capital Inc., Hong Kong, 1993—. Mem. Hong Kong Alliance of Chinese and Expatriates (chmn. 1994—), Assn. Experts for Modernization (pres. 1993-94). Avocations: football, tennis, sailing. Office: Lam & Co Peregrine Tower, Lam & Co Tower Two, Lippo Ctr Ste 3202, Hong Kong Hong Kong

LAM, RINGO WING-KWAN, electrical engineer, researcher; b. Hong Kong, People's Republic of China, July 25, 1971; s. Chun Chiu and Yuen Shan L. BEE, U. Hong Kong, 1993; MPhil, Chinese U., Hong Kong, 1995. Project mgr. Electronic News Media & Pub. Consortium, Hong Kong, 1995-96, Info. Networking Lab, Hong Kong, 1996—; CEO, Wisers Information, Ltd. Founder Hong Kong Devel. & Strategic Rsch. Ctr., 1996. Mem. IEEE, Webmasters Assn. (Hong Kong, chmn., founder). Avocation: hiking. E-mail: ringo@wisers.com. Office: 14/F Luk Kwok Ctr, 72 Gloucester Rd, Wanchai Hong Kong

LAM, SHIU KUM, gastroenterologist, hepatologist, educator; b. Hong Kong, Dec. 9, 1942; s. Biu Yuen Lam and Ngar Ming Mok; m. Winnie Wing Khi Chan, 1969; children: Amy, Bryan, Catrina. MBBS, U. Hong Kong, 1967, MD, 1975. Mem. Royal Coll. Physicians, U.K., 1972, Fellow Royal Coll. Physicians, London, 1983, Edinburgh, 1980, Glasgow, 1990, Fellow Royal Australasian Coll. Physicians, 1990. Sr. lectr. medicine U. Hong Kong, 1977-80, chief of gastroenterology, 1977-81, reader, 1980-84, prof. medicine, 1984—, chief of gastroenterology and hepatology, 1982—, chmn. dept. medicine, 1995—; cons. physician Queen Mary Hosp., Hong Kong, 1980—. Author: Viral Hepatitis B Infection, Vaccine and Control, 1984, Update on Hepatobiliary Diseases, 1996; editor, author: Health of the Elderly in Hong Kong, 1997; chief editor Jour. Gastroenterology and Hepatlogy, 1986—. Vice chmn. Hong Kong Liver Found., 1993—, Hong Kong Digestive Found., 1997—; coun. mem. Beijing Liver Found., 1997—. Recipient Officer of Brit. Empire award 1997; Hong Kong Coll. Physicians fellow, 1993, Hong Kong Acad. Medicine fellow 1993. Mem. Hong Kong Soc. Gastroenterology (pres. 1984-86, 96-98, 2000), Asian Pacific Assn. Gastroenterology. Office: U Hong Kong Dept Medicine, Queen Mary Hosp, Hong Kong Hong Kong

LAM, SIO KUAN, physicist, rsearcher; b. Fujien, China, June 14, 1969; s. Cheng Fong and Wai Chao (Cheong) L.; m. Pui I. Kong, Apr. 29, 1995; 1 child. BSc in Physics, Hua Chiao U., Fukien, China, 1990; MPhil, Hong Kong Poly. U., 1995; PhD, Chinese U Hong Kong, 1998. Lab. technician Macau Workers Childrens Wing Sch., 1990-91; tchr. Pui Ching H.S., Macau, 1991-92; postdoctoral fellow Chinese U. Hong Kong, 1997—. Mem. SPIE, Optical Soc. Am., Phys. Soc. Hong Kong. Avocations: computer programming, photography.

LAM, WAH KIT, internist, pulmonary specialist, educator; b. Hong Kong, China, Dec. 28, 1947; s. Hon Cheung and Jak Nung (Mok) L.; m. Sau Chi Leung, Mar 27, 1974. MB, BS, U. Hong Kong, Hong Kong, 1972; MD, U. Hong Kong, 5, 1986. Med. officer Castle Peak Hosp., Hong Kong, 1973, United Christian Hosp., Hong Kong, 1973-75; lectr. in medicine U. Hong Kong, 1975-84, sr. lectr. in medicine, 1984-89, reader in medicine, 1989-96, prof. of medicine, 1996—; hon. cons. Queen Mary Hosp., Hong Kong, 1984—, chief divsn. respiratory medicine, 1989—; hon. cons. in medicine Hosp. Authority, Hong Kong, 1991—; dep. head dept. medicine U. Hong Kong, 1995—. Editor: Clinical Respiratory Medicine, 1996, 2nd edit., 2000; also contbr. chpt. to book, articles to profl. jours. Mem. Med. Coun., Hong Kong, 1997-2000; med. advisor Hong Kong Asthma Soc., 1989—. Recipient Commonwealth Med. scholarship, Commonwealth Med. Soc. Bd., 1977-79; grantee Rsch. Grant Coun., Hong Kong, 1996. Fellow Am. Coll. Chest Physicians (gov. Hong Kong and Macau chpts. 1996-2000, regent 2000—), Royal Australian Coll. Physicians (Asia-Pacific com. 1995—), Royal Coll. Physicians of Edinburgh (coll. overseas adviser for Hong Kong 1997—), Hong Kong Lung Found. (founding chmn. 1996—), Hong Kong Coll. of Physicians (chmn. examination com. 1992—, chmn. internat. liaison com. 1998—); mem. Hong Kong Med. Assn. (specialists panel on rehab. 1992—). Avocations: travel, classical music. Office: Queen Mary Hosp U Dept Med, Pokfulam Rd, Hong Kong China

LAM, WAI KUEN ALEX, financial controller, accountant; b. Hong Kong, Aug. 6, 1964; s. Cheung and Yuen Ming (Mau) L.; m. Fun Wa Li, Feb. 14, 1993. Profl. Diploma Mgmt. Accountancy, Hong Kong Polytechnic, 1987; MBA, Univ. Wales, Bangor, 1996. Chartered acct. Acct. supr. Albert Y C Lee & Co., Hong Kong, 1987-88; acct. Dodwell Internat. Buying Offices Ltd., Hong Kong, 1988-91; group fin. controller Tillsonburg Co. Ltd., Hong Kong, 1991—; bd. dirs. Champion Alpha Industries Ltd., Hong Kong, Prime Source Holdings Ltd., Hong Kong, Truss Rich Worldwide Co. Ltd. Fellow Assn. Chartered Certified Accts., Inst. Chartered of Mgmt. Accts. (asso. Avocations: property investments, shares trading, driving, travelling, information technology. Home: Palm Springs Wo Shang Wai, House No 16 Geranium Path, Hong Kong China Office: Tillsonburg Res Asia 18 Fl, 8 Lam Lok St Kowloon Bay, Hong Kong China

LA MADRID, MONICA, market researcher; b. Dolores, Argentina, Dec. 5, 1949; d. Cesar Vilgré and Nancy Blondeau; m. Carlos Escudé, Jan. 27, 1977. Lic., Argentine Cath. U., Buenos Aires, 1974; MA, U. Conn., 1985. Project dir. IPSA, Buenos Aires, 1985-88, mgr. surveys divsn., 1988-94; mgr. surveys divsn. AC Neilsen Argentina, Buenos Aires, 1994-97; ptnr. Markwald, La Madrid y Asociados, Buenos Aires, 1997—; founder, bd. dirs. Argentine Soc. Mktg. Rsch. and Pub. Opinion, Buenos Aires, 1996—. Fax: 54-11-4816-0589. E-mail: marklam@impsat1.com.ar. Office: Markwald La Madrid y Asoc, Paraguay 1840, 1121 Buenos Aires Argentina

LAMALFA, SALVADOR, research engineer, consultant; b. Milazzo, Sicily, Italy, Mar. 26, 1951; arrived in Argentina, 1952; s. Antonino and Rosa (De Gaetano) LaM.; m. Maria del Carmen Diaz; 1 child, Diana Elizabeth. Bachellor in Acctg., CENS 36, Bahia Blanca, Argentina, 1983. Electrical technician Argentine Navy, 1964-76; electrical technician Inst. Applied Mechanics (Conicet), Bahia Blanca, 1976-90, rsch. engr., 1976—; asst. prof. Faculty of Engring., U. Tecnologica Nacional, Argentina, 1980—; cons. Empresa de Servicios Electricos, Bahia Blanca, 1984—. Contbr. articles to profl. publs.; inventor balancing machine. Named Spl. Mention Ho. of Reps., Argentina, 1995. Mem. Am. Acad. of Mechanics. Roman Catholic. Avocation: gardening. Home: Santiago del Estero 646, 8000 Bahia Blanca Argentina Office: Inst of Applied Mechanics, Gorriti 43, 8000 Bahia Blanca Argentina

LAMANA DOS SANTOS, LUIZ ALBERTO, plastic surgeon; b. Pocos de Caldas, Brazil, Apr. 18, 1953; s. Paulo dos Santos and Wilma Lamana; m. Marly Amorim Silva, July 1, 1979; children: Luis Alberto Amorim Lamana, Carlos Henrique Amorim Lamana. Diploma, Seminario Nssa. Sra. Esperanca, Pocos de Caldas, Brazil, 1967, Escola Assis Chanteabriand, Sao Paulo, Brazil, 1970; MD, Faculdade Ciencias Medicas, Belo Horizonte, Brazil, 1977; Plastic Surgeon, IPSEMG Hosp., Belo Horizonte, Brazil, 1980. Medical diplomate Faculdade de Ciencias Medicas de Minas Gerais in Belo Horizonte, Brazil. General surgeon Ipsemg Hosp., Belo Horizonte, 1978-79, plastic surgeon, 1978-80; plastic surgeon Santa Rita Hosp., Belo Horizonte, 1979-99, Santa Helena Hosp., Belo Horizonte, 1979-99, Nucleo de Cirurgia Plastica, Belo Horizonte, 1979-99; pres. dir. Nucleo de Cirurgia Plastica, Belo Horizonte, 1979-99; clin. dir. Nucleo de Cirurgia Plastica, Belo Horizonte, 1979-99; adminstr. dir. Biosut Ltda., Belo Horizonte, 1994-99; chief of svc. Nucleo de Cirurgia Plastica, 1984-99. Recipient awards in field. Mem. Brazilian Assn. Plastic Surgery, Assn. Med. and Surgery Laser, others. Roman Catholic. Avocations: diving, mountain biking, tennis, jogging, table tennis. Office: Nucleo de Cirurgia Plastia, Av Prof Cristovan dos Santos, 30320510 Belo Horizonte Brazil

LAMAR, HORACE BEASELY, JR., university dean; b. Mobile, Ala., June 12, 1955; m. Danielle Kennedy; children: Horace Lamar III, Kennedy O'Neal Lamar. BS, Miss. Valley State U., 1977; MA, U. Minn., 1979; PhD in Music Edn., U. So. Miss., 1989. Tchr. music LeFlore H.S., Mobile, Ala., 1979-88; asst. prof. music Ala. A&M U., Normal, 1988-91; asst. prof. music Ala. State U., Montgomery, 1991-95, dean Sch. Music, 1995—. Home: 137 Oldfield Dr Montgomery AL 36117-3937 Office: Alabama State University PO Box 271 Montgomery AL 36101-0271

LAMAR, JASON RANDOLPH, graphic designer; b. Muncie, Ind., June 3, 1974; s. William Gregg and Andrea Lynn LaMar; m. Lisa Marie Brummet, May 5, 1996. BS in Journalism, Ball State U., 1996. Asst. coord. The Ind. Acad. Office Outreach Programs, Muncie, 1996-98, asst. dir. comm. and devel., 1998-99; dir. web svcs. Ohio Wesleyan U., Delaware, 1999—; founder, creative dir. LaMar StudioWorks, Columbus, Ohio. Project dir. (ednl. web sites) Smithsonian Nat. Mus. Natural History, 1997, 98, San Francisco Ex-

ploratorium, 1997, BBC WebGuide, 1998, The Chgo. Field Mus., 1999 (Bonus.com Editor's Choice award 1999), The Newseum, 1998. Web dir. Carter for County Commr., Delaware County, Ohio, 2000. Recipient Coolest Sci. Site Nat. Acad. Press, 1997-98. Avocations: MIDI music composition, creative writing, digital art and illustration. Office: Ohio Wesleyan U Mowry Alumni Ctr Delaware OH 43015

LAMAR, WILLIAM FRED, chaplain, educator; b. Birmingham, Ala., Jan. 4, 1934; s. William Fred Sr. and Everette (Kelley) L.; m. Roberta Anton, Sept. 17, 1955 (dec.); 1 child, Jonathan Frederick; m. Martha Anne Lee, June 7, 1986. BA, U. Ala., 1954; BD, Vanderbilt U., 1957; PhD, St. Louis U., 1972; D Min., Eden Theol. Sem., 1974; grad., Spanish Lang. Sch., Antigua, Guatemala, 1993. Minister United Meth. Ch., Bynum, Ala., 1959-61, Fultondale, Ala., 1961-65; campus minister U. Mo., Rolla, 1965-74; chaplain, prof., dir. overseas missions DePauw U., Greencastle, Ind., 1974-97; dir. United Meth. Com. on Relief Vol. Programs, Travnik, Bosnia, 1996-98; advisor overseas vol. program United Meth. Ch. Ind., Indpls., 1980-88; mem. Eli Lilly Found. study on the future of the ministry, 1989-91; cons. internat. vol. programs United Theol. Sem., Vanderbilt U. Div. Sch. and Westminster Coll., Oxford U., 1989-93; bd. dirs. Ecumenical Ventures, The Philippines, China. Author: (book) Role of the College Chaplain at the Church-Related College, 1984; designer electric utility computer programs, 1979-85. Vice chmn. County Welfare Bd., Rolla; bd. dirs. Sr. Vol. Program Action, Greencastle, 1977-80. Served to 1st lt. U.S. Army, 1957-59. Recipient Award of Honor, Ind. Gov's. Voluntary Action, 1976, Cross of Jerusalem, Episcopal Diocese of Guatemala, 1979, Cross of St. Francis, Inst. de Asuntos Culturales del Peru, 1982, 587th Point of Light award Pres. George Bush, 1991, Vol. award Ind. Nature Conservancy, 1993; Danforth fellow, 1971-72. Mem. Nat. Campus Ministry Assn. (chmn. sci. and ethics network), Nat. Assn. Coll. Chaplains, Assn. Religion in Intellectual Life, Assn. Coll. and U. Religious Advisors (nat. program chair 1993; bd. dirs. Ind. office campus ministry 1988-98), Acad. Sr. Profls. (Eckerd Coll.). E-mail: lamarfm@gte.net. Home and Office: 5565 Escondida Blvd S Saint Petersburg FL 33715-1454

LAMARCHE, PIERRE MARIE EMILE, oil company executive; b. Gomze Andoumont, Liege, Belgium, Jan. 1, 1948; s. Jean-Pierre and Monique (Bosschaert) L.; m. Sabine Germaine Goethals, Apr. 8, 1972; children: Astrid, Diego, Catalina, Damien. Degree in engring., U. Cath. de Louvain, Belgium, 1970; MBA (hon.), Katholieke U. Leuven, Belgium, 1972. Cert. commercial engr. Asst. to indsl. advisor UN Indsl. Devel. Orgn., Lima, Peru, 1972-75; with supply dept. Petrofina, Brussels, 1976-78, supply mgr., 1981-83; supply mgr. Zaire Sep/Petrofina, Kinshasa, 1978-81; sr. trader Marc Rich, Madrid, 1983-86; mng. dir. Hauterat & Watteyne, Liege, 1986-96, Transcor, Brussels, 1989-96; chmn., mng. dir. Petrus, Brussels, 1998—. Office: Petrus, Avenue Louise 391 Box 9, 1050 Brussels Brabant, Belgium

LAMARRE, BERNARD, engineering, contracting and manufacturing advisor; b. Chicoutimi, Que., Can., Aug. 6, 1931; s. Emile J. and Blanche M. (Gagnon) L.; m. Louise Lalonde, Aug. 30, 1952; children: Jean, Christine, Lucie, Monique, Michèle, Philippe, Mireille. BSc, Ecole Poly., Montreal, Que., Can., 1952; MSc, Imperial Coll., U. London, 1955; LLD, St. Francis Xavier U., N.S., Can., 1980; D in Engring. (hon.), U. Waterloo, Ont., 1984; LLD (hon.), U. Concordia, Montreal, 1985; D in Engring. (hon.), U. Montreal, 1985; D in Applied Sci. (hon.), U. Sherbrooke, Que., 1986; D in Bus. Adminstrn. (hon.), U. Chicoutimi, Que., 1987; D in Sci. (hon.), Queen's U., Kingston, Ont., 1987; D in Engring. (hon.), U. Ottawa, Ont., 1988, Tech. U. N.S., 1989, Royal Mil. Coll., Kingston, 1990. Structural and founds. engr. Lalonde-Valois, Montreal, 1955-60, chief engr., 1960-62; ptnr., gen. mgr., pres. Lalonde, Valois, Lamarre, Valois, Montreal, 1962-72; chmn., chief exec. officer Lavalin Group, 1972-91; sr. advisor SNC-Lavalin Inc., 1991-99; chmn. Soc. du Vieux Port de Montreal, Bellechasse Santé, Soc. de la Faune et des Parcs du Quebec (FAPAC); bd. dirs. Telesystems Inc., Tembec Inc., Microcell Inc., Acier Leroux Inc., Capital Internat. CDPQ. Bd. dirs. U. of Montreal, Montreal Design Inst.; chmn. Montreal Mus. Fine Arts. Decorated officer Ordre nat. du Québec, Order of Can.; Athlone fellow, 1952. Fellow Engring. Inst. Can., Can. Soc. Civil Engring.; mem. ASCE, Order Engrs. Que., Mont-Royal Club, St. Denis Club, Laval-sur-le Lac Club. Roman Catholic. Home: 4850 Cedar Crescent, Montreal, PQ Canada H3W 2H9

LAMATA, WILLA GALVE, college dean, accountant; b. Bago, The Philippines, Oct. 24, 1957; d. Wilfredo Jocson and Lucia Galve Lamata. BSBA in Acctg., U.P. in the Visayas, Iloilo, The Philippines, 1978, MM, BM, 1990. CPA, The Philippines. Acctg. clk. U.P. in the Visayas, Iloilo, 1980, chief acctg. svcs. unit, 1981-82, mem. faculty, 1989-90; acct. Poveda Learning Ctr., Iloilo, 1982-85; mem. faculty U. San Agustin, Iloilo, 1985-89, 92—, acad. coord., 1993-95, 98-99, dean coll. of commerce, 1999—. Scholar in pedagogy Teresian Assn., Madrid, Rome, 1991-92. Roman Catholic. Avocations: reading, listening to music, writing poems. Home: 14 General Luna St, Iloilo 5000, The Philippines Office: U San Agustin, General Luna St, Iloilo 5000, The Philippines

LAMAZE, JEAN-HUGHES DE, equity analyst executive; b. Paris, Apr. 11, 1965; s. Jean and Cecile (De Francelieu) De L.; m. Aude de Chassey, May 15, 1993. LLB, U. Paris II-Assas, 1987; diploma, Inst. Superieur de Gestion, Paris, 1988, Ctr. Formation Fin. Analysis, 1992, Franco-Brit. C. of C., 1986; Internat. Exec. Programme, INSEAD, 2000. Trainee analyst Enskilda Securities, London, 1987; trainee fund mgr. Cholet-Dupont, Paris, 1988; equity analyst Enskilda Societe de Bourse, Paris, 1989-96; dir., head French equity rsch. Credit Suisse First Boston, London, 1996—. Head young mems. Parti Republicain, Paris, 1985. Lt. French Light Cavalry, 1988-89. Recipient Nat. Def. medal French State, 1989. Mem. French Soc. Fin. Analysts (diploma 1992), Cercle du Bois de Boulogne. Avocations: theater actor, mountains, politics. Home: 35 Queens Gate Gardens, London SW7 5RR, England Office: Credit Suisse First Boston, One Cabot Square, London E14 4QJ, England

LAMB, CHRISTOPHER JOHN, research scientist; b. York, England, Mar. 19, 1950; s. John Mungall and Eileen Blanche (Marley) L.; m. Jane Susan Wright, Sept. 3, 1970; children: Catherine, William, Donald. BA, U. Cambridge, England, 1972, PhD, 1976. Jr. faculty biochem. U. Oxford, England, 1977-82; staff scientist Salk Inst., La Jolla, Calif., 1982-85, assoc. prof., 1985-92, prof., 1992-98; Regius prof. plant sci. U. Edinburgh, Scotland, 1999; dir. John Innes Ctr., Norwich, England, 1999—; John Innes prof. biology U. East Anglia, Norwich, England, 1999—; tech. founder, co-chair scientific adv. bd. AKKADIX, Inc., San Diego, 1999—. Contbr. articles to profl. jours. Recipient Am. Chem. Soc. Found. award, 1985; ICI Rsch. fellow U. Oxford, 1975-77, Browne Rsch. fellow The Queen's Coll., Oxford, 1977-82, McKnight Found. Rsch. scholar, 1983. Fellow AAAS. Avocations: walking, sushi, wine, swimming. Office: John Innes Ctr Norwich Rsch Park, Norwich NR4 7UH, England

LAMB, JAMES WARNER, biology educator; b. Yakima, Wash., Apr. 21, 1945; s. John Ed and Alama Verna Freeman; m. Mary Sue Sowell, Mar. 15, 1954; children: James David, Lana Gail. BS, N.Mex. State U., 1970, MS, 1975; DSc, London Inst. Applied Rsch., 1972. Constrn. expeditor Internat. Mineral & Chem. Corp., Carlsbad, N.Mex., 1964-68; coordinator introductory biology N.Mex. State U., Las Cruces, 1970-72; prof. biology El Paso (Tex.) C.C., 1972-79, div. chmn., 1977-88; dir. eastern Carribean project HOPE, Barbados, 1979-80; assoc. dean arts and sci. El Paso C.C., 1980-83, prof. biology, 1983-93; assoc. v.p. instrnl. svcs., 1993-95; program dir. Project HOPE, Barbados, West Indies, 1979-80; head instr. biology Lamb's Material Arts, El Paso, 1980—; dean instrn. Santa Fe C.C., 1995-97; dean instructional svcs. Ctrl. Ariz. Coll., Winkelman, 1999—; instr. N.Mex. State U., Las Cruces, 1974-78; speaker in field. Author: Oral Histology and Embryology, 1976, Microbiology and Pharmacology for Dental Assisting, 1985. Trustee Rep. Presdl. Task Force, Washington, 1980-87; state dir. Olympics of the Mind, El Paso and West Tex., 1982-85, bd. dirs., 1982-87; exec. dir. U.S. Combat Martial Arts, Maryville, Mo., 1986-87, bd. dirs. 1987—; bd. dirs. Santa Fe Econ. Devel., 1996-99, Leadership Santa Fe, 1996, 97; mem. San Manuel Focus Future Task Force, 2000—; treas. Ariz. Occupational Adminstrs. Coun., 2000—. Recipient Faculty Excellence award Burlington No. Found., 1993; named one of Top 50 C.C. Tchrs. USA Today, 1993. Mem. Internat. Platform Assn., Assn. C.C.'s Trustees (Outstanding Faculty Western Region award 1993), Tex. Faculty Assn. (v.p. 1986-87), Faculty Assn. El Paso Community Coll. (v.p. 1983-84), Tex. Acad. of Sci., Herpetologist League, U.S. Tae Kwon Do Assn. (instr. 1984—), Sr. C. of C. (bd. dirs. 1999—). Mem. Ch. of Christ. Clubs: Lamb's Martial Arts (El Paso) (master 1980-87). Avocations: fencing, gem collecting. Home: 65731 E Desert Moon Dr Tucson AZ 85739-1685 Office: Ctrl Ariz Coll-Aravaipa Campus 80440 E Aravaipa Rd Winkelman AZ 85292-7068

LAMB, ROBERT EDWARD, diplomat; b. Atlanta, Nov. 17, 1936; s. T.E. and Lois (Harris) L.; m. Lucille Trujillo, Jan. 13, 1962; children: Robert Edward, Anne Gretchen, Michael David. BA in Internat. Rels., U. Pa., 1962. Joined Fgn. Service, Dept. State, 1963; dir. fin. services Dept. State, Washington, 1975-77, dir. passport office, 1977-79; adminstrv. counsellor U.S. Embassy, Bonn, Fed. Republic Germany, 1979-83; asst. sec. of state for adminstrn. Dept. State, Washington, 1983-85; asst. sec. of state Diplomatic Security, 1985-89; U.S. Amb. to Cyprus Cyprus, 1990-93; spl. Cyprus coord., 1993-94; exec. dir Am. Philatelic Soc., State Coll., Pa., 1994—. Pub.: Index of American Philatelic Literature. Served with USMC, 1958-61. Mem. Am. Philatelic Soc. Home and Office: PO Box 8068 State College PA 16803-8068

LAMB, STUART HOWARD, clothing company executive; b. Wakefield, West York, England, Apr. 21, 1948; s. William and Ruth Evelyn (Mellor) L.; m. Gillian Margaret Hadfield, Sept. 15, 1969 (div. Oct., 1974); children: William Robert Stuart, Deborah Jane; m. Jean Lesley Wagstaff, Apr. 14, 1979; children: Ruth Caroline, Charlotte Jayne. Assoc. of Brit. Clothing Inst., Leicester Coll., Leicester, England, 1966. Mgr. production William Lamb Footwear Ltd., Wakefield, West York, England, 1966-67; production dir. William Lamb Footwear Ltd., Wakefield, 1967-69, joint mng. dir., 1969-82, chmn., 1982-83; chmn. Gola Lamb Group, Wakefield, 1983-90; chmn. Austin Footwear Ltd., Wakefield, 1974-96, Gola Ltd., Gibraltar, 1985-90; dep. chmn. Gola Sportswear Internat., Wakefield, 1989-92; chmn. William Lamb Group, 1985—, William lamb Footwear, 1985—, Lamb Logistics, 1992—; Trade Warden of Worshipful Co. of Pattenmakers 1998-2000, mem. Court of Worshipful Co. of Pattenmakers 2000—. Mem. Boot & Shoe Inst. (ABSI), Wakefield Golf Club. Mem. Conservative Party. Mem. Ch. England. Home: Walton Common Farm, Common Ln West York, Walton Wakefield WF26PS, England

LAMB, WILLIS EUGENE, JR., physicist, educator; b. L.A., July 12, 1913; s. Willis Eugene and Marie Helen (Metcalf) L.; m. Ursula Schaefer, June 5, 1939 (dec. Aug. 1996); m. Bruria Kaufman, Nov. 29, 1996. BS, U. Calif., 1934, PhD, 1938; DSc (hon.), U. Pa., 1953, Gustavus Adolphus Coll., 1975, Columbia U., 1990; MA, Oxford (Eng.) U., 1956; MA (hon.), Yale, 1961; LHD (hon.), Yeshiva U., 1965; Dr.rer.nat (hon.), U. Ulm., Germany, 1997. Mem. faculty Columbia U., 1938-52, prof. physics, 1948-52; prof. physics Stanford U., 1951-56; Wykeham prof. physics and fellow New Coll., Oxford U., 1956-62; Henry Ford 2d prof. physics Yale U., 1962-72, J. Willard Gibbs prof. physics, 1972-74; prof. physics and optical scis. U. Ariz., Tucson, 1974—, Regents prof., 1990—; Morris Loeb lectr. Harvard U., 1953-54; Gordon Shrum lectr. Simon Fraser U., 1972; cons. Philips Labs., Bell Telephone Labs., Perkin-Elmer, NASA; vis. com. Brookhaven Nat. Lab. Recipient (with P. Kusch) Nobel prize in physics, 1955, Rumford premium Am. Acad. Arts and Scis., 1953; award Rsch. Corp., 1954, Yeshiva award, 1962; Guggenheim fellow, 1960-61, sr. Alexander von Humboldt fellow, 1992-94. Fellow Am. Phys. Soc., Optical Soc. Am., N.Y. Acad. Scis.; hon. fellow Inst. Physics and Phys. Soc. (Guthrie lectr. 1958), Royal Soc. Edinburgh (fgn. mem.); mem. Nat. Acad. Scis., Phi Beta Kappa, Sigma Xi. Office: U Ariz Optical Scis Ctr PO Box 210094 Tucson AZ 85721-0094

LAMBERG, BROR AXEL, endocrinologist; b. Helsinki, Finland, Mar. 1, 1923; s. Axel and Anna (Perkowsky) L.; m. Carin Olin, Feb. 25, 1924; 1 child, Christel. MD, U. Helsinki, 1949, PhD, 1953. Lectr. in medicine U. Helsinki, 1957-65, assoc. prof., 1965-71, prof. endocrinology, 1971-89; asst. head physician Univ. Hosp., Helsinki, 1962-65; v.p. Med. Commn., Acad. Finland, 1971-73; cons. Nat. Med. Bd., Helsinki, 1980-90; mem. CIBA Found. Adv. Panel, London, 1967-86, Bd. of Finnish Sci. Socs., 1990-92; endocrinology mem. Nat. Bd. Health, 1980-90. Author: Thyroid Diseases, 1967, Swedish edit., 1968; editor: Clinical Endocrinology, I, 1978, II, 1984, III, 1992, History of Goitre and Iodine, 1998; Finnish editor Acta Endocrinologica, 1971-81; editor Transaction of Finnish Med. Soc., 1984-89. Chief Minerva Found. Inst. Med. Rsch., Helsinki, 1959-71; pres. bd. Minerva Found., Helsinki, 1971-95, Signe and Ane Gyllenberg Found., Helsinki, 1979-93; pres. Nordic Insulin Found., Gentofte, Denmark, 1984-89. Lt. Finnish mil., 1941-44. Decorated Liberation Cross IV with swords, comdr. Finnish Lion Order, Polar Stern Order (Sweden); recipient Ayrapaa award Finnish Med. Socs. and Assn., 1979, Nyström award Finnish Soc. for Scis. and Letters, 1999. Mem. Finnish Soc. Nuclear Medicine (hon., pres. 1962-65, Heiskanen award 1973), Finnish Soc. Endocrinology (hon., pres. 1968-71), Finnish Med. Soc. (hon., pres., v.p. 1973-74, Runeberg award and medal 1985), Finnish Soc. Internal Medicine (hon.), Swedish Med. Soc. (hon.), others. Avocations: Rome and Roman culture, music, opera, thyroid history.

LAMBERS, JOHANNES THIEO, biologist, educator; b. Anloo, Drenthe, The Netherlands, Dec. 16, 1950; s. Gezinus Margus and Luchina Jantina (Vos) L.; m. Marion Lesley Cambridge. PhD, U. Groningen, 1979. Lectr. U. Groningen, 1976-79; postdoctoral fellow U. We. Australia, Perth, 1979, U. Melbourne, 1980-81, Australian Nat. U., Canberra, 1981-82; lectr. U. Groningen, 1982-85; prof. biology U. Utrecht, 1985—; prof. agr. U. We. Australia, 1998—. Office: U Utrecht Faculty Biology, U We Australia Faculty Agr, Hacket Dr, 3584 CA Nedlands WA 6009, Australia NL-3584

LAMBERT, ANGELA MARIA, writer, journalist; b. Beckenham, Kent, Eng., Apr. 14, 1940; d. John Donald and Edith Paula Alice (Schroeder) Helps; m. Martin John Lambert (div. 1966); children: Carolyn Ruth, Jonathan Martin; ptnr. Stephen Vizinczey; 1 child, Marianne Jane Vizinczey-Lambert; ptnr. Antony John Price, 1986. Grad. in Philosophy, Politics and Econs., St. Hilda's Coll., Oxford, Eng., 1961. Editor Cassell & Co., London, 1961-62; rsch. asst. Labour Cabinet Min., House of Lords, London, 1964-68; journalist SUN Newspaper, London, 1969-71; reporter Ind. TV News, London, 1972-76, London Weekend TV, 1976-78, Thames TV, London, 1978-89; columnist, interviewer The Independent, London, 1989-96; interviewer The Daily Mail, 1996-2000. Author: Unquiet Souls: 1880-1918, 1984 (Runner-up Whitbread Biog. prize 1984), 1939: The Last Season of Peace, 1989, Love Among the Single Classes, 1989, No Talking After Lights, 1991, A Rather English Marriage, 1993, The Constant Mistress, 1995, Kiss & Kin, 1997, Golden Lads and Girls, 1999, The Property of Rain, 2000. Mem. English P.E.N. (exec. com. 1991-95), Friends of Classics. Labour Party. Anglican. Avocations: reading, writing, talking, travelling, grandchildren. Fax: 0207-244 8297. Home: Flat 4 15 Collingham Rd, London SW5 0NU, England

LAMBERT, CHARLENE MILLIKEN, marketing executive; b. Boise, Idaho, June 6, 1949; arrived in the Netherlands, 1995; d. Charles R. and Audrey M. (Beckstead) Milliken; children: Lisa, Nicolas. B in Modern Langs., St. Mary's Coll., 1971; M in Urban and Regional Planning, U. of Ottawa, Can., 1983. Sr. econ. devel. officer City of Ottawa, 1983-92; nat. dir. Transport 2000 Can., 1993-94; sr. policy analyst Fedn. of Can. Municipalities, Ottawa, 1994-95; lic. and infor. officer City of the Hague, The Netherlands, 1995-97; mktg. mgr. The Hague Region Bus. Corp., 1997—; adj. prof. Webster U., Leiden, The Netherlands, 1997—; founding chmn. Farmers' Markets Ottawa, Ont., 1990-92. Tchr. of the Dutch Ctr. for Refugees, Leiden, Netherlands, 1997—. Mem. Connecting Women, Le Cercle Français, Hong Kong Trade Devel. Coun., Can. Women's Club. Avocations: traveling, Chinese language, fitness, family, history. Home: Witte Rozenstraat 52A, 2311XX Leiden The Netherlands Office: West Holland Fgn Invest Agy, Koningskade 30 POB 66, 2502LS The Hague Netherlands

LAMBERT, DEBORAH NOLAN, library administrator; b. Wakefield, R.I., Oct. 2, 1952; d. Richard M. and Eileen E. Nolan; m. Paul Jeffrey Lambert; 1 child, Ryan R. BA, Wittenberg U., 1974; MLS, U. Pitts., 1975. Libr. Cuyahoga C.C., Cleve., 1976-83, dir. Campus Learning Resource Ctr., 1983-86; coll. dir. ednl. support svcs. Montgomery Coll., Rockville, Md., 1986-90; libr./media specialist Montgomery County Pub. Schs., Rockville, 1990-94, instrnl. tech. specialist, 1994-97; asst. dir. adminstrv. svcs. Wake Forest U. Z. Smith Reynolds Libr., Winston-Salem, 1997—; exec. bd. mem. Acad. Libr. Assn. Ohio, 1984-86, Congress Acad. Libr. Dirs., Md., 1988-90; adv. bd. mem. Cleve. Area Met. Libr. Sys., 1985-86. mem. ALA, Assn. Coll. and Rsch. Librs., Libr. Adminstrn. and Mgmt. Assn., N.C. Libr. Assn. (chair pers. and staff devel. spl. interest group 1999—). E-mail: lamberdn@wfu.edu. Office: Z Smith Reynolds Libr Wake Forest Univ Winston Salem NC 27109

LAMBERT, DIDIER MICHEL, chemistry researcher; b. Brussels, Belgium, May 3, 1966; s. Paul Alexis and Marie Gabrielle (Havelange) L.; children: Romain, Camille. Pharmacist, U. Louvain, Brussels, 1989, PhD in Pharm. Scis., 1994. Rsch. asst. U. Louvain, 1989-91, tchg. asst., 1992-94; rschr. U. Minn., Mpls., 1994-95; asst. prof. U. Louvain, 1995-98, prof., 1998—; cons. Belgian Ctr. of Pharmacotherapeutic Info., Brussels, 1998. Mem. editl. bd. Current Med. Chemistry, 1997-99; contbr. articles to profl. jours. Grantee Royal Belgian Acad. of Medicine, Brussels, 1994; recipient NATO fellowship, 1994-95. Mem. Royal Chem. Soc. of Belgium (bd. dirs. 1994-98), Am. Chem. Soc., Internat. Cannabis Rsch. Soc., N.Y. Acad. of Scis. Avocations: lit. and poetry, soccer, tennis. Office: Cath Univ of Louvain, 73 Aven Mounier CMFA 7340, Brussels 1200, Belgium

LAMBERT, GARY ERVERY, lawyer; b. Providence, Oct. 27, 1959; s. Ervery Eldege and Melitta (Hirsch) L.; m. Lori Keller, Apr. 22, 1995; 1 child, Katherine Elizabeth. BS in Chemistry and Biology, Valparaiso (Ind.) U., 1981; JD with honors, Drake U., 1984. Bar: Iowa 1984, Mass. 1986, U.S. Ct. Mil. Appeals 1986, U.S. Dist. Ct. Mass. 1987, U.S. Ct. Appeals (1st cir.) 1987, U.S. Patent and Trademark Office 1993, U.S. Ct. Appeals (fed. cir.) 1996. Litigator Gallagher & Gallagher, P.C., Boston, 1987-89; owner Law Office of Gary Lambert, Boston, 1989-93; ptnr. Lambert Assocs., PLLC, Boston, 1993—; intellectual property judge advocate, hdqs. USMC, 1997—. Capt. USMC, 1984-87, Japan. Mem. Boston Bar Assn., Boston Patent Law Assn., Am. Intellectual Property Assn., Marine Corps Res. Officers Assn. (life), NRA (life). Republican. Lutheran. Home: 32 Columbia Ave Nashua NH 03064-1601 Office: Lambert Assocs PLLC 92 State St Boston MA 02109-2004

LAMBERT, JEAN MARJORIE, health care executive; b. Bay City, Mich., Mar. 19, 1943; d. Richard William and Fidelis Rena (LeVasseur) L. BA, Madonna U., Livonia, Mich., 1967; MA, Ea. Mich. U., 1975. Cert. in Shiatsu; bd. cert. reflexology. Dir. religious edn. Archdiocese of Detroit, 1970-75, dir. evaluation, 1975-77; assoc. dir. programming Intermedia Found., Santa Monica, Calif., 1977-78; acad. dean St. John Provincial Sem., Plymouth, Mich., 1978-84; asst. dir. quality mgmt. Sisters of Mercy Health Corp., Farmington Hills, Mich., 1984-87; sr. cons. Mercy Collaborative, Livonia, mich., 1987-88; v.p. Mission Mercy Health Sys., Cin., 1988-91, Mission Sisters Providence Health Sys., Springfield, Mass., 1991-99; sr. v.p. Mission Integration Humility of Mary Health Ptnrs., Youngstown, Ohio, 1999—; asst. prof. homiletics St. John Sem., Plymouth, Mich., 1978-85, St. Mary of the Woods Coll., Terre Haute, Ind., summer 1985, St. Meinrad Sem., Ind., summer 1984; bd. dirs. Combined Health Appeal of Mass., Providence Ministries, New Eng. Conf. Cath. Healthcare; bd. dirs. Am. Reflexology Certification Bd. Editor Religious Edn., 1975-77. Nat. Cath. Edn. Assn.-Assn. Theol. Schs. for U.S. and Can. grantee, 1983. Mem. NAFE, Groundwork, Network, Am. Hosp. Assn., Am. Mgmt. Assn., Mental Health Assn., Cath. Health Assn. (bd. dirs. New Eng. Conf.), Acad. Leadership in Cath. Health Care, Providence Ministries (bd. dirs.). Roman Catholic. Avocations: woodcarving, photography, continuing education, shiatsu, reflexology. Office: Humility of Mary Health Ptnrs 1044 Belmont Ave Youngstown OH 44504-1006

LAMBERT, JON KELLY, mechanical engineer; b. Seattle, Nov. 4, 1954; s. William Edward and Irene Myrtle (Paulson) L.; m. Linda Lenore LeMere, July 18, 1980; 1 child, Kelly Renee. Cert. nuclear lead auditor. Nuclear quality control inspector various orgns., 1981-87; dir. quality Tanco, Inc., Houston, 1987; welding engr. Joy Technologies, Inc., Thompson, Tex., 1987; quality inspector Townsend & Bottum Svcs. Group, 1987-88; welding engr. M.K. Ferguson Co., Bridgman, Mich., 1988; quality engr. M.K. Ferguson Co., Aiken, S.C., 1988-90; welding engr. Westinghouse Savannah River Co., Aiken, 1990-95; quality assurance mgr. Mitsubishi Heavy Industries Am., Inc., Newport Beach, Calif., 1995-96; asst. dir. certification, staff engr. Bechtel Internat., Campeche, Mex., 1998—. Mem. Am. Welding Soc. (sr. certification welding insp., mem. sub-com. structural welding code-steel, charter com. stainless steel welding code 1990-96, qualification com. 2000—). Achievements include work on safety of nuclear power plants and defense nuclear facilities.

LAMBERT, KIRSTEN SCHNOOR, public relations executive, writer; b. Chgo., Dec. 26, 1963; d. Walter Karl and Irmgard (von Stockhausen) Schnoor; m. Christopher Jay Lambert, May 25, 1996. BA in Liberal Arts, DePaul U., 1995. Editl. and prodn. asst. Kraft Inc., Glenview, Ill., 1986-89; comm. assoc. Budget Rent A Car, Chgo., 1989-91; spl. events asst. Chgo. Sun-Times, 1992-94; editl. asst. Chgo. Reader, 1994-95; freelancer DonTech Corp., Chgo., 1995-96; comm. mgr. The Sherwood Group, Inc., Northbrook, Ill., 1996-00, Am. Orthopaedic Assn., Rosemont, Ill., 2000—; mgr. Internat. Ctr. for Orthopaedic Edn., Rosemont, 2000—; liaison Am. Acad. Orthopaedic Surgeons, Rosemont, 2000—. Author: Chicago '96 Democratic National Convention Visitors' Guide, 1996; editor newsletter Interactions, 1999 (Circle of Excellence award Am. Soc. Assn. Execs, 1999). Support mgr. Howard Brown Meml. Clinic, Chgo., 1987-91. Mem. Internat. Assn. Bus. Communicators (chpt. membership com. 1989-91). Avocations: writing, music, dancing. E-mail: lambert@aoassn.org. Office: Am Orthopaedic Assn 6300 N River Rd Rosemont IL 60018-4206

LAMBERT, RENE E., gastroenterologist; b. Lyon, France, July 23, 1930; d. Jacques and Valentine (Neuville) L.; m. Claude Mayoux, Apr. 1, 1952; children: Philippe, Olivier, Pierre Gilles, Flavien; m. Annick Chavaillon, 1986; 1 child, Justine. MD, Sch. Medicine of Lyon, 1958. Rsch. fellow Ctr. Nat. Rsch. Sci., Lyon, 1959-63; dir. Ctr. d'epidemiologie, 1978-83; assoc. prof. U. Lyon, 1963-74, prof., 1974-95; chief gastroenterology unit Hosp. E. Herriot, Lyon, 1974—; dir. rsch. unit INSERM, 1964-83; chmn. European Digestive Week, Paris, 1996; sr. advisor Internat. Agy. for Rsch. on Cancer, Lyon, 1999. Author: Les Aspects Recents de l'ulcere Experimental, 1958, La Digestion, 1976, Epidemiologie: Elements pour le Clinicien, 1981, Les Lasers; Applications Medicales, 1985; contbr. articles to profl. jours. Fellow Royal Coll. Physicians; mem. Internat. Soc. Laser Med. Surgery, European Laser Assn., Am. Gastroenterol. Assn., British Soc. Gastro., Soc. France Endoscopie Digestive, French Soc. Gasgro., Am. Soc. GI Endosc. Home: 10 rue Chevalier, Lyon 69003, France Office: Internat Agy Rsch Cancer, 150 Cours A Thomas, Lyon 69003, France

LAMBERT, RICHARD WILLIAM, mathematics educator; b. Gettysburg, Pa., May 1, 1928; s. Allen Clay and Orpha Rose (Hoppert) L.; m. Phyllis Jean Bain, Sept. 2, 1949 (div. May 1982); children: James Harold, Dean Richard; m. Kathleen Ann Waring, Aug. 30, 1982; stepchildren: Gregory Scott Gibbs, LeAnn Marie Gibbs. BS, Oreg. State U., 1952; MA in Teaching Math., Reed Coll., 1962. Instr. Siuslaw High Sch., Florence, Oreg., 1954-55, David Douglas High Sch., Portland, Oreg., 1955-67; instr. Mt. Hood Community Coll., Gresham, Oreg., 1967-87, ret., 1987. NSF grantee, 1959, 60, 62. Mem. Nat. Coun. Tchr. Math., Am. Math Soc., Math. Assn. Am., Am. Math. Assn. of Two Yr. Colls., Oreg. Coun. Tchrs. Math. Democrat. Methodist. Avocations: travel, camping, home improvements, reading. Home: 11621 SE Lexington St Portland OR 97266-5933

LAMBERTON, DONALD MCLEAN, economics educator; b. Casino, Australia, July 29, 1927; s. Leslie Thomas and Isabel Mary Lamberton; m. Lynette Yorke Brookes, Jan. 10, 1949 (dec. Sept. 1963); m. Clare Margaret McSullea, Nov. 20, 1965; children: Hugh, Anna. B in Econs., U. Sydney, Australia, 1949; PhD, U. Oxford, England, 1963. Clk. Bank New South Wales, 1942-45; fin. journalist Sydney Morning Herald, 1949; editor Sydney Stock Exchange, 1950-53; lectr. U. New Eng., Armidale, 1953-57; research studentship Nuffield Coll., Oxford, 1958-60; sr. lectr. U. New South Wales, Sydney, 1960-65, assoc. prof., 1966-69; prof. econs. Case Western Res. U., Cleve., 1969-72, U. Queensland, Brisbane, 1972-89; dep. dir. Centre Internat. Rsch. Communication & Info. Techs., Melbourne, Australia, 1989-92; vis. fellow Australian Nat. U., 1992—; adj. prof. U. Canberra, Australia, 2000—; vis. at Pitts. U., Stanford U., UCLA, Oxford U., U. Tel-Aviv, Deakin U.,

Curtin U., Murdoch U., Massey U., U. Melbourne, East-West Ctr., Honolulu; cons. Orgn. for Econ. Coop. and Devel., Paris, 1978, UNESCO, Paris, 1978, Internat. Telecomm. Union, Geneva, 1985, UN Ctr. for Transnat. Corps., N.Y.C., 1985; mem. bd. govs. Comm. Rsch. Inst. Australia, Canberra, 1984-91. Author: The Theory of Profit, 1963; editor: Economics of Information and Knowledge, 1971, The Information Revolution, 1974, Beyond Competition: The Future of Telecommunications, 1995, Economics of Communication and Information, 1996, The New Research Frontiers of Communications Policy, 1997, Communication and Trade, 1998, Globalisation Employment and Quality of LIfe, 2000; editor: (with others) The Trouble with Technology, 1983, The Cost of Thinking, 1988; coordinating editor Info. Econs. and Policy; gen. editor Prometheus. Mem. Pub. Libraries Inquiry Com., Australia, 1975-76, Indsl. Property Adv. Com., Australia, 1978-83, ASTEC Technol. Change Com. Australia, 1984, Marine Industries Sci. and Tech. Com., Australia, 1988; mem. internat. adv. coun. TODA Inst. for Global Peace and Policy Rsch., 2000. Postgrad scholar Australian Services Canteens Fund, 1957-60; travel grantee Australian-Am. (Fulbright) Ednl. Found., 1966; recipient Scholar award Rockefeller Bellagio Ctr., 1985. Mem. Am. Econ. Assn., Royal Econ. Soc., Econ. Soc. Australia, Am. Soc. Info. Sci., Pacific Sci. Assn. (coun. 1991-95), Internat. Telecomm. Soc. (bd. dirs. 1992—).

LAMBIN, ERIC FRANÇOIS, geography educator; b. Uccle, Belgium, Sept. 23, 1962; s. Jean-Jacques Lambin and Daisy de Doetinghem; m. Régine Anne Geets, Sept. 7, 1989; children: Tatiana, Julie. PhD, U. Louvain, Louvain-La-Neuve, Belgium, 1985, lic. in geography, 1985, DSc, 1988. Vis. scientist Joint Rsch. Ctr., Ispra, Italy, 1989-90; asst. prof. Boston U., 1991-93; expert European Commn., Brussels, 1993-95; prof. U. Louvain, 1995—, chair dept., 2000—; chair land use/land cover change program Internat. Geosphere-Biosphere Program, Internat. Human Dimensions of Global Change, 1999—; mem. mission adv. group European Space Agy., 1997-99. Contbr. numerous articles to profl. publs., chpts. to books. Mem. AAAS, Acad. Royale des Scis. d'Outre-Mer de Belgique. Avocations: horseback riding, jazz, poetry. Office: U Louvain Dept Geography, 3 Pl Pasteur, B-1348 Louvain-la-Neuve Belgium

LAMBIN, PHILIPPE PAUL, physics educator; b. Libramont, Belgium, Dec. 25, 1953. Degree in physics engring., U. Liège, Belgium, 1976, D in Physics, 1981. Rsch. asst. Nat. Found. Sci. Rsch., Brussels, 1977-82, rsch. assoc., 1985-95; asst. prof. physics U. Namur, Belgium, 1982-85, assoc. prof., 1995—.

LAMBLOT, VALERE CHRISTIAN, publishing executive; b. Sousse, Tunisia, Nov. 17, 1940; s. Camille Empedocle and Louise Anna (Forcioli) L.; m. Valerie Anne-Marie Bessis, July 15, 1967; childre: Thomas, Cecile. Diploma in engring., Ecole Superieure Electricite, Paris, 1965. Prof. math. Ecole Normale Des Professeurs, Tunis, 1965-69; cons. Inst. D'Organisation Vente, Paris, 1969-73, Banque Populaire, Paris, 1974-77, Soc. Ge. Restauracion, Paris, 1977-87; exec., pres. Great Events Editions, Paris, L.A., 1987—. Contbr. articles to profl. jours. Home: 79 rue Corot, 92410 Ville D'Auray France Office: Great Events Editions 1925 Century Park E Los Angeles CA 90067-2701

LAMBRECH, RÉGINE M., college program administrator, language educator; b. White Plains, N.Y., Nov. 21, 1950; arrived in France, 1978; d. Matthew André and Winifred Dorothy (Blaney) L. BA, Ladycliff Coll., 1972; MA, Pa. State U., 1975, PhD, 1985. Tchg. asst. Pa. State U., University Park, Pa., 1972-78; vis. prof. French and English U. Lyon (France) II, 1978-79; asst. prof. French and English U. Lyon III, 1979-83; assoc. prof. French and English École Centrale de Lyon, Écully, France, 1983-2000, dir. internat. rels., 1989-2000; dir. internat. edn. Quinnipiac U., Hamden, Conn., 2000—; cons. internat. rels. U. Timisoara, Romania, 1995, Rector of Poly. U. Lodz, Poland, 1993, U. Warsaw, 1994, Rector of U. Salford, Eng., 1991-92, European Commn.'s Task Force for Human Resources, Edn. and Youth, 1995-2000; adv. bd. humanities dept. U. Salford, 1990—; presenter and invited spkr. in field at various confs. and workshops; bd. dirs. Rhone-Alpes Internat. Enterprises, Lyon Internat. Mem. editl. bd. Jour. Profl. Studies, 1996—, Internat. Jour. of Leadership in Edn., 1998—, Jour. for Acad. Leadership, 2000—; book and manuscript reviewer Lang. Planning and Lang. Learning Jour., 1992—; book manuscript reviewer on 2d lang. acquisition, Cambridge U. Press, 1992—; contbr. articles to profl. jours. and conf. procs. Recipient Disting. Alumna award Pa. State U., 1996, Irena Galewska-Kielbasinski award, Tech. Hochschule Darmstadt, Germany, 1993; named Erasmus scholar in residence, French Dept. Trinity College, Dublin, Ireland, 1991; recipient Tchr. of Yr. award Nat. Conservatory of Arts and Profns., 1991. Mem. MLA, NAFSA, Assn. Internat. Educators (overseas ednl. advisors spl. interest group), European Assn. Internat. Edn. (chair internat. rels. mgrs. sect. 1989-94, mem. study abroad and fgn. student advisors/langs. for ednl. mobility profl. sects.; elected bd. lang. educators, chair working group on intercultural issues 1996-98, chair ICT Group), Union des Profs. de Langues Étrangères dans les Grandes Écoles (internat. commn.), Internat. Soc. Intercultural Edn., Tng. and Rsch., Lyon Assn. Dirs. Internat. Rels. (bd. dirs. 1996-2000), Pa. State U. Alumni Club of France (founder, pres. 1985-2000), Phi Sigma Iota, Alpha Mu Gamma, Phi Kappa Phi. Roman Catholic. Avocations: reading, sports, crafts, volunteer work. Home: 6 Bayview Ter New Fairfield CT 06812-3402 Office: Quinnipiac U 275 Mount Carmel Ave Hamden CT 06518-1961

LAMBRECHTSEN, JESS, cardiologist; b. Aalborg, Denmark, June 1, 1965; s. Normann and Jytte (Joergensen) L.; m. Birgitte Von Sehesled, July 31, 1993; children: Jonas, Julie. Cand.Med., Odense (Denmark) U., 1992, PhD, 1999. Cardiology dept. Odense U. Hosp., Odense, 1992; endocrinology dept. Odense Univ. Hosp., 1995-96, internal medicine dept., 1999—; internal medicine dept. Haderslev Hosp., 1993-94. Lt. Danish Air Force, 1992—. Mem. Soc. Internal Medicine, Soc. of Cardiology, Soc. Hypertension. Avocations: volleyball, soccer, cycling, running. Home: Bergsvej, 5230 Odense Denmark Office: Odense Univ Hosp, Kloevervaenget 2, 5000 Odense Denmark

LAMBRI, CLAUDIO, management consultant; b. Cremona, Italy, Oct. 25, 1945; m. Fernanda Zippel; children: Francesco Riccardo. BS in Chem. Engring., Politecnico Milan, Italy, 1970. With Montedison, Paris and Milan, 1972-78; indsl. paper mgr. CRDM, Milan, 1978-80; market mgr. Grace, Milan, 1980-91; gen. mgr. Mead Pack Divsn., Milan, 1991-95; mng. dir. CMB/Crown Cork, Parma, Italy, 1995—. Lt. Italian Army, 1970. Mem. Rotary Club (pres. 1995-96). Avocations: pilot, sailing.

LAMBRIGGER, MARKUS, engineering researcher; b. Basel, Mar. 27, 1960; s. Camille and Paula (Stöckli) L. Ing., ETH Zürich, 1989, Dr.sc.tech., 1992. Rsch. asst. Eidgenössische Technische Hochschule, Zürich, 1989-93; reviewer Polymer Engring. Sci., Zürich, 1996-97, 99—; rsch. asst. Ecole Poly. Fed. Lausanne, Villigen PSI, Switzerland, 1997—; with security Nat. Mus. of Med. History, Zürich, Switzerland, 1994-96, Schweizer Börse SWX, Switzerland, 1999—, GME, Glattbrugg, Switzerland, 1999; expert in radiation protection and transport of radioactive materials. Contbr. articles to profl. jours. Soldier Infantry, 1980-90. Avocations: tropical agriculture, history, ethnologic, environmental care, soccer. Home and office: Im Struppen 12, CH-8048 Zurich Switzerland

LAMCHE, HERBERT ROBERT, biochemist, researcher; b. Mistelbach, Austria, June 22, 1957; s. Robert Erich and Liselotte (Krenn) L.; m. Monika Christa Braunsteiner, July 2, 1981; children: Elisabeth, Markus, Gregor. Diploma in engring., Tech. U., Vienna, 1982, D in Tech., 1983. Postdoctoral fellow U. Minn., 1984-85, Ludwig-Boltzamnn-Inst., Vienna, 1985; rsch. scientist Boehringer Ingelheim Austria, Vienna, 1985—. Inventor coating of intraocular lenses. Pres. Bürgerforum, Alland, 1993—; Sanitäter Austrian Red Cross, Alland, 1992—. Oberleutnant Gardebataillon Wien, 1975-76. Mem. Austrian Biochem. Soc., Clin. Ligand Assay Soc., Katholische Österreichische Studenten Verbindung Kreuzenstein (sr.). Roman Catholic. Avocation: model railroading. Office: Boehringer Ingelheim Austr, Dr Boehringergasse 5-11, A-1121 Vienna Austria

LAMELAS, MARIO NESTOR, retired textile company executive, finance consultant; b. Buenos Aires, Jan. 3, 1930; s. Nestor and Isabel (Santos) L.; m. Sofia Esther Simkin, July 15, 1954; children: Adriana Graciela, Edgardo Nestor. M in Adminstrn., U. Buenos Aires, 1972; degree in Psychosociol. Counselling, Pichon Riviere, Buenos Aires, 1990. Asst. gen. mgr. Banco Central, Buenos Aires, 1946-49; costs chief exec. SNIAFA, Buenos Aires, 1949-55; adminstrn. mgr. Laboratorios Industriales Fisicoelectronicos, Buenos Aires, 1955-68; credit mgr. Philips, Buenos Aires, 1969-73; gen. mgr. Talleres Adabor, Buenos Aires, 1973-75; adminstrn. fin. mgr. SNIAFA, Buenos Aires, 1975-96, adminstrn. fin. counseling, 1996—. Mem. The Planetary Soc., Am. Mgmt. Internat., N.Y. Acad. Scis. Avocations: reading essay books, leasing classical music. Home: La Pampa 2119-9C, 1428 Buenos Aires Argentina

LAMER, ANTONIO, retired Canadian supreme court chief justice; b. Montreal, Can., July 8, 1933; s. Antonio and Florence (Storey) L.; m. Danièle Tremblay; children: Stephane, Melanie, Jean-Frederic. BA, Licentiate in Laws, U. Montreal, 1956; LLD, U. Moncton, 1981, U. Montreal, 1991, U. Toronto, 1992, U. N.B., 1995, Dalhousie U., 1996; D Univ. (hon.), U. Ottawa, 1987. Bar: Que. 1957. Justice Superior Ct. Que., 1969-78, Que. Ct. Appeal, 1978-80; justice Supreme Ct. Can., 1980-99, chief justice, 1990-2000; vice chmn. Nat. Law Reform Commn. Can., 1971-75, chmn., 1976-78; prof. agregé U. Montreal, 1967—; read law with Cutler, Lamer, Bellemare & Assocs.; lectr. U. Montreal, Can. Jud. Conf.; former sr. ptnr. Cutler, Lamer, Bellemare & Assocs.; Que. Bar rep. govt. interdisciplinary com. on structures U. Que.; chmn. Can. Law Reform Commn., 1975; spl. cons. Stikeman Elliott, 2000—; assoc. prof. U. Montreal, 2000. Bd. dirs. Canadian Human Rights Found., 1974. Served with Can. Army Res., 1950, hon. col. 2nd Field Reg. Knight of Justice, Order of St. John, 1993; recipient Order of Merit, U. Montreal, 1991. Mem. Privy Coun. Can., Can. Jud. Coun. (chmn.), Nat. Jud. Inst. (chmn.), Soc. Criminologie Québec (pres. 1974). Office: 50 O'Connor St Ste 914, Ottawa, ON Canada K1P 6L2

LAMKIN, MARTHA DAMPF, lawyer; b. Talladega, Ala., May 20, 1942; d. Keith J. and Neva (Magness) Dampf; m. E. Henry Lamkin Jr., Aug. 28, 1968; children: Melinda Lamkin Skillern, Matthew Davidson. BA in English summa cum laude, Calif. Baptist U., 1964; MA in English and Am. Lit., Vanderbilt U., 1966; JD, Ind. U., 1970. Bar: Ind. 1970. Assoc. Joseph D. Geeslin, Indpls., 1971-72, Lowe, Gray, Steele & Hoffman, Indpls., 1976-82; field office mgr. U.S. Dept. Housing and Urban Devel., Indpls., 1982-87; exec. dir., corp. rep. responsibility and govtl. affairs Cummins Engine Co., Inc., Columbus, Ind., 1987-91; exec. v.p. corp. advancement USA Group, Inc., Indpls., 1991-2000; exec. dir. USA Group Found., Inc., 2000—; pres., bd. dirs. Cummins Engine Found., 1989-91; bd. dirs. Meridian Mut. Ins. Co., Indpls., USA Group, Inc., USA Group Loan Svcs., Inc.; bd. dirs. Citizens Gas & Coke Utility, Inc., chair, exec. com., 1998—. Commr., sec., chmn. Indpls. Human Rights Commn., 1971-79; commr. Indpls. Housing Authority, 1979-82; chmn. exec. com. S.K. Lacy Exec. Leadership, Indpls., 1986-87; chmn. Ind. Leadership Celebration, Indpls., 1985-87; sec. Gov.'s Mansion Commn., Indpls., 1981-89; bd. dirs. Great Indpls. Progress Commn., 1986-87, Indpls. Symphony Orch., 1983-89, 98-99, Indpls. Project, 1986-91, Ind. Fiscal Policy Inst., 1998—, Ind. Colls. Ind., 1997-2000; bd. dirs., sec. COMMIT, Inc., COMMIT Found., 1990-97; chmn. bd. trustees Christian Theol. Sem., Indpls., 1983-93; hon. gov. Richard C. Lugar Excellence Pub. Svc. Series, 1990—; chair, 1997, trustee Indpls. Found., 1992—; mem. exec. com. Mayor's Task Force on Housing, 1987, exec. com., Ind. Sports Corp., 1997-2000; sec., bd. dirs. Indpls. Econ. Devel. Corp., 1997-2000; vice chair, dir. Ctrl. Ind. Cmty. Found.; mem. Hoosier Capitol Girl Scouts Adv. Bd., 1996—. Recipient Presdl. Rank award 1985, Mental Health Initiative Gov. Ind., 1986, Matrix award Women in Communication, 1987. Mem. State Assembly Women (pres. 1977-79), Indpls. Jr. League, Indpls. C. of C. (bd. dirs. 1986-87). Republican. Mem. Christian Ch. (Disciples of Christ). Office: USA Group Found Inc PO Box 7039 (H 765) Indianapolis IN 46207-7039

LAMM, CAROLYN BETH, lawyer; b. Buffalo, Aug. 22, 1948; d. Daniel John and Helen Barbara (Tatakis) L.; m. Peter Edward Halle, Aug. 12, 1972; children: Alexander P., Daniel E. BS, SUNY Coll. at Buffalo, 1970; JD, U. Miami (Fla.), 1973. Bar: Fla., 1973, D.C., 1976, N.Y. 1983. Trial atty. frauds sect. civil div. U.S. Dept. Justice, Washington, 1973-78, asst. chief comml. litigation sect. civil div., 1978, asst. dir., 1978-80; assoc. White & Case, Washington, 1980-84, ptnr., 1984—; mem. Sec. State's Adv. Com. Pvt. Internat. law, Secs. Study Com. on Proposal Hague Conv. on Jurisdiction and the Enforcement of Judgements; arbitrator U.S. Panel of Arbitrators, Internat. Ctr. Settlement of Investment Disputes, 1995—; mem. com. on pvt. dispute resolution NAFTA. Mem. bd. editors Can./U.S. Rev. Bus. Law, 1987-92; mem. editorial adv. bd. Inside Litigation; contbg. editor: Internat. Arbitration Law Rev., 1997—; contbr. articles to legal publs. Mem. Mayor's Commn. on Violence Against Women, 1996-2000; mem. coun. Holy Trinity Parish; bd. dirs. D.C. Appleseed Found.; mem. Frederick Abramson Bd. Found. Fellow Am. Bar Found.; mem. ABA (chmn. young lawyers divsn., rules and calendar com., chmn. house membership com., chmn. assembly resolution com., sec. 1984-85, chmn. internat. litigation com. coun. 1991-94, sect. litigation, ho. dels. 1982—, nomination com. 1984-87, chair 1995-96, past D.C. Cir. mem., standing com. fed. judiciary 1992-95, chmn. com. scope and correlation of work 1996-97, commn. on multidisciplinary practice), Am. Arbitration Assn. (arbitrator, com. on fed. arbitration act), Fed. Bar Assn. (chmn. sect. on antitrust and trade regulation), Bar Assn. D.C. (bd. dirs., sec., found. bd.), D.C. Bar (pres. 1997-98, bd. govs. 1987-93, steering com. litigation sect.), Am. Law Inst. (coun.), Women's Bar Assn. D.C., Am. Soc. Internat. Law, Am. Indonesian C. of C. (bd. dirs.), Am. Uzbekistan C. of C. (bd. dirs., sec., gen. counsel), Am. Turkish Friendship Coun. (bd. dirs., chair), Nat. Women's Forum, Columbia Country Club, Manchester Country Club. Democrat. Home: 2801 Chesterfield Pl NW Washington DC 20008-1015 Office: White and Case 601 13th St NW Washington DC 20005-3807

LAMM, CLAUS, cognitive neuroscientist, psychologist, researcher; b. Lustenau, Vorarlberg, Austria, Dec. 10, 1973; s. Milly Lamm. MS, U. Vienna, Austria, 1997. Rsch. asst. Ludwig-Boltzmann-Inst. for Radiol.-Phys. Tumor Diagnostics, Vienna, 1997-98; rsch. asst. dept. psychology U. Vienna, Brain Rsch. Lab., 1997—. Contbr. articles to profl. jours. Recipient Hon. award Austrian Min. Sci., Vienna, 1997. Mem. Austrian Neurosci. Assn., Austrian Soc. Cognitive Sci., German Soc. Psychology. Avocations: soccer, rock climbing, mountain biking. E-mail: Claus.Lamm@univie.ac.at. Fax: 43-1-427747859. Office: U Vienna Brain Rsch Lab, Liebiggasse 5, A-1010 Vienna Austria

LAMM, FREDDIE RAY, research agricultural engineer; b. Boonville, Mo., Sept. 11, 1955; s. Henry Silas and Mildred Jean (Pfeiffer) L.; m. Donna Lee Gawith, Dec. 31, 1983; children: Elaine MaDonna, Henry Silas IV, Rachel Alison, Sarah Nicole. BS in Agrl. Engring., U. Mo., 1978, MS in Agrl. Engring., 1979; PhD in Engring., Kans. State U., 1990. Registered profl. engr., Kans. Instr. Kans. State U., Colby, 1979-90, asst. prof., 1990-94, assoc. prof. agrl. engring., 1994-2000, prof. agrl. engring., 2000—. Contbr. articles to profl. jours. Mem. Am. Soc. Agrl. Engrs. (chair SW-245 1993-94, Kans. sect. chair 1996-97, Young Mem. of Yr. 1993), Irrigation Assn. (chmn. agrl. irrigation com. 1995-97), Am. Soc. Agronomy, Kans. Acad. Sci., Am. Soc. Plasticulture, Sigma Xi, Alpha Epsilon, Gamma Sigma Delta. Democrat. Baptist. Achievements include research with use of microirrigation on field corn. Avocations: snow skiing, computers. E-mail: flamm@oznet.ksu.edu. Office: Kansas State Univ 105 Experiment Farm Dr Colby KS 67701-1697

LAMMEL, GERHARD, atmospheric chemist, researcher; b. Regensburg, Germany, June 23, 1960; s. Hubert and Barbara (Ernstberger) L.; m. Kirsten Ilchmann, Dec. 9, 1988; children: Kathrin, Marie. Diploma in chemistry, U. Freiburg, Germany, 1985; PhD, Max Planck Inst. for Chemistry, Mainz, Germany, 1988. Rsch. scientist Max Planck Inst. for Chemistry, Mainz, Germany, 1988, Kernforschungszentrum Karlsruhe, Germany, 1988-93; vis. scientist U. Calif., Berkeley, 1992; sci. exec. German Adv. Bd. for Global Change, 1993-98; habilitation environ. chemistry, Stuttgart, 2000. Mem. edit. bd. Umweltwiss Schadstofforschung, 1995—; contbr. articles to profl. jours. Mem. Am. Geophys. Union, Gesellschaft Deutscher Chemiker. Roman Catholic. Avocation: cycling. Office: Max Planck Inst Meteorology, Bundesstr 55, 20146 Hamburg Germany

LAMMERINK, MARC PETER, social scientist, consultant; b. Amersfoort, Utrecht, The Netherlands, Mar. 13, 1949; s. Barend and Elisabeth Roelofske (Byl) L.; m. Mayra Ondina Ordoñez, Nov. 15, 1990; children: Brenda Elisa, Ruben. MSc in Sociol. Economy, The Netherlands State U., Groningen, 1974; MSc in Andragogy, Free U. of Amsterdam, 1981; PhD, U. Nymegen, The Netherlands, 1993. Rschr. Ministry of Agriculture, Nickerie, Surinam, 1974-75; jr. cons. Bout & Ptnrs., Amsterdam, 1975-77; lectr. Free U. Amsterdam, 1977-87; advisor of dep. minister Ministry of Adult Edn., Managua, Nicaragua, 1981-82; project dir. Universidad CentroAmericana, Managua, Nicaragua, 1983-87; sr. cons. ETC Fdn., Leusden, The Netherlands, 1988-90; dir. Forestry Manpower Devel. Cons., Haarlem, The Netherlands, 1990—; project coord. Internat. Water and Sanitation Ctr., The Hague, 1993-98. Author: Aprendiéndo juntos-vivencias en investigacion participativa, 1995; co-author, editor: Approches participatives pour un développement durable, 1998, Some selected examples of Participatory research, 1994; contbr. articles to profl. jours.; presenter in field. Fax: 31-23-5257467. E-mail: fmd.nl@planet.nl. Home: Santpoorterstraat 17, 2023 DA Haarlem The Netherlands

LAMMERS, LAURA BEA, writer, communications executive; b. San Diego, Nov. 22, 1963; d. Lennis Larry and Beatrice Mearlyn Lammers. Student, U. Tulsa, 1981-82; AA sum cum laude, Ocean County Coll., 1993; postgrad., Stockton U., 1994-95. Tech. writer SpaceCom, Gaithersburg, Md., 1984-85; computer tng. cons. Portsmouth, N.H., 1985-89; actress, model Foster Fell Agency, N.Y.C., 1989-92; tech. writer Preferred Behavioral Health, Lakewood, N.J., 1992-96, Zellweger Uster, Knoxville, Tenn., 1997-99, 2000—, Hampton-Tilley Assocs., Knoxville, 1999-2000; dir. content, mktg. Webcortex, Inc., Queens, 2000—; pres., founder CyberNuts, Inc., Knoxville, 1998—; cons. Maximus, Washington, 1997; German translator The Learning Co., Knoxville, 1998; trade show salesperson, N.Y.C., 1989-92. Author, editor: A Hero Borne, Tribute to John Glenn, 1999; artist works includes restoration of Embassy of Kuwait, Washington, 1983; adminstr. editor Alliance for Women in History, 1990-97. Vol. CMC Hosp., Toms River, N.J., 1992-96; fundraiser Hurricane David and Kobe Earthquake Relief; sci. officer region 9 Star Trek Orgon, Tomo River, 1994-97; host Barnes & Noble Women's Poetry Group, 1998-99. Recipient Poetry award Am. Collegiate Poets, 1981, 1st pl. French Extraporancous award Clemson U., 1979. Mem. Nat. Soc. DAR, AAUW, Nat. Assn. Female Execs., Knoxville Assn. Female Execs., Peoria Tribe Okla., Phi Theta Kappa, Padi Scuba (cert. mem.). Avocations: poetry, art, scuba, piano, travel. E-mail: wm.tell.us@apoetborn.com. Office: CyberNuts Inc DBA APoetBorn.Com PO Box 24238 Knoxville TN 37933-2238

LAMO DE ESPINOSA, EMILIO, sociologist, educator; b. Madrid, Spain, Aug. 12, 1946; s. Emilio and MaLuisa (Michels de Champourcin) L.; m. Ana Paloma Abarca, Mar. 14, 1970; children: Juan, Miguel, Jaime. Lic. Law, U. Madrid, 1968, PhD in Law, 1973; PhD in Sociology, U. Calif., Santa Barbara, 1979. Gen. dir. univs. Min. of Edn., Madrid, 1982-85; sec.-gen. Coun. Univs., Madrid, 1985-87; vice-chmn. Inst. Advanced Social Rsch., Madrid, 1987-89; CEO Burke-Emopublica, Madrid, 1989-91; prof. sociology U. Complutense, Madrid, 1982—; dir. Ortega & Gasset U. Inst., Madrid, 1992—; cons. European U. Inst., Florence, 1987-93, European Inst. Edn. and Social Policy, Paris, 1989-92. Author: Sociedades de cultura j sociedades de ciencia, 1996; editor Revista de Occidente, 1979-83, Revista Española de Investigaciones Sociologicas, 1992-96; contbr. articles to profl. jours. Recipient Ordre Des Palmes Academiques, French Govt., 1986, Gran Cruz de Alfonso XEl Sabio, Spanish Govt., 1988. Home: Calle Cinca 23, 28002 Madrid Spain Office: Inst Univ Ortega y Gasset, Calle Fortuny 53, 28010 Madrid Spain

LAMONICA, SERGIO, financial consulting company executive; b. Rome, Sept. 4, 1943; s. Roberto and Teresa (Neri) L.; m. Antonietta Abazia (div. 1970); m. Marilena Ervo Bruschi, Sept. 10, 1999; stepchildren: Giorgia, Ginevra. Degree in econs., U. Naples, Italy, 1966; postgrad., Am. Studies Ctr., Ann Arbor, Mich., 1966; degree in pub. rels. with honors, ISIRP, Rome, 1971; degree in fin. analysis, Bocconi U., Milan, Italy, 1976. CPA; ofcl. state auditor; econ. journalist. Office mng. ptnr. Arthur Andersen, Bologna, Italy, 1982-87; audit practice dir. Italy and Greece Arthur Andersen, Milan, 1987-89; bus. cons. country ptnr. Arthur Andersen MBA, Milan, 1987-89, corp. fin. country ptnr., 1989-91, chmn., mng. dir., 1991-97, chmn., 1997-2000; chmn. adv. bd. Andersen Worldwide, Chgo., 1985-86, mem. Japanese Internat. Network, Tokyo, 1987-93; chmn., mng. dir. Omniconsult, 2000—. Italian edn. coord. Vital Signs, 1997; author: Euro: The Effects on Corporate Businesses, 1998; contbr. articles on bus. to Italian fin. newspaper Il Sole 24Ore, 1990—. Mem. Assn. Italiana Analisti Finanziari (dirs. coun. 1991—), Assn. Nazionale Direttori Amministrazione e finanza (statutory auditor 1994—), Ordine Commercialisti, Ordine Giornalisti, Italian Fedn. Pub. Rels. Profls. Avocations: sailing, skiing, travel, photography, model cars. Home: Vaile Sabotino 19/2, 20135 Milan Italy Office: Omniconsult SRL, Via Andegari 18, 20121 Milan Italy

LAMONSOFF, NORMAN CHARLES, psychiatrist; b. Bklyn., Sept. 16, 1936; s. Isidore and Kate (Wolfe) L.; m. Sheila R. Kaplan, Aug. 27, 1961; children: Karen M., Jacob D. BA, Cornell U., 1958; MD, SUNY, 1962. Diplomate Am. Bd. Psychiatry and Neurology. Medical internship Bklyn. Jewish Hosp., 1963; residency psychiatry Kings County Hosp., Bklyn., 1963-66; sr. supervising psychiatrist St. Vincent's Hosp. of Richmond, Staten Island, N.Y., 1968-70; cons. psychiatrist Staten Island Hosp., 1968-87; dir. psychiatry N.Y.C. Dept. Mental Health and Mental Retardation Svcs., 1970-74; attending psychiatrist Jersey City (N.J.) Medical Ctr., 1974-76; program dir. addiction svcs. unit Jersey City Medical Ctr., 1974-76; medical dir. Somerset County Com. Mental Health Ctr., Somerville, N.J., 1976-83, Helene Fuld Crisis Ctr., Trenton, N.J., 1984-87; chmn. psychiatry Helene Fuld Med. Ctr.; medical dir. Bristol-Bensalem Human Svcs. Ctr., Newportville, Pa., 1987—; clinical supr. residency training The Trenton Psychiatric Hosp., clinical asst. prof. N.J. Coll. Medicine. Contbr. articles to profl. jours. With U.S. Army, 1966-68. Decorated Army Commendation medal; recipient Exemplary Psychiatrist award Bucks County area chpt., Nat. Alliance for the Mentally Ill., 1994. Mem. N.Y. Soc. Clinical Psychiatry, Am. Psychiatry Assn., Am. Medical Assn., Mercer County Medical Soc. Home: 121 Trappe Ln Langhorne PA 19047-1432 Office: 340 E Maple Ave Ste 104 Langhorne PA 19047-2851 Address: PO Box L-27 Langhorne PA 19047

LAMONT, ALICE, accountant, consultant; b. Houston, July 19; d. Harold and Bessie Bliss (Knight) L. BS, Mont. State U.; MBA in Taxation, Golden Gate U., 1983. CPA. Tchr. London Ctrl. H.S., 1974-80; acct. Signetics, Sunnyvale, Calif., 1980-82; propr. Alice Lamont Ltd., 1985—. Mem. Atlanta Hist. Soc., 1985-93, High Mus. Art, 1986-89, Atlanta Botanical Garden, Brit. Am. Bus. Group (mem. com. 1993-97), Friend of Atlanta Opera, Atlanta Opera Guild, Jeannette Rankin Found.; mem. Atlanta organizing com. Nat. Osteoporosis Found., 1997—. Fellow Ga. Soc. CPAs (chmn. Acctg. Inst. 1995-97); mem. AAUW (life mem., audit chmn. 1993-95, mem. scholarship com. 1994—), Atlanta Tax Study Assn., English Speaking Union, Atlanta Woman's Club (co-chair ways and means com. 1985-86, asst. treas. 1986-88, treas. 1990, 92-94), Women's Commerce Club (mem. adv. bd. 1994-98).

LAMPE, LASZLO GYULA, obstetrician-gynecologist; b. Budapest, Nov. 24, 1929; s. Laszlo and Laszlone (Velkei) L.; m. Magdolna Zajacz, Aug. 7, 1954; children: Zoltan, Zsuzsanna. MD, U. Med. Sch., Debrecen, Hungary, 1954; DSc, Acad. Scis., Budapest, 1978. Specialist in ob.-gyn. U. Debrecen, 1954-72, prof. ob.-gyn., 1973—, dir. dept. ob.-gyn., 1973-95, prof. emeritus, 1995—. Editor: Intensive Labor Word, 1973, 86, Obstetrics and Gynecology I, 1981, II, 1984, III, 1987, (with Z. Papp), 4th edit., 1992, Operative Obstretrics-Gynecology, 1987, 2000, (with Á. Szállási) Centenary of the Hungarian Society of Obstetrics and Gynecology, 1996, (with S. Gödény) Therapy in Obstetrics and Gynecology, 1996, (with Á. Szállási) Medicina im Nummis Debrecenien-sis, 1997; mem. editl. bd. 4 Hungarian and 12 internat. med. jours. Mem. 11 gynecol. socs. (hon.). Avocations: music, dogs. Home: Pechy u 3/A, H-4032 Debrecen Hungary Office: Debreceni Orvostudomanyi, Nagyerdei krt 98, H-4012 Debrecen Hungary

LAMPERT, MICHAEL ALLEN, lawyer; b. Phila., May 6, 1958; s. Arnold Leonard and Marilyn (Sternberg) L.; m. Angela Gallicchio, Dec. 6, 1987; 1 child, David Max. AB in Econs. cum laude, U. Miami, Coral Gables, Fla., 1979, postgrad., 1980; JD, Duke U., 1983; LLM in Taxation, NYU, 1984. Bar: Fla. 1983, D.C. 1984, Pa. 1984, U.S. Tax Ct. 1984, U.S. Ct. of Appeals for the Armed Forces 1995; U.S. Dist. Ct. (S. Dist. Fla.), 2000, bd. cert. tax lawyer, Fla. Bar. Assoc. Cohen, Scherer, Cohn & Silverman, P.A., North

Palm Beach, Fla., 1984-88; instr. div. continuing edn. Fla. Atlantic U., Boca Raton, 1988—; prin. Jacobson & Lampert, P.A., Boca Raton, 1988-91; pvt. practice West Palm Beach, 1991—. Mem. editl. bd. Southeastern Tax Alert, 1993-97, Sales and Use Tax Alert, 1997—. Instr., trainer, past chpt. vice-chair, sect. for bd. dirs. ARC, Palm Beach County, Fla.; bd. dirs. Jewish Fedn. Palm Beach County, 1989-91, 97-99; bd. dirs. Jewish Family and Children's Svc. Palm Beach County, 1988—, treas., 1991-94, pres., 1997-99; pres. Jewish Residential and Family Svc., Inc., 1997—; commr. Commn. for Jewish Edn.-Palm Beach, 1997-99; mem. nat. planned giving com. Weismann Inst., Israel; v.p. planned giving Am. Soc. for Tech., Palm Beach. Recipient Young Leadership award, 1988, Safety award ARC, 1989, Cert. of Merit, Am. Radio Relay League, West Palm Beach Club, 1988, Cert. of Appreciation for Leadership, ARC Disaster Svcs., Palm Beach County, 1989, Disaster Svc. award, 1994, Human Resources award, 1993, Tax Law award Legal Aid Soc. of Palm Beach County and Palm Beach County Bar Assn., 1993, Young Leadership award Jewish Fedn. of Palm Beach County, 1998. Mem. Palm Beach Tax Inst. (pres., bd. dirs.), Fla. Bar (exec. coun., tax sect.), Palm Beach County Bar Assn. (chair bus. and corp. continuing legal edn. com. 1989-90, chair legal asst. com. 1988-91, Tax Law award 1993), Legal Aid Soc. of Palm Beach County, Inc. Avocations: aquatics, amateur radio, running. Office: Ste 900 1655 Palm Beach Lakes Blvd West Palm Beach FL 33401-2211

LAMPERT, S. HENRY, dentist; b. Bklyn., Mar. 10, 1929; s. Joseph and Sadie (Bass) L.; m. Jacqueline Adler, Mar. 27, 1955; children: Karen Ann, Beth Robin, Judith Ellen. BA, U. Ill., 1950; DDS, NYU, 1954. Intern in dentistry Mt. Sinai Hosp., N.Y.C., 1954-55; gen. practice dentistry Essex Junction, Vt., 1957-95; ret., 1995; dir. Temporo Mandibular Joint Program, Med. Ctr. Hosp. Vt., Burlington, 1970-76, attending staff 1957-92, peer rev. com., 1978-92; mem. staff Fanny Allen Hosp., Winooski, Vt., 1961-89 ; assoc. prof. Sch. Allied Health Scis., U. Vt., Burlington, 1963-73, clin. instr. Coll. Medicine, 1974-75, clin. instr. dept. oral surgery, 1986-96. Sec., Vt. Bd. Dental Examiners, 1973-76, pres., 1976-77; instr. photography Church St. Ctr. for Cmty. Edn., U. Vt., until 1998; mem. N.E. Regional Bd. Dental Examiners, 1973-84, 96-98, cons. and examiner, 1996; lectr. in field; CPR instr. Vt. Heart Assn.; photographer Essex (Vt.) Reporter, 1997—. Contbr. articles to profl. jours., photographs pub. in numerous mags. and jours. Capt. AUS, 1955-57. Fellow Internat. Coll. Dentists; mem. ADA (standard setting com. of coun. on nat. bd. exams. 1978-81), Champlain Valley (pres. 1961-62), Acad. Operative Dentistry, Vt. Dental Soc., Masons, Rotary, Alpha Omega. Jewish (bd. govs. synagogue 1967-70, 72-73, chmn. bd. edn.). Home: PO Box 667 Essex Junction VT 05453-0667

LAMPERT, SHLOMO IZHAK, marketing and business strategy consultant; b. Ramat-Gan, Israel, Nov. 10, 1939; s. Abraham Aba and Tova (Rotkowitz) L.; m. Zipora Tova Wilner, Aug. 23, 1967; children: Efrat, Ayelet, Anat, Naama, Aviya. BS in Mech. Engring., The Technion, Israel, 1963; M in Indsl. Engring., NYU, 1965; PhD in Bus. Adminstrn., Columbia U., 1971. Asst. prof. mktg. Grad. Sch. Bus. Adminstrn. NYU, 1969-71; lectr. mktg. Jerusalem Sch. Bus. Hebrew U., 1971-77, coord. mkgt. area Jerusalem Sch. Bus. Adminstrn., 1975-76; part time sr. lectr. mktg. Jerusalem Sch. Bus. Adminstrn., 1982-86; founder, coord. MA in Econs.-Bus. Adminstrn. program dept. econs. Bar-Ilan U., 1977-79, sr. lectr. mktg. dept. econs. and bus., 1978-91, vice chair dept. econs. and bus. adminstrn., coord. bus.adminstrn., 1982-84, founding dir. Grad. Sch. Bus. Adminstrn., 1991-95, sr. lectr. mktg. Grad. Sch. Bus. Adminstrn., 1991—, dir. Lorber program for entrepreneurial excellence in Israel, 1999—; bd. dirs. Etgar Co. Mgmt. Investment Portfolios, mem. investment com., 1992-98, chmn. auditing com., 1994-95, acting chmn., 1995-96; bd. dirs. Neviot-Nature of Galilee Ltd., 1997—, Bezeq, Israel Telecomm. Corp., 1993-94, Pele-Phone Comm. Ltd., 1994-95; founding chmn. dept. bus. adminstrn. Coll. Adminstrn., Tel Aviv, Israel, 1973-79; lectr. mktg. (part time) Bar-Ilan U., 1971-77, top mgmt. tng. programs in mktg. The Israeli Mgmt. Ctr., Koor Industries, Tack Tng., Shekem Retail Chain, Tel Aviv, others, 1970-79; founding dean Internat. Sch. Mgmt. Touro Coll., 1995-96, prof., cons., 1996-97; assoc. prof. mktg. Baruch Coll. CUNY, 1979-82, vis. assoc. prof. mktg., 1986-87; cons. computer usage Nat. Mills Divsn. U.S. Industries, Memphis, Tenn., summer, 1964; syss. analyst Computer Applications, Inc., N.Y.C., summer, 1965; project mgr. The Israel Inst. Applied Social Rsch., Jerusalem, 1976-77; sr. mktg. cons. Israeli Aircraft Industries, 1979-80; econ. adviser to comptroller Ministry of Def., Israel, 1979-80; mktg. cons. United Mizrahi Bank, Israel, 1983-86; top project cons. The Clearway Co., Queens, N.Y., 1986-87; first, leading bus. cons. to chief scientist Ministry of Industry and Commerce, Jerusalem, 1985-89; chief bus. cons. UKI Internat., N.Y.C., 1989-90. Co-author Advertising and Promotion-Practices of Full Service Banks, 1970; author: Managers are not Mathematicians, 1977; mem. editl. bd. Jour. City and Region, 1992-95, Jour. Bus. to Bus. Mktg., 1997—; contbr. numerous articles to profl. jours., chpts. to books; internat. patentee the Pollimeter, social sci. scaling device. Grantee The Chief Scientist Office Ministry Industry and Commerce, Israel, 1986-87, 88, 89. Mem. Am. Mktg. Assn., Acad. Mgmt., European Internat. Bus. Acad., Alpha Pi Mu. Jewish. Avocation: sports. Fax: 972-2-5862962. E-mail: lampers@mail.biu.ac.il. Home: 7 Netivei-Am St, Ramot Jerusalem 97552, Israel Office: Bar-Ilan U, Grad Sch Bus Adminstrn, Ramat Gan 52900, Israel

LAMPERT, ZOHRA, actress; b. N.Y.C.; d. Morris and Rose (Eriss) L. BA, U. Chgo.; MA, CUNY; studies with Mira Rostova. Actress: (stage prodns.) Dancing in the Chequered Shade, 1955, Venice Preserv'd, 1955-56, Diary of a Scoundrel, 1956, Major Barbara, 1956, Maybe Tuesday, 1958, Look: We've Come Through, 1961 (Tony nomination), First Love, 1961, Mother Courage and Her Children, 1963 (N.Y. Drama Critics award 1973, Tony nomination), After the Fall, 1964, Marco Millions, 1964, The Natural Look, 1967, Lovers and Other Strangers, 1968, The Sign in Sidney Brustein's Window, 1972, Drinks Before Dinner, 1978-79, Gifted Children, 1983, My Poppa's Wine, 1986, The Diary of Anne Frank, 1987, Mr. Gogol and Mr. Preen, 1991, A Day in New York, 1994-95, Krinsky, 1996, (feature films) Splendor in the Grass, 1961, A Fine Madness, 1966, Bye Bye Braverman, 1968, Let's Scare Jessica to Death, 1971, Opening Night, 1977, Alphabet City, 1984, The Cafeteria, 1986, Fakebook, 1989, Alan and Naomi, 1991, The Eden Myth, 1998 (TV series) Where the Heart is, 1970-71, The Girl with Something Extra, 1973-74, Doctors' Hospital, 1975-76, (TV movies) The Connection, 1972, Ladies of the Corridor, 1975, The Girl, The Gold Watch and Everything, 1979, Izzy & Moe, 1985, (TV spl.) Leonard Bernstein's Carmen for Omnibus; (TV episodes) Better Luck Next Time, 1964, The F.B.I., 1970, Love, American Style, 1972-73, The Bob Newhart Show, 1973, Kojak (Emmy award), Quincey, 1979, others, also radio and TV commls. (Andy award). Recipient Ralph Weiler prize for painting, Louis La Beaume prize for painting Nat. Acad. Design. Mem. Actors' Equity Assn., AFTRA, AGVA, Nat. Acad. N.Y. Address: care David Williams Don Buchwald Agy 10 E 44th St New York NY 10017-3601

LAMPL, YAIR, neurologist; b. Tel Aviv, Israel, Aug. 28, 1946; s. Franz Israel and Sonia (Silverman) L.; m. Yemima Arieli, Aug. 6, 1974; children: Sivana, Nevo Siel. Degree in Math., U. Vienna, Austria, 1974, MD with honors, 1980. Physician Hainburg (Austria) Hosp., 1980; resident in neurology Edith Wolfson Med. Ctr., Holon, Israel, 1984-89, sr. neurologist, rsch. clin. Neurology and neurosci., 1989—. Contbr. articles to profl. jours. Recipient Outstanding Employee award Ministry of Health, Jerusalem, 1990. Mem. AAAS, Israel Med. Assn., Israel Neurol. Soc., Israel Assn. EEG and Clin. Neurophysiology, Israel League for Prevention of Epilepsy, World Fedn. Neurology, Eurpean Neurol. Soc., N.Y. Acad. Sci. Jewish. Avocations: painting, writing poetry. Home: Weidat Katowitz Str 25, 62304 Tel Aviv Israel Office: Edith Wolfson Med Ctr, 58100 Holon Israel

LAMPREIA, JOAQUIM MARTINS, public relations consultant; b. Moura, Portugal, Mar. 7, 1948; s. Joaquim Pedro and Alexandrina (Martins) L.; m. Maria Raquel Melo Sales, Feb. 24, 1975; children: Joaquim Pedro, Filipe. M Comms., Lisbon (Portugal) U., 1979. Pub. rels. officer IATA, Lisbon, 1976-82; freelance journalist Lisbon, 1978-82; gen. mgr. Interpub. Advt. Agy., Lisbon, 1982-83, CNEP Hill and Knowlton, Lisbon, 1984-97; comm. tchr. European U., Lisbon, 1993-94; hon. consul Republic of Rwanda, Lisbon, 1986-97; pub. rels. cons. European Union-DGX, Brussels, 1993-94. Author: Communication Techniques, 1981, Media Relations, 1986, Modern Advertising, 1988, Corporate Communications, 1992. Pres. Apecom. Pub. Rels. Assn., 1989-93. Mem. Gremio Literario. Avocations: tennis, motorcycling, horseback riding, skiing. Home: Lotei, R proj a Av Eng AA Coutinho, 2750 Cascais Portugal Office: CNEP/Omniconsul Edif Omni, Av Duque D'Avila No 141 1E, 1050 Lisbon Portugal

LAMPREIA, LUIZ FELIPE, Brazilian government official. Former amb. to Portugal Govt. of Brazil, sec. gen. Ministry Fgn. Affairs, min. fgn. rels., 1994—. Office: Ministry External Rels, Palácio do Itamaraty 2andar, 70170900 Brasilia DF Brazil*

LAMVIK, JON OFSTAD, hematology educator; b. Tingvell, Norway, May 21, 1929. MD, U. Bergen, Norway, 1955, PhD, 1969. Lectr. The Gade Inst. U. Bergen, Norway, 1961-70; reader Norwegian Inst. Tech. U. Trondheim, 1970-73, prof., 1973-76; prof. hematology U. Trondheim, 1976-96; head divsn. hematology U. Trondheim Hosp., 1971-96; dean faculty medicine U. Trondheim, 1974-78. Author: Antibody Synthesis in Rabbit Blood Lymphocyte Cultures, 1969. Mem. Norwegian Cancer Soc. (bd. dirs. 1975-79), Inst. Cancer Rsch. (chmn. bd. dirs. 1983-89), Soc. Med. Tech. (chmn. bd. dirs. 1992-2000), Royal Norwegian Order Knighthood. Office: Trondheim U Hosp, N-7006 Trondheim Norway

LAMY, M(ARY) REBECCA, land developer, former government official; b. Ft. Bragg, N.C., Nov. 21, 1929; d. Charles Joseph and Sarah Esther (Koonce) L. BA, U. N.C., Greensboro, 1952. Procurement analyst Air Force Mil. Interdept. Purchase Request Mgmt. Office, Washington, 1958-60, procurement and fiscal officer, 1960-68; budget analyst Naval Air Sys. Command, Washington, 1968-69, indsl. specialist, 1969-71; indsl. specialist Armament Devel. and Test Ctr., Eglin AFB, Fla., 1971-74, Def. Logistics Agy., Alexandria, Va., 1974-81; logistics mgmt. specialist Strategic Sys. Project Office, Dept. Navy, Washington, 1981-82; procurement analyst Hdqrs. Dept. Army, Washington, 1982-85. Emeritus mem. Onslow Mus. Found. Bd., Onslow Meml. Hosp. Aux., 1985-91. Recipient Outstanding Performance awards USAF, 1956, 65, 72, 73, Quality award Def. Logistics Agy., 1979, Outstanding Performance award, 1978, 79, Exceptional Svc. award, 1983, 84, 85, Comdr.'s award Hdqrs. Dept. Army, 1985, others. Mem. U. N.C. at Greensboro Alumni Assn.

LAN, ZHANG, conservationist, researcher, educator; b. Shanghai, Aug. 22, 1957; s. Zhang Fu-Sun and Liu Li-Wen; m. Pu Xin, May 4, 1986; children: Xun, Zhang. Student, Shanghai Inst. Arts and Crafts, 1975-78, Shanghai Internat. Trade Inst., 1978-81, Shanghai TV U., 1982-85, Fudan U., 1988. Rsch. asst. Sci. Lab., Shanghai, 1978-85; vice dir. arts restoration and reprodn. dept. Shanghai Mus., 1985-88; chief sr. curator Rsch. Lab. Relics Repairing Tech. Shanghai Hist. Relics Safekeeping Com., 1985-87; dep. editor-in-chief Scis. of Conservation & Archaeology, 1989—; vice-dir., assoc. prof. Rsch. Lab. for Conservation and Archaeology, Shanghai, 1995—; exec. dir. publ. dept. Rsch. Lab. Conservation and Restoration, 1999—; mem. coun. com. for restoration and reprodn. Chinese Cultural Relics Acad., Beijing, 1992—. Editor and author: A Collection of the Shanghai Museum Theses, 1996, Chinese Traditional Art and Craft Technology; dep. editor-in-chief Scis. Conservation and Archaeology (Shanghai prize 1992); contbr. articles to profl. jours. Recipient Cultural Sci. prize Culture Ministry China, 1985. Mem. Assn. Sci. Conservation Hist. Relics China, Internat. Coun. Mus.-Conservation Com. (working group on lacquer and furniture), China Materials Assn., Shanghai Sci. Jour. Editors Assn. (coun. 1992). Avocations: painting, artistic carving, collecting, writing. Home: 1506 No 3 135 Lane, Longcao Rd, Shanghai 200233, China Office: Rsch Lab Conser-Archaeology, 201 Ren Min Da Dao, Shanghai 200003, China

LANATA, CLAUDIO FRANCO, epidemiologist, physician; b. Lima, Peru, Feb. 4, 1951; s. Ernesto F. and Juanita M. (de las Casas) L.; m. Elena Augusta Piazzon, Feb. 21, 1975; children: Fiorella, Cristina, Mariana. MD, Peruvian U. Cayetano Heredia, Lima, 1977; MPH, Johns Hopkins U., 1983. Resident in internal medicine St. Vincent's Med. Ctr., Bridgeport, Conn., 1977-80; fellow in infectious diseases U. Md. Sch. Medicine, Balt., 1980-82; fellow in geog. med. Johns Hopkins U. Sch. Medicine, Balt., 1983; rsch. dir. Nutrition Rsch. Inst., Lima, 1985-88, sr. rschr., 1983—, gen. dir., 1987-93; vis. sr. rsch. fellow London Sch. Hygiene and Tropical Medicine, 1991-92; hon. sr. lectureship London Sch. Hygiene and Tropical Medicine, 1996—; assoc. dept. internat. health Johns Hopkins U., Baltimore, 1986—; dir. maternal and child tng. program Esan Bus. Sch., Lima, 1996-99; mem. steering com. and tech. adv. group WHO, 1986—, also numerous consultancies on health projects; mem., chmn. sci. working group Pan Am. Health Orgn., Washington, 1984-87. Contbr. 13 chpts. to books; author 7 monographs; contbr. 56 articles to profl. jours. Mem. Internat. Epidemiol. Assn. Avocation: tennis. Office: Nutrition Rsch Inst, 18-0191 Lima 18, Peru

LANCAR, REMI, biostatistician, consultant; b. Paris, France, Dec. 9, 1965; s. André and Dorothée (Nahum) L.; m. Sophie Sagues; children: David, Marine, Simon. PhD, U. Paris XI, 1997. Biostatistician Inst. Gustave Roussy, Villejuif, 1992-94, Protocole, Saint Aubin, 1994-95; engr. INSERM, Paris, 1996—. Office: INSERM Svc Commun 4, 27 rue Chaligny, 75571 Paris France

LANCASTER, IAN MICHAEL, editor; b. Manchester, England, Nov. 8, 1948; s. Gabriel and Sarah P. (Lipman) L.; m. Novello Dawn Cawley, July 1977 (div. 1989); m. Anita V. Fox, June 1997; stepchildren: Ben, Zoë. BA with honors, U. Hull, 1971; MBA, Polytech Ctrl. London, 1972. Adminstr. Libr. Theatre, Manchester, England, 1972-73; officer drama, dance East Midlands Arts, England, 1973-77; dir. arts Calouste Gulbenkian Found., U.K., 1977-82; founder, mgr. dir. Third Dimension Ltd., London, 1982-86; exec. dir. Mus. Holography, N.Y.C., 1986-88; mng. dir. Reconnaissance Internat., England, 1989—; mem. arts com. Commn. Racial Equality, England, 1978-82; dir. Vis. Arts Unit, U.K., 1978-82; gen. sec. Internat. Hologram Mfrs. Assn., 1992—. Editor: HoloPack/HoloPrint Guidebook, 1996, 98. Chmn. Northwest Surrey Synagogue, Weybridge, England, 1992-94, 96—. U.S. State Dept. fellow, 1979. Mem. British-Am. Arts Assn. (chmn. 1978-82). Jewish. Avocations: scuba diving, theatre. Office: Reconnaissance Internat, Runnymede Malthouse, Egham TW20 9BD, England

LANCASTER, KENNETH G., lawyer; b. Stafford Springs, Conn., Dec. 6, 1949; s. Talbot Augustin and Helen Collier (McRae) L.; m. Margaret Jane Royer, Aug. 25, 1973; children: Kimberly Jane, John Talbot, Christopher Andrew. BA, U. Miami, 1971, JD, 1974. Bar: Fla. 1974, U.S. Dist. Ct. (so. dist.) Fla. 1975, U.S. Dist. Ct. (mid. dist.) Fla. 1976. Adminstr. Met. Dade County, Miami, Fla., 1971-73; assoc. Robert A. Spiegel, Coral Gables, Fla., 1973-78; sole practice South Miami, Fla., 1978-80; ptnr. Clark, Dick & Lancaster, South Miami, Fla., 1980-87, King & Lancaster PA, South Miami, Fla., 1987—; cons. 1st City Bank Dade County, Miami, 1983-84; dir. U. Miami Bus. Sch. Bd. dirs., v.p. U. Miami Hall Fame, Coral Gables, 1984—, mem. endowment com., 1982—; mem. Atty.'s Title Ins. Fund, 1982—. Mem. ABA, Fla. Bar Assn., Dade County Bar Assn. (Disting. Svc. award 1984), Dade County Attys. Real Property Coun., Hurricane Club/U. Miami (bd. dirs. 1984—, pres. 1996-97). Home: 10241 SW 141st St Miami FL 33176-7005 Office: King & Lancaster PA 5975 Sunset Dr Ste 301 Miami FL 33143-5198

LANCE, DAVID HARRY, investment banker; b. Sydney, NSW, Australia, Nov. 8, 1933; s. Nathan Lance and Mabel Austin; m. Rebecca Eve Lance; children: Jasmine, Monique, Adam. B Econs., U. Sydney, 1952; D Univ., U. Tech., Sydney, 1999. Chmn. Nationwide Resources, Australia, 1995-98, Tech. Transactions, Sydney, 1995—; bd. dirs. See Corp. Ltd., Perth, Australia, Eon Ltd., Perth; founder Aust'n Tech. Awards, Sydney, 1997; adj. prof. U. Tech., Sydney, 1998. Dep. chancellor U. Tech., 1989-98, mem. coun., 1979-98. Named to Order of Australia, 1999. Avocations: reading, family, walking, travel. Home: 13/14 Ross St, Waverton NSW 2060, Australia Office: Tech Transactions LVL 39, Aust Sq 264-278 George St, Sydney NSW 2000, Australia

LANCE, STEVEN, author. BA in English, Upsala Coll., 1976. Dir. mktg. Monmouth County Arts Coun.-Count Basie Theatre, Red Bank, N.J., 1990; entertainment columnist The Two River Times, 1991-93; founder, exec. dir. Silent Running Soc., 1985—; founder, mng. editor (online svc.) www.PlanetShowbiz.com; host Names in the News, WHTG (FM), Eatontown, N.J., 1993-96. Author: Written Out of Television: The Encyclopedia of Cast Changes and Character Replacements, 1945-94, 1996, Written Out of Television: A TV Lover's Guide to Cast Changes 1945-94, 1996; rsch. asst. (Vincent Terrace) Television Character and Story Facts, 1993, (Vincent Terrace) Television Specials, 1995, (James Robert Parish) Rose: Rosie O'Donnell's Biography, 1997, others; actor Star Trek: The Motion Picture, 1980, Stardust Memories, 1981. Fax: 732-364-1705. Office: VEGR 4057 Hwy 9 Howell NJ 07731-3307

LANCELLOTTA, JOHN JERRY-LOUIS, public service administrator; b. Providence, R.I., Aug. 25, 1953; s. Joseph Ralph and Mary Grace (DeGregory) L. AS in Polit. Sci. cum laude, Roger Williams U., 1983, BS in Pub. Adminstrn. cum laude, 1984. academically cert. in paralegal studies, Roger Williams Coll., 1982. Contractor, estimator Ctr. Contractors, West Warwick, R.I., 1975-79; staff trainer econ. dept. City of Warwick, 1982; legis. aide U.S. Senator Pell, Providence, R.I., 1983-85; ombudsman/investigator Atty. Gen., Providence, 1985-91; exec. dir. Jaycee Found., West Warwick, 1991—; advisor Narragonsett Bay Commn., Providence, 1982-89; cons. Mcpl. Affairs, West Warwick, Coventry, R.I., 1979-93. Candidate Town Coun., West Warwick, 1976-92; com. Rep. Dist. 39, West Warwick, 1984-86; mem. Comprehensive Plan Commn., West Warwick, 1990-92; exec. bd. Citizens Adv. Com., v.p. 1979-86; mem. R.I. and Pawtuxet Valley Ch. Couns., 1972-92; 1st tree bd. commr. Town of West Warwick, 1999; cons. Jr. Achievement R.I., 2000. Recipient Letters of Commendation U.S. Pres. Bush and Clinton, 1992-96, Proclamation Gov. of R.I., 1990, 1st Civic Pride citation Town of West Warwick, 1989, Environ. citation Gov. R.I., 1998-99, Svc. Above Self award, Pawtuxet Valley Rotary Internat., 1999. Mem. Am. Soc. Pub. Adminstrn. (contbr. 1984-99, Letter of Excellence 1986), U.S. Jr. C. of C. (officer, amb. 1992), Diocese of Providence and Cmty. Vicariate (Cert. 1988), R.I. Jaycees (exec. bd. 1976-93, gov. 1992), Jr. Chamber Internat. (senator 2000). Democrat. Roman Catholic. Avocations: animal rescue, horticultural digs, walking club, spiritual outings, disabled visitations. Home: 32 River Ave West Warwick RI 02893-1820 Office: Jaycee Found PO Box 348 West Warwick RI 02893-0348

LANCELOT, ALAIN, political science educator; b. Chêne-Bougeries, Switzerland, Jan. 12, 1937; s. Elisée and Suzanne (Perrin) L.; m. Marie-Thérèse Merlet; children: Emmanuel, Anne. MA, Inst. of Polit. Scis., 1958; PhD in Polit. Scis., U. Sorbonne, 1967; state PhD, U. Paris, Sorbonne, 1980. Rschr. Nat. Ctr. for Scientific Rsch., Paris, 1959-67; rsch. dir. Nat. Found. for Polit. Sci., Paris, 1967-99, adminstr., 1987-96; prof. Inst. of Polit. Studies, Paris, 1981-99, dir., 1987-96; mem. justice Constitutional Coun., Paris, 1996—; cons. Sofres, Paris, 1996-99; dir. Ctr. for the Study of French Politica Life, Paris, 1975-87; scientific dir. Interregional Observatory of Politics, Paris, 1985-99. Author many books. Recipient Legion d'Honneur French Govt., 1986, Fed. Merit German Govt., 1995, Merit of the Italian Republic Italian Govt., 1989. Avocation: sailing. Office: Conseil Constitutionnel, 2 Rue de Montpensier, 75002 Paris France

LANCI, LUCA, geophysicist, researcher; b. Fano, Italy, Oct. 5, 1963; s. Pierfranco and Pia (Poli) L.; m. Anna Maria Campani, Oct. 8, 1995. MSc, U. Urbino, 1991; PhD, U. Trieste, 1995. Postdoctoral rschr. Inst. Geophysics/ETH, Zurich, Switzerland, 1995-99; postdoctoral assoc. geology Rutgers Univ., Piscataway, N.J., 1999—. Office: Dept Geological Sci Rutgers Univ 610 Taylor Rd Piscataway NJ 08854-8066

LANCIAI, CHRISTIAN AURELIO, magazine editor, writer; b. Helsingfors, Finland, Sept. 10, 1951; arrived in Sweden, 1955; s. Aurelio and Gunvor Elisabeth (Westerberg) L. Church organist Gothenburg (Sweden) Cath. Ch., 1977-78; organist Jewish Cmty., Gothenburg, 1981-86; publisher, editor Letnany Pubs., Gothenburg, 1996—; freelance piano tchr., Gothenburg, 1973-88. Editor (mag.) The Free Thinker, 1992—; editor, contbr. 75 publs. and books, 1996-99. Democrat. Roman Catholic. Avocation: travel. Home: Ankargatan 2A, S-41461 Göteborg Sweden

LANCIAUX, CONCETTA, consumer goods company executive; b. Accettura, Italy, 1966; d. Giovanni Carestia and Rosa D'Eramo. M Humanities and Comm., U. Cattolica, Milan, Italy, 1966; PhD in Humanities and Social Scis., U. N.C., 1971; exec. MBA, Carnegie Mellon U., 1996. Assoc. prof. humanities and social scis. Carnegie Mellon U., Pitts., 1971-77; European human rels. devel. dir. Tex. Instruments Europe, 1978-80; human resouces dir. Intel Corp., 1980-85; human rels. exec. v.p. Financiere Agache, Paris, 1985-91; human rels. exec. v.p., advisor to pres. LVMH, Paris, 1991—; co-founder Devel. of Mgmt. of Luxury Goods, 1990; chair LVMH-ESSC, 1991; mem. Conf. bd. Europe; sponsor, mem. Euro-Asia Ctr. INSEAD; lectr. French bus. schs. Author: Humanistic and Scholastic Poets, 1981, Reward Strategies, 1990 (Human Rels. Mgr. of Yr. award 1990), Computer-Aided Translation. Mem. Multinat. Cos. Pers. Assn. (pres. 1990-96). Office: LVMH, 54 Ave Montaigne, 75008 Paris France cre

LANCY, RATNASAMY, physiotherapist; b. Pondicherry, India, Nov. 10, 1954; arrived in Brunei, June 14, 1979; s. Ratnasamy Arokiasamy and Honorine Lourdes (Maigumey) Ratnasamy; m. Umadevi Marie Ganesa Pillai, May 14, 1979; children: Rajiv Cyril, Sanjiv Paul. BA, Loyola Coll., Madras, India, 1973; degree in physiotherapy, Christian Med. Coll. & Hosp., Vellore, India, 1976; postgrad. cert. in hydrotherapy, Royal Nat. Hosp., Bath, Eng., 1983. Staff physiotherapist Christian Med. Coll. & Hosp., Vellore, 1976-77, incharge physiotherapist cardiothoracic unit, 1977-78, incharge physiotherapist rehab. inst., 1978-79; incharge physiotherapist Gen. Hosp., Bandar Seri Begawan, Brunei, 1979-83; incharge, head physiotherapist Ripas Hosp., Bandar Seri Begawan, 1983-94, sr., head physiotherapist, 1994—; personal physiotherapist to His Royal Highness Begawan Sultan, Brunei, 1985-86. Sports sec. Students Hostel, Vellore, 1974-76; founder, exec. mem. Adult Disabled's Assn., Brunei, 1984-85, Handicapped Children's Assn., Brunei, 1986-88. Mem. Coun. Professions Supplementary to Medicine-U.K., Indian Assn. Physiotherapists (life mem., treas. Vellore br. 1977-79), Singapore Physiotherapy Assn., Bandar Seri Begawan Indian Assn. (pres. 1986-88). Roman Catholic. Avocations: music, stamp and coin collecting, traveling. Office: Ripas Hosp, Physiotherapy Dept, Bandar Seri Begawan 2680, Brunei

LAND, GEOFFREY ALLISON, science administrator; b. Jeannette, Pa., July 9, 1942; s. Albert E. Jr. and Helene (Matthews) L.; m. Maxine McCluskey, Jan. 22, 1966; children: Kevin Jeffrey, Melissa Allison, Kyle Robert. MS in Biology (Biochemistry), Tex. Christian U., 1970; PhD in Microbiology/Immunology, Tulane U., 1973. Cert. clin. lab. dir. Am. Bd. Bioanalysis. Dir. mycology Wadley Institutes Molecular Medicine, Dallas, 1974-78; dir. mycology, assc. dir. microbiology U. Cin. Med. Ctr., 1978-81; dir. microbiology/immunology Meth. Med. Ctr., Dallas, 1981—, assoc. adminstrv. dir. pathology, 1990—; dir. histocompatibility Stewart Blood Ctr., Tyler, Tex., 1987—; sci. dir. pathology and labs. Meth. Med. Ctr., Dallas, 1993—; adj. full prof. biology Tex. Christian U., Ft. Worth, 1982—. Mem. rev. bd. Jour. Clin. Microbiology, 1980—, editor, 2000—; mem. rev. bd. Am. Jour. Tropical Medicine and Hygiene, 1989—; author: Pictorial Handbook of Medically Important Fungi, 1982, (with others) The Dermatophytes, 1996, Handbook of Applied Mycoses, 1991, Manual of Clinical Microbiology, 1992, Clinical Microbiology Procedures Manual, 1994. Coach Denton (Tex.) Soccer Assn., 1981—; min. Tioga (Tex.) Ch. of Christ, 1985—; chmn.-elect Region 4 histocompatibility com. United Network for Organ Sharing, 1993. Recipient Svc. Above Self award Rotary Club. Mem. Mycol. Soc. Am. (pres. 1990-93, Billy H. Cooper-Meridian award 1992), Tex. Soc. Clin. Microbiology (pres. 1977-79, 81-83), N.Y. Acad. Sci., Am. Soc. Histocompatibility and Immunogenetics (commr. region 2 1995—, author procedure manual 1996—), Am. Soc. Microbiology. Mem. Ch. of Christ. Office: Meth Med Ctr 1441 N Beckley Ave Dallas TX 75203-1201

LAND, RICHARD DALE, minister, religious organization administrator; b. Houston, Nov. 6, 1946; s. Leggette Sloan and Marilee (Welch) L.; m. Rebekah Ruth Van Hooser, May 29, 1971; children: Jennifer, Richard Jr., Rachel. BA, Princeton U., 1969; ThM, New Orleans Bapt. Theol. Sem., 1972; D.Phil., U. Oxford, Eng., 1980. Ordained to ministry So. Bapt. Conv., 1969. Pastor S. Oxford Bapt. Ch., Oxford, Eng., 1972-75; prof. theology and ch. history Criswell Coll., Dallas, 1975-76, acad. dean, 1976-80, v.p. for acad. affairs, 1980-88; pres. ethics and religious liberty commn. So. Bapt. Conv., Nashville, 1988—; mem. exec. com. Nat. Coalition against Pornography, Cin., 1989—; bd. dirs. Bapt. Joint Com. Pub. Affairs, Washington, 1987-91, Nat. Pro-Life Religious Coun., Washington; host nationally syndicated daily

radio program For Faith & Family, 1998—. Cons. editor Criswell Study Bible, 1979. Mem. Gov.'s Task Force on Welfare Reform, Austin, Tex., 1988, Pres.'s Campaign for a Drug-Free Soc., Washington, 1991—; bd. dirs. Nat. Law Ctr., Arlington, Va., 1991—. Recipient Disting. Alumnus award New Orleans Bapt. Theol. Sem., 1997. Mem. Bapt. World Alliance (spl. com. on racism 1992, gen. bd. 1993, v. chmn. christian ethics com. 1995—). Office: Ethics & Religious Liberty Commn 901 Commerce St Ste 550 Nashville TN 37203-3600

LANDAU, ALEXANDR ISAAKOVICH, physicist, researcher; b. Kharkov, Ukraine, Aug. 1, 1933; arrived in Israel, 1995; s. Isaak Vladimirovich and Ada Gudya Iosifovna (Spivakova) L.; m. Valeriya Davidovna Besher, Nov. 3, 1962 (div. Sept. 1963); m. Nadya Viktorovna Shlyapina, Aug. 15, 1965; 1 child, Evgeny. MS, Kharkov State U., 1955, PhD in Physics and Math., 1959, DSc in Physics and Math., 1985. Jr. rsch. fellow Kharkov Inst. Single Crystals, 1955-56; sr. rsch. fellow Kharkov Rsch. Inst. Basic Chemistry, 1960-61; leading rsch. fellow Inst. Low Temperature Physics and Engring. Acad. Scis., Kharkov, 1961-95; cons. dept. engring. materials Ben-Gurion U. of the Negev, Beer-Sheva, Israel, 1995—. Co-author: (in Russian) Phase Equilibria in Multicomponent Systems, 1961, English translation, 1964, (in Japanese) Physica of Metals, 1984, (in Russian) Modern Problems of Low Temperature Plasticity of Materials, 1987. Avocations: computers, television.

LANDAU, ELLIS, gaming company executive; b. Phila., Feb. 24, 1944; s. Manfred and Ruth (Fischer) L.; m. Kathy Suzanne Thomas, May 19, 1968 (div.); children: Rachel, David; m. Yvette Ehr Cohen, Nov. 1, 1992. BA in Econs., Brandeis U., 1965; MBA, Columbia U., 1967. Fin. analyst SEC, Washington, 1968-69; asst. treas. U-Haul Internat., Phoenix, 1969-71; v.p., treas. Ramada, Inc., Phoenix, 1971-90; CFO Boyd Gaming Corp., Las Vegas, Nev., 1990—. Home: 7571 Silver Meadow Ct Las Vegas NV 89117-2986 Office: Boyd Gaming Corp 2950 S Industrial Rd Las Vegas NV 89109-1100

LANDAU, EMANUEL, epidemiologist; b. N.Y.C., Nov. 28, 1919; s. Meyer and Annie (Heller) L.; m. Davetta Goldberg, Sept. 5, 1948; children: Melanie (dec.), Elizabeth. BA, CCNY, 1939; Phd, Am. U., 1966. Supervisory analytical statistician Calif. Dept. Public Health, 1957-59, chief biometry sect., divsn. air pollution, 1959-62; head lab. and clin. trials sect. Nat. Cancer Inst., 1962-65; statis. adviser Nat. Air Pollution Control Administrn., 1965-69; epidemiologist Environ. Health Svc., 1969-71; chief epidemiologic studies br. Bur. Radiol. Health, 1971-74; project dir., sci. cons. Am. Pub. Health Assn., Washington, 1975—; cons., adv. in field, including WHO adv. on air quality criteria, Geneva, 1967, Karolinska Inst., Stockholm, 1968. Contbr. articles to profl. jours. Vol. White House Health Care Reform Corr. With AUS, 1942-46, capt. USPHS (ret.). Decorated Belgian Fourragere; recipient Superior Svc. award HEW, 1963. Fellow Am. Pub. Health Assn., Royal Soc. Health; mem. Soc. Epidemiologic Rsch., Am. Statis. Assn. (chmn. com. on stats. and environ.), Cosmos Club. Democrat. Jewish. Home: 4601 N Park Ave Apt 208 Chevy Chase MD 20815-4575 Office: Am Pub Health Assn 800 I Street NW Washington DC 20001-3710

LANDAU, IDDO, philosopher, educator; b. Jerusalem, Aug. 2, 1958; s. Jacob and Zipora (Marcus) L. BA, Hebrew U., Jerusalem, 1984, MA, 1986; PhD, McGill U., Montreal, Can., 1991. Lectr. Haifa (Israel) U., 1991-97, sr. lectr., 1997—. Contbr. articles to profl. jours. Recipient Alon prize State of Israel, 1992. Avocations: reading, traveling. Office: Dept Philosophy, Haifa Univ, 31905 Haifa Israel

LANDAU, LOUIS I., pediatrician; b. Melbourne, Australia, Aug. 11, 1942; s. Jack and Hilda (Pahoff) L.; m. Miriam Erlich, Jan. 19, 1965; children: Jonathan, Peter. MB BS, Univ. Melbourne, 1965, MD, 1974. FRACP. Resident med. officer Royal Melbourne Hosp., 1966-67; resident med. officer Royal Children's Hosp., Melbourne, 1968-70, rsch. fellow, 1971-72, rsch. fellow, acting dir., dept. thoracic medicine, 1974-76; Uncle Bob's Travel fellow/Med. Rsch. Coun. of Can. McGill U., Montreal, Que., Can., 1973-74; hon. cons., pediatric. thoracic medicine Royal Children's Hosp. and Queen Victoria Med. Ctr., Melbourne, 1977-84; prof. of paediatrics U. Western Australia, 1984-95, exec. dean faculty of medicine and dentistry, 1996—; chmn. Inst. for Child Health Rsch., Perth, Australia, 1990-94; hon. cons., pediatric thoracic medicine, Mercy Materinity Hosp. and Royal Women's Hosp., Melbourne, Australia, 1977-84; vis. fellow Health Scis. Ctr., Tucson, Ariz., 1980-81, Hadassah U. Hosp., Jerusalem, 1980-81; prin. rsch. fellow Royal Children's Rsch. Found., 1981-83; tutor in pediatrics, Ormond Coll./Univ. Melbourne, 1975-80, tutor/sr. assoc., 1975-84, part-time lectr. dept. physiology, 1978-84; vis. prof. Health Scis. Ctr., U. London, 1992, U. Capetown, S. Africa, 1993, U. Bristol, U.K. Author: Cystic Fibrosis, 1984, Respiratory Illness in Children, 1990, Pediatric Respiratory Medicine, 1999; contbr. 200 articles to profl. jours. Fellow Royal Astralasian Coll. Physicians; mem. Australian Coll. Paediatrics, Thoracic Soc. Australian/New Zealand, European Respiratory Soc., Am. Thoracic Soc. Office: Fac of Medicine/Dentistry, U Western Australia, Nedlands 6907, Australia

LANDAU, MICHAEL B., law educator, musician, writer; b. Wilkes-Barre, Pa., July 3, 1953; s. Jack Landau and Florence (Rabitz) Simon. BA, Pa. State U., 1975; JD, U. Pa., 1988. Vis. prof. law Dickinson Sch. Law, Pa. State U., Carlisle; assoc. Cravath, Swaine and Moore, N.Y.C., 1988-90, Skadden, Arps, N.Y.C., 1990-92; assoc. prof. Coll. Law Ga. State U., Atlanta, 1992-99, prof. law, 1999—; pres., founder Balloon-A-Grams of N.Y., N.Y.C., 1981-86, N.Y. Singing Telegrams, 1981-86; vis. prof. law U. Ga. Law Sch., 1998; guest lectr. Johannes Kepler U., Linz, Austria, summer 1994, 95, 96. Contbr. articles to law jours. on copyright, art, patent, entertainment law. Mem. ABA, N.Y. State Bar Assn., Internat. Bar Assn., Vol. Lawyers for Arts, Am. Fedn. Musicians, Am. Intellectual Property Law Assn., Copyright Soc. U.S. Am., Phi Kappa Phi, Omicron Delta Epsilon. Democrat. Avocations: photography, jazz guitar, jazz piano. Office: Ga State U Coll Law University Pla Atlanta GA 30303

LANDAU-CRAWFORD, DOROTHY RUTH, local social service executive; b. Staten Island, N.Y., Oct. 5, 1957; d. Robert August and Dorothy Faith (Schaut) Landau; m. John W. Crawford, Oct. 21, 1989; 1 child, Jacqueline Lauren. AS, SUNY, Farmingdale, 1977; BS in Biology, Wagner Coll., 1979. Sci. tchr. Bais Yaakov, S.I., 1979-81; dental asst. Dr. Marvin Freeman, S.I., 1981-82; office mgr. Dr. Bennett C. Fidlow, S.I., 1982-85; polit. aide to S.I. Borough Pres. S.I. Borough Pres., 1985-89; exec. dir. Richmond Sr. Svcs. Project Share, 1990—; v.p. N.J. Shared Housing Assn., regional dir. Nat. Shared Housing Resouces Ctr., 1995—; environ. chmn. S.I. League for Better Govt., 1984—; pres. Tottenville Improvement Council Inc., Staten Island, 1985—. Dem. candidate N.Y. State Assembly 60th Dist., 1986, dist. leader; dir. cmty. bds. S.I. Borough Pres.'s Office; founder, pres. environ. group S.I.L.E.N.T., S.I., 1985; 1st v.p. 123d Cmty. Coun., L.I., 1986; social chmn. South Shore Dem. Club; founding mem. Friends of Clay Pit Pond Park; mem. Protectors of Pine Oak Woods Inc., Roserio Alliotta Dem. Club, Dem. Orgn. Richmond; trustee S.I. Bd. Leukemia Soc. Am., 1988—, chair Celebrity Waiters Luncheon; spl. election candidate for 51st Councilmatic Dist., 1994. Recipient Cmty. Activist award Office of pres. S.I. Borough, 1987. Mem. NAFE, Bus. and Profl. Women (young careerist for S.I.). Avocations: photography, sports, ceramics, youth programs. Home: 370 Jackson Mills Rd Jackson NJ 08527-4446

LANDAUER, ELVIE ANN WHITNEY, humanities educator, writer; b. Detroit, Dec. 10, 1937; d. Augustus and Leona (Green) Moore; m. Thomas Whitney, 1963 (div. 1978); m. Ernest Landauer, Dec. 31, 1987. BA, Calif. State U., L.A., 1978; MA, San Francisco State U., 1989; postgrad., U. N.Mex. Cert. C.C. tchr. (life). Dep. dir. Calif. Arts Coun., Sacramento, 1976-79; exec. dir. Mothers Emergency Svc., Sacramento, 1979-82; assoc. dir. San Francisco Cmty. Bds., 1982-83; project dir. San Francisco Prevention Project, 1983-86; exec. dir. East Bay Ctr. for Performing Arts, Richmond, Calif., 1987-89; instr. English Calif. C.C.s, Pittsburg, Fremont & Hayward, 1990-93; instr. Am. studies U. N.Mex., Alburg, 1993-94; instr. humanities New Coll., San Francisco, 1994-95; bus. owner Academics of Course!, Books, Berkeley, Calif., 1997—; rschr. L.A. Cmty. Arts Alliance, 1972. Author: Plays: The Disinherited, 1971, The Uptown Mrs. Carrie, 1989; prodr. Meat Theater Co., 1970-72. Bd. dirs. Richmond (Calif.) Arts Coun., 1986-89; workshop coord. Watts (Calif.) Writers Workshop, 1966-69, Sacramento Civic Theater, 1980; project coord. Cmty. Spirit Project, Pasadena, Calif., 1972-75. With USN, 1958-61. Recipient Woman of Yr. award Iota Phi Lambda, Sacramento, 1981. Home: 1317 Arch St Berkeley CA 94708-1824

LANDAUER, MICHELLE DEBORAH, English literature researcher; b. Detroit, July 3, 1969; d. David F. and Fern E. (LeMoult) L.; m. Michael Joseph Burguieres. BA in English Lit., Tex. A&M U., 1991; MA in English Lit., DePaul U., 1995; doctoral candidate, U. Melbourne, Australia, 1996—. Tutor DePaul U., Chgo., 1992, adminstrv. asst., 1992; program coord. Northwestern U., Chgo., 1993-96; edito U. Melbourne, 1996, instr., 1997—; conf. coord. Dept. of English Postgrad. Conf., U. Melbourne, 1997. Contbr. articles to profl. jours. Recipient Undergrad. Rsch. Opportunity award Tex. A&M U., 1990; DePaul U. grantee, 1995, Melbourne U. Postgrad. scholar, 1996—, Melbourne Abroad Postgrad. Travelling scholar U. Melbourne, 1997; rsch. grantee U. Melbourne, 1997, 98. Mem. MLA, Internat. Gothic Assn., N.Am. Soc. for Study of Romanticism, N.E. Am. Soc. for Eighteenth Century Studies, Brit. Assn. for Romantic Studies. E-mail: m.landauer@pgrad.unimelb.edu.au. Office: U Melbourne Dept English, Parkville, Victoria 3052, Australia

LANDEIRA-FERNANDEZ, JESUS, neuroscientist; b. Rio de Janeiro, Oct. 22, 1962; s. Agapito Landeira-Mallón and Maria Mercedes Fernandez-Antello; m. Rosane Zylberberg, Nov. 12, 1988; children: Julia Landeira-Zylberberg, Victor Landeira-Zylberberg. Student, Cath. U., Rio de Janeiro, 1985; MA, U. São Paulo, 1988, UCLA, 1992; PhD, UCLA, 1994. Tchg. fellow Cath. U., Rio de Janeiro, 1984-85, prof., 1995—; prof. U. Guarulhos, São Paulo, 1987-88; from tchg. asst. to rsch. asst. UCLA, 1993-94; head Behavioral Neurosci. Lab., Rio de Janeiro, 1996—; cons. Fundagñ São João Del Rey, Minas Gerais, Brazil, 1994-95, Cath. U., Rio de Janeiro, 1995—; referee Ministry for Sci. and Tech. Brazil, Rio de Janeiro, 1994—, Brazilian Jour. Med. and Biol. Rsch., Rio de Janeiro, 1995—. Contbr. articles to profl. jours. Founder Brazil Today, L.A., 1990. Sec. for Sci. and Tech. Brazil scholar, 1988, Orgn. Am. States scholar, 1989; Sec. for Sci. and Tech. Brazil grantee, 1995. Mem. Soc. for Neurosci., Brazilian Soc. for Neurosci. and Behavior, N.Y. Acad. Sci. Avocations: travel, reading, playing and listening to music. Office: PUC Rio Dept Psychology, Rua Marques Sao Vicente 225, 22453-900 Rio de Janeiro Brazil

LANDER, RUTH A., medical group and association administrator; b. Fitchburg, Mass., Dec. 13, 1948; d. H. Allison and Violet K. (Erickson) Linné; m. C. Stephen Lander, June 28, 1968; children: Timothy, Mary. BA, Ohio State U., 1978; postgrad., Kennedy-Western U., 1995—. Dir. fin. Luth. Svc. Assn. New England, Natick, Mass., 1973-76; gen. mgr. Logos, Columbus, 1976-87; practice adminstr. Columbus Oncology Assocs., Inc., 1987—; sec., treas. Adminstrs. in Oncology Hematology Assembly, Englewood, Colo., 1994-95, legis. liaison, 1994-95, pres.-elect, 1995-96, pres., 1996-97; spkr. on med. group mgmt. issues. Editor Adminstrs. in Oncology Hematology Assembly News, 1994-95; mem. editl. bd. Oncology Issues Mag.; contbr. articles to profl. jours. Mem. Vineyard Christian Fellowship, Westerville, Ohio; grass roots legis. group Ohio Med. Group Mgmt. Assn., Columbus, 1994—. Fellow Med. Group Mgmt. Assn., Am. Coll. Med. Practice Execs. (nat. chair membership devel. com. 1999); mem. Mid-Ohio Med. Group Mgmt. Assn. (pres. 1993-94, sec. 1992-93, program dir. 1991-92, exec. com. 1990-97), Assn. Cmty. Cancer Ctr. (mem. editl. bd. mag.), Ohio Med. Group Mgmt. Assn. (exec. com. 1994—, sec. 1995-96, pres.-elect 1997, pres. 1998), Ohio Oncology Med. Group Mgmt. Assn. (pres. 1997), Ohio State Med. Assn. (mem. group practice task force). Republican. Avocations: reading, computers, crafts, knitting, Bible study. Office: Columbus Oncology Assocs 810 Jasonway Ave Ste A Columbus OH 43214-2329

LANDERS, VERNETTE TROSPER, writer, educator, association executive; b. Lawton, Okla., May 3, 1912; d. Fred Gilbert and LaVerne Hamilton (Stevens) Trosper; m. Paul Albert Lum, Aug. 29, 1952 (dec. May 1955); 1 child, William Tappan; m. 2d Newlin Landers, May 2, 1959 (dec. Apr. 1990); children: Lawrence, Marlin. AB with honors, UCLA, 1933, MA, 1935, EdD, 1953; Cultural doctorate (hon.), Lit. World U., Tucson, 1985. Tchr. secondary schs. Secondary Schs., Montebello, Calif., 1935-45, 48-50, 51-59, 1935-45, 48-50, 51-59; prof. Long Beach City Coll., 1946-47; asst. prof. L.A. State Coll., 1950; dean girls Twenty-Nine Palsm (Calif.) H.S., 1960-65; dist. counselor Morongo (Calif.) United Sch. Dist., 1965-72, coord. adult edn., 1965-67, guidance project dir., 1967; clk.-in-charge Landers (Calif.) Post Office, 1962-82, ret., 1982; participant Yucca Valley Cowboy Poetry and Music Gathering, 1996, 98; grand marshall Yucca Valley Grubstake Parade, 1999. Author: Impy, 1974, Talkie, 1975, Impy's Children, 1975, Nineteen O Four, 1976, Little Brown Bat, 1976, Sio-Go, 1977, Owls Who and Who Who, 1978, Sandy, The Coydog, 1979, The Kit Fox and the Walking Stick, 1980; contbr. articles to profl. jours., poems to anthologies. V.p., sec. Landers Assn., 1965—; sec. Landers Vol. Fire Dept., 1972—; life mem. Hi-Desert Playhouse Guild, Hi-Desert Meml. Hosp. Guild; bd. friends Copper Mountain Coll., 1990-91; bd. dirs., sec. Desert Emergency Radio Svc.; mem. Rep. Senatorial Inner Cir., 1990-92, Regent Nat. Fedn. Rep. Women, 1990-92, Nat. Rep. Congl. Com., 1990-91, Presdl. Task Force, 1990-92; lifetime mem. Girl Scouts USA, 1991. Recipient internat. diploma Creativity award Internat. Pers. Rsch. Assn., 1972, award Goat Mt. Grange No. 818, 1987; cert. of merit for disting. svc. to edn., 1973; Order of Rose, 1978, Order of Pearl, 1989, Alpha Xi Delta; poet laureate Ctr. of Internat. Studies and Exchanges, 1981; diploma of merit in letters U. Arts, Parma, Italy, 1982; Golden Yr. Bruin UCLA, 1983; World Culture prize Nat. Ctr. for Studies and Rsch., Italian Acad., 1984; Golden Palm Diploma of Honor in poetry Leonardo Da Vinci Acad., 1984; Diploma of Merit and titular mem. internat. com. Internat. Ctr. Studies and Exchanges, Rome, 1984; Recognition award San Gorgonio coun. Girl Scouts USA, 1984—; Cert. of Appreciation Morongo Unified Sch. Dist., 1984, 89; plaque for contbn. to postal svc. and cmty. U.S. Postal Svc., 1984; Biographee of Yr. award for outstanding achievement in the field of edn. and svc. to cmty. Hist. Preservation of Am.; named Princess of Poetry of Internat. Ctr. Cultural Studies and Exchange, Italy, 1985; cmty. dinner held in her honor for achievement and svc. to cmty., 1984; Star of Contemporary Poetry Masters of Contemporary Poetry, Internat. Ctr. Cultural Studies and Exchanges, Italy, 1984; named to honor list of leaders of contemporary art and lit. and apptd. titular mem. of Internat. High Com. for World Culture & Arts Leonardo Da Vinci Acad., 1987; named to honor list Foremost Women 20th Century for Outstanding Contbn. to Rsch., IBC, 1987; Presdl. Order of Merit Pres. George Bush-Exec. Coun. of Nat. Rep. Senatorial Com., Congl. cert. of Appreciation U.S. Ho. of Reps.; other awards and certs. Guest of hon. ground breaking ceremony Landers Elementary Sch. 1989, dedication ceremony, 1991. Fellow Internat. Acad. Poets (life), World Lit. Acad.; mem. Am. Pers. and Guidance Assn., Internat. Platform Assn., Nat. Ret. Tchrs. Assn., Calif. and Nat. Assn. for Counseling and Devel., Am. Assn. for Counseling and Devel. (25-Yr. Membership pin 1991), Nat. Assn. Women Deans and Adminstrs., Montebello Bus. and Profl. Women's Club (pres.), Nat. League Am. Pen Women (sec. 1985-86), Leonardo Da Vinci Acad. Internat. (Winged Glory diploma of honor in letters 1982), Landers Area C. of C. (sec. 1985-86, Presdl. award for Outstanding Svcs., Internat. Honors Cup 1992-93), Desert Nature Mus., Whittier Toastmistress Club (Calif.) (pres. 1957), Homestead Valley Women's Club (Landers), Soroptimists (sec. 29 Palms chpt. 1962, life mem. 1983, Soroptimist of Yr. local chpt. 1987-88), Phi Beta Kappa, Pi Lambda Theta (Mortar Bd., Prytanean UCLA, UCLA Golden Yr. Bruin 1983), Sigma Delta Pi, Pi Delta Phi. Home: PO Box 3839 Landers CA 92285-0839

LANDI, GIOVANNI, banking executive; b. Milan, Italy, Mar. 31, 1962; m. Barbara Giacomoni; children: Tomasso, Benedetta. PhD in Econs., Bocconi U., Milan, 1986. Treas. Banca Popolare Veneta, Padua, Italy, 1990-92; chief investigative officer Deutsche Bank Fondi, Milan, 1992-97; head asset mgmt. Banca Commerciale Italiana, Milan, 1997-99, CEO asset mgmt. divsn., 1999—. Office: Banca Commerciale Italiana, C so di Porta Nuova 3/A, 20121 Milan Italy

LANDINO, DANIEL, speech pathologist; b. New Haven, Nov. 11, 1957; s. Albert and Carmel (Pantano) L.; m. Karen Sabino, July 18, 1980; children: DanaMarie, Daniel II. BA, So. Conn. State U., 1979, MS, 1982, postgrad. degree, 1997. Speech and lang. pathologist Bridgeport (Conn.) Pub. Schs., 1982-85, Derby (Conn.) Pub. Schs., 1985—, Novacare, New Haven, 1989-93, Paragon, 1993—, 1998—. Mem. Conn. Speech-Lang.-Hearing Assn. Home: 49 McMahon Ln North Branford CT 06471-1475

LANDIS, RICHARD GORDON, retired food company executive; b. Davenport, Okla., Apr. 5, 1920; s. John William and Venna Marie (Perrin) L.; m. Beth Throne, Nov. 6, 1943; children: Gary Perrin, Dennis, Michael, Kay Ellen. BA, U. LaVerne, 1942; postgrad., Claremont Grad. Sch., 1947; LLD (hon.), U. LaVerne, 1981. Mgmt. Delmonte Corp, San Francisco, 1942-83, pres., 1971-77, pres. & chief exec. officer, 1977-78, chmn. & chief exec. officer, 1978-81; pres. Pacific div. R.J. Reynolds, Inc., San Francisco, 1981-83; former chancellor U. LaVerne, Calif.; bd. dirs. Stanford Rsch. Internat., Menlo Park, Calif. Mem. Commn. of Calif., 1984-90; chmn. Pacific Basin Econ. Coun., 1975-83; officer Boy Scouts Am., 1946—, Invest in Am.; Lt. USAF, 1942-46. Mem. Pacific Union Club, Bohemian Club, Peachtree C. of C. Republican. Avocations: golf, edn. activities, youth programs. Office: 120 Montgomery St Ste 1880 San Francisco CA 94104-4321

LANDIS, ROBERT KUMLER, III, investment banker, lawyer; b. Dayton, Ohio, June 20, 1953; s. Robert Kumler Landis Jr. and Rebecca (McCall) Baird; m. Robin Lee Taylor, June 2, 1979; children: Robert Kumler IV, Taylor McCall, Samuel Tufts. AB, Princeton (N.J.) U., 1975; JD, Harvard U., 1978. Bar: N.Y. 1978. Assoc. Simpson Thacher & Bartlett, N.Y.C., 1978-83; dir. Merrill Lynch & Co., N.Y.C., 1984-94; mng. dir. Schooner Capital Internat., Boston, 1994-96; pres. Northern Lights Investors, LLC, 1996—. Republican. Episcopalian.

LANDIVAR, JORGE ROBERTO, insurance executive, financial analyst; b. Buenos Aires, Feb. 1, 1941; s. Roberto and Natividad (Santos) L.; m. Carmen Elsa Daina (div. Oct. 1976); m. Teresa Fernandez. High Technician in ElectroTechnics, U. Nacional de Tucuman, Argentina, 1962; High Technician in Adminstrn./Orgn., Inst. Superior de Tech. & Sci., Buenos Aires, 1967; High Technician in Commercialization, Centro de Altos Estudidos, Buenos Aires, 1971. Head of maint. Cia. Azucarera Concepción, Tucuman, 1963-64; mng. ptnr. Landivar & Luchesi S.C.A., Tucuman, 1964-69, Equipos y Servicios S.C., Tucuman, 1969-71; comml. chief Seguros B. Rivadavia C.L., various cities, Argentina, 1971-83; pres. Proteccion Patrimonial S.A., Buenos Aires, 1983—; gen. dir. Centro Fed. de Servicios de Fedecamaras (Ctrl. Empresaria del Comercio Minorista), Buenos Aires, 1990—; ofcl. ins. cons. Confederacion General de la Industria de la Argentina, Buenos Aires, 1991—. Gen. sec. Centro Estudiantes Instituto Técnico, Tucuman, 1960-61; pres. Federacion Tucumana de Estudiantes, 1961-62; sec. Asociacion Argentina Asesores de Seguros, Buenos Aires, 1989-91; full mem. Comision de Economia del Comite Nacional de la Union Civica Radical, Buenos Aires, 1993—. Mem. Union Civica Radical. Roman Catholic. Avocations: Chess, Go (card game), target practice (shooting). Office: Proteccion Patrimonial SA, Varela 18 1 5, Buenos Aires 1406, Argentina

LANDMAN, BETTE EMELINE, academic administrator; b. Piqua, Ohio, July 18, 1937; d. Wilson Richard and Lois (Wilson) L. BS, Bowling Green State U., 1959; MA, Ohio State U., 1961, PhD, 1972. From instr. to asst. prof. anthropology Springfield (Mass.) Coll., 1963-67; asst. prof. Temple U., 1967-71; asst. prof. anthropology Beaver Coll., Glenside, Pa., 1971-76, dean, 1976-85, v.p. acad. affairs, 1980-85, acting pres., 1982-83, 85, pres., 1985—. Bd. dirs. Abington (Pa.) Meml. Hosp., 1986-93, 95—, Abington Meml. Hosp. Found., 1993-95; mem. blood donor campaign ARC, chair Pa.-Jersey Region Higher Edn., 1990-91; bd. advisors Coll. Physicians of Phila., 1994—. Recipient Disting. Teaching award Christian R. and Mary F. Lindback Found., 1973; NSF fellow, 1961-63, Wenner-Gren Found. for Anthrop. Rsch. fellow, 1965-66; named Disting. Dau. of Pa., 1992, Educator of Yr. Boy Scouts Am., 1996; Ann. Pa. Am. Coun. on Edn.-NIP award established in her honor, 1992. Mem. Am. Coun. Edn. (state coord. 1980-84, commn. on leadership devel. 1989-94, chmn. 1991-92, bd. dirs. 1993-97), Assn. Am. Colls. (bd. dirs. 1986-91, vice chair 1989-90, chair 1990-91), Assn. Presbyn. Colls. and Univs. (exec. com. 1988-93, 95—, sec. 1989-90, v.p. 1990-91, pres. 1991-92), Pa. Assn. Colls. and Univs. (exec. com. 1992-93), Nat. Assn. Ind. Colls. and Univs. (commn. on campus concerns 1991—, vice chmn. 1992, chmn. 1993), NCAA Divsn III Pres. Coun., Southeastern Pa. Consortium Higher Edn. (chair 1996-98), Sigma Xi, Phi Kappa Phi, Kappa Delta Pi. Office: Beaver Coll Office of Pres 450 S Easton Rd Glenside PA 19038-3215*

LANDMAN, LAWRENCE BRUCE, federal official; b. N.Y.C., Oct. 12, 1958; arrived in Denmark, 1992; s. Raoul Ray and Barbara Joan (Greenberg) L.; m. Helle Lind Christensen, Feb. 22, 1982; children: Elizabeth, Benjamin. BA with honors, SUNY, Stony Brook, 1980; JD, U. Calif., Berkeley, 1984; MBA, Columbia U., N.Y.C., 1990; PhD, Roskilde (Denmark) U., 1999. Bar: N.Y. 1985, N.J. 1988. With Landman & Christensen, N.Y.C., Copenhagen, 1984-95; assoc. prof. Helsingor Business Coll., 1992-94; fellow Roskilde U., 1995-98; pres., CEO Am. C. of C. in Denmark, 1998—; adj. prof. Copenhagen Bus. Sch., 1992-98, Malmö (Sweden) U., 1999—; bd. dirs. Fulbright Commn., Copenhagen; referee market economists dialogue Copenhagen Bus. Sch., 1999; lectr. in field. Author: Doing Business in the United States, Legal Opportunities and Pitfalls, 1997; contbr. articles to profl. jours. Gen. coun. Am. Dem. Abroad, Scandinavia, 1992-95, pres. Copenhagen chpt., 1992-95. Denmark Internat. Student Com. scholar, Copenhagen, 1978. Mem. ABA (subcom. chmn. 1995-97), Licensing Exec. Soc., Am. Club. Democrat. Avocations: jogging, camping, sailing. Office: Am C of C in Denmark, Christians Brygge 28, DK-1559 Copenhagen Denmark

LANDOLT, ARLO UDELL, astronomer, educator; b. Highland, Ill., Sept. 29, 1935; s. Arlo Melvin and Vesta (Kraus) L.; m. Eunice Jean Casper, June 8, 1966; 1 child, Jennifer; stepchildren: Lynda, Barbara, Vicky, Debra. B.A., Miami U., Oxford, Ohio, 1955; M.A., Ind. U., 1960, Ph.D., 1963. Mem. 1st wintering-over party Internat. Geophys. Year, Amundson-Scott South Pole Sta., Antarctica, 1957; asst. prof. physics and astronomy La. State U., 1962-65, asso. prof., 1965-68, prof., 1968—, dir. La. State U. Obs., 1970-88, acting chmn. dept. physics and astronomy, summers 1972-73, pres. faculty senate, 1979-80; program dir. astronomy sect. NSF, 1975-76; mem. governing bd. Am. Inst. of Physics, 1985-91, 95—; guest investigator Kitt Peak Nat. Obs., Tucson, Cerro Tololo Inter-Am. Obs.,Las Campanas Observatory, La Serena, Chile, Dyer Obs., Vanderbilt U., Goethe Link Obs., Ind. U. Rsch. grantee NSF, 1964, 66, 69, 71, 73, 75, 92—, NASA, 1965, 92, Rsch. Corp., 1964, Air Force Office Sci., 1977-87, Space Telescope Sci. Inst., 1985-90, 92; recipient George Van Biesbroeck prize, 1995. Fellow AAAS (sec. Sect. D 1970-78); mem. AAUP, Am. Astron. Soc. (sec. 1980-89, 95—; pres. divsn. IX 2000—), Internat. Astron. Union (sec. U.S. nat. com. 1980-89, 96—, v.p. commn. 25 1979-85, 91—), Royal Astron. Soc. (Eng.), Astron. Soc. Pacific, Am. Polar Soc., Am. Philatelic Soc., The Explorer's Club, Sigma Xi, Pi Mu Epsilon. Office: La State U Dept Physics And Astro Baton Rouge LA 70803-0001

LANDON, WILLIAM J., intelligence officer; b. Menno, S.D., June 23, 1939; s. Helmuth Samuel and Violet A. (McPherson) Neuharth. LLB, Blackstone Sch. Law, 1962, JD, 1968; AA in Bus. Mgmt., Coastline C.C., 1984. Criminal investigator Internat. Acad. Police Sci., Oklahoma City, Southwestern Inst. Criminology, Lawton, Okla.; criminal investigator, intelligence officer ASI divsn. Internat. Investigators and Police, St. John, N.B., Can., 1964-94; intelligence officer, analyst Internat. Investigators & Police, Rapid City, S.D., 1990—. Sponsor Robin Anne Syperda Benedict meml. scholarship Calif. State U., Fullerton, 1990—. With USMC, 1957-65. Mem. Internat. Assn. Study Organized Crime, Internat. Investigators Police Assn., Internat. Assn. Law Enforcement Intelligence Analysts, Assn. Former Intelligence Officers, Am. Soc. Criminology, Nat. Mil. Intelligence Assn. Avocations: martial arts, classical music, fencing.

LANDRAKIS, JOHN, business educator, consultant; b. Piraeus, Greece, Apr. 14, 1960; s. Nickolaos and Maria Landrakis. BA, Queens Coll., N.Y.C., 1982; MS, Polytechnic Inst., N.Y.C., 1985. Dean studies Mac Bus. Studies, Athens, Greece, 1993-98; lectr. U. Indpls., 1999—; cons. Media Strom, Athens, 1994—; instr. Page Found., Athens, 1994—, Am. European Studies, Athens, 1995—, K.E.K. Euroaction, Athens, 1993-97, I.E.K. Domi, Athens, 1993-94, I.E.K. C.G.A., Athens, 1990-93, Coll. Southeastern Europe, Athens, dean, 1987-93, STAS Found., Athens, 1997—, SBS Coll., Athens, 1996—; I.B. instr. Athens Coll., 1996—, prin. lectr. Assoc. Cert. Chartered Accts., 1998—, rep. St.Clements U., Greece. Author: Selection of Exercises in Mathematics, 1990. Sgt. artillery Greek Army, 1985-87. Fellow Soc. Bus. Practitioners (hon. rep. 1996); mem. British Inst. Mgmt., Am. Inst.

Indsl. Engring., Greek Math. Assoc., Greek Economical Assn. Christian Orthodox. Avocations: reading, swimming, horseback riding. Home and Office: Pellis 14 Kiffisia, Athens Greece

LANDRUM, CRAIG NELSON, lawyer; b. Greenwood, Miss., Dec. 29, 1955; s. Malcolm Lamar and Elizabeth Jane (Doolittle) L.; m. Judy Catherine Altman, Jan. 6, 1979; children: Austin Craig, Julia Allison. BS, Miss. State U., 1977; JD, U. Miss., 1980. Bar: Miss. 1980, U.S. Dist. Ct. (no. dist.) Miss. 1980, (so. dist.) Miss. 1980, U.S. Ct. Appeals, 5th circuit, 1980. Assoc. Stennet, Wilkinson & Ward, Jackson, Miss., 1980-85; ptnr. Chunn & Landrum, Jackson, Miss., 1985-89; ptnr., shareholder Heidelberg & Woodliff, Jackson, Miss., 1989-95, Watkins, Ludlam, Winter & Stennis, Jackson, Miss., 1995—; mem. lawyers com. Miss. Bankers Assn., Jackson, 1985—, chmn. 1992-94. Named to Best Lawyers in Am. Woodward & White, 1995-2000. Mem. ABA, Miss. Bar Assn. Office: PO Box 427 Jackson MS 39205-0427

LANDRY, MARK EDWARD, podiatrist, researcher; b. Washington, May 24, 1950; s. John Edward and Daphne (Fay) L.; m. Mary Ann Kotey, Sept. 7, 1974; children: John Ryan, Christopher John, Jessica Marie. D in Podiatry, Ohio Coll. Podiatric Medicine, 1975; MS in Edn., U. Kans., 1982. Diplomate Am. Bd. Podiatric Surgery, Am. Bd. Podiatric Orthopedics and Primary Podiatric Medicine. Gen. practice podiatry Kansas City, Mo., 1977—, Overland Park, Kans., 1980—; clin. asst. prof. U. Health Scis., Kansas City, 1985-98; clin. assoc. prof. Coll. Podiatric Medicine and Surgery U. Osteo. Medicine and Health Scis., Des Moines, 1985-92; clin. instr. Sch. Medicine U. Mo., Kansas City, 1987-95; founder, bd. dirs. Kansas City Podiatric Residency Program, Kansas City, 1982-91; adv. bd. Rockport Shoe Co.; chmn. podiatry dept. Park Lane Med. Ctr., Kansas City, Mo., 1995-97; dir. continuing edn. Kans. Podiatric Med. Assn., 1997—. Contbr. articles to profl. jours. Cons. Mid-Am. Track and Field Assn., Lenexa, Kans., 1978-88; com. chmn. Boy Scouts Am., Overland Park, Kans.; coach Johnson County Soccer League, 1987-90; head coach 6th and 7th grade girls' Cath. Youth Orgn. Basketball, 1995-96, 97; sponsor 8 & 11 Baseball League, 1987-90. 1st lt. USAF, 1975-77. Recipient Pres.'s award Ohio Sch. Podiatric Medicine, 1975; USAF scholar Armed Forces Health Professions, 1973-75. Fellow Am. Coll. Foot Surgeons, Acad. Podiatric Sports Medicine, Am. Coll. Primary Podiatric Medicine & Podiatric Orthopedics; mem. Kans. Podiatric Med Assn. (bd. dirs. 1997—), Brit. Podiatry Assn. (hon.), Am. Bd. Primary Podiatric Medicine (founding dir., bd. examiner 1994—), Holy Cross Social Club (pres. 1983-84), Prairie Life Club, Leukemia Assn. of Am. (team in tng. 1997—, team capt. 1999, K.C. corp. challenge participant 1997-99), K.C. (4th degree 1995—, chancellor 1998, 99), KC Ski Club (trip capt. 1999). Republican. Roman Catholic. Avocations: triathlon training (completed Grand Floridian Ironman competition, 1998, Ironman Fla., 1999), skiing. Home: 8120 W 99th St Overland Park KS 66212-3444 Office: 10550 Quivira Rd Ste 260 Overland Park KS 66215-2375

LANDSAAT, PETER MARINUS, cardiologist, researcher; b. Amsterdam, The Netherlands, Apr. 23, 1964; s. P. and E.F.A. (Titselaer) L.; children: Indy David, Charlie Linde. MD, U. Amsterdam, 1990, cardiologist, 1998. With Acad. Med. Ctr., Amsterdam, 1980-98, Slotervaart Ziekenhuis, Amsterdam, 1998-99, Onze Lieve Vrouwe Gasthins, Amsterdam, 1999—. Capt. Landmacht, 1988-90. Mem. Am. Heart Assn., Netherland Soc. Cardiology. Home: Koningsvalen 64, 1391 AL Abroude The Netherlands Office: Onze Luve Vronwe Baothils, 1 Dosterpark St 279, 1079 HA Amsterdam The Netherlands

LANDSBERG, DENIS NEVILLE, lawyer, consultant; b. Witbank, South Africa, Aug. 24, 1951; s. Melville and Petronella Johanna (Dutoit) L.; m. Penelope Ann Philp, Apr. 2, 1977; 1 child, Robyn. BA, Stellenbosch U., South Africa, 1975; LLB, Stellenbosch U., 1977. Atty. Supreme Ct. of South Africa; conveyancer, commr. of small claims ct., appraiser. Articles clk. Buchanan Boyes, Cape Town, South Africa, 1978-80; ptnr. Groenewald, Landsberg & Pollard, Somerset West, South Africa, 1980-82, Ince & Wood, Stellenbosch, 1983-84; sr. ptnr. Landsberg, Carinus & Brand, Stellenbosch, 1985-91; prin. ptnr. Landsberg & Assocs., Somerset West, 1991-95; pvt. practice; bd. dirs. S.P.C. Group of Cos., Rustenburg, South Africa, Dariada N.V., St. Maarten, Verhoef Internat. Computer Svcs. Inc., U.S., various cos. in South Africa and U.K.; cons. to various internat. corps. Bd. dirs. Stellenbosch Coll., 1990—, Somerset Coll., Parklands Coll.; trustee Tygerberg Zool. Preservation Trust, Cape Town, 1987—; mem. Lawyers for Human Rights, South Africa; sponsor Magendavidadom, Cape Town. Lt. South Africa commandos, 1968-79. Recipient B.G. Heydenrych scholarship, 1976. Mem. Law Soc. of the Cape of Good Hope, Stellenbosch C. of C. (pres.), Round Table Assn. (chmn. 1984-85), Hottentots Holland Beach Sailing Club (commodore 1983-85). Avocations: sailing, hiking, constructing kites. Office: Landsberg & Assocs, 8 Stuart St, Somerset West 7130, South Africa

LANDSBERG, GARY MILLER, law firm investigator; b. Pasadena, Calif., Oct. 13, 1953; s. Henry and Patricia Ann Landsberg; m. Judy E. Caine, Nov. 21, 1979; children: Briana, Nicole. AS, Portland C.C., 1982. Investigator Freelance Legal Inst., Portland, Oreg., 1981-82, Martin, Bischoff, et al, Portland, 1983—; profl. musician and rec. artist, bass player, drummer, 1975-90. Coach/mgr. area youth soccer orgn. Mem. Internat. Soc. Air Safety Investigators. Office: Martin Bischoff et al 888 SW 5th Ave Ste 900 Portland OR 97204-2023

LANDSBERGIS, VYTAUTAS, Lithuanian government official; b. Kaunas, Oct. 18, 1932; s. Vytautas Landsbergis-Žemkalnis and Ona Jablonskyte-Landsbergiene; m. Gražina Ručyte; 3 children. Dep. chmn. USSR Supreme Soviet, Moscow, 1990—; chmn. Supreme Soviet, Vilnius, Lithuania, USSR, Sajudis (Lithuanian Reform Movement); chair Seimas, 1996—. Office: Seimas of Lithuania, Gedimino 53, 2002 Vilnius Lithuania*

LANDSMAN, SAMUEL, food executive, consultant; b. Newark, Dec. 28, 1923; s. William and Eva (Levy) L.; m. Rhoda L., Dec. 6, 1942; children: Eve Sandra, Sonja Anne, Peggy Ann, Jefferey Bernard, Amy Jan, Sheri Michelle. Pres. Garden State Packing Co., Inc., Hammonton, N.J., 1946-60, Va. Farmers Packing Co., Inc., Norfolk, 1954-60, Landsman Packing Co., Inc., Red Hook, N.Y., 1957-80, Landsman Internat., Inc., Aventura, Fla., 1978—, Bartow (Fla.) Holding Co., Inc., 1993—. With U.S. Army Signal Corps, 1942-43. Mem. Inst. Food Technologists. Avocations: numismatics, writing, arts. E-mail: samanro@fla.net.

LANDSTROM, JERONE T., surgeon; b. Miami, Aug. 9, 1952. MD, Wayne State U., 1981. Diplomate Am. Bd. Surgery, bd. cert. in hand surgery. Intern St. John's Hosp., Detroit, 1981-82; resident in gen. surgery Providence Hosp., Southfield, Mich., 1986-90; capt. surgeon USN Res.; fellow Hand and Microsurgery Ctr., Houston, 1995-96. Fellow ACS, Hand Ctr. Office: Ste 212, Guam Medical Plaza, Tamuning 96911, Guam

LANDUYT, WILLIAM M., holding company executive; b. Evergreen Park, Ill., 1955. BBA in Acctg. cum laude, U. Notre Dame. With Small Bus. Dept. Price Waterhouse, N.Y.C., 1977-83, sr. mgr.; asst. treas. Hanson Industries, 1983, controller, 1983-87, v.p. fin., 1987-88, v.p., CFO, 1988-90; assoc. dir. Hanson PLC, 1990-92; fin. dir. on bd. dirs. Hanson PLC, London, 1992-95; pres., CEO Hanson Industries, 1995-96; chmn., CEO Millennium Chemicals, Inc., 1996—. Office: Millennium Chemicals Inc 230 Half Mile Rd Red Bank NJ 07701-5683*

LANDY, BURTON AARON, lawyer; b. Chgo., Aug. 16, 1929; s. Louis J. and Clara (Ernstein) L.; m. Eleanor M. Simmel, Aug. 4, 1957; children: Michael Simmel, Alisa Anne. Student, Nat. U. Mex., 1948; B.S., Northwestern U., 1950; postgrad. scholar, U. Havana, 1951; J.D., U. Miami, 1952; postgrad. fellow, Inter-Am. Acad. Comparative Law, Havana, Cuba, 1955-56. Bar: Fla. 1952. Practice law in internat. field Miami, 1955—; ptnr. firm Ammerman & Landy, 1957-63, Paul, Landy, Beiley & Harper, P.A. and predecessor firm, 1964-94, Steel Hector & Davis, 1994-97; ptnr. firm, chmn. emeritus Internat. Practice Group Akerman, Senterfitt & Eidson, P.A., 1997—; lectr. Latin Am. bus. law U. Miami Sch. Law, 1972-75; also internat. law confs. in U.S. and abroad; mem. Nat. Conf. on Fgn. Aspects of U.S. Nat. Security, Washington, 1958; mem. organizing com. Miami regional conf. Com. for Internat. Econ. Growth, 1958; mem. U.S. Dept. Commerce Regional Export Expansion Council, 1969-74, mem. Dist. Export Council, 1978—; mem. U.S. Sec. State Adv. Com. on Pvt. Internat. Law; dir. Fla. Council Internat. Devel., 1977—, chmn. 1986-87, 99; mem. U. Miami Citizens Bd., 1977—; chmn. Fla. del. S.E. U.S.-Japan Assn., 1980-82; mem. adv. com. 1st Miami Trade Fair of Ams., 1978; dir., v.p. Greater Miami Fgn. Trade Zone, Inc., 1978—; mem. organizing com., lectr. 4 Inter-Am. Aviation Law Confs.; bd. dirs. Inter-Am. Bar Legal Found.; participant Aquaculture Symposium Sci. and Man in the Ams., Mexico City, Fla. Gov's Econ. Mission to Japan and Hong Kong, 1978; mem. bd. exec. advisors Law and Econs. Ctr.; mem. vis. com., internat. adv. bd. U. Miami Sch. Bus.; mem. internat. fin. council Office Comptroller of Fla.; founding chmn. Fla.-Korea Econ. Coop. Com., 1982—, Southeast U.S.-Korea Econ. Com., 1985—; chmn. Expo 500 Fla.-Columbus Soc., 1985-87; founding co-chmn. So. Fla. Roundtable-Georgetown U. Ctr. for Strategic and Internat. Studies, 1982-85; chmn. Fla. Gov.'s Conf. on World Trade, 1984—; gen. counsel Fla. Internat. Bankers Assn.; dir., former gen. counsel Fla. Internat. Ins. and Reins. Assn., chmn. Latin Am. Carribbean Bus. Promotion Adv. Counc. to U.S. Sec. of Commerce and Aid Adminstr; appointee Fla. Internat. Trade and Investment Coun.; mem. steering com. Summit of Ams., 1994—, co-chair post summit planning com.; strategic planning com. Mayor Miami Dade County Internat. Trade Commn. Contbg. editor Econs. Devel. Lawyers of the Ams., 1969-74; contbr. numerous articles to legal jours. in U.S. and fgn. countries. Chmn. City of Miami Internat. Trade and Devel. Com., 1984-86; chmn. internat. task force Beacon Coun. of Dade County, Fla., 1985, dir., chmn., 1991—; bd. dirs., exec. com. Internat. Comml. Dispute Resolution Ctr., Miami Internat. Arbitration and Mediation Inst.; chmn. Comml. Dispute Resolution Ctr. for the Ams., Miami, 1995—; apptd. by Gov. of Fla. to Internat. Currency and Barter Commn., 1986; lectr. U. Miami Inter-Ban course for Latin Am. bankers; steering com. Summit of the Americas, Miami, 1994, co-chair post Summit Planning Com., 1994; co-chair mayor Miami-Dade County Strategic Planning for Internat. Trade, 1998—; co-chair strategic planning com. Mayor of Miami Dade County Internat. Trade Commn.; bd. dirs. Americas Trade Mission Ctr., 2000—; mem. internat. adv. com. Enterprise Fla., 2000—. Named Internat. Trader of Yr., Fla. Council Internat. Devel., 1980, Bus. Person of Yr., 1986; recipient Pan Am. Informatica Comunicaciones Expo award, 1983, Lawyer of Americas award U. Miami, 1984, Richard L. McLaughlin award Fla. Econ. Devel. Coun., 1993; named hon. consul gen. Republic of Korea, Miami, 1983-88, State of Fla., 99—, recipient Heung-in medal (Order of Diplomatic Service), 1986, Ministerial Citation, Min. of Fgn. Affairs, 1988; apptd. Hon. consul Ft. Lauderdale, Fla., 1991-98; apptd. Hon. consul gen. State of Fla., 1999—. Fellow ABA Found. (chmn. com. arrangements internat. and comparative law sect. 1964-65, com. on Inter-Am. affairs of ABA 1985-87); mem. Inter-Am. Bar Assn. (asst. sec.-gen. 1957-59, treas. 11th conf. 1959, co-chmn. jr. bar sect. 1963-65, mem council 1969—, exec. com. 1975—, pres. 1982-84, Diploma de Honor 1987, William Roy Vallance award 1989), Spanish Am. Bar Assn., Fla. Bar Assn. (vice chmn. adminstrv. law com. 1965, vice chmn. internat. and comparative law com. 1967-68, chmn. aero. law com. 1968-69), Dade County Bar Assn. (chmn. fgn. laws and langs com. 1964-65), Internat. Ctr. Fla. (World Trade Ctr., pres. 1981-82), World Peace Through Law Ctr., Miami Com. Fgn. Relations, Inst. Ibero Am. Derecho Aero., Am. Soc. Internat. Law, Council Internat. Visitors, Am. Fgn. Law Assn. (pres. Miami 1958), Bar of South Korea (hon. mem.), Greater Miami C. of C. (bd. govs. 1986—), Colombian-Am. C. of C. (bd. dirs. 1986—), Peruvian-Am. C. of C. (bd. dirs.), Norwegian Am. C. of C. (bd. dirs.), Phi Alpha Delta. Home: 605 Almeria Ave Coral Gables FL 33134-5602 Office: One SE Third Ave 28th Flr Miami FL 33131

LANDY, JOANNE VEIT, foreign policy analyst; b. Chgo., Oct. 15, 1941; d. Fritz and Lucille (Stearns) Veit; m. Seymour Landy, Mar., 1959 (div. 1962); m. Nelson Lichtenstein, Mar., 1972 (div. 1976). BA in History, U. Calif., Berkeley, 1968, MA in History, 1970; MPH, Columbia U., 1982. Dir. N.Y. Met. Office, U. Chgo., N.Y.C., 1977-80; pres. Campaign for Peace and Democracy, N.Y.C., 1982—; exec. dir. Physicians for a Nat. Health Program N.Y.C. Pub. Health Assn., 2000—, Pub. Health Assn., N.Y.C., 2000—; bd. dirs. Human Rights Watch, Helsinki; exec. dir. Physicians for Nat. Health Program N.Y.C.-Pub. Health Assn. N.Y.C. Editor: Peace and Democracy, 1984-1996; mem. editl. bd. New Politics, 1986—. Recipient grant for rsch. and writing John D. and Catherine T. Mac Arthur Fedn., Program on Peace and Internat. Cooperation, Chgo., 1990-91. Mem. Coun. on Fgn. Rels., Phi Beta Kappa. Home: 2785 Broadway Apt 7A New York NY 10025-2850

LANDY, LISA ANNE, lawyer; b. Miami, Fla., Apr. 20, 1963; d. Burton Aaron and Eleonora Maria (Simmel) L. BA, Brown U., 1985; JD cum laude, U. Miami, 1988. Bar: Fla. 1988, U.S. Dist. Ct. (so. dist.) Fla. 1988. Atty. Paul, Landy, Beiley & Harper, P.A., Miami, Fla., 1988-94; atty. Steel Hector & Davis, Miami, Fla., 1994-97, ptnr., 1996-97; ptnr. Akerman Senterfitt & Eidson P.A., Miami, 1997—. Bd. dirs. Miami City Ballet, 1992-97, pres., 1996; bd. dirs. Women in Internat. Trade, Miami, 1992—, pres., 1994; bd. dirs. Orgn. Women in Internat. Trade, 1994—, v.p., 1997, 98, pres. 1998-2000; bd. dirs. Women in Tech. Internat. South Fla, The Next Step Youth Cmty. Ctr., Inc. Mem. ABA, Inter-Am. Bar Assn. (asst. sec. 1997—). Avocations: sports, arts, fluent in Spanish, French.

LANDY, MARK DAVID, anesthesiologist, critical care specialist; b. Brisbane, Australia, Dec. 13, 1956; s. Pete James and Cecily Margaret (O'Connor) L.; m. Lisa Jon Torrens, Sept. 20, 1998; children: Liam, Patrick. MB, BS, U. Queensland, 1979. Anaesthetic registrar Royal Hallamshire Hosp., Sheffield, Eng., 1983-85, Royal Brisbane Hosp., 195-88; v.m.o. Ipswich (Australia) Hosp., 1989; staff anaesthetist Nambour (Australia) Gen. Hosp., 1990-94, staff intensivist, 1996—; sr. registrar intensive care unit Royal Brisbane Hosp., 1994-95. Contbr. articles to profl. jours. Fellow Australia-New Zealand Coll. of Anaesthesiologists, Faculty of Intensive Care of Australia-New Zealand, U. of Queensland Found.; mem. Australia Med. Assn., Australia Soc. Anaesthesiologists, Australian/New Zealand Intensive Care Soc. Office: Nambour Gen Hosp ICU, Dept Anaesthesia Hosp Rd, Nambour 4560, Australia

LANE, BARRY, professional golfer; b. Hayes, Eng., June 21, 1960; m. Stephanie Lane; children: Benjamin, Emma. Profl. golfer, 1976—; mem. European Ryder Cup Team, 1993, Dunhill Cup Team, 1988, 94, World Cup Team, 1988, 94. Winner Equity & Law Challenge, 1987, Jamaica Open, 1983, Bell's Scottish Open, 1988, Mercedes German Masters, 1992, Canon European Masters, 1993, Turespana Open de Baleares, 1994, Andersen Consulting World Championship, 1995. Avocation: cars. Office: IMG Pier House, Strand On The Green, Chiswick W4 3NN, England

LANE, DAVID GERALD, classics educator; b. Nasik, India, Sept. 1, 1942; s. Gerald Richard and Jessie Louise (Young) L. MA with honors, Cambridge U., 1968. Asst. tchr. King Edward VI Sch., Chelmsford, Eng., 1965-88; asst. tchr. Kamuzu Acad., Malawi, 1988-91, head of classics, 1991-97; housemaster Kamuzu Acad., 1989-91, choirmaster, 1989-97. Organist, choirmaster St. John the Baptist, Widford, Herts, 1962-74, St. Nicolas, Witham, Essex, 1974-84, St. Paul's Cathedral, Nicosia, 1998—. State scholarship Ministry of Edn., 1960, Seaman scholarship Corpus Christi Coll., 1960. Mem. Ch. of Eng. Avocations: music, philately, gardening, photography.

LANE, DOROTHY PERSON, nursing educator; b. Springfield, Tenn., Jan. 9, 1933; d. Robert Pearl and Sallie Mai (Griffin) Person; m. Fred. Leon Lane Jr., Aug. 29, 1958; children: Fred Leon III, Robert Person, Michael Wendell. BSN, Meharry Med. Coll., Nashville, 1955; MS in Health Adminstrn., Ctrl. Mich. U., 1988. Cert. HIV counselor. Staff nurse Hubbard Hosp., Nashville, 1955-56; staff nurse, asst. head nurse L.A. County Hosp., 1956-58; instr. Meharry Med. Coll., Nashville, 1958-61; staff nurse operating and emergency rm. St. Thomas Cath. Hosp., Nashville, 1961; staff nurse Murfresboro (Tenn.) Vets. Adminstrn. Psychiatric Hosp., 1961-62; staff nurse VA Med. Ctr. Bklyn., 1962-66, staff nurse in Kidney Dialysis Unit, 1981-88, nurse mgr. med. unit, 1988-89, headnurse med. unit, 1989, cmty. health nurse coord., 1989-92, instr. nursing, coord. career devel., 1992—; insvc. educator Bushwick Home and Hosp. for Aged, Bklyn., 1966; chair side asst., adminstrv. asst. Fred L. Lane Jr. D.D.S., Bklyn., 1966-79; nurse Beth Israel Hosp., N.Y.C., 1979-80; staff nurse Manhattan Kidney Ctr., N.Y.C., 1979-80; retired, 1995; pvt. bus./proprietor, Harper's Lane, Bklyn., 1980-82; adj. prof. nursing N.Y.C. Technol. Coll., 1990-91. Asst. ch. clk. Cornerstone Bapt. Ch., 1989—, instr., tchr. tng. Sunday sch., 1985—; pres. parent assn. Elem. Sch. PS 91, Bklyn., 1976, Stuyvesant High Sch., N.Y.C., 1978-79; mem. exec. com., founder/pres. Troy Ave.- Rutland Rd. Block Assn., 1978—; pres. Manhattan Fedn. H.S. Parents, N.Y.C. High Sch. Parent Assn. Pres., 1978-79; nat. pres. Hansel & Gretel Family Club, 1975-79. Recipient Dedicated Svc. award, Hansel & Gretel Club, 1977-79, cert. of Merit Cmty. Sch. Bd. Bkyn., 1975-76, Ptnrs. in Edn. award N.Y.C. Bd. edn., 1977, Courage award Region II Negro Airmen Internat., 1977, Jumbo award for highest financial contrib. Bklyn. Alumnea chpt. Delta Sigma Theta, Inc., 1985, Recognition award Bus. & Profl. Women's Club of Cornerstone Baptist Ch., Bklyn., 1992, Catherine Alexander Svc. award Bklyn. Alumnea chpt. Delta Sigma Theta, 1993, Religious & Humanitarian award Royal Progressive Club of CBC, Bklyn., 1995, Pres.'s award Meharry Med. Coll., 1955-1980, Bklyn. Veteran Adminstrn. Dir.'s Cert. of Recognition for Outstanding and Dedicated Svc. to the EEO Program, 1993. Mem. Am. Nephrology Nursing Assn. (exec. bd. Big Apple chpt. 1993-95, coun. jour.), Nat. Nephrology Nursing Assn., Nurses Orgn. VA (news reporter 1993-94), Delta Sigma Theta Inc. (Bklyn. alumnae chap.), 1955—. Avocations: reading, flying, needle craft, biking, traveling. Home: 540 Troy Ave Brooklyn NY 11203-1219 Office: VA Med Ctr Bklyn 800 Poly Pl Brooklyn NY 11209-7104

LANE, IAN FRANCIS, vascular surgeon, researcher; b. Birmingham, Eng., May 14, 1952; s. Frank Ernest and Teresa Ellen (Wallace) L.; m. Carol Myhill Morris, Mar. 29, 1980; children: Richard Nicholas, Rebecca Frances. BA, Oxford (Eng.) U., 1973, BM MCh, 1976, DM, 1987, MD, 1988. Intern U. Oxford, 1970-73; resident St. Thomas Hosp. Med. Sch., London, 1973-76; house surgeon St. Thomas' Hosp., London, 1976-77; demonstrator in physiology St. Thomas' Hosp. Med. Sch., London, 1978; resident surg. officer Brompton Hosp., London, 1979-80; lectr. in surgery Charing Cross and Westminster Med. Sch., London, 1982-88; cons. vascular surgeon U. Hosp. Wales, Cardiff, 1988—, clin. dir. surgery, 1993, assoc. med. dir., 1994-99, med. dir., 1999—. Contbr. articles to profl. jours. including Brit. Jour. Surgery, Varicose Vein Surgery; contbr. chpts. to books.; mem. internat. editl. bd. Jour. Vascular Investigation, 1995—. Recipient Finlandia prize Assn. Internat. Vascular Surgeons, Italy, 1987, King Edward VII Travelling award, London, 1988; rsch. grantee Brit. Heart Found., 1995. Fellow Royal Coll. Surgeons Eng., Assn. Surgeons Gt. Britain and Ireland, Royal Soc. Medicine (sec. steering com. venous forum 1996—, sec. 2000—); mem. Vascular Soc. Gt. Britain and Ireland (mem. vascular adv. com. 1994—, mem. coun. 1999—). Avocations: fine art collecting, travel, golf. Office: U Hosp Wales, Dept Surgery, Cardiff CF14 4XW, Wales

LANE, MARGARET ANNA SMITH, real estate property manager, real estate developer; b. Aspinwall, Pa., Nov. 26, 1918; d. Max Charles and Mary Ann (Jones) Smith; m. Frank A. Lane Jr., Feb. 7, 1954; 1 child, Alan Michael. AB, UCLA, 1940; MS, U. So. Calif., 1949. Cert. secondary tchr., Calif. Demonstration and tng. tchr. UCLA and U. Calif., Northridge, 1948-74; pvt. practice Cottonwood, Ariz., 1975—; tchr. dept. chmn. L.A. City Schs., 1948-74; sec.-treas. Silver Hoof, Inc., Sedona, Stone Pine Gallery, Ltd., Sedona. Mem. Pi Gamma Mu. Avocations: Native American cultures, art. Home: PO Box 4289 West Sedona AZ 86340-4289

LANE, ROBERT EDWARDS, political scientist; b. Phila., Aug. 19, 1917; s. Robert Porter and Bess (Edwards) L.; m. Helen Sobol, Nov. 15, 1944; children: Robert Lawrence, Thomas Edwards. BS, Harvard Coll., 1939; PhD, Harvard U., 1950. Instr. to prof. polit. sci. Yale U., New Haven, 1948-85, prof. emeritus, 1985—. Author: Political Ideology, 1962, The Market Experience, 1991, The Loss of Happiness in Market Democracies, 2000; contbr. articles to profl. jours. Capt. USAAF, 1942-46. Fellow Ctr. for Advanced Study in Behavioral Scis., 1956-57, Woodrow Wilson Internat. Ctr., 1970-71, Fulbright-Hays scholar, 1972-73; Netherlands Inst. for Adv. Study fellow, 1982-83; Australian Nat. U. fellow, 1985. Fellow Brit. Acad.; mem. Am. Polit. Sci. Assn. (pres. 1970-71), Policy Studies Orgn. (pres. 1973), Internat. Soc. Polit. Psychology (pres. 1978-79). Democrat. E-mail: roberl.lane@yale.edu.

LANE, ROBIN, lawyer; b. Kerrville, Tex., Nov. 28 1947; d. Rowland and Gloria (Benson) Richards; m. Stanley Lane, Aug. 22, 1971 (div. 1979); m. Anthony W. Cunningham, Nov. 22, 1980; children: Joshua Lane, Alexandra Cunningham. BA with honors in Econs., U. Fla., 1969; MA, George Washington U., 1971; JD, Stetson U. Coll. Law, 1978. Bar: Fla. 1979, U.S. Ct. Appeals (11th cir.) 1981, U.S. Supreme Ct. 1986, U.S. Ct. Appeals (D.C. cir.) 1992, U.S. Ct. Appeals (3rd cir.) N.Y. 1993. Mgmt. trainee internat. banking Gulf Western Industries, N.Y.C.; internat. rsch. specialist Ryder Systems, Inc., Miami, Fla., 1973, project mgr., 1974; assoc. Wagner, Cunningham, Vaughan & McLaughlin, Tampa, Fla., 1979-85; pvt. practice law, 1985—; guest lectr. med. jurisprudence Stetson U. Coll. Law, 1982-91, also mem. exec. coun. law alumni bd. Contbr. articles to various revs. Recipient Am. Jurisprudence award-torts Lawyers Co-op. Fla., 1979; Scottish Rite fellow, 1968-69. Mem. ABA, Acad. Fla. Trial Lawyers (mem. com. 1983-84), Assn. Trial Lawyers Am., Fla. Bar Assn., Fla. Women's Alliance, Omicron Delta Epsilon. Home: 4934 Saint Croix Dr Tampa FL 33629-4831 Office: PO Box 10155 Tampa FL 33679-0155

LANE, ROSALIE MIDDLETON, extension educator; b. Savannah, Ga.; d. Freddie and Willie Blanche (Jones) Middleton; m. Martin Luther Jones, Apr. 24, 1964 (div. July 1977); children: Regina Veronica, Sharon Yolanda; m. Woodie Lane, Sr., Dec. 6, 1985; 1 stepchild, Woodie M., Jr. BA, Western Mich. U., 1989; M in Urban and Regional Planning, Ala. A&M U., 1995. Exec. sec. Curtis Brown, Ltd., N.Y.C., 1959-64; adminstrv. sec. Bronx (N.Y.)-Lebanon Hosp. Ctr., 1971-76; adminstr. IBM Corp., Savannah, Ga. and Huntsville, Ala., 1980-95; extension educator, rschr. educator Ala. Cooperative Extension Sys., Ala. A&M U., Normal, 1995—; past mem. customer interface task force USDA, Washington. Author: (with others) A Directory of Resource for Low Income, Elderly, and Homeless Citizens in North Ala., 1995; author poems. Vol. Coalition/On- At-Risk Minority Males, Huntsville, Ala., 1992; bd. dirs. ARC Minority Initiatives Com., Huntsville, 1994. Mem. NEA, Am. Planning Assn., Com. Minorities in Pub. Transp. Orgn., Alpha Zeta. Presbyterian. Avocations: creative writing, song writing. Office: Ala Cooperative Extension Sys Meridian St Normal AL 35762

LANE, RUSSELL J.M., neurologist, researcher; b. London, May 27, 1949; s. John William and Christine Ruth (Morley) L.; children: Rebecca Louise, Anna Victoria. BS, U. Newcastle upon Tyne (Eng.), 1970, MBBS, 1973, MD, 1984. Accreditation in Neurology, Joint Com. Higher Med. Tng., 1983. House officer Royal Victoria Infirmary, Newcastle upon Tyne, Eng., 1973-74; sr. house officer Newcastle (Eng.) Gen. Hosp., 1974-76; rsch. fellow muscular dystrophy group Gt. Britain Muscular Dystrophy Assn., 1976-78; rsch. fellow, sr. resident in neurology Duke U., 1978-80; Wellcome sr. rsch. fellow clin. scis. Newcastle and Liverpool, Eng., 1980-86; sr. registrar neurology Charing Cross Hosp., London, 1986-89, cons., hon. sr. lectr., 1989—. Editor: Handbook of Muscle Disease, 1996; contbr. articles to med. jours. Fellow Royal Coll. Physicians, Royal Soc. Medicine (hon. sec. sect. neurology 1996-97, hon. treas. 1997—); mem. Assn. Brit. Neurologists. Avocations: piano, guitar, squash, tennis, golf. Office: Charing Cross Hosp Neurosci, Fulham Palace Rd, London W6 8RF, England

LANE, SIMON JOHN, wildlife biologist, researcher; b. Bridport, Eng., May 14, 1967; s. Gerald Peter Foyle and Junita (Ruff) L.; m. Patricia Vazquez-Bahamonde, Sept. 21, 1996. BS, U. Wales, Aberystwyth, 1989; PhD in Ecology, U. East Anglia, Eng., 1994. Rsch. assoc. U. East Anglia, Norwich, Eng., 1989-94; postdoctoral rsch. fellow Nat. Agr. Rsch. Ctr., Tsukuba, Japan, 1994-96, U. Tokyo, 1996-97, Nat. Mus. Natural Scis., Madrid, Spain, 1997-99, U. Newcastle, Australia, 1999—. Contbr. articles to profl. jours. Recipient Marie Curie Postdoctoral Rsch. Tng. grant European Commn., Madrid, 1997-99. Office: Sch of Biol/Chem Scis, Univ Newcastle/Dis Biol Sci, Callaghan NSW 2308, Australia

LANES, ROBERTO L., pediatric endocrinologist, educator; b. Caracas, Venezuela; s. Imre Ianes and Marianne Eylenburg; m. Gloria Gomez, Nov. 8, 1974; children: Anabela, David, Isabela. MD, U. Cen. Venezuela, Caracas, 1973; pediatrician, Beth Israel Med. Ctr., N.Y., 1976; pediat. endocrinologist, Johns Hopkins Med. Ctr., Balt., 1978. Cert. in medicine, Md., N.Y., Venezuela. Attending pediat. endocrinologist Hosp. Cen. Dr. Carlos Arvelo, Caracas, 1979-82, 85-90; attending full-time pediat. endocri-

nologist North Shore Univ. Hosp., N.Y.C., 1982-84; asst. prof. pediats. Cornell Med. Ctr., N.Y.C., 1982-84; full-time staff pediat. endocrinologist Hosp. Clinicas Caracas, 1985-99; prof. postgrad. pediats. and pediat. endocrinology U. Cen. Venezuela, Caracas, 1979-99. Contbr. chpts. to books on pediat. endocrinology, also articles to med. jours. Fellow Am. Acad. Pediat.; mem. Endocrine Soc., Lawson Wilkins Pediat. Endocrine Soc., Venezuelan Endocrine Soc. (sec. 1989-91, pres. 1991-93). Office: Hosp Clinicas Caracas, Ave Panteon San Bernardino, Caracas Venezuela

LANEY, JAMES THOMAS, former ambassador, educator; b. Wilson, Ark., Dec. 24, 1927; s. Thomas Mann and Mary (Hughey) L.; m. Berta Joan Radford, Dec. 20, 1949; children: Berta Joan Vaughan, James T., Arthur Radford, Mary Ruth Laney Reilly, Susan Elizabeth Castle. BA, Yale U., 1950, BD, 1954, PhD, 1966; DD (hon.), Fla. So. Coll., 1977; LHD (hon.), Rhodes Coll., 1979; HHD (hon.), Mercer U., 1980; LLD (hon.), DePauw U., 1985; DD (hon.), Wofford Coll., 1986; LHD (hon.), Millsaps Coll., 1988, Austin Coll., 1990, W.Va. Wesleyan Coll., 1990, Yale U., 1993; DD (hon.), Emory U., 1994; LLD (hon.), U. St. Andrews, Scotland, 1994, Alaska Pacific U., 1994; DD (hon.), Yonsei U., Korea, 1997; LHD (hon.), U. S.C., 1997, Queens Coll., 1998; D in Internat. Affairs, Am. U., 1998; LLD (hon.), Piedmont Coll., 1999; DD (hon.), Kwansei Gakuin U., Japan, 2000; LHD (hon.), LaGrange Coll., 2000. Chaplain Choate Sch., Wallingford, Conn., 1953-55; ordained to ministry Meth. Ch., 1955; asst. lectr. Yale Div. Sch., 1954-55; pastor St. Paul Meth. Ch., Cin., 1955-58; sec. student Christian movement, prof. Yonsei U., Seoul, Korea, 1959-64; asst. prof. Christian ethics Vanderbilt U. Div. Sch., 1966-69; dean Candler Sch. Theology, Emory U., 1969-77, pres. univ., 1977-93; U.S. amb. to Republic of Korea, 1993-97; vis. prof. Harvard Div. Sch., 1974. Author: The Education of the Heart, 1994; (with J.M. Gustafson) On Being Responsible, 1968; author essays. Pres. Nashville Cmty. Rels. Coun., 1966-69; mem. Yale Coun. Com., 1972-77; bd. dirs. Fund Theol. Edn.; chmn. United Bd. Christian Higher Edn. in Asia, 1990-93; bd. dirs. Atlanta Symphony, 1979-91; chmn. bd. overseers com. to visit Harvard Div. Sch., 1980-85; mem. Yale U. Coun. Exec. Com., 1990-93; mem. Carnegie Endowment Nat. Commn. on Am. and the New World; mem. adv. com. Atlanta Project; chmn. so. dist. Rhodes Scholarship Com., 1980-90; bd. dirs. Atlantic Coun., 1987-93. With AUS, 1946-48; mem. tercentenary steering com. Yale U., 1998—. Selected for Leadership Atlanta, 1970-71; recipient Disting. Alumnus award Yale U. Div. Sch., 1979, 93, Kellogg award for leadership in higher edn., 1983, Wilbur Cross medal Yale Grad. Sch., 1996, James Van Fleet award, Korean Soc., 1996, Kangwa medal for disting. diplomatic svc., Rep. Korea, 1997, Dept. Defense medal for disting. pub. svc., U.S. Govt., 1997, 1st Internat. Human Rights award Inst. Human Rights, Korea, 1998; D.C. Macintosh fellow Yale U., 1965-66. Mem. Am. Soc. Christian Ethics, Soc. for Values Higher Edn. (pres. 1987-91), Coun. on Fgn. Rels. (co-chair task force on Korean Peninsula 1997—), Pilgrim Soc., Atlanta C. of C., Commerce Club, Phi Beta Kappa, Omicron Delta Kappa. Office: Emory U Pres Emeritus 1462 Clifton Rd NE Ste 302 Atlanta GA 30322-1000

LANG, BOHUMIR ALFONS, molecular biologist, researcher; b. Vyškov, Moravia, Czechoslovakia, Oct. 19, 1924; s. František and Marie (Rosnerová) L.; m. Jarmila Vyškovská, July 3, 1948; children: Blanka, Helena, Petr. MD, Palacky U., Olomouc, Czech Republic, 1950, PhD, 1964. House officer Polio Rehab. Inst., Velké Losiny, Czech Republic, 1950-54, Tchg. Hosp., Clinic of Neurology, Olomouc, 1955-56; asst. prof. Inst. Med. Chemistry, Olomouc, 1957-68; head clin. biochemistry dept. Brno, Czech Republic, 1969-76; head clin. biochem. dept. Masaryk Meml. Cancer Inst., Brno, 1977-86, rschr., 1987—; prof. Palacky U., Olomouc, 1993—; sci. coun. med. faculty, Olomouc, 1990-99; med. faculty Cons. Inst. Chemistry, Olomouc, 1996—. Co-author: Medical Faculty Textbook, 1975; editor Vnitřní Lékařství, 1969-90, Dialog-Evropa XXI. Pres. Moravian-Silesian Christian Acad., Brno, 1990-99, hon. pres., 2000—. Mem. Czechoslovak Med. Soc. J. E. Purkyně (Deyl prize 1968), Internat. Soc. Neurochemistry, Internat. Soc. Oncodevel. Biology and Medicine, Internat. Union Biochemistry and Molecular Biology, Fed. European Biochem. Soc. Office: Masaryk Meml Cancer Inst, Zluty kopec 7, 656 53 Brno Moravia, Czech Republic

LANG, CHRISTOPHER ANTHONY, irrigation company executive; b. Kabwe, Zambia, Africa, Mar. 6, 1947; arrived in South Africa, 1952; s. Harold James and Eleanor Mable (Opie) L.; m. Kathryn Arnott Cullen, Sept. 1, 1972; children: Bradley James, Janine Kathryn. Matriculation, Oxford Coll., Johannesburg, South Africa, 1965; diploma in Agr., Cedara Agrl. Coll., South Africa, 1970. Ins. clk. Guardian Assce Co., Durban, South Africa, 1960-68; farmer Underberg, South Africa, 1968-69; field officer South Africa Sugar Assn., Durban, 1972-73; agronomist Ubombo Ranches, Swaziland, 1973-82; gen. mgr. Sod Farm, Johannesburg, South Africa, 1982-83; co. dir. Barstone Irrigation Systems, Johannesburg, South Africa, 1983—; bd. dirs. Pine Lake Share Block, Joahannesburg. Contbr. articles to S.A. Sugar Technologists Ann. Congress, 1976, 78. Mem. Turf Irrigation Assn., Internat. Irrigatoin Assn., Royal Johannesburg Golf Club (Hole-in-One award 1975, 94). Avocations: golfing, tennis, squash, spear fishing angling. Office: Barstone Irrigation Sys Ltd, PO Box 6455, Dunswart 1508, South Africa

LANG, DANNY ROBERT, municipal development official; b. St. Louis, June 4, 1955; s. George Robert and V. Arlene (Underwood) L.; m. Diane Marie Martin, Aug. 14, 1976; children: Douglas Gerald, Derek Robert, Darin Kenneth. BS, U. Mo., 1977. Dir. lakes and pks. Lake Saint Louis (Mo.) Cmty. Assn., 1977-80; environ. planner Harland Bartholomew & Assoc., St. Louis, 1980-81, Booker & Assocs., St. Louis, 1981-87; dir. cmty. devel. City of St. Peters, Mo., 1987-95, dir. city devel., 1995—. Dir. deanery planning St. Charles Deanery-St. Louis Archdiocese. Recipient Eagle Scout Boy Scouts Am., 1972. Mem. Am. Planning Assn. (past pres. Mo. chpt. 1992-97, Excellence in Planning awards 1985, 87, 91, 96), Mo. Tax Increment Fin. Assn. (bd. dirs. 1995-97). Roman Catholic. Avocations: coaching little league baseball, stamp collecting. Office: City of St Charles 200 N 2nd St Saint Charles MO 63301-2851

LANG, ERHARD WOLFGANG, physician; b. Giessen, Hessia, Germany, 1964; s. Wolfgang F. and Isolde H. (Gabelick) L.; m. Karen Scheuermann, Sept. 15, 1995; children: Eva, Franziska. MD, Philipps U., Marburg, Germany, 1993, Julius Maximilians U., Wuerzburg, Germany, 1994. Intern Heidelberg/Mannheim (Germany) U., 1992-93; fellow dept. neurosurgery U. Calif. San Diego & San Francisco, 1993-95; resident in neurosurgery Christian Albrechts U., Kiel, Germany, 1995—; cons. DWL Electronics, Inc., GMS Inc., Germany. Contbr. articles to profl. jours. With German mil., 1984-85. Recipient Chemistry Merit award U. Mont., 1982, Rsch. fellow Dept. Neurosurgery at U. Calif. San Diego & The Brain Trauma Found., N.Y.C., 1993-95, Deutsche Forschungsgemeinschaft, Bonn, Germany, 1994-95, 97-2000. Mem. German Assn. of Neurosurgery (jr.). Avocations: dressage riding, skiing, sailing. Office: Christian Albrechts U Dept, Neurosur Weimarer Strasse 8, D-24106 Kiel Germany

LANG, ERIN H., internist, oncologist, hematologist, geriatrician; b. Republic of China, Sept. 13, 1956. MD, Coll. Medicine Nat. Taiwan U., Taipei, 1981. Diplomate Am. Bd. Internal Medicine, Am. Bd. Oncology, Am. Bd. Geriat. Medicine, Am. Bd. Hematology. Intern Brookdale Hosp. Med. Ctr., Bklyn., 1983-84, resident in internal medicine, 1984-86, fellow in hematology/oncology, 1986-87, 88-89; fellow in hematology/oncology St. Lukes-Roosevelt Hosp., N.Y.C., 1987-88; with Hoag Cancer Ctr., Newport Beach, Calif. Office: Hoag Cancer Ctr 4000 W Coast Hwy # 3E Newport Beach CA 92663-2695

LANG, EUGENE MICHAEL, retired technology development company executive; b. N.Y.C., Mar. 16, 1919; s. Daniel and Ida Lang; m. Theresa Volmar, Apr. 15, 1946; children: David A., Jane, Stephen. BA, Swarthmore Coll., 1938; MS, Columbia U., 1940; postgrad., Bklyn. Poly. Inst., 1941-42; LLD (hon.), Swarthmore Coll., 1981, St. Paul's Coll., 1987, Columbia U., 1988, SUNY, 1987, St. Michaels Coll., 1988; LHD (hon.), Coll. New Rochelle, 1986, Bank St. Coll., 1986, New Sch. Social Research, 1987, Trinity Coll., Hartford, Conn., 1988; Dr. Pub. Svc. (hon.), R.I. Coll., 1988, CUNY, 1989, Springfield Coll., Mass., 1989, Yale U., 1989, Hunter Coll., 1990, Hobart Coll., 1990, Glassboro State Coll., 1990; LHD (hon.), Bard Coll., 1991; LLD, Lawrence U., 1991, U. Mo., 1993; LHD (hon.), Whitman Coll., 1993; LHD, Goucher Coll., 1994. Works mgr. Aircraft Screw Products, Inc., N.Y.C., 1941-46; founder, pres. Clark Chem. Co., Long Island City, N.Y., 1946-48; co-founder, exec. v.p. Heli-Coil Corp. (now divsn. of Black & Decker), Danbury, Conn., 1948-52; founder, chmn. REFAC Technology Devel. Corp., N.Y.C., 1952-97, chmn. emeritus, dir., 1997—; sr. v.p., gen. counsel Barrett Resources Corp.; chmn. Electronic Rsch. Assn., Inc., Winsted, Conn., 1978-90; bd. dirs. other U S. and fgn. cos. Patentee. Contbr. articles on internat. bus., small bus. issues, technology transfer and venture capital projects to profl. pubs. Bus. chmn. Citizens for Humphrey-Muskie, N.Y., 1968; trustee, vice chmn. New Sch. Social Rsch., N.Y., 1978—; mng. dir. N.Y.C. Met. Opera Assn., 1978-93; bd. dirs. Columbia U. Grad. Sch. Bus., 1986—; adv. dir. Carnegie-Mellon Grad. Sch. Bus. Adminstrn., 1989—; dir. Mannes Coll. Music, 1989—; chmn. bd. dirs. Swarthmore Coll., Pa., 1981-88, emeritus, 1988—; chmn. Eugene M. Lang Found., "I Have A Dream" Found., emeritus, 1996—; founding donor Eugene Lang Coll., New Sch. Social Rsch.; founder "I Have A Dream" program minority student edn., 1981-96; donor Theresa Lang Children's Ambulatory Ctr. N.Y. Hosp.; guest and cultural honoree Gov. of India, 1996. Recipient George Washington award Am.-Hungarian Fedn., 1982, Community Service award Booth Meml. Med. Ctr., N.Y., 1980, Disting. Service for Trusteeship Assn. Governing Bds., Washington, 1985, Brotherhood award NCCJ, 1985, John Jay award Conf. Ind. Colls. and Univs. of N.Y. State, 1986, Booth award Vols. of Am., 1986 presdl. citations, 1979, 85, Family of Man award nat. Council of Chs., 1986, Hubert H. Humphrey Humanitarian award Nat. Urban Coalition, 1986, Jefferson award Am. Inst. Pub. Service, 1986, Martin Luther King medal of Freedom, N.Y. State, 1987, Human Rights award N.J. Ednl. Assn., 1987, Front Page award N.Y. Daily News, 1987, Leadership award Nat. Urban League, 1987, Carter Humanitarian award NAACP, 1987, Salute award U.S. C. of C., 1987, Horatio Alger award Horatio Alger Found., 1987, Pub. Service award P.R. Family Inst., 1988, Friend of Edn. award NEA, N.Y., 1988, Fisher Disting. Service to Edn. award Council for Advancement and Support of Edn., 1988, Disting. Leadership award United Negro Coll. Fund, 1988, Val-Kill award Eleanor Roosevelt Found., 1988, Finley medal CCNY Alumni Assn., 1988, Evangeline Booth award Salvation Army, 1988, CESPA award Elem. Sch. Prins. Assn., 1989, Meridian award Children's Mus. Indpls., 1989, medal of distinction Barnard Coll., 1989, Leadership award Boston Partnership in Edn., Robie award Jackie Robinson Found., 1990, Point of Light citation President George Bush, Pub. Svc. award Boston Dept. Pub. Edn., 1991, Drum Major award So. Christian Leadership Conf., 1991, Trail Blazer award Assn. Negro Bus. Women, 1991, Community Svc. award U.S. Dept. Justice, 1991, Dodge award YMCA, 1992, S. Henry Smith Pub. Svc. award Alfred U., 1992, Fgn. Trade Leadership award Charlotte World Trade Assn., 1992, Champion of Mentoring award Children's Crusade of R.I., Trustee's award Spelman Coll., 1993, Youth Svc. award Upward, Inc., Nat. Caring award, Recog. award Martin Luther King Com., Norman Vincent Peale award Norman Vincent Peale Fedn., 1994, Goodworks award Theaterworks USA, Botwinick prize Columbia U. Bus. Sch., 1995, Achievement in Edn. award McDonald's Corp., 1995, Excellence in Edn. award Pi Lambda Theta, 1995, The Presdl. Medal Freedom President Bill Clinton, 1996; torch bearer 1996 Olympic Games. Mem. Licensing Exec. Soc., Univ. Club, Century Club, Yale Club, Golden Key (hon. mem. Baruch Coll. chpt.). Home: 912 5th Ave New York NY 10021-4159 Office: REFAC Technology Devel Corp 122 E 42nd St New York NY 10168-0002 Office: Tower 3 Ste 1000 1515 Arapahoe St Denver CO 80202*

LANG, FRIEDER R., psychologist, researcher; b. Constance, Germany, Oct. 1, 1962; s. Gerhard and Ursula (Oberdorfer) L.; m. Gudula Ostrop, July 10, 1998; 1 child, Clarissa A. MA, Tech. U., Berlin, 1990; PhD, Free U. Berlin, 1993. Rsch., tchg. asst. Tech. U., Berlin, 1986-90; pre-doctoral fellow MaxPlanck Inst., Berlin, 1990-93; post-doctoral fellow MaxPlanck Inst., 1993-94; visiting scholar Stanford U., Palo Alto, Calif., 1996; rsch. sci. Free U., Berlin, 1994-99; asst. prof. Humboldt U., Berlin, 1999—. Author: (in German) Managing Support in Old Age, 1994, Psycology & Aging, 1994, 97; contbr. articles to profl. jours. Recipient group award German Soc. Gerontopsychiatry and Psychology, 1997. Mem. APA, German Soc. Psychology, Gerontol. Soc. Am., Internat. NEtwork Personal Relationships, Internat. Soc. Study Personal Relationships. Office: Humboldt Univ, Geschwister-Scholl Str 7, 10099 Berlin Germany

LANG, GORDON, JR., retired lawyer; b. Evanston, Ill., July 27, 1933; s. Gordon and Harriet Kendig Lang; m. Clara Bates Van Derzee, Sept. 26, 1970; children: Elizabeth K., Gordon III, Harriet B. BA, Yale U., 1954; MA in History, U. Ariz., 1958; LLB, Harvard U., 1960. Bar: Ill. 1960. Assoc. Gardner, Carton & Douglas, Chgo., 1960-67, ptnr., 1967-98, ret., 1998; cons., 1999—. Dir. North Side Boys' Clubs, Chgo., 1961-67, Yale Scholarship Trust Ill., 1966-69, pres., 1967; mem. Assocs. Rush-Presbyn.-St. Luke's Med. Ctr., Chgo., 1962—, Assocs. Northwestern U., Evanston, 1970—; dir. Chgo. Youth Ctrs., 1967—, pres., 1982-84; trustee Chgo. Latin Sch. Found., 1978—, pres., 1995—; trustee Groton (Mass.) Sch., 1982-93; dir. United Way of Chgo., 1984-90, United Way/Crusade of Mercy (Met. Chgo.), 1989-95. 1st lt. USAF, 1955-57. Mem. ABA (sect. bus. law), Ill. State Bar Assn., Chgo. Bar Assn. (mem. corp. law com. 1975-98, mem. fin. instns. com. 1985-98), Chgo. Club (former dir. and sec.), Econ. Club Chgo. (former dir. and sec.), Onwentsia Club, Racquet Club Chgo., Chgo. Commonwealth Club, Yale Club Chgo. (former dir., past pres.). Republican. Episcopalian. Avocations: golf, skiing, hiking. E-mail: glang@gcd.com. Home: 1520 N Astor St Chicago IL 60610-1610 Office: Gardner Carton & Douglas 321 N Clark St Ste 3400 Chicago IL 60610-4795

LANG, HEINRICH, chemist, educator; b. Baden-Württemberg, Germany, Mar. 20, 1956; s. Ewald Stephan and Elisabeth (Zimmermann) L.; m. S. Ahrens; 1 child, Florian Jan. Arbitur, Technisches Gymnasium, Ravensburg, Germany, 1976; PhD, U. Konstanz, Germany, 1985; postgrad., MIT, 1985-87; habilitation, U Heidelberg, Germany, 1992. Heisenberg grantee Deutsche Forschungsgemeinschaft, U. Heidelberg, 1992-96; prof. inorganic chemistry Tech. U. Chemnitz, Germany, 1996—; sec. Chemische Gesellschaft zu Heidelberg, 1990-91; vice dean faculty of sci. Tech. U. Chemitz, 1997-00, dean faculty of sci., 2000—. Contbr. over 180 articles to profl. jours., chpts. to books; 6 patents in field. Postdoctoral fellow Deutsche Forschungsgemeinschaft, 1985-86, Heisenberg fellow, 1992-96. Mem. Gesellschaft Deutscher Chemiker, Chemische Gesellschaft zu Heidelberg, Am. Chem. Soc., Gesellschaft der TU Chemmitz. Office: Tech U Inst Chemistry, Strasse der Nationen 62, 09111 Chemnitz Germany

LANG, JAMES RICHARD, education consultant; b. Cleve., Feb. 7, 1945; s. Francis H. and Rachel L. (Boyce) L.; m. Marilyn F. Hosken, July 1, 1967; children: Christopher Charles, James Walter. Salesman Stas. WOHI-AM/WRTS-FM, East Liverpool, Ohio, 1967-68; gen. mgr. Sta. WEIR-AM, Weirion, W.Va., 1969-76; v.p. sales Paperwork Systems, Inc., Bellingham, Wash., 1976-78; v.p. market devel. Sta. Bus. Systems div. Control Date Corp., Greenwich, Conn., 1978-85; mgr. Eaglestone div. Siber Hegner N.Am., Inc., Milford, Conn., 1986-89; dir. mktg. MacMillan/McGraw-Hill, Avon, Conn., 1990-93; pres. Imagination Works, Trumbull, 1993—. Served with USN, 1968-69. Recipient Outstanding Service to Community award Italian Sons and Dads Am., 1970. Mem. Instrument Soc. Am., Direct Mtkg. Assn., Jaycees (Cmty. Svc. award 1975), Internat. Brotherhood of Magicians, Rotary (pres. 1996-97, area rep. 1997-98, asst. gov. dist. 7980 1999—, Man of Yr. 1975, Paul Harris fellow dist. 7980), Fellowship of Rotary Magicians. Methodist. Office: Imagination Works 24 Primrose Dr Trumbull CT 06611-5043

LANG, JOHN JOSEPH, systems engineer, program manager; b. Franklin, Pa., Feb. 24, 1960; s. Robert Andrew and Mary Jane (Wensel) L. BSEE, Marquette U., 1982; MBA, Pepperdine U., 1987. Cert. Project Mgmt. Profl., Project Mgmt. Inst. Mem. tech. staff Hughes Aircraft Co., Fullerton, Calif., 1982-85, sr. project engr., 1991-94; field team leader, test dir. Hughes Aircraft Co., Anaheim Hills, Calif., 1985-88, tech. supr., project engr., 1989-90; project mgr. Hughes Info. Tech. Systems, Riyadh, Saudi Arabia, 1994-97; mgr. engring. programs Raytheon Systems Co., Riyadh, 1997-99; dir. Cambridge Technology Ptnrs., Phoenix, 1999—. Contbr. articles to mags. and profl. jours. Active Am. Cmty. Svcs., Riyadh, 1994-99. Sch. of Bus. and Mgmt. scholar Pepperdine U., 1986. Mem. IEEE, NARAS, N.Y. Acad. Scis., Engring. Mgmt. Soc. (body of knowledge com. 1998-99), Project Mgmt. Inst. Avocations: music, nanotechnology. Office: Cambridge Tech Ptnrs 2425 E Camelback Rd Ste 450 Phoenix AZ 85016-4236

LANG, JOSEPH HAGEDORN, lawyer; b. Cleve., Sept. 30, 1937; s. Carl Frederick and Martha Clotilda (Hagedorn) L.; m. Elsie A. O'Berry, Aug. 8, 1965; children: Joseph H. Jr., Robert Warren, James O'Berry. AA, St. Petersburg Jr. Coll., 1959; BA, Duke U., 1961; JD, U. Fla., 1963. Bar: Fla. 1964, U.S. Dist. Ct. (mid. dist.) Fla. 1965, U.S. Ct. Appeals (5th cir.) 1965, U.S. Supreme Ct. 1975. Assoc. Baynard McLeod & Overton, St. Petersburg, Fla., 1964-69; ptnr. Baynard McLeod & Lang, St. Petersburg, 1969-80; pres. Baynard McLeod & Lang, P.C., St. Petersburg, 1980—. Active Police Cmty. Coun., Cmty. Alliance; chmn. bd. dirs. St. Petersburg Jr. Coll., Pinellas County, 1983—, trustee, 1977-97, chmn., 1982-89, 92-96, chmn. emeritus, 1997—; mem. State Bd. C.C.'s, 1997, vice chmn. 1998-99, chmn., 1999—; vice chmn. Pinellas County Workforce Devel. Bd., 1997-99, sec., 1999—; bd. dirs. Am. Heart Assn. Pinellas Country divsn., 1997—. Named Sch. Adv. Com. Mem. of Yr.; recipient Trustee of Yr. award Fla. Assn. Cmty. Coll., 1993, Bob Graham C.C. Disting. Svc. award, 1994, Trustee Leadership award So. Region, ACCT, 1994, Alumni award St. Petersburg Jr. Coll., 1990. Mem. Fla. Bar Assn., St. Petersburg Bar Assn., St. Petersburg C. of C. (Outstanding Mem. award 1990), Suncoasters Club, Dragon Club, Phi Theta Kappa (Disting. Alumni award 1978). Democrat. Roman Catholic. Office: Baynard McLeod & Lang 669 1st Ave N Saint Petersburg FL 33701-3696

LANG, LOTHAR A., engineer; b. Aschaffenburg, Germany, Feb. 13, 1959; s. Horst and Marianne (Ziegler) L.; m. Judith K. Pfeifroth, July 12, 1985; children: Matthias, Thomas, Christina. BS in Chem. Engring., U. Minn., 1983; Diploma in Chem. Engring., Tech. U. Karlsruhe, 1985; PhD in Chem. Engring., U. Stuttgart, Germany, 1991. Process engr. in cen. R&D tech. Bayer AG, Leverkusen, Germany, 1990-95, prodn. and plant mgr. in silicone base production, 1995-98, head advanced process control, 1998—; adv. bd. PMC Utrecht, Netherlands, 1996-97. Author publs. in field. Finalist Computerworld-Smithsonian, 1995. Mem. Verein Deutscher Ingenieure. Roman Catholic. Avocations: sports, family, travel. Office: Bayer AG, Bldg E41, Leverkusen 51368, Germany

LANGBACKA, RALF RUNAR, theater director, educator, manager; b. Närpes, Finland, Nov. 20, 1932; s. Runar Emanuel and Hulda Emilia (Backlund) L.; m. Birgitta Runa Danielsson, Nov. 5, 1961; children: Thomas, Mats, Nina. MA, Abo Akademi, Turku, Finland, 1956. Artistic dir. Swedish Theatre, Turku, 1960-63; dir. Finnish Nat. Theatre, Helsinki, 1963-65; artistic dir. Swedish Theatre, Helsinki, 1965-67, Turku City Theatre, 1971-77; prof. arts Helsinki, 1979-83, 88-93; mng. dir. Helsinki City Theatre, 1983-87; vis. prof. theatre sci. Abo Akademi, Turku, 1994-97; freelance dir. Finland, Denmark, Germany, Sweden and Norway, 1967-71, 77-83, 88—; mem. State Drama Commn., 1967-70. Author: Teatterikirja (Theatre Book), 1977, Bland annat om Brecht (On Brecht and Others), 1982, rev. edit., 1983, Möten med Tjechov (Meetings with Chekhov), 1986, Denna langa dag, detta korta liv, dikter (This Long Day, This Short Life, poems), 1988, (play) Krocketspelaren (The Croquetplayer), 1990, (play) Olga, Irina och jag (Olga, Irina and I), 1991, Brecht and the Realistic Theatre, 1998; also articles on theatre and lit. Recipient Critics Spurs award Finnish Critics Assn., 1963, Pro Finlandia medal, Order Finnish White Rose, 1973, Henrik Steffens award, 1994; named Prof. of Arts, 1979-84, 88-93, The Finland prize Swedish Acad., 1999. Mem. Finnish Theatre Dirs. Assn. (chmn. 1979-83), Internat. Theatre Inst. (exec. com. 1991-95), Finnish Ctr. Internat. Theatre Inst. (pres. 1983-96). Socialist. Home: Hopeasalmenranta 1B, 00570 Helsinki Finland

LANGBORT, POLLY, retired advertising executive; b. N.Y.C.; d. Julius and Nettie (Berman) L. BA, Adelphi U. Sec. Young & Rubicam, Inc., N.Y.C., media buyer, media planner, 1960-65, planning supr., 1965-70, v.p. group supr., 1970-75, v.p. dir. planning devel., 1975-80, sr. v.p., dir. planning, 1980-85, sr. v.p. direct mktg. and media services Wunderman, Worldwide div., 1985-86, exec. v.p. dir. mktg. & media services, 1986-90; assoc. pub. Lear's Mag., N.Y.C., 1990-91; ret., 1991. Author: DMA Factbook, 1986; contbr. articles to profl. jours. Spl. gifts chairperson Am. Cancer Soc., N.Y.C., 1985-90. Mem. Boca Raton Resort and Club, Boca Pointe Country Club. Avocations: classical music, outdoor activities. Home: 7614 La Corniche Cir Boca Raton FL 33433-6055

LANGDON, SIMON PETER, biologist; b. Chatham, Kent, England, Apr. 2, 1957; s. Reginald Earnest and Jean (Clout) L.; m. Laura Elizabeth Longmuir; 1 child, Sarah Fiona. BA, Oxford U., 1979, MA, 1985; PhD, Aston U., 1983. Staff scientist Imperial Cancer Rsch. Fund/Med. Oncology Unit, Edinburgh, Scotland, 1989—. Editor: (book) Biology of Female Cancers, 1997. NCI rsch. fellow Jules Bordet Inst., Brussels, 1980. Mem. British Assn. for Cancer Rsch., Am. Assn. for Cancer Rsch. Avocation: athletics. Office: ICRF Med Oncology Unit, Western General Hospital, Edinburgh EH4 2XU, Scotland

LANGE, DANIEL H., electronic engineer, researcher; b. Haifa, Israel, May 26, 1966; s. shimon and Ziva (Fiterman) L.; m. Sigal Hotter, Aug. 29, 1989; children: Tomer, Kfir, Maayan. BSc in Elec. Engring., Technion, Haifa, 1989, MSc in Elec. Engring., 1994, ScD in Elec. Engring., 1998. Tchg. asst. Technion, Haifa, 1992-98, rsch. asst., 1994-98, rsch. assoc. in elec. engring., 1998-99. Gutwirth fellow, 1997. Mem. IEEE, Engring. Medicine and Biology Soc. Avocations: science fiction, basketball. Home: Efroni 31 POB 939, Kfar Vradim 25147, Israel Office: HP Labs, Isreal Technion IIT, Haifa 32000, Israel

LANGE, DIANA ISABELL VASHTI, consultant physician psychiatry and public health; b. Sydney, Australia, Dec. 22, 1942; d. Matthew Morrison and Joyce Vashti (Burrell) Williams; m. Stephen John Lange (div. 1984); children: Owen Christopher, Timothy Stephen, Peter Warwick. A., Trinity Coll. Music, London, 1963; MB, B.Surgery, U. Queensland, Australia, 1968; B.Sc., U. Queensland, 1971; M in Health Planning, U. NSW, Australia, 1984. Staff specialist Hornsby Hosp., 1976-78; cons. psychiatrist Westmead Hosp., 1978-81; med. supt. Mt. Druitt Hosp., NSW, 1981-84; dep. dir. med. svcs. Royal Newcastle Hosp., 1984-89; CEO Mater Misericordiae Hosp., Newcastle, 1989-91; chief health officer Queensland Health, 1991-99; cons. vis. psychiatrist regional forensic mental health svc. The Mason Clinic, New Zealand, 2000; chair Queensland Inst. Med. Rsch. Coun., 1991-96. Mem., exec. Nat. Health and Med. Rsch. Coun., Australia, 1997-99. Fellow Royal Australian and New Zealand Coll. Psychiatry, Royal Australanian Coll. Physicians (faculty pub. health medicine), Royal Australian Coll. Med. Adminstrs., Health Svc. Execs. (assoc. 1985—), Vis. Clin. fellow; mem Med. Bd. Queensland (pres. 1991-97), Assn. Med. Supts. (pres.), Nat. Mental Health Promotion and Prevention Com. (founding mem. 1997—), Zonta Internat., Queensland Medico-Legal Soc., Pub. Health Assn. Australia (Elkington Orator 1996), Health Assn. (chmn.), Australian Med. Coun., Natural Pub. Health Partnership Group (founding mem. 1996-99). Fax: 61 (0) 7 33941558. E-mail: dilange@bigpond.com.

LANGE, FREDERICK EDWARD, JR., computer information systems architect; b. Johnstown, Pa., Oct. 21, 1946; s. Frederick Edward and Jean Louise (Huebner) L.; m. Karen Ann Mawson, Mar. 15, 1975; 1 child, Sharon Ann. BA in Social Scis., Cleve. State U., 1969, MA in Econs., 1978. Cert. secondary tchr., Ohio. Vol. Peace Corps, Liberia and Micronesia, 1969-73; tchr. Cleve. Pub. Schs., 1973-74; dir. Westside Inst. Tech., Cleve., 1974-81; systems analyst Case Western Res. U., Cleve., 1982-83; systems engr. Profl. Support, Inc., Brecksville, Ohio, 1983-91; analyst Setpoint, Brecksville, 1991-93; prin. cons. Cap Gemini Am., Beechwood, Ohio, 1994-96; sr. prin. cons. Oracle Corp., Cleve., 1996—; bd. dirs. Zoe, Inc., Cleve., Fast Refund Svc. Editor: Fuel Efficiency and Safety, 1979; contbr. Data Mgmt. Rev. Mem. Richmond Heights (Ohio) Civic League, 1986, Northeast Ohio Returned Vol. Assn. (Beyond War award 1987), Cleve., 1978—, Nat. Peace Corps Assn. Mem. Am. Econs. Assn., Data Processing Mgmt. Assn., Assn. Computing Machinery, Instument Soc. Am. (Dedicated Svc. award 1980), Javelin Class Assn. (fleet capt. 1982-83, sec. 1987-88, commodore 1989-91). Avocations: sailing, gardening, genealogy. Office: Oracle Corp 4850 Lindsey Ln Cleveland OH 44143-2928

LANGE, KLAUS, law educator; b. Dessau, Germany, Aug. 6, 1939; s. Max and Hildegard (Dittrich) L.; m. Angelika Wilkens, Dec. 18, 1970; children: Friederike, Moritz. Diploma-Volkswirt, U. Goettingen, 1965, dr. iur, 1967. Prof. U. Goettingen, 1974-75, U. Bochum, Germany, 1975-78, U. Giessen, Germany, 1978—; dean Law Sch. U., Giessen, 1983-84, v.p. 1989-91. Author: Die Organisation der Region, 1968 (Award), Verkehr und Oeffen-

tliches Recht, 1974, Das Weisungsrecht des Bundes in der Atomrechtlichen Auftragsverwaltung, 1990; editor: Giessener Abhandlungen zum Umweltrecht. Mem. Constitutional Ct. of Hessen, 1984, pres. 1996. Mem. Vereinigung der Deutschen Staatsrechtslehrer, Deutsche Sektion des Internat. Instituts fuer Verwaltungswissenschaften, Vereinigung fuer Rechtssoziologie. Office: Justus Liebig U Giessen, Hein-Heckroth-Strasse 5, D-35390 Giessen Germany

LANGE, MICHAEL CLEMENS ANTON, insurance company executive; b. Houston, May 7, 1963; arrived in England, 1989; married; 2 children. BBA, U. Tex., 1985; cert., N.Y. Inst. Fin., 1988, 89. Underwriter Chubb & Son, Houston, 1985-87; asst. mgr. N.Y. Chubb & Son, N.Y.C., 1987-89; U.K. country mgr. Chubb & Son, London, 1989-94; sr. v.p., head internat. bus. devel. ops. ACE Ltd., London, 1994-99; COO, bd. dirs. ACE European Markets Ltd.-ACE European Markets Reins. Ltd., Dublin, Ireland, 1997; COO, ACE Europe, Middle East and Africa, London, 1999—; mem. Inst. Dirs., London, 1994. Contbr. articles to profl. jours. Mem. Chartered Ins. Inst., City Forum, Harbour Club. Democrat. Avocations: golf, tennis, history.

LANGE, STEFAN FRIEDRICH, physician, researcher; b. Kaiserslautern, Rheinland, Germany, Sept. 22, 1962; s. Guenther and Helga (Dehne) L. Diploma in Medicine, U. Duesseldorf, Germany, 1989, MD, 1994. Rsch. fellow dept. internal medicine Cmty. Hosp. Wuppertal, Germany, 1983-93; intern Cmty. Hosp. Krefeld, Germany, 1988-89; rsch. fellow Ruhr U., Bochum, Germany, 1993-95, asst. prof., 1995—; organizer Congress, 1995. Author: Osteodemsitometrie, 1994. Office: Ruhr U. Bochum, Dept Med Info, Biomet & Epidemiology, 44780 Bochum Germany

LANGEL, ÜLO, biochemist, educator; b. Tartu, Estonia, Mar. 2, 1951; s. Leopold and Alla (Trei) L.; m. Ülle Meister, Aug. 22, 1980; 1 child, Tõnu. BSc, Tartu U., 1974, PhD, 1980; PhD, Tartu U., 1993. From jr. rschr. to lectr. Tartu U., 1974-87; vis. rrshr. Stockholm U., 1987-91, lectr., rschr., 1992-2000; assoc. prof. biochemistry Scripps Rsch. Inst., La Jolla, Calif., 2000—; vis. prof. Tartu U., 1995—. Fellow Internat. Neuropeptide Soc. U.S., N.Y. Acad. Scis. Office: Scripps Rsch Inst Dorris Neurol Rsch Ctr La Jolla CA 92037

LANGEN, KARL-JOSEF, nuclear medicine physician; b. Immerath, Germany, May 2, 1959. MD, U. Aachen, Germany, 1985; phys. nuc. medicine, U. Düsseldorf, Germany, 1989; prof. nuc. medicine, U. Düsseldorf, 1997. Asst. doctor nuc. medicine U. Düsseldorf, 1985-89; scientist, physician nuc. medicine Rsch. Ctr. Jülich, Germany, 1989—. Contbr. articles to profl. jours. Avocation: piano. E-mail: k.j.langen@fz-juelich.de. Fax: 0049 2461 612990. Office: Inst Medicine, Rsch Ctr Jülich, 52426 Jülich Germany

LANGENBECK, KONRAD, retired mechanical engineering educator; b. Leipzig, Saxony, Germany, Jan. 11, 1932; s. Bernhard and Margarete (Degen) L.; m. Annemarie Schloz, mar. 30, 1961; 1 child, Bernhard. Diploma Mech. Engring., Munich Coll. Technology, 1958, D Engring., 1966. Sr. rsch. asst. Lab. of Gears and Gearing Design/Munich Coll. Technology, 1958-66; chief of design and devel. Gears/Vehicles Axles Divsn. Rheinstahl Ag (now Thyssen Industrie AG), Muelheim-R./Kassel, Germany, 1966-72; tech. dir. BHS Works Sonthofen (now BHS Cin. Getriebetechnik), Germany, 1973-75; full prof. mech. engring. and machine design Dir. of Inst. Machine and Gearing Design/U. Stuttgart, Germany, 1975; ret., 1998; dean of the faculty Design and Prodn. Technology, U. Stuttgart, 1979-82; mem. bd. adminstrn., U. Stuttgart, 1984-96. Patentee in field; contbr. articles to profl. jours. Mem. Assn. German Engrs., Assn. Tribology Germany.

LANGENBERG, DONALD NEWTON, academic administrator, physicist; b. Devils Lake, N.D., Mar. 17, 1932; s. Ernest George and Fern (Newton) L.; m. Patricia Ann Warrington, June 20, 1953; children: Karen Kaye, Julia Ann, John Newton, Amy Paris. B.S., Iowa State U., 1953; M.S., UCLA, 1955; Ph.D. (NSF fellow), U. Calif. at Berkeley, 1959; D.Sc. (hon.), U. Pa., 1985, MA (hon.), 1971. Electronics engr. Hughes Research Labs., Culver City, Calif., 1953-55; acting instr. U. Calif. at Berkeley, 1958-59; mem. faculty U. Pa., Phila., 1960-83; prof. U. Pa., 1967-83; dir. Lab. for Research on Structure of Matter, 1972-74; vice provost for grad. studies and research, 1974-79; chancellor U. Ill.-Chgo., 1983-90, U. Md. System, Adelphi, 1990—; maitre de conference associe Ecole Normale Superieure, Paris, France, 1966-67; vis. prof. Calif. Inst. Tech., Pasadena, 1971; guest researcher Zentralinstitut für Tieftemperaturforschung der Bayerische Akademie der Wissenschaften and Technische Universität München, 1974; dep. dir. Nat. Sci. Found., 1980-82. Rschr., contbr. to publs. on solid state and low temperature physics including electronic band structure in metals and semiconductors, quantum phase coherence and nonequilibrium effects in superconductors, sci. and edn. policy and rsch. adminstrn. Recipient John Price Wetherill medal Franklin Inst., 1975, Disting. Contribution to Research Adminstrn. award Soc. Research Adminstrs., 1983, Disting. Achievement Citation, Iowa State Alumni Assn., 1984, Significant Sig award Sigma Chi, 1985; fellow NSF, 1959-60, Alfred P. Sloan Found., 1962-64; Guggenheim Found., 1966-67. Fellow AAAS (pres. 1990), Am. Phys. Soc. (pres. 1993), Sigma Xi. Office: U System Md 3300 Metzerott Rd Adelphi MD 20783-1600

LANGENDORF, DIETER, printing company executive; b. Cologne, Germany, May 16, 1936; s. Fritz and Hildegard L.; m. Barbara (dec. 1988); m. Elisabeth; children: Bettina, Kirstin. Diploma, Tech. U. Berlin, 1961; MS, Stanford U., 1965. V.p. C.G. Brimelkorp, Chgo., 1966-69, Krupp Inst., Elmsford, N.Y., 1969-76; pres. Vloitl Transmission, Allendale, N.Y., 1976-89, BHS Printing Media, Balt., 1989—. Mem. Rotary. Avocation: sailing. e-mail: bhsprint@aol.com. Home: 7 Joel Ct Reisterstown MD 21136-5643 Office: BHS Printing Machinery 30 E Padonia Rd Lutherville Timonium MD 21093-2345

LANGENEGGER, OTTO, hydrogeologist, environmental engineer; b. Arbon, Switzerland, Apr. 22, 1938; s. Robert and Anna (Suhner) L.; m. Dorothea Kloss, June 24, 1967; children: Urs, Thomas. Diploma, Engring. Sch., Winterthur, Switzerland, 1964; PhD, U. Bern, Switzerland, 1973, Century U., Albuquerque, 1998. Hydrogeologist Christoffel Mission, Addis Ababa, Ethiopia, 1974-76; h.s. tchr. Gymnasium Untere Waid, Mörschwil, Switzerland, 1976-79; cons. Electrowatt Engring. Ltd., Accra, Ghana, 1979-81; project officer World Bank UN Devel. Program, Washington, 1981-82; regional project officer World Bank UN Devel. Program, Abidjan, Ivory Coast, 1983-88; lectr. Univ. Applied Scis., St. Gall, Switzerland, 1989—; pvt. practice Gais, Switzerland, 1989—; asst. U. Bern, 1971-72; rsch. asst. Axel Heiberg expdn., Can. Arctic, McGill U., Montreal, Que., 1968. Author: World Bank: GW Quality and Handpump Corrosion in West Africa, 1994; co-author: World Bank: Community Water Supply-The Handpump Option, 1987; contbr. articles to profl. jours. Mem. Am. Chem. Soc., Am. Water Works Assn., Internat. Assn. Hydrogeologists, Nat. Groundwater Assn., Swiss Soc. Engrs. and Architects, Assn. Groundwater Scientists and Engrs., Swiss Gas and Water Industry Assn., Swiss Acad. Natural Scis. Achievements include rsch. in impact of handpump corrosion on water quality, guidelines for application of galvanized equipment for handpumps, mapping of groundwater quality, mapping air pollution by means of snow samples. Home and Office: Roesslistrasse 23, CH-9056 Gais Switzerland

LANGENSCHEIDT, FLORIAN, publisher; b. Berlin, Mar. 7, 1955; s. Karl Ernst and Renate Tielebier-Langenscheidt; m. Gabriele Quandt. PhD, L.M. U., 1982; diploma, Harvard U., 1982; MBA, INSEAD, 1985. Editl. dir. Langenscheidt Pubs., N.Y.C., 1983-84; pub. Polyglott Pubs. Co., Munich, 1985-94, Humboldt Pubs. Co., Munich, 1985-94, Mentor Pub., Munich, 1985-94; co-pub. Baedeker Pubs. Co., 1985-94, APA Pubs. Co.; bd. dirs. Bibliographisches Inst. and F.A., Brockhaus AG, Mannheim, Germany; gen. mgr. Majestic Luftschiffahrtsgesellschaft mbH, Munich, 1987; mem. supr. bd. World-Wide Fund for Nature; chmn. study group initiative future Fed. Pres. Germany. Author: (novel) The Baby, 1975, (book) Glücksmomente, 1991, Wish I May, Wish I Might, 1993, Bei uns zu Hause, 1995, Glück mit Kindern, 1997, 100XMUT Beispielhaftes für das dritte Jahrtausend, 1999; contbr. articles on music and lit. to profl. publs.; dir. concerts. Bd. dirs. Atlantic Brücke, Bonn, Germany, 1990—, Artists for Nature, Munich, 1989—, Children for a Better World. Grantee Studienstiftung des deutschen Volkes, 1974. Mem. Verlegerausschuss of the Börsenverein des deutschen Buchhandels, Munchener Herrenclub. Office: Grüntal 16 3, D-81925 Munich Germany

LANGENWALTER, GARY ALLAN, manufacturing and management consulting company executive; b. Pendleton, Oreg., Jan. 11, 1946; s. Allan Charles and Florine Ruth (Brace) L.; m. Janet Ann Case, Aug. 5, 1972; children: Karl Case, Keith Allan. Diploma, NOIB, Breukelen, The Netherlands, 1966; BA in Mgmt., U. Oreg., 1967; MBA in Mgmt., Mich. State U., 1969. Cert. fellow in prodn. and inventory mgmt.; cert. in integrated resources mgmt. Programmer, analyst Arthur Andersen & Co., Detroit, 1969-72; project mgr. Burroughs Corp., Detroit and Radnor, Pa., 1972-78; mgr. MIS Faultless Caster, Evansville, Ind., 1978-82; mgr. trading ops. Christopher Funk & Co., Lafayette, Ind., 1982-83; mgr. mfg. cons. Peat Marwick Main, Cin. and N.Y.C., 1983-87, Coopers & Lybrand, Boston, 1988; founder, pres. Langenwalter & Assocs., Stow, Mass., 1988-95; founder, pres. Mfg. Cons. Ptnrs., Inc., 1995—; adj. instr. Nichols Coll., Dudley, Mass., 1989-91; seminar leader U. Seminar Ctr., Boston, 1990-91; guest lectr. Bryant Coll., 1991-92, Assumption Coll., 1993, Worcester State Coll., 1993, Suffolk U., 1993, Clark U., 1997—, Northeastern U., 2000—. Co-author: The Handbook of Materials and Capacity Requirements Planning, 1993; author: Repetitive Scheduling Training Aid, 1998, Repetitive Manufacturing Methodologies, 1999, Enterprise Resources Planning and Beyond: Integrating Your Entire Organization, 2000. Mem. adminstrv. coun. St. Matthew's United Meth. Ch., Acton, Mass., 1989-90, 93-95, cert. lay spkr., 1999—; capt. Stow Minutemen, 1990-95; founder Stow Civic Leadership Coun.; pres. Stow Bus. Assn., 1992-94, dir., 1995-96; treas. Troop 1 Boy Scouts Am., 1990-93; mem. Stow Econ. Devel. Coun., 1996-97; mem. So. New Eng. Emmaus Cmty., 1993-99. With U.S. Army, 1969-71. Fellow Am. Prodn. and Inventory Control Soc. (bd. dirs., nat. rep. mfg. specific industry group 1993-98, nat. process industry specific industry group 1999—, pres. Detroit chpt. 1975-76, spkr. internat. conf. 1994-98, spkr. regional chpt. meetings 1979—, instr. repetitive mgmt. 1995-99); mem. Assn. Mfg. Excellence, Assn. Quality and Participation, Beta Gamma Sigma. Home and Office: 22 Seven Star Ln Stow MA 01775-1449

LANGER, BERNHARD, professional golfer; b. Anhausen, Germany, Aug. 27, 1957; m. Vikki Langer; children: Jackie Carol, Stefan Bernhard, Christina Joy. Profl. golfer, 1972—; mem. European Ryder Cup Team, 1981, 83, 85, 87, 89, 91, 93, 95, 97, World Cup Team, 1976, 77, 78, 79, 80, 90, 91, 93, 95, 97; capt. Nissan Cup Team, 1985, 86, Kirin Cup Team, 1987, Four Tours World Championship Team, 1989. Winner 7 German Nat. Opens and 2 German Nat. PGAs, over 50 internat. tournaments including Dunlop Masters, 1980, Colombian Open, 1980, German Open, 1981, 82, 85, 86, Bob Hope Brit. Classic, 1981, Italian Open, 1983, Glasgow Classic, 1983, Johnnie Walker Tournament, 1983, Caslo World, 1983, Irish Open, 1984, 87, Dutch Open, 1984, French Open, 1984, Spanish Open, 1984, Australian Masters, 1985, European Open, 1985, Sun City Challenge, 1985, PGA Championship Eng., 1987, Belgian Classic, 1987, European Epson Match Play, 1988, Peugeot Spanish Open, 1989, German Masters, 1989, Madrid Open, 1990, Benson & Hedges Open, 1991, Heineken Dutch Open, 1992, Honda Open, 1992, Volvo PGA Championship, 1993, European Open, Volvo PGA, 1995, Dunhill Asian Masters, 1996, Italian Open, Benson & Hedges Internat. Czech Open, Linde German Masters, Argentine Masters, 1997; co-winner Lancome Trophy; leader European Order of Merit, 1981, 84; tour victories include Masters, 1985, 93, Sea Pines Heritage Classic, 1985. Avocations: skiing, soccer. Office: PGA European Tour, Wentworth Dr/Virginia Water, Surrey GU25 4LX, England

LANGER, DALE ROBERT, electrical engineer; b. Kenosha, Wis., Dec. 21, 1947; s. Robert M. and Lucile A. (Brandt) L.; m. Sharon L. Bascombe, June 14, 1969; children: Michael J., Michelle M., Marissa K. BSEE, U. Wis., 1975. Electrical design engr. Tex. Instruments, Dallas, 1975-80; prin. engr. Zenith Data Systems, St. Joseph, Mich., 1980-83; sr. tech. fellow Powerware Corp. formerly Exide Electronics, Raleigh, N.C., 1983—. Pres. local br. Aid Assn. for Lutheran, Raleigh, 1995, Dallas, 1980. Mem. IEEE, Assn. for Computing Machinery. Achievements include patents in field of UPS system with improved network communications. Home: 8913 Lindenshire Rd Raleigh NC 27615-3727 Office: Powerware Corp 3201 Spring Forest Rd Raleigh NC 27616-2821

LANGER, GLENN ARTHUR, cellular physiologist, educator; b. Nyack, N.Y., May 5, 1928; s. Adolph Arthur and Marie Catherine (Doscher) L.; m. Beverly Joyce Brawley, June 5, 1954 (dec. Nov. 1976); 1 child, Andrea; m. Marianne Phister, Oct. 12, 1977. BA, Colgate U., 1950; MD, Columbia U., N.Y.C., 1954. Diplomate Am. Bd. Internal Medicine. Asst. prof. medicine Columbia U. Coll. Physicians and Surgeons, N.Y.C., 1963-66; assoc. prof. medicine and physiology UCLA Sch. Medicine, 1966-69, prof., 1969-97, Castera prof. cardiology, 1978-97, assoc. dean rsch., 1986-91, dir. cardiovascular rsch. lab., 1987-97, emeritus prof., 1997—; Griffith vis. prof. Am. Heart Assn., L.A., 1979; cons. Acad. Press, N.Y.C., 1989-97. Author: Understanding Disease, 1999; editor: The Mammalian Myocardium, 1974, 2d edit., 1997, Calcium and the Heart, 1990; mem. editorial bd. Circulation Rsch., 1971-76, Am. Jour. Physiology, 1971-76, Jour. Molecular Cell Cardiology, 1974-97; contbr. more than 200 articles to profl. jours. Capt. U.S. Army, 1955-57. Recipient Disting. Achievement award Am. Heart Assn. Sci. Coun., 1982, Heart of Gold award, 1984, Cybulski medal Polish Physiol. Soc., Krakow, 1990, Pasarow Found. award for Cardiovascular Sci., 1993; Macy scholar Josiah Macy Found., 1979-80. Fellow AAAS, Am. Coll. Cardiology; mem. Am. Soc. Clin. Investigation, Am. Assn. Physicians. Achievements include research on control of cardiac contraction.

LANGER, HORST, financial corporate executive; b. Mar. 16, 1936. Chmn., CEO Siemens Corp. subs. Siemens A.G., Munich, N.Y.C.; dir. U.S. divsn. Med. Osram-Sylvania (part of Siemens family), N.Y.C.; chmn. supervisory bd. Med. Osram-Sylvania (part of Siemens family), Munich. Recipient Fedr. Cross of Merit with Ribbon. *

LANGER, JERZY JÓZEF, chemist, physicist, scientist, educator; b. Bad Harzburg, Germany, Feb. 25, 1946; arrived in Poland, 1946; s. Bronisław and Halina (Cendrowska) L.; m. Anna Rempulska, Feb. 16, 1974; children: Marcin, Krzysztof. BSc, Liceum Ogólnokształcace, Śrem, Poland, 1964; MSc in Chemistry, A. Mickiewicz U., Poznań, Poland, 1969, MSc in Physics, 1972, PhD in Phys. Chemistry, 1974, DSc in Phys. and Theoretical Chemistry, 1989. Asst. lectr. dept. chemistry A. Mickiewicz U., 1969-74, sr. asst. chemistry, 1974-76, adj. in chemistry, 1976-89, asst. prof. chemistry, 1989-96, assoc. prof., 1996—, head organic semiconductor lab., 1984—, mem. senate, 1980; rsch. asst. NIH Gerontology Rsch. Ctr., Balt., 1981; sr. visitor dept. chemistry U. N.C., Chapel Hill, 1981-82; coord. rsch. project within CPBP program, Poland, 1985-90; rsch. fellow dept. chemistry Queen Mary and Westfield Coll., U. London, 1990-92; coord. rsch. project within European Cooperation in Sci. and Tech. Program, 1993-95; organizer internat. confs., 1995, 97, 99. Contbr. articles to profl. pubs.; patentee in field. Recipient award for sci. achievements Ministry of Nat. Edn., Warsaw, 1988, Queen Mary and Westfield Coll., U. London, 1991; Cooperation in Sci. and Tech. rsch. grantee European Union, 1992, rsch. grantee Royal Soc. Chemistry, London, 1994, 95, 96, 99, 2000. Fellow Royal Soc. Chemistry (chartered chemist); mem. AAAS, European Materials Rsch. Soc., Internat. Soc. for Molecular Electronics and Biocomputing, World Assn. Theoretical Organic Chemists, Sigma Xi. Achievements include patents in field; research in molecular electronics and archaeometry. Avocations: music, swimming, walking, bike and car travel. Office: A Mickiewicz U Faculty Chem, Grunwaldzka 6, PL-60780 Poznań Poland

LANGERMANN, JOHN W. R., financial services executive; b. N.Y.C., Aug. 14, 1943. BA with highest honors, Lehigh U., 1965. Ptnr., sales mgr. L.F. Rothschild, Unterberg, Towbin, Boston, 1977-87; sr. v.p. County Nat. West Securities, Boston, 1987-90; v.p. Piper, Jaffray & Hopwood, Boston, 1990-92; sr. v.p. Needham & Co., Inc., Boston, 1993-94; mng. dir. instl. sales Ladenburg, Thalmann & Co., Inc., Boston, 1994-96; mgr. Brown Bros. Harriman & Co., Boston, 1996-99; ptnr. Langermann.com, Boston, 1999—. Mem. Internat. Soc. Security Analysts, Kansas City Soc. Fin. Analysts. Avocations: vintage sports car racing, curling, sculling, wu shu. Address: PO Box 1307 Boston MA 02205-1307

LANGFIELD, RAYMOND LEE, real estate developer; b. Houtzdale, Pa., Jan. 31, 1921; s. Arthur H. and Sadie L. (Morris) L.; m. Helen Deborah Elion, Oct. 15, 1952; 1 child, Joanna Langfield Rose. BS in Indsl. Engring., Pa. State U., 1942. Registered profl. engr., Conn. Chief mgmt. engr. CIT Fin. Corp., N.Y.C., 1947-50; v.p. Mosler Safe Co., N.Y.C., 1950-60; pres. Spicer Fuel Co., Groton, Conn., 1960-86, United Fuel Corp., Groton, Conn., 1962-86, Spicer Gas Co., Groton, Conn., 1982-86, Conn. Hotel Corp., New London, Conn., 1986-94. Mem. Conn. Energy Adv. Bd., Hartford, 1985-87; pres. Grade Arts Ctr., New London, 1985-87. Lt. comdr. USNR, 1941-47. Mem. Southeast Conn. C. of C. (bd. dirs., chmn. bd. 1978-80), Ind. Conn. Petroleum Assn. (chmn. bd. 1973-74, Oil Man of Yr., 1975), New Eng. Fuel Inst. (bd. dirs. 1972-84), Navy League Conn. (bd. dirs. 1985-87). Jewish. Avocations: fresh-water fishing, electronics. Home: 23362 Torre Cir Boca Raton FL 33433-7026

LANGFORD, ROLAND EVERETT, environmental scientist, safety engineer, writer; b. Owensboro, Ky., Apr. 11, 1945; s. John Roland and Mary Helen (Cockriel) L.; m. Son-Hee Shin, Dec. 18, 1971; children: John Everett, Lee Shin. AA, Armstrong State Coll., 1965; BS, Ga. So. Coll., 1967; MS, U. Ga., 1971, PhD, 1974; PhD, U. N.C., 1996. Cert. indsl. hygienist, safety profl.; registered hazardous substances profl., sanitarian, State of Ariz., Nat. Environ. Health Assn.; diplomate Am. Acad. Sanitarians. Instr. Savannah (Ga.) Sci. Mus., 1971-72, Bainbridge (Ga.) Jr. Coll., 1973-74; asst. prof. chemistry Ga. Mil. Coll., Milledgeville, 1975-77; asst. prof. Ga. So. Coll., Statesboro, 1977-78; commd. capt. U.S. Army, 1978, advanced through grades to lt. col., 1992; chief chemistry sect. U.S. Army Acad. Health Scis., Ft. Sam Houston, Tex., 1978-79; sanitary engr. U.S. Army Environ. Hygiene Agy., Aberdeen Proving Ground, Md., 1979-81; comdr. environ. sanitation detachment Taegu, Republic of Korea, 1981-83; environ. sci. officer Ft. Huachuca, Ariz., 1984-88; chief occupl. health rsch. U.S. Army Biomed. R&D Lab., Ft. Detrick, Md., 1991-92; comdr. med. rsch. detachment Walter Reed Army Inst. Rsch., Wright-Patterson AFB, Ohio, 1992-98; preventive medicine officer NATO/IFOR, Zagreb, Croatia, Sarajevo, Bosnia-Herzegovina, 1996-97; chief abiotic processes br. Robert S. Kerr Lab. of U.S. EPA, Ada, Okla., 1998; supt. health and safety Huntsman Corp. Jefferson County Ops., Port Neches, Tex., 1998-2000; mgr. indsl. hygiene Huntsman Corp., Houston, 2000—; mem. panel Comprehensive Assistance to Undergrad. Sci. Edn., NSF, 1975-77; mem. emergency response planning guidelines com. panel Am. Indsl. Hygiene Assn., 1999—; judge Internat. Sci. Fair, San Antonio, 1979; mem. sci. rev. panel NIH, 1986—; adj. faculty St. Leo's Coll., San Antonio, 1978-79, U. Md., Taegu and Pusan, Korea, 1981-83, AFIT, 1993-98, Purdue U., 1995—. Author: International Book of Units and Measurement Systems, 1999; co-author: Hazardous Materials Training Program for International Union of Operating Engineers, 1988, Fundamentals of Hazardous Materials Incidents, 1990, Substance Abuse in the Workplace, 1994; contbr. articles to profl. jours. Active Boy Scouts Am., Ft. Sam Houston, 1978-79; mem. parish coun., lay minister Holy Family Parish, Ft. Huachuca, 1985-88, lay min., lector 1985-88; advisor Med. Explorer Post, Ft. Huachuca, 1986-88; lay minister St. Thomas More Ch., 1988-91, WPAFB Chapel, 1992-98. Fellow Am. Inst. Chemists; mem. AIChE, Am. Soc. Safety Engrs., Am. Acad. Indsl. Hygiene (cert.), Am. Chem. Soc., Nat. Environ. Health Assn. (cert. hazardous materials profl.), Korean Chem. Soc., Royal Asiatic Soc. (bd. dirs. 1982-83), Assn. Mil. Surgeons U.S., Am. Acad. Sanitarians (cert.), Health Physics Soc., Am. Indsl. Hygiene Assn., Am. Acad. Health Physics (assoc.). Republican. Roman Catholic. Avocations: ham radio, oriental studies, photography. Home: 5627 Heather Run Houston TX 77041-6617 Office: Huntsman Corp 3040 Post Oak Blvd Houston TX 77056-6500

LANGGUTH, A(RTHUR) J(OHN), writer, journalism educator; b. Mpls., July 11, 1933; s. Arthur John and Doris Elizabeth (Turnquist) L. BA cum laude, Harvard U., 1955. Corr. Cowles newsletter, 1959; mem. bur. Look Mag. Bur., Washington, 1959; polit. corr. for Presdl. election Valley Times Cowles Publs., San Fernando Valley, Calif., 1960; corr. Calif. gubernatorial election Cowles Publs., 1962; reporter N.Y. Times, Dallas, 1963, N.C., Miss., Ala., 1963; corr. S.E. Asia N.Y. Times, 1964, bur. chief Saigon (Vietnam), 1965; spl. assignment N.Y. Times Mag., 1968, 70. Author: Jesus Christs, 1968, paperback edit., 1969, reissue with new illustrations, 1993, Wedlock, 1972, paperback edit., 1973, Marksman, 1974, Macumba, White and Black Magic in Brazil, 1975, Hidden Terrors, 1978, paperback edit., 1979, Portuguese edit., 1979, Brazilian book club edit., 1983, Russian edit., 1985, Saki, A Life of Hector Hugh Munro, 1981, paperback edit., 1982, Patriots, The Men Who Started the American Revolution, 1988, paperback edit., 1989, audio version, 1989, A Noise of War: Caesar, Pompey, Octavian and the Struggle for Rome, 1994, audio version, 1995, Our Vietnam: The War 1954-1975, 2000; contbr. articles to profl. jours. including The N.Y. Times Mag., N.Y. Times Book Rev., Washington Post Book World, L.A. Times Book Rev., numerous others. Shaw travelling fellow Harvard Coll., 1955-56, fellow John Simon Guggenheim Meml. Found., 1976-77. Mem. Author's Guild. E-mail: langguth@usc.edu. Home: 1922 Whitley Ave Los Angeles CA 90068-3233 Office: U So Calif Asc 102C University Park Los Angeles CA 90089-0001

LANGHAM, NORMA E., playwright, educator, poet, composer, inventor; b. California, Pa.; d. Alfred Scrivener and Mary Edith (Carter) L. BS, Ohio State U., 1942; B in Theatre Arts, Pasadena Playhouse Coll. Theatre Arts, 1944; MA, Stanford U., 1956; postgrad., Summer Radio-TV Inst., 1960, Pasadena Inst. Radio, 1944-45. Tchr. sci. California High Sch., 1942-43; asst. office pub. info. Denison U., Granville, Ohio, 1955; instr. speech dept. Westminster Coll., New Wilmington, Pa., 1957-58; instr. theatre. California U., Pa., 1959, asst. prof., 1960-62, assoc. prof., 1962-79, prof. emeritus, 1979—, co-founder, sponsor, dir. Children's Theatre, 1962-79; founder, producer, dir. Food Bank Players, 1985, Patriot Players, 1986, Noel Prodns., 1993. Writer: (plays) Magic in the Sky, 1963, Founding Daughters (Pa., Nat. DAR awards 1991), Women Whisky Rebels (Pa. Nat. DAR awards 1992), John Dough (Freedoms Found. award 1968), Who Am I?, Hippocrates Oath, Gandhi, Clementine of '49, Soul Force, Dutch Painting, Purim, Music in Freedom, The Moon Is Falling, Norma Langham's Job Johnson; composer, lyricist: (plays) Why Me, Lord?, (text) Public Speaking; co-inventor (computer game) Highway Champion. Recipient Exceptional Acad. Svc. award Pa. Dept. Edn., 1975, Appreciation award Bicentennial Commn. Pa., 1976, Gregg award Calif. U. of Pa. Alumni Assn., 1992, Emeriti Faculty award California U. Pa., 2000. Mem. AAUW (co-founder Calif. br., 1st v.p. 1971-72, pres. 1972-73, Outstanding Woman of Yr. 1986, 97), DAR, Internat. Platform Assn. (poetry award 1993, 94, monologue award 1997), California U. Pa. Assn. Women Faculty (founder, pres. 1972-73), California 150, California Hist. Soc., Pa. Assn. Safety Edn., Washington County Hist. Soc., Dramatists Guild, Ctr. in Woods, Mensa, Alpha Psi Omega, Omicron Nu. Presbyterian (elder). Home: 204 Ellsworth St California PA 15419-1206

LANGLANDS, ROBERT PHELAN, mathematician; b. New Westminster, Can., Oct. 6, 1936; came to U.S., 1960; s. Robert and Kathleen (Phelan) L.; m. Charlotte Lorraine Cheverie, Aug. 13, 1956; children: William, Sarah, Robert, Thomasin. BA, U. B.C., 1957, MA, 1958, DS honoris causa, 1985; PhD, Yale U., 1960; DSc (hon.), McMaster U., 1985, CUNY, 1985; D in Math. (hon.), U. Waterloo, 1988; DSc (hon.), U. Paris, 1989, McGill U., 1991, Toronto U., 1993, U. Montréal, 1997. From instr. to assoc. prof. Princeton (N.J.) U., 1960-67; prof. math. Yale U., New Haven, 1968-72, Inst. Advanced Study, Princeton, 1972—. Author: Euler Products, 1971, (with H. Jacquet) Automorphic Forms on GL (2), 1970, On the Functional Equations Satisfied by Eisenstein Series, 1976, Base Change for GL (2), 1980, Les Débuts d'une Formule des Traces Stable, 1983. Recipient Wilbur Lucius Cross medal Yale U., 1975, Common Wealth award Sigma Xi, 1984, Mathematics award Nat. Acad. Sci., 1988, Wolf prize in math. Wolf Found., 1995-96, la Grande Médaille d'Or de l'Académie des Scis., 2000. Fellow Royal Soc. London, Royal Soc. Can.; mem. NAS, Am. Math Soc. (Cole prize 1982), Can. Math. Soc. Office: Inst Advanced Study Sch Math Olden Ln Princeton NJ 08540

LANGLEY, ROLLAND AMENT, JR., retired engineering technology company executive; b. San Francisco, Aug. 22, 1931; s. Rolland Ament and Kathryn Lee (Beals) L.; m. Pamela Winston, May 15, 1954 (div. 1978); children: Owen C., Cynthia, James R.; m. Chiara Bini-Sexton, Apr. 12, 1978. BS in Engring. and Physics, U. Calif., Berkeley, 1953; MME, U. Pitts., 1961; MBA, Golden Gate U., 1973. Engr. Bettis Atomic Power Lab. of Westinghouse Electric Corp., Pitts., 1957-62; with Bechtel Corp., San Francisco, 1962-71; mgr. refinery and chem. nuclear fuel ops. Bechtel Inc., San Francisco, 1977-78; mgr. projects nuclear fuel ops. Bechtel Nat. Inc.,

San Francisco, 1979-80, mgr. decontamination and restoration nuclear fuel ops., 1980-81; v.p., mgr. nuclear fuels ops. Bechtel Nat. Inc., Oak Ridge, Tenn., 1981-84; sr. v.p., mgr. div. ops., R & D ops. Bechtel Nat. Inc., San Francisco, 1985-89; dep. mgr. Uranium Enrichment Assocs., San Francisco, 1972-76; v.p. Uranium Enrichment Tech. Inc., San Francisco, 1976-77; pres., dir. Bechtel Systems Mgmt. Inc., 1988-90; pres., CEO BNFL Inc., 1990-97, 98-99, also bd. dirs., 1994—; bd. dirs. 21st Century Coatings; trustee, pres. World Mem. Fund-U.S.A., 1993-98; chmn., Pajarito Sci. Corp., 1995-97, bd. dirs.; pres. Pacific Nuclear Coun., 1998-2000; mem. Nat. Acad. Sci. panel on nuclear separation and transmutation, 1992-95. Contbr. articles to profl. jours. Trustee Environ. Sci. and Tech. Inst., 1995-98. Capt. USNR. Recipient Bausch and Lomb Sci. award, 1948. Mem. Naval Res Assn. (past pres. Golden Gate chpt.). Achievements include patents in nuclear fuel and reactor systems design; research on uranium enrichment, nuclear waste disposal, fast breeder reactors, and engineering management. Home: PO Box 208 Middleburg VA 20118-0208 Office: BNFL Inc 10306 Eaton Pl Ste 450 Fairfax VA 22030-2201

LANGLEY, TIMOTHY MICHAEL, minister; b. Shawnee, Okla., Mar. 11, 1954; s. R.V. and Alice Elizabeth (Alcorn) L.; children: Mary Elizabeth, Landon Grant. Student, Okla. U., 1967-71; AS, Acad. Health Scis., San Antonio, 1983; AA, Ft. Steilecoum County Coll., Tacoma, Wash., 1974; postgrad., E. Cen. U., 1976-78. Lic. to ministry S. Bapt. Ch., 1979, ordained, 1985. Min. music/youth Trinity Bapt. Ch., Ada, Okla., 1976-79, 1st Bapt. Ch., Idabel, Okla., 1979-81; min. music/edn. Henderson Hills Bapt. Ch., Edmond, Okla., 1982-83; music evangelist 1s So. Bapt. Ch., Del City, Okla., 1983-85; min. music Potee Park Bapt. Ch., St. Joseph, Mo., 1985-90; min. worship E. Metro Community Ch. So. Bapt. Conv., Aurora, Colo., 1990—; prin. Emanuel So. Christian Sch., Edmond, 1983-84; pres., clinician, composer Day Star Prodns., Aurora, 1985—; v.p. C Bar N Ministries, Gulf Shores, Ala., 1983—; pres. Lynnalynn Ministries Inc., St. Joseph, Mo., 1985-90; founder Mile High Music Conf., Aurora, 1991. Composer religious songs. Liaison sch. bd. Horizon Middle Sch., Aurora, 1990-91. With U.S. Army, 1973-76. Mem. Music Tex., Music Fla., Music Memphis, Mile High Music Conf., Idabel Rotary (music dir. 1979-80). Republican. Avocations: golf, fishing. Home: 17919 E Jarvis Pl Aurora CO 80013-3425 Office: E Metro Community Ch So Bapt Conv 1730 S Abilene St Ste 201 Aurora CO 80012-5658

LANGLINAIS, J. WILLIS, priest, theology educator; b. San Antonio, Aug. 12, 1922; s. J. Willis and Marie Nellie (St. Julien) L. BS, U. Dayton, 1943; STD, U. Fribourg, Switzerland, 1954. Joined Soc. of Mary of St. Louis, 1940; ordained priest Roman Cath. Ch., 1952. Tchr. Cathedral H.S., Belleville, Ill., 1943-44, Provencher H.S., Winnepeg, Man., Can., 1944-46, St. Mary's H.S., St. Louis, 1946-47, Chaminada Coll. Prep. Sch., St. Louis, 1947-48, 55-59; prof., dir. Marynook Novitiate, Galesville, Wis., 1959-63; prof. theology St. Mary's U., San Antonio, 1963—, dean arts and scis., 1964-75, acad. v.p., 1975-81, chaplain Marianist Cmty., 1966-82, 84-98, 99—, chaplain Sch. Bus., 1987—. Contbr. articles New Cath. Ency., 1972, Ency. Dictionary Religion, 1979. Pres. United Svcs. Orgn. South Tex., 1985-87, Holy Rosary Elem. Sch., San Antonio, 1997-99; mem. bd. Tex. Bach Choir; pres. sch. bd. Ctrl. Cath. H.S., 1987-91. Named Champion of Compassion, B'nai B'rith, San Antonio, 1990. Mem. Rotary, Torch Club (pres. 1993-95). Avocations: horticulture, classical music. E-mail: jwillis@alvin.st.marytx.edu. Home and Office: St Mary's U One Camino Santa Maria San Antonio TX 78228

LANGLOIS, JOHN EMILE, lawyer, politician; b. Leicester, Eng., Oct. 31, 1942; s. Emile and Anita Eunice (Bourgaize) L.; m. Patricia Battersby, Jan. 5, 1975; children: Mark, Paul. A.L.B.C., London Bible Coll., 1969; LLB, U. London, 1970, Dip.Th., 1969. Barrister, Gray's Inn, London, 1971; advocate Royal Ct. Guernsey, 1971. Ptnr. Carey Langlois, Guernsey, 1973—; dir. Credit Suisse (Guernsey) Ltd., S.G. Hambros Bank, Guernsey. Contbr. articles to profl. jours., chpts. to books. Dep. States of Guernsey, 1980-84, 94—, conseiller, 1984-94; treas. World Evang. Fellowship, 1980—, chmn. World Evang. Fellowship Religious Liberty Commn., 1992—; chmn. Advocates Internat., Washington, 1996—, Care for Children, 1998—. Fellow Chartered Inst. Arbitrators. Avocations: motor boating, reading, travel. Home: Les Emrais de Bas, Castel Guernsey GY5 7YF, Channel Islands Office: Carey Langlois, 7 New St, Saint Peter Guernsey GY1 4BZ, Channel Islands

LANGLOIS, MARILYN SUE, psychologist; b. Sacramento; d. Winston Alma and Alice Laureen (Flynn) Langlois; divorced; children: Alexandra, Maria. Student, Sacramento State U., 1966-69, New Eng. Conservatory, Boston, 1967-68; M of Psychology, U. Innsbruck, Austria, 1990; PhD in Psychology, U. Vienna, Austria, 1993. Therapist asst. Rehab. Ctr. Psychiatry Univ. Vienna, 1979-87; trainer Assn. for Managerial Psychol. Fischlof, Vienna, 1981-83; mezzo-soprano State Theater, Luzern, Switzerland, 1981-84; music therapist Psychiat. U., Basel, Switzerland, 1986; self-employed psychologist Zurich, Switzerland, 1988-93; dir. Ctr. for the Psychology of Voice, Zurich, 1993—; free-lance concert singer, Switzerland, 1985—; pvt. voice instr., 1994—; choral conductor various choirs, Switzerland, 1990—; voice coach Mixed Choir Zurich, 1993—; presentor in field. Mem. Voice Found., Fedn. of Swiss Psychologists. Avocations: gardening, acting, childrens' theater. Home: Hardturmstr 392, 8005 Zurich Switzerland Office: Inst for Psych and the Voice, Muhleg 12, 8001 Zurich Switzerland

LANGLOIS IMMOOS, MARILYN SUE, psychologist, music therapist, singer, conductor, composer; b. Sacramento, July 21, 1948; arrived in Switzerland, 1981; d. Winston Alma and Alice Laverne (Flynn) L.; m. René Alfred Immoos (div. Mar. 1991); children: Alexandra Immoos, Maria Theresa Immoos; m. Manfred Peter Speiser. Student, Calif. State U., Sacramento, 1966-69, New Eng. Conservatory of Music, Boston, 1967-68, Mozarteum, Salzburg, Austria, 1969-74; magister, U. Innsbruck, Austria, 1990; PhD, U. Vienna, Austria, 1993. Concert singer Vienna, 1974-79; part-time asst. psychotherapist, asst. trainer Psychiat. Rehab. Ctr., Lauzendorf, Austria, 1979-81; part-time managerial psychologist Fischhof Inst. Managerial Psychology, 1979-83; mezzo-soprano City Theater Luzern, Switzerland, 1981-84; music therapist Psychiat. Univ. Clinic Basel, Switzerland, 1986; founder, dir. Ctr. for Psychology of Voice, Zürich, Switzerland, 1988—; tchr. Peoples' Insts. of Higher Edn., Switzerland, 1993—; condr. cmty. and ch. choirs, Switzerland, 1990—, composer, 1993—, freelance concert singer, 1990—; freelance vocal coach Zürich Opera, 1996—; collaborator Children's Choir, Zürich, 1994-96. Author, spkr., singer, pianist: (cassette) Learning to Perceive Your Singing Voice, 1993, (CD and booklet) Good Morning Voice, 1999; author, presenter: (poster) Vocal Pedagogy and Resonance-Therapeutic Principles, 1993. Freelance rschr. Swiss AIDS Help, Zürich and Bern, 1986; freelance counselor for alcohol and drug addiction, Zürich, 1986—; mem., rschr. Orgn. for Parents of Children with ADHD, Zürich, 1999—. Mem. Voice Found., Swiss Fedn. Psychologists, Chow-chow Club. Avocations: acting, cooking, gardening, dog breeding and raising. Home: Hardturmstrasse 392, CH-8005 Zürich Switzerland Office: Ctr for Psychology of Voice, Mühlegasse 12, CH-8001 Zürich Switzerland

LANGMAN, MICHAEL JOHN, medical educator; b. Gravesend, Kent, UK, Jan. 30, 1935; s. John A. and Edith M. L.; m. Rosemary A. Hempton; children: Nicholas J., Suzannah M., Victoria H., Benjamin M. BSc, London U., 1955, MBBS, 1959, MD, 1965, Med.Sci., 1999. Scientific staff Med. Rsch. Coun., UK, 1965-68; from sr. lectr. to Boots prof. therapeutics U. Nottingham, UK, 1968-87; William Withering prof. medicine U. Birmingham, UK, 1987-2000, hon. prof. medicine, 2000—; chmn. Warwicke Ambulance NHC Trust, 2000—; dean faculty medicine U. Birmingham, 1992-98; hon. cons. WHO Collaborating Ctr. for Internat. Drug Monitoring, 1996-98; hon. sr. rsch. fellow European Inst. Oncology, 1996—; non-exec. dir. Birmingham Health Auth., 1992-98. Fellow Royal Coll. Physicians (London). Office: Queen Elizabeth Hosp, Dept Medicine, Birmingham B15 2TH, England

LANGMEIER, MILOS, physiologist; b. Prague, Bohemia, Czech Republic, Feb. 15, 1951; s. Josef Langmeier and Danuska Langmeierova Taborska; m. Marta Lastovkova, Mar. 23, 1974; 1 child, Jan. MD, Charles U., Prague, 1969-75; PhD, Czechoslovak Acad. Scis., Prague, 1981. Med. diplomate. Postdoctoral fellow Czechoslovak Acad. Scis., Prague, 1975-78, rsch. student, worker, 1978-87; asst. prof. Faculty of Medicine/Charles U., 1987-91, assoc. prof., 1991—. Editor: (book) Ontogenesis of the Brain, 1991. Mem. Czech Physiol. Soc., Internat. Soc. for Devel. Neurosci., Internat. Brain Rsch. Orgn., N.Y. Acad. Scis. Office: Inst Physiology/Charles U, First Faculty of Medicine Albertov 5, 128 00 Prague 2, Czech Republic

LANGNER, GERALD, science educator; b. Breslau, Germany, Dec. 2, 1943. Diploma in physics, TU-München, 1971; D natural scis., TU-Darmstadt, 1977. Prof., dept. biology TUD, Darmstadt, 1988—; Heisenberg fellow DFG, Germany, 1983-88; dir. Zool. Inst. of TUD, 1989-90, 96-98; dean TUD dept. biology, 1992-93. Contbr. articles to profl. jours. Mem. Soc. for Neurosci., Soc. for Neuroethology, European Neurosci. Assn., Neurowissenschaftliche Gesellschaft. E-mail: gl@neuro.bio.tu-darmstadt.de. Office: Abteilung fur Neuroakustik, Zool Inst TU Darmstadt, Darmstadt 64287, Germany

LANGSNER, ALAN MICHAEL, pediatric cardiologist; b. N.Y.C., Dec. 21, 1948; s. Herman and Celeste (Prince) L.; m. Hilary Schmidt, Dec. 19, 1971. BA in Psychology, Fairleigh Dickinson U., 1970; MD, U. Autonomia Guadalajara, Jalisco, Mex., 1977; postgrad., NYU, 1977-78. Cert. Am. Bd. Pediat. and Pediat. Cardiology. Resident in pediatrics N.Y. Med. Coll./Met. Hosp. Ctr., N.Y.C., 1978-79, resident in pediatrics-primary care tng. program, 1979-80, chief resident in pediatrics-primary care tng. program, 1980-81; pvt. practice pediatric cardiology N.Y.C., 1983—; attending pediatrics, sr. cons. pediatric cardiology St. Barnabas Med. Ctr., Livingston, N.J., 1983—; assoc. cons. pediatric cardiology St. Vincent's Med. Ctr., S.I., N.Y., 1983—; chief dept. pediatric cardiology Children's Hosp. of N.J. at Newark Beth Israel Hosp., 1999—; cons. pediatric cardiology, clin. assoc. prof. pediatrics NYU Sch. Medicine, N.Y.C., 1983—, S.I. U. Hosp., 1985—; mem. perinatal rev. com., med. bd. St. Barnabas Med. Ctr.; presenter in field. Contbr. articles to profl. jours. Fellow Am. Coll. Caridology, Am. Acad. Pediatrics; mem. AMA, Essex County Med. Soc. Office: 405 Northfield Ave West Orange NJ 07052-3023

LANGTON, JEFFREY H., judge; b. Hamilton, Mont., Apr. 22, 1953; s. Richard L. and N. Louise (Mittower) L.; m. Patricia L. Stanbery, June 17, 1978 (div. Feb. 1999); children: Melanie, Matthew, Stephen, Thomas. BA in history with high honors, U. Mont., 1975, JD, 1978. Bar: Mont. 1978, U.S. Dist. Ct. Mont. 1978. Assoc. Schultz Law Firm, Hamilton, 1978-82; pvt. practice Hamilton, 1982-92; dist. judge 21st Dist. Ct., Hamilton, 1993—; bd. clin. visitors Law Sch., U. Mont., Missoula, 1993-99; Mont. Sentence Review Divsn., 1998—, chmn., 2000; chmn. self represented litigants Mont. Supr. Ct. Commn., 2000—. Author: The Victor Story, 1985. Bd. dirs. Victor Heritage Mus., 1990-95. Named Man of Yr. Victor Booster Club, 1988, 93. Mem. ABA (Mont. del. 1994—), Am. Jud. Soc., Mont. Bar Assn., Mont. Judges Assn. Presbyterian. Avocations: Montana history, fly fishing, environmental issues. Home: 2975 Mittower Rd Victor MT 59875-9542 Office: 21st Jud Dist 205 Bedford St Hamilton MT 59840-2853

LANHER, BERTRAND SIMON, biological spectroscopist, corporate manager; b. Charleville, France, May 27, 1965; came to U.S., 1990; s. Gilbert and Micheline Juliette (Constant) L.; m. Debra Mary Ubbelohde, July 28, 1991. MSc, U. des Scis. et Tech. de Lille, France, 1987; PHD, U. Bourgogne, Dijon, France, 1991. Chemist Helio Jean Didier, Hellemnes, France, 1985; quality assurance/quality control mgr. SRBG-Coca Cola, Fâches Thumesnil, France, 1986-87; rsch. engr. INRA, Poligny, France, 1988-91; product mgr. Nicolet Instrument Corp., Madison, Wis., 1991-92; gen. mgr. Chemometrics Cons., Cottage Grove, Wis., 1992-95; pres., CEO Anadis Instruments USA, Inc., Madison, Wis., 1993-1995; sr. scientist Perstorp Analytical Inc., Silver Spring, Md., 1995-96; gen. mgr. Arden Med., Inc., Monona, Wis., 1997-98; ops. gen. mgr., COO Kemtck Analytical Inc., Albuquerque, N.Mex., 1999—; speaker at confs. in field. Contbr. articles to profl. publs. Musician Dijon Jazz Band, 1987-90, Am. Jazz Express, 1992—. French Govt. grantee, 1990. Mem. AAAS, Assn. Ofcl. Analytical Chemists, Am. Musicians Union, N.Y. Acad. Scis. Roman Catholic. Achievements include patent for monitoring of the kinetics of milk enzymic coagulation usint FT-IR spectroscopy; finding of implementation of algorithms for the automated calibration of FT-IR spectrometers. E-mail: drbear@chorus.net or info@kemtchanalytical.com. Office: Kemtck Analytical Inc 100 S Baldwin St Ste 305 Madison WI 53703-3056

LANIER, MARK MURFEE, law educator, consultant; b. Montgomery, Ala., Oct. 15, 1958; s. Lawrence Howard and Ann Murfee (Sullivan) L.; children: Seth, Lucas, Jessica Lauren. BS, Auburn U., 1987; MS, U. Ala., Birgmingham, 1989; PhD, Mich. State U., 1993. Instr. Mich. State U., East Lansing, 1991-92; asst. prof. Ea. Mich. U., Ypsilanti, 1992-93; asst. prof. U. Ctrl. Fla., Orlando, 1993-98, assoc. prof. criminal justice, 1998—; HIV/AIDS rschr. Fla. Dept. Health, Tallahassee, 1997—; cons. Ctr. for Drug Free Living, Orlando, 1997—. Author: (with S. Henry) Essential Criminology, 1998; editor: (with S. Henry) Defining Crime, 2000; book reviewer Harper Collins, 1998, Waveland Press, 1999, Wadsworth Pub., 1999—. Mem. Am. Soc. Criminology, Acad. Criminal Justice Scis., Women and Criminal Justice (consulting editor 1997—). Avocations: surfing, wake boarding, powerboat racing. E-mail: lanier@pegasus.cc.ucf.edu. Home: 2440 Lake Vista Ct Apt 302 Casselberry FL 32707-6469 Office: Univ Ctrl Fla Dept Criminal Justice Orlando FL 32816-0001

LANIER, WILLIAM LOVEL, JR., anesthesiologist, educator; b. Statesboro, Ga., June 8, 1955; s. William Lovel Sr. and Nancy (Jones) L.; m. Mary Duckworth, July 15, 1978; children: Elizabeth Brooke, William Hudson. BS, U. Ga., 1976; MD, Med. Coll. of Ga., 1980. Resident in anesthesiology Wake Forest U. Med. Ctr., Bowman Gray Sch. Medicine, Winston-Salem, N.C., 1980-83; fellow in neurosurg. anesthesia Mayo Grad. Sch. Medicine, Rochester, Minn., 1983-84; cons. in anesthesiology Mayo Clinic, Rochester, 1984—, prof. anesthesiology, 1995—; Aitken Meml. lectr. U. Western Ont., London, 1993; Marshall Meml. lectr. U. Toronto, 2000; examiner Am. Bd. Anesthesiology, 1994—. Sect. editor Jour. Neurosurg. Anesthesiology, 1988-92; editor-in-chief Mayo Clinic Procs., 1999—. Grantee NIH, 1999. Mem. Am. Soc. Anesthesiologists, Soc. Neurosurg. Anesthesiology and Critical Care (pres. 1993-94), Assn. of Univ. Anesthesiologists (mem. sci. adv. bd. 1998—), First Families of Ga., Phi Beta Kappa, Phi Kappa Phi. Roman Catholic. Avocations: fishing, reading, boating. E-mail: lanier.william@mayo.edu. Office: Mayo Clinic 200 1st St SW Rochester MN 55905-0002

LANIN, ANATOLY GEORGIEVICH, material scientist, researcher; b. Orenburg, Russia, Dec. 30, 1926; s. Georgy Sergeevich Lanin and Alexandra Sergeevna Chirkova; m. Lidia Alexabdrovna Soldatova, June 30, 1950 (div. 1974); children: Irina, Sergey; m. Aliftina Petrovna Zanina, Oct. 4, 1974; 1 child, Miichail. Diploma in energy., Indsl. Inst., Kuiibyshev, Russia, 1948; Candidate of Tech. Sci., U. Moscow, 1959, D Tech. Sci., 1976. Engr. Indsl. Nuclear Assn. MAYAK, Ozersk, Russia, 1948-52, sr. sci. rschr., 1952-62; head lab. Sci. Rsch. LUCH, Podolsk, Russia, 1962-95, prin. scientist, 1995—; asst. prof. Engrng. Tech. Inst., Moscow, 1964-81, mem. phys. coun., 1964—, prof., 1994-97. Author: (with A. Andrievsky G. Rimashevsky) Strength of Refractory Compoinds, 1974, Strength and Thermal Shock Resistance of Industrial Ceramics, also procs. in field; contbr. over 350 articles to profl. jours. Recipient prize Coun. of Ministers, 1985. Mem. Intergovtl. Coun. on Physics of Strength and Plasticity. Home: Oktayabrskaya 5A-100, 142117 Podolsk Russia Office: State Rsch Inst Sci Indsl, Zheleznodorozhnaya 24, 142100 Podolsk Russia

LANITIS, NICHOLAS CONSTANTINE, investments and business executive, author; b. Limassol, Cyprus, Sept. 15, 1917; s. Constantine Panayi and Thereza (Nicolaides) L.; m. Vanda E.M. Lainas, Aug. 21, 1947; children: Hebe, Vladimir, Thereza, Julia. BA, Cambridge (Eng.) U., 1939; MA, Trinity Coll., 1957. Founder, chmn. Lanitis Bros. Ltd., Nicosia, Cyprus, 1943—, Food Products Co., Ltd., Channel Islands, 1986—, Gen. Fin. Corp. Ltd., Bahamas, 1964—, Lanitis Bros. Trading Ltd., Turks and Caicos Islands, 1965—; co-mng. dir. Cyprus Wines and Spirits Co. Ltd., Limassol, 1944-47; dep. contr. supplies Govt. of Cyprus, 1940-42. Author: Rural Indebtedness and Agricultural Co-operation in Cyprus, 1944, rev. edit. 1992, Our Destiny, 1963, also booklets. Founder, 1st chmn. The Cyprus Employers Fedn., 1960-63, Cyprus Productivity Ctr., 1961-63; founder, 1st sec. Social Progress Soc., 1944-47. Trinity Coll. scholar, 1957. Home: Block B, Park Guillemó, Andorra la Vella Andorra Office: PO Box 59 (French PO), 62 Meritxell Ave, Andorra la Vella Andorra

LANNAMANN, RICHARD STUART, executive recruiting consultant; b. Cin., Sept. 4, 1947; s. Frank E. and Grace I. (Tomlinson) L.; m. Katharine Tinkham Scheffler, Sept. 5, 1998; children by previous marriage: Thomas Cleveland, Edward Payne, John Stewart. AB in Econs., Yale U., 1969; MBA, Harvard U., 1973. Investment analyst U.S. Trust Co. N.Y., N.Y.C., 1969-71; rsch. analyst Smith, Barney & Co., N.Y.C., 1973-75, 2d v.p., 1975-77; v.p. successor firm Smith Barney, Harris Upham & Co., N.Y.C., 1977-78, Russell Reynolds Assocs., Inc., N.Y.C., 1978-83; sr.v.p. Mgmt. Asset Corp., Westport, Conn., 1986-87; mng. dir. Russell Reynolds Assocs., N.Y.C., 1983-86, 87—. Trustee Orpheus Chamber Orch. Mem. N.Y. Soc. Security Analysts, Assn. for Invesment Mgmt. and Rsch. Inst., Chartered Fin. Analysts, Riverside Yacht Club, Yale Club of N.Y., Links Club. Home: 21 Willowmere Cir Riverside CT 06878-2503 Office: 200 Park Ave New York NY 10166-0005

LANNE, JACQUES EMMANUEL, editor, monk; b. Paris, Aug. 4, 1923; s. Prosper and Elisabeth (Le Roy Ladurie) L. Diploma, École Hautes Études, Paris, 1956, É Langues Orientales, Paris, 1956; Doctor, U. Neuchatel, Switzerland, 1970. Benedictine monk. Tutor Greek Coll., Rome, 1956-62, rector, 1962-67; prof. theol. faculty St. Anselmo, Rome, 1960-69; cons. Secretariat for Promoting Christianity, Vatican, 1963-88, Oriental Contregation, Vatican, 1964—, Coun. for Promoting Christian Unity, Vatican, 1988—; editor Irenikon Chevetogne, Belgium, 1971-1998. Author: Coptic Liturgy, 1960, Theology of the Church, 1997. Roman Catholic. Fax: 083-21-60-45. E-mail: lanne@monasterechevetogne.com.

LANNOO, GODFRIED JOSEPH KNIGHT, publishing company executive; b. Tielt, Belgium, May 7, 1927; s. Joris Antoine and Maria (De Tavernier) L.; m. Maria Maertens; children: Katrien, Matthias, Wivina, Beatrijs, Karel, Irene. Student, Kortrijk, Belgium; degree in printing sci., Plantin Genootschap, Antwerp, Belgium; student top mgmt. program, Vlerick Sch., Gent, Belgium, 1958. Pres. Lannoo Printers and Pubs., Tielt, 1968-92, Lannoo Pubs., Tielt, 1992—. Past bd. dirs. G.O.M., Bruges, V.E.V., Antwerp, pres. regional br. Flanders; past. bd. dirs. Vlerick Sch. Mgmt., Ghent; mem. Adviser Fgn. Affairs, Book Commn., Flanders. Mem. Vereniging van Uitgevers van Nederlandstalige Boeken (former dir.). Home: Kasteelstraat 99, 8700 Tielt Belgium Office: Lannoo Pubs, Kasteelstraat 97, 8700 Tielt Belgium

L'ANNUNZIATA, MICHAEL FRANK, chemist, consultant; b. Springfield, Mass., Oct. 14, 1943; s. Michael Peter and Irene M. L'Annunziata; m. Maria del Carmen Elena Monge, Mar. 3, 1973; children: Michael O., Helen, Frank E. BS, St. Edward's U., Austin, Tex., 1965; MS, U. Ariz., 1967, PhD, 1970. Rsch. chemist Amchem Products, Inc., Ambler, Pa., 1971-72; rsch. assoc. U. Ariz., Tucson, 1972-73; prof., sect. head U. Chapingo, Mexico, Mexico, 1973-75; rsch. scientist Nat. Inst. Nuclear Rsch., Mexico City, 1975-77; assoc. officer IAEA, Vienna, Austria, 1977-80, 2d officer, 1980-83, 1st officer, head sci. visits program, 1983-86, sr. officer, head fellowships and tng. sect., 1986-91; mng. dir. LMS Internat. Tech. Svcs., Ltd., Coronado, Calif., 1992-95; dir. WorldTech Internat. Tech. Svcs., Oceanside, Calif., 1995-99; pres. The Montague Group, 1999—; bd. dirs. internat. sci. programs Uppsala (Sweden) U.; internat. IAEA cons.; cons., lectr. Forestry Rsch. Inst., Ibadan, Nigeria, 1994, 95, Ministry Edn., Jakarta, Indonesia, 1995, Internat. Sales, Mktg., and Tng., Packard Instrument Co., Meriden, Conn., 1995-2000, Egypt Atomic Energy Authority, Cairo, 1995, 96, Gezira Rsch. Sta., Wad Medani, Sudan, 1995, Ethopian Sci. and Tech. Commn., Addis Ababa, 1996, Nat. Radiation Commsn., Arusha, Tanzania, 1996; vis. lectr. Advanced Sch. Tropical Agriculture, Cardenas, Mexico, 1973, Atomic Energy Commn. of Ecuador, Quito, 1978, Timiryazev Agrl. Acad., Moscow, 1980, 81, Nuc. Rsch. Inst. in Vet. Medicine, Lalahan, Turkey, 1981, IAEA Seilbersdorf Labs., Seibersdorf, Austria, 1978-82, U. Guanajuato, Mex., 1981, Coll. Montecillo, Chapingo, Mex., 1989, Korea Atomic Energy Rsch. Inst., Seoul, 1991, Nat. Atomic Energy Agy., Jakarta, 1991-94, Zhejiang Agrl. U., Hangzhou, China, 1992, Ctrl. Nuc. "La Reina", Santiago, Chile, 1992, Internat. Atomic Energy Agy., Vienna, 1993, Mt. Makulu Ctrl. Rsch. Sta., Lusaka, Zambia, 1994, Office Atomic Energy Peace, Bangkok, 1995, Swedish Radiation Protection Inst., Stockholm, 1996, CIEMAT, Madrid, 1996, Laguna Verde Nuc. Power Plant, Vera Cruz, Mex., 1996, Oak Ridge (Tenn.) Nat. Labs., 1998, Min. Water and Irrigation, Amman, Jordan, 1998, Wyeth-Ayerst, Pearl River, N.Y., 1998, Chem. Industry Inst. Toxicology, Rsch. Triangle Park, N.C., 1998, Los Alamos Nat. Labs., N.Mex., 2000; hon. prof. Zhejiang Agrl. U., 1992. Author: (textbooks) Radiotracers in Agricultural Chemistry, 1979, Radionuclide Tracers, Their Detection and Measurement, 1987; author, editor (with J.O. Legg) Isotopes and Radiation in Agricultural Sciences, Vol. 1, 1984, Vol. 2, 1984, Handbook of Radioactivity Analysis, 1998; contbr. articles to profl. jours. Recipient hon. tchg. diploma, silver plaque Ctrl. U., Ecuador, Quito, 1978. Mem. AAAS, N.Y. Acad. Scis., Am. Nuc. Soc., Sigma Xi, Phi Lambda Upsilon, Gamma Sigma Delta. Roman Catholic. Achievements include discovery of molecular D-chiro-inositol phosphate in soil/plant systems; determination of the biochemical mechanism and pathway involved in the formation of soil chiro-inositol phosphate; elucidated mechanisms of soil organic phosphorus fixation; separation of the radioactive nuclides Sr-90 from soil surfaces after nuclear fallout; first separation of radioactive nuclides Sr-90 and Y-90 by electrophoresis; execution of over 80 fact-finding, planning, and implementation missions to over 60 countries of Asia, Africa, Europe, Latin America, North America, and the Middle East for United Nations, International Atomic Energy Agy. from 1978 to the present; development of several chemical and instrumental techniques for the analysis of radioactive nuclides. E-mail: lannunziata@compuserve.com. Office: The Montague Group PO Box 1471 Oceanside CA 92051-1471

LA NOIRE, ALBERTO, finance administrator, consultant; b. Lima, Peru, Nov. 13, 1963; s. Oswaldo and Elvigia (Neyra) La N. ESAN, Lima, Peru, 1998. Fin. and adminstrn. mgr. Wiese, Lima, Peru, 1998—. E-mail: alanoire@wieserep.com.pe. Office: Wiese Representaciones SA, Carabaya 501, Lima 1, Peru 51

LANQUETOT, E. ROXANNE, special education educator, writer; b. Kansas City, Nov. 29, 1933; d. Myron Lewis and Bonnie (Goldberg) Leiser; m. Guy Alfred Lanquetot, Oct. 3, 1958; 1 child, Serge Normand. Student, Stanford U., 1951-53; cert. of French Pronunciation, Inst. de Phonetique, Sorbonne, Paris, 1954; BS, Columbia U., 1956, MA, 1957; MA, CCNY, 1976; postgrad., CUNY, 1980-83. Asst. tchr. English Lycee Fenelon, Paris, 1960-62; tchr. kindergarten Lycee Francais N.Y., N.Y.C., 1964-65; dir. nursery & kindergarten Lyceum Francais, N.Y.C., 1965-66; tchr. 2d grade P.S. 113 M, N.Y.C., 1966-69; tchr., jr. guidance counselor P.S. 87 M, N.Y.C., 1969-71; tchr. emotionally handicapped P.S. 106, Bellevue Hosp., N.Y.C., 1971-99. Contbr. articles to profl. publs., Newsday, Wall St. Jour., others. Fellow Am. Orthophyschiatric Assn.; mem. Nat. Alliance for Rsch. on Schizophrenia and Depression (mem. leadership coun.). Avocations: creative writing, travel, ballet, classical music, theatre. Home and Office: 315 W 106th St New York NY 10025-3445

LANS, HAKAN A., engineer; b. Stockholm, Nov. 2, 1947; s. Patrik and Maja L.; m. Inga Maria Liefeldt L.; children: Maria, Terese. BS in Elec. Engring., Higher Tech. Coll., Stokholm, 1968; PhD (hon.), U. Uppsala, Sweden. Cons. Swedish Nat. Def. Rsch. Inst., 1970-80; sci. advisor Swedish Aviation Adminstrn. Recipient gold medal Swedish Inventor of Yr., 1990, Internat. Seatrade award, 1993, Gold medal Royal Swedish Acad. Engring. Scis., 1993, Am. Laurels award, 1994, Polhems prize, 1995, Swedish Pilot of Yr., 1995, Large prize Swedish Royal Inst. Tech., 1996, Positive Sweden prize, 1998, Carl August Wicander award, 1998, Thulin award Swedish Soc. Aero. and Astronautics, 1999; named Swedish Aviator of Yr., 1997. Mem. Royal Swedish Acad. Engring. Sci. (elected), Royal Swedish Acad. Def. Scis. Office: GPC Sys Internat, Ringvaegen 56E, 13335 Saltsjobaden Sweden

LANSDALE, H. PARKER, minister, historian, non-profit administrator; b. Worcester, Mass., Mar. 18, 1923; s. Herbert P. Jr. and Marjorie M. (McKay) L.; m. Elizabeth Ann MacCollum, Feb. 25, 1945 (div. Jan. 1976); children: Ann T., Kirk M., Todd A.; m. Dorothy Phillips Deschamps, May 26, 1976; children: Thomas A. Deschamps, Margaret D. Sticklen, Brian P. Deschamps, Patricia S. Deschamps. AB, Oberlin Coll., 1944; BD, Yale Div. Sch., 1950; MA, Yale Grad. Sch., 1953, PhD, 1956. Ordained to ministry Presbyn. Ch. (USA), 1950. Boys work sec. YMCA, New Haven, 1948-56; mem. faculty Yale Div. Sch., 1948-56; assoc. gen. sec. YMCA, Wilmington, Del., 1956-59;

program dir. YMCA Greater N.Y., N.Y.C., 1959-61; gen. sec. YMCA of Greater Bridgeport, Conn., 1961-69; dir. (on loan from YMCA) Higher Edn. Ctr. for Urban Studies, Bridgeport, 1968-77; cmty. liaison (on loan) Bridgeport Area Found.-United Way, Bridgeport, 1977-83; ret., 1983; rsch. assoc. rsch. dept. YMCA U.S.A., 1990—; exec. dir. (on loan) Action for Bridgeport Cmty. Devel., 1964-65; courtesy historian in residence Sarasota-Manatee Campus, U. South Fla.; parish assoc. Hon. Ret. 1st Presbyn. Ch., Sarasota; lectr. in field. Author: History of the Work of the YMCA with Boys (1900-25), 1992; co-editor, author: There is a Tide, 2000; contbr. articles to profl. jours. Bd. dirs. ARC, 1963-70, Bridgeport Model Cities, 1969-74, Park City Hosp., 1970-83, Conn. Health Plan, 1972-80, numerous others; mem. Peace River Presbytery Presbyn. Ch. With USMCR, 1942-46. Fellow N.Am. Fellowship YMCA Retirees, World Fellowship YMCA Retirees; mem. Peace River Presbytery. Democrat. Avocations: history, writing, volunteer service.

LANSDOWNE, KAREN MYRTLE, retired English language and literature educator; b. Twin Falls, Idaho, Aug. 11, 1926; d. George and Effie Myrtle (Avotte) Martin; m. Paul L. Lansdowne, Sept. 12, 1948; children: Michele Lynn, Larry Alan. BA in English with honors, U. Oreg., 1948, MEd, 1958, MA with honors, 1960. Tchr. Newfield (N.Y.) H.S., 1948-50, S. Eugene (Oreg.) H.S., 1952; mem. faculty U. Oreg., Eugene, 1958-65; asst. prof. English Lane C.C., Eugene, 1965-82, ret., 1982; cons. Oreg. Curriculum Study Center. Co-author: The Oregon Curriculum: Language/Rhetoric, I, II, III and IV, 1970; rsch., co-author: Lansdowne Family Genealogy Center Studies, 1995-99. Rep. Calif. Young Neighborhood Assn., 1978—; mem. scholarship com. First Congl. Ch., 1950-70. Mem. MLA, Pacific N.W. Regional Conf. C.C.s, Nat. Coun. Tchrs. English, U. Oreg. Women, AAUW (sec.) Jaycettes, Pi Lambda Theta (pres.), Phi Beta Patronesses (pres.), Delta Kappa Gamma. Home: 2056 Lincoln St Eugene OR 97405-2604

LANSFORD, EDWIN GAINES, accountant; b. Chattanooga, Aug. 20, 1924; s. Frederick Duke Lansford and Edwina (Gaines) Lansford Stone; m. Sue Ann Kemmer, may 29, 1954; children: Virginia Nan, Sue Ann, Edwin Gaines, Jr., James Robert, Frederick Scott. BBA, U. Chattanooga, 1948; LLB, McKenzie Coll., 1958. Mem. Tennessee Bar Assn. Cost acct. Cavalier Corp., Chattanooga, 1948-52; staff acct. O.T. Draewell and H.L. Oakes, Chattanooga, 1952-54; own account and various partnerships Crossville and Chattanooa, 1954-98; v.p. Lansford Kawasaki, Inc., Crossville, 1978—; of counsel Lansford, Stephens & Brummett, CPAs, Pikeville and Crossville, Tenn., 1999—. With U.S. Army, 1943-46, ETO. Mem. AICPA (hon. mem.), NRA, Nat. Assn. Tax Practitioners (bd. dirs. 1996—, treas. 1998—), Tenn. Soc. CPAs (life mem., sec., various coms., pres. Chattanooga chpt. 1962-63, co-founder, 1st pres. Upper Cumberland chpt. 1978-79), Tenn. Shooting Sports Assn. (pres. 1969-71, H.P. Rifle Team 1963-64), Lions (treas. Signal Mountain club 1974-75), Rotary Internat. (all offices and bd. dirs. Crossville noon chpt. 1983—, Paul Harris fellow), Cumberland County C. of C. (bd. dirs. 1976-79), Elks. Methodist. Avocations: hunting, hiking. Office: 92 Rockwood Ave Crossville TN 38555-4610

LANSIMIES, ESKO ANTERO, clinical physiologist, physician, educator; b. Nurmes, Carelia, Finland, Apr. 8, 1941. MD, Turku (Finland) U., 1967, PhD in Clin. Physiology, 1975, cert. specialist in Nuclear Medicine, 1978. Sr. tchr. Turku U., 1968-74; vis. scientist Lund (Sweden) U., 1975; chief physician U. Hosp., Kuopio, Finland, 1976—, prof. clin. physiology, 1998—; mem. ethical bd. Kuopio U., Univ. Hosp., 1993—. Author, editor: (text) Clinical Physiology, 1988, 2d rev. edit. 1994, Clinical Physiology and Nuclear Medicine, 2000; editor: (text) Functional Diagnostics, 1990, 2d rev. edit. 1992; editor-in-chief: Clinical Physiology, 1998—; contbr. numerous articles to profl. jours.; columnist in field. Mem. Health Bd. City of Kuopio, 1989-92, Kuopio Dance Festival, 1991-96; mem. Kuopio Sch. Bd., 1993-2000, City Coun., 1993-2000, v.p. 1995-96. Decorated Knight of White Rose of Finland, Finnish Pres., 1991. E-mail: esko.lansimies@kuh.fi. Office: Kuopio U Hosp, PO Box 1777, FIN70211 Kuopio Finland

LANSKA, DOUGLAS JOHN, neurologist; b. Milw., Aug. 8, 1959; s. Orville Emmanuel Lanska and Margaret Mary (Daly) Kenehan; m. Mary Jo Brook, June 26, 1982; children: Joseph, John, James. BS, U. Wis., 1980; MS, MD, Med. Coll. Wis., 1984; MSPH, U. Ky., 1996. Nat. Bd. Med. Examiners; Diplomate Am. Bd. Neurology, Am. Bd. Psychiatry. Intern in internal medicine U. Hosps., Cleve., 1984-85; resident in neurology U. Hosps. Cleve., 1985-88, instr. neurology, fellow, 1988-89; computer operator C.S.I. Corp., Butler, Wis., 1977-78, computer programmer, 1978, data processing mgr., 1979-82, cons. computer programmer, 1982-84; computer programmer Med. Coll. Wis., Milw., 1982, rsch. asst., 1982-83; assoc. Sanders-Brown Ctr. on Aging, Lexington, Ky., 1989-98; asst. prof. U. Ky. Med. Ctr., Lexington, 1989-93, assoc. prof., 1993-98, prof., 1998; prof. U. Wis., 1998—; cons. Ky. Med. Rev. Bd., Frankfort, 1989-98, Commonwealth Ky. Ctr. for Excellence in Stroke, Lexington, 1989-91, Internal Medicine Ctr. to Advance Rsch. and Edn., Washington, 1991-98, AMA, Chgo., 1991-94, Health Care Financing Adminstrn., Balt., 1991-97, Agy. for Health Care Policy and Rsch., Rockville, Md., 1992-96, Am. Bd. Psychiatry and Neurology, Deerfield, Ill., 1992—, NIH, 1994-95, Scientists in the Schs. Program, 1995-98; staff neurologist VA Med. Ctr., Lexington, 1989-98, Fed. Med. Ctr., Lexington, 1995-98; chief staff VA Med. CTr., Tomah, Wis., 1998—. Contbr. articles to profl. jours. Mem., participant Ky. Physicians Care Program/Life, 1989-98, Leadership VA, 1999. Recipient Drs. Houghton award Wis. State Med. Soc., 1984, Rsch. Svc. award Nat. Inst. on Aging, 1989, Career Investigator Devel. award Nat. Inst. Neurol. Disease, Stroke, 1991. Mem. Am. Acad. Neurology, Am. Neurol. Assn., World Fedn. Neurology, Internat. Soc. for History of Neurology, Phi Beta Kappa, Alpha Omega Alpha. Roman Catholic. Avocations: sailing, basketball, hiking, computer programming, mathematics.

LANSMAN, EMILE CHARLES, publishing executive; b. Jumet, Hainaut, Belgium, Aug. 2, 1947; s. Emile Albert Lansman and Leonia Maria Vermoesen; m. Annick Florine Vandersnickt, Mar. 28, 1980; children: Celine, Arnaud. Lic. psychologist, U. de l'Etat Mons, 1981. Diplomate Psychologue and Pedagogue. Tchr. Ecoles Primaires, Morlanwelz, Belgium, 1966-81; prof. Ecole Normale, Charleroi, Belgium, 1981-85; dir. Theater-Edn. Assn., Belgium, 1985—; dir. Editions Lansman, Carnieres, Belgium, 1989—; adminstr. Ctr. des Ecritures Dramatiques Wallonie-Bruxelles, 1999—. Author: (series) Lea la grenouille, 1992-93; dir. publ. Internat. Drama and Edn. Assn., 1992-95; editor, pub. theater books, 1989—. Decorated chevalier Ordre des Arts et Lettres (France); recipient Prix du Hainaut des Arts de la Scene, 1996. Home: Rue Ferrer 6, B-7141 Carnieres Hainaut, Belgium Office: Editions Lansman, Rue Royale 63, B-7141 Carnieres Hainaut, Belgium

LANT, CHRISTOPHER LOUIS, geographer, educator; b. Albany, N.Y., Feb. 22, 1961; s. Herbert V. and Anne Marie (Rissberger) L.; m. Sandra Gayle Charlson, May 29, 1988; children: Hannah Marie, Helen Grace. BA, SUNY, Albany, 1983; MA, U. Iowa, 1985, PhD, 1988. Asst. prof. geography So. Ill. U., Carbondale, 1988-94, assoc. prof., 1994—, chmn. dept., 1996—. Contbr. to profl. publs.; editor Jour. Am. Water Resources Assn., 1993—. Grantee Iowa State Water Resources Rsch. Inst., 1987-88, Water Resources Ctr., 1991-93, Ill. Groundwater Consortium, 1991-93. Mem. Assn. Am. Geographers (dir. water resources splty. group 1992-95), Soil and Water Conservation Soc., Am. Water Resources Assn. Democrat. Avocations: fishing, basketball. Office: So Ill U Carbondale Geography Faner Hall Carbondale IL 62901-4514

LANTER, SEAN KEITH, software engineer; b. Los Alamos, N.Mex., May 8, 1953; s. Robert Jackson and Norma Esther (Jonas) L.; m. Lauri Jane Willand, July 16, 1977; children: Tully Erik, Sarah Elizabeth, Rachel Erin. BA in Physics, U. Utah, 1974, MSME, 1977; MS in Computer Sci., LaSalle U., 1998. Registered profl. engr., Wash. Sr. engr. Boeing Comml. Airplane Co., Seattle, 1977-82; systems analyst Internat. Submarine Tech. Ltd., Redmond, Wash., 1982-83; engr. software Advanced Tech. Labs., Bellevue, Wash., 1983-84; engr. contract Rho Co., Redmond, 1984-85; sr. tech. staff Cedar Software Inc., Redmond, 1985-87; pres. Connexions Engring. and Software, Woodinville, Wash., 1987-88; pres., chief engr. Connexions Engring., Inc., Woodinville, 1990-95; sys. engr. Microrim Software, Inc., Bellevue, Wash., 1998-99; cons., contract programmer, 1990—. Contbr. articles to profl. jours. Mem. Assn. Computing Machinery, NSPE. Lutheran. Avocations: chamber music, reading, history, baseball. Office: Connexions Engring PO Box 3007 Woodinville WA 98072-3007

LANTERMANN, WERNER, social scientist; b. Dinslaken, Germany, Aug. 13, 1956; s. Heinrich and Marga (Benninghoff) L. Diploma in social sci., U. Duisburg, Germany, 1994. Social scientist Lutherian Ch., Oberhausen, Germany, 1987—; cons. Ministry of Environ., Bonn, Germany, 1990-94, German. Soc. for Prevention of Cruelty to Animals, Bonn, 1990-94. Author: (with Annette Schuster) Papageien-vom Aussterben Bedroht, 1990, Handbuch Papageien, 1994, Papageienkunde, 1999; editor: (with Thomas Arndt) Papageienkunde-Parrot Biology, 1997—; contbr. articles to profl. jours. Hon. presybter Ch. Cmty., Oberhausen, 1980-87; hon. judge Amtsgericht, Oberhausen, 1990-94. Mem. Parrot Rsch. Inst., Ornithol. Soc. Germany. Avocations: gardening, study trips to tropical countries. Home: Drostenkampstreet 15, D-46147 Oberhausen Germany

LANTIGUA, JOSE SALVADOR, computer engineer, consultant; b. Havana, Cuba, Mar. 18, 1953; came to U.S., 1960; s. Jose Gregorio and Hilda Simona (Barrial) L.; m. Pansy Reen Fuller, Mar. 5, 1977; children: Joseph Gabriel, Christina Simone. AA, Miami-Dade C.C., 1973; BA, Northwestern State U. La., 1978, BS, 1979; MA, Pepperdine U., 1980; M Computer Engring., Fla. Atlantic U., 1989. Engr. NASA, Houston, 1973-75; mgr. automation Blue Cross-Blue Shield, Jacksonville, Fla., 1981-83; regional engring. mgr. Victor Techs., Jacksonville, 1983-84; dir. sys. integration Abacus Data, Inc., Jacksonville, 1984-85; cons. engr. IBM, Jacksonville, 1985-93; mng. dir. Furash & Co., Washington, 1993-94; pres. Epi-Tech Corp., Alexandria, Va., 1994-96; v.p. ISS Corp., Stamford, Conn., 1996-97, Renaissance Worldwide, 1997-99; pres., COO Well Credit, Inc., Orange Park, FL, 1999—. Author: Knowledge Rules from Dircted Graphs, 1989; contbr. articles to various publs. Advisor Jr. Achievement, Jacksonville, 1987. Maj. U.S. Army, 1975-80, mem. USAR, 1980—. Mem. IEEE, Am. Assn. for Artificial Intelligence, Assn. for Computing Machinery, Mensa, Phi Theta Gamma. Republican. Roman Catholic. Achievements include development of knowledge acquisition software, business process reengineering methodology, financial application business system architecture. Office: Well Credit Inc PO Box 7078 Orange Park FL 32073-5562

LANTIN, EMMANUEL MACASAET, education educator; b. Manila, Jan. 2, 1934; s. Pedro Torres and Dolores de Gala (Macasaet) L.; m. Myriam Viguier Masson, Oct. 6, 1973; children: François-Emmanuel, Marie-Bernadette. BA, Berchmans Coll., Cebu City, The Philippines, 1957; MA, Ateneo Manila U., Quezon City, The Philippines, 1959; licentiate, U. Innsbruck, Austria, 1965; PhD cum laude, Inst. Cath. de Paris, 1973. Asst. prof. Ateneo Manila U., Quezon City, 1966-67; professorial lectr., asst. to dir. East Asian Pastoral Inst., Quezon City, 1966-67; asst. prof. De La Salle U., Manila, 1973-76, assoc. prof., 1976-92; official del. World Coun. Ch. Seminar, Géneva, 1972; chmn. acad. com. Poveda Learning Ctr., Manila, 1987-88. Author: Christian Mystery and Human Understanding, 1976; editor: Religious Studies Jour.; contbr. articles to profl. jours. Interpreter XIII World Jr. Chess Championship, Manila, 1974, Ali-Frazer World Boxing Championship, 1975; pres. Evansorian Assn., Parañaque, 1985-86. Qui et Qui en Francophonie award Richelieu Internat., Paris, 1986-87, 91-92. Mem. Alliance Française Manila (bd. dirs., sec. 1976-80), Philippine-French Assn. (chmn. scholarship program 1975-80, bd. dirs., treas. 1977-80), Philippine Austrian Cultural Soc. (bd. dirs., treas. 1987-91), Am. Studies Internat., Am. Studies Assn. Philippines (life), Women's Inst. Continual Edn. (TEFL program dir. 1997-98), English Workshop (founder-dir. Ville de Cergy 1998—). Mem. Socialist Party. Roman Catholic. Address: 9 Les Dix Arpents Ocres, 95610 Eragny Sur Oise France

LANTIN, MA MELANIE MANALO, medical communications executive; b. Pateros, Philippines, May 2, 1961; d. Melchor Pascual Manalo and Teresita Guevarra Santos; m. Emmanuel Umali Lantin, Dec. 11, 1988; 1 child, Ma. Czarina Dominque. BSBM, Ateneo de Manila U., 1983; MBA, De La Salle U., Philippines, 1988, Manila U., 1999. Sales exec. Silahis Hotel Manila, Philippines, 1983-87; advt. sales mgr. Medi Media, Makati, Philippines, 1988-91; pres. and CEO Medicomm Pacific, Inc., Pasig, Philippines, 1991—; pres., CEO Medicomm Advt., Inc., Pasig, 1991—. Recipient acad. scholarship Ateneo de Manila U., 1979-83. Mem. Mktg. Execs. of Pharm. Industry (v.p., dir. 1998—), Young Entrepreneur's Orgn. (bd. dirs., fin. chmn.). Office: Medicomm Pacific Inc, GF/2F Jollibee Plz Bldg, Pasig Philippines

LANTIS, DONNA LEA, retired banker, art educator, artist; b. Medford, Oreg., Oct. 12, 1931; d. James Warren Fader and Amy Bell (Crump) Fader-Snyder; m. Victor Earl Lantis, July 9, 1950 (div. Apr. 1975); children: Deborah Ann Hayes, Diana Lorraine Keaton. BS, So. Oreg. U., 1966; postgrad., Otis Art Inst., L.A., 1969; 5th yr. cert., U. Oreg., 1974. Art tchr., Oreg., Tenn., Ky.; cert. banker Am. Inst. Banking. Banker First Nat. Bank, Ashland, Oreg., 1951-62; tchr. art, history Klamath County Sch. Dist., Klamath Falls, Oreg., 1966-68; tchr. art Ashland Sch. Dist., 1968-75; banker First Interstate Bank, Medford, Oreg., 1979-92; supr. student tchrs. So. Oreg. U., Ashland, 1968-75, work with traumatized children, 1968-69. Author illustrated poetry; exhbns. include Oreg. State Fair, So. Oreg. U., Portland, Monmouth Rogue Art Gallery, Medford, Oreg., banks, librs.; dollmaker. Asst. founder lupus support group, Ashland, Oreg., 1977, 78, 79. Elks scholar, 1950, John Dickey Art scholar So. Oreg. U., 1966; recipient Voice of Democracy 1st Place Hon. Mention Broadcasters and Radio Dealers of Am. KWIN, 1949. Mem. AAUW, So. Oreg. Alumni Assn., Libr. of Congress, Women in Arts. Avocations: music, history, writing, gardening, dolls. Home: 604 Newtown St Medford OR 97501-3464

LANTOS, BÉLA, engineering educator; b. Miskolc, Borsod, Hungary, Jan. 8, 1941; s. Béla and Etelka (Sümeghy) L.; m. Gizella Feczko; 1 child, Béla. BSEE, Tech. U. Budapest, 1961; MS in Elec. Engring., Tech. U., Ilmenau, Germany, 1965; MS in Math., Univ. of Scis., Budapest, 1972; PhD, Hungarian Acad. Scis., 1976, DSc, 1994. Asst. lectr. Tech. U., Budapest, 1965-79, assoc. prof., 1979-94, prof. dr.habil., 1994—; cons. Hungarian Elec. Wks. Co., Budapest, 1984-87; rschr. Rsch. Inst. Informatics Karlsruhe, Germany, 1987; expert Hungarian Rsch. Found., Budapest, 1990—; reviewer Hungarian Acad. scis., Budapest, 1996. Author: Robot Control, 1991, 2d edit., 1997; co-author: Advanced Robot Control, 1997. Recipient Book award Hungarian Acad. Scis., 1997; Szechenyi Prof. scholar Hungarian Govt., 1999—. Mem. Internat. Fedn. Automatic Control (tech. com. robotics 1996—, tech. com. non-linear sys. 1996—, tech. com. optimal control 1996—). Home: IV em 12, Bartók Bela ut 3/D, H-1225 Budapest Hungary Office: Tech Univ Budapest, Pazmany Peter setany 1/D, H-1117 Budapest Hungary

LANTRIP, IVOLUE MAY, secretary; b. Cherryvale, Kans., Mar. 13, 1929; d. John Franklin Sanders and Treva Jenneve (Rohrbough) McKinnon; m. Truman Leo Lantrip, July 23, 1949; children: Michael Dennis, Richard Oden. Grad. h.s., Benicia, Calif. Sec. Benicia H.S., 1948-54, 62-67, counselors sec., 1961-62; fin. sec., bookkeeper Benicia Unified Sch. Dist., 1967-71, ret. Author: The American Genealogy of the Lantrip Family, 1994. Mem. DAR (Acalanes chpt. historian 1984-86, 88-90, treas. 1986-88), Carquinez Strait Stitchers Quilt Guild (treas. 1996), Ret. Pub. Employees Assn. of Calif. Avocations: oil painting, china painting, quilting/wearable art, genealogy, travel.

LANTSMAN, MEIR HAIMOVITCH, mathematician; b. Gitomir, USSR, Nov. 17, 1929; arrived in Israel, 1991; s. Haim Mordkovitch and Golda Samuilovna (Levin) L.; m. Maja Borisovna Konstantinopolski, Apr. 14, 1957; 1 child, Elena. PhD in Math., Pedagogical U., Moscow, 1965. Leading engr. Petrochemical Ctr., Moscow, 1956-62; sr. rsch. fellow T-ermal Instruments Rsch. Inst., Moscow, 1962-65; assoc. prof. Corr. Civil Engring. Inst., Moscow, 1966-90. Inventor: 1985, 93, 97. Home: Yair 5/8, Netanya 42487, Israel

LANZA, JOHN FRANCIS, JR., artist, educator; b. Weymouth, Mass., Dec. 31, 1948; s. John Francis and Sadie (Rizzotto) L.; m. Kathy Louise McGill, Aug. 1, 1976; children: Rebecca Elizabeth, Maria Melanie. BA cum laude, Amherst Coll., 1971; MFA, Boston U., 1975. Painting conservator Iso Papo, Brookline, Mass., 1974-86; prof. Art Inst. of Boston, Lesley Coll., 1978—, coord. drawing and sculpture, 1981—, acting dept. illustration dept., 1989, acting dept. chair found. dept., 1998; instr. anatomy Cambridge Ctr. Adult Edn., 1977-85; instr. anatomy and painting South Shore Art Ctr., Cohasset, Mass., 1979-81; instr. Boston Visual Sch., Trieste, Italy, 1988-91, Viterbo, Italy, 1994, Montserrat Coll. Art, Viterbo, 1997; sec., clk. Boston Visual Sch., Dorchester, Mass., 1991-95; jurist South Shore Art Ctr., 1981—; chair curriculum com. Art Inst. of Boston, Lesley Coll., 1985-88, sec., 1988-95, ad hoc faculty com., sec. faculty/staff senate and coun., 1990-99, rep., 1980-88, faculty affairs and acad. policies com., 1999—. Illustrator: Heritage Collection, The Bragging Tortoise, Theme Books, 1989; one-man show at Helen Bumpus Gallery, 1996; exhibited in group shows at Art Inst. Boston, 1979-99, South Shore Art Ctr., 1979-99 (Best Realist award 1988, 2d pl. award for oils 1987), Art Inst. Boston Show, 1980, 84, 90, Boston Visual Sch. Exhibits, 1989, 90, 91, U.S. Extemporaneous Show, 1994, U.S. Extemporaneous Show, Vitorchiano, Italy, 1994, Attleboro Mus., 1998. Libr. vol. Plymouth River Sch., Hingham, Mass., 1988—; worship commn. St. John the Evangelist Ch., Hingham, 1991—. Recipient Disting. Svc. award, Plymouth River Sch., 1998; fellow Amherst Coll. 1969, Boston U., 1973. Avocations: reading, traveling abroad. E-mail: lanzafamily@aol.com. Home: 152 Summer St Hingham MA 02043-1062

LANZAVECCHIA, ANTONIO, immunologist; b. Varese, Italy, Oct. 9, 1951. MD, U. Pavia, 1976. Asst. prof. U. Genoa, Italy, 1981-87; mem. Basel Inst. Immunology, Switzerland, 1983-89; assoc. prof. U. Genoa, 1987-98; permanent mem. Basel Inst. Immunology, 1990-99; vis. prof. immunology U. Siena, Italy, 1999—; dir. Inst. Rsch. in Biomedicine, Bellinzona, Switzerland, 1999—. Recipient medal European Molecular Biology Orgn., 1988, prize Cloetta Found., 1999.

LANZILLO, BERNARDO, neurologist; b. Cardito, Naples, Italy, Nov. 26, 1958; s. Sossio and Anna (Vitagliano) L.; m. Andreina Raucci, Sept. 19, 1987; children: Anna, Caterina. MD, Naples U., 1984. Cons. neurologist F. S. Maugeri, Campoli, 1986—. Mem. Italian Neurologic Soc. Roman Catholic. Avocations: boats, modeling, travel. Home: Via C Battisti 142, 80024 Cardito Naples, Italy Office: F S Maugeri Centro Campoli, Via N Bixio 10, 82030 Campoli Benevent, Italy

LANZINGER, KLAUS, language educator; b. Woergl, Tyrol, Austria, Feb. 16, 1928; came to U.S., 1971, naturalized, 1979; m. Aida Schuessl, June, 1954; children—Franz, Christine. B.A., Bowdoin Coll., 1951; Ph.D., U. Innsbruck (Austria), 1952. Research asst. U. Innsbruck, 1957-67; assoc. prof. modern langs. U. Notre Dame (Ind.), 1967-77, prof., 1977-97, prof. emeritus, 1997—, resident dir. fgn. study program, Innsbruck, 1969-71, 76-78, 82-85; acting chmn. dept. Modern and Classical Languages, U. Notre Dame, fall 1987, chmn. dept. German and Russian, 1989-96. Author: Epik im amerikanischen Roman, 1965, Jason's Voyage: The Search for the Old World in American Literature, 1989. Editor: Americana-Austriaca, 5 vols., 1966-83. Contbr. numerous articles to profl. jours. Bowdoin Coll. fgn. student scholar, 1950-51; Fulbright research grantee U. Pa., 1961; U. Notre Dame summer research grantee Houghton Library, Harvard U., 1975, 81. Mem. MLA, Deutsche Gesellschaft für Amerikastudien, Thomas Wolfe Soc. Home: 52703 Helvie Dr South Bend IN 46635-1215 Office: Dept German Russian Langs & Lits U Notre Dame Notre Dame IN 46556

LANZISERA, VINCENT ANTHONY, microwave engineer; b. Bklyn., Apr. 6, 1933; s. Joseph Crescent and Emma (Uliano) L.; m. Patricia Margaret O'Connell, June 26, 1976; m. Cecelia Russamano, Apr. 7, 1956; 1 child, Joanne. Student, N.Y. C.C., 1957-59, Queens Coll., 1959-64. Tech. Sperry, Greatneck, N.Y., 1956-62; tech. assoc. GTE Labs., Bayside, N.Y., 1962-72, Microwave Assocs., Burlington, Mass., 1972-73; mem. tech. staff GTE Labs., Waltham, Mass., 1973-96, ret., 1996. Inventor in field. Bd. dirs. Cable TV Commn., Northboro, Mass., 1992-93. With USAF, 1952-56. Mem. IEEE, Elks.

LANZKRON, ROLF WOLFGANG, manufacturing company executive; b. Hamburg, Germany, Dec. 9, 1929; came to U.S., 1951, naturalized, 1961; s. Aron Artur and Hanna (Farbstein) L. m. Amy Virginia Yarri, Mar. 5, 1961; children: Paul Joshua, Sophie Miriam, Lisa Rachel. BS, Milw. Sch. Engring., 1953; MS, U. Wis., 1955, PhD, 1956. Registered profl. engr. Calif. Computer designer Univac Sperry Rand, St. Paul, 1956-58; guidance and control systems integrations staff Martin Marietta, Orlando, Fla., 1958-61; systems engr. Martin Marietta, Balt., 1961-68; became chief command and svc. module flight project div. NASA Manned Spacecraft Ctr., Apollo Program, Houston, 1963; graphic ops. mgr. Raytheon Co., Marlborough, Mass., 1968-82, dep. dir. air traffic control, 1982-92, dir. air traffic control, 1992-95; pres. RWL Assocs. Conss., 1995; Registered profl. engr., Calif. With Israeli Army, 1948-51. Recipient NASA Outstanding Achievement award, 1964, Spl. Svc. award, 1966. Mem. AIAA, Am. Math. Soc., IEEE, Am. Mgmt. Assn., Sigma Xi. Fax: 978 282-4897. Office: RWL Assoc Consulting Firm 2 Mallard Way Gloucester MA 01930-3243

LAPADATU, DANIEL ILIUTA, design engineer, researcher; b. Turnu Magurele, Teleorman, Romania, Aug. 17, 1967; s. Gheorghe and Floarea (Vijiala) L.; m. Adriana Maria Cozma, Oct. 22, 1988; 1 child, Monica. BS, UNIREA H.S., Turnu Magurele, Romania, 1985; Engring. Diploma, Poly. Inst., Bucharest, Romania, 1991; MS, Cath. U., Leuven, Belgium, 1992, PhD, 1996. Rschr. Cath. U. Leuven, 1991-96; design engr. SensoNor asa, Horten, Norway, 1996—; mgr. Union Cons. and Devel., Turnu Magurele, Romania, 1997—. Contbr. articles to profl. jours. Tempus grantee European Union, 1991; recipient Mention Internat. Physics Olympiad, 1985, First Prize Nat. Physics Contest, 1987. Mem. IEEE, Electron Device Soc. of IEEE. Achievements include patents for photovolvic etch technique, 1992, micromechanical device for stress release. Avocations: world history, mountain hiking, science fiction. Fax: 47-33035105. E-mail: daniel.lapadatu@sensonor.no. Office: SensoNor asa, Knudsrødveien 7, N-3192 Horten Vestfold, Norway

LA PERGOLA, ANTONIO, legal administrator; b. Catania, Nov. 13, 1931. Degree in Law, U. Catania. Qualified solicitor; specialization in G.b., Holland, U.S. Prof. U. Padua, Italy, U. Bologna, Italy, U. Rome, U. Argentina, U. America; dir. Inst. of Regional Studies CNRS; elected mem. Superior Coun. of the Judiciary, 1976; judge Constnl. Ct., 1978, pres., 1986-87; min. EEC policies Goria Govt., 1987-88, De Mita Govt., 1988-89; mem. European Parliament S-Socialist Group, 1989; chmn. Com. on Energy, rsch. and tech., substitute com. Instnl. Affairs and mem. Del. for Rels. with Ctrl. Am., Mex.; mem., then chmn. Com. on Energy, Rsch., Tech., chmn. Com. on Culture, Youth, Edn. and Media, Com. on Instnl. Affairs, 1992-94; advocate gen. European Ct. Justice, Luxembourg, 1994-99, judge, 1999-; mem. Del. for Rels. with Countries of Ctrl. Am. and Mex. and substitute Del. for Rels.. with Mashreq countries; mem. com. of 3 jurists set up by Prime Min. to devise rules for cleavage of pvt. interest from pub. office, 1994. Office: European Ct of Justice, Blvd Konrad Adenauer, L-2925 Kirchberg Luxembourg*

LAPID, KOTY, economist, researcher; b. Nyrbator, Hungary, Feb. 7, 1949; arrived in Israel, 1971; d. Henrik and Ilona (Lipsitz) Grosz; m. Joshua Lapid, June 28, 1977; children: Eyal, Noa. BSc, Ben Gurion U., Beer Sheva, Israel, 1984, MSc, 1989; PhD, Hungarian Acad. Scis., 1995. Cert. prof. indsl. engr. Rschr. Jerusalem Inst. Israel Studies, 1985-93; lectr. Ben Gurion U., 1985-93; ind. rschr. Budapest, Hungary, 1994—; regional corr. Internat. Asn. Mgmt. Tech., Miami, 1996—, track co-chair 2000, referee Portland Internat. Conf. Mgmt. Engrng. Tech. , Portland, Oreg., 1997—, Acad. Mgmt., N.Y.C., 1997—, organizer sessions Inst. Ops. Rsch. Mgmt. Sci., Providence, 1997—. Author: Technology and Competitiveness, 1997, (booklet) Externalities and Learning Patterns During the Innovation Process, 1994, Innovation and Competitiveness in the Economy, 1996; contbr. articles to profl. jours. and conf. procs., chpts. to books. Elected mem. student coun., Ben Gurion U., 1980-81; co-founder Women's Group for Better Family Relationships and Sex Life, Beer Sheva, 1979-81; mem. Israeli Orgn. Working Women's Rights, Beer Sheva, 1972—. Mem. N.Y. Acad. Scis., Acad. Mgmt. Avocations: textile sculpturing, walking, storytelling, website development. E-mail: korylapid@softblock.net.

LAPIDUS, DENNIS, real estate developer; b. Chgo., Oct. 21, 1942; s. Sidney and Mildred (Karlin) L. BSME, Northwestern U., 1964; MBA, Roosevelt U., 1967. Pres., founder Productive Computer Sys., Chgo., 1980-86, MBI Leasing, Chgo., 1986—. Bd. dirs. Anti-Cruelty Soc., New Century Bank. Productive Computer Sys. named to Inc. Mag. 500 Fastest Growing

Privately Held Cos., 1986. Mem. Ravisloe Country Club, Medinah Country Club. Avocations: golf, basketball. Home: 1941 N Fremont St Chicago IL 60614-5016 Office: MBI Leasing PO Box 146522 Chicago IL 60614-6400

LAPIDUS, LEIF JOSEF, physician; b. Boras, Sweden, Jan. 26, 1950; s. Bengt-Olov and Anna-Lisa (Byk) L.; m. Ulla Margareta Friman, Oct. 28, 1972; children: John, Robert, Daniel. BA, U. Göteborg, Sweden, 1971; MD, U. Göteborg, 1976, PhD, 1985, specialist in internal medicine, 1984. Asst. physician Gen. Hosp., Jönköping, Sweden, 1976-78; postgrad. trainee internal medicine County Hosp., Kungälv, Sweden, 1978-82; rsch. fellow U. Göteborg, 1982-85; assoc. prof. dept. medicine Sahlgren's U. Hosp., Göteborg, 1986—, head physician dept. medicine, 1989—; rsch. mem. Prospective Population Study of Women, Göteborg, 1982—. Contbr. articles to profl. jours. Recipient Annual award Swedish Female Victoria Order, 1991. Mem. Swedish Cardiologists Union. Avocations: photography, golf, tennis, 20th century art. Home: Hyvelspånsgatan 3, S-41680 Göteborg Sweden Office: Dept Medicine, Sahlgren's Univ Hosp, S-41345 Göteborg Sweden

LAPIN, BORIS ARKADIEVICH, pathologist; b. Kharkov, USSR, Aug. 10, 1921; s. Arkady Julievich and Faina (Borisovna) L.; m. Ester Iliinichna Kurdina, June 10, 1944 (dec. 1969); children: Elena B. Lapina, Arkady B. Lapin; m. Lelita Andreevna Yakovleva, Dec. 20, 1969. MD, Moscow 2nd Med. Inst., 1949; PhD, Acad. of Med. Scis., Moscow, 1952, Dr.M.Sci., 1958. Pathologist 13th Clin. Hosp., Moscow, 1950-52; rsch. scientist Med.-Biol. Sta., Acad. of Med. Sci., Sukhumi, Russia, 1952-53; rsch. dir. Inst. Exptl. Pathology and Therapy Acad. of Med. Sci., Sukhumi, 1953-57, dir., 1958-92; dir. Inst. of Med. Primatol. Russian Acad. of Med. Sci., Sochi-Adler, Russia, 1992—; head dept. health Inst. of Exptl. Pathology, Sukhumi, 1957-92; adviser to the presidium Acad. of Med. Sci., 1992—; chair prof. Dept. of Exptl. Pathology Abkhasian State U., 1980-92. Author: Monkey Diseases as a Model of Human Diseases, 1960; co-author: Comparative Pathology in Monkeys, 1963, (with L. Yakoleva) Pathology of Simian Primates, 1972, Nonhuman Primates and Medical Research, 1974; mem. bd. Jour. Med. Primatology, 1972-96, Exptl. Pathology, 1968-90, others; contbr. over 600 articles to profl. jours. Dep. Supreme Soviet of Abkhazia, 1983, Supreme Soviet of Georgia., Tbilisi, 1980; chmn. primate commn. Acad. Med. Sci., 1969—; pres. Russian Found. of Med. Primatology, Moscow, 1995. Lt. Airforce, 1941-44. Recipient Medal of Astronaut Gagarin, 1981, Korolev medal, 1986, V. Timakov prize in virology, 1984, State prize Russia, 1997, also 8 orders, 17 medals; named honored citizen Sochi, Ga., Abkhazia. Mem. Am. Soc. Primatology, German Acad. Natural Sci., Russian Acad. Med. Sci., Russian Acad. Natural Sci., N.Y. Acad. Sci., Intern. Acad. Sci., Russian Sect., correspondent, Internat. Acad. of Astronautics, (corr.), Russian Soc. of Pathologists, Hungarian Soc. of Microbiology (hon. mem.), Internat. Assn. Comparative Leukemia and Related Diseases (v.p. 1977-79, pres. 1979-81), Am. Assn. Advancement Sci., Internat. Primatological Soc., Nat. Geograpic Soc. Avocations: collecting minerals and rosary. Home & Office: Inst Med Primatology, Russian Acad Med Sci, 354376 Sochi-Adler Veseloye, Russia

LAPLANTZ, DAVID MILTON, artist, educator; b. Toledo, June 12, 1944; s. Milton N. LaPlantz and Bernice L. Merle; m. Shereen F. Buckland, Feb. 7, 1970. BS in Edn., Bowling Green State U., 1966; MFA in Metal Smithing, Cranbrook Acad. Art, 1969. Instr. jewelry Inst. Am. Indian Arts, Santa Fe, 1967-68, Flint (Mich.) C.C., 1968-69, Colo. State U., Ft. Collins, 1969-70; asst. prof. art San Diego Sate U., 1970-71; asst. prof. Humboldt State U., Arcata, Calif., 1971-77, prof., 1978—; vis. artist Kent (Ohio) State U., 1977-78. Editor: Jewelry Metalwork Survey 1991: Survey, Visions, Concepts, Communicating, 1991, Jewelry/Metal Work Survey #2: A Way of Communicating, 1992, Jewelry/Metalwork Survey #3: Ideas, Images, Imagemakers, 1993; exhibited in group shows at Oliver Art Ctr., Calif. Coll. Arts and Crafts, Oakland, 1990, Connel Gallery, Atlanta, 1990, Great Am. Gallery, Atlanta, 1990, Ont. (Can.) Crafts Coun.'s Craft Gallery, 1993, Nat. Libr., Ottawa, Can., 1993, Gallery Craft Alliance, St. Louis, 1994, Oakland Mus. Art, 1994, Montgomery Coll. Art Gallery, Rockville, Md., 1996, John Waldron Arts Ctr., Bloomington, Ind., 1998, Eloise Pickard Smith Gallery, U. Calif., Santa Cruz, Calif., 1999; represented in permanent collections Am. Craft Mus., N.Y.C., Calif. Crafts Mus., San Francisco, Nat. Mus. Am. Art, Smithsonian Instn., Washington, Nat. Mus. Modern Art, Kyoto, Japan, Oakland Mus. Art, Ont. Crafts Coun., Toronto, Can., Schmuckmuseum, Pforzheim, Germany. Chairperson, mem. adv. com. Sta. KHSU-FM, Humboldt State U., Arcata, 1992-94. Fulbright scholar 1985. Avocations: motorcycles, custom cars, landscaping. Home: 1957 Bartow Rd Mckinleyville CA 95519-4313 Office: Humboldt State U Art Dept 1 Harpst St Arcata CA 95521-8222

LAPORTE, ADRIENNE AROXIE, nursing administrator; b. Oceanside, N.Y., Sept. 29, 1938; d. Leonide and Grace (Ajamian) LaP. Diploma in nursing, St. John's Episc. Hosp., 1960; BA in Behavioral Scis., Lesley Coll., 1986; MA in Counseling, Liberty U., 1994. RN, N.Y., Fla., Mass., La., Ala.; cert. psychiat./mental health nurse Am. Nurses Credentialing Bd. Supr. Creedmoor State Hosp., Queens Village, N.Y., 1960-66, Taunton (Mass.) State Hosp., 1985-87, Mental Health Resources, Jacksonville, Fla., 1990-92, Staff Builders Home Health Agy., New Bedford, Mass., 1996-99; supr. psychiat. unit Univ. Hosp. of Jacksonville, 1977-79, Parkwood Hosp., New Bedford, 1980-84; dir. nursing Care Unit of Jacksonville Beach, Fla., 1987-90, Bradford Adult & Adolescent, Pelham, Ala., 1992-93, 94-95; program dir. Bowling Green Hosp., Mandeville, La., 1993; therapist Ctr. for Health and Human Svcs., Inc., New Bedford, Mass., 1999—. Lt. col. Nurse Corps U.S. Army, 1966-87, Vietnam. Decorated Bronze Star, Legion of Merit, Armed Forces Res. medal, Army Commendation medal, Combat Readiness medal, Meritorious Svc. medal, Presdl. and Unit citation, Republic of Vietnam Campaign medal, Vietnam Svc. medal. Mem. ACA, VFW, Nurses Soc. on Addictions, Fla. Nurses Assn., Am. Legion, Vietnam Vets. Am., Internat. Soc. Psychiat.-Mental Health Nurses. Home: Pine Hill Acres 47 Little Oak Rd New Bedford MA 02745-2021

LAPORTE, ERIC, computer science educator; b. Saint-Quentin, France, July 9, 1962; s. Jean-Claude and Nicole (Mathez) L. Dr., Ecole Normale Superieure, Paris, 1988; Dr.hab., U. Paris, 1993. Asst. prof. U. Paris, 1989-95; prof. U. Reims, France, 1995-98; rschr., head rsch. team U. Marne-la-Vallée, France, 1991—, prof., 1998—. Author: Phonemic Dictionary of French, 1988. 2nd class Scientific Dept., 1987-88. Scientific prize Philip Morris, 1989. Avocation: counter-tenor. Home: 16 passage de la Main-d'Or, F-75011 Paris France Office: U Marne-la-Vallée, 5 bd Descartes, F-77454 Marne-la-Vallée Cedex 2, France

LAPORTE, YVES MICHEL, neurobiologist; b. Toulouse, France, Dec. 20, 1920; s. Frederic and Yvonne (Grill) L.; m. Beatrice Colomb De Daunant, Sept. 14, 1945; children: Anne, Edmée. MD, Toulouse U., 1947; MD (hon.), Goteborg (Sweden) U., 1990. Asst. Rockefeller Inst., N.Y.C., 1949-51; asst. prof. Med. Sch., Toulouse, 1952-61, prof. physiology, 1961-71; prof. neurophysiology Coll. France, Paris, 1972-91, hon. prof., 1991—; pres. Coll. France, 1980-91. Contbr. articles to profl. jours. With French Army, 1944-45. Mem. French Acad. Scis. Office: Coll France, Place Marcelin Berthelot, 75231 Paris France

LAPTENOK, IGOR NIKOLAYEVICH, publisher; b. Minsk, Belarus, Aug. 31, 1947; s. Nikolai Danilovich and Larisa Vasilyevna (Burko) L.; m. Helen Georgiyevna Pogorelova, Nov. 14, 1975; children: Denis, Anna. Diploma tchr., interpreter, Belarusian Linguistic U., Minsk, 1971; diploma in Journalism, Minsk Higher Sch., 1979. Chief ednl. staff Vysheishaya Shkola Pubs., Minsk, Belarus, 1975-77, 79-87; editor-in-chief, head dept. Belarus State Com. for Pub., Printing and Book Trade, Minsk, 1987-90; dir. Narodnaya Asveta Pubs., Minsk, 1990—. Translator: Your Child from 0 to 3, 1985, Physics II, 1991, Culture and Democracy, 1995; contbr. articles to profl. jours. Mem. Belarusian Assn. Pubs., Printers and Book-Sellers (mem. bd. 1994-96, 98—), State Com. on Press Belarus (bd. dirs. 1996). Avocations: books, collecting stamps, coins, playing chess. Home: 87 Skorina Ave, 220012 Minsk Belarus Office: Narodnaya Asveta, Prospekt Masherova 11, 220600 Minsk Belarus

LAPUENTE, MANUEL, professional soccer coach, former player; b. May 15, 1944. Player Monterrey Team, Mex.; player Puebla Team, Mex., coach; winner Nat. Championship, 1983, 90; player Necaxa Team, Mex., coach; winner Mex. League Title, 1996; player Atlas Team, Mex.; coach Mex. Nat. Team, 1990-91, 97-98; winner Gold Cup, U.S., 1998; coach World Cup, Mexico, 1998. Coached Mex. Soccer Team to U.S. Cup, 1999; winner Copa Am. and Confedn. Cup, 1999. Office: Abraham Gonzalez 74, Col Juarez, CP 06600 Mexico City DF, Mexico*

LARA, CATALINA, biochemist, researcher, educator; b. Montoro, Spain, Feb. 13, 1953; d. Bartolomè and Francisca (Coronado) L.; m. Angel De la Torre; children: Julia, Sergio. PharmM, U. Granada, Spain, 1975; PharmD, 1981. Asst. prof. U. Granada, Spain, 1976-78; fellow U. Calif., Berkeley, 1978-80; rsch. biochemist, 1980-81; postdoctoral fellow U. Sevilla, Spain, 1981-84; adjunct prof., 1984-85, prof., 1985—. Contbr. more than 50 articles to profl. jours. and scientific books. Grantee Spanish Dir. Gen. Sci. and Tech. Investigation U. Sevilla, 1989-92, 1992-95, 1995-98. Mem. Soc. Biochemistry Biol. Molecular, Soc. Physiology Vegetal, Fedn. European Societies of Plant Physiology. Avocations: music, literature, painting. Office: Dept Bioquimica Vegetal y Biologia Molecular, USE Apdo 1095, E-41080 Sevilla Spain

LARA, FRANCISCO, botany educator, researcher; b. Córdoba, Spain, Apr. 9, 1963; s. Antonio Lara and Isabel García; m. María Vegara, Sept. 9, 1995; 1 child, Lucia. Lic. in biology, U. Autónoma Madrid, 1986, PhD in Biology, 1993. Collaborator tchr. Batres Landscape Gardening Sch., Madrid, 1988-95; univ. tchr. CEU Univ. Sch., Madrid, 1993-96; assoc. prof. U. Autónoma Madrid, 1995—. Co-author: Riparian Vegetation of the Jarama Basin, 1995. U. Autónoma Madrid grantee, 1987; Min. Edn. rsch. fellow, 1989. Mem. Internat. Assn. Bryologist, Spanish Soc. Bryology (pres. 1997—). Avocation: outdoor activities. Home: C/Poniente 19, E-28290 Madrid Spain Office: U Autónoma Madrid, Cantoblanco, E-28049 Madrid Spain

LARAGH, JOHN HENRY, physician, scientist, educator; b. Yonkers, N.Y., Nov. 18, 1924; s. Harry Joseph and Grace Catherine (Coyne) L.; m. Adonia Kennedy, Apr. 28, 1949; children: John Henry, Peter Christian, Robert Sealey; m. Jean E. Sealey, Sept. 22, 1974. MD, Cornell U., 1948. Diplomate Am. Bd. Internal Medicine. Intern Presbyn. Hosp., N.Y.C., 1948-49; asst. resident Presbyn. Hosp., 1949-50; cardiology trainee Nat. Heart Inst., 1950-51; rsch. fellow N.Y. Heart Assn., 1951-52; asst. physician Presbyn. Hosp., 1950-55, asst. attending, 1954-61, assoc. attending, 1961-69, attending physician, 1969-75, pres. elect med. bd., 1972-74; faculty Coll. Physicians and Surgeons Columbia U., 1950-75, prof. clin. medicine, 1967-75, spokesman exec. com. faculty coun., 1971-73; vice-chmn. bd. trustees for profl. and sci. affairs Presbyn. Hosp., 1974-75; dir. Hypertension Ctr., chief nephrology divsn. Columbia-Presbyn. Med. Ctr., 1971-75; Master prof. medicine, dir. Hypertension and Cardiovascular Ctr., N.Y. Hosp.-Cornell Med. Ctr., 1975—, chief cardiology div., 1975-95; cons. USPHS, 1964—. Editor-in-chief Am. Jour. Hypertension, Cardiovascular Reviews and Reports; Editor: Hypertension Manual, 1974, Topics in Hypertension, 1980, Frontiers in Hypertension Rsch., 1981; editor Hypertension: Pathophysiology, Diagnosis, and Management, 1990, 1995; editorial bd.: Am. Jour. Medicine, Am. Jour. Cardiology, Kidney Internat., Jour. Clin. Endocrinology and Metabolism, Hypertension, Jour. Hypertension, Circulation, Am. Heart Jour., Procs. of Soc. Exptl. Biology and Medicine, Heart and Vessels. Mem. policy adv. bd. hypertension detection and follow-up program Nat. Heart and Lung Inst., 1971, bd. sci. counselor, 1974-79; chmn. U.S.A.-USSR Joint Program in Hypertension, 1977-93. With U.S. Army, 1943-46. Recipient Stouffer prize Med. Rsch., 1969, J.K. Lattimer award Am. Urol. Assn., 1989, Robert Tigerstedt award Am. Soc. Hypertension, 1990, John P. Peters award Am. Soc. Nephrology, 1990, Lifetime Achievement in Medicine award N.Y. Acad. Medicine, 1993, Disting. Alumnus award Cornell U. Med. Coll., 1993, Bristol Myers Squibb award for disting. achievement cardiovalcular rsch., 1996, Disting. Achievement award Coun. for High Blood Pressure Rsch., Am. Heart Assn., 1999; subject of Time Mag. cover story, 1975; Most Frequently Cited Scientist: Top Ten Advances in Cardiopulmonary Medicine, 1946-75. Fellow Am. Coll. Cardiology; mem. ACP (Master), Am. Heart Assn. (chmn. med. adv. bd. coun. high blood pressure rsch. 1968-72), Am. Soc. Clin. Investigation, Assn. Am. Physicians, Assn. Univ. Cardiologists, Endocrine Soc., Am. Soc. Nephrology, Am. Soc. Hypertension (founder, 1st pres. 1986-88), Internat. Soc. Hypertension (pres. 1986-88), Harvey Soc., Kappa Sigma, Nu Sigma Nu, Alpha Omega Alpha, Country Club of Fla., Shinnecock Hills Golf Club (Southampton, N.Y.). Achievements include research on hormones, renin, aldosterone and electrolyte metabolism and renal physiology, mechanisms of edema formation and on causes and treatments of high blood pressure. E-mail: dczhang@suda.edu.com. Home: 5 Sandpiper Dr Vlg Of Golf FL 33436-5621 Office: NY Hosp-Cornell Med Ctr 525 E 68th St New York NY 10021-4885

LA RAJA, MARIA CRISTINA, psychiatrist, researcher; b. Trieste, Italy, May 2, 1925; d. Vincenzo La Raja and Rita Saraval. Degree in arts, U. Torino, Italy, 1948; degree in medicine, U. Rome, 1975; degree in psychiatry, U. Trieste, 1981. Prof. arts Pio XII Normal Sch., Sondrio, Italy, 1962-64; prof. Italian lang. East Ham Tech. Coll., London, 1966-67; prof. jr. high schs., Rome, 1968-77; asst. physician Villa Napoleon Clinic, Treviso, Italy, 1977-83; psychiat. rschr. U. Rome, 1986-87, 95-96; prof. psychosociology S. Giuseppe Hosp., Rome, 1987; counsellor Italian League Against Tumors, Treviso, 1983-87, co-dir. gazette, 1983-87. Author: (poetry) Due Tempi, 1971; co-author: Psychoanalysis and Religion, 1980-85; journalist cultural transmissions Italian Radio, 1950-60, Vaticano Radio, 1961-70, 92-93. Recipient health award Internat. Acad. Econ. and Social Scis., Rome, 1995. Mem. AAAS, Internat. Acad. Scis. of Nature and Soc., N.Y. Acad. Scis. Home: Via A Foschini 20, 00163 Rome Italy

LARAKI, AZEDINE, prime minister of Morocco; b. Fez, Morocco, 1929. Ph.D., Faculty of Medicine, Paris, 1957. Intern various hosps., Morocco; assoc. med. chief Province of Oujda, Morocco; dir. cabinet Minister of Nat. Edn, Morocco, 1958, Ministry of Pub. Health, 1959; dir. Avicennes Hosp., head respiratory surgery and pneumology, 1967—; prof. Faculty of Medicine, 1967—; minister nat. edn. Morocco, 1977—, vice prime minister, 1985, prime minister, 1986-92; chancellor Al Akhawayn U., Ifrane, Morocco, 1992-96; sec. general Org. Islamic Conf., Jeddah, Saudi Arabia, 1997—; v.p. 4th extraordinary session UNESCO, Paris, 1982; v.p. 23d gen. conf. UNESCO, Sofia, 1985. Address: Office of Prime Minister, Rabat Morocco

LARA-ROSANO, FELIPE, systems engineer; b. Puebla, Mexico, Mar. 22, 1938; s. Jesus and Eva (Rosano) Lara; m. Beatriz Garcia (div. 1970); 1 child, Felipe; m. Guadalupe Elisa Velazquez; 1 child, Rossana. BS in Engring., U. Puebla, 1962; MSc, Nat. Univ. Mex., 1970, PhD, 1973. Project engr. Siemens, Mexico City, 1965-69; assoc. prof. inst. engring. Nat. U. Mex., Mexico City, 1970-75; gen. dir. Barros-Sierra Found., Mexico City, 1975-77; sr. rschr. Nat. U. Mex., 1978—, head grad. dept. sch. engring., 1991-93, dir. Ctr. for Instrumentation Rsch., 1997; cons. Pub. Edn. Ministry, Mexico City, 1980; guest prof. U. Karlsruhe, Germany, 1985. Internat. Inst. Advanced Studies in Sys. Rsch. and Cybernetics fellow, Baden-Baden, Germany, 1992. Mem. N.Y. Acad. Scis. Achievements include planning techniques, simulation models for complex systems and expert systems development for engineering and medicine. Office: UNAM, Apartado 70-418, Coyoacan Mexico City 04510, Mexico

LARA-URBANEJA, JORGE, lawyer; b. Bogota, Colombia, July 9, 1944; s. Alfonso Lara and Luisa Amelia (Urbaneja) de Lara; m. Rosario Lopez, Aug. 22, 1969; children: Eduardo, Jorge Alfonso. BS, Colegio Santiago de Leon de, Caracas, Venezuela, 1961; LLD, Colegio del Rosario, Bogota, 1968; postgrad., Kent Law Sch., Chgo., 1979-80. Adminstrv. mgr. Colminas Ltda., Bogota, 1967-69; assoc. Raisbeck & Raisbeck, Bogota, 1969-73; ptnr. Lar & Lara, Bogota, 1973-79, Baker & McKenzie, Bogota, 1980—; exec. pres. C. of C. Colombia-Venezuela, Bogota, 1976-77, mem. adv. com. 1977—; mem. Profl. Responsibility and Practice Com., Baker & McKenzie, 1996-2000; regional coord. Baker & McKenzie Banking and Fin. Region Practice, 1997; bd. dirs. Coun. Am. Cos. Author: Tracing Assets, Vol. II, 1997; contbg. author: Global Securities Market, 1995-98; contbr. articles to profl. jours. Fracisco de Miranda Order, Govt. of Venezuela, Caracas, 1993. Mem. Country Club of Bogota, Jockey Club of Bogota, Gun Club of Bogota. Avocations: golf, billiards, bridge, music, sea sports. Office: Baker & McKenzie, Calle 35 No 7-25 Piso 4, Bogota Colombia

LARBERG, JOHN FREDERICK, wine consultant, educator; b. Kansas City, Mo., Jan. 21, 1930; s. Herman Alvin and Ann (Sabrowsky) L. AA, Kansas City Jr. Coll., 1948; AB cum laude, U. Mo., 1950, postgrad., 1955-56; MSW, Bryn Mawr Coll., 1961. Cert. social worker. With Westinghouse Electric Corp., 1953-56; dir. House of Industry Settlement House, Phila., 1957-61; asst. to exec. dir. Health and Welfare Coun., Inc., Phila., 1961-66; sr. staff cons., 1966-73, dir. Washington office, 1971-72, Nat. Assembly for Social Policy and Devel., Inc., N.Y.C.; nat. dir. community and patient services Nat. Multiple Sclerosis Soc., N.Y.C., 1974-81, nat. dir. spl. projects, 1981-82; adminstrv. v.p. Fedn. Protestant Welfare Agys. N.Y., 1982-86; sr. advisor, 1986-87; exec. dir. Am. Assn. State Social Work Bds., 1987-89; cons. The Wine Aficionado, N.Y., 1990—. Cons. exec. com. Commn. on Vol. Svc. and Action, 1967-76, cons. Met. N.Y. Project Equality, 1968-73, Encampment for Citizenship, 1973-74, Symphony for UN, 1974-77, Lower Eastside Fam. Union, 1984—, Wielenga Psych. Svc., 1993—, Malignant Hyperthermia Assn. U.S., 1994—, Internat. Fedn. Multiple Sclerosis Socs., 1995—, Nat. Multiple Sclerosis Soc., 1997—; bd. dirs. Health Systems Agy. of N.Y., 1984-86; trustee The Riverside Ch., N.Y.C., 1985-89, worship commn., 1992-94, ordination com., 1993—, chmn., 1996—; bd. dirs., mem. exec. com. Metro Assn. United Ch. of Christ, N.Y., 1993—, dir. N.Y. state coun., 1995—, nat. del. Gen. Synod, 1997; mem. Disciples of Christ/United Ch. of Christ N.Y. State Joint Task Force, 1996—; nat. dir. Coun. Soc. Wk. Edn., 1985-86. Served with AUS, 1951-53. Mem. Acad. Cert. Social Workers (charter), Nat. Assn. Social Workers (chpt. legis. com. 1968-70, nat. publs. com. 1968-71, nat. legal regulation com. 1987-89), Internat. Coun. Social Welfare (internat. com. of reps. 1980-84, U.S. com. for Internat. Coun. Social Welfare, bd. dirs. 1983-90, exec. com. 1983-90), Internat. Fedn. Multiple Sclerosis Socs. (vice chmn. patient services com. 1976-81, chmn. 1981-84, mem. individual and family services com. 1984-97, non-govtl. rep. to UN, 1990-96, rep. to Rehab. Internat. Med. Commn. 1976-81), Nat. Conf. Social Welfare (program com. 1966-73, chmn. combined assoc. groups 1969-70, nat. dir. 1971-73, 83-87), Fedn. of Assns. Regulatory Bds. (nat. dir. 1988-89), Malignant Hyperthermia Assn. U.S. (nat. dir. 1984-93, nat. pres. 1985-89, rep. 10th Quad. World Congr. Anesth. Hague 1992), Am. Acad. Polit. and Social Sci., Nat. Urban League (nat. trustee-at-large 1968), Hawk Mountain Sanctuary Assn., Bryn Mawr Social Work Alumni Assn. (pres. 1963-65), Am. Mus. Natural History, N.Y.C. Citizens Union, N.Y. Mcpl. Art Soc., Phi Beta Kappa Assn. N.Y. (pres. 1980-82), Omicron Delta Kappa, QEBH, Alpha Phi Omega, Alpha Pi Zeta, Pi Sigma Alpha, Alpha Kappa Psi. Home and Office: 400 E 58th St Apt 2F New York NY 10022-2333

LARDIHRE, OLIVIER, astronomer; b. Aox-en-Provence, France, Nov. 10, 1971; s. Bernard Lardihre and Chantal Pellet. Diploma in engring., Nat. Higher Sch. Caen, France, 1995; PhD, U. Provence, Marseilles, France, 1999. Engr. Haute-Provence Observatory, CNRS, St. Michel l'Observatory, France, 1996—. Co-discoverer Hale-Bopp comet, 1997; inventor in field. Mem. Soc. Popular Astronomy. Avocations: photography, computers. Fax: +33495706464. Office: Haute-Provence Observatory, 04870 Saint Michel L'Observatoire France

LARDNER, RING WILMER, JR., author; b. Chgo., Aug. 19, 1915; s. Ring Wilmer and Ellis (Abbott) L.; m. Silvia Schulman, Feb. 19, 1937 (div. 1945); children: Peter, Ann; m. Frances Chaney, Sept. 28, 1946; 1 child, James; stepchildren: Katharine, Joseph. Student, Princeton, 1932-34. Reporter N.Y. Daily Mirror, 1935; press agt. Selznick Internat. Pictures, Culver City, Calif., 1935-37; screenwriter various cos., 1937-82; freelance writer, 1982—. Screenwriter: (with Michael Kanin) Woman of the Year, 1942 (Acad. award 1942), (with Leopold Atlas) Tomorrow the World, 1944, (with Albert Maltz) Cloak and Dagger, 1946, (with Philip Dunne) Forever Amber, 1947, (with Terry Southern) The Cincinnati Kid, 1965, M*A*S*H, 1970 (Acad. award 1970), The Greatest, 1977; author: (novels) The Ecstasy of Owen Muir, 1955, All for Love, 1985, The Lardners: My Family Remembered, 1976; also TV and movie pieces; collaborator Broadway mus. Foxy, 1964. Recipient First Annual Writer's Tribute Nantucket Film Festival, 1998. Mem. Writers Guild Am. (Screen Laurel award 1989, Ian McLellan Hunter Meml. award for lifetime achievement 1992).

LARENTZAKIS, DIMITRIS S., air traffic control engineer; b. Athens, Greece, June 26, 1951; s. Stylianos and Stella (Lascari) L.; m. Vassiliki Stamatelou, Sept. 22, 1991; 1 child, Stella Despina. Degree in electronic engring., Advanced Sch. Electronics Eng., Athens, 1974. Cons. in high fidelity sys. designs and installation Electracoustiki, Athens, 1973-74; computer electronic engr. Graphotechniki, Athens, 1978-80, Control Data Greece Inc., Athens, 1980-83; air traffic control engr. Civil Aviation Authority, Athens, 1983—. Contbr. articles to tech. publs. Dir. Nat. Theater, 1977-78. Mem. IEEE, N.Y. Acad. Scis., Panhellenic Electronic Engr. Assn., Panhellenic Air Traffic Control Engring. Assn., Internat. Fedn. Air Traffic Safety Electronic Assns. Christian Orthodox. Avocations: swimming, snow skiing, electronic designs and construction, gardening. Home: 20 Amissou Str-New Smyrni, 17124 Athens Greece Office: Civil Aviation Orgn, Vas Georgiou 1 Elliniko, 16777 Athens Greece

LARGER, CHRISTIAN FRANÇOIS, advertising agency executive; b. Besançon, Doubs, France, June 10, 1953; s. Jean and Denise (Coillot) L.; m. Elizabeth Mouraret; children: Anne Sophie, Thibault, Flore, Julie. Diploma, Inst. D'Etudes Politiques, Paris, 1975; D Economy, Universite Dauphine, Paris, 1977. Cons. Hay Group, Paris, 1976-79, mgr. devel., 1979-84; CEO Hay Strategy & Orgn., Paris, 1984-88; exec. v.p. Hay France, Paris, 1988-90; mng. dir. Hay Internat. (Human Resources Planning & Devel.), London and Paris, 1990-91; CEO Saatchi & Saatchi Bus. Comm. Group, Paris, 1991—; vice chmn., mng. dir. Altavia Group, St. Ouen, France, 1999—. Author: Pour en Finir Avec La Bureaucratie, 1990, Les Dirigeants Face a l'Evolution de la Communication, 1992, 94, 97. Mem. Institut d'Etudes Politiques (prof., 1983—, mem. exec. bd. 1992—, sci. coun. 1993—, pres. Profl's Assn. 1998), SAR. E-mail: clarger@altavia group.com. Office: Altavia Group, 10 Rue Blanqui, Saint Oven 93406, France

LARGO, DANILO BASNILLO, biology educator; b. Cebu City, The Philippines, Feb. 21, 1961; s. Paz Basnillo Largo; m. Alona Remo, June 8, 1991; children: Ma. Kathryn, Tadahi. BSc, U. San Carlos, Cebu City, 1981, MSc, 1986; MSc, Kochi (Japan) U., 1995; PhD, Ehime U., Matsuyama, Japan, 1998. Rsch. asst. marine biology sect. U. San Carlos, Cebu City, 1981-82, microtechnician dept. biology, 1982-86, part-time instr. dept. biology, 1982-86, asst. prof. dept. biology, 1986-98, prof., dept. chmn. biology, 1998—, sect. head marine biology sect., 1990-92. Asst. editor: Seaweed Resources of the World, 1998; contbr. articles to profl. jours. Recipient Best Poster Presentation award 2nd Asia-Pacific Marine Biotechnology, Phubet, Thailand, 1997; named Most Outstanding Alumni, U. San Carlos, Cebu City, 1999, Outstanding Young Scientist in the Field of Aquatic and Environ. Sci., Nat. Acad. Sci. and Technol., Manila, The Philippines, 1999. Mem. Philippine Assn. Marine Sci., Asian Pacific Phycol. Forum, Phycol. Soc. Am. Roman Catholic. Avocations: playing guitar, singing, gardening. Office: Dept Biology, Univ San Carlos Talamban, Cebu City 6000, Philippines

LARIFLA, DOMINIQUE LUCIEN, Guadeloupean government official, cardiologist; b. Petit-Bourg, Guadeloupe, July 6, 1936; s. Stéphane and Julie (Gillot) L.; m. Simone Plaisir, July 31, 1965; children: Nathalie, Laurent, Pascal, Delphine. MD, U. Montpellier, France, diplome in cardiology. Med. asst., 1970-74, dep. med. hosp. head, 1974—; prof. Ctrl. de Formation et des Soins Infirmiers, Pointe-à-Pitre, Guadeloupe; mayor of Guadeloupe, 1977—; mem. Gen. Coun. of Guadeloupe, 1979—, pres., 1985—; mem. Regional Coun., 1979-83, 86-88; dep. of Guadeloupe, 1988-93, sen. of Guadeloupe, 1995—; rep. to French Senate, Paris, 1999—. Author: Fénestrations valvulaires aortiques, 1968, Aspect du tétanos en Guadeloupe, 1970, Quelques particularités de la fièvre typhoïde en Guadeloupe, 1972, la Siphylis cardiovasculaire en Guadeloupe, 1974, A propos de l'hypertension artérielle en Guadeloupe, 1983. Decorated chevalier L'Ordre Nat. du Mérite, L'Ordre des Arts et des Lettres. Office: Palais du Luxembourg, 15 rue de Vangirard, 75291 Paris Cedex 06, France*

LARIONOV, MIKHAIL GRIGORIEVICH, astrophysicist, researcher; b. Moscow, Apr. 21, 1941; s. Grigorii Lavrenievich and Vera Ivanovna (Patrikeeva) L.; ; Nina Aleksandrovna Dyomina, Oct. 15, 1967 (div. Apr. 1972); 1 child, Nataliya Mikhailovna; m. Larisa Nikolaevna Lesik, June 18, 1973; children: Grigorii Mikhailovich, Anastasiya Mikhailovna. Grad. in Astro-

nomy, Moscow State U., 1964, PhD, 1975. Faculty rsch. asst. Moscow State U., 1964-66; faculty rschr. Sternberg Astron. Inst., Moscow, 1969-78, lab. RATAN-600 chief, 1978-87, faculty rschr., 1987—, mem. coord. coun. radioastronomy complex program, 1990—. Recipient Silver medal for achieved success in developing nat. economy Maj. Com. USSR, 1985. Mem. Internat. Astron. Soc.. Avocations: fishing, playing guitar. Home: Olympiiskaya derevnya, Michurinskii Prospect, 117602 Moscow Russia Office: Sternberg Astron Inst, Universitetskiy Prospect 13, 119899 Moscow Russia

LARIONOV, OLEG ALEKSEEVICH, biologist, researcher; b. Kaliningrad, Russia, Feb. 5, 1952; s. Aleksey Fodorovich and Anna Ivanovna (Mityaeva) L.; m. Olga Georgievna Nickiforova, Aug. 1974 (div. 1976); 1 child, Maria; m. Nadeshda Pavlovna, June 21, 1980; children: Kate, Tania. MSc, Moscow Phys. Engring. Inst., 1975; PhD, Inst. Molecular Genetics, Moscow, 1982. Scientist Inst. Gen. Genetics, Moscow, 1980-86; scientist Inst. Bioorganic Chemistry, Moscow, 1986-88, sr. scientist, 1988-89, head sci. group, 1989—. Patentee in field. Recipient travel grant NATO, 1994, collaborative rsch. grant NATO, 1995. Office: Inst Bioorganic Chemistry, Ul Miklukho Maklaya 16-10, 117871 Moscow Russia

LARK, RAYMOND, artist, art scholar; b. Phila., June 16, 1939; s. Thomas and Bertha (Lark) Crawford. Student, Phila. Mus. Sch. Art, 1948-51, L.A. Trade Tech. Coll., 1961-62; BS, Temple U., 1961; LHD, U. Colo., 1985. Ednl. dir. Victor Bus. Sch., L.A., 1969-71; pub. rels. exec. Western States Svc. Co., L.A., 1968-70; owner, mgr. Raymond Lark's House of Fine Foods, L.A., 1962-67; from exec. sec. to v.p. Physicians Drug and Supply Co., Phila., 1957-61; lectr. L.A. Trade Tech. Coll., 1973, Compton (Calif.) Coll., 1972, Nat. Secs. Assn., Hollywood, Calif., UCLA, U. Utah, Salt Lake City, 1993, others. One-man shows include, Dalzell Hatfield Galleries, L.A., 1968-86, Arthur's Gallery Masterpieces and Jewels, Beverly Hills, Calif., 1971, Dorothy Chandler Pavillion Music Center, L.A., 1974, Honolulu Acad. Arts, 1975, UCLA, 1983, U. Colo. Mus., 1984, Albany State Coll. Art Gallery, Albany, Ga., 1988, Utah Mus. Fine Arts, Salt Lake City, 1989, Mind's Art Gallery, Dickinson U., Dickinson, N.D., 1989, Trinton Mus. Art, Santa Clara, Calif., Greenville (N.C.) Mus. of Art, 1993, Springfield (Mo.) Art Mus., 1995, Washington County Museum of Fine Arts, Hagerstown, Md., 1996, The Peninisula Fine Arts Center, Newport News, Va., 1996, N.C. State U., Raleigh, 1998, others; group exhbns. include, Smithsonian Instn., 1971, N.J. State Mus., Trenton, 1971, Guggenheim Mus., N.Y.C., 1975, Met. Mus. Art, 1976, La Galerie Mauffe, Paris, 1977, Portsmouth (Va.) Mus., 1979, Ava Dorog Galleries, Munich, W. Ger., 1979, Accademia Italia, Parma, 1980, Ames Art Galleries and Auctioneers, Beverly Hills, 1980, Le Salon des Nations at Centre International d'Art Contemporain, Paris, 1983, Tivolio Gallery, Salt Lake City, 1991, Hyatt Regency Hotel, Capitol Hill, Washington, 1993, Alexandria Mus. Art, La., 1998, Hill country Arts Found., Ingram, Tex., 1998, others; represented in permanent collections, Library of Congress, Ont. Coll. Art, Toronto, Mus. African and African Am. Art and Antiquities, Buffalo, Carnegie Inst., numerous others; art commns. for TV and film studios include, All in the Family, Carol Burnett Show, Maude, The Young and the Restless, Universal City Studios, Palace of the Living Arts, Movie Land Wax Mus.; author works in field; author and contbr. more than 50 scholarly treatises on art, edn. and the hist. devel. of Black Ams., chpts. to encyclopedias and textbooks, articles to jours., introductions to mus. exhbn. catalogues. Recipient gold medal Acad. Italia, 1980, also numerous gold medals and best of show awards, 3 presdl. proclamations; award Internat. Platform Assn.; Dr. Raymond Lark Day proclaimed by State of Md., 1994; grantee Nat. Endowment Arts, ARCO Found., Colo. Humanities Program, Adolph Coors Beer Found. Mem. Art West Assn. (pres. 1968-70). Address: PO Box 76169 Los Angeles CA 90076-0169

LARKIN, ANDREW, economics educator; b. Denver, Aug. 22, 1946; s. Leo A. and Maryrose (Ahern) L. BS, Creighton U., 1967; MA, U. Notre Dame, 1969; PhD, U. Nebr., 1982. Asst. prof. St. Cloud (Minn.) State U., 1982-88, assoc. prof., 1988-91, prof. econs., 1991—. Author: To Promote the General Welfare, 1999, Varieties of Economic Experience, 2000. With U.S. Army, 1969-71, Korea. E-mail: larkin@stcloudstate.edu. Home: 2611 Park Dr Saint Cloud MN 56303-1383 Office: St Cloud State Univ 720 4th Ave S Saint Cloud MN 56301-4498

LARKIN, NELLE JEAN, computer programmer, systems analyst; b. Ralston, Okla., July 4, 1925; d. Charles Eugene and Jennivea Pearl (Lane) Reed; m. Burr Oakley Larkin, Dec. 28, 1948 (div. Aug. 1969); children: John Timothy, Kenneth James, Donald Jerome, Valerie Jean Larkin Rouse. Student, UCLA, 1944, El Camino Jr. Coll., 1946-49, San Jose (Calif.) City Coll., 1961-62. Sr. programmer, analyst III Santa Clara County, San Jose, Calif., 1963-69; sr. analyst, programmer Blue Cross of No. Calif., Oakland, 1971-73; sr. programmer, analyst Optimum Systems, Inc., Santa Clara, Calif., 1973-75, Crocker Bank, San Francisco, 1975-77, Greyhound Fin. Service, San Francisco, 1977-78; analyst, programmer TRW, Mountain View, Calif., 1978-79; sr. programer analyst Memorex, Santa Clara, 1979-80; staff mgmt. cons. Am. Mgmt. System, Foster City, Calif., 1980-82; sr. programmer, analyst, project leader Tymeshare, Cupertino, Calif., 1982-83; sr. programmer, analyst Beckman Instruments, Palo Alto, Calif., 1983-89; analyst, programmer U.S. Postal Svc., San Mateo, Calif., 1989—. Mem. Calif. Scholarship Fedn. (life mem. 1943), Alpha Sigma Gamma. Avocations: needlework, camping. Home: 3493 Londonderry Dr Santa Clara CA 95050-6632 Office: US Postal Svc 2700 Campus Dr San Mateo CA 94497-0001

LARKINS, FRANCIS PATRICK, scientist, educator; b. Geelong, Victoria, Australia, Apr. 15, 1942; s. Francis Edward and Cecilia V. (Whelan) L.; m. Valerie Ethelwyn Jones, Sept. 9, 1967; children: Susan Leighanne, Michael Francis. BSc with honors, U. Melbourne, 1962, MSc, 1966, BE, 1966, DSc, 1987; DPhil, Oxford U., 1969. Tutor, lectr. Secondary Tchrs. Coll., Melbourne, Victoria, 1963-65; from lectr. to reader Monash U., Victoria, Australia, 1973-83; chemistry prof., dept. head U. Tasmania, Hobart, 1983-90; dep. vice chancellor rsch., prof. chemistry U. Melbourne, 1990—; acad. dir. rsch. U. Tasmania, Hobart, 1989-90; dir. UNIMELB Ltd., Victoria, 1990-97. Contbr. over 200 articles to profl. jours. Chmn. Victorian Amateur Athletic Assn., Victoria, 1976-82; pres. Fedn. Australian Sci. and Tech. Socs., 1988-89. Fellow Royal Australian Chem. Inst. (pres. 1992), Australian Acad. Tech. Sci. and Engring. (coun. 1993-99, hon. asst. sec. 1994-95, hon. sec. 1995-99, v.p. 2001—), Australian Inst. Physics, Australian Inst. Energy, Australian Acad. Sci. Avocations: running, reading, fishing. Office: U Melbourne, Parkville, Victoria 3010, Australia

LARKINS, RICHARD, college dean, dentistry educator. BS, MD, U. Melbourne; PhD, London U. Clin. tng. in internal medicine and endocrinology Royal Melbourne Hosp.; tchr., rschr. U. Melbourne, Dept. Medicine Royal Melbourne Hosp., 1974-77, Repatriation Gen. Hosp., Melbourne, 1978-83; James Stewart chair medicine U. Melbourne, Royal Melbourne Hosp., 1984-97, dir. dept. diabetes and endocrinology, chmn. divsn. of medicine; prof. U. Melbourne, dean Faculty of Medicine, Dentistry and Health Scis., 1998—; chmn. Nat. Health and Med. Rsch. Coun. Author 5 textbooks; contbr. more than 180 articles to sci. and profl. jours.; mem. editl. bds. for internat. sci. and med. jour. publs. Fellow Royal Coll. Physicians, Royal Australian Coll. Physicians (Eric Susman prize 1982), Australasian Coll. of Physicians (pres., chmn. bd. censors), Endocrine Soc. of Australia (past pres.).

LARMOLA, EERO ANTERO, business educator; b. Helsinki, Finland, Dec. 29, 1937; s. Erkki and Irja (Pernaja) L.; m. Leena Halme, June 1, 1968; children: Seija, Tuula, Kirsti. BS in Econs., Helsinki Sch. Econs./Bus.Adm., 1961, MS in Econs., 1966. Asst. Helsinki Sch. Econs. and Bus. Adminstrn., 1961-67, lectr., 1967-71, sr. lectr., 1971—, rschr., 1979-82, bd. dirs., 1975-81; asst. Helsinki U. Tech., 1966-69; cons. Finnish Hosp. Assn., 1966-76; assoc. prof. Tampere (Finland) U., 1968-69; co. Editor: Liikkeenjohto ja ATK E. Data Processing and Business Administration, 1971. Chmn. Nat. Assn. Univ. Lectrs., 1970-71, vice chmn., 1973-74. Jr. sgt. Finnish Mil., 1957-58. Recipient Knight Cross of 1st Order in Finnish Lion, Pres. of Finland, 1982, medal of 30 years svc. Nat. C. of C., 1991. Mem. Finnish Operation Rsch. Soc., Info. Sci. Rsch. Soc., Nat. Assn. Alumni Bus. Schs. (auditor 1968-86). Avocations: tennis, volleyball, photography. Office: Helsinki Sch Econs/Bus Adm, Runeberginkatu 14-16, 00100 Helsinki Finland

LARMOUR, IAN, pharmacist, pharmacologist; b. Wycheproof, Victoria, Australia, Dec. 24, 1945; s. Rugby Winter and Edith Jessie (McLennan) L.; m. Laurise Zelle Humphreys, May 9, 1972; children: Luke Ian, Paul John. B.Pharmacy, Monash U., Melbourne, Australia, 1969, MS in Pharmacology, 1986. Registered pharmacist, Victoria, Australia. Student, trainee, staff pharmacist Royal Melbourne Hosp., 1968-70; dep. dir. pharmacy Prince Henry's Hosp., Melbourne, 1973-81, dir. pharmacy, 1981-88; mgr. pharm. svcs. Monash Med. Ctr., Melbourne, 1988—; dir. pharmacy svcs. Jessie McPherson Pvt. Hosp., Melbourne, 1988—; sr. mgr. So. Health Care Network Pharmacy Svcs., 1997—; cons. Monash Healthcare Cons., Melbourne, 1994—; mng. dir. Enzal Products & Svcs./Larmour Enterprises, Melbourne, 1994—; lectr. in field; condr. seminars in field; mem. pharm. adv. com. Human Svcs. Dept., Victoria, 1998—. Editor The Encapsulator, 1988—; contbr. numerous articles to profl. jours.; article reviewer The Annals of Pharmacotherapy, 1996—. Chmn. Drug Usage Group, Melbourne Tchg. Hosp., 1993-95, chmn. MTHOUG Health Care Agreement subcom., 1999—; mem. Health & Cmty. Svcs.-Pharm. Issues Working Party, Melbourne, 1995-96; v.p. Surrey Hills Presch. Ctr., Melbourne, 1986, pres., 1988; elder Surrey Hills Uniting Ch., Melbourne, 1985—, mem. parish coun., 1983-88; chmn. Child Accident Prevention Found. Medidump Campaign Com., 1981-84; mem. South Surrey Park Redevel.. Adv. Com. of City of Camberwell, 1986. Lt. Australian Army, 1970-73, capt. Australian Army Reserve, 1973-76. Recipient Samuel Wynn award Prince Henry's Hosp., 1976; Nat. Hosp. Quality Mgmt. Program rsch. grantee, 1994. Fellow Soc. Hosp. Pharmacists Australia (treas. 1975, chmn. 1976-79, Victorian br., Sigma award 1974, Glaxo Medal of Merit 1991); mem. Victorian Hosps. Assn. (pharm. adv. com. 1981—), Pharm. Soc. Australia, Pharm. Def. Pty. Ltd., Hosp. Pharmacists Assn. Victoria, Australian Soc. Parenteral and Enteral Nutrition, Australian Soc. Clin. and Exptl. Pharmacologists, Naval and Mil. Club, Amnesty Internat., Melbourne Cricket Club, Melbourne Football Club. Avocations: reading, writing, gardening, photography, cricket. Office: Monash Med Ctr Dept Pharm, 246 Clayton Rd, Melbourne 3168 VIC, Australia

LA ROCCA, RENATO VINCENZO, medical oncologist, clinical researcher; b. Cin., June 16, 1957; m. Margaret Carolyn Cauthron, Sept. 5, 1987; children: Alessandra, Marcello, Victoria, Chae. MS, Liceo Sci. Statale, Turin, Italy, 1976; postgrad., U. Padua, Italy, 1976-80; MD, Cornell U., 1982. Diplomate Nat. Bd. Med. Examiners, Am. Bd. Internal Medicine, Am. Bd. Oncology. Resident in internal medicine N.Y. Hosp.-Cornell Med. Ctr., N.Y.C., 1982-85; med. oncology fellow medicine br. Nat. Cancer Inst., Bethesda, Md., 1985-88, sr. investigator medicine br., 1988-90; pvt. practice Kentuckiana Med. Oncology Assocs., PSC, Louisville, 1990-97; dir. Kentuckiana Cancer Inst. (KCI), 1997—; clin. assoc. prof. U. Louisville Sch. Medicine, clin. assoc. prof. medicine U. Ky. Coll. Medicine; cons. Jansen Rsch. Found.; spkrs. bur. RPR Pharmaceuticals, Eli Lilly guest rschr. med. br. Nat. Cancer Inst., NIH, Bethesda; mem. steering com. Ky. Cancer Pain Initiative; mem. adv. bd. Hospice Louisville; chmn. cancer com. Jewish Hosp., Louisville. Author: (chpts. in books) Molecular and Cellular Biology of Prostate Cancer, Molecular Foundations Oncology; contbr. articles to profl. jours.; patentee in field. Chairperson Louisville Lung Cancer Symposium, 2000. Recipient USPHS Commendation medal, 1990, Leadership award Am. Cancer Soc., 1995. Fellow ACP; mem. Am. Soc. Clin. Oncology, Am. Assn. Cancer Rsch., European Soc. Med. Oncology, Am. Cancer Soc. (v.p. Ky. divsn.), Am. Coll. Physician Inventors, Am. Pain Soc., Soc. Neuro-Oncology, Jefferson County Med. Soc., Ky. Oncology Soc., Ky. Med. Assn., Ind. Med. Assn., Alpha Omega Alpha. Avocations: sailing, computers, astronomy, skiing, political science. Office: Kentuckiana Cancer Institute PLLC 100 E Liberty St Ste 502 Louisville KY 40202-1427

LAROCK, VICTOR DOUGLAS, engineering executive; b. Uccle, Brabant, Belgium, Nov. 27, 1955; s. Victor Joseph and Vlasta (Jindrak) L. Grad. elec. engr., U. Brussels, 1978. Faculty asst. U. Brussels, 1978-81; design mgr. Soc. de Microélectronique, Loverval, Belgium, 1982-89; tech. mgr. Soc. Anonyme Internat. Telecomms., Brussels, 1989-2000, Alcatel-Bell Space, Hoboken, Belgium, 2000—; lectr. U. Antwerp, Belgium, 1993-97. Editor Revue HF Special Issue, 1999. Mem. IEEE, Royal Inst. for Internat. Rels., Soc. Des Ingenieurs en Telecomms. Avocations: wildlife photography, amateur astronomy. Office: ABSp, Berkenrodelei 75, B-2660 Hoboken Belgium

LAROCQUE, BRETT, account executive; b. Tarrytown, N.Y., Apr. 6, 1967; s. Lawrence and Marjorie LaRocque; m. Jill Christine Joynes, Sept. 17, 1999. Student, Allegheny Coll., 1989. Customer svc. rep. Bank of N.Y., Valhalla, 1989-90; agt. Monarch Fin. Group, White Plains, N.Y., 1990-91; asst. v.p. account exec. Fidelity Nat. Title, White Plains, 1991—. Mem. Friends of Westchester County Med. Ctr. Children's Hosp., Valhalla, N.Y. Named Best Reflection of Masons, Chappaqua, N.Y., 1989. Mem. Real Estate Fin. Assn., Nacore Internat., No. Westchester Bar Assn., Builders Inst. (trustee), Ossining Bar Assn. Avocations: golf, travel, collecting IE Hall of Fame memorobilia, Christmas ornaments. Office: Fidelity Nat Title Ins Fifth Fl 140 Grand St Fl 5 White Plains NY 10601-4831

LA ROCQUE, EUGENE PHILIPPE, bishop; b. Windsor, Ont., Can., Mar. 27, 1927; s. Eugene Joseph and Angeline Marie (Monforton) LaR. BA, U. Western Ont., 1948; MA, Laval U., 1956. Ordained priest Roman Catholic Ch., 1952, consecrated bishop, 1974; asst. parish priest Ste. Therese Ch., Windsor, 1952-54; registrar, then dean men, lectr. Christ The King Coll., U. Western Ont., 1956-64; asst. spiritual dir. St. Peter's Sem., 1964-65; prin., dean King's Coll., 1965-68; pastor St. Joseph's Ch., Rivière-aux-Canards, Ont., 1968-70, Ste. Anne's Ch., Tecumseh, 1970-74; bishop of Alexandria-Cornwall, Ont., 1974—; dean Essex County, 1970-73; trustee Essex County Roman Cath. Separate Sch. Bd., 1972-74; 1st chmn. liaison com. Can. Jewish Congress Can. Coun. Chs. and Can. Cath. Conf. Bishops, 1977-84, mem. pro-life com., 1992-94; pres. Ont. Conf. Cath. Bishops, 1992-96; pres. Fedn. Couns. Priests of Can., 1973-74. Mem. KC (3d degree, chaplain Ont. 1977-87). Address: 222 Montreal Rd, Box 1388, Cornwall, ON Canada K6H 5V4

LA ROSA, GIUSEPPE, accountant; b. Ragusa, Sicily, Italy, Oct. 19, 1946. Degree in applied indsl. scis., Inst. Tecnique Sup. Fribourg, Switzerland, 1981; degree in chartered acctg., Coll. Chartered Acctg., Milan, Italy, 1971. Expert auditor Ministry Trade and Industry. Acct., auditor Milan, 1979-80; statutory auditor Ernst & Young, Milan, 1989-99; pres. La Rosa & Assocs., Milan, 1991—; fiscal adviser Bianchi & Montanari Law Firm, Milan, 1978; fiscal and auditing expert adviser Coopers & Lybrand, Milan, 1974-77. Mem. Brit. C. of C. (Italy), Lion's Club. Avocations: classical music, painting, sailing. Office: La Rosa & Assocs, Via Ponchelli 6, 20129 Milan Italy

LAROTONDA, GERARDO JULIO, veterinary pathologist; b. Buenos Aires, June 28, 1951; s. Donato and Maria Delia (Orengo) L.; m. Monica Vesi, June 4, 1977; children: Julia Lorley, Johanna Paula. DMV, U. Buenos Aires, 1975. With U. Buenos Aires, 1973-75, 75-80, chief practical works, 1980-87, asst. prof. dept. pathology, 1987—. Mem. Soc. Vet. Medicine, Vet. Pathologists Orgn. E-mail: lauet@uol.com.ar. Home: Montes de Oca 929, 1270 Buenos Aires Argentina Office: F C V U BA, Chorroarin 280, 1427 Buenos Aires Argentina

LAROUNIS, GEORGE PHILIP, manufacturing company executive; b. Bklyn., Mar. 19, 1928; s. Philip John and Helen (Cormentelou) L.; m. Mary G. Efthymiatou, Jan. 13, 1958; 1 child, Daphne H. B.E.E., U. Mich., 1950, postgrad. in Law; J.D., N.Y. U., 1954. Electronics engr. in research and devel. Columbia U. Electronics Research Lab., 1952-54; assoc. firm Pennie, Edmonds, Morton, Barrows & Taylor, N.Y.C., 1954-58; fgn. patent atty. Western Electric Co., N.Y.C., 1958-60; asst. dir. Bendix Internat., Paris, 1960; dir. licensing and indsl. property rights Bendix Internat., to 1974; v.p. staff ops. Bendix Europe, 1974-77; v.p. Bendix Internat. Fin. Corp.; v.p. Europe, Middle East and Africa Bendix Corp., Paris, 1977-82; pres. Bendix Internat. Cons. Corp., 1974-86; v.p., group exec. Allied Automotive, 1982-85; pres. Allied-Signal Fibers Europe S.A.; v.p. Allied-Signal Internat., 1985-93; dir. CopyTele, Inc., Delphi Soc., Am. Farm Sch., Greece. Served with U.S. Army, 1946-47. Chevalier French Legion of Honor. Mem. N.Y. Patent Bar Assn., Fed. Patent Bar Assn., Licensing Execs. Soc., Am. C. of C. in France and Greece (dir., pres., exec. com. European Coun.), Polo Club de Paris, Papagou Tennis Club (Athens), Tau Beta Pi, Eta Kappa Nu. Home: 15-17 A Tsoha St, Athens 11521, Greece

LAROUZE, BERNARD, physician; b. Asnieres, France, Feb. 18, 1944; s. Georges Larouze and Huguette Duchaussoy; m. Veronique Barrois, Nov. 1978; children: Anne, Laure, Mathilde. MD, Paris Med. Sch., 1968. Countryside physician French Civil Svc., Algeria, 1968-70; resident Paris Hosps., 1970-76, fellow, 1978-81; rsch. fellow Ctr. Nat. Rsch. Sci., Paris, 1981-89; sr. rschr. Inst. Nat. de la Sante et de Rsch. Med., Paris, 1989—; vis. clin. rsch. fellow ICR, Phila., 1973-76, vis. rsch. physician, 1976-78. Mem. Am. Soc. Tropical Medicine and Hygiene, European Assn. for Study of Liver. Avocation: music. Home: 7 rue Guy de La Brosse, 75005 Paris France Office: INSERM 444 Faculty Med, 27 rue Chaligny, 75012 Paris France

LARRAMENDI, LUIS HERNANDO DE, lawyer; b. Madrid, July 4, 1952; s. Ignacio and Lourdes (Martinez) H.L.; m. Mercedes Varela Villafranca, Oct. 20, 1978; children: Coro, Ignacio, Lourdes. Degree in law, U. Complutense, Madrid, 1974. Bar: Madrid, Europe; cert. translator, English, French. Assoc. J.A. Labat Law Firm, Madrid, 1975-81; advisor Spanish Trademark Office, Madrid, 1981-82; ptnr. Elzaburu Law Firm, Madrid, 1982—; bd. dirs. MAPFRE Ins. Corp., Madrid; chmn. anticounterfetting com. European Cmty. Trademark, European Union, 1997—; pres. of jury History of Carlism Award, 1996—. Author: Horas Vividas, 1998; editor Aportes, 1990-94. CEO Larramendi Found., Madrid, 1987—; v.p. Tavera Hist. Found., Toledo, 1998—. Mem. Assn. Internacional Protection Propriete Intellectual, Internat. Trademark Assn., Lic. Execs. Soc. Mem. Carlist Party. Roman Catholic. Avocations: poetry, mountaineering, history. Home: Diego de Leon 34, 28006 Madrid Spain

LARREA HOLGUÍN, JUAN IGNACIO, archbishop; b. Buenos Aires, Argentina, Aug. 9, 1927; s. Carlos Manuel Larrea and Lola Holguín. D of Law, U. Rome, 1952; D of Canon Law, U. Pontificia, Rome, 1952; Doctor Honoris Causa, Catholic U., Guayaquil, 1994. Bishop Quito, 1960-76, Ibarra, 1978-83; bishop castrense Quito, 1983-88; archbishop Guayaquil, 1988. Author: Derecho Civil del Ecuador, 11 vols., 1964-84, Derecho Internacional Ecuat, 1976, Derecho Constitucional Ec., 1984, Repertorio de Jurisprudencia, 40 vols. Mem., pres. Supreme Electoral Tribunal, Quito, 1956-59; assesor Pres. of Republic, Quito, 1970, Supreme Ct. Justice, Quito, 1971; procurator Caja del Seguro Social, Quito, 1956-62. Recipient Premio Tobar award City of Quito, 1969, Placa de Oro award Orden Nacional Hon. Vasquez, 1990, Gran Cruz award Orden Nacional al Merito, 1994, Premio Espejo, 1999. Mem. Nat. Acad. Langs., Nat. Acad. History, Acad. Abogados Quito, Found. for Ecuadorian Culture.

LARROCA, RAYMOND G., lawyer; b. San Juan, P.R., Jan. 5, 1930; s. Raymond Gil and Elsa Maria (Morales) L.; m. Barbara Jean Strand, June 21, 1952 (div. 1974); children—Denise Anne Sheehan, Gail Ellen, Raymond Gil, Mark Talbot, Jeffrey William. B.S.S., Georgetown U., 1952, J.D., 1957. Bar: D.C. 1957, U.S. Supreme Ct. 1960. Assoc., Kirkland, Fleming, Green, Martin & Ellis, Washington, 1957-64; ptnr. Kirkland, Ellis, Hodson, Chaffetz & Masters, Washington, 1964-67, Miller, Cassidy, Larroca & Lewin, Washington, 1967—. Served with arty. U.S. Army, 1948-49, to 1st lt., inf., 1952-54. Mem. ABA, D.C. Bar, Bar Assn. D.C., The Barristers. Republican. Roman Catholic. Clubs: Congl. Country (Potomac, Md.); University (Washington). Office: 2555 M St NW Ste 500 Washington DC 20037-1302

LARSEN, DAVID WAYNE, telecommunications industry executive; b. Teaneck, N.J., Nov. 27, 1952; s. Robert Louis and Mildred Alfreda (Kraus) L.; m. Victoria Coates, Feb. 18, 1978. BS in Applied Physics, Ga. Tech. U., 1974; ThM, Dallas Theology Sem., 1978, postgrad., 1986-87. Assoc. pastor Clear Lake Cmty. Ch., Houston, 1978-80; sr. pastor Grace Bible Ch., Shawnee, Okla., 1980-86; founder, CEO TIV, Inc., Dallas, Hong Kong, 1987-98; CEO TIV, LLC, Dallas, Hong Kong, Manila, Sydney, Honolulu, 1996—; cons. Malaysia Hotel Assn., Kuala Lumpur, 1995, Hong Kong Hotel Assn., 1996. Home: 4 Spyglass Ct Frisco TX 75034-6807 Office: TIV LLC Ste 300 5300 Town And Country Blvd Frisco TX 75034-6898

LARSEN, ELLEN ERREBO, retired rheumatologist; b. Olgod, Denmark, June 7, 1934; d. Eiler and Emilie (Jessen) Skovbjerg; m. Holger Errebo Larsen, Aug. 10, 1957; children: Karen, Inge, Lars. Registrar County Hosp., Grindsted, Denmark, 1961-62, Mcpl. Hosp., Copenhagen, Denmark, 1962-64, 69-70, County Hosp., Copenhagen, Denmark, 1964-68, U. Hosp., Copenhagen, Denmark, 1968-69; rheumatologist pvt. practice, Copenhagen, Denmark, 1970-72; chief physician Soc. Poliamyelitis, 1972—. Contbr. articles to profl. jours. Mem. Danish Med. Soc., Danish Soc. Rheumatology, Danish Soc. Rehab. Home: Sondersovej 29, 3500 Vaerlose Denmark Office: Soc Poliamyelitis, Tuborgvej 5, 2900 Hellerup Denmark

LARSEN, ERIK, art history educator; b. Vienna, Austria, Oct. 10, 1911; came to U.S., 1947, naturalized, 1953; s. Richard and Adrienne (Schapringer de Csepreg) L.; m. Lucy Roman, Oct. 4, 1932 (dec. 1981); children: Sigurd-Yves, Annik-Eve., Erik-Claude (dec.); m. Anna Gallup Moses, May 8, 1982 (div. Sept. 1986); m. Katharina Ehling, Oct. 21, 1989. Candidate, Institut Superieur d'Histoire de l'Art et d'Archéologie, Brussels, 1931; Licentiate, Louvain (Belgium) U., 1941; Docteur en Archéologie et Histoire de l'Art, 1959; D. honoris causa, Janus Pannonius U., Pécs, Hungary, 1992. Dir., editor-in-chief on semi-ofcl. cultural mission for Belgian Govt. Pictura, art. mag., Brussels, Rio de Janeiro, Brazil, 1946-47; research prof. art Manhattanville Coll. of Sacred Heart, 1947-55; instr. CCNY, 1948-55; lectr, then vis. prof. Georgetown U., 1955-58, assoc. prof. fine arts, 1958-63, prof., 1963-67, head dept. fine arts, 1960-67; prof. history of art U. Kans., 1967-80, prof. emeritus, 1980—; dir. Center for Flemish Art and Culture, 1970-80; cons. old masters' paintings, guest-prof. U. Salzburg, Austria, 1988. Author: books, the most recent being La Vie, Les Ouvrages et Les Eleves de Van Dyck, 1975, Calvinistic Economy and 17th Century Dutch Art, 1979, rev. edit., 1999, Anton van Dyck, 1980, Rembrandt, Peintre de Paysages: Une Vision Nouvelle, 1983, Japanese edit., 1992; Seventeenth Century Flemish Painting, 1985, The Paintings of Anthony van Dyck, 2 vols., 1988, Jan Vermeer. Catalogo completo, 1996 (Am. edit., 1998), Hieronymus Bosch, Catalogo completo, 1998 (Am. edit., 1998); contbr. numerous articles, revs. to profl. publs., newspapers. Mem. Kans. Cultural Arts Commn., 1971-73; mem. Kans. Cultural Arts Adv. Council, 1973-79. Served with Belgian Underground, 1942-45. Decorated knight's cross Order Leopold, knight's cross Order of Crown, officer Order Leopold (Belgium); officer Order of Rio Branco (Brazil), Knight's Cross Mex. Order of Law, Culture, and Peace (Mex.); recipient prix Thorlet, laureate Inst. France, Académie des sciences morales et politiques, 1962; Internat. Hon. Citizen, New Orleans, 1989; named hon. Ky. col., 1977. Fellow Soc. Antiquaries of Scotland; mem. Appraisers Assn. Am., Association des Diplomés en Histoire de l'Art et Archéologie de L'Université Catholique de Louvain, Académie d'Aix-en Provence (France) (corr.), Académie de Mâcon (France) (assoc.), Académie d'Alsace (France) (hon.), Comité Cultural Argentino (hon.), Schweizerisches Institut fuer Kunstwissenschaft (Zurich, Switzerland), Academia di Belle Arti Pietro Vanucci (Perugia, Italy) (hon.), Royal Soc. Arts (London) (Benjamin Franklin fellow); correspondent-academician Real Academia de Bellas Artes de San Telmo (Malága, Spain), Real Academia de Bellas Artes de San Jorge (Barcelona, Spain), Accademia Tiberina (Rome), Académie Royale D'Archéologie de Belgique (fgn. assoc.). Home: 511 S Washington St Beverly Hills FL 34465-4312

LARSEN, GLEN ALBERT, JR., finance educator; b. St. Louis, Nov. 9, 1947; s. Glen Albert Sr. and Jane (Steuby) L.; m. Nancy Ann McMahon, Mar. 30, 1980; children: Erik Paul, Colleen Elizabeth. BS in Ceramic Engring., U. Mo., Rolla, 1970; MS in Materials Engring., Purdue U., 1973; MS in Bus. Adminstrn., Ind. U., 1982, DBA in Fin., 1989. Registered profl. engr., Ill.; CFA. Plant ceramic engr. U.S. Steel Corp.-South Works, 1971-73, gen. foreman constrn. svcs., 1973-74; mgr. tech. svc. Merkle Engrs., Inc., 1974-76; gen. foreman U.S. Steel-Gary (Ind.) Works, 1976-80, asst. supt., 1980-83; pres. G.A. Larsen Co., Homewood, Ill., 1983-86; instr. Ind. U., Bloomington, 1986-89, vis. asst. prof. fin., 1989-90; asst. prof. fin. U. Tulsa, 1990-94, assoc. prof. fin., 1994-96; chairperson undergrad. program, assoc. prof. fin. Ind. U., Kelley Sch. Bus., 1996—; presenter in field. Contbr. articles to profl. jours. 2nd lt. USAR N.G., 1970-76. Mem. Am. Fin. Assn., Fin. Mgmt. Assn. Home: 115 Lynn Ct Zionsville IN 46077-1026 Office: Ind Univ Kelley Sch Bus 801 W Michigan St Indianapolis IN 46202-5199

LARSEN, GWYNNE E., computer information systems educator; b. Omaha, Sept. 10, 1934; d. Melvin and Vernetta (Allen) Bannister; m. John M. Larsen, June 8, 1958; children: Bradley Allen, Blair Kevin, Randall

Lawrence. A in Bus. Adminstrn., Denver U., 1956, MBA, 1975, PhD, 1979; BS, Met. State Coll., 1971. Instr. Met. State Coll. Denver, 1979-81, asst. prof., 1981-85, assoc. prof., 1985-88, prof., 1989—, acting chair computer dept., 1991-92; book reviewer McGraw Hill, 1991, Harcourt Brace Jovanovich, 1991, Macmillan Pub. Co., 1993, Southwestern Pub. Co., 1993; presenter Mountain Plains Mgmt. conf., Denver, 1982, Rocky Mountain Bus. Expo, Denver, 1982, Red Rocks C.C., 1984, Colo.-Wyo. Acad. Sci. conf., 1985, Boulder, 1986, Colorado Springs, 1987; local coord. John Wiley & Sons, Denver, 1982, 83; panel chmn. on office automation Assn. for Computing Machinery, Denver, 1985; spkr. ASTD, 1986, Am. Pub. Works Assn., 1986; participant numerous presentations and confs. Author: (with others) Computerized Business Information Systems Workbook, 1983, Collegiate Microcomputer, 1992, (with Verlene Leeberg) Word Processing: Using WordPerfect 5.0, 1989, Word Processing: Using WordPerfect 5.1, 1991, First Look at WordPerfect 5.1, 1991, First Look at DOS, 1991, First Look at NetWare, 1992, Using WordPerfect for Windows, 1993, (with Marold and Shaw) Using Microsoft Works: An Introduction to Computing, 1993, Using Microsoft Works, An Introduction to Computing, 1993, First Look at WordPerfect 6.0 for Windows, 1994, Using WordPerfect 6.0 for Windows, 1994, Using Microsoft Works for Windows, An Introduction to Computing, 1996, Beyond the Internet, 1996, (with Marold) Using Microsoft Works 4.0, 1997; co-author: Microsoft Office 97 Online Course; apptd. editl. bd. Jour. Mgmt. Sys., 1988, Jour. Microcomputer Sys. Mgmt., 1989, Info. Resources Mgmt. Jour., 1991; mem. editl. rev. bd. Jour. Info. Resources Mgmt. Sys., 1985—, Jour. Mgmt. Info. Sys., 1986—, Jour. Database Mgmt. Sys., Jour. Database Mgmt. Sys., 1987—, Jour. End User Computing, 1990—; contbr. articles to profl. jours. Mem. Info. Resources Mgmt. Assn., Colo.-Wyo. Acad. Scis. Avocations: walking, aerobics, reading detective stories. Home: 8083 S Adams Way Littleton CO 80122-3603 Office: Met State Coll Denver Campus Box 45 PO Box 173362 Denver CO 80217-3362

LARSEN, HENRIK ASLAK, mechanical engineer; b. Odense, Denmark, May 12, 1967; s. Frede Larsen and Lisbet Soholm; 1 child, Sydney Milan. MS, Tech. U. Denmark, 1991. From field engr. to cell leader Dowell Schlumberger, Denmark, Scotland, Norway, Eng., 1991-94; from project engr. to dist. tech. engr. Schlumberger Dowell, Maurice, La., 1995-97; field svc. mgr., Y2K coord. Schlumberger Dowell, Maurice, 1998-99; account mgr. Schlumberger, New Orleans, 1999—. Mem. Danish Engring. Soc., Soc. Petroleum Engr.s. Avocations: music, martial arts, nature. Home: PO Box 750968 New Orleans LA 70175-0968 Office: Schlumberger 1515 Poydras St Ste 2700 New Orleans LA 70112-4516

LARSEN, JAN, science educator; b. Stege, Denmark, June 25, 1965. MSc, Tech. U. Denmark, Lyngby, 1989, PhD, 1994. Assoc. prof. signal processing learning sys. Tech. U. Denmark, Lyngby, 1998—. Rsch. grantee Radio Parts Found., 1994. Mem. IEEE (mem. neural networks signal processing tech. com. 1996-99). Avocation: music. Fax: 45872599. E-mail: il@imm.dtu.dk. Office: Tech U Denmark Bldg 321, Richard Petersen Plads, DK-2800 Lyngby Denmark

LARSEN, JENS CHRISTIAN, mathematician, researcher; b. Copenhagen, Denmark, Jan. 30, 1963; s. Henning and Lilian (Frederiksen) L. MSc, Tech. U. Denmark, Copenhagen, 1988, PhD, 1991. Postdoctoral assoc. Tech. U. of Denmark, Copenhagen, 1991-94, U. Lund, Sweden, 1994-95, U. Copenhagen, 1995-96; asst. prof. Royal Vet. and Agrl. U., Copenhagen, 1997—. Contbr. articles to math. jours. E-mail: jlarsen@dina.kvl.dk. Office: Royal Vet & Agrl U, Thorvaldsensvej 40, DK-1871 Copenhagen Frederiksberg, Denmark

LARSEN, JOHN WESTER, chemist educator; b. Hartford, Conn., Oct. 30, 1940; s. Einar H. and Margaret G. (Graversen) L.; children: Elaine, Kirsten, Sarah. BS, Tufts U., 1962; PhD, Purdue U., 1966. Asst. prof. to prof. U. Tenn., Knoxville, 1968-84; chemist Oak Ridge (Tenn.) Nat. Lab., 1974-84; prof. chemistry Lehigh U., Bethlehem, Pa., 1984-2000; chmn. dept. chemistry Lehigh U., Bethlehem, 1988-91; chemist Exxon Rsch. and Engring. Co., Annandale, N.J., 1984-93. Contbr. over 100 rsch. articles to profl. jours. Recipient Storch award Am. Chem. soc., 1985, Disting. Rsch. Scientist award, 1978. Mem. AAAS, Am. Chem. Soc. Achievements include research on physical-organic chemistry. Office: Lehigh U/Chem Dept 6 E Packer Ave Bethlehem PA 18015-3102

LARSEN, KIMBERT E., journalist; b. Boulder, Colo., June 14, 1941; s. Junius and Dorothy May (Cavanaugh) Larsen. AA, Idaho State U., 1963. Bur. reporter Deseret News, Salt Lake City, 1959-60, Salt Lake Tribune, Salt Lake City, 1960-63; assoc. editor Register Sys. of Newspapers, Denver, 1963-64, Denver, 1966-69; city hall reporter Ind.-Record, Helena, Mont., 1964; editor Western Mont. Register, 1965-66; nat. affairs staff writer Nat. Cath. News Svc., Washington, 1969-70; Billings (Mont.) Gazette, Billings, 1970-90; freelance writer Billings, 1990—; news editor The Harvest, 1999—. Author: The Case for Rimrocks National Monument, 1970; contr. Ecotage!, 1972; mem. editl. bd. The Billings Gazette, 1983-85. Pres. Idaho Young Dems., Pocatello, Idaho, 1963; chmn. Diocesan Pastoral Coun., diocese of Great Falls-Billings, 1995-99, Parish Pastoral Coun. of Holy Rosary Ch. in Billings, 1994-97; bd. dirs. Mont. Cath. Conf., 1999—; mem. Mont. Human Rights Network. Travel grant, Norwegian Royal Ministry of Fgn. Affairs, Oslo, 1980. Mem. Yellowstone Valley Audubon Soc. Democrat. Roman Catholic. Avocations: books, classical music, travel, hiking. Home: 2451 Cascade Ave Billings MT 59102-0535

LARSEN, LAWRENCE BERNARD, JR., priest, pastoral psychotherapist; b. Yonkers, N.Y., Jan. 24, 1937; s. Lawrence Bernard and Astrid Charlotte (Bjorkgren) L.; m. Marion Davidson Hines, Nov. 29, 1968; children: Lawrence Bernard III, Hannah Hines, Sarah Astrid. BA, Trinity Coll., 1958; MDiv, The Gen. Theol. Sem., N.Y.C., 1961; diploma candidate, C.G. Jung Inst., Zurich, Switzerland, 1975; MSW, U. Tenn., 1989; training program, Diocese N.Y. Interim Ministry, 1996. Ordained priest Episcopal Ch., 1961; cert. social worker. Curate Christ Episcopal Ch., Poughkeepsie, N.Y., 1961-63; asst. Episcopal chaplain Vassar Coll., Poughkeepsie, N.Y., 1961-63; vicar All Saints Episcopal Ch., East Hartford, Conn., 1963-66; asst. to rector Trinity Ch., Southport, Conn., 1966-69; chaplain Chatham (Va.) Hall Sch., 1969-72, tchr. bible and religion, 1969-72; Jungian psychotherapist pvt. practice Lookout Mountain, Tenn., 1975-89; priest assoc. Good Shepherd Episcopal Ch., Lookout Mountain, Tenn., 1975-85; interim rector Episcopal Ch. Nativity, Ft. Oglethorpe, Ga., 1985-86; priest-in-charge St. Barnabas Episcopal Ch., Trion, Ga., 1987-89; staff psychotherapist Mid Hudson Consultation Ctr., Wappingers Falls, N.Y., 1989-96; pastoral psychotherapist Northeast Counseling Ctr., Katonah, N.Y., 1989-96; pastoral care coord. Hospice of No. Westchester, Mt. Kisco, N.Y., 1995; interim rector Christ Ch. Tarrytown, N.Y., 1996-97; assoc. priest St. Wilfred's Episcopal Ch., Sarasota, Fla., 1998-99; asst. for pastoral care St. Wilfred's Episc. Ch., 2000—; asst. Episcopal chaplain Vassar Coll., Poughkeepsie, 1961-63; assoc. priest Good Shepherd Episc. Ch., Lookout Mountain, Tenn., 1975-85, faciltator Mutual Study Ministry, 1996-97. Mem. War on Poverty com. U.S. Office Econ. Opportunity, Hartford, Conn., 1965-66. Republican. Avocations: reading, crossword puzzles, politics. Home: 7623 Preserves Ct Sarasota FL 34243-3769

LARSEN, LOREN JOSEPH, retired pediatric orthopedic surgeon; b. Idaho Falls, Idaho, Oct. 10, 1914; s. Charles Wilford and Marie (Jacobsen) L.; m. June Elmer, Mar. 20, 1943; children: Mary Ann, Loren J. Jr. BA, U. Utah, 1939; MD, U. Chgo., 1941. Intern Alameda County Hosp., 1942; resident orthopedic surgery Samuel Merit Hosp., Oakland, Calif., 1943-44; postgrad. tng. U. Calif., 1944-46, San Francisco Gen. Hosp., 1946-47; clin. prof. orthopedic surgery U. Calif., San Francisco, 1957-60; chmn. emeritus dept. orthopedic surgery Children's Hosp., San Francisco, 1957-88; chief of staff emeritus Shriner's Hosp. Crippled Children, San Francisco, 1968-80; pvt. practice San Francisco; cons. orthopedics U.S. Army Letterman Gen. Hosp., San Francisco, 1959—, U.S. Naval Hosp., Oakland, Calif., 1960-75, King Faisal Hosp., Ridyaah, Saudi Arabia, 1968. Contbr. 37 articles to profl. jours. Mem. Scoliosis Rsch. Soc. (founding), Am. Orthopedic Foot and Ankle Soc. (founding). Republican. Achievements include discovery of reporting syndrome, later named Larsen Syndrome; genetic research to determine the location of the chromosome and genes responsible for inheritance characteristics. Home: 437 Twin Lakes Cir Santa Rosa CA 95409-6448 Office: 3838 California St San Francisco CA 94118-1522

LARSEN, PAUL EDWARD, lawyer; b. Rock Springs, Wyo., Jan. 5, 1964; s. Otto E. and Linda K. (Wright) L.; m. Dawn Jannette Griffin, June 25, 1986; 1 child, Quinne Caitlin. BA, U. Oreg., 1986, JD, 1989. Bar: Nev. 1989, U.S. Dist. Ct. Nev. 1989, U.S. Ct. Appeals (9th cir.) 1994. Atty. Lionel, Sawyer & Collins, Las Vegas, Nev., 1989—, chmn. land use and planning divsn., 1995—; gen. counsel Nev. State Democrats, 1996, corp. for solar tech. and renewable resources, 1995-96. Author, editor: Nevada Environmental Law Handbook, 1991, 1st edit., 2d edit., 3rd edit.; contbg. author: Nevada Gaming Law, 2d edit., 1995; contbr. articles to profl. jours. Pres., dir. Desert Creek Homeowners Assn., Las Vegas, 1994-95; atty. Clark County Pro-Bono Project, Las Vegas, 1989-95, Nev. Dem. Party, Las Vegas, 1994. Mem. ABA (vice chair com. natural resources pub. lands sect. 1993-95, bd. dirs. young lawyers divsn. natural resources com. 1992-95, atty. young lawyers divsn. program 1989-90), Nev.-Am. Inns of Ct., Nev. Assn. Gaming Attys., Internat. Assn. Gaming Attys. Avocations: scuba diving, golf, fishing. Office: Lionel Sawyer and Collins 300 S 4th St Ste 1700 Las Vegas NV 89101-6053

LARSEN, PEDER OLESEN, research foundation executive; b. Copenhagen, Sept. 7, 1934; s. Kristoffer Olesen and Vibeke (Nordentoft) L.; m. Lis Nielsen, Mar. 29, 1958; children: Vibeke, Johannes, Karen. Student, U. Copenhagen, 1952-57, Dr.phil., 1969. Asst. prof. Danish Vet. and Agrl. U., Copenhagen, 1958-61, assoc. prof., 1961-68, full prof., 1968-87; dep. permanent sec. Ministry Edn. and Rsch., Denmark, 1987-91; chief exec. officer Danish Nat. Rsch. Found., Denmark, 1991-98; external prof. U. Aarhus, Denmark, 1999—; chmn. Danish Nat. Sci. Rsch. Coun., Denmark, 1973-75, Coun. Rsch. Policy and Planning, Denmark, 1984-87, Danish Nat. Rsch. Found., 1991-98, prorektor Royal Vet. and Agrl. U., 1981-85; mem. CREST, EEC, 1987-91. Author: (book) Research Policy in a Small Country, Danish edit., 1981. With Danish Army, 1957-58. Fellow Royal Danish Acad. Sci. and Letters, Danish Acad. Tech. Scis. Lutheran. Home: Marievej 10 A 2, DK-2900 Hellerup Denmark

LARSEN, RALPH S (STANLEY LARSEN), healthcare company executive; b. Bklyn., Nov. 19, 1938; s. Andrew and Gurine (Henningsen) L.; m. Dorothy M. Zeitfuss, Aug. 19, 1961; children: Karen, Kristen, Garret. BBA, Hofstra U., 1962. Mfg. trainee, then supr. prodn. and dir. mfg. Johnson & Johnson, New Brunswick, N.J., 1962-77; v.p. ops., v.p. mktg. McNeil Consumer Products Co. div. Johnson & Johnson, Ft. Washington, Pa., 1977-81; pres. Becton Dickenson Consumer Products, Paramus, N.J., 1981-83; pres. Chicopee div. Johnson & Johnson, New Brunswick, 1983-85; co. group chmn. Johnson & Johnson, New Brunswick, N.J., 1985-86, vice chmn., exec. com., bd. dirs., 1986-89, chmn. bd., pres., CEO, 1989—, also bd. dirs., mem. exec. com.; bd. dirs. Xerox Corp., AT&T Corp. Mem. Bus. Coun., Bus. Roundtable (policy com.). Republican. Avocations: skiing, boating, art. Office: Johnson & Johnson 1 Johnson And Johnson Plz New Brunswick NJ 08933-0002

LARSEN, RENÉ, conservator, educator; b. Copenhagen, June 15, 1951; s. Christian Alfred and Rigmor Kristine (Madsen) L.; children: Mette Bang, Morten Bang. BS in Conservation, Royal Danish Acad. of Fine Art, 1980, MS in Conservation, 1986; PhD in Biochemistry, U. Copenhagen, 1995. Part-time tchr. Royal Danish Acad. of Fine Arts Sch. of Conservation, Copenhagen, 1980-86, tchr., rschr., 1986-96, rector, 1996—; sci. coord. EEC leather rsch. project, 1991-94, EU leather rsch. project, 1995-96, EU parchment rsch. project, 1996-99. Author, editor: STEP Leather Project, 1994, Fundamental Aspects of the Deterioration of Vegetable Tanned Leathers, 1995, Environment Leather Project, 1997; contbr. numerous articles to profl. jours. Co-founder, bd. dirs. European Network for Conservation-Restoration Edn. (ENCoRE), 1997, chmn., 1998. Fellow Internat. Biog. Assn. (life); mem. AAAS, N.Y. Acad. of Scis., Internat. Coun. of Mus. (com. for conservation), Internat. Inst. of Conservation (nordic group). Office: Royal Danish Acad Fine Arts, Sch Conservation Esplanaden 34, 1263 Copenhagen K, Denmark

LARSEN, SAMUEL HARRY, minister, educator; b. Sterling, Kans., Feb. 3, 1947; s. Harold Julius and Edna Marguerite (Wasson) L.; m. Natalie Louise Mahlow, June 21, 1969; children: Samuel Eric, Kristen Joy, Hans Joseph. BS, U.S. Naval Acad., 1969; MDiv, Covenant Theol. Sem., 1979; D of Ministry, Reformed Theol. Sem., 1989; PhD, Trinity Internat. U., 1998. Ordained to ministry Presbyn. Ch., 1981. Ops. officer USS O'Hare USN, Norfolk, Va., 1969-71; sr. advisor River Interdiction divsn. 42 U.S. Naval Adv. Group, Vietnam, 1971-72; instr. U.S. Naval Acad., Annapolis, Md., 1972-75; pastoral intern Community Presbyn. Ch., Nairobi, Kenya, Africa, 1977-78; officer-in-charge Naval Res. Shipboard Simulator Lab. and Sch., New Orleans, 1979-81; church planter Mission to the World, Brisbane, Australia, 1982-84; team coord. Mission to the World, Queensland, Australia, 1984-86; regional dir. Mission to the World, Australia, 1986-89; squadron chaplain Destroyer Squadron Five, San Diego, 1989-92; chaplain Naval Air Sta. Whidbey Island, Oak Harbor, Wash., 1992-95; acad. mentor Chesapeake Theol. Sem., Linthicum Heights, Md., 1996; asst. prof. missions Reformed Theol. Sem., Jackson, Miss., 1998—; dean Westminster Theol. Coll., Brisbane, 1986-88; del. La. Congress on World Evangelism, Manila, 1989. Pres. Covenant Sem. Student Assn., St. Louis, 1976-77; chaplain Chs. Soccer Assn., Sunshine Coast, Australia, 1984-86; tutor Logan Elem. Sch., San Diego, 1991-92; mem. adv. bd. YMCA, Oak Harbor, 1992-95. Recipient Meritorious Svc. medal Sec. of Navy, 1981, 96. Avocations: chess, astronomy, history, anthropology. Office: Reformed Theol Sem 5422 Clinton Blvd Jackson MS 39209-3004

LARSEN, SØREN EJLING, meteorologist, educator; b. Elsinore, Denmark, Apr. 14, 1943; s. Axel Harry and Margrethe (Hollensen) L.; m. Bodil Wright Thorson, July 28, 1965; children: Lena, Axel. MSc, Danish Tech. U., Denmark, 1968, PhD, 1971. Sci. staff Riso Nat. Labs., Denmark, 1971-76, program head, 1977; vis. prof. U. Wash., Seattle, 1976-77; vis. prof. Navy Postgrad. Sch., Monterrey, Calif., 1984-85, Ctrl. Sch., Nantes, France, 1991-94; adj. prof. geophysics Copenhagen U., 1993—; mem. Panel Marine Rsch., Copenhagen, 1987-95; mem. steering com. EUROTRAC 2, Munich, 1997—; cons. Kuwait Inst. Sci. Rsch., 1991-93; coord. EUROTRAC-ASE, Garmisch, Germany, 1990-95. Contbr. over 300 articles to sci. publs., also chpts. to books; editor books. Mem. Am. Meteorol. Soc., Danish Engring. Soc., Royal Meteorol. Soc. Avocations: gardening, reading, diving, bicycling. Home: Norregardsvej 176, DK-2610 Rodovre CPHGN, Denmark Office: Vea 125, Riso Nat Lab, DK-4000 Roskilde Zealand, Denmark

LARSEN, TROELS, engineering executive; b. Lyngby, Copenhagen, Denmark, May 10, 1953; s. Jørgen and Daga (Lytzen) L.; m. Pia Haudrup Christensen, Jun. 2, 1984; children: Tobias, Josefine. BSc in Engring., Danmarks Ingeniørakademi, Lyngby, 1979. Devel. engr. Ortofon A/S, Valby, Denmark, 1979-83; devel. engr. Philips Electronic, Copenhagen, 1983-87, group leader, 1987-89; project mgr. Philips Radio Communication, Copenhagen, 1989-91, Philips Navigation Systems, Copenhagen, 1991-94; sr. engring. mgr. Process Approval Tech. Nokia Mobile Phones, Copenhagen, 1994-99, mgmt. planning, 1999-2000, bus. human resources mgr., 2000—; project orgn. instr. Dieu, Hørsholm, Denmark, 1992-94. Avocations: wine making, playing guitar, swimming. Office: Nokia Mobile Phones A/S, Frederikskaj, 1790 Copenhagen VS, Denmark

LARSEN, VIBEKE, Danish government official. High commr. Ríkisumboós Maóurin (Danish High Commn.), Tórshavn, Faeroe Islands. Office: Ríkisumbodsmadurin, POB 12 Amtmansbrekkan 4, 110 Thorshavn Faeroe Islands*

LARSON, BRYAN A., lawyer; s. Byron Ancedus and Betty Marilyn Stevenett; m. Kathy Larson; children: Aaron, Adam, Conor, Kaden, Sara, Aubrey. BA, Brigham Young U., 1980, JD, 1983. Bar: Utah 1983. Assoc. Christensen, Jensen & Powell, Salt Lake City, 1983-86, McKay, Burton & Thurman, Salt Lake City, 1986-91; ptnr. Larson, Jenkins & Halliday, Salt Lake City, 1991-95, Larson, Kirkham & Turner, Salt Lake City, 1995-99, Larson, Turner, Fairbanks and Dalby, Salt Lake City, 1999—. Editor newsletter Backtalk, 1995. Mem. ALTA (mem. polit. action com. 1991—), Utah Bar Assn. (com. chmn. 1990-92), Utah Trial Lawyers Assn. (polit. action com. 1991—), Order of Barristers. Mem. LDS Ch. Avocations: boating, snow skiing. Office: Larson Turner Fairbanks & Dalby 4516 S 700 E Ste 100 Salt Lake City UT 84107-8319

LARSON, CHARLES FRED, trade association executive; b. Gary, Ind., Nov. 27, 1936; s. Charles F. and Margaret J. (Taylor) L.; m. Joan Ruth Grupe, Aug. 22, 1959; children: Gregory Paul, Laura Ann. BSME, Purdue U., 1958; MBA summa cum laude, Fairleigh Dickinson U., 1973. Registered profl. engr., N.J. Project engr. Combustion Engring., Inc., East Chicago, Ind., 1958-60; sec. Welding Rsch. Council, N.Y.C., 1960-70, asst. dir., 1970-75; exec. dir. Indsl. Rsch. Inst., Inc., Washington, 1975-99, pres., 1999—; mem. mech. engring. adv. bd. Purdue U. Assoc. editor Jour. Pressure Vessel Tech., 1973-75; mem. bd. advisors Who's Who in Am. Mem. Wyckoff (N.J.) Bd. Edn., 1973-78, pres., 1976-77; reader In Touch Networks, Inc., N.Y.C., 1979-89; chmn. 43d Nat. Conf. on Advancement Rsch. Fellow AAAS; mem. ASME, NSPE, Am. Soc. Assn. Execs., Coun. Engring. and Sci. Soc. Execs., Sigma Xi, Univ. Club, Kenwood Club. Republican. Methodist. Office: Indsl Rsch Inst Inc 1550 M St NW Washington DC 20005-1708

LARSON, DAVID MITCHELL, English studies educator, writer; b. Marshall, Minn., Oct. 21, 1944; s. Clarence I. and Alyce I. Larson; 1 child, Brian. BA, U. Minn., 1966, MA, 1969, PhD, 1973. Prof. English Franklin & Marshall Coll., Lancaster, Pa., 1971-75, Cleve. State U., 1975—. Contbr. editor: Heath Anthology of American Literature, 1990; contbr. author: Encyclopedia of American Literature, 1999; contbr. articles to profl. jours. Mem. Human Rights Campaign, Gay Lesbian Ctr., Cleve.; mem. Interweave, Cleve. City Country Dancers, Brothers' Keepers. Mem. AAUP (pres., 2000—, v.p. Cleve. State U. chpt. 1998-2000, sec. 1994-96). Democrat. Unitarian. Avocations: reading, attending plays, square dancing, camping. Home: 15105 Lake Ave Apt 2 Lakewood OH 44107-1326 Office: Cleve State U Dept English Euclid at East 24th St Cleveland OH 44115

LARSON, JERALD ALLEN, electric utility operations consultant; b. Junction City, Kans., Oct. 2, 1947; s. Bernard A. and Margaret Larson; m. Patricia A. Larson, Dec. 29, 1969; children: Jeffrey, Gregory, Stephanie. BS in Bus., Park Coll., 1988. Ops. supt. Kansas City Power and Light Co., 1983-86, fuel supt., 1986-88, plant mgr., 1988-97, operation svcs. mgr., 1997-99, ops. cons., 1999—; operating cons. KLT Power, Kansas City, 1998. Sgt. U.S. Army, 1967-69, Vietnam. Home: 18998 174th St Tonganoxie KS 66086-5219 Office: Kansas City Power & Light Co 1201 Walnut St Kansas City MO 64106-2117

LARSON, KENNETH ORVILLE, computer engineer; b. Chgo., June 16, 1954; s. Orville Talamadge and Karen Kristine Larson; m. Kathleen Marie Kirkhart, June 14, 1975; children: Coreen, David, Allen. BS in Engring. Graphics, Ill. Inst. Tech., 1975. Designer, draftsman Sargent & Lundy Engrs., Chgo., 1975-76, sect. leader, computer aided design, 1976-87; prin., solution arch., cons. Digital Equipment Corp., Schaumburg, Ill., 1987-96; cons., solution arch. Compaq Computer Corp., Schaumburg, 1996—; mem. CAD adv. bd. Elgin C.C. Mem. ch. coun. St. Andrews Luth. Ch., Chgo., 1980; chmn. bd. edn. St. John Luth. Sch., Chgo., 1983. Mem. ASME. Avocations: computer science, genealogy, home remodeling. Fax: 847-781-6507. Home: 3710 King George Ln Saint Charles IL 60174-7838 Office: Compaq Computer Corp 1124 Tower Rd Schaumburg IL 60173-4306

LARSON, LARRY, librarian; b. El Dorado, Ark., July 18, 1940; s. Willie Lee and Myrtle Elizabeth (McMaster) L.; m. Dorothy Ann Bing, Apr 23, 1966; 1 child, Larisa Ann. BS, Ouachita Baptist U., 1962; MLS, George Peabody Coll., 1967. Asst. librarian, media specialist Hall High Sch., Little Rock, 1962-65; asst. librarian, circulation Ark. Tech. U., Russellville, 1965-67; asst librarian reference Hendrix Coll., Conway, Ark., 1967-73; head librarian U. Ark., Monticello, 1973-75; librarian, dir. N. Ark. Regional Library, Harrison, 1975-85, Ft. Smith (Ark.) Pub. Library, 1985—; mem. adv. bd. Sparks Regional Med. Ctr., 1998—. Bd. dirs. Ft. Smith Hist. Soc., 1986-90, Info. Network Ark., 1997—; treas. bd. dirs. Pub. Awareness Com., Ft. Smith, Ark., 1986—. Mem. ALA, Ark. Libr. Assn. (vice chair membership com. 1968, Disting. Svc. award 1985, chair pub. libr. divsn., 1993), Ark. Libr. Devel. Dist. (chair 1985-87), Ark. Adminstrs. Pub. Librs. (chair 1988-89, del. Ark. govs.' conf. on librs. 1990), Noon Exchange Club., Info. Network Ark. (bd. dirs. 1997—). Democrat. Baptist. Avocations: gardening, woodworking. Home: 3114 S Enid St Fort Smith AR 72903-4445 Office: Ft Smith Pub Libr 3201 Rogers Ave Fort Smith AR 72903-2953

LARSON, LLOYD WARREN, economist; b. Barrett, Minn., Sept. 2, 1920; s. John Arthur and Jennie Constance (Nygren) L.; m. Laurene J. Tibbitts, June 10, 1995; B.A., U. Minn., 1946, M.A., 1947; postgrad. U. Minn., George Washington U. Assoc. prof. history and polit. sci. Carthage (Ill.) Coll., 1948-49; with Dept. Labor, Washington, 1950-78; chief div. state workers' compensation standards, 1974-78; mem. research faculty Cornell U. Sch. Indsl. and Labor Relations, 1979-81; writer, cons. U.S. Task Force on Safety, 1968, Interdeptl. Workers Compensation Task Force, 1974-77, Nat. Commn. on State Workmen's Compensation Laws, 1971-72; pres. dept. labor credit union, 1960-62; officer, mem. exec. bd. local Am. Fedn. Govt. Employees, 1962-73. Served with U.S. Army, 1942-46. Mem. Am. Polit. Sci. Assn., Center for Study of Presidency, Internat. Soc. Polit. Psychology, Nat. Peace Found., Internat. Platform Assn., Am. Legion (past post comdr.), Order Ky. Cols. Lutheran. Author books, reports, bulls., papers in field. Home: 641 Erie St SE Minneapolis MN 55414-3110

LARSON, MARK EDWARD, JR., lawyer, educator, financial advisor; b. Oak Park, Ill., Dec. 16, 1947; s. Mark Edward and Lois Vivian (Benson) L.; m. Patricia Jo Jekerle, Apr. 14, 1973; children: Adam Douglas, Peter Joseph, Alex Edward, Gretchen Elizabeth. BS in Acctg., U. Ill., 1969; JD, Northwestern U., 1972; LLM in Taxation, NYU, 1977. Bar: Ill. 1973, N.Y. 1975, D.C. 1976, Minn, 1982, Tex. 1984, U.S. Dist. Ct. (no. dist.) Ill. 1973, U.S. Dist. Ct. (so. dist.) N.Y. 1975, U.S. Ct. Appeals (2d cir.) 1975, U.S. Ct. Appeals (7th cir.) 1976, U.S. Dist. Ct. D.C. 1977, U.S. Ct. Appeals (D.C. cir.) 1977, U.S. Dist. Ct. Minn. 1982, U.S. Ct. Appeals (8th cir.) 1982, U.S. Tax Ct. 1976, U.S. Supreme Ct. 1976; CPA, Ill. Acct. Deloitte & Touche (formerly Haskins & Sells), N.Y.C., Chgo., 1973-81; atty., ptnr. Larson, Perry & Ward and former firms, Chgo., 1981—; prin. Winfield Fin. Svcs. and affiliates, Chgo., 1986—; adj. faculty U. Minn., Mpls., 1982-83, Aurora (Ill.) U., 1990-98, St. Xavier U., Chgo., 2000—; program chair No. Ill. U.-CPFP, DeKalb, 1996—. Contbr. articles to profl. jours. Mem. ABA, AICPA, AHLA, Am. Assn. Atty.-CPAs. Office: 1212 S Naper Blvd Ste 119 Naperville IL 60540-7349

LARSON, MICHAEL LEN, newspaper editor; b. St. James, Minn., Feb. 3, 1944; s. Leonard O. and Lois O. (Holte) L.; m. Kay M. Monahan, June 18, 1966; children: Christopher, David, Molly. BA, U. Minn., 1966; MBA, Mankato State U., 1986. Mng. editor Paddock Circle Inc., Libertyville, Ill., 1972-74, New Ulm (Minn.) Journal, 1974-76, Republican-Eagle, Red Wing, Minn., 1976-79; mng. editor Mankato (Minn.) Free Press, 1979-84, editor, 1984-95, editor of editl. page, 1995-97; editor Minot (N.D.) Daily News, 1997-2000; bus. editor St. Cloud Times, 2000—; bd. dirs. Minot Area Devel. Corp. d. dirs. Valley Indsl. Devel. Corp., Mankato, 1985-95, also treas.; adv. bd. Mankato State U. Bus. Sch. With U.S. Army, 1966-68, Vietnam. Recipient First Place award for investigative reporting Minn. Newspaper Assn., 1969, 71, 72, 76, 78, First Place award for feature writing, Suburban Newspapers Am., 1974. Mem. Minn. AP (pres. 1988—), Kiwanis. Roman Catholic. Avocation: bicycling. Home: 1808 N Eighth St Sartell MN 56377-1697 Office: St Cloud Times 3000 7th St N Saint Cloud MN 56303-3108

LARSON, RICHARD SMITH, pathologist, researcher; b. Ithaca, N.Y., Aug. 27, 1962; s. Richard Ingwald and Judith Ann (Larsen) L.; m. Blaire Martin, June 4, 1989. AB in Chemistry summa cum laude, U. N.C., 1984; MD, Harvard U., 1990, PhD, 1990. Cert. anatomic and clin. pathologist Am. Bd. Pathology. Pathologist, resident Barnes Hosp., St. Louis, 1990-93; hematopathology fellow Vanderbilt U., Nashville, 1993-96; asst. prof., dir. clin. lab. U. N.Mex., 1996—. Contbr. articles to profl. jours. including Jour. Biol. Chemistry, Procs. NAS, European Molecular Biology Orgn. Jour., Jour. Exptl. Medicine, Jour. Virology, Jour. Cell Biology, Advances in Immunology, Leukocyte Adhesion Molecules, Procs. Cold Spring Harbor Symposia on Quant. Biology, Leukocyte Typing, Cell Regulation, Immunol. Revs., Cardiac Pathology, Diagnostic Molecular Pathology, Am. Jour. Clin. Pathology, Blood, Pediatric Nephrology, Human Path. Cancer Rsch., Jour. Clin. Investigation, others. Recipient Nat. Rsch. Sci. award, 1986-90, 92-93; grantee Am. Cancer Soc., 2000. Mem. Coll. Am. Pathologists (chmn. future tech. com.), Am. Soc. Hematology, Assn. Molecular Pathologists, Southwest

Oncology Group. Phi Beta Kappa. Achievements include several patents including cDNA clone of LFA-1 alpha subunit and anti-inflamatory drugs.

LARSON, STEVEN MARK, physician; b. Tacoma, Wash., Nov. 30, 1941; s. Louis Edward and Evelyn Agusta (Peterson) L.; married; children: Nathan, Justine. BA in Zoology, Univ. Wash., 1963, MD, 1968. Diplomate Am. Bd. Nuclear Medicine, Am. Bd. Internal Medicine. Various positions in field to chief, dept. nuclear medicine NIH, Bethesda, Md., 1983-88; prof. dept. radiology Uniformed Svcs./Univ. Health Scis., Bethesda, 1983-88; attending physician Meml. Hosp./Meml. Sloan-Kettering Cancer Ctr., 1988—; prof. radiology Cornell Med. Coll., N.Y.C., 1988—; chief, Nuclear Medicine Svc., Dept. Med. Imaging Meml. Sloan-Kettering Cancer Ctr., 1988—, chief Radioisotope Svc., Dept. Med. Physics, 1988—, attending physician Div. Hematologic Oncology, 1990—; vis. clinician Brookhaven Nat. Lab., 1990—; cons. FDA, 1973, Nat. Libr. Medicine, 1972—, NIH, 1972-74, Bur. of Drugs/FDA, 1973-82, others. Editorial bd. Jour. Nat. Cancer Inst., 1986—, Hybridoma, 1986—, Jour.: Antibody, Immunoconjugates and Radiopharmaceuticals, 1987—; assoc. editor The Jour. of Nuclear Medicine, 1989—, others; editor-in-chief: Clin. Positron Imaging. Capt. USPHS, 1972-90. Named Outstanding Zoology Undergrad., Univ. Wash., Seattle, 1963, Rockwell Meml. Lectr., U. Iowa Coll. of Medicine, 1985, Disting. AMA Lectr. in Med. Scis., 1986; recipient Smith-Kline Instrumentation prize, 1968, Zetein award in Nuclear Medicine, 1968, Disting. Alumnus award Div. Nuclear Medicine, Johns Hopkins Med. Instns., 1985, Eugene Pendergrass award New Horizons Lectr./Radiol. Soc. North Am., 1986, award from Louise and Lionel Berman Found., Inc., 1990, G.V. Hevesy Lectr. Medal, Hungary, Elis Berven Lecture medal Swedish Soc. Oncology, 1999. Mem. Soc. Nuclear Medicine (chmn. coms. 1973-78, pres. Pacific Northwest chpt. 1982-84), Am. Coll. Nuclear Physicians (regent 1973-75, coms., Ralph Robinson lectureship 1997), Am. Coll. Radiology, N.Y. County Med. Soc., AMA, Am. Soc. Clin. Oncology, Radiol. Soc. N. Am. Independent. Presbyterian. Achievements include development of positron emission tomagraphy for oncology, first "kit" methods for nuclear medicine; discovery of action of gallium-67 citrate, a radiopharmaceutical that binds to the transferrin receptor; research in immunokinetics of radiolabeled anti-tumor antibodies, and application of anti-tumor antibodies to diagnosis and treatment. Office: Meml Sloan-Kettering Cancer Ctr 1275 York Ave New York NY 10021-6094

LARSON, WANDA Z(ACKOVICH), writer, poet; b. Cle Elum, Wash., Aug. 27, 1926; d. Stanley Aloysius and Anele (Valente) Zackovich; m. Glen B. Larson, Nov. 18, 1950 (div. Mar. 1967); children: Karen Holk, Margot Huffman, Lisa Larson Landrey (dec. 1998). BA, U. Wash., 1949. Columnist North Bend Herald, Snoqualmie, Wash., 1955-61, Goldendale (Wash.) Sentinel, 1962-67; news editor West Seattle Herald, 1950-51; editor employee newsletter Alaska Steamship Co., Seattle, 1951; editl. asst. Associated Publs., Portland, Oreg., 1970-72, staff writer, 1974-78; pub., editor Blue Unicorn Press Inc., Portland, 1990—; poet, host program Sta. KOPB, Portland, 1991—. Author: Portlandia, 1991, Miracle at Blowing Rock, 1992, Elisabeth: A Biography, 1997, Our Flag-Born Through Valor, 1999, Bird Woman (Sacajawea), 2000, The Legend of Something More, 2000. Co-recipient 2nd pl. award Poetry Forum Quar., 1990; hon. mention Still Water Press, 1990, Internat. Mss, 1990. Baptist. Avocations: needlework, cooking, humanitarian interests. Home: PO Box 40300 Portland OR 97240-0300

LARSSON, GÖRAN ENGELBREKT, managment consultant; b. Solna, Stockholm, Sweden, Oct. 26, 1943; s. Ture O.C. and Sonja K. (Soderholm) L.; m. Louise U.E.A. Rosencrantz, July 1, 1969; children: Marie, Miklas, Holger, Sophie. MSc, Royal Inst. of Tech., 1967; MBA, Stockholm Sch. of Econs., 1970. Graphics industry systems pres. Ferag Inc., Phila., 1993-94; radio comm. systems pres. Radio Comm. Systems, 1991-95, part owner, chmn., 1991-96; rotary stitchers pres. Tolerans Ingol Sweden AB, 1995-96; computer aided design systems Cadsystem Dataware AB, 1995-97; pres. microlithographic writing systems Micronic Laser Systems, 1996-97; pres. comml. printer Norstedts Tryckeri AB, 1998-99; pres. The Swedish Nat. News Agy., 1999—; vice chmn. software devel. and sales Readsoft AB, 1999—; chmn., part owner rotary stitchers Tolerans Ingol Holding AB, 1999—; chmn. bd. graphics industry sytems Ferag Svenska AB, 1999—; chmn. bd. Newspaper Printing House, 1999—. Sgt. Radio Intelligence Unit, 1962-63. Mem. Royal Swedish Acad. of Engring. Scis. (tech. attaché), Swedish Def. Rsch. Establishment (cons.), Swedish Inst. of Tech. (asst. tchr.), Nobel Inst. of Nuclear Physics. Home: Eddavagen 16, S-18263 Djunholm Sweden

LARSSON, KJELL, Swedish government official. Minister of the environment Govt. of Sweden, Stockholm, 1998—. Mem. Social Democratic Party. Office: Ministry of Environment, Tegelbacken 2, S-103 33 Stockholm Sweden*

LARSSON, PER ERIK ROLAND, biomathematician, statistician; b. Borländ, Sweden, Aug. 4, 1964; s. Roland Ruben and Margareta Anna (Jacobsson) L.; m. Marie Ulla Göthberg, May 14, 1999. PhD, Uppsala (Sweden) U., 1991. Mathematician Pharmacia, Uppsala, 1986-87; cons. Upmath HB, Uppsala, 1988-97; assoc. prof. Uppsala U., 1991-92; biomathematician AstraZeneca, Lund, Sweden, 1992—. Contbr. articles to profl. jours. Mem. Swedish Assn. Statisticians, Swedish Assn. Statisticians in the Pharm. Industry, Slite Golf Club. Avocations: golf, petanque, wine, gardening, cooking. Office: R&D Lund, AstraZeneca, S-22187 Lund Sweden

LARSSON, PER-OLOV, fish biologist, researcher; b. Gagnef, Dalarna, Sweden, Dec. 7, 1941; s. Karl Einar and Linnéa (Norberg) L.; m. Inger Enquist, July 16, 1966 (div. Oct. 1975); children: Maud, Jens; m. Jana Pickova, Apr. 7, 1978; children: Caroline, Thomas, David. BA, U. Stockholm, 1969, MA, 1979, PhD, 1984. Fishery biologist Inst. Freshwater Rsch., Drottningholm, Sweden, 1968-70, Water and Air Pollution Rsch. Inst., Gothenburg, Sweden, 1970-72; head marine biology divsn. Salmon Rsch. Inst., Alvkarleby, Sweden, 1972-83; mgr. Saltvik Aquaculture R&D, Barseback, Sweden, 1983-85; mng. dir. Laxkonsult, Dalby and Brastad, Sweden, 1985—, Leirvik, Norway, 1985—; sr. scientist Inst. Marine Rsch., Lysekil, Sweden, 1988—; dir. Baltic Sea Rsch. Sta., Karlskrona, Sweden, 1999—. Contbr. chpts. to books and articles to profl. jours. Chmn. bd. Nature Conservation Orgn., Lysekil, 1989-93. Mem. Internat. Coun. for the Exploration of the Sea (Swedish rep., mem. various coms.). Office: Inst Marine Rsch, PO Box 4, 45321 Lysekil Sweden

LARTZEV, YURI VASILEVICH, medical researcher, educator; b. Ismailovo, Russia, Mar. 10, 1960; s. Vasiliy Petrovich and Mariya (Kartzeva) L.; m. Olga Nikolaevna Samarina, Mar. 7, 1992. Student, Kuibyshev Med. State U., Samara, Russia, 1977-84; postgrad., Cours Med. U., Samara, 1991-93; MD, Samara State Med. U., 1994. Intern Rwy. Clin. Hosp., Samara, 1983-84; orthopedist Rwy. Hosp., Kinel, Russia, 1984-88; resident Clin. Hosp. Med. U., Samara, 1988-90, mgr. dept. traumatology, 1990-94, asst. prof. traumatology and orthopedics post-diploma tng., 1994—; rschr., rschr. in field. Contbr. articles to profl. jours. Mem. N.Y. Acad. Scis., Russian Assn. Traumatologists-Orthopedists, Russian Arthroscopic Soc. Office: Samara State Med U, Chapaevskaya St 89, 443099 Samara Samarskaya Russia

LARY, BANNING KENT, video producer, publisher; b. Chgo., Aug. 27, 1949; s. Banning Gray and Katherine Lee (Tedrow) L.; m. Janice Ann, Dec. 22, 1974 (div. Aug. 1977); 1 child, Venus Ayn Katherine; m. Valerie Maria Dalli, Dec. 28, 1987; children: Alexandra Lee, Kristin Gray. BJ, U. Tex., 1970. Editor-in-chief Beach & Town, Miami, Fla., 1976-77; gen. contractor Larydome Inc., Miami, 1977-80; exec. dir. Legal Devel. Resources, Austin, 1989—; pres. Promedion, Inc., Austin, 1990—, Am. Multimedia Pubs., Austin, 1996—; dir., 1985—; freelance writer, 1970—; creative troubleshooter, writer, editor various orgns.; video pub., 1987—. Author: Twist of Faith, 1996; writer, prodr., dir. Robbery! The Aftermath, 1988, Ten Commandments of Avoiding Legal Malpractice, 1989, Ten. Procedures for Avoiding Medical Malpractice, 1990, The Belli Tapes: Winning at Trial, 10 vols., 1991, Childproof: Home Safety Checklist, 1991, Webmaster Secret Internet Marketing Strategies, 1999; video prodr. Bad Paper, 1987, Extortion Set, 1988; prodr. The Sexual Harassment Prevention Kit, 1992, Teens-At-Risk Series, 8 vols., 1998, and many others; prodr. numerous TV commls.; contbr. articles to mags.; author: Twist of Faith, 1996; editor: How to Win Your Case in Court, 1996; pub. Do What You Want to Do, 1996, Gold Medal Performance Without Dangerous Steroids, 1997; editor, prodr.: Living Well Past 50, 1998; prodr., dir.: Heroin Story, Please Remember Suzi, 1998 (silver award), Teen Drinking, 1998 (gold award), Human Communications Theory, 1998 (bronze award), Teen Finances (bronze apple), 1999; inventor roller washer II, golf swing muscle articulator. Mem. bd. Alpha Nu House Corp., Austin. Recipient Gold award for video prodn., 1987, silver award, 1988, 91, Prize Stories Anthology award, 1989, O'Henry awards, Best of Austin award Internat. Assn. Bus. Communicators, 1986, 93, Disting. Achievement award Am. Soc. Ind. Security-Video, 1987, 1st pl. U.S.A. Hometown Video Festival, 1991, award of excellence ACTV, 1992, Bronze award Charleston Internat. Film Festival, 1993, Bronze award Worldfest, 1995, Gold award Flagstaff Internat. Film Festival, 1998, Pegasus award, 1998, Crystal award of Excellence, 1999; named to Top 100 Multimedia Prodrs. Am. Mem. Am. Acad. Poets, Tex. Writers League, Austin Writers League, Amnesty Internat., Sigma Chi. Avocations: photography, painting, philosophy, securities analysis, films. Office: Am Visionary Artists PO Box 3551 Austin TX 78764-3551

LARZELERE, KATHY LYNN HECKLER, paralegal; b. Sellersville, Pa., Dec. 4, 1955; d. Harold Tyson and Hannah Ruth (Wile) Heckler; m. Lawrence Sollanek, Nov. 1984 (div.); m. Loel Harry Larzelere, Aug. 27, 1992; 1 stepdaughter, Lindsie M. AAS magna cum laude, Columbus State C.C., 1991. From sales person to dept. mgr. Macy's New York, North Wales, Pa., 1977-83; store mgr. Bathtique, Wilmington, Del., Towson, Md., 1983-86; customer svc. person Marshall Fields, Chgo., 1987; word processor Franklin County Children Svcs., Columbus, Ohio, 1988-89; legal sec., paralegal M. Cohen and Assocs., Columbus, 1989-94; paralegal Calig and Handelman LPA, Columbus, 1994-97, Weltman, Weinberg & Reis, Columbus, 1997—. Author: (poetry) American High School Poets, 1973. Ward coord. Amelia Salerno for City Coun., Columbus, 1993; co-chmn. Columbus Christmas in Apr. Home Amb. Com., Columbus Christmas in Apr. Materials and In-Kind Donations Com. Mem. award Phi Theta Kappa. Mem. Nat. Fedn. Paralegal Asns., Paralegal Assn. Cen. Ohio (writer newsletter The Citator, co-chair student outreach com. 1994-95, chair 1995-97, 1st v.p. 1995-97, 2000—, pres. 1997-99, mem. adv. bd. 1999-2000, chair student outreach com. 1999-2000), Columbus Bar Assn. (assoc.). Lutheran. Avocations: handcrafts, reading, walking, watercolor painting, counted cross-stitch. Home: 2119 Kingsglen Dr Grove City OH 43123-1252 Office: Weltman Weinberg & Reis 175 S 3rd St Ste 900 Columbus OH 43215-5177

LAŠAS, LIUDVIKAS, biomedical engineer, educator; b. Kaunas, Lithuania, June 4, 1933; s. Vladas and Janina (Mackevičaite) L.; m. Danute Terese Mockute, Aug. 14, 1965; children: Lina, Tomas. B in Biotech., Technol. U., Kaunas, 1956; PhD, Technol. U., 1962; DSc, Technol. Inst., St. Petersburg, Russia, 1989. Asst., assoc. prof. Technol. U., Kaunas, 1959-78; head lab. Kaunas Br. Inst. Endocrinology Med. Acad. USSR, Kaunas, 1978-90; dir. Inst. Endocrinology Lithuania, Kaunas, 1990—; dir. rsch. lab. Plant Endocrinic Preparations, Kaunas, 1971-86; prof. Med. Univ., Kaunas, 1993—; dir. Endocrinology Ctr. Lithuania, Kaunas, 1994—; mem. senate, bd. dirs. Med. Univ., Kaunas, 1991—; bd. dirs. Food Inst., Kaunas. Author: Human Growth Hormone, 1982, Obesity and its Treatment, 1998; contbr. over 300 articles to profl. jours. Named Inventor of USSR, 1986. Mem. Internat. Growth Hormone Rsch. Soc., Internat. Soc. Endocrinologists, Internat. Ostioporosis Fedn. (bd. dirs.), N.Y. Acad. Scis. Achievements include 30 patents and inventions. Home: Aukstaiciu 37, 3005 Kaunas Lithuania Office: Inst Endocrinology, Eiveniu 2, 3007 Kaunas Lithuania

LASDUN, DENYS LOUIS, architect; b. Sept. 8, 1914; s. Norman and Julie (Abrahams) L.; m. Susan Bendit, 1954; 3 children. Grad., Rugby Sch.; student, Archtl. Assn.; DA (hon.), U. Manchester, 1966; DLitt (hon.), U. East Anglia, 1974, Sheffield U., 1978. Practiced with Wells Coates, Tecton and Drake; pvt. practice architecture with Peter Softley London, 1960—; Hoffman Wood prof. architecture U. Leeds, London, 1962-63; lectr. U.K., U.S., Europe, China, Hong Kong. Prin. works include housing and schs., London hdqrs. Govt. New South Wales, Australia, luxury flats St. James Pl., London, Royal Coll. Physicians, master plan New U. East Anglia prin. teaching & residential bldgs, Christ's Coll. extension and Fitzwilliam Coll., Cambridge, U. London Law Inst., U. London Sch. Oriental and African Studies, Inst. Edn., project for Courtauld Inst., Nat. Theatre and IBM Central London Mktg. Ctr., South Bank, EEC hdqrs. for European Investment Bank, Luxembourg, Milton Gate; exhibited Royal Acad., London, 1997; designs for Hurva Synagogue, Genoa Opera House; author: Architecture in an Age of Scepticism, 1984; contbr. articles to archtl. jours. Mem. adv. council Victoria and Albert Mus., 1973-83; trustee Brit. Mus., 1975-85; mem. Slade Com., 1976-92; mem. arts panel Arts Council Gt. Britain, 1980-84. Served with Royal Engrs., 1939-45. Decorated mem. Order Brit. Empire, Her Majesty Queen Elizabeth, 1945, comdr. Brit. Empire, 1965, created knight, 1976, Companion of Honour Her Majesty Queen Elizabeth II, 1995; recipient Civic Trust awards class I, 1967, group A, 1969; recipient spl. award Sao Paulo Biennale (Brazil), 1969, awards Concrete Soc., 1977, centanary medal The architects' Jour., 1995, Companion of Honour, Her Majesty Queen Elizabeth II, Inst. of Am. Architects, Bulgaria Gold medal, 1997, Royal Inst. Brit. Architects Trustees medal, 1992; hon. diploma 1st World Bienniale of Architecture, Sofia, 1981; subject of Denys Lasdun: Architecture, City, Landscape (William Curtis), 1994. Fellow Royal Inst. Brit. Archs. (London arch. Bronze medals 1960, 64, Royal Gold medal 1977, London regional award for Nat. Theatre 1978), AIA (hon.), Royal Coll. Physicians (hon.), Royal Inc. Architects Scotland (hon.); mem. Academie d'Arch. Paris, Accademie Nazionale di San Luca (Rome), Bulgarian Inst. Archs. (hon.), Royal Academician, Wolf Found. (prize in arts-arch. 1992). Address: 51 Rowan Rd, London W6 7DT, England

LASER, CHARLES, JR., oil company executive; b. Redford Twp., Mich., July 8, 1933; s. J.C. and Gertrude L.; m. Glenda Johnson, Sept. 27, 1972; 1 child, Susan Faye. Student, Mich. Tech. U., 1952-54, Ctrl. Mich. U., 1959-60; DD (hon.), Palm Beach Theol. Sem. Coll., 1991; LLD (hon.), Northwood U., 2000. With Retail Credit Co., 1958-60; exec. dir. Saginaw County Rep. Com., 1960-65, Rep. Com. D.C., 1967; fin. dir. San Joaquin Rep. Party, Stockton, Calif., 1968; owner Laser Advt., Bay City, Mich., 1969-75; exec. v.p. Vindell Petroleum, Inc., Midland, Mich., 1972-75, Geo Spectra Corp., Ann Arbor, Mich., 1977-86; pres. Laser Exploration Inc., Deerfield Beach, Fla.; task force Domestic Violence, Gov. Jeb Bush, 1999—. Chmn. Genesee County Rep. Com., 1981-82, mem. Broward County Rep. Exec. Com., 1987-88, indsl. bond screening com. Deerfield Beach, 1992; chmn. U.S. Senator Connie Mack Palm Beach County Round Table; bd. dirs. Palm Beach County Libr. Found., Shepherd Care Ministries, Hollywood, Foa., 1991—; adv. com. Tall Pines coun. Boy Scouts Am., mem. adv. bd. Gulf Stream Coun., 1980; mem. gov. prevention adv. com. Juvenile Justice Deliquency, Fla., 1988-96; mem. adv. bd. Humanitarian Soc., 1989—; bd. dirs., life mem. Large Freedoms Found., Valley Forge Broward County, Fla. chpt., 1995—; bd. govs. Northwood U., West Palm Beach, Fla., 1997; chmn. emeritus Fla. Symphonic Pops Orch., 1998; apptd. mem. Task Froce on Domestic Violence. With U.S. Army, 1954-58. Mem. Deerfield Beach C. of C. (v.p.), World Trade Coun. (Palm Beach, Fla. chpt.), Detroit Econ. Club, Bankers Club (Boca Raton), Humanitarian Soc. (adv. bd.), Rep. Men's Club (past pres., v.p. Boca Raton chpt.), Gold Coast Venture Capital Club (Delray Beach chpt.), Palm Beach Roundtable (bd. dirs., chmn. exec. com., sec. 1994-96), Hillsboro Cove Condominium Assn. (pres. 1994), Rotary, Elks. Home: PO Box 8604 1523 E Hillsboro Blvd Apt 131 Deerfield Beach FL 33441-4301

LASH, WILLIAM HENRY, III, law educator, lawyer; b. Jersey City, Jan. 21, 1961; s. William H. Jr. and Vivian G. Lash; m. Sharon K. Zackula, Dec. 31, 1992; 1 child, William H. IV. BA, Yale U., 1982; JD, Harvard U., 1985. Bar: N.J. 1986, Washington 1988. Law clk. Justice Alan B. Handler, Trenton, N.J., 1985-86; assoc. Fried, Frank, Harris et al, Washington, 1986-88, 88-89; counsel to chmn. U.S. Internat. Trade Commn., Washington, 1988; asst. prof. law Western New Eng. Coll., Springfield, Mass., 1989-90, St. Louis U., 1990-93; prof. law George Mason U., Arlington, Va., 1993—; dir. Nostalgia TV Network, Washington, 1993-98, UCS, Carlton Maritime Fund; mem. adv. bd. World TV Program, Washington, 1998; disting. sr. fellow Ctr. for Study of Am. Bus., St. Louis, 1993—; bd. dirs. Virtual Credit Svcs., Carton Maritime Fund.; adj. fellow Citizens for a Sound Economy, 2000—. Author: Regulating Securities, 1996, International Trade Law, 1998. Bd. dirs., treas. Internat. Law Students Assn., 1996; vice chmn. fin. instns. Federalist Soc., Washington, 1997; mem. Va. Commn. for Environ., Richmond, 1996; bd. dirs. Trade Policy Ctr. Cato Inst.; adj. fellow Citizens Sound Economy. Mem. ABA (editl. bd. Bus. Law for Today 1997—), Yale Club N.Y.C. Republican. Lutheran. E-mail: wtoman@aol.com. Office: George Mason U Sch Law 3401 Fairfax Dr Arlington VA 22201-4411

LASHLEY, FELISSA R., dean, nursing educator, researcher; b. N.Y.C., Apr. 6, 1941; d. Jack and Ruth (Dorbin) Lashley; divorced; children: Peter, Heather, Neal. BS, Adelphi Coll., 1961; MA, NYU, 1965; PhD, Ill. State U., 1973. Cert. Am. Bd. Med. Genetics., Am. Coll. Med. Genetics. Dean Sch. of Nursing So. Ill. U., Edwardsville, Ill. Author: Clinical Genetics in Nursing Practice, 1998 (book of yr. award); editor: The Person with AIDS: Nursing Perspectives, 1987 (Book of Yr. award), Tuberculosis: A Sourcebook for Nursing Practice and Women, Children and HIV/AIDS (Book of Yr. award 1993). Mem. ANA (coun. nurse researchers), AAAS, Am. Soc. Human Genetics, Am. Acad. Nursing, Nat. League Nursing, Midwest Nursing Rsch. Soc., N.Y. Acad. Scis., Ill. Nurses Assn., Am. Coll. Med. Genetics, Phi Sigma.

LASHLEY, LENORE CLARISSE, lawyer; b. N.Y.C., June 3, 1934; d. Leonard Livingston and Una Ophelia (Laurie) L.; children: Donna Bee-Gates, Michele Bee, Maria Bee. BA, CUNY, 1956; MSW, U. Calif., Berkeley, 1970, MPH, 1975; JD, U. Calif., San Francisco, 1981. Bar: Calif. 1981. Atty. W.O.M.A.N., Inc., San Francisco, 1982-84; pvt. practice San Francisco Law Office, 1984-87; dep. dist. atty. Monterey Dist. Atty., Salinas, Calif., 1987-89; trial atty. State Bar of Calif., L.A., 1989; dep. dist. atty. L.A. Dist. Atty., 1989; dep. city atty. Office of City Atty., L.A., 1989—; chair, bd. dirs. St. Anthony's Dining Room, San Francisco, 1986-87; sec., bd. dirs. NAAC, Monterey, 1987-88; bd. dirs. Childrens Home Soc., Oakland, Calif., 1966-68. Recipient Cert. of Merit, Nat. Assn. Naval Officers, 1987. Mem. L.A. County Bar Assn. (del. to state bar 1992, 93). Roman Catholic. Avocations: running, reading, animal welfare, volunteer work with people with AIDS. Office: City Atty LA 200 N Main St Ste 1700 Los Angeles CA 90012-4110

LASHLEY, ROBERT H., engineering manager; b. Lawrence, Kans., Nov. 4, 1955; s. Richard H. and Virginia L.; m. Anne Regine Deveaux, Mar. 29, 1980 (div. Feb. 1997); children: Randall H., Scott B. BSEE, U. Calif., Berkeley, 1978, MSEE, 1979. Jr. engr. Ampex Corp., Redwood City, Calif., 1978; mem. tech. staff Apple Computer, Inc., Cupertino, Calif., 1979-83; engr. Gavilan Computers, Campbell, Calif., 1983-84; ptnr., prin. engr. Tech. Assocs., Los Gatos, Calif., 1984-94; founder, sr. engr. The Engring. Dept., Inc., Los Gatos, 1985-89; computer aided engring. mgr. Radius, Inc., San Jose, Calif., 1989-94, G.E.C. Plessey Semiconductors Inc., Scotts Valley, Calif., 1994-97; computer aided design mgr. Sun Microsystems, Inc., Palo Alto, Calif., 1997—. Inventor/patentee Monitor Control Systems and Methods for Monitoring and Controlling Atmospheres in Containers for Respiring Perishables, 1991. Office: 901 San Antonio Rd Palo Alto CA 94303-4900

LASHLEY, VIRGINIA STEPHENSON HUGHES, retired computer science educator; b. Wichita, Kans., Nov. 12, 1924; d. Herman H. and Edith M. (Wayland) Stephenson; m. Kenneth W. Hughes, June 4, 1946 (dec.); children: Kenneth W. Jr., Linda; m. Richard H. Lashley, Aug. 19, 1954; children: Robert H., Lisa Lashley Van Amberg, Diane Lashley Tan. BA, U. Kans., 1945; MA, Occidental Coll., 1966; PhD, U. So. Calif., 1983. Cert. info. processor, tchr. secondary and community coll., Calif. Tchr. math. La Canada (Calif.) High Sch., 1966-69; from instr. to prof. Glendale (Calif.) Coll., 1970-92, chmn. bus. div., 1977-81, coord. instructional computing, 1974-92, prof. emeritus, 1992—; sec., treas., dir. Victory Montessori Schs., Inc., Pasadena, Calif., 1980—; pres. The Computer Sch., Pasadena, 1983-92; pres. San Gabriel Valley Data Processing Mgmt. Assn., 1977-79, San Gabriel Valley Assn. for Systems Mgmt., 1979-80; chmn. Western Ednl. Computing Conf., 1980, 84. Editor Jour. Calif. Ednl. Computing, 1980. NSF grantee, 1967-69, EDUCARE scholar U. So. Calif., 1980-82; John Randolph and Dora Haynes fellow, Occidental Coll., 1964-66; student computer ctr. renamed Dr. Virginia S. Lashley Ctr., 1992. Mem. AAUP, AAUW, DAR (scholarship chair), Calif. Edn. Computing Consortium (bd. dirs. 1979—, v.p. 1983-84, pres. 1985-87), Orgn. Am. Historians, San Marino Women's Club, Colonial Dames, XVII Century (scholarship chair), Nat. Geneal. Soc., New Eng. Hist. Geneal. Soc., Town Hall, World Affairs Coun., Phi Beta Kappa, Pi Mu Epsilon, Phi Alpha Theta, Phi Delta Kappa, Delta Phi Upsilon, Gamma Phi Beta. Republican. Congregationalist. Home: 1240 S San Marino Ave San Marino CA 91108-1227

LASHMAN, L. EDWARD, arbitrator, mediator, consultant; b. New Orleans, June 6, 1924; s. L. Edward and Edith Ruth (Deutsch) L.; m. Elizabeth Gitt Fichman, June 6, 1948 (dec. Aug. 1984); children: Deborah, Rebekah, David W. (dec. Feb. 1993), Judith; m. Joyce Blicher Schwartz, July 25, 1987. Student, U. N.C., 1940-42, Tulane U., 1942-43. Ptnr. Caire Assocs., New Orleans, 1946-51; with CIO and AFL-CIO, 1951-67; asst. to sec., dir. cong. liason HUD, Washington, 1967-69; mng. ptnr. Urban Housing Assocs., Denver, 1969-70; v.p. U. Mass., 1970-75; dir. external affairs, sr. planning counselor Harvard U., Cambridge, Mass., 1975-89; sec. adminstrn. and fin. Commonwealth of Mass., Boston, 1989-91, chmn. Mass. bd. regents pub. higher edn., 1986-88; chmn. Mass. Housing Fin. Agy., Boston, 1977-79, Commonwealth Land Bank, Boston, 1975-77; acting exec. dir. (pro bono) Mass. State Lottery, 1999; contract mediator U.S. Equal Employment Opportunity Commn.; contract arbitrator U.S. Postal Svc. Mem. exec. com. Denver County Dem. Party, 1952-64; chmn. Colo. Urban League, Denver, 1961-63; acting COO (pro bono) Judge Baker Children's Ctr., Boston, 1993-94; dir. Nat. Housing Conf., Washington, 1969-75; v.p. Handel & Haydn Soc., Boston, 1982-84. With U.S. Army, 1943-46, ETO. Mem. Am. Arbitration Assn., Mass. Assn. Mediation Programs, Norfolk and Suffolk County Superior Ct. Mediation Panels, Joint Labor Mgmt. Com. Mediation Panel. Avocations: fly fishing, cooking, photography. Home and Office: 236 Conant Rd Weston MA 02493-1654

LASHMAN, SHELLEY BORTIN, judge; b. Camden, N.J., Aug. 18, 1917; s. William Mitchell and Anna (Bortin) L.; m. Ruth Horn, Jan. 3, 1959; children: Karen E. Lashman Hall, Gail A. McBride, Mitchell A., Christopher R. BS, William and Mary Coll., 1938; postgrad., Columbia U., 1938, 39; JD, U. Mich., 1946. Bar: N.Y. 1947, N.J. 1968. Judge N.J. Workers Compensation, 1981—. With USNR, 1940-70. Mem. Atlantic County Bar Assn., Am. Judges Assn., Atlantic County Hist. Soc., Am. Judicature Soc., Ret. Officers Assn., U.S. Navy League, Fleet Res. Assn., USS Yorktown CV-5 Club, Mil. Order World Wars. Republican. Home fax: 609-653-6686. Office fax: 609-441-3161. Home: 1209 Old Zion Rd Egg Harbor Township NJ 08234-7667 Office: 1333 Atlantic Ave Atlantic City NJ 08401-8201

LASICH, VIVIAN ESTHER LAYNE, secondary education educator; b. Hopewell Twp., Pa., Dec. 17, 1935; d. Charles McClung and Harriette Law (George) Layne; m. William G. Lasich, Apr. 10, 1958; children: C. Laurence, Celeste M., Michelle R. AB, Geneva Coll., 1956; MA in Edn., No. Mich. U., 1970, postgrad. Secondary tchr. Freedom (Pa.) High Sch., 1956-57; elem. educator Gilbert Elem. Sch., Gwinn, Mich., 1967-69; lang. arts educator Gwinn Mid. Sch., 1970-99; ret., 1999; adv. bd. panel Mich. Dept. Edn./Arts, 1976-79; mem. sch. improvement team, 1988-91, 93-94, co-chair, 1995-98; mid sch. concept team, 1992-98, mid sch. at-risk coord. dist. curriculum coord. coun., 1995-96; dist. curriculum strategy action team, 1993-94; dist. profl. devel. strategy action team, 1993-94; mem. sounding bd. Mid. Sch., 1994-98, dist. sch. improvement team, 1994-98; lang. arts curriculum design com., 1997-98; rep. Gwinn Edn. Assn. Mid. Sch., 1995-98. Author: Prophets Without Honor: Teachers, Students, & Trust, 1991. V.p. Marquette (Mich.) Community Theatre, 1962-63 bd. dirs. 1963-74, mem. 1961-92; pres. Marquette Arts Coun. 1973-74, v.p. 1972-73, bd. dirs. 1970-78, mem. 1970-84; pres. Upper Peninsula Arts Coordinating Bd. 1976-78, v.p. 1974-76, bd. dirs. 1978-84; bd. dirs. Mich. Community Theatre Assn. 1972-73; bd. dirs. Mich Community Arts Agys., 1976-79. Recipient Committment to Excellence award Marquette Community Theatre, 1965. Devotion to Arts Development award Upper Peninsula (Mich.) Arts Coord. Bd. 1979. Mem. ASCD, NEA, AAUW, Mich. Edn. Assn., Phi Delta Kappa. Presbyterian. Avocations: rsch., writing, theatrical direction and performance, vocal music. Home: 508 Pine St Marquette MI 49855-3838 Office: Gwinn Area Community Schs Gwinn MI 49841

LASKA, VERA, history educator; b. Kosice, Czechoslovakia, July 21, 1928; came to U.S., 1946; m. Andrew J. Laska, Nov. 5, 1949; children: Thomas Vaclav, Paul Andrew. MA in History, Charles U., 1955; PhD in History, U. Chgo., 1959. Fgn. student counselor U. Chgo., 1955-59; cons. Inst. Internat. Edn., N.Y.C., 1964-66; prof. history Regis Coll., Weston, Mass., 1966—; cons., evaluator Fulbright Commn., Sao Paulo, 1960-64; lectr. in field. Contbr. to 4 books; contbr. around 350 articles and revs. to profl. jours. and newspapers; author: Women in the Resistance and in the Holocaust, 1983, 88, and six other books; columnist in Mass. papers. Chmn., Weston Hist. Comm., 1969-73; mem. Weston Biecentenial Com., 1973-76, Mass. Bicentenial Commn., 1973-77; trustee Weston Pub. Libr., 1984-85; pres. Weston Hist. Soc., 1985-88. Masaryk grantee, 1945-46, Am. Hist. Assn., 1984; Inst. Internat. Edn. fellow, 1946-47, Internat. House fellow, 1947-49; named Outstanding Educator of Am., 1972; recipient Kidger award, 1984, George Washington Honor medal Freedoms Found. of Valley Forge, 1990. Mem. Am. Hist. Assn., New Eng. Hist. Assn., New Eng. History Tchrs. Assn., Czechoslovak Acad. Arts and Scis. in Am., Am. Assn. Fgn. Student Affairs, Masaryk Club. Avocations: travel, reading, people. Home: 50 Woodchester Dr Weston MA 02493-1436 Office: Regis Coll 235 Wellesley St Weston MA 02493-1505

LASKA-MIERZEJEWSKA, TERESA, anthropologist; b. Lodz, Poland, Feb. 19, 1931; d. Jozef and Stanislava (Podebska) Łaska; m. Zbigniew Mierzejewski, Jan. 15, 1959; children: Ann, Maciej. MSc, U. Wroclaw, 1957, DSc, 1966. From asst. to prof. Acad. Physical Edn., Warsaw, Poland, 1958—. Author: Sexual Dimorphism in Men of Black and White Races, 1982, Anthropology in Sport and in Physical Education, 1999; co-author: Biological Indicators of Social Stratification in Rural Population in 1967, 1977, and 1987, 1993, Anthropology/Handbook, 1999; contbg. author: Woman, Sport, Health, 1998; contbr. articles to profl. jours. Avocations: traveling, skiing, gardening. Home: Dembinskiego 4a, 01-644 Warsaw Poland Office: Acad Physical Edn, Acad Physical Edn/Dept Anth, Marymoncka 34, 00-968 Warsaw Poland

LASKIEWICZ, HENRYK ERYK, physical education educator, researcher; b. Gdansk-Wrezeszcz, Pomerania, Poland, Jan. 7, 1929; s. Henryk and Leokadia L.; m. Teresa Ludmila Later, Aug. 10, 1957. Mgr., MS, Acad. Phys. Edn., Warsaw, 1952, Dr. Phys. Edn., 1965, Dr. habil. Phys. Edn., 1972. Academic U. Tchr. Asst. Acad. Phys. Edn., Warsaw, 1953-65, adj., asst. prof., 1965-72; privatdocent H.S. Phys. Ed., Katowice, Szczecin, Poland, 1972-91; assoc. prof. U. Szczecin (Poland), 1991—; dir. Humanist Inst. H.S. Phys. End., Katowice, Poland, 1972-75; vice-dir. Inst. Akademy of Phys. Edn., Warsaw, 1975-1981, Inst. Phys. Culture U., Szczecin, Poland, 1990-93; chief dept. history and orgn. Phys. Edn. U., Szczecin, Poland, 1981-97. Author: Workers Physical Culture in Poland, 1971, The Participation in Physical Culture, 1990, Uprising and Organization Development of Sportmovement, 1993, Overlocal Physical Culture in Organizations in West Pomerania, 1945-1957, 1966, Physical Culture in Wilnius Region, 1900-1939, 1998; editor: Studies of the Institute of Physical Education No. 6, 1990; contbr. numerous articles to profl. jours. Chmn. province bd. Polish Sci. Culture Assn., Szczecin, Poland, 1980-91. Recipient Medal Commn. Nat. Edn. Ministry Edn., 1975, Cavalier Cross - Order of Poland Restitution Polski Coun. of State, 1984. Avocations: music, playing orgel, piano, video-camera expeditions. Office: Inst Phys Culture Univ, al Piastów 40b, 71-065 Szczecin Pomerania, Poland

LASKIN, DANIEL M., oral and maxillofacial surgeon, educator; b. Ellenville, N.Y., Sept. 3, 1924; s. Nathan and Flora (Kaplan) L.; m. Eve Pauline Mohel, Aug. 25, 1945; children: Jeffrey, Gary, Marla. Student, NYU, 1941-42; BS, Ind. U., 1947; MS, U. Ill., 1951. Diplomate Am. Bd. Oral and Maxillofacial Surgery. Mem. faculty U. Ill., Chgo., 1949-84, prof. dept. oral and maxillofacial surgery, 1960-84, head dept., 1973-84, clin. prof. surgery, 1961-84, dir. temporomandibular joint and facial pain research center, 1963-84; prof., chmn. dept. oral and maxillofacial surgery Med. Coll. Va., Richmond, 1984—; dir. temporomandibular joint and facial pain rsch. ctr. MCV, Richmond, 1984—; head dept. dentistry MCV Hosp., Richmond, 1986—; former attending oral surgeon Edgewater, Swedish Covenant, Ill. Masonic, Skokie Valley Community hosps., all Chgo.; former chmn. dept. oral surgery Cook County Hosp., Chgo.; cons. oral surgery to Surgeon Gen. Navy, 1977-83; dental products panel FDA, 1988-92, cons., 1993-95; Francis J. Reichmann Lectr., 1971, Cordwainer lectr., London, 1980, Donald B. Osborn Meml. lectr., 1999. Author: Oral and Maxillofacial Surgery, Vol. I, 1980, Vol. II, 1985; contbr. articles to profl. jours.; editor-in-chief: Jour. Oral and Maxillofacial Surgery, 1972—; mem. editl. bd. Internat. Jour. Oral and Maxillofacial Surgery, 1978-88, Topics in Pain Mgmt., Densat, Internat. Jour. Oral and Maxillofacial Implants, Quintessence Internat., Revista Latino America Cirugia Traumatologia Maxilofacial, Va. Dental Jour., Jour. Dental Rsch.; mem. internat. editl. bd. Headache Quar.; mem. editl. bd. Greek Jour. Oral and Maxillofacial Surgery, Electronic Jour. Dentistry; assoc. editor Odontology. Nat. hon. chmn. peer campaign A.A.O.M.S. Edn. and Rsch. Found., 1990; bd. dirs. Internat. Assn. Oral and Maxillofacial Surgeons Found.; chmn. Nat. Acad. Dentistry, 1997-99; pres.-elect Nat. Acad. of Practice, 1999. Recipient Disting. Alumni Svc. award Ind. U ., 1975, William J. Gies editl. award hon. mention, 1975-77, 80, 88, 90, 91, 93, 95, 1st prize, 1978-79, 84, 87, 89, 92, 96, spl. editl. citation Internat. Coll. Dentists, 1999, Simon P. Hullihen Meml. award, 1976, Arnold K. Maislen Meml. award, 1977, Thomas P. Hinman medallion, 1980, W. Harry Archer Achievement award for rsch., 1981, Heidbrink award, 1983, Disting. Alumnus award Ind. U. Sch. Dentistry, 1984, Rene Lefort medal, 1985, Semmelweis medallion Semmelweis Med. U., 1985, Golden Scroll award Internat. Coll. Dentists, 1986, Internat. award Friends Sch. Dental Medicine, U. Conn. Health Ctr., Donald B. Osborn award, 1991, Achievement medal Alpha Omega, 1992, Norton M. Ross Excellence in Clin. Rsch. award, 1993, Va. Commonwealth U. Faculty award of excellence, 1994; named Zendium Lectr., 1989, Edward C. Hinds Lectr., 1990, Disting. Practitioner Nat. Acads. Practice, 1992, Hon. Diplomate, Am. Soc. Osseointegration, 1992; fellow in gen. anesthesia Am. Dental Soc. Anesthesiology, fellow in dental surgery Royal Coll. Surgeons Eng., Glasgow Royal Coll. Physicians and Surgeons (hon.). Fellow AAAS, Am. Coll. Dentists, Internat. Coll. Dentists, Am. Acad. Implant Prosthodontists (academia), Acad. Internat. Dental Studies (hon.), Internat. Assn. Oral and Maxillofacial Surgeons (hon., exec. com. 1980-95, pres. 1983-86, sec. gen. 1989-95, exec. dir. 1995-99, genl. chmn. 14th Internat. Conf. on Oral and Maxillofacial Surg., 1999); mem. Ill. Splty. Bd. Oral Surgery, ADA (adv. com. advanced edn. in oral surgery 1968-75, cons. Coun. on Dental Edn. 1968-82, mem. Commn. on Accreditation 1975-76), Am. Assn. Oral and Maxillofacial Surgeons (editor Forum 1965-96, AAOMS Today 1996—, disting. svc. award 1972, pres. 1976-77, rsch. recognition award 1978, William J. Gies award 1979, dedication 73d ann. meeting and sci. sessions 1991), Internat. Assn. Dental Rsch., Am. Dental Soc. Anesthesiology (pres. 1976-78), Am. Soc. Exptl. Pathology, Am. Assn. Dental Editors, Royal Soc. Medicine, Brazilian Coll. Oral and Maxillofacial Surgery and Traumatology (hon.), Chilean Soc. Oral and Maxillofacial Surgery (hon.), Hellenic Assn. Oral Surgery (hon.), Sadi Fontaine Acad. (hon.), Internat. Congress Oral Implantologists (hon.), Soc. Maxillofacial and Oral Surgeons South Africa (hon., assoc. life), Am. Dental Bd. Anesthesiology (pres. 1983-92), Nat. Chronic Pain Outreach Assn. (adv. bd.), Japanese Soc. for Temporomandibular Joint (hon.), Am. Soc. Laser in Dentistry (hon. life), Internat. Study Group for the Advancement of TMJ Arthroscopy (hon.), William F. Harrigan Soc., Odontographic Soc., Can. Assn. Oral and Maxillofacial Surgeons (hon.), Hungarian Dental Assn. (hon.), Israel Soc. Oral and Maxillofacial Surgeons (hon.), Sigma Xi, Omicron Kappa Upsilon. Rsch. and publs. on connective tissue physiology and pathology, particularly cartilage and bone metabolism, craniofacial growth, oral maxillofacial surgery, and pathology of temporomandibular joint. Office: Med Coll Va Dept Oral/Maxillofac Surg PO Box 980566 Richmond VA 23298-0566

LASKIN, MARK JEFFREY, psychologist; b. Phila., July 2, 1951; arrived in England, 1984; s. Harold and Lynn G. (Bailer) L.; children: Justin Matthew, Charlotte Jamie. BA, Univ. Va., 1973; MHA, Med. Coll. Va., 1977; MSc, Calif. Western U., 1979, PhD, 1980. Staff assoc. The White House, Washington, 1976-77; pub. health adv. Dept. of State, Latin Am., Caribbean, 1977-79; regional health officer U.S. Embassy, Bridgetown, Barbados, 1979-84; dep. regional dir. Internat. Planned Parenthood Fedn./Western Hemisphere Region, N.Y.C., 1984-85; asst. sec. gen. Internat. Planned Parenthood Fedn., London, 1985-97; prin. The Unicon Clinic, Marlow, Bucks, England, 1997—; trustee Population Concern, London, 1994—, Mgmt. Svcs. for Africa, 2000—. Mem. APA, British Assn. Counselling, Inst. Dirs. Mem. Soc. of Friends. Avocations: skiing, sailing.

LASLEY, CHARLES HADEN, cardiovascular surgeon, health and fitness consultant; b. Lewisburg, Ky., Dec. 16, 1921; s. Marion Grinter and Helen May (Murray) L.; m. Mary Brown, June 14, 1946 (div. 1966); children: Mary Ann, Charles H., Jr., Robert Murray, David Marion; m. Janet Elizabeth Evans, Jan. 28, 1967; children: Tiffany Jean, Phillip Evans. BS in chemistry, biology, U. Fla., 1939-43; MD, Harvard Med. Sch., 1944-47. Diplomate Am. Bd. Thoracic Surgery, Am. Bd. Surgery. Intern in surgery Grady Hosp., Atlanta, 1947-48; asst. resident in surgery Grady Hosp., 1948-49; resident in surgery Gorgas Hosp., Ancon, Canal Zone, 1950; sr., chief resident surgery Gorgas Hosp., 1951, staff surgeon, chief gen. surgery, 1952-53; asst. chief orthopedic surgery USAH Ft. Carson, Colorado Springs, Colo., 1953-54; resident in cardiac surgery City of Hope Med. Ctr., L.A., 1954-55; resident in thoracic, cardiovascular surgery VAH Oteen, Asheville, N.C., 1955-56; pvt. practice thoracic, cardiovascular surgery Morton Plant Hosp., Clearwater, Fla., 1956-79; chief of surgery Morton Plant Hosp., 1971-72, chief thoracic, cardiovascular surgery, 1977-78; med. dir. Longevity Clin., Clearwater, 1977-78; med. cons. Wellness Ctr. Morton Plant Hosp., 1996—; lectr. in field. Author: Veritas, 1996. Jazz drummer Red Suspenders Jazz Band, 1991—; mem. Calvary Bapt. Ch. With US Army, 1949-54. Mem. Am. Assn. for Thoracic Surgery, Am. Coll. of Sports Medicine, Soc. of Thoracic Surgeons, So. Thoracic Surgery Assn., Fla. Soc. of Thoracic and Cardiovascular Surgeons (president 1972), Suncoast Dixieland Jazz Society. Republican. Avocations: distance running (18 marathons and 34 triathlons), triathlons, handball, dixieland jazz. Home: Unit 4 Pelican Pl 672 Poinsettia Rd Belleair FL 33756-1525

LASMÉZAS, CORINNE IDA, veterinarian; b. Paris, Jan. 2, 1968; d. Andre Jean and Marie-Luise (Munding) L. Degree in vet., Vet. Sch. Toulouse, France, 1990; DVM, Faculty Medicine, Toulouse, 1993; PhD in Neurosci., Pierre & Marie Curie U., Paris, 1995. Rschr. CEA, Fontenay-aux-Roses, France, 1996—; tchr. U. Paris, 1998—, U. Paris VII, 1998—; mem. French nat. com. Transmissible Spongiform Enphalopathies, Paris, 1996—. Contbr. articles to profl. jours. Postdoctoral fellow CEA, 1995-96. Avocations: singing, cello, swimming, skiing. Office: CEA Svc Neurovirologie, 60-68 av G Leclerc BP6, 92268 Fontenay-aux-Roses France

LASOK, KAROL PAUL, Queen's counsel barrister; b. London, July 16, 1953; s. Dominik and Sheila May (Corrigan) L.; m. Karen Bridget Griffith, Feb. 21, 1991; children: Frances Katharine Marina, Anna Zofia Christina. MA, Jesus Coll., 1975; LLM, U. Exeter, 1977, PhD, 1986. Legal sec. Ct. Justice European Cmty., Luxembourg, 1980-84; pvt. practice Brussels, 1985-87, London, 1987—. Author: The European Court of Justice: Practice and Procedure, 2d edit., 1994; contbr. chpts. to books; editl. bd. Law & Justice, European Competition Law Rev., Common Market Law Reports. Avocations: walking, music. Office: Monckton Chambers, 4 Raymond Bldg Gray's Inn, WC1R 5BP London England

LASPADA, MARY ANNE, retired medical assistant; b. Boston, Feb. 12, 1930; d. Antonio and Angelina (Prestia) L. Student, Stratford Bus. Sch., 1947-48, Ms Allen's Finishing Sch., 1948. Notary pub., Mass. Typist, stenographer, sec. to pres., treas. Cynthia Mills, Inc., Boston, 1947-51; adminstrv. asst., asst. to chair divsn. psychiatry, adminstrv. dir. acad. affairs psychiatry Boston U. Sch. Medicine, 1951-99; ret., 1999. Mem. Am. Soc. Notaries, Campion Club of Boston (sec. 1989-94, 98-2000, bd. dirs. 1994-2000). Avocations: gardening, reading, dancing, knitting, crocheting.

LASPINAS, PIEDAD NOEL, physician; b. Cebu City, Cebu, Phillipines, Sept. 18, 1919; d. Hilaridn Hernani and Maternidad Trazo (Noel) L. AA, U. Philippines, 1938, MD, 1946. Diplomate Bd. Pediatric Soc., Philippines. Asst. city health officer Cebu City, 1953-76; cons. maternal and child svcs. Dept. of Health Region VII, Cebu City, 1976-80; instr. Coll. of Medicine Gullas, Cebu City, 1981-91; ret.; pvt. practice Cebu City; cons. nursery Cebu Maternity Hosp., Cebu City, 1997-99. Mem. Philippine Med. Assn., Philippine Pediatric Soc., Philippine Women's Med. Assn. Roman Catholic. Avocations: reading, hiking, gardening.

LASRY, JEAN-MICHEL, mathematics educator; b. Paris, Oct. 29, 1947; m. Elisabeth du Boucher; children: Laura, Romain, Julien. M in Econs., U. Paris-Assas, 1970; these d'etat in math., U. Paris IX, 1975. Rsch. fellow Ctr. Nat. Recherche Scientifique, Paris, 1971-78; prof. Paris-Dauphine U., 1978—, chmn. math. dept., 1980-83; cons. Compagnie Bancaire, Paris, 1988-91; mem. exec. bd. Caisse des Depots, 1991-94; CEO Caisse Autonome de Refinancement, 1994-96; global head of rsch., fixed income Bank Paribas, 1997-99, Deputy CEO, Compagnie Parisienne de Reescompte (CPR). Contbr. articles to profl. jours. Mem. Am. Math. Soc., Soc. Mathematiques apliquies et industrielles (bd. dirs.), Soc. Mathematique de France, Assn. Francaise de Finance, Ecole de la Cause Freudienne.

LASS, TERESA LEE, secondary school and special education educator; b. Atlanta, Aug. 30, 1958; d. Houston Lee and Carolyn (Cowan) L.; m. William Gary Carpenter, Oct. 1, 1983 (div. Sept. 1995). BA in German, Studio Art, Art History, Agnes Scott Coll., 1980; MEd, Ga. State U., 1994. Art gall. dir. TPS/Decor Corp., Atlanta, 1978-88; instr. adult literacy State Ga., Dept. Continuing Edn., Atlanta, 1990—; instr. New Tchr. Inst. Ga. State U., Atlanta, 1990-91; instr. staff devel. Dekalb Schs., Decatur, Ga., 1996—; tchr. prodn. and distbn. Warren Tech. Sch., Chamblee, Ga., 1988—, Ptnr. in Edn. liaison, 1994—, chair human rels., 1996—; cons. Ga. Learning Resource Svcs., Atlanta, 1993—. Chmn. Peachtree Arts, High Mus. of Art, Atlanta, 1996-97, sec./liaison 1991-95, sec., 1999—; artistic coord. Habitat for Humanity Artfest, Atlanta, 1996—. Named Tchr. of Yr., 1994-95. Mem. Phi Beta Kappa, Kappa Delta Pi. Baptist. Avocations: travel, reading, art collecting, cooking, writing. Home: 2155 Morris Ave Tucker GA 30084-4510 Office: Warren Tech Sch 3075 Alton Rd Chamblee GA 30341-4301

LASSEN, BETTY JANE, educator; b. Topeka, Kans., Apr. 19, 1923; d. Harvey Leroy and Anna Elizabeth (Day) Rose; m. Emil Lassen Jr., June 5, 1944 (dec. Sept. 1989); 1 child, Emil III. Instr., guide YMCA-YWCA, Albuquerque, 1975-84, U. N.Mex. Continuing Edn., Albuquerque, 1979—, Ft. Lewis Coll. Continuing Edn., Durango, Colo., 1992-93; liaison, asst. coord. San Juan Coll. Elder Hostel, Farmington, N.Mex., 1993-94; owner, pres. Outdoor Adventure Tours, Inc., Albuquerque, 1982—; mem. curriculum com., human svcs. tng. coun. gerontology divsn. continuing edn. U. N.Mex., 1979-82; spkr. in field. Designer ski equipment; contbr. articles, poetry to profl. publs. Vol. instr., guide for disabled Easter Seals Soc., Albuquerque, 1983; vol. campground host Nat. Park Svc., Chaco Canyon Ruins, N.Mex., 1990; campaign vol. Dem. Party, Albuquerque, 1976. Recipient Appreciation award Easter Seals Soc., 1983. Mem. Puerto Del Sol Ladies Golf Assn. (pres. 1976-77), N.Mex. Outfitters/Guides, N.Mex. Cross-Country Ski Club (sec. 1973-76), N.Mex. Mountain Club. Avocations: cross-country skiing, hiking, bicycling, golf, ballroom dancing. Home: 2916 Santa Clara Ave SE Albuquerque NM 87106-2947

LASSEN, JOHN KAI, development and construction company executive; b. Youngstown, Ohio, Mar. 28, 1942; s. Kai Kierulff and Helen Susanne (Elsaesser) L.; m. Marion duPont McConnell, Sept. 26, 1987; children: Christian K., Laura Wick, William duPont, James Tyler. BA, Yale U., 1964; JD, U. Pa., 1967. Bar: Del. 1971, U.S. Dist. Ct. Del. 1972. Ptnr. Morris, Nichols, Arsht & Tunnel, Wilmington, Del., 1977-83, Lassen, Smith Katzenstein & Furlow, Wilmington, Del., 1984-91; pres. Chesapeake Industries, Inc., Wilmington, Del., 1992—; vice-chmn., COO Krapfcandoit Co., Wilmington, Del., 1995-2000; pres. Southern Sr. Devel. Co., Wilmington, Del., 2000—. Lt. UNSR, 1967-70. Mem. ABa, Del. Bar Assn. (chmn. decedents, estate and trusts 1979-81), Del. World Affairs Coun., Soc. Mayflower Descendants (dep. gov. 1990-93), Soc. of Colonial Wars, Friends of Winterthur, Wilmington Club, Wilmington Country Club, Vicmead Hunt Club, Ocean Reef Club, Lincoln Club, Yale Club N.Y.C., Rotary. Episcopalian. Home: Crooked Billet PO Box 3712 3510 Kennett Pike Wilmington DE 19807-3019 Home (summer): Shore Winds 19 Hall Ave Rehoboth Beach DE 19971-2512

LASSEN, LISBETH HJORTH, neurologist; b. Lyngby, Denmark, Dec. 3, 1956; d. Ernst and Valborg (Joergensen) L.; m. Ole Meisner, July 27, 1985; children: Anne-Sophie Meisner, Marie-Louise R. Meisner. MD, Copenhagen U., 1991, PhD, 1998. Physician Gentofte (Denmark) Hosp., 1991-93; rsch. fellow in neurology Glostrup (Denmark) Hosp., 1993-97, clinician dept. neurology, 1997—. Avocation: jogging. Home: Skraenten 8, 2820 Gentofte Denmark Office: Glostrup Hosp Dept Neurology, U Copenhagen, 2600 Glostrup Denmark

LASSLO, ANDREW, medicinal chemist, educator; b. Mukacevo, Czechoslovakia, Aug. 24, 1922; came to U.S., 1946, naturalized, 1951; s. Vojtech Laszlo and Terezie (Herskovicova) L.; m. Wilma Ellen Reynolds, July 9, 1955; 1 child, Millicent Andrea. MS, U. Ill., 1948, PhD, 1952, MLS, 1961. Rsch. chemist organic chems. div. Monsanto Chem. Co., St. Louis, 1952-54; asst. prof. pharmacology, divsn. basic health scis. Emory U., 1954-60; prof. and chmn. dept. med. chemistry Coll. Pharmacy, U. Tenn. Health Sci. Ctr., 1960-90, Alumni Disting. Svc. prof. and chmn., dept. medicinal chemistry, 1989-90, professor emeritus, 1990—; cons. Geschickter Fund for Med. Research Inc., 1961-62; rsch. contractor U.S. Army Med. R & D Command, 1964-67; dir. postgrad. tng. program sci. librarians USPHS, 1966-72; chmn. edn. com. Drug Info. Assn., 1966-68, bd. dirs., 1968-69; dir. postgrad. tng. program organic medicinal chemistry for chemists FDA, 1971; exec. com. adv. council S.E. Regional Med. Library Program, Nat. Library of Medicine, 1969-71; chmn. regional med. library programs com. Med. Library Assn., 1971-72; mem. pres.'s faculty adv. council U. Tenn. System, 1970-72; chmn. energy authority U. Tenn. Center for Health Scis., 1975-77, chmn. council departmental chmn., 1977, 81; chmn. Internat. Symposium on Contemporary Trends in Tng. Pharmacologists, Helsinki, 1975. Producer, moderator (TV and radio series) Health Care Perspective, 1976-78; author: Travel at Your Own Risk-Reflections on Science, Research and Education, 1998, Molecules, Miracles and Medicine, 2000; editor: Surface Chemistry and Dental Integuments, 1973, Blood Platelet Function and Medicinal Chemistry, 1984; contbr. numerous articles to sci. and profl. jours.; mem. editl. bd. Jour. Medicinal and Pharm. Chemistry, 1961, U. Tenn. Press, 1974-77; composer (work for piano) Synthesis in C Minor, 1968; patentee in field. Trustee 1st Bohemian Meth. Ch., Chgo., 1951-52, mem. bd. stewards, 1950-52; mem. ofcl. bd. Grace Meth. Ch., Atlanta, 1955-60; mem. adminstrv. bd. Christ United Meth. Ch., Memphis, 1964-72, 73-75, 77-79, 81-83, 88-90, chmn. commn. on edn., 1965-67, chmn. bd. Day Sch., 1967-68. 1st lt. USAR, 1953-57, capt., 1957-62. Recipient Research prize U. Ill. Med. Ctr. chpt. Sigma Xi, 1949, Honor Scroll Tenn. Inst. Chemists, 1976, Americanism medal DAR, 1976; U. Ill. fellow, 1950-51; Geschickter Fund Med. Research grantee, 1959-65, USPHS Research and Tng. grantee, 1958-64, 66-72, 82-89, NSF research grantee, 1964-66, Pfeiffer Research Found. grantee, 1981-87. Fellow AAAS, Am. Assn. Pharm. Scientists, Am. Inst. Chemists (nat. councilor for Tenn. 1969-70), Acad. Pharm. Rsch. and Sci.; mem. ALA (life), Am. Chem. Soc. (sr.), Am. Pharm. Assn., Am. Soc. Pharmacology and Exptl. Therapeutics (chmn. subcom. pre and postdoctoral tng. 1974-78, exec. com. ednl. and profl. affairs 1974-78), Sigma Xi (pres. elect U. Tenn. Ctr. for Health Sci. chpt. 1975-76, pres. 1976-77, Excellence in Rsch. award 1989), Beta Phi Mu, Phi Lambda Sigma, Rho Chi. Methodist. Achievements include 7 U.S. and 11 foreign patents in field; identification of platelet aggregation-inhibitory specific functions in synthetic organic molecules; design and synthesis of novel human blood platelet aggregation inhibitors, novel compound for mild stimulation of central nervous system activity; research on relationships between structural features of synthetic organic entities, their physicochemical properties and their effects on biologic activity. Home and Office: 5479 Timmons Ave Memphis TN 38119-6932

LASSMANN, GÜNTER, biophysicist, researcher; b. Breslau, Germany, Apr. 2, 1936; s. Hermann and Hildegard (Schilauski) L.; m. Brunhilde Jung, Oct. 28, 1961; children: Holger, Anke. Diploma in physics, U. Leipzig, Germany, 1960, PhD in Molecular Biophysics, 1972. Rsch. scientist Inst. Biophysics Acad. Scis. Germany, Berlin, 1960-72, head dept. magnetic resonance Inst. Molecular Biology, 1972-84, rsch. scientist, 1984-89; project leader Max-Delbrück-Ctr. Molecular Medicine, Berlin, 1989-94; project leader Max-Volmer-Inst. Biophysical Chemistry Tech. U. Berlin, 1994—; rsch. scientist Nat. Inst. of Environ. Health Scis., Rsch. Triangle Pk., N.C., 1990, U. Umea, Sweden, 1992. Co-author: Methods in Protein Analytics, 1996; contbr. articles to profl. jours. Avocation: classical music. Office: Tech U Berlin, Strasse des 17. Juni 135, D-10623 Berlin Germany

LAST, DONALD, conservationist, educator; b. June 19, 1943. BA, Valparaiso U., 1965; MA, U. Wis., 1972, PhD, 1992. Instr. U. Wis. Marinette County, 1967-70; environ. quality agt. Dane County Wis., 1970-76; soil and water conservation specialist U. Wis., Stevens Point, 1976-82, prof., natural resources specialist, 1982—. Office: Coll Natural Resources Rm 204 U Wis Stevens Point WI 54481

LAST, ISIDORE, physicist; b. Ostrov Lubelski, Lublin, Poland, Nov. 3, 1931; s. Bezalel and Dora (Shulman) L.; m. Rosa Drosin, Oct. 21, 1959; 1 child, Mark. MS, Gorki U., USSR, 1954; PhD, Lebedev Phys. Inst., Moscow, 1960. Lectr. Karaganda Mining Inst., Kazachstan, USSR, 1954-57; rschr. Inst. Chemistry, Ufa, USSR, 1958-61, sr. rschr., 1961-74; sr. rschr. Inst. Geophysics, Ufa, 1974-77, Soreq Nuclear Ctr., Yavne, Israel, 1979-96, Tel Aviv U., 1996—; assoc. prof. Bashkirian U., USSR, 1964-77; rsch. fellow SUNY, Buffalo, 1986-87; vis. prof. Barcelona (Spain) U., 1994-95. Author: Radiometric Determination, 1968; contbr. numerous articles to profl. jours. Mem. Seminar of Jewish Refusnics, Moscow, 1974-77; mem. Scientists' Com. for Soviet Jewry, Tel Aviv, 1989-94. Mem. N.Y. Acad. Scis. Avocations: demography, modern history. Home: Yigal Allon Str 23/3, Benei-Beraq 51231, Israel

LASTER, RICHARD, biotechnology executive, consultant; b. Vienna, Austria, Nov. 10, 1923; came to U.S., 1940, naturalized, 1944; s. Alan and Croline (Harband) L.; m. Liselotte Schneider, Oct. 17, 1948; children: Susan Laster Rubenstein, Thomas. Student, U. Wash., 1941-42; BChE cum laude, Poly. Inst. Bklyn., 1943; postgrad., Stevens Inst. Tech., 1945-47. With Gen. Foods Corp., 1944-82; corp. rsch. and devel. Gen. Foods Corp., Hoboken, N.J., 1944-58; ops. mgr. Franklin Baker divsn. Gen. Foods Corp., Hoboken, 1958-64; ops. mgr. Atlantic Gelatin divsn. Gen. Foods Corp., Woburn, Mass., 1958-64; mgr. rsch. and devel. Jell-O divsn. Gen. Foods Corp., White Plains, N.Y., 1967-68, exec. v.p. Maxwell House divsn., 1968-69, pres. Maxwell House divsn., 1969-71, corp. v.p., 1971-73, exec. v.p., 1974-82; also dir. R&D and food-away-from-home Gen. Foods Corp., White Plains, 5, 1975-82; bd. dirs.DNA Plant Tech. Corp., 1982-94, chmn., 1988-94, CEO, 1982-92, pres., 1982-91; mgmt. cons., 1994—; bd. dirs. RiceTec; bd. dirs., chmn. WellGen, Inc. Contbr. articles to profl. publs.; patentee in field. Mem. Sch. Bd., Chappaqua, N.Y., 1971-74, pres., 1973-74; chmn., bd. dirs., 1st v.p. United Way of Westchester, 1978; chmn. adv. com. Poly. Inst. Westchester, 1977; trustee Poly. Inst. N.Y., 1978—; mem. coll. coun. SUNY, Purchase, Purchase Coll. Found., 1986—; mem. corp. N.Y. Bot. Grden; mem. subcom. export adminstrn. Pres.'s Export Coun., 1995; chmn. Westchester Edn. Coalition, 1992—; chmn. Westchester Holocaust Commn., 1994—; chmn. Am. Soc. Plant Physiologists Edn. Found., 1995; mem. New Castle Town Bd. Recipient Disting. Alumnus award, 1996, Disting. Sc. award NCCJ; Poly Inst. N.Y. fellow. Mem. AAAS, AIChE (Food and Bioengrng. award 1972), N.Y. Acad. Scis., Am. Chem. Soc., Am. Inst. Chemists, Tau Beta Pi, Phi Lambda Upsilon. Home: 23 Round Hill Rd Chappaqua NY 10514-1622 Office: Richard Laster 103 S Bedford Rd Mount Kisco NY 10549-3440

LAŠTOVIČKA, JAN, physicist; b. London, Nov. 10, 1944; arrived in Czech republic, 1945; s. Bohuslav and Marie (Bohanesová) L.; m. Marcela Přibylová, dec. 22, 1967; 1 child, Radek. RNDr, Charles U., Prague, Czech republic, 1974; PhD, Czech Acad. Sci., Prague, 1973, DrSc, 1987. Postgrad. Geophys. Inst., Prague, 1967-69, scientist, 1969-94; dir. Inst. Atmospheric Physics, Prague, 1998—; lectr. in field. Contbr. more than 190 articles to profl. jours. With Czech Army, 1966-67. Mem. Am. Geophys. Union, European Geophys. Soc., Internat. Assn. Geomagnetism and Aeronomy (v.p. 1999—). Avocations: hiking, skiing, history. Office: Inst Atmospheric Physics, Bocni II, 14131 Prague 4, Czech Republic

LASTRA, JOSE RAMON, plant virologist, eductor; b. Orense, Spain, May 22, 1939; arrived in Venezuela, 1954, naturalized; s. Ramon and Maria (Rodriguez) L.; m. Ana Maria Mumm, Mar. 3, 1953; children, Ricardo, Daniel, Eduardo, Andres. Degree in Biology, U. Cent. Venezuela, 1966; MSc in Plant Pathology, U. Calif., Berkeley, 1970, PhD in Plant Pathology,

1974. Head plant virus lab IVIC, Caracas, 1974-85; prof. U. Cen. Venezuela, Caracas, 1976-85; head molecular biology lab. CATIE, 1980-87; coord. IPM project CATIE, Turrialba, Costa Rica, 1985-86; dir. ednl. programs CATIE, 1986-94; dir. edn. and capacity bldg. World Wide Fund for Nature-Internat., Gland, Switzerland, 1994-97; dir. regional office for the Ams., Internat. Plant Genetic Resources Inst., Cali, Colombia, 1997—; cons. in field. Mem. Am. Phytopathol. Soc. (pres. Caribbean divsn. 1978), Soc. Latinoamericana de Fitopatologos, Soc. Venezolana de Fitopatologia, N.Am. Assn. Environ. Educators, Phi Beta Kappa. Roman Catholic. Avocations: tennis, philately. Office: PGR care CIAT, AA 6713, 1196 Cali Colombia

LASTRA, ROSA MARIA, law and finance educator; b. Salamanca, Spain, Dec. 2, 1964; d. Saturnino and Rosa (Leralta) L.; m. Mats Göran Kummelstedt, Sept. 19, 1992; children: Alexander, Eric. LLB, Valladolid U., Spain, 1987, MA, 1989; LLM, Harvard U., 1991; PhD, Madrid U., 1991. Cons. Internat. Monetary Fund, Washington, 1992-93; dir. internat. fin. and bus. Columbia U. Sch. Internat. & Pub. Affairs, N.Y.C., 1993-95, asst. prof., 1993-96; fellow internat. fin. and monetary law U. London, Queen Mary and Westfield Colls., London, 1996—, lectr. internat. fin. and monetary law, 1997—; dir. internat. fin. and bus. studies Columbia U. Sch. Internat. and Pub. Affairs, N.Y.C., 1993-95, co-dir. Ctr. Internat. Bus. Edn., 1993-95; asst. dir. London Inst. Internat. Baning, Fin. and Devel. Law, 1996—; assoc. mem. Fin. Markets Group, London Sch. Econs., 1996—. Author: Central Banking and Banking Regulation, 1996. Recipient Fulbright fellowship Harvard, 1990-92, Banco de España grantee for rsch. on ctrl. banking and banking regulation London Sch. Econs., 1990. Office: Queen Mary & Westfield Coll, U London, 339 Mile End Rd, London E1 4NS, England

LAŠTUVKA, ZDENEK, zoology educator, researcher; b. Brno, Czech Republic, Apr. 28, 1955; s. Zdenek and Jitka (Hladíková) L.; m. Anna Václavová, Nov. 22, 1980; children: Jana, Zdenek. M in Natural Scis., U. J.E. Purkynĕ, Brno, Czech Republic, 1979, D in Natural Scis., 1979; PhD, U. Agr., Brno, Czech Republic, 1987. Study stay U. Agr., Brno, Czech Republic, 1980-83; postgrad. study U. Agr., Brno, 1983-85, asst. zoologist, 1986-90, assoc. prof., 1991—. Author, editor: (books) Katalog von Faltern Mährens, 1993, An Illustrated Key to European Sesiidae, 1995, (with A. Lastuvka) Nepticulidae Mitteleuropas, 1997, Checklist of Lepidoptera of the Czech and Slovak Republics, 1998, (with K. Spatenka, O. Gorbunov, I. Tosevski, Y. Arita) Handbook of Palaearctic Macrolepidoptera, Vol. 1 Sesiidae, 1999; also articles. Mem. Czech Entomol. Soc., Czech Zoolog. Soc., Soc. European Lepidopterologica. E-mail: last@mendelu.cz. Office: Mendel U Agr & Forestry Dept Zoology, Zemĕdĕlská 1, 613 00 Brno Czech Republic

LASYS, JOAN, medical nurse, writer, educator, publisher; b. Siauliai, Lithuania, Sept. 1, 1924; arrived in Can., 1948; came to U.S., 1960; d. Joseph-Apolinarius and Elena (Šlapokaite) Barcevičius; m. Bill Lasys, July 31, 1949. RN degree, Lithuanian Red Cross Sch. Nurs, 1945; student, Ariz. State U., 1981-86, Ea. Ariz. Coll., 1981-86. RN, Can., Nebr.; cert. nursing tchr., Ariz. Staff RN St. Mary's Hosp., Montreal, Can., 1949-51, Montreal Gen. Hosp., 1951-53, 1959-60; pvt. duty Nurses Registry, Montreal, 1953-56; Can. civil svc. RN R.H.O. Ctr. Dept. Vets. Affairs, Ottawa, Can., 1956-57, Queen Mary Vets. Hosp., Montreal, 1957-58; staff RN St. Joseph's Hosp., Omaha, 1968-69, Meryvale Hosp., Phoenix, 1969-71, Valley View Hosp., Youngtown, Ariz., 1971-72, Boswell Hosp., Sun City, Ariz., 1972-76; RN Kivel Care Ctr., Phoenix, 1986-93; past v.p. and officer Pine-Strawberry (Ariz.) Health Svcs.; columnist/reporter Payson (Ariz.) Roundup. Pub. (mag.) Small Town U.S.A.; prodr. audio tapes: Time Management, Nursing Communications. Life mem. Pine-Strawberry and Gila County Homemakers, Payson Regional Med. Ctr. Aux. Mem. AAUW. Republican. Roman Catholic. Avocations: writing poetry, public speaking. Home: 506 N William Tell Cir Payson AZ 85541-4050

LASZCZKA, ANDRZEJ KONSTANTY, biologist, journal editor; b. Cracow, Poland, July 7, 1930; s. Czesław and Jadwiga (Brzezinska) L.; m. Barbara Jaszczyszyn, Jan. 28, 1961; 1 child, Artur. Agrl. engr., Jagiellonian U., Cracow, 1953; MS in Animal Sci., Agrl. U., Cracow, 1954, D of Agrl. Scis., 1965; Habilitation, Nat. Rsch. Inst. Animal Prodn., Cracow, 1976; prof. agrl. scis. From asst. to sr. asst. Agrl. U., 1954-62; asst. prof. Exptl. Sta. Balice, Nat. Rsch. Inst. Animal Prodn., Cracow, 1962-72, asst. prof. dept. animal reprodn., 1972-78, assoc. prof., 1978-84, prof., 1984—, dep. head dept., 1980—; Editor-in-chief Annals of Animal Sci., 1986—. Grantee State Com. Sci. Rsch., Cracow, 1992-94, 95-98. Mem. Polish Soc. Animal Sci., Polish Acad. Scis. (mem. com.), Polish Soc. Vet. Scis. (jour. editor, pres. commn. on animal reprodn., physiology and pathology 1972-74), European Soc. for Domestic Animal Reprodn., Polish Andrological Soc. Avocations: photography, mountain travel, travel. Office: Nat Rsch Inst Animal Prodn, Inst Zootech Balice, PL 32083 Balice nr Cracow Krakow, Poland

LASZEWSKI, BOLESLAW TADEUSZ, civic volunteer; b. Gora Ropczycka, Poland, Nov. 22, 1912; s. Jozef and Katarzyna (Totan) L.; m. Sophie Kinel, Sept. 26, 1947 (div. 1968); children: Barbara, Marlena, Dorothy; m. Christine Gaszynski. BSBA, CUNY, 1954; MS, Columbia U., 1956; MA, Jagiellonian U., 1937. Co-founder, hon. pres. Polish Assistance, N.Y.C., 1952—; co-founder, pres., Polish Assn., London, 1945-50; v.p. Worldwide Orgn. Poles Abroad, London, 1947-80; mem. Kostiuszko Found., N.Y.C., 1952—; co-founder, pres. Polish Daily News, N.Y.C., 1970—; pres. Polish Am. Army Veterans Assn., 1985—; exec. dir. Polish Inst. Arts & Scis., N.Y.C., 1986-90; v.p., dir. Polish Am. Congress, 1986-88; pres. Polish Fed. Credit Union, Bklyn., 1985-90. Author: From Army to Civilian Life, 1984, Krakow, 1985, East West Russia—USSR—USA—Poland, 1986.

LASZEWSKI, ZOFIA K., medical administrator; b. Lwow, Poland, Sept. 26, 1922; came to U.S., 1951; d. Zygmunt and Zofia A. (Scheinder) Kinel; divorced, 1964; children: Barbara Elizabeth Laszewski Garner, Marzena Laszewski Ferguson, Dorota Laszewski Polomis. MB BChir, Aberdeen (Scotland) Med. Sch., 1950; postgrad., NYU, 1952-55. Diplomate Am. Bd. Phys. Medicine and Rehab., Internat. Acad. Clin. Nutrition; cert. Am. Coll. for Advancement in Medicine. Rotating intern Muhlenberg Hosp., Plainfield, N.J., 1951-52; dir. phys. medicine and rehab. St. Barnabas Hosp., N.Y.C., 1952-63; attending physiatrist House of Giles the Cripple for Children, Bklyn., 1955-71; clin. prof. phys. medicine and rehab. N.Y. Polyclinic Med. Ctr., N.Y.C., 1957-70, Brown U., Providence, R.I., 1976-88; pvt. practice N.Y. Ctr. of Phys. Medicine and Rehab., N.Y.C., 1969-76; chief cerebral palsy St. Agnes Hosp., Westchester, N.Y., 1961-70; dir. phys. medicine and rehab. Jewish Hosp., Rehab. Ctr., Jersey City, 1969-76; chief rehab. svc. PVA Med. Ctr., Providence, 1976-94; founder, dir. Inst. Preventive and Nutritional Medicine, 1999; dir. phys. medicine and rehab. Lenox Hill Hosp., N.Y.C., 1961-76. Contbr. articles to sci. and med. jours. Recipient numerous awards, including Woman of Yr. award United Cerebral Palsy, 1968, Hands and Heart award VA-Max Cleland, 1988. Mem. ACAM, Am. Congress of Phys. Medicine and Rehab., Polish Med. Soc., N.Y. Acad. Scis. Republican. Roman Catholic. Avocations: tennis, swimming, volleyball. Home: 3 W Prospect St Greenville RI 02828-2108

ŁASZKIEWICZ, RAFAŁ, engineering educator; b. Warsaw, Oct. 24, 1934; s. Antoni and Elżbieta (Litmanowicz) Ł; m. Regina Alwin, Oct. 27, 1974. Postgrad. degree., Politechnika, Warsaw, 1956, PhD, 1965. Tech. rschr. Polish Rlwys. Rsch. Inst., Warsaw, 1955-56; with Polish Rlwys. (PKP), Warsaw, 1956-60; adj. tech. rschr. Polish Rlwys. Rsch. Inst. (COBiRTK), Warsaw, 1960-68, ind. rschr., 1968-74; asst. prof. Politechnika, Radom, Poland, 1971—; lectr. Politechnika, Warsaw, 1967-70; vis. lectr. Politechnika, Katowice, Poland, 1979-80; dep. dir. Tech. Inst., Radom, 1978-81; mem. tech.-econ. coun. Polish Railways, 1990-93; visitor Brit. Coun., 1979, 88; lectr., tech. visitor Deutsche Forschungsgemeinschaft, Germany, 1995; rschr. Dutch and Brit. Rlys., UNTAss., Utrecht, The Netherlands and London, 1970. Author: Freight Traffic on Railways, 1979, Organization of Rail Passenger Transport, 1998; contbr. articles to profl. jours. Mem. Deutsche Verkehrswissenschaftliche Gesellschaft e.V. Home: Ul Malawskiego 3 m 114, 02-641 Warsaw Poland Office: Politechnika Radomska, Ul Malczewskiego 20a, 26-600 Radom Poland

LATERZA, VITO, publisher; b. Bari, Italy, Dec. 11, 1926; s. Giuseppe and Maria (Lembo) L.; m. Antonella Chiarini, Feb. 20, 1929; children: Giuseppe, Federico. Degree in Philosophy, U. Florence, 1948. Pub.'s asst. Casa Editrice Laterza, Bari, Italy, 1949-55, pub., 1955—. Decorated Chevalier des Arts et Métiers (France), Cavaliere del Lavoro della Repubblica Italiana (Italy). Home: Largo Elvezia N 5, 00197 Rome Italy Office: Gius Laterza & Figli SpA, Via di Villa Sacchetti 17, I-00197 Rome Italy also: Via Sparano 162, 70121 Bari Italy

LATHE, ROBERT EDWARD, management and financial consultant; b. Balt., Apr. 8, 1945; s. Warren Calvin Sr. and Margaret Mary (Cavey) L.; m. Hermina Yeghnazarian, Apr. 13, 1967; children: Michelle Gayaneh, Mellina Margaret. MSc in Mgmt., U. Dublin Trinity Coll., 1985. Metrology/field engr. Bendix Field Engring. Corp., Balt., 1967-68; quality assurance supr. space seismology lab. Bendix Aerospace Systems Divsn., Ann Arbor, Mich., 1968-72; programs mgr. Iran Aircraft Industries, Tehran, 1972-76; mgmt. cons. Alexander Proudfoot Co., Chgo., 1977-78; program mgr., field engr. Harris-PRD Electronics Divsn., Syosset, N.Y. & Isfahan, Iran, 1978-80; ops. dir. Airmotive Ireland Ltd., Dublin, 1980-84; project mgr. Handley-Walker Co., Inc., Valencia, Calif., 1986-87; owner, pres. Hyrel Bus. Svcs., Glendale, Calif., 1987-90; fin. planner, investment advisor IDS Fin. Svcs. Inc., Glendale, 1990-94; co-founder, sr. ptnr. Calif. Connection, Glendale, 1994—. Sgt. USAF, 1963-67, Vietnam. Mem. Am. Legion, Internat. Platform Assn. Avocations: microcomputers, public speaking, golf, swimming, ten-pin bowling. Home: 543 Milford St # 4 Glendale CA 91203-1697

LATHON, SHERAINE, clergyman; b. Chicago Heights, Feb. 20, 1952; d. Roosevelt Willingham and Norma L. Cobb; m. Willie Lathon, Jr., June 11, 1983; children: Eric, Christopher. AAS, Prairie State Jr. Coll., 1972; BS, Friends Internat. U., 1992, MS, 1994, PhD, 1997. Ordained to ministry, 1999. Collection mgr. Donnelley Directory, Chgo., 1973-87; ch. adminstr. Liberty Temple Full Gospel Ch., Chgo., 1987—, sr. pastor, 1999—; assoc. prof. Logos Ministerial Tng. Inst., Friends Internat. U. Sec.-treas. Bushido-Kan Acad.; pres. Sheraine Lathon Evangelistic Ministries. Mem. NAFE. Office: Liberty Temple Full Gospel Ch 2233 W 79th St Chicago IL 60620-5803

LATHROP, MITCHELL LEE, lawyer; b. L.A., Dec. 15, 1937; s. Alfred Lee and Barbara (Mitchell) L.; m. Lynn Mara Dalton; children: Christin Lorraine Newlon, Alexander Mitchell, Timothy Trewin Mitchell. BSc, U.S. Naval Acad., 1959; JD, U. So. Calif., 1966. Bar: D.C. 1966, Calif. 1966, U.S. Supreme Ct. 1969, N.Y. 1981; cert. arbitrator, Nat. Arbitration Forum, ARIAS-US. Dep. counsel L.A. County, Calif., 1966-68; with Brill, Hunt, DeBuys and Burby, L.A., 1968-71; ptnr. Macdonald, Halsted & Laybourne, L.A. and San Diego, 1971-80; sr. ptnr. Rogers & Wells, N.Y.C., San Diego, 1980-86; sr. ptnr., exec. com. Adams, Duque & Hazeltine, L.A., San Francisco, N.Y.C., San Diego, 1986-94, firm chmn., 1992-94; sr. ptnr. Luce, Forward, Hamilton & Scripps, San Diego, N.Y.C., San Francisco, L.A., Chgo., 1994—; presiding referee Calif. Bar Ct., 1984-86, mem. exec. com., 1981-88; lectr. law Calif. Judges Assn., Practicing Law Inst. N.Y., Continuing Edn. of Bar, State Bar Calif., ABA, others. Author: State Hazardous Waste Regulation, 1991, Environmental Insurance Coverage, 1991, Insurance Coverage for Environmental Claims, 1992; mem. editl. bd. Def. Counsel Jour., 1997—; editl. bd. Y2K advisor Jour. Ins. Coverage. Western Regional chmn. Met. Opera Nat. Coun., 1971-81, v.p., mem. exec. com., 1971—, now chmn.; trustee Honnold Libr. at Claremont Colls., 1972-80; bd. dirs. Music Ctr. Opera Assn., L.A., sec., 1974-80; bd. dirs. San Diego Opera Assn., 1980—, v.p., 1985-89, pres.-elect, 1993, pres., 1994-96; bd. dirs. Met. Opera Assn., N.Y.C.; mem. nat. steering coun. Nat. Actors Theatre, N.Y. Mem. ABA, N.Y. Bar Assn., Fed. Bar Assn., Fed. Bar Council, Calif. Bar Assn., D.C. Bar Assn., San Diego County Bar Assn. (chmn. ethics com. 1980-82, bd. dirs. 1982-85, v.p. 1985), Assn. Bus. Trial Lawyers, Am. Intellectual Property Law Assn., Assn. So. Calif. Def. Counsel, Los Angeles Opera Assos. (pres. 1970-72), Soc. Colonial Wars in Calif. (gov. 1970-72), Order St. Lazarus of Jerusalem, Friends of Claremont Coll. (dir. 1975-81, pres. 1978-79), Am. Bd. Trial Advocates, Judge Advocates Assn. (dir. Los Angeles chpt. 1974-80, pres. So. Calif. chpt. 1977-78), Internat. Assn. Def. Counsel, Brit. United Services Club (dir. Los Angeles 1973-75), Mensa Internat., Calif. Soc., S.R. (pres. 1977-79), Calif. Club (Los Angeles), Valley Hunt Club (Pasadena, Calif.), Met. Club (N.Y.C.), The Naval Club (London), Phi Delta Phi. Republican. Home: 3355 Valemont St San Diego CA 92106-2430 Office: Luce Forward Hamilton and Scripps 600 W Broadway Fl 26 San Diego CA 92101-3311 also: Citicorp Ctr 153 E 53rd St 26th Fl New York NY 10022-4611

LATHROP, THOMAS ALBERT, language educator; b. L.A., Apr. 18, 1941; s. Donald C. and Ethel M. (Challacombe) L.; BA, UCLA, 1964, MA, 1965, PhD, 1970; m. Constance Ellen Cook, Aug. 30, 1969; 1 child, Aline. Mem. faculty romance langs. UCLA, 1964-66, U. Wyo., 1966-68, Transylvania U., 1973-76, Lafayette Coll., 1976-80; assoc. prof. romance langs. U. Del., Newark, 1980—; editor Juan de la Cuesta Hispanic Monographs, 1978—; co-editor The Cabrilho Press, 1974-89; pres. Linguatext, Ltd., 1989—; asst. editor Cervantes Bull. of the Cervantes Soc. Am., 1980-90. AID grantee, 1968; Nat. Endowment for Humanities grantee, 1976, 81; Gulbenkian Found. grantee, 1973; Del Amo Found. grantee, 1972. Mem. MLA, Cervantes Soc. Am., Internat. Assn. Hispanists, Am. Coun. on Teaching of Fgn. Lang., Am. Assn. Tchrs. Spanish and Portuguese. Author: The Legend of the Siete Infantes de Lara, 1972; (with F. Jensen) The Syntax of the Old Spanish Subjunctive, 1973; Espanol - Lengua y cultura de hoy, 1974; The Evolution of Spanish, 1980; De Acuerdo! and Tanto Mejor, 1986; (with E. Dias) Portugal: Lingua e Cultura, 1978, 2nd edit., 1995, Curso de gramatica historica espanola, 1984, 89, (with E. Dias) Brasil: Lingua e Cultura, 1992, student edit. Don Quijote, others. Home: 270 Indian Rd Newark DE 19711-5204 Office: U Del Dept Lang Newark DE 19716

LATIBEAUDIERE, DERICK MILTON, bank official; b. St. Catherine, Jamaica, June 9, 1951; married; 2 children. BA in Math. and Econs., U. West Indies, 1974, M in Econs., 1975. Economist in Rsch. dept. Bank of Jamaica, Kingston, 1975-78, sr. economist in Monetary and Fgn. Exch. Policy dept., 1978-79; country economist Caribbean Devel. Bank, 1979-83; asst. dir. monetary and fgn. exch. policy Bank of Jamaica, Kingston, 1983-85, dir. econ. policy, 1985-86, sr. dir., econ. adviser and head Econ. Policy and Programming dept., 1986-88, dep. gov. rsch. and econ. programming, 1988-93, with Banking and Mktg. Ops. divsn., 1993-95, sr. dep. gov., 1995-96, gov., 1996—; chmn. bd. dirs. Bank of Jamaica; bd. dirs. Planning Inst. Jamaica, 1988-95, Air Jamaica Ltd., Fin. Sector Adjustment Co., Fin. Instn. Svcs. Jamaica Coll. scholar. Office: Bank of Jamaica, Nethersole Pl PO Box 621, Kingston Jamaica*

LATIF, ABU HAMID, educator; b. Dinajpur, Bangladesh, Apr. 15, 1936; s. Khorshed Ali Ahmed and Begum Hamida Khatun; m. Mamtaz Jahan, Oct. 19, 1968; children: Sumana, Nabina. BA, Dhaka U., 1959, MA, 1960, MEd, 1963; EdD, U. No. Colo., 1968. From lectr. to prof. Inst. Edn. & Rsch. Dhaka U., Bangladesh, 1965—; exec. dir. population edn. programme Min. Edn., Dhaka, 1976-80; dir. Inst. Edn. & Rsch., 1987-90; cons. UNESCO, 1979, 90, 92, World Bank, 1990-92; sec. task force primary and mass edn. Govt. Bangladesh, 1992-93. Author: Nonformal Education, 1984; translator: Talks on American Education, 1968, Adult Education and Development, 1985; contbr. articles to profl. jours. Mem. Bangladesh Forum for Ednl. Devel. (chmn. 1990—), South Asian Forum for Ednl. Rsch. (coord. 1993—), So. Ednl. Rsch. Initiative. Avocations: reading, music, travel. Office: Inst Edn & Rsch, Dhaka U, 1000 Dhaka Bangladesh

LATIFUR RAHAMAN, RASUL BOAKSH, legal profession executive; b. Kushita, Bangladesh, Jan. 1, 1945; arrived in India, Jan. 3, 1945; s. Fazlur Rahman and Rabya Khatun Ruby Rabia Khatun; married; children: Rassel, Boaksel. Diploma, Kushtia Coll., 1963, LLB, 1966; M Commerce, Dhaka U., 1967. Headmaster Talberia High Sch., Kushtia Dist., 1961; head asst. Indsl. Promo Svcs., Dacca, 1966-67; income tax cons. Bangladesh Bar Assn., Segun Bagicha/Dacca, 1967-69; pres. Kushtia Income Tax Bar Assn., 1970-90, Padma Devel., Kushtia, 1980—; chmn. Bangladesh Coms., Padma, Kushtia, 1971—; chmn. Cen. Capital, Padma; leader of party/chmn., Bangladesh Internat. Order Party, Padma, 1980—; trade consulate Bangladesh Trade, Padma, 1980—; chmn. Bazar com., Padma. Mem. Pub. Libr., Kushtia, 1965-66. Office: The Income Tax Bar Assn, B06000 Kushtia Padma, Bangladesh

LATIMER, HUGH SCOT, healthcare consultant, architect; b. Richmond, Va., Mar. 23, 1956; s. Hugh Alfred and Alice Marye L.; m. Nancy Phyllis Tull, Oct. 4, 1980; children: Stephanie Laura, Anne Elizabeth, Carrie Grace. BS, U. Va., 1978; MBA, U. Ill., 1980, MArch, 1981. Lic. architect, Calif. Project mgr. Bank Am.-Corp. Real Estate, San Francisco, 1980-82, mgr. No. Calif. properties, 1985-86; divsn. project mgr. Asia Bank Am.-Corp. Real Estate, Hong Kong, 1982-85; sr. project mgr. Bank Am.-Corp. Real Estate, N.Y.C., 1986-87; sr. cons. health svcs. Hamilton KSA, Boston, 1987-89; mgr. health svcs. Hamilton KSA, Fairfax, Va., 1989-91, prin. health svcs., 1991—, nat. dir. design svcs., 1995-97; nat. dir. design svcs. Hamilton-HMC, N.Y.C., 1997—; spkr. in field. Mem. AIA, Am. Soc. for Healthcare Engring. Office: Hamilton HMC 650 5th Ave New York NY 10019-6108

LATIMER, PAUL JERRY, non-destructive testing engineer; b. Springfield, Tenn., July 21, 1943; s. Paul Daniel and Juanita Inez (Richey) L.; m. Sylvia Susan Cole, June 6, 1966; children: Zachary Nathaniel, Matthew Jason. BS in Physics with honors, U. Tenn., 1966, MS in Physics, 1979, PhD in Physics, 1983. Devel. engr. Oak Ridge (Tenn.) Nat. Lab., 1980-81; faculty rsch. assoc. Ohio State U., Columbus, 1981; rsch. asst. U. Tenn., Knoxville, 1981-83; sr. rsch. engr. McDermott Techs. Inc. R&D divsn. Lynchburg Rsch. Ctr., Va., 1983-98; sr. engr. MAST Automation, Inc., Lynchburg, Va., 1998—. Contbr. articles to profl. jours.; patentee in field. Co-leader cub pack Lynchburg Area coun. Boy Scouts Am., 1983-84; vol. United Way, 1994; mem. Pacer Club for United Way Support, 1993-98. Mem. ASTM, Am. Soc. Metals, Am. Soc. Non-destructive Testing (cert. Level III untrasonic methods), Am. Welding Soc., Sigma Pi Sigma. Avocations: martial arts, hiking, lapidary, mineral collecting. Home: 303 Juniper Dr Lynchburg VA 24502-5661 Office: MAST Automation Inc Innerspec Techs Divsn 4004 Murray Pl Lynchburg VA 24501-5004

LATIMIER, PHIL H., investment banker; b. Paris, Oct. 9, 1953; s. Albert C. and Genevieve Cazauran L.; m. Anne M. Roudier, July 7, 1978; children: Romain-Morgan, Margaux-Joy. MS in Mgmt., MS. in Polit. Sci., Paris U., 1976; Grad., Donald T. Regan Sch. Advanced, Fin. Mgmt., N.Y.C., 1982; MBA, Am. Coll. Paris, 1982; CBA, Inst. Bus. Appraisers, Inc., 1997. Real-estate developer Cogedim - Paribas Group, Paris, 1976-78; mgr. fin. products devel. and corrs. banking Citibank, N.A., Paris, 1978-82; sr. mgr. corp. banking and internat. trade fin. Nat. Bank of Kuwait, Paris, 1982-87; asst. v.p. corp. banking Saudi European Bank, Paris, 1987-89; assoc. cons. in corp. fin. and fin. engring. Group Cie Fin. Edmond de Rothschild, Paris, 1989-91; founding ptnr., pres. Quantum Fin. Intermediation, Paris, 1989—; prof. fin., investment banking and bus. fin. Inst. Superieur du Commerce, Paris, 1993—; assoc. lectr. in internat. fin. Paris-Dauphine U., France, 1994—; Asian devel. bank expert; dir. B.L.L. Prodns., Paris; founding chmn. Culture and Mecenat, Paris; vis. prof. fin. Rutgers U., Tex. A&M, U. San Diego, U. Utah, Ngee Ann Polytech./Singapore, U. Paris, Dauphine, U. Wyo., North Fla. U., Embry-Riddle U.; cons. USAID, BARENTS (KPMG), Washington, Asian Devel. Bank, World Bank. Chair fin. dept. Rennes Internat. Sch. Bus. Mem. Inst. Bus. Appraisers. Avocations: contemporary art and antics.

LATINI, GIUSEPPE, pediatrician; b. Brindisi, Italy, Jan. 8, 1949; s. Nino Latini and Roja Provenzano; m. Anna Del Giudice; 1 child, Benedetta; 2 children: Marco, Fabio. Degree in Medicine, U. Siena, Italy, 1973, Degree in Pediat., 1976; Degree in Neonatology, U. Modena, Italy, 1982. Asst. pediat. clinic U. Siena, 1974-76; asst. pediat. divsn. Hosp., Brindisi, 1977-88, neonatology ICU chief, 1988-97, head pediat. divsn., 1997—. Mem. editl. bd. Biology of the Neonate, 1999. Mem. N.Y. Acad. Scis. Achievements include inventor of new polymers. E-mail: gilatini@tin.it. Fax: 39-831-537861. Home: via M Pagano 10, 72100 Brindisi Italy Office: Azienda Ospedaliera Summa, piazza di Summa, 72100 Brindisi Italy

LATKOVIĆ, IVAN JERONIM, retired internal and nuclear medicine educator; b. Imotski, Dalmatia, Croatia, May 15, 1925; s. Jeronim Josip and Andjela Ivan (Zaradić) L.; m. Sofija Brajša, Nov. 19, 1950; children: Jasna, Vesna. MD, U. Zagreb, Croatia, 1950, specialist in internal medicine, 1959; PhD, U. Zagreb, 1969, specialist in nuclear medicine, 1980. Chief dept. U. Zagreb Clin. Med. Ctr., 1961-90; prof. internal and nuclear medicine U. Zagreb, 1961-91; ret., 1991. Contbr. over 50 articles to Croatian and internat med. jours., including Croatian Med. Jour. Mem. Croatian Med. Assn. Home: Cazmanska 2, 10000 Zagreb Croatia

LATKOVICH, PREDRAG MICHAEL, anatomic and clinical pathologist, educator; b. Split, Croatia, Apr. 27, 1962; came to U.S., 1992; s. Michael and Zorka Latkovich; m. Katarina Latkovich, Jan. 6, 1990; 1 child, Luka. MD, U. Zagreb, Croatia, 1988'. Intern Clin. U. Belgrade, Yugoslavia, 1989-90; resident in anatomic and clin. pathology Berkshire Med. Ctr., U. Mass., Pittsfield, 1994-98; surg. pathology fellow NYU Med. Ctr., N.Y.C., 1998-99; asst. prof. U. Mo. Med. Sch., Kansas City, 2000—. Contbr. articles to profl. jours. Recipient Physician Recognition award AMA, 1998. Fellow Coll. Am. Pathologists (Informatics award 1997), U.S. Can. Acad. Pathology, Am. Soc. Clin. Pathology; mem. Mass. Med. Soc. Avocations: astronomy, hiking, movies. E-mail: latkovich@pol.net. Home: # 203 10215 W 118th Ter Apt 203 Overland Park KS 66210-3609 Office: U Mo Kansas City Dept Pathology 2301 Holmes St Kansas City MO 64108-2640

LATONI, ALFONSO RAFAEL, sociology and political science educator; b. Coral Gables, Fla., Feb. 9, 1958; s. Alfonso and Olga (Rodriguez) L.; m. Carmen Sol Ramirez, Nov. 1, 1996; children: Elena Isabel, Angelica Rocio. BA in Polit. Sci., U. P.R., 1979; MA, Georgetown U., 1981; PhD, Boston Coll., 1993. Rsch. asst. Smithsonian Instn., Washington, 1979; asst. fgn. student advisor Georgetown U., Washington, 1980-81; tchg. fellow dept. sociology Boston Coll., 1982-83; prof. sociology Interam. U. P.R., San German, 1983-86, cons. for planning new courses, 1983-84, assoc. dean studies, 1985-86; prof. sociology and polit. sci. U. P.R., Mayaguez, 1986—, asst. chmn. dept. social scis., 1988-91; faculty rep. bd. dirs. Nat. Collegiate Conf. Assn.-Nat. Model U.N., 1994-96; pres. univ. srch. com. for pres. U. P.R., 1994, faculty srch. com. for chancellor U. PR., Mayaguez, 1996. Mem. Arts and Cultural Workshop, Adjuntas, P.R., 1984—; tchr. Labor inst. for Worker Edn., Mayaguez, 1983; asst. organizer United Elec. Radio and Machine Workers of Am., Boston, 1982; cons. to pres. U. P.R. for faculty rsch. scholarships in the Caribbean, 1994—. Mem. City Commn. for the Endowment of the Arts and Culture, Mayaguez, 1995—. Named to Outstanding Young Men of Am., 1988-91; U. P.R. grad. presdl. scholar, 1979; Boston Coll. grantee, 1982, 83. Mem. Am. Sociol. Assn. (chmn. MOST program 1998—), Soc. for Study of Social Problems, Phi Delta Kappa. Avocations: skiing, camping, hiking, reading, gardening. Home: 531 Ext Villa Fontana Mayaguez PR 00681 Office: U PR Mayaguez Campus Dept Social Sci Mayaguez PR 00681

LATORRE, CRISTIAN FREEMAN, advertising executive; b. Santiago, Chile, Jan. 2, 1965; s. Jorge Ernesto and Maria Patricia (Freeman) L.; m. Maria Olivia Undurraga, Aug. 2, 1997; 1 child, Maria Olivia. Grad., U. Gabriela Mistral, Chile, 1995. Prodn. mgr. Spalding & Bros., Santiago, Chile, 1991-94; comml. mgr. Schupper, S.A., Santiago, Chile, 1994-95; exec. dir. Latorre & Freeman, Santiago, Chile, 1995—. Roman Catholic. Avocations: tennis, rugby, music. Office: Latorre & Freeman, Augusto Leguia N 255 Of 11, Las Condes Santiago, Chile

LATORRE, CRISTINA, microbiologist; b. Barcelona, Spain, Jan. 29, 1948; d. Marcos and Roser L.; m. Ricard Torrella, Feb. 28, 1975; children: Blanca, Jordi. Degree in biology, U. Barcelona, Spain, 1971, degree in pharmacy, 1974, D of Biology, 1990. Investigator Hosp. Del Mar, Barcelona, Spain, 1972-76; prof. microbiology U. Autonoma, Barcelona, Spain, 1972-76; resident Hosp. Bellvitge, Barcelona, Spain, 1976-79; adj. microbiology Hosp. Sant Joan de Deu, Barcelona, Spain, 1979-92, dept. chief microbiology, 1992—. Avocations: skiing, cycling, climbing. Office: Hosp St Jean de Deu, Passeig S Joan de Deu 2, 08950 Barcelona Spain

LATOSIŃSKA, JOLANTA NATALIA, physicist, mathematician, researcher; b. Poznań, Poland, Jan. 5, 1965; d. Henryk Bolesław and Alicja Róża (Konwerska) L. MS in Maths., Adam Mickewicz U., Poznań, 1988, MS in Physics, 1992, PhD in Physics, 1997. Asst. Adam Mickiewicz U., Poznań, 1991-98, tutor, rsch. worker, 1998—. Author: Ency. of Spectroscopy and Spectrometry, 2000; contbr. articles to profl. jours. Fellow Polish Phys. Soc., Best Europe. Avocations: computer science. Office: Adam Mickiewicz U., Umultowska 85, 61-614 Poznań Poland

LATOUR, MIREILLE JACQUELINE ALBERTINE MARIE, physics educator, researcher, consultant; b. Arles, France, Nov. 12, 1938; d. Paul and Alix G. (Bechet) L.; m. Preston Vincent Murphy, Aug. 16, 1997. BSc, U. Montpellier, France, 1959, PhD, 1968, DSc, 1972. Asst. lectr. U. Montpellier, 1960-65, sr. lectr., 1966-80, prof., 1987—; dir. lab. U. Montpellier, 1987—, Erasmus Formation, 1992—, Socrates Formation, 1992—; cons. Lectret SA, Geneva, Switzerland, 1978—, Lectret Precision, Singapore, 1987—, Solvay, Brussels, 1986-93, Ifremer, Brest, France, 1985-95, Nat. Telecomm. Studies Ctr., Lannion, France, 1979-83, Nat. Aerospace Studies and Rsch. Office, Chatillon, France, 1989-94. Author: Electrical Properties of Polymers, 1978, Ferro Electrics Composites and Copolymers, 1995; contbr. over 200 articles to profl. jours.; inventor in field. Fellow Inst. Physics (London); mem. French Acoustical Soc., French Phys. Soc. Avocations: painting, music. Office: U Montpellier II, Pl E Bataillon, 34095 Montpellier France

LATOURRETTE, KATHRYN, family therapist, counselor, artist; b. Camp Atterbury, Ind., Nov. 16, 1942; d. Herbert Cecil and Goldie Ann (Wright) Little; m. Robert William LaTourrette, Dec. 22, 1964; children: Robert Scott, Bradley Talon, Todd Lawson. BS in Elem. Edn. and Psychology, N.Mex. State U., 1964; MS in Counseling, Troy State U., 1985. Lic. marriage and family therapist, N.Mex. Counseling and Therapy Practice Bd. Elem. tchr. Univ. Hills Elem., Las Cruces, N.Mex., 1964-65; substitute tchr. Mesa (Ariz.) Sch. Sys., 1974-75; counselor Las Vegas (Nev.) Rape Crisis Ctr., 1985-86; group facilitator Nev. State Dept. Corrections, Las Vegas, 1985-86; counselor and family therapist Drug Abuse Comprehensive Coordinating Office, Tampa, Fla., 1989-91, Pinon Hills Hosp., Santa Fe, 1991-99; pvt. practice Jefferson Davis, MD, Santa Fe, 1999—; instr. Abuse Shelter, Okinawa, Japan, 1987-89. Works exhibited Albuquerque Art Soc., 1968-71, Old Town Gallery, Alexandria, Va., 1977-78 (Best in Show award 1977), Conquistador Gallery, Taos, N.Mex., 1982-84. Cub Scout leader, Hahn, Germany, 1965-66; hon. chmn. ARC, Okinawa, 1986-88; advisor Kadina Officers Wives Club, Okinawa, 1986-89. Mem. Am. Assn. Marriage and Family Counselors, Gamma Beta Phi. Presbyterian. Avocations: art, hiking, brass rubbing, gardening. Home: 692 La Viveza Ct Santa Fe NM 87501-8999

LATSA, MARINA, chemical engineer, researcher; b. Athens, Greece, June 5, 1973; d. Petros Latsas and Niki Latsa. ChemEngring diploma, Nat. Tech. U. of Athens, 1996, postgrad., 1997—; Grosses Deutsches Sprachdiplom, Goethe Inst., Athens, 1998. Quality control Unilever Hellas, Athens, 1992, quality control, 1994; R&R rschr. Intrasoft, Athens, 1995-96. Avocations: computers, German language, dancing. E-mail: latsa@chemeng.ntua.gr. Home: 72 Heroon Polytechniou Str, Athens 15772, Greece Office: Nat Tech U of Athens, Zografou Campus ChemEngring, Athens 15780, Greece

LATSON, RICHARD CHARLES, audio visual manager; b. Nov. 13, 1947; s. Robert Lee and Ruby (Kent) L.; m. Sherilyn Day (div.). BA in Radio and TV Comm., Tex. Tech U., 1970. Radio-TV broadcaster, 1967-70; TV prodn. specialist Naval Acad., Annapolis, Md., 1974-79; mgr. TV prodn. Walter Reed Army Med. Ctr., Washington, 1979-87; audio visual mgmt. officer Dept. Army, Pentagon, 1987-90; mgr. audio visual prodn. and distbn. program Dept. Def., Alexandria, Va., 1990—; mem. fed. audiovisual com. Office Mgmt. and Budget, Washington, 1990-96; U.S. judge Internat. Mil. Film Festival, Argentina, 1998, U.S. del. to Internat. Mil. Film Festival, Rome, Italy, 1998. Mem. NATO Audiovisual Working Group; chair Dept. Def. Audiovisual Prodn. Awards Program. 1st lt. USAF, 1970-74. Decorated Air Force commendation medal. Mem. NATAS, Am. Nat. Stds. Inst. (image tech. stds. bd. 1990-98, info. sys. stds. bd. 1990—), Photog. and Imaging Mfrs. Assn., Inc. (stds. mgmt. bd. 1992—), Brit. & Commonwealth Soc. of N.Am. (past pres.). Avocations: old time radio programs, big band music, collecting art. Home: 3344 Hewitt Ave Apt 76 Silver Spring MD 20906-5425 Office: Am Forces Info Svc 601 N Fairfax St Ste 230 Alexandria VA 22314-2054

LATTA, THOMAS ALBERT, lawyer; b. Tulsa, Nov. 3, 1931; s. Albert Lloyd and Myrtle Irene (Lay) L.; m. Shirley Elaine Glauser, June 20, 1965 (div. 1985); children: Thomas Albert, John Montgomery, Shannon Elaine. Student, Carnegie Mellon U., 1949-52; BA, U. Tex., 1955; JD, U. Tulsa, 1959. Bar: Okla. 1959, Ariz. 1964, D.C. 1965, Calif. 1974. Pvt. practice San Francisco, 1974, Phoenix, 1975; dir., shareholder Wentworth & Lundin, P.A., Phoenix, 1975-86, San Francisco, 1980-84; of counsel Whitehead, Porter & Gordon LLP, San Francisco, 1997—; mem. Ariz. Bd. Accountancy, Phoenix, 1979-83. Capt. JAGC, USAR, 1959-60. Avocation: sailing. Office: Whitehead Porter & Gordon LLP 220 Montgomery St Ste 1850 San Francisco CA 94104-3419

LATURNUS, FRANK, marine chemist, environmental scientist; b. Rheine/Westfalen, Germany, Oct. 30, 1961; s. Theodor Rolf Hans and Irmgard Ida Dora (Wenderoth) L.; m. Birgit Gisela Kocher, Aug. 2, 1985. Master's degree, U. Bremen, Germany, 1990, PhD, 1993. Asst. prof. Tech. U. Denmark, 1994-95; postdoctoral rschr. U. Antwerp, Belgium, 1995-97; sr. rschr. Risø Nat. Lab., Denmark, 1997-2000; postdoctoral rschr. U. Copenhagen, 2000—; lectr. Tech. U. Bremerhaven, 1990-92. Contbr. chpts. to book, articles to internat. jours. Active mem. Soc. German Reservists, 1983-95. Capt. Air Force, 1981-83, Germany. Recipient Outstanding Poster award, 1993. Mem. German Soc. Chemists, Am. Geophys. Union. Avocations: music, diving, scale modeling. Home: Utterslev Torv 4 2th, DK-2400 Copenhagen NV, Denmark Office: Symbion Sci Pk Lab Mat Sci, Fruebevjvej 3, 2700 Copenhagen Copenhagen 2100, Denmark

LATUSHKO, SERGEI MIKHAILOVICH, astronomer; b. Pochinok, Russia, July 26, 1959; s. Mikhail Philippovich and Lubov Sergeevna (Kulbitskaya) L.; m. Tatiana Alexandrovna, Nov. 3, 1982; 1 child, Marina. MS, Leningrad U., 1985. Rschr. Inst. of Solar-Terrestrial Physics, Irkutsk, Russia, 1985—. Contbr. articles to profl. jours. Avocations: skiing, submarine hunting. Home: Pomialovski 11 28, 664054 Irkutsk Russia Office: Inst Solar-Terrestrial Phys, Lermontov st 128/Box 4026, 664033 Irkutsk Russia

LATYPOV, ROUSTAM KHAFIZOVICH, mathematician, educator; b. Namangan, Uzbekistan, USSR, May 28, 1953; s. Khafiz Latypovich and Liabiba Nazipovna (Mukhamediarova) L.; m. Alsu Faridovna, Jan. 18, 1980; 1 child, Sayeed. Diploma in math., Kazan (Russia) State U., 1975. Asst. prof. Kazan State U., 1975-84, assoc. prof., 1985-95, prof., 1996-99, dean faculty of computer sci., 1999—. Contbr. articles to profl. jours.; patentee in field. Mem. IEEE (test tech. coun. 1995—). Avocations: football, basketball, jazz, classical music. Home: 5-8 Joukovskogo St, 420015 Kazan Russia Office: Kazan State U, 18 Kremliovskaya St, 420008 Kazan Russia

LATYSHEV, LEONID ALEXEYEVICH, aerospace engineer; b. Kharkov, USSR, Nov. 17, 1926; s. Alexey Semenovich Latyshev and Rosaliya Semenovna Karpel.; m. Ada Moiseyevna Goldberg, June 18, 1948; children: Vladimir, Alexander. Engr., Moscow Aviation Inst., 1949, PhD, 1954, D Tech. Sci., 1971, Prof, 1972. Jr. rschr. Moscow Aviation Inst., 1949-54, sr. rschr., 1954-63, prof., 1963-71, full prof., 1971—; supr. Moscow Aviation Inst., 1949-60, scientific head, 1960—, head complex rsch., 1970—. Author: Introduction to Aviation and Space Technique, 1979, Theory of Space Engines, 1967; co-author: (monographies) Electropneumatic Stroboscopic Indicator, 1957, Solar Power Satellites: A Space Energy System for Earth, 1997, (textbook) Theory and Calculations on Power Installations and Electrorocket Propulsion Engines, 1984. Chmn. Moscow Aviation Inst., 1967-68, Coun. of Students Rsch. Work, Moscow Aviation Inst., 1970-83; mem. All-Union Coun. of Student's Rsch. Work, Moscow, 1975-90. Recipient Diploma for Best Scientific Work, Ministry of Higher Edn., Moscow, 1986, prize Coun. of Ministers of USSR, 1990, Meritorius Sci. Worker of Russian Fedn., 1997. Mem. Russian Engring. Acad. (hon.). Avocations: sci., technique and arts, tourism. Office: Moscow State Aviation Inst, Volokolamskoe sh 4, 125871 Moscow Russia

LAU, ANKIE HEUNG-PING, film producer, film director, actress; b. Hong Kong, Canton, China, Apr. 2, 1958; arrived in Germany, 1979; d. Kwok Hin and Yiu Yim (Liu) L.; m. Michael Beilke, Oct. 23, 1979 (div. Sept. 1988); 1 child, Ankie. Diploma, Film Sch., Hong Kong, 1977, Volkhoch Schule Goethe Inst., Düsseldorf, Germany, 1983. Model, actress Film & Foto Prodns., Hong Kong, 1977-84; film acquisition Lau Film Internat., Munich, 1988-98; actress Lau Film Internat., Hong Kong and Europe, 1976-97; pres. Lau Film Internat., Munich, 1989—; dir. Pacific Asia bus. devel. for pharms. Bionorica, Newmarkt, Germany, 1994—; film selection com. Film Festival, Shanghai, 1993—; tchr. secondary sch., Hong Kong, 1975-76; comm. cons. U.S., Germany, China, 1991-99. Scriptwriter, dir., prodr. Last Chance Love, 1997 (Best Fgn. Film 1998); actress leading role Leo Sunnyboy, 1989 (Best Pub. award 1991). Mem. fgn. rep. del. film selection com. Shanghai Internat. Film Festival, 1993—. Mem. Chinese Women in South Germany, Oversea Chinese in Germany for Economy and Trade, New German Prodr. Union. Avocations: music, films, reading, travel, dancing. E-mail: laufilm@aol.com. Office: Lau Film Internat, Postfach 33 06 28, 80066 Munich Bavaria, Germany

LAU, BOBBY WAI-MAN, marketing professional, investment and financial planner, business startup trainer; b. Hong Kong, Dec. 24, 1944; s. Nelson and Ruby (Choy) L.; m. Sharon Tsai. BS in Math., U. Calif., Davis, 1969, MA in Math., 1971; postgrad. in math., Calif. Inst. Tech.; postgrad. in math and computers, UCLA, 1972-75. Ins. agt. Equitable Life Assurance Soc. of U.S., L.A., 1975-80, sr. dist. mgr., 1980-90; pres. Bobby Lau Seminars for Profls., 1979—; chmn. bd. dirs. Success Pension & Ins. Svcs. Corp., dir. internat. fin. rsch., 1994—; pres. World Mktg. Power, 1994—. Contbr. articles to mags. and newspapers. Office: PO Box 80223 San Marino CA 91118-8223

LAU, D.W., dean, science educator. Dean faculty sci. Chinese U. Hong Kong. Fax: 852 2603 5315. Office: Chinese U Hong Kong, Station, New Territories Hong Kong*

LAU, GEORGE KA-KIT, hepatologist; b. N.Y.C., Dec. 7, 1962; s. James and Shirley (Loh) L.; m. Amy Yee-Kwan Kwok; children: Michele, Jerry. MB B of Surgery, U. Hong Kong, 1987, postgrad. Trustee China Internat. Hepatitis Rsch. Found. Fellow Hong Kong Acad. of Medicine; mem. Royal Coll. of Physicians (U.K.). Office: Rm 1838 Blk K Queen Mary, Hosp 102 Pokfulam Rd, Hong Kong Peoples Republic of China

LAU, ISRAEL MEIR, chief rabbi of Israel. Head of the Ashkenzi Community, 1993—. Office: Rechov Hamelech George 58, 58 King George St, 91074 Jerusalem Israel*

LAU, JOHN HON SHING, manufacturing executive; b. China, June 17, 1946; came to U.S., 1973; s. Shui Hong and Mary Au L.; m. Teresa Yu, Sept. 2, 1972; 1 child, Judy M. BS in Civil Engring., Nat. Taiwan U., 1970; MASc in Structural Engring., U. B.C., 1973; MS in Engring. Mechanics, U. Wis., 1974; PhD in Theoretical and Applied Mechanics, U. Ill., 1977; MS in Mgmt., Fairleigh Dickinson U., 1981. Registered profl. engr., N.Y., Calif. Rsch. engr. Exxon Prodn. and Rsch. Co., Houston, 1977; structural specialist Control Data Corp., Sunnyvale, Calif., 1977-78; rsch. assoc. Internat. Paper Co., Tuxedo Park, N.Y., 1978-79; sr. engr. Ebasco Svcs. Inc., N.Y.C., 1979-81, Bechtel Power Corp., San Francisco, 1981-83; MTS Sandia Nat. Lab., N.Mex., 1983-84, Hewlett-Packard Labs., N.Mex., 1984-95; pres. Express Packaging Sys., Inc., Palo Alto, Calif., 1995—. Contbr. articles to profl. jours. and 12 tech. books; assoc. editor for ASME Transaction Jour. Elec. Packaging. Fellow ASME, IEEE; mem. ASM Internat., AAAS, N.Y. Acad. Scis., Sigma Xi. Roman Catholic. Home: 961 Newell Rd Palo Alto CA 94303-2929 Office: EPS Inc 1137 San Antonio Rd Palo Alto CA 94303-4310

LAU, KIM-TEEN, electronics engineer, educator; b. Penang, Malaysia, June 16, 1959; s. Cheng-Chuan Lau and Phaik-Lee Quek. BSEE, Cornell U., 1983, M in Engring., 1984. Design engr. Nat. Semiconductor Corp., Santa Clara, Calif., 1984-85; prodn. engr. Hewlett-Packard, Penang, Malaysia, 1985-86; from lectr. to assoc. prof. Nanyang Technol. U., Singapore, 1986—. Mem. IEEE. Avocations: golf, tennis, badminton, reading, traveling. Office: Nanyang Technol U, Sch EEE, S639798 Singapore Singapore

LAU, MAUREEN TREACY, television producer; b. São Paulo, Brazil, Aug. 29, 1946; came to U.S., 1949; d. John Edward and Catherine (Balzer) Treacy; m. Alberto Lau, Dec. 10, 1975; children: Erin, Maya. BA, Immaculate Heart Coll., Los Angeles, 1968; MA, San Diego State U., 1975. Instr. San Diego Community Coll., 1975-76, Southwestern Coll., San Diego, 1976-78; sr. TV producer San Diego State U., 1978—; owner, pres. Lumina Prodns., Inc., San Diego, 1987—; owner Treacy Lau & Assocs., San Diego, 1987—; media cons. San Diego Mus. Art, 1983-85; mgr. SDSU-TV, 1999—. Producer TV programs including El Politico Honesto, 1979, Age Is A Work Of Art, 1980 (Emmy nomination 1980), Learning Through Play, 1984, Work and Motherhood, 1985. Recipient Best of West award Western Ednl. Soc. for TV, 1980, First Prize Nat. Ednl. Film Festival, San Francisco, 1985. Mem. Nat. Acad. TV Arts and Scis. (gov. and v.p. San Diego chpt. 1985—), Women in Film, Advocates for Women in Academia (founding), Internat. TV Assn. (Merit award 1985). Democrat. Avocation: sailing. Home: 10995 Negley Ave San Diego CA 92131-1815

LAU, MICHELE DENISE, advertising consultant, sales trainer, television personality; b. St. Paul, Dec. 6, 1960; d. Dwyane Udell and Patricia Ann (Yri) L. Student, U. Minn., 1979-82. Pub. rels. coord. Stillwater (Minn.) C. of C., 1977-79; asst. mgr. Salkin & Linoff, Mpls., 1982, store merchandiser, sales trainer, 1982-83; rental agt. Sentinel Mgmt. Co., St. Paul, 1983-84; account exec. Community Svc. Publs., Mpls., 1984-85, frwy. news supr., 1985, asst. sales mgr., 1985-86; asst. sales mgr. St. Paul Pioneer Press Dispatch, 1986-91; pres. Promotional Ptnrs., Eden Prairie, Minn., 1991-96; on-air show host Home Shopping Network, Eden Prairie, 1996—; on-air personality Sta. WCCO II Cable TV Mpls., 1988-89, co-host Afternoon Midwest, 1989-93; co-host Home Shopping Show, host Minn. Voices, Fox 29, 1995; cons. U. Minn. Alumni mag., 1986-89. Author mechandising and sales tng. manuals. Fund-raiser sustaining program YMCA, Mpls., 1986, Jr. Achievement, St. Paul, 1988; cons. Muscular Dystrophy Assn., St. Paul, 1988-89; bd. dirs. St. Paul Jaycees. Mem. NAFE, Nat. Assn. Home Builders, Mpls. Builder Assn. (amb.), Metro-East Profl. Builders Assn. (spl. events com.), Advt. Fedn., The Newspaper Guild, Internat. Platform Assn., Speakeasy Club. Lutheran. Avocations: tennis, golf, aerobics. Home: 4961 Bacopa Ln S Unit 102 Saint Petersburg FL 33715-2621

LAU, SIU KAI, sociology educator; b. Hong Kong, June 7, 1947; s. Keng Por and Wai Sin (Fong) L.; m. Lai Mui Sophie Kwok, July 15, 1972; 1 child, Poon Yung. BS, U. Hong Kong, 1971; PhD, U. Minn., 1975. Lectr. sociology Chinese U. Hong Kong, 1975-83, sr. lectr., 1983-87, reader sociology, 1987-90, prof. sociology, 1990—; dir. Ctr. Hong Kong Studies Chinese U. Hong Kong, 1984-90. assoc. dir. Hong Kong Inst. Asia-Pacific Studies, 1990—, chmn. sociology dept., 1994—; cons. in field. Author: Society and Politics in Hong Kong, 1982; co-author: The Ethos of the Hong Kong Chinese, 1988; contbr. articles to profl. jours. Justice of the Peace, 1999. Mem. Am. Polit. Sci. Assn. Avocations: reading, walking, travel. Office: Chinese U Hong Kong, Dept Sociology, Shatin New Territories Hong Kong

LAUBACH, ROGER ALVIN, accountant; b. Riegelsville, N.J., July 3, 1922; s. Harry and Daisy (Cyphers) L.; Diploma in bus. adminstrn., Churchman Bus. Coll., Easton, Pa., 1941; BS cum laude in Acctg., Rider U., 1949. CPA, N.Y., N.J. Acct. Coopers & Lybrand, CPAs, N.Y.C., 1949-60; asst. to treas. Coca-Cola Bottling Co. N.Y., N.Y.C., 1960-63; mgr. audits and systems Atlantic Rsch. Corp., Alexandria, Va., 1964-65; contr. Ely-Cruikshank Co., Inc., Realtors, N.Y.C., 1965-66, asst. treas., 1966-67, treas., dir., 1967-71; dir. N.Y. Fed. Savs. & Loan Assn., 1970-71; dir. Phila. Acctg. Ctr. Ogden Food Svc. Corp., 1971-72, treas., 1972-77; dir. corp. auditing Ogden Corp., N.Y.C., 1977-79; contr. Burlington County Cmty. Action Program, Burlington, N.J., 1981-84. With U.S. Army, 1942-46; ETO. Decorated Bronze Star, N.J. Disting. Svc. medal, 1998. Mem. AICPA, ARC (vol. bloodmobile 1986—), Inst. Internal Auditors, N.Y. State Soc. CPAs, N.J. Soc. CPAs, Real Estate Bd. N.Y., SAR (registrar, geneal. 1995—, War Svc. medal, Liberty medal), VFW, Am. Legion, 100th Inf. Divsn. Assn., Soc. Colonial Wars, Laubach Family Assn. (book com. 1989-93), Nat. Trust for Hist. Preservation, Bucks County (Pa.) Hist. Soc., Warren County (N.J.) His. Soc. Home: 39 Southgate Rd Mount Laurel NJ 08054-2932

LAUBE, THOMAS, chemist, researcher; b. Berlin, Fed. Republic Germany, Sept. 20, 1952; arrived in Switzerland, 1981; s. Herbert Urbschat and Ingeborg Laube. Diploma in Chemistry, Free U., Berlin, 1980; dissertation, Eidgenössische Technische Hochschule, Zürich, Switzerland, 1984; habilitation, ETH, Zürich, Switzerland, 1988. Asst. ETH, Zürich, Switzerland, 1983-89, privatdozent, 1989—; vis. scientist U. So. Calif., L.A., 1995-96; head lab. Cilag AG, Schaffhausen, Switzerland, 1997—. Contbr. articles to profl. jours. Recipient Silver medal ETH, Zürich, Switzerland, 1984, Ruzicka prize Swiss Univ. Coun., 1988, dozentenstipendium Fund of the Chem. Industry, Frankfurt, Fed. Republic of Germany, 1988. Mem. Am. Crystallographic Assn. Avocation: mathematics.

LAUBER, CHRISTOPHER JOSEPH, sports event promoter; b. Passaic, N.J., Jan. 7, 1958; s. Edward C. and Patricia F. (Donovan) L.; m. Raissa C. Lupjan, May 26, 1985; children: Leah Frances, Nicole Marie. BA with honors, Boston Coll., 1981. Lic. coach U.S. Soccer Assn. Pres. WaterCross Internat., Inc., St. Petersburg, Fla., 1979—; ind. film technician, Boston, 1981-85; freelance photographer, Boston, 1982—; founder, race dir. Fla. Gulf Beaches Marathon, 2000. Founder, organizer World Cup WaterCross Tour, 1983—; exec. producer home video Jet Ski Fever, 1983; assoc. prodr. (film) Making Waves, 1997. Founder, promoter Fla. Gulf Beaches Marathon, 2000. Fla. state freestyle jet ski champion, 1981; named One of Top 10 Leaders in Watercraft Indusry Watercraft World mag., 1996, Coach of Yr. Azalea Youth Soccer Assn., 1997. Mem. Internat. Jet Sport Boating Assn., U.S.A. Track and Field. Avocations: sports, photography, soccer. Home: 6161 7th Ave N Saint Petersburg FL 33710-7015 Office: 6967 Sunset Dr S Saint Petersburg FL 33707-2817

LAUBER, MIGNON DIANE, food processing company executive; b. Detroit, Dec. 21; d. Charles Edmond and Maud Lillian (Foster) Donaker. Student Kelsey Jenny U., 1958, Brigham Young U., 1959; m. Richard Brian Lauber, Sept. 13, 1963; 1 child, Leslie Viane (dec.). Owner, operator Alaska World Travel, Ketchikan, 1964-67; founder, owner, pres. Oosick Soup Co., Juneau, Alaska, 1969—. Treas., Pioneer Alaska Lobbyists Soc., Juneau, 1977—. Mem. Bus. and Profl. Women, Alaska C. of C. Libertarian, Washington Athletic Club. Author: Down at the Water Works with Jesus, 1982; Failure Through Prayer, 1983, We All Want to Go to Heaven But Nobody Wants to Die, 1988. Home: 321 Highland Dr Juneau AK 99801-1442

LAUBER, VOLKMAR, political science educator; b. Wels, Austria, Dec. 8, 1944; s. Josef and Gertrud (Ruby) L.; married; children: Alexander, Elias. LLD, U. Vienna, Austria, 1968; LLM, Harvard U., 1970; D in Polit. Sci., U. N.C., Chapel Hill, 1977. Asst. U. Graz Law Sch., Austria, 1971; vis. lectr. U. South Fla., Tampa, 1976-77; asst. prof. W.Va. Wesleyan Coll., Buckhannon, 1977-82, Johns Hopkins U., Bologna, Italy, 1979-80; prof. polit. sci. U. Salzburg, Austria, 1982—. Author: The Political Economy of France, 1983; editor: Contemporary Austrian Politics, 1996; co-editor: Handbuch des Politischen Systems Österreichs, 1991, 3d edit., 1997, Environmental Policy: The Voluntary Approach, 2000; contbr. articles to profl. jours. E-mail: volkmar.lauber@sbg.ac.at. Home: Waldburgergasse 42, A-5026 Salzburg Austria Office: Inst f Politikwissenschaft, Rudolfskai 42, A-5020 Salzburg Austria

LAUBSCHER, LEEANN, medical and surgical nurse; b. Monticello, N.Y., Apr. 24, 1962; d. Lee Gregory Baumgardt and Carole Ann (Blume) Nicolis; m. Robert Francis Laubscher, Aug. 16, 1986. BSN, Mt. St. Mary Coll., Newburgh, N.Y., 1984; MSN, SUNY, New Paltz, 1996. RN, N.Y. Staff nurse Westchester County Med. Ctr., Valhalla, N.Y., 1984-90; staff nurse VA Hudson Valley Healthcare Sys., 1990-98, nurse mgr. ICU, 1992, women vets. coord., 1995—, patient advocate, 1998—; breast cancer detection awareness educator Am. Cancer Soc., N.Y., 1995—; cmty. educator LENS (Linking Edn., Nursing and Seniors) Project, 1995. Mem. N.Y. State Nurses Assn. (Dist. 12), Soc. Healthcare Consumer Advocacy, Sigma Theta Tau Internat. Nursing Honor Soc. Avocations: reading, needlework, travel. Office: VA Hudson Valley Healthcare Castle Point NY 12511

LAUCHE, HERVÉ MICHEL, oncologist; b. Bordeaux, Gironde, France, July 1, 1952; s. Michel Georges and Simone Marie (Rousseau) L.; m. Eliane Marguerite Vollmer, May 26, 1979; children: Anne-Sophie, Olivier. MD, Med. Sch. Strasbourg, France, 1977. Bd. cert. in oncology and radiation oncology; expert in oncology. Intern U. Hosp. Cancer Ctr., Strasbourg, 1975-77, resident, 1978-79, sr. asst., 1981-87; oncology specialist French Cancer Ctr., Strasbourg, 1987; head dept. oncology Clinique Clementville, Montpellier, France, 1988—; asst. clin. faculty Med. Sch. Strasbourg, 1982-87; clin. rsch. asst. Thermology Lab., U. Strasbourg, 1982-87; pres. Tumors Register of Herault, Montpellier, 1992—. Editor-in-chief Bull. French Soc. Pvt. Oncology, 1989—. With French Mil., 1979-80. Mem. Am. Soc. Clin. Oncology, European Soc. Med. Oncology, European Soc. Therapeutic Radiation Oncology, European Orgn. Rsch. Treatment of Cancer, French Soc. Cancer, French Soc. Radiation Oncology, French Soc. Pvt. Oncology (gen. sec. 1989—). Roman Catholic. Avocations: tennis, skiing, bridge. Office: Clinique Clementville, 25 Rue de Clementville, 34000 Montpellier France

LAUCK, DONNA L., adult psychiatric and mental health nurse; b. Berwick, Pa.; d. Earl Andrew and Catherine Arlene Kreiser; m. Ronald Joseph Lauck, Oct. 21, 1966; 1 child, Ronald Joseph Jr. BSN, U. Pa., 1973, MSN, 1982, DNSc, 1991. RN, Pa; ANA cert. clin. nurse specialist, adult psychiat. and mental health nursing, 1994; founding certificant Nat. Registry of Certified Group Psychotherapists, 1995; BLS instr., Am. Heart Assn.; cert. sexual assault nurse examiner, 1996; diplomate Am. Bd. Forensic Examiners. Oper. room staff nurse Lower Bucks County Hosp., Pa., 1959-60; charge nurse Boron (Pa.) Cmty. Hosp., 1960; part-time staff nurse Barstow (Calif.) Cmty. Hosp., 1960-65; office nurse S.W. French, III, M.D., Barstow, 1960-65; IV team nurse Jefferson Hosp., Pa., 1966; staff nurse critical care unit Presbyn. Hosp., Pa., 1966; head nurse ICU/CCU Meth. Hosp., Pa., 1966-69; head nurse ICU Frankford (Pa.) Hosp., 1970-76; dir. nursing Geriat. and Med. Ctrs., Inc., 1977-79; staff nurse, asst. sr. nurse, charge nurse Friend's Hosp., Phila., 1971-86, relief 11-7 supr., 1971-86; nursing staff devel. specialist Inst. of Pa. Hosp., Phila., 1986-92, clin. nurse specialist, 1992-96; dir. clin. svc. Kirkbride Ctr., Phila., 1997; clin. nurse specialist, sr. nurse in-charge admissions Friend's Hosp., Phila., 1998-2000, sr. nurse therapist Cognitive Behavioral Unit, 2000, clin. nurse specialist, therapist Adult Svcs., 2000—; spkr. in fields of violence, AIDS, stress mgmt., nursing rsch. Chmn. U. Pa. Sch. Nursing fundraising telethon, 1981, 82, active mem. to present; active mem. liaison program for undergrad. freshman students, U. Pa., 1990—, facilitator comm. workshop sr. student nurses, 1999—; adv. bd. West Phila. Coalition of Neighborhoods and Businesses, Advanced Practice Nurses Coun., Pa. Hosp., 1994-96. Mem. Am. Soc. Clin. Hypnosis, Internat. Assn. for Study of Dissociative Disorders, Psychiat. Advanced Practice Nurses of Pa., Ea. Pa. Assn. Nursing Diagnosis (mem. psychiat.-mental health spl. interest group), Presbyn. Hosp. Alumni Orgn., Internat. Soc. of Hypnosis, Am. Coll. Forensic Examiners. Home and Office: 863 Granite St Philadelphia PA 19124-1728

LAUDE, JEAN-PIERRE ROBERT, scientific director; b. Isle Sur Le Doubs, France, June 23, 1940; s. Robert Charles and Andrée Eugenie Augusta (Becker) L.; m. Christine Lucienne Viel, Oct. 22, 1965; children: Jean-Christophe, Vincent, Thomas, Blandine, Marjolaine, Gregoire. Degree in engring., Ecole Superieure d'optique, Paris, 1963; doctorate, Orsay (France) U., 1966. Rsch. worker Ctr. Nat. de la Recherche Sci., Orsay, 1963-66; grating dept. chief Jobin-Yvon, Longjumeau, France, 1966-74, sci. dir., 1974-2000; cons. various, France, 2000—; tchr. U. Paris, Orsay, 1990—, Ecole Nat. Superieure Telecommunications, Paris, 1990-92, Ecole Superieure d'optique, Orsay, 1991—, Inst. Nat. des Telecommunications, Evry, France, 1992-96. Author: Le multiplexage de longueur d'onde, 1992, Wavelength Division Multiplexing, 1993; co-author: Encyclopedie Scientifique et Technique, 1971, Trends in Optical Fiber Metrology and Standards, 1995 ; contbr. articles to profl. jours. Pres. Assn. Culturelle, Saclas, France, 1985—. Recipient medal Ctr. Nat. d'Etudes Spatiales Francais, Photonic Circle of Excellence award, 1995, SPIE Tech. Achievement award, 1997. Mem. OSA, SPIE, SFO, IEEE, ASME. Roman Catholic. Achievements include 40 patents in field. Home: 13 bis rue de Chilly, 91160 Longjumeau France Office: 3 rue des Gravériots, 91690 St Cyr la Rivière France

LAUDER, LEONARD ALAN, cosmetic and fragrance company executive; b. N.Y.C., Mar. 19, 1933; s. Joseph H. and Estée (Mentzer) L.; m. Evelyn

Hausner, July 5, 1959; children: William Phillip, Gary Mark. BS, Wharton Sch., U. Pa., 1954. With Estée Lauder, Inc., N.Y.C., 1958—, exec. v.p., 1962-72, pres., 1972-82, pres., CEO, from 1982, now chmn., CEO; vice chmn. bd. CFTA, N.Y.C., 1976-79. Trustee Aspen Inst. for Humanistic Studies, 1978—, U. Pa., Phila., 1977—; pres. Whitney Mus. Am. Art, 1977—; bd. dirs. Adv. Commn. on Trade Negotiations, Washington, 1983-87; bd. govs. Joseph H. Lauder Inst. Mgmt. and Internat. Studies, 1983—. Lt. USNR, 1955-58. Mem. Chief Execs. Orgn., French-Am. C. of C. in U.S. (coun. frn. relations). Office: Estée Lauder Cos Inc 767 5th Ave New York NY 10153-0023*

LAUDER, VALARIE ANNE, editor, educator; b. Detroit, Mar. 1; d. William J. and Murza Valerie (Mann) L. AA, Stephens Coll., Columbia, Mo., 1944; postgrad., Northwestern U. With Chgo. Daily News, 1944-52, columnist, 1946-52; lectr. Sch. Assembly Svc., also Redpath lectr., 1952-55; freelance writer for mags. and newspapers including New York Times, Yankee, Ford Times, Travel & Leisure, Am. Heritage, 1955—; editor-in-chief Scholastic Roto, 1962; editor U. N.C., 1975-80, lectr. Sch. Journalism, 1980—; gen. sec. World Assn. for Pub. Opinion Rsch., 1988-95; nat. chmn. student writing project Ford Times, 1981-86; pub. rels. dir. Am. Dance Festival Duke U., 1982-83, lectr., instr. continuing edn. program, 1984. Contbg. editor So. Accents mag., 1982-86. Mem. nat. fundraising bd. Kennedy Ctr., 1962-63; bd. dirs. Chapel Hill Mus., Inc., 1996-98. Recipient 1st place award Nat. Fedn. Press Women, 1981, 1st place awards Ill. Women's Press Assn., 1950, 51. Mem. Pub. Rels. Soc. Am. (treas. N.C. chpt. 1982, sec. 1983, v.p. 1984, pres.-elect 1985, pres. 1986, chmn. coun. of past pres., chmn. 25th Ann. event 1987, del. Nat. Assembly 1988-94, S.E. dist. officer, nat. nominating com. 1991, 1st pres.'s award 1993), Women in Comms. (v.p. matrix N.C. Triangle chpt. 1984-85), N.C. Pub. Rels. (mem. Hall of Fame com.), DAR, Soc. Mayflower Desc. (bd. dirs. Ill. Soc. 1946-52), Chapel Hill Hist. Soc. (bd. dirs. 1981-85, 94—, chmn. pub. com. 1980-85, pres. 1996—), Chapel Hill Preservation Soc. (bd. trustees 1993-96, nominating com. 1994), N.C. Press Club (3d v.p. 1981-83, 2d v.p. 1983-85, pres. 1985, 1st pl. awards 1981, 82, 83, 84), Univ. Women's Club (2nd v.p. 1988), The Carolina Club, The Nat. Press Club. Office: U NC Sch Journalism and Mass Comm Cb 3365 Cmn Chapel Hill NC 27599-0001

LAUDRUP, ALEX, lawyer, general manager; b. Copenhagen, Aug. 31, 1946; s. Jens Otto Petersen and Ketty Hansine Laudrup; m. Marion Hanne Pedersen, Oct. 12, 1974; children: Camilla, Nicholas. Degree law, U. Copenhagen, 1972. Bar: Denmark 1975, Ct. of Appeal 1980, Supreme Ct. Denmark 1985. Atty. Skuld/Danske, Copenhagen, 1972-77, sect. mgr., 1978-81; gen. mgr. Shipowners Coun. of Copenhagen, 1982—; atty. Nebelong, Groth-Andersen, Laudrup, 1982-89; atty. Gorrissen & Federspiel, 1989-91, ptnr., 1992—. Contbr. articles to profl. jours. Mem. Internat. Bar Assn., Danish Bar Assn. Home: Falkevang 8, 3450 Allerod Denmark Office: Gorrissen Federspiel et al, HC Andersens Blvd 12, 1553 Copenhagen Denmark

LAUDRUP, MICHAEL, professional soccer player; b. June 15, 1964. Midfielder IF Brondby Football Club, Denmark, 1982-83, Lazio Roma Football Club, Italy, 1983-85, Juventus Football Club, Italy, 1985-89, Barcelona Football Club, Spain, 1989-94, Real Madrid Football Club, Spain, 1994-96, Vissel Kob Football Club, Japan, 1996-97, Ajax Amsterdam Football Club, Holland, 1997-98, Danish Nat. Team; winner Champions League (with Barcelona), 1992. Recipient six Nat. Championships, Juve, Barca, Real, Ajax. Address: Vedbaek Strandvej 464, 2950 Vedbaek Denmark Office: Danish Football Assocs, Indraettens Hus Brondby, DK-2605 Brondby Denmark

LAUER, BERNHARD, museum director; b. Britten, Germany, Jan. 2, 1954; s. Johann Peter and Anna Theresia (Michels) L. D in German, Slavic, Romanic Studies, U. Marburg, Lahn, 1983. Asst. Dpet. Slavic Studies U. Marburg, 1977-83, asst. prof. Dept. Fgn. Langs., 1987-89; exbhn. mgr. Assn. Bros. Grimm, Kassel, Germany, 1984-86; gen. sec. Assn. Bros. Grimm, Kassel, 1990—; mus. dir. Mus. Bros. Grimm, Kassel, 1989—. Author, gen. editor: (yearbook) Jahrbuch der Brueder Grimm Gesellschaft; editor, author: Schriften der Brueder Grimm-Gesellschaft, Ausstellungen im Brueder Grimm-Museum. Mem. Lions Club Kassel. Roman Catholic. Avocations: collecting old books, fine arts, gardening. Office: Brueder Grimm-Museum Kassel, Brueder Grimm-Platz 4A, 34117 Kassel Germany

LAUFER, HANS, developmental biologist, educator; b. Germany, Oct. 18, 1929; s. Sol and Margarete (Freundlich) L.; m. Evelyn Green, Oct. 31, 1953; children: Jessica, Marc, Leonard. B.S., CCNY, 1952; M.A., Bklyn. Coll., 1953; Ph.D. (James fellow), Cornell U., Ithaca, N.Y., 1957. Research and teaching asst. Cornell U., 1953-57; NRC fellow Carnegie Instn. of Washington, 1957-59; asst. prof. biology Johns Hopkins U., 1959-65; assoc. prof. U. Conn., Storrs, 1965-72; prof. U. Conn., 1972—; vis. prof. Karolinska Inst., Stockholm, 1972, Charles U., Prague, 1974, Yale U., 1980, Harvard U., 1987-89; participant Nat. Acad. Scis.-Czechoslovak Acad. exchange program, 1974, 77; ad hoc mem. study sect. tropical medicine NIH, 1981, mem., 1982-85; Conklin Meml. fellow Marine Biology Lab., Woods Hole, Mass., 1956, Lalor fellow, 1962, 63, mem. staff, embryology course, 1968-72, mem. corp., 1962—, corp. trustee, 1978-82, mem. exec. com., 1979-80; vis. scholar Case Western Res. U., 1962; mem. NSF-NATO Fellowship Rev. Panel, 1974, 76. Contbg. author numerous books; assoc. editor Jour. Exptl. Zoology, 1969-73, 90-93, Archives Insect Physiology and Biochemistry, 1983-95, Invertebrate Reprodn. and Devel., 1984-86, mng. editor, 1991—; contbr. numerous articles to profl. jours. Recipient Rsch. Svc. award NIH, 1989, Marcus Singer medal for rsch., 1986, 95; NATO sr. fellow, 1973, fellow Lady Davis Trust, Hebrew U., 1988; Japan Soc. Promotion of Sci. Fell., 1980; Rosenstiel scholar Brandeis U., 1973; Dozor vis. prof., Ben Gurion U., 1997. Fellow AAAS (chmn. sect. biology 1975), Royal Entomology Soc. London (fgn. fellow, elected); mem. Internat. Soc. Devel. Biology, Assn. Rsch. Couns. (nat. bd. on grad. edn. of conf. bd. 1971-75), Am. Soc. Zoology (chmn. divsn. developmental biology 1981-82), Soc. Devel. Biology, Am. Soc. Cell Biology, European Soc. Comparative Endocrinology, Am. Assn. Advancement Aging Rsch., Internat. Soc. Differentiation, Tissue Culture Assn. (coun. 1979-82), World Aquaculture Soc., Conn. Acad. Sci. & Engring. Home: 57 Davis Rd Storrs Mansfield CT 06268-2525 Office: U Conn Dept Molecular & Cell Biology U-125 Storrs Mansfield CT 06268

LAUFER, JACOB, lawyer; b. Munich, Feb. 28, 1949; came to the U.S., 1951; s. Moritz and Felicja (Pruszanowska) L.; m. Clara G. Schwabe, Jan. 27, 1983; children: Samara, Aviva, Mia. BS, CUNY, 1971; JD cum laude, Fordham U., 1974. Bar: N.Y. 1975, D.C. 1975, U.S. Ct. Appeals (2d cir.) 1975, U.S. Dist. Ct. (so. and ea. dists.) N.Y. 1976, U.S. Ct. Appeals (5th cir.) 1979, U.S. Supreme Ct. 1980, U.S. Ct. Appeals (3d cir.) 1985, U.S. Ct. Appeals (D.C. cir.) 1994. Spl. atty. Organized Crime and Racketeering Sect., U.S. Dept. Justice, 1974-77; asst. U.S. atty. So. Dist. N.Y., N.Y.C., 1977-79; of counsel Bartels, Pykett & Aronwald, White Plains, N.Y., 1979-81; ptnr. Bornstein & Laufer, N.Y.C., 1981-85, Laufer & Karish LLP, N.Y.C., 1986—. Mem., contbr. Fordham Law Rev., 1973-74. Mem. D.C. Bar Assn., Bklyn. Bar Assn., Assn. Bar City of N.Y (com. criminal advocacy 1998—). Democrat. Jewish. Notable cases include: Pavelic & LeFlore vs. Marvel Entertainment Group; and Allen vs. National Video, Inc. Avocation: reading. Office: Laufer Halberstam LLP 39 Broadway Rm 1440 New York NY 10006-3003

LAUFER, WILLIAM HERVEY, artist, printmaker; b. Newark, Apr. 2, 1934; s. Edward Basil and Grace (Krudop) L.; m. Guida Miller Jackson, Feb. 14, 1986. Student, Trinity Coll., Hartford, Conn., 1952-53, New Sch. for Social Rsch., N.Y.C., 1971-73; AA, SUNY, Albany, 1973. Commd. ensign USN, 1960, advanced through grades to lt. comdr., 1968, ret., 1973; exhibition artist-printmaker The Woodlands, Tex., 1973—; founder Third Coast Letter Press, 1993—; vis. lectr. in art Stephen F. Austin State U., Nacogdoches, Tex., 1998. Author, artist: Indochina Suite, 1994, Surrogates, 1995, Four Sea Interludes, 1996, P: An Excursus Into Liminal Space, 1997, Laughing Woman, 1998, Judith & Bluebeard: A Little Something for the Millennium, 1999, Voice: Some Music in the Sanskrit Mode, 1999. Mem. Assn. Difusora obra Grafica Internat. (Barcelona, Spain), Guild Bookworkers.

LAUFER-DVORKIN, BATIA, English educator, applied linguist; b. Vilnius, Lithuania, Dec. 30, 1946; arrived in Israel, 1959; d. Rafael and Luba (Furman) Dvorkin; m. Zvy Laufer, Aug. 6, 1968; three children. BA, Haifa U., 1969; MA, Leiden U., 1974; PhD, Edinburgh U., 1986. Lang. tchr. Haifa U., Israel, 1970-74, English as fgn. lang. tchr., 1974-95, from lectr. applied linguistics to assoc. prof. English dept, 1995—. Author: Similar Lexical Forms in Interlanguage, 1991; editor: A Teacher's Grammar of the English Verb, 1992; contbr. articles to profl. jours. Office: Haifa U, English Dept, 31905 Haifa Israel

LAUGHLIN, AUBREY SCOTT, mechanical engineer; b. Laguna Beach, Calif., Mar. 17; s. Aubrey Arlan Laughlin and Julia Francis Abney; m. Susan Rene Rikard, July 23, 1992; children: Aubrey Lee, Laurel Elizabeth. BS in Mech. Engring., McNeese State U., 1985. Registered profl. engr., Tex. Engr. United Gas Pipeline Co., Houston, 1985-89; project engr. Tenneco Energy, Houston, 1989-94, Columbia Energy, Houston, 1994-97; project mgr. Alliance Engring., Houston, 1997—. Bd. mem. Cornerstone Pl. Homeowner's Assn., Katy, Tex., 1997, 98. Winner Mousetrap Vehicle Champion, McNeese State U. Mousetrap Vehicle Champion, 1984, 85, 86. Republican. Baptist. Avocations: golf, tennis, swimming, biking. E-mail: slaughli@alliance-engineering.com. Office: Alliance Engring 16340 Park Ten Pl Houston TX 77084-5142

LAUGHLIN, CHRISTEL RENATE, translator, consultant; b. Berlin, Dec. 18, 1940; came to U.S., 1966; d. Werner Wilhelm and Rosa Ida (Conrad) Friedrich; m. Phillip Edward Laughlin, July 1, 1966; 1 child, Christina Rosa. Cambridge proficiency diploma, Davies's Sch., London, 1960; French lang. diploma, U. Paris, 1961; Italian lang. diploma, Centri Europei Lingua, Florence, Italy, 1961; BA in Translating, U. Geneva, 1964; accredited travel agt., N.Am. Sch. Travel, Newport, Calif., 1976. Mem. touring svc. Swiss Touring Club, Geneva, 1962-63; hostess, interpreter Intercontinental Hotel, Geneva, 1964, Swiss Nat. Exhbn., Lausanne, 1964; exec. sec. Intercom S.A., Geneva, 1964-65, Soc. Luchard, Paris, 1965-66; outside saleswoman Hunnicutt Travel, Ft. Worth, 1974-76; pres. Simon Stevens Laughlin Travel, Ft. Worth, 1976-81; cons., translator K.T. Lendt & Co., N.Y.C., 1969-96; tax acct. Tarrant Operators, Inc., Ft. Worth, 1996-98; market rsch. analyst Power Base, Denver, 1997; cons. Schwartzkopf Cosmetics, Duesseldorf, Germany, 1997; traffic cons. ADAC-Automobil Club Germany, Munich, 1997. Pres. Symphony League Ft. Worth, 1972-74; juror host family, interpreter Van Cliburn Internat. Piano Competition, Ft. Worth, 1973-97; host family interpreter XX World Gymnastics Championships, Ft. Worth, 1979, U.S. Gymnastics Internat., Ft. Worth, 1982. Mem. AAUW, Nat. Assn. Market Rsch. Analysts, Bot. Rsch. Inst. Tex. (sponsor), Arts Coun. Ft. Worth, Modern Art Mus. Fort Worth. Avocations: tennis, skiing, classical music, opera, travel. Home: 6212 Indian Creek Dr Fort Worth TX 76107-3526

LAUGHLIN, ROBERT B., physics educator; b. Visalia, Calif., Nov. 1, 1950; m. Anita Rhona Perry, Apr. 22, 1979; children: Nathaniel David, Todd William. AB in Math, U. Calif., Berkeley, 1972; PhD in Physics, MIT, 1979. Postdoctoral fellow Bell Telephone Labs., 1979-81, Lawrence Livermore Nat. Lab., 1981-82; assoc. prof. physics Stanford (Calif.) U., 1985-89, prof. physics, 1989—, Anne T. and Robert M. Bass prof. Sch. Humanities and Scis., 1992—, prof. applied physics, 1993—; lectr. in field. Contbr. articles to profl. jours. With U.S. Army, 1972-74. IBM fellow, 1976-78; recipient E.O. Lawrence award for physics, 1985, Franklin Inst. medal, 1998; named Eastman Kodak lectr., 1989, Van Vleck lectr., 1994.Nobel Prize Physics 1998. Fellow Am. Phys. Soc. (Oliver E. Buckley prize 1986); mem. AAAS, NAS, Am. Acad. Arts and Scis., Aspen Ctr. Physics. Office: Stanford U Dept Physics Stanford CA 94305

LAUGHLIN, WILLIAM EUGENE, electric power industry executive; b. Sheffield, Ala., May 4, 1936; s. Rawlie Wayne and Nina Louise (Campbell) L.; m. Donna Lynn Blackburn, Jan. 3, 1958; children: Kevin McGregor, Christopher Scott, Laura Shannon, Alison Paige. BS, Auburn U., 1961. Registered profl. and electrical engr., Ala., Tenn., Miss. Elec. engr. Dept. Power, Water and Gas, City of Sheffield, 1961-66; chief engr., asst. mgr. Electric Plant Bd., Bowling Green, Ky., 1966-76; systems mgr. Bowling Green Mcpl. Utilities, 1975-77; gen. mgr. Fayetteville (Tenn.) Electric Systems, 1977-81, Talquin Electric Coop. Inc., Quincy, Fla., 1981—; bd. dirs., v.p. Seminole Electric Coop., Inc., Tampa, Fla.; pres. Fla. Rural Electric Coop. Assn., Tallahassee. Pres. Boys Club, Bowling Green, 1972; v.p. Bowling Green C. of C., 1975, Fayetteville C. of C., 1979; dist. chmn. Boy Scouts Am., Bowling Green, 1972, Fayetteville, 1978; pres. Fayetteville United Way, 1980. Mem. Nat. Rural Elec. Coop. Assn. (mem. regional com., nat. water task force 1995), Am. Water Works Assn., Rotary (bd. dirs. 1986-87, pres. Quincy club 1996-97), Fayetteville 1978-79, Paul Harris fellow), Kiwanis (dir. Bowling Green club 1973-74). Democrat. Mem. Ch. of Christ. Home: 2110 Ellicott Dr Tallahassee FL 32312-3118 Office: Talquin Electric Coop Inc PO Box 1679 Quincy FL 32353-1679

LAULETTA, FRANCISCO, accountant; b. Buenos Aires, Argentina, Nov. 10, 1956; s. Francisco Lauletta and Virginia Teres Benardelli. Diploma in Econs. Sci., U. Kennedy, Buenos Aires. Gen. mgr. Banco de Mendoza, Buenos Aires, Banco Mayo, Buenos Aires, Juncal Bank, Buenos Aires; gen. mgr., connoisseur justice comml., civic and adminstrv. Secures Adminstrn., Buenos Aires; prof. spl. courses for gen. mgrs. Univ. Kennedy, Buenos Aires; prof. Buenos Aires U.; cons. Fass-Yakol Ltd., Buenos Aires, Brevet Sch., Buenos Aires. Author: (books) Judges for Banks, 1985, Judges for Commerces, 1990, Judges for Industries, 1991, Judges for Consulting, 1992. Mem. Brevet Sch., Italian Sch., Spanish Sch., Grad. Sch. Assns. Avocations: photographer, reader, football, tennis, paddle. Home: Manco Capac 1226, 1406 Buenos Aires Argentina

LAULICHT, MURRAY JACK, lawyer; b. Bklyn., May 12, 1940; s. Philip and Ernestine (Greenfield) L.; m. Linda Kushner, Apr. 4, 1965; children: Laurie Hasten, Pamela Hirt, Shellie Davis, Abigail Herschmann. BA, Yeshiva U., 1961; LLB summa cum laude, Columbia U., 1964. Bar: N.Y. 1965, N.J. 1968, U.S. Supreme Ct. 1976. Legal staff Warren Commn., Washington, 1964; law clk. Hon. Harold R. Medina U.S. Ct. Appeals, 1964-65; assoc. Kaye, Scholer, Fierman, Hays & Handler, N.Y.C., 1965-68; ptnr. Lowenstein, Sandler, Brochin, Kohl & Fisher, Newark, N.J., 1968-79, Pitney, Hardin, Kipp & Szuch, Florham Park, N.J., 1979—. Mem. N.J. Consumer Affairs Adv. Com., 1991-93; N.J. Commn. on Holocaust Edn., 1991—, chmn. 1992-95; pres. Jewish Edn. Assn., 1981-84, Jewish Fedn. Metro West, 1996-99; chmn. Cmty. Rels. Com., 1988-91.; exec. comm. Coun. of Jewish Fedn., 1996-99; trustee United Jewish Cmtys., 1999—. Recipient Julius Cohn Young Leadership award Jewish Fedn. Metrowest, 1976. Mem. ABA, N.J. State Bar Assn. (dist. X ethics com. 1986-89, bd. editors N.J. Law Jour. 1986-93), N.J. Lawyer Mag. (chmn. 1993-95). Democrat. Avocations: Jewish studies, communal activities. Home: 18 Crestwood Dr West Orange NJ 07052-2004 Office: Pitney Hardin Kipp & Szuch PO Box 1945 200 Campus Dr Ste 1 Florham Park NJ 07932-1007

LAUMONT, PHILIPPE EMILE, communications executive; b. Liege, Belgium, June 17, 1944; came to U.S., 1957; s. Gustave J. and Germaine (Cattet-Thellier de Poncheville) L.; m. Anne Colton Adams, July 19, 1978; children: Anne Sophie, Julia Adams, Laura Philippa. BA, U. Louvain, Belgium, 1964, MA, 1965; MBA, Columbia U., 1978. Film producer CBS Inc., N.Y.C., 1969-78; pres. Laumont Labs Inc., N.Y.C., 1979—, Laumont Photographics, 1993—, Laumont Editions, 1998—. Mem. Coffee House Club, Ausable Club, Tuxedo Club. Office: Laumont Labs 333 W 52nd St New York NY 10019-6238

LAUN, LOUIS FREDERICK, government official; b. Battle Creek, Mich., May 19, 1920; s. Louis Frederick and Roena (Graves) L.; m. Margaret West, Jan. 25, 1947; children: Nancy, Kathryn Webb, Margaret. BA, Yale U., 1942. Asst. advt. mgr. Bates Fabrics, Inc., N.Y.C., 1946-48; asst. to pres., indsl. and public relations Bates Mfg. Co., Lewiston, Maine, 1948-55; advt. dir., out-of-town sales mgr. Burlington Industries, N.Y.C., 1955-57; gen. merchandising mgr. Celanese Fibers Co., N.Y.C., 1957-60; v.p., dir. mktg. Celanese Fibers Co., 1960-63, exec. v.p. mktg., 1963-64; pres. Celanese Fibers Mktg. Co. div. Celanese Corp., 1964-71, also v.p. corp., 1964-71; asso. adminstr. ops. SBA, Washington, 1973; dep. adminstr. SBA, 1973-77; pres. Am. Paper Inst., N.Y.C., 1977-86; asst. Sec. Commerce for Internat. Econ. Policy Dept. of Commerce, Washington, 1986-89, exec. br. commr., Commn. on Security and Cooperation in Europe, 1988-89; cons. Nat. Exec Svc. Corp, 1989—; U.S. pulp and paper rep. food and agrl. orgns. UN; bd. dirs. Overseas Pvt. Investment Corp., Noranda Aluminum, Inc.; exec. br. mem. Commn. on Security and Cooperation in Europe (Helsinki Commn.). Bd. dirs. N.Y. Bd. Trade, Better Bus. Bur. N.Y., Alliance to Save Energy, Bus. Adv. Com. on Fed. Reports, Citizens Against Govt. Waste; indsl. asst. to chmn. Opportunities Industrialization Ctrs. Am.; nat. adv. coun. SBA; chmn. Republican Industry Workshop program; field dir. Com. for Re-election of Pres., 1972; trustee Taft Sch.; mem. exec. com. President's Pvt. Sector Survey on Cost Control; chmn. Kids to Kids Internat., 1999; bd. dirs. New Castle Hist. Soc., 1999—, Edwin Gould Svcs. for Children, 1997—, United Way of No. Westchester, 1998—. With USMCR, 1942-46. Decorated Bronze Star; recipient Human Rights award Anti-Defamation League, 1968; Achievement award Textile Vets. Assn., 1970; named Young Man of Yr. Lewiston-Auburn C. of C., 1953, Man of Yr. Textile Salesman Assn., 1970, Man of Yr. Fabric Salesmen's Guild, 1971; Gold medal for disting. service SBA, Citation Merit Taft Sch., 1988. Mem. Color Assn. U.S. (sec.), Man-Made Fiber Producers Assn. (chmn. 1967-69), Yale Club (N.Y.C.), Sleepy Hollow Country Club (Scarborough, N.Y.), Met. Club (Washington), Mid-Ocean Club (Bermuda). Fax: 914-238-3023. Home and Office: 25 Spring Ln Chappaqua NY 10514-2607

LAUNDER, BRIAN EDWARD, mechanical engineering educator; b. London, July 20, 1939; s. Harry Edward and Elizabeth Ann (Ayers) L.; m. Dagny Simonsen; children: Katya Jane, Jesper David. BSc, Imperial Coll., London, 1961; SM, MIT, 1963, ScD, 1965; DSc, U. London, 1976, U. Manchester, Eng., 1983; DEng, U. Manchester Inst. Sci./Tech., Eng., 1996; D (hon.), Inst. Nat. Polytech., Toulouse, France, 1999. Chartered engr. Rsch. asst. MIT, Cambridge, 1961-64; lectr. in mech. engring. Imperial Coll., London, 1964-71, reader in fluid mechanics, 1971-76; prof. mech. engring. U. Calif., Davis, 1976-80; prof. mech. engring. U. Manchester Inst. Sci. and Tech., 1980-98, head dept. mech. engring., 1993-95, rsch. prof., 1998—; organizing com. Turbulent Shear Flows Symposium, 1977-97; chmn. environ. strategy group, 1998—. Editor in chief Internat. Jour. Heat and Fluid Flow, 1987—. Fellow ASME, Inst. Mech. Engrs., Royal Soc. London, Royal Acad. Engring. London, Royal Aero. Soc. Avocations: French culture and literature, wine tasting, bicycling, photography. Office: UMIST, Dept Mech Engring PO Box 88, Manchester M60 1QD, England

LAUPSA, HALLSTEIN, publisher; b. Kvam, Norway, Sept. 30, 1947; s. Olav and Solveig (Hilland) L.; m. Torunn Haugen, Aug. 22, 1970; three children. Degree, U. Oslo, 1972, U. Oslo, 1976. Info. mgr. Norwegian Folk H.S., Oslo, 1971-74; tchr. Nissen H.S., Oslo, 1972-75; headmaster Lappish Folk H.S., Karasjok, Norway, 1975-76; editor Det Norske Samlaget, Oslo, 1976-78; tchr. Sagavoll Folk H.S., Gvarv, Norway, 1978-80; publisher H. Aschehoug & Co., Oslo, 1980-87, NKS-Forlaget, Oslo, 1987—. Home: Ellingsrudlia 30, N-1400 Ski Akershus, Norway

LAURA, ANTHONY JOSEPH, lawyer; b. Bklyn., July 15, 1961; s. Andrew J. and Edda V. (DePaola) L.; m. Rosemary B. Marino, Sept. 21, 1986; children: Diana Marie, Amanda Rose. BA, Yale U., 1983; JD, Fordham U., 1986. Bar: N.J. 1986, U.S. Dist. Ct. N.J. 1986, N.Y. 1987, U.S. Dist. Ct. (so. dist.) N.Y. 1987, U.S. Ct. Appeals (3rd cir.) 1993. Assoc. atty. Kelley Drye and Warren, N.Y.C., 1986-87, Morristown, N.J., 1987-89, Parsippany, N.J., 1989-97; ptnr. Reed, Smith, Shaw & McClay, Newark, 1997—; bd. trustee Cmtys. on Cable, Summit, N.J., 1994-97, chair fund distribution com. United Way Summit, New Providence, N.J., 1995-2000, trustee, 1998—. Township committeeman Rep. Com. Union County, Berkeley Hts., N.J., 1994-2000; trustee Runnells Specialized Hosp. Found., 1996-98. Mem. N.J. State Bar Assn. (chair product liability and toxic tort sect. 1999—), The Mory's Assn., Park Ave Club (membership com. 1994-96), Yale Club Ctrl. N.J. Avocation: golf. Office: Reed Smith Shaw & McClay 1 Riverfront Plz Fl 2B Newark NJ 07102-5470

LAURE, PATRICK, medicine educator; b. Rodez, France, Apr. 7, 1961; m. Sylvie Boussuge, Jan. 21, 1992; 1 child, Valentin. MD, L. Pasteur U., Strasbourg, France, 1990; PhD, H. Poincaré U., Nancy, France, 1994. Cert. sports medicine, aerospace medicine, emergency medicine. Asst. Gen. Hosp., Mulhouse, France, 1990-92; physician U. Hosp., Nancy, 1992—; educator H. Poincaré U., Nancy, 1994—; cons. Jeunesse et Sports Ministry, Paris, 1995—; bd. dirs. Ctr. Sociopharmacologie, St. Max, France, 1996—. Author: Le dopage, 1995, Memento de médecine du sport, 1995, Les gélules de la performance, 1997, Dopage et société, 2000. Med. officer French Army Health Svc., 1989-90. Recipient Sports Medicine prize Jeunesse et Sports Ministry, 1997. Mem. Soc. Franc Santé Publique. Avocations: swimming, horseback riding. Office: BP 87, 54132 Saint-Max Cedex, France

LAUREN, RALPH, fashion designer; b. Bronx, N.Y., Oct. 14, 1939; s. Frank and Frieda Lifshitz; m. Ricky Low Beer, Dec. 30, 1964; children: Andrew, David, Dylan. Student, CCNY; DFA (hon.), Pratt U., 1988. Salesperson Brooks Bros., N.Y.C.; asst. buyer Allied Stores, N.Y.C.; rep. Rivetz Necktie Mfrs., N.Y.C.; neckwear designer Polo divsn. Beau Brummel, N.Y.C., 1967-69; founder Polo Fashions, Inc., N.Y.C., 1968—; established Polo Men's Wear Co., N.Y.C., 1968—, Ralph Lauren Womenswear, N.Y.C., 1971—, Polo Leathergoods, 1978—, Polo/Ralph Lauren for Boys, 1978—, Polo/Ralph Lauren Luggage, 1982—, Ralph Lauren Home Collection, 1983—; launched fragrances Polo for Men, Lauren for Women, 1979—; chmn. Polo Ralph Lauren Corp. (flagship store N.Y.C., 65 other stores in U.S. and 140 stores worldwide); launched Safari fragrance for women, 1990, Safari for men, 1992, Polo Sport, 1994. Served in U.S. Army. Recipient Coty Am. Fashion awards, 1970, 73, 74, 76, 77, 81, 84, also Coty Hall of Fame award for Menswear and Womenswear, Tommy award Am. Printed Fabrics Coun., 1971, Neiman Marcus Disting. Svc. award, 1973, Am. Fashion award, 1975, award Coun. Fashion Designers Am., 1981, CFDA Lifetime Achievement award, 1992. Office: Polo Ralph Lauren Corp 650 Madison Ave New York NY 10022-1029

LAURENT, GUY, biology educator; b. Vieux-Genappe, Belgium, Nov. 19, 1950; m. Monique Cornez, Dec. 15, 1973 (div. Mar. 1983); children: Christine, Thierry; m. Nicole Delflasse, Aug. 31, 1991. M in Biology, Free U. of Brussels, 1973, PhD in Biology, 1979; PhD in Pharmacology, Cath. U. of Louvain, Brussels, 1990. Rsch. collaborator Free U. Brussels, 1973-79; fellow NCI, NIH, Bethesda, Md., 1980; rsch. collaborator Cath. U. of Louvain, 1981-85; asst. U. Mons-Hainaut, Mons, Belgium, 1986-89; rsch. assoc. Nat. Fund for Scientific Rsch., Brussels, 1989-93, sr. rsch. assoc., 1993—. Sgt. med. corp., 1977, Brussels. Galien award in Pharmacology, 1984. Avocation: pistol shooting. Home: 32 Ave de Wezembeek, B-1950 Kraainem Belgium Office: UMH Medicine/Histology, 6 Ave du Champ de Mars, B-7000 Mons Belgium

LAURENT, JEAN, credit company executive. MS, U. Wichita. Head of info. systems and orgn. dept. to dep. dir. credit Toulouse Regional Bank, 1970-81; dir. rural devel. Loiret Regional Bank, 1981-84; dep. chief exec. in charge of opers. Ile de France Regional Bank, 1984-93; head devel. and markets divsn. Caisse Nat. de Credit Agricole (CNCA), 1993-94, dept. chief exec., 1994—. Office: Caisse Nat Credit Agricole, 91-93 Blvd Pasteur, 75710 Paris France*

LAURENT, J(ERRY) SUZANNA, technical communications specialist; b. Oklahoma City, Okla., Dec. 28, 1942; d. Harry Austin and M. LaVerne (Barker) Minick; m. Leroy E. Laurent, July 2, 1960; children: Steven, Sandra, David, Debra. AS in Engr. Tech., Okla. State U., 1986. Owner, CEO Technically Write, Mustang, Okla., 1989-95; sr. tech. comms. specialist Applied Intelligence Group, Edmond, Okla., 1995-98, DCA Svcs., Oklahoma City, 1998—. Named One of The Top Ten Business Women in Nation Am. Bus. Women's Assn., 1997. Mem. Soc. Tech. Comm. (Superscript editor 1985, feature editor 1986, v.p., 1985, student chpt. pres. 1986, program coord. Okla. chpt. 1992-93, sec. 1993-94, v.p. 1994-95, state pres. 1995-96, state treas. Okla. chpt. 1998-99, Disting. Chpt. Svc. award 1997, dir./sponsor Region 5 1999—, other honors), Am. Bus. Women's Assn. (Dist. III v.p. 1988-89, conf. gen. chair 1992, editor Smoke Signals 1993-95, chmn. bd. dirs. Help Us Grow Spiritually 1993-95, Bull. award 1977, 81, 83, 84, 93, 95, 97, 98, 99, Nat. Newsletter award, 1999, Woman of Yr. 1977, 96, Bus. Assoc. of Yr. 1983-84, area coun. pres. 1987-89, sec. 1990-91, 98-99, Nat. Newsletter award 1999). Democrat. Baptist. Avocations: reading, public speaking, motivating people, volunteer activities. Home: 347 W Forest Dr Mustang OK 73064-3430

LAURENT, JOHN ANGUS, social sciences educator; b. Caulfield, Victoria, Australia, Feb. 22, 1947; s. Robert Oscar and Gladys Jean (Angus) L. BA, U. Queensland, Australia, 1976, BSc, 1979; BSc (hons.), Griffith U., Queensland, Australia, 1980, PhD, 1984. Cert. tchr. Queensland, Australia. Post doctoral fellow Wollongong (New South Wales) U. Australia, 1984-85; Col. George Johnston scholar U. Sydney, N.S.W., Australia, 1986; tutor in econ. history U. New South Wales, Kensington, 1987-88; lectr. Sch. Edn. U. Tech., Sydney, 1988-90, Griffith U., Nathan, QLD., Australia, 1990—. Co-author (with Margaret Campbell) (book) Charles Darwin in Australasia, 1987; editor: (book) Tom Mann's Social and Economic Writings, 1988; co-editor: (with Philip Candy) (Book) Pioneering Culture, 1994; (with others) Science, Technology and Society: An Introduction. Warden archaeol. br. Office of Aboriginal and Islanders Affairs, Queensland, 1979—. Recipient Griffith U. Post-grad. award, 1981-84. Fellow Sci. Policy Rsch. Ctr., Griffith U., Linnean Soc. London; mem. Hist. of Econ. Thought Soc. Australia, Royal Australian Hist. Soc. Avocations: paleontology, reading, book collecting, travel. Home: 1/84 Rita St, Holland Park QLD 4121, Australia Office: Griffith U Sch of Sci, Kessels Rd, Nathan QLD 4111, Australia

LAURENT, MARC OLIVIER, executive; b. Metl, France, Mar. 4, 1952; s. Michel and Francoise (Roger) L.; m. Agnes George, July 1, 1978; children: Pauline, Timothee, Theodore, Kortense, Bernice. MBA, HEC, France, 1975; PhD, Sorbonne, France, 1981. Dir. IDI, Nevilly, France, 1979-84; exec. dir. CCF, Paris, 1984-93; gen. ptnr. Richschild & Cie, Paris, 1993—; bd. dirs. Moulinex, Paris, Continentale, Paris, Deutsch Innob. Leasing, Paris, Ssainte Genevieve Sch., France. Home: 50 Ave Marceau, 75008 Paris France Office: Rothschild & Cie, 17 Av Natignon, 75008 Paris France

LAURENT, TORVARD CLAUDE, biochemist, educator; b. Stockholm, Dec. 5, 1930; s. Torbern and Bertha E. (Svensson) L.; m. Ulla B. G. Hellsing, Oct. 9, 1953; children: Birgitta, Claes, Agneta. B Medicine, Karolinska Inst., Stockholm, 1950, MD, D Med. Scis., 1958; MD (hon.), Turku (Finland) U., 1993; PharmD (hon.), Bologna (Italy) U., 1994; MD (hon.), Bergen (Norway) U., 2000. Instr. histology and chemistry Karolinska Inst., 1949-52, 55-58; rsch. fellow., assoc. Retina Found., Boston, 1953-54, 59-61; assoc. prof. U. Uppsala, Sweden, 1961-66, prof. med. and physiol. chemistry, 1966-96, chair dept. med. and physiol. chemistry, 1973-77, 87-91, dep. dean. faculty medicine, 1969-72; dep. chmn. Biomedical Ctr., Uppsala, 1973-77, 87-91; vis. prof. biochemistry Monash U, Melbourne, Australia, 1979-80; mem. Swedish Natural Sci. Rsch. Coun., 1968-70, Swedish Med. Rsch. Coun., 1970-77, Nobel Com. of Chemistry, 1992-2000; trustee Nobel Found., 1992—, chmn., 1994—. Contbr. 200 papers. Recipient Anders Jahre Med. prize U. Oslo, 1968, Pharmacia award Pharmacia, Inc., 1986, Eric K. Fernström Med. prize U. Lund, 1989, Björkén prize U. Uppsala, 1990. Mem. Royal Swedish Acad. Scis. (pres. 1991-94), Swedish Biochem. Soc. (sec. 1967-70, chmn. 1972-76), Wenner-Gren Found. (sci. sec. 1993—), Academia Europae, Academia Scientiarum and Artium Europea, Hungarian Acad. Scis., Academia delle Scienze Dell'Instituto di Bologna. Achievements include research in chemistry of connective tissue, physical properties, physiological functions, turnover and medical applications of the polysaccharide hyaluronan (hyaluronic acid), ophthalmic biochemistry, physical chemistry of polysaccharide networks, transport processes in polysaccharide solutions, biochemical separation techniques (e.g. a theory of gel filtration) and methods for cell separation. Office: U Uppsala Inst Med Biochem, BMC Box 582, SE751 23 Uppsala Sweden

LAURETTI, GABRIELA ROCHA, medical educator; b. Ribeirão Preto, Brazil, July 18, 1964; d. Argemiro Lauretti-Filho and Djanira Salles Rocha; m. Newton Lindolfo Pereira, July 17, 1987; children: Thabita, Bibiana. MD, U. São Paulo, 1988, PhD, 1995; MSc, U. Manchester, Eng., 1992. Med. diplomate, pain specialist, anesthesia specialist. Rsch. asst. U. Manchester, 1989-91, resident in anesthesia, 1990-92; cons. in anesthesia U. São Paulo, 1993-94, lectr. anesthesia, 1994—, dir. pain specialization, 1995—; coord. symposiums in pain mgmt. Referee Revista de la Sociedad EspanÕla del Dolor, 1997—, European Jour. Anaesthesiology, 1998; author chpts. in books. Mem. Am. Soc. Reg. Anesthesia, Brazilian Soc. Anesthesia, Brazilian Soc. for Pain Study. Presbyterian. Avocations: reading, classical ballet, dancing. Home: Rua-Campos Sales 330, Ribeirão Prêto Brazil Office: Univ São Paulo Fac Med, Campus Universitário, 14049900 Ribeirão Prêto Brazil

LAURIA, RITA MARIE, media and communications researcher, consultant; children: Carmella, Marcela. BA, U. So. Calif., L.A., 1979; MA, U. N.C., 1987, PhD, 2000. Freelance writer, cons. Chapel Hill, 1982-90; adv. to sec. Dept. Transp. and Comm. Federated States Micronesia, 1990-92; instr. Cape Fear C.C., Wilmington, N.C., 1993-94; dir. global virtual univ. initiative U. N.C., Wilmington, 1998-99; rsch. assoc. Media Interface and Network Design Lab. Mich. State U., Lansing, 1997—. Author: The Law and Regulation of International Space Communications, 1988; contbg. author chpt. book; contbr. articles to profl. jours. and pubs. Recipient endowment Nat. Endowment for Humanities, 1994; Writing and Rsch. grantee Nat. Press Found., 1986. Mem. Assn. U. Women (career devel. fellow, Helen Landers endowment 1996-97). Avocations: skiing, water skiing, weight training, running. E-mail: rlauria@worldnet.att.net.

LAURIDSEN, SØREN TINDGARD, food scientist; b. Esbjerg, Denmark, June 19, 1965; s. Kjaer and Birgit (Tindgard) L. BSc, Tech. U. Denmark, Copenhagen, 1990. Scientist Glostrup U. Hosp., Copenhagen, 1991-95; sr. scientist Danish Vet. Food Adminstrn., Copenhagen, 1995—; tchr. Sch. Hosp. Technicians, Copenhagen, 1999—. Contbr. articles to profl. jours. Mem. Scandinavian Soc. Atherosclerosis Rsch. Avocations: soccer, French wine, golf. Home: Sjaelør Blvd 2 th, DK-2450 Copenhagen Denmark Office: Danish Vet and Food Adminst, Mørkhøj Bygade 19, DK-2860 Søborg Denmark

LAURIN, MICHEL, zoologist; b. St.Jerome, Can., Oct. 26, 1965; s. Roger and Carmelle (Auger) L. BS, U. Montreal, Que., Can., 1988; MS, U. Toronto, Ont., Can., 1990, PhD, 1994; PdF., U. Calif., Berkeley, 1996. Tchg. asst. U. Toronto, Mississauga, 1988-93, lectr., 1994; rsch. assoc. U. Calif., Berkeley, 1994-96; assoc. prof. U. Paris 7, 1996-98; rsch. assoc. Humboldt U., Berlin, 1997-98; scientist Nat. Ctr. Sci. Rsch. (CNRS), Paris, 1998—; referee many scientific socs., 1990—. Editor: Tree of Life, Flagstaff, Ariz., 1996—; contbr. articles to profl. jours. Grad. student rep. Biology Exec. Com. of U. of Toronto, Mississauga, 1991, chair Biology Union of Grad. students, Mississauga, 1991. Recipient Humboldt fellowship Alexander von Humboldt Found., Berlin, 1997, Postdoctoral fellow Nat. Sci. and Engrng. Rsch. Coun. of Can., Berkeley, Calif., 1994, Ramsay Wright award U. Toronto, others. Mem. French Assn. Paleontology, Internat. Soc. Vertebrate Morphologists, Soc. Vertebrate Paleontology, Soc. Systematic Biology. Avocations: ancient history, art history, karate, travel. Office: Univ Paris 7, 2 place Jussieu, 75005 Paris France

LAURINČIK, JOZEF, embryologist, researcher; b. Trenčin, Slovakia, Nov. 6, 1959; s. Jozef and Rozália (Skurková) L.; m. Lubica Hadbábna, Mar. 20, 1982; children: Nada, Jozef. DVM, Košice (Slovakia) Vet. U., 1985; PhD, Slovak Acad. Scis., Bratislava, 1990; D, Hannover (Germany) Vet. U., 1995; docent, Košice Vet. U., 1996; DSc, Slovak Acad. Scis., 1997. Rsch. asst. Rsch. Inst. Animal Prodn., Nitra, Slovakia, 1986-88, rsch. worker, 1988-89, head culture lab., 1989-94; vice dir. Inst. Genetics and Exptl. Biology, Nitra, Slovakia, 1994-97; guest prof. U. Konstantin, Nitra, Slovakia, 1998; invited scientist Royal Vet. and Agrl. U., Copenhagen, 1991-92, 93, guest prof., 1995-97; head in-vitro fertilization lab., Ctr. Assisted Reprodn., Nitra, 1992-94; invited scientist Inst. Animal Breeding and Animal Husbandry, Mariensee, Germany, 1992-99, Vet. U., Vienna, 1994, rsch. coord., 1995-97, 98-99. Author: Morphology of the First Porcine Embryonic Cell Cycle, 1995, Cumulus-Oocyte Maturation and Zygote Development in Cattle, 1997; mem. editl. bd. Vet. Med., 1998; contbr. over 40 articles to scientific jours. Named Master of Future, Ministry Agr., Czechoslovak Republic, 1989; Alexander von Humboldt Found. fellow, 1994, 99; recipient Best Rsch. Paper in Agr. award, Ministry Agr., Slovakia, 1991, 93; recipient rsch. grants Danish Vet. and Agrl. Rsch. Coun., 1991-92, Fed. Ministry Agr., Germany, 1992-93, European Union, 1993, Ministry Rsch., Austria, 1995-97, 98—, Ministry Agr., Slovak Republic, 1997—. Mem. N.Y. Acad. Scis., Interventional Embryo Transfer Soc., European Soc. for Domestic Animal Reprodn., Alexander von Humboldt Club (Bratislava). Office: Rsch Inst Animal Prodn, Hlohovská 2, SK-94992 Nitra Slovakia

LAURITSEN, NIELS, advertising executive; b. Silkeborg, Jutland, Denmark, July 30, 1949. Cert. composing and sales mgr. Advt. dir. Freshwater Mag. Freshwater Soc. Denmark, 1993—. E-mail: niels.lauritsen@ry-bogtryk.dk. Office: Freshwater Soc Denmark, Ry Bogtrykkeri PO Box 29, DK-8680 Brunhoejvej 10, Denmark

LAURITZEN, JONAS GUNNAR KJELDGAARD, lawyer; b. Stockholm, Sweden, June 2, 1942; s. Gunnar K. and Inga K. (Jansson) L.; m. Marianne G. Lauritzen, May 27, 1967 (div. Jan. 1992); children: Christian K., Suzanne K.; ptnr. Birgita Wireen, 1992. Degree, U. Lund, Sweden, 1967. With dist. ct. svc. Mcpl. Ct. at Östersund, Sweden, 1968-69; asst. counsel Advokatfirman Curt Blomqvist, Göteborg, Sweden, 1970-77; ptnr. Advokatfirman Lauritzen & Lagerqvist, Göteborg, 1978-89, Advokatfirman Glimstedt, Göteborg, 1980-84, Advokatfirman Wistrand HB, Göteborg, 1985-97, Berglund O & H Co Advokatbyråkb, Göteborg, 1997—; chmn. Västra avdelningen av Sveriges Advokatsamfund, 1990-96; mem. nat. bd. Av Sveriges Advokatsamfund, 1984-90. Mem. Rotary (pres. 1983-84). Avocation: jazz music (playing drums). Home: Södra Bergavägen 4, S-42931 Kullavik Sweden Office: Berglund Och Co Advokatbyra, Berzeliigatan 14 Box 53166, 40115 Göteborg Sweden

LAURO, SHIRLEY MEZVINSKY, playwright, educator; b. Des Moines, Nov. 18, 1933; d. Phillip and Helen Frances (Davidson) Shapiro; m. Norton Mezvinsky, July 22, 1956 (div. 1967); 1 child, Andrea Mezvinsky; m. Louis Paul Lauro, Aug. 18, 1973. B.S. cum laude, Northwestern U., Evanston, Ill., 1955; M.S., U. Wis., 1957; postgrad. Columbia U., 1970-73. Instr. speech and theater CCNY, N.Y.C., 1967-71; instr. speech, theater and playwriting Yeshiva U., N.Y.C., 1971-76; instr. creative writing Manhattan Marymount Coll., N.Y.C., 1978-79; instr. speech and drama Manhattan Community Coll., N.Y.C., 1978-79; instr. playwriting Tisch Sch. of Arts NYU, 1989—; lit. cons. Ensemble Studio Theater, N.Y.C., 1975-80, prodn. critic, 1975—, mem. council, 1975—. Author novel: The Edge, 1965, Money for Women, 1990 (Barbara Deming award 1990); author plays: The Contest (Nat. Found. for Jewish Culture playwright's award 1981), 1975; The Coal Diamond (Heidemann Prize Actors Theater of Louisville's Festival of New Am. Plays 1980, Best Short Plays of 1980), 1979; Open Admissions-one act version (N.Y. Dramatists Guild Hull-Warriner Playwrights award 1981, Samuel French Playwrights award 1979, Ten Best Plays of 1981 N.Y. Times), 1984; Nothing Immediate (Samuel French playwright's award 1979), 1979; Margargaret and Kit (nomination for Susan Blackburn Prize 1980), 1980; I Don't Know Where You're Coming From at All, 1979; In the Garden of Eden, 1984, Sunday Go To Meetin', 1987; Open Admissions-full length version (Tony nominee, Drama Desk nominee, Theater World award), 1984; Pearls on the Moon (Residency Alley Theater, 1987) 1987, A Piece of My Heart, 1988; author screenplay: Open Admissions (CBS-TV Network) 1988. N.Y. Found. Arts Playwright's fellow, 1985; John Guggenheim Playwrights fellow, 1986; NEA Playwrights fellow, 1987. Mem. PEN, Ensemble Studio Theater, League Profl. Theater Women (v.p.), Dramatists Guild, Authors League, Authors Guild, Writer's Guild. Democrat. Jewish. Office: care Gilbert Parker William Morris Agy 1350 Avenue Of The Americas New York NY 10019-4702*

LAURSEN, FINN, educator; b. Romlund, Denmark, June 17, 1944; s. Laurits and Hedvig (Kristensen) L.; m. Berenice Lara, May 10, 1962; children: Jannik, Itzel. Grad., Aarhus (Denmark) U., 1974; PhD, U. Pa., 1980. Researcher European U. Inst., Florence, Italy, 1977-80; vis. fellow Princeton (N.J.) U., 1980-81; asst. prof. Odense (Denmark) U., 1981-82, assoc. prof., 1982-84; vis. fellow Woods Hole (Mass.) Oceanographic Inst., 1984-85; lectr. London Sch. Econs., 1985-88; assoc. prof. European Inst. Pub. Adminstrn., Maastricht, The Netherlands, 1988-90; prof. internat. politics European Inst. Pub. Adminstrn., 1990-95; prof., dir. Thorkil Kristensen Inst., South Jutland U. Ctr., Esbjerg, Denmark, 1995-98; vis. prof. U. Tsukuba, Japan, 1998-99, Schuman prof. Fudan U., China, 1998-99; prof. internat. politics dept. polit. sci. U. So. Denmark, Odense, 1999—. Author: Superpower at Sea, 1983, L'Europe Bleue, 1987, Danmark og Havretten, 1988, Small Powers at Sea, 1993; editor: Toward a New International Marine Order, 1982, Efta and the EC: Implications of 1992, 1990, Europe, 1992, World Partner?, 1991, The Intergovernmental Conference on Political Union, 1992, The Ratification of the Maastricht Treaty, 1994, The Political Economy of European Integration, 1995, The EU and Central Europe: Status and Prospects, 1996. Recipient Am. Studies award, Fulbright Commn., Copenhagen, 1975, Penfield scholarship, U. Pa., Phila., 1977, J.P. Compton fellowship, Princeton U., 1980. Office: U So Denmark Polit Sci Dept, Campusvej 55, DK 5230 Odense M, Denmark

LAURSEN, GITTE VESTERGAARD, micropalaeontologist, geologist; b. Aarhus, Denmark, Nov. 8, 1964; d. Finn Dalsgaard and Agnes Marie (Vestergaard) Laursen. MSc in Geology, U. Aarhus, 1990, PhD in Geology, 1995. Rsch. assoc. in geology U. Aarhus, 1990-94; micropaleontologist Statoil, Stavanger, Norway, 1994—; gov. Biostratigraphy Seminar, Stavanger, 1998. Contbr. articles to Cushman Found. Spl. Publ., Jour. Micropalaeontology, Bull. soc. Geology France, others. Mem. Cushman Found. for Foraminiferal Rsch. (patron), Brit. Micropalaeontological Soc. (patron), Regional com. of No. Neogene and Paleogene Stratigraphy (corr.). Avocations: riding, shooting, dancing.

LAUSTEN, GUNNAR SCHWARZ, orthopedic surgeon, educator; b. Løgumkloster, Denmark, Sept. 29, 1947; s. Laust and Margarethe (Schwarz) L.; m. Bergliot Boas Thorlacius, Jan. 17, 1970; children: Atarina, Karoline. MD, U. Copenhagen, 1974. House surgeon Base Hosp., Wanganui, New Zealand, 1974-76, County Hosp., Copenhagen, 1976-77; dist. surgeon Base Hosp., Chrhåb, Greenland, 1977-79; registrar RigsHosp., Copenhagen, 1979-85; sr. registrar Rigs Hosp., Copenhagen, 1990-93, Ctrl. Hosp., Hillerød, Denmark, 1985-90; cons. County Hosp., Herlev, Denmark, 1993—; cons. Accident Compensation Bd., Copenhagen, 1986—; lectr. U. Copenhagen, 1990—. Contbr. articles to profl. jours. Fellow Danish Orthop. Soc. Home: Bøgholmen 8, DK 2840 Holte Denmark Office: U Copenhagen, Herlev Hosp Dept Orthop, DK 2730 Herlev Denmark

LAUTERBACH, BERND GUENTER, software engineer, researcher; b. Muenchberg, Germany, May 9, 1961; m. Yumi Kawahara. Diploma, U. Bremen, Germany, 1987, DEng, 1993. Rsch. asst. U. Bremen, 1987-93; software engr. Credis, Ltd., Heidelberg, Germany, 1994-95, SAP AG, Walldorf, Germany, 1995—; session chmn. Internat/ Geosci. and Remote Sensing Symposium, Tokyo, 1993. Contbr. articles to profl. jours. Mem. IEEE. Office: SAP AG, Neurottstr 16, 69190 Walldorf Baden, Germany

LAUTERBACH, MICHAEL ALAN, artist; b. Blue Island, Ill., Sept. 6, 1954; s. Harry Lewis and Donna Rae (Jones) L. AA in Art, U. Wis. Ctr., Rice Lake, 1976; BA in Mid. Eastern & S.W. Asian Studies, U. Minn., 1986, BA in Art, 1988; MFA in Visual Arts, U. Ariz., 1992. Material coord. Bell Helicopter Internat., Isfahan, Iran, 1976-78; expediter, material coord. Raymond Internat., Ju'Aymah, Saudi Arabia, 1978-79; storekeeper Air Base Constructors, Ramat-Matred, Negev, Israel, 1980; artist, 1986—. Exhibited in group shows at U. Tex., San Antonio, 1989, U. Ariz. Mus. Art, Tucson, 1992, Pro Arts, Oakland, Calif. Vol. Bethany Luth. Ch., Mpls., 1997-98. Bush Found. artist fellow, 1996, Park Ave. Armory, 1996. Avocations: travel, music, cooking, meditation, world cultures. Home: 1401 Portland Ave Apt C201 Minneapolis MN 55404-5560

LAUTMANN, RUEDIGER, sociology educator; b. Koblenz, Germany, Dec. 22, 1935; s. Kurt and Sybille (Fischer) L. Referendar Jur., U. Wurzburg, Germany, 1959, JD, 1967; PhD, U. Munich, 1968. Rsch. asst. Sozialforschungsstelle, Dortmund, Germany, 1968-69; rsch. fellow dept. sociology U. Bielefeld, Germany, 1970-71; prof. legal sociology U. Bremen, Germany, 1971-81, prof. gen. sociology, 1982—. Author: Justiz—Die Stille Gewalt, 1972; Seminar: Gesselschaft und Homosexualitaet, 1977, Die Gleichheit der Geschlechter, 1990, Die Lust Am Kind, 1994. Mem. Gesellschaft Fuer Kriminologie (juror 1999—), Deutsche Gesellschaft Fuer Soziologie (editor 1995-99). Home: Holzdamm 41, D-20099 Hamburg Germany

LAUTNER, PETER, historian of ancient philosophy; b. Györ, Hungary, Feb. 11, 1959; s. Istvan and Ilona (Szabo) L.; m. Judit Anka, Aug. 24, 1985; children: Adam, Agoston. PhD, Eötvös U., Budapest, Hungary, 1990. Asst. prof. Eötvös U., 1988-89; fellow Hungarian Acad. Scis., Budapest, 1990-94, sr. fellow, 1994—. Author: (with J. O. Urmson) Simplicius on the Void, 1993, Simplicius on Aristotle's De Animal.l-2.4, 1995, Simplicius on Aristotle's Physics, 1997, (with C. Steel and P. Huby) Simplicius on Aristotle's De Anima, 1997, (with J.O. Urmson) Simplicius on Aristotle's Physics 5, 1998. A.W. Mellon Found. fellow, Athens, 1994, Netherlands Acad. Scis. fellow, 1995-96; fellow at Ctr. for Hellenic Studies, Harvard U., 1996-97. Fellow Inst. Classical Studies (London). Home: Ady Endre u 13, H-2081 Klotildliget Hungary Office: Faculty of Arts Eotvos U., Piarista Koz 1, H-1053 Budapest Hungary

LAUTTENBACH, CAROL, artist; b. New Haven, Conn., Nov. 26, 1934; d. Gustav Fredrick and Wanda M. (Eshner) Stolze; m. Francis John Lauttenbach; children: Daniel M., William J. Grad. with honors, Washington Sch. Art, Chgo., 1967. One-woman shows include Greene Art Gallery, Guilford, Conn., Carriage House Gallery Ltd., Guilford, Gallery 53, Meriden, Conn., John Slade Ely House Gallery, New Haven, Conn. Recipient Prix de Paris award Musee Des Raymon Duncan, France, 1972, 76, 80, award Salon Des Surindependants, Paris, 1981. Mem. Conn. Acad. Fine Arts, New Haven Paint and Clay Club, Shoreline Alliance for Arts, Brush and Palette Club, Provincetown Art Assn., Internat. Soc. Artists, Conn. Clasic Arts, Inc., Arts and Crafts Assn. Meriden (Grumbacher silver medal 1983-84, gold medal 1993). Home: 39 Ridgewood Rd Wallingford CT 06492-2116

LAUTZENHEISER, BARBARA JEAN, insurance executive; b. LaFeria, Tex., Nov. 15, 1938; d. Fred E. and Verna V. L. B.A. with high distinction, Nebr. Wesleyan U., 1960. Actuarial trainee Bankers Life Ins. Co. Nebr., Lincoln, 1960-64, programmer and systems analyst, 1964-65, asst. actuary, 1965-69, assoc. actuary, 1969-70, 2d v.p., actuary, 1970-72, v.p., actuary, 1972-80; sr. v.p. Phoenix Mut. Life Ins. Co., Hartford, Conn., 1980-84; pres. Montgomery Ward Life Ins. Co., Montgomery Ward Ins. Co., Forum Ins. Co., Schaumberg, Ill., 1984-85; prin., CEO Lautzenheiser & Assocs., Hartford, 1986—; spokesperson for ins. industry, witness U.S. Senate and Ho. of Reps. coms., commns. and state legislatures; featured on TV, nat. mags. and newspaper articles; mem. Interim Actuarial Std. Bd., 1986-88, Actuarial Std. Bd., 1989-90; chmn. Com. for Fair Ins. Rates, 1983-86; mem. adv. com. Nat. Assn. Ins. Commrs. Life Disclosure (A) Com. working group, 1993; bd. dirs. LifeUSA Holding Co. Contbr. articles to profl. jours. Mem. Lincoln Electric Sys. Adminstrv. Bd., 1977-79; bd. dirs. Nebr. Wesleyan U., 1977-82, 89-93, Am. Coll., 1987-97. Recipient Young Alumni svc. award Nebr. Wesleyan U., 1971, Corp. Woman award Women Bus. Owners of N.Y., 1983, C.H. Poindexter award for disting. achievement and exceptional svc. to the assn. and ins. industry Nat. Assn. Life Cos., 1989. Fellow Soc. Actuaries (pres. 1982-83, dir. 1975-80, 81-85, exec. com. 1978-80, 81-84, chmn. adminstrn. and fin. com. 1981-82, assoc. editor The Actuary 1992-93, life nonforfeiture task force 1995-96), Conf. Cons. Actuaries 1991— (dir. 1997-98); mem. Am. Acad. Actuaries (dir. 1974-77, chmn. com. on publs. 1980-81, nonforfeiture working group 1994—, disclosure working group 1994—, com. on life ins. 1995-99, co-chair 1998—, life practice coun. vice chair 1998), Soc. of Actuaries Found. (founding trustee 1994-98, trustee emeritus Actuarial Found. 1998—), Nat. Alliance Life Companies (bd. dirs. 1992-95), Nebr. Actuaries Club (dir. 1969-70, 71-74, 92-94, chmn. 1973-74, pres. 1972-73, sec., treas. 1971-72), Life Office Mgmt. Assn. (corp. fin. planning com. 1974-81, chmn. 1976-78), Am. Coun. Life Ins. (risk classification com. 1973-81), Greater Hartford C. of C. (nat. policies panel 1980-84). Home: 17 Huntingridge Dr South Glastonbury CT 06073-3614 Office: Lautzenheiser & Assocs City Place II 185 Asylum St Fl 11 Hartford CT 06103-3611

LAUVEN, PETER MICHAEL, anesthesiologist; b. Leverkusen, Fed. Republic Germany, May 13, 1948; s. Peter Aloysius and Katharina (Oedekoven) L.; m. Anne-Kareen Wetje, Nov. 7, 1970; children: Anne-Laureen, Lars-Peter. Diploma in Chem., U. Bonn, Fed. Republic of Germany, 1970, Dr. rer. nat., 1974, Dr. med., 1979, priv.-dozent, 1985. Teaching asst. Inst. Organic Chem. U. Bonn, Fed. Republic of Germany, 1970-76, scientist Inst. Anaesthesiology, 1976-79, physician, 1979—, anaesthesiologist, 1983—, asst. dir., 1983-85, vice-chmn., 1985-92, prof. of anaesthesia, 1986—, chmn. dept. Anaesthesiology & Surg. ICU, 1993—; mem. German Fed. Drug Admission Com., 1987—. Author, co-editor: Das Zentralanticholinergische Syndrom, 1985, Klinische Pharmakologie und rationale Arzneimitteltherapie, 1992; author, editor: Anasthesie und der Geriatrische Patient, 1989, Postoperative Schmerztherapie, 1991. Recipient scholarship Stipendien Fonds der Chemischen Inst., Frankfurt, 1970, Paul Martini award, Paul Martini Found., Bonn, 1988. Mem. Deutsche Gesellschaft für Anaesthesiologie und Intensiv Medizin, Am. Soc. Anaesthesiology (affiliate), Am. Soc. Regional Anaesthesia, European Acad. Anaesthesiology, European Soc. Regional Anaesthesia, European Soc. Intensive Care Medicine, European Soc. Anaesthesiology. Home: Haendelstr 22, D-33604 Bielefeld Germany Office: Clin Anes and Intensive Care, Teutoburger Str 50, D-33604 Bielefeld Germany

LAUWERS, PHILIP LOUIS, cardiologist; b. Antwerp, Belgium, Oct. 31, 1930; s. Philip V. Lauwers and Francoise E. de Hasque; m. Anne C. de le Court, May 2, 1958; children: Kathleen, Philippe, Christine. MD, U. Louvain, Belgium, 1956. Head dept. cardiology Clinique St. Michel, Brussels, 1962-95; pres. Medici's Group Practice, Brussels, 1975—; chief med. advisor life Axa Royale Belgium, 1975—. Contbr. sci. articles to profl. jours. Fellow Royal Coll. Physicians; mem. Belgian Soc. Cardiology. Office: Medicis Group Practice, 251 Ave de Tervuren, Brussels 1150, Belgium

LAUZON, ROBERTA DIZON, agricultural engineer; b. Paku, Philippines, May 13, 1950; d. Pastor and Egmedia (Orag) Dizon; m. Dominador Lauzon, Dec. 27, 1975; children: Darlyn, Quennie, Doryn Jan, Quensteins, Jose Martin. BS, Visayas State Coll., 1975; MS, U. Phillippines, 1984, PhD, 1992. From rsch. asst. to prof. Visayas State Coll. Agriculture, Philippines, 1975—. Office: ViSCA, Dept Ag Chem & Food Sci, 6521-A Baybay Leyte, Philippines

LAVADO, RAUL SILVIO, soil scientist, educator; b. Lomas de Zamora, Argentina, May 16, 1944; s. Silvestre and Dora Luisa (Rodriguez) L.; m. Olga Josefina Stevens (div. Mar. 17, 1993); children: Julian Alvar, Emiliano Fernan; m. Claudia Alejandra Porcelli, Feb. 26, 1999. Degree in agri. engrng., U. Buenos Aires, 1968; degree in soil fertility, U. Granada, Spain, 1971. Soil rschr. Idevi, Viedma, Argentina, 1968-74; prof. soil sci. U. La Pampa, Santa Rosa, 1974-83, U. Buenos Aires, 1983-86, 1986—; rschr. CONICET, Buenos Aires, 1975—. Contbr. articles to profl. jours. Mem. coun. Nat. Rsch. Coun., Buenos Aires, 1997—. Recipient Vilfrid Baron award Argentinian Acad. Agr., 1995. Mem. Assn. Argentina de la Ciencia del Suelo, Soil Sci. Soc. Am., Internat. Soc. Soil Sci. Home: PAdilla 876, 1414 Buenos Aires Argentina Office: U Buenos Aires Fac Agronomy, Ave San Martin 4453, 1417 Buenos Aires Argentina

LAVAGNA, CHRISTIAN, gastroenterology researcher, scientific consultant; b. Nice, France, Jan. 9, 1964; s. Guy and Emilienne Lavagna. PhD, U Nice, 1996. Cert. molecular and cellular biologist. Sr. rschr. Gastroenterology Lab., Nice, 1993—. Avocations: marathon running, mountain biking. E-mail: czerucka@unice.fr. Office: Lab Gastroenterology, 28 Ave de Valombrose, Nice 06107, France

LAVATELLI, CARLA, sculptor, weaver; b. Rome, Aug. 21, 1928; came to U.S., 1947; U.S. citizen, 1957; Teaching degree, Santa Maria Degli Angeli, Rome, 1946. One-woman shows include Heller Gallery, L.A., 1964, Galleria Carpine, Rome, 1966, Palazzo Cerio, Capri, Italy, 1966, Galleria degli Argenti, Milan, Italy, 1967, Galleria La Vernice, Bari, Italy, 1967, Palm Beach (Fla.) Gallery, 1969, 71, 73, 75, Herbert Kende Gallery, N.Y.C., 1969, Galerie Motte, Geneva, 1970, Benjamin Gallery, Chgo., 1970, Galerie Moos, Montreal, 1970, Alexander Iolas, N.Y.C., 1972, Hakone Mus., Tokyo, 1972, Sari Heller Gallery, Beverly Hills, Calif., 1972, Phillips Collection, Washington, 1974, Gimpel & Weitzenhoffer, N.Y.C., 1976, A. & J. Rose, N.Y.C., 1978; public commns.: Pinacoteca di Stato, Rome, 1968, Palace of H.S.H. Reinier of Monaco, Principaute de Monaco, 1970, Mus. Modern Art Palace Shah of Iran, 1972, Spingold Theater, Brandeis U., Waltham, Mass., Freiburg Botanical Garden, U. Bauamt, Germany, Stanford U., Calif., 1975, Pk. 80 Plz. West, N.J., 1976, Sandoz Pharm., N.J., 1979, Cathedral St. John the Divine, N.Y.C., 1986, 96, 140 Thompson, N.Y.C., 1976-96, Sci. Plz., Brown U., 1985, New Enterprise Assn., San Francisco, 1989, St. Giovanni Battista, Pistoia, Italy, 1991, Vado di Camaiore, Lucca, Italy, Sculpture

Garden, Picasso Mus. Photography, Mougins, 1993, St. Augustine Cloisters, Pietra Santa, Italy, 1994, Cathedral St. John the Divine, N.Y.C., 1996, Stanford U. Med. Ctr., Calif., 1997, The Window of Hope, Vatican City, Rome, 1998, Grace Cathedral, San Francisco, 1998, others; installations: Carla Lavatelli Working Pl. Sculpture Garden, Camaiore Lucca, Italy, 1972—, Woodrow Wilson Bldg. Einstein Inst. Advanced Studies, Princeton U., 1977-79, Pecci Mus., Prato, Italy, 1995, Renoir Mus., Cagnes-Sur-Mer, France, 1995, others. Recipient Gold medal City of Mougins. Home and Studio: Carla Lavatelli Working Pl, Sculpture Garden, 55041 Camaiore Lucca, Italy

LAVAUD, FRANÇOIS POL, allergist, consultant; b. St. Fargeau, France, Apr. 17, 1950; s. Gilbert and Paulette (Gille) L.; m. Sylvie Demonet, Mar. 26, 1977; children: Xavier, Vincent. MD, U. Reims, France, 1976; diploma in allergy and clin. immunology, St. Antoine U., Paris, 1980; M of human biology, St. Pères U., Paris, 1984, D of Human Biology, 1987. Asst. in exptl. medicine Univ. Hosp., Reims, 1980-83, asst. in physiology, 1983-88, tchg. coord. allergology, 1980—, assoc. lectr., 1988—; cons. to industry, 1990—, Internat. Rsch. Inst. Metal Ions, Reims, 1992-98; expert Nat. Survey Aerobiology, France, 1996; bd. dirs. Nat. Commn. Rural Allergy, France, 1998—. Co-author: (with J.M. Dubois de Montreynaud et al.) Pneumology, 1977, (with Ph. Collery et al.) Metal Ions in Biology and Medicine, 1990, vol. III, 1994; chief editor OPA-LEN Med., Paris, 1998—; contbr. articles to med. jours. Town councillor, Rosnay, France, 1995; referee Internat. Ctr. Africans and Elites, Paris, 1996. Mem. French Soc. Allergy and Clin. Immunology (sec. nat. meeting), European Respiratory Soc., Soc. Archeol. Champagne. Avocations: archeology, numismatics, classic cars, skiing. Home: 8 Place Armand Dubois, 51390 Rosnay France Office: Univ Regional Hosp Ctr, 45 Rue Cognacq Jay, 51092 Reims France

LAVEAN, MICHAEL GILBERT, medical device company executive; b. Lansing, Mich., Sept. 17, 1954; s. Gilbert Earl and Barbara Ann (Cowels) LaV.; m. Janet Tlapek, Aug. 21, 1992; 1 child, Madeleine. Student, George Mason U., 1972-76. Polit. staff person various Dem. campaigns, 1972-84; mayor City of Saranac, Mich., 1984-86; polit. cons. Polit. Svcs., Inc., Saranac, 1984—; pres. Polit. Svcs., Inc. (merger with A.& N. of Phila.), Saranac, 1985-91; prin. Allan, Drake and LaVean (merger), Saranac, Mich., 1991-95; chief oper. officer Veos Ltd., St. Helier, Jersey, 1995—, Page Hanes, Saranac, Mich., 1995—; bd. dirs. Page Hanes, Inc., Veos, PLC, Veos, S.A. Co-patentee disposable cervical caps, sustained drug delivery, US and Europe; patentee disposal vaginal device, conception cap and conception kit. Vice-chmn. 5th dist. Dem. Com., Grand Rapids, Mich., 1985-87, chmn., 1987-93, vice-chmn. 3d dist., 1993—; mem. Dem. Electoral Coll., 1988; bd. dirs. United Way of Ionia (Mich.) County, 1986-92; exec bd. dirs. Ionia County chpt. ARC, 1987—. Recipient award for patent "Gynecol. Innovation of the Yr.", Quotidion Pharmacien, 1999. Fellow Internat. Napoleonic Soc. (bd. dirs. 1995—); mem. Napoleonic Soc. Am. (bd. dirs. 1991—, sec. 1995—), Masons. Baptist. Avocation: reading. E-mail: lavean@veos.com. Home: PO Box 31 Saranac MI 48881-0031 also: Le Bois du Gué, 35340 La Bouexiere France also: Veos France, 203-205 Blvd Jean-Janres, F-92100 Boulougne France

LAVELLE, BRIAN FRANCIS DAVID, lawyer; b. Cleve., Aug. 16, 1941; s. Gerald John and Mary Josephine (O'Callaghan) L.; m. Sara Hill, Sept. 10, 1966; children: S. Elizabeth, B. Francis C., Catherine H. BA, U. Va., 1963; JD, Vanderbilt U., 1966; LLM in Taxation, NYU, 1969. Bar: N.C. 1966, Ohio 1968. Assoc. VanWinkle Buck, Wall, Starnes & Davis, Asheville, N.C., 1968-74, ptnr., 1974—; lectr. continuing edn. N.C. Bar Found., Wake Forest U. Estate Planning Inst., Hartford Tax Inst., Duke U. Estate Planning Inst. Contbr. articles on law to profl. jours. Trustee Carolina Day Sch., 1981-92, sec., 1982-85; bd. dirs. The Salvation Army, 1986—; bd. dirs. Western N.C. Cmty. Found., 1986—, sec., 1987-90; bd. advs. U. N.C. Ann. Tax Inst., 1981—. Capt. JAG USAF, 1966-67. Mem. ABA, Am. Coll. Trust and Estate Counsel (state chmn. 1982-85, regent 1984-90, lectr. continuing edn.), N.C. Bar Assn. (bd. govs. 1979-82, councillor tax sect. 1979-83, councillor estate planning law sect. 1982-85, v.p. 1997—), N.C. State Bar (splty. exam. com. on estate planning and probate law 1984-90, chmn. 1990-91, cert. 1987), Rotary. Episcopalian. Clubs: Biltmore Forest Country, Asheville Downtown City. Home: 45 Brookside Rd Asheville NC 28803-3015 Office: 11 N Market St PO Box 7376 Asheville NC 28802-8506

LAVELLE, CHARLES JOSEPH, lawyer; b. Louisville, Aug. 31, 1950; s. James Ronald and Mary Elizabeth (Logan) L.; m. Donna Kay Mulligan, Jan. 21, 1978. BS with high honors, U. Notre Dame, 1972; JD, U. Ky., 1975; LLM in Taxation, NYU, 1977. Bar: Ky. 1975, U.S. Dist. Ct. (wes. dist.) Ky. 1977, U.S. Tax Ct. 1977, U.S. Claims Ct. 1986, U.S. Ct. Appeals (6th and Fed. cirs.) 1986, U.S. Supreme Ct. 1989. Assoc. Greenebaum Doll & McDonald PLLC, Louisville, 1977-82, mem., 1982—; chmn. bar liaison cen. region IRS, Cin., 1989, sec., 1997, bar liaison southeast region IRS; mem. Regional Counsel Adv. Group, Cin., 1988-89. Contbr. articles to profl. jours. Bd. dirs. Ky. Ctr. Pub. Issues, 1992-94; mem. steering com. Ky. Coalition for Edn., 1993-94; mem. Ky. Ltd. Liability Co. Legislation Drafting Com., 1993-94; mem. planning com. Ky. Conclave on Legal Edn., 1995. Secondary Sci. Tng. grant NSF, U. Ga., 1967, rcsh. grantee NSF, U. Notre Dame, 1969. Mem. ABA (tax sect.), Ky. Bar Assn. (chmn. tax sect. 1992-93), Louisville Bar Assn. (chmn. tax com. 1983, 84, vice chmn., treas. tax com. 1980-82), U. Ky. Law Alumni Assn. (bd. dirs. 1986—, pres. 1989-90, treas. 1987-90, 90—), Ky. C. of C. (bd. dirs. 1991—, exec. com. 1997—, chair pub. policy com. 1997-98, health ins. task force, tax com.), Rotary (bd. dirs. 1991-93, 95-97, treas. 1995-97, dist. conf. chair 1994), Notre Dame Club (pres. 1984-86, chmn. 1986-88, Ky. Man of Yr. 1990), Leadership Ky. (vice chmn. membership svcs. 1995-98, alumni bd. dirs. 1992-92, pres. alumni 1993-94, bd. dirs. 1993-98, exec. com. 1995-98). Office: Greenebaum Doll & McDonald PLLC 3300 National City Tower Louisville KY 40202

LAVENSON, SUSAN BARKER, hotel corporate executive, consultant; b. L.A., July 26, 1936; d. Percy Morton and Rosalie Laura (Donner) Barker; m. James H. Lavenson, Apr. 22, 1973; 1 child, Ellen Ruth Stanclift. BA, Stanford U., 1958, MA, 1959; PhD (hon.), Thomas Coll., 1994. Cert. gen. secondary credential tchr., Calif. Tchr. Benjamin Franklin Jr. High Sch., San Francisco, 1960; tchr. French dept. Lowell High Sch., San Francisco, 1960-61; v.p. Monogram Co., San Francisco, 1961-62; creative dir. Monogram Co., N.Y.C., 1973-86; pres. SYR Corp., Santa Barbara, Calif., 1976-89; mng. ptnr. Lavenson Ptnrs., Camden, Maine, 1989—; mem. commn. on co-edn. Wheaton Coll., Norton, Mass., 1985-87; mem. Relais et Chateaux, Paris, 1978-89; cons. World Bank Recruit Divsn., 1993. Author: Greening of San Ysidro, 1977 (Conf. award 1977). Trustee Camden Pub. Libr., 1989-95, v.p. 1991-93; vice chair bd. trustees Thomas Coll., Waterville, Maine; trustee Atlantic Ave. Trust; founding pres. Maine chpt. Internat. Women's Forum, 1991—; mem. Coun. of Advisors Coll. of the Atlantic. Bar Harbor, Maine, 1996—. Mem. Advice Inc., Camden Yacht Club, Stanford Alumni Assn., Com. of 200 (treas. 1985-86), Women's Entrepreneur Corps, Phi Delta Kappa (Stanford U. chpt.). E-mail: susiebl@earthlink.net. Home and Office: 10 Norumbega Dr Camden ME 04843-1746

LAVENTHOL, DAVID ABRAM, newspaper editor; b. Phila., July 15, 1933; s. Jesse and Clare (Horwald) L.; m. Esther Coons, Mar. 8, 1958; children: Peter, Sarah. BA, Yale U., 1957; MA, U. Minn., 1960; LittD (hon.), Dowling Coll., 1979; LLD (hon.), Hofstra U., 1986. Reporter, news editor St. Petersburg (Fla.) Times, 1957-62; asst. editor, city editor N.Y. Herald-Tribune, 1963-66; asst. mng. editor Washington Post, 1966-69; from assoc. editor to pub., CEO Newsday, L.I., N.Y., 1969-86; group v.p. newspapers Times Mirror Co., L.A., 1981-86, sr. v.p., 1987-93, pres., 1987-93; pub., CEO L.A. Times, 1989-93; editor-at-large Times Mirror Co., L.A., 1994-98, cons. editor, 1998-99; editor, pub. Columbia Journalism Rev., 1999—; mem. Pulitzer Prize Bd., 1982-91, chmn., 1988-89; vice-chmn. Internat. Press Inst., 1985-93, chmn., 1993-95. Bd. dirs. United Negro Coll. Fund, 1988, Mus. Contemporary Art, L.A., 1989—, chmn., 1993-97; bd. dirs. Associated Press, 1993-96, Columbia Journalism Sch., 1995—, Nat. Parkinson Found., 1995—, Saratoga Performing Arts Ctr., 1993-96. With Signal Corps AUS, 1953-55. Recipient Columbia Journalism award for Disting. Svc., 1994. Mem. Am. Soc. Newspaper Editors (chmn. writing awards bd. 1980-83), Council Fgn. Relations. Clubs: Century (N.Y.C.), Regency (L.A.). Office: Columbia Journalism Review Columbia Univ 2950 Broadway New York NY 10027-7004

LAVERGE, HENDRIK JOHANNES, finance company executive, investor, consultant; b. Jakarta, Java, Indonesia, Apr. 4, 1941; came to US, 1966; s. Albertus and Juliette (Terwindt) L.; m. Regine A. Schade, Dec. 7, 1968 (div. Dec. 1994); children: Albert Johannes, Claire Antoinette. BA, Willibrord Coll., Zeist, The Netherlands, 1959; LLM, Leiden (The Netherlands) U., 1965. Ptnr. Frick Wellington & Laverge, N.Y.C., 1992—; mng. dir. Valenzuela Capital Ptnrs. LLC, N.Y.C., 1992—; chmn. Devonshire Holding, La Grangeville, N.Y.; bd. dirs. Concordia Agritrading Pte. Ltd., Singapore, 1994—. Dir. Leiden U. Fund., 1995; dir., treas. St. Barnabas Coll., Johannesburg, South Africa, 1990-95; trustee Madison Ave. Presbyn. Ch., N.Y.C., 1975-85. Mem. Union Club N.Y.C. Home: 14 Herb Rd Sharon CT 06069-2326 Office: FW&L 1270 Avenue Of The Americas New York NY 10020-1700

LAVIANO, ALESSANDRO, internist, nephrologist; b. Rome, Apr. 2, 1963; s. Francesco and Maria Clara (Gatt) L. MD, U. La Sapienza, 1988. Chief resident internal medicine U. La Sapienza, Rome, 1989-93; resident in internal medicine U. La Sapienza, 1993, chief resident in nephrology, 1996-99; asst. prof. medicine U. La Sapienza, Rome, 1998—; rsch. fellow in metabolism and nutrition SUNY Health Sci. Ctr., Syracuse, 1994-95; organizing com. XVII Congress of European Soc. Parenteral and Enteral Nutrition, 1994-95; mem. edtl. adv. bd. Nutrition, The Internat. Jour. Applied and Basic Nutritional Scis. 1996—; vis. rsch. asst. prof. SUNY Health Sci. Ctr., Syracuse, 1999—. Contbr. articles to profl. jours. Mem. Jr. Chamber Internat. Chpt. Rome, 1997-98. Cpl. Carabinieri Corps. Italian Army, 1989-90, Rome. U. Rome Sch. Medicine fellow, 1988-93, Am. Inst. for Cancer Rsch. fellow, Syracuse, N.Y., 1995-96, Italian Nat. Rsch. Coun. fellow, 1993; Travel grant NATO, Syracuse, N.Y., Rome, 1994. Mem. AAAS, European Soc. Parenteral and Enteral Nutrition, Italian Soc. Parenteral and Enteral Nutrition, N.Y. Acad. Sci. Roman Catholic. Avocations: modern art, action movies, hiking, soccer. Home: Via Giuseppe Avezzana 31, 00195 Rome Italy Office: U La Sapienza Dept Clin Med, Viale Universita 37, 00185 Rome Italy

LAVIELLE, LISETTE, chemist, researcher; b. Mulhouse, France, Apr. 14, 1941; d. Aloyse and Suzanne (Renn) Muller; m. Jean-Pierre Lavielle, Dec. 28, 1964; children: Anne-Geraldine, Marie-Caroline. Grad. in Chem. Engring., Ecole Nat. Sup. Chimie, Mulhouse, France, 1964; D of Engring., U. Strasbourg, France, 1968; DSc, U. Haute-Alsace, Mulhouse, 1971. Rsch. assoc. Ecole Nat. Sup. Chimie Mulhouse Lab. Physics, Mulhouse, 1964-70; rsch. assoc. mineral chemistry lab. CNRS, Nat. Ctr. Sci. Rsch., Mulhouse, 1971-76; engr. Soc. European Propulsion, Vernon, France, 1978-79; rsch. assoc. macromolecular chem. lab. CNRS, Nat. Ctr. Sci. Rsch., Rouen, France, 1980-81; rsch. assoc. rsch. ctr. phys. chemistry of solid surfaces CNRS, Nat. Ctr. Sci. Rsch., Mulhouse, 1981-94; rsch. assoc. gen. photochem. lab. CNRS, Ecole Nat. Superieure Chimie, Mulhouse, 1995—. Author: (chpt.) Polymer Surface Dynamics, 1987; co-author: (chpt.) Polymer Characterization by Inverse Gas Chromatography, 1989; contbr. articles to profl. jours. Recipient Emilio Noelting prize Ecole Nat. Sup. Chimie, 1964. Mem. Soc. French Physicists, Soc. French Chemists. Roman Catholic. Avocations: music (piano), hunting. Office: CNRS Lab Photochimie Gen, 3 Rue A Werner, 68093 Mulhouse Cedex, France

LAVIGNE, LAWRENCE NEIL, lawyer; b. Newark, June 30, 1957; s. Daniel S. and Alice M. (Melon) L.; m. Benjie Panesh, Oct. 12, 1986; children: Gabriel A., Derek N. BA, Franklin & Marshall Coll., 1979; JD, Seton Hall U., 1982. Bar: N.J. 1982, U.S. Dist. Ct. N.J. 1982, U.S. Ct. Appeals (3d cir.) 1986, U.S. Supreme Ct. 1986, N.Y. 1989. Assoc. Shanley & Fisher, P.C., Newark, 1982-83; ptnr. Hanlon & Lavigne (and predecessor firm), Edison, N.J., 1983—; instr. Am. Inst. Paralegal Studies, Mahwah, N.J., 1985-88. Mem. ABA (litigation sect.), N.J. Bar Assn. (product liability com.), Middlesex County Bar Assn., Trial Attys. N.J., N.J. Def. Assn., Assn. Trial Lawyers Am., Somerset Bar Assn., Worrall F. Mountain Inn of Court (barrister 1991-93), Def. Rsch. Inst. Republican. Jewish. Avocations: tennis, music, computers. Office: Hanlon & Lavigne 10 Parsonage Rd Ste 200 Edison NJ 08837-2429

LAVIGNE, PETER MARSHALL, environmentalist, lawyer, educator; b. Laconia, N.H., Mar. 25, 1957; s. Richard Byrd and D. Jacquiline (Cobleigh) L.; m. Nancy Gaile Parent, Sept. 20, 1979; 1 child, Rhiannon Genevra Lavigne Parent. BA, Oberlin Coll., 1980; MSEL cum laude, Vt. Law Sch., 1983, JD, 1985. Bar: Mass. 1987. History tchr. Cushing Acad., Ashburnham, Mass., 1983-84; rsch. writer Environ. Law Ctr., Vt., 1985; lobbyist Vt. Natural Resources Coun., Montpelier, 1985; exec. dir. Westport (Mass.) River Watershed Alliance, 1986-88, Merrimack River Watershed Coun., West Newbury, 1988-89; environ. cons. Mass., N.H., Vt., and Oreg., 1990—; N.E. coord. Am. Rivers, Washington, 1990-92; dir. river leadership program River Network, Portland, Oreg., 1992-95; dir. spl. programs River Network, Portland, 1995-96; dep. dir. For the Sake of the Salmon, Portland, 1996-97; pres. Watershed Cons., Portland, 1997—; adj. prof. Antioch New Eng. Grad. Sch., Keene, N.H., 1991-92, Portland State U., 1997—; mem. Portland Willamette River Task Force, 1997-99; chair adv. bd. Cascadia Times, Portland, 1995-99, Amigos Bravos, Taos, N.Mex., 1993-98; trustee Rivers Coun. Washington, Seattle, 1993-98; bd. dirs. Alaska Clean Water Alliance, 1995-98, acting pres. 1997-98; adv. bd. Glen Canyon Inst., 2000—; Watershed adv. group Natural Resources Law Ctr. U. Colo., 1995-96; coastal resources adv. bd. Commonwealth of Mass., Boston, 1987-91; adj. assoc. prof. Portland State U., 1997—; Watershed Mgmt. Profl. program dir., Portland State U., 1999—; pres. Cascadia Times Rsch. Fund, 1998-99. Co-author: Vermont Townscape, 1987; contbr. articles to profl. jours. Dir. Mass. League of Environ. Voters, Boston, 1988-92; mem. steering com. N.H. Rivers Campaign, 1988-92; co-founder, co-chair New England Coastal Campaign, 1988-92; EMT South Royalton (Vt.) Vol. Rescue Squad, 1982-86; dir., chairperson Vt. Emergency Med. Svcs. Dist. 8, Randolph, 1984-86; co-founder, v.p. Coalition for Buzzards Bay, Bourne, Mass., 1987; housing renewal commn. City of Oberlin, Ohio, 1980-81; mem. properties com. First Unitarian Ch., 1995. Recipient Environ. Achievement award Coalition for Buzzards Bay, 1988; land use rsch. fellow Environ. Law Ctr., Vt. Law Sch., 1984-85; Mellon found. rsch. grantee Oberlin Coll., 1980. Mem. Natural Resources Def. Coun., River Alliance of Wis., Rivers Network, Idaho Rivers, League of Conservation Voters, Amigos Bravos, Glen Canyon Inst. Democrat. Unitarian-Universalist. Avocations: sea kayaking, mountaineering, woodwork, reading, photography. E-mail: watershed@igc.org. Fax: (503) 232-2887. Home: 3714 SE 11th Ave Portland OR 97202-3724 Office: Watershed Cons PO Box 42162 Portland OR 97242-0162

LAVIN, LAURENCE MICHAEL, lawyer; b. Upper Darby, Pa., Apr. 27, 1940; s. Michael Joseph and Helen Clair (McGonigle) L. BS, St. Joseph's U., Phila., 1962; JD, Villanova (Pa.) U., 1965. Bar: Pa., S.C. Vol. U.S. Peace Corps, Thika, Kenya, 1966-67; atty. Community Legal Svcs., Phila., 1968-70, exec. dir., 1971-79; exec. dir. Palmetto Legal Svcs., Columbia, S.C., 1981-85; dir. Law Coordination Ctr., Harrisburg, Pa., 1985-88, Nat. Health Law Program, L.A., 1988—; chmn. bd. dirs. L.A. Poverty Dept.; bd. dirs., chmn. civil com. Nat. Legal Aid and Defender, Washington, 1976-78. Founding mem. Pa. Coun. to Abolish Death Penalty, Harrisburg, 1986; bd. dirs. L.A. Poverty Dept., 1996—. Mem. ABA, Pa. Bar Assn. (chmn. legal svcs. to pub. com. 1985-88). Democrat. Avocations: reading, arts, acting. Home: 1133 22nd St Santa Monica CA 90403-5721 Office: Nat Health Law Program 2639 S La Cienega Blvd Los Angeles CA 90034-2675

LAVINE, THELMA ZENO, philosophy educator; b. Boston; d. Samuel Alexander and Augusta Ann (Pearlman) L.; m. Jerome J. Sachs, Mar. 31, 1944; 1 child, Margaret Vera. A.B., Radcliffe Coll., 1936; A.M., Harvard U., 1937, Ph.D., 1939. Instr. Wells Coll., 1941-43, asst. prof., 1945-46; asst. prof. philosophy Bklyn. Coll., 1946-51; asst. prof. U. Md., 1955-57, assoc. prof., 1957-62, prof., 1962-65; Elton prof. George Washington U., 1965-85, chmn. dept., 1969-77; Clarence J.Robinson Univ. prof. George Mason U., Fairfax, Va., 1985—; lectr., seminar cons. Inter-Am. Def. Coll., 1975—; exec. bd. Jour. of Speculative Philosophy, 2000—. Author: TV course From Plato to Sartre, 1980, From Socrates to Sartre: The Philosophic Quest, 1984; co-author: History and Anti-History Philosophy, 1989, introduction to Collected Works of John Dewey, Vol. 16, 1990; contbg. author: Philosophy of Paul Ricoeur, 1995, Rorty and Pragmatism, 1996, Reading Dewey, 1998; exec. bd. Jour. of Speculative Philosophy, 2000—; contbr. articles to profl. jours., chpts. to books. Recipient Outstanding Faculty award U. Md., 1965, Outstanding Faculty award George Washington U., 1968, Alumnae Achievement award Radcliffe Coll., 1991; NEH sr. rsch fellow, 1980; Am. Enterprise Inst. Public Policy Research fellow, 1980-81, Va. Found. Humanities fellow, 1990; Herbert W. Schneider award contbns. to Am. Philosophy, 2000. Mem. Am. Philos. Assn. (5th Ann. Romanell lectr. 1991), Soc. Advancement Am. Philosophy (exec. com. 1979-82, pres. 1992-94), Internat. Soc. Sociology Knowledge, Internat. Soc. Polit. Psychology, Metaphys. Soc. Am., Washington Philosophy Club (pres. 1967-68), Washington Sch. Psychiatry, Forum Psychiatry and Humanities (exec. bd.), Cosmos Club, Harvard Club, SOPHIA, Phi Beta Kappa (pres. chpt. 1978-80). Home: 1625 35th St NW Washington DC 20007-2316 Office: George Mason U Robinsons Profs E 207 Fairfax VA 22030

LAVOIPIERRE, ALAIN MAURICE, radiologist, diagnostician; b. Quatre Bornes, Mauritius, May 12, 1951; arrived in Australia, 1966; s. Maurice Jacques and Pauline Marie (Koenig) L.; m. Gail Vicki Webb, July 16, 1983; children: Amanda, Sara. MB,BS, U. Melbourne, Australia, 1974. Intern St. Vincent's Hosp., Melbourne, 1975, radiology registrar, 1977-80, radiologist, 1980-83; jr. resident Royal Children's Hosp., Melbourne, 1976; dir. radiology Fairfield Hosp., Melbourne, 1985-93; dir. CT & ultrasound Cabrini Hosp., Melbourne, 1993—; ptnr. Radclin Med. Imaging, Melbourne, 1983—, chmn., 1995-98; clin. instr. U. Melbourne, 1985-93, Monash U., 1997-98, sr. lectr. 1999—. Author: A Guide to Medical Imaging, 1988, 2d edit., 1993, 3d edit., 1997; co-author: Imaging Guidelines, 1990, 2d edit., 1994, 3d edit., 1997. Fellow Royal Australasian and New Zealand Coll. Radiologists (Victorian convener, pvt. hosps. com. 1996—, joint nuclear medicine credentialling and accreditation com. 2000—, Philips prize 1996); mem. Australian Med. Assn., Radiol. Soc. N.Am. Roman Catholic. Avocations: walking, boating, reading, wine, architecture. Office: Radclin Med Imaging, 183 Wattletree Rd, Malvern Vic 3144, Australia

LAVOLPE, ANTONIO, accountant; b. Baires, Argentina, May 30, 1932; m. Sara Maria Rey; children: Pablo Antonio, M. Alejandra, Cristina. Pub. Acct., U. Buenos Aires, 1957. Ptnr. Estudio Lavolpe & Assocs., Buenos Aires, 1957—; Dir. Sindico Cons., Indunor S.A., others; cons., B.I.D. prof. Universidad Buenos Aires, Universidad Católica Argentina; prof. emeritus U Católica Argentina. Author: Control de Costos En La Construccion, 1981. Fellow Nat. Assn. Accts.; m. Consejo Profesional Ciencias Econ. (v.p. 1970-71, tesorero 1985-89), U. Catolica Argentina Consejo Directivo. Roman Catholic. Office: Estudio Lavolpe & Assocs, Cerrito 1136, 1010 Buenos Aires Argentina

LAVRENKO, VLADIMIR ALEXEYEVICH, chemist; b. Belogorie, Ukraine, Jan. 23, 1933; s. Alexey Pavlovich and Bronislava Nickolayevna (Gayevska) L.; m. Alla Denisovna Panasyuk, Feb. 2, 1962. MS, Kiev Polytech Inst., Ukraine, 1955; PhD, Taras Shevchenko State U., Kiev, 1960; DS in Chemistry, Inst. Problems Materials Sci., Kiev, 1971. Rschr. Inst. Problems Materials Sci., Kiev, Ukraine, 1958-61, sr. rschr., 1961-76; head gen. chemistry dept. Kiev Polytech. Inst., Kiev, Ukraine, 1976-85; head dept. Frantsevich Inst. Problems Materials Sci., Kiev, Ukraine, 1985—; vis. prof. Nat. Tsing Hua U., Hsinchi, Taiwan, 1994; TV lectr. Modern Chemistry Students, Kiev, 1978-80; spkr. 3d Internat. Conf. Advanced Materials, Tokyo, 1993; cons. in field. Author: Recombination of Hydrogen Atoms on Solid Surfaces, 1973; co-author: High-Temperature Oxidation of Metals and Alloys, 1963, Corrosion of High-Performance Ceramics, 1989, Hydride Systems, 1992; contbr. articles to profl. jours. Deputy dir. chemistry dept. Ministry High Edn. Ukraine, Kiev, 1977-85; corr. mem. Acad. Tech. Scis. Ukraine, Kiev, 1992-94. Mem. Engring. Assn. USSR, Internat. Assn. Hydrogen Energy, N.Y. Acad. Scis. Home: Shelkovichnaya st 10 apt 12, 252 021 Kiev Ukraine Office: Inst Problems Materials Sci, 3 Krzhyzhanovsky str, 252 142 Kiev Ukraine

LAVROV, BORIS PAVLOVICH, physics educator, researcher; b. Kirov (now Vjatka), USSR, Dec. 16, 1944; s. Pavel Ivanovich and Marina Borisovna Lavrova; m. Lyudmila Vasil'evna Ipatova, Jan. 23, 1965; 1 child, Peter. Diploma in physics, Leningrad (USSR) State U., 1969, Candidate of Scis, 1975, DSc, 1988. Engr. Inst. Applied Chemistry, Leningrad, 1969; jr. rschr. Inst. Physics, Leningrad State U. (St. Petersburg State U. 1993—), 1972-77, asst. prof. physics, 1977-86; assoc. prof. Leningrad State U. (St. Petersburg State U. 1993—)., 1986-93; prof. St. Petersburg State U., 1993—; cons. Stanford (Calif.) &., 1990-91; cons. Inst. Low Temperature Plasma Physics, U. Geifswald, Germany, 1994—. Author: Determination of Gas Temperature from Intensities of Molecular Bands of H2 and D2, 1978; co-author: Plasma Chemistry, 1984; contbr. over 200 articles to sci. jours. Dep. leader St. Petersburg com. Dem. Party Russia, 1991-93. Grantee G. Soros Found., 1995, Russian Found. Basic Rsch., 1995-97. Mem. Phys. Soc. Russia. Achievements include patent for method of light emission generation in gas discharge and setup for its realization, 1982. Avocations: mushroom hunting, oldtimers. Fax: 7 (812) 428-72-40. E-mail: lavrov@pobox.spbu.ru. Home: Raz'ezshaya 3 Apt 32, 191002 Saint Petersburg Russia Office: St Petersburg State U, Sch Physics Ul'yanovskaya 1, 198904 Saint Petersburg Russia

LAVROV, SERGEI VIKTOROVICH, ambassador; b. Mar. 21, 1950; married; 1 child. Student, Moscow Inst. Internat. Rels. Attaché U.S.S.R. Embassy Sri Lanka, 1972-76; sec. dept. internat. econ. orgns. Ministry Fgn. Affairs, 1976-81; sec., counsellor U.S.S.R. Mission UN, N.Y.C., 1981-88; dept. chief, dept. internat. econ. rels. Ministry Fgn. Affairs, 1988-90, dir. dept. internat. orgns. & global problems, 1990-92, dep. min., 1992-94; permanent rep. Russian Fedn. UN, N.Y.C., 1994—. Office: Russian Perm Mission 136 E 67th St New York NY 10021-6137

LAW, BERNARD FRANCIS CARDINAL, archbishop; b. Torreon, Mex., Nov. 4, 1931; s. Bernard A. and Helen A. (Stubblefield) L. B.A., Harvard U., 1953; postgrad., St. Joseph Sem., St. Benedict, La., 1953, Pontifical Coll. Josephinum, Worthington, Ohio, 1955. Ordained priest Roman Catholic Ch., 1961, consecrated bishop, 1973; editor Natchez-Jackson diocesan paper, Jackson, 1963-68; exec. dir. U.S. Bishops Com. for Ecumenical and Interreligious Affairs, 1968-71, chmn., from 1975; vicar gen. Diocese of Natchez-Jackson, 1971-73; bishop Diocese of Springfield-Cape Girardeau, Mo., 1973-84; archbishop Archdiocese of Boston Brighton, Mass., 1984—; created cardinal, 1985; mem. adminstrv. com. Nat. Conf. Cath. Bishops, from 1975; mem. communication com. U.S. Cath. Conf., 1974, mem. adminstrv. bd., from 1975; mem. Vatican Secretariat for Promoting Christian Unity, from 1976; consultor Vatican Commn. Religious Relations with the Jews, from 1976; chmn. bd. Pope John XXIII Med.-Moral Research and Edn. Ctr., St. Louis, 1980-82; ecclesiastical del. of Pope John Paul II for matters pertaining to former Episcopal priests, 1981. Trustee Pontifical Coll. Josephinum, 1974-85, Nat. Shrine of Immaculate Conception, from 1975; bd. regents Conception (Mo.) Sem. Coll., from 1975. Office: Cardinal's Residence 2101 Commonwealth Ave Brighton MA 02135-3192

LAW, FRANCES ANNE MEYNELL, manager; b. Harrogate, Yorkshire, Eng.; d. Hugo Anthony Meynell and Anne Devine; m. Andrew Millar Law. BA in Econs. with honors, Leeds Met. U., 1989; MBA, Edinburgh U., 1997. Dept. mgr. Callard & Bower, Bridgend, 1989-92; planning mgr. McVitas, Broxburn, 1992-97; sr. cons. Andersons Cons., Sydney, Australia, 1998-99; strategic devel. mgr. St. Regis Paper Co., Maidenhead, Eng., 1999—. Shift leader Crisis, London, 1985-95. Office: St Regis Paper Co, Mill Ln Taplow, Maidenhead SL6 0AF, England

LAW, KWOK-KEUNG, optics scientist; b. Hong Kong, China, Apr. 23, 1958; came to U.S., 1984; s. Wai-kam and Sit-Ying (See) L.; m. Puffin So, Sept. 8, 1991; children: Victoria, William. BSc with honors, Chinese U. Hong Kong, 1981; MS, U. Calif., Santa Barbara, 1987; PhD, U. Calif., 1992. Asst. prof. Northwestern U., Evanston, Ill., 1992-94; sr. rsch. engr. 3M Ctr., St. Paul, 1994-96; co-pres. 168 Inc., Akron, Ohio, 1996-97; tech. staff, project team leader Lucent Technologies, Wichita, Kans., 1997-00; program mgr., dir. Vitesse Semiconductors, Camarillo, Calif., 2000—. Contbr. articles to profl. jours.; patentee in field. Recipient Tau Beta Pi award, 1990.

LAW, NICHOLAS SIMON, publishing executive; b. Guildford, Eng., May 26, 1954; s. Douglas Birch and Erica Rosemary (Bowman) L.; m. Mary Virginia Halliday, Oct. 6, 1979; children: Sarah Catherine, Hamish Simon. Student, Coll. Arts and Tech., Cambridge, 1976. Prodn. dir. Melrose Press/IBC, Cambridge, Eng., 1979-88, chief exec., 1988-93, mng. dir., 1993—; bd. dirs. Wings of Whyteleafe Ltd., Cambridge, 1995—; congress

dir. IBC, Cambridge, 1992—, dir. gen. 1994—. Mem. Soc. Protection Ancient Bldgs. Avocations: windmills, cars, cycling, music, reading. Home: Great Mill House, Aldreth Rd, Haddenham Ely CB6 3PN, England Office: Melrose Press Ltd, St Thomas Place Ely, Cambridge CB7 4GG, England

LAW, PHILLIP GARTH, scientist, Antarctic explorer, educator; b. Tallangatta, Victoria, Australia, Apr. 21, 1912; s. Arthur James and Lillian (Chapman) L.; m. Nel Isabel Allan, Dec. 20, 1941. Student, Ballarat Tchrs. Coll., 1931, Melbourne Tchrs. Coll., 1932; BSc, Melbourne U., 1939, MSc, 1941, Dr. Applied Sci. (hon.), 1962, Dr. Edn. (hon.), 1977, DSc (hon.), 1995. Tutor in physics Newman Coll., U. Melbourne, 1941-45; lectr. physics U. Melbourne, 1943-48; dir. Antarctic divsn. Dept. External Affairs, 1949-66; exec. v.p. Victoria Inst. Colls., 1966-77; chmn. Australian Nat. Com. on Antarctic Rsch., 1966-80; pres. Victorian Inst. Marine Scis., 1978-80; pres. Geog. Soc. N.S.W., 1955-56, Geelong Area Victorian Scouts Assn., 1964—; mem. Victorian Com. for Duke of Edinburgh's Award, 1964-80; pres. Grad. Union, U. Melbourne, 1971-77; mem. com. for natural scis. Australian Adv. Com. for UNESCO, 1972-77; dep. pres. Sci. Mus. Victoria, 1979-82; trustee Specific Learning Difficulties Assn., 1972—; mem. governing coun. Melbourne U., 1959-78, La Trobe U., 1964-74. Sci. Mission for Australian Army to New Guinea, 1944; leader numerous Antarctic expdns., 1949-66; responsible for establishing Australia's three permanent Antarctic Stations and for exploring3000 miles of Antarctic coastline. Author: (with John Bechervaise) ANARE, 1957; Antarctic Odyssey, 1983, The Antarctic Voyage of H.M.A.S. Wyatt Earp, 1995, You Have To Be Lucky, 1995; contbr. articles to profl. jours. Decorated companion Order of Australia, comdr. Order of Brit. Empire; recipient Founders Gold medal Royal Geog. Soc., 1960, Polar medal, 1996, award of merit Commonwealth Profl. Officers Assn., 1957, Gold medal Australian Geog. Soc., 1988. Fellow Australian Acad. Sci., Australian Acad. Technol. Scis. and Engring., ANZAAS, Australian Inst. Physics, Royal Geog. Soc., Royal Soc. Victoria (pres. 1967-69, councillor); mem. Australian New Zealand Sci. Exploration Soc. (pres. 1976-82, patron 1982—), Brit. Schs. Exploring Soc. (patron 1983—), Melbourne Film Soc. (pres. 1972-92).

LAW, THOMAS HART, lawyer; b. Austin, Tex., July 6, 1918; s. Robert Adger and Elizabeth (Manigault) L.; m. Terese Tarlton, June 11, 1943 (div. Apr. 1956); m. Jo Ann Nelson, Dec. 17, 1960; children: Thomas Hart Jr., Debra Ann. AB, U. Tex., 1939, JD, 1942. Bar: Tex. 1942, U.S. Supreme Ct. 1950. Assoc. White, Taylor & Chandler, Austin, 1942; assoc. Thompson, Walker, Smith & Shannon, Ft. Worth, 1946-50; ptnr. Tilley, Hyder & Law, Ft. Worth, 1950-67, Stone, Tilley, Parker, Snakard, Law & Brown, Ft. Worth, 1967-71; pres. Law, Snakard, Brown & Gambill, P.C., Ft. Worth, 1971-90; of counsel Law, Snakard & Gambill, P.C., Ft. Worth, 1990—; gen. counsel Gearhart Industries, Inc., Ft. Worth, 1960-88, Tarrant County Coll. Dist. Chmn. Leadership Ft. Worth, 1974-90; bd. regents U. Tex. System, 1975-81, vice chmn., 1979-81. Lt. USNR, 1942-46. Recipient Nat. Humanitarian award Nat. Jewish Hosp./Nat. Asthma Ctr., 1983; named Outstanding Young Man, City of Ft. Worth, 1950, Outstanding Alumnus, Coll. of Humanities, U. Tex., 1977, Outstanding Citizen, City of Ft. Worth, 1984, Bus. Exec. of Yr., City of Ft. Worth, 1987, Blackstone award for contbns. field of law Ft. Worth Bar Assn., 1990, Disting. Alumnus U. Tex., 1992. Fellow Am. Bar Found., Tex. Bar Found., Am. Coll. Probate Counsel, Tarrant County Bar Found. (founding chmn.); mem. Ft. Worth C. of C. (pres. 1972), Mortar Bd., Phi Beta Kappa, Omicron Delta Kappa, Pi Sigma Alpha, Delta Sigma Rho, Phi Eta Sigma, Delta Tau Delta. Democrat. Presbyterian. Clubs: Ft. Worth (bd. govs. 1984-90), Century II (bd. govs. to 1985), River Crest Country, Exchange (pres. 1972), Steeplechase. Lodge: Rotary (local club pres. 1960). Avocation: numismatics. Home: 6741 Brants Ln Fort Worth TX 76116-7201 Office: Law Snakard & Gambill 3200 Bank One Tower 500 Throckmorton St Fort Worth TX 76102-3859

LAWARE, JOHN PATRICK, retired banker, federal official; b. Columbus, Wis., Feb. 20, 1928; s. John Henry and Ruth (Powles) L.; m. Margery Ann Ninabuck, Dec. 22, 1952; children: John Kevin, Margaret Ann. BA in biology, Harvard U., 1950, grad. Advanced Mgmt. Program, 1975; MA in Polit. Sci., U. Pa., 1951; LHD (hon.), Suffolk U.; D in Polit. Sci. (hon.), Northeastern U. Trainee Chem. Bank & Trust Co., N.Y.C., 1953-54, with credit dept., 1954-56, asst. sec., 1957-60, asst. v.p., 1960-62, v.p., 1962-65, v.p. in charge of mktg. divsn., 1965-68, sr. v.p., 1968-72; sr. v.p. in charge holding co. ops. Chem. N.Y. Corp., 1972-78; pres., dir. Shawmut Corp., 1978-80; pres., dir. Shawmut Bank of Boston N.A., 1978-80, chmn., dir., CEO, 1980-88; ret., 2000; pres., dir. Shawmut Assn. Inc., 1978-80; chmn., CEO Shawmut Bank Boston, 1980-88; mem. bd. govs. FRS, Washington, 1988-95, ret., 1995; pres., dir. Devonshire Fin. Svc. Corp., 1978-88; chmn., treas. Boston Clearing House Assn. Inc., Shawmut Corp. subs.; mem. Internat. Fin. conf.; chmn. Mass. Bankers Assn., 1982-83, Assn. Bank Holding Cos., 1986-87; bd. dirs. Liberty Mut. Ins. Co., mem. compensation com.; adv. dir. Stewart Info. Sys. Corp., 1995—. Trustee, vice chmn., chmn. fin. com. Northeastern U., 1981-88; trustee, mem. fin. com. Mt. Holyoke Coll., 1984-88; chmn. Children's Hosp. Med. Ctr., 1989-91; past chmn., bd. dirs. Mass. Bus. Roundtable; chmn. coord. com. Boston Bus. Leaders Orgn.; chmn. bd. trustees Ctr. Blood Rsch., Boston; chmn. bd. dirs. Alliance for Commonwealth, Boston. Recipient Disting. Citizen award Minuteman Coun. Boy Scouts Am., Chief Exec. Officer of Yr. award Northeastern U. Coll. Bus., Outstanding Citizen award B'nai B'rith-Antidefamation League. Mem. Assn. Bank Holding Cos. (past chmn., dir.). Office: PO Box 30083 Sea Island GA 31561-0083 also: 57 Fairgreen Pl Chestnut Hill MA 02467-2721

LAWAY, NASEER AHMAD, electrical engineering educator, researcher; b. Srinagar, India, Feb. 15, 1960; s. Ghulam Nabi and Mala Bibi (Mam) L.; m. Sumera Sofi, Nov. 1, 1992; children: Saif Ali, Shifa. MSEE, U. Kashmir, India, 1982; M in Engring. with honors, U. Roorkee, India, 1988; PhD, U. Roorkee, 1995. Shift engr. dept. power devel. Jammu and Kashmir Govt., Kashmir, India, 1982-84; lectr. regional engring. coll. U. Kashmir, 1984-90, sr. lectr., 1990-95, asst. prof., 1995—; cons. dept. sci. and tech. J & K Govt., 1995. Contbr. articles to profl. jours. Sec. Tchrs. Assn., Srinagar, 1995—; sec. students affairs Study Cir. for Advancement of Knowledge, Srinagar, 1985-90. Mem. N.Y. Acad. Scis. Moslem. Avocations: reading, hiking, writing poetry, meditation. Home: 25 Pamposh Colony Natipora, Srinagar 190015, India Office: Regional Engring Coll, Srinagar 190006, India

LAWING, JIM L., attorney; b. Oklahoma City, Feb. 19, 1937; s. Oscar Mitchell and Clara Hattie (Williams) L.; m. Karlin Church, Jan. 24, 1964 (div. Dec. 1979); children: Keith Lawing, Kirsten Spinell, Chris Lawing; m. Mary Ann, Sept. 2, 1989; children: Jeff Harper, Jennifer Harper, Curry Harper, Gretchen Flatan, Anne Byne, Andy Newlan. BS, Northeastern State U., Okla., 1959; JD, U. Kans., 1965. Bar: Kans. Atty. Wichita, Kans., 1965—. State rep. Kans. House Reps., 1975-76; chmn. Sedgunk County Dem. Party, Kans., 1993-96; lay reader St. Stephen's Episcopal Ch., 1997—. Democrat. Episcopalian. E-mail: lawing@feist.com. Office: 200 E 1st St N Wichita KS 67202-2111

LAWLER, JOHN GRIFFIN, graphic designer, educator; b. Albany, N.Y., June 11, 1936; s. John Griffin and Elizabeth Moore (Elder) L.; m. Priscilla Jury, 1961 (div. 1974); children: Dawn, Erin; m. Mary T. Flynn, Mar. 4, 1978; 1 child, Sean Flynn. BFA, Pratt Inst., Bklyn., 1963, MFA, 1968. Co-owner Comart, Ayer, Mass., 1957-59; pvt. practice John Lawler & Assocs., N.Y.C., 1959-68, Eau Claire, Wis., 1968-74; pres., CEO Greendoor Graphics & Advt., Eau Claire, 1974—; creator, head graphic design program U. Wis., Eau Claire, 1968-96, prof. emeritus, 1996—; cons. Eau Claire Sch. Dist. Creator sculptures, 1961—. Mem. adv. bd. United Way of Great Eau Claire, Eau Claire Main St Assn.; pres., chmn. bd. Cmty. Learning Ctr., 1971-75; founder Chippewa Valley Communicators Club, 1975; co-founder Western Wis. Ad Club, 1982, pres., 1985-87; chair Neighborhood Plan Commn., 1998-2000. Recipient awards Ad Clubs, Soc. for Mktg. Profl. Svcs., Small Space Newspaper Advt. awards, Internat. Assn. Bus. Communicators, Univ. Design Assn., Wis. Credit Union League and Affiliates, Nat. Health Info. Awards, Smithsonian, 1969—, Vol. of Yr. award Gov. Tommy Thompson, 1994, award Wis. Credit Union League. Avocations: photography, architecture, furniture design, sculpture. Home: 1349 S Farwell St Eau Claire WI 54701-3948 Office: Greendoor Graphics & Advt 309 Main St Eau Claire WI 54701-3617

LAWLESS, ALLYSON, civil engineer; b. Durban, Natal, South Africa, Oct. 1, 1952; d. Mathys Johannes and Peggy Elizabeth (Vanderberg) Greeff; m. Mark Francis Lawless, Aug. 30, 1975; children: Alistair, Kate Louise. BSc in Civil Engring., U. Natal, 1973; MSc, Imperial Coll., London, 1976, Diploma, 1976. Grad. engr. Ove Arup & Ptnrs., Windhoek, S.W. Africa, 1974, Johannesburg, South Africa, 1975; design engr. Conder Midlands, U.K., 1976-78, Mackenzie Cairns & Bothma, South Africa, 1978-79; mng. dir. Allyson Lawless (Pty) Ltd., Johannesburg, 1979—. Named Small Businesswoman of Yr., Sarie/Old Mut., 1988; recipient Silver award Software Export Competition, Computer Svcs. South Africa, 1988. Fellow South African Inst. Civil Engrs. (pres. 2000), Inst. Structural Engrs. (v.p. 1998). Office: Allyson Lawless Pty Ltd, PO Box 73285, Fairland Gauteng 2030, South Africa

LAWLESS, ROBERT WILLIAM, academic administrator; b. Baytown, Tex., Feb. 13, 1937; s. James Milton and Belva Ambaline (Mode) L.; m. Marcella Jane Emmert; children: Christopher, Cheryl, Diana. BS, U. Houston, 1964; PhD, Tex. A&M U., 1968. Instr., asst. prof. Tex. A&M U., College Station, 1967-69; prof., sr. vice chancellor U. Houston, 1969-82; v.p., CFO S.W. Airlines, Dallas, 1982-85, exec. v.p., COO, 1985-89; cons. Tex. Hosp. Assn., Austin, 1966-82, banks, savs. and loans, 1970-72, NASA, 1970; pres. Tex. Tech U. and Tex. Tech. U. Health Scis. Ctr., Lubbock, 1989-96, Univ. Tulsa, Okla., 1996—; ind. dir. Salomon Bros. Asset Mgmt. Co., 1991-2000, Cen. and S.W. Corp., 1991—; chmn. Coun. of Pub. Univ. Pres. and Chancellors, Tex. higher edn. sys., 1993-95, mem. Pres.'s Commn. NCAA, 1994-97, exec. com., 1998—, bd. dirs. divsn. I; dir. Nat. Assn. Ind. Colls. and Univs., Assn. Presbyn. Colls. and Univs. Contbr. articles to profl. jours. Mem. formula adv. com. Tex. State Coordinating Bd., Austin, 1977-89; chmn. bd. dirs. Coll. Football Assn., 1990-92. Recipient Teaching Excellence award U. Houston, 1972, Disting. Faculty award Coll. Bus. Alumni, 1971, Disting. Alumni award Lee Coll., 1984, U. Houston, 1990. Office: Univ of Tulsa 600 S College Ave Tulsa OK 74104-3126

LAWLIS, PATRICIA KITE, air force officer, computer consultant; b. Greensburg, Pa., May 5, 1945; d. Joseph Powell Jr. and Dorothy Theresa (Allshouse) Kite; m. John Charles Ryan, Feb. 6, 1965 (div. 1973); m. Mark Craig Lawlis, Sept. 17, 1976 (div. 1983); 1 child, Elizabeth Marie. BS in Math., East Carolina U., 1967; MS in Computer Sci., Air Force Inst. Tech., 1982; PhD in Computer Sci., Ariz. State U., 1989. Cert. secondary math. tchr. Employment counselor Pa. State Employment Svc., Washington, Pa., 1967-69; math. tchr. Fort Cherry Sch. Dist., McDonald, Pa., 1969-74; commd. 2d lt. USAF, 1974, advanced through grades to lt. col., 1994; data base mgr. Air Force Space Command, Colorado Springs, Colo., 1974-77; computer sys. analyst USAF in Europe, Birkenfeld, Germany, 1977-80; prof. computer sci. Air Force Inst. Tech., Wright-Patterson AFB, Ohio, 1982-86, 89-94; ret. USAF, 1994; computer cons., pres. C.J. Kemp Systems, Inc., Huber Heights, Ohio, 1983—; Ada cons., Ada Joint Program Office, Washington, 1984-94. State treas. NOW, Pa., 1973-74. Recipient Mervin E. Gross award Air Force Inst. Tech., 1982, Prof. Ezra Kotcher award, 1985. Mem. Computer Soc. of IEEE, Assn. Computing Machinery, Tau Beta Pi (v.p. chpt. 1981-82), Upsilon Pi Epsilon. Office: CJ Kemp Systems Inc PO Box 586 Fairborn OH 45324-0586

LAWN, TIMOTHY REGIS, lawyer; b. Phila., Nov. 23, 1962; s. John Joseph and Carolyn Marie (McTamney) L.; m. Arlene Patricia Lawn, Apr. 5, 1991; children: Joshua, Daniel, John, Maureen. BS in Acctg. cum laude, Spring Garden Coll., 1984; JD cum laude, Widener U., 1989. Bar: Pa. 1989, U.S. Dist. Ct. (ea. dist.) Pa. 1990. Assoc. O'Brien & Ryan, Plymouth Meeting, Pa., 1989-96; ptnr. Litvin, Blumberg, Matusow & Young, Phila., 1996—; adj. faculty Temple Univ. Sch. Law.; instr. Nat. Inst. of Trial Advocacy. Chmn. bd. dirs. Dave Palmer Meml. Found., Phila., 1992—. Recipient Am. Jurisprudence awards (2), 1989. Mem. ATLA, ABA, Pa. Bar Assn., Phila. Bar Assn., Pa. Trial Lawyers Assn., Phila. Trial Lawyers Assn. Office: Litvin Blumberg Matusow & Young 1339 Chestnut St Fl 18 Philadelphia PA 19107-3520

LAWNY, FRANCOIS, industrial engineer; b. Rozay en Brie, France, May 29, 1949; s. Edouard and Marie-Rose (Cardoux) Lawny; m. Gilda Chantale Tersiguel, Aug. 25, 1975; children: Thibault, Gauthier, Florine. Degree in engring., Inst Nat Superieur Chimie, Rouen, France, 1973; PhD, U. Compiegne, France, 1975. Engr. Inst. Tech. Surfaces Actives, Compiegne, 1974-78; asst. to rsch. mgmt. Biotrol. Lab., Louvres, 1978-81, head of immunology, 1981-84; project mgr. CNTS, Les Ullis, 1985-89, head diversification, 1989-92; head of immunology Biolog, Plaisir, 1993-94; indsl. devel. mgr. Pierre Fabre Lab., St. Julien, 1995—. Patentee in field. Mem. Am. Chem. Soc. Avocation: mountain sports. Home: 19 Rue des Champs de Chant, 74800 St Sixt France Office: Ctr Immunologie Pierre Fabe, Bp 497, 74164 St Julien Genevois France

LAWRENCE, BELLARMINE VINCENT, oncologist; b. Tiruchy, Tamilnadu, India, Jan. 20, 1942; s. Amaladoss and Mariakolandai (Baby) L.; m. Radhi Lawrence, May 7, 1973; 1 child. MBBS, Stanley Med. Coll., Madras, India, 1964, MD, 1972; Diploma in Internal Medicine, Charleston Area Med. Ctr., W.Va., 1977. Diplomate Am. Bd. Internal Medicine. Tutor in physiology Med. Coll., Tanjore, India, 1965; asst. prof., nephrology medicine Madras Med. Coll., 1972-74, asst. prof. medicine, 1980-87; fellow in oncology Hershey (Pa.) Med. Ctr., 1977-79; prof. medicine Chengalpat Med. Coll., Chengalpattu, India, 1987-88; sr. cons., oncology King Fahd Hosp., Al Quassim, Saudi Arabia, 1988-90; sr. cons., oncology Tamilnad Hosp., Madras, 1990—, med. dir., 1990—; hon. prof. internal medicine and oncology Sri Ramachandra Med. Coll., Porur, Madras, India; cons. oncologist Malar Hosp., Madras. Capt. Indian Army, 1964-69. Recipient Gold medal in Medicine, Stanley Med. Coll., India, 1971, fellowship in medicine Am. Coll. Physicians, 1982, fellow in oncology Hershey Med. Ctr., 1979. Fellow Am. Coll. Physicians; mem. Am. Soc. Clin. Oncology, Assn. of Physicians of India. Avocation: music. Home: 12 IV Main Rd Kamarajnagar, 600041 Madras/Tamilnadu India Office: Tamilnad Hosp, Perumbakkam, 601302 Madras/Tamilnadu India

LAWRENCE, BRUCE CASSELS, composer, artist, music educator; b. Sydney, Australia, Aug. 2, 1932; s. George Feather and Dorothy Agnes (Higgins) L.; m. Denise McGarvie, Jan. 14, 1963; children: Adrian, Julian. Assoc. in music, Sydney Conservatorium, 1958; Licentiate, Trinity Coll., London, 1966. Viola player Tasmanian Symphony Orch., Australia, 1958-59; tchr. Dept. Edn., Sydney, 1960-65; dep. headmaster Aylesbury Music Sch., Buckinghamshire, Eng., 1968-74; examiner Australian Music Exam. Bd., Sydney, 1987—; composer, artist, performing musician, throughout career. Various solo exhbns. painting, Australia; editor: Viola Technique,, 1993; composer: Violin Sight Reading, 1996, (choral music) Salvator Mundi, 1969 (commnd. Arts Coun. Great Britain); compositions include extnsive orchestral, choral, chamber and other instrumental music and songs, and much music for tchg. purposes. Fellow Trinity Coll. London, 1974. Avocations: reading, bushwalking. Home: 38 Bangalla St Warrawee, Sydney NSW 2074, Australia

LAWRENCE, CHARLES EDWARD, JR., lawyer, judge; b. Beaumont, Miss., July 29, 1955; s. Charles Edward and Mattie Mae Lawrence; m. Shirley A. Sutton, June 5, 1977; children: Charles E. III (CJ), Chari E. B, U. So. Miss., 1976; JD, Howard U., 1979. Bar: Miss. 1979. Pvt. practice atty., counselor at law Hattiesburg, Miss., 1979—; mcpl. ct. judge City of Hattiesburg, 1997—; Bd. dirs. BancorpSouth Cmty. Adv. Coun. Contbg. columnist, 1983-85. V.p. Forrest County br. NAACP, Hattiesburg, 1980; councilmember City of Hattiesburg, 1985-97; pres. Hattiesburg City Coun., 1991-97; bd. dirs. Wesley Med. Ctr. Meth. Hosp., Hattiesburg, 1995-97, United Way, Hattiesburg, 1997—. Recipient Svc. award Optimist International, 1986, New Medinah Islamic Retreat, 1996. Mem. ATLA, Miss. Bar Assn., Miss. Mcpl. Judge Assn., Magnolia Bar Assn. (so. dist. rep. 1986-87). Baptist. Avocations: camping, reading, bike riding, photography. Fax: 601-544-9279. Home: 606 John St Hattiesburg MS 39401-3948 Office: 606 1/2 John St Hattiesburg MS 39401-3966

LAWRENCE, CHRISTOPHER JOHN, historian; b. Birmingham, Eng., July 2, 1947; s. Leslie and Nora May (Wilkins) L.; m. Sarah Wolpe, Jan. 1969 (div. 1977); children: Victoria Frances, Samuel Brighton; m. Ghislaine Mary Skinner, Dec. 1986 9div. 2000); children: May Elizabeth, Arthur Frederick. MB ChB, U. Birmingham, 1970; MSc, Imperial Coll., London, 1974; PhD, Univ. Coll., London, 1984. Gen. practitioner Shetland Isles, 1971-72; lectr. Wellcome Inst., London, 1974-94, reader, 1994-99, prof., 1999—. Author: (books) Photographing Medicine, 1988, Medicine in the Making of Modern Britain, 1994. Avocation: resting. Office: Wellcome Inst, 183 Euston Rd, London NW1 2BE, England

LAWRENCE, CHRISTOPHER ROBERT, physicist, researcher; b. Redhill, Surrey, Eng., Feb. 1, 1967; s. Robert Charles and Phyllis Audrey Ivy (Duggins) L.; m. Alexandra Elizabeth Haywood. BSc with honors in Physics, U. Exeter, Eng., 1988, PhD in Physics, 1992. Computer programmer SD-Scicon, Milton Keynes, 1988-89; postdoctoral rschr. Exeter U., 1992-96; prin. scientist DERA, Farnborough, 1996—; cons. physicist CSIRO, Melbourne, Australia, 1993. Contbr. articles to profl. jours., chpts. to books; patentee in field. U.K. MOD Corp. Rsch. fellow, 1998—. Mem. Inst. of Physics. Avocations: squash, cycling, cinema. Office: DERA, Rm 1146 Bldg A7, Farnborough GU14 0LX, England

LAWRENCE, DAVID LONG, radiologist; b. Jamestown, Ky.; s. Marshall Marvin Lawrence and Opal Hilden Long; m. Jeanette Wesley, Jan. 30, 1954 (div. 1990); 1 child, Julia L.; m. Sandra B. Hubbard, Feb. 14, 1992. AB, Centre Coll., Danville, Ky., 1955; MS, U. Ky., 1958; MD, U. Louisville, 1962. Diplomate Am. Bd. Radiology, Nat. Bd. Med. Examiners. Radiologist, v.p. Springfield (Ohio) Radiology, 1971-96; locum tenens cons. Global Med. Staffing, Salt Lake City, 1995—, Vista Med. Staffing, Salt Lake City, 1997—; med. staff Mercy Med. Ctr.; chmn. bd. Missionary Health Svc., 1991. Lt. comdr., USNR, 1966-68. Mem. Am. Coll. Radiology, Clark County Med. Soc. (pres. 1983), Ohio State Med. Assn. (alternate del.). Episcopalian. Avocations: fly fishing, cosmology, mind/brain interface, etymology. E-mail: sandavid@msn.com.

LAWRENCE, JOANNA CLAIR, editor, proofreader; b. Bishops Stortford, Eng., Apr. 1, 1967; d. Peter John and Jane Elizabeth (Seymour) L. BS with honors, U. London, 1989, MPhil, 1993. Clerical asst. Med. Rsch. Coun., Cambridge, Eng., 1985-86; edtl. asst. Plenum Pub. Co., London, 1993-94, commissioning editor, 1994-98; pub. editor Kluwer Acad./Plenum Pubs., London, 1998—; proofreader Chapman and Hall, London, 1996. Office: Kluwer Acad/Plenum Pub Ltd, 101 Back Church Ln, London E1 1LU, England

LAWRENCE, (ROBERT) JOHN, social work educator, consultant; b. Mt. Gambier, South Australia, Australia, Apr. 24, 1931; s. Robert Gribbon and Lucy Evelyn (Butlin) L.; m. Patricia Dean Berry, Aug. 25, 1956; children: David John Lawrence, Peter Michael Lawrence, Ruth Margaret Lawrence Karski. BA (hons.), Dip.Soc.Sci., U. Adelaide, Australia, 1953; BA, Oxford U., Eng., 1956, MA, 1961; PhD, Australian Nat. U., Canberra, 1963. Social worker Commonwealth Dept. Social Svcs., Adelaide, Australia, 1956-58; lectr., sr. lectr. Dept. Social Work U. Sydney, Australia, 1961-68; prof. social work U. New South Wales, Sydney, Australia, 1968-91, head of sch., 1968-82, prof. emeritus, 1991—; vis. lectr. Mich. U., Ann Arbor, 1967; chmn. Faculty Profl. Studies, U. New South Wales, Sydney, 1971-73, 80-81, mem. U. Coun., 1979-81, presiding mem. Social Policy Rsch. Ctr., mgmt. bd., 1990-96; vis. prof. Dept. Social Adminstrn. and Social Work, U. York, Eng., 1974, Sch. Social Work, Rutgers U., New Brunswick, N.J., 1983, Sch. Applied Social Scis., Case Western Reserve U., Cleve., 1983, Sch. Social Work, U. Stockholm, 1990; IASSW rep. UN, New York, 1987, 88. Author: Professional Social Work in Australia, 1965, (govt. report) Responsibility for Service in Child Abuse and Child Protection, 1983, Argument for Action: Ethics and Professional Conduct, 1999; editor: Community Service: Citizens and Social Welfare Organizations, 1966; compiler, editor: Norma Parker's Record of Service, 1969. Mem. Coun. of Aboriginal Legal Svc., Sydney, 1970-74; elected mem. governing bd. Australian Coun. Social Svc., Sydney, 1973-77, v.p. 1976-77; bd. dirs. Benevolent Soc. of New South Wales, Sydney, 1977-86. Recipient Fulbright Sr. award Australian-Am. Ednl. Found., 1967, 83, Moses Disting. Prof. award Hunter Coll., CUNY, 1987-88; Can. Commonwealth fellow Wilfrid Laurier U., Can., 1990; Rhodes scholar Oxford U., 1954. Mem. Internat. Assn. Schs. of Social Work (mem. exec. bd. 1974-82), Internat. Social Svc. Australia (coun. mem. Australian chpt. 1986-95), Australian Assn. Social Workers (life, fed. pres., 1968-70), Order of Australia. Achievements include first professor of social work in Australia, being responsible for first child abuse inquiry in Australia. Avocations: organ playing, gardening.

LAWRENCE, JOHN KIDDER, lawyer; b. Detroit, Nov. 18, 1949; s. Luther Ernest and Mary Anna (Kidder) L.; m. Jeanine Ann DeLay, June 20, 1981. AB, U. Mich., 1971; JD, Harvard U., 1974. Bar: Mich. 1974, U.S. Supreme Ct. 1977, D.C. 1978. Assoc. Dickinson, Wright, McKean & Cudlip, Detroit, 1973-74; staff atty. Office of Judge Adv. Gen., Washington, 1975-78; assoc. Dickinson, Wright, McKean, Cudlip & Moon, Detroit, 1978-81; ptnr. Dickinson, Wright, Moon, VanDusen & Freeman, Detroit, 1981-98, Dickinson Wright PLLC, Detroit, 1998—. Exec. sec. Detroit Com. on Fgn. Rels., 1988—; trustee Ann Arbor (Mich.) Summer Festival, Inc., 1990—; patron Founders Soc. Detroit Inst. Arts, 1979—. With USN, 1975-78. Mem. AAAS, ABA, Am. Law Inst., State Bar Mich., D.C. Bar Assn., Am. Judicature Soc., Internat. Bar Assn., Am. Hist. Assn., Detroit Athletic Club, Econ. Club Detroit, Phi Eta Sigma, Phi Beta Kappa. Democrat. Episcopalian. Office: Dickinson Wright PLLC 500 Woodward Ave Ste 4000 Detroit MI 48226-3416

LAWRENCE, JONATHAN, mechanical engineering researcher, consultant; b. Stockport, Manchester, Eng., Jan. 8, 1970; s. Dorothy (Bullock) L. B Engring., U. Bradford, Eng., 1994; PhD, U. Manchester, 1999. Turner Brooks Andell, Stockport, 1986-91; instrumentation engr. Smurfit, Burnley, Eng., 1992-93; project engr. Brit. Timken, Northampton, Eng., 1995; rsch. assoc. Inst. Sci. and Tech., U. Manchester, 1999—. Contbr. articles to profl. jours., including Materials Sci. and Engring., Jour. Physics. Internat. travel grantee Royal Acad. Engring., 1999. Mem. Instn. Mech. Engrs. (assoc.). Achievements include patents in field. Avocations: sports, travel. Office: U Manchester Inst Sci-Tech, PO Box 88, Sackville St, Manchester M60 1QD, England

LAWRENCE, MARILYN EDITH (GUTHRIE), association executive; b. Auburn, N.Y., Oct. 5, 1946; d. George Nelson and Marjorie Estelle (Field) G.; AAS, SUNY, Morrisville, 1966. Various secretarial positions, 1966-75; exec. asst. Northeastern Retail Lumbermens Assn., Rochester, N.Y., 1975-79, sr. v.p., Wellesley, Mass. and Rochester, 1979-86; placement specialist Renda Personnel Cons., Rochester, N.Y., 1986-89; exec. dir. Oil Heat Inst. Upstate N.Y., Rochester, 1989-92; owner Profl. Bus. Svcs., Newark, N.Y., 1992-94; program dir. Assn. Mgmt. Svc., Rochester, 1992-94; exec. dir. Internat. Mcpl. Signal Assn., 1994-95, Newark, N.Y., exec. dir., 1995—. Mem. Am. Soc. Assn. Execs. Republican.

LAWRENCE, RICHARD DEAN, lawyer; b. Jefferson City, Mo., Sept. 20, 1944; s. Charles Eugene and Edith Lucille (Moore) L.; m. Diana H. McIntyre, Aug. 13, 1967; children: Jennifer, Daniel, Michael, David, Lindsay. AA, U. Cin., 1964, BA, 1967; JD with honors, J.D. Chase Coll. Law, 1971. Bar: Ohio 1971, Ky., 1989, U.S. Dist. Ct. Ohio, U.S. Ct. Appeals. Founder, ptnr., pres. Gustin & Lawrence, 1971—; ptnr., pres. Lawrence, Linder & McGrath, Cin., 1991—; guest lectr. Chase Coll. Law, 1983-87, Ohio Trial Practice Inst., Cin., 1975-77; speaker med. malpractice Ohio Acad. Trial lawyers, Cin. Bar Assn., Ky. Bar Assn. Pres. Washington Hills Assn., Cin., 1977-78; bd. dirs. Hamilton Mut. Ins. Co.; past deacon Pleasant Ridge Presbyn. Ch.; past mem. adminstrv. bd. United Meth. Ch. of Milford. Mem. ABA, Ohio Bar Assn., Cin. Bar Assn., Assn. Trial Lawyers Am., Ky. Bar Assn., No. Ky. Bar Assn., Hamilton County Trial Lawyers Assn., Ohio Acad. Trial Lawyers, Ky. Acad. Trial Attys. Office: Plz Level Ste 120 50 E Rivercenter Blvd Covington KY 41011-1683

LAWRENCE, ROBERT SWAN, physician, educator, academic administrator; b. Phila., Feb. 6, 1938; s. Thomas George and Catherine (Swan) L.; m. Cynthia Starr Cole, July 1, 1960; children: Job Scott, Matthew Swan, Hannah Starr, Jin Sook, Sang Bo. AB magna cum laude, Harvard U., 1960, MD, 1964. Intern, resident in internal medicine Mass. Gen. Hosp., 1964-66, 69-70; surgeon USPHS, 1966-69; asst. prof., then assoc. prof. medicine, chief div. community medicine Med. Sch. U. N.C., 1970-74; dir. divsn. primary care Harvard U. Med. Sch., 1974-91, assoc. prof. medicine, 1980-81, Charles S. Davidson assoc. prof. medicine, 1981-91; chmn. dept. medicine Cambridge

(Mass.) Hosp., 1980-91; adj. prof. NYU Sch. of Medicine, 1992-95; prof. health policy and mgmt. Johns Hopkins Sch. Hygiene and Pub. Health, 1995—, assoc. dean for profl. edn., 1995—, Edyth Schoenrich prof. preventive medicine, 2000—; prof. medicine Johns Hopkins Sch. Medicine, 1996—; mem. com. human rights NAS, 1986-97; chmn. bd. health promotion and disease prevention IOM, 1981-86, chmn. com. health and human rights, 1990-94; chmn. U.S. Preventive Svc. Task Force, HHS, 1984-89, active mem., 1990-96; fellow Ctr. for Advanced Study in Behavioral Scis., 1988-89; dir. health scis. Rockefeller Found., 1991-95. Editor Am. Jour. Preventive Medicine, 1990-92; contbr. articles and chpts. in books. Bd. dirs. Physicians for Human Rights, 1986-91, 97—, pres., 1999—; bd. trustees Tchrs. Coll., Columbia U., 1992-98. Recipient Maimonides prize, 1964, John Atkinson Ferrell prize, 1997. Fellow Am. Coll. Preventive Medicine (Spl. Recognition award 1988); mem. ACP (master), Inst. Medicine, Am. Pub. Health Assn., Soc. Gen. Internal Medicine (pres. 1978-79, Leadership award 1997), Soc. Tchrs. Preventive Medicine (Spl. Recognition award 1993), Phi Beta Kappa, Delta Omega. Home: Highfield House 1112 4000 N Charles St Baltimore MD 21218-1760 Office: Johns Hopkins Sch Hygiene and Pub Health 615 N Wolfe St Baltimore MD 21205-2103

LAWRENCE, RODERICK JOHN, architect, social science educator, researcher, consultant; b. Adelaide, Australia, Aug. 30, 1949; s. Keith and Babette Naomi (Radford) L.; m. Clarisse Christine Gonet, Sept. 30, 1977; children: Xavier Gerard, Adrien Keith, Kevin John. BS with first class hons., Adelaide U., Australia, 1972; MS, Cambridge U., Eng., 1977; PhD, Ecole Poly., Lausanne, Switzerland, 1983. Architect Edwards, Madigan and Torzillo, Sydney, Australia, 1972-74, S. Australian Housing Trust, Adelaide, 1973-76; rsch. scholar St. John's Coll., Cambridge U., Eng., 1975-77; asst. prof. Ecole Poly. Fed., Lausanne, Switzerland, 1978-84; cons. Econ. Commn. Europe, Geneva, 1984—; master tchr. and rschr. U. Geneva, 1984-99, prof. Faculty of Social and Econ. Scis., 1999—; vis. prof. U. Que., Montreal, Can., 1987; vis. fellow Flinders U., Adelaide, 1985; mem. editorial bd. Open House Internat., 1986, Netherlands Jour.; mem sci. adv. bd. on health and environ., WHO, 1994—; cons. Urban Affairs divsn., Environment Directorate, OECD, Paris, 1992—; speaker, guest lectr. various European and Australian univs. Author: Le Seuil Franchi..., 1986, Housing, Dwellings, and Homes, 1987, Better Understanding Our Cities: The Role of Urban Indicators, 1997 ; contbr. articles to profl. jours. and chpts. to books; mem. editl. bd. Architecture and Behavior, 1980, Open House Internat., 1986, Netherlands Jour. of ; guest editor to jours. Nat. Sci Found. Switzerland fellow, 1984. Mem. Internat. Assn. Study of People and their Phys. Surroundings (bd. dirs. 1986—, exec. bd. 1994—, treas. 1994—), Environ. Design Rsch. Assn., People and Phys. Environ. Rsch. Soc., Open House Internat. Assn., Internat. Sociological Assn. (regional editor for newsletter 1988—). Avocations: photography, bushwalking, skiing. Office: Univ of Geneva, 102 Blvd Carl Vogt, 1211 Geneva 4, Switzerland

LAWRENCE, SANFORD HULL, physician, immunochemist; b. Kokomo, Ind., July 10, 1919; s. Walter Scott and Florence Elizabeth (Hull) L. AB, Ind. U., 1941, MD, 1944. Fellow in biochemistry George Washington U., 1941; intern Rochester (N.Y.) Gen. Hosp., 1944-45; resident Halloran Hosp., Staten Island, N.Y., 1946-49; chief med. svce. Ft. Ord Regl. Hosp., 1945-46; dir. biochemistry rsch. lab. San Fernando (Calif.) VA Hosp.; asst. prof. UCLA, 1950—; cons. internal medicine and cardiology U.S. Govt., Los Angeles County; lectr. Faculte de Medicine, Paris, various colls. Eng., France, Belgium, Sweden, USSR, India, Japan; chief med. svc. Ft. Ord Regional Hosp.; chmn. Titus, Inc., 1982—. Author: Zymogram in Clinical Medicine, 1965; contbr. articles to sci. jours.; author: Threshold of Valhalla, Another Way to Fly, My Last Satyr, and other short stories; traveling editor: Relax Mag. Mem. Whitley Heights Civic Assn., 1952—; pres. Halloran Hosp. Employees Assn., 1947-48. Served to maj. U.S. Army, 1945-46. Recipient Rsch. award TB and Health Assn., 1955-58, Los Angeles County Heart Assn., 1957-59, Pres. award, Queen's Blue Book award, Am. Men of Sci. award; named one of 2000 Men of Achievement, Leaders of Am. Sci., Ky. Col., named Hon. Mayor of West Point, Ky. Mem. AAAS, AMA, N.Y. Acad. Scis., Am. Fedn. Clin. Research, Am. Assn. Clin. Investigation, Am. Assn. Clin. Pathology, Am. Assn. Clin. Chemistry, Los Angeles County Med. Assn. Republican. Methodist. Avocations: bridge, comml. pilot, pianist, organist. Home: Whitley Heights 2014 Whitley Ave Los Angeles CA 90068-3235 also: 160 rue St Martin, 75003 Paris France

LAWRENCE, WILLIAM CLARENCE, business executive, lawyer; b. Tuskegee, Ala., Dec. 15, 1945; s. James Clarence and Nellie Mae James Lawrence; m. Audrey Rochelle Diggs Rackley, Dec. 30, 1973 (div. Sept. 1979); 1 child, Kimberly Ann; m. Grace Louise McDonald, June 23, 1984; children: Antoinette, Robert David. BS in Polit. Sci., Tuskegee U., 1968; M in Pub. Adminstrn., St. Mary's U., 1976; JD, Ind. U., 1979; M in Mgmt., U. Dallas, 1993. Tax atty. audit divsn. U.S. Treasury Dept., Indpls., 1979-80; commodities mgr. Cummins Engine Co., Columbus, Ind., 1980-82; staff mgr. GTE Network Svcs. Planning, Stamford, Conn., 1982-86; product mgr.-consumer GTE Product Mgmt., Irving, Tex., 1986-89, group product mgr.-wireless, 1989-92; group product mgr.-devel. GTE Product Mgmt., Irving, 1992-96; group mktg. mgr.-systems GTE Bus. Sales Ops., Irving, 1996-99; pres., CEO Dakiman Co., Highland Village, Tex., 1999—; chmn., bd. dirs. GTE Hdqrs. PAC, Irving, 1995-98. Pres., bd. dirs. Boston Home Childrens Found., Dallas, 1988-93; commr. Planning and Zoning Comm., Highland Village, 1996-99; chmn. Irving Sch. Dist. Improvement Com., 1998—; mem. Tex. State Textbook Rev. Adv. Panel, 2000; city coun. and mayor pro tem Highland Village, 1999-2000; mayor City of Highland Village, 2000-02. Col. USAF Res., 1976—. Mem. ABA (assoc., alternate disputes resolution sect.), New Product Devel. Assn., Project Mgmt. Inst., Alpha Phi Alpha, Phi Alpha Delta. Republican. Baptist. Avocations: golf, racquetball, volleyball. Home: 2800 Woodlake Ct Highland Village TX 75077-6496

LAWRENCE-COX, NANCY NELL, executive secretary, artist; b. Columbus, Miss., Mar. 4, 1934; d. James Edward and Elizabeth Caplinger (Land) Lawrence. BFA, U. Ark., Little Rock, 1983, postgrad., 1983-84. Office boy Miss. State Hwy. Dept., Columbus, 1952-53; clk.-typist FBI, Washington, 1953-54; sec.-automation Little Rock AFB, Ark., 1984—. Exhibited sculptures at U. Ark., 1982 (Best of Show 1981-82), Centre International D'Art Contemporain, 1984, photography at Les Editions Arts et Images du Monde, 1990, Who's Who Internat. Art, Lausanne, Switzerland, 1993. Civic vol. Yes We Can Team 314th Supply Squadron Care Team, 1989-94. Recipient Cert. of Recognition, Jacksonville C. of C., 1991, other awards. Office: 314th Med Support Squadron 1090 Arnold Dr Little Rock AFB AR 72099-4933

LAWRENSON, PETER JOHN, electrical engineer, educator, entrepreneur; b. Prescot, Lancs, Eng., Mar. 12, 1933; s. John and Emily (Houghton) L.; m. Shirley Hannah Foster, 1958; 4 children. BSc, U. Manchester, Eng., 1954, MSc, 1956, DSc, 1971. Registered profl. engr. Rsch. engr. Associated Elec. Industries, Manchester, 1956-61; lectr. U. Leeds, 1961-66, prof., 1966-91, chmn., 1974-84; founder, chmn. Switched Reluctance Drives Ltd., Harrogate, 1980-97, non-exec. dir., 1997—; pres. Instn. Elec. Engrs., 1992-93. Author: Analysis and Computation of Electromagnetic Field Problems, 1993, 95, and others; contbr. over 120 articles to profl. jours.; patentee in field. Recipient James Alfred Ewing Gold medal Instn. Civil Engrs., 1983. Fellow IEEE, Instn. Elec. Engrs. (Faraday medal 1990, others), Royal Acad. Engring., Royal Soc. (Esso Energy Gold medal 1985). Avocations: tennis, chess, bridge, walking, jewelry design. Office: Switched Reluctances Drives Ltd, East Park House Otley Rd, Harrogate HG3 1PR, England

LAWS, GORDON DERBY, lawyer; b. Dallas, Feb. 1, 1949; s. Wilford Derby and Ruby (Whiteleather) L.; m. Barbara Ruth Hill, May 9, 1974; children: Gordon Derby Jr., Stephen Richard, Ruthanne. BA in Econs., Brigham Young U., 1973, JD, 1976. Bar: Utah 1976, Tex. 1986, U.S. Supreme Ct. 1981, U.S. Ct. Appeals (5th cir.) 1982, U.S. Dist. Ct. (we. dist.) Tex. 1987, U.S. Dist. Ct. (so. dist.) Tex. 1991. Trial atty. U.S. Justice Dept., Washington, 1976-81; asst. U.S. atty. Western Dist. Tex., San Antonio, 1981-87, asst. chief, civil divsn., U.S. atty., 1985-87; assoc. Gary, Thomasson, Hall & Marks, Corpus Christi, Tex., 1987-89; ptnr./mem. Gary, Thomasson, Hall & Marks, 1989—; mem. exec. com. Gary, Thomasson, Hall & Marks,1994—. Bishop Ch. of Jesus Christ of Latter Day Saints, Corpus Christi, 1990-95. Avocations: reading, camping. Home: 4158 Eagle Dr Corpus Christi TX 78413-2024 Office: Gary Thomasson Hall & Marks 210 Carancahua Ste 500 PO Box 2888 Corpus Christi TX 78403-2888

LAWS, RICHARD MAITLAND, biology educator, scientist, government agency director; b. Whitley Bay, U.K., Apr. 23, 1926; s. Percy Malcolm and Florence May (Heslop) Laws; m. Maureen Isobel Holmes, June 7, 1954; children: Richard Anthony, Christopher Peter, Andrew David. BA, MA, PhD, ScD, Cambridge U.; DSc (hon.), Bath U. Prin. sci. officer Nat. Inst. Oceanography, Godalming, 1954-61; dir. Nuffield Unit of Tropical Animal Ecology, Uganda, 1961-67, Tsavo Rsch. Project, Kenya, 1967-68; head life scis. divsn. Brit. Antarctic Survey, Natural Environ. Rsch. Coun., Cambridge, 1969-73, dir., 1973-87, dir. Sea Mammal Rsch. Unit, 1977-87; master St. Edmund's Coll., Cambridge, 1985-96. Author: Antarctica: The Last Frontier, 1980; co-author: Elephants and Their Habitats, 1975; editor: Scientific Rsch. in Antarctica, 1977, Life at Low Temperature, 1990, Antarctic Ecology, 1984, Antarctic Nutrient Cycles and Food Webs, 1985, Antarctica and Environmental Change, 1991, Antarctic Seals, 1993, Elephant Seals: Aspects of Population Ecology, Behavior and Physiology, 1994. CBE, Her Majesty The Queen, 1983; recipient Bruce medal Royal Soc. Edinburgh, 1954, Sci. medal Zool. Soc. London, 1965, Polar medal Her Majesty The Queen, 1976. Fellow Royal Soc., Norwegian Acad. Sci. (fgn. mem.), Inst. Biology (v.p. 1973, pres. sci. com. Antarctic rsch. 1990-94), Zool. Soc. London (hon., sec. 1984-88); mem. Soc. Marine Mammalogy (hon. mem.), Uganda Nat. Parks (hon., warden), Brit. Ecol. Soc., Mammal Soc., Am. Soc. Mammalogy. Home: 3 Footpath Coton, Cambridge CB3 7PX, England

LAWSON, ABRAHAM ODARTEY, accountant; b. Accra, Ghana, Aug. 23, 1947; s. Gathrol Lante Lawson and Abigail Ameley Hammond; m. Evelyn Norkor Nortey, Mar. 4, 1978 (div. Oct. 1987); children: Ellis Nii Lante, Prince Nathan Lanquaye; m. Mary Henerietta Myers, Apr. 2, 1998; children: Sydney Nii Lante, Jeffrey Ataa Lante. Diploma in acctg., U. Ghana, Legon, Accra, 1975. Clerical officer IRS, Accra, 1970-73, Jr. tax officer, 1973-75, tax officer, 1975-78; accounts officer Ghana Airways Corp., Accra, 1978-80, sr. accounts officer, 1980-82, asst. acct., 1982-84, acct., 1984—; dist. acct. Ghana Airways Corp., Lagos Sta., 1993-99. Anglican. Clubs: Accra Hearts of Oak (auditor 1977), Football Supporters. Avocations: table tennis, soccer, reading, listening to radio. Office: Ghana Airways Corp, Ghana House, Accra Ghana

LAWSON, BEN F., lawyer, international legal consultant; b. Marietta, Okla., Feb. 7, 1939; s. Woodrow W. and Lennie L. (McKay) L.; m. Diane W. Lawson; children: Nicole, Michael C. BBA, U. Houston, 1965, JD, 1967. Bar: Tex. 1967. Atty. Monsanto/Burmah Oil, Houston, 1967-72; mgr. internat. acquisitions Oxy (formerly Cities Svc. Co.), Houston, 1972-78; gen. atty. Damson Oil Corp., Houston, 1978-81; gen. counsel, v.p. Newmont Oil Co., Houston, 1981-86; pvt. practice internat. law Houston, 1986—; cons. internat., 1987—. Contbr. numerous articles to profl. jours. Staff sgt. USAF, 1959-65. Fellow Houston Bar Found.; mem. ABA, Am. Corp. Counsel Assn. (chmn. oil and gas com. 1986-87). Republican. Avocations: fishing, antiques. Address: 3027 Bernadette Ln Houston TX 77043-1302

LAWSON, CAROLE JEAN, religious educator, author, poet; b. San Antonio, June 18, 1944; d. Albert Joseph and Pearl Nettie (Garner) Fuller; m. James Ray Lawson, Sept. 7, 1962; children: Regina Anne (Lawson) Kacho, Clinton Ray. Founder Love Makes the World Go Around in Peace, Ft. Worth, Tex., 1988—; founder, dir. Healing Thru Love Seminars, Ft. Worth, Tex., 1988—; founder Sunshine 'n Rainbows Stress Overcomers, Ft. Worth, 1985-87; founder, head Omni-Vision Pub. and Prodns., Ft. Worth, 1990-93. Pub. editor Omni Vision newsletter, 1985-93; author: To God Be the Glory, poetry collection, 1988-90, My Rocky Mountain High, 1989, The Reflection of God's Smile, 1991. Sec. Lightly Speaking Forum, Ft. Worth, 1987-89; supporter of publicity Campaign for the Earth, 1990-91; founder, pres. Universal World Investments, Omni Vision Ministries, 1993-99. Named Honorary Mayan Centurian. Mem. Internat. Platform Assn. Home and Office: RR 1 Box 199K Whitney TX 76692-9722

LAWSON, GERALD WILBUR, health facility administrator; b. Brunswick, Md., July 4, 1942; s. Harry Clarkson and Pauline Lawson; m. Becky Ann Pounds, Oct. 26, 1985; children: Darwyn, Sherry Hudson, Holly Jo. Grad. H.S., Frederick, Md., car. Animal caretaker NIH, Bethesda, Md., 1964-65; carpenter NIH, Bethesda, 1965-70, cabinet maker, 1970-73, maintenance inspector, 1973-82, contract inspector, 1982-86, project officer, 1986-93, spl. projects mgr., 1993—; owner home improvement co., Frederick, 1964-78. Pres. Home Owner Assn., Germantown, Md., 1984. Mem. Train Collector's Assn., Elks. Avocation: large scale model railroading. E-mail: lawsong@ors.od.nih.gov. Office: Divsn Space & Facility Mgmt 6120 Executive Blvd Ste 200 Rockville MD 20852-4909

LAWSON, HAROLD WILBUR, computer engineering company executive, consultant; b. Phila., Dec. 13, 1937; s. Harold and Thelma Catherine (Bushey) L.; m. Clara Eleanor Rex, Nov., 1959; 1 child, Catherine Louise; m. Annika Margareta Johansson, Apr., 1987; children: Per Adrian Julius, Jasmine Maria Rebecca. BS, Temple U., 1959; PhD, Royal Tech. U., Stockholm, 1983. Programmer Remington Rand Univac, Phila., 1959-61; mgr. advanced tech. IBM Corp., N.Y.C., 1961-67; prof. computer sci. Poly. Inst. Bklyn., 1967-72; dir. programming rsch. Std. Computer Corp., Costa Mesa, Calif., 1969-70; prof. computer sci. Linkoping (Sweden) U., 1973-88; CEO Lawson Konsult AB, Lidingö, Sweden, 1988—; guest prof. U. Malaya, Kuala Lumpur, 1984, Poly. Barcelona, Spain, 1975-76, Keio U., Yokohama, Japan, 1984, U. Calif., Irvine, 1969-70; prof. computer sci. IBM Belgium, Free U. Brussels, Belgium NSF, Brussels, 1982; chmn. adv. bd. elec. and computers, Incentive AB, Stockholm, 1981-86; head Swedish del. ISO/IEC JTC1 SC7 WG7, 1996—; dir. Link Tech., Stockholm, 1997—. Author: The PL/I Machine, 1969, Understanding Computer Systems, 1979, Parallel Processing in Industrial Real-Time Applications, 1992. Recipient Best Paper award IEEE/Assn. Computing Machinery, Houston, 1975. Fellow IEEE (Disting. Visitor 1991), Assn. Computing Machinery (disting. lectr. 1969-71, 1998—); mem. Internat. Coun. on Systems Engring. Avocations: tennis, gardening, coaching youth sports teams, skiing. Office: Lawson Konsult AB, Björnvägen 7, 181 33 Lidingö Sweden

LAWSON, JACK WAYNE, lawyer; b. Decatur, Ind., Sept. 23, 1935; s. Alva W. and Florence C. (Smitley) L.; m. Sarah J. Hibbard, Dec. 28, 1961; children: Mark, Jeff. BA in Polit. Sci., Valparaiso U., 1958, JD, 1961. Bar: Ind. 1961, U.S. Supreme Ct. 1970, U.S. Dist. Ct. (no., so. dists.) Ind. 1991, Ind. Supreme Ct., Appellate Cts. 1991. Ptnr. Beckman, Lawson LLP, Ft. Wayne, Ind., 1961-84; sr. ptnr. Beckman, Lawson LLP, Ft. Wayne, 1984—; seminar presenter and writer Ind. CLE Forum, Indpls., 1970—, Nat. Health Lawyers Assn., Washington, 1986. Editor-in-chief Indiana Real Estate Transactions; contbr. articles to profl. jours. Mem. Ft. Wayne C. of C., 1975—; small claims ct. judge, Allen County, Ind., 1963-67. Mem. Am. Coll. Real Estate Lawyers. Republican. Lutheran. Avocations: sailing, teaching religious seminars, antique consulting. Office: Beckman Lawson LLP 800 Standard Federal Plaza PO Box 800 Fort Wayne IN 46801-0800

LAWSON, JENNIFER, broadcast executive; b. Birmingham, Ala., June 8, 1946; d. Willie DeLeon and Velma Theresa (Foster) L.; m. Elbert Sampson, June 1, 1979 (div. Sept. 1980); m. Anthony Gittens, May 29, 1982; children: Kai, Zachary. Student, Tuskegee U., 1963-65; MFA, Columbia U., 1974; LHD (hon.), Teikyo Post U., Hartford, Conn., 1991. Assoc. producer William Greaves Prodns., N.Y.C., 1974-75; asst. prof. film studies Bklyn. Coll., 1975-77; exec. dir. The Film Fund, N.Y.C., 1977-80; TV coord. Program Fund Corp. for Pub. Broadcasting, Washington, 1980-83, assoc. dir. TV Program Fund, 1983-89, dir. TV Program Fund, 1989; exec. v.p. programming PBS, Alexandria, Va., 1989-95; broadcast cons. Md. Pub. TV, 1995—, exec. cons., 1996-98, exec. prodr., 1998—; v.p. Internat. Pub. TV, Washington, 1984-88; panelist Fulbright Fellowships, Washington, 1988-90. Author, illustrator: Children of Africa, 1970; illustrator: Our Folktales, 1968, African Folktales: A Calabash of Wisdom, 1973. Coord. Nat. Coun. Negro Women, Washington, 1969. Avocations: painting, reading. Office: 1838 Ontario Pl NW Washington DC 20009-2109

LAWSON, JONATHAN NEVIN, university official; b. Latrobe, Pa., Mar. 27, 1941; s. Lawrence Winters and Mary Eleanor (Rhea) L.; m. Leigh Farley (div.); children: Paul, Joshua, Jacob; m. Pamela Cross. AA, York Coll. Pa., 1962; BFA, Tex. Christian U., 1964, MA, 1966, PhD, 1970. Dir. composition St. Cloud (Minn.) State U., 1971-77, assoc. dean, 1977-81; asst. vice chancellor Minn. State U. System, St. Paul, 1980-81; dean liberal arts Winona (Minn.) State U., 1981-84; dean arts and scis. U. Hartford, West Hartford, Conn., 1984-86; sr. v.p., dean of faculty U. Hartford, 1986-95; v.p. acad. affairs Idaho State U., Pocatello, 1995—. Author: Robert Bloomfield, 1980; editor: Collected Works: Robert Bloomfield, 1971; contbr. articles and papers to scholarly publs; assoc. editor Rhetoric Soc. Quar., St. Cloud, 1974-79. Mem. regional adv. bd. Greater Hartford C.C., 1992-94; trustee Hartford Coll. for Women, 1992-94; mem. acad. affairs com. Idaho Bd. Edn., 1995—; bd. dirs. Bannock County Devel. Corp., 1998—. Mem. Am. Coun. Edn., Coun. Fellows Alumni, Coun. Liberal Learning, Assn. Gen. and Liberal Studies, Assn. Am. Colls., N.E. Assn. Schs. and Colls. (chmn. commn. on instns. higher edn. 1992-95), Asian Studies Consortium (chmn. bd. 1991-94), Pocatello C. of C. (bd. dirs.), Lambda Iota Tau (hon.), Alpha Chi (hon.). Episcopalian. Avocations: fishing, camping, writing, walking. Home: 1401 Juniper Hill Rd Pocatello ID 83204-4921 Office: Idaho State U PO Box 8063 Pocatello ID 83209-0001

LAWSON, SUSAN COLEMAN, lawyer; b. Covington, Ky., Dec. 4, 1949; d. John Clifford and Louise Carter Coleman; m. William Henry Lawson, June 6, 1980; 1 child, Philip. BA, U. Ky., 1971, JD, 1979. Bar: Ky. 1979. Ptnr. Lawson & Lawson, P.S.C., Harlan, 1995—; atty. Stoll, Keenon & Park, Lexington, Ky., 1979-80; atty., Harbert Constrn. Co., Middlesboro, Ky., 1980-81; ptnr. Buttermore, Turner, Lawson & Boggs, P.S.C., Harlan, Ky., 1981-94. Mem. ABA, Ky. Bar Assn., Harlan County Bar Assn. (pres. 1983), Order of Coif. Democrat. Avocation: golf. Fax: 606-573-4992. Home: 511 W Kentucky Ave Pineville KY 40977-1307

LAWSON, THOMAS CHENEY, fraud examiner; b. Pasadena, Calif., Sept. 21, 1955; s. William McDonald and Joan Bell (Jaffe) L.; m. Susan Sullivan; children: Chri stopher, Brittany, Courtney. Student, Calif. State U., Sacramento, 1973-77. Cert. internat. investigator, fraud examiner. Pres. Tomatron Co., Pasadena, 1970-88, Tom's Tune Up & Detail, Pasadena, 1971-88, Tom's Pool Svc., Sacramento, 1975-78, Tomsupply Co., 1975—; mgmt. trainee Permoid Process Co., L.A., 1970-75; prof. automechanics Calif. State U., Sacramento, 1973-75; regional sales cons. Hoover Co., Burlingame, 1974-76; mktg. exec. River City Prodns., Sacramento, 1977-78; territorial rep. Globe div. Burlington House Furniture Co., 1978; So. Calif. territorial rep. Marge Carson Furniture, Inc., 1978-80; pres. Ted L. Gunderson & Assos., Inc., Westwood, Calif., 1980-81; pres., CEO Apscreen, Newport Beach, Calif., 1980—; founder Creditbase Co., Newport Beach, Calif., 1980-89, Worldata Corp., Newport Beach, 1980-89, Trademark Enforcement Corp., L.A., 1985-86; pres. Carecheck, Inc., Newport Beach, 1990—, CEO Badchex, Inc., Newport Beach, 1992—. Mem. editl. rev. bd. The White Paper. Calif. Rehab. scholar, 1974-77. Mem. Christian Businessmen's Com. Internat., Coun. Internat. Investigators, Am. Soc. Indsl. Security (cert., chmn. Orange County chpt. 1990), Nat. Pub. Records Rsch. Assn., Profls. in Human Resources Assn., World Assn. Detectives, Assn. Cert. Fraud Examiners (editl. rev. bd. 1995—), Soc. Human Resource Mgmt., World Investigators Network. Office: 2043 Westcliff Dr Ste 300 Newport Beach CA 92660-5511

LAWSON, THOMAS SEAY, JR., lawyer; b. Montgomery, Ala., Oct. 30, 1935; s. Thomas Seay and Rose Darrington (Gunter) L.; m. Sarah Hunter Clayton, May 27, 1961; children: Rose Gunter, Gladys Robinson, Thomas Seay III. AB, U. Ala., 1957, LLB, 1963. Bar: Ala. 1963, U.S. Supreme Ct. 1969. Law clk. to chief judge U.S. Dist. Ct. (no. dist.) Ala., 1963-64; assoc. Steiner, Crum & Baker, Montgomery, 1964-68; ptnr. Capell, Howard, Knabe & Cobbs P.A., Montgomery, 1968-98; asst. dist. atty. 15th jud. cir. of Ala., 1969-70; ptnr. Cap ell & Howard, P.C., Montgomery, 1999—; mem. lawyers adv. com. U.S. Ct. Appeals, 5th cir. 1978, 11th cir. 1979-82. Pres. The Lighthouse, 1978-79. Lt. USNR, 1957-60. Fellow Ala. Law Found.; mem. ABA, FBA, Ala. State Bar (pres. young lawyers sect. 1970-71), Montgomery County Bar Assn. (pres. 1980), Am. Judicature Soc., 11th Cir. Hist. Soc. (pres. 1999—), Soc. of Pioneers of Montgomery (pres. 1983), Farrah Law Soc. (pres. 1986-88, Outstanding Alumnus award U. Ala. student chpt. 1989), Montgomery Inn of Ct. (master bencher, bd. dirs. 1989-93, chancellor 1991, pres. 1992-93, emeritus 1994—), Ala. Law Inst. (bd. dirs. 1986—), Ala. Law Sch. Found. (trustee 1985—), Montgomery Country Club. Episcopalian. Home: 1262 Glen Grattan Dr Montgomery AL 36111-1402 Office: Capell & Howard PC PO Box 2069 150 S Perry St Montgomery AL 36102-2069

LAWSON, THOMAS VINCENT, wind engineer; b. Soissons, France, Jan. 22, 1925; s. John Boyd and Mary Alexandra (Chambers) L.; m. Pauline Elizabeth Gaunt, Aug. 6, 1948; children: Alexandra Barbara, Theodore Thomas, Charity Jenny, Oscar Charles, Pandora Pauline, Darcie Tabitha. BSc, U. Leeds, U.K.; Diploma, Imperial Coll., London. Lectr. aeronautical engring. U. Bristol, Eng., 1949-62, sr. lectr., 1962-72, reader in indsl. aerodynamics, 1972-83, sr. rsch. fellow, 1983—; cons. in wind engring. Bristol, 1983—; chmn. wind engring. group Engring. Scis. Data Unit Internat., U.K., 1972—, mem. structural vibration group, 1980-90; mem. wind loading com. Brit. Standards Inst. Author: Wind Effect on Buildings, 2 vols., 1980, Wind Loading Handbook: Guide to the Use of BS6399, Part 2, 1996; mem. editl. bd. Jour. Atmospheric Environment, 1965-90, Jour. Aerodynamics and Wind Engring., 1975—. Fellow Royal Acad. Engring., Royal Aero. Soc. Home: Hamel Green House, Pill Nr Bristol BS20 0HF, England Office: U Bristol, Queens Bldg, Dept Aero Engring, Bristol BS8 1TR, England

LAWSON, WILLIAM, otolaryngologist, educator; b. N.Y.C., Nov. 23, 1934; s. Alexander and Sophia (Elkind) L.; m. Miriam Patkin, Nov. 7, 1965; 1 child, Vanessa Ann. BA, NYU, 1956, DDS, 1961, MD, 1965. Diplomate Am. Bd. Otolaryngology, Am. Bd. Cosmetic Surgery, Am. Bd. Facial Plastic Surgery. Intern Mt. Sinai Hosp., N.Y.C., 1965-66, rsch. fellow in otolaryngology, 1969-70, resident in otolaryngology, 1970-73; resident in gen. surgery Bronx (N.Y.) VA Hosp., 1966-67, chief otolaryngology, head and neck surgery, 1974—; prof. Mt. Sinai Sch. Medicine, N.Y.C., 1980—; vice chmn., 1996—; co-dir. Paranasal Sinus Rsch. Lab.; dir. facial plastic surgery clini Mt. Sinai Hosp., N.Y.C.; cons. Nat. Space Biomed. Rsch. Consortium. Author: Paraganglionic Chemoreceptor Systems, 1982, Surgery of the Paranasal Sinuses, 1988, 2nd edit., 1992, External Ear, 1995; contbr. over 200 articles to med. jours., chpts. to books. Capt. M.C., U.S. Army, 1967-69. Fellow ACS, Am. Acad. Facial Plastic and Reconstructive Surgery (svc. awrd), Am. Soc. Head and Neck Surgery, Am. Soc. Maxillofacial Surgeons, Am. Rhinologic Soc., Otologic and Laryngologic Soc., Am. Laryngol. Soc.; mem. Am. Acad. Otolaryngology (svc. award), Am. Bronchoesophagologic Soc. (included in Best Drs. Am., Best Drs. in N.Y.). Avocations: photography, art history, horology. Office: Mt Sinai Med Ctr 1 Gustave L Levy Pl New York NY 10029-6500

LAWSON, WILLIAM HOGAN, III, electrical motor manufacturing executive; b. Lexington, Ky., Feb. 3, 1937; s. Otto Kirsky and Gladys (McWhorter) L.; div.; children: Elizabeth, Cynthia; m. Ruth Stanat, 1995. BSME, Purdue U., 1959; MBA, Harvard U., 1961. Gen. mgr. svc. divsn. Toledo Scale Corp., 1964-68; exec. v.p., COO Skyline Corp., Elkhart, Ind., 1968-85; chmn. bd. dirs., CEO Franklin Elec. Co., Inc., Bluffton, Ind., 1985—, also bd. dirs.; bd. dirs. JSJ Corp., Skyline Corp., Sentry Ins. (a Mut. Ins. Co.); instr. U. Toledo, 1966-67. With U.S. Army, 1961-63. Mem. Harvard U. Bus. Sch. Assn., Ft. Wayne Country Club, Summit Club Ft. Wayne, Harvard Club N.Y.C., Bird Key Yacht Club. Republican. Presbyterian. Home: 7126 Blue Creek Dr Fort Wayne IN 46804-1483 also: 232 Bird Key Dr Sarasota FL 34236-1602 Office: Franklin Electric Co Inc 400 E Spring St Bluffton IN 46714-3798

LAWSON-BAKER, NEIL ANTHONY, dental surgeon; b. Watford, England, Nov. 8, 1938; s. Guthrie Dudley Andrews Baker and Margaret Charlotte Lawson; m. Susan Carol Vetter, Jan. 8, 1972 (div. 1980); m. Auriol Susanna Pace, July 4, 1992; 1 child, Tom. BDS, Guys Hosp., 1963; MB BS, London U., 1969. Sr. ptnr. Dental Clinic, London, 1969—; chmn., CEO L.B.P. Sculpture & Design, London, 1989—. Prin. works include sculpture Ransomes Dock, London, House of Commons, London, London Internat. Fin. Futures and Options Market, London, Beirut U., Byblos, Lebanon, Brit. Gas R & D Ctrs., Reading and Longhborough, Channel Tunnel Inauguration Folkestone, Magna Carta Fountain-Egham, 42-ft. KERIS for Nat. Sports Stadium, Kuala Lumpur, Malaysia, also others. Founder Chearish Fund for Children's Hospices; competitor Around the World in 80 Days Rally, 2000. Recipient Brodie prize in Clin. Surgery, St. Georges Hosp., U. London, 1969. Mem. Arts Club London, Vintage Sports Car Club. Avoca-

tions: horseback riding, horse breeding, opera, ballet, theatre. Office: No 31 Wilton Pl, London SW1X 8SH, England

LAWSON-JOWETT, MARY JULIET, lawyer; b. Mobile, Ala., May 26, 1959; d. William Max Lawson and Perina Juliet (Barich) Franc; m. Adam Geoffrey Jowett; 1 child, Caitlin Victoria Jowett. BA, U. Miss., 1981, JD, 1987. Bar: Miss. 1988, U.S. Dist. Ct. (no. and so. dists.) Miss. 1988. Tchr. Ocean Springs (Miss.) Sch. System, 1981-85; atty. Ronald W. Lewis & Assocs., Oxford, Miss., 1988-89; ptnr. occupl. hearing loss and hand-arm vibration syndrome Scruggs, Millette, Lawson, Bozeman & Dent, P.A., Pascagoula, Miss., 1989—; gen. practice, civil rights and employment law Juliet Jowett, P.A., 1997—; cons. Occupational Hearing Loss, P.A., 1989-96. Contbr. articles to profl. jours. Mem. Walter Anderson Players, Ocean Springs, 1973-96. Mem. ABA, ATLA (chmn. occupational hearing loss litigation group 1990-94), Miss. Trial Lawyers Assn. (editor 1990-92), Magnolia Bar Assn. Democrat. Roman Catholic. Avocations: reading, golf, horseback riding, gardening, acting. Office: Juliet Jowett PA PO Office Drawer 1625 1016 La Fontaine St Ocean Springs MS 39564-4934

LAWTON, WAYNE MICHAEL, mathematician, educator; b. Manchester, Conn., June 6, 1950; s. William John and Marion (Phaneuf) L. BA, Wesleyan U., Middletown, Conn., 1972, PhD in Math., 1972. Mem. tech. staff MRJ, Inc., 1978-80; rsch. engr. Radar and Optics divsn. Environ. Rsch. Inst. Mich., 1980-81; mem. tech. staff image processing sect. Jet Propulsion Lab., Pasadena, 1981-85; sr. project engr. Data Sys. Lab., TRW Def. Sys. Group, Redondo Beach, Calif., 1985-87; founder, chief scientist AWARE, Inc., Cambridge, Mass., 1987-91; sr. scientist Ctr. for Info. Enhanced Medicine, Nat. U. Singapore, Singapore, 1993-97, rsch. assoc. prof. dept. math., 1997—; assoc. prof. math. Nat. U. Singapore, 1999—; cons. Analytic Scis. Corp., Reading, Mass., Lockheed R&D Labs., Palo Alto, Calif.; G.C. Evans instr. dept. math. Rice U., Houston, 1972-74, adj. prof. dept. elec./computer engring., 1988-90; rsch. assoc. dept. math. U. Houston, 1975; asst. prof. math. U. Petroleum and Minerals, Saudi Arabia, 1975-76; lectr. math. Grad. Sch. Scis., Chiang Mai U., Thailand, 1976-78; lectr. UCLA, 1983-84, U. So. Calif., L.A., 1983-84; vis. scientist Harvard/Smithsonian Ctr. for Astrophysics, 1991; adj. prof. Northeastern U., Boston, 1991-92; mem. Inst. Advanced Studies, Princeton, 1974-75. Editor Jour. S.E. Asian Math. Soc., 1997—; contbr. articles to profl. jours.; patentee in field; patentee in field. Thorndike scholar, 1968-72. Mem. IEEE, Am. Math. Soc., Sigma Xi, Phi Beta Kappa. Democrat. Avocations: swimming, aerobics, weightlifting, museums and travel. Home: 16 Hazel Dr Branford CT 06405-5916 Office: Nat U Singapore Dept Math, 2 Science Dr 2, Singapore 117543, Singapore

LAX, PHILIP, land developer, space planner; b. Newark, Apr. 22, 1920; s. Nathan and Beckie (Hirschhorn) L.; m. Mildred Baras, Feb. 15, 1948; children: Corinne, Barbara. B.S., NYU, 1940, postgrad., 1941-42. With Lax & Co., Newark, 1942-77; v.p. Lax & Co., 1950-77; pres. Chathill Mgmt., Inc., 1977—; cons. World Book of Am. Heritage, 1992. Pres. B'nai Brith Ctr., Rochester, Minn., 1965-70, now hon. pres.; trustee Rutgers U. Hillel; pres. B'nai Brith Rutgers U. Hillel Found. Bldg. Corp., 1969—; chmn. United Jewish Appeal, Maplewood, N.J., 1966, 76; mem. N.J. region exec. bd. Anti-Defamation League, mem. nat. community rels. bd.; mem. Gov.'s Conf. on Edn., N.J., 1966, mem. bd. trustees Soc. Friends of Touro Synagogue, Newport, R.I., 1996; v.p. Touro Synagogue, 2000—; bd. dirs. Hebrew Immigration Soc. (HIAS); hon. chair B'nai B'rith Ctr. for Pub. Policy. 1999; mem. Mayor's Budget Com., Maplewood, 1958-59; co-chmn. N.J. Opera Ball, 1977; trustee B'nai Brith Found., Washington, 1967— (Philip Lax Gallery of B'nai Brith History and Archives named for him in Philip Klutznick Mus., Room named in his honor Stern Sch. Econs.); co-chmn. B'nai Brith Internat. Coun., 1979, chmn., 1980-85, hon. chmn., apptd. chmn. internat. coun., 1990; voting del. to Jewish Agy., Jerusalem; ECOSOC mem. UN, representing coordinated Bd. Jewish Orgns.; attended UNESCO Conf. in Mex., 1982, with Internat. Coun. B'nai Brith and U.S.; trustee, mem. exec. com. N.J. sect. NCCJ, 1981; trustee Henry Monsky Found., Washington, 1968—; trustee Leo N. Levi Hosp., Hot Springs, Ark., 1968-71, B'nai Brith World Jewish Ctr., Jerusalem, 1982, Nat. Arthritics Hosp., 1976—, N.Y. Statue of Liberty Centennial Found., Touro Synagogue, Newport, R.I., 1996—; hon. trustee Arts Coun. of Suburban Essex, N.J., 1980, Soc. Friends Touro Synagoague, Newport, 1996; mem. Econ. Devel. Commn., Twp. of Maplewood, 1979—; mem. steering com. to Restore Ellis Island, 1977—; nat. pres. Ellis Island Restoration Commn., 1978—, responsible for planning, funding and operating Family History Ctr. on Ellis Island; appointed to planning team of Statue of Liberty and Ellis Island by Nat. Park Service, Dept. of Interior ; mem. Statue of Liberty/Ellis Island Centennial Commn., Statue of Liberty-Ellis Island Centennial Commn., Com. of Architecture and Restoration of Statue of Liberty-Ellis Island, past chmn.; bd. dirs. Hebrew Immigration Aid Soc. Decorated cavaliere officiale Order of Merit of the Republic of Italy; recipient Found. award B'nai Brith, 1968, Humanitarian award, 1969, Pres.'s Gold medal, 1975; Pro Mundi Beneficio medal Brazilian Acad. Humanities, 1976; Philip Lax chapel at Rutgers U. Hillel named in his honor; named One of 100 Most Influential New Jersey Jews in the 20th Century; room named in honor Stern Sch. Econs., NYU; honored by N.J. State Senate. Mem. Am. Soc. Interior Designers, Nat. Soc. Interior Designers (trustee 1970-73), Am. Arbitration Assn., Am. Jewish Hist. Com. (v.p.), Am. Jewish Hist. Soc. (trustee 1984), Am. Soc. Israel Philatelists, Masons (32 deg.), Shriners, B'nai Brith (v.p. Supreme Lodge 1968-71, internat. bd. govs. 1971—, mem. exec. com. of internat. coun.), NYU Club (founder 1956), Nat. Press Club. Home: 35 Claremont Dr Maplewood NJ 07040-2119 Office: Chathill Mgmt 40 Main St Chatham NJ 07928-2402

LAXMINARAYANA, DAMA, geneticist, researcher, educator; b. Hyderabad, India, Apr. 20, 1953; came to U.S., 1990; s. Kishtaiah and Sathyamma; m. Dara Jayalakshmi; children: Dama Bhargavi, Dama Sriharsha, Dama Vishnupriya. BSc, Osmania U., Hyderabad, 1974, MSc, 1976, PhD, 1982. Jr. sci. asst. dept. genetics Osmania U., 1977-78, lectr. dept. zoology, 1985-90; jr. rsch. fellow Indian Dept. Atomic Energy, 1978-81, postdoctoral fellow, 1982-83, rsch. assoc., 1983-85; postdoctoral fellow dept. medicine Case Western Res. U. Sch. Medicine, Cleve., 1990-91; rsch. assoc. dept. internal medicine Wake Forest U. Sch. Medicine, Winston-Salem, N.C., 1991-94, rsch. instr., 1994-98, rsch. asst. prof., 1998—; conf. presenter in field. Contbr. articles to sci. jours., chpts. to books. Recipient internat. award Tata Meml. Trust, 1985; grantee Univ. Grants Commn. india, 1988-90, Lupus Found. Am., 1993-95, 96-98, NIH, 1999—. Mem. AAAS, Environ. Mutagen Soc. India, India Soc. Cell Biology, Soc. Geneticists and Cytologists India, N.Y. Acad. Scis. Home: 444 Lynn Ave Winston Salem NC 27104-4043 Office: Wake Forest U Sch Medicine Dept Internal Medicine Medical Center Blvd Winston Salem NC 27157-0001

LAY, DONALD POMEROY, federal judge; b. Princeton, Ill., Aug. 24, 1926; s. Hardy W. and Ruth (Cushing) L.; m. Miriam Elaine Gustafson, Aug. 6, 1949; children: Stephen Pomeroy (dec.), Catherine Sue, Cynthia Lynn, Elizabeth Ann, Deborah Jean, Susan Elaine. Student, U.S. Naval Acad., 1945-46; BA, U. Iowa, 1948, JD, 1951; LLD (hon.), Mitchell Coll. Law, 1985. Bar: Nebr. 1951, Iowa 1951, Wis. 1953. Assoc. Kennedy, Holland, DeLacy & Svoboda, Omaha, 1951-53, Quarles, Spence & Quarles, Milw., 1953-54, Eisenstatt, Lay, Higgins & Miller, 1954-66; judge U.S. Ct. Appeals (8th cir.), 1966—, chief judge, 1980-92, senior judge, 1992—; faculty mem. on evidence Nat. Coll. Trial Judges, 1964-65, U. Minn. Law Sch., William Mitchell Law Sch.; mem. U.S. Jud. Conf., 1980-92. Mem. editorial bd.: Iowa Law Rev., 1950-51; contbr. articles to legal jours. With USNR, 1944-46. Recipient Hancher-Finkbine medal U. Iowa, 1980. Fellow Internat. Acad. Trial Lawyers; mem. ABA, Nebr. Bar Assn., Iowa Bar Assn., Wis. Bar Assn., Am. Judicature Soc., Assn. Trial Lawyers Am. (bd. govs. 1963-65, Jud. Achievement award), Order of Coif, Delta Sigma Rho (Significant Sig award 1986, Herbert Harley award 1988), Phi Delta Phi, Sigma Chi. Presbyterian. Office: US Ct Appeals 8th Cir 316 Robert St N Ste 560 Saint Paul MN 55101-1461

LAY, KENNETH LEE, diversified energy company executive; b. Tyrone, Mo., Apr. 15, 1942; s. Omer and Ruth E. (Reese) L.; m. Linda Ann Phillips, July 10, 1982; children: Robyn Anne, Mark Kenneth, Todd David, Elizabeth Ayers, Robert Ray. BA, U. Mo., 1964, MA, 1965; PhD, U. Houston, 1970. Corp. economist Exxon Corp., Houston, 1965-68; asst. prof. and lectr. in econs. George Washington U., 1969-73; tech. asst. to commr. FERC, 1971-72; dep. undersec. for energy Dept. Interior, 1972-74; v.p. Fla. Gas Co. (now Continental Resources Co.), Winter Park, Fla., 1974-76, pres., 1976-79; exec. v.p. The Continental Group, 1979-81; pres., chief operating officer, dir. Transco Energy Co., Houston, 1981-84; chmn., chief exec officer Houston Natural Gas Corp., 1984-85; pres., chief exec. officer, chief operating officer, dir. HNG/InterNorth (now Enron Corp.), Omaha, 1985—, also chmn. bd. dirs., Houston; asst. prof. George Washington U.; bd. dirs. Eli Lilly & Co., Trust Co. West, Compaq Computer Corp.; past chmn. Greater Houston Partnership. Former chmn. bd. regents U. Houston; bd. trustees The H. John Heinz III Ctr. for Sci., Econs. & the Environment, The Bus. Coun., Am. Enterprise Inst.; Houston Host Com. for 1992 Rep. Nat. Conv.; co-chmn. 1990 Houston Econ. Summit Host. Com.; trustee Howard U.; active Resources for the Future. Decorated Navy Commendation award; recipient Pvt. Sector Coun. Leadership award, 1997, Horatio Alger award, 1998; N.A.M. fellow; State Farm fellow; Guggenheim fellow; named one of 25 Top Mgrs. in the World, Bus. Week., 1999; named to Tex. Bus. Hall of Fame, 1997. Mem. Nat. Petroleum Coun., River Oaks Country Club, Phi Beta Kappa. Republican. Methodist. Office: Enron Corp PO Box 1188 Houston TX 77251-1188

LAYAMANUMAN, WITTAYA, chemical company executive; b. Ampur Muang, Nakornsrithammarat, Thailand, Dec. 27, 1963; s. Tong Huad and Jantira Tang; m. Chutima Pupong; 1 child, Watita. BSc in Engring., Prince of Songkia U., Thailand, Republic of China, 1988; MBA, Ramkumhang U., Thailand, 1998. Factory mgr. So. Chems. Co., Ltd., Thailand, 1994—. Home: Chumreonvitee 1603, 80000 Muang Nakornsrithammart, Thailand Office: So Chems Co Nakornskri-, Tungsong 21/3 Moo 8, 80000 Praprom Nakornsrithammart, Thailand

LAYCOCK, ANITA SIMON, psychotherapist; b. Cheyenne, Wyo., Dec. 17, 1940; d. James Robert and Dorothy (Dearmin) Simon; m. Maurice Percy Laycock, June 18, 1965(dec. 1976); 1 child, (dec.). BA, U. Wyo., 1962, MA, 1971. Lic. counselor, Wyo., nationally cert. addiction specialist. Grad. student counselor, psychometrist Wyo. State Prison, Rawlins, 1971-73; counselor, trainer Dept. of Insts. State of Colo., Denver, 1973-75; counselor, tchr. supr. Jefferson County Evaluation-Diagnostic Ctr., Rawlins, 1975-78; psychometrist Wyo. State Penitentiary, Rawlins, 1978-79; counselor, therapist Rocky Mountain Arts and Scis., Cheyenne, 1979-81; counselor, therapist supr., dir. SWARA, Rock Springs, Wyo., 1981-85; therapy dir. St. Joseph Residential Treatment, Torrington, Wyo., 1985-88; dir. psychiatric unit Nat. Med. Enterprises Hill-Haven-Pk. Manor, Rawlins, 1988-89; chief exc. officer Simon-Laycock & Assocs., Rawlins, 1989—; cons. Kids in Distressed Situations, Rawlins, 1990-91, Child Devel. Ctr., Rawlins, 1991—; dir. Pub. Offender and Forensic Mental Health Program, Rawlins, 1988-91. Author: (programs) related to sex offenders. Pres. Cheyenne City Panhellenic, 1965-68. Named Miss Wyo.-Miss Universe, 1960; named Miss Wool of Wyo., 1965. Mem. ACA, Nat. Sex Offenders Counselors, Nat. Assn. Drug and Alcohol Counselors, Pub. Offenders Counselors Assn., Western Corrections Assn., Wyo. Assn. Addiction Specialists (pres. 1988—). Avocations: profl. animal trainer, artist. Office: Simon Laycock & Assocs 1716 Old Yellowstone Rd # 124 Cheyenne WY 82009-9183

LAYCOCK, MARY CHAPPELL, gifted and talented education educator, consultant; b. Jefferson City, Mo., Jan. 11, 1915; d. Alvin E. and Ollie (Harris) Chappell; m. James Charles Laycock, June 22, 1937; children: Charles, Ann, Donald E., Jane. AB, Judson Coll., 1937; MA in Math. Edn., U. Tenn., 1961. Math. tchr. various, 1938-41; math. tchr. Kingsport (Tenn.) Jr. High Sch., 1942; math. coord. Oak Ridge (Tenn.) City Schs., 1956-68, high sch. math. tchr., 1945-68; math. specialist Nueva Ctr. for Learning, Hillsborough, Calif., 1968-98; cons. Hayward, Calif., 1990-97. Author many books including Mathematics for Meaning, The Fabric of Mathematics, Algebra in Concrete, Focus on Geometry, Hands On Mathematics for Secondary Teachers, Weaving Your Way from Arithmetic to Mathematics, 1993, The Magician's Castle Fantasy, 1995; developed documentary Don't Bother Me, I'm Learning, 12 videotapes on teaching manipulatives; contbr. articles to profl. jours. Recipient Calif. Educator award, 1989, Elem. Math. Tchr. award Calif. Math. Coun. and State of Calif., 1989, Award of Recognition Calif. Assn. for the Gifted. 1984. Mem. NEA, Nat. Coun. Tchrs. Math., Oreg. Math. Coun., Calif. Math. Coun. (life), Fla. Math. Coun., Greater San Diego Math. Coun., San Mateo County Math. Coun., Calif. Assn. for the Gifted. Avocation: geometric art. Home and Office: 20655 Hathaway Ave Hayward CA 94541-3740

LAYDER, DEREK, sociology educator; b. Liverpool, Eng., Apr. 28, 1948; s. Roy Austin and Joan (Peters) L. BS in Sociology, Leicester U., 1970; PhD in Sociology, London Sch. Econs., 1976. From tutor to reader in sociology Leicester U., 1973-97, prof. sociology, 1997—. Author: Structure Interaction and Social Theory, 1981, The Realist Image in Social Science, 1990, New Strategies in Social Research: An Introduction & Guide, 1993, Understanding Social Theory, 1994, Methods, Sex and Madness, 1994, Modern Social Theory: Key Debates & New Directions, 1997, Sociological Practice: Linking Theory and Social Research, 1998; contbr. articles to profl. jours. Social Sci. Rsch. Coun. scholar London Sch. Econs., 1970-73. Mem. Brit. Sociol. Assn. Home: 21 Byway Rd Evington, Leicester LE5 5TF, England Office: Leicester U, Dept Sociology, Leicester LE1 7RH, England

LAYMAN, EMMA MCCLOY (MRS. JAMES W. LAYMAN), psychologist, educator; b. Danville, Va., Feb. 25, 1910; d. Charles Harold and Anna (Fisher) McCloy; m. James Walter Layman, Dec. 12, 1936 (dec. May 5, 1978). A.B., Oberlin Coll., 1930; M.A., NYU, 1931; Ph.D., U. Iowa, 1937; L.H.D. (hon.), Iowa Wesleyan Coll., 1981. Diplomate: Am. Bd. Examiners Profl. Psychology. Psychol. examiner Iowa Psychopathic Hosp., Iowa City, 1934-35, 37; clin. psychologist Mich. Children's Inst., Ann Arbor, 1935-36; supr. psychol. services Iowa Bd. Social Welfare, Des Moines, 1937-41; assoc. prof. psychology Woman's Coll., U. N.C., 1947-52; supervisory clin. psychologist Brooke Army Hosp., Ft. Sam Houston, 1952-54; chief psychologist Children's Hosp., Washington, 1954-60; head dept. psychology Iowa Wesleyan Coll., Mt. Pleasant, 1960-75, assoc. prof., 1960-61, prof., 1961-75, emeritus, 1975—, asst. acad. dean, 1964-65, chmn. social sci. div., 1969-75, dir. East Asian Inst., 1963-75, dir. internat. studies, 1970-75; pvt. practice clin. psychology, 1941—; lectr. U. Chattanooga, 1946-47; vis. prof. edn. Duke, summers 1948-50; adj. prof. Am. U., 1954-60; lectr. Howard U., 1956-60; cons. Walter Reed Army Hosp., 1956-60. Author: Mental Health Through Physical Education and Recreation, 1955, Airesboro Castle, 1974, Buddhism in America, 1976, also articles. Vice pres. Oberlin-Wellington bd. Ch. Women United, also mem. Lorain County bd.; pres. Class of 1930, Oberlin Coll., also mem. alumni coun. Lt. USNR, 1943-46. Fellow APA, Acad. Clin. Psychology, Sigma Xi; mem. AAUW, Am. Assn. Chinese Studies, Phi Beta Kappa. Episcopalian. Home: 154 Kendal Dr Oberlin OH 44074-1907

LAYNE, JAMES LEE, small business owner; b. Alliance, Ohio, Oct. 12, 1956; s. Harold James and Olice P. L.; m. Sandra J. Layne, May 20, 1974 (div. Dec. 15, 1991); children: James Lee II, Kyle James. Student, Kent State U., 1975-76. Owner Nat. Auto, Alliance, 1974-89; owner Carnation Constrn., Alliance, 1975-89, Munchy's Bar & Drive Thru, Alliance, 1979—, limo svc., Alliance, 1983-86, Rain Tree Spas, Alliance, 1987-89, Rent-It-Ctr., Sebring, Ohio, 1987-89, Country Barns, Las Vegas, Nev., 1989-91; cons. Stuchell Home Improvement, Alliance, 1991-95, Danny's Paint Svc., Alliance, 1991-95. Mgr. country music singers and songwriters, 1993—. Top area fundraiser Muscular Dystrophy, Alliance, 1988; Best Drug Abuse Poster in Ohio Ohio Sch. Bds., 1968. Mem. William Penn Club, Moose. Avocations: boating, travel, theatre, arts, fine dining. Office: Munchys Bar & Drive Thru 507 Homeworth Rd Alliance OH 44601-9071

LAYSON, WILLIAM MCINTYRE, retired research consulting company executive; b. Lexington, Ky., Sept. 24, 1934; s. Zed Clark and Louise (McIntyre) L. B.S., MIT, 1956, Ph.D., 1961; postgrad., U. Sydney, Australia, 1957-58. Research scientist European Ctr. Nuclear Research, Geneva, 1960-62; research scientist U. Calif., Berkeley, 1962-64; mem. tech. staff Pan Am World Airways, Patrick AFB, Fla., 1964-67; research scientist Gen. Research Corp., Rosslyn, Va., 1967-70; dir. Sci. Applications Internat. Corp., McLean, Va., 1970-98, sr. v.p., chmn. incentives com., 1975-93, coord. def. nuclear programs, 1975-99, chmn. ethics com., 1994-99; ret., 1999; dir. Langley Sch., 1992-97, pres., 1995-97; pres. Layson's Buffalo Trace Farms, 1976—. Fulbright scholar U. Sydney, Australia, 1957-58. Mem. Am. Def. Preparedness Assn. Democrat. Presbyterian (elder). Avocations: church activities, jogging, swimming, skiing. Home: 8301 Summerwood Dr Mc Lean VA 22102-2213

LAYTON, HARRY CHRISTOPHER, artist, lecturer, consultant; b. Safford, Ariz., Nov. 17, 1938; s. Christopher E. and Eurilda (Welker) L.; m. Karol Barbara Kendall, July 11, 1964 (div. Jan. 1989); children: Deborah, Christopher, Joseph, Elisabeth, Faith, Aaron, Gretchen, Benjamin, Justin, Matthew, Peter. LHD, Sussex Coll., Eng., 1969; RE (hon.), PhD (hon.), St. Matthew U., Ohio, 1970, DRE (hon.), 1970; DFA (hon.), DSc (hon.), London Inst. Applied Rsch., Ohio, 1972. Cert. clin. hypnotherapist. Pres., mgr. Poems, Art & Myths; pres., CEO, Layton Studio Graphic Design, L.A.; lectr. ancient art Serra Cath. H.S., Gardena, Calif., 1963-64, L.A. Dept. Parks and Recreation, summers 1962-64; interior decorator Cities of Hawthorne, Lawndale, Compton, Gardena, and Torrance, Calif., 1960-68. One-man shows Nahas Dept. Stores, 1962, 64; group shows include Gt. Western Savs. & Loan, Lawndale, 1962, Gardena Adult Sch., 1965, Serra Cath. H.S., 1963, Salon de Nations, Paris, 1983; represented in permanent collections Sussex Coll., Culver City-Foshey Masonic Lodge, Gt. Western Savs. & Loan; paintings inlcude The Fairy Princess, 1975, Nocturnal Covenant, 1963, Blindas Name, 1962, Creation, 1962; works pub. in Our World's Favorite Gold and Silver Poems, 1991, Our World's Favorite Poems, 1993, World's Best Poems, 1993, Outstanding Poets of 1994, Best Poems of 1995, also others. Elder LDS Ch., Santa Monica, Calif., 1963—. Recipient Editor's Choice award Nat. Libr. Poetry, 1994, 95. Mem. Am. Hypnotherapy Assn., Nat. Notary Assn., Internat. Soc. Artists, Internat. Platform Assn., Am. Security Coun., Soc. for Early Hist. Archaeology, Am. Councilor's Soc. Psychol. Counselors, Salon des Nation Paris Geneva, Ctr. Internat. Art Contemporain, Internat. Soc. Poets (disting.), Internat. Masonic Poetry Soc., Am. Legion, Masons (32d degre), Shriners, KT, Alpha Psi Omega. Republican. Home and Office: Layton Studio Graphic Design Inc 3654 Centinela Ave Apt 10 Los Angeles CA 90066-3147

LÁZÁR, GEORGE, pathophysiologist, researcher; b. Kismarja, Bihar, Hungary, Mar. 12, 1934; s. János and Ágnes (Szilber) L.; m. Elisabeth Husztik, Aug. 15, 1960; children: George, Stephen. MD, Albert Szent-Györgi Med. U., Szeged, Hungary, 1958, Specialist in Lab. Investigation, 1964; PhD, Hungarian Acad. Scis., Budapest, Hungary, 1970, Dr.Med.Scis., 1975. Asst. Albert Szent-Györgyi Med. U., 1958-68, asst. prof., 1968-73, assoc. prof., 1973-77, prof. Inst. Pathophysiology, 1977—; vis. prof. U. Pierre and Marie Curie, Paris, 1989-90. Contbr. more than 200 articles to profl. jours. Res. Officer Hungarian Army. Recipient Literary prize Hungarian Writers' Assn., 1952, Acad. prize Hungarian Acad. Scis., 1974, Szeged-1956 Commemorative medallion City of Szeged, 1997, Albert Szent-Györgyi prize, 1999, medal for Szeged, 2000; named Accomplished Tchr., Ministry of Edn., Budapest, 1976; fellow U. Montreal, 1971-72, U. Groningen, The Netherlands, 1986, INSERM, Paris, 1976, 82, 84, 87. Mem. European Reticuloendothelial Soc. (v.p. 1982-86, bd. dirs. 1984-86), Hungarian Physiol. Soc. (bd. dirs. 1972-80), Hungarian Soc. Chemotherapy (bd. dirs. 1985—). Avocations: hammer-throwing, literature. Home: Petőfi S St 40/B, 6722 Szeged Hungary Office: Albert Szent-Györgyi Med, U Szeged Pharm Ctr, Semmelweis St 1, PO Box 427, PO Box 531, 6701 Szeged Hungary

LÁZÁR, GYULA LEVENTE, anatomist, educator; b. Szend, Komárom, Hungary, Feb. 19, 1938; s. Gyula Lázár and Jolán Hajas; m. Judit Kinga Novotny, June 12, 1965; children: Boglárka, Orsolya, Zsófia. MD, U. Med., Pécs, Hungary, 1962, PhD, 1976; DSc, Acad. Scis., Budapest, Hungary, 1991. Med. diplomate. Jr. lectr. U. Med. Sch. Dept. Anatomy, Pécs, 1962-64, lectr. in anatomy, 1964-75, sr. lectr., 1976-80, reader, 1980-93, prof., 1993—; sec. sci. com. U. Pécs, 1982-88, 99—; gen. sec. Hungarian Anatomical Soc., 1991—; mem. doctoral bd. Hungarian Acad. Scis., 2000—. Contbr. chpts. to books. Recipient Acad. prize Hungarian Acad. Scis., Budapest, 1991; named Master Tchr., 1999; Szechenyi Professorial fellow, 2000—. Mem. Internat. Soc. Vertebrate Morphology, Internat. Brain Rsch. Orgn., European Neurosci. Assn., Hungarian Neurosci. Soc., Hungarian Neuropathol. Soc. Avocations: collecting frog figures and stamps, photography, travel, gardening. Office: Dept Human Anatomy, Szigeti út 12, 7643 Pécs Hungary

LAZAR, IMRE, internist, medical anthropologist; b. Budapest, Hungary, Apr. 5, 1957; s. Imre and Imrene (Toth Erzsebet) L.; m. Edit Balogh, Mar. 17, 1987; children: Csenge Eszter, Csanad Imre, Keve Botond, Kincso Boglarka. MD, Semmelweis U. Medicine, Budapest, 1981; PhD in Behavioral Medicine, Hungarian Acad. Scis., Budapest, 1998. Internist dept. internal medicine Tetenyi Tchg. Hosp., Budapest XI Tetenyi ut iz, Budapest, 1981-91; head dept. psychosomatic medicine St. Imre Hosp., Budapest X Gazdagreti, Budapest, 1991—; dep. head dept. med. anthropology Inst. Behavioral Scis., Semmelweis U. Medicine, Budapest, 1993—; founder/head Ctr. Environ. Anthropology & Behavioral Ecology Cath. Tchr. Tng. Coll., Zsambek, 1998—; invited lectr. Eotvos Lorand U. Scis., Budapest, 1991-92; lectr. Pub. Health Sch., Debrecen, Hungary, 1996—; founding mem. Commn. Ethnic Rels., Internat. Union Anthropol. and Ethnological Soc., 1995. Editor Environment and Medicine, 1994-96, 98—; author: Psychoneuroimmunology, 1991, Behavioral Immunology, 1993, Human Ecology, 1994, Human Ecology I, Cognitive Ecology II, 1998-2000; editor: Basis and Methods of Behavioral Sciences Public Health School, 1996. Head Civil Assn. Rozsavolgy, Budapest, 1992—. Mem. Hungarian Crohn Assn. (coun. mem. 1994—), Hungarian Assn. Social Psychiatry (coun. mem. 1994), N.Y. Acad. Scis. Home: Gerinc /str 60, 1221 Budapest Hungary Office: Inst Behavioral Scis, Nagyvarad Ter 4, 1089 Budapest Hungary

LÁZÁR, ISTVÁN, chemist, educator; b. Hajdúnánás, Hungary, Sept. 15, 1959; s. István and Magdolna (Pomucz) L.; m. Ágnes Irén Józsa, Oct. 31, 1981; children: István, Edina. MS, Kossuth U., Debrecen, Hungary, 1984, PhD, 1988. Asst. prof. I Kossuth U., Debrecen, 1987-92, asst. prof. II of chemistry, 1992-96, assoc. prof., 1996—; rsch. assoc. U. Tex., Dallas, 1989-91, 94. Author: Special and Dangerous Materials, 1995, 2d edit., 1998, General and Inorganic Chemistry, 1998, 2d edit., 2000. Hungarian Acad. Sci. scholar, 1984-87. Avocations: computers, microelectronics, astronomy, badminton. Home: Szligeti u 12 II/7, H-4028 Debrecen Hungary Office: U Debrecen, Egyetem Ter 1, H-4010 Debrecen Hungary

LAZAR, JOHN EDWARD, administrator non-profit organization; b. Bklyn., Mar. 24, 1950; s. John and Elizabeth (Titch) L. BA, St. John's U., Bklyn., 1971; postgrad., Bklyn. Coll., 1972-73; MDiv, Sem. of Immaculate Conception, 1980. Cert. tchr., N.Y.; ordained clergyman Roman Cath. Ch. 1980. English tchr. N.Y.C. Bd. Edn., Bklyn., 1973-79; clergyman Roman Cath. Diocese of Bklyn., 1980-93; pres. POMOC, Inc., N.Y.C., 1981-84; dir. housing Argus Cmty., Inc., Bronx, N.Y., 1993-96; devel. cons. Met. Cmty. Ch., L.A., 1997—; exec. dir. San Fernando Valley Am. Cancer Soc., Sherman Oaks, Calif., 1998—; exec. dir. Peregrinatio Ad Petri Sedem-U.S. Office of Pilgrimages, Vatican City, 1985-86. Author: Outpouring the Spirit: Gay and Lesbian Spirituality in the Judeo Christian Tradition, 1996; TV show host Polish Profiles, 1989-93. Commr. City of West Hollywood (Calif.) Lesbian and Gay Adv. Bd., 1998—, now co-chair; bd. dirs. City Vol. Corps., N.Y.C, 1990-96, Stonewall Dem. Club, L.A., 1997—; v.p. Polish Am. Congress, N.Y.C., 1989-93; co-prodr. civic celebration Bklyn. Outdoor Mus. of Art, 1993; mem. com. Mayor's Planning Com. L.A. Vol. Festival, 1998, 99; chmn. N.Y.C. Comptr.'s Polish Adv. Com., 1982-89, 94-96. Named Hon. Alumnus, Our Lady of the Lake Sem., 1982; recipient Pres.'s award Stonewall Dem. Club, 1998, Commendation award N.Y.C. Comptr., 1995, Citizen of Yr. award Polish Am. World, 1982. Mem. Polish Inst. Arts and Scis. in Am., Inc., So. Calif. Assn. Non Profit Housing, Inc. Democrat. Avocations: bicycling, reading, prestidigitation, downhill skiing. E-mail: JE-Lazar324@aol.com. Home: 1351 N Curson Ave Ph 1 Los Angeles CA 90046-4092 Office: Am Cancer Soc 4940 Van Nuys Blvd Ste 301 Sherman Oaks CA 91403-1742

LAZARCIK, GREGOR, educator, financial research company executive, economist; b. Horna Streda, Slovakia, Mar. 10, 1923; came to U.S., 1953, naturalized, 1958; s. Gaspar and Maria (Rehak) L.; m. Theresa M. Good, Aug. 14, 1971. BS, State Coll., Slovakia, 1945; MS, Coll. Agr., Brno, Czechoslovakia, 1948; cert., Swiss Inst. Tech., Zurich, 1949; AM, U. Strasbourg, France, 1952; LLM, LLD (fellow), U. Paris, 1953; PhD (fellow), Columbia, 1960. Asst. to mgr. Ctrl. Cutter Dairy, Lucerne, Switzerland, 1948-49; controller dairy products Agrl. Syndicate, Hazebruck, France, 1949-50; with Rsch. Project on Nat. Income Columbia U., N.Y.C., 1956-00, sr.

rsch. economist, 1961-70, seminar assoc., 1970—; pres., chmn. bd. L.W. Internat. Financial Rsch., Inc., N.Y.C., 1961-00; lectr. econs. Hunter Coll., CUNY, 1963-64, Columbia U., 1964-68; prof. econs. SUNY, 1968-85, CUNY, 1984—. Author: Le Commerce en Matiere Agricole Entre l'Europe de l'Ouest et l'Europe deL'Est, 1959; co-author: Czechoslovak National Income and Product, 1947-56, 1962, The Performance of Socialist Agriculture, 1963, Scientific Research and its Relation to Earnings and Stock Prices, 1965, Comparison of Agricultural and Nonagricultural Income, 1937, 48-65, 1968, Defense, Education and Health Expenditures and Their Relation to GNP in Eastern Europe, 1978, Economic Growth in Eastern Europe, 1965-82, 1983, Agricultural Output and Productivity in Eastern Europe and Some Comparisons with the USSR and USA, 1985; contbr. to East European Economics Post-Helsinki, 1977, Pressure for Reform in the East European Economics, Joint Econ. Com., U.S. Congress, 1989, The Development of the Private Sector in East Central Europe, 1993, Overview of Transportation Infrastructure in East Central Europe, 1994, The Status of and Prospects for Agriculture in East Central Europe, 1996, Energy in Eastern Europe: Production, Consumption, and Trade, 1970-1987, 1999. Mem. Am. Econ. Assn., Am. Regional Sci. Assn., Assn. Comparative Economic Studies, Am. Assn. Advancement Slavic Studies. Roman Catholic. Address: 100 La Salle St Apt 17-b New York NY 10027-4730

LAZARENKOV, VADIM GRIGORIEVICH, petrography educator; b. Leningrad, USSR, Dec. 17, 1933; s. Grigory Vasilievich and Anastasia Andreevna (Golubeva) L.; m. Tatiana Ivanovna Loginova; 1 child, Tatiana Vadimovna. BS, Mining Inst., Leningrad, 1963, DSc, 1981. Registered engr. Asst. Mining Inst., Leningrad, 1960-67, prof. petrography, 1982—, dean, 1981-85, chief dept., 1984-88; chief dept. Poly. Inst., Conakry Guinea, 1967-71, dean, 1970-71. Author: The feldspathoidic Syenites of Massif Los Guinea, 1975, Formation Analysis of Continent and Ocean Alkaline Rocks, 1988, Platiniferous Mineralization of Ultramafic Zonal and Comatiites Massives, 1992, Geochemistry of Platinum Group Elements, 1996. Recipient medal 200th Anniversary of Mining Sch. Paris, 1983, reward Fund Sores, 1993. Mem. Russian Mineral. Soc. (presidium 1982-87), N.Y. Acad. Scis. Home: Corp 1 App 523, Korablestroiteley b 19, 199226 Saint Petersburg Russia Office: Mining Inst, 21 Line 2, 199026 Saint Petersburg Russia

LAZARESCU, MIHAI MUGUREL, computer scientist, researcher; b. Braila, Romania, Dec. 11, 1973; s. Gabriel Iuliu and Sevastita Lazarescu. BS in Computer Sci. honors first class, Curtin U. Tech., Perth, Australia, 1996, PhD, 2000. Rschr. Curtin U. Tech., 1996-99, lectr., 1998; rschr. Inst. Informatics and Math., U. Bern, Switzerland, 1999—. Contbr. articles to profl. jours.; author procs. Avocations: classical music, history, cycling, running. E-mail: lazaresc@cs.curtin.edu.au. Office: Curtin U Tech, GPO Box U 1987, Perth Australia 6001

LAZAREV, GIRGORY B., engineer; b. Kharkov, Ukraine, May 17, 1938; s. Bentsion G. and Mirra L. (Passel) L.; m. Galina B. Silaeva, Oct. 27, 1967; 1 child, Olga. MSEE, Polytech., Kharkov, Ukraine, 1961; PhD in Elec. Engring., State Inst. Energy, Acad. Sci., Moscow, 1978. Engr. Rsch. Inst. Heavy Elec. Equipment, Kharkov, Ukraine, 1961-65; engr., faculty mem. dept. indsl. elecs. Polytech. Inst., Kharkov, Ukraine, 1965-68; sr. rsch. asst. State Inst. Energy, Moscow, 1968-81; sr. engr., head scientific rsch. Electric Power Rsch. Inst., Moscow, 1981—; tech. dir. ENEL Engring., Moscow, 1992-2000. Author: Over Voltages in the Systems with Thhyristor Convetors, 1979, Electrical Variable Speed Drives of Aucalairy Machinary for Heating Electric Power, 1990. Mem. scientific coun. Elecric Power Rsch. Inst., Moscow, 1984; mem. tech. com. State Stds. Com., Moscow, 1999. Recipient Silver medal Exhbn. Nat. Economy Improvements, Moscow, 1989. Mem. IEEE, N.Y. Acad. Scis. Avocations: reading, family activities, music, art. Office: Elec Power Rsch Inst, 22-3 Kashirskoje Shosse, 115201 Moscow Russia

LAZAREVA, TAT'YANA GENNADIEVNA, physicist, chemist; b. Leningrad, USSR, Nov. 27, 1948; d. Gennadii Mikhailovich and Valeriya Andrianovna (Vdovina) Tyapkini; m. Igor Andreevich Lazarev, Dec. 4, 1970; 1 child, Andrei Igor'evich. Diploma in chemistry, Belarusian U., Minsk, 1971; PhD in Chemistry, Acad. Scis., Minsk, 1986. Jr. rsch. scientist Inst. Gen. and Inorganic Chemistry, Acad. Scis. Belarus, Minsk, 1971-86, rsch. scientist, 1986-90, sr. rsch. scientist, 1990—. Contbr. articles to profl. publs. Mem. Assn. of Mil. Christian Fellowship of Belarus, Minsk, 1996—. Internat. Sci. Found. grantee, 1994-96. Mem. Materials Rsch. Soc. Avocations: travel, Russian classical literature, photography. Home: 1 Lesnaya Str Flat 66, 220056 Minsk Belarus Office: Inst Gen & Inorganic Chem, 9 Surganov St, 220072 Minsk Belarus

LAZARIDES, HARRIS N., food engineering educator; b. Arnea, Chalkidiki, Greece, July 14, 1950; s. Nicolas and Evangelia (Tsaknakis) L.; m. Mary S. Kyriakou, Apr. 22, 1982; children: Nicolas, Spyros. MS in Agr., Aristotelean U., 1973; MSc in Food Sci., U. Minn., 1977; PhD in Food Engring., U. Mass., 1980. Engring. project mgr. Agno Dairy Industry, Thessaloniki, 1980-83; mng. dir. DLE Hellas, Thessaloniki, 1983-85; asst. prof. Thessaloniki Tech. Inst., Thessaloniki, 1985-86; assoc. prof. Aristotelean U. Thessaloniki, 1986-91, prof., 1996—. Contbg. author books; contbr. articles to profl. jours. Vice-pres. Consumer Protection Orgn., Thessaloniki, 1985—. Disting. Student State Scholarship Orgn., Athens, 1968-73. Mem. Inst. Food Technologists. Avocations: marathon runner, mountaineering, fishing, music, travel. Office: Aristotelean U Thessaloniki, PO Box 255, Thessaloniki 54006, Greece

LAZARIDES, MICHAEL, botanist; b. Townsville, Queensland, Australia, Feb. 26, 1928; s. Lazarus and Panayiota (Manicaros) L.; m. Margaret Joan Cooper, Apr. 2, 1956; children: Wayne Michael, Gai Margaret, Brett John. Diploma in agr., Queensland Coll., Gatton, Australia, 1947; MSc, Leicester (Eng.) U., 1967. With Commonwealth Scientific Indsl. Rsch. Orgn., Canberra, Australia, 1949—; liaison officer KEW, London, 1965-66; expert witness Australian Govt., 1975; spkr. in field. Author: The Grasses of Central Australia, 1970, The Tropical Grasses of Southeast Asia, 1980; co-author: The Floras of Central Australia, 1981, Plant Resources of Arid and Semi-Arid Lands, 1985, The Floras of South Australia, 1986, Plant Cell Environment, 1986, The Floras of Perth Region, Western Australia, 1987, The Floras of the Kimberley Region, Western Australia, 1992, Desertified Grasslands, 1992, The Economic Plants of Australia, 1993, The Floras of Ceylon, 1994, Australian Weeds, 1997; contbr. articles to profl. jours. Grantee Smithsonian Inst., 1970, Australian Biol. Resources Study, 1979, 81-82, 89, Australian Nat. Parks Wildlife Svc., 1980, Chinese Acad. Sci., 1990; S.E. Asian Treaty Orgn. fellow, 1970. Mem. Canberra Club (sr., fin. dir. 1997-98). Greek Orthodox. Avocations: photography, philateley, leather crafts, wood crafts. Home: 14 Yapunyah St, Canberra 2602, Australia Office: CSIRO, Clunies Ross St, Canberra 2601, Australia

LAZARIS, ANDREAS, pathologist; b. Paleo Phaliro, Greece, May 21, 1965; s. Christos and Maria (Sigala) L. MD, Athens U., 1989, PhD, 1995. Resident in pathology Hippokration Hosp., Athens, 1990-94; rsch. coord. rsch./immunology lab, 1st propaedic surg. dept. Athens Med. Sch., 1992-93, rsch. fellow dept. pathology, 1992-96; specialist pathologist dept. pathology Volos Gen. Hosp., Greece, 1996-97; lectr. in pathology dept. pathology Med. Faculty of Athens U., 1998—; clin. attachment to dept. of pathology SGH, Glasgow, Scotland, 1999. Translator: (Greek edit.) Pathology, 1995; contbr. articles to profl. jours. With Armed Forces, 1995-96, 2d lt. 1999. Recipient 2d award Union of Med. Armed Forces Scientists, 1994, Award Greek Union of Tumor Markers, 1996, 1st award monograph Sci. Com. of the 24th Annual Hellenic Med. Congress, 1998. Mem. Internat. Acad. Pathology, Gen. Med. Coun. U.K., Hellenic Soc. Anatomic Pathology. Avocations: classical music, theatre. Home: 5 Martinegkou Str, Nea Filothei, GR 11524 Athens Greece

LAZARIS, PAMELA ADRIANE, community planning and development consultant; b. Dixon, Ill., Oct. 13, 1956; d. Michael Christ and Ellen Euridice (Eftax) L.; m. Eugene Dale Monson, Oct. 17, 1987; children: Anthony Edward, Anna Adriane. BFA in Fine Arts, U. Wis., Milw., 1978; MS in Urban and Regional Planning, U. Wis., 1982; MBA, U. St. Thomas, 1992. Analyst planning Wis. Dept. Natural Resources, Madison, 1979-82; asst. city planner City of Albert Lea, Minn., 1982-83; specialist community devel. City of Winona, Minn., 1983-85; dir. community devel. City of Waseca, Minn., 1985-98; assoc. Real Estate Dynamics, Inc., Madison, Wis., 1998-99; prin. Planning Svc. and Solutions, Lake Mills, Wis., 1999—. Vol. spl. events Farmam-Minn. Agrl. Interpretive Ctr., Waseca, 1985-86; mem. Waseca County Econ. Devel. Commn., 1989-98; com. dir. Waseca Area Found., 1989-98; mem. dist. 2 city coun. City of Lake Mills, Wis., 1999—, mem. city plan commn., 1999—. Named one of Oustanding Young Women of Am., 1986. Mem. Am. Inst. Cert. Planners (cert.), Am. Planning Assn. (chpt. bd. dirs. 1986-89), Minn. Planning Assn. (v.p. 1989-90, dist. bd. dirs. 1985-89), Toastmasters (chpt. sgt.-at-arms 1987, ednl. v.p. 1988, 91-98), Lake Mills Area C. of C. Avocations: public speaking, travel, art. Home: PO Box 17 Lake Mills WI 53551-0017 Office: 110 E Madison St Lake Mills WI 53551-1644

LÁZARO, MARÍA ESTER, physician, researcher; b. Buenos Aires, Nov. 16, 1955; d. Emilio Lázaro and Sara Gurny; m. Ricardo Horacio Calvi, Nov. 5, 1981; children: Paula, Emilio Horacio. Physician with honors, U. Buenos Aires, 1978, Splst. in Infectious Diseases, 1984. Med. Diplomate; splst. in internal medicine. Resident in internal medicine Gen. San Martín Hosp., Buenos Aires, 1982, mem. staff infectious diseases svcs., 1985-88; chief infectious diseases unit Hosp. Zonal Bariloche (Río Negro), Argentina, 1988—; coord. STD and AIDS program Hosp. Zonal Bariloche (Río Negro), 1989—; coord. infectious diseases IV Sanitary Zone, Bariloche, 1988—; coord. hantavirus Sec. Pub. Health Río Negro Province, 1986—; temporal cons. hantavirus WHO, 1997; prin. researcher A. Roemmers Found., 1989-90, 97-99; educator to health workers and cmty.; speaker on hantavirus. Contbr. article to profl. jour., chpt. to book. Mem. Argentine Microbiology Assn., Argentine Group for AIDS. Avocations: swimming, yoga, travel, reading. Office: Hosp Zonal Bariloche, Moreno 601, Rio Negro 8400 Bariloche Argentina

LAZAROIU, DUMITRU FELICIAN, engineering educator, consultant; b. Ploiesti, Romania, Jan. 19, 1926; arrived in France, 1983; s. Dumitru and Vasilica (Ionescu) L.; children: Ioana, Mihaela; m. Marcelle Loyaute Lazaroiu (Celine Varenne), Dec. 20, 1986. Gen. cert. scientific edn., Lyceum B.P. Hasdeu, Buzau, Romania, 1944; diploma in Elec. Engring., Polytechnic U., Bucharest, Romania, 1949, PhD in Tech. Scis., 1968. Elec. Engring. diplomate. Univ. asst. Polytechnical U., Bucharest, Romania, 1950-57, asst. prof., 1957-72, prof., 1972-82, 1990; quality mgr. Elscint, Paris, 1984-96; quality cons. internat. Liberal, Paris, 1997—; sr. engr., rschr. Elec. Equipment Industry, Bucharest, Romania, 1949-58; tech. dir. Electronica Works, Bucharest, Romania, 1958-64; gen. dir. Industry Ministry, 1969-72; scientific dir. Electro Tech. Rsch. Inst., Bucharest, Romania, 1964-69; higher edn. and rsch. gen. dir. Edn. Ministry, Bucharest, 1972-75. Author of 26 books in electronics, automation and reliability to include Small Power Electrical Machines, 1976, Noise of Electrical Transformers, 1973, Electrical Servomotors of Small Inertia, 1969; inventor: 9 patents in Romania, U.S., France, Japan and Germany to include Electrical Disk Servomotors with Printed Windings, 1969-75; contbr. over 100 articles to profl. jours. Mem. various anticommunist orgns. of Romanian Exile, Paris, 1983—; cons. for Studies in Modern Quality Mgmt., UN Devel. Program, Bucharest, Romania, 1992-94; cons. for Studies in Quality Rsch. Min. for Rsch. and Tech., Bucharest, Romania, 1995-99. Mem. Nat. Orgn. Engrs. and Scientists of France, European Engr. Assn. Romanian Scientists, Expert for Eastern Countries, N.Y. Acad. Scis. Avocations: history, environment, philately, concerts, museums. Home and Office: 19 rue de Penthievre, 75008 Paris France

LAZAROVICI, PHILIP, pharmacologist, educator; b. Roman, Moldova, Romania, Oct. 1, 1949; arrived in Israel, 1963; s. Leon and Cuta Bracha (Fischler) L.; m. Janina Kapitkovsky, June 3, 1980; children: Lotan, Limor. BSc, Hebrew U., Jerusalem, 1975, MSc, 1976, PhD, 1981. Tchg. asst. Hebrew U., 1974-80, lectr., 1989-94, sr. lectr., 1994—; scientist Volcani Inst., Bet-Dagan, Israel, 1980-82; rsch. fellow CNRS, Marseille, France, 1982; postdoctoral fellow Weizmann Inst., Rehovot, Israel, 1982-84; vis. assoc. NIH, Bethesda, Md., 1985-88; neurosci. advisor Promega, Madison, Wis., 1994-96; sci. cons. Alomone Labs. Jerusalem, 1990—. Editor book series: Cellular and Molecular Mechanisms of Toxin Action, 1997—; co-editor: Biochemical Aspects of Marine Pharmacology, 1996; contbr. articles to profl. jours. Sgt. Zahal, Israel, 1968-71. Recipient Israel Cancer Rsch. award, Montreal, Can., 1990-92, award Nat. Inst. Psychology, 1990-95, Teva Pharm. Co., 1997-98. Mem. Am. Soc. Neurosci., Am. Chem. Soc., Internat. Soc. Toxicology. Jewish. Avocations: chess, fishing, cinema, reading. Home: Moshe Zvi Segal 30/6, Ramot Ghimel Jerusal Israel Office: Hebrew U, Sch Pharmacy, Jerusalem 91120, Israel

LAZAROWITZ, RACHEL HERTZ, education educator, psychologist; b. Haifa, Israel, July 24, 1940; d. Zvi Herman and Batia (Baumflek) Hertz; m. Reuven Lazarowitz, Dec. 2, 1958; children: Nurit, Neer, David. BA, Hebrew U., Haifa, 1971; MA, U. Tex., 1972, PhD, 1974. Cert. tchr. Tchr., counselor Spl. Edn. Sch., Nahariya, Israel, 1960-71; asst. instr. U. Tex., Austin, 1971-74; from lectr. to assoc. prof. Haifa U., 1974-99; vis. prof. CUNY Grad. Ctr., 2000—; vis. prof. U. So. Calif., L.A., 1987-88; acad. dir. womens leadership Haifa U., 1982-85, 94-00, chair devel. and mgmt. edn. sys., 1994-98; acad. head Coop. Learning & Literacy, Haifa, 1985-97; cons. in field. Author: What Happened to Daddy and Mommy, 1979; co-editor: (with N. Miller) Interaction in Cooperative Group, 1992; co-author: Handbook of Interethnic Coexistance, 1998. Project head Jews and Arab ptnrship The Abraham Fund, 1998—; head no. br. Israeli Womens Orgn., Haifa, 1991-95; nat. com. for gender equality Min. Edn., 1994-00, head project for improving Arab sch., Nazereth, 1993-00. Recipient prize for excellent study on the interfaith, Jerusalem, 1979. E-mail: rhertz-lazarowitz@gc.cuny.edu. Home: Kashtan Str # 3, 34984 Haifa Israel Office: Haifa Univ, Faculty Edn, 31905 Haifa Israel also: CUNY Grad Sch and Univ Ctr 365 5th Ave New York NY 10016-4309

LAZARUS, ARNAUD, cardiologist; b. Boulogne Billancourt, France, Nov. 9, 1962; s. Bernard and Claudine (Grimaux) L.; m. Laurence Leconte, May 28, 1988; children: Charlotte, Augustin, Louis. MD, Paris, 1991. Asst. prof. Paris, 1992-94; assoc. Assn. Cardiologic Val D'or, St. Cloud, France, 1994—; cons. in field. Contbr. articles to profl. jours. Mem. French Cardiology Soc., N.Am. Soc. of Pacing and Electrophysiology, N.Y. Acad. Scis., European Working Group on Cardiac Packing, InParys (assoc.). Avocations: tennis, golf. Office: 12 rue Pasteur, 92210 Saint Cloud France

LAZARUS, ARNOLD ALLAN, psychologist, educator; b. Johannesburg, Republic of South Africa, Jan. 27, 1932; came to U.S., 1963; s. Benjamin and Rachel Leah (Mosselson) L.; m. Daphne Ann Kessel, June 10, 1956; children: Linda Sue, Clifford Neil. BA with honors, U. Witwatersrand, Johannesburg, 1956, MA, 1957, PhD, 1960. Diplomate: Am. Bd. Profl. Psychology, Am. Bd. Med. Psychotherapists (fellow), Internat. Acad. Behavioral Medicine, Counseling and Psychotherapy. Pvt. practice clin. psychology Johannesburg, 1959-63, 64-66; vis. asst. prof. dept. psychology Stanford (Calif.) U., 1963-64; prof. psychology Temple U. Med. Sch., Phila., 1967-70; dir. clin. tng. Yale U., New Haven, 1970-72; disting. prof. Rutgers U., New Brunswick, N.J., 1972-98; pres. Ctr. for Multimodal Psychol. Svcs., Princeton, N.J., 1998—; mem. adv. bd. Psychologists for Social Responsibility, 1984—; cons. in field. Author: 15 books including Behavior Therapy and Beyond, 1971, Multimodal Behavior Therapy, 1976, The Practice of Multimodal Therapy, 1981, rev. edit., 1989, In the Mind's Eye, 1984, Martial Myths, 1985, Mind Power: Getting What You Want Through Mental Training, 1987, The Essential Arnold Lazarus, 1991, A Dialogue with Arnold Lazarus, 1991, Don't Believe It For A Minute!, 1993, Abnormal Psychology, 1995, Brief But Comprehensive Psychotherapy, 1997, The 60 Second Shrink, 1997, I Can If I Want To, 2000; editl. bd. sci. jours.; contbr. articles to profl. jours. Recipient Disting. Svc. award Am. Bd. Profl. Psychology, Disting. Career Achievement award Am. Bd. Med. Psychotherapists, Outstanding Contbns. to Mental Health award Psychiat. Outpatient Ctrs. of the Americas, 1991, Disting. Profl. Contbns. award Divsn. Clin. Psychology, Am. Psychol. Assn., 1997. Fellow APA (Disting. Psychologist award divsn. of psychotherapy 1992, 1st Ann. Cummings Psyche award 1996), Am. Bd. Profl. Psychology (diplomate), Internat. Acad. Eclectic Psychotherapists, Acad. Clin. Psychology; mem. Internat. Assn. Marriage and Family Counselors (Disting. Presenter Series award 2000), Am. Acad. Psychotherapy, Assn. for Advancement Psychotherapy, Nat. Acads. Practice in Psychology (disting.), Soc. for Exploration of Psychotherapy Integration, Calif. Psychol. Assn. (Lifetime Achievement award 1999), Assn. Advancement Behavior Therapy (Lifetime Achievement award 1999), Internat. Assn. Marriage and Family Counselors (Disting. Presenter award 2000). Home: 56 Herrontown Cir Princeton NJ 08540-2924

LAZARUS, MARGUERITE (ANNA GILBERT), writer; b. Durham, Eng., May 1, 1916; d. John Jackson and Hannah (Keers) Gascoigne; m. Jack Lazarus, Apr. 3, 1956. BA with honors, Durham (Eng.) U., 1937, MA, 1945. Grammar sch. tchr. Eng., 1941-73. Author: (as Marguerite Gascoigne) The Song of the Gypsy, 1956; (as Anna Gilbert) Images of Rose, 1973, The Look of Innocence, 1975 (Romantic Novelists Assn. award 1976), A Family Likeness, 1977, Remembering Louise, 1978, The Leavetaking, 1979, Flowers for Lilian, 1980, Miss Bede Is Staying, 1982, The Long Shadow, 1984 , A Walk in the Wood, 1989, The Wedding Guest, 1993, The Treachery of Time, 1995 (Catherine Cookson prize), A Hint of witchcraft, 2000. Home: Oakley Cottage, Swainsea Ln, Pickering YO18 8AR, England

LAZARUS, RICHARD J., law educator; b. Urbana, Ill., July 15, 1954; s. David and Betty (Ross) L.; m. Jeannette Lynn Austin, July 9, 1983; children: Samuel William Austin, Jesse Robert Austin. BS, BA, U. Ill., 1976; JD, Harvard U., 1979. Bar: D.C., Ill., Mo. Trial atty. land and natural resources divsn. U.S. Dept. Justice, Washington, 1979-83, asst. solicitor gen., 1986-89; asst. prof. law Ind. U., Bloomington, 1982-86; assoc. prof., then prof. law Washington U., St. Louis, 1989-96; prof. Georgetown U., Washington, 1996—; mem. nat. environ. justice adv. coun. EPA, Washington, 1994-97. Mem. nat. coun. World Wildlife Fund, Washington, 1994—. Woodrow Wilson fellow Woodrow Wilson Ctr. for Internat. Scholars, Washington, 1999-2000. E-mail: lazurus@law.goergetown.edu. Office: Georgetown U Law Ctr 600 New Jersery Ave Washington DC 20057-0001

LAZARUS, VIJAY JOHN, entertainment company executive; b. Pune, India, Nov. 10, 1949; s. John and Gladys (Anand) L.; m. Shirley Janette Fernandes, Apr. 20, 1976; children: Vishaal, Tia, Gaurav. BA in Econs. with honors, Pune U., 1970; MBA, Bajaj Jamnalal Inst., India, 1973. Mgmt. trainee Polydor, India, 1970-71, export exec., 1971-75, sales mgr., 1976-80; mgr. sales & mktg. Music India, 1981-87; v.p. sales & mktg. Polygram, India, 1988-94; pres., mng. dir. Universal (formerly Polygram), India, 1994—; pres. Indian Music Industry, 1994—; chmn. Phonographic Performances Ltd., 1994—; bd. dirs. Fedn. Indian C. of C. and Industry. Mem. Royal Western India Truff Club. Roman Catholic. Avocations: music, cricket. Home: 102, Nargis Dutt Rd, Mumbai 400050, India Office: Universal Music, 16-2, Dr. A. B. Rd, Mumbai 400018, India

LAZEA, VALENTIN, macroeconomist, researcher; b. Huedin, Cluj, Romania, Apr. 26, 1958; s. Emil and Alvina Lazea; m. Mihaela Chirila, May 30, 1985; 1 child, Victor-Florin. Grad. diploma in econs., Acad. Econ. Studies, Bucharest, Romania, 1982; diploma in advanced banking, Giordano dell Amore Inst., Milan, 1991; postgrad. diploma in econs., Sussex U., Brighton, Eng., 1993; diploma in fin. programming, Internat. Mon. Fund Inst., Washington, 1995. Econs. diplomate. Economist Ferrites Plant, Urziceni, Romania, 1982-85, Elec. Machines Plant, Bucharest, 1985-90; sci. rschr. Nat. Inst. for Econ. Rsch., Bucharest, 1990-93; head monetary policy divsn. Nat. Bank Romania, Bucharest, 1993-97, chief economist, 1999—; sec. state Ministry of Fin., Bucharest, 1997-99; assoc. prof. Acad. Econ. Studies, Bucharest, 1996-97; bd. dirs. Deposit Ins. Fund, Bucharest; counsellor to prime min. Govt. of Romania, 2000—; mem. bd. Romanian Ctr. for Econ. Policy. Co-author: Counsellor to the Presidency of Romania, 1994, Presidential Council's Reports, 1996; mem. editl. coll. Oeconomica Quarterly Rev., 1994—; contbr. articles to profl. jours. Candidate parlimentary elections Social-Democratic Party Romania, Bucharest, 1990, 92, mem. dir. com., 1994—, v.p., 1999—. Lt. Romaniana Army, 1977-78. Mem. Romanian Inst. for Free Enterprise. Avocations: traveling, painting, soccer, new-age literature. Home: 1 Corneliu Botez Str Apt 5, Bucharest Romania Office: 25 Lipscani Str, Bucharest Romania

LAZENBY, DAVID WILLIAM, civil engineer, consultant, standardizer; b. Frimley, Surrey, Eng., Oct. 13, 1937; s. George William and Jane (Foster) L.; m. Valerie Ann Kent, Sept. 2, 1961; children: Jonathan Kent, Andrea Jane. Diploma Imperial Coll., U. London, 1960; diploma, City U., London, 1983. With Balfour Beatty, London and Scotland, 1955-62; with Andrews Kent & Stone, London, 1962-97, ptnr., 1972-86, chmn., 1986-94; chmn. Com. Europeenne de Normalisation European Eurocodes Com., 1993-2000; dir. stds. Brit. Stds. Instn., 1998—; v.p. Com. Europeenne de Normalisation (European Stds. Orgn.); mem. coun. Internat. Orgn. for Standardization. Author: Structural Mechanics, 1965, Structural Steelwork, 1966, Cutting for Construction, 1978. Named European Engineer FEANI, 1988. Fellow City & Guilds of London, Instn. Civil Engrs., Instn. Structural Engrs. (pres. 1990-91); mem. Assn. Cons. Engrs. Mem. Ch. of England. Avocations: opera, tennis, golf, good food and wine. Home: Pond Cottage 28 Sanger Dr, Send, Woking GU23 7EB, England Office: British Stds Inst, 389 Chiswick High Rd, London W4 4AL, England

LAZIER, BUDDY, professional race car driver; b. Loveland Pass, Colo., Oct. 31, 1967; m. Kara Flynn, Aug. 31, 1997; 1 child, Robert Flinn. Driver Hemelgarn Racing, 1996; competitor Can. Am. Thundercar Series and Formula Vee. Winner Indpls. 500, 1996; 5th pl. Indy 200 at Walt Disney World; winner 125 cc Colo. Supercross Motorcycle championship, 1985, AIS championships, 1988, 2nd Indpls. 500, 1998, 2nd place Dover 2000, Midas 500 Classic, 2000. Office: Hemelgarn Racine 130 Gasoline Aly Indianapolis IN 46222*

LAZO BARRA, FLORENCIO, import-export executive, rancher, fruit grower; b. Santiago, Chile, Dec. 18, 1942; s. Florencio Lazo and Gertrudis Barra; m. Constanza Reyes Corbeaux, Apr. 27, 1974; children: Juan Enrrique, Sebastian, Florencio, Andres, Bernadita. Degree in architecture, U. Chile, 1965. Pres. Florencio Lazo Cia Ltd., Rancagua, Chile, 1980—; pres. Agricola Naicura Ltd., Rancagua, 1980, Forestal Naicura Rancagua, 1983; v.p. Fedefruta, Santiago, 1989—. Mem. Fedn. Productores de Frutas de Chile (founder 1985, pres. 1988, v.p. 2000—), Club de Polo Cachapoal, Club de Polo Las Mercedes (pres., founder 1995-99), Yacht Club Puerto Moutt. Avocations: polo, sailing, skiing, flying, diving.

LAZORENKO-MANEVICH, REM MIKHAILOVICH, chemist; b. Kamenets-Podolsk, Ukraine, Jan. 11, 1930; s. Mikhail Faddeyevich Lazorenko and Maria Markovna Manevich; m. Natalia Ivanovna Drozdova, Sept. 26, 1953; children: Ekaterina, Mikhail, Vladimir. B, Mendeleyev Inst. Chem. Engr., 1952; PhD, Karpov Inst. Phys. Chemistry, 1963, DSc, 1985. Engr. Chlorine Producing Co., Kemerovo, Russia, 1953-58; rschr. Karpov Inst. Phys. Chemistry, Obninsk, Russia, 1960-86; leading rschr. Karpov Inst. Phys. Chemistry, Obninsk, 1986—. Editl. bd. mem. Elektrokhimiya, 1995—; contbr. articles to profl. jours. Avocation: mini-football. Home: Joliot-Curie St 7 App 7, 249020 Obninsk Kaluga, Russia Office: Karpov Inst Phys Chemistry, State Rsch Ctr Russian Fedn, 249020 Obninsk Kaluga, Russia

LAZZAROTTO, MARCIO, science educator; b. Bento Gongalves, Brazil, Apr. 21, 1970; s. Honorino and Maria Lazzarotto; m. Francine Furtado Nachtigall, Sept. 12, 1992; 1 child, Davi. Cert. in chemistry. Temporary prof. Fed. U. Santa Catarina, Florianopolis, 1996-97; postdoctoral fellow U. Degli Studi di Parma, 1998-99; prof. State U. Ponta Grossa, Brazil, 1999—. Contbr. articles to profl. jours. Avocations: spending time with son, chess. E-mail: mlazzaro@uepg.br. Office: Praga Santos Andrade, s/n, Ponta Grossa 84010270, Brazil

LAZZI, GIANLUCA, electronics engineer, researcher; b. Rome, Apr. 25, 1970; s. Romano and Annamaria (Pastore) L.; m. Dulce Altabella, Mar. 20, 1999. D in Electronics Engring., U. La Sapienza, Rome, 1994; PhD in Elec. Engring., U. Utah, 1998. Registered profl. engr., Rome. Vis. rschr. Nat. Italian Bd. for Nuc. and Alternative Energies, Rome, 1994-95; sci. collaborator U. La Sapienza, Rome, 1994-95; rsch. assoc. U. Utah, Salt Lake City, 1995-98, rsch. asst. prof., 1998—; asst. prof. N.C. State U., Raleigh, 1999—; cons. BCD Sistemi, Rome, 1993-94. Co-author: software packages for the Italian Nat. TV Network, 1988; contbr. articles to profl. jours. Recipient Young Scientist award Internat. Union Radio Sci., 1996, Curtis Carl Johnson Meml. award Bioelectromagnetics Soc., 1996. Mem. IEEE (sr.), Italian Elec. and Electronic Soc. Office: NC State U Dept Elec Computer Engring PO Box 7914 Raleigh NC 27695-0001

LE, KHANH CHAU, mechanical engineering educator; b. Hanoi, Viet Nam, Nov. 17, 1955; arrived in Germany, 1988; s. Khanh Can Le and Tan Nhan Truong; m. Thanh Hoa Nguyen, July 12, 1982; 1 child, Thanh Ly Le. MS, Moscow State U., 1979, PhD, 1983, DSc, 1986; Dr. Habil., Bochum U., Germany, 1996. Head dept. Inst. Mechanics, Hanoi, 1986-88; rsch. fellow Humboldt Found., Bochum, 1988-89; asst. prof. Bochum U., 1989-93, assoc. prof., 1993—. Author: Continuum Modelling of Media with Changeable Microstructure, 1996, Vibrations of Shells and Rods, 1998; contbr. articles to profl. jours. Mem. ASME, Am. Math. Soc., Gesellschaft für Angewandte Math. und Mechanik. Avocations: music, chess. Home: Am Josephsschacht 242, 44879 Bochum Germany Office: Bochum U, Universitatsstr 150, 44780 Bochum Germany

LE, LY NGOC, environmental physicist, educator; b. Hanoi, Vietnam; naturalized, 1988; s. Le Ngoc Can and Phan Thi Chan; m. XuanDung Vu. PhD in Environ. Physics magna cum laude, State Hydromet Inst., St. Petersburg, Russia, 1977. Postdoctoral rsch. assoc. Iowa State U., Ames, 1985-88; scientist III U. Coop. for Atmospheric Rsch. Inst. for Naval Oceanography, Stennis Space Ctr., Miss., 1988-92; sr. rsch. scientist Ctr. for Ocean and Atmospheric Modeling, USM, Stennis Space Ctr., Miss., 1992-93; rsch. prof. Naval Postgrad. Sch., Monterey, Calif., 1993—. Author: Dynamics of the Atmosphere, 1980; contbr. articles to profl. jours. Recipient Rsch. grant Office of Naval Rsch. Mem. N.Y. Acad. Scis., Am. Geophys. Union, Am. Meteorol. Soc., Soc. for Indsl. and Applied Math. Achievements include developments of air-wave-sea coupled model based on a new turbulence concept and of a computer ocean modeling system incorporating a new turbulent closure with a surface wave parameterization and grid generation techniques. Office: Naval Postgrad Sch Dept Oceanography Monterey CA 93943

LE, THAI VAN, lawyer; b. Tan-An, Long-An, Vietnam, June 19, 1946; s. Tieu Van Le and Lung Thi Nguyen; m. Nhu-Nguyen Thi Pham, Feb. 28, 1971; children: Tuan, Nhu-Tuyen Pham. LLB, Saigon (Vietnam) U. of Law, 1971, LLM 1st grade, 1972. Cert. internat. banking tng., forex tng., audit qualification, tchr. Mng. dir. Orient Comml. Bank, Saigon, 1971-75; mgr. Saigon Bank for Industry and Trade, Ho Chi Minh City, Vietnam, 1990-92, Van-Lang U., Ho Chi Minh City, 1995—; lawyer Russin & Vecchi LLP, Ho Chi Minh City, 1994—. Author: Business English, 1998; translator: Commercial Banking, 1991; contbr. articles to profl. publs. Mem. Ho Chi Minh City Lawyers' Assn. (cons. 1990—). Avocations: reading, fishing, hiking. Home: 258/507 Vo Van Tan Dist 3, Ho Chi Minh City Vietnam Office: Russin & Vecchi LLP, 8 Nguyen-Hue 15/F Dist 1, Ho Chi Minh City Vietnam

LE, THANG KIM, computer science educator; b. Dalat, Vietnam, Dec. 10, 1950; arrived in Australia, 1981; s. Ha Kim Le and Dung Thi Bui; m. Cam-Hoa Thi Nguyen, Apr. 26, 1975; children: Thuan Kim, Minh Kim. B Engring., Nat. Inst. Tech., Saigon, Vietnam, 1973; M Engring., U. Newcastle, Australia, 1986; PhD, U. Sydney, Australia, 1991. Asst. lectr. Nat. Inst. Tech., Saigon, 1973-75; lectr. U. Polytechnique, Saigon, 1975-81; commissioning engr. IHI, NSW, Australia, 1982-85; tutor U. Sydney, 1985-87; lectr. U. Canberra, Australia, 1987—. Contbr. articles to profl. jours. and ency.; editor: Jour. Knowledge-based Intelligent Engring. Sys., 1999. Chmn. Van-Hanh Buddhist Family, Australia, 1997—. Mem. IEEE Computer Soc., Vietnamese Buddhist Assn. (Australia; pres. 1984-86). Avocations: bush walking, music, swimming, ping pong, bicycling. Office: U Canberra, Sch Computing, Canberra ACT 2601, Australia

LEA, RICHARD GRAHAM, reproductive immunologist; b. London, Feb. 8, 1963; s. Percy and Elsie Patricia (Chambers) L.; m. Corinne Eliane Giudici, July 18, 1987. BSc with honors, U. East London, 1984; PhD, Sheffield (Eng.) Hallam U., 1988. Fellow McMaster U., Hamilton, Ont., Can., 1988-91; sr. rsch. fellow dept. medicine U. Edinburgh, Scotland, 1991-94, sr. rsch. fellow dept. ob-gyn., 1994-96; sr. rsch. scientist Rowett Rsch. Inst., Aberdeen, Scotland, 1996—. Contbr. chpt. to: Balliere's Clinical Obstetrics and Gynecology, 1989, 91, Annals of New York Academy of Sciences, 1991; contbr. articles to profl. jours. Recipient award for Best Clin. Presentation, Can. Fertility and Andrology Soc., Vancouver, 1989; Rsch. grantee, Novo Nordisk U.K., Savena Trust, Med. Rsch. Coun., Brit. Diabetic Assn., Dr. James Alexander Mearns Trust. Mem. Am. Soc. Reproductive Immunology (New Investigator award 1997), Soc. for Study of Fertility, Brit. Soc. Immunology, Soc. for Endocrinology. Office: Rowett Rsch Inst, Greenburn Rd, Bucksburn, Aberdeen AB21 9SB, Scotland

LEACH, JAMES GLOVER, lawyer; b. Panama City, Fla., Jan. 26, 1948; s. Milledge Glover and Thelma Louise (Hamilton) L.; m. Judith A. Leach, Feb. 26, 1972 (div. 1987); children: Allison, Arica; m. January Parker, Dec. 1997. AS, Gulf Coast Coll., 1968; BA, Duke U., 1970; MBA, Ga. State U., 1974, MI, 1976; JD, Drake U., 1989. Bar: Iowa 1990; CPCU 1977, CLU 1978. Bank officer Bank South, Atlanta, 1972-75; asst. v.p. Johnson & Higgins, Atlanta, 1975-78; pres. Nat. Gen. Ins. Co., St. Louis, 1978-85, AOPA Svc. Corp., St. Louis, 1985-87, Kirke-Van Orsdel Specialty, Des Moines, 1987-89, Gallagher Specialty, St. Louis, 1990-92; prin., dir., counsel Pauli & Co. Inc., St. Louis, 1992-93; sr. v.p. and gen. counsel Am. Safety Ins., Atlanta, 1993-98; vice chair, gen. counsel, dir. Unistar Fin. Svc. Corp., Dallas, 1998—; cons. McDonnell Douglas, St. Louis, 1987; dir. Gateway Ins. Co., St. Louis, 1992; corp. assembly Blue Cross/Blue Shield, St. Louis, 1991-92. Contbr. articles to profl. jours. 1st lt. USAF, 1970-72, Korea. Avocations: pilot, golf. Home: 13907 Montfort Dr Apt 233 Dallas TX 75240-4399 Office: Unistar Fin Svc Corp 4635 McEwen Rd Dallas TX 75244-5308

LEACH, LUANN MARIE, elementary school educator; b. Grand Rapids, Mich., Oct. 27, 1963; d. Robert Allen and Rose Clare (Williams) L. BS, Western Ky. U., 1989; postgrad., U. W. Fla., 1999—. Gymnastics instr. Pensacola (Fla.) Jr. Coll., 1989-90; elem. phys. edn. tchr. Ferry Pass and Beulah Elem. Sch., Pensacola, Fla., 1989-90, Myrtle Grove and Beulah Elem. Sch., Pensacola, Fla., 1990-92, Myrtle Grove and McArthur Elem. Sch., Pensacola, Fla., 1992-93, Myrtle Grove and Lipscomb Elem. Sch., Pensacola, Fla., 1993-95; gymnastics instr. Dmitri Bilozertchev Gymnastics Tng., Pensacola, Fla., 1995; elem. phys. edn. tchr. Lipscomb and N.B. Cook Magnet Sch. for the Performing Arts, Pensacola, Fla., 1995-96; soccer tchr. Lipscomb's After the Bell Program, Pensacola, Fla., 1996; elem. phys. edn. tchr. Oakcrest and Warrington Elem. Sch., Pensacola, Fla., 1996-97, Oakcrest and Ensley Elem. Sch., Pensacola, 1997-98, O.J. Semmes Montessori Acad., 1998-99, O.J. Semmes Montessori Acad. and Hallmark Elem. Sch., 1999—; tutor Beyond the Sch. Day program, substitute tchr. Neighborhood Learning program, 1997-98,; presenter in field. Vol. gymnastics tchr. Ferry Pass, Beulah, Myrtle Grove Elem. Schs., Pensacola, 1989-91; vol. coach Fit to Achieve Teams: Beulah and Myrtle Grove Elem. Schs., Pensacola, 1990-92; vol. tennis coach, coord. 10 teams Pensacola Jr. Tennis Assn., Pensacola, 1993-96; vol. coach Jogging Club for Myrtle Grove and Lipscomb Elem. Schs., Pensacola, 1994-95; Vacation Bible Sch. and Sunday sch. tchr. First Bapt. Ch., Pensacola, Fla., 1996-98; vol. Habitat for Humanity, 1998; 8th grade cheerleading coach Easthill Christian Sch., Pensacola, 1998-99. Recipient Outstanding Elem. Sch. Team Tennis Coach award Pensacola Jr. Tennis Assn., 1993, cert. of achievement for the Model Phys. Fitness Sch. Program Fla. Govs. Coun. on Phys. Fitness and Sports, 1995, awards for cheerleading teams coached. Mem. AAHPERD, ASCD, Fla. Assn. for Health, Phys. Edn., Recreation, Dance and Driver Edn., Escambia County Phys. Edn. Assn. (sec. 1992). Republican. Avocations: violin, art, tennis, interior design. Home: 3421 Riverside Dr Pensacola FL 32514-8172

LEADBETTER, MARK RENTON, JR., orthopedic surgeon; b. Phila., Nov. 7, 1944; s. Mark Renton and Ruth (Protzeller) L.; m. Letitia Ashby, July 28, 1973 (div. June 1990); m. Jan Saker, 1991. BA, Gettysburg Coll., 1967; MSc in Hygiene, U. Pitts., 1970; MD, Temple U., 1974. Cert. ind. med. examiner. Surg. intern Univ. Hosps., Boston, 1974-75, resident in surgery, 1975-76; emergency room physician Sturdy Meml. Hosp., Attleboro, Mass., 1976-78; resident in orthopaedics U. Pitts., 1978-81; orthopaedic physician Rockingham Meml. Hosp., Harrisonburg, Va., 1981-82, courtesy staff, 1982—; pvt. practice, Staunton, Va., 1982—; mem. active staff King's Daus. Hosp., Staunton, 1982—; active staff Samaritan Hosp., Moses Lake, Wash.; courtesy staff Columbia Basin Hosp., Ephrata, Wash.; med. dir. Ind. Med. Examiners. Contbr. articles to med. jours.; patentee safety syringes, safety cannulas, designer of medecal equipment. Mem. AMA, Am. Coll. Sports Medicine, Am. Bd. Ind. Med. Examiners, Acad. Disability Evaluating Physicians, So. Med. Assn., So. Orthopaedic Assn., County Med. Soc., Nat. Futures Assn. (assoc.). Republican. Avocations: flying, skiing, raising bird dogs. Home: 3233 Centralia Alpha Rd Onalaska WA 98570-9610

LEADER, CHRISTOPHER ROBERT, manufacturing executive; b. South Bend, Ind.; s. Robert A. and Dorothy R. L.; m. Linda A. Hoyt; three children. BS in Mech. Engring., U. Notre Dame, 1981; MBA, U. Mich., 1991. Lt. USN, navigator, dept. head USS England (CG-22), San Diego (home port), 1981-85; statis. process control analyst GM, Saginaw, Mich., 1985-87, sr. quality engr., 1987-91; prodn. supt. Ford Motor Co., Avon Lake, Ohio, 1991-93, vehicle evaluation mgr., 1993-94, prodn. mgr., area mgr., 1994; v.p. ops., corp. officer Trek USA Bicycle Corp., Waterloo, Wis., 1994-96, Skyline Corp., Elkhart, Ind., 1997—. Co-author: Quality Engineering Jour., 1989. Lt. USN, 1981-85. Mem. Am. Soc. Quality (sr. mem., cert. quality engr.). Office: Skyline Corp 2520 By Pass Rd Elkhart IN 46515

LEADER, ROBERT JOHN, lawyer; b. Syracuse, N.Y., Oct. 14, 1933; s. Henry John and Dorothy Alberta (Schad) L.; m. Nancy Bruce, Sept. 23, 1960; children: Henry, William, Catherine, Thomas, Edward. AB, Cornell U., 1956; JD, Syracuse U., 1962. Bar: N.Y. 1963. Assoc. Ferris, Hughes, Dorrance & Groben, Utica, N.Y., 1962-64; ptnr. Cole Leader & Elmer, Gouverneur, N.Y., 1964-66, Case & Leader, Gouverneur, 1966—; sec. North Country Hosps. Inc., 1972—; atty. Village of Hermon (N.Y.), 1968—, Town of Gouverneur, 1967-94, Town of Pitcairn (N.Y.), 1974—, Town of Edwards, 1974—, Town of Rossie, 1985—, Town of Fowler, 1978—; corp. counsel Village of Gouverneur, 1973—; counsel Gouverneur Ctrl. Sch. Dist., 1980—; bd. dirs. Gouverneur Savs. and Loan. Trustee Edward John Noble Hosp., Gouverneur, 1972—, Gouverneur Libr., 1973-83, Gouverneur Nursing Home Co., Inc., 1972—, past pres., 1979-81; Republican chmn. Town and Village of Gouverneur, 1969-72; del. N.Y. State Jud. conv., 1981—. Served to capt. USAF, 1956-59. Mem. Rotary (pres. 1988-89). Roman Catholic. Home: 187 Rowley St Gouverneur NY 13642-1220 Office: 107 E Main St Gouverneur NY 13642-1408

LEADER, ROGER JOHN, executive recruiter; b. Hong Kong, Oct. 3, 1956; arrived in Eng., 1992; s. College John and Anna (Mackie) L.; m. Sarah Alexandria Samuels, Nov. 23, 1986; children: Edward, Victoria, Hugo. Educated, Eastbourne (Eng.) Coll., 1973. Mgr. Interfashion Industries Ltd., Hong Kong, 1975-78; regional mktg. mgr. Dunlop/Slazenger Ltd., Hong Kong, 1978-85; mng. assoc. Korn Ferry Internat., Hong Kong, 1985-87; mng. dir. Consulting Group, Hong Kong, 1987-92; cons. Stephens Assocs., London, 1992-93; CEO Leader Fin. Rsch., London, 1993—. Avocations: cresta run, golf, water sports. Home: Rutherfords Stud, Chantry Ln, Andover Hampshire SP11 9ET, England

LEAHY, KEVIN SEAN, energy company strategist; b. Logansport, Ind., Apr. 14, 1958; m. Joyce L. Steiner, 1990. BS in Mech. Engrnig., Purdue U., 1980; MBA, Ind. U., 1987; MPA, Harvard U., 1998. Mech. engr. Commonwealth Edison, Chgo., 1981-82; engr., vol. U.S. Peace Corps, Honduras, 1982-84; asst. dir. microenterprise devel. U.S. Peace Corps, Tirana, Albania, 1993-95; internat. bus. devel. analyst Cummins Engine Co., Columbus, Ind., 1987-89; human rels. mgr. Cummins Engine Co., Columbus, 1989-92; chief strategy officer internat. Cinergy Corp., Cin., 1998—; cons. World Bank, Washington, 1996. Vocalist Plymouth Music Series Chorus, Mpls., 1996-97. Bd. mem. First Call for Help, Columbus, 1992; visitor host Minn. Internat. Ctr., 1996-97. Mem. World Affairs Coun. Avocation: singing. E-mail: leastein@mindspring.com. Fax: 513-287-2037. Office: Cinergy Global Resources 105 E 4th St Ste 710 Cincinnati OH 45202-4015

LEAK, JESSIE ARONOW, anesthesiologist; b. Beaumont, Tex., May 19, 1957. MD, U. Tex. Health Sci. Ctr., 1984. Diplomate Am. Bd. Anesthesiology. Resident in anesthesiology Med. U. S.C., Charleston, 1984-87, fellow in obstet. anesthesiology, pain mgmt., 1987-88; staff anesthesiologist Cape Fear Valley Med. Ctr., Fayetteville, N.C., 1989-98, Highsmith-Rainey Meml. Hosp., Fayetteville, 1988-98; pvt. practice Valley Anesthesia, P.A., Fayetteville, 1988-90; founding ptnr., sec. bd. dirs. Cumberland Anesthesia Assocs., P.A., Fayetteville, 1990-98; asst. prof. anesthesiology U. N.C., Chapel Hill, 1989-94; assoc. prof. divsn. anesthesia, symptom control and palliative care U. Tex. M.D. Anderson Cancer Ctr., Houston, 1998—. Contbr. articles to profl. jours. Active Fayetteville Area C. of C., 1988-98, Fayetteville Area Econ. Devel. Corp., 1996-98. First prize award Am. Soc. Anesthesiologists Art Exhbn., 1999. Mem. AMA, Am. Soc. Anesthesiologists, So. Med. Assn., N.C. Med. Soc., N.C. Soc. Anesthesiology (past pres.), Tex. Soc. Anesthesiologists. Office: U Tex MD Anderson Cancer Ctr Divsn Anesthesiology 1515 Holcombe Blvd # 42 Houston TX 77030-4009

LEAK, NANCY MARIE, artist; b. Takoma Park, Md., Nov. 24, 1931; d. George Morton and Ella (Oberholtzer) Hinkson; m. Thomas Clayton Leak Jr., Dec. 30, 1950; children: Suzanne M. Street, Sharon Leak-Hayden, Stephen, Scott. Grad. h.s., Washington. Co-illustrator: The Kissing Hand, 1993; exhbns. include Olney Art Assn., Internat. Exhbn. of the Miniature, Fla., Ga., Washington, N.J., Cider Painters Am. Nat. Exhbn., Hunterdon Art Ctr., N.J., Sumner Mus., Washington, Gurmukhs Gallery, Aspen Hill, Md., Nev. Miniature Art Soc., Worldwide Miniature Exhbn., Australia, 2000, Hoffberger Gallery, Balt., Ocean City (Md.) Art League, Rockville (Md.) Art League, Md. Printmakers, Worldwide Miniature Exhbn., London, Tasmania, Australia, 2000, Md. Ho. of Dels., Annapolis, NIH, Bethesda, Md., Johns Hopkins Space Telescope Sci. Inst., Balt., Del Bello Gallery, Ont., Can., Rockville Art League, Pinneberg, Germany, Gov's. Mansion, Annapolis, 1999, George Mason U. Art Gallery, Arlington, Va., 2000; participated in numerous juried or invitational exhbns. Recipient numerous awards for art. Mem. Nat. League Am. Pen Women, Md. Printmakers Assn., Miniature Painters, Sculptors & Gravers Soc. Washington, Miniature Art Soc. Fla., Rockville Art League, Olney Art Assn., Cider Painters Am., Miniature Artists Am. Democrat. Methodist. Avocations: crafts, reading, designing notecards, genealogy, photography.

LEAKE, DAVID, bishop; b. Argentina, June 26, 1935; s. William Alfred and Dorothy Violet (Frostick) L.; m. Rachel Yarham, Dec. 31, 1961; children: Andrew, Philip, Judith. Licentiate in Theology, St. Johns Coll., Nottingham, Eng., 1959. From priest to bishop North Argentina Anglican Ch. in Argentina, Salta, 1963-89; bishop Argentina Anglican Ch. in Argentina, Buenos Aires, 1990—. Address: Casilla 4293 Correo Central, 1000 Buenos Aires Argentina Office: Anglican Ch, 25 de Mayo 282, 1002 Buenos Aires Argentina

LEAKE, HEATHER ALISON, pharmacist, educator, minister; b. Oxford, Eng., June 24, 1966; d. John Walgate and Pamela Marjorie (Lancelotte) L. BS with honors, Brighton (Eng.) Poly., 1988; diploma in clin. pharmacy, U. Wales, Cardiff, 1991; MS in Clin. Pharmacy, U. Brighton, 1996. Ordained to ministry, Meth. Ch. Pre-registration pharmacist Northampton (Eng.) Gen. Hosp., 1988-89; resident pharmacist Derbyshire Royal Infirmary, Derby, Eng., 1989-91; sr. clin. pharmacist Brighton Health Care Nat. Health Svc. Trust, 1991-99, prin. pharmacist, 1999—; recognized clin. tchr. U. Brighton, 1992—; part-time lectr. U. Portsmouth, U.K., 1992—; group mem. AIDS Pharmacy Assn. (formerly AIDS Pharmacists Group), 1991—, mem. coord. com., 1996-2000. Contbr. articles to profl. jours. Mem. Guild Hosp. Pharmacists (sec. Sussex group 1991-93), U.K. Clin. Pharmacy Assn., Brit. HIV Assn. Methodist. Avocations: walking, gardening, traveling, cinema, theater. Office: Hove Gen Hosp, Elton John Centre Brighton Gen Hosp, Elm Grove Brighton BN2 3EW, England

LEAKEY, ROGER RICHARD BAZETT, research scientist, consultant; b. Nairobi, Kenya, July 19, 1946; s. Douglas Gray Bazett and Beryl Enid (Jackson) L.; m. Alison Edith Swan, Aug. 16, 1974; children: Andrew David Bazett, Christopher Douglas Bazett. BS with honors, U. Wales, 1970; PhD, U. Reading, Eng., 1974; DS, U. Wales, 1998; NDA, CDA, Newton-Abbot (Eng.) Agrl. Coll., 1967. Chartered biologist, Inst. Biology, 1997. Rsch. scientist Inst. Tree Biology, Edinburgh, Scotland, 1974-75; sr. sci. officer Inst. Terrestrial Ecology, Edinburgh, Scotland, 1975-85, prin. sci. officer, 1985-93; dir. rsch. Internat. Ctr. Rsch. in Agroforestry, Nairobi, Kenya, 1993-97; head tropical ecology Inst. Terrestrial Ecology, 1997—; cons. Food and Agr. Orgn. UN, Italy, 1982, 87, World Bank, U.S., 1985, 87, 89; sec. U.K. Tree Biotech. Liaison Group, 1985-93; dir. Edinburgh Ctr. Tropical Forests, 1999—. Co-author: Domestication of Tropical Trees for Timber and Non-Timber Forest Products, 1994; co-editor: Tropical Trees: Potential for Demestication and the Rebuilding of Forest Resources, 1994, Domestication and Commercialization of Non-Timber Forest Products in Agroforestry Systems, 1996, Cultivating Trees: People and Plants Handbook No. 5, 1999; contbr. over 150 articles to profl. jours. Named Hon. fellow U. Edinburgh, 1987. Fellow Inst. Biology; mem. Internat. Soc. Tropical Foresters, Commonwealth Forestry Assn., N.Y. Acad. Scis., Edinburgh Ctr. Tropical Forests (hon.). Mem. Ch. of Scotland. Avocations: large scale gardening, natural history, photography. Office: Inst Terrestrial Ecology, Bush Estate Penicuik, Midlothian EH26 0QB, Scotland

LEAL, BARBARA JEAN PETERS, fundraising executive; b. Hartford, Ala., Oct. 24, 1948; d. Clarence Lee and Syble (Simmons) Peters; m. Ramon Leal, 1991; children: Michaelle, Jonathan. AA, Enterprise State Jr. Coll., 1970; BA, U. South Fla., 1974; MA, Trinity U., San Antonio, 1975; postgrad., U. Nacional Autonoma de Mex., 1982. Cert. fundraising exec. Instr. San Antonio Coll., 1975; planner Econ. Opportunities Devel. Corp., San Antonio, 1976, Alamo Area Coun. Govts., San Antonio, 1977-82; dir. planned giving Oblate Missions, San Antonio, 1982—; spkr. in field. Author: Paratransit Provider Handbook, 1978; contbg. author: Human Resources to Aging, 1976, Transportation for Elderly Handicapped Programs and Problems, 1978; contbr. articles to profl. publs. Mem. San Antonio chpt. Nat. Com. on Planned Giving; mem. Nat. Cath. Devel. Conf. Named one of Outstanding Young Women of Am., 1985. Mem. Nat. Soc. Fund Raising Execs. (founding mem., past. pres. San Antonio chpt.), Am. Coun. on Gift Annuities, Coun. Advancement and Support Edn. Roman Catholic. Office: Oblate Missions PO Box 96 San Antonio TX 78291-0096

LEA MOND, HAROLD JOSEPH, urban planner; b. Newport News, Va., June 11, 1953; m. Deborah Kelly, Oct. 19, 1991; children: Michael, Kathryn. BA, Wofford Coll., 1976; MPA, Coll. of Charleston, 1981. Planning intern City of Charleston, S.C., 1980, planning technician, 1980-82, planner I, 1982; boarding agt. Harrington and Co., Inc., Charleston, S.C., 1982-83; office and planning mgr. Sigma Engrs., Inc., Charleston, S.C., 1983-86; county planner Berkeley County, Moncks Corner, S.C., 1986—. Mem. AICPA, Am. Planning Assn. (legis. com. S.C. chpt.). Fax: (843) 719-4111. Office: Berkeley County Planning and Zoning 223 N Live Oak Dr Moncks Corner SC 29461-3707

LEAO MONTEIRO, JOSE LUIS BARBOSA, diplomat. Permanent rep. Republic of Cape Verde UN, N.Y.C., 1994—. Office: Republic of Cape Verde Perm Mission to the UN 27 E 69th St New York NY 10021-4917*

LEAPER, DAVID JOHN, surgeon, educator; b. York, Eng., July 23, 1947; s. David Thomas and Gwendoline (Robertson) L.; m. Gillian Margot Fanthorpe, May 31, 1971 (div. July 1992); children: Charles David Edward, Alice Jane Sophia; m. Francesca Ann Hanes, Nov. 4, 1995. MBChB with honors, Leeds Med. Sch., U.K., 1970; MD, Leeds Med. Sch., 1979, ChM, 1982; FRCS, Royal Coll. of Surgeons, Eng., 1975; FRCSEd, Royal Coll. of Surgeons, Edinburgh, 1974. Med. diplomate. Surg. registrar Leeds and Scarborough Hosps., U.K., 1971-75; cancer rsch. campaign fellow Kings Coll. Hosp., U.K., 1976-77; sr. registrar Westminster Hosp., London, 1977-81; prof. surgery U. Hong Kong, 1988-90; sr. lectr. U. Bristol, 1981-95; prof. surgery U. Newcastle-Upon-Tyne, 1995—; Zachary-Cope lectr. Royal Coll. Surgery, Eng., 1999; program dir. Higher Surg. Tng. No. Deanery; profl. rep. specialist adv. com. HIgher Surg. Tng. U.K. Chief editor surg. rsch. comm., 1988-97; editl. bd. British Jour. Surgery, 1992-98; author/editor: International Surgical Practice, 1992; author: (book series) Your Operation, 1993-94; author: Oxford Handbook of Operative Surgery, 1997, Wounds: Biology and Management, 1998. Chmn. Round Table Britain and Ireland, Thornbury, U.K., 1988-89; mem. dept. health/Hosp. Infection Control, U.K., 1992-94; vice-chmn. hosp. ethic com., Bristol, U.K., 1994-95. Recipient Distinction award Nat. Health Svc., U.K., 1993, 97; fellow Med. Rsch. Coun., 1971-72, Rsch. fellow Southwest Region Eng., 1982; rsch. and devel. grantee NHS, 1996, Action Rsch. Fellow ACS (Am. Coll. of Surgs.), Royal Coll. of Surgeons (Glasgow); mem. European Wound Mgmt. Assn. (pres. 1994-95), Royal Soc. Medicine U.K. (v.p. sect. surgery 1985-93), Royal Coll. Surgeons Eng. (mem. court examiners 1992-98, Ethicon Found. award 1976, 82, Hunterian prof. 1981, Zachary-Cope lectr. 1999), Surg. Infection Soc. (recorder 1993-98, pres. 1999—), Surg. Rsch. Soc. (com. mem. 1987-89, European fellow 1976), North of Eng. Surg. Soc., Internat. Soc. Surgery. Office: U Newcastle Upon Tyne Surgery, North Tees NHS Trust, TS198PE Cleveland England

LEAR, ERWIN, anesthesiologist, educator; b. Bridgeport, Conn., Jan. 1, 1924; s. Samuel Joseph and Ida (Ruth) L.; m. Arlene Joyce Alexander, Feb. 15, 1953; children—Stephanie, Samuel. MD, SUNY, 1952. Diplomate Am. Bd. Anesthesiology, Nat. Bd. Med. Examiners. Intern L.I. Coll. Hosp., Bklyn., 1952-53; asst. resident anesthesiology Jewish Hosp., Bklyn., 1953-54; sr. resident Jewish Hosp., 1955, asst., 1955-56, adj., 1956-58, assoc. anesthesiologist, 1958-64; attending anesthesiologist Bklyn. VA Hosp., 1958-64, cons., 1977—; assoc. vis. anesthesiologist Kings County Hosp. Ctr., Bklyn., 1957-80; staff anesthesiologist Kings County Hosp. Ctr., 1980-81; vis. anesthesiologist Queens Gen. Hosp. Ctr., 1955-67; dir. anesthesiology Queens Hosp. Ctr. Jamaica, 1964-67; chmn. dept. anesthesiology Catholic Med. Ctr., Queens and Bklyn., 1968-80; dir. anesthesiology Beth Israel Med. Ctr., N.Y.C., 1981-98; clin. instr. SUNY Coll. Medicine, Bklyn., 1955-58; from clin. asst. prof. to clin. prof. SUNY Coll. Medicine, 1958-80, prof., vice-chmn. clin. anesthesiology, 1980-81; prof. anesthesiology Mt. Sinai Sch. Medicine, 1981-94, Albert Einstein Coll. of Medicine, 1994—; cons. in field. Author: Chemistry Applied Pharmacology of Tranquilizers; contbr. articles to profl. jours. Served with USNR, 1942-45. Fellow Am. Coll. Anesthesiologists, N.Y. Acad. Medicine (sec. sect. anesthesiology 1985-86, chmn. sect. anesthesiology 1986-87); mem. AMA, Am. Soc. Anesthesiologists (chmn. com. on by-laws 1982-83, dir. 1981-97, ho. of dels. 1973-94, editor newsletter 1984-88, chmn. adminstrv. affairs com., 1987-94), N.Y. State Bd. Profl. Med. Conduct, N.Y. State Soc. Anesthesiologists (chmn. pub. relations 1963-73, chmn. com. local arrangements 1968-73, dist. dir. 1972-73, v.p. 1974-75, pres. 1976, bd. dirs. 1972-94, chmn. jud. com. 1977-81, assoc. editor Bulletin 1963-77, editor Sphere 1978-84, Disting. Svc. award 1996), N.Y. State Med. Soc. (chmn. sect. anesthesiology 1966-67, sec. sect. 1977-81), N.Y. County Med. Soc., SUNY Coll. Medicine Alumni Assn. (pres. 1983, trustee alumni fund 1980), Alpha Omega Alpha. Address: 3 Harriman Dr Sands Point NY 11050-1246

LEASURE, ROBERT ELLIS, writer, photographer; b. Lamar, Colo., Oct. 20, 1921; s. Henry Naley and Pansy Margaret (Leatherman) L.; m. Betty Jean Stulck, July 4, 1945; twins: Mary Margaret and David Lee. Grad. high sch., Lamar, Colo. Cryptographer 15th Air Force Air Def. Command, Colorado Springs, Colo., 1946; staff Colorado Springs (Colo.) Post Office, 1946-76; freelancer photographer, writer, 1976—. Author: Black Mountain, 1975; exhibited at Tex. Fine Art Assn. Mem. Colorado Springs Fine Arts Guild.Sgt. U.S. Army, 1942-45. Mem. VFW. Presbyterian. Avocations: nature, art, history, archaeology, literature. Home: 1210 Milky Way Colorado Springs CO 80906-1715

LEATHER, VICTORIA POTTS, college librarian; b. Chattanooga, June 12, 1947; d. James Elmer Potts and Ruby Lea (Bettis) Potts Wilmoth; m. Jack Edward Leather; children: Stephen, Sean. BA cum laude, U. Chattanooga, 1968; MSLS, U. Tenn., 1978. Libr. asst. East New Orleans Regional Libr., 1969-71; libr. Erlanger Nursing Sch., Chattanooga, 1971-75; chief libr. Erlanger Hosp., Chattanooga, 1975-77; dir. Eastgate Br. Libr., Chattanooga, 1977-81; dir. libr. svcs. Chattanooga State Tech. Community Coll., 1981-95, dean libr. svcs., 1996—. Mem. Allied Arts, Hunter Mus., High Mus. Art. Mem. ALA, Southeastern Libr. Assn., Tenn. Libr. Assn. (past chair legislation com.), Chattanooga Area Libr. Assn. (pres. 1978-79), Tenn. Bd. Regents Media Consortium (chair 1994-95), Phi Delta Kappa. Episcopalian. Avocations: reading, needlework, traveling.

LEATON, MARCELLA KAY, insurance representative, business owner; b. Eugene, Oreg., Oct. 9, 1952; d. Robert A. and Wanda Jo (Garner) Boehm; m. Michael G. Schlegel, Aug. 9, 1975; children: Kaellen June, Krystalynn Michele. Grad. high sch., Springfield, Oreg. Sales rep. The Prudential, Novato, Calif., 1973—; bus. owner Marcella Enterprises, Novato, 1983—; owner, operator Meetings Extraordinaire, 1987—; owner Mastermind Escapes, 1990—; ind. travel agt., 1995—. Contbr. articles, poetry to profl.

pubs. Mem. Nat. Assn. Life Underwriters (nat. quality award 1978, 80, 84), Marin Life Underwriters, Nat. Assn. Profl. Saleswomen (founder Marin chpt., pres. 1982-85, 91-93, chmn. 1985-87, nat. v.p. 1985-86, awards and recognition chmn. 1985-88, nat. pres. 1987-90, exec. dir. 1988-91, regional v.p. 1991-92, N.W. region conf. chmn. 1993), Leading Life Producers No. Calif., Million Dollar Round Table (qualifying), Marin Rowing Assn. (travel chmn. 1992-93), President's Club, Western Star Club, Leaders Club. Fax: 415-897-5347. Office: Marcella Enterprises 1929 Benton Ln Novato CA 94945-1747

LEAVELL, LANDRUM PINSON, II, seminary administrator, clergyman, educator; b. Ripley, Tenn., Nov. 26, 1926; s. Leonard O. and Annie Glenn (Elias) L.; m. Jo Ann Paris, July 28, 1953; children: Landrum Pinson III, Ann Paris, Roland Q. II, David E. AB, Mercer U., 1948; BD, New Orleans Bapt. Theol. Sem., 1951, ThD, 1954; DD, MIss. Coll., 1981, Campbell U., 1989. Pastor Union Bapt. Ch., Magnolia, Miss., Crosby Bapt. Ch., Miss.; pastor First Bapt. Ch., Charleston, Miss., Gulfport, Miss., Wichita Falls, Tex., 1963-75; pres. New Orleans Bapt. Theol. Sem., 1975-95; pastor emeritus Frist Bapt. Ch., Wichita Fallas, 1995. Author: Angels, Angels, Angels, 1973, Sermons for Celebrating, 1978, Twelve Who Followed Jesus, 1975, The Devil and His Domain, 1973, For Prodigals and Other Sinners, 1973, God's Spirit in You, 1974, The Harvest of the Spirit, 1976, John's Letters: Light for Living, 1970, Evangelism: Christ's Imperative Commission, 1979, The Doctrine of the Holy Spirit, 1983, Parting Shots, 1995. Mem. Bapt. Joint Com. Pub. Affairs, 1986-91; bd. dirs. Bapt. Cmty. Ministries, New Orleans, 1985-95, ret. 1995. Recipient George Washington Honor medal Freedoms Found., Valley Forge, Pa., 1968. Mem. New Orleans C. of C., Rotary (past pres. Paul Harris fellow). Home: 2100 Santa Fe St #601-2 Wichita Falls TX 76309-3461*

LEAVESLEY, GWENDOLINE MARY, medical sexologist, educator; b. Wigan, Eng., May 5, 1930; arrived in Australia, 1957; d. Horace Dell and Clarice Edith (Kenyon) Clayton; m. James Harrison Leavesley, Aug. 18, 1954 (div. 1985); children: David Ian, James Mark, Anne Kenyon. MB ChB with 1st class honors, U. Liverpool, Eng., 1955. Diplomate Am. Bd. Sexology. Resident med. officer Lancashire Hosp., 1955-57; gen. practitioner in pvt. practice, Perth, Australia, 1958-80; rsch. asst. dept. surgery U. Western Australia, Perth, 1965-67; med. dir. Family Planning Assn. Perth, 1975-95; mem. steering group on quality assurance screening for prevention of cancer of Cerviz Dept. Health, Canberra, Australia, 1991-93; mem. Western Australia Screening Reference Group, 1994-96. Mem. Inaugural Women's Adv. Coun. to Premier Western Australia, 1984-85; bd. dir. Coun. Western Australia Inst. Tech., 1977-79, King Edward Maternity Hosp., Perth, 1985-92, Guardianship and Adminstrn. Western Australia, 1992-96. Fellow Australian Coll. Sexual Health Physicians; mem. Western Australia Sexology Soc. (life). Avocations: gardening, tennis, swimming. Home: 9/20 Kings Park Rd, 6005 West Perth 6005, Australia

LEAVEY, THOMAS EDWARD, international organization administrator; b. Kansas City, Mo., Nov. 10, 1934. BA, Josephinum Coll, 1957; Lic., Cath. Inst., Paris, 1964; MA, Princeton U., 1967, PhD, 1968; cert. in bus. and fin., NYU, U. Tex., U. Va., Duke U., 1969-91. Prof. Tng. and Devel. Inst., Bethesda, Md., 1970-72; dir. Postal Svc. Tng. and Devel. Mgmt. Tng. Ctr., L.A., 1973-75; gen. mgr. employment and placement divsn. USPS Hdqs., 1976-78, 1976-78, dir. postal career exec. svc., 1979; postmaster, sectional ctr. mgr. Charlottesville, Va., 1980; regional dir. human resources cen. region Chgo., 1981; contr. USPS Hdqs., 1982, gen. mgr. internat. mail processing divsn., 1982-87, asst. postmaster gen., sr. dir. internat. postal affairs, 1987-94; dir. gen. internat. bur. Universal Postal Union, Berne, 1995—; prof. Fairleigh Dickinson U., Teaneck, N.J., George Washington U., Washington, 1968-70. Recipient Heinrich von Stephan medal German Ministry of Post and Telecomm., 1997, ASTD award, 1973. Office: Universal Postal Union, Case postale, 3000 Bern 15, Switzerland

LEAVITT, CHARLES LOYAL, English language educator, administrator; b. Randolph, Maine, Apr. 30, 1921; s. Charles Warren Franklin and Alice Mabel (Sparrow) L.; m. Emily Raymond Stewart, June 12, 1951 (dec. 1966); m. Virginia Louise Kracke, Sept. 6, 1969. Diploma in Edn., U. Maine, Farmington, 1941; BS in Edn., U. So. Maine, 1946; MA in English, Boston U., 1947; PhD in English, U. Wis., 1961; MLS, Columbia U., 1969. Cert. tchr. English and history, elem., secondary, coll. Tchr. pub. schs., Vanceboro, Maine, 1941-42; tchr., prin. pub. schs., York Village, Maine, 1945-47; Instr. English and history Endicott Jr. Coll., Beverly, Mass., 1947-48; assoc. prof. English Lyndon State Coll., Lyndon Center, Vt., 1948-53, 54-55; teaching asst. in English U. Wis., Madison, 1953-54, 55-59; instr. Wayne State U., Detroit, 1959-61; assoc. prof. Montclair (N.J.) State Coll. 1961-68; v.p., sec., dir. edn. Universal Learning Corp., N.Y.C., 1968-69; assoc. dir. admissions Sarah Lawrence Coll., Bronxville, N.Y., 1970-71; dir. continuing edn., asst. dean, prof. Bloomfield (N.J.) Coll., 1971-74; chmn. liberal arts, prof. Coll. of Ins., N.Y.C., 1975-86, prof. emeritus, 1987—; adj. prof. English Fairleigh Dickinson U., Teaneck, N.J., 1988-92; lect. N.Y. theater, 1970s. Author: Ten Lit. Study Guides, 1964-66, (book and tape) Guide to London, 1969; cons. editor Monarch Lit. Guides, N.Y.C., 1963-68; contbr. entry to book. Treas. Youth Community Funds, York Village, Maine, 1946-47; asst. scoutmaster Boy Scouts Am., York Village, 1946-47; v.p. Overseas Neighbors, Montclair, 1974-75; tchr. Adult Sch. of Montclair, 1963-68. With USAAF, 1942-45. Named Most Popular Prof., Montclair State Coll., 1967, Prof. of Yr., Coll. of Ins., 1978; yearbook dedications Lyndon State Coll., 1950, Bloomfield Coll., 1974, Coll. of Ins., 1987; Nat. Audubon scholar, Garden Clubs York Village, 1947. Mem. AAUP, MLA, Coll. English Assn., Internat. Platform Assn., Princeton Club (N.Y.C.), Faculty Columbia U. Club, New Eng. Soc. N.Y.C. Club, Kiwanis (trustee Manhattan found. 1989—), Soc. Mayflower Descendants. Republican. Baptist. Home: 93 Stonebridge Rd Montclair NJ 07042-1632 Office: One Insurance Pla 101 Murray St New York NY 10007-2132

LEAVITT, DAVID LIVINGSTONE, architect; b. Omaha, Nebr., Aug. 26, 1918; s. Frederick William and Mattie Louise Knapp Bennett. BA in Architecture, U. Nebr., 1940; M of Architecture, Princeton (N.J.) U., 1942. Assoc. prof. Princeton (N.J.) U., 1941-42; chief designer Raymond and Rado, N.Y.C., Tokyo, 1951-53; instr. in design Columbia U., N.Y.C., 1956, Pratt Inst., Bklyn., 1957-59; dir. architecture and design Hilton Internat., N.Y.C., 1968-76; architectural designer Mr. Bailey Assoc., Athens, 1977-80; hotel design cons. N.Y.C., 1982—. Architectural designer residencies Russel Wright, 1956, Reader's Digest Bldg. Tokyo, 1964, Nanzan U., 1966, U.S. Embassy Housing, Tokyo, 1953. Regents scholarship U. Nebr., 1936. Mem. AIA, Nat. Architects Registration (bd. dirs. 1946-99), Far East Assn. of Architects and Engrs. Avocations: painting, music (piano), reading, swimming, tennis. Home: 118 W 72nd St Apt 903 New York NY 10023-3321 Office: c/o ADA 170 E 61st St New York NY 10021-8551

LEAVY, BRIAN CAHIR, business educator; b. Dublin, Ireland, June 30, 1950; s. Bernard Francis and Mary Elizabeth (Healy) L.; m. Ailish Philomena Molony, Jan. 3, 1974; children: Emer, Eoin. BSc in Physics, Nat. U. Ireland, Galway, 1971, MBA, 1980; PhD, U. Warwick, Eng., 1990. Mfg. engr. Digital Equipment Corp., Galway, Ireland, 1973-81; lectr. Dublin City U., 1981-91, sr. lectr., 1991-94, prof., 1994—, dean Bus. Sch., 1998—. Author: Key Processes in Strategy, 1996; co-author: Strategy and Leadership, 1994; contbr. articles to jours. in field. Mem. Am. Prodn. and Inventory Control Soc. (cert.), Irish Prodn. and Inventory Control Soc. (hon.). Avocations: music, swimming, walking. Office: Dublin City U Bus Sch, Dublin 9, Ireland

LEAVY, HERBERT THEODORE, publisher; b. Detroit, July 10, 1927; s. Morris and Thelma (Davidson) L.; m. Patricia J. Moran, June 20, 1953; children: Karen, Kathryn, Jill, Jacqueline. B.S. in Journalism, Ohio U., 1951. Supervisory editor Fawcett Books, N.Y.C., 1951-60; v.p., editorial dir. Davis Publs., N.Y.C., 1960-69; founder, pres. Internat. Evaluations, Hauppage, N.Y., 1969-70; pub. dir. Countrywide Publs. Inc., N.Y.C., 1970-75; pres. Communications Devel. Co., N.Y.C., 1975-79; editorial dir. Watson-Guptil Publs., N.Y.C., 1979-80; pres. Books from Mags., Inc., Smithtown, N.Y., 1980—, Resumes Unltd., Smithtown, 1984—. Author: 101 Fast Track Resumes, The Pleasure, Executive Handbook, Vegetarian Times Cookbook, McCall's Houseplant and Indoor Landscaping Guide, Working Mother Cookbook, Carpentry, Shoe and Leather Repair at Home, The Complete Book of Beards and Moustaches, Air Conditioning-Repair and Maintenance, Designing and Building Beds, Lofts and Sleeping Areas, Wallcovering, Floor Stripping and Refinishing, Packing and Moving, Recreational Vehicles, Appliance Repair, Plumbing Handbook, Successful Small Farms; numerous others; editor-in-chief: The Ohioan Mag. Ohio U., 1950-51. Acting 1st sgt. USAF, 1945-47. Mem. Sales Exec. Club, Am. Soc. Mag. Editors, Nat. Sporting Goods Assn., Am. Mgmt. Assn., Mag. Advts. Sales Club, Electronics Press Club, U.S. Tennis Ct. and Track Builders Assn., Am. Motorcycle Assn., Am. Horse Council, Authors Guild, Motorcycle Industry Council, Nat. Indoor Tennis Assn., Bus./Profl. Advt. Assn., Sigma Delta Chi. Office: Resumes Unlimited 222 E Main St Ste 107A Smithtown NY 11787-2814

LEBA, MARIA CERES DE LOS REYES, customer service representative; b. Iloilo City, The Philippines, Feb. 17, 1969; d. Santiago Librero De Los Reyes and Cecilia Losaria Librando; m. Percy Lescain Leba, Dec. 30, 1998. BS in Bus. Mgmt., U. of the Philippines, Iloilo City, 1989; M in Mgmt., U. of the Philippines, Visayas, 1992. Rsch. asst. RRDP U. of the Philippines, Iloilo City, 1989-90, rsch. asst. provincial govt. project, 1990-91, coll. dept. staff, 1992; med. rep. Medicus, Iloilo City, 1992; regional rep. Diners Club Internat., Makati City, The Philippines, 1993—; lectr. San Jose Coll., Iloilo City, 1993-95, Iloilo Doctor's Coll., Iloilo City, 1996-98. Youth rep. Mcpl. Govt., Lambunao, Iloilo, The Philippines, 1985-89. Recipient award IWAG Found., Lambunao, The Philippines, 1985, Gerry Roxas Leadership award Gerry Roxas Found., Lambunao, 1985; Coll. scholar 2nd Sem Sch. Devel. Mgmt., U. of the Philippines, 1989. Roman Catholic. Avocations: reading philosophical and religious books, listening to classical and pop songs, tinkering with small things, making assorted crafts. Home: 80 Burgos St, 5042 Lambunao Iloilo, The Philippines

LE BALLOIS, SANDRINE ISABELLE, engineering educator; b. Paris, Mar. 25, 1967; d. Alain and Annie (Raoult) Le B. Degree in elec. engring., Supélec, Gif sur Yvette, France, 1991; PhD, Orsay (France) U., 1994. Rschr. Supélec, Gif sur Yvette, 1991-94; assoc. prof. Cergy U., France, 1994—. Author: (book) Automatique: Systèmes Linéaires et Continus, 1998, (chpt.) Commande Robuste: Développements et Applications, 1996; contbr. articles to profl. jours. Mem. sci. coun. Cergy U., France. Avocations: sailing, music, literature. Office: IUP Génie Electrique, Rue Eragny Neuville Oise, 95031 Cergy-Pontoise France

LE BAS, RONALD WILLIAM ALBERT, assay master, goldsmith company executive; b. Dublin, Ireland, June 3, 1955; s. Ronald Richard Samuel and Alice Mary (Counihan) Le B.; m. Adrienne McCarthy, Jan. 5, 1990; children: Samuel, Hugo. Student, St. Marys Coll., Rathmines, Dublin, 1962-73. Tech. adviser precious metals Irish Govt. Dept. Industry & Commerce; chief exec. Co. of Goldsmiths, Dublin; assay master Ireland, 1988—; tech. expert Vienna Internat. Hallmarking Conv.; rep. Nat. Standard Authority, Internat. Standards Orgn., Tech./Coms. 174, 283 Precious Metals, European Com. Standardization; organizer, chmn. Internat. Conf. Precious Metals and European Consumer, 1992. Chmn. Irish Jewellery Trade 1992 Com. Fellow Huguenot Soc. Great Britain and Ireland; mem. Irish Mgmt. Inst. (cert.) Irish Bus. and Employers Confederation, Internat. Precious Metals Inst., Inc., Union Internat. des Laboratories Independents, European Assay Office Assn. (dep. chmn. 1995, chmn. 1996), The Silver Soc., The London Goldsmiths Co. (assoc.). Avocations: motor racing, hill climbing. Office: Co of Goldsmiths Assay Office, Dublin Castle, Dublin 2, Ireland

LEBDETTER, EUGENE FLOYD, JR., food service executive; b. Charleston, SC, Feb. 5, 1966; s. E. Floyd and Omi Jeannie (Barron) L.; m. Renee Marie, Mar. 17, 1990; children: Eugene III, Zachary Tylor, Damia Hinderson Wimmer. Caterer Barron's Limited, Marietta, Ga., 1984-90; security police USAF, Okinawa, 1990-95; food svc. U.S. Army, Ft. Leavenworth, Kans., 1995-98, Dept. Justice, Marianna, Fla., 1998—; bd. dirs. Barrons Limited, Marietta, Ga., 1988-90; sr. instr. Ga. Hapkido Assn., 1989. Contbr. poetry to Garden of Peace, Nat. Libr. of Poetry, The International Library of Poetry, 1998, America at the Millennium, 2000. Asst. Scout Master, BSA, Marietta, Ga., 1984-87, unit commr. 1988-90, alter server, Catholic Ch., Marianna, Fla., 1998—; camp counselor, dir., commr., Ga. and Okinawa, Japan, 1984-93. Recipient Eagle Scout award, BSA, 1994, Naval Res. Meritorious Svc. Medal, 1988, Navy E award, 1986. Mem. Nat. Eagle Scout Assn., Libr. Congress, Theta Chi. Independent. Roman Catholic. Avocations: painting, reading, law, camping, poetry. Office: Box 7007 11470-045 Marianna FL 32447-7007

LEBEAU, CHARLES, tobacco company executive; b. Diego Suarez, Madagascar, Mar. 6, 1954; s. Simon and Marguerite (Totah) L.; m. Nadia Delume, Feb. 19, 1993; 1 child, Alexander. Bachelor, Chatellerault, France, 1974; degree, Inst. Tech., Tours, France, 1976, Inst. Politics, Paris, 1978; M in Adminstrn. Econ., U. Tours, Tour, 1979. Brand mgr. Seita, Paris, 1979-83, sr. brand mgr., 1984-86, dir. mktg., 1984-89, internat. dir., 1989-95, exec. v.p. internat. devel. divsn., 1995-99, exec. v.p. internat. devel. and cigars divsn., 2000—, sec. gen. Altadis group, 2000—. Avocations: aikido, jogging. Office: Sieta, 53 Quai D'Orsay, 75347 Paris Cedex 7, France

LEBEAU, DANIEL PIERRE, manufacturing professional; b. Jemappes, Hainaut, Belgium, July 10, 1962; s. Pierre Jean Lebeau and Marthe Bastin; m. Pascale Herman, Aug. 22, 1987; children: Claire, Pierre-Yves, Eric. Engr., FPMs, Mons, Belgium, 1984, D in Applied Scis., 1991; Diploma in Mgmt., UCL, Louvain-La-Neuve, Belgium, 1993. Prin. engr. Assn. Euratom-Belgian State, 1984-91; IS devel. supr. Kraft Jacobs Suchard, Namur, Belgium, 1991-94, IS mgr., 1994-96, IS & logistics mgr., 1996, IS mgr. ops., 1996-2000; dir. mgmt. and info. sys. Glaxo Smithkline Biols., Rixensart, Belgium, 2000—; lectr. FPMs, Mons, 1992-96; pres. HEC, Liège, Belgium, 1995, lectr. Contbr. articles to profl. jours. Office: Glaxo Smithkline Biols, Rue de l'Institut 89, 1330 Rixensart Belgium

LEBED, ANDREI G., physicist; b. Dniepropetrovsk, Ukraine, Jan. 29, 1959; s. Gregorii K. and Stella B. (Brusse) L.; m. Nataliia N. Bagmet, Oct. 2, 1991. MS, MIPT, Moscow, 1982; PhD, Landau Inst., Moscow, 1985. Young rschr. Landau Inst., Moscow, 1985-89, rschr., 1990—; rsch. assoc. BNL, Upton, 1989-90; prof. Tohoku U., Sendai, Japan, 1995-97, Osaka (Japan) Prefecture U., 1997-98, Okayama (Japan) U., 1998—; vis. rschr. U. Paris, SUD, Orsay, 1991-93, NHMFL, Tallahassee, 1993-95. Recipient All-Soviet Union Youth League prize in physics, 1990. Achievements include the prediction of "Magic Angles" and new high magnetic field superconducting phase and study of triplet superconductivity. Office: Okayama Univ, Phys Dept, 700 Okayama Japan

LEBEDEV, ALEXANDER ALEXANDROVICH, engineering executive, consultant; b. Arkhangelsk, Russia, Oct. 1, 1959; arrived in South Africa, 1992; s. Alexander Glebovich Lebedev and Henrietta Victorovna (Pavlova) Lebedeva; m. Marina Yurievna Zlotnikova, June 30, 1985; 1 child, Maria. MSc in Engring., Inst. Steel & Alloys, Moscow, 1982, PhD in Engring., 1987. Profl. engr., South Africa. Jr. rschr. Inst. Steel and Alloys, Moscow, 1984-88; jr. rschr. All Russia Inst. Fire Protection Rsch., Balaskikha, 1988-89, sr. rschr., 1989-90, leading rschr., 1990-91; chief specialist Konkord, Moscow, 1991-92; cons. Protection Projects, Johannesburg, South Africa, 1992-93; sr. cons. Xcel Engring. and Mgmt., Pretoria, South Africa, 1993-99; cons. Lebedev Cons., Pretoria, South Africa, 1999—. Contbr. articles to profl. jours. Sr. lt. Russian Def. Force, 1982-84. Mem. Internat. Soc. Computer Simulation, Can. Inst. of Mining, Metallurgy and Petroleum. Avocation: books. Home and Office: PO Box 73621 Lynnwood Ridge, Pretoria 0040, South Africa

LEBEDEV, ANATOLY ALEXEYEVICH, mechanical engineer, researcher; b. Sushchovo, Russia, Feb. 1, 1931; s. Alexey Michaylovich and Evdokiya Grigoriyevna (Komarova) L.; m. Zoya Evgeniyevna (Izvekova) L., Oct. 19, 1931; children: Alexey, Alyona. Diploma in mech. engring., Kiev (Ukraine) Poly. Inst., 1954; PhD, Inst. Problems Material Sci., Nat. Acad. Scis. Ukraine (NASU), Kiev, 1963, DSc, 1973. Rsch. fellow, sr. rsch. fellow Inst. Problems Material Sci. (NASU), 1963-66; sr. rsch. fellow Inst. Problems of Strength (NASU), 1966-71, sr. scientist, 1965—, head of dept., 1971—; lectr. Kiev Poly. Inst., 1972-76, prof., 1976—; dep. chmn. Coun. Mechs. of Solids, NASU, 1963—, dep. chmn. Nat. Com. Ukraine for Theoretical and Applied Mechs., 1993—, chmn. subcom. for standardization of test methods of materials and strength calculations, NASU, 1986—. Author: Phenomenological Principles for Strength Calculations of Structures, (in Russian) 1984; co-author: The Strength of Materials and Structural Elements under Extreme Conditions, 2 vols., (in Russian) 1980 (State prize USSR 1982), (handbook) Mechanical Properties of Structural Materials under Complex Stress State, (in Russian) 1983 (State prize Ukraine, 1997), (handbook) A Reference Book on Strength Calculations of Machine-Building Structures, 1990; mem. editl. bd. (NASU jours.) Strength of Materials, 1971—, Problems of Mech. Engring. and Reliability of Machines, 1990-95, Physico-Chem. Mechs. of Materials, 1994—. Mem. sect. for math. and mechs., Com. for State Prizes of Ukraine, Kiev, 1976-86, 93—, USSR, Moscow, 1976-86. Grantee Internat. Soros Sci. Edn. Program, 1997; recipient Order of Badge honors, Supreme Soviet of USSR, 1971, Hon. deed of Supreme Soviet of Ukraine, 1981. Mem. N.Y. Acad. Scis., Am. Soc. Metals Internat., Russian Acad. Quality, Nat. Acad. Scis. of Ukraine (corr. mem., academician). Avocations: hunting, literature. E-mail: leb@ipp.adam.kiev.ua. Home: 28-B Bazhan Ave Apt 108, 02140 Kiev Ukraine Office: Inst Problems Strength NASU, 2 Timiryazevskaya Str, 01014 Kiev Ukraine

LEBEDEV, BORIS VLADIMIROVICH, physicist, chemist; b. Bolshoye Tumanovo, Russia, Dec. 30, 1935; s. Vladimir Alekseevich and Elizaveta Maksimovna (Boronina) L.; m. Zhanna Vladimirovna Trelina, Nov. 5, 1962; 1 child, Irina Borisovna. Chemist-Rschr., N. Novgorod U., Nizhny Novgorod, Russia, 1963, CandChem Sci, 1968; DrChem Sci, Moscow State U., 1979. Dep. dir. Chem. inst. Nizhny Novgorod U., 1971-86, dir. Chem. Inst., 1986-91, prin. rschr., chief of lab. Chem. Inst., 1994—; exec. mgr. Thermodynamic Sci. Ctr., Nizhny Novgorod, 1994—; prof. chemistry Nizhny Novgorod U., 1966—, Conacry (Guinea) U., 1968-71; invited prof. Laval U., Que., Can., 1990; mem. sci. coun. on chem. thermodynamics Russian Acad. Sci., 1980-95. Author: Thermodynamics of Polymers, 1979; (with B.A. Krentsel) Polymers and Copolymers of Higher-2-Olefins, 1997; Carbyne and Carbynoid Structures, 1999; (with N. N. Smiznova) Chemical Thermodynamics of Polyalkanes and Polyalkenes, 2000; contbr. articles to profl. jours. Decorated Valiant Labour medal, Excellent Labour Successes badge; named Disting. Man of Sci. Mem. N.Y. Acad. Sci. Avocations: classic literature, especially Russian; cultivation of fruits and vegetables. Office: Chem Inst N Novgorod U, Gagarin Prospekt 23/5, 603600 Nizhny Novgorod Russia

LEBEDEV, VYACHESLAV M., judge. Chmn. Supreme Ct. Russian Fedn., Moscow. Office: ul Ilyinka 37, 121260 Moscow Russia*

LEBEDEV, YURI ANATOLIEVICH, physicist; b. Simferopol, Crimea, USSR, Nov. 11, 1945; div. Sept., 1990; 1 child. Diploma in elec. engring., Inst. Petrochem. Industry, Moscow, 1968; diploma in physics, Moscow State U., 1973, PhD, 1977; DSc Physics, Russian Acad. Scis., Moscow, 1993. Engr. Design Office, Moscow, 1968-71; engr. Inst. Petrochem. Synthesis Russian Acad. Scis., Moscow, 1971-72, jr. scientist, 1975-85, sr. scientist, 1985-96, head of lab., 1996—. Co-author: Methods of Contact Diagnostics in Non-Equilibrium Plasma Chemistry, 1981, Plasma Diagnostics, 1994; editor, co-author: Plasma Chemistry, 1998. Mem. Moscow Phys. Soc. (vice-chmn. bd. 1994, mem. editl. bd. jour. 1995), United Phys Soc. Russian Fedn. (vice chmn. bd. dirs. 1998). Avocations: traveling, kayaking. Office: Acad Scis Inst Petrochem, Leninsky Prospect 29, 117071 Moscow Russia

LEBEDOFF, GERIC, legal counsel; b. Antwerp, Belgium, Jan. 16, 1950; s. Robert Louis and Christiane (de Badrihaye) L. Law degree, U. Libre de Brussels, 1973, degree criminology, 1973, internat. law degree, 1974; M of Comparative Law, Mich. State U., 1975. Assoc. Cleary Gottlieb Steen & Hamilton, Paris, 1975-79; counselor IMF, Washington, 1979-81; legal counsel Pechiney, Paris, 1981-87; gen. counsel Valeo, Paris, 1987—; counsel UN, Geneva, 1977-78. Contbr. articles to profl. jours. Mem. Polo de Paris, Polo Club of Chantilly, Royal Golf Club of Belgium. Avocation: Polo. Home: Haras de la Plaine, 77630 St Martin en Biere France Office: Valeo, 43 rue Bayen, 75117 Paris France

LE BERRE, MICHEL, science educator; b. Douarnenez, France, Dec. 8, 1943; s. Henri and Lucie (Harré) Le B.; m. Maryvonne Drou, July 20, 1968; children: Guillaume, Marine. Lic., U. Rennes, France, 1966, PhD, 1970; DSc, U. Lyon, France, 1989. Tchr. Lycée Joss, Douala, Cameroon, 1970-72; asst. U. Constantine, Algeria, 1972-74; maitre asst. INRAA, Biskra, Algeria, 1974-76; asst. prof. U. Lyon, 1976—; sr. cons. UNESCO, Paris, 1985—, sci. advisor Niger Embassy, 1990—. Author: Faune du Sahara, 1991, Rodent and Space, 1991, Biodiversity in Marmots, 1996; co-editor South-South Perspectives, 1994—. Home: 24 rue des Remparts d'Ainay, 69002 Lyon France Office: UCBL1 LSC, 43 Bd d 11.11.1918, 69622 Villeurbanne France

LE BLANC, BART, banker; b. S'Hertogenbosch, The Netherlands, Nov. 4, 1946; arrived in France, 1998; s. Christianus and Joke (Bogaerts) Le B.; m. Gerardine Van Lanschot; children: Godfried Thierry, Annabelle, Claudia. D in Econ. Sci., U. Leiden. Spl. advisor, dep. sec. to Cabinet Prime Min.'s Office, 1973-79; dep. dir.-gen. Civil Svc. at the Home Office, 1979-80; dir.-gen. for the Budget Office of Treasury, 1980-83; dep. chmn. mgmt. bd. F. van Lanschot Bankiers NV, 1983-91; sec. gen. European Bank for Reconstrn. and Devel., London, 1991-94, v.p. fin., 1994-98; dir. internat. fin. Caisse des dépôts et consignations, 1998—; hon. prof. Tilburg U., 1991—. Author numerous books; contbr. articles to profl. jours. Decorated knight Order of Netherlands Lion. Office: 84 Rue De Lille, Paris France

LEBLANC, JOSEPH EDWARD, physicist; b. Kenora, Ont., Can., June 1, 1962; arrived in U.S., 1965; s. Joseph Isaias and Gilda Altagracia (DiFranco) L.; m. Yoshimi Kambe, Nov. 4, 1989; 1 child, Adam. BS in Physics, U. Puerto Rico, 1986; MS in Physics, Calif. State U., Northridge, 1991; D of Engring., Nagoya U., 1996. Lectr. U. Puerto Rico, Mayagüez, 1985-86; mem. tech. staff Hughes Aircraft Co., M.S.G., Canoga Park, Calif., 1986-91; rsch. assoc. Nagoya U., 1996-98, asst. prof., 1998—; English conversation tchr., Japan, 1992-96. Inventor mechanical device; designer, maker furniture. Fellowship Hughes Aircraft Co., 1988; scholarship Combulu Co., 1994. Mem. AIAA, Am. Phys. Soc., Japanese Shock Wave Soc., Japan Soc. for Aeronautical and Space Scis. Democrat. Roman Catholic. Avocations: woodworking, musician, art and history books collector. Home: 17-16 Yobitsugi-Motomachi, Minami-ku, Nagoya 457, Japan Office: Nagoya U Dept Aerospace Eng, Furo-cho Chikusa-ku, Nagoya 464-8603, Japan

LEBLANC, LEONARD JOSEPH, electronics company executive; b. Amherst, N.S., Can., Feb. 4, 1941; came to U.S., 1952 naturalized 1959; s. Edgar Marcel and Mary Catherine (Bourgeois) LeB.; m. Janice May Dittrich, Sept. 11, 1965; children: Bryan, Jeffrey, Steven. B.S., Coll. of Holy Cross, 1962, M.S., 1963; M.S., George Washington U., 1966. Fin. analyst to mgr. Philco-Ford Corp., Blue Bell, Pa., 1966-72; asst. corp. controller Centainteed Corp., Valley Forge, Pa., 1972-73; sr. v.p. fin. Data Tech. Corp., Costa Mesa, Calif., 1973-76; v.p., controller Memorex Corp., Santa Clara, Calif., 1976-82; v.p. fin., treas. Saga Corp., Menlo Park, Calif., 1982-87; exec. v.p. fin. and adminstrn. Cadence Design Systems Inc., San Jose, Calif., 1987-92; sr. v.p. fin. and adminstrn., CFO GTech Corp., West Greenwich, R.I., 1993-94; exec. v.p., CFO, COO Infoseek Corp., Santa Clara, Calif., 1996-97; exec. v.p., CFO Vantive Corp., Santa Clara, 1998-2000; bd. dirs. OpLink Comms., Inc., EBest Inc. Mem. Monte Sereno Archtl. Com., Calif., 1981-93; bd. dirs. Eastfield Children's Ctr., Campbell, Calif., 1984-87. Served to lt.(j.g.) USN, 1963-66. Recipient commendation U.S. Navy Med. Sch., Bethesda, Md., 1966; fellow Coll. of Holy Cross, 1962. Mem. Fin. Execs. Inst. (pres. Santa Clara chpt. 1986-87).

LE BOUILLE, LUCIEN, educator; b. Sevres, France, Sept. 8, 1938; s. Ferdinand and Lucienne (Cornu) LeB.; m. Monique Sénécal, July 16, 1960; 1 child, Jean. Agregation d'anglas, France, 1963, doctorat d'etat, 1979. Tchr. Lycée Alain, Alençon, France, 1963-64, Lycée Fresnel, Bernay, France, 1964-66; lectr. U. Caen, France, 1966-85; prof. U. Caetn, France, 1985—; head English dept. U. Caen, 1986-88. Author: Etudes sur John Fowles, 1978, (with others) Intercultural Encounters, 1999; editor: L'Ente et la Chimere Caen, 1986, Fins de Textes, 1993. Home: 1 Route de Saint Léger, 27300 Saint Leger de Rotes France Office: U de Caen, Esplanade de la Paix, 14032 Caen France

LEBOVITZ, CHARLES NEAL, surgeon; b. Pitts., Jan. 16, 1943; s. Herbert B. and Margaret (Kopelman) L.; m. Rose Linda Benkovitz, Dec. 13, 1975; children: Emily Suzanne, Jeffrey Scott. BS, U. Pitts., 1963, MD, 1966.

Diplomate Am. Bd. Surgeons. Intern in surgery Hosp. of U. of Pa., Phila., 1966-67; resident in surgery Health Ctr. Hosps. U. of Pitts., Pitts., 1967-68, 70-73; pvt. practice surgery Chetlin & Lebovitz Surg. Assocs., Pitts., 1973-94, Premier Surg. Assocs., Pitts., 1994-98; pvt. practice White Oak, Pa., 1998—; clin. asst. prof. surgery U. Pitts., 1973—, med. exec. com., 1993-97; pres. med. staff Braddock Med. Ctr., 1995-97. Lt. comdr. USNR, 1968-70, Vietnam. Fellow Am. Geriatrics Soc; mem. AMA (Pa. and Allegheny County chpts.), Pitts. Surg. Soc., Allegheny County Med. Soc. (med. staff officers group 1993-97), Phi Beta Kappa, Alpha Omega Alpha. Avocations: travel, computers, bicycling. Home: 1046 Lyndhurst Dr Pittsburgh PA 15206-4536 Office: 1220 Lincoln Way Ste 100 White Oak PA 15131-1642

LEBOWITZ, JOEL LOUIS, mathematical physicist, educator; b. May 10, 1930; came to U.S., 1946, naturalized, 1951; m. Estelle Mandelbaum, June 21, 1953 (dec. Dec. 1996); m. Ann Keay Beneduce, June 3, 1999. BS, Bklyn. Coll., 1952; MS, Syracuse U., 1955, PhD, 1956; hon. doctorate, Ecole Poly. Federale, Lausanne, Switzerland, 1977, Clark U., 1999. NSF postdoctoral fellow Yale U., New Haven, 1956-57; mem. faculty Stevens Inst. Tech., Hoboken, N.J., 1957-59; mem. faculty Yeshiva U., N.Y.C., 1959-77, prof. physics, 1965-77, acting chmn. Belfer Grad. Sch. Sci., 1964-67, chmn. dept., 1967-76; George William Hill prof math. and physics, dir. Ctr. for Math. Scis., Rutgers U., New Brunswick, N.J., 1977—. Co-editor: Phase Transitions and Critical Phenomena, 1980, editor Jour. Statis. Physics, 1975—, Studies in Statis. Mechanics, 1973—, Com. Math. Physics, 1973—; contbr. articles to profl. jours. Recipient Boltzmann medal Internat. Union Pure and Applied Physics, 1992, Max Planck Rsch. award, 1993, Delmar S. Fahrney medal Franklin Inst., 1995, Henri Poincare prize Internat. Assn. of Math. Physics/Daniel Iagolnitzer Found., 2000; Guggenheim fellow, 1976-77. Fellow AAAS (Sci. Freedom and Responsibility award 1998), Am. Phys. Soc., N.Y. Acad. Scis. (pres. 1979, A. Cressy Morrison award in natural scis. 1986, Heinz R. Pagels Human Rights of Scientists award 1996); mem. NAS, AAUP, Am. Math. Soc., Phi Beta Kappa, Sigma Xi. Office: Rutgers U Ctr Math Sci Rsch 110 Frelinghuysen Rd Piscataway NJ 08854-8019

LEBRE, MARIA MANUELA A. AZEVEDO, biologist, researcher; b. Lisbon, Portugal, Jan. 28, 1958; d. Ramiro Lourenço and Albertina (Azevedo) A.; m. Francisco Manuel Inácio Guedes Lebre, June 4, 1983; children: Inês, Ana, Guilherme. Grad. Biology, U. Lisbon (Portugal), 1982, MS in Statistics, 1993. Biologist; statistician. Rsch. scientist Rsch. Inst. Fisheries and Sea, Lisbon, Portugal, 1982—; prof. statistics post-grad. Biomed. Sci. Inst. Abel Salazar, Oporto, Portugal, 1996—; Biostatistics educator Portuguese Biologists Assn., Lisbon, 1993-94, Évora (Portugal), 1994. Grantee Overseas Fishery Coop. Found., 1984, French Embassy, 1985, 86. Fellow Portuguese Biologists Assn., Portuguese Statistics Soc.; mem. Internat. Coun. Exploration of Sea. Avocations: scientific illustration, diving, water skiing, horseback riding. Office: IPIMAR, Ave de Brasilia, 1449-006 Lisbon Portugal

L'EBRELLEC, PASCAL, sales executive; b. Fria, Guinea, Oct. 28, 1965; s. Yann and Daniele (Alaouret) L'E.; m. Isabelle Audubert, July 15, 1989; children: Audrey, Helene, Marianne. CPE, U. Cambridge, Eng., 1984; lic. in law, U. Rennes, France, 1985; Laureate, Inst. d'Etudes Politiques, paris, 1987; M European Studies, U. Kent, Eng., 1988. Cert. assoc. acaedmician Internat. Informatization Acad., 1996. Mktg. analyst Thomson-CSF, Bagneux, France, 1989-91, strategic planning mgr., 1992-94, sales mgr., 1995-97, area sales mgr., 1998—. Editor: def. mag. Enjeux Atlantiques, 1989-99. Dep. chief youth sect. French Atlantic Cmty. Assn., Paris, 1987-90. Mem. Centre d Analyse la Sevurite Europeene (assoc.). Roman Catholic. Avocations: strategy games, undersea diving. Office: Thomson-CSF Airsys, 9 rue des Mathurins, 92223 Bagneux France

LE BRUN, JEAN, retired banker; b. Lessines, Hainaut, Belgium, May 4, 1936; s. Victor and Marthe (Deportemont) L. B.Philosophy, Cath. U. Louvain, Belgium, 1957, Lic. in Notary, 1960, PhD in Law, 1959. From asst. to lectr. U. Louvain, 1959—; from advisor to dir. Banking and Fin. Commn., Brussels, 1963—; lectr. FUCAM, Mons, 1968—; mem. mgmt. coun. Office of Control and Assurance, 1983—; ret. Contbr. articles to profl. jours. Home: Ave de Fré 233, 1180 Brussels Belgium

LECA, FRANCINE, cardiologist, surgeon; b. Paris, May 20, 1938; d. Jacques Leca and Yvonne Dutrieux; m. Georges Chetochine; children: Caroline, Orso. Intern Hosp. of Paris, 1964; prof. cardiac surgery, 1979; head dept. cardiac surgery Hosp. N.E.M., Paris, 1984; mem. Commn. Sci. Specialise Insery, 1984-87. Editor: Cardiologie Pratique de l'Enfant, 1976, (film) Chirurgie Cardiaque de l'Enfant, 1976. Recipient Officier de L'ordre Nat. du Merite, 1976, 99, Chevalier de la Legion d'Honneur, 1995. Mem. EACTS, St. Chir Thorac et Cardio Vasculaire, St. Française de Cardiologie. Home: 86 Chemin de Grisy, 78860 St Nom la Breteche Yvelines, France Office: Hosp Necker Enfants Malades, 149 Rue de Sevres, 75015 Paris France

LECAPITAINE, JOHN EDWARD, counseling psychology educator, researcher; b. Nov. 21, 1950; s. Vincent Bernard and Evelyn Lucille LeCapitaine; m. Jessica Dale; 1 child, Katherine Briee. BS, U. Wis., 1973, MS, 1975; D, Boston U., 1980. Diplomate forensic psychologist, psychotherapist; diplomate Am. Psychotherapy Assn. Counseling and sch. psychologist Martin Luther King. Jr. Ctr., Boston, 1976-78; adj. prof. Boston U., 1980-90; rsch. cons. Dept. Mental Health, 1985-90; prof. counseling psychology U. Wis., River Falls, 1990—. Contbr. poetry, fiction, and acad. articles to profl. jours. Recipient Disting. award for Schs. as Devel. Clinics, The Edn. Jour., 1999. Mem. APA, ACA, Inst. Noetic Scis., Internat. Biographical Inst., Nat. Assn. Sch. Psychologists, Internat. Coun. Psychologists, Assn. Play Therapy, Assn. Multicultural Counseling and Devel., Assn. Humanistic Devel. and Edn., Assn. Counselor Edn. and Supervision, Internat. Soc. Poets, Phi Delta Kappa. Avocation: fiction writing, poetry. Home: 731 Lumphrey Ct River Falls WI 54022-3426 Office: U Wis Coll Edn and Grad Studies Dept Couns/Sch Psych 410 S 3rd St River Falls WI 54022-5013

LE CARRÉ, JOHN (DAVID JOHN MOORE CORNWELL), author; b. Poole, Dorset, Eng., Oct. 19, 1931; s. Ronald Thomas Archibald and Olive (Glassy) Cornwell; m. Alison Ann Sharp, Nov. 27, 1954 (div. dissolved 1972); children: Simon, Stephen, Timothy; m. Valerie Jane Eustace, 1972; 1 son, Nicholas. Student, Bern (Switzerland) U., 1948-49, BA in Modern Langs., 1956; hon. doctorate, U. Exeter, 1990, St. Andrews U., 1996, U. Southampton, U. Bath. Tutor Eton Coll., Berkshire, Eng., 1956-58; mem. Brit. Fgn. Service, 1959-64; 2d sec. embassy Brit. Fgn. Service, Bonn, Germany, 1961-63; consul Brit. Fgn. Service, Hamburg, Germany, 1963-64. Author: Call for the Dead, 1960, A Murder of Quality, 1962, The Spy Who Came in From the Cold, 1963 (Mystery Writers of Am. Novel of Yr., 1963, Brit. Crime Novel of Yr. award 1963, Somerset Maugham award 1963), The Looking-Glass War, 1965, A Small Town in Germany, 1968, The Naive and Sentimental Lover, 1971, Tinker Tailor Soldier Spy, 1973, rev., 1978, The Honourable Schoolboy, 1977 (James Tait Black Meml. prize, Crime Writers Assn. gold dagger), Smiley's People, 1980 (televised 1982), The Little Drummer Girl, 1983, A Perfect Spy, 1986, The Russia House, 1989 (Nikos Kasanzakis prize 1991), The Secret Pilgrim, 1991, The Night Manager, 1993, Our Game, 1995, The Tailor of Panama, 1996, Single & Single, 1999. Recipient Somerset Maugham award 1964, Edgar Allen Poe award Mystery Writers Am., 1965, Gold dagger Crime Writers Assn., 1978, Black Meml. award, 1978, The Kazamzakis prize, Greece, 1984, Grand Master award Mystery Writers Am., 1986, Malaparte prize, 1987, Diamond Dagger award Crime Writers Assn., 1988; Lincoln Coll., Oxford hon. fellow, 1984. Office: David Higham Assocs Ltd 175 5th Ave New York NY 10010-7703

LECCE, GIOVANNI, lawyer; b. Milan, Jan. 3, 1941; s. Salvatore and Albertina (Savi) L.; m. Maria Giuseppina Ietto, Apr. 24, 1971; children: Eleonora, Riccardo. JD, U. Degli Studi, Milan, 1965. Pvt. practice patent law Milan, 1966—; procurator Dott. Giovanni Lecce & C. Srl, Milan, 1968—, Ufficio Brevetti Calciati Srl, Milan, 1973—, BRE-MA, Brescia, Italy, 1975-82, Internazionale Brevetti, Reggio Emilia, Italy, 1977—, Studio Nord Brevetti, Bergamo, 1986—, Studio Tutela Brevetti, Crema, Italy, 1981—, Dott. Giovanni Lecce & C. Srl, Brescia, 1992—, Studio Nord Brevetti, Vicenza, 1999—; auditor various cos., Milan, 1986—. Author: Inventions and Industrial Models in Jurisprudence, 1987, The Trademark in Jurisprudence, 1996. Mem. Associazione Tributaristi Italiani, Albo dei Consulenti in Proprietà Industriale, Albo degli Avvocati, Albo dei Revisori dei Conti, Circolo della Stampa, Touring Club. Italiano. Avocations: horse riding, swimming, water skiing, jogging. Office: Dott Giovanni Lecce & C Srl, Via G Negri 10, 20123 Milan Italy

LECHAGO, JUAN, pathologist, educator; b. Barcelona, Spain, Aug. 2, 1942; came to U.S., 1973; s. Angel and Dolores (Xicart) L.; m. Lia Virginia Epstein, Feb. 26, 1966; children: John Patrick, James Bernard, Sarah Angela. B of Humanities, Nat. Coll. Monserrat, Cordoba, Argentina, 1959; MD, Nat. U. Cordoba, 1966; PhD in Pathology, Queen's U., Kingston, Ont., Can., 1971. Diplomate Am. Bd. Pathologists. Staff pathologist Harbor UCLA Med. Ctr., Torrance, Calif., 1973-87; asst. prof. pathology UCLA, 1973-79, assoc. prof. pathology, 1979-85, prof. pathology, 1985-87; prof., vice-chmn. dept. pathology U. Tex. So. Med. Sch., Dallas, 1987-90; chief lab. VA Med. Ctr., Dallas, 1987-90; prof. pathology Baylor Coll. Medicine, Houston, 1990—, prof. medicine, 1998—; dir. morphology Core Ctr. for Study of Inflammatory Bowel Disease, Torrance, 1985-87, Ctr. for Diabetes Rsch., Dallas, 1988-90; dir. surg. pathology svc. The Meth. Hosp., Houston, 1990—. Editor: Cellular Basis of Chemical Messengers in the Digestive System, 1981, Endocrine Pathology Update, 1990, Bloodworth's Endocrine Pathology, 3d edit., 1996; contbr. over 100 articles to profl. jours. NIH grantee, 1974-84, 82-86. Mem. U.S. Can. Acad. Pathology (edn. com. 1973—), Gastrointestinal Pathology Soc. (founding mem.; pres. 1987-88), Latin Am. Pathology Found. (pres. 1994-96), Ctrl. Am. Assn. Pathology (hon.), Argentinian Soc. Pathology (hon.). Achievements include work on ultrastructural and histochemical characterization of the digestive endocrine cells in man and animal species, first immunocytochemical cellular localization of the neuropeptides Bombesin and Ranatensin in animals, first immunolocalization of Granuliberin-like peptide in frog brain, molecular biology of Barrett's esophagus-derived cancer. Avocations: gourmet cooking, wine tasting, music and opera listening, martial arts, 2d degree Black Belt Jujitsu. Office: Dept Pathology Baylor Coll Medicine One Baylor Plz Houston TX 77030

LECHER, BELVADINE (REEVES LECHER), museum curator; b. Plainview, Nebr., Nov. 14, 1921; d. Robert Ancil and Myrtle Ivian (Rodgers) Reeves; m. Raymond Ralph Lecher, June 6, 1943; children: Krissa R. Lecher Randall , Pamela G. Lecher Hersh, Kim N. Lecher. Cert. in Hosp. Adminstrn., St. Louis U., 1967. Sec. Baird Law Office, Gordon, Nebr., 1938-39; cashier, bookkeeper, receptionist Western Pub. Svc. Co., Gordon, 1939-41, Consumers Pub. Power Co., Chadron, Nebr., 1941-45; cashier, bookkeeper, med. records Luth. Hosp. Homes Soc., Crawford, Nebr., 1952-62, adminstr., 1962-70; rate auditor, acct. Ross Transfer, Inc., Chadron, 1970-90; curator, dir. Dawes County Hist. Soc. Mus., Chadron, 1992—. Editor: (newspaper) Golden Age Courier, 1994—, (newsletter) Dawes County Hist. Soc., 1981—; co-editor: (book) Man of Many Frontiers - The Diaries of Billy the Bear Iaeger, 1994. Active Am. Cancer Soc., Dawes County, 1981-2000; bd. dirs. Habitat for Humanity, Chadron, 1993-95; tutor adult basic edn., Chadron, 1990-95. Recipient Cmty. Svc. award Rotary, Chadron, 1985, Good Neighbor award Ak-Sar-Ben/Omaha World Herald, Omaha, 1994, Woman of the Yr. award Chadron Bus. and Profl. Women's Club, Chadron, 1996, Recognition of Vol. Svc. award Am. Legion Aux., Chadron, 1994. Mem. Nebr. Mus. Assn., Nebr. State Genealogy Soc. (query editor 1982-84), Northwest Genealogy Soc. (county dir. 1992-94), Dawes County Hist. Soc. (pres. 1981-92, mus. curator 1992—), DAR (regent, registrar, treas. 1978-97), Area C. of C. (vis. com. 1996—). Republican. Methodist. Avocations: historic and lineage research, reading, writing, handcrafts, hiking. Office: Dawes County Hist Soc 341 Country Club Rd Chadron NE 69337-7329

LE CHEVALIER, THIERRY, medical oncologist; b. Lisieux, France, Aug. 12, 1948; s. François and Jacqueline (Deshayes) Le C.; m. Françoise D'Ornellas, Mar. 2, 1973; children: Isabelle, Clemence, Stanislas, Edouard. MD, U. Paris Sud, 1979. Fellow French Health Assistance, Yaounde, Cameroun, 1973-74; head lung unit Inst. Gustave Roussy, Villejuif, France, 1979—, asst. medicine, 1981-88, chief of unit, 1988-94, chief of svc., 1994—, chmn. clin. trial com., 1998—, head dept. of medicine, 2000—; vis. assoc. prof. Georgetown U., Washington, 1983-84; pres. Lung Group of French Cancer Ctr., 1982—. Assoc. editor Annals of Oncology; contbr. numerous articles to profl. jours. Mem. Am. Soc. Clin. Oncology, European Soc. Med. Oncology, Internat. Assn. for Study of Lung Cancer, French Cancer Soc. Roman Catholic. Home: 10 Square de la Tour, Maubourg, 75007 Paris France Office: Institut Gustave Roussy, rue Camille Desmoulins, 94800 Villejuif France

LECHNER, JON ROBERT, nursing administrator, educator; b. Detroit, Nov. 5, 1957; s. Monroe Stanley and Helen Cecelia (Schneider) L. Cert. in practical nursing, Oakland C.C., Southfield, Mich., 1983; ADN, Mercy Coll. Detroit, 1991, BSN, 1992; MSA, Ctrl. Mich. U., 1998. Cert. EMT; RN, ANCC, Mich. Coord. emergency med. svcs., paramedic William Beaumont Hosp., Royal Oak, Mich., 1979-84, nurse, 1986—, asst. nursing mgr., 1992-97, nursing mgr., 1997—; pastoral assoc. St. Mary's Parish & Sch., Toledo, 1984-86; adj. clin. instr. Oakland C.C., Waterford, Mich., 1993—; cert. BLS instr. Am. Heart Assn., Southfield, 1986—. Vol. Project Health-O-Rama, 1992—, Wellness Networks, Inc., 1992—; voting mem. region I State of Mich. HIV Planning & Prevention Commn., Detroit, 1994—. Mem. Am. Assembly Men Nursing, Am. Assn. Neurosci. Nurses, Acad. Med. Surg. Nurses (charter), Assn. Nurses AIDS Care, Sigma Theta Tau. Democrat. Roman Catholic. Avocations: reading, hiking, walking, cycling, theatre. Home: 28450 Universal Dr Warren MI 48092-2441 Office: William Beaumont Hosp 3601 W 13 Mile Rd Royal Oak MI 48073-6712

LECHNER, PETER, surgeon; b. Steyr, Austria, July 15, 1956; s. Kurt S. and Elfriede (Pienegger) L.; m. Diana K. Radler, Sept. 29, 1975 (div. Dec. 1987); 1 child, Michael; m. Brigitte O. Jesch, Feb. 27, 1988. MD, U. Graz, Austria, 1981; Prof., U. Graz, 1995. Tchg. asst. Inst. of Anatomy/U. Graz, 1977-81; resident 2nd Dept. Surgery/U. Hosp./U. Graz, 1981-88, cons., 1988-95; prof. of surgery U. Graz, 1995—; head of dept. Community Hosp., Klosterneuburg, Austria, 1996—. Author more than 100 scientific publs. and presentations in field. Recipient Rsch. award Am. Cancer Soc., 1997, Outstanding Investor award NIH, 1996. Fellow Am. Coll. Surgeons; mem. N.Y. Acad. Scis. Roman Catholic. Avocations: yacht sailing, fly fishing, piano playing, classical music. Office: Community Hosp, Krentfergasse A2-14, A-3400 Klusterneuburg Austria

LECHNER, ROBERT HANS LEO, telecommunication consultant executive; b. St. Poelten, Austria, Aug. 8, 1946; s. Robert and Anna (Schobel) L.; m. Elisabeth Laimer, 1996; children: Claudia, Thomas. Diploma, Tech. U., Vienna, Austria, 1974. Qualified elec. engr. R & D engr. Siemens, Munich, 1965-75, mgr., 1975-84, dep. dir., 1984-87; sr. dir. Siemens, Vienna, 1987-91; v.p., dir. Ericsson, Vienna, 1991-93; sr. cons. for telecom. adv. svc., Munich, 1993—; mem. adv. bd. Multimedia Info. Tech. GMBH, Vienna, Austria, 1998-99; acting dir. VIAG Interkom, Munich, 1998-99, mem. bd., Venture Select, Munich, 1999—; gen. mgr. Littlefeet Eurp[e, 1999-2000; concept developer Tech. U., St. Poelten, 1993; conf. presenter in field. Inventor over 70 telecommunications system solutions. Decorated knight Order of Holy Sepulchre (Vatican). Fellow Oesterr Verband Elekrotechnik/IEEE, Verband Dt. Elektrotechnik/Informationstechn. Gesellschaft, Austrian Soc. Electricity; mem. Austrian Inst., German Soc. Electricity. Avocations: skiing, playing piano, tennis. Home: Am Steinbuehel 12, A-3071 Boeheimkirchen Austria

LECKEY, ANDREW A., financial columnist; b. Chgo., Sept. 22, 1949; s. Alexander and Ellen (Martin) L. B.A., Trinity Coll., Deerfield, Ill., 1971; M.A. in Journalism, U. Mo., 1975; postgrad., Columbia U., 1978-79, Rutgers U., 1981. Fin. editor Oreg. Statesman, Salem, 1975-76; statehouse reporter Phoenix Gazette, 1976-78; fin. columnist Chgo. Sun-Times, 1979-85, Chgo. Tribune and N.Y. Daily News, 1985—; fin. commentator Sta. WBEZ, Chgo., 1981-83, Sta. WLS-TV, Chgo., 1983—; syndicated fin. columnist Los Angeles Times Syndicate, 1983-85, Tribune Media Services, 1985—. Author: Make Money with the New Tax Laws, 1987. Office: Tribune Media Svcs 435 N Michigan Ave Ste 1500 Chicago IL 60611-4012

LECKIE, CAROL MAVIS, retired state government administrator; b. Watertown, Wis., Feb. 25, 1929; d. Arthur Walter Bessel and Effie Vada (Squires) Downs; m. Ralph Junior Judd, Sept. 27, 1947 (div. Dec. 1952); Children: Russell Howard, Barbara Rae; m. Leonard John Leckie, Sept. 30, 1977 (dec. May 1990); stepchildren: Leonard John, Gordon Armstrong, Lorna Jean. Grad. h.s., Madison, Wis. Mgr. data processing Dept. Justice, State of Wis., Madison, 1971-79, mgr. Records Mgmt. Program, 1979-83, mgr. Typography Sect., 1983-90; ret. Mem. com. State of Wis. Employees Combined Campaign, Madison, 1986, 88-91, co-chair, 1987; co-chair East 1946 Class Reunion Com. Mem. Assn. Records Mgrs. and Adminstrs. (pres. 1983-84), Assn. Career Employees, Bus. Forms Mgmt. Assn. Lutheran. Avocations: travel, church work. E-mail: cmjl106@chorus.net. Home: 5555 Tancho Dr Apt 106 Madison WI 53718-1929

LECKIE, STUART HAMILTON, investment actuary; b. Glasgow, Scotland, May 28, 1945; s. Stuart Morrison and Jean McKinley (McCurdie) L.; m. Rosemary Jean McGregor; children: Rosie, Roy, Victoria, Alexandra. BSc with honors, U. Glasgow, 1967. Actuarial asst. Scottish Mut. Assurance Soc., Glasgow, 1967-70; asst. actuary Lincoln Nat. Ins. Co. Ltd., London, 1970-73; dep. actuary Providence Capitol Ins. Co. Ltd., London, 1973-76; actuary, fin. dir. Swiss Pioneer Life Ins. Co. Ltd., Liverpool, Eng., 1976-79; mng. dir., actuary Sedgwick Employee Benefit Cons. Ltd., Hong Kong, 1979-82; mng. dir., actuary Watson Wyatt Worldwide, Hong Kong, 1982-93, Asia-Pacific chmn., 1994-95; Asia-Pacific chmn. Fidelity Investments, Hong Kong, 1995-97; actuary Stirling Fin Ltd., Hong Kong, 1998—; chmn. Woodrow Milliman China Ltd., 1998—. Contbr. articles to profl. jours.; speaker in field. Mem. Com. Securities and Futures Commn., Hong Kong, 1983—, Ctrl. Policy Unit, Hong Kong, 1989-97; chmn. Hong Kong Rugby Football Union, 1992-96. Decorated officer Order Brit. Empire; Justice of Peace, Hong Kong Govt., 1994; freeman City of London, 1991. Fellow Inst. of Actuaries; mem. Fin. Execs. Inst. Hong Kong (pres. 1981), Actuarial Soc. Hong Kong (pres. 1982-99), Hong Kong Club (chmn. 1997). Protestant Christian. Avocations: sports, travel, gardening. Office: Stirling Fin Ltd Tower 1, 1806 Lippo Ctr 89 Queensway, Hong Kong Hong Kong

LECKIENE, MARGARITA, immunologist, researcher; b. Jerevan, Armenia, Nov. 3, 1955; arrived in Lithuania, 1982; d. Nikolaj Petrosian and Emma Khachaturova; m. Antanas Leckas, Oct. 26, 1983; five children. MS, Yerevan (USSR) State U., 1977; PhD, Inst. Molecular Biology, Moscow, 1983. Tchg. qualification in chemistry and biology. Rsch. assoc. Inst. Biotechnology, Vilnius, Lithuania, 1982—. Contbr. articles to profl. jours.; inventor in field. Recipient Young Investigator award European League Against Rheumatism, 1995. Mem. Armenian Apostolic Church. Avocations: semiotics, psychoanalysis, history, linguistics, art. Office: Inst Biotechnology, Graiciuno no 8, LT-2028 Vilnius Lithuania

LECLAIR, JOHN CLARK, professional hockey player; b. St. Albans, Vt., July 5, 1969. Hockey player Montreal Canadiens, 1987-94, Phila. Flyers, 1995—. Named to ECAC All-Star 2d team, 1990-91, Sporting News All-Star 1st team, 1994-95, NHL All-Star 1st team, 1994-95.

LECLAIR, SUSAN JEAN, hematologist, clinical laboratory scientist, educator; b. New Bedford, Mass., Feb. 17, 1947; d. Joseph A. and Beatrice (Perry) L.; m. James T. Griffith; 1 child, Kimberly A. BS in med. tech., Stonehill Coll., 1968; postgrad., Northeastern U., Boston, 1972-74; MS in Med. Lab. Sci., U. Mass., Dartmouth, 1977. Cert. clin. lab. scientist; cert. med. technologist. Med. technologist Union Hosp., New Bedford, Mass., 1968-70; supr. hematology Morton Hosp., Taunton, Mass., 1970-72; edn. coord., program dir. Sch. Med. Tech. Miriam Hosp., Providence, 1972-79; hematology technologist R.I. Hosp., Providence, 1979-80; asst. prof. med. lab. sci. U. Mass., Dartmouth, 1980-84, assoc. prof. med. lab. sci., 1984-92, prof. med. lab. sci., 1992—; instr. hematology courses Brown U., Providence, 1978-80; cons. bd. R.I. Hosp. Div. Clin. Hematology, Charlton Meml. Hosp., St. Luke's Hosp., VA Med. Ctr., Providence, 1984—, Nemasket Group, Inc., 1984-87, Gateway Health Alliance, 1985-87; chair hematology/hemostasis com. Nat. Cert. Agy. for Med. Lab. Pers. Exam. Coun., 1994-98. Contbr. articles to profl. jours.; contbr. articles to jours and chpts. to books; author computer software in hematology. Reviewer Nat. Commn. Clin. Lab. Scis., 1986-89; chairperson Mass. Assn. Health Planning Agys., 1986-87; bd. dirs. Southeastern Mass. Health Planning Devel. Inc., (1975-88, numerous other offices and coms.); planning subcom. AIDS Edn. (presentor Info Series). Mem. Am. Soc. Clin. Lab. Sci. (editor clin. practice sect. CLS jour.), Am. Soc. Med. Tech. Edn. and Rsch. Fund, Inc. (chairperson 1983-85), Mass. Assn. for Med. Tech. (pres. 1977-78), Southeastern Mass. Soc. Med. Tech. (pres. 1975-76), Alpha Mu Tau (pres. 1993-94). Avocations: choral singing, cooking, reading. Office: U Mass Dept Med Lab Sci Dartmouth MA 02747

LECLANT, JEAN, Egyptologist, archaeologist, philologist; b. Paris, Aug. 8, 1920; s. René Leclant and Laurence Pannier; m. Marie-Françoise Alexandre-Hatvany, July 7, 1988. Cert., U. Paris, Sorbonne, 1945, PhD in Humanities, 1955; PhD honoris causa, Cath. U., Leuven, Belgium, 1991, U. Bologne, Italy, 1992. Prof. Egyptology U. Strasbourg, France, 1953-63, U. Sorbonne, Paris, 1963-79; dir. studies École Pratique des Hautes Études, Paris, 1964—; prof. emeritus Egyptology Collège de France, Paris, 1979-90; dir. Mission Française Archéologique, Ethiopia, 1952-56; mem. archaeol. missions to Sudan, 1960-78, Egypt, 1948-96; mem. Inst. France, Acad. des Inscriptions et Belles-Lettres, Paris, 1974—, perpetual sec., 1983—. Author: Enquêtes sur les Sacerdoces et les Sanctuaires Égyptiens à l'Epoque dite "Ethiopienne, " 1954, French Bibliographical Digest, Archaeology, 1945-1955, I, Egypt and Surrounding Countries, 1956, Dans les Pas des Pharaons, 1958, Montouemhat, Quatrième Prophète d'Amon, Prince de la Ville, 1961, Recherches sur les Monuments Thébains de la XXVe Dynastie, 1965, Inventaire Bibliographique des Isiaca I, 1972, II, 1974, III, 1984, IV, 1991; co-author: Karnak-Nord IV, 1954, Le Temple Haut du Complex Funéraire du Roi Teti, 1972, Kition II, 1976, Le Temple Haut du Complexe Funéraire du Roi Ounas, 1977, La Culture des Chasseurs du Nil et du Sahara, 2 vols., 1980; co-editor: Soleb I, 1966, Soleb II, 1971; dir. series in collection: L'Univers des Formes, I, 1978, II, 1979, III, 1980; founder, dir. (newsletter) Meroitic Newsletter, 1968—; founder, co-dir. (jour.) Annales d'Ethiopie, 1955-72; contbr. numerous articles to profl. jours. Commandment French Navy, 1945-46. Decorated Comdr., Legion of Honor, Comdr., Order of Merit, Comdr., Order of Acad. Palms, Comdr., Order of Arts and Letters, Officer, Imperial Order of Menelik, Ethiopia, Grand Officer, Order of Egyptian Republic; recipient Arakel Nubar Pacha prize Asssn. France-Egypt, 1954, Gold medal for archaeology Acad. of Arch., 1983, Galileo Galilei medal U. Pisa, Balzan prize Fondazione Internat., 1993. Fellow Brit. Acad. Scis. (corr.), Acad. Scis. Vienna (corr.); mem. Inst. d'Égypte, Assn. de l'Academia dei Lincei, Royal Acad. Belgium, Royal Acad. Denmark, Royal Acad. Sweden, Bavarian Acad., Romania Acad., German Archaeol. Inst., Royal Acad. Madrid, Austrian Archaeol. Inst., Acad. Mediterranean Studies, Italian Inst. of Near and Far East (hon.), Acad. Europaea, Russian Acad. Scis. (fgn.), Royal Acad. Historia (Madrid), Am. Philos. Soc., Soc. Asiatique (hon. pres.), Overseas Acad. Scis. (Paris), Acad. Delphinale, Acad. d'Aix-en-Provence, Acad. de Lyon, Acad. de Bordeaux, Acad. de Marseille, Nat. Soc. Antiquarians of France, Internat. Assn. Egyptologists (hon. sec.-gen.), Group for Meroitic Studies (co-pres.), Soc. for Nubian Studies (hon. pres.), Internat. Assn. for History of Religions (v.p.), French Commn. for UNESCO (v.p.), Archael. Rsch. Commn. Overseas, Ministry of Fgn. Affairs. Home: 25 Quai de Conti, 75006 Paris France Office: Inst de France, 23 Quai de Conti, 75006 Paris France

LECLERC, PAUL, library director; b. Lebanon, N.H., May 28, 1941; s. Louis and M. Juliette (Trottier) LeC; m. Judith Ginsberg, Oct. 26, 1980; 1 child, Adam Louis. BS, Coll. Holy Cross, 1963; student, U. Paris, 1963-64; MA, Columbia U., 1966, PhD with distinction, 1969; LHD (hon.), L.I. U., 1994, Coll. of the Holy Cross, 1994, Hamilton Coll., 1995, Union Coll., 1997, Hunter Coll., 1997, Fordham U., 1997. Assoc. prof. French Union Coll., Schenectady, 1969-79, chmn. dept. modern langs. and lit., 1972-77, chmn. humanities div., 1975-77; univ. dean for acad. affairs CUNY, 1979-84; provost and acad. v.p. Baruch Coll., CUNY, 1984-88; pres. Hunter Coll., CUNY, 1988-93; pres., CEO New York Public Library, 1994—; bd. dirs. N.Y. Alliance for Pub. Schs., N.Y.C., 1981-84, El Museo del Barrio, The Feminist Press; pres. N.Y. Tchr. Edn. Conf. Bd., Albany, N.Y., 1983-84. Author: Voltaire and Crebillon Pere, 1972, Voltaire's Rome Sauvée, 1992; co-editor: Lettres d'André Moreliet, vol. I, 1991, vol. II, 1994, vol. III, 1996; contbr. articles to profl. jours. Decorated officier Palmes Académiques, chevalier Legion of Honor (France); grantee NEH, 1971, 79, Am. Coun. Learned Socs., 1973, Ford Found., 1979. Mem. MLA, Am. Soc. for 18th

Century Studies. Office: NY Pub Libr Fifth Ave & 42nd St New York NY 10018

LECLERCQ, GUY, laboratory director; b. La Louvière, Hainaut, Belgium, Mar. 15, 1944; s. Urbain and Denise (Van den Houdt) L.; m. Denise Messenguy, Nov. 21, 1970; children: Régis, Arnaud. DrSc, U. Brussels, 1970. Rsch. fellow, 1968-77; chief Travaux, 1977-93; prof. U. Brussels, 1993—; dir. Lab. Breast Cancer Rsch., Inst. Bordet, Brussels, 1993—. Author: Clinical Interest of Steroid Hormone Receptors in Breast Cancer, 1984; contbr. articles to profl. jours. Recipient prizes Found. Cancérologique St. Michel, Belgium, 1980, Found. Hoyer-Van Cutsem, 1993. Mem. European Orgn. for Rsch. and Treatment of Cancer (mem. receptor and biomarkers group). Office: Lab Cancerologie Mammaire, Inst Bordet, 1 rue Heger, 1000 Brussels Belgium

LE CLOIREC, PIERRE ANDRÉ, environmental engineer, educator; b. Lorient, France, Feb. 11, 1955; s. Félix Louis and Thérèse Eugénie (Anglade) Le C.; m. Claudine Suzette Renaud, Dec. 26, 1980; children: Gildas, Diane. Diploma in Engring., Sch. Chemistry, Rennes, France, 1979; PhD in Chemistry, U. Rennes, 1983, PhD in Physics, 1985. Asst. prof. Sch. Chemistry, U. Rennes, 1982-85; postdoctoral visitor U. N.C., Chapel Hill, 1985-86; assoc. prof. Sch. Chemistry, U. Rennes, 1986-90; rsch. scientist Elf Co., Pau, France, 1989; prof. Mining Sch., Alès, France, 1990-95, Nantes, France, 1995—; rsch. scientist Sch. Chemistry, 1982-90; lab. dir. Mining Sch., 1990-95, rsch. dept. dir., 1995—. Editor: The Volatile Organic Compounds in Environment (in French), 1998; mem. editl. bd. Jour. Environ. Tech., 1996—; contbr. articles to profl. jours.; patentee in field. Sgt. French Engrs., 1980-81. Recipient Prof. Pierre Gineste award, Rennes, 1985, Ademe award, Angers, France, 1996. Mem. Internat. Assn. Water Quality, GRUTTEE, Am. Chem. Soc., Am. Water Works Assn. Home: 19 rue Antoine St Exupery, 44240 La Chapelle Erdre France Office: Ecole des Mines de Nantes, 4 rue Alfred Kastler, 44307 Nantes cedex 03, France

LECOMTE, OLIVIER, property investment executive; b. Saint-Quentin, France, Aug. 7, 1965; s. Gilles Lecomte and Monique La Marre. Grad., Ecole Centrale Paris, 1989. Assoc. Societe Generale, London, 1989-91; v.p. Societe Generale, Paris, 1991, Demachy Worms & Co., Paris, 1992-94; head corp. devel. Unibail, Paris, 1994-95, exec. v.p., 1999—; CEO Espace Expansion, Paris, 1996—; v.p. Conseil Nat. des Ctrs. Commerciaux, Paris, 1996—; mem. Inst. de L'Enterprise, Paris, 1998—. Office: Unibail, 108 Rue de Richelieu, F-75002 Paris France

LE COUSTUMIER, ALAIN, medical microbiologist; b. Vitry Le François, France, May 6, 1956; s. Jacques and Odile (Thivet) Le C.; m. Annick Kawski, June 27, 1979. Grad. in Chemistry, U. Nancy, France, 1978, grad. in Med. Biology, 1983, Cert. Biology of Reprodn. and Devel., 1991; Cert. of Med. Pedagogy, U. Nancy, 1995; postgrad. in Applied Epidemiology, Tufts U., 1991; Cert. on Methods and Markers, U. Tours, France, 1992. Intern Univ.'s Hosps., Nancy, 1979-83; asst. Regional Hosps., Thionville, France, 1983-85; co-dir. Labioma, St. Jean d'Angely, France, 1985-86; praticien Inter Cmty. Hosp. Villeneuve, St. Georges, France, 1986-87; microbiologist Champ Le Roi Hosp., Neufchateau, France, 1987-98; bd. dirs. Coll. Bacteriology, Virology and Hygien French Hosps., 1992—; bd. dirs. Assn. Interns and Past Intern's of Nancy's Univ. Hosps., 1979-82, 93—. Contbr. articles to profl. jours. Mem. Am. Soc. Microbiology, French Soc. Microbiology, Rotary Club. Roman Catholic. Avocations: sailing, skiing tours, cycling. Home: 750 les junies, 46000 Cahors France Office: Lab Hosp, BP269 Cahors 46005, France

LEDBETTER, LINDA CAROL, pension fund executive, professional organization executive; b. Detroit, Dec. 22, 1948; d. Ray Finley Ledbetter and H. Christine Gore; m. Jerome D. Davis, Jan. 20, 1996. BA, Western Mich. U., Kalamazoo, 1966; MEd, La. State U., New Orleans, 1975; PhD, U. New Orleans, 1978; postgrad., Claremont (Calif.) Coll., 1990-91. Cert. tchr., prin., supt., parish/county adminstr., La., Mich., Wis. Tchr. Milw., New Orleans, Detroit, 1970-90; assoc. prof., coll. adminstr. U. New Orleans, 1977-82; prof. La. State U. Law Sch., Baton Rouge, 1977-82; pres., CEO The Neron Group, New Orleans, 1993—; exec. dir. Coun. La. Trustees, 1996—; cons. Nat. Tchr. Ctr., Washington, 1979-83, U.S. Office Edn., Washington, 1979-80, various civic, charitable and polit. groups, 1979-97; internat. conf. spkr., 1989—; provider, sponsor, planner Nat. Pension Fund Conf., 1997—. Contbr. articles to profl. jours., books in field. Mem. exec. coun., v.p. Tchrs. Union New Orleans, 1977-93; del.-at-large Nat. Dem. Conv., Atlanta, 1988; trustee pension fund La. Tchrs. Retirement Sys., 1990-94; bd. govs. Coun. La. Trustees, 1995—, nat. conf. planner and sponsor, 1997—; bd. dirs. La. Soc. Prevention of Cruelty to Animals, New Orleans, 1985-90. Fellow Inst. Politics Loyola U., New Orleans, 1982; named Tchr. of Yr., Jr. Achievement, La., 1990, Outstanding Young Woman of Am., 1980; recipient Spl. Recognition award Exec. Dept. State of La., 1993, cert. of merit Mayor's Office City of New Orleans, 1993. Mem. Women's Profl. Coun. (membership chair 1997), Freedom Found., 100 Club of New Orleans. Avocations: travel, horseback riding, sailing. Home and Office: 33 Neron Pl New Orleans LA 70118-4265

LEDECKY, JAROMIR, metalworking company executive; b. Prague, Czechoslovakia, Aug. 8, 1927; s. Jaroslav and Jarmila (Horčičková) L.; m. Berta Greenwald, Dec. 30, 1956; children: Jonathan, David. BA, Rutgers U., 1949; MBA, NYU, 1962, PhD, 1966. CPA, N.Y. Rschr. Mid-European Rsch. Ctr., N.Y.C., 1953-55; economist Lionel D. Edie & Co., N.Y.C., 1955-66; v.p. economist Quantum Sci. Corp., N.Y.C., 1966-71; sr. v.p., economist Rinfret, Boston, 1971-80; dir. pub. policy and econs. Conoco Oil Co., Stamford, Conn., 1980-82; assoc. prof. U. Conn., Stamford, 1980-82; prof. Marymount Coll., N.Y.C., 1982-85; adj. prof. NYU/GBA, Westchester, N.Y., 1985-87; dir. Legacy Fund Inc., Washington, 1986—; chmn. bd. Vanberk (Czech Republic) Chains Ltd., 1992—. Cpl. U.S. Army, 1950-52. Recipient Aerospace Writers award, N.Y.C., 1961, Founders Day award NYU Trustees, N.Y.C., 1966; Jan Masaryk scholar Masaryk Inst., N.Y.C., 1947. Office: Vamberk Chains Ltd, Dvořákova 426, 517 54 Vamberk Czech Republic also: 2700 Virginia Ave NW Washington DC 20037-1908

LEDEN, IDO LORENS, rheumatologist; b. Lund, Sweden, July 4, 1942; s. Ido E. and Majken (Tornberg) L.; m. Birgitta Elmqvist, Jan. 5, 1968; children: Charlotta, Anna. MB, U. Lund, 1963, MD, 1971. Resident, then chief resident rheumatology dept. U. Lund, 1976-81; head rheumatology sect. Kristianstad (Sweden) Hosp., 1981—. Co-author: Rheumatology, 1994, Rheumatology-Past, Present, Future, 1995; contbr. to Nat. Ency., Bra Böckers Läkarlexikon. Recipient Trafvenfelt silver medal Swedish Soc. Medicine, 1993. Mem. Swedish Soc. for Rheumatology (gen. sec. 1984-90), Scandinavian Soc. for Rheumatology (chmn. 24th congress 1992), Nat. Orgn. Against Rheumatism (bd. dirs. 1982-99). Avocations: history of medicine, paleopathology, collecting topical stamps, bridge, tennis. Home: Bokvägen 27, 291 43 Kristianstad Sweden Office: Kristianstad Hosp, Rheumatology Sect, 291 85 Kristianstad Sweden

LE DENTU, CHARLES, professional association administrator; b. Paris, Aug. 16, 1938; m. Solange de Mathan, June 11, 1966; children: Béatrice, Emmanuel, Charles-Eric. Engr., Ministry Agr., Paris, 1964; Mastere, Inst. Control Gestion, Lyon, France, 1977. Agr. French Ministry Adv., 1963; agr. mgmt. Badische Anilin and Soda Fabrik Ag, France, 1966; internat. rels. mgr. Rhone-Poulenc, Lyon, 1992; founder, pres. French Assn. Diagnostic Industries Agr., Agrofood & Environ., 1994—. Named Officier du Mérite Agricole, Ministry Français de l'Agriculture, Paris, 1999. Mem. French Sea Salt Brotherhood (knight of honour 1999). Roman Catholic. Home: Clos Mirman, 5 rue des Tourterelles, F30132 Caissargues Camargue, France Office: Afidiale, BP n 5, F30132 Caissargues France

LEDERBERG, JOSHUA, geneticist, educator; b. Montclair, N.J., May 23, 1925; s. Zwi Hirsch and Esther (Goldenbaum) L.; m. Marguerite S. Kirsch, Apr. 5, 1968; children: David Kirsch, Anne. BA, Columbia U., 1944; PhD, Yale U., 1947. With U. Wis., 1947-58; prof. genetics Sch. Medicine, Stanford (Calif.) U., 1959-78; pres. Rockefeller U., N.Y.C., 1978-90, univ. prof. Sackler Found. scholar, 1990—; adj. prof. Columbia U., 1990—; mem. adv. com. med. rsch. WHO, 1971; chair adv. bd. Ellison Med. Found., 1997—; mem. bd. sci. advisors Sci. Internat. Applications Corp., McLean, Va., Antigenics, N.Y., Lilly & Co., Cin., Maxygen, Palo Alto, Aviron, Mountain View, Calif.; cons. U.S. Def. Sci. Bd., NSF, NIH, NASA, ACDA. Trustee Camille and Henry Dreyfus Found.; bd. dirs. Chem. Industry Inst. Toxicology, N.C. With USN, 1943-45. Recipient Nobel prize in physiology and medicine for rsch. in genetics of bacteria, 1958, U.S. Nat. Medal of Sci., 1989, Alan Newell award ACM, 1996, John Stearns award N.Y. Acad. Medicine, 1996, Maxwell Finland award NCIH, 1997, Morris Collen award Am. Med. Info. Assn., 1999; sr. scholar Stanford U. Ctr. Internat. Security and Arms Control, 1998—. Fellow AAAS, Am. Philos. Soc., Am. Acad. Arts and Scis., Acad. Universelle Cultures (Paris); mem. Inst. Medicine NAS, Coun. Fgn. Rels., Royal Soc. London (fgn.), N.Y. Acad. Scis. (hon. life gov.), Ordre des Lettres et des Arts (comdr.). E-mail: lederberg@mail.rockefeller.edu. Office: Rockefeller U 1230 York Ave Box 174 New York NY 10021-6399

LEDERER, HERBERT, foreign languages educator; b. Vienna, Austria, June 9, 1921; came to U.S., 1942; s. Hans Lederer and Frida Rosenbaum; m. Eva Marie Hohenberg, June 20, 1948; children: George Kenneth, Barbara Louise. BA, Bklyn. Coll., 1948; MA, U. Chgo., 1949, PhD, 1953. Instr. German U. Chgo., 1949-52; asst. prof. German Wabash Coll., Crawfordsville, Ind., 1952-57; assoc. prof. German Ohio U., Athens, 1957-61, Queens Coll., Flushing, N.Y., 1961-69; prof. German, head dept. Germanic and Slavic langs. U. Conn., Storrs, 1969-89, prof. emeritus, 1989; chief reader German Ednl. Testing Svc., Princeton, N.J., 1964-68; chmn. German test com. Coll. Engrance Examination Bd., N.Y.C., 1967-71; cons. Nat. Endowment for the Humanities, Washington, 1973-75, 90-91. Author: Reference Grammar of the German Language, 1969, Handbook of East German Drama, 1945-85, 1987, Bilingual Plays, 1997; editor Gedichte von Arthur Schnitzler, 1969; assoc. editor Modern Austrian Lit., 1968-80. Rsch. grantee Am. Coun. of Learned Socs., 1968, Cross of Honor for Arts and Letters Austrian Govt., 1976, Rsch. award Internat. Theatre Inst., 1978, 81, 83, 85, Fed. Cross of Merit German Govt., 1987. Mem. MLA (parliamentarian 1972-88), Am. Assn. of Tchrs. of German (exec. bd. 1970-72, 79-82), Am. Coun. for the Study of Austrian Lit. (pres. 1972-80), Assn. of Depts. of Fgn. Langs. (exec. bd. 1976-79, pres. 1978), Kafka Soc. Am. Democrat. Jewish. Avocation: theatre. Home: 143 Separatist Rd Storrs Mansfield CT 06268-2003

LEDERER, PAUL EDWARD, landscape architect; b. Paradise, Nova Scotia, Can., Mar. 2, 1942; came to U.S., 1946; s. Emil and Edith (Kann) L. BS, Rutgers U., 1964; B of Land Architecture, U. Mass., 1965, M of Land Architecture, 1969. Registered landscape architect, Mass., N.J., Va., Md., Ala. Landscape architect John Rahenkamp & Assoc, Phila., 1965, Nat. Park Svc., Phila., 1965, 67-69; landscape architect, planner Nat. Park Svc., Washington, 1969-97; civil engring. aid Soil Conservation Svc., Northampton, Mass., 1967. Mem. Com. of 100 on Fed. City D.C., 1987. Mem. Am. Soc. Landscape Architects, Am. Planning Assn., Nat. Trust for Hist. Preservation, Nat. Park and Recreation Assn. Jewish. Avocations: fine arts, sculpture, collecting classic cars, photography, swimming.

LEDERMAN, FRANK L., scientist, research center administrator; b. Buffalo, Aug. 19, 1949; s. Sol J. and Carol S. (Dankman) L.; m. Daphna Kaplansky, Aug. 8, 1993. BS in Math., Carnegie-Mellon U., 1971, MS in Physics, 1971; MS in Physics, U. Ill., 1972, PhD, 1975. Fellow U. Pa., Phila., 1975; physicist R & D ctr. GE Corp., Schenectady, N.Y., 1976-78, mgr. ultrasound program, 1978-80, mgr. energy systems mgmt. br., 1981-82, acting mgr. liaison ops., 1983-84, mgr. power electronics systems br., 1984-87, mgr. programs and resources, 1988; v.p., dir. rsch. Noranda Inc., Pointe Claire, Que., Can., 1988-91, sr. v.p. tech., 1992-95; v.p., chief tech. officer Alcoa Inc., Alcoa Center, Pa., 1995—. Contbr. articles to profl. jours.; patentee in field. Mem. IEEE, Indsl. Rsch. Inst., Am. Phys. Soc. Home: 4011 Pin Oak Ct Murrysville PA 15668-9799 Office: Alcoa Tech Ctr 100 Technical Dr New Kensington PA 15069-0001

LEDERMAN, LEON MAX, physicist, educator; b. N.Y.C., July 15, 1922; s. Morris and Minna (Rosenberg) L.; m. Florence Gordon, Sept. 19, 1945; children: Rena S., Jesse A., Heidi R.; m. Ellen Carr, Sept. 17, 1981. BS, CCNY, 1943, DSc (hon.), 1980; AM, Columbia U., 1948, PhD, 1951; DSc (hon.), No. Ill. U., 1984, U. Chgo., 1985, Ill. Inst. Tech., 1987. Assoc. in physics Columbia U., N.Y.C., 1951, asst. prof., 1952-54, assoc. prof., 1954-58, prof., 1958-89, Eugene Higgins prof. physics, 1972-79; Frank L. Sulzberger prof. physics U. Chgo., 1989-92; dir. Fermi Nat. Accelerator Lab., Batavia, Ill., 1979-89, dir. emeritus, 1989—; Pritzker prof. sci. Ill. Inst. Tech., Chgo., 1992—; resident scholar Ill. Math. and Sci. Acad., 1998—; dir. Nevis Labs., Irvington, N.Y., 1962-79; guest scientist Brookhaven Nat. Labs., 1955; cons. Nat. Accelerator Lab., European Orgn. for Nuclear Rsch. (CERN), 1970—; mem. high energy physics adv. panel AEC, 1966-70; mem. adv. com. to div. math. and phys. scis. NSF, 1970-72; sci. advisor to gov. State of Ill., 1989-93; chmn. XXIV Internat. Physics Olympiad, 1991-93; co-chair com. on capacity bldg. in sci. Internat. Coun. Sci. Unions, 1994—. Author: Quarks to the Cosmos, 1989, The God Particle, 1993; also over 200 articles. Trustee Univ. Rsch. Assocs., 1967-71, 92—; bd. dirs. Mus. Sci. Industry, Chgo., 1989—, Weizmann Inst. Sci., Israel, 1988—; mem. adv. bd. Sec. of Energy, 1991—. Recipient Nat. Medal of Sci., 1965, Townsend Harris medal CUNY, 1973, Elliot Cresson medal Franklin Inst., 1976, Wolf prize, 1982, Nobel prize in physics, 1988, Enrico Fermi prize, 1992, Rosenblith Lecturer in Science and Technology Nat. Acad. of Sciences, 1995, Joseph Priestly award Dickinson Coll., 1996, Pres.'s medal CCNY, 1993, Heald prize Ill. Inst. Tech., 2000, Pupin Med. award Columbia U., 2000, 34 additional hon. degrees including univs. and acads. in Finland, Eng., Italy, Argentina, Mex., Brazil, Russia and Peru; Guggenheim fellow, 1958-59, Ford Found. fellow European Ctr. for Nuclear Rsch., Geneva, 1958-59, fellow NSF, 1967, Presdl. fellow World Bank, 1996—; resident scholar Great Minds program Ill. Math. Sci. Acad. Fellow AAAS (pres. 1990-91, chmn. 1991-92), Am. Phys. Soc.; mem. NAS (U.S., Argentina, Finland, Mex.), IEEE (hon.), Italian Phys. Soc., Aspen Inst. Physics (pres. 1990-92), Ill. Math. Sci. Acad. (vice chmn. 1985-98), Tchrs. Acad. for Math. and Sci. in Chgo. (co-chmn. 1990—), Coun. of the Am. Phys. Soc., Coun. Advancement Sci. Writing, Bulletin Atomic Scientists (vice chmn. 1989—), comr. White House Fellows Program, 1997-2000. also: Ill Inst Tech BCP Dept Life Scis Bldg 3101 S Dearborn Rm 106 Chicago IL 60616-3793

LEDESMA, JOSE FORTUNATO GAMBOA, health facility executive; b. Iloilo City, The Philippines, Feb. 21, 1947; s. Ramon and Oliva Jurilla (Gamboa) L.; m. Rhodora Roca Regalado, Aug. 2, 1969 (div.); children: Jean Elaine Tricia, Birthday Ann Betsy, Rowena Emma Alicia; m. Evelyn Prudente; children: Michelle Rose, Denise Claudine. BSChemE, U. San Agustin, Iloilo City, 1967; cert. in hosp. adminstrn., Ateneo de Manila U., 1981; MBA, U. of City of Manila, 1983. Med. rep. Beecham Rsch. Labs., Iloilo, 1968-70; territory mgr. Bristol Labs. Philippines, Inc., Iloilo, 1970-76; CEO Iloilo Mission Hosp., 1977-80; mktg. mgr. Tesco Mfg. Corp., Mandaluyong, The Philippines, 1980-81; mgr. St. Luke's Med. Ctr., Quezon City, The Philippines, 1981-86; exec. dir. St. Luke's Med. Ctr., Quezon City, 1986-96, pres./CEO, 1996—; bd. dirs. Philippine Lithotripter, Inc., Manila, Empress Fin. Corp., Manila, Med. Arts Bldg. Corp., Quezon City; bd. dirs., treas. St. Luke's Coll. Medicine, Quezon City, 1994—; cons. on healthcare Office of V.P., Republic of The Philippines. Pres. Loyola Heights Pugad Lawin, Quezon City, 1993, Makati Ctrl. Heart Found., Makati City, The Philippines, 1993—; bd. dirs. Mabuhay Deseret Found., Manila, 1989—; v.p. Lualhati Found. Named Knight Comdr. of Ct. of Honor, Supreme Coun. Scottish Rite Freemasons, The Philippines, 1994. Mem. Am. Coll. Healthcare Execs., Mgmt. Assn. of The Philippines, Fin. Execs. Inst. of The Philippines, Philippine Coll. Hosp. Adminstrs., Makati Bus. Club, Rotary (bd. dirs. Makati Ctrl. chpt. 1993-96, pres. 1998-99), Masons (33d degree, Hon. Inspector Gen. 1999). Avocations: collecting Lladro and crystal figurines, collecting paintings, table tennis, tennis, vintage wines. Home: 102 Maharlika Main St, Taytay Rizal, The Philippines Office: St Luke's Med Ctr, 279 E Rodriguez Sr Blvd, Quezon City The Philippines

LEDGER, SIR PHILIP STEVENS, conductor, musician, educator; b. Bexhill-on-Sea, Sussex, Eng., Dec. 12, 1937; s. Walter Stephen and Winifred Kathleen (Stevens) L.; m. Mary Erryl Wells, Apr. 15, 1963; children: Timothy, Katharine. MA, MusB, Cambridge U., 1961; LLD, U. Strathclyde, 1987. Master of music Chelmsford Cathedral, 1962-65; dir. music U. East Anglia, 1965-73, dean Sch. Fine Arts and Music, 1968-71; condr. Cambridge U. Mus. Soc., 1973-82; dir. music, organist King's Coll., Cambridge U., 1974-82; prin. Royal Scottish Acad. Music and Drama, Glasgow, 1982—; v.p. Aldeburgh Festival; v.p. Cambridge Festival Assn.; chmn. exams. bd. Assoc. Bd. Royal Schs. Music. Editor: Anthems for Choirs 2 & 3, 1973, The Oxford Book of English Madrigals, 1978; composer, editor: The Six Carols with Descants, 1975. Created Knight Bachelor, 1999; decorated comdr. Order Brit. Empire, 1985; recipient Silver medal Worshipful Co. Musicians; John Stewart of Rannoch scholar. Fellow Royal Coll. Music, Royal Coll. Organists (pres. 1992-94, Limpus and Read prizes), Inc. Soc. Musicians (pres. 1994-95), Royal No. Coll. Music, Com. Prin. of Conservatoires (chmn. 1994-98), Brit. Fedn. Young Choirs (chmn. adv. coun.), Royal Soc. Edinburgh; mem. Royal Acad. Music (hon.), Guildhall Sch. Music (hon.), Sette of Odd Volumes Club. Office: Royal Scottish Acad, 100 Renfrew St, Glasgow G2 3DB, Scotland

LEDIN, MARIA EVA, microbiologist, researcher; b. Linköping, Sweden, Apr. 13, 1964; d. Axel Helge and Birgit Viktoria (Quick) W.; m. Tomas Carl Gunnar Ledin, May 9, 1991; children: Johanna, Sofia. BSc, Linköping U., 1988, PhD, 1994. With dept. gen. and marine microbiology Göteborg (Sweden) U., 1994-95; rsch. asst. dept. water and environ. studies Linköping U., 1997-99. Contbr. numerous articles to profl. jours. Home: Blaklintsgatan 13, SE-58246 Linköping Sweden

LEDNICKY, RICHARD, physicist, researcher; b. Vítkovice, Czech Republic, Oct. 14, 1945; s. Jan and Vlastimila (Kolková) L.; m. Tatána Sokolovová, Aug. 18, 1972; children: Denis, Xenie. Student, Czech Tech. U., Prague, 1963-67, Filial of Moscow State U., Dubna, Russia, 1967-68; diplomate physicist, Charles U., Prague, 1969; CSc, Joint Inst for Nuclear Rsch., Dubna, 1973, DrSc, 1990. Rsch. scientist Joint Inst. for Nuclear Rsch., Dubna, 1969-92, Inst. Physics of the Acad. Scis. of the Czech Republic, Prague, 1975—. Contbr. articles to profl. jours. Avocations: football, volleyball, ice-hockey, skiing, table tennis. Home: Počernická 517, 10800 Prague 10 Czech Republic Office: Inst Physics Acad Scis, Na Slovance 2, 18040 Prague Czech Republic

LE DUFF, YVES, science educator, laboratory administrator; b. Loguivy-Plougras, Brittany, France, Aug. 12, 1939; s. François and Marie (Morvan) Le D.; m. Liliane Duval, July 7, 1962; children: Veronique, Marc, Hélène. Grad., U. Paris, 1969, Doctorat es Sciences, 1974. Assoc. prof. U. Paris, 1962-86; prof. U. Angers, France, 1986—, head physics and chemistry dept., 1993-95; dir. Lab. Proprietes Optiques des Materiaux et Applications U. Angers, Nat. Ctr. Sci. Rsch., 1996—. Contbr. articles to profl. jours. Named Chevalier dans L'ordre des Palmes Academiques, 1996. Office: Laboratoire POMA, 2 Boulevard Lavoisier, 49045 Angers France

LEE, ANDREAS, obstetrician, researcher; b. Eggenburg, Austria, Apr. 4, 1963; s. Michael and Edeltraud (Dollesch) L. MD, U. Vienna, 1988, PhD, 1999. Intern Hosp. Eggenburg, Austria, 1988-91; resident dept. prenatal diagnosis U. Vienna, 1992—. E-mail: andreas.lee@atunivie.ac.at. Office: Univ Vienna, Wahringer Gurtel 18-20, A-1090 Vienna Austria

LEE, ANDREW SIU WOO, investment company executive; b. Guangzhou, Guangdong, China, Sept. 12, 1955; s. Ying Yuen and Lai Mui (Chan) L. Diploma in bus. adminstrn., Inst. Bus. Adminstrn., Australia, 1978; diploma in mktg., Inst. Mktg., Eng., 1976. Mgr. credit and mktg. Citibank N.A., Hong Kong, 1981-84; fin. cons. Merrill Lynch (Asia Pacific Ltd.), 1984-88; head of fund mgmt., div. and first investment mgr. Hong Kong Spl. Adminstrv. Region Govt. Land Fund, 1988-92; exec. dir. Capital Asia Ltd., Hong Kong, 1992-93; dep. mng. dir., chief investment mgr. Grand Resources Holdings Ltd., Hong Kong, 1993-94; mng. dir. World Capital Investments Ltd., Hong Kong, 1994-97; CEO China Capital Corp., Applied Biotech. Devel. Co. Ltd., 1998—; exec. dir. Rosin Resources Investment Ltd., 1998—. Mem. Inst. Adminstrv. Mgmt., Chartered Inst. Mktg., Chartered Inst. Secs. and Adminstrs. (assoc.). Address: 2/F Chawan Indsl Centre, 20 Lee St, Chaiwan Hong Kong

LEE, ANG, filmmaker; b. Taiwan, Oct. 23, 1954; m. Jane Lin; 2 children. BFA in Theater, U. Ill., 1980; MFA in Film, NYU, 1984. Dir. films Fine Line, 1985, Sense and Sensibility, 1996 (N.Y. Film Critics Circle award, Boston Film Critics award, Nat. Bd. Rev. award, Golden Bear award, Berlin Film Festival award, nominee Brit. Acad. Film and TV Arts award, nominee Dirs. Guild award, nominee Golden Globe award, all as best dir.); screenwriter (with Hui Ling Wang and James Schamus), Eat Drink Man Woman, 1994 (Best Fgn. Lang. Film award Nat. Bd. Rev., nominee Acad. award for Best Fgn. Lang. Film, nominee Golden Globe award for Best Fgn. Lang. Film, honored for Best Film and as Best Dir. Asian Pacific Film Festival, various Ind. Spirit award nominations), Ride With the Devil, 1999; dir., prodr. films Pushing Hands, 1991 (several Golden Horse award nominations, Taiwan, Spl. Jury prize for Direction, Best Film honors Asian Pacific Film Festival 1992), The Wedding Banquet, 1993 (Asian Am. Media award 16th Asian Am. internat. Film Festival, Golden Bear award Berlin Film Festival, nominee Acad. award for Best Fgn. Lang. Film, nominee Golden Globe award for Best Fgn. Lang. Film, several Ind. Spirit award nominations, Golden Horse awards for Best Film and Best Dir.), The Ice Storm, 1997; The Wedding Banquet and Eat Drink Man Woman included in book: Two Films by Ang Lee, 1994. Address: CAA 9830 Wilshire Blvd Beverly Hills CA 90212-1804

LEE, ANITA YUEN, solicitor; b. Hong Kong, Sept. 6, 1955; d. Chung Ping and Mee Lun (Tse) Lee; children: Charmaine, Sarah, Sharon, Edward. LLB, U. Hong Kong, 1978, postgrad. cert. in law, 1980; diploma in Chinese law, U. East Asia, Macau, 1987. Solicitor, Hong Kong, 1982, Eng. and Wales, 1985, Vic., Australia, 1986, Singapore, 1990. Articled clk. Johnson Stokes & Master, Hong Kong, 1980-82, asst. solicitor, 1982-88, ptnr., 1988—. Mem. exec. com. Hong Kong Family Welfare Soc., 1985-89, mem. foster care adv. com., 1985—; hon. legal advisor N.W. U. Tech. Edn. and Devel. Fund, Shenyang, China, 1991—, Sincere Charitable Found., Hong Kong, 1994. Mem. Hong Kong Fedn. Women Layers (exec. com., hon. treas. 1988-94, hon. membership chmn. 1994-95), Soc. Trust and Estate Practitioners, Hong Kong Jockey Club, Hong Kong Cricket Club, Zonta Club Victoria (bd. dirs.). Avocations: keeping tropical fish, tennis, singing. Office: Johnson Stokes & Master, 10 Chater Rd 17th Fl Princess Bldg, Hong Kong Hong Kong

LEE, ANNE W.M., clinical oncologist; b. Hong Kong, Feb. 21, 1952; d. Fung and Ngo (Chan) L. MBBS, U. Hong Kong, 1976. From med. officer to sr. med. and health officer Inst. Radiology & Oncology Queen Elizabeth Hosp., Hong Kong, 1977-91; cons., chief of svc. clin. oncology dept. Pamela Youde Nethersole Eastern Hosp., Hong Kong, 1993-97; examiner Hong Kong Poly. U., 1992—, Hong Kong Coll. Radiologists, 1995—. Author: Complications of Radiation Therapy in Nasopharyngeal Carcinoma, 1991; contbr. articles to profl. jours. Fellow Royal Coll. Radiologists, Hong Kong Acad. Medicine, Hong Kong Head & Neck Soc. Roman Catholic. Office: Pamela Youde Nethersole Eastern Hosp, 3 Lok Man Rd, Chai Wan Hong Kong China

LEE, ARTHUR VIRGIL, III, biotechnology company executive; b. Detroit, Nov. 24, 1920; s. Arthur Virgil and Emily S. (Burry) L.; m. Elizabeth Hoppin Chafee, Dec. 8, 1945 (div.); children: Arthur C., Sherrill Ann Rosoff, William J., Henry C.; m. Jean Austin LaMothe, Dec. 30, 1967. BA, Williams Coll., 1942; Indsl. Adminstr. (World War II MBA), Harvard Bus. Sch., 1943. With McKesson & Robbins, Inc., Memphis, 1946-47; ops. mgr. Providence div. McKesson & Robbins, Inc., 1947-63, v.p., mgr. Providence div., 1954-59, with Boston div., 1959-63, with Pitts. div., 1963; asst. dean Harvard U. Bus. Sch., Cambridge, Mass., 1964-65, dir. corp. rels., 1965-72, dir. resources, 1972-73; v.p. Lesley Coll., Cambridge, 1973-77; dir. corp. rels. Tufts U., Medford, Mass., 1977-79; pres. Biotec Internat., Ltd., Williamstown, Mass., 1979-95. Bd. dirs. New Eng. Drug Exchange, 1956-63; trustee Am. Coll. Switzerland, 1978-82, Williamstown Theatre Festival, 1984-94, trustee emeritus, 1994—; mem. Weston Town Fin. Com., 1961-66; mem. adv. bd. Coll. Pharmacy, U. R.I., 1957-58. Lt. USNR, 1942-46. Mem. Taconic Golf Club, Yeamans Hall Club (Charleston, S.C.), Alpha Delta Phi. Congregationalist. Home and Office: PO Box 488 Williamstown MA 01267-0488

LEE, B. KYUN, mechanical engineer, educator; b. Taegu, Kyung-Boog, Republic of Korea, Sept. 20, 1952; came to U.S., 1982; s. Jung-Ha and Il-Jin (Kim) L.; m. Misook Park, Oct. 3, 1980; children: Eun-Gi, Nathan. BSME, Young-Nam U., Taegu, 1980; MSME, Oreg. State U., 1984; MA, N.W.

Christian Coll., 1988; PhD, Oreg. State U., 1988; MDiv, New Orleans Bapt. Theol. Sem., 1994. Registered profl. engr., Tex. R&D engr. Hyun-Dai Motor Co., Ulsan, Republic of Korea, 1980-82; engr. Evanite Fiber Co., Corvallis, Oreg., 1987-88; assoc. prof. LeTourneau U., Longview, Tex., 1988—; pastor Sae-Nu-Ree Ch., Dae Jeon City, Republic of Korea, 1996-99; prin. investigator Colt Friction Products, Longview, 1989-90; co-investigator GRACO Children's Products, 1990-91; cons. Stemco Co., Longview, 1990-91; prin. investigator Capacity of Tex., Longview, 1991-94; researcher LeTourneau U., Longview, 1988-96. Author sci. papers. Mem. ASME, Am. Soc. Engring. Edn., Soc. Mfg. Engr., Phi Kappa Phi. Baptist. Avocations: tennis, soccer. Home: Jeon-Ming Dong Expo Apt 302-1302, Dae Jeon City 305-390, Republic of Korea Office: LeTourneau U PO Box 7001 Longview TX 75607-7001

LEE, BAEK RAK, microbiologist, educator; b. Seoul, Korea, Mar. 3, 1962; s. Seok Hee Lee and Jeongok Lin; m. Sun Ae Kim, Jan. 24, 1987; children: Sang Heon, Sang Ji. BS, Seoul (Korea) Nat. U., 1985; MS, Korea Advanced Inst. Sci./Tech, Seoul, 1988, PhD, 1991. Rsch. assoc. U. Wis. Med. Sch., Madison, 1991-93; asst. prof. Inje U., Kimhae, Korea, 1993-98, assoc. prof., 1998—, dir. Inst. Genetic Engring., 1996-98, chmn. dept. microbiology, 1998—; dir. Inst. Molecular Biology Paik Hosp./Inje U., 1998—; vis. assoc. scientist U. Wis., 2000—. Contbr. articles to profl. jours. With Korean Army, 1986. Recipient achievement award Korean Soc. Hypertension, 1995. Mem. Am. Soc. Microbiology, Korean Soc. Molecular Biology, Korean Soc. Applied Microbiology. Avocations: reading, travel. Office: Inje U Dept Microbiology, 607 Obang-dong, Kimhae Kyung Nam 621-749, Korea

LEE, BETTY REDDING, architect; d. Joseph Alsop and Mary (Byrd) Redding; m. Frank Cayce Lee, Nov. 22, 1940 (dec. Aug. 1978); children: Cayce Redding, Clifton Monroe, Mary Byrd (Mrs. Kent Ray). Student La. State U., 1936-37, 37-38, U. Calif. War Extension Coll., San Diego, 1942-43; sudent Centernary Coll., 1937; attended Roofing Industry Ednl. Inst., 1980-82, 84, 86-88, 89-90, 93, Better Understanding Roofing Sys. Inst., 1989. Sheetmetal worker Consol. Vultee, San Diego, 1942; engring. draftsman, 1943-45; jr. to sr. archtl. draftsman Bodman & Murrell, Baton Rouge, 1954-55; sr. archtl. draftsman to architect Post & Harelson, Baton Rouge, 1955-58; assoc. arch. G. Ross Murrell, Jr., Baton Rouge, 1960-66; staff arch. Charles E. Schwing & Assocs., Baton Rouge, 1966-71, Kenneth C. Landry, Baton Rouge, 1971, 73-74; engring., design draftsman Rayner & McKenzie, Baton Rouge, 1972-73; cons. arch. and planner Office Engring. and Cons. Svcs., La. Dept. Health and Human Resources, Baton Rouge, 1974-82; sr. arch. roofing and waterproofing sect. La. Dept. Facility Planning and Control, 1982-96; pvt. consulting practice, Baton Rouge, 1996—; Betty Redding Lee, Architect, 1996; Author Instructions to Designers for Roofing Systems for Louisiana Public Buildings: co-author: Building Owners Guide for Protecting and Maintaining Built-up Roofing Systems, 1981; designed typical La. country store for La. Arts and Sci. Ctr. Mus. Recipient Honor award Schuller/Johns Manville BURSI Group, 1989, 90, 91, 92, 93. Mem. La. Assn. Children with Learning Disabilities, 1967-69, Multiple Sclerosis Soc., 1963—, CPA Aux., 1960-69, PTA, 1953-66; troop leader Brownies and Girl Scouts U.S.A., 1959-60; asst. den mother Cub Scouts, 1955-57. Licensed architect. Mem. ASTM, Nat. AIA, AIA La., AIA Baton Rouge (first Shreveport & Baton Rouge, La. woman architect), DAR, Roofing Industry Ednl. Inst. Alumni Assn. (charter mem.), Constrn. Specifications Inst.(charter mem. Baton Rouge chpt.), Roof Cons. Inst. (profl. mem.), Roof Cons. Inst. (profl. mem.), Jr. League Baton Rouge, Kappa Delta. Republican. Episcopalian. E-mail: brlee@worldnet.att.net. Home and Office: 881 Kenmore Ave Baton Rouge LA 70806-5521

LEE, BLAINE NELSON, executive consultant, educator, author; b. Olympia, Wash., Apr. 3, 1946; s. Elwyn Earl and Thelma Marie (Woods) Reeder; m. Shawny Christian Lee; children: Blaine, Benjamin, Adam, Michal, Joseph, Joshua, Casey, Abraham, Eliza, Gabriel, Celeste, Isaac. BS in Psychology, Brigham Young U., Provo, Utah, 1969, MS in Ednl. Psychology, 1972; PhD in Ednl. Psychology, U. Tex., 1982. Cert. ednl. specialist, secondary edn., ednl. adminstrn. Dir. instrnl. sys. USAF, San Antonio, 1972-75; assoc. prof. USAF Acad., Colorado Springs, Colo., 1975-78; edn. dir. Heritage Sch., Provo, Utah, 1978-81; asst. prof. Utah Valley State Coll., Orem, Utah, 1981-84; pres. Skills for Living, Salem, Utah, 1984-86; v.p. Covey Leadership Ctr., Provo, Utah, 1986-97, Franklin Covey Co., Provo, 1997—; cons. in field. Author: Affective Objectives, 1972, Personal Change, 1982, Stress Strategist, 1986, Principle Centered Leadership, 1990, Power Principle: Influence with Honor, 1997; contbr. articles to profl. jours. High councilman LDS Ch., mem. gen. bd., 1970-72; pres. Provo PTO. Named one of Outstanding Young Men of Am., U.S. C. of C., 1976, 84. Mem. APA, ASTD, Am. Mgmt. Assn., Nat. Spkrs. Assn., Phi Delta Kappa. Avocations: cmty. theatre, choir dir., camping, poetry, soccer coach. Home: PO Box 367 Orem UT 84059-0367 Office: Franklin Covey Co 360 W 4800 N Provo UT 84604-5675

LEE, BONG JIN, mechanical engineer; b. Cheju, Korea, Jan. 13, 1933; Soonkyung Lee and Soonyie Koh; m. Eui Soon Koh, Nov. 8, 1964; children: Yoonchul, Yoonji, Yoonhae. BS, U. Tokyo, 1963; DSc, Inha U., 1974. Head automatic control lab. Korea Inst. Sci. & Technology, Seoul, 1968-74; internat rsch. fellow SRI, Menlo Park, Calif., 1974-75; dir. Precision Machinery Technology Ctr., Seoul, 1975-83; prof. Kangwon Nat. U., Chunchon, Korea, 1983-85; rsch. engr., gen. mgr. prodn. tech. lab. Fanuc Ltd., Oshino, Japan, 1985-90; tech. advisor Fanuc Ltd., 1990—; chief exec. Lee Engring., Korea, 1994—; vis. prof. Seoul Nat. U., 1990-95. Author: System Engineering of Factory Automation, 1990, Management of Japanese High-Tech. Manufacturing Industries, 1992, Management Tailored to Korean Manufacturing Industries, 1994, Re-engineering for Korean Manufacturing Industries, 1995. Mem. Korean Soc. Precision Engring., Soc. Machine Tool Engrs., Korean Engrs. Club, Japan Soc. of Mech. Engrs., Japan Soc. of Precision Engring. Home: 247-2 Nonhyun-Dong, Kangnam ku 135-010 Seoul Republic of Korea

LEE, CHAN-YUN, physicist, process engineer, educator; b. Hwa-Liang, Taiwan, July 19, 1952; came to U.S., 1988; s. Hsiao-Feng and Shu-Yun (Huang) L.; m. Chia-Li Yang, Jan. 13, 1983; children: Yifan E., Ethel Y., Elias Y. BS in Physics, Soochow U., Taipei, Taiwan, 1974; MS, U. So. Calif., 1980; PhD, U. Notre Dame, 1988. Cert. assoc. prof., lectr. Dept. Edn. Asst. prof. physics Tatung Inst. Tech., Taipei, 1982-86, assoc. prof., 1986-88, chmn. physics sect., 1986-88; cons. Tatung Semiconductor Divsn., Taipei, 1985-88; dir. Tatung Natural Sci. Mus., Taipei, 1986-88; lab. instr. U. Notre Dame, Notre Dame, Ind., 1988-94; process engr. Lam Rsch. Co., Fremont, Calif., 1994-96, sr. process engr., 1996-99, mgr. metal etch key accounts, 1998-99; assoc. prof. physics San Jose City Coll., Calif., 1998-99; reginal chief process technologist Silicon Valley Group, 2000—; rsch. asst. U. So. Calif., L.A., 1977-79. Contbr. numerous articles to profl. jours. 2d lt. Chinese Artillery, 1974-76. Recipient Excellent Rschrs. prize Chinese Nat. Sci. Coun., Taipei, 1986, 87, 88, Outstanding Acad. Pub. prize Hsieh-Tze Indsl. Revival Com., Taipei, 1987, 88, 27th Ann. Sci. & Tech. Pers. Rsch. & Study award Chinese Nat. Sci. Coun., 1989. Mem. Chinese Physics Assn. Achievements include development of model of relativistic corrections to semiconducting properties of selected materials, simulated and calculated the dynamical sysceptibility of square lattice antiferromagnets; successfully developed the first large size SAC process in the world on high density plasma TCP etcher with satisfactory yields; designed and constructed a spectrophotometer to measure the absolute photoabsorption cross section of atomic potassium in VUV region. Avocations: moutain hiking, swimming, computer program design, fishing. Home: 471 Via Vera Cruz Fremont CA 94539-5325 Office: Silicon Valley Group Inc 541 E Trimble Rd San Jose CA 95131-1284

LEE, CHARLES ROBERT, telecommunications company executive; b. 1940; married; 5 children. BS in Metall. Engring., Cornell U., 1962; MBA, Harvard U., 1964. Mgr. bus. research U.S. Steel Co., 1964-71; sr. v.p. fin. Penn Ctrl. Corp., 1971-80, Columbia Pictures Industries, 1980-83, GTE Corp., Stamford, CT, 1983-86; sr. v.p. fin. & planning GTE Corp., 1986-89; pres., chief oper. officer GTE Corp., Stamford, CT, 1988-92, COO, chmn., chief exec. officer, 1992—, also bd. dirs.; chmn., co-CEO Verizon Comms., New York, 2000—; bd. dirs. United Techs. Corp., Proctor & Gamble Co., USX Corp.; chair Pres.'s Nat. Security Telecoms. Adv. Com. Trustee Cornell U.; bd. dirs. Stamford Hosp. Found., New Am. Schs. Devel. Corp.; bd. dirs. of the assocs. Harvard Bus. Sch.; adv. com. pres.' commn. Critical Infrastructure Protection. Mem. Fin. Execs. Inst., Nat. Planning Assn. (com. on new Am. realities, trustee), Bus. Roundtable, Stanwich Club, Blind Brook Club, Thunderbird Country Club, Laurel Valley Golf Club. Office: GTE Service Corp 40 Sylvan Rd Waltham MA 02451-1120

LEE, CHIEN-HSIUNG, research scientist, educator; b. Hong Kong, Dec. 1, 1949; s. Ting-Chaing and Ping (Chang) L.; m. Mung-Hsien Wang, Aug. 3, 1974; children: Der-Show, Der-Ye. BS, Chung-Cheng Inst. Tech., Tai-Chi, Taiwan, 1972, MS, 1976; PhD, Purdue U., 1987. Asst. scientist Inst. Nuclear Energy Rsch., Lung Tan, Taiwan, 1976-83, assoc. scientist, 1987—; assoc. prof. Chaio Tung U., Hsinch, Taiwan, 1989—. Editor Nuclear Sci. Jour. Recipient scholarship Nat. Sci. Coun., Taiwan, 1990, 2000, Outstanding Paper award Exec. Yuan, Taiwan, 1994, 97, Outstanding Paper award Chung Hua Nuclear Soc., 1997, 2000. Mem. Chung Hua Nuclear Soc., Sigma Pi Sigma. Avocations: travel, reading. E-mail: chlee@iner.aec.gov.tw. Home: 2-4 Alley 12, Lane 75, Chien-Kuo Rd, Lungtan 32500, Taiwan Office: Inst Nuclear Energy Rsch, PO Box 3-3, Lungtan 32500, Taiwan

LEE, CHIH HSIUNG, communications company executive; b. Tao-Yuan, Taiwan, July 11, 1959; s. Ching Chin and Bih Yuh (Chen) L.; m. Shu Chen Kuo, Nov. 10, 1990; 2 children. BS, Chung-Yuan U., Chung-Li, Taiwan, 1983. Engr. Print Circuit Bd. Yield, Tao-Yuan, 1985-87, Electronics Rsch. and Svc. Orgn., Hsin-Chu, Taiwan, 1987-89; sect. mgr. Taiwan Semicondr. Mfg. Co., Ltd., Hsin-Chu, 1989-98, tech. mgr., 1998—. Contbr. articles to profl. jours.; patentee in field. Served with Taiwanese Navy, 1983-85. Mem. Tai Chi Chuan Assn., Electronic Devices and Material Assn. Avocations: swimming, archery, basketball, volleyball. Office: TSMC, 9 Creation Rd I, Science-Based Indsl Park, 300 Hsin-Chu Taiwan

LEE, CHIH SHENG, engineering educator, researcher; b. Tainan, Taiwan, Feb. 23, 1968; s. Chong Chang Lee and Sue A Ching; m. Shieu Chen Yang, Dec. 15, 1995; children; Yang, Yung. PhD, Nat. Cheng Kung U., 1996. Diplomate environtl. engring. Rsch. asst. Nat. Cheng Kung U., Tainan, 1992-96, rsch. assoc., 1998-99; asst. prof. Kung Shan Inst. of Tech., Tainan, 1999—; Referee dept. environ. protection Govt. of Taiwan, Province, Hantou County, 1998, Govt. of Ping-tong County, 1999, Govt. of Chia-I County, 1998; referee dept. constrn. Govt. of Kaohsiung County, 1999. Referee Jour. of Environtl. Mgmt., 1997-99; contbr. articles to profl. publs. Capt. Dept. of Ocean and Beach Def., 1996-98. Mem. AGU, AWWA, IZZS. Avocation: tennis. Office: Kung Shan Inst of Tech, #949 Da Wan Rd, Yun Kan City Taiwan

LEE, CHI-WEN JEVONS, accounting educator, administrator, columnist; b. Wen-Sen, Yunan, Republic of China, Sept. 28, 1944; came to U.S., 1970; s. Kai-Chang and Fei-Zen (Chen) L.; m. Chin-Shya Lee, July 1971 (div. 1988); children: Spencer, Scott; m. Ching-Chi Chiang, Oct. 1, 1988; children: Stephenie, Stacy. BA, Nat. Taiwan U., 1966; MA, U. Rochester, 1973, PhD, 1977. CPA, N.Y., Ill., Pa., La., cert. mgmt. acct. Asst. prof. Grad. Sch. Bus. U. Chgo., 1980-83; assoc. prof. Wharton Sch. U. Pa., Phila., 1983-88; Freeman prof., assoc. dean Freeman Sch. Bus. Tulane U., New Orleans, 1988—; cons. U.S. Dept. Energy, 1980, ROC Cen. Bank, Taiwan, 1986, PROC Ministry of Constrn., China, 1987. Author of 4 books; contbr. numerous articles to profl. jours. Mem. Am. Acctg. Assn. (com. chair 1984—). Avocations: fishing, travel. Office: Freeman Sch Bus Tulane Univ New Orleans LA 70118-5669

LEE, CHOK-KAU B., physicist, engineer; b. Canton, China, Aug. 6, 1948; came to U.S., 1969; s. Ching Lam and Choi-Ha (Lam) L.; m. Viola Leng Chan, Aug. 30, 1976; 1 child, Sean Yu-Chiu. BS in Elec. Engring., San Francisco State U., 1972; MS in Nuclear Engring., U. Calif., Berkeley, 1973; PhD in Nuclear Engring., UCLA, 1979. Registered profl. engr., Calif. Draftsman ThermXchanger Inc., Oakland, Calif., 1970-73; engr. Nuclear Svcs. Corp., San Jose, Calif., 1973-76; scientist R&D Assocs., Marina del Rey, Calif., 1979-88; sr. scientist Logicon RDA, L.A., 1988—; cons. ThermXchanger, Oakland, 1973-76, Nuclear Svcs. Corp., San Jose, 1976-82. Contbr. articles to Physics of Fluids, Jour. Computational Physics, Shock Waves, Jour. Geophys. Rsch., others. Mem. AAAS, ASME, Am. Phys. Soc., Am. Geophys. Union, Soc. for Indsl. and Applied Math. Avocations: chess, table tennis. E-mail: blee@logicon.com. Home: 222 S Le Doux Rd Beverly Hills CA 90211-3003 Office: Logicon RDA PO Box 471 San Pedro CA 90733-0471

LEE, CHOO HIE, electronic engineering educator; b. Seoul, Nov. 21, 1934; s. In Soo Lee and Kum Soon Jun; m. Young Ia Lim, June 1, 1968; children: Seokhyunn, Sung-Hyun. BS, Seoul Nat. U., 1956; Dr.Eng., Keio U., Tokyo, 1980. Rschr. Inst. of Nat. Def., Seoul, 1956-60; engr. Korea Electirc Power Co., Seoul, 1960-76; rschr. faculty of engring. Keio U., Yohohama, Japan, 1977-80; prof. Kyung Hee U., Suwon, Korea, 1981—; dir. Bus. Affairs of Kyung Hee U., Suwon, 1984-87, Inst. for Laser Engring., 1989—, dean rsch. affairs, 1992-95, dean Engring. Coll., 1995-96. With Navy Inst. of Nat. Def., 1956-59. Fellow Optical Soc. Am.; mem. Optical Soc. of Korea (pres. 1996), Internat. Soc. for Optical Engring. (pres. Korea chpt. 1994-97), IEEE/Lasers and Electro-Optics Soc. Avocations: Orchid growing, listening classical music, field hockey, golf, football. Home: #197-19 Jooan-Dong Nam-ku, Inchon 402-201, Korea Office: Kyung Hee U Elec Engring, #1 Seochon-Ri Kiheung Up, Yongin Si 449-701, Korea

LEE, CHO-SIK, philosophy educator; b. PyongYang, Republic of Korea, Feb. 1, 1935; s. Gye-In and Soon-Duk (Kwak) L.; m. Ok-Young Kim; children: Ji-Aeh, Ji-Ho, Ji-Un, Ji-Yong. BA, Seoul (Korea) Nat. U., 1958, MA, 1962; PhD, Salzburg (Austria) U., 1974. Prof. Seoul (Korea) Nat. Edn. U., 1965-77, Konkuk U., Seoul, 1977-81, Korea U., Seoul, 1981—. Author: Philosophy of Artificial Intelligence, 1993 (Yolam prize 1993). 1st lt. Republic of Korea Air Force, 1958-62. Mem. Korean Philos. Assn. (pres.-elect 1999-2000), Congress Korean Philosophers (organizing com. 1999), Korean Acad. Tchg. Philosophy (pres. 1995—), Korean Assn. Tchg. Philosophy (pres. 1986-92), Korean Soc. for Cognitive Sci. (pres. 1992-94), Soc. Philos. Studies (pres. 1992-94), The Korean Assn. for Logic (pres. 1982-83). Avocation: tennis. Fax: 82-2-364-7855. E-mail: leecs@kuccnx.korea.ac.kr. Home: 93-1 Daesin-dong, Seoul 120-160, Republic of Korea

LEE, CHUNG KUNG, chemical and environmental engineer, educator; b. Changhua, Taiwan, Apr. 11, 1960; s. Shang Chia and Yu Yun (Hsieh) L.; m. Shu Fen Huang, May 9, 1993; children: Nieh Ting, Cheng Che. BS, Nat. Taipei Inst. Tech., 1981; MS, Nat. Ctrl. U., 1988, PhD, 1992. Data processor Taiwan Cement Co. Ltd., Taipei, 1984-86; postdoc. rschr. Nat. Chung Cheng. U., Chiayi, Taiwan, 1992-94; assoc. prof. environ. engring. Van Nung Inst. Tech., Chungli, Taiwan, 1994-98, prof., 1999—. Contbr. articles to profl. jours. With Chinese Army, 1981-83. Mem. Chinese Inst. Chem. Engring., Chinese Inst. Environ. Engring., Phi Tau Phi. Avocations: exercise, music, fishing, reading, cooking. Home: 3d Fl 10 Sublane 16 Ln 373, Teho Rd, Yungho Taipei 234, Taiwan Office: Van-Nung Inst Tech Dept Environ Engring, 63-1 Shuiwei Li, Chungli 320, Taiwan

LEE, CHUNGMIN, educator, linguist; b. Seoul, Korea, Sept. 22, 1939; came to U.S., 1986; m. Hyekyung Park Lee, Dec. 26, 1980; children: Suh-Kyung, Choon-Kyu. BA, Seoul Nat. U., 1963, MA, 1968; PhD, Ind. U., 1973. Asst. prof. to assoc. prof. Seoul Nat. U., 1974-84, prof., 1984—; vis. prof. UCLA, 1986-88, 98—, Linguistic Soc. Am. Linguistic Inst., U. Calif., Santa Cruz, 1991; assoc. dir. rsch., editor lang. rsch. Lang. Rsch. Inst. of Seoul Nat. U., 1976-86; lectr. Cornell U., Ithaca, N.Y., 1988, U. Pa., 2000; dir. Inst. Cognitive Sci., Seoul Nat. U. Author: Abstract Syntax and Korean, 1973, Linguistic Theory & Contemporary Scientific Thoughts, 1986, Dictionary of Linguistics, 1982; contbr. articles to profl. internat. jours. Asan Found. grantee 1984, Fulbright fellow, 1967, NSF fellow, 1971, Ind. U. Cross-Cultural Ford fellow, 1972. Mem. Linguistic Soc. Am., Linguistic Soc. Korea (editorial bd. 1975-78, rep. formal theory grp. current Koean Soc. Lang. and Info. 1988-92), Korean Soc. Analytical Philosophy (steering com. 1979-84), Internat. Pragmatics Assn. (consultation bd. 1986-97, editor Pragmatics 1997—), Korean Soc. Authors (sec. gen. 1984-99, v.p. 2000—), Korean Soc. Cognitive Sci. (editorial bd. 1989, v.p. 1990-94, pres. 1994-96, editl. bd. linguistics and philiosophy 1997—, Jour. East Asian Linguistics 1999—, area editor 1992-98). Office: Seoul Nat U Dept Linguistics, San-51 Sillim-dong, Seoul 151-742, Republic of Korea

LEE, DAI GIL, engineering educator; b. Nonsan, Korea, Jan. 19, 1952; s. Soo Nam and Seon Keum (Kim) L.; m. Og Heui Jeong, Feb. 25, 1978; children: Dong Gyu, Ji Yun. BS, Seoul Nat. U., 1975; MS, KAIST, 1977; PhD, MIT, 1985. Asst. prof. Busan (Korea) Nat. U., 1978-81; prof. KAIST, Taejon, Korea, 1986—; mem. bd. city constrn. City of Taejon, 1997—. Mem. editl. bd. Jour. Composite Structures; contbr. articles to profl. jours. Mem. Korea Soc. Composite Materials, Korea Soc. Mech. Engrs., Korea Soc. Automotive Engrs. Avocation: swimming. Office: Korea Adv Inst Sci and Tech, Gusong-dong Yusong-gu, Taejon 305-701, Republic of Korea

LEE, DANIEL ANDREW, osteopathic physician, ophthalmologist; b. Bklyn., Aug. 20, 1951; s. Jack W. and Lily (Ho) L.; m. Janet Lynne Eng, June 14, 1975 (div. Sept. 1985); children: Jason Matthew, Brian Christopher, Joshua Daniel; m. Kelly Lynne Crego, Sept. 5, 1987; children: Joshua Daniel, Alexandra Nicole Avetkova, Brandon Scott. BS in Psychobiology, SUNY, Stony Brook, 1973; BS in Biology, Westminster Coll., 1973; OD, Pa. Coll. Optometry, 1977; DO, Ohio U., 1984. Cert. in low vision proficiency, ophthalmology; cert. Osteopathic Acad. Opthalmology and Otolaryngology. Instr. Mohawk Valley C.C., Rome, N.Y., 1978-80; pvt. practice optometry Utica, N.Y., 1978-80, Chauncey, Ohio, 1981-84, Dayton, Ohio, 1984—; intern Grandview Hosp., Dayton, 1984, mem. staff, 1984-85, opthalmology resident, 1985—; ophthalmology chief resident, 1987-88; fellow Ophthalmology Corneal Cons. of Ind., Indpls.; chmn. dept. ophthalmology USNH, Okinawa; assoc. prof. ophthalmology Ohio U. Coll. Osteopathic Medicine; cons. Rome Sch. Dist., Ctrl. Assn. for Blind, Utica, Kernan Sch. for Multiple Handicapped, Utica, Dept. of Def. Schs.; credentials chmn. Dayton br. Laser Ctrs. Am.; Amelia Earhart student adv. coun., Vestry-All Soul's Episcopal Ch.; spkr. various profl. orgns. and confs.; mem. curriculum adv. com. Deer Creek Curriculum Rev. Conf., 1982; chief sect. ophthalmology Stouder Meml. Hosp.; instr. Am. Acad. Ophthalmology, 1998, 99; mem. Wells Inst. Study on Dry Eyes Macular Degeneration Cataract Medications; FDA investigator Glaucoma Wick Surgery, Cornea Donor Study. Contbr. articles to profl. jours. Founder Russian Orphanage Fund; mem. adv. bd. ARC, Rome, 1977-80; mem. Mohawk Valley Chinese Cultural Assn., Rome, 1977-80, Dayton Area Chinese Assn., 1985—; nominated People to People Optometry Delegation to People's Republic of China, 1985, India, 1986; co-chmn. Ohio Eye Injury Registry; chmn. pub. health and welfare com. Dayton dist. Acad. Osteo. Medicine; founder Russian Orphanage Fund; cons. Boonshoff Mus. With USAF, 1977-80, to lt. comdr. USNR, 1988-91. Named Lion of Yr., 1999; recipient Melvin Jones award Lions Club Internat. Found., 2000, Leadership award Lion Club Internat. Found., 2000. Fellow Am. Acad. Optometry (LASIK instr.), Osteopathic Coll. Ophthalmology, Otolaryngology, and Head and Neck Surgery; mem. AMA, Am. Cancer Soc. (mem. bd. dirs. Miami County, Troy chpt.), Am. Osteo. Assn. (student rep. nat. com. on colls. 1984), Ohio Osteo. Assn., Am. Acad. Ophthalmology, Pediat. Keratoplasty Soc., Dayton Area Chinese Assn., Gold Key, Montgomery County Med. Soc., Ohio State Med. Assn., Am. Soc. Cataract and Refractie Surgery, Ohio Opthalmological soc. (rep. children's vision stds. com., rep. vision adv. bd. Ohio Dept. Health), Ohio Eyes, Ears, Nose and Throat Assn. Soc. (pres., program chair 1996), Miami County Med. Soc., Internat. Soc. Refractive Keratoplasty, Assn. Contemporary Optholmology, Internat. Soc. Refractive Surgery, C. of C. Huber Heights and Troy, Order of Ea. Star, Beta Beta Beta. Episcopalian. Avocations: hunting, fishing, martial arts, photography, playing mandolin. Home: 1495 Fox Run Troy OH 45373-7550 Office: 7371 Brandt Pike Ste B Huber Heights OH 45424-3200

LEE, DANIEL KAM-LEN, molecular biologist; b. Guangzhou, Guangdong, China, May 1, 1954; m. Wan San Windsor, May 20, 1992; children: Yuet Tung, Yuet Kei. BSc in Biomolecular Sci. with honors, Portsmouth (Eng.) Poly., 1982; PhD in Med. Scis., U. Calgary (Can.), 1988. Technician student med. lab. Tung Wah Group of Hosps., Hong Kong, 1972-75, med. lab. technician II, 1975-79; med. lab. scientific officer Charing Cross Hosp. (Fulham), London, 1980, 81; rsch. biochems. specialist Boehringer Mannheim (China) Ltd., Hong Kong, 1989; med. scientific officer prenatal diagnosis lab. Tsan Yuk Hosp., Hong Kong, 1989; lectr. dept. applied biology and chem. tech. The Hong Kong Poly., 1989-92; asst. prof. dept. applied biology and chem. techn. The Hong Kong Poly. U., 1992—; guest mem. selection bds. Sir Edward Youde Meml. Fellowships and Scholarships, 1995-96, 96-97, 97-98, 98-99, 99-00; lectr. in field. Contbr. numerous articles to profl. jours. Mem. AAAS, Am. Soc. Biochemistry and Molecular Biology, Soc. Chinese Bioscientists in Am., N.Y. Acad. Scis., Hong Kong Soc. Med. Genetics, Hong Kong Soc. Biochemistry and Molecular Biology, Hong Kong Biophysical Soc., Hong Kong Instn. of Sci., Asia Pacific Soc. of Bioscientists, Molecular Medicine Soc., Soc. Chinese Bioscientists Am. Avocations: horseback riding, table tennis. E-mail: bcdlee@inet.polyu.edu.hk. Office: Hong Kong Poly Univ, Dept Applied Biology & Chem Tech, Hung Hom Kowloon Hong Kong China

LEE, DAVID CHANG, physician; b. Seoul, Republic of Korea, Sept. 14, 1940; s. Young C. Lee and Hae W. (Kim) Kim; m. Margaret C. Park, Sept. 10, 1965; children: Edward, Grace, George. MD, Yon-Sei Sch. Med., Seoul, 1965. Diplomate Am. Bd. Otolaryngology. Intern Howard med. Ctr., Washington, 1965-66; resident gen. surgery Roger's Meml. Hosp., Washington, 1966-67; resident otolaryngology St. Louis City Hosp., 1967-70, U. Md. Hosp., Balt., 1970-71; staff physician Ft. Howard (Md.) Vets. Hosp., 1971-73; asst. prof. U. Ill., Chgo., 1973—, Chgo. Osteo. Med. Sch., 1999—; med. staff St. Francis Hosp., Blude Island, Ill., 1973—, Ingall's Meml. Hosp., Harvey, Ill., 1973—. Contbr. articles to profl. jours. Fellow ACS, Am. Acad. Otolaryncology and Head and Neck Surgery; AMA. Presbyterian. Avocations: Tae Kwon Do (3d degree black belt), golf. Office: 5320 159th St Oak Forest IL 60452-4705

LEE, DAVID GEORGE, business manager; b. North Sydney, N.S., Can., Dec. 19, 1947; s. Donald George and Margaret Lillian Lee; children: Kristine, Patricia. BS in Bus. Mgmt., Am. Internat. U., 1980, MBA in Mktg. magna cum laude, 1981. Office mgr., acct. Total Splty. Advt., Toronto, Ont., Can., 1969-73; bus. mgr. Circle One Advt., Toronto, 1973-75; gen. mgr. Ea. Can. Yellow pages Dir., Toronto, 1975-78; bus. adminstr. Laurelbrook (Tenn.) Acad. and Sanitarium, 1981-82; mktg.-devel. dir. Riverside Hosp., Nashville, 1982-83; bus. mgr., devel. dir. Harbert Hills Acad., 1983-84; pres. Supersnacks, Roanoke, Va., 1984-94; gen. mgr. Chilli Peppers Bar & Grill, Roanoke, Va., 1994-2000; mgr. The Point Country Club, Mooresville, N.C., 2000—; cons. in field. Mem. So. Advt. Assn., Southeastern Mktg. Assn., Southeastern Pub. Accts. Assn., Valleybrook Golf and Country Club, Ole Monterey Country Club. Home: 10403 Willow Run Rd Apt 1L Charlotte NC 28210-8457 Office: The Point Country Club Bradley Rd Moonsville NC 28115

LEE, DAVID MALLIN, physicist; b. Bklyn., Jan. 18, 1944; s. George Francis Lee and Winifred Rita (Jones) Wyatt; m. Judith Carol Silliman, Aug. 20, 1966; children: David, Timothy, Karen, Jeffrey, Rebecca. BS, Manhattan Coll., 1966; PhD, U. Va., 1971. Vis. mem. staff Los Alamos (N.Mex) Nat. Lab., 1971-74, mem. staff, 1974-80, 81—; U.S. tech. expert IAEA, Vienna, Austria, 1980-81. Patentee in field. Mem. Am. Phys. Soc., AAAS, Sigma Xi. Democrat. Roman Catholic. Home: 48 Wildflower Way Santa Fe NM 87501-8616*

LEE, DAVID MORRIS, physics educator; b. Rye, N.Y., Jan. 20, 1931; s. Marvin and Annette (Franks) L.; m. Dana Thorangkul, Sept. 7, 1960; children: Eric Bertel, James Marvin. AB, Harvard U., 1952; MS, U. Conn., 1955; PhD, Yale U., 1959. Instr. of physics Cornell U., Ithaca, N.Y., 1959-60, asst. prof. physics, 1960-63, assoc. prof. physics, 1963-68, prof. physics, 1968-97, James Gilbert White disting. prof. phys. scis., 1997—; vis. scientist Brookhaven Nat. Lab., Upton, N.Y., 1966-67; vis. prof. U. Fla., Gainesville, 1974-75, 94, U. Calif., San Diego, La Jolla, 1988; vis. lectr. Peking U., Beijing, China, 1981; chair municipal Joseph Fourier U., Grenoble, France, 1994. Contbr. articles to Phys. Rev. Letters, Phys. Rev., Physica and Nature. With U.S. Army, 1952-54. John Simon Guggenheim fellow Guggenheim Found., 1966-67, 74-75, Japan Soc. Promotion of Scis. fellow, 1977; recipient Sir Francis Simon Meml. prize Brit. Inst. Physics, 1976, Wilber Cross medal Yale U., 1998, shared Nobel prize for physics, 1996. Fellow AAAS, Am. Phys. Soc. (Oliver Buckley prize 1981), Brit. Inst. Physics, Am. Acad. Arts and Scis.; mem. Nat. Acad. Scis. Achievements include codiscovery of superfluid 3He, of the tricritical point of 3He-4He mixtures; co-

observation of spin waves in spin polarized hydrogen gas. Office: Cornell U Physics Dept Clark Hall Ithaca NY 14853-2501

LEE, DENNIS TURNER, civil engineer, construction executive; b. Dallas, Jan. 6, 1941; s. Joseph Thomas and Elizabeth Lee; m. Dianna Christine Ricker, Aug. 8, 1964; children: Christopher Scott, Karen Denise, Suzanne Elizabeth. BSCE, So. Meth. U., 1964; MS in Constrn. Mgmt., Stanford U., 1965. Cert. project mgmt. profl., asbestos contr./supr. Constrn. engr. Kaiser Engrs., Oakland, Calif., 1965-66; project engr. Hoffman Constrn. Co., Portland, Oreg., 1969-76, supt., 1977, project ops. mgr., 1978-84; sr. project mgr. Chanen Constrn. Co., Phoenix, 1985-87, Sundt Corp., Phoenix, 1987-93, Linthicum Constructors, Scottsdale, Ariz., 1993; account exec. Water Purge Sys., Scottsdale, 1994; facilities mgr. InteSys Technologies, Inc., Gilbert, Ariz., 1994-97; project mgr. Motorola New Constrn. Team ICF-Kaiser, Chandler, Ariz., 1998; project mgr. Target Gen., Inc., Phoenix, 1999—; mem. lawyer ethics discipline com. Ariz. State Bar, 1990-93. 1st lt. C.E. U.S. Army, 1966-69. Decorated Army Commendation medal. Mem. ASCE, Project Mgmt. Inst. (pres. 1990-93), Environ. Info. Assn. (bd. dirs. 1992-93), Toastmasters (pres. 1992). Achievements include pioneered use of time lapse movie technology in construction operations; designed jobsite concrete precasting and steam curing plants; pioneered use of lasers in construction. Avocations: hiking, camping, skiing, in-line skating. Home: 8019 E Voltaire Ave Scottsdale AZ 85260-4933

LEE, DO-HOON, computer science educator; b. Koseung, Korea, Sept. 29, 1963; s. Sang-mae and Doo-Sam Lee; m. Eun-Sil Nam, Dec. 13, 1992; children: Na-Kyung, In-Hyup. BS, Pusan (Korea) Nat. U., 1986, MS, 1992, PhD, 1998. Tchg. asst. Pusan (Korea) Nat. U., 1990-92, instr., 1993-94; instr. Miryang Nat. U., South Kyoungsang Province, 1993-94; rschr. Info. & Comm. Rsch. Inst., Pusan, 1994-98; prof. dept. computer engring. Miryang Nat. U., Kyungnam, Korea, 1995—, head dept. computer engring., 1997-98; dir. Inst. Advanced Tech. in Info. and Comm., 1999—. Author: (in Korean) Fundamentals and Applications of Latex, 1994, The Principle and Problems with C, 2d edit., 1999, Computer for Windows 95 and Internet Users, 1998, A New Synthesizing Method for Handwritten Korean Scripts, 1998, The Beta-Velocity Model for Simulating Handwritten Korean Script, 1998; transl.: Discrete Mathematics, 1999. Sgt. Korean Army, 1987-89. Mem. IEEE, Soc. Indsl. and Applied Math., Assn. Computing Machinery, Korea Info. Sci. Soc. Avocations: sea sports, tennis. Office: Miryang Nat U, Comp Eng Dept, Kyungnam 627-702, Republic of Korea

LEE, DONG WOOK, biochemistry and toxicology researcher; b. Seoul, Republic of Korea, Jan. 11, 1950; s. Chong Nak Lee and Na Mee Shin; m. Youn Ja Yu, May 5, 1979; children: Sun Mee Lee, Hang Yeul Lee. B in Engring., Han Yang U., Seoul, 1979; MS in Biochemistry, Chung Ang U., Seoul, 1981, PhD in Biochemistry, 1984. Lectr. Chung Ang U., 1981-86; sr. rschr. Korea Ginseng & Tobacco Rsch. Inst., Taejon, Republic of Korea, 1986-93, prin. scientist, 1994—, dir., 1998—; vis. prof. Chung Ang U., 1987—, U. Tex. Health Sci. Ctr., San Antonio, 1988-90, Hallym U., Chuncheon, Republic of Korea, 1998—. Contbr. numerous articles to profl. jours. and conf. procs. (Excellent Paper award Korean Found. Sci. Tech. Soc. 1993). With Republic of Korea army, 1975-76. Mem. N.Y. Acad. Scis., Internat. Free Radical Assn., Gerontol. Soc. Am., Korean Free Radical Assn., Biochem. Soc. Republic of Korea, Korean Soc. Gerontology (v.p. 1998-99, editor-in-chief 1997-99), Soc. Korean Ginseng, Korean Soc. Tobacco Sci. (editor-in-chief 1997-98, sec. gen. 1999—). Avocations: classical music, golf.

LEE, DOO YONG, engineering educator, researcher; b. Seoul, Korea, Aug. 20, 1962; s. Jang Seok and Myung Hi (Kang) L.; m. Sun Young Yi, Sept. 15, 1995; children: Sun Ho, Chang Ho. BS, Seoul Nat. U., 1985; MS, Rensselaer Poly. Inst., Troy, N.Y., 1987, PhD, 1993. Postdoctoral rsch. assoc. Rensselaer Poly. Inst., Troy, 1993-94; asst. prof. mech. engring. Korea Advanced Inst. Sci. and Tech., Taejon, 1994—. Contbr. articles to profl. jours. Cpl. Korean Air Force, 1987-89. Recipient Charles M. Close Doctoral Prize Rensselaer Poly. Inst., 1993, Baek-Am Paper award Korean Soc. Mech. Engrs., 1999. Mem. IEEE (sr.), Soc. Mfg. Engrs. (sr.). Office: Korea Adv Inst Sci Tech ME Dept, 373-1 Kusong-dong Yusong-gu, Taejon 305-701, Republic of Korea

LEE, DORA FUGH, artist; b. Beijing, China, Aug. 16, 1930; arrived in U.S., 1957; d. Philip and Sarah F.; m. Richard Wen-han Lee; children: April, Sarah, Handel, Helen. Student, Chow Yang Law Sch., Peking, China, 1947; studied Chinese traditional painting, western watercolor, sculpture. Art tchr. Chinese Sch., Tokyo, 1950-53; illustrator CIE Visual sect. U.S. Army, Tokyo, 1953-56; tchr. Chinese calligraphy George Washington U., 1982; tchr. Chinese traditional painting Smithsonian Instn., 1983. One-person exhbns. in Chinese Cultural Ctr., Washington, 1958, Swan Gallery, Plainfield, N.J., 1963, China Inst., N.Y.C., 1964, Stoneman Gallery, Washington, 1966, 70, 72, 74, Franz Bader Gallery, Washington, 1976, 80, 82, 83, 84, 85, 87, 88, 92, 94, Johns Hopkins, Balt., 1985, Pacific Art Club, Hong Kong, 1989, Courtyard Gallery, Beijing, 2000; permanent collections include Smithsonian Inst., Washington, NIH, Bethesda, Md., Nat. Cathedral, Washington, Nat. Portrait Gallery, Washington, Nat. Mus. Women in Arts, Washington, Nat. League Am. PEN Women, numerous others. Mem. Nat. League Am. PEN Women, Am. Watercolor Soc., Washington Watercolor Assn. Home: 6305 Orchid Dr Bethesda MD 20817-5613

LEE, EDNA PRITCHARD, education educator; b. Windsor, N.C., Oct. 6, 1923; d. Peter Bernard and Edna (Smith) Pritchard; m. Mack Lloyd Lee Sr., May 17, 1945 (dec. Nov. 1970); 1 child, Mack Lloyd Jr.; m. Lee Cross, June 1, 1991 (dec. Aug. 1997). BS, State U. N.C., Elizabeth City; MA, NYU, N.Y.C. Cert. N.Y. Adminstr.-Supr. Tchr. elem. schs. Windsor, N.C., 1944-61; tchr. elem. schs. Mohegan Lake, N.Y., 1961-68, asst. prin. elem. sch., 1968-82; dir. basic edn. Peekskill (N.Y.) High Sch., 1969-80; adj. prof. Mercy Coll., Peekskill, 1985—; vice chmn. bd. dirs. Peekskill Area Health Ctr.; bd. dirs. Family Resource Ctr., Montrose Child Care Ctr. Co-author: Syllabus for 4th Grade Social Studies, 1972. Trustee Mt. Olivet Ch., 1993-961 ores, Tee Ettes, 1995—. Named Woman of Yr., NAACP, Peekskill, 1976, Woman Engr. of Yr., Bus. and Profl. Women, Peekskill, 1980; recipient Louis Gregory award Bahai Religion, Peekskill, 1988. Mem. AAUW (v.p. 1970-72), Blacks in Govt., Delta Kappa Gamma, Alpha Kappa Alpha, Tee-Ettes (sec. 1982-88). Avocations: golf, gardening. Home: 101 Dutch St Montrose NY 10548-1517

LEE, EDWARD BROOKE, JR., real estate executive, fund raiser; b. Silver Spring, Md., Oct. 25, 1917; s. E. Brooke Lee and Elizabeth (Wilson) Aspinwall; m. Camilla Edge, Apr. 15, 1944 (div. Feb. 1983); children: Camilla Lee Alexander, E. Brooke III, Kaiulani Lee Kimbrell, Katherine Blair Lee St. John, Richard Henry, Elizabeth Ashe Somerville; m. Deborah Roche, Apr. 30, 1983 (div. Nov. 1997); children: Samuel Phillips II, Regina Blair; m. Brenda Baker Puderbaugh, Feb. 12, 1998; stepchildren: Thomas Ance Puderbaugh, Shawn Michael Puderbaugh, Shannon Lee Puderbaugh. AB, Princeton U., 1940; student, The Infantry Sch., 1942; postgrad. bus. sch., Harvard U., 1957. Cert. real estate broker Md., D.C., Va. Various indsl. positions to nat. account mgr. Scott Paper Co., Phila., 1940-62; comml. broker Shannon and Luchs, Washington, 1962-83, Merrill Lynch Comml. Realty, Washington, 1983-89, Prudential Preferred Properties, Bethesda, Md., 1989-95; pres. E. Brooke Lee Properties, Inc., Montgomery County, Md., 1979—; fund raiser key gifts Nat. Found. for Cancer Rsch., Bethesda, Md., 1985-95; v.p. Ga. Ave. Properties, Montgomery County, Ga.-Conn., Inc., Montgomery County, Conn. Aspen, Inc., Montgomery County, 1962—; sec.-treas. Brooke Lee Family, Inc., Montgomey County, 1962—. Author numerous sales articles for purchasing mags. Chmn. Drug Action Coalition, Inc., fin. v.p., bd. dirs., 1966-70; rep. candidate for Mayor of Washington, 1982, rep. primary candidate for U.S. Senate, State of Md., 1986. Served to capt. airborne inf. U.S. Army, 1943-45, ETO. Named Realtor Assoc. of Yr., Washington Bd. of Realtors, 1984. Mem. Harvard Bus. Sch. Club (pres. 1962, exec. v.p. 1975), Princeton Club of Washington (sec., bd. dirs. 1970-75), Princeton Club of N.Y., Nat. Account Mktg. Assn. (founder, pres. 1959-62). Republican. Episcopalian. Clubs: Metro, Chevy Chase Country (Washington). Lodge: Kiwanis. Avocations: tennis, hunting, swimming, sailing, skating. Home and Office: E Brooke Lee Jr Properties Inc 8806 Connecticut Ave Chevy Chase MD 20815-6737

LEE, EUN JI, linguist, educator; b. Seoul, July 15, 1952; d. Tae Dong and Myung Jung Lee. BA, Yonsei U., Seoul, 1981, MA, 1983; MA, U. Conn., Storrs, 1991, PhD in Linguistics, 1992. Tchg. asst. Yonsei U., Seoul, 1981-82, U. Conn., Storrs, 1988-90; lectr. Yonsei U., Seoul, 1983-84, 92-96, Korea U., Cochiwon, 1993, Kyunghee U., Yongin, 1994-96, Kwukmin U., Seoul, 1994-96, Seoul City U., 1995-96; asst. prof. linguistics Daebul U., Mokpo, Korea, 1996—. Contbr. articles to profl. jours. Sunday sch. tchr. Sajickdong Presbyn. Ch., Seoul, 1980-84; deacon Yanguimwun Presbyn. Ch., Seoul, 19994—, Mokpo Zion Presbyn. Ch., 2000—; trustee Linguistic Soc. Korea, 1997-99. Recipient scholarship U. Conn., Storrs, 1990-92. Mem. Linguistic Soc. Am., Linguistic Soc. Korea, korean Generative Grammar Circle. Presbyterian. Office: Daebul U English Dept, 72 Sanho-Li, Samho-Myen, Cennam Yengam-Kwun 526-890, Korea

LEE, FRANCES HELEN, editor; b. N.Y.C., Jan. 6, 1936; d. Murray and Rose (Rothman) Lee. BA, Queens Coll., 1957; MA, NYU, 1962. Editl. asst. Christian Herald Family Bookshelf, N.Y.C., 1957-62; with Gordon and Breach Sci. Pubs., Inc., N.Y.C., 1964-66, Am. Electric Power Svc. Corp. AEP Operating Ideas, N.Y.C., 1966-69, Indsl. Water Engring. Mag., N.Y.C., 1969-71; directory editor photographic divsn. United Bus. Publs., N.Y.C., 1971-80; editor Am. Druggist Blue Book Hearst Books/Bus. Publs. Group, 1980-81; spl. projects coord. motor manuels Hearst Book Divsn., 1981-82; editor New Price Report, 1982-84, Am. Druggist Blue Book, 1982-88; free-lance editor, cons., 1988—. Supr. Bronx divsn. N.Y. State Civil Defense, 1953-59; mem. com. on N.Y.C. charter revision, Citizens Union, 1975, com. on city mgmt., 1977-92, bd. dirs., co-chmn. com. on N.Y.C. cultural concerns, 1979-97, chmn., 1997-98; vol. N.Y.C. Opera, 1988—. Recipient cert. of honor NYU Alumni Fedn., 1985, Meritorious Svc. award, 1986. Mem. N.Y. Bus. Press Editors (bd. dirs. 1988-90, sec. 1990-91), Women's Equity Action League (chmn. rsch. com.), NYU Alumnae Club (dir. 1976-78, rec. sec. 1978-80, v.p. 1980-82, pres. 1982-84, rep. to bd. dirs. fedn. 1984-86), NYU Alumni Fedn. (dir.-at-large 1986—), Villa-Lobos Music Soc. (sec. 1989-91, treas. 1992-95), NYU Club (bd. govs. 1987-89). Home: 170 2nd Ave New York NY 10003-5754

LEE, FRED STEVEN, telecommunications engineer; b. Wahiawa Oahu, Hawaii, June 7, 1954; s. Michael T. H. and Annette Kimiko (Ozawa) L.; m. Lynn Marie Gray, Aug. 16, 1985; children: Jennifer L. Pearce, Sandra M. Pearce, Christopher M., Nicole M. BSEE, Cornell U., 1975, MSEE, 1976. Head digital task group Watkins-Johnson, Gaithersburg, Md., 1976-78; prin. engr. Fairchild Space and Electronics, Germantown, Md., 1978-82; dir. engring. DAMA Telecom., Rockville, Md., 1982-86, Data Gen. Telecom., Rockville, 1986-87; pres., owner TransDigital Sys., Inc., Rockville, 1987—; cons. COMSAT Labs., Germantown, 1987—. Tiger Cub leader Cub Scouts Pack 178, Rockville, 1992-93. Achievements include patents for distributed switching architecture and high speed communication processing system. Avocations: scuba, backpacking, spelunking. Office: TransDigital Sys Inc 7753 Barnstable Pl Rockville MD 20855-2537

LEE, HAKSIK, marketing educator; b. Moon Kyoung, Republic of Korea, May 29, 1952; s. Mongkyu and Kwinam Lee; m. Youngsook Huh, Oct. 2, 1977; children: Seungjae, Jennie, Jean. B in Engring., Korea U., Seoul, 1976; MBA, Seoul Nat. U., 1979; PhD, Mich. State U., 1987. Mgr. Daewoo Heavy Industries, Ltd., Seoul, 1977-78; prof. Hong Ik U., Seoul, 1987-99; cons. Seoul City Govt., 1989-93, Seoul City R.R. Co., Seoul, 1995-96. Author: Consumer Behavior, 1992, Marketing, 1999; mem. editl. bd. Korean Mktg. Jour., 1998-99; contbr. articles to profl. jours. Mem. Korean Acad. Soc. Bus. Adminstrn. (mem. editl. bd., area editor 1996-98), Korean Mktg. Assn. (bd. dirs. 1995-99), Korean Soc. Consumer Studies (bd. dirs. 1993-97). Avocation: mountain climbing. Fax: 02-333-1735. Home: Mokdong Apt 1307-206, Yangcheon-ku, Seoul 158-076, Republic of Korea Office: Hong Ik U, Mapoku, Seoul 121-791, Republic of Korea

LEE, HAN DONG, prime minister of Korea; b. Kyonggi-do, Korea, Dec. 5, 1934; m. Nam Sook Cho; 3 children. BA, Seoul (Korea) Nat. U., 1958. Judge Seoul Dist. Ct., 1963-69, prosecutor ministry of justice, 1969-74; sr. prosecutor Daejeon Dist. Prosecutor's Office, 1975-77; sr. prosecutor spl. investigations Divsn. Pusan Dist. Prosecutor's Office, 1977-80; sr. prosecutor 1st spl. investigations Seoul Dist. Prosecutor's Office, 1980-81; mem. Nat. Assembly, 1981-2000, vice spkr., 1995; prime min. Republic of Korea, 2000—; chmn. Kyonggi Provincial chpt. Dem. Justice Party, 1983, sec. gen., 1994, floor leader, 1986, 89, rep. four party talks, 1987, mem. ctrl. exec. coun., 1990; del. preparation com. South and North Korea Parliamentary Talks, 1988; floor leader Dem. Liberal Party, 1993, chmn. Kyonggi Provincial chpt., 1994, spl. advisor to party pres., 1996; chief exec. chmn. New Korea Party, 1997; chief exec. chmn. Grand Nat. Party, 1997, v.p., 1998, acting pres., 1998; acting pres. United Liberal Dems., 2000, pres., 2000. With Republic of Korea Army, 1959-63. Recipient Svc. Merit medal, 1976, Order of Svc. Merit with blue stripes, 1989. Office: Residence of Prime Min, 106 Samchung-dong Chongno, Seoul Republic of Korea*

LEE, HARRISON HON, naval architecture librarian, consultant; b. Stockton, Calif., Sept. 20, 1943; s. Hon Bo and Lulu Joyce Lee; m. Estelle Toby Wlosko, May 11, 1980. AA, Stockton (Calif.) Coll., 1967; BA, Stanislaus State Coll., Turlock, Calif., 1969; MA, Sonoma State U., Cotati, Calif., 1973; MS in Libr. Sci., Simmons Coll., 1978. Lectr. Ecole d'Humanite, Reuti, Switzerland, 1973-75; libr. M. Rosenblatt & Son, Inc., N.Y.C., 1978-89; libr. cons. SELF, Stockton, 1989—. Mem. Spl. Libr. Assn., Soc. Naval Archs. and Marine Engrs. Unitarian.

LEE, HEE JUN, sedimentologist, researcher; b. Seoul, South Korea, Nov. 29, 1956; s. Wan Shik and Gye Hoon Lee; m. Sun Ok Kim, Oct. 5, 1985; children: Soo Ah, Kee Hyun. B, Seoul Nat. U., 1980, MSc, 1986, PhD, 1991. Lic. oceanography. Rschr. Korean Ocean Rsch. & Devel. Inst., Ansan, South Korea, 1984-90, sr. rschr., 1991—; group leader Korean Ocean Rsch. & Devel. Inst., Ansan, 1993-95. Contbr. articles to profl. jours. Mem. AAAS, Soc. for Sedimentary Geology, Internat. Assn. Sedimentologists. Office: Korea Ocean Rsch & Devel, Ansan PO Box 29, 425-600 Seoul Republic of Korea

LEE, HEEKWAN, engineering researcher; b. Seoul, Korea, June 15, 1965; s. Hwan-Sik and Kho-Bok Lee; m. Jihye Kwon, May 18, 1994; children: Paul, Cecilia. B Engring., U. Seoul, 1992, M Engring., 1994; PhD Candidate, U. Reading, U.K., 1999—. Cpl. Korean mil. Mem. ASHRAE, Am. Soc. Testing & Materials, Chartered Inst. Bldg. Svcs. Engrs. Office: U Reading, Whiteknights PO Box 219, Reading RG6 6AW, United Kingdom

LEE, HEESOON, pharmacy educator; b. Cheongju, Chungbuk, South Korea, May 15, 1957; s. Taejin and Gesun (Ahn) L.; m. Jungsook Cho, July 24, 1983; children: Jaejoong and P. Jaeyong. BS, Seoul Nat. U., 1981, MS, 1986; PhD, SUNY, Buffalo, 1991. Tchg. asst. SUNY, Buffalo, 1988-90; postdoctoral fellow Rensselaer Poly. Inst., Troy, N.Y., 1991-93; asst. prof. Chungbuk Nat. U., Cheongju, 1993-97, assoc. prof., 1997—. Contbr. articles to Biorganic and Medicinal Chemistry Letters. Recipient Reukjunggicho award Korean Sci. and Engring. Found., 1997. Mem. Pharm. Soc. Korea, Korean Chem. Soc. Office: Chungbuk Nat U Coll Pharm, San 56-1 Gaesin-Dong, Cheongju, Chungbuk 361-763, Korea

LEE, HI YOUNG, physician, acupuncturist; b. Seoul, Korea, Oct. 18, 1941; came to U.S., 1965, naturalized, 1976; s. Jung S. and Hwa J. (Kim) L.; m. Sun M. Lee, June 4, 1965; children: Sandra, Grace, David. M.D., Yon Sei U., Seoul, 1965. Diplomate Am. Bd. Family Practice. Intern Grasslands Hosp., Valhalla, N.Y., 1965-66; resident VA Hosp., Dayton, Ohio, 1966-70; mem. staff Eastern State Hosp., Medical Lake, Wash., 1970-74; practice family medicine, acupuncturist Empire Med. Office, Spokane, Wash., 1974—; active staff St. Lukes Meml. Hosp., Spokane, 1974—, bd. trustees St. Georges Prep Sch., Wash., 1986— ; courtesy staff Deaconess Med. Center, Spokane, 1974—, Sacred Heart Med. Ctr., Spokane, 1974—. Author: Von Recklinghousen's Disease, 1970 (McDermit award); columnist Rainier Forum Korea Post Weekly News, 1996—. Elder First Presbyterian Church, Spokane, 1975. Fellow Am. Acad. Family Practice; mem. ctr. for Chinese Medicine, Spokane County Med. Soc., Nat. Acupuncture Research Soc., Christian Med. Soc. Home: 2006 W Liberty Ave Spokane WA 99205-2570 Office: Empire Med Office 17 E Empire Ave Spokane WA 99207-1707

LEE, HONGKOO, diplomat. M in Polit. Sci., Yale U., D in Polit. Sci. Min. Nat. Unification Republic of Korea Govt., 1988, spl. asst. to pres. polit. affairs, 1990, Republic of Korea amb. to the U.K., 1991, dep. prime min., 1994, prime min. of Korea, 1994-95, Republic of Korea amb. to U.S., 1998—; chmn. New Korea Party; mem. Korean Nat. Assembly. Office: Embassy of the Republic of Korea 2450 Massachusetts Ave NW Washington DC 20008-2850

LEE, HOSUN, physics educator; b. Seoul, Mar. 14, 1961; s. Kun-Jong Lee and Jung-Soon Shin; m. Won-Mi Lee; children: Soo-Jin, Soo-Yeon. BS, Seoul Nat. U., 1983; MA, Brandeis U., 1987; PhD, U. Ill., 1993. Rsch. assoc. Sandia Nat. Lab., Albuquerque, 1993-95; assoc. prof. physics Kyung Hee U., Yong-In, Republic of Korea, 1995—. Mem. Am. Phys. Soc., Korean Phys. Soc. Home: Soo-Ji-Up Jook-Jeon-Ri 501, Dong-Seong Apt 103-1201, Yong-In-Shi Kyung-Ki, Republic of Korea Office: Kyung Hee U Dept Physics, Ki-Heung Up, Seo-Chon-Ri 1, Yong-In Kyung-Ki, Republic of Korea

LEE, HOW CHUEN, manufacturing company executive; b. Swatow, China, Sept. 17, 1948; m. Kam Fung Lau, Mar. 28, 1982; children: Carmen, Graham. BBA, Chinese U. Hong Kong, 1973. Pres. Splendour Internat. Enterprise Co., Ltd., Hong Kong, 1976—, Splendour Handbag (Shenzhen) Co., Ltd., 1983—; mng. dir. Splendour Indsl. Co., Hong Kong, 1976—, Long Fair Handbag Factory, China, 1986—. Editor: The Practice and Theory of Pak Gua Martial Arts, 1994. Pres. Chin Wu Athletics Assn., Hong Kong, 1990—, tchr., 1992—; vice chmn. Advancement Pak Gua Martial Arts Assn., 1980—. Fellow Chartered Inst. Mktg. (U.K.) (diploma). Avocation: Chinese kung fu martial arts. Office: Splendour Int Ent Hin Win Fty, 4/F Flat B How Ming St, 110 Kowloon Hong Kong

LEE, HSIAO YI, medical technology educator; b. Taipei, Taiwan, Feb. 15, 1967; s. Hsin Bern and Yo Mei (Chern) L.; m. Hsin Yi Ma, Jan. 25, 1996. BS in Physics, Nat. Ctrl. U., Chung-Li, Taiwan, 1989, MS in Optical Sci., 1991, PhD in Optical Sci., 1994. Assoc. prof. electronics Da-Hwa Coll., Hsin-Chu, 1996-97; optical engr. Vivitek Co. Ltd., Hsin-Chu, 1996-97, cons., 1997—; assoc. prof. dept. radiol. tech. Yuan-Pei Tech. Coll., Hsin-Chu, 1997-2000; cons. Delta Co. Ltd., Chung-Li, 1999—; asoc. prof. dept. elec. engring., dept. optical engring. Minghsing Inst. Tech., Taiwan, 2000—; cons. Queening Hi-Tech. Corp., Taiwan. Contbr. articles to profl. jours. 2nd lt. Sch. Mil. Sgt., 1994-96. Mem. Soc. of Photo-Optical Instrumentation Engrs. Office: Minghsing Inst Tech, 1 Hsin-Hsing Rd, Taiwan 304, China

LEE, HYERAN, adult education educator; b. Taegu, Korea, Jan. 11, 1961; child of Changkyu Lee and Oksun Park; m. Taemyung Lee, June 29, 1986; children: Hae-Byul, Hae-Sol. BA, Kyung Hee U., Seoul, Korea, 1983; MA, U. Fla., 1992, PhD, 1997. Lectr. Kyung Hee U., Seoul, 1997, prof., 1997-98, head prof., 1998—. Author: A Feature-Based Account of Long-Distance Anaphora, 1997, First Step in Korea, 1999, Exploring Korean, 2000; translator: Comparative Syntax, 1999. Scholar Kyung Hee U., 1979. Fax: 82-2-2201-4475. Office: Kyung Hee U Multi Media Blg, # 1 Secheon-ri, Kihung-up, 499-701 Kyunggido Korea

LEE, HYUNG HOAN, science educator, researcher, director; b. Hapdeog-Up, Repulic of Korea, Nov. 2, 1940; s. Myung K. Lee and Gum Hee Park; m. Sung Ja Choi, Aug. 14; children: Hyun Na, Jae Hoon, Hyun Mi. BS, Konkuk U., Seoul, Republic of Korea, 1965; MS, Yonsei U., Seoul, 1970, Brigham Young U., 1975; PhD, U. Idaho, 1979. Rsch. specialist Sch. Medicine U. Utah, Salt Lake City, 1975-76; assoc. dean, chmn. biology dept. Coll. Sci. Konkuk U., Seoul, 1979-87, prof., dir. Inst. Genetic Engring., 1984-2000, dean acad. affairs, 1988-89, dean acad. rsch., 1992-95, pres. Acad. Life Sci., 1996-98, dean Coll. of Sci., 2000—; advisor Korean Inst. Oriental Medicine, Seoul; chief rschr. Rsch. CTr. Molecular Microbiology Seoul Nat. U. Contbr. articles to profl. jours. With Republic of Korea Army, 1961-63. Recipient award for sci. writing Ministry Sci. and Tech., Korean Govt., 1983, award Edn. Ministry Edn. Korean Govt., 1985, award for acad. achievement Pres. of Konkuk U., 1987, 94, award for acad. or sci. rsch. Korean Soc. BRM, 1996, award for sci. rsch. Korean Soc. Applied Microbiology, 1998, Seoul City Cultural prize, 1998.m. Mem. Am. Soc. Microbiology, Soc. Microbiology, Korean Soc. Virology (mem. bd. com.), Korean Soc. Applied Microbiology (pres. 1999), Kongju U. Alumni (pres. 1985-86), Konkuk U. Biology Dept. Alumni (pres. 1987-88), Korean Soc. Mycology (pres. 1989-90). Avocations: hiking, golf, reading. Home: #3-403 Shindonga Apt, Hangdang 2 dong, Seoul 133-072, Korea Office: Konkuk U Dept Biology, Hwayang, Seoul 143-701, Korea

LEE, HYUNG JONG, physics educator; b. Kwangju, Rep. of Korea, Aug. 3, 1957. PhD, Advanced Inst. Sci. and Tech., Taejon, Rep. of Korea, 1989. Prof. Chonnam Nat. U., Kwangju, 1981—; tech. staff AT&T Bell Labs., Murray Hill, 1985-88, 93-95; invited mem. tech. staff Korea Electronics and Telecomm. Rsch. Inst., Taejon, 1988-90. Fax: 82-62-530-0334. E-mail: hyunglee@chonnam.ac.kr. Office: Chonnam Nat U Dept Physics, Puk-ku Yongbong-Dong, 500-757 Kwangju Republic of Korea

LEE, ILSE M., musician; b. Johannesburg, S. Africa, Apr. 30, 1962; d. Coenrad Hendrik and Barbara Maria (De Villiers) Van Wyk; m. Floyd Denman Lee, July 2, 1994; 1 child, Craig Michael. BMus, U. Witwaterand, 1983; MMus, No. Ill. U., 1986, MMus in composition, 1986; DMA, U. Az., 1989. Prof. music Mont. State U., Bozeman, 1989—; cellist Billings Symphony, 1989—, Grand Teton Music Festival, Jackson, Wy.; pvt. instr. cello. Bd. dirs. Mont. Chamber Music Festival, Bozeman, 1992—. Fellowship, Mont. Arts. Coun., 1990. Mem. Mont. Am. String Tchrs. Assn. (pres.-elect), Music Tchrs. Nat. Assn., Music Educators Nat. Conf. Office: Music Dept MSU-Bozeman Bozeman MT 59717

LEE, IN-HO, physicist; b. Pusan, Republic of Korea, May 23, 1967; s. Cheon-Yong and Jum-Soon (Chang) L.; m. Kyoung-Hee Yeo; 1 child, Hyun-Jihn. BS, Pusan Nat. U., Republic of Korea, 1990; MS, Korea Advanced Inst. Sci., Taejon, 1992, PhD, 1996. Rsch. assoc. Beckman Inst. U. Ill., Urbana, 1996-97, rsch. assoc. materials rsch. lab., 1997; rsch. scientist Postech, Pohang, Republic of Korea, 1998; rsch. fellow Korean Inst. Advanced Study, Seoul, Republic of Korea, 1998—. Contbr. articles to Phys. Rev. Avocation: football. Office: KIAS, Dongdaemun-gu, 207-43 Cheongryangri-dong, Seoul 130-012, Republic of Korea

LEE, JACQUES KIM CHEN, insurance broker; b. Riviere des Anguilles, Mauritius, June 3, 1942; s. Lee Hoi Foo and Suyin (Lim Fat) L.; m. Isabelle Kwee Lam Po Yuen, Aug. 13, 1966; children: Richard, Paul, Michael. Asst. acct. Hertz, London, 1966-68; life underwriter Sun Life Can., London, 1968-74; ins. broker Jaykel Ltd., London, 1974-97; practitioner, lectr. complementary medicine London, 1997—; pres. APWM Credit Union, London, 1976-80; sec. gen. Inst. Mauritian Bus., London, 1986-90; cons. Jaykel Travel Svcs., London, 1976-92. Author: The Nautilus and the Gang of Three, 1983, SEGA: The Mauritian Folk Dance, 1990, The Tongue: Mirror of the Immune System, 1999, Mauritius: Its Creole Language, 1999; editor Mauritian Internat. mag. Magistrate Wimbledon Magistrates Ct., 1988—. Mem. Chartered Ins. Inst. (assoc.). Avocations: homeopathy, conchology, opera, Chinese cooking. E-Mail: jaclee@compuserve.com. Office: Nautilus Pub Co, PO Box 4100, London SW20 0XN, England

LEE, JAE-KEUN, mechanical engineer, educator; b. Kyeongjoo, Kyeongbook, Korea, Oct. 6, 1959; s. Banghee and Okseon (Chang) L.; m. Eunsoon Park, Aug. 9, 1962; children: Meehae, Meeran, Chaejong. BS, Pusan (Korea) Nat. U., 1981; MS, Korea Advanced Inst. Sci/Tech., 1983, U. Minn., 1990; PhD, U. Minn., 1992. Rschr. LG Rsch. Lab., Seoul, 1983-88; rsch. asst. U. Minn., Mpls., 1988-92; rschr. MSP Co., Mpls., 1990-93; prof. Pusan Nat. U., 1993—; cons. Cambridge Filter, Seoul, 1996-97, Jangwoo Machine Co., Pusan, 1996—, KAF Co., 1994—, LG Electronic Co., Changwon, Korea, 1997—. Patentee in field. Mem. Environ. Assn., Pusan, 1993—. Recipient Pres. prize Korean Govt., 1986. Mem. Environtl. Engring. Rsch., Korean Soc. of Mech. Engrs. Avocations: tennis, golf, mountain climbing, listening to music, traveling. Home: Seon Kyeong Apt 309-1203, Kooseodong Kumjeonggoo, Pusan 609-312, Korea Office: Pusan U Sch Mech Engring, San 30 Changjeon Kumjeong, Pusan 609-735, Korea

LEE, JAICHAN, engineering educator; b. Chunchon, Kangwon, Korea, Feb. 15, 1961; s. Hyung Jun Lee and Hyo-Ja Choi; m. Duk Ju Hwang, Apr. 23, 1987; children: Seung Keon, Dong Gun. BS, Seoul (Korea) Nat. U., 1983; MS, Korea Advanced Inst. Sci./Tech, Seoul, 1985; PhD, Rutgers U., 1993. Mem. rsch. staff Samsung Electro-mechs., Suwon, Korea, 1985-87, Samsung Advanced Inst. Tech., Kiheung, Korea, 1987-89; mem. tech. staff Bellcore, Red Bank, 1993-94; asst. prof. Sung Kyun Kwan U., Suwon, 1995-99, assoc. prof., 1999—. Contbr. articles to profl. jours. Mem. Korean Ceramic Soc. (assoc. editor), Korean Materials Rsch. Soc. Avocation: playing guitar. Home: 134-1702 Hanil Town, 440-200 Jowon Dong Suwon Korea Office: Sung Kyun Kwan U, 300 Chunchun Dong, 440-746 Suwon Korea

LEE, JAMES JIEH, environmental educator, computer specialist; b. I-Lan, Taiwan, Aug. 27, 1939; came to U.S.A. 1968; s. Yun Ping and Lien Hwa (Kuo) L.; m. Margie J. Feng, March 31, 1965; 1 child: Jean H. BA, Taiwan Normal U., Taipei, 1962; MA, U. Minn., 1970; PhD in Environ. Scis., Greenwich U. Cert. high sch., univ. tchr., Taiwan. Tchr. I-Lan High Sch., 1962-64; instr. Ta-Tung & Taiwan Normal U., 1964-68; rsch. asst. U. Minn., Mlps., 1968-71, rsch. assoc., 1971-77; computer specialist U.S. Dept. Commerce, Silver Spring, Md., 1977-83; sr. computer system analyst U.S. Pub. Health Svc., Rockville, Md., 1983-92; planning dir. Ctr. for Taiwan Internat. Rels., Washington, 1990—; pres. World Fedn. Taiwanese Assns., 1995-99; deputy adminstr. EPA, Taiwan, 2000—; with Internat. Environ. Protection Assn., Washington, 1988-90, also bd. dirs. 1986—; bd. dirs. Asia Resource Ctr., Washington, 1993—; exec. dir. Constitution Movement for Taiwan, Washington, 1993—; chmn. Formosan Human Rights Assn. Washington chpt., 1976—. Co-author: (with others) Introduction to Human Geography, 1966, Yun-Wu Social Sci., 1971; author: Minnesota Taxing Jurisdictions, 1976, Back to Nature, 1991, Taiwan's Ecological Series, Vols. 1-4, 1995. Bd. dirs. Formosan Assn. Pub. Affairs, Washington, 1982-92. Recipient automation data processing/extramural rsch. USPHS, 1991. Mem. World Watch, Nat. Resource Def. Coun., Am. Solar Energy Soc., Union of Concerned Scientists, World Fedn. Taiwanese Assns. (pres. 1995-99), Sierra Club. Avocations: traveling, hiking. Home: 14306 Parkvale Rd Rockville MD 20853-2530

LEE, JANG GYU, electrical engineering educator, executive; b. Kongju, Chungnam, Korea, May 28, 1946; m. Suk Hie Youn, May 6, 1971; 1 child, Shin Young. BS in Engring., Seoul (Korea) Nat. U., 1971; MS in Elec. Engring., U. Pitts., 1974, PhD in Elec. Engring., 1977. Tech. staff The Analytic Scis. Corp., Reading, Mass., 1977-81, Charles Stark Draper Lab., Cambridge, Mass., 1981-82; asst. prof. dept. control and instrumentation engring. Seoul (Korea) Nat. U., 1982-86, assoc. prof., 1986-92, prof., 1992-95, prof. Sch. of Elec. Engring., 1995—; dir. Automation and Systems Rsch. Inst., Seoul Nat. U., 1996-98, Automatic Control Rsch. Ctr., 1995—. Moderator Weekly TV programs Science 2001, 1991-93, Korean Broadcasting System; co. author: (books) Automatic Controls, 1983, Modern Society and Civilization, 1997. Exec. sec. Christian Ethics Movement of Korea, 1989—. With Korean Army, 1967-68. Mem. IEEE, AIAA, Nat. Acad. Engrs. of Korea (asst. to pres., 1995—), IFAC Tech. Com. in Aerospace. Avocations: reading, running (finished 1980 Boston marathon), Skiing. Home: #13-706 Woosung Apt, Dowha Dong, Mapo-Ku, 121-042 Seoul Korea Office: Seoul Nat U Sch Elec Engrig, Kwanak PO Box 34, 151-600 Seoul Korea

LEE, JAY, foreign language educator; b. Kaohsiung, Taiwan, Dec. 22, 1973; s. Cam Phan and Shu Hsia (Hsieh) L. BA, Baylor U., 1995; MA, Nat. Sun Yat-Sen U., Kaohsiung, 1998. Premier tchr. Cosmos-Kaplan, Kaohsiung, 1997—; lectr. Nat. Sun Yat Sen U., Kaohsiung, 1998—, Nat. Kaohsiung Normal U., 1999—. Mem. Eighteenth Century Studies. Avocation: art deco. Office: Nat Sun Yat Sen U, Dept Fgn Lang, Kaohsiung 804, Taiwan

LEE, JAY HYUN, food company executive; b. Seoul, South Korea, Mar. 19, 1960; s. Meng Hi and Bok Nam (Sohn) L.; m. Hee Jae Kim, Apr. 1, 1984; children: Kyeong Hoo, Seon Ho. BA, Korea U., Seoul, 1984. Mgr. Citibank, Seoul, 1983-85; sr. mgr. Cheil Foods & Chem. Inc., Seoul, 1985-93; exec. dir. Samsung Electronic Co., Seoul, 1993; mng. dir. Cheil Jedang Corp., Seoul, 1993-97, v.p., 1997, vice chmn., 1997—. Recipient Global Leaders for Tomorrow award World Econ. Forum, Davos, Switzerland, 1996. Mem. Koryo Lions Club. Avocations: playing golf, watching movies, listening to music, writing oriental calligraphy. Home: #301 J-One Villa 107-1(2/8), Jangchoong-Dong, Chung-gu, Seoul South Korea Office: Cheil Jedang Corp, 500 5-ga, Namdaemoon-no, Seoul 100-095, South Korea

LEE, JECHUL, dean; b. Kumi, KyungPook, South Korea, Oct. 22, 1967; parents Inho Lee and Sangyoun Han; m. Kyunghee Kim, Jan. 27, 1991; children: Sungdong, Kyudong. Med. diploma, KyungPook Nat. U., 1990, M of Med. Sci., 1992, PhD, 1996. Tchg. asst. Sch. Medicine KyungPook Nat. U., Taegu, 1990-94; chmn. dept. microbiology Coll. Medicine Seonam U., NamWon/ChunPook, 1997—, dean Coll. Medicine, 1998—. Capt. South Korean mil., 1994-97. Grantee Korean Sci. Found., 1998, Korean Rsch. Found., 1998. Mem. Am. Soc. Microbiology, Korean Soc. Microbiology. Avocations: fishing, golf.

LEE, JEE WON, nuclear engineer educator; b. Kobe, Japan, Oct. 29, 1936; s. Won Bok and Bun Kyo (Kwon) L.; m. Heung Boon Ham, June 16, 1971; children: Hyun Mee, Sang Soo. BS in nuclear engr., Han Yang Univ., Seoul, 1963; MS in nuclear engr., Purdue Univ., 1967, PhD in nuclear engr., 1969. Instr. Han Yang Univ., 1970-71; part time instr. Kyong Hee Univ., Seoul, 1972-77, U S Army Edn. Ctr., Korea, 1978-80; asst. prof. DaeYoo Tech. Jr. Coll., Korea, 1978-82, assoc. prof., 1982-88, prof., 1988—; dir. computer ctr. Dae Yoo Coll., 1988-90, Coll. Libr., 1994-96. Author: Unix for Super Users, 1992, Computer Science An Overview, 1995; contbr. articles to profl. jours. With Korean Army Argumenteal U.S. Army, 1959-62. Recipient Citation Min. of Edn., 1990. Mem. IEEE. Avocations: bowling, jogging. E-mail: jwonlee@haksan.dsc.ac.kr. Home: Kang Dong Villa Na 203, Pung Nap Dong Song Pa Ka, Seoul Korea Office: Dong Seoul Coll, Bok Jung Dong 423 Kyong Ki Do, Sung Nam City Su Jung ku, Korea

LEE, JEN-JIANG, engineering executive; b. Taichung, Taiwan, China, June 13, 1952; s. Di-Sen and Lan-Jen Lee; m. Hai-In Wang, Dec. 10, 1983; children: Tiffany, Preston. BS, Nat. Taiwan U., 1974; MS, U. Fla., 1978; PhD, Stanford U., 1984. Staff engr. Motorola, Inc., Austin, 1984-89; process engring. mgr. SGS-Thomson Microelectronics Corp., Carrollton, Tex., 1989-94; process mgr. Lam Rsch. Corp., Fremont, Calif., 1994-95; process devel. mgr. Texas Instruments, Inc., Dallas, 1995-96; divsn. dir. United Microelectronics Corp., Hsin-Chu, Taiwan, 1996—. Deacon Austin Chinese Ch., 1988-89. Mem. IEEE. Achievements include co-patent Barrier Metal Formation for Sub-micron Integrated Circuits Fabrication. Fax: 886-3-592-2839. Office: United Microelectonics Corp, #3, Li-Hsin Rd 2, Hsin-Chu City 300, Taiwan

LEE, JIANN-DER, electrical engineer educator; b. Tainan, Taiwan, June 6, 1961; s. Lo-Jen and Shan (Wang) L.; m. In-Jen Chang, May 15, 1988; 3 children. MS, Nat. Cheng Kung Univ., Tainan, 1988, PhD, 1992. Instr. Kuna-Shan Tech., Tainan, 1988-92; assoc. prof. Chang Gung U., Tao-Yuan, Taiwan, 1992—; cons. Nan-Jung Elec. Co., 1988-92, Imaging Tech. Co., 1992—. Author: Introduction to Computer Science, 1991 (Best Textbook prize 1992). Recipient Best Paper award Acer Co., 1992, 99. Mem. IEEE, IAPR, N.Y. Acad. Scis. Office: Chang Gung U Dept Elec Engring, 259 Wen-Hua 1st Rd, 333 Tao-Yuan Taiwan

LEE, JIMMY CHE-YUNG, city planner; b. Canton, China, May 29, 1946; came to U.S., 1969.; s. Che Dui and Fong-Lee (Leung) L.; m. Annie On-lin Chan, Nov. 29, 1970 (div. 1987); m. Eileen Oi Ping Cheung, Dec. 16, 1987 (div. 1990); m. Sara Yeuk Siu, June 21, 1994. Grad., Sir. Robert Black Coll. Edn., Hong Kong; BA, U. Tex., 1973, MA, 1975. Tchr. English and Chinese Asbury Meth. Primary Sch., Hong Kong, 1966-69; asst. mgr. Trader Vic's Restaurant Dallas Hilton Inn, 1971-75; planner Dallas County Community Action Agy., 1975, dir. projects and resource devel. div., 1975—; pres. U-Asia Corp., Hong Kong, 1975; owner Dragon Inn Restaurant, 1975; contr. food and beverage div. Plaza of Am. Hotel, 1979-82; comptr. Carlyle Hotels & Restaurants Inc., Harold Farb Cos., 1982; founder, chief exec. officer Lee & Lee Fine Linens, Inc., 1982—; v.p. Asiatex Inc., 1987—, Titan Real Estate Devel. & Investment Group, Inc., 1993—; bd. dirs. Crown Chpt. Nat. Bank Dallas. Pres. North Tex. Cantonese Assn., 1986-88, hon. pres., 1989—; dir. Dallas chpt. Friends of Hong Kong and Macau; v.p., dir. North Tex. Chinese Culture Divination Soc. Mem. Am. Inst. Planners (assoc.), Tex. Assn. Community Action Agys., Hong Kong Registered Tchrs. Assn., Oakcliff C. of C. Baptist. Home: 10115 Chisholm Trl Dallas TX 75243-2511

LEE, JIN-HAK, ophthalmologist; b. Seoul, Korea, Oct. 11, 1945; s. Byung-Gi and Song-Mo (Chung) L.; m. Kyung-Eun Choo; children: Chae-Jin, Chae-Sun, Chae-Won. MD, Seoul Nat. U., 1972, PhD, 1981. Diplomate Nat. Bd. Ophthalmology. Intern Seoul Nat. U. Hosp., 1972-73, Resident in ophthalmology, 1973-77, from asst. to assoc. prof., 1983-93; instr. Seoul Nat. U., 1980-83, prof., 1993—, chmn., 1998—; dir. eye bank Seoul Nat. U. Hosp., 1985-95, dir. social work svc., 1995-96; dir. hosp. news monthly, 1996—. Author: Ophthalmology, 1986, Biological Science of Human, 1993; editor in chief Seoul Nat. U. Hosp. News Monthly, 1997—; mem. editl. bd. Korean Jour. Ophthalmology, 1989. Maj. Korean Air Force, 1977-81. Kresge Eye Inst. fellow, Detroit, 1983-84; named Med. Essayist of Yr., Euhak Shin-mun, 1995. Mem. Korean Ophthalmol. Soc., Am. Soc. Cataract and Refractive Surgery, Assn. for Rsch. in Vision and Ophthalmology. Methodist. Home: Apt Seo Hyun Dong, 216-1501 Sibum Woo Sung, 463-050 Sung Nam Republic of Korea Office: Seoul Nat Univ Hosp Dept Opthalmology, 28 Yeungun-Dong, 110-744 Seoul Republic of Korea

LEE, JIN-SUK, energy researcher; b. Seoul, Feb. 21, 1957; s. Yong-Seo and Ok-Ju (Kim) L.; m. Hye-Sung Cho, Jan. 7, 1989; 2 children. BS, Korea U., 1980, MS, 1982; PhD, Lehigh U., 1987. Sr. rschr. Korea Inst. Energy Rsch., Taejeon, 1987-98, prin. rschr., 1998—. Contbr. articles to profl. jours.; inventor in field. Recipient scholarship Korean Ministry Edn., 1982-87, fellowship Lehigh U., 1986-87. Mem. Internat. Solar Energy Soc. Avocations: sightseeing, mountain climbing, skiing, bowling. Office: KIER, 71-2 Jang-dong Yuseong-ku, 305-343 Taejeon Korea

LEE, JINTAE, computer science educator, researcher; b. Kangrim, Kangwondo, Korea, Dec. 12, 1957; s. Hag-Ui and Ok-Soon (Kim) L.; m. Hyun-Sook Kim, Aug. 18, 1990; children: John, Sung-Un. BS, Seoul (Korea) Nat. U., 1981; MS, Korea Advanced Inst. Sci. & Tech., Seoul, 1983; DSci, U. Tokyo, 1993. Cert. computer engr. level 1. Sr. rschr. Korea Inst. Sci. & Tech., Seoul, 1983-89; visiting rschr. George Washington U., Washington, 1998-99; assoc. prof. U. Aizu, Aizu-Wakamatsu, Japan, 1993—. Inventor modeled painting brush; contbr. articles to profl. jours. Recipient Excellent Rschr. award Syss. Engring. Rsch. Inst., Seoul, 1989. Mem. IEEE Computer Soc., Info. Processing Soc. Japan, Korea Info. Sci. Soc. Avocations: music, tennis, swimming. Home: C303 1-17-25 Matsunaga, Aizu-Wakamatsu 965-0001, Japan Office: U Aizu, Tsuruga, Ikki-machi, Aizu-Wakamatsu 965-8580, Japan

LEE, JIUNG, electrical engineer; b. Seoul, Korea, Sept. 27, 1968. BS, U. Wis., 1989, MS, 1991, PhD, 1996. Postdoctoral fellow Argonne (Ill.) Nat. Lab., 1996-97; integration engr. Micron Display Tech., Boise, Idaho, 1997—. Contbr. articles to profl. jours.; patents pending. Mem. IEEE, Soc. Info. Display. Office: Micron Display 3000 S Denver Way Boise ID 83705-5287

LEE, JOHN NING-YUEAN, academic administrator; b. Sept. 2, 1945; m. Ya Ling Wu; children: Ming Shu Lee, Ming Chia Lee. BS in Agr. Chemistry, Nat. Taiwan U., 1971, MS in Biochem. Nutrition, 1975, PhD in Biochem. Nutrition, 1978; postgrad., Kans. State U., 1981. Assoc. prof. Fu Jen Cath. U., Taipei, Taiwan, 1978-83, prof. dept. nutrition and food scis., 1983-89, dean Coll. of Human Ecology, 1994-2000, pres., 2000—; dean Office of Student Affairs Nat. Coll. of Phys. Edn. and Sports, Taiwan, 1990-94. Active numerous civic orgns. and pvt. enterprises. Fellow Assn. of Aerobic Exercises (ROC), Assn. of Sports Medicine (ROC), Chinese Home Econs. Soc., Assn. of Phys. Edn. (ROC); mem. Nutrition Soc. of Taiwan (pres.), Assn. of Food Scis. and Technology (ROC), Assn. of Biochemistry (ROC), Formosan Med. Assn. E-mail: fjdp2098@mails.fju.edu.tw. Office: Fu Jen Cath Univ, 510 Chung Cheng Rd, Hsinchung/Taipei Taiwan*

LEE, JONG SEH, civil engineering educator, researcher; b. Namwon, Korea, Oct. 31, 1954; s. Kyo Hwan and Hyo Nam (Ryu) L.; m. Kyung Sook Ore, Jan. 7, 1985; children: Brian Seohyun, Suemin Jasmine. BS, Yonsei U., Seoul, Korea, 1981; MS, U. Pa., 1983; PhD, Princeton U., 1988. Rsch. asst. U. Pa., Phila., 1981-83, Princeton (N.J.) U., 1983-88; asst. prof. Clarkson U., Potsdom, N.Y., 1988-94, assoc. prof., 1994-96, adj. rsch. prof., 1996—; prof. Hanyang U., Ansan, Korea, 1995—; chmn. Internat. Symposium on Mechanics of Electromagnetic Materials and Structures, Charlottesville, 1993; mem. internat. sci. com. Internat. Conf. on Structural Dynamics, Vibration, Noise and Control, '97, Hong Kong, 1995. Chief editor Mechanics of Electromagnetic Materials and Structures, 1993; editor Internat. Jour. Applied Electromagnetics and Mechanics, 1994—, Reliability, Stress Analysis and Failure Prevention Aspects of Composite and Active Materials, 1994; assoc. editor-in-chief Jour. Korean Soc. Civil Engrs., 1997—. Recipient fellowship Internat. Tel. & Telegraph/Inst. Internat. Edn., 1981, Initiation award NSF, 1989, rsch. grants NSF, 1992, 93, 94, 95. Mem. ASCE (sec. adv. composites com. 1994—, control group mem. elasticity com. 1995—), ASME (joint com. on constitutive equations 1992—, co-chmn. symposium at Internat. Mech. Engring. Congress and Expn. 1994), Earthquake Engring. Soc. Korea (bd. dirs. 1996—), Korea Computational Structural Engring. Inst. (bd. dirs. 1998—, sec. gen. 1998—), Korean Soc. Civil Engrs. (chmn. pub. rels. com. 1999—). Home: 14-108 Samho Apt, Seoul Republic of Korea Office: Hanyang Univ, 396 Daehak-Dong, Ansan 425-791, Republic of Korea

LEE, JONG-HO, electronics engineer; b. Kyungnam, Korea, Apr. 12, 1966; parents Ki-Yeon Lee and Zeung-Im Kim; m. Eun-Kyung Lee, Nov. 19, 1994; children: Dong-Jin, Kyung-Joo. BS, Kyungpook Nat. U., 1987; MS, Seoul Nat. U., 1989, PhD, 1993. Rsch. engr. Seoul Nat. U., 1993; instr. Wonkwang U., Iksan, Korea, 1994-95; postdoctoral rschr. MIT, Cambridge, Mass., 1988-99; asst. prof. Wonkwang U., 1996-2000; prof. Wonkwang U., Iksan, Korea, 2000—. Mem. IEEE, Korean Inst. Telematics & Electronics. Office: Wonkwang U Sch EE, 344-2 Shinyong-Dong, Iksan Korea 570-749

LEE, JONG-HYEON, computer and communications security researcher, mobile communications researcher; b. Seoul, Dec. 15, 1966; s. Sang-Rok and Soon-Ryeon (Kim) L.; m. Young-Hee Koo, Nov. 2, 1994; children: Seung-Yeon, Seung-Yoon. BS in Math., Sogang U., Seoul, 1989; MS in Math., Pohang Inst. Sci. and Tech., Korea, 1991; PhD in Computer Sci., U. Cambridge, Eng., 2000. Teaching asst. dept. math. Pohang (Republic of Korea) Inst. Sci. and Tech., 1989-91; rsch. asst. Computer Lab. U. Cambridge, 1998-99; computer asst. officer Newnham Coll., Cambridge, Eng., 1998-2000; mem. tech. staff mobile com. protocol sect., mobility mgmt. sect. Electronics and Telecom. Rsch. Inst., Taejon, Republic of Korea, 1991-96; sr. mem. tech. staff in mobility mgmt. sect. Electronics and Telecom. Rsch. Inst., Taejon, 1996-97; pres., CEO Filonet Corp., Vancouver, B.C., Can., 2000—; engring. cons. Mirae Corp., Cheon-an, Korea, 1994-99; co-founder SoftForum, Inc.; pres. Filonet Korea, Inc., Seoul, Korea, 2000—; mem. supervisory bd. ecom-monitor.com Inc., Czech Republic, 2000—. Author: (with Y-H Koo) Modern Cryptology, 1997, (with R.J. Anderson, B. Crispo, C. Manufavas, V. Matyas and F.A.P. Petitcolas) The Global Trust Register, 1998, The Global Internet Trust Register, 1999, (with S. Katzenbeisser and F.A.P. Petitcolas) Information Hiding Techniques for Steganography and Digital Watermarking, 2000; mem. editl. adv. bd. Computer & Communications Security Reviews (pub. by Anbar Electronic Intelligence), 1999-2000. Mem. AAAS, IEEE, Am. Math. Soc., Math. Assn. Am., Planetary Soc., Korean Inst. Comm. Scis., Soc. Indsl. and Applied Math, Cambridge Philosophical Soc., Assn. for Computing Machinery. Avocations: racquetball, tennis, mountain climbing, designing software package, swordsmanship (kendo). Home: Wolfson College, Univ Cambridge, Cambridge CB3 9BB, England Office: Filonet Corp, 500-666 Burrard St, Vancouver, BC Canada V6C 3P2

LEE, JONGMIN, physicist, researcher; b. Seoul, May 15, 1943; s. Yunsei and Toowol Lee; m. Youngsook Kim, Aug. 14, 1973; children: Eunjoo, Eunah, Sungho. BS, Seoul Nat. U., 1966, MS, 1970; PhD, Korea U., Seoul, 1980. Rsch. asst. Seoul Nat. U., 1966-68; lectr. Korea Mil. Acad., Seoul, 1970-73; dept. head Agy. for Def. Devel., Taejon, 1973-86; v.p. Korea Atomic Energy Rsch. Inst., Taejon, 1986—; vis. prof. Han Nam U., Taejon, 1990—, Chung Nam U., Taejon, 1994—, Korea U., Seoul, 1995—. Contbr. over 210 articles to profl. jours.; patentee in field. Decorated Mokryon for Nat. Outstanding Scientist, Korean Govt., 1991; named Outstanding Scientist of Yr., Ministry of Sci. and Tech., 1987; recipient Significant Achievements in Sci. award, 1989, Scientist of Month award Ministry Sci. and Tech., 1997. Fellow Korean Phys. Soc. (divsn. chmn. optics and quantum electronics 1992-94, Best Paper of Yr. 1985), Optical Soc. Korea (life, divsn. chmn., treas. 1994-96, v.p. 1997-99, pres. 2000—), Korean Nuclear Soc. (life); mem. Korean Inst. Telematics and Electronics (life), Korea Accelerator and Plasma Rsch. Assn. (gen. sec. 1990—), Korean Chem. Soc. (life), Korean Sensors Soc. (life), Laser Soc. Japan, Optical Soc. Am., European Optical Soc., Internat. Soc. Optical Engring. Avocation: amateur radio. Home: 393-15 Doryongdong, Yusongku Taejon 305-340, Republic of Korea Office: Korea Atomic Energy Rsch Inst, PO Box 105, Yusong Taejon 305-600, Republic of Korea

LEE, JOOH, business science educator; b. Seoul, Apr. 28, 1948; m. Rebecca C. Lee, Aug. 1987; 1 child, David M. MS in Mgmt., Colo. State U., 1982; PhD in Bus. Adminstrn., U. Miss., 1987. Prof., dept. chmn. Rowan U., Glassboro, N.J., 1988—. Mem. Phi Kappa Phi, Beta Gamma Sigma, Sigma Beta Delta. Methodist. Office: Rowan U Coll of Bus Glassboro NJ 08028

LEE, JOON-HYUN, engineering educator; b. Seoul, South Korea, May 15, 1956; s. Soo Kyung Lee and Bong Soon Ahn; m. Hyun Soon Kim, Dec. 30, 1984; children: Jeho, Keunho. BS, Pusan (Korea) Nat. U., 1983; MSc, Tohoku U., Sendai, Japan, 1985, PhD, 1988. Rsch. scientist Northwestern U., Evanston, Ill., 1988-90; asst. prof. Pusan Nat. U., 1990-94, assoc. prof., 1994—; guest rsch. prof. U. Wash., Seattle, 1993-94; vis. assoc. prof. Northwestern U., 1996-97; group leader Materials Strength Group, Pusan, 1990—; cons. LG Electronics Ltd., Changwon, Korea, 1997—, Hyundai Heavy Industry, Ulsan, Korea, 1994-97. Author: Statics, 1992; editor Procs. Internat. Workshop on Safety, 1995. Recipient Outstanding Asian Middle-Ager Rsch. award Japanese Soc. Materials Sci., 1997. Fellow Korea Soc. for Nondestructive Testing (Best Paper award 1994, divsn. chmn. 1994—); mem. Am. Soc. for Nondestructive Testing, AECM (internat. adv. com. 1992-94). Avocations: tennis, golf. Home: 103-1702 Dae-Rim Apt, Zwa-Dong Haeundae-Gu, Pusan 612-030, Korea Office: Pusan Nat U, Sch Mech Engring, Pusan 609-735, Korea

LEE, JOSEPH SHING, economics educator; b. Shanghai, China, Nov. 28, 1939; came to U.S., 1963; s. Winston D.K. and Annie (Liu) L.; m. Margaret Chen Lee, Oct. 30, 1966; children: Pauline Chen, Baldwin Joseph. BS, Nat. Taiwan U., 1962; MS, U. Mass., 1966, PhD, 1970. Instr. Gannon U., Erie, Pa., 1968-70; asst. prof. Mankato (Minn.) State U., 1970-72, assoc. prof., 1972—, prof. econs., 1975—; vis. prof. Nat. Taiwan U., 1973-74; cons. China Steel Corp., Taiwan, 1980; dir. Ctr. Internat. Labor Studies, 1989—; trustee Found. for Rsch. on Open Space, Taiwan, 1990—; v.p. Chung-Hua Inst. for Econ. Rsch., Taiwan, 1992. Bd. dirs. Inter-Faculty Orgn., St. Paul, 1986-90; vis. rsch. fellow Inst. of Econs., Academia Sinica, Taiwan, 1991-92. Mem. Am. Econs. Assn., Indsl. Relations Res. Assn., Internat. Indsl. Relations Assn. Home: 5224 Lochloy Dr Minneapolis MN 55436-2024

LEE, JOUNG-BINN, minister of foreign affairs and trade; b. Dec. 16, 1937; married; 2 children. Law degree, Seoul (Korea) Nat. U., 1960. With Min. Fgn. Affairs, 1959—, 3d sec. Korean Embassy to Swiss Confedn., 1965-70, dir. edn. and tng. divsn. Inst. Fgn. Affairs, 1970-71, dir. mid. divsn., 1974-76, dir. UN divsn., 1976-78, dir.-gen. policy coord. office planning and mgmt., 1978, dir. gen. Mid. East Affairs Bur., 1979-80, asst. min. polit. affairs, 1989-91, chancellor Inst. Fgn. Affairs and Nat. Security, 1995-96; 1st sec. Korean Permanent Observer Mission UN, N.Y.C., 1970; consul-gen. Korean Consulate Gen., Chgo., 1980-83; ambassador extraordinary and pleinpotentiary Kingdom of Nepal, 1983; ambassador extraordinary and plenipotentiary Sweden, 1986-89, Republic of India, 1991-95; sec. for polit. affairs Pres. of Korea, 1984-86. Pres. Korea Found., 1998. Recipient Diplomatic Order 2d class Kuwait, 1980, King Abdul Aziz medal of Saudi Arabia, 1980, Commdr. Grand Cross, Royal Order of Polar Star of Sweden, 1989, Order of Svc. Merit with yellow stripes, 1998. Office: Min Fgn Affairs and Trade, San 8 Hannam-dong, Yongsan-ku Seoul Korea*

LEE, JU-HONG, engineering educator; b. Tou Cheng, Taiwan, Dec. 7, 1952; s. Ching-Jung and A-Sen (Fong) L.; m. Shiow-Huey Liaw, Dec. 30, 1989; children: Song-Ya, Wang-Hsin. BS, Nat. Cheng-Kung U., 1975; MS, Nat. Taiwan U., 1977; PhD, Rensselaer Polytech. Inst., 1984. Vis. assoc. prof. Nat. Taiwan U., Taipei, 1984-86, assoc. prof., 1986-89, prof., 1989—; vis. prof. U. Md., Balt., 1996—. Contbr. articles to profl. jours. Recipient Outstanding Rsch. award Nat. Sci. Coun., 1992, 93, 94, Disting. Rsch. award, 1999, 99. Avocations: music, reading, gardening, jogging. Office: Dept Elec Engring, Nat Taiwan Univ, Taipei 106, Taiwan

LEE, JUNGHO, botanist, researcher; b. Seoul, Sept. 4, 1958; s. Suk-Bong Lee and Pyung-Sook Kang; m. Sun-Young Rieh, May 3, 1994; children: Lee, Yonu. BS in Agr., Seoul Nat. U., 1982, MSc in Horticultural Sci., 1984, BA in Botany, 1989; MA in Botany, U. Tex., 1994; PhD in Botany, Tex. A&M U., 1997. Postdoctoral fellow Tex. A&M U., College Station, 1998, U. Zurich, Switzerland, 1998-2000, U. Mass., Amherst, 2000—. 2d lt. Samsa Mil. Acad., 1984-85. Mem. AAAS, Am. Soc. Plant Taxonomy, Phycol. Soc. Am. Office: Biology Dept, Univ Massachusetts, 8008 Amherst Switzerland

LEE, JUNG-HOON, electrical engineer, educator; b. Pohang, South Korea, Feb. 1, 1966; s. Sang-Su Lee and Wall-Sun Baek. BSc, Kyoungpook Nat. U., 1988; MS, Korea Advanced Inst. Sci. Tech., Seoul, 1990; PhD, Korea Applied Inst. Sci. Tech., Taejon, 1995. Rsch. asst. Korea Advanced Inst. Sci. & Technology, Taejon, 1990-92; prof. Gyeongsang Nat. U., Chinju, Korea, 1995—. Avocations: cinema, squash. Home: 249-3 Sang Dae-Ri, ChoungHa-Moon Book-kug, Pohang City Kyeong 791-920, South Korea Office: Gyeongsang Nat U, 900 Gazwa-dong, Chinju South Korea 660-701

LEE, JYH-JONE, mechanical engineering researcher; b. Tainan, Taiwan, Oct. 7, 1960; s. Chun-shen and Jwo-In (Lin) L.; m. Sunny Lu, Apr. 2, 1994; 1 child, Ya-Chi. BS in Mech. Engring., Cheng-Kung U., Tainan, 1982, MS in Mech. Engring., 1984; PhD in Mech. Engring., U. Md., 1991. Instr. Army Mil. Sch., Feng-Sun, Taiwan, 1984-86; assoc. rschr. Mech. Industry Rsch. Lab, Indsl. Tech. Rsch. Inst., Hsin Chu, Taiwan, 1986; rsch. asst. U. Md., College Park, 1987-91; rsch. engr. Mech. Industry Rsch. Lab, Indsl. Tech. Rsch. Inst., 1991-94, project leader, 1994-98; asst. prof. Dept Mechanical Engrg., Nat. Taiwan Univ., Taipei, Taiwan, 1998—. Contbr. articles to scientific jours.; inventor, internat. patentee in field. Mem. Chinese Soc. Mech. Engrs. Avocations: swimming, classical music. Home: 2F-1 # 56 Lane 269, Roosevelt Rd Sect 3, 116 Taipei Taiwan Office: ME Dept Nat Taiwan Univ, 1 Roosevelt Rd Sec 4, Taipei 106, Taiwan

LEE, KANG S., artist, educator; b. Seoul, Korea, June 5, 1937; came to U.S., 1967; d. Kee Young and Young Sook (Choy) L.; m. Frank James Sheppard (dec. 1990); m. James C. Brown, Apr. 17, 1999. BFA, Univ. Hong Ik, Seoul, 1963; postgrad., Univ. Colo., 1968-70; MA, Univ. Phoenix, 1989. Cert. tchr. Mgr. advt., presentation J.C. Penney, Colorado Springs, 1970-79; dist. merchandise presentation mgr. J.C. Penney, Denver, 1980-85; prof. Pikes Peak C.C., Colorado Springs, 1991—; prof. Univ. Colo., Colorado Springs, 1992—; chairperson bd. dirs. Sheppard Arts Inst. and World Culture Ctr., Colorado Springs, 1998—. Exhibited in group shows Nat. Art Exhibition, Seoul, 1962-66 (Creative Excellence awards); one-woman shows include Ft. Carson Gallery, 1967, Colo. Coll., 1968, J.C. Penney Gallery, 1972, 73, 75. Judge mktg. and distributive edn. Colo. and Nat., 1975-86; v.p. Friendship Force Internat., 1990-98, pres., 1998; coord. Internat. Cultural Celebration, Colorado Springs, 1993-95; mem. Common Ground Arts and Cultural, Colorado Springs, 1994—, sr. adv. com. colorado Springs, 1995—; deacon First Presbyn. Ch., Colorado Springs; sr. svcs. adv. com. Colo. Springs Sr. Ctr., Colorado Springs. Recipient 6 Corporation awards, 1974-79. Republican. Avocations: nature, birds, animals, plants, gardening. Home: 4590 Kashmire Dr Colorado Springs CO 80920-7616

LEE, KANG YONG, mechanical engineering educator; b. Busan, South Korea, Jan. 19, 1947; s. Koon Hyung and Doo Yun Lee; m. Un Soo Cheong, Feb. 27, 1973; children: Seung Yon, Jae Won. BS, Yonsei U., Seoul, South Korea, 1969, MS, 1971; PhD, W.Va. U., 1978. From asst. prof. to prof.

Yonsei U., 1980—, assoc. dean, 1989-91; mem. editl. bd. Material Sci. Forum, Switzerland, 1996—. Author: Introduction to Elasticity and Plasticity, 1993, Material Behavior of Material, 1994; editor: Fracture and Strength '90, 1991; editor-in-chief newsletter Yonsei Prof. Coun., 1994-96. chmn. exec. com. Fracture and Strength, Seoul, 1990. Mem. Korean Soc. Mech. Engrs. (gen. sec. 1993, acad. prize 1988, v.p. 2000—), Korean Soc. Automotive Engrs. (chmn. com. car body in Korea 1995-96, 99—), Korean Soc. for Nondestructive Testing (auditor 2000—), Nat. Acad. Engring. Korea (assoc.). Avocations: travel, mountain-climbing. Office: Yonsei U, Dept Mech Engring, Seoul 120-749, South Korea

LEE, KA-SUEN, electronic engineer, researcher; b. Hong Kong, Jan. 13, 1969; s. Hung Lee and Ping-Sin Lo. BSc in Applied Physics, Hong Kong Bapt. U., 1993; MPhil in Electronic Engring., Chinese U. Hong Kong, 1995, PhD in Electronic Engring., 1998. Rsch. asst. Sylva Industries Ltd., Hong Kong, 1989; engr. trainee Respironics (H.K.) Ltd., Hong Kong, 1990; grad. asst. Chinese U. Hong Kong, 1993-98, postdoctoral fellow dept. electronic engring., 1999; vis. scholar Chinese U. Hong Kong, 2000; electro-optics designer JDS Uniphase Corp. Hdqs., Can., 2000—. jour. reviewer, Inst. Elec. Engrs. (IEE), U.K., 1998, 2000, Chapman and Hall, U.K., 1999, Elsevier Sci., The Netherlands, 1999. Contbr. articles to profl. jours. Mem. IEEE, Optical Soc. Am., Hong Kong Profl. Tchrs. Union. Avocations: classical music, photography, hiking, tennis. Office: JDS Uniphase Corp, 570 West Hunt Club Rd, Ottawa, Canada K2G 5W8

LEE, KELLEY, international health researcher; b. Vancouver, B.C., Can., May 5, 1962; arrived in U.K., 1986; d. Monty M.Y. and Elizabeth B.Q. (Mah) L.; m. Andrew Scott Gilmore, July 16, 1994; children: Jennifer Anne Lee Gilmore, Alexander Scott Lee Gilmore. BA in Internat. Rels. and English Lit., U. B.C., Vancouver, 1984; MPA, U. Victoria, Can., 1986; MA in Internat. Rels., U. Sussex, Brighton, Eng., 1987, DPhil in Internat. Rels., 1992. Rsch. officer Ministry of Lands, Parks and Housing, Govt. of B.C., 1985, Dept. Consumer and Corp. Affairs, Govt. of Can., 1986; tutor internat. rels. Sch. European Studies U. Sussex, Eng., 1989; rsch. fellow dept. pub. health and policy London Sch. Hygiene and Tropical Medicine, U. London, 1992-94, sr. lectr. global health policy, 1994—; lectr. in field; external examiner, vis. lectr., Liverpool Sch. Tropical Medicine, U. Liverpool, 1995—; vis. lectr. Ctr. Rsch. on Drugs and Health Behavior Charing Cross Hosp., London, 1994-98; chair WHO scientific adv. group on globalization and health, 1999—. Author: (with others) Cooperation for Health Development: Extrabudgetary Funded in the World Health Organization, 1995, Cooperation for Health Development: The World Health Organisation's Support to Programmes at Country Level, 1997, Global Telecommunications Regulation: A Political Economy Perspective, 1995, Historical Dictionary of the World Health Organization, 1998; contbr. numerous articles to profl. publs., chpts. to books. Scholar U. Victoria, 1985-86, Queen Elizabeth II B.C. Centennial scholar, 1986-88; doctoral fellow Social Scis. and Humanities Rsch. Coun. Can., 1986-89, postdoctoral fellow, 1993-95; grantee UN Population Fund, 1994-95, Econ. and Social Rsch. Coun. U.K., 1994-97, Govts. Australia, Can., Italy, Norway, Sweden and U.K., 1996-97, ODA/ESCOR, 1997, WHO-Internat. Clearinghouse on Health Sector REform, 1997. Fellow Royal Soc. for Protection of Birds; mem. Brit. Internat. Studies Assn., Acad. Coun. UN Sys., Internat. Studies Assn. Office: London Sch Hygiene/Trop Med, Keppel St, London WC1E 7HT, England

LEE, KI-NAM, medical educator; b. Pusan, South Korea, Mar. 29, 1956; parents Byung-Yong Lee and Kae-Wha Kim; m. Ju-Ri Jeong, Jan. 25, 1985; 1 child, Seong-Eun. MB, Pusan Nat. U., 1981, MM, 1984, PhD, 1991. Cert. in medicine. Dir. Chinju (South Korea) Med. Ctr., 1985-90; asst. prof. Dong-A U. Coll. Medicine, Pusan, 1991-94, assoc. prof., 1996—; rsch. fellow U. Calif., San Francisco, 1995-96. Contbr. papers to profl. jours. Capt. Army, 1985-88. Mem. Soc. Thoracic Radiology, Korean Radiol. Soc., Korean Soc. Thoracic Radiology, Pusan Radiol. Soc. (sec.). Avocations: golf, mountain climbing. Fax: 051 253 4931. E-mail: kinamlee@chollian.net. Home: 102-1108 Bando Bora Apt, Dangni-Dong, Saha-Ku Pusan 604-010, South Korea Office: Dong-A U Coll Medicine, 3-1 Ga Seo-Ku, Pusan 602-040, South Korea

LEE, KIYONG, linguistics educator; b. Cheju, Republic of Korea, July 19, 1937; s. Sanghoon Lee and Sook Park; m. Jungja Ha, Jan. 12, 1969; children: Sue-en, Ghang, Jeun. AB, St. Louis U., 1963; MA, Chonnam Nat. U., Kwangju, Republic of Korea, 1967; PhD, U. Tex., Austin, 1974. Assoc. prof. linguistics Chung-Ang U., Seoul, Republic of Korea, 1977-82; prof. linguistics Korea U., Seoul, Republic of Korea, 1982—; dir. Rsch. Inst. Lang. and Info., Korea U., 1993-95; dir. Audio-Visual Edn. Ctr., Korea U., 1988-89; Fulbright vis. scholar, CSLI, Stanford (Calif.) U., 1989; vis. prof. Tenri U., Japan, 1998-99; mem. rev. com. on Korean lang. and info. Republic of Korea Ministry Info. and Tourism, chmn., 1997-2001. Author: On Montague Grammar, 1985, Language and the World: Formal Semantics, 1998, Tense and Modality: Possible Worlds Semantics, 1998, Situation and Information: Situation Semantics, 1998, Computational Morphology, 1999; co-author: Introduction to English Grammar: Generative Grammar, 1986, A Basic Study for the Design and Applications of Korean Database, 1995, Computational Semantis and Its Applications, 1996. Deutscher Akademischer Austauschdienst e.V. scholar, Erlangen-Nürnberg U., 1994. Mem. Linguistic Soc. Korea (pres. 1990-92), Korean Soc. Cognitive Sci. (pres. 1989-90). Home: Banpo apt 62-105, Banpo-bon-dong, Socho-gu, Seoul 137-049, Republic of Korea Office: Korea U Dept Linguistics, Anam-dong, Songbuk-gu, Seoul 136-701, Republic of Korea

LEE, KI-YOUNG, research scientist; b. Seoul, Republic of Korea, Jan. 1, 1958; s. Hwoe-Soon Lee and Jung-Sook Jung; m. Eun-Ae Jang, Sept. 19, 1987; 2 children. BS, Seoul Nat. U., 1981; MS, Korea Advanced Inst. Sci/Tech., 1983; postgrad., U. Vt., 1993; PhD, U. Newcastle (Australia), 1994. Materials sci. engr. Sect. mgr. Daewoo Heavy Industries Ltd., Incheon, Republic of Korea, 1983-89; vis. scientist KFA-IFF, Jülich, Germany, 1992; rsch. scientist KAIST, Taejon, Republic of Korea, 1994-95; prin. rsch. scientist Battery Rsch. Inst. LG Chem. Rsch. Park, Taejon, 1996—. Recipient LG Rsch. and Devel. award, 1999, Chang Young Shil award, 1999. Office: LG Chem Rsh Park, 104-1 Moonji-Dong, Yusong Taejon 305-380, Republic of Korea

LEE, KUAN YEW, Singapore government official; b. Singapore, Sept. 16, 1923; s. Lee Chin Koon and Chua Jim Neo; m. Kwa Geok Choo, 1950; 3 children. Student, Raffles Coll., Singapore; BA with spl. distinction, Cambridge (Eng.) U., 1949; LLD (hon.), Royal U. Cambodia, 1965, Hong Kong U., 1970, U. Liverpool, 1971; LL.D. (hon.), U. Sheffield, 1971. Barrister-at-law, hon. bencher Middle Temple, London, 1969. Adv., solicitor, 1951—; sec.-gen. People's Action Party, 1954-92; prime minister Govt. of Singapore, 1959-90, sr. minister Prime Minister's Office, 1990—; adv. trade unions, 1952; Singapore rep. to Parliament of Malaysia, 1963-65; elected to bur. Socialist Internat., 1967; mem. internat adv. coun. Inst. Internat. Studies. Decorated companion of Honour, 1970, grand cross Order St. Michael and St. George, U.K., 1972, Bintang Adi Pradana (Indonesia), 1973, Order of Sikatuna (Philippines), 1974, Most Hon. Order of the Crown of Johore, 1984; named Hon. Freeman, City of London, 1982; Hon. fellow, Fitzwilliam Coll., Cambridge, 1969. Avocations: jogging, swimming. Office: Prime Minister's Office, Istana Annexe Orchard Rd, Singapore 238823, Singapore*

LEE, KUN CHANG, management information systems educator; b. Taejon, Republic of Korea, Apr. 2, 1959; s. Hyuk Lee and Kyung Bong Hwang; m. Sun Yang Kwon; children: Lee Eun Sung, Lee Jae Sung, Lee Min Sung. BA, Sung Kyun Kwan U., Seoul, Republic of Korea, 1982; MS, Korea Advanced Inst. Sci. Tech., Seoul, 1984, PhD, 1988. Dir. BoRam Investment Mgmt. Co., Seoul, 1988-90; assoc. prof. Kyonggi U., Suwon, Republic of Korea, 1990-94; prof. Sung Kyun Kwan U., Seoul, 1995—; reviewer Fuzzy Sets and Sys., 1988—. Author: Accounting Information Systems, 1998, Management Information Systems, 1999; contbr. articles to profl. jours. including Decision Support Sys., Expert Sys., Intelligent Sys. in Acctg. Fin. and Mgmt. Mem. Christian Univ. Fellow Laborers Assn. Mem. IEEE, Assn. Computing Machinery. Avocations: reading, climbing. Home: Chu Yop 2 Dong, Koyang Korea Office: Sung Kyun Kwan U Sch Bus, Hong Kong U Sci and Tech, Clear Water Bay Hong Kong

LEE, KUN-HEE, executive; b. Taegu, Korea, Jan. 9, 1942; m. Ra Hee Hong Lee; 4 children. Degree in econs., Waseda U., Tokyo, 1965; MBA, George Washington U., 1966. With Tong-Yang Boradcasting Corp., Korea, 1966-78; vice chmn. Samsung Corp., Korea, 1978-87; chmn. Samsung Group, Korea, 1987-98, Samsung Elecs. Co., Korea, 1997—; vice chmn. Korea-Japan Econ. Com., 1981—; vice chmn. Fedn. Korean Industries, 1987—. Author: Read the World, with Your Own Thinking, 1997. Dir. Korean Youth Assn., 1982—; chmn. Korea Sports Assn. for Disabled, 1998—; hon. pres. Korean Amateur Wrestling Fedn., 1997—, pres., 1982-96; hon. pres. Korean Olympic Com., 1996—; mem. Internat. Olympic Com., 1996—, Korean Organizing Com. for 2002 FIFA World Cup, Korea/Japan, 1996—. Avocations: gold, equestrian sports, table tennis, movies, classical music. Office: Samsung Group, 250 Taepyung-10 2-ka, Seoul 100-742, Korea*

LEE, KUN-HONG, chemical engineering educator; b. Milyang, Kyungbuk, Republic of Korea, Nov. 23, 1956; s. Chung-Soon and Kyung-Ok Lee; m. Hee Sook Chung, 1982; children: Young Hwa, Tae Hee. BS, Seoul Nat. U., Republic of Korea, 1979; MS, Kaist, Seoul, 1981; PhD, U. Del., 1986. Process engr. Chon Engring. Co., Seoul, 1981-82; postdoctoral fellow U. Del., Newark, 1987-88; asst. prof. Pohang (Republic of Korea) U. of Sci. and Tech., 1987-92, assoc. prof., 1992-2000, prof., 2000—; vis. scientist U. Dortmund, Germany, 1986; vis. prof. Kyushu U., Fukuoka, Japan, 1992; invited prof. INRS-Energie et Materiaux, Varennes, Can., 1995—. Recipient Simgang award Korean Inst. Chem. Engrs., 1993. Mem. AAAS, AIChE, Korean Inst. Chem. Engrs. (edtl. bd. 1993—, life), Membrane Soc. Korea (life), MRS, Electrochem. Soc., Korean Sensor Soc. (life), Am. Carbon Soc. Avocations: skiing, travel, mountain climbing. Office: Pohang U Sci and Tech, San 31 Hyoja-dong, Pohang Kyungbuk, Republic of Korea

LEE, KUNWOO, mechanical engineer, educator, consultant; b. Seoul, Korea, Dec. 11, 1955; s. Chongho and Soonwan (Jeung) L.; m. Whaae Koo, June 4, 1979; children: Young-hee, Young-eun, Sang-hyun. BS, Seoul (Korea) Nat. U., 1978; MS, MIT, 1981, PhD, 1984. Rsch. asst. MIT, Cambridge, 1980-83; asst. prof. U. Ill., Urbana, 1984-86; asst. prof. Seoul Nat. U., 1986-90, assoc. prof., 1990-95; vis. assoc. prof. MIT, 1993-94; prof. Seoul Nat. U., 1995—. Author: (in Korean) Mechanical Drafting, 1992, (in Korean) Computer Graphics and CAD, 1994, (in English) Principles of CAD/CAM/CAE Systems, 1999; contbr. articles to profl. jours. With Korean Army, 1978-79. Recipient Bak Am Paper award Korea Soc. Mech. Engrs., 1987. Mem. Soc. CAD/CAM Engrs. Korea (v.p. 1995—), Korean Fedn. Sci. and Tech. Socs. (dir. 1996—), Korean Soc. Precision Engring., 1996—. Achievements include patent in clamping device for rotary table. Office: Seoul Nat Univ San 56-1, Shinlim-Dong Kwanak-Gu, 151-742 Seoul Republic of Korea

LEE, KYOUNG, microbiologist, educator; b. Namji, Kyongnam, Korea, Aug. 20, 1962; s. Sam-Suk Lee and Duk-Man Kim; m. Hyo-Kyung Lee; children: Inwon, Ha-Min. BS, Seoul (Korea) Nat. U., 1985; MS, Korea Advanced Inst. Sci. & Tech., Seoul, 1987; PhD, U. Iowa, 1995. Rsch. scientist Korea Inst. Sci. and Tech., Seoul, 1987-90; postdoctoral rschr. U. Iowa, Iowa City, 1996-97; asst. prof. Changwon (Korea) Nat. U., 1997—. Contbr. articles to profl. jours. Grantee Korea Sci. and Engring. Found., 1999, Korea Rsch. Found., 1999. Fellow Korean Soc. for Applied Microbiology, Microbiol. Soc. of Korea; mem. Am. Soc. Microbiology. Avocations: tennis, mountain climbing, reading. Office: Changwon Nat U, 9 Sarim-dong, Changwon Kyongnam 641-773, Korea

LEE, LANSING BURROWS, JR., lawyer, corporate executive; b. Augusta, Ga., Aug. 27, 1919; s. Lansing Burrows and Bertha (Barrett) L.; s. Natalie Krug, July 4, 1943; children: Melinda Lee Clark, Lansing Burrows III, Bothwell Graves, Richard Hancock. BS, U. Va., 1939; postgrad., U. Ga. Sch. Law, 1939-40; JD, Harvard U., 1948. Bar: Ga. 1947. Corp. officer Ga.-Carolina Warehouse & Compress Co., Augusta, 1957-89, pres., CEO; co-owner Ga.-Carolina Warehouse; pvt. practice, Augusta. Chmn. bd. trustees James Brice White Found., 1962—; sr. warden Episcopal Ch., also chancellor, lay min.; sr. councillor Atlantic Coun. U.S.; bd. dirs. Med. Coll. Ga. Found. Capt. USAAF, 1942-46. Fellow Am. Coll. Trust and Estate Counsel; mem. Ga. Bar Found., Harvard U. Law Sch. Assn. Ga. (pres. 1966-67), Augusta Bar Assn. (pres. 1966-67), Soc. Colonial Wars Ga., State Bar Ga. (former chmn. fiduciary law sect.), U.S. Supreme Ct. Hist. Soc., U. Va. Thomas Jefferson Soc. Alunni, Internat. Order t. Luke the Physician, Augusta Country Club, Harvard Club Atlanta, President's Club Med. Coll. Ga. Office: First Union Bank Bldg 699 Broad St Ste 904 Augusta GA 30901-1448

LEE, LESLIE WARREN, marketing executive, public speaker; b. Mpls., Nov. 21, 1949; s. Adolph Orlando and Eunice Celia (Akerson) L.; m. Kathleen Karen Frie, June 2, 1973; children: Megan Christine, Maren Elisabeth, Matthew Warren. BA in History magna cum laude, Augsburg Coll., Mpls., 1971. CLU, ChFC. Dir. YMCA, Mpls., 1971-73; dist. sales mgr. Chrysler Mtr. Corp., Marshfield, Wis., 1973-75; agt. Northwestern Mut. Life, Marshfield, 1975-81; mgr. advanced underwriting The Rural Cos., Madison, Wis., 1981-83; advanced life mktg. specialist Am. Family Ins., Madison, 1983-95; nat. sales dir., v.p. mktg. Flexsystem, Madison, 1995-98; instr. Dept. Bus., U. Wis., Madison, 1981-82, Dept. Econs., U. Wis., Stevens Point, 1978-81; lectr. in field; cons. in litigation involving life ins. Mem. Nat. Assn. Inst. & Fin. Advisors, Madison Assn. Life Underwriters, Nat. Spkrs. Assn., Nat. Assn. Ins. and Fin. Advisors, Wis. Profl. Spkrs. Assn., Soc. Fin. Svc. Profls. Republican. Lutheran. Avocation: philately. Office: Motivation and Tng for Arena Life PO Box 620305 7522 E Hampstead Ct Middleton WI 53562-3609

LEE, LEWIS SWIFT, lawyer; b. Dallas, Nov. 19, 1933; '. Lenoir Valentine and Margaret Louise (Clendon) L.; m. Frances Ann Childress, Mar. 16, 1956; children; Frances Ann Lee Webb, Lewis S. Jr., George Childress, Lenoir Valentine Lee II. AB, U. South, 1955; postgrad., Washington & Lee U., 1954-55; MA, Emory U., 1956, JD, 1960. Bar: Fla. 1960, U.S. Dist. Ct. (so. and mid. dists.) Fla., U.S. Ct. Appeals (5th and 11th cirs.). Trainee Citizens & So. Nat. Bank, Atlanta, 1956, 58-59; assoc. Adair, Ulmer, Murchison, Kent & Ashby, Jacksonville, Fla., 1960-63; shareholder Ulmer, Murchison, Ashby & Ball, Jacksonville, 1963-95; of counsel LeBoeuf, Lamb, Greene & MacRae, LLP, Jacksonville, 1996-99, Martin, Ade, Birchfield & Mickler, PA, Jacksonville, 2000—; gen. counsel Fla. Rock Industries, Inc., Jacksonville, 1972—, Patriot Transp. Holdings, Inc., Jacksonville, 1989—; dir. Fla. Sch. Book Depository, Jacksonville, 1990—. 1st lt. AUS, 1956-58. Mem. ABA, Jacksonville Bar Assn., Ponte Vedra Inn & Club, Timuquana Country Club, Fla. Yacht Club, The River Club, The Heritage Club. Republican. Epsicopalian. Avocations: hiking, skiing, swimming, hunting, travel. Home: 3733 Ortega Blvd Jacksonville FL 32210-4347 Office: Martin Ade Birchfield & Mickler PA One Independent Sq Ste 3000 Jacksonville FL 32202

LEE, LIANG-SUN, chemical engineering educator; b. Chaotun, Nantou, Taiwan, Mar. 10, 1943; s. Chao-Kon and A-lan (Chang) L.; m. Ping Chen, Jan. 19, 1947; 1 child. BS, Nat. Taiwan U., 1965, MS, 1969; PhD, U. Okla., 1973. Assoc. prof. Nat. Ctrl. U., Chungli, Taiwan, 1976-80, dept. head, 1981-86, prof., 1980—, vice dean Engring. Coll., 1999—; vis. scholar MIT, Cambridge, Mass., 1985-86, Purdue U., West Lafayette, Ind., 1986; dir. Energy Conservation Task Force, Taipei, Taiwan, 1988-91; cons. Indsl. Tehc. Rsch. Inst., Hsinchu, Taiwan, 1995—. Contbr. articles to profl. jours. Advisor Dem. Progress Party, Taoyan, Taiwan, 1999. 2d lt. Taiwan Army, 1965-66. Mem. Chinese Inst. Engrs., Chinese Inst. Chem. Engrs. (v.p. 1997-98). Avocations: classical music, reading, tennis. Office: Nat Ctrl U, Dept Chem Engring, Chungli 32054, Taiwan

LEE, LOU-CHUANG, dean, science educator. Dean coll. sci. Nat. Cheng Kung U., Tianan City, Taiwan. Fax: 886-6-237-8377. Office: Nat Cheng Kung U, 1 Ta-Hsueh Rd, Tainan City Taiwan*

LEE, LUNG-SHENG, industrial technology educator, government adviser; b. Nantou, Taiwan, Republic of China, May 15, 1954; s. Chiou-Ming and Yuh-Shiow (Chang) L.; m. Chun-Chin Lai, Mar. 29, 1980; children: Yu-Hao, I-Chia. BS, Nat. Taiwan Normal U., Taipei, 1978, MS, 1980; PhD, Ohio State U., 1991. Tchr. Taiwan Provincial Tauyuan Sr. Vocat. Sch., 1977-78; instr. Nat. Taipei Inst. Tech., 1982-84; instr. Nat. Taiwan Normal U., Taipei, 1984-86, assoc. prof., 1986-93, prof., 1993—; sec. gen. Indsl. Tech. Edn. Assn., Taiwan, 1995—; adviser Ministry Edn., Taiwan, 1997—. Author: Issues in Technology Education and Vocational Education, 1996, Trends in Technology Education and Vocational Education, 1997, Prospect of Technology Education and Vocational Education, 1998, Outlook of Technology Education and Vocational Education, 1999, Cross-Century of Technology and Vocational Education, 1999, Promotion of Technology and Workforce Education, 2000—; author, chief editor: Technol. and Vocat. Edn., 1996—; chief editor Living Tech. Edn. Monthly, 1995—. 2d lt. Taiwan Army Ordnance, 1980-82. Mem. ASCD, Chinese Vocat. Edn. Assn. (standing trustee), Assn. Curriculum and Instrn. (trustee), Internat. Tech. Edn. Assn. (Leader to Watch award 1996), Am. Career and Tech. Assn., Phi Tau Phi. Buddhist. Avocations: reading, jogging, music. Office: Nat Taiwan Normal U Indsl, 162 Hoping E Rd Sec 1, 106 Taipei Taiwan, Republic of China

LEE, MARCIA ELLEN, insurance agent; b. Framingham, Mass., Mar. 27, 1949; d. Robert F. and Lois Ann (Walker) Reeves; m. William G.T. Lee, Nov. 8, 1994. Grad. high sch., Scotia, N.Y. Cert. gen. agt.; acredited customer svc. rep.; errors and omissions cert. trainer. Account exec. Nat. Mortgage and Fin. Co. Ltd., Honolulu, 1980-82; ind. ins. agt. Ins. Specialist of Hawaii, Inc., Honolulu, 1982-89, Beck, Kudlich & Swartman, Inc., Honolulu, 1989-90; pres., mgr. Mutual Gen. Underwriters, Inc., Honolulu, 1990-95; area mgr., gen. agt., regional mgr. Conseco Health Ins. Co., Honolulu, 1995—; exec. v.p. Internat. Ins. Alliance, Inc. Pres. Kapiolani Jaycees, Honolulu, 1984-86; trustee Honolulu Theater for Youth, 1997—. Recipient Warrior Club Recruitment award Hawaii Jaycees, Honolulu, 1984, 85; named 1st female chpt. pres. Hawaii Jaycees, Honolulu, 1984, pres. of month, 1985, Outstanding Young Woman of Am., 1985, ABI Woman of Yr., 1992; Po'okela award Hawaii State Theatre Coun., 1998. Mem. Hawaii Ind. Ins. Agts. Assn. (conv. chmn. 1987-89, edn. chmn. 1989-91, v.p. 1990, pres.-elect 1991, pres. 1992, Disting. Svc. award 1989), Honolulu Execs. Assn., Amb. Coun. Plz. Club. Avocations: golfing, walking, knitting. Address: Marcia E Lee Assocs 3210 Wauke St Honolulu HI 96815-4449

LEE, MARGARET ANNE, psychotherapist, social worker; b. Scribner, Nebr., Nov. 23, 1930; d. William Christian and Caroline Bertha (Benner) Joens; m. Robert Kelly Lee, May 21, 1950 (div. 1972); children: Lawrence Robert, James Kelly, Daniel Richard. AA, Napa Coll., 1949; student, U. Calif., Berkeley, 1949-50; BA, Calif. State Coll., Sonoma, 1975; MSW, Calif. State U., Sacramento, 1977. Diplomate clin. social worker; lic. clin. social worker, Calif.; lic. marriage and family counselor, Calif.; tchr. Columnist, stringer Napa (Calif.) Register, 1946-50; eligibility worker, supr. Napa County Dept. Social Services, 1968-75; instr. Napa Valley Community Coll., 1978-83; practice psychotherapy Napa, 1977—; oral commr. Calif. Dept. Consumer Affairs, Bd. Behavioral Sci., 1984-90; bd. dirs. Project Access, 1978-79. Trustee Napa Valley C.C., 1983—, v.p. bd., 1984-85, pres. bd., 1986, 90, 95, clk., 1988-89; bd. dirs. Napa County Coun. Econ. Opportunity, 1984-85, Napa chpt. March of Dimes, 1957-71, Mental Health Assn. Napa County, 1983-87; vice chmn. edn. com. Calif. C.C. Trustees, 1987-88, chmn. edn. com., 1988-89, legis. com., 1985-87, bd. dirs., 1989-99, 2d v.p., 1991, 1st v.p., 1992, pres., 1993; mem. student equity rev. group Calif. C.C. Chancellors, 1992; bd. dirs. C.C. League Calif., 1992-95, 1st v.p., 1992; appointed mem. Nape County Paratransit Coord. Coun., 1999—. Recipient Fresh Start award Self mag., award Congl. Caucus on Women's Issues, 1984; named Woman of distinction, Soroptimist Internat. and Sunrise Clubs of Napa, 1997. Mem. NASW, Calif. Elected Women's Assn. Edn. and Rsch. Democrat. Lutheran. Office: 1100 Trancas St Napa CA 94558-2908

LEE, MARGARET NORMA, artist; b. Kansas City, Mo., July 7, 1928; d. James W. and Margaret W. (Farin) Lee; PhB, U. Chgo., 1948; MA, Art Inst. Chgo., 1952. Lectr., U. Kansas City, 1957-61; cons. Kansas City Bd. Edn., Kansas City, Mo., 1968-86; guest lectr. U.Mo.-Columbia, 1983, 85, 87, 89, 91, 93-95, 97; one-woman shows Univ. Women's Club, Kansas City, 1966, Friends of Art, Kansas City, 1969, Fine Arts Gallery U. Mo. at Columbia, 1972, All Souls Unitarian Ch. Kansas City, Mo., 1978; two-Woman show Rockhurst Coll., Kansas City, Mo., 1981 exhibited in group shows U. Kans., Lawrence, 1958, Chgo. Art Inst., 1963, Nelson Art Gallery, Kansas City, Mo., 1968, 74, Mo. Art Show, 1976, Fine Arts Gallery, Davenport, Iowa, 1977; represented in permanent collections Amarillo (Tex.) Art Center, Kansas City (Mo.) Pub. Library, Park Coll., Parkville, Mo. Mem. Coll. Art Assn. Roman Catholic. Contbr. art to profl. jours.; author booklet. Home and Studio: 4109 Holmes St Kansas City MO 64110-1127

LEE, MENG-LUEN, pediatrician; b. Changhua, Taiwan, Feb. 1, 1959; s. Hsu-Chiang Chang and Hsien-Ju Lee; m. Hui-Chen Chu, June 11, 1990; children: Szu-Yi, Chen-Ching. MD, China Med. Coll., Taichung, Taiwan, 1984. Fellow in pediatric cardiology Nat. Taiwan U. Hosp., Taipei, 1991-93; resident in pediat. Changhua Christian Hosp., 1987-91, mem. vis. staff, 1993—, dir. pediatric ICU, 1995—. Contbr. articles to med. jours., including Am. Jour. Cardiology, Pediatric Cardiology, Acta Paediatrica, Internat. Jour. Cardiology, Pediatric Pulmonology, Jour. Thoracic Imagin, Respiratory Medicine, Acta Paediatrica Sinica, Jour. Formosan Med. Assn. Grantee Nat. Sci. Coun., Taiwan, 1999. Avocations: travel, house decorating, playing Chinese chess, writing Chinese brush, reading comics. Office: Changhua Christian Hosp, 135 Nanhsiao St, Changhua 50050, Taiwan

LEE, MICHAEL, leasing company executive, real estate company executive; b. Chgo., Nov. 26, 1953; s. Joseph A. and Mildred M. Kathrein; m. Victoria Lee; children: Jane Emily, Joseph Andrew, Theodore Michael, Elizabeth Grace, Fay Golda. BS in Acctg., U. Nebr., 1978; M in Mgmt., Northwestern U., 1985. CPA, Ill.; lic. real estate broker, pilot. Tax mgr. Touche Ross & Co., Chgo., 1978-84; corp. contr., v.p. Lettuce Entertain You Enterprises, Chgo., 1984-86; pres., CEO Kathrein Leasing Co., Chgo., 1983—; also bd. dirs.; pres., chief exec. officer Empire Real Estate Investment Co., Chgo., 1986—; bd. dirs., speaker Nat. Speakers Bur., N.Y.C., 1985-94; cons. Fla. Investor, Inc., Cocoa, 1986—. Author: (how-to book) Real Estate Comparative Analysis, 1986. Bd. dirs. Revenue Crusade of Mercy, United Way, Chgo., 1980. Mem. AICPA, Cert. Mgmt. Accts. Assn. (cert.), Cert. Internal Auditors Assn. (cert.), Nat. Assn. Realtors, Young Pres.'s Orgn., Northwestern U. Alumni Assn., Mensa. Avocations: aviation, lecturing. Home: 7601 N Eastlake Ter Chicago IL 60626-1421

LEE, MICHAEL HAN, video communication professional, researcher; b. Seoul, Rep. of Korea, Feb. 4, 1956; arrived in Australia, 1990; s. Jin-Pyo Lee and Jung-Suk Ryoo; m. Hyang Bog Lee, Apr. 1, 2000. B of Engring., Konkuk U., Seoul, 1979; M of Engring., Yonsei U., Seoul, 1981; PhD, U. Western Australia, Nedlands, 1995. Rschr. Korea Atomic Energy Rsch. Inst., Taejon, 1981-90; assoc. lectr. U. Western Australia, 1995, rsch. fellow, 1996-98; rsch. scientist Mediaware Solutions, Canberra, Australia, 1999-2000; rsch. scientist Math. and Info. Scis. Commonwealth Sci. Indsl. Rsch. Orgn., 2000—. Contbr. articles to profl. jours. Mem. fgn. qualification com. IE Australia, Canberra, 1996—. Univ. scholar U. Western Australia, 1992-94. Mem. IEEE (mem. coms.). Avocations: photography, guitar, classical music, archery. E-mail: michael.lee@cmis.csiro.au. Fax: 61-2-6216-7111. Office: GPO Box 664, Canberra ACT 2601, Australia

LEE, MIKE MYUNG-OK, engineering educator; b. Chonju, Chonbuk, Republic of Korea, Dec. 10, 1959; s. Jeong-Whan and Cha-Nam (Shim) L.; m. Eun-Mi Lee, Apr. 28, 1990; 1 child, Jeong-Hee. BS, Chonbuk Nat. U., 1981, Ariz. State U., 1983; MNS, Ariz. State U., 1987, PhD, 1988. Sr. rsch. engr., mem. tech. staff Motorola, Inc., Mesa, Ariz., 1988-95; indsl. fellow U. Tokyo, 1992-94; prof. engring. Dongshin U., Naju, Republic of Korea, 1995—; dir. IDEC, Dongshin U., 1997—; tech. advisor MyCAD, Inc., Seoul, Republic of Korea, 1997—, Hichips Co., Kwangju, Republic of Korea, 1998—; CEO HiMEMS Telecom. Co., Naju, 1997—. Author: Semiconductor Fundamentals and Multimedia IC Designs, 1997. Mem. IEEE (sr.), IEEK, IEICE. Avocations: golf, reading, tennis, travel. Office: Dongshin Univ, 252 Daeho-Dong, Chonnam Naju 520-714, Republic of Korea

LEE, MILES, management consultant; b. Shenyang, Liaoning, China; s. Jinzhen and Shufang (Wong) L; m. Qi Luo, July 6, 1982; 1 child, Steven S. BA, Sichuan U., Chengdu, China, 1982; postgrad., Niagara Coll., Welland, Ont., Can., 1983-85. Asst. engr. Rsch. Inst. Indsl. Automation and Instrumentation, Chongqing, China, 1982-83; translator, lectr. in bus. adminstrn. China/Can. Enterprise Mgmt. Tng. Ctr., Chengdu, 1985-89; dir. project coordinating office Sino-Am. CTRP Project/GE, Shenzhen, China, 1989-93; dep. gen. mgr. Shenzhen Yulian Indsl. Co., 1993-94; dep. dir.

Modern World Econ. Rels. Rsch. Assocs., Beijing, China, 1994-95; asst. CEO, Shenzhen ZongCheng Group, 1995—; cons. Internat. Edn. Cons. Co., Ltd., Hong Kong, 1998-99; chmn. Leemiles Cons. Assocs., Shenzhen, 1998. Translator: Western Classical Management Theory, 1995, others; editor: China Finance Research, 1999. Avocations: swimming, cycling, reading, jazz.

LEE, MIN-KYO, lawyer; b. Seoul, Korea, Feb. 28, 1957. BA, Seoul Nat. U., 1979, LLM, 1982; LLM, Duke U., 1984, JD, 1987, SJD, 1990. Bar: D.C., Pa. Lawyer Skadden, Arps, Slate & Flom, Washington, 1987-89, Kim & Change, Seoul, 1990—. Office: Kim & Chang 6F Seyang Bldg, 223 Naeja-Dong Chong-ku, Seoul 110-072, Korea

LEE, MOON HO, materials science educator; b. Koryong, South Korea, June 6, 1954; s. Jae-Sun and Oak-Soon (Jun) L.; m. Dong-Sook Lee, Oct. 15, 1958; children: Joo-Oak, Joo-Sook, Joo-Hyun. BS in Electronic Engring., Seoul Nat. U., 1976; MS in Materials Sci., Korea Advanced Inst. Sci/Tech., Seoul, 1978, PhD in Materials Sci., 1981. From asst. prof. to prof. Yeungnam U., Kyungsan, Korea, 1981—; assoc. dean Grad. Sch. Yeungnam U., Kyungsan, 1993-94, head dept. appl. electronics, 1996—, dir., res. inst. biomed. electronics, 1999—; rschr. Korea Inst. Sci. and Tech., Seoul, 1985-86; vis. prof. Pa. State U., State College, 1986-87, adj. prof., 1996-98; councillor Ministry of Sci. and Tech., Seoul, 1993-94; pres. EMO Co. Ltd., 1998—, chair rsch. and devel. group, 1999—. Councillor, Teagu City, Korea, 1990-93. Mem. Korea Nat. Acad. Engring. Home: Jisandong 1257-1, Yeungnam # 102-1305, Taegu City Republic of Korea Office: Yeungnam U Dept Metallurg Engring, Daedong 214-1, 712-749 Kyungsan Republic of Korea

LEE, MOON-KYU, industrial engineer, educator; b. Yesan, Choong-Nam, South Korea, Apr. 3, 1957; s. Kwi-Young and Kyung-Ye (Kim) L.; m. Hee-Sook Jeon; children: Yoo-Jin, Jin-Hyung. BS, Seoul Nat. U., 1979; MS, Korea Adv. Inst. Sci. and Tech, 1981, PhD, 1989. With Daewoo Engring. Co. Ltd., Seoul, 1981-83, asst. supr., 1983-84; vis. asst. prof. Rutgers U., Piscataway, N.J., 1991-93; asst. prof. Keimyung U., Taegu, South Korea, 1989-92, assoc. prof., 1992-97, prof. dept. indsl. engring., 1997—; cons. Yujin Electro-Circuit Sys., Taegu, 1996—, Dasol Automation, Taegu, 1997—, Ryucheon Co., Ltd., Dalseong, South Korea, 1998—. Contbr. articles to profl. jours. Mem. Korean Inst. Indsl. Engrs. (dir. 1995-96), Korean Soc. Maint. Engrs. (councilor 1996—), Inst. Indsl. Engrs., Korean Ops. Rsch. and Mgmt. Sci. Soc. Avocations: Go, tennis. Home: Pooreun-Maeul Apt 102-803, Dalseo-gu Ekok-dong 1330, Taegu 704-140, Republic of Korea Office: Keimyung Univ Indsl Engring, Dalseo-gu Shindong-dong 1000, 704-701 Taegu Republic of Korea

LEE, MYOUNG-BOK, electric engineering educator, researcher; b. Ulsan, Kyung-Nham, Republic of Korea, June 25, 1959; s. Dae-O Lee and Im-Sun Kim; m. Kwang-Sook Jang, May 9. 1985; 1 child, Jung-In. 0BS, Kyungpook Nat. U., Taegu, Republic of Korea, 1982, MS, 1984; PhD, Liverpool (Eng.) U., 1996. Tchg. asst. Kyungnham U., Masan, Republic of Korea, 1985-86; rschr. Korea Inst. Sci. and Tech., Seoul, 1986-92; prof. Kyungpook Nat. U., 1998—. Sunday sch. tchr. Presbyn. Ch., Taegu, 1999—. Achievements include patent for electron beam lithography system and its application for multilayer. Avocations: tennis, research, Bible study, consulting. Fax: 82-53-950-5505. E-mail: mblee@ee.knu.ac.kr. Home: Hwasung Apt 102-203, Pokhyun-Dong, Pookgu, Taegu 702-022, Republic of Korea Office: Kyungpook Nat U Sch Elect-, Elec Eng 1370, Sankyuk-Dong, Pookgu Taegu 702-701, Republic of Korea

LEE, MYUNG WOO, financial secretary, accountant; b. Yong-chon, Pyungbuk, Korea; came to U.S., 1972, naturalized; s. Sung S. and Sea (Oh) L.; m. Chan Soo Kim, Nov. 15, 1960; children: Francis S., Sang-Gil P., Monica E. BS in Bus. Adminstrn., Chung-Ang U., Seoul, Korea, 1960; MBA in Fin., Oklahoma City U., 1994. CPA; Series 6 stock broker. Chief acct., bd. mem. Hwa Sung Ind. Co. Ltd., Seoul, 1965-72; owner, operator Broadway Texaco, Walters, Okla., 1976-80; support person GM Small Car Divsn., Oklahoma City, 1979—; mgr. Mike's Donut, Oklahoma City, 1981-83, Lee's Cleaners, Oklahoma City, 1984-92; fin. sec. UAW Local 1999, Oklahoma City, 1995-98; owner Lee's CPA, Moore, Okla., 1999—. v.p. Chung Ang Econ. Rsch. Club, Seoul, 1958-60; bd. mem. Korean Soc. Oklahoma City, 1996; treas. North Cleve. County Dem. Club, Moore, Okla., 1997; chmn. election com., Korean Soc. of Oklahoma City, 1998; parish council chair Korean Martyrs Cath. Ch., Oklahoma City, 1998-2000. Mem. Okla. Soc. Public Acct., Am. Inst. Cert. Public Acct. Avocations: swimming, table tennis, golf. Fax: 405-528-7273. Home: 801 S Bouziden Dr Moore OK 73160-7324

LEE, PATRICIA, lawyer, diploma; b. Honolulu. Cert., U. Paris, 1964; MA, Columbia U., 1966; PhD, Northwestern U., 1973; JD, U. Hawaii, 1979. Ptnr. Goodsill Anderson Quinn & Stifel, Honolulu, 1979—; hon. consul Consulate of France, 1997. Office: France Hon Consulate 1099 Alakea St 1800 Alii Pl Honolulu HI 96813-4511

LEE, PATSY L., English educator, legal representative; b. Cash, Ark., June 6, 1940; d. Miller and Grethel Burden; m. Norman Dean Lee, Aug. 19, 1962; children: Eric, Lisa. M in Edn., Ark. State U., Jonesboro, 1962. Tchr. English Grants, N.Mex., 1962-65, Indio (Calif.) H.S., 1965-66, Raymond Cree Jr. H.S., Palm Springs, Calif., 1967-77, Palm Springs H.S., 1977—. Mem. Calif. Tchrs. Assn., Delta Kappa Gamma (sec. 1991-96). Home: 206 Loch Lomond Rd Rancho Mirage CA 92270-5603 Office: Palm Springs HS 2401 E Baristo Rd Palm Springs CA 92262-7127

LEE, PETER C.Y., engineering educator; b. Hankow, Hupei, China, Sept. 29, 1934; came to U.S., 1959; s. Paul P.W. Lee and Pei-Chiu Wang; m. Fui-Tseng Huang, May 28, 1961; 1 child, Andrew Wen-Tsen. BSCE, Nat. Cheng-Kung U., Tainan, Taiwan, 1957; MSCE, Rutgers U., 1961; MS in Engring. Mech., Columbia U., 1965, ScD, 1965. Alfred P. Sloan fellow dept. civil and environ. engring. Princeton (N.J.) U., 1965-66, asst. prof., 1966-72, assoc. prof., 1972-76, prof., 1976—, dir. grad. studies dept. civil and environ. engring., 1972-77, 81-82, 1989-90; vis. prof. Inst. Applied Mech. Nat. Taiwan U., spring 1989;. Contbr. articles to profl. jours. Mem. IEEE (C.B. Sawyer Meml. award Internat. Frequency Control Symposium 1980), AAAS, ASCE, ASME, Acoustical Soc. Am., Ultrasonics, Ferroelectrics and Frequency Control Soc. Avocations: tennis, golf, travel. E-mail: lee@princeton.edu. Office: Princeton U Dept Civil Environ Engring Princeton NJ 08544-0001

LEE, PREM KUMAR DEVASAHAYAM, engineering executive; b. Madras, Tamilnadu, India, Mar. 15, 1945; s. Moses Thomas and Ida Ranie (Devasahayam) L.; m. Lalitha Raja, May 18, 1972; children: P. Chitra Daniel, Neeta C., Asha C. Assoc. membership Inst. Engrs., Instn. Mech. Engrs., India, 1966; IMechE, Instn. Mech. Engrs., 1967; BD, Serampore, India, 1982. Dep. dir. inspector RDSO, Madras, 1975-79; dep. regional mgr. RITES, Bangalore, India, 1979-82; dep. chief mech. engring. Indian Railways, Madras, 1982-85; gen. mgr. India Govt. Mint, Calcutta, 1986-88, Security Printing, Hyderabad, 1988; regional rep. Haggai Inst., Hyderabad, 1988-98, exec. dir. internat. advancement, 1998—, vice pres., 2000—. Author: Add to Your Faith Excellence, 1994. Mem. Inst. Engrs., Amer. Soc. of Tng. and Devel., Amer. Mgmt. Assn. Avocations: bible study. Home and Office: Somajiguda, 83 Sangeethnagar, Hyderabad 500082, India

LEE, RAPHAEL CARL, plastic surgeon, biomedical engineer; b. Sumter, S.C., Oct. 29, 1949; s. Leonard Powell and Jean Maurice (Langston) L.; m. Kathleen Kelley, Feb. 11, 1983; children: Rachel, Catherine. BS, U. S.C., 1971, ScD (hon.), 1999; MS, Drexel U., 1975; MD, Temple U., 1975; ScD, MIT, 1979. Diplomate Am. Bd. Plastic Surgeons, Am. Bd. Surgery. Chief resident gen. surgery U. Chgo. Hosps., 1980-81; chief resident plastic surgery Mass. Gen. Hosp., 1982-83; assoc. in surgery Brigham and Women's Hosp., 1984-89; assoc. surgeon The Children's Hosp., 1985-89; dir. Electrical Trauma Rsch. Program, 1991—; med. dir. U. Chgo. Burn Unit, 1991-97; asst. prof. surgery Harvard Med. Sch., 1984-89; VanTassel asst. prof. of elec. and bioengring. MIT, 1983-89, asst. prof. bioengring. and surgery Harvard MIT, Divsn. Health Scis. and Tech., 1983-89; prof. plastic surgery, medicine, anatomy and organismal biology U. Chgo., 1992—; chmn. bd. dirs. Avocet Polymers Techs., Inc., 1996—. Author: Electrical Injury, Multidisciplinary Approach, 1994, Occupational Electrical Injury, 1999; editor: Electrical Trauma, Pathophysiology, 1992; assoc. editor Bioelectromagnetics, 1993—; contbr. more than 200 articles to profl. jours. Recipient Alumni Achievement award Class of 1975 Temple Med. Sch., 1995, Searle Scholar award The Searle Found., 1985-88, Disting. Engring. Sch. Alumnus award U. S.C., 1998, award for advancing safety and health Am. Electric Power Assn.; named Ams. 100 Brightest Young Scientists Sci. Digest, 1984; MacArthur Prize fellow John D. and Catherine T. MacArthur Found., 1981-86. Fellow ACS (Schering Scholar in Surgery 1978), Am. Inst. Med. and Biol. Engring.; mem. IEEE, AAAS, Am. Burn Assn. (Lindberg award), Am. Phys. Soc., Am. Soc. for Cell Biology, Am. Assn. Plastic Surgeons (James Barrett Brown award 1988), Biophys. Soc., Nat. Med. Assn. (plastic surgery sect chmn. 1989-91), Soc. for Phys. Regulation in Biology and Medicine (pres. 1995), Soc. of Univ. Surgeons, Surg. Biology Club III, Tau Beta Pi, Alpha Omega Alpha, Sigma Xi. Achievements include 12 patents. Office: U Chgo Hosps Pritzker Sch Medicine-Surgery MC6035 5841 S Maryland Ave Chicago IL 60637-1463

LEE, RAYMOND, chemist; b. San Bernardino, Calif., Aug. 31, 1950; s. Stephen S. and Dorris Elaine (Human) L.; m. Ronda Lou Geary, July 26, 1986; children: RayLynne, Rebecca, Ronald. BS in Chemistry, U. Calif., Riverside, 1972; postgrad., San Diego State U., 1972-79. Rsch. engr. Solar Turbines Internat., San Diego, 1978-81; rsch. mgr. Internat. Harvester, Elk Grove Village, Ill., 1981-83; rsch. mgr. Imi-Tech. Corp., Elk Grove Village, 1983-84, dir. R&D, 1984-89, chemist, 1989-91; sr. R&D chemist Ethyl Corp., Baton Rouge, 1991-93; R&D specialist Ethyl Corp./Albemerle Corp., Baton Rouge, 1993-96; sr. R&D specialist Albemarle Corp., Baton Rouge, 1996—. Deacon Elk Grove Bapt. Ch., Elk Grove Village, 1986-89, Istrouma Bapt. Ch., Baton Rouge, 1996—. Recipient Certs. of Recognition Nat. Aeronautics and Space Adminstrn.-Johnson Space Ctr., (3), 1980, (4), 1982. Mem. Am. Chem. Soc. Republican. Baptist. Achievements include 36 patents for polyimide foam products and processes. Avocations: skiing, golfing, tennis, gardening, woodworking. Home: 18554 Wildlife Way Dr Baton Rouge LA 70817-3993 Office: Albemarle Corp PO Box 341 Baton Rouge LA 70821-0341

LEE, RICHARD FRANCIS JAMES, evangelical clergyman, media consultant; b. Yakima, Wash., Sept. 13, 1967; s. Richard Francis and Dorothy Aldean (Blackwell). Diploma, Berean Coll., Springfield, Mo., 1989; BA, U. Wash., Seattle, 1990; JD, Gonzaga Sch. Law, 1997; postgrad., Fuller Theol. Seminary. Lic. clergyman; ordained Assemblies of God, So. Calif. Dist., 1999. Lic. clergyman N.W. dist. Assemblies of God, Seattle, 1989. Author: Tell Me the Story, 1982, The Crimson Detective Motion Picture, 1996. Named Most Likely to be President, Franklin High Sch., Seattle, 1986. Pentecostal. Avocations: collector, writer, itinerant speaker, filmmaker. Home: 262 N Los Robles Ave Apt 105 Pasadena CA 91101-1534 Office: Evangel Outreach Ministries 2604 E Boone Ave Spokane WA 99202-3718

LEE, RONSON KWOK KEUNG, accountant; b. Hong Kong. B.Bus., U. So. Queensland, Australia. Cert. practicing acct., Australia. Prin. Chin & Tong, CPAs, Hong Kong; bd. dirs. R & A Assocs. Ltd. Fellow Taxation Inst. Australia; mem. Australian Soc. CPAs (cert.), Hong Kong Soc. Accts. Office: Chin & Tong, 100 Nathan Rd Tung Ying Bld, Tslmshatsui Kowloon, Hong Kong

LEE, RUBY BEI-LOH, multimedia and computer systems architect; b. Singapore; came to the U.S., 1970, naturalized, 1996; m. Howard F. Lee, July 27, 1974; children: Patrick, Josephine. AB in Computer Sci. and Comparative Lit. with distinction, Cornell U., 1973; MS in Computer Sci., Stanford U., 1975, PhDEE, 1980. Asst. prof. elec. engring. Stanford (Calif.) U., 1980-81; lead architect Hewlett Packard Co., Palo Alto, Calif., 1982-84, lead designer microprocessors, 1984-86; project mgr. Hewlett Packard Co., Cupertino, Calif., 1987-90, chief arch. computer sys. architecture, multimedia, security, 1991-97; chief arch. Security Architecture, Cupertino, Calif., 1997-98; Forrest G. Hamrick prof. elec. engring. Princeton (N.J.) U., 1998—; cons. assoc. prof. elec. engring. Stanford U., 1990-95, cons. prof., 1995-98. Designer PA-RISC (Precision Architecture Reduced Instrn. Set Computer) architecture, Multimedia Acceleration EXtensions (MAX) architecture; contbr. articles to profl. jours.; inventor, patentee in field, including 19 U.S. patents and 63 Foreign ones. Mem. IEEE (mem. exec. com., mem. tech. com. on microprocessors, mem. program com. Compcon conf. San Francisco 1991-97, program chairperson Hot-Chips Symposium, Stanford 1992-93, mem. editl. bd. IEEE Micro and Spectrum, guest editor spl. issues IEEE MICRO 1994, 96), Assn. for Computing Machinery, Phi Beta Kappa, Alpha Lambda Delta. Methodist. Office: Princeton U Dept Elec Engring Princeton NJ 08544-0001

LEE, SANG MOON, management educator; b. Seoul, Republic of Korea, Apr. 1, 1939; came to U.S., 1961; s. Chang Woo Lee and Duck Soon Bahng; m. Joyce A. Sturm, Mar. 16, 1991; children: Tosca Lee Phillips, Amy L. BA in Econs., Seoul Nat. U., 1961; MBA, Miami U., Oxford, Ohio, 1963; PhD, U. Ga., 1969; PhD (hon.), U. Tirana, Albania, 1998. Prof. Va. Poly. Inst., Blacksburg, 1968-76; disting. prof., chair U. Nebr., Lincoln, 1976—; cons. Omaha Pub. Power, 1983-86, Ssang Yong Corp., Seoul, 1984-97; project dir. U.S. Agy. Internat. Devel., 1991—. Author: Operations Management, 1995, Management Science, 4th edit., 1995, World-Class Organization, 1996. Recipient Valley Forge Levey award Freedoms Found., 1995. Fellow Acad. Mgmt., Pan Pacific Bus. Assn. (pres. 1985—), Decision Scis. Inst. (pres. 1984-85). Republican. Office: U Nebr 209 CBA Lincoln NE 68588

LEE, SANG UK, electrical engineer, educator; b. Seoul, Korea, Aug. 11, 1949; s. Sun Joong and No Mi (Chung) L.; m. Joo Won Ban, June 2, 1977; children: Yoo Min, Seong Min. BS, Seoul Nat. U., 1973; MS, Iowa State U., 1976; PhD, U. So. Calif., 1980. Rschr. KIST, Seoul, 1973-74; rsch. engr. GE, Lynchburg, Va., 1980-81; MTS M/A co., Rockville, 1981-83; asst. prof. Seoul Nat. U., 1983-87, assoc. prof., 1987-93, prof., 1993—; dir. Inst. New Media and Comms., Seoul Nat. U., 1998—. Assoc. editor IEEE Transitions on Circuits and Systems for Video Technology; mem. editl. bd. Jour. Visual Comm. and Image Representation, 1998—; contbr. articles to profl. jours. including IEEE, Signal Processing and Pattern Recognition, among others. Mem. IEEE (sr.), Phi Kappa Phi. Home: Hanyang Apt 43-403, Upgujeong-Dong Kangnam, Seoul Korea Office: Seoul Nat U Sch Elec Engr, Shinlim-Dong, Kwanak-ku, Seoul 151-742, Korea

LEE, SANGHACK, economist, educator; b. Seoul, Korea, Feb. 11, 1958; s. Yongwoo and Byungsook (Kim) L.; m. Kyunghee Kim, Aug. 26, 1984; children: Juyon, Wonhyong. BA in Econs. with honors, Seoul Nat. U., 1976-80; PhD in Econs., U. Buffalo, 1989. Economist Bank of Korea, Seoul, 1980-85; rsch. instr. U. Buffalo, 1989-90; assoc. rsch. fellow Korea Inst. Internat. Econ. Policy, Seoul, 1990-91; asst. prof. econs. Kookmin U., Seoul, 1991-95, assoc. prof., 1995-2000, prof., 2000—. Contbr. articles to profl. jours. Spl. merit fellow U. Buffalo, 1986-88. Mem. Korea Internat. Econ. Assn. (mem. bd. editors 1993—). Avocation: go. Office: Kookmin U, 861-1 Jeongnung-dong, 136-702 Seoul Republic of Korea

LEE, SANG-HO, economist, researcher; b. Kwangju, South Korea, Oct. 15, 1966; s. Hyun-Soo and Hwa-Ja L.; m. Min-Ok Yoon, Oct. 4, 1992; children: Jin-Yong, Jin-Heok. BS, Korea U., Seoul, 1989; MS, Korea Adv. Inst. Sci. & Tech., Seoul, 1991; PhD, Korea Adv. Inst. Sci. & Tech., Taejon, Korea, 1995. Postdoc. Elec. and Telecomm. Rsch. Inst., Taejon, Korea, 1995; lectr. Chonam Nat. U., Kwangju, Korea, 1996-98, asst. prof., 1998—; cons. Com. Pub. Prices, Kwangju, Korea, 1996-98. Contbr. articles to profl. jours. Mem. Am. Econ. Assn., Korean Econ. Assn. Avocations: basketball, tennis. Office: Chonnam Nat U Dept Econs, 300 Yongbong-dong, Kwangju 500-757, Republic of South Korea

LEE, SEUNG GU, geochemist, researcher; b. Seoul, Republic of Korea, Nov. 27, 1960; s. Nam Young and Cheon Seop (Sim) L.; m. Kyung Hee Kim, Apr. 23, 1994. BS, Seoul (Korea) Nat. U., 1983, MS, 1985; DSc, U. Tokyo, 1991. Rschr. Korea Ocean R & D Inst., Ansan, 1985-86, U. Tokyo, 1991-92, Korea Inst. Geology, Mining and Materials, Taejon, Republic of Korea, 1992—. Contbr. articles to profl. jours., including Geochim Cosmochim Acta, Geochem. Soc., Sci. Fellow Japanese Sci. Tech. Assn. Home: Eunchorong Apt 507, 908-3 Dunsandong Seogu, Taejon 302-173, Republic of Korea Office: Korea Inst Geology Mining, 30 Kajungdong Yusongku, Taejon 305-350, Republic of Korea

LEE, SHENG YEN, writer; b. Xinyang, Henan, China, Dec. 28, 1924; s. Yi-San and Qin-Yuan (Gan) L.; m. Winnie Cho, Aug. 25, 1949; 1 child, Yin May. BS in Chemistry, Nat. Northeastern U., 1946; PhD in Chemistry, U. Colo., 1964. Chemist inspector Agrl. Inspection Bur., Taiwan, 1948-51; lang. interpreter Chinese Army, Taiwan, 1951-53; chem. engr. Agrl. Chem. Works, Kaohsiung, Taiwan, 1953-59; chemist Polymer Corp., Ltd., Sarnia, Ontario, Can., 1965-68; chemist, supr. Harry Diamond Labs., U.S. Army, Adelphi, Md., 1969-79; chemist Goddard Space Flight Ctr., NASA, Greenbelt, Md., 1979-91; editor Chinese Am. Forum, Inc., Silver Spring, Md., 1984-99; prof. hon. Xinyang Tchrs. Coll., 1991. Founder, bd. chmn. Chinese Am. Forum, 1984-2000; patentee in field; contbr. sci. papers to profl. publs. Named Inventor-of-the-yr. finalist NASA, 1990. Avocations: reading, travel, swimming, writing. Home: 15100 Interlachen Dr Apt 201 Silver Spring MD 20906-5694

LEE, SHEW KUHN, retired optometrist; b. Balt., Apr. 24, 1923; s. Mong Har and Gum Tuey (Wong) L. OD, Ill. Coll. Optometry, 1949; postgrad. Cath. U. Am., 1957, Md. U., 1959; m. Florence Gin Toy, Oct. 29, 1949; children: Wayson Perry, Davin Jeffrey. Pvt. practice optometry, Washington, 1949-88; ret., 1988. Lectr. D.C. Traffic Safety Sch.; v.p. D.C. Bd. Optometry, 1959-65; mem. D.C. Bd. Examiners in Optometry, 1973-84, sec., 1974; mem. Eye Bank Council; vision rsch. cons. HEW, 1973. Bd. dirs. Eye Bank and Rsch. Found., Washington Hosp. Center. 2d Lt. USAR, 1943-45. Decorated Purple Heart, Bronze Star medal with oak leaf cluster; recipient Meritorious Pub. Svc. award Govt. of D.C., 1965. Mem. Am. Optometric Assn. (life, pres. joggers 1968—, Disting. Svc. award 1974), Am. Legion (life, citation of merit 1954, post comdr. D.C. 1960), D.C. Optometric Soc. (sec. 1956-57), Lees Assn. (trustee), Chinese Consol. Benevolent Assn. (founder), Flying Optometrist Assn. Am. (bd. dir. 1974—), Beta Sigma Kappa. Lion (charter pres. Chi-Am. 1960, zone chmn. 1961, dep. dist. gov. 1963, hon. mem. Capitol Hill, Washington Host, Extension award 1960, 75, Presdl. Banner award 1975). Rsch. publs. in field. Home: 2939 Mckinley St NW Washington DC 20015-1217

LEE, SHUIT-TONG, physicist; b. Shaodong, China, Jan. 28, 1947; s. Kuk-Chuen and Hai L.; m. Anna Leun Yee Tang, Aug. 18, 1971 (dec. Sept. 1989); two children. BSc, Chinese U. Hong Kong, 1969; MSc, U. Rochester, 1971; PhD, U. Br. Columbia, 1974. Postdoctoral assoc. U. Calif., Berkeley, 1974-76; from sr. rsch. scientist to sr. rsch. scientist Eastman Kodak Co., Rochester, N.Y., 1976-94; assoc. prof. City U. Hong Kong, 1994-96, prof. materials sci., 1996—; chair materials sci., 1996—; acting head, dept. physics and materials sci. City U. Hong Kong, 1998-99; dir. Ctr. Super-Diamond and Advanced Films, 1998—. Office: Dept Physics Materials Sci, City Univ Hong Kong, Hong Kong China

LEE, SINGH YAN ROBERT, neonatologist; b. Hong Kong, July 25, 1964; s. Wan Loy and Yim Chun (Kam) L.; m. Lai Hung Chan, Mar. 22, 1992; 1 child, Hok Ling. MBBS, U. Hong Kong, 1989. Med. officer dept. pediatrics Princess Margaret Hosp., Hong Kong, 1990-96, sr. med. officer, 1996—. Author reports. Fellow Hong Kong Acad. Medicine; mem. Royal Coll. Physicians U.K. Avocation: travel. Office: Princess Margaret Hosp, Lai King Hill Rd, Kwaichun, Hong Kong China

LEE, SOOGAB, aerospace engineering educator; b. Pusan, Republic of Korea, Sept. 29, 1960; m. Mi-hwa Song; children: Seung-geol, Seung-youn. BS, Seoul Nat. U., 1983, MS, 1985; PhD, Stanford U., 1992. Rsch. scientist NASA Ames Rsch. Ctr., Calif., 1992-95; asst. prof. aerospace engring. Seoul Nat. U., 1995—. Mem. AIAA (sr.), Am. Helicopter Soc. (tech. com.), Acoustical Soc. Am., Korean Soc. Noise and Vibration (exec. bd. 1999—). Office: Seoul Nat U Dept Aero Eng, San 56-1, Shillimdong, Kwanak Seoul 151-742, Republic of Korea

LEE, STEVEN WILSON, sporting goods manufacturing company executive; b. Olympia, Wash., Nov. 17, 1950; s. Marvin Wilson and Nathalie Jeanne (Reisman) L.; m. Bibianna Maria Johanna Bouwkamp, Apr. 1, 1977 (div. 1979); m. Gail Ann Dymsza, May 23, 1988; 1 child, Courtney McKinney. AA in physical edn., Foothill Jr. Coll., Los Altos Hills, Calif., 1971; BA in physical edn., U. Calif., Berkeley, 1975. V.p. Hind-Wells, Inc., San Luis Obispo, Calif., 1977-80; nat. sales mgr. Sub-4, Inc., Fountain Valley, Calif., 1980-81; nat. dir. sales and mktg. Sasaki Am., Inc. subs. Sasaki Corp., Carson (Calif.), Osaka (Japan), 1982-86; v.p. Packaging Industries Group, Inc., Hyannis, Mass., 1986-87; pres., chief exec. officer Lee Enterprises Worldwide Inc., Parkland, FLa., 1990—; bd. dirs. SecondWind Products, Inc., Paso Robles, Calif., 1994—, pres., 1994—. V.p./bd. dirs. Mashpee (Mass.) Shores Homeowners Assn., 1989-90; active Citizens of Parkland Focus Group, 1991, Cypress Head Homeowners Assn., 1991—; bd. dirs. Parkland Homeowners Assn., 1991-93, v.p., 1993-95, bd. dirs. St. Jude's Children's Rsch. Hosp./ A.F. Best Securities Charity Golf, 1990-95; adv. bd. dir. parks and recreation City of Parkland, 1993—; with Broward Econ. Devel. Coun., 1993-97, sports devel. com., 1994—. Mem. Am. Mgmt. Assn., Nat. Sporting Goods Assn., Sporting Goods Mfg. Assn., Nat. Recreation and Parks Assn., U.S. Master Swimming, Nat. H.S. Coaches Assn. (All Am. Water Polo champion 1969), Nat. C. C. Coaches Assn. (All Amer. Water Polo champion 1971), Nat. Collegiate Athletic Assn. (nat. water polo champion 1973, 74), Am. Legion, Broward County C. of C., U. Calif. Bear Backers, Optimist Club (v.p. Parkland chpt. 1993-95), U. Calif. Berkeley Alumni Assn. (life), Boca Grove. Democrat. Roman Catholic. Avocations: golf, boating, swimming, stamp collecting, camping. Home: PO Box 970020 Coconut Creek FL 33097-0020 also: 1398 S Ocean Blvd Pompano Beach FL 33062-7154 also: 13 Redwood Cir Mashpee MA 02649-2041

LEE, STEWART S., political scientist; b. Pyung Yang, Korea, Sept. 7, 1935; s. Mu-sung and Bock-nai (Kim) L.; m. Young-ja Lee, Sept. 10, 1963; children: Edwin, Jane, Richard. BA, Westminster Coll., New Wilmington, Pa., 1959; MA, Rutgers U., 1960, PhD, 1967. Prof. polit. sci. Muhlenberg Coll., Allentown, Pa., 1963—, dir. East Asian studies, 1971-76; prin. Korea Sch. of Lehigh Valley, Allentown, 1998—. Author: Korean-Japanese Discord, 1975; contbr. articles to profl. jours. Mem. Korean Assn. of Greater Lehigh Valley (pres. 1972-74, founder). Democrat. Home: 935 Beverly Dr Allentown PA 18103-3723 Office: Muhlenberg Coll Dept of Polit Sci Allentown PA 18104

LEE, SU KIM, language educator; b. Kuala Lumpur, Malaysia, Apr. 25, 1955; d. Koon Liang Lee and Kwee Hoon Foo; m. Kam Hoong Lee, June 2, 1984; 1 child, Jan Ming. BA with honors, U. Malaya, Kuala Lumpur, 1977, Diploma in Edn., 1978; MEd, U. Malaya, 1983. Tchr. English lang. Pa'Badol Secondary Sch., Kelantan, Malaysia, 1979, Nat. U. Malaysia, Bangi, Selangor, 1979-85, 85-96; assoc. prof. Nat. U. Malaysia, Bangi, 1996—; trainer in comm. skills, grammar, resource person Malaysian Inst. Mgmt., Kuala Lumpur, 1991-96. Author: Malaysian Flavours, 1996, (resource textbook) Explorations: Process-Based Writing Tasks in English, 1994, Manglish: Malaysian English at Its Wackiest!, 1998; columnist: English lang. newspaper The Star, 1993-96. Mem. TESOL (USA, Albert H. Marckwardt travel award 1998). Avocations: creative writing, reading, travel, theatre, music. Home: 8 SS 18/5A, Subang Jaya Selangor, Malaysia also: 880 Tully Rd Apt 94 Houston TX 77079-5425 Office: Nat U Malaysia, Faculty Lang Studies, Bangi Selangor, Malaysia

LEE, SUN BOK, biochemical engineering educator; b. Cheong Ju, Chung Buk, Korea, Dec. 23, 1953; s. Won Ku and Moon G. (Yeon) L.; m. Young Ran Cho, Oct. 6, 1981; children: Jae Won, Ji Won. BS, Seoul (Korea) Nat. U., 1976; PhD, Korea Adv. Inst. Sci. Tech., Seoul, 1981. Cert. biochem. engring. Rsch. fellow Calif. Inst. Tech., Pasadena, 1981-83; asst. prof. Korea Adv. Inst. Sci. Tech., Seoul, 1983-88; head enzyme technol. lab. Genetic Engring. Rsch. Inst., Seoul, 1988-89; assoc. prof. biochem. engring. Pohang (Korea) U. Sci. Tech., 1989-96, prof. biochem. engring., 1996—; head dept. chem. engring., 1998—; vis. prof. U. Calif., Davis, 1985. Author: Biocatalysis in Organic Solvent, 1991, Bioprocess Kinetics of Recombinant Culture, 1991; exec. editor Biotechnology and Bioprocess Engineering, 1995—; mem. editl. bd. Jour. Molecular Catalysis B: Enzymatic, 1995—. Mem. adv. bd. Pohang City Coun., 1991—. Recipient govt. fellowship Korea Adv. Inst. Sci. Tech., Seoul, 1976, postdoctoral fellowship Korea Sci. and Engring. Found., Seoul, 1981, Govt. award Ministry Sci. and Tech., Seoul, 1988. Mem. Am. Inst. Chem. Engrs., Am. Soc. Microbiolgoy, Korean Inst. Chem. Engrs., N.Y. Acad. Scis. Achievements include patents for separation of aminoglycoside antibiotics, enzymatic synthesis of cephalexin, L-trytophan fermentation, enzymatic synthesis beta-lactam antibiotics; findings on quantitative description of gene expression kinetics, enzyme kinetics in anhydrous

media. Office: Pohang U Sci Tech, San 31 Hyoja-dong, Pohang 790 784, Republic of Korea

LEE, SUNG HO, psychiatrist; b. Seoul, June 28, 1934; s. Suk K. Lee and Chung Won Kim; m. Myung H. Lee, Nov. 17, 1959; children: Benjamin, May. Student, Yonsei U., 1953-55, MD, 1959; MSc, Ohio State U., 1967; postgrad. med. cert., UCLA, 1968. Diplomate Am. Bd. Psychiatry and Neurology, Korean Bd. of Psychiatry and Neurology. Psychiat. resident Brentwood Psychiat. Hosp., VAMC, L.A., 1967-68, Ohio State U. Hosp., Columbus, 1965-67; neurology resident Cin. Gen. Hosp., 1964-65; psychiat. resident Yonsei U. Hosp., Seoul, 1960-62, staff psychiatrist, 1968-69; chief psychiatrist Ewha U. Hosp., Seoul, 1969-70; clin. dir. unit B Broughton State Hosp., Morganton, N.C., 1970-71; chief psychiatrist VA Med. Ctr., Dayton, Ohio, 1971-79; staff psychiatrist Eastway Cmty. Mental Health Ctr., Dayton, 1975-95; med. dir. South Cmty. Inc., Centerville, Ohio, 1990-95; pvt. practice Dayton, 1975-95; chief psychiatrist Kyung Hee Pundang CHA Gen. Hosp., Seoul, 1995-96; staff psychiatrist Accord Behavioral Healthcare, Dayton, 1996—; staff psychiatrist, dep. med. dir. Eastway Corp., Dayton, 1996—; cons. psychiatrist South Cmty Inc., Centerville, 1980-90, Dayton Mental Health Ctr., 1975-95, Eastway Cmty. Mental Health Ctr., 1975-79; assoc. clin. prof. Wright State U., Dayton, 1979—, asst. clin. prof., 1975-79; prof. Kyung Hee U., 1975-76; asst. clin. prof. Ohio State U., Columbus, 1971-75; asst. prof. Ewha U. Coll. of Medicine, 1969-70; instr. Yonsei U. Coll. of Medicine, 1968-69, 1961-64. Home: 7706 Normandy Ln Dayton OH 45459-4118 Office: Eastway Behavioral Health 600 Wayne Ave Dayton OH 45410-1122

LEE, SUNGHO H., education educator, consultant, dean; b. Kyonggi-do, Rep. of Korea, Nov. 3, 1946; s. Kiwon and Imae (Song) L.; m. Hwadong Kim, Feb. 17, 1973; children: Haichung, Haiseok. BA, Yonsei U., Seoul, Rep. of Korea, 1970, MA, 1975; student, Ruhr U., Bochum, Germany, 1976-77; EdD, George Washington U., 1980. Instr. Yonsei U., 1975-76, asst. prof., 1981-85, assoc. prof., 1986-90, prof., 1991—, dean Coll. Edn., 1998-2000, dean Grad. Sch., 2000—; asst. min. Ministry of Edn., Rep. of Korea, 1993; dir. univ. evaluation Korean Coun. for Univ. Edn., Korea, 1983-90; mem. Presdl. Commn. 21st Century, 1989-93. Author: Shaking Parents and Straying Children, 1997 (award Chosun Daily Newspaper Co. 1997); co-author: Scientific Development and Higher Education, 1989 (award NSF 1986), Academic Profession in the World, 1995, Teaching Methods in Schools, 1999; contbr. chpts. to books. Cons. New Cmty. Devel. Movement Assn., Korea, 1996-99; mem. Nat. Commn. UNESCO, Korea, 1993-95; bd. trustees Nat. Inst. Curriculum Devel., 1998-99; mem. nat. adv. com. for edn. policy, Korea, 1996-99; mem. standing com. Presdl. Com. for Rebuilding Korea, 1998—. Sgt. US I Corps., 1970-73. Rsch. grantee Nat. Assn. Trade and Tech. Schs., 1980; recipient award Carnegie Found., 1992, Order of Svc. Merit award Pres. of Korea, 2000. Mem. Korean Soc. for Study Edn. (bd. trustees 1981-83, 86-90, 98—), Korean Higher Edn. Assn. (bd. trustees 1994—). Evangelical. Avocation: golf. Office: Yonsei U Dept Edn, Shinchon-dong 134, Sodaemoon-ku Seoul 120-749, Korea

LEE, TAEK SEUNG, educator; b. Seoul, Korea, Apr. 13, 1966; s. Kang Soo and Hong Ja (Jung) L.; m. Soo Yeon Kim. BS, Seoul Nat. U., Korea, 1988, MS, 1990, PhD, 1994. Rwch. assoc. U. Mass., Lowell, 1995-97; with Korea Inst. Sci. & Tech., Seoul, 1994-95. Contbr. articles to profl. jours. 2d lt. Korean Army, 1990-91. Mem. Am. Chem. Soc., Korean Chem. Soc., Polymer Soc. Korea. Avocations: exercise, skiing, golf, photography. Office: Chungnam Nat U, Dept Textile Engring, Taejon 305-764, Korea

LEE, TENG-HUI, president of Republic of China; b. Sanchih, Taiwan, Jan. 15, 1923. Degree, Kyoto Imperial U., Japan, 1945; BS, Nat. Taiwan U., 1949; MA, Iowa State U., 1953; PhD, Cornell U., 1968. Asst. prof. Nat. Taiwan U., 1949-55, assoc. prof., 1956-58; rsch. fellow Taiwan Cooperative Bank, 1953; specialist, econ. analyst dept. of agriculture & forestry Taiwan Provincial Govt., 1954-57; specialist Joint Commn. on Rural Reconstruction, 1957-61; sr. specialist, cons., 1961-70; chief Rural Econ. Divsn. Joint Commn. on Rural Reconstruction, 1970-72; prof. Nat. Chengchi U., 1958-78; min. without portfolio, 1972-78; mayor Taipei City, 1978-81; gov. Taiwan Provincial Govt., 1981-84; v.p. Repub. of China, 1984-88, pres., 1988-2000; hon. chmn. Taiwan Rsch. Inst., 2000—. Author: The Road to Democracy: Taiwan's Pursuit of Identity, Agricultural Development and Its Contributions to Economic Growth in Taiwan, An Analytical Review of Agricultural Development in Taiwan, Intersectoral Capital Flows in the Economic Development of Taiwan, Initial Conditions of Agriculture and Development Policy, Process and Pattern of Growth in Agriculture Production of Taiwan, Agricultural Diversification and Development, On the Problems of Agriculture Price Policy and Price Level. Office: Taiwan Rsch Inst Fl 30, JungJeng E Rd, Danshuei Jen Taipei 251, Taiwan, Republic of China

LEE, THOMAS CHAN, communication educator; b. Showkung, Shandong, China, Aug. 8, 1925; s. Chun Chao Lee and Marry chang; m. Wen Ying Lee, Aug. 24, 1957; children: Shih-Queen, Shih-Ning; m. Jih Lin, Aug. 4, 1983; m. Cheng Fu, Dec. 22, 1992; children: Jolinta, Joshowa, Jean. B Law, Nat. Chengchi U., Nanking, China, 1948; MA, Nat. Chengchi U., Taipei, Taiwan, 1956; postgrad., Stanford U., 1964. Lectr. Nat. Chengchi U., Taipei, 1956-59, assoc. prof., 1959-62, prof. comm., 1962—, dean Grad. Sch. Journalism, 1981-87; vis. scholar Columbia U., N.Y.C., 1983. Author: A History of World Journalism, 1966 (Scholarly achievement award, Gold Medallion Min. Edn. 1967), Comparative Journalism, 1972 (Commn. Theory prize 1974), Comparative Television Systems, 1974, International Communications, 1977, Space Communication, 1979; drafter Taiwan broadcasting law, press code, TV code. Chmn. Rosalind Found., Taipei, 1986-99, Chinese Culture Found., Taipei, 1989-95; mem. standing com. Chinese Comm. Edn. Assn., Taipei, 1969-88; cons. China Times, Press Coun., Govt. Info. Office, Tapei; promoter Dem. Comm. Sys., Press Freedom, Two Party Democracy and Repealing Martial Law, Taiwan, 1983. Maj. Chinese Army, 1943-44. Rsch. fellow, Grantee Nat. Sci. Coun., 1959-84; grantee Taiwan Power Co., 1991-92, Fgn. Affairs Inst., 1995-96. Mem. World Peace Profs. Assn. (gov. 1986-99). Mem. National Party. Achievements include establishing the first PhD program in Journalism at Nat. Chengchi University (Taiwan) in 1982. Avocations: music, travel, tennis.

LEE, THOMAS HONG-CHI, historian, educator; b. Chang-Hua, Taiwan, Mar. 5, 1945; s. Chia-sung and Chiung-Hua (Shih) L.; m. Hsiang Nina Chen, June 19, 1971; children: Jennifer Ining, Jonathan Iming. BA, Nat. Taiwan U., Taipei, 1968; PhD, Yale U., 1975. Lectr. Chinese U. Hong Kong, 1974-84, sr. lectr., dir. internat. Asian studies program, 1984-91, reader, 1991; prof. dept. history City Coll. N.Y., CUNY, 1991—, chmn. Asian studies dept., 1992-96, dir. Asian studies program, 1996—. Recipient fellowship Whiting Found., 1973-74, rsch. grant Harvard-Yenching Instn., 1981-82, sr. scholar rsch. grant Chiang-Ching-Kuo Found., 1997-98. Mem. Assn. Asian Studies, Am. Hist. Assn., Chinese Am. Acad. and Profl. Soc. (pres., dir. 1999). Office: City Coll NY CUNY Dept History 138th St at Convent Ave New York NY 10031

LEE, THOMAS TEHWEN, neurosurgeon; b. Tainan, Taiwan, Dec. 27, 1967; s. Chang Kuei and Shiu-Hoa Shu L.; m. Margaret Yu, Aug. 31, 1993. BA, U. Calif., Berkeley, 1989; MD, UCLA, 1993. Diplomate Nat. Bd. Medical Examiners. Resident neurosurgeon U. Miami - Jackson Meml. Med. Ctr., 1993-94; attending neurosurgeon Neurosurgeons of New York, White Plains, N.Y., 1999—; med. edn. liaison Congress of Neurol. Surgeons, Park Ridge, Ill.; com. mem. edn. com. of Congress of Neurol. Surgeons, Park Ridge. Contbr. articles to profl. jours., chpt. to books in field. Mem. med. response team Championship Auto Racing Team, 1995-99. Mem. AMA, N.Am. Spine Soc., Am. Assn. Neurol. Surgeons, Golden Key, Phi Beta Kappa. Avocations: movie poster collection, swimming, tennis, target shooting. E-mail: ThomasTLee@aol.com. Office: Neurosurgeons of New York 222 Westchester Ave Ste 202 White Plains NY 10604-2926

LEE, TIMOTHY EARL, international agency executive, paralegal; b. Seattle, May 23, 1947; s. Charles Augusta and Esther Letty (Young) L.; m. Marcia Lea Wulff, July 6, 1968 (div. May 1976); children: Vincent Dean, Dante' Claude; 1 stepson, Kevin Paul McCorkle; m. Jayne Elizabeth Ashley, Apr. 28, 1984 (div. Apr. 1995). Cert., Ivy Tech., 1981, Am. Inst. Paralegal Studies, 1988. Mgr. Gen. Fin. Corp., Evanston, Ill., 1970-74, FBT Capital Corp., South Bend, Ind., 1974-76; owner Lee's Internat. Investigative Rsch. Agy., Ft. Wayne, Ind., 1978—. Mem. Heritage Foun., Citizens Against Govt. Waste; spl. adv. Allen Superior Ct. With U.S. Army, 1966-68, Vietnam. Recipient Cert. of Appreciation, DAV, 1968. Mem. VFW, Ind. Assn. Pvt. Detectives (v.p. N.E. region Ind. 1984—), Ind. Sheriff's Assn., Ft. Wayne Allen County Security Assn., Coun. for Inter-Am. Security, Nat. Security Ctr., Nat. Def. Inst., 27th Field Artillery Assn. (v.p., founding father), Am. Legion, Vietnam Vets, Internat. Platform Assn., Concord Coalition. Home: 8516 River Canyon Dr Fort Wayne IN 46835-1015

LEE, TONG HUN, economics educator; b. Seoul, Nov. 20, 1931; came to U.S., 1955, naturalized, 1968; s. Chong Su and Yun (Lee) L.; m. Yul Jah Ahn, June 11, 1960; children: Bruce Keebeck, James Keewon. BS, Yonsei U., 1955; PhD, U. Wis., 1961. Asst. prof. econs. U. Tenn., Knoxville, 1962-64; assoc. prof. U. Tenn., 1964-67; prof. econs. U. Wis., Milw., 1967-96, chmn. dept. econs., 1978-82; disting. prof. econs. Ajou U., Suwon, Korea, 1997—. Author: Interregional Intersectoral Flow Analysis, 1973; contbr. articles to profl. jours. NSF grantee, 1965-67, 73-75. Mem. Am. Econ. Assn., Am. Fin. Assn., Am. Statis. Assn., Econometric Soc. Home: 55 W Delaware Pl Apt 1021 Chicago IL 60610-6073 Office: Ajou U Sch Bus Adminstrn, 5 Wonchon-Dong Paldal-Gu, Suwon 442-749, Republic of Korea

LEE, TON-JU, Korean language and literature educator; b. Tamyang, Chonnam, Republic of Korea, Nov. 8, 1937; s. Sung-ho Lee and Jae-hi Han; m. Kyung-ja Kim; 1 child, Kyung-geun. BA, Chonnam Nat. U., Kwangju, 1960, MA, 1963, PhD, 1980. From instr. to prof. Korean lang. and lit. Chonnam Nat. U., 1966—, dean student affairs, 1981-84, dean acad. affairs, 1987-88, dean Coll. Humanities, 1995-97, dean grad. sch., 2000—; vis. prof. Chenggung Nat. U., Tainan, Taiwan, 1978-79, Tsukuba (Japan) U., 1986-87, Fudan U., Shanghai, 1998-99. Author: Introduction to Chinese Characters, 1979, 2d edit., 1992, Chonnam Dialects, 1979, The Studies of Sino-Korean of Hunmong-Jahoe, 1990, Understanding of Chinese Historical Phonology, 1995. With Korean Army, 1961-62. Decorated Medal of Pomegranate (Republic of Korea); recipient cultural award Chonnam Province, 1979. Fellow Gokkugo Gakkai, Chosen Gakkai; mem. Korean Lang. Soc. (trustee 1986—), Soc. Korean Linguistics (vice dir. 1988-90), Soc. Korean Lang. and Lit. (bd. dirs. 1991-92). Avocation: jogging. Office: Chonnam Nat U, 300 Yongbong-dong, Kwangju Republic of Korea

LEE, TSUNG-DAO, physicist, educator; b. Shanghai, China, Nov. 25, 1926; s. Tsing-Kong L. and Ming-Chang (Chang); m. Jeannette Chin, June 3, 1950; children: James, Stephen. Student, Nat. Chekiang U., Kweichow, China, 1943-44, Nat. S.W. Assoc. U., Kunming, China, 1945-46; PhD, U. Chgo., 1950; DSc (hon.), Princeton U., 1958; LLD (hon.), Chinese U., Hong Kong, 1969; DSc (hon.), CCNY, 1978. Research assoc. in astronomy U. Chgo., 1950; research assoc., lectr. physics U. Calif., Berkeley, 1950-51; mem. Inst. for Advanced Study, Princeton (N.J.) U., 1951-53, prof. physics, 1960-63; asst. prof. Columbia U., N.Y.C., 1953-55, assoc. prof., 1955-56, prof., 1956-60, 63—, adj. prof., 1960-62, Enrico Fermi prof. physics, 1963—, Univ. prof., 1984—; Loeb lectr. Harvard U., Cambridge, Mass., 1957, 64. Editor: Weak Interactions and High Energy Nutrino Physics, 1966, Particle Physics and Introduction to Field Theory, 1981. Decorated grande ufficiale Order of Merit (Italy); recipient Albert Einstein Sci. award Yeshiva U., 1957, (with Chen Ning Yang) Nobel prize in physics, 1957, Ettore Majorana-Erice-Sci. for Peace prize, 1990. Mem. NAS, Acad. Sinica, Am. Acad. Arts and Scis., Am. Philos. Soc., Acad. Nazionale dei Lincei, Acad. Sci. China. Office: Columbia U Dept Physics Pupin Hall W 538 120th St Rm 829 New York NY 10027

LEE, WILDA, engineer; b. Taiwan, June 23, 1967; came to U.S., 1982; p. Sam Sen-Hao and Amy Chun-Hsiang Lee. B in Engring., SUNY, Stony Brook, 1991; MS in Mech. Engring., Purdue U., 1993. With Allied Signal, Inc., Lynn Haven, Fla.; engr. Dana Corp., Caldwell, Ohio, Albany Internat., Tumwater, Wash.; sr. quality analyst Pratt & Whitney, East Hartford, Conn. Mem. ASME, Soc. Women Engrs., Lions. Avocations: flying, music, outdoor adventures, reading, travel. E-mail: leewy@pureh.com. Office: Pratt & Whitney MIS 102-32 400 Main St East Hartford CT 06108-0968

LEE, WILLIAM JOHNSON, lawyer; b. Jan. 13, 1924; s. William J. and Ara (Anderson) L. Student, Akron U., 1941-43, Denison U., 1943-44, Harvard U., 1944-45; J.D., Ohio State U., 1948. Bar: Ohio 1948, Fla. 1962. Research asst. Ohio State U. Law Sch., 1948-49; asst. dir. Ohio Dept. Liquor Control, chief purchases, 1956-57, atty. examiner, 1951-53, asst. state permit chief, 1953-55, state permit chief, 1955-56; asst. counsel, staff Hupp Corp., 1957-58; spl. counsel City Attys. Office, Ft. Lauderdale, Fla., 1963-65; asst. atty. gen. Office Atty. Gen. State of Ohio, 1966-70; administr. State Med. Bd. Ohio, Columbus, 1970-85; mem. Federated State Bd.'s Nat. Commn. for Evaluation of Fgn. Med. Schs., 1981-83; mem. Flex 1/Flex 2 Transitional Task Force, 1983-84; pvt. practice law, Ft. Lauderdale, 1965-66; acting municipal judge, Ravenna, Ohio, 1960; instr. Coll. Bus. Adminstrn., Kent State U., 1961-62. chmn. legal aid com. Portage County, Ohio, 1960. Mem. Editl. bd. Ohio State Law Jour., 1947-48; contbr. articles to profl. jours. Mem. pastoral relations com. Epworth United Meth. Ch., 1976; troop awards chmn. Boy Scouts Am., 1965; mem. ch. bd. Melrose Park (Fla.) Meth. Ch., 1966. Served with USAAF, 1943-46. Mem. ATLA, Exptl. Aviation Assn. S.W. Fla., Franklin County Trial Lawyers Assn., Am. Legion, Fla., Columbus, Akron, Broward County (Fla.) bar assns., Delta Theta Phi, Phi Kappa Tau, Pi Kappa Delta. Home: Apple Valley 704 Country Club Dr Howard OH 43028-9530

LEE, WON JAY, radiologist; b. Seoul, Korea, Feb. 2, 1938; came to U.S., 1965; s. Kang Sei and Choon Ja (Park) L.; m. Moon Jung, Feb. 24, 1968; children: Julie, Lisa, Jennifer. MD, Yonsei U., Seoul, 1962. Diplomate Am. Bd. Radiology, Am. Bd. Nuclear Medicine. Intern Wyckoff Heights Hosp., Bklyn., 1965-66; resident in radiology NYU Med. Ctr., N.Y.C., 1966-69; fellow, asst. radiologist L.I. Jewish Med. Ctr., New Hyde Park, N.Y., 1969-71, staff radiologist, 1975-82, chief uroradiology, 1983—; assoc. radiologist Binghamton (N.Y.) Gen. Hosp., 1971-75; asst. prof. SUNY, Stony Brook, 1975-86, assoc. prof. radiology, 1987-89; prof. radiology Albert Einstein Coll. Medicine, 1989—; vis. prof. diagnostic radiology Yonsei U. Coll. Medicine, Seoul, 1996—; cons. in field. Asst. editor: Jour. Endourology, 1987-96; assoc. editor: Jour. Korean-Am. Med. Assn., 1995-98, editor-in-chief, 1999—; contbr. chpts. to books and articles to profl. jours. First lt. Republic of Korea Army M.C., 1962-65. Recipient Sci. Paper award Soc. Uroradiology, 1994, Clin. award Can. Assoc. Radiologists, 1979, Disting. Svc. award Yonsei U. Col. Med. Alumni Assn., 1998. Fellow Am. Coll. Radiology, Cardiovasc. and Interventional Radiology (emeritus), Soc. Uroradiology; mem. Assn. Univ. Radiologists, Am. Roentgen Ray Soc. (Merit award 1983), Radiol. Soc. N.Am., Korean-Am. Med. Assn. (chmn. sci. and edn. divsn. 1996), Korean Radiol. Soc. N.Am. (pres.-elect 1998), Severance Alumni Assn. Am. (pres. 1997),. Democratic. Methodist. Avocations: gardening, golf, travel. Home: 15 Lucille Ln Huntington Station NY 11746-5848 Office: LI Jewish Med Ctr 270-05 76th Ave New Hyde Park NY 11040-1433

LEE, WOO JONG, logistics company executive; b. Seoul, Jan. 27, 1948; s. Moon Suk and Moo Sung (Chung) L.; m. Hyun Sun Lee, Oct. 26, 1975; children: Young Ki, Sekyung. BA in Polit./Diplomatic Sci., Korea U., 1974. Cargo mgr. Korean Air, Dhahran, Saudi Arabia, 1978-80, Taipei, 1981-84; sales mgr. Korean Air, Seoul, 1985-86; rep. Burlington Air, Seoul, 1987-89, pres., 1990-97; resp. dir. BAX Global, Seoul, 1998—; dir. Korean Internat. Freight Forwarding Assn., Seoul, 1997—. Mem. Rotary (chief mem. internat. com. 1998). Avocations: golf, tennis, music. Office: 4F Seong Ji Bldg, 373-4 Hapjung Dong Mapoku, Seoul Korea

LEE, YEONHEE, research scientist; b. Seoul, Korea, Feb. 24, 1961; d. Chunwoo and Yongsun (Won) L.; m. Jaecheul Kim, May 17, 1987 (dec. Oct. 1992); 1 child, Jihyeon; m. Duk Bin Jun, May 6, 2000; children: Hyoungwoo Brian, Hyounglak David. BS, Korea U., Korea, 1984, MS, 1986; PhD, U. Pitts., 1993. Lab. tech. U. Pitts., 1988-89, rsch. asst., 1990-93; fellow Argonne (Ill.) Nat. Lab., 1994-95; sr. rsch. scientist Korea Inst. Sci. Tech., Seoul, 1995—. Mem. editl. bd, Korean Soc. Analytical Sci., 1998—; contbr. articles to profl. jours. Postdoctoral fellow Argonne (Ill.) Nat. Lab., 1994-95. Mem. Am. Chem. Soc., Am. Vacuum Soc., Signa Xi. Avocations: tennis, music, piano, kendo, skiing. Office: Advanced Analysis Ctr KIST, 39-1 Haweolgok Dong, Seoul 136-791, Korea

LEE, YIU BUN, engineering educator; b. Taishan, Guangdong, China, Nov. 18, 1970; s. Tsang Yuen Lee and Mo Wan Wong; m. Man Chu Leung, May 12, 1996. B Engring., Chinese U. Hong Kong, 1993, PhD in Info. Engring., 1997. Rsch. engr. Advanced Network Sys. Lab. Chinese U. of Hong Kong, 1993-94, software architect, 1994-96, project mgr., 1996-97, vis. asst. prof. dept. info. engring., 1997-98; asst. prof. computer sci. dept. Hong Kong U. of Sci. and Tech., 1998-99; asst. prof. info. engring. Chinese U. Hong Kong, 1999—; asst. prof. dept. info. engring., CUHK, 1999—. Contbr. articles to profl. jours.; patentee in field. Mem. IEEE, Assn. Computing Machinery. Avocations: classical music, high-fidelity audio. Office: Chinese U Hong Kong, Dept Info Engring, Clear Water Bay Shatin Shatin Hong Kong NT, China

LEE, YONG JIN, electrical engineer; b. Seoul, Korea, Nov. 27, 1964; came to U.S., 1983; s. Chul Choo and Sung Sook (Hong) L.; m. Soenkyung Pak, Dec. 27, 1992. BSEE, Stanford U., 1987, MSEE, 1990, MS in Engring. Mgmt., 1992, AB in Econs., 1990, PhD in Elec. Engring., 1994. Engr. Daewoo Electronics, Seoul, Korea, 1986; mem. tech. staff Tex. Instruments, Dallas, 1992-94; chief scientist CVC Products, Fremont, Calif., 1994, dir., chief scientist, 1994—. Senator Associated Students of Stanford (Calif.) U., 1988. Recipient F.E. Terman award Stanford U., 1987, Korean Honor scholarship South Korean Govt., 1990. Mem. IEEE, Tau Beta Pi, Phi Beta Kappa. Achievements include invention of Acoustic Temperature and Film Thickness Monitor, Sensor for Measuring the Temperature of Ambient over Silicon Wafer, Photoacoustic Oscillator Sensor for Temperature and Film Thickness Measurements, Multizone Real-Time Emissivity Correction System for semiconductor processing, advanced illuminator for rapid thermal processing, gas delivery system for chemical vapor deposition, advanced physical vapor deposition systems. Home: 781 Rosewood Dr Palo Alto CA 94303-3638 Office: CVC Products 3100 Laurelview Ct Fremont CA 94538-6535

LEE, YONG-HWAN, agricultural biology educator; b. Jungsun, Kangwon, Republic of Korea, July 29, 1961; s. Doyun Lee and Jungok Cho; m. Sujeong Lee; 1 child, Hyunkyung Caroline. BSc, Seoul Nat. U., Suwon, Republic of Korea, 1983; MS, Suwon, Seoul Nat. U., 1985; PhD, La. State U., 1991. Rsch. asst. La. State U., Baton Rouge, 1988-91; vis. asst. prof. Clemson (S.C.) U., 1991-93; sr. scientist LG Chem. Ltd., Seoul, 1993-95; tchg. assoc. dept. agrl. biology Seoul Nat. U., 1985-88, asst. prof., 1985-99, assoc. prof., chmn. dept., 1999—. Author: The Rice Blast, 1999; editor: Plant Pathology Jour., 1999; contbr. articles to sci. jours. Recipient award for best presentation Soybean Promotion Bd., Tenn., 1990. Mem. Am. Phytopath. Soc., Korean Soc. Molecular Biology, N.Y. Acad. Scis. Avocations: hang gliding, fishing, shooting. Home: Saebyul Apt 201-101, Kyunggi Dalan-Anyang 431-058, Republic of Korea Office: Seoul Nat U, Seodun-Dong, Kyunggi Suwon 441-744, Republic of Korea

LEE, YONG-JOO, sociologist, educator; b. Seoul, South Korea, July 16, 1958; s. Hae-Myong and Bo-Young Lee; m. Im-Ok Hwang, Aug. 8, 1987; 1 child, Samuel Lee. BA, Sogang U., Seoul, 1982; MBA, U. Mont., Missoula, 1987; MA, Mich. State U., 1990, PhD, 1994. Asst. prof. Mich. State U., East Lansing, 1994; instr. Sogang U., Seoul, 1995-99; asst. prof. Nanyang Technol. U., Singapore, 2000—. Co-author: Capitalism and Development, 1994. With Korean Army, 1982-84. Mem. Am. Sociol. Assn., Korean Sociol. Assn. Office: Nanyang Bus Sch Divsn Mgmt, Nanyang Technol U, Singapore 639798, Singapore Address: 98 Nanyang Crescent, Block M #07-04 637665, Singapore

LEE, YOUNG HAE, engineering educator; b. Kyungju, S. Korea, Nov. 11, 1954; s. Jang Yong Lee and Hu Nam Chu; m. Do Geum Kim, May 17, 1977; 1 child, Ji Young. BS, Korea U., Seoul, 1977; MS, U. Ill., 1983, PhD, 1986. Engr. Daewoo Heavy Industries Ltd., Seoul, Republic of Korea, 1977-81; asst. prof. Hanyang U., Seoul, Republic of Korea, 1986-90, assoc. prof., 1991-95, prof. indsl. engring., 1996—; vis. prof. Osaka (Japan) U., 1990-91, Purdue U., 1997—. Author: Introduction to Manufacturing Automation, 1995; co-author: (in Korean) Engineering Statistics, 1989, (in Korean) System Stimulation, 1995; assoc. editor: Jour. Korean CAD/CAM Soc., 1995-96. Mem. steering com. Nation Policy Inst., Seoul, Republic of Korea, 1995—. Lt. Korean Mil., 1977-81. Recipient Kyeongbang award Kyeongbang Found., 1975. Mem. Korean Inst. Indsl. Engrs. (sr., dir. 1991-94), Soc. Mfg. Engrs. (sr.), Inst. Ops. Rsch. and Mgmt. Sci. (sr.), Korea Soc. Simulation (v.p. 1995—), Korean Commerce At light Speed/Electronic Commerce Soc. (dir. 1996—), Korean Ops. Rsch./Mgmt. Sci. Soc. (dir. 1996—), Korean Forum for Info. Soc. (mem. steering com. 1996—). Achievements include patent for an algorithm for path optimization in surface mounters. Home: Hyundai Apt 417-1201, Seohyun-dong Pundang-gu, Seongnam Kyunggi-do 463-050, Republic of Korea Office: Hanyang U, Dept Indsl Engring, 133-791 Seoul Republic of Korea

LEE, YOUNG HWAN, chemistry educator; b. Seoul, Republic of Korea, Jan. 8, 1949; s. Kyung Sun Lee and Jung Jae Kim; m. Chung Sim Baik, Feb. 22, 1985; 1 child. BS, Korea U., 1973; MS, So. Ill. U., 1976; PhD, Clarkson U., 1982. Rsch. assoc. Case Western Res. U., Cleve., 1980-81; sr. rschr. KIST, Seoul, 1981-84; asst. prof. chemistry Kyung-won U., Sung-Nam City, Republic of Korea, 1984-87, prof. chemistry, 1988—; cons. Seoul Chem. Co., Ltd., An-San City, Republic of Korea, 1988—. Patentee in field. Rsch. grantee Korean Inst. Tech., 1989-93, Seoul Chem. Co., 1988-97, Korean Govt., 1995—. Mem. Korean Chem. Soc. Avocation: travel. Fax: 82-2-537-4238. E-mail: leeyh@mail.kyungwon.ac.kr. Home: Dongkwang Villa 201, Banpo-Dong, Seo-cho-ku Seochoku Seoul Republic of Korea Office: Kyung-won U, Kyung-Ki-Dong, Sung-Nam City Republic of Korea

LEE, YUAN TSEH, chemistry educator; b. Hsinchu, Taiwan, China, Nov. 29, 1936; came to U.S., 1962, naturalized, 1974; s. Tsefan and Pei (Tasi) L.; m. Bernice Wu, June 28, 1963; children: Ted, Sidney, Charlotte. BS, Nat. Taiwan U., 1959; MS, Nat. Tsinghua U., Taiwan, 1961; PhD, U. Calif., Berkeley, 1965. From asst. prof. to prof. chemistry U. Chgo., 1968-74; prof. emeritus U. Calif., Berkeley, 1974—, also former prin. investigator Lawrence Berkeley Lab., 1974-97; pres., v.p. Academia Sinica, Taiwan, 1994—. Contbr. numerous articles on chem. physics to profl. jours. Recipient Nobel Prize in Chemistry, 1986, Ernest O. Lawrence award Dept. Energy, 1981, Nat. Medal of Sci., 1986, 90, Peter Debye award for Phys. Chemistry, 1986; fellow Alfred P. Sloan, 1969-71, John Simon Guggenheim, 1976-77; Camille and Henry Dreyfus Found. Tchr. scholar, 1971-74, Harrison Howe award, 1983. Fellow Am. Phys. Soc.; mem. NAS, AAAS, Am. Acad. Arts and Scis., Am. Chem. Soc. Office: Acad Sinica Pres Office, 128 Academia Rd Sec 2, Nankang Taipei 11529, Taiwan

LEE, YUAN-PERN, chemistry educator, science faculty administrator; b. Hsin-Chu, Taiwan, Jan. 25, 1952; s. Tseh-Fan Lee and Pei Tsai; m. Su-Yuen Fu; children: Yi-Ju, Yi-Chuan. BS, Nat. Taiwan U., Taipei, 1973; PhD, U. Calif., Berkeley, 1979. Rsch. assoc. NOAA/Environ. Rsch. Labs., Boulder, Colo., 1979-81; assoc. prof. chemistry Nat. Tsing Hua U., Hsin-Chu, 1981-85, prof. chemistry, 1985—; adj. rsch. fellow Academia Sinica, Taipei, 1988—; dir. Regional Analytical Instrument Ctr., Hsin-Chu, 1991—; nat. chair prof. Min. Edn., 1997—. Contbr. articles to profl. jours. Outstanding scholar, Found. Advancement Outstanding Scholarship, Taiwan, 1995—; recipient 16th Wu Shan-Liang Found. award, Taipei, 1993, Scholar award in basic sci. Ministry Edn., Taipei, 1990, Scholar medal Chinese Chem. Soc., 1996. Fellow Am. Physics Soc.; mem. Sigma Xi. Avocations: tennis, badminton, classical music. Home: 57 Lin-Sheng Rd 9th Fl, Hsin-Chu 300, Taiwan Office: Nat Tsing-Hua U Dept Chem, 101 Sect 2 Kuang-Fu Rd, Hsin-Chu 30013, Taiwan

LEE, YU-MAY, molecular biologist, educator; b. Taipei, Taiwan, June 15, 1961; parents Rei-Cheng Lee and Sien-Fu (Bai) L.; m. Wuh-Liang Hwu, Nov. 9, 1986; children: Yi-Hsuan, Tzui-Hao. MS, Yang-Ming U., 1986; BS, Nat. Taiwan U., 1983, PhD, 1992. Tchg. asst. Yang-Ming U., 1983-84; asst. rsch. fellow Acad. Sinica, Taiwan, 1986-95, assoc. rsch. fellow, 1995—; lectr. Inst. Biochem. Sci., Nat. Taiwan U., 1997—. Contbr. articles to profl. jours. Recipient Excellent Rsch. award Nat. Sci. Coun., Taiwan, 1988—. Avocations: music, reading, cooking. E-mail: yml6120@gate.sinica.edu.tw. Fax: 886-2-27889759. Office: Inst Biol Chemistry, Acad Sinica, Nankong Taipei 115, Taiwan

LEE, YUN BAE, computer science educator; b. Mokpo, Korea, May 29, 1952; s. Joo Han and Yoen Ae (Cho) L.; m. Jung Sook Kim, Sept. 28, 1980. BS, Kwang Woon U., 1980; MS, Kwang Woon Grad. Sch., 1983; D, Soongsil Grad. Sch., 1993. Chief Coll. of Industry Chosun U., Kwangju, Korea, 1993-95, head dept. computer sci., 1997-99, dean Coll. of Info. Sci., 1997—; prof. computer sci. Chosun U., Kwangju, 1999—; adv. com. Kwangju Dist. City, Korea. Author: Expert Systems, 1995, Intro of Computer Science, 1997, Intro of Computer Science and Application, 1998, Computer Science and Application, 2000, Understanding of Multimedia and Application, 2000. Mem. IEEE Korea Coun., Korean Info. Sci. Soc., Korea Info. Processing Soc., The Korea Database Soc., Korean Inst. Maritime Info. and Comm. Scis. Avocations: writing, reading, tennis, golf. Office: Chonsun U Sch Computer Engr, 375 Seosuk-dong Dong-ku, 501-759 Kwangju 501-759, Republic of Korea

LEE, ZUK-NAE, psychiatry educator, psychotherapist, dean; b. Hab-Chun, Kyungnam, Republic of Korea, Feb. 5, 1940; s. Sang-Yong and Yeum-Chun Song-Lee; m. Young-Hee Kwon-Lee, May 7, 1968; children: Kyung-Im, Sung-Lim. MD, Kyungpook U., Taegu, Republic of Korea, 1965; Lic. in Philosophy, Zurich U., Switzerland, 1986, PhD, 1990. Lic. psychiatrist. Intern Korean First Army Hosp., Taegu, 1965-66, resident, 1966-70; dir. Non-San Army Hosp., 1970-71, 102 Korean Army Hosp., Natrang, Vietnam, 1971-72; psychiat. rschr. Hdqs. for Rsch., Seoul, 1972-73; teaching staff Med. Coll. Chungnam U., Taechun, Republic of Korea, 1973-74; tng. candidate Jung Inst., Zurich, 1974-78; asst. prof. Med. Coll., Kyungpook U., 1978-82, assoc. prof. psychiatry, 1982-90, prof., 1990—; chmn., dir. dept. Kyungpook U. Hosp., 1994-98; dean Kyungpook Nat. U. Sch. Medicine and Grad. Sch Pub. Health, 1998—. Chief editor: Shim-Song Yon-Gu, 1986—. Served to maj. Korean mil., 1982-83. Mem. Korean Acad. Psychotherapists (pres. Taegu br. 1988-89), Korean Assn. Psychotherapists (exec. com. 1984—), Korean Soc. Analytical Psychology (tng. analyst 1978—, v.p. 1986-88, pres. 1988-91), Inst. for Human Sci. (exec. com. 1987-89), Korean Neuropsychiatric Assn. (pres. Taegu br. 1988-89). Avocation: mountain climbing. Home: 50 Samduk-Dong 1-Ka Chung-Ku, Taegu 700-411, Republic of Korea Office: Kyungpook U Hosp, 52 Samduk-Dong Chung-Ku, Taegu 700-412, Republic of Korea

LEEB, CHARLES SAMUEL, clinical psychologist; b. San Francisco, July 18, 1945; s. Sidney Herbert and Dorothy Barbara (Fishstrom) L.; m. Storme Lynn Gilkey, Apr. 28, 1984; children: Morgan Evan, Spencer Douglas. BA in Psychology, U. Calif.-Davis, 1967; MS in Counseling and Guidance, San Diego State U., 1970; PhD in Edn. and Psychology, Claremont Grad. Sch., 1973. Assoc. So. Regional Dir. Mental Retardation Ctr., Las Vegas, Nev., 1976-79; pvt. practice, Las Vegas, 1978-79; dir. biofeedback and athletics Menninger Found., Topeka, 1979-82, dir. children's div. biofeedback and psychophysiology ctr. The Menninger Found., 1979-82; pvt. practice, Claremont, Calif., 1982—; dir. of psychol. svcs. Horizon Hosp., 1986-88; dir. adolescent chem. dependency and children's program Charter Oak Hosp., Covina, Calif., 1989-91; founder, chief exec. officer Rsch. and Treatment Inst., Claremont, 1991—; lectr. in field. Contbr. articles to profl. jours. Mem. Am. Psychol. Assn., Calif. State Psychol. Assn. Office: 937 W Foothill Blvd Ste D Claremont CA 91711-3358

LEECH, GEOFFREY NEIL, English language educator; b. Gloucester, Eng., Jan. 16, 1936; s. Charles Richard and Dorothy Eileen (Foster) L.; m. Frances Anne Berman, July 29, 1961; children: Thomas, Camilla. BA, U. Coll. London, 1959, MA, 1963, PhD, 1968; PhD (hon.), Lund (Sweden) U., 1987. Asst. lectr. U. Coll. London, 1962-64, lectr., 1965-69; reader Lancaster (Eng.) U., 1969-74, prof., 1974-96, rsch. prof., 1997—, co-dir. unit computer rsch. English lang., 1984-95, chmn. inst. English lang. edn., 1985-90, chair univ. ctr. corps. rsch. lang., 1995—; hon. prof. Beijing Fgn. Studies U., 1994—. Author: Semantics: The Study of Meaning, 1981, Principles of Pragmatics, 1983; co-author: Style in Fiction, 1981, A Comprehensive Grammar of the English Language, 1985; author, editor over 20 books. Harkness fellow MIT, 1964-65, British Acad. fellow, 1987—, U. Coll. London fellow, 1989—. Mem. Acad. Europea, Norske Videnskaps Acad. Liberal Democrat. Anglican. Avocations: music, piano, organ. Office: Dept Linguistics, Lancaster Univ, Lancaster LA1 4YT, England

LEECH, SALLY See KEMP, SARAH

LEECH, STEWART ANDREW, accounting educator, researcher; b. Melbourne, Australia, July 21, 1946; s. Norman Charles and Matilda Mavis (Mitchell) L.; m. Susan Mary Klein, Aug. 27, 1977. BCom, U. Melbourne, 1970; MEc, U. Tasmania, Hobart, Australia, 1976. Sr. tutor U. Melbourne, 1970-72; sr. lectr. U. Sydney, 1979-80; lectr. U. Tasmania, 1973-79, sr. lectr., 1980-84, reader in acctg., 1985-92, prof. acctg., 1992-2000; prof. acctg. and bus. info. sys. U. Melbourne, 2000—. Co-author: Introduction to Accounting Method, 1984, The TAC System, 1985; contbr. articles to Abacus, Acctg. Edn., Acctg. and Fin., Jour. Bus. Fin. and Acctg., Internt. Jour. Acctg., Brit. Acctg. Rev., others. Australian Rsch. Coun. grantee, 1994, 99; Inst. Chartered Accts. grantee, 1994-95. Mem. Am. Acctg. Assn. (chairperson info. sys. sect. 1998-99), Univ. Club. Avocations: tennis, golf, antiques, history, travel. Home: 153 Wellington St, 3101 Kew Victoria, Australia Office: U Melbourne, Parkville, Victoria 3010, Australia

LEEDER, STEPHEN ROSS, dean, medical educator; b. Grafton, Australia, Dec. 13, 1941; s. Norman Montague and Winifred Ruth (Long) L.; m. Dorothy Muriel Evans, Jan. 12, 1967 (div. 1986); children: Nicholas John, Robert Stephen; m. Katharine Marjorie Esson, Sept. 30, 1989; 1 child, James Esson. BSc in Medicine, U. Sydney, 1964, MBBS, 1966, PhD, 1974. FRACP, FFPHM, FAFPHM. Resident Royal North Shore Hosp., Sydney, 1966-67, 1969-70; rsch. scholar U. Sydney, 1971-73; lectr. St. Thomas Hosp., London, 1974-75; asst. prof. McMaster U., Hamilton, Ont., Can., 1975-76; prof. community medicine Newcastle U., 1976-85; prof. pub. health and community medicine Westmead Hosp./Sydney U., 1985-97; dean of medicine U. Sydney, Australia, 1997—; chmn. assessment sub-com., 1976-79, others; dir. of Asian and Pacific Ctr. for Clin. Epidemiology, Newcastle, 1982-85, others; med. officer Tinsley Hosp., Baiyer River, Papua New Guinea, 1968; vis. med. officer thoracic medicine Royal Newcastle Hosp., 1976-85, Wallsend Dist. Hosp., 1977-83, Westmead Hosp., NSW, 1986—; adv. in cmty. health Hunter Regional Office, NSW Health Commn., 1976-85; mem. Better Health Commn., 1984-86, 88-91; expert adviser to Nat. Program for Better Health, 1988-92; pres. Pub. Health Assn. of Australia, 1985-88, 94-98; chmn. rsch. ethics com. Western Sydney Area Health Svc., 1995—, others. Mem. Australasian Epidemiol. Assn. (pres. 1991-95), others. Office: U Sydney, Faculty of Medicine, 2006 Sydney Australia

LEEDS, HAROLD MITCHELL, computer consultant, director; b. Bklyn., May 11, 1954; s. William Arten and Sylvia Leeds; m. Harriet Jane Weiss, Feb. 16, 1992; children: Matthew, Todd. BA, Ohio State U., 1976. Technician Network One, Hollywood, Fla., 1980-85; sr. ops. mgr. Worldcom, Boca Raton, 1985-96; dir. ops. Facility Works, Fort Worth, Tex., 1996-97. Bd. dirs. Big Bros. and Sisters, Boys and Girls Clubs, Casa Manana Theatre, Fort Worth; mem. North Tex. Workforce Devel. Coun., Forth Worth C. of C. Econ. Devel. and Small Bus. couns. Mem. Rotary (Fort Worth). Republican. Avocations: tennis, golf, snorkeling. Fax: (817) 339-1138. E-mail: hleeds@morrownet.com. Home: 7937 Morning Ln Fort Worth TX 76123-1925 Office: Single Source Commn 201 Main St Ste 600 Fort Worth TX 76102-3110

LEEDS, KAREN, sales executive, marketing professional; b. Flushing, N.Y., Aug. 29, 1955; d. Robert Sol and Roberta Vera L.; m. Phillip M. Markham, Sept. 21, 1979 (Apr. 1993). Student, Fla. State U., 1973-76. Mgr. sales adminstr. dbx, Inc., Newton, Mass., 1980-86; mktg. mgr. Nat. Teledata Corp., Norwell, 1986-88; ind. mfrs. rep. The Winters Group, Boston, 1988-93; v.p. sales and mktg. Future Primitive, Scottsdale, Ariz., 1993—. Vol. Hospice of the Valley, Phoenix, 1999. Office: Future Primitive 4841 N Scottsdale Rd Ste 205 Scottsdale AZ 85251-7612

LEEDY, GENE ROBERT, architect; b. Isaban, W.Va., Feb. 6, 1928; s. Cecil Hudgins and Ethyl (Ferguson) L.; m. Kathryn Hoge, 1950 (div. 1958); 1 child, Robert; m. Marjorie Ingram, 1960; children: Helen Knight, Saffie Ellerman, Ingram. BArch, U. Fla., 1950. Registered architect, Fla. Pvt. practice Winter Haven, Fla., 1955—; adj. prof. U. Fla., 1979—; founder Sarasota Sch.; archtl. design cons. Alfred A. Yee & Assocs., Honolulu, 1965—; mem. various award jurys; vis. critic and lectr. U. Fla., 1975, 76, 77, 78, 79; lectr. in field. Contbr. articles to profl. jours.; works pub. in various mags., newspapers, books, profl. jours. Mem. archtl. adv. coun. Coll. Arch., U. Fla., 1986; chmn. award com. Hillsborough County Planning Commn., Tampa, 1989. 1st lt. USAF, 1951-54. Recipient Award of Merit, Fla. Assn. Architects, 1957, 62, award House and Home mag., 1956, Award of Excellence for house design Archtl. Record, 1965, Award of Merit, Prestressed Concrete Inst., Chgo., award for comml. bldg. renovation Orlando Mag., 1987; Disting. Alumni award Coll. Arch., U. Fla., 1993, numerous others. Fellow AIA (Award of Honor for Design 1988, Lifetime Achievement award of honor 1988). Home: 1518 Drexel Ave NE Winter Haven FL 33881-4439 Office: Gene Leedy Architect, FAIA 555 Avenue G NW Winter Haven FL 33881-4039

LEEDY, WALLACE CURTIS, former educator; b. Dinuba, Calif., Nov. 15, 1924; s. Walter Boston Leedy and Stella Eunace Fields; m. Barbara Mace, July 1, 1945 (dec. June 1999); 1 child, Dawn Caroline Leedy Guest. BA, Fresno State Coll., 1951; Tchr. Cert., 1952. Cert. tchr. secondary sch. Tchr. L.A. City Schs., 1952-56, N.Am. Aviation, 1956-85; ind. rschr., writer social behavioral sci. and biology. Mem. Social Sci. Honor Soc., Edn. Honor Soc., Arabian Horse Assn. of San Fernando Valley (past pres.). Avocations: Arabian horses. Home: 1400 Victoria Ave Apt 120 Oxnard CA 93035-2113

LEEK, BARRY FRANK, veterinarian, educator; b. Birmingham, England, Apr. 13, 1935; s. Frank and Evelyn (Greenwood) L.; m. Fiona Alexandra King Jack, July 9, 1970; 1 child, Aidan. B of Veterinary Medicine & Surgery, U. Edinburgh, 1958, BSc, 1960, PhD, 1967. From asst. lectr. to lectr. U. Edinburgh, Scotland, 1958-72; prof. Univ. Coll. Dublin, Ireland, 1972—. Fellow Royal Acad. Medicine (Ireland); mem. Royal Coll. Vet. Surgeons, Physiol. Soc. Avocations: horseback riding, hiking, beekeeping, bird watching. Office: Vet Coll Ireland, Ballsbridge, Dublin 4, Ireland

LEEK, DIANE WEBB, nurse; b. St. Louis, Dec. 19, 1956; d. Paul Benedict and Bessie Marie (Brenneison) Webb; m. Gregory Leek, Apr. 4, 1992; children: Jon, Cliff. AS in Nursing, Maryville Coll., 1978; BSN, St. Louis U., 1982, MSN, 1994. RN, Mo.; cert. case mgr.; cert. legal nurse cons. Staff nurse Jewish Hosp., St. Louis, 1978-82; critical care staff nurse St. Luke's Episcopal Hosp., Houston, 1983-84; staff nurse, emergency room Meml. Hosp., South Bend, Ind., 1984; staff nurse, trauma emergency rm. Med. Ctr. Hosp., San Antonio, 1985-88; tchr. asst. U. Tex. Health Sci. Ctr., San Antonio, 1988; utiliation rev. coord. Group Health Plan, St. Louis, 1988-90; trauma staff nurse emergency rm. Barnes/Jewish Hosp., St. Louis, 1988-97; nurse cons. Aetna Life & Casualty, 1991-93; case mgr. cons. St. Paul Fire & Marine Ins., 1993-97; mgr. health care cons. Ernst & Young, 1997-98; mgr. legal nurse cons. RGL Gallagher LLP, St. Louis, 1998—. Contbg. author: Case Management Practice Guidelines, 1996. Vol. RN supr. ARC, San Antonio, 1987. Recipient Pres. award for Excellence and Achievement Group Health Plan, 1990. Mem. Case Mgmt. Soc. St. Louis (sec., bd. dirs. 1994, pres. 1997), Am. Assn. Legal Nurse Cons. (newsletter editor 1999, bd. dirs. 1999), Sigma Theta Tau (award for Acad. Excellence 1994). Republican. Roman Catholic. Avocations: classical music, piano, needlepoint, crafts, photography. Home: 1209 Crested View Dr Saint Louis MO 63146-5518

LEEK, JAY WILBUR, management consultant; b. Albany, Ind., Apr. 24, 1928; s. Cecil and Hazel (Lindley) L.; m. Geneva Adams, June 30, 1948; children: Roderick Jay, Stacy LeAnn, Scott Lee, Timothy Lane, Debra Jan, Marilynn Sue, James Jay. BS in Indsl. Engring., Pacific Western, 1969, MS in Mgmt., 1976, D in Bus. Adminstrn., 1980. Registered profl. engr., Calif. Mgr. Nutone, Inc., Cin., 1951-53, Bulova Watch Co., N.Y.C., 1953-59, Martin Marietta Corp., Orlando, Fla., 1959-75; v.p. Northrop Corp., L.A., 1975-80; pres., COO Philip Crosby Assocs., Winter Park, Fla., 1980-87, also bd. dirs.; mgmt. cons., Ft. Myers, 1987-91; pres., CEO Carchi-Resources, Inc., Ocala, Fla.; bd. dirs. So. Bank, Longwood, Fla., Electro-World, Orlando. Author: Workmanship Standards, 1974; co-author: (with others) AMA Management Handbook, 1986, Quality Management Handbook, 1986. Trustee Orlando Sports Inc., 1985-87, Fla. State Univ. Found., Tallahassee, 1986-96; bd. dirs. Fla. Citrus Sports Assn., Orlando, 1984-90. With USN, 1944-46. Recipient Academician award Internat. Acad. for Quality, Grobenzell, Fed. Republic Germany, 1985; named to Wall of Fame, Am. Mgmt. Assn., 1979. Fellow Am. Soc. Quality Control (pres. 1980-81), Black Diamond Ranch Country Club, Country Club of Ocala, Sapphire Lakes Country Club, Masons, Shriners. Republican. Fax: 352-861-8922. Home: 3095 SW 53d St Ocala FL 34474-5802 Office: 303 SE 17th St Ste 307 Ocala FL 34471-4423

LEEKLEY, MARIE VALPOON, secondary education educator; b. Honolulu, Mar. 28, 1941; d. Amil Richard and Florence Haruko (Soken) V.; m. John Darwin Leekley, Jr., June 26, 1965; children: Katherine Joan, Tracy Ann Kehaunani. BS, Carroll Coll., Waukesha, Wis., 1963; MEd, Nat. Coll. Edn., Evanston, Ill., 1990; postgrad., Marquette U. Dir. Christian edn. Kamehameha Sch. for Girls, Honolulu, 1963-64; elem. tchr. Milw. Pub. Schs., 1965-67; vol. Marianas Edn. Dept. Peace Corps, Saipan, Mariana Islands, 1967-69, dist. coord. tchr. edn., 1969-71; tchr. Ethan Allen Sch. for Boys, Wales, Wis., 1977-96; tchr. adult basic edn. Waukesha County Tech. Coll., Pewaukee, Wis., 1977—. Mem. Menomonee Falls (Wis.) Pub. Schs. Bd. Edn., 1990—; bd. dirs. Comprehensive Ednl. Svcs. Agys., West Allis, Wis., 1991-96. Recipient vol. appreciation award Greater Menomonee Falls Com., 1991, Boardmanship award Wis. Assn. Sch. Bds., 1991, 92, 93; named Edn. Leader of Yr. AAUW, 1996. Mem. ASCD, Correctional Edn. Assn., Nat. Sch. Bd. Assn., Wis. Assn. Adult and Continuing Edn., Wis. Vocat. Assn., Wis. Edn. Assn. Methodist. Home: W148N7590 Woodland Dr Menomonee Falls WI 53051-4522 Office: Waukesha County Tech Coll 327 E Broadway Waukesha WI 53186-5008

LEEKPAI, CHUAN, prime minister of Thailand, lawyer; b. Muang Dist., Trang Pr., Thailand, July 28, 1938. LLB, Thammasat (Thailand) U., 1962; D Polit. Sci. (hon.), Srinakharinwirot U., 1985, Ramkhamhaeng U., 1987; LLD (hon.), U. Philippines, 1993, Vongechavalitkul U., 1998; LittD in Painting (hon.), Silpakorn U., 1994; LittD (hon.), Nat. U. San Marcos, Lima, Peru, 1999. Barrister, Thailand, 1964. Mem. Thai Ho. of Reps., Bangkok, from 1969, spkr., 1986-88; dep. min. justice Dept. Justice, Bangkok, 1975-76, min. justice, 1976-80; min. to Office of Prime Min., Bangkok, 1976; min. commerce, Bangkok, 1980-81, min. agr. and coops., 1981-83, 90, min. edn., 1983-86, min. pub. health,, 1988-89, dep. prime min.,, 1989-90, prime min.,, 1992-95, 97—, also min. def., 1997—, leader of opposition,, 1995-97; vis. lectr. forensic medicine dept. Chulalongkorn U. Faculty Medicine. Mem. coun. Silpakorn U., Kasetsart U., Srinakharinwirot U., Thammasat U.; v.p. coun. Prince of Songkhla U. Decorated knight grand cross 1st class and knight grand cordon Most Noble Order of Crown of Thailand, knight grand cross 1st cross and knight grand cordon spl. class Most Exalted Order of White Elephant, grand companion 3d class, higher grade and knight grand comdr. 2d class, higher grade Most Illustrious Order of Chula Chom Klao (Thailand), Order of Sukatuna spl. class, Raja (The Philippines), grand cross Order of Sun (Peru), grand cross Order of Christ (Portugal), gran cruz Jose Dolores Estrada, Batalla de San Jacinto (Nicaragua). Buddhist. Office: Secretariat of Prime Min, Government House, Bangkok 10300, Thailand

LEELARASAMEE, AMORN, medical educator; b. Bangkok, Aug. 26, 1948; s. Yothin and Yuvadee Leelarasamee; m. Imjai Leelarasamee, 1973; children: Jinda, Yodmanee, Patara. BSc, Mahidol U., Bangkok, 1970, MD, 1972; cert. in internal medicine, Thai Med. Coun., Bangkok, 1976; MS, U. Newcastle, Australia, 1989. Mem. med. staff Siriraj Hosp. Mahidol U., Bangkok, 1976-79, asst. prof. internal medicine, 1979-84, assoc. prof. internal medicine and infectious disease, 1984-95, dir. clin. epidemiology unit, 1990-97; fellow in infectious disease U. Calif., San Diego, 1981, prof. medicine and infectious disease, 1995—; chmn. sci. com. 2d Western Pacific Congress on Infectious Disease and Chemotherapy, 1989-91; vice chmn. task force for multicenter study of investigation and therapeutic guideline for pyrexia of unknown origin in Thailand, Ministry of Pub. Health, Bangkok, 1990-93, mem. nat. expert com. on standardization of drug therapy for urinary tract infection, 1986-88, mem. com. communicable diseases commn., 1989-94, head Office for R&D Faculty of Medicine Siriraj Hosp., 1996—, among others. Pres., editor-in-chief Assn. Infectious Disease of Thailand, Bangkok, 1984-2000. Mem. Assn. Infectious Disease Thailand (pres. 1996-99, editor-in-chief 1989-2000). Office: Siriraj Hosp, Dept Medicine Prannok Rd, Bangkok 10700, Thailand

LEEMANS, CHARLES REINIER, otolaryngologist, head and neck surgeon; b. Rotterdam, The Netherlands, Aug. 21, 1959; s. Karel Willem Leemans and Antoinetta Petronella Stoovi; m. Letta Boudientje Van der Have. MD, Erasmus U., Rotterdam, 1985; PhD, Vrije U., Amsterdam, 1992. Cert. in medicine, otolaryngology. Resident in gen. surgery Andreas Hosp., Amsterdam, 1985-86; resident in otolaryngology Univ. Hosp. Vrije Universiteit, Amsterdam, 1987-92, fellow in head and neck surgery, 1992-93, asst. prof. otolaryngology-head and neck surgery, 1994-98, assoc. prof. otolaryngology-head and neck surgery, 1998—; fellow in plastic surgery Canniesburn Hosp., Glasgow, Scotland, 1993-94; fellow in head and neck surgery Netherlands Cancer Inst./Antoni van Leeuwenhoek Hosp., Amsterdam, 1994; mem. oper. rm. com. Univ. Hosp. Vrije Universiteit, Amsterdam, 1996—. Contbr. articles to med. jours. Hans Wyder fellow European Sch. Oncology, Milan, 1991, fellow in head and neck oncology Dutch Cancer Soc., Amsterdam, 1992-94. Fellow Royal Soc. Medicine, Am. Head and Neck Soc. (corr.); mem. Netherlands Soc. Otorhinolaryngology and Cervico-facial Surgery (sec. working party on head and neck surgery and oncology 1996—). Fax: 31 20 4443688. E-mail: chr.leemans@azvu.nl. Home: P C Hoofstraat 50-2, 1071 CA Amsterdam The Netherlands Office: U Hosp Vrije Universiteit, PO Box 7057, 1007 MB Amsterdam The Netherlands

LEEMPOEL, PETER J. B., dentist; b. Hilversum, The Netherlands, July 11, 1947; s. André M. C. and Maria (Brölmann) L.; m. Maria J. Th. A. Schellekens, July 25, 1970; children: Sebastiaan, Astrid. Dental degree, U. Nijmegen, The Netherlands, 1970, PhD, 1987. Staff prosthodontist dept. prosthodontic dentistry Nijmegen, 1970-76, sr. staff prosthodontist, assoc. prof. dept. Occlusal Reconstruction, 1976—; sr. staff prosthodontist dept. prosthodontic dentistry Brussels, 1982-83; mem. bd. dept. Occlusal Reconstruction, Nijmegen, 1978-82, prosthetic dentistry, Nijmegen, 1974-75; v.p. bd. Faculty Dentistry, Nijmegen, 1979-80, substitute pres. bd., 1980. Author: De Prothetische Behandeling van een Patient met een Edentate Bovenkaak en een Gedeeltelijk Betande Onderkaak, 1986, Die prothetische Versorgung eines Patienten mit zahnlosem Oberkiefer und teilbezahntem Unterkiefer, 1986, Levensduur en Nabehandelingen van Kronen en Conventionele Bruggen in de Algemene Praktijk, 1987. Mem. Fedn. Dentaire Internat., Assn. Nederlandse Tandartsen. Office: St Canisiussingel 21, 6511 TG Nijmegen The Netherlands

LEEPA, ALLEN, artist, educator; b. N.Y.C., Jan. 9, 1919; s. Harvey and Esther (Gentle) L. Student (scholar), The New Bauhaus Sch., 1937-38; scholar, Hans Hofmann Sch., 1938-39; B.S., Columbia U., 1942, M.A. (scholar), 1948, Ed.D., 1960. Art instr. Hull Sch., Chgo., 1937-38, Bklyn. Art Center, 1939-40, Met. Mus., N.Y.C., 1940-41, St. Marks Center, N.Y.C., 1941-42; draftsman Acrotorque Co., Conn., 1942, Glen Martin Aircraft, N.Y.C., 1942-44; prof. art Mich. State U., 1945-84, ret. prof. emeritus; mem. Leepa Gallery of Fine Art, Tarpon Springs, Fla., 1987-90. Author: The Challenge of Modern Art, 1949, 95, Abraham Rattner, 1974; contbr.: (anthologies) The New Art, 1966, 68, The Humanitites in Contemporary Life, 1960, Minimal Art; art editor: The Centennial Rev. Arts and Scis. Jour., 1959-62; one man shows Artists Gallery, N.Y.C., 1953, La Cours D'Ingres, Paris, 1961, Artists Mart, Detroit, 1969, Duke U., 1981; group shows include Mus. Modern Art, N.Y.C., 1953, VII Bienal, São Paulo, Brazil, 1963, Prado Mus., Madrid, Spain, 1956, Detroit Inst. Arts, 1948, 50, 56, 80, Pa. Acad. Fine Arts, 1951, 63; represented in permanent collections Mich. State U., Grand Rapids (Mich.) Mus., South Bend (Ind.) Mus.; lifetime work Tampa Mus. Fine Art, Leepa/Rattner Mus. Fine Arts St. Petersburg (Fla.) Jr. Coll. Fulbright award to Paris, 1950-51; Ford Found. grantee Brazil, 1970; recipient numerous prizes for paintings including: 1st prize statewide mural competition, Mich., 1983; 1st prize abstract painting Guild Hall Mus., East Hampton, N.Y., 1985. Mem. Mich. Acad. Arts, Scis., Letters. Office: Mich State U Art Dept East Lansing MI 48823

LEERBERG, PER, accountant; b. Nexø, Denmark, Nov. 7, 1938; s. Carl and Sine Frederikke (Nielsen) Mortensen; m. Christina Stephansen, Dec. 17, 1966 (div. July 1974); children: Sisse, Pernille; m. Susanne Calundan, Feb. 21, 1979; 1 child, Marie Wedel. Grad., Bus. Sch. Aalborg, Denmark, 1961. Acct. Stroybergs, Aalborg, Denmark, 1956-59, Heier, Aalborg, Denmark, 1959-60, Aalborg Mcpl., 1960-66; mng. dir. discotheque " The Cat", Aalborg, 1966-72, "King Arthur", Aalborg, 1966-68; mng. dir. restaurant "The Golden Lion", Aalborg, 1969-70; mng. dir. Bispe Shopping Ctr., Aalborg, 1972-74, Leerberg Investments, Aalborg, 1974—; pres. East Park Jazz Club, Aalborg, 1956-66, Aalborg Movie Club, 1962-68; lisence Movie Theatre; founder, dir. Nordj.JazzRadio.com. Author: The Totality in Carl Th. Dreyers Production, 1964, Jazzarchives-Live Recordings, 1956-72, (CD recordings) Sound Pictures in Jazzmusic in Aalborg, 1994, Earl Hines Live, Aalborg, Denmark, 1965, 94. Avocations: sound-recording, jazz music, classical music, movies, science. Home and office: Rughaven 15, DK-9000 Ålborg Denmark

LEES, ALFRED WILLIAM, writer, former magazine editor; b. Kansas City, Kans., June 12, 1926; s. Alfred Whitaker and Blanche (Pontius) L. BA, Stanford U., 1950. Editor, writer Home Craftsman, N.Y.C., 1953-59, Family Handyman, 1960; editor, writer Popular Sci., N.Y.C., 1960-62, sr. editor, writer, 1967-71, group editor, reader activities, 1972-88; editor, writer Popular Mechanics, 1962-66; home care columnist Cosmopolitan, 1965-67; dir., judge nat. ann. design competition Am. Plywood Assn., Tacoma, 1976-86; pres. Nat. Assn. Home and Workshop Writers, 1990-92. Author: Leisure Homes, 1980, 67 Prizewinning Plywood Projects, 1984; co-author: Wood Finishing and Painting, 1955, DIY Projects for Your Own Backyard, 1978, 2d edit., 1984, What's Wrong with My Car?, 1990, Decks and Sunspaces, 1991, Longtime Companions, 1999. With USAAF, 1944-45. Mem. Dutch Treat Club. Presbyterian. Avocations: world travel, photography. Home: 140 Nassau St Apt 9B New York NY 10038-1526

LEES, SIR DAVID, business executive; b. England, Nov. 23, 1936; s. D.M. and C.D.M. L.; m. Edith Mary Bernard; children: Jeremy, Virginia, Justin. Cert., London Bus. Sch., 1967. Clk. Binder Hamlyn & Co., London, 1957-62; sr. audit clk. Handley Page Ltd., London, 1962-63; chief acct. Handley Page Ltd., 1964-68; fin. dir. Handley Page Aircraft Ltd., 1969; chief acct., dep. controller, then dir., sec., controller GKN Sankey Ltd., London, 1970-76; group fin. exec. GKN plc (formerly GKN Ltd.), London, 1976-77; gen. mgr. fin. GKN plc (formerly GKN Ltd.), 1977-82, fin. dir., 1982-87, group mng. dir., chmn. designate, 1987-88, chmn., chief exec., 1988-97, chmn., 1997—; bd. dirs. GKN (U.K.) plc., United Engring. Ltd.; dir. Bank of England, 1991—; non-exec. dir. Courtauld's plc, 1991-98, non-exec. chmn. 1997-98; mem. Midlands Indsl. Coun., 1988-96; ex-officio mem. mgmt. bd. and gen. coun. Engring. Employers' Fedn., 1987—, mem. policy com., v.p., 1988-89, sr. dep. pres., 1989-90, pres., 1990-92, v.p., 1994—; chmn. coun., econ. and fin. policy com., 1988-94, mem. president's com. Confederation Brit. Industry, 1988-96, mem. fin. and gen. purposes com., 1994—; mem. NEDO Engring. Industry sector group, 1988-92; mem. Listed Cos. adv. group, 1990-97. Bd. govs., Shrewsbury Sch.; dir. Royal Opera House, 1998—. Fellow Royal Soc. Encouragement of Arts, Mfrs. and Commerce; mem. Soc. Bus. Economists (pres.), European Round Table. Avocations: golf, music, opera, walking. Office: GKN plc, Redditch, Worcestershire B98 0TL, England

LEES, WILLIAM GLENWOOD, finance executive, retail executive; b. Flat River, Mo., Nov. 18, 1916; m. Mary Louise Meier, Aug. 22, 1937; children: Graham (dec.), Van P.G. Grad. high sch., Flat River, 1934. Office clk. Schramm Grocery Co., Flat River, 1934-36; asst. mgr. Wetterau Grocery Co., Desloge, Mo., 1936-39; owner Lees Food Market, Flat River, 1939-48, Lees Tom Boy Store, Farmington, Mo., 1948-55; pres. Lees Shopping Ctr. Inc., Farmington, 1955-80, So. Acceptance Corp., Inc., Farmington, 1961-98; ret., 1998; pres. Lees Home Furnishings Inc., Farmington, 1980—. Pres. Presbyn. Home for Children, Farmington, 1958-70; v.p. Camp Penuel, Inc., Ironton, Mo., 1977—; elder Presbyn. Ch., Farmington, 1958-70, Penuel Fellowship,Ironton, 1977—. With U.S. Army, 1943-46. Mem. C. of C. (bd. dirs. 1956-58), Masons, Shriners (pres. 1963). Republican. Avocations: golf, travel. Home: 18 Airline Dr Farmington MO 63640-1106

LEET, RICHARD HALE, oil company executive; b. Maryville, Mo., Oct. 11, 1926; s. Theron Hale and Helen Eloise (Rutledge) L.; m. Phyllis Jean Combs, June 14, 1949; children: Richard Hale II, Alan Combs, Dana Ellen. B.S. in Chemistry, N.W. Mo. State Coll., 1948; Ph.D. in Phys. Chemistry, Ohio State U., 1952. Rsch. chemist Standard Oil Co., Whiting, Ind., 1953-64; dir. long-range and capital planning, mktg. dept. Am. Oil Co., Chgo., 1964-68; mgr. ops. planning, mfg. dept. Am. Oil Co., 1968-70; regional v.p. Am. Oil Co., Atlanta, 1970-71; v.p. supply Am. Oil Co., Chgo., 1971-74; v.p. planning and adminstrn. Amoco Chems. Corp., Chgo., 1974-75; v.p. mktg. Amoco Chems. Corp., 1975-77, exec. v.p., 1977-78, pres., 1978-83; dir. Amoco Corp., Chgo., 1983-91, vice chmn., 1991-92; retired, 1992; bd. dirs. emeritus Gt. Lakes Chem., Vulcan Materials Corp., ITW, Landauer, Inc. Former chmn. bd. mgrs. Met. YMCA, Chgo.; former pres. Boy Scouts Am.; former chmn. bd. Am. Indsl. Health Coun.; former bd. visitors Emory U., 1970-71; hon. v.p. found. bd. Ohio State U; trustee Brenau U. With USNR, 1944-46. Mem. Am. Chem. Soc., Soc. Chem. Industry (exec. com.), Am. Petroleum Inst. (bd. dirs.), Société Industrielle de Chemie, Chem. Mfrs. Assn. (dir.), Phi Sigma Epsilon, Gamma Alpha. Office: Lighthouse Acres 3631 Lantern Dr Gainesville GA 30504-5420

LEETS, PETER J., consulting firm executive; b. London, Mar. 12, 1946; came to U.S., 1948; s. Earl Edward and Doris Eileen L.; m. Anne E. Shahinian, May 15, 1982. BS in Mktg., Ind. U., 1969. Salesman Ortho Pharm. Corp., Raritan, N.J., 1969-74; account mgr. Revlon Inc., Indpls., 1974-76; regional dir. Revlon Inc., Cleve., 1976-79; field sales mgr. Revlon Inc., Bay Village, Ohio, 1979-83; nat. field sales mgr. Binney & Smith, Bethlehem, Pa., 1983-85; v.p., dir. sales Dell Pub. Co., Inc., N.Y.C., 1985-87; exec. v.p. Geneva Corp., Irvine, Calif., 1987-88; pres. Geneva Cos., Costa Mesa, Calif., 1988-90; exec. v.p. Exec. Assets Corp., Irvine, Calif., 1990-91; pres. Exec. Assets Corp., 1992-94; reg. mng. prin. Right Mgmt. Cons., Irvine, Calif., 1994—; bd. dirs. Career Beginnings, Career Transition Ptnrs., Constl. Rights Found., Prof. Coaches Mentors Assn. Chairperson Orange County Econ. Outlook Conf.; bd. dirs. Forum for Corp. Dirs., PIHRA Found., Chapman U. Fellow Outplacement Inst.; mem. Internat. Assn. Career Mgmt. Profls. (bd. dirs.), Ind. U. Alumni (life), Delta Chi. Office: Right Mgmt Cons Inc 3333 Michelson Dr Ste 400 Irvine CA 92612-1684

LEFEBVRE, ARTHUR HENRY, mechanical engineer, educator; b. Long Eaton, Eng., Mar. 14, 1923; came to U.S., 1976; s. Henri and May (Brown) L.; m. Elizabeth Marcella Betts, Dec. 20, 1952; children: David Ivan, Paul Henry, Anne Marie. B.Sc., Nottingham U., 1946; Ph.D., Imperial Coll., London, 1952, D.Sc., 1975; D.Sc., Cranfield Inst. Tech., 1989. Combustion engr. Rolls Royce, Derby, Eng., 1952-61; prof. aircraft propulsion Cranfield Inst. Tech., Eng., 1961-71; prof., head Sch. Mech. Engring. Cranfield Inst. Tech., 1971-76; prof., head Sch. Mech. Engring., Purdue U., West Lafayette, Ind., 1976-80; Reilly prof. combustion engring. Sch. Mech. Engring., Purdue U., 1980-93, emeritus Reilly prof. combustion engring., 1993—; cons. on combustion to various cos., Britain, Europe and U.S.A.; mem. propulsion and energetics panel Adv. Group Aero. Research and Devel., 1972-76. Author: Gas Turbine Combustion, 1983, Atomization and Sprays, 1989; contbr. tech. articles to profl. jours.; patentee combustion equipment. Fellow Royal Aero. Soc., Instn. Mech. Engrs., Royal Soc. Arts, ASME (Gas Turbine award 1984, R. Tom Sawyer award 1984, Internat. Gas Turbine Inst. scholar award 1995, Aircraft Engine Tech. award, 1996), Royal Acad. Engring.; mem. AIAA (Propellants and Combustion award 1990). Home: Low Furrow, Pebworth, Stratford-upon-Avon CV37 8XW, England

LEFEBVRE-BRION, HÉLÈNE, chemical physicist; b. Saint-Dié, France, Sept. 14, 1928; m. Roland Lefebvre, Mar. 20, 1959; children: Alain, Marc. Doctorat es scis., Univ. Paris, 1958. Dir. of rsch. Ctr. Nat de la Recherche Scientifique, Paris, 1977; organizer of workshops on molecular spectroscopy, Paris, 1969-79; lectr. Internat. Winter Sch., Trieste, Italy, 1973, Physics Summer Sch., Canberra, Australia, 1992, course for grad. students, Paris, 1959-76. Author: Perturbations in the Spectra Of Diatomic Molecules, 1986; editorial bd. Jour. of Chemical Physics, 1996-99. Avocation: linguistics. E-mail: helene.lefebvre-brion@ppm.u-psud.fr. Office: Lab de Photophysique Moleculaire Univ Paris, Batiment 213, 91405 Orsay Cedex, France

LEFELHOCZ, IRENE HANZAK, nurse, business owner; b. Cleve., Nov. 10, 1926; d. Joseph J. and Gisella Elizabeth (Biro) Hanzak; m. Joseph R. Lefelhocz, Aug. 7, 1948; 1 child, Joseph R. III. RN, St. Luke's Hosp. Sch. Nursing, 1948; BSN, Case Western Res. U., 1963; MEd, John Carroll U., 1971; MSN, Case Western Reserve U., 1973. RN, Ohio, Ala. Adminstrv. cons. The Episcopal Kyle Home, Gadsen, Ala., 1986-88; pres., mgr. The Joseph House, Gadsen, 1989-97; nurse cons. Ala. Dept. Health, Montgomery, Ala., 1988-90; supr., evening and night nurse adminstr. Riverview Med. Ctr., Moragne Park, Gadsden; counselor Sch. Nursing Holy Name of Jesus Med. Ctr, 1990-92; psychology therapist, counselor to inpatient population Mountain View Hosp., Gadsden, 1994-97, mem. spkrs. bur. Mem. allocations com. United Way, Etowah County; active numerous other community orgns.; bd. dirs., vice chmn. Etowah County chpt. ARC. Mem. NEA, Ohio Edn. Assn., ARC (past pres.). Office: Mountain View Hosp 3001 Scenic Hwy Gadsden AL 35904-3047

LEFEVRE, THIERRY, cardiologist, educator; b. St.-Germain En laye, France, Apr. 10, 1957; s. Marcel and Monique (Thiel) L. MD, Necker U., 1985, cert. in cardiology, 1988. Cert. echocardiologist. Fellow in cardiology Hôpital Poissy, d'Argenteuil, Gonesse, Pontoise, Paris, 1985-88; rsch. fellow in cardiology Montreal Heart Inst., Can., 1989-90; cardiologist UCVI-Clinique Hartmann and Hôpital Pontoise, Neuilly and Pontoise, France, 1990-95; chief cath. lab. Inst. Hosp. Jacques Cartier, Massy, France, 1995—. Mem. editl. com. Etudes Cardiovasculaires, 1994-97; contbr. articles to profl. jours. Capt. French Mil., 1986. Rsch. grantee Regional Assn. Cardiology, 1988. Fellow European Soc. Cardiology; mem. Am. Heart Assn., Soc. Française Cardiologie, Working Group Coronary Circulation, Soc. Cardiac Angiography and Intervention, 1998. Avocations: tennis, skiing, sailing, funboard. Fax: 33 1 60 13 4603. Office: Inst Hosp Jacques Cartier, Avenue du Noyer Lambert, 91300 Massy France

LEFFLER, CAROLE ELIZABETH, mental health nurse, women's health nurse; b. Sidney, Ohio, Feb. 18, 1942; d. August B. and Delores K. Aselage; children: Veronica, Christopher. ADN, Sinclair Community Coll., Dayton, Ohio, 1975. Cert. psychiat. nurse coord. Nurse Grandview Hosp, Dayton, 1961-76; substitute sch. nurse Fairborn (Ohio) City Schs., 1981-82; dir. nursing Fairborn Nursing Home, 1983; psychiat. nurse coord. Dayton Mental Health Ctr., 1984—; mem. exec. bd. 1199; chmn. disaster mental health com. ARC Ohio. Vol., instr., disaster health nurse ARC, chmn. State of Ohio disaster mental health com.; officer, leader, camp nurse for Girl Scouts, Boy Scouts; Ch. Parish Coun. Recipient Fleur de Lis award Girl and Boy Scouts, Svc. award ARC, Fairborn Mayor's Cert. of Merit for Civic Pride, State of Ohio Govs. award Innovation Ohio. Mem. ANA, Ohio Nurses Assn. Home: 3020 N Dayton Lakeview Rd New Carlisle OH 45344-8505

LEFKO, JEFFREY JAY, hospital administrator; b. St. Paul, July 15, 1945; s Morris and Dorothy (Mindell) L.; m. Philomena M. Corno, Mar. 6, 1970 (div. Dec. 1984); children: Melissa Ann, Benjamin Scott, Ellen Rachael; m. Mary Wilson, Jan. 10, 1986 (div. June 1989); m. Susan H. Shockley, Jan. 5, 1990. BSBA with distinction, U. Nebr., 1967; M in Hosp. Adminstrn., Washington U., St. Louis, 1969. Adminstrv. resident St. John's Mercy Hosp., St. Louis, 1968-69; nat. fellow Health Services Adminstrn. Am. Hosp. Assn.-Blue Cross Assn., Chgo., 1969-70; v.p. planning/ops. Meth. Hosp. of Ind., Indpls., 1970-75; v.p. Jewish Hosp., St. Louis, 1975-78; v.p. planning Greenville (S.C.) Hosp. System, 1979-88; exec. cons. The Lash Group, Greenville, 1988-90; v.p. planning Union Meml. Hosp., Balt., 1990-93; v.p. planning and mktg. St. Joseph Med. Ctr., Balt., 1993-98; exec. v.p. Am.'s Dr., Inc., 1998—, Americasdoctor.com, 1998-2000; v.p. e-bus. HCIASachs, Inc., 2000—; adj. instr. Washington U., 1976-78; guest lectr. Duke U., Univ. S.C., Clemson U., Ind. U.; instr. Furman U., Greenville, 1982-84, Med. Univ. of S.C. 1989. Contbr. articles to profl. jours.; contbr. to (book) Guide to Strategic Planning for Hosps., 1981; mem. edit. bd. Health Care Strategic Mgmt., 1984—. Mem. Am. Hosp. Ass. (pres. Soc. for Hosp. Planning and Mktg. 1984-85), Am. Coll. of Health Care Execs., Carolinas Soc. of Hosp. Planning (founding mem.), Innocents Soc., Beta Gamma Sigma. Lodge: Rotary. Avocations: coaching boys' baseball, basketball clubs, reading, tennis, baseball card collecting. Office: HCIASachs 300 E Lombard St Baltimore MD 21202

LEFKOVITS, ALBERT MEYER, dermatologist; b. N.Y.C., June 30, 1937; s. Aaron Melchoir and Muriel (Mark) L.; A.B., Cornell U., 1958; M.D. (Lederle research fellow), N.Y. Med. Coll., 1962; m. Cheryl Beth Kornberg, Apr. 25, 1971; children—Ari Nathan, Lauren Blair. Intern, Newark Beth Israel Hosp., 1962-63; resident in dermatology Kings County Hosp. Center, SUNY, Downstate Med. Center, Bklyn., 1963-65; chief resident dermatology Mt. Sinai Hosp., N.Y.C., 1965-66, research fellow in dermatology, 1966-67, asst. attending physician, 1966—; practice medicine specializing in dermatology, N.Y.C., 1966—; asst. attending physician Beekman-Downtown Hosp., N.Y.C., 1968-75; instr. dermatology Mt. Sinai Sch. Medicine, 1966-68, clin. asso. dermatology, 1968-73, asst. prof., 1974, acad. council, 1973-78, 1886—; instr. dermatology N.Y. Med. Coll., 1966-69. Alumni fund-raising chmn. Horace Mann Sch., 1976-78; treas. Mt. Sinai Alumni, 1988-90, sec., 1991-93, v.p., 1993-95, pres. 1995-97. Served to maj. M.C., AUS, 1969-71. Recipient Fredrick Wise Dermatology award N.Y. Acad. Medicine, 1965, Torch of Liberty award Anti-Defamation League, 1987, Maimonides award Keren Or Found. for Handicapped Blind Children, 1994; mem. med. adv. bd. Skin Cancer Found. Mem. Harvey Soc., Soc. Investigative Dermatology, Dermatology Found., Soc. Tropical Dermatology, Am. Acad. Dermatology (task force on therapeutics and FDA liaison com., comm. coun., physicians practice com.), Am. Acad. Dermatology (comm. coun., physicians practice com.), AMA, Internat. Soc. Human and Animal Mycology, Mycology Soc. Ams., N.Y. Acad. Sci., Am. Physicians Fedn. (trustee, exec. com.), Jewish Chautaugua Soc. (life), Dermatology Soc. Greater N.Y. (pres., chmn. physicians advocacy com.), N.Y. State Med. Soc., Cornell Alumni Assn. N.Y. (bd. govs. 1974-76) Med. Adv. Bd. Skin Cancer Found., 1986—. Jewish (dir. congregation Emanu-El men's club). Clubs: Harmonie, Town, Cornell (N.Y.C.), Friar's, Lawrence Yacht (fleet surgeon 1982-83, sec. 1984, treas. 1985, commodore 1987). Address: 1040 Park Ave New York NY 10028-1032

LEFLOCH, PHILIPPE GERARD, mathematician; b. Rennes, France, Aug. 17, 1962; s. Gerard and Michelle (Paugam) LeF.; m. Claire Elisabeth Laborie, Feb. 25, 1984; children: Olivier, Aline, Bruno. PhD, Ecole Polytech. France, 1988; habil., U. Paris VI, 1990. Rschr. Ecole Polytech., Palaiseau, France, 1987—; dir. rsch. CNRS, 1999—; Courant instr. NYU, 1990-92, asst. prof. U. So. Calif., L.A., 1992-93, assoc. prof., 1993-94; vis. position Inst. Math. Applications, Mpls., 1989, 95; sci. visit Calif. Inst. Tech., 1995, 96, Inst. Advanced Studies, Italy, 1995, 97. Contbr. articles to profl. jours. Grantee Air Force Office, 1993, NSF, 1992-95, Career award, 1995. Mem. Am. Math. Soc., Soc. Math. Applications, Soc. Indsl. and Applied Math. Office: Ctr Math Applications, Ecole Polytechnique, 91128 Palaiseau France

LEFLON, JACQUES PAUL BENOÎT, manufacturing executive; b. Compiègne, France, June 8, 1935; s. Pierre and Marthe (Willepote) L.; m. Monique Demouy, Apr. 26, 1960; children: Isabelle, Thierry, Olivier. Grad., Inst. Polit. Studies, Paris, 1957; JD, Faculty of Law, Paris, 1959. Staff, fin. dept. Pechiney, Paris, 1962-72; group v.p. Pechiney Ugine Kuhlmann, Paris, 1972-75; pres. Aluminum Pechiney, Paris, 1976-81; exec. v.p. Pechiney, Paris, 1982-86; sr. v.p. Internat. Pechiney, Paris, 1987—; chmn. Union Confederations Industrie Employers Europe World Trade Orgn. Working Group, Brussels, 1997—. Decorated Chevalier, Legion of Honor, 1994. Avocations: skiing, sailing. Office: Pechiney, 7 Place du Chancelier Adenauer, F-75218 Paris Cedex 16 France

LEFRANC, MARIE-PAULE, immunogenetics educator, researcher; b. Oignies, France, Mar. 6, 1943; d. Jean Brasselet and Paule Despret; m. Gérard Lefranc, June 29, 1968; children: Anne-Christelle, Eric, Bénédicte, Isabelle, Anne-Cécile. MS, U. Lille, France, 1963; Agregation in Natural Scis., Ecole Normale Supérieure, Paris, 1966; postgrad., U. Calif., Berkeley, 1966-67; PhD, U. Paris, 1980, U. Montpellier, France, 1984. Cert. in biol. scis. Rsch. scientist Ctr. Tech. Tropical Forests, Cotonou, Bénin, 1963-64; jr. lectr. Cath. U., Lille, 1964-65; prof. biology Lycée F. de Coulanges, Strasbourg, France, 1967-68; prof. natural scis. French Embassy, Beirut, 1968-75; sr. lectr. biochemistry U. Monastir, Tunisia, 1976-81; sr. lectr. U. Montpellier, 1981-84; European Molecular Biology Orgn. fellow, rsch. scientist Med. Rsch. Coun., Cambridge, Eng., 1984-85; prof. immunogenetics U. Montpellier, 1985—; dir. Lab. Immunogénétique Moléculaire, Univ., Nat. Ctr. Sci. Rsch., Montpellier, 1985—, mem. nat. com. Nat. Ctr. Sci. Rsch., 1991-95; vis. prof. U. Monastir, 1981-84, U. Beirut, 1992—; initiator, coord. Internat. ImMunoGeneTics Database, Montpellier, 1991—. Contbr. articles to profl. jours. Recipient Rosen prize of cancerology Found. of Med. Rsch., Paris, Silver medal of Paris, 1988, Regional prize Assn. for Devel. of Rsch. for innovation-rsch.-enterprise, 1994; Fulbright fellow U. Calif., Berkeley, 1966-67. Mem. French Soc. Genetics (sci. coun. 1993—), French Soc. Immunology (coun. mem. 1987-91), French Soc. Hematology (sci. coun. 1993—), French Soc. Biochemistry, Molecular Biology (sci. coun. 1995—), Assn. of Rsch. sur la Polyarthrite (pres. sci. coun. 1993-95). Avocations: skiing, reading, swimming. Office: LIGM IMGT IGH, 141 rue de la Cardonille, 34396 Montpellier Cedex 5, France

LEFTON, HARVEY BENNETT, gastroenterologist, educator, author; b. Cleve., May 17, 1944; s. Nat L. and Edith (Waintrup) L.; m. Paulette Lipkowitz, Aug. 24, 1968; children: Allison Rachel, Daniel Adam. BS, U. Pitts., 1966; MD, Jefferson Med. Coll., Phila., 1970. Cert. Nat. Bd. Med. Examiners, Am. Bd. Internal Medicine, Am. Bd. Gastroenterology. Intern medicine Cleve. Clinic, 1970-71, resident internal medicine, 1971-72, fellow gastroenterology, 1972-74; chief gastroenterology Scott AFB, Belleville, Ill., 1974-76; asst. clin. prof. medicine Med. Coll. Pa., Phila., 1976-78, assoc. clin. prof. medicine, 1978-81, clin. prof. medicine, 1981—; chief gastroenterology Frankford Hosps., Phila., 1997—, pres. med. staff, 1998—; cons. gastroenterology Friends Hosp., Belmont Psychiat. Hosp., Pa., 1980—. Contbr. articles to profl. jours. Maj. USAF, 1974-76. Named Outstanding Vol. Physician, Med. Coll. Pa., 1994. Fellow ACP, Am. Coll. Gastroenterology, Coll. Physicians Phila.; mem. Am. Soc. Gastroenterology Endoscopy, Pa. Soc. Gastroenterology (sec. 1998—), Frankford Hosp., Omicron Delta Kappa. Home: 559 Long Ln Huntingdon Valley PA 19006-2935 Office: 2 Bala Plz Ste Il 22 Bala Cynwyd PA 19004-1501

LEGASPI, BENEDICTO CRUZ, JR., banker, realtor; b. Manila, May 3, 1955; s. Benedicto Carlos and Remedios (Cruz) L. BS in Mgmt., Ateneo de Manila U., Quezon City, The Philippines, 1976; postgrad., Asian Inst. Mgmt., 1997. Rschr. Manila Banking Corp., Makati City, The Philippines, 1976; asst. treas. Bancom Devel. Corp., Makati City, 1978-81; credit analyst Far East Bank and Trust Co., Makati City, 1976-78, from mgr. to 1st v.p., 1981-93, 1st v.p., chief credit officer, 1993-97, sr. v.p., 1997—; dir. Far East Bank Leasing Corp., 1998—; Philippine Bankers Assn. rep. Philippine Indsl. Restructuring Program Makati City, 1991-97; bd. dirs. Feb Leasing Corp. Mem. Am. Mgmt. Assn., Philippine Chamber Commerce and Industry (co. rep. 1994—), Garment Bus. Assn. Philippines, Makati Sports Club. Roman Catholic. Home: 375 HV de la Costa St, Makati MM 1227, The Philippines Office: Far East Bank and Trust Co, Senator Gil Puyat Ave, Makati MM 1200, The Philippines

LEGATES, JOHN CREWS BOULTON, information scientist; b. Boston, Nov. 19, 1940; s. Eber Thomson and Sybil Rowe (Crews) LeG.; m. Nancy Elizabeth Boulton, Apr. 28, 1993. BA in Math., Harvard U., 1962. Edn. svcs. mgr. Telcomp Dept. Bolt Beranek & Newman, Cambridge, Mass., 1966-67; v.p. Washington Engring. Svcs., Cambridge, 1967-69; v.p., co-founder Cambridge Info. Systems, 1968-69; v.p., founder Computer Adv. Svc. to Edn., Wayland, Mass., 1966-72; exec. dir. Educom Interuniversity Communications Coun., Boston, 1969-72; founder, mng. dir. Program on Info. Resources Policy Harvard U., 1973—, founder, pres. Ctr. Info. Policy Rsch., 1978—; mem. Arpanet NWG, core Arpanet/Internet design team, 1970-72; U.S. del. First World Conf. on Computer comms., Amsterdam, 1970; cons. in field. Contbr. articles to profl. jours. Bd. dirs. Nat. Telecommunications Conf., Washington, 1979. Kent fellow, 1964. Mem. NAS/NRC (telecommunications privacy, reliability and integrity panel), IEEE, Nat. Sci. Found., Soc. for Values in Higher Edn., Nashoba Valley Hunt Club (pres. 1974-80). Unitarian. Avocations: sailing, fox-hunting, mountaineering, classical music. Home: PO Box 6331 Lincoln MA 01773-6331

LEGEAIS, JEAN-MARC J., ophthalmologist; b. Montreuil, France, Aug. 20, 1959; s. Joseph and Jeanine (Guyot) L.; m. Sylvie Massucchetti, May 26, 1984; children: Sophie, Elodie, Thomas. MD, U. Paris, 1984, PhD, 1995. Resident Assistance Public, Paris, 1989; fellow Hotel Dieu Hosp., Paris, 1989; rsch. fellow Bascom Palmer Eye Inst., Miami, 1991; researcher INSERM, Paris, 1993—; cons. France Chirurgie Instrument, Paris, 1991-96; assoc. prof. Hotel Dieu Hosp., 1993-95, prof., 1997; adj. asst. prof. U. Miami, 1997; prof. Hotel-Dieu Paris Hosp., U. Paris, 1998. Patentee in field. Mem. Am. Acad. Ophthalmology, Am. Soc. Cataract & Refractive Surgery. Office: Hotel Dieu de Paris Hosp, 1 Place Parvis Notre Dame, 75004 Paris France

LEGER, DAMIEN FRANCOIS, neurophysiologist, researcher, consultant; b. Neuilly, France, Aug. 13, 1959; s. Jacques H. and Chantal M. (Duval-Arnould) L. Internat des Hôpitaux de Paris, U. Paris V, 1985, MD, 1989; PhD in Pub. Health, U. Paris VI, 1989. Med. resident U. Paris VI (Pierre et Marie Curie), Paris, 1985-88; cons. WHO, Geneva, 1989, Coun. of Europe, Copenhagen, 1989; asst. prof. Hôtel-Dieu, Paris, 1990-94, dir. Sleep Ctr., 1995—; vis. asst. prof. Stanford U., Palo Alto, Calif., 1989-90; cons. Nat. Commn. on Sleep, Washington, 1990, Securité Routière, Paris, 1992—. Co-editor four books; redactor in chief Sommeil et Vigilance, 1994—; contbr. articles to profl. jours. Recipient Prix Ernest Duffo, Garantie Medico-Chirugicale, Paris, 1990, Prix de Prévention Médicale, Prévention Routière, Paris, 1992, Prix Generation 2000, 1998. Mem. Soc. Hygiene (sec. 1992), Soc. Française de Recherche sur le Sommeil, European Sleep Rsch. Soc., Am. Sleep Disorder Assn. Home: 26 Ave Montaigne, 75008 Paris France Office: Hotel Dieu de Paris, 1 Pl Parvis Notre-Dame, 75004 Paris France

LEGER, JEAN-YVES, communication company executive; b. Montreuil, France, Nov. 15, 1948; s. Marcel and Yvonne (Nourry) L.; m. Jan Francoise, Sept. 25, 1971 (div. Sept. 1998); 1 child, Jean-Francois. Scis. econ., U. Paris, 1971, scis. politiques, 1972, fin. analyst degree, 1974. Fin. analyst CCBP, Paris, 1972-75, corp. fin. officer, 1975-77; fin. mgr. Danone, Paris, 1977-86, investor's rels. and comm. mgr., 1986-91; fin. comm. mgr. LVMH, Paris, 1991-93; mng. dir. FRI, Paris, 1993-95; ptnr. EURO RSCG OMNIUM, Paris, 1995—. Mem. Soc. Franç des Anoclip tes Financiers, Cercle de liaison des Informateurs Financiers en France (chmn. 1987-93), Entreprises et Medias. Home: 32 rue de Saussure, 75017 Paris France Office: Euro RSCG OMNIUM & Assocs, 84 rue de Villiers, 92683 Levallois-Perret France

LEGER, PHILIPPE, legal administrator; b. 1938. Mem. judiciary Min. of Justice, 1966-70; head of and subsequently tech. advisor Pvt. office of Min. for Living Stds., 1976; tech. advisor Pvt. Office of Garde des Sceaux, 1976-78; dep. dir. criminal affairs and reprieves Min. Justice, 1978-83; sr. mem. Ct. of Appeal, Paris, 1983-86; dep. dir. Pvt. Office of Garde des Sceaux, Min. for Justice, 1986; pres. Regional Ct. Bobigny, 1986-93; head pvt. office Ministre d'État, the Garde des Sceaux, Min. for Justice, 1993-94; advocate gen. Ct. Appeal, Paris, 1993-94; assoc. prof. René Descartes U., Paris, 1988-93; advocate gen. Ct. Justice, Luxembourg, 1994—. Office: European Ct of Justice, Blvd Konrad Adenauer, L-2925 Kirchberg Luxembourg*

LEGGAT, PETER ADRIAN, public health physician, medical educator; b. Brisbane, Queensland, Australia, Dec. 2, 1961; s. Bruce William and Frances Winifred (Hage) L.; m. Ureporn Kedjarune, Nov. 25, 1993. B in Med. Sci. with distinction, U. Queensland, 1985, MB, BChir, 1987; diploma in clin. nutrition, Internat. Acad. Nutrition, 1988; diploma in edn., U. So. Queensland, 1989; diploma in tropical medicine and hygiene, Mahidol U., Thailand, 1990; M in Med. Edn., U. Dundee, Scotland, 1992; cert. addiction studies, Curtin U., 1992; diploma in industrial health, U. Otago, New Zealand, 1993; DSc, Somerset U., Eng., 1993; grad., Corporate Dirs. Assn., New England, 1996; corp. dirs. grad. diploma, U. New England, 1996; MPH, U. Otago, New Zealand, 1998, postgrad. cert. in travel medicine. Cert. safety exec., safety mgr., safety specialist and safety and security dir. World Safety Orgn.; registered med. practitioner, specialist in pub. health medicine, Queensland; vocationally registered med. practitioner, Commonwealth Dept. Health. NHMRC med. undergrad. scholar U. Queensland Med. Sch., 1984-85, clin. tutor/specialist tutor/lectr. dept. social/prev. med., 1985-89; med. officer Dept. Vets. Affairs, Repatriation Gen. Hosp., Greenslopes, Queensland, 1988-89; attached def. officer Australian Embassy, Bangkok, 1990; med. officer Dept. Def., Townsville, 1990-91; sr. lectr. dept. pub. health and tropical medicine James Cook U., Townsville, 1992-98, dep. head dept., 1997-2000, assoc. prof., 1999—; dir. gen. World Safety Orgn., 1997-99, mem. internat. bd. dirs., 1989-99, dep. dir.-gen., 1993-97; cons. Anton Breinl Ctr., James Cook U., 1991, assoc. dean, mem. faculty biomed. and health scis., 1995-97, acad. advisor, 1998—; vis. med. officer dept. def. Townsville, 1992—; ofcl. accredited rep., liaison officer (World Safety Orgn.) to UN Econ. and Social Commn. for Asia and the Pacific, 1994-2000; vis. prof. Prince of Songkla U., Hatyai, Thailand, 1995—; dir. R&D in Tropical Medicine, 1996—; vis. prof. U. Witwatersrand Dept. Cmty. Health, Johannesburg, South Africa, 2000—; presenter in field. Editor: International Directory of Training in Tropical Medicine, 1994—, The Inaugural Ashdown Oration and Convocation, 1994, Dictionary of Tropical Medicine for Health Professionals, 1995, Asia-Pacific Safety Directory, 1996—, Annals of the Australasian College of Tropical Medicine Inc., 1995—, Primer of Travel Medicine, 1996, 2d edit., 1998; contbr. over 150 articles to profl. jours. Hon. sec. Townsville-Thuringowa Local Med. Assn. and voting del. to Queensland br. Australian Med. Assn., 1992-96, pres., 1996—; chmn. Stately Ct. Body Corporate, Townsville, 1993—; commr. for declarations Dept. Justice, Queensland, 1997-98, justice of peace, 1998—. Lt. Royal Australian Army Med Corps, 1987-88, capt., 1988-91; lt. col. Australian Army Res., 1999—; corps med. officer, Northern Corps St. John Ambulance, Australia, 2000—. Named World Safety Person of the Yr., World Safety Orgn., 1988, Internat. Man of the Yr. Internat. Biog. Centre, U.K., 1992-93, Disting. Leadership award Am. Biog. Inst., 1993, Ednl. award World Safety Orgn., 1992, Australian Coll. Occupational Medicine prize, 1984, Award of Merit, U. Queensland, 1986; J.G. Hunter rsch. fellow, 1995-96. Fellow Australasian Coll. Tropical Medicine (hon. sec. 1991-96, pres. 1996-98, councillor, acting hon. sec. 1999-2000, v.p. 2000—, Presdl. medallion 1998, medal 2000, Ednl. award 2000), Australian Inst. Co. Dirs., Australasian Faculty Pub. Health Medicine, Royal Australasian Coll. Physicians, Royal Soc. Tropical Medicine and Hygiene, Australian Coll. Rural Remote Med., Safety Inst. Australia; mem. Royal Australasian Coll. Med. Adminstrs., Royal Australian Coll. Gen. Practitioners, Australian Med. Assn., New Zealand Soc. Travel Med., South African Soc. Travel Medicine, Australian Coll. Edn. Roman Catholic. Avocations: stamp collecting, coin collecting, badminton, chess. Office: James Cook U, Sch Pub Health/Tropical Medicine, Townsville QLD 4811, Australia

LEGGETT, SIMON JAMES, tourism company executive; b. Great Bentley, Essex, Eng., Sept. 21, 1945; arrived in Papua New Guinea, 1967; s. Duglas Allen and Irene May (Mann) L.; m. Àiline Òfa-Ki-Tonga Naitoko, July 17, 1989; 1 child, Leilani Meresini. Leaving Cert., Parthfield Coll., Essex, 1960. Hon. Brit. consulate. Salesman Oldfields, Australia, 1965-67; mgr. Rabaul Shipping & Stevdoring, Papua New Guinea, 1967-68; asst. collector customs Australian Customs Dept., Papua New Guinea, 1968-74; co. dir. Seabreeze Enterprise Pty. Ltd., Rabaul, Papua New Guinea, 1974—; chmn. ENB Tourist Bd., Rabual, 1986-94, mem., 1984—. Chmn. Red Cross Internat., Rabaul, 1995-96. 2d officer Brit. Navy, 1960-61. Named Mem. of the Order of the Brit. Empire, 1999. Mem. United Ch. Avocations: scuba diving, game fishing, chess, reading, bush walking.

LEGLER, APRIL ARINGTON, librarian, educator; b. Gary, Ind., Apr. 20, 1946; d. James Berry Arington and Charlotte Bushong Arington Canine; m. Theodore Rex Legler II, Aug. 26, 1967; children: Melinda, Sara, Tad. AB in Comparative Lit., Ind. U., 1968, MLS, 1971. Various capacities in pub. and acad. librs., 1961-70; head librarian Math., Physics and Astronomy Libr. Ind. U. Librs., Bloomington, 1970-71; instr. Big Bend C.C., Berlin, Germany, 1986-88, Midlands Tech. Coll., Columbia, S.C., 1988-91, U. Md., Heidelberg, Germany, 1992; instr. Schiller Internat. U., Heidelberg, 1991-92, head libr., 1992-95; career counselor Ind. U. Kelley Sch. of Bus., 1997-99; course mgr. I.U. Kelley Sch. of Bus., 1999—. Author monograph. Life mem. Girl Scouts U.S., 1979—, instr. adult leader devel., 1983-85, bd. dirs. Congaree coun., Columbia, 1989-91, bd. dirs. North Atlantic, Europe, 1992-95; adult mem. Boy Scouts Am., 1973—, instr. adult leader devel., 1973-92; instr. outdoor living skills Am. Camping Assn., 1985-87; vol. ARC. Recipient Silver Beaver award Boy Scouts Am., 1987, Congaree award Girl

Scouts U.S., 1991. Mem. German-Am. Women's Club (v.p. 1992-93), Am. Found. for Visual Awareness (Ind. state trustee 1996-98, Ind. state sec. 1998—), Ind. U. Alumni Assn. (life), Ind. U. Women's Club (2nd v.p. 1999-00, program chair 2000—), Beta Phi Mu, Psi Iota Xi (treas. 1999—). Avocations: poetry, needlework, gourmet cooking. Home: 4630 Chatham Dr Bloomington IN 47404-1319

LE GOC, MICHEL JEAN-LOUIS, business educator; b. Toul, France, May 12, 1921; s. Yves and Suzanne (Badie) Le G.; m. Jacqueline Grapin, Apr. 6, 1971; children: Yves, Isabelle, Jean, Brigitte, Claire, Julien. Engring. degree, French Air Force Acad.; Sup. Educ. of Polit. Econ. and Pub. Law, PhD in Mgmt. Sci. summa cum laude. Surveyor European Defense Community, 1951-55; with fin. div. then procurements div. French Nat. Aeronautic Bd., 1955-57; gen. sec. European econ. issues Elec. Mfrs. Assn., 1957-60; co-founder, cons. Eurofinex, 1960-65; sr. v.p. devel. Cegos, 1965-71; founder, cons. Interfinexa, Geneva, 1971-86; prof. econs. U. Geneva, 1973-85; prof. internat. bus. Am. U. Washington, 1997—; ptnr. Air Cons., Geneva; spl. advisor H.H. Shamarpa Rinpoche, Delhi, India. Author: The Concentration of Enterprises, The Imperatives of Success; contbr. articles to profl. jours. Res. mem. supervisory agy. French Armed Forces. Served to gen. Free French Air Force, World War II. Named to Pres. Swiss br. Légion d'Honneur, Commandeur; decorated Croix de Guerre, Médaille de la Résistance, Médaille des Evadés, others. Mem. USAF Assn., Assn. Free French Air Force, Assn. Profs. Univ. Geneva, PEN Club, Club Alpin, Cosmos Club Washington, Lions Club. Office: 4745 Massachusetts Ave NW Washington DC 20016-2345

LE GOFF, PIERRE YVES, chemical engineering educator; b. Brest, France, Feb. 8, 1923; s. Joseph and Jeanne (Lariviere) Le G.; m. Jacqueline Gerard, Aug. 1, 1949; 1 child, Herve. Degree in chem.engring., U. Nancy, France, 1947, PhD, 1955. Asst. lectr. U. Nancy, France, 1947-54, lectr., 1954-57, sr. lectr., 1957-59; prof., chair Inst. Nat. Polytech. Lorraine, Nancy, France, 1959-93, prof. emeritus, 1993—; dir. engring. dept. U. Nancy, 1964-80, dir. rsch. lab., 1980-96. Named Commandeur de la Legion d'Honneur. Home: 22 Rue de la Croix Gagnee, 54000 Nancy France Office: Lab Genie Chem, 1 Rue Grandville, 54000 Nancy France

LEGON, FAUSTINO JUAN, lawyer, educator; b. Buenos Aires, Sept. 25, 1941; s. Faustino and Maria Erilda (Hargouas) L.; m. Maria Cecilia Cullen, Sept. 15, 1966; children: Cecilia, Ana, María de la Paz. Degree in law, Cath. U., Argentina, 1964. Admitted to bar 1965. Judge Nat. Civil Ct. Appeal, Buenos Aires; prof. civil law Nat. U. Buenos Aires Law Sch., Argentine Cath. U. Law Sch., Buenos Aires; mem. consulting com. Nat. Ministry Justice for Family Trial Cts., Buenos Aires. Rep. Salvador U., Orgn. Universidades Catolicas de America Latina; mem. several civil law congresses. Mem. Buenos Aires Bar Assn., Cath. Lawyers Corp. Argentina. Office: Piso 8, Marcelo T de Alvear 1381, C 1058AAU Buenos Aires Argentina

LEGOVIC, TARZAN, ecologist; b. Pula, Istra, Croatia, May 10, 1951; s. Orlando Legovic and Lina Labinac. BS, U. Rijeka, Croatia, 1973; MS, U. Toronto, Can., 1976; PhD, U. Zagreb, Croatia, 1979. Vis. scientist EAWAG-ETH, Zurich, Switzerland, 1980, Politechnico Milano, Milan, 1991; with Inst. Ecology, Athens, Ga., 1985-87; rsch. prof. R. Boskovic Inst., Zagreb, 1991—; vis. prof. Internat. Ctr. Mediterranean Agrl. Studies, Zaragoza, Spain, 1986, Nat. Inst. Ocean and Fish, Alexandria, Egypt, 1988, U. P. et M. Curie, Paris, 1993, Ctr. Advanced Studies, Blanes, Spain, 1994-95, U. Innsbruck, Austria, 1998, U. Kassel, Germany, 2000. Contbr. more than 100 articles to sci. jours. Recipient R. Boskovic Nat. sci. discover prize, Republic Croatia, 1990. Mem. Croatian Soc. Computer Simulation (pres. 1996-2000), Internat. Soc. Ecol. Modelling (v.p. 1997—). Achievements include co-author of comprehensive software package to control pollution and eutrophication in surface waters. E-mail: legovic@rudjer.irb.hr. Office: R Boskovic Inst, PO Box 180 Bijenicka 54, HR100002 Zagreb Croatia

LE GRAND, HOMER, academic dean; married; three children. BA in History/Chemistry, U. N.C., 1966; PhD in History of Sci., U. Wis., 1971. Asst. prof. history Va. Polytechnic Inst. and State U., 1970-74; lectr. to sr. lectr., assoc. dean Faculty of Arts U. Melbourne, 1975-89; assoc. in geology U.E.R. des Scis. de la Terre, U. de Lille I, Villeneuve d'Ascq, France, 1980-81; reader, head dept. of history and philosophy of sci., dean U. Melbourne, 1990-93, prof. and dean, Faculty of Arts, 1994-99; prof., dean Faculty of Arts Monash U., 1999—; mem. Internat. Commn. on the History of Geol. Scis., 1998—, steering com. for history, Am. Geophys. Union, 1995—. History editor: Transactions of the American Geophysical Union, 1997-99; mem. editl. bd.: Australasian Studies in History and Philosophy of Sci., 1981—; mem. nat. adv. bd. Australian Sci. Archives Project, 1996—; contbr. articles to profl. jours. Mem. Australian Acad. of Scis. (nat. com. for history and philosophy of sci. 1984-87, 89-95), Geol. Soc. of Australia, History of Eart Scis. Soc., Sigma Xi, others. Office: Monash Univ, Clayton Campus, Victoria 3800, Australia

LE GUIN, URSULA KROEBER, writer; b. Berkeley, Calif., Oct. 21, 1929; d. Alfred Louis and Theodora (Kracaw) Kroeber; m. Charles A. Le Guin, Dec. 22, 1953; children: Elisabeth, Caroline, Theodore. BA, Radcliffe Coll., 1951; MA, Columbia, 1952; 9 hon. degrees. Vis. lectr. or writer in residence numerous workshops and univs., U.S. and abroad. Author: Rocannon's World, 1966, Planet of Exile, 1966, City of Illusion, 1967, A Wizard of Earthsea, 1968, The Left Hand of Darkness, 1969, The Tombs of Atuan, 1970, The Lathe of Heaven, 1971, The Farthest Shore, 1972, The Dispossessed, 1974, The Wind's Twelve Quarters, 1975, A Very Long Way from Anywhere Else, 1976, Orsinian Tales, 1976, The Word For World is Forest, 1976, The Language of the Night, 1979, rev. edit., 1992, Leese Webster, 1979, Malafrena, 1979, The Beginning Place, 1980, Hard Words, 1981, The Eye of the Heron, 1983, The Compass Rose, 1982, King Dog, 1985, Always Coming Home, 1985, Buffalo Gals, 1987, Wild Oats and Fireweed, 1988, A Visit from Dr. Katz, 1988, Catwings, 1988, Solomon Leviathan, 1988, Fire and Stone, 1989, Catwings Return, 1989, Dancing at the Edge of the World, 1989, Tehanu, 1990, Searoad, 1991, Fish Soup, 1992, A Ride on the Red Mare's Back, 1992, Blue Moon Over Thurman Street, 1993, Wonderful Alexander and the Catwings, 1994, Going Out With Peacocks, 1994, A Fisherman of the Inland Sea, 1994, Four Ways to Forgiveness, 1995, Unlocking the Air, 1996, (with Diana Bellessi) The Twins, The Dream, 1997, Lao Tzu: Tao Te Ching: A Book About the Way and the Power of the Way, 1997, Steering the Craft, 1998, Jane on Her Own, 1999, The Sixty Odd, 1999, The Telling, 2000; also numerous short stories, poems, criticism, screenplays. Recipient Jupiter award 1975, Lewis Caroll Shelf award 1979, Internat. Fantasy award 1989, Howard D. Vursell award Am. Acad. Arts and Letters, 1991, Pushcart prize, 1991, Boston Globe-Hornbook award for excellence in juvenile fiction, 1968, Nebula award (novel) 1969, (novel and story) 1975, (novel) 1990, (story) 1996, Hugo award (novel) 1969, (novel) 1973, (story) 1974, (novel) 1975, (story) 1988, Gandalf award, 1979, Kafka award, 1986, Newbery honor medal, 1972, Nat. Book award, 1972, H.L. Davis award Oreg. Inst. Literary Arts, 1992, Hubbub annual poetry award, 1995, Asimov's Reader's award, 1995, James Tiptree Jr. award, 1995, Retrospective award, 1996, 97, Theodore Sturgeon award (story), 1995, Locus Readers award (story), 1973, 84, 95, 96, Prix Lectures-Jeunesse award, 1987, Robert Kirsch/L.A. Times Lifetime Achievement award, 2000. Mem. NARAL, Amnesty Internet. USA, Environ. Def. Fund, Nat. Resources Def. CTEE, Planned Parenthood Fedn. of Amer., Oreg. Nature Conservancy, Sci. Fiction Research Assn., Sci. Fiction Writers Assn., Authors League, PEN, Writers Guild West, Phi Beta Kappa. Office: care Virginia Kidd Lit Agy PO Box 278 Milford PA 18337-0278 also: care Matthew Bialer William Morris Agy 1350 Avenue Of The Americas New York NY 10019-4702

LEGUM, JEFFREY ALFRED, automobile company executive; b. Balt., Dec. 16, 1941; s. Leslie and Naomi (Hendler) L.; m. Harriet Cohn, Nov. 10, 1968; children: Laurie Hope, Michael Neil. Student, The Park Sch., 1959; BS in Econs., Wharton Sch. U. Pa., 1963; grad., Chevrolet Sch. Merchandising and Mgmt., 1966. With Park Circle Motor Co., Balt., 1963—, exec. v.p., 1966-77, pres., 1977—; pres., dir. Legum Chevrolet-Nissan, 1977-89; ptnr. Pkwy. Indsl. Ctr., Dorsey, Md., 1965-91; ltd. ptnr. Circle Ltd. Partnership, Glen Burnie, Md., 1991; v.p., dir. P.C. Parts Co., 1967—, pres., 1995—; v.p. Westminster Motor Co. (Md.), 1967-72, pres., dir., 1972-97; pres. One Forty Corp., Westminster, Md., 1972-97; dir., exec. com. United Consol. Industries, 1970-73; dist. chmn. Chevrolet Dealers Coun., 1975-77; chmn. Washington zone, 1982-83. Chmn. transp. div. Associated Jewish Charities, Balt., 1966-69; bd. dirs. Assoc. Placement Bur. (Jewish Vocat. Svc.), Balt., 1964-76, v.p., 1972-76, Preakness Celebration, Inc., 1988-89; mem. adv. bd. The Competitive Edge, Albuquerque, 1977-81; mem. investment com. Balt. Hebrew Congregation, 1980—, bd. electors, 1990-93, Md. Svc. Acad. Review Bd., 1975-77, bus. adv. bd. to Atty. Genl., 1985-87, Balt. Mus. Art, 1992—, fine arts accessions com., 1992—, chaired legal panel, 1996-99, investment com., 1992—, chmn., 1995-96, exec. com., 1993, fin. com., 1995—, contbr., 1994-96, sec., treas., 1996—, pres.'s com. U. Toronto, 1983—; trustee The Park Sch. Balt., 1979-94, chmn. investment com., 1980-96, mem. exec. com., chmn. fin. com., treas., 1981-91, mem. sr. adv. bd., 1994—, The Legum Found., 1967—; trustee, mem. fin. com. Johns Hopkins Med. Insts., 1997—; adv. coun. Wilmer Eye Inst., The Johns Hopkins Hosp., 1991—; mem. inst. rev. bd. for human subjects rsch. Johns Hopkins Bayview Med. Ctr., 1992-98; mem. steering com. Govt. House Trust, 1996—. Recipient award of honor Assn. Jewish Charities of Balt., 1967, 68, Cadillac Master Dealer award, 1980-88, 91, Cadillac Pinnacle of Excellence award, 1986, Young Pres.'s Orgn. Cert. Appreciation, 1984, Nissan Nat. Merit Master award, annually 1979-89, Sales Giant award Automotive News, 1987, Minute of Gratitude The Park Sch. Bd. Trustees, 1994. Mem. Young Pres. Orgn. (pres.'s forum 1977-92), World Pres.' Orgn., Benjamin Franklin Assocs., Johns Hopkins Assocs., Md. Hist. Soc. (exec. com. Library of Md. History 1981-90), Chesapeake Pres.' Orgn., Suburban Club (Balt. County), U. Pa., Center Club, U. Toronto Faculty Club (hon.). Home: 10 Stone Hollow Ct Baltimore MD 21208-1860 Office: 1829 Reisterstown Rd Baltimore MD 21208-6320

LEGWAILA, LEGWAILA JOSEPH, ambassador; b. Botswana, Feb. 2, 1937; s. Madume John and Morongwa (Serumula) L.; m. Sept. 20, 1975; children: Lorato, Neo, Thembile. BA, U. Calgary, Alta., Can., 1972; MA, U. Alta., 1973. Sch. head tchr., 1958-66; asst. prin. Botswana Min. Fgn. Affairs, Gaborone, 1973-74; sr. pvt. sec. to pres. of Botswana, 1974-80; Botswana amb. to UN N.Y.C., 1980—, Botswana amb. to Cuba, 1982—; high commr. to Guyana, 1981—, to Jamaica, 1982—; dep. spl. rep. of the UN Sec. Gen. for Namibia, 1989-90; spl. rep. of the OAU sec. gen. South Africa, 1992-94; pres. UN Security Coun., 1995, 96. Author: (with others) Safari to Serowe, 1971. Recipient Presdl. Order of Honour (PH), 1991. Mem. United Congl. Ch. South Africa. Avocations: golf, walking, reading. Office: Permanent Mission of Botswana 103 E 37th St New York NY 10016-3002*

LEH, SIU-CHUAN YU, otolaryngologist; b. Manila, Aug. 22, 1934; s. Choon-Cheng Gui Leh and Le-Siek Yu; m. Benita Ong, Apr. 6, 1958; children: Shirley, Frederick, Sandra, Patrick. AA, U. Santo Tomas, The Philippines, 1955, MD, 1959. Diplomate Am. Bd. Otolaryngology-Head and Neck Surgery, Philippine Bd. Otolaryngology-Head and Neck Surgery. Sect. head Chinese Gen. Hosp., Manila, 1969—, dep. med. dir., 1989—. Recipient Bronze medal Office of the Pres. Rep. of the Philippines, Manila, 1969. Mem. Philippine Bd. Otolaryngology and Head and Neck Surgery (pres. 1997—), Philippine Acad. Head and Neck Surgery (founder), Philippine Soc. Otolaryngology Head and Neck Surgery (ex-pres. 1988-89). Home: 38 Brixton Hills Ext, Quezon City 1100, The Philippines

LEHERISSEL, HERVE, lawyer; b. Paris, May 7, 1953; s. Andre and Annie (Van De Poll) L.; m. Anne Crebassa, Dec. 20, 1980; children: Sophie, Arnaud. Diploma, Polit. Studies Inst., Paris, 1973; law degree, U. Paris 7, 1974; postgrad., Ecole Nat. Adminstrn., 1978. Head office dir. tax rulings bur. Min. of Fin., France, 1978-83; dep. fin. officer Commr. Atomic Energy, France, 1983-86; dep. commr. tax legislation svc. Svc. de la Legis. Fiscale, Paris, 1987-91; ptnr. Archibald Andersen, Paris, 1991—. Author: Slavery Games or Citizenship, 1985. Nat. del. Club 89, Paris, 1983-86. Roman Catholic. Home: 18 Bis Ave, Marechal Douglas Haig, 78000 Versailles France Office: Archibald Andersen, 41 Rue Ybry, 92576 Neuilly-sur-Seine France

LEHERTE, LAURENCE, chemist, educator; b. Namur, Belgium, Aug. 8, 1964; d. Jean-Pierre and Marie-Therese (Alexandre) L.; m. Pierre Dahin. MS, Fac. U. N.D. Paix, Namur, 1986, PhD, 1990. Rsch. asst. Fac. Univ. N.D. Paix, Namur, 1988-91; postdoctoral fellow Queen's U., Kingston, Ont., Can., 1991-93, Cambridge Crystallographic Data Centre, Eng., 1993; rsch. fellow Fac. Univ. N.D. Paix, Namur, 1993-94, prof. asst. chemistry, 1994è. Contbr. articles to profl. jours. Avocations: drawing, karate. Office: Fac Univ N-D Paix, Rue de Bruxelles 61, 5000 Namur Belgium

LEHMAN, CYNTHIA LEIGH, educator; b. Sunbury, Pa., Nov. 25, 1968; d. William Franklin Lehman and Sarah Elizabeth Stimmel. BA, Shippensburg U., 1991; MA, Temple U., 1995, PhD, 1997. Rsch. asst. Temple U., Phila., 1992-96, tchg. asst., 1993-97; asst. prof. Ea. Ill. U., Charleston, 1997—; editl. asst. Jour. Black Studies, Phila., 1993—. Author (book chpt.) Handbook of Intercultural Communication, 1999. Black history cons. Carl Sandburg Elem. Sch., Charleston, Ill., 1997—. Mem. AAUW, Am. Hist. Assn., Nat. Coun. Black Studies.

LEHMAN, DENNIS DALE, chemistry educator; b. Youngstown, Ohio, July 15, 1945; s. Dale Vern and Coryn Eleanor (Neff) L.; m. Maureen Victoria Tierney, July 19, 1959 (div. Mar. 1981); children: Chris, Hillary; m. Kathleen Kim Kuchta, May 15, 1983. BS, Ohio State U., 1967; MS, Northwestern U., 1968, PhD, 1972. Prof. chemistry, chmn. dept. Chgo. City Colls., 1968—; prof. chemistry Northwestern U., Evanston, Ill., 1974-98, lectr. biochemistry Med. Sch., Chgo., 1979-90, lectr. chemistry, 1998; cons. Chgo. Bd. Edn. Author: Chemistry for the Health Sciences, 1981, 8th edit., 1998, Laboratory Chemistry for the Health Sciences, 1981, 8th edit., 1998. Mem. AAAS, Am. Chem. Soc., Sigma Xi. Home: 5918 Tomlinson Dr Mchenry IL 60050-1715 Office: Chgo City Colls 30 E Lake St Chicago IL 60601-2403

LEHMAN, JULIE AIMÉE, secondary education educator; b. Coldwater, Kans., Jan. 22, 1969; d. John Wilbur and Helen Louise (Lohrding) L. BA in English, St. Mary of the Plains Coll., 1991. Secondary English cert. Kans. State Bd. Edn. English tchr. grades 7-8 Sacred Heart Cathedral Sch., Dodge City, Kans., 1992-94; English tchr. grades 9-12 Lenora (Kans.) H.S., 1994-97; English tchr. grades 7-12 Ashland (Kans.) H.S., 1997-2000; English instr. Colby (Kans.) C.C., 1995-97, Dodge City (Kans.) C.C., 1997-2000. Adviser: Wildcat, 1994-97 (Taylor Pub. Award of Merit 1997). Active Dodge City (Kans.) Roundup, Inc., 1991—. Mem. NEA, Nat. Coun. Tchrs. English, Nat. Fedn. Interscholastic Speech and Debate Assn., Kans. Speech Comm. Assn. Republican. Methodist. Avocations: reading, gardening, rodeo. Home: PO Box 783 Ashland KS 67831-0783

LEHMAN, NILES E., science educator; b. Larkspur, Calif., June 3, 1962; s. Larry M. Lehman and Barbara A. Miller; m. Debra J. Decker, June 26, 1993; 1 child, Anya J. BS in Chemistry, U. Calif., Berkeley, 1984, MA in Biochemistry, 1986; PhD in Biology, UCLA, 1990. Postdoctoral fellow Scripps Rsch. Inst., San Diego, 1990-93, U. Oreg., Eugene, 1993-95; asst. prof. Calif. State U., Long Beach, 1995-97, SUNY, Albany, 1997—; mem. adv. bd. Jour. Molecular Evolution, Palo Alto, Calif., 1995—. Contbr. articles to profl. jours. Rsch. grantee NSF, 1999, NASA, 1999. Mem. AAAS, Internat. Soc. Study Origins Life, Genetics Soc. Am., Soc. Study Evolution. Avocations: skiing, badminton. Office: SUNY 1400 Washington Ave Albany NY 12222-1000

LEHMAN, TOM (THOMAS EDWARD LEHMAN), professional golfer; b. Austin, Minn., Mar. 7, 1959; m. Melissa; children: Rachael, Holly, Thomas. Student, U. Minn. Profl. golfer PGA, 1982—. Named Ben Hogan Tour Player of Yr., 1991; named to Pres. Cup team, 1994; ; won Reflection Ridge, Gulf Coast Classic, S.C. Classic, Santa Rosa Open, The Meml. Tournament, 1994, Colonial Invitational, 1995, Brit. Open, 1996, The Tour Championships, 1999, Phoenix Open, 2000. Office: Signature Sports Group Box 109601 801 Park Ave Minneapolis MN 55404-1136

LEHMANN, INES, bank executive, economist, consultant; b. Moscow, Mar. 23, 1959; d. Klaus and Svetlana (Kuprijanova) Kirshner; m. Jürgen Lehmann, May 31, 1980; children: Katja, André. MS in Econ., Moscow State U. Internat. Rels, Moscow, 1982; cert. in econ., London Sch. Econs., Berlin, 1994; cert. bus. adminstrn./project mgmt., BBW Acad., 1997. Ofcl. rep. Ministry Fin., Berlin, 1982-85, Econ. Commn., Berlin, 1985-90; sales mgr. Fried Krupp, Essen, Germany, 1990-93; sr. mgr. Treuhand Osteuropa Beratungsgesellschaft, Berlin, 1994-98; sr. bank mgr. Raiffeisen Zentralbank, Vienna, 1999—. Author: Inflation in COMECON Countries, 1983. Avocation: diving. Home: An der Kolonnade 2, D-10117 Berlin Germany Office: Raiffeisen Zentralbank, Am Stadtpark 9, A-1030 Vienna Austria

LEHMANN, JAN ERIK, urologist, researcher; b. Kiel, Germany, Jan. 29, 1967; s. Volker and Katrin (Wiese) L.; m. Irene Agnes Louise Hölscher, Aug. 16, 1997; children: Nils, Ole. MD, Free U. Berlin, 1995. 1st yr. surg. resident Moabit Hosp., Berlin, 1995-96; resident in urology U. Kiel, 1997—; tchg. asst. anatomy U. Hamburg, Germany, 1991-92. Composer, performer music scores for 5 amateur drama prodns. Theater AG, Harburg, Germany, 1986-90; author, planner improvements of historic war monument in Hamburg (3d prize 1986). Vol. Am. Field Svc., Hamburg, 1985-92, Amnesty Internat., Berlin, 1994-96, German Med. Student Exch., Berlin, 1994, Med. Student Body, U. Hamburg, 1990-91. Recipient study and travel grants Studienstiftung d. Dt. Volkes, 1990-95, Deutsche Forschungsgemeinschaft, 1999—, Young Investigator award European Soc. Magnetic Resonance in Medicine and Biology, 1996, 2d prize German Soc. Radiology, 1997, Poster award European Assn. Urology, 1999. Mem. German Soc. Urology. Lutheran. Avocations: cross-country bicyling, hiking, piano. Office: U Kiel Klinik Urologie, Arnold-Heller-Str 7, 24105 Kiel Germany

LEHMANN, KLAUS-DIETER, library director; b. Breslau, Germany, Feb. 29, 1940; s. Kurt and Charlotte (Maennchen) L.; m. Lieselotte Maria Schiep, June 4, 1965; children: Lutz, Lisa. Diploma in Physics, U. Cologne, Mainz, 1967; Diploma in Libr. Sci., Libr. Sch. Frankfurt, Germany, 1970; prof., U. Frankfurt, 1986. Libr. State/Univ. Libr., Darmstadt, 1970-73, City/Univ. Libr., Frankfurt, 1973-87; dir.-gen. Nat. Libr., Frankfurt, 1988—; pres. Stiftung Preussicher Kulturbesik, Berlin, 1999—; prof. U. Frankfurt, 1986—; cons. in field. Author: Bibliotheca Publica, 1985; editor Zeitschrift Bibliothekswesen; co-editor Alexandria Jour.; contbr. articles to profl. jours. Decorated Chevalier, Ordre Palmes Academiques, Paris, 1990, Fed. Cross of Merit, Bonn, 1996. Mem. Acad. Sci. Mainz, Conf. European Nat. Librs., Preussischer Kultur-Besitz (chmn. divsn. profl. coms.), Internat. Fedn. Libr. Assns. and Instns. (exec. bd. dirs.), Coun. Libr. and Info. Resource (European commn. preservation and access).

LEHMANN, STEFFEN, financial counsulting company executive; b. Giessen, Hesse, Germany, Aug. 6, 1960; s. Alfred and Christel Lehmann; m. Ulrike Ehrhardt, May 30, 1998. Econs. and bus. adminstrn. diploma, Justus-Liebig-U., Giessen, 1986. Contr. Schunk Group (Germany), Giessen, 1986-91; mgr. 3i Deutschland Gesellschaft für Industriebeteiligungen mb, Frankfurt am Main, Germany, 1991-98; CEO, Mezzanine Mgmt. Beteiligungsberatung GmbH, Frankfurt am Main, 1998—. With German Army, 1979-81. Fellow 3i Nexus Club; mem. Econs. Club Rhein-Main, Frankfurt Pvt. Equity Club. Avocations: golf, skiing, family. Office: Mezzanine Mgmt Beteil GmbH, Myliusstrasse 45, 60323 Fankfurt am Main Hesse, Germany

LEHMANN, THOMAS CHRISTIAN, physician, surgeon, consultant; b. Buelach, Switzerland, Jan. 8, 1949; s. Walter and Hedwig Elsa (Senn) L.; m. Madeleine Buri; children: Dominik, Joël, Alexandra, Joachim, Annouk, Noëmi. MD, Berne (Switzerland) U., 1976. Diplomate Swiss Assn. Physicians. Surg. staff Oberdiessbach, Switzerland, 1977; internal medicine staff Sanitorium, Braunwald, Switzerland, 1978; pediat. surg. staff Berne U. Hosp., 1979-81; med. staff Dept. Rehab., Berne, 1981-86, Berne U. H osp., 1986-92, Polio Ctr. Wittigkoten Hosp., Berne, 1992—; med. cons. Swiss Group of Interests for Late Effects of Poliomyelitis, Fribourg, 1990—. Author, editor: Poliomyelitis-Die Spaetfolgen, 1988-2000; contbr. numerous profl. jours. and conf. procs. Home: Koenizbergstr 13, CH-3097 Liebefeld Switzerland Office: Krank Wittigkoten Polio Ctr, Jupiterstr 65, CH-3000 Berne 15 Switzerland

LEHMANN, WINFRED PHILIPP, linguistics educator; b. Surprise, Nebr., June 23, 1916; s. Phillip Ludwig and Elenore Friederike (Grosnick) L.; m. Ruth Preston Miller, Oct. 12, 1940; children: Terry Jon, Sandra Jean. BA, Northwestern Coll., Watertown, Wis., 1936; MA, U. Wis., 1938, PhD, 1941; LittD (hon.), SUNY, Binghamton, 1985; DHL (hon.), U. Wis., 1995. From instr. to asst. prof. Wash. U., 1946-49; from assoc. prof. to prof. U. Tex., 1949-63, Ashbel Smith prof. linguistics, 1963-83, Louann and Larry Temple prof. humanities, 1983-86, prof. emeritus, 1986—, chmn. dept. Germanic langs., 1953-65, chmn. dept. linguistics, 1965-72, dir. Linguistics Rschr. Ctr., 1961—; Jawaharlal Nehru Meml. lectr., New Delhi, 1981; dir. Georgetown English lang. program, Ankara, Turkey, 1955-56; chmn. linguistics del. People's Republic of China, 1974, co-chmn. Social Sci./Humanities Planning Commn., 1981. Author: (with L. Faust) A Grammar of Formal Written Japanese, 1951, Proto-Indo-European Phonology, 1952, The Alliteration of Old Saxon Poetry, 1953, The Development of Germanic Verse Form, 1956, Historical Linguistics: An Introduction, 1962, 3d edit., 1992, Descriptive Linguistics: An Introduction, 1972, 2d edit., 1976, Proto-Indo-European Syntax, 1974, (with R.P.M. Lehmann) An Introduction to Old Irish, 1975, Linguistische Theorien der Moderne, 1981, Language: An Introduction, 1982, Gothic Etymological Dictionary, 1986, Die Gegenwaertige Richtung der Indogermanistischen Forschung, 1992, Theoretical Bases of Indo-European Linguistics, 1993, Residues of Pre-Indo-European Active Structure and Their Implications for the Relationships among the Dialects, 1995; editor: Language and Linguistics in the People's Republic of China, 1974, Syntactic Typology, 1978, (with Yakov Malkiel) Perspectives on Historical Linguistics, 1982, Language Typology, 1985, Language Typology: Systematic Balance in Language, 1987, (with H.J.J. Hewitt) Typological Models in Reconstruction, 1988, (with Esther Raizen and H.J.J. Hewitt) Biblical Hebrew, 1999; contbr. articles to profl. jours. Chmn. bd. dirs. Center for Applied Linguistics, 1973-78. 1st lt. Signal Corps AUS, 1942-46. Decorated Comdr.'s Cross, Order Merit Fed. Republic Germany, 1987; recipient Jakob Grimm prize, 1975, Pro bene Meritis award, U. Tex., 1987; fellow Fulbright Found., Norway, 1950-51, Guggenheim Found., 1972-73. Mem. MLA (exec. coun. 1977-80, pres. 1987), Linguistic Soc. Am. (pres. 1973), Am. Coun. Learned Socs. (sec. bd. 1977-86, Harry H. Ransom award teaching excellence 1983), Danish Acad. Scis. Lutheran. Home: 3800 Eck Ln Austin TX 78734-1613 *Died Apr. 3, 2000.*

LEHMBERG, ROBERT HENRY, research physicist; b. Phila., Dec. 4, 1937; s. Henry and Marguerite Elenore (Schock) L.; m. Norma Geder, Dec. 29, 1966; 1 child, Karl Robert. BSc, Pa. State U., 1959; MSc, U. Ariz., 1961; PhD, Brandeis U., 1968. Rsch. physicist Naval Air Devel. Ctr., Warminster, Pa., 1966-72, Naval Rsch. Lab., Washington, 1972—; chmn. program com. Conf. on Lasers and Electro-Optics, Washington, 1991. Contbr. articles to profl. jours.; patentee in field. Fellow Am. Phys. Soc. (Excellence in Plasma Physics Rsch. award 1993); mem. AAAS, IEEE, Sigma Xi. Achievements include development of optical beam smoothing techniques for laser fusion, optical design of the Naval Research Laboratory's Nike laser facility, and research in nonlinear optics, excimer laser physics and laser-plasma interaction physics. Office: Naval Rsch Lab Plasma Divsn 4555 Overlook Ave SW Washington DC 20375-0001

LEHMKUHL, URSULA, history educator; b. Bocholt, Germany, May 20, 1962; d. August Heinrich and Radegunde Lehmkuhl; m. Wolfgang J. Helbich, May 16, 1988; children: Elisabeth, Peter. MA in History, Ruhr-U., Bochum, Germany, 1985, PhD in History, 1990, habilitation in polit. sci., 1997. Asst. prof. internat. rels. Ruhr-U., Bochum, 1994-98, prof., 1996-98; prof. N.Am. history U. Erfurt, Germany, 1999—; advisor German Assn. Polit. Sci., Darmstadt, Germany, 1997—. Author: Canada's Opening Moves Toward Asia, 1990, Theories in International Relations, 1996, Pax Anglo-Americana, 1999; editor: Enemy Images in American History, 1997. Recipient Faculty Rsch. award Can. Govt., 1997; Dissertation fellow German Hist. Inst., 1987-88; Rsch. fellow Deutsche Forschungsgemeinschaft, 1994, 95; fellow German Rsch. Assn., 1995-96. Mem. German Assn. Am. Studies, Soc. Historians Am. Fgn. Rels., Orgn. History Can. Avocations: violin, viola, skiing. Fax: 49-361-737-4419. Home: Cumbacher Str. 6, 99880 Schnepfenthal, Thuringia Germany Office: U Erfurt, Nordhauserstr. 63, Thuringia D-99086, Germany

LEHN, JEAN-MARIE PIERRE, chemistry educator; b. Rosheim, Bas-Rhin, France, Sept. 30, 1939; s. Pierre and Marie (Salomon) L.; m. Sylvie Lederer, 1965; 2 children. Grad., U. Strasbourg, France, 1960, PhD, 1963;

PhD (hon.), U. Jerusalem, 1984, U. Autonoma, Madrid, 1985, U. Göttingen, 1987, U. Brussels, 1987, U. Herakliou, Greece, 1989, U. Bologna, 1989, Charles U., Prague, 1990, U. Twente, 1991, U. Sheffield, 1991, U. Athens, 1992, U. Polytech. Athens, 1992, Poly. U. Bucharest, 1994, Ill. Wesleyan U., 1995, U. Montreal, 1995, Bielefeld U., 1998, USTC, Hefei, 1998, Southeast U., Nanjing, 1998, Weizmann Inst., Rehovoth, 1998; applied Scis., U. Brussels, 1999. Various positions Nat. Ctr. Sci. Rsch., France, 1960-66; postdoctoral rsch. assoc. Harvard U., Cambridge, Mass., 1963-64; asst. prof. U. Strasbourg, France, 1966-69; assoc. prof. U. Louis Pasteur of Strasbourg, 1970, prof. of chemistry, 1970-79; prof. Coll. France, Paris, 1979—; vis. prof. chemistry Harvard U., 1972, 74, E.T.H., Zurich, Switzerland, 1977, Cambridge (Eng.) U., 1984, Barcelona (Spain) U., 1985, Frankfurt (Fed. Republic Germany) U., 1985-86; Heinrich-Hertz Gast prof. Karlsruhe U., 1989; Woodward vis. prof. Harvard U., Cambridge, Mass., 1997; Newton-Abraham vis. prof. Oxford U., 1999-2000. Contbr. over 530 articles to sci. publs. Recipient Bronze, Silver and Gold medals, Ctr. Nat. Sci. Rsch. (CNRS), Gold medal Pontifical Acad. Sci., 1981, Paracelsus prize Swiss Chem. Soc., 1982, von Humboldt prize, 1983, Nobel Prize for Chemistry, 1987, Karl-Ziegler prize, 1989, Bonner Chemiepreis, 1993, Ettore Majorana-Erice-Sci. for Peace prize, 1994, Gold medal Soc. Acad. Arts, Scis., Lettres, 1995, Davy medal Royal Soc., 1997, Lavoisier medal SFC, 1997, A.R. Day award, 1998, others; decorated commandeur Légion d'Honneur, officier Order Nat. du Mérite, Ordre pour le Mérite for Scis. and Arts. Mem. AAAS (fgn. hon.), Inst. de France, Deutsche Acad. der Naturforscher Leopoldina, Acad. Nazionale dei Lincei, NAS (fgn. assoc.), Royal Netherlands Acad., Am. Philos. Soc. (Phila., fgn. mem.), Acad. Europaea, Acad. Wissenschaften Literalur-Mainz, Acad. Wissenschaften, Göttingen, Yougoslav Acad. Arts and Scis. Zagreb., Indian Acad. Scis., Polish Acad. Scis., Royal Acad. Scis. Letters & Fine Arts (Belgium), Acad. Arts & Scis. P.R., Acad. Scis. Ukraine, Inst. Grand Ducal (Luxembourg), Acad. Roumaine, Royal Soc., Korean Acad. Sci. and Tech., The Czech Learned Soc., 3d World Acad. Scis., Pintifical Acad. Scis., Acad. Scis. Torins, Royal Irish Acad., Russian Acad. Scis. Home: 6 rue des Pontonniers, 67000 Strasbourg France Office: Coll France, 11 pl Marcelin Berthelot, 75005 Paris France also: U Louis Pasteur, 4 rue Blaise Pascal, 67000 Strasbourg France

LEHNE, CARLOS J. A., nephrologist; b. Mexico City, June 4, 1941; arrived in Germany, 1987; s. Carlos and Rita (Garcia-Mulia) L.; m. Patricia Alexander, Aug. 17, 1967; children: Carlos, Walter. BS, Autonomous Nat. U. Mex., 1959, MD, 1967. Cert. in internal medicine, Germany; cert. in nephrology, Mex., Germany. Intern, resident dept. nephrology Nat. Inst. Cardiology, Mexico City, 1969-71; fellow dept. internal medicine, nephrology Michael Reese Hosp., Chgo., 1972-74; clin. rsch. fellow medicine Mass. Gen. Hosp., Boston, 1974-75; head transplant unit renal divsn. Gen. Hosp. I.M.S.S., Mexico City, 1976-85; cons. nephrology, chmn. transplants Humana Hosp., Mexico City, 1986-87; rschr. clin. dialysis membranes Pharm. Industry Ober Ursel Taunus, Germany, 1988; asst. physician internal medicine Med. Univ. Lübeck, Germany, 1989; med. dir. nephrology Dialysis Ctr., Nordhorn, Germany, 1990—; postgrad. instr. nephrology Dialysis, Nordhorn, 1996—; assoc. prof. postgrad. divsn. nephrology Autonomous Nat. U. Mex., 1981-85; tutelar prof. renal transplantation Gen. Hosp., Instituto Mexicano Seguro Social, Mexico City, 1983-85, chmn. transplantation com., 1983-85. Contbr. articles to profl. jours. Mem. N.Y. Acad. Sci., European Renal Assn., Mex. Soc. Nephrology. Avocations: astronomy, music, astrophysics. Home and Office: Kokenmühlenstrasse 11, 48529 Nordhorn Germany

LEHNER, URBAN CHARLES, journalist; b. Grand Rapids, Mich., May 10, 1947; s. Urban Edward and Angeline Grace (Marcy) L.; m. Anne Marie Eding, May 2, 1969 (div. 1976); m. Nancy Ellen Leonard, June 28, 1980; 1 child, Alicia Ann. AB in history, U. Mich., 1969; JD, Georgetown U., 1979. Staff reporter The Wall Street Jour., N.Y.C., Phila., Chgo., Washington, 1969-80; bur. chief The Wall Street Jour., Tokyo, 1980-83, Detroit, 1983-85; mng. editor The Wall Street Jour. Europe, Brussels, 1985-87; bur. chief The Wall Street Jour., The Asian Wall Street Jour., Tokyo, 1988-92; editor The Asian Wall Street Jour., Hong Kong, 1992-97; exec. editor Dow Jones Asia, 1997-98; pub., exec. editor Asian Wall St. Jour., 1998—. Editor: Let's Talk Turkey (About Japanese Turkeys) And Other Tales from the Asian Wall Street Journal, 1996. Lt. (j.g.) USNR, 1970-72. Recipient Citation for Excellence with Alan Murray for Strained Alliance Overseas Press Club, 1991. Mem. Fgn. Corrs. Club Japan. Office: The Asian Wall St Jour, 25/F Ctrl Plz 18 Harbour Rd, GPO Box 9825 Hong Kong China

LEHNER-QUAM, ALISON LYNN, library administrator; b. Oak Harbor, Wash., Apr. 25, 1960; d. Paul Elias and Johanna Marie (Vinson) Q.; m. Matthias Karl-Eugen Lehner, Oct. 3, 1997; 1 child, Peter Elias Bernhard Lehner. BA, U. Wash., 1983; cert. tech. theater, Yale U., 1985; MS in Libr. Sci., Columbia U., 1991. Freelance costumer various prodns. N.Y.C., 1984-90; cataloging asst. Fashion Inst. of Tech., N.Y.C., 1986-91; intern Bank St. Sch., N.Y.C., 1991; asst. dir. Columbia Children's Lit. Inst., N.Y.C., 1990; libr. dir. Lincoln Ctr. Inst., N.Y.C., 1991—; project dir. Arts Edn. Reference Window on the Work, 1992—. Pub. mgr.: (periodical) The Institute View, 1996—, Lincoln Ctr. Inst., 1999. Vol. mgr. Lincon Ctr. Inst., N.Y.C., 1995—. Recipient Dirs.' Emeriti award Lincoln Ctr. for Performing Arts, 1997; scholar Sch. Libr. Svcs., Columbia U., 1989, 90. Mem. ALA, N.Y. Arts in Edn. Roundtable (steering com. 1995-98), Theater Libr. Assn., Beta Phi Mu (bd. dirs. Theta chpt. 1997—, v.p. 1994-96). Avocations: reading, the arts.

LEHNERT, BO PETER, physicist, educator; b. Stockholm, Mar. 30, 1926; s. Edwin Berthold and Greta Maria Elisabet (Dorch) L.; m. Ann-Marie Elisabeth Kronqvist, Aug. 18, 1989. MSc, Royal Inst. Tech., Stockholm, 1950, DSc, 1955. Asst. prof. Royal Inst. Tech., 1955-63; from assoc. prof. to prof. Swedish Atomic Rsch. Coun., Stockholm, 1963-90; prof. Royal Inst. Tech., 1990—. Author: Electromagnetic Phenomena in Cosmical Physics, 1958, Dynamics of Charged Particles, 1964, Extended Electromagnetic Theory, 1998. Capt. Swedish Royal Tank Guards, 1947-66. Recipient Celsius gold medal Royal Soc. Sci., 1974, medal of His Majesty the King of Sweden, 1996; fellow Alpha Found. Inst. for Advanced Study. Fellow Inst. Math. and its Applications; mem. European Phys. Soc. (chmn. plasma physics divsn. 1969-72), Swedish Euratom Assn. (head Swedish rsch. unit 1980-92), Royal Swedish Acad. Sci. (Edlund prize 1962), Royal Swedish Acad. Engring. Sci., N.Y. Acad. Scis. Avocations: downhill skiing, windsurfing, languages, classical and folk music. Home: Morbydalen 22, S-182 52 Danderyd Sweden Office: Royal Inst Tech, Valhallavagen, S-100 44 Stockholm Sweden

LEHR, CLAUS-MICHAEL, biopharmaceutics and pharmaceutical educator; b. Merzig, Saarland, Germany, Oct. 2, 1961; s. Karl and Helene (Walther) L.; m. Christine Schaal, Mar. 27, 1987; children: Johanna, Saskia, Felix. Degree in Pharmacy, U. Hamburg, Germany, 1987; PhD, Ctr. for Biopharm. Scis., Leiden, The Netherlands, 1991. Postdoctoral fellow U. So. Calif., L.A., 1991-92; rsch. assoc. Leiden Amsterdam Ctr. for Drug Rsch., The Netherlands, 1992-93; assoc. prof. U. Marburg, Germany, 1993-95; prof., head dept. biopharmaceutics/pharm. tech. U. Saarland, Saarbrücken, Germany, 1995-98; co-chmn. German-Am. Frontiers of Scis., 1997—. Mem. editorial bd. Jour. of Drug Targeting, European Jour. of Pharmaceutics and Biopharmaceutics; assoc. editor European Jour. Pharm. Biopharm., 1998—; contbr. more than 50 articles to sci. jours., books. Served with German Navy, 1981-82. Mem. Am. Soc. Pharm. Scientists, Controlled Release Soc. (young investigator award 2000), Deutsche Pharmazeutische Gesellschaft, Arbeitsgem.f.Pharm. Verfahrenstechnik (bd. govs. 1998—), European Fed. Pharm. (mem. coun. 1999). Avocations: sailing, piano, drums. Office: Univ Saarland, Dept Biopharm Pharm Tech, 66123 Saarbrücken Germany

LEHRER, MERRILL CLARK, retail store executive; b. Queens, N.Y., May 24, 1955; s. Stanley and Laurel Lehrer; m. Elisabeth Pine, Oct. 24, 1984. BA in Communications magna cum laude, Adelphi U., 1976. Asst. buyer Lafayette Electronics, Syosset, N.Y., 1976-78; dept. mgr. Abraham & Straus, Massapequa, N.Y., 1978-80; dept. mgr., assoc. buyer, buyer Rich's, Atlanta, 1980-84, sr. buyer, 1984-88; mng. editor USA Today mag., Valley Stream, N.Y., 1988-89; buyer Burdine's, Miami, Fla., 1989; sr. buyer, v.p., gen. mdse. mgr. Office Depot, Delray Beach, Fla., 1989-97; divsnl. mdse. mgr. Petco, San Diego, Calif., 1997—. Contbr. articles to USA Today. Office: Petco 9125 Rehco Rd San Diego CA 92121-2270

LEHRER, STANLEY, magazine publisher, editorial director, corporate executive; b. Bklyn., Mar. 18, 1929; s. Martin and Rose L.; m. Laurel Francine Zang, June 8, 1952; children: Merrill Clark, Randee Hope. BS in Journalism, N.Y. U., 1950; postgrad. in edn, San Antonio Coll., 1952. Editor and pub. Crossroads mag., Valley Stream, N.Y., 1949-50; youth service editor Open Road mag., N.Y.C., 1950-51; mng. editor School & Society, N.Y.C., 1953-68, v.p., 1956-68; pub. School & Society Books, N.Y.C., 1963-86; pres., pub. School & Society mag., N.Y.C., 1968-72; founder, pres., pub. Intellect mag., N.Y.C., 1972-78, editl. dir., 1974-78; founder, pres., pub., editl. dir. USA Today, Valley Stream, N.Y., 1978-99; pres., pub., editorial dir. Newsview newsletter, 1979-99, Your Health newsletter, 1980-99, The World of Sci. newsletter, 1980-99; cons. Child Care Publs., N.Y.C., 1955. Prodr., commentator: (WBAI-FM radio program) Report on Eucation, N.Y.C., 1960-61; guest spkr. Midwestern Writers' Conf., Chgo., 1950, Writers and Artists Group Nat. Music Camp, Interlochen, Mich., 1950, World of the Little Magazine, WNYC-AM, N.Y.C., 1977, Titanic Symposium Mariners' Mus., Newport News, Va., 1998; author: John Dewey: Master Educator, 1959, Countdown on Segregated Education, 1960, Religion, Government, and Education, 1961, A Century of Higher Education: Classical Citadel to Collegiate Colossus, 1962, Automation, Education, and Human Values, 1966, Conflict and Change on the Campus: The Response to Student Hyperactivism, 1970, Leaders, Teachers, and Learners in Academe: Partners in the Educational Process, 1970, Education and the Many Faces of the Disadvantaged: Cultural and Historical Perspectives, 1972, Titanic: Fortune & Fate, 1998; contbr. articles to nat. mags., newspapers and profl. jours.; exhibited Stanley Lehrer maritime collection on transatlantic ships at N.Y. Yacht Club, 1983, on Cunard Line's 150th anniversary at Forbes Mag. Galleries, N.Y.C., 1989-90, on French Line's Normandie at French Embassy, N.Y.C., 1992, and Bass Mus. Art, Miami, Fla., 1993, on Ships of State: The Great Transatlantic Liners, PaineWebber Art Gallery, N.Y.C., 1994-95, on the Wreck of the Titanic, Nat. Maritime Mus., London, 1994-95, on S.O.S. Safety on Ships: Learning from New York's Maritime Tragedies, Water Street Gallery, Seamen's Church Institute, N.Y.C., 1996, on Titanic: Fortune & Fate at the Mariners' Mus., Newport News, Va., 1998; on Titanic: The Artifact Exhibition at World Trade Center, Boston, 1998; on Titanic: the Exhibition, Union Depot, St. Paul, 1998-99, on Blue Ribband: Quest for Speed Across the Atlantic, U.S. Courthouse, N.Y.C., 1999, on Titanic: The Experience, Tropicana, Atlantic City, NJ, 1999, on Titanic, Better Living Ctr., Toronto, Can., 1999-2000; on Titanic: The Artifact Exhibit, Fair Park, Dallas, 2000; on Titanic: The Exhbn., Mus. Sci. & Industry, Chgo., 2000, on Titanic, Tropicana, Atlantic City, 2000; life jackets for Broadway musical Titanic, Lunt-Fontanne Theatre, N.Y.C., 1997 (based on Stanley Lehrer Titanic Collection); photographs and artifacts from Stanley Lehrer maritime collection featured in books and videos: On Board The Titanic, 1996, Lost Liners, 1997, Titanic: Legacy of the World's Greatest Ocean Liner, 1997, Titanic: Fortune & Fate, 1998; Nat. Geog. Soc. booklet on Titanic, 1998, Eyewitness: Titanic, 1999, Molly Brown: Unraveling the Myth, 1999, Titanica (video), 1998. V.p. Garden City Park (N.Y.) Civic Assn., 1961-63; treas. Citizens' Com. Edn., Garden City Park, 1962; mem. nat. jr. book awards com. Boys' Clubs Am., 1954; mem. nat. hon. com. for Richard H. Heindel Meml. Fund, Pa. State U., 1979-80. With Signal Corps, U.S. Army, 1951-53. Recipient non-fiction awards Midwestern Writers Conf., Chgo., 1948. Mem. New Hyde Park (N.Y.) C. of C. (dir. 1961-62), Titanic Hist. Soc., S.S. Hist. Soc. Am., Titanic Internat., Soc. Advancement of Edn. (treas. 1953-99, trustee 1963-99, pres. 1968-99), Ocean Liner Mus. (N.Y.C.), Psi Chi Omega. Home: 82 Shelbourne Ln New Hyde Park NY 11040-1044

LEHRLING, TERRY JAMES, real estate broker; b. Wellington, Kans., Feb. 23, 1950; s. Phillip James and Phyllis Cecele (Capps) L.; student U. Ariz., 1969-70, Pima Community Coll., 1970-71; m. Virginia Lucille Bogart, Feb. 27, 1971; children—Eric Terry, Adam James, Nicholas Justin. Sales exec., San Xavier Realty & Trust Co., 1972; residential sales mgr. 1st Realty & Investment Co., Inc., Tucson, 1973; founder, broker Terry J. Lehrling & Assos., Tucson, 1974—; founder Teleco Product Devel. and Mktg., Tucson, 1976—; broker Red Carpet Realtors, Tucson, 1976—; founder Teleco Realty & Devel., 1978; founder, pres. Number One Mktg. Group, Tucson, 1978—; asst. mgr. Shadron Bus. Brokerage, 1983—; v.p. Am. Bus. Enterprises, 1983—; founder, chief exec. officer Legal Research Assocs., 1983—. Mem. Pima County Parks and Recreation Commn., 1973—, chmn., 1976—; mem. Democratic Precinct Com., 1972—, Ariz. Com., 1972—; bd. dirs. Pima Community Coll., 1970; del. Dem. Regional Conv., 1976; bd. dirs. Met. Youth Council, 1977, chmn. bd., 1978-79; pres. bd. dirs. Hudlow Kindergarten, 1977; chmn. Ariz. Supreme Ct. Foster Care Rev. Bd. No. 5, 1979-83, mem. state bd., 1980—, mem. C.A.T.S. com. Central Ariz. Project; bd. dirs., active mem. Tucson Boys' Chorus, 1985—; pres. Dietz. PTA, 1983-84; mem. Autocap Bd. for Pima County Atty. and Ariz. Automobile Assn., 1996; vice chmn. noise reduction task force Mayor and Coun., City of Tucson, 1996. Recipient copper letter for cmty. svc. Mayor of Tucson, 1980, Copper Plaque Pima County Bd. Suprs., 1991. Mem. Ariz. Parks and Recreation Assn. Club: DeMolay. Home: PO Box 30304 Tucson AZ 85751-0304 Office: PO Box PO Box 18536 Tucson AZ 85731-8536

LEHTIMÄKI, PENTTI JOHANNES, military and political scientist; b. Hämeenkyrö, Finland, June 26, 1936; s. Eino Vihtori and Anni Sofia (Jokinen) L.; m. Tuulikki Marja-Liisa Satuli, Nov. 24, 1962; children: Jouni, Maunu. Commd. officer, Mil. Acad., Helsinki, Finland, 1961; student, U.S. Army Career Course, 1966; M in Polit. Sci., U. Helsinki, 1970; gen. staff officer, War Coll., Helsinki, 1973. Councillor, mil. rep. Finnish UN Mission, N.Y., 1981-84; chief of staff Karelian Brigade, Valkeala, Finland, 1984-86; comdr. Seinäjoki (Finland) Mil. Dist., 1986-89; chief sect. gen. staff FDF, Helsinki, 1989-92, chief personal def. forces, 1993-96; chief coord. Estonian Project, Finland, Estonia, 1996—; bd. mem. AssCherishing the Memory of Death of War, 1998—. Editor: Tietoja Maanpuolustuksesta, 1980. Pres. Assn. of the Relatives of Fallen Soldiers, 1998—. Maj. gen. FDF, 1993-96. Recipient Mil. Merit medals, Finland, 1991, Estonia, 1998; named Knight first class Order of the White Rose of Finland, 1984, Comdr. first class Order of the Lion of Finland, 1996. Mem. Mil. Sociol. Soc. Finland (chmn. 1994—), Mol. Shooting Assn. (chmn. 1995—). Avocations: political and military history, hunting, sports. Home: Pohjoiskaari 8 B 49, 00200 Helsinki Finland Office: Pääesikunta, Fabianinkatu 2, 00130 Helsinki Finland

LEHTINEN, VELI-HANNU, automation engineer; b. Helsinki, Finland, Dec. 29, 1959; s. Veikko Anselm and Kaisa Maija (Hannu) L.; m. Mari Johanna Karkkainen, May 12, 1989. BA, Myllykosken Lukio, Finland, 1978; MSc, Helsinki U. Tech., 1983, D in Tech., 1994. Rsch. scientist Tech. Rsch. Ctr. Finland, Espoo, 1983-85; devel. engr. ASEA Robotics Ab, Vasteras, Sweden, 1985-87; rsch. scientist VTT Automation, Espoo, 1987-95, sr. rsch. scientist, 1996-97, group mgr. on mobile robotics, 1998—; lectr. robotics Helsinki U. Technology, Espoo, 1988-97. Served in Finnish Air Force, 1978-79. Mem. Robotic Soc. Finland (bd. dirs. 1991-93), Finnish Soc. Automation (editl. bd. 1992—). Avocations: judo, alpine skiing, dogs. Home: Mechelininkatu 21 A 11, 00100 Helsinki Finland Office: VTT Automation, Otakaari 7 B, Espoo 02044, Finland

LEHTMETS, LEMMIK, electrical engineer; b. Luusika, Estonia, Feb. 10, 1948; s. Paul and Amanda (Altdorf) L.; m. Enda Rahni, June 25, 1951; 1 child. BS, Tallinn Poly. Inst., Estonia, 1971, MBA, 1971. Engr. Meat Factory, Paide, Estonia, 1971-72; state employee Estonia, Tallinn, 1972-91; exec. dir. Silves Enterprise Inc, Tallinn, 1991-93; mgr. Addinol Mineralöl GmbH, Tallinn, 1994-97; CEO Atto Bus. Contacts Ltd., Tallinn, 1991-99, ONAKO EESTI Ltd., Tallinn, 1999—. Office: Randvere Tee 118, 11913 Tallinn Estonia

LEHTOKANGAS, MIKKO ILMARI, technology researcher and educator; b. Tampere, Finland, Nov. 26, 1969. MSc, Tampere U. Tech., 1993, Licentiate of Tech., 1994, DrTech, 1995. Rsch. asst. Tampere U. Tech., 1992-93, rsch. scientist, 1993-95, sr. rsch. scientist, 1996-99; project mgr. TNokia Rsch. Ctr., Tampere, 1995-96; rsch. fellow Acad. of Finland, Helsinki, 1997—; Finland rep. COST 249, Belgium, 1996—; docent Helsinki U. Tech., 1999—. Contbr. articles to profl. jours. Acad. of Finland rsch. grantee, 1997. Mem. IEEE, IEEE Signal Processing Soc., Internat. Neural Network Soc., Finnish Assn. Grad. Engrs. E-mail: mikkol@cs.tut.fi. Office: Tampere U Tech, Hermiankatu 12 C, Tampere Finland 33720

LEHTONEN, HANNU VÄINO TAPANI, educator; b. Helsinki, Finland, July 1, 1950. MSc, U. Helsinki, 1973, PhD, 1981. Rschr. Water Conservation Lab., Helsinki, 1972-73; rschr. Finnish Game and Fisheries Rsch. Inst., Helsinki, 1973-83, sr. rschr., 1983-95; prof. U. Helsinki, 1995—. Contbr. over 400 articles to profl. jours. Avocations: fishing, hiking, nature. Home: Peukaloisenpolku 3, 02660 Espoo Finland Office: Univ Helsinki, PO Box 27, 00014 Helsinki Finland

LEHTONEN, HEIKKI ANTERO, social studies educator; b. Tampere, Finland, July 26, 1943; s. Vaito Artturi and Rebekka Elisabet (Oja) L.; m. Tellervo Elisabet Lahtinen, May 20, 1967; children: Timo Artturi, Kai Antero, Jan Olavi. D in Social Scis., U. Tampere, 1983. Assoc. prof. U. Tampere, 1985-98, prof., 1998—. Author: (in Finnish) The Forms of Use and Reproduction of Labour Force, 1983, Community, 1990, Social Policy as Moral Economy, 1996. Mem. Westermarck Soc., Finnish Assn. of Social Policy. Office: Dept Social Policy/Social W, U Tampere, FIN33014 Tampere Finland

LEIB, STEPHEN LOUIS, internist; b. N.Y.C., Dec. 27, 1961; arrived in Switzerland, 1963; s. George Leib and Ursula (Stauffacher) Rüegger; m. Barbara Marianne Fischer, June 12, 1999. MD, U. Basel, Switzerland, 1989; postgrad., U. Zürich, Switzerland, 1989-91. Cert. internal medicine, cert. infectious diseases. Asst. physician U. Zürich, 1990-91; asst. physician U. Basel, 1991-94, cons. infectious diseases, 1996-97; rsch. fellow U. Calif., San Francisco, 1994-96; attending physician, group leader meningitis rsch. U. Bern, Switzerland, 1997—. Contbr. chpts. to books and articles to profl. jours. Fellow Swiss NSF, 1989, 94, 95. Mem. Swiss Assn. Physicians, Swiss Soc. for Infectious Diseases. Avocations: Alpine skiing, snowboarding, turtle breeding, gardening. Office: Univ Bern Inst Med Micro, Friedbühlstr 51, 3010 Bern Switzerland

LEIBACHER, JOHN WILLIAM, astronomer; b. Chgo., May 28, 1941; s. George W. and Irene Leibacher; m. Lise H. Ouvrard, Dec. 21, 1976. AB, Harvard U., 1963, PhD, 1971. Postdoctoral fellow U. Colo., Boulder, 1970-71; scientist Laboratoire de Physique Stellaire et Planetaire, Paris, 1972-74, Lockheed Rsch. Lab., Palo Alto, Calif., 1975-81; astronomer Nat. Solar Obs., Tucson, 1982—, dir., 1988-93; dir. Global Oscillation Network Group Project, Tucson, 1984—. Address: PO Box 26732 Tucson AZ 85726-6732

LEIBETSEDER, JOSEF LEOPOLD, nutritionist, educator; b. Linz, Austria, Mar. 7, 1934; s. Josef and Pauline (Brandner) L.; m. Hedwig Vana, May 23, 1959; children: Florian, Veronika, Valentin, Sebastian. DVM, U. Vet. Medicine Vienna, 1958; PhD, U. Vet. Medicine, 1963, Dr honoris causa. Asst. prof. U. Vet. Medicine, Vienna, Austria, 1958-72; assoc. prof. U. Calif., Davis, 1972-73; assoc. prof. U. Vet. Medicine, Vienna, 1974, full prof., head, 1975-97, rector, 1995—. Co-author: Supplements to Lectures and Practice in Animal Nutrition, 1989; editor, co-author: Nutrition of Monogastric Animals, 1993; editor: (jours.) Ernährung Nutrition, 1992-97, Wiener Tierärztliche Monatsschrift, 1989-94. Mem. feedstuff com. Ministry of Agr., 1975-93; chem. com. Ministry of Ecology Youth and Family, 1988—, SCAN, 1997—. Recipient Sandoz award, 1972, Gustav Fingerling award Deutsche Landwirtschafts-Gesellschaft, 1987. Mem. Austrian Nutrition Soc. (pres. 1991-96), European Soc. Vet. and Comp. Nutrition (pres. 1992-94), Vet Assn. (v.p. 1986-98). Roman Catholic. Office: Inst Nutrition, Veterinarplatz 1, A-1210 Vienna Austria

LEIBOVICI, VERA, dermatologist, educator; b. Tirgu-Mures, Romania, June 25, 1953; arrived in Israel, 1980; d. Emeric and Agness (Blau) Lax; m. Marcel Leibovici, Apr. 19, 1975; children: Aviva, Edward. MD, U. Medicine, Tirgu-Mures, 1978; specialization in dermatology, Hadassah U. Hosp., Jerusalem, 1986. Intern, then resident Hadassah U. Hosp., 1978-86, instr. dermatology, 1984-87, lectr., 1987—. Contbr. articles to Jour. Am. Acad. Dermatology, Clin. and Exptl. Dermatology, European Jour. Dermatology. Mem. Am. Acad. Dermatology, Internat. Soc. Dermatology (tropical, geog. and ecologic sect.), Internat. Soc. Cosmetic Dermatology. Avocations: music, classic literature. Office: Hadassah Univ Hosp, PO Box 12018, 91120 Jerusalem Israel

LEIBY, ROBERT E., county agricultural agent; b. Allentown, Pa., Sept. 25, 1953; s. Earl R. and Gladys M. Leiby; m. Christina A. Leiby, Apr. 24, 1980 (div. Sept. 1997); 1 child, David. BS, Delaware Valley Coll., Doylestown, Pa., 1975; MEd, Pa. State U., 1982. County agrl. agt. Pa. Stat U. Lehigh County, Allentown, 1981—, county extension dir., 1986—; cons. U.S. AID, Swaziland, 1990, 91; treas. Spanish Ctr., Allentown, 1989-99; cons., vol. ACDI/VOCA, Moscow, 1999. Weekly columnist The Morning Call, 1981—. Mem. Nat. Assn. County Agrl. Agts. (Disting. Svc. award 1993), Potato Assa. Am., Pa. Assn. County Agrl. Agts., Pa. Plant Food and Protectant Edn. Soc. (bd. dirs. 1995-97). Mem. United Ch. of Christ. Avocation: outdoors. E-mail: rleiby@psu.edu. Office: Pa State U 4184 Dorney Park Rd Allentown PA 18104-5728

LEICH, JOHN, civil engineer, management executive; m. Sharon Anne Carter, Feb. 14, 1976; children: Stefanie, Mark. BCE, U. Sydney, Australia, 1975; MBA, U. Tech., Sydney, 1992. Gen. mgr. Ken on Concrete, Hong Kong, 1992—; mgmt. exec. Shiu on Corp., Hong Kong, 1992—; chmn. Far East Cement Co., Hong Kong, 1998—, Environment Com., Hong Kong, 1998-99. Recipient Hong Kong Quality award The Hong Kong Mgmt. Assn., 1998. Mem. Hong Kong Jockey Club, Royal Hong Kong Yacht Club. Avocations: golf, tennis, reading and research. Home: 9 Hosking St, Balmain East NSW 2041, Australia also: Mid-levels, 22E Block 2 58 Conduit Rd, Hong Kong Hong Kong Office: Ken on Concrete Co Ltd, 38 Tai Kok Tsui Rd, Kowloon Hong Kong

LEICHT, ERNST NIKOLAUS, physician, consultant; b. Budapest, Hungary, Nov. 23, 1934; s. Otto Herbert and Elisabeth Franziska (Kossow-Geronnay) L.; m. Irina Marianne Lenuweit Leicht, Dec. 20, 1983; 1 child, Hans Benno. MD, U. Graz, Austria, 1961; prof.'s degree, U. Saarland, Homburg, 1992. Asst. Dept. Pharmacology U. Tübingen, Germany, 1961-62; intern Dept. Surgery District Hosp., Heidenheim, 1962; intern Dept. Internal Medicine Dist. Hospital, Lüneburg, 1963; Dept. Gynecology Sanderbusch, 1963-64; asst. Dept. Internal Medicine U. Mainz, 1964-68; resident Dept. Internal Medicine U. Saarland, Homburg, 1968, emeritus, 2000—; endocrinologist, Homburg/Saar, 2000—. Author: Radioimmunoassay of Parathyroid Hormone, 1982. Recipient Claude Bernard award Salvia Co., Homburg, 1977, Albert Knoll award Knoll Co., Ludwigshafen, 1982. Mem. German Soc. Endocrinology, German Soc. Internal Medicine, United Leukodystrophy Found., N.Y. Acad. Scis. Roman Catholic. Office: Eisenbahnstrasse 52, D-66424 Homburg/Saar Germany

LEIDLMAIR, ADOLF, geographer; b. Linz, Austria, June 5, 1919; s. Adolf and Viktoria (Lettner) L.; m. Elizabeth LaFleur, Sept. 2, 1950; 1 child, Karl. PhD, U. Innsbruck, Austria, 1950. Asst. U. Tübingen, Germany, 1951-57; asst. prof. U. Tübingen, 1958-62; prof. U. Karlsruhe, Germany, 1963-66, U. Bonn, Germany, 1967-69, U. Innsbruck, Austria, 1969-89; prof. emeritus U. Innsbruck, 1989—. Author: Die Formentwicklung im Mitter Pinzgau, 1956, Bevölkerimg und Wirtschaft in Südtirol, 1958, Hadramaut, Bevölkerung und Wirtschaft im Wandel der Gegenwart; editor: Tirol Atlas; editor Landeskunde Österreich, 1983. Gr. silbernes Ehrenzeichen f. Verdienste u.d. Republik Österreich, 1986, Fr. v. Wieser medaille Mus.Ferdinand eum Innsbruck, 1988, Fr. v. Hauer medaille Österreichischen Geographischen Gesellschaft, 1989, Ehrenzeichen d. Landes Tirol, 1989. Mem. Austrian Acad. Sci. Home: Kaponsweg 17, A6065 Thaur Austria

LEIER, CARL VICTOR, internist, cardiologist; b. Bismarck, N.D., Oct. 20, 1944; married; 3 children. Grad., Creighton U., 1965, MD cum laude, 1969. Diplomate Am. Bd. Internal Medicine, Cardiovascular Medicine, Critical Care Medicine, Geriatric Medicine, Electrocardiography, Nat. Bd. Med. Examiners; lic. med., surgical Nebr., med. Ohio. Intern Ohio State U. Coll. Medicine, Columbus, 1969-70, med. resident (instr.) dept. medicine, 1971-73, chief resident (instr.), 1973-74, fellowship divsn. cardiology, 1974-76; pathology resident dept. pathology St. Vincent Hosp., Worcester, Mass., 1970-71; trainee NIH Tng. Grant, 1974-75; asst. prof. medicine cardiology dept., Ohio State U. Coll. Medicine, Columbus, 1976-80, asst. prof. pharmacology, 1976-80, assoc. prof., 1980-84, faculty mem. grad. sch., 1980—, dir. rsch. divsn. cardiology, 1980-83, James W. Overstreet prof. of

medicine, 1983—, prof. of medicine divsn. cardiology, 1984—, prof. pharmacology, dept. pharmacology, 1984—, dir. divsn. cardiology, 1986-98; hosp. procedures com. Ohio State U. Hosps., 1973-74; mem. pharmacology and therapeutics com. Ohio State U. Hosps., 1976-80; mem. rsch. com. ctrl. Ohio chpt. Am. Heart Assn., 1977-84, bd. trustees, 1979-88, exec. rsch. com., 1979-84, vice chmn. rsch. com., 1980-82, chmn. rsch. peer rev. com., 1982-84, v.p., 1984-86, pres. elect, 1986-88; numerous other coms.; cons. cardiorenal adv. bd. Smith-Kline Labs., 1982-85, com. on cardio-vascular rsch. and devel., 1982-85., AMA on Drugs and Tech., 1985—, FDA Cardiorenal adv. com. 1986-92, Lilly-Elanco devel. ractopamine, 1989; mem. ad hoc adv. com. on carvedilol in congestive heart failure, Smith, Kline and Beacham Pharms., 1991, ad hoc adv. com. on PDEI devel., McNeil Pharms., 1991, ad hoc adv. com. for clin. trials on Ibopamine, Zambon Pharms., 1993, sci. adv. com. Ohio State Univ. Brain Tumor Rsch. Ctr., 1993—, data safety monitoring bd., Otsuka Vesnarinone Trials, 1993— mem. chmn. Annual Sci. Sessions of the Am. Coll. of Cardiolog, 1996-97; vis. prof., lectr. and presenter at numerous sci. confs., insts. in U.S. and internationally. Editor: (book) Cardiotonic Drugs, 1986, 2d rev. edit., 1991; co-author: (with H. Boudoulas) CardioRenal Disorders and Diseases, 1986, 2d edit., 1992 (with J. Vincent) Critical Care Medicine: Recent Advances in Cardiovascular Medicine, 1990; contbr. more than 40 chpts. to other medical books and almost 200 articles to peer reviewed jours. including: Vascular Surgery, Archives of Internal Medicine, Circulation, Brit. Heart Jour., Jour. Electrocardiology, Clinical Pharmacologic Therapy, Chest, Am. Jour. Medicine, Jour. Cardiovascular Pharmacology, Am. Heart Jour., Geriatrics, Annals of Internal Medicine and others; editor in chief Congestive Heart Failure: Index and Revs., 1988—; mem. editorial bds. of ten medical jours. concerned with heart diseases, the review bds. of others including New Eng. Jour. Medicine, Internat. Jour. Cardiology, Jour. of Lab. and Clin. Medicine. Recipient Upjohn award, 1969, Lange Scholar award, 1969, Golden Apple Student Tchg. award, 1973, 75, Young Investigator award Ctrl. Ohio Heart Chpt., Am. Heart Assn., 1976-78, Rsch. Recognition award, 1978; named One of Best Doctors of Columbus, Columbus Monthly, 1992. Fellow Am. Coll. Clin. Pharmacology, Coun. on Clin. Pharmacology, Am. Heart Assn., Am. Coll. Cardiology, Am. Coll. Physicians, Coun. on Geriatric Cardiology; mem. AAAS, Ohio State Med. Assn., Am. Fedn. for Clin. Rsch., Ctrl. Soc. for Clin. Rsch., Am. Soc. Clin. Investigation, Assn. Univ. Cardiologists, Internat. Soc. for Heart Rsch., Internat. Soc. Cardiovascular Pharmacotherapy, Assn. Profs. of Cardiology. Office: Ohio State U Med Ctr Divsn Cardiology 1654 Upham Dr Columbus OH 43210-1250

LEIFER, MICHAEL, educator; b. London, Nov. 15, 1933; s. Nathan and Rose (Leperer) L.; m. Frances Phyllis Shwartz, Aug. 1, 1955; children: Simon, Richard, Jeremy. BA, U. Reading, England, 1956; PhD, U. London, 1959. Lectr. politics U. Adelaide, Australia, 1959-63, U. Hull, England, 1963-69; lectr. internat. rels. London Sch. Econs., 1969-74, reader, prof., 1974-89, pro-dir., 1991-95, dir. Asia rsch. ctr., 1996—; co-chair European Coun. for Security Cooperation in the Asia-Pacific. Author: Cambodia: The Search for Security, 1967, Indonesia's Foreign Policy, 1983, Asean and the Security of South-East Asia, 1989, 90, Dictionary of the Modern Politics of South-East Asia, 1995, 96; editor: Asian Nationalism, 2000. Disting. fellow Ctr. Strategic and Internat. Studies, Indonesia, 1996. Mem. Internat. Inst. Strategic Studies, Inst. Def. and Strategic Studies Singapore (bd. dirs. 2000). Avocations: music, walking. Office: London Sch Econs & Polit Sci, Houghton St, London WC2A 2AE, England

LEIFERT, WAYNE RICHARD, cardiac electrophysiologist; b. Adelaide, Australia, Sept. 7, 1969; s. Klaus and Lola Ruth (Kramer) L. Cert. Med. Lab. Sci., South Australian Inst. Tech., 1990; Dip.Med.Lab.Sci., U. of South Australia, 1992; BSc with honors, Flinders U. of South Australia, 1997. Tech. officer CSIRO, Adelaide, 1988-97; tchg. assoc. U. Adelaide, 1998—; secretariat-asst. Internat. Congress of Nutrition, Adelaide, 1992-93; student rsch. co-supr. CSIRO/U. Adelaide, 1997—. Contbr. articles to profl. jours. Recipient W.R. O'Dell award Australian Inst. Med. Scientists, 1993, W.G. Nayler prize Internat. Soc. for Heart Rsch., 1998, travel award, 1997. Mem. Australian Soc. for Med. Rsch. (Ross Wishart Meml. award 1999), Am. Oil Chemists Soc., Internat. Soc. for Heart Rsch. (exec. com. 1997—, state rep.). Nutrition Soc. Australia. Home: PO Box 291, Gumeracha 5233 SA, Australia Office: CSIRO Health Scis andNutrition, PO Box 10041, Adelaide SA 5000, Australia

LEIFSSON, BJORGVIN RUNAR, biology educator; b. Reykjavik, Iceland, July 22, 1955; s. Leifur Jonsson and Maria Bjorgvinsdottir; m. Eyvor Gunnarsdottir, Sept. 17, 1976; children: Hilmar Dui, Sigurdur Jon, Erla Maria. BS, U. Iceland, Reykjavik, 1979, MS, 1996. Biology educator Akranes (Iceland) Coll., 1979-86; biology rschr. Akureyri (Iceland) Natural History Mus., 1986-87; biology educator Husavik (Iceland) Coll., 1987—; curriculum mgr. Husavik Coll., 1989-93; marine biology rschr. Town of Husavik, 1996. Editor The Natural History of Skagafjordur, 1987; contbr. articles and reports to jours. Grantee Icelandic Tchrs. Union Sci. Fund, Reykjavik, 1993, Ministry Edn., Reykjavik, 1993, Ednl. Fund Govt. Employees, Reykjavik, 1993, Icelandic Rsch. Fund for Grad. Students, Reykjavik, 1994. Mem. Icelandic Natural History Soc., Icelandic Coll. Tchrs. Union, Govt. Employees Union, Husavik Bridge Club (chmn. 1987-93, 96—). Mem. Left Green Alliance. Avocations: bridge, mountain driving, reading, music. E-mail: brl@ismennt.is. Fax: 354-464-1638. Home: Asgardsvegur 5, 640 Husavik Iceland Office: Husavik Coll, Storigardur 10, 640 Husavik Iceland

LEIGH, HOYLE, psychiatrist, educator, writer; b. Seoul, Korea, Mar. 25, 1942; came to U.S., 1965; m. Vincenta Masciandaro, Sept. 16, 1967; 1 child, Alexander Hoyle. MA, Yale U., 1982; MD, Yonsei U., Seoul, 1965. Diplomate Am. Bd. Psychiatry and Neurology. Asst. prof. Yale U., New Haven, 1971-75, assoc. prof., 1975-80, prof., 1980-89, lectr. in psychiatry, 1989—; dir. Behavioral Medicine Clinic, Yale U., 1980-89; dir. psychiat. cons. svc. Yale-New Haven Hosp., 1971-89; chief psychiatry VA Med Ctr., Fresno, Calif., 1989—; prof., vice chmn. dept. psychiatry U. Calif., San Francisco, 1989—, head dept. psychiatry, 1989—; cons. Am. Jour. Psychiatry, Archives Internal Medicine, Psychosomatic Medicine. Author: The Patient, 1980, 2d edit., 1985, 3d edit., 1992; editor: Psychiatry in the Practice of Medicine, 1983, Consultation-Liaison Psychiatry: 1990's & Beyond, 1994, Biopsychosocial Approaches in Primary Care: State of the Art and Challenges for the 21st Century, 1997. Fellow ACP, Internat. Coll. Psychosomatic Medicine (v.p.), Am. Acad. Psychosomatic Medicine; mem. AMA, AAUP, World Psychiat. Assn. Avocations: reading, music, skiing. Office: U Calif Dept Psychiat 2615 E Clinton Ave Fresno CA 93703-2223

LEIGH, JAMES, epidemiologist, researcher; b. Sydney, NSW, Australia, Jan. 29, 1944; s. William Richard and Jean Arthur (Baxter) L.; m. Carole Marion Day, Jan. 27, 1967; children: Julia Marion, Antonia Jane, Claudia Mary. MB BS, U. Sydney (Australia), 1967, PhD, 1972; postgrad., Monash U., Melbourne, Australia, 1974; MSc, U. Sydney, 1980, MA, 1981, MD, 1992. Resident med. officer St. George Hosp., Sydney, 1967; rsch. fellow U. Sydney, 1968-70; lectr. U. Birmingham (Eng.), 1971-72; staff specialist Monash U., Melbourne, 1973-74; dir. computer svcs. NSW Health, Sydney, 1975-78; rschr. med. divsn. Joint Coal Bd., Sydney, 1978-88; head epidemiology dept. NIOHS, Sydney, 1988—, head rsch. unit, 1998—; vis. scientist Nat. Ctr. Sci. Rsch., Strasbourg, France, 1982; chmn. Faculty Occupational Medicine, NSW, 1988-96, councillor, 1993-94; vis. prof. Finnish IOH, Helsinki, 1994; sr. lectr. U. Sydney, 1988—; cons. ILO, Indonesia, 1996—, Geneva, Switzerland, 1997. Editor: Scandinavian Jour. Work Environ. Health, 1994; author (book chpts.) Source Book on Asbestos, 1994-96; contbr. articles to profl. jours. Fellow Faculty of Occuptl. Medicine Royal Australasian Coll. of Physicians, Faculty of Public Health Medicine Royal Australasian Coll. of Physicians; mem. Australian Math. Soc., Brit. Computer Soc., Internat. Epidemiol. Assn., Killara Tennis Club. Avocations: tennis, golf, music, Wagner, piano. Home: 5 Nelson Rd Lindfield, Sydney NSW 2070, Australia Office: NOHSC, 92 Parramatta Rd Camperdown, Sydney NSW 2050, Australia

LEIGH, MARGIE, mortgage company administrator; b. Campbellsville, Ky., June 6, 1946; d. Bennie Lawrence and Evelyn Garnetta (Seay) DeWitt; children: Susan Leigh, Tracy Lynne. Grad. in elem. edn., Western Ky. U., 1968; postgrad., U. Ky., Lexington, 1986, U. Ky., Elizabethtown, 1988. Real estate agt. Nat. Realtors Assn., Elizabethtown, Ky., 1986-92; mortgage originator Nat. Bankers Assn., McLean, Va., 1993—; br. mgr. Old Kent Mortgage Co. Mem. adv. bd. Hardin County Sch., Elizabethtown, 1985-87. Recipient Apple award Elizabethtown Sch. Sys., 1985; named to Order of Ky. Cols. Mem. Order Ea. Star. Republican. Baptist. Avocations: golf, tennis, writing.

LEIGH, MIKE, film director; b. Salford, England, Feb. 20, 1943; s. A.A. and P.P. (Cousin) L.; m. Alison Steadman, 1973; 2 children. Student, Royal Acad. Dramatic Art, London, Camberwell Sch. Arts and Crafts, Cen. Sch. Art and Design, London Film Sch. Director: (plays) The Box Play, 1965, My Parents Have Gone to Carlisle, The Last Crusade of the Five Little Nuns, 1966, Nenaa, 1967, Individual Fruit Pies, Down Here and Up There, Big Basil, 1968, Epilogue, Glum Victoria and the Lad with Specs, 1969, Bleak Moments, 1970, A Rancid Pong, 1971, Wholesome Glory, The Jaws of Death, Dick Whittington and His Cat, 1973, Babies Grow Old, The Silent Majority, 1974, Abigail's Party, 1977, Ecstasy, 1979, Goose-Pimples, 1981 (George Devine award 1973, Critics' Choice Best Comedy award London Evening Std. 1981, Critics' Choice Best Comedy award Drama London 1981), Smelling A Rat, 1988, Greek Tragedy, 1989, (feature films) Bleak Moments, 1971 (Golden Leopard award Locarno Film Festival 1972, Golden Hugo award Chgo. Film Festival 1972), Abigail's Party, 1977, High Hopes, 1988 (Internat. Critic's prize Venice Film Festival 1988, Best Film Coup de Coeur Geneva 1989, Peter Sellers Best Comedy Film award London Evening Std. 1990), Life is Sweet, 1990, Naked, 1993 (Best Dir. award Cannes Internat. Film Festival 1993), Secrets and Lies, 1996, Career Girls, 1997, Topsy-Turvy, 1999, Topsy-Turvy, 1999, (TV films) A Mug's Game, Hard Labour, 1972, The Permissive Society, The Birth of the 2001 F.A. Cup Final Goalie, Old Chums, Probation, A Light Snack, Afternoon, 1975, Nuts in May, 1976, Knock for Knock, 1976, The Kiss of Death, 1977, Abigail's Party, 1977, Who's Who, 1978, Grown Ups, 1980, Home Sweet Home, 1981, Meantime, 1983, Four Days in July, 1984, The Short and Curlies, 1987, (radio play) Too Much of a Good Thing, 1979. Address: Peters Fraser & Dunlop, Drury House 34-43 Russell, London WC2B 3HA, England

LEIGH, VINCENTA M., health administrator; b. N.Y.C., June 27, 1947; d. Emanuel and Ines Masciandara; m. Hoyle Leigh, Sept. 16, 1967; 1 child, Alexander. BA, Lehman Coll., 1968; MSN, Yale U., 1973. Psychiat. clinician Jacobi Hosp., Bronx, N.Y., 1971; pediatric nurse Conn. Mental Health Ctr., New Haven, 1971-73; instr. in psychiat. nursing Yale U., New Haven, 1973-77; asst. dir. mental health nursing edn. Conn. Valley Hosp., Middletown, 1980-81; nurse coord. Inst. of Living, Hartford, Conn., 1981-85, asst. dir. nursing, 1985-89; asst. clin. profl. psychiatry U. Calif., San Francisco, 1989—; coord. Intensive outpatient program Kaiser Permanente, Fresno, Calif., 1996—. Contbr. articles to profl. jours. Mem. ANA, Am. Psychosomatic Soc., Internat. Coll. Psychosomatic Medicine, Am. Orthopedic Assn., Jr. League. Avocations: piano, reading, trombone, skiing.

LEIGHNINGER, DAVID SCOTT, cardiovascular surgeon; b. Ohio, Jan. 16, 1920; s. Jesse Harrison and Marjorie (Lightner) L.; m. Margaret Jane Malony, May 24, 1942; children: David Allan, Jenny. BA, Oberlin Coll., 1942; MD, Western Res. U., 1945. Intern Univ. Hosps. of Cleve., 1945-46, resident, 1949-51, asst. surgeon, 1951-68; rsch. fellow in cardiovascular surgery rsch. lab. Case Western Res. U. Sch. Medicine, Cleve., 1948-49, 51-55, 57-67, instr. surgery, 1951-55, sr. instr., 1957-64, asst. prof., 1964-68, asst. clin. prof., 1968-70; resident Cin. Gen. Hosp., 1955-57; practice medicine specializing in cardiovascular surgery Cleve., 1957-70; pvt. practice medicine specializing in cardiovascular and gen. surgery Edgewater Hosp., Chgo., 1970-82, staff surgeon, also dir. emergency surg. svcs., 1970-82; staff surgeon, also dir. emergency surg. svcs. Mazel Med. Ctr., Chgo., 1970-82; emergency physician Raton, N.Mex. and Trinidad, Colo., 1982-85; assoc., courtesy, or cons. staff Marymount Hosp., Cleve., Mt. Sinai Hosp., Cleve., Geauga Cmty. Hosp., Chardon, Ohio, Bedford Cmty. Hosp. (Ohio), 1957-70. Contbr. numerous articles to med. jours., chpts. to med. texts; spl. pioneer rsch. (with Claude S. Beck) in physiopathology of coronary artery disease and CPR; developed surg. treatment of coronary artery disease; developed vein graft bypass in late 1940s; (with Claude S. Beck) achieved 1st successful defibrillation of human heart; 1st successful reversal of fatal heart attack; provided 1st intensive care of coronary patients. Tchr. tng. courses in CPR for med. personnel, police, fire and vol. rescue workers, numerous cities, 1950-70. Served to capt., M.C., AUS, 1946-48. Recipient Chris award Columbus Internat. Film Festival, 1964, numerous other awards for sci. exhibits from various nat. and state med. socs., 1953-70; USPHS grantee, 1949-68. Fellow Am. Coll. Cardiology (emeritus), Am. Coll. Chest Physicians; mem. Mont Reid Surg. Soc. (Cinn.).

LEIGHTON, JACK RICHARD, small business owner, former educator; b. Boise, Idaho, May 10, 1918; s. Ralph Waldo and Lucia Marie (Strub) L.; m. Helen Louise Wirtenberger, July 24, 1942; 1 child, James Carl. Student, U. Wash., 1938-39; BS, U. Oreg., 1941, MS, 1942, PhD, 1954; postgrad., U. Iowa, 1950. Dir. phys. edn. and athletics Montpelier (Idaho) H.S., 1941-42; exec. asst. phys. medicine rehab. svc. Vancouver (Wash.) VA Hosp., 1946-50; assoc. prof. phys. edn. Pa. State U., State College, 1952-53; assoc. prof. Ea. Wash. U., Cheney, 1953-56, prof., 1956-81, dir. divsn. health, phys. edn., recreation and athletics, 1953-81; pres. Leighton Flexometer Co. Inc., Spokane, Wash., 1985—; Mem. com. on secondary sch. health and phys. edn. Idaho Dept. Edn., Boise, 1942; cons. state adv. com. on sch. activity and phys. edn. Wash. Dept. Pub. Instrn., Olympia, 1954-55, mem. com. on phys. edn. curriculum guide, 1957-58. Author: Physical Education for Boys, 1942, Objective Physical Education, 1946, Progressive Weight Training, 1961, Fitness, Body Development & Sports Conditioning Through Weight Training, 1983; assoc. editor Rsch. Quar. AAHPERD, 1960-63, Jour. Health, Phys. Edn. and Recreation, 1967-68; editor Jour. Assn. for Phys. and Mental Rehab., 1963-67; mem. editl. bd. Am. Corrective Therapy Jour., 1972-79; contbr. articles to profl. jours., chpts. to books; patentee instrument to measure range of joint motion. Mem. Ea. Wash. U. Retirees Bd., 1996-99; mem. Spokane County Cmty. Svcs. Devel. Disabilities Adv. Bd., 1999—. With AUS, 1942-46. Fellow Am. Coll. Sports Medicine; mem. AAHPERD (necrology com. 1955-58, chmn. fitness sect. 1960-61, mem. rsch. coun., com. to study purpose and propose revisions of structure and procedures gen. divsn. 1960-61; mem. N.W. dist. honor awards com. 1955-57, 76-79, chmn. 1976-77, mem. constn. com. 1957-60, chmn. rsch. sect. 1957-58, v.p. phys. edn. 1957-58, chmn. fitness sect. 1963-64, pres. 1971-72), Wash. Assn. Health, Phys. Edn. and Recreation (phys. fitness steering com. 1955-57, constn. com. 1957-58, chmn. tchr. tng. sect. 1956-57, phys. fitness steering com. 1957-59, v.p. ea. dist. 1957-58, pres. 1959-60), Spokane United Sch. Groups (Ea. Wash. U. rep. 1957-60), Spokane Area C. of C. (small bus. coun. 1993—), Phi Delta Kappa, Phi Epsilon Kappa. Home and Office: 1321 E 55th Ave Spokane WA 99223-6311

LEIGHTON, JAMES NORTHING, oil company executive; b. Victoria, Hong Kong, Oct. 22, 1957; s. Basil Frank and Isabel Dora (Day) L. BA in Polit. Sci., Newcastle U., Eng., 1979; MBA, Nantes (France) U., 1987. Supr. Halliburton, Fahud, Oman, 1980-84; divsn. mgr. Petrometalic, Cambrai, France, 1987-94; mktg. dir. Drillflex, Rennes, France, 1994—; lectr. Lille (France) U., 1992-94. Contbr. articles to profl. jours.; 2 patents in field. Mem. Soc. Petroleum Engrs., Exiles Club London. Avocations: paragliding, squash, swimming, bridge, gastronomy. Office: Drillflex, 29 Rue Lavoisier, 35230 Noyal Chatillon, France

LEIGHTON, LAWRENCE WARD, investment banker; b. N.Y.C., July 1, 1934; s. Sidney and Florence (Ward) L.; m. Mariana Stroock, June 21, 1959; children: Sandra L. Galvin, Michelle S. Wykoff. BSE, Princeton U., 1956; MBA, Harvard U., 1962. V.p. Kuhn Loeb & Co., N.Y.C., 1962-69, Clark, Dodge & Co., Inc., 1970-74; dir. Norton-Simon, Inc., 1974-78; ltd. ptnr. Bear, Stearns & Co., 1978-82; mng. dir. Chase Investment Bank, 1983-88; pres., CEO Union d'Etudes et d'Investissements Mcht. Bank of Credit Agricole, 1989-93; vice-chmn. 2I, Inc., 1993-94; mng. dir. LM Capital Corp., 1994-96; sr. advisor Bentley Assocs., LP, 1997—; dir. Corp. Renaissance Group, 1994-2000; chmn. Princeton Schs. Com. of N.Y., 1965-85. Mem. exec. com. Princeton U. Alumni Coun., 1975-80; mem. exec. com. alumni coun. The Lawrenceville Sch., 1999—; vice-chmn. nat. schs. com. Princeton U., 1980—; chmn. Harvard Bus. Sch. Fund of N.Y., 1964-65; mem. nat. fin. com. Pete DuPont for Pres., 1986-88; trustee Waterford Inst., 1985—. Lt. (j.g.) USN, 1957-60. Mem. Stanwich Club (Greenwich, Conn.), Princeton Club of N.Y. (scholarship com. 1970—, bd. govs. 1989-96), Coral Beach and Tennis Club (Bermuda). Avocations: flying, golf, photography. Home: 1088 Park Ave New York NY 10128-1132 Office: Bentley Assocs 101 Park Ave Rm 2101 New York NY 10178-2101

LEIGHTON, ROBERT BRUCE, investment company executive; b. London, Feb. 28, 1956; s. David Straun Robertson and Helen Margaret (House) L.; m. Doreen Bernadette Jones, Dec. 6, 1991. BA with honors, U. Calgary, Can., 1977; MA in African Politics, U. London, 1980; MBA, Harvard Bus. Sch., 1984. Analyst Credit Lyonnais, Calgary, 1980-82; from officer trade fin. to asst. supr. The Bank of Nova Scotia, Toronto, Can., 1984-88; sr. fin. officer Export Devel. Corp., Ottawa, Can., 1988-90; investment officer Internat. Fin. Corp., Washington, 1990-96; resident rep. Internat. Fin. Corp., Brazil, 1996—; bd. dirs. PISA, Jaguarive, CRP Caderi, Porto Alegre. Rep. Can. Crossroads Internat., Calgary, 1981-83; sponsor Foster Parents Plan, Toronto, 1979-91. Recipient Prix d'Honneur Banff Ctr., Alberta, Can., 1978. Mem. Inst. Fin. Execs., Harvard Bus. Sch. Club Brazil, Commonwealth Inst. Avocations: running, scuba, hiking, clarinet. Home: 1818 H St NW # Ifc-res Washington DC 20433-0001 Office: Internat Fin Corp, Rua Guararapes 2064, 04561004 Sao Paulo Brazil Address: Leighton % World Bank 1818 H St NW # Ifc Washington DC 20433-0001

LEIGHTON, ROBERT JOSEPH, state legislator; b. Austin, Minn., July 7, 1965; s. Robert Joseph Sr. and JoAnn (Mulvihill) L. BA, U. Minn., 1988; JD, U. Calif., Berkeley, 1991. Minn. state rep. Dist. 27B, 1995—. Presdl. and Waller scholar U. Minn., 1988. Mem. ABA, Minn. Bar Assn., Minn. Trial Lawyers Assn., Phi Beta Kappa. Home: 900 4th St NW Austin MN 55912-2001 Office: Leighton Meany Cotter & Enger 601 N Main St Austin MN 55912-3319

LEIKOLA, ANTO HEIKKI ALBERT, history of science educator; b. Helsinki, Finland, June 8, 1937; s. Erkki Ensio and Elli (Suolahti) L.; m. Helka Leena Marjatta Huttunen, Feb. 21, 1959; children: Markus, Anna. Cand. Phil., U. Helsinki, 1959, Mag. Phil., 1960, Lic. Phil., 1961, PhD, 1964. Asst. dept. zoology U. Helsinki, 1960-63, 73-85; rsch. asst. State Commn. Natural Sci., Helsinki, 1964-68; head nonfiction dept. Werner Söderström Pubs., Helsinki, 1968-72; acting prof. history of sci. U. Oulu, Finland, 1980, 83; sr. rschr. U. Helsinki, 1984-85, prof. history of sci., 1988-97; lectr. devel. biology U. Helsinki, 1972-88; lectr. history of sci. U. Oulu, 1980—, U. Helsinki, 1998—. Co-author: History of the University of Helsinki, 1987-91; author (with others) biology textbooks, several collections of essays; translator numerous books from various langs. into Finnish; contbr. essays, revs., articles and sci. papers to profl. publs. Exec. bd. dirs., adv. bd. Finnish Cultural Found., Helsinki, 1968-91; exec. bd. dirs. World Wildlife Fund, Helsinki, 1977-86; mem. Finnish UNESCO Commn., Helsinki, 1987-95; chmn. citizens' del. for Martti Ahtisaari's presdl. campaign, 1993-94. Decorated 1st Class Knight, Order of White Rose of Finland, 1973, Commendatore, Ordine Al Merito della Repubblica Italiana, 1993, Officer Three Stars Order of Republic of Latvia, 1997, Comdr., Order of Lion of Finland, 1997; recipient Finnish State award for sci. popularization, 1969, 80, Kansanvalistusseura award, 1974, Werner Söderström Lit. Found. award, 1978, Kordelin Found. Lit. award, 1985, Finnish Nonfiction Writers' Warelius award, 1988. Mem. Internat. Acad. History of Sci., Finnish Soc. History of Sci. and Ideas (chmn. 1976-97), Finnish Soc. Scis., Latvian Acad. Sci. (fgn.). Mem. Green League. Avocation: nature photography. Home: Pölkönhovintie 135A, FIN77350 Montola Finland

LEIMALA, RAIMO JUHANI, chemical engineering administrator; b. Turku, Finland, Aug. 21, 1942; s. Kaino Gabriel and Saida Lahja (Anttila) L.; m. Ritva Tellervo Laakso; children: Tuire Birgit, Tarja Margit. MS in Chem. Engring., Åbo Acad., Turku, 1967. Rsch. chemist Outokumpu Oy, Pori, Finland, 1969-72; oper. engr. Outokumpu Oy, Harjavalta, Finland, 1973-79; dept. engr. Outokumpu Oy, Pori, 1979-81, supt., 1981-88; sr. rsch. metallurgist Outokumpu Rsch. Oy, Pori, 1988-92, devel. mgr., 1993—; Phone: 358 2 626 5030. Contbr. articles to profl. jours.; patentee in field. Mem. Mining and Metall. Soc. Finland. Office: Outokumpu Rsch Oy, PO Box 60, FIN28101 Pori Finland

LEIN, FILIP MARCEL, banker; b. Courtrai, Belgium, May 23, 1961; s. Frans Hendrik and Nicole (Cottenier) L.; m. Janet Jarman, June 29, 1996. LLB, Cath. U. Louvain-Courtrai, Belgium, 1981; Licentiate Law, Cath. U. Louvain, Belgium, 1984; MA in Internat. Bus., Sophia U., Tokyo, 1987. Analyst Merrill Lynch, Tokyo, 1987-89, assoc. investment banking, 1989-91; v.p. equity capital markets Merrill Lynch, Tokyo, N.Y.C. and London, 1992-94; dir. equity capital markets Merrill Lynch, London, 1995-98; joint head equity capital markets Merrill Lynch Japan, 1999—. Author: Department Stores in Japan, 1987. Avocations: tennis, windsurfing, shorinji kempo. Office: Merrill Lynch, 1-1-3 Chiyoda-Ku, Tokyo 100-8180, Japan

LEINDLER, LASZLO, mathematics educator; b. Kecskemét, Hungary, Oct. 1, 1935; s. János Leindler and Eszter Végh; m. Margit Zsitva, Oct. 4, 1958; children: László, Zoltán. PhD, Jozsef Attila U., Szeged, Hungary, 1964. Asst. prof. math. U. Szeged, 1962-65, assoc. prof. math., 1965-68, prof. math., 1968—, chmn. dept. math., 1978-98; dean U. Szeged, 1972-75, dep. rector, 1975-78, 84-87; dir. Bolyai Inst. Szeged, 1978-85. Author (monograph) Strong Approximation by Fourier Series, 1985. Mem. Hungarian Acad. Sci. (v.p. math. sect. 1976-90), Bolyai Math. Assn. Avocations: soccer, tennis, walking. E-mail: leindler@math.u-szeged.hu. Home: Balfasor 16, H-6726 Szeged Hungary Office: U Szeged, Aradi Vertanuk Tere 1, H-6720 Szeged Hungary

LEINFELLNER, WERNER HUBERTUS, education educator; b. Graz, Austria, Jan. 17, 1921; came to U.S., 1966; s. Hubertus L. and Maria (Woschner) L.; m. Elisabeth Rupertsberger, Oct. 28, 1960; 1 child, Ruth. MA, U. Vienna, 1946, PhD, 1959; Dr honoris causa, Coll. de France, Paris. Asst. prof. Inst. Advanced Studies, Vienna, 1962-66; lectr. U. vienna, 1962-66; prof. philosophy U. Nebr., 1967-86; guest prof. U. Basle (Switzerland), 1966; vis. prof. U. Heidelberg, 1973, U. Vienna, 1976, Tech. U., Vienna, 1976, 80—; mng. editor Theory and Decision Libr., U. Canberra, 1992, U. Taipei, 1993; co-dir. Boltzmann Inst. U. Graz, 1993—. Editor-in-chief jour. Theory and Decision, 1970—; editor: jour. Wisenschaftsforschung, 1990—; author: (books) Structure and Construction of Scientific Theories, 1965, Introduction into Philosophy of Science and Epistemology, 3d edit., 1978, The Rise of Theories: An Analysis of the Critical Thinking of Antiquity, 1966; co-author: Forschungslogik der Sozialwissenschaften, 1973, Ontology, System Theory and Semantics, 1978; co-editor: Recent Developments in the Methodology of the Social Sciences, I, 1974, II, 1978, Decision Theory and Social Ethics, 1978, Wittgenstein and His Impact on Contemporary Thought, 1977, Ludwig Wittgenstein Dictionary, 1977, Language and Ontology, 1981, M. Allais, His Work, 1990, Game Theory and Rationality, 1997; contbr. articles to profl. jours. Recipient prize Korner Found., Vienna, 1963, 66, Austrian Disting. award for Rsch.: Intelligence and Evolution, 1990. Mem. Philosophy Sci. Assn., Assn. Symbolic Logic, Philosophy Soc. Vienna, Kuratorium Inst. Sci. and Arts, Am. Philos. Assn., Nebr. Acad. Scis. (chmn.), Assn. Philos. Jour., Editors, Austrian Wittgenstein Soc. (v.p. 1976—), Internat. Conf. Utility and Risk Theory (pres. 1982—), Hauer Gesellschaft, Paulus Soc. (cons. bd.), Nebr. Acad. Sci. (sect. chmn.), Vienna Circle Inst. (cons. bd.), Internat. Wittgenstein Symposia (v.p. 1977-80, chmn. 1980), European Acad. Scis. and Arts, Russian Acad. Sci. Office: Boltzmann Inst Sci/U Graz, Mozartgasse 14, A 8010 Graz Austria

LEINIEKS, VALDIS, classicist, educator; b. Liepaja, Latvia, Apr. 15, 1932; came to U.S., 1949, naturalized, 1954; s. Arvid Ansis and Valia Leontine (Brunaus) L. BA, Cornell U., 1955, MA, 1956; PhD, Princeton U., 1962. Instr. classics Cornell Coll., Mount Vernon, Iowa, 1959-62, asst. prof. classics, 1962-64; assoc. prof. classics Ohio State U., 1964-66; assoc. prof. classics U. Nebr., Lincoln, 1966-71, prof. classics, 1971—, chmn. dept. classics, 1967-95, chmn. program comparative lit., 1970-86, interim chmn. dept. modern langs., 1982-83. Author: Morphosyntax of the Homeric Greek Verb, 1964; The Structure of Latin, 1975; Index Nepotianus, 1976; The Plays of Sophokles, 1982, The City of Dionysos, 1996. Contbr. articles to profl. jours. Mem. AAUP, Am. Classical League, Classical Assn. Middle West and South, Am. Philol. Assn. Republican. Home: 2505 A St Lincoln NE 68502-1840 Office: U Nebr Dept Classics Lincoln NE 68588-0337

LEINO, DEANNA ROSE, business educator; b. Leadville, Colo., Dec. 15, 1937; d. Arvo Ensio Leino and Edith Mary (Bonan) Leino Malenck; 1 adopted child, Michael Charles Bolan. BSBA, U. Denver, 1959, MS in Bus. Adminstrn., 1967; postgrad., C.C. Denver, U. No. Colo., Colo. State U., U. Colo., Met. State Coll. Cert. tchr., vocat. tchr., Colo. Tchr. Jefferson County Adult Edn., Lakewood, Colo., 1963-67; tchr. bus., coord. coop.

office edn. Jefferson H.S., Edgewater, Colo., 1959-93, ret., 1993; sales assoc. Joslins Dept. Store, Denver, 1978—; mem. ea. team. clk. office automation Denver Svc. Ctr., Nat. Park Svc., 1993-94; wage hour technician U.S. Dept. Labor, 1994—; instr. C.C. Denver, Red Rocks, 1967-81, U. Colo., Denver, 1976-79, Parks. Coll. Bus., (now Parks Jr. Coll.), 1983-98, Front Range C.C., 1998-2000; dist. advisor Future Bus. Leaders Am. Author short Story. Active City of Edgewater Sister City Project Student Exch. Com.; pres. Career Women's Symphony Guild; treas. Phantoms of Opera, 1982—; active Opera Colo. Assocs. and Guild, I Pagliacci; ex-officio trustee Denver Symphony Assn., 1980-82. Recipient Disting. Svc. award Jefferson County Sch. Bd., 1980, Tchr. Who Makes a Difference award Sta. KCNC/Rocky Mountain News, 1990, Youth Leader award Lakewood Optimist Club, 1993; inducted into Jefferson H.S. Wall of Fame, 1981; named to Jefferson County Hall of Fame, 2000. Mem. NEA (life), Colo. Edn. Assn., Jefferson County Edn. Assn., Colo. Vocat. Assn., Am. Vocat. Assn., Colo. Educators for and about Bus., Profl. Secs. Internat., Career Women's Symphony Guild, Profl. Panhellenic Assn., Colo. Congress Fgn. Lang. Tchrs., Wheat Ridge C. of C. (edn. and scholarship com.), Federally Employed Women, Tyrolean Soc. Denver, Delta Pi Epsilon, Phi Chi Theta, Beta Gamma Sigma, Alpha Lambda Delta. Republican. Roman Catholic. Avocations: decorating wedding cakes, crocheting, sewing, music, world travel. Home: 3712 Allison St Wheat Ridge CO 80033-6124

LEIS, HENRY PATRICK, JR., surgeon, educator; b. Saranac Lake, N.Y., Aug. 12, 1914; s. Henry P. and Mary A. (Disco) L.; m. Winogene Barnette, Jan. 8, 1944; children: Henry Patrick III, Thomas Frederick. BS cum laude, Fordham U., 1936; MD, N.Y. Med. Coll., 1941. Diplomate Am. Bd. Surgery. Intern Flower and Fifth Ave Hosps., N.Y.C., 1941-42, resident, 1943-44, 46-49, attending surgeon, chief breast service, 1960-81; resident in surgery Kanawa Valley Hosp., Charleston, W.Va., 1942-43; attending surgeon, chief breast svc. Met. Hosp., N.Y.C., 1960-81, emeritus chief breast svc., 1982—; attending surgeon Coler Meml. Hosp., N.Y.C., 1960-76; chief breast surgery Cabrini Hosp. Med. Ctr., 1978-85, cons. breast surgery, 1985—; emeritus surgeon Lenox Hill Hosp., N.Y.C., 1980-83; hon. mem. surg. staff Lenox Hill Hosp., N.Y.C., 1984—, Drs. Hosp., N.Y.C.; hon. mem. surg. staff, cons. breast surgery Breast Ctr. Grand Strand Regional Med. Ctr., Myrtle Beach, S.C., 1985—; attending surgeon Westchester County Med. Ctr., 1977-81, emeritus surgeon, 1982—; clin. prof. surgery U. S.C. Sch. Medicine, Breast Surg. Oncology, Columbia, 1985-2000, prof. emeritus, 2000—; hon. dir. breast cancer ctr., cons. in breast surgery Winthrop Univ. Hosp., Mineola, 1971—; cons. in breast surgery VA Hosp., Columbia, S.C., 1985—; breast surg. oncologist Carolina Cancer Ctr., 1997—; cons. in breast surgery St. Claires Hosp., N.Y.C., 1979; attending surg. staff Richland Meml. Hosp., Columbia, 1986-90; clin. prof. surgery, 1960-81, prof. emeritus, 1982—, co-dir. Inst. Breast Diseases, 1978-82, emeritus, 1982—, chief breast svc. N.Y. Med. Coll., 1960-81, emeritus, 1982—; cons. in breast surgery SUNY Div. Rehab., 1965—, Med. and Surg. Specialists Plan N.Y.; mem. Am. Joint Com. on Breast Cancer Staging and End Results; v.p. N.Y. Met. Breast Cancer Group, 1975-76, pres., 1977-79; cons. Med. Advs. Selective Svc. System, N.Y.C. Alumni trustee N.Y. Med. Coll., 1971-76; adv. coun. Fordham Coll. Pharmacy, 1968; bd. dirs. Hall Fame and Mus. Surg. History and Related Scis. Author: Diagnosis and Treatment of Breast Lesions: The Breast, 1970, Management of Breast Lesions, 1978, Breast Cancer: Conservative and Reconstructive Surgery, 1989, Breast Lesions: Diagnosis and Treatment, 1988; co-editor: Breast; hon. editor Internat. Surgery Jour.; mem. editorial bd. jour. Senolgia, 1982—, Breast: An Internat. Jour.; contbr. articles to profl. jours. Mem. Women's Cancer Task Force of S.C. Capt. M.C., AUS, 1944-46, PTO. Decorated knight Grand Cross Equestrian Order Holy Sepulchre Jerusalem, knight Mil., Order of Malta, Knight Noble Co. of the Rose; recipient award of Merit Am. Cancer Soc., 1969, 87, cert. and award for outstanding and devoted services to indigent sick City N.Y., 1965, Dr. George Hohman Meml. medal, 1936, N.Y. Apothecaries medal, 1936, Internat. cert. merit for disting. service to surgery, 1970, award of merit N.Y. Met. Breast Cancer Group, 1976, medal of Ambrogino (Italy), 1977, Service award of Honor N.Y. Med. Coll., 1969, medaille d'Honneur (France), medal of City of Paris, 1979, Silver Palm Jerusalem award 1996, citation for svcs. to indigent sick in S.C.; Henry P. Leis, Jr. Breast and Women's Ctr. named in his honor, Grand Strand Reg. Med. Ctr., Myrtle Beach, S.C., 1999. Fellow ACS (cancer liaison physician Surgeons commn. on Cancer 1988-98, emeritus cancer liaison physician commn. on Cancer 1999—, Cancer Liaison Physician Merit award Grand Strand Regional Med. Ctr., 1988-98), Peruvian Acad. Surgery (hon.), Am. Acad. Compensation Medicine, Am. Soc. Clin. Oncology, Am. Assn. Cancer Rsch., Am. Geriats. Soc., Indsl. Med. Assn., Internat. Coll. Surgeons (1st v.p. 1973-74, pres. 1977-78, v.p., chmn. coun. examiners U.S. sect. 1962-68, pres. 1971, Svc. award of honor 1971), Internat. Paleopathology Assn. (founder), N.Y. Acad. Medicine, N.Y. Coun. Surgeons, Royal Soc. Health (Eng.); mem. AMA, AAAS, AAUP, Am. Cancer Soc. (com. breast cancer), Am. Med. Writers Assn., Am. Soc. Breast Diseases and Breast Surgeons, S. Carolina Women's Cancer Coalition, Breast Surgical Cons. of Carolina Cancer Ctrs. (mem. profl. edn. and risk factors coms.), Am. Profl. Practice Assn., Assn. Am. Med. Colls., Am. Coll. Radiology (com. mammography and breast cancer), Assn. Mil. Surgeons U.S., Am. Soc. Breast Diseases, Am. Soc. Breast Surgeons, Cath. Physicians Guild (pres. N.Y. 1970-78), Gerontol. Soc., Internat. Platform Assn., N.Y. Cancer Soc., N.Y. County Med. Soc., N.Y. Surg. Soc., Pan Am Med. Assn. (v.p. N.Am. sect. on cancer 1967—), Pan Pacific Surg. Assn. (v.p. 1980, Res. Officers Assn. U.S., Soc. Acad. Achievement (mem. editl. bd. 1969—), Nat. Consortium Breast Ctrs. (bd. dirs. 1991-96), Soc. Med. Jurisprudence, Soc. Nuc. Medicine Surg. Soc. N.Y. Med. Coll., WHO, World Med. Assn., Alumni Assn. N.Y. Med. Coll. (gov. 1960—, pres. 1971), Assn. Mil. Surgeons U.S., Catholic War Vets. Assn., VFW, Hollywood Acad. Medicine (hon.), Alpha Omega Alpha, Phi Chi; hon. mem. Argentine Soc. Mammary Pathology, Argentina Cardiac and Thoracic Surg. Soc., Ecuador Med. Assn., Mo. Surg. Soc., Venezuela Surg. Soc., Italian Surg. Soc., S.C. Oncology Soc., So. Med. Assn. Club: Surf, Rotary. Lodge: K.C. (4th deg.).

LEISING, DAVID MICHAEL, industrial engineer; b. Buffalo, Jan. 18, 1950; s. Lawrence Valentine and Patricia (Masterson) L.; m. Mary Kathleen Coyle, July 19, 1969; 1 child, Michelle. AAS, Jamestown (N.Y.) C.C., 1977; BS, Rochester Inst. Tech., 1992. Indsl. engr. Weber Knapp Co., Jamestown, 1977-99; steam engr. Chautauqua Belle. With USN, 1969-73. Mem. ASME, Am. Assn. Indsl. Engrs., Waltonians (bd. dirs. 1993-94). Roman Catholic. Avocations: hunting, fishing, carpentry, camping, sailing. Home: 94 Lister St Jamestown NY 14701-2742

LEISING, GUENTHER, physicist, educator; b. Gleisdort, Styria, Austria, Nov. 22, 1952; s. Walter and Maria (Schlintl) L.; m. Denise Janda, Apr. 5, 1975. Dipl.Ing., Tech. U., Graz, Austria, 1978, Dr.Tech., 1983, Univ. Dozent, 1989. Rschr. Tech. U., Graz, 1983-89, univ. dozent, 1989-96, prof. solid state physics, 1996—; vis. prof. U. Nantes, France, 1989, U. Paderborn, Germany, 1994; cons. tech. U., graz, 1983-97; dir. Adres OEG, Graz, Lumitech OEG, St. Martin, Austria, SDS GmbH, Obdach, Austria. Reg. editor Synthetic Metals, 1997—, Phys. Status Solidi, 1997—; contbr. articles to profl. jours.; patentee in field. Mem. grazer Kunstverein, Graz, 1997, Verein der freunde der Neuen Gallerie, Graz, 1997. Recipient Fritz Kohlrausch award Austrian Phys. Soc., 1988. Mem. Austrian Phys. Soc. (bd. dirs. 1997—), Internat. Soc. Optical Engring., Materials Rsch. Soc. Avocations: tennis, travel, literature, music, art. Home: St Peter Hauptstrasse 33A, A-8042 Graz Styria, Austria Office: Tech U Graz/Solid State Physics, Petersgasse 16, A-8010 Graz Styria, Austria

LEISS, WILLIAM CARL, communication educator; b. Jamaica, N.Y., Dec. 28, 1939; came to Can., 1968, naturalized, 1979; s. William Carl and Ethel Bertha (Walter) L.; m. Marilyn Ann Lawrence, Sept. 23, 1973. B.A. in History, Fairleigh Dickinson U., 1960; M.A. in History, Brandeis U., 1963; Ph.D. in Philosophy, U. Calif.-San Diego, 1969. Asst. prof. polit. sci. U. Regina, Sask., Can., 1968-73; assoc. prof. sociology U. Toronto, Ont., Can., 1975-76; prof. polit. sci., prof. Faculty Environ. Studies, York U., Downsview, Ont., 1973-75, 76-79; prof. communication Simon Fraser U., Burnaby, B.C., Can., 1980—, chmn. dept., 1980-85; cons. to Can. provincial and nat. govt. depts., agys. Author: The Domination of Nature, 1972, The Limits to Satisfaction, 1976; Social Communication in Advertising, 1986, C.B. Macpherson, 1988, Under Technology's Thumb, 1988. Editor: Ecology versus Politics in Canada, 1979. Woodrow Wilson fellow, 1960; Can. Council grantee, 1969, 71, 73, 76, 79, 82, 83, 85, 86-88. Mem. Can. Communication Assn. (pres. 1982-83)., pres., The Royal Society of Canada. Office: Simon Fraser U, Dept Communication,, Burnaby,, BC Canada V5A 1S6*

LEISTNER, MARIA-VERENA HELENE, literary scholar; b. Leipzig, Germany, Dec. 19, 1938; d. Werner Theodor and Helene Lina (Scheffel) Schoch; m. Bernd Siegfried Leistner, Aug. 3, 1965; 1 child, Saskia. B in German and History, Karl Marx U., 1962, PhD, 1972. Tchr. grammar sch., Zschopau, Germany, 1962-65; sr. lectr. Karl Marx U., Leipzig, Germany, 1965-71, 74-93, U. Skopje, Macedonia, 1971-74; free-lance scientist, 1993—. Author: Wilhelm Muellers Schwabenreise 1827, 1994; editor: Wilhelm Mueller: Werke, Tagebuecher, Briefe, 1994; contbr. articles to profl. jours., chpts. to books. Home: Brockhausstrasse 61, 04229 Leipzig Germany

LEISTNER, OTTO ALBRECHT, botanist, scientific editor, researcher; b. Leipzig, Saxony, Germany, Apr. 21, 1931; s. Erich Franz and Gertrud Katharina (Kutzsch) L.; m. Mariette Zeiler, Aug. 25, 1973; children: Elke, Ninette. BSc in Botany and Zoology, U. Stellenbosch, Republic of South Africa, 1951, MSc in Botany, 1954, DSc in Botany, 1964. Bot. survey officer Bot. Rsch. Inst., Pretoria, Republic of South Africa, 1955-63, head flora rsch., 1976-85, head biosystematics/publs., 1985-89, head publs. sect., 1990-96, editl. cons., 1996—; South African liaison officer Royal Bot. Gardens, Kew, Eng., 1964-67; curator Nat. Herbarium, Pretoria, 1967-76; sec., mem. adv. com. for bot. rsch. Min. Agr., Pretoria, 1973-89. Author: The Plant Ecology of the Southern Kalahari, 1967, Southern African Place Names, 1976; editor: (book series) Flora of Southern Africa, 1979-97, (journal series) Bothalia, 1986-97, Flowering Plants of Africa, 1990-97, Memoirs of the Bot. Survey of South Africa, 1986-94, Strelitzia, 1995-97; contbr. over 80 articles to profl. publs. Fellow Linnean Soc. London; mem. Namibia Sci. Soc. (corr.), South African Assn. Botanists (editl. cons. 1987—). Avocations: music, nature. Home: 194 Griselda St, 0184 Pretoria Gauteng, South Africa Office: Nat Bot Inst 2 Cussonia Rd, Pvt Bag 101, 0001 Pretoria Gauteng, South Africa

LEITCH, SHIRLEY ROSE, management consultant, educator, dean; b. Auckland, New Zealand, Aug. 6, 1960; d. Courtney William and Violet Constance (Gwilliam) L. BA, U. Auckland, New Zealand, 1981, MA with honors, 1983, PhD, 1986. Asst. lectr. U. Auckland, 1981-85; exec. asst. Min. Women's Affairs, 1985-87; lectr. Victoria U. Wellington, 1988, Massey U., 1989; assoc. prof., assoc. dean U. Waikato, 1990—. Author: News Talk, 1990; contbr. articles to profl. jours. including Australian Jour.a Comms., Pub. Rels. Rev., Media Internat. Australia. Mem. Australian and New Zealand Comm. Assn. (v.p. 1998, pres. 1999), Pub. Rels. Inst. New Zealand, Internat. Comm. Assn. Avocation: sport horses. Office: U Waikato Mgmt Sch, Pvt Bag 3105, Hamilton New Zealand

LEITE, CLELIO DINIS FERREIRA, physicist; b. Lisbon, Portugal, Apr. 1, 1964; s. Jorge Martins and Maria Teresa (Almeida) L.; m. Maria João Parreira, Sept. 18, 1999; 1 child, Carolina Quina. BS in Mil. Sci., Naval Acad., 1984; MS in Physics, NPGS, 1995. With Portugal Navy, 1987-90, advanced through grades to lt. comdr., 1990—; missile program mgr., 1994—; bd. dirs. Horizontal Directional Drilling, Portugal. Mem. SPIE, APEE, AIAA (Missile Design award 1993), Assn. Old Crows. Roman Catholic. Avocations: astronomy, tennis, cigars, golf, watersports. Office: Marinha-Dir Navios, BNL Alfeite, 2800 Almada Portugal

LEITE, EUGÉNIO OSCAR LUIS, ophthalmology educator, researcher; b. Vila Pery, Mocambique, Portugal, Jan. 11, 1955; s. Sebastião and Maria Adelaide Reis (Batista) L.; m. Conceicao Ferreira, Dec. 19, 1977; children: Filipe Miguel Ferreira, Ruben Dinis Ferreira. Medicine, Coimbra (Portugal) U., 1978, Ophthalmology, 1988, PhD in Ophthalmology, 1999. Med. diplomate. Rsch. asst. Ophtalmic Rsch. Ctr. U. Coimbra, 1983, invited asst. ophthalmology, 1990; clin. asst. dept. ophthalmology U. Hosp. Coimbra, 1990, cons. dept. ophthalmology, 1994. Mem. Internat. Soc. Ocular Fluorophotometry (gen. sec. Europe, Africa 1988-94, bd. dirs. 1994), Cirurgia Implanto Refractiva Portugal (gen. sec. 1996-98, Refractive CIRP-Iolab award 1990, 94), Nat. Coun. Tech. Exercise Medicine (cons. 1997), European Soc. Cataract and Refractive Surgeons, European Soc. Engring and Medicine, Internat. Intra-Ocular Implant Club, European Soc. Cataract Refractive Surgery (European De Jong award 1994), Lions Club (v.p. Coimbra 1997-98, pres. 1998-99), Rowing Sect. Coimbra U. (dir. 1996—). Roman Catholic. Avocations: golf, tennis, sailing. Home: Rua Miguel Torga, Urb Qta Alpões Lt 3, 2o Dto Coimbra 3030-765, Portugal Office: Edificio Avenida, Av Sá da Bandeira 33-35, Piso 5 Sala 519-520 Coimbra 3000, Portugal

LEITE, ISABEL CRISTINA, dentist; b. Juiz de Fora, Brazil, July 23, 1970; d. Abel da Silva Leite and Maria Alice Gonçalves. Grad., Escola Estadual Anexa Edn., Juiz de Fora, 1985, Inst. Edn., Juiz de Fora, 1988; degree in odontology, Faculty Odontology, Juiz de Fora, 1993; MSc, FIOCRUZ, Rio de Janeiro, 1997; postgrad., FIOCRUZ, 2000—. Asst. prof. Faculty Odontology, 1996-2000, Faculty Fonoaudiology, 2000—; pvt. practice pedodontics Juiz de Fora, 1998—; corr. médico expert Soc. Iberoamericana de Info. Cientifica. Home: Ave Barão do Rio Branco, 1519/201 Juiz de Fora, Minas Gerais 36035000, Brazil

LEITE, JOÃO PEREIRA, neurologist, scientist; b. Ribeirão Preto, Brazil, Feb. 4, 1961; s. José Venâncio and Odila (Pereira) L.; m. Claudia Beatriz Pena, Nov. 13, 1992; children: Luiz Felipe, João Henrique. MD, U. Sao Paulo, 1984. Prof. U. Sao Paulo Sch. Medicine, 1998—. Mem. Soc. Neurosci., Am. Epilepsy Soc., Brazilian Neurophysiology Soc., Brazilian League Epilepsy. Office: U Sao Paulo Dept Neurology, Campus Universitario, Ribeirao Preto SP 14049900, Brazil

LEITE, JOÃO VERDI CARVALHO, aerospace executive; b. Alfenas, Brazil, June 25, 1935; s. João Soares and Maria Conceição (Carvalho) L.; m. Sonia Regina Brasil, July 17, 1965; 1 child, João Brasil Carvalho. Degree in aero. engring., Inst. Tech. Aero., São José Dos Campos, Brazil, 1958; DSc in Aerospace Rsch., Internat. U. Found., 1989. Registered aero. engr. Pres. dir. Avibras Aerospacial S/A, São José Dos Campos, 1974—; chmn., CEO Tectran S/A São José Dos Campos, 1982—, Powertronics S/A, São José Dos Campos, 1983—, Avibras Found. for Edn. and Work, São José Dos Campos, 1983—; chmn., dir. Avibras Internat. Ltd., Jersey, Channel Islands, 1989—; chmn., dir. Avibras Divisao Aerea e Naval, Jacarei, SP, 1995; adviser CEBEU (Brazil-US Enterprise Coun.), CEBRU (Brazil-UK Enterprise Coun.). Patentee in field. Mem. AIAA (sr.), Am. Soc. for Metals, Exptl. Aircraft Assn., Seaplane Pilots Assn., Assn. of U.S. Army, N.Y. Acad. Scis., Rotary Club, Soc. Automotive Engrs. Brasil. Avocations: experimental aircraft and helicopter pilot, diving, parachuting. Office: Avibras Aerospacial S/A, Rod Dos Tamoios Km 14 #278, 12300-000 Jacareí Brazil

LEITE, SERGIO DE QUEIROZ BOGADO, nuclear engineer; b. Rio de Janeiro, Brazil, July 26, 1951; s. Onofre and Martha (de Queiroz) L.; m. Helinea Almeida, July 7, 1977; children: Daniel, Felipe. BSc, Catholic U., 1974; MSc, Army Inst. Engring., Rio de Janeiro, 1977; PhD, N.C. State U., 1981. Lectr. Catholic U., Rio de Janeiro, 1975-76, N.C. State U., Raleigh, 1980-81; rschr. Aerospace Tech. Ctr., Sao Jose dos Campos, Brazil, 1981-89; project mgr. Jaakko Poyry Engring., Sao Paulo, Brazil, 1989-90, Emgepron, Sao Paulo, 1990-95; sr. rschr. Nat. Nuclear Energy Commn., Rio de Janeiro, 1995—, reactor coord., 1998-99. Home: Rua Gal Pereira da Silva, 87/2202, 24220030 Niterói RJ, Brazil Office: Nat Nuclear Energy Commn, Rua Gal Severiano 90, 22294900 Rio de Janeiro RJ, Brazil

LEITE, SERGIO ROBERTO DE ANDRADE, chemistry educator, researcher; b. Salvador, Bahia, Brazil, May 2, 1948; s. Floriano de Oliveira and Semiramis (de Andrade) L.; m. Clarice Queico Fujimura, Jan. 9, 1982; children: Mônica Fujimura, Daniel Fujimura. Med. degree, U. Sao Paulo, Brazil, 1971, BSc in Chemistry, 1975, PhD in Chem. Physics, 1983; MS in Food Sci., U. Campinas, Brazil, 1979. Prof. Chemistry Inst., U. Estadual Paulista, Araraquara, Brazil, 1981—, dir. chemistry course, 1989-91, dir. campus acad. chamber, 1990-91, head gen. and inorganic chemistry dept., 1998-2000; adviser Regional Chemistry Coun., Sao Paulo, 1995-98. Contbr. articles to sci. jours., including Chem. Physics Letters, Can. Jour. Chemistry, Brazilian Jour. Med. Biol. Rsch., Jour. Brazilian Chem. Soc., Spectrochimica Acta. Fellow Brazilian Assn. for Devel. Sci., Brazilian Chem. Soc.; mem. Araraquara Ecol. Soc. (pres. 1983-87), N.Y. Acad. Scis. Roman Catholic. Avocations: astronomy, collection minerals, gardening. Home: PO Box 586, Av Marcelo Scaraficci, 14801970 Araraquara SP, Brazil Office: UNESP Inst Chemistry, PO Box 355, 14801970 Araraquara SP, Brazil

LEITES, BARBARA L. (ARA LEITES), artist, educator; b. Hamilton, Ohio, June 3, 1942; d. Wilbur Frank and Alice Marie (Butts) Mayer; m. William Michael Whitley, Oct. 29, 1972 (div. Nov. 1977); 1 child, Rachel; m. Andre Leo Leites, Dec. 15, 1981 (div. Mar. 2000); children: David, Bevin; 1 stepchild, Daniella. BFA, Miami U., Oxford, Ohio, 1964, MFA, 1967. Tchr. Madison Elem. Sch., Hamilton, 1964-65; tchr. art and humanities Key West (Fla.) H.S., 1967-70, tchr. adult edn. in art, 1968-70; isntr. Fla. Keys Jr. Coll., Key West, 1969-70; co-dir. Kleinert Gallery, Woodstock, N.Y., 1977-80; self employed artist under the name Ara Leites, 1981—; bd. dirs. Woodstock Guild of Craftsmen, 1978-79; instr. drawing and painting, divsn. head visual arts Georgiana Bruce Kirby Preparatory Sch., Santa Cruz, Calif., 1998—. Exhibited at Gallery El Ciruello, Tepoztlan, Mex., Club 209 Gallery, Cuernavaca, Mex., Black Sheep Art Gallery, Eng., Westminster Gallery, London, Cin. Art Mus., Dayton Art Inst., Springfield (Mo.) Art Mus., Miami U.; U.S. nat. exhbns. of over 150 shows and 60 awards including Rocky Mountain Nat., Watercolor USA, Adirondacks Nat., Nat. Watercolor Soc., Am. Watercolor Assn., Audubon Artists, Am. Watercolor Soc., Phila. Watercolor Club, Allied Artists, N.Y.C., Calif. Nat. Watercolor Soc.; subject of articles in publs. Mem. AAUW, Internat. Soc. Exptl. Artists (signature), Am. Artists Profl. League (signature), Nat. Watercolor Soc. (signature), Nat. Soc. Painters in Casein and Acrylic (signature), Nat. Acrylic Painters Assn. (signature), Watercolor USA Honor Soc. (signature), Ky. Watercolor Soc. (signature), Tex. Watercolor Soc. (signature), Ga. Watercolor Soc. (signature), Miss. Watercolor Soc. (signature), Phila. Watercolor Club Soc. (signature), Audobon Artists (signature), Watercolor Club Soc., Delta Delta Delta Alumnae Assn. Republican. Avocations: gardening, carpentry, skiing, snowboarding, surfing. Home: 168 Oxford Way Santa Cruz CA 95060-6447

LEITES, IOSIF L., chemist, researcher, consultant; b. Moscow, Russia, Nov. 19, 1933; s. Leizer V. and Vera A. (Selitskaya) L.; m. Ljudmila K. Kazantseva, Nov. 11, 1960; 1 child. Degree in Engr. Chem. Technology, MHTI, Moscow, 1956; PhD, NIFHI, Moscow, 1963; prof., GJAP, Moscow, 1980. Sci. collaborator GIAP, Moscow, 1956-64, elder sci. collaborator, 1964-65, chief of lab., 1965-96, cons., 1996—. Author, editor: Technological Gases Purificaiton, 1969, 2d edit., 1977, Theory and Practice of Energy Saving Chemical Technology, 1988; author articles. E-mail: leites@chat.ru. Home: Donetskaya St 12-84, 109652 Moscow Russia

LEITMAN, HAROLD N., telecommunications industry executive; b. Everett, Mass., Feb. 22, 1918; s. Max and Lee (Mogul) L.; m. Shirley Bloom, Dec. 23, 1945 (dec. Sept. 25, 1987); children: Valerie Russell, Daniel Leitman; m. Joyce Zeeve, April 27, 1990. Student, U. Fla., 1935-37. Pres. TT Systems Corp., N.Y.C., 1975—, chmn., 1980—; pres. subs. of Goodyear Tire, Akron, Ohio, 1950-52, subs. of B.F. Goodrich, Akron, 1952-54. With USAF, 1941-45. Jewish. Home: 58 Talcott Rd Rye Brook NY 10573-1421 Office: TT Stystems Corp 7 Daeu Plaza Yonkers NY 10701

LEITNER, GREGORY MARC, lawyer; b. Chattanooga, Apr. 19, 1957; s. Paul Revers and Suzanne Joy Leitner; m. Sheryl Leitner; children: Gregory Marc, Ashley Meredith. BA cum laude, Memphis State U., 1978; JD, U. Tenn., Knoxville, 1980. Bar: Tenn. 1981, U.S. Dist. Ct. (ea. dist.) 1981, U.S. Ct. Appeals (6th cir.) 1983, U.S. Ct. Appeals (11th cir.) 1988. Ptnr. Leitner, Warner, Moffitt, Williams, Dooley, Carpenter & Napolitan, Chattanooga, 1986—. Mem. ABA, Tenn. Bar Assn., Pi Sigma Alpha, Phi Delta Phi. Republican. Methodist. Avocations: politics, international politics, history. Home: 6259 Forest Trl Signal Mountain TN 37377-2807

LEITSCH, WALTER, historian, educator; b. Vienna, Austria, Mar. 26, 1926; s. Josef and Antonie (Pedajas) L.; m. Ludmilla Kunčič, Dec. 24, 1940; children: Alexander, Marie Thérèse, Markus Anton. PhD, U. Vienna, 1954; diploma, Inst. for Research of Austrian History, Vienna, 1956. Asst. Inst. Ea. European History, Vienna, 1955-56, asst. prof., 1956-64; ofcl. Ministry of Edn., Vienna, 1964-65; chmn. Inst. Ea. European History, 1965-96; full prof. U. Vienna, 1965-96. Author: Moskau und die Politik des Kaiserhofes, 1960; co-author: Das Institut für osteuropäische Geschichte, 1983; editor monograph series Wiener Archiv für Geschichte des Slawentums und Osteuropas, 1966—. Recipient hon. gold medal of municipality of Vienna, 1986. Mem. Austrian Acad. Scis. Home: Formanekgasse 10, A-1190 Vienna Austria Office: Inst osteuropaische Gesch, U AAKH Spitalgasse 2-4/H 3, A-1090 Vienna Austria

LEITZMANN, CLAUS, retired nutritionist, writer; b. Dahlenburg, Germany, Feb. 6, 1933; s. Wilhelm and Thyra (Garbers) L.; m. Ilse Wachenhusen; children: Peter, Michael, Rita, Heidi. BSc, Capital U., 1962; MSc, U. Minn., 1964, PhD, 1967. Rsch. asst. molecular biology inst. UCLA, 1967-69; asst. prof. biochemistry Mahidol U., Bangkok, Thailand, 1969-71; vis. prof. Malnutrition Rsch. Ctr., Chiang Mai, Thailand, 1971-74; from rsch. assoc. to head dept. Inst. Nutrition U. Giessen, Germany, 1974-95; ret., 1995. Author: Human Nutrition, 1988, Wholesome Nutrition, 1994, Dictionary of Nutrition, 1996, Vegetarian Diet, 1996, Phytochemicals, 1999, Nutrition in Prevention and Therapy, 2000. Mem. German Soc. Nutrition. Avocations: travel, writing, reading, gardening, jogging. Home: Doerrenbergweg 24, 35321 Laubach Germany Office: U Giessen, Wilhelmstrasse 20, 35392 Giessen Germany

LEJEUNE, MICHEL, university administrator, lawyer; b. Tienen, Belgium, May 24, 1938; s. Alexander and Marie-José (Mosmans) L. PhB, Louvain U., Belgium, 1958, LLD, 1967. Lectr. Makerere U., Uganda, 1976-82, Dundee U., Scotland, 1983-85; prof. U.C.L. U., Belgium, 1985-90; pres. ct. appeals Mechelen Ct., Belgium, 1988-92; vice-chancellor Uganda Martyrs U., Uganda, 1992—; guest prof. Fribourg (Switzerland) U., 1986-91. Translator, editor: English Penitential Literature, 1991; contbr. articles to profl. jours. Mem. Am. Soc. Law and Medicine, Canon Law Soc. Am., N.Y. Acad. Scis. Roman Catholic. Avocations: music, sports, woodworking. Fax: 00-256-481-21898. E-mail: vcumu@afsat.com. Home and Office: Uganda Martyrs U, PO Box 5498, Kampala Uganda

LEJOSNE, ROGER, retired English language educator; b. Paris, July 2, 1933; s. Albert and Cecile (Bennet) L.; m. Jacqueline Secondi, July 26, 1962; 1 child, Pierre. BA, Ecole Normale Superieure, Saint-Cloud, France, 1955; MA, Ecole Normale Superieure, Saint Cloud, France, 1956, agregation d'anglais, 1958; LittD, Sorbonne, Paris, 1979. Asst. lectr. U. Lille, France, 1964-71; reader U. Paris, Sorbonne, 1971-83; prof. U. Amiens, France, 1983-94, emeritus prof., 1994—. Author: La Raison Dans L'Oeuvre De John Milton, 1981; editor: Le Quatrieme Pouvoir en Grande Bretagne, 1990, Educations Anglo Saxonnes, 1992, 95, 97, Mariages a la mode Anglo Saxonne, 1995. Ensign French Navy, 1958-60. Recipient Ordre des Palmes Acad. French Min. Edn., 1986, Ordre des Palmes Acad. Officer French Min. Edn. 1993. Mem. Soc. Anglicistes de l'Enseignement Superieur. Home: 227 rue de strasbourg, 77350 Le Mee Sur Seine France

LEKE BETECHUOH, CASIMIR, administrator, policy expert; b. Essohattah-Fontem, Cameroon, 1955; s. Boniface and Josepher (Alekenkeng) B.; m. Mchangeh Agatha Funkeng; children: Nchapbanu Gwendoline, Fonkeng Clarence. Grad., U. Taounde, Cameroon, 1979, PTT, Taounde, 1980; diploma, KDD, Tokyo, 1993. Chief sect. DTT, Douala, Cameroon, 1980-84; chief telecom. agy. PTO, Buea, Cameroon, 1984-85; chief telecom. agy. PTO, Yaounde, Cameroon, 1986-88, chief svc. accts., 1988-89, sub-dir. telecom exploration, 1989-96; mgr. promotion RASCOM, Cameroon, 1996—. Contbr. articles to profl. jours. Roman Catholic. Avocations: reading, music, football, dancing, cooking. Home: OH Bp 2091, Abidjan 04, Cote d'Ivoire Office: RASCOM, 010 Bp 3628, Abidjan 01, Cote d'Ivoire

LEKNER, JOHN, physicist, educator, researcher; b. Prague, Czech republic, May 13, 1938; arrived in N.Z., 1948; s. Joseph and Anne (Nejedla) L.; m. Marjorie Anne Austin, Oct. 12, 1966; children: Poppy Louise, Dayton Joseph. BSc, U. Auckland, N.Z., 1960, MSc, 1962; PhD, U. Chgo., 1967; MA (hon.), U. Cambridge, Eng., 1968. Postdoctoral fellow U. Libre de Brussels, 1966-67; dir. studies in physics Emmanuel Coll., Cambridge, Eng., 1968-73; demonstrator U. Cambridge, 1968-73; sr. lectr., then reader Victoria

U. of Wellington, N.Z., 1973-91, chmn. dept. physics, 1993-95, prof. theoretical physics, 1991—; vis. prof. U. Minn., Mpls., 1990, 92, U. Wash., Seattle, 1996; mem. bd. dirs. Carter Obs., Wellington, 1997—. Mem. editl. com. Devel. in Electromagnetic Theory and Applications, 1987—; author: Theory of Reflection, 1987; contbr. articles to profl. jours. Recipient Sidey medal Royal Soc. N.Z., 1997, fellow, 1991; Emmanuel Coll. fellow, 1968-73. Fellow Cambridge Philos. Soc. Avocations: mountain climbing, gliding. Office: Victoria U of Wellington, PO Box 600, Wellington 6001, New Zealand

LEKOTA, MOSINOA GERARD PATRICK, federal official, writer; b. Senekal, Aug. 13, 1948; married. Student, U. of the North. Permanent organizer South African Student's Orgn., 1974-75; imprisoned, 1974-82; publicity sec. United Dem. Front, 1983; imprisoned, 1988; ANC convenor South Natal, 1990; elected ANC Nat. Exec. Com. and Nat. Working Com., 1991, ANC Chief of Intelligence, 1991; sec. ANC Electoral Commn., 1992; premier Free State Provincial Govt., 1994-96; chairperson Nat. Coun. of Provinces, 1997—, min. of def., 1999—. Mem. African Nat. Congress. Office: Ministry of Def, Pvt Bag X427, Pretoria 0001, South Africa*

LELE, SMITA SATISH, chemical engineer, educator; b. Sankeshwara, Karnataka, India, Jan. 15, 1955; d. Gajanan Bajirao and Sunita Gajanan (Joshi) Godbole; m. Satish Vithal Lele, May 29, 1977; 1 child, Nilesh. B-ChemE, U. Dept. Chem. Tech., Mumbai, India, 1977-79, MChemE, 1981, PhD in Tech., 1990. Rsch. assoc. Hindustan Lever Ltd., India, 1977-79; project coord. Demech, India, 1982-84; assoc. lectr. U. Dept. Chem. Tech., Mumbai, 1980-82, lectr., 1986-90, reader in biochem. engring., 1991—; cons. Alfa Laval (I), India, 1995-96; vis. rsch. fellow U. Pitts., 1998. Inventor in field; contbr. articles to profl. jours. Mem. Indian Women Scientist' Assn. (joint sec. 1995-97), Third World Orgn. for Women in Sci., Italy, Assn. Food Scientists and Technologists India (convenor student activities), Indian Inst. Chem. Engrs. Hindu. Avocations: career counseling, activites related to science and technology for high school students, study of Hindu philosophy. E-mail: sslele@fft.udct.ernet.in. Home: J-22 Sector 7 Vashi Navi, Mumbai 400703, India

LELEK, ANTONIN, fishery scientist; b. Brno, Czech Republic, Oct. 11, 1933; s. Antonin Lelek and Anna (Drahoradova) Lelkova; m. Marta Lokvencova, July 4, 1959; children: Martina, Karolina. Diploma, U. Agr., Brno, 1957; PhD, Acad. Sci./Charles U., Prague, 1961. Sr. rschr. Acad. Sci., Czech Republic, 1957-68; sr. lectr. U. Ghana, 1965-67; fishery biologist FAO, Rome, 1968-71; sr. rschr. Biol. Anstalt, Helgoland, Germany, 1971-73, Nat. Mus. and Rsch. Inst., Senckenberg, Germany, 1974—; prof. U. Gottingen, Germany, 1983—; cons. WHO, GENF, 1991-93; vis. prof. U. Guelph, Can., 1989, various banks and firms. Author: (books) Threatened Fishes of Europe, 1987, The Rhine in the Past and Future, 1992; editl. bd.: Jour. Fish Biology, 1969-87, Environmental Biol. of Fish, 1978—, Fish Ecology, 1989—. Lt. Artillery, Brno, 1952-56. Avocations: skiing, hunting, tennis. Office: Forschungsinstitut Senckenb, Senckenberganlage 25, D-60325 Frankfurt Germany

LELEUX, JOHN ALLEN, retired protective services official; b. Kaplan, La., Sept. 28, 1937; s. Lionel Isadore and Beulah (Bonvillian) L.; m. Mary Ann Higginsbotham, Nov. 12, 1960; children: Brenda Ann Arceneaux, Julie Marie Comeaux. Student, La. State U., Eunice, La. State U., Baton Rouge. Fire driver Crowley (La.) Fire Dept., 1957-67, fire capt., 1967-75, .ire chief, 1975-99; ret. Mem. plumbing and elec. bd. City of Crowley, 1975—, safetyman, 1975-99. Mem. Army N.G., 1959. Mem. Crowley Firemen's Assn. (sec.-treas. 1999—), La. Fire Chiefs Assn. (pres. 1987-88), Internat. Assn. Fire Chiefs (S.W. divsn. pres. 1990-91), La. State Firemen's Assn. (pres. 1994-95), Acadia Parish Fire Protection Assn. (1st acting sec. 1989), Am. Legion, Woodmen of the World. Democrat. Roman Catholic. Avocations: camping, guitar, fishing. Home: 1213 William Ave Crowley LA 70526-3045

LELIÈVRE-BERNA, EDDY, physicist, researcher; b. Amiens, Somme, France; s. Jean and Marie-Odile Lelièvre-Berna; m. Brigitte Giraud, Aug. 27, 1994; children: Mileva, Wilhem. Diploma in physics and engring., Inst. Nat. Poly. Grenoble, France, 1990; postgrad., Higher European Rsch. Course for Users of Large Exptl. Syss., Grenoble, 1993; M in Fundamental Physics, U. Joseph Fourier, Grenoble, 1990, PhD in Physics, 1994. Cert. in polarized neutron scattering and magnetism. Engr. Commissariat a l'Energie Atomique Bruyères le Châtel, 1990-91; physicist Inst. Laue Langevin, Grenoble, 1994—; sec. Workshop on Polarized Neutrons for Condensed Matter Investigations, Grenoble, 1998; ILL specialist Inst. Laue Langevin, Grenoble, 1998-2000. Contbr. articles to profl. jours. and procs. Pres. Coop. de l'Inst. Nat. Poly. Grenoble, 1989. Mem. French Soc. Neutron Users. Fax: 33 476207648. E-mail: lelievre@ill.fr. Office: Inst Laue Langevin, 6 rue Jules Horowitz, 38042 Grenoble France

LELKES, MIKLOS, epidemiologist, health educator; b. Budapest, Hungary, June 10, 1938; s. Miklos and Irma (Gonczlik) L.; m. Gizella Hohmann, Apr. 30, 1966; children: Gizella Virág, Miklos Zsolt. MD, Semmelweis U., Budapest, 1962; M in Hygiene and Infectious Disease Epidemiology, Inst. Postgrad. Med. Edn., Budapest, 1966, M Health Edn., 1985; PhD, Tudomanyos Minosito Bizottsag, Budapest, 1983. Prof.'s asst. Semmelweis U., 1962-72, adj., 1973-81, head physician, 1981-86, head dept. Inst. Hygiene and Epidemiology, hon. asst. prof., 1987—. Author: (with others) Practice of Hygiene and Epidemiology of Infectious Diseases, 1972, 2nd edit., 1974, 3rd edit., 1976, 4th edit., 1981; author, editor: Medical Work and Health Education, 1974; author: Some Infectious Diseases and Their Prevention, 1975, Egészségnevelés, 1980, Vilmon Gyula, 1980. Recipient Bronze medal Hungarian Red Cross, 1971, Silver medal, 1982, Gold medal, 1987. Avocations: writing, cooking. Home: II Törökvész ut 95, B ep IX em 53, H-1025 Budapest Hungary Office: Semmelweis U, Nagyvarad ter 4 Pf 370, H-1445 Budapest Hungary

LELL, EBERHARD, retired inorganic chemist; b. Linz, Austria, Oct. 3, 1927; came to U.S., 1957; s. Wilhelm and Margarete (Sigel) L.; m. Edith Döller, May 26, 1962; children: Christoph, Bertrand, Claudia. Dipl.Ing., T.U., Graz, Austria, 1952; PhD, T.U., Stuttgart, Germany, 1956. Asst. prof. T.U., Stuttgart, 1956-57; sr. scientist Bausch & Lomb Inc., Rochester, N.Y., 1957-69, Itek Corp., Lexington, Mass., 1969-74; project mgr. Voest-Alpine, Linz, 1975-91, ret., 1991. Contbr. articles to Progress in Ceramic Sci., Can. Jour. Physics, Physics and Chemistry of Glasses, Jour. Am. Ceramic Soc., Applied Physics, Am. Ceramic Soc. Bull. Mem. Gesellschaft Österreichischer Chemiker, Export Club Linz, Austrian Sr. Expert Pool. Home: Knabenseminarstrasse 47, Linz A-4040, Austria

LELONG, PIERRE, auditor; b. Paris, May 22, 1931; s. Marcel and Jeanne (Maistrasse) L.; m. Catherine DeMargne; children: Claude Odier, Olivier, Martin, Marc, Antoine. Licencié en droit, U. Paris, 1952; Diplomá, Inst. Politiques, 1952; Ancien éleve de l'Ecole Nat. d'Adminstrn., Paris, 1957. Adminstr. Ministry of Fin. and Economic Affairs, France, 1958-62; advisor economic affairs Prime Minister Pompidou, France, 1962-67; gen. mgr. Agrl. Intervention Bd., France, 1967-68; mem. French Nat. Assembly, France, 1968-74; sec. of state Posts and Telecommunications, France, 1974-75; mem. Ct. of Auditors, Paris, 1975-77; mem. EEC Ct. of Auditors, Luxembourg, 1977-81, 84-90, pres., 1981-84; conseiller-maitre French Ct. of Auditors, Paris, 1990-94, pres. de chambre, 1994-2000; pres. Adv. Com. on Secret Def. Matters, Paris, 1999; pres. adv. com. on armament purchases Consultative Commn. Nat. Def. Secret, Paris, 2000—. Decorated grand croix Ordre de la Couronne de Chene (Luxembourg), officer Legion of Honor (France).. Home: 130 Rue de Rennes, 75006 Paris France Office: Commn Consultative Sec Def Nat, 35 rue St Dominque, 75007 Paris France

LELORD, GILBERT FRANCOIS, physiologist and psychiatrist; b. St. Etienne de Montluc, France, Jan. 24, 1927; s. Auguste Marie and Henriette Anne (Metayer) L.; m. Angele Lea Maitre (dec. Dec. 1992); children: Christophe, Francois. Agregation physiology, Univ. Paris, 1970; PhD, Faculty of Scis., Paris, 1967; MD, Faculty of Medicine, Paris, 1956. Chief resident Hosp. La Salpetriere, Paris, 1956-58; researcher Nat. Ctr. Scientific Rsch., Paris, 1958-69; chief dept. psychiatry Hosp. Bretonneau, Tours, France, 1964-70; physiology prof. Univ. Francois Rabelais, Tours, France, 1970-79; chmn. dept. neurophysiology Hosp. Univ. Tours, 1979-87; chief of team #3 Unit Inserm 316, Tours, 1987-93; com. mem. Inserm Paris, 1976-80, 87-91; mem. European group Child Psychiatry Rsch., WHO, 1985-91; mem. scientific com. Autism-Europe, Luxembourg, 1987-95, mem. scientific com. Nat. General Delegation Sci. Rsch., 1977; mem. editorial bd. Jour. Autism and Development Disorders, 1987-96. Author articles to on clin. psychiatry, cerebral imagery, genetics, therapeutics in childhood autism. Mem. com. mental diseases Min. of Health, Paris, 1978, com. mem. handicap Min. of Rsch., Paris, 1988. Lt. French Air Force, 1952-53. Recipient Baillarger award Acad. of Medicine, Paris, 1974, Chevalier of the Legion of Honour Min. of Edn. & Sci., Paris, 1993. Mem. Lions Club, N.Y. Acad. Scis., Internat. Soc. Biological Psychiatry. Roman Catholic. Avocation: equitatory hunting. Home: 2 Ferdinand Dubreuil Str, 37000 Tours France Office: Hosp Bretonneau, 2 Bd Tonnele, 37044 Tours France

LE LOUARN, CLAUDE, plastic surgeon; b. Paris, Sept. 6, 1947; s. Joseph Yvon and Jeanine Leone (Calin) Le L.; m. Sylvie Daniele Marie Motte Flipo, June 1986; children: Raphaële, Floriane. Degree in biology and sport medicine, U. Limoges, France, 1976; postgrad., U. Paris VI, 1978, cert. in microsurgery, 1979. Qualified in gen. surgery Ordre des Medecins, 1980, competency in plastic reconstructive and aestetic surgery, 1982; diplomate French Bd. Plastic and Reconstructive Surgery, 1981. Resident in plastic surgery St. Louis Hosp., Paris, 1977, Foch Hosp., Paris, 1978; pvt. asst. in plastic surgery Office of Dr. Paul Tessier, Paris, 1979; asst. in plastic surgery St. Antoine Hosp., Paris, 1980-85; pvt. practice aesthetic plastic surgery Paris, 1982—; plastic surgeon Found. Adolphe de Rothschild, Paris, 1981—. Developed various surg. treatments and techniques in field of plastic surgery. Mem. Internat. Soc. Aesthetic and Plastic Surgery, Soc. Française de Chirurgie Plastique Reconstructive et Esthetique. SOFCEP (bd. dirs. 1994—). Roman Catholic. Avocations: fitness, skiing, archery, opera, theater. Home and Office: 59 Rue Spontini, 75116 Paris France

LEM, RICHARD DOUGLAS, painter; b. Nov. 24, 1933; s. Walter Wing and Betty (Wong) L.; m. Patricia Ann Soohoo, May 10, 1958; 1 child, Stephen Vincent. BA, UCLA, 1958. One-person shows include Gallery 818, L.A., 1965; exhibited in group shows Lynn Kottler Galleries, N.Y.C., 1973, Palos Verdes Art Gallery, 1968, Galerie Mouffe, Paris, 1976, Le Salon des Nations, Paris, 1984, numerous others; represented in permanent collections; writer, illustrator: Mile's Journey, 1983, 2d edit., 1995, I'm Dying, but I'm Not Sick. The Final Journey, 1999; cover illustrator: The Hermit, 1990, The Hermit's Journey, 1993. with AUS, 1958-60. Address: 1861 Webster Ave Los Angeles CA 90026-1229

LEMAIRE, JEAN-PHILIPPE ETIENNE, spine surgeon; b. Epernay, France, June 19, 1950; s. Robert Fernand Marcel and Annie Renee (Floc) L.; m. Valerie Marie Odile Barbarin, Oct. 28, 1995; children from previous marriage: Sebastien, Julie. MD, Med. U., Dijon, France, 1979, postgrad., 1981, 83. Fellow Med. U., Dijon, 1981-85, resident in surgery and orthopedic surgery, 1975-80; resident Med. U., Marseille, France, 1979; vis. resident Children's Hosp., Boston, 1980, Med. U., Toronto, 1980; spine surgery cons. Univ. Hosp., Dijon, 1983-85; spine surgeon pvt. hosp., Dijon, 1986—; guest lectr. Coll. de France, Paris, 1992. Patentee in field. Mem. French Scoliosis Soc. (pres. 1996-99), French Soc. Orthopedica nd Traumatologic Surgery, European Soc. Spine, Internat. Soc. Rsch. and Study of Spine (sci. com. 1998), N.Y. Acad. Scis. Avocation: classical music. E-mail: jplemaire@ipac.fr. Office: Point Medical, Rond Point de la Nation, Dijon 21000, France

LEMAIRE, MARC, educator, researcher; b. Paris, Oct. 18, 1949; s. Jacques and Monique (Mazoyer) L.; m. Elda Kreutzer, Apr. 5, 1990; children: Jules, Jacques, Jean. Student chem. engring., CNAM, Paris, 1979; DEA, U. Paris VI, 1980, PhD in Chimie Organique, 1982. Postdoctoral fellow U. Gronigen, The Netherlands, 1983; chemist Roussel-UCLAF, Romainville, France, 1972-79; asst. prof. CNAM, France, 1979-89; prof. 2d class Lyon U., 1989-92, prof. 1st class, 1992—; dir. Laboratoire de Catalyse et Synthese Organique UCBL/CNRS, Lyon, 1999—; dir. catalyse DEA UCBL, Lyon, 1992-99, dir. chimie organique, 1991—; mem. nat. com. CNRS Sect. 16, Paris, 1994-99. Contbr. articles to profl. publs.; inventor in field. Recipient Medaille Berthelot French Acad., 1999, Prix Paul Langevin, 1999, Prix de Chimie Organique due CNAM, 1977. Fellow Societe Francaise Chimie (organic divsn.), ACS. Office: 43 Boulevard du 11, Novembre 1918, 69622 Vilembanne France

LEMAIRE, MAURICE, engineering educator; b. Auneau, France, May 4, 1946; s. Paul and Marie-Jo (Perrotin) L.; m. Monique Hilaire, Aug. 17, 1968; children: Isabelle, François, Cécile, Pierre. Degree in civil engring, Nat. Inst. Applied Sci., Lyon, France, 1968; D Engring., U. Lyon I, 1971, DS, 1975. Cert. civil and mech. engr., France. Assoc. prof. Nat. Inst. Applied Sci., Lyon, 1969-75; prof. U. Clermont, Clermont Ferrand, France, 1975-91, French Inst. Advanced Mechanics, Clermont Ferrand, 1991—; dir. Civil Engring. Lab., Clermont Ferrand, 1975-91, Mech. Engring. Lab., 1991—; expert Ministry of Edn. and Rsch., Paris, 1980—; prof. Ecole Nationale des Travaux Publics de l'Etat, Lyon, 1976-89. Editor: Applications of Statistics and Probability, 1995; contbr. articles to sci. jours. Mem. Internat. Conf. on Applications of Stats. and Probability, Assn. Profs. in Mechanics, Assn. Profs. in Civil Engring. Avocations: biking, photography. Office: Inst Français Mech Adv, IFMA BP 265, 63 175 Aubière Puy de Dôme, France

LE MAISTRE, CHARLES AUBREY, internist, epidemiologist, educator; b. Lockhart, Ala., Feb. 10, 1924; s. John Wesley and Edith (McLeod) LeM.; m. Joyce Trapp, June 3, 1952; children: Charles Frederick, William Sidney, Joyce Anne, Helen Jean. BA, U. Ala., 1943, LLD (hon.), 1971; MD, Cornell U., 1947; LLD (hon.), Austin Coll., 1970; DSc (hon.), U. Dallas, 1978, Southwestern U., 1981; D honoris causa, U. Guadalajara (Mex.), 1989. Intern, then resident medicine N.Y. Hosp., 1947-49; rsch. fellow infectious diseases Cornell U. Med. Coll., 1949-51, mem. faculty, 1951-54, asst. prof. medicine, 1953-54; mem. faculty Emory U. Sch. Medicine, 1954-59, prof. preventive medicine, chmn. dept., 1957-59; prof. medicine U. Tex. Southwestern Med. Sch., 1959-78, assoc. dean, 1965-66; vice chancellor health affairs U. Tex. System, Austin, 1966-68; exec. vice chancellor U. Tex. System, 1968-69, dep. chancellor, 1969-70, chancellor, 1971-78, prof. medicine, 1978-96; pres., internist, prof. medicine U. Tex. M.D. Anderson Cancer Ctr., 1978-96; cons. epidemiology Communicable Disease Center, USPHS, 1953-69; cons. medicine VA, 1954-59; area med. cons. VA (Atlanta area), 1958-59; vis. staff physician Grady Meml. Hosp., Atlanta, 1954-59, Emory U. Hosp., 1954-59; sr. attending staff mem. Parkland Meml. Hosp., Dallas, 1959-66; med. dir. chest div. Woodlawn Hosp., Dallas, 1959-65; mem. Surgeon Gen.'s Adv. Com. Smoking and Health, 1963-64, AMA-Edn. Research Found. com. research tobacco and health, 1964-66; chmn. Gov. Tex. Com. Tb Eradication, 1963-64; cons. internal medicine Baylor U. Med. Center, Dallas, 1962-66, St. Paul Hosp., Dallas, 1966; cons. div. hosp. and med. facilities USPHS, 1966; mem. N.Y.C. Task Force on Tb, 1967; cons. Bur. Physician, HEW, 1967-70; mem. grad. med. edn. nat. adv. com. Health Resources Adminstrn., 1977-80; mem. Tex. Legislature Dept. Health, Edn. and Welfare, 1967, Tex. Legislature Com. on Organ Transplantation, 1968, Carnegie Commn. on Non-Traditional Study, 1971-73; mem. bd. commrs. Nat. Commn. on Accrediting, 1973-76; mem. joint task force on continuing competence in pharmacy Am. Pharm. Assn.-Am. Assn. Coll. in Pharmacy, 1973-74; mem. exec. com. Legis. Task Force on Cancer in Tex., 1984-86; adv. bd. 6th World Conf. on Smoking and Health. Contbr. med. jours.; contbg. author: A Textbook of Medicine, 10 and 11th edits, 1963, Pharmacology in Medicine, 1958; Translating author: The Tubercle Bacillus, 1955; mem. editorial bd. Am. Rev. Respiratory Diseases, 1955-58. Mem. President's Commn. White House Fellows, 1971; chmn. subcom. on diversity and pluralism Nat. Council on Ednl. Research, 1973-75; bd. dirs. Assn. Tex. Colls. and Univs., 1974-75; mem. devel. council United Negro Coll. Fund, 1974-78; mem. nat. adv. council Inst. for Services to Edn., 1974-78; mem. exec. com. Assn. Am. Univs., 1975-77; mem. Project HOPE com. on Health Policy, 1977; chmn. steering com. Presbyn. Physicians for Fgn. Missions, 1960-62; mem. Ministers Cons. Clinic, Dallas, 1960-62; trustee Austin Coll., 1979-83, Stillman Coll., 1978-84; bd. dirs. Ga. Tb Assn., 1955-59; bd. dirs. Damon Runyon-Walter Winchell Cancer Fund, 1976-85, chmn. exec. com., v.p., 1978, pres., 1979-83; trustee Biol. Humanics Found., Dallas, 1973-82; chmn. health manpower com. Assn. Am. Univs., 1975-78; sec. Council So. Univs., Inc., 1976-78, pres., 1977-78; hon. life trustee Menninger Found.; Host com. Houston Econ. Summit, 1990. Recipient Cornell Univ. Alumni of Distinction award, 1978, Disting. Alumnus award U. Alabama Sch. Medicine, 1982, Pres.' award Am. Lung Assn., 1987, Gibson D. Lewis award for Excellence in Cancer Control Tex. Cancer Coun., 1988, award of Honor Am. Soc. Hosp. Pharmacists, 1988, Svc. to Mankind award Leukemia Soc. Am. Tex. Gulf Coast chpt., 1991, People of Vision award Tex. Soc. to Prevent Blindness, 1991, Outstanding Tex. Leader award 7th Ann. John Ben Sheppard Pub. Leadership Forum, 1991; Inst. Religion's Caring Spirit Tribute, 1993, AMA Disting. Svc. award, 1995, Ala. Acad. of Honor, 1998, Disting. Svc. award NASA, 1998, Charles A. LeMaiste Clinic Bldg. U. Tex. M.D. Anderson Cancer Ctr., Houston, 197, Ted C. Mars award Am. Cancer Soc., :998, Medal of Honor, 1998; named Houstonian of Yr. Houston Sch. for Deaf Children, 1987; named to Ala. Healthcare Hall of Fame, 1999. Mem. AMA, (Disting. Svc. award 1995), NASA, NIH (chair joint adv. com. behavioral rsch. 1992), Am. Thoracic Soc. (past v.p.), So. Thoracic Soc. (past pres.), Nat. TB Assn., Tex. Med. Assn., Ga. Med. Assn., Soc. Assn. Oncology (bd. dirs.), Am. Cancer Soc. (tex. bd. dirs. 1977-89, med. and sci. com. 1974, chmn. study com. on tobacco and cancer 1976, pub. edn. com. 1976-87, chmn., mem. various nat. coms., v.p., pres. 1986, med. dir.-at-large 1977-89), Houston C. of C. (dir. 1979-89), Philos. Soc. Tex. (pres. 1980-81), Greater Houston Ptnrship (bd. dirs. 1989-96), Alpha Omega Alpha. Presbyterian. Home: 7 Bristol Grn San Antonio TX 78209-1846

LEMANSKA, MIRIAM, mathematician, researcher; b. Lodz, Poland, May 11, 1920; arrived in Israel, 1959; d. Pinkus and Laja (Spitzberg) Lemanski; 1 child, Alexander Lemanski. MSc, Lodz U., 1952; DSc, Technion, Haifa, Israel, 1967. Tchr. Lyceum, Lodz, 1946-52; prelector Tchrs. Acad., Lodz, 1951-54; sr. asst. Lodz U., 1953-57; rsch. worker I.B.J. (Nuclear Rsch. Inst.), Warsaw, Poland, 1956-58; rschr. Soreq Nuclear Rsch. Ctr., Yavne, Israel, 1960-85, part-time rschr. and cons., 1985—. Contbr. articles to sci. jours., including Jour. Nuclear Energy, Jour. Applied Math. Physics, Internat. Jour. Impact Engring. Recipient award Atomic Commn. and State Coun., Warsaw, 1958; testimonial of recognition Saraq Nuclear Rsch. Ctr. and Israel Atomic Energy Commn., 1999. Fellow Israel Nuclear Soc. Avocation: listening to music. Office: Soreq Nuclear Rsch Ctr, 81800 Yavne Israel

LE MAROIS, OLIVIER, utilities executive; b. Roanne, Loire, France, June 5, 1961; s. henri Le Marois and Antoinette du Cauzi de Nazelle; m. Elodie Thabard, July 2, 1988; children: Stanislaus, Marguerite. Degree in Engring., Ecole Poly., Paris, 1985. Civil servant Industry Dept., France, 1988-91; adviser Prime Min., France, 1991-92, Environ. Min., France, 1992-93; mgr. Compangie Ginirale des Eaux, France, 1993-96; sr. exec. v.p. Dalkia Energy subsidiary of Vivendi, France, 1996—; econs. tchr. Inst. des Scis. Politques, Paris, 1988-91. Ensign French Marines, 1982-85. Avocations: sailing, bridge. E-mail: olemarois@dalkia.com. Fax: 33 1 46 53 20 70. Home: 102 Rue de la Tour, 75116 Paris France Office: Dalkia, 33 place Ronde, 92981 Paris La Difense France

LEMAY-DOAN, CATRIONA, speed skater; b. Saskatoon, Can., Dec. 23, 1970; married. Student, U. Calgary. Mem. Can. Nat. Women's Speed Skating Team, 1989—. Recipient Gold medal women's speed skating 500 meters, Olympic Games, Nagano, Japan, 1998, Bronze medal women's speed skating 1000 meters, 1998. Avocations: soccer, track and field, golf, horses. Office: Canadien Speed Skating Assoc, 2781 Lancaster Rd Ste 402, Ottawa, ON Canada K1B 1A7*

LEMBO, FRANK RALPH, educator; b. Ittabena, Miss., Oct. 25, 1920; s. Ralph Lembo and Eura Gay Smith. BA in Music, La. State U., 1942; MusM, Cin. Conservatory, 1947. Tchr. SW Tex. State U., San Marcos, Tex., 1948-52, U. Colo., Boulder, 1960, Grants (N. Mex.) High Sch., 1968-69, Santa Fe (N. Mex.) High Sch., 1970-90. Author: (poetry) Words in Mild Breezes, 1949, Raindust, 1950, funeral Song, 1998. William Frederick Poet grantee Publisher William F. Poet, 1949. Presbyn. Avocations: philatelist, orchid grower. Home: 1896 Lorca Dr Acoma Pk 38 Santa Fe NM 87505

LEMENS, WILLIAM VERNON, JR., banker, finance company executive, lawyer; b. Austin, Tex., Oct. 26, 1935; s. William Vernon and Lylia (Engberg) L.; m. Jean Lemens, May 31, 1959; children: William Vernon III, Shandra Christine. BA, U. Tex., 1958, LLB, 1962, JD, 1962. Bar: Tex. 1962; lic. real estate broker, Tex. Pvt. practice Austin, 1962—; pres. Standard Fin. Co., Austin, 1963-67, First State Loan, Austin, 1967—; chief exec. officer Southwest Computer Svcs., Inc., Austin, 1965—; pres., chief instr., mgmt. cons. Decision Dynamics, Inc., Austin, 1965-75; exec. v.p., atty. Northwest Savs. Assn., Austin, 1975-78; chmn. bd. First State Bank, Jarrell, Tex., 1975-87; pres., chief exec. officer First Am. Fin. Co., Ft. Worth, 1982—, Eagle Bank, Jarrell, 1987—. Author: Elements of Objective Orientation, 1971, SSAM-The Power of Perfect Decisions, 1972, Successful Financial Institution Operation, 1978, National Standard Financial Company Operations, 1981. Pres. Ballet Austin, 1967, Southwest Regional Ballet Assn., 1968; deacon Univ. Bapt. Ch., Austin, 1979—. Mem. State Bar Tex., Austin Bd. Realtors, Tex. Fin. Inst. (bd. dirs. 1975—), Tex. Consumer Fin. Asns. (bd. dirs. 1995—). Office: 1509 Guadalupe St Ste 200 Austin TX 78701-1608

LEMESIS, GUNTIS VICTOR, telecommunications company executive; b. Jekappils, Latvia, May 17, 1943; came to U.S., 1950; s. Alberts and Alma Lemesis; m. Mara Kalva, Aug. 2, 1979 (div. 1988); m. Susan Durden, Aug. 26, 1989. BA, Wesleyan U., 1966. Compensation specialist Honeywell, Inc., Phoenix, 1978-79, human resources planning specialist, 1979-80; mgr. benefits planning Honeywell, Inc., Mpls., 1980-82; dir. compensation & benefits United Airlines, Elk Grove Village, Ill., 1982-86; dir. compensation & mgmt. resources Contel Corp., Atlanta, 1986-91; v.p. compensation GTE Corp., Stamford, Conn., 1991-93; dir. compensation & human resources planning Sci.-Atlanta, Inc., Norcross, Ga., 1993—; instr. Am. Compensation Assn., Scottsdale, Ariz., 1985—; mem. exec. adv. panel Acad. Mgmt., Boston, 1997—. Co-author: Determining Compensation Costs, 1992, Compensation Guide, 1993; mem. editl. bd. Executive Compensation Reports, 1999—. Mem. employee benefits com. U.S. C. of C., Washington, 1981-86. Recipient 1st pl. Pub. Utilities Advt. Assn., 1972, 1st pl. Ariz. Assn. Bus. Communicators, 1974. Mem. Am. Compensation Assn., Soc. Human Resources Mgmt. Republican. Methodist. Avocations: music, wine collecting, amateur photography, chess. Office: Sci Atlanta Inc 1 Technology Pkwy S Norcross GA 30092-2967

LEMKE, HERMAN ERNEST FREDERICK, JR., retired elementary education educator, consultant; b. Argo, Ill., July 13, 1919; s. Herman and Augusta Victoria (Statt) L.; m. Geneva Octavene Davidson, Sept. 5, 1942; children: Patricia, Herman E.F. III, Gloria, John, Elizabeth. BA, George Peabody Coll., 1949, MA, 1952. Cert. social sci. tchr., Tenn., elem. tchr., Calif. Tchr. Cadd Parish Sch., Shreveport, La., 1950-55, Pacific Sch. Dist., Sacramento, 1956-58, Sacramento Sch. Dist., 1958-89; part-time tchr. Sacramento County Sch., 1974-84; substitute tchr., 1989—. Co-author: Natural History Guide, 1963, (field guide) Outdoor World of Sacramento Region, 1975; contbr. articles to profl. jours. Asst. dist. Commn. Boys Scouts Am., Shreveport, 1954, cubmaster, 1954; leader 4-H Club, Shreveport, 1950-54; elder Faith Luth. Ch., Fair Oaks, Calif., 1981-88. Recipient Scouter award, Boy Scouts Am., Shreveport, 1954, Honorary Svc. award Am. Winn Sch. PTA, 1982, Calif. Life Diploma Elem. Schs., 1961. Mem. Calif. Congress Parents Tchrs. Inc. (life). Democrat. Avocations: backpacking, coin collecting, stamp collecting, antiques, fishing. Home: 7720 Magnolia Ave Fair Oaks CA 95628-7316

LEMKE, SHERRY ELLEN, therapist; b. Mpls., Sept. 8, 1946; d. Henry Lloyd Oscar Dietz and Virginia Jean (Aument) Hennis; m. Ronald Herbert Erwin, July 31, 1965; children: Lorra Jeanne Prabhakar, Peter Christian, Kirra Lynne. BM, DePaul U., 1980; MA, Roosevelt U., 1987. Lic. clin. profl. counselor, Ill.; cert. addictions specialist; nat. cert./registered music therapist; Carl Orff cert. for music profls. in edn. Music therapist, instr. Arlington Heights, Ill., 1980—; family therapist Luth. Child and Family Svcs., Arlington Heights, 1987-94; family therapist, dir. Crossroads Comty. Counseling, Arlington Heights, 1994—; mem. adv. bd. for pers. No. Ill. Dist. of Mo. Synod Luth. Ch., Hillside, Ill., 1994—. Recipient Monetary award Webb Found., 1994-99, monetary grantee, 1995. Mem. ACA, Am. Assn. Christian Counselors, Ill. Mem. Counseling Assn., Christian Profl. Women's Group at Crossroads Comty. Counseling (founder), 116/120 Eastman Women's Group (co-founder), Cen. Bus. Dist. Lutheran. Achievements include cofounding new theory model Therapy within the Christian Context. Avocations: playing piano, reading. Office: Crossroads Comty Counseling 120 W Eastman St Ste 102 Arlington Heights IL 60004-5948

LEMLE, ALFRED, pulmonologist; b. Frankfurt, Germany, Sept. 9, 1936; s. Henrique and Margot (Rosenfeld) L.; m. Miriam Milla, July 5, 1959; children: Bruno, Marina. MD, U. Fed. Do Rio de Janeiro, Brazil, 1960. Asst. prof. U. Fed., Rio De Janeiro, Brazil, 1965-75, assoc. prof., 1976-84; prof. pneumology U. Fed., Rio De Janeiro, 1985—. Author: (books) Provas De Funcao Pulmonar Na Pratica Diaria, 1994, Tratamento Ambulatorial ne Brasil. V.p. Assn. Religiosa Israelita, 1981-94, pres., cons., 1985-86; head med. svcs. S. Martinho Found., Rio De Janeiro, 1991-92. Recipient Premio Fernandes Figueira, Acad. Nat. De Medicina, 1980, Homenagem, Uniao Beneficiente Ispalita, 1999. Fellow Am. Coll. Chest Physicians; mem. Soc. Brasil Pneumology, Clube Caicaras. Jewish. Avocations: theatre, tennis, jewish studies. Home: Rua Nascimento Silva 178, Apt 501, 22421020 Rio De Janeiro Brazil Office: Av Ataulfo de Paiva 135, Sala 1518, 22449900 Rio De Janeiro Brazil

LEMLE, ROBERT SPENCER, lawyer; b. N.Y.C., Mar. 6, 1953; s. Leo Karl and Gertrude (Bander) L.; m. Roni Sue Kohen, Sept. 5, 1976; children: Zachary, Joanna. AB, Oberlin Coll., 1975; JD, NYU, 1978. Bar: N.Y. 1979. Assoc. Cravath, Swaine & Moore, N.Y.C., 1978-82; assoc. gen. counsel Cablevision Sys. Corp., Woodbury, N.Y., 1982-84, v.p., gen. counsel, 1984-86, sr. v.p., gen. counsel, sec., 1986-94, exec. v.p., gen. counsel, sec., 1994—; vice chmn. Madison Sq. Garden, 1999—; bd. editors Cable TV and New Media Law and Fin., N.Y.C., 1983-99, bd. dirs. Cablevision Systems Corp., 1988—. Bd. trustees L.I. Children's Mus., 1990—, pres., 1996—; bd. trustees Oberlin Coll., 1996—. Mem. ABA, N.Y. State Bar Assn. Avocation: real estate. Office: Cablevision Systems Corp 1111 Stewart Ave Bethpage NY 11714-3581

LEMMON, JACK (JOHN UHLER LEMMON, III), actor; b. Boston, Feb. 8, 1925; s. John Uhler, Jr. and Mildred LaRue (Noel) L.; m. Cynthia Boyd Stone, May 7, 1950; 1 child, Christopher; m. Felicia Farr, Aug. 17, 1962; 1 child, Courtney. Grad., Phillips Andover Acad., 1943; BS, BA, Harvard U., 1947. Pres. Jalem Prodns., N.Y.C., 1952—. Appeared in summer stock, 1940-48, radio, TV shows, 1948-52; including TV series That Wonderful Guy, 1950; summer replacement: Toni Twin Time, 1950; appeared in TV series: The Adlibbers, 1951, Couple Next Door, 1951-52, Heaven for Betsy, 1952; appeared on Broadway in: Room Service, 1953, Face of A Hero, 1960, Tribute, 1979 (Broadway Drama Guild award); other stage appearances Idiot's Delight, 1970, Juno and the Paycock, 1975, Long Day's Journey Into Night, 1986; appeared in films: Mister Roberts (Acad. award best supporting actor), It Happened to Jane, You Can't Run Away From It, Fire Down Below, Cowboy, Operation Madball, Bell Book and Candle, Some Like It Hot, The Apartment, The Wackiest Ship in the Army, Notorious Landlady, Irma La Douce, Under The Yum Yum Tree, Days of Wine and Roses, Good Neighbor Sam, How to Murder Your Wife, The Great Race, The Fortune Cookie, Luv, The Odd Couple, The April Fools, The Out-of-Towners, The War Between Men and Women, 1972, Avanti, 1972, Save the Tiger, 1973 (Acad. award best actor), The Front Page, 1974, The Prisoner of 2d Avenue, 1975, Alex & the Gypsy, 1976, Airport, 1977, The China Syndrome, 1978 (Best Actor Cannes Film Festival), Tribute, 1980, Buddy Buddy, 1981, Missing, 1981 (Best Actor Cannes Film Festival), Mass Appeal, 1984, Macaroni, 1985, That's Life, 1986, Dad, 1989, JFK, 1990, The Player, 1992, Glengarry Glen Ross, 1992, Short Cuts, 1993, Grumpy Old Men, 1993, Getting Away with Murder, 1995, The Grass Harp, 1995, Grumpier Old Men, 1995, My Fellow Americans, 1996, Hamlet, 1996, Getting Away with Murder, 1996, A Weekend in the Country, 1996, Out to Sea, 1997, The Odd Couple II, 1998; TV appearances include: The Entertainer, 1975 (Emmy award nomination), 'S Wonderful, 'S Marvelous, 'S Gershwin, 1972 (Emmy award), The Murder of Mary Phagan, 1988, A Life in the Theatre, 1993, For Richer, For Poorer, 1992, Puppies for Sale, 1997, 12 Angry Men, 1997, Inherit The Wind, 1999 (Golden Globe award), The Long Way Home, 1998. Ensign USNR, 1945-46. Recipient Lifetime Achievement award, Am. Film Inst., 1988, D.W. Griffith award, 1987, Kennedy Ctr. Honors, 1996. Clubs: Hasty Pudding (pres. 1945-46), Delphic (v.p. 1945-46), Dramatic (v.p. 1945) (Harvard U.); Players (N.Y.C.). Office: CAA c/o Scott Landis 9830 Wilshire Blvd Beverly Hills CA 90212-1804

LEMOINE, MICHEL JULES, research scientist, educator; b. Neuilly, France, Mar. 7, 1937; s. Henri and Gabrielle (Besnard) L.; m. Armelle Marie Guidon, Aug. 25, 1960; children: Gwenola, Loeiz, Gael, Hervelina. Lic. de Lettres, Sorbonne U., Paris, 1958, diplome d'etudes superieures, 1959, PhD, 1981. Tchr. Foyer St-Georges, Meudon, France, 1960-62; bibliographe, 1962-84; ingénieur d'études Centre Nat. de la Recherche Scientifique, Paris, 1984-88, ingénieur de recherche, 1988-97; mem. com. Nat. de la Recherche Scientifique, Paris, 1978-83; bd. dirs. U. Paris, 1978-83; instr. U. Catania, Italy, 1987, 92, 95, 97, 2000, Nat. U., Pusan, South Korea, 1995, U. Sarah Lawrence, Paris, 1981-97. Author: L'ile Morte, 1983, William of Saint-Thierry, de Natura Corporis et Animae, 1988, Théologie et platonisme au XIIe, Intorno a Chartres, 1998; editor in chief Cahiers Universitaires Catholiques, 1986-93; contbr. articles to profl. jours. Mem. Conv. des Instns. Républicaines, Paris, 1967-69. Recipient medaille du Centre Nat. de la Recherche Scientifique, 1998. Mem. Soc. Internat. pour L'ètude de la Philosophie Mèdievale, Assn. Internat. D'ètudes Patristiques, Soc. Nat. des Antiquaires de France. Roman Catholic. Avocations: water painting, poetry, choir. Home: 1 Sq Pergolese, 78150 Le Chesnay France Office: Com du Cange, 23 Quai de Conti, 75006 Paris France

LEMOINE, SERGE, educator, museum director; b. Laon, Aisne, France, Mar. 8, 1943; s. Daniel and Madeleine (Dollé) L.; m. Marianne Le Pommeré, Dec. 24, 1966; children: Marie, Louise. Degree, U. Dijon, France, 1975; D es Lettres, U. Paris Sorbonne, 1985. Maitre de conf. U. Dijon, 1969-86; prof. Sch. of the Louvre, Paris, 1982-87; dir. Mus. of Grenoble, France, 1986—; prof. U. Paris Sorbonne, 1989—; conseiller artistique pour la Bourgogne, 1969-81; mem. Comml. des Dations, Paris, 1994—. Author: Piet Mondrian et de Stijl, 1987, Art Constructif, 1992, Aurelie Nemours, 1989, Francois Morellet, 1996. Decorated chevalier Order of Merit, officier Order Acad. Palms, chevalier Order Arts and Letters (France), chevalier Order Legion of Honor; recipient Grand prix Nat. des Musées, 1996. Mem. AICA, SHAF, ICOM/CIMAM. Home: 1 rue du Gen de Beylié, 38000 Grenoble France also: 33 ave Trudaine, 75009 Paris France Office: Musée de Grenoble, 5 Pl de Lavalette, 38000 Grenoble France

LEMON, ROBERT WAYNE, electronics executive, consultant; b. Brisbane, Queensland, Australia, Mar. 5, 1963; s. Kenneth Reginald and Winnifred Dorothy (Connell) L. AS in Elec. Engring., Southbank TAFE, Brisbane, Australia, 1995. Apprentice Brisbane City Coun., 1979-83, traffic signal technician, 1983-95, supervising officer, 1995-96; dir. Chameleon Electronics Pty. Ltd., Brisbane, 1996—; cons. Brisbane City Coun., 1996-98. Named Sportsman of Yr., Brisbane Sporting Car Club, 1985. Mem. Planetary Soc., Greenpeace. Avocations: astronomy, creation of the universe, UFO sightings and abductions, computers, reading. Office: Chameleon Electronics Pty, PO Box 533, Ashgrove Brisbane QLD 4060, Australia

LEMONNIER, ERIC, psychiatrist, researcher; b. Paris, Dec. 31, 1959; s. Jean-Claude Topic Lemonnier and Antoinette (Perraud) Pone; m. Jana Smutna, Mar. 29, 1997. MD, Cochin, Paris, 1993. Asst. Hosp. Pitie-Salpetriere, Paris, 1993-97, Hosp. U. Brest, France, 1997—. Co-author: Traite de Medecine Interne, 1996; contbr. articles to med. jours. Pres. Cultural Assn. Clapotido, Paris, 1995—. Avocation: sailing. Home: 12 Rue Richelieu, F-29200 Brest France Hosp.: Hosp U Brest, F-29820 Bohars France

LEMOS DE SOUSA, MANUEL JOAO, geology educator, researcher; b. Porto, Portugal, Nov. 10, 1937; s. Joao Wengorovius Sousa and Berta Alves Lemos. Grad. in geology, U. Porto, 1965, PhD, 1975, Agregation, 1977. Asst. U. Porto Faculty Scis., 1965-75, asst. prof. geology, 1975-79, prof., 1979—, head rsch. dept. geology, 1994—; expert for coal conversion European Union, Brussels, 1993—; pres. Internat. Com. for Coal and Organic Petrology, 1995-999; organizer 4 internat. congresses. Mem. edit. bd. Internat. Jour. Coal Geology, 1995-98; editor 7 books; contbr. over 100 articles to sci. jours. Lt. Portuguese Army, 1960-64. Mem. Royal Acad. Scis. (Madrid) European Acad. Arts, Scis. and Humanities. Fax: (351) 22 332 5937. E-mail: mlsousa@fc.up.pt. Office: U Porto Faculty Scis, Praca de Gomes Teixeira S/N, 4099-002 Porto Portugal

LEMUS-DESCHAMPS, LILIA LEMUS, research scientist; b. Mexico City, Nov. 23, 1952; arrived in Australia, 1988; d. Gabriel and Esther (Hidalgo) L.; m. Renato Deschamps; children: Paola, Laura. BSc, Nat. U. Mexico, 1978, MSc, 1984; PhD, U. Melbourne, Australia, 1994. Assoc. rsch. scis. faculty Nat. U. Mexico, 1977-80, rsch. fellow, 1983-84, 84-88, lectr., 1984-88; asst. U. Melbourne, Australia, 1988-94; rsch. fellow Meteorology Cooperative Rsch. Ctr. and Bur. Meteorology, Melbourne, 1994—. Contbr. articles to profl. jours. Mem. AAAS, Australian Metoeology and Oceanography, N.Y. Acad. Scis. Office: Bur Meteolology Coop Rsch, Ctr GPO Box 1289 1C, Melbourne 3001 VIC, Australia

LEN, MICHAEL WAI HIN, psychological consultant; b. Honolulu, Oct. 7, 1946; m. Vera Hind (dec. Oct. 1995). Student, U. Md., 1965-68; BA in Social Scis., U. Hawaii, 1970, MSW, 1976; PhD in Psychology, Union Inst. Grad. Sch., Cin., 1978. Cert. counselor; accredited marriage and family counselor; lic. Meth. lay preacher, New Zealand. Program dir. counselor svcs. United Way-John Howard Assn., Honolulu, 1971-79; asst. prof. criminal justice Chaminade U., Honolulu, 1979-81; exec. dir. Dept. Navy's Family Svc. Ctr., Barbers Point, Hawaii, 1981-89; counseling supr., chaplain Meth. Mission, Christchurch, New Zealand, 1991-92; residential cons. Winford Manor Priory, Bristol, Eng., 1993-97, The Little Ctr. for Interfaith and Intercultural Learning, 1998—; practicum instr. U. Hawaii Sch. Social Work, 1977-89; psychology supr. Calif. Behavioral Scis. Examiners, 1988-90; equal employment specialist Dept. Navy, Barbers Point, Hawaii, 1987-89. Mission interpreter United Ch. Bd. World Ministries, Asia, India, 1979; dir. Diamond Head Mental Health Ctr., Honolulu, 1977-81; v.p. Hawaii Coun. Chs., Honolulu, 1981-84; dir. Alzheimer's Disease Assn., Honolulu, 1982-89, Home and Family Soc., Christchurch, New Zealand, 1991-93. With U.S. Army, 1964-68. Group study exch. fellow Rotary Found. Internat., Eng., 1982. Mem. NASW (peace and internat. social welfare com. 1982-89), Psychology and Psychotherapy Assn. Eng., Masons (master mason Honolulu), Bristol (Eng.) Psychotherapy Assn., Rotary. Avocation: master Tai Chi Chuan and Chi Kung.

LENAERTS, KOEN, judge; b. Mortsel, Belgium, Dec. 20, 1954; m. Kris Grimonprez; 6 children. Student, U. Namur, U. Leuven, Harvard U. Asst. prof. Leuven U., 1979-82, assoc. prof., 1982-83, prof. European Communities law, 1983; prof. European Insts. Coll. Europe, Bruges, Belgium, 1984-89; law clk. to Judge R. Joliet Ct. Justice European Communities, 1984-85; judge Ct. 1st Instance European Communities, Luxembourg, 1989—; vis. prof. U. Burundi, 1983, 86, U. Strasbourg, 1986-89, Harvard U., 1988-89. Author: "The Negative Implications" of the Commerce Clause and "Preemption" Doctrines as Federalism Related Limitations on State Power: a Historical Review, 1978, Le juge et la constitution aux Etats-Unis d'Amérique et dans l'ordre juridique européen, 1988, Two Hundred Years of U.S. Constitution and Thirty Years of EEC Treaty: Outlook for a Comparison, 1988; (with P. Van Nuffel) Constitutional Law of the European Union, 1999; (with D. Arts) Procedural Law of the European Union, 1999; contbr. articles and reviews to profl. jours. Office: Ct 1st Instance European Communities, Palais de la Cour de Justice, L-2925 Luxembourg Luxembourg

LENARD, GEORGE DEAN, lawyer; b. Joliet, Ill., Aug. 26, 1957; s. Louis George and Jennie (Helopoulos) L.; m. Nancy Ilene Sundquist, Nov. 11, 1989. BS, Ill. State U., 1979; JD, Thomas Cooley Law Sch., 1984. Bar: Ill. 1984, U.S. Dist. Ct. (no. dist.) Ill. 1984, U.S. Ct. Appeals (6th cir.) 1998, U.S. Supreme Ct. 1990, Mich. 1998, Ariz. 1999. Asst. states atty. Will County States Attys. Office, Joliet, 1984-88; pvt. practice law Joliet, 1988—. Mem. ABA, ATLA, Nat. Assn. Criminal Def. Lawyers, Ill. State Bar Assn., Chgo. Bar Assn., State Bar Ariz., State Bar Mich., Phi Alpha Delta (Isaac P. Christiancy chpt.). Avocation: golf. Office: 81 N Chicago St Ste 206 Joliet IL 60432-4383

LÉNÁRD, LÁSZLÓ CSABA, physiology educator, neuroscientist; b. Pecs, Hungary, Oct. 26, 1944; s. Jozsef and Margit (Balint) L.; m. Sarolta Angela Mesko, Sept. 27, 1969; children: Laszlo, Kata, Miklos. MD, Pecs U., 1969; PhD, Hungarian Acad. Sci., 1980, DMsc, 1989. Rsch. fellow Neurophysiology Rsch. Group, Pecs, 1970-80; Hungarian Acad. Scis. sr. scientist Inst. Physiology Pecs U., 1981-88; rsch. adviser Pecs U. Med. Sch., 1989-90, prof., chmn. Inst. Physiology, 1990—, dir. Neurophysiol. Rsch. Group Inst. Physiology, 1990—; adj. prof. dept. zoology Janus Pannonius U. Pecs., 1990-97; mem. food and water intake commn. Internat. Unions Physiol. Socs., 1993-98, chmn. 1998—. Contbr. articles to profl. jours. Recipient Pro Scientia award for Rsch. Edn., Hungarian Acad. Scis., 1989, 93; Edn. Master, Nat. Com. for Tech. and Devel., 1993. Fellow Internat. Behavioral Neurosci. Soc. (Eurasian rep., mem. coun. 1992-94, co-chair program com. 1995-97, chair 1997-98, pres. elect 1998, pres. 1999-2000); mem. Hungarian Neurosci. Soc. (pres. 1993-97), Hungarian Physiol. Soc. (v.p. 1989-98), Hungarian Acad. Scis. (pres. neurobiology com. 1995-97, cons. mem. biology divsn. 1997—), Internat. Brain Rsch. Orgn. (governing coun. 1995-97), European Brain and Behavior Soc. (coun. 1997—). Office: Inst Physiology Pecs U Med Sch, Szigeti Str 12, H-7643 Pécs Hungary

LENAS, PARIS PROCOPIOU, mechanical engineer; b. Nicosia, Cyprus, Apr. 2, 1936; s. Procopios and Marie (Peonidou) L.; m. Mary Theodoulou, June 1, 1943; children: Pavlina, Marios. Diploma Mech. Engring., London Poly., 1958; postgrad., U. Toronto, 1967. Registered profl. engr., Cyprus. V.p., mgr. Lenas & Charalambides, Nicosia, 1960-66, Newform Furniture Co., Nicosia, 1969-74; mng. dir. MKL Ltd., Nicosia, 1969-74; sr. ptnr., pres. GEMAC Cons., Nicosia, 1969—. Mem. Ho. of Reps., Nicosia, 1976-81; chmn. Cyprus Stock Exch., 2000—. Fellow Brit. Inst. of Mgmt.; mem. Cyprus Profl. Engrs. (founder), ASHRAE, Assn. Energy Engrs., Brit. Inst. Mgmt., Solon, Rotary (chmn. 1988—), Cyprus C. of C. (v.p. 1996—). Mem. Democratic Rally Party. Greek Orthodox. Lodges: Rotary (chmn. 1988—), Solon. Avocations: fishing, hunting, tennis. Home: 4 Metochiou St, PO Box 24199, Nicosia 1702, Cyprus Office: GEMAC, 73 Prodromos St, Nicosia Cyprus

LENCEK, RADO LUDOVIK, Slavic languages educator; b. Mirna, Slovenia, Oct. 3, 1921; came to U.S., 1956; s. Ludovik Ivan and Kati (Jaksa) L.; m. Nina A. Lovrencic, May 4, 1946; children: Bibi-Alice, Lena-Maria. Student, U. Ljubljana, Slovenia, 1940-45, U. Padova, Italy, 1946-47; tchg. diploma, Inst. Magistrale, Gorizia, Italy, 1947; MA in Linguistics, U. Chgo., 1959; PhD in Slavic Langs., Harvard U., 1962. Asst. prof. Inst. Magistrale Sloveno, Gorizia-Trieste, Italy, 1944-55; editor USIS, Trieste, Italy, 1951-54; asst. prof. U. Ill., Urbana, 1962-65; from asst. prof. to prof. Slavic langs. Columbia U., N.Y.C., 1965-92, prof. of langs. emeritus, 1992—; assoc. Averell Harrinan Inst. for Advanced Study of the Soviet Union and of the Inst. on East Cen. Europe, 1966—; vis. assoc. prof. NYU, 1969-72; vis. prof. Yale U., 1974, U. Ill., Urbana, 1977; coord. Nat. Com. Serbo-Croatian Teaching Materials, 1982-94; U.S. coord. for Cooperation Project on Slavistics, 1983—; active U.S.-USSR Commn. on the Humanities and Social Scis., Inst. East Ctrl. Europe; participant Internat. Congs. of Slavists Prague, 1968, Warsaw, 1973, Zagreb-Ljubljana, 1978, Kiev, 1983, Sofia, 1988, Bratislava, 1993; coord. Columbia U. Program in Slavic Cultures, organized symposia Columbia U., 1974, 84, Prato di Resia, Italy, 1979, Northwestern U., 1980, U. Chgo., 1984, Acad. of Scis. USSR, Moscow, 1987, Am. Assn. Tchrs. of Slavic and East European Langs. Annual Convention, San Francisco, 1991, Toronto, Can., 1993; mem. adv. bd. Slovenski jezik-Slovene Linguistic Studies, 1994—; mem. faculty Sch. of Internat. Affairs, 1966—. Author: Ob Jadranu, Ethnographic Studies, 1947, The Verb Pattern of Contemporary Slovene, 1966, A Bibliographical Guide to Slavic Civilizations, 1966, An Outline of the Course on Slavic Civilizations, 1970, 2d edit., 1978, The Structure and History of Slovene Language, 1982, Slovenes, The Eastern Alpine Slavs, and Their Cultural Heritage, 1989, The Correspondence Between Jan Baudouin de Courtenay (1845-1929) and Vatroslav Oblak (1864-96), 1992, Izbrane Razprave in Eseji (selected papers and essays), 1996; editor: (with others): Xenia Slavica, Gojko Ruzicic Festschrift, 1975, The Dilemma of the Melting Pot: The Case of the South Slavic Languages, 1976, To Honor Jernej Kopitar, 1780-1980, 1982, A Bibliography of Recent Literature on Macedonian, Serbo-Croatian and Slovene Languages, 1990; coeditor: Who's Who of Slovene Descent in the United States, 1992, 2d rev. edit., 1995, 3d edit., 1998; editor U.S. Info. Svcs. Bull., Trieste, Italy, 1951-54, others; editor (series) Papers in Slovene Studies, 1975-76, editl. com., editor book revs. Slovene Studies, 1979—; editl. com. Folia Slavica, 1976-89, Nationalities Papers, 1979-98, Geschichte, Kultur und Geisteswelt der Slowenen, Munich, 1982-91, Beiträge zur Kenntnis Südosteuropas, Munich, 1983-91, Münchner Zeitschrift für Balkankunde, 1983-91, Geschichte, Kultur und Geisteswelt der Südslaven, Munich, 1990; mem. coun. jours. Slavistična revija, 1991—; contbr. numerous articles in field of Slavic linguistics and cultures to scholarly jours. and proceedings of internat. confs., symposiums: "Kopitar's Understanding of Historical Evolutionary Trends of Older Slovene Written Texts," 1996, (selected papers) Izbrane razprave in eseji, 1996, "Sociolinguistic Components of Adam Bohoric's Concept of his Literacy Standard of Written Slovene," 1996, "An Attempt of Stratification of Early Slovene Christian Terminology of the Oldest Eastern Alpine Slavic Texts," 1996, "Matija Murko's Letters in Baudouin's Manuscript Collectanea of the Archives of the Russian Academy of Sciences in St. Petersburg," 1997, "Jan Baudouin de Courtenay-Vatroslav Oblak's Master and Teacher," 1997; contbr. papers and essays to profl. jours. Fulbright fellow, 1986; named Amb. of Rep. of Slovenia for Sci. by Ministry for Sci. and Tech. of Rep. of Slovenia, 1995; grantee NSF, 1974, 79, Japan Soc. for Promotion Sci., 1989, Internat. Rsch. Exchs. Bd., 1971, 72, 83, 85, 94; recipient Lit. prize for publ. of Who's Who of Slovene Descent in U.S. 1995 Soc. Slovene Intellectuals of Trieste (Italy), 1996. Fellow Am. Coun. Learned Socs., Bulgarian Acad. Scis.; mem. Slovenska Kulturna Akcija (Buenos Aires), Slavists' Assn. Slovenia (hon. Ljubljana chpt. 1989—), Linguistic Soc. Am., Linguistic Circle N.Y., Am. Assn. Advancement Slavic Studies, Am. Assn. Tchrs. Slavic and East European Langs. (Disting. Scholarly Career award 1994), Soc. Slovene Studies (founder, pres. 1973-83, editor SS Newsletter 1973-77, editor Letter 1978-83, dir. Rsch. and Documentation Ctr., Columbia U., Inst. East Ctrl. Europe 1988—); corresponding mem. Slovene Acad. Scis. and Arts in Ljubljana, European Acad. Scis. and Arts in Salzburg, Acad. Scis. and Arts in Belgrade, Prague, Cracow, and Moscow, Fulbright Assn.; mem. Am. Slovene Cong. (orgnl. com. 1993-94, acad. advisor to its coun. on acad. activities 1994—). Home: 560 Riverside Dr New York NY 10027-3202 Office: Columbia U 420 W 118th St New York NY 10027-7213

LENDINARA, PATRIZIA, humanities educator; b. Amelia, Italy, Mar. 28, 1946; d. Pierantonio and Silvia (Silvani) L.; m. Ciro Piedimonte, Mar. 7, 1971; children: Camilla, Fabio. Degree in Eng. Lang. and Lit., Istituto U. Orientale, Napoli, Italy. Prof. in charge Germanic philology, faculty lettere U. Palermo, Italy, 1979—, assoc. prof., 1984—, prof. Germanic philology, faculty magisteero, 1990—. Editor: (with M.C. Ruta) Per una storia della semiotica: teorie e metodi, 1981; (with L. Melazzo Feor and Neah. Scritti di Filologia Germanica in memoria di Augusto Scaffidi Abbate, 1983; co-editor Schede Medievali, 1979—, Anglo-Saxon England, 1992—, Quaderni di Lingue e Letterature Straniere. Fac. di Magistero, Università degli studi di Palermo, 1992-93; editor Quaderni di Lingue e Letterature Straniere. Fac. di Magistero, Università degli Studi di Palermo, 1989-90, 92, 93, La Memoria. Annali della Fac. di Lettere e Filosofia dell' Università di Palermo, 1991; contbr. articles to profl. jours. Mem. Internat. Soc. Anglo-Saxonists (officer 1985-87, 2nd v.p. 1987-91, 1st v.p. 1993-95, pres. 1996-97), Officina di Studi Medievali (pres. 1992—), Associazione dei docenti Italiani di Filogia Germanica (pres. 1996—), Circolo Semiologico Siciliano, Soc. Italiana di Glottologia, Internat. Saga Soc., Soroptimists Club, Centro di Studi linguistici e filologici siciliani, Circolo Glottologico Sicialiano, Classiconorrena. Avocations: skiing, tennis, drawing, cooking. Office: U Palermo Faculty Sci, Piazza I Florio N 24, 90144 Palermo Italy

LENDL, MARKUS, engineering educator; b. Nuremberg, Germany, Aug. 7, 1966; m. Andrea Loges, Sept. 12, 1991; children: Christian, Nils. Diploma in engineering, U. Erlangen, Nuremberg, 1991, D Engring., 2000. Rschr. Siemens AG, Erlangen, 1991; rschr. dept. theoretical founds. of elec. engring. U. Erlangen, 1991—, lectr., 1996—. Sci. fellow German Govt., 1991-92. Mem. IEEE (engring. medicine & biology sci.). Avocation: sports. Office: U Erlangen, Cauerstr 7, D-91058 Erlangen Germany

LENDVAI, FERENC L(EIMDÖRFER), philosophy educator; b. Mezöberény, Hungary, July 2, 1937; s. Imre and Róza Emilia (Soós) Leimdörfer; m. Mária Horváth, May 15, 1962; 1 child, Dávid Péter. MA, Eötvös U., Budapest, 1961; PhD, Hungarian Acad. Scis., Budapest, 1980, DSc, 1994. Asst. Semmelweis U., Budapest, 1961-71; lectr., sr. lectr. Eötvös U., Budapest, 1971-88; sr. lectr. Inst. Philosophy Hungarian Acad. Scis., Budapest, 1988-92; prof. philosophy U. Miskolc (Hungary), 1992—. Author: A Short History of Philosophy, 1974, 81, 85, 95, A History of the Thought, 1983, 84, 89, Protestantism and Revolution, 1986, A Hungarian Philosopher, 1993, Philosophical Vademecum, 1995, Concepts on Central Europe, 1997; editor-in-chief Hungarian Rev. of Philosophy, 1984—. Mem. Assn. for the City of Budapest. Mem. Hungarian Philos. Assn., Internat. Assn. of Tchrs. of Philosophy, Internat. Fichte Assn., Internat. Lukács Assn. Affiliated Social-Liberals. Calvinist. Avocations: films, photography, stamps, traveling. Office: U Miskolc Fac Arts, Dept Philosophy, Egyetemvaros Miskolc Hungary

LENEWEIT, GERO STEPHAN, physicist, researcher; b. Göppingen, Germany, Dec. 26, 1968; s. Reinhold Heinz and Irene Margarethe (Dieckfoss) Trenkel; m. Kathrin Leneweit, Jan. 17, 1994; children: Raja, Raul. Diploma in Physics, U. Göttingen, Germany, 1995, D of Natural Scis., 1999. Sci. employee Tech. U., Darmstadt, Germany, 1996-99; head dept. C.G. Carus-Inst., Niefern, Germany, 1999—. Office: Carl Gustav Carus Inst, Am Eichhof, D-75223 Niefern Germany

LENEY, GEORGE WILLARD, consulting engineer; b. Nov. 13, 1927; s. Bert and Iva Irene (Skoog) L.; m. Arax G. Tefankjian, June 25, 1955 (dec. Aug. 1983); children: Sara Ann, Janet Ellen, John Alan, Ruth Alison. BS, U. Mich., 1950, MS, 1952, MA, 1955. Tchg. fellow U. Mich., 1951-53, 53-55; geophysicist Gulf Oil Co., Harmarville, Pa., 1955-56; chief geophysicist Hanna Mining Co., Cleve., 1956-64; staff geophysicist Shell Oil Co., Houston, 1964-66; chief geologist H.K. Porter Co., Inc., Pitts., 1966-76; cons., 1976-77, 81-86; regional geologist U.S. Dept. Energy, 1977-81; air pollution adminstr. Allegheny County Health Dept., Pa., 1986-97; v.p., bd. dirs. Pacific Asbestos Corp., 1970-75. With USN, 1946-48. Recipient Robert Peele Meml. award AIME, 1965 for pioneering work in geophysical exploration of iron ore. Mem. Soc. Econ. Geologists, Am. Inst. Mining Engrs., Soc. Exploration Geophysicists, Geologic Soc. Am., Pa. Acad. Sci., Air and Waste Mgmt. Assn. Achievements include being principally noted for technical achievements in mineral exploration and mining geophysics, including discovery of the Pilot Knob iron ore body in Missouri. Career included work with the Geological Survey of Canada on canoe reconnaissance in Labrador and the Northwest Territories. Organized and carried out minerals exploration programs for asbestos, iron ore, base metals, gold, oil and gas, and uranium in the U.S., Canada, Brazil and Cameroon; established a second career in air pollution, becoming recognized in the fields of emissions inventory and ozone planning. Address: 5335 Tomfran Dr Pittsburgh PA 15236-2477

LENG, MARGUERITE LAMBERT, regulatory consultant, biochemist; b. Edmonton, Alta., Can., Sept. 25, 1926; came to the U.S., 1950; d. Joseph Edouard and Marie (Kiwit) Lambert; m. Douglas Ellis Leng, June 18, 1955; children: Ronald Bruce, Janet Elaine, Douglas Lambert. BSc in Honours Chemistry, U. Alta., 1947; MSc, U. Sask., 1950; PhD, Purdue U., 1956. Rsch. asst. U. Mich. Med. Rsch. Inst., Ann Arbor, 1950-53; with agrl. dept. Dow Chem. Co., Midland, Mich., 1956-59, 66-76, with health and environ. scis. dept., 1976-86, mgr. internat. regulatory affairs, 1986-90; pres., cons. Leng Assocs., Midland, 1991—. Editor: Pesticide Chemist and Modern Toxicology, 1981, Agrochemical Environmental Fate Studies: State of the Art, 1995; contbr. articles to profl. jours., chpts. in books and encys. Life ins. med. rsch. fellow Equitable Life Assurance Co., 1949-50. Fellow Am. Inst. Chemists (bd. dirs. 1991-97); mem. Am. Chem. Soc. (agrochems. divsn. fellow 1976, chmn. 1981, program chmn. 1980, alt. councilor 1984-91, councilor 1992—), Internat. Soc. for Study Xenobiotics, Soc. Environ. Toxicology and Chemistry. Avocations: international travel, family activities, foreign languages. Home and Office: 1714 Sylvan Ln Midland MI 48640-2538

LENGAUER, WALTER OSKAR FRANZ, material scientist, educator; b. Stadl-Paura, Austria, Jan. 22, 1958; s. Walter Franz and Hermine Maria (Gollner) L.; m. Barbara Christine Diller, Dec. 6, 1997; children: Lukas Clemens, David Jakob, Chiara Magdalena Lengauer. Dipl.Ing., Tech. U. Vienna, Austria, 1984, Dr. Engring., 1987. Asst. prof. Tech. U. Vienna, 1984-93, assoc. prof. chemistry, 1993—. E-mail: wl@metec3.tuwien.ac.at. Home: Weinberggasse 12, A-2100 Leobendorf Austria Office: Technical Univ of Vienna, Vienna U of Tech, Getreidemarkt 9/161, A-1060 Vienna Austria

L'ENGLE, MADELEINE (MRS. HUGH FRANKLIN), writer; b. N.Y.C., Nov. 29, 1918; d. Charles Wadsworth and Madeleine (Barnett) Camp; m. Hugh Franklin, Jan. 26, 1946; children: Josephine Franklin Jones, Maria Franklin Rooney, Bion. A.B., Smith Coll., 1941; postgrad., New Sch., 1941-42, Columbia U., 1960-61; holder 19 hon. degrees. Tchr. St. Hilda's and St. Hugh's Sch., 1960—; mem. faculty U. Ind., 1965-66, 71; writer-in-residence Ohio State U., 1970, U. Rochester, 1972, Wheaton Coll., 1976—, Cathedral St. John the Divine, N.Y.C., 1965—. Author: The Small Rain, 1945, Ilsa, 1946, Camilla Dickinson, 1951, A Winter's Love, 1957, And Both Were Young, 1949, Meet the Austins, 1960, A Wrinkle in Time, 1962, The Moon by Night, 1963, The 24 Days Before Christmas, 1964, The Arm of the Starfish, 1965, The Love Letters, 1966, The Journey with Jonah, 1968, The Young Unicorns, 1968, Dance in the Desert, 1969, Lines Scribbled on an Envelope, 1969, The Other Side of the Sun, 1971, A Circle of Quiet, 1972, A Wind in the Door, 1973, The Summer of the Great-Grandmother, 1974, Dragons in the Waters, 1976, The Irrational Season, 1977, A Swiftly Tilting Planet, 1978, The Weather of the Heart, 1978, Ladder of Angels, 1980, A Ring of Endless Light, 1980, Walking on Water, 1980, A Severed Wasp, 1982, And It Was Good, 1983, A House Like a Lotus, 1984, Trailing Clouds of Glory, 1985, A Stone for a Pillow, 1986, Many Waters, 1986, Two-Part Invention, 1988, A Cry Like a Bell, 1987, Sole Into Egypt, 1989, From This Day Forward, 1988, An Acceptable Time, 1989, The Glorious Impossible, 1990, Certain Women, 1992, The Rock That Is Higher: Story As Truth, 1993, Anytime Prayers, 1994, Troubling a Star, 1994, Penguins and Golden Calves, 1996, A Live Coal in the Sea, 1996, Glimpses of Grace, 1996, Wintersong, 1996, Mothers and Daughters, 1997, Friends for the Journey, 1997, Bright Evening Star: Mystery of the Incarnation, 1997. Pres. Crosswicks Found. Recipient Newbery medal, 1963, Sequoyah award, 1965, runner-up Hans Christian Andersen Internat. award, 1964, Lewis Carroll Shelf award, 1965, Austrian State Lit. award, 1969, Bishop's Cross, 1970, U. South Miss. medal, 1978, Regina medal, 1985, Alan award Nat. Coun. Tchrs. English, 1986, Kerlan award, 1990, Margaret Edwards award, 1998; collection of papers at Wheaton Coll. Mem. Authors Guild (mem. council), Authors League (mem. council), Writers Guild Am. Episcopalian. Home: 924 W End Ave Apt 95 New York NY 10025-3544 Office: Cathedral Libr St John the Divine 1047 Amsterdam Ave New York NY 10025-1747 also: care Random House Children's Media 1540 Broadway New York NY 10036-4039

LENGY, JACOB ISRAEL, parasitologist, educator; b. Tel Aviv, Mar. 14, 1928; s. Herman Meyer and Shulamith (Leader) L.; m. Sima Hassidoff, Feb. 11, 1958; children: Orith, Amnon, Assaf. BA, Colo. U., 1951; MSc in Biology, Wyo. U., 1957; PhD summa cum laude, Hebrew U., Jerusalem, 1961. Cert. med. technologist. Grad. teaching asst. dept. biology Wyo. U., Laramie, 1955-57; grad. rsch. fellow dept. parasitology Hebrew U., 1958-60; teaching asst. dept. microbiology Tel Aviv U., 1960-61, from instr. to lectr. dept. microbiology, 1961-63, sr. lectr., 1963-66, assoc. prof. Med. Sch., 1966-72, prof. parasitology Med. Sch., 1972-96, prof. emeritus, 1997—, head sect. parasitology Med. Sch., 1972—, chmn. dept. human microbiology Med. Sch., 1981-85, 89-91; cons. in parasitology Ichilov Mcpl. Hosp., Tel Aviv, 1966—, Zamenhoff Cen. Sick-Fund Lab., Tel Aviv, 1964-91. Author: Guidelines to Parasitology, 1986; contbr. numerous articles to med. jours. Staff sgt. USAF, 1951-53. Grantee Ford Found., 1965, Israel Ministry of Health, 1975, 77, Joint Israel-Egypt Peace Fund, 1988, Zukerman Clin. Parasitology Fund, 1982—. Mem. AAAS, Am. Soc. Parasitologists, N.Y. Acad. Scis., Israel Soc. Parasitology (co-founder, dep. chair 1978-79, chmn. 1980-83), World Fedn. Parasitologists (Israeli rep. 1978-85). Avocations: chess, classical music, TV and radio musical quizzes. Home: 12 Oppenheimer St, Tel Aviv Israel Office: Tel Aviv U at Ramat Aviv, Sackler Sch Medicine, Dept Human Microbiology Tel Aviv Israel

LENGYEL, GYÖRGY, sociologist, educator; b. Budapest, Hungary, Mar. 20, 1951; s. György and Éva (Machati) L. MA in Econs., Karl Marx U. of Econs., Budapest, Hungary, 1975, U. D in Econs., 1977; MA in History and Sociology, L. Eötvös U. Arts, Budapest, Hungary, 1981; PhD in Sociology, Hungarian Acad., Budapest, Hungary, 1991. Rsch. fellow City Archives, Budapest, Hungary, 1975-78, Karl Marx U. of Econs., Budapest, Hungary, 1978-91; chmn., dept. sociology Budapest U. Econs., Hungary, 1991—. Author: Entrepreneurs, Bankers, Merchants, 1989; editor: Hungarian Economy and Society during World War II, 1992, The Transformation of the Economic Elite, 1997; co-editor: The Spread of Entrepreneurship in Eastern Europe, 1996, Elites after State Socialism, 2000; chmn. editl. bd. Hungarian Sociol. Rev., 1999—; contbr. articles to profl. jours. Mem. European Sociol. Assn. (exec. com. 1999—), Internat. Sociol. Assn. (dep. chmn. rsch. com. on economy and society, 1994—), Hungarian Acad. Scis. (com. sociology 1993—, com. human resources 1994—). Office: Budapest U Econ Sci, Fövam ter 8, 1093 Budapest Hungary

LENGYEL, JENő FERENC, electrical engineering executive; b. Büdszentmihály, Hungary, June 30, 1948. Grad. in Elec. Engring., Tech. Univ. Budapest, 1976. Cons. Nat. Bur. Measurements, Hungary, 1973-76; civil tchr. engring. Mil. Coll. Hungary, Budapest, 1977-78; sci. advisor Rsch. Inst. Measuring Instruments, Budapest, 1978-84; owner Lexica Gmk., Budapest, 1984—; lectr. in field. Mem. Sci. Soc. Measurement and Automation, Am. Internat. Club Hungary (v.p.), Nat. Geographic Soc., European Fedn. of Nat. Engring. Assn., C. of C. and Industry (Budapest), Hungarian Amateur Radio Soc. Avocations: swimming, cycling. Home: Kakukk út 8/A, Budapest 1126, Hungary Office: Lexica Gmk, Kakukk ú 8/A, Budapest 1126, Hungary

LENGYEL, LASZLO, surgeon, medical administrator; b. Wolfsberg, Austria, Dec. 4, 1945; s. Imre Lengyel and Ilona Bodnár; m. Judit Krajczár, July 4, 1971; children: Robert, Csongor, Szabolcs. MD, Debrecen Med. Sch., 1971, diploma in surgery, 1975; diploma in oncology, Nat. Cancer Inst., Budapest, 1984. Resident Debrecen U., 1971-75, cons., 1976-87; head surg. dept. Tchg. Hosp., Berettyoujfalu, 1987—. inventor breast screening sys., 1985, early results breast screening, 1997, late results breast screening, 1997. Mem. ESSO, EPHA. Avocations: music, photography, surfing. Home: Komlossy u 17, H-4032 Debrecen Hungary Office: Tchg Hosp, Orban B ter 1, H-4101 Berettyoujfalu Hungary

LENK, CARLA M., business executive, educator; b. Milw., Sept. 25, 1938; d. Chester Paul and Dorothy Marie Dombrowski; widowed; children: Elizabeth, Jeanette, Andrew. BS, U. Wis., Milw., 1960, MS, 1975. CEO Forward Svcs. Corp., Madison, Wis., 1994; pres. Wis. Bus. Procurement Assn., Wisconsin Rapids, Wis., 1981-88; dir. Small Bus. Devel. Ctr., Whitewater, Wis., 1987—. Mem. Nat. Contract Mgmt. Assn. (sec. 1988-89), South Ctrl. World Trade Assn. (pres. 1988-90, exec. dir. 1990—), Wis. Dist. Export Coun., Wis. Women's Entrepreneurs, Rotary (Atkinson). Office: U Wis-Whitewater 800 W Main St Whitewater WI 53190-1705

LENK, RICHARD WILLIAM, JR., history educator; b. Hackensack, N.J., Aug. 29, 1936; s. Richard William and Eleanor Marion (Haenschen) L.; BA cum laude, Fairleigh Dickinson U., 1959; PhD, NYU, 1969. Lectr., L.I. U., 1964-65, Bklyn. Coll., 1965-67; instr. N.Y. U., summer 1968; lectr. Hunter Coll., N.Y.C., 1969; asst. prof. Bergen C.C., Paramus, N.J., 1969-73, assoc. prof., 1973-80, prof. history, 1980-98, prof. emeritus, 1998 . Trustee, Bergen County Hist. Soc., 1977-80, pres., 1980-83; mem. Hackensack Tercentenary Com. for N.J., 1962-64; historian City of Hackensack, 1999—. Mem. Am. Hist. Soc., Orgn. Am. Historians, Archaeol. Inst. Am., N.Y. Hist. Soc., N.J. Hist. Soc., Assn. Ancient Historians. Contbr. articles to profl. jours. Office: Dept Social Scis Bergen Community Coll 400 Paramus Rd Paramus NJ 07652-1508

LENKEI, PETER, structural engineering educator, consultant; b. Budapest, Hungary, May 25, 1933; s. Kalman and Borbala (Straszer) L.; m. Gizella Malek, Feb. 1, 1935; children: Peter, Gabor. Structural Engr., Moscow U., 1956, PhD in Structural Engring., 1965; DSc, Hungarian Acad. Sci., 1984. Registered structural engr., Hungarian Chamber of Engrs. Structural design engr. Pecs (Hungary) Uran Co., 1956-62; rsch. fellow, head dept., divsn. dir. Hungarian Insts. Bldg. Rsch., Budapest, 1963-87; head Pecs Poly., 1987-92, prof., 1987-95; vice rector sci. affairs Janus Pannonius U., Pecs, 1995-97, prof. structural engring. Coll. Engring., 1995—, Szechenyi prof. structural engring., 1999—; mem. adminstrv. coun. Euro-Internat. Concrete Com., Lausanne, Switzerland, 1980-97; mem. Hungarian Accreditation Com., Budapest, 1994-97; mem. presidency Hungarian Chamber Engrs., Budapest, 1997—; sr. ptnr. Lenkei Consult Ltd., Pecs, 1997—; mem. Mechanics Commn., Hungarian Acad. Scis., 1978—. Contbr. over 140 articles to profl. jours. on reinforced concrete structures; co-author 2 inventions. Chmn. Lions Club Pecs, 1994-95; zone chmn. Hungarian Lions Clubs, 1995-96. Recipient Lorand Eötvös prize Min. Constrn., Budapest, 1987, Baranya medal Baranya County Coun., Pecs, 1989, M. Pollack Golden medal Pecs Poly., 1993, Szent-Györgyi Albert prize Ministry Edn., Budapest, 2000. Mem. Hungarian Acad. Engring., Russian Acad. Arch. and Constrn. Sci. (fgn. mem.), N.Y. Acad. Scis. Avocation: old Hungarian history. Office: Pecs Univ, Boszorkany u 2, H-7624 Pécs Hungary

LENMAN, BRUCE PHILIP, historian, educator; b. Aberdeen, Scotland, Apr. 9, 1938; s. Jacob Philip and May (Wishart) L. MA in History with 1st class honors, Aberdeen U., 1960; MLitt, U. Cambridge, 1965, LittD, 1986. Asst. prof. U. Victoria, B.C., Can., 1963; lectr. Queen's Coll., Dundee, Scotland, 1963-67, U. Dundee, 1967-72; lectr. U. St. Andrews, Scotland, 1972-78, sr. lectr., 1978-83, reader, 1983-92, prof. of modern history, 1992—; James Pinckney Harrison prof. history Coll. William and Mary, Williamsburg, Va., 1988-89; Bird prof. history Emory U., Atlanta, 1998; mem. humanities com. Coun. for Nat. Acad. Awards, London, 1985-87. Author: From Esk to Tweed, 1975, Economic History of Modern Scotland, 1977 (Scottish Arts Coun. award 1977), The Jacobite Risings 1689-1746, 1980 (Scottish Arts Coun. award 1980), Scotland 1746-1832, 1981, The Jacobite Clans of the Great Glen, 1984, The Jacobite Clause, 1986, The Eclipse of Parliament, 1992, England's Colonial Wars, 2000, Britain's Colonial Wars, 2000; co-author: (with John S. Gibson) The Jacobite Threat, 1990; editor: Chambers Dictionary of World History, 1993, rev. edit., 2000. Brit. Acad.-Newberry Library fellow, 1982, John Carter Brown Library fellow, 1984, Mellon fellow Va. Hist. Soc., 1990, Mayers fellow Huntington Libr., 1996, Folger Libr. fellow, 1997. Fellow Royal Hist. Soc.; mem. Am. Soc. for 18th Century Scottish Studies, Am. Soc. for 18th Century Studies, Soc. for History of Discoveries, Hakluyt Soc. Clubs: Royal Commonwealth (London); New Golf (St. Andrews). Avocations: golf, hill walking, swimming, Scottish country dancing, badminton. Office: U St Andrews Dept Modern History, St Katharine's Lodge, Saint Andrews KY16 9AL, Scotland

LENNARD, JOHN CHEVENING, literature educator; b. Bristol, Avon, Eng., June 16, 1964; s. Michael Briart and Joan Kathleen L. BA, New Coll., Oxford, Eng., 1985; PhD, New Coll., 1990; MA, Washington U., St. Louis, 1986. Tutor Open U., Bristol, 1990-91, Royal Holloway & Bedford New Coll., Surrey, Eng., 1990-91; fellow, dir. of studies in English Trinity Hall, Cambridge, Eng., 1991-98; Newton Trust lectr. Faculty of English, Cambridge, 1993-98; examiner Faculty of English, Cambridge, 1993-98. Author: (books) But I Digress: The Exploitation of Parentheses in English Printed Verse, 1991, The Poetry Handbook, 1996. Leverhulme rsch. fellow, 1999-00. Avocations: walking, film, folk and blues, environment. Office: c/o Trinity Hall, Cambridge CB2 ITJ, England

LENNARD-JONES, JOHN EDWARD, retired gastroenterologist; b. Bristol, Eng., Jan. 29, 1927; s. John Edward and Kathleen Mary Lennard-Jones; m. Verna Margaret Down, Feb. 19, 1955; children: David, Peter, Andrew, Timothy. BA, Corpus Christ Coll., Cambridge, Eng., 1947, MA, 1951; MB, BChir, U. Cambridge, 1953, MD, 1965; DSc (hon.), U. Kingston, 1999. Mem. med. rsch. coun. indsl. medicine and burns unit Birmingham Accident Hosp., 1947-48; house surgeon, house physician U. Coll. Hosp., London, 1953-54; sr. house officer Manchester (Eng.) Royal Infirmary, 1954-55; registrar Ctrl. Middlesex Hosp., 1956-58, sr. registrar, 1961-63, mem. med. rsch. coun. gastroenterology rsch. unit, 1963-74; registrar, mem. med. rsch. coun. dept. clin. rsch. U. Coll. Hosp., London, 1958-61, cons. physician, 1965-74; prof. gastroenterology Royal London Hosp., 1974-87; cons. gastroenterologist St. Mark's Hosp., London, 1965-92; ret., 1992; chmn. Brit. Assn. for Parenteral and Enteral Nutrition, 1991-95, Sir Halley Stewart Trust, 1997—. Joint author: Clinical Gastroenterology, 1968, Inflammatory Bowel Disease, 1992, Constipation, 1994; contbr. articles to profl. jours. Cir. steward Meth. Ch., London, 1986-92. Fellow Royal Coll. Physicians London, Royal Coll. Surgeons London, U. Coll. London, Royal Soc. Medicine London (hon.); mem. Nat. Assn. for Colitis and Crohn's Disease (hon. life pres. 1992—), Brit. Soc. Gastroenterology (hon., hon. sec. 1965-70, pres. 1983, chmn. clin. svcs. com. 1986-90), Digestive Disorders Found. (pres. 1992—), Swedish Soc. Gastroenterology (hon.), Swiss Soc. Gastroenterology (hon.) Netherlands Soc. Gastroenterology (hon.), South African Soc. Gastroenterology (hon.), French Soc. Coloproctology (hon.). Methodist/Anglican. Avocations: gardening, ornithology, golf. Home: 72 Cumberland St, Woodbridge 1P12 4AD, England

LENNGREN, CARL ANDERS, transportation executive; b. Karlskoga, Örebro, Sweden, Aug. 28, 1954; s. Carl Einar and Gunnel (Holmgren) L. MS, Royal Inst. Tech., Stockholm, 1983; PhD, Royal Inst. Tech., 1990; MS in Civil Engring., U. Wash., 1986. Rschr. Swedish Nat. Rd. Adminstrn., Borlänge, 1984-89; cons. Vägundersökningar Aktiebolag, Stockholm, 1990; postdoc. assoc. U. Minn., Mpls., 1991-93; chief rschr. Road Survey Tech.-Sweden, Solna, 1993-96; cons. VV Konsult, Vanersborg, Sweden, 1996—; cons. Minn. Dept. Transp., Maplewood, 1991-92, Prodn. West, Vanersborg, 1993-95, World Bank, Changsha, China, 1996; lectr. Dept. Transport, Harare, Zimbabwe, 1994. Valle scholar, 1984, Wallenberg scholar, 1986. Mem. Internat. Soc. Asphalt Pavements (founding), Internat. Soc. Optical Engring., Planetary Soc., Assn. Asphalt Paving Technologists. Avocations: photography, astronomy. Home: Bokgatan 32, 46252 Vanersborg Sweden Office: VV Konsult, Box 1200 Regementsgatan 15, 46228 Vanersborg Sweden

LENNON, DOUGLAS RAYMOND, management information systems executive; b. Shepparton, Victoria, Australia, Nov. 12, 1942; s. Alan and Muriel Violet (Gilchrist) L.; m. Leslie Doris Lorimer, June 23, 1979; children: Susan Joye, Tania Gaye, Kim Toinette Dolan, Keryn Simone Gibson, Brent Andrew Leahy, Jared Kent Leahy. Scheduling mgr. Australia Dept. of Def., Canberra, 1967-70; Victorian ops. mgr. NCR, Melbourne, 1970-73; sr. systems analyst Ansell Internat., Melbourne, 1973-75, EDP mgr., 1975-88; project coord. Ansell Internat., Europe, 1989-90; internat. project leader Ansell Internat., Europe, Australia, 1990-92; European info. sys. mgr. Ansell GmbH, Munich, 1992-98; global projects mgr. Ansell Internat., Australia, 1998—; dir. Global Year 2000 Initiative, 1999-2000; IT dir. Asia Pacific mktg. region Ansell, 2000—. Mem. IEEE, Australian Computer Soc. Office: Ansell Internat, 530 Springvale Rd, Glen Waverley 3150, Australia

LENNON, STEPHEN JOHN, research scientist, executive; b. Pietermaritzburg, S. Africa, Mar. 25, 1959; s. Peter Joseph and Joan Margaret (Arbuckle) L.; m. Julie Dawn Fisher, Dec. 18, 1982; children: Shannon, Russell. BS, U. Natal, Durban, 1980; MS, U. Witwatersrand, Johannesburg, S. Africa, 1982, PhD, 1985. Rschr. CSIR, Pretoria, 1985-86; corrosion scientist Eskom, Johannesburg, 1986-89, scientific investigations, 1989-93, rsch. mgr., 1993-99, acting head tech., 1999, sr. gen. mgr. tech., 1999—; chmn. Power Inst. of Ea. and So. Africa, 1997—; mem. Coun. for the Environment, S. Africa, 1993-95; chmn. Energy Sector Foresight, 1997—. Editor: (books) Global Climate Change and South Africa, 1996; contbg. author: (book) Air Pollution and its Impacts on the SA Nighveld, 1996, IPCC Working Group III; contbr. articles to profl. jours. Chmn. Sch. Governing Body, Johannesburg, 1996—; lead Nat. Facilities Rev., Pretoria, 1997; mem. Systemwide Rev., S. African Govt., 1998. Lt. S. African mil., 1984-86. Mem. Nat. Sci. Tech. Forum (chmn. 1999—), others. Avocations: cycling, reading, music, family. Office: Eskom, PO Box 10011, Johannesburg 2000, South Africa

LENOIR-FREAUD, NOËLLE, French government official; b. Neully sur Seine, France, Apr. 27, 1948; d. André and Madeleine (Kahn) Freaud. Degree in pub. law, U. Paris, 1971; diploma, Inst. Polit. Sci., Paris, 1972; PhD (hon.), U. Suffolk, 1993. Prin. adminstr. French Senate, 1972-82; dir. regulatory matters Nat. Commn. Data-Processing and Liberty, 1982-84; legal advisor Coun. of State, 1984—, prosecutor contentious and other govt. bus. sect., 1988; mem. Constnl. Ct., Paris, 1992—; chair bioethics adv. com. UNESCO, 1992-98, spl. councellor of the gen. dir., 1998—; chair group of advisors on ethical implications of biotech. European Commn., 1994-97, pres. European Group of Ethics in Sci. and new Techs. European Union; mayor Valmondois, Dept. of Va. d'Oise, 1989-95; spl. adviser on law relating to bioethics and life scis. to Prime Min. of France, 1990-91; dir. pvt. office Keeper of the Seals and Min. of Justice, 1988-90; mem. cons. forum on biotech. EU-US, 2000; expert FAO, 2000. Author: La Transparence Adminstrative, 1987, Les normes internat. de la Bioéthique, 1998, La justice de Daumier a nos jours, 1999; contbr. articles to profl. jours. Pres. Friends of Honorè Daumier, 1994—. Mem. Soc. of Gray's Inn (hon. master of bench), Am. Law Inst., European Group on Ethics in Sci. and New Techs. of European Union (pres. 1998). Home: 28 Boulevard Raspail, 75007 Paris France Office: Conseil Constitional, 2 rue Montpensier, 75001 Paris France

LENTINI, JOSEPH CHARLES, government agency management analyst; b. Washington, Oct. 2, 1943; s. Joseph and Pearl (Crosman) L.; m. Colleen Gail Sargent, Dec. 5, 1983; children: Randolph, Lois, Steven, Suzanne, Richard. AA cum laude, Prince Georges C.C., Largo, Md., 1977; BS cum laude, U. Md., 1982; MS in Pub. Adminstrn., Am. U., 1991; CIO cert., IRM Coll., 1997. Owner, operator N.Am. Van Lines, Ft. Wayne, Ind., 1974-79; materiel bus. adminstr. E-Systems, Inc., Falls Church, Va., 1979-81; adminstrv. mgr. MA/COM, Inc., Rockville, Md., 1981-83; computer specialist VA, Washington, 1983-89; web master, mgmt. analyst, IRM expert EPA, Washington, 1989—. Mem. adv. com. Nat. Multiple Sclerosis Soc., Washington, 1993-95. Served with USN, 1961-69. Decorated Purple Heart, Presdl. Unit citation, 1967. Mem. ASPA, DAV, Assn. Fed. Info. Resources Mgrs., Armed Forces Comm. and Electronics Assn., Am. Legion, Fleet Res. Democrat. Avocations: biking, camping, reading, judo, music. Home: 12632 Maryland Rte 216 Highland MD 20777-9731 Office: EPA # 3615 1200 Pennsylvania Ave NW # 3615 Washington DC 20460-0001

LENTNER, HOWARD HENRY, political scientist; b. Detroit, Sept. 8, 1931; s. Frank Richard and Millicent Marie (Kelley) L.; m. Margaret Nancy Taylor, Aug. 23, 1958 (div. 1983); children: Tarah (dec.), J Talar, Leseh. BS, Miami U., 1958; MA, Syracuse U., 1959, PhD, 1964. Instr. polit. sci. Western Res. U., 1962-63, asst. prof., 1963-68; assoc. prof., chmn. dept. polit. sci. McMaster U., Hamilton, Ont., Can., 1968-72; assoc. prof. CUNY Baruch Coll. and Grad. Sch., N.Y.C., 1973-76, prof., 1977—, exec. officer PhD program polit. sci., 1979-82. Author: Foreign Policy Analysis: A Comparative and Conceptual Approach, 1974, State Formation in Central America: The Struggle for Autonomy, Development, and Democracy, 1993, International Politics: Theory and Practice, 1997; co-editor: Power in Contemporary Politics: Theories, Practices, Globalizations, 2000. Served with U.S. Army, 1953-55. Mem. Am. Polit. Sci. Assn., Internat. Studies Assn., Northeastern Polit. Sci. Assn., Internat. Polit. Sci. Assn. Office: 17 Lexington Ave New York NY 10010-5518

LENTON, ROBERTO LEONARDO, research facility and environmental administrator; b. Buenos Aires, Feb. 28, 1947; s. Leonard Gersham and Katie (McCulloch) L.; m. Julia Anne Frend, June 11, 1971; children: Alexandra, James, Christopher, Jessica. Civil Engr., U. Buenos Aires, 1971; SM in Civil Engring., MIT, 1973, PhD in Water Resources Systems, 1974. Planning asst. Ministry Pub. Works, Buenos Aires, 1970-71; vis. rsch. engr. MIT, Cambridge, 1971-72, rsch. asst., 1972-74, asst. prof., 1974-77; project specialist Ford Found., New Delhi, 1977-80, program officer, 1980-83; program officer Ford Found., N.Y.C., 1983-86; dep. dir. gen. Internat. Irrigation Mgmt. Inst., Kandy, Sri Lanka, 1986-87; dir. gen. Internat. Irrigation Mgmt. Inst., Colombo, Sri Lanka, 1987-94; dir. sustainable energy and environ. divsn. UN Devel. Programme, N.Y.C., 1995—. Co-author: Applied Water Resources Systems Planning, 1979. Bd. dirs., treas. Am. Embassy Sch., New Delhi, 1981-83; bd. dirs. Overseas Children's Sch., Colombo, 1989-93. Mem. ASCE, Am. Geophys. Union, Centro Argentino Ingenieros. Avocations: windsurfing, tennis, running. Home: 48 Rye Rd Rye NY 10580-2231 Office: UN Devel Programme One UN Plz New York NY 10017

LENTZ, DEBORAH LYNN, telemetry, thoracic surgery, and intensive care nurse; b. Greenport, N.Y., Oct. 24, 1971; d. Stanley Antone Jr. and Linda Ann (Bernhard) C.; m. Stephen C. Lentz III, Dec. 1993; children: Stephen C. IV, Victoria A. Cert. LPN, Harry Ward Tech. Ctr., Riverhead, N.Y., 1989; ADN, SUNY, Alfred, 1991. RN, N.Y.; cert. BLS, ACLS. LPN San Simeon By the Sound, Greenport, 1989-91; RN Meml. Sloan Kettering Cancer Ctr., Manhattan, N.Y., 1991-92, L.I. Jewish Hosp., New Hyde Park, N.Y., 1992-94; nurse Ctrl. Suffolk Hosp., 1994-97; CCU, med. ICU nurse Stony Brook (N.Y.) U. Hosp., 1997—. Mem. N.Y. State Nurses Assn. Roman Catholic. Avocations: music, animal and nature lover. Home: 11815 Sound Ave # 2 Mattituck NY 11952-3180

LENTZ, EDWARD ALLEN, consultant, retired health administrator; b. Superior, Wis., May 30, 1926; s. Otto Albert and Martha Mary Ann (Gruhel) L.; m. Margaret Ann Denier, May 30, 1952; 1 child, Elizabeth Ann Clark. BS, U. Cin., 1951; MHA, Wayne State U., Detroit, 1957. Asst. dir. Pub. Health Fedn., Cin., 1954-57; dir. health planning United Cmty. Coun., Columbus, Ohio, 1957-62; asst. dir. Columbus Hosp. Fedn., 1962-65; assoc. exec. dir. Ohio Hosp. Assn., Columbus, 1965-69; exec. dir. Health Planning Assn. of Ohio River Valley, Cin., 1969-70; asst. prof. grad. program in health svcs. adminstrn. Coll. of Medicine, Ohio State U., Columbus, 1970-72, adj. assoc. prof. preventive medicine, 1957—; dep. dir. med. care adminstrn. Ohio Dept. Health, Columbus, 1972-75; pres., CEO Med. Advances Inst., Columbus, 1975-79; v.p. corp. devel. Mt. Carmel Health System, Columbus, 1979-95; cons. Mt. Carmel Health System, 1995-97; cons. cmty. health planning USPHS; bd. dirs. Scioto Valley Health Sys. Agy. Contbr. articles to profl. jours. Mem., chair Ohio Dept. Human Svcs./Ohio Med. Care Adv. Com., Columbus, 1975—; bd. dirs., vice chair Netcare Corp., Columbus, 1989—. Served with USN, 1944-46; 1st lt. U.S. Army, 1951-53, Korea. Recipient Spl. Citation for hosp. planning and mktg. in Ohio and Delbert L. Pugh Conf., Ohio State U. Coll. Medicine and Ohio Hosp. Assn., 1991. Fellow Am. Pub. Health Assn. (bd. dirs., vice chmn. bd. trustees 1979-83); mem. Ohio Pub. Health Assn. (pres. 1969-70), Am. Assn. Areawide Planning Agencies (pres. 1969-70), Ohio Hosp. Assn. Soc. for Hosp. Planning and Mktg. (pres. 1987-88), Columbus Rotary (com. chair). Presbyterian. Avocations: fishing, photography, tennis. Home: 585 Keyes Ln Worthington OH 43085-3503

LENTZ, MARY A., lawyer, educator; b. Cleve., May 17, 1942; d. Edward G. and Agnes D. (O'Brien) L. BA, Ursuline Coll., Cleve., 1964; MA, Georgetown U., 1968; JD, Cleve. State U., 1973. Bar: Ohio 1973, Pa. 1984, U.S. Dist. Ct. (no. and ea. divsns.) Ohio 1974, U.S. Ct. Appeals (6th dist.) 1975, U.S. Ct. Appeals (D.C. cir.) 1986, U.S. Supreme Ct. 1977; cert. secondary tchr., Ohio. Tchr. Cleve. Pub. Schs., 1965-74; legal counsel Ohio State Dept. Edn., Columbus, 1974-76; asst. pros. atty. criminal divsn. Cuyahoga County, Cleve., 1976-78; atty., ptnr. Weston, Hurd, Fallon, Paisley & Howley, Cleve., 1978-92; atty. in pvt. practice Cleve., 1992-95; ptnr. Walter & Haverfield, Cleve., 1995-99; chief atty. office civil rights U.S. Dept. Edn., Cleve., 1999; pvt. practice Chagrin Falls, Ohio, 1999—; lectr. and presenter in field. Editor Ohio Sch. Jour., 1977—; author quar. periodical Pvt. Sch. Law Digest, 1982-89. Dir. Sch. Safety and Security Acad., Cuyahoga C.C., Cleve., 1997-99; dir. Inst. for Sch. Resource and Security Officers, Ashland (Ohio) U., 1998—. Recipient Master Tchr. award Jennings Found., 1970, Appreciation award Westlake Police Dept., 1996, Appreciation award Cuyahoga County C.C., 1997, Appreciation award Cleve. Pub. Schs. Divsn. Safety and Security, 1997, FBI Dir.'s Cmty. Leadership award, 1999. Mem. ABA, Ohio State Bar Assn., Greater Cleve. Bar Assn., Geauga (Ohio) Bar Assn., Pa. Bar Assn., D.C. Bar ASsn.

LENTZ, THOMAS LAWRENCE, biomedical educator, dean, researcher; b. Toledo, Mar. 25, 1939; s. Lawrence Raymond and Kathryn (Heath) L.; m. Judith Ellen Pernaa, June 17, 1961; children: Stephen, Christopher, Sarah. Student, Cornell U., 1957-60; MD, Yale U., 1964. Instr. in anatomy Yale U. Sch. Medicine, New Haven, 1964-66, asst. prof. anatomy, 1966-69, assoc. prof. cytology, 1969-74, assoc. prof. cell biology, 1974-85, prof. cell biology, 1985—, asst. dean for admissions, 1976-2000, assoc. dean for admissions, 2000—, vice chmn. cell biology, 1992—; mem. cellular and molecular neurobiology panel NSF, 1987-88, mem. cellular neurosci. panel, 1988-90; mem. neurology B-1 study sect. Nat. Inst. Neurol. Disorders and Stroke, NIH, 1996, 98; mem. exptl. virology study sect. Nat. Inst. Allergy and Infectious Disease, NIH, 1997, 98. Author: The Cell Biology of Hydra, 1966, Primitive Nervous Systems, 1968, Cell Fine Structure, 1971; contbr. over 100 articles to sci. publs. Vice chmn., chmn. Planning and Zoning Commn., Killingworth, Conn., 1979—; active Killingworth Hist. Soc. Recipient Conn. Fedn. Planning and Zoning Agys. award, 1995, Citizen of Yr. award Killingworth Lions Club, 1993; fellow Trumbull Coll., Yale U.; grantee NSF, 1968-92, Dept. Army, 1986, NIH, 1987—. Mem. AAAS, Am.

Soc. Cell Biology, Soc. for Neurosci., N.Y. Acad. Scis., Appalachian Mountain Club (trails com., Warren Hart award, Pychowska award, White Mountain Four Thousand Footer Club), Fla. Trail Assn., Appalachian Trail Conf., Mt. Washington Obs., Wonalancet Out Door Club, Alpha Omega Alpha. Republican. Mem. United Ch. of Christ. Achievements include study of primitive nervous systems, identification of neurotoxin binding site on the acetylcholine receptor, identification of cellular receptor for rabies virus. Office: Yale U Sch Medicine Dept Cell Biol 333 Cedar St PO Box 208002 New Haven CT 06520-8002

LENZ, GUY, NATO official; b. Petange, Luxembourg, Jan. 28, 1946; m. Liliane Wetz, 1970; children: Isabelle, Véronique. Student, U. Liege, 196-66; grad., French Mil. Acad., 1969. Commd. 2d lt. Belgian Armed Forces, 1969, advanced through grades to col., 1998, early assignments from platoon leader to dep. comdr., 1969-90; head of group inspections, verifications and observations Belgian Armed Forces, Luxembourg City, 1990-91; mission comdr. Belgian Armed Forces, Turkey and Iraq, 1991-93; mil. advisor to Luxembourg delegation to NATO, 1993-95; perm. rep. to NATO Mil. Com. Brussels, 1995-98; Luxembourg mil. del. Western European Union, 1995-98; chief of staff Luxembourg Army, 1998—. Decorated Knight Order of Orange de Nassau, Knight Order of Civil and Mil. Merit of Adolphe de Nassau, Comdr. Order of the Couronne de Chêne. Office: NATO Hdqrs, Blvd Leopold III, 1110 Brussels Belgium*

LENZ, PAUL REUBEN, health care company executive, physician; b. Brno, Czech Republic, Oct. 15, 1934; came to U.S., 1962; s. Stanislav Shlomo and Mila (Wiener) L.; m. Gloria Jean Spitzer, Jan. 15, 1968; children: Deborah, Dawn, William. MD, Hebrew U., Jerusalem, Israel, 1958. Chief of nephrology Kaplan Hosp., Rehovoth, Israel, 1968-70; nephrologist, internist GHA, Washington, 1970-72, regional dir., 1972-75; med. dir. Rutgers Comty. Health Plan, N.J., 1975-90; pres. Garden State Med. Group, N.J., 1981-96; CEO Medicover, 1997—. Editor: Reengineering Health Care, 1997. Capt. res. Israeli Army, 1968-70. Mem. Am. Coll. Physician Execs. (disting. fellow). Avocations: skiing, bicycling, photography, arts and crafts. Office: Medicover, 10 Sapienzynska St, 00-215 Warsaw Poland

LENZI, GUIDO, diplomat; b. Bucharest, Romania, Jan. 10, 1941; s. Alfredo and Elvira (Baratelli) L.; m. Elisabetta Fortis, Apr. 14, 1969; children: Alessia, Jacopo. Grad. in law, U. Florence, 1963. Joined Italian Fgn. Svc., Rome, 1964; with Dept. Cultural Rels. of Fgn. Ministry, Italian Fgn. Ministry, 1966-68; 2nd sec. Italian Embassy, Italian Fgn. Svc., Algiers, 1968-70; with permanent mission of Italy Vienna, 2000—; Italian consul Lausanne, Switzerland, 1970-72; with Asia Dept. Fgn. Ministry, 1972-73, head of secretariat polit. dept., 1973-76; counsellor Italian Embassy, London, 1976-80; 1st counsellor Italian Embassy, Moscow, 1980-83; head NATO Desk Fgn. Ministry, 1983-87; diplomatic advisor Min. of Def., 1987-89; minister plenipotentiary Italian Mission to UN, N.Y.C., 1989-93; dep. chief Cabinet of Min. of Fgn. Affairs, 1993-94; diplomatic advisor Pres. of Senate, 1994-95; dir. Inst. Security Studies of Western European Union, 1995-99; mem. Inst. Strategic Studies, London. Roman Catholic. Avocations: travel, photography, theater, classical music. Office: Permanent Mission of Italy, Strohgasse 142, 1030 Vienna Austria

LENZI, MARK, Olympic athlete, springboard diver; b. Huntsville, Ala., July 4, 1968; s. William S. and Mary Ellen L. BS in Gen. Studies, Ind. U., 1990. Mem. U.S. National Diving Team, 1989-93, 95; Olympic springboard diver Barcelona, Spain, 1992, Atlanta, 1996; now diving coach U.S. Diving Team, Indpls.; nat. spokesperson Learn To Fly program Nat. Air Transp. Assn. Recipient Gold medal springboard diving Olympics, Barcelona, 1992, Bronze medal springboard diving Olympics, Atlanta, 1996, 17 internat. titles, 7 nat. titles, 2 World Cups. Achievements include first person to score over 100 points on a single dive; first American to complete a forward 4 1/2 somersault in national competition. Avocations: reading, drawing, hunting and fishing. Office: c/o US Diving Inc 201 S Capitol Ave Ste 430 Indianapolis IN 46225-1026*

LEO, MAGGIE PENINA, librarian; b. Ann Arbor, Mich., June 18, 1957; d. Thomas and Margaret (Roebuck) Black; John Francis Leo (div. 1994). B in Libr. Sci., U. Wales, 1989, dip. libr., 1998. Dep. libr. Kent Inst., England, 1990-93; dep. libr. Loughborough Coll. Art & Design/Loughboro Tech. Coll., England, 1993-94, libr., 1994-98. E-mail: m.leo@lboro.ac.uk. Office: Loughborough U, Pilkington Libr, LE113TU Loughborough England

LEOGRANDE, WILLIAM MARK, political science educator, writer; b. Utica, N.Y., July 1, 1949; s. John James and Patricia Ann (Ryan) LeoG; m. Martha J. Langelan. AB, Syracuse U., 1971, MA, 1973, PhD, 1976. Asst. prof. Hamilton Coll., Clinton, N.Y., 1976-78; dir. polit. sci. Am. U., Washington, 1980-82, asst. prof. polit. sci., 1978-83, assoc. prof., 1984-89, prof., 1989—, chair dept. govt., 1992-96, dean Sch. Pub. Affairs, 1997-99; mem. profl. staff U.S. Senate, 1982-83, cons., 1984-85. Author: Cuba's Policy in Africa, 1980; editor: (with Morris Blachman) Confronting Revolution: Security Through Diplomacy in Central America, 1986, (with Louis Goodman) Political Parties and Democracy in Central America, Our Own Backyard: The United States in Central America, 1998; dir. Latin Am. Rsch. Rev., 1982-86, World Policy Jour., 1983-93. Dir. svc. com. Unitarian-Universalist Ch., Boston, 1983-86; mem. staff Michael Dukakis Presdl. Campaign, 1988. Council Fgn. Relation Internat. Affairs fellow, 1982-83, Pew Faculty fellow, 1994-95. Mem. Coun. Fgn. Rels., Am. Polit. Sci. Assn., Latin Am. Studies Assn. (exec. council 1984-87). Democrat. Home: 7215 Chestnut St Bethesda MD 20815-4051 Office: Am U Sch Pub Affairs Ward Cir Washington DC 20016

LEON, ALBERTO EDEL, chemistry educator, researcher; b. Villa Maria, Cordoba, Argentina, Oct. 24, 1961; s. Edel Pedro and Nilda Emilia (Leuca) L.; m. Maria Susana Miozzo; children: Malena, Julian Alberto. BS, U. Nac. Cordoba, 1985; PhD, U. Nac. La Plata, 1995. Aux. de primera faculty U. Cordoba, 1985-89, jefe trabajos practicos, 1989, prof. adjunto, 1999—; rschr. Ceprocor, Cordoba, 1999. Contbr. articles to profl. jours. including Cereal Chemistry. With Argentinian Army, 1980-81. Grantee Assn. Esp. Coop. Internat., 1996, U. Nac. Cordoba, 1995, Min. Edn., 1998. Mem. Am. Assn. Cereal Chemists. Home: Chaneton 418, 5016 Cordoba Argentina Office: Fac Ciencias Agropecuarias, Valparaiso 5/N CC 509, 5000 Cordoba Argentina

LEON, NELSON, genetics educator, endocrinologist; b. Izmir, Turkey; s. Rafael and Donna L. Medicine Degree, Istanbul U., Turkey, 1948. Med. Diplomate. Asst. 2d Med. Clinic, Istanbul, Turkey, 1950-51, Hosp. Moncorvo Filho, Rio de Janeiro, 1952; first med. clinic faculty medicine São Paulo U., Brazil, 1953-63, mem. Lab. Genética, 1961-91, asst., 1989—; ret., 1991; rschr. Inst. Butantan, São Paulo, 1972—. Author: Miroirs Embués, 1977; contbr. articles to profl. jours. Res. officer Mil. Hqrs., 1949-50. Recipient Lab. Farm. V. Amato award São Paul Med. Assn., 1959, grantee in field. Mem. AAAS, Brazilian Soc. Endocrinology and Metabolism, Bioscis. Inst. (bd. dirs.), N.Y. Acad. Scis., Brazilian Press Assn. Avocations: engraving, drawing, collection of cigarette cards, linguistics, fgn. langs. Home: Apt 122, Rua da Consolaçao 2764, 01416 000 São Paulo Brazil Office: Inst Butantan, PO Box 65 Av Vital Brazil 1500, 05503900 São Paulo Brazil

LEON, ROLANDO LUIS, lawyer; b. Ponce, P.R., Oct. 18, 1952; s. Luis Manuel and Patricia (Cruz) L.; m. Jznet Williams, May 20, 1994; children: Brandon Alexandre, Bryan Christopher, Lauren Patricia. BA in Govt., U. Tex., Arlington, 1972; JD, Tex. Tech. U., 1975; MS in Pub. Adminstrn., Golden Gate U., 1979. Bar: Tex. 1976, U.S. Ct. Mil. Appeals 1977, U.S Dist. Ct. (we., so. dists) Tex. 1981, U.S. Ct. Appeals (5th cir.) 1985; cert. in personal injury and civil trial law Tex. Bd. Legal Specialization, 1985; cert. civil trial advocacy Nat. Bd. Trial Advocacy, 1990. Ptnr. Thornton, Summers, Biechlin, Dunham & Brown LC, Corpus Christi, Tex., 1980-99; mng. ptnr. Barker, Leon, Fancher & Matthys, LLP, Corpus Christi, 2000—. Editor: Tex. Tech. U. Law Rev., 1974-75. Lt. USN, 1976-80. Mem. ABA, Tex. Bar Assn., Assn. Trial Lawyers Am. Office: Barker Leon Fancher & Matthys LLP Ste 1200 555 N Carancahua St Corpus Christi TX 78478

LEON, VLADIMIR, physicist, researcher; b. Caracas, Venezuela, June 20, 1944; s. Carlos Augusto and Maria Guadalupe (Bencomo) L.; m. Blanca Rosa Marmol, July 20, 1963; children: Carlos Augusto, Camilo, Vladimir, Mariana. Degree in physics, U. Ctrl. Venezuela, Caracas, 1968; MPh, Yale U., 1972, PhD, 1975. Rschr. Nat. Inst. Sci. Rsch., Caracas, 1971-86; rschr. rsch. and devel. ctr. Venezuelan Oil Industry, PDVSA/INTEVEP, Caracas, 1986—; editor Acta Cientifica Venezolana, Caracas, 1974-77. Contbr. articles to profl. jours. Mem. AAAS, N.Y. Acad. Scis., Am. Vacuum Soc., Venezuelan Assn. for Advancement of Sci. Office: Intevep SA, PO Box 76343, Caracas 1070A, Venezuela

LEONARD, CRAIG B., technology company executive; b. Alton, Ill., Nov. 19, 1959; s. Thomas C. and Irma M. (Bartels) L.; m. Lynn D. Gauger, Aug. 8, 1981 (dec. 1996); m. Crystal D. Young, Feb. 28, 1998; children: Whitney Nichole, Nicholas Craig, Morgan Qiu Jing. BS in Indsl. Mgmt., Purdue U., 1981; postgrad., N.H. Coll., Northeastern U. Indsl. engr. GM, Framingham, Mass., 1981-82; mfg. program mgr. Lockheed Sanders, Nashua, N.H., 1982-85, program mgr., 1985-92; mgr. programs Steinbrecher, Burlington, Mass., 1992-95, dir. devel. programs, 1995-96; dir. Greater China Comverse Network Sys., Wakefield, Mass., 1996-98; dir. Greater China Converse Asia Pacific, Ltd., Hong Kong, China, 1998—. Republican. Lutheran. Home: #2143 Twr 6, 88 Tai Tam Reservoir Rdtes, Repulse Bay Hong Kong China Office: Comverse Asia Pacific Ltd 2701, 27/F Ctrl Plz 18 Harbour Rd, Wanchai Hong Kong China

LEONARD, GRAHAM DOUGLAS, priest; b. Greenwich, Eng., May 8, 1921; s. Douglas and Emily Mabel (Cheshire) L.; m. Vivien Priscilla Swann, Jan. 2, 1943; children: James Vivian, Mark Meredith. Student, Balliol Coll., Oxford, 1940-41; MA, Balliol Coll., 1947; student, Westcott House, 1946-47; DD, Episcopal Theol. Sem., 1974; D.Cn.L (hon.), Nashotah House, 1983; STD (hon.), Siena Coll., 1984; LLD (hon.), Simon Greenleaf Sch. Law, 1987; DD (hon.), Westminster Coll., Fulton, 1987; DLitt (hon.), Coun. for Nat. Acad. Awards, 1989. Ordained priest Roman Cath. Ch., 1994. Curate Ardleigh, 1947-52, vicar, 1952-55; dir. edn. Diocese of Albans, 1958-62; gen. sec. Nat. Soc. and Sec. Ch. of Eng. Schs. Coun., 1958-62; archdeacon of Hampstead, rector St. Andrew Undershaft, 1962-64; bishop Willesden, 1964-73; bishop of Truro, 1973-81, bishop of London, 1981-91, ret., 1991; mem. Privy Counsel, 1981; dean Her Majesty's Chapels Royal, 1981-91; prelate Most Excellent Order of Brit. Empire, 1981-91; chmn. Ch. of Eng. Bd. for Social Responsibility, 1976-83; chmn. Bd. Edn., 1983-89; mem. House of Lords, 1977-91; mem. Polytechs. and Colls. Funding Coun., 1989-93; John Findley Green Found. lectr. Westminster Coll., Mo., 1987; Hensley Henson lectr. U. Oxford, Eng., 1991-92. Capt. Royal Army, 1941-45, Freeman, London, 1970. Decorated knight comdr. Royal Victorian Order, 1991; recipient Prelate of Honour of His Holiness, 2000. Home: 25 Woodlands Rd, Witney, Oxford OX8 6DR, England

LEONARD, GUY MEYERS, JR., international holding company executive; b. Bluefield, W.Va., Sept. 22, 1926; s. Guy Meyers and Mabel (Bonham) L.; m. Pat Kirby, June 28, 1949; children: Calvin David, Dinah Lynn. AB, BS, Morris Harvey Coll., 1949; BDiv, Southwestern Bapt. Sem., 1952; STM, Harvard U., 1957. Commd. ensign USN, 1952, advanced through grades to capt., 1968, ret., 1972; dir. R&D Ency. Britannica Ednl. Corp., Chgo., 1972-76; pres. Communication Programming Svcs., inc., Charleston, S.C., 1976—; pres., CEO First Don Trading Co., 1982—; chmn., CEO Transocean Ltd., Internat. Holding Co., 1982-86; pres. GHL, Inc., Pacific Rim, Africa, 1991—; cons. drug control programs for schs., cons. Ency. Britannica, Home Mission Bd. and Brotherhood Commn. So. Bapt. Conv. Sec., U.S. Power Squadron, Charleston, 1969; chmn. Spl. Commn. on Drug Abuse for Armed Forces, 1970-72; active Conn. coun. Boy Scouts Am., 1959-62; chmn. stewardship com. Episc. Diocese of S.C., 1994-95; bd. dirs. CWA Found. Ch. Adv. Bd. CWA. Bd. dirs. CWA Found. Served with USN, 1943-72. Decorated Legion of Merit, Meritorious Svc. medal, Navy Commendation medal, Disting. Svc. medal; recipient Disting. Svc. award City of Louisville, 1963. Mem. Harvard Club S.C., C. of C., Trident Chamber (Charleston), Navy League U.S., Ret. Officers Assn., Kiwanis (spl. projects chmn. 1964-65). Achievements include the design and prodn. with Harvard U. and sta. WGBH, Boston, mediated coll. curriculum leading to BS degree for use by naval personnel.

LEONARD, JAMES PATRICK, writer, editor, communications consultant, instructor; b. Boston, July 6, 1968; s. James Joseph and Kathleen Helen Leonard; m. Elizabeth Anne Kearns, June 5, 1999. Student, Nat. U. Ireland, Galway, 1989; BA, Boston College, 1990, MA, 1998. Sr. editor/writer Cahners Publ., Reed-Elsevier, Inc., Newton, Mass., 1990-1995; freelance writer, editor, media consultant, project mgr., 1995—; tech. editor, mng. editor, dir. Aberdeen Group, Inc., Boston, 1998—; freelance instr., ESL tutor, 1995-98; adj. instr. and lectr. Boston College, 1996-98, Aquinas Coll., Newton, Mass., 1999, Suffolk U., Boston, 1999—; instr., publ. cons. Pine Manor Coll., Chestnut Hill, Mass., 1997—. Asst. editor: Eire-Ireland, 1996—; contbr: Encyclopedia of the Irish in America, 1999, secondary sch. textbooks, 1999, contbr. to profl. jours. Mem. MLA, Internat. Assoc. for Study of Anglo-Irish Lits. (annual conf. presenter, 1996, 97), Am. Conf. Irish Studies, Boston Coll. Alumni Assoc. Career Adv. Network (vol.). Roman Catholic. Avocations: internat. travel, hiking, music. Office: Aberdeen Group Inc One Boston Place 29th Fl Boston MA 02108

LEONARD, JEFFREY S., lawyer; b. Bklyn., Sept. 14, 1945; m. Maxine L. Bortnick, Dec. 28, 1967; children: Deborah, Jennifer. AB in History, U. Rochester, 1967; JD, U. Ariz., 1974. Bar: Ariz. 1974; U.S. Dist. Ct. Ariz. 1974, U.S. Ct. Appeals (9th cir.) 1974, U.S. Supreme Ct. 1985. Law clk. to judge U.S. Dist. Ct. Ariz., 1974-75. Mem. editl. bd. Ariz. Law Rev., 1973-74. Mem. Order of Coif. E-mail: jleonard@lck.net. Office: Leonard Collins & Kelly PC Two Renaissance Sq 40 N Central Ave Ste 2500 Phoenix AZ 85004-4405

LEONARD, JOSEPH HOWARD, association organization executive; b. Cambridge, Md., Oct. 20, 1952; s. Joseph Francis and Catherine (Hill) L.; m. Jacquelyn Lee McCall, June 7, 1975 (div. Dec. 1981); m. Margaret Ann Shenton, June 26, 1982; children: Stephanie Kristina, Jacquelyn Margaret. BA in Psychology, Salisbury State U., 1976; MA in Rehab. Counseling, Gallaudet U., 1979; postgrad., Washington Coll., Chestertown, Md., 1984, 88, U. Md., 1986-87, San Diego State U., 1996, Johns Hopkins U., 1998. Cert. profl. counselor, Md. Staff electrician John W. Tieder, Inc., Cambridge, Md., summers 1973-74; prodn. supr. W.H. Leonard & Sons, Inc., Seward, Md., summers 1968-70, 75; instr., program coord. Dorchester Devel. Unit, Inc., Cambridge, 1976-77; rehab. counselor Tex. Rehab. Commn., Austin, 1979; instr. Am. Sign Lang., developmental disabilities Chesapeake Coll., Wye Mills, Md., 1979—; case mgr., coord. spl. programs Dorchester County Health Dept., Cambridge, 1979-90; ind. interpreter Am. Sign Lang. Md., 1979—; exec. dir. Deaf Ind. Living Assn., Inc., Salisbury, Md., 1990—; adj.faculty, interpreter tng. program Catonsville (Md.) C.C., 1995—; v.p. bd. dirs. Deaf Ind. Living Assn., Inc., Md., 1984-90; trustee Md. Sch. for the Deaf, 1985—, pres., 1996—; mem. adv. bd. Devel. Disabilities program Chesapeake Coll., 1986-90; mem. Gov.'s Commn. on the Hearing Impaired, Md., 1984-90; surveyor Applied Rsch. and Evaluation U., U. Md., 1988-89; bd. dirs. Md. Assn. Cmty. Svcs.; mem. mental health adv. com. for deaf and hearing impaired, Md., 1990—. Contbr. articles to profl. jours. Asst. scoutmaster Boy Scouts Am., Cambridge, 1973-78; v.p. bd. dirs. Dorchester County Family YWCA, 1985; pres. bd. dirs. Dorchester Assn. for Devel. Disabled, 1979-88; bd. dirs. Eastern Shore Ctr. Ind. Living, 1998—; pres. Trappe Little League Baseball and Softball Assn., 2000—. With USN, 1970-73, with USCGR, 1975-86. Recipient Founder's award Gallaudet U., 1993, Disting. Svc. award Md. Assn. of the Deaf, 1995. Mem. Am. Deafness and Rehab. Assn., Am. Assn. Mental Retardation, Nat. Assn. Deaf, Registry of Interpreters for the Deaf (bd. dirs. Potomac chpt. 1996—), Md. Assn. for Retarded Citizens, Chi Sigma Iota, Psi Chi, Rho Sigma Chi. Roman Catholic. Avocations: woodcarving, backpacking, canoeing, sailing, scuba diving. Home: 29972 Holly Acres Rd Trappe MD 21673-1612 Office: Deaf Ind Living Assn Inc PO Box 4038 Salisbury MD 21803-4038

LEONARD, JUSTIN (JUSTIN CHARLES GARRET LEONARD), professional golfer; b. Dallas, June 15, 1972. Bus. degree, U. Tex., 1994. Profl. golfer PGA, 1994—; mem. nat. teams Walker Cup, 1993, Pres.'s Cup, 1996, 98, Ryder Cup, 1997, 99, Dunhill Cup, 1997, World Cup, 1997. Won U.S. Amateur Championship, 1992, NCAA Championship, 1994, Buick Open, 1996; only golfer in history to win 4 straight Southwest Conf. titles; Kemper Open, 1997; British Open, 1997; The Players Championship, 1998. Office: c/o PGA Box 109601 100 Avenue Of Champions Palm Bch Gdns FL 33418-3653

LEONARD, MARY EILEEN, medical technologist, educator; b. Charleston, S.c., Jan. 9, 1925; d. Edward Andrew and Honora Elizabeth (Price) L. Attended, Barry U., Miami, Fla., 2 yrs.; BS, Coll. of Charleston, 1945; postgrad. in Med. Tech., Med. U. S.C., 1947. Med. technologist Med. U. S.C., Charleston, 1946-79, Roper Hosp., Charleston, 1979—; chmn. adv. com. Trident Tech. Coll., Charleston, 1992—. Recipient awards and scholarships. Mem. West Ashley Civitan (bd. dirs. 1998—). Roman Catholic. Home: 1538 Dunnes Ln Charleston SC 29407-5013 Office: Roper Hosp 316 Calhoun St Charleston SC 29401-1125

LEONARD, RICHARD LAWRENCE (DICK LEONARD), writer, journalist; b. London, Dec. 12, 1930; s. Cyril and Kate (Whyte) L.; m. Irène Heidelberger, Mar. 29, 1963; children: Mark, Miriam. MA in Polit. behavior, U. Essex, U.K., 1969. Tchg. cert. U. London, 1953. Tchr. Hertfordshire County Coun., 1953-55; dep. gen. sec. Fabian Soc., London, 1955-60; journalist and broadcaster various pubs. and BBC, 1960-68; sr. rsch. fellow U. Essex, 1968-70; mem. Parliament U.K. House of Commons, 1970-74; asst. editor The Economist, London and Brussels, 1974-86; journalist, cons., prof. Ctr. for European Policy Studies, Brussels, 1980—, sr. advisor, 1994-99; vis. prof. Free U. Brussels, 1988-96; mem. Spkr.'s Conf. on Electoral Law, 1972-74; Brussels and EC correspondent Observer, 1989-96. Asst. editor The Economist, 1974-85; author: Guide to the General Election, 1964, Elections in Britain, 1968, The Backbencher and Parliament, 1972, Paying for Party Politics, 1975, BBC Guide to Parliament, 1979, The Socialist Agenda, 1981, World Atlas of Elections, 1986, Pocket Guide to the EEC, 1988, Elections in Britain Today, 1991, The Economist Guide to the European Union, 1992, 6th edit., 1998, Replacing the Lords, 1995, Eminent Europeans, 1996, Crosland and New Labour, 1998, The European Reader, 2000; contbg. editor: Europe mag., 1992—; contbr. articles to profl. jours. Labour Party. Avocations: walking, book reviewing, family pursuits. Home: 32 Rue des Bégonias, 1170 Brussels Belgium Office: Center European Policy Stud, 1 Place du Congrés, 1000 Brussels Belgium

LEONARD, THOMAS MICHAEL, university program director, educator; b. Elizabeth, N.J., Nov. 8, 1937; s. Edward Carroll and Amelia Teckla (Chap) L.; m. Yvonne Ann-Marie Clements, Aug. 13, 1960; children: Thomas Jr., Robert, Randall, Edward, David, Stacy. BS, Mt. St. Mary's Coll., Emmitsburg, Md., 1959; MA, Georgetown U., 1963; PhD, The Am. U., Washington, 1968. Sales exec. Weston Instruments, Newark, 1959-60; tchr. social studies Balt. County Bd. Edn., Towson, Md., 1960-62; instr. to assoc. prof. history St. Joseph Coll., Emmitsburg, 1962-73; assoc. prof. to prof., dir. internat. studies U. North Fla., Jacksonville, 1973—; bd. dirs. N.E. Fla. Export Trading Co.; vis. prof. Inst. Advanced Studies, Guadalajara, Mex., 1978, Mt. St. Mary's Coll., Emmitsburg, winter interterms, 1979-84, U. San Diego, Guadalajara, summer 1992; Fulbright lectr. Inst. Juan XXIII, Bahía Blanca, Argentina, 1984; adj. instr. U. Fla., 1980—; cons. U.S. Dept. Edn., 1996-97. Author: Day By Day: The Forties, 1977, United States and Central America, 1944-49: Perceptions of Political Dynamics, 1984, Central America and United States Policies: Guide to Issues and Sources, 1985, Castro and the Cuban Revolution, 1999, (with others) Day By Day: The Seventies, 1988, Central America and the United States: The Search for Stability, 1991, Panama and the United States: Guide to Issues and Sources, 1993, Guide to Archival Material in the United States on Central America, 1994, The United States and Latin America, 1850-1903: Establishing a Relationship, 1998; contbr. numerous chpts. to books, articles to profl. jours. Rsch. grantee numerous orgns. including Franklin D. Roosevelt Presdl. Libr., 1991, U. North Fla., 1993, Andrew W. Mellon Found., 1994; grantee U.S. Dept. Edn., 1998-2000. Avocations: travel, reading, sports. Home: 1104 Pond View Ct Jacksonville FL 32259-2950 Office: U North Fla St John's Bluff Rd Jacksonville FL 32224

LEONARD, VENELDA HALL, writer; b. Tifton, Ga., Jan. 7, 1914; d. Alonza Clayton and Bessie Lee (Shiver) Hall; m. James W. Leonard, June 14, 1931; children: James W. Leonard, Jr., Doris Delle Carr, Joan Le Mai Kyser. AA, Gulf Coast C.C., Panama City, Fla., 1964; BS, Fla. State U., 1965, MS, 1966. Instr. English, journalism Mosley H.S., Panama City, Fla., 1969-78; instr. remedial English Gulf Coast C.C., Panama City, 1979. Author: Sourwood, 1995. Mem. Phi Theta Kappa. Home: 2302 Country Club Dr Lynn Haven FL 32444-1994

LEON DUB, MARCELO, chemicals executive, entrepreneur; b. Quito, Ecuador, Mar. 30, 1946; arrived in Colombia, 1946; s. Jorge E. and Helen (Dub) Leon Fernandez-Salvador; m. Patricia Gomez, Dec. 19, 1974; children: Mateo, Nicolas, Manuela. Diploma in chem. engring., U. Nacional, Bogota, Colombia, 1968; MBA, Harvard U., Boston, 1972. Tecnico Dept. Nacional De Planeacion, Bogota, 1968-70; gen. mgr. Aknaz Colombiana, S.A., Bogota, 1972-74; co. gen. mgr. Quimica Comml. Andina, S.A., Bogota, 1974-96, Distribuidora Andina S.A., Bogota, 1976—; bd. dirs. Quala, S.A., Bogota, Sociedad Agricola De Dibulla, Ltd., Bogota, Minomet C.A. e.m.a., Valencia, Venezuela. Bd. dirs. Corporacion Sindrome de Down, Bogota, 1988-92, Fundacion Recreacion Y Cultura, Bogota, 1990-95, Coinvertir, Bogota, 1998—. Mem. Young Pres. Orgn. (membership chmn. 1988-89, chmn. 1992, area v.p. 1993-94), Group of Fifty (Washington), MIT and Harvard Club, Bogota Country Club (bd. dir.s 1990-91), Chicala. Office: Distribuidora Andina SA, Calle 12 A No. 68C-25, Bogota Colombia

LEONE, AURELIO ANTONIO, physician, researcher; b. Rome, July 21, 1942; s. Oreste and Matilde (Centaro) L.; m. Elena Archilli, Jan. 10, 1968; children: Oreste Maria, Aldo, Francesco Maria. Degree in medicine, U. Rome, 1966, cert. in cardiology, 1969; cert. in internal medicine, U. Pise, 1972; cert. in hygiene and preventive medicine, U. Genoa, 1977. Asst. chair pathol. anatomy U. Rome, 1966-69; rschr. in clin. physiology Med. Sch. U. Pise, 1969-73; asst. prof. cardiology City Hosp., La Spezia, 1973-87; chief divsn. medicine City Hosp., Pontremoli, 1987-99; chief med. divsn. City Hosp., Massa, Italy, 1999—. Editor: Hospital Care, 1981, The Elderly-Medical Aspects, 1985, Drug Addiction, 1984, Sudden Death, 1986. Fellow Royal Soc. Health (Eng.); mem. Am. Soc. Hypertension, N.Y. Acad. Scis., Geriatric Cardiology, Eques Sancti Gregorii Magni, Lions Club. Home fax: 39-0187-676346; Office fax 39-0585-493352.

LEONG, ADRIAN FRANCIS PENG KHEONG, colorectal surgeon, consultant, educator; b. Sydney, Australia, Oct. 25, 1959; arrived in Singapore, 1960; s. James Hin Seng and Kathleen Kim Tai (Foo) L.; m. Moira Chin Ai Goh, Oct. 9, 1988; children: Samantha, Evan, Alastair, Micaela. MB, BS, Nat. U. Singapore, 1983, MSurg, 1988. Registrar Birmingham (Eng.) Gen. Hosp., 1991, Basingstoke Gen. Hosp., U.K., 1991-92; hon. clin. asst. St. Mark's Hosp., U.K., 1992-93; med. officer Singapore Gen. Hosp., 1985-88, registrar, 1989-90, sr. registrar, cons. in colorectal surgery, 1992—; clin. instr. Nat. U. Singapore Med. Faculty, 1989—, assoc. prof., sr. cons., head colorectal surgery svc. Nat. U. Hosp., 1999—; clin. adminstrv. Basingstoke Large Bowel Cancer Screening Programme, 1991-92; instr. advanced trauma life support ACS, 1993—; lectr. advanced surgery Sch. Postgrad. Medicine, Singapore, 1993—; dir. Singapore Polyposis Registry, 1996—; mem. standing adv. com. Postgrad. Med. Inst., 1996—. Contbr. articles to med. jours., including Brit. Jour. Surgery, Diseases of Colon and Rectum, Internat. Jour. Colorectal Diseases. Vol. physician Singapore Cancer Soc., 1993—. Maj. Singapore Armed Forces, 1993—. Grantee Pub. Svc. Commn., Singapore, 1978; fellow Ministry Health, Singapore, 1991, travel fellow World Congresses Gastroenterology, 1994. Fellow Royal Coll. Surgeons (Edinburgh), Acad. Medicine (Singapore). Roman Catholic. Avocations: music, golf. Office: Nat Univ Hosp Dept Surgery, 5 Lower Kent Ridge Rd, Singapore 119074, Singapore

LEONG, ANTHONY SIEW-YIN, pathologist, researcher, educator; b. Singapore, Jan. 24, 1945; arrived in Australia, 1975; s. Hee-Siong and Jackie Jiak-Lung (Tan) L.; m. Wendy Guat-Wah Ooi, June 30, 1970; children: Franz Joel, Wen-Ming, Trishe Yu-Ming. MB BS, U. Malaya, 1969; MD, U. Adelaide, Australia, 1981. Postdoctoral fellow U. Washington, Seattle, 1971-73; lectr. pathology U. Malaya, 1973-75; cons. pathologist Queen Elizabeth Hosp., Adelaide, 1975-80, Sullivan, Nicolaidese & Ptnrs., Brisbane, Australia, 1980-81; dir. surg. pathology Inst. Med. and Vet. Sci., Adelaide, 1981-96; clin. prof. pathology U. Adelaide, 1981-96; prof. anatomical and cellular pathology Chinese U. Hong Kong, 1996-98; med. dir. Hunter Area

Pathology Svcs., Newcastle, Australia, 1999—; prof. anatomical pathology U. Newcastle, 1999—. Author: Essential Oncology of the Lymphocyte, 1987, Cancer Explained, 1991, Basic Histotechnology, 1996, Manual of Diagnostic Antibodies, 1998; editor: Applied Immunohistochemistry for the Surgical Pathologist, 1994, Principles and Practice of Medical Laboratory Science, Vol. 2, 1997, Hepatocellular Carcinoma-Contemporary Diagnosis and Management, 1999; mem. editl. bd. Pathology, Cell Vision, Chinese Jour. Pathology, others. Fellow China Med. Bd., 1971. Mem. Indonesian Soc. Clin. Oncology (internat. advisor 1996—), Internat. Acad. Pathology (pres. 1996-98). Avocations: jazz and classical music, tennis, golf. Office: Hunter Area Pathology Svcs, Locked Bag 1 Hunter Mail Ct, Newcastle NSW 2310, Australia

LEONG, CHOON-CHIANG, business educator; b. Singapore, Dec. 24, 1942; s. Koon-Koi Leong and Soong-Yong Low; m. See-Ching Chong, Nov. 3, 1970; children: Chee-Sian, Chee-Wei, Chee-Yee, Chee-Yeow. MS, U. Wash., 1967; BBA, U. Hawaii, 1972. Exec. dir. Regent Hotel, Kuala Lumpur, Malaysia, 1972-88; project dir. SMI Hotels & Resorts, Singapore, 1988-90; assoc. prof. Nanyang Technol. U. Sch. Accountancy and Bus., Singapore, 1991—; expert UN Indsl. Devel. Orgn., Vienna, Austria, 1994—; chmn. bd. Sedunia Travel Svcs., 1980-88; mem. coun. Pacific Asia Travel Assn., San Francisco, 1982-86. Assoc. editor 5 internat. travel and tourism jours. Chmn. culture and edn. Nanyang Hakka Clan Fedn., Singapore, 1991—; chmn. organizing com. World Hakka Clan Reunion, Singapoe, 1996. Fellow Brit. Inst. Mgmt.; mem. Harvard Bus. Sch. Alumni Club Malaysia (pres. 1986-87). Bhudist. Office: Nanyang Technol U Sch, Accountancy-Bus Nanyang Ave, Singapore 639798, Singapore

LEONG, HELEN VANESSA, systems programmer; b. Chgo., Dec. 14, 1949; d. Linton and Sue Lin (Hong) L.; m. Stephen Occhiuzzo, Aug. 28, 1993. BS in Liberal Arts/Math., Ill. Inst. Tech., 1971. Computer sys. analyst Ill. Bell Tel., Chgo., 1971-76; commd. ensign USN, 1977, advanced through grades to lt. comdr., 1992; pers. officer NAS Glenview, Ill., 1977-78; pub. affairs officer NAS Glenview, 1979-80; computer sys. analyst Space and Naval Warfare Sys. Command, Washington Navy Yard, Washington, 1980-83; program mgr. asst. Dept. of Navy (OP-942) Pentagon, Washington, 1983-86; joint action officer Office Joint Chiefs of Staff (J-6), Pentagon, Washington, 1986-87; exec. officer Naval Regional Data Automation Ctr., Newport, R.I., 1987-89; sys. programmer Stanford (Calif.) Health Svcs., 1989-97, PKS Info. Svcs., 1997—. mem. Svc. Acad. Adv. Bd. Frank Wolf, Tenth Dist., Va., 1985-87; chairperson energy com. Skyline Condo Assn., Falls Church, Va., 1986. Decorated Navy Achievement medal, 1982, Joint Commendation medal, 1987, Navy Commendation medal, 1989, Nat. Def. medal, 1992. Mem. NAFE, Nat. Sys. Programmers Assn. Avocations: downhill skiing, ice skating, roller blading, knitting, reading. Office: Stanford Health Svcs PKS Info Svcs 11707 Miracle Hills Dr Omaha NE 68154-4457

LEONG, JOHN CHI-YAN, orthopaedic surgeon, educator; b. Hong Kong, July 10, 1942; s. Kam-Leng and Doris Lai-Che (Cheung) L.; m. Annie On-Pok Hsu, Jan. 11, 1969; children—Jonathan Jit-Man, Julian Jit-Hung. B.S., M.B., U. Hong Kong, 1965. Intern, U. Hong Kong-Queen Mary Hosp., 1965-66, resident, 1966-70; asst. lectr. U. Hong Kong, 1966-67, lectr., 1967-75, sr. lectr., 1975-81, prof. orthopaedic surgery, 1981—, dean Faculty of Medicine, 1985-90; hon. registrar Nuffield Orthopaedic Ctr., Hong Kong, 1975-81; cons. orthopaedic surgeon United Christian Hosp., Hong Kong, 1967-80, Duchess of Kent Children's Hosp., Hong Kong, 1975—, Hong Kong Army, 1982-97; vis. prof. U. Calif.-San Francisco, 1979; C. Howard Hatcher vis. prof. Syanford U., 1987; speaker in field. Corr. editor Acad. Jour., 1983—; contbr. articles to profl. publs., chpts. to books. Fellow Brit. Orthopaedic Assn., Western Pacific Orthopaedic Assn. (pres. 1992-95); mem. Societe Internat. de Chirurgie Orthopedique et de Traumatologie, Scoliosis Research Soc. Clubs: Royal Hong Kong Golf, Royal Hong Kong Jockey, Hong Kong Country. Office: Univ Hong Kong,, Dept Orthopaedic Surgery,, Hong Kong Hong Kong

LEONG, SZE HIAN, finance company executive, financial planner; b. Singapore, Singapore, Nov. 23, 1953; s. Nee Kian Leong and Ah Foong Choy; m. Yong Wah Lou, Dec. 15, 1980; 1 child, Yui Ern. MSM, Am. Coll., 1985, MS in Fin. Svcs., 1989; MS in Fin. Planning, Coll. for Fin. Planning, 1992; OPM, Harvard U., 1996. CFP, ChFC, chartered mutual fund couns., affiliate Securities Inst. of Australia, fellow Australian Ins. Inst., master fellow Life Mgmt. Inst., chartered life underwriter, fellow Inst. Chartered Secretaries and Admins., mem. chartered Inst. of Transport. Mng. dir. Dicken Pte Ltd., Singapore, 1979—; chmn. Inst. Adminstrv. Mgmt., Singapore, 1983-85; lectr. Edith Cowan U., Western Australian Coll. of Advanced Educ., Singapore, 1987, Singapore Coll. Ins., 1988-92; adv. exec. MBA program, Golden Gate U., Singapore, 1987-88. Author: Life Insurance & Investment Products, 1988; contbr. articles to profl. jours. Trustee Singapore Profl. Ctr., 1985-96; chmn. Com. Continuing Edn., Singapore, 1987—; Jamaican consul to Republic of Singapore; hon. cons. devel. to Ctr. Clobal Nonviolence. Recipient Worldwide Subject award Australian Ins. Inst., 1983, Lord of Newsham, Yorkshire. Fellow Soc. Will Writers; mem. Am. Soc. Pension Actuaries, Chartered Ins. Inst. (chartered insurer), Chartered Inst. Mktg. (mem. coun. 1996—). Avocations: military history, non-traditional education, tennis. Home: 59 Walmer Dr, 555077 Singapore Singapore Office: Dicken Pte Ltd, 371 Alexandra Rd 10-10, 159963 Singapore Singapore

LEONHARDT, JÜRGEN HANS KARL, philologist; b. Lahr, Baden, Germany, Aug. 12, 1957; s. Fritz and Ilse (Rindt) L.; m. Ursula R. Knittel, Mar. 31, 1995. PhD, U. Munich, 1985, PhD habilitation, 1994. Cert. prof. classical philology. Asst. prof. U. Munich, 1986-92; prof. U. Rostock, Germany, 1994-97, U. Marburg, Germany, 1997—. Author: Dimensio Syllabarum, 1989, Phalloslied und Dithyrambos, 1991, Cicero's Kritik der Philosophenschulen, 1999; editor: Melanchthon und das Schulbuch des 16 Jahrhunderts, 1997. E-mail: leonharj@mailer.uni-marburg.de. Office: U Marburg, Wilhelm-Röpke St 6D, D-35032 Marburg Germany

LEONHARDT, RUDOLF WALTER, editor; b. Altenburg, Thuringia, Germany, Feb. 9, 1921; s. Rudolf Emil and Paula Luise L.; m. Ulrike Pauline Zoerb, June 18, 1949; children: Joachim Rudolf, Doerte Susanne, Timm Christopher. State exam., U. Bonn, 1950, PhD, 1950. Asst. lectr. U. Cambridge, 1948-50; programme asst. BBC, London, 1950-55; sub-editor DIE Zeit, Hamburg, 1955-57, cultural editor, 1957-73, dep. editor-in-chief, 1973-91. Author 20 books, translator of and contbr. to many publs., contbr. articles to profl. jours. Mem. PEN Club of Germany. Office: Die Zeit, 1 Speersort, 20095 Hamburg Germany

LEONI, FRANCESCO, political science educator; b. Tufo, Avellino, Italy, Aug. 8, 1932; s. Annibale and Egidia (Polcari) L. Degree, U. Rome, 1961. Assoc. prof. U. Cassino, Italy, prof.; charged prof. U. Teramo, Italy; chmn. Inst. S. Piov, Rome, 1961—; rector U. S. Piov, Rome, 1997. Author: Magazine of Political Studies, 1989. Decorated Chevalier, Pres., Italy; named commentator, Constantinian Order, Naples, Italy, S. Silvestro's Order, Vatican. Roman Catholic. Home: Piazza Navona 93, 00186 Rome Italy Office: Free Stuty Univ S Piov, Via delle Sette Chiese 139, 00147 Rome Italy

LEONIDOPOULOS, GEORGIOS, electrical, computer and electronics engineer, educator, researcher; b. Kalamata, Messinia, Greece, Apr. 18, 1958; s. Panayiotis and Helene (Pratte) L. Diploma in Elec. and Computer Engring., Patra (Greece) U., 1981; postgrad., Iowa State U., 1982, Wayne State U., 1983; MS in Electronic and Elec. Engring., Strathclyde U., Glasgow, Scotland, 1984, PhD, 1988. Cert. and Licentiate engr., Greece. Trainee elec. engr. Pub. Electricity Co. of Greece, Kalamata, 1979; tchg. asst. Strathclyde U., Glasgow, Scotland, 1984-87; Engring. educator secondary sch., Kalamata, Greece, 1991-94; prof. engring. Inst. Tech., Kalamata, Greece, 1994-97; prof. engring. elec. engring. dept. Inst. Tech., Lamia, Greece, 1997—; researcher in field; examiner for postgrad. scholarships, inst. adminstrv., various other work; expert evaluator European Commn.'s sci., rsch. and devel. programs. Contbr. rsch. articles to profl. jours. and publs, referee rsch. articles; patentee in field. With Greek Army 1989-90. Grantee Schilizzi Found., 1987, Empeirikeion Found., 1994. Mem. IEEE (Power Engring. Soc., Computer Soc.), N.Y. Acad. Scis., Internat. Assn. for Advancement of Modelling and Simulation Techniques in Enterprises. Christian Orthodox. Avocations: swimming, bicycling, athletics. Home and Office: Kilkis 11, GR-24100 Kalamata Messinia, Greece Office: Inst Tech, Dept Elec Engring, 35100 Lamia Greece

LEONIE, ANDREW DRAKE, III, judge, lawyer; b. Loma Linda, Calif., Dec. 13, 1952; s. Andrew and Norma Lou Leonie; m. Jamie Lorraine Chism, June 16, 1995; children: Andrew, Aaron, Rachel. BS, Western Ill. U., 1972; MA, U. Ill., 1974; JD, St. Mary's U., 1977; postgrad., Andrews U., 19985. Bar: Tex., U.S. Dist. Ct. (so. dist.) Tex., U.S. Dist. Ct. (no. dist.) Tex., U.S. Supreme Ct. Assoc. Smith, McIlheran, Lauderdale & Jones, Weslaco, Tex., 1977-79; ptnr. Jones, Marsh, Rodriguez, Welch & Leonie, McAllen, Tex., 1980-85; asst. atty. gen. Atty. Gen. Tex., Dallas, 1987-94; pvt. practice Dallas, 1994-95; judge, family law ct. master 1st Jud. Region Tex., Dallas, 1995—; mediator Christian Conciliation Svc., McAllen, Tex., 1984—; advisor Tex. Senate Com. on Family Law Issues, 1996; bd. advisors Iverson Inst. Ct. Reporting; mem. transition com. Tex. Atty. Gen. John Cornyn, 1998-99; mem. child support legis. com. Tex. Sunset Commn., 1999. Contbr. article to profl. jour., chpt. to book. Mem. exec. com. Rockwall (Tex.) Rep. Party, 1989-98; commr. planning and zoning commn. City of Rockwall, 1990-92; bd. dirs. Tex. Rural Legal Aid, 19805. Recipient Pro Bono award Rockwall County Bar Assn., 1995. Mem. Am. Jud. Soc., Tex. Bar Assn. (chair mcpl. judges sect.), Dallas Bar Assn. (mem. judiciary com., ethics com. 19945), Hidalgo County Bar Assn. (sec. bd. dirs. 1977-82), Christian Legal Soc., Rotary (pres. Rockwall (Tex., Rotarian of Yr. 1991, Breakfast Club). Republican. Episcopalian. Avocations: running, gardening, religious history. Home: 4617 Lakepointe Ave Rowlett TX 75088-6862 Office: First Jud Region Tex George Allen Civil Cts Bldg 600 Commerce St 7th Fl Dallas TX 75202-4616

LEONOVICH, ANATOLY SERGEEVICH, physicist, researcher; b. Irkutsk, Russia, July 18, 1957; s. Sergey Innokent'evich and Ekaterina Vasil'evna (Nikitina) L.; m. Ludmila Maksimenko, Aug. 8, 1980; children: Natal'ya, Vitaly. Diploma, Irkutsk State U., 1979; Cand. Sci., Inst. Solar-Terrestrial Physics, Irkutsk, 1986; DSc, Irkutsk, 2000. Jr. rsch. fellow Inst. Solar-Terrestrial Physics, Russian Acad. Scis., 1985-89; sr. rsch. worker Russian Acac. Scis., 1989—. Contbr. articles to sci. jours. Grantee Internat. Sci. Found., 1994, 95, Russian Found. for Fundamental Rsch., ž1995, 96, 97. Avocation: travel. Fax: (7-395-2) 46-25-57. E-mail: leon@iszf.irk.ru. Home: Lermontova 333V Apt 47, 664033 Irkutsk Russia Office: Inst Solar-Terrestrial Phys, Lermontova 126, 664033 Irkutsk Russia

LEON-PORTILLA, MIGUEL, historian, educator; b. Mexico City, Mex., Feb. 22, 1926; s. Miguel and Luisa (Portilla) L.; m. Ascension Hernandez Treviâo, May 2, 1965; 1 child, Marisa. BA, Loyola U., L.A., 1948, MA, 1951; PhD, Nat. U. Mex., 1956; PhD (hon.), So. Meth. U., 1980; DHL (hon.), U. Tel Aviv, 1987, So. Calif. U., 1989, Toulouse U., France, 1990, Colima U., San Andres, 1994, U. La Paz, Bolivia, 1994, Brown U., 1996. Sec. Interam. Indian Inst., Mexico City, 1955-58, asst. dir., 1958-60, dir., 1960-66; prof. faculty philosophy Nat. U. Mex., 1957—, dir. Inst. Hist. Rsch., 1966-76; researcher emeritus Inst. Hist. Rsch. Nat. Univ. Mexico, Mexico City; sec.-gen. Internat. Congress Americanists, Mexico City, 1962; disting. lectr. Am. Anthrop. Assn., 1974. Author: La Filosofia Nahuatl estudiada en sus fuentes, 8th edit., 1997, Vision de las Vencidos, 13th edit., 1992, Broken Spears-Aztec Account of Conquest of Mexico, 10th edit., 1994, Aztec Thought and Culture, 1964, 9th edit., 1986, Le Crepuscule des Azteques, 1965, Trece Poetas del Mundo Azteca, 1967, Pre-Columbian Literatures of Mexico, 1969, Testimonios Sudcalifornianos, 1970, Religion de los Nicaraos, 1972, Time and Reality in the Thought of the Maya, 1972, The Voyages of Francisco de Ortega to California, 1932-36, 1972, Historia Natural y Cronica de la Antiqua California, 1973, Il Rovescio della Conquista, Testimoniaze Asteche Maya e Inca, 1974, Anthropology and the Endangered Cultures, 1976, New Light on the Sources of Torquemada's Monarchia Indiana, 1979, Native Mesoamerican Spirituality, 1980, Toltecayotl, Aspectos de la Cultura Nahuatl, 1980, The Natural History of Baja California, 1980, The Testaments of Culhuacan, 1984, La Pensée Azteque, 1985, Time and Reality in the Thought of the Maya, 1988; editor: Monarquia Indiana (Father Juan de Torquenada), 1975, Hamnotzejim Jazon, 1976, Culturas en peligro, 1976, Indian Place Names in Baja California, 1977, Los manifiestos en nahuatl de Emilian Zapata, 1978, Native Mesoamerican Spirituality, Ancient Myths, Discourses, Stories, Doctrines, Hymns, Poems from the Aztec, Yucatec, Quichè-Maya, and Other Sacred Traditions, 1980, The Natural History of Baja California, 1980, Place Names in Nahuatl: Their Morphology, 1981. Bd. regents Nat. U. Mex., 1976-86; amb. of Mex. to UNESCO, 1987-92, permanent del., Paris, 1987-92. Decorated Order of Great Cross, Alfonso X the Wise (Spain); recipient Elias Sourasky prize in Humanistic Rsch. Mex. Sec. Edn., 1966; recipient Serra award of the Ams., 1978, Nat. prize in Social Scis. Govt. of Mex., 1981, Gamio award, 1983, Raphael Heliodoro Valle prize in History, 1984, Nat. U. Mex. prize, 1994; Guggenheim fellow, 1969; Fulbright fellow, 1975. Mem. NAS (fgn.), Mex. Acad. History (pres. 1996), Royal Spanish Acad. Lang., Smithsonian Coun., Am. Hist. Assn. (hon.), Socièté des Americanistes de PAris, Inst. Different Civilizations, Sociedad Mexicana de Antropologia, Am. Anthrop. Assn., El Colegio Nacional Mex., Royal Acad. Letters of Extremadura. Home: Coyoacán, 103 Alberto Zamora, 04000 Mexico City Mexico Office: Ciudad U, Inst de Investig Históricas, 04510 Mexico City Mexico*

LEONTIDOU, LILA (TRIANTAFYLLIA), humanities educator; b. Athens, Greece, Apr. 29, 1948; d. Jason and Afroditi (Poulakou) L. Diploma in Archt. Engring., Nat. Tech. U., Athens, 1971, cert. in urban and regional planning, 1972; MSc in Geography, London Sch. Econs./Polit. Sci., 1973; PhD, U. London, 1981. Lectr. Aristotle U., Thessaloniki, Greece, 1975-81; devel. planner, 1982-87; assoc. prof. Nat. Tech. U., Athens, 1986-93; sr. lectr. Kings Coll., London, 1993-97; prof. U. Aegean, Lesvos, 1997—; contractor, project coord. Western Athens plan Ministry Environment, Regional Planning and Pub. Works, 1983-86; coord. European Union Targeted Socio-Econ. Rsch. Project on Social Exclusion on European Union Borders, 1997-2000. Author: Cities of Silence: Working-class Space in Athens and Piraeus, 1909-1940, 1989, The Mediterranean City in Transition: Social Change and Urban Development, 1990; author, editor: Launching Greek Geography on the Eastern European Border, 2000, European Geographies, 2000, Mediterranean Tourism, 2000; contbr. articles to profl. jours., chpts. to textbooks. Expert on Mission UN E.C.E., Geneva, Switzerland, 1985-87; rep. Nat. Ctr. Social Rsch., Brussels, 1989-91; steering com. Univs. of Capital Cities Network, Amsterdam, The Netherlands, 1991-94; chair organizing com. Internat. Geo-Symposium of the Aegean, 1999; Greek rep. standing com. for the social scis. European Sci. Found., Strasbourg, France, 1994-99. Sr. fellow Johns Hopkins U., Balt., 1986; Empirikion Found. scholar, Athens, 1987. Mem. Inst. Brit. Geographers, London Sch. Econs. Soc., Assn. Greek Planners, Assn. Greek Architects, Forum Civil EUROMED, Hellenic Found. Urban History and Planning. Achievements include establishment of first geography degree course in Greece, serving as first chair of first degree-awarding department of geography in Greece. Avocations: swimming, music, reading, photography, travel. E-mail: leontidou@geo.aegean.gr. Home: 11-13 Ravine St, 115 21 Athens Greece

LEONTIEF, RUDOLF GEORIEVICH, economics educator; b. Khabarovsk, USSR, Dec. 2, 1940; s. Georgy Afansievich and Lidia Ivanovna L.; m. Inna Yurievna Klochko, Aug. 7, 1971; children: Andrey, Natalia. Splst. diplomate, Khabarovsk State U. Tech., USSR, 1966, Acad. Civil Aviation, St. Petersburg, USSR, 1976; Candidate of sci. (tech.), Far Ea. Br. Russian Acad. Sci., Vladivostock and Moscow, 1980, D in Econs., 1992; Sr. Researcher (hon.), Russian Acad. Scis., 1987, Prof. Econs. (hon.), 1994. Engr., mgr. diplomate. Chief passenger freightage handling dept. Far Ea. Mgmt. Civil Aviation, Khaborovsk, 1966-82, econ. dir., 1987-91; asst. prof. Khabarovsk State U. Tech., 1980-83, prof., 1987-94; asst. prof. Far Ea. U. Transp., 1983-87; prof. Khabarovsk State Acad. Econs. and Law, 1994-99; dean Far Ea. Faculty Moscow Consumers' Co-ops. U., 1994-95; adviser to gov. Khabarovsk Terr. Adminstrn., 1991-93; gen. dir. Joint Stock Co. Check Investment Fund "Ea. Net Work", Khabarovsk, 1993-94. Author: Formation of the United Regional Transport's System, 1986 (Moscow Nauka award 1987), Regional Corporation in the Sphere of Telecommunication: Organizing Aspect, 1999 (Vladivostock Dalnauka award 1999); contbr. articles to profl. jours. Pres. Khabarovsk Terr. Football Union, 1991-93; cand. in dep. State Duma Fedn. Meeting Russian Fedn., Khabarovsk, 1995. Mem. Russian Acad. Scis. (acad. sec., head lab. Communter Ctr. far ea. br. 1983-87, chief researcher Commuter Ctr. far ea. br. 1995-99), Russian Geographical Soc., Russian Acad. Transport (academician), N.Y. Acad. Scis., Far Ea. Acad. Social adn Econ. Scis. (academician, 1st v.p. 1998-99), Khabarovsk Terr. Club Economists (pres. 1991-98, prof. econs. 1994). Avocations: singing tenor, football, fencing, tennis, refereeing. Home: 6-61 Dzerjinskogo str, 680000 Khabarovsk Russia Office: 65 Kim Yu Chen St, 680063 Khabarovsk Russia

LEÓN VILLEGAS, BRAULIO RAFAEL, bishop; b. Leon, Guanajuato, Mex., Mar. 26, 1943; s. Juan Rafael León Chávez and Manuela Villegas Macías. Grad. in Theology, Gregorian U., Rome, 1970, grad. in Canon Law, 1972. Spiritual advisor Diocesan Sem., León, 1973-83; chancellor Diocesis of León, 1983-90; bishop Diocesis of La Paz, 1990-99, Ciudad Guzman, Jal. Roman Catholic. Home: Portal Ramon Corona # 26, Centro Apdo Postal # 86, 49000 Guzman Jal, Mexico

LEON YEBRA, CARLOS, physics educator, researcher; b. Madrid, Spain, June 5, 1968; s. Luis Leon and Pilar Yebra. Degree in Physics, Universidad Complutense Madrid, 1991, PhD in Physics, 1997. Tng. cons. Telefonica, Madrid, 1990—; asst. tchr. Universidad Complutense Madrid, Madrid, 1992—. Contbr. articles to profl. jours. Mem. Spanish Royal Soc. Physics. Office: Universidad Complutense, Facultad De Ciencias Fisica, 28040 Madrid Spain

LEOPOLD-WILDBURGER, ULRIKE, mathematician educator; b. Graz, Austria, June 23, 1949; s. Karl and Margarete Wildburger; children: Astrid, Armin. MS, U. Graz, 1972, PhD, 1975, Habil., 1982. From lectr. to asst. U. Graz, Austria, 1973-89, prof. math. and stats., 1989—; head dept. U. Graz, 1996—; guest lectr. U. Klagenfurt, Austria, 1986; guest prof. U. Zürich, Switzerland, 1988-89, U. Minn., Mpls., 1991, U. St. Gallen, Switzerland, 1998—. Mem. Austrian Math. Soc., Austrian Statis. Soc., Austrian O.R. Soc. (pres. 1993-97), German O.R. Soc., Fond fur Iordering Wisscuschaftliche Forschung (coun. mem.). Avocations: swimming competitions, skiing racing. Home: Viktor-Kaplang 30, A8045 Graz Austria Office: Graz U Dept Stats and Math, Univ Strasse 151E, A8010 Graz Austria

LEO WEE-HIN TAN, university administrator, biology researcher, science educator; b. Singapore, Oct. 19, 1944; s. Kok Soon and Maisie (Chan) T.; m. C.C. Wong, Nov. 14, 1976; children: Lionel J.J., Lester T.J. BSc with honors, U. Singapore, 1969, PhD, 1974. Lectr. U. Singapore, 1974-81; sr. lectr. Nat. U. of Singapore, 1982-86; dir. Singapore Sci. Ctr., 1982-91; assoc. prof. Nanyang Tech. U., Singapore, 1991, prof. biology, 1992—; dean Sch. of Sci. Nat. Inst. Edn., Singapore, 1991-2000, dir., 1994—; chmn. Nat. Youth Achievement Award coun., 1995—. Chmn. Alexandra Hosp. Medifund Com., Singapore, 1993—; mem. Citizens Consulatative Com., Clementi Constituency, Singapore, 1981—; chmn. Nat. Parks Bd., 1998—. Decorated Gold Pub. Adminstrn. medal Govt. of Singapore, 1988, Pub. Svc. medal, 1995, Nat. Green Leaf award, 1997, Nat. Sci. and Tech. medal, 1999. Fellow Singapore Inst. Biology; mem. Fedn. Asian Sci. Acads. and Socs. (treas. 1994-98, pres. 1999—), Singapore Nat. Acad. Sci. (pres. 1992—), Singapore Inst. Biology (pres. 1991-94), Rotary Internat. (Jurong Town Club, pres. 1987-88). Roman Catholic. Office: Nat Inst Edn NTU, 1 Nanyang Walk, Singapore Singapore

LE PAILLEUR, CLAUDE, physician; b. Paris, Oct. 22, 1938; s. Maurice Le Pailleur and Josephine Marceau; m. Eugenie Buisson, June 4, 1983. MD, U. Paris, 1970. Physician, cons. Necker Hosp., Paris, 1971—. Contbr. articles to profl. jours. Avocations: perfumed orchid flowers, chess, fishing. Home: 28 rue Vaneau, F-75007 Paris France Office: Hospital Necker, 149 rue de Sevres, 75743 Paris Cedex 15, France

LE PAIR, CORNELIS, research organization executive, retired; b. Leiden, The Netherlands, Mar. 2, 1936; s. Cornelis and Louisa (Wijnnobel) Le P.; m. Hendrika Gijsbertha Schroten, Dec. 17, 1962 (div. 1989); children: Djamila, Jean-Philippe; m. Lioubov Bytchikhina, Feb. 9, 1993; 1 child, Elena. BSc in Physics and Math., Leiden U., 1957, MSc in Exptl. Physics, 1960, PhD in Low Temperature Physics, 1965; Dr. in Tech. Scis. honoris causa, Tech. U., Delft, 2000. Rsch. assoc. Leiden U., 1961-65; asst. prof. Am. U., Beirut, 1965-68; dep. dir. Found. for Fundamental Rsch. on Matter, Utrecht, The Netherlands, 1968-82; rsch. assoc. NSF, Washington, 1971; CEO Tech. Found. Stichting Voor Technische W., Utrecht, 1981-99, ret.; advisor Ministry of Sci. and Edn., Bangkok, 1985-86, Swiss govt., 1995,98; mem. Def. Rsch. Coun., Delft, The Netherlands, 1996-99, Gen. Energy Coun., The Hague, The Netherlands, 1991-99; chmn. monitoring team Joint European Semi-conductor Silicium Initiative, European Union, 1990-96; inspector Eureka Project Micro-electronics Devel. European Applications, 1995-99; mem. Def. Rsch. Coun., 1996-99; chmn. ICT task force, 2000—. Editor: Physics in the Netherlands, 2 vols., 1982; contbr. numerous articles to profl. jours., 97 newspaper cols. Mem. S&T com. VVD (Liberal polit. party), 1991-99; mem. Pac. Socialist Party, 1961-65. Recipient Highest Merit award Royal Netherlands Acad., 1988; decorated Ridder Order of Netherlands Lion, 1995. Mem. Netherlands Soc. Coastal Navitation, Internat. Soc. Scietometrics, EPS, Hollandsche Maatschappij Wetenschappen (dir. 1990), Engring. Acad. Amsterdam, Gesellschaft Wissens Forschung Germany (hon.). Mem. Liberal Party. Avocation: ocean sailing. Home: Smient 27, 3435 VJ Nieuwegein The Netherlands

LEPANE, VIIA, chemistry educator; b. Tallinn, Estonia, May 25, 1962; d. Juho and Malle (Virkoja) L. Diploma in analytical chemistry, Tartu U., Estonia, 1985; MS, Tallinn Tech. U., Estonia, 1992. Sr. lab. asst. Tallinn Tech. U., Estonia, 1985-87, tchg. asst., 1991-96, lectr., 1996—; vis. scientist U. Gothenburg, Sweden, 1990, 94-96. Contbr. articles to profl. jours. Leader Tallinn Tech. U., 1992—. Grantee Johnson Found., Sweden, 1990, Nordic Coun. of Ministers, 1994, Knut and Alice Wallenberg Found., Sweden, 1995. Mem. Estonian Chem. Soc., N.Y. Acad. Scis. Avocations: swimming, cycling, nature. Office: Tallinn Tech Univ, Ehitajate tee 5, 19086 Tallinn Estonia

LE PAPE-GARDEUX, CLAUDE MARCEL, communications executive; b. Nanterre, France, May 28, 1963; s. Bernard Henri Le Pape and Michele Marie-Louise (Berthet) Gardeux; m. Anne Suzanne Collinot, June 24, 1988; children: Camille Helene, Simon Pierre, Alexandre Henri. M in Computer Sci., U. Paris XI, 1984, PhD in Computer Sci., 1988; degree in mgmt., Coll. des Ingenieurs, Paris, 1988; postgrad., Stanford U., 1988-90. Software developer Ilog SA, Gentilly, France, 1991-95; rsch. scientist Bouygues SA, St.-Quentin-en-Yvelines, France, 1995-98; dir. R&D Bouygues Telecom, Velizy, France, 1998—. Contbr. numerous articles to profl. jours., chpts. to books. Mem. Am. Assn. Artificial Intelligence, Inst. for Ops. Rsch. and Mgmt. Sci., Soc. Math. France. Avocations: opera, classical music, books, poetry. Home: 14 rue de Turin, F-75008 Paris France Office: Bouygues Telecom, 51 ave de l'Europe, F-78944 Velizy France

LEPECKI, WITOLD PIOTR STEFAN, nuclear engineer; b. Warsaw, Poland, May 2, 1936; arrived in Brazil, 1939; s. Zbigniew and Zofia Jadwiga (Kłaczyńska) L.; m. Maria Lucia Torres, Apr. 1963 (div. 1970); 1 child, Andre; m. Regina Maria Moraes, Nov. 30, 1975; children: Cristina, Leopoldo. Degree in civil engring., Univ Fed. Minas Gerais, B. Horizonte, Brazil, 1958, MSc in Nuclear Engring., 1960; D of Reactor Physics, U. Paris, 1965. Head reactor engring. divsn., head thorium group Radioactive Rsch. Inst., B. Horizonte, 1966-70; head reactors and planning divsn. Nat. Nuclear Energy Commn., Rio de Janeiro, 1970-72; exec. asst., supt. gen. to tech. devel. dir. Nuclebras, Rio de Janeiro, 1972-76; dir. NUSTEP, Essen, Germany, 1977-79; supt. Nuclen, Rio de Janeiro, 1980-91; spl. assessor Eletronuclear (formerly Nuclen), Rio de Janeiro, 1991—; mem. internat. nuclear safety adv. group to dir. gen. Internat. Atomic Energy Agy, Vienna, 1985-91. Co-editor: Introductory Course to Nuclear Generation, 1968. Counselor energy coun. Comml. Assn. Rio de Janeiro. Recipient Nat. Order of Merit Pres. of France, 1974, Nat. Order of Sci. Merit award Pres. of Brazil, 1998. Fellow Am. Nuclear Soc. (chmn. Latin Am. sect. 1983-84); mem. Nat. Acad. Engring (Brazil), Internat. Nuclear Energy Acad. Avocation: astronomy, history of nuclear energy. Office: Eletronuclear, rua Candelária 65, 20090021 Rio de Janeiro Brazil

LE PECQ, JEAN-BERNARD RENE, biotechnologist, business executive; b. Mondoubleau, France, June 15, 1939; s. Eugene and Renee (Fenu) Le P.; m. Elisabeth Helene Jouvet, Feb. 25, 1965; 1 child, Nathalie. Pharmacist, U.

Paris, 1961, PhD, 1965. Postdoctoral fellow Calif. Inst. Tech., 1965-66, Stanford (Calif.) U., 1966-68; maitre de recherche CNRS, France, 1968-72; prof. U. Paris, 1972-89, chmn. dept. biochemistry, 1979-82; sr. v.p. rsch. Rhone Poulenc Rorer, Vitry, France, 1990-98; founder AP Cells Inc., 1998—; vis. scientist U. Tokyo, 1988; dir. Lab. Molecular Pharmacology, Cancer Inst., Villejuif, France, 1972-89. Author: Chimiotherapie Anticancereuse, 1978; contbr. more than 150 articles to sci. jours.; patentee antitumor drugs. Lt., Health Svc., French Navy, 1963-64. Recipient prix Lacassagne, Ligue Nat. contre le Cancer, 1990, prix Griffuel, Assn. Recherche Cancer, 1985, prix H. Fouley, Nat. Acad. Medicine, 1979. Mem. French Acad. Sci. (corr. mem.), Comite Application Academie des Scis., Acad. Nat. Pharm. Avocations: tennis, collecting Asian art. Home: 37 Sq St Charles, 75012 Paris France also: 675 Olive St Menlo Park CA 94025-5744 Office: AP Cells Inc 1014 Hamilton Ct Menlo Park CA 94025-1423

LE PEN, JEAN-MARIE, politician; b. La Trinité-sur-Mer, Morbihan, France, June 20, 1928; s. Jean-Marie Le Pen and Anne-Marie Hervé; m. Pierrette Lalanne, 1960 (div.); 3 children. Grad., Coll. des Jésuites St.-François-Xavier, U. de Paris. Editor polit. sect. Caravelle, 1955; nat. del. for Union de défense de la jeunesse française; dep. 1st sector, then ind. dep. La Seine; mem. Groupe d'union et de fraternité at Nat. Assembly, 1958-62; gen. sec. Front nat. combattant, 1956, Tixier Vignacour Com., 1964-65; dir. Soc. d'études et de rels. publigues, 1963—; pres. Front nat., 1972—; mem. Nat. Assembly, 1986-88; pres. groupe des droites européennes au Parlament Européen, 1984—; mem. European parliament, Bussels, Belgium; presdl. candidate, 1988. Author: Les Français d'abord, 1984, La France est de retour, 1985. Sub-lt. 1st fgn. bn. paratroopers, Indochina, 1954. Decorated Croix de la Valeur militaire (France). Home: 8 parc de Montretout, F-92210 Saint-Cloud France Office: 6 rue de Beaune, 75007 Paris France Home: 8 Parc de Montretout, 92210 Saint-Cloud France*

LE PENSEC, LOUIS, French politician; b. Mellac, France, Jan. 8, 1937; s. Jean and Marie-Anne (Hervé) De P., July 27, 1963; m. Colette Le Guilcher, July 27, 1963; 1 child, Olivier. Ed., Faculty Letters-Econ. Scis., Rennes, France, Faculty Letters Paris. Pers. officer Nat. Soc. for Study and Constrn. Airplane Engines, 1963-66, Soc. Indsl. Vehicles and Mech. Equipment, 1966-69; instr. pers. mgmt., legal scis. teaching and rsch. unit U. Rennes, 1970-73; mayor City of Mellac, 1971—; dep. from Finistère, Nat. Assembly, Paris, 1973-81, 83-88; councillor for Finistère, 1976-81, min. for sea,, 1981-83, min. overease depts. and territories,, 1988—, min. agr. and fisheries, until 1998; mem. Senate, Paris, France, 1998—; mem. steering com. Parti Socialiste, 1977, mem. Exec. Bur., 1979; v.p. Coun. European Communes, 1980; lst v.p. for Europe, Coun. European Communities, 1983-88; head ASEAN Mission for External Trade. Avocations: reading, tennis, the sea. Office: Ministry of Agr & Fisheries, 78 Rue de Varenne, 75700 Paris France*

LEPIE, ALBERT HELMUT, chemist, researcher; b. Malapane, Silesia, Germany, Aug. 6, 1923; came to U.S., 1963; s. Albert and Emilia (Zachlod) L.; m. Claire Kortz, 1956 (div. 1964); 1 child, Karin. Degree in chem. engring., Staatliche Ing. Schule, Essen, Germany, 1953; diploma in chemistry, Tech. Hochschule, Aachen, Germany, 1959; D in Natural Scis., Tech. Hochschule, Munich, Germany, 1961. Chem. engr. Pahl'sche Gummi & Asbest, Düsseldorf, 1953-59; chemist Deutsche Versuchanstalt für Luftfahrt, Munich, 1961-63; rsch. chemist U.S. Naval Propellant Plant, Indian Head, Md., 1963-64; rsch. chemist Naval Weapons Ctr., China Lake, Calif., 1964-95, ret., 1995; chmn. mech. properties panel Joint Army, Navy, NASA, and Air Force Interagy. Rocket Propulsion, 1977-84. Inventor air curtain incinerator for energetic materials and fiber peal force measurement device, flywheel high rate tensile tester for viscoelastic materials. Recipient Joint Army, Navy, NASA, and Air Force award, 1984, William B. McLean award Naval Weapons Ctr., 1988. Mem. Am. Chem. Soc. (sec. China Lake chpt. 1968, 69), China Lake Astron. Soc., Sigma Xi. Roman Catholic. Avocations: astronomy, computer programming, motorcycling. Home: 121 S Desert Candles St Ridgecrest CA 93555-4218

LEPIK, ÜLO, applied mechanical engineering educator; b. Tartu, Estonia, July 11, 1921; s. Rudolf and Elfriede (Pajo) L.; m. Aino Punga, Sept. 8, 1951; children: Rein, Toivo, Piia. Candidate, Tartu U., 1952, PhD in Structural Mechanics, 1958. Asst. Tartu U., 1947-54, docent, 1954-60, prof. theoretical mechanics, 1960-92, prof. emeritus, 1992—. Author: (textbooks in Estonian) Theoretical Mechanics, 1971, (with J. Engelbrecht) The Chaos Book, 1999; (monograph) Optimal design of nonelastic structures under dynamic loading, (in Russian) 1982; contbr. numerous articles to profl. jours. Recipient Award Order of the Arms of Estonia, 1998. Mem. Estonian Acad. Scis., Polish Soc. Theoretical and Applied Mechanics (hon.), German Soc. Applied Math. and Mechanics, German Soc. Structural and Multidisciplinary Optimization. Avocations: bridge, skiing tours, swimming. E0mail: ylepik@ut.ee. Home: Lunin Str 3, 50406 Tartu Estonia Office: Tartu U Inst Appl Math, Vanemuise 46, 51014 Tartu Estonia

LEPKE, CHARMA DAVIES, musician, educator; b. Delavan, Wis., Oct. 1, 1919; d. Ithel B. and Florence Mary (Jones) Davies; m. John Richard Lepke, Dec. 22, 1949 (div. July 1974). BA, Wellesley Coll., 1941, MA, 1942; MMusic, Am. Conservatory of Music, Chgo., 1946. Piano tchr., organist Fairfax Hall Jr. Coll., Waynesboro, Va., 1942-44; piano tchr. U. Nebr., Lincoln, 1946-50; ch. organist Trinity Methodist, Unitarian, Lincoln, 1946-50; missionary Am. Bd. Congl. Ch., Durban, Johannesburg, South Africa, 1950-56; ch. organist, choir dir. Congl. United Ch. of Christ, Oconomowoc/Sheboygan, Wis., 1957-70; organist Coloma, Mich., 1970-73; ch. organist Brick Bapt. Ch., Walworth, Wis., 1974, United Meth. Ch., Delavan, 1974-77, Congl. United Ch. of Christ, Delavan, 1977—. Music editor revised Zulu hymnal Amagama Okuhlabelela, South Africa, 1951-56; composer preludes for organ, piano pieces, song and anthem. Recipient 1st prize for song Wis. Fedn. Music Clubs, 1960, others. Mem. Am. Guild of Organists, Music Tchrs. Nat. Assn., Wis. Alliance for Composers, Delavan Musical Arts Soc. (founder, pres.), Phi Beta Kappa. Congregationalist. Home: 223 W Geneva St Delavan WI 53115-1626

LEPLOW, BERND, psychologist, researcher; b. Rostock, Germany, Sept. 9, 1953; s. Hans-Joachim Leplow and Ruth (Kegel) Maerz. Diploma in psychology, U. Hamburg, Germany, 1981, PhD, 1988; habilitation, U. Kiel, Germany, 1994. Asst. in med. psychology Univ. Hosp. Hamburg, Germany, 1981-86; asst. in psychology U. Kiel, Germany, 1987-94, asst. prof. psychology, 1995-97; substitute prof. psychology U. Halle, Germany, 1997-99; prof. U. Halle, 1999—. Civil svc., hosp., Schortens/Wilhelmshaven, Germany, 1974-75. Mem. N.Y. Acad. Scis., German Soc. Psychology, German Soc. Behavioral Medicine, German Soc. Psychophysiology and its Applications. Avocations: sailing, literature, politics, arts. E-mail: b.leplow@psych.uni-halle.de. Home: An der Pekükirche 5, 06120 Halle/S Germany Office: U Halle Dept Psychology, Brandbugweg 23, 06120 Halle/S Germany

LEPLYANIN, GENNADI VIKTOROVITCH, chemistry technology researcher; b. Alma-Ata, Kazakhstan, Russia, Aug. 25, 1938; s. Viktor Ivanovitch and Vera Andreevna (Markina) L.; m. Ludmila Ivanovna Maksimova, May 23, 1980; 1 child, Elena Gennadyevna. Engr., Inst. Chem. Tech., Leningrad, Russia, 1960; D in Chemistry, Russia, 1979, prof., 1984. Cert. engr. Laborant Inst. Organic Chemistry, Kazan, Russia, 1960-65; engr. Inst. Chem. Sci., Alma-Ata, Kazakhstan, 1965-69; docent Inst. Industry, Pavlodar, Kazakhstan, 1969-71; chief of lab. Inst. Organic Chemistry, Ufa, Russia, 1971-94; vice-dir. Inst. Organic Chemistry, Ufa, 1986-91; chief of lab. Russian Forest Chem. Rsch. Inst., Moscow, 1994—. Contbr. articles to profl. jours.; inventors in field. Mem. N.Y. Acad. Sci. Office: Russian Forestry Chem Rsch Inst, Zavodskaya St 10, 141250 Ivanteevka City Moscow, Russia

LEPONIEMI, ARVI KALEVI, economist, educator; b. Jamijarvi, Finland, July 18, 1926; s. Oskari and Aleksandra (Myllykangas) L.; m. Hilkka Tuulikki Marikainen, Dec. 26, 1956; 2 children. MA, U. Turku, 1949; D of Social Scis., U. Helsinki, 1966. Scientist, sci. dir. Kyosti Haataja Found., Helsinki, 1961-68; prof., docent Helsinki Sch. Econs. and Bus. Adminstrn., 1966-91, pres., 1981-90, reg., 1991; assoc. prof. U. Helsinki, 1968-73. Editor-in-chief Finnish Econ. Jour., 1990-94; editor books, monographs, and articles in profl. jours. Recipient Fulbright Rsch. award U. Pa., 1962-63. Mem. Finnish Acad. Sci. and Letters (awards 1977, 80), Finnish Soc. Econ. Rsch., Finnish Econ. Assn. (pres. 1974). Avocations: history, literature. Home: Niittyranta 21, 00930 Helsinki Finland

LEPPÄNIEMI, ARI KALEVI, surgeon, educator; b. Kokkola, Ostrobotnia, Finland, May 30, 1954; s. Olavi Kalervo and Anna Margareta (Niemi) L.; m. Eija Helinä Riikonen, Aug. 12, 1987; children: Ville Oskari, Kaapo Santeri. Med. Lic., U. Helsinki, Finland, 1980, specialist in surgery, 1987, specialist in gastroenterology, 1992, docent in surgery, 1995. Resident in surgery 2d dept. surgery Helsinki U. Hosp., 1981, 85-87, sr. resident in gastroenterology, 1990-91; asst. surgeon Kuusankoski Dist. Hosp., Finland, 1982-83; attending surgeon, asst. prof. 2d dept. surgery Helsinki U. Hosp., 1991-94, 96-98, chief emergency surgery and surg. ICU, 1999—; sr. house officer Abmadu Bello U., Zaria, Nigeria, 1983-84; field surgeon Internat. Com. Red Cross, Thailand, 1985, Kenya, 1986, Pakistan, 1992; chief surgeon UN Devel. Program, Tuvalu, Ctrl. Pacific, 1988-89; vis. asst. prof. Uniformed Svcs. U., Bethesda, Md., 1994-95. Author: (books) Trauma to the Parenchymatous Abdominal Organs, 1991, Abdominal Trauma in War and Disaster, 1995; contbr. about 120 articles to profl. jours. Recipient Red Cross award Finnish Red Cross, Helsinki, 1987, Commendable Svc. medal, Univormed Svcs. U., Bethesda, Md., 1996. Mem. Am. Assn. for Surgery of Trauma, Internat. Surgical Soc., Ambroise Pare Internat. Mil. Surg. Forum (asst. sec. 1995-97, sec. 1997-99, pres.-elect 1999—). Avocations: jazz saxophone, tennis, karate. Home: B 45, Munkkiniemen puistotie 18, 00330 Helsinki Finland Office: Helsinki U Hosp Surg 2, Haartmaninkatu 4, 00290 Helsinki Finland

LEPPIK, ILO E., neurologist, educator; b. Tartu, Estonia, Aug. 18, 1942; s. Elmar Emil and Lilly (Hanson) L.; m. Margaret Ann White, June 18, 1967; children: Peter, David, Karina. BS, Haverford (Pa.) Coll., 1964; MD, U. Pa., 1968. Diplomate Am. Bd. Neurology and Psychiatry, Am. Bd. Clin. Neurophysiology. Rsch. fellow Montreal (Que.) Neurol. Inst., McGill U., 1974-76; asst. prof. neurology U. Minn., Mpls., 1976-80, assoc. prof. neurology, 1980-87, prof. neurology, 1987-89, clin. prof. neurology, 1989—, clin. assoc. prof. pharmacy, 1986-89, clin. prof. pharmacy, 1987—; dir. rsch. MINCEP Epilepsy Care, Mpls., 1990—. Author: Contemporary Diagnosis and Management of the Patient with Epilepsy, 1993, 4th edit., 1998; editor books in field; contbr. articles to profl. jours.; founding editor Jour. Epilepsy Rsch., 1987—. Bd. dirs. Am. Bd. Clin. Neurophysiology, 1992-94. Maj. USAF, 1969-71. Fellow Am. Acad. Neurology; mem. Am. Epilepsy Soc. (pres. 1992-94, treas. 1983-86), Ctrl. Soc. Neurol. Rsch. (pres. 1991-92), Assn. Neurologists of Minn. (pres. 1983-89), Epilepsy Found. Am. (chmn., profl. adv. bd. 1989-91, bd. dirs. 1982-92). Republican. Unitarian. Achievements include devel. of new drugs for treatment of epilepsy. Avocation: cross country skiing. Office: MINCEP Epilepsy Care 5775 Wayzata Blvd Minneapolis MN 55416-1222

LEPSCHY, ANNA LAURA, Italian language educator; b. Turin, Italy, Nov. 30, 1933; d. Arnaldo Dante and Gemma Celestina (Segre) Momigliano; m. Giulio Ciro Lepschy, Dec. 20, 1962. BA, Oxford U., 1955, BLitt, 1961. Jr. fellow in Italian U. Bristol, UK, 1957-59; from asst. lectr. to lectr. U. Reading, UK, 1959-67; from lectr. to prof. U. Coll., London, 1967—; chair com. for equal opportunities U. Coll. London, 1990-93, chair Soc. Italian Studies, 1989-95. Author: (with G.C. Lepschy) The Italian Language Today, 1992; author: Tintoretto Observed, 1983, Narrativa e Teatro fra due secoli, 1984, Varietà linguistiche e pluralità di codici nel Rinascimento, 1996, Davanti a Tintoretto.Una storia del gusto attraverso i secoli, 1998, (with G.C. Lepschy) L'Amanuense analfabeta e atri saggi, 1999. Mem. Soc. for Italian Studies, Assn. for Study of Modern Italy, Soc. for Pirandello Studies, Comparative Lit. Assn., Assn. Internat. Study Italian Lang. and Lit. Avocation: swimming. Office: Univ Coll London, Gower St, London WC1 E6BT, England

LEPUCKI, RICHARD JOHN, engineer; b. Aug. 28, 1949. B in Engring., Stevens Inst. Tech., 1971; post grad., U. Akron, 1975-76. Prin. engr. Babcock and Wilcox, R & D, Alliance, Ohio, 1971-97; project mgr. Seifert Tech., Massillon, Ohio, 1997—. Home: 2326 Rutgers St NW North Canton OH 44720-5757

LE QUEMENT, PATRICK GILLES-MARIE, automotive executive; b. Marseilles, France, Feb. 4, 1945; s. Jean Paul and Gladys Edna (Read) le Q.; m. Monique Monfort, Apr. 27, 1968; children: Laurent, Maxime, Guillaume. BA with honors, Birmingham (Eng.) Inst. Art, 1966; degree in bus. adminstrn., Danbury (Eng.) Coll., 1971; doctoral degree, U. Ctrl. Eng., Birmingham, 1996. Designer Simca Chrysler, Paris, 1966-67, Ford Motor Co., Dunton, Eng., 1968; design exec. Ford Trucks, Dunton, 1976-79; chief designer Ford AG, Cologne, Germany, 1981-85; dir. design Volkswagen AG, Düsseldorf, Germany, 1985-87; v.p. design Renault SA, Paris, 1987-94, sr. v.p. quality and corp. design, 1995-99; sr. v.p. corp. design, 1999—. Decorated Nat. Order of Merit, Legion of Honor (France); recipient Grand prix de la Creation Indsl., Govt. of France, 1992. Fellow Chartered Soc. Designers; mem. Automobile Club France. Avocations: architecture, fine arts, literature, travel, fine cars. Office: Renault Techno Ctr Svc 1600, 1 Avenue du Golf, F78288 Guyancourt France

LE QUÉRÉ, JEAN FRANÇOIS MARIE, scientific instrumentation researcher; b. Pabu, France, Apr. 7, 1933; s. Yves Marie and Yvonne Marie Rose (Ollivier) Le Q.; m. Jacqueline Marie Le Colas, Mar. 26, 1964; children: Anne Marie, Isabelle Marie, Jean-Yves Marie, Blandine Marie. Upper tech. diploma, Nat. Conservatory Arts-Trade, Paris, 1965, engr. physicist grad., 1968; DEng, U. Pierre and Marie Curie, Paris, 1983. Electrician Regie Renault, Paris, 1950-61; lab. technician, Paris, 1961-65, lab. upper rsch. technician,, 1965-68; engr. physicist U. Paris 6, 1968-72, engr. rschr., 1972-96; mem. faculty U. Paris 7, 1972-94, engr. rschr., 1972—. Contbr. articles to profl. jours. With French Army, 1953. Mem. Assn. Tchg. (pres. 1996). Home: 22 rue Pierre Brossolette, 93160 Noisy le Grand France

LEQUESNE, MICHEL GABRIEL, educator, rheumatologist; b. Neuilly, Seine, France, Dec. 20, 1924; s. Yvonne Lequesne; m. Jacqueline Delafontaine, June 8, 1948 (dec. Apr. 1964); children: (twins) Pascal and Berengere, Constance. m. Michele Natasha Le Cerf, Oct. 19, 1991. French Baccalaureat, Lycee Buffon, Paris, 1941. Resident Paris Hosps., 1950-54; asst. Clinique of Prof. de Seze, Paris, 1955-69; chief rheumatology dept. Hosp. Leopold Bellan, Paris, 1969-94, cons. physician, 1995—; assoc. prof. Coll. Med. Paris Hosps., 1979—. Author: Diseases of the Hip in Adult Life, 1967, Methodology for the Clinician, 1989; editor: Evaluation of the Locomotor Apparatus Imaging, 1994, Hip Diseases Imaging, 1999; contbr. over 420 articles to profl. jours. Capt. French Army, 1944-45. Avocations: modern painting, sailing, submarine diving. Home and Office: 33 Rue Guilleminot, 75014 Paris France

LEQUEU, BRUNO, biologist, consultant; b. Chalon, France, Nov. 6, 1957; s. Claude and Monique (Deschamps) L.; m. Catherine Langlois, May 2, 1987; children: Jean Baptiste, Hélène, Pierre. Cert. in immunology, U. Lyon, France, 1982; cert. in parasitiology, U. Lyon, 1984; cert. in haematology, U. Marseille, 1983; PharmD, Dijon, France, 1983; cert. in bacteriology and virology, U. Besancon, 1984. With hosp. industry, 1981-84, with pharm. industry, 1984-85; project chief Founier Labs., Dijon, France, 1984-85; dir. clin. labs., cons. Point Med., Dijon, 1985—. Author: Vitamin A, 1990, The Vitamins, 1992, From Nutrients to Drugs, 1992. Mem. French Soc. Biology, French Soc. Vitamins. Avocations: sculpture, radioastronomy, entomology. Office: Lab Clos, Rond Point Nation, 21000 Dijon France

LERAAEN, ALLEN KEITH, financial executive; b. Mason City, Iowa, Dec. 4, 1951; s. Myron O. and Clarice A. (Handeland) L.; m. Mary Elena Partheymuller, Apr. 14, 1978. BBA in Data Processing and Acctg., No. Ariz. U., 1975. CFA. Data processing supr. Stephenson & Co., Denver, 1978-81, contr., 1981-85, arbitrageur, trader, 1985-88, v.p., 1985-90, exec. v.p., portfolio mgr., 1990—; v.p., sec. bd. dirs. Circle Corp., Denver, 1985—; v.p. StarTek, Inc., Denver, 1997—. Mem. Assn. Investment Mgmt. and Rsch., Denver Soc. Security Analysts. Avocation: flying. Home: 5692 S Robb St Littleton CO 80127-1942 Office: 100 Garfield St Fl 4 Denver CO 80206-5597

LERMAN, ZVI, economist, researcher; b. Harbin, China, Dec. 17, 1941; arrived in Israel, 1953; s. Joseph and Bronislava (Kleismer) L.; m. Edna Ben-Jacob, Apr. 15, 1962; children: Hagar, Hagit, Nati, Omer. BSc, Hebrew U., Jerusalem, 1963, MBA, 1975, PhD, 1984. Chief editor Israel Program for Sci. Translations, Jerusalem, 1960-67; asst. mng. dir. Keter Pub. House, Jerusalem, 1967-75; rschr. Jerusalem Inst. of Mgmt., 1977-83; lectr. The Hebrew U., Jerusalem, 1986-91, sr. lectr., 1992—; cons. World Bank, Washington, 1988—, FAO, Rome, 1995—, Govt. of Ukraine, 1995-97; vis. prof. U. Minn., St. Paul, 1989-90, U. Toronto, Ont., Can., 1984-86. Author: Agricultural Reform in Russia: A View from the Farm Level, 1996, Land Reform in Ukraine: The First Five Years, 1997, Land Reform and Farm Restructuring in Moldova, 1998, Private Agriculture in Armenia, 2000; contbr. articles to profl. jours. Fellow Woodrow Wilson Ctr., 1999—. Mem. Internat. Assn. Agrl. Econs., European Assn. Agrl. Econs., Am. Assn. Agrl. Econs. Jewish. Avocations: gardening, travel. E-mail: lerman@agri.huji.ac.il. Fax: 972-2-5701686. Home: 57 Ha'alon Str, 90836 Har-Adar Israel Office: Hebrew U Faculty Agr, Dept Agrl Econs and Mgmt, 76100 Rehovot Israel

LERNER, ALEXANDER ROBERT, association executive; b. Chicago, Ill., June 26, 1946; s. Peter Lerner and Lillian Orlinsky Joseph; m. Marianne Ryan, Apr. 21, 1979; 1 child, Lindsey Anne. BS, No. Ill. U., 1970. Adminstrv. asst. Gov. of Ill., 1970-72; adminstrv. asst. speaker Ill. Ho. of Reps., Springfield, 1973-74; asst. dir. pub. affairs div. AMA, Chgo., 1974-75; dir. Ill. State Med. Soc., Chgo., 1975-78; pres. Govtl. Affairs, Inc., Chgo., 1978-81; chief exec. officer Ill. State Med. Soc. and Ins. Svcs. Inc., Ill. State Med. Inter Ins. Exch., Chgo., 1981—. Chmn. Ill. Sports Facilities Authority, 1992—. Mem. Am. Assn. Med. Soc. Execs., Am. Soc. Assn. Execs., Chgo. Soc. Assn. Execs., Assn. Forum Chgo., Union League Club, Chgo. Yacht Club, Michigan Shores Club, Execs. Club of Chgo., Conway Farms Golf Club. Avocations: nautical antiques, presidential history, travel, golf. Office: Ill State Med Soc 20 N Michigan Ave Chicago IL 60602-4811

LERNER, ALFRED, real estate and financial executive; b. N.Y.C., May 8, 1933; s. Abraham and Clara (Abrahmson) L.; m. Norma Wokloff, Aug. 7, 1955; children: Nancy Faith, Randolph David. BA, Columbia U., 1965. Chmn. bd., chief exec. officer Multi-Amp Corp., Dallas, 1970-80, Realty Refund Trust, Cleve., 1971-90; pres., chief exec. officer Refund Advisers, Inc., 1971—, Town & Country Mgmt. Corp., 1979-93; chmn., dir. Equitable Bancorp., Balt., 1981-90; chmn., bd. dirs. Prog. Corp., Cleve., 1988-93; chmn., CEO, pres. MBNA Corp., Newark, 1991—; chmn., CEO Town & Country Trust, 1993—; owner, chair Cleveland Browns, 1998-; chmn., bd. dirs. MNC Corp., Balt., 1991-93. Trustee Columbia U., Case Western Res. U.; pres. Cleve. Clinic. 1st lt. USMCR, 1955-57. Mem. Young Pres. Orgn., Beechmont Club (Cleve.), Harmonie Club (N.Y.C.). Jewish. Home: 19000 S Park Blvd Cleveland OH 44122-1853 Office: MBNA Corporation 1100 N King St Wilmington DE 19884-0001

LERNER, HERBERT J., retired accountant; b. Newark, Aug. 19, 1938; s. Morris David Lerner and Evelyn L. (Shapiro) Kaplan; m. Dianne Joan Prag, Aug. 23, 1959; children—Joy Ellen, Mark Allen. B.S., Rutgers U., 1959; LL.B., Georgetown U., 1963. Bar: D.C. 1964; C.P.A., D.C. With Ernst & Young, Washington, 1963-96; ptnr. Ernst & Young, 1970-83, 83-89; vice chmn. tax Ernst & Asbest Young, Washington, 1990—; nat. dir. tax policy and standards Ernst & Young; ret.; mem. IRS Commrs. Adv. Group, 1982-83, 96-98; treas., trustee Am. Tax Policy Inst., 1990-97. Author: (with others) Federal Income Taxation of Corporations Filing Consolidated Returns, 4 vols., 1975, with ann. supplement thru 1997; contbr., editor pvt. letter rulings column Jour. Taxation. Mem. AICPA (exec. com. tax divsn. 1979-82, 85, 89, past chmn., bd. dirs., co-chmn. nat. conf. lawyers and CPAs), ABA, George Town Club.

LERNER, JENNIFER SUSAN, psychology educator; b. New Rochelle, N.Y., Apr. 16, 1968; d. Edward and Joan Lerner; m. Brian Paul Gill, June 27, 1998. BA in Psychology, U. Mich., 1990; MA in Psychology, U. Calif., Berkeley, 1994, PhD in Psychology, 1998. Rsch. program coord. U. Mich., Ann Arbor, 1990-92; postdoctoral fellow UCLA, 1998-99; asst. prof. Carnegie Mellon U., Pitts., 1999—. Contbr. articles to profl. jours. Predoctoral fellow NSF, 1992-95; postdoctoral fellow Nat. Inst. Mental Health, 1998. Mem. APA (Conf. Travel award Sci. Directorate 1994), Am. Psychol. Soc., Soc. for Personality and Social Psychology (Conf. Travel award 1994, 95), Assn. for Consumer Rsch., Soc. for Judgement and Decision Making, Mortar Bd. Avocations: dogs, walking, reading, dancing. E-mail: jlerner@andrew.cmu.edu. Office: Dept Social & Decision Scis Carnegie Mellon Univ Pittsburgh PA 15213

LERNER, RICHARD, hematologist; b. Lodź, Poland, Oct. 18, 1947; s. Aleksander and Irena (Iberal) L.; m. Nina G. Unterberger, Apr. 1, 1972; children: Martin, Mikael. MD, U. Lund, Sweden, 1974; PhD, Karolinska Inst., Stockholm, 1993. Med. specialities internal medicine and hematology. Intern Serafimer Lasarett Hosp., Stockholm, 1974-75; resident dept. medicine Stockholm Söder Hosp., 1976-80, cons. in medicine and haematology, 1982-96; asst. prof. dept. hematology Huddinge (Sweden) Hosp., 1996—. Mem. Swedish Soc. Hematology (bd. dirs. 1993-96), Swedish Med. Soc., European Haematology Assn. Avocation: books. Office: Dept Hematology, Huddinge Univ Hosp, 14186 Stockholm Sweden

LERNER-LAM, EVA I-HWA, transportation executive; b. N.Y.C., Dec. 27, 1954; d. Sau-Wing and Jean (Lu) Lam; m. Arthur Lawrence Lerner-Lam, Sept. 4, 1977; children: Timothy Chi-Wen, Matthew Ta-Wen, Katherine I-Wen. AB, Princeton U., 1976; MS, MIT, 1978. Asst. planner County of San Diego, San Diego, 1977-78; dir. transp. planning group PRC Toups/Voorhies, La Jolla, Calif., 1978-79; assoc. planner Orange County Transit Dist., Garden Grove, Calif., 1979-80; assoc. planner San Diego Met. Transit Devel. Bd., 1980, sr. planner, 1981, dir. planning and ops., 1982-84; gen. mgr. Regency Motors, Montclair, N.J., 1984-85; asst. v.p., dir. planning and adminstrn. The Dah Chong Hong Trading Corp., N.Y.C., 1985-88; prin., cons. The Palisades Cons. Group Inc., Tenafly, N.J., 1988—; transport sys. advisor Economist Confs. Group, 1994—; co-founder ChinaTransport.net, 2000—; mem. coun. on Fgn. Rels., 1996—, bd. adv. ENO Transp. Found., 1997—; chair Transit Cooperative Rsch. Program Transit-IDEA, Transp. Rsch. Bd., 1998—; bd. dirs. Transit Stds. Consortium, Inc. Founder, coord. Asian-Am. Admissions Vols. Group, Princeton, N.J., 1985—; chmn. bd. dirs. Si-Yo Music Soc. Found., N.Y.C., 1988—; bd. dirs. Princeton U., 1984-88, founder, bus. mgr. and condr. Princeton U. Jazz Ensemble, 1973-76; mem. Coun. on Fgn. REls., 1996—; bd. advisors Eno Transp. Found., 1997—. Outstanding student fellow State Farm Cos., Princeton, 1974; recipient Outstanding Achievement award Tribute to Women in Industry, San Diego, 1983; named Auto Dealer of Yr., N.J. Living Mag., 1985. Mem. NSF (transp. rsch. bd.), ASCE (vice chmn. planning com. urban transp. divsn. 1987-91, vice chairperson exec. com. 1991-92, chmn. exec. com. 1992-93, Frank M. Masters Transp. Engring. award 1998), Am. Planning Assn., Inst. Transp. Engrs. (best paper award 61st ann. meeting 1991, Innovative Intermodal Solutions for Urban Transp. award 1993, Ivor S. Wisepart Engr. award 1995), IVHS Am. (founding mem.), Asian Alumni of Princeton (mem. exec. com. Beijing 2000—, Outstanding Achievement award 1988), Campus Club (bd. dirs. 1984-94), San Diego Princeton Club (pres. 1983-84). Avocations: piano, swimming, running, bicycling, hiking.

LERNØ, FINN J(EFF), lawyer; b. Copenhagen, Apr. 27, 1953; s. Poul and Djuta B. (Nielsen) L.; m. Susanne Raackmann L., Aug. 23, 1980; children: Frederik, Kathrine. Student Criminology, Internat. Law, Calif. State U., Northridge, 1976; LLM, U. Copenhagen, 1979. Assoc. Poul Schmith Law Firm, Copenhagen, 1979-85; sr. assoc. The Law Offices of Erik Münter, Copenhagen, 1985-88, The Law Offices of Bornstein & Grønborg, Copenhagen, 1988-90; ptnr. The Law Offices of Koch-Nielsen & Grønborg, Copenhagen, 1990-96, The Law Offices of Plesner & Grønborg, Copenhagen, 1997—. Lead author: The Commentaries to the Stamp Duty Act, 1985, supplement 88, 2d edit., 1994. Mem. Internat. Bar Assn. (editor newsletter of com. S 1997—, publs. officer com. S 1999—). Avocations: modern art, tennis, soccer.Fax: 4533120014. E-mail: fl@pglaw.dk. Office: Plesner & Grønborg, 34 Esplanaden, 1263 Copenhagen K, Denmark

LE ROUX, GERARD EDOUARD, financial consultant, author; b. Paris, June 23, 1938; s. Edouard Paul and Therese Cyprienne (Fabre) Le R.; m. Mariane Bayle, May 7, 1965 (div. 1980); children: Desiree, Ariane; m. Maya Obradovic, June 18, 1991; children: Helene Theresa, Clara. Student, Johns Hopkins U., Balt., 1956-59. Analyst Lehman Bros., N.Y.C., 1964-66; mgr.

for Europe First Boston Corp., Zürich, Switzerland, 1966-69; dir. Bank Guyerzeller, Zurich, 1969-71; ptnr. Bank Franck & Cie, Geneva, 1971-80; fin. cons. Geneva, 1980, fin. mgr., 1981—. Author: Fumée Verte, 1982, The Treasure of the Condors, 1983, Dollarium Tremens, 1984, Fumée Rouge, 1988, Jaune, 1991, The Three Alchemists, 1996, Cocoa (mus. comedy); columnist Geneve Home Info. newspaper. With French Army, 1960-62. Decorated Maltese Cross Order of Merit, Rome, 1978, Cross of Merit of Savoia, Order of St. Maurice and Lazzare, Rome, 1982, Order of Humanitarian Exploits, Paris, 1978. Mem. Golf Club of Geneva, Club Nautique Geneva, Mktg. Comm. Exec. Internat. Club, Eagle Ski Club Gstaad, Maxim Bus. Club, Swiss Acad. Gourmets, Internat. Acad. Gastronomy, Piping Rock Club (Locust Valley, L.I., N.Y.), Knight of Malta. Roman Catholic. Avocations: writing, tennis, skindiving. Home: 10 Place de la Taconnerie, CH-1204 Geneva Switzerland Office: 7 rue Versonnex, CH-1207 Geneva Switzerland

LE ROUX, JOEL, electrical engineering educator; b. Doue la Fontaine, France, Sept. 8, 1949; s. Alain and Francine (Cillart) Le R.; m. Line Fioramonti, July 12, 1982; children: Roland, Melanie. Engr., Nat. Sch. Telecommunications, 1972; D, Nice U., 1985. Asst. prof., researcher Nat. Sch. Telecommunications, Paris, 1972-82; rsch. engr. Idate Inst., Montpellier, France, 1982-84, CNET Microelectronics Ctr., Grenoble, France, 1984-87; prof. U. Nice (France), 1988—. Contbr. papers to profl. pubs. Mem. IEEE, EURASIP. Avocation: mountain hiking. E-mail: leroux@essi.fr. Office: U Nice I3S Les Algorithmes, Euclide 2000 Rte Lucioles, 06560 Sophia Antipolis France

LE ROUX, PIERRE FRANCOIS, telecommunications industry executive; b. Bordeaux, France, Dec. 12, 1942; s. Francois Pierre and Marguerite Alice (Thierry) Le R.; m. Catherine Anne Matet, Dec. 4, 1975; children: Guillaume, Jean, Nicolas. Student, Ecole Poly., 1962-64; ed., ENSAE, 1965-67, IEP, Paris, 1965-67. Mgr. INSEE, Paris, 1967-71; prof. ENSAE, Paris, 1971-73; exec. Office of Budget, Paris, 1973-78; advisor Minister of Fin. and Economy, Paris, 1978-81, deputy dir., 1981-83; CFO Cit-Alcatel, Paris, 1983-86; CFO Alcatel, Paris, 1987-96, exec. v.p., 1989-97, human resources dir., 1998—. Decorated chevalier Legion of Honor. Home: 3 rue Pasteur, 78110 Le Vésinet France Office: Alcatel, 54 rue La Boetie, 75008 Paris France

LEROY, MISS JOY, model, designer; b. Riverdale, Ill., Sept. 8, 1927; d. Gerald and Dorothea (Wingebach) Reasor. BS, Purdue U., 1949. Model, sales rep. Jacques, Lafayette, Ind., 1950; book dept. sales rep. Loebs, Lafayette, 1951-52; window trimmer Marshall Field's and Co., Evanston, Ill., 1952-53; sales and display rep. Emerald Ho., Evanston, 1954-55; model, narrator, designer J.L. Hudson Co., GM Corp., Coca Cola Co., Hoover Vacuum Co., Jam Handy Orgn., Am. Motors Corp., Speedway Petroleum Corp., Ford Motor Co. Auto, Tractor & Implement Divsn.-The Sykes Co., Detroit, 1956-61; tour guide, model The Christian Sci. Publ. Soc., spl. events coord. Prudential Ins. Co., model Copley 7, Boston, 1962-70. Author: Puzzits, 1986—. Founding angel Asolo Theatre, Sarasota, 1960s; mem. Ft. Lauderdale Internat. Film Festival, 1990, Mus. of Art, 1978, Fla. Conservation Assn., Rep. Senatorial Com. Inner Cir., 1990, (disting. 20th Century Republican Leader, 1998, Millennium Medal of Freedom, 1999, Millennium medal of honor 2000, Hallmark medal of honor, Presdl. Seal of Honor), Rep. Presdl. Roundtable, 2000, Congl. Com., 1990, Nat. Trust for Hist. Preservation, 1986, Fla. Trust for Hist. Preservation, 1987, Nat. Park Trust; one of founding friends 1000 Friends of Fla., 1991; mem. Rep. Presdl. Task Force, 1993; founding mem. Rep. Campaign Coun., 1994, Grand Club Rep. Party Fla., 1996. Recipient Internat. Order of Merit, 2000, Presdl. Seal of Honor, 2000, Order of Internat. Ambs., 2000, Rep. Millennium medal of Honor, 2000. Fellow Order of Internat. Fellowship (Woman of Yr. 1996-98); mem. Nat. Parks and Conservation Assn., Ellis Island Found. (charter), Duke of Gloucester Soc., Am. Queen Inaugural Soc., Stratford Shakespearean Festival of Can., USS Constn. Mus. (charter mem. 1993), Libr. of Congress (assoc.), Purdue U. Alumni Assn. (pres.'s coun.), Wilderness Soc., Magic Kingdom Entertainment Club, Maupintour Travelers Club, Heritage Found. (Internat. Woman of Yr. 1996-97), Soc. Honorary Mariners, Heralds of Nature Soc., Ducks Unltd., Paddlewheel Steamboatin' Soc. Am., Cunard World Club, Skald Club, Seabourn Club, The Crystal Soc., The Cousteau Soc., Nat. Corvette Owners Assn., Corvette Club, Coastal Conservation Assn., Captain's Cir., Intravler Club, Zeta Tau Alpha. Avocation: travel, art, education, design. Home: 2100 S Ocean Ln Apt 2104 Fort Lauderdale FL 33316-3827

LE ROY LADURIE, EMMANUEL BERNARD, historian, educator; b. Moutiers-en-Cinglais, France, July 19, 1929; s. Jacques and Leontine (Dauger) Le Roy Ladurie; m. Madeleine Pupponi, Sept. 7, 1955; children: Anne, François. Student, Coll. St.-Joseph, Caen, France, Lycee Henri IV, Paris; D of Letters, degree in teaching; student, Lycee Lakanal, Sceaux, France; Doctorate (hon.), U. Geneva, U. Mich., 1978, U. Leeds Hall, 1981, U. Leicester, Eng., 1982; U. East Anglia, 1985; Doctorate (hon.), U. Albany, 1986; U. York, 1986; Doctorate (hon.), U. Oxford, Eng., 1993, U. Haifa, Israel, 1993, U. Montreal, 1993; H.E.C., Paris, 1999. Prof. Lycee de Montpellier, France, 1953-57; attache de recherche Centre National de la Recherche Scientifique, Paris, 1957-60; asst. prof. Faculty des Lettres de Montpellier, 1960-63; maitre-asst. Ecole Pratique des Hautes Etudes, Paris, 1963-65, dir. d'etudes, 1965-69; head of conf., lecturer Faculte des Lettres, Paris, 1969-70; prof. UER Geographie et Sciences de la Societe, Paris, 1970-73; prof. history Coll. de France, Paris, 1973-98, prof. emeritus, 1998—; pres. sci. coun., dir. Bibliotheque Nationale, Paris, 1987-94. Author: Les Paysans de Languedoc, 1966, Histoire du Climat depuis l'An Mil, 1967, 2d edit., 1983, Times of Feast, Times of Famine: A History of Climate Since the Year 1000, 1971, Le Territoire de l'Historien, 2 vols., 1973, 78, Montaillou, village occitan de 1294 à 1324, 1975, Montaillou, 1978, Carnival in Romans, 1979, Le Carnaval de Romans, 1579-1580, 1980, Histoire de la France urbaine, Tome III, 1981, Paris-Montpellier PC-PSU, 1945-1963, 1982, La Sorcière de Jasmin avec fac-similé de l'éd. originale bilingue (1842), de la Françouneto de Jasmin, 1983, L'Etat royal, 1987, L'Ancien Régime, 1991, Le Siècle des Platter, (1499-1628), Le mendiant et le professeur, 1995, L'historien, le chiffre et le texte, Fayard, 1997, Saint-Simon ou le Système de la Cour, Fayard, 1997, Le Voyage de Thomas Platter, 2000. Named comdr. French Legion of Honor, Art et Lettres; recipient Silver medal Ctr. Nat. Recherche Sci., 1966. Fellow The British Acad. (corres.); mem. Acad. of Scis., Morales and Politics, Am. Acad. Scis. Roman Catholic. Office: Coll de France, 11 Place Marcelin Berthelot, 75005 Paris France

LERSCH, DELYNDEN RIFE, computer engineering executive; b. Grundy, Va., Mar. 22, 1949; d. Woodrow and Eunice Louise (Atwell) Rife; m. John Robert Lersch, May 9, 1976; children: Desmond, Kristofor. BSEE, Va. Poly. Inst. & State U., 1970; postgrad., Boston U., 1975—. With Stone & Webster Engring. Corp., 1970-91; elec. engr., supr. computer applications Stone & Webster Engring. Corp., Boston, 1978-80, mgr. computer graphics, 1984-87, mgr. engring. sys. and computer graphics, 1984-87, divsn. chief info. techs., 1987-90, v.p., 1990-91; chief ADP officer Univ. Rsch. Assocs., 1991-94, 97-99, also bd. dirs., 1997-99; dir. Global Elec. Security & Bus. Continuity, CARE Pvt. Mortgage Ins. Sys. Corp.; acct. mgr. Perot Sys. Corp., Dallas, 1994—. Author: Cable Schedule Information Systems As Used in Power Plant Construction, 1973, 2d edit., 1975, Information Systems Available for Use By Electrical Engineers, 1976; contbr. articles in field of computer-aided design and engineering. Grantee Mass. Solar Energy Rsch., 1978; honored for contbns. to constrn. industry Engring. News Record Mag., 1983. Mem. IEEE (sr.), Assn. Women in Sci., Soc. Women Engrs. (sr.), Women in Sci. and Engring., Energy Communicators, Nat. Computer Graphics Assn., Profl. Coun. New England, Women in Energy (dir. Mass. chpt. 1978, New Eng. region 1979), LWV, Rotary (Rotarian of yr. 1993-94). Congregationalist. Club: Boston Bus. and Profl. Women's. Home: Seis Lagos 503 Riva Rdg Wylie TX 75098-8264 Office: Perot Sys Corp 12377 Merit Dr Ste 1100 Dallas TX 75251-2200

LERVIK, JOHN MARKUS, research scientist; b. Sunndal, Norway, Aug. 17, 1969; s. Bjørn Arnold and Sigrid Helga (Erstad) L.; m. 209se Helene Laukli, May 27, 1995; 1 child, Anne Siri. MSc, Norwegian Inst. Tech., Trondheim, Norway, 1992; PhD, Norwegian U. Sci. & Tech., Trondheim, Norway, 1996. Sr. rsch. scientist NERA Rsch., Norway, 1997; chief tech. officer Fast Search & Transfer, Norway, 1997—. Inventor image compression method; contbr. articles to profl. jours. Mem. IEEE, ACM. Avocations: literature, cross country skiing, wine, orienteering. Home: Abyfaret 36, N-1392 Vettre Norway Office: Fast Search & Transfer, Brynsveien 3B, N-0667 Oslo Norway

LÉRY, LOUIS, physician, consultant; b. Lyon, France, July 5, 1941; s. Aime and Emilienne (Montriond) L.; m. Nicole Lothoz, Sept. 16, 1967; children: Damien, Blandine, Vincent. MD, Faculty of Medicine, Lyon, 1970, Splty. in Occupl. Medicine, 1969, Splty. in Immunology, 1975. Head dept. Inst. Pasteur, Lyon, 1973-97; asst. prof. Med. U., Montreal, 1992—; physician Hosp. Cariology, Lyon, 1971—; asst. prof. Med. U. Pub. Health, Lyon, 1997—. Co-author: Accidents Thérapeutiques Medicamment, 1970. Recipinet medal Vet. Soc. Pathology, 1991, GMC prize, 1998. Mem. N.Y. Acad. Scis., Nat. Assn. Occupl. Medicine and Hosp. Pers. (pres. 1999), Health, Ethics and Freedom (prs. 1999). Office: Cardiology Hosp, BP Lyon-Montchat, 69394 Lyon France

LESACA, REYNALDO MENDOZA, civil, sanitary and environmental engineer, mathematician, consultant; b. Lipa City, Batangas, The Philippines, Nov. 28, 1922; s. Jose and Rosario (Mendoza) L.; m. Florinda Jacob; children: Albert, Reynaldo Jr., Evelyn, Robert, Florinda, John, Karl, Bertrand. BS in Civil Engring. cum laude, U. Philippines, Manila, 1943, MS in Math., 1958; MS in Sanitary Engring., U. N.C., 1948; DEng, Johns Hopkins, 1955; MS in Biology, U. Rochester, 1961. Registered civil engr., sanitary engr., environ. planner The Philippines. Prof. pub. health U. Philippines, Manila, 1943-63; commr. Nat. Poll. Contr. Commn., Manila, 1968-76; regional dir., rep. UN environment program Bangkok, Thailand, 1976-83; sr. advisor on environment Philippine Senate, Manila, 1987-91; pres. Technics, Evaluation, Simulation and Testing Cons., Inc., Manila, 1994-95; free-lance environ. engring. cons. Manila, 1994—; dir. TEST Conss., Inc., Manila, 1985-95; dir., stockholder Asian Inst. Strategic Studies, Manila, 1996—; corp. sec. Asian Inst. Strategic Studies Rsch. Found., Inc., Manila, 1998—; chair bd. sanitary engring. Profl. Regulation Commn., Manila, 1998—. Contbr. articles to profl. jours., chpts. to books. Dir. Haribon Found. for Nat. Resources Conservation, Manila, 1984-97, Nat. Integration Protection Areas, Manila, 1994-97. Recipient Centenary award Sci. and Tech., Adriatico Centennial Commn., 1969, Cert. of Merit award Assn. Govt. Civil Engrs. of the Philippines, 1969, Disting. Alumni award Nat. Def. Coll. The Philippines, 1975, Achievement award Nat. Rsch. Coun. Philippines, 1989; Spl. fellow Woodrow Wilson Internat. Ctr. Scholars, Washington, 1972, East-West Ctr.'s Environment and Policy Inst., Hawaii, 1983; named Outstanding Sanitary Engr., Profl. Regulation Commn., Philippines, 1984. Fellow Philippines Assn. Advancement of Sci., Philippine Soc. Sanitary Engrs.; mem. Philippine Assn. Environ. Assessment Profls. (bd. dirs.), Mensa Philippines (chmn.), Toastmasters Internat., Phi Kappa Phi. Roman Catholic. Avocation: flying radio-controlled model planes and helicopters. Home: Area 1 U Philippines Campus, 59 Mabini St, Diliman Quezon City, Manila 1101, The Philippines

LESACK, BEATRIZ DÍAZ, secondary education educator; b. Arequipa, Peru, Dec. 2, 1948; came to U.S., 1977; d. Jésus Heradio Díaz Vargas and Elisa (Huamán) Díaz Peralta; m. Federico Vera Ponce de León, May 22, 1965 (div. 1977); 1 child, Edson Giovanni; m. Leo Pap Dorn, Oct. 27, 1977. BS in Spanish, San Agustin U., 1974; MS in Gen. Edn., SUNY, New Paltz, 1978-81, postgrad. Cert. elementary and secondary tchr., French and Spanish lang. tchr., N.Y. Tchr. Spanish Huguenot Nursery Sch., New Paltz, N.Y., 1983; tchr. elem. bilingual Ellenville (N.Y.) Sch. Dist., 1984-85; tchr. Spanish Poughkeepsie (N.Y.) Sch. Dist., 1985-86, Liberty (N.Y.) Sch. Dist., 1986-88, Fla. Unified Sch. Dist., Fla., N.Y., 1988-89; tchr. Spanish-French Hyde Park (N.Y.) Sch. Dist., 1989-91; tchr. Spanish Greenburgh Eleven Unified Sch. Dist., Dobbs Ferry, N.Y., 1991—, Copake-Taconic Hills Sch., Hillsdale, N.Y., 1995-96, FDR Sch., Bristol Twp., Pa., 1996-97; tax examiner U.S. Treasury, 1998-99, rschr., 1999—; substitute tchr. Newburgh, Wallkill, Onteora Sch. Dists., Poughkeepsie, N.Y., 1982-83; exec. sec. Hotels and Restaurants Assn., Arequipa, 1972-73; mem. asst. Radio Club Dr. Oscar Guillen, Arequipa, 1971; tax examiner U.S. Treasury, 1998-99, rsch., 1999-2000. Fund chairman Dem. Com., New Paltz, 1991-92; mem. fundraising com. Multicultural Edn., New Paltz, 1992; mem. Mid. Sch. Steering Com., 1989-91, Multicultural Edn. Com., 1991—, steering com. Maurice Hinchey Nat. Bilingual Edn., 1980—; candidate for Phila. Bd. Edn., 2000. Fulbright Hays fellow to Dominican Rep., 1991; faculty grantee SUNY, 1978, 83-84. Mem. NAFE, Am. Assn. Tchrs. Spanish, N.Y. Fgn. Lang. Tchrs. Assn. (pres.), N.Y. Union Tchrs., Faculty Wives and Women (pres. 1989-92). Avocations: photography, video production, handicrafts, reading, golf. Home: 5411 Vicaris St Philadelphia PA 19128-2823 Office: Greenburgh Eleven Unified Sch Dist PO Box 501 Dobbs Ferry NY 10522-0501

LESAFFRE, ODILE RAMETTE, librarian; b. Valenciennes, France, Oct. 7, 1949; d. Jean and Micheline (Fievet) Ramette; m. Thierry Lesaffre, Feb. 23, 1980. DSc, U. Paris, 1979. Libr. Ecole d'Architecture de Lille, 1973—. Roman Catholic. Avocations: arts, ceramic & tiles, kites, travel.

LESCHINSKY, ACHIM WILHELM, education educator; b. Mühlhausen, Germany, Apr. 8, 1944; s. Heinz B. and Anne Marie E. (Böttger) L.; children: Tobias, Moritz. PhD, U. Hamburg, Germany, 1976; Habilitation, Free U., Berlin, 1983. Cert. tchr. Sic. asst. U. Hamburg, 1970-73; scientist Max Planck Inst. Human Devel. & Edn., Berlin, 1973-92; prof. Humboldt U., Berlin, 1992—; guest lectr. Meiji U., Tokyo, 1988; hon. prof. Free U., Berlin, 1988-96. Author: Schule im Historischen Prozess, 1976, 2nd edit., 1982, Vorleben oder Nachdenken?, 1996; co-author, co-editor: Das Bildungswesen in Der Bundesrepublik Deutschland, 1979, 2nd edit., 1990, 4th edit., 1994, Zwischen zwei Diktaturen, 1997; co-author, co-editor: Die Schule als moralische Anstalt, 1999, Comprehensive School Experiment Revisited: Evidence from Western Europe, 1990, 2d edit., 1999; editor: Die Institutionaliserung von Lehren und Lernen, 1996. Mem. German Soc. Edn.

LESCHONSKY, BERND, molecular biologist, educator; b. Friedrichshafen, Baden-Württemberg, Germany, June 26, 1968; s. Eberhard and Gisela L. Vordiplom, U. Cologne, Germany, 1990; diploma, U. Regensburg, Germany, 1994; PhD magna cum laude, 2000. Biologist Inst. Med. Microbiology, Regensburg, Germany. Contbr. articles to profl. jours. Tennis instr. Wuerttembergischer Tennis-Bund, Friedrichshafen, 1986-87, Regensburg, 1992; ski instr. H. Pircher Ski Sch., Reschen, Italy, volleyball instr. Regensburg, 1994. Scholar Keystone Symposia, Park City, Utah, 1998. Mem. Assn. for Germany Virology, Internat. Soc. Antiviral Rsch. (scholar 1998). Avocations: tennis, volleyball, skiing, reading, sailing.

LESCOT, PAUL EDMOND, mathematics educator; b. Toulouse, France, Dec. 3, 1967; s. Jean-Claude Edmond and Jeannine Madeleine (Roy) L. Agrégation, Ecole Normale Supérieure, 1987; DEA, U. Paris VI, 1987, PhD, 1993. Allocataire moniteur normalien U. Paris, 1989-92, tchg. and rsch. asst., 1992-96; maître de confs. U. de Picardie, 1996—. Contbr. articles to profl. jours. V.p., sec. gen. Assn. des Anciens Mem. de Jeunes Vocations Artistiques, Littéraires et Scientifiques, Paris, 1988-94; mem. adminstrn. coun. Assn. des Anciens Elèves du Lycée Louis-le-Grand, 1996—, dep. sec.-gen. 1998—. Recipient 3d prize Concours Général (Math.) 1983 and 3d prize Internat. Math. Olympiad, 1983. Mem. Assn. for Symbolic Logic, Assn. des Joueurs d'Echecs par Correspondance. Roman Catholic. Avocations: 20th century history, violin, correspondence, chess, jiu-jitsu. Office: U de Picardie, 48 rue Raspail, 02100 Saint-Quentin France

LESCUYER, BRUNO MARIE, insurance company executive, educator; b. Uccle, Belgium, Sept. 3, 1954; (parents French citizens); s. Pierre Marie and Solange Marie (Thomas) L.; m. Claire Marie Sauteron, Apr. 9, 1983; children: Baudouin, Sophie, Ombeline, Charlotte. Grad., Poly. Sch., Paris, 1977; postgrad., Nat. Sch. Bridges and Roads, Paris, 1977-79. Mgmt. cons. Andersen Cons., Paris, 1979-83; fin. dir. Lucmaire Group, Paris, 1983-86; overseas mgr. AXA, Paris, 1986-89; dir., actuary AXA, London, 1989-92; head chmn.'s cabinet AXA, Paris, 1992-93; mng. dir. for internat. ops. Athena, Paris, 1993-96; mgr. dir. for Europe and Africa, UAP, Paris, 1996-97; chmn., CEO, AUXIA, Paris, 1997—; lectr. U. Assas, Paris, 1992—. Bd. dirs. La Providence, children's sch., Paris, 1997—. Officer French Navy, 1974-77. Mem. French Inst. Actuaries, Brit. Inst. Actuaries (assoc.), State Français. Roman Catholic. Avocations: tennis, golf, skiing. Home: 1 Ave Rodin, 75116 Paris France Office: AUXIA, 23 Rue Truffaut, 75017 Paris France

LESHCHENKO, DMITRII DAVIDOVICH, physicist, mathematician, educator; b. Odessa, Ukraine, Feb. 6, 1949; s. David Samoilovich Belfor and Lidia Dmitrievna Leshchenko; m. Helen Abramovna Rosanova, Dec. 3, 1988; 1 child, Dariya. DSc in Physics and Math., Odessa State U., 1971. Assoc. prof. theoretical mechanics Odessa State Acad. Refrigeration, 1982-96, prof. theoretical mechanics, 1997-99; head of chair of theoretical mechanics, prof. Odessa State Acad. of Civil Engring. and Architecture, 1999—. Contbr. articles to profl. jours. Named Soros assoc. prof., 1995. Mem. N.Y. Acad. Scis. E-mail: leshchenko d@mail.ru. Home: Dvoryanskaya Str 6 apt 5, 65026 Odessa Ukraine Office: Odessa State Acad Civil Eng, Didrikhson Str 4, 65029 Odessa Ukraine

LESH-LAURIE, GEORGIA ELIZABETH, university administrator, biology educator, researcher; b. Cleve., July 28, 1938; d. Howard Frees and Josephine Elizabeth (Taylor) Lesh; m. William Francis Laurie, Aug. 16, 1969. BS, Marietta Coll., 1960; MS, U. Wis., 1961; PhD, Case Western Reserve U., 1966. Asst. prof. SUNY, Albany, 1966-69; asst., then assoc. prof. Case Western Reserve U., 1969-77, asst. dean, 1973-76; interim dir. Cleve. State U., Ohio, 1980; prof., chairperson Cleve. State U., 1977-81, dean grad. studies, 1981-86, dean arts and scis., 1986-91, interim provost, v.p. academic and student affairs, 1989-90; vice chancellor acad. and student affairs U. Colo., Denver, 1991-95; interim chancellor U. Colo., 1995-97, chancellor, 1997—; cons. in field; reviewer numerous granting agencies, profl. jours., 1968—; advanced placement exam. Edn. Testing Service, Princeton, N.J., 1982-83. Contbr. sci. articles to profl. pubs. Trustee Marietta Coll., Ohio, 1980-84, 85-95; mem. city/univ. interchange com., Cleve., 1983-91. Fellow NSF, NIH; grantee NIH, Am. Cancer Soc., Am. Heart Assn., Research Corp., 1968—; recipient Wright fellowship Bermuda Biol. Station; named among AAUW Women of Distinction; named to Girl Scouts Women's Leadership Cir. Fellow AAAS; mem. Am. Soc. Zoologists, Soc. Devel. Biology, Am. Soc. Cell Biology, Phi Beta Kappa. Home: 1761 E Phillips Ave Littleton CO 80122-3260

LESIEUR, MARCEL ROBERT, mathematician; b. Poitiers, France, July 12, 1945; s. Leonce Ernest and Edith Marie (Rapilly) L.; m. Catherine Lipietz, July 19, 1969 (div. 1981); children: Stephanie, Juliette Mariasine; m. Patricia Doctrovee Samba, Dec. 12, 1992; children: Guillaume, Alexandre. Degree in engring., Ecole Poly., Paris, 1968; MS, U. Paris VI, 1969, PhD, 1970; DSc, U. Nice, France, 1973. Rsch. scientist CNRS, Paris, 1969-71, Nice, 1971-76; assoc. prof. Nat. Poly. Inst., Grenoble, France, 1976-84, 1st class prof., 1984-91, exc. class prof., 1992; sr. mem. Inst. Univ. de France, Grenoble, 1995—; vis. prof. U. So. Calif., L.A., 1982-83; head rsch. group Inst. de Mecanique, Grenoble, 1983-85; dir. French computational fluid dynamics program CNRS, 1988-92; chmn. French turbulence rsch. program CEA/CNRS, France, 1996-97. Author: Turbulence in Fluids, 1987, 2d edit., 1990, 3d edit., 1997), La Turbulence, 1994; editor: Turbulence and Coherent Structures, 1990, Computational Fluid Dynamics, 1996, Turbulence and Determinism, 1998. Lt. French Navy, 1968-69. Recipient Thorlet award Acad. Sci., 1985, Spl. Prize Seymour-Cray France, 1989, Great prize Marcel Dassault Acad Sci., 1998. Mem. French Mechan. Soc., French Phys. Soc., EUROMECH. Achievements include identification of coherent vortices in turbulence numerical simulations; discovered very fast models for turbulence computations. Office: LEGI/IMG, BP 53, 38041 Grenoble Cedex 9, France

LESIOW, TOMASZ, educator; b. Walbrzych, Poland, Nov. 27, 1953; s. Stanislaw and Elzbieta (Hutter) L.; m. Danuta Kaczor; children: Hanna, Martyna. Grad., Acad. Econs., Wroclaw, Poland, 1977, PhD, 1986. Asst. prof. U. Econs., Wroclaw, Poland, 1977-86, adj. prof., 1986—; vis. prof. Ohio State U., Columbus, 1995. Mem. Polish Food Tech. Soc. Avocation: local and mountain guide. Home: Drzewieckiego 52/23, 54-129 Wroclaw Poland Office: U Econs, ul Komandorska 118/120, 53-345 Wroclaw Poland

ŁĘSKI, JACEK MAREK, biomedical educator, researcher; b. Gliwice, Poland, July 1, 1963; s. Tadeusz and Anna (Chmiak) L.; m. Iwona Wanda Fortunka, Dec. 12, 1987; children: Izabela, Agata. MSc, Silesian Tech. U., Gliwice, 1987; PhD, Silesian Tech. U., 1989, DSc, 1995. Jr. asst. Silesian Tech. U., Gliwice, 1987-88; sr. asst. Silesian Tech. U., 1988-89, asst. prof., 1989-95, assoc. prof., 1995-97, prof., 1998—; bd. dirs. MEDEA Corp., Gliwice. Author: A New Possibility of Non-Invasive Electrocardiological Diagnosis, 1994; co-author: Digital Biomedical Signal Processing, 1993, Fuzzy and Neuro-Fuzzy Intelligent Systems, 2000; contbr. articles to profl. jours. Mem. Solidarity Trade Union, Gliwice, 1989. Roman Catholic. Avocations: music, photography. Home: Wroclawska 15/7, 44-100 Gliwice Poland Office: Silesian Tech U, Akademicka 16, 44-100 Gliwice Poland

LESKIEN, HERMANN ADALBERT, library director; b. Koenigsberg, Germany, Dec. 23, 1939; s. Bruno and Maria (Rikowski) L.; m. Marga Schmidt, June 19, 1965 (div.); children: Cosima, Titus; m. Elisabeth Heinrich, May 24, 1993. PhD, U. Wuerzburg, Germany, 1966. Lic. libr. Acquisition dept. head U. Libr., Wuerzburg, 1967-73; dir. U. Libr., Bamberg, Germany, 1973-79, U. Libr. Munich, 1979-92; dir. Bavarian State Libr., Munich, 1992—, dir. gen., 1999—. Avocations: classical music, hiking, cycling. Home: Graubuendener Str 55, D-81475 Munich Germany Office: Bayerische Staatsbibliothek, D-80328 Munich Germany

LEŠKO, VLADIMÍR, philosopher, researcher, educator; b. Prešov, Slovak Republic, Mar. 15, 1950; s. Ján and Helena (Cehel'ská) L.; m. Terézia Timková, June 2, 1973. Magister, Faculty Philosophy, Prešov, 1973; PhD, Slovak Acad. Sci., Bratislava, 1983. Chair dept. Faculty Philosophy, 1986-88, vice-dean, 1994-96; vice rector U. Prešov, 1997—. Author: History of Philosophy, 1986, 2d edit., 1993, 3d edit., 1994, 4th edit.,ú1996, History of Atheism, 1987, History of Russian and Soviet Philosophy, 1988, Philosophy of History of Philosophy, 1999; editor: Nietzsche and Present, 1994, Descartes and Present, 1996, Philosophy of History of Philosophy, 1998. Czech Acad. Soc. grantee, 1995. Slovak Acad. Soc., 1997. Avocations: classical music, tennis, soccer. Home: Gen Svobodu 4, 08101 Presov Slovakia Office: Katedra filozofie FF PU, 17 novembra 1, 08001 Presov Slovakia

LESLE, LUTZ, journalist; b. Cuxhaven, Germany, Jan. 17, 1934; s. Erich and Luise (Winckler) L.; m. Dietlind Petzold, Apr. 24, 1941 (div. 1979). Diploma, Poly. Sch. Librarianship, Hamburg, Germany, 1967; PhD, U. Hamburg, 1983; Prof., Music Acad. Lübeck, 1992. Chief libr. Pub. Music Libr. of Hamburg, 1968-83; music acad. lectr. Music Acad. of Lübeck, 1984—. Author: (books) Emergency Case Music Criticism, 1981, The Music Critic - Judge or Promoter? 1984; contbr. articles to revs. and newspapers. Mem. Free Acad. Arts, Hamburg, 1973. Mem. Brahms Soc. Hamburg, Mahler Soc. Hamburg. Avocations: playing piano and flute, biking. Office: Music Acad Lübeck, Grosse Petersgrube 17-29, D-23552 Lübeck Germany

LESLEY, ULF KARL GUSTAV, marketing professional; b. Vasteras, Sweden, Apr. 5, 1961; s. Torsten and Kerstin L.; m. Eva Lesley. BSBA, Lund U., Sweden, 1987; MSEE, Lund Inst. Technology, Sweden, 1987. Sr. mgr. bus. support Ericsson Telecom AB, Australia, 1992-93, sr. mgr. customer mktg., 1993-95; dir. global mktg. Ericsson Telecom AB, Sweden, 1995-99; dir. mktg. comm. and branding GSM & WCDMA Ericsson Radio Sys. AB, Stockholm, 1999—. Office: Ericsson Radio Sys AB, Kista, S-164 80 Stockholm Sweden

LESLIE, EVELYN, psychotherapist; b. Covington, La., Apr. 7, 1944; d. Calvin and Elizabeth Johnson; m. Reo Leslie, Jr., Feb. 15, 1992; children: Twilonda, Gregory. BA in Psychology, Chapman U., 1988; MA in Psychology, Regis U., 1994; student. Lic. psychologist, Colo. Pvt. practice various, 1988-93; asst. dir., psychotherapist Family Therapy/Play Therapy Inst., Denver, Colo., 1993—; bd. dirs. Colo. Assn. Psychotherapists. Mem. Internat. Assn. Play Therapy, Am. Assn. Marriage and Family Therapy. Baptist. Avocations: reading, meditation, music. Office: Family Therapy Play Therapy Inst 1777 S Bellaire St Ste 327 Denver CO 80222-4318

LESLIE, JOHN, artist, designer, photographer, sculptor; b. Phila., July 11, 1923; s. John Joseph and Mary Kathryn (Bauermees) L.; m. Kathryn Elizabeth Frame, Feb. 4, 1946 (div. 1948); m. Mary Frances Huggins, Apr. 2, 1950; children: Karol Ann, John Joseph III, Mary Lee. Grad. comml. art, Murrell Dobbins Tech., Phila., 1941; postgrad., Fleisher Art Meml., Phila.,

1939-42; postgrad, Phila. Museum Sch. Indsl. Art, 1944; postgrad., Phila. Music Acad., 1965-67, Pa. State U., 1982—. Staff artist Phila. Daily News, 1942; founder, creative dir. Graphic Ad Displays, Inc., Phila., 1944; artist/muralist Bonwit Teller, Phila., 1944-46; collaborative designer fashion show stage sets and Gimbel Bros. Thanksgiving Day Parade, Phila., 1945; pres., art dir. Duplex Display and Mfg. Co., Inc., Phila., 1947-54; pres., designer Leslie Creations, Inc., Lafayette Hill, Pa., 1954-65; pres., founder Mail Order Methods, Inc., Lafayette Hill, 1954-67; pres. World Treasures, Seven Seas House, Inc., Lafayette Hill, 1960-65; founder, creative dir. Kopy Kat Inc. with 150 franchised instant printing ctrs., Fort Washington, Pa., 1968-77; art dir. designer Jesse Jones Industries, Inc., Phila., 1978-79; co-founder, art dir. Galerie Marjolé, Inc., Sanatoga, Pa., 1987-89, lectr. ltd. edition prints, 1987—; fine art spokesman radio, TV, 1989—; guest spkr. Hundred Million Club, N.Y.C., 1963; stage set designer Bessie V. Hicks Sch., Dramatic Arts, Phila., 1944-46. Patentee U.S. Kopy Kat, Inc. trademark; prin. works include site selection Jeanes Meml. Libr., Lafayette Hill, Pa., 1967; executed murals Phila. Savs. Fund Soc., Phila. Eagles Football Team, E.F. Houghton Co., 1945-53; originator of 3-Ds (3-dimensional collages of paper-sculpture, painted artwork and layered composition bd.), 1940s; originator/designer first giant 3-D Dioramic Collages in U.S., 1940's; created wrought iron and chromed steel functional metal sculptures, 1954-79; designer the Crystal Mall concept (a climate-controlled atrium enclosing entire existing downtown shopping dists.), 1990; designer U.S. WWII Vets. Meml. Hall of Honor, 1996; artworks in U.S. Embassy, Paris, J.F.K. Libr., Boston, Woodmere Art Mus., Pa. Acad. Fine Arts, Phila., Mus. Art, and many other U.S. museums; first artist to use tissue paper as papier maché sculptural medium, 1940s; released 3 ltd. edit. lithographic prints and many fine art photographs, 1988—; designer homes and avant garde furniture including first ocean front A-Frame home on Atlantic coast, first lakeside French Provencial home Port Charlotte, Fla; designer Mannequettes for dept. store windows; creator Plasti-Coils, 1940-50; inventor Showoff cabinet and Room Divider Record Screen, a 3-way folding screen, to file, store, and display LP record albums and video discs, 1954-63; designer the Skyscraper chromed steel functional metal sculpture, 1978; exhibited in shows at Art Expo N.Y.C., 1988, Ursinus Coll., Collegeville, Pa., 1983, Phila. Sketch Club, 1987, Englewood Art Guild Fine Art Photo Expos, Fla., 1996—; contbr. weekly column "Lasting Impressions" to Herald, Englewood, Fla., 2000—. Pres., founder Ctrl. Citizens Com., Inc. (limiting strip mining in residential areas), Whitemarsh Twp., Pa., 1960-75; active Big Bros. Am., Phila., 1957-65, YMCA Indian Guides, Montgomery County, Pa., 1965-68; conservationist, animal rights activist Am. Anti-Vivisection Soc., 1959—; mem. Arts and Humanities Coun. of Charlotte County, Fla.; pres. Lions, Lafayette Hill, Pa., 1960-70. With 8th Armored Divsn. Tank Corps., U.S. Army, 1943. Named Citizen of Week Montgomery Newspapers, 1978; recipient Direct Mail Leaders award Direct Mail Advt. Assn., 1957, 60, Artistic Merit award Playboy Mag., 1958, Japanese Graphic Arts Industry award, 1975, King of Prussia Fine Arts award Upper Merion Cultural Ctr., 1966, Disting. Svc. award Citizens Com. on Pub. Edn., Phila., 1981, Walter Emerson Baum Award for An American Impressionist Painting, Sellers Mus., Bucks County, Pa., 1995; inducted into Artist's Hall of Fame Murrell Dobbins Tech., Phila., 1988; presented artist's proof to French World Cup Soccer Champions, Paris, 1998. Mem. Woodmere Art Mus. (Phila.), Boca Grande Fla. Art Alliance, Englewood (Fla.) Photographers Assn., Les Amis de Veterans Francais, N.Y. Oil Pastel Assn., Nat. Amvets., 8th Armored Divsn. Assn. Roman Catholic. Avocations: collecting antique photographs, pottery, opera, jazz. Studio: Blueberry Hill 6318 Zeno Cir Pt Charlotte FL 33981-7304

LESLIE, LISA DESHAUN, professional basketball player; b. Gardena, Calif., July 7, 1972. Grad., U. So. Calif., 1994. Basketball player USA Women's Nat. Team, 1996, L.A. Sparks WNBA, 1997—; mem. gold medal winning 1994 Goodwill Games Team. Named 1993 USA Basketball Female Athlete of Yr.; recipient gold medal Atlanta Olympics, 1996; named MVP 1st WNBA All-Star Game, 1999. Office: Los Angeles Sparks Great Western Forum POB 10 3900 W Manchester Blvd Inglewood CA 90306-0010

LESLIE, MAE SUE, writer; b. Forrester, Ark., Dec. 22, 1940; d. Doyle Joseph and Ruby Estelle (Stewart) Davis; m. Gerald Robert Leslie, Sept. 2, 1967; children: Neal R., Denise. Student, Instituto Allende, San Miguel Allende, Mex., 1960-61; BA in Journalism, Sam Houston State U., 1966. Cert. nursing home social worker, Tex. Sec. Am. Gen. Ins. Co., Houston, 1966-67; social worker Harris County, Houston, 1968; sec. temp. agys.. Houston, 1977-81; freelance writer, 1981—. Author: (novel) Canadian Capers, 1998; author of three childrens books and screenplay; freelance cartoonist. Pianist, Sunday sch. tchr. Riverside (Tex.) Bapt. Ch., 1963-65. Recipient 3d pl. for article Fla. State Writing Competition, 1994, 2d pl. for short story Manuscripts Guild, 1994, 3d pl. for nonfiction, 1994. Mem. Nat. Writer's Union, Houston Screenwriters, Nat. Honor Soc. for Journalism Students. Democrat. Baptist. Home: 802 Carol St Bellaire TX 77401-4713

LESLIE, ROBERT LORNE, lawyer; b. Adak, Ala., Feb. 24, 1947; s. J. Lornie and L. Jean (Conelly) L.; children: Lorna Jean, Elizabeth Allen. BS, U.S. Mil. Acad., 1969; JD, U. Calif., San Francisco, 1974. Bar: Calif. 1974, D.C. 1979, U.S. Dist. Ct. (no. dist.) Calif. 1974, U.S. Ct. Claims 1975, U.S. Tax Ct. 1975, U.S. Ct. Appeals (9th and D.C. cirs.) 1974, U.S. Ct. Mil. Appeals 1980, U.S. Supreme Ct. 1980. Commd. 2d lt. U.S. Army, 1969, advanced through grades to maj., 1980; govt. trial atty. West Coast Field Office, Contract Appeals, Litigation and Regulatory Law divsns., Office JAG, Dept. Army, San Francisco, 1974-77; sr. trial atty., team chief Office of Chief Trial Atty., Dept. of Amry, Washington, 1977-80; ptnr. McInerney & Dillon, Oakland, Calif., 1980—, 1980—; lectr. on govt. contracts CSC, Continuing Legal Edn. Program; lectr. in govt. procurement U.S. Army Material Command. Served to col. USAR, ret. Decorated Purple Heart, Silver Star. Mem. ABA, Fed. Bar Assn., Associated Gen. Contractors, The Beavers. Office: McInerney & Dillon Ordway Bldg Fl 18 Oakland CA 94612-3610

LESLIE, WILLIAM BRUCE, history educator; b. Orange, N.J., July 21, 1944; s. William and Annette (Riedell) L.; stepmother, Dorothy Kaul; children: William Andrew, Sarah Acton. BA, Princeton U., 1966; PhD, Johns Hopkins U., 1971. Asst. prof. history SUNY, Brockport, 1970-79, assoc. prof., 1979-96, prof., 1996—; vis. prof. Jordanhill Coll., Scotland, 1972, dir. grad. studies in history, 1984-90, 97-99; co-dir. SUNY Social Sci. Program, London, 1978-79, 82-83, 89; cons. Regents Coll., ETS, AP Exams., Fulbright, Scandinavian Selection. Author: Gentlemen and Scholars, 1993; mem. editl. bd. History of Higher Edn. Ann., 1991—; contbr. articles and revs. to profl jours. Fulbright scholar, Denmark, 1996-97. Mem. Orgn. Am. Historians, Am. Hist. Assn., History of Edn. Soc., Adirondack Mountain Club, Western Monroe Hist. Soc., Princeton Club N.Y. Democrat. Avocations: camping, travel, gardening. Office: SUNY History Dept Brockport NY 14420-2956

LESNIEWSKI-LAAS, MAREK, lawyer; b. Warsaw, Poland, July 2, 1950; came to U.S., 1965; s. Jerzy and Maria Jadwiga (Czerski) Lesniewski; m. Elizabeth Trechsel, July 3, 1979; children: Christopher, Alicia, Nicholas, Alexandra. AB, Bowdoin Coll., Brunswick, Maine, 1973; JD, Boston U., 1976. Self employed lawyer, prin. Boston, 1977; asst. atty. gen. Office of Atty. Gen. Mass., Boston, 1985-91; dep. commr., gen. counsel Commonwealth of Mass. Dept. Med. Security, Boston, 1991-96; v.p. legal affairs The Stanton Group, Boston, 1996—; lectr. legal continuing edn. seminars and health care confs., Boston, 1987-92. Hon. consul Republic of Poland, 1994—. Mem. Consular Corps Boston, Union Club Boston, Ancient and Hon. Artilery Co. Mass., Am. Assn. Polish-Jewish Studies (dir.), Polish Am. Congress. Avocations: sailing, photography, travel, shooting sports. E-mail: marek@shore.net. Office: Consulate of Poland 1 Faneuil Hall Boston MA 02109-1646

LESNIKOVICH, ANATOLY IVANOVICH, chemist, researcher, educator; b. Rachkovichy, Belarus, Apr. 3, 1941; s. Ivan Onufrievich and Lubov Gerasimovna (Moros) L.; m. Larisa Aleksandrovna Krogol, Jan. 19, 1968; children: Cyril, Julia. Diploma, U. Minsk, Belarus, 1965, candidate sci., 1970, DSc, 1986. Worker State Farm, Rachkovichy, 1957-59; asst. U. Minsk, 1966-70, sr. tchr., 1970-77, asst. prof., 1977-78, head lab., 1978-90, vice rector, 1990-96; 1st dep. chmn. State Higher Attestation Com. Belarus, 1996-2000; chmn. State Com. Sci. & Tech., 2000—; part-time engr. U. Minsk, 1963-65, part-time rschr., 1965-78, part-time asst. prof., 1978-85, part-time full prof., 1985-96; part-time head dept. gen. chemistry and methods chemistry tchg., 1996—. Author: Correlations in Contemporary Chemistry, 1989; inventor fire-retardant composition, 1992; editor: Reports of Belarussian State U., 1990-97; contbr. articles to profl. jours. Mem. Acad. Sci., Internat. Acad. Higher Sch., Acad. Edn. Belarus. Avocations: handicrafts, reading, gardening. Home: Voronjanskogo St 3/1 k9, 220039 Minsk Belarus Office: Belarussian Akac Sci, Akademicheskaia Str 1, 220072 Minsk Belarus

LESOT, PHILIPPE GEORGES JULIEN, chemist, researcher, educator; b. Paris, Oct. 7, 1967; s. Jean Louis and Daniele (Lecureaux) L. B in Chemistry, U. Paris XI, 1989, M in Organic Chemistry, 1990, High Studies diploma in Chemistry, 1991, PhD in Chemistry, 1995. Rschr. U. Southampton, U.K., 1995-96; asst. prof. chemistry U. Paris XI, Orsay, 1996-97; rschr. Nat. Ctr. Sci. Rsch., Orsay, 1997—. Contbr. articles to profl. jours. Mem. bd. dirs. Inst. Tech., Orsay, 1986-88. With French Artillery, 1991-92. Recipient award Royal Soc. London, 1995, grant U. Southampton, 1995-96. Avocations: astronomy, astrophysics, photography of nature. Office: Univ Paris SUD bat 410, Lab OrganicChemistry, 91405 Orsay Cedex, France

LESS, ANTHONY ALBERT, retired naval officer; b. Salem, Ohio, Aug. 31, 1937; s. Joseph Anthony and Mildred Gertrude (Bair) L.; m. Leanne Carol Kuhl, Mar. 3, 1962; children: Robyn, Pamela, Theresa, Christina. BS in Chemistry, Heidelberg Coll., 1959. Designated naval aviator. Commd. ensign USN, 1960, advanced through grades to vice adm., 1991, ret., 1994; comdg. officer USS Wichita (AOR-1), 1979-81, USS Ranger (CV-61), 1982-83; chief of staff Comdr. 7th Fleet, Yokosuka, Japan, 1983-84; dir. Polit. Mil Br. JCS, Washington, 1985-87; comdr. Carrier Group One, Pacific, 1987-88, Mid. East Force, Manama, Bahrain, 1988-89; dir. Plans and Policy Navy Staff, Washington, 1989-91; comdr. Naval Air Force Atlantic Fleet, Norfolk, Va., 1991-94; pres. Assn. Naval Aviation, Washington, 1995; cons. Kaman Aerospace, Bloomfield, Conn., 1994—; v.p. K-Max mil. ops. Kaman Aerospace Corp., Bloomfield. Mem. Assn. Naval Aviation (pres. 1994), Soc. Naval Engrs. Roman Catholic. Avocations: racquetball, farming, reading. Office: K-Max Mil Ops Kaman Aerospace Blue Hills Ave Bloomfield CT 06002

LESSARD, ARNOLD FRED, international business executive; b. Newburyport, Mass., Oct. 9, 1923; s. Fred Soloman and Azilda Mary (Goodreau) L.; m. Francine Colette Treutenaere, June 30, 1975; 1 son, Arnaud Alfred. Diploma in acctg., Burdett Coll., 1943; BS with honors, Boston U., 1949; MA with honors, Columbia U., 1951; postgrad., Georgetown U., 1953-56, George Washington U., 1953-56. Head pers. devel. divsn. Nat. Security Agy., 1951-56; cons. Booz, Allen & Hamilton, Inc., N.Y.C., 1956-59, assoc., 1959-61, v.p., 1961-69, regional v.p., 1969-71; chmn. bd. Resources Engring. & Mgmt. Internat., London and Denver, 1971-78; v.p., dir. Chase World Info. Corp. (Chase Manhattan Bank), N.Y.C., 1978-79; with Sears Roebuck & Co., 1983—; dir. for Europe, Middle East and Africa, Sears World Trade, Washington, 1983-84, sr. v.p. Internat. Planning and Analysis Ctr., 1984-85; founding chmn. Internat. Coal Exploration Symposium, London, 1975; pvt. sector and banking advisor West and Ctrl. Africa, U.S. Agy. for Internat. Devel., Abidjan, Ivory Coast and Paris, 1985-89; nat. banking and pvt. sector advisor U.S. Agy. for Internat. Devel., Kinshasa, Zaire, 1989-92; dep. exec. dir. Uganda Investment Authority, Kampala, Uganda, 1992-95; sr. internat. project cons. UNDP, UNCTAD, USAID, The World Bank, 1995—. Served with USAAF, 1943-46; served to capt. USAF, 1951-53. Mem. Inst. Mgmt. Consultants (founding mem., cert. mgmt. cons., regional v.p. Europe 1971-78), Soc. for Pers. Adminstrn., Acad. Mgmt., Export Fin. Group, U.S. C. of C., Phi Delta Kappa, Pi Gamma Mu, Kappa Delta Pi, Reform Club (London). Office: 23 Pleasant St Newburyport MA 01950-2622

LESSER, IAN O., foreign affairs expert; b. Oct. 22, 1957. Ba in Internat. Politics, U. Pa., 1979; MSc in Internat. Rels., The London Sch. Econs., 1980; MA in Law, Diplomacy, Tufts U., 1982; PhD in Internat. Politics, Oxford U., 1988. Sr. fellow The Atlantic Coun. of U.S., Washington, 1980-81; staff cons. Internat. Energy Assocs. Ltd., Washington, 1982-83; sr. fellow Ctr. Strategic and Internat. Studies, Washington, 1985-88; sr. analyst Nat. Security Rsch. Divsn. RAND, Santa Monica, Calif., 1989-94; assoc. dir. strategy and doctrine program Project Air Force RAND, Santa Monica, Calif., 1996-98; sr. internat. policy analyst RAND, Santa Monica, Calif., 1996—; mem. policy planning staff U.S. Dept. State, Washington, 1994-95. Author: Mediterranean Security, 1992, Security in North Africa: Internal and External Challenges, 1993, Turkey's New Geopolitics, 1993, A Sense of Siege: The Geopolitics of Islam and the West, 1994, Strategic Exposure: Proliferation Around the Mediterranean, 1996, Sources of Conflict in the 21st Century, 1998. Mem. Coun. Foreign Rels., Pacific Coun. Internat. Policy, Internat. Inst. Strategic Studies, Atlantic Coun. (councillor). Office: Rand Corp 1700 Main St Santa Monica CA 90401-3297

LESSER, JULIAN (BUD LESSER), film producer, historian; b. San Francisco, Jan. 18, 1915; s. Sol Leonard and Fay (Grunauer) L.; m. Genee Kobacker, 1938 (div. 1952); m. Betsy Bamberger, Jan. 24, 1955 (div. Jan. 1980); children: Stephen, Belinda, David; m. Helene Feinberg, Aug. 8, 1983. BA, Stanford U., 1936; postgrad. Grad. Sch. Bus., Harvard U., 1937. Salesman J.E. Brulatour & Co., Eastman Raw Films, Hollywood, Calif., 1937-39; chair Def. Coun. Film Bur., L.A., 1941-42; v.p. Sol Lesser Prodns., L.A., 1947-58; pres. Royal Prodns., L.A., 1950-80; presenter in field. Journalist/historian niche periodicals, 1985—. Maj. USMCR, 1942-49. Mem. USMC Combat Corrs. (bd. dirs. 1996-98, pres. L.A. chpt. 1999&, Dickson award 1994). Office: 396 Saddlehorn Trl Palm Desert CA 92211-3295

LESSER, LAURENCE, musician, educator; b. Los Angeles, Oct. 28, 1938; s. Moses Aaron and Rosalyne Anne (Asner) L.; m. Masuko Ushioda, Dec. 23, 1971; children—Erika, Adam. AB, Harvard U., 1961; student of Gaspar Cassadó, Germany, 1961-62; student of Gregor Piatigorsky, 1963-66. Mem. faculty U. So. Calif., Los Angeles, 1963-70, Peabody Inst., Balt., 1970-74; mem. faculty New Eng. Conservatory Music, Boston, 1974—, pres., 1983-96, pres. emeritus, 1997—; former vis. prof. Eastman Sch. Music, Rochester, N.Y.; vis. prof. Toho Gakuen Sch. Music, Tokyo, 1973-95; performed with New Japan Philharm., Boston Symphony, London Philharm., L.A. Philharm. and Marlboro, Spoleto, Casals, Santa Fe and Banff festivals; rec. artist; overseer emeritus Boston Symphony Orch. Trustee emeritus WGBH Ednl. Found.; mem. adv. coun. Chamber Music Am. Recipient prize Tchaikovsky Competition, Moscow, 1966; Fulbright scholar, 1961-62; Ford Found. grantee, 1972. Mem. Am. Acad. Arts and Scis., Harvard Mus. Assn., Tavern Club, Phi Beta Kappa, Pi Kappa Lambda, Sigma Alpha Iota. Jewish. E-mail: llesser@rcn.com. Home: 65 Bellevue St Newton MA 02458-1918 Office: New Eng Conservatory Music 290 Huntington Ave Boston MA 02115-5018

LESSEVA, MAGDALENA IVANOVA, microbiologist, researcher, consultant; b. Lovetch, Bulgaria, May 15, 1958; d. Ivan Charalampiev and Violeta Petkova (Dimitrova) L.; m. Kiril Assenov Ivanov, Sept. 17, 1977; 1 child, Viliana Kirilova. MD, Med. Acad., Sofia, 1982, PhD Degree in Microbiology, 1987. Dist. physician Regional Hosp., Pernik, Bulgaria, 1982-84; microbiologist Inst. Pirogov, Sofia, 1987-88, asst. clin. microbiology, 1988-91, chief asst., 1991-98, assoc. prof., 1999—; cons. in antibiotics Glaxo Office, Sofia, 1992-94; cons. Nat. Drug Inst., Sofia, 1997-98; presenter in field. Contbr. articles to profl. jours. Mem. N.Y. Acad. Scis., Bulgarian Assn. Scientists, European Burns Assn., European Soc. Chemotherapy, Bulgarian Med. Doctors Assn. Mem. Eastern Orthodox. Avocations: history, computative knowledges, swimming, tourism, growing flowers. Home: 6 Iskar St, 1000 Sofia Bulgaria Office: Sci isnt Emergency Medicine, 21 Macedonia Blvd, 1606 Sofia Bulgaria

LESSEY, SAMUEL KENRIC, JR., foundation administrator; b. Newark, Oct. 9, 1923; s. Samuel Kenric and Ruth (Turner) Lessey. BS, U.S. Mil. Acad., 1945; student, Vanderbilt U., 1945; LLB, Harvard U., 1951; postgrad., Washington U. Law Sch., 1951-52, U. Md., 1951-53; MBA, Harvard U., 1956; postgrad., Air War Coll., 1974-75. Bar: N.Y., U.S. Dist. Ct. D.C., U.S. Ct. Claims, U.S. Tax Ct., U.S. Ct. Mil. Appeals, U.S. Ct. Appeals (D.C. cir.), U.S. Supreme Ct. Commd. USAF, 1945, advanced through grades to brig. gen., active duty, 1942-54, 76-78; with USAFR, 1954-83; v.p., bd. dirs. Nat. Aviation Corp. Investment Trust, 1957-68; v.p. Shearson Hammill and Co., Inc., 1968-74; moblzn. asst. to dir. Fed. Emergency Mgmt. Agy., 1979-82; insp. gen. U.S. Synthetic Fuels Corp., 1982-86; dir. Selective Svc. System, 1987-91; Dir. Nat. Stroke Assn. 1991—, chmn. of bd. 1994—. civilian aide to sec. of Army 1992. Decorated Legion of Merit with Oak Leaf Cluster, Army Outstanding Civil Svc. award, Selective Svc. Disting. Svc. medal, WWII Victory medal, Occupation medal, Nat. Def. Svc. medal, Am. Campaign medal, UN Svc. medal, Air Force Outstanding Unit award; Korean Svc. medal. Mem. AIAA, IEEE, Aerospace Analysts Soc. (past pres.), Am. Fighter Pilots Assn., Air Force Assn. (past v.p. Iron Gate chpt.), Am. Astronautical Soc., Am. Def. Preparedness Assn., Am. Helicopter Soc. (N.H. pres.), Assn. U.S. Army, Aviation Space Writers Assn., Elec. and Electronic Analysts Group, Fin. Analysts Fedn., N.Y. Soc. Security Analysts, Mil. Order of World Wars, Res. Officers Assn., Am. Assoc. Royal Acad. Arts, Def. Orientation Conf. Assn. (dir.), Wings Club (past bd. dirs.), Nat. Aviation Club, N.Y. Athletic Club, Lincoln's Inn Soc., Harvard Club (N.Y.C.), Capitol Hill Club, Army & Navy Club. Avocations: skiing, tennis, swimming, traditional jazz, antiques. Home: Brimstone Corner PO Box 57 Hancock NH 03449-0057 Office: Nat Stroke Assn 9707 E Easter Ln Englewood CO 80112-3754

LESSING, DORIS (MAY), writer; b. Kermanshah, Persia, Oct. 22, 1919; d. Alfred Cook Tayler and Emily Maude McVeagh; m. Frank Charles Wisdom, 1939 (div. 1943); m. Gottfried Anton Nicholas Lessing, 1945 (div. 1949); children: John W. (dec.), Jean W., Peter L. Educated in, So. Rhodesia; DLitt (hon.), Princeton U., 1989, Durham U., 1990; D Fellow in Lit., Sch., Eng. Am. Studies, U. East Anglia, 1991; DLitt (hon.), Warwick U., 1994; LittD (hon.), Bard Coll., 1994, Harvard U., 1995, Open Univ., 1999, Univ. London, 1999. Author: (novels) The Grass is Singing, 1950, Five Short Novels, 1953, Retreat to Innocence, 1959, The Golden Notebook, 1962 (Prix Medicis Award for work translated into French, 1976), Children of Violence, 5 vols., 1964-69, Briefing For a Descent Into Hell, 1971, The Summer Before the Dark, 1973, The Memoirs of a Survivor, 1975, Shikasta, 1979, Marriages Between Zones Three, Four and Five, 1980, The Sirian Experiments, 1981 (Booker McConnell Prize nominee, 1981), The Making of the Representative for Planet 8, 1982, Documents Relating to the Sentimental Agents in the Volyen Empire, 1983, The Diaries of Jane Somers (Diary of a Good Neighbour, 1983, and If the Old Could..., 1984, pub. under pseudonym Jane Somers), The Good Terrorist, 1985 (W.H. Smith Lit. Award, 1986; Palermo Prize, 1987; Premio Internazionale Monello, 1987), The Fifth Child, 1988, The Libretto of the Making of the Representative for Planet 8, 1988, The Fifth Child, 1988, Playing the Game, 1995, Love, Again, 1996, Mara and Dann, 1999, Ben, In The World, 2000; (nonfiction) Going Home, 1968, In Pursuit of the English, 1961, Particularly Cats, 1967, Prisons We Choose to Live Inside, 1987, The Wind Blows Away Our Words...and Other Documents Relating to the Afghan Resistance, 1987, Particularly Cats and More Cats...And Rufus, 1991, African Laughter: Four Visits to Zimbabwe, 1992; (autobiography) Under My Skin: Volume One of My Autobiography, to 1949, 1994, Walking in the Shade: Volume Two of My Autobiography, 1949-62; (short stories) This Was the Old Chief's Country, 1952, The Habit of Loving, 1957, A Man and Two Women, 1963, African Stories, 1965, The Temptation of Jack Orkney and Other Stories, 1978, The Story of a Non-Marrying Man, 1972, Collected African Stories, 1978, This Was Old Chief Country, 1952, The Sun Between Their Feet, 1981, London Observed: Stories and Sketches (U.K.)/The Real Thing (U.S.), 1992; (collections) To Room 19 (Collected Stories Vols. 1 and 2), 1978, The Doris Lessing Reader, 1990; (plays) Each in His Own Wilderness, 1958, Play with a Tiger, 1973, The Singing Door, 1973; (essays) A Small Personal Voice, 1974; (poetry) Fourteen Poems, 1959; (libretto for opera with music by Philip Glass) The Making of the Representative for Planet 8, 1988; also newspaper reports. Recipient Somerset Maugham award Soc. of Authors, 1954, Austrian State prize for European Lit., 1981, Shakespeare prize, Hamburg, 1982, Grinzane Cavour award, Italy, 1989; named Woman of Yr. Norway, 1995, awarded Premi Internatl. Catalunya, 1999. Fellow MLA (hon.); mem. Nat. Inst. Arts and Letters., Am. Acad. Arts & Letters (assoc. mem. 1974), Inst. Cultural Rsch. (Companion of Honor 2000). Office: care Jonathan Clowes Ltd, 10 Iron Bridge House, Bridge Approach, London NW1 8BD, England

LESTER, MARK CHARLES, neurosurgeon; b. Pitts., Sept. 23, 1952. AB, Cornell U., 1973; MD, U. Pitts., 1977; postgrad., Matie Wharton Exec. MBA, Program, 2000—. Diplomate Am. Bd. Neurol. Surgery. Intern gen. surgery U. Health Ctr. Hosps., Pitts., 1977-78, resident in neurological surgery, 1978-83; neurosurgeon Allentown, Pa., 1983—; chief, Divsn. Neurol. Surgery Lehigh Valley Hosp., Allentown, 1992—, co-med. dir. trauma/neuro ICU, 1998—, vice-chmn. for opers., dept. surgery, 1999—, med. dir. oper. rm., 1999—; clin. assoc. prof. Pa. State Coll. of Medicine, Hershey, Pa., 1995—; head sect. neurotrauma Lehigh Valley Hosp., Allentown, 1991—; clin. assoc. prof. Pa. State Coll. of Medicine, Hershey, Pa., 1995—; adj. clin. asst. prof. Hahnemann U., Phila., 1988—. Fellow Am. Coll. Surgeons; mem. Am. Assn. Neurolog. Surgeons, AAAS. Office: Neurosurg Assocs of Lehigh Valley Physician Group 1240 S Cedar Crest Blvd Ste 308 Allentown PA 18103

LESTER, NITA CLARE, education educator; b. Toowoomba, Queensland, Australia, May 5, 1954; d. David and Clare Cecily (Heiner) Phillips; m. Phillip Stanley Lester, May 5, 1975; children: Elton, Brooke. Degree in edn., U. Queensland, 1974, degree in arts, 1977, degree in sci., 1984; grad. diploma in applied sci., U. So. Queensland, 1994, MEd, 1995. Cert. tertiary lectr. primary through secondary tchg.; qualified justice of the peace. Tchr. secondary and primary edn. Edn. Dept., Australia, 1974-89; univ. lectr. U. So. Queensland, 1990—; rural edn. rschr., 1992—; Waterlily rschr. So. Queensland U. and Myall Park Bot. Garden, 1994—; cons. rural edn., Queensland, 1987—; amb. to China Ednl. Adminstrs., Australia, 1994—; cons. to local govts., 1992—; Queensland rep. Craft Bd. of Australia, 1985—; panel mem. Nat. Heritage Found., 1998—. Author: (book) Teaching in Multi-grade Classrooms, 1996, also children's book, 1999, natural resources botany book, 2000; contbr. articles to profl. jours. Chmn. Myall Park Bot. Garden, 1988—; pres. numerous civic groups, drama groups, and sporting orgns., 1976—; treas. Nat. Network of Plant Conservation, 1999—. Rsch. grantee various industries and univs., 1991-98; winner Elaine Brough Bursary, 1998. Mem. Australian Coun. Ednl. Adminstrs., Australian Coun. Edn., Queensland Arts Coun. (life). Anglican. Avocations: helping children, botanical art, sailing, writing, reading.

LESTHAEGHE, RON JEAN, sociologist, educator; b. Ostend, Belgium, June 2, 1945; s. August Lesthaeghe and Leonie Demeulemeester; m. Hilary J. Page, Dec. 25, 1971; children: David, Claire. Licence in Social Scis., Ryks U., Ghent, Belgium, 1967; PhD in Social Scis., 70; MA in Sociology, Brown U., 1968. Rsch. assoc. Ctr. Population Family Studies, Brussels, 1970; lectr. Vrye U., Brussels, 1971-77, prof. demography, 1978—; rsch. assoc. office population rsch., Princeton (N.J.) U., 1971-72; regional rep. Population Coun., N.Y. and Lagos, Nigeria, 1975-76; dean faculty econs. and social scis., Vrye U., Brussels, 1989-92; cons. NAS, Washington, 1984, 87, 89-93, King Baudouin Found., Brussels, 1981-83, others. Author: The Decline of Belgian Fertility, 1800-1970, 1978; co-author: Child-Spacing in Tropical Africa: Traditions & Change, 1980, La Formation Des Familles, Etude Prospective, 1995; editor: Reproduction and Social Organization in Sub-Sahara Africa, 1989. Recipient Colson Chair, Inst. Sci. Polit. Paris, 1987-91, Le Clercq Chair, U. Louvain, Belgium, 1995-96; Franqui chair U. Antwerp, 1998-99. Mem. Population Assn. Am., Internat. Union Sci. Study of Population, European Assn. Population Studies, European Soc. Population Econs., Belgian Acad. Arts and Scis., Acad. Europaea, Belgian Acad. Overseas Scis. (assoc.), Dutch Acad. Scis. (foreign mem.). E-mail: rlestha@vub.ac.be. Office: Vrye U, Pleinlaan 2, B 1050 Brussels Belgium

LESTIENNE, PATRICK PIERRE, molecular biologist; b. Roubaix, France, Oct. 5, 1950; s. Joseph Pierre and Brigitte Therese (Eeckman) L.; m. Catherine Marie Trouvé, July 7, 1973 (div. 1991); children: Vincent, Laetitia, Amelie. BTS, ESTBA, Paris, 1972; M in Biochemistry, U. Louis Pasteur, 1974, DEA in Biochemistry, 1975, PhD, 1978, DSc, 1980. Chargé rsch. Poly. Sch., Palaiseau, France, 1980-83, Stanford (Calif.) U., 1983-85; chargé rsch. Pasteur Inst., Paris, 1985-86, Angers, France, 1986-88; dir. rsch. Pasteur Inst., Angers, 1988-97, Bordeaux, France, 1997—. Author: Mitochondrial Diseases, 1998; contbr. articles to profl. jours. Mem. AAAs, European Soc. Human Genetics, Soc. French Genetics. Office: U Bordeaux 2, 146 Leo Saignat, 33076 Bordeaux France

LESTIENNE, REMY, neuroscientist; b. Toulouse, France, May 13, 1941; s. Gerard and Denise (Tiberghien) L.; m. Bernadette Courouble; children:

Catherine, Marion. PhD, U. Paris, 1967. Dir. Ctr. Studies & Documentation U. Sci. & Technology, Cairo, 1976-77; attache Amb. to France, Algiers, Algeria, 1981-85, Washington, 1990-94; sr. rschr. Inst. Neuroscis. CNRS, Paris, 1994—. Author: The Children of Time, 1995, The Creative Power of Chance, 1998. Mem. Internat. Soc. Study of time (pres. 1998—). Home: 65 Rue du Javelot, 75013 Paris France Office: Inst Neurosci, 9 quai St Bernard, 75005 Paris France

L'ESTRANGE, ALEXANDER WILLIAMSON HUME, manufacturing company executive; b. Walcha, NSW, Australia, Feb. 16, 1955; s. Alexander Ernest and June Christina (Bowman) L'E.; m. Susan Nicole Boothroyd, Mar. 5, 1983 (div. Jan. 1990); m. Narelle Gai Harris, Mar. 9, 1991; children: Alexander, Edward. Degree in Elec. Engring., Sydney (Australia) Tech. U., 1978. Refrigeration mechanic Snow Master, Leichhardt, Australia, 1975-78; grazier Family Property, Walcha, Australia, 1979-80; mng. dir. Betetec Industries, Ballina, Australia, 1980—. Inventor in field. Mem. Soc. Audio Engrs., Chamber Mfrs. Avocations: golfing, reading, listening to music, traveling, wine collecting. Office: Betetec Industries Pty Ltd, 17 DeHavilland Crescent, Ballina 2478 NSW, Australia

LET, FRED VAN, technical director; b. The Hague, The Netherlands, Sept. 3, 1949; m. Ank Barendse, Sept. 13, 1974; children: Bart, Sanne. MS, Tech. U., Delft, The Netherlands, 1975. Sr. cons. ATEL, Almere, The Netherlands, 1975-80; group mgr. CASEMA, Rijswijk, The Netherlands, 1980-85, tech. dir., 1985-98; dir. Competence Ctr. on Broadband Tech. CASEMA, Rijswijk, 1999—. Office: NV CASEMA, PO Box 2500 BD, The Hague The Netherlands

LETALICK, ALF DIETMAR, scientist; b. Linköping, Sweden, Apr. 9, 1957; s. Hans F.E. and Gunborg L. (Strid) L.; m. M.M. Jeanette Haglund, July 5, 1997. MSc, Linköping (Sweden) U., 1981; PhD, Chalmers U., Gothenburg, Sweden, 1991. Rsch. engr. FOA, Linköping, 1981-85, scientist, 1986-92, sr. scientist, 1993—; expert evaluator of proposals European Union, Brussels, 1999. Chmn. Komkyrkans Kammarorkester, Linköping, 1987-89; chmn. Lihkören, Linköping, 1992-95, Sjötomta Samfällighetsförening, Ekängen, 1998—. Mem. IEEE, Internat. Soc. Optical Engring., Optical Soc. Am. Avocation: music. Office: FOA, PO Box 1165, SE-58111 Linköping Sweden

LETHADEVI, GOVINDAN, biochemist; b. Trivandrum, Kerala, India, May 11, 1936; d. K. Govindan and Kannan Bhavani; m. Kochukrishnan Hrishikesan; children: Lekha Hrishikesan, Geetha, Arun. MBBBS, Trivandrum Med. Coll., 1958, MD in Biochemistry, 1964. Tutor Med. Coll., Trivandrum, 1960-64, asst. prof., 1964-72, assoc. prof., 1973-80, prof., 1981-88, dir., prof., 1989-91; dir. clin. biochemistry G.G. Hosp., Trivandrum, 1992—. Mem. Assn. Clin. Biochemists of India (life). Avocations: reading, stitching, cooking. Home: Pournemy Vikas Ln 66, Trivandrum Kevala State 695037, India

LETHBRIDGE, ROBERT DAVID, French language educator, university official; b. N.Y.C., Feb. 24, 1947; s. Albert and Muriel Alice (De Saram) L.; m. Vera Lenore Laycock, Jan. 2, 1970; children: Jonathan Andrew, Tamsin Jane. BA, U. Kent at Canterbury, Eng., 1969; MA, McMaster U., Can., 1970; MA (hon.), Cambridge (Eng.) U., 1973, PhD, 1974. Tchg. fellow Fitzwilliam Coll. Cambridge U., 1973-94, sr. tutor, 1982-92, lectr. French, 1980-94; prof. French lang. and lit. U. London, 1994—, head dept. Royal Holloway, 1995-96, vice prin. Royal Holloway, 1997—; mem. bd. mgmt. Brit. Inst. in Paris, 1994—; mem. exec. com. Rsch. Ctr.: Intertextualitées littéraires et artistiques, Sorbonne, Paris III, 1995—. Author: Maupassant: "Pierre et Jean,,' 1984; mem. editl. bd. Les Cahiers naturalistes, 1987—, Romance Studies, 1999—; editor: Zola and the Craft of Fiction, 1990, Artistic Relations: Literature and the Visual Arts in Nineteenth-Century France, 1994, Maupassant conteur et romancier, 1994, Emile Zola works Germinal, 1993, L'Assommoir, 1995, Pot-Bouille, 2000; contbr. articles to profl. jours., including French Studies, Modern Lang. Rev., Australian Jour. French Studies, Les Lettres Romanes, Spectator, Les Cahiers Naturalistes, Revue d' Histoire Littéraire de la France. Chmn. regional arbitration panel Ministry Agr., U.K., 1976-79. Decorated chevalier des Palmes Académiques (France); life fellow Fitzwilliam Coll., Cambridge U., 1994. Mem. Soc. for French Studies, Emile Zola Soc. (v.p. 1993), Assn. Univ. Profs. and Heads Dept. French (nat. exec. 1995-98). Home: 35 Warbeck Rd, London W12 8NS, England Office: U London, Royal Holloway, Egham TW20 0EX, England

LETOUBLON, FRANCOISE VUILLEMIN, Greek language and literature educator, researcher; b. Pontarlier, Doubs, France, Jan. 24, 1966; d. Jules and Suzanne (Pagnier) V.; m. Christian Letoublon, Aug. 8, 1969; children: Antoine, Alice, Nicolas. B in Philosophy, Paris, 1962, lic. lettres, 1967; M in Lettres Classiques, Sorbonne U., Paris, 1969, D in Lettres Classiques, 1981. Prof. Agregée Lycée Simone, 1969-70; attachée recherche CNRS, 1970-77, chargé recherche, 1977-80; maitre asst. U. Grenoble, 1980-88; prof. U. Stendhal, Grenoble, 1988-92; chargee de conf. U. Stendhal, 1992—. Mem. Assn. Qualité de la Sci. Francaise. Office: U Stendhal, UFR de Lettres, F-38040 Grenoble Cedex 9, France

LETSIE, III (MOHATO SEEISO), King of Lesotho; b. Morija, July 17, 1963; s. King Moshoeshoe II and Princess Tabitha 'Masentle. BA in Law, Nat. U. Lesotho, 1984; diploma, U. Bristol, 1986; student, Wye Coll., London, 1987-89, U. Cambridge, 1989. Prin. chief Matsieng, 1989-90; mem. Maseru City Coun., 1989-90, Nat. Constituent Assembly, 1989-90; coronated King of Lesotho, 1990—. Office: Royal Palace, PO Box 524, Maseru 100, Lesotho*

LETSOU, GEORGE VASILIOS, cardiothoracic surgeon; b. Boston, 1958; s. Vasilios George and Helen (Valacellis) L.; m. Jane Elizabeth Carter, June 1, 1985; children: Christopher George, Philip Taylor, John Carter. AB magna cum laude, Harvard U., 1979; MD, Columbia U., 1983. Diplomate Am. Bd. Surgery, Am. Bd. Thoracic Surgery. Resident in gen. surgery Yale-New Haven Hosp., 1983-88, chief resident and instr. surgery, 1987-88, clin. fellow in cardiothoracic surgery, 1988-89, Cystic Fibrosis Found. fellow cardiopulm. transplantation, 1988-89, Winchester scholar in cardiothoracic surg. rsch., 1989-90, resident in cardiothoracic surgery, 1990-91, chief resident in cardiothoracic surgery, 1991-92; attending surgeon Yale U., New Haven, 1992-95, instr. surgery, 1987-88, 91-92, asst. prof. surgery, 1992-95; attending surgeon Yale-New Haven Med. Ctr., 1992-95, Meth. Hosp., Ben Taub Hosp., Houston, 1995—; assoc. prof. surgery Baylor Coll. Medicine, Houston, 1995-99; attending surgeon Meml.-Hermann Hosp., Houston, 1998—; assoc. prof. surgery, chief cardiac surgery U. Tex., Houston, 1999—. Mem. AMA, ACS, Am. Coll. Cardiology, Am. Coll. Chest Physicians, Soc. Thoracic Surgeons. Fax: 713-500-0650. E-mail: George.V.Letsou@uth.tmc.edu. Office: Univ Tex-Houston Cardiothoracic Surgery 6431 Fannin St # 1214 Houston TX 77030-1501

LETTA, ENRICO, Italian government official; b. Pisa, Italy, Aug. 20, 1966. Min. EU Policy, Rome, 1998—; now min. industry and external trade. Office: Via Molise 2, 00187 Rome Italy*

LETTAU, THOMAS GUNTER, horticultural engineer; b. Erfurt, Germany, June 27, 1968; s. Gunter and Luise (Goglin) L.; m. Ramona Gleichmar; children: Luisa, Charlotte. Diploma, Humboldt U. Berlin, 1995. Cert. assessor, Erfurt, 1997. Rschr. Humboldt U. Berlin, 1997-98; cons. Erfurt Exptl. Sta., 1998-99; dept. head Office of Agr., Soemmerda, Germany, 1999—. With German Inf., 1989-90, Berlin. Protestant. Home: Am Angerberg 7, D-99094 Erfurt Germany Office: Humboldt U, Albrecht-Thaer-Weg 5, D-14195 Berlin Germany

LETTIN, ALAN WILLIAM, orthopaedic surgeon; b. London, Jan. 6, 1931; s. Frederick and Louisa Marion (Tabberer) L.; m. Patricia Jean Plumb, Sept. 19, 1953; children: Jennifer Ann (dec.), Nicholas Alan, Jonathan Frederick, Timothy William. BSc, U. Coll. London, 1952, MB, BChir, 1956; MS, U. London, 1967. Lic. Royal Coll. Physicians. House physician U. Coll. Hosp., London, 1955-56, house surgeon, 1956-57, casualty-surg. officer, 1959-60, surg. registrar, 1960-62; sr. house officer Royal Nat. Orthop. Hosp., London, 1962-63, orthop. registrar, orthop. sr. registrar, cons. orthop. surgeon, 1969-93; cons. orthop. surgeon St. Bartholomews Hosp., London, 1967-95, Middlesex & Univ. Coll. Hosp., London, 1993-94; hon. cons. Dr. Barnardos Homes, 1967-71; lectr. U. London. Author: Fundamental Anatomy for Operative Orthopaedic Surgery, 1991; contbr. articles to profl. jours. Freeman City of London, 1973—; master Worshipful Co. of Barbers, London, 1990. Flight lt. RAF, 1957-59. Fellow Royal Coll. Surgeons Eng. (coun. mem., 1984-96, v.p. 1994-96); mem. Inst. Brit. Surg. Technicians (hon.), Brit. Orthopaedic Assn. (sr. fellow, pres. 1993-94, Sir. Robert Jones Gold medal 1967), Gen. Osteopathic Coun. Avocations: gardening, photography, woodworking, home improvement. Home: Moat Farm, Swan Ln, Cretingham, Woodbridge 1P13 7AZ, England

LETTOW, CHARLES FREDERICK, lawyer; b. Iowa Falls, Iowa, Feb. 10, 1941; s. Carl Frederick and Catherine (Reisinger) L.; m. Sue Lettow, Apr. 20, 1963; children: Renee, Carl II, John, Paul. BS in Chem. Engring., Iowa State U., 1962; LLB, Stanford U., 1968. Bar: Calif. 1969, Iowa 1969, D.C. 1972, Md. 1991. Law clk. to Hon. Ben C. Duniway U.S. Ct. Appeals (9th cir.), San Francisco, 1968-69; law clk. to Hon. Warren E. Burger U.S. Supreme Ct., Washington, 1969-70; counsel Council on Environ. Quality, Washington, 1970-73; assoc. Cleary, Gottlieb, Steen & Hamilton, Washington, 1973-76, ptnr., 1976—; pres. Busy Way Farms, Inc., 1989—. Contbr. articles to profl. jours. Trustee Potomac Sch., McLean, Va., 1983-90, chmn. bd. trustees, 1985-88. 1st lt. U.S. Army, 1963-65. Mem. ABA, Am. Law Inst., D.C. Bar Assn., Iowa Bar Assn., Order of Coif. Club: University. Office: 2000 Pennsylvania Ave NW Washington DC 20006-1812

LETTS, LINDSAY GORDON, pharmacologist, educator; b. Warragul, Victoria, Australia, Jan. 9, 1948; came to U.S., 1987; m. Barbara Dawn Hawkey, Sept. 13, 1969; children: Michelle Maree, Kathryn Jane, David Gordon. BS, Monash U., Australia, 1971; PhD, Sydney U., 1980. Tutor Sydney (Australia) U., 1976-80; rsch. scientist Royal Coll. Surgeons Eng., London, 1980-82; sr. rsch. fellow Merck Frosst Can. Inc., 1982-87; dir. pharmacology Boehringer Ingelheim Pharms., Inc., Ridgefield, Conn., 1987-93; v.p. rsch. NitroMed Inc., Cambridge, Mass., 1993-96, chief sci. officer, sr. v.p. R&D, 1997—; adj. assoc. prof. Yale U. Sch. Medicine, New Haven, 1991-94. Editor Mediators of Inflammation, 1992-98, Pulmonary Pharmacology and Therapeutics, 1992—; sect. editor Prostaglandins, 1986—; editor Inflammation Rsch., 1994—. Bd. dirs. Nat. Inst. for Community Health Edn., Quinnipiac Coll., Hamden, Conn., 1990-94, Conn. United Rsch. Excellence, Wallingford, 1991-94. Mem. Inflammation Rsch. Assn. (bd. dirs. 1992—, pres. 1996-98). Office: NitroMed Inc 12 Oak Park Dr Ste 2 Bedford MA 01730-1426

LEU, HSI-MUH, academic administrator. Pres. Nat. Taiwan Normal U., Taipei. Office: Taiwan Normal U, 162 E Ho Ping Rd Sec 1, Taipei 10610, Taiwan*

LEU, IOAN CORNELIU, writer; b. Medgidia, Romania, July 21, 1932; s. Ioan Constantin and Valentina (Sora) L.; m. Rodica Novac, Apr. 18, 1956; children: Vlad, Tudor. Grad., Coll. Constantza, Romania, 1950. Writer, journalist, 1950—, pub., 1960—, movie, TV prodr., 1965—, prof. personalism, 1990—. Author: Dracula's Complaint, 1976 (Nat. award), The Way to Damascus, 1995 (Acad. award), others. Sec. gen. Bishop Grigorie Found.; pres. Romanian Agrarian Movement; pres. Nat. Coun. Village Intellectuals. Mem. PEN, Cinematographers Union, Journalists Union, Inst. Intenat. Jacques Maritain, Assn. Europeanne Enseignants. Home: 126 Blvd Dacia, 70267 Bucharest Romania

LEU, NELU ION, engineering educator; b. Sutesti, Romania, Feb. 1, 1944; s. Alicsandru and Elena (Mircea) L.; m. Georgeta Surdeanu, Nov. 1, 1970; children: Elena Madalina, Ioana Smarandita. Degree in engring., Mining Surveying U., Petrosani, Romania, 1968; D in Engring., Tech. U., Petrosani, Romania, 1974, photogrammetry expert, 1984; surveying expert, Min. Justice, Bucharest, Romania, 1990. Lt. Romanian Army, 1969—; surveying engr. Rsch. Finding Oil, Romania, 1968-71; design engr. City Hall, Bucharest, 1971-72; prof. engring. Agrl. Scis. Vet. Med. U., Bucharest, Romania, 1972—; prof. Tech. U., Bari, Italy, 1993-94, Min. Agr., Bucharest, 1993-97, Master of Sci. Bucharest, 1994-97. Author: From Foot to Satellite Measuring, 1981, Surveying & Photography, 4 Vols., 1982-86, Terestrial Measurements for Agriculture, 1990, Management for Urbanism, 1996. Regional leader Nat. Christian Party, 1994-97; handball referee, rugby referee. Mem. Coms V ISPRS (pres. 1984-94), Coms. VI ISPRS (pres. 1994-97), SNPh Arch. Romania Orthodox. Avocations: agriculture, farming. Home: Ion Paun Pincio, 73306 Bucharest Romania Office: Agricultural U, Marasti Bd 59, 70000 Bucharest Romania

LEUBERT, ALFRED OTTO PAUL, international business consultant, investor; b. N.Y.C., Dec. 7, 1922; s. Paul T. and Josephine (Haaga) L.; m. Celestine Capka, July 22, 1944 (div. 1977); children: Eloise Ann Cronin, Susan Beth; m. Hope Sherman Drapkin, June 4, 1978 (div. 1982). Student, Dartmouth Coll., 1943; BS, Fordham U., 1946; MBA, NYU, 1950. Account mgr. J.K. Lasser & Co., N.Y.C., 1948-52; controller Vision, Inc., N.Y.C., 1952-53; controller Old Town Corp., 1953-54, sec., controller, 1954-56, sec.-treas., 1956-57, v.p., treas., 1957-58; dir. subsidiaries Old Town Corp. (Old Town Internat. Corp., Old Town Ribbon & Carbon Co., Inc.), Mass. and Calif., 1955-58; v.p., controller Willcox & Gibbs, Inc., N.Y.C., 1958-59; v.p., treas. Willcox & Gibbs, Inc., 1959-65, pres., dir., CEO, 1966-76; founder, pub., pres. Leubert's Compendium of Bus. (Fin. and Econ. Barometers), 1978-82; pres. Alfred O.P. Leubert Ltd., 1981-82, chmn. CEO, 1993—; chmn., CEO Solidyne, Inc., 1982; chmn. bd., pres., CEO, dir. Chyron Corp., 1983-91; dir. K & E Real Estate Ltd., China, 1994-96; chmn. bd. CEO Leubert & Co. (H.K.) Ltd., 1994-98; dir. Laser-Pacific Media Corp., 1995-96; chmn. bd., CEO, bd. dirs. Chyron Group (U.K.) Ltd., 1985-89; dir. Isis Interactive Inc., 1996—; dir., vice chrmn. Advanced Definition Systems, Inc., 1996-97; chmn. bd., CEO, bd. dirs. CMX Corp., 1983-91; bd. dirs. Aurora Sys., 1988-91; dir. Avid Nordic AB, 1997—; strategic advisor PlasmaNet, Inc., 1999—, Tru-You.Com, Inc., 2000—, d-Merc.Com, Inc., 2000—, Dir. Media, Inc., 2000—; CEO, dir. CGS Units, Inc., 1988-90, chmn. bd., 1989-90; bd. dirs. Digital Svcs. Corp.; vice chmn. bd. dirs. CMX Laser Sys., Inc., 1988-93; instr. accountancy Pace Coll., 1955-57. Bd. dirs. United Fund of Manhasset, 1963-69, pres., 1964-65; bd. dirs. Actor's Studio, 1972-76; adv. bd. St. Anthony's Guidance Clinic, 1967-69. Served to 1st lt., inf. USMCR, 1943-46. Decorated Bronze Star; recipient Humanitarian award Hebrew Acad., N.Y.C., 1971. Mem. AICPA, N.Y. State Soc. CPAs, Fordham U. Alumni Assn., N.Y. Athletic Club. Roman Catholic. Home and Office: 1 Lincoln Plz New York NY 10023-7129

LEUENBERGER, MORITZ, federal official; b. Biel, Sept. 21, 1946. Law degree, U. Zurich. Bar: Zurich 1972. Pvt. practice, 1972-91; mem. governing coun. Canton of Zurich, Justice and Interior Portfolios, 1991-95; chief Fed. Dept. of Environ., Transp., Energy and Comm., Bern, Switzerland, 1995—. Pres. Social Dem. Party of Zurich, 1972-80; mem. city coun., 1972-83; mem. nat. coun. Ho. of Reps., 1979-95. Social-Democrat. Office: Bundeshaus Nord, Kochergasse 10, CH 3003 Bern Switzerland

LEUNG, ANGELA, marketing executive; b. Hong Kong, Dec. 14, 1958; d. T.L. and L.P. (Pang) L. Rschr. SRH, Hong Kong, 1978-82; rsch. mgr. AGB McNair, Hong Kong, 1982-86; assoc. dir. Frank Small, Hong Kong, 1986-92; mng. dir. Asia Mkt. Intelligence, Hong Kong, 1992—; cons. Procter & Gamble, Guang Zhou, China, 1992. Mem. MRS U.K., ESOMAR. Office: Asia Mkt Intelligence Ltd, 9/F Leighton Ctr/77, Causeway Bay Hong Kong

LEUNG, BEATRICE KIT FUN BENEDICT, political studies educator; b. Hong Kong, Aug. 15, 1938; d. Benedict Kwai Wah and Anna Mo Ying (Chan) L. BA, U. Hong Kong, 1966, MA, 1983; PhD, London Sch. Econs./Polit. Sci., 1988. Entered Sisters of Precious Blood, Roman Cath. Ch., 1957—. Secondary sch. educator, 1957-79; exec. sec., rschr. Holy Spirit Study Ctr., 1979-85, Hong Kong, 1988-90; lectr. Hong Kong Shue Yan Coll., 1990-92, Asia (Macau) Internat. Open U., 1989-93; asst. prof. U. Macau, 1992-93; assoc. prof. Lingnan U., Hong Kong, 1993-95, sr. lectr., program dir., 1995-99; rsch. assoc. Ctr. Asian Studies, U. Hong Kong, 1989—. Author: Sino-Vatican Relations: Problems of Conflicting Authority, 1992, (in Chinese) Relations Between Vatican and Chinese Communist Party, 1995; editor: Christianity in China: Foundation of Dialogue, 1993, Church and State Relations in 21st Century Asia, 1996. Rsch. fellow Ctr. asian Pacific Studies, Lingman U., 1994—; Rsch. Grant Coun. grantee, Hong Kong, 1994; German Mission scholar, 1985-88. Home: Sisters of Precious Blood, 86 Un Chau St, Kowloon Hong Kong Office: Lingnan Univ No 8, Castle Peak Rd, Tuen Mun Hong Kong

LEUNG, CHUN FAI, civil engineer, educator; b. Kowloon, Hong Kong, Nov. 23, 1954; s. Chung Leung and Choi Siu Yip; m. Anna Tan, Mar. 24, 1984; children: Wanling, Weiwen, Liwen. B in Engring., U. Liverpool, 1997, PhD, 1981. From lectr. to assoc. prof. Nat. U. Singapore, 1981—; cons. Econ Piling, Singapore, 1988-99, Fugro Cons., 1999-2000, Maritime and Port Authority, Singapore, 1997-98, Bintan Internat. Resorts, Indonesia, 1996-97. Grantee Port Singapore Authority, 1992-97, Nat. Sci. & Technology Bd., Singapore, 1995-99. Mem. Instn. Civil Engrs. UK, Instn. Engrs. Singapore, Internat. Soc. Soil Mechs. and Geotech. Engring. Tech. Com. Avocations: tennis, bridge, jogging, traveling. Office: Nat U Singapore Civil Eng, 10 Kent Ridge Crescent, Singapore 119260, Singapore

LEUNG, CHUN-YING, surveyor, consultant; b. Hong Kong, Aug. 12, 1954; s. Chung-en and Sau-tse (Keung) Liang; m. Ching-yee Tong; children: Chuen-yan, Chai-yan, Chung-yan. BS in Valuation & Estate Mgmt., Bristol Poly., Eng., 1977; D Bus. Adminstrn. (hon.), U. West of Eng., 1998, Hong Kong Poly. U., 1999. Fellow Hong Kong Inst. Surveyors, Royal Instn. Chartered Surveyors. Assoc. Jones Lang Wootton, Hong Kong, 1977-93; mng. dir. C.Y. Leung & Co., Hong Kong, 1993-99; chmn. DTZ Debenham Tie Leung Co Ltd, Hong Kong, 2000—. Sec. gen. Basic Law Consultative Com., 1988-90; vice chmn. Preparatory Com. for the Adminstrv. Region, Nat. People's Congress of China, 1996-97; mem. exec. coun. HKSAR, 1997-99, provisioanl legis. coun., 1997-99. Mem. Hong Kong Inst. Surveyors (past pres.). Office: DTZ Debenham Tie Leung Co, Jardine House Rm 1001, Hong Kong Hong Kong

LEUNG, ERWIN KA-YUE, engineer; b. Hong Kong, May 4, 1955; s. George Man-Wai and Yuk Chun (Ho) L.; m. Shirley Xiao-Hong Wang, Feb. 8, 1995. MS in Indsl. Engring., U. Hong Kong, 1987, MSEE, 1995; post-grad. in bus. info. tech., City Polytechnic of Hong Kong, 1989. Chartered elec. engr., U.K. Avionics overhaul engr. Hong Kong Aircraft Engring. Co., Ltd., 1983-88, sr. avionics overhaul engr., 1988-90, avionics overhaul supt., 1990-99; dir. engring. Asia Standard (Hong Kong) Ltd., 1999—; tech. cons. Express Fire Engring. Co., Ltd., Hong Kong, 1995—; dir. Rapid Strides Co., Ltd., Hong Kong, 1982—. Coord. for the candidate of election, Legis. Coun., Hong Kong, 1995. Mem. Hong Kong Instn. Engrs., Instn. Elec. Engrs. (corp. mem.), IEEE, World Wide Fund for Nature, The Planetary Soc. Roman Catholic. Office: C 28 2/F San Po Kong Plaza, 33 Shung Ling St, San Po Kong Kowloon Hong Kong

LEUNG, JIN PANG, behavioral psychologist; b. Guangzhou, China; s. Kai Fat and Yun Nui (Lai) L.; m. Lai Yee To; 1 child, Tina Leung. BA with honors, Massey Univ., 1981, PhD, 1984. Postdoctoral fellow Canterbury Univ., Christchurch, New Zealand, 1984-85; assoc. prof. The Chinese Univ. of Hong Kong, Shatin, 1985—; cons. Suen Mei Tng. Ctr. for the Deaf, Kowloon, Hong Kong, 1987-91; dir. Wai Ji Christian Svc., 1997—. Assoc. editor Bull. of the Hong Kong Psychol. Soc., 1990—, Jour. Psychology in Chinese Soc., 2000—; contbr. articles to profl. jours. Fellow Hong Kong Psychol. Soc. (mem. exec. com. 1986-88, pres. 1997-99), Am. Psychol. Assn. (affiliate mem.). Avocations: music, sports, reading. Office: Psychology Dept, Chinese Univ of Hong Kong, Shatin Hong Kong

LEUNG, KARL RICHARD PING HUNG, computer scientist; b. Hong Kong, May 22, 1961; s. Wai and Chung Ha (Law) L.; m. Iman Siu Kuen Yau, Apr. 23, 1994. Diploma in Computing Studies, Hong Kong Poly., 1985, Higher Diploma in Computing Studies, 1987; MPhil in Computer Sci., U. Hong Kong, 1992; PhD in Computer Sci., U. Hong Hong, 1997. Chartered engr., Engring. Coun. U.K. Analyst programmer East Asia Computer Co., 1983-85; freelance analyst, 1985-88; project mgr., rsch. asst. dept computer sci. Hong Kong U., 1988-89, software engr., 1989—; software engr. Hong Kong Poly./Haking Wong Tech. Inst., 1990—; hon. asst. prof. dept. computer sci. and info. sys. U. Hong Kong, 2000—; hon. info. tech. advisor Manicon Tech. Ltd., 2000—; indsl. cons. Hong Kong Inst. Vocat. Edn., 1998—; coord. computer dance rsch. group Hong Kong Poly., 1990—, Hong Kong Acad. Performing Arts, 1990—, Hong Kong U., 1990—, demonstrator dept. computer sci., 1987-89, demonstrator extra mural studies, 1988-89; coord. computer music rsch. group U. Hong Kong, 1990—, Shatin Tech. Inst., 1990—, City Poly. Hong Kong, 1990—, Hong Kong Poly. U., 1990—, lectr., 1990—, asst. prof. II, 1995—; prin. lectr. dept. computing and math. Hong Kong Inst. Vocat. Edn., 1998—; asst. lectr. dept. computing Hong Kong Poly., 1990, workshop tchr. dept. computing studies, 1989-90; organizer Internat. Computer Sci. Conf., 1992, Internat. Symposium on Algorithms and Computation, 1993, Internat. Computer Sci. Conf., 1995; tech. cons. Hong Kong Soc. for the Blind, 1995—; presenter in field. Contbr. articles to profl. jours. Swimming and life saving instr. YMCA, 1985—; swimming instr. Hong Kong Sport Assn. for the Mentally Handicapped, 1984—; tchr. Childrens Computer Club, 1983; swimming, life saving and synchronized swimming instr. Hong Kong Govt., 1982—; live saving and synchronized swimming instr. Tsuen Wan Life Saving Assn., 1978-82; dancer Inspired Dance Co., 1990—, hon. info. sys. mgr., 1990-91; hon. sec. Fedn. Synchronized Swimming Assn., Hong Kong, 1980-82; hon. tech. cons. Hong Kong Soc. for Blind, 1995—; Hong Kong conv. amb. Hong Kong Tourist Assn., 1994—. Vis. fellow UN Univ. Internat. Inst. for Software Tech., 1995—, French Nat. Rsch. Inst. in Computer Sci. and Control, 1997. Mem. IEEE (com. mem. Hong Kong sect. computer chpt. 1991—, sec. 1994, vice chair 1995—), Assn. Computing Machinery, Hong Kong Instn. Engrs., Hong Kong Computer Soc. (edn. and tng. com. mem., sec. open system special interest group 1991), Brit. Computer Soc. (edn. sub-com. mem. Hong Kong sect. 1990-91), Australian Computer Soc., Hong Kong Instn. Engrs., Asia Pacific Software Engring. Conf. (steering com. 1994—). Avocations: computer science research, performing arts, water sports, hiking. Office: Hong Kong Poly Univ, Dept Computing, Hong Kong China

LEUNG, LUP BONG LAWRENCE, training company executive; b. Hong Kong, Oct. 13, 1961; s. Cheuk and Chi Hoi (Loo) L.; m. Eva Wong, May 25, 1996. BA, Hong Kong Bapt. U., 1984; MBA, U. East Asia, Macau, 1992. Bus. exec. Marubeni Hong Kong Ltd., 1984-85; rep. Marubeni Corp., Shanghai, 1985-87; mgr. Dharmala Group, Hong Kong, 1987-88; comml. officer Commn. for Can., Hong Kong, 1988-96; v.p. Top Human Tech. Inc., Vancouver, B.C., Can., 1996—; mng. dir. Top Human Tech. Ltd., Hong Kong, 1997—; dir. Hang On Tai Co. Ltd., Hong Kong, 1992-97; v.p. Aristotle Capital Inc., Vancouver, B.C., 1996-97, Top Human Tech. (Shouzha) Ltd., vice chmn. Chmn. Assn. of Round Tables in Hong Kong, 1993; founding mem. Talent of People Found., Hong Kong, 1995. Mem. Hong Kong Gen. C. of C., Chinese Gen. C. of C., Can. C. of C., Total Quality Forum, Internat. Golf & Yacht Club, Aberdeen Boat Club, Mission Country Club. Avocations: golf, swimming, boating. Fax: 852 2528-6622. E-mail: lawrence@tophuman.com. Home: A3 17/F Grandview Tower, 130 Kennedy Rd, Hong Kong China Office: Top Human Tech Ltd, 7C One Cap Pl 18 Luard Rd, Hong Kong China

LEUNG, PO SING, physiology educator; b. Macao, Jan. 10, 1961; s. Kwok Bun Leung and Kam Luen Fok; m. Wan Chun Hu, July 29, 1988; children: May, Yan. BSc, Nat. Taiwan Normal U., Taipei, 1987; PhD, Queen's U. Belfast, No. Ireland, 1993. Higher Cert. in water pollution control. Insp. Environ. Protection Dept., Hong Kong, 1987-90; postdoctoral fellow Queen's U. Belfast, 1993-94, Japan Sci. and Tech. Agy., 1994-95, Chinese U. Hong Kong, 1995-96; asst. prof. physiology dept. Chinese U., Hong Kong, 1996-98; assoc. prof. dept. physiology Chinese U., 1998—. Contbr. articles to sci. jours., including Cellular and Molecular Endocrinology, Jour. Endocrinology, Jour. Membrane Biology, Biochimica et Biophysica Acts; mem. editl. bd. Jour. of Pancreas. Grantee Hong Kong Rsch. Grants Coun., 1997-99, 2000-2002, Germany-Hong Kong Joint Rsch. Scheme, 1997-99, 99-2000. Mem. Endocrine Soc., Biochem. Soc., Chinese Physiol. Soc., N.Y. Acad. Scis. Avocations: reading, jogging, table tennis. E-mail: psleung@cuhk.edu.hk. Office: Chinese U Hong Kong Fac Med, Dept Physiology, Shatin NT, Hong Kong

LEUNG, WING TAI, youth organization executive; b. Hong Kong, Hong Kong, Oct. 4, 1949; s. Tack Ming Leung and Yuet Ling Tam; m. Kit Ngar Lo, Aug. 14, 1976; children: Horasis, Joshua, Gabriel. MA in Theol. Studies, Gordon-Connell Theol. Sem., South Hamilton, Mass., 1976; MA,

Bowling Green State U., 1977; MFA, U. So. Calif., L.A., 1983; PhD, Regent U., 1994. Tchr. Queen Elizabeth Sch., Hong Kong, 1972-74; dir. audio-visual dept. Breakthrough, Hong Kong, 1978-97, assoc. gen. sec., 1986—; gen. mgr. Breakthrough Youth Village, 1995—; adj. prof. China Grad. Sch. Theology, Hong Kong, 1980, Regent U., Virginia Beach, 1992-94; cons. Inst. Studies in Asian Chs. and Culture, Manila, 1981—; plenary spkr. Internat. Christian Media Conf., Holland, 1986; program prodr. First Youth Festival Hong Kong Govt., 1989; founding mem., sec. Electronic News Media and Pub. Consortium, Hong Kong, 1995—; chair com. on info. age Chinese Coordination Ctr. of World Evangelism Congress, Hong Kong, 1995-96. Exec. prodr., dir. (multivision/presentation) Gen, 1984, (tv series) Generation 21, 1989; exec. prodr. (interactive exhbn.) Peace Hi-Touch Exhbn., 1985, (tv series) Quest for Metropolis, 1990; chief editor Inst. for Exec. Devel., Hong Kong, 1996. Mem. Speech Comm. Assn., Hong Kong Inst. for Exec. Devel., Internat. Comm. Assn., Phi Alpha Ki. Avocations: fishing, hiking, reading, photography. Home: 13-B On Ting Terr G Floor, Shatin Hong Kong Office: Breakthrough, 33 A Kung Kok Shan Rd, Shatin Hong Kong

LEUNG, WOON-FONG WALLACE, mechanical and chemical engineer, scientist; b. Hong Kong, Jan. 25, 1954; s. Shing-Lam and So-Wan (Cheung) L.; m. Stella Po-Chun Cheng, June 25, 1978; children: Jessica, Jeffrey. SB, Cornell U., 1977; MSME, MIT, 1978, ScD, 1981. Cons. Water Purification Assoc., Cambridge, Mass., 1979-80; rsch. engr. Gulf Rsch. & Devel. Co., Harmarville, Pa., 1981-83; sr. engr. Gulf Rsch. & Devel. Co., Houston, 1983-84; project leader Schlumberger Tech., Sugarland, Tex., 1984-86; dir. process tech. Baker Process, South Walpole, Mass., 1986—; dir. Solid/Liquid Separation for Process Industries course and Centrifuge course Ctr. for Profl. Advancement. Author: Industrial Centrifugation Technology, 1998, Perry and Green's Chemical Engineering Handbook on Centrifugation, 7th edit., 1995, Handbook of Separation Techniques, 3d edit., 1995; editor: System Approach to Separation and Filtration Process Equipment, 1993, Advances in Filtration and Separation Technology vol. 13a, 13b, 1999; assoc. editor Fluid-Particle Separation Jour., 1990-92; inventor in field; lectr. in field; contbr. articles to profl. jours. Organizer MIT Chin. Students Club Concert, 1991. Recipient Cedric Ferguson medal AIME, Soc. Petroleum Engrs., Dallas, 1987, Baker Hughes Tech. Achievement award, Houston, 1992. Mem. Am. Men and Women of Sci., ASME, AIChE, Am. Filtration and Separation Soc. (bd. dirs. 1992-98, chmn. centrifuge network, 1990—, ann. conf. chair and organizer 1993, 99, Engring. Merit award 1992, soc. chmn. 1999—), Soc. Petroleum Engrs., Soc. Rheology. Achievements include 31 patents on centrifugal separation; findings on petroleum production and well "skin" testing, aquifer water flow, centrifuge, rotating flow, rheological behavior of non-Newtonian fluid, ultrafiltration and lamella sedimentation. E-mail: wfleung@aol.com; wallace.leung@bakerhughes.com. Home: 11 Ames Dr Sherborn MA 01770-1056 Office: Baker Process 100 Neponset St South Walpole MA 02071-1037

LEUNG, YEE HONG, communications engineer, researcher; b. Singapore, Aug. 4, 1955; arrived in Australia, 1968; s. Wai Sun and Hing Hang (Tsang) L.; m. Yoon Fong Chin, May 8, 1982; children: Jee Yun, Jee Ming. BEng, U. Western Australia, Perth, 1977, PhD, 1986. Rsch. scientist Def. Sci. and Tech. Orgn., Adelaide, Australia, 1986-88; lectr. U. Western Australia, 1988-94; rsch. fellow Curtin U. Tech., Perth, 1994—. Contbr. articles to sci. jours., including Applied Math. and Optimization, IEEE Trans Signal Processing. Grantee Australian Rsch. Coun., 1989—, rsch. grantee Def. Sci. and Tech. Orgn., 1996-97. Mem. IEEE (chmn. signal processing chpt. Western Australia chpt. 1998—). Baptist. Avocation: classical music. Office: Australian Telecomm Rsch Inst, Curtin U Tech, Bentley WA 6102, Australia

LEUNG, YIU CHEONG, engineering educator; b. Hong Kong, Sept. 11, 1959; s. Man Hin and Shuet Ngan (Mak) L.; m. Betty Shuk Kwan Kwong, Oct. 1, 1988; children: Hoi Ki, Hoi Yeung. BSc in Engring., U. Hong Kong, 1982, PhD, 1988. Environ. engr. Kong Kong Elec. Co. Ltd., 1987-93; assoc. prof. U. Hong Kong, 1993—, chmn. environ. engring. program, 1998—. Contbr. over 80 articles to profl. jours. Fellow Inst. Mech. Engrs., Inst. Energy, Hong Kong Inst. Engrs. Office: U Hong Kong Dept Mech Engr, Pokfulam Rd, Hong Kong China

LEUNG, YIU WING, computer science educator; b. Hong Kong, 1967; s. Lo Chong and Choy Chu (Cheng) L.; m. Yvonne L.Y. Tsang, July 12, 1997. BSc, Chinese U. Hong Kong, 1989, PhD, 1992. Asst. prof. Hong Kong Poly. U., 1993-97; assoc. prof. computer sci. Hong Kong Bapt. U., 1997—; external examiner City U. of Hong Kong, Open U. of Hong Kong, Ctrl. Queensland U. Australia, 1998—. Mem. editl. rev. com. IEEE Tranasactions on Instrumentation and Measurement, 1996-98; paper reviewer IEEE and ACM jours., 1991—; external assessor to assess earmarked rsch. grant proposals, Hong Kong, 1994—; contbr. over 50 articles to profl. jours. Mem. IEEE (sr.). Office: Hong Kong Bapt U, Dept Computer Sci, Kowloon Hong Kong China

LEUPP, CAROL ANNE, retired elementary education educator; b. Delta, Ohio, Jan. 5, 1940; d. Marvin Lester and Mildred Christine (Fauble) Cook; m. Harold Roger Leupp, Mar. 23, 1962; children: Sarah Leupp Corbett, Christopher John, Melissa Anne. BS in Edn., Bowling Green State U., 1961; MEd, U. Toledo, 1966. Tchr. Sylvania (Ohio) Schs., 1961-62, Delta (Ohio)/Pike/York Schs., 1966-67, Olivet Christian Nursery Sch., Sylvania, 1974-76; reading tutor adult literacy program Toledo, 1988-91; reading tutor Sprinfield Schs., Holland, Ohio, 1991-2000. Leader Girl Scouts U.S., Sylvania, 1979-82; dir. Ch. Sch. Edn., Youth Handbell Choir, Sylvania, 1970-87; mem. Friends Libr.-Lucas County, Toledo, Sunset Ho. Aux., Toledo. Mem. AAUW (Toledo pres. 1986-88, Ohio pres. 1996-98, mem. program com. 1999—). Republican. Lutheran. Avocations: reading, playing piano, tennis, golf, collecting children's books. Home: 239 Stone Oak Ct Holland OH 43528-9256

LEURQUIN, ERIC X., market risk management auditor, finance educator; b. Uccle, Brussels, Belgium, Jan. 12, 1966; s. Philippe Leurquin and Laure-Elisabeth Lorent; m. Anne Geraets; 1 child, Elise. MS in Engring. in Logistics, Cath. U. Louvain, Belgium, 1989; MSEE, U. C. of Louvain, Belgium, 1988; MBA in Fin., U. Chgo., 1991. Cert. internal auditor. Engr. Honeywell, Belgium, 1989-90; auditor Petrofina, Belgium, 1992-93, acctg., 1993-94; fund mgr. Bank Brussels Lambert, Belgium, 1994-98; market risk mgmt. auditor BBL-ING, Brussels, 1999-2000, euro coord., 2000—; prof. fin. Inst. Cooremans, Belgium, 1999—, HEC Liege, Belgium, 2000—. Contbr. articles to newspapers. Recipient FMC Corp. prize for outstanding achievement, 1991; Belgian Am. Ednl. Found. scholar, 1990. Mem. Inst. Internal Auditors. Roman Catholic. Avocations: travel, theater, tennis. Home: Rue de Rixensart 45 A, B-1332 Genval Belgium Office: BBL, Av Marnix 24, B-1000 Brussels Belgium

LEUSCHNER, RUTH MARIA, biologist; b. Basel, Switzerland, Sept. 20, 1922; d. Alfred Robert Leuschner and Pauline Maria Leuschner-Rörich. Diploma in higher tchg., U. Basel, 1967, PhD, 1973. guest spkr. found. congress Italian Assn. Aerobiology, 1985; presenter various profl. confs. Editor: (with G. Boehm) Advances in Aerobiology, 3rd Internat. Conf. on Aerobiology, Basel, 1986; contbr. revisions, transl. to German: Allergies: Questions and Answers (G. Thieme), 1988; contbg. author: Atlas of European Allergenic Pollens, 1974, Swiss Atlas of Health Resorts and Spas, 1984, Atlas of Mould in Europe, 1984; contbr. weekly column, Orientation for Allergy Sufferers, to Basler Zeitung, 1979—; contbr. chpts., articles to profl. publs., including jours., procs. and books in field; presenter radio broadcasts. Rsch. grantee Swiss Nat. Found. Sci. Rsch., 1973, 77, 80. Fellow European Assn. Climatotherapy (mem. com. 1980-96, hon. pres. Swiss working group on aerobiology); mem. Internat. Assn. Aerobiology (hon., founding, officer 1974-90), Swiss Assn. Aerobiology (hon.), Basel Bot. Soc. (mem. com. 1974-96, editor jour. Bauhinia 1977-79). Mem. Reformed Ch. Switzerland. Achievements include research on airborne particles, including dust particles from the Sahara desert, particles collected in the Burkard trap, on the Cantonial Hosp., fungal spores and inorganic particles in the air at various recording sites; measurements of the effectiveness of different air purifying apparatus on pollen in enclosed environments; monitoring and initial identification of the presence of Ambrosia (ragweed) in Basel and Nyon; Avocations: microscopy, botany. Home: Thannerst 5, CH-4054 Basel Switzerland Office: Divsn Dermatology/Allergy, Dept Forschung, Hebelstr 20, CH-4031 Basel Switzerland

LEUTSCHER, PETER DEREK CHRISTIAN, tropical medicine physician; b. Heemsted, The Netherlands, Oct. 8, 1960; s. Jakob Kos Leutscher and Elise Leth; m. Karen Meyer, Jan. 9, 1993; children: Kristian, Markus, Daniel, Nikoline. MD, U. Aarhus, 1989; PhD, U. Copenhagen, 1998. Intern Broenderslev Hosp., Denmark, 1989-91; anesthesiologist, internist Silkeborg Hosp., Denmark, 1991-93; med. officer U.S Peace Corps, Antananarivo, Madagascar, 1994—; cons. physician U.S. Embassy, Antananarivo, 1995—; temporary advisor WHO, Annecy, France, 1997. Mem. Danish Med. Assn., Danish Soc. Tropical Medicine. Office: Inst Pasteur de Madagascar, BP 1274 Antananarivo Madagascar

LEUTY, GERALD JOHNSTON, osteopathic physician and surgeon; b. Knoxville, Iowa, July 23, 1919; s. John William and Mable Reichard (Johnston) L.; m. Martha L. Weymouth, Jan. 24, 1940 (div. 1957); children: Maxine Joanne, Robert James, Gerald Johnston Jr., Karl Joseph; m. Norma Jean Hindman, Dec. 30, 1969; children: Barbara Jayne, Patrick Jack. AB, Kemper Mil. Sch., Boonville, Mo., 1939; postgrad., Drake U., Des Moines, 1944-45; DO, Des Moines Coll. Osteopathy, 1949; embalmer, Coll. Mortuary Sci., St. Louis, 1941. Mortician/embalmer Cauldwell-McJihon Funeral Home, Des Moines, 1939-40; aero. engr. Boeing Aircraft Co., Wichita, Kans., 1941-42; osteopathic physician and surgeon Knoxville (Iowa) Ostepathic Clinic, 1949-56; dir. Leuty Osteopathic Clinic, Earlham, Iowa, 1957-77; osteopathic physician and surgeon in pvt. practice Santa Rosa, Calif., 1977—; prof. clin. med. Western U. Health Svcs., Pomona, Calif., 1985—. Mem. Iowa's Gov. Blue Med. Adv. Bd., 1972-77. With U.S. Army, 1942-46. Named Physician of the Yr., 6th Dist. Iowa Ostepathic Soc., 1975, Disting. Leadership award, Am. Biog. Inst., 1988, others. Fellow Internat. Co.. Angiologists; mem. Am. Ostepathic Assn. (ho. of dels., life mem. 1989), Iowa Osteopathic Soc. (pres. 6th dist. 1974), Soc. Osteopathic Physicians, No. Calif. Osteopathic Med. Soc. (pres. 1981), Osteopathic Physicians and Surgeons of Calif. (pres. 1982), Am. Acad. Osteopathy (chmn. component socs. com. 1988, pres. Calif. divsn. 1987, pres. No. Calif. divsn. 1989, 91-93, 95), North Coast Osteopathic Med. Assn. (pres. 1992), Am. Med. Soc. Vienna (life mem.), Am. Legion (6th dist. comdr. 1974-75), Lions (pres. 1946). Republican. Presbyterian. Avocations: photography, travel. Home: 5835 La Cuesta Dr Santa Rosa CA 95409-3914

LEUWER, MARTIN KARL, anesthesiologist; b. Bonn, Germany, Feb. 10, 1954; s. Winfried and Ruth (Pirkel) L.; m. Gertrud Haeseler. MD, Johann-Wolfgang-Goethe U., Frankfurt am Main, Germany, 1979, Dr.med., 1982; Dr.med.habil., Medizinische Hochschule, Hannover, Germany, 1994, Prof., Pers. Chair Anesthesia and Intensive Care Medicine, 1999-2000. Registrar Mil. Hosp., Giessen, Germany, 1979-82; registrar U. Clinic, Frankfurt/Main, Germany, 1982-86, cons., 1987-93; vice-head univ. dept. anesthesiology I Hannover Med. Sch., 1993-2000; prof., chmn. anesthesia U. Liverpool, Eng., 2000—. Author: Muscle Relaxants in Children, 1996; editor: Interdisziplinäre Intensivmedizin, 1999; patentee in field. Rsch. grant Riese Found., Frankfurt/Main, 1986; recipient Best Poster award Ctrl. European Anesthesia Congress, Interlaken, 1991, Best Free Paper award Neuroanesthesia Soc. Gt. Britain and Ireland, Bochum, 1996, Heller-Mager-von Schroetter award, 1999. Mem. Anaesthetic Rsch. Soc., German Assn. for Anesthesiology and Intensive Medicine, European Soc. Anesthesiologists (subcom. pharmacology 1997—). Avocations: piano, sailing, skiing, horse riding, gardening. Fax: 44-151-706 5884. Office: U Liverpool Dept Anesthesia, Duncan Bldg Daulby St, Liverpool L69 3GA, England

LEV, ELISE L., nurse; m. Joseph Lev, June 11, 1961; children: Joyce, Andrew. BS, Adelphi Coll., 1962; EdD, Columbia U., 1986. Assoc. prof. Coll. New Rochell (N.Y.); asst. prof. Coll. Nursing Rutgers U. Contbr. articles to profl. jours. Postdoctoral fellow U. Pa., Phila., Henry Rutgers Rsch. fellow Rutgers U. Mem. ANA (adult psychiat. mental health nursing, clin. specialist), Coun. Nurse Researchers, Sigma Theta Tau (Disting. Lectr.).

LEVANDOWSKI, BARBARA SUE, educational administrator; b. Chgo., Mar. 16, 1948; d. Earl F. and Ann (Klee) L.. BA in Edn. and Spanish, North Park Coll., 1970; MS in Elem. Edn., No. Ill. U., 1975, degree in curriculum and supervision/instruction, 1977, EdD, 1979. Cert. elem. tchr.; cert. secondary tchr.; cert. in adminstrv. with supt. endorsement; cert. senior reviewer, Ill. Tchr. Round Lake (Ill.) Sch. Dist., 1970-75; tchr. Schaumburg (Ill.) Sch. Dist., 1975-87, asst. prin., 1977-87; prin., staff devel. dir. Dist. 200 Northwood Elem. Sch., Woodstock, Ill., 1987-94, dir. curriculum and instrn., 1994—; curriculum cons. Spring Grove (Ill.) Sch. Dist., 1980-81; instr. various courses, Schaumburg, 1984-86; dir. Einstein Sch. Writing Project, 1986-87; dir. Dist. 200 Thinking Skills Task Force, 1988—; co-instr. Dist. 200 Teaching Thinking Skills Across the Curriculum, 1992—, dir. curriculum and instrn.; chair north ctrl. assn. visitation team Huntley Sch. Dist., 1989; presenter various confs. Mem. editorial bd. Ill. Sch. R & D Jour., 1981—; contbr. articles to profl. jours. Mem. staff Round Lake Park Dist., 1973—; chair Computer/Tech. Strategic Action Team, Woodstock, 1988-89. Recipient numerous awards for excellence in teaching, Those Who Excel award State of Ill., 1979; fed. grantee. Mem. NAESP, NAFE, Am. Biog. Inst. Rsch. Assn. (bd. dirs. 1985—, publs. com. 1983), Nat. Staff Devel. Coun., ASCD (inservice presenter 1984-86, presenter state and nat. conv. 1989—), Nat. Coun. of States for InSvc., Ill. Staff Devel. Coun., Ill. Assn. for Supervision and Curriculum Devel. (chair research com. 1982), Ill. Computer Educators, Inst. for Ednl. Rsch. (editorial bd. advisors, co-chair effective teaching characteristics observation 1990—, Omega award), Ill. Prin. Assn., Phi Delta Kappa, Delta Kappa Gamma. Home: 426 Normandie Ln Round Lake IL 60073-3711 Office: Woodstock Sch Dist 200 227 W Judd St Woodstock IL 60098-3126

LEVANON, HAIM JONATHAN, chemist, educator; b. Jerusalem, Mar. 20, 1938; s. Jacob and Rachel (Masseioff) L.; m. Hedva Bilogrotzky, Nov. 11, 1963; children: Jacob, Asaf, Rachel. BSc, Hebrew U., Jerusalem, 1963, MSc, 1965, PhD, 1969. Rsch. assoc. Washington U., St. Louis, 1969-72; lectr. Hebrew U., Jerusalem, 1972-75, sr. lectr., 1975-79, assoc. prof., 1979-83, prof., 1983—; dir. The Farkas Ctr. for Light-Induced Processes, Jerusalem, 1991-99; pres. Israel Chem. Soc., Jerusalem, 1984-87; bd. dirs. Israel Chems., 1988-94, TAMI Ctrl. Rsch. Facility of Israel Chems.; chmn. Israel Oceanographic and Limnological Rsch. Ltd., chmn. five internat. sci. confs. Editor-in-chief Israel Jour. Chemistry, 1987—; contbr. articles to profl. jours. Chmn. Assn. Profs. for Polit. and Economical Strength in Israel, Jerusalem, 1991-93. Sgt. Infantry-Israel Def. Force, 1956-58. Recipient Max Planck Rsch. award Alexander von Humboldt and Max Planck Gesellschaft, Germany, 1992; Willstätter lectr. German Chem. Soc., Germany, 1994. Avocation: carpentry. Home: 14 Leshem St, 90805 Mevasseret Zion Israel Office: Hebrew Univ Jerusalem, Dept Phys Chemistry, 91904 Jerusalem Israel

LEVASHOV, MIKHAIL IVANOVICH, laboratory administrator, researcher; b. Ishimbay, Russia, Oct. 7, 1953; s. Ivan Fedorovich and Vera Ivanovna (Ruleva) L.; m. Larisa Grigorivna Konoval, Mar. 3, 1979; children: Oleg, Igor. MD, Med. Inst., Kyibyshev, Russia, 1978; Candidate Med. Scis., Med. Inst., Kyibyshev, 1984; DMS, Inst. Physiology, Kiev, Ukraine, 1994. Cert. gen. therapy, clin. pulmonology. Therapist Zlatoust (Russia) Regional Hosp., 1978-79; jr. rschr. Med. Inst., Kyibyshev, 1979-84, asst., 1984-85; rschr. A.A. Bogomoletz Inst. Physiology, Kiev, 1986-87; sr. rschr. R.E. Kavecky Inst. Oncology Problem, Kiev, 1987-95; leading rschr. A.A. Bogomoletz Inst. Physiology, Kiev, 1995—; cons. Hosp. Nat. Acad. Scis., Kiev, 1987-99; head lab. Sci. Ctr., NORT, Nat. Acad. Scis., Kiev, 1995. Patentee in field. Mem. N.Y. Acad. Scis., Internat. Respiratory Care Clab, Physiology Soc. Ukraine. Orthodox Christian. Avocations: tourism, reading, writing. Home: Lunacharsky St 24 Apt 364, 02002 Kiev Ukraine Office: AA Bogomoletz Inst Physiol, Bogomoletz St 4, 01024 Kiev Ukraine

LEVASSEUR, LEE ALLAN, fine artist; b. Hartford, Conn., Apr. 8, 1950; s. Euclid Roland and Beatrice Marie (Daigle) LeV.; m. Evelyn M. Tucker, June 30, 1973 (div. Mar. 1986); 1 child, Robert Aaron. BS in Art Edn., So. Conn. State U., 1973. Cert. art tchr. K-12. Artist Organic Surrealism, Branford, Conn., 1989—; prodr., dir. Organic Surrealism, Branford, 1991; custom picture framer APN Gallery, Branford, Conn., 1990-92, Off the Wall Gallery, Madison, Conn., 1992-93; archival picture framer Northlight Gallery, Branford, 1995—; co-prodr., dir. "America 500" Quintcentennial, Buenos Aires, New Haven, Boston, N.Y.C., 1992; lectr. Rotary, Guilford, Conn., 1990. Exhibited Internat. Festival of Arts and Ideas, New Haven, 1999. Recipient Cert. of Excellence Artitudes Internat. Art Competition, N.Y.C., 1989, Blue Ribbon Branford (Conn.) Festival, 1991, Prize E SoHo Internat. Art Competition, 1992, First Pl. Mixed Media, Cheshire Art League, 2000. Mem. Shoreline Alliance of Artists, Art Coun. New Haven (Conn.), Branford C. of C. Democrat. Roman Catholic. Avocations: hiking, herbalism, camping, gardening, environmental conservator. Office: Organic Surrealism 525 E Main St Trlr 40 Branford CT 06405-2930

LEVCOVICI, SANDA MARIA, engineering educator, researcher; b. Rostoride Vede, Teleorman, Romania, Sept. 4, 1944; d. Paraschiv and Maria (Panait) Tuchel; m. Teodor Levcovici, Dec. 2, 1967; children: Bogdan George, Cristian. Diplomate engr., U. Dunarea de Jos, 1967, doctor of engring., 1998. Engr. Galati, Romania, 1967-68; rsch. engr. Siden SA, Galati, 1968-70; design engr. ICPPAM SA, Galati, 1970-72; asst. lectr. U. Dunarea de Jos, Galati, 1978-78, lectr., 1978-98, asst. prof., 1998—; profl. concillium Sci. of Materials, U. Dunarea de Jos, 1990-99; mem. non-conventional technologies Filial From Galati of Roumanien Acad., 1997-99. Author: Low Cycle Fatigue and Elastoplastic Behavior of Materials, 1998; contbr. articles to profl. jours.; patentee in field. Avocations: travelling, books, classical music. Home: Barbosi No 39 Bl B6, AP 46 Micro 17, 6200 Galati Romania Office: U Dunarea de Jos of Galati, Domnfasca No 47, 6200 Galati Romania

LEVEEN, ROBERT FREDERICK, radiologist; b. Jersey City, July 24, 1946; s. Harry Henry and Jeanette Lois (Rubricius) LeV.; m. Sandra Sue Hickstein, May 28, 1974; children: Emily, Rob. BA, Grinnell Coll., Iowa, 1968; MD, U. Nebr., Omaha, 1974. Diplomate Am. Bd. Radiology. Intern dept. surgery U. Washington, 1974-75; resident in radiology Coll. Medicine U. Nebr., 1975-78; asst. prof. radiology U. Nebr. Med. Ctr., Omaha, 1978-80; from asst. prof. radiology to assoc. prof. U. Pa., Phila., 1980-90; research assoc. VA Med. Ctr., Phila., 1980-83; clin. investigator VA Med. Ctr., 1985-90; coordinator, angiography research U. Pa., Dept. Radiology, 1985-90; assoc. prof. radiology U. Nebr. Med. Ctr., 1991-99; chief radiology svc. VA Med. Ctr., Omaha, 1991-99; assoc. prof. U. Fla., Gainesville, 1999—. Recipient Career Devel. award, VA, 1985; Stauffer award, Assn. U. Radiologists, 1986. Fellow Am. Coll. Radiology; mem. Soc. Cardiovascular and Interventional Radiology, Radiologic Soc. N.Am., Assn. U. Radiologists, Nebr. Radiolog. Soc. (pres. 1998-99). Presbyterian. Office: U Fla Coll Medicine Dept Radiology PO Box 100374 Gainesville FL 32610-0374

LEVENE, SHIRLEY SCHECHTER, psychotherapist; b. N.Y.C., Oct. 10, 1917; d. William and Edith (Herman) Goldsmith; m. Jack Levene, Nov. 1983; children: Judith Schechter Lasko, Ruth Schechter Rubinow. BA, Vassar Coll., 1938; MS, Columbia U., 1942; cert. analytic group psychotherapy, Postgrad. Ctr. Mental Health, 1968, cert. supervision of individual and group therapy, 1971. Psychotherapist Family Consultation Svc., Eastchester, N.Y.; pvt. practice psychotherapist White Plains, N.Y. Contbr. articles to profl. jours. Fellow AGPA; mem. NASW (diplomate), Eastern Group Psychotherapy Soc. (past pres.), N.Y. Soc. Clin. Social Work Psychotherapists (diplomate N.Y. State cert. social worker). Home and Office: 111 Miles Ave White Plains NY 10606-3816

LEVENS, JOSEPH DAVID, investment company executive; b. Boston, July 13, 1957; s. Frederick M. and Ruth R. (Raphael) L.; m. Beth Anne Wolfson, July 27, 1986; 1 child, Samuel L. BA Polit. Sci., U. Mass., 1979; MPA, Syracuse U., 1981. Adminstrv. asst. UN, Geneva, 1977, 78; grad. asst. Syracuse U., N.Y., 1979-81; cons. Info. Bus., Cambridge, Mass., 1980; rsch. asst. Operation Drake, Sulawesi, Indonesia, 1980; sr. cons. Booz Allen & Hamilton, Washington, 1981-84; sr. mgmt. analyst Gen. Electric, Lynn, Mass., 1984-86; prin. Am. Mgmt. Sys. Inc., Cambridge, 1986-94; dir. Fidelity Investments, Boston, 1994—. Author: (with others) Personnel Management in Government, 1981. Bd. dirs. U. Mass. Alumni Bd., Amherst, 1985-87; mem. troop 182 com. coun. Boy Scouts Am., 1985—. Avocations: cross country skiing, scuba diving, photography, hiking, gardening.

LEVENSON, ALAN BRADLEY, lawyer; b. Long Beach, N.Y., Dec. 13, 1935; s. Cyrus O. and Jean (Kotler) L.; m. Joan Marlene Levenson, Aug. 19, 1956; children: Scott Keith, Julie Jo. AB, Dartmouth Coll., 1956; BA, Oxford U., Eng., 1958, MA, 1962; LLB, Yale U., 1961. Bar: N.Y. 1962, U.S. Dist. Ct. D.C. 1964, U.S. Ct. Appeals (D.C. cir.) 1965, U.S. Supreme Ct. 1965. Law clk., trainee div. corp. fin. SEC, Washington, 1961-62, gen. atty., 1962, trial atty., 1963, br. chief, 1963-65, asst. dir., 1965-68, exec. asst. dir., 1968, dir., 1970-76; v.p. Shareholders Mgmt. Co., L.A., 1969, sr. v.p., 1969-70, exec. v.p., 1970; ptnr. Fulbright & Jaworski, Washington, 1976—; lectr. Cath. U. Am., 1964-68, Columbia U., 1973; adj. prof. Georgetown U., 1964, 77, 79-81, U.S. rep. working party OECD, Paris, 1974-75; adv. com. SEC, 1976-77; mem. adv. bd. Securities Regulation Inst., U. Calif., San Diego, 1973—, vice chmn. exec. com., 1979-83, chmn., 1983-87, emeritus chmn., 1988—; mem. adv. coun. SEC Inst., U. So. Calif., L.A., Sch. Acctg., 1981-85; mem. adv. com. Nat. Ctr. Fin. Svcs,. U. Calif.-Berkeley, 1985-89; mem. planning com. Ray Garrett Ann. Securities Regulation Inst. Northwestern U. Law Sch.; mem. adv. panel to U.S. compt.-gen. on stock market decline, 1987, panel of cons., 1989-98; mem. audit adv. com. GAO, 1992—. Mem. bd. editl. advisors U. Iowa Jour. Corp. Law, 1978—; Bur. Nat. Affairs adv. bd. Securities Regulation and Law Report, 1976—; bd. editors N.Y. Law Jour., 1976—; bd. advisors, corp. and securities law advisor Prentice Hall Law & Bus., 1991-95; contbr. articles to profl. jours.; mem. adv. bd. Banking Policy Report. Trustee, chair audit com. SEC Hist. Soc. Recipient Disting. Service award SEC, 1972; James B. Richardson fellow Oxford U., 1956. Mem. ABA (adv. com., fed. regulation securities com., task force rev. fed. securities laws, former chair subcom. on securities activities banks), Fed. Bar Assn. (emeritus mem. exec. com. securities law com.), Am. Law Inst., Practicing Law Inst. (nat. adv. com. 1974, adv. com. ann. securities reg. inst.), AICPA (pub. dir., bd. dirs. 1984-91, fin. com. 1984-91, chmn. adv. coun. auditing standards bd. 1979-80, future issues com. 1982-85), Nat. Assn. Securities Dealers (corp. fin. com. 1981-87, nat. arbitration com. 1983-87, gov.-at-large, bd. govs. 1984-87, exec. com. 1986-87, long range planning com. 1987-90, chmn. legal adv. bd. 1988-93, spl. com. governance and structure 1989-90, numerous adv. coms.), Transparency Internat. (bd. dirs.). Home: 12512 Exchange Ct S Potomac MD 20854-2431 Office: Fulbright & Jaworski LLP 801 Pennsylvania Ave NW Washington DC 20004-2615

LEVENSPIEL, OCTAVE, engineering educator; b. Shanghai, China, July 6, 1926; came to U.S., 1947; s. Abraham and Elizabeth (Greenhouse) L.; m. Mary Josephine Smiley; children: Bekki, Barney, Morris. BS in Chemistry, U. Calif., Berkeley, 1947; MS in Chem. Engring., Oreg. State Coll., 1949, PHD in Chem. Engring., 1952; DSc (hon.), Nat. Poly. Inst., Lorraine, France, 1987; PhD (hon.), Nancy, France, 1987, Colo. Sch. Mines, 2000. Profl. engr., Oreg. Asst. prof. Oreg. State Coll., Corvallis, 1952-54; asst. prof. Bucknell U., Lewisburg, Pa., 1954-56, assoc. prof., 1956-58; assoc. prof. Ill. Inst. Technology, Chgo., 1958-62, prof., 1962-68; prof. Oreg. State U., 1969-91, prof. emeritus, 1991—. Author five textbooks. Mem. AIChE, Nat. Acad. Engring., Am. Chem. Soc. E-mail: octave@che.orst.edu. Office: Oregon State Univ Chem Engring Dept Gleeson 103 Corvallis OR 97331

LEVEQUE, JEAN AMEDEE, physicist, educator; b. Angers, France, July 10, 1963; s. Jean Amedee and Nadia Leila (Mostefai) L. BS, U. Nantes, France, 1986, M of Elec. Engring., 1987; postgrad. degree in elec. engring., U. Grenoble, 1990, PhD in Physics, 1993. Lectr. U. Nancy, France, 1991, asst. lectr. physics, 1993—. Contbr. numerous articles to profl. jours. Fellow Club of Elec. Engring. Assn., N.Y. Acad. Scis; mem. IEEE. Avocations: reading, music, art, long walks. Office: Green UHP, U Nancy BP 239, 54506 Vandoeuvre France

LEVEQUE, MICHEL, SR., diplomat; b. Algiers, France, July 19, 1933; s. Raymond and Suzanne (Lucchini) L.; m. Georgette Van de Kerchove, Oct. 25, 1955; children: Valerie, Beatrice, Michel Jr. BS in Law, U. Paris, 1957; diploma, Ecole Nationale France d'outre-Mer, Paris, 1958. Counsellor Ministry of Planning, Ivory Coast, 1960-63, counselor, 1960-63; with dept. atomic affairs Ministry of Fgn. Affairs, 1963-64; 1st sec. French Embassy, Moscow, 1964-68; with dept. Am.can affairs Ministry of Fgn. Affairs, Paris, 1968-69; counselor French Embassy, Sofia, Bulgarai, 1969-72; with dept. staff Ministry Fgn. Affairs, Paris, 1972-74; counselor French Embassy, Tunisia, 1974-78; chief rsch. sect. NATO, Brussels, 1978-82; dep. dir. African Affairs Ministry Fgn. Affairs, Paris, 1982-85; amb. Tripoli, Libya, 1985-89; under sec. of state for African Affairs, 1989-91; amb. Rabat, Morocco, 1991-

93, Brasilia, Brazil, 1993-94, Algiers, Algeria, 1994-97; min. of state Principality of Monaco, 1997-2000. Lt. French army, 1958-60. Decorated Croix de la Valeur Militaire, Officier de l'Ordre National du Mérite, Officier de l'Ordre National del la Légion d'Honneur; named Life Amb. of France, 1996. Home: 57 Rue de l'Université, Paris 7, France Office: French Embassy Office Min State, BP 522, MC 98015 Monaco Monaco also: 3 rue Sahnoun, Rabat Morocco*

LEVER, ANDREW MICHAEL LINDSAY, physician, consultant, educator; b. Trincomalee, Sri Lanka, June 23, 1953; arrived in U.K., 1953; s. Ivor Lindsay Douglas and Sylvia Marion (Tannock) L.; m. Elizabeth Ann O'Donnell, July 24, 1981; children: Robert Andrew, Jonathan Patrick, Gillian Elizabeth. BSc in Biochemistry, U. Wales, Cardiff, 1975, MB, BS, 1978, MD, 1987. Med. position U. Hosp. Wales, 1978-79, U. Newcastle, Eng., 1979-80; med. position Clin. Rsch. Ctr., London, 1980-82, rsch. fellow, 1983-85; Wellcome trust lectr. Royal Free Hosp., London, 1985-88; rsch. fellow Dana-Farber Cancer Inst., Boston, 1988-89; physician, sr. lectr., cons. St. George's Hosp., London, 1989-91; reader in infectious diseases Cambridge U., 1991—. Editor-in-chief Jour. Infection; contbr. articles to profl. jours.; inventor HIV-based viral vector sys. Med. Rsch. Coun. grantee, 1989—. Fellow Royal Coll. Physicians, Royal Coll. Physicians Edinburgh, Acad. Med. Scis.; mem. AAAS, Royal Coll. Physicians Scotland, Assn. Physicians Gt. Britain, Med. Rsch. Soc., Brit. Infection Soc., Royal Coll. Pathologists. Office: Addenbrooke's Hosp, Dept Medicine, Cambridge CB2 2QQ, England

LEVERINGTON, DAVID, astronomy writer, retired engineering executive; b. Lincoln, Eng., Nov. 13, 1941; s. John Arthur and Phyllis Mary (Atkinson) L.; m. Christine Rosemary McMullen, Apr. 26, 1969; children: Mark Robert, Claire Elizabeth, Rebecca Alexandra. BA, Oxford U., Eng., 1963, MA, 1967; PhD, Open U., Eng., 1997; FBIM, Brit. Inst. Mgmt., Eng., 1988. Rsch. physicist ICI Fibres, Eng., 1963-67; rsch. physicist Brit. Aircraft Corp., Eng., 1967-69, project mgr. space studies, 1969-71, design mgr. Geos Spacecraft, 1971-77; programme mgr. Meteosat Spacecraft European Space Agy., France, 1977-80; head of spacecraft engring. Brit. Aerospace Space Systems Ltd., Eng., 1981-85, tech. exec., 1985-87, exec. dir. engring., gen. mgr., 1987-89, project dir. personal comms. network, 1989-90, orgn. devel. dir., 1989-91, dep. mng. dir. Brit. Aerospace Comm., 1991-92; writer, 1993-94, 98—; dir. Satellite Mgmt. Internat., Ltd., 1991-92, dir. Bishopsgate Systems Ltd., Eng., 1991-92. Author: A History of Astronomy From 1890 to the Present, 1995; contbr. articles to profl. jours. Fellow Royal Astron. Soc. Avocations: photography, philately, modern history classical music, sports. Home: Green Acre, Langley Upper Green, Saffron Walden CB114RY, England

LEVERKUS, C. ERICH, banker; b. Duisburg, Germany, Mar. 15, 1926; s. C. Otto and Paula (Siebert) L.; m. Ingrid Nottebohm, Aug. 18, 1952; children: Juliane Brumberg, Johannes, Joachim, Jakob, Justus. Diploma Volkswirt, U. Tuebingen, Germany, 1955, Dr.Rer.Pol., 1957. Chmn. Vereinigte Utramarinfabriken AG, Bensheim, Germany, 1957-72; mng. ptnr. Wilhelm Ree Jr., Hamburg, Germany, 1961-86; gen. ptnr. Leverkus & Co., 1987—. Author: Nordelbishce Pastorenfamilien und ihre Nach Kommen, 1973, Beautiful Lakes of the Canadian Rockies, 1979, Alberta's Forestry Trunk Road, 1979, Freier Tausch und Fauler Zauber, 1990, Wie der Neandertaler in Seinem Namen Kam, 1999, Evolution und Feist, 1999. Chmn. Versammlung Eines Ehrbaren Kaufmanns zu Hamburg e.V., 1982-90. Knight of Justice, Johanniterorden. Mem. Rotary, Uebersee Club. Lutheran. Office: Leverkus & Co, Schauenburgerstrasse 55, D-20095 Hamburg 1, Federal Republic of Germany

LEVERTON, ROGER FRANK, business executive; b. Apr. 22, 1939; s. Frank Arthur and Lucia Jean (Harden) L.; m. Patricia Jones, 1962 (dissolved); 2 children; m. Marilyn Williams, 1992. FCA, Haberdashers Askes Sch., 1962. With Black & Decker Mfg. Co., 1968-84; European dir., gen. mgr. Black & Decker Mfg. Co., France, 1978-81; v.p. So. Europe Black & Decker Mfg. Co., 1981-84; chief exec. MK Electric Group (now Pillar Elec. PLC), 1984-89; pres., chief exec. Indal Ltd./RTZ Corp. PLC, 1989-92; chief exec. Pilkington PLC, Merseyside, Eng., 1992-97; chmn. Haden MacLellan Holdings plc, 1997—; non-exec. dir. Smiths Industries PLC, 1994—, bd. dirs. Avocations: tennis, golf, skiing, theatre. Office: Smiths Industries Plc, 765 Finchley Rd, London NW11 8DS, England also: HMH, Haleworth House, Tite Hill, Surrey Egham TW20 0LR, England*

LEVETON, IAN SINCLAIR, civil engineer; b. Birmingham, Eng., Nov. 27, 1942; came to U.S., 1953; s. Eric Karl and Zena (Altman) L. BA in Physics and Econs., NYU, 1965; cert. of achievement, Orange Coast Coll., Costa Mesa, Calif., 1990. Computer programmer trainee Bklyn. Union Gas Co., 1969; computer programmer Elizabeth Arden Sales Corp., N.Y.C., 1970; electronics expeditor Bendix Navigation & Controls, Teterboro, N.J., 1971; inventory control supr. Roman Products Inc., South Hackensack, N.J., 1972; nuclear mech. engr. Pub. Svc. N.J., Newark, 1973; mech. engr. Chemplant Designs divsn. DuPont, N.Y.C., 1974-78, Holmes and Narver, Inc., Orange, Calif., 1978-82; tech. writer nuclear safety So. Calif. Edison, Rosemead, Calif., 1983-85; civil engr. tech. City of Santa Ana, Calif., 1985—; cons. Islian Assocs., Teaneck, N.J., 1970-71. Mem. Teaneck Bicentennial Com., 1976; coord. United Way, City Pub. Works Agy., Santa Ana, 1992. Mem. KP (sec. 1974-76). Avocations: tennis, boating, reading, music, traveling. Home: 19302 Steven Ln Huntington Beach CA 92646-2711

LEVETT, MICHAEL JOHN, insurance company executive; b. Cape Town, South Africa, June 6, 1939; m. Mary Gillian Aston, 1966; 3 children. Attended, Christian Brothers Coll., Cape Town, U. Cape Town. Joined Old Mutual, 1959; seconded to, now dept. chmn. Mutual & Fed. Ins. Co. Ltd., 1971, mng. dir., 1985—, chair, 1990-99; dir. Barlow Rand Ltd., Cen. Africa Bldg. Soc., Zimbabwe, S. African Breweries Plc, Nedcor Ltd. Avocation: skiing. Office: Old Mutual Plc, 57 Berkeley Sq, London W1X 5DH, England

LEVEY, MICHAEL (VINCENT), art historian, author; b. London, Eng., June 8, 1927; s. O.L.H. and Gladys Mary (Milestone) L.; grad. with 1st class honours in English lang. and lit., Exeter Coll., Oxford, 1950; DLitt (hon.) Manchester U.; m. Brigid Brophy, June 12, 1954; 1 dau., Katharine Jane. Asst. keeper Nat. Gallery, London, 1951-66, dep. keeper, 1966-68, keeper, from 1968, dep. dir., 1970-73, dir., 1973-86. Slade prof. fine art Cambridge U., 1963-64, Oxford U., 1994-95; Wrightsman lectr. N.Y. U., 1968; hon. fellow Exeter Coll., Oxford, 1973. Served as capt. King's Shropshire Light Inf., attached Edn. Corps, 1945-48. Decorated Lt. Victorian Order; knight batchelor. Fellow Brit. Acad., Royal Soc. Lit.; mem. Ateneo Veneto (fgn.). Author: National Gallery Catalogues, 1956, 59, 71; Painting in XVIIIth Century Venice, 1959, rev. edit., 1994; From Giotto to Cézanne, 1962; Dürer, 1964; Later Italian Pictures in the Royal Collection, 1964, rev. edit., 1991; Rococo to Revolution, 1966; Early Renaissance (Hawthornden prize 1968), 1967; Concise History of Western Art, 1968; Painting at Court, 1971; The Life and Death of Mozart, 1971; Art and Architecture in 18th Century France, 1972; High Renaissance, 1975; The World of Ottoman Art, 1976; The Case of Walter Pater, 1978; (exhbn. catalogue) Sir Thomas Lawrence, 1979; Tempting Fate (fiction), 1982; An Affair on the Appian Way, 1985, Giambattista Tiepolo, 1986 (Banister Fletcher prize 1987), Men at Work, 1989, Painting and Sculpture in France 1700-1789, 1992, Florence: A Portrait, 1996, others. Editor: Pater's Marius the Epicurean, 1985. Home: 36 Little Ln, Louth Lincolnshire LN11 9DU, England*

LEVI, LESTER WRIGHT, retired religion educator; b. Soddy, Tenn., Sept. 17, 1928; s. Lester and Ora Nitia (Wright) L.; m. Mary Jane Houston, Sept. 3, 1949 (dec. July 1991); children: Lester Sr., Cynthia, Charles; m. Mary Ethel Derryberry, Apr. 30, 1994. BA, Carson Newman Coll., 1949; BD, So. Bapt. Theol. Sem., 1953; MS, Vanderbilt U., 1958. Minister various chs. Tenn. and Ky., 1949-63; asst. prof. Mid.-Tenn. State U., Murfreesboro, 1961-90. Baptist. Avocations: stock market, square dancing, hiking, photography. E-mail: lwlevi@aol.com. Home: 1510 Jones Blvd Murfreesboro TN 37129-2049

LEVI, RICHARD J., neurologist, clinical neuroscientist; b. Stockholm, Aug. 31, 1958; s. Lennart and Isabella (Weitman) Levi; m. Yvonne Freund, May 3, 1988; children: Rebecca, Jacqueline, Alexander. MD, Karolinska Inst., Stockholm, 1983; PhD, Karolinska Inst., 1996. Cons. in neurology South Hosp., Stockholm, 1986-91, Frosunda Rehab. Ctr., Stockholm, 1988—; chief physician Spinalis Spinal Injuries Unit Karolinska Hosp., Stockholm, 1996-99, assoc. prof. clin. neurosci., 1999; chief physician Frosunda Ctr., 1999—; cons. in clin. neurology Karolinska Inst., 1990, cons. in physiatry, 1992, mem. exec. bd. WHO Collaborating Ctr. for Neurotraumatology, 1995—. Author: Acute Diagnostics, 1988; co-author: A Book About the Brain, 1995, Spinalis Handbook, 1995. Chmn. Nat. Swedish Coun. for Spinal Injuries, 1996—; v.p. Swedish Magen David Adom, Stockholm, 1996—. Mem. Internat. Med. Soc. of Paraplegia, Swedish Med. Assn., Scandinavian Med. Soc. of Paraplegia, Am. Spinal Injury Assn., N.Y. Acad. Scis. Avocations: literature, music, sports. Office: Frosunda Ctr, Frosundanks Allé 13, S-16970 Solna Sweden

LEVI, SHALOM, chemist, company director, inventor; b. Fegra, Yemen, Oct. 20, 1945; arrived in Israel, 1949; s. Ihia and Bracha Levi; m. Nechama Sokoler, Nov. 16, 1947 (div. Jan. 1986); 1 child, Liad. BS in Physics and Chemistry, Hebrew U., Jerusalem, 1969, MS in Organic Chemistry, 1971, diploma of tchg., 1972, PhD in Chemistry, 1977. Cert. sr. chemist, sr. rschr. Tchg. asst. Hebrew U., 1969-77; postdoctoral fellow McGill U., Montreal, Can., 1977-79; rsch. assoc. SUNY, Stony Brook, 1979-80; dept. dir. indsl. toxicology Tel Aviv U., 1980-83; sr. rschr. Ben-Gurion U., Beer-Sheva, Israel, 1983—; ionizing radiation inspector Ministry of Labor, Jerusalem, 1987-89, sci. cons., 1986-91; sci. cons., chief chemist Auto-Part Ltd., Tel Aviv, 1991-92; chem. industry sci. cons., Beer-Sheva, 1992—; sci. cons. H.O.P. Engring., Tel Aviv, 1995—; dir. 2 high-tech. cos. in agr. and environ. protection. Contbr. numerous sci. papers and reports to profl. jours. including Clin. Biochemistry, Indsl. Hygiene and Toxicology, Chem. Ecology, others; inventor and patentee in field. Recipient 12 grants and awards Israeli, European, and Am. funds; grantee Moria Fund, 1991-93, Beare Found., 1991-94, Rashi Found., 1994-96. Mem. Am. Chem. Soc., Sci. Rsch. Soc. of N.Am., N.Y. Acad. Scis., Sigma Xi. Avocations: music, dancing, traveling, sports, philosophy. Home: 21/4 Hacotel Hamaravi, 84280 Beer-Sheva Israel also: PO Box 738, 84106 Beer Sheva Israel

LEVI, VICKI GOLD, picture editor, historical consultant, actress, author; b. Atlantic City, Sept. 16, 1941; d. Albert and Beverly Valentine Gold; m. Alexander Hecht Levi, May 31, 1970; 1 child, Adam Hecht Levi. Student, Montclair State Coll., 1959-60, New Sch. Social Rsch., N.Y.C., 1970-73, Sch. Visual Arts, N.Y.C., 1972, Lee Strass Berg Sch. Acting, N.Y.C., 1961. Actress Atlantic City, N.Y.C and L.A., 1945—; asst. to pres. Family Fare, Inc., N.Y.C., 1966; advt. rep. Cosmopolitan Mag., N.Y.C., 1967; publicity dir. Misty Harbor, Ltd., N.Y.C., 1968; freelance picture researcher, 1972—; contbg. picture editor Esquire Mag., N.Y.C., 1980—, Mirabella Mag., N.Y.C., 1991—, Atlantic City Mag., 1988—, New Woman Mag., 1995—; story cons. Alvin Cooperman Prodns., N.Y.C., 1985—; hist. cons. various Atlantic City, N.Y.C., 1994—; lectr. on Atlantic City, 1979—; guest exhibitor Internat. Ctr. Photography, N.Y.C., 1979; guest exhibitor and lectr. Cooper Hewitt, N.Y.C., 1980; guest curator Songwriters Hall of Fame, N.Y.C., 1979; guest lectr. Mcpl. Art Soc., N.Y.C., 1979; co-founder Atlantic City Hist. Mus., 1985—, bd. dirs., exhibit dir., 1995—; hist. cons. Toast to Times Square Com., N.Y.C., 1988—; curator Atlantic City Playground of the Nation, Atlantic City Hist. Mus., 1994; co-curator Charles K. Doble's Atlantic City, 1994, Images of African Americans in Atlantic City, 1995, Seventy-Five Years of Miss America in Pictures, 1995, The Al Gold Years, 1996, Bettmann on the Boardwalk, 1997, 360 Degrees of Atlantic City, 1998, Stompin' at the Shore, 1999, Atlantic City Hist. Mus., 1996, Noyes Mus. Through the Lens, 1998, Up From the Boardwalk, Down by the Sea, 1998; bd. dirs. Hecht-Levi Found.; preliminary judge Miss America, 1997. Co-author: Atlantic City: 125 Years of Ocean Madness, 1979, rev. edit., 1994, Live and Be Well: A Celebration of Yiddish Culture in America, 1982, rev. edit., 2000, You Must Have Been a Beautiful Baby, 1992; columnist Phila. Bull., The Way It Was, 1980; prodr., dir. (hist. video) Boardwalk Ballyhoo, 1992 (Am. Assn. State and Local History award 1995, Atlantic City Tourism Coun. Resolution award 1995, Tourism Advocacy award Greater Atlantic City Region Tourism Coun. 1996); rschr.: Miss America, The Dream Lives On, 1995; hist. cons. (prodn.) Atlantic City Experience, 1995, (Broadway prodn.) Having Our Say, 1995, Time and Again; hist. image cons. (PBS prodn.) I Hear America Singing, 1996; hist. rschr. (Disney World prodn.) BoardWalk Resort, 1996, (Broadway prodn.) Steel Pier (hist. cons.), 1998, (Broadway prodn.) The Civil-War, 1999 (hist. pictoral editor). Reviewer of grants, Nat. Endowment for Humanities, Washington; preliminary judge Miss Am., 1997. Recipient Author's Citation, N.J. Inst. Tech., Divsn. Continuing Edn., 1980, Senate Resolution, N.J. State Senate, 1979, Outstanding Achievement award, Atlantic City Women's C. of C., 1981, Proclamation from mayor of Atlantic City, 1981, Encore award, 2000; named An Atlantic City Treasure, Atlantic City Women's C. of C., 1989; named to Atlantic County Woman's Hall of Fame, 1997. Mem. NATAS (Emmy judge 1987-89, spl. events com. 1989-90), SAG, Am. Fedn. TV and Radio Artists, Am. Soc. Picture Profls. (bd. dirs. 1984). Democrat. Jewish. Avocations: world travel, memorabilia collecting. Home and Office: 211 Central Park W New York NY 10024-6020

LEVI, YOEL, orchestra conductor; b. Sotmar, Rumania, Israeli, Aug. 16, 1950; naturalized U.S. citizen, 1987; m. Jacqueline; 3 children. MA in Violin and Percussion, U. Tel Aviv, 1975; grad. degree, Jerusalem Acad. Music, 1976; studied with, Mendi Rodan; Diploma, Guildhall Sch. Music and Drama, London, 1978; studied with Franco Ferrara, Siena, Acad. Santa Cecilia, Rome and Kiril Kondrashin, Hilversum. Percussionist Israel Philharmonic Orch., 1975, conducting asst., 1978-80; resident condr. Cleve. Orch., 1980-84; music dir. Atlanta Symphony Orch., 1988—; guest condr. N.Am. and European orchs. Albums include The Artistry of Yoel Levi: The Telarc Collection, Vol. 8; recs. with Angel-EMI, Schwann, Telarc. Recipient 1st prize Condrs. Internat. Competition, Besancon, 1978. Office: care Harold Holt Ltd, 31 Sinclair Rd, London England W14 ONS also: Atlanta Symphony Orchestra 1293 Peachtree St NE Atlanta GA 30309-3571*

LEVIE, W. IAIN E., lawyer; b. Aberdeen, Scotland, July 9, 1963; came to U.S., 1989; s. David Stuart Craigen and Mary Mowatt Ross (Mackie) L.; m. Jarisa Nicolle Levie, May 12, 1991 (div. May 1998). MA, U. Aberdeen, 1984; LLM, U. Wash., 1990. Bar: Calif. 1991, Oreg. 1991. Trainee solicitor Peterkins, Aberdeen, 1984-88; atty. Milbank Tweed Hadley & McCloy, L.A., 1990-91, Lane Powell Spears Lubersky, Portland, Oreg., 1991-97, Davis Wright Tremaine, Portland, 1997—; dean-elect Oreg. Consular Corps, Portland, 1996—; H.M. hon. counul U.K. Govt., London, 1996—. Author (manual) Federal Civil Litigation, 1996. Mem. Oreg. Def. Counsel, Fed. Bar Assn., Multnomah Bar Assn. Avocations: climbing, skiing, reading, travel. Office: Davis Wright Tremaine 1300 SW 5th Ave Ste 2300 Portland OR 97201-5682

LEVIEN, ROGER ELI, strategy and innovation consultant; b. Bklyn., Apr. 16, 1935; s. Abraham Mark and Rosalind (Horowitz) L.; m. Carla Johanna Sherow, Oct. 9, 1960; children: Royce Adam, Alisa Tova. BS, Swarthmore Coll., 1956, MS, 1958; PhD, Harvard U., 1962. Mem. rsch. staff RAND Corp., Santa Monica, Calif., 1960-67, head sys. scis. dept., 1968-71; dir. Washington domestic program RAND Corp., Washington, 1971-74; program leader Internat. Inst. Applied Sys. Analysis, Laxenburg, Austria, 1974-75, gen. dir., 1975-81; dir. strategic sys. analysis Xerox Corp., Stamford, Conn., 1981-85, corp. v.p. strategy office, 1985-92, corp. v.p. strategy and innovation, 1992-97; adj. prof. UCLA, 1970-81; mem. adv. bd. Carnegie-Bosch Inst., Pitts., 1995—, Poly. U., Bklyn., 1995-97; bd. dirs. Brown & Sharpe, North Kingstown, R.I. Author: The Emerging Technology, 1972, Research and Development Management, 1975, Taking Technology to Market, 1997, (chpt. in book) The Civilizing Currency, 1992. Bd. dirs. Nat. Corp. Theatre Fund, N.Y.C., 1985—, Conn. Grand Opera and Orch., Stamford, 1994—. Recipient Ehrenkreuz First Class in Arts and Sci. award Austrian Govt., 1982. Mem. Mfrs. Alliance Coun. on Strategy (chmn. 1990-91), Coun. Planning Execs. (conf. bd.), Coun. on Mgmt. of Innovation and Tech. (chmn. conf. bd. 1996-97), Phi Beta Kappa, Sigma Xi, Tau Beta Pi. Avocations: skiing, photography, collecting North American Indian art, musical theater. Office: Strategy and Innovation Cons 2 River Ln Westport CT 06880-1925

LEVI-MONTALCINI, RITA, neurobiologist, researcher; b. Turin, Italy, Apr. 22, 1909; came to U.S., 1947; naturalized, 1956; d. Adamo Levi and Adele Montalcini. MD, U. Turin, 1936. Asst. in neurology Inst. Anatomy, Neurology Clinic, Turin Sch. Medicine, 1936-37; researcher Neurol. Inst. Brussels, 1939; with Allied Health Svc., Italy, 1944-45; resident, assoc. zoologist Washington U., 1947-51, assoc. prof., 1951-58, prof., 1958-81; prof. emeritus Washington U., St. Louis, 1977; dir. neurobiology rsch. program CNR (Nat. Rsch. Coun.), Rome, 1961-69, dir. cellular biology lab., 1969-79, guest prof. cellular biology lab., 1979-89; guest prof. inst. neurobiology CNR (Italian Nat. Rsch. Coun.), Rome, 1989—; pres. Inst. della Enciclopedia Italiana Treccani; pres. Ency. Italiana, 1993, Italian Nat. Commn. of United World Colls., 1993. Author: In Praise of Imperfection: My Life and Work, 1988. Recipient Albert Lasker Med. Rsch. award, 1986, Nobel prize Physiology-Medicine, (with Stanley Cohen) for work on chem. growth factors which control growth and devel. in humans and animals, 1986, Lewis S. Rosenstiel award, U.S. Nat. Medal of Sci. Mem. AAAS, Soc. Devel. Biology, Am. Assn. Anatomists, Tissue Culture Assn., NAS, Pontifical Acad., Nat. Acad. dei Lincei, Harvey Soc., Am. NAS, Belgian Royal Acad. Medicine, NAS of Italy, European Acad. Scis., Arts and Letters, Acad. Arts and Scis. of Florence. Office: Inst of Neurology CNR, viale Marx 15, 00137 Rome Italy*

LEVIN, ALLEN JAY, lawyer; b. Bridgeport, Conn., May 27, 1932; s. Simon H. and Adele Miriam (Rossinoff) L.; m. Judith Ann Rubinstein, Aug. 18, 1957 (div. 1987); children: Jennifer Suzanne, Miriam Adele, David Newmark, Michael Aaron; m. Gabrielle Hasson-Azar, Feb. 24, 1995. BA, NYU, 1954; postgrad., Boston U., 1954-55; JD, U. Miami, 1957. Bar: Fla. 1957, Conn. 1958, U.S. Dist. Ct. Conn. 1960, U.S. Dist. Ct. (so. dist.) Fla. 1962, U.S. Dist. Ct. (mid. dist.) Fla. 1969, U.S. Ct. Appeals (11th cir.) 1981, U.S. Supreme Ct. 1982. Small claims ct. judge County of Charlotte, Punta Gorda, Fla., 1962-72; legal counsel Port Charlotte-Charlotte Harbor (Fla.) Fire Control Dist., 1965-86; mcpl. judge City of North Port, Fla., 1973-76, city atty., 1977-87; pvt. practice Charlotte, Fla.; legal counsel Charlotte County Habitat for Humanity, Inc. Mem. ABA, Fla. Bar Assn. (probate law com. real property probate and trust law sects.), Charlotte County Bar Assn., Port Charlotte-Charlotte County C. of C., Port Charlotte-Charlotte County Bd. Realtors (assoc.), Elks, Kiwanis (youth svcs. chmn. Port Charlotte club 1986—, pres. 1984-85, 98-99, lt. gov.-elect divsn. 18 Fla. dist. 1999-2000, lt. gov. 2000—). Avocation: stamp collecting. Home: 125 Graham St SE Pt Charlotte FL 33952-9153 Office: 3440 Conway Blvd Ste 1A Pt Charlotte FL 33952-7050

LEVIN, ALLEN JOSEPH, lawyer; b. Lewistown, Pa., Jan. 17, 1948; s. Norman Lewis and Dorothy Sanford (Herbster) L.; m. Mary Gwendolyn McAdoo, Aug. 14, 1974. Cert., Ecole d'art Americaines, Fontainebleau, France, 1968; BA, Dickinson Coll., 1969; JD, Dickinson Sch. Law, 1974. Bar: Pa. 1974, U.S. Supreme Ct., U.S. Ct. Appeals (3d cir.), U.S. Dist. Ct. (mid. dist.) Pa. Assoc. Brugler & Levin Law Offices, Lewistown, 1974-80, ptnr., 1980-2000; ptnr. Levin Law Offices, Lewistown, 2000—; counsel Mifflin County Ind. Devel. Corp., Lewistown, 1978—, Mifflin County Ind. Devel. Authority, Lewistown, 1980—; pres. Pa. Sch. Bd. (mid-west sch. dist.) Solicitors Assn., Harrisburg, 1989; v.p., assoc. gen. counsel Pocono Mountain R.R., Scranton, Pa., 1994-96; pres. Lewistown Ctrl. R.R. Co., Mt Union Connecting R.R. Co. pres. Greater Lewistown Corp., 1983-95, v.p., 1995-99. Recipient Outstanding Svc. to Edn. award Pa. Sch. Bds. Assn., 1989. Mem. Pa. Bar Assn., Mifflin County Bar Assn. (pres. 1992-93), Juniata Valley C. of C. (pres. 1983-85), Rotary Club Lewistown, Elks (# 663). Jewish. Avocations: fishing, reading. Home: 9 N Grand St Lewistown PA 17044-2040 Office: Levin Law Offices 27 West 3d St Lewistown PA 17044-0231

LEVIN, BORIS WULFOVICH, geophysicist, researcher, administrator; b. Moscow, Aug. 26, 1937; s. Wulf Khaimovich and Elena Samuilovna (Nepomnjaschaja) L.; m. Elena Vasilievna Sasorova, May 4, 1959; 1 child, Dasha. Dipl. Engr., Moscow, 1959; Dipl. Sr. Rschr., Russian Acad. Scis., Moscow, 1980; PhD, Skochinsky Inst. Mining, Moscow, 1970; DSc in Physics and math., Inst. Geosystem, Moscow, 1990. Rsch. scientist Skochinsky Inst. Mining, Moscow, 1961-70; leader engr. Inst. Optics and Phys. Measurement, Moscow, 1970-71; head seismology sta., head lab. Sahkalin Inst. Russian Acad. Sci., Yushno-Sakhalinsk, 1971-80; leader scientist Skochinsky Inst. Mining, 1980-90, State Oceanographic Inst., Moscow, 1990-93; dir. geoscis. dept. Russian Found. Basic Rsch., Moscow, 1993—; chief scientist State Oceanographic Inst., 1993-94; lab. head Shirshov Inst. Oceanology, Russian Acad. Sci., 1994—; prof. physics Moscow State Mining U., 1995—. Editor: Tsunamis in the mediterranean Sea 2000 B.C.-1991 A.D., 1997; contbr. articles to profl. jours. Russian Found. Basic Rsch. grantee, 1993; Internat. Assn. Promotion grantee, 1997. Mem. Am. Geophys. Union, Internat. Geodesic Geophysics Union (internat. tsunami com.), Russian Nat. Tsunami Commn. (chmn.). Avocations: mountain climbing, skiing, songwriting. Home: 2-3-91 Sumskoj proezd, 113208 Moscow Russia Office: Russian Found Basic Rsch, 32-a Leninsky prospekt, 117334 Moscow Russia

LEVIN, GERALD M., media and entertainment company executive; b. Phila., May 6, 1939; m. Barbara J. Riley. BA, Haverford Coll., 1960; LLB, U. Pa., 1963; LLD (hon.), Tex. Coll., 1985; LLD (hon.), Middlebury Coll., 1994; LHD (hon.), U. Denver, 1995. Assoc. Simpson, Thacher & Bartlett, N.Y.C., 1963-67; gen. mgr., chief operating officer Devel. and Resources Corp., N.Y.C., 1967-71; rep. Internat. Basic Economy Corp., Tehran, Iran, 1971-72; v.p. programming Home Box Office, N.Y.C., 1972-73, pres., chief exec. officer, 1973-76, chmn., chief exec. officer, 1976-79; group v.p. video Time Inc., N.Y.C., 1979-84, exec. v.p., 1984-88, vice chmn., dir., 1988-90; vice chmn., dir. Time Warner Inc., N.Y.C., 1990—, chief oper. officer, 1991-92, pres., co-chief exec. officer to chmn. and CEO, 1992—, chmn., CEO; trustee emeritus Hampshire Coll.; bd. dirs. N.Y. Stock Exch., Inc. Bd. dirs., treas. N.Y. Philharm., Ctr. for Comm., A Living Meml. to the Holocaust—Mus. of Jewish Heritage. Mem. The Aspen Inst., N.Y. City Partnership, Nat. Cable TV Ctr. and Mus., Coun. on Fgn. Rels., The Trilateral Commn., Corp. Governance Task Force of the Bus. Roundtable, Phi Beta Kappa. Office: Time Warner Inc 75 Rockefeller Plz # 2919 New York NY 10019-6908*

LEVIN, HARVEY JAY, financial institution design and construction specialist, developer, auctioneer; b. Fitchburg, Mass., Apr. 27, 1936; s. Abe and Ila L.; children: Kimberly, Tara, Robin, Vanessa. Student, Brandeis U., Boston U., U. Md., Ind. U.; BBA in Fin., U. Mass., 1960; MA in Econs., U. N.H., 1970; PhD, LaSalle U.; PhD in Philosophy Bus. Mgmt., 1996. Lic. real estate broker, Mass., N.H., R.I.; lic. comml. pilot; lic. auctioneer, Maine, Mass., N.H., Vt., Fla. Accredited Auctioneer Real Estate, CAI. Pres. Central Tool Warehouse, Leominster, Mass., 1959-66; dir. mktg. and sales Spacemakers, Canton, Mass., 1970-72, New Eng. Homes, Biddeford, Mass., 1973-74; gen. mgr. Great No. Homes, Boston, 1966-70; cons. svc. mgr. Bank Bldg. Corp., St. Louis, 1974-80; v.p. Shelter Resources, Birmingham, Ala., 1972-73, Fin. Concepts, Natick, Mass., 1980-85; pres. Am. Bank Design, Inc., and Credit Union Bldg. Corp., Portsmouth, N.H., Harv Levin, Inc., Auctioneers, 1986—; cons. Republic Homes, Truro, Can., 1974. Author, lectr. personal and profl. seminars. Chmn. sch. bldg. com. Kensington, N.H., 1985; pres. Pheasant Run Condominium Assn., 1993-95; chairperson Parents Fund, U. N.H., 1993-95, pres.-elect Parents Coun., 1995. Served with U.S. Army, 1955-57. Recipient Award of Honor, Bank Bldg. Corp. of Am., 1976, 1st Place Design award Bank Bldg. Corp. of Am., 1977, Best Mktg. and Sales Plan award Automation in Housing Assn., 1972, FMHA award for Best Elderly Housing Project (Hazel Dell Apts., Alfred, Maine); named Hon. Lt. Col. Aide-de-Camp by Gov. of Ala., 1978. Mem. Aircraft Owners and Pilots Assn., Phi Sigma Kappa. Clubs: The River (Kennebunkport, Maine); Hampton River Boat, Portsmouth Power Squadron, Wentworth By the Sea Country Club. Lodge: Masons. Office: Harv Levin Inc & Am Bank Design Inc & Credit Union Bldg Corp 6 Greenleaf Woods Dr Unit 102 Portsmouth NH 03801-7410

LEVIN, HERBERT, diplomat, foundation executive; b. N.Y.C., Jan. 14, 1931; s. Sol and Kate (Gottlieb) L.; m. Cornelia Rose, Feb. 21, 1954; children: Martha, Jonathan C. BA, Harvard U., 1952; MA, Fletcher Sch. Law Diplomacy, 1956. Internat. economist Dept. of State, 1956-58; Chinese lang. and area tng. Taichung, Taiwan, 1959-61; econ. officer Am. Consulate Gen., Hong Kong, 1961-64; polit. officer Am. Embassy, Taipei, 1964-67, Tokyo, 1967-70; staff mem. East Asia Nat. Security Coun., 1970-71; deputy dir. Japanese affairs Dept. of State, 1971-74; deputy chief mission Am. Embassy, Dar-es-Salaam, 1975-77, Colombo, 1977-79, New Delhi, 1979-81; asst. nat. intelligence officer East Asia East and South Asia Nat. Intelligence Coun., 1981-83; staff mem. policy planning coun. Dept. State, 1983-85; staff

dir. subcom. Asian and Pacific Affairs Ho. Reps., 1985; diplomat-in-residence, dir. studies Asia Found., San Francisco, 1986-88; spl. asst. Office of Sr. Rep. for Strategic Tech. Policy Dept. State, 1988-90, exec. asst. to amb.-at-large and spl. asst. to sec. of state for non-proliferation and nuclear energy affairs, 1990-91; spl. advisor to UN under-sec. gen. Ji Chaozhu N.Y.C., 1991-94; exec. dir. Am.-China Soc., N.Y.C., 1994-99; adviser U.S. Del. to 14th Gen. Assembly of UN, 1985. With U.S. Army, 1953-55, U.S. Fgn. Svc. 1956-91. Fellow Ctr. Internat. Affairs, Harvard U., 1974-75. Fellow Am.-China Forum, Atlantic Coun. (assoc. sr.); mem. Am. Fgn. Svc. Assn. (life), Asia Soc., Assn. Asian Studies (life), Coun. Fgn. Rels., Fairbank Ctr. for East Asian Rsch. Harvard U. (assoc. in rsch.), UN Assn. N.Y. (bd. dirs.), Harvard Club N.Y., Cosmos Club, Dar-es-Salaam Yacht Club (life), Sri Lanka, Hill Club (life), Hong Kong Cricket Club (life), Lake Mansfield Trout Club (life). Home (summer): Box 93 Long Meadow Hill Calais VT 05648-0093

LEVIN, JUDITH MARIA, health science association administrator; b. July 23, 1953. BS, George Mason U., 1990; M in Social Sci., Syracuse U., 1999. Cons. to internat. not-for-profit orgns., Washington, 1981-91; program specialist Fogarty Internat. Ctr. NIH, Bethesda, Md., 1991—.

LEVIN, LEONID A., computer science educator; b. Dnepropetrousk, Ukraine, Nov. 2, 1948; s. Anatoly A. and Anna Levin; m. Larissa V. Lastovetskaya, Sept. 3, 1977; children: Rebecca A., Naomi T., Andrei J. MA in Math., Moscow U., 1970, postgrad., 1972; PhD, MIT, 1979. Rschr. MIT, Cambridge, Mass., 1978-80; prof. Boston U., 1980—; vis. prof. U. Calif., Berkeley, 1986, Calif. Inst. Tech., Pasadena, 1987, Hebrew U., Jerusalem, 1993-94; math. lab. asst. NAS, Inst. Info. Transmission, Moscow, 1972-73; rsch. scientist Moscow U., 1970-72. Guggenheim Found. fellow, 1993-94; NSF rsch. grantee, 1980—. Jewish. Home: 460 Commonwealth Ave Newton MA 02459-1333 Office: Boston U Computer Sci Dept 111 Cummington St Boston MA 02215-2411

LEVIN, MARK JAY, photography director, lighting designer, cinematographer; b. Mpls., July 30, 1957. BA, U. Wis., 1979. Lighting dir., cameraman Sta. WHA-TV, Madison, Wis., 1978-79, NBC, 1980, ABC, Hollywood, 1982-89; dir. photography Columbia Pictures TV, 1989-93; dir. photography comedy, dramatic, music, variety, news and talk format prodns. Concepts in Light, Burbank, 1991—, IFA West, 1994-98, Disney TV, 1994-99; lighting dir. Bob Booker/Universal TV, 1984, Platypus Prodn., 1983-85, Dick Clark Prodn., 1982-83, Sta. KABC-TV, 1984-86; dir. photography Amos Prodn., 1982; pres. Concepts in Light, Burbank, Calif.; dir. photography Walt Disney TV, 1994—, NBC Prodns., Burbank, 1997—. Lighting designer, dir. photography numerous TV series spls. and CD Rom games including The New Love American Style, 1985, Charmed Lives, 1986, Sweet Surrender, 1986, The Charmings, 1986-87, Facts of Life, 1987, Women in Prison, 1987-88, Who's the Boss ?, 1985-92 (6 Emmy award nominations 1986-91, Emmy award 1989), The Martin Short Show, 1994, Treasure Quest CD Rom 1995, Who Makes You Laugh ?, 1995, Kelsey Grammer's Look at Parenthood, 1995, Unhappily Ever After 1994-99, Cleghorne, 1994-95, High School USA, 1996, 98, General Hospital, 1984-89, 91, 92, Living Dolls, 1989, Faerie Tale Theater, 1983-85 (Ace award 1983), American Bandstand, 1983-86, The Love Boat Spl., 1984, Home Movies, 1982, The Love Connection, 1984-85, ABC's World News Tonight, 1984-86, Married With Children, Nat. Cerebral Palsey Telethon, 1985, 87, 89, One of the Boys, 1989, numerous local prodns.; dir. of photography Married People, 1990, Guys Next Door, 1990; lighting designer Up With People, 1990, Countdown, 1990, The Summer X-Games for ESPN, 1997—; dir. of photography Rap Tap, 1991, Vinnie and Bobby, 1992, Hangin' with Mr. Cooper, 1992, The Hannigans, 1992, City Guys, 1997-99; (pilot) Country Comfort, (pilot) Beakmans World, 1992, Letting Go, 1992, Hangin' With Mr. Cooper, 1992-93, George, 1993, (pilot) Family, 1993, Who Makes You Laugh?, 1994, The Martin Short Show, 1994, The Jerry Springer Show, 1994—, The Dirs. Round Table, 1994, Romance Theatre, 1994, Bill Cosby-In Concert, 1994, 98, Christmas from the Los Angeles Music Ctr., 1995-98, The Iceman Cocketh (pilot), 1996, It Ain't Easy (pilot), 1996, Starz, 1996, City Guys, 1997, Lou Rawls in Concert, 1999; contbg. editor Lighting Dimensions mag., 1980-85; author: Cosmos the Space Ship, News Lighting; contbr. articles to Internat. Photographers Mag. Active Big Bros. of Greater L.A., 1984-91; mem. adv. bd. Coll. of Letters and Scis. U. Calif., Pamona, U. So. Calif. Dept. of Neurology. Recipient ACE award for Lighting Design in a Dramatic Presentation, 1983, Patriotic Svc. award U.S. Dept. of the Treasury, 1984, Outstanding Excellence award Am. Soc. Lighting Designers, 1988-91, Outstanding Artistic Achievement (4), 1989, Emmy award Outstanding Lighting Dir. for a Series (prime time), 1989. Mem. Internat. Photographers Guild (IATSE local 600), Internat. Assn. Lighting Designers (assoc.), Am. Soc. of Lighting Designers, Internat. Assn. Theatrical Stage Employees, World Underwater Fedn., Nat. Assn. Broadcast Employees and Technicians, Soc. Operating Cameramen, Profl. Assn. Diving Instrs. (divemaster), Soc. TV Lighting Dirs. (Can.), Nat. Assn. Underwater Instrs. (divemaster), Soc. Motion Picture and TV Engrs. Office: Concepts in Light 859 N Hollywood Way Ste 172 Burbank CA 91505-2814

LEVIN, MICHAEL MARTIN JOHN, political science educator; b. Douglas, Isle of Man, Eng., Oct. 4, 1940; m. Patricia Dora Montes (div. 1978); 3 children. BA, Leicester U., Eng., 1964; PhD, Leicester U., 1971; MSc, London U., 1965. Tutorial asst. U. Leicester, Eng., 1965-66; asst. lectr. U. Leeds, Eng., 1966-67; lectr. U. Wales, Aberystwyth, 1967-88; lectr., sr. lectr. U. London, 1988—. Author: Marx, Engels & Liberal Democracy, 1989, The Spectre of Democracy, 1992, The Condition of England Question, 1998. Home: 38 Westwood Pk, London SE23 3QH, England Office: Univ London Goldsmiths Coll, Lewisham Way, London SE14 6NW, England

LEVIN, MURRAY SIMON, lawyer; b. Phila., Feb. 8, 1943; s. Sidney Michael and Eva (Goldstein) L.; m. Jalond Marie Robinson, June 9, 1968; children—Adrianne Lesley, Alexandra Amber-Rose. BA, Haverford Coll., 1964; MA, Harvard U., 1968, LLB, 1968; cert., Hague Internat. Acad. Law, 1967. Bar: Pa. 1968, U.S. Dist. Ct. (ea. dist.) Pa. 1970, U.S. Ct. Appeals (3d cir.) 1970, U.S. Supreme Ct. 1979. Instr. English Harvard U., 1965-68; law clk. to U.S. Dist. Ct. Judge, 1968-70; instr. govt. Haverford Coll., 1970-71; litigation ptnr. Pepper, Hamilton LLP, Phila., 1970—, mem. firm exec. com., 1993-95; overseas lectr., U.K., Sweden, Germany, Senegal, Kenya, Cameroon, Morocco, Israel, Vietnam, 1988—; law seminar speaker. Weekly commentator radio Sta. WCAU Dick Clayton Show, TV program Morningside, 1973-76; weekly host, interviewer Sta. WHYY, 1974-79; TV commentator O.J. Simpson trial, 1995; contbr. articles to profl. jours. Chmn. Phila. Coun. Expt. in Internat. Living, 1968-70; mem. Phila. Urban Coalition Housing Task Force, 1968-80; chmn. coll. divsn. Allied Jewish Appeal, 1968-70; pres. Ctrl. Phila. Reform Dems., 1973-74; bd. dirs. Grad. Hosp. Phila., 1976-96, Friends Ctrl. Sch., 1988-96, divsn. Fgn. Policy Rsch. Com. Mid. East Coun., 1992-94, Mid. East Forum, 1994—; candidate for Dem. Party nomination for U.S. Senate from Pa., 2000. Root-Tilden fellow, 1964. Mem. ABA, Pa. Bar Assn. (ho. of dels.), Phila. Bar Assn. (young lawyers exec. bd. 1973, bd. govs. 1985-88, zone del. 1988—, chmn. profl. guidance com. 1989-92, co-chmn. internat. human rights com. 1990-91), Phila. Trial Lawyers Assn., Assn. Internat. des Jeunes Avocats Brussels (bd. dirs. 1981-85, 1st Am. pres. 1985-88), Union Internationale des Avocats Paris (advisor to pres., mem. exec. com. 1993—, pres. Am. chpt. 1995-97, congress pres. 1997), Am. Law Inst., Am. Judicature Soc., Phi Beta Kappa. Office: Pepper Hamilton LLP 3000 2 Logan Sq 18th & Arch Sts Philadelphia PA 19103-2799

LEVIN, NORMAN LEWIS, biology educator; b. Hartford, Conn., Mar. 31, 1924; s. Joseph and Fannie (Sosin) L.; m. Shirley Alleen Ginsberg, Sept. 1950; children: Faye Deborah, Alan Jeffrey. BS, U. Conn., 1948, MS, 1949; PhD, U. Ill., 1956. Teaching asst. U. Ill., Champaign, 1953-56, instr. zoology, 1956-57; vis. asst. prof. biology Westminster Coll., Fulton, Mo., 1957-58, asst. prof., 1958-60; fellow in tropical medicine Sch. of Medicine La. State U., 1959; instr. biology Bklyn. Coll., 1960-64, asst. prof., 1964-71, assoc. prof., 1971-76, prof., 1976—, dep. chmn. dept., 1983—, emeritus prof., 1996; mem. evaluation panel NSF, Washington, 1968, 71, 74; reader advanced placement exams. Ednl. Testing Svc., Princeton, N.J., 1978-84. Contbr. articles to profl. jours. With AUS, 1942-45, PTO. Fellow AAAS; mem. Am. Soc. Parasitologists, Am. Soc. Zoologists, Am. Soc. Tropical Medicine and Hygiene, Am. Microscopical Soc., Helminthological Soc. Wash., Sigma Xi, Phi Sigma. Avocations: photography, reading, hiking. Summer: PO Box 142 Becket MA 01223-0142 Office: CUNY Bklyn Coll Ave H and Bedford Ave Brooklyn NY 11210

LEVIN, RICHARD CHARLES, university president, economist; b. San Francisco, Apr. 7, 1947; s. D. Derek and Phylys M. (Goldstein) L.; m. Jane Ellen Aries, June 24, 1968; children: Jon, Daniel, Sarah, Rebecca. BA, Stanford (Calif.) U., 1968; LittB, Oxford (Eng.) U., 1971; PhD, Yale U., 1974; LLD (hon.), Princeton U., 1993, Harvard U., 1994; D in Civil Law (hon.), Oxford U., 1998. With Yale U., New Haven, 1974—, pres., 1993—, chmn. econs. dept., 1987-92, Frederick William Beinecke prof. econs., 1992—, dean Grad. Sch., 1992-93; rsch. assoc. Nat. Bur. Econ. Rsch., Cambridge, Mass., 1985-90; program dir. Internat. Inst. Applied Sys. Analysis, Vienna, 1990-92; mem. exec. com. Consortium on Financing Higher Edn.; trustee Tanner Lectures on Human Values; cons. numerous law and bus. firms. Trustee Hopkins Sch., New Haven, 1988-95. Yale-New Haven Hosp., 1993—, Univs. Rsch. Assn., 1994-99; bd. dirs. Yale-New Haven Health Svcs. Corp., Inc., 1993—; mem. bd. on sci., tech. and econ. policy Nat. Rsch. Coun.; mem. The William and Flora Hewlett Found. Fellow Merton Coll. Oxford U., 1996. Fellow Am. Acad. Arts and Scis.; mem. Am. Econ. Assn., Econometric Soc. Democrat. Jewish. Office: Yale U Office of Pres 105 Wall St New Haven CT 06511-6608

LEVIN, ROGER MICHAEL, lawyer; b. N.Y.C., Oct. 20, 1942; s. Harold F. and Blanche M. (Tarr) L. BA in Polit. Sci., U. Chgo., 1964; MA with distinction in polit. sci., U. Calif.-Berkeley, 1966; JD, NYU, 1969. Bar: N.Y. 1970, D.C. 1982, U.S. Dist. Ct. (so. and ea. dists.) N.Y., 1971, U.S. Ct. Appeals (2d cir.) 1971, U.S. Ct. Appeals (D.C. cir.) 1979, U.S. Customs Ct. 1974, U.S. Tax Ct. 1981, U.S. Ct. Customs and Patent Appeals 1974, U.S. Supreme Ct. 1974. Personal asst. to U.S. rep. Dept. State, Quang Nam Province, South Vietnam, 1966; asst. to dir. Nr. East/South Asia Bur. Office Internat. Security Affairs, Office Sec. of Def., Washington, 1967. Rsch. editor NYU Jour. Internat. Law and Politics. Fulbright scholar U. Sri Lanka, 1964-65; Woodrow Wilson fellow U. Calif.-Berkeley, 1966; named Best Oralist, Jessup Internat., Law Moot Ct. Regional Competition, NYU, 1969. Office: 15 E 90th St New York NY 10125-0001

LEVIN, SHANA, psychology educator. BA in Psychology summa cum laude, U. Calif., Berkeley, 1990; MA in Psychology, UCLA, 1993, PhD in Psychology, 1996. Postdoctoral rschr. UCLA, 1996-98; asst. prof. psychology Claremont (Calif.) McKenna Coll., 1998—. Ad hoc reviewer Personality and Social Psychology Bull., Polit. Psychology; contbr. chpts. to books and articles to profl. jours. UCLA Alumni fellow, 1991-93, Lady Davis Grad. fellow Lady Davis Fellowship Trust, Hebrew U., Jerusalem, 1993-94; grantee Sigma Xi, 1995. Mem. APA, Am. Psychol. Soc., Internat. Soc. Polit. Psychology, Soc. for Personality and Social Psychology, Soc. for the Psychol. Study of Social Issues, Calif. Alumni Assn. (life), Phi Beta Kappa. Avocations: volleyball, crossword puzzles, movies, international travel. Office: Claremont McKenna Coll 850 Columbia Ave Claremont CA 91711-3901

LEVIN, VICTOR JACOVLEVICH, geologist, researcher; b. Gorky, Vitebsk, USSR, Oct. 20, 1934; s. Jacov Davidovich L. and Silvia Lvovna (Gitlovskaja) Olginskaja; m. Iraida Aristidovna Charlampova, Apr. 10, 1957; children: Maria, Tatjana. Engr.-geologist, Mining Inst., Sverdlovsk, USSR, 1957; PhD, Acad. Scis., Sverdlovsk, USSR, 1969. Main geologist parties of geol. expedition, Cheljabinsk, USSR, 1957-69; head petrologies lab. Ilmen res. Acad. Scis., Miass, USSR, 1969-75; mem. editl. coun. Ural Branch Acad. Scis., 1971-75; main geologist Ctrl. party Ural Geol. Mapping Expedition, Ekaterinburg, Russia, 1975—, curator rare metals, 1995—; mem. editl. coun. Ural Geol. Mapping Expedition, Ekaterinburg, 1997—; mem. Ural Petrography Coun., Ekaterinburg, Russia, 1974—. Author: Alkaline Province of Ilmene-Vishnevy Mountains, 1974; co-author: Depth's Structure and Metallogeny of Mobile Belts, 1990, Orogenic Granitoids Magmatism of Ural, 1994, Alkaline-Carbonatite Complexes of Ural, 1997. Recipient Hon. Prospecting of Depths award Ministry Natural Resources; named Hon. Geologist Russia Fedn., Pres. Russia Fedn., 1999. Mem. Internat. Acad. Mineral Resources, Internat. Assn. Genesis Ore Deposits, N.Y. Acad. Scis. Avocations: fishing, gardening. Office: AO Ural Geol Mapping Exped, 55 Vainera str, 620014 Ekaterinburg Russia

LEVIN, WILLIAM EDWARD, lawyer; b. Miami, Fla., June 13, 1954; s. Harold A. and Phyllis (Wolfson) L.; m. Mary Catherine Egan, June 25, 1994; 1 child: Sean Alexander. Student, Conn. Coll., 1972-74; BA, Emory U., Atlanta, 1976; JD, U. Miami, 1979. Bar: Fla. 1979, Calif. 1982; lic. real estate broker, Calif. Distbr. N.Y. Times, Atlanta, 1975-76; legis. intern Congressman William Lehman, Washington, 1974; law clk. Superior Ct. Hillsborough County, Tampa, Fla., 1974; legal asst./law clk. U. Miami Sch. Law, 1977-78; law clk. Shevin, Shapo & Shevin, Miami, 1977-79; assoc. Law Offices of John Cyril Malloy, Miami, 1979-82; assoc./ptnr. Flehr, Hohbach, Test, Albritton & Herbert, San Francisco, 1982-87; ptnr. Cooper, White & Cooper, San Francisco, 1987-88; pvt. practice trademark and copyright law San Francisco, 1988-92, Irvine, Calif., 1993-96; broker/sole proprietor Levin Realty, San Francisco, 1987-92; of counsel Goldstein & Phillips, San Francisco, 1988-91, Hawes & Fischer, Newport Beach, Calif., 1992-93, Gauntlett & Assocs., Irvine, Calif., 1995-96; mng. partner Levin & Gluck, Laguna Beach, Calif., 1996-97; mng. ptnr. Levin & Hawes, Laguna Beach, Calif., 1997—; co-chmn. trademark com. San Francisco Patent & Trademark Assn., 1985-86; moot ct. judge Giles Rich Moot Ct. Competition, San Francisco, 1986; ofcl. arbitrator Am. Arbitration Assn., 1987-96; mem. exec. com. L.A. Complex Inns of Ct., 1994-96; lectr. in field. Author: Trade Press Protection, 1996; mem. editorial bd. Trademark World, London, 1987-90, Trademark Reporter, 1987-89, 93—, Trademark Reporter Task Force, 1994-97, San Francisco Atty., 1986-89; mem. adv. bd. United States Patents Quarterly, 2000—; contbr. articles to profl. jours. Adminstrv. bd. Californians for Missing Children, San Francisco, 1989-92, Hebrew Inst. Law, San Francisco, 1986-88; atty's. steering com. Jewish Cmty. Fedn., San Francisco, 1987-88; fin. com. Temple Emanu-el, San Francisco, 1985-86; bd. dirs. Ctr. 500, Orange County Performing Arts Ctr. Support Group, 1996, Anti-Defamation League Orange county and Long Beach Region, 1998—; trustee Shir Ha Ma'lot Temple, 1997—. Mem. ABA, Internat. Trademark Assn., Orange County Bar Assn., Orange County Patent Law Assn., Am. Intellectual Property Law Assn. Democrat. Jewish. Avocations: biking, skiing, gardening.

LEVIN, ZEV, atmospheric sciences laboratory director, educator; b. Haifa, Israel, Dec. 17, 1940; s. Baruch and Sara (Warman) L.; m. Susan M. Warshaw, Aug. 22, 1965; children: Rami, Tamar. BS, Calif. State U., L.A., 1966; PhD, U. Wash., 1970. Prof. Tel Aviv U., 1971—; NRC sr. rsch. assoc. NASA-Ames, Moffett Field, Calif., 1981-82, NASA-Goddard, Greenbelt, Md., 1992-93; v.p. R&D, dean rsch. Tel Aviv U., 1987-92, chair prof., 1994—; chmn. bd. Ramot Ltd., Tel Aviv U., 1987-92, exec. bd. Ramot Ltd., 1987—, acad. senate, 1984—, exec. com. acad. senate, 1987-97; vis. prof. Inst. Atmospheric Physics, Zurich, Switzerland, 1999; dir. Porter Sch. for Environ. Scis./Tel Aviv U., 2000—. V.p. Internat. Cloud Physics Commn., 2000—. Sgt. Israel Def. Forces, 1959-61. Mem. Am. Meterol. Soc., Am. Geophysics Union, Israel Aerosol Rsch. Assn. (pres. 1999—). Avocations: tennis, squash, swimming. E-mail: zev@hail.tau.ac.il. Office: Tel Aviv Univ, Geophysics Planetary Sci, 69978 Tel Aviv Israel

LEVINA, AVIVA, chemist, researcher; b. Riga, Latvia, Aug. 4, 1966; d. Boris and Hana (Poris) L. MSc in Chemistry, Riga Tech. U., 1988, PhD in Chemistry, 1992. Rschr. Riga Tech. U., 1988-93, U. Sydney, Australia, 1995—; postdoctoral fellow U. Reims, France, 1994. Contbr. articles to profl. jours.; patentee in field. Mem. Royal Australian Chem. Inst. E-mail: levina a@chem.usyd.edu.au. Office: U Sydney, Sch Chemistry, Sydney 2006 NSW, Australia

LEVINE, ALAN, lawyer; b. Middletown, N.Y., Jan. 17, 1948; s. Jacques and Florence (Tananbaum) L.; m. Nancy Shapiro, June 7, 1971; children: Emily Jane, Malcolm Andrews. BS in Econs., U. Pa., 1970; JD, NYU, 1973. Bar: N.Y. 1974, U.S. Dist. Ct. (so. dist.) N.Y. 1974, U.S. Dist. Ct. (ea. dist.) N.Y. 1980, U.S. Tax Ct. 1980, U.S. Ct. Appeals (2d cir.) 1975. Law clk. U.S. Dist. Ct. (so. dist.) N.Y., N.Y.C., 1973-75; asst. U.S. atty. U.S. Attys. Office, so. dist. N.Y., Dept. Justice, N.Y.C., 1975-80; assoc. Kronish, Lieb, Weiner & Hellman, N.Y.C., 1980-82, mem., 1982—, co-mng. ptnr., 1997—. Chmn. bd. dirs. Park Ave. Synagogue, N.Y.C., 1993—; bd. dirs. Jewish Theol. Sem. Rabbinical Sch., MYF Legal Svcs. Inc., 1990-93; law chmn. N.Y. County Rep. Com., 1991-93. Recipient Atty. Gen. Dirs. award U.S. Dept. Justice, 1980, Torch of Learning award Am. Friends Hebrew U., 1995. Fellow Am. Bar Found., Am. Coll. Trial Lawyers; mem. ABA (ho. of dels. 1983-84, chmn. spl. com. for youth edn. for citizenship, 1988-91, vice chmn. white collar crime com. 1996—), N.Y. State Bar Assn. (chmn. com. on citizenship edn. 1979-84, ho. of dels. 1982-84, award of achievement 1984), Sunningdale Country Club (bd. trustees 1988-90 Scarsdale, N.Y.), Mask and Wig Club (Phila.). Republican. Jewish. Home: 1185 Park Ave New York NY 10128-1308 Office: Kronish Lieb Weiner & Hellman 1114 Avenue Of The Americas New York NY 10036-7703

LEVINE, AMIHUD, rabbi; b. Balfuria, Israel, May 14, 1946; s. Moshe and Ester (Epshtein) L.; m. Hinda Haddasah Laufer; children: Hana, Bluma, Moshe, Sarah, Jacob. MA, Tel Aviv U., 1979, Tel Aviv U., 1984. Ordained rabbi, 1970. Lectr. Tel Aviv U., 1977-81; rosh yesiva Netania, 1982—; editor Oraita Megazin, Netania, 1978—; lawyer Netania, 1984—. Editor: Oraita, 1978—. Maj. Israel Army, 1969-73. Home: PO Box 245, 42102 Netanya Israel

LEVINE, ANN MEBANE, university administrator; b. Reidsville, N.C., Oct. 14, 1943; d. Clark Cornelius and Nantce (Weaver) Mebane; m. Arnold Jules Levine, June 17, 1967 (dec. Dec. 1990); children: Cynthia Levine Crouch, Melissa F. BA, Mary Baldwin Coll., 1965; MA, Emory U., 1967. Instr. Morris Brown Coll., Atlanta, 1967-68; adminstv. asst. Faculty & Course Devel. Internat. Studies W.Va. U., Morgantown, 1980-93, asst. dir. Faculty & Course Devel. Internat. Studies, 1993—. Mem. Svc. League Morgantown, W.Va. Univ. Club, Campus Club W.Va. U. Democrat. Unitarian. Office: WVa U Dept Polit Sci Morgantown WV 26506-6317

LEVINE, HAROLD, lawyer; b. Newark, Apr. 30, 1931; s. Rubin and Gussie (Lifshitz) L.; children: Brenda Sue, Linda Ellen Levine Gersen, Louise Abby, Jill Anne Levine Lipari, Charles A., Cristina Gussie, Harold Rubin II; m. Cristina Cervera, Aug. 29, 1980. BS in Engring., Purdue U., 1954; JD with distinction, George Washington U., 1958. Bar: D.C. 1958, Va. 1958, Mass. 1960, Tex. 1972, U.S. Patent Office 1958. Naval arch., marine engr. U.S. Navy Dept., 1954-55; patent examiner U.S. Patent Office, 1955-58; with Tex. Instruments, Inc., Attleboro, Mass., 1959-77; asst. sec. Tex. Instruments, Inc., Dallas, 1969-72, asst. v.p. and gen. patent counsel, 1972-77; ptnr. Sigalos & Levine, Dallas, 1977-93; prin. Levine & Majorie LLP, Dallas, 1994—; chmn. bd. Vanguard Security, Inc., Houston, 1977—; chmn. Tex. Am. Realty, Dallas, 1977—; lectr. assns., socs.; del. Geneva and Lausanne (Switzerland) Intergovtl. Conf. on Revision, Paris Pat. Conv., 1975-76. Editor George Washington U. Law Rev., 1956-57; mem. adv. bd. editors Bur. Nat. Affairs, Pat., Trdmk. and Copyright Jour.; contbr. chpt. to book and articles to profl. jours. Mem. U.S. State Dept. Adv. Panel on Internat. Tech. Transfer, 1977. Mem. ABA (chmn. com. 407 taxation pats. and trdmks. 1971-72), Am. Patent Law Assn., Dallas Bar Assn., Assn. Corp. Pat. Csl. (sec.-treas. 1971-73), Dallas-Ft. Worth Patent Law Assn., Pacific Indsl. Property Assn. (pres. 1975-77), Electronic Industries Assn. (pres. pat. com. 1972), NAM, Southwestern Legal Inst. on Patent Law (planning com. 1971-74), U.S. C. of C., Dallas C. of C., Kiwanis, Alpha Epsilon Pi, Phi Alpha Delta. Republican. Jewish. Office: Levine and Majorie LLP 12750 Merit Dr Ste 1000 Dallas TX 75251-1219

LEVINE, JACK, artist; b. Boston, Jan. 3, 1915; s. Samuel Mayer and Mary (Grinker) L.; widowed; 1 child, Susanna Levine Fisher. AFD, Colby Coll., Waterville, Maine, 1956. One-man shows include Downtown Gallery, N.Y.C., 1938, Artists, 1942, Mus. Modern Art, N.Y.C., 1943; exhibited in group shows at Jeu de Paume, Paris, 1938, Carnegie Internat. exhbns., 1938-40, Artists for Victory, Met. Mus., N.Y.C., 1942, retrospective at Jewish Mus., N.Y.C., 1978-79, Bklyn. Mus., 1999; represented in permanent collections Mus. Modern Art, Met. Mus. Art, N.Y.C., William Hayes Foggs Mus., Harvard U., Addison Gallery, Andover, Mass., Mus. Vatican, D.C. Moore Gallery, N.Y. With AUS, 1942-45. Mem. Am. Acad. Arts and Letters (pres., chancellor), Inst. Arts and Letters (pres. 1993), Nat. Acad. Design, Century Club.

LEVINE, JAMES ANDREW, endocrinologist; b. London, Nov. 20, 1963; came to U.S., 1992; s. Eric Anthony and Jemma Ann Levine; children: Ariella Rosie, Yae Talia. BSc, Royal Free Hosp. Sch. Medicine, London, 1985, PhD, 1988, MB BChir, 1991. Lic. physician, Minn. Intern Royal Free Hosp. Sch. Medicine, London, 1992-95; resident in internal medicine Mayo Clinic, Rochester, Minn., 1995-98, fellow in endocrinology, 1998-99, cons., 1999—. Contbr. numerous articles to med. jours. Chmn. STOP drug abuse prevention program. Recipient 1st prize Brit. Nutrition Found., 1985, 1st prize in ob-gyn., 1989, 1st prize Coun. on Alcoholism, Royal Coll. Physicians, 1989, 1st prize for poster presentation 11th Congress of European Soc. of Parenteral and Enteral Nutrition, 1989, Stuart Mills prize in tropical medicine, 1990, Glynn Morgan prize and medal Cardiology and Chest Medicine, 1991, Emlyn Williams prize in surgery, 1991, Gant medal in surgery, 1991, William and Edith Ryman prize in gen. practice, 1991; winner Nat. Am. Coll. Physicians Assoc.'s Clin. Vignette Competition, 1995, Nat. Am. Coll. Physician Assoc.'s Rsch. Competition, 1996; Elmore Med. Rsch. scholar U. Cambridge, 1987-88; Sir John Cass fellow, 1986-87. Fax: 507-284-5745. E-mail: levine.james@mayo.edu. Office: Mayo Clinic 200 1st St SW Rochester MN 55905-0002

LE VINE, JEROME EDWARD, retired ophthalmologist; b. Pitts., Mar. 23, 1923; s. Harry Robert and Marian Dorothy (Finesilver) L.; m. Marilyn Tobey Hiedovitz, Apr. 14, 1957; children: Loren Robert, Beau Jay, Janice Lynn. B.S., U. Pitts., 1944; M.D., Hahnemann Med. Sch., Phila., 1949; postgrad. in ophthalmology U. Pa., 1951-52. Diplomate Am. Bd. Disability Cons., Am. Bd. Quality Assurance & Utilization Rev. Intern, St. Francis Hosp., Pitts., 1949-50; resident in ophthalmology Jefferson U. Med. Sch. Hosp., Phila., 1952-54; ophthalmologist Leech Farm VA Hosp., Pitts., 1955-59; chief eye dept. Stanocola Clinic, Baton Rouge, 1959-64; sole practice medicine specializing in ophthalmology, Baton Rouge, 1959-86; cons. La. State U., East La. State Hosp. Infirmary, Villa Feliciana Geriatric Hosp., disability dept. Social Security Adminstrn., div. blind La. State Pub. Welfare dept.; mem. staff Our Lady of the Lake Hosp., Baton Rouge Gen. Hosp., Women's Hosp.; instr. spl. edn. U. Southeastern La., 1971. Mem. Am. Bd. Quality Assurance and Utilization Rev., 1990. Served with MC, AUS, 1942-44. Fellow Am. Geriatric Soc., Royal Soc. Health; mem. AMA, La. State Med. Soc., East Baton Rouge Parish Med. Soc., 6th Dist. Med. Soc., New Orleans Acad. Ophthalmology, So. Med. Assn., La. Med. Soc., Baton Rouge Parish Med. Soc., Pi Lambda Phi, Phi Delta Epsilon. Democrat. Jewish. Office: PO Box 66787 Baton Rouge LA 70896-6787

LEVINE, MARILYN MARKOVICH, lawyer, arbitrator; b. Bklyn., Aug. 9, 1930; d. Harry P. and Fannie L. (Hymowitz) Markovich; m. Louis L. Levine. June 24, 1950; children: Steven R., Ronald J., Linda J. Morgenstern. BS summa cum laude, Columbia U., 1950; MA, Adelphi U., 1967; JD, Hofstra U., 1977. Bar: N.Y. 1978, U.S. Dist. Ct. (so. and ea. dists.) N.Y. 1978, D.C. 1979, U.S. Supreme Ct. 1982. Sole practice Valley Stream, N.Y., 1978—; contract arbitrator bldg. svc. industry, N.Y.C., 1982—; panel arbitrator retail food industry, N.Y.C., 1980—; arbitrator N.Y. dist. cts., Nassau County, 1981—; mem. Nat. Acad. Arbitrators, 1992—. Panel arbitrator Suffolk County Pub. Employee Relations Bd., 1979—, Nassau County Pub. Employee Relations Bd., 1980—, Nat. Mediation Bd., 1986—; mem. adv. council Ctr. Labor and Industrial Relations, N.Y. Inst. Tech., N.Y., 1985—; counsel Nassau Civic Club, 1978—. Mem. ABA, N.Y. State Bar Assn., D.C. Bar Assn., Nassau County Bar Assn., N.J. Bd. Mediation (panel arbitrator), Am. Arbitration Assn. (arbitrator 1979—), Fed. Mediation Bd. (arbitrator 1980—). Home and Office: 1057 Linden St Valley Stream NY 11580-2135

LEVINE, MELVIN CHARLES, lawyer; b. Bklyn., Nov. 12, 1930; s. Barnet and Jennie (Iser) L. BCS, NYU, 1952; LLB, Harvard U., 1955. Bar: N.Y. 1956, U.S. Supreme Ct. 1964. Assoc. Kriger & Haber, Bklyn., 1956-58, Black, Varian & Simons, N.Y.C., 1959; sole practice N.Y.C., 1959—; devel. multiple dwelling housing; dir. Am. ORT Nat. Cabinet; mem. Am. ORT Nat. Campaign Com.; trustee Bramson ORT Coll.; mem. housing ct. adv. coun. N.Y. State Unified Ct. Sys.; mem. ind. dem. jud. screening panel N.Y.C civil ct. judges; mem. Character and Fitness Com., First Jud. Dept. Trustee Jewish Ctr. of the Hamptons, Bramson Ort Coll. Recipient N.Y.

Ort Scholarship Fund Cmty. Achievement award. Mem. N.Y. County Lawyers Assn. (co-chair civil ct. practice sect., civil ct. com., housing ct. com., uniform housing ct. rules com., liaison to Assn. Bar City of N.Y. on selection of housing, civil and criminal ct. judges, com. on jud., task force on tort reform, Civil Ct. Practice Sect. Disting. Svc. award), Assn. Bar of City of N.Y. (adj. mem. jud. com.). Democrat. Jewish. Home: 146 Waverly Pl New York NY 10014-3848 Office: 271 Madison Ave Ste 1404 New York NY 10016-1001

LEVINE, MICHAEL ELIAS, law educator, executive; b. N.Y.C., Apr. 8, 1941; s. Morris and Sara (Meltzer) L.; m. Carol June Stover, June 2, 1967; children: Sara Rebecca, Anna Rachel. BA in Philosophy, Reed Coll., 1962; JD, Yale U., 1965, grad. in Econs., 1965. Atty. CAB, Washington, 1965-66; spl. asst. C.C. U.S. Task Force Econ. Growth and Opportunity, 1966-67; law and econs. fellow U. Chgo. Law Sch., 1967-68; asst. prof. law U. So. Calif. Law Ctr., 1968-70, assoc. prof. law, 1970-72, prof. law, 1972-84, William T. Dalessi prof. law, 1985-87; Gen. George Rogers Clark prof. mgmt. studies Sch. Mgmt. Yale U., New Haven, 1987-90, William S. Beinecke prof. mgmt. studies, dean Sch. Mgmt., 1990-92; vis. prof. Duke U., 1972-73; Henry R. Luce prof. law and social change in tech. soc. Calif. Inst. Tech., Pasadena, 1973-83; on leave Calif. Inst. Tech., U. So. Calif., 1977-79, 81-83; dir. Bur. Pricing and Domestic Aviation, CAB, 1978, gen. dir. internat. and domestic aviation, 1979; exec. v.p. mktg. Continental Airlines, 1981-82; pres., CEO N.Y. Air, 1982-84; exec. v.p. mktg. Northwest Airlines, St. Paul, Minn., 1992-94, exec. v.p. mktg. and internat., 1994-99; adj. prof. law Harvard Law Sch., 1999—; chmn. Rohn Industries, Inc., 1999—; mgmt. intern Def. and Fgn. Affairs Orgn. exec. office Pres. Bur. Budget, 1964; vis. prof. Duke U., 1972-73; acad. visitor London Sch. Econs. and Polit. Sci., 1977; vis. lectr. Inst. Air and Space Law, McGill U., 1978; mem. U.S. Aviation Safety Commn., 1987-88; mem. adv. panel airport and air traffic ctrl. sys. office tech. assessment, 1980-81; pub. cons. subcom. administrv. practice and procedure U.S. Senate, 1974-75, Commonwealth PR, 1974, Nat. Sci. Found., 1975-77, Calif. Air Resources bd., 1976, Energy Resources Conservation and Devel. Commn., Calif., 1976, U.S. Interstate Commerce Commn., 1980, U.S. Civil Aeronautics bd., 1977, 1980, Port Authority N.Y. and NJ, 1984-85, Nat. Coun. Pub. Works Improvement, 1987-88, Corp. and Consumer Affairs Canada, 1988-89, U.S. Dept. State, 1989-91, OECD, 1991-92; chmn. Rohn Industries, Inc., 1999—. Contbr. articles on air transp. regulation, theories of legal process and regulatory behavior; contbr. other articles to scholarly jours. and books; referee Jourbal Law and Economics, Journal of Law, Economic and Organization, others. Bd. trustees Ctr. Law Pub. Interest, L.A., 1971-76; mem. edit. adv. panel Environ. Law Reporter, 1971-77; trustee Wenner-Gren Found. for Anthrop. Research, 1983-89, Reed Coll., 1984—; bd. dirs. Institut du Transport Aerien, Paris, 1984—, UNR Personal Injury Plaintiffs Trust asbestos bankruptcy, 1989—. Recipient award for excellence and disting. public service CAB, 1979, Vis. scholar Inst. Advanced Legal Studies, 1977. Fellow Nat. Acad. Pub. Adminstrn., 1997—; mem. Assn. Am. Law Schs. (exec. coun. sect. on antitrust and econ. regulation 1974-78, 87-91), U.S. Aviation Safety Commn., 1987-88, Nat. Acad. Scis. Com. on airline svc. and saftey deregulation, 1989-91.

LEVINE, NAOMI BRONHEIM, university administrator; b. N.Y.C., Apr. 15, 1923; d. Nathan and Malvina (Mermelstein) Bronheim; m. Leonard Levine, Apr. 11, 1948; 1 dau., Joan. BA, Hunter Coll., 1944; LLB, Columbia, 1946, JD, 1970. Bar: N.Y. 1946. With Scaadrett, Tuttle & Chalaire, N.Y.C., 1946-48, Charles Gottleib, N.Y.C., 1948-50; with Am. Jewish Congress, 1950-78, exec. dir., 1972-78; v.p. to sr. v.p. external affairs NYU, 1978—; asst. prof. law and police sci. John Jay Coll., N.Y.C., 1969-73, L.I. U., 1965-69. Author: Schools in Crisis, 1969, The Jewish Poor-an American Awakening, 1974, Politics, Religion and Love, 1990; mem. editl. bd. Columbia Law Rev., 1945-46. Bd. dirs. Jewish Cmty. Rels. Coun., Am. Women's Econ. Devel. Council; trustee N.Y. UJA-Fedn. Named to Hunter Coll. Hall of Fame, 1972. Office: NYU External Affairs 70 Washington Sq S New York NY 10012-1091

LEVINE, SANFORD HAROLD, lawyer; b. Troy, N.Y., Mar. 13, 1938; s. Louis and Reba (Semegren) L.; m. Margaret R. Appelbaum, Oct. 29, 1967; children: Jessica Sara, Abby Miriam. AB, Syracuse U., 1959, JD, 1961. Bar: N.Y. 1961, U.S. Dist. Ct. (no. dist.) N.Y. 1961, U.S. Dist. Ct. (we. dist.) N.Y. 1979, U.S. Dist. Ct. (ea. and so. dists.) N.Y. 1980, U.S. Ct. Appeals (2d cir.) 1962, U.S. Supreme Ct. 1967. Law asst. to assoc. judge N.Y. Ct. Appeals, Albany and to justice N.Y. Supreme Ct., 1962-66, N.Y. Ct. Appeals, Albany, 1964; asst. counsel N.Y. State Temporary commn. on Constl. Conv., N.Y.C., 1966-67; assoc. counsel SUNY System, Albany, 1967-70, dep. univ. counsel, 1970-78, acting counsel, 1970-71, acting univ. counsel, 1978-79, univ. counsel and vice chancellor legal affairs, 1979-97, prof. Sch. of Edn., dir. program in edn. and law, 1997—; adj. prof. Sch. of Edn. State U. N.Y., Albany, 1992-97; mem. paralegal curriculum adv. com. Schenectady County Community Coll., 1975—. Editl. bd. Syracuse U. Law Rev., 1960-61; editl. adv. bd. Jour. Coll. and Univ. Law, 1977-81. Fellow Am. Bar Found., N.Y. Bar Found., State Acad. for Pub. Adminstrn.; mem. ABA (ho. dels. 1987-89), N.Y. State Bar Assn., Albany County Bar Assn., Nat. Assn. Coll. and Univ. Attys. (exec. bd. 1979-82, bd. dirs. 1982-89, pres. 1986-87), Am. Soc. Pub. Adminstrn., Am. Health Lawyers Assn. Home: 1106 Godfrey Ln Schenectady NY 12309-2712

LEVINE, STEVEN ALAN, real estate appraiser, environmental consultant; b. Cin., Aug. 28, 1951; s. E. Pike and Beverly Rae (Friedman) L. BA with honors, U. Cin., 1975; postgrad., George Washington U., 1975-77. Appraiser Real Estate Evaluators and Cons., Cin., 1969-75; program asst. U.S. Renegotiation Bd., Washington, 1975; assessor D.C. Govt., Washington, 1976-77; emergency mgmt. specialist Fed. Emergency Mgmt. Agy., Washington, 1977-80; v.p. Am. Res. and Appraisal Ctr., Cin., 1980-82; pres. Steven A. Levine & Assocs., Inc., Cin., 1982—; v.p., exec. v.p. Nat. Assn. Environ. Risk Auditors, 1995—; cons. U.S. Army, 1982—, U.S. Dept. Interior. Author: Environmental Challenges Can Create Work for Real Estate Appraisers, Environmental Liabilities Affecting Real Estate, Kuwait: An Environmental Nightmare, The Renegotiation of Defense Contracts, Military Installation Real Property Management, Property Tax Relief Measures for the Elderly. Mem. Forum for Urban Studies, Washington, 1977, The Appraisal Found. (bd. trustees ethics, policies and procedures com., 1997; co-chmn. emerging issues com., 1998; co-chmn. mem. com., 1999—). Sgt. USAF, 1969-75. Named to Hon. Order Ky. Cols., Louisville, 1979; named lt. col. aide-de-camp Staff of Gov. of Ga., Atlanta, 1979, lt. col. aide-de-camp Staff of Gov. of Ala., Montgomery, 1983. Mem. Nat. Assn. Environ. Risk Auditors (v.p., exec. dir., cert. environ. risk assessor, rep. Appraisal Found. Adv. Coun.), Am. Assn. of Cert. Appraisers. Jewish. Avocations: running, classical music, golf, reading, interior design. Office fax: 513-674-0680. Home: 3073 Buell Rd Cincinnati OH 45251-4505 Office: 6645 Colerain Ave Cincinnati OH 45239-5539

LEVINE, THOMAS JEFFREY PELLO, lawyer; b. Santa Monica, Calif., Mar. 6, 1952; s. Allan Lester and Shirley Elaine (Pello) L.; m. Margaret Louise Adlon, Aug. 27, 1977; children: Marissa, Matthew, Molly. Student, U. Denver, 1970-71, Calif. State U., Northridge, 1971-73, Uppsala U., Sweden; BA, Calif. State U., Sacramento, 1974; JD, Southwestern U., 1977; postgrad., Yale U., 1999. Bar: Calif. 1977, U.S. Dist. Ct. (cen. dist.) Calif. 1978. Ptnr. Levine & Levine, L.A., 1977-83; staff atty. Fed. Deposit Ins. Corp., Newport Beach, Calif., 1983-85; v.p., assoc. counsel Imperial Bank, Inglewood, Calif., 1985-88; v.p., counsel Community Bank, Pasadena, Calif., 1988; gen. counsel, sr. v.p., sec. Calif. Commerce Bank, Banamex USA Bancorp, L.A., 1988—; legal affairs com. mem. Calif. Bankers Assn., San Francisco, 1990—; chmn. Am. Bankers Assn. Bank Counsel Com. 1993-97. Dir. Angelino Heights Historic Preservation Assn., L.A., 1985-95; sec., dir. Carroll Ave. Restoration Found., L.A., 1979-87; dir. Wilshire C. of C., L.A., 1982. Mem. L.A. County Bar Assn., Braemar Country Club (bd. govs. 1979-83). Jewish. Avocations: running, golf, Aztec history, historic preservation. Office: Banamex USA Bancorp 2029 Century Park E Fl 42 Los Angeles CA 90067-2901

LEVINSEN, HENRIK, biologist, researcher; b. Hillerod, Denmark, Oct. 9, 1968; s. Jorgen and Benthe (Thiesen) L.; m. Sanne Kortbek Sandal, May 7, 1994; children: Ane, Ida. MS, U. Copenhagen, 1995, PhD, 2000. Rsch. asst. Nat. Environ. Rsch. Inst., Roskilde, Denmark, 1998. Author rsch. papers in field. Office: Nat Environ Rsch Inst, Frederiksborgevej 399, 4000 Roskilde Denmark

LEVINSON, BARRY L., film director; b. Balt., Apr. 6, 1942. Ed., Am. U., Washington. film writer, actor: Silent Movie, 1976, High Anxiety, 1978; writer: ...And Justice for All, 1979, Inside Moves, 1980, Best Friends, 1982, Unfaithfully Yours, 1984; dir.: The Natural, 1984, Young Sherlock Holmes, 1985, Good Morning Vietnam, 1987, Rain Man, 1988 (Academy award 1989, Dirs. Guild Am. award 1989); screenwriter, dir.: Diner, 1982, Tin Men, 1987, Avalon, 1990 (Writers Guild Am. award 1990); co-prodr., dir. Bugsy, 1991, Disclosure, 1994, Wag the Dog, 1997, Sphere, 1998; co-writer, dir., prodr. Toys, 1992; prodr. Donnie Brasco, 1997; writer, dir., prodr. Jimmy Hollywood, 1994 (also actor), Sleepers, 1996, Liberty Heights, 1999; actor: Quiz Show, 1994; dir., exec. prodr. (TV) Homicide: Life on the Street, 1993 (Emmy award, Outstanding Individual Achievement in Directing in a Drama Series, 1993, Peabody award 1993); exec. prodr. (TV) Oz, 1997; dir, and prodr., The Beat, 2000 (TV). Mem. Dirs. Guild Am., Writers Guild Am. Address: c/o Baltimore Pictures 4000 Warner Blvd Bldg 133 Burbank CA 91522-0001

LEVINSON, JERROLD, humanities educator; b. Bklyn., July 11, 1948; s. Max and Paula (Forster) L.; m. Alicia Janet Greene, Aug. 2, 1970 (div. June 1981); m. Karla Ruth Hoff, July 14, 1985; 1 child, Melanie Augusta Hoff. BS in Philosophy and Chemistry, MIT, 1969; PhD in Philosophy, U. Mich., 1974. Vis. prof. State U. N.Y., Albany, 1974-75; prof. U. Md., College Park, 1976—; vis. prof. U. London, 1991, Johns Hopkins U., 1993, U. de Rennes, France, 1998, U. Canterbury, New Zealand, 1999, Columbia U., 2000. Editor: Aesthetics and Ethics, 1998; author: Music, Art and Metaphysics, 1990, Pleasures of Aesthetics, 1996, Music in the Moment, 1998, L'Art la Musique, et Histoire, 1998; contbr. articles to profl. jours. Fellow NEH, 1980. Mem. Am. Soc. Aesthetics (v.p./pres. 1999-02), British Soc. Aesthetics, Am. Philos. Assn. Democrat. Jewish. Avocations: racket sports, baroque recorder, francophonie. E-mail: JL32@umail.umd.edu. Office: Univ Md Dept Philosophy Skinner Bldg College Park MD 20742-0001

LEVINSON, NANETTE SEGAL, international relations educator, administrator; b. Boston, Nov. 8, 1946; d. Oscar and Rose (Menicks) Segal; m. Peter Joseph Levinson, Mar. 30, 1968; children: Sharman Risa, Justin David. AB cum laude, Harvard U., 1968, EdM, 1969, EdD, 1979. Asst. prof. Am. U., Washington, 1980-86, dir. advanced tech. mgmt. program, 1983-88, assoc. prof., 1986—, assoc. dean sch. internat. svc., 1988—; cons. David Taylor Naval Ship Rsch. and Devel. Ctr., 1984-86, Xerox Corp., Leesburg, Va., 1986-91; chair bd. dirs. Nat. Conf. on Advancement of Rsch., 1992-93, bd. dirs., 1996—; bd. dirs. Women's Fgn. Policy Group, 1997-2000, mem. adv. coun., 2000—; bd. dirs. Transatlantic Info. Exch. Svcs., sec.-gen., 1997-99; vis. scholar Ritsumeikan U., Kyoto, Japan, 1993. Contbr. numerous articles to profl. jours. Bd. dirs. Joint Bd. on Sci. and Engring. Edn., Washington, 1982-85; co-chair The Rsch. Project on Women Leaders in Internat. Affairs, 1995-99. Mem. Internat. Studies Assn., Am. Polit. Sci. Assn., Internat. Assn. for Media and Comm. Rsch. Office: Am U Office of Dean 4400 Massachusetts Ave NW Washington DC 20016-8071

LEVINSON, PETER JOSEPH, lawyer; b. Washington, June 11, 1943; s. Bernard Hirsh and Carlyn Virginia (Krupp) L.; m. Nanette Susan Segal, Mar. 30, 1968; children: Sharman Risa, Justin David. AB in History cum laude, Brandeis U., Waltham, Mass., 1965; JD, Harvard U., 1968. Bar: Hawaii 1971, U.S. Supreme Ct. 1975. Summer supr. Harvard Legal Aid Bur., Cambridge, Mass., 1968; research asst. Harvard Law Sch., 1968-69; teaching fellow Osgoode Hall Law Sch., York U. (Can.), 1969-70, research assoc., 1969-70, asst. prof., 1970-71; dep. atty. gen. State of Hawaii, 1971-75; vis. fellow Harvard U., 1976-77; ptnr. Levinson and Levinson, Honolulu, 1977-79; spl. asst. to dir. Office Program Support, Legal Services Corp., Washington, 1979; cons. Select Commn. on Immigration and Refugee Policy, Washington, 1980-81; minority counsel subcom. on immigration, refugees and internat. law com. on judiciary, U.S. Ho. of Reps., Washington, 1981-85, minority counsel subcom. monopolies and comml. law, 1985-89, minority counsel subcom. econ. and comml. law, 1989-95, counsel com. on judiciary, 1995—. Trustee, Hawaii Jewish Welfare Fund, 1972-75, chmn. fund drive, 1972; trustee Temple Emanu-El, Honolulu, 1973-75; mem. alumni admissions council Brandeis U., 1978-82. Recipient award of merit United Jewish Appeal, 1974. Mem. Hawaii State Bar Assn. (chmn. standing com. on continuing legal edn. 1972, chmn. standing com. on jud. adminstrn. 1979), ABA, Am. Judicature Soc. Contbr. articles to profl. jours. Office: B353 Rayburn House Office Bldg Washington DC 20515-0001

LEVINSON, ROBERT ARLEN, computer science educator, consultant; b. Mpls., Oct. 30, 1958; s. Morton William and Chernie Rae (Braufman) L. BS in Math., BS in Computer Sci., U. Minn., 1981; PhD, U. Tex., 1984. Tech. support analyst Minn. Gas Co., Mpls., 1975-79; tchg. asst. U. Minn., Mpls., 1980-81; grad. rsch. fellow dept. chemistry U. Tex., Austin, 1983-85; asst. prof. U. Calif., Santa Cruz, 1986-93, assoc. prof., 1993—; contract programmer U. Minn. Computing Ctr., Mpls., 1979-81; vis. prof. FMC Corp., Santa Clara, Calif., 1989-90; cons. Textwise, Syracuse, N.Y., 1995-97, Stock Sci., 1999-2000. Editor: Conceptual Structures, Applications, Implementation and Theory, 1995, procs. 3d Internat. Conf. on Conceptual Structures, 1995; editl. bd.: Multi-Senser Info. Fusion jour., 2000-2001; pubs. chair Second Internat. Conf. on Multisource-Multisensor Info. Fusion, 1999. Grantee NSF, Washington, 1989-94, grad. fellow, 1979-83; grantee NASA, Ames, Calif., 1986-87. Avocations: chess, sports, stock market investments. Fax: (831) 459-4829. E-mail: levinson@cse.ucsc.edu. Home: 41 Grandview St Apt 1507 Santa Cruz CA 95060-6800 Office: U Calif 225 Applied Scis Santa Cruz CA 95064

LEVINSON, SHAUNA T., financial services executive; b. Denver, Aug. 1, 1954; d. Charles and Geraldine D. Titus; m. Kenneth L. Levinson, Dec. 21, 1986. BA cum laude, U. Puget Sound, 1976; M Bank Mktg. with honors, U. Colo., 1986. Cert. fin. planner. Fin. planning analyst Swift and Co., Chgo., 1977-79; from credit analyst to asst. v.p. Ctrl. Bank of Denver, 1979-84; v.p. fin. svcs. First Nat. Bank S.E. Denver, 1984-94; dir. mktg. First Nat. Banks, 1991-94; pres., CEO Fin. Directions, Inc., Denver, 1994—; CEO Levinson Resources, Inc., Denver, 1994—. Contbr. articles to profl. jours. Chmn. human resources com., mem. adminstrv. coun. Jr. League of Denver, 1983—; mem. cmty. assistance fund, placement adv. com.; fundraiser Women's Libr. Assn. U. Denver, 1990-94, 96—, Good Shepherd Cath. Sch., 1986-95, Jewish Cmty. Ctr., Denver, 1990-95, St. Mary's Acad., 1995-99 Theodor Herzl Day Sch., 1996-99; mem. Denver Campus for Jewish Edn., 2000—. Recipient Gold Peak award Am. Bankers Assn.-Bank Mktg. Assn., 1987; named Businessperson of Week Denver Bus. Jour., 1995. Mem. Jr. League Denver, U. Denver Pioneer Hockey, St. Andrews Soc. (life), Crestmoor Gardeners (treas. 1994-2000), Betty Baur Lambert Soc. (life), Kappa Alpha Theta (Chgo. NW alumnae 1977-79, Denver alumnae 1980—), Phi Kappa Phi, Phi Chi Theta. Office: 1624 Market St Ste 475 Denver CO 80202-1518

LEVISAY, LEESA DAWN, music educator, composer; b. Fort Worth, Tex., Mar. 30, 1959; d. Earl Lee and Dawn Estelle (Langley) Hall; m. Charles Glen Levisay, Apr. 14, 1984; children: Laura, Leah, Chad. MusB, Tarleton State U., 1982, MBA, 1983. Grad. asst. dept. fine arts and speech, asst. condr. choirs Tarleton State U., Stephenville, 1982-83; piano tchr. Tarleton State U., Stephenville, Tex., 1983; ins. underwriter Carter, Metsger, & Jones, Inc., Stephenville, 1984-85; piano, vocal instr. Stephenville, 1985—; co-owner A Musical Spectrum - Sch. Music, Stephenville, 1999—; mem. Cross Timbers Fine Arts Coun. Bd. Dirs., Stephensville, 1989-90; adjuctor piano competition Music Tchrs. Assn., Weatherford, Tex., 1990-96, Ft. Worth, 1991-92, Abilene, Tex., 1992-93; composer Concert Master Pub. Co., Dallas, 1993—; condr., composer Nat. Group Piano Tchrs. Assn., 1994; guest condr. The Keynote Studio, Dallas, 1996-97; guest composer, condr. Nat. Piano Tchrs. Inst., So. Meth. U., Dallas, 1997; adjudicator vocal judge Tarleton State U., 1998. Composer, arranger Christmas Collection, 1993, Canon in D-Pachelbel, 1996; composer Laura's Song, 1994. Singer Cross Timbers Civic Chorale, Stephenville, 1982-99; com. mem. Cross Timbers Habitat for Humanity, Stephenville, 1997-99. Mem. Nat. Piano Tchrs. Guild, Music Tchrs. Nat. Assn. (cert. profl. music tchr.), Tex. Music Tchrs. Assn., Cross Timbers Music Tchrs. Assn. (ensemble dir. 1985-97), Early Childhood Music and Movement Assn. (cert. early childhood music level 1), Stephenville C. of C. Presbyterian. Avocations: crafts, church work, gardening, reading. Office: A Musical Spectrum - Sch Music 495 N Harbin Dr Stephenville TX 76401-2861

LEVISON, STEVEN WILLIAM, scientist, educator; b. Bklyn., Aug. 6, 1961; s. Fredric Eliot and Carol Furgatch Levison; m. Teresa Lynne Wood, July 26, 1996. BS, U. Rochester, 1983; PhD, U. N.C., 1990. Postdoctoral fellow Columbia U., N.Y.C., 1990-93; asst. prof. Pa. State U., Hershey, 1993-99, assoc. prof., 1999—. Mem. editl. bd. Devel. Neurosci., 1999; contbr. articles to profl. jours. Rsch. grantee NIH, Bethesda, Md., 1994, 98, 98, Nat. Multiple Sclerosis Soc., N.Y., 1998. Mem. Am. Soc. for Neurochemistry (pres. Susquehanna Valley chpt. 1999), Soc. for Neurosci. Democrat. E-mail: slevison@psu.edu. Fax: 717-531-0714. Home: 835 Verden Dr Hummelstown PA 17036-9700 Office: Pa State Coll Medicine PO Box 850 Hershey PA 17033-0850

LEVI-STRAUSS, CLAUDE, educator; b. Brussels, Nov. 28, 1908; s. Raymond and Emma (Levy) Levi-S.; m. Dina Dreyfus, 1932; m. 2d, Rose-Marie Ullmo, 1946; 1 son, Laurent; m. 3d, Monique Roman; 1 son, Matthieu. Agrègè de Philosophie, Sorbonne, Paris, 1931; DLitt, U. Paris, 1948; PhD (hon.), U. Brussels, 1962, Oxford U., 1964, Yale U., 1965, U. Chgo., 1967, Columbia U., 1971, Stirling U., 1972, U. Nat. du Zaire, 1973, U. Uppsala, 1977, Johns Hopkins U., 1978, Laval U., 1979, U. Nat. Mexico, 1979, Visva Bharati U., India, 1980, Harvard U., 1986, Montreal U., 1998. Prof. U. Sao Paulo, Brazil, 1935-38; vis. prof. New Sch. for Social Rsch., N.Y., 1941-45; cultural counsellor French Embassy, Washington, 1946-47; assoc. curator Musee de l'Homme, Paris, 1948-49; dir. studies Ecole Pratique des Hautes Etudes, Paris, 1950-82; prof. Coll. de France, 1959-82; mem. French Acad., 1973. Publs. include La Vie familiale et sociale des Indiens Nambikwara, 1948, Les Structures elementaires de la parente, 1949 (The Elementary Structures of Kinship 1969), Race et histoire, 1952, Tristes Tropiques, 1955, English edit., 1973, A World on the Wane, 1961, abridged edit. of Tristes Tropiques, Anthropologie structurale Vol. 1, 1958, Vol. 2, 1973 (Structural Anthropology, Vol. 1, 1964, Vol. 2, 1977), Le Totemisme aujourd'hui, 1962 (Totemism, 1963), La Pensee sauvage, 1962 (The Savage Mind, 1966), Le Cru et le cuit, 1964 (The Raw and the Cooked 1970), Du Miel aux cendres, 1967 (From Honey to Ashes, 1973), L'Origine des manieres de table, 1968 (The Origin of Table Manners, 1978), L'Homme nu, 1971 (The Naked Man, 1981), La Voie des Masques, 1975 (The Way of the Masks, 1982), Le Regard èloignè, 1983 (The View from Afar, 1985), Paroles données, 19984 (Anthropology and Myth 1987), La Potiere jalouse, 1985 (The Jealous Potter, 1987), De Près et de loin, 1988 (Conversations with Claude Levi-Strauss, 1991), Histoire de Lynx, 1991 (The Story of Lynx, 1995), Regarder ècouter Lire, 1993 (Look, Listen, Read, 1993), Saudades do Brasil, 1994 (A Photographic Memoir, 1995), Saudades de São Paulo, 1996, relevant publs. include: Conversations with Levi-Strauss (ed. G. Charbonnier), 1969; by Octavio Paz: On Levi-Strauss, 1970; Claude Levi Strauss: An Introduction, 1972, Marcel Henaff: Claude Levi-Strauss, 1998. Decorated grand croix de la Legion d'Honneur, 1991, commandeur Ordre Nat. du Merite, 1971. Corr. mem. Royal Acad. Netherlands, Norwegian Acad., Brit. Acad., Nat. Acad. Scis., Am. Acad. and Inst. Arts and Letters, Am. Philos. Soc., Royal Anthropol. Inst. Gt. Britain, London Sch. African and Oriental Studies. Home: 2 rue des Marronniers, 75016 Paris France

LEVIT, JAY J(OSEPH), lawyer; b. Phila., Feb. 20, 1934; s. Albert and Mary Levit; m. Heloise Bertman, July 14, 1962; children: Richard Bertman, Robert Edward, Darcy Francine. AB, Case Western Res. U., 1955; JD, U. Richmond, 1958; LLM, Harvard U., 1959. Bar: Va. 1958, D.C. Ct. Appeals 1961, U.S. Supreme Ct. 1961. Trial atty. U.S. Dept. Justice, Washington, 1960-64; sr. atty. Gen. Dynamics Corp., Rochester, N.Y., 1965-67; ptnr. Stallard & Levit, Richmond, Va., 1968-77, Levit, Mann & Halligan, Richmond, 1978—; instr. U. Mich. Law Sch., Ann Arbor, 1964-65; adj. assoc. prof. U. Richmond Law Sch., 1974-77; adj. lectr. Va. Commonwealth U., Richmond, 1970-85; lectr. in field. Contbg. editor The Developing Labor Law-Bur. Nat. Affairs, 1974—. Mem. ABA (labor com.), Va. Bar Assn. (labor com., Chair's award for extraordinary contbns. to labor and employment law sect. 1999), Fed. Bar Assn. (labor com.). Avocations: art collecting, jogging, swimming, travel. Home: 419 Dellbrooks Pl Richmond VA 23233-5559 Office: Levit Mann & Halligan 1301 N Hamilton St Richmond VA 23230-3959 also: Levit Mann & Halligan 127 Thompson St Ashland VA 23005-1511

LEVIT, WILLIAM HAROLD, JR., lawyer; b. San Francisco, Feb. 8, 1938; s. William Harold and Barbara Janis Kaiser L.; m. Mary Elizabeth Webster, Feb. 13, 1971; children: Alison Jones Baumler, Alexandra Bradley Kovacevich, Laura Elizabeth Fletcher, Amalia Elizabeth Webster, William Harold, III. BA magna cum laude, Yale U., 1960; MA Internat. Rels., U. Calif., Berkeley, 1962; LLB, Harvard U., 1967. Bar: N.Y. 1968, Calif. 1974, Wis. 1979. Fgn. service officer Dept. State, 1962-64; assoc. Davis Polk & Wardwell, N.Y.C., 1967-73; assoc. ptnr. Hughes Hubbard & Reed, N.Y.C., L.A., 1973-79; sec. and gen. counsel Rexnord Inc., Milw., 1979-83; ptnr., dir., chair internat. practice group Godfrey & Kahn, Milw., 1983—; substitute arbitrator Iran-U.S. Claims Tribunal, The Hague, 1984-88; lectr. Practicing Law Inst., ABA, Calif. Continuing Edn. of Bar, State Bar of Wis. Contbr. to: Mergers and the Private Antitrust Suit: The Private Enforcement of Section 7 of the Clayton Act, 1977. Bd. dirs. Wis. Humane Soc., 1980-90, pres., 1986-88; bd. dirs. Vis. Nurse Corp., Milw., 1980-90, chmn., 1985-87; bd. dirs. Vis. Nurse Found., 1986-95, chmn., 1989-91; bd. dirs. Aurora Health Care Inc., 1988-93, Wis. Soc. to Prevent Blindness, 1981-91, Columbia Coll. Nursing, 1992—, vice chair, 1998—, Aurora Health Care Ventures, 1993—, chmn., 1998-2000; adv. bd. Med. Coll. Wis. Cardiovasc. Rsch. Ctr., 1994—, chmn., 1999—; rep. Assn. Yale Alumni, 1976-79, 81-84, 90-93; pres. Yale Club So. Calif., 1977-79; mem. neutral advisor panel and franchise, and ins. panels panels CPR Inst. for Dispute Resolution. Ford Found. fellow U. Pa., 1960-61, NDEA fellow U. Calif., Berkeley, 1961-62. Mem. ABA, Am. Law Inst., Am. Soc. Corp. Secs. (pres. Wis. chpt. 1982-83, dir. 1981-92), Am. Arbitration Assn. (comml. panel 1977—, internat. panel 1997—), Assn. Bar City N.Y., State Bar Calif. (com. on continuing edn. of bar 1977-79), Los Angeles County Bar Assn. (ethics com. 1976-79), State Bar Wis. (dir. internat. bus. transactions sect. 1985-92, dist. 2 bd. attys. profl. responsibility com. 1985-94, chmn. 1993-94), Bar Assn. 7th Cir. (2d v.p. 2000—), Am. Br. Internat. Law Assn., Nat. Assn. Security Dealers (panel arbitrators 1988—), Chartered Inst. Arbitrators (London), N.Y. Stock Exch. (panel arbitrators 1988—), N.Am. Coun. London Ct. of Internat. Arbitration, Am. Soc. Internat. Law, Inst. Jud. Adminstrn., Milw. Club, Milw. Athletic Club, Town Club, Phi Beta Kappa. E-mail: walevit@gklaw.com. Office: 780 N Water St Ste 1200 Milwaukee WI 53202-3512

LEVITAN, MAX FISHEL, geneticist, anatomy educator; b. Tverai, Telsiu Aps, Lithuania, Mar. 1, 1921; came to U.S., 1928; s. Solomon Leib Hannah (Siev) L.; m. Beth Sheva German, Oct. 25, 1947; children: Eve Leah Gerber, Sara Ann, Marjorie Ruth Gross. AB, U. Chgo., 1944; MA, U. Mich., 1946; PhD, Colmubia U., 1951. Asst. in zoology Columbia U., N.Y.C., 1946-49; assoc. prof. biology Va. Poly. Inst., Blacksburg, 1949-55; asst. prof. anatomy Woman's Med. Coll. Pa., Phila., 1955-58, assoc. prof., 1958-60, prof. anatomy and med. genetics, 1960-66, acting chmn. anatomy dept., 1964-66; prof. biology, chmn. dept. George Mason U., Fairfax, Va., 1966-68; assoc. prof. anatomy Mt. Sinai Sch. Medicine, CUNY, N.Y.C., 1968-70, prof. anatomy, 1970—, prof. human genetics, 1995—. Author: Textbook of Human Genetics, 1971, 3rd edit. 1988; contbng. author: Clinical Genetics, 1973, Genetics and Biology of Drosophila, 1982, Drosophila Inversion Polymorphism, 1992, Encyclopedia of Human Biology, 1992, 1997, Encyclopedia of Science and Technology, 1992, 1997, Genetics of Natural Populations, 1995; assoc. editor Evolution, 1977-79; contbr. articles to profl. jours. Named Edward Everett Just Meml. lectr. Howard U., Washington, 1968; recipient Rsch. Career Devel. award NIH, 1963. Fellow AAAS; mem. Genetics Soc. Am., Soc. for Study of Evolution, Am. Soc. Naturalists, Sigma Xi (sec. VPI chpt. 1954-55, sec.-treas. Mt. Sinai chpt. 1975—). Jewish. Achievements include rsch. in linkage disquilibria in inversion systems, unique chromosomal breakage factor, suppressor systems in evolution. E-mail: max.levitan@mssm.edu. Home: 1212 5th Ave New York NY 10029-5210 Office: Mt Sinai Sch Medicine CUNY 1 Gustave L Levy Pl New York NY 10029-6500

LEVITAN, YURI SEMENOVICH, physics researcher, educator; b. Moscow, June 4, 1941; s. Semen Arkadievich and Rachel Aronovna (Levina) L.; m. Olga Ivanovna Trantina, May 4, 1974; 1 child, Alexandra. Degree in mech. engring., Moscow Aviation Inst., 1966, PhD, 1978. Engr. Moscow Aviation Inst., 1966-71, jr. rsch. worker, 1971-79, tchr. physics, 1979—, sr. rsch. worker, 1980—; cons. in field. Author: Low Temperature Plasma vol.

1, 1990, Instabilities and Turbulence in Low Temperature Plasma, 1994; contbr. articles to profl. jours.

LEVITAS, JOSEPH, aerospace engineer, researcher, educator; b. Daugavpils, Latvia, USSR, Aug. 12, 1955; arrived in Israel, 1971; s. Reuven and Raisa (Belkina) L.; m. Sarit Auerbach (div. 1992); 1 child, Jonathan. BSc in Aerospace Engring., Technion U., Haifa, Israel, 1982, MSc in Aerospace Engring., 1988, DSc in Aerospace Engring., 1992. Engr. Israel Aircraft Industry, Lod, 1982-83; instr. Technion U., Haifa, 1985-92, rschr., 1992-93; lectr. Brauda Coll., Karmiel, 1994-2000; rsch. engr. VSoft, Yoqneam, 1996—; cons. Nanomotion, Yoqneam, 1993-94, 97-2000, Elbit, Haifa, 1995-96. Contbr. articles to profl. jours. including Jour. Applied Mechanics, Jour. Sound and Vibration, Internat. Jour. Non-Linear Mechanics, Fuzzy Sets and Sys. Staff sgt. Israel Def. Force (Paratroops), 1974-77. Miriam and Aaron Gutwirth fellow Technion-Israel Inst. Tech. Avocations: reading, exercising, dramatic acting, dancing, phycology. Office: VSoft, Hi-Park, Region No 7 Bldg 1, Yoqneam Israel

LEVITAS, VALERY, mechanics educator, researcher; b. Kiev, Ukraine, Apr. 3, 1956; arrived in Germany, 1993; s. Ilya and Shanna (Beresina) L.; m. Ludmila Borodyanskaya, Aug. 25, 1978 (div. 1992); 1 child, Oleg; m. Natasha Danekina, Jan. 20, 1993; 1 child, Roman. MSc with honors, Inst. Tech., Kiev, 1978; PhD, Inst. Superhard Materials, Kiev, 1981; DSc, Inst. Elect. Machine Bldg., Moscow, 1988; D of Engring. Habilitation, U. Hannover, Germany, 1995. Cert. engr. Jr. rschr. Inst. for Superhard Materials, Kiev, 1981-84, leader rsch. group, 1982-95, sr. rschr., 1984-89, leading rschr., 1985-95; vis. rschr. Inst. Problems of Mechanics, Moscow, 1985; vis. and rsch. prof. U. Hannover, Germany, 1992, 93-99; assoc. prof. Tex. Tech. U., Lubbock, 1999—; cons. Inst. for Superhard Materials, Kiev, 1995—; dir. Firm Strength, Kiev, 1990-92; spkr. in field. Author: (books) Large Elastoplastic Deformations of Materials at High Pressure, 1987, Thermomechanics of Phase Transformations and Inelastic Deformations in Microinhomogeneous Materials, 1992, Large Deformations of Materials with Complex Rheological Properties at Normal and High Pressure, 1996; bd. editors: (jour.) High Pressure Physics and Tech., 1996—; mem. editl. adv. bd.: (jour.) Superhard Materials, 1990—. Recipient medal Ukrainian Acad. Scis., 1984, Disting. Paper award Internat. Jour. Engring. Sci., 1995, Richard von Mises award Soc. Applied Math. and Mechanics, 1998; Humboldt Rsch. fellow, 1993-95. Mem. ASME, Internat. Assn. for Advancement of High Pressure Sci. (exec. com. 1993—), Soc. Engring. Sci. Office: Tex Tech U Dept Mech Engring Lubbock TX 30167

LEVITCH, JOSEPH See LEWIS, JERRY

LEVITE, ALLAN EUGENE, administrative assistant; b. Chgo., Oct. 29, 1947; s. Louis and Rose Levite. BSBA, Roosevelt U., 1970. Sales adminstr. Hammer Storage Solutions, Newark, Calif., 1992-97; adminstv. asst. Socket Comm., Newark, 1997-99; support analyst Superior Cons., San Francisco, 1999-2000. Author: Guilt, Blame and Politics, 1998; contbr. articles to profl. jours. Libertarian. Office: Stanyan Press PMB # 226 915 Cole St San Francisco CA 94117-4315

LEVITIN, GREGORY, electrical engineer; b. Kharkov, Ukraine, Sept. 19, 1959; arrived in Israel, 1990; s. Simon and Nelia (Abolnikov) L.; m. Irena Osovsky, Sept. 27, 1981; 1 child, Viktor. MS, Polytech. U. Kharkov, 1982; BS in Math., State U. Kharkov, 1986; PhD, Rsch. Inst. Metalworking Mach., Moscow, 1989. Software engr. Inst. Indsl. Automation, Kharkov, 1982-86; sr. rsch. assoc. Hydraulics Rsch Inst., Kharkov, 1989-90; postdoctoral rschr. Israel Inst. Tech., Haifa, 1991-93; engr., expert Israel Electric Corp., Haifa, 1993—; adj. lectr. Israel Inst. Tech., Haifa, 1994—. Contbr. articles to profl. jours. Mem. IEEE (sr.), Ops. Rsch. Soc. Israel. Office: Israel Electric Corp, PO Box 10, 31000 Haifa Israel

LEVITIN, JOSEPH, physicist, researcher; b. Konotop, Ukraine, USSR, Mar. 8, 1948; arrived in Israel, 1990; s. Lev and Izabela (Vurgapht) L.; m. Ludmila Levitin; 1 child, Mark. MSc, Polytechnic Inst., Leningrad, USSR, 1972; PhD, Hydrometeorol. Inst., Leningrad, USSR, 1979. Sr. engr. Electric Power Sta. Inst., Leningrad, 1972-81; scientist Chem. Inst., Leningrad, 1981-88; head of group Vacuum Equipment Inst., Riga, 1988-90; scientist Israel Meteorol. Svc., Bet Dagan, Israel, 1991—. Contbr. articles to profl. jours. Avocations: travel, sailing, theatre, books. E-mail: jlevitin@yahoo.com. Office: Israel Meteorol Svc, 50250 Bet Dagan Israel

LEVITIN, VALIM VLADIMIR, physicist, educator, researcher; b. Kharkov, Ukraine, Oct. 25, 1930; s. Vladimir Feodor Feldman and Victoria (Ephraim) Levitina; m. Lydia Michael Ignatovich, Jan. 17, 1953; 1 child, Victor Valim. PhD, Kharkov U., Ukraine, 1953; degree in physics and math., Urals U., Sverdlovsk, 1961; DSc, Inst. Met. Phys., Moscow, 1983. Rsch. engr. Metall. Works, Satka, 1953-55; sr. rsch. worker Inst. Ferrous Metals, Sverdlovsk, 1955-62; phys. lab. chief Inst. Alloy Steels, Zaporozhye, Ukraine, 1962-82; prof. physics Zaporozhye State Tech. U., Zaporozhye, Ukraine, 1982—; prof. in physics dept. Supr. Comm. Cert. Scis., Moscow, 1984; tchr. Tech. Secondary Sch., Satka, 1953-55, Gymnasium, Zaporozhye, 1995—. Contbr. more than 110 articles to profl. jours.; patentee in field. Mem. N.Y. Acad. Scis. Avocations: classical music, theater, literature, English, chess. Home: 4-14 Relyefnaya Str, 69065 Zaporozhye Ukraine Office: Zaporozhye Tech Univ., 64 Zhukovsky Str, 69063 Zaporozhye Ukraine

LEVITSKY, MELVYN, former ambassador, professor; b. Sioux City, Iowa, Mar. 19, 1938; s. David and Mollie (Schwartz) L.; m. Joan Daskovsky, Aug. 12, 1962; children: Adam, Ross Josh. BA, U. Mich., 1960; MA, U. Iowa, 1963. Polit. officer U.S. Embassy, Moscow, 1972-75; officer-in-charge Soviet-U.S. bilateral relations Dept. State, Washington, 1975-78, dep. dir. UN polit. affairs, 1978-80, dir. UN polit. affairs, 1980-82, dep. asst. sec. for human rights and humanitarian affairs, 1982-83; dep. dir. Voice of Am., Washington, 1983-84; dep. assoc. dir. broadcasting USIA, Washington, 1983-84; U.S. amb. to Bulgaria, 1984-87; exec. sec., spl. asst. to sec. Dept. State, Washington, 1987-89, asst. sec. state internat. narcotics matters, 1989-94; U.S. amb. to Brazil Dept. State, Brasilia, 1994—; prof. Internat. Relations & Pub. Adminstrn. Maxwell School of Citizenship & Pub. Affairs, Syracuse U., Syracuse, NY; Disting. Fellow of the Global Affairs Inst. Syracuse U., Syracuse, NY. Recipient Meritorious Honor award Dept. State, 1968, Superior Honor award Dept. State, 1975, 82, Presdl. Meritorious Svc. awards, 1986-91. Mem. Am. Fgn. Service Assn. Office: Maxwell School of Citizenship & Pub Affairs Syracuse U Syracuse NY 13244-0001*

LEVITSKY, MIKHAIL LVOVITCH, economics educator; b. Moscow, July 27, 1944; s. Lev Grigorievitch and Valentina Konstantinovna (Semionova) Epshtein; m. Margarita Leontievna, Aug. 12, 1966; 1 child, Elena Mikhailovna. MS, Tech. U., 1966; PhD, Inst. of History and Theory of Pedagogies, 1986. Head Social and Econ. Rsch. Lab., Moscow, 1978-90; head dept. econ. Moscow State Pedagogical U., 1990—, dean faculty econ. mgmt., 1998—. Author: Methods and Models to define Economic Efficacy of National Education, 1990, Financial and Economic Activities of Schools, 1997; editor-in-chief Magister, 1996; contbr. articles to profl. jours. Vice dir. econ. coun. Ministry of Edn., 1993-97. Lt. Air Force, 1968-70. Grantee Tempus, 1993. Mem. N.Y. Acad. Sci., Acad. of Mgmt. Edn. and Culture, Russian State Acad. Edn. Avocations: alpine skiing, travelling.

LEVITT, B. BLAKE, medical and science writer; b. Bridgeport, Conn., Mar. 25, 1948; d. John Joseph and Beatrice Rozanski Blake; m. Andrew Levitt, Dec. 20, 1968 (div. May 1977); m. Jon P. Garvey, Nov. 19, 1983. BA in English magna cum laude, BA in History summa cum laude, Quinnipiac Coll., 1972; postgrad., Yale U., 1988. Instr. English as fgn. lang. U. Khon Kaen, Thailand, 1968-69; market researcher Lyons Bakeries Ltd., London, summer 1971; traffic mgr., copywriter Provocatives Advt. Agy., Danbury, Conn., 1976-78; tech. writer tng. divsn. Jack Morton Prodns., N.Y.C., 1978-82; freelance feature and med. writer Litchfield County Times, New Milford, Conn., 1982-85, N.Y. Times, N.Y.C., 1985-89; freelance writer med. and sci. books, 1989—. Author: Electromagnetic Fields: A Consumer's Guide to the Issues and How to Protect Ourselves, 1995 (Will Solimene Book Award of Excellence 1996), 50 Essential Things to Do When the Doctor Says It's Infertiltiy, 1995; co-author: (with John R. Sussman M.D.) Before You Conceive, The Complete Pre-Pregnancy Guide, 1989 (Will Solimene Book Award of Excellence 1991); contbr. articles to N.W. Hills Mag., New Eng. Monthly, Con. Mag. Founding mem., bd. dirs. Warren (Conn.) Land Trust, 1989-91, Lake Watch, Inc., Lake Watch Ednl. Inst., 1996—; trustee Berkshire-Litchfield Environ. Coun., 1999—; mem. Dem. Town Com., Warren, 1993—; vice chmn. zoning bd. appeals Town of Warren, 1993-95. Mem. Nat. Assn. Sci. Writers, Bioelectromagnetics Soc., Am. Med. Writers Assn., Author's Guild, Author's League. Avocations: architectural design and renovation, reading, hiking, gardening.

LEVITT, BRIAN MICHAEL, consumer products and services company executive, lawyer; b. Montreal, Que., Can., July 26, 1947; s. Eric and Rya Levitt; m. Claire Gohier, Jan. 25, 1992; children: Marie-Anne, Katherine. BASc, U. Toronto, Ont., Can., 1969, LLB, 1973. Spl. asst. to provost U. Toronto, 1969-73; dir. interpretation Anti-Inflation Bd. Govt. Can., Ottawa, 1975-76; assoc. Osler, Hoskins & Harcourt, Toronto, 1976-79, ptnr., 1979-91; pres. Imasco Ltd., Montreal, 1991—, COO, 1993—, CEO, 1995—, also bd. dirs.; bd. dirs. First Fed. Savs. & Loan Assn., Rochester, N.Y., CT Fin. Svcs., Inc., Westbury Can. Life Ins. Co., BCE, Inc., Montreal, Bell Can.; mem. adv. bd. faculty mgmt. McGill U., Montreal. Contbr. articles to profl. jours. Bd. dirs. Montcrest Schs.; mem. adv. coun. Soc. Ednl. Visits and Exchanges in Can. Mem. ABA (bus. law subsect.), Can. Bar Assn., Law Soc. Upper Can., Caledon Ski, Toronto Club, Mt. Royal Club, Donalda Club, Mt. Bruno Country Club. Avocation: skiing, riding, sailing. Office: BCE Inc Bur 3700, 1000 Rue de Gauchetiere W, Montreal, PQ Canada H3B 4Y7*

LEVITT, HARRY, speech and hearing scientist; b. Johannesburg, South Africa, May 19, 1937; came to U.S., 1964; s. Boris and Thelma (Kagan) L.; m. Eleanor Claire Sosnow, June 15, 1969; 1 child, David Avrum. BSc, U. Witwatersrand, Johannesburg, 1958; PhD, Imperial Coll. Sci. and Tech., London, 1964. Tech. staff mem. AT&T Bell Labs., Murray Hill, N.J., 1964-69; assoc. prof., prof., disting. prof. CUNY, 1969-2000; cons. AT&T Bell Labs., 1980—, BBN, 1970—, Audimax, 1970—, various univs.; reviewer NIH, NSF, Office Edn., VA, 1970—. Sr. editor: Sensory Aids for Hearing Impaired, 1989; invited editor: Jour. Comm. Disorders, Jour. Rehab., Rsch. and Devel., 1980—; patentee in field; contbr. numerous articles to profl. jours. Beit fellow, 1960-63; fellow Acoustical Soc. Am., 1970, Am. Speech and Hearing Assn., 1980; recipient Nat. Winner for Computing to Aid the Handicapped Johns Hopkins, 1981, N.Y.C. Mayor's award for contbns. to sci. and tech., 1999. Achievements include introducing computer assisted adaptive testing to the field of audiology; developed first digital hearing aid. Home: 998 Sea Eagle Loop Bodega Bay CA 94923-0610 Office: CUNY Grad Sch 365 5th Ave New York NY 10016-4334

LEVITT, JAREN, real estate corporation officer; b. N.Y.C., Mar. 19, 1946; s. Seymour and Harriet (Finorsky) L.; children: Jaden, Janna; m. Theresa Julyun Kim, Oct. 16, 1995. BS in Psychology and Biology, Syracuse U., 1965; MS in Clin. Psychology, U. Tex., 1967; PhD in Clin. Psychology, UCLA, 1974. Spl. asst Mayor's Office, N.Y.C., 1968-71, Pres. U.S., Washington, 1971; pres. Med. Cons. Internat., Woodland Hills, Calif., 1973-78; mktg. dir. vacation planning Playboy Internat., McAffe, N.J., 1978-80; regional mktg. dir. Gen. Devel. Co., Miami, Fla., 1981-88, asst. v.p., 1988; v.p. Cen. Region and Far East Gen. Devel. Co., Norridge, Ill., 1988-90; pres. Am. Real Estate Devel. Corp. Gen. Devel. Co., Fla.; pres. Global Acquisition and Devel. Corp., 1990-95; pres. Stone Trend Internat., Inc., Sarasota, 1995—, owner; owner RoadWarriorTrading.com; cons. substance abuse projects to bus. and fgn. govts., 1968-78. Contbr. articles to profl. jours. Mem. Heritage Found. Republican. Jewish. Avocations: scuba, skiing, skydiving, tennis, flying. Office: 6244 Clark Center Ave Bldg 3 Sarasota FL 34238-2752

LEVITZKY, MICHAEL GORDON, physiology educator, researcher; b. Elizabeth, N.J., Jan. 3, 1947; s. Edward and Shirley (Worfman) L.; m. Ellen Marie De Roxtro, June 27, 1969 (div. Dec. 18, 1984); m. Elizabeth Gouaux, Mar. 13, 1985; children: Edward Benjamin, Sarah Elizabeth. BA, U. Pa., 1969; PhD, Union Coll, 1975. Physiology instr. Albany (N.Y.) Med. Coll., 1974-75; asst. prof. physiology La. State U. Health Scis. Ctr., New Orleans, 1975-80, assoc. prof. physiology, 1980-85, prof. physiology, 1985—, prof. anesthesiology, 1991—; adj. prof. pediats. Tulane U. Sch. Medicine, New Orleans, 1990—, adj. prof. physiology, 1991—; dir. basic sci. curriculum La. State U. Med. Sch., 1998—. Author: Pulmonary Physiology, 5th edit., 1999; co-author: Cardiopulmonary Physiology in Anesthesiology, 1997, Introduction to Respiratory Care, 1990. Grantee NIH, 1976-78, 78-86. Mem. Am. Physiol. Soc. (edn. com. 1988-91, Arthur C. Guyton Tchr. of Yr. 1998), Am. Thoracic Soc., Coun. Sci. Editors, N.Y. Acad. Scis., Soc. for Exptl. Biology and Medicine, Sigma Xi. Office: La State U Health Scis Ctr 1901 Perdido St New Orleans LA 70112-1328

LEVY, ALBERT, family physician; b. Stanleyville, Congo, Nov. 8, 1948; came to U.S., 1977; s. Moise and Eugenie J. (Menache) L.; children: Antonia G., Eric M. MD, Fed. U. Brazil, Rio de Janeiro, 1973, MS in Field Medicine, 1976. Diplomate Am. Bd. Family Physicians, Am. Bd. Family Practice, Am. Bd. Geriatric Medicine. Chief family medicine sect. Our Lady of Mercy Hosp., Bronx, N.Y., 1989-96; pvt. practice family medicine Manhattan Family Practice, N.Y.C., 1990—; physician Montefiore Med. Ctr., Bronx, 1994—; asst. clin. prof. dept. family medicine Albert Einstein Coll. Medicine, Bronx, N.Y., 1994—; asst. prof. N.Y. Med. Coll., Valhalla, N.Y., 1994—; asst. prof. medicine Mt. Sinai Sch. Medicine, 1999—; with Beth Israel Med. Ctr., 1986, St. Luke's/Roosevelt Med. Ctr., 1986, Lenox Hill Hosp., 1995, Mt. Sinai Med. Ctr., 1999. Fellow Am. Acad. Family Physicians, Royal Soc. Medicine, (Eng.), N.Y. Acad. Medicine; mem. AMA, Am. Geriatric Soc., World Orgn. Nat. Colls./Acads. Family Physicians, N.Y. Acad. Scis., Med. Soc. State of N.Y., N.Y. County Acad. Family Physicians (v.p. 1992), Soc. Tchrs. Family Medicine. Jewish. Avocations: tennis, opera, travel, wind surfing. Home: 311 Wilton Rd Westport CT 06880-1426 also: 25 Sutton Pl S New York NY 10022-2441 Office: Manhattan Family Practice 911 Park Ave New York NY 10021-0337

LEVY, ARNOLD S(TUART), real estate company executive; b. Chgo., Mar. 15, 1941; s. Roy and Esther (Scheff) L.; m. Eva Cichosz, Aug. 8, 1976; children: Adam, Rachel, Deborah. BS, U. Wis., 1963; MPA, Roosevelt U., 1970. Dir. Neighborhood Youth Corps, Chgo., 1966-68; v.p. Social Planning Assn., Chgo., 1968-70; planning dir. Office of Mayor Chgo., 1970-74; dep. dir. Mayor's Office Manpower, Chgo., 1974-75; sr. v.p. Urban Investment & Devel. Co., Chgo., 1975-93; pres., CEO Stone-Levy, LLC, Chgo., 1994—; mem. S-L Hospitality Group, LLC, 1995—; pres. JMB/Urban Hotels, Hotel and Resort Devel. Group, JMB/Urban Devel. Co., 1985-93; bd. dirs. Hostmark Mgmt. Group, Inc.; mem. Urban Land Inst. Pres. Ark, Chgo., 1970-72, Parental Stress Svcs., Chgo., 1978-79; past lectr. DePaul U., Roosevelt U., Loyola U.; v.p. Inst. Urban Life, Chgo., 1983—. Co-editor: The Professionals' Guide to Commercial Property Development, 1988. Bd. dirs. Mus. Broadcast Communications, Chgo. Coun. of Urban Affairs, Am Shalom, pres. Ill. Humane Soc. ; steering com. Radio Hall of Fame; chmn. Spertus Inst. Jewish Studies, Glencoe Plan Commn., Carlton Club (Chgo.), Twin Orchard Club. Home: 535 Park Ave Glencoe IL 60022-1501 Office: Stone-Levy & Co LLC 630 Dundee Rd Ste 220 Northbrook IL 60062-2750

LEVY, AVI, mechanical engineering educator; b. Tel-Aviv. BS, Ben-Gurion U., Beer-Sheva, Israel, 1990, PhD, 1995. Rsch. asst. Two Phase Flow Inst. of Applied Rsch./Ben-Gurion U. of Negev, Beer-Sheva, 1989-90, tchg. asst. Control Theory and Linear Systems, 1990-95; rsch. fellow bulk solids handling Ctr. for Indsl. Bulk Solids Handling, Glasgow, U.K., 1995-97; sr. lectr. mech. engring. multiphase transport sys. and energy process lab. Ben-Gurion U. the Negev, Israel, 1997—; vis. rschr. Sch. of Mech. Engring., U. Witwatersrand, Johannesburg, 1992. Office: Ben-Gurion U of Negev, Dept Mech Engring, Beer Sheva Israel

LEVY, BERNARD-HENRI, writer; b. Beni-Saf, Algeria, Nov. 5, 1948; s. André and Ginette Levy; 2 children. Student, Ecole Normale Superieure, Paris. War corr. Daily Combat, 1971-72; lectr. in epistemology U. Strasbourg, 1973; lectr. in philosophy Ecole Normale Supérieure, 1973; mem. Françoise Mitterand's Group of Experts, 1973-76; editor nouvelle philosophie series Editions Grasset, 1973; editor Idées sect. Quotidien de Paris; co-founder Action Int. contre la Faim, 1980; founder, dir. Règle du Jeu, 1991—; pres. commn. avancés sur réceltes au cinéma, 1992—. Author: Les Indes Rouges, 1973, La Barbarie à Visage Humain, 1977, Le Testament de Dieu, 1979, L'Idéologie Française, 1981, Questions de Principe, 1983, Le Diable en tête (Prix Médicis) 1984, Impressions d'Asie, 1985, Questions de Principe Deux, 1986, Eloge des Intellectuels, 1987, Les Dernier jours. de Charles Baudelaire (Prix Interallié), 1988, Questions de Principe Trois, 1990, Les Années 80 De Stella, 1990, Les Aventures de la Liberté, 1991, Piet Mondrian, 1992, Piero Della Francesca, 1992, Les Bronzes de César, 1991, (play) Le Jugement Dernier, 1992, (documentary) Un Jour dans la Mort de Sarajevo, 1993, Questions de Principe Quatre, 1993, Les Hommes et les Femmes, avec Françoise Giroud, 1993; prodr. 4 Heures sur les Aventures de la Liberté, 1991; author, prodr. (with Alain Ferrari) Bosna!, 1995, La Pureté Dangereuse, 1995, Question de Principe Cinq, 1996, Le Lys et la Cendre, 1996, (film) Le Jour et la Nuit, 1997, Comédie, 1997, Avec Salman, 1999, Le Siede de Sartre, 2000. Avocations: skiing, judo, water skiing. Address: 61 rue des Saint-Pèeres, 75006 Paris France

LEVY, D.A. FINER, social services administrator; b. New Haven, Mar. 15, 1957; d. Kenneth Leslie Finer and Anna Rosa Beltramello Finer; m. Gordon Herman Levy, Aug. 2, 1987; 1 child, Benjamin. BSW, So. Conn. State Coll., 1979; MSW, Fordham U., 1981. Lic. clin. social worker Acad. Cert. Social Workers. Counselor State of Fla., West Palm Beach, 1981-83; juvenile counselor II-residential Palm Beach County, West Palm Beach, 1983-87, juvenile counselor II, 1987-94, youth affairs coord., 1994-99; program dir. Children's Home Soc., West Palm Beach, 1999—. Mem. code enforcement bd. Village of Palm Springs, Fla., 1995—. Named Outstanding Young Women Am., 1988. Mem. NASW (mem. com. on inquiry 1990-98, chair com. on inquiry 1998—, Social Worker of the Yr. 1990), Orgn. Ednl. Resources and Technol. Tng.-Women's Am. Home: 453 Palo Alto Dr Palm Springs FL 33461-1517 Office: Childrens Home Soc 2100 46th St West Palm Beach FL 33407

LEVY, DANIEL, economics educator; b. Tschakaia, Georgian Republic, Georgia, Nov. 13, 1957; came to U.S., 1983; s. Shabtai and Simha (Leviashvili) L.; m. M. Sarit Adler, Spet. 10, 1981; children: Avihai, Eliav. BA, Ben-Gurion U., Beer-Sheva, Israel, 1982; MA, U. Calif., Irvine, 1989, PhD, 1990. Lectr. U. Minn., Mpls., 1983-88, St. Olaf Coll., Northfield, Minn., 1986-88, The Coll. St. Catherine, St. Paul, 1987-88; prof. Pepperdine U., Irvine, 1989-90, U. Calif., Irvine, 1990-91, Union Coll., Schenectady, N.Y., 1991-92, Emory U., Atlanta, 1992—; computer software programmer Mac Cartuli, 1989. Contbr. articles to profl. jours. Treas. Minn. Student Orgn., 1984-85. Mem. Am. Econ. Assn., Soc. Econ. Dynamics and Control, Econometric Soc., Western Econ. Assn., Mensa. Avocations: basketball, tennis, chess, computers, piano. Office: Emory U Dept Economics Atlanta GA 30322-0001

LEVY, DAVID, Israeli politician; b. Rabat, Morocco, 1937; came to Israel, 1957; married; 12 children. Ed. secondary sch. Dep. mayor, mem. mcpl. coun. Knesset, Israel, 1964-77; mem. labor and social affairs com. Knesset, Beit She'an, Israel, 1969-73; mem. house com. Knesset, Jerusalem, Israel, 1973-77; minister immigrant absorption Knesset, Israel, 1977-79, minister construction and housing, 1979-81, dep. prime minister, 1981-84, minister foreign affairs, 1984-90, vice premier, minister foreign affairs, 1990-92, mem., 1992-96, dep. prime minister, minister foreign affairs, 1996—; Likud candidate for sec. gen., 1977, 81, now chmn. Likud party; mem. Israeli Knesset, 1969—, min. of immigrant absorption, 1977-78, min. of constrn. and housing, 1978-90, dep. prime min., 1981-92, 96—, min. fgn. affairs, 1990-92, 96—; with Gesher Party, 1996—. Founder, chmn. Gesher party, 1995. Office: Office Dep Prime Min Ministry Fgn Affairs, Hakirya Romena, Jerusalem 91950, Israel

LEVY, ELIAHOU, quality assurance consultant; b. Alexandria, Egypt, Dec. 3, 1930; s. Mordekhay and Rina (Mizrahi) L.; m. Aviva Troygut, Mar. 13, 1956; children: Rina, Michal, Eyal. Degree, Cranfield Inst. Tech., Eng., 1991. Cert. maintenance engr., quality system mgmt. assessment profl. Squadron shop chief Israeli Air Force, 1952-55; tech. supt. Israel Aircraft Industries, 1956-68, quality assurance mgr., 1969-86; quality assurance cons. Gen. Mgr., Israel, 1987—. Recipient Chief of Staff award Peruvian Air Force, 1970. Avocations: computer, boat sailing. Office: Matass Ltd, PO Box 53222, 61531 Tel Aviv Israel

LEVY, EZRA CESAR, aerospace scientist, real estate broker; b. Habana, Cuba, Sept. 22, 1924; s. Mayer D. and Rachel Levy; m. Gaynor D. Popejoy, 1980; children from previous marriage: Daniel M., Diana M. Levy Friedman, Linda R. Levy Brenden. MS, UCLA, 1951. Sect. head Douglas Aircraft Co., Santa Monica, Calif., 1951-54; dept. head Lockheed Aircraft Co., Van Nuys, Calif., 1954-56, Librascope, Glendale, Calif., 1956-57, Radioplane, Van Nuys, 1957-58; asst. dept. mgr. Space Tech. Labs., Redondo Beach, Calif., 1958-60; asst. divsn. dir. TRW, Redondo Beach, Calif., 1960-74; now real estate broker, owner Jaunty Real Estate, Glendale, Calif., 1984—; rschr. EKG analysis Heart Rsch. Found., 1953-68; spl. traffic cons. South Bay Cities, 1960-65. Author: Laplace Transform Tables, 1958, Selling Your Property?, 1995, Sample Contractual (Real Estate) Terms, 1996, A Glossary of Real Estate Terms, 1998, 2d edit., 2000; contbr. articles to profl. jours. With U.S. Army, 1944-46. Mem. Temple City C. of C. (pres. 2000—, bd. dirs. 1992-97), Masons (past master and sec.). Democrat. Jewish. Avocations: art, music, philately. Home: 1935 Alpha Rd Apt 102 Glendale CA 91208-2146 Office: Jaunty Real Estate 1935 Alpha Rd Unit 102 Glendale CA 91208-2146

LEVY, HAROLD DAVID, psycholinguist; b. Rochester, N.Y., Aug. 25, 1938; s. Barnet Lewis and Ada Sylvia (Zimmerman) L.; m. Jan Patricia Schwartz, Mar. 3, 1959 (div. 1961); 1 child; m. Natalie Miller, Nov. 27, 1969 (div. 1982); 1 child; m. Judy Weiner, Sept. 9, 1987. BS in Gen. Studies, U. Rochester, 1969, MA in Edn., 1971. Permanent cert. to teach French, grades 7-12. Sociotherapist Convalescent Hosp. for Children, Rochester, 1971-72; tutor spl. edn. City Sch. Dist., Rochester, 1973-83; editor, ednl. dir. Operaton Friendship, Rochester, 1983-88; pvt. tutor home and social agencies Rochester, 1982-91; vol. and activities asst. therapist Genesee Hosp., Rochester, 1983-93; dramatics instr. Hochstein Music Sch., Rochester, 1972; lang. tchr. Harley Sch. and Talmudical Inst. Upstate N.Y., 1974-75. Author: Forced Categories: A Taxonomy for Languages, 1971, Languages: Their Common Elements, 1990, Language Learning by Slices, 1990, Linguistics: The Binary System, 1990, Psycholinguistic Interpretation of Names as Language Field Universals, 1995, Lexical Transformations: The Brain's Code, 1996, The Psycholinguistic Development of Terminal Information Systems, 1997; contbr. articles to sci. jours. Avocations: jazz piano, mental health education, nutrition. Home: 111 East Ave Apt 719 Rochester NY 14604-2542

LEVY, JEROME HENRY, ophthalmic surgeon; b. N.Y.C., Sept. 12, 1942; s. Louis and Lee (Boockvar) L.; B.A. magna cum laude, Syracuse U., 1963; M.D., SUNY, Bklyn., 1966; m. Elizabeth DeJesus; children: Linda, David, Jaslyn. Intern, Kings County Hosp., Bklyn., 1966-67; resident in ophthalmology Manhattan Eye, Ear and Throat Hosp., N.Y.C., 1968-70, chief resident, 1970-71, attending surgeon, 1971—, coordinator phacoemulsification tng., 1971—, also prin. investigator YAG laser; practice medicine specializing in ophthalmic surgery, Bronx, N.Y., 1971—; attending surgeon Manhattan Eye, Ear and Throat Hosp.; surgeon dir. N.Y. Eye Surgery Ctr. Diplomate Am. Bd. Ophthalmology. Fellow Am. Acad. Ophthalmology and Otolaryngology, Am., Internat. colls. surgeons; mem. AMA, Am. Intraocular Lens Soc., N.Y. Intraocular Lens Implant Soc. (pres.), Contact Lens Soc. Ophthalmologists, N.Y. State, Bronx County med. socs., Ophthalmic Laser Surg. Soc., Manhattan Ophthal. Soc., Phi Beta Kappa, Phi Kappa Phi. Contbr. articles to profl. publs. Home: 200 E 65th St New York NY 10021-4451 Office: 1101 Pelham Pky N Bronx NY 10469-5411

LEVY, KENNETH ST. CLAIR, barrister, psychologist, criminologist, accountant; b. Brisbane, Australia, Dec. 23, 1949; s. Francis and Grace (Ferguson) L.; m. Veronica Mary Forster, Jan. 7, 1978; children: Clare, Gregory. BA, U. Queensland, Australia, 1978; B in Commerce, U. Queensland, 1980, PhD, 1994; LLB, Queensland Inst. Tech., 1986. Barrister at Law High Ct. Australia, Supreme Ct. Queensland; registered tax agt., Queensland. Numerous mgmt. and organizatioal positions, 1974—; dep. dir.-gen. Dept. Justice, Queensland, 1989—; mem. bd. mgmt. Australian Inst. Criminology, 1991—, Criminology Rsch. Coun., Australia, 1991—. Found. mem. Rental Bond Authority, 1989-90; pres. Alternative Dispute Resolution Coun., 1994—; mem. Ctr. for Crime Policy and Pub. Safety Adv. Com., Griffith U., 1995-97. Lt. Col. Army Res. Fulbright scholar, 1995.

Fellow CPA Australia (dep. chmn. disciplinary com. Queensland divsn. 1992—, Queensland divisional coun. 1995-2000, chmn. 2000, applications com. 1996, dep. chair 1997, v.p. prof. devel. 1996-97, dep. pres. 1998, pres 1999—); mem. APA, Australian Psychol. Soc., Bar Assn. Queensland (spl.), Coll. Forensic Psychology, United Svcs. Club. Avocations: music, reading, travel.

LEVY, LESLIE ANN, business researcher, consultant, professor, software producer; b. N.Y.C., Dec. 25, 1941; d. Paul and Ruth Candace (Tachna) Bauman; m. Marc Gersan Gerard Levy, Oct. 1962 (div.); children: Benjamin Gerard, Remy Marcel Gerard. BA in Philosophy summa cum laude in philosophy, Smith Coll., 1962; MBA, Harvard U., Boston, 1976, DBA, 1980. Cert. French Fashion Acad., 1964. Tchg. asst. in philosophy UCLA, 1962-63; asst. prof. mgmt. policy Case Western Res. U., Cleve., 1981-84; pres., dir. Commonwealth Collaborative, Inc., Cambridge and Sarasota, Fla., 1976-99; pres., CEO Acad. for Corp. Governance, Fordham U. Grad. Sch. Bus., 1990-91; pres., dir. Inst. for Rsch. on Bds. Dirs., Sarasota, 1983—; dir. Inst. Assocs., Sarasota, 1997-99; pres., dir., treas., sec. DirectorsData, Inc., 1999—; sr. rsch. asst. Harvard Sch. Bus. Adminstrn., Boston, 1979-81; engring., fin., mktg. and mgmt. positions Honeywell Info. Sys., Boston, 1971-74, 75; author, cons., lectr. on corp. governance, bds. dirs., and alignment of bd. structure, processes, and leadership with co. bus. in large and small corps. Contbr. articles to profl. jours.; prin. author, acad. editor: Director Motivation: Incentives and Disincentives to Board Service, 1996; author case studies; contbr. regular column From the Institute, Directors and Boards, 1996-97; author (spl. report) Separate Chairmen of the Board: Their Roles, Legal Liabilities, and Compensation; editor, contbg. author: Boards of Directors Part II, Harvard Bus. Sch. Divsn. Rsch.; prodr. bd. and governance related software, 1996—. Mem. Boston and Tampa Bay Com. on Fgn. Rels. Acad. Corp. Governance rsch. fellow; Fulbright scholar. Mem. Am. Soc. Corp. Secs., Nat. Assn. Corp. Dirs., Acad. Mgmt. (article reviewer), Boston Computer Soc., Nat. Investor Rels. Inst., Inst. of Dirs., Federalist Soc., Women in Pensions, Fla. Women's Alliance. So. Fin. Assn., Harvard Club of Sarasota, Am. Jewish Com., Am. Jewish Congress, Nat. Coun. Jewish Women. Avocations: hiking, art history, construction.

LEVY, MARVIN DANIEL, retired professional football coach, sports team executive; b. Chgo., Aug. 3, 1929. BA, Coe Coll., 1950; MA, Harvard U., 1951. High sch. coach St. Louis, 1951-52; asst. football coach Coe Coll., Cedar Rapids, Iowa, 1953-55; asst. coach, then head coach U. N.Mex., 1956-59; head coach U. Calif., Berkeley, 1960-63, Coll. William & Mary, Williamsburg, Va., 1964-68; asst. coach Phila. Eagles, NFL, 1969, Los Angeles Rams, NFL, 1970, Washington Redskins, NFL, 1971-72; head coach Montreal (Que., Can.) Alouetts, Can. Football League, 1973-77, Kansas City (Mo.) Chiefs, NFL, 1978-82, Chgo. Blitz, U.S. Football League, 1984; head coach Buffalo Bills, NFL, 1986—, v.p., 1995—. Office: Buffalo Bills Rich Stadium 1 Bills Dr Orchard Park NY 14127-2296*

LEVY, MATTHEW DEGEN, investment banking technology and operations company executive, consumer products business development and planning executive, management consultant; b. N.Y.C., Dec. 5, 1958; s. Herbert Monte and Marilyn (Wohl) L.; m. Laura Ann Goldin, Aug. 20, 1989; children: Ely Samuel, Philip Benjamin. BA magna cum laude and spl. honors, Tufts U., 1980; MBA, Yale U., 1983. Rsch. assoc. State St. Cons., Boston, 1980-81; cons. to vice chmn. Yankelovich, Skelly & White, Inc., Stamford, Conn., 1982; staff fin. analyst IBM Corp., White Plains, N.Y., 1983-86; co-founder, COO White, Skelly, Yankelovich Cons. Group, Inc., Greenwich, Conn., 1986-93; area dir. and mng. cons. Renaissance Strategy Group, N.Y.C., 1993-95; dir. bus. planning and devel. Sara Lee Corp., N.Y.C., 1995-97; v.p. global ops. Salomon Bros. Inc., N.Y.C., 1997; v.p. tech. and ops. Salomon Smith Barney Inc., N.Y.C., 1997-98; v.p. info. tech. Goldman Sachs, N.Y.C., 1999—; cons. Yale Sch. Mgmt. Alumni Assn., 1989; bus. mgr., anchorman WMFO Radio, Medford, Mass., 1977-80; co-instr. course on decision-making Tufts U., 1977. Contbr. articles to mags. Bd. dirs. DOROT, N.Y.C., 1986-97, pres. bd., 1991-94; mem. allocations com. United Way of Greenwich, 1984-86; bd. dirs. Am. Jewish World Svc., N.Y.C., 1997—. Home: 160 Riverside Dr Apt 8C New York NY 10024-2111 Office: Goldman Sachs 180 Maiden Ln Fl 4 New York NY 10038-4958

LEVY, MAYER BASIL, advertising company executive, video specialist; b. Johannesburg, South Africa, July 1, 1949; s. Norman Max and Bessie Ella (Contius) L.; m. Doreen Sandra Kaplan, Nov. 25, 1979; 3 children (2 by previous marriage). Std. 9 degree, Damelin Coll., Johannesburg, 1967. Sales mgr. Cinemark Advt., Johannesburg, 1981-82, 82-90; owner Shamdor Prodns., Johannesburg, 1990-94; CEO, mng. dir. Plasmedia Advt. (Pty.) Ltd., Johannesburg, 1994—, Take 5 Film 7 Video Svcs. Ltd., Johannesburg, 1999—. With South African Air Force Security Divsn., 1968, Pretoria. Avocations: cinema memorabilia (owner of private museum), classical and rock music, movies. Office: PlasMedia Advt (Pty) Ltd, PO Box 438, 1600 Isando South Africa

LEVY, PIERRE-YVES, microbiologist, health facility administrator; b. Marseille, France, Mar. 8, 1962; s. Gabriel and Jacqueline (Rispy) L.; m. Anne Sibourg, July 24, 1993; children: Julien, Alice. DEA in Cellular Biology, U. Scis., Marseille, 1987; MD, U. Medicine, Marseille, 1989, DESC in Infectious Diseases, 1990. Fellow Univ. Hosp., Marseille, 1985-89; dir. Lab. Casamance, Aubagne, France, 1989—; cons. clin. microbiology Univ. Hosp., Marseille, 1989—. Contbr. articles to profl. jours. Mem. Am. Soc. Microbiology. Jewish. Avocations: tennis, piano. Office: LABM La Casamance, 33 Bd des Farigoules, 13400 Aubagne France

LEVY, ROGER LAURENCE, computer and telecommunications executive; b. Melbourne, Victoria, Australia, Dec. 1, 1948; s. Robert Samuel and Muriel Eileen (Rhook) L.; m. Margaret Mary French, Aug. 25, 1975; children: Jesinta Eileen, Rebecca Mary. Diploma in elec. engring., Footscray Inst. Tech., Melbourne, 1968, diploma in electronic engring., 1969; BEngring (1st class honors), U. Melbourne, 1973, MEngring Sci., 1975; grad. Internat. Bus. Mgmt., Inst. Internat. Studies, Tokyo, 1982. Chartered electronics engr. Sr. engr. Telecom Australia, Melbourne, 1968-79; chief engr. G. Close & Assocs., Melbourne, 1979-81; gen. mgr. engring. NEC Australia Pty. Ltd., Mulgrave, Australia, 1981-84; group gen. mgr. NEC Australia Pty. Ltd., Mulgrave, 1984-86; chief exec. Labtam Internat. Pty Ltd., Braeside, Victoria, 1986; mng. dir. Levy Mgmt. Svcs. Pty Ltd., 1986—; group mgr. Telstra Corp., 1994—; mng. dir. Forensic Tech. P/L, 1997—. Pub. Svc. Bd. scholar Govt. Australia, 1975; found. fellow Australian Inst. Co. Dirs. Fellow Australian Inst. Mgmt., Radio and Electronics Engrs. Australia; mem. IEEE (sr.), Am. Mgmt. Inst., Kt. St. J.

LEVY, THIERRY PIERRE (LEVY-MANNHEIM), lawyer; b. Neuilly, France, Aug. 4, 1971; s. Philippe Edmond and Claire Jeannie (Amedee.Mannheim) L. LLM cum laude, Paris XI, 1992; PhD cum laude in Law and Economics, Paris IX, 1993; Hautes Etudes Commls., Bus. Sch., 1992. CAPA. Assoc. Moquet Borde et al., Budapest, Hungary, 1995-96, Paris, 1996-98; assoc. Norton Rose, Paris, 1998-2000, Freshfields, Paris, 2000—. Mem. HEC Lawyers, Young Leadership. Jewish. Avocations: Scrabble, violin. Home: 143 rue de Saussure, 75017 Paris France Office: Freshfields, 69 bd Haussmann, 75008 Paris France

LÉVY-GARBOUA, LOUIS JACQUES, economics educator; b. Cairo, Egypt, Sept. 27, 1945; arrived in France, 1948; s. Victor A. and Hettie R. (Ades) L.; m. Evelyne S. Koch, June 14, 1987; 1 child, Simon. Degree in engring., Ecole Poly., Paris, 1967; degree in stats. and econs., Nat. Sch. Stats. and Econs., Paris, 1969; diploma, U. Paris-Pantheon Sorbonne, 1970, D of Econs., 1972. Sr. rsch. assoc. Ctr. of Rsch. and Study of Conditions of Life, Paris, 1969-88; asst. prof. U. Brest, France, 1974-76; prof. U. Paris, Villetaneuse, France, 1976-81; disting. prof. U. Paris-Pantheon Sorbonne, Paris, 1981—; dir. rsch. team Nat. Ctr. Scientific Rsch., Paris, 1977-85, dir. lab. applied microeconomics, 1986-91; founder, coord. Jour. Applied Microeconomics Ann. Conf., 1984—; mem. exec. bd. U. Paris-Pantheon Sorbonne, 1989-93, dir. Ecole Doctorale, 1991-95; apptd. mem., counsel dept. scis. Nat. Ctr. Scientific Rsch., Paris, 1996—; mem. scientific coun. of observatory of student life, 1994—; apptd. mem. scientific coun. Dept. of Agrl. Econ. and Sociology of the Nat. Inst. for Agronomic Rsch., 1998—. Author: Economique de l'Education, 1979; editor: Sociological Economics, 1979; contbr. articles to profl. jours. Recipient Ordre Nat. Merite, 1995. Mem. Am. Econ. Assn., European Econ. Assn., French Econ. Assn. (Award 1973). Avocations: trips, opera, reading. Fax: 33 14278 7545. Home: 24 Rue du Renard, 75004 Paris France Office: U Paris-Pantheon Sorbonne, 106-112 bvd de l'Hopital, 75013 Paris France

LEVY-LEBOYER, CLAUDE, research scientist, consultant; b. Paris, June 16, 1928; d. Rene and Helene (Lambert) Gugenheim; m. Maurice Levy-Leboyer; children: Marion, Antoine. MA in Psychology, Sorbonne, Paris, 1949, PhD in Psychology, 1965; PhD honoris causa, U. Surrey, 1992. Prof. U. Rouen, France, 1968-70; rschr. CNRS, Paris, 1952-68; prof. U. Paris V, 1970-96, v.p., 1980-92; cons. Min. of Rsch., Paris, 1994-98; CEO Inst. Rsch. Psychol. Travail, 1973—. Author 20 books; contbr. articles to sci. jours. Recipient Francqi prize Francqi Found., 1986. Mem. Internat. Assn. Applied Psychology (past pres., Disting. Svc. award 1990). Office: Inst Rsch Psychol Travail, 64 rue Pergolèse, 75116 Paris France

LEVY-MYERS, HELEN JULIA, newspaper sales professional; b. Long Branch, N.J., July 26, 1959; d. Herman Joseph and Betty Nan (Levy) O. BA, Brandeis U., 1981. With mktg. research Morgan-Grampan Pub. Co., Boston, 1981-84; sales rep. Worcester County Newspapers, Shrewsbury, Mass., 1984-87, TABLOID Newspapers, Newton, Mass., 1987-90; in advt. Finvest, Moscow, 1990-91; sales mgr. Boston Parents Paper, 1991-94; pub. Parent Weekly, 1995—. Campaign mgr. Fran Cooper Election Com., Cambridge, Mass., 1983; campaign chairperson Cambridge Civic Assn. Election Com., 1987, v.p., 1988-89. Democrat. Jewish. Home: 1754 Wainwright Dr Reston VA 20190-3443

LEW, SALVADOR, radio station executive; b. Camajuani, Las Villas, Cuba, Mar. 6, 1929; s. Berko and Clara (Lewinowicz) L.; 1 child, Esther Maria. JD magna cum laude, U. Havana, 1952. Editor Sch. Mural Newspaper, Camajuani, Cuba, 1941-43; pres. youth sect., nat. sect. Cuban People's Party, 1948-53; Lat. Am. cons. Waltes, Moore & Costanzo, Miami, 1961-72; news dir. Sta. WMIE and Sta. WQBA, Miami, 1961-70; gen. mgr., news dir. Sta. WRHC, Miami, 1973-89; host talk show, 1989—; pres. adv. bd. Cuba Broadcasting, 1992; sr. cons. Everet Clay Assocs., 1989—. Trustee, dir. United Way, 1985—. Recipient Lincoln Marti award Sec. HEW, 1964, FBI award for cmty. svcs., 1983, cmty. svc. awards arious orgns. Mem. Cuban Lawyers Assn., Exile. Jewish. Home: 2863 SW 23rd St Miami FL 33145-3309

LEWALD, JOERG, neurobiologist; b. Bochum, Germany, Nov. 25, 1959; s. Georg and Hildegard (Katzorrek) L. Diploma in Biology, Ruhr-Univ., Bochum, 1985, Dr. rer.nat., 1989. Scientist biol. faculty U. Bochum, 1985-92; scientist Inst. fuer Arbeitsphysiologie, Dortmund, Germany, 1993-96; scientist psychol. faculty U. Bochum, 1996-98; scientist Inst. fuer Arbeitsphysiologie, Dortmund. Contbr. articles to profl. jours. Recipient Lederle award, 1998. Mem. German Neurosci. Soc. Berlin. Office: Inst f Arbeitsphysiologie, Ardeystr 67, D-44139 Dortmund Germany

LEWALLEN, WILLIAM MARVIN, JR., ophthalmologist; b. McGregor, Tex., Aug. 31, 1927; s. William M. and Lois Pauline (Sherrill) L.; m. Katherine Louise Mosley, June 12, 1947 (div. Nov. 1985); children: Margaret Anne, William Michael, Susan, Cynthia. BS, Southern Meth. Univ., 1944; MD, Southwestern Med. Coll. Tex., 1947. Diplomate Am. Bd. Otolaryngology, Am. Bd. Ophthalmology. Internship Baylor Univ., Dallas, 1947-48; residency otolaryngology Southwestern Medical Coll., Dallas, 1948-50; residency ophthalmology Jefferson Davis Hosp., Houston, 1953-54; pvt. practice Pueblo, Colo., 1955—; asst. clin. prof. Univ. Colo. Medical Sch., Denver, 1956-99; cons. Colo. State Hosp., Pueblo, 1956-99, U.S. VA Hosp., Ft. Lyon, Colo., 1956-99; chief ophthalmology St. Mary-Corwin Hosp., 1970-72, exec. com., 1970-74; bd. dirs. Republic Nat. Bank, Centenial Banks Pueblo & Blende. Contbr. articles to profl. jours. Bd. dirs. YMCA, Pueblo, 1958-60; pres. bd. dirs. Rocky Mountain Coun. Boy Scout Am., 1960-72; mem. sch. bd. Pueblo Sch. Bd. Dist. 60, 1959-71, pres. sch. bd., 1967-69; chmn. bd. dirs. Pueblo Blvd. Bank, 1979-93; pres. Rotary Club, 1975-76, dir., 1974-77. Lt. comdr. U.S. Navy, 1950-52. Fellow Am. Acad. Ophthalmology. Republican. Protestant. Avocations: bicycling, fishing, hiking, skiing. Fax: (719) 545 1951. Home and Office: 205 Dunsmere Ave Pueblo CO 81004-1026

LEWANDOWSKI, JERZY BOLESLAW, economist, educator; b. Lódź, Poland, Aug. 14, 1948; s. Jan and Lucyna L.; m. Halina Maria Mordawska, Dec. 6, 1975; 1 child, Karolina. MS, Tech. U. Lodz, 1974, DSc, 1980. Head dept. prodn. mgmt. Tech. U. Lodz, 1990, vice-dean faculty mgmt. and orgn., 1990-92, 97-99, 2000—, prof., 2000—, chief editor sci. bull., 1992; rector Coll. Econs., Lodz, 1994-95; quality com. Nat. Econ. Chamber, Warsaw, 1994, chmn. ergonomics and occupl. safety com., 1996. Author: Ergonomics, 1995, Maintenance Management, 1997, Total Quality Management-Quality, Ergonomics, Occupational Safety, Environmental Protection, 1998, Management Information Systems in Enterprise, 1999, Occupational Safety Management in Enterprise, 2000, Environmental Management in Enterprise, 2000; co-author: The Ergonomics of Manual Work, 1993, Human Aspects of Advanced Manufacturing, 1996. Roman Catholic. E-mail: j.lewandowski@wip.pw.edu.pl. Home: Skalna 63, 92-007 Lódź Poland Office: Tech U Lódź, Piotrkowska 266, 90-361 Lódź Poland

LEWANDOWSKI, WŁODZIMIERZ WIKTOR, chemist, researcher; b. Puznøwka, Poland, Apr. 12, 1946; s. Władysław and Romana (Pachowska) L.; m. Maria Filipowicz, June 28, 1969; 1 child, Hanna. Master dept. chemistry, Warsaw (Poland) U., 1971, PhD, 1978, DSc, 1988. Prof. Agrl. U. Warsaw, 1992-97, head dept. gen. chemistry, 1992-96; prof. Bialystok Tech. U., Warsaw, 1998—, rschr. Drug Inst., 1998—; head dept. chemistry Bialystok U., Warsaw, 1998—. Co-author books; contbr. articles to sci. jours., including Vibrational Spectroscopy, Internat. Jour. Quantum Chemistry, others. Scholar Marquette U., Milw., 1988-89. Mem. N.Y. Acad. Scis. Avocation: sports. Office: Bialystok Tech U, Zanveunofa 29, 15 435 Bialystok Poland

LEWEKE, ROBERT WAYNE, communication educator; b. Roanoke, Va., Apr. 25, 1963; s. Clifford Samuel and Betty (Weaver) L.; m. Cheryl Shelor, Apr. 23, 1988; 1 child, Rachel Anne. BA, Va. Poly. Inst. and State U., 1992, MA, 1994; PhD, U. N.C., Chapel Hill, 1999. Dist. mgr. circulation Roanoke Times, 1987-91; asst. prof. dept. comm. Pikeville (Ky.) Coll., 1999—. Vol. tutor Literacy Coun., Orange County, N.C., 1997. Rubinstein scholar, 1998. Mem. Assn. for Edn. in Journalism and Mass Comm., Nat. Comm. Assn., Kappa Tau Alpha. Libertarian. Avocations: bicycling, racquetball. Home: 261 Sycamore St Pikeville KY 41501-1113 Office: Pikeville College 147 Sycamore St Pikeville KY 41501-9042

LEWEY, SCOT MICHAEL, gastroenterologist; b. Kansas City, Mo., Sept. 10, 1958; s. Hugh Gene and Janice Vivian (Arnold) L.; children: Joshua Michael, Aaron Scot, Rachel Anne; m. Jennifer L. Hill, Feb. 3, 1997. BA in Chemistry, William Jewell Coll., 1980; DO, U. Health Scis., 1984. Diplomate Am. Bd. Internal Medicine, Am. Bd. Gastroenterology, Am. Bd. Pediat. Commd. 2d lt. U.S. Army, 1980, advanced through grades to lt. col., 1994; resident internal medicine and pediat. William Beaumont Army Med. Ctr., El Paso, Tex., 1985-89; asst. chief pediat. svc. Irwin Army Hosp., Ft. Riley, Kans., 1989-90; asst. chief dept. medicine Irwin Army Hosp., Ft. Riley, 1990, chief emergency med. svcs., 1990; comdr. F co. 701st support bn. 1st inf. Operation Desert Shield Operation Desert Storm U.S. Army, Saudi Arabia, 1990-91; chief dept. pediatrics Munson Army Hosp., Ft. Leavenworth, Kans., 1991-92, chief dept. medicine, 1992-93; fellow in gastroenterology Fitzsimons Army Med. Ctr., Aurora, Colo., 1993-95, staff gastroenterology svc., 1995-96; chief gastroenterology svc. Evans Army Hosp., Ft. Crason, Colo., 1996-98; ret., 1998; adult and pediat. gastroenterologist Meml. Hosp., Colorado Springs, Colo., 1998—; clin. instr. medicine U. Colo. Health Scis. Ctr. Sch. Medicine. Decorated Bronze Star; named Outstanding Young Man of Am.; recipient Jr. Scientist Rsch. award William Baumont Soc. of Army Gastroenterologists, 1994. Fellow ACP, Am. Acad. Pediat.; mem. AMA (Physician Recognition award), Am. Coll. Gastroenterology, Am. Osteo. Assn., Am. Gastroenterol. Assn., Am. Soc. Gastrointestinal Endoscopy, Assn. Mil. Osteo. Physicians and Surgeons. Republican. Mem. Christian Ch. Avocations: racquetball, running, genealogy, reading. Fax: 719-632-4468. Office: Gastroenterology Assocs of Colorado Springs 1699 Medical Center Pt Colorado Springs CO 80907-5700

LEWI, ELIAS, geophysicist; b. Addis Ababa, Showa, Ethiopia, Aug. 25, 1960; s. T. Mariam Lewi and Tenaye Fekade; m. Menen Ashenafi, Mar. 5, 1994; children: Elias Yonatan, Elias Mahlet. BSc, Addis Ababa U., 1983; MTech., Roorkee U., 1988; PhD, Tech. U. Darmstadt, 1997. Geophysicist EIGS, Addis Ababa, 1983-91; rsch. asst. IPG, Darmstadt, Germany, 1997-98. Contbr. articles to profl. jours. Fax: 620515 (251 1). Office: GeoMET Plc, PO Box 578 Code 1110, Addis Ababa Ethiopia

LEWIN, LEIF GUNNAR TORBJORN, educator; b. Orebro, Sweden, Mar. 28, 1941; s. Torbjorn E. and Astrid A.M. (Karlsson) L.; m. Barbro M. Goranson, June 30, 1964; children: Anna, Magnus, Karin. PhD, U. Uppsala, Sweden, 1967. Johan Skytte prof. U. Uppsala, Sweden, 1972—, dean social sci. faculty, 1991-99; vice rector U. Uppsala, 1999—; cons. in field. Contbr. articles to profl. jours. Mem. Academia Europaea, Swedish Assn. Univ. Tchrs. (chmn. 1986-90). Home and office: Skytteanum Box 514, SE-75120 Uppsala Sweden

LEWIN, LEIF I., finance director; b. Gothenburg, Sweden, Apr. 1, 1936; s. Anders L. and Elisabeth L.; m. Britt-Marie; children: Lena, Asa, Olof, Lotta, Lisbeth. MA in Social Scis., U. Uppsala, 1959. Rsch. officer OK, Oljekonsumenternas Förbund, Stockholm, 1961-69, asst. to chief exec. officer, 1969-77, chief exec. officer, 1977-84; chief exec. officer KF, Kooperativa förbundet, Stockholm, 1984-92; chmn. bd. dirs. Swedbank, Sparbanken Sverige, Stockholm, 1992-95.

LEWIN, MENACHEM, chemistry educator; b. Sokoly, Poland, Mar. 26, 1918; s. Ytzchak and Fryda (Bialodworski) L.; m. Rachel Joachimowicz, Sept. 29, 1944; children: Dorith, Ytzchak, Yehudith. MS in Chemistry, Hebrew U., 1945, PhD in Phys. Chemistry, 1947. Rsch. officer Israel Air Force, Tel Aviv, 1948-50; chief rsch. officer Rsch. Coun. of Israel, 1950-54; dir. Israel Fiber Inst., Jerusalem, 1954-86; prof., chmn. divsn. polymer and textile chemistry Grad. Sch. Applied Sci. and Tech., Hebrew U., Jerusalem, Israel, 1969-88; rsch. prof. Polytechnic U., Bklyn., 1984—; cons. Govt. of Brazil, Rio, 1977, 82, 89, Colgate-Palmolive, U.S., 1988, 92, DuPont Co., U.S., 1984-96, L'Air Liquid, Rhone-Poulene, France, 1991-94; interim chmn. Conf. Polymers Advanced Techs., Jerusalem, 1987, Oxford, 1993, Pisa, 1995, Leipzig, 1997, Tokyo, 1999; chmn. Conf. Recent Advances in Flame. Editor-in-chief: Internat. Jour. Polymers for Advanced Technologies, 1989—; editor: (book series) Fiber Science and Technology, 1978—; author and editor 29 books on polymer and fiber and flame; contbr. articles to profl. publs.; holder 28 patents in U.S., Europe, Japan and Israel. Hon. citizen City Coun., Jerusalem, 1993—; co-chmn. Am. Academics for Israel's Future, 1994—; exec. com. Psi-Profs. for a Strong Israel, Jerusalem, 1992—. Lt. Israeli Air Force, 1948-50. Recipient Habif prize U. Geneva, 1959. Fellow Acad. Wood Sci. Jewish. Home: 1 Shmaryamu Levin St, 96664 Jerusalem Israel Office: Polytechnic Univ 6 Metrotech Ctr Brooklyn NY 11201-3840

LEWINER, JACQUES, physicist; b. Vic sur Cere, France, Aug. 9, 1943; s. Maurice and Fanny (Esterowitz) L.; m. Colette de Botton, Oct. 16, 1968; children: Elisabeth, France, Thomas. PhD, U. Paris. Rsch. assoc. Catholic U., Washington, 1967-69, CNRS, Paris, 1969-73; prof. ESPCI, Paris, 1973—; sci. dir. ESPCI, 1987—. Contbr. articles to profl. pubs. Recipient prize for Innovation French Pres. Republic, 1988, Laureate prize French Acad. Scis., 1990. Mem. Am. Physical Soc., French Physical Soc., Soc. Elec. Engrs. Achievements include 140 patents in field. Home: 7 av de Suresnes, 92210 Saint-Cloud France

LEWINSON, DINA, cell biologist, anatomist, researcher, educator; b. Jerusalem, Feb. 17, 1935; d. Etienne and Sharlotte (Holdheim) Basch; m. Shlomo Peter Lewinson, Dec. 27, 1956; children: Ayeleth, Talyah, Yael, Oded. MSc, Hebrew U., 1957; DSc, Technion U., 1979. Unit dir. Kupat Holim, Haifa, Israel, 1956-70; lab. dir. Elisha Hosp., Haifa, 1971-72; rsch. asst. Technion U., Haifa, 1972-74, instr., 1975-79, lectr., 1979-84, sr. lectr., 1984—. Avocation: classical music. Office: Technion U Faculty Med, 31096 Haifa Israel

LEWIS, ALEXANDER INGERSOLL, III, lawyer; b. Detroit, Apr. 10, 1946; s. Alexander Ingersoll Jr. and Marie T. (Fuger) L.; m. Gretchen Elsa Lundgren, Aug. 8, 1970; children: Jennifer L., Katherine F., Elisabeth M., Alexander Ingersoll IV. BA with honors, Johns Hopkins U., 1968; JD cum laude, U. Pa., 1971. Bar: Md. 1972, U.S. Dist. Ct. Md. 1972, U.S. Ct. Appeals (4th cir.) 1975, U.S. Supreme Ct. 1976, D.C. 1982. Assoc. Venable, Baetjer & Howard, LLP, Balt., 1972-75, 78-80, ptnr., 1981—, head estate and trust practice group, 1993-99, sr. ptnr. estate and trust practice group, 1993—; asst. atty. gen. State of Md., 1975-77; cons. subcom. on probate rules, standing com. on rules and procedures Md. Ct. Appeals, 1976—; mem. Md. Gov.'s Task Force to Study Revision of Inheritance and Estate Tax Laws, 1987-88; lectr. Md. Inst. Continuing Profl. Edn. Lawyers, 1978—, Nat. Bus. Inst., 1986-87, 92-99, Cambridge Inst., 1986-90, Nat. Law Found., 1988-99. Contbr. articles to legal jours. Vice chmn. Md. Gov.'s Task Force on Long-Term Fin. Planning for Disabled Individuals, 1990-94. 1st lt. U.S. Army, 1972. Fellow Am. Coll. Trust and Estate Counsel (state laws coord. for Md. 1991—); mem. ABA, Md. Bar Assn. (chmn. probate reform and simplification com. estates and trusts coun. 1984-86, sec. 1987-88, chmn. 1989-90, com. on laws 1994-98), D.C. Bar Assn., Bar Assn. City Balt., Balt. Estate Planning Coun., Johns Hopkins Club. Republican. Roman Catholic. Avocations: canoeing, camping, tennis. Home: 922 Army Rd Ruxton MD 21204-6703 Office: Venable Baetjer & Howard LLP 1800 Two Hopkins Plz Baltimore MD 21201

LEWIS, ANDRÉ LEON, artistic director; b. Hull, Que., Can., Jan. 16, 1955; s. Raymond Lincoln and Theresa L. Student, Classical Ballet Studio, Ottawa, Royal Winnipeg (Man.) Ballet Sch., 1975; studies with David Moroni, Arnold Spohr, Rudi van Dantzig, Jiri Kylian, Peter Wright, Hans van Manen, and Alicia Markova, among others. Mem. corps de ballet Royal Winnipeg (Man.) Ballet, 1979-82, soloist, artistic coord., 1984-89, interim artistic dir., 1989-90, assoc. artistic dir., 1990-96, artistic dir., 1996—; staged Danzig's Romeo and Juliet, Teatro Comunale, Florence, Italy, Greek Nat. Opera, Athens. Dancer, soloist (ballets) Song of a Wayfarer, Fall River Legend, Nuages Pas de Deux, Lento A Tempo E Appassionatto, Nutcracker, Four Last Songs, Romeo and Juliet, Belong Pas de Deux, Ectasy of Rita Joe, (TV and films) Fall River Legend, Giselle, Heartland, Romeo and Juliet, The Big Top, Firebird; performed at many events including the opening Gala performance of the Internat. Ballet competition in Jackson, Miss., Le Don Des Etoiles, Montreal, a spl. gala honoring Queen Beatrix of Holland and at a Gala performance in Tchaikovsky Hall, Moscow; appeared as a guest artist throughout N.Am., the Orient and USSR. Avocation: listening to opera. E-mail: ballet@rwb.org. Office: Can Royal Winnipeg Ballet, 380 Graham Ave, Winnipeg, MB Canada R3C 4K2

LEWIS, BASIL STANLEY, cardiologist, researcher, consultant; b. Springs, South Africa, Jan. 17, 1946; s. Philip and Bluma (Levin) L.; m. Noga Sara Amitai, May 24, 1977; children: Yair, Noam, Eran, Nir. MB, BChir, U. Witwatersrand, Johannesburg, South Africa, 1968, MD, 1977. Diplomate Bd. Internal Medicine, Bd. Cardiology. Med. officer Wentworth Hosp., Durban, South Africa, 1971-73; mem. staff Johannesburg Hosp., 1975-76; sr. staff cardiologist, assoc. prof. Hadassah-Hebrew U., Jerusalem, 1976-84; dir. cardiac catheterization VA Med. Ctr., L.A., 1992-95; prof. medicine UCLA, 1992-95; dir. cardiology, prof. medicine Lady Davis Carmel Med. Ctr., Technion U. Sch. Medicine, Haifa, Israel, 1995—. Editor: Heart Failure: Mechanisms and Management, 1991; editor Jour. of Heart Failure, 1993—; contbr. numerous articles to profl. jours. Lt. South African Def. Forces, 1970. H.J. Mirisch fellow Cedars-Sinai Med. Ctr., L.A., 1986; recipient Morris C. Bender award Israel Scis. Assn., 1976. Fellow Royal Coll. Physicians, European Soc. Cardiology, Am. Coll. Cardiology; mem. Internat. Soc. Heart Failure (founder, chmn. 1989), Israel Heart Soc. (exec. com. 1983-84). Jewish. Home: 18 Freud St, 34753 Haifa Israel Office: Lady Davis Carmel Med Ctr, 7 Michal St, 34362 Haifa Israel

LEWIS, BENJAMIN PERSHING, JR., pharmacist, public health service officer; b. Danville, Ky., June 2, 1942; s. Benjamin Pershing Lewis and Juanita Elizabeth (Garner) Applewhite; m. Patricia Marlene Glover, Aug. 7, 1968; children: Laura Denise, Jason Matthew. BS in Pharmacy, Auburn U., 1966, MS in Pharmacy, 1972; PhD in Health Svcs. Mgmt., Century U., L.A., 1989. Registered pharmacist, Ky., Ala. Instr. Auburn (Ala.) U. Sch. Pharmacy, 1972-73, now affiliate asst. prof.; commd. lt. comdr. USPHS,

1976, advanced through grades to capt., 1985; pharmacy officer Bur. Drugs FDA, Rockville, Md., 1976-82, health scientist adminstr. orphan products devel., 1982-87, AIDS coord., 1987-89; spl. asst. to assoc. dir. Ctr. Biologics Evaluation-Rsch. FDA, Bethesda, Md., 1989-92; dir. regulatory ops. divsn. of emerging transfusion transmitted diseases FDA Ctr. Biologics Evaluation and Rsch., Rockville, Md., 1993—; adj. prof. San Diego State U., 1998. Co-author: Veterinary Drug Index, 1982; editor: FDA Role in AIDS, 1988, The International Ramifications of Drug Development, 1988, Report of the Criticism Task Force on Career Development, 1989; co-editor: Poliovirus Attenuation: Molecular Mechanisms and Practical Aspects, 1993, Combined Vaccines and Simultaneous Administration, 1995; contbr. articles to profl. jours. Officer U.S. Army, 1972-76. Recipient letter of appreciation Sec. Md. Dept. Econ. and Employment Devel., 1991. Mem. COA of USPHS, Regulatory Affairs Profl. Soc. (Cert. Appreciation 1993), Am. Pharm. Assn., Am. Acad. Pharm. Rsch. and Sci., Sigma Xi. Methodist. Home: 24137 Newbury Rd Gaithersburg MD 20882-4009 Office: FDA Ctr Biols Eval and Rsch HFM 310 1401 Rockville Pike Rockville MD 20852-1448

LEWIS, BETTE LOUISE, school principal; b. Chandler, Ariz.; m. Gladstone S. Lewis (dec. 1987); 1 child, Clinton H. BA, Marymount Coll., 1964; MA, U. Md., 1970. Cert. tchr., adminstr., supr., Md. Tchr. Palos Verdes (Calif.) Peninsula Unified Sch. Dist., 1963-65; tchr. Prince George's County Pub. Schs., Upper Marlboro, Md., 1965-69, vice-prin., 1969-72, prin., 1972—. Recipient Washington Post Dist. Ednl. Leadership Award, Prince George's County C. of C. Outstanding Adminstr. Award, Prince George's County Public Schools Outstanding Adminstr. Award, Sigma Sigma Sigma Alumna Achievement Award. Fellow Inst. Devel. Ednl. Activities (asst. dir. 1990); mem. ASCD, Am. Assn. Sch. Adminstrs., Nat. Assn. Secondary Sch. Adminstrs., Nat. Middle Sch. Assn., Md. Middle Sch. Assn., Md. Assn. Secondary Sch. Adminstrs., Rotary Internat., Sigma Sigma Sigma. Roman Catholic. Avocations: classical music, ballroom dancing, tennis, gardening, antiques. Office: Martin Luther King Jr Mid Sch 4545 Ammendale Rd Beltsville MD 20705-1113

LEWIS, BRIAN, Olympic athlete; b. Sacramento, Calif., Dec. 5, 1974. Placed 2nd JUCO Indoor 200 meter, 1994, winner Modesto Relays, 1996, placed 3rd Paris Grand Prix, 1997, placed 3rd Goodwill Games, 1998, winner Edwardsville Grand Prix, 1998, placed 2nd Birmingham 60 meters, 1998, placed 2nd 100 meters USA Outdoors, 1999, placed 2nd 200 meters USA Indoors, 2000, placed 4th USA Olympic Trials, 2000; winner Gold medal 4x100 meter relays Sydney, 2000. Ranked no. 10 in world Track and Field News, 1998, # 4, 1999. Office: USA Track and Field Team One RCA Dome Ste 140 Indianapolis IN 46225*

LEWIS, CARL (FREDERICK CARLTON LEWIS), Olympic track and field athlete; b. Birmingham, Ala., July 1, 1961; s. Bill and Evelyn (Lawler) L. Student, U. Houston. Competed in Europe and U.S.; track meets include: Nat. Collegiate Athletic Assn. indoor championships, Baton Rouge, La., 1981, Nat. Outdoor Championships, Knoxville, Tenn., 1982, Nat. Sports Festival, 1982, Athletic Congress Outdoor Championships, Indpls., World Championships, Helsinki, 1983, Millrose Games, N.Y., 1984, Summer Olympics, 1980, 1984, 88, 92, 96; recorded album Break it Up, 1986. Recipient James E. Sullivan award best amateur athlete, 1981, Jesse Owens award, 1982, Athlete of Yr. award Assoc. Press Sports, 1983; named World Athlete of the Decade Track & Field News, 1980-89, U.S. Athlete of the Yr., 1981, 82, 83, 84, 87, 88, 91, World Athlete of the Yr., 1982, 83, 84; winner 1 Bronze medal Pan Am. Games, 1979, 2 Gold medals, 1981, 1 Gold medal World Cup, 1981, 3 Gold medals World Championships, 1983, 9 Gold medals Olympics, 1984, 88, 92, 96, 1 Silver medal, 1988; named to U.S. Olympic Hall of Fame, 1985; world record holder in 4x100 relay, 1981, 83, 84, 91, 92, in 4x200 relay, 1989, 100 meter dash, 1991; Am. record holder in 4x100 relay, 1981, 83, 84, 90, 91, in 200 meter dash, 1983, 100 meter dash, 1987, 88, 91, 4x200 relay, 1989; world and Am. indoor record holder in long jump, 1981, 82, 84, in 60 yd. dash, 1983. Office: Carl Lewis Internat Fan Club PO Box 57-1990 Houston TX 77257-1990

LEWIS, CECIL DWAIN, minister; b. Dayton, Ohio, June 30, 1929; s. Clyde Dexter and Ina Candice (Harmon) L.; m. Jacqueline Ann Jones, July 29, 1951; children: Cynthia Lewis Parker, Constance Lewis Bunker. BA, Bob Jones U., 1951; MDiv, Grace Theol. Sem., Winona Lake, Ind., 1957; MA, Chapman Coll., 1972; postgrad., U.S.A. Chaplain Sch., 1973; PhD, Calif. Grad. Sch. Theology, Rosemead, 1991. Ordained to ministry Bapt. Ch., 1950. Asst. pastor Riverside Bapt. Ch., Decatur, Ill., 1951-54; pastor 1st Bible Ch., New Castle, Ind., 1961-64, Faith Baptist Ch., Flint, Mich., 1964-66; commd. 1st lt. U.S. Army, 1966, advanced through grades to lt. col., 1980; chaplain U.S. Army, various places in U.S. and Vietnam, 1966-86; ret. U.S. Army, 1986; pastor Harmony Bapt. Ch., Waynesville, Mo., 1988-89; adj. prof. Drury Coll., 1984-90, John Brown U., 1992-93. Author: Training for Lay Leaders, 1981; tech. advisor, writer: (film) In Beginning, 1980; developer tng. programs for U.S. Army chaplaincy, 1978-82; contbr. articles to profl. jours. Chaplain Siloam Springs (Ark.) Police Dept. and Fire Dept.; bd. regents Liberty U., Linchburg, Va. Decorated Bronze Star (2), Air Medal, Meritorious Svc. medal, Valorous Unit award, Presdl. Unit Citation, Vietnamese Cross of Gallantry, Army Commendation award for heroism. Mem. VFW (life), Vietnam Vets. Am. (life), Am. Assn. Marriage and Family Therapists, Ret. Officers Assn. (life), Siloam Springs Country Club (bd. dirs.). Home: 706A Meghan St Siloam Springs AR 72761-5516

LEWIS, CHARLES ARLEN, software company executive; b. Columbus, Ga., Nov. 7, 1943; s. Harlin B. and Dorothy A. (Elliott) L.; m. Linda L. McDowell, Dec. 5,1964; 1 child, Bryan C. Security trader White & Co. Investments, St. Louis, 1964-67; dist. sales mgr. Horizon Corp., Overland Park, Kans., 1967-73; mgr. U.S. Realty & Investment Co., St. Louis, 1973-75; fin. cons. Profesco, Inc., St. Louis, 1975-77; pres., CEO Am. Econ. Svcs., Ltd., St. Louis, 1977-82, Nat. Investment Corp., St. Louis, 1982-88; pres., CEO Le Bryan Corp., Washington, 1988-93, bd. dirs.; pres., CEO Integrated Mgmt. Sys., Inc., Lancaster, Calif., 1994-99, also chmn. bd., 1994-99; CEO CPI Techs. Corp., Palmdale, Calif., 1999—; also chmn. bd. CPI Techs. Corp., Palmdale, 1999—; bd. dirs. Grimm Fin. Resources Inc., McLean, Va., Elliott, McDowell & Davis, Ltd., St. Louis. Columnist Orthodontic Products mag., 1997—. Adv. bd. mem. Child Find Internat., St. Louis, 1987-88; chmn. bd. World Practical Taekwondo Fedn., Hong Kong, 1986—. 2d lt. U.S. Army, 1961-64. Recipient Disting. Svc. award Hong Kong Taekwondo Assn., 1982, Outstanding Svc. award World Practical Taekwondo Fedn., 1984, 87, Humanitarian award World Jungyae Moosul Fedn., 2000. Avocations: flying, golf.

LEWIS, CORINNE HEMETER, psychotherapist, educator; b. N.Y.C., Nov. 28, 1925; d. Leslie Hall and Frances Pope Hemeter, m. Aug. 22, 1947 (div. 1984); children: Anne Marie, Richard Allyn, Timothy Hall; m. Ceylon S. Lewis Jr., Aug. 6, 1999. BSN, U. Pitts., 1947; MSW, U. Okla., 1978. Diplomate in clin. social work. Staff nurse St. Joseph's Hosp., Buckhannon, W.Va., 1947; head nurse Myer's Clinic, Phillipi, W.Va., 1948; clin. instr., supr. Allegheny Valley Hosp., Tarentum, Pa., 1949; coord. psychiat. nursing edn. Hillcrest Med. Ctr., Tulsa, 1966-67; clin. staff mem. Tulsa Psychiat. Ctr., Tulsa, 1968-77; tchr. principles personality devel. Hillcrest Med. Ctr., Tulsa, 1966-75; supr., interns in psychotherapy Tulsa Psychiat. Ctr., 1971-77; pvt. practice psychotherapist Tulsa, 1978—; dir. Drug Day Hosp., Tulsa Psychiat. Ctr., 1969, dir. nursing, 1970-71; adminstrv. cons. Family and Children's Svcs., Tulsa, 1978; renal dialysis unit cons. Hillcrest Med. Ctr., 1978; dir. Am. Cancer Soc. funded program Tulsa Psychiat. Ctr., 1977-79, cons. to dept. internal medicine, Tulsa Med. Coll., 1977-98. Jr. bd. mem. Women's Assn., Tulsa Boys Home, 1957-59; mem. Mental Health Assn. Tulsa, 1968-83, bd. dirs., 1982-83; vol. Jr. Assn., Tulsa Boys Home, 1958-59, Children's Med. Ctr., 1953-56; bd. dirs. Nursing Svc. Inc., Tulsa, 1982-83. Mem. Nat. Assn. Social Workers, Acad. Cert. Social Workers, Sigma Theta Tau. Democrat. Presbyterian. Avocations: classical music, reading. Home: 2300 Riverside Dr Apt 8F Tulsa OK 74114-2403

LEWIS, DAVID THOMAS ROWELL, solicitor; b. Hong Kong, Nov. 1, 1947; s. Thomas Price Merfyn Lewis; m. Theresa Susan Poole, July 25, 1970; children: Suzannah, Thomas. MA in Law, Oxford U., 1969. Qualified solicitor, Eng., 1972. Trainee Norton Rose, London, 1969-72, solicitor, 1972-76, ptnr., 1977—; mng. ptnr. Norton Rose, Hong Kong, 1979-82, head corp. fin., 1989, head profl. resources, 1994, sr. ptnr., 1997—; mem. Law Soc. Legal Practice Bd., 1996-2000. Gov. Oxford Brookes U., 1996—, Dragon Sch., Oxford, 1987—. Named One of Top 40 under 40 Young Businessmen of the Yr. (U.K.) Business mag., 1986; hon. fellow Jesus Coll., 1998, Oxford. Mem. London Law Soc. (co. law com. 1982-96), Hong Kong Law Soc. (co. law com. 1979-82), Hong Kong Club, Achilles Club, Oxford U. Athletic Club. Avocations: keeping fit, collecting maps, travel. Office: Norton Rose, Kempson House Camomile St, London EC3A 7AN, England

LEWIS, DELANO EUGENE, ambassador, former broadcast executive; b. Arkansas City, Kans., Nov. 12, 1938; s. Raymond Ernest and Enna (Wordlow) L.; m. Gayle Carolyn Jones; children: Delano Jr., Brian, Geoffrey, Phillip. BA, U. Kansas, 1960; JD, Washburn U., 1963; LHD (hon.), Marymount U., 1988; D of Humane Letters, Bowie State U., 1992; D of Pub. Svc., George Washington U., 1991; DHL (hon.), Barry U., 1994, Kent State U., 1995, Lafayette Coll., 1996; LLD (hon.), Nova Southeastern U., 1997; DFA (hon.), So. Ill. U., 1997. Staff atty. U.S. Dept. of Justice, Washington, 1963-65, EEOC, Washington, 1965-66; assoc. dir., country dir. U.S. Peace Corps., Nigeria, Uganda, 1966-69; legis. asst. Sen. Edward Brooke Mass., Washington, 1969-71; adminstrv. asst. Congressman Walter Fauntroy, Washington, 1971-73; mgr. pub. affairs Chesapeake & Potomac Telephone Co., Washington, 1973-76, asst. v.p., 1976-83, v.p., 1983-88, pres., 1988-93; pres., CEO Nat. Public Radio, Washington, 1994-98; amb. to South Africa Dept. of State, Pretoria, South Africa, 1995—; bd. dirs. Guest Svcs., Inc., Black Entertainment TV, Colgate-Palmolive, Halliburton Co., Eastman Kodak Co. Pres. Greater Washington Bd. Trade, 1988; chmn. Mayor's Transition Com., 1978, D.C. Youth Employment Adv. Coun., 1992; co-chair D.C. Vocational Edn. and Career Opportunities Com., 1991, NPR Found.; mem. emeritus bd. Washington Performing Arts Soc., 1990—, Nat. Bd. AFRICARE, 1990—; bd. dirs. Lincoln Theatre; trustee The Menninger Found., 1996. Named Washingtonian of Yr. Washingtonian mag., 1978, Man of Yr., Greater Washington bd. trustees, 1992; recipient Pres. medal Cath. U., Washington, 1978, Tree of Life award NCCJ, 1989, Social Responsibility award George Washington U. Sch. Bus., 1990, Spl. award Women of Washington, Disting. Alumni Citation U. Kans.; Disting. Leadership award Amnesty Internat., 1997, US Media Spotlight award, 1997. Mem. Kans. Bar Assn., D.C. Bar Assn., Georgetown Club. Democrat. Roman Catholic. Avocations: jogging, tennis, racquetball. Office: US Embassy, 877 Pretorius St, Arcadia Pretoria 0001, South Africa

LEWIS, DENISE, Olympic athlete; b. Birchfield, England, Aug. 27, 1972. Winner Bronze medal heptathlon Atlanta, 1996; winner heptathlon European Championship, 1998, winner heptathlon Commonwealth Championship, 1998, winner Silver medal heptathlon World Championships, 1999; winner Gold medal heptathlon Sydney, 2000. Became only Brit. woman to win track and field medal in Atlanta, 1996. Office: Brit Athletic Fedn, 225a Bristol Rd, Edghaston, Birmingham B5 7UB, England*

LEWIS, DOROTHY MILLIGAN, academic administrator; b. Rochester, N.Y., Dec. 15, 1943; d. Ralph Andrews and Gladys (Jones) Milligan; m. Gary Maujer Lewis, April 6, 1968 (div. 2000); 1 child, Heather Michelle. BA, Hartwick Coll., 1965; MEd, Harvard U., 1984, EdD, 1994. Math. and eng. tchr. U.S. Peace Corps., Komenda, Ghana, West Africa, 1966-69; dir. financial and bus. affairs Harvard Divinity Sch., Cambridge, Mass., 1981-85; dir. adminstrv. svcs. Harvard Grad. Sch. Design, Cambridge, Mass., 1986-88; asst. dean for adminstrv. planning Harvard U., Cambridge, Mass., 1989-91, asst. dean finance, 1991-95; dir. budget State Colls. Colo., Denver, 1996-98; dir. budget and fiscal planning U. Colo., Denver, 1998—; v.p. Komenda Publishing Co., Boulder, 1995-99. Mem. Clamshell AntiNuclear Alliance, Cambridge, 1978-84; co-chair Caretakers of Aging Parents, Cambridge, 1988-91; co-mgr. Metro. Meals Program, Cambridge, 1989-95; campaign mgr. Cambridge Sch. Com., 1985, 87. Recipient Disting. Alumni award Hartwick Coll., Oneonta, N.Y., 1998. Mem. Assn. Inst. Rsch., Soc. Coll. and Univ. Planners, Hartwick Coll. Alumni Assn. (v.p. 1993-95, bd. dirs. 1990-99, pres. 1995-97). Democrat. Mem. Unitarian Ch. Avocations: skiing, reading, hiking. E-mail: dottie.lewis@cudenver.edu. Home: 8113 S Humboldt Cir Littleton CO 80122-2989 Office: Univ Colo at Denver 1250 14th St # 720 Denver CO 80202-1702

LEWIS, DUNCAN JAMES, company executive; b. London, Apr. 28, 1951; s. Geoffrey Albert and Monica Jean (Daragon) L. MA, Cambridge (Eng.) U. Dir. planning STL/ICL, London, 1982-85; dir. svcs. Brit. Telecom, London, 1985-90; mng. dir. Cable & Wireless, London, 1990-94; chief exec. Mercury T'Comms, London, 1994-96, Grandad Media Group, London, 1996-97; mng. dir. Equant N.V., Amsterdam, The Netherlands, 1998—; bd. dirs. Cheek By Jowl, London, Farming on Line, U.K., Lazawood, Croydon, Eng. Avocation: theatre. Office: Equant AV, Gatwickstraat 2133, 1043 Amsterdam The Netherlands

LEWIS, EDWARD B., biology educator; b. Wilkes-Barre, Pa., May 20, 1918; s. Edward B. and Laura (Histed) L.; m. Pamela Harrah, Sept. 26, 1946; children: Hugh, Glenn (dec.), Keith. B.A., U. Minn., 1939; Ph.D., Calif. Inst. Tech., 1942; Phil.D., U. Umea, Sweden, 1982; DSc, U. Minn., 1993. Instr. biology Calif. Inst. Tech., Pasadena, 1946-48, asst. prof., 1949-56, prof., 1956-66, Thomas Hunt Morgan prof., 1966-88, prof. emeritus, 1988—; Rockefeller Found. fellow Sch. Botany, Cambridge U., Eng., 1948-49; mem. Nat. Adv. Com. Radiation, 1958-61; vis. prof. U. Copenhagen, 1975-76, 82; researcher in developmental genetics, somatic effects of radiation. Editor: Genetics and Evolution, 1961. Served to capt. USAAF, 1942-46. Recipient Gairdner Found. Internat. award, 1987, Wolf Found. prize in medicine, 1989, Rosenstiel award, 1990, Nat. Medal of Sci. NSF, 1990, Albert Lasker Basic Med. Rsch. award, 1991, Louisa Gross Horowitz prize Columbia U., 1992, Nobel Prize in Medicine, 1995. Fellow AAAS; mem. NAS, Genetics Soc. Am. (sec. 1962-64, pres. 1967-69, Thomas Hunt Morgan medal), Am. Acad. Arts and Scis., Royal Soc. (London) (fgn. mem.), Am. Philos. Soc., Genetical Soc. Great Britain (hon.). Home: 805 Winthrop Rd San Marino CA 91108-1709 Office: Calif Inst Tech Divsn Biology 1201 E California Blvd Pasadena CA 91125-0001

LEWIS, EDWIN LEONARD, III, lawyer; b. Phila., Nov. 24, 1945; s. Edwin Leonard Jr. and Nancy (Hoffman) L.; m. Elisabeth C. Bacon, Oct. 6, 1984; children: Katharine Bacon, Caroline Huffington. BA, Lafayette Coll., 1967; JD, Temple U., 70. bar: Pa. 1970, Ill. 1995. Assoc. MacElree, Platt & Harvey, West Chester, Pa., 1970-73; asst. gen. counsel Fidelity Mut. Life, Phila., 1973-76; sr. atty. Atlantic Richfield Co., Phila., 1976-83; v.p. law Wells Fargo Alarm Svcs., King of Prussia, Pa., 1983-91; v.p., gen. counsel, sec. Borg Warner Protective Svcs., Parsippany, N.J., 1991-95, Borg Warner Security Corp., Chgo., 1995-97; pres. Atlantic Legal Found., N.Y.C., 1998-2000; v.p., gen. counsel Am. Sci. and Engring., Inc., Billerica, Mass., 2000—; pub., editor Science in the Courtroom Review, 1998. Capt. M.I., USAR, 1970-76. Mem. Am. Corp. Counsel Assn., Phila. Bar Assn., Nat. Fedn. Ind. Bus. Legal Found. (legal adv. bd. 2000—). Avocations: marathon running, tennis, golf, sailing. Home: 59 Delafield Island Rd Darien CT 06820-6012 Office: Am Sci & Engring 829 Middlesex Turnpike Billerica MA 01821

LEWIS, F.L, electrical engineer; b. WÜrzburg, Germany, May 11, 1949; s. Frank L. and Ruth Evangeline Shirley L.; m. Galina; children: Christopher, Roman. BEE, Rice U., 1971, MEE, 1971; MS in Aerospace Sys., U. West Fla., 1977; PhD in Elec. Engring., Ga. Inst. Tech., 1981. Registered profl. eng., Tex. Commd. ensign USN, 1971, advanced through grades to lt.; from asst. prof. to prof. Ga. Inst. Tech., Atlanta, 1981-90, prof., 1990; endowed prof. U. Tex., Arlington, 1990—; adj. prof. Ga. Inst. Tech., Atlanta, 1990—. Author: Optimal Control, 1986, 2d edit. 1995, Optimal Estimation: With an Introduction to Stochastic Control Theory, 1986, (with B.L. Stevens) Aircraft Control and Simulation, 1992, Applied Optimal Control and Estimation: Digital Design and Implementation, 1992, Control of Robot Manipulators, 1993, High-Level Feedback Control with Neural Networks, 1998, (with S. Jagannathan and A. Yesildirek) Neural Network Control of Robot Manipulators and Nonlinear Systems, 1998; author 20 book chpts.; contbr. 130 articles to profl. jours.; mem. editl. bd. Internat. Jour. Intelligent Control and Sys., 1995—, Circuits, Sys., and Signal Processing, 1995—, Internat. Jour. Control, 1995-98; active confs. Recipient Frederick E. Terman award Am. Soc. Eng. Educators, 1989. Fellow IEEE (program com. 1993, program chmn. 1994, 95, gen. chmn. 1996, outstanding chpt. award 1994, outstanding svc. award 1994); mem. AAAS, Soc. Indsl. and Applied Math., Fulbright Found., Sigma Xi (Mona A. Ferst award 1981). E-mail: flewis@control-s.uta.edu. Fax: 817-272-5989. Office: Automation and Robotics Rsch Inst The Univ Texas at Arlington 7300 Jack Newell Blvd S Fort Worth TX 76118-7115

LEWIS, GEORGE DOUGLAS, federal agency administrator; b. Louisa, Ky., Mar. 23, 1941; arrived in England, 1978; s. Douglas Putnam and Charlene (Moore) Lewis; m. Maureen Mary Darby, Aug. 20, 1966; 1 child, Karen Mary. BA, Morehead State U., 1967; MBA, Wright State U., 1971; postgrad., Air U., 1975. Contracting officer USAF, Dayton, Ohio, 1967-69, br. chief, 1969-73, divsn. chief, 1973-77; dep. comdr. USAF, Madrid, 1977-78, Upper Heyford, England, 1978-90; exec. dir. U.S. Army Contracting Agy., London, 1990-93; ret., 1993. Contbr. articles to profl. jours. With USAF, 1959-65. Recipient award for meritorius civilian svc. USAF, 1993. Mem. Nat. Contract Mgmt. Assn., Assn. Old Crows. Home: 4 Westminster Croft, Brackley NN13 7ED, England

LEWIS, GERALD JORGENSEN, judge; b. Perth Amboy, N.J., Sept. 9, 1933; s. Norman Francis and Blanche M. (Jorgensen) L.; m. Laura Susan McDonald, Dec. 15, 1973; children by previous marriage: Michael, Marc. AB magna cum laude, Tufts Coll., 1954; JD, Harvard U., 1957. Bar: D.C. 1957, N.J. 1961, Calif. 1962, U.S. Supreme Ct. 1968. Atty. Gen. Atomic, La Jolla, Calif., 1961-63; ptnr. Haskins, Lewis, Hugent & Newnham, San Diego, 1963-77; judge Mcpl. Ct., El Cajon, Calif., 1977-79, Superior Ct., San Diego, 1979-84; assoc.. justice Calif. Ct. of Appeal, San Diego, 1984-87; dir. Fisher Scientific Group, Inc., 1987-98, Bolsa Chica Corp., 1991-93, Gen. Chem. Group, Inc., 1996—; of counsel Lathan & Watkins, 1987-97; adj. prof. evidence Western State U. Sch. Law, San Diego, 1977-85, exec. bd., 1977-89; dir. Invesco Mutual Funds, 2000—; faculty San Diego Inn of Ct., 1979—, Am. Inn of Ct., 1984—. Cons. editor: California Civil Jury Instructions, 1984. City atty. Del Mar, Calif., 1963-74, Coronado, Calif., 1972-77; counsel Comprehensive Planning Orgn., San Diego, 1972-73; trustee San Diego Mus. Art, 1986-89; bd. dirs. Air Pollution Control Dist., San Diego County, 1972-76. Served to lt. comdr. USNR, 1957-61. Named Trial Judge of Yr. San Diego Trial Lawyers Assn., 1984. Mem. Am. Judicature Soc., Soc. Inns of Ct. in Calif., Confrerie des Chevaliers du Tastevin, Order of St. Hubert (knight comdr.), Friendly Sons of St. Patrick (Irishman of Yr. 2000), The Irisn 50 Aztec Big 50, Bohemian Club, La Jolla Country Club (dir. 1980-83), Prophets, The K Club (County Kildare). Republican. Episcopalian. Home: 6505 Caminito Blythefield La Jolla CA 92037-5806 Office: Latham & Watkins 701 B St Ste 2100 San Diego CA 92101-8197

LEWIS, GORDON CARTER, customer service administrator; b. Billings, Mont., June 14, 1960; s. Gene Eskil and Vanda (Carter) L. Student, U. Utah, 1978-79, 81-82; AA, LDS Bus. Coll., 1984; BBA, Nat. Coll., Denver, 1986. Market rsch. interviewer Colo. Market Rsch. Svcs. Inc., Denver, 1984-87, 93-94; mgmt. trainee Yellow Front Stores, Aurora, Colo., 1987; auditor, 1987-93; computer office coord. US EPA, Denver, 1989-91; store mgr. Trans Pacific Stores, Denver, 1994-97; with Apple One Employment, Salt Lake City, 1997-99; Microsoft customer care svc. bus. acct. Convergus Customer Mgmt. Group, Inc., Salt Lake City, 1999—. Ch. leadership, 19795, bowling league officer. Mem. Assn. Govt. Accts., Am. Bowling Congress, Am. Philatelic Soc. Republican. Mem. LDS Ch.

LEWIS, GORDON RICHARD, lawyer; b. Rockford, Ill., June 12, 1949; s. H. Walter and Elizanne (Hanitz) L.; m. Jo Andrea Fetter, Aug. 5, 1972; children: Kathleen McHugh, Anne Elizabeth. BS in Environ. Sci., Mich. State U., 1971; JD, U. Mich., 1974. Assoc. atty. Warner Norcross & Judd LLP, Grand Rapids, Mich., 1974-79, ptnr., 1979—; dir. Bay Plastics Machinery Corp., Bay City, Mich., 1997—; dir., sec. Scheer Bay Co., Bay City, 1998—. Dir. Little Manistee Watershed Conservation Coun., Irons, Mich., 1996—. Named to Best Lawyers in Am., Woodward-White, 1994—. Mem. Indian Club (dir., sec. 1986—), Kent Country Club. Avocations: fly fishing, golf, hunting. Office: Warner Norcross & Judd LLP 111 Lyon St NW Grand Rapids MI 49503-2406

LEWIS, HAROLD ALLEN, childcare company executive; b. Bronx, Oct. 1, 1945; s. Barney and Bess S. (Feifer) L.; B.B.A., Hofstra U., 1970; M.B.A., N.Y.U., 1971; m. Helene A. Lipitz, May 25, 1968; children—Lyn C., Franci K. Asso. mgr. fin. planning and analysis Dun & Bradstreet Corp., N.Y.C., 1975-77, mgr. budgets/forecasts, 1977-78; mgr. strategic planning Reuben H. Donnelley Corp., N.Y.C., 1978-79; mgr. treasury ops. Dun & Bradstreet, N.Y.C., 1979-80; v.p. fin./planning Corinthian Broadcasting Corp., N.Y.C., 1980-85; v.p. fin. and adminstrn. Thomas Cook Travel, USA, 1985-86, sr. v.p., 1986, pres., 1986-89; chief oper. officer U.S. Travel Systems Inc., 1989-91; pres., chief exec. officer Childtime Learning Ctrs., 1991; mem. dean's exec. coun. Frank G. Zarb Sch. Bus., Hofstra U. With Army N.G., 1966-71. Mem. Hofstra U. Alumni Assn., NYU Alumni Assn. Home: 6659 Pleasant Lake Ct West Bloomfield MI 48322-4711

LEWIS, JERRY (JOSEPH LEVITCH), comedian; b. Newark, Mar. 16, 1926; s. Danny and Rae Levitch; m. Patti Palmer, 1944 (div.); children: Gary, Ron, Scott, Chris, Anthony, Joseph; m. Sandra Pitnick, 1983; 1 child, Danielle Sara. Edn., Irvington (N.J.) High Sch.; DHL (hon.), Mercy Coll., 1987. Prof. cinema U. So. Calif.; pres. JAS Prodns., Inc., P.J. Prodns., Inc. Began as entertainer with record routine at Catskill (N.Y.) hotel; formed comedy team with Dean Martin, 1946-56; performed as a single, 1956—; formed Jerry Lewis Prodns. Inc., prod., dir., writer, star, 1956; films include: My Friend Irma, 1949, My Friend Irma Goes West, 1950, At War with the Army, 1950, That's My Boy, 1951, Sailor Beware, 1951, The Stooge, 1952, Jumping Jacks, 1952, Scared Stiff, 1953, The Caddy, 1953, Money From Home, 1953, Three Ring Circus, 1954, Living it Up, 1954, You're Never Too Young, 1955, Artists and Models, 1955, Partners, 1956, Hollywood or Bust, 1956, The Delicate Delinquent, 1957, The Sad Sack, 1957, The Geisha Boy, 1958, Rockabye Baby, 1958, Don't Give Up the Ship, 1959, Li'l Abner, 1959, Visit to a Small Planet, 1960, The Bellboy, 1960, Cinderfella, 1960, The Ladies Man, 1961, It's Only Money, 1962, The Errand Boy, 1962, It's a Mad, Mad, Mad, Mad World, 1963, The Nutty Professor, 1963, Who's Minding The Store, 1963, The Patsy, 1964, The Disorderly Orderly, 1964, The Family Jewels, 1965, Boeing-Boeing, 1965, Three On A Couch, 1965, Way ... Way ... Out, 1966, The Big Mouth, 1967, Don't Raise the Bridge, Lower the Water, 1968, Hook, Line and Sinker, 1969, One More Time, 1969, Which Way To the Front?, 1970, Hardly Working, 1981, King of Comedy, 1983, Smorgasbord, 1983, Slapstick, 1984, To Catch A Cop, 1984, How Did You Get In?, 1985, Cookie, 1989, Arrowtooth Waltz, 1991, Mr. Saturday Night, 1992, Arizona Dream, 1993, Funny Bones, 1995; appeared on Broadway in Damn Yankees, 1995, on tour, 1995—; author: The Total Film-Maker, 1971, Jerry Lewis in Person, 1982; principal TV appearances include master of ceremonies ann. Labor Day Muscular Dystrophy Telethon, 1966—. Comdr. Order of Arts & Letters, France, 1984; nat. chmn. Muscular Dystrophy Assn. Recipient most promising male star in TV award Motion Picture Daily's 2nd Ann. TV poll, 1950, (as team), one of TV's 10 money making stars award Motion Picture Herald - Fame poll, 1951, 53-54, 57, best comedy team award Motion Picture Daily's 16th annual radio poll, 1951-53, Nobel Peace Prize nomination, 1978. Mem. Screen Producers Guild, Screen Dirs. Guild, Screen Writers Guild. Office: Jerry Lewis Films Inc 3160 W Sahara Ave # 16C Las Vegas NV 89102-6003 also: William Morris Agy Inc 151 S El Camino Dr Beverly Hills CA 90212-2704

LEWIS, JONATHAN JOSEPH, surgical oncologist, molecular biologist, educator; b. Johannesburg, South Africa, May 23, 1958; s. Myer Philip and Maisie (Bagg) L.; m. Nanci Lynn Vicedomini, May 20, 1990. MB BCH, Witwatersrand U., Johannesburg, 1982; PhD, Yale U., 1990. Registrar in surgery Witwatersrand U. Sch. Medicine, 1982-87; postdoctoral assoc. Yale U. Sch. Medicine, New Haven, Conn., 1987-90; chief resident, surgery Yale U. Sch. Medicine, New Haven, 1990-92; fellow dept. surgery Meml. Sloan-Kettering Cancer Ctr., N.Y.C., 1992-94, attending surgeon, 1994—, asst. mem., 1994-99, assoc. mem., 1999—; chief med. officer Antigenics Inc., N.Y.C., 2000—; asst. prof. surgery Cornell Univ. Med. Coll., 1994-99, assoc. prof., 1999—; chief med. officer Antigenics Inc., N.Y.C., 2000—. Contbr. articles to profl. jours. Recipient Abelheim medal Med. Coun., 1982, Trubshaw medal Coll. of Surgeons, Johannesburg, 1984; Winston fellow Sloan-Kettering Inst., 1994-95. Fellow ACS, Royal Coll. Surgeons; mem. Am. Soc. Cell Biology, Am. Assn. Cancer Rsch., Am. Soc. Clin. Oncology (Young Investigator award 1994), Assn. Acad. Surgeons, Soc. Surg. Oncology, N.Y. Acad. Scis. Jewish. Achievements include research in oncogenes, growth factors, signal transduction, immunotherapy, gene therapy. Office: Antigenics 630 5th Ave New York NY 10111

LEWIS, JORDAN DAVID, management consultant, author, international speaker, educator; b. Chgo., Aug. 9, 1937; s. Murray Robert and Ruth (Weinstein) L.; m. Lynn Lopata, Sept. 20, 1964; children: Matthew Michael, Katherine Anne. B.S.Engring. in Physics., U. Mich., 1960, B.S. Engring. in Math, 1960, M.S. Engring. in Instrumentation (fellow), 1963, M.S. Engring. in Nuclear Engring., 1963, Ph.D. in Thermonuclear Physics, 1966. Instr. physics U. Mich. at Dearborn, 1962-64, research asst., 1964-66; with Battelle Devel. Corp., Columbus, Ohio, 1966-72; asst. mgr. devel. dept. Battelle Devel. Corp., 1968-70, mgr. gen. operations, 1970-72; dir. applied tech. programs Batelle Columbus Labs., Columbus, 1972; dir. presdl. tech. and econ. policy program Nat. Bur. Standards, Washington, 1973-77; exec. dir. A.T. Internat., Washington, 1977-79; mgmt. cons., 1979—; sr. lectr. Wharton Sch., U. Pa.; U.S. del. to OECD, Paris; advisor strategic alliance to internat. corps.; fellow World Econ. Forum, Geneva, 1993, 94, 96, 98; chmn. Fed. Task Force on Energy Intensive Products, 1975. Author: Partnerships for Profit: Structuring and Managing Strategic Alliances, 1990, The Connected Corporation: How Leading Firms Win Through Customer-Supplier Alliances, 1995, Trusted Partners: How Companies Build Mutual Trust and Win Together, 2000; editor: (with Lynn L. Lewis) Industrial Approaches to Urban Problems, 1972; guest columnist Wall St. Jour., N.Y. Times; contbr. articles to newspapers and profl. jours. Co-chmn. Columbus Outdoor Summer Concerts, 1968-70; chmn. bd. dirs. Columbus Inner-City Econ. Devel. Corp., 1969-71. AEC fellow, 1964-66. Fellow AAAS (mem. council; chmn. indsl. sci. sect. 1975); mem. Am. Econs. Assn., Sigma Xi. Home: 3707 33rd Pl NW Washington DC 20008-3201

LEWIS, JUDITH SUSANNA, artist; b. Ithaca, Ohio, Apr. 16, 1940; d. Kenneth William and Mildred Pauline Coates; m. Harry Robert Lewis, Aug. 18, 1967; children: Lucianna Doré, Brishen Marie. BS, Miss. State Coll. for Women, 1962; MS, Ind. U., 1966. Cert. tchr., Miss., Ind. Elem. tchr. Seymour (Ind.) Cmty. Schs., 1963-74. One-woman show Shaker Seed Box Co. Gallery, Mariemont, Ohio, 1991; group exhbns. include So. Ind. Ctr. for the Arts, Seymour, 1997, Madison (Ind.) Fine Arts Gallery, 1998, Hoosier Salon Gallery, Indpls., 1999-2000, Columbia Club, Indpls., 2000; painted murals in elem. schs. and pub. bldgs.; represented in permanent collection The Honeywell Found., Inc., Wabash, Ind., Rushville (Ind.) Art Ctr., Japanese Govt. Recipient 1st place award Madison Art Club Exhibit, Ind., 1999, 1st place and best of show, Brown County Art Gallery Patrons Show, Nashville, Ind., 1998, 99, Merit award Ind. Heritage of the Arts, 1999, Merit award and Purchase award Hoosier Salon, 2000. Mem. So. Ind Ctr. for the arts, Hoosier Salon, Plein Air Painters, Ind. Heritage of the Arts, Southside Art League, Brown County Art Gallery Assn. Avocations: travel, writing, photography, plays and musicals. Home and Studio: 602 N Walnut St Seymour IN 47274-1539

LEWIS, JULIANHART, developmental biologist, author; b. London, Aug. 12, 1946; s. Aubrey Julian and Hilda North (Stoessiger) L.; m. Sherry Lee Granum, 1983; Emma R., Sarah N., Rebecca E. BA in Physics, Oxford (Eng.) U., 1967, D Philosophy, Theoretical Physics, 1971. Fellow Royal Soc. Exch. Inst. for Phys. Problems, Moscow, 1970-71; rsch. asst. Middlesex Hosp. Med. Sch., London, 1971-78; lectr. in anatomy King's Coll., U. London, 1978-86; sr. scientist Imperial Cancer Rsch. Fund, 1986—; vis. assoc. prof. U. Calif., San Francisco, 1987-88; rsch. lectr. Dept. Zoology U. Oxford, 1989—; hon. prof. dept. anatomy and developmental biol. Univ. Coll. London, 1999—; principal scientist Imperial Cancer Rsch. Fund. Author (with B. Alberts and others): (book) Molecular Biology of the Cell, 1985, 2d edit. 1989, 3d edit. 1994, Essential Cell Biology, 1998. Office: Imperial Cancer Rsch Fund Vertebrate Dev, 44 Lincoln's Inn Fields, London WC2 A3PX, England

LEWIS, KENNETH D., banker; b. 1947. BA, Ga. State U., 1969. Pres. NCNB Nat. Bank Fla., 1986-88, NCNB Tex., Dallas, N.C., 1988-90, Gen. Bank NationsBank, Atlanta, Ga., 1991-93, NationsBank Corp., Charlotte, N.C., 1993-99; pres., COO Bank of Am. Corp., Charlotte, 1999—; bd. dirs. Health Mgmt. Assocs., Naples, Fla. Past chmn. bd. United Way of Cen. Carolinas Inc., Charlotte; dir. Homeownership Edn. and Counseling Inst.; vice chmn. bd. of trustees Nat. Urban League; chmn. Arts and Sci. Coun. campaign dr., Charlotte, 1998; bd. dirs. Presbyn. Hosp. Found., Charlotte. Office: Bank of Am Corp Ctr 100 N Tryon St Fl 58 Charlotte NC 28255-0001

LEWIS, KIM, microbiologist; b. N.Y.C., Feb. 3, 1953; s. Tom John Lewis and Fainna Solasko; m. Tanya Genina, May 20, 1986; children: Alexandra, Maria. BS, Moscow U., 1976, PhD, 1980, D of Biology, 1984. Rschr. Moscow U., 1976-79, sr. rschr., 1979-84; rsch. assoc. U. Wis., Madison, 1987-88; asst. prof. MIT, Cambridge, Mass., 1988-94; assoc. prof. U. Md., Balt., 1994-97, Tufts U., Medford, Mass., 1997—. Contbr. numerous papers to profl. jours. Rsch. grantee NSF, 1992, 94, ACS, 1992, NIH, 1996, 99, 2000, Dept. Energy, 1997. Mem. Am. Soc. Microbiology. Avocations: reading, art, music. Office: Tufts U 4 Colby St Medford MA 02155-6013

LEWIS, KIRK MCARTHUR, lawyer; b. Schenectady, N.Y., Jan. 3, 1957; s. David MacArthur and Eleanor Burrows (Smith) L.; m. Barbara Jean Lewis, June 12, 1982; children: John Christopher, Kerry Elizabeth. BS, Cornell U., 1979; JD, Syracuse U., 1985. Bar: N.Y. 1986, U.S. Dist. Ct. (no. dist.) N.Y. 1988, U.S. Dist. Ct. (ea. dist.) N.Y. 1991, U.S. Ct. Appeals (2d cir.) 1989. Jud. clk to Hon. Conrad K. Cyr U.S. Dist. Ct. Maine, Bangor, 1985-87; assoc. DeGraff, Foy, Holt, Harris, Mealey & Kunz, Albany, N.Y., 1987-92, ptnr., 1993-98; gen. counsel Schenectady Assn. Retarded Citizens, 1999—; mem. Village of Scotia Planning Bd., 1999—. Bd. dirs. Schenectady (N.Y.) Assn. for Retarded Citizens, 1990-98. Mem. ABA, N.Y. State Bar Assn. Home: 30 Washington Rd Scotia NY 12302-2413 Office: Schedy ARC PO Box 2236 Schenectady NY 12301-2236

LEWIS, LOIDA NICOLAS, food products holding company executive; b. The Philippines, Dec. 23, 1942; m. Reginald Lewis, 1969. BA, St. Theresa's Coll., 1963; LLB, U. Philippines, 1967. Immigration atty. N.Y.C.; with Immigration and Naturalization Svc.; chmn., CEO TLC Beatrice Internat., N.Y.C., 1994—. Author: How the Filipino Veteran of World War II Can Become a U.S. Citizen (According to the Immigration Act of 1990), 1991, One Hundred One Legal Ways to Stay in the U.S.A.: or, How to Get a Green Card According to the Immigration Act of 1990, 1992, How to Get a Green Card: Legal Ways to Stay in the U.S.A., 1993. Office: TLC Beatrice Internat 9 W 57th St Fl 39 New York NY 10019-2701

LEWIS, MARGO, talent agent; b. Bklyn., Dec. 19, 1937; d. Vito and Gemma (Baccari) Crocitto. Keyboard player Goldie & the Gingerbreads, N.Y.C., 1963-68, Blythe Spirit, N.Y.C., 1969-72, various groups, N.Y.C., 1972-74, Isis, N.Y.C., 1974-80; pres., CEO Talent Cons. Internat., Ltd., N.Y.C., 1988—; v.p. mktg. Women In Music, N.Y.C., 1990-93. Mem. NARAS (N.Y. chpt. bd. govs. 1995—, v.p. 1996—, chairperson music events com. 1996—, alternative trustee 1996-97, trustee 1997—), Women In Music (adv. bd. 1993—). Home: 210 Gair St Piermont NY 10968-1058 Office: Talent Cons Internat Ltd 1560 Broadway # 1308 New York NY 10036-1518

LEWIS, MARK JAMES, tennis coach; b. Auckland, New Zealand, May 27, 1961; s. James and Marcia Gabrielle (Hart) L.; m. Ann Maree Chambers; children: Tyler Jordan, Amber Montana. Student, St. Peter's Coll., Auckland, New Zealand, 1976-77. Cert. New Zealand Profl. Tennis Coaches Assn. Profl. tennis player, 1979-84; mem. Davis Cup Team, New Zealand, 1980-81; mktg. exec. Fin Sports, New Zealand, 1985-86; head coach Iphitos Tennis Club, Munich, 1988-93; pvt. coach Michael Stich, Germany, 1990-94; coach, mgr. Auckland Tennis Inc., 1997—; Fed. Cup capt. New Zealand Tennis, 1999—. Mem. Internat. Club of New Zealand.

LEWIS, MARTIN EDWARD, shipping company executive, foreign government concessionary; b. Chgo., Dec. 27, 1958; s. Martin Luther and Anna Adlene (Gaines) L. BA, Johns Hopkins U., 1981; postgrad., Rush Med. Coll., 1983-85. Chmn. bd., chief exec. officer Internat. Financier Inc., Chgo., 1987—; co. rep. Assn. S.E. Asia Nations Secretariat Gen., Jakarta, Indonesia, 1995—; co. rep. OPEC, Vienna, 1988—, Supreme Coun. States of Cooperation Coun., Summit Confs. Countries of Cooperation Coun. for Arab States of Gulf, Secretariat Gen., Riyadh, Saudi Arabia, 1989—; corp. amb. plenipotentiary GM Overseas Ops., N.Y.C., 1977, Adam Opel, Russelsheim, Fed. Republic Germany, 1977. Mem. Asia Soc., Japan Soc. Republican. Avocations: golf, tennis, yachting, scuba diving.

LEWIS, PATRICK ALBERT, diplomat; b. St. Johns, Antigua, Nov. 27, 1938; m. Michele Lewis. BA in History, Hampton Inst., 1966; MA in History, U. Cin., 1968, PhD in History, 1974. Asst. prof. history U. Cin., 1971-73; from asst. prof. to prof. history Hampton Inst., 1973-84, dir. ethnic studies, 1976-84; advisor to dep. prime min. Antigua and Barbuda Lester B. Bird, 1984-87; min.-counsellor Antigua and Barbuda UN, 1987-91; amb. Antigua and Barbuda to U.S. Washington, 1991-95; amb. Antigua and Barbuda to UN, 1995—; lectr. in field. Editor Hampton Inst. Jour. Ethnic Studies, 1976-84; contbr. numerous articles to profl. jours. Office: Permanent Mission of Antigua & Barbuda to UN 610 5th Ave Rm 311 New York NY 10020-2403*

LEWIS, RALPH JAY, III, management and human resources educator; b. Balt., Sept. 25, 1942; s. Ralph Jay and Ruth Elizabeth (Schmeltz) L. BS in Engring., Northwestern U., 1966; MS in Adminstrn., U. Calif., Irvine, 1968; PhD in Mgmt., UCLA, 1974. Rsch. analyst Chgo. Area Expressway Surveillance Project, 1963-64, Gen. Am. Transp. Co., Chgo., 1965-66; assoc. prof. mgmt. and human resources mgmt. Calif. State U., Long Beach, 1972—; cons. Rand Corp., Santa Monica, Calif., 1966-74, Air Can., Montreal, Que., 1972-73, Los Angeles Times, 1973;. Co-author: Studies in the Quality of LIfe, 1972; author instructional programs, monographs; co-designer freeway traffic control system. Bd. dirs. Project Quest, Los Angeles, 1969-71. Mem. AAAS, APA, The World Future Soc., Soc. of Mayflower Descendants, SAR (Ill. Soc.), Beta Gamma Sigma. Democrat. Office: Calif State U Dept Human Resources Mgmt Long Beach CA 90840-0001

LEWIS, RICHARD M., lawyer; b. Gallipolis, Ohio, Dec. 11, 1957; s. Denver E. and Mary Esther (Mobley) L.; m. Cheryl F. Hickman (div.); m. Diane K. Williams, Apr. 26, 1986. BA in Polit. Sci., Ohio State U., 1979; JD, Capital U., 1982. Bar: Ohio 1982, U.S. Dist. Ct. (so. dist.) Ohio 1984, U.S. Supreme Ct. 1986, U.S. Ct. Appeals (6th cir.) 1999; cert. civil trial advocacy Nat. Bd. Trial Advocacy. Pvt. practice law, 1982-83; assoc. Mary Bone Kunze, Jackson, Ohio, 1983-85; pvt. practice law Jackson, 1985-86; ptnr. Ochsenbein, Cole & Lewis, Jackson, 1986-96, Cole & Lewis, Jackson, 1996—; lectr. in field; expert witness. Mem. ABA, Assn. Trial Lawyers Am., Ohio State Bar Assn., Jackson County Bar Assn. (past pres.), Ohio Acad. Trial Lawyers (bd. trustees 1993—, budget com. 1993-94, supreme ct. screening com. 1994, vice-chairperson family law com. 1994-95, chairperson-elect family law com. 1995—, chairperson family law com. 1995-96, exec. com., chair mem. com. 1996-97, co-chair regional CLE seminars 1997, exec. com. 1998-99, chair ADOPT task force 1998). Home: 603 Reservoir Rd Jackson OH 45640-8714 Office: Cole and Lewis 295 Pearl St Jackson OH 45640-1748

LEWIS, ROBERT DAVID, ophthalmologist, educator; b. Thomasville, Ga., Aug. 27, 1948; s. Ralph N. and E. Margaret (Klaus) L.; m. Cathleen Ann Polster, May 26, 1996. BS, St. Louis Coll. Pharmacy, 1971; MD, St. Louis U., 1975. Diplomate Am. Bd. Ophthalmology; registered pharmacist. Intern, Cardinal Glennon Hosp. Children, St. Louis, 1975-76; resident St. Louis U., 1976-79; practice medicine specializing in ophthalmology, St. Louis, 1979—; dir. pediatric ophthalmology St. Louis U., 1980-82, 85, asst. prof., 1980-88, assoc. prof., 1988-97, clin. prof. ophthalmology, 1998; pres. St. Louis Ophthalmological Soc., 1991-92; dir. pediatric ophthalmology Cardinal Glennon Hosp. for Children, St. Louis, 1980-82, 85; mem. adv. bd. Delta Gamma Found. for Visually Handicapped Children. Recipient St. Louis U. Award for Teaching, 1982. Fellow ACS; mem. AMA, Mo. Med. Assn., St. Louis Med. Soc., Am. Acad. Ophthalmology, Contact Lens Assn. Ophthalmology, Internat. Assn. Ocular Surgeons, Am. Intraocular Implant Soc., St. Louis Ophthalmol. Soc. (pres. 1991-92), Am. Bd. Club. (pres. 1991-92). Office: 12700 Southfork Rd Ste 205 Saint Louis MO 63128-3201 also: 3915 Watson Rd Saint Louis MO 63109-1251

LEWIS, ROBERT DAVID GILMORE, retired editor; b. Chgo., Jan. 16, 1932; s. James Lee and Betty (Ryden) L.; m. Georgia Demopoulos, Aug. 4, 1956 (div. July 1988); children: Peter, Sarah, Mary, John, Elizabeth, Daniel, Susan; m. Jacqueline Mc Gregor, July 15, 1988; children: Jill, Katy, Sara. BA, Mich. State U., 1955. Reporter, city editor Galesburg (Ill.) Register-Mail, 1955-59; reporter, bus. editor Kalamazoo Gazette, 1960-64; state capitol corres. Booth Newspapers, Lansing, Mich., 1964-66; Washington corres. Booth Newspapers, Washington, 1966-87, Newhouse Newspapers, Washington, 1987-91; sr. editor Am. Assn. Retired Persons Bull., Washington, 1991-99, ret., 1999. Bd. visitors Les Aspin Ctr. for Govt., Marquette U., 1996—. Mem. Soc. Profl. Journalists (chmn. freedom info. com. 1978-83, sec.-treas., pres.-elect then pres., 1983-86, Wells Meml. Key award 1980), White House Corres. Assn., Nat. Press Club (chmn. bd. govs. 1975-77), Sigma Delta Chi Found. (bd. dirs. 1986-88), Cosmos Club, Supreme Ct. Hist. Soc., U.S. Capitol Hist. Soc., Catherine Filene Shouse Legacy Cir. of the Wolf Trap, Found. for the Performing Arts. Avocations: antique furniture collecting, fishing. Home: 301 Constitution Ave NE Washington DC 20002-5921

LEWIS, ROBERT EDWIN, JR., pathology immunology educator, researcher; b. Meridian, Miss., Mar. 11, 1947. BA in Biology and Chemistry, U. Miss., 1969, MS in Microbiology, 1973, PhD in Pathology, 1976; specialty tng., Barnes Hosp., U. Miami Med. Ctr., U. Tenn. Ctr. for Health Scis., City of Memphis Hosps., St. Jude Children's Research Hosp. Instr. pathology, anesthesiology U. Miss. Med. Ctr., Jackson, 1976-77, asst. prof. pathology, 1977-84, asst. prof. anesthesiology, 1977-85, asst. dir. clin. immnuopathology lab., 1978-81, assoc. dir. tissue typing lab., 1980-84, dir. paternity testing lab., 1981—, assoc. dir. clin. immunopathology lab., 1981-84, asst. prof. nurse anesthesiology, 1981-85, assoc. prof. pathology, 1984-91, prof., 1991—, dir. clin. immunology, tissue typing lab., 1984—, mem. grad. council, 1981—, prof., 1991—. Co-author: Illustrated Dictionary of Immunology, 1995, Atlas of Immunology, 1999; editor: (with J.M. Cruse) Concepts in Immunopathology, Vols. 1-8, 1985-91, The Year in Immunology-1984-85, 1985, The Year in Immunology-1986-87, 1987, The Year in Immunology-1988, 1989, The Year in Immunology-1989-90, 1990, Progress in Experimental Tumor Research, Vol. 32, 1987, Contributions to Microbiology and Immunology, Vol. 8, 1986, Vol. 9, 1987, Vol. 10, 1989, Vol. 11, 1989, The Year in Immunopathology, 1987, Complement Profiles, Vol. 1, 1992; sr. editor Pathology and Immunopathology Research, 1982-90, Immunologic Research, 1981—, Transgenics, 1993—, Experimental and Molecular Pathology, 1999—; series editor Concepts in Immunopathology, The Year in Immunology, Contributions to Microbiology and Immunology; vol. editor Progress in Experimental Tumor Research; immunology editor Dorland's Illustrated Medical Dictionary, 26th and 27th edits.; dep. editor-in-chief Pathobiology, 1990-98; contbr. chpts. to books. Am. Cancer Soc. grantee, NIH grantee, Wilson Found. grantee, 1990-95. Fellow Royal Soc. Health; mem. AAAS, Am. Assn. Pathologists, Am. Assn. Immunologists, Clin. Immunology Soc., Can. Soc. Immunology, Reticuloendothelial Soc., Am. Soc. Microbiology, Am. Soc. Histocompatibility and Immunogenetics (co-chmn. publs. com. 1987-2000, chmn. 2000—), Exptl. Biology and Medicine, N.Y. Acad. Scis., Miss. Acad. Scis., Sigma Xi. Office: U Miss Med Ctr Pathology Dept Dept Pathology 2500 N State St Jackson MS 39216-4500

LEWIS, ROBERT JOHN CORNELIUS KOONS, university library director, consultant; b. Feb. 15, 1938; s. Frank Ashby and Dorothy Elaine (Koons) L.; m. Martha Marie Popejoy, Dec. 22, 1957 (div. 1964); 1 child, Stephen Ashley; m. Helena Barbara Vaughn Schumacker, Sept. 11, 1968 (div. 1976); children: Matthew, Randolph; m. Marguerita S. Kris, July 28, 1985. BA in History of Religion, George Washington U., 1961, MA in Secondary Edn., 1966; MS in L.S., Cath. U. Am., 1974. Intelligence analyst CIA, Washington, 1958-62; tech. libr. supr. Bell Aerospace, Tucson, 1968-70; info. officer Ambionics Inc., Washington, 1970-73; law libr. Patton, Boggs & Blow, Washington, 1973-75; rsch. George Washington U., Washington, 1976-78; libr. dir. Benjamin Franklin U., Washington, 1979—; Oriental art cons. Silverman Galleries, Alexandria, Va., 1978—; libr. dir. Cushman, Darby & Cushman, 1988-90, Nat. Geneal. Soc., 1990-93; libr. Met. Club, 1994—. Author, compiler: Brief History of the Rose Mount Branch of the Surles (Searles) Lewis Family of Virginia, 1976, collected poems: Quatrains based on the Love Poems of the 6th Dalai Lama and other poems, 1979, Lewis Patriarchs of Early Va. and Md., 1989, rev. edit., 1991, rev. 3d. edit., 1998, Welsh Family Coats of Arms, 1995. With U.S. Army, 1963-65. Awarded title of Gyalwa Karma Lozang Dondrup, by Kalu Rinpoche of Darjeeling, 1977; hon. grantee of arms Coll. of Arms, London, 1998. Mem. ALA (pres. com. 1982), Assn. Former Intelligence Officers, Spl. Librs. Assn., Nat. Geneal. Soc. (councilor 1990-93), Soc. Geneal. of London, Jamestowne Soc., The Augustan Soc., Mahikari of Am. Club, Subud Club, Theosophical Soc. Club, Sigma Phi Epsilon. Episcopalian. Home: 18612 Sage Way Germantown MD 20874-2041 Office: Met Club Libr 1700 H St NW Washington DC 20006-4601

LEWIS, ROBERT LEE, lawyer; b. Oxford, Miss., Feb. 26, 1944; s. Ernest Elmo and Johnice Georgia (Thirkield) L.; children: Yolanda Sherice, Robert Lee Jr., Dion Terrell, Viron Lamar, William Lovell. BA, Ind. U., 1970, JD, 1973; M in Pub. Service, West Ky. U., 1980. Bar: Ind. 1973, Ky. 1979, U.S. Ct. Claims, U.S. Ct. Internat. Trade, U.S. Tax Ct., U.S. Ct. Mil. Appeals, U.S. Ct. Appeals (fed. cir.), U.S. Supreme Ct. Sole practice Evansville, Ind., 1973-75, Gary, Ind., 1980—; atty., army officer U.S. Army, Ft. Knox, Ky., 1975-78; appellate referee Ind. Employment Security Div., Indpls., 1978-80. Mem. adv. com. Vincennes (Ind.) U., 1983—; bd. dirs. Opportunities Industrialization Ctr., Evansville, 1973-75. Served to sgt. JAGC, USMC, 1962-66, Vietnam, sgt. U.S. Army, 1975-78, lt. col. USAR. Named Ky. Col. Mem. ABA, Ind. Bar Assn., Ky. Bar Assn., Nat. Bar Assn., Ind. Bd. Realtors, Ind. U. Alumni Assn., Phi Alpha Delta. Methodist. Home and Office: 2148 W 11th Ave Gary IN 46404-2306

LEWIS, RONALD HUGH, religious organization administrator; b. London, June 13, 1930; s. Alec and Toba (Ash) L.; m. Doreen Rose MacDonald; children: Macdonald Hugh, Kirstine Joy Greenwood. BA, U. Wales, 1951. Min. Presbyn. Ch., Jarrow, Eng., 1959-63, Harlow, Eng., 1963-72; min. United Reformed Ch., Redcar, Eng., 1972-90, Blackburn, Eng., 1990-95; exec. sec. Internat. Messianic Jewish Alliance, Kent, Eng., 1979-99, hon. sec. Europe, 2000—; cons. Presbyn. Ch. Eng., 1962-72, United Reformed Ch., 1972-00. Co-editor, contbr. Christians and Jews in Britain, 1983; editor, author Messianic Jew (formerly Hebrew Christian), 1979-98. With Royal Artillery, 1952-54. Avocations: Scottish country dancing, walking, jazz and classical music appreciation. Fax: 01254 387462. E-mail: ronlewis@surfaid.org. Home: 11 Beetham Ct, Clayton Le Moors BB5 5GB, England Office: PO Box 163, Ramsgate CT11 8GJ, England

LEWIS, SHARON LARUE (SHARI HAYES), clinical medical assistant, travel agent; b. Eugene, Oreg., Nov. 12, 1943; d. Lawrence Earl and Marjorie Ann (Smith) Crook; m. Lorin Donald Lewis (div. 1977); children: Kevin Earl Lewis, Randall Bruce Lewis, Gregory Steven Lewis; 1 foster child, Deborah Jo Bull Plume; m. Richard David Hayes, Mar. 17, 1984 (div. 1999); 1 child, David Sean Gregory; stepchildren: Heidi O'Malley, Heather Angela. Student, U. Oreg., 1962-63, Chemeketa C.C., Salem, Oreg., 1972, Lane C. C., Eugene, Oreg., 1981-83. Cert. med. asst.-clin., 1973; ltd. radiology permit holder, Oreg., 1982. Exec. sec. to Dean Arthur Esslinger U. Oreg. Sch. Health, Phys. Edn. and Recreation, 1961-69; asst. in radiation therapy to Margaret Thompson, MD, Salem Meml. Hosp., 1970-71; med. asst., office mgr. Daniel DiIaconi, MD, Surgeon, Carl H. Matthey, MD, family practice, 1970-79, Daniel Usdin, MD, Cardiologist, Jacksonville, Fla., 1979-80; med. asst., ltd. x-ray permit holder Clifford Bre Miller, MD, and Richard Oehler, MD, family practice, Eugene, Oreg., 1980-85; med. asst., limited x-ray tech. Terry Copperman, MD, family practice, Eugene, Oreg., 1981-95; clin. med. asst., clin. offic mgr., transcriptionist R. Garr Cutler, MD, plastic/reconstructive and hand surgeon, Eugene, Oreg., 1985-95; adminstrv. asst., med. asst. Lewis Thompson, MD, plastic/reconstructive and hand surgeon, Tulsa, Okla., 1995-96; head nurse Cornerstone Family Medical Clinic, Tulsa, 1997-99; clin. med. asst., patient coord. Paul Angelchik M.D. Plastic and Reconstructive Surgeon, Glendale, Ariz., 2000—; travel agent Uniglobe Magic Carpet, 1989-98; crafter jewelry Shari's Original Designs, Eugene, 1990-93. Appeared in Eugene Opera, 1983-85, Main Stage Theater, Eugene, 1982. Host U. Oreg. fgn. student program, 1982-95; bd. dirs. Oreg. Repertory Theatre, Eugene, 1984-85, Plan Loving Adoptions Now, Internat. Adoption Agy., McMinnville, Oreg., 1994-95; foster parent to 29 foster children, 1968-72; spkr., counselor foster parent support groups, Lane County, Oreg., 1967-70; dir. children's choir Liberty Gardens Bible Ch., Salem, Oreg., 1968-72, tchr. Sunday sch., 1960-95; dir. Jet Cadets children's group, Salem, 1969-72; mem. PTA, 1970—. Named Med. Asst. Yr. Marion and Polk Counties of Medical Assistants, 1977, Lane County, 1990, State of Oreg., 1991. Mem. Assn. Plastic Surgery Nursing Assn., Am. Assn. Med. Assts. (mem. edn. com., house of dels. State of Oreg. 1971-72, 89, v.p. Lane chpt. med. assts. 1988, pres. 1989), Tulsa County Medical Assistants, Doll Dreamers UFDC (sec. 1993-94), Doll Study Club of Tulsa. Avocations: doll collecting, opera, the arts, travel, raising boxers. Home: 850 S River Dr Unit 1115 Tempe AZ 85281-4664

LEWIS, SHARYN LEE, sculptor; b. Carmel, Calif., July 31, 1946; d. William Albert and Hazel Elisabeth Lewis; m. Robert John Western, Mar. 22, 1986. Asst. art tchr. Benin (Nigeria) Coll., 1974-76; comml. artist KTT Art Svc., Campbell, Calif., 1976-77; graphic artist, illustrator Intersil Corp., Santa Clara, Calif., 1977-80; sr. artist, graphic designer Pro-Log Corp., Monterey, Calif., 1980-83; freelance graphic designer Monterey, Calif., 1983-92, sculptor, 1992—. Sculptor: exhibitions include: Mystic Maritime Gallery, Mystic Seaport, Conn., 1995-96, 97-98, 99 2000, Big Horn Galleries, Carmel, Calif., 1995-96, Fifth Ann. Loveland (Colo.) Sculpture Invitational, 1996, Monterey Peninsula Art Found. Ann. Members Show, 1997, Monterey Mus. of Art, 1998, 99, 2000; also in many private collections in U.S. Mem. Internat. Sculpture Ctr., Washington, Nat. Sculpture Soc., N.Y.C., Nat. Mus. Women in Art, Washington, Met Mus. of Art, N.Y.C., Monterey Mus. of Art. E-mail: WestRim@mbay.net.

LEWIS, SHERMAN RICHARD, JR., investment banker; b. Ottawa, Ill., Dec. 11, 1936; s. Sherman Richard and Julia Audrey (Rusteen) L.; m. Dorothy Marie Downie, Sept. 9, 1967; children: Thomas, Catherine, Elizabeth, Michael. AB, Northwestern U., 1958; MBA, U. Chgo., 1964. With investment dept. Am. Nat. Bank & Trust Co., Chgo., 1961-64; v.p. Halsey, Stuart & Co., N.Y.C., 1964-70, v.p. in charge corp. fin. dept., 1970-73; v.p. C.J. Lawrence & Sons, N.Y.C., 1970; ptnr. Loeb, Rhoades & Co., N.Y.C., 1973-76, ptnr. in charge corp. fin. dept., 1975-76, exec. v.p., bd. dirs., 1976-77, pres., co-chief exec. officer, 1977-78; vice chmn., co-chief exec. officer Loeb Rhoades, Hornblower & Co., N.Y.C., 1978-79; pres. Shearson/Am. Express Inc., N.Y.C., 1979-82, vice chmn., 1983-84; vice chmn. Shearson Lehman/Am. Express Inc., 1984-85, Shearson Lehman Bros. Inc., 1985-87, Shearson Lehman Hutton Inc., 1988-89; co-chief exec. officer, vice chmn., chmn. exec. com. Lehman Bros., 1990; vice chmn. Shearson Lehman Bros. Holdings, Inc., N.Y.C., 1990-93, Lehman Bros. Holdings, Inc., Lehman Bros., Inc., 1993—. Mem. Pres.'s Commn. on Housing, 1981-82, Pres.'s Coun. on Internat. Youth Exch., 1982-88; trustee Northwestern U., 1992—, regent, 1990-97; mem. bd. visitors Weinberg Coll. Arts and Scis., Northwestern U., 1981—, chmn., 1990-96; mem. coun. Grad. Sch. Bus., U. Chgo., 1991—; bd. dirs. The Korea Soc., U.S.-Greece Bus. Coun., N.Y. Eye and Ear Infirmary, U.S. Japan Bus. Coun. Commd. officer USMC, 1958-61. Mem. Coun. on Fgn. Rels., The Pilgrims, Bond Club, Univ. Club, Quogue Field Club, Shinnecock Yacht Club, Quantuck Beach Club. Office: Lehman Bros Inc 3 World Financial Ctr New York NY 10285-0001*

LEWIS, STUART WESLIE, surgeon; b. Bellefield, Mandeville, Jamaica, Oct. 23, 1938; came to U.S., 1959; s. Phillip Augustus and Ivy Hyacinth (Glegg) L.; m. Cordia L. Beverley; children: Camille, Hope Louise, Denise, Hara. BA, NYU, 1965; MD, Harvard U., 1974. Dir. Youth in Action, Neighborhood Youth Corps, Bklyn., 1966-69; resident in surgery NYU Med. Ctr.-Bellevue Hosp., N.Y.C., 1974-76; resident in surgery SUNY Downstate Med. Sch.-Kings County Hosp., Bklyn., 1976-79, chief surg. resident, 1979-80; pres. Monad Med. Svcs., Bklyn., 1981—; asst. v.p., med. dir. N.Y.C. Transit Authority, Bklyn., 1989—; adj. prof. NYU Med. Sch.; adj. prof. environ. medicine NYU; sr. advisor Orthop. Indsl. Occupl. Ctr., Hosp. for Joint Diseases, N.Y.C. Chair David Dodge Bedford Stuyvesant Neighborhood House, Bklyn., 1990—; chmn. Bedford Stuyvesant Restoration Corp.; mem. Friends of Edn. Mus. of Modern Art N.Y.; bd. mem. Herbert Birch Svcs., N.Y.C. Recipient Marcus Garvey award Com. to Honor Marcus Garvey, Bklyn., 1991, Recognition award Cen. Bklyn. Coord. Coun., 1992. Mem. Med. Execs., 100 Black Men. Avocations: reading, computer hacking. Address: CLB Med Svcs PC 1085 Park Ave New York NY 10128-1168

LEWIS, THELMA AGNES, medical laboratory scientific officer; b. Bartica, Guyana, Mar. 19, 1933; d. Edward Albert and Zuleika Fredrica (Peters) L. Gen. Cert. of Edn., U. London, 1960; scientist, Inst. Med. Tech., 1964; Higher Nat. Diploma Home Economics, Poly Tech North London, 1988; Ordinary Nat. Diploma, Hotel Catering & Inst. Ops., 1992; Diploma in Pub. Health & Hygiene, U. London, 1992; Diploma in Pastoral Ministry, Westminster Sem., 1992. Mem. nursing staff St. Joseph Mercy Hosp., Guyana, 1951-55; sr. med. lab. tech. London, 1966-85; bus. partnership catering Commonwealth Secretariat, London, 1988-91; parish asst. St. Anselm Roman Cath. Ch., London, 1995—; assoc. Sisters of Mercy; advisor to Nat. Coun. Lay Assns., 1993—; med. lab. sci. officer in hematology, blood group serology, histopathology, exfoliate cytology. Author: (information leaflet) Sickle Cell Anemia, 1976, (book) Herbs and Spices, 1995. Chairperson Aid to Guyanese Group, London, 1983—. Mem. Assn. Guyanese Nurses & Allied Professions (v.p. 1993—), Commonwealth Countries League, Brit. Caribbean Assn. Roman Catholic. Achievements include research on ophthalmology, dentistry and museum skills. Avocations: reading good books, theatre, dining out, meeting people, sports. Home: 28 Noyna Rd, London SW17 7PH, England Office: St Anselm Cath Ch, 9 Tooting Bec Rd, London SW17, England

LEWIS, VICTOR BRADLEY, philosopher, educator; b. Wayne, Mich., Feb. 20, 1965; s. Earl Clifford and Rachael Louise Hudson; m. Jody Vaccaro Lewis, July 10, 1999. BA, U. Md., 1987; MA, U. Notre Dame, 1989, PhD, 1997. Asst. prof. philosophy Cath. U. Am., Washington, 1997—; cons. editor Communio: Internat. Catholic Rev., 1998—. Mem. Am. Philos. Assn., Am. Cath. Philos. Assn., Soc. Ancient Greek Philosophy, Soc. Greek Polit. Thought. Roman Catholic. E-mail: lewisb@cua.edu. Office: Cath U Am Sch Philosophy Washington DC 20064-0001

LEWIS, W. WALKER, strategic and financial advisory company executive; b. Middletown, Ohio, Sept. 15, 1944; s. W. Walker Jr. and Emily S. (Spivy) L.; m. Ellen Anschuetz, Mar. 30, 1970; children: Walker, Alexandra (Sasha), Morgan. AB, Harvard U., 1967. Mgr. Boston Cons. Group, 1970-72; chmn. Strategic Planning Assocs., Washington, 1972-92; pres. Avon Products, N.Y.C., 1992-94; mng. dir. Kidder Peabody, N.Y.C., 1994-95; sr. advisor Dillon Read & Co., N.Y.C., 1995-97; chmn. Devon Value Advisers, N.Y.C., 1997—. Mem. Coun. on Fgn. Rels., Washington Inst. Fgn. Affairs. Office: Devon Value Advisers 399 Park Ave Unit 19 New York NY 10022-4616

LEWIS, WAYNE WALTON, industrial engineer; b. Summerville, Ga., Mar. 5, 1951; s. Calvin Tipton and Annie Marie (Robbins) L.; m. Dianne Stone, Dec. 14, 1973 (div. June 1976); 1 child, Christopher Wayne; m. Marie Hardwick Mercer, July 8, 1991; 1 child, Jonathan Michael. AS in Bus. Adminstrn., Kennesaw State U., 1982, BBA in Bus. Adminstrn., 1987; AA in Psychology, Floyd Coll., 1986; A in Specialized Tech. in Indsl. Engring, Pa. State U., 1997. Jr. indsl. engr. Riegel Textile Corp., Trion, Ga., 1971-73; asst. indsl. engr. E.T. Barwick Industries, Barnwell, S.C., 1973-75; tech. svcs. supr. Pharr Yarns of Ga., Rome, 1975-95, Image Industries, Rome, 1995—; mem. adv. bd. Berry Coll., Rome, Ga., 1991-93. Mem. campaign activities com. Ga. Ho. of Reps., Rome, 1978-98. Mem. Inst. Indsl. Engrs. (pres. 1973-98, Highest Growth award 1987), Grtr. Rome Engring. Assn. Republican. Methodist. Avocations: golf, tennis, lawn- and landscaping. Home: 26 Windrush Dr NW Rome GA 30165-9787 Office: Image Industries 243 Huffaker Rd NW Rome GA 30165-1941

LEWIS, WILLIAM JOHN, aerospace engineer; b. Moncton, N.B., Can., Sept. 3, 1959; s. Ronald Lloyd and Marion Elizabeth (Dodge) L.; m. Shane Andrea Martin, July 16, 1983; children: Theodore William Dodge, Benjamin Peter Dodge. B in Engring., Royal Mil. Coll., Kingston, Ont., Can., 1981, M in Nuclear Engring., 1988; MBA, U. Man., Winnipeg, Can., 1985; B in Edn., Queen's U., Kingston, 1990, MEd, 1991; PhD in Nuclear Engring., Pacific Western U., 1992. Registered profl. engr., Ont. and Man. Commd. 2d lt. Can. Air Force, 1981; advance through grades to maj., 1994—; aerospace engring. officer Dept. Nat. Def., Winnipeg, 1982-85, Ottawa, Ont., 1985-86; maintenance analysis officer Dept. Nat. Def., Trenton, Ont., 1991-94, aerospace engring. officer, 1994-97; aerospace engring. officer Dept. Nat. Def., Ottawa, Ont., 1997—; lectr. engring. Royal Mil. Coll., 1985-88, asst. prof., then assoc. prof., 1988-91, adj. prof., 1991—; cons., pres. Software Aide, Kingston and Trenton, 1985—; mem. postgrad. adv. bd. Royal Mil. Coll., 1988-91. Contbg. author: Neutron Radiography, 3rd edit., 1990, 5th edit., 1997, Radiation Measurements and Applications, 1991. Scout leader Boy Scouts Am., 1994—. Grantee, Chief of Rsch. and Design, Ottawa, 1986—; recipient Can. 125 medal Govt. of Can., 1993, Can. Order of Mil. Merit, Govt. Can., 1999. Mem. AIChE, Am. Soc. for Engring. Edn., Can. Soc. Chem. Engring., Can. Soc. for Non-destructive Testing, Can. Neutron-Radiography Assn. (mem. conf. organizing com. 1990), Can. Nuclear Soc. (conf. organizing com. 1991), Masons, Shriners. Mem. United Ch. of Can. Achievements include design, installation and commission of world's first neutron radiography facility using small research reactor as neutron source; pioneer in investigation of advanced metal ceramics and composite aircraft flight controls using neutron radiography. Avocations: outdoor activities, visiting family cottage, recreational vehicles, hunting, fishing. Home: 85 Hansen Ave, Kanata, ON Canada K2K 2M2 Office: Royal Mil Coll Can Chem Eng, PO Box 17000 Stn Forces, Kingston, ON Canada K7K 5L0

LEWIS-GRIFFITH, DOROTHY ELLEN, music educator, pianist; b. High Point, N.C., July 7, 1932; d. Fleet and Foda Lee (Blakeley) Lewis; m. David Griffith, Dec. 12, 1959 (div. 1967); children: Dorothy Lewis, David Fleet; m. Adrian Lafayette Shuford, Jr., July 28, 1985. BS, Juilliard Sch., 1954, MS, 1955; D Mus. Arts, Johns Hopkins U., 1978. Grad. asst. Peabody Conservatory, Johns Hopkins U., Balt., 1971-72; assoc. prof. music Valdosta State U., U. Ga. System, 1974-86; artist-in-residence Shuford Sch. Performing Arts, Catawba Coll., Salisbury, N.C., 1986—; vis. prof. U. Wis., Superior, summer 1972, Steinway Artists Roster. N.Y. debut Town Hall, 1965, recitals at Abraham Goodman House, 1983, Weill Hall at Carnegie Hall, 1992; concerts in Germany, France, Brazil, Peoples Republic of China; soloist with Atlanta Symphony, Brevard Music Festival Orch., N.C. Symphony, Winston-Salem Symphony, Orchestre de la Cité Universitaire, Paris., Kunming, Yunnan (China) Symphony; recs. include Starer Sonata, Ginastera Sonata, 1965, A Christmas Celebration at the Piano, 1978, George Gershwin: A Piano Solo Album, 1994; contbr. to EPTA Music Jour. and New Grove Dictionary Am. Music and Musicians revised edit., New Grove Dictionary of Opera. Bd. dirs. Charlotte (N.C.) Symphony, 1963-65, Lowndes Art Commn., Valdosta, 1975-78, N.C. Symphony, Raleigh, 1988-90, N.C. Sch. Arts, 1994—; mem. Jr. League Charlotte. Recipient diploma Geneva Internat. Piano Competition, 1956, winner Brevard (N.C.) Music Festival Concerto Competition, 1965; Fulbright-Hays grantee, 1955, rsch. grantee Valdosta State Coll., 1983. Mem. Music Tchrs. Nat. Assn., Sigma Alpha Iota. Avocations: gardening, swimming.

LEWIS MILL, BARBARA JEAN, school psychologist, educator; b. Sacramento, Sept. 12, 1959; d. William Vasse and Mary Allene (Bridges) Lewis; m. Thomas Steven Mill, Oct. 17, 1981; 1 child, Thomas William. BA, U. Calif., Davis, 1981; MA, U. Calif., Santa Barbara, 1984. Pupil pers. svcs. credentials; cert. basic and sch. psychologist; cert. behavioral intervention case mgr. Pub. rels. asst. Coll. Agrl. and Environ. Scis., U. Calif., Davis, 1979-81; adminstrv. asst. libr. U. Calif., Santa Barbara, 1981-84; sch. psychologist intern Ventura (Calif.) County Supt. of Schs. Office, 1984-85, sch. psychologist, 1985-91; sch. psychologist Rio Sch. Dist., Oxnard, Calif., 1985, Ojai (Calif.) Sch. Dist., 1991-92, Santa Paula (Calif.) Sch. Dist., 1991-2000, Ventura (Calif.) Unified Sch. Dist., 2000—; coord. Primary Intervention Program, Santa Paula (Calif.) Sch. Dist., 1992-94; mem. planning com. Dropout Prevention/Outreach Program, Grace Thille Sch., Santa Paula, 1994. Mem. adv. bd. Pleasant Valley Rainbow Girls, Camarillo, Calif., 1986-89; bd. dirs. Strawberry Patch Presch., Oxnard, 1995-96; v.p. Rose Ave. Sch. PTA, 1997-98; co-pres. Hueneme Swimming Assn., 1998—; bd. dirs., asst. coach Channel Islands Aquatics, 1999—. Mem. ASCD, Nat. Assn. Sch. Psychologists (nat. cert. sch. psychologist), Internat. Reading Assn., Calif. Assn. Sch. Psychologists (Outstanding Sch. Psychologist region IV 1998; region VIII rep. 2000—), Ventura County Assn. Sch. Psychologists (exec. bd. 1987-91, 93-94, dir. pub. rels. 1991-93, 94-96, pres.-elect 1997-98, pres. 1998-99, past pres. 1999-2000, Outstanding Sch. Psychologist 1989, Meritorious Svc. award 1993), Hueneme Swimming Assn. (co-pres., bd. dirs. 1998—), Order Ea. Star, Rainbow for Girls (life, state officer Grand Scribe 1979). Avocations: parent education and outreach, conservation, creative arts, historical preservation, health and fitness.

LEWIS-RODRIGUEZ, PAMELA SUSAN, academic advisor; b. Flushing, N.Y., Oct. 22, 1970; d. Jorge Enrique Rodriguez II and Anne Yvonne Northrup; m. Robert J. Lewis Jr., May 23, 1998; 1 child, Anniston Quinn Lewis Rodriguez. BA, Purdue U., 1993, MS in Edn., 1997. Acad. advisor, adj. prof. L.I. U., C.W. Post Campus, Brookville, N.Y., 1997-99; acad. planner CUNY Queens Coll., 1999; acad. advisor Met. C.C., 1999—. Mem. Am. Coll. Personnel Assn., Nat. Acad. Advising Assn., Nat. Assn. Student Personnel Adminstrs. E-mail: peanutz9@aol.com. Home: 12104 Stonegate Dr Apt 302 Omaha NE 68164-5242

LEWY, JOSEF E., education educator; b. Berlin, Oct. 20, 1927; s. Eliezer E. and Natalie (Perlman) L.; m. Aliza Weinberg, Dec. 25, 1949; children: Efrat, Nitsa, Yuval. BSc, The Hebrew U., Jerusalem, 1955, tchrs. diploma, 1955; MA, Tel-Aviv and Bar-Ilan U., 1971; PhD, Bar-Ilan U., 1987. Tchr. various secondary schs., Israel, 1952-64; tchr., head tchr. Tchr. Tng. Coll., Israel, 1955-64; expert UNESCO, Lagos, Nigeria, 1964-65; inspector, head dept. Ministry Edn., Israel, 1966-79, head pre-acad. studies, 1978-79, chief supr., 1979-84; sr. lectr. Bar-Ilan and Hebrew Univs., Israel, 1972—; visitor, lectr. The Brit. Coun., 1979, 81, 82, 88, 91, 95; assoc. prof. Touro Coll. Grad. Sch., Jerusalem, 1991-99; planner reform of assessment in secondary and higher edn. Ministry Edn. and Univs., Israel, 1995-99; mem. inter-univs. com. for the introduction of alternative tchg. and assessment in Israeli H.S. planning, steering and assessing, 1996-99; mem. chief scientist's methodol. com. for the state-wide feedback of the edn. sys. in Israel, 1999-2000; mem. com. for the introduction of tchrs.' self assessment in H.S. Author: Evaluation of Achievement in Jewish Studies, 1988, Studies in Educational Administration, 1989, Achievements in Learning-Evaluation and Measurement, 1990, Reform and Changes in Matriculation Exams, 1991. Mem., chair various coms. The Soc. for the Preservation of Nature, Israel, 1955-95. Grantee The Brit. Coun., London, 1988, 91, 95. Mem. Am. Ednl. Rsch. Assn., Comparative and Internat. Edn. Soc., European Assn. for Rsch. on Learning and Instrn. Avocations: nature preservation, ornithology. Home: 1 Epstein St, 96555 Jerusalem Israel

LEYDEN, MICHAEL JOSEPH, II (LEI JIE MING), communications executive; b. Feb. 26, 1950; m. Ivy Zhong Yu Xu, Nov. 1991. AA in Econs., Wenatchee Valley Coll., 1970; USVI, U. V.I., 1971; BA in Philosophy and Psychology, Ctrl. Wash. U., 1972; MA in Philosophy, Wash. State U., 1974; various mktg. diplomas, U. Hawaii, 1975-89; DBA, Newport U., Utah and Beijing, 1997. Corp. mgr., tng. dir. Colwell Bankers-Davenport Inc., Wenatchee, Wash., 1977-81; v.p. sales and mktg. John's Real Estate and Securities Corp., Bellevue, Wash., 1981-82; pres., founder Aero-Brokers Inc., Honolulu, 1983-86; gen. mgr. Tadashi & Sons Ltd., Truk Islands, Micronesia, 1987; CEO, adminstrv. and fin. mgr. Zorro's Pizza and Italian Restaurants, Honolulu, 1988; gen mgr. Coast Enterprises of Hawaii Inc., Honolulu, 1990; exec. v.p., gen. mgr. Eternity Internat. Trade Devel. Co., Ltd., Honolulu, China-U.S., 1992-93; prof. Sch. Internat. Bus. Nankai U., Tianjin, China, 1994; prof. dept. internat. politics Sch. Internat. Rels. Beijing U., 1995; prof. dept. econ. and mgmt. Qinghua (Tsinghua) U., Beijing, 1996; internat. bus. affairs dir. Michael Trading and Cons. Co. Ltd., Beijing City, 1997; prof. dept. econ. and mgmt. Shanghai U., People's Republic of China, 1998; dean, adminstrn. and devel. Coll. of Marshall Islands, Majuro, Micronesia, 1998; project dir., coord. not for profit orgn., Honolulu, 1999—; spl. asst. to commr. edn. and rsch., statistician No. Marianas Islands Pub. Sch. Sys., 1989. Chmn., mem. Shanghai Am. C. of C. Edn.-Pub. Com., 1997-99; mem. Tianjin and Beijing C. of C., 1995, 96. Mem. Am. Mgmt. Assn. (mem. pres. club 1980, 87, 92), N.Ctrl. Wash. Oriental Rug Soc. (editor Oriental Textile 1977-80), Royal Philatelic Soc. London, Am. Philatelic Soc., China Stamp Soc., N.C. Wash. Writers Guild, Executive Club of Honolulu (sec. 1987), Collectors Club, Lions, Honolulu Downtown Club, St. Augustine's By the Sea. Fax: 808-735-9736. E-mail: michaelleyden@yahoo.com. Home: 3662-A Hilo Pl Honolulu HI 96816-3318 Office: ABI Comm Group Svcs Co PO Box 22124 Honolulu HI 96823-2124

LEYDON, DEBRA JEAN, food products executive; b. Bridgeport, Conn., Mar. 24, 1954; d. Thomas George and Joan Marie (Stewart) L. Materials specialist, receiving mgr. StorageTek Corp., Louisville, Colo., 1979-85; warehouse mgr. McData Corp., Broomfield, Colo., 1985-87; warehouse supr. Melco Industries, Westminster, Colo., 1987-92; master scheduler SPM/Denver, 1993-94; corp. warehouse mgr. Walker Component Group, Denver, 1994-95; materials mgr. DTM Products, Niwot, Colo., 1995-97; ops. mgr. Avalon Imaging, Boulder, 1997-99; pres., CEO Rocky Mountain Land & Sea Food Co., 1999—. Mem. Big Sisters, Denver, 1985-90. Mem. Am. Prodn. Inventory Control Soc. Home: 676 Monroe St Denver CO 80206-4451

LEYDORF, FREDERICK LEROY, lawyer; b. Toledo, June 13, 1930; s. Loftin Herman and Dorothy DeRoyal (Cramer) L.; m. Mary MacKenzie Malcolm, Mar. 28, 1953; children: Robert Malcolm, William Frederick, Katherine Ann, Thomas Richard, Deborah Mary. Student, U. Toledo, 1948-49; B.B.A., U. Mich., 1953; J.D., UCLA, 1958. Bar: Calif. 1959, U.S. Supreme Ct. 1970. Assoc. Hammack & Pugh, L.A., 1959-61; ptnr. Willis, Butler, Scheifly, Leydorf & Grant, L.A., 1961-81, Pepper, Hamilton & Scheetz, L.A., 1981-83, Hufstedler & Kaus, L.A., 1983-95; lectr., cons. Calif. Continuing Edn. of Bar, 1965-92; mem. planning com. Probate and Trust Conf., U. So. Calif., 1984-92. Contbg. author: California Non-Profit Corporations, 1969; contbr. articles to profl. jours. Chmn. pub. adminstr.-pub. guardian adv. commn. Los Angeles County Bd. Suprs., 1972-73; v.p. J.W. and Ida M. Jameson Found., 1995—, bd. dirs., 1967—; bd. dirs. Western Ctr. on Law and Poverty, Inc., 1980-82, L.A. Heart Inst., 1988-90; mem. legal com. Music Ctr. Found., 1980-95; mem. lawyers adv. coun. Constl. Rights Found., 1982-85; mem. devel. adv. bd. U. Mich. Sch. Bus. Adminstrn., 1984-90; mem. adv. bd. UCLA-CEB Estate Planning Inst., 1979-92; Lt. USNR, 1953-55. Mem. Libbey H.S. Hall of Fame (Toledo), 1999. Mem. ABA, L.A. County Bar Assn. (bd. trustees 1973-75), State Bar Calif. (chmn. conf. dels. 1977, Alumnus of Yr. award, conf. of dels. 1983, mem. exec. com. estate planning, trust and probate law sect. 1979-80), L.A. County Bar Found. (pres. 1977-79, bd. dirs. 1975-87), Internat. Acad. Estate and Trust Law (v.p. N.Am. 1978-82), Life Ins. and Trust Coun. L.A. (pres. 1983-84), UCLA Law Alumni Assn. (pres. 1982), L.A. World Affairs Coun. (mem. internat. cir.), Chancery Club (pres. 1991-92), Jonathan Club, Laguna Hills Golf Club, Sunrise Country Club (Rancho Mirage, Calif.), Phi Delta Phi, Phi Delta Theta. Republican. Lutheran. Home: 75 Majorca Dr Rancho Mirage CA 92270-3826

LEYNAUD, GERARD LOUIS, surgeon; b. Aubenas, France, Jan. 10, 1944; s. Paul Joseph Leynaud and Jeanne Marie Roques; m. Francoise Marie Robin, July 1972; children: Andeol, Jourdaine, Mayeul, Olympe. Grad., Marseille Med. Faculty, Digestive Endoscopy, 1991, Hepatic Surgery, 1995. Cert. med. dr. Intern Hosp. Marseille, 1973, chief clinic, asst., 1977, surgeon, 1981; hosp. chief svc. Hosp. Marseille, Aix en Provence, France, 1983. Contbr. articles to profl. jours. Mem. European Soc. for Surg. Oncology, Coll. Francaise de Chirurgie Generale, Viscerale et Digestive. Avocations: history, genealogy, numismatics. Home: 28 Av Marx Dormoy, 03100 Montlucon France Office: Clinique St Francois, 7 rue Pierre Troubat, 03100 Montlucon France

LEZAL, DIMITRIJ, materials scientist, researcher, educator; b. Prague, Czech Republic, June 28, 1933; s. Frantisek and Berta (Janouskova) L.; 1 child, Tomas. Diplng, Tech. Chem. U., Prague, 1958, PhD, 1965; DrSC, Acad. of Scis., Prague, 1989. Rschr. CKD Semicondrs., Prague, 1958-69; scientist Inst. of Radioelectronics Acad. of Sci., Prague, 1969-80, scientist Inst. of Glass and Ceramic Materials, 1980-94, dir. Inst. Glass and Ceramic Materials, 1989-94; scientist Lab. of Inorganics Materials Acad. of Sci. and ICT, Prague, 1994—. Author: Semiconductor Technology, 1965, Non-Crystalline Semiconductors; author monographs; bd. editors Jour. Ceramics-Silikáty; contbr. articles to profl. jours. UNESCO scholar, 1979. Mem. Internat. Soc. for Optical Engring., Nat. Soc. Laser-Optics in Medicine, N.Y. Acad. Scis. Roman Catholic. Avocations: sports, tennis, history. FAX: 2 66009330. E-mail: lezal@llc.cas.cz. Home: Sleska 127, 130 00 Prague 3, Czech Republic Office: AS & ICT Lab Inorganic Materials, 250 68 Řež Czech Republic

LI, ARTHUR KWOK CHEUNG, surgery educator; b. Hong Kong, June 23, 1945; s. Fook Shu and Tse Ha (Woo) L.; m. Diana Chester, July 24, 1974; children: Man Ying, Alexander, Man Chun, Peter. BA, Cambridge U., 1966, MBBChir, 1969, MA, 1970, MD, 1981, DSc (hon.), 1999, DLitt (hon.), 1999. Surg. registrar St. Mary's Hosp., 1973-75; sr. surg. registrar Royal Free Hosp., 1975-77; clin. and rsch. fellow Harvard Med. Sch., 1977-80; cons. surgeon Royal Free Hosp., 1980-82; prof., chmn. dept. Chinese U., Hong Kong, 1982—, dean surgery Faculty of Medicine, 1992-95, vice chancellor, 1996—; bd. dirs. Union Hosp., Bank of East Asia., Glaxo Wellcome, China Mobile plc, Hong Kong; chmn. Regal Hotel Group Plc. Mem. editl. bd. Sci. and Med. Jours. Internat.; contbr. numerous articles to profl. jours. Mem. prep. Com. for Hong Kong spl. adminstrv. region of Nat. People's Congress; mem. Chinese People's Polit. Consultative Conf. Fellow Royal Coll. surgeons; mem. Basic Law Consultative com., Hong Kong Affairs Advisors, Hong Kong Jockey Club, Hong Kong Country Club, Hong Kong Club, Kowloon Club. Office: Chinese U Hong Kong, Vice Chancellor's Office, Shatin NT, Hong Kong

LI, BAO QING, scientific researcher; b. Shanghai, China, Dec. 17, 1942; s. Jin Shui and Cui Qin (Yu) L.; m. Zhen Ying Fang, Apr. 25, 1973; 1 child, Hui. BS, East China U. Sci. and Tech., Shanghai, 1964; PhD, Free U. Brussels, Belgium, 1990. Rsch. fellow Inst. Coal Chemistry, Chinese Acad. Scis., Taiyuan, 1964-80, rsch. asst., 1981-86, assoc. prof., 1992-93, prof., 1994—, chief Coal Chemistry Lab., 1992-98; vis. prof. Strathclyde U., Glasgow, Kyoto U., Kyoto, 1994, Pa. State U., University Park, 1997; guest prof. Shandong U. Sci. and Tech., Jinan, China, 1994-97; chmn. IOC 10th ICCS, Taiyuan, China. Editor: (with Z.Y. Liu) Prospects for Coal Science in the 21st Century, 1999; mem. editl. bd. Fuel Processing Tech., 1996—, Jour. Fuel Chemistry and Tech., 1995—; contbr. articles to profl. jours.; patentee in field. State Coun. grantee, 1993. Mem. Shanxi Chemistry Soc. Avocation: music. Office: Inst Coal Chemistry/CAS, 27 Taoyuan Nan Rd, 030001 Taiyuan, Shanxi 030001, China

LI, CHANGAN, entomologist, educator; b. Xian, China, Mar. 14, 1936; s. Jiliang and Shuzhen Li; m. Wenju Guo, May 1, 1971; 1 child, Hao. BS, NanKai U., TianJin, China, 1960. Prof. dept. biology Shanxi U., Taiyuan, China, 1986—; cons. Assn. Wild Animals Reservation, Shanxi, 1993-97, Juvenile Sci. Popularization Assn., Shanxi, 1990-93. Contbr. articles to profl. jours. Mem. AAAS, Zoological Assn. China (dir. 1994—), Entomological Assn. China (diplomate), Nat. Geog. Soc., N.Y. Acad. Scis. Avocations: reading, music, sports, Beijing opera. Office: Shanxi U Dept Biology, Wucheng Rd No 36, Taiyuan 030006, China

LI, CHENG-CHANG, academic administrator; b. Chang-Hua County, Taiwan, Oct. 2, 1936. BS in Agronomy, Nat. Chung Hsing U., 1960; MS, Internat. Rice Rsch. Inst., U. Philippines, 1966; PhD, U. Calif., Davis, 1975. Rsch. technician Taiwan Provincial Dept. Agr. and Forestry, 1962-64; rsch. scholar Internat. Rice Rsch. Inst./Coll. of Agr., U. Philippines, 1964-66; instr. genetics dept. agronomy Nat. Chung Hsing Univ., Taiwan, 1967-71; assoc. prof. genetics dept. agronomy Nat. Chung Hsing Univ., 1971-76, prof. genetics dept. agronomy, 1976—, chmn., 1985-90, dean Coll. of Agr., 1990-96, pres., 1997—; vis. prof. Tokyo Univ. of Agrl. Contbr. over 123 papers to publs. in field; author: (books) Glossary of Genetics by Chinese, 1984, Rice Genetics and Breeding by English, 1991. Recipient Excellence Rsch. awards Nat. Sci. Coun., Taiwan, 1967—; appointed vice-dir. to lead Chinese Agrl. Tech. Mission in Saudi Arabia, 1982; recipient Excellence Achievement in Agrl. Rsch. award U. Calif., Davis, 1991. Mem. Asian Crop Sci. Assn. (pres. 1995—), Asian Assn. of Agrl. Colls. and Univs. (pres. 1992-96), others. Office: National Chung Hsing Univ, 250 Kuo Kuang Rd, Taichung/Taiwan Republic of China

LI, DAO-LUN, pediatrician, educator; b. Meixian, Guandong, China, Nov. 25, 1936; s. Tse-Nan and Bau-Yin (Hau) L.; m. Ai-Yuan, Oct. 31, 1959; 5 children. MD, Guang Xi Med. Coll., Guang Xi, China, 1959; hon. chmn. of Dong Hu Rsch. Station, Human Body Applying Sci. Applying Hong Shan Dist., Wu Han City, 1989-99. Cert. pediatrician. Physician People's Hosp., Guang Xi, China, 1959-65; physician in charge People's Hosp. of Ping Le County, Guang Xi Zhuang Zhu, 1965-84; physician Tai Shan Hosp., Tai Shan, China, 1985-92, physician, dir., 1994-99; prof. Sun Yat Sen Univ., Guan Dong, China, 1994-99, acupuncturist, Chinese Herbology of the Assn. of the Chinese, New York, 1996-99. Author: The World Traditional Med. (book), 1996, contbr. papers in field,contbr. articles to profl. jours. Recipient, Best Paper on World Traditional Med., 1996, The First Internat. Conf. & Exhibition on Ethnic Med. Cert. of Best Papers, 1997, Thesis Compilation of the First Internat. Traditional Therapy Acad. Conf., Cert. of Excellent Thesis, 1996, Recognition of Disting. Achievements, Popular Works by Centuries World Celebrities, The Volumes: Chinese Sci. and Culture. Mem. Assn. of Chinese Herbalists, 1998—. Inventor: Magnetic Anesthesia, 1978, The First Internat. Conf. Exhibition on Ethnic Med., 1997, The First Internat. TRaditional Therapy, China, 1996, Internat. Symposium on Ped. Pain, 1991, 7th World Congress on Pain (treatment with miniature needle knife), France, 1993.Avocations: medical rsch. for pain, acupuncture, chess. Office: Tai Shan People's Hosp Peds, 20 Gee Yon Rd, 529200 Tai Shan Guan Dong, PRC China

LI, DAVID WAN-CHENG, cell biologist; b. Heng Shan, Peoples Republic of China, Sept. 2, 1960; came to the U.S., 1986; s. Xi-Lin and Xin-Tao (Guo) L.; m. Lilly Liu, June 17, 1986; children: Flora, Jesse. BS, Hunan Normal U., 1982, MS, 1985; PhD, U. Wash., 1992. Adj. prof. biology Hunan Normal U., Chang Sha, People's Republic of China, 1995—; tchg. asst. U. Alta., Edmonton, Can., 1986; tchg. and rsch. asst. U. Wash., Seattle, 1986-92; rsch. scientist Columbia U., N.Y.C., 1992-95, asst. prof. ophthalmology, 1996-98; asst. prof. molecular biology UMDNJ-Sch. Medicine, Stratford, 1998—. Contbr. articles to profl. jours. Exec. pres. June 4th Found., Seattle, 1990-92, bd. dirs., 1989—. Mem. AAAS, Am. Soc. Cell Biology, Am. Soc. Biochemistry and Molecular Biology, Soc. Devel. Biology, Internat. Soc. Eye Rsch., N.Y. Acad. Sci., Assn. for Rsch. in Vision and Ophthalmology. Achievements include devel. of a set of biol. stds. for the hybrid yue carp and its parents; identification of pair of duplicated genes coding for two different isoelectric forms of insect pigment protein and cloning of these genes; discovery of a common cellular mechanism for stress induced non-congenital cataract formation in humans and animals. Home: 1000 W Atlantic Ave Apt 88 Laurel Spgs NJ 08021-3054 Office: U Medicine and Dentistry NJ Dept Molecular Biology 2 Med Ctr Dr Sci Ctr Rm 347 Stratford NJ 08084

LI, DENGFENG, computer engineering educator; b. Bobai, Guangxi, China, Nov. 11, 1965; s. Jixing and Aifang (Liu) L.; m. Wei Fei, June 19, 1992; 1 child, Nuo. BS, Nat. U. Def. Tech., Changsha, China, 1983, MS, 1990; DSc, Dalian (China) U. Tech., 1995. Tchg. asst. Dalian Naval Acad., 1990-92, lectr., 1993-95, assoc. prof., 1996-98, prof., 1999—, dir. dept. mil. ops. rsch., 1999—; dir. China Mil. Ops. Rsch. Inst., 1995—, Evaluation Com. of Acad. Degree, Dalian, 1999—. Author: Fuzzy Many Person Multiobjective Decision Makings and Games, 1999, Differential Games and Applications, 1998 (China Books award 1999). Recipient sci. and tech. advance awards Ministry of Nat. Edn. China, 1998, 99. Avocations: reading novels, appreciating music, playing volleyball. Home and Office: Dalian Naval Acad, No 667 Jiefang Rd, Dalian 116018, China

LI, DEXIN, physicist; b. Xiuyan, Liaoning, China, Oct. 31, 1960; s. Hongyan and Shumei Li; m. Peiheng Yuan, Apr. 8, 1986; 1 child, Yuan. BS, Jilin U., Changchun, China, 1982; M Engring., Northeast U., Shenyang, China, 1985; MS, Tohoku U., Sendai, Japan, 1992, DSc, 1995. Asst. Northeast U., Shenyang, 1982-88, lectr., 1988-90; postdoctoral fellow Tohoku U., Sendai, 1995-96, asst., 1996—. Contbr. articles to profl. jours. Mem. Phys. Soc. Japan. Avocation: table tennis. Home: Onuki 843, Tohoku U Hostel 2-1-1, Oarai 311-1311, Japan Office: Tohoku U Inst Material Rsch, Narida 2145-2, Narida 2145-2, Oarai 311-1313, Japan

LI, DING, plasma physicist, researcher, educator; b. Tongcheng, Anhui, China, Feb. 9, 1957; s. Bicai Li and Youyun Pan; m. Yinqiu Song, Aug. 16, 1985; 1 child, Xinyi. BS, U. Sci. and Tech. China, Hefei, 1982, MS, 1984; PhD, Chinese Acad. Scis., Hefei, 1988. Asst. prof. U. Sci. and Tech. China, 1984-85; internat. sci. cooperation fellow Commn. European Cmtys., Rsch. Ctr. Juelich, Germany, 1989-92; rsch. fellow Inst. Plasma Physics, Chinese Acad. Scis., Hefei, 1992, assoc. prof., 1992-96, prof., 1996-97, dep. head

physics experiment divsn., 1994-97; guest scientist Rsch. Ctr. Juelich, 1996-97; prof. U. Sci. and Tech. China, Hefei, 1997—, head dept. modern physics, 1998—, asst. pres., 2000—. Contbr. articles to profl. jours. Grantee Nat. Sci. Fund for Disting. Young Scholars, 1995. Mem. German Phys. Soc., European Phys. Soc., Chinese Physics Soc., Am. Physics Soc. Avocations: calligraphy, collecting coins and stamps. Office: U Sci and Tech China Dept, Modern Physics PO Box 4, Hefei 230027, China

LI, EDDIE HERBERT, applied physicist, educator, engineer; b. Hong Kong, Feb. 6, 1957; s. Kwok-Keung Lee and Julia Yuk-Ying (Yeung) L.; m. Elaine Yuemin Pak, Sept. 1998; children, Victoria G., Elizabeth C. BS, Wash. State Coll., 1979; MS, Wasington U., St. Louis, 1981; Diploma BTM, Profl. Bus. and Tech. Mgmt., 1986; MPhil, U. Hong Kong, 1990; PhD, U. Surrey, Eng., 1992. Chartered engr., chartered physicist, chartered mathematician. Head Pi Mu Epsilon Tutoring Ctr., Washington, 1978-81; sr. instr. Matteo Ricci Coll., Hong Kong, 1981-82; engr., sci. officer K.K. Co., Hong Kong, 1981-82; dir. Assn. for Engring. and Med. Svcs., 1985-91, 96—, chmn., 1987-90; rschr. Hong Kong Poly., 1983; sr. instr. Hong Kong Bapt. Coll., 1984-88; civil svc. examiner Govt. of Hong Kong, 1984-90; cons. K.K. Co., Hong Kong, 1985-87; mng. ptnr. HAL Computer Cons., Hong Kong, 1987-88; lectr. applied math. City. U. Hong Kong, 1988-89; vis. rsch. faculty dept. applied sci. City U. Hong Kong, 1990-96; OPTO group leader elec. and electronic engring. U. Hong Kong, 1994—; life dep. gov. Am. Biog. Inst. Rsch. Assn., 1989; hon. life advisor Internat. Biog. Ctr. Adv. Coun., U.K., 1989; vis. sr. fellow U. Surrey, U.K., 1998-2001. Author: Differential Equations, 1980, Non-linear Optics, 1999; editor Internat. Jour. Otptoelectronics, 1994—; assoc. editor, IEEE Jour. Quantum Elecs.; contbr. articles to profl. jours. Fellow Royal Statis. Soc., Inst. Mgmt. Specialists, Brit. Soc. Commerce, Soc. Comml. Tchrs., Inst. Math. and Its Applications, Inst. of Physics; mem. AIAA, SPIE (chair Hong Kong chpt. 1998—), IEEE (sr.; J. Langham Thompson premium prize 1992), Internat. Assn. Math. Physics, Am. Math. Soc., Am. Phys. Soc., Raffles, Y's Men's Club Hong Kong. Office: U Hong Kong Dept Elec Engr, Pokfulam Rd, Hong Kong China

LI, FENGKUI, research scientist; b. Handan City, Hebei, China, Apr. 20, 1968; s. Jianxin and Yunzhi Li; m. Lanying Qi, Oct. 18, 1994. BS, Beijing U. of Chem. Tech., 1990; MS, Tianjin U., China, 1993; PhD, Chinese Acad. Scis., 1996. Cert. engring. Rsch. assoc. Pohang (Korea) U. Sci. and Tech., 1996-97, Chinese Acad. Scis., Beijing, 1997-98, Iowa State U., Ames, 1998—. Recipient several outstanding rsch. and paper awards; grantee Iowa Soybean Promotion Bd., 1999. Mem. Am. Chemical Asoc., Internat. Plastic Soc., Sigma Xi. E-mail: fkli@iastate.edu. Home: 209 S Oak Ave Apt 129 Ames IA 50010-6950 Office: Iowa State U Chemistry Dept Ames IA 50011-0001

LI, FULDA FULDIEN, lawyer, educator, arbitrator; b. Taipei, Taiwan, Jan. 4, 1952; s. Kuang Ming and Yung Fang (Kao) L.; m. Pamela Fann, Oct. 26, 1979; children: Gi-hong, Gi-kuen. LLB, Chinese Culture U., Taipei, 1974, PhD in Law, 1984; LLM, Soochow U., Taipei, 1977. Editor Taiwan Comml. Press, Taipei, 1974-75; vis. scholar Yale U. Law Sch., New Haven, 1984-85; prof. law Chinese Culture U., Taipei, 1978-92; mng. ptnr. Cha & Pan, Taipei, 1992-94; mng.ptnr. Li & Ptnrs., Taipei, 1995—; counselor, mem. Ministry of Transp. and Comm., Taipei, 1991-97; counselor, lectr. China External Trade Devel. Coun., Taiwan, 1990—; arbitrator, mem. Comml. Arbitration Assn., Taipei, 1989—; counselor, dir. Ministry of Edn., Taipei, 1989—; dir. Hwa Kang Legal Found., Taipei, 1988; founder, pres. Young Patriot Found., Taipei, 1987; dean, founder law dept. Sch. Law, Shin Hsin U., 1995—; mem. Com. Appeal Affairs, Exec., Yuan, 1999—. Author: Legal Problems Arising from Container Transportation, 1981; Study on the Hamburg Rules, 1978, 84, Law Change and Social Change, 1984, Joint Venture Regulations, PRC, 1989, Taiwanese Investment in Mainland China, 1991, Economic Contract Law, PRC, 1993; author, editor: Introduction to Law, 1987, Legal Knowledge for Teenagers, 1991, Joint Venture Regulations and Licensing Operations, 1994, Introduction to Jurisprudence, 1995, Introduction to IPR, 1999. Mem. ctrl. com. KMT, Taipei, 1993. Named Disting. alumnus Chinese Culture U., 1979. Mem. Am. C. of C. in Taipei, Am. Internat. Law Soc., China Comparative Law Soc. (com. head 1984), Bar Assn. Taipei, Pvt. Internat. Law Soc., ROC Comml. Arbitration Assn., Phi Tau Phi. Avocation: reading. E-mail: advocate@law.com.tw. Office: Li & Ptnrs 7F-5 50 Sec 1, Sing Sheng S Rd, Taipei 100, Taiwan

LI, GENXI, bioelectrochemist; b. Jining, Shangdong, China, Feb. 9, 1965; s. Benheng and Guixiang (Feng) L.; m. Lingjun He, Dec. 31, 1991. BA in Polymer Chem., Nanjing (China) U., 1988, MA in Analytic Chem., 1991, PhD in Analytic Chem. with honors, 1994. Instr. Nanjing U., 1994-96, assoc. prof., 1996-2000, prof., 2000—, chair dept. biochemistry, 2000—; vis. scholar Munich (Germany) U., 1998, Tohoku U., Japan, 1999, Harvard U., 2000. Contbr. articles to profl. jours. Fellow Chinese Chem. Soc., Chinese Biochem. Soc. Avocation: music. E-mail: genxili@nju.edu.cn. Home: 8 Danfeng St, 210008 Nanjing China Office: Nanjing Univ Dept Biochem, 22 Hankou Rd, 210093 Nanjing China

LI, GUANGZE, pharmacologist, researcher; b. Chengdu, Sichuan, China, May 17, 1950; came to the U.S., 1994; s. Tingyuan Li and Yizhong Tang; m. Yin Liu, July 28, 1982; 1 child, Yang. BS, Harbin (China) Med. U., 1978, MD, 1987; PhD, Shanghai Second Med. U., 1992. Asst. prof. Harbin Med. U., 1978-89, assoc. prof., 1989-93, vice chair dept., 1993; rschr., vis. scholar Wright State U., Dayton, Ohio, 1994—. Author: Textbook of Pharmacology, 1987, 94, Taurine, 1999; mem. editl. bd. Exptl. Pharmacology, 1993-94. Recipient 2nd prize of sci. Progress Sci. and Tech. Award Jury, Shanghai, 1993, Heilongjian, China, 1994, first prize of sci. Progress Edn. Com., Heilongjiang, 1994. Mem. AAAS, Soc. Pharmacology China (Best Sci. Paper award 1987), Soc. Physiology China, Soc. for Neurosci., N.Y. Acad. Sci. Avocations: volleyball, pingpong, soccer, basketball, chess. E-mail: guangze.li@wright.edu. Office: Wright State U Emergency Med Dept 3525 Suthern Blvd Kettering OH 45429

LI, GUOHUA, epidemiologist, educator; b. Hubei, Mianyang, China, Jan. 11, 1963; s. Juxian Li and Fulan Xie; m. Xiaoying Ma, Dec. 15, 1987; children: Roland, Susan. MD, Beijing Med. U., 1984; MPH, Tongji Med. U., Wuhan, China, 1987; PhD, Johns Hopkins U., 1993. Lectr. Tongji Med. U., Wuhan, 1987-89; rsch. assoc. Johns Hopkins U. Sch. Hygiene and Pub. Health, Balt., 1992-95; asst. prof. Johns Hopkins U. Sch. Medicine, Balt., 1995-97, assoc. prof., 1997—; mem. adj. faculty Johns Hopkins U. Sch. Hygiene and Pub. Health, 1995—. Co-author: Injury Fact Book, 2d edit., 1992; contbr. articles to profl. jours. Trustee Howard County Chinese Sch., Columbia, Md., 1998—. Recipient FIRST award Nat. Inst. on Alcohol Abuse and Alcoholism, 1995, Roche Epidemiology prize, 1999; grantee Nat. Inst. on Aging, NIH, 1997—, Nat. Inst. on Alcohol Abuse and Alcoholism, 1999—, Alcoholic Beverage Med. Rsch. Found., 1997-99, Ins. Inst. for Hwy. Safety, 1999—. Mem. Am. Pub. Health Assn., Aerospace Med. Assn., Soc. Acad. Emergency Medicine, Soc. Epidemiologic Rsch. Avocations: reading, writing, walking, team sports. Home: 4742 Leyden Way Ellicott City MD 21042-5989 Office: Johns Hopkins U 600 N Wolfe St Baltimore MD 21287-0005

LI, GUOQIANG, engineering educator, researcher; b. Rongcheng, China, Apr. 1, 1963; came to U.S., 1997; s. Zhensheng and Guiying Li; m. Deying Zhao, Aug. 10, 1989. BS, Hebei U. Tech., China, 1985; MS, Beijing Poly. U., China, 1988; PhD, S.E. U., China, 1997. Cert. supervising engr. for civil engring., China. Lectr. Hebei U. Tech., Tianjin, China, 1988-91; asst. prof. Hebei U. Tech., 1991-95, assoc. prof., 1996-97; rsch. asst. prof. La. State U., Baton Rouge, 2000—; supervising engr. Hebei Dept. Transp., Shijiazhuang, 1992-93;. Co-author: (book) Expressway Management, 1997; contbr. articles to profl. jours. Fellow Soc. Chinese Transp. Profls. in the U.S., Tianjin Soc. Civil Engrs. (1st prize paper 1987); mem. ASME, Soc. Plastics Engrs. Avocations: sports, classical music, pop music, climbing, cooking. E-mail: lguoqi1@lsu.edu. Office: Composite Lab Dept Mech Engring La State U Baton Rouge LA 70803-0001

LI, GUOSONG, mechanical engineering educator; b. Gaoyou, Jiangsu, China, May 9, 1965; s. Jiqing and Guixiang (Xu) L.; m. Aibin Liu, Mar. 24, 1993. BSc, Jiangsu Inst. Tech., Zhenjiang, China, 1985; MSc, Jiao Tong U., Shanghai, 1988, D Engring., 1991. Asst. prof. Jiao Tong U., Shanghai, 1991-92, assoc. prof. mech. engring., 1993—, dep. dir. mfg. engring. divsn. dept. mech. engring., 1994—; mem. youth commn. Prodn. Engring. Instn., 1992—. Contbr. articles to profl. jours. Recipient Grade 2-prize for sci. and tech. progress The State Commn. of Edn. of People's Republic of China, Shanghai, 1993. Mem. AIAA, ASME, Soc. Mfg. Engrs., Chinese Mech. Engring. Soc. Avocations: classical music, Chinese chess, philosophy, fishing. Home: 24248 Woodham Rd Novi MI 48374 Office: Hourglass Solutions Inc Ste 424 17199 N Laurel Park Dr Livonia MI 48152

LI, HONG-JUN, chemistry researcher; b. Jing Jiang, Jiang Su, China, Mar. 7, 1964; arrived in Japan, 1995; s. Pin-Zhen Li and Mei-Fang Tiao; m. Hiroko Furuta Ri. BS, Nanjing (China) U., 1986, MS, 1989; PhD, Tokyo U., 1998. Cert. chem. engring. Chem. rschr. Nanjing U., 1989-95; with Chugai Technos Co., Ltd., 1999—. Home: 196-2-403 Minoridai, Matsudoshi Chiba 270-2231, Japan Office: Tokyo Univ, 4-6-1 Komaba Meguro-ku, Tokyo 153-0041, Japan

LI, HONGMIN, crystallographer, research scientist; b. Hegang, China, Nov. 19, 1968; came to U.S., 1995; s. Yan and Shoulan L.; m. Zhong Li, July 18, 1994; children: Tiarhao, Tian Ling. BSc, Peking U., Beijing, 1990; MSc, Inst. Biophysics, Beijing, 1993, PhD, 1995. Rsch. scientist U. Md. Biotech. Inst., Rockville, 1995-2000; rsch. scientist Wadsworth Ctr., N.Y. State Dept. Health, Albany, 2000—. Contbr. articles to profl. jours.; book reviewer in field. Recipient Pres. award Chinese Acad. Scis., Beijing, 1995. Mem. AAAS, Am. Crystallography Assn. Avocations: basketball, soccer, fishing, table tennis. E-mail: lih@wadsworth.org. Office: Ctr for Advanced Rsch Biotech 9600 Gudelsky Dr Rockville MD 20850 Office: Wadsworth Ctr NY Dept Health Empire State Plz PO Box 509 Albany NY 12201-0509

LI, HONG-NAN, civil engineering educator; b. Shenyang, China, Aug. 29, 1957; m. Suyan Wang; children: Li, Chen. BS, Shenyang Archl. Inst., China, 1982; MS, Inst. Engring. Mechs., Harbin, China, 1987, PhD, 1990. Postdoctoral asst. Dalian U. Technology, China, 1990-92; rsch. assoc. Va. Tech. U., Blacksburg, 1992-94; prof., head dept. Shenyang Archl. & Civil Engring. Inst., 1994—. Author: Fundamentals of Structures Resistant to Earthquake, 1996, Theory and Design of Structures to Multiple Seismic Input, 1998; author, co-editor: Design of High Rise Building Structures, 1998; contbr. articles to profl. jours. Fellow Archl. Soc. China, Soc. Civil Engring. China. Avocations: drawing, reading, hiking, singing. Office: Shenyang Archl Inst, 17 E Wenhua Rd, 110015 Shenyang China

LI, JACKIE SAU-MAN, education consultant; b. Hong Kong, Oct. 8, 1964; d. Kim-Ming and Yuk-Bing (Ng) L.; m. Man-Lung Wong, Oct. 10, 1983; children: Yat Long, Yat Chun, Yat Hei. BA, Bard Coll., 1986; MA in Criminal Justice, SUNY, 1987, MS in Ednl. Psychology, 1988, MS in Ednl. Adminstrn., 1990. Asst. lectr. City U. Hong Kong, 1992-96; mgr. human resources Waly Interior Products Ltd., Hong Kong, 1996-97; edn. cons. Kinwell Group Ltd., Hong Kong, 1997—. Mem. APA, Hong Kong Psychol. Soc., British Psychol. Soc., Hong Kong Psychotherapy Soc., Hong Kong Soc. Child Protection, Ctr. Child Devel., Internat. Assn. Play Therapy. Avocations: reading, swimming. Office: 1/F 2 Heung Yip Rd, Wong Chuk Hong Hong Kong

LI, JING RONG, neurosurgeon, educator, consultant; b. Shang Hang, Fujian, China, Sept. 11, 1929; s. Kok Tai Li and Yu Chun Hwang; m. Xuan Mei Chen, Feb. 10, 1959 (dec. Feb. 1985); children: Gang, Qiang, Qiong Hui, Chen Peng; m. Zhi Ying Chen, Nov. 8, 1991. BS, Beijing Med. U., 1956. Neurologist Hsiang Ya Hosp. of Hunan Med. U., Changsha, China, 1956-60, neurosurgeon, 1961-86; neurosurgeon Rsch. Inst. Neuroscis., Guangzhou (China) Med. Coll., 1986—, prof., 1988—, vice dir., 1989-95; cons. Hsiang-Qian Ry. Campaign Hdqs. Hosp., Zhijiang, China, 1971-74; editor, supr. neurology and neurosurgery Fgn. Med. Scis., Changsha, 1978-83, cons. editor, 1986. Cons. editor Jour. Guangzhou Med. Coll., 1988-98, Chinese Jour. ENT and Skull Base Surgery, 1995; contbr. articles to med. jours., including Chinese Med. Jour. Fellow Guangzhou Neurosurg. Assn.; mem. Chinese Med. Assn. in Guangdon, Guangzhou Overseas Chinese Assn. (vice chmn. 1988—), Malaysia Ipoh Yok Choy and Perak Girl's Sch. Alumni Assn. (chmn. Guangzhou 1993—). Avocations: travel, exercise, chess, photography, reading. Office: Guangzhou Med Coll Neurosci, 250 Chang Gang Don Rd, Guangdon Guangzhou 510260, China

LI, JINGHAI, science educator; b. Jingle, Shanxi, China, Oct. 25, 1956; s. Maocai Li and Chun Lan Gao; m. Lan Lu, Apr. 22, 1986; 1 child, Yue. Bachelor's degree, Harbin Inst. Tech., 1982, Master's degree, 1984; PhD, Chinese Acad. Scis., Beijing, 1987. Rsch. fellow Chinese Acad. Coal Scis., Beijing, 1984-85; rsch. assoc. CCNY, N.Y.C., 1987-88, Swiss Fed. Inst. Tech., Zurich, 1988-90; assoc. prof. Inst. Chem. Metallurgy, Beijing, 1990-92, prof., 1992—, dep. dir., 1995—. Author: Particle-Fluid Two-Phase Flow, 1994 (Nat. Nature Sci. award 1995); patentee in field; contbr. articles to profl. jours. Recipient Nature Sci. prize 1st class Academia Sinica, 1989, 93, Nat. Nature Sci. prize 2d class Com. of Sci. and Tech. of China, 1989, Chinese Young Scientist 3d class prize, 1996, Disting. Young Scholar prize, Hong Kong Qiushi Sci. & Tech. Found., 1996; named Excellent Scientific Rschr. China, 1997. Mem. Chinese Acad. of Sci. Office: Inst of Chem Metallurgy, PO Box 353, 100080 Beijing China

LI, KA-SHING, property developer; b. 1928; m. Chong Yuet-ming; 2 children. LLD (hon.), U. Hong Kong, 1986, U. Calgary, Can., 1989; D Degree (hon.), Beijing U., 1992; D Social Sci. (hon.), Hong Kong U. Sci. and Tech., 1995. Salesman toy mfg. co., 1942-50; founder Cheung Kong Plastics Factory, 1950; chmn. Cheung Kong (Holdings) Ltd., Hong Kong, 1972—, Hutchison Whampoa Ltd., Hong Kong, 1979—; mem. preliminary working com. of preparatory ocm. Hong Kong Spl. Adminstrv. Region, 1993, mem. preparatory com. to oversee handover of Hong Kong in 1997, 1995; mem. Drafting Com. for Basic Law; owner, shareholder numerous cos. Local adviser China, 1992—. Named Hon. Citizen, Cities of Shantou, Guangzhou, Shenzhen, Nanhai, Foshan, Jiangmen, and Chaozhou; recipient Businessman of Yr. award DHL/SCMP, 1990, Comdr. of Order of Brit. Empire, Comdr. of Order of Crown, Belgium. Mem. Royal Hong Kong Jockey Club. Avocations: golf, boating. Office: Hutchison Whampoa Ltd, 10 Harcourt Rd 22nd Fl, Hong Kong China

LI, KE'AN, chemistry educator; b. Yancheng, Jiangsu, China, Jan. 22, 1945; s. Rubao and Hehua (Yang) L.; m. Xiaoqing Duan, May 8, 1971; 1 child, Xueping. BS, Peking (China) U., 1970. Asst. dept. chemistry Peking U., Beijing, 1970-83, lectr., 1983-90, assoc. prof., 1990-95, prof. chemistry, 1995—, dean ednl. adminstrn. divsn., 1996—; cons. CPPX, Shandong, China, 1983—. Author: Concised Handbook of Analytical Chemistry, 1981, Numerical Methods in Analytical Chemistry, 1991, Basic Experiments of Analytical Chemistry, 1995, Olimpic Chemistry, 1995; editor Chemistry jour., 1994—, Analytical Sci. Acta, 1998—. Recipient Tchg. award Edn. Min., Beijing, 1990-96, Peking U., 1991—; Rsch. Fund grantee Natural Sci. Found. Com., Beijing, 1993—. Mem. Chemistry Soc. China. Avocations: walking, swimming, climbing, reading. Home: Bldg 319, Yenbei Yuan Apt 109, Beijing 100091, People's Republic of China Office: Peking Univ, Coll Chemistry/Molec Eng, Beijing 100871, People's Republic of China

LI, KEQIN, computer scientist, educator; b. Shanghai, China, May 26, 1963; s. Guoxing and Zongfen (Gu) L.; m. Ling Gao, May 21, 1987; children: Andrew, Charlotte, Christina. BS in Computer Sci., Tsinghua U., 1985; PhD in Computer Sci., U. Houston, 1990. Instr. U. Houston, 1987-88, rsch. asst., 1988-90; asst. prof. SUNY, New Paltz, 1990-96, assoc. prof., 1996-99, prof., 1999—. Assoc. editor-in-chief Internat. Assn. of Sci. and Tech. for Devel. jour., 1996-99; co-editor: Parallel Computing Using Optical Interconnections, 1998; co-editor conf. procs.; contbr. numerous articles to profl. jours. Recipient Best Paper award Internat. Conf. on Parallel and Distributed Processing Techniques and Applications, 1996, 49th Nat. Aerospace and Electronics Conf., 1997, Internat. Parallel and Distributed Processing Symposium, 2000. Mem. IEEE (sr.), IEEE Computer Soc., Assn. of Computing Machinery, Soc. for Indsl. and Applied Math., Internat. Assn. of Sci. and Tech. for Devel. Achievements include pioneered research on processor allocation and job scheduling in partitionable mesh connected systems which has inspired substantial subsequent research by numerous researchers and has created a very active and productive resarch area in parallel computing; co-inventor linear array with a reconfigurable pipelined bus system computing model which is now more and more popular in parallel computing using optical interconnections. Home: 21 Robin Rd Poughkeepsie NY 12601-5619 Office: SUNY 75 S Manheim Blvd New Paltz NY 12561-2499

LI, KUAN-TE KEVIN, business educator, restaurateur, consultant; b. Taipei, Taiwan, Dec. 12, 1968; came to U.S., 1990; s. Michael and Mei Lee. MA in Orgnl. Change, Hawaii Pacific U., 1999, MA in Human Resources, 1999, MBA, 1999. Founder, owner Ko Chia Hsiang Restaurant, Taipei, 1988—; exec. asst. Empire Constrn. Ltd., Taipei, 1991-95; instr. Kapi'olani C.C., Honolulu, 1999—; owner Li-Empire Internat., Honolulu, 1999—; mem. TIM banquet planning com., Hawaii Pacific U., Honolulu, 1998-99. Mem. Rep. Nat. com., Hawaii, 1995-98. Mem. Am. Mgmt. Assn., Am. Mktg. Assn., Urban Land Inst. Avocations: reading, exercise, music, travel. E-mail: Li-Empire@hotmail.com. Office: Li-Empire Internat Ltd 1255 Nuuanu Ave Apt 2104 Honolulu HI 96817-4010

LI, KUO-TSENG, chemical engineer, educator; b. Chia-Yi, Taiwan, Sept. 23, 1953; s. Shiang and Tang Li; m. Cheng-Chin Lin, June 2, 1989; children: Yen Der, Yen Hsing. BS, Tunghai U., 1976; MS, SUNY Buffalo, 1981; PhD, Carnegie-Mellon U., 1985. Asst. prof. U. Detroit, 1985-90; mgr. Catalyst Rsch. Ctr., Tou-Fen, Taiwan, 1990-93; assoc. prof. Tunghai U., Taichung, Taiwan, 1993-96, prof., 1996—; cons. Catalyst Rsch. Ctr., Tou-Fen, 1993-94; vis scholar Northwestern U., 1998-99. Contbr. articles to profl. jours.; holder 12 patents. Recipient Rsch. award Nat. Sci. Coun., 1996-99. Mem. Chinese Inst. Chem. Engrs., Am. Chem. Soc. Avocations: tennis, basketball. Office: Dept Chem Engring, Tunghai Univ, Taichung 40704, Taiwan

LI, KWOK YING ROWLAND, company executive; b. Hong Kong, Nov. 20, 1956. BA, Ctrl. Pacific Coll., Australia, 1986; MBA, Newport U., 1990. Key accounts mgr. R.J. reynolds Tobacco Co., 1989-91; sales mgr. Tai Koo Sugar, 1991-94; mktg. dir. Reebok China, 1994-95; bus. mgr. Philips (HK) Ltd., 1995-97; gen. mgr. Supra (HK) Ltd., 1997—; gen. mgr., mktg. and sales dir. Guangmei Foods Co. Ltd., Guangzhou, China, 1997—. Mem. Chartered Inst. Mktg., Inst. Mgmt., Profl. Bus. and Tech. Mgmt. Inst., Australian Mktg. Inst.

LI, LEI, mathematics and computer science educator; b. Yan Cheng, Jiangsu, China, May 1, 1961; parents Guo Ming Li and Feng Xian Qian; m. Jie Hu, Dec. 26, 1986; 1 child, Jiayi Li. MS, Xi'an (China) Jiaotong U., 1986, DSc, 1989; D of Engring., Tohoku U., Sendai, Japan, 1994. Tchr. Haitong H.S., Yancheng, China, 1980-83; asst. prof. Xi'an Jiaotong U., 1985-87, lectr., 1987-89; postdoctoral fellow Hirosaki (Japan) U., 1989-90, asst. prof., 1990-92; assoc. prof. Aomori (Japan) U., 1992-97, Yamaguchi (Japan) U., 1997—; adj. prof. Beijing Inst. Applied Physics and Computational Maths., 1995-98; rsch. vis. prof. SUNY, Stony Brook, 1999-2000; mem. program com. Japan-China Symposium: Scies. and Techs. in 21st Century, U. Tokyo, 1999; chair exec. com. 3d Western Japan Symposium on Indsl. and Applied Maths., Yamaguchi, Japan, 1999; dir. Chinese Acad. Sci. and Engring. in Japan, Tokyo, 1997—; conf. chair First Intern Conf. Info., Fukuoka, Japan, 2000. Co-author: (books) Queuing Theory and Design of Computer Systems, 1995, Fast Algorithms and Parallel Signal Processing, 1999, 500 Keywords in Modern Sciences, 1999; editor: Jour. Advanced Sci. and Tech., 1997—; editor-in-chief: INFORMATION: An International Interdisciplinary Jour., 1997—. Recipient Computer Software Papers Internat. prize Hitachi To. Ltd., 1990; Sasakawa Sci. Rsch. Found. grantee Japan Sci. Soc., 1990-91, sci. rsch. grantee Japan Ministry of Edn., 1995, 98-00. Mem. IEEE Computer Soc., Soc. for Indsl. and Applied Maths., Info. Processing Soc. Japan, Japan Soc. for Indsl. and Applied Maths. Avocations: fishing, swimming, taking trips, reading. Fax: 81 839 335768. E-mail: lilei@sci.yamaguchi-u.ac.jp. Office: Yamaguchi U Faculty of Sci, Yoshida 1677-1, Yamaguchi 753-8512, Japan

LI, MAOQIANG, material scientist; b. Shanghai, China, July 2, 1942; s. Changren Li and Jiaji Zhu; m. Ping Wu, May 30, 1976. BS, Beijing Inst. Bldg. Industry, 1965; PhD, Pa. State U., 1984. From technician to engr. Rsch. Inst. Bldg. Materials, Beijing, 1965-81; sr. engr. China Bldg. Materials Acad., Beijing, 1984-88; vis. scholar Pa. State U., 1989-90; prof., prin. engr. China Bldg. Materials Acad., Beijing, 1990—. Mem. IEEE, Chinese Ceramic Soc., Am. Ceramic Soc. Home: Hepingli 7Qu 7-1-301, 100013 Beijing China Office: China Bldg Materials Acad, West Bldg Guanzhuang, 100024 Beijing China

LI, MENG RU, mathematics educator; b. Kai Feng, Henan, China, Feb. 20, 1944; s. Xie Shan Li and Wen Ying Han; m. Qin Chun Shi, Jan. 11, 1969; children: Shi Rui, Li Zhen. MS, Zhengzhou (China) U., 1981. Lectr. Zhengzhou U., 1983-86, assoc. prof., 1987-93, prof., 1994—; mem. coun. higher math. workship, China, 1992—; reviewer math. revs., U.S., 1989—. Author: Calculus, 1994; contbr. articles to profl. jours. Recipient Educator of Excellence award Zhengzhou City Trade City, 1994, Achievements in Tchg. Govt. of Henan Province, 1996. Mem. Am. Math. Soc., Henan Math. Soc. Office: Dept Math Zheng U, 75 Da Xue Rd, Zhengzhou Henan 450052, China

LI, MENGFENG, molecular biologist, virologist, educator; b. Guiyang, Guizhou, China, Oct. 4, 1964; came to U.S., 1993; s. Qiaoxin Li and Youchun Zhu; m. Qing Zeng, Feb. 20, 1992; 1 child, Cindy. MD, Sun Yat-Sen U. Med. Sci., 1986, PhD, 1991. Investigator Nat. Lab. Molecular Virology and Genetic Engring., Beijing, 1991-93; vis. rsch. investigator Cancer Inst. U. Pitts., 1993-97, asst. prof., 1997—. Author: Advances in Molecular Virology, E-C Dictionary of Molecular Biology and Biotechnology, Medical Molecular Virology and Application, Encyclopedia of Medical Diagnosis, Progress in Techniques of Medical Molecular Microbiology, Rsch. Trends in Immunology; contbr. articles to profl. jours. Mem. Am. Assn. Cancer Rsch., Soc. Natural Immunity. Achievements include discovering new members of human interferon family and making them applicable in medicine; discovering oncogenic effects of a retrovirus in melnocytes; designing and constructing encaphaline directed tumor-targeting interferon molecules; anti-angiogenic therapy of cancer. Office: Univ Pitts Cancer Inst 200 Lothrop St # W907 Bst Pittsburgh PA 15213-2546

LI, MI, physics educators, engineer; b. Dingxiang, Shanxi, China, May 4, 1937; s. Keda and Yinchan Hu L.; m. Dongyun Jiang, Nov. 17, 1969; children: Yichuan, Yishan. BS, Peking U., Beijing, 1960. Cert. engr. Asst. prof. Beijing Inst. Maching Bldg., 1960-70; engr. to sr. engr. Beijing Rsch. Inst. of Automation for Machine Bldg. Industry, 1974-90; sr. engr., prof. Beijing U. Sci. and Tech.; physicist Microtron Designing Group, Beijing, 1976-78, Project 87, Beijing, 1978. Contbr. articles to profl. jours. Mem. The Chinese Phys. Soc., Chinese Materials Rsch. Soc. Office: Beijing U Sci/Tech Dept Phy, No 30 Xueyuan Rd, Beijing 100083, China

LI, MING-FU, physicist, educator, electrical engineer; b. Shanghai, China, Sept. 26, 1937; s. Zu-Yi and Tong-Yun (Guan) L.; m. Xing-Zhen Qian, Apr. 16, 1969; children: Li, Hao-Hua. BS, Fudan U., Shanghai, China, 1960. Assoc. prof. to prof. Grad. Sch. Chinese Acad. Scis., Beijing, China, 1978-90, Nat. U. Singapore, 1991—; adj. prof. Fudan U., Shanghai, 1989-91, Inst. Semiconductors Chinese Acad. Scis., Beijing, 1990-92, Chinese U. Sci. and Tech., Hefei, 1989-92; divsn. head micro-electronics Nat. U. Singapore, 1997—; vis. scholar Case Western-Reserve U., Cleveland, 1979, U. Ill., Urbana, 1979-81; vis. scientist U. Calif. Berkeley, 1986-87, 90-91. Author: (books) Modern Semiconductor Quantum Physics, 1994, Semiconductor Physics, 1991. Contbr. to over 100 articles to profl. jours. Recipient Disting. Achievement award, Chines Acad. Scis. Mem. IEEE (sr.), Inst. of Engrs. Singapore. Avocations: swimming, music, literature, painting. Office: Dept Electrical Engring, Nat Univ Singapore, 119260 Singapore Singapore

LI, MINGQI, plant physiologist; b. Victoria, Can., Apr. 20, 1920; arrived in China, 1925; s. Dore Li and Yizhen Chen; m. Pengru Xu, Oct. 25, 1952 (dec. July 1986); children: Naifu, Naiyi. BS, Lingnan U., Guangzhou, China, 1950. Asst. Lingnan U., Guangzhou, 1951-52; asst. S. China Agrl. Coll., Guangzhou, 1953-56, instr., 1956-78, prof., 1978—; cons. S. China Botanical Inst., Chinese Acad. Sci., Guangzhou, 1983-85, mem. acad. com., 1984-87. Author: Fruit Physiology, 1989 (Advancement Sci. tech. award Bur. Higher Edn. 1991); assoc. editor: Basic Biochemistry, 1985 (Excellent Textbook award Min. Agr. China 1992); contbr. over 80 articles to profl. jours. Recipient Excellent Tchg. award Bur. Higher Edn. Guangdong Province, 1982, Best Tchr. award Min. Agr. Forestry and Fishery, 1983-84, Nat. Edn. Commn. China, 1989, others. Mem. AAAS (internat.), N.Y. Acad. Sci., Chinese Soc. Plant Physiologists (mem. coun. 1983-88), Chinese Soc. Biochemistry Molecular Biology, Chines Soc. Botany. Avocations: reading,

music, gardening. Office: Coll Biol Tech, S China Agrl U Wushan, Guangzhou 510642, China

LI, OGG, educator; b. Seoul, Korea, Nov. 8, 1928; arrived in France, 1956; s. Yin and Kyung Hi (Koh) L.; m. Yim Soun Kim, Aug. 3, 1958; children: Dominique, Philippe, Françoise. BA, Yonsei U., Seoul, 1952, MA, 1954; PhD in History, U. Paris, 1968, Doctorat D' Etat, 1977. Teaching asst. Yonsei U., Seoul, 1954-56; lectr. U. Paris, France, 1956-59, Ecole Nat. des Langues Orientales, Paris, 1959-69; assoc. prof. Ecole Pratique des Hautes Etudes, Paris, 1970-82; assoc. prof. Univ. de Paris (France) 7, 1970-83, prof., 1983-94, dir. dept. Korean studies, 1970-94, prof. emeritus, 1994—; prof. emeritus Kyonggi (Korea) Univ., 1994—; dir. Ctr. for Korean Studies, Coll. of France, Paris, 1970-92; pres. European Assn. for Korean Studies, Paris, 1980-82. Author: Histoire de la Corée, 1969, Recherche Sur L'Antiquité Coréenne, 1980, La Corée des Originesà Nos Jours, 1988, La Mythologie Coreenne et son Expression Artistique, 1996. Recipient Comdr. de L'Ordre des Palmes Academiques, France, 1986, Comdr. of Merite, South Korea, 1988, Chevalier de l'Ordre Nat. du Merite, France, 1996. Home: 15 rue Nicolas Fortin, 75013 Paris France Office: Univ de Paris 7, 2 Place Jussieu, 75005 Paris France

LI, PAI-CHI, electrical engineering educator, consultant; b. Keelung, Taiwan, Republic of China, Nov. 11, 1965; s. Wen-Jing and Pei-Ching (Hsiao) Li; m. Shu-Chin Ma, Oct. 6, 1995. BS, Nat. Taiwan U., 1987; MS, U. Mich., 1990, PhD, 1994. Mem. tech. staff Acuson Corp., Mountain View, Calif., 1994-97; asst. prof. Nat. Taiwan U., Taipei, Republic of China, 1997-98, assoc. prof., 1998—; cons. Biostar, Taipei, Republic of China, 1997, Skylark, Tao-Yuan, Republic of China, 1998, ITRI, Hsin-Chu, Republic of China, 1997-98. Contbr. articles to profl. jours.; patentee in field. Pvt. tutor Taipei, 1983-87. 2d lt. Republic of China Army, 1987-89. Recipient Rsch. award Nat. Sci. Coun., 1998, 99. Mem. IEEE. Avocations: guitar, golf, hiking, basketball, reading. Office: Dept EE Nat Taiwan U, No 1 Sec 4 Roosevelt Rd, Taipei 106 ROC, Taiwan

LI, PENG, biologist, researcher; b. Jiangxi, China, Oct. 26, 1965; d. Tian Lang Li and Zhu Ying Chen; m. Sheng Cai Lin; children: Jason Ye Lin, Jackie Jin Lin. BSc, Beijing Normal U., 1987; PhD, U. Calif., San Diego, 1995. Rsch. fellow Inst. Molecular and Cell Biology, Singapore, 1996-97, prin. investigator, 1998—; rsch. assoc. Howard Hughes Med. Inst., Dallas, 1997-98. Contbr. articles to profl. jours. Recipient Young Scientist award Nat. Sci. and Tech. Bd., Singapore, 1999. Home: 61 Mount Sinai Dr 06-02, Kamehameha Rise, Singapore 277113, Republic of Singapore Office: Inst Molecular/Cell Biology, 30 Medical Dr, Singapore 117609, Republic of Singapore

LI, PING, psychologist, educator; b. Yongxing, Hunan, China, Dec. 22, 1962; s. Kuang-Guo and Xiao-Ying (Zhang) L.; m. Lee Yong Tan, May 2, 1992; 1 child, Jessie. BA, Peking U., Beijing, 1983, MA, 1986; PhD, U. Leiden, The Netherlands, 1990. Asst. lectr. Peking U., 1986; asst. prof. Chinese U., Hong Kong, 1992-96; asst. prof. dept. psychology U. Richmond, Va., 1996-99; assoc. prof. dept. psychology U. Richmond, 2000—; postdoctoral fellow U. Calif., San Diego, 1990-92, McDonnell-Pew Ctr., San Diego, 1992; vis. scholar Max Planck Inst., The Netherlands, 1995, 98, 99. Contbr. articles to profl. jours. Human Frontier Sci. Program rsch. fellow, 1990-92, McDonnell-Pew Ctr. postdoctoral fellow, 1992; chinese U. Direst Rsch. grantee, 1992-96; recipient award NSF, 1999—. Mem. Psychonomic Soc., Cognitive Sci. Soc., Internat. Neural Network Soc. Roman Catholic. Avocations: reading, swimming, travel. Home: 2821 Ambergate Ter Midlothian VA 23113-2176

LI, QI, economics educator, researcher; b. Beijing, Aug. 12, 1956; came to U.S., 1986; s. Xiyan Li and Shizhen Yan; m. Zhenjuan Liu, May 16, 1983; children: Kathy Li, Kevin Li. BS, Peking U., Beijing, 1982; MS, Nankai U., Tianjing, China, 1985; PhD, Tex. A&M U., 1991. From asst. prof. to prof. U. Guelph, Ont., Can., 1991-99, Ind. U., Bloomington, 1993; prof. econ. Tex. A&M U., College Station, 1999—. Contbr. articles to sci. publs., including Econometrica, Nonparametric Stats., others.; assoc. editor Econometrics Theory, 1997—, Jour. Nonparametric Stats., 1999—; co-editor Annals of Econs. and Fin., 2000—. Recipient Ont. Premier's Rsch. Excellence award, Ont. Govt., 1999. Fellow Jour. Econometrics; mem. Econmetrica Soc., Am. Statistical Assn. Avocation: playing basketball. E-mail: qi@econ.tamu.edu. Office: Tex A&M U Dept Econ College Station TX 77843-0001

LI, QIN, research scientist; b. Zhengzhou, Henan, China, Nov. 7, 1963; p. Shouchang and Wenxiang Li; m. Dan Lu, Dec. 3, 1990; 1 child, Yiran. BS, Wuhan (China) U., 1981, MS, 1985; PhD, U. Wash., 1996. Asst. tchr. Wuhan U., 1988-91, asst. prof., 1991-93, assoc. prof., 1993-96; rsch. asst. U. Wash., Seattle, 1996-2000; rsch. scientist U. Calif., Santa Barbara, 2000—. Contbr. chpts. to ency. and articles to profl. jours. Recipient 1st award sci. and tech. advancement State Edn. Commn. China, 1990. Mem. Chinese Inst. Electronics (sr.). E-mail: qli@icess.ucsb.edu. Office: ICESS Univ Calif Santa Barbara CA 93106

LI, QING, economics educator; b. Shanghai, Peoples Republic China, Aug. 8, 1968; m. Wayne Way; children: Adam, Ally. MA, Univ. Houston, 1992, PhD, 1995. Asst. prof. Wichita (Kans.) State Univ., 1995—. Contbr. articles to profl. jours. Recipient rsch. grants Barton Sch. Bus., 1997, 99. E-mail: li@twsuvm.uc.twsu.edu. Office: Wichita State Univ Dept Econ 1845 Fairmount St Wichita KS 67260-0001

LI, QISHU, English educator; b. Kunming, Yunnan, China, Nov. 6, 1945; s. Fakuan Li and Zhiwen Jin. MA in English, Sichuan Inst. Fgn. Langs., Chongqing, China, 1982, Longwood Coll., 1992. Chief interpreter, translator China Export Co., Beijing, 1973-78, Yunnan Airlines, China, 1985; prof., chair English dept. Yunnan Inst. Nationalities, Kunming, China, 1982-89, prof. English, v.p.; sr. rschr. Va. Ctr. of Humanities, Charlottesville, 1989-90; tchr. Chinese culture Tandem Sch., Charlottesville, 1989-90; adj. prof. Chinese culture Longwood Coll., Farmville, Va., 1990-91. Mem. Yunnan Soc. Fgn. Langs. (vice dir. 1999—), Yunnan Translators Assn. (mem. coun. 1999—). Avocations: reading, music, swimming, bridge. Office: Yunnan Inst Nationalities, English Dept, 650031 Kunming Yunnan China

LI, RONGBAI, agricultural studies educator, researcher; b. Huazhou, Guangdong, China, Dec. 22, 1957; s. Jinzhao and Huijuan (Liang) L.; m. Yanping Wei, July 13, 1984; 1 child, Chengwei. BSA, South China Agrl. Coll., Guangzhou, 1982; MS in Plant Breeding, G. Ballabh Pant U. Agr./Tech., Pantnagar, India, 1996; PhD in Genetics and Plant Breeding, G. Ballabh Pant U. Agr./Tech., 1999. Technician Hubian Sta. for Agro-Technology Ext., Huazhou, 1975-78; asst. prof. Guangxi Acad. Agrl. Scis., Nanning, China, 1982-94; assoc. prof. Guangxi Acad. Agrl. Scis., Nanning, 1995-99, prof., 2000—. Leader China 7th Five-year Program rsch. project Evaluation of Genetics of Cold Tolerance in Wild Rice, 1986-90 (Sci. & Tech. award 1991); leader China Nat. Sci. Found. rsch. project Study on Anther Culture of Superior Wild Rice Resources, 1986-90 (Sci. & Tech. award 1991); leader China 7th Five-year Program rsch. project Identification and Evaluation for Disease and Insect Resistance in Eight Kinds of Foodgrain Crop Resources, 1986-90 (China Nat. Scientific Achievement award 1983, Award of Improvement of Sci. and Tech. China Ministry of Agr. 1993); leader China 7th and 8th Five-year Programs rsch. project Maintenance, Evaluation and Utilization of Rice Genetic Resources in China, 1986-95 (Award of Improvement of Sci. and Tech. China Ministry of Agr. 1997); leader China 7th and 8th Five-year Programs rsch. project Propagation, Maintenance, Identification and Evaluation of Wild Rice Genetic Resources, 1986-95 (Guangxi Sci. and Tech. award 1996); leader China 7th, 8th and 9th Five-year Programs rsch. project Natural Reservation of Wild Rice as National Germplasm, 1986-2000 (Sci. and Tech. award 1998; leader rsch. project Technique of Unpollinated Ovary Culture and Its Utilization in Rice Improvement, 1994-96 (Guanxi Sci. and Tech. award 1998); leader China Nat. Rsch. Found. rsch. project Genetic Study on Resistance of Wild Rice Resources to a Serious Insect Pest, Brown Planthopper, 1993-98 (Guangxi Sci. and Tech. award 1999). Recipient 10 Excellent Young Scientist awards Guangxi State Govt., Nanning, 1997, Trans-century Excellent Young Talents award Chinese Govt., 1999. Mem. China Genetics Soc., China Genetic Resources Soc., N.Y. Acad. Scis. Avocations: photography, music, reading, cooking, walking. Office: Guangxi Acad Agrl Scis, Nanning, Guangxi 530007, Peoples Republic of China

LI, SHIBO, medical genetics educator; b. Changchun, Jilin, People's Republic of China, Nov. 3, 1959; came to U.S., 1987; s. Yuliang and Zhongju (Gu) L.; m. Ying Zhao, May 18, 1985; 1 child, Lingshen. MD, Norman Bethune U. Med. Scis., Changchun, 1984. Resident, chief resident dept infectious disease First Teaching Hosp. of Norman Bethune U. Med. Scis., Changchun, 1984-87; postdoctoral fellow dept. lab. medicine and dept. genetics Yale U. Sch. Medicine, New Haven, 1987-93; clin. cytogenetic fellow, adj. asst. prof. U. South Ala. Coll. Medicine, Mobile, 1993-96, asst. prof., 1996—. Contbr. articles to profl. jours. Fellow Ministry of Pub. Health, People's Republic of China, 1987. Mem. AAAS, Assn. Chinese Geneticists in Am. (postdoctoral fellow ann. award 1990), Am. Human Genetics Soc. Home: 13504 Fox Creed Dr Oklahoma City OK 73131 Office: BSEB Rm 224 941 Stanton L Young Blvd Oklahoma City OK 73104-5019

LI, SHIZHI, materials scientist, educator; b. Nanjing, Jiangsu, China, Mar. 12, 1932; s. Liyan Li and Fulin Xie; m. Yaqing Wu, Oct. 18, 1962; children: Fan, Shitau. Degree in engring., U. Sci. and Tech., Beijing, 1955. Cert. materials sci. educator, China. Asst. engr. Inst. Metals Rsch. Academia Sinica, Shanyang, China, 1955-58; engr. inst. Atomic Energy Academia Sinica, Beijing, 1959-73; prof. materials sci. Qingdao (China) Inst. Chem. Tech., 1973—; mem. com. Coun. Gas-Phase Deposition, Wuhan, China, 1988—; guest scientist U. Zurich, Switzerland, 1988; guest prof. Inst. Chemistry of Info. Recording Tech. U. Munich, 1992-93. Patentee in field (recipient Gold medal Eureka, Brussels World Fair for Invention 1988, 3d Nat. Prize for Invention 1989, 1st prize for improvement in sci. and tech. Ministry of Chem. Industry 1989). Mem. standing com. Com. Shandong Province of Chinese People's Polit. Consultive Conf., Jinan, 1988—. Avocations: reading, travel, cooking, swimming, Taiji. Home: Shangqiu Rd 7 Unit 3 No 203, Qingdao 266045, China Office: Qingdao Inst Chem Tech, Zhengzhou Rd 53, Qingdao Shandong 266042, China

LI, SHOUROU, physician, researcher; b. Beijing, China, July 3, 1922; d. Yuangquan and Desheng (Ding) Li; m. Jiateng Zhao; children: Xin Zhao, Yizuan Zhao. MD, Nanking Ctrl. Univ. Med. Coll., 1947. Med. diplomate. Residnet Tchg. Hosp. Ctrl. Univ. Med. Coll., Nanking, China, 1947-52; vis. physician Tchg. Hosp. 5th Mil. Med. U., Nanking, 1952-54, Tchg. Hosp. 1st Mil. Med. U., Changchun, 1954-58, Tchg. Hosp. N. Bethune Med. U., Changchun, 1958-78; vice chief physician 2d Tchg. Hosp. N. Bethune Med. U., Changchun, 1978-79, chief physician, prof., 1979—. Author: Chinese Obstetrics and Gynecology, 1999; vice-editor: Atlas of Congenital Malformations-Birth Defects Monitored in China, 1998; author articles. Named Family Planning Advanced Worker, Nat. Family Planning Office, 1991, Provincial Pub. Health Advanced Worker, Provincial Pub. Health Bur., 1977, Nat. Women and Children's Health Care Advanced Worker, Ministry Pub. Health, 1997. Avocations: television, music, travel, photography, walking. Home: 34 Yong Chang Hu Tou 304, 130021 Changchun China Office: 2 Tchg Hosp/N Bethune Med U, 18 Zi Qiang St, 130041 Changchun china

LI, SHU-GUANG, geochemistry educator, researcher; b. Xianyang, Shanxi, China, Feb. 15, 1941; s. Pei-ren and Rui-xia (Zhang) L.; m. Yi-zhi Chen, Feb. 13, 1972; 2 children. Grad., U. Sci. and Tech. China, Beijing, 1965. Asst. U. Sci. and Tech. China, Beijing, 1965-78; lectr. U. Sci. and Tech. China, Hefie, 1978-83, assoc. prof., 1987-93, prof., 1993—; vis. scientist MIT, Boston, 1983-86. Contbr. articles to profl. jours. including Sci. in China, Precambrian Rsch., Geochimet Cosmochim Acta, Chem. Geology, Internat. Geol. Review and Jour. Geology. Recipient award Acad. Sci. China, 1982, 95, 96, 97. Mem. Nat. Natural Sci. Found. China. Avocation: Taijiquan. E-mail: lsg@ustc.edu.cn. Office: U Sci and Tech in China, Dept Earth and Space Scis, Hefei Anhui 230026, China

LI, SHUJIE, mathematician; b. Harbin, China, June 27, 1940; s. Zuotian and Yuzhen (Jin) L.; m. Huiyan Wang, Mar. 8, 1967; children: Di, Chong. Grad., Kirin U., Chang Chun, China, 1963. Prof. Inst. Math. Acad. Sinica, Beijing, 1988—; chmn. functional analysis sect. Inst. Math. Acad. Sinica, 1994—; vis. scientist Courant Inst. NYU, 1979-81; vis. prof. Internat. Ctr. for Theoretical Physics, Trieste, Italy, 1986, Internat. Sch. for Advanced Studies, Trieste, 1987. Contbr. 70 articles to profl. jours. Recipient Natural Sci. prize Acad. Sinica, 1988, 96. Mem. Chinese Math. Soc. Office: Inst Math Acad Sinica, 100080 Beijing China

LI, SHUSHEN, science administrator, environmental scientist; b. Panshan, Liaoning, China, June 2, 1937; s. Hongjiang and Siqin Li; m. Guifen Jin; 1 child, Jinbo. B, Haerbin (China) Tech. U., 1963. Pilot researcher Beijing Inst. Indsl. Hygiene, 1964-65; rsch. asst. No. 7 China Indsl. Hygiene Inst., Taiyuan, 1965-78, engr., 1978-97; assoc. researcher, standing dep. dir. gen. Radiation Protection Inst. Nuclear Industry, Taiyuan, 1987-90; researcher, standing dep. dir. gen. China Inst. Radiation Protection, Taiyuan, 1990-99; sr. advisor China Inst. Radiation Protection; mem. Expert Rev. Com. Chinese Nuclear Environment, 1993—; researcher in field. Author: Guideline of Safety Assessment for Shallow land Disposal of Low Level Radioactive Waste, 1993; chief editor: Proceedings of the First Nat. Symposium on EIA, 1997. Named Expert with Outstanding Contribution China Nat. Nuclear Cooperation, 1990, Receiver Spl. Govt. Subsidies State Coun., 1992, Excellent Spls. Shanxi Provicne Provincial Govt., 1996. Mem. China Assn. Environ, Assessment (pres. 1996—), Internat. Assn. Impact Assessment. Avocations: reading, walking. Office: China Inst Radiation Prot, 270 Xuefu St, 030006 Taiyuan Shanxi, China

LI, STAN ZIQING, electrical and computer engineer, educator, researcher; b. Zhuzhou, Hunan, China, Aug. 18, 1958. B in Engring., Hunan U., Changsha, China, 1982; M in Engring, Nat. U. of Defense Tech., Changsha, China, 1985; PhD, U. Surrey, Eng., 1991. Lectr. Nat. U. of Defense Tech., China, 1985-88; rsch. fellow U. Surrey, Eng., 1990-91; rsch. fellow Nanyang Tech. U., Singapore, 1991-94, lectr., 1994-97, sr. lectr., 1997-99, assoc. prof., 2000—, rschr., 2000—. Author: (book) Markov Random Field Modeling in Computer Vision, 1995; editor: (book) Recent Developments in Computer Vision, 1996; also contbr. articles to profl. jours., chpts. to books. Recipient scholarship The Brit. Coun., 1988-91; Excellent Paper award First Asian Conf. on Computer Vision, Japan, 1993. Mem. IEEE (sr.). Avocations: swimming, music, reading, tennis. Fax: 86 10 8809-7305. E-mail: szli@microsoft.com. Office: Microsoft Rsch China, 5/F Beij Sigma Ctr 49 Zhichun Rd, Beijing 100080, People's Republic of China

LI, TAIWU, marine biologist, educator; b. Fuyu County, Jilin, China, Dec. 9, 1955; s. Jiyao and Xiulian (Zhang) L.; m. Xiurong Su, May 1, 1982; 1 child, Yanyan. BS, N.E. Normal U., Changchun, China, 1982, MS, 1984; PhD, East China Normal U., Shanghai, 1991. Lectr. Liaoning Normal U., Dalian, China, 1984-88; assoc. prof. Liaoning Normal U., Dalian, 1991-93, prof., 1996-99; prof. marine biology Ningbo (China) U., 1999—; vice dir. Aquacultural Disease Control Com., Dalian, 1996-99. Contbr. articles to profl. jours. Mem Chinese Polit. Consultative Com., Dalian, 1998—. Recipient Sci. and Tech. Advanced award Liaoning Province, 1997, Dalian City, 1999. Fellow Internat. Abalone Assn., Internat. Shellfisheries Assn.; mem. Chinese Oceanography and Limnology ASsn. (dir.), Ecologies Assn. Inst. of Oceanography/Chinese Acad. Scis. Avocations: reading, computer, playing basketball. E-mail: twli@263.net. Office: Marine Biotech/Ningbo U, Ningzhen Rd, Ningbo, Zhejiang 315211, China

LI, TIANQING, retired university administrator; b. Xinhui, Guangdong, China, Oct. 4, 1924; s. Zhaoxian and Yuhua (Ni) L.; m. Huiyan Liang; 1 child, Vincent Weicheng. BS, Zhejiang U., China, 1946; D (hon.), U. Macau, 1995. Assoc. prof. Lingnan U., Guangzhou, China, 1951-52, Zhongshan U., Guangzhou, 1952; assoc. prof. Engring. Inst. Nat. Def., Harbin, China, 1952-60, prof., 1960-65; prof. Jinan U., Guangzhou, 1965-70, South China Normal U., Guangzhou, 1970-73, Zhongshan U., Guangzhou, 1973-78; dean of studies Jinan U., Guangzhou, 1978-82, v.p., 1982-84; v.p. Shenzhen (China) U., 1984-86; vice rector U. East Asia, Macau, 1988-91; acting rector U. Macau, 1991, rector, 1992-94, ret., 1994; dir. Audison New Energy Power Plant, Xinjiang, 1997—; mem. coun. U. Macau, 1995—; mem. Edn. Coun., Macau, 1991-94; hon. vice chmn. Guangzhou Sci. and Tech. Advancement Fund, Guangzhou, 1992—; mem. nat. com. Chinese People's Polit. Consultative Conf., Beijing, 1993-98. Bd. trustees Pui Ching Comml. Coll. Recipient Outstanding Leadership award Oklahoma City U., 1985, Highest Honors award Soka U., Tokyo, 1993. Mem. Guangdong Nuc. Sci. Soc. (former chmn.), Nuc. Physics Soc. (former bd. dirs.), Guangdong Higher Edn. Soc. (former v.p.), Guangdong Translation Soc. (former v.p.), Zhuhai Sci. and Tech. Macau Assn. (hon. pres.). Home: Rua de Pedro Coutinho 29, Kings Ct 28-D, Macau Macau

LI, TIEN-YIEN, mathematics educator; b. Hunan, China, June 28, 1945; came to the U.S., 1969; BS, Nat. Tsing Hua U., Taiwan, 1968; PhD, U. Md., 1974. Instr. U. Utah, Salt Lake City, 1974-76; asst. prof. Mich. State U., East Lansing, 1976-79, assoc. prof., 1979-83, prof., 1983-98, univ. disting. prof., 1998—. Contbr. articles to profl. jours. Guggenheim fellow, 1995. E-mail: li@math.msu.edu. Home: 6439 E Island Lake Dr East Lansing MI 48823-9715 Office: Dept Math Mich State Univ East Lansing MI 48824

LI, WU HU, material engineer researcher; b. Wangcheng, Hunan, People's Republic of China, Nov. 23, 1967; s. Qi Xuan and Chun Hua (Sun) L.; m. Xiao Ning Wang; 1 child, Oliver Zhi Yu. BSc with honors, Xiamen U., People's Republic of China, 1989, PhD, 1994. Postdoctoral fellow Hong Kong U. of Sci. and Tech., 1995-96, U. Liverpool, U.K., 1996-98, Inst. of Materials Rsch. and Engring., Singapore, 1998—. Contbr. articles to profl. jours. Mem. Electrochem. Soc. Inc. Office: Inst Materials Rsch/Engring, 3 Research Link, Singapore 117602, Republic of Singapore

LI, XIANKUI, research scientist; b. Fushun County, Sichuan, China, Oct. 10, 1956; m. Xiaolong Tan, Sept. 9, 1999; 1 child, Rachel T. Lee. BSc, S.W. Agrl. Coll., Chongqing, 1982; MS, Beijing Agrl. U., 1994; PhD in Molecular Biology & Biochemistry, Peking U., Beijing, 1992. Postdoctoral scientist Harvard Med. Sch., Boston, 1992-93; rsch. scientist U. Leuven, Belgium, 1989-92, 93-95; postdoctoral scientist Childrens Hosp. L.A., 1995-96; rsch. assoc. U. So. Calif., L.A., 1996-98; rsch. scientist House Ear Inst., L.A., 1998—. Contbr. rsch. papers to sci. jours. Sci. and Tech. grantee Commn. of European Cmtys., 1989-90, 90-91; internat. rsch. fellow U. Leuven, 1991-92. Mem. AAAS, Am. Soc. Cell Biology. E-mail: suntiger@hotmail.com.

LI, XIAO DONG, architect, educator; b. Beijing, Apr. 3, 1963; s. Zhimo Li and Baozhu Wang; m. Xi Wang, Apr. 29, 1990. BArch, TsingHua U., Beijing, 1984; PhD, Delft U./Eindhoven U. Tech., The Netherlands, 1993. Tchg. asst. TsingHua U., Beijing, 1984-89; architect de Architekten Cie, Amsterdam, The Netherlands, 1993-97; architect, ptnr. Leex Architecture & Urban Devel., Delft, The Netherlands, 1995-97; advisor ING Group, The Hague, The Netherlands, 1996-97; lectr. sch. architecture Nat. U. Singapore, 1997—; cons. in field. Rsch. fellow Delft U. Tech., 1989-91, scholar, 1989; rsch. scohlar Eindhoven U. Tech., 1991. Avocations: taijii, badminton, travel. Office: Nat U Singapore, 10 Kent Ridge Rd, Singapore 119620, Singapore

LI, XIAO WU, metallurgical engineering educator, researcher; b. Jingdezhen, Jiangxi, China, Aug. 8, 1969; s. Wen Yao and Shu Zhen (Zheng) L.; m. Yang Liu, July 16, 1998; 1 child, Ruo Xuan. BSc, Jiangxi U., Nanchang, China, 1992; M in Engring., Inst. Metal Rsch., Chinese Acad. Scis., Shenyang, 1995, DEng, 1998. Asst. prof. State Key Lab. Fatigue and Fracture of Materials Inst. Metal Rsch., Chinese Acad. Scis., 1998—, rsch. assoc.; rschr. dept. materials sci. and engring. Osaka (Japan) U., 2000—. Translator: The Guiness Ency., 1999.; contbr. or co-contbr. articles to sci. jours. and procs. Post-doctoral fellow Japan Soc. for the Promotion of Sci. Avocations: Chinese calligraphy, computers, music, sports, table tennis. Office: Osaka U Grad Sch Engring, 2-1 Yamuda-Oka Suita, Liao Nng Shenyang 110015, China

LI, XING SHENG, mechanical engineering educator; b. Jingdezhen, China, Jan. 20, 1959; s. Gong Yi and Yi Wen (Shu) L.; m. Fang Fang, Dec. 30, 1983 (div. Feb. 1993); 1 child, Jie Li; m. Feng Zhi Wang, Sept. 21, 1993; 1 child, Anna Li. BS in Engring., Jiangxi Poly. U., 1982; MS in Engring., Guangxi U., 1985; PhD, Curtin U. Tech., Perth, Australia, 1994. Lectr. Jingdezhen Ceramic Inst., 1985-89; rsch. fellow Curtin U. Tech., Perth, 1989-90; sr. rsch. scientist, project leader divsn mfg. sci. & tech. Commonwealth Sci. and Indsl. Rsch. Orgn., Brisbane, 1994—. Editor: (books) Advanced Ceramic Tools for Machining Application I, 1994, Advanced Ceramic Tools for Machining Application II, 1995; contbr. articles to profl. jours. Mem. ASME, Assn. Profl. Engrs., Scientists and Mgrs. Australia. Avocations: basketball, photography, collecting stamps. Home: 23 Penarth St, Runcorn QLD 4113, Australia Office: CSIRO Divsn Mfg Tech, 2643 Moggill Rd Pinjarra Hills, Brisbane QLD 4069, Australia

LI, YANMIN, physicist, banker; b. Rizhao, China, Oct. 25, 1959; arrived in Germany, 1994; s. Jiankai and Jiansan (Guo) L.; m. Liwen Gao, Dec. 26, 1983; children: Cong, Ying. BSc, Qufu Normal U., 1982; MSc, Northeast U., 1984; PhD, Inst. Physics, Beijing, 1987. Lectr. Northeast U., Shenyang, China, 1987; rsch. fellow Inst. Theoretical Physics, Beijing, 1988-89, Internat. Ctr. Theoretical Physics, Trieste, Italy, 1989-91, U. Warwick, Coventry, U.K., 1991-94, Max-Planck-Inst., Dresden, Germany, 1994-95, U. Warwick, Coventry, 1995-97, Imperial Coll., London, 1998-99; banker Tokyo-Mitsubishi Internat. plc., London, 1999—. Mem. Am. Phys. Soc., China Ctr. for Advanced Sci. and Tech. Avocations: table tennis, swimming, basketball, chess. Home: 52 Rokeby Gardens, Woodford Green IG8 9HR, England Office: Tokyo-Mitsubishi Internat, 6 Broadgate, London EC2M 2AA, England

LI, YAO-EN, chemical engineer; b. Shanghai, People's Republic of China, Oct. 24, 1958; m. Yi-Yin Ku, May 15, 1959; children: Kory, Katherine. MS, U. Ill., Chgo., 1986, PhD, 1988. Scientist Am. Air Liquide, Countryside, Ill., 1988-89, sr. scientist, 1989-2000; rsch. investigator Abbott Labs., Chgo., 2000—. Contbr. more than 20 articles to AIChE Jour., Jour. of Catalysis, Jour. Phys. Chemistry, Catalysis Letter, Vacuum; patentee in field. James scholar U. Ill., Chgo., 1984; grad. fellow U. Ill., Chgo., 1985-87; recipient Rsch. and Devel. award, 1997. Mem. AIChE, Am. Chem. Soc., Tau Beta Pi. Achievements include the invention & developing the first membrane - based perfluorcarbon compound recovery commercial process in the world, inventor of a hydrogen chloride purification process, invention of several metal surface passivation processes.

LI, YOU-CHUN, geneticist; b. Hanyuan, Sichuan, China, May 22, 1963. BS, Sichuan Agrl. U., Ya An, China, 1984, MS, 1987; PhD, U. Haifa, Israel, 2000. Wheat geneticist and breeder Inst. of Crop Rsch./Sichuan Acad. Agrl. Scis., Chengdu, China, 1987-94; assoc. prof. Marine U. of Zhanjiang, China, 1994-95; head rsch. programs inst. Crop Rsch., Sichuan Acad. of Agrl. Scis., Chendgu, 1990-94, Marine U., Zhanjiang, 1994-95. Contbr. articles to profl. jours. Recipient acad. awards Sichuan Agrl. U., 1988-94. Mem. Israeli Soc. Plant Scis., Assn. of Genetics in China, Assn. of Agrl. Scis. of China. Office: Inst Evolution, Mount Carmel, Haifa 31905, Israel

LI, YU-CHUAN, dean; b. Taipei, Taiwan, Apr. 26, 1966. MD, Taipei Med. Coll., 1991; PhD, U. Utah, 1994. Bd. cert. dermatologist. Assoc. prof. dept. pub. health Taipei Med. Coll., 1995-97, assoc. prof. dept. hosp. adminstrn., 1997-98; dir. info. ctr. Taipei Med. Coll. Hosp., 1995-96; dean Grad. Inst. of Med. Informatics Taipei Med. Coll., 1998—; bd. dirs. Nat. Health Rsch. Inst., Taipei, Dept. of Health, Health Informatics Policy and Strategy Bd.; Inst., Taipei, Dept. of Health, Health Informatics Symposium in Taiwan, 1998, IT cons. chair scientific com. Med. Infomatics Symposium in Taiwan, 1998, IT cons. Wan-Fang Hosp., Taipie, 1997-98, Nat. Taiwan U. Hosp., 1996—; adj. assoc. prof. Nat. Def. Med. Ctr., 1998—, Sch. of Medicine, Nat. Taiwan U., 1996—; attending physician Dept. Dermatology, Wanfang Hosp., 1999—, Taipei Med. Coll. Hosp., 1999—; dir. Taipei Med. Ctr. Ctr. for Biomed. Infomatics, 1995—. Adv. editl. Handbook of Medical Informatics, 1997—; editl. bd. Dept. Health Informatics Policy and Strategy Bd., 1998—, Internat. Jour. of Med. Informatics, 1998—, Jour. of Med. Informatics, 1998—; contbr. numerous articles to profl. jours. Recipient Rsch. prize Nat. Sci. Coun., 1996, 99. Mem. Taiwan Med. Informatics Assn. (bd. dirs. 1997—), Taiwan Assn. of Med. Informatics (bd. dirs. 1997—), Healthcare Info. Mgmt. Systems Soc., Am. Med. Informatics Assn. E-mail: jack@tmc.edu.tw. Office: Inst Med Info Taipei Med, No 250 Wu Hsin St, 110 Taipei Taiwan, Republic of China

LI, YUFENG, engineer; b. Ruicheng, Shanxi, China, Apr. 29, 1959; s. Liansheng and Dangdang (Liu) L.; m. Danzhu Lu, June 4, 1985; children: Linda,

Steven. BS, Jiaotong U., 1982; MS, U. Wis., 1984, PhD, 1988. Postdoctoral rsch. scientist CMRR/U. Calif., San Diego, 1988-90; sr. adv. engr. Seagate Tech., Bloomington, Minn., 1990-95; sr. engring. mgr. Samsung Info. Systems Am., San Jose, Calif., 1995-98; prin. engr. Iomega Corp., Milpitas, Calif., 1998-99; sr. prin. engr. Read-Rite Corp., Milpitas, Calif., 1999—. Author chpt. to engring. handbook; contbr. articles to profl. jours. Recipient Math. Competition award Xi'an Jiaotong U., 1978. Mem. ASME (Best Paper award 1993). Achievements include major scientific/engineering contributions that include discovering the inherent shortcomings of optical profilometer in measuring non-homogeneous material and proposed the dual-wavelength solution; establishing the interface stiction theory with surface roughness and liquid film; theorized the I-beam strain gauge measurement system; conceiving the discrete laser-bump texture for tribiological application; demonstrated the accurate measurement of flash temperature with an MR head in nanoseconds; inventing the standard for flying height calibration down to nanometers; developing the model for the efficient utilization of desiccant in packaging. Office: Read-Rite Corp 345 Los Coches St Milpitas CA 95035-5428

LI, ZHENGANG, molecular geneticist; b. Tsingtao, China, Aug. 1, 1935; s. Peixun and Min (Wang) L.; m. Qiuying Wu, July 3, 1962 (dec. 1989); children: Jie Li, Chunsheng Li; m. Rongqi Zhai, May 21, 1993; 1 child, Jiarui. Grad., Peking Normal U., 1956, postgrad., 1959. From lectr. to doctoral tutor U. Sci. & Technology China, Hefei, 1978—. Office: U Sci & Tech China Dept Biology, Jinzhai Rd #96, 230027 Hefei China

LI, ZHI-PING, mathematician, educator; b. Beijing, June 25, 1955; s. Zhao-Liu and Xin-Zhen Li; Jian Li, Oct. 1, 1984; 1 child, Yi-Han. BSc, Xi'An Jiaotong U., China, 1982; MSc, Peking U., Beijing, 1984, PhD, 1987. Lectr. math. Peking U., 1987-88, assoc. prof., 1993-97, prof., 1997—; rsch. assoc. Heriot-Watt U., Edinburgh, Scotland, 1988-90; rsch. fellow Brunel U., London, 1991-93. Contbr. articles to profl. jours. Mem. Computer Math. Soc. Beijing, Computational Math. Soc. of China (councillor). Office: Peking U, Sch Math Sci, 100871 Beijing China

LI, ZHU, human resources director; b. Beijing, July 15, 1937; d. Zhu Xing Pu and Zhang Shu Wan; m. Ma Wei Zhang; children: Zhu Jinno, Ma Biao. Bachelor's degree, Hankai U., Tianjin, China, 1954. Editor China Today, Beijing, 1955-71; VIP USIA, Washington, 1988; dir. divsn. Inst. World Econs. and Politics, 1988-93; spl. asst. Golden State Im. and Ex. Co., Beijing, 1996-97; dir., sr. cons. Golden State (Holding) Group Corp., Beijing, 1997—; vis. fellow Oxford (Eng.) U., 1984, Columbia U., N.Y.C., 1991, UCLA, 1992, Washington Inst. for Near East Policy, 1991; prof. polit. sci. Chinese Acad. Scis.; spl. rsch. fellow Ctr. for 3d World Studies; program officer Brit. Coun., 1986; mem. del. ASEAN countries, Singapore, 1989, NIRA Conf., Tokyo, 1993; dep. head del. UMEMO, Soviet Union, 1990. Author: (books) The History of Relationship Between Russia and Middle East, 1986, A Survey of Middle East, 1990; revisor: (book) The Language of Trade, 1999. Named Hon. Alumni of Queen Elizabeth House, 1985, Excellent Worker of Inst. of World Econs. and Politics, 1993; recipient Key of City of Freeport, Ill., 1992, Permanent Spl. State award Chinese Govt., 1993. Mem. Am. C. of C., Western Returned Scholars. Avocations: music, movies.

LI, ZONGQUAN, materials scientist; b. Da County, Sichuan, China, Feb. 3, 1942; s. Shuzhai Li and Zhengshu Wu; m. Aili Zhang, Feb. 3, 1972; 1 child, Zinan Li. BS, Sichuan U., Chengdu, China, 1964; postgrad. Inst. Metal Rsch., Academia Sineca, Shenyang, China, 1968. Rsch. asst. Inst. Metal Rsch. Academia Sineca, 1968-76, rsch. assoc., 1976-81; rsch. assoc. Inst. Solid State Physics, Hefei, China, 1981-85; vis. scholar Argonne (Ill.) Nat. Lab., 1985-87; assoc. prof. Inst. Solid State Physics, Hefei, 1987-94; prof. materials sci. Zhejiang U., Hangzhou, China, 1994—. Mem. Anhui Assn. Electron Microscopy (co-chmn. 1987-94). Office: Dept Math Sci & Engring, Dept Math Sci and Engring, Zhejiang U, Hangzhou 310027, China

LIAKOS, JAMES CHRIST, business manager; b. Washington, Feb. 10, 1933; s. Christ and Xantippe (Franks) L.; m. Alexandra Avayanos, Jan. 1, 1956 (div. Jan. 1960); 1 child, Stephanie; m. Roberta Sue Katzman, May 31, 1963. B Comml. Scis., Benjamin Franklin U., 1956. Supr. acctg. dept. Bakery & Confectionery Union Industry Internat. Welfare and Pension Funds, Washington, 1955-66; adminstrv. asst. Am. Physiol. Soc., Bethesda, Md., 1966-76, asst. bus. mgr., bus. mgr., 1985—. With U.S. Army, 1953-54, ETO. Mem. Nat. Soc. Pub. Acctg., Am. Soc. Assn. Execs. Greek Orthodox. Home: 11001 Lopa Ln North Potomac MD 20878-2542 Office: Am Physiol Soc 9650 Rockville Pike Bethesda MD 20814-3998

LIAN, HANS JACOB BIORN, Norwegian diplomat; b. Mar. 21, 1942; married; 2 children. Lic. in Econ. Scis., Neuchatel, Switzerland, 1967. With Norwegian Ministry Fgn. Affairs, Oslo, 1967; exec. officer polit. dept. (Soviet Union and Ea. Europe) Norwegian Ministry Fgn. Affairs, Oslo, Belgium, 1972-73; sr. exec. officer Norwegian Ministry Fgn. Affairs, Oslo, 1979-80, head divsn. dept. external econ. affairs, 1980-82, head divsn. polit. dept. for NATO and security policy, 1982-85, dir. gen. dept. polit. affairs, 1992-94; 2d sec. Norway's permanent del. to NATO, Brussels, $D, 1970-72; 1st sec. Norway's del. to Conf. on Security and Cooperation in Europe, 1973-75; 1st sec. Permanent Mission Norway to UN Office, Geneva, 1975-79; min.-counsellor Del. Norway to Conf. on CSBMs and Disarmament in Europe, Stockholm, 1980-82; amb., head Norwegian del. to negotiations on confidence and security bldg. measures, Vienna, Austria, 1988-92; permanent rep. Norway to UN, N.Y.C., 1984-98, NATO, Brussels, 1998—. also: NATO Hdqs, Blvd Leopold 111, 1110 Brussels Belgium*

LIAN, HANS JACOB BJØRN, Norwegian diplomat, NATO official; b. Norway, Mar. 31, 1942; married; 2 children. Degree in econs., Switzerland, 1967. With Norwegian Ministry of Fgn. Affairs, 1967-70; 2d sec., Norway's Permanent Delegation to NATO Norwegian Ministry of Fgn. Affairs, Brussels, 1970-72; exec. officer polit. dept. Soviet Union and Eastern Europe Norwegian Ministry of Fgn. Affairs, 1972-73; 1st sec. of Embassy, Norway's delegation to Conf. Security and Cooperation in Europe, 1973-75; 1st sec. permanent Mission of Norway to UN, 1975-79; sr. exec. officer polit. dept. Norwegian Ministry of Fgn. Affairs, 1979-80, head of divsn., dept. external econ. affairs, 1980-82, head of divsn., polit. dept. NATO, security policy, 1982-85; minister-counsellor Delegation of Norway to Conf. on CSBMs and Disarmament in Europe, Stockholm, 1985-88; amb., head of Norwegian delegation to CSCE Vienna, 1988-92; amb., head of delegation to negotiation on conventional armed forces in Europe, 1988-90; dir. gen., dept. polit. affairs Norwegian Ministry of Fgn. Affairs, 1992-94; permanent rep. of Norway to UN N.Y.C., 1994-98; permanent rep. of Norway to NATO Brussels, 1998—. Office: NATO Hdqrs, Blvd Leopold III, 1110 Brussels Belgium

LIANCHU GU, electrical engineering educator; b. Shanghai, Feb. 15, 1926; s. Houtian and Cuilian (Cai) G.; m. Liying Han, Jan. 1, 1954; 1 child, Congzhong. BS, Qing Hua U., 1950. Asst. prof. Qing Hua U., Beijing, 1950-54, lectr., 1954-61, assoc. prof., 1961-85, prof., 1985—, dir. lab., 1953-61, dir. tchg. groups, 1961-86, dir. univ. libr., 1986-92, dep. mng. dir. Power Electronics Ctr., 1992—. Author: Design of Thyristors, 1975; author, editor: High Power Thyristors, 1976, Series of Power Electronics, 1988, Data and Selection Manual of Chinese Power Semiconductor Devices, 1995. Cons. Mcpl. Govt., Beijing, 1983-97. Mem. Soc. Power Electronics-Chinese Electrotechnical Soc. (vice chmn. 1980—), Beijing Soc. Power Electronics (hon. chmn. 1995—), Coun. Libis. Soc. Avocations: chorus, swimming, basketball, running. Office: Qing Hua U Libr, Qinghuayuan W Suburb, Beijing 100084, China

LIANG, DONG-CAI, biophysicist, educator; b. Guangzhou, China, May 29, 1932. BS, Zhong-shan U., China, 1955; PhD Inst. Organo-Element Compounds, Acad. Scis., USSR, 1960. Head x-ray crystal structure analysis group Inst. Physics Chinese Acad. Sci., Beijing, 1960-65, chief Peking insulin structure group, 1967-70; dep. head divsn. ocean physics Inst. South Sea Chinese Acad. Sci., Guangzhou, 1970-78; head divsn. protein crystallography Inst. Biophysics Chinese Acad. Sci., Beijing, 1978-83, dir. Inst. Biophysics, 1983-86; vice-chmn. Nat. Natural Sci. Found. China, Beijing, 1986-95; dep. chief editor Sci. in China, Chinese Sci. Bull., 1996—; v. chmn. Nat. Natural Sci. Found., 1986-95, adv. 1995-98, chmn. inspection com. 1998—. Fellow The Third World Acad. Scis.; mem. Chinese Acad. Scis. Office: Chinese Acad Scis, Inst Biophysics 15 Datun Rd, 100101 Beijing China

LIANG, HUA, research scientist; b. Jiangzi, China, Dec. 20, 1965; s. Bi Yao and Cong Lan (Huang) L.; m. Yong Guang, Sept. 29, 1995. BS, Nanchang U., China, 1985; MS, Northwestern Poly. U., China, 1987; PhD, Inst. of Systems Sci., China, 1992. Asst. fellow Nanchang Inst. of Aero. Tech., China, 1987-89; rsch. assoc. Inst. of Systems Sci., Beijing, China, 1992-95, assoc. prof., 1995—; Humboldt rsch. fellow Humboldt Univ., Berlin, Germany, 1996—. Contbr. numerous articles to profl. jours. Recipient Excellent Youth award Inst. of Systems Sci., Beijing, 1993, 94, Sci. & Tech. Progress 2nd prize Shanxi Province, 1995, 2nd Class award State Stats. Bur., 1996, 97. Mem. Am. Math. Soc. Office: Inst of Systems Sci, Chinese Acad of Sci, Beijing 100080, China

LIANG, JEROME ZHENGRONG, radiology educator; b. Chongqing, China, June 23, 1958; came to U.S., 1981; BS, Lanzhou U., China, 1982; PhD, CUNY, 1987. Rsch. instr. Albert Einstein Coll. Medicine, Bronx, N.Y., 1986-87; rsch. assoc. Duke U. Med. Ctr., Durham, N.C., 1987-89; asst. med. rsch. prof. Duke U. Med. Ctr., 1990-92; asst. prof. SUNY, Stony Brook, 1992-97, assoc. prof., 1997—, co-dir. biomedical engring., 1998—. Contbr. articles to profl. jours. Grantee Soc. Thoracic Radiology, 1994-95, ADAC Rsch. Lab., 1994-95; recipient NIH awards 1990-94, 95—, AHA award, 1996—, N.Y. State Biotech award 1996-98, E-Z-EM award, 1997-98. Mem. Assn. Chinese-Am. Sr. Profls., Inc. (trustee 1994—). Achievements include devel. of Bayesian image processing, quantitative emission computed tomography, tissue segmentation from magnetic resonance images, virtual endoscopy, virtual realities in radiology. Avocations: swimming, fitness, tennis. Office: SUNY Stony Brook Dept Radiology 4th Fl Brk Rm 092 Stony Brook NY 11794-0001

LIANG, SHIDONG, physicist, educator; b. Shunde, China, Nov. 20, 1958; s. Zijiu Liang and Wenying Chen; m. Danhong Chen; 1 child, Liqi. MPhil, Shanghai Inst. Nuclear Rsch., China, 1990; PhD, U. Hong Kong, 1999. Tchg. asst. U. Foshan, China, 1990-92, lectr., 1992-93; lectr. Guangzhou (China) Normal U., 1993-96, 99—; tchg. asst. U. Hong Kong, China, 1996-99. Contbr. articles to profl. jours. Mem. Chinese Phys. Soc., Hong Kong Phys. Soc. Office: Inst Physics, Academia Sinica, Nankang Taipei 11529, Taiwan

LIANG, TIAN, Olympic athlete; b. Chongqing, China, Aug. 26, 1979. Placed 2nd to Dmitry Sautin World Championships, 1998, co-winner Gold medal in platform diving World Cup, 1999; winner Gold medal platform diving Sydney, 2000. Office: Swimming Assn People's Rep China, 9 Ti Yuguan Rd, Beijing 100061, China*

LIANG, WEI, technology educator; b. Jiaocheng, Shanxi, China, Nov. 18, 1963; parents Yulin Liang and Chunlian Hou; m. Xuemei Li, Oct. 17, 1985; 1 child, Xingzhong. BSc, Taiyuan (China) U. Tech., 1985, MSc, 1991; PhD, Harbin Inst. Tech., 1997. Cert. tchr. Technician Fenyang, Shanxi, 1985-88; asst. Taiyuan U. Tech., 1991-92, lectr., 1992-96, prof., 1996—; pres. Electron Microscopy of Shanxi, Taiyuan, 1997; mem. Electron Microscopy China, Beijing, 1996. Contbr. articles to profl. jours.; patentee in field. Avocations: singing songs, table tennis, volleyball, playing cards. Fax: 86 351 6041237. E-mail: liangwei@public.ty.sx.cn. Office: Taiyuan U Tech, 79 W Yingze St, Taiyuan Shanxi 030024, China

LIANG, WEIWEN, biological researcher; b. Fuzhou, Fujian, China, Nov. 15, 1967; came to U.S., 1992; s. YongQian and Lianjin (Dai) L., m. Xiaohong Pan, Feb. 16, 1999;. BS, Shanghai Med. U., China, 1990; PhD, W. Va. U., 1998. Scientist Fuda Pharms., Fuzhou, 1990-92; rsch. asst. W. Va. U., 1993-98; rsch. assoc. U. Pitts., 1998—. contbr. articles to profl. jours.; Inventor biochimia of biophysic action. Mem. Am. Assn. Pharm. Rsch. (named outstanding rechr. 1996), Am. Assn. Advanced Sci.; Controlled Release Soc.; assoc. mem. Soc. Gene Therapy, Sigma Xi Soc. (named outstanding rechr. 1996). E-mail: Wel6t@Pitt.edu. Home: 3424 Ward St Pittsburgh PA 15213-4318 Office: University of Pittsburgh Dept of Pharmacology W1316 Bst Pittsburgh PA 15261-0001

LIANG, WENJIE, chemist, educator; b. Tianjin, China, June 5, 1930; s. Baosen and Xiuzhen (Xie) L.; m. Qiushui Yang, Jan. 1958; children: Yue, Jin. B, U. Tsinghua, Peking, China, 1952; M, Inst Petroleum, Peking, China, 1956. Lectr. Inst. Petroleum, Peking, 1956-78; assoc. prof. Inst. Petroleum, Dongying, 1979-85; prof. U. Petroleum, Dongying, 1986—. Author: (books) Chemistry of Petroleum, 1995, Chemistry of Heavy Oils, 1999; co-author: (book) Petroleum Refining Engineering, 1999. Avocation: reading.

LIANG, XIN-GANG, science researcher, educator; b. Fushun, Liaoning, China, Feb. 2, 1962; s. Zuo-Shan Liang and Yan Lu; m. Xu Wang, Feb. 23, 1988. Bachelor's degree, U. Sci. and Tech. of China, Hefei, 1985, PhD, 1991. Cert. tchr. diploma, assoc. prof. diploma. Lectr. Tsinghua U., Beijing, 1991-93, assoc. prof., 1994-98, prof., 1998—, dir. Inst. Engring. Thermophysics, dept. engring. mechanics; visitor dept. mech. engring. U. Calif., Berkeley, 1997-98; assoc. dir. engring. thermophysics divsn., dept. engring. mechanics Tsinghua U., Beijing, 1995-97. Contbr. articles to profl. jours. Avocations: badminton, go, soccer. Office: Tsinghua U, Dept Engring Mechanics, 100084 Beijing China

LIANGQUAN, GE, nuclear geophysicist; b. Anqing, Anhui, China, July 8, 1962; s. Ge Xianzhao and Zhang Yunzhi; m. Zhuang Li; 1 child, Ran. BS, Chengdu (China) Coll. Geology, 1983, MS, 1987; PhD, China U. Geoscis., Beijing, 1995. Technician 263d Geol. Team, China, 1983-84; lectr. Chengdu Coll. Geology, 1987-92; postdoctoral rschr. Chengdu U. Tech., 1995-97, assoc. prof., 1997-98; prof. Chengdu U. Tech., Sichuan, China, 1998—; vice dir. Open Rsch. Lab. Applied Nuclear Tech. in Geoscis., Sichuan, China, 1997—. Author: In-Situ X-Radiation Sampling, 1997, X-Ray Spectrometry, 1997; editor: Handbook of Software for Micro-Computer, 1995, Engineering and Environmental Geophysics for the 21st Century, 1997; contbr. articles to profl. jours. Recipient award Ednl. Found. of Internat. Engring. and Tech., 1996. Mem. Sichuan Assn. Nuclear Scis., Sichuan Assn. Geology. Office: Dept Nuclear Tech, 1 Erxianqiao Dong San Rd, Chengdu Sichuan 610059, China

LIANKE, SUN, electrical engineer, educator; b. Qingzhou, Shandong, China, Nov. 26, 1944; m. Liu Guizhen; children: Lipeng, Limin. BS, Shandong U., 1970. Diplomate electronic sci., engring. Lctr. Shandong U., Jinan, China, 1982-88; assoc. prof. Shandong U., Jinan, 1989-96, prof., 1997—; deputy dir. Inst. Crystal Materials, Jinan, 1993; pres. Coretech Crystal Co., Jinan, 1994; bd. mem. Optical Coun. Shandong Optical Soc., Jinan, 1996—. Office: Shandong U, 27 Shanda Nan Rd, Jinan 250100, China

LIAO, CHUN-CHEN, dean, science educator. Dean coll. sci. Nat. Tsing Hua U., Taiwan, China. Office: Nat Tsing Hua U, 101 Sect 2 Kuang Fu Rd, Taiwan China*

LIAO, LIH-YIH, nuclear engineer, researcher; b. Taichung, Taiwan, June 24, 1954; s. Chia-Shiang Liao and Fun-Ley Chen; m. Shu-Ying Lu, Nov. 1, 1982; children: Tommy, Howard, Gerry. BS, Tsing Hua U., Hsinchu, Taiwan, 1976, MS, 1978; PhD, MIT, 1985. Asst. scientist Inst. Nuc. Energy Rsch., Lung Tan, Taiwan, 1978-85, assoc. scientist, 1985-96, scientist, 1996—; commr. com. on appraisal, Inst. Nuc. Energy Rsch., 1991-92, commr. com. on nuc. safety, 1992-96. Co-author: Artificial Intelligence and Other Innovative Computer Applications in the Nuclear Industry, 1987; contrbr. articles to profl. jours., including (jour.) Nuc. Tech., Nuc. Engring. and Design, Nuc. Sci. Jour. (best paper of yr. 1995). Recipient Class A Rsch. award Nat. Sci. Coun. Taiwan, 1992. Mem. Am. Nuc. Soc. (Taiwan sect.), Chung Hua Nuc. Soc. Office: Inst Nuclear Energy Rsch, PO Box 3-3, Lungtan Taiwan

LIAO, MARTHA, geneticist; b. Leeds, Eng., Feb. 9, 1948; came to U.S., 1967; d. Chung-Chou and Shirley Liao; m. Haojiang Tian, Mar. 18, 1991. BA, Bryn Mawr Coll., 1970; PhD, U. Pa., 1974. Inst. fellow Eleanor Roosevelt Inst., Denver, 1979-86; asst. prof. U. Colo. Health Scis. Ctr., Denver, 1982-88; sr. fellow Eleanor Roosevelt Inst., Denver, 1986-94; assoc. prof. dept. pediat. U. Colo. Med. Sch., Denver, 1988-95; chmn. sci. adv. bd. Cancer League of Colo., Denver, 1989-91; reviewer VA Merit Rev. Bd., Washington, 1988-92; vis. assoc. prof. Albert Einstein Coll. Medicine, Bronx, N.Y., 1992-96; presenter in field. Contbr. articles to Porceedings NAS. Pres. Asian Performing Arts Colo., Denver, 1986—; chmn. rev. com. Denver Cultural Dist., 1989-91; bd. dirs. Asian Arts Assn., Denver Art Mus., 1989-91. Rsch. scholar to China NAS, 1981-82; Rsch. grantee NSF, 1984-86, Am. Cancer Soc., 1981-82, NIH, 1980-94. Mem. Am. Soc. Human Genetics, Am. Soc. for Cell Biology, AAAS, Soc. Chinese Bioscientist in Am. (rep. Denver 1988—), Assn. Chinese Geneticists in Am. (sec. 1989-91). Achievements include research in human chromosome 12 by molecular and cell genetics, human protein and its gene that helps AIDS virus multiply in humans. Fax: 212-336-9487. E-mail: marthaliao@aol.com. Home: 7205 S Gaylord St Apt K Littleton CO 80122-1603 Office: 150 Columbus Ave Apt 18D New York NY 10023-5969

LIAO, TA-HSIU, biochemistry educator; b. Taipei, Taiwan, Feb. 22, 1942; s. Hsin-Zu and A-Men (Hsieh) L.; children: Cinderella, Richard. BS, Nat. Taiwan U., Taipei, 1964; PhD, UCLA, 1969. Fellow Rockefeller U., N.Y.C., 1970-73, asst. prof., 1973-74; asst. prof. Okla. State U., Stillwater, 1974-78, assoc. prof., 1978-82, prof., 1982-85; prof. biochemistry Nat. Taiwan U., Taipei, 1985—, assoc. dean, 1988-91, dir. Inst. Ctr., 1991-95, dir. Inst. Biochem., 1996—. Grantee NIH, 1975-80, Nat. Sci. Coun. Taiwan, 1985—. Mem. AAAS, The Protein Soc., Am. Soc. for Biochemistry and Molecular Biology, Taiwan Soc. for Biochemistry and Molecular Biology (pres. 1999—), Rotary (past pres. Taipei Southsea). Office: Nat Taiwan Univ Coll Medicine, No 1 Sec 1 Jen-Ai Rd, Taipei Taiwan

LIAO, YAN BIAO, optics educator; b. Nanchang, Jiangxi, China, Nov. 7, 1935; s. Cheng Xian Liao and Hui Ying Hong; m. Su Ying Wu, Aug. 15, 1959; children: Xiang, Ming. BS, Wuhan (China) U., 1957. Head optical lab. Tsinghua U., Beijing, 1958-68, head sect. of physics, 1969-74, head laser physics and tech. lab., 1975-88, head opitcal fiber sensors lab., 1981—, prof. optics, 1988—; prof. Nat. Def. Sci. and Tech. U., Changsha, China, 1995—, Beijing Glass Rsch. Inst., 1983-86; chmn. Sino-Japanese Internat. Conf. on Optic Fiber Sensors, Beijing, 1988; chmn. internat. confs. SPIE, Wuhan, 1992, Beijing, 1996. Author: A Survey of Overseas Electronic Industry, 1986 (Sci. and Tech. Progess award 1988), Physical Optics, 1986, Optical Waveguide Sensors: Principles and Technology, 1998, Optical Waveguide Sensors: Principle and Technology, 1998, Fiber Optics, 2000; editor Chinese Jour. Lasers, 1988—; patentee fiber device, method for measuring fiber. Recipient Nat. Sci. and Tech. Progress award Nat. Sci. and Tech. Com., 1988, Nat. Sci. and Tech. Invention award Nat. Sci. and Tech. Com., 1992, Outstanding Achievement award State Coun., Beijing, 1992. Mem. Optical Fiber Sensor Soc. China (chmn. 1992—), Chinese Optical Soc., Chinese Instrument and Meter Soc. Chinese Communist. Avocations: collecting stamps, swimming. Home: Tsinghua U, High II-1306, 100084 Beijing China Office: Tsinghua U, Dept Electronic Engring, 100084 Beijing China

LIAPIS, CHRISTOS DEMETRIOS, surgery educator; b. Kalabaka, Greece, Feb. 13, 1947; s. Demetrios and Helen (Kariofilli) L.; m. Vicky A. Galanis, Feb. 19, 1977; children: Demetrios, Andreas. MD, Athens (Greece) U., 1972. Cert. gen. surgery, cert. vascular surgery. Clin. instr. surgery, clin. fellow vascular surgery Ohio State U., Columbus, 1978-80; rsch. fellow surgery Harvard U., Boston, 1980-81; lectr. Athens U. Med. Sch., 1982-89, asst. prof., 1989-95, assoc. prof., 1995—; pres. Greek Angiological Soc., 1994-96; gen. sec. Greek Surg. Soc., 1996-97; examiner European Diploma Vascular Surgery, 1998, 99; mem. bd. European Sch. Vascular Surgery, 1998; gen. sec.-treas. divsn. and bd. for vascular surgery Union Européenne des Médecins Spécialistes, 1999—. Lt. Greek Army Med. Corp., 1972-75. Recipient Physicians Recognition award AMA, 1981. Fellow ACS, Internat. Cardiovasc. Soc., European Soc. for Vascular Surgery. Office: 131 Vas Sofias Ave, 115 21 Athens Greece

LIAUBA, DANUTE, music educator; b. Amsterdam, N.Y., Aug. 19, 1955; d. Vytautas and Adele Staskevicius; m. Rimas Liauba, Sept. 6, 1981. BS in Music Theory, Nazareth Coll., Rochester, N.Y., 1976; postgrad., Eastman Sch. Music, 1979-80; MusM in Musicology, Ind. U., 1982. Cert. tchr. music, N.Y. Lectr. Bucknell U., Lewisburg, Pa., 1981-83, U. Akron, Ohio, 1987—; pvt. practice instr. music Medina, Ohio, 1987—; vis. lectr. Vytautas Magnus U., Kaunas, Lithuania, 1992. Co-author: Music of the Spheres, 1986, Curlionis: Painter and Composer, 1994. Mem. Music Tchrs. Nat. Assn., Ohio Music Tchrs. Assn. (pres. Akron chpt. 1995-97), Tuesday Musical Club (chair concert lecture 1999—). Avocations: skiing, scuba diving, travel. Home and Office: 3344 Forest Lake Dr Medina OH 44256-8733

LIBAI, DAVID, lawyer, educator, member of Parliament; b. Tel Aviv, Israel, 1934. DCL, U. Chgo.; LLM, Hebrew U., Jerusalem. Dep. state atty. Govt. Israel, 1961-65; former dir. Inst. Criminology and Criminal Law Tel Aviv Univ., dean of students, 1969-73; mem., press council Israeli Parliament, Jerusalem, 1984—; mem. com. constn., law and justice, 1984-92, 96—, house com., 1984-88; chair state comptroller com. 1984-92. Author: The Laws of Arrest and Release, 1978; contbr. articles to profl. jours. Chmn. constl. com. Labour Party; former chmn. Israel-Britain Parliamentary Friendship Assn. Mem. Israel Bar Assn. (pres. 1982-84).

LIBBEY, JAMES K., education educator; b. Holden, Mass., May 16, 1942; s. Russell J. and Narcissa E. L.; m. Joyce M. Holmes, Dec. 28, 1963. BA, Miami U., Oxford, Ohio, 1964, BSEd, 1967; MA, Ea. Ky. U., 1971; PhD, U. Ky., 1976. Tchr. St. Michael Sch., Brookville, Ind., 1964-67; clk., typist U.S. Army, Bad Kreuznach, Germany, 1968-70; instr. U. Ky., Lexington, 1973-74; asst. prof. Ea. Ky. U., Richmond, 1974-79, assoc. dean, 1979-86; rschr. Flagler Coll., St. Augustine, Fla., 1986-93; assoc. prof. Embry-Riddle Aeronautical U., Daytona Beach, Fla., 1993—; cons. So. W. Va. C.C., Logan, W.Va., 1975, University Press of Ky., Lexington, 1982, Miami U., Oxford, 1986. Author: (books) Alexander Gumberg and Soviet - American Relations, 1977, Dear Alben: Mr. Barkley of Kentucky, 1979, American - Russian Economic Relations, 1989, Russian - American Economic Relations, 1999. Co-chmn. Food Bank, Richmond, 1975-80; hope builder Habitat for Humanity, St. Augustine, Fla., 1992—; active Green Peace Action, 1986—. With U.S. Army, 1968-70, Germany. Grantee U. Ky., 1972, NEH, 1979, Kennan Inst. for Advanced Russian Studies, 1999. Mem. Am. Assn. Advancement of Slavic Studies, Soc. for Historians of Am. Fgn. Rels., Assn. for Gen. and Liberal Studies (exec. coun. mem. 1980-83, 94-97). Democrat. Roman Catholic. Avocations: walking, reading, travel, model building. Home: 258 Deltona Blvd Saint Augustine FL 32086-7355 Office: HU/SS Dept Embry-Riddle Aero Univ Daytona Beach FL 32114-3900

LIBBRECHT, GASPAR JOSEPH, civil engineer, educator; b. Roeselare, Belgium, Mar. 22, 1930; s. Pascal Leonard Libbrecht and Euphrasia Maria Vansteenkiste; m. Edna Deleu, July 15, 1961 (div. July 1993); children: Mieke, Katrien, Jan. Civil engr., U. Gent, 1955. Engr. Siemens, Brussels, 1957-58; prof. Katholieke Industriële Hogeschool, Oostende, Belgium, 1958-95; consulting engr. Roeselare, 1965—; prof. Katholieke Hogeschool Brugge Oostende, Brugge, Belgium, 1995-2000. Author: Computation of Machinery, 1961, Electrical Machinery, 1970, Control and Regulation, 1975, Servomechanism, 1975. Mem. Koninklijke Vlaamse Ingenieurs Vereniging, Koninklijke Vereniging Belgische Elektrotechnici, Order Architects Brussels. Avocation: recreational activities. Home: Mandeldreef 38, B 8800 Roeselare Belgium

LIBEN, ASEFA, judge. Pres. Supreme Ct. of Ethiopia, Addis Ababa, Ethiopia. Office: care Ethiopian Embassy 2134 Kalorama Rd NW Washington DC 20008-1647 also: Supreme Ct, PO Box 6166, Addis Ababa Ethiopia*

LIBENSKY, STANISLAV, art educator; b. Sezemice, Czech Republic, Mar. 27, 1921; s. Emil and Hedvika (Mizlerova) L.; m. Jaroslava Brychtova, Apr. 1963; children: Jaroslav, Milos, Alena. MFA, Acad. Applied Art, Praha, Czech Republic, 1963-87; D (hon.), Royal Coll. Art, London, 1994, U. Suntherland, Eng., 1999, R.I. Sch. Design, 2000, Royal Coll. Art; DA (hon.), U. Suntherland G. Britanien; DFA (hon.), RISD. Prof., chair dept. glass Acad. Applied Art, Praha, 1963-87; chair Czech Glass Artists Union, Prague, 1989-92, Czech Artist Union, Prague, 1968-69, lectr., Ohio State, Berkeley, Pilchuck Glass Sch. (established Libensky award); exhbns. include

IUC Hall, Paris, 1962-64, Prague Castle, 1964-69, River of Life Expo, Osaka, 1967-70, Cornin Mus., N.Y., 1978-80, Chapel Horsvskytyn, 1990-91, Corning Inc. Bldg., N.Y.C., 1991-93, Kioi Hall, Tokyo, 1994-95, Kameoka, Kyoto, Japan, 1998, Sao Paulo, 1965, Rio de Janeiro, 1966, Finland, 1984, Zurich, 1990, Yokohama, 1995, Nat. Gallery, Prague, 1989, Am. Craft Mus., N.Y., 1996, Brno, Czech Republic, 1996, Venezia Palazzo Ducale, 1996, Lausane Museé des Art, 1997, Bergamo Piazza Vecchia, 1998, Prague Carolinum, 2000. Decorated chevalier Order Arts and Letters (France); recipient Grand Prix Expo 58 Brussels; Gold medal VIII Biennale Sao Paulo, Brasil, 1966, Herder prize Vienna, Austria, 1975; Libensky award est. in his name at Pilchuck Glass Sch.

LIBERATI, DIEGO, electronic engineering educator, scientist; b. Milan, Dec. 10, 1958; s. Omar and MariaLaura (Barzaghi) L. BS, Einstein Coll., Milan, 1977; PhD in Electronic Engring., Polytech U., Milan, 1983; D of Rsch. in Biomed. Engring. (hon.), Italian Ministry Sci. Rsch., Rome, 1988. Cert. engr. Prof. French Einstein Coll., Milan, 1978-91; prof. computer sci. Radiotechnic Inst., Milan, 1982-83; sr. exec. scientist Italian Nat. Rsch. Coun., Milan, 1984—; prin. sr. scientist Italian Nat. Rsch. Coun., Genoa, 1997—; prof. math. modeling Politechnic U., Milan, 1987-90, prof. signal processing, 1990-94; prof. microelectronics Univ., Perugia, Italy, 1989-92; prof. instrumentation lab. Univ., Milan, 1991-95; chief scientist NRC, Genoa, Italy, 1999—; vis. scientist NYU, 1986, 87, Univ. Calif. Berkeley, 1988, 89, 92, 93, 95. Contbr. articles to profl. jours. Pres. Internat. Movement of Catholic Intellectuals, Milan, 1992-95; pres. regional coun. Lombardia St. Vincent De Paul Soc., Milan, 1984-88, mem. gen. internat. coun., Paris, 1995—. Recipient Youth Leadership award Rotary Internat., 1997; Machine Vision fellow Internat. Ctr. for Mech. Studies, Udine, Italy, 1988. Fellow Italian Electrical Assn. (sec. Biomed. Engr. Soc. 1991—, Milan prize 1987), Italian Assn. for Automation (sci. coms. 1996—, pres. sci. com. 1997); mem. Milan Commerce and Industry Chamber (expert for inovation 1994—, Innovation Plaza award 1994). Fax: 39-010-6475-200. E-mail: liberati@ice.ge.cnr.it. Home: via Vittorio Veneto 49/1, 16036 Recco Genova Italy Office: Istituto Cir Elettronici, via De Marini 6, 16149 Genova Italy

LIBERMAN, IAKOV L'VOVICH, engineering educator, humanities educator; b. Alapaevsk, Russia, Jan. 29, 1944; s. Lev Abramovich and Vera Iakovlevna L.; m. Nina Il'inichna Gorbunova, June 11, 1977; 1 child, Maria. Diploma in mech. engring., Ural State Tech. U., Ekaterinburg, Russia, 1965, PhD in Tech. Scis., 1970; cert. tchr. jewish history and lit., Bar Ilan U., Ramat-Gan, Israel, 1992. Asst., sr. lectr. Ural State Tech. U., Ekaterinburg, 1965-72, assoc. prof. machine bldg. dept., 1972—, assoc. prof. philol. dept., 1991—, head Jewish Studies Lab., 1994—; rector Ural Jewish People's U., Ekaterinburg, 1995—; academician Acad. Authors Sci. Discoveries and Inventions, Moscow, 1998—; assoc. academician Internat. Info. Acad., Montreal, Can., 1998—. Author: Combinatoric Scales in Automatic Systems, 1973, Automatic Machines for Inspection and Sorting, 1983, Statistical Coding of Information of Controlling Programs as a Method of Increase of DNC System's Reliability, 1988, Principles of Construction and Development's Prospect of Monitoring System for Metalcutting Machine-Tools, 1989, Increase of Technological Reliability of Automatic Machines for Inspection and Sorting, 1991, Isaak Babel Through Jewish Eyes, 1996, How to Translate Poems, 1996, Monitoring Systems for Metallcutting Machine-Tool, 2000; author, compiler, poem-translator: From Medieval Jewish Poetry, 1991, From Hebrew Poetry, 1993, Thirty-Three Centuries of Jewish Poetry, 1997, Music for Poems of Medieval Jewish Poets, 2000; contbr. articles to profl. jours. Named hon. mem. Writer's Union of Israel. Mem. Sverdlovsk Region's Soc. Jewish Culture (lectr.), Sverdlovsk Region's Assn. Jewish Studies, N.Y. Acad. Scis., Acad. Technol. Scis. (counsellor 1997—), Profl. Union of Workers of H.S. and Sci. Establishments, UNESCO Club. Achievements include 51 patents in field. Home: Apt 99, 20 Syromolotova St, 620072 Ekaterinburg Russia Office: Ural State Tech U, Mira St 19, Ekaterinburg 620002, Russia

LIBERSKI, PAWEL PIOTR, medical educator; b. Zgierz, Poland, Nov. 25, 1954; s. Benon and Krystyna (Lesser) L.; m. Maria Respondek. MD, Med. Acad. Lodz, Poland, 1979, PhD, 1982. Asst. dept. neurol. Med. Acad. Lodz, Poland, 1979-83, asst. prof., 1983-86, 89-93, prof., chmn., 1993—, prof. chmn. dept. molecular biology; vis. scientist LCNSS, NIH, Bethesda, 1991, 93, courtesy assoc., 1995-96, 97, 98; vis. scientist Neurol. Inst. U. Vienna, Austria, 1991-2000, Ctr. Vet. Lab., Weybridge, England, 1992, 93, 95. Author: The Enigma of Slow Viruses: Facts & Artefacts, 1993; author, editor: Light and Electron Microscopic Neuropathology of Slow Virus Disorders, 1993, (with MJ Mossa Kowski) Tumors of the Nervous System, Transmissible Sponigiform Encephalopathies, 2000; contbr. articles to profl. jours. Vis. fellow LCNSS, NIH, Bethesda, Md., 1986-89. Mem. AAAS, Assn. Polish Neuropathologists (v.p. 1993-96, 99—), N.Y. Acad. Scis., Am. Assn. Sci. Avocation: rare books. E-mail: ppliber@psk2.am.lodz.pl. Home: Podgorna 45m3, 93-272 Lodz Poland Office: Dept Mol Biol Czecho, Slowacka St 8/10 Pl, 92-216 Lodz Poland

LIBMAN, ELENA SOLOMONOVNA, ophthalmologist, researcher; b. Moscow, Sept. 15, 1928; d. Solomon Markovich and Tsirlya Aronovna (Cheprakova) L.; m. Boris Moiseevich Guekht, Aug. 22, 1950; 1 child, Alla B. Guekht. MD, 2nd Moscow Med. Inst., 1952; Ophthalmologist, Ctrl. Inst. Postgrad. Tng., Moscow, 1957; PhD, Ctrl. Inst. Postgrad. Tng., 1963; D of Med. Sci., Moscow Ophthalmol. Inst., 1974; Prof., Ctrl. Inst. Evaln. Working Capacity, Moscow, 1978. Ophthalmologist City Hosp., Chimkent, USSR, 1952-55; dep. chief physician Moscow Eye Hosp., 1955-67; head ophthalmol. dept. Ctrl. Inst. Evaln. Working Capacity, Moscow, 1967—; mem. World Coun. Blind, 1978. Author: Gainful Employment of the Blind, 1979 (Gold Medal Exhibn. Achievements of People's Economy 1981), Blindness in Russia, 1988, Actual Objectives of Social Ophthalmology, 1982; contbr. 350 articles to profl. jours. Recipient Gold Medal Govt. of Russia, 1986, 90; named Honored Scientist Russian Fedn. Supreme Soviet Russian Fedn., 1989. Mem. Russian Acad. Med. and Tech. Scis. (academician), Russian Acad. Natural Scis. (academician), Internat. Acad. Informatization (dep.), Ophthalmol. Soc. Russia (chairwoman commn. 1976, dep. chairwoman 1990), N.Y. Acad. Scis., All-Russian Ophthalmol. Soc. E-mail: a.shpak@g23.relcom.ru. Home: Prospect Mira 118 apt 138, 129164 Moscow Russia Office: CIETIN, I Susanin Str 3, 127486 Moscow Russia

LIBOWITZKY, EUGEN, mineralogist, crystallographer; b. Vienna, Austria, Nov. 26, 1962; s. Eugen and Hedwig (Bausback) L.; m. Petra Kolowratnik, May 9, 1987; children: Simon, Lukas. MSc, U. Vienna, 1986, PhD, 1989. Asst. U. Vienna, Austria, 1989-94; postdoctoral rschr. U. Berne, Switzerland, 1994-95, Calif. Inst. Technology, Pasadena, 1995-96; from univ. asst. to asst. prof. U. Vienna, 1996—. Assoc. editor European Jour. Mineralogy, 1998—. Mem. Austrian Mineralogy Soc., Mineralogy Soc. Am., Mineralogy Assn. Can. Roman Catholic. Avocations: music, sports, traveling, family. Office: Inst Mineralogy U Vienna, Althanstr 14, A-1090 Vienna Austria

LIBRESCU, I. LIVIU, aeromautical and mechanical engineer, researcher; b. Ploiesti, Romania, Aug. 18, 1930; came to U.S., 1985; s. Isidor and Mina (Finkelstein) L.; m. Marilena Semian, Apr., 1966; children: Joseph, Lionel. B in Aero. Engring., Poly. Inst., Bucharest, Romania, 1952, MS, 1953; PhD, Acad. Scis. Romania, Bucharest, 1969; PhD (hon.), Poly. U., Bucharest, 2000. Prin. rsch. worker Inst. Fluid Mechanics Acas. Scis., Bucharest, 1953-69, Inst. Aerospace Constrns., Bucharest, 1970-75; prof. aero. mech. engring. Tel-Aviv U., 1979-86; prof. Va. Poly. Inst. and State U., Blacksburg, 1985—; vis. prof. Terza U. degli Studi, Rome, 2000; rschr. NASA Larc, Air Force Office of Sci. Rsch., NATO Rsch Office; lectr. in nat. and internat. confs.; organizer symposia and sessions with nat. and internat. confs.; reviewer for more than 40 jours. Author: Elasto-Statics and Kinetics of Anisotropic and Heterogeneous Shell-Type Structures, 1975; co-author: Random Vibrations and Reliability of Composite, 1992, Thermal Stresses IV, 1996, Series on Stability, Vibration and Control of Systems, vol. 4, 1997; contbr. over 250 articles to profl. jours.; adv. bd. editors Solid Mechs. Archives, 1975—; mem. editl. bd. Jour. Thermal Stresses, 1998, Internat. Jour. Non-Linear Mechs., 1997—, Jour. Thin-Walled Structures, 1999—; author of monographs; guest editor ASME. Recipient Traian Vuia prize Romanian Acad. Sci., 1972, Dean's award Excellence in Rsch., Va. Poly. Inst. and State U., 1999. Fellow Acad. Engring. Armenia, 1999; mem. Internat. Soc. Interaction Mechanics and Maths., N.Y. Acad. Sci., Commn. Astronautics Romanian Acad. Scis. Achievements include research that has resulted in seminal contributions brought within the disciplines: aeroelasticity, composite material structures, classical/non-classical shell, plate and beam theories, non-linear structural stability, unsteady magnetoaerodynamics, unsteady supersonic aerodynamics with chemical reactions, smart structures, vibration feedback control of aeronautical structures. E-mail: librescu@vt.edu. Office: Va Poly Inst and State U MC 0219 Dept Engring Blacksburg VA 24061

LIBROVÁ, HANA, sociologist; b. Brno, Czechoslovakia, Nov. 26, 1943; d. Ludvik and Otilie Nechuta; m. Jaromir Libra, Sept. 25, 1971; 1 child, Bohdana. BS in Biology, U. Brno, 1967; PhD, U. Komenského, 1984. Rsch. scientist Microbiology Inst., Trebon, Czechoslovakia, 1967-68; from asst. to prof. dept. sociology U. Brno, 1968—; founder environ. humanities Masaryk U. Author: Love to the Landscape?, 1988, Social Need and Value of the Landscape, 1987, The Colourful and the Green, 1994. Mem. Soc. Sustainable Living. Home: Tvrdeho 22, 602 00 Brno Czech Republic Office: Masaryk U Dept Environ, Gorkeho7, 602 00 Brno Czech Republic

LICALZI, MICHAEL CHARLES, county official; b. Washington, May 12, 1949; s. Phillip S. Licalzi and Arlene L. (Hemphill) Webb; m. Patricia Ann Roth, Nov. 28, 1970; 1 child, Michael Scott. AAS in Computer Info. Systems, No. Va. C.C., 1990; BBA, Averett Coll., 1995. Wireman Traffic Signal Supply Corp., Alexandria, Va., 1973-91; field troubleshooter Hawkins Electric Co., Inc., College Park, Md., 1973-80; traffic signal field tech. Arlington County, Va., 1980—. Bd. dirs. Internat. Mcpl. Signal Assn. Edn. Found., Ft. Worth, 1995. With USN, 1967-71. Mem. Am. Pub. Works Assn., Mid. Atlantic Signal Assn. (pres. 1985-95), Am. Legion. Avocations: youth football refereeing, umpiring baseball, coaching softball, football. Office: Arlington County Traffic 4300 29th St S Arlington VA 22206-2211

LICHEM, WALTHER G., diplomat; b. Villach, Carinthia, Austria, Mar. 13, 1940; s. Walther J. and Friederike (Wedenigg) L.; m. Maria Teresa Medeiros; children: Matthias, Jûrgen, Maria Emilie, Roland. JD, U. Graz, Austria, 1963; MA, U. N.C., 1967; diploma, Inst. for Higher Studies, Vienna, Austria, 1966. UN secretariat Fed. Ministry for Fgn. Affairs, N.Y., 1965-74; consul gen. Austraian Consulte Gen.Affairs, Ljubljana, Yugoslavia, 1976-80; Austrian amb. to Chile Fed. Ministry for Fgn. Affairs, Vienna, 1980-84; dep. dir. gen. for devel. coop. Fed. Ministry for Fgn. Affairs, Vienna, Yugoslavia, 1985-89; dep. dir. gen. for polit. affairs Fed. Ministry for Fgn. Affairs, Vienna, Chile, 1989-93; Austrian amb. to Can. Fed. Ministry for Fgn. Affairs, Vienna, 1993-2000, dir. internat. orgns., 2000—; chmn. European com. on North-South Campaign Coun. of Europe, Strasbourg, 1986-88; rapporteur IV World Water Congress, 1982; chmn. Interpress Svc., Rome; vice chmn. Ind. Commn. for Human Rights Edn. Mem. Internat. Assn. for Water Law. Lutheran. Office: Fed Ministry Fgn Affairs, Ballhauspl 2, A-1014 Vienna Austria

LICHON, MICHAEL JOHN, environmental scientist, chemist; b. Hobart, Tasmania, Australia, Oct. 18, 1962; s. Franciszek and Tatiana (Maganov) L. BS, U. Tasmania, Hobart, 1983, BSc with honors, 1984, PhD, 2000. Analyst U. Tasmania, Hobart, 1980-82; rsch. asst. E-Z Co., Hobart, 1981-82; geol. asst. Mines Dept., Hobart, 1983; chem. rschr. ICI Australia, Melbourne, 1983-84; food scientist Def. Dept., Scottsdale, Australia, 1985-91; rschr. U. Tasmania, 1991—. Contbg. author: Handbook of Food Analysis, 1996, Ency. Analytical Chemistry, 2000; editor Illuminations, 1992-2000; referee Jour. Chromatography, 1993-96; contbr. articles to profl. jours. Leader Venturer Unit, Scottsdale, 1987; rschr. Wilderness Soc., Hobart, 1992-97. Rsch. scholar Aberboyle Commonwealth, Tasmania, 1991-94. Mem. Royal Australian Chem. Inst., Australian Inst. Food Sci. and Tech., Mole Creek Caving Club (founding pres. 1991-2000). Humanist. Avocations: wilderness photography, cave exploration, wine making, music, water sports. Home: Cascades, 311C Strickland Ave Cascade, Hobart TAS 7004, Australia Office: U Tasmania Dept Plant Sci, GPO Box 252-55, Hobart TAS 7001, Australia

LICHT, CHRISTOPH, medical professional; b. Karlsruhe, Baden, Germany, July 17, 1964; s. August and Anna-Elisabeth (Zimmermann) L.; m. Ulrike Hantel, Apr. 14, 1993; children: Johann-Christoph, Anna, Benedikt. Abitur, Bismarck-Gymnasium, Karlsruhe, 1983; student, U. Essen, U. Heidelberg, U. Freiburg. Cert. pediatrician. Trainee in pediat. Children's Hosp., U. Cologne, 1992-99; postdoctoral rsch. fellow in nephrology U. Tex. S.W. Med. Ctr., Dallas, 1999—. Roman Catholic. Home: 10529 Sandpiper Ln Dallas TX 75230-4218 Office: 5323 Harry Hines Blvd Dallas TX 75390-7208

LICHT, RASMUS WENTZER, psychiatrist; b. Holstebro, Jutland, Denmark, May 26, 1953; s. Orla Wentzer and Else (Lund) L.; m. Ruth Helene Birnbaum, June 9, 1984; children: Lea, Troels. MD, U. Aarhus, Denmark, 1981, PhD, 1999. Registrar Hosp. Rånders, Denmark, 1981-83, Hosp. Horsens, Denmark, 1983-85; sr. registrar County of Aarhus Adminstrn., 1985-86; registrar Mcpl. Hosp. Aarhus, 1986-88; sr. registrar Psychiatric Hosp. Aarhus, 1988-95, chief psychiatrist, 1995—; head Mood Disorders Rsch. Unit, Psychiat. Hosp. Aarhus, 1999; rsch. fellow U. Tex., 1998; cons. County Aarhus Dept. Social Rehab. Contbr. articles to profl. jours. Mem. Danish Soc. Psychiatrists, Scandinavian Soc. Psychopharmacology, Am. Psychiat. Assn. Avocations: tennis, books, music. Office: Psychiat Hosp Aarhus, Skovagervej 2, 8240 Risskov Denmark

LICHTENBERG, PAUL THOMAS, business consultant; b. Detroit, July 30, 1961; s. Harold Fred Lichtenberg and Nörma Lee Boyd; m. Julie Anderson, Dec. 27, 1986; children: Boyd, Samuel, Axel, Grace. BS, Mich. State U., 1983; MBA, Denver U., 1992. Rental/sales mgr. A.I.S. Continental, Richmond, Mich., 1986-90; rental mgr. Mercy Svcs., Frederick, Colo., 1990-92; sr. cons. Thompson Assocs., Ann Arbor, Mich., 1992—. Missionary Ch. of Jesus Christ of Latter-day Saints, New Zealand, 1984-86, 1st councilor, Ann Arbor, 1998—. Scholar Nat. Home Builders Assn., 1991. Mormon. Avocations: swimming, squash, reading. E-mail: paulltaresearch.com. Home: 1035 Long Lake Dr Brighton MI 48114-9641

LICHTENTHALER, FRIEDER WILHELM, chemist, educator; b. Heidelberg, Germany, Jan. 19, 1932; s. Wilhelm and Emma (Hick) L.; m. Evemaria von Infeld, Apr. 15, 1966; children: Matthias, Johannes, Kathrin. Diploma Chemistry, U. Heidelberg, 1956, D in Natural Scis., 1959; DSc (hon.), Kossuth Univ., Debrecen, Hungary, 1993. Rsch. fellow dept. biochemistry U. Calif., Berkeley, 1959-62; habilitation Technische Universität Darmstadt, Germany, 1963, assoc. prof., 1969-72, prof., 1972—; vis. prof. Keio U., Tokyo, 1973, Kyoto U., 1976, Tongji U., Shanghai, 1981, U. Calif., Berkeley, 1985, Yokohama U., 1992. Editor: (monograph) Carbohydrates as Organic Raw Materials, 1991; contbr. over 200 articles to sci. jours. Recipient Sugar Rsch. award Sugar Processing Rsch. Inst., New Orleans, 1994. Fellow Royal Soc. Chem.; mem. Gesellschaft Deutscher Chemiker, Am. Chem. Soc., Chem. Soc. Japan, European Carbohydrate Orgn. (pres. 1985-87). Home: Am Willgraben 5, D-64367 Mühltal Germany Office: Inst Organische Chemie, Petersenstrasse 22, D-64287 Darmstadt Germany

LICHTER, IVAN, surgeon; b. Oudtshoorn, S. Africa, Mar. 14, 1918; s. Goodman and Sarah (Mierowsky) L.; m. Lily Heather Lloyd, Mar. 14, 1951; children: David Gordon, Jonathan Lloyd, Barry Michael, Shelley. MBBCh, Witwatersrand U., Johannesburg, S. Africa, 1940. Medical diplomate. Cons. thoracic surgeon Pneumoconiosis Bur., Johannesburg, 1952-60; thoracic surgeon Rietfontein Hosp., Johannesburg, 1952-60, Boksburg-Benoni Hosp., Boksburg, S. Africa, 1952-60, Otago Hosp. Bd., Dunedin, New Zealand, 1961-84; assoc. prof. surgery U. Otago, Dunedin, 1961-84; med. dir. Te Omanga Hospice, Lower Hutt, New Zealand, 1986-93; examiner in cardio-thoracic surgery Royal Australasian Coll. of Surgeons, 1974-84; mem. Acad. of Hospice Physicians, 1991—. Author: Communication in Cancer Care; contbg. author: Oxford Textbook of Palliative Medicine, 2d edit., 1998, Palliative Care: The Management of Far Advanced Illness, 1984, Ethical Dilemmas in Cancer Care, 1989; contbr. articles to profl. jours. Capt. S. African med. corps, 1942-45. Mem. Order of New Zealand, HM Queen Elizabeth II, Eng., 1997. Fellow Royal Coll. of Surgeons, Royal Australasian Coll. of Surgeons, Australiasian Chpt. Palliative Medicine (hon.). Avocations: hobbies, reading, music, walking. Home: 41 Kitchener Rd, AK 1309 Milford Auckland, New Zealand

LICHTER, PETER, geneticist, researcher; b. Mannheim, Germany, Oct. 16, 1957; m. Annerose Christine Trabold, Aug. 23, 1982; children: Christian, Markus. Diploma in biology, U. Heidelberg, Germany, 1983, PhD in Biology, 1986, degree in molecular human genetics, 1994. Postdoctoral scientist dept. genetics Yale U., New Haven, 1986-90; head project group German Cancer Rsch. Ctr., Heidelberg, 1990-92, head divsn. orgn. of complex genomes, 1992—. Contbr. articles to profl. jours.; mem. editl. bd. Chrom. Rsch., 1993-96, Cytogenet. Cell Genetics, 1993—, GATA, 1990-97, Comp. and Funct. Genomics, 2000—; assoc. editor Internat. Jour. Cancer. Recipient Walther und Christine Richtzenhain Found. award, 1993, Karl Freudenberg award Acad. Scis., 1991; fellow Studienstiftung des Deutschen Volkes, 1981-86, European Molecular Biology Orgn., 1986-87, Deutsches Forschungsgemeinschaft, 1987-89. Mem. Soc. Human Genetics (award 1992), European Assn. Cancer Rsch., German Cancer Soc. Achievements include development of in situ hybridization techniques and their application in clinical diagnostics and cell biology, structure of the cell nucleus. Office: German Cancer Rsch Ctr, Im Neuenheimer Feld 280, 69120 Heidelberg Germany

LICHTIG, LEO KENNETH, health economist; b. Bklyn., Oct. 20, 1953; s. Samuel and Alyne Norma (Strauss) L.; m. Susan Mary Walsh, May 15, 1977; children: Brielle Joy, Danica Jill. BS, MS, Rennselaer Poly. Inst., 1974, PhD, 1976. Asst. prof. SUNY, Albany, 1976-77; project specialist, econometrician N.J. State Dept. Health, Trenton, 1977-82; dir. utilization econs. and rsch. Empire Blue Cross/Blue Shield, Albany, 1982-90; v.p. rsch. and demonstration Health Care Rsch. Found., Albany, 1982-90; v.p. Network, Inc., Randolph, N.J., Latham, N.Y., 1990-94; sr. v.p., chief info. officer Network, Inc., Somerset, N.J., 1994—, Latham, N.Y., 1994—; pvt. practice cons., Latham, 1982-90; mem. nat. diagnosis related group steering com. health care fin. adminstrn. Yale U., Washington, 1979-81; mem. adj. faculty Russell Sage Grad. Sch. Health Adminstrn., Albany, 1986-94, Union Coll. Grad. Mgmt. Inst., Schenectady, N.Y., 1991-92; expert reviewer Health Care Financing Adminstrn., Washington, 1987, 89. Author: Hospital Information Systems for Case Mix Management, 1986; contbg. editor (newsletter) Nat. Report on Computers & Health, 1982-85; contbr. articles to profl. jours. Mem. tech. adv. com. Statewide Planning and Rsch. Coop. System, N.Y. State Dept. Health; mem. N.Y. State Universal Data Specifications Task Force, 1998—. Mem. Assn. for Health Svcs. Rsch., Am. Statis. Assn. (com. on privacy and confidentiality 1981-84, subcom. on quality and productivity measures 1988-90), Healthcare Fin. Mgmt. Assn. Avocation: Arthurian legends. Office: Network Inc 270 Davidson Ave Somerset NJ 08873-4140

LICHTMAN, ALLAN JAY, historian, educator, consultant; b. Bklyn., Apr. 4, 1947; s. Emanuel and Gertrude Louise (Cohen) L.; m. Katherine Martin Crane, June 6, 1970 (div.); 1 child, Kara Martin; m. Shelia Bradford, 1980 (div.); m. Karyn Lynn Strickler, June 8, 1991; 1 child, Samuel Allan. BA magna cum laude, Brandeis U., 1967; PhD, Harvard U., 1973. Dir. forensics Brandeis U., Waltham, Mass., 1968-71, Harvard U., Cambridge, Mass., 1971-72; asst. prof. history The Am. U., Washington, 1973-77; assoc. prof. history The Am. U., Washington, 1977-78, prof. of history, 1978—, assoc. dean faculty and curricular devel. coll. arts & scis., 1985-87, chair dept. history, 1997—; instr. Brandeis U., 1970; cons. Smithsonian Instn., 1974-79, John Anderson campaign for Pres., 1980, George Washington U., 1983, U.S. Dept. Justice, Washington, 1983—, V.P. Albert Gore, Jr., Washington, 1994-95; advisor Ted Kennedy for Pres. campaign, 1980; cons., commentator NBC spl. project on the history of the Am. Presidency; news cons. CBS; polit. commentator NBC News Nightside, Voice of Am., USIA, Am.'s Talking Cable Network; expert witness Com. for Civil Rights Under Law, 1983—, U.S. Dept. Justice, 1983—, pvt. attys., 1986—, various state, mcpl. and county jurisdictions, 1986—, ACLU, 1987—, So. Poverty Law Ctr., 1990, Legal Def. Fund, 1991, Puerto Rican Legal Def. and Edn. Fund, 1991—, NAACP, 1993-94, Reform Party, 1996, 2000, Reuters News Svc., 1996, 2000; columnist Montgomery Jour., Rockville, Md., 1990-98; columnist Montgomery Gazette, Gaithersburg, Md., 1998—; appeared on various radio and TV programs; spkr. at more than 50 confs. Author: Your Family History: How to Use Oral History, Personal Family Archives, and Public Documents to Discover Your Héritage, 1978, Prejudice and the Old Politics: The Presidential Election of 1928, 1979, The Keys to the White House, 1996; co-author (with Valerie French) Historians and the Living Past: The Theory and Practice of Historical Study, 1978, (with Laura Irwin Langbein) Ecological Inference, 1978; co-editor (with Joan Challinor) Kin and Communities: Families in America, 1979, (with Ken DeCell) The 13 Keys to the Presidency, 1990; series editor: Studies in Modern American History, 2000—; contbr. articles to profl. jours. and popular mags. Tchg. fellow Harvard U., 1969-73; rsch. grantee Am. U., 1978, 82; recipient Outstanding Young Men of Am. award U.S. C. of C. 1979-80, Top Spkr. award Nat. Conv. Internat. Platform Assn., 1983, 84, 87; Sherman Fairchild Distinguished Visiting scholar Calif. Inst. Tech., 1980-81; defeated twenty opponents on TIC TAC DOUGH, 1981. Mem. Am. Historian Assn., Orgn. Am. Historians, Social Sci. History Assn., Fed. City Club, Phi Alpha Phi, Phi Beta Kappa. Democrat. Jewish. Home: 9219 Villa Dr Bethesda MD 20817-3365 Office: The Am Univ Washington DC 20016

LICHTSTEIN, DAVID, physiologist, researcher; b. Lodz, Poland, July 13, 1949; arrived in Israel, 1957; s. Chaim and Miriam (Sandler) L.; m. Esther Lipshitz, Nov. 2, 1970; children: Ehud, Tamar, Gideon. BSc, Hebrew U., Jerusalem, 1970, MSc, 1972, PhD, 1977. Postdoctoral fellow Roche Inst. Molecular Biology, Nutley, N.J., 1977-79; from asst. prof. physiology to assoc. prof. Hebrew U. Med. Sch., 1979-95, prof., 1995—, chmn. neurobiology tchg. divsn., 1982-85; vis. scientist NICHD, NIH, Bethesda, Md., 1985-86; chmn. dept. physiology, Hebrew U. Med. Sch., 1992-96; chmn. Inst. Med. Scis., 1999—. Contbr. articles to profl. publs. Grantee Inst. Psychobiology, 1981, Nat. Acad. Scis., Israel, 1982-83, 86, 88, Israel-U.S.A. Binat. Found., 1994—. Mem. Internat. Neurochemistry, Soc. Neuroscis., Am. Soc. Hypertension (pres.), Israel Soc. for Physiology and Pharmacology (pres. 1995-99). Home: 22 Propes St, Jerusalem 97735, Israel Office: Hebrew U Hadassah Med Sch, PO Box 12272, Jerusalem 91120, Israel

LICKINDORF, ELISABETH TERESA, English educator, freelance journalist; b. London, Apr. 24, 1948; arrived in South Africa, 1977; d. Stansilaw and Teresa Ludwiga (Giedroyć) L. BA, U. Cape Town, South Africa, 1969, BA with honors, 1970; MPhil, U. Oxford, England, 1973, DPhil, 1986. Lectr. U. Witwatersrand, South Africa, 1977-81, Rand Afrikaans U., South Africa, 1982-94; prof., dept. head U. Port Elizabeth, South Africa, 1995-98. Editor: Shakespeare's Macbeth, 1987. Mem. Human Scis. Soc. South Africa (mgmt. com., chair 1993-95, 97-2000), Assn. Univ. English Tchrs. South Africa (chair 1991-96). Roman Catholic. Avocations: reading, watching movies, walking.

LIDBURY, BRETT ANDREW, research virologist and immnologist; b. Waratah, NSW, Australia, Nov. 23, 1963; s. Ronald and Glenda May (Phillips) L. BS, U. Newcastle, NSW, 1989, BS with honours, 1990; PhD, Australia Nat. U., Canberra, 1993. Cert. med. lab. technologist. Rsch. scientist Australian Inst. Mucosal Immunology, Newcastle, 1994-95; postdoctoral fellow Faculty Sci., Australian Nat. U., 1995-96; lectr. sch. human & biomed. sci. divsn. sci. and design U. Canberra, Australia, 1996—. Contbr. articles to sci. jours., including Archives Virology, Cytokine, Immunology and Cell Biology, Lymphokine and Cytokine Rsch., Jour. Infectious Disease. Mem. Australasian Soc. Immunology. Avocations: sports, guitar, mandolin. Office: U Canberra Divsn Sci Design, Sch Human and Biomed Sci, Canberra ACT 2601, Australia

LIDDELL, JANE HAWLEY HAWKES, civic worker; b. Newark, Dec. 8, 1907; d. Edward Zeh and Mary Everett (Hawley) Hawkes; AB, Smith Coll., 1931; postgrad. in art history, Harvard U., 1933-35; MA, Columbia U., 1940; Carnegie fellow Sorbonne, Paris, 1937; m. Donald M. Liddell, Jr., Mar. 30, 1940; children: Jane Boyer, D. Roger Brooke. Pres., Planned Parenthood Essex County (N.J.), 1947-50; trustee Prospect Hill Sch. Girls, Newark, 1946-50; mem. adv. bd., publicity and public relations chmn. N.J. State Mus., Trenton, 1952-60; sec., then v.p. women's br. N.J. Hist. Soc.; women's aux. prodn. chmn. Englewood (N.J.) Hosp., 1959-61; pres. Dwight Sch. Girls Parents Assn., 1955-57; v.p. Englewood Sch. Boys Parents Assn., 1958-60; mem. Altar Guild, women's aux. bd., rector's adv. council St. Paul's Episcopal Ch., Englewood, 1954-59; bd. dir. N.Y. State Soc. of Nat. Soc. Colonial Dames, 1961-67, rep. conf. Patriotic and Hist. Socs., 1964—; bd.

dirs. Huguenot Soc. Am., 1979-86, regional v.p., 1979-82, historian, 1983-84, co-chmn. Tercentennial Book, 1983-85; bd. dirs. Soc. Daus. Holland Dames, 1965-82; nat. jr. v.p. Dames of Loyal Legion, USA; bd. dirs., mem. publs. com. Daus. Cin., 1966-72; bd. dirs. Ch. Women's League Patriotic Service, 1962—, pres., 1968-70, 72-74; bd. dirs., chmn. grants com. Youth Found., N.Y.C., 1974—; chmn. for Newark, Smith Coll. 75th Ann. Fund, 1948-50; pres. North N.J. Smith Club, 1956-58; pres. Smith Coll. Class 1931, 1946-51, 76-81, editor 50th anniversary book, 1980-81. Author: (with others) Huguenot Refugees in the Settling of Colonial America, 1982-85; contbr. The Dutch Contribution to the Development of Early Manhattan, 1969. Recipient various commendation awards. Republican. Mem. Colonial Dames Am. (N.Y.C. chpt.). Clubs: Colony, City Gardens, Church (N.Y.C.); Jr. League N.Y.; N.Y. Jr. League; Needle and Bobbin, Nat. Farm and Garden . Editor: Maine Echoes, 1961; research and editor asst., Wartime Writings of American Revolution Officers, 1972-75.

LIDMAN, TOMAS ERIK, national librarian; b. Stockholm, June 30, 1948; s. Ivar and Gunhild (Andersson) L.; m. Kerstin Gårdbro, Aug. 19, 1972; children: Erica, Carl-Fredrik, Charlotte. PhD, U. Stockholm, 1979. Asst. libr. Royal Libr., Stockholm, 1971-79; sr. libr. Stockholm U. Libr., 1979-80; head dept. Delegation for Sci. Info., Stockholm, 1980-84; libr. Nordic Mus., Stockholm, 1984-85; dir. Nat. Libr. Psychology and Edn., Stockholm, 1985-92; libr. Stockholm U. Libr., 1992-95; nat. libr. Royal Libr., Stockholm, 1995—; chmn. U. Borås, 1998—. Author: Party Politics in the House of Nobility in the 19th Century, 1979, Libraries in Sweden, 1990; co-author: Litteratursociologi, 1995; editor: Svenska Antikvariat, 1986. Mem. Swedish Assn. Bibliophiles (pres. 1992-97), Swedish Assn. Rsch. Librs. (pres. 1989-94), Scandinavian Fedn. Rsch. Librs. (pres. 1992-94). Avocations: art, music, sports, travel. Office: Royal Libr, PO Box 5039, S-10241 Stockholm Sweden

LIDMAR-BERGSTRÖM, KARNA HELENA, physical geographer, researcher, educator; b. Halmstad, Sweden, Apr. 26, 1940; d. Rudolf Edvard and Inga (Malmgren) Lidmar; m. Jan Lennart Bergström, June 11, 1966; children: Johan, Helena. MS, Lund (Sweden) U., 1964, PhD, 1982. Asst. Lund U., 1961-65, 1968-82, rsch. asst., 1982-88, rschr., lectr., 1988-89, asst. prof., 1990; rschr. Stockholm U., 1989-93, rschr., lectr., 1994-2000, prof., 2000—; mem. editl. adv. bd. Scottish Geog. Mag., Glasgow, 1996—, Norwegian Jour. Geography, 2000—. Author: Pre-Quaternary Geomorphological Evolution in Southern Fennoscandia, 1982; editor spl. issue Geografiska Annaler, 1988, Geomorphology, 1995. Mem. Brit. Geomorphology Rsch. Group, Swedish Soc. for Anthropology and Geography (Alfort prize 1985). Office: Stockholm U, Dept Phys Geography, SE-10691 Stockholm Sweden

LIDON, FERNANDO JOSÉ CEBOLA, education educator; b. Elvas, Alentejo, Portugal; s. José Frederico Mourato and Isidora Conceicão Rica Cebola L.; m. Filomena Cruz Guerreiro Mira, Aug. 15, 1990; children: Marta Mira, Sara Mira, Sofia Mira. Grad. biology, U. Evora, Portugal, 1984; grad. in biochemistry, U. Lisboa, Portugal, 1989; M of Biology, U. Nova Lisboa, Portugal, 1991, PhD in Biochemistry, 1994; PhD in Plant Biochemistry, U. Wis., 1998. Tchr. U. Evora, 1981-82; h.s. tchr. Evora, 1983-87; prof. U. Nova Lisboa, 1987—; rschr. Estacao Agronomica Nacional, Oeiras, Portugal, 1989-99. Contbr. articles to profl. jours. Avocation: fishing.

LIDSTONE, HERRICK KENLEY, JR., lawyer; b. New Rochelle, N.Y., Sept. 10, 1949; s. Herrick Kenley and Marcia Edith (Drake) L.; m. Mary Lynne O'Toole, Aug. 5, 1978; children: Herrick Kevin, James Patrick, John Francis. AB, Cornell U., 1971; JD, U. Colo., 1978. Bar: Colo. 1978, U.S. Dist. Ct. Colo. 1978. Assoc. Roath & Brega, P.C., Denver, 1978-85, Brenman, Epstein, Raskin & Friedlob, P.C., Denver, 1985-86; shareholder Brenman, Raskin & Friedlob, P.C., Denver, 1986-94; mem. Friedlob Sanderson Raskin Paulson & Tourtilott, LLC, Denver, 1995-98, Norton Lidstone, P.C., Englewood, Colo., 1998—; adj. prof. U. Denver Coll. Law, 1985-2000; spkr. in field various orgns. Editor U. Colo. Law Rev., 1977-78; co-author: Federal Income Taxation of Corporations, 6th edit.; contbg. author: Legal Opinion Letters Formbook, 1996, supplement, 1999; contbr. articles to profl. jours. Served with USN, 1971-75, with USNR, 1975-81. Mem. ABA (Am. Law Inst.), Colo. Bar Assn., Arapahoe County Bar Assn., Denver Assn. Oil and Gas Title Lawyers. Avocation: fluent Spanish language. Office: Norton Lidstone PC 5445 Dtc Pkwy Ste 850 Englewood CO 80111-3076

LIDSTONE, JOHN GRAHAM, geographer, educator; b. Sittingbourne, Eng., Apr. 21, 1947; s. Stanley James and Clare L.; m. Heather Barrett Norris, Aug. 29, 1970; children: Christopher, Anna. BSc in Econs., London U., 1971, MA, 1977, PhD, 1985. Tchr. geography, environ. and social studies various h.s., England, 1971-83; lectr. Brisbane Coll. Advanced Edn., Australia, 1984-90; sr. lectr. Queensland U. Tech., Brisbane, 1991—; dir. Ctr. Applied Environ. Social Edn. Rsch., Brisbane, 1992-96, assoc. prof. edn., 1999—; exec. sec. Internat. Geographical Union Commn. on Geographical Edn., 1992-2000. Mem. Royal Geog. Soc. Queensland (councillor, chair edn. com. 1993—). Office: Queensland U Tech Fac Edn, Victoria Park Rd, Red Hill Australia 4059

LIE, TSCHONG-SU, medical educator; b. Seoul, Korea, Feb. 20, 1929; arrived in Germany, 1959; s. Kysup and Lymson (Soe) L. Med. exam., U. Düsseldorf, Germany, 1962, PhD in Medicine, 1964; PhD in Sci. (hon.), Konkuk U., Seoul, 1976; PhD in Law (hon.), Hanyang U., Seoul, 1993. Asst. dept. surgery Bethesda Hosp., Duisburg, Germany, 1963-64, City Hosp., Wuppertal, Germany, 1964-66; univ. asst. Surg. Univ. Clin., U. Bonn, Germany, 1967-70, docent, 1970-75, chief dept. transplantation, 1975—; life prof. U. Bonn, 1975—. Author: Liver Transplantation, 1974, Acites, 1994, Dealing with Liver Disease; editor: Microsurgery, 1978; contbr. articles to profl. publs. Chmn. Inst. for Liver Disease Rsch., Bonn, 1993—, Prof. Dr. T.S. Lie's Med. Rsch. Found., Seoul, 1989—. Mem. Internat. Transplantation Soc., Internat. Soc. Artificial Organs, European Soc. Surg. Rsch., Internat. Soc. Lymphology, Internat. Microsurg. Soc., German Soc. Surgery, German-Korean Soc. Medicine (pres. 1992—). Home: Falkenweg 6, 53359 Rheinbach Merzbach, Germany Office: Inst for Rsch Liver Disease, Adolfstr 9-11, 53111 Bonn Germany

LIE, YU-CHUN DONALD, electrical engineer; b. Taipei, Taiwan, Apr. 25, 1965; came to U.S., 1989; s. Kuo-Chin and Shu-Ling (Kung) L.; m. Ching-Wen Wendy Yang, Aug. 26, 1995; 1 child, Paul Emmanuel. BSc, Nat. Taiwan U., Taipei, 1987; MSc, Calif. Inst. Tech., 1990, DPhil, 1995. Cert. engr.-in-tng., Calif. Comm., electronics, rsch. officer Taiwanese Army, 1987-89; head tchg. and rsch. asst. Calif. Inst. Tech., Pasadena, 1990-95; sr. process devel. engr. Rockwell Semiconductor Sys., Newport Beach, Calif., 1995-97, staff engr., 1997-99; mem. tech. staff, advisory engr., RFIC designer Silicon Wave Inc., San Diego, 1999-2000; advisory engr., scientist analog/RFIC designer IBM Microelectronics, Encinitas, Calif., 2000—; summer intern Motorola Inc., Phoenix, 1994, Jet Propulsion Lab., Pasadena, Calif., 1993. Contbr. over 30 articles to profl. jours., chpts. to books, internat. confs. Rotary Internat. scholar, Evanston, Ill., 1989-90; recipient Grad. Student award Internat. Union Material Rsch. Soc., 1994, various scholarships and contests. Mem. IEEE. Baptist. Achievements include patents on designing semiconductor circuits, devices and materials.

LIEBAU, FREDERIC JACK, JR., investment manager; b. Palo Alto, Calif., Sept. 30, 1963; s. Frederic Jack and Charlene (Conrad) L.; m. Carol Platt. BA, Stanford U., 1985. Press aide Office of V.P., Washington, 1982; intern L.A. Times, 1983; analyst Capital Rsch. Co., L.A., 1984-86; ptnr., portfolio mgr. Primecap Mgmt. Co., Pasadena, Calif., 1986—; owner Liebau Farms. Office: Primecap Mgmt Co 225 S Lake Ave Ste 400 Pasadena CA 91101-3093

LIEBENBERG, ALGERNON CHARLES, civil engineer; b. Bredasdorp, We. Cape, S. Africa, Dec. 13, 1926; s. Louis Wilhelm and Johanna Martha (Loxton) L.; m. Francina Salomina Jurgens, Oct. 6, 1951; children: Wilhelm, Franciscus, Deon, Louis, Annette. BS Engring., U. Cape Town, 1948, PhD, 1965, DSc in Engring. (hon.), 1995. Chartered profl. engr. S. Africa, U.K. Asst. design engr. A F Bisschop Cons. Engrs., Cape Town, 1949-50; rsch. asst. civil engring. dept. U. Cape Town, 1951-52; sr. ptnr. A C Liebenberg Cons. Engr., Cape Town, 1951-54; sr. ptnr. Liebenberg & Stander, Cape Town, 1954-93, cons., 1993—; chmn. local and regional bds. of PERM Bldg. Soc., Cape Town, 1970-92; mem. Civil Engring. Adv. Coun., Bldg. Industries Adv. Coun., Sci. Adv. Coun., 1988-90, Bd. Nuclear Accelerator Ctr., Faure, 1991-94. Author: Concrete Bridges: Design and Construction, 1992; co-author: Handbook of Structural Concrete, 1983, Bridge Aesthetics Around the World, 1991; contbr. articles to profl. jours. Recipient Order for Meritorious Svc. (Gold) Chancery of Orders, State Pres. of South Africa, Fedn. Internat. de la Précontrainte medal, 1997. Fellow Acad. Engrs. of South Africa (founder, pres. 1991), Royal Acad. Engring. U.K. (fgn. mem.), South Africa Inst. Civil Engrs. (hon., pres. 1976, Gold medal 1993); mem. ASCE (life), South African Assn. Cons. Engrs. (hon., pres. 1969-70), Assn. Sci. and Tech. Soc. of South Africa (Gold medal 1983), South African Inst. Archs. (hon.). Achievements include identification and analysis of arch action in concrete slabs; devel. of a stress-strain function (non-linear) for concrete, analytical procedure to determine interaction between shear walls and frames in tall bldgs., risk analysis of bridges subjected to flooding, suspended by cables method of constructing large concrete arch bridges; identified planar force in stairs; responsibility for design of several large span concrete bridges and tall buildings in South Africa. Home: Silverhurst Est Constantia, Western Cape 7806, South Africa

LIEBERMAN, ABRAHAM NATHAN, physician, medical administrator; b. Bklyn., July 8, 1938; s. Usher and Esther (Nosenchuk) L.; m. Ina Lieberman, Feb. 14, 1965; children: Wendy, Unice, Usher, Mike. AB, Cornell U., 1959; MD, NYU, 1963. Diplomate Am. Bd. Psychiatry and Neurology. Intern Cin. Gen. Hosp., 1963-64; resident, chief resident in neurology Bellevue Hosp. Med. Ctr.-NYU, N.Y.C., 1964-67; staff neurologist USAF Hosp., Tachikawa, Japan, 1967-69; fellow in pharmacology NYU Med. Ctr., N.Y.C., 1969-70, from instr. to prof. neurology, 1970-89; attending physician Univ. Hosp., N.Y.C., 1970-78; attending physician Bellevue Hosp., N.Y.C., 1970-89, assoc. dir. EEG, 1973-79; attending physician Manhattan VA Hosp., 1972-89; chief Movement Disorders Barrow Neurol. Inst., 1989—; attending physician St. Joseph's Hosp., Phoenix, 1989-98; cons. NeuroSci. Inst. Good Samaritan Hosp., L.A., 1993-98; nat. med. dir. Muhammad Ali Ctr. Excellence Nat. Parkinson Found., Miami, Fla., 1997—; reviewer Archives of Neurology, Annals of Internal Medicine, Annals of Neurology, JAMA, Jour. Pharmacology and Exptl. Therapeutics, Med. Letter, Movement Disorders, New Eng. Jour. Medicine, Neurology; mem. pharm. med. adv. bd., cons. Adria Labs., 1988-91, Boehringer Ingelheim, 1992-96, Elan Pharms., 1990-92, Janssen Pharms., 1990-92, Merck, Sharpe & Dohme, 1983-89, Pharmacia, 1991—, Smith Kline Beecham, 1995—, SIBIA, 1994—, Novartis (formerly Sandox), 1985—, Eli Lilly, 1996—, Hoffman LaRoche, 1993—, Dupont Pharma, 1995—; presenter papers at confs., symposiums, and seminars; lectr. in field. Editor-in-chief Neuroviews Trends in Clin. Neurology, 1985-89, Neurology Forum, 1990-96; mem. editl. bd. Parkinsonism and Related Disorders, 1995—; contbr. numerous articles to profl. jours. including Neurology, JAMA, Jour. Neurol. Neurosurgery Psychiatry. Recipient numerous awards; grantee Nat. Cancer Inst., 1969-71, 72-75, 76-79, Merck, Sharp and Dohme, 1971-72, 75, Sterling Winthrop, 1971, Schering Corp., 1972-75, Nat. Inst. Neurol. and Communicative Disorders and Stroke, 1972-83, Servior Labs., 1973-75, Eli Lilly Corp., 1977-80, 79-80, 97—, Schering AG, 1979-82, Hoffman La Roche, 1982-85, 92-94, 94—, Sandoz, 1983-85, Janssen Pharms., 1984-86, Syntho Labs., 1985, Am. Home Products, 1985-87, FIDIA, 1985-87, Somerset Pharms., 1986-89, Adria Labs., 1990-92, Elan Pharms., 1990-92, Synergan, 1993-95, Smith Kline Beecham, 1993-97, MDS Harris and Scherer, 1997—, Novartis, 1997—, PSG, 1997—, Merrill-Trust, 1972, Bendheim Found., 1986-89, John and Evelyn Kossak Found., 1989-96, Frank and Donna Stanton Found., 1992-95, Wallace Found., 1994-96, among others. Fellow Am. Acad. Neurology; mem. Am. Neurol. Assn., Movement Disorder Soc., World Fed. Neurology Rsch. Coun., Internat. Tremor Found. (med. adv. bd. 1993—), Parkinson's Disease Study Group. Office: Nat Parkinson Found 1501 NW 9th Ave Miami FL 33136-1407

LIEBERMAN, DOUGLAS LIONEL, scriptwriter, software writer; b. Detroit, Mich., Dec. 14, 1946; s. Barnard Leon and Mary Elizabeth (McKinney) L.; m. Beverly Anne Berneman,. AB, Columbia U., 1968; MFA, Art Inst. Chgo., 1972. Mem. Cranbrook Sch., Bloomfield Hills, Mich., 1968-70; mem. faculty Art Inst. Chgo., 1970-74; lectr. Northwestern U., Evanston, Ill., 1978-86, Loyola U., Chgo., 1984-86; pres. Rocket Riter, Inc., Skokie, Ill., 1988—; assoc. Hewitt Assocs., Lincolnshire, Ill., 1999—; bd. chmn. Imagination Celebration, Chgo., 1973-74. Author: (play) Contemporary Children's Theatre, 1973; editor: Pre-Med: Foundation of a Medical Career, 1968; scriptwriter documentaries including Choosing One's Way (Hugo award Chgo. Film Festival 1994), 1993. Jem. bd. edn., dist. 69, Skokie, Ill.; chmn., bd. dirs., Halevi Choral Soc., Chgo. Recipient silver medal awards N.Y. FilmFestival, 1979, 1982, bronze medal, 1984, 9 Golden Eagle awards CINE Film Festival, Washington, D.C., 1982, 1985-86, 1989-90, 1992, 1st and 2d place Western Film Showcase, Canada, 1990, Creative Excellence award U.S. Indsl. Film Festival; named Favorite Tchr. Detroit News, 1968. Avocations: piano, orchids, tropical fish. Office: Hewitt Assocs 4 Overlook Pt Lincolnshire IL 60069-4302

LIEBERMAN, EUGENE, lawyer; b. Chgo., May 17, 1918; s. Harry and Eva (Goldman) L.; m. Pearl Naomi Feldman, Aug. 3, 1947; children: Mark, Robert, Steven. LLB, DePaul U., 1940, JD, 1941. Bar: Ill. 1941, U.S. Supreme Ct. 1963. Mem. firm Jacobs and Lieberman, 1954-60; sr. ptnr. Jacobs, Lieberman and Aling, 1960-74; spl. hearing officer U.S. Dept. Justice, 1967-78; hearing officer Ill. Pollution Control Bd., 1973—; pvt. practice Chgo. Contbr. articles to profl. jours. With U.S. Army, 1942-45. Recipient 1st in State award Moot Ct. Championship, 1940, gold award Philatelic Exhbn., Taipei, 1981, gold award World Philatelic Exhbn., Melbourne, 1984, Meritorious Svc. medal, bronze arrowhead award, others. Mem. Ill. State Bar Assn. (sr. counselor 1991), Chgo. Bar Assn., Appellate Lawyers Assn., Chgo. Philatelic Soc. (pres. 1964-68), Ill. Athletic Club. Home: 801 Leclaire Ave Wilmette IL 60091-2065

LIEBERMAN, JOSEPH ALOYSIUS, III, physician, educator; b. Allentown, Pa., Oct. 15, 1938; s. Joseph Aloysius and Marie Catherine (McDermott) L.; m. Judith Ann Dees, July 23, 1966; children: Lila, Lucy, Joseph IV, Karl. BS, Georgetown U., Washington, 1960; MD, Jefferson Med. Coll., Phila., 1964; MA in Pub. Health Rutgers U., 1989, Health Policy Fellow, Inst. of Med. Nat. Acad Scis., 1988-89 Diplomate Am. Bd. Family Practice. Family physician Sr/Jr Partnership, Allentown, 1967-68; pvt. practice, Allentown, 1968-71; sr. ptnr. West End Med. Group, Allentown, 1971-77; faculty Robert Wood Johnson Med. Sch., Piscataway, N.J., 1977-91, prof., chmn. dept. family medicine, 1982-91; clin. prof. family medicine Jefferson Med. Coll. Thomas Jefferson U., 1991—, chmn. dept. family and cmty. medicine Christiana Care Health Sys., 1991—. Contbr. articles to profl. jours. Capt. USAF, 1965-67. Recipient Exceptional Merit award U. Medicine and Dentistry of N.J., 1979-82. Republican. Roman Catholic. Office: Christiana Care Health Sys Dept Family & Cmty Medicine PO Box 1668 Wilmington DE 19899-1668

LIEBERMAN, LESTER ZANE, engineering company executive; b. Newark, July 4, 1930; s. Herman P. and Cecile A. (Ashenfeld) L.; m. Judith Mazor, Aug. 11, 1957; children—Susan, Jane. BS in Mech. Engring., Newark Coll. Engring., 1951, postgrad., 1953-58; DHL (hon.), Clarkson U., 1991. Registered profl. engr., N.J., Pa. Pres. Crest Engring. Inc., Newark, 1955-60; chmn., pres. Atmos Engring. Co. Inc., Kenilworth, N.J., 1960-78; pres., CEO, Clarkson Industries, Inc., N.Y.C., 1978-90; real estate investment and development Dowel Assoc., 1990—; partner, cons. Construction HUAC, 1990—; bd. dirs. Lazard Fund, Cives Steel Corp. Trustee Clarkson U., Potsdam, N.Y.; chmn. Beth Israel Med. Ctr., Newark, 1970-96, NBI Healthcare Found. N.J., 1996—, N.J. Healthcare Found., 1996—. Named Alumnus of Yr., Newark Coll. Engring., 1980; recipient Friendship award Best Friends Newark, 1999, Humanitarian award St. Barnabas's Burn Found., 1999, Citizens award N.J. Acad. Medicine, 2000. Mem. ASHRAE (pres. 1964-65), Nat. Soc. Profl. Engrs., N.J. Soc. Profl. Engrs., Assn. Energy Engrs., Am. Acad. Environ. Engrs. (diplomate), Mason., Mountain Ridge Country Club (N.J.), Stockbridge Country Club (Mass.), Cornell Club (N.Y.), Morristown Club, Tau Beta Pi (Key award 1982). Jewish. Lodge: Masons. Avocations: skiing, sailing, tennis, golf. Home: Spring Valley Rd Morristown NJ 07960-7011 Office: 1500 Mount Kemble Ave Morristown NJ 07960-6799

LIEBERMAN, LYNN I., psychologist; b. Chgo., Dec. 20, 1953; d. Morris and Teresa (Kneller) L. BA, U. Kans., 1973; MS, U. Mo., Columbia, 1975; PhD, U. Mo., Kansas City, 1990. Lic. psychologist, Kans., Mo., Nebr., B.C. Russian resettlement counselor Jewish Vocat. Svc., Kansas City, 1977-78; employment devel. specialist City of Kansas City, 1978-82; therapist Rsch. Mental Health Ctr., Kansas City, 1986-88; psychologist Western Mo. Mental Health Ctr., Kansas City, 1989—; cons. Long-Term Care Physicians, Kansas City, 1987-89, Golden Years, Missino, Kans., 1995-97; presenter, lectr. Internat. Schizophrenia Conf., 1996, 98. Participant Operation Cross Roads Africa, Ivory Coast, 1973; com. mem. Kansas City Balley Guild, 1991-94; mem. Friends of Ailey, Kansas City, 1996-99. NDFL fellow Cornell U., Ithaca, N.Y., 1972. Mem. Baha'i Faith. E-mail: lynnlee@prodigy.net. Office: Western Mo Mental Health Ctr 600 E 22d St Kansas City MO 64108

LIEBERMAN, MARK JOEL, lawyer; b. Chgo., Apr. 12, 1949; s. Eugene and Pearl Naomi (Feldman) L.; m. Kathleen; children: Amy, Kevin. BA, DePaul U., 1971, JD, 1974. Bar: Ill. 1974, Calif. 1980, Tex. 1989. House counsel Mercantile Fin. Corp., Chgo., 1974-80; sr. atty. Assocs. Comml. Corp., Chgo., 1981-84; v.p., asst. gen. counsel Assocs. Comml. Corp., Dallas, 1984—; spkr. in field. Contbr. articles to profl. jours. Mem. ABA, Calif. State Bar Assn. Republican. Jewish. Avocation: woodcarving. Office: Assocs Comml Corp 300 E Carpenter Fwy Irving TX 75062-2727

LIEBERS, RALF THORSTEN, mathematician, educator; b. Radeberg, Saxony, Germany, Dec. 8, 1961; s. Dieter and Margarete (Härtel) L.; m. Simone Albrecht, May 18, 1980 (div. 1985); children: Daniel, Kristin; m. Constanze Prignitz, Mar. 11, 1989; children: Mark Norman, Carrie-Sue. M in Math., Tech. U., Dresden, 1988, M in Math. Informatics, 1988; M in Math. Informatics, Tech. U., Dresden, 1989; PhD, Mining Acad., Freiberg, 1993. Sci. asst. Inst. Geoscis., Freiberg, 1989-92, rschr., 1992-93; rsch. prof. Inst. Planetary Geodesy, Dresden, 1993-95; rschr. Inst. Statistics in Econs., Dresden, 1996-97; mgr. faculty medicine Tech. U. Dresden, 1997—; vis. rschr. Geol. Survey, Lawrence, Kans., 1992; co-worker Statis. Office, Dresden, 1984-89, cons., Freiberg, 1989-93; reviewer Internat. Ass. for Math. Geology, 1994—, Slovakian Statis. Soc., 1994—. Co-editor: Geostatistical Glossary, 1992; contbr. articles to profl. jours. Mem. Hist. Soc., Radeberg, 1976-80, Hist. Assn., Dresden, 1984-89; pres. Young Mathematicians, 1989-91. Bn. comdr. German Air Force, 1980-83. Mem. Internat. Assn. Math. Geology, Am. Math. Soc., Soc. Indsl. and Applied Math. Avocations: sports, postal stamps, American Native, poems. Home: Am Birkenwaldchen 9, 01900 Bretnig-Hauswalde Germany Office: Tech U Dresden Fac Med Assn Clin Rsch Mgmt, Haus 40 Fetscherstr 74, 01307 Dresden Germany

LIEBERS, VERENA IRIS GISELA, immunologist; b. Berlin, May 31, 1961; d. Gottfried and Ilse (Lenski) L. PhD, U. Munich, 1992. Scientist Klinikum Grosshadern, Munich, Germany, 1989-90; BGFA, Bochum, Germany, 1990—. Avocations: painting, writing, sports, reading. Office: BGFA, Burkle de la Camp Pl 1, 44789 Bochum Germany

LIEBERT, ULRIKE, political scientist, educator; b. Weimar, Thuringen, Germany, Jan. 30, 1951; d. Günther and Ursula (Kleekottka) L.; m. Frances Tierra Morata; m. David Bathrick; 1 child, Tilmann. MA, U. Munich, 1977; PhD, European U. Inst., Florence, 1983; Habil., U. Heidelberg, Germany, 1994. Rschr. European U. Inst., Florence, 1984-88; vis. prof. U. Brcelona, 1988-89; asst. prof. U. Heidelberg, 1989-90, 91-95, U. Mannheim, 1990-91; vis. assoc. prof. Cornell U., Ithaca, N.Y., 1995-97, adj. prof., 1997—; prof. dept. polit. sci. U. Bremen, 1997—, chmn. dept. govt., 1998-99; co-dir. rsch. sect. European Investigation; dir. rsch. project on gener politics EU, 1999—. Author books in German. Mem. Deutsche Vereinigung Politik-Weissenschaft (steering com. 1994-97, co-dir. comp. democratization, 1995—, co-dir. European investigation, 1997—), Am. Polit. Sci. Assn. E-mail: liebert@uni-bremen.de. Office: Univ of Bremen, FB8 Polit Sci, 28334 Bremen Germany

LIEBERTZ-GRUEN, URSULA, philologist, educator; b. Bonn, Germany, Jan. 13, 1948; d. Ludwig and Maria (Weis) Gruen. Grad., U. Cologne (Germany), 1971, PhD, 1976. Vis. prof. U. Bayreuth (Germany), 1983-84, U. Madison (Wis.), 1991-92; prof. philology U. Cologne, 1987-95, U. Kassel (Germany), 1995-98, U. Mannheim (Germany), 1998—. Author: Zur Soziologie des amour courtois, 1977, Seifried Helbling, Satiren kontra Habsburg, 1981, Das andere Mittelalter, Erzählte Geschichte und Geschichtserkenntnis um 1300, 1984, Ordnung im Chaos, Studien zur Poetik der Bettine Brentano-von Arnim, 1989; editor Deutsche Literatur, Eine Sozialgeschichte, vol. 1; contbr. articles to profl. jours. Office: U Mannheim Sem Philologie, Schloss EW 239, D-68131 Mannheim Germany

LIEBES, RAQUEL, import/export company executive, educator; b. San Salvador, El Salvador, Aug. 28, 1938; came to the U.S., 1952, naturalized, 1964; d. Ernesto Martin and Alice (Philip) L.; m. Richard Paisley Kinkade, June 2, 1962 (div. 1977); children: Kathleen Paisley, Richard Paisley Jr., Scott Philip. BA, Sarah Lawrence Coll., 1960; MEd, Harvard U., 1961; MA, Yale U., 1963, postgrad., 1963-65; PhD, Oxford U., 1994. Tchg. fellow in Spanish Sarah Lawrence Coll., Bronxville, N.Y., 1958-60; econ. tchg. fellow Yale U., New Haven, 1964-65, instr. Spanish dept., 1964-66; exec. stockholder Import Export Co., San Salvador, 1968-89, also bd. dirs.; adj. prof. Am. U., Washington, 1989-91, dept. fgn. lang. and linguistics dept., fgn. studies Georgetown U., Washington, 1989-93; lectr. and conf. participation in Latin Am. art. Contbr. glossary of Spanish med. terms. Hon. consul Govt. of El Salvador, 1977-80; docent High Mus. of Art, Atlanta, 1972-77; vol. Grady Hosp., Atlanta, 1966-71; instr. Spanish for med. drs. Tucson Med. Ctr., 1966-71; chmn. Atlanta Coun. for Internat. Visitors, 1966-71; mem. Outreach Group on Latin Am., The White House, Washington, 1982-86; founding mem. John Kennedy Ctr. for Performing Arts, 1980—; mem. Folger/Shakespeare Libr., Smithsonian Inst., Agape, El Salvador; founding mem. Agape, El Salvador, 1981—, Concultura, El Salvador, 1999—, Libr. of Congress, Washington. Econ. fellow Yale U., 1964-65; Corcoran Mus. Art fellow, 1984-85; Smithsonian Mus. awardee, 1981-96. Mem. MLA, AAUW, Am. Biog. Inst., Rsch. Assn. (hon. consul of El Salvador, dep. gov. 1978-80, bd. advisors 1994), Jr. League of Washington, Harvard Club, Yale Club. Republican. Avocations: comparative literature, languages, international business, English literature, Shakespeare. Office: V I P Sal # 148 PO Box 52-5364 Miami FL 33152-5364

LIEBMAN, NINA R., economic developer; b. Toledo, Ohio, May 27, 1941; d. Jules Jay and Phyllis Gertrude (Kasle) Roskin; m. Theodore Liebman, Oct. 27, 1968; children: Sophie, Hanna, Tessa. Student, U. Marseilles, Aix-en-Provence, France, 1959-60, Skidmore Coll., 1960-61, NYU, 1961-63; cert. labor negotiator, Cornell U., 1993. Pub. info. officer Young Adult Inst., N.Y.C., 1978-81; U.S.A. dir. Rhone-Alps Econ. Devel. Assn., N.Y.C. and Lyon, France, 1981-85; internat. mktg. specialist N.Y. State Dept. Econ. Devel., N.Y.C., 1985-89, chief internat. programs, 1989-95; cons. Russian Fedn. Housing project The World Bank, 1995, cons. Russian Cmty. Social Infrastructure project, 1997; exec. dir. Nat. Assn. Export Cos., 1997-99, Internat. Cons. Svcs., 2000—. Co-author: Biz Speak: A Dictionary of Business Terms, Slang and Jargon, 1986. Vol., trained mediator Bklyn. Mediation Ctr.; mem. internat. adv. coun. Eisenhower Found.; mem. internat. adv. bd. Nat. Minority Bus. Coun., Bklyn. Philharmonic Chorus. Fellow Eisenhower Exch. Fellowship Program, 1993. Mem. UN Assn., Alliance Am. and Russian Women (bd. dirs.), U.S. Com. for UN, Devel. Fund for Women, Bklyn. Heights Assn., Mcpl. Arts Soc. Democrat. Jewish. Avocation: choral singing.

LIEBMANN, SEYMOUR W., construction consultant; b. N.Y.C., Nov. 1, 1928; s. Isidor W. and Etta (Waltzer) L.; m. Hinda Adam, Sept. 20, 1959; children: Peter Adam, David W. BSME, Clarkson U., 1948; grad., Indsl. Coll. Armed Forces, 1963, U.S. Army Command and Gen. Staff Coll., 1966, U.S. Army War Coll., 1971. Registered profl. engr., N.Y., Mass., Ga. Area engr. constrn. divsn. E.I. DuPont de Nemours & Co., Inc., 1952-54; constrn. planner Lummus Co., Inc., 1954-56; prin. mech. engr. Perini Corp., 1956-62; v.p. Boston Based Contractors, 1962-66; v.p. A.R. Abrams, Inc., Atlanta, 1967-74, pres., 1974-78, also bd. dirs.; founder Liebmann Assocs., Inc., Atlanta, 1979—; mem. nat. adv. bd. Am. Security Coun. Author: Military Engineer Field Notes, 1953, Prestressing Miter Gate Diagnoals, 1960; contbr. articles to publs. Mem. USO Coun., Atlanta, 1968—, v.p., 1978, mem. exec. com., 1975-79; mem. Nat. UN Day Com., 1975; sr. army coord., judge Sci. Fair, Atlanta Pub. Schs., annually, 1979-88, 92—; asst. scoutmaster troop 298 Atlanta area coun. Boy Scouts Am., 1980-87, Explorer

advisor, 1982-86, unit commr., 1985, dist. commr. North Atlanta Dist., Atlanta Area Coun., 1988-90, asst. coun. commr., 1990-95, mem. faculty Commrs. Coll., 1985-88, 92, mem. North Atlanta Dist. com., BSA, 1996—; mem. alumni adv. com. Clarkson Coll. Tech., 1981—, alumni bd. govs., 1983-94, Disting. Alumni Golden Knight award, 1983; mem. exec. com., zoning chmn. neighbor planning unit "A" City of Atlanta, 1982—, chmn., 1988, 95, 96, 97, 98, 99, 2000, vice-chmn., 1989; pres. West Paces/Northside Neighborhood Assn., 1991—; apptd. civil engr. mem. to City of Atlanta Water and Sewer Appeals Bd., 1992—; apptd. mem. to Mayor's Bond Oversight Com. City of Atlanta, 1995-96. Col. AUS Ret. Corps Engrs., 1948-52, Korea, Germany. Decorated Legion of Merit, Meritorious Svc. medal, USAR medal; elected to Old Guard of Gate City Guard, 1979; recipient cert. achievement Dept. Army, 1978, Bronze DeFleury medal U.S. Army Engr. Regiment, 1997, USO Recognition award, 1979, Order of Arrow award Boy Scouts Am., 1983, 87, Scouters Key Boy Scouts Am., 1988, North Atlanta Dist. Merit award, 1989, Silver Beaver award, 1991, Disting. Commn. award, 1991, Engring. Profl. award Am. Inst. Plant Engrs., 1987; named Met. Atlanta Engr. of Yr. in Pvt. Practice, 1991. Fellow Soc. Am. Mil. Engrs. (bd. dirs. 1986—, chmn. readiness com. 1986-88, program chmn. Atlanta post 1980-81, v.p. 1982, pres. 1983, program chmn. 1988, nat. meeting, asst. regional v.p. for readiness So. region 1991—, Nat. award of Merit 1982-83, Atlanta post Leadership award 1988, life dir. Atlanta Post 1994, elected nat. dir. 1994-97, James Lucas Chair Atlanta Post 1994, life mem., program chmn. S.Ea. regional site tng. conf. 1999); mem. ASTM, NSPE, Am. Cons. Engrs. Coun. (state and nat. pub. rels. coms., nat. ethics com., state legis. liaison com.), Am. Concrete Inst., Soc. 1st U.S. Inf., Res. Officers Assn. (life), U.S. Army War Coll. Found. (life), Nat. Def. U. Found., U.S. Army War Coll. Alumni Assn. (life), Ga. Soc. Profl. Engrs. (bd. dirs. Buckhead chpt., state ethics com.), Met. Atlanta Engrs. (chmn. week 2000 awards com.), Engrs. Club Boston, Assn. U.S. Army (v.p. exec. com. local chpt. 1998-2000), Def. Preparedness Assn., Am. Arbitration Assn. (panel arbitrators 1979—, constrn. adv. com. 1984—), Cobb C. of C., Downtown Atlanta Kiwanis, Atlanta C. of C. (mil. affairs com. 1999), Mil. Order World Wars, Order of Engr., Army Engr. Assn. (life), Appalachian Trail Conf., Benyton Mackaye Trail Assn., Ga. Conservancy, Atlanta Hist. Soc., NRA, Masons (32 degree), Shriners, Nat. Sojourners, Heroes of '76, Elks, Civitan. Republican. Jewish. Home: 3260 Rilman Dr NW Atlanta GA 30327-2224 Office: Ste 700 210 Interstate North Pkwy SE Atlanta GA 30339-2111

LIEBOWITZ, LARRY ARNOLD, chemical engineer; b. Bklyn., June 19, 1944; s. Max and Estelle L. BChemE, CCNY, 1965; MChemE, NYU, 1968. Engring. group leader MEPCO divsn. NV Philips, Morristown, N.J., 1965-68; product mgr. Nytronics, Inc., Berkeley Heights, N.J., 1968-71; engring. mgr. KDI Pyrofilm Corp., Whippany, N.J., 1971-75; pres. LAL Technol. Corp., East Brunswick, N.J., 1975—; founder, CEO Advanced Materials Tech. Corp. Inventor split plate constrn. to promote flux cancellation for reduced inductance in multilayer capacitor chips, buried layer chip architecture for chips in microwave applications, SAFETURF (artificial turf engineered to reduce leg injuries). Mem. Soc. Plastics Engrs. (chmn. elec. and electronic divsn. 1970-71), Am. Chem. Soc., Am. Ceramics Soc. Achievements include devel. of monolithic multilayer ceramic capacitors, superior ceramic materials and chip structures and mfg. techniques for electronic components and microcircuits which allow their use at microwave frequencies and high speed wireless comm. applications, log-slope method of predicting high-frequency performance of electronic devices, water based binders for electronic ceramics, replacing ones based on environment unfriendly volatile organic solvents; rsch. in high temperature superconductor materials. Home and Office: PO Box 412 East Brunswick NJ 08816-0412

LIEBSCHER, JÜRGEN, chemistry researcher and educator; b. Freital, Germany, Oct. 4, 1945; s. Heinz and Marianne (Bürger) L.; m. Sonnhilde Damm, July 5, 1976; children: Manuela, Hannes, Tobias. MS, Tech. U., Dresden, Germany, 1969, PhD in Organic Chemistry, 1973, DS in Organic Chemistry, 1977. Lectr. Tech. U., Dresden, Germany, 1969-77, sr. lectr., 1977-79; assoc. prof. Addis Abab U., Ethiopia, 1979-82; dozent Humboldt U., Berlin, 1982-92, prof., 1992—. Contbr. over 170 articles to profl. jours. Mem. German Chem. Soc., Internat. Soc. Heterocycloc Chemistry. Office: Inst Chemistry, Hessische Str 1-2, 10115 Berlin Germany

LIEBSCHER, KLAUS, stock exchange executive, banker. Pres. Vienna (Austria) Stock Exch.; chmn. Raiffeisen Zentralbank Österreich AG, Vienna; pres. Anstvison Nat. Bank; now pres. Ctr. Bank Austria, Vienna. Office: Vienna Stock Exch, 9 Otto Wagner Platz 3, A-1011 Wien Austria also: Raiffeisen Zentralbank Österreich AG, Am Stadtpark 9, A-1030 Vienna Austria*

LIEDY, WERNER, engineering educator; b. Böhl, Germany, June 11, 1951. Diploma in physics, U. Karlsruhe, Germany, 1978, D Chem. Engring., 1985. Asst. U. Karlsruhe, 1978-85; process engr. BASF Tech. Devel., Ludwigshafen, Germany, 1985-93, head drying team, 1988-91, head high pressure processing team, 1991-93; prof., lectr. U. Applied Sci., Frankfurt, Germany, 1993—; cons. in field, 1994—. Contbr. articles to profl. jours.; patentee process for formulation of granules for hämodialysis. Office: Fachhochschule Frankfurt, Kleistrasse 3, 60318 Frankfurt Germany

LIEF, HAROLD ISAIAH, psychiatrist; b. N.Y.C., Dec. 29, 1917; s. Jacob F. and Mollie (Filler) L.; m. Myrtis A. Brumfield, Mar. 3, 1961; Caleb B., Frederick V., Oliver F.; children from previous marriage: Polly Lief Goldberg, Jonathan F. BA, U. Mich., 1938; MD, NYU, 1942; cert. in psychoanalysis, Columbia Coll. Physicians and Surgeons, 1950; MA (hon.), U. Pa., 1971. Intern Queens Gen. Hosp., Jamaica, N.Y., 1942-43; resident in psychiatry L.I. Coll. Medicine, 1946-48; pvt. practice N.Y.C., 1948-51; asst. physician Presbyn. Hosp., N.Y.C., 1949-51; asst. prof. Tulane U., New Orleans, 1951-54, assoc. prof., 1954-60, prof. psychiatry, 1960-67; prof. psychiatry U. Pa., Phila., 1967-82, prof. emeritus, 1982—; dir. div. family study U. Pa., 1967-81; dir. Marriage Council of Phila., 1969-81, Ctr. for Study of Sex. Edn. in Medicine, 1968-82; mem. staff U. Pa. Hosp., 1967-81, Pa. Hosp., 1981—; clin. prof. psychiatry Jefferson Med. U., 1994—. Author: (with Daniel and William Thompson) The Eighth Generation, 1960; Editor: (with Victor and Nina Lief) Psychological Basis of Medical Practice, 1963, Medical Aspects of Human Sexuality, 1976, (with Arno Karlen) Sex Education in Medicine, 1976, Sexual Problems in Medical Practice, 1981, (with Zwi Hoch) Sexology: Sexual Biology, Behavior and Therapy, 1982, (with Zwi Hoch) International Research in Sexology, 1983, Human Sexuality With Respect to AIDS and HIV Infection, 1989; contbr. numerous articles to publs. Bd. dirs. Ctr. for Sexuality and Religion, chmn., pres., 1998-2000; mem. adv. bd False Memory Syndrome Found., 1992—; mem. La. State Commn. Civil Rights, 1958-67. Maj. M.C. U.S. Army, 1943-46. Commonwealth Fund fellow, 1963-64; recipient Gold Medal award Mt. Airy Hosp., 1977, Lifetime Achievement award Phila. Psychiat. Soc., 1992, Gold Medal, World of Assn. Sexology, 1999; named practitioner of yr. Phila. County Med. Soc., 1998. Fellow Phila. Coll. Physicians, Am. Psychiat. Assn. (50 yr. life), N.Y. Acad. Scis., AAAS, Am. Acad. Psychoanalysis (charter, past pres.), Am. Coll. Psychiatrists (founding), Am. Coll. Psychoanalysts (charter); mem. AMA, Am. Assn. Marriage and Family Therapists, Sex Info. and Edn. Coun. U.S. (past pres.), Group Advancement Psychiatry (life), Am. Soc. Adolescent Psychiatry, Am. Psychosomatic Soc., Assn. Psychoanalytic Medicine (life), Am. Psychoanalytic Assn., Internat. Psychoanalytic Assn., Internat. Acad. Sex Rsch., Soc. Sci. Study of Sex, Am. Soc. Sex Educators, Counselors and Therapists, Soc. Sex Therapists and Rschrs., World Assn. Sexology (past v.p.), Soc. Exploration of Psychotherapy Integration (adv. bd.), Pa. Med. Soc., Phila. Med. Soc., Columbia Club, Mich. Club of Greater Phila., Penn Club of N.Y., Sigma Xi, Al pha Omega Alpha, Phi Eta Sigma, Phi Kappa Phi. Home: 840 Montgomery Ave Bryn Mawr PA 19010-3344 Office: 987 Old Eagle School Rd Ste 719 Wayne PA 19087-1708

LIEJON, BRITTA, Swedish deputy minister of justice. Dep. min. justice Ministry Justice, Stockholm. Office: Ministry of Justice, Rosenbad 4, S-10333 Stockholm Sweden*

LIEM, MIKE SWAN LIANG, physician, researcher; b. Rozenburg, The Netherlands, Dec. 24, 1967; s. Hwie Thjan and Djoen Ie L. MD, U. Leiden, The Netherlands, 1992; PhD cum laude, U. Trecht, The Netherlands, 1997. Rsch. fellow Duke U., Durham, 1989-90; urology resident Ctrl. Military Hosp., Utrecht, The Netherlands, 1992-93; clin. rsch. fellow U. Utrecht, The Netherlands, 1993-97, resident in surgery, 1997—; mng. coord. Clin. Trial Bur., U. Utrecht, The Netherlands, 1993-96. 1st Lt. Navy, 1992-93. Recipient Hippocrates award, 1991, Incentive prize Human Related Rsch., Univ. Hosp. Utrecht, 1995, 1st prize Human Related Rsch., Univ. Hosp. Utrecht, 1998, Schoenmaker award Best PhD Thesis Dutch Surg. Assn., 1998, 1st and 2nd prize Best Resident Article in BMC Jour., 1999, others; contbr. articles to profl. jours. Roman Catholic. Avocations: classical music, cooking, history. Office: Univ Hosp Utrecht, Heidelberglaan 100, 3584 CX Utrecht The Netherlands

LIEN, FUE-SANG, mechanical engineer; b. Taipei, Taiwan, Apr. 13, 1960; arrived in Can., 1997; s. Lung-Hui Lien and Su-Huei Lin; m. Hui-Hsiang Chen, Apr. 13, 1987; children: Chi-Chen, Chi-Wen. BSc, Cheng-Kung U., Tainan, Taiwan, 1982, MSc, 1984; PhD Inst. Sci. and Tech., U. Manchester (Eng.), 1992. Lectr. Taipei Inst. Tech., 1986-88; rsch. asst. U. Manchester Inst. Sci. and Tech., 1988-92, rsch. assoc., project officer, 1992-96, lectr., 1996-97; asst. prof. mech. engring. U. Waterloo (Can.), 1997—; tech. mgr. FLAIR unit U. Manchester Inst. Sci. and Tech., 1994-96. Office: Dept Mech Engring, Dept Mech Engring, U Waterloo, Waterloo, ON Canada N2L 3G1

LIENEMANN, DELMAR ARTHUR, SR., accountant, real estate developer; b. Papillion, Nebr., May 17, 1920; s. Arthur Herman and Dorothea M. (Marth) L.; m. Charlotte Peck, Jun 17, 1944 (dec. Mar. 1995); children: Delmar Arthur Jr., David (dec.), Diane, Douglas, Dorothy, Daniel, Denise. BS, U. Nebr., 1941. CPA, Nebr. Acct. Wickstrom Supply, Lincoln, Nebr., 1941, L.L. Coryell & Sons, Lincoln, 1942, Lester Buckley, CPA, Lincoln, 1943-45; pvt. practice Lincoln, 1945—. Pres., v.p., sec., treas., bldg. chmn., charter mem. Christ Luth. Ch., Lincoln, 1949-70; co-commr. Lancaster County, Lincoln, 1954-58; pres. Lincoln Symphony Orch. Found., 1984—, Ethel S. Abbott Charitable Found. Mem. AICPA, N.E. Soc. CPA, Colo. Soc. CPA, Tex. Soc. CPA, Sertoma (sec.-treas. Lincoln chpt. 1952-68, Internat. Sertoman of Yr. 1962), Hillcrest Country Club, Nebr. Club, Nebr. Chancelors Club, Nebr. Touchdown Club, Nebr. Power Club, Nebr. Rebounders Club. Republican. Avocation: travel. Office: PO Box 81407 Lincoln NE 68501-1407

LIENHARD, MARC, theology and church history educator; b. Colmar, Alsace, France, Aug. 22, 1935; s. Jean and Elisabeth (Graff) L.; m. Annemarie Guerrier, July 6, 1961; children: Michel, Fritz, Pierre, Thomas. MTh, U. Strasbourg, France, 1959, ThD, 1965, Doctorat d'Etat, 1971. Ordained to ministry Lutheran Ch., 1963. Pastor Ch. of the Augsbourg Confession of Alsace and Lorraine, Bischheim, Uhrwiller, France, 1963-68; rsch. prof. Ecumenical Inst., Strasbourg, 1968-73; prof. faculty of Protestant theology U. Strasbourg, 1973-97—, dean faculty of Protestant theology, 1991-96; pres., dir. Ch. of the Augsburg Confession of Alsace and Lorraine, Strasbourg, 1997—; dir. Group for Rsch. on Non-conformists of 16th Century, Strasbourg, 1975-97. Author: Foi et vie des protestants d'Alsace, 1981, Luther: Witness to Jesus Christ, 1982, Un temps, un ville, une Réforme, Studien zur Reformation in Strassburg, 1990, Martin Luther, Un temps, une vie, un message, 3d edit., 1991, Au Coeur de la foi de Luther: Jesus Christ, 1991, Le Foi vécue, 1997, others; editor: La Foi des Eglises Luthériennes, Confessions et catéchismes, 1991, Martin Bucer and Sixteenth Century Europe, 1993, Martin Luther, La passion de Dieu, 1999, Martin Luther, Oeuvres, vol. I, Pléiade, 1999. Pres. assn. of pupuls parents Gynmase Jean Sturm, Strasbourg, 1980-84. Sgt. French Mil., 1959-61. Mem. Acad. Scis. Mainz, Germany (corr.). Avocations: music, walking, skiing, volleyball. Home: H 1 rue Martin Luther, 67000 Strasbourg France Office: Ch of the Augsburg, H 1b Quai Saint-Thomas, 67081 Strasbourg France

LIESEN, KLAUS, gas industry executive; b. Cologne, Germany, Apr. 15, 1931. Law student, U. Marburg (Germany), U. Cologne (Germany), U. Göttingen (Germany); D, 1957. With Unilever, Fed. Ministry Econ. Affairs, Germany; numerous mgmt. positions Ruhrgas AG, Essen, Germany, 1963, chmn. exec. bd., 1976—; chmn. supervisory bd. Volkwagen, AG. Mem. Fed. Assn. German Gas and Water Industries (first v.p.), Initiativkreis Ruhrgebiet, Donors Assn. for Promotion of Scis. and Humanities in Germany (chmn. bd. 1987—). Office: Ruhrgas AG, Huttropstr 60, D-45138 Essen Germany*

LIETAVA, PETER, nuclear physicist; b. Piestany, Slovakia, Oct. 15, 1964; s. Milan and Monika (Wohlsteinová) L. PhD, Comenius U., 1987. Safety assessment mgr. Nuclear Rsch. Inst., Plc., Řež, Czech Repblic, 1987—. Home: u Cukrovaru 1065, CZ-27801 Kralupy Czech Republic Office: Nuclear Rsch Inst plc, Waste Mgmt Dept, CZ-25068 Rez Czech Republic

LIETZEN, JOHN HERVY, human resources executive, health agency volunteer; b. Kansas City, Kans., July 17, 1947; s. Walter Edwin and Kathleen Mae (Griffith) L.; children: Gwendolyn Therese, Anne Gabrielle, Sarah Kathleen. BS, Mo. Valley Coll., 1974; MS, U. Mo., 1976; postgrad, U. Nebr., 1982-88. With Union Pacific R.R., 1971—; yard condr. Union Pacific R.R., Kansas City, Kans., 1971-77; pers. officer Union Pacific R.R., Omaha, 1977-78; pers. dir. Union Pacific R.R., Cheyenne, Wyo., 1978-79, sr. tng. officer dept. claims, 1979-83, mgr. staffing, 1983-84, mgr. affirmative action, 1984-86; human resources tng. and devel. cons. Union Pacific R.R., Omaha, 1986-89, 94—, Salt Lake City, 1989-94. Bd. dirs. Berkshire Village, Kansas City, 1976-77; mem. bd. ministries Valley View Meth. Ch., Overland Park, Kans., 1976-77; pastor and staff rels. com. Hanscom Pk. United Meth. Ch., 1980-81, lay leader, 1983; asst. leader Wyo. coun. Girl Scouts U.S.A., Cheyenne, 1978-79, asst. leader, Omaha, 1980-89, Salt Lake, 1989—, bd. dirs. Great Plains Girl Scout Coun., 1987-89; exec. bd. Nebr. affiliate Am. Diabetes Assn., 1981-89, pres. Midlands chpt., 1982-84, mem. planning and orgn. com., 1986-87, bd. dirs. Utah affiliate, 1990-94, co-founder Omaha Insulin Pump Club, 1986; loaned exec. United Way of Midlands, 1984. Sgt. U.S. Army, 1968-71, Germany. Mem. ASTD, Am. Soc. Pers. and Guidance Assn., Adult and Continuing Edn. Assn. Nebr. (mem. planning com. 1982-84), Nat. Soc. for Performance and Instrn. Republican. Office: 1416 Dodge St # Pf2 Omaha NE 68179-0001

LIEVENS, PETER F.A., physicist, researcher; b. Geel, Belgium, July 7, 1963; s. Josephus Lievens and Hilda Vandenbergh; m. Min I.F. Berghmans, Aug. 19, 1988. Lic. in physics, K.U. Leuven, Belgium, 1985, PhD, 1991. Sci. collaborator Inst. Nuclear and Radiation Physics K. U. Leuven, 1985-90, postdoctoral rschr. FWO Lab. Solid State Physics/Magnetism, 1993—; fellow PPE divsn. CERN, Geneva, 1991-92. Contbr. numerous articles to profl. jours., including Phys. Rev. Letters, Phys. Rev., Physics Letters, Europhysics Letters, Chemical Physics Letters, Jour. Chemical Physics, Jour. Physics, Nuclear Instruments and Methods, Hyperfine Interactions, others. Mem. Belgian Phys. Soc., European Phys. Soc., Am. Assn. Advancement Sci. Home: Pastorijstraat 6B, B-2440 Geel Belgium Office: K U Leuven, Celestijnenlaan 200D, B-3001 Leuven Belgium

LIEVORE, RUSTON, pathologist, consultant; b. Colatina, Brazil, July 6, 1963; s. José Anselmo and Edith Pereira (Cardoso) L. Grad., U. Fed. do Espirito Santo, Vitória, Brazil, 1989. Med. diplomate; residence fo gen. physician diplomate, residence of clin. pathology diplomate, speciality of clin. pathology diplomate. Gen. physician Hucam-U. Fed. do Espirito Santo, Vitória, 1990-91; clin. pathologist Hosp. and Clinics-U. de São Paulo, Brazil, 1992-94; clin. pathologist, immunohematology chief Blood Bank of Hucam, Vitória, 1995—; clin. pathology, tech. dir. Pathology Lab., Vitória, 1995—. Contbr. articles to profl. jours. Mem. AAAS, Am. Soc. for Microbiology, Am. Assn. for Clin. Chemistry. Roman Catholic. Avocations: reading, listening to classical music, painting, traveling, drawing. Home: Rua Miguel Jantorno 279, 29043220 Vitória Brazil

LIEW, SOO CHIN, research scientist; b. Alor Setar, Kedah, Malaysia, Oct. 24, 1957; s. Yim Heng Liew and Loo Wah Lin; m. Peh Yean Cheah; children: Kaiyang, Kaiyi. BSc with honors, U. Sains Malaysia, Penang, 1982; PhD, U. Ariz., 1989. Rsch. scientist dept. radiology U. Calif., San Francisco, 1989-90; tchg. fellow dept. physics Nat. U. Singapore, Singapore, 1990-95, rsch. scientist Ctr. Remote Imaging, Sensing and Processing, 1995—, head rsch. Ctr. Remote Imaging, Sensing and Processing, 1998—; prin. investigator EO-1 sci. team NASA, 2000—, European Space Agy., 2000—. Contbr. articles to profl. jours. Mem. IEEE, Inst. Physics Singapore. Fax: 65-7757717. Home: Blk 27, Dover Crescent # 13-29, 130027 Singapore Republic of Singapore Office: Nat U Singapore, Blk S17, Level 2 Lower Kent Ridge Rd, 119260 Singapore Republic of Singapore

LIEWENDAHL, BO KRISTIAN, clinical pathologist, nuclear physician; b. Helsinki, Aug. 21, 1941; s. Ernst August and Irina (Semenov) L.; 1 child, Kari Peter Nikolai. MD, U. Helsinki, 1966, PhD, 1968. Med. diplomate. Resident dept. clin. chemistry Helsinki U. Hosp., 1966-69, resident dept. medicine, 1969-72, cons. lab. dept., 1974-82; asst. prof., docent U. Helsinki, 1977-96, prof., 1996—; chief physician divsn. nuclear medicine Helsinki U. Hosp., 1983-99; NIH postdoctoral fellow U. Calif., San Francisco, 1972-73; vis. scientist U. Wis., Madison, U. Va., Charlottesville, 1982; dir. nuclear medicine rsch. group Minerva Inst. Found., Helsinki, 1977—; sec. gen. Minerva Found., 1997—; sec. European Thyroid Assn. Congress, Helsinki, 1976; pres. European Nuclear Medicine Congress, Helsinki, 1984; chmn. European Congress Clin. Chemistry, Tampere, Finland, 1995; pres. Scandinavian Congress of Nuclear Medicine, Helsinki, 1998; del. nuclear medicine sect. European Union Med. Spltys., 1994—; del. European Bd. Nuclear Medicine, 1995—. Author, editor Scandinavian Jour. Clin. Lab. Investigation, 1986-97; bd. editors European Jour. Nuclear Medicine, 1991—; contbr. over 400 articles to profl. jours. Recipient J.W. Runeberg Prize Finnish Med. Soc., 1969, Ann. Lecture Prize Finnish Med.Soc., 1973, T. Heiskanen Meml. Prize Finnish Radiol. Soc. and Finnish Nuclear Medicine Soc., 1985, Gold medal Minerva Found., Helsinki, 1989. Mem. European Assn. Nuclear Medicine (del. 1988-95, mem. organizing com. congress in Copenhagen 1996, Congress prize 1991), European Thyroid Assn., Finnish Soc. Nuclear Medicine (pres. 1996-98, hon. mem. 1999), World Fedn. Nuclear Medicine and Biology (del. 1988—), Soc. Nuclear Medicine N.Y., N.Y. Acad. Scis. Lutheran. Achievements include thyroid function tests, particularly accurate assays for free thyroid hormone concentrations in blood; nuclear medicine procedures for diagnosis of oncological, hematological and neurological diseases. Office: Minerva Found, Stockholmsgatan 2, 00250 Helsinki Finland

LI-FENG, ZHANG, chemist, researcher; b. Luzi, Hunan, China, Nov. 3, 1968; arrived in Singapore, 1996; s. Zhang Guan-Wen and Shi Fu-Yu; m. Chen Lei, Sept. 16, 1996. BS, Wuhan (China) U., 1990, MS, 1993, PhD, 1996. Rsch. engr. Nat. U. Singapore, 1996-99; sr. chemist Environ. Tech. Inst., Singapore, 1999—. Contbr. articles to sci. publs., including Jour. Chromotography A, Tetrahedron Letters; patentee in field. Home: Blk 707 06-339 Clementi W, Singapore 120707, Singapore Offfice: Environ Tech Inst NTU GC, Innovation Ctr Unit 237, Singapore 639798, Singapore

LIFLYAND, ELIJAH, mathematician; b. Donetsk, Ukraine, Apr. 10, 1952; arrived in Israel, 1991; s. Raphael Y. and Ida D. (Fishman) L.; m. Irina Stolbun; 1 child, Olga. MA, U. Donetsk, 1974; PhD, Inst. Applied Math. Donetsk, 1982. Programmer Computer Ctr., Donetsk, 1976-81; sr. rschr. Coal Inst., Donetsk, 1981-89; assoc. prof. Tech. U. Donetsk, 1989-91; rschr. Technion, Haifa, Israel, 1992; sr. rschr. Bar-Ilan U., Ramat-Gan, Israel, 1992—; programmer Donetsk, 1976-89; mathematician Tech. U. Donetsk, 1984-91, Bar-Ilan U. Ramat-Gan, 1992—. Contbr. articles to profl. jours. With Soviet Army, 1974-75. Fellow Ministry Adoption, Israel, 1995. Mem. European Math. Union, Israel Math. Union, Am. Math. Soc. Avocations: chess, tennis, languages. Office: Dept Math & Computer Sci, Bar-Ilan Univ, 52900 Ramat-Gan Israel

LIFSCHULTZ, PHILLIP, financial and tax consultant, accountant, lawyer; b. Oak Park, Ill., Mar. 5, 1927; s. Abraham Albert and Frances Rhoda (Siegel) L.; m. Edith Louise Leavitt, June 27, 1948; children: Gregory, Bonnie, Jodie. BS in Acctg., U. Ill., 1949; JD, John Marshall Law Sch., 1956. Bar: Ill. 1956; CPA, Ill. Tax mgr. Arthur Andersen & Co., Chgo., 1957-63; v.p. taxes Montgomery Ward & Co., Chgo., 1963-78; fin. v.p., contr. Henry Crown & Co., Chgo., 1978-81; prin. Phillip Lifschultz & Assocs., Chgo., 1981—; exec. dir. Dodi Orgn., 1987-90; v.p. Altra Travel, Northbrook, Ill., 1975—; pres. Great Lakes Shoe Co., Bannockburn, Ill., 1996—. Mem. adv. coun. Coll. Commerce and Bus. Adminstrn. U. Ill., Urbana-Champaign, 1977-78; chmn., Civic Fedn. Chgo., 1980-82; chmn. adv. bd. to Auditor Gen. of Ill., 1965-73; project dir. Exec. Service Corps of Chgo., Chgo. Bd. Edn. and State of Ill. projects, 1980-87. With U.S. Army, 1945-46. Mem. Ill. Bar Assn., Chgo. Bar Assn., Am. Inst. CPA's, Ill. CPA Soc., Am. Arbitration Assn. (comml. panel 1983-94), Nat. Retail Merchants Assn. (chmn. tax com. 1975-78), Am. Retail Fedn. (chmn. taxation com. 1971), Standard Club. Home and Office: 442 Kelburn Rd Apt 123 Deerfield IL 60015-4370

LIGETI, ERZSÉBET KATALIN, physiology educator; b. Budapest, Hungary, July 17, 1950; d. Gèza István and Alice (Reviczky) L. MD, Semmelweis Med. U., Budapest, 1974, PhD, 1980; DSc, Hungarian Acad. Scis., Budapest, 1990. Rsch. asst. Semmelweis Med. U., Budapest, 1974-82, asst. prof., 1982-89, assoc. prof., 1989-93, prof. physiology, 1993—; vis. scientist Centre D'Études Nucleaires, De Grenoble, France, 1983-84, 88; Humboldt fellow U. Heidelberg, Germany, 1990-91; vis. scientist Boston Biomed. Rsch. Inst., 1994. Co-author: Physiology for Pharmaceutical Students, 1989, Medical Physiology, 1992, 94; contbr. articles to profl. jours. Recipient award for excellent work Hungarian Ministry of Edn., Budapest, 1987, Excellent tchr. award Semmelweis Med. U., Budapest, 1990, Acad. Prize Hungarian Acad. Sci., 1996. Mem. Biochem. Soc. (London), European Soc. Clin. Investigation. Avocations: hiking, travel, classical music. Office: Semmelweis Med U Dept Physiology, PO Box 259, H-1444 Budapest 8, Hungary

LIGGIANS, RHONDA LEIGH, publishing company executive; b. Cin., Oct. 22, 1959; d. Velma Anita (Carter) Smith; m. Tyrone William Liggians, Apr. 28, 1980; children: Janelle, Lamar, Ashley, Shauntel, Shawn, Shannon. BA, Capital U., Bexley, Ohio, 1981; MPA, CUNY, 1995. Cataloger, libr. Capital U. Libr., Bexley, Ohio, 1977-81; account clk. Dept. Adminstrv. Svcs., Columbus, Ohio, 1983-85, acct., 1985-90; v.p. Chief Cornerstone Prodns. Inc., 1995—; v.p. Chief Cornerston Prodns., Inc. Sunday sch. tchr.; choreographer, adminstr. teen and adult praise and worship dance ministry. Mem. Pi Phi Epsilon (chaplain 1980-81), Alpha Kappa Alpha, Pi Alpha Alpha. Mem. Full Gospel Ch. Avocations: teaching Sunday school; jazz, tap and ballet dancing. Home: 1117 Manor Ave Apt 1H Bronx NY 10472-3908

LIGHT, ALFRED ROBERT, lawyer, political scientist, educator; b. Dec. 14, 1949; s. Alfred M. Jr. and Margaret Francis (Asbury) L; m. Mollie Sue Hall, May 28, 1977; children: Joseph Robert, Gregory Andrew. Student, Ga. Inst. Tech., 1967-69; BA with highest honors, Johns Hopkins U., 1971; PhD, U. N.C., 1976; JD cum laude, Harvard U., 1981. Bar: D.C. 1981, Va. 1982. Tax clk. IRS, 1967; lab technician Custom Farm Svcs. Soils Testing Lab, 1968; warehouse asst. State of Ga. Mines, Mining and Geology, 1970; clk.-typist systems mgmt. div., def. contract adminstrv. Def. Supply Agy., Atlanta, 1971; rsch. and teaching asst. dept. polit. sci. U. N.C., Chapel Hill, 1971-74; rsch. asst. Inst. Rsch. in Social Sci., 1975-77; program analyst Office of Sec. Def., 1974; asst. prf. polit. sci., rsch. scientist Ctr. Energy Rsch. Tex. Tech. U., Lubbock, 1977-78; rsch. asst. grad. sch. edn. Harvard U., 1978-79; assoc. Butler, Binion, Rice, Cook & Knapp, Houston, summer 1980; Bracewell & Patterson, Washington, summer 1980, Hunton & Williams, Richmond, Va., 1981-89; of counsel, 1989-93, 95-96; assoc. prof. St. Thomas U. Sch. Law, Miami, Fla., 1989-93; prof., 1993—; interim dean, 1993-94; bd. advisors Toxics Law reporter, Bur. Nat. Affairs, Washington, 1987—. Contbr. articles to profl. jours. Charter mem. West Broward Cmty. Ch. Capt. USAR, 1971-85. Grantee NSF, Inst. Evaluation Rsch., U. Mass., Ctr. Energy Rsch., Tex. Tech. U., 1977-78; recipient Julius Turner award Am. Polit. Sci. Assn., 1977. Mem. ABA (vice-chmn.) tort and ins. practice sect. 1988-97, nat. res. and environ. sect. 1993-95, chmn. 1995—), Fed. Bar. Assn., Va. Bar Assn., Richmond Bar Assn., Phi Beta Kappa, Phi Eta Sigma. Democrat. Home: 1042 Woodfall Ct Fort Lauderdale FL 33326-2832 Office: St Thomas U Sch Law 16400 NW 32nd Ave Opa Locka FL 33054-6459

LIGHT, JOHN RICHARD, sculptor; b. Kalamazoo, Oct. 11, 1940; s. Richard Light and Rachel Mary (Upjohn) L.; m. Frances Mary Hesser, June 21, 1969; 1 child, Aimee Upjohn. BA, Yale U., 1962. Asst. advt. mgr. Verson Allsteel Press Co., Chgo., 1967-68; pub. relations copywriter Barton Brands, Chgo., 1970; investment cons. Chgo., 1972-86; sculptor, 1986—. Editor: Impact Machining, 1968; exhbns. include Skokie (Ill.) Fine Arts Commn., 1991, Iron Feather Gallery, Sedona, Ariz., 1993, Auburn (Calif.)

Art Ctr., 1994, Art Guild, Farmington, Conn., 1995, Art at Parkview Hills, Kalamazoo, 2000; represented in permanent collections Goulandris Mus. Cycladic Art, Athens, Greece, Horvath Med. Sch., Cambridge, Mass., Nat. Gallery Art, Washington, Nat. Mus. Ireland, Dublin, Pushkin Mus. Art, Moscow, U. Chgo., Yale U., New Haven. Bd. dirs. Juvenile Protective Assn., Chgo., 1975—, Kalamazoo Child Guidance Clinic, 1969—, Lakeside Boys and Girls Home, 1979—. Recipient Distinguished Service award Publicity Club Chgo., 1972. Mem. Internat. Sculpture Ctr., Nat. Sculpture Soc., Publicity Club (Chgo.) (dir. 1975-77, mgr. club publs. 1972-73, chmn. seminar com. 1976-77), Kiwanis (Kalamazoo and Chgo.). Roman Catholic. Home: 4020 Old Field Trl Kalamazoo MI 49008-3339 Office: Light Sculpture Studio 616 Comerica Bldg Kalamazoo MI 49007-4716

LIGHT, JOHN ROGER CHARLES, publisher; b. Hornchurch, Essex, Eng., June 5, 1943; s. William Charles and Betty Irene (Horner) L.; m. Marilyn Grime, Mar. 25, 1967; children: Katherine Ann, Mark Edward, Roger Alan. BS, U. Durham, Eng., 1965, PhD, 1968. Rsch. chemist Monsanto SA, Zürich, Switzerland, 1968-69; rsch. asst. U. Bristol, Eng., 1969-70; sci. officer The Radiochem. Centre, Amersham, Eng., 1970-72; adminstr. Queen Mary Coll., London, 1972-96, hon. lectr., 1986-96; pub. Photon Press, Berwick-upon-Tweed, Eng., 1986—; indexer Elsevier, Oxford, Eng., 1995-99; lectr. writing, 1990—; examiner U. London, 1980-93. Author: (novel) The Well of Time, 1981, (novel) Death on Dorado, 1992, (novel) The Lords of Hate, 1997, (collected poems) Lines of Light, 1994, children's book series (8 titles), 1989, 90; (poems for children) Are These Rhymes Nonsense, 1998; editor: (poetry anthology) Mystery of the City, 1997. Union rep. Assn. Univ. tchrs., London, 1972-86, Inst. Profl. Civil Servants, Amersham, 1970-72. Mem. Northumberland and Durham Family History Soc. Avocations: genealogy, climbing, gardening, reading, music. E-mail: photon.press@cwcom.net. Home & Office: 37 The Meadows, Berwick-Upon-Tweed, Northumberland TD15 1NY, England

LIGHT, PAMELA DELAMAIDE, interior designer; b. Pittsburg, Kans., Sept. 16, 1950; d. Jack Riley and Pearl Darlene (Nelson) Delamaide; m. Kenneth Layne Light, July 25, 1970 (div. Apr. 1974); m. F. Dennie Pimental, Nov. 2, 1985. Student, Ohio U., 1968-70; BS in Environ. Design, Ball State U., 1973. Interior design apprentice Jon Wilding Studio, Anderson, 1970-71; interior designer Suniland Office Furniture, Houston, 1973-83; furniture rep. Reeves, Rice & Lights, Houston, 1983-84; interior designer H.O.K., San Francisco, 1986-87; sr. project designer, prin. Interior Archs., San Francisco, 1987-88; sr. designer, project mgr. Leason Pomeroy Assoc., Orange, Calif., 1988-90; sr. designer, v.p. Whisler-Patri, 1990-93; v.p. Reel Grobman, 1993-94, HOK, 1995—; cons. Front to Back, Houston, 1982-84. Mem. Archtl. Found. L.A. (exec. bd. 1995—), Inst. Bus. Designers (v.p. programs 1983, pres. South Tex. chpt. 1985, pres. No. Calif. chpt. 1987, nat. v.p. membership 1990), People for Ethical Treatment of Animals, Citizens for Animal Protection, Houston Humane Soc. Republican. Methodist.

LIGHT, WILLIAM RANDALL, lawyer; b. Lynchburg, Va., Sept. 11, 1958; s. John Leftwich and Patricia (Wilson) L.; m. Lisa Burcher, Apr. 27, 1991; children: William Randall II, Madeline Gibson. BA, Emory and Henry Coll., 1980; JD, Nova U. Bar: Va. 1985, U.S. Dist. Ct. (we. dist.) Va. 1985, U.S. Ct. Appeals (4th cir.), U.S. Supreme Ct. Assoc. Killis T. Howard, a profl. corp., Lynchburg, 1984-98; pvt. practice Lynchburg, 1998—; spl. justice Commonwealth of Va. 24th Jud. Dist., Lynchburg, 1987—; adj. prof. Lynchburg Coll., 1989, 91. Bd. dirs. Lynchburg Mental Health Assn.; vice chmn. Rep. com. City of Lynchburg, 1986-90, acting chmn., 1990-91; vestry St. Paul Episcopal Ch., Ecclesiastical Ct. Episcopal Diocese of Southwestern Va. Maj. Va. Def. Force. Mem. ABA, Lynchburg Bar Assn. (v.p. young lawyers sect. 1984-88, pres. 1989-90), Va. Trial Lawyers Assn., Amherst County-Nelson County Bar Assn., Masons (Master 1991), Phi Alpha Delta. Republican. Episcopalian. Home: 1804 Mobile Rd Lynchburg VA 24503-2434 Office: William R Light PC 1011 Court St PO Box 309 Lynchburg VA 24505-0309

LIGHTFOOT, ALBERT J., clergyman; b. Birmingham, Ala., July 2, 1926; s. Albert and Odessa Lightfoot; m. Catherine Kidd; children: Calvin, Cornelius, Reggie, Ronald, Phillip, Nedra, Phyllis. Student, U. Mich., 1960-62, Liberty Bible Coll., 1965-68, Union Bapt. Sem., 1975. Ordained to ministry Bapt. Ch., 1965. Organizer, pastor New Hope Bapt. Ch., Ann Arbor, Mich., 1965—, also gen. supt. Sunday sch., trustee clk., deacon, organizer Kangaroo Day Care Program; moderator Huron Valley Dist. Assn., 1996; mem. Wolverine State Conv., Nat. Bapt. Conv. USA Inc.;. Mem. Ypsilanti-Ann Arbor Vicinity Ministerial Alliance (pres.). Home: 700 Braeside Pl Ann Arbor MI 48103-6149 Office: New Hope Bapt Ch 218 Chapin St Ann Arbor MI 48103-3390

LIGHTFOOTE, MARILYN MADRY, molecular immunologist; b. Jacksonville, Fla.; d. Arthur Chester and Janie (Cowart) Madry; m. William Edward Lightfoote II, Oct. 23, 1971; 1 child, Lynne Jan-Maria. BA in Chemistry magna cum laude, Fisk U.; MS in Biochemistry, Georgetown U.; PhD in Microbiology and Immunology, U. Va., 1983. Staff fellow Lab. Immunogenetics Nat. Inst. Allergy Infectious Diseases, NIH, Bethesda, Md., 1983-85, staff fellow Lab. Immunoregulation, 1985-87; rsch. faculty dept. biochemistry George Washington U., 1987-90; molecular immunologist HHS Ctr. Devices and Radiol. Health FDA, Rockville, Md., 1990-97; dir. divsn. life scis. HHS, CDRH, FDA, Rockville, Md., 1998—; Graves meml. lectr. biology dept. N.C. A&T Coll., Greensboro; NSF tng. fellow U. Va., 1979-83; presenter various orgns., workshops and symposiums. Author: Biology of Light, 1992; issue editor Immunomethods, 1992-93. Dir. fund raising Jack and Jill of Am., Reston, Va., 1986-90; dir. Project Lead, Links Inc., Reston, 1990; mem. vestry St. Paul's Episcopal Ch., Alexandria, Va., 1987-90, 95-98; pres. auxiliary to D.C. chpt. Nat. Med. Assn., 1998—; mem. Commn. on Ministry Episcopal Coun. of Va., 1999—. Mem. AAAS, Am. Assn. Immunology, Mortarboard, Links (pres. Reston chpt. 1997—), Sigma Xi. Achievements include development and characterization of cell lines for study of HIV virus; first isolation and publication of amino acid analysis of HIV Reverse Transcriptase. Home: 827 Swinks Mill Rd Mc Lean VA 22102-2124 Office: FDA Ctr Devices and Radiol Health HHS 12709 Twinbrook Pkwy Rm 2 Rockville MD 20852-1719

LIGNEREUX, YVES GUY, veterinary anatomy educator; b. Algiers, Algeria, Apr. 15, 1952; s. Yvon Pierre and Simone Jeanne (Teyssier) L.; divorced; children: Louis, Pierre. DVM, Nat. Vet. Sch. of Toulouse, France, 1976; Agrégation, Ecoles Nats. Véterinaires, 1983; Doctorate, Paul Sabatier U., Toulouse, 1986. Asst. Nat. Vet. Sch., Toulouse, 1976-78, maître-asst., 1978-86, 89-92; asst. prof. Nat. Vet. Sch., Algiers, 1987-89; asst. prof. Nat. Vet. Sch., Toulouse, 1992-98, prof., 1998—. Author more than 100 articles on vet. anatomy, archaeozoology and paleopathology. Mem. Nat. Soc. for Protection of Nature, World Assn. Vet. Anatomists (pres. internat. com. on tchg. of vet. anatomy 1991—), Assn. Archeologies (pres. 1998—). Roman Catholic. Avocations: reading history and natural sciences, gardening, drawing. E-mail: yves.lignereux@free.fr. Home: 32 rue Dominique Clos, 31300 Toulouse France Office: Ecole Nat Vet, 23 chemin des capelles, 31076 Toulouse France

LIGON, PATTI-LOU E., real estate company executive, educator; b. Riverside, Calif., Feb. 28, 1953; d. Munford Ernest and Patsy Hazel L. BS, San Diego State U., 1983; BBA, Nat. U., San Diego, 1983, MA in Bus. Adminstrn., 1984. Cert. profl. counselor. Escrow asst. Cajon, Calif., 1978-79, Summit Escrow, San Diego, 1979-81; escrow officer Fidelity Nat. Title, San Diego, 1982-84, Dawson Escrow, San Diego, 1984; owner, property mgr., investment adviser Ligon Enterprises, San Diego, 1980—, cons., 1982—. Chmn. com., alumnae and assocs. San Diego State U., 1983-85; chmn. com. San Diego Zool. Soc., 1985; pres. Friends of Symphony, Riverside, Calif., 1978. Recipient commendation City and County of Honolulu, 1981. Mem. NAFE, Nat. Notary Assn., Calif. Escrow Assn., Am. Home Econs. Assn., Internat. Platform Assn., Calif. Bus. Edn. Assn., Jr. League of San Diego, Spinster Club (pres. 1981), Univ. Club (San Diego), Sigma Kappa (pres. 1974, v.p. sorority corp. 1976—). Republican. Methodist. Avocations: racquetball, clothing design, photography, travel. Home and Office: Ligon Enterprises PO Box 1642 La Mesa CA 91944-1642

LIGTHART, LEO PETRUS, electrical engineering educator; b. Rotterdam, The Netherlands, Sept. 15, 1946; s. Anton A. and Maria Ligthart; m. Ine E. Versaevel, Oct. 3, 1969; children: Remco, Eveline, Ilse-Faran, Leontine. BSc, Delft U. Tech., The Netherlands, 1967, MSc, 1969, PhD in Engring., 1985; D (hon.), Moscow State Tech. U. of Civil Aviation, 1999. Student asst. Delft U., 1968-69, scientist, 1969-88, prof. electronic sys. for positioning and radar, 1988-92, prof. microwave transmission, radar and remote sensing, 1992—, dir. Internat. Rsch. Ctr. for Telecom. Transmission, 1994—; postdoctoral fellow Chalmers U., Gothenburg, Sweden, 1976-77; cons. Getronics/K&H, Delft, 1987-97, Intercai, Utrecht, The Netherlands, 1992-96; radiocomm. advisor SRR, Rotterdam, 1989-91; Netherlands rep. COST, European Union, Brussels, 1972—. Co-author: Advanced Antenna Technology, 1982, Direct and Inverse Methods in Radar Polarimetry, 1992, Review of Radio Science 1990-1992, 1993; patentee for polarizer for radar waves. Fellow Instn. Elec. Engrs. (student councilor Delft 1991—, Blumlein Brown Willans Premium award 1982); mem. IEEE (sr.), Internat. Union Radio Scientists (corr.). Avocation: sailing. Office: Delft U IRCTR, Mekelweg 4, 2628 CD Delft The Netherlands

LIHUI, ZHENG, Olympic athlete. Winner Gold medal gymnastics all around Sydney, 2000. Office: Chinese Gymnastics Assn, 9 Tiyuquan Rd, 100763 Beijing China

LIJEWSKI, TEOFIL ZYGMUNT, geographer, educator; b. Poznan, Poland, Feb. 3, 1930; s. Antoni and Aniela (Przybylska) L.; m. Teresa Maria Kiedrowska, Sept. 3, 1957; children: Pawel, Izabela. Grad., U. Poland, Poznan, 1955; Doctorate, Inst. Geography, Warsaw, Poland, 1961. Planner Urban Bur. City of Warsaw, 1955-59; asst. Inst. Geography Polish Acad. Scis., Warsaw, 1958-61, lectr., 1961-67, head dept., 1966-78, asst. prof., 1967-80, extraordinary prof., 1980-88, ordinary prof., 1988—; head Warsaw sect. Polish Geog. Soc., 1984-87. Author: Commuting in Poland, 1967, Geography of Transportation in Poland, 1977, Industrialization of Poland 1945-75, 1978, Austria, 1987; co-author: Lexicon of Polish Towns, 1998. Mem. Polish Geog. Soc., Polish Tourist Soc. Avocations: traveling, sightseeing, photography. Home: Prosta 2 m 154, PL 00850 Warsaw Poland Office: Inst Geography, Twarda 51/55, PL 00818 Warsaw Poland

LIJNEN, HENRI ROGER, biochemistry educator; b. Houthalen, Belgium, Dec. 1, 1952; s. Victor August and Maria (Gijbels) L.; m. Ingrid Claes, Apr. 10, 1978; children: Koen, Tine. MS in Chemistry, U. Leuven, Belgium, 1974, PhD in Biochemistry, 1978. First asst. U. Leuven Sch. Medicine, 1978-85, work leader, 1985-87, lectr., 1987-89, assoc. prof., 1989-92, sr. lectr., 1992-95, prof. biochemistry, 1995—; sec. gen. XI Congress, Internat. Soc. Thrombosis and Haemostasis, 1987, program chmn. XII Congress Fibrinolysis, 1994, chmn. fibrinolysis subcom., 1990-92. Contbr. chpts. to books; assoc. editor Thrombosis and Haemostasis, 1993—. Recipient Dr. Karel Verleysen prize Royal Acad. Medicine, Belgium, 1994. Mem. Internat. Soc. Thrombosis and Haemostasis, Internat. Soc. Fibrinolysis and Thrombolysis (bd. dirs. 1992—, prize 1996), Belgian Soc. Thrombosis and Haemostasis, Dutch Soc. Thrombosis and Haemostasis. Avocations: sports, literature. Office: UZ Gasthuisberg, Herestraat 49, B 3000 Leuven Belgium

LIKHTERMAN, LEONID BOLESLAVOVITCH, neurologist, researcher; b. Sebastopol, Crimea, USSR, Oct. 6, 1931; s. Boleslav Vladimirovitch Likhterman and Sarra Evseevna Brusilovskaja; m. Zoja Ivanovna Kirnose, Apr. 11, 1958; 1 child, Boleslav. MD, Med. Inst., Simpheropol, USSR, 1956; PhD, Neurosurgery Inst., Moscow, 1962, DMS, 1972. Cert. neurologist. Neurologist Psychoneurol. Ctr., Aktjubinsk, 1956-58; aspirant Neurosurgery Inst., Moscow, 1958-62, sr. scientist, 1984—; sr. scientist Traumatology Inst., Gorky, USSR, 1962-73; sci.-patent head Traumatology Inst., Gorky, 1973-84; chief Thermovision Ctr., Gorky, 1983-84; acad. bd. Sec. Expert Com., Moscow, 1987-91. Editor, author: (book) Clinical Manual on Head Injury, 1998; author: (monographs) Combined Head Injury, 1977 (diploma Russian Acad. Med. Scis. 1978), Clinical Diagnosis of Cerebral Tumours, 1979, Ultrasound Tomography and Thermography in Neurosurgery, 1983. Recipient Russian State Prize Laureate, 1995. Mem. European Acad. Multidisciplinary Neurotrauma, N.Y. Acad. Scis. Avocations: traveling, fine arts, swimming. Home: Fadeev Str 5-21, 125047 Moscow Russia Office: Burdenko Neurosurgery Inst, Fadeev Str 5, 125017 Moscow Russia

LIKHTEROV, LEV, engineer; b. Gomel, Soviet Union, Aug. 23, 1940; arrived in Israel, 1987; s. Emmanuel and Judith Likhterov; m. Anna Eshchin, July 25, 1970; children: Emma, Simona. MSc, Shipbuilding Inst., 1963; PhD, Kriloff Rsch. Inst., 1971. Sr. engr. Design Bur. Propeller, Moscow, 1963-73; head of sector Moscow Br. of Giprorybflot, Moscow, 1973-78; sr. engr. Spl. Design Bur., Moscow, 1978-87; rsch. engr. Ben-Gurion U., Beer-Sheva, Israel, 1988—. Co-author: Vertical Axis Propellers, 1973; contbr. articles to profl. jours. Home: 23 Mark Hassman St, 84000 Beer-Sheva Israel Office: Ben Gurion U of Negev, PO Box 653, 84105 Beer-Sheva Israel

LIKIS, FRANCES ESTES, nurse midwife, nurse practitioner; b. Opelika, Ala., Dec. 12, 1970; d. Kenneth James and Katherine Seibels (Russell) L.; m. William Alexander Blue, Sept. 5, 1998. BS cum laude, Vanderbilt Univ., 1993, MSN, 1994; nurse-midwifery cert., Frontier Sch. Midwifery, 2000. Family nurse practitioner Cen. Care Medical Ctrs., Nashville, 1995-96, United Neighborhood Health Svcs., Nashville, 1995-99; sexual assault examiner Met. Nashville Gen. Hosp., Nashville, 1995—; adj. instr. Vanderbilt Univ. Sch. Nursing, 1997—; mem. Nat. Health Svc. Corps, 1997-99; emer. contraception vis. faculty Assn. Reproductive Health Profls., Washington, 1999—. Recipient KittyErnest scholarship Frontier Sch. Midwifery & Family Nursing, Hyden, Ky., 1999. Mem. Middle Tenn. Advanced Practice Nurses (co-pres. 1997—), Assn. Reproductive Health Profls., Tenn. Nurses Assn., Am. Coll. Nurse-Midwives, Am. Coll. Nurse Practitioners, Internat. Assn. Forensic Nurses. E-mail: flikis@midwives.org.

LIKPHAI, CHAUN, prime minister of Thailand; b. Muang District, South Thailand, July 28, 1938. BA in Law, Thammasat U.; MA, Thai Bar Assn.; PhD (hon.), Ramkhamhaeug U., Srinakharinwirot U. Dep. min. of justice, 1975, min. prime min.'s office, min. of commerce, min. of agr. and cooperatives, 1982-83, 90-91, min. of edn., 1983-86, spkr. Ho. of Reps., 1986-88, min. of pub. health, 1988-89, dep. prime min., 1989-90, prime min., 1992-95, 97—; mem. Ho. of Reps., 1969, 75, 76, 79, 83, 86, 88, 92, 95; v.p. U. Coun., Prince of Songkhla U., Kasetsart U., Bangkok; mem. univ. coun. Silpakorn U., Bangkok, Srinakharinwirot U., Bangkok, Thammasat U., Bangkok; lectr. forensic medicine sect. Faculty of Medicine, Chulalongkorn U., Bangkok. Deocrated Grand Champion Most Illustrious Order of Chula Chom Klao, 1996, Knight Grand Cordon (spl. class) Most Exalted Order of the White Elephant, 1980, 82, Most Noble Order Crown of Thailand, 1979, 81. Office: Govt Ho, Thanon Nakhon Pathom, Bangkok 10300, Thailand*

LILAN, ZHU, Chinese government official. Chemistry, Odessa U, 1956. Scientist Chem. Inst., Chinese Acad. Sci., 1956-86; v. chair State Sci. and Tech. Commn., Beijing, 1986-98; chmn. State Commn. for Sci. and Tech., Govt. of China, Beijing, 1998—. Editor Sci. and Edn. for a Prosperous China, 1995. Mem. Communist Party. Address: State Commn Sci and Tech, 15/B Fuxing Lu Hai Dian Qu, Beijing China 100763*

LILANI, PANKAJ MAGANLAL, financial controller; b. Bombay, Aug. 25, 1960; s. Maganlal M. and Jasumati M. Lilani; m. Mamta Janaj Merchant, Apr. 23, 1994; 1 child, Master Varun. B of Comm., Mulund Coll. Commerce, Bombay, 1982. Chartered acct. cert. cost acct. Head costing dept. Nat. Textiles Corp. (South Maharashtra) Ltd., Bombay, 1986-87; acct. Tabuk (Saudi Arabia) Agrl. Devel. Co., 1989-91; asst. fin. contr. Union Transporting & Contracting Co. Wade Adams LLC, Duba, United Arab Emirates, 1992-96; fin. contr. Hilal Bil Badi & Ptnrs. Contracting Co. WLL, Abu Dhabi, United Arab Emirates, 1996—. Fellow Inst. Chartered Accts. India, Inst. Cost and Works Accts. India. Office: HILALCO, PO Box 28177, Abu Dhabi United Arab Emirates

LILJEGREN, JAN RAGNAR GUSTAF, group company executive; b. Gothenburg, Sweden, July 31, 1929; s. Ragnar Gustaf Oscar and May Gunvor Ann-Margret (Petré) L.; m. Harriet Thyra Wahlén, Apr. 25, 1965; children: Harriet Mikaela, Harriet Camilla, Carl Jonas; 1 child by previous marriage, Per Johan Gustaf. Student, London, Paris, 1948-49; BS, Stockholm Sch. Econs., 1972; LLB, Stockholm U., 1974, IFL, 1987. Mgr. Nyman & Schultz Travel Bur., Stockholm, 1956-62; sales mgr. AB Nyman & Schultz, Stockholm, 1962-64; dir. AB Nyman & Schultz, Stockholm, 1963-64; gen. sales mgr. Vingresor AB, Gothenburg, Sweden, 1964-67; mng. dir. AB Finnlines Ltd., Stockholm, 1967-75; mng. dir. Tidningsstatistik AB (Swedish Audit Bur. of Circulations), Solna, Sweden, 1976-80, fin. exec., 1981-86; fin., legal and adminstrv. exec. TURATOR (TS Forvaltn AB), Sollentuna, 1986-93, group staff exec., 1993-94; mng dir. Media Rsch. AB, Media & Market Info. AB, 1988-95; mng. dir. Travel Rsch. Testologen AB, 1986-95; mng. dir. Media Vision AB, Marknadssociologen AB, 1991-95, adv. group mem., 1994—; mng. dir. Reklamstatistik AB (Advt. Stats. Ltd.), 1976-80; chmn. Lingmerths Travel Bur., Eksjo, 1981-85, SAM Bus Tour Operators AB, Stockholm, 1982-84; chmn. Flygresebyran AB, Stockholm, 1984-85, Air Travel Sweden AB, Stockholm 1984-85, Alandia Cruise Line GmbH, Alandia Tour Svc. GmbH, Lubeck, Germany, 1986—; exec. ScanConcepts Stockholm, HB, 1986—, CEO, 1994—; educator Travel Edn. Ctr., IATA/UFTAA Authorized Tng. Ctr., Stockholm, 1985—; Scandinavian rep. Heinrich Vogel Fachzeitschriften GmbH, Verlagsgruppe Bertelsmann Internat., Munich, 1994—; vice chmn. Jarfalla local govt. bd. technics and resources, 1995-99; sr. coord. Scandinavia, Sea Cloud Cruises GmbH, Hamburg, 1997—; legal advisor Netcheck internet project, Stockholm, 1996—; chmn. tenant Owners' Soc., Gjutaren, Järfälla, 1999—. Author: Turistens Uppslagsbok, 1963, Försäljningslära, 1969; co-author: Hur man reser i Europa, 1953, Hur man reser i Beneluxländerna, 1954; contbr. to Check-in, Travelmag., Sweden, 1996—. Hon. chmn. Stockholm Travel Bur. Salaried Employees Assn., 1957; mem. planning commn. Psychol. Def., Nat. Bd. Psychol. Def., 1979-90; mentor Stockholm Sch. Econs., 1994—; vice-chmn. ednl. inst. Medborgarskolan, Solna, 1999—. Capt. Swedish Army Res. Decorated Hanseatenkreuz; recipient Lubeck award, 1989. Mem. Stockholm Mktg. Assn. (bd. dirs. 1976-79), Stockholm Skalclub, Internat. C. of C. (nat. mktg. com. 1976-80), Snackevarp Presidium, Swedish Market Rsch. Assn., Market Law Assn., KOGGE, North European Cooperation Group, The Alumni Assn. of Stockholm Sch. Econs., Travel Industry Srs. Sweden, Jarfalla Fedn. of Conservatives (bd. dirs., vice-chair), Jarfallas Ch. Cmtys. (bd. dirs.), Alandia Jazz, The Blue Banana Network of Baltic Sea Area. Home and Office: Mantalsvägen 8, SE 17550 Jarfalla Sweden

LILJESTRÖM, CHEDDI, lawyer; b. Kungälv, Sweden, Sept. 15, 1954; s. Lars Övind and Rita (Laxèn) L.; m. Hillevi Liikamaa, Aug. 17, 1991; children: Didrik, Hampus. LLM, Uppsala (Sweden) U., 1979; MCJ, NYU, 1981, LLM, 1982. Asst. in penal law U. Uppsala, 1977-80; legal rsch. instr. NYU Sch. Law, N.Y.C., 1981-82; intern UNITAR, UN, N.Y.C., 1981-82; assoc. Wetter & Wetter Advokatbyrå, Stockholm, 1982-83; judge Stockholm Dist. Ct., 1983-85; assoc. Rydin & Carlsten Advokat AB, Stockholm, 1985-88; corp. legal counsel Scandinavian Airlines System, Stockholm, 1988-93; ptnr. Söderlund & Ptnrs. Advokatbyrå, Stockholm, 1993-95, Liljeström Lundquist Advokatbyrå, Stockholm, 1996—. Fulbright scholar, 1980. Mem. ABA, N.Y. Bar Assn., Internat. Bar Assn., Swedish Bar Assn. Avocations: travel, tennis, wine collection, family activities. Office: Liljeström Lundquist Advokatbyrå, Birger Jarlsgatan 16, 114 34 Stockholm Sweden

LILL, ROLAND, biochemist; b. Oehringen, Germany, Oct. 9, 1955; s. Rolf and Ilse (Doebele) L.; m. Angelika Haag; children: Michael, Daniel, Sandra. Diploma in chemistry, U. Munich, Germany, 1981, D, 1986. Rsch. scientist U. Munich, Germany, 1981-87, sr. rschr., 1990-96; prof. U. Marburg, Germany, 1996—. Postdoctoral fellow U. Calif., L.A., 1987-89. Avocations: hiking, music, volleyball. Office: Inst Zytobiologie, Robert-Koch-Str 5, 35033 Marburg Germany

LILLEY, PETER BRUCE, government official; b. Aug. 23, 1943; s. Arnold Francis and Lilian (Elliott) L.; m. Gail Ansell, 1979. Grad., Dulwich Coll., Clare Coll., Cambridge U. M.P. St. Albans, 1983-97; econ. sec. Her Majesty's Treasury, 1987-89, fin. sec., 1989-90; sec. of state for trade and industry Her Majesty's Govt. Treasury, London, 1990-92; sec. state for social security Her Majesty's Govt. Treasury, 1992-97; M.P. for Hitchin and Harpenden, 1997—, shadow chancellor of Exchequer, 1997-98, dep. leader of the opposition, 1998-99. Office: House of Commons, London SW1A 0AA, England

LILLEYMAN, JOHN STUART, paediatric hematologist, oncologist educator; b. Sheffield, Eng., July 9, 1945; s. Ernest and Frances (Johnson) L. MBBS, St. Bartholomew's, London, 1968, DSc in Medicine, 1996. Rsch. fellow Welsh Nat. Sch. of Medicine, Wales, 1972-74; cons. hematologist Sheffield (Eng.) Children's Hosp., 1975-95; prof. pediatric hematology and oncology St. Bartholomew's and Royal London Sch. Medicine, 1995—; chief exec. Clin. Pathology Accreditation, Eng., 1992-97. Editor: (book) Paediatric Haematology, 1999; author: (book) Childhood Leukaemia-The Facts, 1994, 2d edit., 1999; editor Jour. of Clin. Pathology, 1986-92. Fellow Royal Coll. Physicians, Royal Coll. Pathologists (v.p. 1993-96, Disting. Svc. medal 1991, pres. 1999—), Inst. Biomed. Sci. (hon.), Coll. of Pediats. and Child Health; mem. Brit. Soc. for Haematology, Assn. Clin. Pathologists (U.K., pres. 1998-99). Office: Royal London Hosp, Dept Ped Hematol and Oncol, London E1 1BB, England

LILLIEHÖÖK, DANIEL, physicist; b. Farsta, Stockholm, Sweden, Nov. 10, 1971; s. Fred Marttinen and Marika Lilliehöök; m. Birgitta Maria Johansson, Aug. 14, 1993 (div. Jan. 1997). MS, Stockholm U., 1995, PhD, 2000. Contbr. articles to profl. jours. including Phys. Rev. B. L. Namowitsky's study grantee Stockholm U., 1995. Avocation: singing. Home: Skrakgrönd 9 8tr, 12349 Farsta Sweden Office: Fysikum, Box 6730, 11385 Stockholm Sweden

LILLIEHÖÖK, J(OHAN) BJÖRN O(LOF), health science association administrator; b. Stockholm, Feb. 12, 1945; s. Nils Olof and Barbro (Brandel) L.; m. E. Margareta Setterberg, Sept. 7, 1968; children: Veronica, Lovisa, Alexandra. LLB, U. Stockholm, 1969. Dist. judge's assessor Dist. Ct. Sollentuna and Farentuna, Solna, Stockholm, Sweden, 1969-72; prin. clk. Swedish Nat. Bd. Immigration, Stockholm, 1972-73; dir., v.p., head regional office Swedish Employers' Confederation, Stockholm, 1973-90; sec.-gen., chief exec. officer Swedish Heart Lung Found., Stockholm, 1990—; chmn. Stockholm New Enterprise Ctr., 1987-90; chair Nordic Assn. in Stockholm, 1993-2000; trustee. bd. dirs. King Oscar II's Jubilee Found., Stockholm, 1994—; bd. dirs., mem. mgmt. exec. F.O.F. Rsch. and Progress Found., Stockholm, 1996—, chmn., 2000—. Chmn. fund raising com., mem. exec. com. Internat. Union Against Tb and Lung Disease, Paris, 1994-99; mem. exec. bd. World Heart Fedn., Geneva, 1995-99; mem. European Heart Network Coun., Brussels, 1996—; mem. bd., mgmt. exec. com. Hässelby Found., 1993-2000; v.p. Internat. Non-Govtl. Coalition Against Tobacco, Paris, 1998—; chmn. mgmt. com. European Heart Health Initiative, Brussels, 1997—; chmn. steering com. Nordic-Baltic Project Against Tuberculosis in the Baltic States, 1996—. Mem. Internat. Soc. for Labour Law and Social Security, Kollegiet, Sallskapet, SvD Exec. Club, Rotary (bd. dirs. Stockholm club, pres. 1989-90). Lutheran. Avocations: fishing, hunting, skiing, skating, photography. Office: Swedish Heart Lung Found, Riddargatan 18, SE 11451 Stockholm Sweden

LILLY, ARNYS CLIFTON, JR., physicist; b. Beckley, W.Va., June 3, 1934; s. Arnys Clifton and Ella Vay (McKeehan) L.; m. Agnes Madeline Micou, June 9, 1956; children: Gregory Alan, Diane Renee, James Clifton. BS in Petroleum Engring., Va. Poly. Inst., 1957, PhD in Physics, 1989; MS in Physics, Carnegie-Mellon U., 1963. Rsch. physicist Gulf Rsch. and Devel. Co., Pitts., 1957-65; prin. scientist Philip Morris Rsch. Ctr., Richmond, Va., 1965—, research fellow, 1984, dir. tech. assessment, 1988, v.p. tech. assessment, 1996. Mem. Am. Phys. Soc., Sigma Xi. Contbr. articles to physics jours.; patentee in field. Home: 9641 Waterfowl Flyway Chesterfield VA 23838-8905 Office: Philip Morris Rsch Ctr 4201 Commerce Rd Richmond VA 23234-2269

LILLY, JOHN RICHARD, II, prosecutor; b. Phila., July 20, 1962; s. John Richard Sr. and Elizabeth Anne (Brown) L.; children: John Richard III, Cameron Lewis. BA, Geoge Washington U., 1987; JD, U. Balt., 1991. Bar: Md. 1992, U.S. Dist. Ct. Md. 1995. Law clk. 7th Jud. Cir. Md., Upper Marlboro, 1991-92; asst. state's atty. State's Atty.'s Office Prince George's County Md., Upper Marlboro, 1992-98; asst. atty. gen. Md. Atty. Gen.'s Office, Balt., 1998—; adj. prof. U. Balt. Sch. Law. Comments editor U. Balt. Jour. Environ. Law. Chmn. Oakland Mills Village Bd., Columbia, Md., 1990-92; pres. St. Stephen's Area Civic Assn., Crownsville, Md., 1994-95. Lt. USNR, 1988—. Mem. Anne Arundel Bar Assn. Avocations: tennis, sailing, reading, photography. Home: 1306 Eva Gude Dr Crownsville MD 21032-2102 Office: Md Atty Gen's Office Environ Crimes Unit 2500 Broening Hwy Baltimore MD 21224-6601

LILLY, WESLEY COOPER, marine engineer, ship surveyor; b. Phila., May 23, 1933; s. Richard Gladstone and Margaret Jane L.; m. Barbara Joan

Newton, June 18, 1935 (div. Nov. 24, 1978); children: Pamela Lynn, Barbara Joan. BS in Engring., Pa. Mil. Coll., 1956-61. Apprentice machinist Phila. Naval Shipyard, 1951-53, prodn. shipbuilding, 1955-66, planning, design divsn., 1966-68; mem. shipbuilding testing specifications staff Naval Weapons Svc. Office, 1968-70; procurement prodn. Navy Dept. Navsea, Washington, 1970-86; pres., owner Marine Assocs., Amelia Island, Fla., 1972—; pres., founder Saturn Marine Engring., St. Augustine, Fla., 1986—; programmer Basic, Fortran, and Cobol rev. bus. computech programs. Inventor, patentee in field. Served with U.S. Army, 1953-55. Mem. Soc. Naval Archs. and Marine Engrs. (chmn. com. for small and medium shipyards/shipbuilding), Tech. Exch. Marine Profls., Antique Outboard Motor Club Internat., Amelia Island PC Users Group, Amelia Island Computer Club. Episcopalian. Avocations: accounting, computers, cruising, sailing. E-mail: abcmarine2@hotmail.com.; abcmarine@nassnet.com. Home: 2757 1st Ave Fernandina Beach FL 32034-2345 Office: Marine Assocs Fernandina Beach FL 32034

LIM, CHWEE-TECK, mechanical engineer, educator; b. Singapore, Sept. 5, 1965; parents Ah-Lay Lim and Kim-Suan Tan. B in Engring., Nat. U. Singapore, 1990; PhD, U. Cambridge, 1996. Mech. engr. Singapore Technologies Aerospace, 1990-92; asst. prof. Nat. U. Singapore, 1996—. Mem. ASME (faculty advisor 1999—), Inst. Engrs. Singapore, Nat. U. Singapore Soc. Avocations: swimming, reading, cycling, golf. Office: Nat U Singapore Mech Engrin, 10 Kent Ridge Crescent, Singapore 119260, Singapore

LIM, DUCK-HO, economics educator, university dean; b. Kwang-Ju, Republic of Korea, Mar. 28, 1953; s. Ki-Ju Lim and Pan-Rae Kwon; m. Young-Eun Jang, June 13, 1982; children: Hee-Rock, Su-Min. BA, Hanyang U., Seoul, Republic of Korea, 1982; PhD in Econs., Rice U., 1987. Prof. econs. Hanyang U., Ansan, Republic of Korea, 1988—, dean continuing edn. program, 1997-98, dean Office Student Affairs, 1999—. Author: Microeconomics, 1994, Principles of Economics, 1998; contbr. articles to profl. jours., including Jour. Urban Econs., Korean Econ. Rev. Mem. Civic Soc. for Econ. Justice (pres. 1998—), New Edn. Soc. (pres. 1998—). Avocations: tennis, basketball, movies. Office: Hamyang U, 1271 Sal Dong, Kyonggi Ansan 425-791, Republic of Korea

LIM, HYUN-CHIN, sociologist; b. Seoul, Korea, Apr. 26, 1949; s. Keun Soo and Bok Soun (Chung) L.; m. Sun-Hee Youm. BA, Seoul Nat. U., 1971, MA, 1973; PhD, Harvard U., 1982. Asst. to prof. Seoul Nat. U., Korea, 1982—; dir. Inst. Social Devel. of Policy Rsch., Seoul, 1995-99; vis. prof. Duke U., Durham, N.C., 1997; rsch. fellow Cen. for East Asisn Studies, U. Chgo., 1989-90; rsch. assoc. Cen. Internat. Affairs., Harvard U., Cambridge, Mass., 1980-82. Editor: Korean Social Sci. Jour., 1998—; editl. mem. Contemporary Sociology, 1999—; Author: (books) Comparative Sociology, 1999, Korean Development in A Global Age, 1998, Third World Developments, 1993, Modern Korea & Dependency Theorys, 1987. V.p. Nana Assn. for Nat. Policy, 1997-98. Cpt. Army, 1973-76. Recipient Fulbright Scholar, 1994-95, rsch. fellowship, U. Chgo., 1989-90, Harvard-Yenching fellow, Harvard U., 1976-82. Mem. Am. Sociological Assn., Internat. Political Sci. Assn., Assn. for Asian Studies. Avocations: fishing, travel, tracking. Office: Seoul Nat U Kwanak-ku, Shimnim-Pong Sum 51, 151-742 Seoul Korea

LIM, JOSEPH DY, oral surgeon; b. Manila, Nov. 2, 1948; s. Celestino Yu and Soledad (Dy) L.; m. Giok Leng Cua, Nov. 10, 1974; children: Joseph Oliver, Alistair Bryan, Kenneth Lester, Mark Andrew. DMD cum laude, U. of the East, The Philippines, 1974. Pres. Filipino-Chinese Dental Found., Inc., 1982-83; mng. dir. Internat. Dental Supply, Inc., Manila, 1982—; pvt. practice Manila, 1975—; pres. Coll. Oral Implantology of The Philippines, 1997—; adviser Found. Oral Implant Rsch. of the Philippines, Inc.; co-chmn. trade exhibits Asian-Pacific Dental Congress, 1994; organizing chmn. 12th Internat. Oral Implant Symposium, Manila, 1995; chief Philippine del. 14th Asian-Pacific Dental Congress, Seoul, Republic of Korea, 1989; Philippine del. 16th Asian-Pacific Dental Congress, Kuala Lumpur, Malaysia, 1993; bd. dirs., internat. adv. bd. Implant Dentistry Rsch. and Edn. Found. of Internat. Congress Oral Implantologist. Editl. cons. MDS Digest, 1989; contbr. sci. articles to profl. jours. Chmn., team leader Civic Action, Filipino-Chinese Dental Found., Inc., 1981—; pres. Metro Manila Health Group-Dr. Puring Rocamora Meml. Found. Recipient Disting. Svc. award Filipino-Chinese Dental Found., Inc., 1982, Outstanding Achievement award Grace Alumni Assn., Inc., 1995. Fellow Philippine Coll. Oral Maxillo-Facial Surgeons, Internat. Coll. Dentists, Internat. Assn. Oral and Maxillofacial Surgeons, Asian Oral Implant Acad. (hon., pres. 1996-98), Internat. Congress Oral Implantologist (diplomate, v.p. Asian-Pacific sect., chmn. Asia-Pacific sect. 1998—, Edn. award 1995); mem. ADA (assoc.), Philippine Dental Assn. (auditor 1982-83, 92-93, 94-95, trustee 1988-89, chmn. trade exhibits 1982-89, Presdl. award of merit 1983, Spkr.'s Bur. 1992—), Soc. Assn. Execs. Philippines (founding), Manila Dental Soc. (pres. 1989-90, organizer CIVAC team 1982—), U. of the East Dental Alumni Inc. (bd. dirs. 1993—), Fedn. Dentaire Internat. (co-chmn. trade exhibits 1986), Asian-Pacific Dental Fedn., Asian Oral Implant Acad., Assn. Asian Oral Mixillo-Facial Surgeons, Internat. Assn. Dental Rsch., Asian Acad. Craniomandibular Disorders, Assn. Dental Practitioners of Philippines (pres. 1993—), Oral Implantology Ctr. Study Club (founding), Am. Acad. Implant Dentistry, Acad. Osseointegration. Avocations: reading, swimming, bowling, horseback riding, golf. Office: Tytana Pla Ste 821, Pla Lorenzo Ruiz Binondo, Manila The Philippines also: Ortigas Ctr Complex, Jollibee Ctr Bldg Ste 202, Pasig, Metro Manila The Philippines

LIM, KOON SANG, engineering executive; b. Singapore, Jan. 8, 1954; s. Poh Lim and Sieweng Chan; m. Sweehong Tan, May 6, 1984; 1 child, Mingyu. M Engring., Nat. Inst. Applied Scis., Lyon, France, 1979. Chartered engr. Brit. Engring. Coun. Rsch. engr., head dept. Def. Sci. Orgn., Singapore, 1979-81; mng. dir. Info. Engring. Svcs. Pte. Ltd., Singapore, 1981-91; group chief tech. officer Logic Group, Singapore, 1992-94, CEO, 1994—; chmn. s/w subcom. Singapore Fedn. Computer Industry, 1988-91; mem. econ. planning com. Singapore Ministry Trade and Industry, 1990-91; mem. adv. bd. Nat. Computer Bd., Singapore, 1989-91, Inst. Sys. Scis., Singapore, 1989-91. Lt. Logistics Res., 1973—. Overseas scholar Singarore Pub. Svc. Commn. and French Govt., 1973-79. Mem. IEEE, Brit. Computer Soc., Assn. for Computing Machinery. E-mail: kslim@singnet.com.sg. Home: 149 Hougang St 11 #10-138, 530149 Singapore Singapore Office: Bangkok Bank Bldg, 180 Cecil St #15-03, Singapore 069546, Singapore

LIM, LAY-HOOI, plastic and reconstructive surgeon, consultant; b. Georgetown, Penang, Malaysia, Aug. 20, 1960; d. Beng-Seng Lim and Seok-Tin Soo; m. Meow-Foong Yoong, May 19, 1984. MB, BS, U. Malaya, Kuala Kumpur, Malaysia, 1984. House officer Ipoh Gen Hosp., 1984-85; rotations in gen. surgery, pediat., orthopaedics, others gen. hosps., Alor Setar & Kuala Lumpur, 1985-88; registrar gen. surgery Gen. Hosp., Kuala Lumpur, 1989; registrar in plastic surgery Kuala Lumpur Hosp., 1990, Royal Adelaide (Australia) Hosp., 1991-92, Westmead, Auburn and Camperdown Hosps., Sydney, Australia, 1993; locum cons. plastic surgeon Royal Victoria Infirmary, Newcastle-upon-Tyne, Eng., 1994; cons. plastic surgeon, head unit Penang Hosp., 1995—. Contbr. articles to med. jours., including Malaysian Jour. Surgery, Brit. Jour. Plastic Surgery, Australian-New Zealand Jour. Surgery, Plastic and Reconstructive Surgery. Fellow Royal Coll. Surgeons (Edinburgh), Royal Australasian Coll. Surgeons; mem. Malaysian Assn. Plastic Surgeons, Nat. Soc. of Aesthetic Plastic Surg. Avocation: scuba diving. Office: Penang Hosp Dept Plastic-, Recon Surgery, Residency Rd, Penang 10990, Malaysia

LIM, LICARION GOREMBALEM, fraternal organization administrator; b. Lavezares, Philippines, June 7, 1944; s. Venancio Valenteros and Norberta (Gorembalem) L.; m. Perla Galias, June 26, 1972; children: Lerwin, Yvette Marie, James Licarion, Laurean Paul. BA in Pre-Medicine, U. of Tacloban, 1967. Sci. h.s. tchr. St. Anthony's Acad., Llorente, Philippines, 1967-69, Salvacion Inst., Lavazares, Philippines, 1969-71; first aid and swimming instr. Philippine Nat. Red Cross, Catarman, Philippines, 1972-79; fraternal counselor K.C. Fr. Martires Coun., Catarman, 1989-91; grand knight K.C. Fr. Matires Coun., Catarman, 1989-91; dist. dep. K.C. Dist. #36, Catarman, 1991-93; state ins. promotion chmn. K.C. Visayas Jurisdiction, Cebu City, Philippines, 1994-95; ways and means provincial dir. K.C. Northern Samar Area, Catarman, Philippines, 1995-96; area mgr. K.C. Fraternal Assn. of the Philippines, Inc., Manila, 1982—; mcpl. councilor Local Govt. Unit, Lavezares, 1995—. Radio comm. to serve humanity Kabalikat Civicom, 1997—; mem. health and sanitation Local Govt. Unit, 1995-98; campaign against drug abuse Philippine Nat. Red Cross, Catarman, Philippines, 1972-78; chmn. com. law Sangguniang Bayan Local Govt. , 1995—. Recipient Fr. George J. William, SJ award, 1982-87, Cmty. and Edn. Svc. award, 1996, Outstanding Mcpl. Councilor of the Philippines award, 1998. Mem. K.C. (grand knight and dist. dep. 1977-93, State Dep. award 1993). Roman Catholic. Avocations: basketball, table tennis, swimming, reading, dancing. Home: 816 San Isidro St, Lavezares 6404, Philippines Office: Gen Luna Cor, Sta Potenciana Sts, Intramuros 1002, Philppines

LIM, OOI-KONG, hotel executive; b. Kuala Lumpur, Malaysia, Mar. 24, 1950; s. Lim Foo-Yong and Chu Yin-Mooi. Degree, Lewis Hotel/Motel Sch., N.Y.C., 1972. Exec. dir., gen. mgr. Hotel Merlin Inc., Hong Kong, 1975—; bd. dirs. Maple Ltd., Singapore, Banguan Sdn. Bhd., Kuala Lumpur, Lim Foo Yong Sendirian Berhad, Kuala Lumpur, Chulan Realty Sdn. Bhd., Kuala Lumpur; pres. Hotel Merlin Inc., San Francisco. Decorated knight His Royal Highness Sultan Kelantan, 1988. Recipient Seri Mahkota award H.R.H. Sultan of Kelantan, 1982, Jaksa Perdamai award His Royal Highness, Sultan of Kelantan, 1985. Mem. Malaysian Assn., Am. Hotel and Motel Assn. Club: Royal Selangor Golf. Avocation: aeronautics. Home: # 21 Lorong Bukit Pantai Lapan, Bukit Pantai 59100 Kuala Lumpur Malaysia Office: Lim Foo Yong Holdings, Sdb Bhd 18A Jalan P Ramlee, 50250 Kuala Lumpur Malaysia

LIM, PETER HUAT-CHYE, surgeon, consultant; b. Kuala Lumpur, Malaysia, Jan. 28, 1950; s. Lim Boon-Hor and Foo Hooi-Ean; m. Tan Choo-Hee, 1978; children: Lim, Norman Thuan-Siew. BS, MB, U. Singapore, Singapore, 1975, MD in surgery, 1980; D in urology, U. Coll. London, 1988. Intern Tan TockSeng & Toa Payoh Hosp., Singapore, 1975-76; medical officer Ministry of Health Hosp., Singapore, 1977-79; registrar in surgery Tao Payoh Hosp., Singapore, 1980-84, sr. registrar in urology, 1985-86, cons. urological surgery, 1987-90, head, div. of urology, 1991-93, sr. cons., head, 1994—, chief dept. urology, 2000—; vis. cons. Nat. U. Hosp., 1998—; chmn. Asia-Pacific Continence Adv. Bd., 1998—; clin. lectr. Nat. U. Singapore, 1999—; adj. prof. Edith Cowen U., Australia, 2000—; med. dir. Urology Ctr. Glenagles Hosp. Contbr. articles to profl. jours. Hon. medical adv. Disabled People's Assn., Singapore, 1990—, Handicapped People's Assn., Singapore, 1991—. Fellow Singapore Urological Assn. (pres. 1994-95), Internat. Coll. Surgeons (hon. sec. 1993-95, pres. 1996—); mem. Soc. Continence (pres. 1991—), Acad. Medicine, British Assn. of Urological Surgeons, Am. Urological Assn., Internat. Continence Soc. (continet custodian 1995—), Asean Soc. Female Urology (pres. 1998—). Roman Catholic. Avocations: swimming, filming, photography. Home: 178 Taman Permata, Singapore 2057, Singapore Office: New Changi Hosp, 2 Simei St 3, Singapore 529889, Singapore

LIM, PIN, physician, educator; b. Penang, Malaysia, Jan. 12, 1936; m. Shirley Loo-Lim, Mar. 21, 1964; children: Jui, Jiun, Elaine Hsuen. MBBChir, U. Cambridge, 1963, MA, 1964, MD, 1970; DSc (hon.), U. Hull, 1999. Registrar diabetic dept. King's Coll. Hosp., London, 1965; med. officer Ministry Health, Singapore, 1965-66; lectr. to assoc. prof. medicine Nat. U. Singapore, 1966-77, prof., head dept. medicine, 1978-81, dy vice-chancellor, 1979-81, vice-chancellor, 1981—; fellow Royal Infirmary, Edinburgh, England, 1970; chmn. Genetic Modivication Adv. Com.; mem. Nanyang Tech. U. Coun.; bd. dirs. Overseas Union Bank, PharmBio Growth Fund Pvt. Ltd.; bd. govs. Inst. Policy Studies, Singapore Internat. Found.; bd. advisors Mendaki. Founder, pres. Endocrine and Metabolic Soc. Singapore; overseas advisor Royal Coll. Physicians London; mem. U. Melbourne Coun., DuPont ASEAN Adv. Coun., Nat. Wages Coun. Recipient Republic Singapore Pub. Adminstrn. gold medal, 1984, Republic Singapore Meritorious Svc. award, 1990, Friend Labour award Nat. Trade Union Congress, 1995; Eisenhower fellow, 1982; Queen's scholar, 1957. Fellow ACP, Royal Coll. Physicians, Acad. Medicine Singapore, Royal Australasian Coll. Physicians, Royal Coll. Surgeons Edinburgh (hon.), Coll. Gen. Practitioners Singapore (hon.), Royal Australian Coll. Ob-Gyn. (hon.), Royal Coll. Physicians and Surgeons Glasgow (hon.), Royal Coll. Dentists (U.S.A.), Royal Coll. Surgeons Edinburgh (hon.); mem. Singapore Med. Assn., Acad. Medicine (past master), British Med. Assn., Singapore Profl. Centre. Home: 2 Jalan Harum, 268476 Singapore Singapore Office: Nat U Singapore Dept Med, 5 Lower Kent Ridge Rd, 119074 Singapore Singapore

LIM, RAMON (KHE-SIONG), neuroscience educator, researcher; b. Cebu City, The Philippines, Feb. 5, 1933; came to U.S., 1959, naturalized, 1973; s. Eng-Lian and Su (Yu) L.; m. Victoria K. Sy, June 21, 1961; children: Jennifer, Wendell, Caroline. AB, U. Santo Tomas, Manila, 1953; MD cum laude, U. Santo Tomas, 1958; PhD in Biochemistry, U. Pa., 1966. Diplomate Am. Bd. Psychiatry and Neurology. Rsch. neurochemist U. Mich., Ann Arbor, 1966-69; asst. prof. biochemistry U. Chgo., 1969-76, assoc. prof. Brain Rsch. Inst., 1976-81; prof. dept. neurology U. Iowa, Iowa City, 1981—, dir. divsn. neurochemistry and neurobiology, 1981—; career investigator VA, 1983. Mem. editl. bd. Internat. Jour. Devel. Neurosci., 1984-91, Neurochem. Rsch., 1997—; contbr. articles to sci. jours. Grantee NIH, 1971—, NSF, 1979—, VA, 1981—; recipient 3d prize Art Assn. Philippines, 1957; named Outstanding Overseas Young Chinese, Fedn. Overseas Chinese Orgns., 1961. Mem. Am. Soc. Biochem. Molecular Biology, Internat. Soc. Neurochemistry (vis. lectorship 1986), Am. Soc. Neurochemistry, Soc. Neurosci., Am. Soc. Cell Biology. Avocations: calligraphy, painting, writing, music. Achievements include research in isolation and characterization of regulatory brain proteins; growth and differentiation of brain cells; brain chemistry and molecular biology. Home: 118 Richards St Iowa City IA 52246-3516 Office: U Iowa Iowa City IA 52242

LIM, SALLY-JANE, insurance and financial consultant, diversified financial services company executive; b. Manila; came to U.S., 1990; d. Teddy and Sonia (Yii) L.; children: Robin Michael, Rodney Jovin, Romelle Gavin Lim Velasco. AB-BSC magna cum laude, Coll. of Holy Spirit, Manila, The Philippines. CPA, The Philippines; Life Underwriters Tng. Coun. Fellow (LUTCF). Treas-contr. Ky. Fried Chicken, Makati, Philippines, 1968-73; ins. rep. Insular Life Assurance Co., Makati, 1972-82; project analyst Pvt. Devel. Corp. of Philippines, Makati, 1972-78; account exec. Genbancor Devel. Corp., Makati, 1978-80; risk mgr. Filcapital Devel. Corp., Makati, 1978-82; pres. and gen. mgr., ins. broker Sally-Jane Multiline Insce. Consulting, Inc., Manila, 1978-90; real estate broker Sally-Jane Realty, Inc., Manila, 1980-90; ins. rep. and v.p. Macaulay Club Sun Life of Can., 1982-91; rep. Prudential Ins. Co. of Am., Prudential Property & Casualty Ins. Co., Prudential HealthCare; registered rep. Pruco Securities Corp., L.A. Dist., South Pasadena, Calif., 1990-91, Asian Pacific Dist., Calif., 1991-98; ind. ins. broker John Hancock Life Ins. Co., CNA Life, Conseco Life, Calif., 1998—; registered rep. John Hancock Variable Life Ins. Co./Signator Investors, Inc, 1999—. Flagbearer The Philippines Opening Ceremonies, Million Dollar Round Table 58th Ann. Meeting, San Francisco, 1985; guest fashion model A Company of Women Carnegie's Highlands Golf & Country Club, Idaho, 1999. Recipient Bronze trophy Most Outstanding Ins. Sales Exec. of the Philippines Consumers' Union of the Philippines, Manila, 1983, 88, Plasma 1 Million trophies Dept. Ins. the Philippines, 1988, 89, Young Achiever award Young Achiever Found., Quezon City, Philippines, 1988, Golden Scroll award Philippine Ednl. Youth Devel., Inc., Quezon City, 1988, Twelve Outstanding Profl. Svc. (T.O.P.S.) awards Nat. Achievement Rsch. Soc., Manila, 1988, Lahing Kayumanggi award Outstanding Lady Bus. Exec., Sons and Daughters Charity, Inc., the Philippines, 1988, Internat. Quality award (IQA) (Five Yrs. Qualification) Life Ins. Mktg. and Rsch. Assn., Hartford, 1989, Young Famous Celebrity Mother's trophy Golden Mother/Father Found., Quezon City, 1990, Recognition of Excellence cert., Merit award County of L.A., 8th Ann. Women of Achievement awards San Gabriel Valley YWCA, 1992, 1998 Grand Achievement award For Profl. Sector, People's Choice awards Atened U., the Philippines, cert. recognition, 1998, Parangual ng Bayan awardee, Nat. Consumers Coun., the Philippines, 1998, numerous others. Mem. Million Dollar Round Table (life), Nat. Assn. Ins. and Fin. Advisors, Calif. Assn. Ins. and Fin. Advisors, Arcadia C. of C., Asian Bus. Assn., Filipino-Am. C. of C., Greater Pasadena Assn. Ins. and Fin. Advisors, Chinese C. of C. (bd. dirs. L.A. 1992—). Avocations: Broadway musicals, ballet, fashion shows, concerts, ballroom dancing. Home and Office: 1006 Royal Oaks Dr Ste A Monrovia CA 91016-3737

LIM, SANG HO, materials engineer; b. Sangjoo, Korea, Dec. 22, 1959; s. Shin Chul and Yoon Shim (Kim) L.; m. Yeon Ok Cho; children: Jean Soo, Jean Sun. BS, Korea U., 1981; MS, Korea Advanced Inst. Sci., 1983; PhD, U. Newcastle, 1989. Rsch. scientist Korea Inst. Sci. & Technology, Seoul, 1983-86; nat. rsch. fellow Commonwealth Scientific Indsl. Rsch. Orgn., Syndey, Australia, 1990; from sr. rsch. scientist to prin. rsch. scientist Korea Inst. Sci. & Technology, 1990—. Mem. IEEE, Korean Magnetics Soc., Korea Inst. Metals & Materials. Achievements include accurate and fast calculation of phase diagrams and thermodynamic properties by Monte Carlo method; development of giant magnetostrictive materials with excellent field sensitivity at low magnetic fields and microdevices using the materials. Office: KIST Thin Film Tech Rsch Ct, 39-1 Hawolgok-dong, Sungbuk-gu Seoul Republic of Korea

LIM, SANG SEOK, electrical engineering educator, systems analyst; b. Young Joo, Republic of Korea, Mar. 15, 1955; s. Chang Hak and Woo Hoon (Lee) L.; m. Yeon Hee Lee, June 10, 1982. BS, Hankuk Aviation U., Seoul, Korea, 1976; M of Applied Sci., U. Ottawa, Can., 1984, PhD, 1990. Profl. electronics engr. Rschr. Agy. Defense Devel., Daejeon, Korea, 1976-82; lectr. U. Ottawa, 1989-90; rsch. assoc. Royal Mil. Coll., Kingston, Can., 1990-92; rsch. scientist Defence Rsch. Establishment Ottawa, 1992-95; assoc. prof. Hankuk Aviation U., 1995—; sr. sys. analyst Computing Concepts, Ottawa, 1992-95; project mgr. Inter-Techno Co., Kimpo, Korea, 1995-97; prin. investigator Korea Airport Authority, Seoul, 1996. Author: Avionics, 1997; contbr. articles to profl. jours. including Internat. Jour. Sys. Scis., Signal Processing, Dynamics and Control, Elec. Power Sys. Rsch. Jour. Mem. IEEE, Korean Inst. Comm. Scis., Korea Navigation Inst. (sec. 1996-98). Avocations: hiking, travel, camping, golf. Office: Hankuk Aviation U, 200-1 Whajun-dong, Koyang-si 412 791, Republic of Korea

LIM, WEI SHI, business educator, researcher; b. Singapore, Dec. 23, 1967; d. Ju Kim and Tan Wah Tay. BSc with honors, Nat. U. Singapore, 1990; postgrad. diploma in edn., Nanyang Tech. U., Singapore, 1991; PhD, London Sch. Econs., 1996. Asst. prof. Nat. U. Singapore, 1992—; cons. Singapore Pouls, 1999, Singapore Internat. Monetary Exch., 1997. Pub. Svc. Commn. scholar, 1986, Overseas Postgrad. scholar, 1993, Internat. scholar Soc. Instrument and Control Engring. of Japan, 1996. Office: Nat U Singapore Dept Bus, 15 Law Link, Singapore S11 7591, Republic of Singapore

LIM, YONG CHING, engineering educator, researcher; b. Tokai, Kedah, Malaysia, Apr. 6, 1953; arrived in Singapore, 1982; s. Wee Cheng Lim and Swee Foong Kim; m. Ah Geok Tan, Aug. 7, 1977; children: Chau Sian, Yu Xian. BSc, U. London, 1977, PhD, 1980. Rsch. assoc. Naval Postgrad. Sch., Monterey, Calif., 1980-82; lectr. Nat. U. Singapore, 1982-86, sr. lectr., 1986-93, assoc. prof., 1993-99, prof., 1999—. Contbr. articles to profl. jours. Fellow IEEE (Norman Hayes Meml. award 1990, Guillemin-Cauer award 1996). Office: Dept Elec Engring, Nat U Singapore, Singapore 119260, Singapore

LIMAN, ADRIAN MAC, political scientist; b. Bucharest, Romania, Aug. 12, 1944; s. Horia and Clara (Shwarz) L.; m. Pilar Rubio, Apr. 17, 1971 (div. Sept. 1982); children: Adriana Isabel, Sarah Daniela; m. Jacqueline Liman, May 12, 1984. Student, Jazykova Skola, Prague, 1964. Corr. El Pais, Washington, 1976; spokesman to the sec. gen. OAS, Western Europe, 1977; European Econ. corrs. La Vanguardia, Geneva, 1973-84; spl. corrs. El Independiente, Mid. East, 1987-90; internat. spokesman Barcelona Olympic Games, Barcelona, 1991-92; head of Arab world unit CIDOB Found., Barcelona, 1995-97; cons. to Spanish Cos. and NGOs in Jordan, West Bank, Gaza Strip, 1993—; sr. cons. to the EU Bus. Orgns., Middle East, 1993—; expert Coun. of Europe Mid. East Peace Process Task Force, Starbourg, 1996; trustee Inst. Ciencia y Soc. (INACS), Madrid, 1997-2000; lectr. in field. Author: (books) Cronicas palestinas, 1989, Las tramas secretas de la guerra del Golfo, 1990, Palestina, 1993, De la nacion de refugiados al Estado-nacion, 1995, Europa siglo XXI, 1997, Via Dolorosa, 1999; contbr. articles to profl. jours. Mem. Mid. East Studies Assn. of Am., Asn. Pro Europa Agustin Arguelles, Acad. of Polit. Sci. Avocations: lit., music, ancient civilizations, religious studies. Office: PO Box 14766, 28080 Madrid Spain

LIMAN, ELLEN, painter, writer, arts advocate; b. N.Y.C.; d. David and Gertrude (Edelman) Fogelson; m. Arthur Liman, Sept. 20, 1959 (dec.); children: Lewis, Emily, Doug. BA, Barnard Coll., 1957; student, N.Y. Sch. Interior Design, 1959. In pub. rels. Tex McCrary, Inc., 1957; interior designer Malanie Kahane Assocs., 1958-60; cons. on grants to the arts The Joe and Emily Lowe Found., 1975-92, pres./trustee, 1993—; exec. asst. Adv. Commn. for Cultural Affairs, N.Y.C., 1981-82; dir. spl. projects, dir. City Gallery for N.Y.C. Dept. Cultural Affairs, 1980-84; chair N.Y.C. Adv. Commn. for Cultural Affairs, 1991-93. Author: The Money Savers Guide to Decorating, 1972, Decorating Your Country Place, 1973, Decorating Your Room, 1974, The Spacemaker Book, 1977, The Collecting Book, 1980, Babyspace, 1984, others; contbr. editor: Kid Smart Mag., 1995-96; contbr. articles to nat. mags. Founding trustee Internat. Ctr. of Photography, 1973—; trustee The Jewish Mus., 1974—, hon. trustee, 1993—; trustee The Ctr. for Arts Info., 1985-86, Mus. Am. Indian, 1998—, Westchester Coun. on Arts, 1994—; mem. N.Y.C. Commn. for Cultural Affairs, 1986-89; bd. dirs. Art Table, Inc., 1987-90, Trust for Cultural Resources, 1993-96, Am. Fedn. of Arts, 1994—; adv. bd. mem. Nat. Acad. Design, 1998—.

LIMANOVA, NATALYA IGOREVNA, engineering educator, researcher; b. Samara, Russia, Feb. 1, 1963; d. Igor Alexeevich and Evelina Vasilievna (Fedotova) L.; m. Alexey Rudolfovich Shishkin, July 26, 1984; children: Pavel Alexeevich Shishkin, Ludmila Alexeevna Shishkina. Degree in engring., Samara State Aviation Inst., 1986; postgrad., Aerospace U., Samara, 1989-92. Engr. Aviation Inst., Samara, 1986-89; asst. prof. Pedagogical U., Togliatty, Russia, 1992—. Author: (poetry) Light and Shadows, 1994, 5 Minutes Before Birth, 1997; contbr. articles to profl. jours.; patentee in field. Mem. Internat. Soc. Optical Engring. Avocations: writing poetry, philosophy, literature, philology. Office: Pedagogical U, 13 Korolyova Blvd, 445859 Togliatty Russia

LIMANTOUR, PHILIPPE, computer science research executive, educator; b. Abidjan, Ivory Coast, Aug. 30, 1966; s. Jean-François and Anna (Morvan) L. Grad. computer sci. engr., Engr. Sch. in Computer Sci., Paris, 1990; higher studies degree in image art, Jussieu U., Paris, 1991; PhD, Orsay U., Paris, 1994; mgmt. degree, Conservatoire Nat. Arts Metier, Paris, 1998. Cert. in real time 3D computer graphics and multimedia engring. R & D engr. Videosystem, Paris, 1991-93; R & D project dir. Medialab, Paris, 1993-96; R & D rendering engr. Alias Wavefront/SGI, Paris, 1997-98; mng. dir., tech. dir. Sim Team, Paris, 1998-99; v.p. mktg. and devel. Cril Telecom, Paris, 1999-2000; mng. dir. Quantic Dream, Paris, 2000—; instr. computer graphics Ecole Superieure d'Info. Elec. Automatique, 1990—; lectr. virtual reality and multimedia Ecole Superieure d'Info. Elec., Paris, 1994—; multimedia expert EEC, Brussels, 1997—. Mem. IEEE, Assn. for Computing Machinery, N.Y. Acad. Scis., AIR-ESIEA Assn. (founder, chmn. 1986-90). Avocations: rugby, sailing, scuba diving, travel. Office: Quantic Dream, 11 Rue Sainte Felicite, 75015 Paris France

LIMÃO VIEIRA, PAULO MANUEL ASSIS LOUREIRO, physicist, researcher; b. Guarda, Portugal, Dec. 1, 1970; s. Alberto Limão Vieira Fonseca Oliveira and Maria Alice Araújo Assis Loureiro Limão Vieira. Degree, U. Nova de Lisboa, Lisbon, Portugal, 1994; MSc, U. Nova de Lisboa, 1999; postgrad., Univ. Coll. London. Rsch. fellow Ctr. Molecular Physics, Lisbon, 1993-94, rschr., 1993—; univ. asst. U. Nova de Lisboa, 1995—, supervisor grad. students, 1995—; rschr. Cefitec, Lisbon, 1995—. Mem. Portuguese Phys. Soc., European Phys. Soc., Portuguese Assn. Phys. Engrs. (v.p.). Roman Catholic. Avocations: reading, swimming, travel. Office: Ctr Molecular Physics, IST-Ave Rovisco Pais, 1049-001 Lisbon Portugal

LIMB, BEN QUINCY, lawyer; b. Taejon, Korea, Nov. 28, 1936; came to U.S., 1964; s. Tong-shik and San-jong (Lee) L.; m. Mary Shinkawa, Feb. 4, 1968; children: Amy, Lisa. BA, Korea U., 1961; MA, Seton Hall U., 1969; JD, N.Y. Law Sch., 1984; PhD, St. John's U., 1979. Bar: N.Y. 1985, U.S. Ct. Appeals (fed. cir.) 1988, U.S. Ct. Internat. Trade 1988, U.S. Supreme Ct. 1991. Pvt. practice N.Y.C., 1985-93; counsel Abraham & Silver, N.Y.C., 1994-96; sr. advisor Bae, Kim & Lee, Seoul, Korea, 1998—; speaker nation-

ality law and human rights The Law of the World Conf., 1987; anniversary lectr. Han Nam U., Taejon, Republic of Korea, 1991; spkr. in field. Pres. Korean Inst. for Human Rights, Washington, 1989-91; chair Asian Pacific Am. Com. for Dem. Nat. Conv., 1992. Recipient Appreciation award Assn. of Korean Christian Scholars in North Am., L.A., 1988, Outstanding Pro Bono award N.Y. County Lawyers Assn., 1997, Lifetime Achievement award N.Y. Law Sch. Asian Am. Alumni Assn., 1998. Mem. ABA, Fed. Bar Assn., N.Y. State Bar Assn. (bd. dirs. 1997—), N.Y. County Lawyers Assn. (bd. dirs. 1997-99), Korean-Am. Lawyers Assn. of N.Y. (pres. 1989-91), N.Y. Law Sch. Alumni Assn. (bd. dirs. 1987—), Am. Immigration Lawyers Assn. (co-chmn. N.Y. chpt. ethics 1988-89), Korea Bar assn. (lectr. annual seminar, Seoul 1988), Asian Am. Bar Assn. of N.Y. (bd. dirs. 1994—, pres. 1996-97), Internat. Assn. Korean Lawyers (sr. v.p. 1989-90, 94-95, special leadership award 1998). Fax: 82-2-3404-0006. E-mail: benlimb@hotmail.com. Office: Bae Kim & Lee, 647-15 Yeoksam-dong, Kangnam-gu Seoul 135-723, Korea

LIMB, HAN HUI, small business owner; b. Hong Kong, Oct. 24, 1937; s. Peng Kwi and Pak Kiang (Chan) L.; m. Yuk-yan Kwok, Apr. 7, 1962; 1 child, Rebecca Yee Lee. B of Commerce, United Coll. of Hong Kong, 1960. Owner, mgr. Handart Embroideries, Hong Kong, 1960—. Hon. treas. Inc. Owners of Good View Ct., Hong Kong, 1986—. Recipient scholarship Mencius Ednl. Found., Hong Kong, 1956. Mem. Christian Ch. Avocations: reading, classical music. Home: A7 Good View Ct, 21 Robinson Rd, Hong Kong Hong Kong Office: Handart Embroideries, Handart Embroideries, 27 Cameron Rd/Tsim Sha Tsui, Kowloon Hong Kong

LIMBACH, JUTTA, judge; b. Berlin, Neukölln, Mar. 27, 1934; married: 3 children. With SPD, 1962, mem. commn. for domestic and legal policy, party exec., 1987—; prof. FU Berlin, 1971; prof. legal sociology U. Heidelberg, 1974; judge, chmn. of second senate Fed. Constl. Ct., Germany, 1994, pres., 1994—. Contbr. articles to profl. jours. Office: Bundesverfassungsgericht, Schlossbezirk 3, D-76131 Karlsruhe Germany*

LIMBRUNO, UGO, cardiologist; b. Rome, Jan. 5, 1961; s. Alfonso and Adriana (Delfico) L.; m. Cristina Fioretti; 1 child, Luca. MD, U. Rome, 1985; PhD, Scuola Superiore, Pisa, Italy, 1989. Resident cardiology U. Pisa, 1988, interventional cardiologist, 1992—. Contbr. articles to profl. jours. Vol. ARC, Rome, 1983. Fellow Italian Soc. Cardiology. Avocation: sailing. Office: Cisanello Hosp, Cardiac and Thoracic Dept, 56124 Pisa Italy

LIMET, RAYMOND ROBERT, cardiovascular surgeon; b. Flemalle-Haute, Belgium, Mar. 9, 1943; s. Valere and Josette (Steyls) L. MD, U. Liege, 1968, PhD, 1979. Rsch. assoc. Baylor, Houston, 1969-70, 73-74; resident IV ICM, Montreal, Can., 1974-75; charge de cours U. Liege, Belgium, 1979-86, prof., 1986—; pres. Dept. Surgery, Chu, Liege, 1986—. Mem. Belgian Soc. of Surgery, Academie Royale Medicine Belgium. Office: Chu Sart Tilman, 4000 Liege Belgium

LIMHAISEN, MOHAMMED ABDULRAHAM, banker; b. Al Sulfi, Saudi Arabia, Dec. 29, 1949; s. Abdulrahman Abdul Mohsin; m. Modhi Nasir Abdulaziz Al Nowaiser, June 14, 1978; children: Sarah Mohammed, Abdulrahman Mohammed, Majed Mohammad, Mounirah Mohammad, Hossah Mohammad. BS, Wash. State U., 1973, BS in Chemistry, 1974; MBA, N.W. Mo. State U., 1975. Credit officer Chase Manhattan Bank, 1976-77; loan officer, project mgr. Saudi Indsl. Devel. Fund, Saudi Arabia, 1977-78, controller gen., 1980; asst. gen mgr. United Saudi Comml. Bank, Riyadh, Saudi Arabia, 1983-86, corp. sec., 1983—; gen. mgr. Saudi Investment Bank, Riyadh, Saudi Arabia, 1988-89; mng. dir. Nat. Co. for Mfg. Food Stuff and Mktg. Ltd., Riyadh, 1989—; chmn. bd. dirs. Riyadh Internat. Med. Co.; bd. dirs. Saudi So. Dairy Co., Riyadh, Saudi Shares Registration Co., Riyadh., Nat. Co. Mfg. Food Stuff, Riyadh. Mem. Am. Mgmt. Assn., Arab Bankers Assn., Minninger Found. Club: Equestrian (Riyadh). Avocations: jogging, squashing, swimming, camping, reading. Home: PO Box 56013, Riyadh 11554, Saudi Arabia Office: PO Box 3533, Riyadh 11481, Saudi Arabia

LIMING, PENG, medical educator; b. Chengou, Sichuan, China, May 29, 1959; s. Peng Huhal and Shao Wenshu; m. Wang Jing, May 1, 1985; 1 child, Xin. BS, Chongqing Med. U., 1986, MD, 1991. Technician 1st Hosp., Neijiang, People's Republic China, 1986-88; tchr. 1st Hosp., Chengdu, People's Republic China, 1991-94, 95-96, assoc. prof., 1998—; rsch. scientist Flinders Med. Ctr., Adelaide, Australia, 1998—; dir. Chinese Clin. Medicine, Sichuan, People's Republic China, 1998—, STT, Beijing, 1999—. Editor: The Fundamental and Clinical of Apoptosis, 1998, Automation and Its Application, 1999; contbr. articles to profl. jours. Mem. Internat. Soc. Thrombosis, Chinese Clin. Lab., Chinese Clin. Medicine. Avocations: soccer, music, writing. Office: Dept Lab Med, 1st Univ Hosp WCUMS, Chengdu Sichuan 610041, Peoples Republic China

LI-MIN JIA, electrical engineering educator, control engineer; b. Altai, Xinjiang, China, Jan. 18, 1963; s. Hou-Nio and Xin-Er (Lie) J.; m. Xiao-Xia Song; 1 child, Rei-Yian Jia. BEE with honors, Shanghai Tiedao U., 1984; MEE, China Acad. Railway Scis., Beijing, 1987, PhD in Elec. Engring., 1991; diploma in French, Beijing U. Fgn. Langs., 1988; diploma in English with honors, Applied Scholastics Internat., U.S., 1990. Diplomate French, English, Internat. Bus. Rsch. asst. China Acad. Railway Scis., Beijing, 1984-87, rsch. engr., 1987-92, assoc. rsch. prof., 1992-94, resident prof., 1994—, dir. rsch. ctr. of intelligent tech., 1996—; vice chief engr. Beijing Capital Sci. and Tech. Group Co. Ltd., 1995—; pres., gen. mgr. Beijing Shouke Software and Sys. Integration Co., Ltd., 1996—; exec. chmn. Young Scientist Forum of China, 1996—; vis. prof. U. NSW, Australia, 1993, SUNY Buffalo, 1994, Found. Rsch. and Devel., South Africa, 1994, Rand Afrikaans U., 1994, Stellenboch U., South Africa, 1994; adj. prof. Polytech U. Ctrl.-So. China, Changsha, 1995—, Xi'an Jiaotong U., China, 1995—, Shanghai U., 1995—, Beijing Polytech U., 1995—, Northern Jiaotong U., 1999—; mem. rsch. team applicaton of rlwy. automation technologies to underground rail transp. syss. Mettall. Ministry China, 1983-86, mem. study on parameters of rlwy. track circuits, 1985-87; project dir. universal approach to the knowledge representation in intelligent control-fuzzy timed petri net based approach Nat. Scis. Found. China, 1990-91, fuzzy cell mapping based approach to the modelling and control of complex dynamical syss., 1992-94, intelligent control of high speed trains Nat. Scis. Found. and Rlwy. Ministry of China, 1993-95, intelligent traffic control software for CTC ctr. of high speed rlwys. Rlwy. Ministry of China, 1996-97, theory and implementation of multivariable fuzzy controller Rlwy Scis. Found. China, 1993-95; project. co-dir. intelligent rlwy. traffic control of high speed trains Nat. Scis. Found. China and Rlwy. Ministry China, 1993-95, fuzzy logic control integrated in the inops DCS syss. Beijing Municipality, 1995-96, study on safety syss. structure of high-speed rlwy. Rlwy. Ministry China, 1996-97; sub-project dir. on-board syss. and associated key equip. rsch. Nat. Planning Com. China, 1996-97; nat. expert State Coun., China, 1999. Contbr. articles to profl. jours., conf. papers; spkr. in field. Recipient excellent paper award China Assn. Scis. and Tech., 1995, Beijing Assn. Scis. and Tech., 1995, Beijing Outstanding Young Scientist award Beijing Assn. Scis. and Tech. and Beijing Mcpl. Govt., 1995, 99, excellent contrbn. award Rwy. Ministry China, 1996, Outstanding Young Scientist award Rwy. Ministry of China, 1996, one of Top 100 Young Experts in China, Pers. Ministry Sci. and Tech. Commn. of China, 1997. Mem. Internat. Fedn. Automatic Control, China Assn. Automation (excellent paper award 1995), China Rlwy. Soc. (Excellent paper award 1987, 95, 96, 98). Achievements include establishment of fuzzy multiobjective optimal control theory, fuzzy cell mapping based theory for dealing with complex syss. and methodology of distributed traffic control through fuzzy decision making, leadership in the rsch. and devel. of intelligent techniques for rlwys. automation, initiator of rlwy. intelligent automation rsch. field. Office: China Acad Rlwy Scis, 2 Daliushulu Haidian Dist, Beijing 100081, China

LIMONERO, JOAQUIM TIMOTEO, psychologist, educator; b. Sabadell, Barcelona, Spain, Sept. 23, 1964; s. Salvador Limonero and Isabel Garcia; m. Maria José Gómez, Oct. 25, 1996. MA, U. Autonoma Barcelona, 1990, PhD, 1994. Rsch. fellow psychology U. Autonoma Barcelona, 1991-93, asst. prof. psychology, 1993-97, assoc. prof., 1997—. Contbr. articles to profl. jours. Mem. Spanish Soc. for Study of Anxiety and Stress, Catalano-Balear Soc. of Palliative Care. Avocations: travel, walking. E-mail: Joaquin.Limonero@uab.es. Office: U Autonoma Barcelona, Faculty of Psychology, 08193 Bellaterra Barcelona Spain

LIMÓN ROJAS, MIGUEL, Mexican government official; b. Veracruz, Mex., Dec. 17, 1943. BA in Law, Nat. Autonomous U., 1967. Lawyer, 1968—; dep. dir. demographics, population Ministry of Govt. of Mex., 1971, dir. demographics, population, 1973; pvt. sec. to undersec. to pres., prof. constl. law Govt. Mex., 1970, advisor to sec. edn., negotiator nat. ednl. plan, 1982-88, undersec. population and migration, 1988-93, sec. agrarian reform, 1993-94, sec. pub. edn., 1995—; dir. Inst. Indigenous Peoples, 1983-88; dir. dept. humanities, Autonomous U.; acad. sec. U. Pedagógica Nat. Mem. Instl. Revolutionary Party. Office: Office of the Secretariat 2nd Fl Sec Pub Edn, Obrego Num 28Av Rep Argentina y Gonzalez, Mexico City 06029, Mexico*

LIMPAKARNJARAT, KHANCHIT, epidemiologist; b. Muang, Thailand, Mar. 19, 1954; s. Mongkang Lim and Samorn (Nettakul) Limpakarnjanarat; m. Pimporn Chamnannark, Oct. 25, 1979; children: Sivapong, Chris. BSc, Chulalongkorn U., Bangkok, 1974, MD, 1976; MPH, Emory U., 1985. Cert. in epidemiology Ministry Pub. Health, Thailand, in epidemic intelligence svc. Ctrs. for Disease Control and Prevention. Physician Phan Dist. Hosp., Chiang Rai, Thailand, 1977-79; acting chief FETP Diven. Epidemiology, Ministry Pub. Health, Bangkok, 1985-90; chief epidemiol. manpower Dept. Epidemiology, Ministry Pub. Health, Bangkok, 1987-89; acting chief viral and rickettsial disease br. Divsn. Gen. Communicatble Disease, Ministry Pub. Health, Bangkok, 1985-87; chief evaluation br. Dept. Epidemiology, Ministry Pub. Health, Bangkok, 1989-90; adj. dir. HIV/AIDS Collaboration, Nonthaburi, Thailand, 1990—; cons. WHO, Vientaine, 1986-89; mem. collaborating ctr. for tng. and rsch. on HIV/AIDS, Nonthaburi, Thailand, 1998-99; mem. Com. on Improvement of Epidemiology for Disease Control, Nonthaburi, 1998. Mem. editl. bd. Thai AIDS Jour., 1997—. Mem. Med. Virology Assn. Thailand (mem. exec. com. 1999—), Thailand Med. Rsch. Coun., Thailand Med. Assn., Preventive Medicine Assn. Thailand. Home: 60/540 Pracha-Ruamjai Rd, Sai Gong Din Tai, Klong Samwa Bangkok, Thailand Office: HIV/AIDS Collaboration, Min Pub Health DMS 6 Bldg, Nonthaburi 11000, Thailand

LIMPAPHAYOM, PIMAN, business educator; b. Bangkok, Thailand, Apr. 4, 1966; s. Manas and Pimpa Limpaphayom; m. Julanita Chaiprapal, Aug. 21, 1998. BEd, Chulalongkorn U., Bangkok, 1986; MBA, U. So. Miss., 1987; PhD, U. R.I., 1998. Asst. prof. Shippensburg (Pa.) U., 1992-93; instr. U. R.I., kingston, 1994-96; vis. asst. prof. U. New Haven, West Haven, Conn., 1997-98; dean of bus. Asian U. Sci. and Tech., Chonburi, Thailand, 1998—; mgmt. cons. Rasa Devel. Corp., Bangkok; cons. Asian Devel. Bank, Manila, 1998-99. Contbr. articles to profl. jours. Recipient CBA Instrnl. Excellence award U. R.I., 1995, Sportsmanship award South County Tennis Assn., 1997. Mem. Royal Bangkok Sports Club. Avocations: tennis, golf. Office: Asian U Sci and Tech, 89 Hwy 331, Chonburi Thailand 20260

LIMPER, ANDREAS ALBERT, engineering educator; b. Altenhundem, Germany, Apr. 4, 1956; s. Alfons Peter and Maria (Schlueter) L.: m. Brigitte Josefine Schwellenbach, Sept. 9, 1980; children: Max, Alex, Felix. Diploma engring., Rheinisch Westfalische Tech Ho, Aachen, Germany, 1981, PhD, 1982; PhD, Rheinisch Westfalische Tech Ho, Aachen, Germany, 1992. Rschr. Inst fur Kumststoff Verarbeitung, Aachen, 1981-85, head ext. dept., 1985-87; head R&D Battenfeld Ext. Tech., B. Oeynhausen, Germany, 1987-89; gen. mgr. tech. Werner & Pfleiderer, Freudenberg, Germany, 1989-95; prof. U. Paderborn, Germany, 1995—; mem. sci. com. Kautschuk Gummi, 1998—; mem. sci. bd. Deutsches Inst. fur Kautschuktechnik, 1999. Editor, author: Kautschukverarbeitung, 1989; contbr. articles to profl. jours. Mem. VDI-Beirat Elastomertechnik, Deutsche Kautschuk Gesellschaft (E. Konrad medal 1997). Achievements include 25 patents for different machines for plastics/rubber processing. Avocations: reading, playing guitar, sports. Home: Malerwinkel 4, 57258 Freudenberg Germany Office: U Paderborn, Pohlweg 47, 33098 Paderborn Germany

LIMPERT, JOHN H., JR., fund raising executive; b. Bklyn., May 14, 1933; s. John H. and Sophia (Douropoulos) L.; A.B., Harvard U., 1955, postgrad., 1955-56; children: Alexandra Michelle, John Harold III. Public relations mgr. Frankfort Distillers Co. div. Seagram, N.Y.C., 1959-63; account exec. McCann-Erickson, Inc., N.Y.C., 1963-65, account dir., 1965-68; v.p. Ted Bates & Co., Inc., N.Y.C., 1968-71; mgr. lectrs. and speakers Keedick Lecture Bur., Inc., N.Y.C., 1971-73; dir. membership and devel. Mus. Modern Art, N.Y.C., 1973-83, dir. devel., 1983-86; v.p. for devel. and mktg. The N.Y. Bot. Garden, 1986-88; v.p. devel. Lincoln Ctr. for the Performing Arts Inc., 1988-89; assoc. fund counsel Charles H. Bentz Assocs., Inc., N.Y.C., 1990—; —; trustee Children's Aid Soc., 1966-74, Festival Orch. and Chorus, 1967-69, Schola Cantorum, 1963-65; bd. dirs. Assoc. Harvard Alumni, 1967-69, 73-74; bd. dirs. Bronx C. of C., 1988-91; vestryman Grace Episcopal Ch., Plainfield, 1992-95; bd. dirs. NY chpt., Nat. Soc. Fund Raising Execs., 1989-93. With U.S. Army, 1956-58. Cert. fund raising exec. Office: 1111 Park Ave Plainfield NJ 07060-3006

LIN, CHENG-SHING, entomology curator, researcher; b. Hsinchu, Taiwan, May 11, 1943; s. Yeh-Mao and Wu-Mei Lin; m. Mei-Huei Kung, June 4, 1973; children: Shih-Fan, Ya-Fan. BS, Chung-Hsing U., Taichung, Taiwan, 1967; MS, N.D. State U., 1973; PhD, U. Hawaii, 1979. Curator Taiwan Mus., Taipei, 1980-84; assoc. prof. Hung-Hsing U., Taichung, Taiwan, 1981-91; assoc. prof. Tunghai (Taiwan) U., 1984-90, prof., 1991—; curator Nat. Mus. Natural Sci., Taichung, 1984—; dir. dept. zoology Taiwan Mus., 1980-84; dir. divsn. collection and rsch. Nat. Mus. Natural Sci., 1986-89, 94-96. Author: Plants Resistant to Insects, 1987; chief editor Jour. Taiwan Mus., 1982-84. Mem. edn. com. YMCA, Taichung, 1984-86; vice chmn. entomology com. Chinese Animal Protection Soc., Taipei, 1984; elder Lishing Presbyn. Ch., Taichung, 1995-97. 2d lt. Chinese Air Forces, 1967-68. Recipient Excellent Svc. award Ministry of Edn., Taichung, 1992. Mem. Lepidopterist's Soc. (v.p. 1994), Entomol. Soc. Japan, Japan Heterocerists' Soc., Chinese Entomol. Soc. (sec. gen. 1999-2000). Avocations: table tennis, Bible study, stamp collecting, gardening. Home: 366-6 Du-Hsing Rd, Taichung 400, Taiwan Office: Nat Mus Natural Sci, 1 KuanChien Rd, Taichung 400, Taiwan

LIN, CHERN SHENG, optics science educator, researcher; b. Feng Sheng, Taiwan; s. I Feng Lin and Der Cheng Chen; m. May Ya Lee, Dec. 24, 1988; children: Lin, Chi Chin. M Mechanics, Taiwan U., Taipei, 1988; PhD in Optical Sci., Ctrl. U., Chung Li, Taiwan, 1994. Engr. Lien Ho Shipbldg. Co., Kau Shiung, Taiwan, 1984, China Shipbldg. Co., Kau Shiung, Taiwan, 1985; instr. Chung Chiu Inst., Yang Lin, Taiwan, 1988-89; instr. China Inst. Tech., Taipei, 1989-94, assoc. prof., 1994-95; assoc. prof. dept. automatic control engring. Feng Chia U., Tai Chung, Taiwan, 1995-2000, prof., 2000—; rschr. CTS Co., Kau Shiung, 1984; computer cons. Author: Precision Measurement 1990 (excellent author award 1990), Optoelectronic Technology, 1990, Photonics in Measurement, 1993, Application of Precision Measurement, 1994, Application of Dsp, 1996, Digital Image and Speech Processing, 1997, Introduction to Photonics, 1999. 2d lt. Taiwan Army, 1982-84. Recipient B prize Nat. Sci. Coun. Taiwan, 1994, A prize, 1997, 98 (dragon award), 99, Excellent price TIC Sci. and Tech. Contest, 2000. Avocations: swimming, chess, table tennis. Office: Tjing Ling Indsl Rsch, 130 Keelung Rd Sec 3, Taipei 32054, Taiwan

LIN, CHIEN-CHIH, hospital administrator, thoracic surgeon; b. Hualien, Taiwan, Dec. 28, 1954; s. Hsing and Ying (Chen) L.; m. Suh-Fang Cheng; children: Bor-Shiuan, Bor-Ting, Yen-Ling, Wen. MD, Kaohsiung Med. Coll., 1970. Resident Kaohsiung Med. Coll., 1983-87, chief resident, 1987-88; vis. staff Kaohsiung Med. Coll. Hosp., 1988-89; vis. staff dept. surgery Tainan Mcpl. Hosp., 1989-90, chief dept. surgery, 1990-96, dep. dir. med. affairs, 1996—. Contbr. articles to profl. jours. European Jour. Surgery, Surg. Laparoscopy & Endoscopy. 2d lt. Taiwanese Army, 1981-83. Mem. Surg. Assn. Rep. of China, Thoracic and Cardiovasc. Assn., Chinese Assn. Soc. of Laparoendoscopic Surgs., Endoscopy Surgery, Surg. Soc. Gastroenterology. Avocations: reading, swimming, jogging, climbing, traveling. Home: 11 Zanell, Wen-Hwa 10 St, 711 Gui-Jen Hsing Tainan, Taiwan Office: Tainan Mcpl Hosp, 670 Chung Te Rd, 701 Tainan Taiwan

LIN, CHIH-MIN, electrical engineer, educator; b. Chang-Hua, Taiwan, Mar. 2, 1959; s. Chaur-Ching and Suh-Chih (Wu) L.; m. Hsiu-Hui Wang, Apr. 18, 1986; children: Lo-Yi, Yu-Chen. Bachelors Degree, Chiao-Tung U., Hsin-Chu, Taiwan, 1981, Masters Degree, 1983, PhD of Electronic Engring., 1986. Deputy sect. head Chung-Shan Inst. Sci. and Tech., Tao-Yuan, Taiwan, 1986-92; assoc. prof. Chiao-Tung U., Hsin-Chu, 1987-89, Chung-Yuan U., Tao-Yuan, 1990-92; assoc. prof. Yuan-Ze U., Tao-Yuan, 1993-96, prof., 1997—. Contbr. articles to profl. jours. Recipient Invention award Ministry of Edn., Taiwan, 1986, Nat. medal Ministry of Nat. Def., Taiwan, 1990, Rsch. award Nat. Sci. Coun., Taiwan, 1994, 96, 97, 98. Mem. IEEE Control Sys. Soc. (sr. mem., dep. chmn. Taipei sect. 1999), Automatic Control Soc. (coun. mem. 1994). Avocations: music, travel. Office: Yuan-Ze U Elec Engr, 135 Far-East Rd, Chung-Li Tao-Yuan 32026, Taiwan

LIN, CHII RUEY, engineering educator; b. Taipei, Taiwan, May 6, 1955; s. Rong Tian and Bao Chai (Chen) L.; m. Ming Yue Chen, Mar. 23, 1980; children: Jun Yong, Wei Ting, Jun Quan. Diplomate, Nat. Taipei U. Tech., 1975; BS, Nat. Taiwan U. Sci. and Tech., 1982, MS, 1987; PhD, Nat. Chiao Tung U., 1998. Tchg. asst. Nat. Taipei U. Tech., 1979-87, lectr., 1987-92, assoc. prof. dept. mech. engring., 1992-99, prof., 2000—, dir. Affiliated Inst. Continuing Edn., 1999—; commr. Min. Econ. Affairs, Taipei, 1997, Vocat. Tng. Bur., Taipei, 1998, Nat. Std. Tech. Com., Taipei, 1999; cons. in spl. projects Wah Lee Indsl. Corp., Taipei, 1997. Contbr. articles to profl. jours. 2d lt. Chinese Marine Corps, 1975-77. Recipient Nat. Svc. Medal grade II, Exec. Yuen, 1989, 99; Nat. Sci. Coun. grantee, 1991, 92. Mem. AAAS, Chinese Soc. Mech. Engring., Chinese Soc. Materials, Chinese Foundrymen's Assn., Taiwan Assn. Thin Film Coatings Tech. Avocations: climbing, hiking, swimming, music, writing. E-mail: erlin@ntut.edu.edu. Home: 2d flr #9 Lan 197 Sec 1, Chung-Yang N Rd, Taipei Peitou 102, Taiwan Office: Nat Taipei Univ of Tech, #1 Sec 3 Chung-Hsiao E Rd, Taipei 106, Taiwan

LIN, CHII-JENG MARK, physician, researcher; b. Chia-Yi, Taiwan, Republic of China, Oct. 16, 1957; s. Chong-Mou and Yu-Jen (Chen) L.; m. Nai-Wen Austin Kuo, July 19, 1984; 1 child, Cheng-Wei. MD, Nat. Taiwan U., Taipei, 1982; PhD, Nat. Cheng Kung U., Tainan, Taiwan, 1998. Resident Nat. Taiwan U. Hosp., Taipei, 1984-89; attending staff Nat. Cheng Kung U., Tainan, 1989-90, lectr., 1990-96, assoc. prof., 1996—; cons. CBL, Taipei, 1991—. Inventor in field. Lt. Taiwan Army, 1982-84. Recipient Outstanding Youth award Tainan Youth Assn., 1997, Best Tchr. award Nat. Cheng Kung U. Med. Sch. Student Assn., 1996-99. Mem. Orthopedic Rsch. Soc., Pediat. Orthop. Soc. N.Am., Pediat. Orthop. Soc. Avocations: fiddler, golf, swimming, choir, badminton. Office: Orthopedics NCKUMC, 138 Sheng-Li Rd, Tainan Taiwan 704, Republic of China

LIN, CHIN-TENG, engineering educator; b. Tainan, Taiwan, Dec. 22, 1963; s. Ming-Te and Yu-Lu (Kuo) L. BS, Nat. Chiao-Tung U., 1986; MS, Purdue U., 1989, PhD, 1992. Rsch. asst. Purdue Intelligent Automation Lab., West Lafayette, Ind., 1989-91; postdoctoral rsch. assoc. in elec. engring. Purdue U., West Lafayette, 1992; assoc. prof. dept. computer and info. sci. Nat. Chiao-Tung U., Hsinchu, Taiwan, 1992-93, assoc. prof. dept. control engring., 1993-97, prof. dept. elec. and control engring., 1997—; dep. dean R&D office Nat. Chiao-Tung U., Hsinchu; cons. Indsl. Tech. Rsch. Inst., Hsinchu, 1993—, Chung-Shan Inst. Sci. and Tech., Lung-Tan, Taiwan, 1993—, Best Sys. Co., Ltd., Taichung, Taiwan, 1998—. Author: Neural Fuzzy Control Systems with Structure and Parameter Learning, 1994, Neural Fuzzy Systems: A Neuro-Fuzzy Synergism to Intelligent Systems, 1996. Recipient Grand Excellent award DSP Design Challenge, 1996, 97, Outstanding Rsch. award Nat. Sci. Coun. Taiwan, 1997, 99, Outstanding Elec. Engring. Prof. award Chinese Inst. Elec. Engring., 1997; grantee Nat. Sci. Coun. Taiwan, 1998. Mem. IEEE (sr., v.p. robotics and automation Taipei chpt., Most Notable Paper award 1992), Chinese Fuzzy Systems Assn. (exec. coun. 1993—), Tau Beta Pi, Eta Kappa Nu. Avocations: badminton, tennis, music. Home: F7 No 64 Ln 476, Kung-Fu Rd Sec 1, Hsinchu Taiwan Office: Nat Chiao-Tung U Dept Control Engring, 1001 Ta-Hsueh Rd, Hsinchu Taiwan

LIN, CHOUNG-MIN, dentist, educator; b. Chia-Yi, Taiwan, Apr. 27, 1948; s. Chin-Sheng and Pien-Pien (Cheng) L.; m. Sophia Su-Fen Hwang, Sept. 20, 1981; 1 child, Leanne. DMD, Taipei (Taiwan) Med. Coll., 1972; PhD, Tokyo Dental Coll., 1979. Cert. dentist. Instr. Tokyo Dental Coll., 1979-82; pvt. practice Dr. Lin & Partners Dental Office, Taipei, 1980—, also bd. dirs.; assoc. prof. Taipei Med. Coll., 1980-1992, Yang-Ming Med. Coll., Taipei, 1986-1992. Lt., R.O.C. airforce, 1972-1973. Recipient Appreciation award U. So. Calif., 1986, Peter K. Thomas award, 1986. Master Gnathology Internat. Acad. Gnathology (Asian sect. 1986); fellow Internat. Coll. Dentists, Pierre Fauchard Acad; mem. Assn. Gnathology R.O.C.(founder, pres. 1984-1988), Chinese Acad. Aesthetic Dentistry (founder, pres. 1994-1996), Internat. Acad. Gnathology (v.p. 1986-1994 Asian sect.), Asian Acad. Aesthetic Dentistry (pres. 1994-1996), Am. Assn. of Orthodontists, Internat. Coll. of Prosthodontists, Acad. of Osseointegration. Avocations: meditation practice, jogging, music. Office: Dr Lin and Ptnrs Dental Office, 5F 60 Tien-Mu West Rd, 111 Taipei Taiwan

LIN, CHUN, chemistry researcher; b. Fuzhou, Fujian, People's Republic of China, Dec. 3, 1969; came to U.S., 1993; BS, U. Sci. Tech. of China, Hefei, 1992; PhD, Fla. Inst. Tech., 1997. Rsch. assoc. dept. chemistry Tex. A&M U., College Station, 1997—. Mem. AAAS, Am. Chem. Soc. (outstanding grad. student Orlando sect. 1995). Achievements include pioneering the study of metal-metal bonded supramolecular chemistry, 1997—, initiating the study of linear free energy relationship in dinuclear compounds, 1993-97. Avocations: classical music, photography, movies, internet, cooking. E-mail: chunlin@lmsb.tamu.edu. Office: Tex A&M U Dept Chemistry PO Box 30012 College Station TX 77842-3012

LIN, FAA-JENG, electrical engineer, educator, consultant; b. Tai-Chung, Taiwan, Aug. 31, 1961; s. Jenn-Shyan and Yuh-Chen (Kuo) L.; m. Huey-Ju Jane, Jan. 21, 1962; two children. BS, Nat. Cheng-Kung U., Tainan, Taiwan, 1983, MS, 1985; PhD, Nat. Tsing-Hua U., Hsinchu, Taiwan, 1993. Asst. rschr. Chung-shan Inst. Sci. and Tech., Taiwan, 1985-89; instr. Lien-Ho Inst. Tech., Taiwan, 1989-90; assoc. prof. Chung-Yuan Christian U., Taiwan, 1993-98, prof., 1998—; cons. Indsl. Tech. Rsch. Inst., Hsinchu, 1996—. Contbr. articles to profl. jours. including IEEE. Capt. Taiwan Army, 1985-89. Grantee Nat. Sci. Coun., 1994-99. Mem. IEEE (sr.). Home: No 21 Alley 1 Ln 42, Bair-Nian 2nd St 325, Lung-Tan Tao-Yan, Taiwan Office: Chung Yuan Christian U, Dept Elec Engring, 32023 Chung-Li Tao-Yuan, Taiwan

LIN, FRANK CHIWEN, computer science educator; b. Shanghai, China, Aug. 28, 1936; came to U.S., 1953; s. Elmer C. and Virginia (Chang) Ling; m. Margareta Lundgren, Mar. 8, 1968 (div. Aug. 1979); children: Ulrika Lin, Sigrid Lin; m. Helen M. Baldado, Mar. 17, 1987. BECE, Yale U., 1957; postgrad., U. Goettingen, Germany, 1958; PhD in Theoretical Physics, Yale U., 1965; postgrad., Polytech. U. N.Y., 1980-82. Rsch. assoc. dept. theoretical physics Chalmers Tech. U., Goeteborg, Sweden, 1965-70; asst. to pres. Biomed. Scis. Inc., Fairfield, N.J., 1971-75; instr. physics, engring., and computer sci. L.B. Wallace State Jr. Coll., Andalusia, Ala., 1976-84; assoc. prof. computer sci. Western Conn. State U., Danbury, 1984-85; prof. computer sci. U. Md., Princess Anne, Md., 1986—; vis. prof. physics Nat. Taiwan U., Taipei, 1970. Author: Elementary FORTRAN with Scientific and Business Applications, 1983, Structured BASIC for Mini- and Micro-Computers, 1985; (play) First Degree Murder, 1997; contbr. articles to profl. jours. Prin. investigator numerous grants, 1981-93. Mem. IEEE (treas./sec. local chpt. 1989-90, vice-chmn. local chpt. 1990-91), Assn. Computing Machinery, Yale Sci. and Engring. Assn., N.Y. Acad. Scis., Am. Assn. for Artificial Intelligence, Internat. Neural Network Soc., Am. Med. Informatics Assn., Tau Beta Pi. Avocation: classical music. Address: Inst Computacao, Rue Passo da Patria 156 Bloc E, 24210-240 Niteroi Rio de Janeiro Brazil

LIN, FUNG J., physician; b. Lo-Tung, Taiwan, July 12, 1954; s. Hong T. and Hsiau M. (Chen) L.; m. Mei L. Chang, June 20, 1980; 1 child, Chiy Y. MB, Kaohsiung Med. Coll., Taiwan, 1979; MPH, Johns Hopkins U., 1983. Resident Cathay Gen. Hosp., Taipei, Taiwan, 1981-82; resident Mackay Meml. Hosp., Taipei, 1983-86, attending, 1986-92; rsch. fellow Vancouver (B.C., Can.) Gen. Hosp., 1992-93; sr. attending Mackay Meml. Hosp., Taipei, 1993—; lectr. China Med. Coll., Tai-Chung, 1996—; statis. cons. Thoracic Soc. Republic of China, Taipei, 1993—. Contbr. rsch. articles to profl. jours. Cons. Asthma Friend Soc., Taipei, 1995—, Pneumoconsisis Claim Assn., Taipei, 1997—. Lt. Army Command, 1979-81. Rsch. grantee Nat. Sci. Couns., 1995-96, Health Dept. of Exec. Yuan, 1996. Fellow Am. Coll. Chest Physicians; mem. Am. Thoracic Soc., European Respiratory Soc. Buddhist. Avocations: swimming, golf, computer games, coin collecting,

reading. Office: Mackay Meml Hosp, 92 Sect 2 Chung-San N Rd, 10449 Taipei Taiwan

LIN, GUANG YONG, educator; b. Jieyang, China, Sept. 17, 1964; s. Hua Shan and Xiu Yin (She) L.; m. Chi Miao Xu, Mar. 9, 1995. BS, Harbin Inst. Tech., China, 1986, MS, 1989, PhD, 1993; postgrad., U. Utah, 1996—. Lectr. South China U. Tech., Guangzhou, China, 1993-95, assoc. prof., 1995—; dir. Inorganic Materials Rsch. Lab., South China U. Tech., Guangzhou, 1995—. Vis. scholar INSA de Lyon, France, 1996. Mem. Am. Ceramic Soc., Internat. Union Materials Rsch. (Chinese com. 1995—). Home: 133 S 900 E Apt 22 Salt Lake City UT 84102-4175 Office: U Utah 122 S Ctrl Campus Rm 304 Dept Material Sci & Engrng Salt Lake City UT 84112

LIN, HO-MU, engineering educator; b. Kaohsiung, Taiwan, July 12, 1938; s. Chao-Wu and Dean-Su L.; m. Su-Jung Wang, 1972; children: Eugene Ted, Jeffrey Eugene. BS, Nat. Taiwan U., 1962; Postgrad. Diploma, Tokyo Inst. Tech., 1966; PhD, Okla. State U., 1970. Sr. lectr., rsch. assoc. Okla. State U., 1970-73; rsch. fellow Rice U., 1974-75; tech. dir., sr. engr. Thermodynamics Rsch. Lab. Purdue U., 1975-87, sr. fellow, 1988-94; spl. chair Nat. Taiwan U., 1994, Nat. Taiwan Inst. Tech., 1994-97; prof., chmn. Nat. Taiwan U. Sci. and Tech., 1997—; sr. scientific adviser BIOS Indsl., Can., 1987—; cons. EXXON Rsch. and Engring. Co., 1984-85; sr. adviser Biotech. Svc. Internat., Can., 1984-87; spl. chair Nat. Sci. Coun., Taiwan, 1994-97. Editor (hon.) Jour. Chinese Inst. Chem. Engrs., Vol. 27 (No. 4), 1996, mem. editl. bd., 1997—;internat. monitor Jour. Chem. Engring. Japan, 1998—; contbr. 150 articles to tech. jours., 2 chpts. to books; patentee in field. Fellow UNESCO, 1965-66; recipient award Am. Petroleum Rsch. Funds, 1968, Rsch. Achievements award EXXON, Chevron, Amoco, 1983-87. Mem. Chinese Inst. Chem. Engrs. (bd. dirs. 1997—, editor (hon.) Chem. Engring. Vol. 45 1996), Am. Chem. Soc., AIChE, AAAS. Avocations: sports, gardening. Home: 3303 Hunter Rd West Lafayette IN 47906-5392 Office: Nat Taiwan U Sci & Tech, 43 Kee-Lung Rd Sec 4, Taipei 106, Taiwan

LIN, HUI QIANG, pharmacologist; b. Zhanjiang, Guangdong, China, Apr. 21, 1950; arrived in Australia, 1988; s. Liang Lin and Ai-Qing Chen; m. Xiao Ying Huang; 1 child, Mark. MB, Guangdong Med. Coll., Zhanjiang, China, 1982; PhD, U. Sydney, Australia, 1995. Tchg. asst. Guangdong Med. Coll., Zhanjiang, 1982-84, South China Normal U., Guangzhou, 1984-88; rsch. asst. dept. psychology U. Sydney, 1991-93, pharmacologist dept. pharmacology, 1995-99; leader in pharmacology, radiopharm. divsn. Australian Nuclear Sci. & Tech. Orgn., Sydney, 1999—; rschr. in/or tchr. pharmacology, physiology and psychology. Contbr. articles and papers to profl. jours. Mem. Australian Soc. Clin. and Exptl. Pharmacologists and Toxicologists. Avocations: soccer, table tennis, visual arts, classical music, ancient Chinese poetry. Office: Radiopharm R&D ANSTO, Pvt Mail Bag 1, Menai NSW 2234, Australia

LIN, JADE CHEN, art society administrator, dance educator, artist; b. Hong Kong, June 1, 1938; came to U.S., 1978; d. Toby Chen and Louise Yao; m. Eddy Lin, July 8, 1960; 1 child, Tony. MusB, Nat. Taiwan Normal U., 1962. Founder Am. Chinese Art Soc., 1984, exec. dir., 1984—; artistic dir. Traditional Chinese Dance Troupe, 1986—; condr. Children Angel Chorus, 1989-97; instr. ACAS Dance Studio, 1996—. Bd. advisors Newton (Mass.) Pride Com., 1996—. Recipient Pride of Newton award Newton Pride Com., 1995. Mem. New Eng. Piano Tchr. Assn., Mass. Music Tchr. Assn. Avocations: music, dance. Office: Am Chinese Art Soc 111 Truman Rd Newton MA 02459-2640

LIN, JAMES K., technology company executive, educator; b. Shanghai, China, Sept. 22, 1941; s. Hua Kun Lin and Sho Cheng Chiang; m. Ellen Lin; children: Vincent, Geoffrey, Charles. BS, Nat. Taiwan U., Taipei, 1965; MS, Pratt Inst., 1969; postgrad., U. Pa.; PhD, U. Southwestern La., 1977; DSc, U. Am., 1977. Sr. analyst, engr. mgr. RCA Global Comms., N.Y.C., 1975-77; mgr. timesharing ctr. CDC Taiwan, Taipei, 1977-81, sales mgr. country mktg., 1981-85; country mgr. CDC China/Hong Kong, Beijing, 1985-89; dep. gen. mgr. WANG Labs., Taipei, 1989-92; regional dir. EDS Asia, Hong Kong, 1992-94; gen. mgr. ABB China Ltd., Hong Kong, 1994—; prof. (part time) CUNY, 1973-74; spkr. in field. Mem. Chinese Academic and Profl. Assn. in Am. (pres. 1975-77), Chinese-Am. Assn. China (exec. dir. 1995-97), Am. C. of C. in China, Am. High Tech. Forum in China (treas. 1987-89), Comm. Network Assn. (exec. dir. 1992-94), Open Sys. Assn. Taiwan (mng. supr. 1989-91, Excellent Performances 1990). Avocations: swimming, basketball, music, travel. Home: 5257 Purdue Ave Culver City CA 90230-5349 Office: ABB China Ltd South Tower, 14 East Third Ring Rd N, 100026 Beijing China

LIN, JEN-KUN, biochemistry educator; b. Chia-Yi, Taiwan, Republic of China, Dec. 4, 1935; parents: You-Chuen and Sha (Ho) Chen; m. Shoei-Yn Lin-Shiau, Nov. 2, 1962; children: Jung-Shin, Cheng-Yen, Tsu-Wei. BS in Pharmacy, Nat. Taiwan U., 1958, MS in Biochemistry, 1961; PhD in Oncology, U. Wis., Madison, 1968. Mem. faculty Nat. Taiwan U., Taipei, Republic of China, 1962—; prof. biochemistry Nat. Taiwan U., 1973—; research assoc. U. Wis.-Madison, 1968-69, vis. prof., Forgaty Internat. fellow, 1975-76; vis. scientist Lab. Molecular Oncology, Nat. Cancer Inst.-NIH, Frederick, Md., 1984; dir. students Coll. Medicine, Nat. Taiwan U., 1979-83. Editor Sci. Monthly, 1970—, proceedings Nat. Sci. Council, Republic of China, 1980—; co-editor Molecular Biology Neoplasia, 1985. Recipient Acad. award Chung-Shan Sic. and Art Found., Taipei, 1982, Outstanding Professorship award Ministry Edn., Taipei, 1983-85, Outstanding Investigator award Nat. Sci. Coun., Taipei, 1985-87, 87-89, 89-91, Acad. award Ministry Edn. Medicine, 1987. Mem. Formosan Med. Assn. (outstanding thesis award 1963, 72), Chinese Biomed. Soc. (pres. 1987-88), Chinese Oncol. Soc., Chinese Toxicol. Soc. (pres. 1991-94), Am. Assn. Cancer Rsch., N.Y. Acad. Scis., Sigma Xi. Buddhist. Club: Taita Tennis (Taipei). Avocations: tennis, hiking, mountain climbing. Office: Nat Taiwan U Inst Biochemistry Coll Medicine, Number 1 Se-t 1 Jen ai Rd, Taipei 100, Taiwan

LIN, JIANYI, physicist, educator; b. Longhai, Fujian, China, Dec. 20, 1943; arrived in Singapore; s. Suoren Lin and Lujin Hong; m. Shimei Hou; children: Dakun, Jingkun. BSc, Xiamen U., China, 1966; PhD, Stanford U., 1991. Asst. lectr. Xiamen U., 1973-81, lectr., 1983-85; rsch. scientist Nat. U. Singapore, 1991-93, lectr., 1994-95, sr. lectr., 1995-98, assoc. prof., 1999—; vis. scientist Bradford U., 1981-83. Contbr. over 60 articles to profl. jours. Office: Dept Physics, Nat U Singapore, Singapore 119260, Singapore

LIN, JIIN-HUEY CHERN, engineering educator; b. Kaoshung, Taiwan, Republic of China, Feb. 19, 1949; d. Fen-Fu and Chung-Lin Lin Chen; m. Luh-Yuan Lin, July 5, 1973; children: Albert Isaac, Alice. BS in Physics, Chung Yuan Christian U., Taiwan, 1970; MS in Physics, N.E. La. U., 1974; PhD in Biomaterials, Northwestern U., 1983. Vis. specialist Nat. Yang-Ming U., Taipei, Tawian, 1984-85; asst. prof. Northwestern U., Chgo., 1985-89, vis. prof., 1996-97; vis. prof. Nat. Cheng-Kung U., Tainan, Taiwan, 1987-88, assoc. prof., 1989-95, prof., 1995—; strategic com. Nat. Sci. Coun., Taipei, 1997-99. Jour. reviewer Dental Materials, Liverpool, U.K., 1995—, Jour. of Materials Chemistry and Physics, Liverpool, 1997—; contbr. numerous articles to profl. jours.; inventor in field. Recipient Excellent Rsch. award Nat. Sci. Coun. of Republic of China, 1990-99, over 30 rsch. grants, 1990-99; rsch. grantee Nat. Health Rsch. Inst., 1994-99. Fellow The Acad. of Denal Materials; mem. Soc. of Biomaterials, Soc. of Dental Materials, Chinese Bioengring. Soc., Am. Ceramic Soc. Home: 911 Tower Rd Winnetka IL 60093-1935 Office: Nat Cheng-Kung U, #1 Da-Sha Rd, Tainan 70101, Taiwan

LIN, JIKEN, banking educator; b. Hongzhon, China, May 15, 1930; s. Yingdong Lin and Huiying Li; m. Qi Run Zhuge, Nov. 30, 1954; children: Ling, Hong. BS, Nankai U., Tanjin, China, 1952. Asst. prof. Liaoning U., Shenyang, China, 1952-59; asst. prof. Liaoning Coll. Fin. and Econs., Dalian, China, 1959-78, assoc. prof., 1978-81; prof. banking Dongbei U. Fin. and Econs., Dalian, 1981—, supervising prof. for doctorate, 1986—, head Fin. Rsch. Inst., 1989—; cons. Bank of Hongda, Dalian, 1988—; mem. Nat. Com. for Fin. Text Books, 1988—; mem. acad. degree appraisal com. Ministry Fin., 1990—. Author: Circulation of Money in Socialist Society, 1964, Law of Circulation of Money, 1965, Circulation of Money and Plan of Bank, 1981, Issue of Money in Socialist System, 1984 (award Ministry Nat. Fin. 1985), Adjustment and Management of Circulation of Money, 1986 (award Govt. of Dalian Cityt 1987), Management of Circulation of Money, 1987 (award Govt. of Dalian City 1988), Stabilizing of Money, 1990 (award Govt. of Liaoning Province 1991), Money and Banking in Socialist Society, 1993 (award People's Bank China 1995), Treatise on Stabilizing Money, 1995 (continuation, 1997), Money Supply, 1996; contbr. more than 90 articles to newspapers and profl. jours. Named Excellent Tchr., Govt. of China, 1989, Excellent Specialist, Govt. of Dalian City, 1992, Govt. of Liaoning Province, 1995. Mem. China Inst. Fin. (bd. dirs., acad. com. 1978—). Office: Dongbei U Fin and Econs, Dept Banking, Dalian 116025, China

LIN, JOU-WEI, physician; b. Taipei, Taiwan, Mar. 3, 1968; s. Chen-Shan and Pai-Ho (Wang) L.; m. Ai-Tzu Li, Dec. 28, 1997; 1 child, Christine Iris. MPH, Harvard Sch. Pub. Health, 1995; MD, Nat. Taiwan U., 1993; PhD, Columbia U., 1999. Clin. intern Nat. Taiwan U., Taipei, 1992; resident in internal medicine Nat. Taiwan Univ. Hosp., 1993-94; rsch. asst. Columbia U., N.Y.C., 1995-98, postdoctoral fellow, 1999—. Contbr. articles to profl. publs., confs. Recipient Best Resident award Nat. Taiwan Univ. Hosp., 1994. Mem. Soc. Nuclear Medicine, Am. Med. Informatics Assn., IEEE. Avocations: computer programming, image processing, music, tennis. Office: Coll of Phys/Surgeons of Columbia Divsn Cardiology 622 W 168th St # P&s953 New York NY 10032-3720

LIN, JUCHUI RAY, polymer scientist; b. Taoyuan, Taiwan, China, Apr. 25, 1947; came to U.S., 1974; s. Pai-Liang and Mai (Wang) L.; m. Jing-Fang Wang, Dec. 24, 1975; children: Amy Monica, Audrey Alice. BS in Chemistry, Nat. Taiwan Normal U., 1972; MS in Chemistry, Southwest Tex. State U., 1977; PhD in Macromolecular Sci., Case Western Res. U., 1985. Tchr. Taipei Gimmei Jr. High Sch., Taiwan, 1971-73; lab. instr. Nat. Ctrl. U., Chungli, Taiwan, 1973-74; cons. Polytronics, Inc., Cleve., 1983-85; chemist Sohio Rsch. Ctr., Warrensville Heights, Ohio, 1983, DPJ Rsch. Ctr., SCM Corp., Strongville, Ohio, 1984-86; sr. scientist Spectrum Control Rsch. Ctr., Erie, Pa., 1986-88; tech. mgr. Koch Membrane Systems, Inc., Wilmington, Mass., 1989-93; mgr. ion-exch. membrane technology Ionics, Inc., Watertown, Mass., 1993—. Author youth sci. books Youth Ency., 1970, also papers in field. Mem. AIChE, Am. Chem. Soc., Soc. Plastics Engrs. Avocation: community service. Achievements include patents in field of conductive polymers, electrical active polymers, resings and coatings, elastomers, encapsulations for electronics, potting, ceramics, polymer blends, polymer surface modifications, membrane formulations, membrane processes; pioneer and inventor of self-assembly surface coating technology. E-mail: jlin@ionics.com. Office: Ionics Inc 65 Grove St Watertown MA 02472-2882

LIN, KAIMING, editor; b. Fuzhou, China, July 23, 1923; s. Heyi and Zhoudi (Chen) L.; m. Xiasheng Wu, Oct. 15, 1951; three children. BA, Xiamen U. Editor, reporter, commentator Tianjin Daily, China, 1950-70; cadre Tianjin Paper Corp., 1971-81; mng. chief editor Mgmt. & Adminstrn. monthly, Tianjin, 1982-85; chief editor Press of Econ. Outlook Round the Bohai Sea, Tianjin, 1986—; dep. sec. gen. Bohai Sea Rim Econ. Info. Soc., Tianjin Econ. Info. Soc.; dir. Asia-Africa Devel. and Exch. Soc. of China. Mem. Tianjin Tennis Club, Tianjin Aquatics Club. Avocations: swimming, tennis, ballroom dancing. Home: 2-4-301 Kehaili Yingshuidao, Nankai Qu Tianjin 300191, China Office: Econ Outlook Round the Bohai Sea, 39 Youyi Lu Hexi Qu, 300201 Tianjin China

LIN, LEE, physics educator; b. Taipei, Taiwan, June 27, 1958; s. Chung-Teh and Shu-Fen (Chen) L. BSc, Nat. Taiwan U., Taipei, 1980; M in Physics, U. Calif., San Diego, 1984, PhD in Physics, 1989. Postdoctoral rschr. Desy Theory Group, Hamburg, Germany, 1989-91, U. Muenster, Germany, 1991-94; assoc. prof. Nat. Chung Hsing U., Taichung, China, 1994—. Contbr. articles to jours. in field. Served with Taiwanes mil., 1980-82. Mem. Am. Phys. Soc. Avocations: Beijing opera, tennis, badminton. Office: Nat Chung Hsing U, 250 Kuo Kuang Rd, Taichung 40227, Taiwan

LIN, LI CONG, mathematics educator; b. Chaozhou, Guangdong, China, June 25, 1935; s. Jie Ju Lin and Su Fang Zhuang; m. Jie Zhen Zhang, Aug. 16, 1963; children: Saying, Jinghui, Ye Xin. Student, South China Normal U., Guangzhou, 1954-58, East China Normal U., Shanghai, 1964-65, Xiamen (China) U., 1979-80. Lectr. Hainan Tchrs. Coll., Haikou, China, 1978-84; dean math. dept. Hanshan Tchrs. Coll., Chaozhou, China, 1984-88; assoc. prof. math. Hanshan Tchrs. Coll., Chaozhou, 1986-92, v.p., 1988-95, chief editor jour., 1989-98, prof. math., 1992—; dir. com. math. tchg. and rsch. Nat. Secondary Specialized Schs., 1984-86; vice chmn. Shantou (China) Math. Soc., 1989-95. Contbr. articles to profl. jours.; inventor in field. Fellow Chinese Math. Soc. (dir. of Guangdong br. 1991-95); mem. AAAS, N.Y. Acad. Scis. Home and Office: Hanshan Tchrs Coll, Chaozhou 521041, Peoples Republic of China

LIN, LIANG PING, chemist, educator, consultant, researcher; b. Ping-Tung, Taiwan, Republic of China, June 4, 1934; s. Ping-Hsiang and Tsao (Shirota) L.; m. Ling Jean Kao, Aug. 30, 1968; children: Hsiu-Yuan, Ming-Haou. BS in Agr., Nat. Taiwan U., Taipei, 1958, MS in Agrl. Chemistry, 1960; MA in Microbiology, U. Tex., 1964; PhD in Microbiology, La. State U., 1966. Rsch. scientist II in microbiology U. Tex., Austin, 1962-63, tchg. asst. in microbiology, 1963-64; grad. asst. in microbiology La. State U., 1964-66; postdoctoral rsch. assoc. in microbiology and pub. health Mich. State U., East Lansing, 1966-69; prof. agrl. chemsitry Nat. Taiwan U., Taipei, 1971—; vis. prof. Mich. State U., East Lansing, 1976-77, vis. specialist, 1985-86; tech. cons. YSK Internat. Co., Kyoto, Japan, 1991—; vis. prof. Marine Biotech. Inst., Kamaishi, Japan, 1966; tech. cons. Bylo Industry Co., Kanagawa, Japan, 1999—. Author: Soil Microbiology, 1986 (Best Design award 1988); contbr. aritlces to profl. jours.; patentee chlorella algae cultivation and prodn. spl. algae. 2nd lt. Chinese Army, 1960-62. Grantee Nat. Sci. Coun., 1970—, Nat. Agrl. Coun., 1980—. Mem. Internat. Fedn. Sci. and Electron Microscopy (adv. com. 1998—), Chinese Chem. Soc., Am. Soc. for Microbiology, Chinese Agrl. Chemistry, Electron Microscopy Soc. A., Chinese Soc. Microbiology, Chinese Inst. Food Sci. and Tech., Biomass Energy Soc. China, Bioindustry Devel. Assn., Electron Microscopy Soc. Rep. China, N.Y. Acad. Scis., Japan Soc. Electron Microscopy, Chinese Soc. Phycology, Asia-Pacific Soc. Applied Physiology, Japanese Soc. Microbial Ecology, Internat. Soc. for Microbial Ecology. Avocation: photography. Home: No 22 5 Ally 30 Ln, Chou-Shan Rd, Taipei Taiwan 106, Republic of China Office: Nat Taiwan U Dept Agrl Chem, No 1 Sec 4 Roosevelt Rd, Taipei Taiwan 106, Republic of China

LIN, LIN, stock broker, insurance agent; b. Jan. 29; d. Boabing Lin and Qiuou Huang; m. Hua-Yun Xiao, Dec. 24, 1984 (div. Feb. 1994); children: Alexander Ronghui, Elizabeth Rong Fong. BA, Wuhan (China) Geol. U., 1983; BS, San Francisco State U., 1993. Clk. U.S. Post Office, San Francisco, 1986-99; broker WMA Securities, Daly City, Calif., 1997—. Mem. Chinese Engring. Soc. E-mail: linlin@dotplanet.com. Office: WMA Securities 333 Gellert Blvd Ste 250 Daly City CA 94015-2614

LIN, MARIE MA-LI, pathologist, immunohematologist, educator; b. I-Lan, Taiwan, May 30, 1938; d. Sing-Chen Lin and Makino Yoshitake; children: Thomas Wei-Tao Chu, Steven Wei-Song Chu; m. Theodore Kay. MD, Kaohsiung (Taiwan) Med. Coll., 1964; MS, Nat. Taiwan U., Taipel, 1967. Resident pathology Nat. Taiwan U. Hosp., Taipei, 1964-69, instr. pathology, 1969-76, assoc. prof. pathology, 1976-78; resident pathology Med. Branch U. Tex., Galveston, 1972-73, 78-81; dir. med. lab. Mackay Meml. Hosp., Taipei, 1981-98, dir. Immunohematology Reference Lab., 1992—; dir. transfusion med. lab. Nat. Health Rsch. Inst., Taipei, 1992-95; prof. Nat. Taiwan U. Hosp., 1987—, Kaohsiung Med. Coll., 1988—; pres. Taiwan Soc. Blood Transfusion, Taipei, 1990-96; mem. blood transfusion adv. com. Dept. Health, Taipei, 1988—. Author: Procedure Manual for Blood Banks, 1983, Transfusion Medicine, 1990, 2d edit, 1997; contbr. articles to profl. jours. Artist Greenfield Art Assn., Taipei, 1964-78, Homerun Art Assn., Taipei, 1990—. Recipient Su-Wei award Ministry Edn., Taipei, 1980, Wang Ming-Ning Found. award, 1992, Helena Rubinstein award for women of sci. nominee, 1998; grantee Nat. Sci. Coun. and Dept. Health, 1984—. Fellow Coll. Am. Pathologists (diplomate); mem. Internat. Soc. Blood Transfusion (councilor London 1992-96, pres. 10th regional congress western pacific region, 1999). Avocations: painting, writing, music, classical Chinese literature. Office: Mackay Meml Hosp, 92 Sec 2 Chung-San N Rd, Taipei Taiwan

LIN, MAW-WEN, petroleum industry executive, researcher; b. Taipei, Taiwan, Republic of China, Dec. 24, 1946; s. Po-Huang and Li-Hui (Shen) L.; m. Kai-Chi Ho, Mar. 27, 1977; 1 child, Yuan-Kae. BS, Tamkang U., 1970; MS, Tenn. Tech. U., 1974; PhD, Nat. Chiao Tung U., Taipei, 1995. Rsch. asst. Ministry of Interior, Taipei, 1971-72; sr. planner R&D divsn. Chinese Petroleum Corp., Taipei, 1974-79, sect. chief planning divsn., 1980-88, sr. specialist, 1989-90, dep. dir., 1990-91, dir. info. sys. divsn., 1991—; lectr. Fu Jen Cath. U., Taipei Hsien, 1975-82, assoc. prof., 1992—; assoc. prof. Tamkang U., Taipei Hsien, 1983-92, Nat. Open U., Taipei Hsien, 1995—. Author: Times Series Analysis and Forecasting, 2d edit., 1991; contbr. articles to profl. jours. Mem. exec. com. Chinese Nat. Party, Taipei, 1990—; mem. Cmty. Adminstrn. Com., Taipei, 1993-96. 2d lt. Air Force Gen. Hdqrs., 1970-71. Recipient Successful Enterprise Mgr. award Republic of China, 1995, Outstanding Info. Application Sys. award, 1991, Outstanding Info. Talents award, 1993, Excellent Talents award Ministry of Econ. Affairs, 1980. Mem. Chinese Mgmt. Assn., Chinese Energy Econ. Assn. (founding mem. 1984—), Chinese Open Sys. Assn. (supr. 1997). Buddhist. Avocations: music, jogging, mountaineering, philately, basketball. Office: Chinese Petroleum Corp, 83 Chung-Hwa Rd Sect 1, Taipei 10031, Taiwan

LIN, MEEI-YN, food microbiology/biotechnology educator; b. Chai-Yi, Taiwan, May 19, 1964. BS, Nat. Chung Hsing U., Taichung, Taiwan, 1986; MS, U. Minn., 1990, PhD, 1992. Rsch. asst. U. Minn., St. Paul, 1988-92, postdoctoral rschr., 1993; assoc. rsch. fellow Devel. Ctr. for Biotech., Taipei, Taiwan, 1993; assoc. prof. Chia Nan Coll. Pharmacy, Tainan, Taiwan, 1993-95; assoc. prof. dept food sci. Nat. Chung Hsing U., 1995—; cons. Home-Well Bio-Tech. Co., Ltd., Taiwan. Contbr. articles to rsch. publs. Mem. Am. Dairy Sci. Assn., Gamma Sigma Delta (U. Minn. chpt.). Office: Nat Chung Hsing U D Food Sc, 250 Kuokuang Rd, Taichung 402, Taiwan

LIN, NENG-PAI, management educator, consultant; b. Tainan, Taiwan, June 1, 1953; m. Su Chen Hung; children: Eva, Joanna. BA in Engring., Nat. Taiwan U., 1975; PhD in Mgmt., Ohio State U., 1989. Mgr. Dynasty Devel. Co., Taipei, 1978-81, Yan-Zan Constrn. Co., Taipei, 1982-83, Fu-Tsu Constrn. Co., Taipei, 1983-86; assoc. prof. Nat. Taiwan U., Taipei, 1989-99, prof., 1994-99, chair, 1995-98, dean Coll. Mgmt., 1999—; cons. Taipei City Govt., 1996—, Dept. Rapid Transit Systems, Taipei, 1996—, San-Chai Devel. Co., Taichung, 1994-95, Chau-Chen Constrn. Co., Taipei, 1990-92. Editor: Red Book of Taipei Rapid Transit System, 1995; contbr. articles to profl. jours. Recipient Stan Hardy award Decision Scis. Inst., U.S., 1993, 95, Best Paper award Chinese Mgmt. Assn., 1993. Office: Nat Taiwan U Coll Mgmt, 6F 50 Ln 144 Keelung Rd 4, Taipei Taiwan

LIN, PING, mechanical engineer; b. Guangdong Province, China, Feb. 1, 1957; cmae to U.S., 1990; m. Qing Xiu Zhang, 1985; children: Jeffrey Y., Jessica Y. BS in Engring., Beijing Inst. Tech., 1982; MS in Mechanics, Northeastern U., Boston, 1992. Mfg. engr. Shanghai Machinery Co., 1982-84; mech. engr. People's Bank China, Beijing, 1984-86, engring. mgr., 1987-90; sr. project engr. Watts Regulator Co., North Andover, Mass., 1993-97; sr. mech. engr. MKS Instruments, Inc., Andover, Mass., 1997—; tchg. asst. Northeastern U., Boston, 1992-93. Recipient Nat. Engring. Excellence award Acad. Conf. Sci. Tech. China, 1986. Mem. ASME, Phi Kappa Phi. Achievements include 2 patents, 1 patent pending; research in fluid dynamics, thermal dynamics, mechanics and materials.

LIN, SHOUYUAN, science educator; b. Shanghai, China, June 21, 1932; s. Keshu Lin and Xihe Zheng; m. Molin Gu, Oct. 1, 1959; 1 child, Nanzhi. Bachelor, S.E. U., Nanjing, China, 1953. Cert. sr. engr. and prof. Engr. Nanjing Rsch. Inst. Electronics Tech., 1960-80, sr. engr., 1981-86, prof., 1987—, dep. chief engr., 1978-97; dir. Nat. Lab. Antenna and Microwave Tech., Nanjing, 1995—; part-time prof. Nanjing U. Post and Telecom., 1996—. Chmn. editl. bd. Modern Radar, 1985—; mem. editl. bd. Electronic Sci. and Tech. Rev., Beijing, 1994—; contbr. articles to profl. jours. Recipient New Product award Ministry of Industry, Beijing, 1956, Excellence Achievement award State Econ. Com., Beijing, 1984, Outstanding Contbn. award The State Coun., China, 1992. Fellow Chinese Inst. Electronics (com. mem. Microwave Soc. 1981-89, standing com. mem. Radar Soc. 1985-97); mem. IEEE (sr.), Acad. Com. State Key Lab of Electromagnetic Wave Propagation. Avocations: fine arts, collecting stamps and coins. Home: Bldg 13-1-201, 3 Ding-Huai Men, Nanjing 210013, China Office: Nanjing Rsch Inst Elec Tech, 1 Ding-Huai-Men, Nanjing 210013, China

LIN, SHUAN-PEI, pediatrician, geneticist, educator; b. Taichung, Taiwan, Oct. 1, 1955; s. Ta-Yaw Lin and Su-Cheng Lee; m. May-Chih Grace Hsu; children: Yu-Shuan, Kevin Shane. MD, Kaohsiung (Taiwan) Med. Coll., 1980. Cert. pediat. specialist, med. genetics specialist, pediat. emergency and critical care medicine, family medicine, pediat. endocrinology and metabolism. Attending physician, instr. dept. pediat. MacKay Meml. Hosp., Taipei, 1986—; dir. dept. pediat. MacKay Meml. Hosp., Taitung, Taiwan, 1988-89; lab. dir. dept. med. rsch. MacKay Meml. Hosp., Taipei, 1993—, sr. attending physician, 1993—, dir. divsn. biochem. genetics dept. med. rsch., 1995—, dir. divsn. genetics dept. pediatrics, 1997—; cons. Taipei Inst. Pathology, 1992—; med. cons. Ctr. for Exam. and Assessment of Mentally Retarded Children, Taipei City Govt., 1998—; hon. cons. Home of Health Care Med. Web, 1998—; lectr. China Med. Coll., Taichung, Taiwan, 1995—, Nat. Taipei Coll. Nursing, 1997—; vis. prof. Yale U. Med. Sch., 1989-91. Author: Caring for Children Age 0-6, 1996, How to Take Good Care of Your Baby in Illness, 1998; contbr. articles to profl. jours., chpts. to books. Supr. Down's Syndrome Assn. Republic of China, Taipei, 1991—; trustee Down's Syndrome Found. Republic of China, Taipei, 1998—; vol. cons., Kaohsiung Life Line, 1976-79, counselor Child Welfare League Found. Republic of China, Taipei, 1994—; hon. sponsor Taiwan Achondroplasia Assn., 1998—; hon. bd. dirs. Taiwan Mucopolysaccharidoses Assn., Taipei, 1996—; hon. sponsor Taiwan Waardenburg's Syndrome Assn., 1996—; med. counselor Taiwan Albinism Assn., 1996; counselor Chinese Assn. Med. Consultation and Svcs., 1997—; bd. dirs. Taiwan Found. for Rare Disorders, 1999—; med. counselor Taiwan Osteogenesis Imperfecta Assn., 2000—; com. mem. Com. Deliberation Rare Disorders and Orphan Drugs, Dept. Health, Exec. Yuan Taiwan Ctrl. Govt., 2000—; med. counselor Prep. com. Taiwan Wilson's Disease Assn., 2000—. Mem. Soc. Med. Genetics-Taiwan Pediat. Assn., Soc. Endocrinology and Metabolism-Taiwan Pediat. Assn., Formosan Med. Assn., Chinese Taipei Assn. Family Medicine, Am. Soc. Human Genetics, European Soc. Human Genetics, Taiwan Soc. Human Genetics (bd. dirs. 1999), Taiwan Osteogenesis Imperfecta Assn. (med. counselor 2000—), Formosa Toastmasters Club (founding mem.). Fax: 886-2-2543-3642. E-mail: zsplin@ms2.mmh.org.tw. Office: MacKay Meml Hosp, 92 Sec 2 Chung San N Rd, Taipei 10449, Taiwan

LIN, SHU-KUN, chemist, researcher; b. Hanchuan, Hubei, China, Mar. 24, 1957; s. Yin-Han and Fu-Zhen (Wang) L.; m. Ming Ye, Oct. 1, 1985 (div. May 1988); 1 child, Qian-Qian; m. Feng Zhang, Jan. 1, 1994; 1 child, Di-Fan. BSc, Wuhan (China) U., 1982; MSc, Academia Sinica, Lanzhou, China, 1985; PhD, ETH, Zürich, Switzerland, 1992. Rsch. scientist Academia Sinica, Lanzhou, 1985-86; rsch. asst. U. Louisville, 1987-89, ETH, Zürich, 1989-92; rsch. assoc. Ciba, Basel, Switzerland, 1993-95; pres. Molecular Diversity Preservation Internat., Basel, 1995—. Editor-in-chief Molecules, 1996—. Mem. Am. Chem. Soc., Swiss Chem. Soc. Avocations: ballpen collection, travel. E-mail: Lin@mdpi.org.

LIN, SONG-SUN, dean. Dean coll. sci. Nat. Chiao Tung U., Hsinchu, Taiwan. Office: Nat Chiao Tung U, 1001 7A Hsueh Rd, Hsinchu 30050, Taiwan*

LIN, THOMAS WEN-SHYOUNG, accounting educator, researcher, consultant; b. Taichung, Republic of China, June 3, 1944; came to U.S., 1970; s. Ju-chin and Shao-chin (Tseng) L.; m. Angela Kuei-fong Hou, May 19, 1969; children: William Margaret. BA in Bus. Adminstrn., Nat. Taiwan U., Taipei, 1966; MBA, Nat. Chengchi U., Taipei, 1970; MS in Acctg. and Info. Systems, UCLA, 1971; PhD in Acctg., Ohio State U., 1975. Cert. mgmt. acct., Calif. Internal auditor Formosa Plastics Group, Taipei, 1967-69, spl. asst. to the pres., 1969-70; asst. prof. U. So. Calif., L.A., 1975-80, assoc. prof., 1980-86, prof. acctg., 1986-90, acctg. cir. prof., 1990—, dir. doctoral studies acctg., 1982-86; cons. Intex Plastics, Inc., Long Beach, Calif., 1979-81, Peat, Marwick, Mitchell, L.A., 1982, City of Chino, Calif., 1982; bd.

dirs., audit com. chmn. FCB Taiwan Calif. Bank, 1997—. Author: Planning and Control for Data Processing, 1984, Use of Mathematical Models, 1986, Advanced Auditing, 1988, Using Accounting Information in Business Planning, Product Costing, and Auditing, 1991, Cost Management: A Strategic Emphasis, 1999; assoc. editor Internat. Jour. Bus., 1997—; mem. editl. bd. Taiwan Mgmt. Acctg., Quarterly Jour. Bus. and Econs., Am. Jour. Math. and Mgmt. Scis., Chinese Acctg. Rev., Hong Kong Jour. Bus. Mgmt., 1988—; contbr. articles to profl. jours. Bd. dirs. U. So. Calif. Acctg. Circle, L.A., 1986-88, 93-99, Taiwan Benevolent Assn. Am., Washington, 1986-89; pres. Taiwan Benevolent Assn. Calif., L.A., 1986-88, Chinese Am. Faculty Assn. So. Calif., 2000—. 2d lt. China Army, 1966-67. Recipient cert. appreciation L.A. City Mayor Tom Bradley, 1988, Congressman Martinez award for outstanding community svc., 1988; Faculty Rsch. scholar U. So. Calif. Bus. Sch., L.A., 1984-87. Mem. Am. Acctg. Assn. (bd. dirs. 1986-88), Chinese Acctg. Profs. N.Am. (founding pres. 1976-80), Inst. Cert. Mgmt. Accts. (cert. of disting. performance 1978), Inst. Mgmt. Accts. (coord. 1984—, Author's trophy 1978, 79, 81, 87), Inst. Mgmt. Scis. Republican. Baptist. Avocation: gardening. Home: PO Box 8023 Rowland Hghts CA 91748-0023 Office: U So Calif Leventhal Sch Acctg Univ Park Acc 109 Los Angeles CA 90089-0001

LIN, TUNG YEN, civil engineer, educator; b. Foochow, China, Nov. 14, 1911; came to U.S., 1946, naturalized, 1951; s. Ting Chang and Feng Yi (Kuo) L.; m. Margaret Kao, July 20, 1941; children: Paul, Verna. BS in Civil Engring., Chiaotung U., Tangshan, Republic of China, 1931; MS, U. Calif., Berkeley, 1933; LLD, Chinese U. Hong Kong, 1972, Golden Gate U., San Francisco, 1982, Tongji U., Shanghai, 1987, Chiaotung U., Taiwan, 1987. Chief bridge engr., chief design engr. Chinese Govt. Rys., 1933-46; asst., then assoc. prof. U. Calif., 1946-55, prof., 1955-76, chmn. div. structural engring., 1960-63, dir. structural lab., 1960-63; chmn. bd. T.Y. Lin Internat., 1953-87, hon. chmn. bd., 1987-92; pres. Inter-Continental Peace Bridge, Inc., 1968—; cons. to State of Calif., Def. Dept., also to industry; chmn. World Conf. Prestressed Concrete, 1957, Western Conf. Prestressed Concrete Bldgs., 1960; chmn. bd. Lin Tung Yen, China, 1993—. Author: Design of Prestressed Concrete Structures, 1955, rev. edit., 1963, 3d edit. (with N.H. Burns), 1981, (with B. Bresler, Jack Scalzi) Design of Steel Structures, rev. edit., 1968, (with S.D. Statesbury) Structural Concepts and Systems, 1981, 2d edit., 1988; contbr. articles to profl. jours. Recipient Berkeley citation award, 1976, NRC Quarter Century award, 1977, AIA Honor award, 1984, Pres.'s Nat. Med. of Sci., 1986, Merit award Am. Cons. Engrs., Coun., 1987, John A. Roebling medal Bridge Engring., 1990, Am. Segmental Bridge Inst. Leadership award, 1992, Outstanding Paper of Yr. award Internat. Assn. Bridge and Structural Engring., 1993, Lifetime Achievement award Asian Am. Archs. and Engring. Assn., 1993, Outstanding Achievement award AAAE Assn. of So. Calif., Prix Albert Caquot award Assn. Française pour Construction, 1995; fellow U. Calif. at Berkeley; named Alumnus of Yr. U. Calif. Alumni Assn., 1994. Mem. ASCE (hon., life, Wellington award, Howard medal, OPAL award), Nat. Acad. Engring., Chinese Acad. Sci., Academia Sinica, Internat. Fedn. Prestressing (Freyssinet medal), Am. Concrete Inst. (hon.), Prestressed Concrete Inst. (medal of honor), Chinese Acad. Sci., Chi Epsilon (nat. hon.). Home: 8701 Don Carol Dr El Cerrito CA 94530-2734 Office: 315 Bay St San Francisco CA 94133-1923

LIN, WEI, information technologist; b. Beijing, May 8, 1967. BS, U. Sci. and Tech. Beijing, 1990; MS, U. Singapore, 1996. Software engr. Lujia Computer, Beijing, 1990-94; info. sys. assoc. Am. Internat. Assurance (AIG Co.), Singapore, 1995-97; analyst developer ING Barings, Singapore, 1997-98; cons. Credit Suisse 1st Boston, N.Y.C., 1998-99; sr. analyst developer Goldman, Sachs & Co., N.Y.C., 1999—; conf. presenter in field. Team mem. Goldman Sachs Cmty. Tamwork, N.Y.C., 1999, 2000. Mem. IEEE. E-mail: william.lin@gs.co. Office: Goldman Sachs & Co One New York Plz 48th Fl New York NY 10004

LIN, WILLIAM BING-TSANG, accountant; b. Changhwa, Taiwan, Republic of China, Dec. 4, 1941; s. Shui-Tsai and Pei (Wu) L.; m. Shui-Lien Yen, Nov. 23, 1967; children: Kai-cheng, Kai Min. BBA, Nat. Taiwan U., 1966; M of Accountancy, U. Mo., 1971; postgrad., Asian Inst. of Mgmt., 1972. CPA, Taiwan. Clk. Internat. Comml. Bank of China, Taipei, 1960-68; audit mgr. Arthur Andersen, Taipei, 1968-70, 71-74; vice chmn. Deloitte & Touche, Taipei, 1975—; lectr. of auditing Nat. Taiwan U., 1968—; asst. prof. acctg. Soochow U., Taipei, 1968—; sub.-com. mem. Econ. Reform Com. Exec. Yuan, Taipei, 1985. Exec. editor Internal Auditor, 1988-96. Recipient Alumni Achievement award Asian Inst. of Mgmt. Alumni Assn., 1993. Mem. Internal Auditors Assn. of Republic of China (chmn. 1988-92), Nat. Fedn. of CPAs Assn. (chmn. ethics com. 1991-94), Acctg. R&D Found. (vice chmn. auditing stds. com. 1985—). Home: 2d Fl No 46, Hsin Hai Rd Sec 1, Taipei Taiwan Office: Deloitte & Touche 7th Fl No 102, Kuang Fu S Rd, Taipei 104, Taiwan

LIN, XI, biomedical researcher; b. Beijing, China, May 17, 1965. B, Beijing U., China, 1987; MD, Peking Union Med. Coll., 1991; PhD, U. Md. Sch. Medicine, 1996. Postdoctoral rsch. assoc. Howard Hughes Med. Inst./Baylor Coll. Medicine, Houston, 1997—. Author rsch. publs. in field. Mem. Soc. Neurosci. Fax: 713-798-8728. E-mail: xlin@bcm.tmc.edu. Office: Howard Hughes Med Inst/Baylor BCM 225 One Baylor Plz Rm T807 Houston TX 77030

LIN, XIANSHU, electrical engineering educator; b. Fuzhou, Fujian, China, Jan. 20, 1937; m. Wenhua Yan, Feb. 20, 1963; children: Yan, Dongyu. BS, Xián (China) Jiao U., 1959. Engring. diplomate. Vis. scholar Wis. U., Milw., 1981-83; assoc. prof. Grad. Sch. North China Inst. Electric Power, Beijing, 1987-92, prof., 1992—. Contbr. articles to profl. jours. Recipient Sci. Progress award Ministry of Electric Power Industry, China, 1995. Office: North China Elec Power Univ, Beijing 100085, China

LIN, XIAO-PING, medical scientist, physician; b. Tianjin, China, Feb. 8, 1955; d. Ming-Chuan and Xian-zhi (Zeng) L.; m. Qing-sheng Wang, Jan. 17, 1990. MD, Tianjin Med. U., 1980. Rsch. asst. Tianjin Cancer Hosp., 1980-87, asst. prof., 1988-95, assoc. prof., 1996—; vis. WHO/IARC, Lyon, France, 1992, U.S., 1993-94. Contbr. articles to profl. jours. Chinese Jour. Clin. Nutrition, Chinese Jour. Cancer Rsch., Chinese Jour. Clin. Oncology, and Chinese Jour. Hematology (Tianjin Sci. award 1989). Recipient Progressive Sci. award Nat. Com. Sci., 1990. Mem. Chinese Med. Assn., Chinese Assn. Preventive Medicine, Chinese Anti-Cancer Union. Avocations: classical music, volleyball, hairstyle design, tennis, dance. Office: Tianjin Cancer Hosp, Huan Hu Xi Rd, Tianjin 300060, China

LIN, XIHONG, statistician; b. Helong jiang, China, Nov. 3, 1967; came to U.S., 1989; d. Rujin Lin and Tong tai Xu; m. Hai Meng, Dec. 26, 1991; 1 child, William. BS in Applied Math., Tsinghua U., 1989; MS in Stats., U. Iowa, 1991; PhD in Biostats., U. Wash., 1994. Tchg. asst. U. Iowa, 1989-91; rsch. asst. U. Wash., 1991-94; asst. prof. U. Mich, 1994-99, assoc. prof., 1999—; prin. investigator Nat. Cancer Inst., 1997. Mem. Internat. Biometrics Soc. (assoc. editor Biometrics 1997; chair Ea.-N.Am. Region of Internat. Biometric Soc. Conf. Program 2000), Am. Statis. Assn. (assoc. editor jour. 1999). Avocations: music, tennis. E-mail: xlin@sph.umich.edu. Office: University of Michigan Department of Biostatistics 1420 Washington Hts Ann Arbor MI 48109-2009

LIN, XIN, optoelectronics researcher; b. Nanjing, Jiangsu, China, Apr. 20, 1962; d. Aifeng and Shuqin (Wang) L.; m. Erlin Ye, Oct. 11, 1990. BS, Optical & Fine Mech. Inst., China, 1983; MS, Chinese Acad. Sci., 1990; PhD, Shizuoka U., Japan, 1996. Engr. Huaxi Corp. of Optoelectronics, Chengdu, China, 1983-87, Huanan Corp. of Optoelectronics, Wuzhou, China, 1990-92; rsch. Shizuoka U., Hamamatsu, Japan, 1992-93, Yamaha Corp., Hamamatsu, Japan, 1996; domestic rsch. fellowship Electrotech. Lab., Tsukuba, Japan, 1997-2000; domestic rsch. fellow Nat. Agrl. Rsch. Ctr., Tsukuba, Japan, 2000—. Contbr. articles to profl. jours. Recipient Daheng Found. Prize for Study of Optics Chinese Acad. of Sinica, 1990. Mem. AAAS, Optical Soc. of Am., Internat. Soc. for Optical Engring., Japan Soc. Applied Physics. Avocations: reading, art. Home: 2-16-15 Takezono, Haitsu Tanaka 202, Tsukuba 305-0032, Japan Office: Nat Agrl Rsch Ctr, 3-1-1 Kannodai, Tsukuba 305-8666, Japan

LIN, YUE SHAN, physician, consultant; b. Taipei, Oct. 10, 1952; s. Zu-Sen Lin and Lin-Yeh Chen; m. Yin-Feng Chou, Apr. 15, 1989; children: Ming-Yi, Ming-Jei, Ming-shein. B in Pharmacy, Taipei Med. Coll., 1975; B in Medicine, Chen-Kung U., Taiwan, 1989. Pharmacist; Obstetrician-Gynecologist. Propagandist Taiwan Cyanamid Co., Ltd., Taipei, 1977-80; mgr. Lin Teh-Yung Co., Ltd., Taipei, 1981-84; resident Cheng-Kung U. Hosp., Tainan, Taiwan, 1989-93, vis. staff, 1993-95; vis. staff Chi-Mei Found. Hosp., Tainan, Taiwan, 1995—. 2nd lt. Taiwanese Army, 1975-77. Mem. Am. Assn. Gynecologic Laparoscopists, Ob-Gyn. Assn. Republic of China, Internat. Gynecologic Cancer Soc. Office: Chi-Mei Found Hosp, 901 Chung Hwa Rd, Yung-Kang Tainan Taiwan

LIN, YUNG-ZEN, pediatrician; b. Kaoshong, Taiwan, June 30, 1956; s. Jin-Yuan and Su-chi (Wang) L.; m. Meng-chuan Hung, May 26, 1984; children: Hsin-Chia, Hsin-Chin. MD, Med. Coll. Nat. Taiwan U., 1981. Resident in pediatrics Nat. Taiwan U. Hosp., Taipei, 1983-87, fellow in allergy and immunology, 1987-88; lectr. Med. Coll. Nat. Taiwan U. Hosp., Taipei, 1995—; vis. staff dept. pediatrics Taipei Mcpl. Chung Hsiao Hosp., 1988—; vis. staff dept. pediatrics Nat. Taiwan U. Hosp., 1988-96; dir. dept. pediat. Taipei Mcpl. Chung Hsiao Hosp., 1996—. Contbr. articles to profl. jours. Lt. Taiwanese Army, 1981-83. Recipient Pediatric Overseas Pub. award Mead Johnson, 1988, 90, Rsch. award Govt. of Taipei, 1989, 91, 92, 95, 96; Nat. Sci. Com. grantee, 1995, 98. Avocation: sports.

LIN, ZHENGDE, physician; b. Fuzhou, Fujian, China, Jan. 14, 1949; s. Junze and Qiyun (Zheng) L.; m. Zhou Fang; 1 child, Zhewen. Grad., Peking (China) U., 1992. Physician Heling Hosp., Fuzhou, 1975—. Author: The Use of Laser Irrodiation at Ashih Point for Anesthesia in Drawing a Tooth, 1991, The Inquire of Nd: YAP laser Indication Muscul Pteryideus Externus Spasm, 1992, One-filling Method of Acute and Chronic Pulpits using Nd:YAP Laser Cauterizing Medicine, 1992, Nd: YAP Laser Therapy Recurrent Oral Ulceration, 1996; contbr. articles to profl. jours. Mem. Zhongshan Clin. Medicine Assn. for Rsch. Shanghai. Chinese Peasant and Worker Dem. Party. Avocation: literature. Home: Gong-yuan Rd No 28, 350007 Fuzhou China Office: Heling Hosp, Liu-yi South Rd No 84, 350007 Fuzhou China

LIN, ZHENGPING, engineering executive; b. YuYao City, Zhejiang, People's Republic of China, Feb. 1, 1933; s. Xuezhi and Yunqing (Min) L.; m. Qing Pan, Feb. 17, 1973; children: Xiaomei, Gang. BS, Chiao-Tong U., Shanghai, 1953; diploma Sr. Engr., Ministry High Edn. State Coun., 1990. Cert. sr. engr. of prof. grade, People's Republic of China; cert. transformer elec. design, Australia. Engr. Design & Rsch. Ins. No. 8 MEEI, Shengyang, 1953-60; chief of design divsn. 220 kV Baoding Transformer Works, 1960-85; chief engr., dep. dir. No. 1 Hefei Transformer Works, 1985-93; engring. mgr., chief engr., tech. dir. Hefei ABB Transformer Co., 1993-95; sr. cons. Sys. Sales Rep., Inc. USA, Lyndonville, Vt., 1995-97; chief rep. Shanghai office Weidmann Sys. Internat., Inc., Lyndonville, Vt., 1998—. Contbr. articles to profl. jours. Mem. IEEE (sr. mem.), N.Y. Acad. Scis., Energy Resource Rsch. Assn. (coun. bd. dirs. 1990). Avocations: classical music, Chinese handwriting, painting. Home: 1219 Inwood Ter Fort Lee NJ 07024-1721 Office: Weidmann Sys Internat Inc PO Box 1388 Indsl Pky Lyndonville VT 05851

LIN, ZHIPING, electrical engineer, educator, researcher; b. Shantou, Guangdong, China, Aug. 8, 1958; s. Maoxing Lin and Qiaoxin Zeng; m. Long Li, Mar. 27, 1991; 1 child, Kelvin. B in Engring., South China Inst. Tech., Canton, 1982; PhD, U. Cambridge, Eng., 1987. Postdoctoral rschr. U. Calgary, Can., 1987-88; assoc. prof. Shantou U., 1988-93; tech. dir. Age D'Or Tech. Svcs. P/L, Singapore, 1993; sr. engr. DSO Nat. Labs., Singapore, 1993-99; assoc. prof. Nanyang Tech. U., Singapore, 1999—. Contbr. articles to profl. jours.; mem. editl. bd. Internat. Jour. Multidimensional Systems and Signal Processing, 1993—; inventor in field. Mem. IEEE. Avocation: swimming. Office: NTU Sch of EEE, Blk 52 Nanyang Ave, 639798 Singapore Singapore

LIN, ZONE-CHING, engineering educator; b. Taipei, Taiwan, Republic of China, Jan. 22, 1951; m. Shaw-Jen Lin; 2 children. BS, Nat. Cheng Kung U., Tainan, Taiwan, 1973; MS, Nat. Taiwan U., Taipei, 1975; PhD, Purdue U., 1984. Assoc. prof. Chung-Shan Inst. Sci. and Tech., Taiwan, 1977-89; prof. mech. engring. Nat. Taiwan U. of Sci. and Tech., Taipei, 1989—, chmn. dept. mech. engring., 1994-98, dean Coll. Engring., 1998—; cons. Adminstrn. of Econ. Affairs, Taipei, 1990—. Editor Jour. of Engineeers of the Chinese Inst., Jour. of the Chinese Soc. of Mech. Engrs. 2d lt. Army, 1973-75. Recipient Outstanding Rsch. award Nat. Sci. Coun., 1998. Fax: 886-2-2737-6460. E-mail: zclin@mail.ntust.edu.tw. Office: Nat Taiwan U Sci and Tech, 43 Keelung Rd Sect 4, 106 Taipei Taiwan, Republic of China

LIN, ZONG-CHI, mathematician educator; b. Yong-Tai, Fuzhou, China, May 14, 1930; s. Xue-Ping and Jiu-Mei (Chen) L.; m. Yu-Gui Huang, Aug. 27, 1957; children: Su-Rong, Su-Zhong. Dipl., Xia-Men U., 1956; postgrad., Beijing Fgn. Lang. Coll., 1958-60; Assoc. D of Math. & Physics, Moscow U., 1964. Teaching asst. Xi-An (China) Air Coll., 1956-57; from teaching asst. to assoc. prof. Fujian Normal U., Fuzhou, 1957-85, prof., 1986—. Co-author: Reference Book of New Mathematics, 1982, Theory and Application on Nonlinear Singular Perturbation, 1989, Perturbation Methods in Applied Math, 1994; editor: Annals of Differential Equations of China, 1988—; editorial com. Applied Math. and Mechanics, 1989—; contbr. articles to profl. jours. Recipient Sci. and Tech. Advancement prize Fujian Provincial Govt., 1979, 84, 86. Mem. Acad. Com. Fujian Province (math. sect.), Acad. Study Sincularly Perturbed Theory of China (vice-chmn. 1987—), Coun. of Fujian Systematic Engring., Fujian Overseas and Returned Scholars Assn., Math. Soc. China. Home: Duihu Rd Cangshan Dist, Rm 402 Bldg 2 Shida Yiyuan, Fuzhou 350007, Fujian China Office: Fujian Normal U, Math Dept, Fuzhou Fujian 350007, China

LIN, ZONGLI, electrical engineering educator; b. Fuqing, Fujian, China, Feb. 24, 1964; came to U.S., 1989; s. Changming Lin and Yuyan Chen; m. Jian K. Lin, June 22, 1992; children: Tony, Vivian. BS, Xiamen U., Fujian, 1983; M Engring., Chinese Acad. Space Tech., Beijing, 1989; PhD in Elec. Engring., Wash. State U., 1994. Engr. Chinese Acad. Space Tech., 1983-86; asst. prof. applied math. SUNY, Stony Brook, 1994-97; asst. prof. elec. engring. U. Va., Charlottesville, 1997—. Author: Low Gain Feedback, 1998; contbr. over 50 articles to sci. jours. Recipient young investigator award Office Naval Rsch., 1999. Mem. IEEE (sr.). E-mail: zl5y@virginia.edu. Office: U Va Dept Elec Engring Charlottesville VA 22903

LIÑÁN, AMABLE, aeronautical engineering educator; b. Noceda, Leon, Spain, Nov. 27, 1934; s. Paulino and Jacinta (Martínez) L.; m. Rosa Maria Gutierrez-Vidarte, May 21, 1965; children: Ignacio, F. Javier, Ana. Grad. in Aero. Engring., U. Politecnica, Madrid, 1960, Calif. Tech. Inst., 1963; Doctor (hon.), U. Carlos III, Madrid, 1994; D in Aero. Engring., U. Politecnica, 1996; Doctor (hon.), U. Zaragoza, Zaragoza, Spain, 1999. Rsch. engr. INTA, Madrid, 1960-76; asst. prof. U. Politecnica, 1961-65; prof. fluid mechanics Sch. Aero. Engring. U. Politecnica, Madrid, Conn., 1965—; dir. propulsion dept. U. Politecnica, Madrid, 1998—; vis. prof. U. Mich., Ann Arbor, 1973-74; prof. adj. Yale U., New Haven, Conn., 1997—. Recipient award in sci. and tech. rsch. Principe De Asturias, 1993, Castilla and Leon, 1995, Gold medal Combustion Inst., 1994. Mem. Real Academia De Ciencias De Espana, Acad. Ingenieria De Espana. Office: Escuela TS Ingenieros Aero, Pl Cardenal Cisneros 3, 28040 Madrid Spain

LINCICOME, DAVID RICHARD, biomedical and animal scientist; b. Champaign, Ill., Jan. 17, 1914; s. David Rosebery and Olive Iola (Casper) L.; m. Dorothy Lucile Van Cleave, Sept. 1, 1941 (dec. Nov. 1952); children: David Van Cleave, Judith Ann; m. Margaret Stirewalt, Dec. 29, 1953. BS, MS with high honors, U. Ill., 1937; PhD in Tropical Medicine, Tulane U., 1941. Diplomate (emeritus) Am. Bd. Microbiology; diplomate Am. Coll. Animal Physiology; cert. animal scientist Am. Registry Profl. Animal Scientists. Asst. instr. U. Ill., 1937; asst. instr. tropical medicine Tulane U. Med. Sch., 1937-41; asst. prof. parasitology U. Ky., 1941-47, U. Wis. Med. Sch., 1947-49; sr. rsch. parasitologist Du Pont Co., 1949-53; from asst. prof. to full prof. biol. Scis. Howard U., 1953-70; vis. sci. NIH, 1965-66; founder, registrar, Jacob Sheep Conservancy, 1988-96, bd. dirs., 1990-97, pres., 1996; vis. scholar Nat. Agrl. Libr., USDA, 1990-92; guest scientist USDA Exp. Sta., Beltsville, Md., 1978—, Naval Med. Rsch. Inst., 1954-62. Founder, editor Exptl. Parasitology, 1949-76; editor Transactions of the Ky. Acad. Sci., 1946-49, Transactions of the Am. Microscopical Soc., 1970-71, Internat. Rev. Tropical Medicine, 1953-63; founder Virology, 1950, Advances in Vet. Sci., 1952. Lt. col. Med. Svc. Corps, U.S. Army, World War II, PTO. Recipient Anniversary award Helminthological Soc., 1975; rsch. grantee NIH, 1958-68. Fellow AAAS, Explorers Club (nat., N.Y.); mem. Helminthological Soc. (pres. 1958, emeritus), Am. Physiol. Soc. (emeritus), Soc. Invertebrate Zoology (emeritus), Am. Soc. Zoologists (emeritus), Am. Soc. Parasitologists, Am. Soc. Cell Biology, Am. Microscopical Soc. (emeritus), Royal Soc. Tropical Medicine (emeritus), Am. Soc. Tropical Medicine (emeritus), Am. Goat Soc. (bd. dirs. 1990-96), Am. Dairy Goat Assn. (founder., 1st sec. rsch. found. 1979, bd. dirs. 1972-87), Nat. Pygmy Goat Assn. (bd. dirs. 1976-92, pres. 1979), Natural Colored Wool Growers Assn. (bd. dirs. 1988-94), Jacob Sheep Breeders Assn., Jacob Sheep Soc. (Eng.), Nat. Tunis Sheep Registry (bd. dirs. 1991-93, sec. 1991-92), Soft-coated Wheaten Terrier Club of Am. (mem rescue com. 1993-97, mem. health com. 2000—), Greater Washington D.C. Area Soft-Coated Wheaten Terrier Club (founder, pres. 1991-92, bd. dirs. 1999—), Am. Livestock Breeds Conservancy (bd. dirs. 1994-97), Va. State Dairy Goat Assn. (founder, pres. 1976, Friend of VSDGA award 1999), Midwestern Conf. Parasitologists (founder, 1st sec. 1949), Soc. Exptl. Biology & Medicine (sec. D.C. chpt. 1996, emeritus), Univ. Ill. Found., Univ. Ill. Pres. Coun., Ut Prosim Soc. (Va. Poly. Inst. and State U.), Va. State Dairy Goat Assn. (founder), Greater Washington Area Soft-Coated Wheaten Terrier Club, Phi Beta Kappa, Sigma Xi (pres. Howard U. chpt. 1962). Achievements include breeding of two rare and endangered breeds of sheep, Jacob and Tunis, early breeder of West African Pygmy Goats and a rare dog, the Soft-coated Wheaten Terrier; founder and first sec. The Rsch. Found. of the Am. Dairy Goat Assn.; founder Midwestern Conf. of Parasitologists; founder four sci. jours. Exptl. Parasitology, Internat. Rev. Tropical Medicine, Virology, and Advances in Vet. Sci. E-mail: wheaten@bellatlantic.net and sheepman@monumental.com. Home: PO Box 13 4419 Cambria Ave Garrett Park MD 20896

LINCKE, GERHARD MARTIN, chemistry educator; b. Gelsenkirchen, Germany, Feb. 24, 1929; s. Friedrich and Lotte (Springorum) L.; m. Gerda Bauer, Dec. 19, 1959; children: Barbara, Dorothea, Ursula. Diploma, U. Tuebingen, Germany, 1956, DPhil, 1959. Head lab. Sachtleben, Duisburg, Germany, 1960-63; mem. faculty Ingenieurschule, Krefeld, Germany, 1964-71; prof. Fachhochschule Niederrhein, Krefeld, Germany, 1971-94; retired, 1994. Contbr. articles to profl. jours. Mem. Gesellschaft Deutscher Chemiker. Avocations: history, natural sciences. Home: Selder 39, D-47918 Toenisvorst Germany Office: FH Niederrhein, Frankenring 20, D-47798 Krefeld Germany

LINCOLN, ALEXANDER, III, financier, lawyer, private investor; b. Boston, Dec. 1, 1943; s. Alexander Jr. and Elizabeth (Kitchel) L.; m. Isabel Fawcett Ross, Dec. 27, 1969. BA, Denver U., 1967; JD, Boston U., 1971. Bar: Colo. 1972, U.S. Ct. Appeals (10th cir.) 1972, U.S. Supreme Ct. 1979. Atty. Dist. Ct. Denver, 1973-78, Colo. Ct. Appeals, Denver, 1978-80; mng. ptnr. Alexander Lincoln & Co., Denver, 1980—. Mem. Colo. Bar Assn. (fin. com. 1975-76), Colo. Soc. Mayflower Descendants (life, bd. dirs. 1975—), Order of Founders and Patriots (life). Republican. Avocations: skiing, mountain climbing, horticulture. Home and Office: 121 S Dexter St Denver CO 80246-1052

LINCOLN, ANNA, company executive, foreign languages educator; b. Warsaw, Poland, Dec. 13, 1932; came to U.S., 1948; d. Wigdor Aron and Genia (Zalkind) Szpiro; m. Adrian Courtney Lincoln Jr., Sept. 22, 1951; children: Irene Anne, Sally Linda, Allen, Kirk. Student, U. Calif., Berkeley, 1949-50; BA in French and Russian with honors, NYU, 1965; student, Columbia Tchrs. Coll., 1966-67. Tchr. Waldwick (N.J.) H.S., 1966-69; chmn. Tuxedo Park (N.Y.) Red Cross, 1969-71; pres. Red Cross divsn. Vets. Hosp.; pres. China Pictures U.S.A. Inc., Princeton, N.J., 1994—; prof. fgn. rels. Fudan U., Shanghai, 1994—, prof. English and humanitarian studies, 1996—; adv. bd. guidance dept. Waldwick (N.J.) H.S., 1966-69; hon. bd. dirs. Shanghai Fgn. Lang. Assn., 1994; hon. prof. Fudan U., Shanghai, 1994; leader seminars pm Chinat at top univs., 1996—. Author: Escape to China, 1940-48, 1985, Chinese transl., 1985, The Art of Peace, 1995, Anna Lincoln Views China, 2000; publ.: China Beyond the Year 2000 and the Nature of Love, 1997, Anna Lincoln Views China, 1999; co-dir. (TV docudrama) Escape to China 1941-48, 1998. Hon. U.S. Goodwill amb. for peace and friendship, China, 1984, 85, 86, 88; founder Princeton-Lincoln Found., Inc., 1985—. Named Woman of Yr. Am. Biog. Soc., 1993; recipient Peace Through the Arts prize Assn. Internat. Mujeres en las Artes, Madrid, 1993. Mem. AAUW, Women's Coll. Club (publicity chmn. 1991-96), Lit. Coll. Princeton, Present Day Club. Avocations: reading, swimming, bridge, seminars, ballroom dancing. Home and Office: China Pictures USA Inc 550 Rosedale Rd Princeton NJ 08540-2315

LINCOLN, BRUCE KENNETH, anthropology and history of religions educator; b. Phila., Mar. 5, 1948; s. William D. Lincoln and Geraldine (Kovsky) Grossman; m. Louise Hassett Lincoln, Apr. 17, 1971; children: Martha, Rebecca. BA, Haverford Coll., Pa., 1970; MA, U. Chgo., 1973, PhD, 1976. Asst. prof. Humanities and religious Studies U. Minn., Mpls., 1976-79, assoc. prof., 1979-84, prof., 1984-94; prof. history of religion, anthropology, classics U. Chgo., 1993—; vis. prof. U. Siena, 1984-85, U. Uppsala, 1985, Novosibirsk State Pedagogical Inst., 1991, U. Copenhagen, 1998. Author: Priests, Warriors and Cattle: A Study in the Ecology of Religions, 1981, Emerging from the Chrysalis: Studies in Rituals of Women's Initiation, 1981, Myth, Cosmos, and Society: Indo-European Themes of Creation and Destruction, 1986, Discourse and the Construction of Society: Comparative Studies of Myth, Ritual and Classification, 1989, Death, War, and Sacrifice: Studies in Ideology and Practice, 1991, Authority: Construction and Corrosion, 1994, Theorizing Myth: Narrative, Ideology and Scholarship, 1999; editor: Religion, Rebellion, Revolution, 1985; contbr. articles to profl. jours. Grantee Am. Coun. Learned Soc. Travel, 1979, Rockefeller Found. Rsch. Conf. 1981, A,. Coun. of Learned Soc. Rsch., 1982-83, Guggenheim Meml. Found. Rsch., 1986. Home: 5735 S Dorchester Ave Chicago IL 60637-1726 Office: Univ of Chgo 1025 E 58th St Chicago IL 60637-1509

LINCOLN, EDWARD PALMER, biologist, research scientist; b. N.Y.C., Oct. 23, 1930; s. James Rufus and Helen (Palmer) L.; m. Gloria Reyes Capco, May 31, 1968; children: Edward Palmer Jr., Laura Capco. AB, U. Ariz., 1953, MS, 1961, PhD, 1972. Scientist dept. agrl. and biol. engring. U. Fla., Gainesville, 1973—, prof. dept. agrl. and biol. engring., 1984—. Prodr. (documentary) Jungle Road; author: Somatic Characterization, 1972; contbr. articles to profl. jours. Sgt. U.S. Army, 1953-55. Mem. AAAS, Nat. Geographic Soc., N.Y. Acad. Sci. Achievements include co-discovery of an internally predatious fish in the Amazon River. Home: 809 SW 21st Ave Gainesville FL 32601-8419 Office: Dept Agrl and Biol Engring U Fla Gainesville FL 32601

LINCOLN, JIMY, small business owner; b. Dec. 9, 1971. BS in Bus. Mgmt., Ga. Inst. Tech., 1997. Owner 3d Team Sports, Lithonia, Ga., 1995—. Home: 2350 Cobb Pkwy SE Apt 16A Smyrna GA 30080-2735 Office: 811 Bristol Way Lithonia GA 30058-8253

LINCOLN, PATRICK JOHN, hemogeneticist, educator; b. Rougham, England, May 30, 1939; s. Percy and Hylda (Asker) L.; m. Christine Bullock, Mar. 19, 1966 (div. June 1971). BSc, U. Leicester, 1960; PhD, U. London, 1967. Scientific officer Blood Transfusion Svc., London, 1960-65; from rsch. asst. to hon. fellow, reader emeritus St. Bartholomew's/Royal London Sch. Medicine & Dentistry, 1965—. Co-author: Blood Group Serology, 5th edit., 1977, 6th edit., 1988; editor: (with J. Thomson) Forensic DNA Profiling Protocols, 1998, (with B. Olaisen and B. Brinkmann) Progress in Forensic Genetics 7, 1998 (with G. Sensabaugh and B. Olaisen) Progress in Forensic Genetics 8, 2000; assoc. editor Forensic Sci. Internat., 1982-99, cons. assoc. editor, 1999—; assoc. editor Transfusion Medicine, 1991-98; sci. editor Medicine Sci. and the Law, 1995—; editor Forensic Sci. Rev., 1989—; med. editl. bd. Legal Medicine, 1999—; contbr. chpts. to books, articles to profl. jours. Fellow Royal Coll. Pathologists, Royal Soc. Medicine London; mem. Internat. Soc. Forensic Haemogenetics (treas. 1987-99), Br. Acad. Forensic Scis. (pres. 1991-92), British Blood Transfusion Soc. (pubs. com. 1993-99). Avocations: walking, gardening, music, travel, complementary therapies. Office: St Barts/, Royal London Sch Medicine, Turner St, London E1 2AD, England

LIND, PEHR ANDERS RUNE MICHAEL, oncologist; b. Gothenburg, Sweden, Dec. 10, 1960; s. Rune Nils and Gerd Louvisa (Samuelsson) L. Med. Licentiate, U. Uppsala, Sweden, 1987, MD, 1989; PhD, Karolinska Inst., Stockholm, 1999. Specialist in oncology and radiotherapy. Dr. King Gustaf the V's Jubilee Clinic, Gothenburg, Sweden, 1989, Radium Hemmet Karolinska Hosp., Stockholm, 1990, Stockholm South Hosp., 1990-94; sr. cons. Huddinge U. Hosp., Stockholm, 1994—; sr. rsch. assoc. dept. radiation oncology Duke U., Raleigh, N.C., 2000. Editor: (jour.) Swedish Uro-Oncology, 1993-95; contbr. rsch. articles to profl. jours. Lt. Swedish Army, 1980. Mem. Swedish Soc. Oncology, Swedish Soc. Uro-Oncology, Swedish Norwegian Testicular Cancer Group. Conservative. Lutheran. Avocations: mountaineering, fishing, hunting. Home: Brännkyrkag 99-2, 117 26 Stockholm Sweden Office: Huddinge U Hosp, Södra Stockholms Oncol, 141 57 Huddinge Sweden

LINDAHL, ANDERS HARALD, medical educator; b. Stockholm, Jan. 24, 1954; s. Harald Sven and Helvig Marianne (Samuelsson) L.; m. Carin Ingrid Ericsson, May 29, 1981; children: Carl, Carolina, Anna Maria. MD, U. Gothenburg, Sweden, 1979, PhD in Physiology, 1986. Bd. cert. in clin. chemistry. Rschr. U. Gothenburg, 1982-86; rsch. fellow Harvard Med. Sch., Boston, 1988-89; resident Sahlgrens U. Hosp., Gothenburg, 1989-93, assoc. prof. clin. chemistry, 1994-2000, prof., 2000—. Contbr. articles to profl. jours.; patentee in field. Recipient Biotech. award Am. Acad. Anti Aging Medicine, 1994, award Lundberg Found, 1996, Jublee prize Swedish Med. Assn., 1995. Mem. Endocrine Soc. U.S., Orthopedic Rsch. Soc. U.S., N.Y. Acad. Scis., Scandinavian Physiol. Soc., Swedish Endocrine Soc., Internat. Cartilage Repair Soc. (bd. dirs.). Avocations: golfing, sailing, skiing. Office: Sahlgrens U Hosp Inst Lab M, Dept Clin Chem/Transf Med, S-41345 Göteborg Sweden

LINDAHL, ANNE KARIN, surgeon, researcher; b. Oslo, May 31, 1960; d. Rolf and Ingeborg (Kleppa) L.; children: Line, Mari. MD, U. Oslo, 1986, PhD, 1992, postgrad. in Health Adminstrn., 1997-98. Rsch. fellow The Norwegian Cancer Assn., 1988-92; fellowship in gen. surgery and vascular surgery Aker Hosp., U. Oslo, 1988-92, 93-97; mem. com. and bds. med. faculty U. Oslo, 1988-97; vis. scientist Emory U., Atlanta, 1992-93; vascular surgeon Aver Hosp., 1993-99, Nat. Hosp., 1999-2000; sr. cons. Islo Ctr. Vascular Surgery, 2000—. Author: Kvinne og lege, 1984. Recipient 1st award Oslo Vascular Biology Club, 1991, Unger-Vetlesen Legacy, Channel Island, Jersey, 1992, Nedron prize, Oslo, 1993. Mem. Internat. Soc. Vascular Surgery, Internat. Soc. Thrombosis and Haemostasis, Norwegian Surg. Soc., Am. Heart Assn. (Travelling award 1993). Office: Oslo Ctr Vascular Surgery, Aller U Hosp, Oslo Norway

LINDAHL, GÖRAN, manufacturing and engineering executive; b. Umea, Sweden, Apr. 28, 1945; arrived in Switzerland, 1987; s. Sven Amandus and Frida Johanna (Johansson) L.; m. Kristina Gunnarsdotter, Mar. 13, 1971; children: Mattias, Anna-Stina. Grade in Astronomy, U. Gothenburg, 1970; MEE, Chalmers U. Tech., 1971, DSc in Engring. (hon.), 1993. Various positions ASEA, Ludvika, Sweden, 1971-77, mgr. high voltage testing lab., 1977-80, mgr. mktg. and sales for transformers, 1980-83, pres. transformers bus. area, 1983-85; pres. Asea Transmission, Vasteras, Sweden, 1985-86; exec. v.p., mem. group mgmt. ASEA AB, Vasteras, 1986-87; exec. v.p., mem. group mgmt. bus. segment power transmission ABB Asea Brown Boveri Ltd., Zurich, 1988-96; responsible for Asia Pacific, India, 1992-94, Mid. East, North Africa, 1994-96; pres., CEO ABB Ltd., Zurich, 1997—. Office: ABB Ltd, Affolternstrasse 44, CH-8050 Zurich Switzerland

LINDAHL, OLOF ANTON, biomedical engineering researcher, educator; b. Örnsköldsvik, Sweden, Nov. 16, 1955; s. Carl and Ann-Marie Kristin (Forsgren) L.; m. Mona Barbro Katarina Karlsson; 1 child, Emma. MS, Linköping (Sweden) U., 1979, PhD, 1993. Cert. clin. engr. at level of MS. Clin. engr. U. Hosp. No. Sweden, Umeå, 1979; rsch. engr. Umeå U., 1980-82; R & D mgr. U. Hosp. No. Sweden, 1982-93; project coord. Uminova Ctr., Umeå, 1988—; faculty clin. engring. U. Hosp. No. Sweden, 1994-96, assoc. prof., 1996—, vis. prof., 1999; bd. mem. RSA Co., Ltd., Umeå, 1994-97; dep. bd. mem. Uminova Found., 1994-97; del. of Gen. Assembly of Internat. Fedn. Med. and Biol. Engring., 1989—; sec., v.p. Med. Tech. and Med. Physics Found., 1990—. Contbr. articles to profl. scientific jours., including Acta Physiol. Scandinavia, Jour. Med. Engring. and Computing, others. Devel. grantee Swedish Nat. Bd. Tech. Devel., 1985, rsch. grantee Swedish Nat. Bd. Indsl. and Tech. Devel., 1996, 97; travel grantee Wallenberg Found., 1995, Anna Cederborg Found., 1991. Mem. Swedish Soc. Med. Tech. and Med. Physics (pres. 1989-90). Avocations: hunting, fishing, reading. Office: Umeå U, Uminova Ctr, S-90187 Umeå Sweden

LINDAUER, JEROME IRA, chemist; b. N.Y.C., Feb. 13, 1941. BS, Columbia U., 1965, MS, 1967. V.p. Internat. Flavors & Fragrances, N.Y.C., 1967—. Patentee in field (26). Mem. Soc. Cosmetic Chemists, Cosmetic, Toiletry, Fragrance Assn. Office: Internat Flavors & Fragrances 650 Highway 36 Hazlet NJ 07730-1704

LINDBERG, FREDRIK, surgeon; b. Nyköping, Sweden, Feb. 13, 1962; s. Jean and Berit (Nilsson) L.; m. Chamilla Steinvall, Feb. 17, 1996. MD, Karolinska Inst., Stockholm, 1989. Intern, resident Skellefteå Hosp., Sweden, 1989-96, cons. surgeon, 1997—. Lt. Swedish AFR, 1982—. Mem. European Assn. for Endoscopic Surgery, Swedish Surg. Soc. E-mail: fred-lind@sverige.nu. Home: Måbärsgatan 58, Ursviken Sweden 932 37 Office: Dept Surgery, Skellefteå Lasarett, Skellefteå Sweden 931 86

LINDBERG, GUNNAR, physician, scientist; b. Vaxholm, Sweden, Nov. 27, 1941; s. Lennart and Kajsa L.; m. Arja von Ritter, June 19, 1975. BE, Teknikum, Gothenburg, Sweden, 1967; MD, Gothenburg U., 1978; PhD, Lund (Sweden) U., 1992. Asst. physician Gothenburg County Coun., 1976-78, Malmöhus County Coun., Lund, 1979-83; cons. indsl. medicine Kristianstad (Sweden) County Coun., 1984; cons. cmty. medicine Värmland County Coun., Karlstad, Sweden, 1985-88; sr. physician Ctr. Pub. Health Rsch., Karlstad, 1989-95; clin. epidemiologist The NEPI Found., Malmö, Sweden, 1995—; assoc. prof. family medicine Lund U., 1994—. Contbr. numerous papers, articles to profl. jours. Swedish Nat. Assn. Heart and Chest Diseases grantee, 1990; Swedish Med. Rsch. Coun. grantee, 1995. Mem. Am. Heart Assn., Swedish Soc. Medicine (grantee 1994). Home: Storgatan 43, SE-240 30 Marieholm Sweden Office: The NEPI Found, Med Rsch Ctr, Malmö U Hosps, SE205 02 Malmö Sweden

LINDBERG, LARS OLAV, anesthesiologist, intensivist, consultant; b. Nässjö, Sweden, Aug. 27, 1956; s. Pär and Eisa Lindberg; m. Eva Larsson, June 7, 1997; 1 child, Andreas. MD, U. Umeå, Sweden, 1981; PhD, U. Lund, Sweden, 1996. Intern Ctrl. Hosp., Gällivare, Sweden, 1981-82; resident Regional Hosp., Östersund, Sweden, 1982-83; resident Univ. Hosp., Lund, 1983-86, locum cons., 1988-93, cons., 1996—; cons. Univ. Hosp., Malmö, Sweden, 1994-96; interim dir. adult and pediat. cardiothoracic ICU Univ. Hosp., Lund, 1988-93. Inventor in field. Scholar Brit. Jour. Anesthesia, 1988. Mem. Swedish Med. Assn., Soc. Critical Care Medicine, European Soc. Heart and Lung Transplantation. Fax: 46-0-46-176050. Home: Hästskovägen 18, S-24657 Barsebäck Sweden Office: Dept Anesthes/Int Care, Univ Hosp Lund, S-221 85 Lund Sweden

LINDBERG, UNO MÅRTEN, biologist educator; b. Silbodal, Sweden, May 19, 1939; s. Edvin Manfred and Karin Elisabet (Lundberg) L.; m. Ann Margret Röhstö, May 30, 1962; children: Anna Karin, Rebecka. MD, PhD, Karolinska Inst., 1967. Prof. Stockholm U., 1981—; vis. prof. Princeton (N.J.) U., 1988-89. Eleanor Roosevelt Postdoctoral fellow Internat. Union Against Cancer, 1969; Fulbright fellow, 1995-96. Mem. Swedish Royal Acad. Sci., Am. Soc. for Cell Biology, European Cytoskeletal Forum, Biophys. Soc. Office: Stockholm U, WGI Cell Biology, S-10691 Stockholm Sweden

LINDBLAD, INGA-BRITT ELISABETH, communications educator; b. Umeaa, Sweden, Jan. 6, 1945; d. Helge Karl and Ragnhild Elisabeth (Oehman) Gidlund; m. Anders Olof Albert Lindblad, July 14, 1970; children: Jenny, Johan. MA, Umeå U., 1972, PhD, 1985. Qualied secondary sch. tchr. Umeå, Sweden, 1972-76; sr. lectr. Dept. of Scandinavian Langs., Sweden, 1977-93; rsch. fellow Dept. of Media and Comms., Sweden, 1989-93; head of dept. media and comm. Umea U., 1993—; mem. humanistic faculty bd. Umeå U., Sweden, 1993-96, mem. undergrad. program com. of the humanistic faculty. Contbr. articles to profl. jours. Mem. Norrmjole Golf Club. Avocations: golf, downhill skiing, sailing, traveling. Home: Hyggesv 13F, S-90346 Umeå Sweden Office: Media/Comms Studies, U Umeå, S-90187 Umeå Sweden

LINDBLAD, MICHAEL JAN TORSTEN, jewelry producer; b. Degerfors, Sweden, July 30, 1952; s. Torsten Ruthstrom and Marianne Ingrid (Lilja) Littorin; m. Nettipa Somwong, Mar. 12, 1989; 1 child, Chanon Jon Michael. BS, U. Gothenburg, Sweden, 1980. Managing dir. Jatomi Jewelry, Gothenburg, Sweden, 1982-89, Degerfors, Sweden, 1989—; managing dir. Precious Products Co., Ltd., Bangkok, Thailand, 1990; gemologist Asian Inst. of Gemological Scis., 1990. Mem. Thai Gems and Jewelry Assn., Thai C. of C. Office: Precious Products Jewelry Co Ltd, Soi Sunthorn5 Soi Petchkasem69, Bangkok 10160, Thailand

LINDBLOM YLANNE, SARI A., educational researcher, conference manager; b. Helsinki, Finland, May 6, 1960; d. Seppo O. and Anneli M. (Johanson) L.; m. Kari T. Ylanne, Nov. 28, 1981; children: Jonne, Joonas, Julius. MA, U. Helsinki, 1986, Licentiate of Philosophy, 1998, PhD, 1999. Legalized psychologist. Researcher Faculty of Medicine U. Helsinki, 1987-98, conf. mgr. Devel. of Studies, 1998—; dir. Nat. Med. Sch. "Learning-from-Text" test Design Bd., Helsinki, 1987—; sec. Nat. Med. Sch. Entrance Examination Bd., Helsinki, 1997-99. Author: Studying in a Traditional Medical Curriculum - Study Success, Orientations to Studying and Problems that Arise, 1999; editor abstract. Mem. Finnish Psychol. Assn., Am. Ednl. Rsch. Assn., European Assn. Rsch. on Learning and Instrn. Avocations: sports, music. Office: U Helsinki Devel of Studies, PO Box 3, Helsinki 00014, Finland

LINDBORG, KEIHAN, food technologist; b. Tehran, Iran, Sept. 21, 1963; arrived in Sweden, 1988; d. Nasser Mani and Fari Dayani; m. Anders Lindborg, Oct. 1, 1994; 1 child, Daniel. BSc, U. Tenn., 1988; PhD, U. Lund, Sweden, 1995. Cert. food engr. Food technologist Nestle R & D Ctr., Bjuv, Sweden, 1995—; presenter in field. Contbr. articles to profl. jours. including Cereal Chemistry, Jour. Food Sci. Am. Trans. Nordic Rheology Soc. Mem. Inst. Food Technologists, Am. Assn. Cereal Chemists. Avocations: travel, cooking. Home: Frostgatan 78, S-26035 Ödåkra Sweden Office: Nestle R & D Ctr, Box 520, S-267 25 Bjuv Sweden

LINDE, LUCILLE MAE (JACOBSON), motor-perceptual specialist; b. Greeley, Colo., May 5, 1919; d. John Alfred and Anna Julia (Anderson) Jacobson; m. Ernest Emil Linde, July 5, 1946 (dec. Jan. 27, 1959). BA, Colo. State Coll. of Edn., 1941, MA, 1947; EdD, U. No. Colo., 1974. Cert. tchr. Calif., Colo., Iowa, N.Y.; cert. ednl. psychologist; guidance counselor. Dean of women, dir. residence C.W. Post Coll. of L.I. Univ., 1965-66; asst. dean of students SUNY, Farmingdale, 1966-67; counselor, tchr. West High Sch., Davenport, Iowa, 1967-68; instr. grad. tchrs. and counselors, univ. counselor, researcher No. Ariz. U., Flagstaff, 1968-69; vocat. edn. and counseling coord. Fed. Exemplary Project, Council Bluffs, Iowa, 1970-71; sch. psychologist, counselor Oakdale Sch. Dist., Calif., 1971-73; sch. psychologist, intern Learning and Counseling Ctr., Stockton, Calif., 1972-74; pvt. practice rsch. in motor-perceptual tng. Greeley, 1975—; rschr. ocumeter survey Lincoln Unified Sch. Dist., Stockton, 1980, 81, 82, Manteca (Calif.) H.S., 1981; spkr. Social Sci. Edn. Consortium, U. Colo., Boulder, 1993; mem. Monday Morning steering com. House Spkr. Newt Gingrich, 1997-98; mem. Attention Disorder Advocacy Group, 1997-2000; attend seminars for ADD and ADHD, alleviating lag/dysfunctional in neural system noted, 1997-98, 1998-99, presenter seminars in field. Author: Psychological Services and Motor Perceptual Training, 1974, Guidebook for Psychological Services and Motor Perceptual Training (How One May Improve in Ten Easy Lessons!), 1992, Manual for the Lucille Linde Ocumeter: Ocular Pursuit Measuring Instrument, 1992, Motor-Perceptual Training and Visual Perceptual Research (How Students Improved in Seven Lessons!), 1992, Effects of Motor Perceptual Training on Academic Achievement and Ocular Pursuit Ability, 1992; inventor ocumeter, instrument for measuring ocular tracking ability, 1989, target for use, 1991; patentee in field. Mem. Rep. Presdl. Task Force, 1989-96, trustee, 1991-92, charter mem., 1994—, life mem., 1994-95; mem. Rep. Nat. Com., 1990, 93-2000, Rep. Nat. Com. on Am. Agenda, 1993, Nat. Rep. Congl. Com., 1990, 92, 93, 95-2000, Nat. Fedn. Rep. Women, Greeley Rep. Women, 1996-2000; advisor Senator Bob Dole for Pres.; charter mem. Rep. Newt Gingrich's Speaker's Task Force, Senator Phil Gramm's Presdl. Steering Com.; at-large- del. Rep. Platform Planning Com.; team leader Nat. Rep. Rapid Response Network, Campaign America, 1996; active Heritage Found. (certificate as honored mem. leadership adv. bd., 1998-2000), Christian Bus. Men's Assn., Friends U. N.C. Librs., Citizens Against Govt. Waste, 1996-2000, Concerns of Police Survivors, 1996-98, Nat. Assn. of Police Orgn., elected to Libr. of Congress Nat. membership, 1997-99. Recipient Presdl. medal of merit and lapel insignia, 1990, Nat. Rep. Senatorial Com., 1991-2000, cert. of appreciation Nat. Rep. Congl. Com., 1992, 95, lapel pin Rep. Senatorial Inner Circle, 1990-96, Rep. Presdl. commemorative honor roll, 1993, Rep. Senatorial Freedom medal, 1994, Rep. Legion of Merit award, 1994, 96, Rep. Congl. Order of Freedom award, 1995, Senatorial Inner Cir. Lapel Pin, 1998, Lapel Pin award RNC, 1996, Leadership citation Rep. Senatorial Inner Cir./ Rep. Nat. Conv., 1996, Legion of Merit Rep. Presdl. exec. com., 1996, Honor cert. House Spkr. Newt Gingrich, 1996, conservative leadership award Young Am.'s Found., 1999; named to Rep. Nat. Hall of Honor, 1992. Mem. AAUP, NAFE, Nat. Assn. Sch. Psychologists and Psychometrists (spkr. conf. 1976), Rep. Senatorial Inner Cir. (name engraved on Ronald Wilson Reagan Eternal Flame of Freedom, 1995, on the Nat. Rep. Victory Monument, Washington, 1996, Rep. Sen. Inner Cir. Conv. Medallion 1996, RNC Mems. Only pin 1996), 20th Century Rep. Leader, Rep. Sen. Inner Cir., 1998, The Smithsonian Assocs., Ronald Reagan Presdl. Libr. and Mus., Bush Presdl. Libr. and Mus., Nat. Trust for Hist. Preservation, Internat. Platform Assn., Friends of Newt Gingrich, 1998-99, Independence Inst., Assn. Children Learning Disabilities (spkr. internat. conv. 1976), Libr. of Congress Assn., 1999, CHADD (Chldrn. and Adults with Attention Deficit Disorder), Learning Disabilities Assn. of Colorado, Natl. Fragile X Found., Fraxa Rsch. Found., 1999, Pi Omega Pi, Pi Lambda Theta. Avocations: music, archtl. design. Home: 1954 18th Ave Greeley CO 80631-5208

LINDE, TORBJORN G.S., physician; b. Skovde, Sweden; s. Gunnar S.R. and Gerd L. (Arvidsson) L.; m. Helena T. Furster, Aug. 9, 1986; children: Henrik, Ebba, Ulrika, Hedvig. MD, U. Uppsala, Sweden, 1987, PhD, 1994. Medical diplomate. Resident in internal medicine Nephrology, Uppsala, 1987—. Home: Dept Internal Medicine, U Hosp, SE-75185 Uppsala Sweden

LINDEGAARD, JACOB CHRISTIAN, oncologist, researcher; b. Frederiksberg, Copenhagen, Aug. 19, 1959; s. Olav Christian and Hanne Egelund (Christensen) L.; m. Lisbeth Moesgaard Thomsen, Aug. 5, 1989; children: Anders Christian, Anne Marie, Morten Peter. MD, Aarhus (Denmark) U., 1988, DMSc, 1993. Asst. prof. Danish Cancer Soc., Aarhus, 1988-91; resident med. dept. Viborg (Denmark) Hosp., 1991; resident in hematology Aarhus U. Hosp., 1991-92, sr. resident in oncology, 1993; resident in surgery Odder Hosp., 1992-93; sr. resident in oncology Copenhagen U. Hosp., 1996-97, Aarhus U. Hosp., 1997—. Contbr. numerous articles to profl. jours. With Danish Army, 1979-80. Fellow European Soc. for Therapeutic Radiology and Oncology, Nordic Soc. Gynecologic Oncology. Office: U Hosp Dept Oncology, Dept Oncology, DK-8000 Århus Denmark

LINDEGAARD, KARL-FREDRIK, neurosurgeon, educator; b. Oslo, Norway, Sept. 11, 1946; s. Karl Fredrik and Ingrid Anne (Gundersen) L. MD, U. Oslo, 1971, PhD, 1989. Cert. specialist in neurosurgery. Resident Nat. Hosp., Oslo, 1975-89, neurosurgeon, 1989-97, chief pediatric neurosurgery, 1991-93, chief neurovascular surgery, 1997—; prof. neurosurgery U. Oslo, 1999—. Contbr. chpts. to handbooks, more than 60 articles to profl. jours. Recipient HM The King of Norway Gold medal U. Oslo, 1986, Monrad-Krohn award for neurosci. rsch., 1995. E-mail: lindega@online.no. Office: Rikshospitalet, Oslo Norway N-0027

LINDEGAARD, KIRSTEN KELSTRUP, retired advocate; b. Aarhus, Denmark, Mar. 31, 1938; d. Sigurd Thomsen and Agnete (Kelstrup) Wegener-Thomsen; m. Kaj Louis Hendriksen, Mar. 30, 1970 (div. Nov. 1983); children: Birgitte Steenbeck, Thorbjørn Henriksen, Karsten Henriksen; m. Hans Lindegaard, May 12, 1984. Gen. cert., Kolding, Denmark, 1958; med. student, U. Copenhagen, 1959-63, grad. in law, 1974, degree in psychology, 1994. Apptd. Superior Ct., 1978. With Lab. Rigshospitalet, Copenhagen, 1963-64; lawyer Copenhagen, 1974-84. Co-author: My Mother Died—My Father Died, 1999. Mem. N.Y. Acad. Scis. Avocations: painting, drawing, playing piano. Home: Le Pujet, 09000 Serres Sur Arget France

LINDELL, ERIC WILLIAM, lawyer; b. Seattle, Aug. 29, 1960; s. Bill and Jan Lindell; m. Marisa Velling, Nov. 16, 1991; 1 child. BA, Ctrl. Washington U.; JD, Willamette U., 1987. Bar: U.S Dist. Ct. Trial atty. Soc. Counsel Representing Accused, Seattle, 1989-95; atty. Leer & Moore PS, Seattle, 1995-96; ptnr. Wieck Lindell, PLLC, Issaquah, Wash., 1997—. Named Super Lawyer Wash. Law and Politics Mag., 1999. Mem. Assn. Trial Lawyers of Am., Wash. State Bar Assn., Wash. State Trial Lawyers Assn., Wash. Assn. Criminal Def. Attys. Office: Wieck Lindell PLLC 175 NE Gilman Blvd Issaquah WA 98027-2904

LINDELL, HENRY NILS, research chemist; b. Jakobstad, Finland, Apr. 21, 1952; s. Rainer Algot and Raili Teresia (Kuorikoski) L.; m. Anne Sinikka Yli-Pentti, Oct. 4, 1980; children: Thomas, Christian. BSc, Åbo (Finland) Acad., 1977, MSc, 1979, Lic Phil, 1983, PhD, 1991. Head analytical lab. Enso Rsch. Ctr., Imatra, Finland, 1980-86, lab. mgr., 1986-91, sr. scientist, 1991-93, rsch. mgr., 1993-98; rsch. dir. Stora Enso Rsch., 1999—; project chmn. Nordic Industry Fund, Oslo, 1994-97; mem. work groups European Standardization Com., 1994—. Contbr. articles to sci. jours. Mem. Assn. Finnish Chem. Socs. (bd. dirs. sensory rsch. divsn. 1992-94). Avocations: music, travel. Office: Stora Enso Oyj, Rsch Ctr Imatra, FIN-55800 Imatra Finland

LINDEMANN, KURT, wholesale distribution executive. CEO, Edeka Zentrale, Hamburg, Germany; now chmn. bd. mgmt. AVA Allgemeine Handelsgesellschaft der Verbraucher AG, Hamburg. Office: New York Ring 6, 22297 Hamburg Germany*

LINDEMULDER, LAURIE, piano educator, concert pianist; b. Detroit, Jan. 22, 1938; d. Ralph Leslie and Wilmine (Vanderveen) L.; m. Charles Thomas Harris, Jan. 15, 1966; children: Leslie Law Harris, Charles Jason Harris. MusB, U. Mich., 1959; MusM, U. Mich., 1961. Mem. faculty Kingswood Sch. Cranbrook, Bloomfield Hills, Mich., 1959-60, Detroit Inst. Musical Art, 1962-65, Detroit Cmty. Music Sch., 1962-65; self-employed, 1966-81; mem. faculty Wayne County C.C., Detroit, 1969-71; pianist Theater on Wheels, Houston, 1981-83; mgr., tchr. Loftis Music Studios, Houston, 1987-91; tchr. Houston Conservatory of Music, Houston, 1990-92; self-employed private studio, Houston, 1989—; tchg. artist Tex. Inst. Arts in Edn., Houston, 1996—; founding mem. Music For a While Concert series, Grosse Pointe Woods, Mich., 1978-81; originator Arts Always, Houston, 1984-86; musician piano duet team with Alice Ellison, Detroit, 1963-94, with Norman Shack, Houston, 1994-2000; musician two piano team with Sheila Johnstone Ferrendelli, 2000—. Vol. dir. camera person First Presbyn. Ch. Houston; founding sec. Cy-Fair Assn. for Edn. Academically Talented, 1984; chmn. Cultural Arts Com., Houston, 1984-86. Travel grantee Cultural Arts Coun. Houston, 1999. Mem. Music Tchrs. Nat. Assn., Nat. Piano Tchrs. Guild, Houston Music Tchrs. Assn. (v.p., program chmn. 1994-97, pres.-elect 1997-98, pres. 1998-2000), Bayou City Federated Music Club (founding pres. 1995—), The Tuesday Musical Club (Houston, 1990—). Home and Office: 4507 Richmond Ave Houston TX 77027-6709

LINDEN, HENRY ROBERT, chemical engineering research executive; b. Vienna, Austria, Feb. 21, 1922; came to U.S., 1939, naturalized, 1945; s. Fred and Edith (Lermer) L.; m. Natalie Govedarica, 1967; children by previous marriage: Robert, Debra. BS, Ga. Inst. Tech., 1944; MChemE, Poly. U., 1947; PhD, Ill. Inst. Tech., 1952. Chem. engr. Socony Vacuum Labs., 1944-47; with Inst. of Gas Tech., 1947-78, various rsch. mgmt. positions, 1947-61, dir., 1961-69, exec. v.p., dir., 1969-74, pres., trustee, 1974-78; various acad. appointments Ill. Inst. Tech., Chgo, 1954-86, Frank W. Gunsaulus Disting. Prof. chem. engring., 1987-90, McGraw prof. energy and power engring. and mgmt., 1990—, interim pres., CEO, 1989-90, interim chmn., CEO Ill. Inst. Tech. Rsch. Inst., 1989-90; COO, GDC, Inc., Chgo., 1965-73; CEO Gas Devel. Corp. subs. Inst. Gas Tech., Chgo., 1973-78, also bd. dirs.; pres., dir. Gas Rsch. Inst., Chgo., 1976-87, exec. advisor, 1987—. Author tech. articles; holder U.S. and fgn. patents in fuel tech. Recipient award of merit oper. sect. Am. Gas Assn., 1956, Disting. Svc. award, 1974, Gas Industry Rsch. award, 1982, R&D award Nat. Energy Resources Orgn., 1986, Homer H. Lowry award for excellence in fossil energy rsch. U.S. Dept. Energy, 1991, award U.S. Energy Assn., 1993, Walton Clark medal Franklin Inst., 1972, Bunsen-Pettenkofer-Ehrentafel medal Deutscher Verein des Gas und Wasserfaches, 1978, Alumni medal Ill. Inst. Tech., 1995, Lifetime Achievement award The Energy Daily jour., 1996; named to Hall of Fame, Ill. Inst. Tech., 1982, Engring. Hall of Fame Ga. Tech., 1996. Fellow AIChE (Ernest W. Thiele award 2000), Inst. Energy; mem. NAE, Am. Chem. Soc. (recipient H.H. Storch award, chmn. divsn. fuel chemistry 1967, councilor 1969-77), So. Gas Assn. (hon. life). Office: Ill Inst Tech PH 135 10 W 33rd St Ph 135 Chicago IL 60616-3730

LINDENBAUM, JEFFREY OWEN, radiologist; b. Dec. 21, 1958. MD, PhD, Albert Einstein Coll., 1988. Resident Columbia Presbyn. Med. Ctr., N.Y.C.; chmn. dept. radiology Wayne (N.J.) Gen. Hosp., 1998—; pres. Preakness Radiol. Assocs., Wayne, 1998—. Cardiovascular & Interventional Radiology fellow Columbia Presbyn. Med. Ctr. Home: 16 Beaver Ridge Rd Morris Plains NJ 07950-1901

LINDENBAUM, S(EYMOUR) J(OSEPH), physicist; b. N.Y.C., Feb. 3, 1925; s. Morris and Anne Lindenbaum; m. Leda Isaacs, June 29, 1958. AB, Princeton U., 1945; MA, Columbia U., 1949, PhD, 1951. With Brookhaven Nat. Lab., Upton, N.Y., 1951-96, sr. physicist, 1963-96, sr. physicist emeritus, 1996—, group leader high energy physics research group, 1954-89; vis. prof. U. Rochester, 1958-59; Mark W. Zemansky chair in physics CCNY, 1970-95, Mark Zemansky prof. emeritus of physics, 1995—; cons. Centre de Etudes Nucleaire de Saclay, France, 1957, CERN, Geneva, 1962; head CCNY Experimental High Energy and Nuclear Physics Rsch. Group, 1970—; dep. for sci. affairs ERDA, 1976-77. Author: Particle Interaction Physics at High Energies, 1973; scriptwriter, narrator, sci. prodr. (multi-screen, audio-visual slide show) Atom Smashing, Atom Smashers: Fifty Years, 1977; contbr. articles to profl. jours. Fellow Am. Phys. Soc.; mem. N.Y. Acad. Scis., AAAS. Achievements include discovering nucleon isobars dominated high energy particles interactions, isobar model; inventor on line computer technique in scientific experiments; proved experimentally that Einstein's special theory of relativity was correct down to subnuclear distances one hundredth the radius of a proton; discovered the glueball states predicted by quantum chromodynamics. Office: Brookhaven Nat Lab Dept Physics Upton NY 11973

LINDENCRONA, G., academic administrator. Pres. Stockholm U. Office: Stockholm U, 10691 Stockholm Sweden*

LINDEN HIRSCHBERG, ANGELICA MARIE CECILIA, obstetrics and gynecology researcher; b. Stockholm, Jan. 3, 1959; d. Miguel Rey Betancourt and Anne-Marie Linden; m. Jurek Hirschberg, June 28, 1992; children: Julia Rebecka, Daniel Isak. Degree in medicine, Karolinska Inst., Stockholm, 1984, MD, 1989. Postdoctoral rsch. fellow, asst. physician Huddinge Hosp., Stockholm, 1989-93; assoc. prof., rsch. physician Karolinska Inst., 1993—; head dept. clin. rsch. dept. ob-gyn. Karolinska Hosp., 1998—. Contbr. articles to profl. jours. Swedish Med. Rsch. Coun. grantee, 1995—. Mem. Swedish Soc. Medicine, Fedn. Scandinavian Socs. Ob-gyn., Swedish Soc. Ob-gyn. Avocations: music, theater, ballet. Office: Karolinska Hosp, Dept Ob-Gyn, SE 17176 Stockholm Sweden

LINDEQUE, BAREND GERHARDUS, obstetrics and gynecology educator; b. Springs, South Africa, Nov. 2, 1953; s. Petrus Johannes and Dorithea Cecilia (Malan) L.; children: Barend Gerhardus, Michelle, Corlia. MBChB, U. Pretoria, 1976; M Medicine cum laude, U. Stellenbosch, 1984, MD, 1989. Med. officer Provincial Adminstrn., Pretoria, South Africa, 1977-80; registrar U. Stellenbosch (South Africa), 1980-84, specialist, 1984-85, sr. specialist, 1987-89; prof., head dept. ob-gyn. U. Pretoria, 1990—; vis. prof. Zimbabwe, 1993, U. Witwatersrand, South Africa, 1989; examiner U.

Witwatersrand, U. Cape Town, U. Stellenbosch, U. Orange Free State U., U. Natal, 1989—, Coll. Medicine South Africa, 1990-96, councillor, 1995-, registrar 1999—, hon. registrar, 1998—, chmn. curriculum com. faculty of medicine, 1995—. Editor Obstetrics and Gynaecology Forum, 1991—, Gynaecology Self Ednl. Programme, 1995—; mem. editl. bd. South African Jour. Obstetrics and Gynaecology, 1995—; contbr. chpts. to books and articles to profl. jours. Elder Dutch Reformed Ch., Pretoria, 1991-92. Capt. South African Med. Svcs., 1978-80. Recipient Lennon Gold medal South African Soc. Med. Oncology, 1992, medal for exceptional achievement U. Pretonia, 1998—; fellow Gynaecol. Oncology Dept. Newcastle, Eng., 1985-86; South African Med. Rsch. Coun. scholar, 1985-86. Mem. South African soc. Ob-gyn. (coun. mem. 1991-96, 98—, pres. 1999—), South African Soc. Gynaecol. Cancer (pres. 1994—), South African Acad. Sci. and Art, Cancer Assn. South Africa, Internat. Gynaecol. Cancer Soc. Avocations: reading, botany, bulldogs. Home: 1436 Walter Ave Waverley, Pretoria 0186, South Africa Office: U Pretoria, Dept Ob-gyn, Pretoria 0001, South Africa

LINDER, RIKARD B.A., physician; b. Boras, Sweden, Apr. 27, 1963; s. Bengt M.W. and Ulla B. (Norlen) L.; m. Susanne B.Klerck, Mar. 20, 1993; childre: Blanca, Julius, Elsa. MD, UMEA, Sweden, 1990. Interventional cardiologist Karolinska Hosp., Stockholm, 1992—. Contbr. articles to profl. jours. Lt. Swedish Navy, 1990—. Mem. European Soc. Cardiology. Lutheran. Avocations: skiing, biking, literature, music. Home: Rudsjovagen 82, S-13147 Nacka Sweden Office: Karolinska Hosp, Dept Cardiology, S-17176 Stockholm Sweden

LINDERHOLM, HÅKAN PER GUSTAF, physiology educator; b. Jönköping, Småland, Sweden, June 11, 1919; s. Gustaf Ernst Rickard and Märta (Tehler) L.; m. Anita Margit Estelle Dalton, Mar. 24, 1951; children: Per, Annika, Mats, Johan, Helena. MD, Uppsala (Sweden) U., 1949, PhD, 1952. Asst. prof. Uppsala U., 1952-55, Karolinska Inst., Stockholm, 1956-59; rsch. fellow NIH, Phila., 1958-59; prof., head dept. clin. physiol. med. faculty Umeå (Sweden) U., 1959-85, dean medicine faculty, 1969-72, prof. emeritus, 1985—; chmn. Commn. on Clin. Physiology IUPS, 1986-97; mem. Nordic Coun. Arctic Med. Rsch., 1969-85, chmn. Nordic Coun. Arctic Med. Rsch., 1972-75. Author: Active Transport of Ions, 1952, publs. related to physiology and clin. physiology, 1949-95; editor: In Honor of Torgny Sjöstrand, 1967, Circumpolar Health 1987, 1987. Fellow Internat. Acad. Chest Physicians and Surgeons; mem. Swedish Assn. Clin. Physiology, Scandinavian Assn. Clin. Physiology and Nuclear Medicine, Swedish Assn. Physiology, Finnish Assn. Clin. Physiology (hon.). Home: Fridhemsvägen 5, S-903 37 Umeå Sweden Office: Umeå U, Dept Clin Physiology, S-901 85 Umeå Sweden

LINDERMAN, JEANNE HERRON, priest; b. Erie, Pa., Nov. 14, 1931; d. Robert Leslie and Ella Marie (Stearns) Herron; m. James Stephens Linderman; children: Mary Susan, John Randolph, Richard Webster, Craig Stephens, Mark Herron, Elizabeth Stewart. BS in Indsl. and Labor Rels., Cornell U., 1953; MDiv magna cum laude, Lancaster Theol. Sem., 1981; postgrad., clin. pastoral edn., Del. State Hosp., New Castle, 1981. Ordained priest, Episcopal Ch. Mem. pers. staff Hengerer Co., Buffalo, 1953-55; chaplain Cathedral Ch. St. John, Wilmington, Del., 1981-82; priest-in-charge Christ Episcopal Ch., Delaware City, Del., 1982-87; vicar Christ Episcopal Ch., 1987-91; assoc. rector St. Andrew's Episcopal Ch., Wilmington, Del., 1991-95, priest in charge, 1995-96; assoc. priest for pastoral care The Episc. Ch. of Sts. Andrew and Matthew, 1998—; chair human sexuality task force, Diocese of Del., 1981-82, mem. clergy compensation com. and diocesan coun., 1982-86, pres. standing com., 1991—, com. on constitution and canons, 1989, designer and leader religious/spiritual retreats. Author, editor hist. study papers. Bd. dirs. St. Michael's Day Nursery, Wilmington, 1985-88; mem. secondary schs. com. Cornell U., bd. dirs., chmn. pers. com. Geriatric Svcs. of Del., 1989-96, sec. bd., 1993-96. Mem. Episcopal Women's Caucus, Del. Episcopal Clergy Assn., Nat. Assn. Episcopal Clergy, DAR (v.-regent Caesar Rodney chpt. 1996—), Mayflower Soc. (elder, surgeon 1983-95), Dutch Colonial Soc. Del., Stoney Run Questers (pres.), Cornell Women's Club Del. (pres. 1966), Women of St. James the Less (pres. 1972-73), Women's Witnessing Cmty. at Lambeth, Patriotic Soc. in Del. (sec.-treas. conv. 1965-68), Chi Omega. Republican. Avocations: history, genealogy, travel. Home: 307 Springhouse Ln Hockessin DE 19707-9691 Office: The Episcopal Ch of Sts Andrew and Matthews Eighth And Shipley St Wilmington DE 19801

LINDEROTH, BENGT GÖSTA, neurosurgeon; b. Stockholm, July 5, 1943; s. Gösta Ludvig and Ingrid Marianne (Olsson) L.; 1 son, Carl; m. Eva Birgitta Lindholm, Mar. 4, 1992. BA, U. Stockholm, 1967, PhD, 1973; MD, Karolinska Inst., Stockholm, 1980, D in Med. Sci., 1992. Rschr. dept. psychology U. Stockholm, 1967-74, lectr., 1971-80, asst. prof., 1975-80, study councelor dept. psychology, 1973-80; sr. neurosurgeon Karolinska Hosp., Stockholm, 1988-94, assoc. prof. neurosurgery, 1994—; adj. prof. Okla. City U., 1999—. Chief contbr. chpts. to textbooks and more than 75 articles to profl. jours. Recipient two awards for outstanding report Scandinavian Assn. for the Study of Pain, Cezanne award Groupe Francais de Neurostimulation et Patologie Vasculaire, Aix-en-Provence, 1990. Mem. Swedish Neurosurgery Soc. (bd. mem. and sci. sec. 1994-97), European Soc. Stereotactic and Functional Neurosurgery (bd. mem. 1994-98), Internat. Neuromodulation Soc. (bd. mem. 1996-2000), World Soc. Stereotactic and Functional Neurosurgery (bd. dirs. 1997—). Avocations: playing classical and pop guitar and keyboard, art, travel, biology, reading. Home: Vintervägen 36, S-16954 Solna Sweden Office: Dept Neurosurgery, Karolinska Hosp, S-171 76 Stockholm Sweden

LINDFIELD, KIMBERLY CARMEN, neuroscientist, researcher; b. Utica, N.Y., Oct. 31, 1969; d. Carmen Carl and Georgia Carol Lindfield; m. John Bernrd Collins, July 6, 1991. BS, Syracuse U., 1991; MA, Brandeis U., 1993, PhD, 1995. Asst. rsch. prof. Sch. Medicine Boston U., 1998—; rsch. psychologist Boston VAMC, 1996—, clin. grand rounds coord., 1996—. Contbr. articles to profl. jours. Grantee NIH, 1998. Mem. APA, Am. Psychol. Sci., Soc. for Neurosci. Avocations: photography, hiking, gardening. Office: DVAMC-151-A 150 S Huntington Ave Boston MA 02130-4817

LINDGREEN, PAUL THEODOOR CAROLUS, business economist; b. The Hague, Netherlands, June 23, 1947; s. Ronald Theodoor and Euphemia Maria (Perizonius) L.; m. Zeljka Matijasic; children: Marko Paul, Ronald Alexander. Bachelor's degree, Zagreb U., 1973, Master's degree, 1976. Zagrebacki Velesajam Zagreb Int-Trade Fair Philips Gloeilampen Fabriek, 1975; Philips Gloeilampen fabriek Zogreb, 1976; contr. Mcpl. Social Security Orgn., The Hague, 1976-79, Cin. Milacron, Vlaardingen, The Netherlands, 1979-94; liaison officer, negotiator Former Yugoslavia, 1994; contr. Gak Nederland BV, Amsterdam, The Netherlands, 1995-2000, Dutch Relief and Rehab. Agy., The Hague, The Netherlands, 2000—; cons. to starting bus. Organizer, coord. various humanitarian activities, The Netherlands and former Yugoslavia. Liaison officer 11 Airmobile Brigade for UN in Bosnia, 1994. Avocations: bicycle building and design, vintage car consulting. Home: Sint Martinuslaan 37, 2273 AP Voorburg The Netherlands

LINDGREN, CHARLOTTE HOLT, English language educator; b. Ipswich, Mass., Jan. 5, 1924; d. Hilmer Harold and Edith Grace (Whittier) L.; m. Donald James Winslow, Aug. 11, 1978. AB, Boston U., 1945, AM, 1947, PhD, 1961; MA (hon.), Emerson Coll., 1967. Tchr. Pinkerton Acad., Derry, N.H., 1945-46, Medfield (Mass.) H.S., 1947-49; adminstrv. asst. Boston Univ., 1949-60; prof. Emerson Coll., Boston, 1960-89, chmn. english dept., 1965-80, prof. emerita, 1989—; co-leader Emerson Abroad Program, 1966-78; corporator Lasell Coll., Auburndale, Mass., 1997—. Co-author: William Barnes Dorset Engravings, 1986 (Mansell-Playdell award 1986), Gerald Warner Brace: Writer, Sailor, Teacher, 1998; editor: The Love Poems and Letters of William Barnes, 1986; contbr. articles to History Today, Dorset Yr. Book, T. Hardy Jour. Mem. Thomas Hardy Soc., William Barnes Soc., Herman Melville Soc., Women in Arts, Phi Beta Kappa. Avocations: photography, book reviewing. Home: 23 Maple St Auburndale MA 02466-2404

LINDGREN, GUNILLA KARIN, social science educator, researcher; b. Sollefteå, Sweden, Apr. 21, 1940; arrived in England, 1992; d. Sven Arthur and Eina Ingeborg (Granbäck) Westin; m. Carl Ingemar Lindgren, 1962 (div. 1972); children: Carl Fredrik Ingemar, Katarina Maria Irene; m. James Mourilyan Tanner, Apr. 4, 1992. Cert. elem. tchr., Stockholm Inst. Edn., 1964; BA in Edn., Psychology, Sociology, Stockholm U., 1972; PhD, U. Stockholm, 1979, docent, 1982. Elem. sch. tchr. Stockholm, 1963-68; rsch. asst. Pedagogical Ctr., Stockholm, 1969-72; rsch. asst. Stockholm Inst. Edn., 1972-78, project leader, 1978-81, sr. lectr., 1981-94, acting prof. edn., 1986-94, personal prof. edn., 1994-91, full prof., 1999—; cons. Epidemiology Rsch. Ctr. & Sch. Pub. Health, U. Tex., Houston, 1993-95; mem. Commn. European Communities project Europe against Cancer, 1992—. Contbr. articles to profl. jours.; mem. editl. bd. Annals of Human Biology, 1982—. Treas. Univ. Tchrs. Assn., Sweden, 1981-85. Vis. fellow WHO Collaborating Ctr. for Phys. Growth and Psychosocial Devel., U. London, 1992—; grantee Nat. Bd. Edn., Stockholm, 1978-82, 82-85, Bank of Sweden Tercentenary Found., Stockholm, 1986-90. Mem. Swedish Academics Ctrl. Orgn., Internat. Assn. Human Auxology (mem. exec. com.). Avocations: golf, opera, concerts, gardening, literature.

LINDGREN, J. RALPH, philosophy educator, writer; b. Oak Park, Ill., Oct. 8, 1933; s. J. Francis Lindgren and Leona G. Toussaint; m. Shirley A. Tryon, Dec. 27, 1958; children: Thomas, Michael, David, Timothy, Kathryn. BS, Northwestern U., 1959; MA in Philosophy, Marquette U., 1961, PhD in Philosophy, 1963. Instr. Coll. Holy Cross, Worcester, Mass., 1962-64, asst. prof. philosophy, 1964-65; asst. prof. philosophy Lehigh U., Bethlehem, Pa., 1965-69, assoc. prof. philosophy, 1969-79, prof. philosophy, 1979-95, William Wilson Selfridge prof. philosophy, 1985-88, Clara H. Stewardson prof. philosophy, 1989-95; prof. emeritus, 1995; vis. scholar U. Pa. Sch. Law, Phila., 1977-78, Oxford (Eng.) U., 1986. Author: The Social Philosophy of Adam Smith, 1973, Sex Discrimination in Higher Education, 1984, The Law of Sex Discrimination, 1984, 88; editor: The Early Writings of Adam Smith, 1967, Horizon of Justice, 1995, Law and Ritual, 1997, Semiotics and the Human Sciences, 1998. With U.S. Army, 1953-55. Mem. Internat. Assn. Philosophy of Law and Social Philosophy (exec. bd. 1981-83, 89-91), Nat. Soc. Philosophy and Pub. Affairs (exec. bd. 1987), Internat. Assn. Semiotics of Law. Democrat. Avocations: genealogy, gardening, photography. E-mail: jrl3@lehigh.edu. Office: Lehigh U Dept Philosophy 15 University Dr Bethlehem PA 18015-3057

LINDGREN, KARL-AUGUST JOHANNES, physiatrist, general practice physician; b. Lovisa, Finland, Feb. 19, 1949; s. Kaj August and Elna Linnea (Strömberg) L.; m. Veronica Helena Haglund, Nov. 11, 1972; children: Tommy, Niklas. MD, U. Helsinki, 1975; specialist in gen. practice, U. Kuopio, Finland, 1982, specialist in phys. medicine and rehab., 1988, competence in adminstrn., 1995. Gen. practitioner Nilsia-Rautavaara Kansanterveys Kuntainliitto, Finland, 1976-84; rehab. physician Siilinjärven Kuntoutumiskeskus, Finland, 1984-87; specialist in phys. medicine and rehab. U. Kuopio Hosp., 1987-97; physician in chief Rehab. Ctr. Orton, Helsinki, Finland, 1998—. Contbr. articles on thoracic outlet syndrome, low back pain and whiplash to med. jours. Mem. Am. Acad. Phys. Medicine and Rehab. (corr.), Inernat. Assn. for Study Pain. Avocations: ornithology, drawing, downhill skiing. Home: Hagbacksvagen 15 B4, 02120 Espoo Finland Office: Rehab Ctr Invalid Found, Tenholantie 10, 00280 Helsinki Finland

LINDGREN, NELLY NAILA, linguist, educator, researcher; b. Leningrad, USSR, Jan. 16, 1957; d. Farhulla and Minera (Kumacheva) Bekyashev; m. Svenolov Lindgren, Jan. 27, 1980; children: Kaj, Sanja. DPhil, Leningrad State U., 1980; PhD, Stockholm U., 1990. Rsch. asst. Acad. Scis. of USSR, Leningrad, 1978-80; rsch. assoc. Stockholm U., 1981-89, researcher, 1994-97, assoc. prof., 1998—; researcher Karlstad (Sweden) U., 1990-93. Author: An Accentological Study of a 17th Century North Russian Manuscript, 1990; contbr. articles to profl. jours. Grantee Royal Swedish Acad. Scis., 1982, Found. for Danish-Swedish Cooperation, 1996, Bank of Sweden Tercentenary Found., 1997—. Mem. Assn. Scandinavian Slavists and Baltologists, Swedish Com. for Byzantine Studies. Home: Apelgården Lundsberg, SE-68891 Storfors Sweden Office: Ersta Skondal U Coll, Dept Theology PO Box 4619, SE-11691 Stockholm Sweden

LINDH, ANNA, Swedish government official; b. Enskede, Stockholm, June 19, 1957. BA in Law, U. Uppsala, 1982. Mem. parliament Swedish Govt., Stockholm, 1982-85, chmn. Govt. Coun. on Alcohol and Drug Policy, 1986-90; vice-mayor, mem. Stockholm City Coun., 1991-94; min. environment Swedish Govt., Stockholm, 1994-98, min of foreign affairs, 1998—; mem. Mcpl. Coun., Enköping, 1977-79; ct. clk. Stockholm Dist. Ct., 1982-83. Chmn. Social Dem. Youth League, Uppsala, 1977-80, pres. 1984-90; mem. exec. com. social Dem. Party, 1991—; chmn. Stockholm City Culture com., Leisure Svcs. Com, Stockholm City Theater, 1991-94. Office: Ministry for Fgn Affairs, Gustav Adolfs torg 1, S-103 39 Stockholm Sweden

LINDH, PERNILLA, judge; b. Malmo, Sweden, Oct. 8, 1945; d. Helmer and Wilma (Sauer) L. LLM, U. Lund, 1971. Jr. judge Ct. First Instance, Trollhattan, Sweden, 1971-74, Ct. Appeal, Stockholm, 1974-76; judge Ct. First Instance, Stockholm, 1976-77; mem. presdl. cabinet Ct. Appeal, Stockholm, 1977-78; head sect. Chancellor of Justice, Stockholm, 1978-80; judge Ct. Appeal, Stockholm, 1980-81; councillor Min. Commerce, Stockholm, 1981-83; councillor Min. Fgn. Affairs, Stockholm, 1986-86, dir., 1986-87, undersec. legal affairs, amb., 1987-94; judge Ct. First Instance European Cmtys., Luxembourg, 1994—. Home: 24-28 rue Goethe, L-1637 Luxembourg Luxembourg Office: European Cmty Ct Justice, Boulevard Konrad Adenauer, Kirchberg L-2925, Luxembourg*

LINDHOLM, ALFONS SETH MIKAEL, engineering educator; b. Karis, Nyland, Finland, July 29, 1916; s. Karl Emil and Elin Hilma (Tenlenius) L.; m. Freja Ingeborg Rantanen, Feb. 1, 1942; children: Ingeborg, Ulla-Maria, Anders, Thomas. MSc, Åbo Acad., Finland, 1945; PhD, Chalmers U. Tech., Gothenburg, Sweden, 1965. Cert. in electrochem. power sources. Prodn. mgr. Kopparfors Corp., Fors, Sweden, 1947-49; head electrochem. sch. EKA AB, Gothenburg, Sweden, 1949-50; sr. master Tech. Sch., Borås, Sweden, 1951-62; rschr. lectr. Chalmers U. Tech., Gothenburg, 1962-65; head rsch. dept. TUDOR AB, ESB (USA), Nol, Sweden, 1964-74; assoc. prof. Royal U. Tech., Stockholm, 1974-86; cons. VARTA Ltd., TUDOR AB, Stockholm, 1982—. Contbr. rsch. reports to profl. publs. Capt. Finnish Army, 1939-44. Recipient disting. medals and crosses. Mem. AAAS, N.Y. Acad. Scis. Evangelical Lutheran. Avocations: literature, poetry, carpentry, outdoor activities. Home: Herserudsvägen 2C, 18134 Lidingö Sweden

LINDHOLM, DWIGHT HENRY, lawyer; b. Blackduck, Minn., May 27, 1930; s. Henry Nathanial and Viola Eudora (Gummert) L.; m. Loretta Catherine Brown, Aug. 29, 1958; children: Douglas Dwight, Dionne Louise, Jeanne Marie, Philip Clayton, Kathleen Anne. Student, Macalester Coll., 1948-49; BBA, U. Minn., 1951, LLB, 1954; postgrad., Mexico City Coll. (now U. of Ams.), 1956-57. Bar: Minn. 1954, Calif. 1958. Sole practice Los Angeles, 1958-65, 72-81, 84—; ptnr. Lindholm & Johnson, Los Angeles, 1965-69, Cotter, Lindholm & Johnson, Los Angeles, 1969-72; sole practice Los Angeles, 1972-81; of counsel Bolton, Dunn & Moore, Los Angeles, 1981-84. Mem. Calif. Republican Central Com., 1962-63, Los Angeles Republican County Central Com., 1962-66; bd. dirs. Family Service Los Angeles, 1964-70, v.p., 1968-70; bd. dirs. Wilshire YMCA, 1976-77; trustee Westlake Girls Sch., 1978-81; hon. presenter Nat. Charity League Coronet Debutante Ball, 1984; bd. dirs. Calif. State U.-Northridge Trust Fund, 1989-93; bd. dirs. Queen of Angeles/Hollywood Presbyn. Med. Ctr., 1990-98; chmn., CEO Queen of Angels, Hollywood Presbyn. Found., 1997—; bd. dirs., corp. sec. QueensCare, 1998—. Served as capt. JAG Corps USAF, 1954-56. Recipient Presdl. award Los Angeles Jr. C. of C., 1959. Mem. Calif. Bar Assn., L.A. County Bar Assn., Wilshire Bar Assn. (bd. govs. 1989-91), Internat. Genealogy Fellowship of Rotarians (founding pres. 1979-86), Calif. Club, Ocean Cruising Club Eng. (Newport Harbor port officer), Rotary (dir. 1975-78), Delta Sigma Pi, Delta Sigma Rho, Delta Theta Phi (state chancellor 1972-73). Presbyterian. Avocations: sailing, offshore cruising. Office: 3580 Wilshire Blvd Fl 17 Los Angeles CA 90010-2501

LINDHOLM, RICHARD THEODORE, economics and finance educator; b. Eugene, Oreg., Oct. 5, 1960; s. Richard Wadsworth and Mary Marjorie (Trunko) L. m. Valaya Nivasananda, May 8, 1987. BA, U. Chgo., 1982, MA, 1983, PhD, 1993. Ptnr. Lindholm and Osanka, Eugene, 1986-89; ptnr. Lindholm Rsch., Eugene, 1989—, owner, 1995—; owner The Lindholm Co., 1995—; guest lectr. Nat. Inst. Devel. Adminstrn., Bangkok, Thailand, 1989; pres. Rubicon Inst., Eugene, 1988—; adj. asst. prof. U. Oreg., Eugene, 1988—. Campaign co-chmn. Lane C.C. Advocates, Eugene, 1988; coord., planner numerous state Rep. Campaigns, Oreg., 1988—; campaign mgr. Jack Roberts for Oreg. State Labor Commn., 1994; mem. staff Oreg. Senate Rep. Office, 1989-90; precinct committeeperson Oreg. Rep. Party, 1987-92, 94—; bd. dirs. Rubicon Soc., Eugene, 1987—, pres., 1993-98. Republican. Lutheran. Home: 3335 Bardell Ave Eugene OR 97401-8021

LINDHOLM, ROBERT MCCLURE, lawyer; b. St. Louis, June 14, 1935; s. Arthur William and Hazel Ann (McClure) L.; m. Susan Sloan Lewis, 1965 (div. 1980); children: Melissa McClure, Christina Walton; m. Joyce Helen Mrkvicka, Mar. 28, 1981. BA in Radio and TV Prodn., U. Mo., 1957, LLB, 1964. Bar: Mo. 1964. Law clk. U.S. Dist. Ct., Kansas City, Mo., 1964-65; jr. ptnr. Bryan, Cave, McPheeters & McRoberts, St. Louis, 1965-68; legal counsel Ralston Purina Co., St. Louis, 1968-70, asst. dir. bus. devel., 1970; asst. sec., asst. gen. counsel ITT Hamilton Life Ins. Co., St. Louis, 1970-72; asst. atty. gen. State of Mo., Jefferson City, 1972-94; photog. cons. Outdoor Am. mag., Arlington, Va., 1989—; photographer, owner Outdoors, 1994—; photography instr. Writer, photographer mag. articles conservation subjects, 1970—; producer photographic essays conservation subjects, 1970—; photographer: (book, William Least-Heat-Moon) River Horse, 1995. Trustee Voyagers Outward Bound Sch., Ely, Minn., 1969-76; dir. Stream, Mo. Outward Bound Adaptation, St. Louis, 1970-78, Mo. chpt. Nature Conservancy, St. Louis, 1986-98, Ctrl. Kans. chpt., 1998—, Wilderness Edn. Assn., Saranac Lake, N.Y., 1985-92; mem. bd. Ling Concert Series, 2000—; mem. Lindsborg Arts Coun., 1998—. Ist lt. USMC, 1957-60. Recipient Citizens award Am. Fisheries Soc., Mo. chpt., 1983, Ansel Adams award Sierra Club, 1986, Disting. Alumnus award U. Mo. Arts and Scis., 1997. Mem. Outdoor Writers Assn. Am., Mo. Bar Assn. (chmn. environ. law com. 1977), Mo. Conservation Fedn. (Conservationist of the Yr. 1988), Great Lakes Outdoor Writers Assn., Mo. Coalition for Edn. Outdoors, Izaak Walton League (ethics chmn. Mo. chpt., Nat. Conservation award 1989, Nat. Svc. award 1990), Kiwanis. Methodist. Avocations: canoeing, running, reading, fine music, camping. Home: 505 S Cherry St Lindsborg KS 67456-2520

LINDHOLM, SVEN OLLE RAGNAR, physician; b. Jonkoping, Sweden, June 17, 1946; s. Thor Olof and Maj Wihlhelmina (Andersson) L.; m. Gabriella Alexandra Meyer, Apr. 9, 1978; children: Erik, Gustav, Karl. MD, U. Lund, Sweden, 1973. Physician Landstinget, Vaggeryd, Sweden, 1977-88; med. officer Foretaqshalsov, Vaggeryd, 1988-92; physician Svegholm AB, Vaggeryd, 1993—. V.p. Conservative Party, Vaggeryd-Skillingaryd, Sweden, 1989-92. Mem. Rotary. Avocations: politics, history, forestry. Home: 2 S Agatan, 56731 Vaggeryd Sweden Office: Svegaholm AB, S Agatan 2, 56731 Vaggeryd Sweden

LINDHORST, THISBE KERSTIN, chemistry educator; b. Munich, Nov. 19, 1962; children: Moritz, Justus. BSc, U. Munich, 1985; MSc, U. Munster, Germany, 1988; PhD, U. Hamburg, Germany, 1991, pvt. dozent, 1998. Lectr. organic chemistry U. Hamburg, 1993—, asst. prof., 1998—, head rsch. group, 1993—, lectr. organic chemistry, 1998—; presenter in field; participant profl. congresses. Author 3 books; contbr. numerous articles to profl. publs. Recipient travel award German-Am. Frontiers of Sci. Symposium, 1998, award Karl-Ziegler Endowment, chemistry prize of Acad. of Scis. in Göttingen. Mem. Soc. German Chemists, German Chem. Soc., Soc. German Natural Scientists and Physicians, Soc. German Nat. Rschrs. and Med. Doctors, Liebig Soc. for Organic Chemistry, Soc. of Assocs. of Dept. of Organic Chemistry of Tech. U. Braunschweig. Avocations: art, sports. Fax: 49 40 4123 4325. E-mail: tklind@chemie.uni-hamburg.de. Office: Univ Hamburg, Martin-Luther-King-Pl 6, D-20146 Hamburg Germany

LINDL, TONI, biotechnologist, educator; b. Berching, Bavaria, Germany, June 9, 1941; s. Franz Xaver and Walburgis (Hutter) L.; m. Marie Luis Wallraven, Feb. 24, 1972. Diploma, U. Freiburg, Germany, 1971, PhD, 1975. Rsch. asst. U. Freiburg, 1972-75; asst. lectr. U. Constance, Germany, 1975-79; assoc. rschr. U. Bonn, Germany, 1979-81; mgr. Inst. Applied Cell Culture, Munich, 1981-90; prof. Coll. High Edn., Freising, 1990—; Bd. dirs. Inst. Applied Cell Culture. Author: Cell and Tissue Culture, 3rd edit., 1994. Active German Found. for Alts. to Animal Testing, Frankfurt, 1993. With German Army Svc., 1962-64. Avocations: classical music, tennis, chess, travel. Office: Inst Applied Cell Culture, Inc 6, Balan St, D-81669 Munich Bavaria, Germany

LINDLEY, COREY BART, sales professional; b. Provo, Utah, June 5, 1964; s. Earl Leishman and Marilyn (Jensen) L.; m. Janis Farnsworth, Apr. 24, 1987; children: Erica, Robyn, Megan, Devin, Haley, Brady. BS in Acctg., Brigham Young U., 1987; MBA, Utah State U., 1991. Acct. Deloitte & Touche, Salt Lake City, 1987-90; controller NuSkin Internat., Provo, 1990-94, internat. mng. dir., 1994-96; CFO NuSkin Enterprises, Provo, 1996-99, exec. v.p., 1999—. Mem. AICPAs, Utah Assn. CPAs. E-mail: clindley@nuskin.com. Office: NuSkin Enterprises 75 W Center St Provo UT 84601-4432

LINDLEY, DAVID, mechanical engineer; b. June 26, 1939; s. William and Millicent (Caine) L.; m. Dorothy Turnock, July 14, 1962; children: Simon David (dec.), Nicolas Rhys, Jonathan Peter, Sarah Jane. BSc, U. Salford, 1962; PhD, U. Wales, 1966; cert. advanced engring. design, U. Cambridge, 1967. Apprentice, mgr. Pump Exptl. Dept. Mather & Platt Ltd., Manchester, Eng., 1955-63; head Turbo Machinery Aerothermodynamics Dept. CEGB, 1967-70; sr. lectr. mech. engring. U. Canterbury, New Zealand, 1970-78; mgr. Energy Sys. Group Jet Propulsion Lab. Calif. Inst. Tech., 1975-76; mng. dir. Wind Energy Group Ltd., 1979-91; dir. Taylor Woodrow plc Group Cos., 1984-91; mng. dir. Nat. Wind Power Ltd., Buckinghamshire, Eng., 1991-96, Lindley and Assocs., Buckinghamshire, 1996—; chmn. Brit. Wind Energy Assn., 1982, 94; mem. Adv. Coun. for R&D for Fuel and Power, 1986-92; dir., pres. European Wind Energy Assn., 1986-89; mem. Renewable Energy Adv. Group, London, 1991-92; vis. prof. Loughborough U. Tech., 1994—, U. Nottingham, 1997—; Royal Acad. Engring. vis. prof. De Montfort U., 1994—; academician The Russian Internat. Higher Edn. Acad. Scis., 1994. Recipient James Watt medal Inst. Civil Engrs., 1987, Stephenson medal U. Newcastle, 1989, Melchett medal Inst. Energy, 1990, BWEA Industry award, 1995, BWEA Pres. award, 1996; named Officer of Brit. Empire, 1997. Fellow Instn. Mech. Engrs., Royal Acad. Engring., Royal Meteorol. Soc.; mem. AIAA, ASME. Avocations: walking, skiing, sailing, photography, reading. Office: Lindley and Assocs Woodfield, Farm Ln, Jordans, Beaconsfield Bucks HP9 2UP, England

LINDNER, DANIEL GEORGE, program analyst; b. Bethlehem, Pa.; s. George K. and Lorraine E. Lindner; m. Jenny Lindner; children: Eric, Alexander. BA in Govt., BA Econs., Lehigh U., 1977; MBA, George Washington U., 1984. Cert. profl. contracts mgr. Nat. Contract Mgmt. Assn. Sports announcer WLRN Radio, Bethlehem, 1973-74; sports dir., announcer WLTN-TV, Bethlehem, 1973-77; contract negotiator Naval Regional Contracting Office, Phila., 1977-80; contract specialist Strategic Sys. Program Office, Washington, 1980-86; staff aide Office of Asst. Sec. of the Navy, Arlington, Va., 1986-90; contracting officer Dept. of the Navy, Arlington, 1990-94; deployment mgr., program analyst Std. Procurement Sys. Program Office, Fairfax, Va., 1994-99; chmn. tech. working group and procurement working group Std. Procurement Sys. Program Office, Fairfax, 1999—. Contbr. articles to profl. jours. Usher, mem. fin. com. Emmanuel Luth. Ch., Vienna, Va., 1989-98; counselor Fairfax (Va.) County Teen Living Program, 1993—; big bro. Big Bros. Am., Fairfax, 1995-96; coach Fairfax County Adult Volleyball League, 1994-95. Mem. Distributive Edn. Clubs Am. (judge regional and state competitions 1998—), Lehigh U. Alumni Assn. (recruiter 1989—, bd. mem. Washington chpt. 1993-97, dep. dir. campaign for preserving the vision 1994, dir. Lehigh Wrestling Club, 1995—). Avocations: travel, sports and history research, running, hiking. E-mail: lindner dan@hotmail.com. Office: Dept of Def PO Box 3814 Merrifield VA 22116-3814

LINDNER, UDO KLAUS, medical director; b. Stuttgart, Germany, Dec. 22, 1949; m. Klaus and Margarethe (Eisele) L.; m. Jeannette Barbara Sosna, July 9, 1979; Thomas, Christopher. MD, U. Heidelberg, 1976, specialist for internal medicine, 1982. Postdoctoral asst. physiology Heidelberg, 1976-78; postdoctoral fellow Med. U. Hosp., Heidelberg, 1978-82; sat down specialist Villingen, Germany, 1983-90; editor-in-chief Springer Pub. House, Villingen, 1990-97; program dir. medicine Springer Ltd. Co., 1998—. Author: ECG in Emergency Cases, 1997, Interpretation of ECG, 7 edits., 1999; contbr. ar-

ticles to profl. jours. Pres. European City Partnership, Villingen, 1985-95. Mem. German Soc. Internal Medicine, German Soc. Med. Journalists, Heidegger Philos. Soc. Avocations: literature, philosophy, classic music, playing clarinet. Home: Herrenweg 56, 69151 Neckargemuend Germany Office: Springer Pub House, Tiergartenstr 17, 69121 Heidelberg Germany

LINDO, J. TREVOR, psychiatrist, consultant; b. Boston, Feb. 12, 1925; s. Edwin and Ruby Ianty (Peterson) L.; m. Thelma Elaine Thompson, Sept. 22, 1962. BA, NYU, 1946; cert. in pre-clin. studies, U. Freibourg, Switzerland, 1953; MD, U. Lausanne, Switzerland, 1957. Lic. psychiatrist, N.Y., Conn. Clin. instr. Columbia U., N.Y.C., 1965-75, asst. clin. prof., 1975-82, assoc. clin. prof., 1982-85; attending psychiatrist Bedford-Stuyvesant Cmty. Mental Health Clinic, Bklyn., 1976-86, med. dir., 1986—; attending psychiatrist Harlem Hosp. Ctr., N.Y.C., 1964-75; vis. psychiatrist Interfaith Hosp., Bklyn., 1976-85; psychiat. cons. Bklyn. Bur. Cmty. Svc., 1980, Marcus Garvey Manor, Bklyn., 1982-86; candidate Nat. Bd. Forensic Examiners, 1995. Co-chairperson com. Dr. Thomas Matthew, N.Y.C., 1974. With U.S. Mcht. Marine, 1947-51. Fellow Am. Coll. Internal Physicians; mem. Nat. Med. Assn., Am. Psychiat. Assn., Provident Clin. Soc. (v.p. 1980-82, parliamentarian 1982—), Bklyn. Psychiat. Soc., Black Psychiatrists of Am. Avocations: travel, African art, sailing, swimming. Office: 1265 President St Brooklyn NY 11213-4237 also: Bedford Stuyvesant Cmty Mental Health Ctr 1406 Fulton St Brooklyn NY 11216-2606

LINDON, JEROME, publishing company executive; b. Paris, France, June 9, 1925; s. Raymond and Therese (Baur) L.; student Lycée Pasteur a Neuilly/Seine, 1936-39; Baccalauréat Lycée Mignet á Aix-en-Provence, 1942; m. Marié Rosenfeld Annette, July 1, 1947; children—Irène, André , Mathieu. Prés., dir.-gen. Editions de Minuit, Paris, 1948—. Office: Editions de Minuit, 7 rue Bernard Palissy, 75006 Paris France

LINDPAINTNER, KLAUS, pharmaceutical executive; b. Innsbruck, Tirol, Austria, Feb. 13, 1955; m. Lyn Singer; children: Julia, Eva. BS, Akademisches Gymnasium, Innsbruck, 1973; MD, U. Innsbruck, 1979; MPH, Harvard Sch. Public Health, 2000. Diplomate Am. Bd. Internal Medicine with subspecialty in cardiovascular diseases, Am. Bd. Med. Genetics with subspecialty in molecular genetics. Head pre-clin. cardiovascular rsch. F. Hoffmann - La Roche, Basel, Switzerland, 1997-98; head, v.p. Roche Genetics, F. Hoffmann - La Roche, Basel, 1998—. Mem. editl. bd.: Jour. Hypertension, 1994—, Hypertension, 1995—, Circulation, 1996—; assoc. editor: Jour. of Molecular Medicine, 1994—; contbr. numerous articles to profl. jours. Recipient Karl Freudenberg award U. Heidelberg, Germany, 1990, Rsch. Career Devel. award NIH, 1994, Okamoto Silver medal for Hypertension Rsch., 1994. Fellow Am. Coll. Physicians, Am. Coll. Cardiology, Coun. for Clin. Cardiology, Am. Coll. Med. Genetics; mem. Human Genome Orgn. Office: F Hoffmann La Roche Ltd, Grenzacherstrasse, CH 4070 Basel Switzerland

LINDQUIST, LOUIS WILLIAM, artist, writer; b. Boise, Idaho, June 26, 1944; s. Louis William and Bessie (Newman) L.; divorced; children: Jessica Ann Alexandra, Jason Ryan Louis. BS in Anthropology, U. Oreg., 1968; postgrad., Portland State U., 1974-78. Researcher, co-writer with Asher Lee, Portland, Oreg., 1977-80; freelance artist, painter, sculptor Oreg., 1980-91, 98-99; assoc. mem. of Com. for Sci. Investigation of Claims of the Paranormal, Skeptical Inquirer jour. Sgt. U.S. Army, 1968-71, Vietnam. Mem. AAAS, NRA Am., Am. Anthropol. Assn., N.Y. Acad. Scis., Acad. Am. Poets, Petersen's Sportsmen's Soc., N.Am. Hunting Club (life). Democrat. Avocations: reading, beachcombing, listening to classical, jazz and native North American music. Home and Office: PO Box 991 Bandon OR 97411-0991

LINDQUIST, RICHARD JAMES, portfolio manager; b. East Orange, N.J., June 22, 1960; s. Chester Edward and Rose Theresa (Grosso) L.; m. Clare Jacangelo, June 21, 1987; children: Matthew Cole, Kimberly Rose. BS, Boston Coll., 1982; MBA, U. Chgo., 1986. CFA; chartered investment counselor. Investment rsch. analyst N.Y. Life Ins. Co., N.Y.C., 1982-84; bond trader, v.p. T. Rowe Price Assocs., Inc., Balt., 1986-88; portfolio mgr., v.p. Prudential Ins. Co. Am., Newark, 1989; mng. dir., portfolio mgr. CS 1st Boston Investment Mgmt., N.Y.C., 1989-95, Credit Suisse Asset Mgmt., N.Y.C., 1995—. Mem. Assn. Investment Mgmt. & Rsch., Fin. Analysts Fedn., Inst. CFAs, Investment Coun. Assn. Am., N.Y. Soc. Security Analysts, N.Y. Athletic Club, Spray Beach Yacht Club, Boston Coll. Club, Sea Oaks Country Club. Avocations: golf, cycling, chess. Office: Credit Suisse Asset Mgmt One Citicorp Ctr 153 E 53rd St Fl 58 New York NY 10022-4611

LINDQVIST, GUNILLA, education educator; b. Uppsala, Sweden, Sept. 22, 1942; d. Lars and Margareta (Franzen) Kjellman; m. Jan Lindqvist; children: Jonas Alwall, Jesper Alwall, Klas Hermodsson, Sara Hermodsson, Alexander Lindqvist. PhD, U. Uppsala, 1995. Prefect U. Karlstad, Sweden, 1978-81; sr. lectr. U. Karlstad, Karlstad, 1995—; rschr. Dept. Ednl. Sci., Karlstad, 1995—. Author: (book) From Facts to Fantasy, 1989, Alone in the Big, Wide World, 1992, The Aesthetics of Play, 1995, The Possibilities of Play, 1996, Vygotsky and School, 1999. Office: Dept Ednl Sci, Univ Karlstad, 65188 Karlstad Sweden

LINDROS, ERIC BRYAN, professional hockey player; b. London, Ont., Can., Feb. 28, 1973; s. Carl and Bonnie L. Student, York U., Toronto. With Detroit Compuware, 1989—, Phila. Flyers, 1992—; mem. Canadian Olympic Team, 1992, Cup All-Star team, 1989-90, OHL All-Star team 1990-91, NHL All-Star team, 1992-93; player NHL All-Star game, 1992-93. Recipient Plus/Minus award Canadian Hockey League, 1990-91, Red Tilson trophym 1990-91, Eddie Powers Meml. trophy, 1990-91; named Most Valuable Player World Jr. Hockey Championships, 1990, Most Valuable Player Ont. Jr. Hockey Assn., 1991, Player of the Year Canadian Hockey League, 1990-91, Hart Trophy, 1995, Lester B. Pearson Award, 1995, Nat. Hockey League. Office: c/o Philadelphia Flyers 3601 S Broad St One Corestates Complex Philadelphia PA 19148-4107

LINDSAY, DALE RICHARD, research administrator; b. Bunker Hill, Kans., Aug. 9, 1913; s. Charles Edwin and Iva (Missimer) L.; m. Sybil Anne McCoy, June 6, 1937; children—Martha Lou Lindsay Cover, Judith Anne Lindsay Clapp, Patricia Dale. A.B., U. Kans., 1937, M.A., 1938; Ph.D., Iowa State Coll., 1943. Entomologist Dept. Agr., summers 1937-39; teaching fellow, instr., research asso. Iowa State Coll., 1938-43; commd. officer USPHS, 1943—, scientist dir., 1955; assigned malaria control in war areas, 1943-45; entomologist charge operations Communicable Disease Center Activies, Pharr, Tex., 1945-48; chief Thomasville (Ga.) field sta., 1948-53; chief program evaluation sect., div. research grants NIH, 1953-55, asst. chief div., 1955-60, chief div., 1960-63; dep. to gen. dir. Mass. Gen. Hosp., Boston, 1963-65; spl. asst. to chancellor health scis. U. Calif. at Davis, 1965-67, asst. chancellor research and health scis., 1968-69; asso. commr. sci. FDA, 1969-71; asso. dir. med. and allied health edn. Duke U., 1971-75; asst. dir. for sci. coordination Nat. Center for Toxicol. Research, Jefferson, Ark., 1975-76; adj. prof. medicine U. Ark. Med. Sch., 1975-76; asso. dept. family and community medicine U. Ariz., 1977-82; Agrl. bd. Nat. Acad. Sci.-NRC, 1970-73; mem. exec. com., public trustee Nutrition Found., 1972-76, Environ. and Agrl. Found., 1974-79; chmn. sci. adv. bd. Nat. Center for Toxicol. Research, 1972-74. Fellow AAAS, Am. Public Health Assn.; mem. Entomol. Soc. Am. (gov. bd. 1958-62), Commd. Officer Assn. USPHS (treas. nat. exec. com. 1959-61) , Sigma Xi, Phi Kappa Phi, Gamma Sigma Delta.

LINDSAY, FRANKLIN ANTHONY, business executive, author; b. Kenton, Ohio, Mar. 12, 1916; s. Harry Wyatt and Ruth (Andrews) L.; m. Margot Coffin, Dec. 17, 1948; children: Catherine, Alison (dec.), John Franklin. A.B., Stanford U., 1938; postgrad., Harvard U., 1946. With Columbia div. U.S. Steel Corp., 1938-39; exec. asst. to Bernard Baruch, U.S. del. UN Atomic Energy Commn., 1946; cons. Ho. of Reps. Select (Herter) Com. on Fgn. Aid, 1947-48, ECA, Paris; rep. to exec. com. OEEC, 1948-49; with CIA, 1949-53; with pub. affairs program Ford Found., 1953-56; prin. McKinsey & Co., Inc., N.Y.C., 1956-61; exec. v.p., dir. Itek Corp., Lexington, Mass., 1961-62, pres., dir., 1962-75, chmn. bd., 1975-81, chmn. exec. com., 1981-83; chmn. Engenics, Inc., Menlo Park, Calif., 1983-85; trustee emeritus Com. Econ. Devel.; rsch. Assoc. Inst. Politics, Harvard U., 1967-71; cons. 2d Hoover Commn., 1954, The White House, 1955; mem. Rockefeller Spl. Studies Panel Econ. Policy, 1956, Gaither Com. Nat. Security Policy, 1957; asst. staff dir. President's Com. World Econ. Policy, 1958; mem. President Elect's Task Force on Disarmament, 1960; dir. Com. for Nat. Trade Policy, 1956-71; adv. coun. dept. econs. Princeton U., 1961-64; mem. Wilson Ctr. Adv. coun. Smithsonian Instn., 1980-94; trustee Bennington Coll., 1963-73; chmn. bd. trustees Edn. Devel. Ctr., 1967-73; mem. vis. com. dept. econs. Harvard U., 1976-80; mem. President's Adv. Com. on Trade Negotiations, 1976-79; bd. dirs. Nat. Bur. Econ. Rsch., 1976-93, mem. exec. com., 1980—, chmn. 1983-86; mem. adv. coun. Gas Rsch. Inst., 1977-83; vice chmn. energy and raw materials, bus. and industry adv. com. OECD, 1977-82, chmn. 1980, mem. adv. bd. Pub. Agenda Found., 1978-84; mem. NRC Commn. Engring. Systems, 1978-84, panel on balancing nat. interest NAS, 1985-87; bd. dirs. Resources for the Future, 1978-86; assoc. Ctr. for Internat. Affairs, Harvard U., 1988-96; vis. scholar Woodrow Wilson Ctr. for Scholars, Washington, 1987-88, 90; adj. prof. Internat. Mgmt. Inst., Kiev, Ukraine, 1993-96; mem. standing policy group on Russia and Eurasia, The Atlantic Coun. of the U.S., 1996—; mem. steering com. Nat. Security Program, Kennedy Sch. Govt., Harvard U., 1994—. Author: New Techniques of Management Decision Making, 1958, Beacons in the Night: War and Revolution in Yugoslavia 1941-45, 1993; contbg. author: Preparing Tomorrow's Business Leaders Today, The Conscience of the City, Removing Obstacles to Economic Growth; contbr. articles on nat. and fgn. policy to profl. jours. Vis. scholar Woodrow Wilson Ctr. for Scholars, Washington, 1987-88, 90. Lt. col. AUS, 1940-45; with guerrilla forces 1944-45, Europe (OSS); chief U.S. Mil. Mission to Yugoslavia, 1945. Decorated Legion of Merit; recipient Gold Freedom medal Republic of Slovenia. Mem. Nat. Planning Assn. (vice chmn. com. arms control 1959-62), Coun. Fgn. Rels., Inst. Strategic Studies (London), Com. for Econ. Devel. (trustee 1967—, vice chmn. 1974-88, mem. rsch. and policy com. 1968—), Can.-Am. Com., Hudson Inst. (pub. mem.), Saturday Club (Boston), Century Club (N.Y.), Phi Beta Kappa, Tau Beta Pi.

LINDSEY, JOANNE M., flight attendant, poet; b. Peoria, Ill., Aug. 27, 1936; d. George Edward and Elsie Rosetta (Mann) L.; m. Aug. 1959 (div. 1961). AA, El Camino Coll., Torrance, Calif., 1958. Exec. adminstrv. sec. Space Tech. Labs. (formerly Ramo-Woolridge), Hawthorne, Calif., 1958-64; flight attendant Am. Airlines, L.A., 1964—. Contbr. poems to anthologies. Attended People to People Amb. Program's So. African Tour of Women Writers, 1998. Recipient 5 Poetry Editor's Choice awards in anthologies Nat. Libr. Poetry, 1996, 97, 98. Mem. AAUW, Acad. Am. Poets, Audie Murphy Rsch. Found., Internat. Soc. Poets, L.A. World Affairs Coun.. Avocations: gardening, writing, skiing, mountain biking, home refurbishing. Home: 846 American Oaks Ave Newbury Park CA 91320-5572

LINDSEY, JONATHAN ASMEL, development executive, educator; b. Bulloch County, Ga., June 9, 1937; s. Joel Wesley and Ethel Iora (Stickland) L.; m. Edythe Annette Loewer, Apr. 3, 1965; children—Julianna Elizabeth, Jonathan Edward. A.B., George Washington U., 1961; B.D., So. Bapt. Sem., Louisville, 1964; Ph.D., So. Bapt. Sem., 1968; M.S.L.S., U. Ala., 1975. Assoc. prof., librarian Judson Coll., Marion, Ala., 1967-77; assoc. dean, librarian Meredith Coll., Raleigh, N.C., 1977-83; librarian Baylor U., Waco, Tex., 1983-89, dir. found. devel., 1989-95; dir donor info./recognition, 1995—. Author: (monographs) Free To Be, 1975, Change and Challenge, 1978, Professional Ethics and Librarians, 1985, Performance Evaluation: A Management Basic, 1986; editor: N.C. Libraries (H.W. Wilson award 1981), 1979-83, Publications in Librarianship, 1988-93; contbr. articles and book revs. to profl. publs. Mem. Waco Peace Alliance, PTA. Mem. ALA, Nat. Soc. Fund Raising Execs., Coun. for Advancement and Support of Edn., Tex. Libr. Assn. Home: 8265 Mosswood Dr Waco TX 76712-2407 Office: Baylor U PO Box 97026 Waco TX 76798-7026

LINDSEY, LINDA LEE, sociology educator; b. St. Louis, Aug. 16, 1947; d. Robert Houston and Ruth Margaret (Weimert) L. BA in Sociology and Edn., U. Mo., 1969; MA, Case Western Res. U., 1972, PhD in Sociology, 1974; MA in Counseling, St. Louis U., 1983. Cert. lifetime secondary social sci. tchr., Mo. Asst. prof. sociology John Carroll U., Cleve., 1973-78; mktg. rsch. supr. Southwestern Bell, St. Louis, 1978-79; assoc. prof. St. Louis Coll. Pharmacy, 1979-86; adj. assoc. prof. social thought and analysis Washington U., St. Louis, 1981—; prof. sociology Maryville U., St. Louis, 1986—; cons. Fact Finders Mktg. Rsch., 1982—; rep. Women's Program Coun. St. Louis, 1983—; rschr. Third World Women, Washington U. and Maryville U., 1990—; spokesperson Am. Stop Smoking Campaign, St. Louis, 1996—; presenter World Congress Sociology, 1978, UN Conf. on Women, Beijing, 1995; program evaluator Asian Studies devel. program East-West Ctr., 1999-2000. Author: Gender Roles: A Sociological Perspective, 1997; co-author: Sociology: Social Life and Social Issues, 2000; also articles. Trustee Children's Survival Fund, Carbondale, Ill., 1985-96; mem., chairperson advocacy com., bd. dirs. Luth. Family and Children's Svcs., St. Louis, 1992—; feedback supr. health focus group Med. Sch. St. Louis U., 1986—. Japanese culture fellow NEH, 1995; fellow Keizai Koho Ctr., Tokyo, 1990; NSF fellow Harvard U., 1989; Malone fellow Nat. Coun. U.S.-Arab Rels., Jordan, 1988; Fulbright fellow, India, 1981, Pakistan, 1986, India Inst., 1999; NEH summer Seminar awardee, Asian Studies Deveil. Program summer Inst. award to Korea, 2000. Mem. Am. Sociol. Assn. (presenter 1995), Nat. Coun. Internat. Health, World Affairs Coun., Sociologists for Women in Soc., Midwest Sociol. Soc. (presenter 1979—), Mo. State Sociol. Soc. (pres. 1994-95, conf. presenter 1997-99). Democrat. Lutheran. Avocations: international travel, swimming, speaking, writing. Home: 29 Algonquin Wood Pl Saint Louis MO 63122-2013 Office: Maryville Univ 13550 Conway Rd Saint Louis MO 63141-7299

LINDSEY, ROBERTA LEWISE, music researcher, historian; b. Munich, Apr. 23, 1958; d. Fred S. and Elsie E. (White) L. BMus, Butler U., 1980, MMus, 1987; PhD, Ohio State U., 1996. Pres., owner Profl. Typing Svcs., Indpls., 1980-84; mktg. specialist Merchants Mortgage Corp., Indpls., 1985-87; exec. asst. Ind. Arts Commn., Indpls., 1988-90; GTA Ohio State U., Columbus, 1990-94, music libr. asst., 1991-93, student coord. music in Ohio festival, 1993, vol. tutor coord., 1994-95; lectr. Ohio State U., Marion, 1995; rsch. editor Ind. High Tech. Directory, 1995-97; lectr. Ind. U. Sch. Music, 1998; vis. asst. prof. Ind. U. Sch. Music, Indianapolis, 1999—; rep. Susan Prter Meml. symposium Ohio State U., Columbus, 1995; vis. rsch. fellow Am. Music Rsch. Ctr., 1997; presenter Am. Musicol. Soc. Midwest conv., 1998, Soc. Am. Music Nat. Conv., 2000, Am. Musicol. Soc. Midwest Conv., 2000, Copland 2000: A Centennial Fest, 2000; co-presenter Tech. Music Appreciation Symposium, 1999. Book reviewer Ohioana Jour.; contbg. editor: Lenten Devotional, 2000; contbr. articles to profl. jours. Reader Ctrl. Ind. Radio Reading, Inc., Indpls., 1985-90; co-founder, mem. Grad. Music Students Assn., Ohio State U., Columbus; mem. multicultural diversity com. Coun. of Grad. Students, Columbus, 1992, mem. orgns. and elections com., 1992, co-chair orientation com., 1993; pre-concert lectr. Carmel Symphony Orch., 1998; mem. Inst. Rep. for the Arts, 1999—; adv. bd. Eiteljorg Mus., 1999—. Sinfonia Rsch. grantee Sinfonia Found., 1993; recipient Grad. Student Alumni Rsch. award Ohio State U., 1993. Mem. Soc. Am. Music, Am. Musicol. Soc., Coll. Music Soc., Soc. Ethnomusicology, Am. Music Rsch. Ctr., Classic Ragtime Soc.

LINDSTRÖM, CAJ-GUNNAR, asset management company executive; b. Karis, Nyland, Finland, Apr. 18, 1942; s. Holger Gunnar and Ilse (Ahlfors) L.; m. Ritva Virtanen; children: Carina, Ronny, Katja. MBA, Åbo (Finland) Acad. U., 1968, D Mgmt. Sci., 1971. Lectr. Åbo Acad. U., 1969-72, prof. mgmt. sci., 1972-92; mng. dir. Åbo Acad. Found., 1993—; rector Bus. Sch. Åbo Acad. U., 1974-80, rector, 1982-88; head of divsn. Swedish Nat. Bd. of Univs. and Colls., Stockholm, 1990-92; bd. dirs. Aktia Bank, Helsinki. Chmn. bd. Verdandi Assurance Co., Åbo, 1997—; bd. dirs. Partek Oyj Abp, Finland, 1998—; mem. Royal Nerwegian Hon. Coun., 1994—. Home: Kankas Gård, 21250 Masku Finland Office: Åbo Acad Found, Auragatan 8, 20100 Åbo Finland

LINDSTROM, CLAS GUNNAR, physician; b. Linkoping, Sweden, Feb. 23, 1940; s. Berndt Gunnar and Ingrid (Kuhla) L.; m. Britta Anna Egberg, Dec. 30, 1972; children: Lars, Linus, Jonas. Med. Cand., U. Lund, Sweden, 1960, PhD, 1978, Med. Lic., 1967. Pathologist cert., 1971. Asst. demonstrator, rsch. asst. U. Lund, 1962-63, 67-81, univ. lectr., 1982-88, clin. tchr., 1988-94; cons. U. Hosp. Mas, Malmo, Sweden, 1971-94, sr. physician, 1994-99; univ. lectr. U. Lund, 1994-99, ret., 1999; dir. studies, U. Lund, 1981-83, 86-98; cons. Medscand, Malmo, 1971-95. Inventor in field. Mem. Swedish Assn. Pathology (pres. edn. com. 1992-95, sec. edn. com. 1988-92), European Assn. Pathology, Swedish Med. Assn.

LINDSTROM, ERIC EVERETT, ophthalmologist; b. Helena, Mont., Nov. 28, 1936; s. Everett Harry and Nan Augusta (Johnson) L.; m. Nancy Jo Alexander, July 24, 1960; children: Laura Ann, Eric Everett. BS, Wheaton Coll., 1958; MD, U. Md., 1963; MPH, Harvard U., 1966. Diplomate Am. Bd. Preventive Medicine, Am. Bd. Ophthalmology. Intern Madigan Army Med. Ctr., Tacoma, 1963-64; resident in aerospace medicine Sch. Aerospace Medicine, Brooks AFB, Tex., 1966-68; resident in ophthalmology Brooke Army Med. Ctr., Ft. Sam Houston, Tex., 1972-75; surgeon 12th combat aviation group U.S. Army, Vietnam, 1968-69; chief profl. svcs. and aviation medicine Beach Army Hosp., Ft. Wolters, Tex., 1969-72; asst. chief ophthalmology clinic Madigan Army Med. Ctr., Tacoma, 1975-76; now with Lindstrom Eye Clinic; med. dir. Palo Pinto County (Tex.) Mental Health Clinic, 1970-72; ret.; cons. Tex. State Rehab. Com., 1971-72; chmn. bd. trustees South Cen. Regional Med. Ctr.; sr. aviation med. examiner, FAA; flight surgeon Miss. ANG. Deacon First Bapt. Ch., Laurel, 1978—; bd. dirs. Laurel Salvation Army, Good Shepherd Clin., Laurel. Decorated Bronze Star, Air medal with 2 oak leaf clusters, Meritorious Svc. medal. Fellow ACS, Am. Coll. Physician Execs., Am. Coll. Preventive Medicine, Aerospace Med. Assn. (assoc.), Am. Acad. Ophthalmology; mem. AMA, FAA (sr. aviation med. examiner), Am. Acad. Cataract and Refractive Surgery, New Orleans Acad. Ophthalmology, Miss. Med. Assn. (trustee), Miss. Hosp. Assn. (bd. govs.), Miss. EENT Assn., South Miss. Med. Soc., So. Med. Assn., La.-Miss. EENT Assn., Flying Physicians Assn., Soc. Mil. Ophthalmologists, Soc. USAF Flight Surgeons, Alliance Air N.G. Flight Surgeons, Aircraft Owners and Pilots Assn., Kiwanis, Nu Sigma Nu. Home: 809 Cherry Ln Laurel MS 39440-1651 Office: Lindstrom Eye Clinic PO Box 407 Laurel MS 39441-0407

LINDSTRÖM, LARS ERNST SIMON, education educator; b. Lund, Sweden, Sept. 8, 1943; s. Henning and Ruth (Håkansson) L.; m. Barbara Kucha, July 13, 1996; children: Simon, Amanda. BA, Lund U., 1966, MA, 1970; PhD in Edn., Stockholm U., 1986. Lic. psychologist, Sweden. Lectr. Stockholm Sch. Social Work, Sweden, 1973-76; asst. prof. U. Coll. Arts, Crafts, and Design, Stockholm, 1976-90; rsch. assoc. Stockholm Inst. Edn./Stockholm U., 1990-94; prof. edn. Stockholm Inst. Edn., 1995—; cons. The Municipality of Stockholm, 1975-80; vis. scholar Harvard U., Cambridge, Mass., 1991; chmn. Nordic Network Rschrs. in Visual Arts Edn., 1994-97; project coord. Comenius 3.1 program European Union, 1997-99; vis. prof. Linköping (Sweden) U., 1999; sci. adviser Nat. Swedish Bd. of Health and Welfare; mem. gov. bd. Stockholm Inst. Edn. Author: Managing Alcoholism, 1992; editor: Nordic Visual Arts Research, 1998, The Cultural Context, 2000; contbr. articles to profl. jours. Lutheran. Home: Urbergsvägen 20, S-16764 Bromma Sweden Office: Stockholm Inst Edn, Box 34103, S-10026 Stockholm Sweden

LINDSTRÖM, TORBJÖRN HANS, endocrinologist, researcher; b. Örebro, Närke, Sweden, Nov. 9, 1952; s. Hans Gustaf and Birgit Ingeborg (Wrane) L.; m. Margareta Anna Bachrach, Aug. 6, 1983; children: Gustaf, Victor, Björn. MD, Uppsala (Sweden) U., 1978; specialist in Internal Medicine, Linköping (Sweden) U., 1985, specialist in Endocrinology, 1986, PhD, 1993. Diplomate Nat. Bd. Health and Welfare Sweden. Intern Norrköping (Sweden) Hosp., 1978-80; resident U. Hosp., Linköping, Sweden, 1980-85; mem. staff Norrköping (Sweden) Hosp., 1978-80; specialist U. Hosp., Linköping, Sweden, 1980-85. Contbr. articles to profl. jours. Mem. European Assn. Study Diabetes, Scandinavian Soc. Study Diabetes, Swedish League Against Hypertension. Avocations: numismatics, dark ages. Office: Dept Endocrinology, The University Hosp, SE-58185 Linköping Sweden

LINDTEIGEN, SUSANNA, rancher, state official; b. Bismarck, N.D., Oct. 3, 1947; d. Casper J. and Lillian Rose (Gross) Kraft; m. Richard Lindteigen; children: Robin Lee, Rhonda Wendy. BS, Mary Coll., 1979; MPA, U. N.D., 1981. Bookkeeper Cen. Bottling Co., Bismarck, 1966-71; office mgr. Jobbers Warehouse/Allied Van Lines, Bismarck, 1971-72; account clk. Hwy. Patrol, Bismarck, 1972-75, per. sec., 1976-78; legal sec. Pub. Svc. Commn. State of N.D., Bismarck, 1979-80, grants and contracts officer Pub. Svc. Commn., 1980-91; acct. technician The Falkirk Minig Co-N.Am. Coal Corp., 1999—; office asst. The Falkirk Mining Co.-N.Am. Coal Corp., 1999. Sec. Dist. 8 Rep. Exec. Com., 1995-98, chmn., 1997-98, 2000—; senate edn. com. clk. N.D. Legislature, 1997; temp. program asst. USDA Farm Svc. Agy. McLean County, 1998-99; mem. ho. human svcs. com. clk. N.D. Legislature, 1999. Recipient Excellence in Pub. Svc. award Gov. of N.D., 1987, South McLean County Soil Conservation award, 1994. Mem. Pheasants Forever, Westerners Club. Republican. Avocations: reading, gardening. Home and Office: 1037 14th Ave NW Turtle Lake ND 58575-9447

LINDUP, WILLIAM EDWARD, pharmacologist, educator; b. Shrewsbury, Shropshire, Eng., July 18, 1944; s. Edward Dennis and Elizabeth May (Jones) L.; m. Joan Mary Cooper, July 10, 1971; children: Anna, Ruth, Lucy. B Pharmacy, U. Wales, Cardiff, 1965; PhD, U. Surrey, Guildford, Eng., 1971. Toxicologist Glaxo Rsch., Fulmer, Eng., 1965-66; rschr. St. Mary's Hosp. Med. Sch., London, 1966-67; rschr. U. Surrey, Guildford, 1967-69, lectr., 1970-73; lectr. dept. pharm. therapeutics U. Liverpool, Eng., 1974-80, sr. lectr., 1980—; cons. Procter & Gamble, 1974-79. Mem. editl. bd. British Jour. Pharmacology, 1981-88, Xenobiotica, 1989-95, Jour. Pharmacy Pharmacology, 1990—, British Jour. Clin. Pharmacology, 1995—; contbr. articles to profl. jours. Grantee Med. Rsch. Coun., 1985-88, Assn. Internat. Cancer Rsch., 1995—, Wellcome Trust, 1998—. Mem. Royal Pharm. Soc. Great Britain, Biochem. Soc., British Pharm. Soc., British Toxicology Soc. Avocations: music, family activities. Office: U Liverpool Dept Pharm, Therapeutics, PO Box 147, Liverpool L69 3BX, England

LINERT, WOLFGANG, chemist, educator; b. Vienna, Austria, Aug. 9, 1955; s. August and Ermelinde (Schöber) L.; m. Maryse Valin, Nov. 4, 1993; 2 children. Degree in engring., HBLVA, Vienna, 1975; diploma in engring., Tech. U., Vienna, 1979, D Tech. in Chemistry, 1981. Asst. Tech. U., 1975-89, lectr., docent, 1989-96, Univ. prof. chemistry, 1996—; leader sci. group Tech. U., 1991; mem. mgmt. and tech. coms. sci. European Union Orgs. Author: Physico-Chemical Applications of NMR, 1996, Chromotropic Materials, 1998; contbr. over 200 articles to profl. jours. Recipient Rudolf Wegscheider prize Austrian Acad. Sci., 1993, Sandoz prize for chemistry, Vienna, 1994. Mem. Accademia Peloritana dei Pericolanti (corr.), Austrian Chem. Soc. (chmn. br.). Office: TU Vienna Inst Inorg Chem, Getreidemarkt 9, A-1060 Vienna Austria

LINFORD, SANDI FELICITY, electronics company executive; b. Johannesburg, South Africa, Mar. 3, 1961; d. George Henry and Theresa Mary (Jurgason) L. Cert. in Bus. Mgmt., South African Chartered Inst., 1989. Shipping officer Oilseeds Bd., Durban, South Africa, 1980-88; asst. group sec. Frame Group Ltd., Durban, 1988-89, group sec., 1989-92; co. sec. Power Techs. Ltd., Johannesburg, 1992-94; group sec. Allied Electronics Corp. Ltd., Johannesburg, 1994—. Assoc. mem. Chartered Inst. Bus. Mgmt. Avocations: reading, wildlife, conservation, travel. Home: PO Box 961, Ferndale 2160, South Africa Office: Allied Electronics Corp Ltd, Brakpan and Van Dyk rds, Boksburg 1459, South Africa

LING, CAROLINE JANE, press officer; b. Lancashire, Eng., Apr. 21, 1965. Jour. Proficiency, Richmond Coll., Sheffield, Eng., 1989. Reporter Citizen Newspaper Group, Lancashire, 1986-88, news editor, 1988-89; feature writer Brighton Evening Argus, Sussex, Eng., 1989-93; press officer West Midlands Police, Eng., 1993-94, Midlands Electricity, West Midlands, 1994—. Mem. Inst. Pub. Rels. (assoc.). Avocations: reading, writing, restoring, furniture. Office: Midlands Electricity GPU Co, Whittington Hall, B62 8BP Worcester WR5 2RB, England

LING, CHUNG-MEI, retired pharmaceutical company executive; b. Wen-Ling, Zhejiang, China, May 5, 1931; came to U.S., 1960; s. Hsin-Sao Ling and San-Mei Juan; m. Amy Hsieh; children: Dori, Ellen. BS, Nat. Taiwan U., 1958; MS, Ill. Inst. Tech., 1962, PhD, 1965. Head virology lab. Abbott Labs., North Chicago, Ill., 1968-81, rsch. fellow, 1978-84, mgr. rsch. and devel., 1981-84; founder, chmn. bd. dirs., chief sci. officer Gen. Biologicals Corp., Hsinchu, Taiwan, 1984-88, hon. chmn. bd., 1991—; prof. Nat. Tsing-Hua U., Hsinchu, 1991-93; asst. prof. Ill. Inst. Tech., Chgo., 1965-68; sci. specialist Nat. Inst. Preventative Medicine, Taipei, Taiwan, 1984-85; chief sci.

cons. KangLing Biotech. Corp., Hsinchu, 1988—. Contbr. articles to profl. jours; patentee in field; inventor Hepatitis B diagnostics. Fellow Am. Acad. Microbiology; mem. Am. Soc. Biol. Chemists, Am. Clin. Chem., Sigma Xi. Avocations: sight-seeing, singing, interior design. Office: 5901 Sun Blvd Ste 202 Saint Petersburg FL 33715-1161

LING, FENG, engineer, scientist; b. Suzhou, Jiangsu, China, July 10, 1971; s. Zhongxi Ling and Limin Kong; m. Jun Lu, May 16, 1996. BS, Nanjing (China) U. Sci./Tech., 1993, MS, 1996; PhD, U. Ill., 2000. Cert. engring. Rsch. asst. Nanjing U. Sci. and Tech., 1993-96, U. Ill., Urbana, 1996-2000; sr. engr., scientist Motorola Inc., Tempe, Ariz., 2000—. Contbr. articles to profl. jours. Mem. IEEE, Phi Kappa Phi. Achievements include research on fast electromagnetic modeling of multilayer microstrip antennas and circuits, hybridization of SBR and MoM RF integrated circuits, RF module and package. Avocations: sports, music, travel. E-mail: fengling@ieee.org Fax: 480-413-4511. Office: 2100 E Elliot Rd # El727 Tempe AZ 85284-1806

LING, FRANCIS CHI-CHUNG, physicist, physics lecturer; b. Hong Kong, Hong Kong, Oct. 2, 1966; s. Kui and Ying-kun (Lo) L.; m. Amy Ngar-ling Lee, May 7, 1969. BSc with honors, U. Hong Kong, 1990, MPh, 1994, PhD, 1996. Chartered physicist. Tchg. asst. U. Hong Kong, 1990-93, 94-96, hon. asst prof., 1996—; scientific officer Hong Kong Govt., 1993. Contbr. articles to profl. jours. Sir Edward Yonde fellow Sir Edward Yonde Meml. Fund Coun., 1995, 96. Avocations: pop music, badminton, table tennis, swimming, football. Office: Dept Physics U Hong Kong, Pokfulam Rd, Hong Kong China

LING, GUO CAN, fluid mechanics educator, scientist; b. Shanghai, Dec. 25, 1938; s. Ling Geng Sheng and Wei Lun Ting; m. Niu Jia Yu, Oct. 22, 1966; children: Yan, Hua. Grad. dept. aerodynamics, Beijing U. Aero/Astronautics, 1960. Tchr. dept. mechanics China U. Sci. and Tech., Beijing, 1961-73; rsch. assoc. Ministry Aerospace Industry, Beijing Inst. Aerodynamics, Beijing, 1974-78; assoc. prof., vice-dir. dept. fluid mechanics Inst. Mechanics, Chinese Acad. Scis. (CAS), Beijing, 1979-84; sr. acad. visitor dept. aeronautics Imperial Coll. Sci. and Tech., London, 1985-86; prof., dir. dept. fluid mechanics, vice-dir. Lab. for Nonlinear Mechanics of Continuous Media, CAS, Beijing, 1987-97, prof., vice-chmn. acad. com., 1997-99; vice chmn. acad. com. State Key Lab. for Nonlinear Mechancs, CAS, 1999—; prof. dept. engring. mechanics Tsinghua (China) U., 1999—; prof. Inst. Applied Math. and Mechanics, Shanghai (China) U., 1999—; vice-chief editor aerodynamics br. China Encyclopedia Press, Beijing, 1982-85; mem. editl. com. ACTA Aeronautica and Astronautica, Beijing, 1988—; standing mem. editl. com. ACTA Mechanica Sinica, China, N.Y.C., 1992—; mem. editl. com. Jour. Hydrodynamics, Shanghai, 1989—. Mem. editl. bd. Jour. Advancements in Mechanics, 1996—; mem. editl. com. ACTA Aerodynamica Sinica, 1998—; reviewer Zentralblatt für Mathematik; contbr. articles to profl. jours. Recipient 2d Class Achievement award in sci. and tech. Chinese Acad. of Scis., 1982, 2d Class Achievement award in nature sci., 1989, 1st Class Spl. Allowance for life State Coun. China, 1992—. Mem. Internat. Soc. of Offshore and Polar Engrs., N.Y. Acad. Scis., Chinese Soc. Theoretical and Applied Mechanics. Avocation: classical music. Office: Inst Mechanics Chinese Acad Scis, LNM Zhong Guan Cun Rd, Beijing 100080, China

LING, JIAN, researcher, consultant; b. Chongqing, China, July 6, 1954; came to the U.S., 1994; s. Guangquan Ling and Shufang Xu; m. Huilian Wu, Dec. 10, 1982; 1 child, Yun. BS, Chongqing U., 1982; MS, Fla. Internat. U., 1996, PhD, 1999. Mech. engr. Jiangyou Power Plant, Sichuan, China, 1982-85; asst. prof. Chongqing U., 1988-94, head tchg. and rsch. divsn. in thermal engring., 1992-94; rsch. asst. Fla. Internat. U., Miami, 1994-97, tchg. asst., 1997-99, rsch. assoc., 1999—; cons. Jiangyou Power Plant, Sichuan, 1988-94. Co-author: Industrial Steam Turbine, 1994; contbr. articles to profl. jours. Mem. ASME (assoc.). E-mail: jlingol@fiu.edu. Office: Fla Internat Univ 3725 EAS Bldg 10555 W Flagler St Miami FL 33174-1630

LING, ROBERT MALCOLM, banker, publishing executive; b. Akron, Ohio, July 6, 1931; s. Howard George and Catherine Zola (Smith) L.; m. Lois Claire Fisher Ling, Nov. 1, 1992; children: Shelly, Robert Jr., Amy, Beth, Patricia. BA in Journalism, Mich. State U., 1952. Asst. pres. Dike-O-Seal, Inc., Chgo., 1955-56; gen. mgr. Vollwerth Marquette (Mich.) Co., 1956-58, pres., 1958-75; pres. Vandco Incorp., Marquette, 1975-85, Cable American Corp., Rancho Cordova, Calif., 1985-89, Romali Holdings, Inc., Rancho Cordova, Calif., 1989—; chmn. Gold River Bank, Fair Oaks, Calif., 1990-92, Sacramento Safety Ctr., Inc., 1996—; publisher Grapevine-Independent newspaper, Rancho Cordova, Calif. Mayor City of Marquette, 1980-83, City of Rancho Cordova, Calif., 1986-87. Capt. U.S. Army, 1952-55. Republican. Home: 6032 Puerto Dr Rancho Murieta CA 95683-9313 Office: Romali Holdings Inc 3338 Mather Field Rd Rancho Cordova CA 95670-5966

LING, WEI, mechanical engineering. MS in Mech. Engring., Washington State U., 1996, MS in Computer Sci., 1999, PhD, 1999. Mech. engr. Electric Locomotive Rsch. Inst., Zhuzhou, Hunan, China, 1990-94; mem. tech. staff Lucent Tech., Inc, Holmdel, N.J., 1999—. Contbr. articles to profl. jours. E-mail: wling@lucent.com.

LING, XIAOPING, computer engineer, educator; b. Shanghai, China, Mar. 2, 1961; arrived in Japan, 1983; s. Liangming Ling and Suzhen Ji; m. Xianglong Wang, Oct. 13, 1991; 1 child, Lijia. BSc, Zhongshan U., Guangzhou, China, 1983; M in Engring., KEIO U., Yokohama, Japan, 1987, PhD in Engring., 1994. Rschr. Kanagawa Inst. Tech., Atsugi, Japan, 1994—; lectr. Tokyo Kougei U., Atsugi, Japan, 1998—. Contbr. articles to profl. jours. including The Jour. of Supercomputing. Mgr. Personal Computer User's Application Tech. Assn., Tokyo, 1988-93. Mem. IEEE, Inst. Electronics, Info. and Comm. Engrs. (com. mem. 1998), Info. Processing Soc. Japan. Avocations: flower arrangement, reading, photo, trival. E-mail: ling@ic.kanagawa-it.ac.jp. Fax: 81(46) 242-8490. Office: Kanagawa Inst Tech, 1030 Shimoogino, Atsugi 243-0292, Japan

LINGA, VENKATESWAR RAO, microbiologist, educator; b. Pallegudem, India, Feb. 3, 1955; s. Rangaiah and Subhadramma (Mikkilineni) L.; m. Arundathi Mikkilineni, June 14, 1978; children: Prakash, Prathima. BS, Osmania U., Hyderabad, India, 1976, MS, 1978, PhD, 1984. Asst. prof. Osmania U., 1978-85, sr. asst. prof., 1986-90, assoc. prof., 1991-98, head dept. microbiology, 1998—; cons. Divi's Labs., Inventa Chems., Usha Internat. Ltd., Hyderabad, 1998-99, Ctrl. Water Commn. Engrs., Hyderabad, 1997; head, chmn. dept. microbiology Nizam Coll., Hyderabad, 1985-90; dir. Sr. A.P. Govt. Coll. Tchrs. Tng. Program, Hyderabad, 1998-99. Author: Applied Microbiology, 2000; contbr. articles to profl. jours. Preceptor Shree Ram Chandra Mission, Hyderabad, 1996—. Mem. Am. Soc. Microbiology, Assn. Microbiologists of India (life), Indian Sci. Congress Assn. (life). Avocation: reading spiritual literature. Home: H # 16-11-741/B/13/103, Moosarambagh, Hyderabad AP 500036, India Office: Osmania U, Dept Microbiology, Hyderabad AP 500007, India

LINGEL, NADA JO, optometry educator; b. Great Falls, Mont., May 15, 1957; d. Donald Stanley and Anna Marie (Lorang) L.; m. Dennis Lynn Smith, May 27, 1989. BS, Pacific U., 1979, D of Optometry, 1981, MS, 1988. Cert. of residency in hosp. based optometry. Pvt. practice Hillsboro, Oreg., 1981-84; asst. prof. optometry Pacific U., Forest Grove, Oreg., 1984-90, assoc. prof., 1990-96, prof., 1996—, asst. dean clin. affairs Coll. Optometry, 1993-96; rsch. optometrist, clinic mgr. Cornea and Contact Lens Rsch. Unit, Sydney, NSW, Australia, 1987-88; consulting and attending dr. VA Med. Ctr., Portland, Oreg., 1994—. Author: (with others) Clinical Ocular Pharmacology, 1995, Clinical Optometric Pharmacology and Therapeutics, 1996; mem. editl. rev. bd. Jour. Optometric Edn., 1991—. Recipient 1st Annual Innovation in Edn. award Assn. Schs. and Colls. Optometry, 2000; named Best Instr., Phi Theta Upsilon, 1991. Fellow Am. Acad. Optometry; mem. Am. Optometric Assn. (mem. coun. optometric edn. 1995—, Continuing Optometric Recognition award 1996, 97, 98, 99, 2000), Oreg. Optometric Assn. (mem. quality assessment appeal bd. 1994—), Beta Sigma Kappa. Avocations: watercolor painting, bicycling. Office: Pacific U Coll Optometry 2043 College Way Forest Grove OR 97116-1797

LINGLE, CRAIG STANLEY, glaciologist, educator; b. Carlsbad, N.Mex., Sept. 11, 1945; s. Stanley Orland and Margaret Pearl (Ewart) L.; m. Diana Lynn Duncan, Aug. 21, 1972; 1 son, Eric Glenn. BS, U. Wash., 1967; MS, U. Maine, 1978; PhD, U. Wis., 1983. Nat. rsch. coun. resident rsch. assoc. Coop. Inst. for Rsch. in Environ. Scis., U. Colo., Boulder, 1983-84, rsch. assoc., 1984-86; program mgr. polar glaciology divsn. polar programs NSF, Washington, 1986-87; cons. Jet Propulsion Lab., Pasadena, Calif., 1987-88; nat. rsch. coun. resident rsch. assoc. NASA Goddard Space Flight Ctr., Oceans and Ice Branch, Greenbelt, Md., 1988-90; rsch. assoc. prof. Geophys. Inst., U. Alaska, Fairbanks, 1990-2000, acting dir. Alaska synthetic aperture radar facility, 1997-98, rsch. prof. geophysics, 2000—. Contbr. articles to profl. jours. Recipient Antarctic Svc. medal of U.S., NSF, 1987, Rsch. Project of Month award Office of Health and Environ. Rsch., U.S. Dept. Energy, 1990, Group Achievement award NASA, 1992. Mem. AAAS, Internat. Glaciological Soc., Am. Geophys. Union, Sigma Xi. Avocations: downhill and cross-country skiing, canoeing, hiking. Office: U Alaska Geophys Inst PO Box 757320 Fairbanks AK 99775-7320

LINHART, JOSEPH WAYLAND, retired cardiologist, educational administrator; b. N.Y.C., Feb. 7, 1933; s. Joseph and Myrla Watson (Wayland) L.; m. Marilyn Adele Voight, Sept. 1, 1956; children: Joseph, Mary-Ellen, Richard, Jennifer, Donna-Lisa, Daria. BS, George Washington U., 1954, MD, 1958. Diplomate Am. Bd. Internal Medicine with subspecialty in cardiovascular diseases. Intern Washington Hosp. Ctr., 1958-59; resident George Washington U. Hosp., Washington, 1959-60, Duke U. Hosp., Durham, N.C., 1961; fellow Duke U. Hosp., Durham, 1960, 62-63, Nat. Heart Inst./Johns Hopkins Hosp., Bethesda/Balt., Md., 1963-64; asst. prof. medicine U. Fla., Gainesville, 1964-67; clin. assoc. prof. U. Miami, Fla., 1967-68; assoc. prof. medicine U. Tex., San Antonio, 1968-71; prof., dir. cardiology Hahnemann Med. Coll., Phila., 1971-75; prof., chmn. dept. medicine Chgo. Med. Sch., 1975-79, Oral Roberts U., Tulsa, 1979-83; prof. medicine U. South Fla., Tampa, 1983-92; prof., regional chmn. medicine Tex. Tech. U., Odessa, 1992-93; prof. medicine La. State U., Shreveport, 1993-97; chief med. svc. VA Med. Ctr., Shreveport, 1993-97, acting chief of staff, 1996-97; ret., 1997; cons. in cardiology and med./legal questions. Contbr. articles to profl. jours.; author 4 books. Mem. med. adv. com. YMCA, Niles, Ill., 1976-79; bd. govs. Phila. Heart Assn., 1972-75; mem. rsch. coun. Okla. Heart Assn., Tulsa, 1980-83. Fellow ACP, Am. Coll. Cardiology; mem. AAAS, Planetary Soc., Nat. Space Soc., Astron. Soc. of Pacific, Alpha Omega Alpha. Republican. Avocations: astronomy, history, model building, organ playing, music. Home: 625 Red Cedar Ct NE Saint Petersburg FL 33703-6203

LINK, GERHARD GOTTFRIED, botany educator; b. Kaköhl, Plön, Germany, Nov. 29, 1948. M in Biology and Chemistry, U. Hannover, Germany, 1972, PhD in Botany and Biochemistry, 1974; Habil., U. Freiburg, Germany, 1982. Rsch. assoc. dept. sci. U. Hannover, 1974-76; rsch. assoc. Biological Labs. Harvard U., Cambridge, Mass., 1976-79; rsch. assoc. dept. biology U. Freiburg, 1979-82; prof. plant cell physiology and molecular biology U. Bochum, Germany, 1985—; vis. asst. prof. Plant Molecular Biology Lab. Rockefeller U., N.Y.C., 1982-83. Contbr. articles to profl. jours. including Cell, EMBO Jour., and Procs. of NAS, also chptrs. to books. Recipient Habilitanden-Stipendium, Deutsche Forschungsgemeinschaft, 1979-82, Heisenberg Rsch. Career Devel. award, 1982-85, rsch. fellow, 1976-78; European Molecular Biology Orgn. long-term fellow, 1978-79. Mem. Internat. Soc. Plant Molecular Biology, Internat. Assn. for Plant Tissue Culture, Assn. Biochemistry and Molecular Biology, Deutsche Botanische Gesellschaft, Am. Soc. Plant Physiologists. Office: U Bochum Plant Physiology, Universitaetsstr 150, D-44780 Bochum ND2/72, Germany

LINK, HENRY JOSEPH, environmental engineer; b. Hartford, Conn., Feb. 19, 1946; s. Frank Joseph and Veronica (Schwegler) L. BSME, MIT, 1967; postgrad., Hartford Grad. Ctr., 1968. Registered profl. engr., Conn. Rsch. engr. United Techs. Corp., East Hartford, Conn., 1968-72, Met. Dist. Commn., Hartford, 1978; environ. engr. CE Maguire, Wethersfield, Conn., 1972-73; various positions, 1973-77; environ. engr. Conn. Health Dept., Hartford, 1978—; dir., cons. Resource Recovery Sys., Essex, Conn., 1978—; bd. dirs., v.p. Performance Automotive, Glastonbury, Conn., 1970—; bd. dirs. Lightstat, New Hartford. Bd. dirs. Hartford Ballet, 1982—, MIT Club of Hartford, 1990—. Mem. World Affairs Coun. (bd. dirs.), Wadsworth Atheneum, Hillstead Mus., New Britain Mus., Sigma Xi. Avocations: tennis, viewing performing or visual arts. Home: 45 Mountain St Hartford CT 06106-4240

LINK, PATRICK JAMES, electrical engineer; b. May 26, 1953. AAS, Milw. Sch. Engring., 1974, BS in Elec. Engring. Tech., 1976. Field svc. engr. Allis-Chalmers, Milw., 1976-80; devel. engr. Siemens, Roswell, Ga., 1980-86; sys. support engr. Allen-Bradley Co., Baton Rouge, La., 1986-92; regl. svc. mgr. ABB Indsl. Systems, Inc., 1992-96; drives cons. ABB Automation Inc., Duluth, Ga., 1996-99; drive cons. ABB Automation Inc., Duluth, GA, 1996-99; pres. Adjustable Speed Drive Svcs., Inc., 1999—, 1999—. Home: 921 Sundew Dr Alpharetta GA 30005-4277

LINK, ROBERT JAMES, lawyer, educator; b. Washington, May 25, 1950; s. Robert Wendell and Barbara Ann (Bullock) L.; m. Cheryl Ann Brillante, Apr. 22, 1978; children: Robert Edward, Holden James. BA, U. Miami, 1972, JD, 1975. Bar: Fla. 1975, U.S. Dist. Ct. (mid. dist.) Fla. 1980, U.S. Ct. Appeals (5th cir.) 1980, U.S. Ct. Appeals (11th cir.) 1981, U.S. Supreme Ct. 1984, U.S. Dist. Ct. (no. dist.) Fla. 1989. Asst. pub. defender City of Miami, Fla., 1975-78, City of Jacksonville, Fla., 1978-82; ptnr. Greenspan, Goodstein & Link, Jacksonville, 1982-84, Goodstein & Link, Jacksonville, 1984-85; pvt. practice, Jacksonville, 1985-88; assoc. Howell, Liles & Milton, Jacksonville, 1988-89; ptnr. Pajcic & Pajcic P.A., 1990—; guest instr. U. Miami, 1976, U. Fla., 1979-88, Stetson U. Law Sch., 1984, Jacksonville U., 1987-88, U. North Fla., 1991. Atty. legal panel ACLU, Jacksonville, 1982-88. Mem. Fla. Bar Assn. (chmn. com. for representation of indigents criminal law sect. 1980, cert. criminal trial lawyer 1989), Jacksonville Bar Assn. (criminal law sect.), Nat. Assn. Criminal Def. Lawyers (vice-chmn. post conviction com. 1990), Fla. Pub. Defender Assn. (death penalty steering com. 1980-82, instr. 1979-89). Democrat. Methodist. Avocations: sailing, fishing, diving, softball. Home: 3535 Carlyon St Jacksonville FL 32207-5836 Office: 1900 Independent Dr Jacksonville FL 32202-5023

LINKOHR, ROLF, physicist; b. Stuttgart, Baden-W, Germany, Apr. 11, 1941; s. Helmut and Margarete (Straub) L.; m. Christel Schlotmann, Feb. 25, 1972; children: Birgit, Katharina. Physicist, U. Stuttgart, 1966; Dr. rer. nat., U. Munich, 1969. Rschr. Deutsche Automobil GmbH, Germany, 1970-79; mem. European Parliament, 1979—; pres., founder Sci. and Technol. Options Assessment, Brussels, 1985-94. Contbr. articles to profl. jours. Pres. European-LatinAm. Inst., Madrid, Spain, 1994—, European Energy Found., Brussels. Decorated Order: Officier de la Légion d'Honeur, France, 1998. Avocations: languages, history. Home: Asangstrasse 219A, 70329 Stuttgart Germany Office: European Parliament, 97-113 rue Wiertz, B-1047 Brussels Belgium

LINKOV, ALEXANDER MIKHAILOVICH, mechanical engineer, educator; b. Novokuznetsk, Kemerovo, Russia, Jan. 10, 1940; s. Mikhail Pavlovich Menkovich and Eugenia Alexandrovna Maslinkova; m. Eugenia Nikovaevna Ivanova, Aug. 5, 1970; children: Mary, Anastasia. MSc cum laude, Mech. U., Leningrad, Russia, 1963; DSc, State U., Leningrad, 1969, D of Phys. Math., 1977. Head of theoretical group All-Russian Inst. for Rock Mechanics and Mining Surveying, St. Petersburg, 1968-84; prof., head dept. Acad. Engring. Econs., St. Petersburg, 1984-93; chief scientist Inst. Problems Mech. Engring., St. Petersburg, 1993—; vis. prof. U. Minn., 1992, 94, 97; invited rschr. Coun. for Sci. and Indsl. Rsch., South Africa, 1996-97; chief scientist part-time VNIMI, 1994—. Author: Dynamic Phenomena in Mines and the Problem of Stability, 1994, Complex Variables Boundary Integral Equations of Elasticity Theory, 1999; co-author: Theory of Protective Seams, 1976, Mechanics of Rock and Outbursts, 1983. Recipient Internat. Schlumberger award for fundamental rsch. in rock mechanics, 1994. Mem. Internat. Assn. Boundary Element Methods, St. Petersburg Sci. Soc., Russian Counsel on Geodynamics, N.Y. Acad. Sci. Home: 32-1-68 Sofiyskaya St, 192236 Saint Petersburg Russia Office: Inst Problems Mech Engring, 61 Bol'shoy Prospect VO, 199178 Saint Petersburg Russia

LINN, CAROLE ANNE, dietitian; b. Portland, Oreg., Mar. 3, 1945; d. James Leslie and Alice Mae (Thorburn) L. Intern, U. Minn., 1967-68; BS, Oreg. State U., 1963-67. Nutrition cons. licensing and cert. sect. Oreg. State Bd. Health, Portland, 1968-70; chief clin. dietitian Rogue Valley Med. Ctr., Medford, Oreg., 1970—; cons. Hillhaven Health Care Ctr., Medford, 1971-83; lectr. Local Speakers Bur., Medford. Mem. ASPEN, Am. Dietetic Assn., Am. Diabetic Assn., Oreg. Dietetic Assn. (sec. 1973-75, nominating com. 1974-75, Young Dietitian of Yr. 1976), So. Oreg. Dietetic Assn., Alpha Lambda Delta, Omicron Nu. Democrat. Mem. Christ Unity Ch. Avocations: sewing, needlecrafts, cooking, swimming, skiing. Office: Rogue Valley Med Ctr 2825 E Barnett Rd Medford OR 97504-8332

LINN, JAMES ELDON, II, insurance company executive; b. Kokomo, Ind., Sept. 6, 1943; s. James Eldon and Mary Jane (Smith) L.; m. Pamela Ann Moser, Sept. 6, 1968 (div. 1986); 1 child, Aaron Moser; m. Annalee Shriner, Nov. 20, 1986 (dec. Apr. 1998); stepchildren: Kris Firestone, Adam Firestone. BS in Bus. Adminstrn., Pacific Western U.; Assoc. Acctg., Lane Tech. Inst. CLU, Chartered Fin. Cons. Mgr. meat A & P, Indpls., 1961-63, Safeway, L.A., 1963-65; agy. mgr. Farm Bur. Ins., Lafayette, Ind., 1967-95; agt., owner Allstate Ins. Premier Svc. Agt., Brooksville, Fla., 1996—; instr. Life Underwriting Tng. Coun. Pres. West Cen. chpt. Kidney Found., Lafayette, 1981-83; bd. mem., sustaining membership chmn. Greater Lafayette YMCA, 1987-92; pres. Greater Lafayette YMCA Found., Inc., 1990-95. Sgt. U.S. Army, 1965-67. Mem. Am. Coll. Life Underwriters, Ind. Assn. Life Underwriters (pres. 1985-86, chmn. ethics com. 1991-95), Lafayette Soc. CLUs (pres. 1982-83), Nat. Assn. Life Underwriters (vice chmn. polit. involvement com. 1987-89), Internat. Soc. Financiers (cert. 1988), C. of C. (membership com. 1990-91), Farm Bur. Pres. Club (life), Frm Bur. Gov.'s Club (life), Hernando E. Rotary (sec. 1997—). Republican. Methodist. Avocation: jogging. Office: Premier Svc Agt Allstate Ins 31134 Cortez Blvd Brooksville FL 34602-7548

LINNANE, ANTHONY WILLIAM, biochemistry educator; b. Sydney, NSW, Australia, July 17, 1930; s. William Patrick and Irene (Broadstock) L.; m. Judith Ann Neil, 1956 (div. 1979); children: Ruth Adele D., Nicholas Anthony S.; m. Daryl Ann Skurrie, May 1980. PhD, U. Sydney, 1956, DSc, 1972. Dir. Ctr. for Molecular Biology and Medicine Epworth Med. Ctr., Melbourne, Australia, 1983; prof. biochemistry Monash U., Melbourne, 1965-94, head dept. biochemistry, prof. emeritus, 1996—; hon. prof. dept. medicine U. Melbourne. Contb. articles and abstracts to profl. jours. Pres. Australian Biochem. Soc., 1974-76, Fedn. Asian & Oceanian Biochemists, 1977-87, 12th Internat. Congress of Biochemistry, 1982. Fellow Australian Acad. Sci., Royal Soc. (London); mem. Internat. Union Biochemistry and Molecular Biology (treas. 1988-98), Moonee Valley Racing Club, Victoria Amateur Turf Club, Victoria Racing Club, Athenaeum Club. Avocations: tennis, reading, horse-racing. Home: 24 Myrtle Rd, Canterbury 3126, Australia Office: Ctr Molecular Biology/Med, Monash U 185-187 Hoddle St, Richmond Vic. 3121, Australia

LINNARTZ, JEAN-PAUL MARIE GERARD, electrical engineer; b. Heerlen, The Netherlands, Sept. 10, 1961; s. Martinus Johannes and Anna Petronella Snijders Linnartz; m. Henriette Gea Smid, Jan. 7, 1993; children: Jasper, Ferdinand. MSc cum laude, Eindhoven U. Tech., The Netherlands, 1986; PhD in Elec. Engring. cum laude, Delft U. Tech., The Netherlands, 1991. Rsch. scientist Netherlands Orgn. Applied Rsch., The Hague, The Netherlands, 1987-88; asst. prof. elec. engring. Delft U. Tech., 1988-91, assoc. prof. elec. engring., 1994; asst. prof. elec. engring. U. Calif., Berkeley, 1991-95; rsch. scientist Philips Rsch., Eindhoven, 1995-98, sr. scientist, 1998-2000, prin. scientist, 2000—; cons. various radio broadcasters, 1990-95; adj. asst. prof. U. Calif., Berkeley, 1995-98; editor-in-chief Wireless Communication, The Interactive Multimedia CD ROM, 1995—. Author: Narrow Band Land Mobile Radio Networks, 1993; contbr. articles to profl. jours. Recipient Veder Prize Netherlands Electronics and Radio Soc., 1991. Office: Philips Rsch Nat Lab, Holstlaan 4 WY61, 5656AA Eindhoven The Netherlands

LINNECAR, PETER CHARLES ROLAND, financial services company executive; b. Croydon, Surrey, Eng., Mar. 3, 1953; s. Douglas Roland and Joan Kathleen (Robins) L.; m. Carolyn Mary Claire Love, Aug. 21, 1976; children: Benjamin, Stephen, Amy. BA with honors, Cambridge (Eng.) U., 1975, MA with honors, 1978; Cert. of Edn., Oxford (Eng.) U., 1976; Doctorate (hon.), All Nations, Benin, Nigeria, 1996; MA in Ch. Sch. Edn., Cheltenham and Gloucester Coll, 1998. Cert. tchr.; cert. fin. planner. Tchr. Bray's Grove Sch., Harlow, Eng., 1976-78; London mgr. Nat. Mut. Life, 1978-84; mng. dir. Macartney & Dowie Fin. Svcs. Ltd., Romford, Eng., 1984—, Macartney & Dowie Investment Mgmt. Plc, Romford, 1991—; bd. dirs. Baynes Roland Ins. Brokers, Alive U.K.; vice prin. Peniel Acad., Brentwood, 1982—; mem. com. ATL, Essex, Eng., 1995—. Editor: Fireside Talks about Brentwood, 1993. Sr. pastor Peniel Pentecostal Ch., Brentwood, 1995. Fellow Inst. Sales and Mktg. Mgmt.; mem. Brit. Inst. Mgmt. Pentecostal. Avocations: youth work, reading, education studies. Office: Macartney & Dowie Fin Svcs, Magellan House/57 Mawney Rd, Romford Essex RM7 7HL, England

LINO, MARISA ROSE, diplomat; d. Luigi and Vida (Bego) L. BA in Polit. Sci., Portland State U., 1971; MA in Internat. Affairs, George Washington U., 1972; postgrad., U. Zagreb, Yugoslavia, 1972-73; cert. in advanced engring. studies, MIT, 1982. Rotational officer Dept. State, Lima, Peru, 1975-77; watch officer ops. ctr. Dept. State, Washington, 1977-78, staff asst. policy planning staff, 1978-79; econ./comml. officer Dept. State, Baghdad, Iraq, 1979-81; info. systems officer Dept. State, 1982-83; adminstrv. officer Dept. State, Rome, 1983-85; econ. counselor Dept. State, Damascus, Syria, 1986-88; refugee coord. Dept. State, Islamabad, Pakistan, 1988-90; consul gen. Dept. State, Florence, Italy, 1990-93, mem. sr. exec. seminar, 1993-94, dep. exec. sec. of state, 1994-96; U.S. amb. Republic of Albania, 1996-99; sr. inspector Office Inspector Gen., Washington, 1999-2000; sr. negotiator for base access and borden sharing Polit. Mil. Affairs Bur., Washington, 2000—. Exhibited in group show of watercolor monotypes, Province of Florence, 1993. Mem. Am. Fgn. Svc. Assn. Avocations: tennis, sailing, hiking. Office: Polit Mil Affairs Bur Washington DC 20520-0001

LINS, ROMULO CAMPOS, mathematics educator; b. Rio de Janeiro, Aug. 21, 1955; s. Cláudio de Medeiros and Alda (Campos) L.; m. Abigail Fregni, June 10, 1988; children: Daniel, Julia, Camila. BEd in Math., U. São Paulo (Brazil), 1986; PhD in Math. Edn., U. Nottingham (Eng.), 1992. Assoc. prof. math. UNESP, Rio Claro, Brazil, 1992—; mem. editorial bd. Revista Quadrante, Lisbon, Portugal, 1994—, Revisto Uno, Barcelona, Spain, 1994—, Jour. Math. Tchrs. Edn., The Netherlands, 1997—. Author: Perspectivas em Álgebra e Arithmética Para O Século XXI, 1997. Gertrude Cropper scholar U. Nottingham, 1991. Mem. Brazil Soc. Math. Edn. (pres. 1995-98), Am. Math. Soc., Brazil Soc. Applied Math. Avocations: listening to jazz music. Office: Dept Math, Av 24-A 1515, 13506700 Rio Claro Brazil

LINS, WOLFGANG, physicist, consultant; b. Bludenz, Austria, May 13, 1968; s. Rainer and Astrid Lins; m. Regina Ehrenbrandtner; 1 child, Maximilian. MS in Physics, U. Vienna, 1998. Engr. Coun. Europeen pour la Recherche Nucléaire, Geneva, 1987-89; journalist Austrian Broadcasting Corp. ORF, Vienna, 1989-90; engr. Austrian Coop. with Russian Space Lab MIR, Vienna, Austria, 1990; office mgr. Nuc. Adv. Bd. of the Fed. Chancellor, Vienna, 1991-92; rsch. assoc. U. Vienna, 1991—; cons. Red Cross Ambulance Svc., Lower Austria, 1997—; dir. Emergency Med. Svc. Comm. Ctr., Red Cross Ambulance Svc., Klosterneuburg, Austria. EMT-Defibrillation Austrian Red Cross Ambulance Svc., Lower Austria, 1991—. With Emergency Med. Svc., 1995-96. E-mail: wl@rettung.at. Fax: 43-1-4082868. Office: U Vienna, Strudlhofgasse 4, A-1090 Vienna Austria

LINSCHITZ, HENRY, chemist, educator; b. N.Y.C., Aug. 18, 1919; s. Joseph and Mindel (Margulies) L.; m. Suzanne Ruth Hodes, Aug. 28, 1964; 1 son, Joseph Martin. B.S., Coll. City N.Y., 1940; M.A., Duke U., 1941, Ph.D., 1946. Mem. research staff Explosives Research Lab., Bruceton, Pa., 1943; sect. leader Los Alamos Lab., 1943-46; research fellow Inst. Nuclear Studies, U. Chgo., 1946-48; from asst. prof. to asso. prof. Syracuse U., 1948-57; prof. chemistry Brandeis U., 1957—; vis. scientist Brookhaven Nat. Lab., 1955-56; Fulbright vis. prof. Hebrew U., 1961; mem. adv. com. space biology NASA, 1959; mem. study sect. biophys. chemistry NIH, 1962-66; mem. com. photobiology Nat. Acad. Scis., 1965—. Mem. steering com. United Campuses to Prevent Nuclear War; co-chair Ctr. Campus Organizing, 1998-2000. Guggenheim fellow Weizmann Inst., Rehovot, Israel, 1971-72. Fellow

Am. Acad. Arts and Scis., AAAS; mem. Am. Chem. Soc. Spl. research photochemistry, photobiology, chem. kinetics. Home: 35 Riverside Dr Waltham MA 02453-2409

LINSTEN, MAGNUS OLOF, engineering executive; b. Kungälv, Sweden, Dec. 5, 1961; s. Per Thorsten and Solveig Lilly Margareta (Ekström) L.; m. AnnCharlotte Lena Palmqvist, Jan. 29, 1994; children: Erik, Emma. MSc, Chalmers U. Tech., Gothenburg, Sweden, 1985, lic. in engring., 1991. Devel. engr. Eka Nobel AB, Bohus, Sweden, 1985-86, 91-94; rsch. engr. Conteka BV, Bohus, 1986-90; mgr. R & D Eka Chems. AB, Bohus, 1994-2000; R & D mgr. Akzo Nobel Functional Chem., Stenungsund, Sweden, 2000—. Patentee in field. Avocations: choral singing, playing cello. Office: Akzo Nobel Functional Chem, S-44485 Stenungsund Sweden

LINTACKER, MARCEL ALPHONSE SIDNEY, finance company executive, consultant; b. St. Niklaas, Flanders, Belgium, Apr. 28, 1926; s. Joseph Ferdinand L. and Leonie Rose Foubert; m. Maria Magdalena Gyselinck, Aug. 17, 1946 (dec. Aug. 1995); 1 child, Huguette. Indsl. Engr. A1, Tech. Inst., Antwerp, Belgium, 1946. With rail ways, Belgium, 1946-53; prodn. mgr. PRB, Belgium, 1953-56, EXSA, Peru, 1956-63; owner, mgr. Belgian Mfg. Co., Peru, 1964-71; owner, gen. mgr. SIPOPSA, Peru, 1971-90, Globimpex, Peru, 1991—; owner, pres. IFIRCO, Panama and Peru, 1996—; bd. dirs. PAIX, Peru; bd. dirs., cons. ACG-Holdings, Peru; cons. Profl. Status, Peru, 1986—; mandate ARVIA, France, 1996—; advisor fgn. trade Belgian Embassy, Peru; chmn., CEO Flanders Mining Corp., Peru, 1998. Hon. Belgian consul, Iquitos, Peru, 1971-88; dean Consular Corps, Iquitos, 1972-85. Decorated 6 Highest Gold Medals WWII Def. Ministry of Belgium, 1946-55, Officer in the Crown Order King of Belgium, 1993. Mem. Internat. Soc. Financiers USA (cert. internat. financier), Oxford Club, Lions (zone chmn. 1964—, Gold Key 1985). Roman Catholic. Avocations: fishing, hunting, recreational activities. Fax: 51-1-4471878. Home: Av Mons Roca y Bologna 762, Miraflores, Lima Lima 18, Peru Office: IFIRCO 2nd Fl, Av Mons Roca y Bologna, Miraflores Lima 18, Peru

LINTERN, MELVYN JOHN, geochemist, researcher; b. Birmingham, Eng., Feb. 11, 1957; arrived in Australia, 1980; s. Robert John and Elsie Marion (Raybould) L.; m. Suzanne Patricia Roe, Feb. 2 18, 1990. BS in Zoology, U. Nottingham, England, 1978. Rsch. geochemist CSIRO, Perth, Australia, 1987—. Author: Portable Digital Voltammeter for Field Analysis of Trace Metals, 1984. Avocations: golf, chess, natural history.

LINTERS, ADRIAAN J. J. A., heritage consultant, lecturer; b. Hasselt, Flanders, Belgium, Apr. 24, 1951. Lic. in history, U. Ghent, Belgium, 1973. Dr. bd. KLEIO Heritage Commn., Wevelgem, Flanders, Belgium; sci. dir. Conservare nv European Heritage Forum, also sci. dir. webpage; rschr., lectr. dept. architecture St. Lukes' Sch. Higher Edn. for Scis. and Arts, Ghent, also in charge rsch. program on indsl. archaeology and bldg. history; lectr. on conservation scis.; bd. dirs. Internat. Coun. on Monuments and Sites of Flanders and Belgium, Europa Nostra Belgium; chmn. Flaxvallei Heritage Truste, 1993; mem. Belgian jury Henry Ford Conservation Awards, 1984—; mem. Royal Commn. Hist. Monuments and Landscapes for Flanders, 1993—, Accreditation Commn. for Mus. in Flanders, 1998—. Author: Industrial Architecture in Belgium, 1986, Industrial Archaeology in Flanders, 1987, De Vlasvallei Industrieel Erfgoed in de Leievallei in West-Vlaanderen en Département Nord-Pas de Calais, 1994, Wie is Wie van het Cultureel Erfgoed in Nederland en Vlaanderen, 1994, Ency. Momumentenzorg, 1994; contbr. over 300 articles on care of monuments, indsl. archaeology and preservation and presentation of cultural heritage to profl. publs. Mem. Flemish Assn. for Indsl. Archateology (founder, chmn. 1978—). Office: Kleio Heritage Cons, Vlamingstraat 4, B-8560 Wevelgem Flanders, Belgium

LINWOOD, RUSSELL JOHN, Australian army officer and state official; b. Bundaberg, Queensland, Australia, Dec. 1, 1952; s. Colin Desmond and Thelma Shirley (Kleidon) L.; m. Judith Ann Heron, Dec. 14, 1973; children: Grant, Mark, Rebecca. BA in Mil. Studies, U. NSW, Sydney, Australia, 1973; B Ednl. Studies, U. Queensland, Brisbane, 1982; MS, Fla. State U. Cert. IV in quality mgmt. assessment. Commd. officer Australian Army, 1970, advanced through grades to lt. col., 1987; numerous positions through comdr. officer 1st Recruit Tng. Bn., 1970-92; dir. ednl. svcs. Queensland Ambulance Svc., Brisbane, 1992-94, 96-97, asst. commr., 1994-95, mgr. spl. projects, 1997—, quality coord., 1997-99. Author: Shoot To Win, 1993, The Making of a Sniper, 1980 (best work award 1980); also articles. Leader Boy Scouts Australia, Canberra and Wagga, 1987-91; mem. Australia Day Coun., 1992-95; mem., chmn. curriculum adv. coms. Univ. and Tech. Coll. Level, Brisbane, 1994-98. Decorated Def. Force Svc. medal; recipient Australia Day achievement medal Queensland Dept. Emergency Svcs., 1995; Blamey scholar Royal Mil. Coll., 1973. Fellow Australian Inst. Mgmt. (assoc.), Australian Coll. Health Svc. Execs. (assoc.); mem. Australian Inst. Ambulance Officers. Mem. Uniting Ch. Avocations: military history, precision military shooting, playing guitar, public speaking, reading. Office: Queensland Ambulance Svc, GPO Box 1425, Brisbane Qld 4001, Australia

LIONS, JACQUES LOUIS, mathematician, educator; b. Grasse, France, May 2, 1928; s. Honore Antoine and Anne (Muller) L.; m. Andree Olivier, Aug. 21, 1950; 1 child, Pierre Louis. Degree in math., Ecole Normale Superieure, Paris, 1950; Dr es Sci., U. Paris, 1954; Dr (hon.), U. Liege, 1973, U. Madrid, 1976, U. Fudan, 1981, U. Goteborg, 1984, Heriot Watt U., Edinburgh, 1982, Poly. U. Madrid, 1988, St. Jacques de Compostella, 1994, U. Malaga, U. Santiago-Chile, 1997, Hebrew U., Jerusalem, 1997, Jian Tong U., Shanghai, 1998, Jian Jong U., Xian, 1998, BUAA, Beijing, 1998, U. Mex., 1998, U. Ctrl. Fla., 2000. Mem. faculty U. Nancy, France, 1954-62, U. Paris, 1962-73; prof. Coll. de France, Paris, 1973-98, hon. prof., 1999—; prof. Ecole Poly., Paris, 1967-86; pres. Inst. Nat. de Rsch. en Informatique et en Automatique, 1980-84, Ctr. Nat. Etudes Spatiales, 1984-92; high sci. advisor DASSAULT industry, 1993—; pres. sci. bd. France Telecom, 1998—; sci. advisor ELF; chmn. sci. adv. com. Pechiney; bd. dirs. St. Gobain Pechiney Dassault Sys., Thomson Multi Media. Author: Les Inequations en Mecanique et en Physique, 1969, Some Methods in the Mathematical Analysis of Systems and of their Control, 1981, Controle des Systemes distribues Singuliers, 1983, others. Decorated comdr. Order Nat. de la Legion d'Honneur, G.O. Merite Nat. Awd., 1999, Order of the Rising Sun, Gold and Silver Star, 1998; recipient Japan prize, 1991, Harvey prize, 1991, Space award Aviation Week and Space Tech., W.T. and Idelia Reid prize SIAM, 1998, Lagrange prize, 1999, Hilbert Medal, 2000. Fellow Tata Inst. of Fundamental Rsch.; mem. Acad. des Scis. (pres. 1997-98), Pontificial Acad. Scis.; fgn. mem. Acad. Royale de Liege, Acad. Scis. Lombardie, Acad. Brasileira de Ciencias, Russian Acad. Scis., Ukraine Acad. Scis., Acad. Royale Belgium, Georgian Acad. Sci., Am. Acad. Arts and Scis., Internat. Acad. Astronautics, Acad. Sci. of Chile, Acad. Europae, Portugal Acad. Scis., Acad. Soc. Argentina, Royal Soc. London, Nat. Acad. Sci. U.S., Third World Acad. Sci., Royal Spanish Acad., Korean Acad. Sci. and Tech., Chinese Acad. Scis., Nat. Acad. Lincei. Office: Coll de France, 3 Rue d'Ulm, 75231 Paris Cedex 05, France

LIONS, PIERRE LOUIS, mathematician; b. Grasse, Alpes, France, Aug. 11, 1956; s. Jacques Louis and Andree Marie (Olivier) L.; m. Lila Laurenti, Dec. 1, 1979; 1 child, Dorian Come. DSc, U. Paris VI, 1979; Doctor honoris causa, Heriot and Watt U., Edinburgh, 1995, City U., Hong Kong, 1999. Supr. normal sch. Paris, 1975-78; prof. U. Paris-Dauphine, France, 1979—; pres. evaluation com. Inst. Nat. Recherche en Informatique on Automatique, 1997; prof. Polytech. Sch., Palaiseau, France, 1984—; cons. Cisi, Paris, 1979-97, Cea-Dam, Paris, 1982-96, Cognitech, Santa Monica, 1990-96, CRS4, Cagliari, 1994-97, CAR (CDC), Paris, 1995-2000, BNP-Paribas, 2000—, Pechiney, Saint-Jean de Maurienne, 1995-97, Aerospatiale (Espace et Defense), Mureaux, 1996—; conf. spkr. Internat. Congress Mathematicians, Warsaw, Poland, 1983, Kyoto, Japan, 1990, Zurich, 1994; dir. Ceremade, Paris, 1991-97; bd. dirs. Alcatel-Alsthom; mem. Sci. Coun. of Def., 1998—. Contbr. articles to profl. jours. Decorated chevalier Legion of Honor (France); recipient prizes IBM-France, Philip-Morris, Ampere, Dusteau-Blutet, Fields medal, 1994. Mem. French Acad. Scis., Acad. Europea.

LIOSSI, CHRISTINA, health psychologist, researcher; b. Athens, Greece, Sept. 14, 1969; d. Epaminondas and Ioanna Liossi. BA in Psychology with honors, U. Sunderland, Eng., 1993, PhD, 1999. Lic. health psychologist. Lectr. health psychology dept. psychology U. West of Eng.., Bristol, 1999—. Contbr. articles to profl. jours. Mem. Internat. Assn. for Study of Pain, European Assn. for Palliative Care, Brit. Psychol. Soc. Avocations: classical guitar, swimming, kung fu, fencing, languages. Office: U West of Eng St Matthias Campus, Oldbury Court Rd, Fishponds Bristol BS16 2JP, England

LIOU, ERIC JEIN-WEIN, orthodontist, researcher; b. Taipei, Taiwan, Dec. 27, 1961; s. Mao-Fa and May-Chei (Lin) L.; m. Karen Chu, Oct. 11, 1998. DDS, Taipei Med. Coll., 1986; MS, U. Ill., Chgo., 1997. Diplomate orthodontist. Attending staff Chang Gung Meml. Hosp., Taipei, 1993-95, asst. prof., 1997—; rsch. fellow Craniofacial Ctr., U. Ill., Chgo., 1995-97, head, 1999—. Co-editor Bull. Dentists Assn. Taipei, 1994-95; contbr. articles to profl. jours.; patentee in field. Recipient B.F. and Helen E. Dewel Clin. Orthodontic award, 1998. Mem. Taiwanese Assn. Craniofacial Anomalies and Cleft Lip and Palate (treas. 1998), Am. Cleft Lip and Palate and Craniofacial Assn., World Fed. Assn. Orthodontists, Taiwanese Assn. Orthodontists, Taiwanese Assn. Cleft Lip/Palate and Craniofacial Anomalies. Avocations: movies, sports. Office: Chang Gung Meml Hosp, 199 Tung-Hwa N Rd, Taipei 105, Taiwan

LIOUBIMTSEVA, ELENA, geography educator; b. Moscow, Apr. 17, 1966; arrived in Belgium, 1996; d. Youriy and Lidya (Arjuzina) L.; m. Valery Klassen (div. Jan. 1997); m. Jack Mangala Munuma; 1 child, Alexandre. MSc, Moscow State U., 1989, PhD, 1994; postgrad., Oxford (Eng.) U., 1992-93. Lectr. Moscow State U., 1993-95; rschr. CNRS, Marseille, France, 1995, U. Louvain, Belgium, 1996-97; fellow U. Oxford, 1998-99; asst. prof. Ctrl. Wash. U., Ellensburg, 1999—; expert Internat. User Com. Vegetation, 1994—; expert image interpreter Internat. Geosphere-Biosphere Program, 1998. Contbr. articles to profl. jours. Grantee Soros Found., 1992; fgn. scholar Internat. Assn. Landscape Ecology, 1999. Mem. RZA, Assn. Devel. Talldetection, Russia Geography Soc., Internat. Assn. Landscape Ecol., Assn. pour le Devel. de Teledection. Russian Orthodox. Avocations: music, travel, jogging, dancing. Home: 1900 Brooklane St Apt K4 Ellensburg WA 98926-3492 Office: Ctrl Wash Univ Ellensburg WA 98926

LIPA, JERZY JOZEFAT, plant protection educator; b. Bychawa, Lublin, Poland, Nov. 14, 1932; s. Jan and Wanda (Sprawka) L.; m. Izabella Szczechowska, Oct. 9, 1936; children: Iwona, Jerzy, Artur. BSc, U. Warsaw, 1953, MSc, 1955; PhD, Agrl. U., 1962, DSc, 1967. Rsch. asst. Inst. Plant Protection, Pulawy, Poland, 1953-57; lab head Inst. Plant Protection, Poznan, Poland, 1961-67, assoc. prof., 1967-71, prof., dept. head, 1972—, chmn. sci. coun., 1995—; rsch. assoc. U. Calif., Berkeley, 1957-60; vis. prof. CIMMYT, Mex., 1989, Agrl. Rsch. Ctr., Jokioinen, Finland, 1990, ETSIAM, Cordoba, Spain, 1992, U. de Navarra, Pamplona, Spain, 1997; scientific coun. IB-PAN, Poznan, 1995—. Author: Insects as Enemies of Farmer, 1965, An Outline of Insect Pathology, (with others) Microbial Control of Insects and Mites, 1971; editor Quarantine Pests for Europe, 1995;. Fellow Polish Acad. Scis., Royal Swedish Acad. Agrl. Sci., Ukrainian Acad. Agrl., Sci., Russian Acad. Agrl. Sci.; chmn. Plant Protection Com. Poland, Entomological Soc. of Finland (hon. mem.), Polish Entomological soc. (hon. mem.), Russian Entomological Soc. (hon. mem.). Roman Catholic. Avocations: summer garden work, winter hunting. Home: Heweliusza 6/17, 60-281 Poznan Poland Office: Inst Plant Protection, Miczurina 20, 60-318 Poznan Poland

LIPATOV, YURI SERGEI, chemist; b. Ivanovo, Russia, July 10, 1927; s. Sergei Michael and Garriet Vladimir (Zalgaller) L.; m. Tatiana Esper Sosnina, July 1, 1947; 1 child, Sergei. Grad., Moscow Oil Inst., Russia, 1949; PhD, Physico-Chem. Karpov Inst., Russia, 1954, DS, 1963. Jr. rschr. L.Y. Kazpov Inst., Moscow, 1954-59; head lab. Acad. Scis., Minsk, Russia, 1959-64; dir. Inst. Macromolecular Chemistry, Kiev, Ukraine, 1964-85, head lab. phys. chemistry, 1985—. Contbr. articles to profl. jours. Mem. Nat. Acad. Sci., Acad. Creative Endeavours, N.Y. Acad. Scis. Avocations: Russian poetry, classical music. Fax: (38044) 552-40-64. E-mail: lipatov@imchem.kiev.ua. Home: 15 A Lipskaya St, 01 021 Kiev Ukraine Office: Inst Macromolecular Chemistry, 48 Kharkov Shaussee, 02160 Kiev Ukraine

LIPCON, CHARLES ROY, lawyer; b. N.Y.C., Mar. 20, 1946; s. Harry H. and Rose Lipcon; m. Irmgard Adels, Dec. 1, 1974; children: Lauren, Claudia. BA, U. Miami, 1968, JD, 1971. Bar: Fla. 1971, U.S. Dist. Ct. (so. dist.) Fla. 1971, U.S. Ct. Appeals (5th cir.) 1972, U.S. Supreme Ct. 1976, U.S. Ct. Appeals (D.C. cir.) 1980, U.S. Dist. Ct. (so. dist.) Tex. 1982, U.S. Ct. Appeals (11th cir.) 1994, U.S. Dist. Ct. Colo. 1999. Pvt. practice Miami, Fla., 1971—; lectr. U. Miami Sch. Law. Author: Help for the Auto Accident Victim, 1984, Seaman's Rights in the United States When Involved in An Accident, 1989; contbr. articles to profl. jours. Named Commodore of High Seas, Internat. Seaman's Union. Mem. ABA, ATLA, Fla. Bar Assn., Fla. Trial Lawyers Assn., Dade County Bar Assn., Dade County Trial Lawyers, Fla. Admiralty Trial Lawyers Assn., Mensa. Office: 2 S Biscayne Blvd Ste 2480 Miami FL 33131-1803

LIPKIN, MARTIN, physician, scientist; b. N.Y.C., Apr. 30, 1926; s. Samuel S. and Celia (Greenfield) L.; m. Joan Schulein, Feb. 16, 1958; children—Richard Martin, Steven Monroe. A.B., NYU, 1946, M.D., 1950. Diplomate Nat. Bd. Med. Examiners. Practice medicine specializing in internal medicine, gastroenterology and neoplastic diseases N.Y.C.; mem. staff N.Y. Hosp., Meml. Hosp. for Cancer and Allied Diseases, 1972-96; prof. medicine Cornell U. Med. Coll., 1978—, prof. Grad. Sch. Med. Scis., 1978—; mem. and attending physician Meml. Sloan-Kettering Cancer Ctr., 1985-96; dir. clin. rsch. Strang Cancer Prevention Ctr., N.Y.C., 1996—; vis. physician Rockefeller U. Hosp., 1981—; hon. lectr. Israel Med. Assn. and Gastroenterology Soc., 1982; nominator Nobel Prize for Physiology and Medicine, 1982; bd. dirs., officer The Med. Ednl. and Sci. Found. of N.Y.; bd. dirs. Internat. Soc. Cancer Chemoprevention; chmn. bd. Irving Weinstein Found. Mem. editorial bd. Cancer Rsch., Internat. Jour. Oncology, World Jour. Gastroenterology; editor: Gastrointestinal Tract Cancer, 1978, Inhibition of Tumor Induction and Development, 1981, Gastrointestinal Cancer: Endogenous Factors, 1981, Calcium, Vitamin D and Prevention of Colon Cancer, 1991, Cancer Chemoprevention, 1992; contbr. articles to profl. jours. Served as officer USN, 1953-55. Recipient NIH career devel. award, 1962-71; Albert F.R. Andresen ann. award and lectr. N.Y. State Med. Soc., 1971, medallion Nat. Cancer Ctr. Rsch. Inst., Tokyo, 1976, U. Padua, Italy, 1978. Fellow ACP, Am. Coll. Gastroenterology; mem. Med. Soc. State of N.Y. (chmn. sci. program com. 1990-91, chmn. edn. com. 1991-99), Am. Soc. Clin. Investigation, Am. Physiol. Soc., Am. Assn. Cancer Rsch., Am. Gastroenterol. Assn., Soc. for Exptl. Biology and Medicine, Harvey Soc. Office: 1230 York Ave New York NY 10021-6307

LIPKIN-SHAHAK, AMNON, Israel government official; b. Tel Aviv, 1944; married; 5 children. Grad., Israel Def. Force Command and State Coll., Nat. Def. Coll., Israel; degree in gen. history, Tel Aviv U. With Israel Def. Force, 1962—, apptd. to Ctrl. Command, 1983, head intelligence br., 1986, apptd. dep. chief of gen. staff, 1991, chief of gen. staff, 1995—; dep. min. tourism and min. transp. Govt. of Israel, Jerusalem. Paratroop comdr. Six Day War, 1967; dep. paratroop brigade comdr. Yom Kippur War, 1973. Decorated 2 Medals of Valor. Office: PO Box 1018, 24 King George St, 91000 Jerusalem Israel•

LIPKOWSKI, JANUSZ STANISŁAW, chemistry educator, researcher; b. Warsaw, Poland, Feb. 3, 1943; s. Otton Robert and Jadwiga Elzbieta (Cybulińska) L.; m. Krystyna Romanowska, Sept. 22, 1964 (div. 1975); 1 child, Piotr; m. Ewa Elzbieta Radoszewska, Feb. 25, 1984. MS, U. Warsaw, Poland, 1965; PhD, Inst. Phys. Chemistry Acad Sci, Warsaw, 1972, DSc, 1983, prof., 1990; Doctorate (hon.), Russian Acad. Scis., 1997. Asst. U. Warsaw, 1965-67; sr. rsch. asst. Inst. Phys. Chemistry, Warsaw, 1973-78, dept. head, 1978—, assoc. prof., dep. dir., 1983-92, prof. chemistry, 1990—, dir., 1992—; prof. Sch. of Scis., Warsaw, 1993—. Author: (with others) Crystallography of Supramolecular Compounds, 1995, Comprehensive Supramolecular Chemistry, 1996. Recipient award for outstanding sci. activity Polish Acad. Scis., Warsaw, 1983, Golden medal of merit State Com., Warsaw, 1984. Fellow Polish Chem. Soc. (chmn. Warsaw divsn. 1986-89), The Soc. for Promotion and Propagation of Scis; mem. Warsaw Soc. Scis (corr.), Polish Acad. Scis. (corr.). Avocation: photography. Home: Złota 63a, 00 819 Warsaw Poland Office: Inst Phys Chemistry, Kasprzaka 44, 01 224 Warsaw Poland

LIPMAN, IRA ACKERMAN, security service company executive; b. Little Rock, Nov. 15, 1940; s. Mark and Belle (Ackerman) L.; m. Barbara Ellen Kelly Couch, July 5, 1970; children: Gustave K., Joshua S, M Benjamin. Student, Ohio Wesleyan U., 1958-60; LLD (hon.), John Marshall U., Atlanta, 1970; LLD (Hon.), Northeastern U., Boston, 1996. Salesman, exec. Mark Lipman Svcs. Inc., Memphis, 1960-63; v.p. Guardsmark, Inc., Memphis, 1963-66; pres. Guardsmark, Inc., 1966—, CEO, 1968—, chmn. bd., 1968—; bd. dirs. Nat. Coun. on Crime and Delinquency, 1975—, chmn. fin. com., treas., 1978-79, vice chmn. bd. dirs., 1982-86, chmn. exec. com., 1986-93, chmn. bd. dirs., 1993-94, chmn. emeritus, 1993—, hon. chmn. 1997—; bd. dirs. Greater Memphis Coun. Crime and Delinquency, 1976-78, entrepreneurial fellow Memphis State U., 1976; mem. environ. security com., pvt. security adv. coun. Law Enforcement Assistance adminstrn., 1975-76; mem. conf. planning com. 2d Nat. Law Enforcement Explorer Conf., 1980. Author: How to Protect Yourself From Crime, 1975, 3d edit., 1989, 4th edit., 1997; contbr. numerous articles to profl. jours., mags. and newspapers. Bd. dirs. Memphis Jewish Cmty. Center, 1974, Memphis Shelby County unit Am. Cancer Soc., 1980-81, Memphis Orchestral Soc., 1980-81, Memphis Jewish Fedn., 1974-83; chmn. Shelby County com. U.S. Savs. Bonds, 1976; mem. president's coun. Memphis State U., 1975-79;, mem. visual arts coun., 1980-82; Memphis met. chmn. Nat. Alliance Businessmen, 1970-71; mem. task force Reform Jewish Outreach, Union Am. Hebrew Congregations, 1979-83; mem. young leadership cabinet United Jewish Appeal, 1973-78, mem. S.E. regional campaign cabinet, 1980; exec. bd. Chickasaw council Boy Scouts Am., 1978-81; bd. dirs., exec. com. Tenn. Ind. Coll. Fund, 1979; trustee Memphis Acad. Arts, 1977-81; mem. president's club Christian Bros. Coll., 1979-89; bd. dirs. Future Memphis, 1980-83, 83-86; nat. trustee NCCJ, 1980-92, exec. com., 1981-92, nat. Jewish co-chmn., 1985-88, nat. chmn., 1988-92, hon. chmn., past nat. chmn. nat. conf. Christians and Jews, 1992—; bd. dirs. Memphis chpt., 1980-85, life bd. dirs. Memphis chpt. 1985—; group II chmn. for 1982 campaign United Way Greater Memphis, 1981; v.p. exec. com. Internat. Coun. Christians and Jews, 1992-94; bd. govs. United Way of Am., 1992-99, bd. gov.'s liaison, 1991-92, chmn. ethics com., 1992-97, mem. exec. com., 1992-97, co-chmn. vol. involvement com., 1992—, mem. strategic planning com., 1994-96, diversity com., 1997-99; chmn. UWLC steering com. 1995-96; mem. Alexis de Tocqueville Soc. Nat. Leadership Coun., 1992-97, mem. emeritus, 1998—, mem. Second Century Initiative Vol. Involvement com., 1987-91; chair Task Force on Critical Markets, 1987-91, mem. exec. cabinet, 1990-91; trustee Memphis Brooks Mus. Art, 1980-83, Yeshiva U.; trustee Simon Wiesenthal Ctr., 1982—, chmn. campaign com., 1983-92, mem. fin. and audit com., 1993—, exec. com., 1994—; bd. dirs. Nat. Alliance against Violence, 1983-85, Nat. Ctr. Learning Disabilities, 1989-94, United Way of Greater Memphis, 1984-85, gen. campaign chmn., 1985-86; founder, bd. overseers B'nai Brith, 1980; bd. dirs. Tenn. Gov.'s Jobs for High Sch. Grads. Program, 1980-83; trustee Ohio Wesleyan U., 1988-97; vice chmn. spl. task force on endowment growth Ohio Wesleyan U., 1990-97; mem. bd. overseers Wharton Sch., U. Pa., 1991—, devel. com., 1995—, exec. adv. bd. Zicklin Ctr. Bus. Ethics Rsch., 1997—; assoc. trustee U. Pa., 1991—; mem. exec. com. Am. Israel Pub. Affairs Com., 1991—; bd. trustees Com. for Economic Devel., 1999—; adv. bd. dirs., Tenn. Titans, 1999—. Recipient Humanitarian of Yr. award NCCJ, 1985, Outstanding Cmty. Sales award Sales and Mktg. Execs. Memphis, 1987, Jr. Achievement Master Free Enterprise award, 1987, Alexis de Tocqueville Soc. award, 1995; one of 10 cited as Best Corp. Chief Exec. of Achievement, Gallagher Pres.'s Report, 1974. Mem. Internat. Assn. Chiefs Police, Am. Soc. Criminology, Internat. Soc. Criminology, Am. Soc. Indsl. Security (cert. protection profl.), 100 Club, B'nai B'rith, Econ. Club (bd. dirs. 1980-85, v.p. 1983-84, pres. 1984-85, chmn. exec. com. 1984-85). Republican.

LIPMAN, MICHEL, writer, former lawyer; b. San Francisco, June 11, 1913; s. Maurice and Frances Lipman; m. Clayre Lipman, Nov. 15, 1940. AA, San Jose State U., 1932; JD, Hastings Coll. Law, 1937. Bar: Calif. 1938, U.S. Dist. Ct. 1938. Corp. counsel Calif. Nurses Assn., San Francisco, 1969-71; pub. rels. dir. State Bar of Calif., San Francisco, 1971-76; v.p. Aeronautics, Inc., Burlingame, Calif., 1976-80; writing cons. Bank of Am., San Francisco; condr. better writing seminars for various clients, San Francisco. Author: (instrn. manual) Safety Practices for Standard Oil Supervisors, (pharmacy publs.) Looking Better Through Plastic Surgery, Medical Law & Ethics, 1993, (with Angelo Capozzi) Change of Face, (with Herman Schwartz) Guidebook for the Hospital Patient; editor 12-set series annotated young people's books, 1971-72; writer, prodr.: (daily radio show) Point of Law, 1953—; creator Point of Law game; contbr. articles to profl. jours. Recipient 1st Ann. award of the bar Bar Assn. San Francisco, 1954, George Washington Honor medal Freedom Found. of Valley Forge, 1953-54, 55, Silver Microphone award Advt. Group, 1999. Avocations: collecting books and stock certificates, pistol shooting. Office: Universal Concepts 719 Battery St San Francisco CA 94111-1501

LIPNITSKY, ANATOLY VASILIEVICH, microbiologist; b. Baku, Azerbaijan, June 9, 1937; s. Vasili Evstafievich and Ludmila Alekseevna Rozenblatt; m. Tatjana Vasilievna Gordienko, Jan. 5, 1963; children: Sergey, Aleksey. First degree candidate, Rostov-on-Don U., Russia, 1966; MD, Saratov U., 1976. Lic. doctor, microbiologist. Physician, postgrad. Antiplague Rsch. Inst., Rostov-on-Don, Russia, 1962-65; jr. rschr. Antiplague Rsch. Inst., Volgograd, Russia, 1965-70, sr. rschr., 1970-72, lab. chief, 1972—, vice dir., 1993—; staff Antiplague Station, Jadrat, Azerbaijan, 1960-62. Author papers. Mem. N.Y. Acad. Scis., Volgograd Club of Doctors. Avocation: gathering mushrooms. Home: Shebelinskaya St 51-10, 400075 Volgograd Russia Office: Antiplague Rsch Inst, Golubinskaya St 7, 400131 Volgograd Russia

LIPOLDOVÁ, MARIE, immunogeneticist; b. Tabor, Czech Republic, Jan. 20, 1955; d. Rudolf and Anastazie (Pavlínová) L. MSc, Khakov State U., 1979; PhD, Inst. Molecular Genetics, Czech Republic, 1983. Vis. rsch. fellow ICRF, London, 1985-87; from staff mem. to sr. scientist, lab. head Inst. Molecular Genetics, Prague, 1987—. Fellow Br. Soc. Immunology, Czech Soc. for Immunology, Soc. Leukocyte Biology, Czech Soc. Biochem. and Molecular Biology, The Genetical Soc. Avocations: opera, classical music. Office: Inst Molecular Genetics, Fleming NáM 2, 16637 Prague Czech Republic

LIPONSKI, WOJCIECH ADAM, Anglosaxon cultures historian, sport historian; b. Sosnowiec, Poland, Dec. 16, 1942; s. Stefan and Janina (Bitner) L.; m. Alexandra Hoffmann, Oct. 18, 1966 (div. Feb. 1986); 1 child, Joanna; m. Romana Bieganska, Mar. 10, 1986; 1 child, Seweryn. MA in Philology, Adam Mickiewicz U., Poznan, Poland, 1967, PhD in History of Culture, 1972, DLitt, 1977. Asst. dept. Polish lit. Adam Mickiewicz U., 1967-68, adj. prof. Inst. English, 1973-77, assoc. prof., 1977-91, vice dir. Inst. English, 1985-88, 91—, prof., 1991—; prof. Phys. Edn. Acad., Poznan, 1991—; chmn. Polish-Anglosaxon Rels., Adam Mickiewicz U., 1978—; vis. lectr. State U. Fla., Gainesville, 1975-76; lectr. Internat. Olympic Acad., Ancient Olympia and Athens, Greece, 1992-94, expert Internat. Olympic Com., Lausanne, Switzerland, 1986; expert Orgn. Com. of 1988 Olympic Games, Seoul, Korea, 1986-89, attended the Presidium of Neophilological Com. of the Polish Acad. of Scis., 1999—. Author: Poland and Britain (in Polish), 1978, Humanistic Encyclopedia of Sport (in Polish), 1987, Origins of Civilization in the British Isles (in Polish), 1995, History of Polish Sport, 1997; founder, editor-in-chief Polish-Anglosaxon Studies periodical, 1987—; editor-in-chief Studies in Phys. Culture and Tourism periodical, 1994—, East European Rep. of Internatl. Jour. of the Hist. of Sport, London, 1989—. Athlete Polish Nat. Track and Field Team (400m and 4x400m run), 1963-67; v.p. Solidarity's Com. Olympism For All, Gdansk, Poland, 1990-92; v.p. Polish Olympic Com., Warsaw, 1991-92; expert Polish Parliament, Warsaw, 1989-91. With Polish Army Infantry, 1966—. Recipient Olympic Laurel in lit. Polish Olympic Com., 1972, Medal in sport-sci.-culture Internat. Olympiade Vereinigung, Munich, 1988, Medal of Nat. Edn. Commn., Polish Ministry Edn., 1993. Mem. Internat. Soc. Anglo-Saxonists, Polish Assn. Authors Zaiks, Comite Internat. Pierre De Coubertin and others. Roman Catholic. Avocations: recreational running, music, lexicography. Home: Osiedle Lokietka 10A/10, 61-616 Poznań Poland Office: Adam Mickiewicz U Inst English, Al Niepodlegloscí 4, 61-874 Poznań Poland

LIPPE, PAOLO, oncologist, researcher; b. Bergamo, Lombardy, Italy, Apr. 29, 1964; s. Claudio and Concetta (Ardizzone) L.; m. Emanuela Ferretti, Sept. 27, 1998. MD, U. Bari (Italy), 1995; Postgrad. Specialization, Med. Oncology Sch., Ancona, Italy, 1999. Fellow in tng. Oncology Dept., Avezzano, Italy, 1992-93, Ancona, 1996-99; oncologist Oncology Divsn., Ancona,

1999; oncology unit S. Croce Hosp., Fano, Italy, 2000—. Contbr. articles to profl. jours. Mem. Assn. Italiana Oncologi Medici. Roman Catholic. Avocation: musician. Fax: 0039-0721-882396. Office: Oncologia Medica, Ospedale S Croce, 61032 Fano Marche, Italy

LIPPENS, MAURICE, finance company executive. CEO Fortis, Brussels, 1996—. Office: Fortis, 53 Blvd Emile Jacqmain, 1000 Brussels Belgium

LIPPER, KENNETH, investment banker, author, producer; b. N.Y.C., June 19, 1941; s. George and Sally (Hollander) L.; m. Evelyn Rebecca Gruss, June 12, 1966; children: Joanna Helene, Daniella, Tamara, Julie. BA, Columbia U., 1962; JD, Harvard U., 1965; LLM, NYU, 1966; postgrad., Faculté de Droit et Economique, Paris, 1967. Bar: N.Y. 1965. Assoc. Fried, Frank, Harris, Shriver & Jacobson, N.Y.C., 1967-68; dir. industry policy Office Fgn. Direct Investment, Washington, 1968-69; assoc., ptnr. Lehman Bros., N.Y.C., 1969-75; mng. dir., ptnr. Salomon Bros., N.Y.C., 1976-82; dep. mayor City of N.Y., 1983-85; chmn. Lipper & Co., 1986—; adj. prof. internat. affairs Sch. Internat. and Pub. Affairs, Columbia U., N.Y.C., 1976-83; mem. adv. bd. Fed. Res. Bank N.Y., 1994—, Chase Manhattan Bank, 1994—. Author: (novel) Wall Street, 1987 and chief tech. advisor movie, 1987; author, screenwriter, producer City Hall, 1996; produer film and play The Winter Guest, 1997, The Last Days, 1998; pub. Lipper Viking Penguin Biograph. Series, 1997—. Mem. adv. bd. John F. Kennedy Sch. Govt., Harvard U., 1994—; bd. dirs. New Holland N.V., 1997—, Lincoln Ctr. Performing Arts, 1995—, Sundance Inst., 1997—. Recipient medal of distinction City of N.Y., 1985. Mem. Internat. Inst. Strategic Studies, Coun. Fgn. Rels., Econ. Club N.Y., Century Assn., Phi Beta Kappa. Office: Lipper & Co 101 Park Ave Rm 6R New York NY 10178-0002

LIPPERT, CHRISTOPHER NELSON, dentist, consultant; b. N.Y.C., Apr. 17, 1952; s. Raymond Joseph and Shirley Ann (Nelson) L.; m. Valerie Jo Schlager, Nov. 4 1989. BS, U. Cin., 1975; DDS, Emory U., 1979. Dentist John W. Regenos DDS, Inc., Cin., 1979-87; pres., dentist Lippert & Wilkes DDS, Inc., Cin., 1987—; cons. Teret's Syndrome Found., Cin., 1983—, Health Am., Cleve., 1985-90; lectr. Ohio State U., 1981-89. Bd. dirs. Creekwood Condominiums, Cin., 1985-86. Mem. ADA, Am. Acad. Fixed Prosthodontists, Ohio Dental Assn., Ohio Acad. Practice Adminstrn., Cin. Dental Soc. (peer rev. com. 1985—), Midwest Med. Found. (bd. dirs. 1984-88), Phi Eta Sigma, Sigma Alpha Epsilon, Psi Omega. Avocations: sailing, fishing, restoration of classic cars.

LIPPERT-RASMUSSEN, KASPER, philosopher; b. Copenhagen, Jan. 16, 1964; s. Frits and Lisbeth (Lippert) Rasmussen; m. Alice Petersen, Mar. 10, 1990; children: Cecilie, William, Hannah. MA in History and Philosophy, U. Essex, Eng., 1990; Magister of Polit. Sci., U. Aarhus, Denmark, 1990; PhD, U. Oxford, Eng., 1995. Carlsberg scholar U. Copenhagen, 1995-97, assoc. prof. philosophy, 1997—. Mem. editl. com. Utilitas, 1999—; contbr. articles to profl. jours. Office: Univ Copenhagen, NJalsgade 80, 2300 Copenhagen Denmark

LIPPIETT, RICHARD JOHN, military officer; b. Bognor Regis, Sussex, England, July 7, 1949; s. Vernon Kingsbury Lippiett and Katherine Fedora Irene (Sabine) Langston-Jones; m. Jennifer Rosemary Wratislaw Walker, May 1, 1976; children: Louisa, Marc, Oliver. Grad., Royal Coll. Def. Studies, 1993. Commd. Brit. Royal Navy; advanced through grades to rear adm. Royal Navy, 1997; naval asst. 1st sea lord MOD, London, 1988-91; dep. flag officer Surface Flotilla, Portsmouth, 1993-95, commodore, RN sch. maritime ops., 1995-97; flag officer sea tng. Surface Flotilla, Plymouth, 1997-99; chief staff Allied Naval Forces Southern Europe, 1999—; comdr. HMS Shavington, 1976-77, HMS Amazon, 1986-87, HMS Norfolk, 1991-92, HMS Dryad, 1995-97, FOST, 1997-99. Author: The Type 21 Frigate, 1988. Decorated mem. Brit. Empire. Avocations: music, gardening, sailing. Office: HQ Comnav South NATO, London BFPO 8, England

LIPPINCOTT, PHILIP EDWARD, retired paper products company executive; b. Camden, N.J., Nov. 28, 1935; s. J. Edward and Marjorie Nix (Spooner) L.; m. Naomi Catherine Prindle, Aug. 22, 1959; children: Grant, Kevin, Kerry. BA, Dartmouth Coll., 1957; MBA with distinction, Mich. State U., 1964. With Scott Paper Co., Phila., 1959-94, staff v.p. corp. planning, 1971, div. v.p., consumer products mktg., 1971-72, corp. v.p., mktg., 1972-75, sr. v.p., mktg., 1975-77, v.p., group exec. packaged products div., 1977, dir., 1978-94, pres., COO, 1980-94, chief exec. officer, 1982-94, chmn., 1983-94; ret., 1994; chmn. bd. Campbell Soup Co., 1999—; bd. dirs. Campbell Soup Co., Exxon Corp.; trustee Penn Mut. Life Ins. Co. Chmn. bd. trustees Fox Chase Cancer Ctr., Phila.; mem. The Bus. Coun. Capt. U.S. Army, 1957-59. Mem. Pine Valley Country Club, Stone Harbor Country Club, Park Meadows Country Club, Kappa Kappa Kappa, Pi Sigma Epsilon, Beta Gamma Sigma. Mem. Society of Friends.

LIPPITT, ELIZABETH CHARLOTTE, writer; b. San Francisco; d. Sidney Grant and Stella L. Student Mills Coll., U. Calif.-Berkeley. Writer, performer own satirical monologues, nat. and polit. affairs for 85 newspapers including Muncie Star, St. Louis Globe-Dem., Washington Times, Utah Ind., Jackson News, State Dept. Watch. Singer debut album Songs From the Heart; contbr. articles to 85 newspapers including N.Y. Post, L.A. Examiner, Orlando Sentinel, Phoenix Rep., The Blue Book; author: 40 Years of American History in Published Letters 1952-1992. Mem. Commn. for Free China, Conservative Caucus, Jefferson Ednl. Assn., Presdl. Adv. Commn. Recipient Congress of Freedom award, 1959, 71-73. Mem. Amvets, Nat. Trust for Hist. Preservation, Am. Security Coun., Internat. Platform Assn., Am. Conservative Union, Nat. Antivivisection Soc., High Frontier, For Our Children, Childhelp U.S.A., Free Afghanistan Com., Humane Soc. U.S., Young Ams. for Freedom, Coun. for Inter.-Am. Security, Internat. Med. Corps, Assn. Vets for Animal Rights, Met. Club, Olympic Club. Home: 2414 Pacific Ave San Francisco CA 94115-1238

LIPPMAN, MURIEL MARIANNE, biomedical scientist; b. N.Y.C., Oct. 16, 1930; d. Louis George and Erna (Hirsch) L. BA, Syracuse U., 1951; MS, U. Pa., 1955; postgrad., Tufts U., 1965-66, Yale U., 1966-67; PhD, U. Chgo., 1970. Chmn. sci. dept. St. Agnes H.S., Rochester, N.Y., 1957-59, Nazareth Acad., Rochester, 1959-63; asst. prof. biology, rsch. dir. Nazareth Coll., Rochester, 1963-65; scientist Retina Found., Boston, 1965-66; vis. scientist Karolinska Inst., Stockholm, 1967; assoc. prof. biology Seton Hall U., South Orange, N.J., 1970-71; sr. staff fellow Nat. Cancer Inst., Bethesda, Md., 1971-76; sr. scientist Food and Drug Adminstrn. Bur. Med. Devices, Silver Spring, Md., 1976-77; sr. staff scientist Nat. Acad. Scis., Washington, 1977-78; dir. scientific planning and review Clement Assocs., Washington, 1978-79; pres. ERNACO, Inc., Silver Spring, 1979—; adj. prof. biology Am. U., Washington, 1981-83; vis. prof. Cook Coll., Rutgers State U., N.J., 1985-86; adj. prof. anatomy Frederick (Md.) C.C., 1991, No. Va. C.C., Sterling, 1992-96; vis. prof. biology U. Md., 1996, 97. Contbr. articles to profl. jours. Mem. Human Relations Commn. Montgomery County, Md., 1982-83. Recipient numerous grants and fellowships including Cancer Rsch. grantee Damon Runyon Found., 1964, Am. Cancer Soc. grantee, 1969-70, Biomedical rsch. grantee Evans Found., 1984-91, Nat. Heart, Lung and Blood Inst. NIH, 1986-87; U.S. Pub. Health fellow, 1965-66, KC Rsch. fellow, 1967, Danforth Teaching fellow U. Chgo., 1970; Teaching Excellence award Rochester Acad. Scis., 1963. Mem. Am. Med. Writers Assn., Drug Info. Assn., Sigma Xi. Office: ERNACO Inc PO Box 6522 Silver Spring MD 20916-6522

LIPPONEN, PAAVO, Finnish prime minister; b. Turtola, Finland, Apr. 23, 1941. Journalist, 1963-67; sec. rsch. and internat. affairs, head polit. sect. Finnish Social Dem. Party, 1967-79, chair Helsinki dist., 1985-92, mem. party com., 1987-90, mem. party coun., 1990-93, chair, 1993—; sec. to prime min. Govt. of Finland, Helsinki, 1979-82, mem. parliament, 1983-87, 91—, spkr. parliament, 1995, prime min., 1995—; head Finnish Inst. Internat. Affairs, 1989-91; chair supervisory bd. Outokumpu Oy, 1989-91; mem. Helsinki City Coun., 1985-94. Office: Office of Prime Min, Box 23, FIN-00023 Govt Finland

LIPPONEN, PERTTI KALEVI, physician, researcher; b. Kuopio, North-Savo, Finland, Oct. 16, 1959; s. Kauko Ilmari and Anna-Liisa (Takkinen) L.; m. Sirpa Helena Aaltomaa, Dec. 20, 1994; children: Olli Matias, Leevi Oskari, Siiri Serafiina. Physician, U. Kuopio, Finland, 1984, MD, 1990, Docent in Cytometry, 1992. Gen. practitioner Finland, 1982-90; rschr. U. Kuopio, 1987—, docent, sr. lectr., 1992—; asst. chief physician City of Kuopio, 1993—; referee in several cancer jours.; lectr. scientific mtgs. in field, Europe, 1989—. Contbr. articles to profl. jours. Treas. North-Savo Med. Assn., Kuopio, 1994-97, pres. 1997—. Rsch. grantee Finnish Urol. Assn., 1990, Finnish Cancer Soc., 1992-95, North Savo Cultural Soc., 1990. Mem. Finnish Med. Assn. (Duodecim bd. dirs. 1999—), Finnish Cytometric Soc., Breast Cancer Rsch. Group. Avocations: painting, photography, travel, writing. Home: Lohkaretie 13 A 10, 70700 Kuopio Finland Office: Univ Kuopio, Dept Path/PO Box 1627, 70210 Kuopio Finland

LIPSCOMB, OSCAR HUGH, archbishop; b. Mobile, AL, Sept. 21, 1931; s. Oscar Hugh and Margaret (Saunders) L. STL, Gregorian U., Rome, 1957; PhD, Cath. U. Am., 1963. Ordained priest Roman Cath. Ch., 1956; consecrated bishop Roman Cath. Ch., 1980. Asst. pastor Mobile, 1959-65; tchr. McGill Inst., Mobile, 1959-60, 61-62; vice chancellor Diocese of Mobile-Birmingham, 1963-66, chancellor, 1966-80; pastor St. Patrick Parish, Mobile, 1966-71; lectr. history Spring Hill Coll., Mobile, 1971-72; asst. pastor St. Matthew Parish, Mobile, 1971-79, Cathedral Immaculate Conception, Mobile, 1979-80; adminstr. sede vacante Diocese of Mobile, 1980, now archbishop; pres. Cath. Housing Mobile, Mobile Senate Priests, 1978-80; chmn. com. on doctrine Nat. Conf. Cath. Bishops, 1988-91. Author articles, papers in field. Chmn. bd. dirs. Mobile Mus., 1966-88, Ala. Dept. Archives and History, 1979—, chmn., 1999—; chmn. bd. dirs. Cath. U. Am., Washington, 1983-98, Spring Hill Coll., Mobile, 1982—; chmn. NCCB Com. on Ecumenical and Interreligious Affairs, 1993-96, Cath. Common Ground Initiative, 1996—, chmn. com. on the liturgy, 1999—; chmn. bd. govs. N.Am. Coll., Rome, 1982-85. Mem. Am. Cath. Hist. Assn., So. Hist. Assn., Ala. Hist. Assn. (pres. 1971-72, exec. com. 1981-88), Hist. Mobile Preservation Soc., Lions. Address: PO Box 1966 36633 400 Government St Mobile AL 36602-2332

LIPSCOMB, WILLIAM NUNN, JR., retired physical chemistry educator; b. Cleveland, Ohio, Dec. 9, 1919; s. William Nunn and Edna Patterson (Porter) L.; m. Mary Adele Sargent, May 20, 1944; children: Dorothy Jean, James Sargent; m. Jean Craig Evans, 1983; 1 child, Jenna. BS, U. Ky., 1941, DSc (hon.), 1963; PhD, Calif. Inst. Tech., 1946; DSc (hon.), U. Munich, 1976, L.I. U., 1977, Rutgers U., 1979, Gustavus Adolphus Coll., 1980, Marietta Coll., 1981, Miami U., 1983, U. Denver, 1985, Ohio State U., 1991; Transylvania U., 1992. Phys. chemist Office of Sci. R&D, 1942-46; faculty U. Minn., Mpls., 1946-59, asst. prof., 1946-50, assoc. prof., 1950-54, acting chief phys. chemistry div., 1952-54, prof. and chief phys. chemistry div., 1954-59; prof. chemistry Harvard U., Cambridge, Mass., 1959-71, Abbott and James Lawrence prof., 1971-90, prof. emeritus, 1990—; mem. U.S. Nat. Commn. for Crystallography, 1954-59, 60-63, 65-67; chmn. program com. 4th Internat. Congress of crystallography, Montreal, 1957; mem. sci. adv. bd. Robert A. Welch Found.; mem. rsch. adv. bd. Mich. Molecular Biology Inst.; mem. adv. com. Inst. Amorphus Studies; mem. sci. adv. com. Nova Pharms., Daltex Med. Svc., Gensia Pharms., Binary Therapeutics. Author: The Boron Hydrides, 1963, (with G.R. Eaton) NMR Studies of Boron Hydrides and Related Compounds, 1969; assoc. editor: Jour. Chemical Physics, 1955-57; contbr. articles to profl. jours.; clarinetist, mem.: Amateur Chamber Music Players. Guggenheim fellow Oxford U., Eng., 1954-55; Guggenheim fellow Cambridge U., Eng., 1972-73; NSF sr. postdoctoral fellow, 1965-66; Overseas fellow Churchill Coll., Cambridge, Eng., 1966, 73; Robert Welch Found. lectr., 1966, 71; Howard U. distinguished lecture series, 1966; George Fisher Baker lectr. Cornell U., 1969; centenary lectr. Chem. Soc., London, 1972; lectr. Weizmann Inst., Rehovoth, Israel, 1974; Evans award lectr. Ohio State U., 1974; Gilbert Newton Lewis Meml. lectr. U. Calif., Berkeley, 1974; also lectureships Mich. State U., 1975, U. Iowa, 1975, Ill. Inst. Tech., 1976, numerous others; also speaker confs.; Recipient Harrison Howe award in Chemistry, 1958; Distinguished Alumni Centennial award U. Ky., 1965; Distinguished Service in advancement inorganic chemistry Am. Chem. Soc., 1968; George Ledlie prize Harvard, 1971; Nobel prize in chemistry, 1976; Disting. Alumni award Calif. Inst. Tech., 1977; sr. U.S. scientist award Alexander von Humboldt-Stiftung, 1979; award lecture Internat. Acad. Quantum Molecular Sci., 1980. Fellow Am. Acad. Arts and Scis., Am. Phys. Soc.; mem. NAS, Am. Chem. Soc. (Peter Debye award phys. chemistry 1973, chmn. Minn. sect. 1949-50), Am. Crystallographic Assn. (pres. 1955), The Netherlands Acad. Arts and Scis. (fgn.), Math. Assn. Bioinorganic Scientists (hon.), Academie Europeenne des Sciences, des Arts et des Lettres, Royal Soc. Chemistry (hon.), Phi Beta Kappa, Sigma Xi, Alpha Chi Sigma, Phi Lambda Upsilon, Sigma Pi Sigma, Phi Mu Epsilon. Office: Harvard U Dept Chemistry & Chem Biol 12 Oxford St Cambridge MA 02138-2902

LIPSKY, BURTON G., lawyer; b. Syracuse, N.Y., May 29, 1937; s. Abraham and Pauline (Leichtner); m. Elaine B. Mannheimer, July 27, 1967; 1 child, Erika S., m. Carol S. Samberg, Feb. 4, 1973; 1 child, Andrew H. BBA, U. Mich., 1959; JD summa cum laude, Syracuse U., 1962. Bar: N.Y. 1962, U.S. Supreme Ct. 1967. Trial atty. U.S. Dept. Justice, Washington, 1962-67; assoc. Kaye, Scholer, Fierman, Hays & Handler, N.Y.C., 1967-72; ptnr. Delson & Gordon, N.Y.C., 1972-87, Lipsky & Stout, N.Y.C., 1991-96; pvt. practice, N.Y.C., 1996—. Mem. bd. visitors Syracuse U. Coll. of Law, 1989—; sec.-treas., dir. Robert Mapplethorpe Found., Inc., 1988—. Mem. ABA, N.Y. Bar Assn., Order of Coif, Justinian Soc., Am. Contract Bridge League (life master). Office: 777 3rd Ave New York NY 10017-1401

LIPSKY, IAN DAVID, mechanical engineering executive; b. Bklyn., May 26, 1957; s. Eugene Herman and Janet Dorothy (Heller) L.; m. Cheryl Joy Weinberg; 1 son, Ethan Maxwell. BS in Marine Engring., Maine Maritime Acad., 1979; MBA, U. San Francisco, 2000. Registered profl. engr., Calif.; lic. engring. contractor, Calif.; lic. U.S. Coast Guard, Merchant Mariners Document steam & motor vessels, 1979. Third asst. engr. Interlake Steamship Co., Cleve., 1979-81; port engr. Exxon Internat. Co., Florham Park, N.J., 1981-84; prodn. supr. Alfred Conhagen Inc. Calif., Hercules, 1984-87, gen. mgr., 1987-89, v.p., 1989—. Mem. Soc. Naval Architects & Marine Engrs., Marine Port Engrs. N.Y., Inst. Marine Engrs. (London), Port Engrs. San Francisco, Nat. Soc. Profl. Engrs. Democrat. Jewish. Avocations: golfing, running, triathlons. Home: 153 Koch Rd Corte Madera CA 94925-1263 Office: Alfred Conhagen Inc Calif 3900 Oregon St Benicia CA 94510-1102

LIPSKY, LINDA ETHEL, business executive; b. Bklyn., June 2, 1939; d. Irving Julius and Florence (Stern) Ellman; m. Warren Lipsky, June 12, 1960 (div. Sept. 1968); 1 child, Phillip Bruce; m. Jerome Friedman, Jan. 17, 1988. BA in Psychology, Hofstra U., 1960; MPS with hon. in Health Care Adminstrn., Long Island U., 1979. Child welfare social worker Nassau County Dept. Social Service, N.Y., 1960-64; adminstr. La Guardia Med. Group of Health Ins. Plan of Greater N.Y., Queens, 1969-72; cons. Neighborhood Svc. Ctr., Bronx, N.Y., 1973-78; dir. ODA Health Ctr., Bklyn., 1978-82; pres. Millin Assocs., Inc., Nassau, N.Y., 1982—. Mem. Health Care Fin. Mgmt. Assn., Nat. Assn. Community Health Ctrs., Nat. Assn. Female Execs., Cmty. Health Ctrs., Assoc. of N.Y., Hofstra U. Alumni Assn. (mem. senate 1984—, chairperson membership com. 1985—), Pi Alpha Alpha. Republican. Jewish. Avocations: cooking, writing, reading. Office: Millin Assocs Inc 521 Chestnut St Cedarhurst NY 11516-2244

LIPSON, ANDREI GRIGORIEVICH, physicist; b. Voronezh, Russia, Dec. 3, 1956; s. Grigory A. Lipson and Natalia P. Popova; m. Natalia O. Dorofeeva, Dec. 20, 1985; 1 child, Maria. M, Voronezh State U., 1979; PhD, Russian Acad. Sci., 1986. Rschr. Inst. Phys. Chemistry Russian Acad. Sci., Moscow, 1987—; guest rschr. NHE-Lab., Sapporo, Japan, 1997-98. Recipient grants Internat. Sci. Found., 1993, 94. Russian Orthodox. Avocations: swimming, soccer. Home: 25 Polikarpova St Apt 92, 125284 Moscow Russia Office: Russian Acad Sci, 31 Leninsky prospekt, 117915 Moscow Russia

LIPTAY, GEORGE, chemist, educator; b. Budapest, Hungary, Feb. 12, 1932; s. Aladar and Maria (Bognar) L.; m. Gabriella Palik, Aug. 9, 1958; 1 child, Gabriella. MSc, Tech. U. Budapest, 1954, PhD, 1963; CSc, Hungarian Sci. Acad., 1970, DSc, 1994. Asst. prof., first asst., assoc. prof. Tech. Univ. Budapest, 1954-92, prof., 1992—. Editor: (series) Atlas of Thermoanalytical Curves I-V, 1971-76; regional editor Thermal Analysis Jour., 1972-91; mem. adv. bd. Jour. Thermal Analysis, 1969—. Pres. Hungarian Chem. Soc., Analytical sect., 1995—, Than Karoly award, 1984; pres. Hungarian Sci. Acad. Thermoanalytical sub-com., 1990—. Mem. European Symposium of Thermal Analysis and Calorimetry, European Soc. Thermal Analysis, Calorimetry Thermodinamics and Chem. Reactivity (nat. rep. 1992—). Avocations: music, sports, travel. Home: Andrassy ul 20, H-1061 Budapest Hungary Office: Tech Univ Budapest, St Gellert Ter 4, H-1521 Budapest Hungary

LIPTON, JACKIE F., artist, educator; b. N.Y.C., Jan. 23, 1950; d. Victor Samuel and Helen Duberstein Lipton; m. John Christopher Bolton, Oct. 17, 1990. BA, Fordham U., 1978; postgrad., Sch. Visual Arts, N.Y.C., 1993-94; MFA, Milton Avery Grad. Sch. Arts, Annandale-on-Hudson, N.Y., 1994. Arts specialist P.S. 162, N.Y.C., 1994—. Exhibited in group shows West Chelsea Open Art Studio Festival, 1997, 98, 99, Drawings at the Westbeth Gallery, N.Y.C., 1999, Art Resources Transfer Gallery, 1999, others; peer studio artist Art REsources Ctr. of Whitney Mus. Am. Art, N.Y.C., 1973-75; gallery artist Condeso/Lawler, 1983-88. Grantee Pollock-Krasner Found., 1985-86, 86-87, 99—; fellow Macdowell Colony, 1988, Cummington Cmty. of the Arts, 1990, Va. Ctr. for Creative Arts, 1991, 93, 95, 97, 99-2000. Home: 55 Bethune St Apt D1003 New York NY 10014-2010 Studio: 526 W 26th St Rm 619 New York NY 10001-5523

LIPUKHIN, YURI VIKTORDVICH, investment company executive; b. Novokaznetsk, Russia, June 10, 1936; s. Viktor Illarionovich and Tatiana Vasilievna L.; m. Raisa Ivanovna Boldyreva, Dec. 7, 1962; children: Viktor Yurievich, Tatiana Yurievna. Grad., Inst. Steel & Alloys, Moscow, 1959. Roller, foreman Iron & Steel World, Sherepovets, Russia, 1959-71, supt. cold rolling shop, 1972-77, head prodn., 1978-79, chief engr., 1979-81, dir., 1981-89; dir. gen. Severstal joint stock co. Iron & Steel World, Sherepovets, Russia, 1989-93, chmn. bd. dirs., 1993—. Contbr. articles to profl. jours., including Steel, Metallurgist; inventor in field (125). Mem. Pub. Movement "Our Home is Russia". Avocations: swimming, gliding, water-sports, fishing, driving. Office: Severstal joint stock co, 30 Mira St, 162600 Cherepovets Russia

LIPUT, ANDREW LAWRENCE, lawyer; b. Trenton, N.J., June 28, 1962; s. Andrew and Bernice Helen L.; m. Jacquelyn Anne Liput, Jan. 11, 1997; 1 child, Mallory. BA, Drew U., 1984; JD, Fordham U., 1987. Bar: N.J., 1987, N.Y., 1988, Conn., 1996. V.p., gen. cousel Parssine Group, Inc., N.Y.C., 1988-91; sr. lawyer Hartman, Buhrman & Winnicki, Paramus, N.J., 1991-93; v.p., gen. counsel Marjam Supply Co., Inc., Bklyn., 1993-96; ptnr. Liput & Speregen, Huntington, N.Y., 1996—; adj. prof. Felician Coll., Lodi, N.J., 1994-97; assoc. prof. Suffolk C.C., Long Island, N.Y., 1998—; trust officer, Neighborhood Cleaners Assn., N.Y.C., 1998—, Metropolitan Package Store Assn., Westchester, N.Y., 1997—. Contbr. articles to profl. jours. Pres., dir. Bridge the Gap!, Long Island, 1999—, councilman, No. Plainfield, N.J., 1988-89. Mem. U.S. Rowing Assn., Aircraft Owners & Pilots Assn., N.Y. State Bar Assn., N.J. State Bar Assn., Conn. Bar Assn. Republican. Avocations: rowing, flying, reading, world travel. Office: Liput & Speregen RC 790 New York Ave Huntington NY 11743-4499

LIPWORTH, SIR (MAURICE) SYDNEY, bank executive, solicitor; b. May 13, 1931; s. Isidore and Rae Lipworth; m. Rosa Liwarek, 1957; 2 children. B in Commerce, LLB, U. Witwatersrand, Johannesburg, South Africa. Admitted solicitor, Johannesburg 1955; bar: South Africa 1956, Inner Temple 1991. Non-exec.dir. Liberty Life Assn. Africa Ltd., 1956-64; barrister Johannesburg, 1956-64; dir. Abbey Life Assurance Group, 1968-70; dir. Allied Dunbar Assurance Plc (formerly Hambro Life Assurance), 1971-88, joint mng. dir., 1980-84, dep. chmn. bd. dirs., 1984-87; chmn. bd. dirs. Dinbar Bank, 1983-88; mng. dir. Allied Dunbar Unit Trusts, 1983-85, chmn. bd. dirs., 1985-88; dir. J. Rothschild Holdings Plc, 1984-87, BAT Industries Plc, 1985-88, Carlton Comm. Plc, 1993—; dir. Zeneca Group Plc, 1994—, chmn. bd. dirs., 1995—; dep. chmn., sr. ind. non-exec. dir. Nat. Westminster Bank Plc (merged with Royal Bank Scotland), London, from 1993; chmn. Fin. Reporting Coun., London, 1993—; mem. Gen. Coun. of Bar, 1992-94. Contbr. chpts. and articles on investment, life ins., pensions and competition law to profl. publs. Chmn. Monopolies and Mergers Commn., 1988-93; mem. Senate Salaries Rev. Body, 1994—; mem. Com. on Fin. Aspects of Corp. Governance, 1994-95; mem. adv. panel Break Through Breast Cancer Res. Trust, 1990—; trustee Allied Dunbar Charitable Trust, 1971—; trustee Philharm. Orch., 1982—, dep. chmn. trustees, 1986-93, chmn. trustees 1993—; trustee Royal Acad. Trust, 1988—; gov. Contemporary Dance Trust, 1981-87, Sadler's Wells Found., 1987-90; hon. mem. Queen's Coun./, 1993. Hon. bencher Inner Temple, 1989. Mem. Bar Assn. for Commerce, Fin. and Industry (chmn. 1991-92). Avocations: tennis, music, theatre. Office: Holborn Hall, 100 Gray's Inn Rd, London WC1X 8AL, England*

LIRITZIS, IOANNIS GEORGE, physicist, educator, researcher; b. Dephi, Phokis, Greece, Nov. 2, 1953; s. George Yiannis and Martha (Alexiou) L. BSc in Physics, Patras (Greece) U., 1975; PhD in Physics, Edinburgh (Scotland) U., 1979. Rsch. assoc. Patras U., 1980-82, Rsch. Ctr. for Astronomy and Applied Math., Acad. Athens, Greece, 1989-99; with Ministry Culture, Atjems, 1983-99; prof. dept. Mediterranean studies Aegean U., Rhodes, Greece, 1998—, dir. Lab. Archaeometry, 2000—; vis. scientist dept. geology McMaster U., Hamilton, Ont., Can., 1977; vis. rschr. U.K. Atomic Energy Rsch. Establishment, Harwell Nuc. Tracer Unit, 1982, Rsch. Lab. for Archaeology and History of Art, Oxford (Eng.) U., 1983; archaeometrist Ministry of Culture and Sci., Athens, 1984-89; rsch. collaborator Nuc. Rsch. Ctr., Demokritos, Athens, 1984-90; vis. prof. Bordeaux III U., 1995; dir. Lab. of Archaeometry, 2000—. Author: Archaeometry: Dating Techniques in Archaeology, 1986, Archaeomagnetism in Greece and Geomagnetic Field Variations in British Lake Sediments Sionce 7000 BC, 1991 (prize Acad. Athens 1991), Radioactivity Alert, 1991, The Mystery of the Greek Pyramidals, 1998; co-author: A Global Archaeointensity Data Bank, 1992; contbr. numerous articles to profl. jours. Com. mem. Hellenic Student's Union, Edinburgh U., 1977-78; co-founder, pres. Delphic Amphictionia, Delphi, 1982-83, Acad. Delphic Studies, Athens, 1991—; founder So. European Conf. on Archaeometry, 1984. With Nat. Svc. Tech. Corp. Recipient Royal Soc. London award, 1976-77, 82, 86, Russell Trust award, 1977, 79, 83, Brit. Coun. award, 1982, UNESCO award, 1984, 95-97, award Onassis Found., 1987-88, 99-20002; Edinburgh U. scholar, 1978-79. Fellow Royal Astron. Soc. Gt. Britain, Royal Geog. Soc. Gt. Britain, N.Y. Acad. Scis.; mem. Inst. Physics Gt. Britain, Internat. Astron. Union, Planetary Soc., Hellenic Astron. Assn., Hellenic Archaeometry Assn., So. European Archaeometry Conf. (founder, conf. organizer, sec. 1984, 91). Greek Orthodox. Avocations: archaeology, guitar, philosophy. Office: U of Aegean, Dept Mediterrnanean Studies, 85100 Rhodes Greece

LIS, ANTHONY STANLEY, retired business administration educator; b. Easthampton, Mass., Aug. 11, 1918; s. Anthony Stanley and Anna Barbara (Kaczmarczyk) L.; m. Jane Ann Mikus, June 25, 1951 (dec.); children: Anthony, Judith A., Patricia Ann, Sandra J.; m. Sophie A. Pobieglo, June 24, 1983. BS, Mass. State Coll., Salem, 1950; MS, Okla. State U., 1951; PhD, U. Minn., 1961. Asst. prof. Okla. State U., Stillwater, 1951-55; assoc. prof. U. Tulsa, 1956-62; mem. faculty U. Okla., Norman, 1962-86, prof. bus. adminstrn., 1967-86, prof. emeritus, 1986—; vis. prof. Central Sch. Planning/Stats., Warsaw, Poland, 1984; del. II Congress Scholars of Polish Descent, Warsaw, 1979, III Congress, 1989 ; cons. to numerous bus. and govtl. agencies. Served with U.S. Army, 1937-40, 1942-46. Decorated Bronze Star; recipient Superior Profl. and Univ. Service award U. Okla., 1981; Summer fellow Found. Econ. Edn., 1954. Mem. Am. Bus. Comm. Assn., Polish Am. Hist. Assn., Delta Pi Epsilon, Beta Gamma Sigma, Delta Sigma Pi. Roman Catholic. Lodge: Lions. Home: 1827 Peter Pan St Norman OK 73072-5837

LISAK, ROBERT PHILIP, physician, researcher, educator; b. Bklyn., Mar. 17, 1941; s. Irving Arthur and Sylvia Lillian (Kadish) L.; m. Deena Freda Penchansky, Aug. 2, 1964; children: Ilene Ann, Michael Loren. BA, NYU, 1961; MD, Columbia U., 1965; MA (hon.), U. Pa., 1976. Diplomate Am. Bd. Neurology. Intern in medicine Montefiore Hosp. and Med. Ctr., Bronx, 1965-66; rsch. assoc. NIMH, Bethesda, Md., 1966-68; resident in medicine Bronx Mcpl. Med. Ctr., 1968-69; resident in neurology Hosp. of the U. of Pa., Phila., 1969-72; with Sch. of Medicine U. Pa., Phila., 1972-87, prof. neurology Sch. of Medicine, 1980-87, vice chmn. dept. neurology Sch. of Medicine, 1985-87; prof., chmn. dept. neurology Sch. of Medicine Wayne State U., Detroit, 1987—; mem. adv. bd. Guillain-Barre Syndrome Internat., Wynnewood, Pa., 1985—; mem. med. adv. bd. Myasthenia Gravis Found., Chgo., 1988—, Nat. Multiple Sclerosis Soc., N.Y.C., 1988—. Co-author:

Myasthenia Gravis, 1982; mem. editl. bd. Jour. Neuroimmunology, 1984-98, Muscle and Nerve Jour., 1981-86, 92-95, 98—, Neurology, 1981-86, Annals of Neurology, 1990-95, Jour. Peripheral Nervous Sys., Clin. Neuropharm., 1997—; editor-in-chief Jour. Neurol. Sci., 1998—; contbr. articles to profl. jours. With USPHS, 1966-68. Fulbright rsch. scholar, London, 1978-79; recipient Disting. Teaching award U. Pa., 1985, Drs. award Myasthenia Gravis Found., 1991. Fellow Am. Acad. Neurology (sci. issues com. 1987-93); mem. Am. Neurol. Assn. (membership com. 1989-91, chmn. 1990-91, sci. program com. 1994-96), Internat. Soc. Neuroimmunology (exec. com. 1987-91, 95—, sec.-treas. 1991-95), Am. Assn. Immunologists, Soc. for Neurosci., Norwegian Neurol. Assn., Royal Soc. Medicine. Office: Wayne State U Sch Medicine 6E-UHC 4201 St Antoine Detroit MI 48201

LISANTI, VIVIANA, communications executive; b. Buenos Aires, Argentina, Dec. 27, 1958; d. Jose and Belma Nansy (Garcia) L.; m. Santiago Juan Tenor, Dec. 26, 1987 (div. 1997); 1 child, Rodrigo Jose. BA in Philosophy, U. Catolica, Argentina, 1978. Translator/prodn. sec. SEA Cinenatogratica, Buenos Aires, Argentina, 1985-86; translator Telearte, Buenos Aires, 1986-91; acquisitions exec. Artear, Buenos Aires, 1991-94; head acquisitions Telefe, Buenos Aires, 1994-99. Mem. Argentine Exec. Women Assn. Avocations: photography, reading. Office: Telefe-TV Federal, Pavon 2444, Buenos Aires Argentina

LISBOA-FARROW, ELIZABETH OLIVER, public and government relations consultant; b. N.Y.C., Nov. 25, 1947; d. Eleuterio and Esperanza Oliver; m. Jeffrey Lloyd Farrow, Dec. 31, 1980; 1 child, Hamilton Oliver Farrow; 1 stepchild, Maximillian Robbins Farrow. Student pvt. schs., N.Y.C. With Harold Rand & Co. and various other pub. rels. firms N.Y.C., 1966-75; dir. pub. rels. N.Y. Playboy Club and Playboy Clubs Internat., 1975-79; pres., CEO Lisboa Assocs., Inc., N.Y.C., 1979—; founder, pres. Lisboa Prodns., Inc., Washington, 1994—. Counselor Am. Woman's Devel. Corp. Sec. Nat. Acad. Concert and Cabaret Arts; mem. nat. adv. coun. SBA, 1980-81, apptd., 1994—; exec. dir. Variety Club of Greater Washington Children's Charity, Inc., 1985-90; bd. dirs. Variety Myoelectric Limb Bank Found., 1990-91; trustee Hispanic Coll. Fund, 1995—, vice chair, 1996—; chairperson bd. trustees Southeastern U., 1997—; mem. adv. bd. Indsl. Bank, N.A., 1996; bd. dirs. Bell Multicultural H.S. Recipient Disting. award of Excellence SBA, 1992, Women Bus. Enterprise award U.S. Transp. Nat. Hwy. Transp. Safety Adminstrn., 1994, Civic Cmty. Achievement Black Bus. and Profls. Network, 1999, Excellence in Entrepreneurship award Dialogue on Diversity, Inc., 1995, Women of Distinction award Nat. Conf. Coll. Women Student Leaders, 2000, Applause award Women's Bus. Enterprise Nat. Coun., 2000; named Pub. Rels. Woman of Yr., Women in Pub. Rels., 1992, Hispanic Bus. Woman of Yr., Nat. Hispanic Bus. Coun., 1996, Hispanic of Yr. in Bus., La Nacion Newspaper, 1997, Presdl. medal Sistema U. Ana G. Méndez, U. Metropolitana, San Juan, P.R., 1999, Entrepreneur of Yr., Hispanic Mag., 1999, Bus. Woman of Yr. N.Y. State Fedn. Hispanic Cs. of C. Mem. U.S. Hispanic C. of C. (vice chair 1999, Nat. Hispanic Businesswoman of Yr. 1996, bd. dirs. 1998), D.C. C. of C. (pres. 2000), Small Bus. Adv. Coun., U.S. C. of C. (Blue Chip Enterprise award 1993), Advt. Coun., Am. Heart Assn., Hispanic Bus. and Profl. Women's Assn., Ibero-Am. C. of C. (bd. dirs. 1993, v.p. 1995, pres. 1997, pres. 1998, adv. chair 1999, Small Bus. award 1993, corp. of yr. award 2000), City Club Washington. Office: 1317 F St NW Washington DC 20004-1105

LISCHINSKY, ADRIANA LEONOR, chemist; b. Buenos Aires, Argentina, Sept. 15, 1953; d. Israel and Gloria (Jospe) L. Bachellor, Nat. Buenos Aires, 1971; lic. in chemistry, U. Buenos Aires, 1976, PhD in Chemistry, 1983; MSc in Physiology, U. Western Ont., 1982. Rsch. asst. Polychaco, Buenos Aires, 1984-86; regualtory affairs cons. Argentina, 1986-90; regulatory affairs cons. Connaught, Toronto, Can., 1991-92; regulatory affairs assoc. Hoechst, Buenos Aires, 1994-96; cons. Buenos Aires, 1996; regulatory affairs mgr. Pfizer, Buenos Aires, 1997—. Contbr. articles to profl. jours. Fellowship Comm. of Scientific Rsch., 1977-79. Avocation: golf. Home: Malabia 2363, 1425 Buenos Aires Argentina Office: V Loreto 2477, Buenos Aires 1425, Argentina

LISE, CLAUDE, government official of Martinique, physician, politician; b. Martinique, Jan. 31, 1941. Mem. Gen. Coun., Martinique, 1980—, pres., 1992—; senator Gen. Coun., Martinique, 1995—; rep. French Senate; dep. Socialist Party Martinique, 1988-93; 3d asst. mayor, Fort-de-France, Martinique, 1983—. Mem. Parti Progressiste Martiniquais. Office: Conseil Gén Martinique, 20 ave des Caraïbes BP, 97264 Fort-de-France France

LISETSKII, FEDOR NIKOLAEVICH, geographer, educator; b. Nikolayev, Russia, Aug. 3, 1958; s. Nikolai Fedorovich and Alexandra Mironovna (Koieva) L.; m. Anna Sokratovna, Apr. 27, 1979; 1 child, Olga; m. Natalia Borisovna Kulikova, July 16, 1982; 1 child, Mary. Cand.Sc. in Geography, Mechnikov State U., Odessa, Russia, 1984, Dr.Sc. in Geography, 1994. Postgrad. fellow Mechnikov State U., Odessa, 1980-83, asst., 1983-85, asst. prof., 1985-95; prof. geography Belgorod (Russia) State U., 1995—, head faculty of geoecology, 1998—; dep. dir. South Centre of Agroecology, Odessa, 1994-95, Inst. Natural Scis., Belgorod, 1997—, dep. vice-rector of Sc. Work, 1999—. Co-author: Conception of Formation of Agrolandscapes, 1992, Landscape Agriculture, 1993, Basis of Landscape-Ecological Agriculture, 1994; author/editor: Conception and Programme "Eco-Vorskla-2005, 1997. Recipient Laureat and prize for best work in ecology field South Centre of Investigation and Social Initiatives, 1990. Mem. Internat. Soc. Soil Sci., European Soc. for Soil Conservation, Russian Geog. Soc. (chmn. Belgorod dept. 1996—), Peter Acad. Sci. and Art (corr.). Avocation: stamp collecting. E-mail: liset@bsu.edu.ru. Home: Nekrasova str 17-V Apt 77, 308007 Belgorod Russia Office: State Univ of Belgorod, 12 Studencheskaya, 308007 Belgorod Russia

LISHER, JAMES RICHARD, lawyer; b. Aug. 28, 1947; s. Leonard B. and Mary Jane (Rafferty) L.; m. Martha Gettelfinger, June 16, 1973; children: Jennifer, James Richard II. AB, Ind. U., 1969, JD, 1975. Bar: Ind. 1975, U.S. Dist. Ct. (so. dist.) Ind. 1975, U.S. Supreme Ct. 2000. Assoc. Rafferty & Wood, Shelbyville, Ind., 1976, Rafferty & Lisher, Shelbyville, Ind., 1976-77; dep. prosecutor Shelby County Prosecutor's Office, Shelbyville, 1976-78; ptnr. Yeager, Lisher & Baldwin, Shelbyville, 1977-96; pvt. practice, Shelbyville, 1996—; pros. atty. Shelby County, Shelbyville, 1983-95, pub. defender, 1995—. Speaker, faculty advisor Ind. Pros. Sch., 1986. Editor: (manual) Traffic Case Defenses, 1982, First Law Office, 1998. Bd. dirs. Girls Club of Shelbyville, 1979-84, Bears of Blue River Festival, Shelbyville, 1982-98; pres. Shelby County Internat. Rels. Coun., 1997-99. Recipient Citation of Merit, Young Lawyers Assn. Mem. ATLA, Nat. Assn. Criminals, State Bar Assn. (bd. dirs.), Ind. Pub. Defender Assn., Ind. State Bar Assn. (bd. dirs. young lawyer sect. 1979-83, bd. dirs. gen. practice sect. 1996-98, treas. 1997-98, vice-chmn. 1998-99, chmn.-elect 1999-2000), Shelby County Bar Assn. (sec.-treas. 1986, v.p. 1987, pres. 1988), Ind. Prosecuting Attys. Assn. (bd. dirs. 1985-95, sec.-treas. 1987, v.p. 1988, pres. 1990), Masons, Elks, Lions. Democrat. Home: 106 Western Trce Shelbyville IN 46176-9765 Office: 407 S Harrison St Shelbyville IN 46176-2170

LISHER, JOHN LEONARD, lawyer; b. Indpls., Sept. 19, 1950; s. Leonard Boyd and Mary Jane (Rafferty) L.; m. Mary Katherine Sturmon, Aug. 17, 1974. B.A. with honors in History, Ind. U., 1975, J.D., 1975. Bar: Ind. 1975. Dep. atty. gen. State of Ind., Indpls., 1975-78; asst. corp. counsel City of Indpls., 1978-81; assoc. Osborn & Hiner, Indpls., 1981-86; ptnr. Osborn, Hiner & Lisher, 1986—. Vol. Mayflower Classic, Indpls., 1981—; pres. Brendonwood Common Inc.; asst. vol. coord. Marion County Rep. Com., Indpls., 1979-80; vol. Don Bogard for Atty. Gen., Indpls., 1980, Steve Goldsmith for Prosecutor, Indpls., 1979, 83, Sheila Suess for Congress, Indpls., 1980. Recipient Outstanding Young Man of Am. award Jaycees, 1979, 85, Indpls. Jaycees, 1980. Mem. ABA, Ind. Bar Assn., Indpls. Bar Assn. (membership com.), Assn. Trial Lawyers Am., Ind. U. Alumni Assn., Hoosier Alumni Assn. (charter, founder, pres.), Ind. Trial Lawyers Assn., Ind. Def. Lawyers Assn., Ind. U. Coll. Arts and Scis. (bd. dirs. 1983-92, pres. 1986-87), Wabash Valley Alumni Assn. (charter), Founders Club, Presidents Club, Phi Beta Kappa, Eta Sigma Phi, Phi Eta Sigma, Delta Xi Alumni Assn. (charter, v.p., sec., Delta Xi chpt. Outstanding Alumnus award 1975, 76, 79, 83), Delta Xi Housing Corp. (pres.), Pi Kappa Alpha (midwest regional pres. 1977-86, parliamentarian nat. conv. 1982, del. convs. 1978-80, 82, 84, 86, trustee Meml. Found. 1986-91. Presbyterian. Avocations: reading; golf; jogging; Roman coin collecting. Home: 5725 Hunterglen Rd Indianapolis IN 46226-1019 Office: Osborn Hiner & Lisher PC 8500 Keystone Xing Ste 480 Indianapolis IN 46240-2460

LISI, VIRNA (VIRNA PIERALISI), actress; b. Ancona, Italy, Nov. 8, 1937; m. Franco Pesci; 1 child. Theater debut: I Giacobini, Piccolo Teatro, Milan; films include Scandali segreti, La romagnola, Come uccidere vostra moglie, La donna del giorno, 1956, Duel of the Titans, 1962, Eva, 1962, How to Murder Your Wife, 1965, Casanova 70, 1965, Signore e signori, 1965, Made in Italy, 1965, Not With My Wife You Don't, 1966, Assault on a Queen, 1966, The 25th Hour, 1966, The Girl and the General, Arabella, 1967, Better a Widow, 1967, Le dolci signore, 1967, Tenderly, 1968, L'albero di Natale, 1969, The Christmas Tree, 1969, The Secret of Santa Vittoria, 1969, La Statua, 1971, Giochi particolari, 1971, Il bel mostro, 1971, Roma bene, 1971, Barbablù, 1972, Il serpente, 1973, Zanna Bianca, 1973, Il ritorno di Zanna Bianca, 1977, Al di là del bene e del male, 1977, Ernesto, 1978, La cicala, 1979, I Love N.Y., 1987, The Boys of Via Panisperna, 1988, Merry Christmas, Happy New Year, 1989, La Reine Margot, 1994 (Best Actress award Cannes Internat. Film Festival), (film) Follow Your Heart, 1996, (TV mini-series) Deserto di fuoco, 1991, (TV) Cristallo di Rocca, 1999. Address: care of VMA, 20 Avenue Rapp, 75007 Paris France also: Via Salaria 396, 1-00199 Rome Italy*

LISIENKOV, IVAN DMITRIEVICH, economist, agricultural engineer, researcher; b. Smolensk, Russia, Aug. 31, 1931; s. Dmitrii Sergeevich and Anna Trogimovna (Trogimova) L.; m. Nina Grigorjevna Chernyshenko, Oct. 6, 1959; 1 child, Sergei Ivanovich. Mech. engr., Electromech. Inst., Moscow, 1954; D in Econs., Inst. Agrl. Prodn., Moscow, 1977. Honorable economist, Russian Fedn., Moscow, 1981, Academician, Internat. Prodn. Informatization Acad., Moscow, 1996. Mech. engr. tractor sta., Ruza, Russia, 1954-58; master, shop supt. mech. plant, Harkov, Ukraine, 1958-61; chief engr., mgr. Agrotechnik, Kaliningrad, Russia, 1961-65; head of dept. State Agro-indsl. Com., Moscow, 1965-91; gen. dir. Inst. Computer Tech., Moscow, 1987—; lectr. Inst. Agrl. Prodn., Moscow, 1978-87; dir. Inst. Mechanization and Electrofication of Agriculture, Moscow, 1969—; mem. coun. Vets.-Engrs. of Agriculture, Moscow, 1995—. Author: Cost Price Planning, 1968; author, editor: Methodology of Measuring and Calculation of Labor Consumption and Machine Repair, 1975, Planning and Management of Repair Enterprises, 1972, 81; contbr. over 50 articles to profl. jours. Mem. Comsomol Dist. Bur., village of Ostashkovo, Moscow Dist., 1955-58, Party Dist. Bur., Pushkino, Moscow Dist., 1964-65; mem. Presidium Agrl. Trade Union, Moscow, 1978-86; pres. Nat. Assn. Wholesale Food Mkts., Moscow, 1995—. Recipient medal for Labor Valor, Supreme Coun., Moscow, 1945, 70, 75, Vet. of Labor medal, 1988. Mem. Hunters and Anglers of Moscow, Countrymen Assn. (coun. mem. 1997—). Avocations: farming, historical and belles-lettres literature, hunting in Siberia. Home: Soviet Army, 127018 Moscow Russia Office: CNII ASU agroservice, B. Sadovaja, 103001 Moscow Russia

LISINENKO, IGOR, government official; b. Orzhitsa, Poltava, Ukraine, May 18, 1962; s. Vasily and Alla (Kozarenko) L.; m. Irina Mironenko, Aug. 26, 1986. B, Mil. U., Moscow, 1988, D in Econ., 1995; postgrad., Moscow Internat. Bus. Sch., 1997-99. Officer USSR Armed Forces, 1980-89; mktg. dir. Avers Corp., Moscow, 1990-91; pres. May Tea & Coffee Corp., Moscow, 1991-97; dep. Moscow City Duma, 1997-99; dep. chmn. parliamentary com. State Duma Parliament of Russian Fedn., 1999—; prof. econs. Mil. U., Moscow, 1997-99. Recipient Krasnaya Zvezda award Govt. USSR. Mem. Russian Acad. Natural Scis. (corr.), Russian Tea & Coffee Assn. (pres. 1996), Russian Union Industrialists and Entrepreneurs (v.p. 1998). Office: State Duma Russian Fedn, 2 Georgievsky Pereulok, 111020 Moscow 103265, Russia

LISOVSKA, EVITA, English educator; b. Riga, Latvia, July 3, 1974; d. Ojars and Dzintra (Stilbina) Smiltens; m. Ainars Lisovskis, May 22, 1994; 1 child, Ilze. B in English Philology, U. Riga, 1996. Guide, translator, interpretor Riga Motormuseum, 1993-95; English tchr. Riga Commerce Sch., 1995—. Avocations: literature, gardening, psychology, computers. Home: Vaidavas 13-45, Riga LV-1084, Latvia Office: Riga Commerce Sch, Salaspils 14, Riga LV-1057, Latvia

LISOVSKY, FJEDOR VIKTOROVICH, physicist; b. Semipalatinsk, Kazakhstan, Nov. 12, 1940; s. Viktor Dmitrievich and Anna Evmen'evna (Lopata) L.; m. Anna Fjedorovna Zhukova, Apr. 5, 1959; 1 child, Sergei Fjedorovich. Candidate Phys. and Math. Scis., Moscow Inst. Physics & Tech., 1968; D in Phys. and Math. Scis., Donetzk Inst. Physics & Tech., Ukraine, 1980; prof. solid state physics, Russian Acad. Scis., Moscow, 1995. Jr. sci. staff mem. Inst. Radio Engring. and Electronics, Acad. Scis. USSR, Moscow, 1965-70; sr. sci. staff mem. Inst. Radio Engring. and Electronics, Acad. Scis. USSR, Fryazino, Moscow, 1970-86; leading sci. staff mem. Inst. Radio Engring. and Electronics, Acad. Scis. USSR, Fryazino, 1986-92, prin. sci. staff mem., head rsch. group, 1992—. Author: Physics of Cylindrical Magnetic Domains, 1979; co-author: Elements and Devices on Cylindrical Magnetic Domains, 1987, (with I.K. Kalugin) English-Russian Dictionary of Electronics, 1987; co-author, co-editor: (with L.I. Antonov) Magnetism and Magnetic Materials, 1997. Dep. Moscow Regional Soviet, 1987-89. Mem. Russian Acad. Scis. (mem. sci. coun. on magnetics 1996—, head magnetic films sect. sci. coun. on magnetics 1996—). Avocations: foreign languages, tourism, fishing, hunting, singing, playing guitar. E-mail: lisf@dataforce.net. Home: Apt 80, Baykal skaya str 23, 107207 Moscow Russia Office: Inst Radio Engring RAS, Vvedensky Sq 1, 141120 Fryazino Moscow, Russia

LISOWITZ, GERALD MYRON, neuropsychiatrist; b. Johnstown, Pa., May 28, 1930; s. Charles Gerson and Tillie (Cohen) L.; m. Amelia Josephine Rozzando, Mar. 1, 1976 (div. June 1967); children: Mara, Scott, Laurie, Carlyn, Linda. BS magna cum laude, U. Pitts., 1953, MD, 1955. Diplomate Am. Bd. Neurology in Psychiatry. Intern Montefiore Hosp., Pitts., 1955-56; psychiat. resident, teaching fellow Western Psychiatric Inst. & Clinic, 1956-59; psychoanalytic trainee Phila. Psychoanalytic Inst., 1958, Pitts. Psychoanalytic Inst., 1962-72; clin. instr. dept. psychiatry Sch. Medicine U. Pitts., 1961-80; pvt. practice gen. psychiatry, 1969—; ptnr. Psychiat. Assocs., Pitts., 1969-83; cons. in field; mem. staff Montefiore U. Hosp., U. Pitts. Med. Sch., St. Francis Gen. Hosp., Pitts., Westmoreland Hosp., Greensburg, Pa.; chief neuropsychiatry U.S. Army Hosp., Ft. Lee, Va.; founder Mental Health Clinic; sr. staff Western Psychiat. Inst., U. Pitts. Med. Sch.; clin. dir. drug and alcohol rehab. St. Francis Gen. Hops., Pitts.-Monroeville, 1990; staff Montefiore U. Hosp., Pitts. Contbr. articles to profl. jours. Bd. dirs., advisor Westmoreland County Mental Health Dept., Greensburg, 1970-85. Capt. U.S. Army, 1959-61. Recipient rsch. award Ciba-Geigy, 1980. Mem. AMA, Am. Psychiat. Assn., Am. Assn. Clin. Psychiatrists, Pa. Med. Soc., Pa. Psychiat. Assn., Westmoreland County Med. Soc., Western Pa. Psychiat. Soc. (pres. 1985-89), Phila. Psychiat. Assn., Pitts. Psychiat. Soc., Pitts. Med. Forum, Phi Delta Epsilon, Phi Beta Kappa. Avocations: music, golf, chess. Home: 3 Foxwood Ln Greensburg PA 15601-9551

LISS, NORMAN, lawyer; b. New York, May 7, 1932; m. Sandra Hirsch, Feb. 28, 1959. BS, NYU, 1952, LLB, 1955. Bar: N.Y. 1955, U.S. Dist. Ct. (so. dist.) N.Y. 1961, U.S. Dist. Ct (ea. dist.) N.Y. 1962. Assoc. Booth, Lipton & Lipton, New York, 1956-57, Seymour Detsky, New York, 1957-58; pvt. practice New York, 1958—; cons. to Portugal Re-Cultural Events in U.S.; represented Norway in N.Y. proceedings to clear records of sailors arrested during 900th anniversary of Leif Ericson Voyage; jour. chair UJA Trial Lawyers USCG Acad. Law Day, 1987, 89, 94, 98. Contbr. articles to profl. jours. Chmn. Bronx County Bar div. United Jewish Appeal, Hist. Documents Exhbn., Operation Sail, 1986, USCG Acad. Law Day, 1987, 89; chmn. devel. Ellis Island Restoration Commn.; counsel N.Y. State Statue of Liberty Centennial Com., Mayor's Handicapped Citizens Adv. Bd., N.Y.C., Coun. on Arts; mem. Bronx County 350 Commn., N.Y.C. Commn. for Presdl. Conv.; rep., counsel N.Y.C. Com. on Bicentennial of U.S. Constitution; cons. Soc. Congl. Medal of Honor; commd. lt. col. N.Y. Guard Judge Advocate Gen. Unit; bd. dirs. Anti Defamation League; trustee Am. Jewish Hist. Soc. Recipient Disting. Humanitarian award Inst. of Applied Human Dynamics, Meritorious Pub. Svc. award USCG, 1989; named Man of Yr. Am. Jewish Congress, Man of Yr. Kinneret Sch., 1985. Mem. ABA, N.Y. Bar Assn., Bronx County Bar Assn., Am. Arbitration Assn. (panel arbitrators), Assn. Trial Lawyers Am., Law Day Outreach Com., NYU Alumni Assn. (adv. coun.). Home: 2727 Palisade Ave Bronx NY 10463-1018 Office: 200 W 57th St New York NY 10019-3211

LIST, GUDULA, psychology educator; b. Leipzig, Germany, Dec. 21, 1938; m. Guenther List. PhD, U. Konstanz, Germany, 1972. Prof. psychology Päd. Hochschule, Reinland, 1976-80; prof. linguistics Erz. Wiss Hochschule, Rheinland-Pfalz, 1980; prof. psychology U. Cologne, 1985—. Office: Univ Cologne, Univ Cologne, Herbert Lewin str 2, 50931 Cologne Germany

LISTE, HARTMUT, language professional, researcher; b. Aug. 20, 1947. Diplom-Philologe, Humboldt U. Berlin, 1971, PhD, 1975. Sci. asst., lang. educator Humboldt U., Berlin, 1974—. Author: Taschenlehrbuch Tschechisch, 1980, 2nd edit. 1983, 3rd edit. 1985, 4th edit. 1987, 5th edit. 1990 (1st new rev. edit.), Taschenwörterbuch Tschechisch-Deutsch, 1986, 2nd edit. 1987, 3rd edit., 1990. Home: Schivelbeiner Str 26, 10439 Berlin Germany

LISTER, BRUCE ALCOTT, food scientist, consultant; b. Bklyn., Dec. 23, 1922; s. James Alan and Georgana Martha (Hunt) L.; m. Doris Ann Jonassen, May 20, 1990. BSChemE, Columbia U., 1943, MSChemE, 1947; cert. in Food Tech., MIT, 1952; PhD (hon.), Hofstra U., 1998. From lab. asst. to div. rsch. dir. General Foods Corp., Hoboken, N.J. and White Plains, N.Y., 1943-62; from mgr. tech. svcs. to v.p. corp. affairs Nestle Foods Corp., White Plains and Purchase, N.Y., 1962-88; exec. dir., chmn. tech. com., bd. dirs. Tea Assn. U.S.A., N.Y.C., 1980-91; cons. food industry Baldwin, 1989—; pres. Internat. Hydrolyzed Protein Coun., Washington, 1979-90; trustee cacao biogenetic rsch. project Pa. State U., State College, 1988-89; chmn. stds. regulations com. Nat. Coffee Assn., N.Y.C., 1968-88, tech. com. Chocolate Mfrs. Assn., McLean, Va., 1972-88; U.S. del., chmn. tea com., mem. coffee com. Internat. Stds. Orgn.; U.S. del., full commn., chocolate, soup, dietary foods, labeling coms. Codex Alimentarius; U.S. del., tea com. UN Commn. on Trade and Devel.; mem. govt. rels. com. Internat. Bottled Water Assn., 1987. Pres., v.p., bd. dirs., fin. chmn. Bethany Meth. Home, Bklyn., 1969—; treas., dir. Coun. Against Drug Abuse, Baldwin, 1969—; trustee, lay leader, fin. chmn. First Ch. Baldwin, United Meth., 1972—; mem. Nassau County Bd. Social Svcs., 1972-74; chmn. Nassau County Bd. Health, Mineola, N.Y., 1975-2000; pres., v.p., bd. dirs. R&D Assocs. U.S. Mil., 1966-76; vice chair, mem. adv. bd., chair scholarship com., cons. for new sci. bldg. Hofstra U., Hempstead, N.Y., 1982—, mem. engring. dept. adv. bd. 1999—, mem. acad. affairs com., 2000—; pres. Rep. Club, Baldwin, 1967-68; mem. engring. sch. adv. bd. Columbia U., 1999—. Lt. (j.g.) USNR, 1944-46. Named Man of Yr., Baldwin Rep. Club, 1968, Nassau County (N.Y.) Sr. Citizen of Yr., 2000; recipient Hon. doctorate Nat. Assn. Food Equip. Mfrs., 1973, Cert. Appreciation for Patriotic Civilian Svc. U.S. Army, 1975. Fellow Am. Inst. Chemists; mem. AIChemE (profl.), Am. Chem. Soc. (emeritus), Inst. Food Technologists (emeritus, chmn. internat. div. 1985-88, mem. awards com. 1989, mem. codex com. 1996—, chair codex com. 1998—, liaison to Codex Alimentarius 1989-93), Phi Tau Sigma (nat. pres. 1989-90), Tau Beta Pi, Sigma Xi, Phi Lambda Upsilon. Achievements include patents in food formulations; working with NASA to supply menu items for all space missions from Mercury thru Shuttle. Fax: (516) 223-0224.. Home: 1976 Oakmere Dr Baldwin NY 11510-2739

LISTER, (MARGOT) RUTH, social science educator; b. Huddersfield, Yorkshire, U.K., May 3, 1949; d. Werner Bernard and Daphne (Carter) L. BA in Sociology with honors, Essex (Eng.) U., 1979; MA in Multi-Racial Studies, Sussex (Eng.) U., 1981; Doctorate (hon.), Manchester (Eng.) U., 1987. Legal rsch. office staff Child Poverty Action Group, London, 1971-75, asst./dep. dir., 1975-79, dir., 1979-87; prof., head dept. applied social studies Bradford (Eng.) U., 1987-93; prof. social policy Loughborough (Eng.) U., 1994—. Author: The Exclusive Society: Citizenship and the Poor, 1990, Women's Economic Dependency and Social Security, 1992, Citizenship: Feminist Perspectives, 1997. Vice chair Nat. Coun. Voluntary Orgns., London, 1991-93; mem. Commn. on Social Justice, London, 1992-94, Opsahl Commn. on Future No. Ireland, Belfast, 1992-93; comdr. Brit. Empire, 1999. Mem. Acad. of Learned Socs. for the Social Scis. (founding academician). Fax: 01509-223944. E-mail: m.r.lister@lboro.ac.uk. Office: Dept Social Scis, Loughborough Univ, Loughborough LE11 3TU, United Kingdom

LISTERUD, BRIAN (LOWELL LISTERUD), choir director, music educator; b. Duluth, Minn., Mar. 20, 1951; s. Lowell Fred Listerud and Carol May (Tuttle) Alseth; m. Christine Joyce Gunvaldson, Aug. 24, 1973 (div. May 1998); children: L. Jason, Bjorn C., Solveig C. BS, Mankato State U., 1973; MMus, Ariz. State U., 1979, postgrad., 1984—; postgrad., U. Mont., 1985-89. Cert. tchr., Mont.; nat. registered music educator. Dir. Presbyn. Ch. Choir, Wolf Point, Mont., 1974-79; tchr. music Wolf Point H.S., 1974-79; dir. handbell choir Trinity Luth., Phoenix, 1989-90; dir. choral activities Great Falls (Mont.) H.S., 1979-80; dir. Random Ringers Handbells, Missoula, Mont., 1986—; dir. choirs Big Sky H.S., Missoula, 1980—; dir. Aesirian Alumni Choir, Missoula, 1991—; instr. Yung Network Coll., Beijing, 1998; adjudicator Mont. H.S. Assn., 1979—; clinician dist. music festivals and honor choirs; clinician N.W. Music Educators Regional Conf., Billings, Mont., 1979, N.W. Music Educators Nat. Conf., Portland, Oreg., 1987, 93, Am. Choral Dirs. Assn., Spokane, 1982, Portland, 1984, Louisville, 1989, Internat. Choral Dir. Exch., Germany, 1988, Sweden, 1992, Argentina, 1994. Dir. several concerts; contbr. articles to profl. jours. Mem. Mont. Arts Coun., Helena, 1985-89. Recipient scholarships, letters of commendation, awards. Mem. Am. Choral Dirs. Assn. (Mont. pres. 1987-89), Mont. Music Edn. Assn. (bus. mgr. 1980-85, historian 1999-2000), Mont. Edn. Assn. (faculty rep. 1985-87), Internat. Fedn. Choral Music, Am. Guild of English Handbell Ringers (state chmn. 1992-94, clinician, historian N.W. region 1997, N.W. chair elect 1998), Nat. Assn. Tchrs. Singing, Mankato State U. Alumni Assn., Ariz. State U. Alumni Assn., Sons of Norway (pres. Normendon lodge 1997-98), Good Samaritans, Carpenters for Christ, Phi Mu Alpha (pres. Lambda Tau chpt. 1972-73). Presbyterian. Avocations: music, travel, building, running, tennis. Office: Big Sky Sch 3100 South Ave W Missoula MT 59804-5106

LISZI, JÁNOS, physical chemist, educator; b. Kispest, Budapest, Hungary, Apr. 30, 1940; s. János Liszi and Mária Kokavecz; m. Jánosné Liszi Dec. 23, 1963; children: Katalin, János. Degree in chem. engring., U. Veszprém, Hungary, 1963. Asst. prof. U. Veszprém, 1963-75, prof., 1975—, vice rector, 1986-89, rector, 1989-95, head of dept., 1990—. Author or co-author 5 books; contbr. numerous sci. papers to profl. publs. Avocations: swimming, fungi, music, traveling, Italy. Office: U Veszprém, Egyetem Str 10, H-8200 Veszprém Hungary

LITCHFIELD, JEAN ANNE, nurse; b. Gary, Ind., Oct. 6, 1942; d. Donald Kleine and Helen Louise (Sweet) Eller; m. Norman E. Stone, Dec. 27, 1965 (div. Aug. 1973); children: Diana, David, Julie; m. Frank Litchfield, Jan. 26, 1974. Lic. practical nurse, Ind. U. Vocat. Tech. Coll., 1973; AS in Biology, Richland C.C., 1991; BSN, Millikin U., 1993; MSN, Ind. State U., 1995. RN, Ind., Ill. Nurse asst. St. Anthony Hosp., Terre Haute, Ind., 1960-73, nurse, 1973-93; charge nurse psychiatric ward St. Mary's Hosp., Decatur, Ill., 1993-99; instr. allied nursing and health divsn. Richland C.C., Decatur, 1995—; mem. student welfare com. Millikin U., Decatur, 1991-92. Recipient 1st place art award 1984, 85, 86, 2d place art award 1984, 85, 2d place County Fair, 1985, Gold Poet award World of Poetry, 1989, Silver Poet award, 1990, Outstanding Innovations in Tchg. and Learning award Richland C.C., 1997, 98, Excellence in Nursing award Decatur Area Task Force Nursing, 2000; named Most Caring Nurse St. Mary's Hosp. 1990, Clara Compton scholar, St. Mary's Hosp., 1993, 94, scholar Am. Legion, 1992. Mem. Internat. Platform Assn., Barn Colony Artists (treas. 1986-88), Phi Theta Kappa, Beta Sigma Phi (treas. 1976-78), Alpha Tau Delta (treas. 1991-92, pres. 1992-93), Sigma Theta Tau Internat. Home: 1680 N 30th St Decatur IL 62526-5416

LITKOUHI, CYRUS, pediatrician, consultant; b. Shiraz, Fars, Iran, Jan. 31, 1946; arrived in United Arab Emirates, 1984; s. Fatolah and Mahin (Mojalali) L.; m. Marie Lydie Lamarque, July 10, 1976; children: Daniel, Shahin, Shahram. MB, BChir, Dow Med. Coll., Karachi, Pakistan, 1972; Diploma in Tropical Medicine and Hygiene, U. London, 1974; Diploma in Tropical Child Health, U. Liverpool, Eng., 1976. Diploma in Child Health Royal Coll. Physicians, London, 1976. Sr. house officer, registrar, sr. registrar Nat. Health, London, Liverpool, 1973-80; cons. pediatrician Tehran (Iran) U., 1980-82; pediatrician Nat. Health Svc., London, 1982-84; head pediat. dept. Alzahra Hosp., Sharjah, United Arab Emirates, 1984-86; cons. pediatrician Alghurair Ctr., Dubai, United Arab Emirates, 1986—; lectr. NHS, London, 1977-80; cons., tchg. examiner Tehran U., 1980-82. Editor

(health column) Weekend Mag., 1987-89. Regional Co. for Devel. scholar Govt. Iran, 1965-71. Mem. Royal Coll. Physicians (U.K.), Brit. Med. Assn., Emirate Med. Assn., Iranian Med. Assn. Avocations: reading, swimming, traveling. Home and Office: Alghurair Ctr, PO Box 6999, Dubai United Arab Emirates

LITMAN, BRIAN DAVID, communications executive; b. Kansas City, Mo., May 9, 1954; s. Marvin Wilbur and Louise Diane (Raskin) L. BJ, U. Mo., 1977. Promotion mgr. Atlanta br. CBS/Columbia Records, Atlanta, 1977-78; promotion mgr. CBS Records, Cleve., 1978-79; dir. mktg. Am. TV and Communications (subs. Time, Inc. Cable), Pitts., 1980-81; account mgr. Group W Satellite Communications, Stamford, Conn., 1981-82; dir. nat. accounts Hearst/ABC/NBC, N.Y.C., 1985-86; mng. dir. western divsn. Hearst/ABC/NBC, L.A., 1986-90; pres. Entertainment and Comm. Holdings Orgn., West Hollywood, Calif., 1990-94; v.p. U.S. West/Interactive Video Enterprises, San Ramon, Calif., 1994-95; chmn. Entertainment & Comms. Holdings Orgn.; CEO Advanced Multimedia Products, 1997—; chmn., CEO PlayMedia Sys. Inc., 1997—; chmn. Continuum Group, 1998—, PlayMedia Labs., 1998—, Subband Software, 2000—. Former dir. editorial bd. Emmy mag. Mem. L.A. World Affairs Coun., 1991—. Mem. Acad. TV Arts and Scis. (chmn. cable com. 1989-91), Hollywood Radio and TV Soc., L.A. Advt. Club, U.S.-Russia Trade and Econ. Coun. Office: Continuum Group PO Box 16298 Beverly Hills CA 90209-2298

LITMAN, ROSLYN MARGOLIS, lawyer, educator; b. N.Y.C., Sept. 30, 1928; d. Harry and Dorothy (Perlow) Margolis; m. S. David Litman, Nov. 22, 1950; children: Jessica, Hannah, Harry. BA, U. Pitts., 1949, JD, 1952. Bar: Pa. 1952. Practiced in Pitts., 1952—; ptnr. firm Litman and Litman, 1952—; adj. prof. U. Pitts. Law Sch., 1958—; permanent del. Conf. U.S. Circuit Ct. Appeals for 3d Circuit; past chair dist. adv. group U.S. Dist. Ct. (we. dist.) Pa., 1991-94, mem. steering com. for dist. adv. group, 1991—; chmn. Pitts. Pub. Parking Authority, 1970-74; mem. curriculum com. Pa. Bar Inst., 1986—, bd. dirs., 1972-82. Bd. dirs. United Jewish Fedn., 1999—, cmty. rels. com., co-chair ch./state com.; bd. dirs. City Theatre, 1999—. Recipient Roscoe Pound Found. award for Excellence in Tchg. Trial Advocacy, 1996, Disting. Alumnus award U. Pitts. Sch. Law, 1996; named Fed. Lawyer of Yr., We. Pa. Chpt. FBA, 1999. Mem. ABA (del., litigation sect., anti-trust health care com.), ACLU (nat. bd. dirs., Marjorie H. Matson Civil Libertarian award Greater Pitts. chpt. 1999), Pa. Bar Assn. (bd. govs. 1976-79), Allegheny County Bar Assn. (bd. govs. 1972-74, pres. 1975), Allegheny County Acad. Trial Lawyers (charter), Order of Coif. Home: 5023 Frew St Pittsburgh PA 15213-3829 Office: 3600 One Oxford Centre Pittsburgh PA 15219

LITOVCHENKO, VOLODYMYR GRYGOROVYCH, physicist; b. Kiev, Ukraine, Dec. 24, 1931; s. Grygorii Gavrylovich and Alexandra Karpovna (Pamiatka) L.; m. Natalia Mitrofanovna Tkach; children: Lesia, Ekaterina. Diploma with honors, U. Kiev, 1955; PhD Inst. Semiconductors, Ukranian Acad. Scis., Kiev, 1961, DSc, 1971. Prof. Kiev U., 1974; dep. phys. sec. Ukranian Acad. Scis., Kiev, 1990-98, chmn. dist. commn. on semiconductors, 1990—. Author: Optical Parameters of Semiconductors, 1987, Surface EL-C Transport of Semiconductors, 1991; mem. editl. bd. Sci. Jours. Physics, 1987—; contbr. articles to sci. publs. Soros prof., 1997. Fellow SPIE, Electrochem. Soc.; mem. Internat. Soc. Optical Engring., Union Radio Sci. Internat. E-mail: lvg@div9.semicond.kiev.ua. Home: Stritenska 17 App 24, 03028 Kiev Kiev, Ukraine Office: Inst Semiconductor Physics, Prospect Nauki, 03025 Kiev Kiev, Ukraine

LITSCHMANN, JIRI, electronics educator; b. Brno, Czech Republic, Dec. 31, 1932; s. Frantisek and Emilie (kristkova) L.; m. Libuse Jachova, Oct. 17, 1957; children: Tomas, Martina, Ales. Engr., Czech Tech. U., Prague, 1956. Asst. prof. Czech Tech. U., 1956-57; doctor Acad. Scis., Prague, 1958; chief of rsch. group Steel Works, Ostrava, Czech Republic, 1959-65; assoc. prof. Mining U., Ostrava, 1964, head of Inst. Automation, 1965-72, prof., 1990; with Inst. Electronics, Ostrava, 1988—; vice-dean Inst. Electronics, 1991. Author: (conf. proceedings/texts) Numerical Control of Servomechanisms, 1970, Hardware and Programming of a NC-System, 1972, others, (textbooks) Logical Circuits I, 1980, Logical Circuits II, 1987, Mikrocomputers, 1978, Multicomputer Systems, 1984. Avocations: theatre, touring, skiing. Office: Technical Univ Ostrava, ulice 17 listopadu, CZ70833 Ostrava Czech Republic

LITSTER, ANNETTE LORNA, veterinarian; b. Brisbane, Queensland, Australia, Dec. 20, 1959; d. Arthur Robert and Lorna Merle (Toomey) Kruger; m. James Donald Litster, Jan. 3, 1980; children: Samuel James, Rachel Tilly, Angus James. B in Vet. Sci., U. Queensland, 1982. Registered vet. surgeon. Sr. clinician Creek Road Cat Clinic, Mt. Gravatt, Queensland, 1989-2000; clinician Stone Lane Vet. Hosp., Shepreth, Eng., 1992; invited vis. veterinarian Dept. Cardiology, Phila., 1998; clin. tutor in small animal medicine U. Queensland, Brisbane, 1998—; invited lectr. and examiner U. Queensland, Brisbane, 1999; examiner Australian Coll. Vet. Scientists Membership Exams, Sydney, 1999. Contbr. articles to profl. jours. Mem. Australian Coll. Vet. Scientists. Anglican. Avocations: reading, travel.

LITT, MORTON HERBERT, macromolecular science educator, researcher; b. N.Y.C., Apr. 10, 1926; s. Samuel Bernard and Minnie (Hertz) L.; m. Lola Natalie Abrahamson, July 7, 1957; children: Jonathan S., Jennifer A. B.S., CCNY, 1947; M.S., Bklyn. Poly. Inst., 1953, Ph.D., 1956. Turner and Newall fellow U. Manchester, Eng., 1956-57; sr. research fellow N.Y. State Coll. Forestry, Syracuse, N.Y., 1958-59; sr. scientist Allied Chem. Corp., Morristown, N.J., 1960-64, assoc. dir. research, 1965-67; assoc. prof. Case Western Res. U., Cleve., 1967-76, prof. macromolecular sci., 1976—; cons. in industry and govt. Patentee in field. Fellow Am. Inst. Physics; mem. AAAS, MRS, Am. Chem. Soc., Chem. Soc. London, J. Polymer Sci. Polymer Chem. (adv. bd.), Electrochemical Soc. Home: 2575 Charney Rd Cleveland OH 44118-4402 Office: Case Western Res U Kent H Smith Bldg Cleveland OH 44106-7202

LITTBRAND, BO, oncologist; b. Stockholm, Sweden, June 6, 1936; s. Anders and Margaret (Holslein) L.; m. Inger Brunér, Mar. 8, 1959; children: Bernt, Kristna, Hakan, Gunnar, Yvonne, Karin; m. Juliana Denehamp, June 19, 1989. MD, Karolinska Inst., Stockholm, Sweden, 1964; PhD, Karolinska Inst., 1971. Cons. Karolinska Inst., 1974-76; prof., chmn. dept. oncology Umeå U., Sweden, 1976—; dean Umeå U., 1987-93; Head clin. oncology Umeå Hosp., 1976-99; chmn. Cancer Rsch. Found., Umeå, 1989-99, chmn. Trust Hosp., Umeå, 1992—; bd. dirs., Cafonden, 1988. Contbr. articles to profl. jours. Avocations: literature, stamp collecting, horse betting, photo. Office: Dept Oncology, Umeå U, S 90185 Umeå Sweden

LITTLE, CHARLES GORDON, radiophysicist; b. Liuyang, Hunan, China, Nov. 4, 1924; s. Charles Deane and Caroline Joan (Crawford) L.; m. Mary Zughaib, Aug. 21, 1954; children: Deane, Joan, Katherine, Margaret, Patricia. BSc with honors in Physics, U. Manchester, Eng., 1948; PhD in Radio Astronomy, U. Manchester, 1952. Jr. engr. Cosmos Mfg. Co. Ltd., Enfield, Middlesex, Eng., 1944-46; jr. physicist Ferranti Ltd., Manchester, Lancashire, Eng., 1946-47; asst. lectr. U. Manchester, 1952-53; prof. dept. geophysics U. Alaska, 1954-58, dep. dir. Geophys. Inst., 1954-58; cons. Ionosphere Radio Propagation Lab. U.S. Dept. Commerce Nat. Bur. Standards, Boulder, Colo., 1958-60, chief Upper Atmosphere and Space Physics divsn., 1960-62, dir. Central Radio Propagation Lab., 1962-65; dir. Inst. Telecommunication Sci. and Aeronomy, Environ. Sci. Services Adminstrn., Boulder, Colo., 1965-67; dir. Wave Propagation Lab. NOAA (formerly Environ. Sci. Services Adminstr.), Boulder, Colo., 1967-86; sr. UCAR fellow Naval Environ. Prediction Research Facility, Monterey, Calif., 1987-89; George J. Haltiner rsch. prof. Naval Postgrad. Sch., Monterey, 1989-90. Author numerous sci. articles. Recipient U.S. Dept. Commerce Gold medal, 1964, mgmt. and sci. research awards NOAA, 1969, 77, Presdl. Meritorious Exec. award, 1980. Fellow IEEE, Am. Meteorol. Soc. (Cleveland Abbe award 1984); mem. NAE, AIAA (R.M. Losey Atmos. Sci. award 1992). Address: 4907 Country Club Way Boulder CO 80301-3656

LITTLE, DECLAN JOSEPH, environmental researcher; b. Limerick, Ireland, Mar. 18, 1964; s. Edward J. and Una (O'Briain) L. B in Agrl. Sci., Univ. Coll. Dublin, 1988, PhD, 1994. Postdoctoral rschr. Univ. Coll. Dublin, 1993-98; project dir. Woodlands of Ireland, 1998-2000; project ecologist People's Millennium Forests Project Coillte Teoranta, the Irish Forestry Bd., Wicklow, 2000—. Coord. Millennium Native Woodland Initiative. Mem. Irish Genetic Resources Conservation Trust, Environ. Scis. Assn. Ireland, Conservation Vols. Ireland, Soil Sci. Soc. Ireland. Office: Coillte Rsch Divsn, Dublin Rd, Newtownmountkennedy Wicklow, Ireland

LITTLE, GAYLE ANNE, neonatal nurse practitioner; b. Coronado, Calif., Sept. 14, 1951; d. Edward William and Lorraine Catherine (Puetz) Campbell; m. James Lovell Little Jr., Aug. 7, 1971 (div. June 1984); children: Wendy Catherine, Christy Marie. Diploma, St. Luke's Hosp. Sch. Nursing, San Francisco, 1971; student, San Francisco City Coll.; ASN, Grossmont Coll., 1972; BSN, San Diego State U., 1985; MS in Neonatal Nurse Practitioner, U. Md., 1995. RN, Calif., Md., Oreg.; cert. BCLS instr., newborn resuscitation instr., newborn resuscitation regional trainer, pediatric advanced life support instr. Phys. therapy asst. St. Luke's Hosp., 1970-71; lic. vocat. nurse Coronado Hosp., 1971; grad. nurse med.-surg. units Sharp Meml. Hosp., San Diego, 1972, staff nurse newborn nursery, relief charge nurse GYN surgery, 1972-73, staff nurse per diem women's maternity-surg. unit, 1973-77, staff nurse cardio-vascular observation unit, 1977-78, clin. nurse I spl. care nursery, 1978-83, clin. nurse IV level II nursery, 1986, clin. nurse III level II and level III NICU, 1983-93; dapa officer, edn. officer Naval Hosp. San Diego, 1988, staff nurse NICU, 1989, staff nurse pediatric unit, 1989-90, NICU/pediatric clin. cons., 1990-91; clinic charge nurse Navy Clinic Persian Gulf War, Bahrain, 1991; evening nurse supr. Naval Hosp. Camp Pendleton, Calif., 1992, asst. charge/charge nurse nursery, 1992-93, customer rels. program mgr., 1993-94; staff nurse per diem med., surg., spl. care and NICU Children's Hosp. San Diego, 1992-94; full ptnr. NICU U. Md. Med. System, Balt., 1994-95; CNIII, CRS Sharp Mary Birch Women's Ctr., 1995-97; neonatal nurse practitioner U.S. Naval Medicine Ctr., 1996-99; LCDR, NC, neonatal nurse practitioner Emanuel Children's Hosp., 1997—; instr. phys. edn. U. San Diego, 1984; mem. edn. com. Sharp Meml. Hosp., 1986, mem. policy and procedure com., 1986, mem. std. care plan com., 1987; mem. stds. com. Naval Hosp. San Diego, 1989, mem. nurse corps ball com., 1990; change of command coord. USN, Bahrain, 1991; mem. stds. com. Naval Hosp. Camp Pendleton, 1993, mem. health care planning and access QMB com., 1994. Lt. USN, 1988-95, Persian Gulf War, 1991; with Naval Nurse Corps Res., 1994—, Lt. comdr. USN, 1995—. Decorated Navy Commendation medal. Mem. AWHONN (cert. neonatology), VFW, Nat. Assn. Neonatal Nurses, Assn. Mil. Surgeons U.S., Fleet Res. Assn. Democrat. Roman Catholic. Avocations: gardening, reading, walking, movies. Home: 530 C Ave Coronado CA 92118-1825

LITTLE, JOHN WILLIAM, plastic surgeon, educator; b. Indpls., Mar. 12, 1944; s. John William Jr. and Naida (Jones) L.; m. Patricia Padgett Lea, May 26, 1969 (div. 1974); m. Teri Ann Tyson, Feb. 28, 1981 (div. 1982). AB, Dartmouth Coll., 1966, B in Med. Scis., 1967; MD, Harvard U., 1969. Diplomate Am. Bd. Med. Examiners, Am. Bd. Surgery, Am. Bd. Plastic Surgery. Intern Case Western Res. U., Cleve., 1969-70, resident in surgery, 1970-74, resident in plastic surgery, 1973-75; fellow in plastic surgery U. Miami, 1975-77; asst. prof. Georgetown U., Washington, 1977-82, assoc. prof., 1982-87, prof., 1987-92, clin. prof., 1992—, dir. div. plastic surgery, residency tng. program, plastic surgeon-in-chief univ. hosp., 1979-92; dir. Nat. Capital Tng. Program in Plastic Surgery affiliated hosps. Georgetown U. and Howard U., 1988-92; dir. Georgetown Plastic Surgery Fellowship in Breast and Aesthetic Surgery, 1990-92; pvt. practice Washington, 1992—; prof. postgrad. edn. in plastic surgery Internat. Soc. Aesthetic Plastic Surgery, 1999—; chief plastic surgery Medlantic Ctr. for Ambulatory Surgery, Inc., 1993—, mem. med. adv. bd., 1993—; cons. Nat. Cancer Inst., NIH, Bethesda, Md., 1977-92, Washington VA Med. Ctr., 1981-92, Reach to Recovery program Nat. Capital chpt. Am. Cancer Soc., 1981—, RENU program in breast reconstrn., 1982; specialist site visitor plastic surgery residency rev. com. Accreditation Coun. for Grad. Med. Edn., 1982—; vis. lect. various insts.; bd. govs. Nat. Endowment for Plastic Surgery, 1995—. Adv. editor Plastic and Reconstructive Surgery, 1997—, manuscript reviewer Plastic and Reconstructive Surgery, Annals of Plastic Surgery; assoc. editor Surgery of the Breast: Principles and Art, 1998; contbr. numerous articles to med. jours., numerous chpts. to books. Bd. dirs. Triann reconstructive surgery teams to Caribbean and S.Am., Georgetown Tissue Bank, 1986-88, Operation Luz del Sol; founder, pres., med. dir. Reconstructive Surgeons Vol. Program; bd. dirs. Washington Summer Opera Theater; trustee Washington Opera, 1993—, artistic com., 1994—; Domingo Circle, 1995—. Mem. AMA, ACS (coord. plastic surgery audiovisual program Ann. Clin. Congress 1988-90, 92-93, bd. govs., Met. Washington chpt. councillor 1985-94, chmn. sci. program com. 1990-91, v.p. 1991-92, pres. 1992-93, bd. govs. 1998—), Nat. Capital Soc. Plastic Surgeons (sec. treas. 1982-83, pres. 1984-85), Am. Soc. Plastic and Reconstructive Surgeons (audiovisual program dir. ann. meeting 1984-86, strategic planning com. 1987-96, fin. com. 1989-94, conv. policy com. 1993-96, ops. com. 1993-96, chmn. 1994-95, spokesperson network steering com. 1994-96, bd. dirs. 1994-96, exec. com. 1995-96, spokesperson 1998—, rep. to IPRAS 1999—), Am. Assn. Plastic Surgeons (co-chmn. various coms.), Plastic Surgery Ednl. Found. (bd. dirs. 1985-97, devel. com. 1991—, chmn. 1997-2000, chmn. various coms., rep. to Coun. Plastic Surg. Orgns. 1989-95, parliamentarian 1992-93, v.p. 1993-94, pres. adv. coun. 1993-96, commr. various commns., pres.-elect, 1995, pres. 1995-96, Maliniac fellow 1998—), Med. Soc. D.C. (chmn. plastic surgery sect. 1985), D.R. Millard Surg. Soc. and Ednl. Found. (pres. 1985-87), Am. Cleft Palate Assn., Am. Soc. Maxillofacial Surgeons, Washington Acad. Surgeons (coun. 1988-90), Am. Soc. Aesthetic Plastic Surgery, NE Soc. Plastic Surgeons (chmn. various coms., v.p. 1991-92, pres. 1992-93, historian 1994-99), Internat. Soc. Aesthetic Plastic Surgery (chmn. bylaws com. 1990-93, 95-97, parliamentarian 1990-93, mem. membership com. 1993-97, chmn. 1993-95, sec. gen. 1997-2000, rep. to IPRAS 1997-2000, prof. postgrad. edn. in aesthetic plastic surgery, others), Am. Alpine Workshop in Plastic Surgery (founder, pres. 1991-92, historian 1995—), Internat. Confedn. Plastic Reconstructive and Aesthetic Surgery (mem. exec. com. 1997-2000, coun. dels. 1999—), Nat. Endowment Plastic Surgeons (bd. govs. 1995—), Internat. Plastic, Reconstructive and Aesthetic Surgery Found. (bd. dirs. 1999—, ednl. program com. chmn. 1999—, vice chmn. devel. com. 1999—, publs. and videotape com.). Republican. Presbyterian. Home: 3030 K St NW Ph 212 Washington DC 20007-5107 Office: 1145 19th St NW Ste 802 Washington DC 20036-3700

LITTLE, MARK MCKENNA, financial management executive; b. Hoisington, Kans., Mar. 30, 1957; s. Freed Sebastian Little and Jana Vaye (Jones) Hansen; m. Peggy Louise Kelly, June 24, 1988; 1 child, McKenna Louise. B of Gen. Studies, Tex. Christian U., 1980. Account exec. Liberty Mut. Ins. Co., San Antonio, 1981-83; cons. M. Little Fin. Enterprises, San Antonio, 1983-89; chmn., chief exec. officer Wall St. Svcs., Inc., San Antonio, 1989—; pres., CEO Waterhouse Fin. Mgmt. Group, Inc., 1995—; mem. bd. advs. Clear Lake Nt. Bank, 1996-97. Bd. dirs. Mental Health Assn. in Greater San Antonio, United Way, 1988-92, pres., chmn., 1990, KLRN TV Cmty. Adv. Bd., San Antonio, 1990-94, pres., 1992-93; bd. dirs. N.E. Ind. Sch. Dist., chmn. bond com., 1998; bd. dirs. Kids Involvement Network, San Antonio, 1990—, chmn., 1990-93; bd. dirs. N.E. Ind. Sch. Dist.-Wide adv. bd., 1991-98, pres., 1991-92; del., bd. dirs. Jaycees Internat., Taipei, Taiwan, 1983; elected del. Tex. State Rep. Conv., 1992, White House Conf. Small Bus., 1995; trustee N.E. Ednl. Found.; vice chair allocations panel United Way, San Antonio, 1994; apptd. del. U.S. SEC-Govt. Forum on Small Bus. Capital Formation, 1995-2000; del., program co-chair Tex. Gov.'s Conf. on Small Bus., 1996; apptd. del. Congl. Small Bus. Summit, Washington, 1998; mem. World Affairs Coun., 1992-93. Recipient Edith Caldwell award Tex. Cmty. Edn. Assn., 1995, Jayne Nelson award, 1998, Citizen of Yr.-Cmty. Involvement award Nat. Cmty. Edn. Assn., 1999. Mem. San Antonio Area Coun. Pres., North San Antonio C. of C. (bd. dirs. 1991—, vice chmn. bd. 1991-92, 95, chmn. bd. 1997), San Antonio Jaycees (bd. dirs. 1982-83), North San Antonio Toastmasters (pres. 1990-91), Delta Tau Delta (Larry Abrahms award). Office: Wall St Svcs Inc 2313 Lockhill Selma Ste 216 San Antonio TX 78230

LITTLE, PAUL STEPHEN, general practice physician, researcher; b. Cheltenham, Eng., May 20, 1958; s. Peter Dennistoun and Betsy Ann (Carter) L.; m. Alison Mary Bridges, July 2, 1988; children: Joseph, Ella-Beth. BA, Oxford (Eng.) U., 1981; MBBS, London U., 1984, MD, 1992. Mem. Royal Coll. Physicians, London, 1989, Mem. Royal Coll. Gen. Practitioners, 1992. Rsch. fellow, primary med. care Southampton (Eng.) U., 1993, Wellcome tchg. fellow, 1993-97, clin. scientist Med. Rsch. Coun., 1998—. Anglican. Avocations: music, walking, films. Office: U Southampton Primary Med C, Aldermoor Health Ctr, Southampton SO16 5ST, England

LITTLE, R. DONALD, architect, administrator; b. Gastonia, N.C., Mar. 18, 1937; s. Coy Marshall and Stella May (Pruett) L.; m. Jacqueline Beatrice Mandel, June 10, 1967 (dec. Mar. 1995); Linda Lee Stoner; Sept. 7, 1999; children by previous marriage: Tina June Whitman, Diana Dawn Little, Laura Marie Van Meel; stepchildren: Keith, Don. BA, U. Md., 1972, BS in Architecture, 1981, MArch, 1983. Blood bank and med. technologist Dr. Oscar B. Hunter Meml. Lab., Washington, 1961-66; biol. lab. technologist Naval Med. Rsch. Inst., Bethesda, Md., 1966-68; blood bank and med. technologist, supr. Ctrl. Lab. Doctor's Hosp., Washington, 1959-79; jr. architect VVKR Inc., University Park, Md., supr. architect; br. head design divsn. Naval Surface Weapons Ctr., Silver Spring, Md., 1981-87; supr. architect, chief facility engring. br. Agrl. Rsch. Svc., USDA, 1987-96; area adminstrv. officer BARC Rsch. Svc., USDA, Beltsville, Md., 1996—. With USN, 1956-61. Mem. Am. Assn. Blood Banks, Am. Soc. Med. Technologists. E-mail: spirit77@bellatlantic.net. Home: 13417 Rich Lynn Ct Highland MD 20777-9790 Office: BARC Rsch Svc/USDA Bldg 003 Rm 203 BARC-W 10300 Baltimore Ave Beltsville MD 20705-2325

LITTLE, RICHARD ALLEN, mathematics and computer science educator; b. Cochocton, Ohio, Jan. 12, 1939; s. Charles M. and Elsie Leanna (Smith) L.; children from previous marriage: Eric, J. Alice, Stephanie; m. Laura Ann Novosel, June 15, 1991. BS in Math. cum laude, Wittenberg U., 1960; MA in Edn., Johns Hopkins U., 1961; EdM in Math., Harvard U., 1965; PhD in Math. Edn., Kent State U., 1971. Tchr. Culver Acad., Ind., 1961-65; instr., curriculum cons. Harvard U., Cambridge, Mass. and Aiyetoro, Nigeria, 1965-67; from instr. to assoc. prof. Kent State U., Canton, Ohio, 1967-75; from assoc. prof. to prof. Baldwin-Wallace Coll., Berea, Ohio, 1975—, dept. chair, 1978-83; mathematician/educator Project Discovery Ohio Bd. Regents, 1992-96; vis. prof., math. Ohio State U., Columbus, 1987-88, 92-95; lectr. various colls. and univs.; pres. Cleve. Collaborative on Math. Edn., 1986-87, bd. dirs. 1985—. Contbr. articles to profl. jours. Bd. dirs. Canton Symphony Orch., 1973-75; Sunday sch. tchr. Bethany English Luth. Ch., Cleve., 1991—; bd. deacons Holy Cross Luth. Ch., Canton, 1968-74, chmn., 1971-74. Recipient Strosacker Excellence in Tchg. award and Student Senate Faculty Excellence award Baldwin-Wallace Coll., 1999. Mem. Nat. Coun. Tchrs. Math. (profl. devel. and status adv. com. 1987-90, program com. ann. meeting 1997), Ohio Coun. Tchrs. Math. (pres. 1974-76, v.p. 1970-73, sec. 1982-84, dir. state math. contest 1983-92, Christofferson-Fawcett award 1990), Ohio Math. Educators Leadership Coun. (pres. 1990-91, bd. dirs. 1988-92), Greater Canton Coun. Tchrs. Math. (pres. 1969-70), Math. Assn. Am. (pres. Ohio sect. 1983-84, editor 1977-83). Avocations: hiking, tennis, handball. E-mail: rlittle@bw.edu. Office: Baldwin-Wallace Coll Dept Math & Computer Sci 275 Eastland Rd Berea OH 44017-2005

LITTLEFIELD, ROY EVERETT, III, association executive, legal educator; b. Nashua, N.H., Dec. 6, 1952; s. Roy Everett and Mary Ann (Prestipino) L.; m. Amy Root; children: Leah Marie, Roy Everett IV, Christy Louise. BA, Dickinson Coll., 1975; MA, Catholic U. Am., 1976, PhD, 1979. Aide U.S. Senator Thomas McIntyre, Democrat, N.H., 1975-78, Nordy Hoffman, U.S. Senate Sergeant-at-arms, N.H., 1979; dir. govt. rels. Nat. Tire Dealers and Retreaders Assn., Washington, N.H., 1979-84; exec. dir. Svc. Sta. and Automotive Repair Assn., Washington, N.H., 1984—; exec. v.p. Svc. Sta. Dealers of Am., 1994—; cons. Internat. Tire and Rubber Assn., 1984; mem. faculty Cath. U. Am., Washington, 1979—. Author: William Randolph Hearst: His Role in American Progressivism, 1980, The Economic Recovery Act, 1982, The Surface: Transportation Assistance Act, 1984; editor Nozzle mag.; contbr. numerous articles to legal jours. Mem. Nat. Dem. Club, 1978—. Mem. Am. Soc. Legal History, Md. Hwy. User's Fedn. (pres.), Nat. Hwy. User's Fedn. (sec.), Nat. Capitol Area Transp. Fedn. (v.p.), N.H. Hist. Soc., Kansas City C. of C., Capitol Hill Club, Phi Alpha Theta. Roman Catholic. Home: 1707 Pepper Tree Ct Bowie MD 20721-3021 Office: 9420 Annapolis Rd Ste 307 Lanham Seabrook MD 20706-3061

LITTLEFORD, WILLIAM DONALDSON, retired publishing executive; b. Ft. Thomas, Ky., Aug. 4, 1914; s. Roger Seiter and Marjorie (Donaldson) L.; m. Mariana Weber, May 8, 1936 (dec. Feb. 1958); children: Anne, Michael; m. Marian Hastings Towne, Aug. 20, 1958; children: Joseph M. Towne, Marian Towne. Student, U. Cin.; grad. advanced mgmt. program, Harvard U., 1951. With Billboard Pub., Inc., Cin., 1934-85; gen. mgr. Billboard Pub., Inc., 1943-58, pres., 1958-76, chmn. bd., 1976-85, chmn. emeritus, 1985-99; dir. Littleford Bros., Inc., Advt. Coun.; dir. Am. Bus. Press, 1954-65, chmn. bd., 1960-61; dir. Audit Bur. Circulations, 1959-67, Mag. Pubs. Assn., 1967-85, 2d Class Mail Publs., 1962-70, Pensord Press Ltd., Wales, U.K., 1969-86, United Color Press, Dayton, Ohio, 1970-87, Viegues Conservation and Hist. Trust, 1987-98. McAllister fellow Northwestern U., Chgo., 1987; named to the Pub. Hall of Fame, 1989; established William D. Littleford Found. for Corp. Cmty. Svc., 1998. Mem. Beta Theta Pi, Harvard Club (N.Y.C.). Episcopalian. Office: 43 Hedge Row Rd Princeton NJ 08540-5054

LITVAK KING, JAIME, archaeologist; b. Mexico City, Dec. 10, 1933; s. Abraham and Eugenia (King) L.; m. Elena Kaninski, 1954 (div. 1968); m. Carmen Aguilera, 1972 (div.); 1 child, Noemi. Licenciatura, Escuela Nacional Antropologia, Mex., 1962; MA, U. Mex., 1963, PhD, 1971. Rschr. Inst. Nacional de Anthropologia, Mex., 1962-66, head Computer Ctr. Mus., 1966-68; rschr. U. Mex., 1968-73, head anthrop. sect., 1973, dir. inst. anthrop. rsch., 1973-85, mem. exec. bd., 1983—; mem. coun., dir. gen. academic projects, 1985-86, coord. Libr. Inst. Anthrop. Rsch., 1993—; prof. emeritus Nat. Sys. Rschrs., 1998—; chmn. dept. anthropology U. Ams., Puebla, 1986-88; Mellon prof. humanities Tulane U., New Orleans, 1988; guest prof. U. Tex., El Paso, 1994-95; dir. bd. Inst. Nacional Indigenista, Mexico, 1975—; chmn. anthropology U. Ams., 1986-89. Author: Cihuatlán y Tepecoacuilco, 1971, Arqueologia y Derecho en Mexico, 1978, Secuencia Cultural del Valle de Mexico, 1982, Ancient Mexico, Todas las Piedras tienen, Una Introduccion A La Arqueologia, El Valle de Xochicalco, 1970; adv. editor Editl. Alhambra, 1982-90. Recipient mención honorifica Escuela Nacional de Antropologia, 1963, U. Mexico, 1970, Fray Bernardino de Sahag n Mexican Nat. Ward for Anthropology, 1970. Fellow Mexican Anthrop. Soc. (sec. 1971-76, 82-83), Soc. Archaeol. Sci., Am. Archaeol. Assn., Am. Archaeology Soc.; mem. Sci. Rsch. Acad. Mex. (nat. rschr. award 1984). Office: Inst Investig Antropoligicas, Ciudad Universitaria, 04510 Mexico City Mexico

LITVIN, YURIY ANDREYEVICH, geochemist, researcher; b. Poltava, Ukraine, Feb. 28, 1937; s. Andrey Leontyevich and Anna Moiseyevna (Morokhovets) L.; m. Svetlana Vasilyevna Yantsen, Jan. 9, 1970; children: Maxim, Vladimir, Vadim. MSc, Moscow State U., 1960; PhD, Moscow Acad. Science, 1968, DSc, 1989. Rsch. scientist National Inst. Mineral Synthesis, Moscow, 1960-70; leading rsch. scientist Russian Acad. Scis., Moscow, 1970—; vis. scientist SUNY, Stony Brook, 1991, vis. prof., 1993; vis. prof. U. Coll. London, 1997-99; prof. High Pressure Edn. & Rsch. Ctr., Moscow, 1997-2000; vis. prof. U. Paris, 1999; dir. High Pressure Edn. & Rsch. Ctr., Moscow, 1997—. Author: (book) Physical Chemistry of the Deep Earth's Melts, 1991; Editor and author: (book) Experiments at High Gas and Solid Medium Pressures, 1978, Problems of High Pressure Solid Medium and Hydrothermal Experiments, 1982, Moderm Methods of Experimental Mineralogy, 1985; contbr. articles to profl. jours. Mem. Am. Geophysical Union, Russian Geochem. Union & Mineralogical Soc. Avocation: downhill skiing. Office: Inst Experimental Min, Russian Acad Scis, 142432 Chernogolovka Russia

LITVINOV, VICTOR MICHAILOVICH, chemistry researcher; b. Moscow, July 16, 1950; arrived at The Netherlands, 1992, naturalized, 1997; s. Michail Sergeevich and Klavdia Vasilievna (Boikova) L.; m. Tatiana Vasilievna Fursova, Nov. 2, 1973; 1 child, Svetlana Victorovna. M, Moscow Acad. Fine Chem. Tech., 1973; PhD, Inst. Organoelement Compounds, Moscow, 1978. Researcher scientific coun. high strength and heat resistant polymer material at the Presidium Acad. Scis. USSR, Moscow, 1978-86, researcher, sr. researcher Inst. Synthetic Polymer Materials, 1986-92; researcher DSM Rsch. B.V., Geleen, The Netherlands, 1992—; Lectr. in field. Contbr. about 50 articles to profl. jours. Fellow Max-Planck Inst. Polymer Rsch., 1988, Alexander von Humboldt fellow, 1990-91, German Sci.

Found. fellow, 1992. Avocations: reading, music, gardening. Office: DSM Rsch BV Dept PAC-MC, PO Box 18, 6160 MD Geleen The Netherlands

LITZMAN, OTTO, physics educator; b. Vyskov, Czech Republic, Apr. 19, 1926; s. Ludvik and Anna (Holubova) L.; m. Libuse Frejkova, Dec. 21, 1955 (div. 1992); children: Jiri, Irena. RNDr, Masaryk U., Brno, Czech Republic, 1952; PhD, Charles U., Prague, 1958. Asst. Faculty of Sci. Masaryk U., 1951-55, 58-61, docent, 1961-66, extraordinary prof., prof., 1966—, head dept. theoretical physics, 1959-62, 64-72, head dept. solid state physics, 1972-81, vice-dean Faculty of Sci., 1961-64; Author: (with M. Sekanina) Groups in Physics, 1982; contbr. more than 60 articles to sci. jours. Mem. Union of Czech Mathematicians and Physicists. Avocations: history, classical music. Office: Faculty of Sci Dept Theor Physics, Kotlarska 2, 611 37 Brno Czech Republic

LIU, ALCOTT K.P., accountant, business consultant; b. Linyuen, Guangdong, China, Mar. 30, 1944; s. Hau Shui and Yat Chun (Chow) L.; m. Margaret So, Apr. 12, 1978; 1 child, Derrick. Traffic officer Cathay Pacific Airways, Hong Kong, 1963-65; audit trainee Sanford Yung & Co., Hong Kong, 1965-67, Coopers & Lybrand, Melbourne, 1967-73; audit sr. Fell & Starkey, Melbourne, 1973-75; audit supr. Coopers & Lybrand, Hong Kong, 1975-76; fin. contr. Rediffusion TV, Hong Kong, 1976-78; propr. Alcott K.P. Liu & Co., Hong Kong, 1978-87, ptnr., 1987—. Co-author: Choosing the Right Business Form and Structure, 1991. Hon. treas. Bishop Hall Prevocational Sch. Coun., 1985-99. Fellow Inst. Chartered Accts. in Australia, Inst. Chartered Secs. and Adminstrs. (London), Inst. Internal Auditors, Inc., Inst. Dirs. (London), Lions, Hong Kong Jockey Club, Fgn. Corrs. Club. Avocations: golf, tennis, swimming, table tennis. Office: Alcott KP Liu & Co, 168 Gloucester Rd, Hong Kong China

LIU, BAO CHEN, engineering educator; b. Tianjin, China, Dec. 25, 1934; m. Shou Cheng Yuan, Nov. 7, 1967; 1 child, Ji Hong Yuan. BS, Tsinghua U., Beijing, 1959, MS, 1961, PhD, 1964. Asst. prof. Tsinghua U., 1975-89, prof., 1990—; vis. prof. Nat. U. Singapore, 1995-97, City U. Hong Kong, 1995-98, Nat. Chung Kung U., Tainen, Taiwan, 1998-99. Author: Modern Photomechanics, 1990 (Sci. Press award 1990), Measuring Technique of Experimental Fracture and Damage Mechanics (Mech. Engrng. Press award 1994); contbr. about 150 tech. papers to profl. jours. Grantee, China, 1975—. Mem. Chinese Soc. Theoretical and Applied Mechs., Chinese Soc. Aeronautics and Astronautics, N.Y. Acad. Scis. Avocations: reading, sports and pring. E-mail: dembcliu@pku.edu.cn. Home: Apt 105-203 Peking U, Cheng Ze Yuan, Beijing 100871, China Office: Tsinghua U, Dept Mech Engrng, Beijing 100084, China

LIU, BEN-CHIEH, economist; b. Chungking, China, Nov. 17, 1938; came to U.S., 1965, naturalized, 1973; s. Pei-juang and Chung-su L.; m. Jill Jyh-huey, Oct. 2, 1965; children—Tina Won-ting, Roger Won-jung, Milton Won-ming. B.A., Nat. Taiwan U., 1961; M.A., Meml. U. Nfld., 1965, Washington U., St. Louis, 1968; Ph.D., Washington U., St. Louis, 1971. Economist Chinese Air Force and Central Customs, Taiwan, 1961-63; resource economist Canadian Land Inventory and Forest Services, Nfld., 1963-65; research project dir. St. Louis Regional Indsl. Devel. Corp., 1968-72; prin. econs. Midwest Research Inst., Kansas City, Mo., 1972-80; mgr. Energy and Environ. Systems Div., Argonne (Ill.) Nat. Lab., 1980-81; prof. econs., assoc. dir. rsch. Oklahoma City U., 1981-82; prof. mgmt., mktg. and info. systems Chgo. State U., 1982—; pres. Liu & Assocs., Inc., 1982—; vis. prof. econs. U. Mo., 1970-78, Nat. Taiwan U., 1991-92; Fulbright prof., dir. Internat. Enterprises Inst., Nat. Dong-Hwa U., Taiwan, 1997-98; dean Coll. Bus., Chung-Yuan Christian U., Taiwan, 2000—; cons. UN, NSF; mem. Gov. Thompson's Adv. Com. on Agrl. Export, 1985-87, Congressman Fawell's Adv. Com. on Sci. and Tech., 1985-98; commr. Nat. Commn. on Librs. and Info. Svcs., 1991-94. Author: Interindustrial Structure Analysis: An Input-Output Study for St. Louis Region, 1968, The Quality of Life in the United States, 1970, Rating, Index and Statistics, 1973, Quality of Life Indicators in U.S. Metropolitan Areas, 1975, Physical and Economic Damage Functions for Air Pollutants by Receptors, 1976, Earthquake Risk and Damage Functions, An Integrated Model, 1981, Income, Energy and Quality of Life: An Information Systems Approach to Decisions, 1988; mem. editorial bd.: Internat. Jour. Math. Social Sci, Am. Jour. Econs. and Sociology, Hong Kong Jour. Bus. Mgmt., Internat. Jour. of Bus.; Internat. Jour. Mgmt.; contbr. articles to profl. jours. Recipient rsch. study award Am. Indsl. Devel. Coun., 1969—, Fulbright Scholar awards, 1992, 96, Faculty Meritorious awards Chgo. State U., 1983, 86, 89, 90, Disting. Prof. Advancement Increase awards, 1990, 96, Outstanding Rsch. award Nat. Sci. Coun., 1997-98; U.S. Econ. Devel. Adminstrn. fellow, 1967-68; Korean Govt. scholar, 1963-65; Fulbright scholar Mgmt. Devel. Inst., Delhi U., 1992. Fellow Am. Statis. Assn. (com. mem.); mem. Am. Econ. Assn. (com. mem.), Econometric Soc., Royal Econ. Soc., Internat. Statis. Instn., Assn. for Social Econs. (com. mem.), Tax Inst. Am., Chinese Acad. and Profl. Assn. (pres. 1984-85), Chinese Econ. Assn. in N.Am. (pres. 1988-90), Chinese Am. Profs. Assn. (pres. 1996—). Home: 5360 Pennywood Dr Lisle IL 60532-2032 Office: Chgo State U Chicago IL 60628

LIU, BENLI, organic chemist; b. Shashi, Hubei, China, Sept. 1, 1962; s. Chenjin Liu and Zingxiu Cheng; m. Lihua Yang; 1 child, Cong. BSc, Ctrl. China Normal U., Wuhan, 1983, MSc, 1986; PhD, Leiden (The Netherlands) U., 1991. Lectr. Ctrl. China Normal U., 1986-88; postdoctoral rschr. Ariz. State U., 1991-92, Kyoto (Japan) U., 1992-93; rsch. assoc. Nard Inst., Ltd., Amagasaki, Japan, 1993—; YPG Japan coord. FIP, 1998. Contbr. articles to profl. jours.; patentee method for quinone synthesis. Fellow Japan Soc. for Promotion of Sci.; mem. AAAS, Internat. Pharm. Fedn., Kinki Chem. Soc. Japan. Avocations: fishing, driving. Office: Nard Inst Ltd, 2-6-1 Nishinagasu, Amagasaki Hyogo 660-0805, Japan

LIU, CHANGNIAN, medical educator; b. Tianjin, China, Jan. 15, 1950; came to the U.S., 1985; s. Wenbo Liu and Fengqin Lu. MD, Tianjin Med. U., 1978; PhD, U. Nebr., 1990. Oncologist dept. chemotherapy/immunotherapy Tianjin Cancer Inst., 1978-80; urologist Tianjin Med. U. Hosp., 1980-85; vis. scholar Northwestern U. Med. Ctr., Chgo., 1985-87; rsch. scientist ImmunoGen, Inc., Cambridge, Mass., 1992-96; asst. prof. U. Nebr. Med. Ctr., 1996—; presenter in field. Editor: Guide for Cancer Prevention and Therapy, 1995, Manual of Practical Oncologic Clinical, 1996; contbr. articles to profl. jours. Mem. AAAS, Am. Assn. for Cancer Rsch. E-mail: cliu@unmc.edu. Office: U Nebr Med Ctr 600 S 42nd St # 986395 Omaha NE 68198-1002

LIU, CHANGSHENG, science company executive; b. Daye, Hubei, China, June 26, 1967; s. Kehong Liu and Guizhen Ji; m. Jiangchao Qian, Dec. 23, 1994; 1 child, Yulai. Bachelor's degree, Hubei U., Wuhan, China, 1989; Master's degree, East China U. Sci. and Tech., Shanghai, 1992, Doctorate, 1996. Polit. instr. gen. party br. biochem. dept. East China U. Sci. and Tech., Shanghai, 1992-93, vice min. Inst. Tech. Chemistry and Physics, 1993-98; gen. dir. Shanghai Rebone Co. Ltd., 1998—. Inventor in field; contbr. articles to profl. jours. Vice sec. gen. Shanghai Club for Young Stars of Sci. and Tech., 1996—. Recipient Highest award of Shanghai Invention Competition, Shanghai Commn. Sci. and Tech., 1998, Gold medal World Chinese Invention Fair, Hong Kong Productivity Coun., 1998; named one of 10 News Persons of Transcen. Elite, Nat. Commn. Sci. and Tech., 1999. Mem. Chinese Particle Soc., Chinese Bioengrng. Soc., Chinese Biomaterial Soc., N.Y. Acad. Sci. Communist. Avocations: tennis, basketball. Office: Shanghai Rebone Co Ltd, Mei Long Rd 130 PO Box 112, Shanghai 200237, China

LIU, CHAO-HAN, electrical engineering educator, academic administrator; b. Liuchou, China, Jan. 3, 1939; came to U.S., 1961; s. Kuo-Yung and Wan-Fang (Chung) L.; m. Tsuei-Chu Mong, Aug. 3, 1963; children: Alice, Robert. BSEE, Nat. Taiwan U., 1960; PhD, Brown U., 1965. Rsch. assoc. U. Ill., Urbana, 1965-66, asst. prof. elec. engring., 1966-70, assoc. prof., 1970-74, prof., 1974-93; pres. Nat. Ctrl. U., Chung Li, Republic of China, 1990—; sci. sec. sci. com. on solar terrestrial physics Internat. Coun. Sci. Unions, 1981-94, pres. 1994—; co-chmn. World Ionosphere-Thermosphere Studies, 1987-90; NSC chair prof. Nat. Taiwan U., 1981, Ctrl. U., Taiwan, 1989-90, NSC Disting. lectr., 1988. Author: (with others) Theory of Ionospheric Waves, 1972; assoc. editor: IEEE Trans. on Antenna and Propagation, 1980-87; contbr. numerous articles to profl. jours. Fellow IEEE (Outstanding Achievement award 1968); mem. Am. Phys. Soc., Am. Geophys. Union, Acad. Sinica (academician 1998), Internat. Sci. Radio Union. Home: 2406 Burlison Dr Urbana IL 61801-6627 Office: Nat Ctrl U, Chung-Li Taiwan*

LIU, CHAO-MIN, biochemist, biotechnology researcher; b. Min-hsiung, Taiwan, Aug. 9, 1936; came to U.S., 1963; s. Shin-ruh and She-O (Yu) L.; m. Sharon Shih, Aug. 10, 1969; children: Franklin, Daniel. BS, Nat. Taiwan U., 1958, MS in Phytopathology, 1960; MS in Biochemistry, U. Wis., 1967, PhD in Biochemistry, 1969. Rsch. asst. Nat. Taiwan U., Taipei, 1961-62; instr. biochemistry Taipei Med. Coll., 1962-63; rsch. asst. U. Wis., Madison, 1963-69; rsch. assoc. Waksman Inst., New Brunswick, N.J., 1970-72; sr. scientist Hoffmann-La Roche Inc., Nutley, N.J., 1972-79, rsch. fellow, 1979-85, rsch. investigator, 1985-91, rsch. leader, 1991—. Contbr. over 40 articles to profl. jours. including Jour. Antibiotics, Jour. Biol. Chemistry, Antimicrobial Agts. and Chemotherapy, Jour. Am. Chem. Soc.; mem. editl. bd. Jour. Antibiotics, 1992—. Life mem. Art Students League N.Y. Fellow Am. Acad. Microbiology; mem. Am. Chem. Soc., Soc. Indsl. Microbiology, European Soc. Animal Cell Tech., Am. Soc. Microbiology. Achievements include 21 U.S. patents on new antibiotics and processes for their production; discovery of ionomycin as a Ca++ ionophore; discovery of antibiotic X-14868A as an anti-coccidial agt. trade name Cygro. Avocations: oil painting. Home: 36 Rockledge Pl Cedar Grove NJ 07009-1627 Office: Hoffmann-La Roche Inc 340 Kingsland St Nutley NJ 07110-1199

LIU, CHENG-TSUNG, electrical engineering educator; b. Taichung, Taiwan, Jan. 26, 1961; s. Hsin-Han and Shou-Chin (Hung) L.; m. Yuan-I Hsieh, Jan. 30, 1992. MSEE, Kans. State U., Manhattan, 1984; PhD, Purdue U., 1988. Registered profl. engr., Taiwan. Instr. Purdue U., West Lafayette, Ind., 1987-88; assoc. prof. Nat. Sun Yat-Sen U., Kaohsiung, Taiwan, 1988—, dir. Computer Ctr., 1997-98. Contbr. numerous articles to profl. jours. 2d lt. Chinese Navy, 1980-82. Mem. IEEE (sr.), Chinese Inst. Engrs. (sr., Disting. Young Engr. award 1998). Avocations: music, travel. Office: Nat Sun Yat-Sen U, Dept Elec Engring, Kaohsiung 804, Taiwan

LIU, CHI, lawyer; b. Guiyang, China, Apr. 2, 1963; s. JiLin Liu and Guo Hua Jia. LLB, Beijing U., 1984; LLM, Temple U., 1988. Legal asst. Epstein Becker & Green, P.C., N.Y.C., 1988-92; Chinese law counsel Shook Lin & Bok, Singapore, 1992-94; sr. assoc. Haiwen & Ptnrs., Beijing, 1994-96; ptnr. Gong Cheng Law Office, Beijing, 1996-98, Xin Ji Yuan Law Office, Beijing, 1998—. Mem. ABA, N.Y. State Bar Assn., All China Bar Assn., Beijing Bar Assn. Avocations: tennis, squash, horseback riding, golf, cycling. Office: Fuhua Mansion # 5B Block D, No 8 N Chaoyang Men St, Beijing 100027, China

LIU, CHIA-YIH, psychiatrist, researcher; b. Nan-Tow, Taiwan, Apr. 14, 1958; s. Ning-Yen and Liau-Dan Liu; m. Chwen-Hwa Lu, May 4, 1991; 1 child, Shawn. MD, Yang Ming Med. Coll., Taipei, Taiwan, 1983. Intern Vets. Gen. Hosp., Taipei, 1982-83, resident, 1985-89, attending psychiatrist, 1990-92; clin. instr. Yang Ming U., 1990-93, Def. Med. Coll., Taipei, 1991-92; attending psychiatrist Chang Gung Meml. Hosp., Taoyuan, Taiwan, 1992—; instr. Chang Gung U., Taoyuan, Taiwan, 1994-97, asst. prof., 1997-2000, assoc. prof., 2000—; inpatient unit chief, Chang Gung Meml. Hosp., 1993-97, res. tng. dir. dept. psychiatry, 1993-98, chmn. dept. psychiatry, 1999—. Contbr. articles to profl. jours. Mem. Am. Psychiat. Assn., Taiwan Soc. Psychiatry. Avocations: fine arts, music, tennis, baseball. Office: Chang Gung Meml Hosp, Dept Psych # 5 Fuh-Hsing Rd, Kuei-San 333, Taiwan

LIU, CHUNG-HO, aeronautical engineering educator; b. Hsinchu, Taiwan, Feb. 16, 1957; s. Guang-Luh and Yuh-Jing (Lin) L.; m. Huei-Jen Chen; children: Chih-Han, Chih-Lin. BS in Aeron. Engring., Chung Cheng Inst. Tech., Taoyuan, Taiwan, 1980; MSc, Nat. Chiao-Tung U., Hsinchu, Taiwan, 1984; PhD in Aeronautics, Imperial Coll., London, 1995. Teaching asst. Chung Cheng Inst. Tech., Taoyuan, 1980-82, lectr., 1984-91, dept. adminstr., 1985-86, dept. coord., 1986-87, assoc. prof., 1995—; cons. in field. Contbr. articles to profl. jours. Disting. Tchr. scholar Min. Nat. Defense, Taipei, Taiwan, 1991-95. Mem. Aero. & Astron. Soc. Taiwan, Chinese Soc. Defense Sci. & Tech., Chinese Soc. Mech. Engrs. Office: Chung Cheng Inst Tech, Dept Aero Engring, Taoyuan 335, Taiwan

LIU, CHUN-LEI, radar meteorologist; b. Fuyang, China, Oct. 5, 1963; s. Yi-Kuan and Qin-De (Zhang) L.; m. Lili Ge, Sept. 7, 1986; children: Mary, Jimmy. BSc, Univ. Sci. & Tech. of China, 1985, MSc, 1987; PhD, UMIST, 1991. Rsch. fellow Univ. Plymouth, U.K., 1990-92, UMIST, U.K., 1992-95, Univ. Reading, U.K., 1995—. Contbr. articles to profl. jours. Recipient Sino-British friendship scholarship British Coun. & Chinese Edn. Coun., 1986. Mem. IEE, EGS. Avocations: sports, fishing. Office: Univ Reading dept Meteorolg, RG 6 6BB Reading United Kingdom

LIU, CHUN-MING, cardiologist; b. Hsiung Shien, Hopei, China, Nov. 5, 1930; s. Tah-Fu and Yu-Ming Liu; m. Wen-Chuan Ma, Apr. 13, 1974. MD, Nat. Def. Med. Ctr., Taipei, Taiwan, 1955. Med. diplomate Internal Medicine Adult Cardiology. Resident, then chief, dir Air Force Gen. Hosp., Taipei, 1955-77; enlisted Chinese Air Force, 1976, advanced through grades to col., 1976; comdr. Air Force Hosp., Taichung, Taiwan, 1977-85; resigned Chinese Air Force, 1986; dir. Taichung Vets. Gen. Hosp., 1986-88; resident Clark Air Force Hosp., Clark AFB, The Philippines, 1962-63; trainee Sch. Aerospace Medicine, Brooks AFB, San Antonio, 1975-76; rsch. fellow in medicine Mass. Gen. Hosp., Boston, 1988-90; staff physician China Med. Ctr., Taipei; vis. fellow in flight simulation MIT, Cambridge, 1988; cons. cardiology Chine Med. Coll., Taichung, 1979—; dept. dir. Country Hosp., Taipei, 1991-92; cons. aviation medicine Airline Pilots Assn., China, 1995—; physician Ming Chuan U., 1997—. Guest editor Army Med. Jour., 1979. Mem. aerospace medicine del. to former USSR, Citizen Amb. Program, 1990. Col. M.C. Chinese Air Force, 1976-85. Mem. Am. Soc. Echocardiography, Aerospace Med. Assn., Soc. Magnetic Resonance, N.Y. Acad. Scis., Paul D. White Soc. Avocations: baseball, swimming, golf. Office: China Med Ctr, 202, Ta-An Rd, SEC1, Taipei 106, Taiwan

LIU, CHUN-YAN, chemist, researcher; b. Yingkou, Liaoning, China, Apr. 24, 1947; s. Yong-quan and Su-qing (Hu) L.; m. Xue-fu Cui, Jan. 31, 1977; 1 child, Cui Jia. Diploma, Nankai U., Tianjin, 1975. Asst. Inst. of Photographic Chemistry, Chinese Acad. Sci., Beijing, 1975-87, asst. prof., 1988-91, assoc. prof., 1992-95, prof. chemistry, 1996—; vis. scholar Inst. Phys. and Theoretical Chemistry, U. Erlangen, Germany, 1986-88, 90; vis. prof. dept. chemistry U. Guelph, Can., 1997. Contbr. articles to profl. jours. Recipient 2d grade award for advancement of sci. and tech. Chinese Acad. Scis., 1985. E-mail: cyliu@ipc.ac.cn. Home: Dewai Beishatan, Jia 3 Datun Rd, Beijing 100101, China Office: Inst Photog Chemistry CAS, Dewai Beishatan, Beijing 100101, China

LIU, DE LI, agronomist; b. Wusheng, Sichuan, China, Dec. 7, 1955; arrived in Australia, 1984; s. Xue-Wen Liu and Lan-Xiu Xiang; m. Ya-Wei Huang, July 19, 1984; children: Chang, Xi, Yang. B in Agr. Sci., S.W. Agr. U., Chongqing, China, 1982; PhD, U. New England, Armidale, NSW, Australia, 1991. Postdoc. fellow Bur. Sugar Experiment Sta., Bundaberg, Qld., Australia, 1990-93; rsch. officer Bur. Sugar Experiment Sta., Bundaberg, 1993-97; sr. rsch. agronomist NSW Agriculture, Wagga Wagga, Australia, 1997—; PhD examiner U. New England, Armidale, 1993, 95, 96. S.W. Agr. Univ. scholar, 1985-86, U. New England scholar, 1987-90. Mem. Australian Soc. Agronomy, Australian Sugar Cane Technologists, Am. Soc. Agronomy, Modelling and Simulation Soc. Australian Inc. Home: 7 McKeown St, Wagga Wagga NSW 2650, Australia Office: NSW Agr, Wagga Wagga Agr Rsch Inst, Wagga Wagga NSW 2650, Australia

LIU, ERJIA, materials engineering educator, researcher; b. Harbin, China, Aug. 22, 1954; s. Shixiong Liu and Jianzhi Meng; m. Meixian Yu, Dec. 9, 1982; 1 child, Zhe. BSc in Engring., Harbin U. Sci. and Tech., 1982; MSc in Engring., Harbin Inst. Tech., 1987; PhD in Engring., Cath. U. Leuven, Belgium, 1997. Technician Harbin Trolleybus Co., 1971-78; asst. Harbin U. Sci. and Tech., 1982-84, lectr., head of lab., dep. dir. sect., 1987-92; vis. scientist Cath. U. Leuven, 1992-93; assoc. prof. Harbin U. Sci. and Tech., 1993—; Vis. Scientist grantee China State Edn. Commn., 1992; PhD scholar Cath. U. Leuven, 1993; rsch. fell. Nanyang Technol. U., 1997; asst. prof. Nanyang Technol. U., 1999. Editor: (book) Proceedings of 1st Conference on Materials Science and Technology in Belgium, 1996; contbr. articles to profl. jours. Mem. ASME Internat., Chinese Soc. Materials Sci. and Tech. in Belgium (coun. mem., dep. dir. 1996-97). Avocations: swimming, music, traveling. Fax: 65-7911859. E-mail: mejliu@ntu.edu.sg. Home: Blk # 11-05, 100 Nanyang Crescent, Singapore 637819, Singapore Office: Nanyang Technol U Sch MPE, 50 Nanyang Ave, 639798 Singapore Singapore

LIU, FAWANG, mathematics educator; b. Fuzhou, China, July 10, 1949; s. Yongkun and Gui Ying (Fu) L.; m. Yizhen Zhao, Sept. 16, 1951; children: Ming, Yi. BS in Computational Math., Fuzhou U., 1975, MS in Computational Math., 1982; PhD in Computational Math., Trinity Coll. Dublin, Ireland, 1991. From assoc. lectr. to assoc. prof. Fuzhou U., 1975-88; rsch. asst. Trinity Coll. Dublin, 1988-91; rsch. fellow U. Coll. Dublin, 1991; postdoctoral rsch. fellow/rsch. fellow Queensland U. Tech., Brisbane, Australia, 1991-98; rsch. fellow U. Queensland, Brisbane, Australia, 1998-2000, 2000—. Contbr. articles to profl. jours. Recipient award Natural Sci. Assn. Fujian Sci. and Tech., 1988, award Australian Rsch. Coun., 1997, grant Australian Rsch. Coun., 1997. Mem. Math. Soc. Australia, Am. Math. Soc., Assn. Microwave Power Europe, Statis. Soc. Australia, Australian and New Zealand Indsl. and Applied Math. Soc. Avocations: swimming, travelling, reading. Office: Queensland U Tech Math Scis, GPO Box 2434, Brisbane Qld 4001, Australia

LIU, FENGHAI, engineer; b. Baotuo, China, Aug. 11, 1967; s. Erren Liu and Yuhua Zhou; m. Xiulan Chang, Aug. 12, 1992; 1 child, Tong. B in Electronic Engring., Tsinghua U., Beijing, 1990, M in Electronic Engring., 1992. Prof. asst. Tsinghua U., Beijing, 1992-94, lectr., 1994-97, assoc. prof., 1997—; guest researcher TEch. U. Denmark, Lyngby, 1997-98. Contbr. articles to profl. jours.; inventor temperature controller. Mem. IEEE, Assn. Chinese Students and Scholars in Denmark. Avocations: sports, music, stamp collecting. Office: Rsch Ctr COM, DTU Bldg 344, Lyngby DK-2800, Denmark

LIU, GANG, electronics engineer, researcher; b. Anyang, Henan, China, Apr. 3, 1961; s. Hauyue and Zhufang (Xu) L.; m. Weiqi Weng, Dec. 17, 1988; 1 child, Yujia. BSEE, Xidian U., Xi'an, 1982, MSEE, 1985; PhD in Electronic Engring., Shanghai U., 1995. Rsch. engr. Communication, Telemetry and Telecontrol Rsch. Inst. Ministry, Shijiazhuang, China, 1985-92; assoc. prof. Fudan U., Shangai, 1995-96; postdoctoral fellow U. Ky., Lexington, 1996—, rsch. scientist, 2000—. Editor: Generalized Function Theory, 1995. Nat. Sci. and Tech. award Ministry Machines and Electronics Industry China, 1990. Mem. AAAS. Fax: 606-257-3092. E-mail: Gangliu@pop.uky.edu. Office: U Ky Dept Electrical Engring 453 Anderson Hl Lexington KY 40506-0001

LIU, GUI-RONG, mechanical engineer, educator; b. Hunan, China, Feb. 3, 1958; arrived in Singapore, 1993; s. Zhicheng and Zhenfong (Fu) L.; m. Zuona Wang, Feb. 11, 1985; children: Yun, Kun. BEng, Hunan U., China, 1981; MEng in Aero. and Astronautics, Beijing U., 1984; PhD, Tohoku U., Japan, 1991. Asst. engr. Qiqihaer Machinery, China, 1981-82; tchr. asst. Beijing U. Aeronautics and Astronautics, 1984-87; rsch. assoc. Tohoku U., 1991; postdoctoral fellow Northwestern U., 1991-93; rsch. scientist Nat. U. Singapore, 1993-95, lectr., 1996-97, sr. lectr., 1998, assoc. prof., 1999—; dep. program dir. R&D Program on Underwater Shock Tech.; program dir. Ctr. for Computational Mechanics, Singapore, Computational Fluid Dynamics Industry Program, 1996—; divsn. dir. Inst. High Performance Computing, Singapore, 1998—; dir. Centre for Advanced Computations in Engring. Sci., 1998—; part-time cons. Def. Sci. Orgn., Singapore, 1995—, Def. Material Orgn., Singapore, 1995—. Translator: Stress and Strain Analysis, 1990; contbr. articles to profl. jours. Mem. Internat. Comty. for Composites Engrng. Avocations: bridge, travel.

LIU, GUOQUAN, materials scientist, educator; b. Le-Ling, Shandong, China, May 4, 1952; s. Benxian and Fengying (Zhang) L.; m. Hongxiang Li, July 25, 1978; 1 child, Yuqiang. Diploma, Beijing U. Iron/Steel Tech., 1976; M of Engring., U. Fla., 1983, PhD, 1984. Courtesy asst. prof. U. Fla., Gainesville, 1981-83; mem. tchg. staff Beijing U. Iron and Steel Tech., 1976-81, lectr., mem. staff, 1984-87, assoc. prof., 1987-91, prof., 1991—, dep. dir. acad. divsn. Grad. Sch., 1993-95, dir., standing vice dean Grad. Sch., 1995-2000; mem., sec.-gen. acad. degrees com. U. Sci. and Tech., Beijing; prof. Baosteel Co., Shanghai, China, 1996—. Author: Stereology, 1989 (Excellent Sci.-Tech. Book award 1990); mem. standing editl. com. Rare Metals, 1989—; mem. editl. com. Chinese Jour. Stereology and Image Analysis, 1996—; contbr. more than 60 articles to profl. jours. Mem. People's Congress, Haidian Dist., Beijing, 1991-98; mem. steering com. for engring. postgrad. edn. Ministry Metall. Industry of China, 1997—; mem. nat. steering com. Ministry Engring. Edn., 1998—. Recipient 1st prize for Chinese Young Educators, Fok Ying Tung Edn. Found., 1989, Top prize for excellent educators Baosteel Edn. Found., 1994, Nat. Excellent Educator award State Edn. Commn. China, 1995, Excellent Young Scientist award Ministry Metall. Industry China, 1997. Mem. Chinese Mech. Engring. Soc. (coun. mem. 1991-96, standing coun. 1996—), Chinese Soc. for Stereology (standing coun. 1988—, v.p. 1999—), Internat. Soc. for Stereology (regional rep. 1990-96, 99—), Chinese Soc. for Acad. Degrees and Grad. Edn. (coun. mem. 1996—). Avocations: hiking, painting. Office: U Sci and Tech Beijing, U Sci and Tech Beijing, Sch Materials Sci & Engring, 100083 Beijing China

LIU, HSIN-FU, medical science researcher; b. Taipei City, Taiwan, Sept. 4, 1961; s. Yen-Ming and Pi-Ying Lin. MSc, U. Louvain, Belgium, 1991, PhD, 1996. Postdoctoral fellow U. Louvain, 1996, Brussels, 1997-99; prin. investigator Mackay Meml. Hosp., Taipei, Taiwan, 1999—. Contbr. articles to profl. jours. Recipient award for best free comm. Euroliver Found., Brussels, 1998. Mem. Am. Soc. Microbiology. Avocations: photography, hiking, bird watching. Home: 31-3 Ln 167 Sec 2, Pa-Teh Rd, 10401 Taipei Taiwan Office: Mackay Meml Hosp/Med Rsch, Min-Sheng Rd 45, 25115 Taipei-Tamshui Taiwan

LIU, HUNG-CHING, medical educator; b. June 18, 1942; arrived in U.S., 1965; d. Chin-Hai and Su-Ein (Chiang) Ou; m. Dar-Biau Liu, Dec. 20, 1969; children: Warrick, Benson. BSc, Taiwan Normal U., 1965; PhD, Wayne State U., 1969. Rsch. assoc. U. Wis., Madison, 1970-73; asst. prof. State Univ. Campinas, Sao Paulo, Brazil, 1973-77; rsch. assoc. N.Y. State U., Stony Brook, N.Y., 1977-83; rsch. asst. prof. Eastern Va. Medical Sch., Norfolk, Va., 1983-88; asst. prof. Cornell Univ. Medical Coll., N.Y., 1988-92, assoc. prof., 1992—; dir. Reproductive Endocrine Lab. Cornell U. Med. Coll., 1988—; cons. Sec. of Dept. Health, Taipei, Taiwan, 1990—; mem. editl. bd. Early Pregnancy Biol. and Med., Cherry Hill, N.J., 1994—; pioneer work in the field of reproductive medicine, in vitro fertilization. Contbr. numerous articles to profl. jours. Recipient first prize for Best Paper award, The Am. Fertility Soc., 1986, Poster Prize award, 1988; named Top Four Paper of Yr. Am. Soc. Rep. Medicine, 1996, SART Prize Paper, 2000, Scientist award ESHRE, 1997, 2000, Prize poster presentation ASRM, 1999. Mem. The Soc. Study of Reproduction, The Am. Fertility Soc. Republican. Avocations: music, travel, coin collecting, reading. Office: Cornell U Med Coll 515 E 71st St Rm S500 New York NY 10021-4873

LIU, JI CHYUN, electrical engineering educator, consultant; b. Taipei, Taiwan, June 21, 1951; s. Long Fong and Yu Ching (Young) L.; m. Huey Ling Wang, Oct. 31, 1981; 1 child, Claire. BSEE, Chung Cheng Inst. Tech., Ta-Hsi, China, 1974, MSEE, 1981, PhD, 1993. Instr. Chung Cheng Inst. Tech., 1981-88, assoc. prof., 1993-98, prof., 1998—; cons. Indsl. Tech. Rsch. Inst., Hsinchu, China, 1998—, Visionetics Intenrat., Hsinchu, 1999—. Patentee in field. Col. Army of Taiwan, 1974-97. Mem. IEEE, Assn. of Old Crows, Armed Forces Comm. Electronic Assn. Avocation: jogging. Home: Thai Ming St 50-6, 33509 Ta-Hsi, Tao-Yuan Taiwan Office: Chung Cheng Inst Tech, Yuan Shu Lin, 33509 Tai-Hsi, Tao-Yuan Taiwan

LIU, JIAN GUO, geologist; b. Tianshui, Gansu, China, Apr. 13, 1951; s. Yumin and Zhen (Qiao) L.; m. Qun Zhao, Oct. 2, 1980; 1 child, Jia Ji-a. BSc, Xi-an Mining Inst., 1978; MSc, China U. Geoscis., Beijing, 1982; PhD, Imperial Coll., London, 1991. Asst. lectr. Xi-an Mining Inst., 1978-79; lectr. China U. Geoscis., Wuhan, 1982-88; rsch. assoc. Imperial Coll., London, 1991-96, rsch. fellow, 1996—. Contbr. articles to profl. jours. Recipient Jerald J. Cook Meml. award 9th ERIM Thematic Conf., 1993, GRSS, 1999, prize paper award IGARSS, 1999. Mem. Geol. Remote Sensing Group U.K. Avocations: model making, photography. Home: Flat 17

Arrow Ct, 84 W Cromwell Rd, London SW5 9QT, England Office: Imperial Coll TH Huxley Sch, Prince Consort Rd, London SW7 2BP, England

LIU, JIANKANG K., freshwater biologist, research scientist; b. Wujiang County, Jiangsu, China, Sept. 1, 1917; s. Zhen-Qi and Shu-Liu (Tao) Liu; m. Yun-Mei Wu, May 26, 1990 (dec.); children: Jun, Di-Xin, Xianping, Xinxing. BSc, Soochow U., Suzhou City, China, 1938; PhD, McGill U., Montreal, Que., Can., 1947. Rsch. asst. Inst. Zoology, Academia Sinica, Beibei, Chongqing, China, 1939-41, rsch. assoc., 1942-44, assoc. scientist, 1945; assoc. rschr. Lab. Exptl. Cell Rsch., Woods Hole, 1947-48; sr. scientist Inst. Hydrobiology, Chinese Acad. Scis., Shanghai, 1950-54; sr. scientist Inst. Hydrobiology, Chinese Acad. Scis., Wuhan, 1954—, dep. dir., 1979-82, dir., 1983-86, hon. dir. emeritus, 1987—. Author: (chpt.) Lakes and Reservoirs, 1984; editor: Cultivation of Chinese Freshwater Fishes, 3rd edit., 1992, Ecological Studies on Lake Donghu, 1990. Vice-chmn. Hubei Com. of Chinese People's Polit. Consultative Conf., Wuhan, 1993-97. Mem. Chinese Acad. Scis. (academician; medal 1989), Chinese Soc. Oceanology and Limnology (v.p. 1979-96, hon. pres. 1997—), Chinese Ichthyological Soc. (hon. pres. 1989—), Hubei Assn. Sci. and Tech. (hon. pres. 1991—), N.Y. Acad. Scis. Home: Apt 26-4 East, Shui Sheng Cun, Luojiashan, Wuhan Hubei 430072, China Office: Inst Hydrobiology, Chinese Acad Scis Luojiashan, Wuhan Hubei 430072, China

LIU, JIAN-XIN, science educator; b. Fuyang, Zhejiang, China, Nov. 6, 1958; parents Wenxiao Liu and Yuying Jiang; m. Adi Yuan, July 24, 1982; 1 child, Ling Liu. BSc, Zhejiang Agrl. U., Hangzhou, China, 1982; MSc, Hokkaido U., Sapporo, Japan, 1985, PhD, 1988. Lectr. Zhejiang Agrl. U., Hangzhou, China, 1988-91, assoc. prof., 1991-94, dir. animal nutrition sect., 1992-93, assoc. dean Coll. Animal Scis., 1993-94, dean Coll. Animal Scis., 1994-99; prof. Zhejiang U., Hangzhou, 1994—; postdoctoral fellow Rowett Rsch. Inst., Scotland, 1995-96; Humboldtian U. Kiel, Germany, 1999-00; cons. Pingyang (China) Prefectural Govt., 1996—, Pinghu (China) Prefectural Govt., 1997—; chief investigator kinetics of digestion and efficient utilization of roughages in ruminants rsch. project, 1993 (3d class award 1995). Co-editor: (book) Manipulation of Agriculture by Chemicals, 1993; editor-in-chief: Zhejiang Jour. Animal Sci. Mem. Zhejiang Provincial Union of Youth, Hangzhou, 1994-98. Recipient Edn. award Huoyingdong Found. for Edn., 1992, Specific Allowance cert. China State Coun., 1993—; named Excellent Youth Tchr., 1991. Mem. China Soc. Animal Nutrition (standing bd. dirs. 1996—), China Assn. Animal Sci. & Vet. Medicine (bd. dirs. 1996—), Zhejiang Soc. Animal Sci. & Vet. Medicine (pres. 1998—).

LIU, JIMING, computer scientist; b. Shanghai; s. Y.Z. Liu and X.D. Cai; m. Meilee Chan, 1986; children: Isabella, Bernice. BS, East China Normal U., 1983; MA, Concordia U., 1987; M in Engring., McGill U., 1990, PhD, 1994. Rsch. assoc. Kentek Rsch. Ctr., Can., 1988; engr. software Virtual Prototypes Inc., Montreal, Can., 1989-91; cons. InfoAutomation, Montreal, 1991-93; asst. prof. Hong Kong Bapt. U., 1993-97, assoc. prof., 1997—; sr. rsch. agt. Computer Rsch. Inst., Montreal, 1991-93, vis. fellow, 1995. Contbr. articles to profl. jours. Mem. IEEE (sr.; Computer Soc., Robotics and Automation Soc.), Assn. Computer Machinery (exec. com. Hong Kong chpt. 1994-95). Avocations: travel, movies, reading.

LIU, JIN-HAO, educator; b. Guangdong, China, May 16, 1959; m. Rosa M. Lai, Oct. 1, 1985; children: Sheila, Laurin. PhD, U. Calgary, Can., 1991. Rsch. scientist Agr. and Agri-Food Can., Alta., 1996-97; asst. prof. Academia Sinica, Taipei, Taiwan, 1998—. Contbr. articles to profl. jours. Mem. Am. Soc. Plant Physiologist. Achievements include patent in field. E-mail: liujh@hotmail.com and liujh@gate.sinica.edu.tw. Fax: 886-2-2651-5600. Office: IBS Academia Sinica, 128 Academia Sinica Rd, Nankang Taipei 115, Taiwan

LIU, JIN-KING, geoscience scientist, researcher; b. Chang-Hwa Hsien, Taiwan, June 2, 1954; s. Ma-Hsiang and Chuang Hsiu (Chuang) L.; m. Fung-Jin Lin, May 10, 1981; children: Yao, Hsau-Wen. BSc, Nat. Cheng-Kung U., Tainan, Taiwan, 1977; MSc, U. London, 1985. ITC soil survey diploma; ISO 9000 lead assessor; Battelle R&D mgmt. Rsch. asst. Mining Rsch./Svc. Orgn., Indsl. Tech. Rsch. Inst., Hsin-Chu, Taiwan, 1977-81; asst. rschr. Mining Rsch./Svc. Orgn., Indsl. Tech. Rsch. Inst., Hsin-Chu, 1981-84; assoc. rschr. Energy and Mining Rsch./Svc. Orgn., Inds. Tech. Rsch. Inst., Hsin-Chu, 1984-87, rschr., 1988-89; rschr. Energy & Resources Labs., Indsl. Tech. Rsch. Inst., Hsin-Chu, 1989-91, rschr., mgr., 1991—; com. mem. Nat. Land Info. Promotion Com., Min. of Econs. Affairs, Taipei, Taiwan, 1994—, Rev. Com. for Slopeland Devel., Mioli, Taiwan, 1995—. Contbr. articles to profl. jours. Mem. Nat. Land Info. Com. Agrl. Council, Exec. Yuen, Taiwan, 1994—. Fellow Chinese Inst. Engrs., Chinese Inst. Mining and Metallurgy Engrs.; mem. Chinese Soil and Water Conservation, Chinese Soc. Photogrammetry and Remote Sensing (dir. 1994-98), Chinese Geog. Info. Assn. (dir. 1995—). Avocations: hiking, internet browsing, reading, writing, speaking. Home: 8F-2 882 Sec 2 Guang-Fu Rd, Hsinchu 300, Taiwan Office: Energy & Resources Lab ITRI, 195-6 Sec 4 Chung-Hsing Rd, Hsinchu Hsien 310, Taiwan

LIU, JIYU, engineering educator; b. Liuyang, Hunan, China, May 22, 1936; s. Mingjun and Qizhen (Tang) L.; m. Ainan Zhang; 1 child, Zhongmou. BS, Wuhan tech. U. Surveying/Map, 1961, PhD, 1983. Faculty Wuhan Tech. U. Surveying and Mapping, 1961-70, assoc. prof., 1979-84, prof., 1987—; specialist Laotian Mapping Bur., Vientiane, Laos, 1977-78; vis. scholar Institut für Angewandte Geodäsie, Frankfurt, Germany, 1985-86; assessment specialist Nat. Awards on Sci. and Tech. Advancements, Beijing, 1997—. Chief author: The Principle and Application of Global Positioning System, 1993 (2d award 1995), Lecture Notes for Visiting Scholars, 1997; editl. bd. Navigation, 1995—; contbr. over 128 articles to profl. jours. With Chinese Army, 1971-76. State Coun. subsidy, 1996; 1st award of excellent tchg. results of nationwide univs. GPS Satellite Navigation, 1997, 2d award of sci. and tech. advancements of nat. grades of China, GPS Photogrammetry, 1999. Fellow Chinese Inst. Electronics (dir. navigation com.); mem. AAAS, N.Y. Acad. Scis., Chinese Soc. Geodesy, Photogrammetry and Cartography (dir. geodesy com. 1989—). Avocations: reading, chinese boxing. Email: jyliu@wtusm.edu.cn. Office: Wuhan Tech U Surveying, 129 Luoyu rd, Wuhan 430079, China

LIU, JUN MING, physicist, materials science educator; b. Daye City, China, Dec. 14, 1964; s. Hen You Liu and Gu Gui Xu; m. Hong Lin Liu, Aug. 1, 1988; 1 child. BS, Huazhong U. Sci. and Tech., Wuhan, China, 1984, MS in Engring., 1987; PhD in Engring., Northwestern Poly. U., Xian, China, 1989. Postdoctoral asst. Nanjing (China) U., 1990-92, lectr., 1992; vis. rschr. Göttingen (Germany) U., 1992-93; assoc. prof. physics Nanjing U., 1993-94, 96-97, prof. physics, 1999—; vis. rschr. Nat. U. Singapore, 1997-98. Author: Encyclopedia of Materials Science, 1995; contbr. articles to physics jours.; patentee in field. Humboldt fellow Hahn-Meitner-Inst., Berlin, 1994-96. Mem. Chinese Phys. Soc., Chinese Metallurgy Soc. Avocations: music, computer games, smoking. Office: Nanjing U Dept Physics, Hankor Rd No 22, Jiangsu Nanjing 210093, China

LIU, JUN-PING, biochemist; b. Hui-Nan, China, Feb. 5, 1957; arrived in Australia, 1987; s. Ming-Han and Yu L.; m. He Li, Oct. 20, 1991; children: Anna, Anthony. MD, Bethune Med. U., China, 1980, M of Med. Sci., 1985; PhD, Monash U., Australia, 1991. Lectr. Beijing Med. U., China, 1985-87; rsch. officer John Hunter Hosp., Newcastle, Australia, 1991-95; sr. scientist Newcastle Mater Hosp., Australia, 1995-96; rsch. fellow Baker Med. Rsch. Inst., Melbourne, Australia, 1996—, sr. rsch. fellow, 2000—. Recipient A.W. Campbell award Australian Neurosci. Soc., 1995, Inaugural Postdoctoral award Nat. Assn. Rsch. Fellows, Australia, 1995, Servier award Endocrine Soc. Australia, 1996, Australian Life Sci. award, 1996. Mem. Australian Soc. Med. Rsch., Endorcine Soc. Am., Internat. Soc. Neurochem., Soc. Neurosci., Am. Assn. for Cancer Rsch. Office: Baker Med Rsch Inst, Comml Rd, Prahran 3181, Australia

LIU, KENNEDY TAT-YIN, accountant; b. Hong Kong, Dec. 11, 1961; s. Hin-Shum and Yuet-Ling (Yau) L.; m. Connie Yuk-Chun Au, Oct. 21, 1989. Profl. Diploma in Accountancy, Hong Kong Poly., 1984; MBA, U. Warwick, Eng., 1993. CPA, Hong Kong; chartered cert. acct. U.K., chartered sec., U.K. Staff acct. Arthur Andersen & Co., Hong Kong, 1984-86, sr. acct., 1986-89, mgr., 1989-90, sr. mgr., 1990-93, gen. mgr., 1993-94, ptnr., 1994—. Fellow Hong Kong Soc. Accts. (coun. 1999—, editl. bd. 1994—, exam. bd. 1998—, PRC tech. com. 2000—, adv. panel on acctg. standards 2000—, adv. com. on listing and takeover regulations 2000—, registration and practising com. 2000—, acct. amb. 2000—, Gold medal 1983, named Young Acct. of Yr. 1999), Assn. Chartered Cert. Accts. (U.K.), Inst. Chartered Secs. and Adminstrs. (U.K.), Hong Kong Inst. Co. Secs. (tech. com. 1995-96). Avocations: travel, tennis, music, golf. Home: Apt 15-B Mcdonnell House, 8 Mcdonnell Rd, Hong Kong SAR, China Office: Arthur Andersen & Co, 21/F Edinburgh Tower, 15 Queen's Rd Ctrl, 21/F Edinburgh Tower Hong Kong SAR, China

LIU, LUKE HSIEN-TANG, bishop; b. Xianxian, Hebei, China, Dec. 21, 1928; s. Peter S.T. and Maria L. PhB, St. Joseph Coll., Manila, 1954, BTh, 1958; D in Canon Law, Urban U., Rome, 1960; MA, Lumen Vitae, Brussels, 1961. Prin. St. Francis Xavier H.S., Taiwan, 1965-81, chmn. bd., 1981—; chmn. bd. St. Peter H.S., Taiwan, 1983—, Stella Matutina Girls' Sch., Taiwan, 1983—, Stella Matutina Primary Sch., Taiwan, 1983—, Sedes Sapientiae Primary Sch., Taiwan, 1983—; bd. dirs. Cath. U. of Fujen, Taiwan, 1983—; chmn. bd. Mater Misericordiae Hosp., Taiwan, 1995—; cons. Religion for the Mcpl. Govt., Hsinchu, Taiwan, 1983—, Religion for the Provincial Govt., 1992-94. Chair St. Joseph Home for Alzheimer Diseased, 1997, Home for the Aged, 1998—, Children's Ctr., 1985—, 70 Catholic kindergartens, 1984—, Commn. Clergy, 1982—. Recipient award Ministry of Edn., Taiwan, 1970, 73, 75, 78, 81. Roman Catholic. Avocations: swimming, jogging, reading, walking, hiking. Office: Diocesis Hsinchuensis, 156-1 Chungcheng Rd, Hsinchu 300, Taiwan

LIU, LUMEI, chemistry researcher; b. Cheng-du, China, Apr. 20, 1939; came to U.S., 1985; d. Feng-Wu Liu and Zon-sheiw Lue; m. Dezhao Wang, Aug. 1, 1961; children: Yu Wang, Xin Wang. Bachelor, Beijing Normal U., 1959, PhD, 1988. Asst. prof. Beijing Normal U., 1959-82; TV lectr. Dept. Chinese Edn., Beijing, 1979-83; assoc. prof. Beijing Normal U., 1988-89; postdoctoral dept. chemistry U. Houston, 1989-92, rschr. Superconductor Ctr., 1992-96, rsch. assoc. Materials Ctr., 1996—; vis. scholar U. Houston, 1985-87. Author: Inorganic Chemistry, 1990; contbr. articles to profl. jours. Named one of Women at Their Best, Glamour Mag., Dec. 1999. Mem. Chinese Assn. Profl. Sci. and Tech. E-mail: lLiu@pop.uh.edu. Office: Univ Houston Dept Chemistry Calhoun 4800 Houston TX 77204-0001

LIU, LUN ZU, chemist, educator; b. Beijing, China, Mar. 17, 1938; s. Jing Xuan Liu and Zhen Tang Wang; m. Ru Zhen Cao, Mar. 28, 1967; children: Chong, Jin. B, Nankai U., 1963. Assoc. prof. Inst. Elements Nankai U., Tianjin, China, 1963-79; vis. scholar Rutgers U., Piscataway, N.J., 1980-82; prof. Inst. Elements Nankai U., Tianjin, 1983—; cons. Coun. Sci. and Tech., Tianjin, 1990—. Author: Organophosphorus Chemistry, 1991; inventor in field. Recipient 1st award tchg. Tianjin Govt., 1993. Mem. Internat. Coun. Main Group Chemistry. Avocations: sports, opera, music. Home: Nankai Univ, SW Village 42-2-504, 300071 Tianjin China Office: Nankai Univ Inst Elements, Nankai Univ Inst Elements, 94 Weijin Rd, Tianjin China

LIU, MARGARET M., fabric company executive; b. China, July 24, 1946; d. I-Yung and K-Ming (Huan) L.; m. Shau-Chung Hu, Feb. 14, 1984; 1 child. Z.G. BA, Christian Coll., Taipei, Taiwan, 1974; MBA, Lincoln U., 1983; BBA, Nat. Acad. Mgmt., Taipei, 1980. Dir., pres. Am. Hubei Assoc., N.Y.C.; dir. Nat. Acad. Mgmt., Taipei; dir., pres. China Natural Fabric Corp., Bklyn.; hostess TV and radio program Computer and You, China TV Co., Cen. Radio Sta., 1970-73. Mem. Nat. Rep. Congl. Com. Recipient award Fend Chia U., Taipei, Taiwan Internat. Conf. on Computerized Bus. Simulations, 1976, Taiwan Merchants Assn. N.Y., Inc. Home: 1025 45th St Apt 1D Brooklyn NY 11219-1904 Address: PO Box 190716 Brooklyn NY 11219-0716

LIU, MAW-SHUNG, physiologist, dentist; b. Taiwan, Republic of China, Feb. 2, 1940; came to U.S., 1968; s. Chao-Tung and Chian (Hwang) L.; m. Min-Chau Chang, Sept. 15, 1966; 1 child, Chien-Ye. DDS, Kaohsiung Med. Coll., Taiwan, 1964; PhD, U. Ottawa, Can., 1976. Cert. by Coun. Nat. Bd. Dental Examiners. Intern in pathology U. Ky., Lexington, 1968-69; instr. physiology La. State U. Med. Ctr., New Orleans, 1974-76, asst. prof., 1976-78; assoc. prof. Sch. of Medicine, Wake Forest U., Winston-Salem, N.C., 1978-82; prof. St. Louis U. Sch. Medicine, 1982—; vis. prof. Beijing Med. U., 1984—, Zhejiang Med. U., 1986, Kaohsiung Med. Coll., 1989—, Chang Gung Med. Coll., 1989—; mem. surgery, anesthesiology and trauma study sect. NIH, 1988-92. Mem. editl. bd. Circulatory Shock, 1982-93, Shock, 1993—; contbr. over 90 articles and 90 papers to profl. jours. Named hon. prof. Nanjing Med. Univ., 1984, Hunan Med. Univ., 1988; grantee Nat. Heart Lung and Blood Inst., Inst. Gen. Med. Sci., 1977—. Mem. Internat. Soc. Heart Rsch., Am. Physiol. Soc., The Shock Soc. Achievements include significant contribution to the understanding of pathophysiology of myocardial and hepatic dysfunction during shock, sepsis and trauma. Office: St Louis U Sch Medicine Dept Pharm and Physiol Sci 1402 S Grand Blvd Saint Louis MO 63104-1004

LIU, MEIGEN, physiatrist; b. Tokyo, Jan. 30, 1955; s. Shyujin and Kazuko (Kaku) L.; m. Kuniko Yamamoto, May 23, 1981; children: Sayaka, Fumio. MD, Keio U., Tokyo, 1979, D in Med. Sci., 1989. Resident Keio U. Hosp., Tokyo, 1979-81, Keio Tsukigase Rehab. Ctr., Amagi, Japan, 1981-83, Minn. U. Hosp., Mpls., 1984-85; chief Higashisaitama Nat. Hosp., Hasuda, Japan, 1985-93; dir. dept. Saitama Prefecture Gen. Rehab. Ctr., Ageo, Japan, 1993—; lectr. Keio U., 1985—. Author: Functional Evaluation of Stroke Patients, 1996; contbr. articles to profl. jours.; editor-in-chief: Japanese Jour. Rehab. Medicine, 1995—; editor: (video) Pulmonary Rehabilitation, 1997, Jour. Clin. Rehab., 1995—. Recipient Most Impressive Presentation award Assn. Japanese Physiatrists, Tokyo, 1993. Mem. Japanese Acad. Rehab. Medicine (councilor), Internat. Rehab. Medicine Assn., Japanese Soc. Prosthetics and Orthotics. Avocations: field watching, photography, computers. Home: 3131-6 Kurohama, Hasuda 349-0101, Japan Office: Saitama Prefecture Gen Rehab Ctr, 148-1 Nishikaiduka, Ageo 362, Japan

LIU, MIN-SHAN, mechanical engineer, educator, administrator; b. Taipei, Taiwan, China, Mar. 8, 1956; child of Bing-Nan Liu and Cheue-Chyn Yan; m. Chien-Chi Lin, Jan. 10, 1984; children: Kevin, Jin-Yu, Jih-Yun. B, Feng-Chia U., Taichung, China, 1979; MS, Stevens Inst. Tech., 1983; PhD, U. Okla., 1988. Assoc. prof. Feng-Chia U., Taichung, 1988—, chmn. machine workshop, 1995-98, chmn. dept. mech. engring., 1998—; cons. Smart Masters Mgmt. Consulting Co., Taipei, China, 1998—, Taiwan Footwear Rsch. Inst., Taichung, 1999; bd. dirs. Yang Shyue-Chou Mech. Fund. Author: Basic Computer Concept, 1995 (Lit. Achievement Feng-Chia U. 1996), Computer Program Design, 1998 (Lit. Achievement Feng-Chai U. 1999), Computer Aided Design, 1999; co-editor Feng Chai Jour., 1994. 2d lt. Chinese Marine Corps, 1979-81. Avocations: stamp collecting, traveling, badminton, swimming. Fax: 886-4451-6545. Office: Feng Chai U Dept Mech Engr, No. 100, Wen-Hua Rd, Taichung 407, China

LIU, NIAN HUA, physicist, educator; b. Ji-an, China, Feb. 5, 1957; m. Suping Liu, Jan. 1, 1982; 1 child, Zhe. PhD, Tongji U., 1994. Lectr. Ji-an Normal Coll., China, 1981-91; prof. Nanchang U., China, 1994—. Communist. Office: Nanchang U Inst Material Sc, #235 E Nanjing Rd, 330047 Nanchang China

LIU, PETER DONG-GUANG, business company director; b. Taipei, Taiwan, Apr. 27, 1953; arrived in Japan, 1987; BSBA, Boston U., 1975, MBA, 1978. Mng. dir. Eisho Trading Co., Kasumigaura Devel. Co., Tokyo, 1987—; pres. China Sports Devel. Enterprise Ltd., Taipei, 1988—, Tamsui (Taiwan) Enterprise Co., Ltd., 1992—; exec. v.p. Coquihalla Devel. Corp., Vancouver, B.C., Can., 1992—; auditor Fedn. Internat. Des Quilleurs, Homasassa, Fla., 1993—, World Tenpin Bowling Assn., Kuala Lumpur, Malaysia, 1993—; vice-chmn. Chinese Coun. Adv. Policy Studies, Tapei, 1992—. Patentee floppy disk punch, 1984, anti-glare coating, 1985, transmission enhancement, 1985, headlight glare control, 1989. Chmn. fundraising com. Dems. Abroad in Japan, Tokyo, 1988. Mem. Asia Soc. (pres. 1969-71), Can. Soc. in Taiwan, Am. C. of C. in Taiwan, Am. C. of C. in Japan, Boston Computer Soc., Tokyo Am. Club. Avocations: skiing, golf, traveling, reading, computers. Office: Eisho Trading Co Ltd, 5-29-15 Shiba Minato-ku, Tokyo 108, Japan

LIU, QINGCAI, educator; b. Chong Qing, China, May 14, 1959; s. Hong Ying L. and Ynju Jiang; m. Jing Lin, July 17, 1985; 1 child, Lin. M, Chongqing U., China, 1984, PhD, 1995. Asst. prof. Chongwing U., China, 1984-92, assoc. prof., 1993-96, prof.. prof., 1997—; program officer Edn. Min. China, Beijing, 1997-98; vis. U. Calif., San Diego, 1999—; tech. advisor Dashan Iron and Steel, Inc., China, 1996—. Author: The Fundamental of Resources Sunthesize Utilization, 1998. Mem. Southwest Metallurgy and Chem. Engring. Soc. (chmn. 1991-97). Office: Inst Mat Sci & Engring, 174 Sapinba St, Chongqing 400044, China

LIU, RANG-SU, physics educator; b. Henyang, Hunan, China, Feb. 18, 1935; s. Bi-yueng Liu and Chi-Cheng Wei; m. Ji-yong Li, May 25, 1942; children: Hai-rong, Qiang. Grad., Hunan U., Changsha, 1964. Technician Shanghai Elec. Apparatus Rsch. Inst. Ministry of Machinery Industry, Shanghai, 1964-71; technician Xiangxiang Chem. Factory, Hunan, 1971-79; lectr. dept. basic courses Hunan U., Changsha, 1979-86, assoc. prof. dept. physics, 1986-92, prof. dept. physics, 1992—, dir. Inst. Physics for Functional Materials, 1994—; vis. prof. U. Waterloo, Can., 1990-92, U. NSW, Australia, 1998; reporter Intelligent Processing and Mfg. of Materials '97 Internat. Conf., Gold Coast, Australia, 1997; keynote spkr. IPMM Internat. Conf., Honolulu, 1999. Contbr. numerous papers and articles to profl. jours.; inventor in field. Recipient Prize of Progress of Sci. and Tech., Edn. Com. of Hunan Province, 1987; grantee Nat. Natural Sci. Found. China, 1993, 96, 99, Ministry of Machinery Industry, China, 1992. Mem. Chinese Phys. Soc., Chinese Materials Rsch. Soc., Intelligent Processing and Mfg. of Materials (prog. com. mem. 1999-2001). Avocations: sports, climbing, writing. Office: Hunan U, Hunan U, Dept Physics, Changsha Hunan, China

LIU, RHONDA LOUISE, librarian; b. Honolulu; d. David Yuk Fong Liu and Shirley May Chong Liu. BA, U. Hawaii at Manoa, Honolulu, 1974, M of Libr. Info. Studies, 1991; grad., FBI Citizens Acad., 1998. Remote regions/homwork ctrs. outreach libr. Alu Like Native Hawaiian Libr. Project, 1992; libr. II Hawaii State Libr., 1992; fgn. expert libr. studies in English program Beijing Fgn. Studies U., 1992-93; info. specialist Savs. & Cmty. Bankers of Am., Washington, 1993-94; staff specialist III Md. State Dept. Edn., Md. State Libr. for Blind and Physically Handicapped, Balt., 1995-99; reference libr. George Washington U. at Mt. Vernon Coll., Washington, 2000; libr. asst. Legis. Reference Bur. Libr., 1989-90; asst. rschr. Legis. Info. Sys. Office, 1984-85; ESL tutor Keimei Gakuen, Tokyo, 1979; exhibit facilitator Smithsonian Instn., 1999; asst. project mgr. serial records holding conversion project/LSSI Libr. of Congress, Washington, 2000; with Head Start Pubs. Mgmt. Ctr., washington, 1999. Active State Libr. for Blind and Physically Handicapped, 1994-99, Md. State Dept. Edn. Employees' Adv. Coun., 1998-99; sec. Coalition Opposed to Violence and Extremism, State of Md., 1997-99; v.p., sec. U. Hawaii Sch. Libr. and Info. Studies, 1990-91. Alu Like Native Hawaiian Libr. fellow, 1990-91; Kamehameha Schs./Bishop Estate scholar, 1991. Mem. Internat. Platform Assn., U. Hawaii Alumni Assn., U. Hawaii Sch. Lib. and Info. Studies Alumni Assn., Kamehameha Schs. Alumni Assn. (East Coast region), Spl. Librs. Assn., Libr. Congress Asian Am. Assn., Spl. Librs. Assn., Assn. Am. Med. Colls. Avocations: gourmet cooking, multi-cultural activities, overseas travel, hula.

LIU, RONG, physician, researcher; b. Beijing, Aug. 18, 1960; d. Qingcheng Liu and Huija Xie. BS, Beijing Med. U., 1982; MS, Peking Union Hosp., Beijing, 1986; MD, U. Basel, Switzerland, 1993. Cert. physician. Resident in internal medicine Peking Union Hosp., Beijing, 1983-87, chief resident in endocrinology, 1987-88; rsch. fellow Sandoz AG, Basel, 1988-90, U. Hosp., Basel, 1991-95; sr. rschr. U. Eye Hosp., Basel, 1996—. Contbr. articles to profl. jours. Sandoz Ltd. rsch. grantee, Basel, 1991-93. Mem. WWF, Swiss Connective Tissue Soc., Assn. Rsch. Vision and Opthalmology. Home: Aessere Lange Herd 1, CH-4142 Munchenstein Switzerland Office: U Eye Hosp Basel, Mittlere Strasse 91, CH-4012 Basel Switzerland

LIU, RONG FANG (RACHEL LIU), transportation engineer, consultant; b. Shijiazhang, China, May 24, 1963; d. Yutian Liu and Shuangshuang Zhang; m. Lu Zhong, Sept. 22, 1987; children: Lyndall, Charlie. BS in Geography, Beijing U., 1984; MS in Planning, Fla. State U., 1991; PhD in Engring., U. South Fla., 1996. Profl. engr., Ohio. Pub. transp. specialist Fla. Dept. Transp., Tallahassee, 1991-93; rsch. assoc. Ctr. Urban Transp. Rsch., Tampa, Fla., 1993-95; project mgr. Woolpert LLP, Dayton, Ohio, 1995-98, Parsons Brinkernhoft, Inc., N.Y.C., 1998—. Author: Urbanology, 1987. Mem. ASCE, Am. Planning Assn., Inst. Transp. Engrs. (transp., rsch., bd. 1994—). Avocations: travel, model trains, photography. E-mail: liur@pbworld.com. Office: PB Transit & Rail Systems Inc Two Gateway Ct Newark NJ 07102

LIU, RUI-YUAN, physicist, researcher; b. Wuxi, Jiangsu, China, Nov. 15, 1941; s. Yun-Chi and Ya-Qin (Xue) L.; m. Jian-Min Ma, Jan. 29, 1968; children: Hei-Feng, Hei-Gang. BS, U. Sci. and Tech. of China, Beijing, 1963; MS, Inst. Electronics, Beijing, 1966. Engr. China Rsch. Inst. Radiowave Propagation, Xinxiang, 1965-80, dep. chief engr., 1982-85, dep. dir., prof., 1985-91; vis. scientist Rutherford Appleton Lab., Chilton, U.K., 1980-82; prof., head upper atmospheric sci. divsn. Polar Rsch. Inst. China, Shanghai, 1991—; guest prof. Wuhan (China) U., 1993—; mem. Nat. Com. on Antarctic Rsch., China, 1986-94; nat. rep. Solar-Terrestrial and Astronomy Study Working Group, Sci. Com. on Antarctic Rsch., 1988—. Contbr. articles to profl. jours. Recipient Sci. and tech. Progressing awards Dept. Electronics Industry, 1985. Fellow Chinese Inst. Electronics; mem. Chinese Soc. Space Rsch. (mem. coun. 1987). Office: Polar Rsch Inst China, 451 Jinqiao Rd, Shanghai 200129, China

LIU, RU-SHI, chemist, educator; b. Tainan, Taiwan, Apr. 6, 1959; s. Tao-I and Chin-lien (Chou) L.; m. Shu-Fen Hu, Jan. 7, 1982; children: Yun-Ching, Yun-Ping. BS, Soochow U., Taipei, Taiwan, 1981; MS, Tsing Hua U., Hsinchu, Taiwan, 1983, PhD, 1990; PhD, U. Cambridge, Cambridge, Eng., 1992. Assoc. rschr. Material Rsch. Labs. Indsl. Tech. Rsch. Inst., Hsinchu, 1983-86, rsch. scientist, rsch. mgr., 1987-92, sr. rsch. scientist, rsch. mgr., 1993-95; assoc. prof. dept. chemistry Taiwan U., Taipei, 1995-99, prof. dept. chemistry, 1999—. Internat. adv. editor Dalton Trans., 1998-2000; contbbr. articles to profl. jours.; approximately 30 patents in field. Recipient Excellent Young Person prize Govt., Taipei, 1989, Outstanding Rsch. award Indsl. Tech. Rsch. Inst., Hsinchu; named excellent inventor Govt., Taipei, 1995. Mem. Chinese Chem. Soc. (Excellent Young Chemist award 1998), Chinese Soc. Material Sci. Fax: 886-2-23636359. Office: Nat Taiwan U Dept Chemistry, Roosevelt Rd Sect 4, Taipei Taiwan

LIU, RUTH WANG, educator, researcher; b. China, Feb. 25, 1945; d. James D. and Anna H. Wang; m. C.Y. Liu, Feb. 21, 1975; children: Brian, Lora. BS, Union Coll., 1966; MS, U. Calif., San Francisco, 1967; EdD, U. Tenn., 1997. Asst. prof. Sch. of Nursing Loma Linda U., Calif., 1968-72; clin. nurse specialist Cmty. Mental Health, San Francisco, 1972-75; adminstr. Chattanooga Women's Laser Ctr., 1976-95; coord. East Tenn. Consortium for Higher Edn. U. Tenn., 1998—; postdoctoral rsch. assoc. U. Tenn., Knoxville, 1998-2000; dir. Institutional Rsch. and Planning So. Adventist U., Collegedale, Tenn., 2000—; adj. prof. So. Adventist U., Collegedale, Tenn., 1996—, cons. 1975; lectr., rschr., cons., 1990—; cons. Taiwan Adventist Hosp., Taipei, Taiwan, 1974, Atlantic Union Coll., South Lancaster, Mass., 1970; adv. bd. Kiddie Kampus, Collegedale, 1994—. Contbr. articles to profl. jours. Exec. com. Ga. Cumberland Conf. of Seventh-Day Adventists, Calhoun, Ga., 1997—; adv. bd. Seventh-day Adventist Ch., Collegedale, 1999—. Mem. Sigma Theta Tau, Phi Kappa Phi. Seventh-day Adventist. Avocations: music, swimming, hiking.

LIU, SHING HWA, pharmacy educator, pharmacologist; b. Taichung, Taiwan, July 12, 1960; s. Tong Pei Liu and Fu Mei (Yang) Liu-Yang; m. Shiau Hui, May 2, 1992; 1 child. BS, China Med. Coll., Taichung, 1984; PhD, Nat. Taiwan U., Taipei, 1991. Lic. pharmacist. Tchg. asst. Taiwan U., Taipei, 1985-91, instr., 1991-93, assoc. prof., 1993-99, prof., 1999—; cons. Taipei Tchg. Ctr., 1993—, Patent and Trademark Office, Taipei, 1993—; fellow Joint Ann. Conf. Biomed. Sci., 1994-96. Contbr. articles to profl. jours. Recipient Nat. Sci. Coun. award, 1993—. Mem. Pharmacol. Soc. Taiwan, Toxicol. Soc. Taiwan. Buddhist. Avocations: music, reading, walkabouts. Fax: 886-2-23410217. Office: Nat Taiwan U Inst Toxicol, Jen-Ai Rd 1st Sect # 1, 10018 Taipei Taiwan

LIU, SI-KWANG, veterinary pathologist; b. Kwangsi, China; came to U.S., 1959; s. Yeeshao and Shinmei (Yeh) L.; m. Sing-ping Chueh, Dec. 20, 1961; children: Davis, Ernest, Diana, Phillip. DVM, Chinese Vet. Coll., Anshun Kweichow, 1950; PhD, U. Calif., Davis, 1964. Chief veterinarian Taitung Agrl. Rsch. Sta., Taiwan, 1951-56; instr., chief Nat. Taiwan U. Vet. Hosp., Taipei, 1956-59; rsch. asst. U. Calif. Sch. Vet. Med., Davis, 1959-64; pathologist, sci. fellow N.Y. Zool. Soc., Bronx, 1964-88, 88—; pathologist, chief, sr. staff mem. Animal Med. Ctr., N.Y.C., 1964-97; fellow in pathology VA Gen. Hosp., Bronx, 1965-68; sr. pathologist, chmn. dept. pathology Animal Med. Ctr., N.Y.C., 1997-98; from asst. assoc. prof. to prof. N.Y. Med. Coll., N.Y.C., 1966-90; sr. pathologist, assoc. dir. Caspary Rsch. Inst., N.Y.C., 1998—; cons. Pig Rsch. Inst., Taiwan, 1984—; vis. expert Nat. Sci. Coun., Taipei, 1976, 83, 88, 91; vis. prof. Nat. Taiwan U., Taipei, 1976, 88, 91, Nat. Chung Hsing U., Taichung, Taiwan, 1983; adj. prof. medicine Cornell U. Med. Coll., N.Y.C., 1998—; condr. some 300 lectrs., acad. presentations, and discussions in biomed. and sci. confs., U.S. and abroad. Author: An Atlas of Cardiovascular Pathology, 1989; contbr. more than 250 articles to Jour. Vet. Med. Assn., Am. Jour. Pathology, others. Elder Presbyn. Ch. of Newtown, Elmhurst, N.Y., 1970-80. Recipient rsch. award Ralston Purina Co., 1982, Feline Disease award Cornation, 1984, Rsch. Excellence award Beecham, 1986, comparative pathology award Chinese Pathology Soc., 1989, Outstanding Svc. award N.Y.C. Vet. Assn., 1991, Outstanding Svc. award N.Y. State Vet. Medicine Soc., 1991, Rsch. award Japanese Vet. Cardiol. Soc., 1992, Rsch. and Svc. award Chinese Vet. Med. Assn., 1992, award Chinese Vet. Med. Assn., 1993, 95, Postgrad. Edn. award Chinese Vet. Med. Assn., 1995, Rsch. Excellence in Cardiovasc. Diseases award Pig Rsch. Inst., Taiwan, 1995, Disting. Svc. award Animal Med. Ctr., 1999. Mem. Internat. Acad. Pathology, Internat. Skeletal Soc., Internat. Cardiovascular Pathology Soc., N.Y. Acad. Scis., Am. Vet. Med. Assn., Vet. Med. Assn. N.Y.C. (hon.), N.Y. State Vet. Medicine Soc. Office: Animal Med Ctr 510 E 62nd St New York NY 10021-8314

LIU, SUNG-PAN, Taiwanese government official. Mem. legis. Yüan Govt. of Taiwan, Taipei. Office: Legis Yüan, 12F 3-1 Chi-nan Rd, Taipei Taiwan

LIU, T. CHENG-YI, biophysicist; b. Dazhu, Sichuan, China, Oct. 3, 1963; s. Zheng-Chang and De-Shu (Cai) L.; m. Mian Tang, July 5 1993; 1 child, Tang Yi-Fei. BS in Chemistry, Nanjing (China) U., 1983; MS in Phys. Chemistry, Jilin U., Changchun, China, 1986; D of Laser Tech., Huazhong U. Sci. and Tech., Wuhan, China, 1993; Postdoctor of Biophotonics, South China Normal U., Guangzhou, China, 1995. Asst. prof. phys. chemistry Huazhong U. Sci. and Tech., 1986-88; assoc. prof. physics South China Normal U., Guangdong, 1995-99, prof. biophysics, 1999—. Contbr. articles to profl. jours. Avocations: theoretical research on time, running, cold shower. Office: South China Normal Univ, Lab Light Transmission Opti, Guangdong 510631, China

LIU, TAI-FENG, physiologist; b. Shenyang, Liaoning, China, May 22, 1930; s. Dingbin and Cunyi (Yao) L.; m. Hui Lan Li, Aug. 6, 1956; children: Li, Jian, Rong. Bachelor, Peking U., 1953. Asst. Peking U., Beijing, 1953-60, lectr., 1960-79, assoc. prof., 1979-85, prof., 1985—; head sect. of physiology Peking U., 1986-90; chmn. com. of degree Coll. of Life Scis., 1993—. Author: Electrophysiology of Myocardium, 1988 (Prize for Textbook 1989), Electrophysiology of Myocardiac Cells, 2000. Mem. Internat. Soc. for Heart Rsch. (coun. Chinese sect. 1988-96), Methods and Findings in Exptl. and Clin. Pharmacology (contbg. editor 1991—), N.Y. Acad. Scis. Avocations: Chinese medicine, reading novels. E-mail: swltf@pku.edu.cn. Home: Bldg 42 Apt 410 Peking U, Zhong guan yuan, Beijing China Office: Coll of Life Scis, Peking Univ, Beijing 100871, China

LIU, TA-TSAI, former military officer, maritime consultant; b. Nanchang, Kiangsi, Republic of China, Sept. 24, 1929; s. Chia Liu and Shun-Yin Wang; m. Chun-Pin Chen,. Oct. 12, 1967; children: Shu-Yao, Shu-Shun. BS, Naval Acad., Tso-ying, Taiwan, 1949; MA, Naval War Coll., Newport, R.I., 1966, Armed Forces Indsl. Coll., Washington, 1974. Commd. Taiwanese Navy, 1949, advanced through grades to vice-admiral, 1984; dir. plan and program Ministry Nat. Def., Taipei, 1969-70; v.p. Def. Inst. Tech., Tao-Yuan, Taiwan, 1974-76; comdr. 192d Squadron Command, Tso-Ying, 1976-79, 2d Naval Dist., Peng-Hu, Taiwan, 1979-82; comdt. Naval Command and Staff Coll., Taipei, 1982-86; vice min. Ministry of Def., Taipei, 1987-88; dep. comdr.-in-chief Combined Svc. Forces, Taipei, 1988-90; advisor Ministry of Def., 1990-95; chmn. Inst. Maritime Affairs and Policy, 1997-99; sr. advisor Sandalwood Culture Found., Puli, Taiwan, 1993—; observer SEAPOL Conf., Bangkok, 1992, SEAPOL Conf., Kuala Lumpur, Malaysia, 1993, Asia-Pacific Def. Conf., Singapore, 1994, ISPA Conf., Boston, 1994, SEAPOL Tri-Regional Conf., Bangkok, 1994; spkr. Ctr. for Strategic Studies, U. Pretoria, South Africa, 1988. Author: The Direction of Naval Warfare, 1983, The Seapower Essays of VADM Liu Ta-Tsai, 1996; editor: (monographs) Chinese Seapower Symposium, I, 1990, II, 1992; pub. monthly naval mag., 1986. Recipient Order of Loyalty and Diligence, Ministry Nat. Def., 1984, Spl. Cravat of Order of Resplendent Banner, Ministry Nat. Def., 1986, Medal of the Armed Forces, Ministry Nat. Def., 1990, Disting. Svc. Medal, Ministry Nat. Def., 1990. Fellow Soc. for Strategic Studies (sr. rsch. fellow); mem. U.S. Naval Inst. Avocations: swimming, golf, classical music, reading, sight-seeing. Home: Sec 1, 5F 27 Ln 197 Chih-Yu Rd, Shihlin Taipei 111, Taiwan

LIU, TAY-JIAN, mechanical and nuclear engineering educator, researcher; b. Taichung, Taiwan, China, July 20, 1953; s. Po-Liang Liu; m. Chiu-Hsia Ma, Mar. 6, 1982; 1 child, Yen-Ting. BS, Chung-Cheng Inst. Tech., 1976, MS, 1980; PhD in Mech. Engring., Northwestern U., 1989. Engr., asst. researcher Inst. Nuclear Energy Rsch., Lungtan, Taiwan, 1980-85; vis. scholar Northwestern U., Evanston, Ill., 1985-89; assoc. researcher Inst. Nuclear Energy Rsch., Lungtan, 1989—, project mgr., 1991—; assoc. prof. Chung-Yuan Christian U., Chung Li, Taiwan, 1990-96; presenter numerous confs. Contbr. articles in fields of nuclear engring. and thermal-hydraulics to profl. jours. Recipient Nat. Sci. Coun. scholarship, Taiwan, 1992, 98, Outstanding Research award Nat. Exec. Yuan, Taiwan, 1994, Profl. Technique award Inst. of Nuclear Energy Rsch., Taiwan, 1996, 97, Outstanding Project award Taiwan Power Co., 1997, 98. Mem. China Soc. Mech. Engrs., Chung Hua Nuc. Soc. (Best Paper award 1996, 97, 98, 2000), Chung Hua Solar Energy Soc. Avocations: badminton, movies, music, jogging. E-mail: tjliu@iner.aec.gov.tw. Home: 5F #70 Ln 370 Min Tzu Rd, Lungtan 32500, Taiwan Office: Inst Nuclear Energy Rsch, 1000 Wenhua Rd Chiaan, Lungtan 32500, Taiwan

LIU, TIAN-HUA, engineering educator; b. Taoyuan, Taiwan, Nov. 26, 1953; s. Yuan-Shing and Dau Liu; m. Li-Yu Lin, Jan. 16, 1957; children: Shiuan-Jr., Shiuan-Hung, Shiuan-Fu. BS, Nat. Taiwan Inst. Tech., Taipei, 1980, MS, 1982, PhD, 1989. Instr. Nat. Taiwan Inst. Tech., Taipei, 1984-89, assoc. prof., 1989-96, prof. dept. elec. engring., 1996—; vis. scholar U. Wis., Madison, 1990-91; cons. TAI-AN Co., Taipei, 1992-94. Contbr. articles to profl. jours. Lt. Taiwan Army, 1974-76. Recipient A Class Rsch. award Nat. Sci. Coun., Taipei, 1984, 85, 96. Mem. IEEE (sr.). Avocations: swimming, hiking, reading. Office: Nat Taiwan Inst Tech, 43 Keelung Rd, Sect 4, Taipei 106, Taiwan

LIU, VINCENT W(EN-CHUNG), lawyer, educator; b. Keelung, Taiwan, Jan. 14, 1955; s. Chuen-Yeh and Shwu-Neu (Chen) L.; m. Stella S.C. Lu, Nov. 12, 1981; 1 child, Scott C. LLB cum laude, Fu-Jen Cath. U., Taipei, Taiwan, 1978; LLM, U. London, 1985. Assoc. Antony Su, Taipei, 1978-79, Huang & Assocs, Taipei, 1979-86, Tsar & Tsai Law Firm, Taipei, 1986-87, Stephen S. Lee & Assocs., Taipei, 1987-89; sr. ptnr. Lin Liu & Wei Law Offices (formerly Ko Lin & Wei Law Offices), Taipei, 1989—; lectr. dept. law Fu-Jen Cath. U., 1986—/. Contbr. articles to profl. jours. Fellow Soc. Advanced Legal Studies London (assoc.); mem. Chartered Ins. Inst. London, Internat. Bar Assn., Lawasia, Inter-Pacific Bar Assn., Taipei Bar Assn., Keelung Bar Assn., Kaohsiung Bar Assn. Fax: 886-2-87730880. E-mail: liuncotw@ms31.hinet.net. Office: Lin Liu & Wei Law Offices, 7th Fl No 107 Sect 4 Jen Ai Rd, Taipei 106, Taiwan

LIU, WEIHONG, art critic; b. China, Dec. 31, 1956; naturalized, 1997; MA, Wachong Tchr. U., Wuhan, China, 1981, PhD, 1983; MA, Bridgeport U., 1995. Rschr. Iron-Road Tech. Acad., 1983-84; assoc. prof. dept. art history TV U., 1984-86, Sarega Edn. Coll., 1986-90; dir. The Weih Fine Arts Appraisal, Inc., 1991—; chmn. dept. contemporary art Soho Fine Arts Inst., 1998—; art cons. Nat. Edn. Inst., N.Y.C., 1996—, Internat. Art League, N.Y.C., 1998—, China Acad. Arts and Famous Figures, 1996—, Windsor (Conn.) Gallery, 1998—; hon. dean Acad. Oriental Arts, 1999—; sr. hon. advisor Sin-shenzou Art Gallery, Singapore, 1997—; hon. lifetime curator Xubozong Mus. Art, China, 1997—. Author: (texts) Contemporary Art, 1986, Abstract Art, 1988, (plays) The Song of Teachers, 1975 (award of excellent play), Unfathomable Enigma, 1993, The Day of Wedding, 1996; editor-in-chief: Comtemporary Art Am., 1999; art exhibited in group shows at Ringwood (N.Y.) Arts Assn., 1997 (3d pl.), Suburban Art League, Woodbury N.Y., 1997, 98 (award of merit 1997, 98), Queens (N.Y.) Artists Alliance, 1998 (Best in Show), AQA Gallery, Queens, 1998 (People's Choice award), Manhattan Art Internat., N.Y.C., 1998 (Artist Showcase award), Singapore Internat. Art competition, 1998 (award of excellence), Famous Figures Works Exhbn. of Arts Circles, China, 1998 (Silver medal). Named One of 100 Outstanding Artists in China, 1998; recipient Omega award Ringwood Manor Assn. Arts, 1998, 1st prize award Nat. Art League, N.Y., 2000. Mem. Singapore Arts Inst. (sr. hon. academician), Assn. Art Historians, Playwrights Assn., Coll. Art Assn., Appraisers Assn. Am. (cert.), Allied Artists Am. Fax: 718-846-6540. Home: 94-46 85th Rd Apt 2H Woodhaven NY 11421

LIU, WEN CHAU, electrical engineer, educator; b. Yurn-Lin Hsien, Taiwan, June 21, 1957; s. Jier and Chun Hua (Guo) L.; m. Lee Fen Yang, Jan. 31, 1985; 1 child, I-Ping. BS, Nat. Cheng-Kung U., 1979, MS, 1981, PhD, 1986. From rsch. asst. to assoc. prof. Nat. Cheng-Kung U., Tainan, Taiwan, 1979-92; prof. Nat. Cheng-Kung U., Tainan, 1992—; tech. expert elec. engring., China, 1979—, electronic engring., China, 1982—. Patentee in field; contbr. articles to profl. jours. 2d lt. Taiwanese Army, 1986-88. Recipient Acad. Rsch. award Xerox Found., 1994, Acer Found., 1996, 97, 98. Mem. IEEE, Chinese Inst. Engrs. (Excellent Young Engr. award 1994), Chinese Inst. Elec. Engring., Phi Tao Phi. Home: 9 Alley 15 Ln 153, Lin-Shen Rd Sec 1, Tainan 70101, Taiwan Office: Nat Cheng-Kung U Elec Engr, 1 University Rd, Tainan 70101, Taiwan

LIU, WENSEN, acoustical engineer, researcher; b. Nanan, Fujian, China, 1963; came to U.S., 1993; s. Yanghan L. and Fuzhi H.; m. Jing Wu, 1994; 1 child, Joanna. BS, Xiamen U., China, 1983; MS Inst Acoustics, Chinese Acad. Scis., Beijing, China, 1986; PhD, U. Calif., San Diego, 1998, San Diego State U., 1998. Rsch. engr. Shangai Acoustics Lab., China, 1986-93, U. Calif., San Diego, 1998-99; acoustical engr. KSC Industries Inc., San Diego, 1999—. Office: KSC Industries Inc 8653 Avenida Costa Norte San Diego CA 92154-6218

LIU, WU-TSE, virologist, educator; b. Changhua, Taiwan, May 18, 1938; s. Yi-Lang and Ch'au-tau Ch'eng L.; m. Chan-fei Lin Oct. 15, 1967; children: Yi-hsiung, Yi-wen. BS, Nat. Taiwan U., 1962, MS, 1968; PhD, Cath. U. Leuven (Belgium), 1979. Teaching asst. Nat. Taiwan U., Taipei, 1963-66, lectr., 1968-70; vis. fellow NIH, Bethesda, Md., 1974-76; rsch. assoc. Katholic Universiteit te Leuven, 1976-78; assoc. prof. Nat. Yang-Ming Med. Coll., Taipei, 1978-82; prof. Nat. Yang-Ming U., Taipei, 1982—. Editor-in-chief Jour. of Biomed. and Lab. Sci., 1992-96. Mem. Assn. of Lab. Medicine (pres. 1982-88), Chinese Soc. Microbiology (pres. 1999-01), Assn. AIDS (ROC) (pres. 1996-00). Home: 155 Li-nung St 2nd Sec, 11221 Taipei Taiwan Office: Nat Yang-Ming Univ, 11221 Taipei Taiwan

LIU, XIAO, ophthalmologist, biologist; b. Shanghai, China, Feb. 11, 1967; s. Benren Liu and Ke Hu. MD, Shanghai Med. U., China, 1990; PhD, Kyoto U., Japan, 1999. Ophthalmologist Huadong Hosp., Shanghai, China, 1990-94, Nagata Eye Hosp., Ikoma Gen. Hosp., Japan, 1995-98; predoctoral rsch. fellow Northwestern U. Med. Sch., Chgo., 1998-99; postdoctoral rsch. fellow Doheny Eye Inst., U. So. Calif. Keck Sch. Medicine, L.A., 1999—. Recipient Eye Rsch. award Meml. Eye Rsch. Fund, Tokyo, 1994, Travel award Japan Med. Assn., 1995, Toyobo Bio-tech. Travel award, Tokyo, 1997, Eye Rsch. award, China-Japan Med. Assn., 1998. Mem. N.Y. Acad. Scis., Assn. Rsch. in Vision and Ophthalmology, Assn. Online Ophthalmologists. Avocations: writing, stamp collecting. Fax: 323-442-6655. E-mail: xiaoliu@hsc.usc.edu. Office: Doheny Eye Inst 1355 San Pablo St # 401 Los Angeles CA 90033-1088

LIU, XUYI, oncologist, educator, researcher; b. Nanjing, Jiangsu, China, Feb. 10, 1934; d. Dun Zheng Liu and Jing Cheng; m. Bang Zheng Li, May 1, 1965. MD, Chinese Med. U., Shenyang, 1958. Resident in ob-gyn Third Hosp. for Women and Children Chinese Med. U., Shenyang, Liaoning, 1958-60; resident, assoc. chief physician in internal medicine First Hosp. of Nanjing Med. Coll., Nanjing, Jiangsu, 1961-69; resident in oncology Nanjing Ctr. Hosp., 1970-74; resident, prof., advisor dir. internal medicine Beijing Inst. for Cancer Rsch., Beijing Med. U., 1975—; attending physician Inst. Cancer Rsch., Beijing, 1978-82, assoc. chief physician, 1983-87, chief physician, dir. internal oncology dept., 1988—; prof. oncology Beijing Med. U., 1990—; vis. scholar, vis. assoc. prof. pharmacology Thomas Jefferson Med. Coll., Pa., 1985-86; vis. scholar in pharmacology Med. Ctr. George Washington U., Washington, 1986-88. Contbr. articles to med. jours., including Cancer, Pharmacology and Clinics of Chinese Materia Medica, Chinese Jour. Clin. Oncology. Recipient award of sci. and technol. progress Beijing Sci. Com., 1994, nat. key projects award Nat. Sci. Com., 1996. Mem. China Anti-Cancer Assn. (chemotherapy program com. 1990—, oncology chemo-com. commisar), China Pharm. Com. (award 1994). Avocations: classical music, history novels. Office: Beijing Med U Sch Oncology, No 52 Fu-cheng Rd, Beijing 100036, China

LIU, YANPEI, mathematician; b. Tianjin, China, Feb. 1, 1939; s. Wanxin and Cuiyun (Tian) L.; m. Fengxiou Li, July 1, 1967; children: Ying, Fang. Grad., U. Sci. and Tech. China, Beijing, 1963. Rsch. assoc. prof. Academia Sinica, Beijing, 1980-85, rsch. prof., 1986—; PhD advisor Nat. State Coun., Beijing, 1989—; prof. North Jiaotong U., Beijing, 1994—; vis. scholar U. Waterloo, Ont., Can., 1982-84; vis. rsch. scientist Rutgers U., New Brunswick, N.J., 1987, 91; vis. prof. U. Rome, 1989, 92; vis. disting. prof. U. Cin., 1997. Author: Embeddability in Graphs, 1995, Enumerative Theory of Maps, 1999, (in Chinese) Rectilinear Embeddings: Theory and Methods, 1994, (in Chinese) Theory of Rectilinear Layouts, 1996, Transportation Networks: Theory and Methods, 1998; editor: Discrete Math in China, 1993; co-editor: (in Chinese) Handbook of Operations Research Fundamentals, 1999. Home: North Jiaotong U, 801 Tower 2, 100044 Beijing China Office: North Jiatong U, Dept Math, Xizhimen Wai, 100044 Beijing China

LIU, YI-HUA, physics educator; b. Yantai, Shandong, Peoples Republic of China, Dec. 2, 1939; s. Cheng-gong and Xiu-ying (Yu) L.; m. Shu-zhi Zhang, Apr. 11, 1968; children: Bao-hong, Bao-qing. BS, Shandong U., Jinan, China, 1964, MS, 1967. Lectr. Shandong U., Jinan, 1967-92, prof., 1992—; vis. scholar Colo. State U., Ft. Collins, 1980-81. Mem. editl. bd. Jour. Magnetic Materials and Devices, 1997—; translator: Junction Circulators, 1977, Interactions on Metal Surfaces, 1985; co-author: A Dictionary of Solid State Physics, 1995; inventor CoFeNiNbSiB amorphous soft magnetic films (Gold award 1993). Recipient Progressing Sci. and Tech. award State Edn. Commn. of China, 1988, 95, Shandong Province, 1992, 94, Top Notch Pers. on Profl. Tech. award, 1995. Mem. Chinese Electronics Inst. (sr.), Chinese Applied Magnetism Inst. (com. 1992—), Nat. Magnetic Metrological Tech. (com. 1997—). Avocations: radio and electronics, taijiquan sport, swimming. Office: Shandong U, Hongjialou No 5, Jinan Shandong 250100, Peoples Republic of China

LIU, YI-XUN, reproductive biologist, researcher; b. Si-An-Tai, Shandong, China, May 5, 1936; s. Si-Pong Liu and Gua-Zhen Zhou; m. Xue-Kun Zhao; 1 child, Guo-Li. Bachelor's degree, Fudan U., Shanghai, China, 1963; PhD, Academia Sinica, Beijing, 1966. Rsch. assoc. Inst. Zoology, Beijing, 1967-73; postdoctoral fellow Imperial Cancer Rsch. Fund, London, 1974-76; from asst. to assoc. prof. Inst. Zoology, Acad. Sinica, Beijing, 1977-90; postdoctoral prof. U. Calif., San Diego, 1984-86; prof., dir. Inst. Zoology Acad. Sinica, Beijing, 1990—; vis. prof. U. Umeå, Sweden, 1989-92, 98-99, Babraham Inst., Leicester U., 1995-97, 99-2001; prof. cons. mem. Nat. Natural Sci. Found. China, Beijing, 1993-98, 2000-02; vice-dir., prof. State Key Lab. Reproductive Biology for Family Planning, Beijing, 1992-96; mem. scientific com. Nat. Commn. of Family Planning; project holder, advisor initiative implantation rsch. WHO/Rockfeller Found., 1999—. Mem. editl. bd.: Human Reproduction (Oxford); assoc. editor: Developmental and Reproductive Biology, 1991—; mem. editl. bd.: Acta Physiol. Sinica, Jour. Reproductive Medicine, Reproduction and Contraception, Andrology, Basic Med. Scis. and Clinics; contbr. over 140 articles to profl. jours. including Acta Physiol. Sinica, Biology of Reproduction, Endocrinology, Jour. Biol. Chem. Recipient 2d Grade of Natural Sci. award Chinese Acad. Scis., 1984, 85, 92, 93, 95, 97, 1st grade of Natural. award, 1997; named Disting. Internat. Referee of Stature, U. Leicester; postdoctoral fellow Rockefeller Found., N.Y. Population Coun., 1984-86, prof. fellow Swedish Med. Rsch. Coun., 1989-90, Royal Soc. U.K., 1995-97, 99-01. Fellow Chinese Acad. Scis.; mem. AAAS, Chinese Soc. for Reproductive Biology (vice-chmn. 1990-99, chmn. 2000—), Nat. Com. Endocrinology, Reproduction and Metabolism (vice-chmn. 1995—), Soc. for Study of Reproduction (U.S.), N.Y. Acad. Scis. Achievements include coordinating gene expression of tissue type plasminogen activator by granulosa cells and its inhibitor-type-1 by theca cells in the ovary induces ovulation. Fax: 86 10 62588461. E-mail: liuyx@panda.ioz.ac.cn. Office: Inst Zoology Academia Sinica Dept Endocrinology, Inst Zoology Acad Sinica, 19 Zhongguancun Lu/Key Lab, Haidian Beijing 100080, China

LIU, YONG CHENG, chemist, educator; b. Ningbo, Zhejiang, China, Apr. 22, 1963; s. Xiqing and Caihua (Ou) L.; m. Jianghong Qian. PhD in Chemistry, Fudan U., Shanghai, 1996. Asst. prof., dir. Ningbo U., 1991-93; asst. prof. chemistry Fudan U., Shanghai, 1993—; dir. Ningbo Membrane Rsch. Ctr., 1989-93. Contbr. articles to profl. jours.; patentee in field. Recipient 1st prize of sci. and tech. Ningbo U., 1991-93, 3d prize of sci. and tech. Zhejiang Province, 1994-96, Ministry Edn., China, 1999, Unilevel prize Fudan U., 1996. Mem. AAAS, Am. Chem. Soc., Internat. Union Pure and Applied Chemistry, Shanghai Chem. Soc. Avocations: music, sports, novels. Office: U Ark Poultry Sci Bldg Dept Poultry Sci Fayetteville AR 72701

LIU, YONG-YU, molecular biologist; b. Weinan, Shannxi, China, Jan. 2, 1957; came to U.S., 1997; s. Zhen-Rong and Miao-Yuan (Shi) L.; m. Min-Hong Dai, June 15, 1985; 1 child, Xiao-Tian. MD, Suzhou Med. Coll., China, 1984; PhD, Shanghai U. of TCM, 1989. Postdoctoral fellow U. Rome, 1993-96, U. Man., Winnipeg, 1996-97; postdoctoral fellow John Wayne Cancer Inst., Santa Monica, Calif., 1997-99, jr. mem., 1999-2000, asst. mem., 2000—; asst. prof. Suzhou Med. Coll., 1989-93. Contbr. articles to profl. jours.; inventor in field. Mem. AAAS, The Endocrine Soc. (assoc.), Am. Assn. for Cancer Rsch., Am. Soc. for Biochemistry and Molecular Biology. Office: John Wayne Cancer Inst 2200 Santa Monica Blvd Santa Monica CA 90404-2302

LIU, YUEFEI, cardiologist, researcher; b. Changsha, China, July 17, 1959; arrived in Germany, 1989; s. Dongquan Liu and Fengying Cao; m. Lijuan Zhou, July 23, 1988; children: Sizhou, Anna. BA, Hunan Med. U., Changsha, 1983; MS, Hunan Med. U., 1986; MD, U. Ulm, 1992. Resident Xiangya Hosp., Changsha, 1983-87, cardiologist, 1987-89; physician, scientist U. Ulm, Germany, 1989—. Author, editor: Cardiovascular Syndromes, 1996; contbr. articles to profl. jours. Recipient Advancement of Sci. award, 1987. Mem. AAAS. Avocations: chess, go, table tennis. Home: Wilhelmstr 1, D-89231 Neu Ulm Germany Office: Univ Ulm Sports Medicine, Steinhövelstr 9, D89070 Ulm Germany

LIU, YUNCAI, computer vision and image processing specialist; b. Jining City, Shandong, China, Jan. 6, 1948; came to U.S., 1984; arrived in Singapore, 1992; s. Yao dong and Leng Ken (Kong) L.; m. Ping Xin, Dec. 25, 1975; 1 child, Dali. BS, Shandong U., 1974, MS, 1981; PhD, U. Ill., 1990. Elec. engr. Shandong TV & Broadcasting Bd., China, 1974-78; lectr. Shandong U., China, 1981-84; rsch. asst., rsch. assoc. U. Ill., Urbana, 1985-92; sys. cons. Sumitomo Electric Ltd., Singapore, 1992-95, chief cons., rschr., 1995-2000; prof. Shanghai Jiao Tong U., 2000—. Contbr. articles to profl. jours. Mem. IEEE, Intelligent Transp. Soc. Am. Achievements include invention of automatic digital map database generation. Office: Shanghai Jiao Tong U, 1954 Hua Shan Rd, Shanghai 200030, Peoples Republic of China

LIU, YUNG HSIEN, obstetrician, gynecologist, embryologist; b. Kaohsiung, Taiwan, Jan. 2, 1962; s. Chen Hsiung and Yeo Mei (Lin) L.; m. Li Chin Chang, Nov. 10, 1990; children: Yu Ming, Yu Ting, Chun Yen. MB, Kaohsiung (Taiwan) Med. Coll., 1988. Diplomate Taiwan Bd. Ob/gyn. Resident Kaohsiung Med. Coll. Hosp., 1990-94, vis. staff, 1994-98; embryologist staff, gametes and embryos micromanipulation Artificial Reproductive Tech. Lab., Kaohsiung Med. Coll., 1994-98; vis. staff Infertility Clinic, Yuan's Gen. Hosp., 1998-99, dir. IVH Prog., chief OBS/GYN, Dept. Yuan's Genl. Hosp. Mem. AAAS, Assn. Ob/gyn. Taiwan, European Soc. Human Reprodn. and Embryology, Am. Soc. for Reproductive Medicine, N.Y. Acad. Scis. Avocations: music, travelling, art. Home: 169 Howjinn West Rd, Nan Tze Kaohsiung 811, Taiwan Office: Kaohsiung Med Coll, 162 Cheng Kung Rd, Kaohsiung 807, Taiwan

LIU, YUNG SHENG, physicist, research and development executive; b. Anhwei, China, Sept. 23, 1944; came to U.S., 1967; naturalized, 1981; s. Hsin-chi and Li-wen (Wang) L.; m. Ming Lee, Nov. 22, 1969; children: Alan, Jenny. BS, Nat. Taiwan U., 1966; PhD, Cornell U., 1973. Rsch. scientist GE Rsch. Ctr., Schenectady, 1972-98; dep. gen. dir. ITRI Optoelectronics and Sys. Labs, Hsinchu, Taiwan, 1998—; vis. scientist UCLA, 1969; cons. Aerospace Bus. Group, Gen. Electric Co., Binghamton, N.Y., 1977—; adj. prof. physics SUNY, Albany, 1986. Contbr. articles to sci. and profl. jours. Patentee in field of lasers and electro-optics. Mem. adv. com. Hudson Valley Cmty. Coll., Troy, N.Y., 1982—; mem. Congl. Adv. Bd., 1982—; prin. Chinese Sch., Albany, N.Y., 1985. Grantee USAF, Office Naval Rsch., U.S. Army; recipient outstanding achievement award GE Co., 1977, managerial award, 1984, 97, 90, patent medal award, 1986, 89. Fellow Optical Soc. Am., Physics Soc. China; mem. SPIE, IEEE (sr.), Am. Phys. Soc., Sigma Xi, Cornell Club (treas. 1974-75), Chinese Cmty. Club (Albany). Office: OES/ITRI, 167-2 Kuang Ming New Vill 4, 310 Chutung Hsinchu Taiwan Republic of China

LIU, ZHENQUN, inorganic materials and ceramics educator; b. Linchuan, Jiangxi, China, May 5, 1922; s. Yun-qing and Liang-jin (Wu) L.; m. Mingqing Liao, July 30, 1945; children: Li-tian, Li-ren, Li-cai, Li-wen, Ting-Ting, Yuan-Yuan. Grad., Nat. Zhong-Zheng U., China, 1945. Prof. South China U. Tech., Guangzhou, Guangdong, 1961—, v.p., 1981-82, pres., 1982-92; mem. Sci. Consulting Com., Guangdong Province, 1991—; dir. Ceramics Soc., China, 1960-90, Materials Soc., China, 1991—. Author: Kilns and Furnaces of Silicate Industry, 1960, Kilns of Ceramic Industry, 1978, Thermo Equipments of Ceramic Industry, 1982, Kilns and Thermotechnique of Ceramic Industry, 1992. Dep. 6th and 7th Nat. People's Congress, Beijin, 1983-92. Recipient Model Worker award Nat. Edn. System, 1989, 2d award Nat. Constrn. Materials Dept., 1992. Home and Office: South China U of Tech, Guangzhou Guangdong 510641, China

LIU, ZHIXIONG, electron physics scientist; b. Yuyao, Zhejiang, China, Oct. 16, 1936; s. Chengqing Liu and Yuechang Xia; m. Jibing Jiang, Nov. 6, 1967; one child. MS, Peking U., Beijing, 1962. Electronics diplomate. Asst. Peking U., Beijing, 1962-78, lectr., 1978-85, assoc. prof., 1985-93, prof., 1993—. Contbr. articles to profl. jours. Recipient 2nd place Sci. and Tech. Progress prize The State Edn. Com., Beijing, 1995. Mem. Inst. Electronics. Avocations: photography, reading novels, cooking. Office: Dept Electronics, Peking Univ, Beijing 100871, China

LIU, ZIE-YONG, company executive; b. Guilin, Guanxi, People's Republic of China, Jan. 13, 1944; arrived in Singapore, 1953; s. How-Wu Liu and King-yee Leung; m. Gaik-eng Khoo; children: Kang, Fei, Chen, JueJi. BA, Ngee Ann Coll., Singapore, 1966. Dir. Welcome Ent. Ltd., Taipei, Taiwan, 1972-75; chmn. Waycome Enterprises (S) Pte Ltd., Singapore, 1972-79, East Wellsum Industries (S) Pte Ltd., Singapore, 1979—; chmn. Nanjing (People's Republic of China) Sanyi Feed Additive Co., 1991—, Warren Garment Industry, Ltd., Teinjin, People's Republic of China, 1991—, P.T. East Nusantara Indonesia, Jakarta, 1991—, Jirong Amino Acid, Hebei, People's Republic of China, 1992—, Wellsum Holding Pte Ltd., Singapore, 1995—, East Wellsum Biochem. (Nanjing) Ltd., China, 1996. Avocations: poetry, collecting Chinese printing and calligraphy. Office: E Wellsum Ind (S) Pte Menara Batavier 14 Fl, Jln KH Mas Manysur Kav 126, Jakarta 10220, Indonesia

LIU, ZI-KUI, materials science and engineering educator; b. Xiang Dong Tungsten Mine, Cha-Ling, China, Jan. 21, 1963; came to the U.S., 1996; s. Kecai Liu and You Ling Song; m. Weiming Huang; children: Erik, David. BS, Ctrl. South U. Tech., Changsha, China, 1982; MS, U. Sci. and Tech., Beijing, 1985; PhD, Royal Inst. Tech., Stockholm, 1992, docent, 1996. Tchg. staff U. Sci. and Tech., Beijing, 1985-87; rschr. Royal Inst. Tech., Stockholm, 1992-96; rsch. assoc. U. Wis., Madison, 1996-98; sr. rsch. scientist Questek Innovations LLC, Evanston, Ill., 1998; asst. prof. Pa. State U., University Park, 1999—. Assoc. editor CALPHAD; contbr. articles to profl. jours. Bd. mem. Chinese Lang. Sch., Madison, 1996-98. Recipient 3rd pize China Nat. Key Projects, Ministry Metallurgy, China, 1988; China State Coun. expert lecturing scholar, 1998, Career award NSF, 1999. Mem. The Mineral, Metals and Materials Soc. (tech. coms. on alloys phases, nuc. materials and edn., TMS Young Leader 1998), Am. Soc. Metals (alloy phase diagram, tech. com. thermodynamics and phase equilibria), Materials Rsch. Soc., Sigma Xi. Avocation: tennis, skiing, squash, golf. E-mail: zikui@psu.edu. Office: Pa State Univ 222 Steidle Bldg University Park PA 16802-5006

LIUKKO, ANNE PĀIVI KRISTIINA, psychiatric and medical nurse; b. Lahti, Finland, May 29, 1957; d. Lasse Paavo Antero and Marja-Lea (Luhtanen) L. Practical nurse's diploma, Helsinki 4th Inst. Nursing, Finland, 1980; student, U. Helsinki, 1995—. RN with splty. in internal, surg., and psychiat. nursing; lic. practical nurse, group counselor. Nurse's aide, practical nurse Lahti City Hosp., 1977-78; practical nurse 1st dept. medicine Helsinki Univ. Cen. Hosp., 1980-81, practical nurse dept. radiotherapy, 1981-85; healthcare asst. Health Ctr. of City of Helsinki, 1986; relief nurse, receptionist Helsinki Deaconess Inst., 1986; practical nurse Sanatorium Hahlama Venofeshlit, Israel, 1988, Helsinki Jewish Hosp., 1988, Helsinki Univ. Cen. Hosp., 1991; nurse Red Cross Security Svc., Helsinki, 1995—; therapist, counsellor Helsinki Saalem Ch., 1996—; group counselor Helmi R.Y., Helsinki, 1998—; rsch. work Aurora Karamzin and Helsinki Deaconness Inst., 1980, Somali refugees in the Finnish Health Care Sys., 1994, Women's Internat. Zionist Orgn., 1994; project work female genital mutilation victims, 1994; group counselor Helsinki Psychiat. Patients Assn. Vol. worker Kibbutz Ma'ale Hahamisha, Israel, 1983-84, 85-86; pvt. vol. nurse Ma'on Netanya, Israel, 1989-90; mem. Amnesty Internat., Helsinki, 1994—, Red Cross, Helsinki, 1995—, Internat. Christian Embassy, Finland, 1991—, Finnish Health Care and Social Union, 1991—; mem. bd. execs. Morris Cerurro World Evangelism, 1992—. Recipient Pilgrim of Jerusalem award, 1995. Mem. AAAS, Finnish Group Psychotherapy Assn., Gospel Bus. Men's Fellowship Internat., N.Y. Acad. Scis., The Women's Internat. Zionist Orgn. Avocations: music, reading, gym, traveling, dancing. E-mail: annli@dlc.fi. Office: Lapinlahdenkatu 25C, 00180 Helsinki Finland

LIVERGOOD, ROBERT FRANK, prosecutor; b. Akron, Ohio, Dec. 20, 1957; s. Robert Burton and Rita Veronica (Haidnick) L.; m. Sandra Anne Ko, Aug. 5, 1983; children: Robert Santos, Jacob Christopher, Sarah Nicole. BA, St. Louis U., 1981, M in Health Adminstrn., 1983, JD, 1988. Bar: Mo. 1988, Ill. 1989, U.S. Dist. Ct. (ea. dist.) Mo. 1989, U.S. Dist. Ct. (so. dist.) Ill. 1989. Dir. market rsch. St. Joseph's Hosp. Kirkwood, Mo., 1983-85; assoc. Husch & Eppenberger, St. Louis, 1988-90; asst. prosecuting atty. Office of the Prosecutor, Clayton, Mo., 1990—. Editor St. Louis U. Law Jour., 1986-87, mng. editor, 1987-88. Vol. lawyer Voluntary Lawyers Program, St. Louis, 1988-90; spkr. St. Louis (Mo.) County and Mcpl. Police Acad., 1993-94. Mem. ABA, Ill. State Bar Assn., Bar Assn. Met. St. Louis. Avocations: martial arts, amateur radio. Office: Office of the Prosecutor 100 S Central Ave Clayton MO 63105-1732

LIVERIS, MARCUS, retired university administrator; b. Perth, Western Australia, May 15, 1931; s. Apostolos Constantine and Maria (Andros) L.; m. Leonie Beth Wood; children: Paul, Alexander, Maria-Eleni. BSc, U. Western Australia, 1952, PhD, 1965; D of Tech. (hon.), Curtin U., 2000. Lectr. Perth (Western Australia) Tech. Coll., 1956-65; fellow Nat. Rsch. Coun. of Can., 1965-66; head dept. chemistry Western Australian Inst. Tech., 1967-69, asst. dir. applied scis., 1970-74; dep. vice chancellor, v.p. health scis. Curtin U. Tech., Perth, Western Australia, 1987-97; pres. Asia-Pacific Acad. Consortium Pub. Health, 1993-99; chmn. bd. dirs. Royal Perth Hosp., 1985-97. Pres. Cancer Found. of Western Australia, 1990-95, Australian Hosp. Assn., 1992-93. Named to Order of Brit. Empire, Queen of Eng., 1982, Western Australian Citizen of Yr. (professions category) 1985. Fellow Australian Coll. Edn., Royal Australian Chem. Inst. Home: 28 Kalari Dr, City Beach Western Australia

LIVERS, THOMAS HENRY, fundraiser for nonprofit organizations; b. Louisville, Sept. 15, 1946; s. Henry Edgar and Katherine (Ellison) L.; m. Karen Culter, June 13, 1970 (div. June 1988); children: Zehra Livers Hudson, Floyd Forrest; m. Beverly Morgan Dennis, June, 1996; children: Eric, Jarrett Dennis. BA, U. Louisville, 1970; postgrad., Butler U., Indpls., U. Conn., Bridgeport. Cert. fund raising exec. Elephant zookeeper Louisville Zoo, 1968-70; curator Indpls. Zoo, 1970-72; zoo dir. Breadsley Park Zoo, Bridgeport, 1972-75; exec. dir. East Bay Zool. Soc., Oakland, Calif., 1975-77; zoo supt. Lafayette Zool. Park, Norfolk, Va., 1977-82; exec. dir. Nature Ctr. of Charlestown, Devault, Pa., 1982-85, Cmty. Health Task Force, Phila., 1985-86; regional dir. Nat. Soc. to Prevent Blindness, Harrisburg, Pa., 1986-89; exec. dir. Nat. Kidney Found., Ind., 1990-92; mortgage broker, loan officer Louisville, Ky., 1992-94; dir. devel. Holy Rosary Acad., Louisville, Ky., 1994-96, Presbyn. Cmty. Ctr., Louisville, 1996-98, Cedar Lake Found., LaGrange, Ky., 1998-2000, Bridgehaven, Inc., Louisville, 2000—; cons. Conn. Gen. Assembly, Hartford, Conn., 1973-75; bd. dirs. Ind. Organ Donors Adv. Bd., Indpls., 1990-92. Writer newspaper column Phoenixville News, 1983-85; contbr. articles to mags. Bd. dirs. earth day Louisville Zoo, Louisville Audubon Soc., Louisville Nature Ctr., Kentuckiana Children's Ctr. Mem. Nat. Soc. Fund Raising Execs. (cert.), Focus Louisville, U. Club Louisville, Exch. Club U.S. (hon. life). Avocations: oil painting, gardening, reading, writing, travel. Office: Bridgehaven Inc 2204 Dixie Hwy Louisville KY 40210-2244

LIVI, IVAN DAVID, retired educational administrator; b. Belle Vernon, Pa., June 17, 1920; s. Attilio Ausilio and Maria (Lazzari) L.; m. Annabelle Rigotti, Apr. 14, 1945; 1 child, Darla. Student, U. Pitts., 1958-64. Technician Mid-States Aviation, Northbrook, Ill., 1945-51; instr. Pitts. Inst. of Aero., 1951-54, dir. tng., 1954-64, v.p., 1964-72, exec. dir., 1972-78, pres., 1978-95; ret., 1995; pres. Aviation Tech. Edn. Coun., Harrisburg, Pa., 1975-77. Contbr. articles to profl. jours. Recipient Award of Excellence FAA, 1989, Clifford Ball award Aero Club of Pitts., 1990, Award of Excellence Profl. Aviation Maint. Assn., 1991. Mem. Pa. Assn. Pvt. Sch. Adminstrs. (pres. 1977-79). Avocations: music, science, astronomy. Home: 210 Melvin Dr Pleasant Hill PA 15236*

LI VIGNI, SHANA MARGARET VERONICA REICHL, disc jockey; b. Camp Lejeune, N.C., Apr. 10, 1953; d. Karl Otto and Veronica Mary (Steiner) Reichl; m. John Rocky Livigni, July 3, 1978 (divorced); children: Stephen, Anthony, Jilly. Student, Western Mich. U., 1971-74; eminence degree, Pasadena City Coll. Disc jockey Stas. WYYY, WMUK-FM, WIDR-FM, Kalamazoo, 1971-74, Sta. KWBB, Wichita, Kans., 1974, Sta. KFRC, San Francisco, 1974-76, Sta. KHJ, Hollywood, Calif., 1976-78, Sta. KEZY-AM-FM, Anaheim, Calif., 1978-80, Sta. KROQ-FM, Pasadena, Calif., 1980, Sta. KLOS-FM, L.A., 1980-86, Sta. KLSX-FM, L.A., 1987-95; asst. program dir., music dir., on-air personality KPCC-FM 89.3, Pasadena, 1996—; instr. radio internship courses Pasadena City Coll.; spkr. numerous radio forums, TV shows and newspapers, San Francisco, L.A., 1974—; spkr. on entertainment and radio industry various seminars, colls. and high schs.; TV guest various programs; instr. Inside Radio UCLA Ext., summer 1994, 95; instr. radio mentoring and internship program Pasadena City Coll., 1996—; instr. radio comm. L.A. County Office of Edn.'s Regional Occupl. Program, 1996—; radio cons. KAZN-AM 1300, Pasadena, 1997—; pres., founder All-Star Prodns., 1993—. Fundraiser, on-air disc jockey Cystic Fibrosis, Childrens Hosp. L.A., 1978, 84-88, Muscular Dystrophy Assn., L.A., 1975, 88, Rock Relief for Africa, L.A., 1985, Vietnam Vets. Am. Fund, L.A., 1988; active Glendale C. of C., YMCA. Recipient outstanding svc. award L.A. County Bd. Suprs., 1986. Mem. AFTRA. Avocations: writing, cooking, music, swimming. Office: KPCC-FM 1570 E Colorado Blvd Pasadena CA 91106-2003

LIVINGOOD, WILSON S., law enforcement official; b. Phila., Oct. 1, 1936; s. Clarence S. and Louise S. L.; m. Mari Louise Vatter, Feb. 21, 1998; stepchildren: Sarah, Elizabeth, Anne. BS in Police Adminstrn., Mich. State U., 1961. Spl. agt. U.S. Secret Svc., Dallas, 1961-69, spl. agt. in charge, 1969-86; deputy asst. dir. U.S. Secret Svc., 1986-89, exec. asst. to dir., 1989-95; sgt. at arms U.S. Ho. of Reps., Washikngton, 1995—; bd. dirs. Fed. Law Enforcement Tng. Ctr., Glynco, Ga. With USN, 1954-57. Mem. Nat. Sheriffs Assn., Internat. Assn. Chiefs of Police (exec. com. 1993-99), Belle Haven Country Club (past bd. dirs.). Episcopalian. Avocations: tennis, running, skiing, sailing, golf. Office: US Ho of Reps H-124 The Capitol Washington DC 20515-0001

LIVINGSTON, CAROLYN HARRIS, music educator; b. Cookeville, Tenn., Jan. 7, 1936; d. Frazier and Myrtle (Lee) H.; m. Frank W. Medley, Jr., June 28, 1955 (dec. Dec. 1967); children: Frank, Jane, Jennifer Medley Martin; m. Jesse B. Livingston, Sept. 1, 1969 (dec. Jan. 1993); stepchildren: Jeffrey, Patrick, Laura Livingston Nuttle; m. Burton Zitkin, May 29, 2000. Student, U. Md., 1957-58; BS, Tenn. Tech. U., 1959; MEd, U. Fla., 1981, PhD, 1986. Tchr. music pvt. practice, Bowie, Md., 1960-68; music specialist Prince Georges City Schs., Bowie, Md., 1968-69; tchr. music pvt. practice, Gainesville, Fla., 1970-80; dir. choirs 1st Luth. Ch., Gainesville, Fla., 1976-83; music specialist Putnam County Schs., Cookeville, Tenn., 1984-86, Memphis City Schs., 1986-87; asst. prof. U. R.I., Kingston, 1987-93, assoc. prof., 1993-99, dir. grad. studies in music, 1997-99, prof., 1999—. Mem. editl. bd. Bulletin Hist. Rsch. Music Edn., 1990—, Jour. Hist. Rsch. Music Edn.; contbr. articles to profl. jours. Founder, dir. U. R.I. Childrens Chorus, 1993-99. Mem. Music Educators Nat. Conf., History Spl. Rsch. Interest Group (vice-chair 1997-99, chair 1999-01), Music Tchrs. Nat. Assn., R.I. Music Tchrs. Assn. (pres. 1992-94), Sigma Alpha Iota, Pi Kappa Lambda, Kappa Delta Pi, Phi Kappa Phi. Lutheran. Avocations: needlework, gardening, travel. E-mail: musiced@uri.edu. Home: 31 Rosemary St Cranston RI 02920-8157 Office: U RI Dept Music Kingston RI 02881

LIVINGSTON, JEFFERY C., history educator; b. Dayton, Ohio, Aug. 20, 1957; s. Charles Hugh and Nancy Carol Livingston; m. Julie Ann Archer, June 6, 1987; children: Jade, Levi. BA, Miami U., Oxford, Ohio, 1980; MA, U. Toledo, Ohio, 1985, PhD, 1989. Prof. history Calif. State U., Chico, 1989—, campus master tchr., 1999—; prin. investigator North State History-Social Sci. Project, Chico, 1995—; cons. U.S. Dept. Edn. Jacob Javits Fellowship, Washington, 1993-95, Calif. Commn. on Tchr. Credentialing, 1994-95. Contbr. numerous articles to profl. jours. Vol., mem. program coun. KZFR Cmty. Radio, Chico, 1997—; mem. Chico Peace and Justice Ctr., 1997—. Mem. Orgn. Am. Historians, Soc. for Historians of Am. Fgn. Rels., ACLU, Amnesty Internat., Phi Alpha Theta, Phi Kappa Phi, Phi Eta Sigma. Avocations: sports, music, travel. E-mail: jlivingston@csuchico.edu. Home: 721 Brookwood Way Chico CA 95926-1732 Office: Calif State U History Dept Chico CA 95929-0001

LIVINGSTON, MARGERY ELSIE, missionary, clinical psychologist; b. Petoskey, Mich., Oct. 29, 1940; d. David Eugene and Beryl Mae (Herrington) L. BS with honors, Taylor U., Upland, Ind., 1962; MA with high honors, Wheaton (Ill.) Coll., 1983; student, U. Paris Sorbonne, 1970. Lic. psychologist, Pa. Tchr. Waterford (Mich.) Sch. Sys., 1962-64; ednl. missionary, county dir. BCM Internat., Union County, N.J., 1965-69; ednl. missionary BCM Internat. and AIM Internat., Albertville and Paris, France, 1969-70; ednl. missionary, technician BCM Internat. and AIM Internat., Watsa, Democratic Republic of Cong, 1970-81; counselor, therapist BCM Internat./AIM Internat. Amani Counseling Ctr., Nairobi, Kenya, 1983-84; organizer, dir. counseling dept., counselor, cons. BCM Internat., Upper Darby, Pa., 1985-97; organizer, dir. mem. care ministries BCM Internat., Upper Darby, 1998-2000, mem. care ministries, cons., 2000—; guest lectr. Bunia (Dem. Rep. Congo) Theol. Sem., 1984, Adi (Dem. Rep. Congo) Bible Inst., 1978, Aru (Dem. Rep. Congo) Bible Inst., 1978, Todro (Dem. Rep. Congo) Bible Inst., 1980; organizer/facilitator Missions and Mental Health-East, Mt. Bethel, Pa., 1995-97; guest lectr. Communauté Evangelique Ctr. de l'Afrique Chs., Dem. Republic of Congo, 1991; spkr. in field. Editor: Commit Thy Way, 1994; author: (Bible study series) Living in Community, 1980; contbr. articles to profl. jours. Spkr., adj. staff Rockford (Mich.) Bapt. Ch., 1965—, Haven Reformed Ch., Kalamazoo, Mich., 1978—, Clinton Hill Bapt. Ch., Union, N.J., 1965—, Silvercrest Bapt. Ch., Waterford, Mich., 1966—, First Congl. Ch., Rockford, Mich., 1985—, North Plainfield (N.J.) Bapt. Ch., 1988—; facilitator Bible Club work, Zaire, 1985—. Billy Graham Evangelistic Assn. scholar, 1981-83. Mem. APA (assoc.), Am. Assn. of Christian Counselors (spkr. regional conf. 1999), Assn. N.Am. Missions, Christian Therapists Bible Study, Episcopal Bible Study. Baptist. Avocations: poetry, clarinet, walking, aerobic weight-lifting, swimming. Office: 237 Fairfield Ave Upper Darby PA 19082-2206 Regional Office: BCMI Western Mich 710 Baldwin St Jenison MI 49428-9706

LIVINGSTON, MYRAN JAY, author, film writer, director and producer; b. N.Y.C., Mar. 19, 1934; s. Myran Jabez and Anne Josephine (White) L.; m. Elizabeth Rasmussen, July 28, 1956 (div. May 1971); 1 child, Lisa Browning; m. Bernice Helen Beck, Nov. 8, 1971; children: Simon Jabez, Sarah Gustine. Student, Kenyon Coll., 1952-56, U.C.L.A., 1957-58. Writer/dir. CBS TV Network, L.A., 1956-64, McCann-Erickson, San Francisco, 1965-71, Eastman Kodak, Rochester, N.Y., 1980-83; owner, operator Promethean Prodns., L.A., 1983-96; guest lectr. Coll. of Marin, San Francisco, 1972-73, Loyola Marymount U., L.A., 1979, Rochester Inst. of Tech., 1982. Author: (novels) The Prodigy, 1979, The Synapse Function, 1985,. Tchr. in comml. prodn. San Francisco Women in Advertising, 1976, The Del Monte Corp., San Francisco, 1970, Van Nuys (Calif.) H.S., 1980, Mira Catalina Sch., Palos Verdes, Calif., 1986. Recipient 7 Golden Eagle awards Coun. on Internat. Theatrical Events, 1982-84, 1st place Gold Camera award U.S. Indsl. Film Festival, 1984, CLIO for "Most Beautiful Spot" award Bullocks, 1978, 4 Telly Silver and Bronze awards 14th and 17th Ann. Competition, 1993,96. Mem. Writer's Guild of Am., The Author's Guild. Episcopalian. Avocations: classical piano, songwriting. Home and Office: Promethean Prodns 12459 Centerville Rd Chico CA 95928-8329

LIVINGSTONE, TRUDY DOROTHY ZWEIG, dancer, educator; b. N.Y.C., June 9, 1946; d. Joseph and Anna (Feinberg) Zweig; m. John Leslie Livingstone, Aug. 7, 1977; 1 child, Robert Edward. Student, Charles Lowe Studios, N.Y.C., 1950-52, Nina Tinova Studio, N.Y.C., 1953-56, Ballet Russe de Monte Carlo, N.Y.C., 1956-57, Bklyn. Coll., 1964-66; BA in Psychology cum laude, Boston U., 1968, MEd, 1969; postgrad., Serena Studios, Carnegie Hall Ballet Arts, N.Y.C., 1973-74. Tchr. Millis (Mass.) Pub. Schs., 1969-72, Hebrew Acad. Atlanta, 1974-76; profl. dancer various orgns. including Rivermont Country Club, Jewish Community Ctr., Callanwolde Performing Arts Ctr., Atlanta, 1974-84; founder, owner, instr. dance Sasha Studios, Atlanta, 1974-77; owner Trudy Zweig Livingstone Studios, Wellesley, Needham, Mass., 1987-88, Palm Beach, Fla., 1989—; judge dance competition Atlanta Council Run-Offs, 1976. Vol. League Sch., Bklyn., 1965, Kennedy Meml. Hosp., Brighton, Mass., 1969, Nat. Affiliation for Literacy Advances, Santa Monica, Calif., 1982. Mem. Am. Alliance for Health, Phys. Edn., Recreation and Dance, Poets of the Palm Beaches, L.A. Athletic Club, Wellesley Coll. Club, Governor's Club (West Palm Beach). Avocation: writing poetry.

LIWANAG, RODEL MORA, minister; b. Casiguran, Aurora, The Philippines, Apr. 18, 1955; came to the U.S., 1992; s. Benjamin Curitana and Eledina Mora Liwanag; m. Josephine Cuenca, Feb. 10, 1980 (dec. Nov. 1998); children: Jashen Mark, Jaminelli Joyce, Jasher Jan, Jether Joy Amor. BA in Religion, Adventist U. of Philippines, Silang, 1980; M in Pastoral Studies, Adventist Internat. Inst., Silang, 1990. Ordained pastor Seventh-day Adventist Ch., 1986. Dist. pastor Seventh-day Adventist Ch., Manila, 1980-92; ch. pastor Seventh-day Adventist Ch., San Angelo, Tex., 1993-96; dist. pastor Seventh-day Adventist Ch., Dalhart, Tex., 1996-98, Abilene, Tex., 1998—; mem. exec. com., bd. dirs. Texico Conf. and Texico Conf. Assn., Amarillo, 1996—. Chaplain Coon Meml. Hosp., Dalhart Ministerial Alliance, 1997-98. Named Outstanding Pastor, Clark Air Base, Pampanga, The Philippines, 1991. E-mail: rmliwanag@empmail.com. Home: 4401 Ridgemont Dr # 1212 Abilene TX 79606-8703 Office: 4909 Canyon Dr Amarillo TX 79110-2329

LIZARDOS, EVANS JOHN, mechanical engineer; b. N.Y.C., Mar. 25, 1936; s. John George and Pearl (Arapoudis) L.; m. Helen Samaras, May 15, 1960; children: John E., Paul E., Lynn Lizardos Bloecker. B in Mech. Engring., Poly. U., Bklyn., 1960. Lic. profl. engr., N.Y. Draftsman Clinton Bogert Assocs., N.Y.C., 1953-56; designer Guy B. Panero, N.Y.C., 1956-60; assoc. Piccirillo & Brown, N.Y.C., 1960-65; pres., CEO Lizardos Engring. Assocs., Albertson, N.Y., 1965—. Contbr. chpts. to books and articles to profl. jours. treas. L.I. Heart Coun., 1992-94, chmn. bd., 1994-98; contbr. Guide Dog Assn. for Blind. Fellow ASHRAE (bd. govs. 1974-75, rec. sec. 1975-76, v.p. 1977-78, pres. 1978-79, chmn. handbook); mem. Cons. Engrs. Coun. N.Y. State (pres. 1986-87), Assn. Energy Engrs. (charter), Am. Solar Energy Soc., ASME, Am. Soc. Plumbing Engrs. (charter, chpt. sec. 1975-77), Constrn. Specification Inst. (profl.), Internat. Dist. Heating and Cooling Assn., Inst. Noise Control Engring., Instrument Soc. Am. (sr.), Internat. Solar Energy Soc., Nat. Fire Protection Assn., NSPE, Refrigeration Engrs. and Techs. Assn. (mem.-at-large). Greek Orthodox. Avocations: model railroading, running. Office: 200 Old Country Rd Mineola NY 11501-4235

LIZT, SARA ENID VANEFSKY, lawyer, educator; b. USSR, Mar. 10, 1913; came to U.S., 1921; d. Max and Yocheved (Koval) Vanefsky; widowed. LLB, CUNY, Bklyn., 1941, LLM, 1962. Bar: N.Y. 1946, U.S. Dist. Ct. (so. and ea. dists.) N.Y. 1946. Pvt. practice Bklyn., 1946—; prof. CUNY, Bklyn., 1966-80. Address: 2060 E 19th St Brooklyn NY 11229-3943

LJØSTAD, TORSTEIN TORBERG, retired airline company executive; b. Oslo, Apr. 6, 1930; s. Kjetil and Margit (Loftesnes) L.; m. Vivi Synnøve Søgaard, Sept. 15, 1955; children: Pål Torstein, Bård Even. Cand.jur., U. Oslo, 1955; MA in Polit. Sci., Columbia U., 1957. Sec. Ministry of Fgn. Affairs, Oslo, 1957-59; sec. Scandinavian Airlines, Stockholm, 1959-64, dir. fgn. affairs, 1964-69; area mgr. Mid. East Scandinavian Airlines, Beirut, Lebanon, 1969-73; regional mgr. East Europe Scandinavian Airlines, Stockholm, 1973-74, v.p. cargo, 1974-80, v.p. fgn. affairs, 1980-82; pres. Norwegian Airlines, Oslo, 1982-97. Author: Chartering of Aircraft, 1957; contbr. articles to profl. jours. Lt. Norwegian Army Res. Mem. Internat. C. of C. (air transport com. 1982-97), Norwegian Aero Club (coun. 1984—). Avocations: skiing, golf, phys. tng., mountain hiking. Home: Åsstubben 27, 0381 Oslo Norway

LJUBIĆ, SPOMENKA, physician, researcher; b. Gjurgjevac, Croatia, July 4, 1959; d. Petar and Smiljka (Fuček) L. MD, Med. Faculty, Zagreb, Croatia, 1982, MS, 1987. Clin. drug investigator Pliva Co., Zagreb, Croatia, 1982-88; internist Vuk Vrhovac U. Clinic, Zagreb, 1994—. Contbr. articles to profl. jours. Mem. European Assn. for the Study of Diabetes, Croatian Soc. for Clin. Pharmacology and Therapy. Avocations: music, literature, traveling. Home: Donji Prečac 30, 10000 Zagreb Croatia Office: Vuk Vrhovac U Clinic, Dugi Dol 4A, 10000 Zagreb Croatia

LLANOS, LUIS SOCORRO, retired public administrator, mediator, arbitrator, public affairs consultant; b. St. Croix, V.I., June 30, 1940; s. Felix and Eulogia (Encarnacion) L.; m. Joycelyn Louise Bough, Oct. 23, 1964; children: Elaine Eulogia Schuster, Luis Socorro, Eric Andre Farid. Cert. adminstrv. law, U. Nev., Reno, 1984; cert. occupl. safety and health mgmt., U. So. Calif., 1984; BS, Western States U., 1986, MBA, 1993; cert. labor rels. studies, Cornell U., 1988; cert. stratgic leadership, Duke U., 1991; cert. mediation theory and practice, Ctr. for Dispute Resolution, 1993; cert. arbitration, VI-PERB, 1994; cert. mediation, U. Mo., 1994. Cert. hazard control mgr. Compliance officer Divsn. Occupl. Safety and Health V.I. Dept. Labor, 1973-74, chief compliance officer, 1974-76, supervisory compliance officer, 1976-77, asst. dir., 1977-80, asst. commr.-OSH, 1980-87, asst. commr. labor, 1987-89, commr. of labor, 1989-94; served on V.I. Bd. of Tax Rev., 1979-89, V.I. Pub. Employees' Rels. Bd., 1983-89, Vocat. Edn. Adv. Coun., 1984-89, V.I. Territorial Emergency Mgmt. Coun., 1989-94, Gov.'s Overall Econ. Devel. Com., 1990-94, V.I. Water and Power Authority, 1991-94. Elected mem. Holy Cross Parish Coun., St. Croix, 1982; mem. Holy Cross choir, 1958; sec. V.I. Wage Bd., 1991-94, V.I.-PERB, 1989-94; chmn. Labor Task Force, Turnbull-James '98 Transition Team, 1998. Served with U.S. Army, 1962-64. Recipient recognition certs. U.S. Dept. Labor-OSHA, V.I. Labor-Mgmt. Com., U.S. Bur. Labor Statistics, Hispanos Unidos, Fed. Mediation and Conciliation Svc., others. Fellow Acad. Polit. Sci., 1994-98; mem. Am. Pub. Health Assn., Am. Arbitration Assn., KC, (charter St. Croix, treas. 1974-75). Democrat. Roman Catholic. Avocations: photography, classical guitar, choir, woodwork. Office: PO Box 850 Kingshill VI 00851-0850

LLENA, REY LAPICEROS, secondary education educator, consultant; b. Canla-On, The Philippines, May 25, 1960; came to U.S., 1990; s. Bonifacio de la Cruz Llena and Maxima Pueblos Lapiceros; m. Suzalin Dinawanao Ramos, June 25, 1983; children: Shari May, Reinalyn, Czarina, Rey Ramos. BS in Chemistry, Silliman U., Dumaguete, The Philippines, 1980; MS in Water Chemistry, U. Wis., 1992. Cert. chemistry and sci. tchr., N.Y. Mem. faculty dept. chemistry Silliman U., 1980-81; environ. chemist Philippine Geothermal Project, Dumaguete, 1981-82, environ. officer, 1983-88; environ. analyst Philippine Nat. Oil Co., Manila, 1982-83, ecologist, 1988-89, environ. planner, 1989-90; environ. specialist Planning Rsch. Corp.-EMI, Chgo., 1992-93; tchr. math. and sci. N.Y.C. Bd. Edn., 1995—; aromatherapy cons.; founder, CEO Ylang Ylang Philippines Inc. and Clean Aramotic Natural Environ. Systems (CANES), Inc.; dream interpreter and numerologist, 1993-95. Named Outstanding Tchr. of Yr. N.Y.C., 1997. Mem. ASCD, Natural Oils Rsch. Assn., Air and Waste Mgmt. Assn., United Fedn. Tchrs. (chpt. leader 1995—). Roman Catholic. Avocations: aromatherapy, webpage development, grant proposal writing. E-mail: ReyLlena@aol.com. Office: Ylang Ylang Philippines Inc 6126 Riverdale Ave Bronx NY 10471-1009

LLERANDI PHIPPS, CARMEN GUILLERMINA, nutritionist and dietitian; b. Aguadilla, Puerto Rico, Jan. 6, 1958; came to U.S., 1979; d. Pablo Manuel Llerandi Alum and Carmen Estela (Santana Phipps) Llerandi; m. June 21, 1981 (div. 1990); 1 child, Paul Gabriel Vallejo Llerandi. BA, Glasboro (N.J.) State Coll., 1984; postgrad., Loma Linda (Calif.) U., 1994—. Lic. and registered dietitian. Pub. health nutritionist Sa Lantic Health Svc., Hammonton, N.J., 1989-90; clin. mgmt. dietician Clifton T. Perkins Psychiat. Hosp., Jessup, Md., 1990-91; adminstrv. clin. dietician Brownsville (Tex.) Med. Ctr., 1991-93; clin. dietician, pediatric outpatient clin. dietitian Loma Linda U. Childrens Hosp., 1993-95; nutrition cons. Rio Grande Valley Midway House, Inc., Harlingen, Tex., 1993—; chief adminstrv. sect. Jerry L. Pettis VA Med. Ctr., Loma Linda, 1995—; MPH Health Edn. and Promotion Edn. Loma Linda U., 2000-; mem. bd. dietetic and nutrition depts. U. Tex., 1991-93. Mem. Am. Dietetic Assn., Am. Assn. Diabetes Educators, Seventh Day Adventist Dietetic Assn., Nutrition Edn. Assn. Office: Jerry L Pettis Meml Vets Med Ctr 11201 Benton St Loma Linda CA 92357-1000

LLEWELLYN, DAVID THOMAS, financial services educator; b. London, U.K., Mar. 3, 1943; s. Alfred George and Elsie Alexander (Frith) L.; m. Wendy Elizabeth James, Sept. 19, 1970; children: Mark, Rhys. BSc in Econs., London Sch. Econs., 1964. Economist Unilever NV, Rotterdam, Holland, 1964-65, HM Treasury, London, 1965-68; lectr. Nottingham U., U.K., 1968-73; economist Internat. Monetary Fund, Washington, 1973-76; prof. money, banking Loughborough U., U.K., 1976—; cons. Harlow Butler Ueda, London, 1981-99, Garban Intercapital P.C., 1999—; mem. adv. bd. Halifax Bldg. Soc., 1987-93; pub. interest dir. Personal Investment Authority, London, 1994—; mem. internat. adv. bd. Italian Bankers Assn.; mem. exec. bd. European Fin. Mgmt. Assn.; mem. adv. bd. NCR Fin. Solutions Group, 1996. Author: International Financial Integration, 1980, Evolution of Financial Systems, 1985, Regulation of Financial Systems, 1986, Surveys of Monetary Economics, 1992, Financial Regulation: Why, How and Where Now?, 1997, The New Economics of Banking, 1999. Mem. Societe Universitaire Europeene Recherches Financieres, 1998-99, pres., 2000—. Fellow Royal Soc. Arts, Chartered Inst. Bankers. Avocations: boating, music, cooking, international travel. Office: U Loughborough, Dept Econs E0800, Loughborough Leics LE11 3TU, England also: Hameau des Pins Les Hauts Golf, Villa 10 760 chemin de la Tire, 06250 Mougins France

LLEWELYN-EVANS, ADRIAN, solicitor; b. Wales, Aug. 5, 1953; s. Henry and May (Morris) E.; m. Catherine Ruth Forster, July 28, 1979; children: Edward, Thomas, Hugh. LLB with hons., U. Durham, Eng., 1976. Solicitor, 1979; accredited mediator. Solicitor Linklaters & Paines, London, 1979-82, Burges Salmon, Bristol, Eng., 1982-84; ptnr. Burges Salmon, Bristol, 1984—, head litigation, 1990—. Contbr. articles to profl. jours. Fellow Chartered Inst. Arbitrators; mem. Internat. Bar Assn., Law Soc. Avoca-

tions: gardening, hill walking, music, fishing. Office: Burges Salmon Narrow Quay, Narrowquay House, Bristol BS1 4AH, England

LLORENS, EMILIO, industrial engineer, economist; b. Buenos Aires, June 14, 1911; s. Manuel Llorens and Maria Palau; m. Felicia Maria Flugel, Dec. 6, 1936 (dec. 1984); children: Ana, José, Luis, Emilio, Maria Isabel. Grad. in indsl. engring., Nat. U. Buenos Aires, 1934. Sec. Inst. Econ. Transp., Buenos Aires, 1935-43; dir. Indsl. Ministry, Buenos Aires, 1943-47, Inst. Econ. Studies Alejandro Bunge, Buenos Aires, 1948-51; mgr. Inst. Argentino Promoción Intercambio, Buenos Aires, 1952-55, Inst. Econ. Promotion, Buenos Aires, 1955-62, Centro Industriales Siderúrgicos, Buenos Aires, 1962-85; regional sec. L.Am. Inst. Iron and Steel, Buenos Aires, 1962-95; econ. counselor Argentine Embassy, Washington, 1952, fin. counselor, 1958-60. Author: Geografic Economica Argentine, 1936, Annuario Geografico, 1939-42, El consumo de alimentos en América del Sur, 1941, Politica Industrial, 1947. Fellow Centro Argentinode Ingenieros, Consejo Profesional Ingenieria Industrial. Roman Catholic. Home: España 923, 1834 Temperley BA, Argentina Office: ILAFA, Maipu 663 5 A, 1006 Buenos Aires Argentina

LLOYD, ALEX, lawyer; b. Atlantic, Iowa, Aug. 13, 1942; s. Norman and Ruth (R.) L.; m. Jacqueline Roe, Aug. 24, 1963; children: Erin, Andrea, John, Peter. BA in Econs., Colby Coll., 1964; LLB, Law Sch., Yale U., 1967. Bar: Conn., U.S. Dist. Ct. (Conn.), U.S. Ct. Appeals (2d cir.), U.S. Tax Ct., U.S. Supreme Ct. Assoc. Shipman & Goodwin, 1967-72, ptnr., 1972—, chmn. mgmt. com., 1985-96; bd. dirs. Hartford Hosp., Conn. Health System, Inc., Conn. Bar Found., VNA Health Care, Inc., Vis. Nurse and Home Care, Inc. Recipient Charles J. Parker award Conn. Bar Assn., Dist. Svc. award Conn. Legal Svcs. Fellow Am. Bar Found., Conn. Bar Found.; mem. ABA, Am. Soc. of Hosp. Attys., Conn. Bar Assn. Avocations: golf, boating, fishing, raquet sports, piano. Office: Shipman & Goodwin 1 American Row Hartford CT 06103-2833

LLOYD, BRENDA AVERIL, bank executive, educator; b. Bulawayo, Zimbabwe, Sept. 16, 1963; d. Tom Alexander and June Patricia (Staal) Buys; m. Selwyn Phillip Lloyd, July 5, 1986; children: Dylan, Amanda, Denver. BSc in Econs. with honors, U. Zimbabwe, Harare, 1984; MA in Econs., U. Botswana, 1994. Tutor U. Zimbabwe, Harare, 1983-84; grad./mgmt. trainee Barclays Bank, Harare, 1985-87; lectr. Botswana Poly. Coll., Gaborone, 1987-92; dir., CEO Botswana Inst. Bankers, 1994—, fellow, 1998—; part-time lectr. Barclays Bank, Gaborone, 1987-91, Std. Chartered Bank, Gaborone, 1987-97; coord. So. African Devel. Cmty. Banking Edn. and Tng. Subcom. Mem. joint forum for productivity awareness Botswana Nat. Productivity Ctr., Gaborone, 1995-98, vice chmn. productivity awareness com., 1997—; mem. tech. econs. com. U. Botswana, Gaborone, 1996-98; chmn. pub. edn. program on banking Bank Botswana, 1996-98. Mem. Botswana Inst. Bankers. Avocations: reading, gardening, music, traveling. Office: Botswana Inst Bankers, P/BAG 00404, Gaborone Botswana

LLOYD, BRIAN EDMUND, engineering educator; b. Hawthorn, Victoria, Australia, June 30, 1929; s. Benjamin Frederick and Rose Veronica (Wray) L.; m. Elizabeth Gertrude Ince, Feb. 9, 1952; children: Brendan, Christopher, Martin, Rosemary. Student, St. Joseph's Coll. Geelong, 1945; DipEE, Gordon Inst. Tech., 1952; MA, U. Melbourne, 1986, PhD, 1989. Electrical engr. Ford Motor Co., Geelong, 1950; electrical engr. Australian Cement Ltd., Geelong, 1951-54, Hydroelectric Commn. of Tasmania, 1955-57; electrical engr. Melbourne & Met. Bd. Works, 1957-72, mgr. Sci. & Tech. Svcs., 1972-84; dir. EPM Consulting Group, 1986-94; adj. prof. Sch. Engring. and Tech. Deakin U., 1994—; nat. pres. Instn. Engrs. Australia, 1993-94; dep. chmn. Victoria Post-Secondary Accreditation Bd., 1987; chmn. TAFE Accreditation Bd., 1983-87; chmn. dirs. TAFE Nat. Ctr. for R & D, 1982-85; chmn. Victoria Divsn. Instn. Engrs. Australia, 1981, dep. pres., 1992, v.p., 1989-91; mem. Nat. Coun. Instn. Engrs. Australia, 1973-95; mem. State Coun. Tech. Edn. of Victoria, 1977-80; chmn. Curriculum Bd., 1973-83. Author: (books on Australia history) Gold at the Ten Mile, 1978, 95, Gold at Harrietville, 1982, Rutherglen, History of Town and District, 1985, A Gallant Life, the Story of an Old Soldier, 1992, ltd. edit., 1998, Tales of the Ten Mile: Ballybeg to the Bush, 1995, (with Howard Combes) Gold at Gaffneys Creek, 1981, (with Bertha Mac Smith) Letters of John Maxwell, 1982, (with Kathy Nunn) Bright Gold, 1987, (with Mabel Justice) Justice of Jamieson: An Irish-Australian Family in the Days of Gold, 1992, (books on engring.) The Education of Professional Engineers in Australia, 1968, Engineers in Australia: A Profession in Transition, 1991, (with others) The Education of Professional Engineers in Australia, 1962, Engineering Manpower in Australia, 1979, Manpower and Education for the Water Industry, 1981, Labour Market Roles of Professional Engineers, 1986, New Pathways in Engineering Education, 1989, Professional Engineers in Australia: Population Analysis, 1990, Professional Engineers in Australia: Protections of Supply, 1991, Skills for the Future: Engineers and Scientists Achieving Enterprise Performance, 1992, Professionalism, Liability and Risk in Engineering Practice, 1994, Status and Reward: The History of Industrial Representation of Professional Engineers in Australia 1946-96, A Gallant Life: The Story of an Old Soldier, 1998; contbr. articles to profl. jours. Named mem. Order of Australia, 1984. Fellow Instn. Engrs. Australia (hon.); mem. Assn. Profl. Engrs. Australia (disting. life mem., hon. gen. sec. 1972, hon. gen. treas. 1964-66, fed. coun. 1966-73, mem. Victoria br. com. 1959), Royal Automobile Club Australia. Roman Catholic. Avocations: writing Australian history. Home: 13 Connor St, Brighton East 3187, Australia

LLOYD, CECIL RHODES, pediatric dentist; b. Corpus Christi, Tex., Aug. 18, 1930; s. Cecil Rhodes Hilbun and Cidney W. (Linxwiler) Lloyd; m. Donna Mae Thomas, Dec. 31, 1955 (div. 1973); children: James Michael, Leigh Ann, Lisa Kendall; m. Glenda Sue Williams, Dec. 31, 1979; children: Lauren Cecily, Sutton Rhodes. Student, La. State U., 1949, La. Tech. Inst., 1950, Centenary Coll., 1952-54; DDS, Loyola U., New Orleans, 1958. Pvt. practice pediatric dentistry, Shreveport, La., 1958—; cons. in pediatric dentistry Barksdale AFB, La., 1970—; mem. staff and surg. com. Christus Schumpert Hosp., Shreveport. Chmn. Cen. YMCA, Shreveport, 1974, met. bd., 1969, Ind. Bowl Football Classic, Shreveport, 1984, 85, Fellowship Christian Athletes, 1986; bd. dirs. Riverside Hosp., Bossier, La., 1982-84; pres.-elect Sports Found., 1989, pres., 1990; founder Sports Mus. of Champions, Shreveport-Bossier; interim mem. Shreveport City Coun., 1990. With USMC, 1950-52. Named Southwestern Handball Hall of Fame, 1996. NW La. Dental Assn., La. Dental Assn., ADA, Am. Acad. Pediatric Dentistry, La. Bd. Dentistry (pres., 1969-70, 77-78, 83-84), Ark.-La.-Tex. Dental Congress (chmn. 1979-80). Republican. Baptist. Avocation: theatre. Office: 927 Shreveport Barksdale Hwy Shreveport LA 71105-2205

LLOYD, GEORGE PETER, retired government administrator; b. London, Sept. 23, 1926; arrived in Bermuda, 1987; s. Thomas Ingram Kynaston and Bessie Nora (Mason) L.; m. Margaret Harvey, Apr. 22, 1957; children: David Kynaston, John Charles, Susan Mary. BA, MA, King's Coll., 1951. Dist. officer Kenyan Govt., 1951-60; prin. Colonial Office, Eng., 1960-61; colonial sec. Seychelles Govt., 1961-66; chief sec. Fiji Govt., 1966-70; sec. security Hong Kong Govt., 1971-74; dep. gov. Govt. Bermuda, 1974-81; gov. Govt. Cayman Islands, 1982-87; non-exec. dir. various world wide shipping cos., Bermuda, 1990-96, Internat. risk Mgmt. Group, Bermuda, 1989-96. Chmn. Bermuda Festivals Ltd., 1987-99; trustee Bermuda Maritime Mus., 1987-97, Bermuda Festival Trust, 1996—. Lt. King's Royal Rifle Corps, Eng., 1945-48. Named Companion of Order St. Michael Queen Elizabeth II, Eng., 1965, Companion of Royal Victorian Order, 1983. Mem. Corquet Club Bermuda (pres. 1995—). Avocations: croquet, geneaology, gardening, needlepoint, traveling. Home: PO Box HM 553, Hamilton HM CX, Bermuda

LLOYD, JOHN ANTHONY, research scientist, consultant; b. Gisborne, New Zealand, Oct. 11, 1949; s. Kevin Lancelot and Elizabeth Hazel (Robertson) L.; m. Lynette Jean Jensen, Apr. 21, 1990; 1 child, Kate. BSc, U. Auckland, New Zealand, 1970, MSc, 1971. Scientist New Zealand Forset Rsch. Inst., Rotorua, 1971-84; sr. scientist PAPRO, Rotorua, 1984-97, Forest Rsch., New Zealand, 1997—; bd. dirs. Rotorua RC (Ind.). Contbr. numerous articles to profl. jours.; patentee in field. Mem. Australasian Pulp and Paper Tech. Assn. (New Zealand com. 1974—, DuPont Bleaching award 1994), New Zealand Inst. Chemistry. Avocations: science, thoroughbred horse breeding. E-mail: John.Lloyd@forestresearch.co.nz. Office: Forest Rsch, Sala St, Rotorua New Zealand

LLOYD, JOHN ANTHONY, analyst; b. Woking, Surrey, Eng., Sept. 2, 1965; s. Robert Edward and Janice Anne (Harrop) L. BSc in Physics with honors, U. Manchester, 1988, MSc in Microprocessor Engring., 1990, PhD in Computation, 1996. Software engr. Syntek Ltd., Manchester, 1989-90; lectr. U. Manchester Inst. Sci. and Tech., 1993-96; neural scientist Neural Technologies Ltd., Petersfield, 1996-97; v.p. Credit Suisse First Boston, London, 1997—. Avocations: rock climbing, sailing, skiing. Office: Credit Suisse First Boston, One Cabot Sq, London England

LLOYD, JOSEPH WESLEY, physicist, researcher; b. N.Mex., Jan. 31, 1914; s. William Washington and Mattie May (Barber) L.; m. Lenora Lucille Hopkins, Jan. 24, 1944 (dec. June 1969); 3 children (dec.); m. Ruth Kathryn Newberry, Nov. 19, 1988 (dec. May 2000); children: Kathryn Ruth Jordan, Mary Evelyn Jordan. Student, Pan Am. Coll., 1942. Plumber Pomona, Calif., 1951-57; plumber, pipefitter Marysville, Calif., 1957-79; ret., 1979; ind. researcher in physics and magnetism, Calif., 1944—. With CAP, 1944-45. Mem. Ch. of Christ.

LLOYD, LEONA LORETTA, judge; b. Detroit, Aug. 6, 1949; d. Leon Thomas and Naomi Mattie (Chisolm) L.; 1 stepson, Joseph Andersen. BS, Wayne State U., 1971, JD, 1979. Bar: Mich. 1981, U.S. Dist. Ct. (ea. dist.) 1981, U.S. Supreme Ct. 1988, U.S. Cir. Ct. (6th cir.) 1983. Speech, drama tchr. Detroit Bd. Edn., 1971-75; instr. criminal justice Wayne State U., Detroit, 1981; sr. ptnr. Lloyd and Lloyd, Detroit, 1982-92; prin. asst., corp. counsel City Detroit Law Dept., 1992-94; judge 36th Dist. Ct., Detroit, 1994—. Co-author, dir. (gospel musical) Freedom Song, 1991. Wayne State U. scholar, 1970, 75; recipient Fred Hampton Image award, 1984, Kizzy Image award, 1985, Nat. Coalition of 100 Black Women Achievement award, 1986, Community Svc. award Wayne County exec. William Lucas, 1986, Merit Black Law Student Assn. cert. U. Detroit, 1986, Spirit of Detroit award, 1991, Martin Luther King Keep This Dream Alive award, 1995, Special Tribute award State of Mich., 1995, Resolution award County of Wayne, 1995, Appreciation cert. City of Detroit, 1995, Bar Assn. award, 1995, B'nai B'rith Barristers award, 1995, Testimonial Resolution award Detroit City Coun., 1995, Woman of Yr. award African Am. Awards Coun., 1996, African Am. Sheroes award Drusilla Farwell Mid. Sch., 1997, Cmty. Pride award Greater Grace Temple, 2000; named to Black Women Hall of Fame. Mem. ABA, NARAS, Wolverine Bar Assn., Mich. State Bar, Mary McLeon Bethune Assn. Office: 421 Madison St Ste 3067 Detroit MI 48226-2358

LLOYD, MATTHEW DAVID, entrepreneur, actor; b. Solihill, Birmingham, Eng., July 16, 1975; s. Michael Thomas and Doreen Anne (Tawn) Holland. Proprietor, mgr. Holland Lesiure, 1993-97; freelance actor, 1997—; gen. asst. FastTrack Cons. Svcs., 1988-91. Served with Royal Navy, 1991-98. Mem. ROSPA, The Inner Circle, British Horse Soc., The Writers Club, First Drop. Home and Office: Waverly Rd, Poskitt House Apt 31, TA6 3R2 Bridgwater England

LLOYD, MICHAEL JEFFREY, recording producer; b. N.Y.C., Nov. 3, 1948; s. John and Suzanne (Lloyd) Sutton; m. Patricia Ann Varble, Sept. 6, 1980; children: Michael, Christopher, Jeni, Deborah. Student, U. So. Calif. V.p. artists and repertoire MGM Records, Inc., 1969-73; ind. record producer, 1973—; pres. Heaven Prodns., 1975—, Michael Lloyd Prodns., 1979—, Taines-Lloyd Film Prodns., 1984-85; music dir. TV series Happy Days; music dir. Kidsongs, Living Proof, NBC-TV movie, Kidsongs Videos; prodr. Love Lines, NBC-TV movie Swimsuit; pres., co-founder MV Online, 2000—; guest lectr. UCLA, Pepperdine U.; judge Am. Song Festival. Composer: (music for feature films) Tough Enough, If You Could See What I Hear, Dirty Dancing, All Dogs Go to Heaven, (music and lyrics) Rudolph the Red Nose Reindeer- The Movie, 1998, Coyote Ugly; composer music for 8 Movies of the Week, 12 TV spls., 28 TV series and 39 feature motion pictures. Recipient 51 Gold Album awards, 24 Platinum Album awards, 26 Gold Single awards, 2 Platinum Single awards, 3 Grammy awards, 41 Chart Album awards, 100 Chart Single awards, 10 Broadcast Music Inc. awards, 1 Am. Music award, 1 Dove award, 2 Nat. Assn. of Record Minets. Mem. ASCAP (12 awards), Am. Fedn. Musicians, Screen Actors Guild, Nat. Assn. Rec. Arts and Scis., AFTRA.

LLOYD, ROBERT ANDREW, opera singer; b. Southend-on-Sea, Eng., Mar. 2, 1940; m. Sandra Watkins (div.); 4 children; m. Lynda Hazell Powell, 1992. Grad., Keble Coll., Oxford, Eng., 1962, London Opera Ctr. Schoolmaster London Pub. Schs., 1962-63; lectr. internat. affairs Bramshill Police Coll., 1966-68; prin. bass Sadlers Wells, London Coliseum, 1969-72, Royal Opera House, Covent Garden, London, 1972-83; comdr. Brit. Empire, 1991—; hon. fellow Keble Coll.; vis. prof. Royal Coll. Music, 1996—. Debut as Fernando in Fidelio, London U. Opera; recs. for EMI, Decca, Philips, Telarc, Erato, Chandos; film of Parsifal, Bluebeard's Castle (Prix Italia); frequent radio talks and TV presenter; Met. debut in Barber of Seville, 1988 Boris Godunov at Kirov, St. Petersburg, 1990; San Francisco debut, 1975, Chgo., 1990, Dallas, 1998; regular appearances Salzburg Festival; created role of Tyrone in the opera Tower by Alun Hoddinatt. Mem. conservatoires adv. group to Higher Edn. Funding Coun., 1994-98. Recipient Buenos Aires Fgn. Artist of Yr. award, 1997, Charles Santley award, 1997, Chaliapan Commemoration Medal, St. Petersburg, 1998. Mem. Royal Acad. Music (hon.). Office: Lies Askomas Askonas Holt Lonsdale Chamb, 27 Chancery Ln, London WC2A 1PF, England

LLOYD, SALLY-HEATH FAHNESTOCK, artist; b. Glen Cove, N.Y., Aug. 22, 1942; d. J. Sheridan Fahnestock and Margaret Fahnestock Lewis; m. Douglas Wray Lloyd, Jr., March 9, 1964; children: Wendy, Douglas. AA, St. Mary's Coll. of Md., 1962; BFA, Ariz. State U., 1989. Studio artist Scottsdale, Ariz., 1989—. Mem. Soc. No. Am. Goldsmiths, Am. Craft Coun., Ariz. Designer Craftsmen (juried mem., state bd. pres. 1997-99), Ariz. Masterworks Chorale, Ariz. State U. Nelson Art Mus., Phoenix Art Mus. Avocations: hiking, choral singing, travel. E-mail: sallyheath@lloydtardis.com. Home and Studio: 23645 N 83rd Pl Scottsdale AZ 85255-3508

LLOYD-DAVIES, BRIAN, educator; b. Barry, United Kingdom, May 17, 1933; came to Central African Republic, 1981; s. Ivor John and Gladys Helena (Lloyd) D. BA (hons.), Durham Univ., U.K., 1955, diploma, 1956; PhD, Tenn. Univ., 1974; diploma, Surrey Univ., U.K., 1982. Univ. lectr. Univ. Bangui, Cen African Republic, 1981—. Avocations: reading, listening to music, Bible, church. Home: B P 1933, Bangui Cen African Republic Office: Univ Bangui, Ave des Martyrs, Bangui Cen African Republic

LLOYD-HUGHES, SIR TREVOR DENBY, retired journalist, public affairs consultant; b. Guiseley, England, Mar. 31, 1922; s. Elwyn and Lucy (Denby) Lloyd-H.; m. Ethel Marguerite Ritchie, May 9, 1950 (div. May 5, 1971); children: Katharine, Richard; m. Marie-Jeanne Moreillon, May 18, 1971; children: David (dec.), Annabelle. MA, Jesus Coll., Oxford, 1947. Asst. inspector taxes Her Majesty's Inland Revenue, Manchester, England, 1948; sub editor Liverpool Daily Post, England, 1949; polit. corr. Liverpool Echo, 1950, Liverpool Post, 1951-64; press sec. Prime Min., London, 1964-69; chief info. adviser Govt. England, London, 1969-70; chmn. Lloyd-Hughes Assocs., London, 1970-89; internat. cons. in pub. affairs; mem. Cir. of Wine Writers, 1961-75, chmn., 1972-73, dir. Trinity Internat. Holdings plc, 1978-91. Founder Oxford U. Opera Club, 1946.

LLOYD-JONES, SIR (PETER) HUGH (JEFFERD), Greek language educator; b. St. Peter Port, Guernsey, Eng., Sept. 21, 1922; s. William and Norah Leila (Jefferd) Lloyd-J.; m. Frances E. Hedley, 1953 (div. 1981); children: Edmund Stephen, Ralph Alexander, Antonia; m. Mary R. Lefkowitz, 1982. MA, Oxford (Eng.) U., 1947; DHL (hon.), U. Chgo., 1970; PhD (hon.), U. Tel Aviv, 1984, Thessalonica U., 1999. Author: The Justice of Zeus, 1971, 2d edit., 1983, Blood for the Ghosts, 1982, Classical Survivals, 1982, (with P.J. Parsons) Supplementum Hellenisticum, 1983, (with N.G. Wilson) Sophoclis Fabulae, 1990, (with N.G. Wilson) Sophoclea, 1990, Academic Papers, 2 vols., 1990, Greek in a Cold Climate, 1991, Sophocles, 3 vols., 1994-96, (with N.G. Wilson) Sophocles: Second Thoughts, 1997; others; translator Oresteia (Aeschylus), 1970. With Brit. Army, 1942-46. Fellow Jesus Coll., Cambridge (Eng.) U., 1948-54; fellow and E.P. Warren praelector in classics Corpus Christi Coll., 1954-60; Regius prof. Greek, Oxford U., 1960-89; vis. prof. Yale U., 1964, 67, U. Chgo., 1972, Harvard U., 1976; Sather prof. U. Calif., Berkeley, 1969. Fellow Brit. Acad.; mem. Am. Acad. Arts and Scis. (hon. fgn.), Acad. Athens, Nordrhein-Westfälische Akademie, Accademia di Archeologia, Lettere e Belle Arti, Naples, Bayerische Akademie, Am. Philos. Soc. Address: 15 W Riding St Wellesley MA 02482-6914 also: Christ Ch, Oxford OX1 1DP, England

LNENICKA, WADE SHERIDAN, purchasing official, councilman; b. Kansas City, Mo., Nov. 1, 1951; s. William Joseph and Georgia Marie (Eriksen) L.; m. Robin Ann Brown, June 22, 1985. BS in Mgmt., Ga. Tech., 1973; MBA, U. Mich., 1978; grad. with honors, U.S. Army Command and Gen. Staff Coll., 1983; grad., Nat. Def. U., 1991. Cert. purchasing mgr. Nat. Assn. Purchasing Mgmt., Inc.; accredited purchasing practitioner Nat. Assn. Purchasing Mgmt. Bus. mgr. Wink Davis Equipment Co., Inc., Atlanta, 1978-79; order control supr. Printpack Inc., Atlanta, 1980-82, purchasing supr., 1982-87, purchasing mgr., 1987—; mem. Smyrna (Ga.) City Coun., 1988—. Mem. civic adv. com. Emory-Adventist Hosp. Home Health, 1997—, Emory-Adventist Hosp. Sr. Oasis, 1998—; bd. dirs. Ridge Assisted Living, Inc. at Ridgeview Inst., 1998—; mem. adv. bd. Small Cities newsletter, 1998—. 1st lt. U.S. Army, 1973-76; maj. USAR, 1976-95. Mem. Am. Legion, Nat. Intercollegiate Lacrosse Officls Assn., U.S. Intercollegiate Lacrosse Assn., U.S. Lacrosse, Cobb Mcpl. Assn. (sec. 1992, treas. 1993, v.p. 1994, pres. 1995). Avocations: bridge, lacrosse, military history, politics. Home: 3950 Glenhurst Dr SE Smyrna GA 30080-5896 Office: Printpack Inc PO Box 43687 Atlanta GA 30336-0687

LO, FU-CHEN, economist, educator; b. Chia-yi, Taiwan, May 8, 1935; s. Chian-Tien and Tan-Baih Lo; m. Vickie Chin-fun Mao, June 15, 1962; children: Theadore Tse-shin, David Tse-yen. BA, Nat. Taiwan U., 1958; MA, Waseda U., Tokyo, 1963; PhD, U. Pa., 1968. Chief comparative studies UN Ctr. Regional Devel., Nagoya, Japan, 1973-80; sr. rsch. fellow East-West Ctr., Honolulu, 1981-82; affiliated faculty U. Hawaii, Honolulu, 1981-84; rsch. coord. Asia and Pacific Devel. Ctr., Kuala Lumpur, Malaysia, 1985-89; prin. acad. officer UN U., Tokyo, 1990-95, dep. dir./prof. Inst. Advanced Studies, 1995-2000, prof. emeritus Inst. Advanced Studies, 2000—; dir. Modern Culture Found., 2000—; vis. prof. U. Pa., Phila., 1982-84; founder, organizer Future of Asian-Pacific Economy Conf., 1985-89; bd. dirs. Taiwan Soc., 1991-94; founder, pub. Taiwan Tribune, N.Y., 1981-87. Author: Growth Pole Strategy and Regional Development Policy, 1978, Asian and Pacific Economy Toward the Year 2000, 1987, Global Adjustment and the Future of Asia-Pacific Economy, 1989, Emerging World Cities in Pacific Asia, 1995. Founding mem., ctr. com. mem. World United Formosans for Independence, N.Y., Taipei, 1970—; bd. dirs. Amnesty Internat., Tokyo, 1975-77; founding mem., bd. dirs. Formosan Assn. for Pub. Affairs, 1982. Grantee Toyota Found., 1977-78, Internat. Devel. Ctr. Japan, 1993-94, Environment Agy. of Japan, 1995-96. Mem. Am. Econ. Assn., Japan Soc. for Internat. Devel. (founding mem.), Internat. Geog. Union (founding mem., mem. working group on urbanization in developing countries). Office: Tapei Econ & Cultural, 5-20-2 Shirokanedai, Minato-ku Tokyo 108-0071, Taiwan

LO, GIN HO, gastroenterologist; b. Yun-Lin County, Taiwan, Dec. 4, 1954; s. Ta Chu and Liaw Yu (Liaw) L.; m. Ying Yang, Jan. 23, 1983; children: Jung, Yang. BS, Kaohsiung (Taiwan) Med. Coll., 1980. Resident in internal medicine Vets. Gen. Hops., Taipei, Taiwan, 1982-86, chief resident, 1986-87, attending physician, 1987-90; attending physician divsn. gastroenterology Vets. Gen. Hops., Kaohsiung, 1990-97, chief divsn. gastroenterology, 1997—. Author: (in Chinese) Liver Cirrhosis, 1996, Diagnosis and Treatment of Hepatitis, 1999, Treatment of Hepatoma, 1999. Recipient Top Rsch. award Nat. Sci. Coun., Taipei, 1996, 97, 98. Mem. Taiwan Gastroenterol. Soc., Chinese Taipei Soc. Ultrasound in Medicine, China Med. Assn. Avocations: tennis, golf. Office: Vet Gen Hosp Kaohsuing 386, Ta-chung 1st Rd, 813 Kaohsiung Taiwan

LO, HOI-KWONG, research scientist; b. Hong Kong, Mar. 21, 1967; arrived in U.S., 1989; s. Lee-Gun Lo and Chung-Chun Liu. BA in Math., Trinity Coll., Cambridge, U.K., 1989; MS in Physics, Caltech, 1991, PhD in Physics, 1994. Mem. Inst. for Advanced Study, Princeton, N.J., 1994-96; rsch. cons. Hewlett-Packard Labs., Bristol, U.K., 1996-97; sr. mem. tech. staff Hewlett-Packard Labs., Bristol, 1997-99; chief scientist, sr. v.p. R&D MagiQ Techs., Inc., N.Y.C., 1999—. Co-editor, co-author: Introduction to Quantum Computation and Information, 1998. Prince Philip scholar Friends of Cambridge U., Hong Kong, 1986. Mem. Am. Phys. Soc. Achievements include co-inventor and patentee quantum cryptographic system with reduced data loss. Office: Maagid Techs Inc 275 7th Ave Fl 26 New York NY 10001-6708

LO, HSIAO SHIH, structural engineer; b. Tangshan, China, Mar. 18, 1922; arrived in Hong Kong, 1950; s. Chung Cheng and Wen Yu (Lee) L.; m. Rita Ching, May 18, 1947; children: Ann Lo, Jeannie Lo, William Lo. Diploma civic engring., Jiao Tung U., China, 1943, British Inst. of Engring., 1957. Registered structural engr., Hong Kong. Air traffic control officer Jinan Airport, Republic of China, 1948-49; engr. Kao Hua Engring. Co., Ltd., Shanghai, 1950-51, Project FEC 197, Kadena U.S. Airbase, Okinawa, 1952-53; foreman Water Supply Dept., 1955; asst. inspector of works Kai Tak Airport Devel. Schmeme, 1956-57; resident engr., 1970-80, Tuen Mun New Town Devel., 1980-84; resident architect Discovery Bay High Rise Bldgs., 1985; sr. engr. Cardo Scott Cons., China, 1989; structural cons. for bridge works, 1990; sr. structural engr. Greg Wong & Assocs. Ltd., 1991; mgr. Crystal Palace Ice Rink, 1992; cons. M.H. Wong Architect & Assocs. Ltd., Kowloon, Hong Kong, 1993—, Maurice Lee & Assocs., Ltd., Hong Kong, 1996-98; with AGS Cons., 1998—; cons. U. Shing Engring. Co., 1999, Slope Engring., Ltd., 1999, Techwell Engring., Ltd., 1999. Designer steel movable blast fences for testing jet engines, Lai Chi Kok Hwy. Bridge, 1961, infrastructures for Kwai Chung Devel. Scheme, 1962, Sham Tseng reclamation and seawalls, 1963, Esso Nga Chau Terminal, Esso mainland bulk plant, 1965, Tsuen War Pier, 1966, Kai Tak Airport Runway Extension Report, 1967, Portal J of Plover Cover Water Scheme, 1968, My Thuan bridge, Vietnam, 1969. Mem. ASCE (life), Soc. of Engrs. (London), Coun. of Engring. Instns. (chartered engr.), Instn. of Structural Engrs., Hong Kong Instn. of Engrs. Home: 29 A Lee Po Bldg, 3 Tsing Ho Square, Tuen Mun Hong Kong China Office: Cons Civil and Structural, PO Box 98482, Kowloon Hong Kong China

LO, KAM WAH, research scientist; b. Hong Kong, Oct. 4, 1961; arrived in Australia, 1992; s. Ching Nin and Mei Kwan (Chui) L.; m. Kit Ping Li, Mar. 19, 1992. BSc, U. NSW, Sydney, Australia, 1983, BEngring., 1985, PhD, 1989. Rsch. assoc. U. NSW, Sydney, 1988-89; lectr. Hong Kong Polytechnic, 1989-92; rsch. scientist Def. Sci. and Tech. Orgn., Adelaide, 1992-93, Sydney, 1995-99; sr. rsch. scientist, 1999—; microwave engr. Commonwealth Sci. and Indsl. Rsch., Sydney, 1993-95; cons. Def. Sci. and Tech. Orgn., Adelaide, Australia, 1992. Contbr. articles to profl. jours. U. NSW scholar, 1985-88; Rsch. grantee U. and Poly. Grant Com. Mem. IEEE (sr.), U. NSW Union (life). Avocations: movies, karaoke, swimming, travel. Office: DSTO Maritime Ops Divsn, PO Box 44 Pyrmont, 2009 Sydney Australia

LO, LESLIE NAI-KWAI, educator; b. Canton, China, Aug. 23, 1949; s. Tai-man Lo and In-Lim Leong; m. Michelle Marie Vosper, July 31, 1982; children: William, Pierce. BA, U. Oreg., 1972; M of Internat. Affairs, Columbia U., 1977, EdD, 1982. Founding dean faculty edn. Chinese U. Hong Kong, 1991-97, dir. Hong Kong Inst. Ednl. Rsch., 1994—, head teaching devel. unit, 1995—, prof. dept. ednl. adminstrn. & policy, 1995—, head grad. divsn. edn., 1997—; guest prof. U. Peking, China, Nanjing U., China, East China Normal U., Ctrl. China Normal U., Capital Tchrs. U., China, others, 1994—. Editor: Research and Endeavours in Moral and Civic Education, 1996; contbr. articles to profl. jours. Fellow Hong Kong Ednl. Rsch. Assn., 1998. Mem. Bd. Edn. Hong Kong, Curriculum Devel. Coun. Hong Kong, Profl. Actions & Cultures Teaching (neternat. dir. 1999). Avocations: reading, sports. Office: Hong Kong Inst Ednl Rsch, Chinese U Hong Kong, Shatin Hong Kong

LO, SHANG-LIEN, environmental engineering educator; b. Kaohsiung, Taiwan, Aug. 17, 1953; s. Kuo-Liaen and Xin-Chou (Chen) L.; m. Kuo Chu Tsao; children: Chung-Yi, Chung-Yu. BS in Civil Engring., Nat. Taiwan U., Taipei, 1975, MS in Environ. Engring., 1978, PhD in Environ. Engring., 1983. Diplomate environ. engring., hydraulic engring., indsl. hygiene. Instr. Nat. Taiwan U., Taipei, 1979-83, assoc. prof., 1983-85, 87-89, prof. environ. engring., 1989—, dir., 1996; postdoctoral rschr. Stanford U., 1985-87; mem.

bd. Consumers' Found. Republic of China, Taiwan, 1994—; chmn. bd. Chinese Inst. Environ. Engring., Taiwan, 1996. Author: Environmental Mathematics, 1991 (Outstanding Textbook award Ministry of Edn. 1992), Water Supply Engineering, 1995, Sewerage Engineering, 1997; editor in chief Jour. Chinese Inst. Environ. Engring., 1992-96 (Best Jour. award Nat. Sci. Coun. 1994, 95); editor, regional editl. com. Asia and Western Pacific, Water Rsch., 1997—. Chmn. bd. Feng and Lin Environ. Found., Taipei, 1997—. With Taiwan Nat. Guard, 1984—. recipient Outstanding Tchg. awards Ministry Edn., Republic of China, Taipei, Taiwan, 1989, 93, 99, Outstanding Rsch. awards Nat. Sci. Coun., Republic of China, Taipei, 1993, 95, 97, 99, Excellent Rsch. awards Nat. Sci. Coun., Republic of China, Taipei, 1990, 91, 92. Mem. Chinese Inst. Engrs. (Best Acad. Dissertation award 1993), Chinese Inst. Environ. Engring. (Best. Acad. Dissertation award 1991), Chinese Inst. Civil and Hydrualic Engring. (Best Acad. Dissertation award 1992). Avocations: bridge, basketball, baseball, camp, music. Home: 7F No 7 Lane 58 Wen-Chou St, Taipei Taiwan Office: Nat Taiwan U Grad Inst, Environ Engring 71 Chou-Shan Rd, Taipei Taiwan

LO, TUNG-BIN, research biochemist, administrator; b. Puli, Nantou, Taiwan, Feb. 15, 1927; s. Yin-Han and Wen (Su) L.; m. Su-Shia Wu; children: Su-Shun, Su-Huey, Su-Hao. BS, Nat. Taiwan U., Taipei, 1949; DSc, Tohoku U., Sendai, Japan, 1960. Jr. rsch. chemist U. Calif., Berkeley, 1959-61; prof. Nat. Taiwan U., Taipei, 1964-95, dean Coll. of Scis., 1978-84, dean of acad. affairs (provost), 1984-90; rsch. fellow Acad. Sinica, Taipei, 1972—, v.p., 1993-96; pres. Coll. Entrance Exam. Ctr., Taipei, 1992—; councilor Acad. Sinica, Taipei, 1978—; vis. prof. U. Calif. San Francisco, 1968-69. Author: (with others) Proceedings Nat. Acad. Sci., U.S., 1991; contbr. numerous articles to profl. jours. Elected mem. Acad. Sinica, Taipei, Taiwan, 1986. Avocations: tennis, golf, travel, classical music. Office: Coll Entrance Exam Ctr, 237 Zhou Shan Rd, Taipei Taiwan

LO, WAI KIT, engineering researcher; b. Hong Kong, Nov. 3, 1970; s. Kam Chu Lo. B.Engring., Chinese U. Hong Kong, 1994, MPh, 1996. Engring. trainee Motorola Semiconductors (Hong Kong) Ltd., 1992-93; grad. asst. Chinese U. Hong Kong, 1994-95, project coord., 1997—; electronic design engr. KMY Instruments LLC, San Jose, 1996-97. Inventor in field. Croucher found. studentship, 1994-96. Mem. IEEE, Inst. Elec. Engrs. Office: Chinese Univ Hong Kong, Dept Elec Engring, Hong Kong China

LO, WEN-LIN, dermatologist; b. Kaohsiung, Taiwan, Jan. 1, 1958; s. Jhi-Yuan and Chung-Hwa (Wang) L.; m. Yung-Jung Ho, March 7, 1987. MD, Nat. Yang-Ming Med. Coll., 1982. Resident in dermatology Vets. Gen. Hosp., Taipei, 1984-89, attending physician, 1989-91; attending physician Chutong (Taiwan) Vets. Hosp., 1991-93, sect. chief, 1993-94; pvt. practice Taipei, 1994—; lectr. Nat. Yang-Ming Med. Coll., Taipei, 1989-91. Assoc. editor: Dermatologica Sinica, 1990; contbr. articles to profl. jours. 2nd lt. Chinese Army, 1982-84. Fellow Am. Acad. Dermatology; mem. Asian Dermatol. Assn., Internat. Soc. Dermatology, Chinese Dermatol. Soc. (Rsch. paper award 1986, 87), Laser Medicine Soc. Office: 2/F # 2 Ln 14 Chung Shan N Sec 7, Taipei 111, Taiwan

LO, YEE ON, composer; b. Chong Qing, Si Chuan, China, Sept. 29, 1945; came to U.S., 1966; p. Kei-Pak and Bih-Tang Lo. AB, U. Calif., Berkeley, 1972, MS, 1979; PhD, Stanford U., 1987. Composer Wings II: Portrait, Dream I - Shattered, When That Call Shudders 'cross..., Duo Concertant - Le Conte du Troubador, The Interrupted Serenade, Three Postludes, Dreams-Sequence, River Through Time. Recipient Program Music prize Bourges Concours Internat., Bourges, France, 1997. Mem. ASCAP (awards 1997, 98, 99), Audio Engring. Soc., Assn. for Computing Machinery, Math. Assn. Am. Fax: 650-329-9655. E-mail: acoustic@netcom.com. Home and Office: PO Box 62 Palo Alto CA 94302-0062

LO, YU-LUNG, engineering educator; b. Taipei, Taiwan, Oct. 4, 1962; s. Ying-Hwa Lo and Hsiu-Chin Chung; m. Chiu-Yi Li, Sept. 7, 1997. BS, Nat. Cheng Kung U., Tainan, Taiwan, 1985; MS, U. Md., 1992, PhD, 1995. Asst. engr. Yue-Loong Motor Engring. Ctr., Taoy-Yuan, Taiwan, 1987-89; rsch. asst. U. Md., College Park, 1989-95; engr. Indsl. Tech. Rsch. Instn., Hsin-Chu, Taiwan, 1996; lectr. Nat. Cheng Kung U., Tainan, 1996-97, asst. prof., 1997-99, assoc. prof., 1999—; part-time asst. prof. Nat. Chung Cheng U., Chia-Yi, Taiwan, 1999; invited spkr., sect. chair Inst. Smart Structures and Systems/Internat. Optical Engring. Soc. conf., 1999. Contbr. articles to profl. jours.; patentee in field. Served with Taiwanese Air Force, 1985-87. Rsch. award Nat. Sci. Coun., Taiwan, 1996, 98, Rsch. Creative award, 1998. Mem. Internat. Soc. Optical Engring. Avocations: fishing, playing ball, hiking. Office: Nat Cheng Kung U, Dept Mech Engring, Tainan 701, Taiwan

LOACH, KENNETH, film director; b. Nuneaton, England, June 17, 1936; s. John Loach; m. Lesley Ashton, 1962; 5 children (1 dec.). Student, St. Peter's Hall, Oxford, Eng. Trainee drama dept. BBC, 1963; freelance film dir., 1963—. Dir. (films) Poor Cow, 1967, Kes, 1969, In Black and White, 1970, Family Life, 1971, Black Jack, 1979, Looks and Smiles, 1981, Fatherland, 1986, Hidden Agenda, 1990 (Cannes Jury prize 1990), Riff-Raff, 1991 (European Film the Yr.), Raining Stones (Cannes Jury prize 1993), Ladybird, Ladybird, 1994 (Berlin Critic prize), Land and Freedom, 1995 (European Film of Yr. 1995), Carla's Song, 1996, My Name is Joe, 1998, Bread and Roses, 2000; dir. (TV films) Diary of a Young Man, 1964, Three Clear Sundays, 1965, The End of Arthur's Marriage, 1965, Up the Junction, 1965, Coming Out Party, 1965, Cathy Come Home, 1966, In Two Minds, 1966, The Golden Vision, 1969, The Big Flame, 1970, After a Lifetime, 1971, The Rank and File, 1972, Days of Hope, 1975, The Price of Coal, 1977, The Gamekeeper, 1979, Auditions, 1980, A Question of Leadership, 1980, The Red and the Blue, 1983, Questions of Leadership, 1983, Which Side are You On?, 1984, The View from the Woodpile, 1988, Time to Go, 1989, Dispatches: Arthur Scargill, 1991, The Flickering Flame, 1996, Another City, 1998. Office: Parallax Pictures Ltd, 7 Denmark St, London WC2H 8LS, England

LOADER, JAMES ALFRED, religious studies educator, minister; b. Pretoria, South Africa, July 12, 1945; arrived in Austria, 1997; s. Leonard James and Reina Gertruida (Rattray) L.; m. Catharina Elizabetha Vorster, Dec. 2, 1972; children: Benjamin, Reina-Marie. MA, U. Pretoria, 1971, DLitt, 1973; ThD, U. Groningen, The Netherlands, 1975, U. South Africa, Pretoria, 1984. Ordained to ministry Reformed Ch. of South Africa, 1970. Lectr. U. Pretoria, 1968-71, sr. lectr., 1971-78, prof., 1979-80; prof. U. South Africa, Pretoria, 1980-97, U. Vienna, Austria, 1997—; cons. Nat. Pks. Bd., Pretoria, 1988-97. Author: Polar Structures in the Book of Qohelet, 1979, A Tale of Two Cities, Sodom and Gomorrah in the Old Testament, Early Jewish and Early Christian Traditions, 1990 (Teyler prize for theology 1989), Das Buch Ester, 1992; editor: Wiener Alttestamentliche Studien, 1998—; co-editor: Old Testament Essays, 1983-93; columnist Beeld Daily Newspaper, Johannesburg, South Africa, 1981-97. Bd. dirs. Lynnwood Sch., Pretoria, 1986-96; mem. Reforum for dismantling of Apartheid, Pretoria, 1982-90. Recipient award for acad. excellence Unisa, Pretoria, 1989, 91, 95, award for outstanding svc. to conservation and environ. edn. Nat. Pks. Bd. of South Africa, 1991. Mem. Brit. Soc. Old Testament Study, European Theol. Soc., South African Soc. for Old Testament Study (gen. sec. 1974-92). Avocations: classical music, ecology, jogging. Office: U Vienna Faculty Theology, Rooseveltplatz 10, A-1090 Vienna Austria

LOARIE, THOMAS MERRITT, healthcare executive; b. Deerfield, Ill., June 12, 1946; s. Willard John and Lucile Veronica (Finnegan) L.; m. Stephanie Lane Fitts, Aug. 11, 1968 (div. Nov. 1987); children: Thomas M., Kristin Leigh Soule. BSME, U. Notre Dame, 1968; Student, U. Minn., 1969-70, U. Chgo., 1970-71, Columbia U., 1978. Registered profl. engr., Calif. Prodn. engr. Honeywell, Inc., Evanston, Ill., 1968-70; various positions Am. Hosp. Supply Co., Evanston, Ill., 1970-83, pres. Heyer-Schulte divsn., 1979-83; pres. COO Novacor Med. Corp., Oakland, Calif., 1984-85, also bd. dirs.; pres. ABA Bio Mgmt., Danville, Calif., 1985-87; chmn., CEO Keravision, Inc., Fremont, Calif., 1987—; founder, chmn., med. device CEO Roundtable, 1993—; asst. prof. surgery Creighton U. Med. Sch., Omaha, 1986-94; speaker in field. Contbr. articles on med. tech. and pub. policy to Wall St. Jour., others. Bd. dirs. Marymount Sch. Bd., 1981-84; bd. dirs. United Way Santa Barbara, 1981-84, assoc. chairperson, 1982-83, treas., 1983. Named One of 50 Rising Stars: Exec. Leaders for the 80's Industry Week mag., 1983. Mem. Assn. for Rsch. in Vision and Ophthalmology, Contact Lens Assn. Ophthalmology, Health Industry Mfrs. Assn. (spl. rep. bd. dirs. 1993-96, bd. dirs. 1997—, exec. com. 1997—, treas. 1998-00, chmn.-elect 2000—), Am. Entrepreneurs for Econ. Growth, Med. Tech. Leadership Forum, Calif. Healthcare Inst. (bd. dirs. 1998—, exec. com. 2000—). Roman Catholic. Achievements include leading development of Intacs corneal ring segments for treatment of nearsightedness (named One of Top 10 Medical Advances by Health Magazine/CNN 1999). Avocations: snow skiing, backpacking, oil painting, the arts. Office: KeraVision Inc 48630 Milmont Dr Fremont CA 94538-7353

LOBACHEV, VITALY VLADIMIROVICH, physics educator; b. St. Petersburg, Russia, Jan. 20, 1960; s. Vladimir Aleksandrovich and Galina Pavlovna (Habarina) L. Engr. Full Specialist diploma, Baltic State Tech. U., St. Petersburg, 1983, postgrad. course diploma, 1988, PhD of Engring. Sci., 1990. Engr. Baltic State Tech. U., St. Petersburg, 1983, chief computers, 1984-87, rschr., 1988, asst. educator, 1989-91, assoc. prof., 1992—, vice-dean aerospace faculty, 1990—; mem. Educators Trade Union, Baltic State Tech. U., St. Petersburg, 1989-97. Co-author: Physical Gasdynamic: Experimental Simulation and Diagnostics, 1986, Handbook: Methodical of Laboratory Papers on Computer Numerical Simulation, 1986, Plasma Generators and Their Power Supply Systems, 1987, Handbook: Mathematics Methods and Models for Computer Calculations, 1992, Optical Resonators-Science and Engineering, 1998; inventor in field; contbr. articles to profl. jours. Mem. Gardening Soc., Inventors Soc.. Sci. Counsel Baltic State U. Avocations: classical music, upright piano, singing, flowers, Russian bathhouse. Office: Baltic State Tech U, 1st Krasnoarmeyskaya 1, 198005 Saint Petersburg Russia

LOBAO, JOAO CORTEZ DE, economist; b. Lisbon, Portugal, June 27, 1962; s. Antonio Cortez and Maria Craveiro Lopes L.; m. Maria Mathias, Jan. 16, 1988; children: Martin, Mathilde, Tomas, Beatriz. Economist, U. Autonoma Lisboa, 1988; postgrad., NYU, 1997. Journalist Expresso, Portugal, 1988-92, editor, 1992-95; analyst Friends Ivory & Sime, N.Y.C., 1996-97, fund mgr., 1997-99; head sales Cisf Dealer, Lisbon, 1999—. Author: Guia da Poupança Investment Guide, 1991 (Best Seller 1991). Avocation: sailing. Office: Cisf Dealer Av Jose Malhoa, Lote 1686 5 Andar, 1070 Lisbon Portugal

LOBAS, LEONID GRYGOROVYCH, mechanics educator; b. Trushivtsi, Ukraine, Aug. 20, 1938; s. Grygorii Stepanovych and Ievdokiya Avramivna (Goncharenko) L.; m. Lyudmyla Genadiivna Kamyshanska, Oct. 31, 1968; children: Lada, Vladyslav. PhD, Nat. Acad. Scis., Kiev, Ukraine, 1963, prof., 1995; DSc, St. Petersburg State U., 1985. Engr. Inst. Mechanics Nat. Acad. Scis., Kiev, 1960-64; sr. rschr. Inst. Mechanics Nat. Acad. Scis., 1978-95; assoc. prof. Kiev Poly. Inst., 1965-77; head dept. theoretical and applied mechanics Kiev Rlwy. Transport Inst., 1996—; Author: Nonholonomic Models of Vehicles, 1986, Mechanics of Multilink Systems With Rolling, 2000; co-author: (with A.A. Martynyuk and N.V. Nikitina) Dynamics and Stability of the Motion of Vehicles, 1981, (with V.G. Verbitskii) Qualitative and Analytical Methods in Vehicle Dynamics, 1990; contbr. articles to profl. jours. Mem. Nat. Com. of Ukraine of Theoretical and Applied Mechanics, N.Y. Acad. Scis. Home: 27 Entuziastiv St Apt 88, 02147 Kiev Ukraine Office: Kiev Rlwy Transport Inst, Street Lukashevycha 19, 03049 Kiev Ukraine

LOBAY, IVAN, mechanical engineering educator; b. Koltuny, Ukraine, Oct. 4, 1911; came to U.S., 1961, naturalized, 1968; s. Stephan and Clementina (Maret) Lobay; m. Halyna Makarenko, Apr. 25, 1943; children: Maria Ivanna, Halyna Blahoslava. Mech. Engr., Inst. Tech., Brno, Czechoslovakia, 1940, Cen. U. Venezuela, Caracas, 1956. Registered profl. engr., Conn. Engr., designer Erste Bruenner Maschinenfabriksgesellschaft, Brno, 1940-41; asst. prof. dept. mech. engring. Inst. Tech., Lviv, Ukraine, 1942-43; sci. asst. dept. mech. engring. Inst. Tech., Brno, 1943-45; engr. san. and civil engring. Ministry San. Affairs, Caracas, Venezuela, 1948-59; prof. dept. civil engring. U. Santa Maria, Caracas, 1957-60; prof., chmn. divsn. tech. machines & prodn Cen. U. Venezuela Mech. Engring. Sch., Caracas, 1956-62; prof. dept. mech. engring. U. New Haven, West Haven, 1963-77, 83-84, prof. emeritus, 1984—; prof. gas sect. Inst. Algerien du Petrole, Boumerdes, Algeria, 1977-82; cons. Ministry of Edn., Ukraine, Kyiv, 1993. Author: Lecciones de Elementos de Maquinas, No. 3, 1960, No. 2, 1961, Estudio Sobre Descarga de Aguas de Lluvia, 1962, Free Lateral Discharge from an Open Triangular Channel, 1993, Education of Engineering Squads in USA, 1996, Workload of University Professors in USA, 1996, Faculty in Higher Education in USA, 1997, Governance in Higher Education in USA, 1999, Memoirs, 1999. With U.S. Army, 1945-47. Decorated Hramota and Cross of Merit Bukovynian Battalion, 1995; recipient Hramota award Govt. in Exile of Ukrainian Nat. Republic, 1992. Mem. AAUP, AAAS, ASME, NSPE, Conn. Soc. Profl. Engrs., N.Y. Acad. Scis., Ukrainian AAUP, Ukrainian Engrs. Soc. Am., Coll. Engrs. Venezuela, Assn. Profs. U. Ctrl. Venezuela, Acad. Engring. Scis. Ukraine. Home: 873 Orange Center Rd Orange CT 06477-1712

LÖBEL, ELISABETH, scientific researcher in linguistics; b. Balingen, Germany, Apr. 19, 1946; d. Herbert and Maria (Jenter) Wolfsteller; 1 child, Barbara Kristina. AD, Fachhochschule, Cologne, Germany, 1972; MA, U. Cologne, 1977, PhD in Gen. Linguistics, 1984, habilitation in Gen. Linguistics, 1996. Asst. dept. gen. linguistics U. Cologne, 1977-81, sci. rschr. dept. gen. linguistics, 1986-89, 95—; sci. rschr. dept. gen. linguistics U. Düsseldorf, Germany, 1991-95. Mem. Generative Linguistics in Old World, Societas Linguistica Europaea, Deutsche Gesellschaft für Sprachwissenschaft, Gesellschaft für Gebärdensprache und Kommunikation Gehörloser e.V. Avocations: sailing, hiking, violin. Home: Schenkspfad 9, D-51105 Cologne Germany Office: U Koln Inst Sprachwissenschaft, Meister-Ekkehart-Str 7, D-50923 Cologne Germany

LOBEL-ANGEL, MEREDITH ANNE, lawyer; b. San Francisco, Nov. 7, 1956; d. Charles I. and Julia V. Lobel; m. Frank P. Angel; 1 child, Fiona. BA, Stanford U., 1978, MA in Latin Am. Studies, 1979, MA in French, 1982, JD, 1983; postgrad., U. Paris, 1977-78. Bar: Calif. 1983, N.Y. 1984, D.C. 1985. With firm Chadbourne, Parke, Whiteside & Wolff, 1983-85, Kadison, Pfaelzer, Woodard, Quinn & Rossi, L.A., 1985-86, Tenenbaum & Ardi, L.A., 1986-87; with Viacom Prodns. Inc., Universal City, Calif., 1988-90; sole pracitioner Malibu and Hillsborough, Calif., 1990-96; dir. legal affairs Inscape, L.A., 1996-97; gen. counsel Graphix Zone Inc., L.A., 1997, Allstate Comms., Inc., Chatsworth, Calif., 98, Dream Works, L.L.C., 1998-99; dir. bus. devel. Riffage.com, 1999—; hon. consulate of Luxembourg, 1993—; arbitrator Los Angeles County Superior and Mcpl. Cts., 1994-96; judge pro tem small claims divsn. Malibu Mcpl. Ct., 1993-94; land trust dir. People for Parks, 1995-97. Mem. bd. visitors Stanford Law Sch., 1996-97. Contbr. chpts. to books, articles to profl. jours. Home: 2961 Valmere Dr Malibu CA 90265-2971

LOBERT, JÜRGEN MICHAEL, research chemist; b. Tauberbischofsheim, Germany, Mar. 24, 1958; came to U.S., 1991; s. Helmut Wilhelm Heinz and Irmgard Elisabeth (Ochs) L. Diploma, Tech. Hochschule, Darmstadt, Germany, 1985; PhD, Johannes Gutenberg U., Mainz, Germany, 1990. Rsch. asst. Tech. Hochschule, Darmstadt, 1984-85; vis. scientist Hahn Meitner Inst., Berlin, 1986; rsch. chemist Max Planck Inst., Mainz, 1986-91; rsch. assoc. NOAA, CMDL, Boulder, 1991-96; project scientist Scripps Inst. Oceanography, La Jolla, Calif., 1997—. Contbr. articles to profl. jours. Mem. Am. Geophys. Union, European Geophys. Soc. Avocations: skydiving, computer graphics, music, worldwide web publishing, outdoors. Home: PO Box 2226 La Jolla CA 92038-2226 Office: C4/SIO/U Calif San Diego 9500 Gilman Dr # 0239 La Jolla CA 92093-5004

LOBINGER, FREDERICH JOSEF, bishop; b. Passau, Bavaria, Germany, Jan. 22, 1929; arrived in South Africa, 1956; s. Hermann Lobinger and Martha Schreiner. D in Missiology, Theology Faculty, Muenster, Germany, 1971. Missionary Roman Cath. Ch., South Africa, 1956-70; dir. pastoral dept. Lumko Inst., South Africa, 1970-86; bishop Aliwal Diocese, South Africa, 1986—. Author: How Much Can Lay People Do?, 1973, Towards Non-Dominating Leadership, 1980. Chmn. Peace Com., Aliwal North, 1993-95. Avocation: mountaineering. Office: 24 Young St, PO Box 27, Aliwal North 5530, South Africa*

LOBO, CRISPINO SIMON, economist; b. Mombasa, Kenya, Sept. 3, 1956; arrived in India, 1970; s. Arcanjo Eugenio and Maria Angela Lobo. BA in Psychology, U. Pune, India, 1979; B of Philosophy, Inst. Philosophy & Religion, India, 1982; MA in Econs., Gokhale Inst. Politics/Econs., Pune, 1985; B of Theology, Vidyajyoti Inst. Rel. Studies, New Delhi, 1989. Program coord. Indo German Watershed Devel. Program, Maharashtra, India, 1989—; mng. trustee, exec. dir. Watershed Orgn. Trust, Ahmednagar, India, 1993—; mem. NGO Task Force for World Bank Funded Project, Govt. Maharashtra, 1998; mem. State-Level Working Group for Prep. of State Forestry Plan, Maharashtra, 1995; mem. regional sanctioning com. Indo-German Social Svc. Soc., Pune, India, 1997—; mem., trustee Social Ctr., Ahmednagar, 1992—. Co-author: (book) The Rain Decided to Help Us, 1995; team leader: (documentary videos) Your Future Is in Your Hands, 1995, Water Gives Life, 1998, other videos on watershed devel. and women's empowerment. Mem. Dist. Literacy Mission, Ahmednagar. Avocations: painting, music, traveling, reading. Office: WOTR-Paryavaran, Market Yard Rd, Ahmednagar India

LOBOCKI, MIECZYSLAW HENRYK, psychologist, educator; b. Starogard, Poland, Aug. 18, 1929; s. Jan and Zofia (Lapka) L. MA, Cath. U., Lublin, Poland, 1956. Tchr. Grammar Sch., Swidnik, Poland, 1957-58; asst. Cath. U., Lublin, Poland, 1958-62; asst. Maria Curie-Sklodowska U., Lublin, Poland, 1962-68, asst. prof., 1968-77, assoc. prof., 1977-86, prof., 1986—, vice dean, 1982-87; vice dir. Inst. Pedagogics, Lublin, 1978-81; mem. Ctrl. Cmty. Awarding Scientific Titles, Warsaw, Poland, 1991-93. Contbr. articles to profl. jours., 20 books. Inspector juvenile deliquents County Ct., Lublin, 1958-68. Mem. Polish Psychol. Soc., Polish Pedagogical Soc., Scientific Soc. Cath. U. Avocations: gardening, classical music, trips. Home: Skrzetuskiego 6/26, 20-628 Lublin Poland Office: Inst Pedagogiki, Narutowicza 12, 20-004 Lublin Poland

LOBODA-CACKOVIC, JASNA, physicist, researcher, artist, sculptor; b. Homec, Slovenia, Mar. 29, 1935; arrived in Germany, 1970; d. Peter and Jelena (Zrinski) L.; m. Hinko Cackovic, July 28, 1962. Diploma, U. Zagreb, Croatia, 1960, MSc, 1964; PhD, Max Planck Inst./U. Zagreb, Croatia, 1970; promotion work, Fritz-Haber-Inst., Max-Planck-Gesellsch., Berlin, 1970. Cert. scientist. Scientist Atom Inst. Ruder Boskovic, Zagreb, Croatia, 1960-71; hon. asst. U. Zagreb, Croatia, 1961-65; scientist Fritz-Haber Inst. der Max-Planck-Gesellschaft, Berlin, 1965-67, 70-97. Sculptures, reliefs and paintings in (journals) Der Künstler No. 1-7, 1988-90, Kunstblatt No. 1 and 2, 1995, Kunst-Aktuell No. 2 and 9, 1995, 99, Kunst-Aktuell, Art Frankfurt, 1996, Meisterwerke zeitgenössischer Kunst, 1998, Meisterwerke Künstler unserer Zeit, 1999, (books) Allgemeines Lexikon der Kunstschaffenden in der Bildenden und Gestaltenden Kunst des Ausgehenden XX, Jahrhunderts, Band 3, 1993, Dokumenta Artis, 1995, 99, Meister Bildender Künste, Band 3, 1996, 4, 1999Modern Artists 3D-Art, 1996, and numerous catalogs; exhbns. in Germany, Austria, France, Monaco, Switzerland, croatia, Luxembourg and in the Internet, 1998, 99; permanent representation Bildhauergalerie Plinthe, Berlin, 1987-95; contbr. over 65 sci. articles to profl. jours. and books. Recipient Euro medal in gold Art and Culture Exhbn., Zürich, Switzerland, 1989, Euro art plaquette Paris Exhbn., 1989, three Euro hon. prizes Berlin Exhbn., 1993, Dresden, Germany, 1994, Baden-Baden, Germany, 1995, prizes for sculptor, 5th Offener Kunstpreis, Bad Nauheim, Germany, 1995, for sculpture, photography and graphics 6th Offener Kunstpreis, 1st Internat. Virtueller Internet Kunstwettbewerb, 1998; Grantee Atom Inst. Ruder Boskovic, Zagreb, Croatia, 1965-66, Deutsche Forschungsgemeinschaft, Germany, 1966, Deutscher Akademischer Austauschdienst, Germany, 1966-67, Alexander von Humboldt Stiftung, Bad Godesberg, Germany, 1970-71. Mem. Internat. Biog. Assn. Avocations: literature, music, astrophysics. Home and Studio: IM DOL 60, 14195 Berlin Germany

LOBO-GUERRERO U., ALBERTO, geologist, consultant; b. Bogotá, Colombia, Oct. 3, 1942; s. Alberto Lobo-Guerrero D. and Sofía Uscátegui M.; m. Beatriz Sanz S., Apr. 8, 1967; children: Alberto, Andrés, María Camila, Luis Ernesto, Nicolás. Degree in Geology, Univ. Nacional de Colombia, 1964; MSc in Geology, Stanford U., 1968. Geologist Richfield Oil Corp., Bogotá, 1965, Servicio Geológico Nacional, Bogotá, 1966-69; geologist, cons. Lobo-Guerrero Geología Ltd., Bogotá, 1970-76, 80-86, 1989—; supt. mining Cemento Samper S.A., Bogotá, 1976-80; gen. dir. Ingeominas, Bogotá, 1986-88. Mem. Geol. Assn. Nat. Univ. (pres. 1976), Soc. Colombiana de Geologia (pres. 1982-84), Internat. Assn. Engring. Geology, Soc. Colombiana de Geotecnia, Internat. Assn. Hydrogeologists. Avocations: tennis, reading. Office: Lobo-Guerrero Geologia Ltd, AA100777 Santa Fè de Bogotá Colombia

LOBRANO, STEPHEN DAVID, lawyer; b. Baton Rouge, Nov. 28, 1947; s. Thomas Skinner Jr. and Villa Rose (Virgets) L.; m. Cynthia B. Lobrano, May 27, 1972; children: Stephen David Jr., Lauren Carrie. BBA, Loyola U., New Orleans, 1972; JD, Tulane U., 1975. Bar: Fla., U.S. Ct. Appeals (11th cir.). Clerk to Hon. Bryan Simpaon U.S. Cir. Ct., Jacksonville, Fla., 1975-76; assoc. Mahoney Hadlow & Adams, Jacksonville, 1976-80; ptnr. Bledsoe Gallagher Mikals & Schmidt, Jacksonville, 1980-81, Knight Kincaid Poucher & Lobrano, Jacksonville, 1981-83, Lobrano & Kincaid PA, Jacksonville, 1983—; dir. Koger Equity Inc., Jacksonville, 1989-91, Chattanooga Group, Inc, Tenn., 1996-98. Editor (articles) Tulane Law Rev., 1974-75. Bd. dirs. Jacksonville Art Mus., 1986-90, Jacksonville Zool. Soc., 1979-90. Mem. River Club, Timuquana Country Club. Republican. Episcopalian. E-mail: lobrano@bellsouth.net. Office: Lobrano & Kincaid PL 4325 Yacht Club Rd Jacksonville FL 32210-8317

LOCH, JOHN ROBERT, educational administrator; b. Aug. 25, 1940; s. Robert Addison and Mary Virginia (Beck) L. Student, Waynesburg Coll., 1958; AB, Grove City Coll., 1962; postgrad., Pitts. Theol. sem., 1962; MEd, U. Pitts., 1966, PhD, 1972; cert., Harvard U., 1984. Cert. program planner. Asst. to dean of men, program planner U. Pitts., 1963-64, dir. student union, 1964-70, dir. student affairs rsch., 1970-71, dir. suburban ednl. svcs. Sch. Gen. Studies, 1971-75; dir. continuing edn. and pub. svc. Youngstown (Ohio) State U., 1975-82, dir. univ. outreach, 1990—; chief adminstrv. officer Metro Coll., 1996-98; assoc. mem. grad. faculty, 1980-95; rsch. assoc. Pres.'s Commn. on Campus Unrest, 1970; bd. dirs. Park Vista Retirement Comty., 1993-99, chmn. program com., 1994-95, vice chair bd. dirs., 1995-96, mktg. com., 1999—; trustee Ohio Presbyn. Retirement Comtys., 1993-99, mem. program com., 1993-99. Trustee Mahoning Shenango Area Health Edn. Network, 1976-91, Career Devel. Ctr. for Women, 1978-80; trustee Youngstown Area Arts Coun., 1980-85, pres., 1981-83; bd. dirs. Protestant Family Svcs., 1981-83; active Older Adults Task Force, Mahoning County, 1992-96; trustee Mahoning County RSVP, 1983-89, chmn. evaluation com., 1983-84, chmn. pers. com., 1984-85, chmn. bd. trustees, 1986-87; coord. fund raising Nat. Unity Campaign, Mahoning County, 1980; state chmn. Young Rep. Coll. Coun. Pa., 1960. Mem. AAUW, Assn. Continuing Higher Edn. (chair-elect region VI 1997-98, chair 1998-99), Adult Edn. Assn. USA, Nat. U. Continuing Edn. Assn., Ohio Coun. Higher Continuing Edn. (pres. 1979-80), Ohio Continuing Higher Edn. Assn. (hon. life mem., co-chmn. constn. com. 1982, v.p. state univs. 1984-85, pres.-elect 1985-86, pres. 1986-87, historian 1988-96, chair awards and honors com. 1989-92, editor Voluntary Continuing Edn. Requirements 1993-95, Spl. Svc. award 1989), Ohio-Pa. Higher Edn. Network (chair 1989-90), Learning Resources Network (Univ. Coun. Gt. Lakes rep. 1996—), Youngstown Traffic Club (hon. life mem.), Youngstown Club, Kiwanis (dir. 1981-82), Youngstown Dist., Purchasing Mgrs. Assn., Omicron Delta Kappa, Kappa Kappa Psi, Phi Kappa Phi (pres. 1980-81, pres. 1994-95, 96-97, Disting. Mem. award 2000), Alpha Phi Omega, Alpha Sigma Lambda, Phi Delta Kappa. Presbyterian. Home: 242 Upland Ave Youngstown OH 44504-1849 Office: Met Coll Southwoods Commons 100 De Bartolo Pl Youngstown OH 44512

LOCHBIHLER, FREDERICK VINCENT, lawyer; b. Chgo., Jan. 30, 1951; s. Frederick Louis and Marion Helen (Rutkauskas) L.; m. Darlene Gotfryde Wantuch, Nov. 8, 1952; 1 child, Frederick Karlman. AB in Govt. summa cum laude, U. Notre Dame, 1973; JD with honors, U. Chgo., 1976. Bar: Ill. 1976, U.S. Dist. Ct. (no. dist.) Ill. 1977, U.S. Ct. Appeals (7th cir.) 1980, U.S. Ct. Appeals (8th cir.) 1981, U.S. Supreme Ct. 1982, U.S. Dist. Ct. (ctrl. dist.) Ill. 1983, U.S. Dist. Ct. Ariz. 1991. Assoc. Chapman and Cutler, Chgo., 1976-84, ptnr., 1984—. Mem. Phi Beta Kappa, Order of Coif. Avocations: military history, literature, travel. Home: PO Box 72 Golf IL 60029-0072 Office: Chapman and Cutler 111 W Monroe St Ste 1700 Chicago IL 60603-4006

LOCHHEAD, ROBERT BRUCE, lawyer; b. St. Louis, June 20, 1952; s. Angus Tulloch and Matilda Evangeline (Thurman) L.; m. KLynn Walker, June 21, 1974; children: Robert, Richard, Cynthia, Melinda, Rebekah, Elizabeth. BA, Brigham Young U., 1975; JD, Columbia U., 1978. Bar: D.C. 1979, Utah 1980, U.S. Dist. Ct. Utah 1980, U.S. Ct. Appeals (10th cir.) 1980, U.S. Supreme Ct. 1986. Law clk. to judge U.S. Ct. Appeals (10th cir.), Salt Lake City, 1978-79; assoc. Hogan & Hartson, Washington, 1979-80, Larsen, Kimball, Parr & Crockett, Salt Lake City, 1980-82; shareholder Parr, Waddoups Brown, Gee & Loveless, Salt Lake City, 1982—; judge pro tem Small Claims Ct., Salt Lake City, 1985-88; mem. panel of arbitrators U.S. Bankruptcy Ct., Dist. Utah, 1995—. Harlan Fiske Stone scholar, 1976-78. Mem. ABA, Am. Bankruptcy Inst. Mormon. Home: 492 N Flint St Kaysville UT 84037-9777 Office: Parr Waddoups Brown Gee & Loveless 185 S State St Ste 1300 Salt Lake City UT 84111-1537

LOCHMILLER, KURTIS L., real estate entrepreneur; b. Sacramento, Dec. 30, 1952; s. Rodney Glen and Mary Margaret (Frauen) L.; m. Mariye Susan Mizuki, Nov. 9, 1951; children: Margaux Sian, Chase Jordan. BA in Econs. and Fin., U. Denver, 1975. Dist. sales mgr. Hertz Truck Div., Denver, 1975-76; drilling foreman Shell Oil, Alaska, Mont., Colo., 1976-79; pres., owner Kurtex Mortgage & Devel. Co., Denver, 1979—, Kurtex Properties Inc., Denver, 1980-86; pres., chief exec. officer Kurtex Inc., Denver, 1981—, Bankers Pacific Mortgage, Denver, 1980—, Bankers Fin. Escrow Corp., Denver, 1984—, Northwest Title & Escrow, Denver, 1984—; pres., chief exec. officer Steamboat Title, Steamboat Springs, Colo., 1985—, First Escrow, Denver, 1986—, Fidelity-Commonwealth-Continental Escrow, Denver, 1984—; pres. Colonnade Ltd., Denver, 1981-88; pres., bd. dirs. Breckridge (Colo.) Brewery. V.p., founder Colfax on the Hill, Denver, 1984; mediator, arbitrator Arbitrator/Mediation Assn., Denver, 1986; mem. Police Athletic League, Denver, 1988. Recipient Pres. Spl. Achievement/Founder award Colfax on the Hill, Denver, 1984, Spl. Mayor's award, City & County of Denver, 1985. Mem. Nat. Assn.of Real Estate Appraisers, Internat. Brotherhood of Teamsters, Colo. Mortgage Bankers Assn., Mortgage Banking Assn., Denver C. of C., Phi Beta Kappa, Omicron Delta Epsilon. Clubs: U.S. Karate Assn. (Phoenix) (3d degree Black Belt), Ferrari (Portland). Lodge: Internat. Supreme Council Order of Demolay. Avocations: collecting cars, karate, fishing, art collecting. Home: 1 Carriage Ln Littleton CO 80121-2010 Office: Bankers Fin Escrow Corp 9655 E 25th Ave Ste 101 Aurora CO 80010-1056

LOCHRIDGE, STANLEY KEITH, cardiovascular and thoracic surgeon; b. Tupelo, Miss., Jan. 24, 1947; s. Oscar Wendell and Willie Lou (Stidham) L.; m. Catherine Louise Jones, Oct. 2, 1983; children: Kirby, Kristin, Erin. BS, U. Ala., Tuscaloosa, 1968; MD, U. Ala., Birmingham, 1972. Diplomate Am. Bd. Surgery, Am. Bd. Thoracic Surgery. Intern and resident Carraway Meth. Med. Ctr., Birmingham, Ala., 1972-76; cardiac fellow U. Iowa Hosps., Iowa City, 1976-78; cardiac surgeon CardioThoracic Surgeons, P.C., Birmingham, 1978-89, Norwood Clinic, P.C., Birmingham, 1989—. Major, U.S. Army N.G., 1972-79, Birmingham. Fellow ACS, Am. Coll. Cardiology, Am. Coll. Chest Physicians; mem. Internat. Cardiovasc. Soc., Soc. Thoracic Surgeons, So. Soc. Thoracic Surgeons, Alpha Omega Alpha. Republican. Methodist. Avocations: hiking, boating, skiing. Office: Norwood Clinic PC 1528 Carraway Blvd Birmingham AL 35234-1991

LOCHTER, ANDRÉ, biosciences researcher; b. Alpen, NRW, Germany, Nov. 9, 1962; s. Helmut and Gertrud (Overmeyer) L. BS, U. Mainz, Germany, 1986; MS, U. Heidelberg, Germany, 1989; PhD in Bioscis., Swiss Fed. Inst. Tech., Zurich, 1993. Jr. scientist U. Heidelberg, 1988-90, Coll. of France, Paris, 1990, Ecole Normale Supérieure, Paris, 1991; scientist Swiss Fed. Inst. Tech., 1991-93, Lawrence Berkeley (Calif.) Nat. Lab., 1994-97; sr. scientist Ctr. for Clin. and Basic Rsch., Ballerup, Denmark, 1998-99; chief bus. devel. officer OsteoPro A/S, Herlev, Denmark, 2000—. Contbr. articles to sci. jours., including Molecular Biology of Cell, Jour. Cell Biology, Seminars in Cancer Rsch., Jour. Neurosci. Fellow Found. German People, 1991, European Molecular Biology Orgn., 1994, Breast Cancer Rsch. Program, Calif., 1996. Office: OsteoPro A/S, Osteopark, Herlev Hovedgade 207, DK-2730 Herlev Denmark

LOCIGNO, PAUL ROBERT, public affairs executive; b. Cleve., Sept. 17, 1948; s. Paul Robert and Anna Mae (Zingale) L.; m. Ki Cho Rim; children: Paul III, Tammy, Robert. AA, Cuyahoga C.C., Parma, Ohio, 1974; BA, Case Western Res. U., 1976; postgrad., Cleve. State U., 1977-78. Part-time faculty Cuyahoga Community Coll., 1979-83; vice-chmn. Presdl. Inaugural Labor Com., Washington, 1980-81; vice-chmn. labor com. Presdl. Inaugural Com., Washington, 1984-85; legis. agt. Internat. Brotherhood of Teamsters, Washington, 1977-90, dir. govt. internat. affairs, 1983-89; dir. Asian/Pacific br. Internat. Brotherhood of Teamsters, Taipei, Taiwan, 1985-88; spl. rep. of chmn. Hill & Knowlton Pub. Affairs Worldwide, Washington, 1989-91; pres., founding ptnr. Rollins Internat. Ltd., Alexandria, Va., 1997—; CEO Ganeden Biotech Inc., San Diego; bd. dirs. Nanjing Ya Dong Corp. Mem. Pres.'s Export Coun., 1988-89; mem. Asia adv. com. Bicentennial of U.S. Constitution, 1990; bd. govs. Am. League for Exports and Security Assistance, 1989; mem. Nat. Commn. for Employment Policy, Washington, 1981-86; bd. dirs. Children's Right Coun., Washington, 1997—. With USMC, 1968-70, Vietnam. Republican. Roman Catholic. Avocations: archery, golf, fishing. Home: 15100 Hawksbill Ct Woodbridge VA 22193-5831 Office: Ganeden Biotech Inc 1228 Euclid Ave Ste 900 Cleveland OH 44115-1845

LOCK, CHRISTOPHER PETER, English educator; b. London, Jan. 15, 1949; s. Eric and Kathleen (Wheelan) L.; m. Takako Mashiba, Aug. 25, 1995. BA, Pacific Western U., 1994, postgrad., 1997—. Archt. and bldg. draftsman Townsville Airport, Queensland, Australia, 1979-80; ESL instr. Osaka, Japan, 1980-84; head edn. ATTY Lang. Inst., Osaka, 1984-90; mgr. Anglo Continental Tip-Top Sch. English, Osaka, 1990-92; ESL instr. Osaka U. Arts Jr. Coll., Chiyoda Jr. Coll., Osaka, 1992—; ESL and lit. instr. Osaka U. Fgn. Studies, 1995—, ESL instr. Osaka Prefectural U., 2000—. Mem. Japan Assn. Lang. Tchrs., Soc. Archl. Illustration, Oxford Club. Avocations: photography, writing, art. Home: Tanimachi 7 chome, 5-5-401 Chuo-ku, Osaka 542-0012, Japan Office: Osaka U Fgn Studies, 8-8-1 Aomatani Higashi, Minoo-shi Osaka 562, Japan

LOCKE, AUSTIN SIMON, sports physician; b. Goulburn, NSW, Australia, Aug. 3, 1951; s. Austin James and Norma Mary (White) L.; m. Robyn Petula Clarice (div. Dec. 6,1992); m. Melissa Hewitt, Nov. 26, 1994; children: Tobias, Austin, Bronte Rose. B of Med. Sci., U. Tasmania, Hobart, Australia, 1972, MB BS, 1975. Med. Bd. Queensland. Resident Princess Alexandra Hosp., Brisbane, Australia, 1976-77; registrar Principle Alexandra Hosp., Brisbane, Australia, 1978-79; gen. practice Brisbane, Australia, 1979-90; cons. Australian Inst. Sport, Brisbane, Australia, 1989—; sports physician Brisbane, Australia, 1991—; med. coord. Australian Inst. Sport, Brisbane, Australia, 1991—, Queensland Acad. Sport, Brisbane, Australia, 1992—; nat. sci./med. com. Squash, Australia, 1993—, Diving, Brisbane, 1993; cons. nat. teams for canoeing, ice skating and diving; reviewer Internat. Jour. Sports Medicine, Denmark, 1996. Contbr. articles to profl. jours. Bd. dirs. Sports Medicine Australia, Brisbane, 1985-89; nat. bd. mem. Australian Coun. Sports Physicians, 1990-95, exec. mem., 1990-92, pres. 1990-95. Fellow Royal Australian Coll. Gen. Practitioners, Australian Coll. Sports Physicians (v.p. 2000—), Australian Sports Medicine Fedn.; mem. Brisbane Polo Club, Brisbane Golf Club. Avocations: skiing, sailing, golf, cycling. Home: 75 Bribane Corso, Brisbane 4103, Australia Office: Sunnybank Med Clinic, 6 Woodsiana St, Brisbane 4109, Australia

LOCKE, JENNIFER LYNNE, mortgage services professional; b. Milw., Apr. 8; d. Sandra Ellen Schleier; m. Jerry Lee Locke, Aug. 8, 1998. Student, Alverno Coll., 1999—. Teller Bank One, Germantown, Wis., 1996, Norwest Bank, Grafton, Wis., 1997; bookseller Harry W. Schwartz Bookshop, Mequon, Wis., 1998; consumer loan processor Mut. Savs. Bank, Milw., 1999; mortgage servicer Wauwatosa (Wis.) Savs. Bank, 2000—. Mem. Milw. Symphony Orch. Chorus, 1999-00. Scholar Ozaukee (Wis.) Chorus, 1996. Avocations: swimming, reading, thinking. E-mail: lockejl@alverno.edu. Home: 305 N 60th St Milwaukee WI 53213-4221

LOCKE, WILLIAM, retired endocrinologist; b. Morden, Man., Can., Mar. 16, 1916; s. Corbet and Ruby Louise (Brown) L.; m. Katherine Elizabeth Acer Russell, Sept. 29, 1945 (dec.). MD, U. Man., Winnipeg, 1938; MS in Medicine, U. Minn., 1947. Diplomate Am. Bd. Internal Medicine. Intern Winnipeg (Man., Can.) Gen. Hosp., 1937-38; fellow in medicine Mayo Found., Rochester, Minn., 1938-40, 46-48; rsch. fellow Harvard U., Boston, 1948-50; staff Ochsner Clinic, New Orleans, 1950-2000, sr. cons., 1987-2000; clin. prof. medicine Tulane U., New Orleans, 1968-86, prof. emeritus, 1986-2000, ret., 2000; sec. Alton Ochsner Med. Found., New Orleans, 1950—; pres. med. staff Ochsner Found. Hosp., New Orleans, 1954-55, trustee, 1978—; cons. in endocrinology Ochsner Found. Hosp., New Orleans, 1998—. Author, editor: Hypothalmus and Pituitary in Health and Disease, 1972; contbr. chpts. to books and articles to profl. jours. Lt. comdr. RCNVR, 1940-46. NIH grant, 1958-62. Fellow ACP; mem. Am. Diabetes Assn., Endocrine Soc., Sigma Xi. Republican. Episcopalian. Home: 150 Broadway St Apt 1104 New Orleans LA 70118-7612 Office: Ochsner Clinic 1514 Jefferson Hwy New Orleans LA 70121-2483

LOCKETT, LANDON JOHNSON, retired linguistic educator, researcher; b. Ft. Benning, Ga., May 22, 1929; s. Landon Johnson and Roberta Blye (Davies) J.; m. Carol Yvonne Ramsay, Aug. 11, 1990. BA, U. Tex., 1954, LLB, 1957, PhD, 1968; M of Comparative Law, So. Meth. U., 1959. Bar: Tex. Atty. Raymond M. Hill and Assocs., Houston, 1957-61; NDEA fellow U. Tex., Austin, 1962-65, instr. Portuguese, 1965-69, asst. prof. Portuguese lang. & linguistics, 1969-75; assoc. prof. linguistics Univ. Fed. Rio Grande North, Natal, Brazil, 1982-83; vis. prof. linguistics Pontificia Univ. Cath. Rio Grande South, Porto Alegre, Brazil, 1970, Univ. Autonoma Guadalajara, Mex., 1976-77, Univ. Fed. Rio Grande North, 1978-82; conservation rschr., advocate. Author: O Uso do Infinitivo num Corpus de Portugues Coloquial Brasileiro, 1969; contbr. articles to profl. jours. Cadet U.S. Cadet Corps, 1948-50. Recipient Nancy benedict Meml. award Native Plant Soc. Tex., 1994. Mem. Tex. Acad. Sci., Tex. State Hist. Assn. Achievements include discovery of wild population of Sabal mexicana palm trees 200 miles north of what was believed to be northern limit of range; led successful effort to protect unique population of apparent Sabal mexicana X, minor hybrid palms. Home: 3210 Stevenson Ave Austin TX 78703-2242

LOCKETT-EGAN, MARIAN WORKMAN, advertising executive; b. Murray, Ky., May 5, 1931; d. Otis H. Workman and Myrtle A. (Jones) Jordan; m. Gene Potts, Jan. 6, 1947 (div. Feb. 1962); children: Reed Nasser, Jennifer Anglin, George M. Potts, Cynthia Klenk; m. Barker Lockett, Oct. 11, 1963 (div. Dec. 1972); 1 child, Stephen R.W.; m. Douglas S. Egan Jr., Feb. 14, 1981. BA, Murray State U., 1962. Asst. media dir. Noble-Dury & Assocs., Nashville, 1963-64; asst. rsch. dir. Triangle Publs., Phila., 1964-66; assoc. media dir. Lewis & Gilman, Phila., 1966-72; v.p. advt. media Scott Paper Co., Phila., 1972-83; pres. DMS Communications Inc., Ardmore, Pa., 1983—; exec. dir. The Media Sch., N.Y.C., 1983-85, 87—; mem. TV com. Assn. Nat. Advertisers, N.Y.C., 1977-83; guest lectr. Wharton U., Phila., 1981-82, 85, 86, 87; Gannet vis. prof. Sch. Journalism, U. Fla., Gainesville, 1982. Guest editor Media decisions, 1981. Trustee Meth. Hosp. Found., Phila., 1973-87; pres. Broadcast Pioneers of Phila., 1994-96. Mem. Broadcast Pioneers (pres. 1994-96), TV and Radio Advt. Club (pres. 1973). Republican. Episcopalian. Avocations: sailing, tennis. Home: 45 Llanfair Cir Ardmore PA 19003-3342

LOCKHART, CHARLES FREDRICK, dentist; b. Mpls., Nov. 9, 1943; s. Walter Lawrence and Lua Jane (Bates) L.; m. Leonora Pennell, Oct. 24, 1998; children: Kendra Paige, Charles Davidson. Student, U. Iowa, 1961-63, Northwestern U., 1967-68; BS in Dentistry, U. Ill., Chgo., 1971, DDS with honors, 1973. Ptnr. Northview Dental Assocs., Ltd., Northfield, Ill., 1974-85; gen. practice dentistry Chgo., 1985-90; ptnr. Town Centre Dental Group, 1990—; pres. Sutra, Ltd., Chgo., 1980—. Editor Pulse Newsletter, 1974-75. Served with USN, 1964-67. Fellow Acad. Gen. Dentistry (master, del. 1979—, sec. 1985—, v.p. 1987, council on dental care 1985—), Acad. Continuing Edn. (charter, 1979, coun. on legis. 1989); mem. ADA, Ill. State Dental Soc., Chgo. Dental Soc., Ill. Acad. Gen. Dentistry (bd. dirs. 1979—, pres. elect 1988, pres. 1989), U. Ill. Alumni Assn. (life), Internat. Platform Assn., U.S. Curling Assn. (bd. dirs. 1987—, v.p. Buffalo Grove, Ill. chpt. 1989—), Caviste-Chaine Des Rotisseurs, Psi Omega, Delta Chi, Omicron Kappa Upsilon. Methodist. Club: North Shore Country (Glenview, Ill.), Wine Label Circle (London). Lodge: Knights of the Vine (master councillor 1982—). Avocations: wine, curling, racquetball. Home: 1561 Winnetka Rd Glenview IL 60025-1821 Office: 4748 N Milwaukee Ave Chicago IL 60630-3646 also: 636 Church St Evanston IL 60201-4508

LOCKHART, MADGE CLEMENTS, educational organization executive; b. Soddy, Tenn., May 22, 1920; d. James Arlie and Ollie (Sparks) Clements; m. Andre J. Lockhart, Apr. 24, 1942 (div. 1973); children: Jacqueline, Andrew, Janice, Jill. Student, East Tenn. U., 1938-39; BS, U. Tenn., Chattanooga and Knoxville, 1955, MEd, 1962. Elem. tchr. Tenn. and Ga., 1947-60, Brainerd H.S., Chattanooga, 1960-64, Cleveland (Tenn.) City Schs., 1966-88; owner, operator Lockhart's Learning Ctr., Inc., Cleveland and Chattanooga, 1975—; co-founder, pres. Hermes, Inc., 1973-79; co-founder Dawn Ctr., Hamilton County, Tenn., 1974; apptd. mem. Tenn. Gov.'s Acad. for Writers. Author poetry, short stories and fiction; contbr. articles to profl. jours. and newspapers. Pres. Cleveland Assn. Retarded Citizens, 1970, state v.p., 1976; pres. Cherokee Easter Seal Soc., 1973-76, Cleveland Creative Arts Guild, 1980; bd. dirs. Tenn. Easter Seal Soc., 1974-77, 80-83; chair Bradley County Internat. Yr. of Child; mem. panel for grants Coun. Govts. S.E. Tenn. Devel. Dist., 1990-92; mem. Internat. Biog. Centre Adv. Coun., Cambridge, Eng., 1991-92; mem. mayor's com. Mus. for Bradley County, Tenn., 1992—. Recipient Service to Mankind award Sertoma, 1978, Gov.'s award for service to handicapped, 1979; mental health home named in her honor, Tenn., 1987. Mem. NEA (life), Tenn. Edn. Assn., Am. Assn. Rehab. Therapy, S.E. Tenn. Arts Coun., Cleveland Edn. Assn. (Service to Humanity award 1987). Mem. Ch. of Christ. Clubs: Byliners, Fantastiks. Home: 3007 Oakland Dr NW Cleveland TN 37312-5281

LOCKHART-MURE, DAVID See RENTON, RIGHT HON. LORD

LOCKIE, ANDREW CAMERON KNIGHT, physician; b. Glasgow, Scotland, May 14, 1938; s. Andrew Cameron and Isabel Mary (Knight) L.; m. Rosemary Catherine Campbell Lockie; children: Andrew David MacKenzie, Shona Mary Campbell, Angus Cameron. BS in Pharmacology (hon.), Edinburgh U., 1964; MBChB, Edinburgh Med. Sch., 1966. Squadron leader Royal Air Force, 1967-72; gen. med. practitioner Stratford Upon Avon, United Kingdom, 1972-98; sr. fellow in travel medicine dept. pub. health U. Glasgow, 1998—. Co-author: Inection, 1994; edtl. adv.: Practitioner Mag., 1978—; contbr. chpts. in field. Decorated mem. Order Brit. Empire. Fellow Royal Coll. Gen. Practitioners, Royal Coll. Physicians (Edinburgh), Royal Geog. Soc., Royal Soc. Tropical Medicine; mem. Royal Coll. Physicians (London), Internat. Soc. Travel Medicine, Brit. Med. Assn., Brit. Travel Health Assn. (chmn.).

LOCKLIN, KENNETH ROBERT, international venture capitalist, merchant banker; b. N.Y.C., May 29, 1949; s. Wilbert Edwin and Olga Maria (Osterwald) L.; m. Helen D. Weiland, Sept. 10, 1983; children: Kayla Weiland, Connor Weiland. BA in Psychology and History, Yale U., 1972. Mgmt. trainee Hartford (Conn.) Nat. Bank, 1972-73, fin. analyst, 1973-74, sr. fin. analyst, 1974; v.p. project devel. Equator Bank Ltd., Hartford, 1974-81, v.p. corp. fin., 1982-83; exec. dir. Equator Adv. Svcs. Ltd., Hartford, 1983-85; chief adminstr. officer Equator Holdings, Nassau, Bahamas, 1986; founder, mgr. Africa Growth Fund, L.P., Washington, 1987-91; pres. Advantage Fin. Svcs., Inc., Storrs, Conn., 1990-97; mng. dir. EIF Group, Washington, 1997—; founder, mgr. Renewable Energy and Energy Efficiency Fund, Washington, 2000—; sr. advisor, dir. environ. investment and fin. A.T. Internat., Washington, 1991-97; bd. dirs. Washington, Sch. for Field Studies, Boston, NESEA, Greenfield, Mass. Mem. Internat. Wilderness Leadership Found., Nature Conservancy, N.E. Sustainable Energy Assn., Club of 1000. Office: EIF Group 2000 L St NW 2d Fl Rd Washington DC 20005

LOCKLIN, RONALD MAURICE, software executive; b. Albion, Mich., June 9, 1958; s. Maurice George and Alice Ann Locklin; m. Lisa Jeanne Robinson, May 26, 1991; children: Matthew Joseph, Benjamin Samuel. BA summa cum laude, Colgate U., 1980; MBA, Dartmouth Coll., 1984. Assoc. Mercer Cons., Lexington, Mass., 1984-88; dir. Bull S.A., Paris, 1988-94; v.p. Digital Equipment, Maynard, Mass., 1995-98, Compaq Computer, Houston, 1998-99, PTC, Waltham, Mass., 1999-2000, Openpages, Westford, Mass., 2000—. Contbr. articles to profl. jours. Mem. Assn. Strategic Alliance Profls., Phi Gamma Delta, Phi Beta Kappa. E-mail: locklin@banet.net. Home: 463 Massachusetts Ave Acton MA 01720-2933

LOCKSPEISER, NANCY FLANDERS, artist, designer; b. Boston, Oct. 9, 1941; d. Louis Hequembourg Flanders Jr. and Florence Lucille Reiter; m. Lester Lockspeiser, Oct. 3, 1969; children: Tai Mara, Brett Louis. BA, Cornell U., 1963; postgrad., U. Colo., 1972-73. Copywriter Cabot, Cabot & Forbes, Boston, 1963-69; copywriter, acting art dir. N.Y. State Urban Devel. Corp., N.Y.C., 1969-72; pub. rels., promotion Hugh Stubbins & Assocs., Cambridge, Mass., 1973-75; art dir., designer Children's Diabetes Found., Denver, 1976-92; prin. Lockspeiser Graphic Design, Denver, 1976—. Commd. print Dr. Henry Kissinger, 1979, Rocky Mountain Hebrew Acad., 1979, Ctrl. City Opera Ho. Assn., 1981, Nat. Multiple Schlerosis, 1989. Guest lectr. Denver Audubon Soc., 1977; mem. Denver Art Mus. Alliance Contemporary Art, 1978—, Guild Children's Diabetes Found., Denver, 1979—, Nat. Mus. Women Arts, 1981—; artist Denver Sister Cities Internat., 1998—, Arthritis Found., Nat. Multiple Schlerosis. Recipient Halo award Denver Advt. Fedn., 1997. Mem. Acad. Am. Poets. Home and Office: 770 Lafayette St Denver CO 80218-3503

LOCKTON, DAVID BALLARD, business executive; b. Indpls., Mar. 28, 1937; s. Richard Curtis and Violet (Ballard) L.; m. Mary Shullenberger, Aug. 1961 (div. Dec. 1969); children: Jennifer Anne, Mary Wendell; m. Kathy Austin, Apr. 3, 1971; 1 child, Richard A. BA, Yale U., 1959; JD, U. Va., 1962; postgrad., Stanford U., 1972. Ptnr. Lockton and Scopelitis, Inc., Indpls., 1965-70; founder, pres., chief exec. officer Ontario (Calif.) Motor Speedway, 1968-71; chief exec. off., publisher, owner Calif. Bus. Mag., L.A., 1972-75; pres., chief exec. officer Lola Grand Prix, Ltd., L.A., 1976-79; founder, chief exec. officer Data Broadcasting, Inc., San Mateo, Calif., 1980-85; chmn., founder, CEO Interactive Network, Inc., 1986-99; pres. Lockton Ventures, 1996—; co-founder, bd. dirs. A.Z.L. Resources, Inc., 1964-75; creator, developer Internat. Race of Champions (IROC) TV Racing Series, 1972—, co-founder, chmn. Repair Shop Systems, Inc., 1986; nationwide lectr. on entrepreneurship and info. tech. Patentee in interactive TV and wireless data. Dir. U.S. Auto Club, 1967-70. Recipient Meritorious Svc. award Soc. Automotive Engrs., 1970. Mem. Jonathan Club (L.A.), Crooked Stick Golf Club (co-founder) (Indpls.), Carmel Valley Ranch, Penrod Soc. (co-founder, Indpls.). Republican. Episcopalian. Avocations: jazz piano, golf. Office: Lockton Ventures 405 El Camino Real Ste 423 Menlo Park CA 94025-5240

LOCKWOOD, HELSHI, advertising executive; b. East Orange, N.J., May 18, 1941; d. Warren Sewell and Ann Frances (Gleason) L.; m. Bertram A. Tunnell Jr., Dec. 13, 1969 (div. Oct. 1976); children: Bertram A. III, Tory Lockwood; stepchildren: John, Mark, Tracy, Wendy, Jan, Kate; m. William B. Hewson Jr., May 30, 1981; 1 child, Charles W.; stepchildren: William B. III, Andrew L., Elizabeth S. BA, Pa. State U., 1963. Promotion asst. Vogue Mag., London, 1963-64; advt. sales rep. Brides Mag., London, 1964-65; west coast mgr. Status Mag., L.A., 1965-67; asst. advt. mgr. Status Mag., N.Y.C., 1968-69; advt. sales rep. Eye Mag., N.Y.C., 1967-68; N.Y. mgr. Phil. and Boston Mags., N.Y.C., 1969-76; v.p. Metro Mag., N.Y.C., 1976-78; exec. v.p., ptnr. Catalyst Communications, N.Y.C., 1978-80; account mgr. Dun's Rev., N.Y.C., 1980-82; ea. advt. dir. Dun's Bus. Month, N.Y.C., 1982-84, advt. dir., 1984-85; dir. nat. accounts Chgo. Mag., N.Y.C., 1986; ea. advt. mgr. Mediatex Nat. Sales, N.Y.C., 1987-88, v.p., nat. sales dir., 1989-94, v.p., mng. dir., 1994-98; pres. Emmis Pub. Nat. Sales (acquired by Emmis Comm.), N.Y.C., 1998—. Deacon Brick Ch., N.Y.C., 1983. Mem. Advt. Women N.Y. Republican. Presbyn. Home: 8 Hanson Rd Darien CT 06820-2502 Office: Ennis Publ Nat Sales 60 E 42d St Ste 1103 New York NY 10165

LOCSIN, ENRIQUE LOPEZ, company executive; b. Manila, Jan. 28, 1946; s. Teodoro M. and Rosario (Lopez) L.; m. Susan Romualdez. Student, Letran Coll., Manila, La Salle Coll., Bacolod City, The Philippines, Asian Inst. Mgmt., Makati City, The Philippines, Alexander Hamilton Inst. Pres. Queen Seven Merchant, The Philippines, 1982—; pres., gen. mgr. Philippines Free Press, The Philippines, 1986—, LR Publs., Inc., The Philippines, 1988—; pres. El Crown Merchant, Inc., The Philippines, 1997—, Today Newspaper, The Philippines, 1999. Agt. Nat. Bur. Investigation, Manila. Mem. Makati Sports Club, Alabang Country Club, Manila Club. Avocations: golfing, football, bowling. Office: Unit D-2 2d FL DPSI Bus Ctr, 210 Nicanor Garcia St, Bel-Air Makati The Philippines

LOCUFIER, PATRICK CLAUDE, city planner; b. Lille, France, May 10, 1954; s. Emile and Irma Elli (Braun) L. Diploma in Geography, UFR, Villeneuve, France, 1980; M of City Planning, MIT, 1983; MBA, Harvard U., 1985. Mgr. Transports Ouvrie, Lesquin, France, 1973-75; fin. advisor European Union Bank, Paris, 1975-76; inst. agt. Caisse Familiale-Vie, Lille, France, 1977-78; free-lance sales Cambridge, Mass., 1983-89; constrn. promoter, city planner Biotic Constns., Brussels, 1989—, Lambersart, France, 1989—. Author: Urbanisme, Construction Geobiologie et Kabbale, 1997; translator numerous books. Comdr. French Army Res., 1972—. Mem. Copywriters Coun. Am. Avocations: Kabbalah, scientific research. E-mail: biotic.constructions@gofornet.com. Home and office: Biotic Constrns, 85 Ave de la Liberté, F-59831 Lambersart Cedex, France

LODAYA, JAICHAND NARSHI, manufacturing company consultant; b. Bombay, India, Jan. 16, 1934; s. Narshi Hirji and Champubai (Munvar) L.; m. Sarla Jaichand Dhulla, Mar. 24, 1962; children: Dhanesh J., Jatin J. B of Engring., V.J.T.I., 1961; diploma in postgrad. studies fuel tech., Portsmouth Coll. of Tech., 1967. Sr. instrumentation engr. Mukand Ltd., Bombay, 1960-71; sr. divsn. mgr. ISPL Industries Ltd., Bombay, 1971-86; cons. HMG Packagings Pvt. Ltd., Bombay, 1987-91, gen. mgr., 1991-97; chief cons. Thermo Indsl. Cons., Bombay, 1997—. Contbr. articles to profl. jours. Scholarship Nanavati Trust, 1952, Vardhman Jetsey scholarship St. Xavier's Coll., 1952. Fellow Inst. of Energy, Indo-Japanese Assn. (life), Instrument Soc. of Am.; mem. Inst. of Measurement and Control (life), The Coun. of Engring. Instns. (chartered engr. 1976), Automobile Assn. of India. Avocations: photography, postage stamps, coin collecting, reading, hiking. Home: Bedeshwar Flat 8 31 MG Rd, Ghatkopar East, Bombay 400 077, India Office: Thermo Indsl Consultants, Bedeshwar Flat 8 31 MG Rd, Ghatkopar East Bombay 400 077, India

LODDE, GORDON MAYNARD, health physics consultant; b. Lafayette, Ind., Aug. 19, 1933; s. Herman Morris and Eva Grace (Robinson) L.; m. Nancy Jean Caldwell, Aug. 21, 1955; children: Gordon A., Bruce C., Melissa J. BS, Purdue Univ., 1958; MS, Univ. Rochester, 1964. Health physist U.S. Army, 1959-79; health physics cons. Porter Cons., Ardmore, Pa., 1979-84; cons. engr. GPU Nuclear, Middletown, Pa., 1984-94; health physics cons. Mt. Joy, Pa., 1994—; Contbr. chpt to book: Handbook for Management of Radiation Protection Programs, 1992. Contbg. author: Ency. Occupl. Health and Safety, 1997. Scoutmaster Boy Scouts Am., White Sands, N.Mex., 1967-70, Edgewood, Md., 1975-79; Post adv. Boy Scouts Am., 1976-80. With U.S. Army Med. Svc. Corp., 1959-79. Decorated Army Commendation medal with two oak leaf clusters, 1960, 63, 68, Legion of Merit, 1979; recipient award of Merit Boy Scouts Am., 1976, Silver Beaver award, 1978. Mem. Health Physics Soc., Am. Nuc. Soc., Am. Conf. of Gov. Hygienists, Am. Indsl. Hygiene Assn., Am. Assn. Physicists in Medicine, N.Y. Acad. Scis. Home and Office: 742 Ferndale Rd Mount Joy PA 17552-9384

LODGAARD, SVERRE, nuclear disarmament researcher; b. Tröndelag, Norway, Apr. 6, 1945; s. Emil Andreas and Ingeborg (Morseth) L.; m. Ingrid Eide, July 9, 1969; 1 child, Christian Eide. Magister, U. Oslo, 1971. Rsch. fellow Norwegian Endowment for Sci. and Humanities, 1972-73; univ. scholar U. Oslo, 1973-77; dir. rsch. Internat. Peace Rsch. Inst., Oslo, 1974-76; researcher, 1977-80, Stockholm Internat. Peace Rsch. Inst., 1980-86; dir. Internat. Peace Rsch. Inst., 1987-92, Norwegian Inst. Internat. Affairs, 1997—; Mem. Norwegian Govt.'s Adv. Coun. on Arms Control and Disarmament, 1972-92. Author: Nuclear Disengagement in Europe, 1983, No First Use, 1984, Overcoming Threats to Europe, 1987, Naval Arms Control, 1990; contbr. articles to profl. jours. Mem. Internat. Pugwash Coun., Coun. UN Univ. for Peace. Lutheran. Home: Ivar Aasens vei 22, N-0373 Oslo Norway Office: Norwegian Inst Internat Affairs, P O B 8159 Dep., 0033 Oslo Norway

LODGE, DAVID JOHN, English literature educator, author; b. Jan. 28, 1935; s. William Frederick and Rosalie Marie (Murphy) L.; m. Mary Frances Jacob, 1959; 3 children. BA with honours, Univ. Coll., London; MA, U. London; PhD, U. Birmingham, Eng. With Brit. Coun., London, 1959-60; asst. lectr. modern English lit. U. Birmingham, 1960-62, lectr., 1963-71, sr. lectr., 1971-73, reader, 1973-76, prof., 1976-87, hon. prof., 1987—; vis. assoc. prof. U. Calif., Berkeley, 1969. Author: The Picturegoers, 1960, Ginger, You're Barmy, 1962, The British Museum Is Falling Down, 1965, Out of the Shelter, 1970, rev., 1985, Changing Places, 1975, How Far Can You Go?, 1980, Small World, 1984 (televised 1988), Nice Work, 1988 (adapted to TV 1989), Paradise News, 1991, Therapy, 1995, Home Truths, 1999; (plays) The Writing Game, 1991, Home Truths, 1998; (criticism) Language of Fiction, 1966, The Novelist at the Crossroads, 1971, The Modes of Modern Writing, 1977, Working with Structuralism, 1981, Write On, 1986, After Bakhtin, 1990, The Art of Fiction, 1992, The Practice of Writing, 1996. With RAC, 1955-57. Recipient fiction prize Yorkshire Post, 1975, Hawthornden prize, 1976, Whitbread Book of Yr. award, 1980, Book of Yr. award Sunday Express, 1988; Henfield writing fellow U. East Anglia, 1977; named to Chevalier l'Ordre des Arts et des Lettres, 1997. Fellow Royal Soc. Lit. Avocations: tennis, television, cinema. Office: care U Birmingham, Dept English, Birmingham B15 2TT, England

LODHI, MALEEHA, diplomat; b. Nov. 15, 1952. BSc in Econs., London Sch. Econs. and Polit. Sci., 1976, PhD, 1980. Lectr. in pub. adminstrn. Quaid-e-Azam Univ., Islamabad, Pakistan, 1979-80; instr. in politics and sociology London Sch. Econs. and Polit. Sci., 1980-85; from assoc. editor to editor The Muslim, Islamabad, 1985-90; editor The News, Pakistan, 1990-93; amb. to U.S. Govt. Pakistan, Washington, 1994—. Author: Pakistan's Encounter with Democracy, 1994, The External Dimension, 1994; contbr. articles to profl. jours. Recipient Journalistic award All Pakistan Newspaper Soc., 1994; named one of hundred global pacesetters Time Mag., 1994. Fellow Pakistan Inst. Devel. Econs. Office: Embassy Pakistan 2315 Massachusetts Ave NW Washington DC 20008-2898

LODICO, CHERYL MADELINE, secondary education educator; b. Bklyn., Aug. 24, 1944; d. Philip and Helen (Kutner) Miller; m. Nicholas Joseph Micucci, Feb. 13, 1969 (dec. Aug. 1987); m. Emanuel Joseph Lodico, Jan. 15, 1989; stepchildren: Diana Lynn, William Maurice. BA, Cortland State Coll., 1966; MS in Edn. in English, Queens Coll., 1971. Permanent cert. to teach English grades 7-12. English tchr. grade 9 Jerusalem Ave. Jr. H.S. North Bellmore, L.I., N.Y., 1966; English tchr. grades 7, 8, 9, also grade 6 gifted Lawrence Middle Sch., L.I., 1966-96; ret., 1996; tchr. ECC Acad., Bayside, N.Y., 1997-98; writer, 1998—; sponsor, editor Creative Writing Club. Contbr. articles to profl. jours.; author of poetry. Mem. Nat. Coun. Tchrs. English. Home: 14712 15th Dr Whitestone NY 11357-2509

LODICO, YVONNE C., lawyer, consulatant; b. Phila., Nov. 12, 1957; d. Lawrence Lodico and Joann (Lee) Sohn; 1 child, Sebastian Karl Lodico Konecsay. MIPA, Columbia U., N.Y.C., 1983; JD, Am. U., Washington, 1989; LLM, NYU, 1994. Liaison officer UN, Luanda, Angola, 1992-93; legal advisor, pol. officer UN, N.Y.C., 1989-92; legal adv. UN, Maputo, Mozambique, 1994-95, N.Y.C., 1995-96; dir. Galileo Inst. for Global Coop., N.Y.C., 1997—; legal officer, asst. to dir. UN Angola, 1995-96; lectr. human rights law U. Melbourne. Recipient award N.Y. State Bar Assn. Mem. ABA, UN Assn., N.Y.C. Bar Assn., Internat. Bar Assn. Episcopal. Avocations: cinema, running, painting. Home: 21 W 88th St Apt 4 New York NY 10024-2551

LODINOVA-ZADNIKOVA, RAJA, pediatrician; b. Tel-Aviv, Palestine, Aug. 25, 1929; arrived in Czech Republic, 1930; d. Artur and Rosa (Abramowitz) Engländer; m. Lodin Zděnek, June 30, 1951 (div. 1973); children: Henčlová, Kateřina, Lodin Michal; m. Milos Źadník, Sept. 29, 1979. MD, Charles U., 1953, pediatrics degree 1st, 1957, PhD, 1963, pediatrics degree 2d, 1970. Pediatrician Inst. Care Mother and Child, Prague, Czech Republic, 1954—; pediatrician Gen. Hosp., Prague, 1954-57; rsch. worker Cedars Sinai Med. Ctr., L.A., 1968-69. Contbr. chpts. in books and articles to profl. jours. Mem. European Soc. Pediatric Rsch., Soc. Mucosal Immunology, Soc. Pediatrics, N.Y. Acad. Scis. Office: Inst Care Mother and Child, Podolské nábř 157, 147 10 Prague 4, Czech Republic

LODOLO, ELIZABETH JACOBA, research scientist; b. Pretoria, Gauteng, South Africa, Dec. 25, 1962; d. Gert Hendrik and Minnie Agnes (Gilliland) Jansen van Rensburg; m. Andrea Fabio Lodolo, June 25, 1988; children: Romina Bianca, Gina Daniella. BSc, U. Pretoria, 1984; BSc with honors, U. Witwatersrand, South Africa, 1986, MSc cum laude, 1989; PhD, U. Stellenbosch, South Africa, 1999. Rschr. CSIR, South Africa, 1986-92; rschr. South African Breweries, Sandton, 1992-94, sr. rschr., 1994—; mem. biotech. adv. com. Technikon, Pretoria, 1998-99; mem. adv. panel Nat. Rsch. Found., 1999. Contbr. numerous papers to profl. jours. Recipient Presdl. award MBAA, 1999. Mem. South African Soc. Microbiology. Avocations: ballet, music, aerobics. Office: South African Breweries, PO Box 782178 65 Park Ln, Sandown Sandton 2146, South Africa

LODWICK, GWILYM SAVAGE, radiologist, educator; b. Mystic, Iowa, Aug. 30, 1917; s. Gwylim S. and Lucy A. (Fuller) L.; m. Maria Antonia De Brito Barata; children by previous marriage: Gwilym Savage III, Philip Galligan, Malcolm Kerr, Terry Ann. Student, Drake U., 1934-35; B.S., State U. Iowa, 1942, M.D., 1943. Resident pathology State U. Iowa, 1947-48, resident radiology, 1948-50; fellow, sr. fellow radiologic and orthopedic pathology Armed Forces Inst. Pathology, 1951; asst., then asso. prof. State U. Iowa Med. Sch., 1951-56; prof. radiology, chmn. dept. U. Mo. at Columbia Med. Sch., 1956-78, research prof. radiology, 1978-83, interim chmn. dept. radiology, 1980-81, chmn. dept. radiology, 1981-83, prof. bioengring., 1969-83, acting dean, 1959, assoc. dean, 1959-64; assoc. radiologist Mass. Gen. Hosp., 1983-88, radiologist, 1988-91; hon. radiologist Mass. Gen. Hosp., Boston, 1991—; vis. prof. dept. radiology Harvard Med. Sch., 1983-93; cons. in field; vis. prof. Keio U. Sch. Medicine, Tokyo, 1974; chmn. sci. program com. Internat. Conf. on Med. Info., Amsterdam, 1983; trustee Am. Registry Radiologic Technologists, 1961-69, pres., 1964-65, 68-69; mem. radiology tng. com. Nat. Inst. Gen. Med. Scis., NIH, 1966-70; com. radiology Nat. Acad. Scis.-NRC, 1970-75; chmn. com. computers Am. Coll. Radiology, 1965, Internat. Commn. Radiol. Edn. and Info., 1969-73; cons. to health care tech. div. Nat. Ctr. for Health Services, Research and Devel., 1971-76; dir. Mid-Am. Bone Tumor Diagnostic Ctr. and Registry, 1971-83; adv. com. mem. NIH Biomed. Image Processing Grant Jet Propulsion Lab., 1969-73; nat. chmn. MUMPS Users Group, 1973-75; mem. radiation study sect. div. research grants NIH, 1976-79, mem. study sect. on diagnostic radiology and nuclear medicine div. research grants, 1979-82, chmn. study sect. on diagnostic radiology div. research grants, 1980-82; mem. bd. sci. counselors Nat. Library of Medicine, 1985, chmn. 1987-89; dir. radiology Spaulding Rehab. Hosp., 1986-92. Adv. editorial bd. Radiology, 1965-86, cons. to editor, 1986-91; adv. editorial bd. Current/Clin. Practice, 1972-88; mem. editorial bd. Jour. Med. Systems, 1976—, Radiol. Sci. Update div. Biomedia, Inc., 1975-83, Critical Revs. in Linguistic Imaging, 1990; mem. cons. editorial bd. Skeletal Radiology, 1977-92, Contemporary Diagnostic Radiology, 1978-80; assoc. editor Jour. Med. Imaging, 1988—. Served to maj. AUS, 1943-46, ETO. Decorated Sakari Mustakallio medal Finland; named Most Disting. Alumnus in Radiology, State U. Ia. Centennial, 1970; recipient Sigma Xi Research award U. Mo., Columbia, 1972, Gold medal XIII Internat. Conf. Radiology, Madrid, 1973, Founder's Gold medal Internat. Skeletal Soc., 1990. Fellow AMA (radiology rev. bd. coun. med. edn., coun. rep. on residency rev. com. for radiology 1969-74), Am. Coll. Radiology (co-chmn. ACR-NEMA standardization com. 1983-90, NEMA Med. Tech. Leadership award 1995); mem. NAS Inst. Medicine, Am. Coll. Med. Informatics (founding), Nat. Acad. Practice in Medicine, Radiol. Soc. N.Am. (3d v.p. 1974-75, chmn. ad hoc com. representing assoc. scis. 1979-87, chmn. assoc. scis. com. 1981-87), Assn. Univ. Radiologists, Mo. Radiol. Soc. (1st pres. 1961-62), Salutis Unitas; hon. mem. Portuguese Soc. Radiology and Nuclear Medicine, Tex. Radiol. Soc., Ind. Roentgen Soc., Phila. Roentgen Ray Soc., Finnish Radio. Soc. (ho.), Rotary, Harvard of Boston Club, Cosmos, Alpha Omega Alpha. Home: 3900 Galt Ocean Dr Apt 307 Fort Lauderdale FL 33308-6622

LOEB, JOHN LANGELOTH, JR., investment counselor; b. N.Y.C., May 2, 1930; s. John Langeloth and Frances (Lehman) L.; children: Nicholas, Alexandra. Grad., Hotchkiss Sch., 1948; A.B. cum laude, Harvard, 1952, M.B.A., 1954; LL.D. (hon.), Georgetown U. With Loeb, Rhoades & Co., N.Y.C., from 1956; gen. ptnr., mem. mgmt. com. Loeb, Rhoades & Co., 1964-73, mng. ptnr., pres., 1971-73, ltd. ptnr., 1973-84; chmn. bd. Holly Sugar Co., Colo., 1969-71; amb. to Denmark Copenhagen, 1981-83; chmn. John L. Loeb, Jr. Assocs., N.Y.C., 1984—; U.S. del. to 38th session Gen. Assembly of UN; spl. advisor environ. matters to Gov. Nelson A. Rockefeller, 1967-73; chmn. Gov. N.Y. Coun. Environ. Advisors, 1970-75; pres. Winston Churchill Found., 1981—; trustee Ednl. Testing Svc., Princeton, N.J., 1986-93. Trustee Montefiore Hosp. and Med. Ctr. Mus. City N.Y., 1962-94, John and Frances L. Loeb Found., 1957-98; mem. Harvard vis. com. Loeb Drama Ctr., 1988-94; mem. N.Y. State Coun. on the Arts, 1996—; pres. John L. Loeb Jr. Found., 1963—. Lt. USAF, 1954-56. Lord of the Manor of Brinsley; Decorated Grand Cross of the Order of Dannebrog (Denmark); recipient Lee Max Friedman award Am. Jewish Hist. Soc., Disting. Patriot award SAR; Hon. Comdr. of the Most Excellent Order of the Brit. Empire. Mem. Downtown Assn. (N.Y.C.), Harvard Club, Century Country Club, Sleepy Hollow Club (Westchester, N.Y.), Buck's Club, Brooks's Club, Hurlingham Club (London), Royal Danish Yacht Club (Copenhagen), Lyford Cay Club (Nassau, Bahamas). Home: Ridgeleigh 194 Anderson Hill Rd Purchase NY 10577-2101 Office: John L Loeb Jr Assocs Inc 50 Broad St Rm 1137 New York NY 10004-2307

LOEHWING, RUDI CHARLES, JR., publicist, radio broadcasting executive, journalist; b. Newark, July 26, 1957; s. Rudy Charles Sr. and Joan Marie (Bell) L.; m. Claire Popham, Sept. 4, 1987; children: Aspasia Joyce, Tesia Victoria, Rudi Douglas, Anna Marie, Samantha Diane, Ian Ryan. Student, Biscayne U., 1975, Seton Hall U., 1977, Hubbard U., 1980. Announcer radio sta. WHBI FM, N.Y.C., 1970-72; producer Am. Culture Entertainment, Belleville, N.J., 1973-74; exec. producer Am. Culture Entertainment, Hollywood, Calif., 1988-94; CEO Broadcaster's Network Internat., Hollywood, U.K., Calif., also U.K., 1989—, Broadcaster's Network Internat., Ltd., Hollywood, also U.K.; bd. dirs. First Break, Hollywood, also U.K., 1988—. Author: Growing Pains, 1970; dir. exec. producer TV documentaries and comml. advertisements, 1983; patentee in field. Devel. dir. Tricentennial Found., Washington, 1989-90; bd. dirs. Civic Light Opera of South Bay Cities, 1998—, Tax Edn. Assn., Just Say No to Drugs, L.A., 1989, Hands Across the Atlantic, Internat. Country Top 10, The Rock of Russia, Job Search, Hollywood, U.K. and Russia. Named Youngest Comml. Radio Producer and Announcer for State of N.Y., Broadcaster's Network Internat., 1972. Mem. Nat. Press Club, Broadcasters Network Assn. (bd. dirs. 1977—), Profl. Bus. Comms. Assn. (founder 1989), BNI News Bur. (chmn. 1991—), Civic Light Opera of South Bay Cities (bd. dirs. 1996—). Avocations: flying, music, writing, photography, martial arts (recipient awards). Office: Broadcasters Network Internat Ltd 2624 Medlow Ave Ste B Los Angeles CA 90065-4617

LOELIGER, JUERG, food company executive, educator; b. Sorengo, Switzerland, July 16, 1943; s. Rudolf and Dora (Erismann) L.; m. Annemarie Sonderegger, Aug. 24, 1968; 1 child, Daniel. MS, Swiss Fed. Inst. Tech., Zurich, 1967; PhD in Chemistry, Fribourg (Switzerland) U., 1970. Postdoctoral U. Fribourg, 1970-72, King's Coll., London, 1972, MIT, Cambridge, Mass., 1972-74; rsch. chemist Nestle Rsch., Lausanne, Switzerland, 1974-90; dir. food sci. rsch. Nestle, Lausanne, Switzerland, 1991-96; dep. dir. Nestle R & D, Kemptthal, Switzerland, 1996—; prof. food sci., U. Lausanne, 1992—. Author: Rancidity in Foods, 1989, Free Radicals and Food Additives, 1991. Mem. local parliament Corseaux twp., Switzerland, 1983—; elder, Evang. Ch. Mem. AFECG, AOCS, IFT. Mem. Evangelical Ch. Office: Nestle R & D Ctr, CH-8310 Kemptthal Switzerland

LOENGARD, RICHARD OTTO, JR., lawyer; b. N.Y.C, Jan. 28, 1932; s. Richard Otto and Margery (Borg) L.; m. Janet Sara Senderowitz, Apr. 11, 1964; children: Maranda C., Philippa S.M. AB, Harvard U., 1953, LLB, 1956. Bar: N.Y. 1956, U.S. Dist. Ct. (so. dist.) N.Y. 1958. Assoc. Fried, Frank, Harris, Shriver & Jacobson, predecessor firms, N.Y.C., 1956-64, ptnr., 1967-97; of counsel Fried, Frank, Harris, Shriver & Jacobson, N.Y.C., 1997—; dep. tax legis. counsel, spl. asst. internat. tax affairs U.S. Dept. Treasury, Washington, 1964-67; mem. Commerce Clearing House, Riverwoods, Ill. Editl. bd. Tax Transaction Libr., 1982-94; contbr. articles to profl. publs. Fellow Am. Coll. Tax Counsel; mem. ABA, N.Y. State Bar Assn. (exec. com. tax sect. 1984—, sec. 1994-95, vice chair 1995-97, chair 1997-98), Assn. Bar City N.Y. Office: Fried Frank Harris Shriver & Jacobson 1 New York Plz New York NY 10004-1980

LOENNING, PER, bishop; b. Bergen, Norway, Feb. 24, 1928; s. Per and Anna (Strømø) L.; m. Ingunn b.Bartz-Johannessen, Aug. 5, 1929; children: Per Eystein, Jan Tore, Ingunn Margrete, Dag Audun. Candidate theology, Free Theol. Faculty, Oslo, 1949; ThD, U. Oslo, Norway, 1955, PhD, 1959; LittD (hon.), St. Olaf Coll., Northfield, Minn., 1986. Asst. pastor Lilleborg Luth. Ch., Oslo, 1951-53; lectr. Oslo Tchr.'s Tng. Coll., 1954-64; dean Bergen Cathedral, Norway, 1964-69; bishop of Borg Fredikstad, Norway, 1969-75, resigned as bishop, 1975; prof. history Christian Thought U. Oslo, Oslo, 1977; research prof. Inst. Ecumenical Research, Strasbourg, France, 1981-87; bishop of Bergen Norway, 1987-94; chmn. Norwegian Pastors' Assn., 1962-64; vis. prof. U. Aarhus, Denmark, 1976. Author: The Dilemma of Contemporary Theology, Off the Beaten Path, Pathways of the Passion, Der begreiflich Unergreifbare, Creation: An Ecumenical Challenge?, 40 other books on theology, philosophy, and religious devotion, 1954—. Active Norwegian Parliament, Oslo, 1957-65; mem. Sch. Bd. Oslo, 1960-64; mem. Nat. Broadcasting Council, 1968-77. Recipient Pax Christi award St. John's U., Collegeville, Minn., 1975. Mem. Royal Norwegian Soc. Scis., Norwegian Acad. Scis. and Humanities. Avocations: skiing, swimming, outdoors. Home: Løvenskiolds Gate 19a, N-0260 Oslo 2, Norway

LOESCH, ANDRZEJ WITOLD, biologist; b. Nowy Sacz, Poland, July 20, 1950; s. Seweryn Jerzy and Maria Aleksandra (Szczepanowska) L.; m. Vivienne Jane Richards, June 1, 1989; 1 child, Aleksander Owain. MSc in Zoology, Jagiellonian U., Cracow, Poland, 1974, DSc, 1988; PhD, Polish Acad. Scis., Warsaw, 1980. Jr. rsch. asst. Polish Acad. Scis., Cracow, 1975; postgrad. fellow Polish Acad. Scis., Warsaw, 1976-79, sr. rsch. fellow, 1979-82, asst. prof., 1982-92; hon. rsch. fellow Univ. Coll. London, 1983-95, sr. rsch. fellow, 1995—, asst. tchr. histology, 1997—; mem. sci. coun. Med. Rsch. Ctr., Polish Acad. Scis., Warsaw, 1987-89. Contbr. over 80 articles to profl. jours., chpts. to books. Recipient Sci. award Polish Neuropathologists Assn., 1985. Mem. N.Y. Acad. Scis. Roman Catholic. Avocations: countryside walking, skiing, astronomy, cooking. Office: U Coll London Dept Anatomy, Gower St, London WC1E 6BT, England

LOETE, STEVEN DONALD, pilot; b. Tacoma, Aug. 21, 1959; s. Donald Kenneth and Ida Lorraine (Buck) L.; 1 child, Samantha; m. Jodi Christine Barnett, 1998; 1 child, Tiffani. BA, Pacific Luth. U., 1984. Pilot contracting office USAF, Williams AFB, Ariz., 1985; flight instr. Clover Park Tech. Coll., Tacoma, 1986, 99; charter pilot Stellar Exec., Chandler, Ariz., 1986-87; pilot, airline capt. Maui Airlines, Guam, 1987; airline capt., checkairman Westair Airlines, Fresno, Calif., 1987-98; airline pilot Air Wis., 1998—; owner Northwestern Properties; corp. pilot Exec. Jet Mgmt., Cin., 1999—. Contbr. Save the Children, 1988-90; mem. Angel Flight, U. Puget Sound, 1981-83; bd. dirs. aviation adv. com. Clover Park Tech. Coll., 1991—. 1st lt. USAF, 1983-93. Mem. Airline Pilots Assn. (chmn. organizing com. 1989, chmn. coun. 1989-91). Republican. Methodist. Avocations: racquetball, fishing. Home and Office: Box 760 Spanaway WA 98387

LOEVINGER, LEE, lawyer, science writer; b. St. Paul, Apr. 24, 1913; s. Gustavus and Millie (Strouse) L.; m. Ruth Howe, Mar. 4, 1950; children: Barbara L., Eric H., Peter H. BA summa cum laude, U. Minn., 1933, JD, 1936. Bar: Minn. 1936, Mo. 1937, D.C. 1966, U.S. Supreme Ct., 1941. Assoc. Watson, Ess, Groner, Barnett & Whittaker, Kansas City, Mo., 1936-37; atty., regional atty. NLRB, 1937-41; with antitrust div. Dept. Justice, 1941-46; ptnr. Larson, Loevinger, Lindquist & Fraser, Mpls., 1946-60; assoc. justice Minn. Supreme Ct., 1960-61; asst. U.S. atty. gen. charge antitrust div. Dept. Justice, 1961-63; commr. FCC, 1963-68; ptnr. Hogan & Hartson, Washington, 1968-85; of counsel Hogan & Hartson, 1986—; v.p., dir. Craig-Hallum Corp., Mpls., 1968-73; dir. Petrolite Corp., St. Louis, 1978-83; U.S. rep. com. on restrictive bus. practices Orgn. for Econ. Coop. and Devel., 1961-64; spl. asst. to U.S. atty. gen., 1963-64; spl. counsel com. small bus. U.S. Senate, 1951-52; lectr. U. Minn., 1953-60; vis. prof. jurisprudence U. Minn. (Law Sch.), 1961; professorial lectr. Am. U., 1968-70; chmn. Minn. Atomic Devel. Problems Com., 1957-59; mem. Adminstrv. Conf. U.S., 1972-74; del. White House Conf. on Inflation, 1974; U.S. del. UNESCO Conf. on Mass Media, 1975, Internat. Telecomms. Conf. on Radio Frequencies, 1964, 66. Author: The Law of Free Enterprise, 1949, An Introduction to Legal Logic, 1952, Defending Antitrust Lawsuits, 1977, Science As Evidence, 1995; author first article to use term: jurimetrics, 1949; contbr. articles to profl. and sci. jours.; editor, contbr.: Basic Data on Atomic Devel. Problems in Minnesota, 1958; adv. bd. Antitrust Bull., Jurimetrics Jour. Served to lt. comdr. USNR, 1942-45. Recipient Outstanding Achievement award U. Minn., 1968; Freedoms Found. award, 1977, 84. Fellow Am. Acad. Appellate Lawyers; mem. ABA (del. of sci. and tech. sect. to Ho. of Dels. 1974-80, del. to joint conf. with AAAS 1974-76, co-chair 1990-93, liaison 1984-90, 93-98, chmn. sci. and tech. sect. 1982-83, coun. 1986-89, standing com. on nat. conf. groups 1984-90), AAAS, Minn. Bar Assn., Hennepin County Bar Assn., N.Y. Acad. Sci., D.C. Bar Assn., FCC Bar Assn., Broadcast Pioneers, U.S. C. of C. (antitrust coun. 1980-94), Am. Arbitration Assn. (comml. panel), Atlantic Legal Found. (adv. coun.), Cosmos Club (pres. 1990), City Club (Washington), Phi Beta Kappa, Sigma Xi, Delta Sigma Rho, Sigma Delta Chi, Phi Delta Gamma, Tau Kappa Alpha, Alpha Epsilon Rho. Fax: 202-637-5910. Home: 5600 Wisconsin Ave Apt 17D Chevy Chase MD 20815-4414 Office: Hogan & Hartson 555 13th St NW Ste 800E Washington DC 20004-1161

LOEVINGER, ROBERT, retired research physicist; b. St. Paul, Minn., Jan. 31, 1916. BA, U. Minn., 1936; MA, Harvard Coll., 1938; PhD, U. Calif., Berkeley, 1947. Asst. physicist The Mt. Sinai Hosp., N.Y.C., 1947-56; asst. prof. Stanford U. Med. Sch., Palo Alto, Calif., 1957-65; chief dosimetry sect. Internat. Atomic Energy Agy., Vienna, 1965-68; dosimetry group leader Nat. Inst. Stds. and Tech., Washington, 1968-88. Recipient William D. Coolidge award Am. Assn. Physicists in Medicine, 1995. Home: 316 New Mark Esplanade Rockville MD 20850-2734*

LOEW, JONATHAN L., lawyer; b. Chgo., May 24, 1956; s. Andrew and Rita L.; m. Margarite Primozich, Sept. 8, 1950; children: Zachary, Vanessa, Jacob. BA in Philosophy, Ripon Coll., 1978; JD, DePaul U., 1981. Bar: Ill. 1982, U.S. Dist. Ct. (no. dist.) Ill. 1982, U.S. Ct. Appeals (7th cir.) 1991, U.S. Supreme Ct. 1993. Assoc. Maryniak & Steere, Chgo., 1982-83, Berman, Fagel, Haber, Maragos & Abrams, Chgo., 1983-86; assoc., ptnr. Spitzer, Addis, Susman & Krull, Chgo., 1986-98; ptnr. Katz, Randall, Weinberg & Richmond, Chgo., 1998—. Contbr. articles to profl. jours. Mem. Chgo. Bar Assn., Appellate Lawyers Assn. Office: Katz Randall Weinberg & Richmond 333 W Wacker Dr Ste 1800 Chicago IL 60606-1329

LOEWE, RAPHAEL JAMES, retired humanities educator; b. Calcutta, India, Apr. 16, 1919; Arrived in England 1920.; s. Herbert M.J. Loewe and Ethel Victoria Hyamson; m. Chloe Klatzkin, Mar. 19, 1952; children: Elisabeth Talbot, Camilla Verry. Degree, Cambridge (Eng.) U., 1941, Oxford (Eng.) U., 1950. Lectr. in Hebrew Leeds (Eng.) U., 1949-54; bye-fellow Caius Coll., Cambridge, 1954-57; vis. prof. Brown U., Providence, 1963-64; from lectr. to prof. Univ. Coll., London, 1965-82. Author: Solomon Ibn Gabirol, 19889; editor, translator: Omar Khayyam (Hebrew translation), 1982, The Rylands Haggadah, 1988; former editor Jour. of Jewish Studies; contbg. editor Ency. Judaica, Jerusalem. Former warden Spanish and Portuguese Jews' Congregation, London; former pres. Soc. for Old Testament Study, Eng., Jewish Hist. Soc. Eng. Lt. Brit. mil., 1941-46. Fellow Royal Asiatic Soc., London Soc. Antiquaries; mem. Brit. Assn. for Jewish Studies (pres. 1998). Jewish. Avocations: translating English, Latin and Hebrew poetry, travel. Home: 50 Gurney Dr, London N2 0DE, England

LOEWENSTEIN, WERNER RANDOLPH, physiologist, biophysicist, educator; b. Spangenberg, Germany, Feb. 14, 1926; came to U.S., 1957; naturalized, 1965.; s. Siegfried and Adele (Muller) von Loewenstein; m. Birgit Rose, Oct. 7, 1971; children: Claudia, Patricia, Harriett, Stewart. BS, U. Chile, 1945, PhD, 1950. Instr. physiology U. Chile, Santiago, 1951-53, assoc. prof., 1955-57; fellow in residence Wilmer Inst., Johns Hopkins U., Balt., 1953-54; rsch. zoologist UCLA, 1954-55; asst. prof. physiology Columbia U. Coll. Physicians and Surgeons, N.Y.C., 1957-59, assoc. prof., 1959-66, prof., 1966-71, dir. cell physics lab., 1963-71; prof. physiology and biophysics, chmn. dept. U. Miami (Fla.) Sch. Medicine, 1971-95, prof., chmn. emeritus, 1995—; dir. lab. cell comm. Marine Biol. Lab., Woods Hole, 1995—; Block lectr. U. Chgo., 1960; lectr. Royal Swedish Acad. Sci., 1966; Max Planck lectr., 1967, Claude Bernard lectr., Coll. de France, 1970; Fulbright disting. prof., 1970, USSR Acad. Sci. lectr., Leningrad, 1975; Humboldt lectr., 1988, Humbolt lectr., Munich, 1988, Lauger lectr., Konstanz, 1991, Hillarp lectr., Munich, 1993; mem. Pres. Ford's Biomed. Rsch. Adv. Panel, 1975-77, USAF Sci. Adv. Panel, 1982-86. Author: The Touchstone of Life, 1999, Penguin Books, 2000; editor Biochimica et Biophysica Acta, 1967-74; editor in chief Jour. Membrane Biology, 1969—; editor Handbook of Sensory Physiology, 51 vols., 1971-77; contbr. numerous articles on membrane biophysics, physiology of intercellular communication, neurophysiolog and cancer rsch. to profl. jours. Kellogg internat. fellow in physiology, 1953-55; Commonwealth Fund internat. fellow, 1967; NSF, NIH Rsch. grantee. Mem. N.Y. Acad. Scis.; mem. Am. Physiol. Soc., Biophys. Soc., Soc. Gen. Physiologogists, The Harvey Society, Soc. Neuroscience, Marine Biol. Lab. Woods Hole (corp. mem.), Quisset Yacht Club, Coconut Grove Sailing Club, Royal Key Biscayne Tennis and Racquet Club. Office: Marine Biol Lab Lab Cell Comm 7 M B L St Woods Hole MA 02543-1015

LOEWENTHAL, NESSA PARKER, communications educator; b. Chgo., Oct. 13, 1930; d. Abner and Frances (Ness) Parker; m. Martin Moshe Loewenthal, July 7, 1951 (dec. Aug. 1973); children: Dann Marcus, Ronn Carl, Deena Miriam; m. Gerson B. Selk, Apr. 17, 1982 (dec. June 1987). BA in Edn. and Psychology, Stanford U., 1952. Faculty Stanford Inst. for Intercultural Communication, Palo Alto, Calif., 1973-87; dir. Trans Cultural Svcs., San Francisco, 1981-86, Portland, Oreg., 1986—; dir. dependent svcs. and internat. edn. Bechtel Group, San Francisco, 1973-81, internat. edn. cons., 1981-84; mem. adv. com. dept. internat. studies Lesley Coll., Cambridge, Mass., 1986—; mem. Oreg. Ethics Commns., 1990—; mem. Bay Area Ethics Consortium, Berkeley, 1985-90; chmn. ethics com. Sietar Internat., Washington, 1987—, mem. governing bd., 1992-95; mem. faculty Summer Inst. for Internat. Comms., Portland, Oreg., 1987-97; core faculty Oreg. Gov.'s Sch. Svc. Leadership, Salem, 1995-97. Author: Professional Integration, 1987, Update: Federal Republic of Germany, 1990, Update: Great Britain, 1987; author, editor book series Your International Assignment, 1973-81; contbr. articles to profl. jours. Mem. equal opportunity and social justice task force Nat. Jewish Coun. on Pub. Affairs; bd. dirs. Kids on the Block, Portland, Portland Jewish Acad., 1996—, Portland Ashkalon Sister City Assn.; bd. dirs., co-chair ethics com. Soc. Humanistic Judaism, 1996-99; task force on Racism and Violence, Portland, Oreg.; mem. Lafayette (Calif.) Traffic Commn., 1974-80; bd. dirs. Ctr. for Ethics and Social Policy, 1988-91; mem. exec. bd. and planning com. Temple Isaiah, Lafayette, 1978-82; bd. dirs. Calif. Symphony, Orinda, 1988-90; mem. exec. com. overseas schs. adv. com. U.S. Dept. State, 1976-82; bd. dirs. Jewish Fedn. Oregon; mem. cmty. rels. com. Portland Jewish Fedn.; mem. Nat. Jewish Cmty. Rels.; mem. Task Force on Racism, Ethnicity and Pub. Policy, 1998—. Named Sr. Interculturalist, Sietar Internat., 1986. Mem. ASTD (exec. bd. internat. profl. performance area 1993-97, 99), Soc. for Intercultural Edn. Tng. and Rsch. (chmn. 1986-87, nomination com. 1984-86, co-chmn. 1989-90, chmn. ethics com. 1989-98, governing bd. 1992-95), World Affairs Coun., Portland City Club. Democrat. Avocations: photography, swimming. Office: TransCultural Svcs 3185 SW Underwood Rd Portland OR 97225

LOEWER, JOHANNES K., virologist, educator; b. Vienna, Austria, Nov. 20, 1944; s. Karl and Margarete (Reihs) Löwer; m. Roswitha M.H. Schieb; children: Cornelia, Bettina, Alexander. MD, U. Würzburg/Tübingen, 1969; MSc in Biochemistry, U. Tübingen, 1975; Habil Med. virology, U. Frankfurt, 1990, Pvt. Dozent, 1990. Postdoctoral fellow Friedrich Miescher Lab., Tübingen, 1976-80; scientist Paul Ehrlich Inst., Frankfurt, 1981—, head cytology sect., 1982-91, dep. dir., 1991-99, head human virology divsn., 1988—, acting dir., 1999—, prof. med. virology, 1999—; mem. blood products adv. com. Fed. Min. Health, mem. Sci. Com. on Medicinal Products and Med. Devices, European Com., Brussels./B. Mem. Soc. for Virology (com. mem. virus safety commn.), Internat. Assn. Biol. Standardization (v.p. 1996-2000), Soc. for Biol. Chemistry, German AIDS

Soc., Soc. German Scientists and Physicians. Office: Paul-Ehrlich Inst, Paul-Ehrlich-Str 51-59, D-63225 Langen Hessen, Germany

LOEWY, ERICH HANS, bioethicist, educator; b. Vienna, Austria, Dec. 31, 1927; s. Oskar W. and Gertrude A. (Commenda) L.; m. Roberta A. Springer, Mar. 8, 1974; children: Oliver, Tom, David. BA, NYU, 1950; MD, SUNY, Syracuse, 1954. Sr. instr. Case Western Res. U., Cleve., 1960-77; asst. prof. Albany (N.Y.) Med. Coll., 1977-81, U. Conn., Harford, 1981-84; assoc. prof. bioethics U. Ill., Peoria and Chgo., Ill., 1984-91, prof., 1991—; prof. and endowed alumni assn. chair of bioethics assoc. dept philosophy U. Calif., Davis, 1996—; cons. in field. Author: Moral Dilemmas in Medicine, 1987, Textbook of Medical Ethics, 1989, Suffering and the Beneficent Community: Beyond Libertarianism, 1991, Freedom and Community: the Ethics of Interdependence, 1992, Ethische Fragen in der Medizin, 1995, Textbook of Health Care Ethics, 1996, Moral Strangers, Moral Acquintance and Moral Friends: connectedness and its conditions, 1996, (with Roberto Springer Loewy) The Ethics of Terminal Care: Orchestrating the End of Life, 2000; contbr. numerous articles to profl. jours. Capt. AUS, 1955-57. Mem. ACP, Soc. Health and Human Values (faculty assoc. chair), European Soc. Philos. Medicine and Health Care, Am. Soc. Bioethics and Humanities, Physicians for Social Responsibility. Avocation: music. Home: 11465 Ghirardelli Ct Gold River CA 95670-7864 Office: U Calif Davis UCDMC-PSSB 2400 4150 V St Sacramento CA 95817-1460

LOFGREN, ERIK LOYD, professional society executive; b. Peoria, Ill., Mar. 5, 1970; s. Frank Gösta and Theo Rae Lofgren. BS in Mktg., Drake U., 1992. Registration coord. Smith, Bucklin & Assocs., Chgo., 1993-94; airborne infantry team leader U.S. Army, Vicenza, Italy, 1994-99; inventory control analyst Alpha Enterprises, Tucson, Ariz., 1998-99; mems. svcs. mgr. Regulatory Affairs Profls. Soc., Rockville, Md., 1999—. Cpl. U.S. Army, 1994-98. Republican. Methodist. Office: 12300 Twinbrook Pkwy Ste 350 Rockville MD 20852-1639

LOFLAND, GARY KENNETH, cardiac surgeon; b. Milford, Del., Mar. 5, 1951; s. Joseph Sudler and Doris Louise (Peters) L.; m. Janice Marie Show, Feb. 3, 1979; children: Kiernan Sudler, Glennis Kathleen. BA cum laude, Boston U., 1969, MD cum laude, 1975. Diplomate Am. Bd. Surgery, Am. Bd. Thoracic Surgery; lic. physician, Va., N.Y., Mont., N.C. Intern, jr. asst. resident in surgery Duke U. Med. Ctr., Durham, N.C., 1975-81; rsch. fellow dept. surgery Duke U. Med. Ctr., Durham, 1979-81, sr. asst. resident in surgery, 1981-84, chief resident in surgery, 1984-85, teaching scholar in cardiac surgery, 1985-86; sr. registrar in cardiothoracic surgery Hosp. for Sick Children, London, 1986-87; dir. cardiovascular surgery Children's Hosp. of Buffalo, 1987-88; asst. prof. surgery SUNY, Buffalo, 1987-88; assoc. prof. surgery/pediatrics, Med. Coll. Va., Richmond, 1988-94, dir. pediatric cardiac surgery/med. dir. cardiac surgery ICU, 1988-94; clin. prof. surgery Georgetown U., Washington, 1994-97; dir. Columbia/HCA Ctr. Congenital Heart Disease, Richmond, 1994-97; dir. cardiovascular surgery Children's Mercy Hosp., Kansas City, Mo., 1997—; clin. prof. surgery U. Mo. Kansas City Sch. Medicine, 1997—, Joseph Boon Gregg chair sect. cardiac surgery. Editorial rev. bd. Progress in Pediatric Cardiology, Year Book of Thoracic Surgery; contbr. articles to profl. jours. Pres. Am. Heart Assn., Richmond; mem. bd. trustees Transplant Found. Lt. comdr. USPHS, 1977-79. Recipient Univ. Hosp. Trustees award, Boston, 1975; HEW/USPHS commendation medal, 1979. Mem. AMA, Am. Heart Assn., Assn. for Acad. Surgery, Internat. Soc. for Heart Transplantation, Med. Soc. Va., Richmond Acad. Medicine, Richmond Surg. Soc., So. Thoracic Surg. Assn., Soc. for Thoracic Surgeons, Congenital Heart Surgeons Soc., , Alpha Omega Alpha. Home: PO Box 126 Crozier VA 23039-0126 Office: Children's Mercy Hosp Divsn Cardiovascular Surgery 2406 Gillham Rd Kansas City MO 64108

LOFTFIELD, ROBERT BERNER, biochemistry educator; b. Detroit, Dec. 15, 1919; s. Sigurd and Katherine (Roller) L.; m. Ella Bradford, Aug. 24, 1946 (dec. Dec. 1990); children: Lore Loftfield DeBower, Eric, Linda, Norman, Bjòrn, Curtis, Katherine, Earl. Allison Dinsdale, Ella-Kari. BS, Harvard U., 1941, MA, 1942, PhD, 1946. Research assoc. MIT, Cambridge, 1946-48; research assoc. to sr. research assoc. Mass. Gen. Hosp., Boston, 1948-64; asst. to assoc. prof. biochemistry Harvard U. Sch. Medicine, Boston, 1948-64; prof. biochemistry Sch. Medicine U. N.Mex., Albuquerque, 1964-90, chmn. dept. biochemistry, 1964-71, 78-90, prof. emeritus, 1990—. Contbr. articles on protein biosynthesis and enzymology to profl. jours. Served as corp. U.S. Army, 1945-46. Fellow Damon Runyon Fund, 1952-53, Guggenheim Found., 1961-62; Fulbright fellow, 1977, 83; sr. fellow NIH, 1971-72. Mem. AAAS, Am. Soc. Biol. Chemists, Am. Chem. Soc., Am. Assn. Cancer Research, Biophys. Soc., Marine Biol. Lab. Lutheran. Avocations: sailing, hiking, camping, skiing. Home: 707 Fairway Rd NW Albuquerque NM 87107-5718 Office: U NMex Sch Medicine Dept Biochemistry Albuquerque NM 87131-0001

LOFTUS, ALBERT, author, paralegal; b. Albany, N.Y., Apr. 28, 1952; s. William and Helen Loftus. AA, El Centro Coll., Dallas, 1999. Registered paralegal. Sr. paralegal Dallas; gen. mgr. Smith Limousine Co., Inc., N.Y.C., 1985-89. Author: (novels) Con Respeto/With Respect: Thrill Killing in Dallas, 1997, Divine Animals, 1998; playwright: The Mourning Mass, 1977, Fantasy Children, 1978. Mem. Nat. Shakespeare Co., N.Y.C.; appointed mem. Limousine Bd. N.Y.C. Taxi and Limousine Commn., 1987-89. Recipient 1st prize League for Innovation lit. competition, North Lake Coll., 1998. Mem. Nat. Fedn. Paralegal Assn., Assn. Legal Adminstrs., Nat. Assn. Legal Assts., Dallas Area Paralegal Assn., State Bar of Tex (Legal Assts. divsn.), The Dramatists Guild, Playwright's Unit, The Pub. Theater, Phi Theta Kappa. Home and Office: 901 Cove Holw Irving TX 75060-6743

LOFTUS, ELIZABETH F., psychology educator; b. L.A.; d. Sidney and Rebecca Fishman; m. Geoffrey Loftus, June 30, 1968 (div. Jan. 1991). BA, UCLA; MA, Stanford U., PhD; DSc (hon.), Miami U.; D (hon.), Leiden U.; LLD (hon.), John Jay Coll. Criminal Justice; DSc (hon.), U. Portsmouth, Eng. Prof. U. Wash., Seattle, 1973—. Author: Eyewitness Testimony, 1979, 2d. edit., 1996, Witness for the Defense, 1991, Myth of Repressed Memory, 1994. Office: U Wash Guthrie Hall Seattle WA 98195

LOFVANDER, MONICA BRITT, physician; b. Uppsala, Sweden, Feb. 3, 1949; d. Per-Axel and May-Britt (Bergefors) L.; m. Ake Lennart Weyler; children: Axel, Elin, Erik. MD, Linkoping U., 1974; PhD, Karolinska Inst., Stockholm, 1997. Gen. practitioner Rinkeby Health Ctr., Stockholm, 1980—; coord. postgrad. tng. in Western Stockholm, 1992—; rsch. fellow Inst. Family Medicine, Stockholm, 1993—; cons. Nat. Health Ins., Stockholm; lectr. general practice, Karolinska Inst., Stockholm. Author: Humanities and Medicine, 1996, Diagnostics of Traumatized Refugees, 1995, Rehabilitation of Young Immigrants, 1998; contbr. articles to profl. jours. Home: Spanga Kyrkvag 592, S-16372 Spanga Stockholm Sweden Office: Rinkeby Health Centre, Skarbygrand 3, S-16372 Spanga Stockholm Sweden

LOGAN, HENRY VINCENT, transportation executive; b. Phila., Nov. 7, 1942; s. Edward Roger and Alberta L.; m. Mary Genzano, Sept. 28, 1963; children: Michele Leah, Maureen Laura, Monica Lynn. BS in Commerce, DePaul U., 1975; M in Mgmt., Northwestern U., 1984. Successively supr. corp. acctg., asst. mgr. gen. acctg., mgr. gen. acctg., dir. corp. acctg. and taxes TTX Co., Chgo., 1962-70, contr., 1970-78, dir. fin. planning, 1978-83, mng. dir., fin. adminstr., 1983-85, CFO, v.p., 1985-88, sr. v.p. fleet mgmt., 1988—; bd. dirs. Calpro, Co., Mira Loma, Calif., RailGon Co., Chgo. Treas. TTX Co. Polit. Action Com., Chgo., 1980; vol Sch. Dist. 87 Task Force, Glen Ellyn, Ill., 1986. Hon. fellow U. Denver Intermodal Transp. Inst., 1999. Mem. Nat. Freight Transp. Assn., Intermodal Assn. N.Am. (chmn. legis. com. 1992-94), Rlwy. Supply Assn. (bd. dirs., treas., sec., v.p., chmn. fin. com.), Union League Club (mem. reception com. 1987-92, fin. com. 1993-95), Medinah (Ill.) Country Club, Willoughby Golf Club, Fla. Republican. Roman Catholic. Avocations: golf, music, reading, bicycling. Home: 812 Abbey Dr Glen Ellyn IL 60137-6130

LOGAN, JAMES SCOTT, SR., federal agency administrator; b. Stanford, Ky., June 18, 1948; s. James M.H. and Lillian Elizabeth (Givens) L.; m. Rose Marie Helm, Aug. 31, 1968; children: James Matthew, Tasha Marie. AA, Columbia (Mo.) Coll., 1990, BS/BA cum laude, 1992; postgrad., U. Colo., 1992—. Unit adminstr. USAR, Lakewood, Colo., 1972-82; continuity of govt. planner Fed. Emergency Mgmt. Agy. Region VIII, Lakewood, 1983-90, tech. hazards program specialist, 1991-92, sr. tech. hazards program specialist, 1992-95; team leader state and local programs Fed. Emergency Mgmt. Agy. Region VIII, Lakewood, Colo., 1995—; emergency analyst Office of Regional Dir., Denver, 1995—, dir. preparedness tng. and exercises divsn., 1998—; chmn. bd. dirs. Rocky Mountain Human Svcs. Coalition, 1995-99, bd. dirs. 1998—, pres., 1998-99. Mem. NAACP, Denver, 1992; mem. NCOA NCO Assn., Denver, 1979—; mem. citizen's adv. com. polit. sci. dept. U. Colo., Denver; chmn. bd. dirs. Rocky Mt. Human Svcs. Coalition, 1995—, pres., 1998-99; bd. dirs. City Club Denver, 2000. With U.S. Army, 1968-71, Vietnam, USAR, 1972. Decorated Legion of Merit. Mem. VFW, Am. Legion, Denver City Club, Pi Sigma Alpha. Democrat. Baptist. Avocations: reading, computers, political science. Home: 16952 E Bates Ave Aurora CO 80013-2243 Office: FEMA Region VIII PO Box 25267 Bldg 710A Denver CO 80225-0267

LOGAN, JOHN STEPHENS, retired internist, gastroenterologist, archivist; b. Ballynure, Antrim, Northern Ireland, Oct. 26, 1916; s. John Beatty Logan and Catherine Holland; m. Mary Sinclair Irwin, Sept. 21, 1940; 5 children. MB, BChir, Queen's U., Belfast, Northern Ireland, 1939, MD, 1946; postgrad., U. Pa., 1950-51. Cons. physician Royal Victoria Hosp., Belfast, 1951-82, archivist; mem. Med. Appeal Tribunal No. Ireland; expert witness in med. cases; br. med. officer Brit. Petroleum Co. Contbr. numerous articles to med. jours. Mem. South Belfast Assn.—Ulster Unionist Party; mem. Ulster Unionist Coun., Royal Brit. Legion, Northern Ireland, Burma Star Assn., Northern Ireland; elder Presbyn. ch. Lt.-col. Royal Army M.C., 1940-46. Fellow Royal Coll. Physicians London, Ulster Med. Soc.; mem. Assn. Physicians of Gt. Britain and Ireland, Brit. Soc. Gastroenterology. Avocations: country life, book collections. Home: 27 Myrtlefield Park, BT9 6NF Belfast Northern Ireland

LOGAN, LEE ROBERT, orthodontist; b. L.A., June 24, 1932; s. Melvin Duncan and Margaret (Seltzer) L.; m. Maxine Nadler, June 20, 1975; children: Chad, Casey. BS, UCLA, 1952; DDS, Northwestern U., 1956, MS, 1961. Diplomate Am. Bd. Orthodontics. Gen .practice dentistry Reseda, Calif., 1958-59; practice orthodontics Northridge, Calif., 1961—; pres. Lee R. Logan DDS Profl. Corp.; mem. med. staff Northridge Hosp.; owner Maxine's Prodn. Co.; owner Maxine's Talent Agy.; guest lectr. UCLA, U. So. Calif., dir dental edn. Northridge Med. Ctr. Contbr. articles to profl. jours. Served to lt. USNR, 1956-58. Recipient Nat. Philanthropy award, 1987, 1st Pl. winner Autistic Jogathon, 1981-2000; named (with wife) Couple of Yr., Autistic Children Assn., 1986. Mem. ADA, San Fernando Valley Dental Assn. (pres. 1998), Am. Assn. Orthodontists, Pacific Coast Soc. Orthodontists (dir., pres. so. sect. 1974-75, chmn. membership 1981-83), Foudn. Orthodontic Rsch. (charter mem.), Calif. Soc. Orthodontists (chmn. peer rev. 1982-93), G.V. Black Soc. (charter) Angle Soc. Orthodontists (pres. 1981-82, bd. dirs. 1982-2000, nat. pres. 1985-87), U. S.C. Century Club Fraternity, Xi Psi Phi, Chi Phi. Home: 4830 Encino Ave Encino CA 91316-3813 Office: 18250 Roscoe Blvd Northridge CA 91325-4226

LOGAN, SAMUEL ROBERT, chemist, educator; b. Coleraine, No. Ireland, Sept. 4, 1935; s. Samuel and Margaret (Stewart) L.; m. Renée Alice Tannahill, Apr. 6, 1972; children: Bruce, Alan Curtis. BSc, Queen's U. of Belfast, No. Ireland, 1956, PhD, 1959, DSc, 1992. Chartered chemist. Rsch. assoc. Ind. U., Bloomington, 1959-61; ICI rsch. fellow U. Leeds, Eng., 1961-64; lectr. in chemistry U. Strathclyde, Glasgow, Scotland, 1964-68; sr. lectr. chemistry New Univ., Coleraine, U.K., 1968-71, reader in chemistry, 1971-84, dean Sch. Phys. Scis., 1982-84; reader in chemistry U. Ulster, Coleraine, 1984-2000; vis. fellow U. Bordeaux, France, 1973, Hahn-Meitner Inst., Berlin, 1985; vis. lectr. U. Canterbury, Christchurch, N.Z., 1978. Author: Fundamentals of Chemical Kinetics, 1996, Physical Chemistry for the Biomedical Sciences, 1998; contbr. articles to profl. jours. Fellow Royal Soc. Chemistry (London); mem. European Photochem. Assn. Avocations: hillwalking, administrating rugby football. Office: Univ of Ulster Sch of ABCS, U Ulster Sch Biomed Scis, Cromore Rd, Coleraine BT52 1SA, Northern Ireland

LOGAN, THOMAS WILSON STEARLY, SR., priest; b. Phila., Mar. 19, 1912; s. John Richard and Mary (Harbison) L.; m. Hermoine Hill, Sept. 3, 1938; 1 son, Thomas Wilson Stearly. AB, Lincoln U., 1935, LLH (hon.), 1985; cert., Gen. Theol. Sem., 1938; STM, Phila. Divinity Sch., 1941; DD, Va. Sem., 1988; LLH (hon.), St. Augustine Coll., 1984; D of Sacred Theology, Episcopal Sem., Cambridge, Mass., 1994. Ordained priest Episcopal Ch., 1938. Vicar St. Philip Ch., N.Y.C., 1938-40, St. Michael's and All Angels Chs., Phila., 1940-45; rector Calvary Ch., Phila., 1945-84, rector emeritus, 1984—; pres. worker's conf. Episcopal Ch., 1951-61; canon St. Mary's Cathedral, Phila.; dean Schykill (Pa.) Deanery; former pres. Hampton (Va.) Mins. Conf., 1960-61; mem. diocesan coun.; police chaplain; chaplain Phila. Gen. Hosp.; S.T.D. Gen. Theol. Sem., N.Y.C., 1998. Bd. dirs. YMCA, Black Mus., Phila.; trustee Haverford State Hosp.; pres. Downington (Pa.) Sch.; life mem. Lincoln (Pa.) U. Mem. NAACP (life), Alpha Phi Alpha (life), Masons (33 degree, past grand master Pa.), Shriner (imperial chaplain). Home: 46 Lincoln Ave Yeadon PA 19050-2822

LOGAN, VINCENT PAUL, bishop; b. Bathgate, Scotland, June 30, 1941; s. Joseph and Elizabeth (Flannigan) L. Student, St. Andrews Coll., Drygrange, 1958-64; diploma in religious edn., Corpus Christi Coll., London, 1967. Ordained priest Roman Cath. Ch., 1964. Asst. priest St. Margaret's, Edinburgh, Scotland, 1964-66; chaplain St. Joseph's Hosp., Rosewell, 1967-77; priest St. Mary's, Ratho, 1977-81; religious edn. adviser Archdiocese St. Andrews & Edinburgh, 1967-70, dir. religious edn., 1970-81, episcopal vicar for edn., 1977-81; bishop Diocese of Dunkeld, Dundee, Scotland, 1981—; pres. priestly formation commn. Scottish Cath. Bishops Conf., Scotland, 1983, pres. vocations commn., 1982-88; chmn. Joint Commn. Bishops and Conf. Religious, Scotland, 1991—, Chesters Coll. Consultative Coun., 1984-89; religious adv. com. BBC and IBA, 1984-89; chmn. bd. govs. St. Andrew's Coll. Edn., Glasgow, Scotland, 1987-91; mem. Scottish religious adv. com. BBC, 1997—; apostolic visitator Sems. Eng. and Wales, 1993, Sems. Malta and Gozo, 1998-99. Co-author: (with Mary Macpherson) I Learn to Pray, 1979, My Prayers for Every Day, 1980, My Book of Prayers, 1980. Pres. Jubilee 2000 Nat. Com., 1996—. Decorated knight comdr. Order Holy Sepulchure Jerusalem. Mem. Order of Malta (magistral chaplain 1985, convental chaplain 1991). Home: Bishops House, 29 Roseangle, Dundee DD1 4LS, Scotland Scotland Office: Diocesan Ctr, 24-28 Lawside Rd, Dundee DD3 6XY, Scotland

LOGANI, MAHENDRA KUMAR, biomedical physics educator; b. Sialkot, Punjab, India, May 15, 1941; came to U.S. 1968; s. Khem Chand and Kartar Devi L.; m. Shashi Prabha, May 16, 1968; children: Anupma L. Kulkarni, Deependra K. BS, Aligarh (India) U., 1957, MS, 1961, PhD, 1967. Lectr. in chemistry Dharam Samaj Coll., Aligarh, 1961-64; postdoct. fellow Smith Coll., Northampton, Pa., 1968-69; rsch. assoc. Temple U., Phila., 1969-72, asst. prof. dermatology, 1972-77, assoc. prof. dermatology, 1977—, prof. biomed. physics, 1994—; vis. scientist Oak Ridge (Tenn.) Nat. Lab, 1981-82, Nagoya (Japan) U., 1980, U. Padova (Italy), 1980; co-investigator Nat. Inst. Environ. Health; prin. investigator NIH, 2000—. Contbr. articles to profl. jours., chpt. to book. Pres. India Cultural and Religious Ctr., Phila., 1985—; v.p. Coun. Indian Orgns., Phila., 1996-98, vice-chmn., 1998-00. Postdoct. fellow Sloan Found., 1968-69. Mem. ACS, Am. Oil Chemists' Soc., AAAS, Bioelectromagnetic Soc., Sigma Xi. Avocations: gardening, jogging, music. Home: 3261 Farragut Ct Bensalem PA 19020-1822 Office: Temple U Sch Medicine 3440 N Broad St Philadelphia PA 19140-5104

LOGANOVSKY, KONSTANTIN NIKOLAYEVICH, neuropsychiatrist; b. Kiev, Ukraine, Nov. 26, 1966; s. Nikolai Grigorievich and Eugenia Nikolayevna (Lisovskaja) L.; m. Tatiana Konstantinovna Dmitrenko, Oct. 3, 1992. MD, Kiev Med. U., 1989; Neuropsychiatrist, Sci. Ctr. Radiation Medicine, Kiev, 1994; PhD in Neuropsychiatry, Kiev Inst. Adv. Med. Studies, 1993. Cert. psychiatrist of the highest category Acad. Med. Scis. of Ukraine. Resident dept. neurology All-Union Sci. Centre for Radiation Medicine, Kiev, 1989-91, postgrad., 1991-94; prin. investigator WHO Pilot Porject Brain Damage in Utero, 1993—, sr. scientist, 1994-97, leading scientist, 1997—; project mgr. internat. project Mental Health Effects in Children exposed in utero as a result of the Chernobyl accident, 1998—; sec. Ukrainian Med. Jour., 1997—, Internat. Jour. Radiation Medicine, 1999—; prin. investigator internat. project Data Base on Psychol. Disorders in Ukrainian Liquidators of the Chernobyl Incident, 2000—; coach LUNDBECK Psychopharmacol. Products in Ukraine, 2000—. Author: (with A.K. Napreyenko) Ecological Psychiatry, 1997, (with A.I. Nyagu) Neuropsychiatric Effects of Ionising Radiation, 1998, (T.K. Loganovskaja) Schizophrenia Spectrum Disorders in Persons Exposed to Ionizing Radiation As a Result of the Chernobye Accident, 2000; contbr. articles to profl. jours. Lt. Res. Med. Svc., Kiev, 1989. Cabinet of Ministers scholar, 1997-98. Mem. Internat. Orgn. Psychophysiology, Internat. Soc. for Neuroimaging in Psychiatry, Am. Neuropsychiat. Assn. Avocations: fine arts, classical and jazz music, Internet browsing, international travel. E-mail: kosti@morion.liev.ua. Home: Apt 173, 16D Heroes of Stalingrad, 04210 Kiev Ukraine Office: Sci Ctr Radiation Medicine, 53 Melnikov St, 04050 Kiev Ukraine

LOGET, OLIVIER MARCEL, toxicologist, ophthalmologist; b. Nantes, France, Aug. 3, 1961; s. Henri Gabriel and Nicole Josiane (Lusseau) L.; m. Florence Marcelle Le Goëc, May 29, 1993; children: Capucine and Valentin (twins). Vet. diplomate, rsch. cert., Vet. Sch., Nantes, 1989; D in Vet. Medicine, Med. U., Nantes, 1990; postgrad. cert. in ophthalmology, Vet. Sch., Toulouse, France, 1992; postgrad. cert. in statis. analysis, P & M Curie U., Paris, 1994; postgrad. cert. in lab. animal sci., Vet. Sch., Lyon, France, 1995. Lic. lab. animal rschr. Dir. internal study Synthelabo Rsch., Porcheville, France, 1986-89; vet. biologist French Army, Amiens, 1989-90; vet. medicine physician SDF Desmaris, Bourges, France, 1990-91; study dir. Hazleton France, L'Arbresle, 1992-93, Pharmakon Europe, L'Arbresle, 1993-96; sr. toxicologist Ctr. Internat. Toxicology, Evreux, France, 1996-99; sr. toxicologist pharmaceuticals divsn. F. Hoffmann-La Roche Ltd./, 1999—; cons. in electrophysiology Synthelabo Rsch., Paris, 1989-90; cons. French Soc. Studies and Rsch. in Vet. Ophthalmology, Paris, 1995—; tchr. Vet. Sch., Lyon, 1994-95, Toulouse, 1996—. Author: Ocular Toxicology, 1995, Advances in Ocular Toxicology, 1997; contbr. articles to profl. jours. Capt. French mil., 1989-90. Recipient Organizer's Congratulations award Internat. Micropig Symposium, Paris, 1992. Mem. Internat. Soc. Ocular Toxicology, Internat. Soc. Vet. Ophthalmologists, Internat. Primatology Soc., Eurotox., European Soc. Lab. Animal Veterinarians. Avocations: chess, horsemanship, windsurfing, photography. Home: 32 rue Turenne, F-68350 Brunstatt France Office: F Hoffmann-La Roche Bld 073, Pharma Precl R & D Toxicology, CH-4070 Basel Switzerland

LOGHIS, CONSTANTINE, obstetrician/gynecologist, educator; b. Athens, Greece, July 20, 1944; s. Dimitrios and Anthousa L. MD, U. Athens, 1971, DSc, 1988. Pub. svc. physician Kesari, Corinth, Greece, 1971-72; tgn. gen. surgery, ob-gyn. Gen. Hosp., Athens, 1972-76; resident in ob-gyn., registrar U. Athens, 1976-88, lectr., asst. prof. ob-gyn., 1990—. Mem. Hellenic Soc. Ob-Gyn, Hellenic Soc. Ultrasound in Medicine and Biology, Hellenic Soc. Pediat. and Adolescent Gynecology, Hellenic Soc. Perinatal Medicine, Hellenic Soc. Fetal-Maternal Medicine, Hellenic Soc. Gynecol. Endocrinology, Hellenic Soc. Gynecol. Urology, N.Y. Acad. Scis. Office: U Athens Dept Ob-Gyn, 76 Vas Sophias Ave, GR 11528 Athens Greece

LOGINOV, ANDREI VASILIEVITCH, physicist; b. Leningrad, Russia, Sept. 20, 1947; s. Vasili Egorovitch and Taisiya Michailovna (Schuchtina) L.; m. Margarita Petrovna Editkina, Sept. 4, 1970; 1 child, Nikolai Andreevitch. DS, Vavilov State Optical Inst., St. Petersburg, Russia, 1995. Jr. rschr. Vavilov State Optical Inst., Leningrad, Russia, 1970-82, sr. rschr., 1982-91; leading rschr. Vavilov State Optical Inst., St. Petersburg, Russia, 1991—; prof. Inst. Fine Mechanics and Optics Tech. U., St. Petersburg, 1999—. Office: Vavilov State Optical Inst, 199034 Saint Petersburg Russia

LOGINOV, BORIS MIKHAILOVICH, mathematician, educator; b. Kaluga, Russia, June 22, 1953; s. Mikhail Andreevich and Nadejda Georgievna (Erokhiha) L.; m. Vera Victorovna Rogova, Dec. 2, 1987; 1 child, Maria. BS in Physics, Moscow State U., 1974, MS in Physics, 1976, postgrad., 1978-81, PhD in Phys. Math. Scis., 1982, Dr. of Scis., 1988. Asst. Kaluga br. Moscow State Tech. U., 1976-78, 82-83, dozent, 1982-89, prof., higher math chair, 1989-90, head of chair info. tech. and applied math., 1990—; cons. Sci. Prodn. Unification S. Lavorhkin, Kaluga br., 1991-95. Author: Dislocation Movement in the crystals with Dislocation Forest, 1988, Principles of Partial Differential Equations, 1990, Numerical Methods for Mathematical Physics Equations, 1992. Mem. N.Y. Acad. Scis., Russian Acad. Natural Scis. Avocations: swimming, travel. Home: Kibalchicha 4 100, 248012 Kaluga Russia Office: Moscow State Tech Univ, Bajenova 4, 248600 Kaluga Russia

LOGINOV, BORIS VLADIMIROVICH, mathematician, educator, researcher; b. Termez, Surh Darya, Uzbek, Nov. 14, 1938; arrived in Russia, 1993; s. Vladimir G. and Anna O. (Gorbatenko) L.; m. Nina V. Magnitskaya, Oct. 3, 1967; 1 child, Julia. Grad. in Mechanics and Math., Tashkent (Uzbek) State U., 1961, candidate in Physics and Math. Sci., 1965; D in Physics and Math. Sci., Lomonosov Moscow State U., 1983; prof. Romanovsky Math. Inst., Acad. Sci. Uzbekistan, 1992. Asst chair math. analysis Tashkent (Uzbek) State U., 1964-66, sr. sci. contbr. differential equations dept., 1966-85; head applied math. dept. Romanovsky Math Inst., Tashkent, Uzbek, USSR, 1985-93; prof. chair higher math. Ulyanovsk (Russia) Tech. U., 1993—; prof. chair mechanics and control Uylanovsk (Russia) State U., 1994—; prof. chair algebra and geometry Ulyanovsk (Russia) State Pedagogical U., 1996—. Contbr. numerous essays and articles to internat. math. jours., 1985—. Decorated to order Sign of Honour, 1987; grantee Novosibirsk U., 1996-97, 98-99, Russian Found. Fund, 1996-97. Mem. Am. Math. Soc., Gesellschaft fur Angewandte Math. and Mechanics. Avocation: mountain travel. Home: Corp 2 Apt 35, L Shevtsova str 54.b, 432027 Ulyanovsk Russia Office: Ulyanovsk State Tech U, Severny Venets Str 32, 432027 Ulyanovsk Russia

LOGINOV, YURI YURIEVICH, physicist; b. Krasnoyarsk, Russia, Jan. 1, 1954; s. Yuri Georgievich and Klavdia Ignatievna (Vladimirova) L.; m. Nadeshda Michailovna Ribiakova, Nov. 16, 1974; children: Vladimir, Svetlana. Student, Krasnoyarsk U., 1976; PhD, U. Gorkii, Russia, 1983; DSc, U. Nishnii-Novgorod, Russia, 1997. Rschr. Krasnoyarsk U., 1976-84, sr. rschr., 1984-85, sr. lectr., 1985-91, reader/docent, 1991-94, vice prorector sci., 1994-97, Soros assoc. prof., 1995, 98, head exptl. dept. Faculty Physics, 1997-99; rector Lesosibirsk Pedagogical Inst., Krasnoyarsk Univ., 1999—. Contbr. articles to sci. jours. Kapitza fellow Royal Soc., U.K., 1994. E-mail: loginov@wood.krasnet.ru. Home: Gusarova 50, Kv 28, 660130 Krasnoyarsk Russia Office: Krasnoyarsk Univ, Svobodnii 79, 660041 Krasnoyarsk Russia

LOGINOVSKY, OLEG VITALYEVITCH, state agency administrator; b. Chelyabinsk, Russia, Dec. 13, 1948; s. Vitaly Deamidovtich Loginovsky and Valentina Ilynichna (Mihaleva) Loginovskaya; m. Alina Sergeevna Zinkevitch; 1 child, Arseny Olegovitch. Engring. degree, Chelyabinsk Polytech. Inst., Russia, 1972; candidate of tech. scis., Moscow Engring. & Bldg. Inst., 1984; D in Tech. Scis., Moscow Mountain U., 1995. Leading engr. Rsch. Inst. Sys. Acad. of Scis. Russia, Chelyabinsk, 1972-74; postgrad. Chelyabinsk Polytech. Inst., 1974-77; chief designer Project and Design Bur., Chelyabinsk, 1978-90; head adminstrv. dept. computer works Chelyabinsk Region Adminstrn., 1990-93; prof. computer dept. Chelyabinsk State Tech. U., 1994-96; head info. sys. and techs. adminstrv. dept. Chelyabinsk Region Adminstrn., 1996—; v.p. Ural Dept. Internat. Acad., Chelyabinsk, 1994—; chmn. South Ural Regional Ctr. Russian Acad. Natural Scis., Chelyabinsk, 1997—, Sci. Coun. Ural Acad., 1998—. Author: Urban Structure Automation Design and Management, 1996, Management and Modeling in Social and Economic Systems, 1997; contbr. articles to profl. jours. Candidate Adminstrn. of Chelyabinsk, 1996. Mem. Russian Acad. Natural Scis. (badge of honour for disting. svcs. 1997), N.Y. Acad. Scis., Italian Acad. Econ. Scis., Internat. Informatization Acad., Internat. ACad. Natural and Social Scis. (Peter Great medal for disting. svcs. in renascence of sci. and econ. in Russian 1996). Avocations: sport, books. Home: Timiryazeva St 29-37, Chelyabinsk 454000, Russia Office: Adminstrn of Chelyabinsk, Revolution Sq 4, Chelyabinsk 454113, Russia

LOĞOĞLU, GÜLAY, medical educator; b. Konya, Turkey, Apr. 16, 1955; d. Ayhan and Yurdagul (Büyükoktar) M.; m. Nihat Loğoğlu, Mar. 5, 1986. MD, Hacettepe U., Ankara, Turkey, 1979; specialist in physiology, Çukurova U., Adana, Turkey, 1990. Gen. practitioner Ofcl. Health Ctr., Ankara, 1979-81; resident dept. pub. health Hacettepe., Ankara, 1981-83; physician pvt. clinic Ankara, 1983-86; physician Family Planning Ctr., Adana, 1986-88; resident faculty medicine dept. physiology Çukurova U., Adana, 1988-90, asst. prof. faculty medicine dept. physiology, 1990-94, as-

soc. prof. faculty medicine dept. physiology, 1994-2000; prof. fac. med. Dept. Physiology, 2000—. Contbr. articles to profl. jours. Mem. Fertility and Embryo Engring. Assn., Assn. for Protection of Environment and Consumer, Kemalist Idea Assn., Nat. Geographic Soc., Chamber of Physicians, Turkish Assn. Physiol. Scis., N.Y. Acad. Sci. Avocation: music. Office: Çukurova U Faculty Medicine, Dept Physiology, 01330 Adana Turkey

LOGOTHETIS, JOHN ACHILLEAS, neurologist, psychiatrist, consultant; b. Thessaloniki, Greece, Feb. 2, 1925; s. Achilleas and Maria (Rizou) L.; m. Thalia N. Kalambokidis, Nov. 25, 1956; children: Nicholas, Michael, Maria. MD, Thessaloniki Med. Sch., 1950; PhD, Minn. Postgrad. Med. Sch., 1957. Diplomate Am. Bd. Psychiatry and Neurology; cert. neurology Greek Bd. Neurology and Psychiatry. Resident in neurology U. Minn. Med. Sch., Mpls., 1951-55, instr. neurology, 1955-59, from asst. prof. to assoc. prof., 1959-67, prof., 1967-72; prof. neurology-psychiatry U. Thessaloniki Med. Sch., 1973-92, prof. emeritus, 1992—; dir. dept. neurology Hennepin County Gen. Hosp., Mpls., 1956-58; cons. neurology Hastings (Minn.) Hosp., 1960-67, VA Hosp., Mpls., 1955-59, VA Hosp., Hot Springs, S.D., 1957-68, VA Hosp., St. Cloud, Minn., 1961-68. Author: (textbooks) Textbook of Neurology, 1978, 2d edit., 1988, 3d edit., 1996, Textbook of Psychiatry, 1975, 2d edit., 1981; contbr. articles to profl. jours. including Neurology, Jour. Lancet, Am. Jour. Medicine. With Greek Army, 1967-69. Recipient Physician's Recognition award AMA, 1971. Mem. Am. Acad. Neurology (E. Weir Mitchell award 1955), Greek Neurol. Assn. (hon. pres. 1994—). Home: 21 Leoforos Nikis, 54623 Thessaloniki Greece

LOGOTHETIS, NICKOLAS, management consultant, researcher, educator; b. Kavala, Macedonia, Greece, Aug. 19, 1952; s. John and Helen (Papadopoulou) L.; m. Elena Nicolaidou, Dec. 29, 1985; children: John, Antigoni. Diploma in Math., Patras Coll., Greece, 1975; MSc in Stats., U. Sheffield, Eng., 1977; PhD, U. Nottingham, Eng. Chartered statistician, England. Rsch. advisor London Sch. Econs., 1980-84; head of stats. GE Co., London, 1985-88; sr. cons. Brit. Telecom, London, 1989-91; mng. dir. TQM Hellas, Athens, Greece, 1991—; sr. vis. rsch. fellow City U., London, 1987-90; councillor, supr. MBA program Brit. Consul, Athens, 1994—. Author: (books) Probability Distributions, 1985, Quality Through Design, 1989, Managing for Total Quality, 1992; also contbr. articles to profl. jours.; mem. editl. com. Applied Stats., 1987-90, Internat. Jour. TQM, Eng., 1988-90. V.p. Overseas Students Bur., U. Nottingham, 1978-79, pres. 1979-80. With Greek Army, 1988. Named EFQM representative Fedn. of Greek Industries, Athens, 1992, Unconditional Consultant, Cyprus Inst. Tech., 1993. Mem. Greek Orthodox Ch. Avocations: music, tennis, basketball, chess, reading. Office: TQM Hellas, Mavili 3, 11141 Athens Attiki, Greece

LOGUNOV, ANATOLY ALEKSEYEVICH, theoretical physicist, educational administrator; b. Obsharovka, Russia, Dec. 30, 1926. Ed., Moscow State U.; hon. doctorate, U. Belgrade, U. Berlin, Bratislava U., U. Havana, U. Prague, Sofia U., various Japanese univs. Mem. faculty Moscow State U., 1951-56; dep. dir. for rsch. Theoretical Physics Lab., Joint Inst. for Nuclear Rsch., Dubna, 1956-63, prof., 1961; dir. Serpukhov Inst. for High Energy Physics, Protvino, Moscow, 1963-74, rsch. leader, 1974—; dir. State Rsch. Ctr. Serpukhov Inst. for High Energy Physics, 1993—; mem. Russian Acad. Scis., 1972—, v.p., 1974-91; rector Moscow State U., 1977-92; prof. Inst. Fundamental Rsch. in Molise, Italy, 1995. Mem. editl. bd. Asia Pacific Peace Forum, 1995—; chief editor Science and Humankind, 1977-91, Theoretical and Math. Physics, 1989—; contbr. numerous articles to profl. jours. Dep. USSR Supreme Soviet, 1978-89. Decorated Hero of Socialist Labour, Order of Lenin(4), Order of Honour, Order of Merit III; Order of Pole Star (Mongolia); Order Yugoslavian Banner with ribbon; comdr. Order of Merit (Poland); recipient Lenin prize, 1970, USSR State prizes, 1973, 84, Golden Medal of Merit for Sci. and Humankind, Czechoslovakia, Lyapunov medal, Gibbs medal, numerous others. Office: State Rsch Ctr, Inst High Energy Physics, RU142284 Protvino, Moscow Russia

LOH, CHENG YEAN, company executive; b. Penang, Malaysia, July 23, 1943; d. Boon Siew Loh and Lay Wah Ong; m. Puay Huat Tan; children: Khenghwee, Kheng Ju, Jukok, Ju Nguan. Dir. Boonsiew Sdn. Bhd., Penang, 1967; mng. dir. Kah Motor Co., Singapore, 1974-95, Boonsiew Singapore, 1974-95; vice chmn. Boonsiew, Malaysia and Singapore, 1989-95; mng. dir. Bayview Internat., Singapore, 1992—; group chmn. Oriental Holdings Berhad, Malaysia, 1995—; chmn. Boon Siew Group of Cos., Malaysia, 1995—; bd. dirs. Tasek Corp., Malaysia, Kah Australia, Kah New Zealand; exec. chmn. Kah Motor Co Sdn Bhd, Malaysia and Singapore, 1995—. Vice gov. Tun Sardon Found., Penang, 1995. Avocations: tennis, golf. Office: Kah Motor Co, 75 Bukit Timah Rd, Singapore 258640, Singapore

LOH, GERHARD, librarian; b. Leipzig, Saxony, Germany, Jan. 24, 1937; s. Artur and Gertrud (Kuhn) L.; m. Elke Martina Teichmann, Feb. 20, 1964; children: Andre, Gerald, Hjalmar. Libr., Fachschule, Leipzig, Germany, 1956; Diploma Okonom, Univ. Leipzig, 1970, PhD, 1983; PhD, U. Berlin, 1990. Libr. U. Leipzig, 1956-70, scientific asst., 1970-75, leader of dept. catalogues, 1975-87, vice-dir., 1987-90, leader of dpe. econs., law, sports, 1990—. Author: Volkerschlacht bei Leipzig, 1963, Internationale Bibliographie der Antiquariats-Auktions- und Kunstkataloge, 1960-96, Bibliographie der Antiquariats-Auktions-und Kunstkataloge, 1975-96; co-editor: Zeitschriftenbestandsverzeichnis der Universitatsbibliothek Leipzig, 1977-89, Verzeichnis der Kataloge von Buchauktionen und Privatbibliotheken aus dem deutschsprachigen Raum, 1995-99, Die europaeischen Privatbibliotheken und Buchauktionen, 1997-2000, others. Office: Universitatsbibliothek, Beethovenstrasse 6, Saxony Leipzig D-04107, Germany

LOH, HORNG-HAI, electrical engineering educator; b. Taipei, Taiwan, Jan. 17, 1960; s. Liang-Chai and Hsiu-Yueh (Chang) L.; m. Hsiu-Chi Tsui; children: Alan, Anna, Julie. BSEE, Nat. Taipei Inst. Tech., 1980; MSEE, U. S.C., 1985; PhD, N.C. State U., 1991. Assoc. prof. Nat. Yunlin U. Sci. and Tech., Touliu, Yunlin, Taiwan, 1992—. Author: Introduction to Microcomputer, 1996. Chmn. Nat. Yunlin Inst. Tech. Consumer Orgn., 1993. Mem. IEEE Computer Soc., Tau Beta Pi, Eta Kappa Nu. Office: Nat Yunlin Inst Tech, Touliu Yunlin, Taiwan

LOH, WOLFGANG F.W., virologist, biotechnologist, consultant; b. Duesseldorf, Germany, Oct. 16, 1940; s. Friedrich and Helga (Bredt) L.; m. Gunhild Balzer, Oct. 9, 1971; children: Wulf-H., Ian-Ch. Diploma in biology, U. Wuerzburg, 1969; PhD, U. Erlangen, 1973; postgrad., BBS, 1990-94; GMP-mng., 1991-94, cert. in pharm. medicine, 1996. Cert. auditor. Postdoctoral fellow Inst. for Clin. Virology and Immunology U. Wuerzburg, 1973-77; head dept. biotech., immunology, med. scis. R&D clin. rsch. numerous pharm. cos., Germany, 1977-88; ind. cons., mng. dir. Immune Biotec Pharma Consulting, Friedrichsdorf, 1989—; pres., mng. dir. BiolmmunPharma GmbH, Friedrichsdorf, 1993—; mem. steering group of pharm. industry on BSE, 1992—. Contbr. more than 30 articles to profl. jours. Mem. Assn. Gene Diagnosis (bd. dirs. 1996-98), Fed. Assn. Pharm. Industry (v.p. biotech. sect. 1997—), ABAS (pres. 1999—). Avocations: sailing, classical music. Office: IBP Consulting/BIP Loh GmbH, Im Dammwald 27, D-61381 Friedrichsdorf Germany

LOHEAC, FRANCIS PAUL, insurance association executive; b. Gourin, France, Jan. 12, 1934; s. Paul Edouard Loheac and Anne Marie Lefebvre; divorced; 1 child, Laura. Degree in law, U. Paris, 1956, degree in literature, 1957; diploma in econs., Ecole Nat. France d'Outre-Mer, 1958. Asst. to dir., lectr. Instit des Hautes Etudes d'Outre-Mer, Paris, 1961-63; adminstr. Ministry of Fin. and Econ. Affairs, Paris, 1963-65; comml. attaché French Embassy, Caracas, Venezuela, 1965-68; comml. counsellor French Embassy, London, 1968-74; dir. French Ins. Assn., Paris, 1974-86; CEO, sec. gen. Comite Europeen Assurances, Paris, 1987-2000; participant many internat. confs. Contbr. articles to profl. jours., profl. revs. Lt. French Military, 1958-60. Recipient Grosses Goldenes Ehrenkreuzeichen for Svcs. Rendered to Austrian Republic.; named Officer Nat. Order of Merit, France. Mem. Automobile Club of France. Avocations: music, literature, walking.

LOHIYA, NIRMAL KUMAR, zoology educator; b. Bhilwara, Rajasthan, India, Dec. 25, 1946; s. Kalyan Mal and Sharda Devi Lohiya; m. Rajeshwari Goyal, Feb. 11, 1977; children: Namrata, Vaibhav. BSc, U. Rajasthan, Jaipur, India, 1968, PhD, 1975; MSc, Birla Inst. Tech. and Sci., Pilani, India, 1970. Asst. prof. U. Rajasthan, Jaipur, 1970-85, assoc. prof., 1985-97, prof. zoology, 1997—, head dept., 1996-99, hon. dir. Sch. Life Scis., 1998; mem. ICMR Task Force on Hormonal Contraceptives; asst. warden Gokhale Hostel, U. Rajasthan, Jaipur, 1976-80; organizing joint sec. All India Inter-Varsity Basketball, 1974-75, 77-78; convener basketball Univ. Studies in Sci., U. Rajasthan, Jaipur, 1972-76, 83-84, 85-86, 88-89; local head dept. zoology U. Maharaja's Coll., Jaipur, 1987-90; convener bd. studies zoology U. Rajasthan, 1998; presenter rsch. papers at seminars and confs. Author: Cell Biology, Heredity and Evolution; corr. editor Asian Jour. Andrology, 1999; contbr. chpts. to books and over 125 rsch. papers to nat. and internat. jours. Pres. Parent-Tchrs. Soc., Kendriya Vidyalaya No. 1, Jaipur, 1994-95; coord. Univ. Grants Comm. Spl. Assistance Programme, 1994, UGC-Com. for Strengthening Infrastructure in Sci. and Tech., 1998-99. Recipient Career award U. Grants Commn., 1980-83, Nahar Sanman Puraskar for edn., 1990, ISEER award for outstanding rsch. in med. scis., 1998. Mem. Primatological Soc. India (life, treas. 1982, gen. sec. 1986), Electron Microscope Soc. India (life, exec. com. 1986), Internat. Primatological Soc. (sec. Australasia 1988-92), Indian Soc. Study Reprodn. and Fertility (founder, life, mem. exec. com. 1995, 97), Soc. Advancement Contraception, Lab. Animal Sci. Assn. India (founder, life), Soc. Andrology (life), Indian Sci. Congress Assn., Indian Soc. Gen. and Comparative Endocrinology. E-mail: lohiyank@hotmail.com. Office: U Rajasthan, Dept Zoology, Jaipur 302004, India

LOHMANN, LESLIE JOHN, employee benefit consultant, actuary; b. Buffalo, May 12, 1950; s. George and Elizabeth Amy (Nichols) L.; m. Mary Katherine Biesel, Oct. 7, 1983 (div. Oct. 1988); m. Shiyoko Ruth Ouchi, Oct. 16, 1994; 1 child, Aiyanna Celestine. BSc, LeMoyne Coll., Syracuse, N.Y., 1970; postgrad., U. Waterloo, Ont., Can., 1976-77. Enrolled actuary; cert. computing profl. Actuary Am. Gen. Life, Houston, 1980-81, Great So. Life, Houston, 1981-82, Reed Stenhouse, Houston, 1982-85; sr. cons. Towers Perrin, Houston, 1985-90; sr. actuary Towers Perrin, Tokyo, 1990-91; pres. Lohmann Internat. Assocs., Tokyo, 1991—. Contbr. articles to profl. jours. Vestry mem. St. Alban's Ch., Tokyo, 1994-97; mem. Houston Ballet Ambs. II, Houston, 1985-91. 1st lt. N.Y. Army Nat. Guard, 1970-77. Fellow Soc. Actuaries, Can. Inst. Actuaries, Conf. Cons. Actuaries, Life Mgmt. Inst.; mem. Am. Acad. Actuaries, Am. C. of C. in Japan (com. vice chair 1993), Can. C. of C. in Japan, Granite Club (Toronto), Tokyo Canadian Club (bd. mem. 1991). Nippon Sei Kokai. Avocations: travel, skiing, snorkeling. Home and Office: Lohmann Internat Assocs, 8-4-11-501 Kitamachi Nerima-ku, Tokyo 179-0081, Japan

LOHRAY, BRAJ BHUSHAN, pharmaceutical executive; b. Khagaria, Bihar, India, Jan. 1, 1954; s. Kamakhya Prasad and Kameswari Devi (Prasad) L.; m. Vidya Pai, May 6, 1980; children: Bharath, Uma. BS, J.B. Coll., Assam, India, 1975; MS, Gauhati U., Assam, India, 1977; PhD in Organic Chemistry, Indian Inst. Tech., Kanpur, 1983. Alexander von Humboldt fellow U. Würzburg (Germany), 1984-85; postdoct. fellow Reinische Westfalrische Technische, Aachen, Germany, 1985-88; rsch. assoc. M.I.T., Cambridge, Mass., 1988-89; sr. scientist Nat. Chem. Lab., Pune, India, 1989-94; v.p. Dr. Reddy's Rsch. Found., Hyderabad, India, 1995-99; pres. Zydus Rsch. Ctr., Ahmedabad, India, 1999—; pres. Zydus Rsch. Ctr., Ahmedabad, India. Mem. Indian Chem. Soc., Am. chem. Soc., German Chem. Soc. Avocations: reading, hiking, driving. Home: 34 Goyal Palace Bodek Dev, 380 054 Ahmedabad Gujarat, India Office: Zydus Rsch Ctr, Gandhinagar-Sorkhy Hwys, 380 053 Ahmedabad Gujarat, India

LOHRLI, ANNE, retired English language educator, writer; b. Bake Oven, Oreg., Feb. 9, 1906; d. Gottfried and Anna (Hüsser) L. BA, Occidental Coll., L.A., 1927, MA, 1928; MA, Columbia U., 1932; PhD, U. So. Calif., 1937. Tchr. L.A. city schs., 1937-45; prof. English N.Mex. Highlands U., Las Vegas, 1945-65; vis. prof. U. Trieste, 1954. Compiler: Household Words, List of Contributors, etc., 1973; contbr. some 40 articles in Dickensian, Princeton U. Libr. Chronicle, Victorian Studies, Pacific Historian, others, 1963-94. Mem. Phi Beta Kappa, Phi Kappa Phi. Home: 901 Marlene St Apt 3 Ukiah CA 95482-5987

LOHSE, ANDREA, business and competition law educator; b. Kellinghusen, Germany, Apr. 28, 1964; d. Peter and Erika (Bräuss) L. Grad., Christian-Albrechts U., Kiel, Germany, 1988, PhD in Law, 1991; second state exam., State Schleswig-Holstein, Germany, 1993. Rsch. asst. Christian-Albrechts-U., 1984-89, adminstrv. asst., 1990-93, acad. asst., 1993-94; asst. in civil, bus., and competition law Free U. Berlin, 1994—; trainee Commn. European Cmty., Brussels, 1989-90; lectr. Acad. Savs. Banks of Schleswig-Holstein, 1991-94. Author: Joint Ventures in EEC Competition Law, 1992 (Faculty award Christian-Albrechts-U.); contbr. articles, revs. to profl. publs. Asst. youth welfare issues Protestant Ch. in Germany, 1979-83. State Schleswig-Holstein scholar, 1989-90, scholar U. Assn. Schleswig-Holstein, 1992; recipient Honor furtherance award Hermann-Ehlers-Found., 1992. Mem. Assn. Young Civil Law Acads. Avocations: music, psychology, astrology, mystics, physics. Home: Uhlenweg 30A, 75548 Kellinghusen Germany Office: Freie U Berlin, Boltzmannstrasse 3, 14195 Berlin Germany

LOHSE, EDUARD, religion educator; b. Hamburg, Germany, Feb. 19, 1924; s. Walther and Mina (Barrelet) L.; m. Roswitha Flitner, July 18, 1952; children: Regula, Martin, Ansgar. D Theology, U. Göttingen, Germany, 1949; Dr.Theol.Habil., U. Mainz, Germany, 1953, Dr.theol. (hon.), 1961; Dr.theol. (hon.), Mühlenberg Coll., 1979, U. Glasgow, Scotland, 1983. Prof. New Testament U. Kiel, Germany, 1956-64, U. Göttingen, 1964-71; bishop of Hannover Evang.-Luth. Ch. of Hannover, 1971-88, Bishop emeritus, 1988—; pres. Coun. of Evangelical Ch. in Germany, 1979-85. Author: The New Testament Environments, 1976, The Formation of the New Testament, 1981, Theological Ethics of the New Testament, 1991. Rector magnificus U. Göttingen, 1969-71; Abt zu Loccum, 1977-2000. Lt. German Navy, 1942-45. Recipient Niedersachsenpreis für Kultur Country Niederssachsen, 1979, Edith-Stein prize Kuratorium Edith-Stein-Gesellschaft, 1995. Mem. Acad. Scis., United Bible Socs. (pres. 1988-96). Lutheran. Home: Ernst Curtius Weg 7, D37075 Göttingen Germany

LO IACONO, ANTONIO, psychologist, psychotherapist, educator; b. Ricadi, Calabria, Italy, Jan. 17, 1945; s. Francesco Lo Iacono and Anna Scozzarro. Psychology degree, U. La Sapienza, Rome, 1970; bioenergetic analysis, Internat. Inst. Biol. Analysis, N.Y.C., 1976; M in Sexology, Med. Sch. Rome, 1978. Diplomate in psychology and psychotherapy. Work psychologist Ente Nazionale Prevenzione Infortuni, Perugia, 1971-72; ednl. psychologist Opera Nazionale Maternità e Infanzia, Frascati, 1973-74; expert judge The Ct., Rome, 1978-90; cons. psychologist S. Eugenio Hosp., Rome, 1978-91; prof. Med. Sch. Rome, 1978—; coord. Coordinamento Regionale Operatori Socio Sanitari, Rome, 1990-95; chmn. Applied Soc. Assn. Assn. Italiana Psicologia Applicata, 1980—; drug addiction officer coord. Assessorato Sanità, Rome, 1988-92; immigration officer sec. Ass. Servizi Sociali, Rome, 1992-94. Author: (books) La Commedia dell'esclusione, 1977, Burnout, 1991, Sailing: Therapeutic Poems, 1994 (Trophy Cup 1995), Drammautogeno: Psychotherapy Art, 1998. Counselor Comm. Sanità Ordine Psicologi Rome, 1977-99; chmn.-elect Italian Soc. Psychology, Rome, 1998—. Lt. Italian Mil. Police, 1969-70. Recipient Trophy award Lioness Club-Caserta, 1987, Plate award Cir. Nautico Capt. Achab, 1989, Tevercxpo 95, 1995. Mem. Centro Italiano Disturbi alimentari Psicogeni (hon. chmn. 1998), Internat. Assn. Human Rels. (hon.), Internat. Inst. Biol. Analysis, Mare Aperto Sailtherapy (vice-chmn. 1988-92), Emergency Psychology Assn. (vice-chmn. 1998-2000). Avocations: theater, poetry, sailing, windsurfing, horse riding. Home: Via Tagliamento 76, 00198 Rome Italy

LOIN, E. LINNEA, retired social work administrator; b. Middletown, Conn., Nov. 20, 1942; d. Alfred William Skinner and Ada Patricia Moore; m. Peter Michael Loin, Sept. 16, 1972. BA, U. Conn., 1965. Social worker State of Conn., Middletown and Hartford, 1964-69; case supr. State of Conn., Hartford, 1969-74; program supr. State of Conn., Hartford, Manchester and, Rockville, Hartford, 1984-90, Willimantic, 1990-97; ret., 1997; state liaison Nat. Ctr. for Child Abuse and Neglect, Washington, 1985-90. Editor: Connecticut's Children, 1985, Common Ground, 1987-89. Avocations: swimming, walking, reading, travel, water sports. Home: 29 Cowles Rd Willington CT 06279-1705

LOINGER, ANGELO GIUSEPPE, physicist, educator; b. Verona, Veneto, Italy, Apr. 1, 1923; s. August Loinger and Wanda Remondini; m. Carla Enrica Colombo, Mar. 6, 1950; children: Guido, Eugenio. D in Physics, U. Bologna, Italy, 1947. Full prof. U. Messina, Italy, 1961, U. Pavia, Italy, 1961-67, U. Milan, 1967-96; ret. Contbr. articles to profl. jours. Recipient Premio F. Somaini, Fondazione F. Somaini, 1970. Mem. Istituto Lombardo Accademia di Scienze e Lett.

LOIZOU, LOIZOS NIKOLAOU, secondary school administrator, educator; b. Asha, Cyprus, Apr. 21, 1953; s. Nikolaos and Margarita Dimitriou (Kashieris) L.; m. Evangelia George Proufa, July 31, 1977; children: Panayiotis, Margarita-Ismini. BA, Sch. of Philosophy, 1977, MA in Clin. Psychology/Devel. Psychology, 1992, PhD in Devel. Psychology, 1996, PhD in History of Art, 1997—. Tchr. Midshipmen Public Sch., Salamis Athens, 1977-78; tchr. deaf-mutes Deaf-Mutes Pvt. H.S., Athens, 1978-80; tchr. Kivotos Public H.S., Kivotos-Grevena, Greece, 1980-82, Public Sr. H.S. Grevena, Greece, 1982-84; head master Karpero Public H.S., Karpero-Grevena, Greece, 1984-89, Intercultural Pub. H.S., Thessaloniki, Greece, 1993-98; prof. extraordinaire, Dept. Psychology U. Crete, Katerini, 1999-2000. Contbr. articles to profl. jours. Scholarship State Scholarship's Instn., 1973-77. Mem. Greek Psychol. Soc., European Assn. for Rsch. Learning and Istrn., Am. Psychol. Assn. Christian Orthodox. Avocations: parapsychology, Oriental philosophies, music, computers, chess. Home: 25 Kolokotronis St, 55337 Triandria Greece Office: HS Supr's Office, Tsaldari 10, Katerini Greece

LOJDA, LADISLAV, veterinarian; b. Litohor, Moravia, Czechoslovakia, Jan. 18, 1926; s. František and Anna (Kratochvílová) L.; m. Jiřina Lojdová, Sept. 8, 1951; children: Ladislav, Zdeněk. DVM, U. Vet. Sci., Brno, Czechoslovakia, 1950, Candidat Scienciarum, 1968. Vet. gen. practitioner Kutná Hora, Czech Republic, 1950-54, Telč, Czech Republic, 1954-56; specialist reprodn. domestic animals/artificial insemination M. Krumlov, Czech Republic, 1956-58; region vet. specialist Brno, 1958-62; rsch. worker Vet. Rsch. Inst., Brno, 1962-68, sr. rsch. worker, 1968-92; adviser animal reprodn. State Vet. Adminstrn., Praha, Czech Republic, 1958-68, adviser vet. genetics, 1968-92. Author: Heredopathology of Reproduction in Domestic Animals, 1971; (with others) Methods of Chromosomal Study, 1977, Fertility and Reproductive Disorders in Cattle, 1980, Quo vadis medicina veterinaria, 1986, Mastitis in cattle, 1987, Cytogenetics of Animals, 1989, Vademecum for veterinary physicians, 1991, Health and diseases in calfs, 1991, History and perspectives of genetic prevention in veterinary medicine, 1996. Dep. of mayor City Dist. Brno-Obřany, 1991-94. Fellow Genetic Soc., Cytogenetic Soc., Czechoslovak Biol. Soc. Home: Lišti 7, 614 00 Brno Moravia, Czech Republic Office: Vet Rsch Inst, Brno 621 32, Czech Republic

LÖJDQUIST, HUGO, electronics company executive, mechanical engineeer; b. Tierp, Sweden, Mar. 20, 1958; s. Per-Hugo and Ulla Löjdquist; m. Ulla-Karin Berg, Apr. 29, 1984; children: Jakob, Louise, Axel. Student, Lvkas, Gothenburg, Sweden, 1979, Worcester Poly. Inst., 1981-82; MSc, Royal Inst. Tech., Stockholm, 1984. Rotation engr. LM Ericsson, Stockholm, 1984-85; project mgr. factory projects Ericsson Telecom., Stockholm, 1985-86, mktg. mgr., 1986-90; mgr. customer support Ericsson Radio Systems AB, Stockholm, 1990-91, dir. customer support, 1991-92, dir. ops., 1992-94; v.p. mobile networks Compañia Ericsson SACI, Buenos Aires, 1995-98; pres. Ericsson de Chile SA, Santiago, 1999—. Office: Av Vitacura 2808, 10143 Correo Ctrl Santiago Rch-Las Condes, Chile

LOKA, HANY, engineering executive, educator; b. Cairo, Nov. 6, 1966; s. Samir and Adoree (Shawky) L.; m. Malak Wahba, Jan. 9, 1997. BSc, Cairo U., 1989, MSc, 1993; PhD, U. Toronto, Can., 1998. Asst. lectr. Cairo U., 1989-93; design engr. Siemens Egypt, Cairo, 1990-93; tchg. asst. U. Toronto, 1994-98, rsch. asst., 1993-98; v.p. Egyptian Engring. & Trading Co., Cairo, 1998—; asst. prof. Cairo U., 1998—; cons. Siemens Egypt, 1998—. Contbr. articles to profl. jours. Treas., bus. com. Nile Assn. Ontario, Can., 1995-97. Univ. of Toronto Open fellowship U. Toronto, 1993-97, Info. Tech. Rsch. Ctr., 1997-98; recipient Cairo U. Outstanding Performance award, 1984-89. Mem. IEEE, OSA, Egyptian Soc. of Engrs. (doctorate mem.). Avocation: soccer, track and field. Home: 32 Falaky St Apt 61, Cairo Egypt Office: Egyptian Engring/Trading, 3(B) Mohamed Haggag #6, Cairo Maarouf, Egypt

LOKESH, BELUR R., biochemist, researcher; b. Secunderabad, India, Feb. 29, 1952; s. Ramaswamy and Indira Iyengar; m. Pushpa Rangaswamy, Nov. 15, 1989. BSc, Bangalore U., India, 1970, MSc, 1972; PhD, Indian Inst. Sci., Bangalore, 1977. Post doctoral fellow U. Iowa, Iowa City, 1977-80; rsch. scientist Sandoz Rsch. Inst., Vienna, Austria, 1980-83; rsch. assoc. II Cornell U., Ithaca, 1983-89; scientist EI CFTRI, Mysore, 1989-94, scientist EII, 1994—; editor: J. Food Sci. & Tech., Mysore, 1996-98, editor-in-chief, 1999—. Mem. Rotary Central Dist. 3180, Mysore, 1996—. Recipient Dr. J.C. Ghosh medal Indian Inst. Sci., 1976-77. Mem. Soc. Biological Chemist (life), Nutrition Soc. India, Assn. Food Scientists & Technologists. Avocations: stamp collection, listening to classical music, travelling. Office: Dept Biochem & Nutrition, Cen Food Technol Rsch I, 570013 Mysore-Karnataka India

LOKEY, FRANK MARION, JR., broadcast executive, consultant; b. Ft. Worth, Oct. 15, 1924; s. Frank Marion Sr. and Corinne (Whaley) L. Student, Smith-Hughes Evening Coll., 1955-59. Announcer, newscaster, disc jockey, morning personality Stas. WAPI, WBRC and WSGN, Birmingham, Ala., 1941-52; pres. Sta. WRDW-TV, Augusta, Ga., 1952-55; asst. gen. mgr., mgr. sales, news anchor Sta. WLW-A TV (now WXIA-TV), Atlanta, 1955-66; co-owner, gen. mgr. Sta. WAIA, Atlanta, 1960-62; S.E. news corr., talk show host CBS News N.Y., N.Y.C., 1960-66; asst. to owner, gen. mgr. Sta. WBIE-AM-FM, Atlanta, 1962-64; asst. to pres., gen. mgr. Stas. KXAB-TV, KXJB-TV, KXMB-TV, Aberdeen, Fargo, Bismarck, S.D., N.D., 1966-67; exec. v.p., gen. mgr. St. WEMT-TV, Bangor, Maine, 1967-70; pres., gen. mgr. Stas. KMOM-TV, KWAB-TV, Odessa-Midland, Big Spring, Tex., 1970-75; exec. v.p., gen. mgr. Sta. KMUV-TV (now named KRBK-TV), Sacramento, Calif., 1975-77; CEO Lokey Enterprises, Inc., Sacramento, L.A., El Centro, Calif., 1977—, also chmn. bd. dirs.; cons., troubleshooter 18 TV stas. nationwide, 1977—; cons., actor 6 movie prodn. cos., Hollywood, Calif., 1980—; cons., outside dir. Anderson Cons., Manhattan, L.I., N.Y., 1981—; network talk show host/news corr. for 7 news orgns. worldwide, 1984—; bd. dirs. Broadcast Audience Behavior Rsch., Manhattan, 1986—, mem. inner circle, 1986—; owner/franchiser The Party Place; motivational spkr. creator, originator approach to real estate mktg.; prodr. swing dance parties, LA., Palm Spring, Calif., Las Vegas, Nev. Hon. mem. Imperial County Bd. Suprs., El Centro, 1986—, El Centro City Coun., 1987—. Mem. Am. Legion. Baptist. Avocations: producer big bands parties, movie acting, ancient history, tracing family tree. Home and Office: 2709 Us Highway 111 Imperial CA 92251-9772

LOKIETEK, WLADYSLAW ZYGMUNT, orthopedist; b. Tertre, Hainaut, Belgium, Aug. 8, 1941; s. Wladyslaw and Teresa (Palaszewska) L.; m. Suzanne Christiaens, July 6, 1967; children: Sophie-Claude Marie, Wladyslaw-François Sabine, Ludmila-Cecile-Lucie, Catherine-Pierre Marie. MD, U. Louvain, Belgium, 1968, PhD, 1982. Intern St. Boniface Hosp., Winnipeg, Man., Can., 1967-68; rsch. fellow Columbia U., N.Y.C., 1971-72; pediatric orthop. resident A.I. DuPont Inst., Wilmington, Del., 1972-73; chief orthop. unit scoliosis Cath. U. Louvain, 1973, chief orthop. ward, 1983, assoc. prof., 1982-90, prof., 1990—; chief orthopediat. rsch., 1982—, acad. prof., 1998; coord. Belgian-Polish Orthop. Coop., 1992; mem. Bur. Groupe Etude Scoliosis, France, 1980; cons. med. rel. U. Cracow, Poland, 1992; organizer orthop. coop. UCL, Cracow, 1992. Assoc. editor Jour. Pediatric Orthop., 1987; contbr. numerous articles to pediatric jours. Mem. Scoliosis Rsch. Soc. (U.S.), European Pediatric Orthopediat. Soc., Belgian Assn. Pediatric Orthopediat. (pres. 1997). Avocations: history. Office: St Luc Univ Hosp, Ave Hippocratic 1200, Brussels Belgium also: Cath U Louvain, Dept Orthopediat, Mont-Godinne Belgium

LØKKETANGEN, ARNE, information science educator; b. Drammen, Norway, Feb. 2, 1954; s. Erik and Lise (Dahlgaard) L.; m. Torill Merete Eide, July 2, 1982 (div. 1996); children: Erik, Marius. BSc, U. Manchester, Eng., 1975; MSc, U. Oslo, 1978; PhD, U. Bergen, 1995. Cons. Garex A/S, Oslo, 1978-82, Telox A/S, Oslo, 1982-88; asst. prof. Molde Coll., Norway, 1988-95, assoc. prof., 1995—; rschr. SINTEF, Oslo, 1995—. Co-author: Metaheuristics: State of the Art 1995, 1995; asst. editor Jour. Heuristics, 1995; contbr. articles to profl. jours. Home: Skrenten 1f, N-6411 Molde Norway Office: Molde Coll, Britveien 2, N-6400 Molde Norway

LOKMER, STEPHANIE ANN, international business development consultant; b. Wheeling, W.Va., Nov. 14, 1957; d. Joseph Steven and Mary Ann (Mozney) L. BA in Comm., Bethany Coll., 1980; cert., U. Tübingen, Germany, 1980, Sprach Inst., Tübingen, 1980. V.p. Wheeling Coffee and Spice, W.Va., 1981—; pres. Lokmer & Assocs., Inc., McLean, W.Va., 1986—. Bd. dors. Am. Found. of Ivory Coast. Mem. Pub. Rels. Soc. Am., World Affairs Coun., Counselors Acad., Zeta Tau Alpha. Republican. Roman Catholic. Avocations: tennis, reading, flying, politics.

LOKTEV, VADIM MIKHAILOVICH, physicist, researcher; b. Kiev, Ukraine, May 3, 1945; s. Mikhail S. Loktev and Aleksandra I. Bondareva; m. Veronica I. Zakharovskaya; 1 child, Loktev Ivan. MS in Physics, Kiev U., 1968; PhD in Physics, Inst. Physics, Ukraine, 1971; DSc, Inst. Theoretical Physics, Ukraine, 1983. Jr. rschr. Bogolyubov Inst. Theoretical Physics, Kiev, 1971-74, sr. rschr., 1974-83, head lab., 1983-92, head dept., 1992—; lectr. Kiev U., 1983-98, Intnal Solomon U., Kiev, 1996-98; head chair Nat. Tech. U . Ukraine, Kiev, 1998—. Co-author: Cryocrystals, 1983, Long-Range Impurity States in Magnetic Cyrstals, 1987; editor: Fundamental Problems of High-Tc Superconductivity, 1989, High-Tc Supercoductivity, 1992. Recipient State Prizes in sci. Govt., Kiev, 1977, 90, annual award in sci. Nat. Acad. Sci., Kiev, 1985. Mem. Am. Phys. Soc., Phys. Soc. Ukraine, Nat. Acad. Scis. Ukraine, European Acad., N.Y. Acad. Scis. Avocations: literature, recreational activities, basketball. Office: Bogolyubov Inst Th Physics, Metrologichna Str 14b, 03143 Kyiv Ukraine

LOLAS, ANTHONY JOSEPH, SR., health and environmental business executive; b. Detroit, Mar. 27, 1942; s. Charles and Doris (Rutkowski) L.; m. Marilyn Ruth Hickey, June 7, 1967 (div. Jan. 1989); children: Anthony J. Jr., Nicole E.; m. Patricia Smith Dod, Dec. 9, 1995. BS in Engring. Mgmt., USAF Acad., 1967; MBA in Bus. Ops. Analysis, UCLA, 1968; EdS in Adminstrn. and Supervision, Troy State U., 1980; PhD in Adminstrn. and Leadership, U. S.C., 1994. CEO Bus. Svcs., Charleston, S.C., 1980-91; chief bus. mgmt. S.C. Dept. Health and Environ. Control, Columbia, 1992—; cons. various cos., Charleston, 1973-89; adj. prof. computer resource mgmt. Webster U., 1993—. Author: (books) Education Objectives, 1980, Crisis in Confidence, 1994. Cons., advisor Future Bus. Leaders, Charleston, 1994-96. Lt. col. USAF, 1967-90. Decorated D.F.C., Meritorious Svc. medal, 4 Air medals. Mem. S.C. Govt. Assn. Purchasing Ofcls., S.C. Fleet Mgmt. Assn., Profl. Risk Mgmt. Assn., Judo Assn. Am. (life), Mensa, S.C. C. of C. (issues com.). Home: 4700 Carter Hill Dr Columbia SC 29206-4604 Office: DHEC Bus Mgmt 2600 Bull St Columbia SC 29201-1797

LOMAKIN, EUGENE VICTOROVICH, mechanician, educator; b. Baku, Azerbaijan, USSR, Jan. 17, 1945; s. Victor Vasilievich and Valentina Ivanovna (Kiporova) L.; m. Marina Alexandrovna Gamrat-Kurak, Aug. 30, 1980; 1 child, Natalie. MS in Mechanics, Lomonosov Moscow State U., 1968, PhD in Physics and Math., 1971, assoc. prof., 1977, DSc in Physics and Math., 1989, prof., 1995. Mech. and math. diplomate. Lectr. faculty mechanics and math. Lomonosov Moscow State U., 1971-77, assoc. prof. faculty mechanics and math., 1977-93, prof. faculty mechanics and math., 1993—, acting dir. dept. theory plasticity faculty mechanics/math., 1994—; rsch. scientist Inst. Graphite, Moscow, 1972-76; sr. rsch. scientist Rsch. Ctr. Molniya, Moscow, 1977-91, Geol. Inst. Russian Acad. Scis., Moscow, 1990-92. Author: (with I.M. Kershtein, V.D. Klyuschnikov, S.A. Schesterikov) Experimental Fracture Mechanics, 1989; contbr. sci. articles to profl. jours. Grantee Internat. Sci. Found., 1994-95, Russian Found. for Basic Rschs., 1993—, Competition Ctr. for Natural Scis., 1998—. Mem. Sci. Mechanics Moscow (sci. sec. 1998—). Home: Novoyasenevsky Ave 40-3-480, 117463 Moscow Russia Office: Lomonosov Moscow State U, Faculty Mechs and Math, 119899 Moscow Russia

LOMAN, MARY LAVERNE, retired mathematics educator; b. Stratford, Okla., June 10, 1928; d. Thomas D. and Mary Ellen (Goodwin) Glass; m. Coy E. Loman, Dec. 23, 1944; 1 child, Sandra Leigh Loman Easton. BS, U. Okla., 1956, MA, 1957, PhD, 1961. Grad. asst., then instr. U. Okla., Norman, 1956-61; asst. prof. math. U. Ctrl. Okla., Edmond, 1961-62, assoc. prof., 1962-66, prof., 1966-93, prof. emeritus, 1993—. NSF fellow, 1965-67. Mem. Math. Assn. Am., Nat. Coun. Tchrs. Math., Okla. Coun. Tchrs. Math. (v.p. 1972-76), Higher Edn Alumni Coun. Okla., VFW Aux., Delta Kappa Gamma. Home: 2201 Tall Oaks Trl Edmond OK 73003-2325

LOMBARD, ALAIN, conductor, artistic director; b. Paris, Oct. 4, 1940. Studied with Line Talleul and Gaston Poulet, Paris Conservatoire. Asst. to prin. condr. Lyon Opera, 1961-65; condr. N.Y. Philharmonic, 1966; musical dir. Miami Opera, 1966-74, Met. Opera, 1967; dir. Strasbourg Philharmonic, 1972-83; artistic dir. Orchestre Nat. Bordeaux-Aquitaine, France, 1988-99; internat. orch. touring condr. Pieter G. Alferink Artists; guest condr. Schveningen Festival, Holland, Hamburg Opera, L'Orchestre de Paris, others. Debuted at age 11 with the Pasdeloup Orch.; recordings include Mozart's cosi fan Tutte, Berlioz Symphonie Fantastique, Harold in Italy and Romeo et Juliette, Verdi Requiem, Prokokiev Violin Concertos (Amoyal) and Ballet Suites, Bartók Concerto for Orchestra and Miraculous Mandarin, Ravel Piano Concerto, Queffelec, Daphis et Chloë No. 2, Gounod Romeo et Juliette; conducted Die Zauberflote at Bordeaux, 1992. Recipient gold medal Dimitri Mitropoulos Competition, 1966. Office: care Pieter G Algerink Mgmt, Apollolaan 181, 1077 Amsterdam The Netherlands also: care Orch Nat Bordeaux Aquitaine, BP 95, F 33025 Bordeaux France*

LOMBARDI, DENNIS M., lawyer; b. L.A., May 15, 1951; s. Peter Joseph and Jean (Nelson) L.; m. Suan Choo Lim, Jan. 9, 1993; children: Alexis Jeanne, Erin Kalani. BA, U. Hawaii, 1974; JD summa cum laude, U. Santa Clara, 1977. Bar: Calif. 1977, U.S. Dist. Ct. Hawaii, 1981. Assoc. Frandzel & Share, Beverly Hills, Calif., 1977-79; pvt. practice Capistrano Beach, Calif., 1979-81; ptnr. Case, Bigelow & Lombardi, Honolulu, 1982—. Office: Case Bigelow & Lombardi 737 Bishop St Fl 26 Honolulu HI 96813-3201

LOMBARDO, DAVID DOMENIC, human resources executive; b. West Reading, Pa., Nov. 20, 1939; s. Anthony D. and Mary A. (Piscitello) L.; m. Maryann V. Widnick, Jul. 12, 1969; children: Michelle Ann, David Anthony. BA in Polit. Sci., Albright Coll., 1961; MA in Internat. Rels., N.Y. Univ., 1964, PhD in Human Resources, 1978. Pers./ind. rels. specialist U.S. Atomic Energy Commn., N.Y., 1967-71; chief employee/labor rels. U.S. Social Security Adminstrn., Flushing, N.Y., 1971-73, chief pers., 1973-77; chief. recruit & placement Libr. of Congress, Washington, 1977-90, chief human resources ops., 1990-95; adj. prof. mgmt., human rels. Univ. Md., College Park, 1987—; dir. human resources Anne Arnndel Co. Publ. Schs., Annapolis, Md., 1995—; mem. rsch. com. Soc. for Human Resource Mgmt., Alexandria, Va., 1993—. Pres. Crofton Civic Assn., Crofton, Md., 1984-88, chmn., 1990-92. With U.S. Army, 1963-65. Mem. Acad. of Mgmt., Am. Assn. of Sch. Pers. Admin., Ind. Rels. Rsch. Assn., Md. Assn. of Sch. Pers. Admin. (pres. 1998-99), Md. Negotiation Svc., Soc. For Human Resource Mgmt., Annapolis Soc. Human Resource Mgmt. (founding pres. 1999-2000). Office: Anne Arundel Co Pub Schs 2644 Riva Rd Annapolis MD 21401-7305

LOMBARDO, FREDRIC ALAN, pharmacist, educator; b. New Castle, Pa., May 11, 1948; s. Valentine Frank and Clara Eleanor (Cugini) L.; m. Loretta D. Patts, May 22, 1971; children: Alan John, Lauren Beth, Leslie Anne. BS in Pharmacy, Duquesne U., 1971, PharmD, 1974; MS, Fla. Inst. Tech., 1979. Registered pharmacist, Pa., Va., D.C., Tex.; cert., Am. Coll. Clin. Pharmacists; bd. cert. in pharmacotherapy, nutritional support and oncology. Resident in hosp. pharmacy Mercy Hosp., Pitts., 1973; commd. 2nd lt. U.S. Army, 1974, advanced through grades to lt. col., 1993; chief clin. pharmacy support svc. Brooke Army Med. Ctr., Ft. Sam Houston, Tex., 1980-85; chief outpatient pharmacy svc. Walter Reed Army Med. Ctr., Washington, 1985-86, chief cancer treatment sect., chief hematol.-oncol. pharmacy, 1986-92; resigned active duty entered U.S. Army reserve, 1993; sr. clin. pharmacy supr. Nat. Heart, Lung and Blood Inst., NIH, Bethesda, Md., 1992-95; asst. prof. clin. and adminstrv. pharmacy sci. Howard U., Washington, 1995—, asst. prof. psychiatry Coll. Medicine, assoc. prof. cmty. medicine and family practice; asst. prof. U. Md.; asst. prof. pharmacology Cath. U., Washington, 1995—, H. Lee Med. Sch., USUHS, Bethesda, 1995—, Howard U. Cancer Ctr., Ctr. for Sickle Cell Disease, 1995—, asst. dir. Cancer Ctr., 1997; prof. Foun. Advancement Edn. in Sci., Grad. Sch. NIH, 1996—; mem. Mid-Atlantic Oncology Adv. Group, Washington, 1997. Co-host Ask the Pharmacy Doctor program Sta. WRC-980, Washington, 1997—; guest various TV and radio programs. Active Urban Health U., Urban Family Inst., Washington, 1996-97. Lt. col., USAR, 1993—. Rsch. grantee Ortho-McNeil Pharm., Washington, 1996-97. Mem. Am. Pharm. Assn. (cert. in pharmacotherapy, cert. in nutrition support, oncology), Am. Soc. Health Profession, Nat. Pharm. Assn., Am. Legion, KC. Democrat. Roman Catholic. Avocations: military history, mathematics. Home: 13503 Apple Barrel Ct Herndon VA 20171-4006 Office: Howard Univ Coll Pharmacy and Pharm Sci 2300 4th St NE Washington DC 20002-1220

LOMBARDO, GAETANO (GUY LOMBARDO), venture capitalist; b. Salemi, Italy, Feb. 4, 1940; came to U.S., 1947; s. Salvatore and Anna Maria L.; Sc.B. with honors, Brown U., 1962; Ph.D. in Physics, Cornell U., 1971; m. Nancy B. Emerson, Sept. 2, 1967 (div. 1993); children: Nicholas Emerson, Maryanne Chilton. Sr. staff Arthur D. Little Inc., Cambridge, Mass., 1967-77; v.p. logistics Morton Salt Co., Chgo., 1977-78; dir. logistics and distbn. Gould Inc., Chgo., 1978-80; corp. dir. Bendix Corp., Southfield, Mich., 1980-82; group v.p. Bendix Indsl. Group, 1982-84; founder, pres., chief exec. officer Comau Productivity Systems, 1984-86; pres. Nelmar Corp., 1983-90; chmn., chief exec. officer Courtesy Mfg. Co., Elk Grove, Ill., 1988—; pres. Poplar Industries, Inc., 1989—; CEO New Eng. Miniature Ball, Norfolk, Ct., 1997—; vis. prof. ops. mgmt. Boston U., 1973. Contbr. articles on physics and bus. mgmt. to profl. jours. Office: Courtesy Mfg Co 1300 Pratt Blvd Elk Grove Village IL 60007-5777

LOMBARDO, MICHAEL JOHN, lawyer, educator; b. Willimantic, Conn., Mar. 25, 1927; s. Frank Paul and Mary Margaret (Longo) L.; children: Nancy C., Claire M. BS, U. Conn., 1951, MS, 1961, JD, 1973. Bar: Conn. 1974, U.S. Dist. Ct. Conn. 1975, U.S. Supreme Ct. 1979, U.S. Ct. Appeals (2d cir.) 1980. Div. controller Jones & Laughlin Steel Corp., Willimantic, 1956-67; adminstrv. officer health ctr. U. Conn., Hartford, 1968-69; dir. adminstrv. svcs. South Central Community Coll., New Haven, 1969-70; asst. dir. adminstrn. Norwich (Conn.) Hosp., 1970-77; asst. atty. gen. State of Conn., Hartford, 1977-92; pvt. practice, Willimantic, 1992—; adj. asst. prof. U. Hartford, 1961-70; adj. prof. bus. Old Dominion U., 1973-81; adj. lectr. in law and bus. Ea. Conn. State U., 1973—, disting. adj. faculty, 1990. Vol. Windham Ctr. (Conn.) Fire Dept. Sgt. U.S. Army, 1945-46, 1st lt. USAFR, 1951-53, col. USAFR, 1953-87, col. USAF ret., 1987. Decorated Air Force Meritorious Svc. medal, 1980; named Disting. Mil. Grad., U. Conn., 1950. Mem. AAUP, VFW, ATLA, Internat. Platform Assn., Retired Officers Assn., Conn. Bar Assn., Windham County Bar Assn., Assn. Trial Lawyers Am., Mensa Internat., Am. Legion, Lions (bd. dirs. Willimantic chpt. 1960-64). Home: 35 Oakwood Dr Windham CT 06280-1520 Office: 6 Storrs Rd Ste 2 Willimantic CT 06226-4006

LOMBET, ALAIN, biochemist, researcher; b. Paris, Sept. 3, 1951; s. Gabriel and Estelle (Giraud) L.; m. Francoise Prin, July 14, 1974; children: Sylvain, Marie-Cecile, Matthieu. M degree, U. Nice, 1975, DSc, 1985. Tchr. Nice, 1976-80; attache de recherche INSERM, Nice, 1980-84, charge de recherche, 1984-87; rsch. scientist Servier, Suresnes, 1987-92; project leader Servier, Croissy, 1992-95; charge de recherche INSERM, Paris, 1995—. Contbr. more than 50 articles to profl. jours. including Biochemistry, Jour. Biol. Chemistry, Pharm. Chemistry, among others; patentee in field. Elder Evang. Ch., 1990. Mem. Soc. Neuroscis. Avocations: theology, mineralogy, climbing. Office: INSERM U339 Hop St Antoine, 184 rue du Fg St Antoine, 75571 Paris Cedex 12, France

LOMHOLT, NIELS FINSEN, pharmacologist; b. Copenhagen, Mar. 16, 1932; s. Svend and Gudrun (Finsen) L.; m. Bodil Elizabeth Parkes, June 29, 1955 (div. Nov. 1978); children: Margrethe Lomholt Kemp, Thorkild Finsen Lomholt; m. Hanne Dorthe Graabek Jensen, Nov. 25, 1978 (dec. Apr. 1993); 1 child, Trine; m. Hanne Flinker, Mar. 15, 1997. MD, U. Copenhagen, 1961. With dept. anesthesiology U. Copenhagen, 1963-65, asst. prof. dept. pharmacology, 1968-99. Patentee in field. U. Copenhagen Dept. Anesthesiology scholar, 1965-68. Home: Lars Nielsens Vej 4, DK 2970 Horsholm Denmark Office: Dept Pharmacology, Blegdamsvej 3, DK 2200N Copenhagen Denmark

LOMONOSOV, VALERY VICTOR, physicist, researcher; b. Moscow, Nov. 18, 1939; s. Victor Iliy and Alexandra Vasily (Kopteva) L.; m. Tatiyna Alexandr Komarovskaiy; children: Alexandr Valery, Michael Valery. BSc, Moscow Engring. Physics Inst., 1963; DSc, Moscow U., 1971. Rschr. IV Kurchatov Atomic Energy Inst., 1963-85, head lab., 1985-88; asst. prof. Moscow Phys. Tech. Inst., 1982-85, assoc. prof., 1986—; bd. dirs. Relcom Alpha, Moscow; dir. expedition AES, Chernobil, Russia, 1986-88; reviewer in field. Contbr. articles to profl. jours. Named to Order of Courage, Russia, 1997. Mem. Nuclear Soc. Avocations: classical quantum mechanics, travel. Home: Komsomolsky pr-t 41-70, 119270 Moscow Russia Office: Russian Rsch Ctr Kurchatov, Inst Kurchatov Sq, 123182 Moscow Russia

LOMONTE, BRUNO, microbiology educator; b. Napoli, Italy, Oct. 6, 1958; arrived in Costa Rica, 1968; s. Giuseppe Lomonte and Rosa Vigliotti; m. Margarita Ramirez, Aug. 27, 1983; children: Irene. Lic., U. Costa Rica, 1981, MSc, 1986; PhD, U. Göteborg, Sweden, 1994. Cert. microbiologist-immunologist. Fulbright rschr. U. Wis., 1986-87; prof. U. Costa Rica, San José, 1991—. Recipient Nat. Sci. award Costa Rican Govt., 1986, Young Scientist award Third World Acad. Scis., Costa Rica, 1997. Mem. Internat. Soc. Toxinology, Am. Soc. Microbiology. Office: Inst Clodomiro Picado, Univ de Costa Rica, San José Costa Rica

LOMPSCHER, JOACHIM, retired psychologist; b. Chemnitz, Sachsen, Germany, Nov. 7, 1932; s. Paul and Jenny (Zudkowitz) L.; m. Flura Dawliewna Achunowa; children: Gudrun, Katrin, Peter. Diploma Pedagogics, Sch. Edn., Moscow, 1955; EdD, Sch. Edn., Leningrad, USSR, 1958; EdDsc, U. Leipzig, Germany, 1970. Asst. prof. Humboldt U., Berlin, 1958-62; rsch. team leader Cen. Pedagogical Inst., Berlin, 1962-70; prof. ednl. psychology Aka. Ednl. Scis., Berlin, 1971, rsch. team leader, 1971-90; prof. psychol. didactics U. Potsdam, Germany, 1993-97; ret., 1997; vice-dir. Inst. Ednl. Psychology, Acad. of Ednl. Scis., Berlin, 1970-89, dir., 1989-90. Editor: Jour. Psychology for Praxis/Soc. Psychology of German Democratic Republic, 1983-90; co-editor: (book) Cognitive and Motivational Aspects of Instruction, 1982, Teaching and Learning Problems in Tertiary Education, 1996; editor/author: Psychological Analyses of Learning Activity, 1989, Learning and Development from a Cultural-Historical Viewpoint: What Has Vygotsky to Say Today?, 1996; co-editor/author: Living, Learning and Working in Elementary School, 1997, Learning Activity and Development, 1999. Mem. German Soc. Psychology, Am. Ednl. Rsch. Assn. Avocations: music, belles lettres, travel, swimming. E-mail: jlomp@rz.uni-potsdam.de.

LONDERO, FRANCO, gynecologist; b. Gemona, Udine, Italy, Jan. 7, 1947; s. Pietro and Domenica Londero; m. Nevia-Agnese Garzitto, Mar. 8, 1975; 1 child, Ambrogio-Pietro. Degree in medicine and surgery, U. Trieste, Italy, 1974, diploma in ob-gyn, 1978, diploma in nephrology, 1988; diploma in oncology, U. Ancona, Italy, 1982; resident, Inst. Dexeus, Barcelona, 1990. Registrar Gen. Hosp., San Vito, Pordenone, Italy, 1976-77, San Bonifacio, Verona, 1977-78; registrar Gen. Hosp., Gemona, 1978-89, sr. registrar, 1989-97, coord. perinatal medicine, 1993—; coord. perinatal medicine Monfalcone, 1998—. Co-author: Our History, 1990, The Fortresses of North-East, 1992, The Birth of Fascism, 1998; contbr. articles to profl. jours. Town councillor City of Artegna, Udine, 1985-90; councillor Cmty. of Gemona, 1985-90. Mem. Storie Dai Longobarz, Natura-Habitat-Salute, Mitteleuropa, N.Y. Acad. Scis. Avocations: archeology, history. Home: Borgo Aplia, 33011 Artegna Italy Office: Ospedale Civile, S Polo, 34074 Monfalcone Italy

LONDNER, MAURICIO VLADIMIRO, biologist, immunologist, researcher, educator; b. Buenos Aires, Nov. 7, 1931; s. Nachman and Juana Sara (Aufgang) L.; m. Zulema Ethel Sack, June 15, 1957; children: Matilde, Horacio, Guillermo. Pharmacist, U. Litoral, Rosario, Argentina, 1961; M in Biochemistry, U. Rosario, Argentina, 1965, PhD in Biochemistry, 1969. Rschr. Inst. Med. Investigation, Rosario, 1965-71; sr. lectr. dept. physiology Faculty Medicine, Rosario, 1967-74, assoc. prof. dept. biochemistry, 1975-76; sr. rschr. U. Rosario, Argentina, 1971-75, dir. rsch., 1975-77; assoc. prof. dept. parasitology Hebrew U., Jerusalem, 1977-90; vis. prof. dept. biomembranes Weizmann Inst., Rehovot, Israel, 1991-95; mem. Cons. Com. Med. Edn., Rosario, 1971-73; sci. cons. Rsch. Coun. U. Rosario, Argentina, 1974-77, Lorente S.A., Madrid, 1987-90, Melotec Sociedad Anonima, Barcelona, Spain, 1992-99. Editor: Immunology of Infectious Diseases, 1978; contbr. articles to profl. jours. Pres. Argentine Soc. Immunology, Buenos Aires, 1974-75, Israeli Soc. Protozoology, Jerusalem, 1980-84; mem. Internat. Union Immunol. Soc., 1976-77. Recipient first prize in immunology Soc. Leprology, Argentina, 1977. Fellow Royal Soc. Tropical Medicine Hygiene; mem. Am. Soc. Tropical Medicine Hygiene, Spannish Soc. Tropical Medicine, Am. Assn. for Clin. Chemistry, Soc. Parasitology. Jewish. Achievements include first publication on transfer of tumor immunity with ribonucleic acid; first to isolate and purified the glycosyl phosphatidy inositol antigens of the protozoan parasite Leishmania. Avocations: photography, tennis. Fax: 34 93 589 1968. E-mail: mlondner@navegalia.com. Home: Apartado 195 St, Sant Cugat, 08190 Barcelona Spain

LONDON, ANDREW BARRY, film editor; b. Bronx, N.Y., Jan. 1, 1949; s. Max Edward and Nellie (Steiner) L. BA in Cinema magna cum laude, U. So. Calif., 1970. Represented by Mont. Artists, Santa Monica, Calif. Prin. works include: (features) Big Eden, 2000, The Meteor Man, 1993, F/X 2, 1991, Rambo III, 1988, Planes, Trains and Automobiles, 1987, Link, 1986, Cloak & Dagger, 1984, Psycho II, 1983, The True Story of Eskimo Nell, 1975, (TV shows) The Soul Collector, 1999, A Memory in My Heart, 1999, Murder at 75 Birch, 1999, Before He Wakes, 1997, Perfect Crime, 1997, Divided By Hate, 1997, The Crying Child, 1996, Evil Has a Face, 1996, Don't Talk to Strangers, 1994, Day of Reckoning, 1993, Mortal Sins, 1992, Running Delilah, 1992, True Tales, 1992, Sweet Poison, 1991, Tales from the Crypt, 1989-90, Beauty and the Beast Pilot, 1987, The Christmas Star, 1986; sound editor: Wolfen (MPSE Golden Reel award 1982), Hammett, Roadgames, Psycho II, I'm Dancing As Fast As I Can, Perfect, Protocol, Coal Miner's Daughter, The Long Riders, others. Mem. Acad. Motion Picture Arts and Scis., Motion Picture Sound Editors (Golden Reel award 1982), Phi Beta Kappa. Office: 3085 St George St #3 Los Angeles CA 90027-2532

LONDON, RAY WILLIAM, consultant, mediator, arbitrator, researcher; b. Burley, Idaho, May 29, 1943; s. Loo Richard and Maycelle Jerry (Moore) L. AS, Weber State Coll., 1965; BS, 1967; MSW, U. So. Calif., 1973; PhD, 1976, Exec. MBA, 1989; postgrad. cert. dispute resolution, Pepperdine Law Sch., 1993; LLM, Strathcylde Sch. Law, 2000. Diplomate: Am. Bd. Psychol. Hypnosis (dir. 1984-97, pres. 1989-97, forensic and ethics divsn.), Am. Acad. Behavioral Med., Internatl. Acad. Med. and Psychol. (dir. 1981-90, pres. 1981-85), Am. Bd. Profl. Neuropsychology, Am. Bd. Adminstrv. Psychol., Am. Bd. Examiners Clinic Social Work, Am. Bd. Profl. Psychol., NASW Clin. Social Work Bd., Am. Bd. Psychol. Specialties, Am. Bd. Forensic Med., Am. Acad. Pain Mgmt., Am. Acad. Experts in Traumatic Stress, Am. Bd. Forensic Examiners; cert. Soc. Med. Analysts; cert. mgmt. cons., profl. cons. to mgmt.; registered internat. cons. Registry of Arbitrators. Congrl. asst. U.S. Ho. of Reps., 1964-65; rsch. assoc. Bus. Advs., Inc., Ogden, UT, 1965-67; dir. counseling and cons. svcs. Meaning Found., Riverside, Calif., 1966-69; mental health and mental retardation liasion San Bernandino Cty. Social Svcs., San Bernandino, CA, 1968-72; clin. trainee VA Outpatient Clin., Los Angeles, CA, 1971-72, Childrens Hosp. of L.A., 1972-73; clin. fellow, 1973-74; clin. trainee Reiss David Child Study Ctr., Los Angeles, 1973-74, L.A. Cty. - U. So. Calif. Med. Ctr., 1973; group facilitator conflict resolution Benjamin Rush Ctr., Orange, CA, 1973-75; psychologist Orange Police Dept., Calif., 1974-80; COO London Assocs. Internat., 1974-80; clin. and consulting psychology postdoctoral intern Orange Cty. Mental Health, Orange, CA, 1976-77; postdoctoral fellow U. Calif. - Irvine-Calif. Coll. Med., 1978; cons. to pub. schs., agys., hosps., bus. Natl. and Internatl., 1973—; cons. qualitative-quantitative rsch., dispute resolution and assessment Santa Ana, Calif., 1974—; pres. bd. govs. Human Factor Programs, 1976-86; CEO Human Studies Ctr., 1987—; pres., CEO London Resolve Orgn. Behavioral-Crisis-Devel. Info. and Knowledge, Conflict Resolution, Change and Rsch. Cons., 1980—; rsch. affil. Ctr. for Crisis Mgmt., U. So. Calif. Grad. Sch., Bus. Adminstrn., 1988-90; presenter nat. and internat. lectures, seminars and workshops; mem. faculty UCLA, U. So. Calif., Calif. State U., U. Calif., Irvine, Calif. Coll. Med., Internat. Cong. of Psychosomatic Med., Internat. Coll.; rsch. assoc. Nat. Commn. for Protection of Human Subjects of Biomed. and Behavioral Rsch., 1976; rschr. E-commerce, info. tech., info. security, intellectual property, defective software law, liability in info. age, Internet telecomm. law U. Strathclyde Sch. Law, 1998—. Editor Internatl. Bull. Med. and Psychol., 1980-90, A.B.C.D. Report, 1988—, Behavioral Med., Australian Jour., 1980, Internat. Bull. Conflict Resolution, 1993—; editor-in-chief LondonResolve.com., LondonMedArb.com., LondonForensic.com., LondonResearch.com.; adv. editor, Internat. Jour. Clin. and Exptl. Hypnosis, 1981-92, mng. editor, 1991-97, assoc. editor, 1992-97; cons. editor, Internatl. Jour. Psychosomatics, 1984-90; Experimentalle und Klinische, 1987—; pub.: London Behavioral Med. Assessment, 1982, A Behavioral-Crisis-Devel. newsletter, ABCD newsnote; prodr.: TV Series Being Human, 1980; contbtg. author World Book Ency. and books; contbr. articles to profl. jours. Recipient Congl. recognition U.S. Ho. of Reps., 1978, Morton Prince Awd., 1993; named scholar laureate Erickson Advanced Inst., 1980. Fellow Inst. for Soc. Scientists Rsch. Coun., Inst. for Social Influence Studies, Soc. Clin. Social Work (dir. 1979-80), Royal Soc. Health, Am. Coll. Forensic Psychol., Soc. Clin. and Exptl. (bd. dirs. 1985-97, treas. 1987-89); mem. ABA (assoc., ethics and tech. coms.), Assn. Internet Rschrs., Soc. for Computers in Psychology, Qualitative Rsch. Cons. Assn., Arbitration Trained World Intellectual Property Orgn., Soc. Profls. in Dispute Resolution, So. Calif. Mediation Assn., Calif. Dispute Resolution Coun., Profl. Mediation Assn., Toastmasters, Phi Delta Kappa, Delta Sigma Rho, Tau Kappa Alpha, Pi Rho Phi, Lamda Iota Tau. Office: London Resolve 17955 Sky Park Cir Ste E Irvine CA 92614-6373

LONDON, ROBERT JAMES, fraternal organization administrator; b. Cleve., July 16, 1961; s. Norton Jay and JoAnn London; m. Nanci L., Feb. 16, 1991; children: Brian, Danielle. BSBA, Bowling Green State U., 1983. Assoc. dir. Lambda Chi Alpha, Indpls., 1983-87; bus. broker Ind. Bus. Brokers, Indpls., 1987-90; v.p. ops. Lambda Chi Alpha, 1990—. Facilitator Impact Leadership, Indpls., 1995—; organizer N.Am. Food Drive, Indpls., 1993—; coach 1st Bapt. Athletic Little League. Mem. Am. Soc. Assn. Execs., Ind. Soc. Assn. Execs., Fraternity Execs. Assn., Indpls. Ambs. (v.p. edn. 1987-88). E-mail: blondon@lambdachi.org. Office: Lambda Chi Alpha Internat Fraternity 8741 Founders Rd Indianapolis IN 46268-1389

LONE, FAROOQ AHMAD, scientist, researcher; b. Anantnag, Kashmir, India, Mar. 11, 1963; s. Ghulam Hassan Lone and Sarwa Begum; m. Maqsooda Khan, Oct. 23, 1988; children: Aatif, Kashif. BSc, Govt. Degree Coll., Anantnag, India, 1981; MSc in Botany, Kashmir U., Srinagar, India, 1983, MPhil, 1984, PhD, 1987. Diploma in computer applications. Lectr. edn. dept. J&K Govt., Anantnag, 1986-91, dist. sci. and tech. coord. sci. and tech. dept., 1992, lectr. higher edn. dept., 1992-93, sci. officer sci. and tech. dept., 1993-95, dep. dir. sci. and tech., 1995-96, joint dir. sci. and tech., 1996-2000, dir. sci. and tech., 2000—. Author: Palaeoethnobotany, 1993; contbr. articles to profl. jours., rsch. papers. Recipient Young Scientist award J&K Govt., Srinagar, 1993, Best Paper award Muslim Assn. for Advancement Sci., Aligarh, 1993. Mem. Nat. Edn. and Rsch. Soc. (vice chmn. 1996—), Palaeobotanical Soc., Blood Transfusion Soc. Muslim. Avocations: gardening, photography, cricket, social work. Home: Custodian Flats, Old Gagribal Rd, Srinagar 190001, India Office: Sci and Tech Dept, Old Secretariat, Srinagar 190009, India

LONERGAN, JAMES BARRY, priest; b. Ticonderoga, N.Y., July 8, 1939; s. James McKee and Yvonne Virginia (Thibault) L.;. BA, SUNY, Garrison, N.Y., 1962; M in religious edn., Univ. San Diego, 1985. Colonel U.S. Army, 1972-96; priest Roman Catholic Ch., Hudson Falls, N.Y., 1997—; tchr., retreat dir. Roman Cath. Ch., Washington, 1967-70, missionary, British Columbia, 1970-72. Decorated Legion of Merit, Meritorious Svc. medal with eight Oak Leaf Clusters, Army Commendation medal with two Oak Leaf clusters, Armed Forces Expeditionary medal, Nat. Defense Svc. medal, Army Overseas medal. E-mail: jblonergan@cs.com. Office: The Church of Saint Mary's Saint Paul's 11 Wall St Hudson Falls NY 12839-1314

LONERGAN, THOMAS FRANCIS, III, criminal justice consultant; b. Bklyn., July 28, 1941; s. Thomas Francis and Katherine Josephine (Roth) L.; m. Irene L. Kaucher, Dec. 14, 1963; 1 son, Thomas F. BA, Calif. State U., Long Beach, 1966, MA, 1973; MPA, Pepperdine U., L.A., 1976; postgrad., U. So. Calif., L.A., 1973-76. Dep. sheriff Los Angeles County Sheriff's Dept., 1963-70; U.S. Govt. program analyst, 1968—; fgn. service officer USIA, Lima, Peru, 1970-71; dep. sheriff to lt. Los Angeles Sheriff's Office, 1971-76, aide lt. to div. chief, 1976-80; dir. Criminal Justice Cons., Downey,

Calif., 1977—; cons. Public Adminstrv. Service, Chgo., 1972-75, Nat. Sheriff's Assn., 1978, 79; cons. Nat. Inst. Corrections, Washington, 1977-89, coordinator jail ctr., 1981-82 ; tchr. N. Calif. Regional Criminal Justice Acad., 1977-79; lectr. Nat. Corrections Acad., 1980-83; spl. master Chancery Ct. Davidson County, Tenn., 1980-82, U.S. Dist. Ct. (no. dist.) Ohio, 1984-85, Santa Clara Superior Ct. (Calif.), 1983-89, Calif. Supreme Ct., 1984-87; U.S. Dist. Ct. Ga., Atlanta, 1986-87, U.S. Dist. Ct. (no. dist.) Calif., 1982-93—, U.S. Dist. Ct. (no. dist.) Idaho, 1986, U.S. Dist. Ct. Oreg. 1986, U.S. Dist. Ct. Portland 1987, U.S. Dist. Ct. (no. dist.) Calif. 1984-89, 95-97. Author: California-Past, Present & Future, 1968; Training-A Corrections Perspective, 1979; AIMS-Correctional Officer; Liability-A Correctional Perspective; Liability Law for Probation Administrators; Liability Reporter; Probation Liability Reporter; Study Guides by Aims Media. Mem. Nat. Sheriff's Assn. Roman Catholic.

LONG, CHARLES FARRELL, insurance company executive; b. Charlottesville, Va., Nov. 19, 1933; s. Cicel Early and Ruth Elizabeth (Shifflett) L.; m. Ann Tilley, May 28, 1960; children: C. Farrell, Linda. CLU; chartered fin. analyst. Founder, pres. Casualty Underwriters, Inc., Charlottesville, 1959-72, Group Underwriters, Inc., Charlottesville, 1959—; trustee P.A.I. Ins. Trust. Mem. Assay Commn. of U.S., 1975; bd. dirs. Am. Heart Assn.; mem. U. Va. Student Aid Found. With USN, 1954-58. Mem. Ctrl. Va. Estate Planning Coun., Am. Soc. CLUs, Ctrl. Va. CLUs Assn. (dir.), Va. Press Assn., Inland Press Assn. Chgo., Million Dollar Round Table, Farmington Country Club. Creator Queen's medal for Queen Elizabeth, 1976. Home: 1400 W Leigh Dr Charlottesville VA 22901-7719 Office: Madison Park Charlottesville VA 22903

LONG, CLARENCE DICKINSON, III, lawyer; b. Princeton, N.J., Feb. 7, 1943; s. Clarence Dickinson and Susanna Eckings (Larter) L.; children: Clarence IV, Andrew, Amanda, Victoria, Stephen. BA, Johns Hopkins U., 1965; JD, U. Md., 1971; postgrad., Judge Adv. Gen.'s Sch., 1979-80. Bar: Ct. Appeals Md. 1972, U.S. Dist. Ct. D.C. 1972, U.S. Ct. Mil. Appeals 1975, U.S. Supreme Ct. 1976, N.C. 1978, U.S. Ct. Claims 1982, U.S. Ct. Appeals (fed. cir.) 1990. Asst. state's atty. Balt., 1973-74; trial atty., trial team chief Office Chief Trial Atty. Contract Appeals Divsn., U.S. Army, Washington, 1980-84; chief atty. Def. Supply Svc., Washington, 1984-87; trial team chief contract appeals divsn. U.S. Army, Washington, 1987-92; sr. atty. Sec. Air Force, Office of Gen. Counsel, Washington, 1992—. Contbr. articles on Am. Civil War to various periodicals. Lt. col. U.S. Army. Decorated Silver Star, Soldier's medal, Bronze Star, Purple Heart (2), Meritorious Svc. medal (2), Army Commendation medal (2), Cross of Gallantry with gold star, Combat Infantryman's badge, Legion of Merit. Mem. D.C. Bar Assn., N.C. Bar Assn., BCA Bar Assn. (bd. govs.), Federalist Soc., Grant Monument Assn. (bd. govs.). Federalist Soc. Home: PO Box 640 Bowling Green VA 22427-0640

LONG, CLIVE GARRY, clinical psychologist, medical administrator; b. Bury St. Edmunds, England, June 23, 1950; s. Arthur George and Jean (Foster) L.; m. Philippa Shadrach, Jan. 2, 1999. BA with honors, U. Sussex, Brighton, Eng., 1971; diploma in criminology, U. Cambridge (Eng.), 1972; MSc, U. Leicester, Eng., 1977; PhD, U. Birmingham, Eng., 1995; D. Clin. Psych., U. Leicester, Eng., 2000. Chartered clin. psychologist, registered psychotherapists United Kingdom Coun. Psychotherapy. Trainee psychologist Leicester Health Authority, 1975-78; clin. psychologist Coventry (Eng.) Health Authority, 1978-87; cons. psychologist St. Andrews Hosp., Northampton, Eng., 1987-89, head psychology, 1989—, clin. dir. acute divsn., 1996—. Contbr. 32 articles to profl. jours., 3 chpts. to books. Fellow Brit. Psychol. Soc. (diploma in clin. psychology 1979). Avocations: squash, tennis, art deco, wine. Office: St Andrews Hosp, Billing Road, Northampton NN1 5D4, England

LONG, FRANK LESLIE, economist; b. Linden, Demerara, Guyana, Jan. 5, 1945; s. Edwin and Irma (McGowan) L.; children: Fasiledes, Nathaniel. MBA, U. P.R., 1971; postgrad. diploma, The Hague, 1972, M of Social Sci., 1974; MS, Oxford U., 1975; PhD, U. Basel, 1977; postdoctoral study, Oxford U., Yale U. Economist UN Conf. Trade and Devel., Geneva, 1975-77; vis. fellow Queen Elizabeth House Oxford U., Eng., 1977-79, 81-82, Wolfson Coll., 1996-98; dir. tech. policy Nat. Sci. Coun. Guyana, 1979-81; advisor Govt. of Guyana, 1979-81; vis. fellow Yale U., New Haven, Conn., 1982-85, dir. Tech. and Devel. Project, 1982-83, Grad. Sch. for Social Scis., U. Guyana, 1985-92; sr. advisor Internat. Ctr. for Pub. Enterprises, Yugoslavia, 1982; spl. advisor to sec. gen. African, Caribbean and Pacific Group States, Secretariat, Brussels, 1983—; professorial fellow Inst. Devel. Studies, 1985-92; spl. adviser to pres. Guyana, 1985-92; internat. cons., envoy UN, 1992-94; chief adv. Govt. Tajikstan, 1994—; mem. Internat. Expert Group on Pub. Enterprises, Internat. Expert Group on Small Enterprises and Indsl. Devel., OECD-UNIDO; cons. in field. Author: Ragnar Frisch, Planning Studies, 1972, Restrictive Business Practices, 1981, Economic Development in the Caribbean, 1983, Employment Effects of Multinational Enterprises in Export Processing Zones in the Caribbean, 1986, Twin Plant Investment and Multinational Enterprises, 1987, Social and Economic Consequences of Expert Processing Zones, 1988; editor: The Political Economy of ACP-EEC, 1979; mem. editorial bd. Pub. Enterprises; contbr. numerous articles to profl. jours. Mem. Royal Econ. Soc., Soc. for Caribbean Studies, Wolfson Coll. (sr.), Internat. Parliament Safety and Peace (Italy, dep.). Clubs: Oxford Soc., Oxford Union, Oxzford and Cambridge Univ. (Eng.). Home: 14 Hamilton Ter Montclair NJ 07043-1606

LONG, HOANG NGOC, physicist, educator, researcher; b. Thaibinh, Vietnam, Dec. 21, 1952; s. Tuu Ngoc Hoang and Lien Thi Nguyen; m. Lai Kim Loan, Feb. 10, 1981; children: Giang, Anh. MSc, St. Petersburg U., 1978; PhD, Inst. Physics, Hanoi, Vietnam, 1986. Cert. theoretical particle physicist. Rschr. Inst. Theoretical Physics, Hanoi, 1980-96; head high energy physics divsn. Inst. Physics, Hanoi, 1997—; organizer Internat. Sch. Particle Physics, Hanoi, 1995—. Nishina Meml. Found. grantee, 1993, Japan Soc. Promotion Sci. grantee, 1998, DAAD grantee, 1999. Mem. Recontre Vietnam. Avocations: chess, tourism, pop music. Fax: 84-4-8349050. Office: Inst Physics, Thu Le, Badinh, Hanoi 10000, Vietnam

LONG, JUDITH ANN, nurse anesthetist; b. Warrensburg, Mo., Sept. 30, 1944; d. Ernest Edwin and Pansy Orene (Maxwell) L. A of Nursing, Coll. of Med. Arts, 1970; degree in nurse anesthesia, Ohio State U., 1974; BA in Health Adminstrn., Ottawa (Kans.) U., 1984; postgrad., 2000—. Staff nurse Kettering (Ohio) Med. Ctr., 1970-72; staff nurse anesthetist St. Lukes Hosp., Duluth, Minn., 1974-76, dir. anesthesia dept., 1979-85; staff nurse anesthetist St. Mary's Duluth Clinic, Duluth, 1986—; mem. adv. dept. design St. Mary's Med. Ctr. Duluth, 1994-96. Author: (novel) Last Mass of Knight Templars, 1998. Adoptive sponsor Christian Found. for Children, Colombia, 1996—, Nairobi, Kenya, 1997—. Mem. Am. Assn. Nurse Anesthetists, Minn. Assn. Nurses, Lake Superior Writers, Benedictine Oblate. Republican. Roman Catholic. Avocations: gardening, sailing, biking, tennis, sporting clays. Office: St Mary's Duluth Clinic 407 E 3d St Duluth MN 55805

LONG, KENNETH D., marketing research administrator; b. Cleve., Mar. 13, 1952; s. Donald C. and Gertrude J. L.; m. Marian H. Long, Nov. 17, 1979; children: Steven, Kristen. BA in psychology, Ohio State Univ., 1974; MBA, Cleve. State Univ., 1984. Interviewer Princeton Survey Rsch. Ctr., Princeton, N.J., 1975; rsch. analyst Penton Media, Inc., Cleve., 1975-78, mgr. of mktg., econ. analysis, 1978-88, dir. info. svcs., 1988-93, dir. rsch. svcs., 1993-99; dir. rsch. ops. The Pat Henry Group, Cleve., 2000—; speaker at confs. Editor: Industry Inquiry Trends, 1998; contbr. articles to profl. jours. Mem. Am. Mktg. Assn., Nat. Assn. Bus. Econs., Phi Beta Kappa. Avocations: music, running. E-mail: k d long@hotmail.com. Office: The Pat Henry Group 230 W Huron Rd Cleveland OH 44113-1418

LONG, MAXINE MASTER, lawyer; b. Pensacola, Fla., Oct. 20, 1943; d. Maxwell L. and Claudine E. (Smith) M.; m. Anthony Byrd Long, Aug. 27, 1966; children: Deborah E., David M. AB, Bryn Mawr Coll., 1965; MS, Georgetown U., 1971; JD, U. Miami, 1979. Bar: Fla. 1979, U.S. Ct. Appeals (5th cir.) 1980, U.S. Dist. Ct. (so. dist.) Fla. 1980, U.S. Ct. Appeals (11th cir.) 1981, U.S. Dist. Ct. (mid. and no. dists.) Fla. 1987. Law clk. to U.S. dist. judge U.S. Dist. Ct. (so. dist.) Fla., Miami, 1979-80; assoc. Shutts & Bowen, Miami, 1980-90, of counsel, 1990-92, ptnr., 1992—. Mem. Fla. Bar Assn. (cert. bus. litigator, mem. bus. litigation cert. com. 1995-99, vice chair, 1996-97, past chair bus. litigation com., exec. coun. bus. law sect.), Dade County Bar Assn. (mem. fed. cts. com., recipient pro bono award/Vol. Lawyers for the Arts 1989). Office: Shutts & Bowen 201 S Biscayne Blvd Ste 1500 Miami FL 33131-4308

LONG, MICHAEL ALAN, musician; b. Chgo., Oct. 14, 1945; s. Irving Robert and Libby (Zasser) L.; m. Isola Charlayne Jones, Aug. 3, 1989 (div. Oct. 1995). BA in English, Ariz. State U., 1967; MusM, Phila. Inst. Music, Kharkov Ukraine, 1993; Mus D, Philharm. State Inst. Music, Kharkov, Ukraine, 1997. Artist in residence Ariz. State U., Tempe, 1968-73; investment banker Bancom Fin. Corp., Phoenix, 1972-83; edn. dir. U.S. Office Econ. Opportunity, Phoenix, 1969-72; pres. Solaris Classics, Phoenix, 1997—; internat. mgr. Russian Fed. Orch., Moscow, 1995-00; artist adv. U.S. Coun. of the Arts, Phoenix, 1970-75; cons. Ministry of Culture of Republic of Ukraine; vis. prof. Philharm. Inst., Kharkov, 1997-00; internat. mgr. State Symphony of Russian Republic; cons. concerts in field, worldwide. Classical recordings include Hovhaness Symphony for Guitar, Music of the Royal Courts, Hovhaness Mystery of the Holy Martyrs, Tristeza de Amor, Partitas of J.S. Bach; writer, prodr., performer Mr. Cobb's Corner, 1978, PBS TV series In Concert, CBS series Perimeter; dramatist: Il Valentino, 1996, Don Carlos, 1997. Recipient Best Documentary Sound Track, U.S. Coun. of the Arts, 1969, Internat. Gold medal Swedish Arabian Horse Assn., Stockholm, 1982, Gold Medal Premio Roma, 5 Grammy award nominations. Jewish. Avocations: weightlifting, collecting books and art, ancient numismatics, breediing horses. Office: 3550 N Central Ave Ste 701 Phoenix AZ 85012-2109

LONG, MICHAEL JOHN, public health sciences educator, researcher; b. Oxford, Eng., Jan. 30, 1932; s. George Henry and Annie Maud (Carpenter) L.; m. Elizabeth Caroline Johnston (div. Mar. 1984); children: Adrian, Sean, Ashley; m. Mary Ann Lescoe, May 26, 1984. BLS, U. Okla., 1971, MA in Econs., 1973; PhD, U. Mich., 1978. Asst. prof., dir. grad. program dept. cmty. medicine Wayne State U., Detroit, 1977-82; assoc. prof., dir. health adminstrn. program Ea. Mich. U., Ypsilanti, 1982-86; prof., assoc. chmn. dept. health adminstrn. Med. U. S.C., Charleston, 1986-88; prof., chmn. dept. health policy and adminstrn. Pa. State U., State Coll., 1988-91; prof., dir. grad. program dept. health adminstrn.-cmty. med. U. Edmonton, Alta., Can., 1991-94; prof., chmn., MPH dir. dept. health svcs. orgn. and policy Wichita (Kans.) State U., 1994-96, prof. dept. pub. health scis., 1996—; faculty cons. W.K. Kellogg sponsored Health Adminstrn. Baccalaureate Curriculum, Washington, 1986-87; cons. Ont. Coun. on Grad. Studies, Can., 1991-94; inaugural lectr. Calgary (Alta.) WHO Ctr. Series in Mental Health, 1993. Author: The Medical Care System: A Conceptual Model, 1994, Health and Healthcare in the United States, 1998; also articles. Dissertation grantee Nat. Ctr. for Health Svcs. Rsch., 1977. Avocations: running, reading, household remodeling. Fax: 316-978-3025. E-mail: long@chp.tw-su.edu. Home: 1223 N Rutland Wichita KS 67206 Office: Wichita State U Dept Pub Health Scis 1845 Fairmount St Wichita KS 67260-0001

LONG, PETER ROBERT, broadcast executive; b. Geelong, Australia, Mar. 13, 1946; s. Robert George and Mavis Mary (Lawry) L.; m. Helen Ann Ball, July 16, 1969; children: Tully Robert Long, Darcy Peter Long. Radio and TV cert., Royal Melbourne Inst., 1966, higher edn. cert., 1977. Chartered Engr. Maintenance supr. TV Internat., London, 1972-73; sr. engr. Rank Video Labs., London, 1973; maintenance supr. Armstrong Audio & Video, Melbourne, Australia, 1973-75; asst. chief engr. Victorian Broadcasting Network, Bendigo, Australia, 1975-87; chief engr. Southern Cross Communications, Bendigo, Australia, 1987-88, network chief engr., 1988-89; dir. engring. Southern Cross Broadcasting, Bendigo, Australia, 1990—; area mgr. Comsyst Pty Ltd., Melbourne, Australia, 1992-93; regional engring. mgr. Galaxy Pty Ltd., Melbourne, 1993-95; area mgr. Austar Pay TV Pty Ltd, Bendigo, 1995-97; mng. dir. Satellite Connect Victoria Pty Ltd, Bendigo, 1997—; mem. Spectrum Working Party, Fedn. Australian TV Stations, 1987—, Ind. Engring. Com., 1989—. Mem. Bendigo Scuba Club, Bendigo, Australia, 1986—, Maritime Archeol. Assn. Victoria, Melbourne, 1986—, Queenscliffe Lifeboat Preservation Soc., 1987—. Mem. Soc. Motion Picture TV Engr., Audio Engring. Soc., Inst. Radio & Electronic Engrs., Australian Inst. Mgmt. Avocations: writing, scuba diving, fishing, repairing antiques, woodworking. E-mail: sateon@hitech.net.au. Home: 30 Barkly St, 3550 Bendigo Australia Office: Southern Cross Broadcasting, Satellite Connect Victoria, Lot 3 Philips Dr, Bendigo Victoria 3555, Australia

LONG, ROBERT EMMET, author; b. Oswego, N.Y., June 7, 1934; s. Robert Emmet and Verda (Lindsley) L. BA, Columbia Coll., 1956; MA, Syracuse U., 1964; PhD, Columbia U., 1968. Instr. SUNY, Cortland, 1962-64; asst. prof. Queens Coll., CUNY, N.Y.C., 1968-71; writer, 1971—. Author: The Great Succession: Henry James and the Legacy of Hawthorne, 1979, The Achieving of the Great Gatsby, 1979, Henry James: The Early Years, 1983, John O'Hara, 1983, Nathanael West, 1985, Barbara Pym, 1986, James Thurber, 1988, James Fenimore Cooper, 1990, The Films of Merchant Ivory, 1991, Ingmar Bergman: Film and Stage, 1994, The Films of Merchant Ivory: Newly Updated Edition, 1997; editor numerous books; contbr. articles to profl. jours. and popular mags. Democrat. Episcopalian. Avocations: films, theater, ballet, jazz, travel. Address: 254 S 3rd St Fulton NY 13069-2356

LONG, ROBERT GLENDON, pediatrician; b. Hartford, Conn., Mar. 7, 1937; s. Glendon Rodney and Alice (Owen) L.; m. Judith Rogers, June 18, 1966; children: Elizabeth Ann Long Turner, David, Daniel, Rebecca Long Helsby. BA, U. Conn., 1959; MD, Albany Med. Coll., 1964. Diplomate Am. Bd. Pediats. Resident in pediats. U.S. Army Tripler Gen. Hosp., Honolulu, 1967; chief pediats. U.S. Army Kue Gen. Hosp., Okinawa, Japan, 1968-70; dir. Hoa Khanh Children's Hosp., Danang, Vietnam, 1970-75; med. dir., pediatrician Logefeil Meml. Hosp., Taitung, Taiwan, 1977-98; pediatrician Quang Nam Gen. Hosp., Tamky, Vietnam, 1998-2000, Logefeil Meml. Hosp., Taitung, 2000—. Mem. missionary TEAM, Wheaton, Ill., 1977—. Lt. col. U.S. Army, 1963-70. Recipient award for svc. to Vietnamese, Vietnamese Govt., 1972, award for svc. in remote area Taiwan, 1990. Fellow Am. Acad. Pediats.; mem. AMA, Christian Med. and Dental Soc. Avocations: photography, writing. Home: 1221 Brookview Station Rd Castleton On Hudson NY 12033-9741 Office: Logefeil Meml Hosp, 350 Kaifeng St, Taitung 950, Taiwan

LONG, ROBERT LEROY, retired utilities executive, consultant; b. Renovo, Pa., Sept. 9, 1936; s. John Leroy and Mary Geraldine (Olmstead) L.; m. Ann Gullborg, Sept. 2, 1957; children: Beth, Jeff, Mark. BSEE, Bucknell U., 1958; MS in Engring., Purdue U., 1959, PhD in Nuclear Engring., 1962. Rsch. assoc. exp. reactor physics Argonne Nat. Lab., 1960-62; reactor specialist nuclear effects br. White Sands (N.Mex.) Missile Range, 1962-65; from asst. prof. to prof. nuclear engring. U. N.Mex., Albuquerque, 1965-78, asst. dean., 1972-74, chmn. chem. and nuc. engring. dept., 1974-78; with GPU Service Corp. (name now GPU Nuc. Corp.), Parsippany, N.J., 1978-96; mgr. generation productivity dept. GPU Service Corp. (name now GPU Nuc. Corp.), 1978-79, dir. reliability engring. dept., 1979-80, dir. tng. and edn., 1980-82; v.p. nuclear assurance GPU Service Corp. (name now GPU Nuc. Corp.), Parsippany, N.J., 1982-87, v.p. planning and nuclear safety, 1987-89; v.p. corp. svcs. GPU Nuc. Corp., Parsippany, 1989-93, v.p. svcs., 1993-95, v.p. nuclear svcs., 1995-96; recovery officer, v.p. human resources N.E. Nuc. Energy Co., 1998—; with rsch. partic. Sandia Corp., 1965-78; cons. White Sands Missile Range Fast Burst Reactor Facility, 1965-78, Sandia Lab., Albuquerque, 1965-70, Con Edison, N.Y.C., 1970-73, Electric Power Rsch. Inst., Palo Alto, Calif., 1976-78, NSF, U.S. Dept. Energy, others; rsch. assoc. nuc. rsch. divsn. Atomic Weapons Rsch. Estab., Eng., 1966-67; mem. Nuc. Stewardship, LLC. Contbr. articles to profl. jours. Served to capt. U.S. Army, 1962-64. AEC fellow, 1958-59; recipient Disting. Engring. Alumnus award Purdue U., 1993. Fellow Am. Nuc. Soc. (chmn. edn. divsn. 1974-75, chmn. nuc. engring. dept. heads com. 1975-76, chmn. No. N.J. chpt. 1986-87, 88-89, v.p., pres.-elect 1990-91, pres. 1991-92, Pioneer in Nuc. Tng. award 1999); mem. Soc. for Risk Analysis, Nuc. Energy Inst., Am. Soc. Engring. Edn. Presbyterian. Avocations: church school teaching, woodworking, reading, choir, model garden railroading. Home: 9615 Elena Dr NE Albuquerque NM 87122-3866

LONG, SUSAN DIANE, management educator; b. Croydon, Eng., July 21, 1948; d. Leonard Henry and Marjorie (Canter) Freake; m. Michael Grant Long, Sept. 9, 1982; children: Taraschne, Jason, Cable. BA with honors, Melbourne (Australia) U., 1971, PhD, 1987; MEd, Monash U., Melbourne, 1977. Registered psychologist, socio-analyst. Lectr. Prahran Coll., Victoria, Australia, 1973-79, Victoria Coll., 1979-87; sessional lectr. Melbourne U., 1987-89; child psychologist Jewish Ctr., Victoria, 1987-89; sr. lectr. Swinburne U., Hawthorn, Victoria, 1990-93, assoc. prof., head dept., 1994-96, prof., 1998—; mem. adv. bd. Monash U., 1996—; pvt. practice orgnl. cons., Melbourne, 1980—. Author: A Structural Analysis of Small Groups, 1992, Hebrew translation, 1996; co-editor jour. Socio-Analysis, 1999; author, editor numerous papers, articles in field. Named Hon. Sr. Lectr., Monash U., 1994—. Fellow Australian Inst. Socio-Analysis; mem. Internat. Soc. Psychol. Study of Ops. (pres. elect.), Australia and New Zealand Acad. Mgmt. Avocations: academics, writing, blacksmithing, horseback riding. Office: Swinburne U Grad Sch Mgmt, PO Box 218, Hawthorn Victoria 3121, Australia

LONG, THAD GLADDEN, lawyer; b. Dothan, Ala., Mar. 9, 1938; s. Lindon Alexander and Della Gladys (Pilcher) L.; m. Carolyn Wilson, Aug. 13, 1966; children: Louisa Frances, Wilson Alexander. AB, Columbia U., 1960; JD, U. Va., 1963. Bar: Ala. 1963, U.S. Dist. Ct. (no. dist., so. dist., mid. dist.) Ala., U.S. Ct. Appeals (11th cir., 5th cir.), U.S. Supreme Ct. Assoc. atty. Bradley, Arant, Rose & White, Birmingham, Ala., 1963-70; ptnr. Bradley, Arant, Rose & White, Birmingham, 1970—; adj. prof. U. Ala., Tuscaloosa, 1988—, Samford U., Birmingham, 1999—, Cumberland Law Sch., 1999—. Co-author: Unfair Competition Under Alabama Law, 1990, Protecting Intellectual Property, 1990; mem. editl. bd. The Trademark Reporter; contbr. articles to profl. jours. chmn. Columbia U. Secondary Schs. Com. Ala. Area, 1975—, Greater Birmingham Arts Alliance, 1977-79; trustee, pres. Birmingham Music Club, 2000—; trustee Oscar Wells Trust for Mus. Art, Birmingham, 1983—, Canterbury Meth. Found., 1993—, sec., 1993—; chmn. Entrepreneurship Inst. Birmingham, 1989; vice chmn., trustee Sons Revolution Found., Ala., 1994—; pres. Birmingham-Jefferson Hist. Soc., 1995-97; trustee Birmingham Music Club Endowment, 1995—; mem. Birmingham Com. Fgn. Rels. Mem. U.S. Patent Bar, Internat. Trademark Assn., Am. Law Inst., Ala. Law Inst., Birmingham Legal Aid Soc., Ala. Bar Assn. (chmn., founder bus. torts and antitrust sect.), Biotechnology Assn. of Ala., Inc. (sec. 1998—), U. Va. Law Alumni (chmn. Birmingham chpt. 1984-89), S.R. (pres. 1994-95), Gen. Soc. S.R. (gen. solicitor 1994-2000), Am. Arbitration Assn., Order of the Coif, Omicron Delta Kappa. Republican. Methodist. Avocations: travel, writing, table tennis. Home: 2880 Balmoral Rd Birmingham AL 35223-1236 Office: Bradley Arant Rose & White 2001 Park Pl Ste 1400 Birmingham AL 35203-2736

LONG, TIMOTHY SCOTT, chemist, consultant; b. Racine, Wis., Dec. 20, 1937; s. Leslie Alexander and Esther (Sand) L.; m. Karen M. Koniarski, July 13, 1985; children by previous marriage: Corinne, Christine. BS in Chemistry, Winona State U., 1975. Staff chemist IBM, Rochester, Minn., 1962-77; adv. chemist IBM, Harrison, N.Y., 1977-80, IBM Instruments, Inc., Danbury, Conn., 1980-81; mgr. Midwest Instrument Ctr. IBM Instruments, Inc., Chgo., 1981-85; mgr. corp. environ. engring. IBM, Stamford, Conn., 1985-89; industry cons. IBM, White Plains, N.Y., 1989-92; environ. cons. Geraghty & Miller, Inc., Rochelle Park, N.J., 1992-94, Indpls., 1994-97; mem. World Environ. Ctr., N.Y.C., 1985-89; adv. bd. Coop. Ctr. Rsch. in Hazardous and Toxic Substances, Newark, 1985-89. Author: Testing for Prediction of Material Performance, 1972, Methods for Emissions Spectrochemical Analysis, 1977, 2d edit., 1982; contbr. articles to Applied Spectroscopy, Plating, Polymer Engring. and Sci. Mem. ASTM (com. emission spectroscopy), Soc. Applied Spectroscopy (chmn. Minn. sect. 1976-77), Soc. Plastics Engrs. (bd. reviewers 1975-76). Achievements include demonstration of world's first application using ion chromatography in the analysis of indsl. waste water. Home: 2 Calle Final Placitas NM 87043-9214

LONG, XIANGCUN TONY, physicist; b. LiLing, China, June 7, 1964; s. Hanyi and Qifu (Wang) L.; m. Bei Feng, Mar. 19, 1997. BS, Hefei U. Tech., China, 1984; MS, Inst. Physics/Chinese Acad. Sci., Beijing, 1991; PhD, U. New Mex., Albuquerque, 1997. Asst. rschr. Inst. Physics/Chinese Acad. Scis., Beijing, 1987-91; scientist U. New Mex., Albuquerque, 1998—. Reviewer: Applied Physics Letters, Optics Letters; inventor in field. Mem. Optical Soc. Am. Avocations: sports, chess. Fax: 505-272-7801. E-mail: longx@chtm.unm.edu. Office: CHTM U New Mex 1313 Goddard St SE Albuquerque NM 87106-4343

LONG, YING CAI, chemist, educator, researcher; b. Shanghai, China, Feb. 1, 1939; s. Yu Sheng and Shu Lan (Chen) L.; m. Shen Ping Shao. BSc in Chemistry, Shandong U., 1960. Asst. dept. chemistry Shandong U., 1960-75; asst. Dept. Chemistry, Fudan U., 1975-79, lectr., 1979-85, assoc. prof., 1985-96, prof., 1996—, PhD supr., 1998—; vis. assoc. prof. Brown U., Providence, 1986-87; vis. scientist Brookhaven Nat. Lab., 1987-88. Contbr. articles to profl. jours.; patentee in field. Recipient Sci. and Tech. award State Edn. Commn., 1995, 98. Mem. Internat. Zeolite Assn. Avocations: classical music, fishing. Office: Fudan U Dept Chemistry, 220 Handan Rd, Shanghai 200433, China

LONGHETTO, ARNALDO, physics educator; b. Turin, Italy, June 28, 1939; s. Egidio and Maria (Bonda) L.; m. Elena Lapenna, Sept. 15, 1969; children: Stefano, Marcello. Degree in Physics, U. Turin (Italy), 1962. Sr. researcher Italian Electricity Bd., Turin, 1965-76, mgr., 1976-81; prof. gen. physics U. Turin, 1981-89, prof. atmospheric physics, 1989—; dir. Inter-U. Ctr. Atmospheric and Hydrospheric Physics, Italy, 1992—, Nat. Consortium Atmospheric and Hydrospheric Physics, Italy, 1997—, drought and desertification internat. project World Lab., Geneva, 1991—, Internat. Sch. Climatology E. Majorana Ctr. for Scientific Culture, Erice, Italy, 1989—. Editor: Il Nuovo Cimento-sect. C-Geophysics and Space Physics (an Europhysics Internat. Jour. of Physics); mem. internat. editl. bd.: Atmospheric Environment, Acta Meteorologica Sinica, Advances in Atmospheric Scis. Lt. Italian Air Force, 1964-65. Mem. Italian Phys. Soc., Am. Meteorol. Soc., Royal Meteorol. Soc. Home: Lungo Po Antonelli 207, I-10153 Turin Piemonte, Italy Office: U Turin Dept Gen Physics, Via Pietro Giuria 1, I-10125 Turin Piemonte, Italy

LONGHI, ROBERT LEONARD, chief financial officer; b. Melbourne, Victoria, Australia, Oct. 30, 1957; s. Guido and Anna (Mascolo) L.; m. Paola Pernaselci, July 18, 1991; 1 child, Elizabeth Anne. B in Econs., Latrobe U., Melbourne, Australia, 1979; Grad. Diploma in Acctg., Victoria Coll., Melbourne, Australia, 1984. CPA. Audit mgr. Coopers & Lybrand, Rome, 1986-92; chief acct. Janssen Farmaceutici, Rome, 1992-94; mfg. controller Janssen-Cilag, Latina, Italy, 1994-95; CFO co. dir. Warner Village Cinemas SpA, Rome, 1995—. Mem. Associazione Italiana per Ricerca del Cancro, World Wildlife Fund, Australian Soc. Cert. Practicing Accts., Medecins sans Frontiers. Roman Catholic. Avocations: writing poetry, photography, reading, swimming, squash. Home: Via Filippo Turati N 12, 00040 Ariccia Italy

LONGIN, PIERRE E., government affairs consultant; b. Lyons, France, Feb. 20, 1938; s. Emile P. and Lucie P. (Girard) L.; m. Francoise Anne L. Duflot, June 26, 1965; children: Marie Blandine, Pierre Henri, Francois, Laurent. Student, Commerce de Lyon, 1962; postgrad., D'Etudes Europennes Turin, 1964. Mgr. sales Durand & Co., U.K., 1966-69; gen. mgr. J&J, France, 1969-74; dir. pub. affairs Merck & Co., Europe, 1974-84, Monsanto Europe-Africa, 1984-89; mng. ptnr. Longin & Assocs., Brussels, Belgium, 1990—. Mem. Internat. Pub. Affairs Forum (chmn. 1980), Automobile Club France, Club Royal Gaulois Brussels. Office: Longin & Assocs, 67 Ave Des Nerviens, 1040 Brussels Belgium

LONGIN, THOMAS CHARLES, education association administrator; b. Lewistown, Mont., Nov. 17, 1939; s. Charles Otto and Anne Dorothy (Vavrovsky) L.; m. Nancy Tillinghast; children: Kevin C., Teresa L., Karl T., Anne M. BA in History, Carroll Coll., 1962; MA in History, Creighton U., 1965; PhD in Am. History, U. Nebr., 1970. Instr. Carroll Coll., Helena, Mont., 1965-67; asst. prof. Va. Poly. Inst. and State U., Blacksburg, 1970-73; asst. prof., then assoc. prof. Ithaca (N.Y.) Coll., 1973-82, dean humanities and scis., 1976-82, provost, 1985-96; v.p. acad. affairs Seattle U., 1982-85; v.p. programs and rsch. Assn. of Governing Bds., Washington, 1997—. Office: Assn of Governing Bds 1 Dupont Cir NW Ste 400 Washington DC 20036-1136

LONGMAN, ANNE STRICKLAND, special education educator, consultant; b. Metuchen, N.J., Sept. 17, 1924; d. Charles Hodges and Grace

Anna (Moss) Eldridge; m. Henry Richard Strickland, June 22, 1946 (dec. 1960); m. Donald Rufus Longman, Jan. 20, 1979 (dec. 1987); children: James C., Robert H. BA in Bus. Adminstrn., Mich. State U., 1945; teaching credentials, U. Calif., Berkeley, 1959; postgrad., Stanford U., 1959-60; MA in Learning Hand, Santa Clara U., 1974. Lic. educator. Exptl. test engr. Pratt & Whitney Aircraft, East Hartford, Conn., 1945-47; indsl. engr. Marchant Calculators, Emeryville, Calif., 1957-58; with pub. rels. Homesmith, Palo Alto, Calif., 1959-62; cons. Right to Read Program, Calif., 1978-79; monitor, reviewer State of Calif., Sacramento, 1976-79; tchr. diagnosis edn. Cabrillo Coll., Aptos, Calif., 1970-79; lectr. edn. U. Calif., Santa Cruz, 1970-79; cons. Santa Cruz Bd. Edn., 1970-79; reading rschr. Gorilla Found., Woodside, Calif., 1982—; bd. mem. Western Inst. Alcoholic Studies, L.A., 1972-73; chmn. Evaluation Com., Tri-County, Calif., 1974; speaker Internat. Congress Learning Disabilities, Seattle, 1974; ednl. cons. rsch. on allergies, 1993—. Author: Word Patterns in English, 1974-92, Cramming 3D Kids, 1975—, 50 books for migrant students, 1970-79; contbr. articles on stress and alcoholism and TV crime prevention for police, 1960-79. Founder Literacy Ctr., Santa Cruz, 1968-092; leader Girl Scouts U.S.A., San Francisco, 1947-50; vol. Thursday's Child, Santa Cruz, 1976-79, Golden Gate Kindergarten, San Francisco, 1947-57. Recipient Fellowships Pratt & Whitney Aircraft, 1944, Stanford U., 1959. Mem. Internat. Reading Assn. (pres. Santa Cruz 1975), Santa Clara Valley Watercolor Soc., Los Altos Art Club (v.p. 1992), Eichler Swim and Tennis Club. Republican. Episcopalian. Avocations: watercolor painting, travel, drama. Home and Office: 153 Del Mesa Carmel Carmel CA 93923-7950

LONGO, DANIEL ROBERT, health services researcher, medical educator; b. Jersey City, N.J., Feb. 20, 1952; s. Frank and Rose (Liguori) L.; m. Karen Ann Ludy, Sept. 4, 1976; children: Gregory Seton, Alexis Seton. BS cum laude, Villanova U., 1974; M of Hosp. Adminstrn., George Washington U., 1976; ScD in Health Policy Mgmt., Johns Hopkins U., 1982. Cons. Am. Hosp. Assn. Hosp., Chgo., 1980-82; dir., multi-hosp. systems project Joint Commn. Healthcare Orgns., Chgo., 1982-85; dir. rsch. Joint Commn. Healthcare Orgns., 1984-86; asst. exec. dir. quality mgmt. Ancilla Systems Inc., Chgo. Applied Healthcare Group, 1986-87; v.p. quality assurance Hosp. Assn. N.Y. State, Albany, 1987-89; pres. Hosp. Rsch. Ednl. Trust, Chgo., 1989-92; assoc. prof. family and cmty. medicine Sch. Medicine U. Mo., Columbia, 1992-99, prof. family and cmty. medicine, 1999—; bd. dirs. Inst. on Quality of Care and Patterns of Practice, 1991-92, Assn. Health Svcs. Rsch., Washington, 1990-92; adv. com., Quality Improvement Task Force, Chgo., 1988-92; liaison com., Inst. Medicine, Washington, 1990-91; adj. faculty Columbia U.; vis. scholar Northwestern U., Evanston, Ill., Johns Hopkins U., Balt., 1991-93, St. Louis U., 1992—; quality of care advisor Mo. Dept. Health, 1993—. Author: Integrated Quality Assessment, 1989, Inventory of External Data, 1990; editor: Quantitative Methods in Quality Assurance, 1990; contbr. articles to profl. jours. Lt. USNR, 1975-79. Rsch. fellow Sisters Mercy Health Corp., 1983-87. Mem. Am. Pub. Health Assn. (program chmn. 1987), Assn. Health Svcs. Rsch. (bd. dirs. 1990-93), Soc. Tchrs. Family Medicine (Best Rsch. Paper Yr. award 1997). Home: Ridley Wood Columbia MO 65203 Office: U Mo Sch Medicine Health Sci Ctr # Ma306 Columbia MO 65212-0001

LONGO, PASQUALE, chemistry educator; b. Giffoni sei Casali, Italy, Feb. 19, 1955; s. Francesco and Maria (Pisano) L.; m. Maria Infante, Aug. 26, 1984; children: Marianna, Francesco, Raffaele. Degree in chemistry, U. Napoli, 1979. Chemistry tchr. H.S., Avellimo, 1981-84; asst. prof. U. Salerno, 1984-92, assoc. prof., 1992—; vice dir. Chemistry Dept. U. Salermo, 1992-95; chmn. Pres. of Faculty Degree Bd., Salermo, 1996-98. Mem. Italian Chem. Soc., Reactivity and Catalysis (scientific com. of comsorzio). Avocations: soccer, bridge. Office: U Salermo Chemistry Dept, Via S Allende, Baromissi 84081, Italy

LONGUET-HIGGINS, H. CHRISTOPHER, chemist, researcher; b. Lenham, Eng.; s. Henry Hugh and Albinia Cecil (Bazeley) Longuet-H. MA, Oxford (Eng.) U., 1949, DPhil, 1947; D (hon.), York U., Essex U.; D in Music (hon.), Sheffield U.; D of Sci. (hon.), Bristol U., Sussex U. Prof. King's Coll., London, 1952-54, Cambridge (Eng.) U., 1954-67; rsch. prof. Edinburgh (Scotland) U., 1967-74; rsch. prof. Sussex (Eng.) U., 1974-88, emeritus prof., 1988—. Author: Mental Processes, 1987. Bd. govs. BBC, 1979-84. Recipient Harrison prize Chem. Soc. London, 1947, Naylor prize London Math. Soc. Fellow Royal Soc. London, Royal Soc. Edinburgh; mem. U.S. Nat. Acad. Scis. (fgn. assoc.), Am. Acad. Arts and Scis. Avocation: music.

LONGWELL, HARRY, oil company executive; b. Bunkie, La., July 20, 1941. Degree in petroleum engring., La. State U., 1963. Engr. drilling Exxon Mobil Corp., New Orleans; mgr. ops. Exxon Mobil Corp., Corpus Christi, 1974; mgr. ops. Exxon Mobil Corp., L.A., 1974, divsn. mgr., 1977; mgr. ops. dept. prodn., v.p. Exxon Mobil Corp., Houston, 1980-85; v.p. exploration and prodn. in Europe Exxon Mobil Corp., London, 1986; exec. asst. Exxon Mobil Corp., N.Y.C., 1986; v.p. exploration and prodn. Exxon Mobil Corp., Florham Park, N.J., 1987, exec. v.p., 1990; pres. Exxon Co., U.S.A., 1992; sr. v.p., dir. Exxon Mobil Corp., Irving, Tex., 1995—. Mem. Nat. Action Coun. for Minorities in Engring. (exec. com. bd. dirs.), United Way of Met. Dallas (bd. dirs.), Bd. Visitors U. Tex. M.D. Anderson Cancer Ctr. (exec. com.), Dallas Area Habitat for Humanity (adv. bd.). Mem. U.S.-China Bus. Coun. (exec. com. bd. dirs.). Office: Exxon Mobil Corp 5959 Las Colinas Blvd Irving TX 75039-4202

LÖNNQVIST, BARBARA, Russian language and literature educator; b. Espoo, Finland, June 15, 1945; d. Hjalmar and Edith (Kajander) L.; m. Jockum Aniansson, Mar. 28, 1980; children: Boel Maria, Ruth Cecilia. MA, U. Helsinki, 1973; PhD, U. Stockholm, 1979. Asst. prof. Russian lit. U. Stockholm, 1983-89; prof. Russian lang. and lit. Åbo Akademi U., 1989—, dean of faculty of humanities, 1994-96; mem. coun. Åbo Akademi U., 1994-96. Editor Russica Aboensia, 1994—; author: Xlebnikov and Carnival, 1979; contbr. articles to profl. jours. Recipient Translator's award Samfundet De Nio, 1988, Svenska Akademien, 1995. Mem. Swedish Writers Union, Swedish PEN Club. Lutheran. Office: Åbo Akademi U, Vänrikinkatu 3, FIN20500 Åbo Finland

LÖNNROTH, KNUT, medical educator; b. Göteborg, Sweden, July 11, 1964. Univ. med. degree, Karolinska Inst., Stockholm, 1992; M of Med. Sci., U. Newcastle, Australia, 1997. Registered med. dr., Sweden. Physician Vasa Hosp., Göteborg, 1990, Stockholm County Coun., 1990-92, Danderyd Hosp., Stockholm, 1992-97; rsch. asst. Karolinksa Inst., Stockholm, 1993-97; lectr. U. Newcastle, 1996, Nordic Sch. Pub. Health, Göteborg, 1997—; rschr. Göteborg U., 1997—. Author: (book chpt.) Health Care in Sweden, 1998, (proc. chpt.) Private-Public Mix in Health Care in Vietnam, 1999, Public Health in Private Hands, 2000; contbr. papers to med. jours. Office: Nordic Sch Pub Health, Post Box 12133, SE-40242 Göteborg Sweden

LONSKY, VLADIMÍR, cardiac surgeon; b. Hradec Králové, Czechoslovakia, Dec. 25, 1953; s. Vladimír and Vera (Brzobohata) Lonská; m. Ivana Kudrnáčová, Mar. 31, 1978; children: Ondřej, Kateřina. MD, Charles U., Czech Republic, 1979, PhD, 1998. Cert. gen. surgeon, cardiac surgeon. Houseman dept. gen. surgery U. Hosp., Hradec, Králove, 1979-83, registrar dept. thoracic surgery, 1983-85; sr. registrar U. Dept. Cardiac Surgery, Hradec, 1985-90, cons. cardiac surgeon, 1990—; sr. lectr. of surgery Charles U., Hradec, 1989—; responsible chief of perfusion dept. U. Dept. Cardiac Surgery, U. Hosp. Hradec, 1991—. Fellow Am. Coll. Chest Physicians, Europea Assn. Cardio-Thoracic Surgeons, European Bd. Thoracic and Cardiovascular Surgeons/Brussels. Avocations: skiing, biking, sports. Office: Univ Hosp, Dept Cardiac Surgery, 500 05 Hradec Králové Czech Republic

LONZA RICCI, LAURA, researcher; b. Trieste, Italy, June 4, 1970; d. Italo and Nevia Hofer Lonza; m. Renzo Luigi Ricci, June 27, 1999. BA, U. Trieste, 1994; MSc, U. Libre, Brussels, Belgium, 1997; postgrad., Inst. Superior Tecnico, Lisbon, Portugal. Intern UN, N.Y.C., fall 1992; practitioner Federecio d'Entitats Locales des Illes Boleares, Palma de Mallorca, Spain, 1994-95; asst. Promoting Operational Links with Integrated Svcs., Brussels, 1996-97, coord., 1997-99; rschr. Inst. for Prospective Tech. Studies-Joint Rsch. Centre, Seville, Spain, 1999—. Editor, co-author: POLIS Newsletter, 1997-99; contbr. articles and reports to profl. jours. Avocations: sailing, swimming. Fax: 34 954 488 279. E-mail: laura.lonza@jrc.es. Office: IPTS-JRC, WTC Isla de la Cartuja s/n, 41092 Seville Spain

LOO, MARCUS HSIEU-HONG, physician, educator; b. N.Y.C., Aug. 12, 1955; s. David Wei and Patricia (Pai) L.; m. Donna C. Wingshee, Oct. 3, 1987; children: Christopher, Courtney. BSEE with distinction, Cornell U., 1977, MD, 1981. Diplomate Am. Bd. Urology. Asst. attending urologist N.Y. Hosp.-Cornell Med. Ctr., N.Y.C., 1988—; clin. asst. prof. urology Cornell U. Med. Coll., N.Y.C., 1994-2000, clin. assoc. prof. urology, 2000—; admissions com. Cornell U. Med. Coll.; mem. operating bd. Columbia Cornell Care, LLC. Author: The Prostate Cancer Source Book, 1998. Mem. oper. bd. Columbia Cornell Care L.L.C. Fellow Am. Coll. Surgeons; mem. AMA, IEEE, Am. Assn. Clin. Urologists, Am. Urol. Assn., Soc. Internat. Urology, Cornell U. Med. Coll. Alumni Assn. (bd. dirs.), Chinese Am. Med. Soc. (pres., bd. dirs. 1990-97), Fedn. Chinese Am. and Chinese Can. Med. Socs. (bd. dirs., v.p.), Tau Beta Pi, Eta Kappa Nu, Phi Tau Phi. Office: 53 E 70th St New York NY 10021-4941

LOO, WING YAN MICHAEL, import/export executive, sales and marketing agent; b. Guangzhou, China, Dec. 12, 1948; s. H.T. Loo and H.Y. Li; m. Y.L. Lam; children: M.L., H.W. PDip in Engring., Hong Kong Poly. U., 1994; MA in Internat. Bus. Mgmt., City Univ. Hong Kong, 1998. Mgr. P.T. Tridaya Inc., 1975-86, Sumitomo Corp., 1986-94; dir., owner Fruition Enterprises, Hong Kong, 1994—. Mem. British Inst. Mgmt., Inst. Indsl. Mgrs., Hong Kong Inst. Mktg. Avocations: touring, camping. Office fax: 27703953. Office e-mail: 96360640@alumni.cityu.edu.hk. Home: GPO Box 12174, Hong Kong China

LOOCKERMAN, WILLIAM DELMER, educational administrator; b. Phila., Feb. 24, 1939; s. William Delmer and Kathleen (Cullen) L.; m. Alice Clara Winnemore, June 9, 1962; 1 child, Alice B. BS in Health and Phys. Edn., West Chester (Pa.) State U., 1962, MS in Health and Phys. Edn., 1967; EdD in Phys. Edn., Temple U., 1970; cert. sch. dist. adminstr., Niagara U., 1974. Tchr. Upper Darby (Pa.) Schs., 1965-68; teaching assoc. Temple U., Phila., 1968-70; asst. prof. SUNY, Buffalo, 1970-73; dir. health, phys. edn. and recreation Orchard Park (N.Y.) Cen. Schs., 1973-81; registered sch. bus. adminstr. Springville (N.Y.) Griffith Inst. Cen. Sch. Dist., 1981—; adj. asst. prof. Niagara U., Niagara Falls, N.Y., 1975-77; adj. prof. Canisius Coll., Buffalo, 1979-81; statewide rep. Group 491 Ins. Safety Program, Albany, N.Y., 1983—, trustee, 1991—, mem. exec. com., 1991—, chair, 1996—; vice chmn. Statewide Safety Com., 1995—; spkr. local, state, nat. and internat. meetings. Contbr. articles to profl. jours. Capt. USNR ret. Recipient spl. honor award N.Y. State Coaches Assn., 1980, honor award N.Y. State Assn. Health, Phys. Edn. and Recreation, 1979, conf. dedication, 1980. Mem. Internat. Assn. Sch. Bus. Ofcls. (mem. choir 1989—, song leader Opening Gen. Session 1997, appreciation award 1990, 94), N.Y. State Sch. Bus. Ofcls. (chpt. exec. com. 1983-85), AMVETS, Naval Order U.S. (chpt. comdr. 1987-96, companion to gen. coun. 1997-99, Naval Res. Assn. (chpt. pres., budget/fin. com. 1995—, v.p. 1997-99, treas. 1999—, mem. nat. adv. com . 1987—), Am. Legion; mem. WNY Armed Forces Week com. 1980—), Springville Cmty. Choir 1997. Republican. Episcopalian. Avocation: woodworking. Home: 7643 Lewis Rd Holland NY 14080-9625 Office: Springville Griffith Inst 307 Newman St Springville NY 14141-1599

LOOK, MELVIN CHEE MENG, surgeon; b. Singapore, Singapore, Feb. 20, 1965; s. Yew Seng Look and Swee Choo Lim; m. Wei Lyn Yang, Dec. 6, 1996. MB BS, Nat. U. Singapore, 1989. Vis. clin. fellow Nat. Cancer Ctr. Hosp., Tokyo, 1996-97; cons. Tan Tock Seng Hosp., Singapore, 2000—; vis. specialist Nat. Cancer Ctr., Singapore, 1999; mem. Nat. Com. for Cancer Care, Min. Health, 1998; vice chmn. Experimental Surgery Lab. Tan Tock Seng Hosp., 1999. Contbr. articles to profl. jours.; mem. editl. com. Med. Digest, 1999, Gutviews, 1999. Vol. Singapore Cancer Soc., 1998. Capt. Singapore Navy, 1991-92. Recipient fellowship in upper gastrointestinal tract surgery Min. Health, 1996. Mem. Gastroenterology Soc. Singapore. Avocations: music, sailing. Office: Tan Tock Seng Hosp DeptSurg, 11 Jalan Tan Tock Seng, Singapore 308433, Singapore

LOOMIS, EDWARD WARREN, writer, educator; b. Newport News, Va., Aug. 8, 1924; s. Arthur Kirkwood and Ethel (Morgan) L.; m. Ruth Fetzer, July 6, 1924 (dec. Feb. 1975); children: Jessica, Andrea, Abby; m. Mary I. O'Connor, Jan. 1, 1976. AB in English, Case Western Res. U., 1947; MA in English, PhD in English, Stanford U., 1959. Instr. English U. Ariz., Tucson, 1955-59; acting chancellor Deep Springs Coll., Calif., 1962-64; prof. U. Calif., Santa Barbara, 1959-87. Author: End of a War, 1958, The Charcoal Horse, 1959, Men of Principle, 1963, Clean and Sober, 2000, Romeo and Juliet in L.A., 2000, Heroic Spain, 2000; also stories. With U.S. Army, 1943-45, ETO. Home: 6591 Camino Venturoso Goleta CA 93117-1525

LOOMIS, HOWARD KREY, banker; b. Omaha, Apr. 9, 1927; s. Arthur L. and Genevieve (Krey) L.; m. Florence Porter, Apr. 24, 1954; children: Arthur L. II, Frederick S., Howard Krey, John Porter. AB, Cornell U., 1949, MBA, 1950. Mgmt. trainee Hallmark Cards Inc., kansas City, Mo., 1953-56; sec., contr., dir. Mine Svc. Co. Inc., Ft. Smith, Ark., 1956-59; contr., dir. Electra Mfg. Co., Independence, Kans., 1959-63; v.p., dir. The Peoples Bank, Pratt, Kans., 1963-65, pres., 1966—; pres., dir. Gt. Plains Leasing Inc., Pratt, 1966-80, Ctrl. States Inc., Pratt, 1970-76; pres. Krey Co. Ltd., Pratt, 1978-99, chmn., dir. 1999—; fin. chmn. Econ. Lifelines, Topeka; bd. dirs. All Ins. Inc., Pratt, Kans. Wildscape Found. Past pres. Pratt County United Fund; past chmn. Cannonball Trail chpt. ARC; bd. dirs., past comdg. gen. Kans. Cavalry; past pres. Kanza coun. Boy Scouts Am. With U.S. Army, 1950-52. Mem. Kans. C. of C. and Industry (past transp. chmn., dir., v.p.), Pratt Area C. of C. (past pres., bd. dirs.), Kans. Bankers Assn. (past bd. dirs.), Fin. Execs. Inst., Park Hills Country Club (past pres.), Elks, Rotary, Sigma Delta Chi, Chi Psi. Republican. Presbyterian. Home: 502 Welton St Pratt KS 67124-1357 Office: The Peoples Bank 222 S Main St Pratt KS 67124-2713

LOOMIS, IAN MORTON, engineering educator; b. Wickham-Woodbridge, Eng., June 17, 1965; came to U.S., 1966; BS with honors, N.Mex. Inst. Mining & Tech., 1987; MS, Va. Poly. Inst. and State U., 1995, PhD, 1997. Registered profl. engr., N.Mex. Mining engr. Dravo Engring. Cos., Inc., Carlsbad, N.Mex., 1987-88; engr. Westinghouse Electric Corp., Carlsbad, 1988-91, sr. engr., 1991-93; grad. rsch. asst. Va. Poly. Inst. Tech. and State U., Blacksburg, 1993-97; rsch. assoc. Va. Poly. Inst. Tech. and State U., 1997—, vis. asst. prof., 1997—. Editor: (book/directory) Virginia Coal (ann.), 1997, 98; presenter at symposia. Fellow Mine Ventilation Soc. of South Africa; mem. Soc. for Mining, Metallurgy & Exploration (Outstanding Grad. Student paper 1996). Achievements include 1st reported investigation of continuous monitoring of natural ventilation pressure in underground mines. Office: Dept Mining & Minerals Engring Va Poly Inst & State U 100 Holden Hall Blacksburg VA 24061

LOOMIS, JAMES COOK, educator, navigator; b. Long Beach, Calif., Sept. 22, 1935; s. Joseph Gray and Elizabeth Cook L.; children: Gannon, Megan Leslie Loomis Powers. BS, U. Calif., 1958, MA, 1961; postgrad., U. Mich., 1962. Dept. head math. Culver City (Calif.) H.S., 1962-70; dir. Cetacean Rels. Soc., Maui, Hawaii, 1976-98, Planetary Healing Pageants, Maui, Hawaii, 1976-98; Fellshp., Mental Health Rsch. Inst., Genetic Algorithms, under John Holland and dir. J.G. Miller, Living Systems; spkr., U Hawaii Matsunaga Peace Inst., 1st Global Peace Rsch. Conf., 1994, SHE PEACE: A World Peace Beachgame; Creating Future Friendly ECO-GEO-CEO's; mem., Proj. Jonah Grant, 1976, Deep Breathold diving Dolphin Entertainer; creator, Y2Kaper FOANA-TUNUP-HAS Flags of All Nations and The United Nations Underwater Parade Honoring All Species for the Global Millenuium Television network 2001, 24 hr. Broadcast. Author: Saving The Cosmos ('il Tuesday), 1995, Strange Fluke, 1990 (1st prize Maui Writers Conf. 1994). Address: PO Box 958 Paia HI 96779-0958

LOOMIS, NORMA IRENE, marriage and family therapist; b. Dunlap, Ind., May 6, 1941; d. Edwin Clifford and Lucille DeVere (Hall) Dick; m. Edwin Dale Loomis; children: William Dale, James Vernon. BS in Edn., Western Mich. U., 1973, MA in Edn., 1976; PhD in Christian Counseling, Rocky Mountin Inc., 1990. Cert. marriage and family therapist. Tchr. Cassopolis (Mich.) Schs., 1973—; counseling Christian Counseling Svcs., Goshen, Ind., 1985—; presenter Elkhart (Ind.) Pub. Schs., 1992-95, Middlebury (Ind.) Pub. Schs., 1992-94, Elkhart Ct., 1995-97; pres. Champion Reality Inc., Elkhart, 1983—. Contbr. articles to profl. publs.; author tchg. materials Hot Shots Prodns. Mem. Cmty. Corrections Adv. Bd., Elkhart County, 1994—; pres. Juniper Beach Assn., Mears, Mich., 1985-96, Women in Action, Elkhart, 1985-94. Mem. ACA, Am. Mental Health Counselors Assn., Ind. Counselors Assn. for Alcohol and Drug Abuse, Am. Assn. Christian Counselors, Christian Assn. Psychol. Studies. Republican. Mem. Bretheran Ch. Avocations: swimming, boating, bowling, crafts. Home: 22650 Lake Shore Dr Elkhart IN 46514-9570 Office: Christian Counseling Svcs 333 E Madison St Goshen IN 46526-3429

LOOMIS, WESLEY HORACE, III, former publishing company executive; b. Kansas City, Mo., July 29, 1913; s. Wesley Horace, Jr. and Mary (Gary) L.; m. Mary Bradford Paine, Apr. 17, 1937 (dec. Feb. 1998); children: Mary Elizabeth (Mrs. R.M. Norton), Jonathan Lee (dec.), Frederick Pierson. Grad., Hackley Sch., Tarrytown, N.Y., 1931; B.S. in Engring. and Bus. Adminstrn, MIT, 1935. Indsl. engr. Automatic Elec. Co., Chgo., 1935-42; pres. Loomis Advt. Co., 1946-55, Gen. Telephone Directory Co., Des Plaines, Ill., 1956-78; v.p. Dominion Directory Co., Vancouver, B.C., 1956-64; pres. Dominion Directory Co., 1964-78, Courtnay Pty., Ltd., Adelaide, Courtnay Pty. Ltd. S.A. Australia, Directories (Australia) Pty., Ltd., Melbourne, Australia, Gen. Telephone Directory Co. C por A, Santo Domingo, 1971-78, Directorio Telefonico Centroamericano, S.A., 1972-78; dir. Directorio Telefonico de El Salvador (SA). Pres. Episc. Charities 1969-70, dir., 1962-83, now life trustee; trustee emeritus U.S. Naval Acad. Found., Annapolis, Md.; bd. dirs. Traveler Aid Soc. Met. Chgo./Immigrants' Service League, 1957-80, pres., 1960-61; chmn. Travelers Aid Internat., Social Service Am., 1973-77; bd. dirs. Travelers Aid Assn. Am., 1977-82, pres., 1978-80; pres. Ind. Telephone Hist. Found., 1967-81, trustee, 1981-98; trustee emeritus Colby-Sawyer Coll., New London, N.H., sec., 1976-81; mem. corp. devel. com. M.I.T., 1979-81; trustee Ill. Bus. Hall of Fame, 1981-83; bd. dirs., trustee, chmn. planning com. Mote Marine Lab., Sarasota, Fla., 1983—. Served to lt. col., Ordnance AUS, 1942-46. Decorated hon. mil. mem. Order Brit. Empire; laureate Am. Nat. Bus. Hall of Fame, 1980; recipient APPY award of excellence Yellow Pages Pubs. Assn., 1998; elected to Ind. Telephone Hall of Fame, 1981, Calif. chpt., 1990. Mem. Ind. Telephone Pioneers Assn. (pres. 1964-66), Racquet Club (Chgo.), Field and Bird Key Yacht (Sarasota), Masons (32 deg.), Phi Gamma Delta. Republican. Episcopalian (warden). Home: 700 John Ringling Blvd Apt 305 Sarasota FL 34236-1542

LOONG, LEE HSIEN, government executive; b. Feb. 10, 1952; widowed; 4 children. BA in Math. & Computer Sci., U. Cambridge, England, 1974; MA in Pub. Adminstrn., Harvard U., 1980. Elected MP, Teck Ghee, 1984, 88; min. State of Trade and Industry, Defense, 1985-90; deputy prime min., 1990—; elected MP, Ang Mo Koi, 1991; min. trade & industry, 1990-92, chmn. min. fin. com., 1994—; 1st asst. sec. gen. PAP. Brig. gen. Singapore Armed Forces, 1971-84. Office: Office of Prime Min, Istana Annexe Orchard Rd, Singapore 238823, Singapore*

LOOR, FRANCIS, immunologist, educator; b. Mons, Belgium, Dec. 20, 1941; s. Louis and Mireille (Duhameau) L.; m. Josiane Carton, Mar. 9, 1965; children: Chantal, Patrice. BSc, Free U. Brussels, 1963, DSc, 1969. Rsch. fellow Belgian Nat. Funds for Sci. Rsch., Brussels, 1963-76; mem. Basel Inst. Immunology, Switzerland, 1970-79; assoc. prof. immunology, medicine U. Mons, 1976-80; prof., chair immunology Louis Pasteur U., Strasbourg, France, 1980—; rsch. fellow Sandoz Pharms., Ltd., Basel, 1979-80; rsch. cons. Transgene, Strasbourg, 1980-83, Sandoz Pharms. Ltd., Basel, 1980-96, Novartis Pharms., Ltd., Basel, 1996—. Editor: B and T Cells in Immune Recognition, 1977; contbr. over 150 articles on immunology, membrane biology, oncology and pharmacology to profl. jours., chpts. to books. Avocations: landscape gardening, hiking. Office: Strasbourg 1 Univ, Rte du Rhin 74 BP 24, F-67401 Illkirch France

LOOS, JOHN THOMPSON, business owner; b. West Palm Beach, Fla.; s. John T. and Margaret (Browning) L.; children: Amy, John, Melissa. BSBA, U. Fla., 1970. Co-founder, v.p., bd. dirs. Am. Mktg. and Mgmt., Inc., Ft. Lauderdale, Fla., 1970-78; pvt. practice real estate investor Ft. Lauderdale, 1978—; bd. dirs. DiMar Industries, Davie, Fla.; pres. Historic Brickell Devel. Corp., 1st Lauderdale Investments-Di-Mar Properties. Active Ft. Lauderdale Riverwalk Com., 1987-91, Jud. Nominating Commn., Broward County, Fla., 1988-92; bd. dirs. Broward County YMCA, 1982—, past pres.; bd. dirs., vice-chmn., chmn. North Broward Hosp. Dist., 1989-93; bd. dirs., vice-chmn. Downtown Devel. Authority, Ft. Lauderdale, 1990, 93, 96, chmn., 1990-94, active, 1988-2000; chmn., Cmty. Svcs. Bd., Ft. Lauderdale, 1986-90; bd. dirs. North Lauderdale-Progreso Devel. Dist., 1990-91, Broward County Planning Coun., 1993-95, Broward County Charter Rev. Com., 1994-96, Broward County Partnership for the Homeless, 1997-98; bd. dirs. Downtown Coun. Named Downtowner of Yr. Ft. Lauderdale, 1997. Republican. Home: PO Box 399 Fort Lauderdale FL 33302-0399

LOOS, KATJA URSULA, chemist; b. Frankfurt, Germany, Feb. 11, 1971; d. Georg Aloysius and Gertrud (Staib) L. Diploma in chemistry, U. Mainz, Germany, 1996. Scientific rschr. U. Mainz, Germany, 1996, U. Bayreuth, Germany, 1997—. Co-author: (chpt.) Alberto Ciferris Supramolecular Polymers, 2000. DAAD Studies fellow, U. Mass., 1993-94, U. Rio Grande do Sul, Brasil, 1998; recipient Poster award Makromolekulares Kolloquium, Freiburg, 1999. Roman Catholic. Home: Hattersheimer Str 14, 65779 Kelkheim Germany Office: U Bayreuth, Mc II, 95440 Bayreuth Germany

LOOSE, RODNEY STEWART, FBI agent; b. West Reading, Pa., Nov. 6, 1948; s. Stewart Henry and Kathryn Marse Loose; m. Suzanne Marse Ludlum, Sept. 28, 1997. BS in Edn., Millersville U., 1970; MS in Criminal Justice Mgmt., West Chester U., 1985; grad., FBI Nat. Acad., 1991. Commd. 2d lt. USMC, 1970, advanced through grades to maj., ret., 1996; indsl. security specialist Def. Logistics Agy., Reading, Pa., 1974-76; civilian criminal investigator U.S. Army, New Cumberland, Pa., 1976-79; personnel security investigator Def. Investigative Svc., Harrisburg, Pa., 1980-84; spl. agt. FBI, Richmond, Va., 1984-87, N.Y.C., 1987—. Mem. FBI Agts. Assn.

LOOSER, DONALD WILLIAM, academic administrator; b. Lufkin, Tex., June 14, 1939; s. William E. and Mildred H. (Wageneck) L.; m. Elsa Jean Albritton, Aug. 20, 1966; 1 child, William Gregory. B in Music Edn., Baylor U., 1962, MusB, 1962; MusM, Northwestern U., 1963; PhD, Fla. State U., 1972. Instr. Miss. Coll., Clinton, 1963-64; asst. prof. Houston Bapt. U., 1964-68, asst. to pres., 1968-72, dean gen. edn., 1972-77, v.p. adminstrv. affairs, 1977-83, v.p. acad. affairs, 1983—; pres. Conf. Deans Faculties and Acad. V.P.s, 1985-86; participant Harvard U. Inst. Edn. Mgmt., 1985; mem. adv. bd. Tex. Edn. Agy., Austin; mem. innovation in undergrad. edn. panel So. Regional Edn. Bd., Atlanta; pres. Nat. Conf. Acad. Deans, 1990-91. Mem. editorial adv. bd. Audio-Visual Inst. Mag.; contbr. articles to profl. jours.; rec. artist A Jubilant Song, 1983. Mem. adv. bd. Houston Symphony Orch., Houston Grand Opera, S.W. Consortium on Internat. Study, Dallas; staff Tallowood Bapt. Ch., 1965-88; pianist Second Bapt. Ch., Houston, 1988-98. Mem. Am. Assn. Higher Edn., Houston Philos. Soc., Rotary, Phi Delta Kappa, Omicron Delta Kappa, Pi Kappa Lambda, Kappa Delta Pi.

LOPACIUK, STANISLAW KAZIMIERZ, physician, educator; b. Podbielskie, Poland, Jan. 4, 1935; s. Jozef and Bronislawa (Zuk) L.; m. Halina Maria Zywicka, Sept. 25, 1926; 1 child, Lopaciuk Margaret. MB, Warsaw Med. Sch., 1958, MD, 1964, PhD in hematology, 1972. Rsch. assoc. Inst. of Hematology, Warsaw, 1956-67, asst. prof., 1967-72, assoc. prof., 1972-80, prof. medicine, 1983—; cons. hematologist Ministry of Public Health, Kuwait, 1980-82; WHO fellowship Oslo U., Norway, 1966; vis. scientist Dept. Pathology, U. N.C., Chapel Hill, 1974-75. Author 2 med. books; contbr. chpts. to books and articles to profl. jours.; mem. editl. com. Acta Haematologica Polonica, 1980—, Haemostasis, 1989-96; editor Thrombosis Rsch., 1990-95. Mem. Polish Acad. of Scis. (com. clin. pathophysiology 1990—), Polish Coll. of Lab. Medicine, Internat. Soc. of Hematology, Polish Soc. of Hematology and Blood Transfusion. Roman Catholic. Home: Gimnastyczna 46, 02-632 Warsaw Poland Office: Inst Hematology/Blood Trans, Chocimska 5, 00-957 Warsaw Poland

LOPATA, HELENA ZNANIECKA, sociologist, researcher, educator; b. Poznan, Poland, Oct. 1, 1925; d. Florian Witold and Eileen (Markley) Znaniecki; m. Richard Stefan Lopata, Feb. 8, 1946 (wid. July 1994); chil-

dren: Theodora Karen Lopata-Menasco, Stefan Richard. B.A., U. Ill., 1946, M.A., 1947; Ph.D., U. Chgo., 1954; DSc (hon.), Guelph U., Can., 1995. Lectr. U. Va. Extension, Langley AFB, 1951-52, DePaul U., 1956-60; lectr. Roosevelt U., 1960-64, asst. prof. sociology, 1964-67, assoc. prof., 1967-69; prof. sociology Loyola U., Chgo., 1969-97, prof. emerita, 1997—, chmn. dept. sociology, 1970-72, dir. Center for Comparative Study of Social Roles, 1972—; mem. NIMH Rev. Bd., 1977-79; mem. Mayor's Council Manpower and Econ. Devel., 1974-79; mem. adv. com., chair tech. com. White House Conf. on Aging, 1979-81; adv. council Nat. Inst. Aging, 1978-83. Author: Occupation: Housewife, 1971, Widowhood in an American City, 1973, Polish Americans: Status Competition in an Ethnic Community, 1976, (with Debra Barnewolt and Cheryl Miller) City Women: Work, Jobs, Occupations, Careers, Vol. I, America, 1984, Vol. II, Chicago, 1985, City Women in America, 1986, (with Henry Brehm) Widows and Dependent Wives: From Social Problem to Federal Policy, 1986, Polish Americans, 1994, Circles and Settings: Role Changes of American Women, 1994, Current Widowhood: Myths and Realities, 1996; adv. editor: Sociologist Quar., 1969-72, Jour. Marriage and Family, 1978-82, Symbolic Interaction, 1989—, Sociol. Inquiry, 1996—; mem. editl. bd. Am. Sociologist, 1996; editor: Marriages and Families, 1973, (with Nona Glazer and Judith Wittner) Research on the Interweave of Social Roles: vol. I, Women and Men, 1980, (with David Maines) vol. 2, Friendship, 1981, (with Joseph Pleck) vol. 3, Families and Jobs, 1983, vol. 4, Current Research on Occupations and Professions, 1987, vol. 5, 1987, Widows: The Middle East, Asia and the Pacific, 1987, Widows: North America, 1987, (with Anne Figert) Current Research on Occupations and Professions: Vol. 9: Getting Down to Business, 1996, Current Research on Occupations and Professions, 1999, Current Research on Occupations and Professions: Jobs in Context: Index and Settings: Vol. 10, 1998, (with David Maines) Friendship in Context, 1990, (with Kevin Henson) Unusual Occupations, 2000; adv. bd. Symbolic Interaction, 1977-89, 92—; contbr. articles to profl. jours. Bd. overseers Wellesley Ctr. of Rsch. and Women, 1979-84. Recipient Research award Radcliffe Coll., 1982; grantee Chgo. Tribune, 1956, Midwest Coun. Social Research on Aging, 1964-65, Adminstrn. on Aging, 1967-69, 68-71, Social Security Adminstrn., 1971-75, also 1975-79, Indo-Am. Fellowship Program: Coun. for Internat. Eschange Scholars, 1987-88, Rsch. Stimulation grantee Loyola U. Chgo., 1988, 92, Am. Coun. Learned Soc. travel grant, 1995, Internat. Rsch. Exchange Bd. short term travel grant, 1995; named Faculty Mem. of Yr., Loyola U., 1975. Fellow Midwest Coun. for Social Rsch. on Aging (pres. 1969-70, 91-92, postdoctoral tng. dir. 1971-77), Ill. Sociol. Assn. (pres. 1969-70), Gerontol. Soc. Am. (chmn. social and behavioral sci. sect. 1980-81, Mentoring award 1995), Internat. Gerontol. Assn.: mem. Soc. for Study Social Problems (chmn. spl. problems com. 1971, v.p. 1975, coun. 1978-80, pres. 1983, Disting. Scholar award family div. 1989), Am. Sociol. Assn. (coun. 1978-81, chmn. sect. family 1976, chmn. sect. sex roles 1975, Sorokin awwards com. 1970-73, publs. com. 1972-73, nominations com. 1977, chmn. sect. on aging 1982-83 (Disting. Career award, 1992 Section on Aging), Cooley-Blumer awards com., 1984, Jessie Bernard awards com. 1984-86, disting. scholarly publ. awards selection com. 1988-89, awards policy com. 1990-92, co-chair com. on internat. sociology, 1992-95, chmn. History of Sociology sect., 2000), Soc. for the Study of Symbolic Interaction (mem 1977—, Mead award for Life Time Achievement, 1993, Feminist Mentoring award 1999), Internat. Sociol. Soc. (com. on family rsch., bd. dirs. 1991-94, com. on work 1972—, rsch. com. on aging 1990—), Midwest Sociol. Assn. (state dir. 1972-74, pres. 1975-76, chair 1994—, publs. com. 1993-95), Nat. Coun. Family Rels. (Burgess award 1990, chair internat. sect. 1991-93), Polish Inst. of Arts and Scis. in Am. (dir. 1976-82, with Zbigniew Brzezinski, Bronislaw Malinowski award in social scis. 1995), Polish Welfare Assn. (bd. dirs. 1988-91), Internat. Inst. Sociology, 1994—, Sociologists for Women in Society (mem. task force alternative work patterns, pres. 1993-94, adv. editor Gender and Soc. 1993-94). Office: Loyola U Dept Sociology 6525 N Sheridan Rd Chicago IL 60626-5385

LOPATA, VASILI IVANOVICH, artist; b. Nova Basan, Ukrainien, Apr. 28, 1941; s. Ivan Mykolayovich and Hanna Antonivna Lopata; m. Regina V. Lopata, Sept. 23, 1969; 1 child, Olga V. Lopata. MA, Acad. of Arts, Kyiv, Ukraine, 1970; PhD, USSR Acad. of Arts, Moscow, 1972. cons. Radyansky Pismennik, Kyiv, 1967, Radyanska Shcola, Kyiv, 1968-89, Dnipro, Kyiv, 1970-88, Veselka, Kyiv, 1970-93, Tavria, Simpheropol, Ukraine, 1972, Melbourne, Australia, 1974, Molodaya Gvardiya, Moscow, 1976, Voronezh, Russia, 1980; author design of Ukrainian currency Govt. of Ukraine, 1991-92. Illustrator, designer Pobratimy, 1972 (2d prize 1972), Poltava, 1980 (2d prize 1980), Ballady, 1982 (2d prize 1982), Topolya, 1984 (1st prize 1984), Slovo O Polku Igorevim, 1986, 1989 (1st prize 1986), History of Ukraine, 1993 (1st prize 1993), The Lord is the Strength of His People, 1996; over 600 woodcuts, linocuts and etchings; artist portrait John Paul II, 1993 (Privet Gift from his holyness 1993); painter numerous oils, pastels, watercolors; author: Somewhere Within My Heart, Hope and Disappointment; contbr. articles to profl. jours.; work collected in numerous museums. With Soviet Army, 1961-64. Recipient First Pl. Book-Plate Competition, London, 1989, Shevchenko prize laureate Govt. of Ukraine, 1992, First prize Prominvestbank, 1998; honored citizen City Hall of Winnipeg, Can., 1990, City Hall of Brundon, Can., 1990; honored artist of Ukraine, 1979, Order of Honor, Govt. of Ukraine, 1988. Mem. Union of Artists of Ukraine. Avocations: collector old and new prints and books. Home: 1800 22nd Ave Apt 103 San Francisco CA 94122-4449

LOPATIN, SERGEY DMITRIEVICH, microelectronic scientist, electrochemist; b. Belarus, USSR, July 11, 1964; came to U.S., 1996; s. Dmitri and Mariya Lopatin; m. Marina Polyanskaya, Dec. 21, 1997; children: Valentin, Dima, Kim. MS, Radioengring. Inst., Minsk, USSR, 1988; PhD, U. Comp. Sci./Radioelectronics, Minsk, Belarus, 1994. Engr. Integral Semiconductor Inc., Minsk, Belarus, 1988-92; scientist Acad. Scis., Minsk, 1992-94; sr. scientist U. Computer Sci. and Radioelectronics, Minsk, 1994-96; vis. scientist Cornell U., Ithaca, N.Y., 1996-97; sr. engr. Advanced Micro Devices, Sunnyvale, Calif., 1997—; instr., lectr Berkeley U., Burlingame, Calif., 1998; lectr. in field. Contbr. numerous articles to profl. jours. Grantee SEMATECH, 1996-97, DARPA, 1997. Mem. IEE, Materials Rsch. Soc., Electrochem. Soc. Achievements include patents in field. Avocations: travel, fine arts, family activities, sports. Home: 1000 Kiely Blvd Apt 66 Santa Clara CA 95051-4842 Office: Advanced Micro Devices 1 Amd Pl # Ms160 Sunnyvale CA 94085-3905

LOPE, HANS-JOACHIM, romance philology educator; b. Wuppertal, Germany, Apr. 19, 1939; s. Willy and Gunhild (Hahne) L.; m. Marie-Thérèse Bouteiller, Nov. 17, 1964 (div. 1973); 1 child, Bettina; m. Brigitte Erven, Sept. 17, 1979. Doctor, Cologne (Germany) U., 1967; prof., Aix-la-Chapelle, Germany, 1973. Asst. prof. Aix-la-Chapelle, Germany, 1967-73, prof., 1973-74; ordinarius Philipps U., Marburg, Germany, 1974—. Author: José Cadalso, 1973, Französische Literaturgeschichte, 1974, 3d edit., 1990, Karl der Kühne, 1995, Federico II de Prusia y los españoles, 2000; editor Studien und Dokumente zur Geschichte der Romanischen Literaturen, 1975—. Recipient Chevalier des Palmes Académiques, France. Avocations: cats, yachting. Office: Philipps Univ FB 10, Wilhelm-Röpke Str 6D, D-35037 Marburg Hessen, Germany

LOPE-BLANCH, JUAN M., philology educator, researcher; b. Madrid, July 17, 1927; arrived in Mexico, 1951; s. Eduardo Lope and Juana Blanch; m. Paciencia Ontañon, Dec. 18, 1951. Doctorado en Filologia, U. Madrid, 1951; Doctorado en Letras, U. Nat., Mexico City, 1964. Prof. ayudante U. Madrid, 1950-51; prof. titular U. Nat., Mexico City, 1953—; investigator El Colegio de Mexico, Mexico City, 1954—; vis. prof. Stanford (Calif.) U., 1972, 83, Georgetown U., Washington, 1965-66, U. Calif., Berkeley, 1982, U. Ariz., Tucson, 1986. Author: El Concepto de Oracion en Linguistica, 1979, Análisis Gramatical del Discurso, 1983, 87, Estudios de Historia Linguistica Hica, 1990; author, dir.: (6 vols.) Atlas Linguistico de Mexico, 1991—; contbr. articles to profl. jours. Recipient Decoration of the Order of Andrés Bello, Venezuela, 1980, award in humanities Mexican Autonomous Nat. U., 1987, Recognition for Sci. Activity, State U. Campinas, São Paulo, 1990, Commandery of the Order of Isabel la Católica, Spain, 1990, Nat. Sci. and Arts award in lit. and linguistics Mexican Govt., 1985, Great Cross of the Order of Alfonso X el Sabio, Spain, 1999. Mem. Soc. de Linguistique Romane, Assn. Internat. Hispanists, De La Alfal (pres. 1987—), Academia Argentina de Letras (corr.), Academia Chilena de la Lengua (corr.). Avocations: sailing, photography, tennis, traveling.

LOPES, ARTUR OSCAR, mathematician, researcher; b. Rio de Janeiro, Oct. 10, 1950; s. Sergio Oscar and Leda (Sperb) L.; m. Silvia Regina Costa, Mar. 24, 1973; 1 child, Daniel. BS, Fed. U. Rio de Janeiro, 1972; MS, Inst. Pure and Applied Math, Brazil, 1974; PhD in Math., IMPA, Brazil, 1977. Prof. Fed. U. Rio Grande do Sul, Porto Alegre, Brazil, 1985—; assoc. Internat. Ctr. Theoretical Physics, Trieste, Italy, 1986—. Contbr. rsch. articles to profl. publs. Mem. Soc. Brasileira Math. Home: Rua Jaragua 125 Apt 702, 90450140 Porto Alegre RS, Brazil Office: Fed U Rio Grande do Sul Inst Math, Ave Bento Goncalves 9500, 91500000 Porto Alegre RS, Brazil

LOPES, HENRIQUE JORGE CRISTO, business marketing educator; b. Lisbon, Oct. 7, 1962; s. Luciano Lopes and Natercia Cristo Lopes; divorced; children: Francisco, Miguel. Degree in psychology, ISPA, Lisbon, 1991; MBA in Mktg., UCP, 1995, M in Mgmt., 1997. Paramedic tchr. CUP, Lisbon, 1981-83; tchr. h.s. Lisbon, 1983-91; treasury asst. Ford, Lisbon, 1991-93, finance and mktg. dir., 1993-95; lectr. U. Cath. Portuguese, Lisbon, 1995—; sr. ptnr. Sharen, Lisbon, 1997—; cons. Railways, Lisbon, 1996-99, MSD, Lisobn, 1995-97; project dir. U. Cath. Portuguese, Lisbon, 1995—, postgrad. dir., 1996—. Bus. columnist, newspapers and mags.; author: Customer Analysis, 2000; contbr. articles to profl. jours. Mem. N.Y. Acad. Scis., Acad. Mgmt. Scis., SPM. Avocations: collecting old sci. materials, cooking. Home: Ave Bomb Vol 41 6 Esd, 1495-02 Alges Portugal Office: Univ Cath Portuguesa, R Palma de Cima, 1600 Lisbon Portugal

LOPES, MYRA AMELIA, educational administrator; b. Nantucket, Mass., July 9, 1931; d. Leo Joseph and Mary Ellen (Moriarty) Powers; m. Curtis Linwood Lopes, June 25, 1955; children: Dennis, Sherry, Kathy, Curtis, Becky. BS, Bridgewater, 1954; diploma, Inst. Children's Lit., 1982, N.Y. Inst. Journalism, 1984. Cert. elem. educator, Mass. Tchr. Fairhaven (Mass.) Sch. Sys., 1954-58; prin. Sheri Ka Kindergarten, Fairhaven, 1960-76; market promotion Store Sys., New Bedford, Mass., 1976-82; writer Fairhaven Sch. Sys., 1987-95, fund raiser, reading promoter, 1987-92. Author: Look Around You, 1990, Looking Back, 1991, Seeing It All, 1992, But Then There Was More, 1993, Captain Joshua Slocum: A Centennial Tribute, 1994, Captain Slocum's Life Before and After the Spray, 1997, The Rogers Legacy, 1997, The Castle on the Hill, 1998, My Town, 1999. Bd. dirs. Fairhaven Improvement Assn., 1986-98, chair membership, 1986-96, pres., 1990-93; bd. dirs. YWCA, New Bedford, 1982-88, chair cmty. rels., 1982-83, nominating chair, 1983-84, chair pers. bd., 1984-88; trustee Millicent Libr., 1993—; bd. govs. Am. Biog. Instn., 1997—; bd. dirs. Fairhaven H.S. Hall of Fame, 1999—. Named to Hall of Fame, Fairhaven H.S., 1997; named Woman of Yr., New Bedford Std.-Times and cmty., 1999. Mem. Rotary (bd. dirs. 1998-99, v.p. 2000—, Paul Harris fellow 2000), Joshua Slocum Soc. Internat. (historian 1997-2000). Democrat. Roman Catholic. Avocations: gardening, reading, walking, crafts, music. Home: 71 Fort St Fairhaven MA 02719-2811

LOPES, SÔNIA GODOY BUENO CARUALHO, writer, educator; b. São Paulo, Apr. 9, 1955; d. Plínio and Lecticia (Godoy Bueno) Carvalho Lopes; m. Carlos Eduardo Rogério, Mar. 18, 1982; chidlren: Bruno, Felipe. BS, U. São Paulo, 1977, MS, 1983, PhD, 1991. Writer Editora Saraiva, São Paulo, 1978—, Editora Atual, São Paulo, 1996-99; tchr., rschr. U. São Paulo, 1988—. Author: Biology—Auto Instructive, Vol. 1 (Cytology), 1978, Vol. 2 (Embryology and Histology), 1978, Vol. 3 (Genetics), 1978, Vol. 4 (Invertebrates), 1978, BIO-Blue Version (Cytology, Embryology and Histology, 1983, BIO-Green Version (Genetics, Evolution and Ecology, 1984, BIO-Yellow Version (Biodiversity), 1985, (with Plínio Carvalho Lopes) Complete Biology Course, 1987, BIO-Volume I (Cytology, Embryology and Histology), 1992, 97, BIO-Volume 2 (Biodiversity), 1992, 97, BIO-Volume 3 (Genetics, Evolution and Ecology), 1992, 97, General Biology, 1994, 98, (with Ana Maria Machado) The Support of Life, 1996, The Life, 1996, The Human Life, 1996, The Matter and the Life, 1996; contbr. numerous articles to profl. jours.

LOPES CARDOZO KINDERSLEY, LYDIA HELENA (LIDA) (LYDIA HELENA (LIDA) KINDERSLEY), letter cutter and designer, publisher; b. Leiden, The Netherlands, July 22, 1954; arrived in Eng., 1976; d. Paul Lopes Cardozo and Ottoline van Hemert tot Dingshof; m. David Guy Barnabas Kindersley, Nov. 17, 1986 (dec. 1995); m. Graham F. Beck, July 7, 1998. Student, Royal Acad. Fine Arts, The Hague, The Netherlands, 1972-76. Letter cutter David Kindersley's Workshop, Cambridge, Eng., 1976—, ptnr., 1981—; sole proprietor The Cardozo Kindersley Workshop (formerly David Kindersley's Workshop), Cambridge, 1995-98; ptnr. with Graham F. Beck in Cardozo Kindersley Workshop Cambridge, 1998—; typeface designer EMI Group, 1996-97; lectr. various locations, Gt. Britain, Europe, U.S. Co-author, illustrator: Letters Slate Cut, 1990; co-author, editor: Lasting Letters, 1992; author, editor: A Guide To Commissioning Work, 1996; co-author: Letters for the Millennium, 1999, Kindersley at Addenbroke's Hospital, 2000; lettering works on display on various locations worldwide including British Libr., Brit. Mus., St. Paul's Cathedral, Westminster Abbey. Sch. gov. Impington Village Coll., Cambridge, 1996—, assoc. Clare Hall, Cambridge, 1998-2000. Mem. Wynkyn de Worde Soc. (chmn. 1988), Double Crown Club, Assn. Typographique Internationale. Home and Office: Cardozo Kindersley Workshop, 152 Victoria Rd, Cambridge CB4 3DZ, England

LOPEZ, DAVID TIBURCIO, lawyer, educator, arbitrator, mediator; b. Laredo, Tex., July 17, 1939; s. Tiburcio and Dora (Davila) L.; m. Romelia G. Guerra, Nov. 20, 1965; 1 child, Vianei López Robinson. Student, Laredo Jr. Coll., 1956-58; BJ, U. Tex., 1962; JD summa cum laude, South Tex. Coll. Law, 1971. Bar: Tex. 1971, U.S. Dist. Ct. (so. dist.) Tex. 1972, U.S. Ct. Appeals (5th cir.) 1973, U.S. Dist. Ct. (we. dist.) Tex. 1975, U.S. Ct. Claims 1975, U.S. Ct. Appeals (fed. cir.) 1975, U.S. Supreme Ct. 1976, U.S. Dist. Ct. (ea. dist.) Tex. 1978, U.S. Ct. Appeals (11th cir.) 1981, U.S. Ct. Appeals (9th cir.) 1984; cert. internat. com. arbitrator Internat. Ctr. for Arbitration; mediator tng. Atty.-Mediator Inst. Reporter Laredo Times, 1958-59; cons. Mexican Nat. Coll. Mag., Mexico City, 1961-62; reporter Corpus Christi (Tex.) Caller-Times, 1962-64; state capitol corr. Long News Svc., Austin, Tex., 1964-65; publs. dir. Interam. Regional Orgn. of Workers, Mexico City, 1965-67; nat. field rep. AFL-CIO, Washington, 1967-71; publs. dir. Tex. chpt. AFL-CIO, Austin, 1971-72; pvt. practice Houston, 1971—; adj. prof. U. Houston, 1972-74, Thurgood Marshall Sch. Law, Houston, 1975-76; mem. adv. com. nat. Hispanic ednl. rsch. project One Million and Counting Tomas Rivera Ctr., 1989-91; mem. adv. bd. Inst. Transnat. Arbitration; charter mem. Resolution Forum Inc.; mem. adv. bd. South Tex. Ctr. Profl. Responsibility; mem. nat. panel of neutrals JAMS/ENDISPUTE, 1996—. Bd. dirs. Pacifica Found., N.Y.C., 1970-72, Houston Community Coll., 1972-75; mem. bd. edn. Houston Ind. Sch. Dist., 1972-75. With U.S. Army. Mem. ABA (newsletter editor Lawyers Conf., jud. divsn.), FBA, ATLA, Tex. Bar Assn. (com. on pattern jury changes), Houston Bar Assn. (com. on alternative dispute resolution), Internat. Bar Assn., Interam. Bar Assn., Bar of U.S. Fed. Cir., Mex.-Am. Bar Assn., Inter-Pacific Bar Assn., Tex.-Mex. Bar Assn. (chair labor com.), Hispanic Bar Assn., World Assn. Lawyers (chair internat. law sect.), Am. Judicature Soc., Indsl. Rels. Rsch. Assn., Sigma Delta Chi, Phi Alpha Delta. Democrat. Roman Catholic. Home: 28 Farnham Ct Houston TX 77024 Office: 3900 Montrose Blvd Houston TX 77006-4908

LOPEZ, ERNESTO MIGUEL CARRANZA, physicist; b. Lima, Peru, Apr. 14, 1932; s. Justo Vilca and Maria Carrion (Carranza) L. MS in Physics, Fed. U. Rio de Janeiro, Brazil, 1965; D, Joseph Fourier Grenoble I, Grenoble, France, 1971. Assoc. prof. Nat. U. Trujillo, Peru, 1962-63; assoc. prof. Nat. U. Engring., Lima, Peru, 1966-73, prof. physics, 1973-92; emeritus prof. Nat. U. Engring., Lima, 2000; chief physics lab. Nat. U. Engring., Lima, Peru, 1977-81, chief grad. sch., faculty scis., 1984-85, dean faculty scis., 1985-87, chief internat. rels. office, 1987-89, dir. gen. rsch. inst., 1989-91. Mem. Peruvian Soc. Physics, Internat. Ctr. Theoretical Physics, Nat. Acad. Scis. Avocations: reading, classical music, walking. E-mail: elopez@fc-uni.edu.pe. Office: Nat U Engring, Av Tupac Amaru 210, 31139 Lima 25, Peru

LOPEZ, GENARO, biology educator; b. Brownsville, Tex., Jan. 24, 1947; s. Genaro Velasco and Carmen (Coronado) L.; m. Lee Cecelia Tole, June 23, 1972; children: G. Daniel, Adriana. BS, Tex. Tech. U., 1970; PhD, Cornell U., 1975. Rsch. asst. Cornell U., Ithaca, N.Y., 1970-75; state extension entomologist Tex. Agr. Extension Svc., College Station, 1975-76; instr. biology Tex. Southmost Coll., Brownsville, 1976—; rschr. mercury levels in Snook at Port of Brownsville. Contbr. articles to profl. jours. Mem. Gulf Coast Coalition for Pub. Health, Brownsville, 1982—. With USNG, 1970-76. Writing grantee NSF, 1980. Mem. Gulf Coast Conservation Assn., Gorgas Sci. Soc. (faculty sponsor), Nat. Wildlife Assn., Phi Theta Kappa (sponsor hon. soc. 1985). Episcopalian. Avocations: fishing, custom rod building, Volvo restoration, classical guitar. Home: 110 Ebony Ave Brownsville TX 78520-8012 Office: U Tex 86 Ft Brown St Brownsville TX 78520-4956

LOPEZ, GERARDO DANIEL, engineering consulting company executive; b. Rosario, Argentina, May 16, 1951; s. Juan and Lidia Esther (Gonzalez) L.; m. Susana Graciela Gervasio, May 16, 1978; children: Javier Alejandro, Mariana Beatriz, Diego Julian. Proficiency in English, U. Mich., 1968, U. Cambridge (Eng.), 1969; chem. tech., ENET Ner 7, Rosario, Argentina, 1969; degree in chem. engring., Nat. Tech. U., Rosario, Argentina, 1976. Production supr. Cindelmet S.A., Rosario, Argentina, 1976-77, Metcon S.A., Villa Constitucion, Argentina, 1977-79; materials engr. Ingar, Santa Fe, Argentina, 1980-83, chief materials dept., 1984-86, projects mgr., 1986—; prof. Nat. Tech. U., Santa Fe, Argentina, 1986—, vice-dean, 1988-89; cons. Cyted, Latin Am., Spain, 1986—; vis. lectr. various univs., Argentina, Spain, Portugal, Brazil, Chile, Costa Rica, 1986—; expert advisor at law courts on materials sci. and engring., 1995—; bd. dirs. Argentine Assn. Chem. Engring. Co-author, editor: Ethanol from Lignocellulosics, 1992; editor: III Symposium on Corrosion, 1986; co-editor: I Binational Meeting on Corrosion, 1988; contbr. numerous articles to tech. and profl. jours. Recipient 1st prize for excellence IADE Argentina, 1998; Spanish Ministry Sci. and Edn. grantee, 1988-89. Mem. Argentine Assn. Corrosion (founding mem., pres. 1986-92), Argentine Affiliate Section of NACE (founding mem., v.p. 1985-87), Argentine Standards Inst. (com. mem., cons. 1984-85), Nat. Assn. Corrosion Engring. (internat. rels. com. 1991), Inst. for Integrated Edn. (founding mem.). Avocations: writing, tennis. Office: Ingar, Avellaneda 3657, 3000 Santa Fe Argentina

LOPEZ, HUGO FERREIRA, materials engineering, educator; b. Luis Potosi, Mex., Dec. 10, 1952; came to U.S., 1980; s. Francisco and Maria (Ferreica) L.; m. Emilia Dearbeloa, Mar. 22, 1981; children: Jessica Emilia, David Joseba. BA in Indsl. Engring., Saltillo (Mex.) Tech., 1975; MS in Metallurgy Engring., Ohio State U., 1982, PhD in Metallurgy Engring., 1983. Rsch. prof. Saltillo Tech.; asst. prof. U. Wis., Milw., assoc. prof.; prof.; chair materials dept. U. Wis., Milw. Contbr. articles to profl. jours. Mem. Nat. Assn. Corrosion Engrs. (bd. dirs. Latin Am.). E-mail: hlopez@uwm.edu. Office: Univ Wis Milw 3200 N Cramer St Milwaukee WI 53211-3029

LOPEZ, JESUS MARTINEZ, artist; b. Mexico City, Mar. 21, 1953; s. Lorenzo and Dolores Martinez Lopez. Student, U. Mich., 1996—, Lake Forest Coll., 1997—, Sch. of Art Inst. of Chgo., 1992-95. Registered architect, Mexico City. Visual artist, pres./founder Lopez's Gallery Internat., Benton-Harbor, Mich., 1980—; educator Lopez's Photonics Studio, Benton harbor, 1996—; pres. Lopez's Gallery Internat., pres., 1989—; program dir. Lopez's Photonics Studio, Benton Harbor, 1995—; artist-in-residence Richard Hunt Studio Ctr., Benton Harbor, 1996—; ind. rschr. Sch. of the Art Inst. of Chgo., 1992-95. Artist: Full Paralax 360-Degree Hologram (prototype) 1995, Pulse Color Hologram (concept) 1996, Large Format Lippman Photography, 1999, Transmition Color Hologram with Movement, 2000. Active Richard Hunt Studio Ctr., 1996, City of Benton Harbor Art-Walk, 1997, Making Kids Art Fair, 1997, others. Mem. Internat. Soc. Photo-Optical Instrumentation Engrs., Soc. for Imaging Sci. and Technology. Roman Catholic. Avocation: nature. Office: Richard Hunt Studio Ctr 258 Territorial Rd Benton Harbor MI 49022-3436

LOPEZ, NANCY, professional golfer; b. Torrance, Calif., Jan. 6, 1957; d. Domingo and Marina (Griego) L.; m. Ray Knight, Oct. 25, 1982; children: Ashley Marie, Erinn Shea, Torri Heather. Student, U. Tulsa, 1976-78. Author: The Education of a Woman Golfer, 1979. 'irst victory at Bent Tree Classic, Sarasota, Fla., 1978; named AP Athlete for 1978; admitted to Ladies Profl. Golf Assn. Hall of Fame, 1987, to PGA World Golf Hall of Fame, 1989; named Rolex Rookie of Yr., 1978, Rolex Player of Yr., 1978, 79, 85; recipient Vare Trophy, 1978; winner Sunstar Classic, 1979, Sahara Nat. ProAm, 1979, Women's Internat., 1979, Coca-Cola Classic, 1979, Women's Kemper Open, 1980, Sara Coventry, 1980, Rail Charity Classic, 1980, Ariz. Copper Classic, 1981, Colgate Dinah Shore, 1981, J&B Scotch Pro-Am, 1982, 83, Mazda Japan Classic, 1982, Elizabeth Arden Classic, 1983, Uniden LPGA Invitational, 1984, Chevrolet World Championship Women's Golf, 1984, Chrysler-Plymouth Charity Classic, 1985, LPGA Championship, 1985, Mazda Hall of Fame Championship, 1985, Henredon Classic, 1985, Portland PING Championship, 1985, Sarasota Classic, 1987, Cellular One-PING Golf Championship, 1987, Mazda Classic, 1988, Ai Star/Centinela Hosp. Classic, 1988, Chrysler-Plymouth Classic, 1988, Mazda LPGA Championship, 1989, Atlantic City Classic, 1989, Nippon Travel-MBS Classic, 1989, MBS LPGA Classic, 1990, Sara Lee Classic, 1991, Rail Charity Golf Classic, 1992, PING-Cellular One LPGA Golf Championship, 1992, Youngstown-Warren LPGA Classic, 1993, Chick-fil-A Charity Championship, 1997, others. Mem. Ladies Profl. Golf Assn. (Player and Rookie of Yr. 1978). Republican. Baptist. Achievements include winning 48 LPGA Tour events, 3 maj. championships. Office: care Internat Mgmt Group 1 Erieview Plz Ste 1300 Cleveland OH 44114-1715

LOPEZ, REMI, architect; b. Paris, Mar. 21, 1939; s. Raymond and Simonne (Pillet) L.; m. Claire Le Roy, May 2, 1964; children: Caroline, Cedric, Charlotte, Julie. Architect's diploma with distinction Ecole Des Beaux-Arts, Paris, 1966. Collaborator architect's office, London, 1961, Hamburg, W.Ger., 1962, Raymond Lopez Architecture Office, Paris, 1962-66; sr. ptnr. Remi Lopez et Associes-Architects and Planners, Paris, 1966—; prof. design health facilities Ecole Nationale de la Sante Publique, Rennes, France, 1981-95. Architect numerous housing devels., ednl. and cultural facilities, hosps., office bldgs., refurbishings, France, shopping center Odienne, Ivory Coast, 1972, Amiri hosp., Kuwait, 1981, pilot indsl. and tech. inst., Jeddah, Saudi Arabia, 1980, postal centers, Riyadh, Jeddah and Dammam, Saudi Arabia, 1982, color TV center, Jeddah. Decorated officier Ordre National du Merite, Ordre Arts et Lettres (France). Mem. Academie d'Architecture, Cercle d'etudes architecturales, Regional Council Order Architects (treas. 1978-82, v.p. 1982-84, pres. 1984-86), Nat. Council Order Architects (pres. 1986-90, 92-96), Nat. Geog. Soc. (life), European Coun. Architects (pres. 1989). Office: Remi Lopez et Associés, 242 Blvd Raspail, 75014 Paris France

LOPEZ, REYNALDO GALVEZ, lawyer, partner, educator; b. Manila, The Philippines, Sept. 26, 1960; s. Rodolfo A. and Lourdes G. (Galvez) L. BA in Polit. Sci., U. Santo Tomas, 1981, LLB, 1985, LLM, 1989. Bar: The Philippines. Lawyer human rights Presdl. Com. Human Rights, Manila, 1986; lawyer rsch., br. clk. Regional Trial Ct. Br. 125, Kalookan City, The Philippines, 1987-89; assoc. Syquia Law Offices, Makati City, The Philippines, 1989-90; exec. asst., asst. chief rsch. and investigation Dept. Fgn. Affairs, Manila, 1990; sr. ptnr. Ochoa Lopez Law Offices, Quezon City, The Philippines, 1991-98; prof., coord. polit. sci. dept. U. Santo Tomas, Manila, 1994—; prof. law Arellano Law Found., Pasay City, The Philippines, 1992—. Prodn. coord. Where Jesus Had Walked, 1987; asst. dir., performer Silong-Tanglaw, 1990; prodn. asst. Sharing in the City, 1986-88. Chair Totus Tuus Eighty-One Movement, 1995—. Recipient Gold Leadership award Ust AB Pax Romana, 1981. Mem. ABA, Integrated Bar of The Philippines, Philippine Polit. Sci. Assn. (Plaque of Recognition 1994). Avocations: billiards, swimming, basketball, singing, theatre. Office: Univ Santo Tomas, Espana, Manila The Philippines

LOPEZ, SUE ANN, nursing educator, nurse; b. Statesboro, Ga., June 25, 1955; d. Donald Ashley and Jean Marie (Black) Coleman; m. Terry Lynn, Oct. 9, 1977 (div. Aug. 1991); children: Stephen, Brian, Matt; m. John Lopez Jr., July 3, 1992. BSN, Valdosta (Ga.) State Coll., 1976; MSN, Med. Coll. Ga., Augusta, 1977. RN, Ga., Tex. RN Bulloch Meml. Hosp., Statesboro, Ga., 1976-82; clin. specialist Dr. Robert H. Swint, Statesboro, Ga., 1982-89; nursing instr. Ga. Southern U., Statesboro, Ga., 1989-94, South Plains Coll., Levelland, Tex., 1994—. Mem. Sigma Theta Tau. Avocations: reading, archeology. Home: 215 Hicks Pl Levelland TX 79336-4823

LOPEZ AYALA, JORGE NAPOLEON, economist, financial consultant; b. La Paz, Bolivia, Sept. 18, 1939; s. Armando Jose and Maria Isabel (Ayala) Lopez; m. Rosario Perez, July 21, 1964 (div. May 1970); children: Maria Del Rocio, Jose Luis, Guadalupe Del Pilar; m. Irma Crespo, June 16, 1976; children: Jorge Napoleon Jr., Miguel Angel. M of Econs., San Andres U., La Paz, Bolivia, 1964; MBA, Syracuse U., 1966. Cert. economist. Gen. mgr. Urdini Motors, La Paz, 1965-70, Bolivian Am. Tobacco, La Paz, 1970-72; v.p. Bolivian Am. Bank, La Paz, 1972-74; fin. mgr. Municipalidad, La Paz, 1975-79; gen. mgr. Fensa Bolivia S.A., La Paz, 1979-86; cons. World Bank, La Paz, 1987—; prof. Bolivian Cath. U., La Paz, 1986—. Mem. Amigos De La Ciudad, 1964; founder Comite Civico Pro La Paz, 1976. Served to col. Bolivian Mil., 1977-78. Recipient medal Municipality, La Paz, 1978, Gold medal Argentin Army, 1981, Gold medal Bolivian Army, 1992. Mem. Am. Mgmt. Asn., Economist Coll. Roman Catholic. Avocations: swimming, soccer, reading, travel. E-mail: Nalloaya@zuper.net. Home: PO Box 5111, Achumani St 12 No 43, La Paz Bolivia Office: FNDR, PO Box 12613, Av 20 De Octubre No 2038, La Paz Bolivia

LOPEZ-CACHERO, MANUEL, economist, educator; b. Madrid, Spain, Mar. 4, 1940; s. Manuel Lopez and Aurora Cachero; m. Cruz Zafra, Dec. 16, 1966; five children. BA, U.C.M., 1964. Dean ICADE, Madrid, 1979-81, CCEE, Madrid, 1981-84, RCU Maria Cristina, Escorial, Spain, 1989-95; prin. U. Alfonso X., Villanueva, Spain, 1995—.

LOPEZ CANIS, FRANCISCO JOSE, association executive; b. Malaga, Spain, Oct. 4, 1938; s. Jose and Felisa (Canis Matute) L.; m. Isabel Lopez-Bago, Dec. 5, 1967; children: Patricia, Reyes, Myriam, Francisco. Student, Faculty of Law, Madrid. Advt. mgr. Colgate Palmolive S.A., Madrid; promotion mgr. Occidente Pub. Co., Madrid; gen. mgr. Dimsa Pub. Co., Madrid; pres. Gourmets Group, Madrid. Editor Club de Gourmets mag., Gourmetabaco mag.; author: Gourmetour and Gourmet Wine of Spain. Mem. Press Assn. Avocations: music, fine arts. Office: Gourmets Group, Claudio Coello 52, 28001 Madrid Spain

LOPEZ-DAVILA, LIANA ESTHER, radiologist; b. San Juan, P.R., July 1, 1963; d. Eliud Lopez-Velez and Yvonne Davila-Chacon; m. Agustin Antonio Rodriguez-Gonzalez, May 1, 1993; children: Agustin Andres, Claudia Sofia. BA, Smith Coll., 1985; MD, U. P.R., San Juan, 1990. Diplomate Am. Bd. Radiology, Nat. Bd. Med. Examiners. Intern in surgery Boston Med. Ctr., 1990-91; radiology resident Beth Israel Med. Ctr., N.Y.C., 1991-94, chief resident in radiology, 1994-95; body imaging fellow Tufts-New Eng. Med. Ctr., Boston, 1995-96; staff radiologist Somascan, Hato Rey, P.R., 1996—. Fellow Radiol. Soc. N.Am.; mem. AMA, Roentgen Ray Soc., Colegio de Medicos-Cirujanos de P.R. Home: 1924 Calle Sauco San Juan PR 00927-6718 Office: Somascan PO Box 364683 San Juan PR 00936-4683

LOPEZ-GOMEZ, JULIAN, mathematician, educator; b. Sacedon, Spain, Sept. 11, 1959; s. Julian López-Orejón and Rosa Gómez-Gónzalez; m. Marcela Molina-Meyer, Dec. 31, 1996; 1 child, Julián López-Molina. BS, Complutense U., 1981. Assoc. prof. U. Complutense, Madrid, Spain, 1986—; assoc. prof. U. Poly. Madrid, 1986; prof. U. Nacional Litoral, Santa Fe, Argentina, 1988, U. Buenos Aires, 1989, U. Zurich, 1994, U. de Bahia Blanca, Argentina, 1998, U. Seville, 1999; rschr. Heriot-Watt U., Edinburgh, Scotland, 1994-95. Author: Estabilidad y bifurcacion de Equilibrios, Aplicaciones y Metodos Numericos, 1988; contbr. articles to profl. jours. Avocations: reading history, arts, walking, hiking. Office: U Complutense de Madrid, Dept Applied Maths, 28040 Madrid Spain

LOPEZ-GUEVARA, CARLOS ALFREDO, lawyer; b. Pocri, Panama, Jan. 7, 1929; s. Santiago Lopez Montenegro and Erundina (Guevara) Lopez; m. Rosa Elena Navarro, Dec. 23, 1954; children: Carlos Alfredo (dec.), Juan Alexis, Pedro Antonio, Alina Del Carmen, Santiago Emilio, Nina Emilia. Degree in law and polit. sci., Panama U., 1954; M of Comparative Law, NYU, 1961; ML, Harvard U., 1957, SJD, 1964. Ptnr. Fábrega, López & Pedreschi, Panama, Panama, 1958-88; prof. law U. Panama, 1964-68; sr. ptnr. Fábrega, López and Barsallo, Panama, 1988-93, Lopez, Lopez and Assoc., Panama, 1994—; min. fgn. affairs Rep. of Panama, 1968-69; spl. amb. for Panama Canal treaty negotiations Govt. Panama, 1971-78, amb. to U.S.A., Can., 1978-80. Author: A Canal Without A Canal Zone. Pres. Labor Party, Panama, 1990-94, Panama-Israel Cultural Inst., 1979-92. Recipient Commendatore award Rep. of Italy, 1975, Harold Weil medal NYU, 1984. Fellow Panama Execs. Orgn., Panama Maritime Law Commn., Rotary. Avocations: ping pong, swimming, theater, opera, classical music. Home: Calle Elida Diaz # E-18, 7 Panama Panama Office: Lopez Lopez and Assoc, PO Box 1754, 9-A Panama Panama

LOPEZ LOZANO, CARLOS, bishop; b. Madrid, May 25, 1962; s. Carlos and Maria Josefa (Lozano) L.; m. Ana Rodriguez Domingo. Degree in history, Autonomous U., Salamanca, 1984; degree in theology, United Evangelical Seminary, Madrid, 1985, Pontifical U., Salamanca, 1991. Acct. Bible Soc. Spain, Madrid, 1987-90; asst. to Bishop Spanish Reformed Episcopal Ch., Madrid, 1990-91; parish rector Spanish Reformed Episcopal Ch., Salamanca, 1991-95, archdeacon, 1992-94, gen. vicar, 1994-95; bishop Spanish Reformed Episcopal Ch., Madrid, 1995—. Author: (books) Intro. to the Psalms, 1987, Study on the Temptations of Christ, 1989, Beginings of Iere, 1991. Home: Beneficencia 18, 28004 Madrid Spain

LOPEZ-MURPHY, RICARDO HIPOLITO, economist; b. Buenos Aires, Aug. 10, 1951; s. Juan Jose Lopez-Aguirre and Brigida Murphy; m. Norma Ruiz Huidobro; children: Pablo, Analia, Ezequiel. MA, U. Chgo., 1980. Prof. U. La. Plata (Argentina), 1975—; cons. IMF, Buenos Aires, 1984-88; chief economist FIEL, Buenos Aires, 1990—; min. of defense Government of Argentina, Buenos Aires, 2000S. Mem. Assn. Argentina Economics. (sec. 1995). Roman Catholic. Office: FIEL, Cordoba 637 Fl 40, 1054 Buenos Aires Argentina*

LOPEZ RODRIGUEZ, NICOLAS DE JESUS CARDINAL, archbishop; b. Barranca, La Vega, Dominican Republic, Oct. 31, 1936; s. Perfecto Ramón López Salcedo and Delia Ramona (Rodríguez) de López. BST, Santo Tomás de Aquino Seminario Pontificio; Licenciatura en Ciencias Sociales, St. Thomas in Urbe Pontifical U., Rome; PhD (honoris causa), Cath. U. Santo Domingo, 1991, Cath. Pontifical U., 1991. Ordained priest Roman Cath. Ch., 1961. Vicario cooperador de la Catedral Diocese of La Vega, 1961-63, canciller, sec. Curia Diocesana, 1966, párroco de la Catedral, 1969, vicario de pastoral, pro-vicario gen., 1970, vicario gen., 1976; bishop Diocese of San Francisco de Macoris, 1978; met. archbishop of Santo Domingo Dominican Republic, 1981; cardinal Roman Cath. Ch., 1991; rector Univ. Nordestana de San Francisco de Macorís, 1979-84. Decorated Orden del Mérito de Duarte, Sánchez y Mella; de la Gran Cruz de Isabel La Católica (Spain). Office: Archbishopric of Santo Domingo, Isabel Le Católica #55, PO Box 186 Santo Domingo Dominican Republic

LÓPEZ-SASTRE, JUAN ANTONIO, chemistry educator, researcher; b. Valladolid, Spain, May 18, 1939; s. Juan López-Anglada and Carmen Sastre-Lago; m. Cristina Romero-Ávila, Sept. 18, 1970; children: Cristina, Enrique-José, Rocío, Juan Antonio. B, La Inmaculada, Valladolid, 1956; lic, U. Valladolid, 1961, DSc, 1967. Asst. prof. U. Valladolid, 1962-65, 68, prof., 1981—; assoc. prof. U. Granada, Spain, 1968-71, 73-81; postdoctoral fellow U. Alta., Edmonton, Can., 1971-73; head of dept. U. Valladolid, 1986-89, 91-95, mem. bd. govs., 1993-95; chem. engr. oil refinery, Tenerife, Canary Islands, 1965; indsl. dir. plastics co., Valladolid, 1966-68; cons., Valladolid, 1986-95. Author: Cereal Straw as an Energetic Alternative for the "Castellano-Leonesa" Region, 1984, Louis Joseph Proust, The Present, The Future, 1990, The Use of the Residues of the Wine Industry in "Castilla y León", 1994, Vegetable Oils as Combustible for Engines, 1995; contbr. articles to profl. jours. Candidate Spanish Senate for C.D.S. Party, Valladolid, 1986, candidate European Parliament, 1987; head pres.'s cabinet in local parliament, Cortes of Castilla y León, Spain, 1989-91. Recipient rsch. award Gajade Ahorros Provincial, Valladolid, 1967; grantee Juan March Found., Spain, 1967; rsch. fellow U. Alta., 1977. Mem. Spanish Chem. Soc., Nat. Chemistry Assn. Roman Catholic. Avocations: swimming, travel, lecturing, music.

LOPEZ TRIACA, RUBEN OSVALDO, stress analysis consultant; b. Buenos Aires, June 7, 1943; s. Antonio Lopez and Ofelia Triaca; m. Maria Iturralde, Mar. 1, 1972; children: Alejandro Ruben, Maria de Los Angeles, Maria Cecilia. Bachiller Nacional, Cap. J.J. Urquiza, Buenos Aires, 1960; Aero. Engr., La Plata U., 1968. Asst. prof. La Plata U., 1967-75; prof. Nat. Technol. U., Buenos Aires, 1974-77, Del Centro U., Olavarria, 1972-77, La Plata U., 1975-77; rschr. Nat. Inst. Indsl. Tech., 1974-77; stress analysis cons. Industria Metalurgicas Pescaramona, Mendoza, ARgentina, 1977-94; dir. Ingenieria u Computacion SA Mendoza, 1982—; gen. mgr. MAC Ingenieria SRL, Mendoza. Fellow Organizacion de Los Estados Americanos; mem. Aero. Engrng. Nat. Coun., Argentine Assn. Computational Mechanics (founder), De Campo Club. Roman Catholic. Avocations: sports, stamp collecting. Home: Necochea 370,, Godoy Cruz 5501,, Mendoza Argentina Office: MAC Ingenieria SRL, Necochea 370, 5501 Godoy Cruz Mendoza Argentina

LOPEZ TRUJILLO, ALFONSO CARDINAL, archbishop; b. Villahermosa, Colombia, Nov. 8, 1935. Ordained priest Roman Catholic Ch., 1960. Instr. maj. sem., Colombia; pastoral coordinator Internat. Eucharistic Congress, Bogota, Colombia, 1968; vicar gen. of Bogota, 1970-72; consecrated bishop of Boseta, 1971; aux. bishop of Bogota, 1971-72; sec.-gen. CELAM, 1972-78, pres., 1979-83; organizer 1979 Puebla Conf.; apptd. coadjutor archbishop of Medellin (Colombia), from 1978; archbishop of Medellin, 1979; elevated to Sacred Coll. of Cardinals, 1983; pres. Bishop's Conf., Pontifical Coun. for the Family. Mem. Social Communications Commn. Latin Am. Address: Piazza S. Calisto 16, 00153 Rome Italy*

LOPOT, FRANTIŠEK, biomedical engineer; b. Červená Voda, Bohemia, Czech Republic, Sept. 30, 1950; s. František and Libuše (Šimku) L.; m. Olga Hladečková, Nov. 6, 1977; children: František, Tereza. Diploma in engring., Czech Tech. U., Prague, 1973, PhD, 1978. Dialysis technician Gen. Univ. Hpsp., Prague, 1973-78, clin. engr., 1978—; lectr. Charles U. Med. Sch., Prague; prin. investigator several dialysis-related rsch. projects. Author: Principles of Dialysis Technology, 1987, 2d edit., 1990; contbr. articles to profl. jours.; editor: Water Treatment, 1988; contbg. author, editor: Urea Kinetic Modelling, 1990. Mem. European Dialysis and Transplant Nurses Assn.-European Renal Care Assn. (Gold medal 1996, pres. 26th conf. 1997, editor jour. 1990-95, com. 1980-82, 84-88, chair tech. group 1998—), Internat. Soc. Blood Purification, Internat. Soc. for Artificial Organs, European Soc. for Artificial Organs, Czech Soc. for Biomed. Engring. (vice chmn. 1998—), Czech Nephrol. Soc. (exec. com. 1999—). Roman Catholic. Avocations: bicycling, farmer house renovation. Fax: 420-2-20513555. E-mail: 106111.2267@compuserve.com and f.lopot@vfn.cz. Office: Gen Univ Hosp Dept Medicine, Šermířská 5 Strahov, 16900 Prague Czech Republc

LOPP, MARGUS, chemist; b. Kuressaare, Saaremaa, Estonia, Sept. 11, 1949; s. Joann and Lembi (Kindlam) L.; m. Annika Mits, Sept. 6, 1972; children: Marge, Nele, Neeme. Diploma in chemistry, Tartu U., Estonia, 1973; PhD, Inst. Chemistry, Estonia, 1981. From rschr. to dir. rsch. Inst. Chemistry, Tallinn, Estonia, 1973-91; prof. chemistry Tallinn Tech. U., 1997—; dept. head Inst. Basic and Applied Chemistry, Tallinn Tech. U., 1992—, dir., 1997—; docent of chemistry U. Helsinki, Finland, 1995—. Patentee in field. ISF grantee, 1994-95; recipient Silver medal Moscow Exbn. Sci. and Tech., Moscow, 1986, Estonian Sci. State award Estonian Acad. Scis., 1987. Mem. Estonian Chem. Soc. (v.p. 1987—). Home: Trummi 32s, 12617 Tallinn Estonia Office: Inst Chemistry, Akadeemia TEE15, 12618 Tallinn Estonia

LOPREATO, JOSEPH, sociology educator, author; b. Stefanaconi, Italy, July 13, 1928; came to U.S., 1951; s. Frank and Marianna (Pavone) L.; m. Carolyn H. Prestopino, July 18, 1954; (div. 1971); children: Gregory F., Marisa S. Schmidt; m. Sally A. Cook, Aug. 24, 1972 (div. 1978). BA in Sociology, U. Conn., 1956; MA in Sociology, Yale U., 1957, PhD in Sociology, 1960. Asst. prof. sociology U. Mass., Amherst, 1960-62; vis. lectr. U. Rome, 1962-64; assoc. prof. U. Conn., Storrs, 1964-66; prof. sociology U. Tex., Austin, 1968—; chmn. dept. sociology U. Tex., 1969-72; vis. prof. U. Catania, Italy, 1974, U. Calabria, Italy, 1980; mem. steering com. Council European Studies, Columbia U., 1977-80; chmn. sociology com. Council for Internat. Exchange of Scholars, 1977-79; mem. Internat. Com. Mezzogiorno, 1986—; Calabria Internat. Com., 1988—. Author: Italian Made Simple, 1959, Vilfredo Pareto, 1965, Peasants No More, 1967, Italian Americans, 1970, Class, Conflict and Mobility, 1972, Social Stratification, 1974, The Sociology of Vilfredo Pareto, 1975, La Stratificazione Sociale negli Stati Uniti, 1945-1975, 1977, Human Nature and Biocultural Evolution, 1984, Evoluzione e Natura Umana, 1990, Mai Più Contadini, 1990, Crisis in Sociology: The Need for Darwin, 1999; contbr. articles to profl. jours. Mem. Nat. Italian-Am. Com. for U.S.A. Bicentennial; mem. exec. com. Congress Italian Politics, 1977-80. Served to cpl. U.S. Army, 1952-54. Fulbright faculty research fellow, 1962-64, 73-74; Social Sci. Research Council faculty research fellow, 1963-64; NSF faculty research fellow, 1965-68; U. Tex. Austin research fellow, 1973-74, spring 1985, spring 1993; Guido Dorso award for U.S.A., Italy, 1992. Mem. AAAS (behavioral sci. rsch. prize com. 1992-94), Internat. Sociol. Assn., European Sociobiolog. Soc., Evolution and Behavior Soc., So. Sociol. Soc. (assoc. editor Am. Sociol. Rev. 1970-72, Social Forces 1987-90, Jour. Polit. and Mil. Sociology 1980—), Internat. Soc. Human Ethology. Catholic-Episcopalian. Home and Office: 1801 Lavaca St Apt 10A Austin TX 78701-1307

LOPUSZANSKI, JAN TADEUSZ, physicist, educator, retired; b. Lwów, Poland, Oct. 21, 1923; s. Wladyslaw Jakób and Janina Maria (Kuzmicz) L.; m. Halina Emilia Pidek, July 14, 1956 (div. 1968); 1 child, Maciej; Barbara Zaslonka, Apr. 14, 1969. MA, U. Wroclaw, Poland, 1950; PhD, Jagellonian U., Cracow, Poland, 1955. From asst. to assoc. prof. U. Wroclaw, 1947-68, full prof., 1968-95; retired, 1995; vice dean math., physics, chemistry faculty U. Wroclaw, 1957-58, dean, 1962-64; vis. prof. U. Utrecht, 1958, NYU, 1960-61, Inst. Advanced Study, Princeton, 1964-65, SUNY, Stony Brook, 1970-71, U. Göttingen, 1984, 91-92; dir. Inst. Theoretical Physics, Wroclaw, 1970-84. Author: Fizyka Statystyczna, 1969, An Introduction to the Conventional Quantum Field Theory, 1976, Rachunek Spinorow, 1985, An Introduction to Symmetry and Supersymmetry in Quantum Field Theory, 1991, The Inverse Variational Problem in Classical Mechanics, 1999; mem. editl. bd. Reports on Mathematical Physics, Progress in Physics; contbr. over 100 articles to profl. jours. Decorated Chevalier Cross Order Polonia Restituta, Officer Cross Order Polonia Restituta. Mem. Polish Acad. Scis. (permanent), Polish Acad. Arts and Scis. in Crackow (corr.), Polish Phys. Soc., Assn. of Mems. of Inst. for Advanced Study Princeton, Internat. Assn. Mathematical Physics, Internat. Union Pure and Applied Physics. Roman Catholic. Office: U Wrocław Inst Theor Physic, Pl Max Born 9, 50204 Wrocław Poland

LORCH, AMNON, lawyer; b. Tel Aviv, Israel, Mar. 29, 1953; s. Netanel and Erika (Frost) L.; m. Deborah Bigio, Apr. 10, 1984; children: Ariel, Shani, Amir. BA, Hebrew U., Jerusalem, 1978. Cert. advocate, 1980. Mgr. YHCA Swimming Pool, Jerusalem, 1976-77; political aid to Bar-Lev The Knesset, Jerusalem, 1977-81; intern Y. Arnon & Co. Law Firm, Jerusalem, 1978-80, lawyer, 1980—, ptnr., 1984—; legal adv. Labor Faction The Knesset; dir. Nat. Oil Corp., Israel, 1988-91, Tahal Consulting Engring. Ltd., Israel, 1989-93; chmn. bd. dirs. Tahal Ltd., Israel, 1993-96, East Jerusalem Devel. Co., 1993-99. Co-author: Lexico For Legal Terms, 1991; judicial commentator: (daily newspaper) Davar, 1990-94. Mem. The Israeli Bar Assn. Mem. Labor Party. Office: Yigal Arnon & Co, Hilel 31 POB 69, 91000 Jerusalem Israel

LORD, JOHN ROBERT (HRH JOHN ROBERT LORD, PRINCE OF JUDAH), computer consultant; b. Vancouver, Wash., Mar. 24, 1954; s. John Gerald (Yakeh IX) and Betty Jane Lord. AA in Mgmt., U. Md., Iwakuni, Japan, 1979; BS in Mgmt., Pepperdine U., 1986. Programmer analyst Hughes Aifcraft Co., Fullerton, Calif., 1981-82, Allergan Pharms., Irvine, Calif., 1982-83; sr. systems analyst Crocker Nat. Bank, Manhattan Beach, Calif., 1983-85; lead systems analyst Transam. Occidental Ins. Co., L.A., 1985-89; ptnr., cons. Constrn. Fin. Svcs.,, West Bloomfield, Mich., 1989-91; owner, cons. Lord Cons., Ocean Park, Wash., 1991—; cons. computer project El Centro Hosp., L.A., 1985. Founder Torch Tape Ministries, Ocean Park, 1974, Trees for L.A. Internat. Airport, 1985, No Graffiti, Playa del Rey, Calif., 1985; congl. candidate Rep. Party, Wash., 1992. Recipient Community award Pres. Ronald Reagan, 1985, Letter of Appreciation, City of L.A., 1986, Vol. award Vols. of L.A., 1985, 86. Baptist. Avocations: shortwave radio, religion, politics, history, genealogy.

LORD, JOHN VERNON, art educator, illustrator; b. Glossop, Eng., Apr. 9, 1939; s. Herbert Vernon and Isabel Marjorie (Smith) L.; m. Lorna Deanna Trevelyan, Oct. 20, 1962; children: Rachel Joanna, Katie Ruhamah, Corin Derry. Dipl. associateship, Salford Sch. Art, Lancashire, Eng., 1960; DLitt, Cen. Sch. Art & Crafts, London, 1961. Freelance illustrator London & Brighton, U.K., 1961-70; lectr. Brighton Coll. Art, Sussex, Eng., 1961-70; sr. prin. lectr., head dept. visual comm. Brighton Polytech., Sussex, 1970-81, 84; prof. illustration U. Brighton, Sussex, 1986-97, head sch. design, 1997—. Author/illustrator: The Giant Jam Sandwich, 1972, The Runaway Roller Skate, 1973, Mr. Mead and His Garden, 1974, Miserable Aunt Bertha, 1979, The Doodles and Diaries of John Vernon Lord, 1986; illustrator: The Nonsense Verse of Edward Lear, 1984 (winner of Redwood Burn award 1985), Aesop's Fables, 1989 (winner of W.H. Smith award 1990), Myths and Legends of the British Isles, 1998. Mem. Soc. Authors. Avocations: music, walking, reading, travel.

LORD, RICHARD DENNIS, photographer; b. Cleve., June 22, 1951; s. James Nelson and Esther (Pollock) L.; m. Patricia L. Michelsen, July 14, 1974 (div. Apr. 1987); children: Tanya, Michele, Arthur. BA, Boston U., 1973, MA, 1975; postgrad., U. Copenhagen, 1974-75. Pres. The Mgmt. Group, N.Y.C., 1987-91; pvt. practice photographer N.Y.C., 1991—; lectr. NYU, N.Y.C., 1989, Seton Hall U., West Orange, N.J., 1989-90, Pace U., White Plains, N.Y., 1990-91; cons. in field, 1986-90. Author: The Management Reports, 1987, The Non Profit Problem Solver, 1989. Trustee City and County Sch., N.Y.C., 1986-88; mem. Hells Kitchen Neighborhood Assn., N.Y.C. Mem. Advt. Photographers of Am., Am. Soc. Media Photographers, United Meth. Assn. Comm., Phi Beta Kappa. Office: 408 W 34th St Apt 2E New York NY 10001-2340

LORD, ROBERT WILDER, retired editor and writer; b. Keene, N.H., May 14, 1917; s. Edward Brown Lord and Alice Maria Buffum; m. Helen Burgess, Aug. 31, 1940 (div. 1965); children: Rowena Lord Soteros, Robert W. Jr., Richard E.B.; m. Barbara Lillian Joanni, June 24, 1967. AB with honors, Middlebury Coll., 1939; MA, NYU, 1964. Chartered Life Underwriter, Am. Coll., Bryn Mawr, Pa., 1944. Writer Prudential Ins. Co. of Am., Newark, 1939-44; editor Flitcraft, Inc., Oak Park, Ill., 1944-48; editor, v.p. Flitcraft A.M. Best Co., N.Y.C., 1948-65; editor, v.p. Communication Channels, N.Y.C., 1966-74; freelance writer N.Y.C., 1974-96; ret., 1996; cons. to ins. orgns.; dir. ins.-connected corps. and ins. co. Author: Running Conventions, Conferences, and Meetings, 1981; former editor 25 books, mags. and newsletters; contbr. numerous articles to ins. publs., newspapers, and mags. Former mem. nominating com. L.I. Sch. Bd.; active in neighborhood orgns. in N.Y.C. to protect environment and preserve landmark status of Greenwich Village area. Mem. Soc. Fin. Svc. Profls., Buffum Family Assn., Wilder Assn., Soc. Mayflower Descendants, Soc. Colonial Wars, Sons of the Revolution (bd. mgrs.), Sons of Union Vets. of the Civil War, Sons Confederate Vets., Navy League of U.S., Masons. Avocations: military history, languages, coins, books, military relics, travel. Home: 61 Jane St Apt 12P New York NY 10014-5138

LORD, ROGER JOHN, immunologist; b. Mt. Isa, Queensland, Australia, Mar. 26, 1966; s. John Russell and Noela Mary (Roberts) L.; m. Jane Fiona Corlis, Sept. 19, 1992. Assoc. Diploma Applied Sci. with distinction, Queensland U. Tech., 1987, B of Applied Sci., 1992; PhD, Dokkyo U., Tokyo, 1996. Chartered biologist. Rsch. asst. Queensland Inst. Med. Rsch., Brisbane, 1986-92; rsch. officer U. Queensland, Brisbane, 1993-96; rsch. fellow U. Wales Coll. Medicine, Cardiff, U.K., 1997-2000; lectr., lab. head, disciple of surgery U. Tasmania, Hobart, Australia, 2000—. Contbr. articles to profl. jours. Br. officer Australian Aid for Ireland, Brisbane, 1990-92. Named Young Queenslander of Yr., State Govt., Brisbane, 1991, Young Achiever award for Sci. and Tech., Dept. Bus., Industry and Regional Devel., 1992; recipient Young Investigator award Sandoz Pharm., Sydney, 1996. Mem. Australian Inst. Biology (credentials com. 1994-95), N.Y. Acad. Scis., Transplantation Soc. Australia & New Zealand, British Soc. for Immunology, Inst. Biology (U.K.). Labor. Methodist. Avocations: photography, reading, travel, entomology, bush walking. Office: Univ Tasmania Head Surgical Rsch Lab, U Tasmania Head Surg Rsch, GPO Box 252-28, Disc of Sur, Hobart TAS 7001, Australia

LORDI, KATHERINE MARY, lawyer; b. Jersey City, N.J., Mar. 24, 1949; d. Peter G. and Hilde E. (Illy) L. AB, Trinity Coll., Washington, 1971; JD, Fordham U., 1975. Bar: N.J. 1975, U.S. Supreme Ct. 1983, U.S. Dist. Ct. N.J. 1975, U.S. Ct. Appeals (3rd cir.) 1989. Clk. Friedman & D'Allessandro, East Orange, N.J., 1974-75; assoc., 1975-76; pvt. practice Bloomfield, N.J., 1976—; adj. instr. Coll. St. Elizabeth, Convent Station, N.J., 1978-86, adj. prof., 1986—; legal adviser Mcpl. Ct. Clks. Assn., 1977-84. Notes editor: Fordham Urban Law Jour., 1974-75. Trustee Cath. Family and Cmty. Svcs, 1980—, v.p., 1986—; mem. adv. bd. Acad. St. Elizabeth, Convent Station, N.J., 1980-84; mem. Essex County Adv. Bd. Status on Women, 1983-92, chmn., 1985-88, co-chair, 1990-92; trustee New Sch. for arts, 1988-89, League for Family Svc. of Bloomfield and Glen Ridge, N.J., 1986—, pres. 1991-94. Fellow Royal Soc. Encouragement of Arts, Mfrs. and Commerce; mem. ABA, N.J. Bar Assn., Essex County Bar Assn., Bloomfield Lawyers Club (pres. 1983-84), Bloomfield C. of C. (trustee 1986-94, v.p. legis. 1990-94). Roman Catholic. Office: 54 Fremont St Bloomfield NJ 07003-3428

LORDOS, CONSTANTINOS GEORGE, diversified group executive, member Parliament of Cyprus; b. Famagusta, Cyprus, Mar. 1, 1940; s. George Demetrios and Andrianie Constance (Pouyouros) L.; m. Marianna G. Constantinides, Jan. 2, 1966; children: George, Andrew, Alexander-Demetrios. BA with honors in Arch., U. London, 1963. Arch. Lordos & Lordos, Famagusta, 1963-66; prodn. dir. G.D. Lordos & Sons, Ltd., Famagusta, 1966-69; mng. dir. Lordos Hotels, Ltd., Famagusta, 1969-74; chmn. Lordos-Hellas, S.A., Athens, 1975-80; also chief exec. Lordos Orgn., Cyprus, Greece, U.K., 1976—; chmn. Lordos Group Ltd., 1983—; dir. 39 pub./pvt. cos.; works include mcpl. bldgs., numerous hotels, large residential complexes; mem. central governing com. Democratic Rally Party, Cyprus, 1976—; mem. Parliament of Cyprus, 1981, 85—. Contbr. articles to newspapers. Mem. Cyprus Employers and Industrialists Fedn. (hon. pres., chmn. 1975), Cyprus Archs. Assn., World Pres.'s Orgn. Greek Orthodox. Achievements include research on prefabrication of buildings. Office: PO Box 24160, 1701 Nicosia Cyprus

LORD ROSENTHAL, SHIRLEY, cosmetics magazine executive, novelist; b. London, Aug. 28; came to U.S., 1971; d. Francis J. and Mabel Florence (Williamson) Stringer; m. Cyril Lord; m. David Anderson; m. A.M. Rosenthal, June 10, 1987; children: Mark, Richard. Matriculation, S.W. Essex Coll., London, 1948. Reporter London Daily Mirror; fiction editor Woman's Own, 1950-53; features editor Good Taste mag., 1953-56; features, fiction editor Woman and Beauty, 1956-59; women's editor Star Evening newspaper, 1959-60, London Evening Standard, 1960-63, London Evening News, 1963-68; beauty editor Harper's Bazaar, London, 1963-71, N.Y.C., 1971-73; beauty, health editor Vogue mag., Condé Nast Publs., N.Y.C., 1973-75; v.p. corp. rels. Helena Rubinstein, N.Y.C., 1975-80; beauty dir. Vogue mag., 1980-94, contbg. editor, 1994—; chairwoman media coun. The Am. Acad. Dermatology, 1995—; corp. v.p. content iBeauty.com, 1999—. Syndicated Field columnist on beauty, health; author 3 beauty books; also novels: Golden Hill, 1982; One of My Very Best Friends, (Lit. Guild Selection), 1985; Faces, 1989; My Sister's Keeper, 1993, The Crasher, 1998. City commr. Craigavon City, No. Ireland, 1963-68. Address: 132 W 36th St New York NY 10018-6903 also: 131 E 66th St New York NY 10021-6129

LORELLI, MICHAEL KEVIN, consumer products and services executive; b. N.Y.C., Apr. 17, 1951; s. Domenic and Effie (Stankevich) L.; m. Judith Bryant; children: Karen, Elizabeth. BE, NYU, 1972, MBA in Mktg., 1973. Dir. mktg. Clairol Co., N.Y.C., 1973-81, v.p., gen. mgr. divsn. Almay cosmetics, 1983-84; v.p., gen. mgr. internat. div. Playtex, Stamford, Conn., 1981-84; v.p. mktg. Apple Computer, Cupertino, Calif., 1984-85; exec. v.p. Pepsi-Cola Co., Somers, N.Y., 1985-88; pres. Pepsi-Cola East, Somers, N.Y., 1989-92, Pizza Hut Internat., 1993-95; pres. America's divsn. Tambrands, Inc., White Plains, N.Y., 1995-96; pres. Bryant Ptnrs. L.L.C., 1997-99; v.p., chief devel. officer Air Express Internat., Darien, Conn., 1999—. Author: (children's book) Traveling Again, Dad?. Bd. dirs. Trident Internat., Inc., Closure Inc., Keep Am. Beautiful, Rosenbluth Travel, Am. Health Found.; trustee Sarah Lawrence Coll., Madison Sq. Boys and Girls Club. Republican. Roman Catholic. Avocations: flying, golf, running.

LOREN, SOPHIA, actress; b. Rome, Sept. 20, 1934; d. Riccardo Scicolone and Romilda Villani; m. Carlo Ponti, Apr. 12, 1967; children: Carlo Ponti, Edoardo. Student, Scuole Magistrali Superiori. Films include E Arrivato l'Accordatore, 1951, Africa sotto i Mari, La Favorita, La Tratta Delle Bianche, 1952, Aida, Tempi Nostri, Ci Troviamo in Gellera, La Domenica Della Buona Genti, Il Paese dei Campanelli, Un Giorno in Pretura, Due Notti con Cleopatra, Pelegrini d'Amore, Attila, Carosello Napoletano, 1953, Miseria e Nobilta, Gold of Naples, Woman of the River, Too Bad She's Bad (Best Actress award Buenos Aires Festival), 1954, Lucky To Be A Woman, Sign of Venus, The Millers Wife, Scandal in Sorrento, 1955, Pride and Passion, Boy on a Dolphin, Legend of The Lost, 1957, Desire Under the Elms, Houseboat, The Key (Best Actress award Japan), 1958, That Kind of Woman, Black Orchid, 1959 (Best Actress Venice Festival, David Di Donatello award Italy, Victoire Popularity award France), Heller in Pink Tights (Best Actress Rapallo Festival Italy), It Started in Naples, A Breath of Scandal, The Millionaires, 1960, Two Women, (11 Best Actress awards including Oscar, Hollywood, Di Donatello award, Cannes Film Festival, N.Y. Critics, Golden Globe, Brit. Film Acad., others from Ireland, Japan, Belgium, Spain, France, W. Ger., also other awards), El Cid, Madame, Bocaccio 70, 1961, The Condemned of Altona, Five Miles to Midnight, 1962, Yesterday, Today and Tomorrow, (Best Actress Di Donatello award, Golden Globe award), 1963, The Fall of the Roman Empire, Marriage Italian Style, 1964 (Best Actress Di Donatello award, Golden Globe award, Alexander Korda award Brit. Film Inst., others), Operation Crossbow, Lady L, Judith, 1965, Arabesque, A Countess From Hong Kong, 1966, Happily Ever After, Ghosts, Italian Style (Best Fgn. Actress Diploma USSR), 1967, More Than A Miracle, (Ramo d'Oro award Italy, other awards), 1968, Sunflower (Best Actress Di Donatello award), 1969, The Priest's Wife, 1970, Lady Liberty, White Sister, 1971, Man of La Mancha, 1972, The Voyage (Di Donatello award), 1973, Brief Encounter, The Verdict, 1974, The Cassandra Crossing, A Special Day, 1977, Firepower, 1978, Brass Target, 1979, Blood Feud, 1981, Grumpier Old Men, 1995, Messages, 1996, Soleil, 1997, Destinazione Verna, 1999; TV film appearances include Sophia Loren: Her Own Story, 1980, Angela, 1982, Aurora, 1985, Mother Courage, 1986, The Fortunate Pilgrim (Best Actress of Yr. for TV mini-series), 1987, La Ciociara, 1989, Ready to Wear (Prêt-à-Porter), 1994. Recipient numerous awards including Nastro d'Argento, Italy, 14 Bambi and Bravo Popularity awards, Fed. Republic Germany, 3 Prix Uilenspigoel Fiamingo award, Belgium, Popularity awards Am. Legion, Tex. Cinema Exhibitors, 4 Snosiki Popularity awards, Finland, 2 Best Actress awards Bengal Film Journalists Assn., India, Box-Office Favourite Medal, Italy, Helene Curtis award, U.S.A., Simpatia Popularity award, Italy, Rudolph Valentino Screen Svcs. award, Italy, Best Actress award Moscow Film Festival, Hon. Acad. award, 1990; named Most Popular Actress in Italy. Address: c/o La Concordia Ranch 1151 Hidden Valley Ranch Rd Thousand Oaks CA 91361

LORENÇO, SERGIO OLIVEIRA, biology educator; b. Rio de Janeiro, Apr. 27, 1970; s. Florencio and Iracema (Oliveira) L. BS, U. Fed. Rural Rio de Janeiro, 1991; PhD, U. São Paulo, Brazil, 1996. Rschr. U. Fed. Rio de Janeiro, Rio de Janeiro, 1997-98; prof., rschr. UFF, Niterói, Brazil, 1998—; referee FACEPE, Recife, Brazil, 1999—, CNPq, Brasilia, Brazil, 1997—. Contbr. articles to profl. jours. Avocations: poetry, soccer, reading about culture, history and geography. Office: UFF Dept Biologia Marinha, Caxia Postal 100466, 24001970 Niterói RJ, Brazil

LORENSON, ROBERT LAWRENCE, sculptor, art educator; b. Cedar Falls, Iowa, July 9, 1969; s. David Lawrence and Lois (Johnson) L. BFA, U. No. Iowa, 1991; MFA, No. Ill. U., 1994. Prof. art Loyola U., Chgo., 1994-96, Harper Coll., Palatine, Ill., 1996-97, No. Ill. U., DeKalb, 1997-99, Bridgewater (Mass.) State Coll., 1999—; bd. dirs. Sarasota (Fla.) Season of Sculpture, 1998-99. E-mail: rlorenson@bridgew.edu. Office: Bridgewater State Coll Art Dept School And Summer Sts Bridgewater MA 02325-0001

LORENTE, MIGUEL, theoretical physics educator; b. Madrid, Mar. 29, 1931; s. Jose Maria Lorente and Teresa Paramo. Philosophy lic., U. Comillas, Madrid, 1956; physics licenciate, U. Complutense, Madrid, 1961, D in Physics, 1971; theology lic., U. Deusto, Bilbao, Spain, 1965; M in Physics, St. Louis U., 1968. Ordained Roman Cath. priest Soc. of Jesus., 1964. Prof. interino U. Complutense, Madrid, 1968-78, prof. titular, 1978-87; catedrático U. Oviedo, Spain, 1987—; prof. adjunto U. Comillas, Madrid, 1968-77, prof. agregado, 1977—; vis. rschr. Boston U., 1972-74; vis. prof. So. Ill. U., Carbondale, 1983, 85, 86, Tech. U., Clausthal, Germany, 1987-92, U. Tübingen, Germany, 1993-99. Contbr. articles to profl. jours. Mem. Am. Phys. Soc., Real Sociedad Española De Fisica y Quimica, Assn. Interdisciplinar Jose de Acosta. Avocations: playing piano and organ, musical accoustics, hiking, playing chess. Home: C/ Doctor Casal 9, E-33001 Oviedo Asturias, Spain Office: U Oviedo Dept Fisica, Ave Calvo Sotelo 18, E-33007 Oviedo Asturias, Spain

LORENTE HERRERA, JUAN B., publishing executive; b. Jeres Marquesado, Granada, Spain, Oct. 11, 1960; s. Antonio Lorente Lorente and Encarnación Herrera Morales. Bachelor's, INUP, Barcelona, Spain, 1994; MBA, Pacific Western U., L.A., 1990. Dir. telemarketing Ediciones Atrium, Barcelona, 1980-92; product mgr. Editorial Marin, Barcelona, 1992-93; editor, product mgr. Idea Books, Barcelona, 1993—; publisher Libr. Agrl, Idea Wood, other titles Idea Books, 1998—; ptnr., pres. pub. group Mr. Jorge Fernandez Pardo. Mem., collaborator Ayuda en Accion, Barcelona, 1992. With Spanish Army, 1980-82. Avocations: handcrafts, sports, nature. Office: Idea Books SA, Rosellón 186 lo 4a, 08008 Barcelona Spain

LORENTZEN, FRIDTJOF, water transportation executive; b. Oslo, Dec. 10, 1929; s. Frithjov Hunter and Else (Bache) L.; m. Karin Holmboe Stenersen, Oct. 20, 1962; children: Lorentzen, Fridtjof Henrik, Else Victoria, Karin Caroline. BA, Harvard U., Cambridge, Mass., 1952, MBA, 1954. Mgr. F.H. Lorentzen A/S, Oslo, 1957-62, joint CEO, 1962-87, CEO, 1987—; vice chmn. A/S Rosshavet, Sandefjord, Norway, 1987-91, also bd. mem.; chmn. Ross Offshore, Oslo, 1991-92; vice-chmn. Transocean Drilling, Tananger, Norway, 1994-96; bd. dirs. Transocean Offshore Inc., Houston, 1996-2000. Bd. dirs. Norwegian Export Coun., Oslo, 1981-83; vice-chmn. Opera Fund, Oslo, 1989-97. Named Comdr. Lion Order of Finland, 1989, 3d Grade Order of Sacred Treasure, Japan, 1992. Mem. Baltic and Internat. Maritime Coun. (pres. 1995-97), No. Def. Club (chmn. 1983-97), Norwegian Shipowners' Assn. (pres. 1980-81), The Norwegian Veritas (coun. 1993—), Internat. Shipping Fedn. (v.p. 1979-80), Intertanko (coun. 1985-99), Japan-Norway Soc. (pres. 1985-2000), Unitas Mut. Ins. Club (chmn. coun. 1989-97).

LORENZ, ALBERT, illustrator, educator; b. N.Y.C., Dec. 9, 1941; s. Albert Carl and Josephine (Thomas) L.; m. Maureen McCartney, Oct. 17, 1965; children: Margaret, Kirsten. BArch, Pratt Inst., 1965; MArch, Columbia U., 1969; postgrad., Princeton U., 1971. Prin. Albert Lorenz Studio, Floral Park, N.Y., 1969—; mem. faculty Pratt Inst., Bklyn., 1972—, mem. faculty continuing edn., 1978-80, coord. media, 1980—, disting. prof., 1989-90; lectr. Tuskegee Inst., 1972, U. of South, 1972, Auburn U., 1972, U. La., 1972, U. Ala., 1973, Tulane U., 1973, N.Y. Inst. Tech., 1985-86. Author, illustrator: Illustrating Architecture, 1985, Architectural Illustration Inside and Out, 1988, Drawing In Color, 1991, Trace, 1993, Metropolis, 1996, Metropolis, 1996 (Prix Nautile de Cristal 1996), House, 1998 (Vernacular Arch award 1999), Buried Blueprints, 2000; illustrator: ABC to ZOGG, 1977, The Dictionary of American English, 1983, The Terra Beyond, 1984, The Bible for Students, 1988; exhbns. include Mus. Modern Art, 1974, Nat. Gallery Art, 1975, Pratt Inst., 1977, Soc. Typographic Arts 100, 1980, Art Dirs.' Show, 1985, 91, N.Y. Soc. Renderers, 1987, Soc. Illustrators, 1987, 90, 91, Illustrators Art Show, 1990; work included in numerous books, jours. and mags. Recipient Design award Progressive Arch., 1973, Outstanding Illustration award Soc. Publ. Designers, 1976, award Chgo. Pub.'s Guild, 1976, ANDY award Merit Advt. Club N.Y., 1980, Exceptional Achievement award PRINT, 1981, award of Excellence Comm. Arts Mag., 1985, DESI award Graphic Design USA, 1985, 1st Pl. award Nat. Newspaper of Admissions Mktg., 1991, Gold medal Soc. Illustrators of L.A., 1995, 96; Kinne Traveling fellow Columbia U., 1969. Mem. AIGA (cert. excellence 1978-83), Assn. Collegiate Schs. Arch., Nat. Inst. Archtl. Edn., Soc. Illustrators (edn. com. 1990-91, cert. merit 1982, 90, 91, lectr. 1988, silver medal 1993), Soc. Illustrators N.Y. (pres. 1999—, gold medal 1996). Roman Catholic. Avocations: golf, tennis. Home and Studio: 49 Pine Ave Floral Park NY 11001-2318

LORENZ, JOHN DOUGLAS, college official; b. Talmage, Nebr., July 2, 1942; s. Orville George and Twila Lucille (Larson) L.; m. Alice Louise Hentzen, Aug. 26, 1967; 1 child, Christian Douglas. BS, U. Nebr., 1965, MS, 1967, PhD, 1973. Systems analyst U. Nebr., Lincoln, 1967-73; asst. prof. Kettering U., Flint, Mich., 1973-74, assoc. prof., 1974-78; prof. GMI Engrng. and Mgmt. Inst., Flint, Mich., 1978—, dept. head, 1984-87, asst. dean, 1986-88, provost, dean faculty, 1988-92, Richard L. Terrell prof. acad. leadership, 1990—, v.p. for acad. affairs, provost, 1992—; cons. GM, Detroit, 1973-82, various orgns. Contbr. articles to profl. jours. Judge Internat. Sci. and Engring. Fair, various locations, 1989—. Mem. NSPE, Soc. Mfg. Engrs. (sr.), So. Automotive Engrs., Accreditation Bd. for Engring. and Tech., Am. Soc. Engring. Edn., Antique Auto Racing Assn., Model Engine Collectors Assn., Antique Model Race Car Club. Home: 8165 Shady Brook Ln Flushing MI 48433-3007 Office: Kettering U 1700 W 3rd Ave Flint MI 48504-4898

LORENZ, PASCAL P., electrical engineer; b. Thionville, France, July 23, 1965; s. Alfred W. and Josephine M. (Wechtler) L. MA, U. Nancy, France, 1990, PhD, 1994. Rschr. WORLDFIP, Nancy, France, 1990-94; rschr., engr. ALCATEL, Paris, 1994-95; lectr. U. Haute Alsace, Colmar, France, 1995—. Contbr. articles to profl. jours. Mem. IEEE, ACM. Office: U Haute Alsace, 34 Rue du Grillenbreit, 68008 Colmar France

LORENZEN, LEENDERT, chemical engineer, educator, consultant; b. Virginia, Free State, South Africa, Nov. 11, 1960; s. Jan Frederik George and Maria Jacoba (Buytendach) L.; m. Lynn Rust, July 7, 1984; children: George, Ninette. B in Engring., U. Stellenbosch, South Africa, 1982, M in Engring., 1985, PhD in Engring., 1993; exec. devel. program, Bus. Sch. U. Stellenbosch, South Africa, 1999. Registered profl. engr. Engring. Coun. South Africa; registered chartered engr. British Engring. Coun. Rsch. metallurgist Anglo Am., South Africa, 1984-86, sr. rsch. metallurgist, 1986-87, plant production supt., 1987-88; sr. engr. Somchem, South Africa, 1988-90; sr. lectr., assoc. prof. U. Stellenbosch, South Africa, 1990-95, prof., dept. head, 1995—; rsch. fellow U. Melbourne, Australia, 1997; dir. Ctr. Process Engring. U. Stellenbosch, 1999—; cons. various internat. mining houses and chem. industries, 1992—, Anglo Am., 1990—, De Beers, 1992—, Techpros, 1998—. Contbr. over 40 articles to profl., internat. jours.; presented 53 papers at internat. confs., 35 at nat. confs.; prepared 22 reports for cons.; completed 30 acad. thesis; patentee: for diagnostic and jet leaching methods. Chmn. fin. com. Civic Soc., Somerset, South Africa. Fellow Inst. for Chem. Engrs. (Brit.), South Africa Inst. for Mining and Metallurgy, South African Inst. Chem. Engring.; mem. Inst. for Waste Mgmt., South African Soc. for Enology & Viticulture. Avocations: sports, coin collecting. Home: 2 Muscadelle St, Western Cape Somerset West 7130, South Africa Office: U Stellenbosch Chem Engr, Pvt Bag XI Matieland, Stellenbosch West Cape 7602, South Africa

LORENZO, HORACIO DANIEL, pharmaceutical industry executive; b. Buenos Aires, Mar. 9, 1956; s. Angel and Josefa (Saragó) L.; m. Alicia Monica Barcia, July 7, 1983; children: Maria Laura, Pablo Daniel. BS, LaSalle U., Buenos Aires, 1973; MD, Sch. of Medicine, Buenos Aires, 1981. Staff physician ID Hosp. F.J. Muniz, Buenos Aires, 1981-91; resident in infectious diseases Sch. of Medicine, Buenos Aires, 1981-84; cons. in infectious diseases Sanatorio Alberti, Buenos Aires, 1985-92; internal medicine head Clinica Vulcano, Buenos Aires, 1991-93; intensive care unit head Clinica Gimenez, Buenos Aires, 1987-91; med. advisor Bayer Labs., Buenos Aires, 1991-92; clin. rsch. dir. Pfizer Labs., Buenos Aires, 1993-96, team leader in antiinfectious diseases, 1996-98; med. dir. Pharmacia & Upjohn, Buenos Aires, 1998—; hon. faculty I.D. Sch. Medicine, buenos Aires, 1984-86. Contbr. articles to profl. jours. Mem. AAAS, Am. Soc. Microbiology, L.Am. Soc. Pediat. Infectology, Internat. Soc. for Interferon Rsch. Avocations: aerobics, soccer, reading, walking, computers. Home: Gorosito 1246, 1661 Bella Vista Buenos A, Argentina

LORENZO, JUAN C., pathologist; b. Barcelona, Sept. 4, 1943; s. Tomas F. Lorenzo and Natividad M. Roldan; 1 child, Tomas. BA, U. Barcelona, 1959, MD, 1965. Diplomate Am. Bd. Anatomic pathology. Chief of surg. pathology Barcelona Hosp., 1976—; prof. U. Barcelona Sch. Medicine, 1993—. Mem. IAP, ISS, SEAP. Office: ICH, Ave Hosp Miletar 151, 08023 Barcelona Spain

LORENZO, NICHOLAS FRANCIS, JR., lawyer; b. Norfolk, Va., Nov. 22, 1942; s. Nicholas and Jean W. L.; m. Patricia C. Connare, Sept. 7, 1968; children: Nicholas Michael, Matthew Christopher. BA, St. Francis Coll., 1964; JD, Duquesne U., 1968. Bar: Pa. 1968, U.S. Dist. Ct. (we. dist.) Pa. 1969, (mid. dist.) Pa. 1977, U.S. Ct. Appeals (3d cir.) 1983, U.S. Supreme Ct. 1976. Pres. Lorenzo and Lundy, PC, Punxsutawney, Pa., 1979-81; pvt. practice Punxsutawney, 1981-90; prin. Lorenzo and Gianvito PC, Punxsutawney, 1990-98, ptnr., 1999—; instr. Sch. Continuing Edn., Pa. State U., 1969-73. Bd. dirs. Punxsutawney Area Hosp., 1972-74; mem. parish coun. S.S.C.D. Roman Cath. Ch., 1978-84, pres., 1979-84; bd. dirs. dist. coun. Boy Scouts Am., 1982-84. Mem. ABA, ATLA, Nat. Bd. Trial Advocacy (civil cert.), Pa. Bar Assn., Pa. Bar Inst. (bd. dirs. 1988-94), Pa. Trial Lawyers Assn. (bd. govs.), West Pa. Trial Lawyers Assn., Jefferson County Bar Assn. (v.p. 1980-82, pres. 1982-84), Punxsutawney Country Club, KC, Elks, Eagles, Rotary (pres. Punxsutawney 1973). Home: 180 Monticello Dr Punxsutawney PA 15767-2614 Office: 410 W Mahoning St Punxsutawney PA 15767-1908

LORENZO FRANCO, JOSÉ RAMÓN, Mexican government official; b. Apizaco, Tlaxcala, Mexico, Jan. 2, 1935. Student, Naval Staff Sch., Mexico, Navy War Coll., U.S. Joined Mexican Navy, 1952, adj., chief tech. dept. naval edn., chief of staff naval zone, dir. gen. Ctr. of Navy Capacities, dir. Ctr. for Higher Naval Studies, comdr. of Naval Region, insp., comptr. gen.; Sec. of the Navy Govt. of Mexico, 1995—. *

LORHO, CHRISTIAN KORDJO, technician engineer; b. Penyi, Volta, Ghana, July 20, 1954; s. Atsu Moses and Ama (Ahiabli) L.; m. Faustine Lagoh, June 13, 1987; children: Worlanyo, Sitsofe. Artisan Electricity Corp., Accra, Ghana, 1981-84; technician trainee Electricity Corp., Accra, 1984-85, technician engr., 1985-87; craft instr. Electricity Corp., Tema, Ghana, 1987-95; acting tech. instr. Electricity Corp., Tema, 1995-96, tech. instr., 1996—; maintenance officer Electricity Corp., Accra, 1984-87, trainer, Tema, 1987—. Sec. Church, Accra, 1987-91; fin. sec. Penyi Benevolent Soc., Accra, 1987—. Mem. Ghana Instn. Technician Engrs. Mem. African Episcopal Methodist Zion Church. Avocations: indoor games, watching television, reading novels. Office: Electricity Corp Tng Sch, PO Box CO2090, Tema Ghana

LORIA, ANTONIO, scientist, consultant; b. Mexico City, Nov. 19, 1969; s. Antonio Loria-Melo and Margarita (Perez-Herrasti) Perez-Loria; m. Elena V. Panteley. BSc in Engring., Inst. Tech. Estudios Superiore, Monterrey, Mexico, 1991; MSc, U. Tech. Compiegne, France, 1993, PhD, 1996. Asst. rschr. U. Twente, Enschede, The Netherlands, 1997; assoc. rschr. Norwegian U. Sci. and Tech., Trondheim, Norway, 1997, U. Calif., Santa Barbara, 1998; permanent asst. rschr. Ctrl. Nat. de la Recherche Scientifique, Grenoble, France, 1999—; cons. Grupo Indsl. Bimbo, Mexico City, 1991—; lectr. Norwegian U. Sci. and Tech., Trondheim, 1997, U. Calif., Santa Barbara, 1998. Author: Passivity Based Control of El Systems, 1998. Mem. IEEE. Achievements include co-author of laser meter. Avocations: photography, history of science, humor. Office: LAG-ENSIEG, BP 46, 38402 St Martin d Heres France

LORIMER, CLARK D., small business owner; b. Williamsport, Pa., Feb. 27, 1947; s. Clark and D. Jean Lorimer; children: Craig A., Duane C. Owner AGS Electrical, Williamsport, Muncy, Pa., 1968—. With USNR, 1965-68. Mem. NRA (life). Avocations: fishing, boating, hunting.

LORIMER, SIR DESMOND, retired chartered accountant; b. Belfast, Ireland, Oct. 20, 1925; s. Thomas Berry and Sarah (Robinson) L.; m. Patricia Doris Samways, Mar. 12, 1957; 2 daus. DSc, U. Ulster, 1987, Queens U., Belfast, 1993. Sr. ptnr. Harmood Banner Smylie & Co., Belfast, 1960-74; chmn. No. Ireland Electricity, Belfast, 1991-94, Lamont Holdings, Belfast, 1973-96, No. Bank Ltd., Belfast, 1986-97, Old Bushmills Distillery Co. Ltd., Belfast, 1986-98; dir. Irish Distillers Group PLC, Belfast, 1986-98. Avocations: golf, gardening. Home: 6A Circular Rd W Cultra, Hollywood BT18 0AT, Northern Ireland Office: Purdys Lande, Newtownbreda, Belfast BT8 7AR, Northern Ireland

LÖRINCZE, PETER L., economist; b. Budapest, Hungary, Feb. 9, 1948; s. Lajos and Erzsebet (Vehovszky-Emerich) L.; m. Katalin Kovacs, May 13, 1989; 1 child, Tamas. MBA, U. Econs., Budapest, 1970. Desk offier Min. Fin., Budapest, 1970-71, C. of C., Budapest, 1971-74; economist GM, N.Y.C., 1974-75; dep. dir. Gen. Min. Fgn. Trade, 1975-81; sec. gen. Hungarian C. of C., 1981-89; chief comm. counsellor Rome, 1989-92; dir. cons. Deloitte & Touche, Budapest, 1992-95, mng. ptnr., 1995-99; bd. mem., zone leader Deloitte & Touche Ctrl. Europe, Budapest, 1999-2000, zone chmn., regional aid program coord., pub. sector industry program leader, 2000—. Recipient award Labour Presdl. Coun., 1985. Avocations: tennis, cross-country, skiing, collecting rare books. Office: Deloitte & Touche Ctrl Europe, Nador 21, 1051 Budapest Hungary

LORING, RICHARD WILLIAM, psychotherapist; b. Bronx, N.Y., May 26, 1928; s. William Maurice and Jeannette Edith (Bass) L.; B.A., DePauw U., 1952; M.A., Ind. U., 1954; Ph.D., Columbia Pacific U., 1982; m. Janet Teetor, Aug. 22, 1953; children—Steven, David, Lynne. Psychiat. social worker Richmond (Ind.) State Hosp., 1954-56; asst. dir. Tippecanoe County Mental Health Center, Lafayette, Ind., 1956-62; exec. dir. Venango County Mental Health Center, Oil City, Pa., 1962-71; adminstr. Mental Health/Mental Retardation Authorities, Oil City, 1970-71; dir. Venango Human Services Center, Franklin, Pa., 1971-75; clin. program dir., dir. consultation and edn. Erie County Mental Health Dept.; pvt. practice psychotherapy, Oil City, 1976—; mem. staff dept. psychiatry Oil City Hosp., sr. psychotherapist Vets. Adminstrn. Vietnam Vets. Outreach Program, 1986—; part-time prof. sociology DePauw U., 1956-62; part-time prof. psychology Pa. State U., 1968-69; field prof. U. Pitts., 1969-74; prof. sociology Clarion State Coll., part-time, 1972-73; part-time prof. mental health counseling Gannon Coll., 1975, clin. advisor Physician Asst. Preceptorship, 1986-95; spl. cons. Corps Chaplains, U.S. Army, 1971-75; mem. profl. adv. com. Crippled Children and Adults Com., 1971-75; mem. profl. adv. com. Clarion State Coll. Sch. Nursing, 1981-94 . Bd. dirs. Pa. Mental Health Assn., 1969-77, mem. exec. com., 1973-77; del., mem. task force White House Conf. on Aging, 1971; del. Nat. Conf. on Mental Health, 1975; bd. dirs. Franklin Light Opera Co., 1970-74; chmn. project rev. com. Venango Regional Comprehensive Health Planning, 1973-75; chmn. Gt. Lakes Forum on Primary Prevention in Mental Health, 1976; chmn. N.W. Pa. Family Planning Council, 1974; mem. N.W. region steering com. Pub. Com. for Humanities in Pa., 1971-74. Served with AUS, World War II. Named Boss of Yr., Ft. Venango chpt. Nat. Secs. Assn., 1972. Fellow Am. Assn. Social Psychiatry; mem. ACA, Psychiat. Outpatient Centers Am. (exec. sec. 1966-74), Am. Pub. Health Assn., Am. Assn. Mental Health Counseling, Am. Coll. Clinic Adminstrs. Editor: Selected Papers of Psychiatric Outpatient Centers, 1967; Psychiatric Outpatient Centers and Low Income Populations, 1968. Home: 406 W 7th St Oil City PA 16301-3040 Office: Venango Int Med Assocs U Pitts Med Ctr 1 Memorial Dr Oil City PA 16301-1341

LORITO, MATTEO, biology educator; b. Salerno, Campania, Italy, Mar. 8, 1961; s. Paolo and Annamaria (Aievoli) L.; m. Sheridan Lois Woo, Mar. 10, 1994. PhD, U. Siena, Italy, 1988. Rsch. asst. U. Siena, 1988-89; rsch. fellow U. Naples, Italy, 1989-90, asst. prof., 1994—; rsch. fellow Cornell U., Geneva, N.Y., 1990-93; cons. Bioworks Inc., Geneva, 1994—; rsch. fellow Nat. Coun. Rsch., Italy, 1995—. Author: Triehoderma e Gliocladium, 1998; patentee in field; contbr. articles to profl. jours. Rep. U. Naples, 1995-98. Recipient CNR fellowship Nat. Coun. Rsch., Rome, 1991, fellowship Orgn. Econ. Coop. and Devel., Brussels, 1995, Fulbright fellowship, 1997. Mem. Am. Phytopath. Soc., MPMI Internat. Orgn., Italian Phytopath. Soc. Avocations: tennis, windsuring, computing, travel. Office: U Naples, Viale Universita 100, 80055 Portel Naples, Italy

LORSCHEIDER, ALOISIO CARDINAL, archbishop; b. Linha Geraldo, Brazil, Oct. 8, 1924. Joined Franciscan Order, Roman Cath. Ch., 1942; ordained priest, 1948; prof. theology The Antonianum, Rome; dir. Franciscan Internat. House of Studies; consecrated bishop of Santo Angelo (Brazil), 1962; archbishop of Fortaleza (Brazil), 1973—, Aparecida, 1995; elevated to Sacred Coll. of Cardinals, 1976; pres. Latin Am. Bishops Conf., 1975; gen. sec. Brazilian Bishops Conf., 1968-71, pres., 1971-79. Address: Curia Metropolitana, CP 05 Torre da Basilica 48, 125700 Aparecida SP, Brazil*

LOS, CORNELIS ALBERTUS, economist, portfolio risk manager, educator; b. Purmerend, The Netherlands, Dec. 14, 1951; arrived in U.S., 1977; s. Klaas and Adriaantje (Nieuwland) L.; m. Diane Nichols, June 10, 1979 (div. 1984); 1 child, Francesca R.E.; m. Elizabeth M. Ten Houten, June 18, 1986 (div. 1991); 1 child, Marguerita E.A.; m. Rose Lee Haubenstock, May 5, 1994. Candidatus cum laude (fellow), U. Groningen, 1974, Doctorandus, 1976; rsch. student London Sch. Econs., Sch., Slavonic & E. European Studies, 1975-76; diploma, Inst. Social Studies, The Hague, 1977; MPhil, Columbia U., 1980, PhD, 1984. Tchg. asst. Columbia U., N.Y.C., 1978-80, preceptor, 1979, instr., 1980-81; economist Fed. Res. Bank of N.Y., N.Y.C., 1981-85, sr. economist, 1985-87; sr. economist Nomura Rsch. Inst. Inc., 1987-90; chief U.S. economist NMB Postbank Group/ING Bank/ING Capital, N.Y.C., 1991-93; assoc. prof. banking and fin. Nanyang Tech. U., Singapore, 1995-99; assoc. prof. fin. U. Adelaide, Australia, 2000—; adj. lectr. Hunter Coll., N.Y.C., 1980, CCNY, 1980-81; adj. prof. Baruch coll., N.Y.C., 1985-86; rsch. assoc. ctr. for Math. Sys. Theory, U. Fla., Gainesville, 1986-92; pres. EMEPS Assocs. Inc., 1986—; lectr. numerous profl. confs., U.S. and fgn. countries; cons. Worldbank, 1994—, Inter-Am. Devel. Bank, 1994—, Asian Devel. Bank, 1996—. Contbr. articles to profl. jours. including Jour. Banking & Finance, Jour. Multinat. Fin. Mgmt., Jour. of Am. Stats. Assn., Jour. Bus. and Econ. Stats., The Am. Statistician, Ea. Econ. Jour., Computers & Math. with Applications, Jour. Performance Measurement, Asian Asset Mgmt. Bd. dirs. The Netherland-Am. Found., Inc., 1991-95; mem. acad. bd. Nanyang Tech. U., 1997-2000. Recipient lady Van Renswoude of The Hague Found. awards, 1974-75; MAOC Countess Van Bylandt Found. award, 1976; Scholten Cordès Found. awards, 1976-77; Fulbright-Hays scholar, 1977. Fellow Am. Coll. Forensic Examiners (life), London Goodenough Trust; mem. Australasian Inst. Banking and Fin. (sr. assocs. 1999—), AIMR, IEEE, Math. Assn. Am., The Econometric Soc., Internat. Assn. Fin. Engrs., Internat. Assn. for Math. and Computer Modeling, Am. Statis. Assn., Am. Econ. Assn., Am. Fin. Assn., Am. Math. Soc., N.Y. Acad. Sci., Singapore Soc. Fin. Analysts, Grad. Faculties Alumni Columbia U., Nanyang Bus. Sch. Alumni Assn., Internat. House (N.Y.C.) (world sponsor), Nat. Econ. Club, Columbia Univ. club (Singapore) (found. treas.). Avocations: Russian and Chinese literature, Central Asian history, yoga, jogging, hiking, photography. Home: 12A Flemington St, Adelaide SA 5063, Australia Office: Adelaide Univ Sch Econs, Napier Bldg G56, Adelaide SA 5005, Australia

LOS, MAREK JAN, scientist, physician; b. Tarnow, Poland, May 23, 1965; s. Kazimierz and Kazimiera (Wrona) L.; m. Wioletta Mikos, June 18, 1972; 1 child, Anetta Daria. MB, U. Krakow, Poland, 1991; MD, U. Heidelberg, Germany, 1995. Scientist U. Freiburg, Germany, 1994, German Cancer Rsch. Ctr., Heidelberg, 1995-97; project leader U. Tuebingen, Germany, 1997-99, U. Muenster, Germany, 1999—; cons. Current Drugs Ltd., London, 1998—; med. mktg. advisor Enzyme Systems Products, Dublin, Calif., 1998—; diagnostic products cons. Evotec, Hamburg, Germany, 1998.

Author: (chpt.) Natural Killer Cell Protocols, 2000; contbr. articles to profl. jours.; patentee in field. Recipient Rsch. grant Bio-Regio, 1997-99, SFB U. Tuebingen rsch. grant, 1999—. Mem. Am. Assn. Cancer Rsch., Polish Med. Assn. Germany. Avocations: cycling, canoe tours, Ju-Do, cross-country skiing. Office: Univ Muenster, Roentgenstr 21, D-48149 Muenster Germany

LOSADA-PAISEY, GLORIA, psychologist; b. Havana, Cuba, Apr. 20, 1957; came to U.S., 1962; d. Manuel Benito and Maria del Pilar (Fernandez) Losada; m. Timothy John Henry Paisey, June 4, 1983 (div. June 1989); 1 child, Monica Paisey. BA, Fla. Internat. U., 1980; D Psychology, Nova U., 1984. Lic. psychologist, Conn. Pre-doctoral psychology fellow Yale U., New Haven, 1983-84; clin. psychologist State of Conn. Dept. Mental Retardation Southbury Tng. Sch., Southbury, Conn., 1984-86, State of Conn. Dept. Mental Retardation New Haven Ctr., New Haven, 1986-88; dir. psychol. svcs. State of Conn. Dept. Mental Retardation Region 6, Waterford, Conn., 1988-92; clin. psychologist Conn. Dept. Children and Youth Svcs., Middletown, Conn., 1992-97, State of Conn. Dept. of Mental Health and Addiction Svcs., Middletown, 1997—; pvt. practice psychology, Waterbury, 1986—; dir. treatment program for mentally retarded offenders Southbury Tng. Sch., State of Conn., 1984-86. Mem. APA. Democrat. Roman Catholic. Avocations: ballet, classical music, jazz, contemporary dance. Office: 1389 W Main St Ste 106 Waterbury CT 06708-3115

LOSANO, GIANNI ALBERTO, cardiovascular physiologist, educator; b. Pinerolo, Piedmont, Italy, July 25, 1934; s. Angelo and Teresa (Pesando) L.; m. Maria Paola Pazé, July 29, 1967; children: Nicoletta, Roberta, Francesca. MD, U. Torino, Italy, 1959. vis. prof., dean Med. Coll. U. Liberia, Monrovia, 1969-71. Resident internal medicine U. Torino, 1964, resident cardiology, 1966, asst. prof, 1963-69, assoc. prof, 1969-73, prof. physiology, 1973—, head dept. human anat. physiology, 1993-95; vis. prof. U. Liberia, Monrovia, 1969-71; pres. sci. and technol. archive U. Torino. Author: (with F. Francini) Fisiologia dell 'Uomo, 1985, 2d edit., 1993, Come funziona il Cuore, 1987, (with M. Marzilli and M. Ferrari) Il Circolo Coronarico, 1997; assoc. editor Jour. Biol. Rsch., 1994—; contbr. articles to profl. jours. Mem. City Coun., Pinerolo, 1975-85, 96-98; active Democratic Party of the Left. 1st lt. Italian Army Health Svc., 1960-61. WHO fellow, Geneva, 1977; recipient Study Visit award Royal Soc. London, 1991, Pinarolium prize Assn. Pro Pinerolo, 1995. Mem. AAAS, Italian Soc. Exptl. Biology (pres. 1991-95), Italian Soc. Physiology, Italian Soc. Human Nutrition, Physiol. Soc. London, Internat. Soc. Toxinology, Italian Soc. for Cardiovascular Rsch. (v.p. 1996—), European Biomed. Rsch. Assn., N.Y. Acad. Scis., Acad. Med. Torino, Assn. Riva-Rocci (hon.). Roman Catholic. Avocations: cycling, hiking. Home: Via Rossi 3, 10064 Pinerolo Piedmont, Italy Office: U Torino Physiology Divsn, Corso Raffaello 30, 10125 Torino Piedmont, Italy

LOSKUTOV, IGOR GRADISLAVOVICH, agricultural industry executive; b. St. Petersburg, Russia, Mar. 17, 1956; s. Gradislav Petrovich and Nina Alexeevna (Lebedeva) L.; m. Natalia Pavlovna Chikova, Oct. 15, 1982; 1 child, Zinaida Igorevna. BS, St. Petersburg State U., 1978; PhD, Vavilov Inst. Plant Industry, St. Petersburg, 1985. Jr. rsch. fellow Vavilov Inst. Plant Industry, St. Petersburg, 1984-88, rsch. fellow, 1988-94, sr. rsch. fellow, 1994—, curator of oat collection, 1999—; vis. scientist Iowa State U., Ames, 1991; lectr. St. Petersburg State U., 1998—. Author: (book) Vavilov and His Institute: A History of the World Collection of Plant Genetic Resources in Russia, 1999; contbr. articles to profl. jours. Mem. Avena Working Group/IPGRI/Rome, Internat. Oat Com. Office: Vavilov Inst Plant Industry, 44 Bolshaya Morskaya, 190000 Saint Petersburg 190000, Russia

LOSONCZY, HAJNA, internist, hematologist, educator; b. Pécs, Baranya, Hungary, Aug. 19, 1941; d. István and Mária (Füzy) L.; m. Lajos Vereczkei, July 28, 1962; 1 child, András. MD, PhD, U. Med. Sch. Pécs, Hungary, 1965. Specialist in internal medicine, 1970, specialist in hematology, 1994. Resident First Dept. Internal Medicine, U. Med. Sch. Pécs, 1965-70, asst., 1970-83, first asst., 1983-90, assoc. prof., 1990-95, full prof., 1995—. Editor, author: Trends in Hemostasis, 1995; contbr. chpt. to book and articles to profl. jours. Mem. Internat. Duna League Against Thrombosis, Hungarian Med. Assn., Hungarian Hematol. Assn. (pres.), Internat. Soc. Hematology. Avocations: music, reading, traveling. Office: U Pécs Faculty Medicine, 1st Dept Medicine Ifjúság u 13, 7624 Pécs Hungary

LOSOS, JONATHAN B., biologist, educator; b. St. Louis, Dec. 7, 1961; s. Joseph Otto and Carolyn Losos; m. Melissa Stamm, May 24, 1998. AB, Harvard U., 1984; PhD, U. Calif., Berkeley, 1989. Asst. prof. dept. biology Washington U., St. Louis, 1992-97, assoc. prof., 1997—; dir. Tyson Rsch. Ctr., 2000—. Contbr. over 75 articles to profl. jours. Recipient Theodosius Dobzhansky prize Soc. for Study of Evolution, 1991, David Starr Jordan prize Jordan Prize Com., 1988; Packard Found. fellow, 1994. Mem. Nature Conservancy (bd. trustees Mo. 1996—). Avocations: ice hockey, nature watching. Home: 7311 Northmoor Dr Saint Louis MO 63105-2111 Office: Washington Univ Dept Biology PO Box 1137 Saint Louis MO 63188-1137

LOSOWSKY, MONTY SEYMOUR, physician, medical educator; b. London, Aug. 1, 1931; s. Myer and Dora (Gottlieb) L.; m. Barbara Malkin, Aug. 15, 1971; children: Kathryn, Andrew. MB, ChB, Leeds U., Eng., 1955, MD, 1961. House officer Leeds Gen. Infirmary, 1955-56; registrar St. Margaret's Hosp., Epping, 1957-59; asst. externe Hosp. St. Antoine, Paris, 1960-61; rsch. fellow, med. unit Harvard U., Boston, 1961-62; from lectr. to reader in medicine, univ. dept. medicine Leeds Gen. Infirmary, 1962-69; prof. medicine, head dept. clin. medicine U. Leeds, 1969-96, dean sch. medicine, 1989-94; 1989-94; gov., chmn. med. adv. bd. Brit. Liver Trust; gov., chmn. med. adv. coun. Coeliac Soc.; sci. gov. Brit. Nutrition Found. Co-author: The Liver and Biliary System, 1984; contbg. editor Gut Defences in Clinical Practice, 1986, others. Trustee Thackray Med. Mus., Leeds. Fellow Royal Coll. Physicians; mem. Brit. Soc. Gastroenterology (coun. mem., edn. com. 1991-94, nominations com. 1991-94, pres. 1993-94), Royal Soc. Medicine, Assn. of Physicians of Great Britain and Ireland. Avocations: golf, watching cricket, walking, medical history. Home: Southview Ling Ln, Leeds LS14 3HT, England Office: St James's Univ Hosp, Univ Dept Medicine, Leeds LS9 7TF, England

LOSSER, MARIE-REINE MARTHE, anesthesiologist, researcher; b. Selestat, Alsace, France, June 12, 1964; d. François Hubert and Anne-Marie Losser. MD, U. Paris XIII, 1993, PhD, 1998. Cert. in anesthesiology and intensive care, Paris, 1993. Anesthesiologist Hosp. Lariboisiere, Paris, 1995—; residentpub. assistance Paris Hosp. Mem. French Soc. Anesthesia Reanimation, European Soc. Intensive Care Medicine, French Coll. Anesthesia Reanimation. Avocations: opera, jazz, natural history. Office: Montreal Gen Hosp Dept Anesthesia, 687 Pine Ave, Montreal, PQ Canada HSA 1A4

LOSSOVSKY, EUGENE KAZIMIROVICH, research scientist, science administrator; b. Smolensk, Russia, Aug. 2, 1931; s. Kazimir Semenovich Lossovsky and Bronislava Samuelovna Kozhuhina; m. Regina Igorevna Lutcenko, June 1, 1931; 1 child, Igor. Engr. in geophysics and geology, State U., Kiev, Ukraine, 1954; PhD, Inst. Geophysics, Acad. Sci., Kiev, 1964, DSc, 1977. Tech. mgr., head seismic crew Ministry of Geology, Leningrad, USSR, 1954-58; rsch. worker Inst. Geology, Acad. Sci., Kiev, 1959-60, sr. rsch. worker, 1964-81, head of seismic lab., 1981-90, head of theory and interpretation dept., 1990—; asst. dir. Inst. Geophysics, Acad. Sci., Kiev, 1966-77. Author: Multiples in Multilayered Media and Reliability of Deep Seismological Reconstructions, 1974 (State Nat. prize 1984); contbr. articles to profl. jours. Mem. Internat. Eurasian Acad. Sci. (corr. mem.). Achievements include research in theory of seismic prospecting, probabilistic theory of random drilling for hydrocarbon deposits, philosophy of geological science, ecology of natural sci. prodn. and study the sys. of flows of geophysical info. Avocations: philosophy of science, history, classical music, Russian poetry, German classic philosophy. Home: 85 Vernadsky Ave Apt 23, 03142 Kiev Ukraine Office: Inst Geophysics Acad Sci, 32 Palladin Ave, 03142 Kiev Ukraine

LOTAS, JUDITH PATTON, advertising executive; b. Iowa City, Apr. 23, 1942; d. John Henry and Jane (Vandike) Patton; children: Amanda Bell, Alexandra Vandike. BA, Fla. State U., 1964. Copywriter Liller, Neal, Battle and Lindsey Advt., Atlanta, 1964-67, Grey Advt., N.Y.C., 1967-72; creative group head SSC&B Advt., N.Y.C., 1972-74, assoc. creative dir., 1974-79, v.p., 1975-79, sr. v.p., 1979-82, exec. creative dir., 1982-86; founding ptnr. Lotas Minard Patton McIver, Inc., N.Y.C., 1986—. Active scholarship fund raising; bd. dirs. Samuel Waxman Cancer Rsch., Found., N.Y.C., 1981-88; fundraiser Nat. Coalition for the Homeless, N.Y.C., 1986—. Recipient Clio award, Venice Film Festival award, Graphics award Am. Inst. Graphic Artists, 1970, Effie award, Grad. of Distinction award Fla. State U., 1993; named Woman of Achievement, YWCA, One of Advt.'s 100 Best Women Ad Age, 1989. Mem. Advt. Women N.Y. (1st v.p. 1984-87, bd. dirs. 1981-87, Advt. Woman of Yr. 1993), The Ad Coun. (mem. creative rev. bd. 1994—, bd. dirs. 1995—), Partnership Drug-Free Am. (mem. creative rev. bd.), Women's Venture Fund (bd. dirs. 1995—), Kappa Alpha Theta. Democrat. Home: 45 E 89th St New York NY 10128-1251

LOTAY, NIRMAL SINGH, telecommunication professional; b. Nairobi, Kenya, Mar. 29, 1970; s. Gurbachan Singh and Balwant Kaur (Sira) L. Recipient awards Birkbeck Coll., London, 1996, others. Mem. Inst. Mgrs. (chmn. 1998—), Sikhs in Eng. (fin. exec. 1997—). Mem. Labour party. Avocations: marathon running, media, stock market. Home: 53 Lincoln Rd/Forest Gate, London E78 CPN, England Office: BT Plc, BT labs/Martlesham/Ipswich, Suffolk England

LOTHA, STEPHEN, science educator; b. Lakhuti, Nagaland, India, Aug. 6, 1956; s. Penathung and Chumoni (Yanthan) Humtsoe; m. Nyanbeni Yanthan, Nov. 10, 1989; children: Chumbenthung, Meriyani, Desmond. BSc, N.E. Hill U., Shillong, India, 1979, MSc, 1985; PhD, N.E. Hill U., 1999. Asst. tchr. h.s., Lakhuti, India, 1980-82; lectr. Kohima (India) Sci. Coll., 1985-94, sr. lectr., 1994-98, reader, 1999—. Contbr. articles to profl. jours. Sch. scholar Nagaland Govt., 1964, tchr. fellow, 1995; Rsch. grant Union Grant Commn., 1996. Mem. Indian Tchrs. Physics Assn., Solid State Nuc. Track Detectors. Avocations: sports, music, hunting, fishing, trekking.

LOTHIAN, SCOTT THOMAS, clinical pharmacist; b. Highland Park, Ill., Oct. 19, 1958; s. David Rogers and Margorie Jane L.; m. Barbara Alice Wallace, June 13, 1981; children: Ryan Scott, Patrick Cameron, Andrew Wallace. BS in Pharm. Scis., Purdue U., 1981. Pharmacist Ill. Masonic Med. Ctr., Chgo., 1981-83; oncology clin. pharmacist Northwestern Meml. Hosp., Chgo., 1983-92, oncology clin. pharmacist, coord., 1992-94, analgesic dosing svc. pharmacist, 1994—. Author: Formulary of Similar Drug Products, 1982; editor: Bone Marrow Transplantation, 1996; contbr. articles to profl. jours. Grantee Nat. Cancer Inst., 1994-97. Mem. Am. Pharm. Assn., Am. Pain Soc., Masonic Lodge (life). Avocations: sports, coaching, church choir, computer. E-mail: slothian@nmh.org. Office: Northwestern Meml Hosp 251 E Huron St Chicago IL 60611-2908

LOTT, IRA TOTZ, pediatric neurologist; b. Cin., Apr. 15, 1941; s. Maxwell and Jeneda (Totz) L.; m. Ruth J. Weiss, June 21, 1964; children: Lisa, David I. BA cum laude, Brandeis U., 1963; MD cum laude, Ohio State U., 1967. Intern Mass. Gen. Hosp., Boston, 1967, resident in pediatrics, 1967-69, resident in child neurology, 1971-74; clin. assoc. NIH, Bethesda, Md., 1969-71; from clin. rsch. fellow to asst. prof. Harvard Med. Sch., Boston, 1971-82; clin. dir. Eunice Kennedy Shriver Ctr. for Mental Retardation, Waltham, Mass., 1974-82; assoc. prof. U. Calif., Irvine, 1983-91, prof., 1992—, chmn. dept. pediat., 1990-2000, dir. clin. neurosci. devel., 2000—; chmn. dept. pediatrics U. Calif., Irvine, 1990-2000 , dir. pediatric neurology, 1983—, clin. neuroscience devel., 2000—; pres. Prof. Child Neurology, Mpls., 1992—. Editor: Down Syndrome-Medical Advances, 1991; contbr. articles to profl. jours. Sec., treas. Child Neurology Soc., Mpls., 1987-90. Lt. comdr. USPHS, 1969-71. NIH grantee, 1974—; recipient Career Devel. award Kennedy Found., 1976. Fellow Am. Acad. Neurology; mem. Am. Pediatric Soc., Am. Neurol. Assn., Nat. Down Syndrome Soc. (sci. acad. bd. 1985—), Western Soc. for Pediatric Rsch. (councillor 1989-91). Achievements include research in relationship of Down Syndrome to Alzheimer's disease, neurometabolic disease, extracorporeal membrane oxygenation in infants. Office: U Calif Irvine Med Ctr Dept Pediatrics 101 The City Dr S # 2 Orange CA 92868-3201

LOTT, JASON EDWARD, community service coordinator; b. Lansing, Mich., Feb. 6, 1973; s. James Louis and Mary Jo Lott. BS, Western Mich. U., 1997. Resident advisor Western Mich. U., Kalamazoo, 1993-94, tchg. asst., asst. residence hall dir., 1994-97, hall stores coord., 1995-97; residence hall area coord. Lake Superior State U., Sault Saint Marie, Mich., 1997—; advisor Pride Group, Sault Saint Marie; com. mem. GLACUHO, Chgo. Choreographer: Cypriot, 1995, The Cottage, 1996, Symmetry is for Easy Chairs, 1996, Survivors, 1997. Regional rep. Mich. Dance Coun., Detroit, 1997—; com. mem. Am.'s Promise, Sault Saint Marie, 1998. Mem. Gt. Lakes Assn. Coll. and Univ. Housing Officers (sexual orientation issues com. mem. 1997—). Methodist. Avocations: dance, music, reading, astrology. Office: Lake Superior State U 650 W Easterday Ave Sault Sainte Marie MI 49783-1643

LOTTA, TOM (ANTHONY TOM LOTTA), artist; b. Rochester, N.Y., Mar. 28, 1924; s. Joseph and Julia (Roncone) L.; m. Rosemary Alionello, June 18, 1949; children: Tom, Karen. AS, Rochester Inst. Tech., 1950. Freelance artist Rochester, 1951—. Committeeman Rep. Cen. Com., Greece, N.Y., 1970—. Sgt. U.S. Army, 1943-45. Named to Boxing Hall of Fame, Can., 1977, Rochester Boxing Hall of Fame; recipient numerous awards for paintings, 50 awards in the arts. Mem. Am. Watercolor Soc., Soc. Illustrators, Rochester Art Club (pres. 1976-77). Roman Catholic. Studio: 1337 Beach Ave Rochester NY 14612-1846

LOTTERMOSER, WERNER ERNST, physicist; b. Braunschweig, Germany, Apr. 27, 1955; s. Werner Wolf and Anna Luise (Schreiner) L.; m. Claudia Hoffmann, Nov. 2, 1990; children: Albrecht, Annemarie. Diploma in Physics, U. Frankfurt, Germany, 1981, PhD, 1986; Habilitation, U. Salzburg, Austria, 1996. Rsch. asst. U. Frankfurt, 1982-86; rsch. asst. U. Salzburg, 1987-92, asst. prof., 1992-96, assoc. prof., 1996-97, prof., 1997—; neutron rsch. Inst. Laue-Langevin, Grenoble, France, 1982-86. Author: (book) The Single Crystal Mossbauer Spectroscopy..., 1996. Mem. German Soc. Crystallography. Avocations: music, inline skating, mountain hiking, skiing. Office: Inst Mineralogy, Hellbrunnerstrasse 34/III, A-5020 Salzburg Austria

LOTTES, PATRICIA JOETTE HICKS, foundation administrator, retired nurse; b. Balt., Aug. 18, 1955; d. James Thomas and Linda Belle (Cadd) Hicks; m. Jeffrey Grant Gross, Aug. 18, 1979 (div. 1981); m. William Melamet Lottes, Sept. 10, 1983 (div. 1997). Diploma in practical nursing, Union Meml. Hosp., 1978. Staff nurse Union Meml. Hosp., Balt., 1978-79, critical care nurse, 1979-81; vis. critical care nurse Balt., 1981-84; head nurse Pharmakinetics, Inc., Balt., 1984-85; dir. Arachnoiditis Info. and Support Network, Inc., Ballwin, Mo., 1991—, dir. nat. support groups, 1992—; nat. support group leader Arachnoid, 1993—. Sec., treas. O'Fallon (Mo.) Elks Ladies Aux., 1989-91, treas., 1991-92, incorporator, 1991, bd. dirs., 1991-94; co-chairperson 303d Field Hosp., U.S. Army Family Support Group, St. Louis, 1990-94. Mem. Nat. Disaster Med. Systems (assoc.), Elks Benevolent Trust, Elks Nat. Home Perpetual Trust. Republican. Baptist. Avocation: quilting. Home: 606 Barbara Dr O'Fallon MO 63366-1306

LOTTI, FERRUCCIO, marketing professional; b. Turin, Piedmont, Italy, Apr. 28, 1951; s. Renato and Maria Margherita (Costa) L.; 2 children: Giovanni, Costanza. Degree in Mktg. and Bus. Adminstrn., SDA, Turin, 1974; degree in Econ., LUISS, Rome, 1978. Advt. mgr. Fiat Auto, Turin, 1977-81; group product mgr. Schiapparelli Farm, Turin, 1981-84; mktg. mgr. Boehringer Ingelheim, Florence, Italy, 1984-90; gen. mgr. Promogold, Italy, 1991-93; pvt. practice mktg. OTC Internat. Cons., Florence, Berlin, 1993—; cons. OTC bus. devel. Berlin-Chemie AG, Germany, 1995—, head OTC divsn., 1996—; pvt. practice OTC Internat. Cons. Menanni Group, Florence, Italy, 1999—. Avocations: skiing, tennis, photography, mountain climbing.

LOTTI, TORELLO M., dermatologist, educator; b. Pieve A Nierole, Pistoia, Italy, Apr. 23, 1953; s. Olinto Lotti and Ada Lombardi; m. Anna Maria Bonelli, Sept. 29, 1979; children: Francesco, Jacopo. MD, U. Florence (Italy), 1978. Prof. dermatology U. Florence, Italy, 1991—; adj. prof. dermatology and cell biology Thomas Jefferson U., Phila., 1995—; dir. dermatol. sect. Montecatini Terme, 1990—; dir. Jour. Current, Parma, Italy, 1991, Jour. European Acad., Amsterdam, 1992; cons. dermatologist U. Siena, 1991; fellow ednl. ctr. Tulane U., 1996. Guest editor Skin Cancer, 1995; co-editor Sclero Derma, 1995, Balneology & Spas, 1996. Recipient Gold medal Brazil Ministry of Health, 1995. Fellow Accademia Medicea; mem. Italian Soc. Tissue Repair (pres. 1996—), European Acad. Dermatology (bd. dirs. 1992), Internat. Soc. Dermatology (sec. gen. 1999—), Sezione Dermatologia (pres. 1996), Rotary Club (v.p. 1994). Roman Catholic. Avocations: golf, sailing. Home: 23 Via Dante Alighieri, 51016 Montecatini Terme Pistoia, Italy Office: 16 Via E Simoncini, 51016 Montecatini Terme Italy

LOTWALA, BHUPENDRA TULSIDAS, finance executive, tax consultant; b. Mumbai, India, Dec. 12, 1944; came to U.S., 1967; s. Tulsidas Jadavji and Jaya Tulsidas Lotwala; m. Harshada Bhupendra, Apr. 15, 1973; children: Raj, Dhir. B of Comm., U. Bombay, 1966; MBA, Pace U., 1971. Asst. contr. Meml. Hosp., Phoenix, 1973-79; contr. Desert Hosp., Palm Springs, Calif., 1979-84, Eisenhower Med. Ctr., Rancho Mirage, Calif., 1984-89; prin. BTL Tax Svc., Palm Desert, Calif., 1989—; CFO Cmty. Health Found., L.A., 1994—; bd. dirs. Clinic Mut. Ins. Co., Nashville. Author, dir. play, 1977. Fellow Healthcare Fin. Mgmt. Assn. (Follmer award 1994), India Cultural Assn. (pres. 1993-96). Hindu. Avocations: reading, writing, chess, tennis. E-mail: blotwala@chfela.org. Home: 40-365 Sagewood Dr Palm Desert CA 92260

LOTZ, JEAN-PIERRE, oncologist; b. Luneville, Lorraine, France, Jan. 2, 1958; s. Jean and Monique (Bochent) L.; m. Veronique Fasano, May 30, 1981; children: Aurélia, Sébastien. MD, Faculte de Paris, 1987. Resident Paris Hosps., 1982-87; intern Tenon Hosp., Paris, 1987-91, resident in oncology, 1991-93, hosp. practioner, bone marrow transplant program coord., 1993-99, prof. medicine, 1999; prof. of medicine. Contbr. articles to profl. jours. Lt. French mil., 1985. Mem. Am. Soc. Clin. Oncology, Soc. Francaise de Greffe de Moelle, European Bone and Marrow Transplantation Group. E-mail: jean-pierre.lotz@tnn.ap-hop-paris.fr. Home: 12 Ter Rue Juillet, 75020 Paris France Office: Hosp Tenon, 4 Rue de Chine, 75020 Paris France

LOTZE, MARTIN PHILIPPE, neuroscience researcher; b. Munich, Mar. 31, 1962; s. Albert and Sigrid (Boden) L.; m. Gabriele Seggewies, Sept. 5, 1997. MD, Ludwig Maximillian U., Munich, 1992, U. Munich, 1996. Asst. physician Univ. Hosp., Munich, 1992-94; asst. neurologist Neurologic Hosp., Aibling, Germany, 1994-95; med. asst. for psychiatry Psychiat. Hosp., Regensburg, Germany, 1995-96; med. asst. in neuroradiology Sect. Exptl. Ctrl. Nervous Sys., Tübingen, Germany, 1996-98; neurologic asst. Neurologic Univ. Hosp., Tübingen, 1998; sci. asst. Inst. for Med. Psychology, Tübingen, 1998—. Contbr. articles to med. jours., including Cortex, Restorative Neurology and Neurosci., Nature Neurosci., Jour. Cognitive Neurosci., Neurologic, Neuro Report. Postdoctoral grantee Volkswagen Found., 1998. Avocation: reorganization of the human motor system. E-mail: martin.lotze@uni-tuebingen.de. Office: Inst for Med Psychology, Gartenstrasse 29, D-72074 Tübingen Germany

LOU, DER-CHYUAN, computer science educator, researcher; b. Chiayi, Taiwan, Republic of China, Mar. 18, 1961; s. Jing-Chen Lou and Tsai-Hwang; m. Suts Hwang, Mar. 29, 1987; children: Yuan-Fu, Yuan-Yaw. BS in Elec. Engring., Chung Cheng Inst Tech., Taoyuan, Taiwan, 1987; MS in Elec. Engring., Nat. Sun Yat-Sen U., Kaohsiung, Taiwan, 1991; PhD in Computer Sci., Nat. Chung Cheng U., Chiayi, Taiwan, 1997. Platoon leader Marines, Kaohsiung, Taiwan, 1981-83; staff, 1983-84; teaching asst. Chung Cheng Inst. Tech., Taoyuan, Taiwan, 1987-89; instr., 1991-93, assoc. prof., 1997—. Contbr. articles to profl. jours. Lt. col. Marines, 1981—, Taiwan. Recipient Rsch. award Nat. Sci. Coun., Republic of China, 1992, 1993. Mem. Phi Tau Phi. Home: 110-48 Lutso Giuntoli, Chiayi 600, Taiwan Office: Dept Elec Engring Chung Cheng Inst Tech, Taoyuan, Taiwan 335, Republic of China

LOU, HANS CHRISTENSEN, neuropediatrician, medical educator; b. Frederiksberg, Denmark, Jan. 26, 1939; s. Regnar Christensen and Margrethe Lou; m. Louise Lange, 1963 (div. 1967); 1 chld, Thora; m. Hanne R. Køser, Mar. 9, 1969; children: Niels, Astrid, Ida. MD, Copenhagen, 1963, DSc, 1973. Bd. qualified in neurology and pediatrics. Chmn. dept. neurology Roskilde Hosp., Denmark, 1979-83; chmn. dept. neuropediatrics J.F. Kennedy Inst., Copenhagen, 1983—; prof. devel. neurology U. Copenhagen, 1993-98; vis. asst. prof. pediatric neurology U. Calif., San Francisco, 1981; cons. Rsch. Coun. Switzerland, 1990, NIH, 1992. Author: Developmental Neurology, 1983; editor: Brain Lesions in the Newborn, 1994; contbr. articles to profl. jours. Bd. dirs. Elsass Found. Recipient Segawa award Japanese Neuropediatric Soc., 1994. Mem. Internat. Child Neurology Assn. (bd. dirs. 1982-94), Child Neurology Soc. (meritorious mem.), European Pediatric Neurology Soc. (bd. dirs. 1994-97). Avocations: musician, tennis, skiing, history of art and science. Home: Keilstruplund 44, DK-3460 Birkerod Denmark Office: John F Kennedy Inst, Gl Landevej 7, DK-2600 Glostrup Denmark

LOUARGAND, MARC ANDREW, real estate executive, financial consultant; b. San Francisco, July 3, 1945; s. Andrew Louargand and Edna Antoinette McNeil (dec.); m. Elizabeth A. Warner, June 18, 1966 (div. Oct. 1978); m. J. R. McDaniel, Feb. 14, 1986. BA, U. Calif., Santa Barbara, 1967; MBA, UCLA, 1974, PhD, 1982. Asst. prof. Calif. State Polytech. U., Pomona, 1975-77; assoc. prof. Calif. State U., Northridge, 1977-83, U. Mass., Boston, 1983-88; sr. lectr. Ctr. for Real Estate Devel. MIT, Cambridge, 1986-93; 2d v.p., sr. officer Mass. Mut. Life Ins. Co., Springfield, Mass., 1993-94; mng. dir. Cornerstone Real Estate Advisors, 1993—; chmn. Mile Square Farm Inc., Vt. Only of Mile Square Farm; cons. in field. Author: CRE2000: Managing the Fifth Strategic Resource, Study Guide to Financial Management, 1986, (with others) Principles and Techniques of Appraisal Review, 1980, Handbook of Real Estate Portfolio Management; assoc. editor Jour. Real Estate Lit., Jour. Real Estate Portfolio Mgmt., Jour. Corp. Real Estate; contbr. articles to profl. jours. Bd. dirs. Beverly Glen Assn., Bel Air, Calif., 1973-77, Citronia Homeowners Assn., Northridge, Calif., 1978-83; chmn. Carlisle (Mass.) Bd. Assessors, 1985-93. Mem. Nat. Coun. Real Estate Investment Fiduciaries (chair portfolio strategy com.), Am. Real Estate Soc. (dir.). Republican. Avocations: tree farming, skiing, building restoration. Home: 32 Longmeadow St Longmeadow MA 01106-1015

LOUBET, EMMANUELLE, multimedia-broadcasting producer, director, writer; b. Limoges, France, Mar. 20, 1958; arrived in Japan, 1986; Doctor, U. Sorbonne, France, 1985. Author Ed. Larousse, Paris, 1980-81; author ARD German Broadcasting Network, 1981-86, prodr., 1986—; ind. prodr. OCORA, Paris, 1988, Internat. Inst. Comparative Music Studies, Berlin, 1991-96; soundscape project prodr. Citizen Group, Osaka, Japan, 1994-96; instr. digital sound design, Kobe (Japan) Electronic Coll., 1997—; multimedia projects leader Kobe Electronic Coll., 1999-2000; guest rschr. Nat. Ctr. Sci. Info. Systems, Tokyo, 1993-96, also bd. dirs. Author and prodr. radiophonic and multimedia art (various awards). Founder FeMPek (Female Independent Media Prodrs. Kansai), 1996—. Recipient Kokoku Dentsu prize Electronic Comm. Advt. Agy., Tokyo, 1999; DAAD grantee, Berlin, 1981-82, Broadcasting Prodn. grantee Housou Bunka Found., Tokyo, 1987, 91. Mem. World Forum Acoustic Ecology (founding mem.), Writer's League and Broadcasting Authors Assn. of Japan, Interactive Soc. Electronic Arts. Avocations: field recordings, socio-ethnic rsch., acoustic design, interactive multimedia art. Fax: 81 729 247735. E-mail: eloubet@gol.com. Office: K-SounD, Higashi-Taishi 2-5-26, Yao-shi Osaka-Fu 581-0062, Japan

LOUBET, JEFFREY W., lawyer; b. Mt. Vernon, N.Y., May 12, 1943; s. Nathaniel R. and Joan (Fleischer) L.; m. Susan Maria Thom, Aug. 29, 1972 (div. Dec. 1997); 1 child, Thom Carlyle; m. Yvonne Phelps, Feb. 26, 1998. BA, Colgate U., 1965; JD, St. John's U., 1968; LLM in Taxation, N.Y. U., 1970. Bar: N.Y. 1968, U.S. Tax Ct. 1969, U.S. Dist. Ct. (so. dist.) N.Y. 1969, N.Mex. 1976, U.S. Dist. Ct. N.Mex. 1977. Assoc. Poletti, Freidin, Prashker, Feldman & Gartner, N.Y.C., 1969-76; ptnr. Modrall, Sperling, Roehl, Harris & Sisk, Albuquerque, 1976-94; counsel Rodey, Dickason, Sloan, Akin & Robb, Albuquerque, 1994-2000; pvt. practice Albuquerque, 2000—; lectr. N.Mex. Estate Roundtable, Albuquerque, 1979—; vis. prof. Estate and Gift Tax U. N.Mex., Albuquerque, 1988-89. Contbr.

articles to profl. jours. Mem. Lovelace Respiratory Rsch. Inst. Estate Planning Adv. Coun., 1993—; mem. adv. bd. on charitable giving Albuquerque Cmty. Found., 1995—; bd. dirs. Wheels Mus. Masters World Record Holder, high hurdles and decathlon. Fellow Am. Coll. Trust and Estate Counsel (mem. estate and gift com.); mem. ABA (chair N. Mex. property tax com.), N.Mex. Estate Planning Coun., Greater Albuquerque C. of C. (chair tax task force, 1992, chair state govt. com., 1993), YMCA (mem. bd. dirs.). Avocations: track & field, skiing, fly fishing. Home: PO Box 3754 Albuquerque NM 87190-3754 Office: Loubet Law Firm 6301 Indian School Rd NE Albuquerque NM 87110-8103

LOUBET, RENÉ PIERRE EMMANUEL, pathologist; b. Limoges, France, Sept. 30, 1925; s. Felix and Marcelle (Lacoste) L.; m. Mary Anne Dagorne; children: Emmanuelle, Marie Pascale. Grad., Med. Sch. Limoges; Phese Doct., Fac Med Paris, 1951. Dir. Lab. Ctr. Regional Blood Transfusion, 1952-56; chief anatomy/pathology Limoges Faculty Medicine, Limoges, 1952-58; prof. U. Paris, Paris, 1961-65; prof., chair anatomy/pathology divsn. Limoges Faculty Medicine, Limoges, 1961-90; prof., chief of svc. CHU Dupuytren Faculty Medicine, Limoges, 1959-90, chief svc. pathology electron microscopy, 1975-90, cons. pathologist, 1990-93, prof., chief svc., 1993—; cons. pathology CHU, 1990-93, Medecin chef svc. honoraire, 1993; mem. Commn. Nat. d'Appel qualification en Anatomie et Cytologie pathologiques humaines, 1990; instr. biblical Hebrew Faculty of Medicine, 1989; pres., founder univ. group for biblical Hebrew studies, 1990. Contbr. numerous articles to profl. jours. Médecin lt.-col. res. French Mil., 1945. Mem. Soc. Anatom de Paris, Soc. Cancer, French Soc. Hematology, French Soc. Gynecology, Gynecopathology French Soc. (v.p. 1996, hon. pres. 1999), Internat. Acad. Pathology (past pres.). Achievements include research in pathologic endocrine ovary and uterus; role of the vascularization in the senescence ovary. Home: 08 rue Leon Sazerat, 87000 Limoges France

LOUBRIEU, GEORGES LOUIS, radiologist, neurologist, consultant; b. Limoges, France, June 20, 1948; s. Jean and Marie Therese (Leniaud) L.; m. Fabienne Achari, Aug. 30, 1973, 1 child, Johanne. MD, U. Tours, France, 1976; diploma, U. Paris-Sud, 1988. Resident in neurology, gen. medicine, neurosurgery Hosp. Tours, 1973-77; substitute chief svc. Hosp. Ctr. Dreux, France, 1977-78; asst. neurology svc. Regional Hosp. Tours, 1977-81, asst. neuroradiology svc., 1981, asst. prof., 1977-81, med. attaché, 1981-86; physician Centre Hospitalier, Bourges, France, 1986—, chief radiology, 1995—; presenter numerous confs.; v.p. Pub. and Pvt. Assn. for Magnetic Resonance Imaging in Berry, 1992—. Contbr. articles to med. jours., including French Pediatric Archives, Rev. Internal Medicine, Annals Surgery. Mem. Coll. d'Enseignement Post U. Radiology, French Radiology Soc., French Neuroradiology Soc., Western soc. Radiol. Imagery. E-mail: gloubrieu@coremail.com. also: 4 Ave Jean Jaures, 18000 Bourges France Office: Centre Hospitalier, 145 Ave F Mitterrand, 18016 Bourges France also: 4 Ave Jean Jouies, 18000 Bourges France

LOUBSER, JOHANNES ALBERTUS, religious studies educator; b. Cape Town, South Africa, July 25, 1949; s. Coenraad Hendrik and Marie Mavis (Vos) L.; m. Minnie Jeanne Le Roux; children: Coenraad, Jacques, Johannes, Sanmari. BA cum laude, U. Stellenbosch, South Africa, 1971, BA in Greek cum laude, 1974, B.Th., 1975, MA in Greek cum laude, 1975, D.Th. in New Testament, 1980; Diploma in German Lang. and Culture, Goethe-Inst., Balubeuren, West Germany, 1975; Lic. in Theology cum laude, 1977; postdoct., U. South Africa, 1992-94. Ordained min. Dutch Reformed Ch. Asst. min. Rhenish Dutch Reformed Mission Ch. (Coloureds), Stellenbosch, South Africa, 1977-78; min. Dutch Reformed Ch., Brenthurst, So. Transvaal, 1978-82, Cape Town, 1982-89; prof. New Testament, head dept. biobliological studies U. Zululand, South Africa, 1990—. Author: The Apartheid Bible, 1987, Introduction to the new Testament: A study guide for the Hueguenot Bible Institute, 1988, The Fork in the Road, Meditation on the Guidance of the Holy Spirit, 1988, Ten Biblical Themes. Study Guide for the Huegenot Bible Institute, 1989, Live with Christ, 1989, Hoor God my Gebed?, 1989; translator God's Promise to Children, 1987; mem. editl. bd. Neotestamentica, 1992-98; contbr. numerous articles to profl. and religious jours. Internat. scholar Rotary Internat., 1974-75; grantee NZAV, 1982, Ctr. for Sci. Devel., 1996, 98, grant rsch. com. U. Zululand, 1998. Mem. South African Acad. Religion (pres. 1998—), South African Acad. Sci. and Art (exec. mem. human scis. faculty bd.), New Testament Soc. South Africa, Bibl. Studies Soc. South Africa, Theol. Soc. South Africa, Am. Acad. Religion, Literator Soc., Ctr. Intergroup Studies. Avocations: cultural tourism, home cooking, art films, hiking. Home: PO Box 123/59 Raphia Cres, Mtunzini 3867, South Africa Office: Pvt Bag X1001, Kwadlangezwa 3886, South Africa

LOUCHEV, OLEG ANATOLIEVICH, researcher, consultant; b. Moscow, June 12, 1960; arrived in Japan, 1995; s. Anatolii Pavlovich and Galina Michailovna (Mednikova) L.; m. Irina Olegovna Baum, Nov. 18, 1958; children: Dmitrii, Alexandra. MS, Moscow Inst. Chem. Engring., 1982; PhD, Turkmenistan Acad. Scis., Ashkhabad, 1986. Cert. applied physics. Rschr. Inst. Solar Energy, Ashkhabad, 1983-86, Rsch. Ctr. for Technol. Lasers, USSR Acad. Scis., Troitsk, Moscow, 1987-89; sr. rschr. Rsch. Ctr. for Technol. Lasers, USSR Acad. Scis., Troitsk, 1992-94, Energy Inst., Moscow, 1990-91; scii. & tech. agy. rsch. fellow Nat. Inst. for Rsch. in Inorganic Materials, Tsukuba, Japan, 1995-96; Ctr. of Excellence rsch. fellow Nat. Inst. for Rsch. in Inorganic Materials, Tsukuba, 1997—. Contbr. articles to profl. jours. Recipient Leniski Komsomol award for achievements in sci. and tech., Moscow, 1986, Sci. and Tech. Agy. Fellowship award Sci. and Tech. Agy. Japan, Tsukuba, 1995. Avocation: photography. E-mail: loutchev@nirim.go.jp. Fax: 81 298 52 7449. Office: Nat Inst Rsch Inorganic Mat, 1-1 Namiki, Ibaraki 305-0044, Japan

LOUCK, JAMES DONALD, physicist, researcher; b. Grand Rapids, Mich., Dec. 13, 1928; m. Margaret (Carolyn) Marsh, 1960; children: Samuel, Thomas, Joseph. BS, Ala. Poly. Inst., Auburn, 1950; MS, Ohio State U., 1952, PhD, 1958. Staff mem. Los Alamos (N.Mex.) Sci. Lab., 1958-60, 63-83, lab. fellow, 1983-90; assoc. rsch. prof. Auburn (Ala.) U., 1960-63; lab. assoc., ret. fellow, 1991—; hon. prof. Nankai U., Tianjin, China, 1996—, hon. dir. ctr. combinatorics, 1998—; pres. Nicholas C. Metropolis Math. Found., 1998—. Co-author: Quantum Theory of Angular Momentum, 1981, The Racah-Wigner Algebra in Quantum Theory, 1981, Symbolic Dynamics of Trapezoidal Maps, 1986; assoc. editor Annals of Combinatorics, 1996—; adv. bd. Jour. Molecular Spectroscopy, 1975-85; mem. editl. bd. Jour. Math. Physics, 1989-91; contbr. over 100 articles to profl. jours. Lt. (j.g.) USN, 1952-55. Mem. AAAS, Am. Phys. Soc. Achievements include discovery and development of numerous mathematical advances in physical applications of symmetry methods and their combinatorial interpretations. Avocations: woodworking, fishing, yardwork. Home: 54 Wildflower Way Santa Fe NM 87501-8616

LOUČKA, TOMÁŠ, chemistry educator; b. Prague, Czech Republic, Dec. 11, 1943; s. Premysl and Emilie Loučka; 2 children: Lucie, Jan. Student, Chem. Tech. U., 1962-67; PhD, CSc, Czechoslovak Acad. Sci., 1967. Researcher Heyrovsky's Inst. Polarography, Prague, 1970-73; researcher Rsch. Inst. Inorganic Chemistry, Usti n.L., 1973-86, dir. rsch., 1986-90, chief dept., 1990-93; vice dean U. J.E. Purkyne, Faculty of Environment, Usti n.L., 1993-96, docent in chemistry, 1996—, vice rector, 1998-99, dean faculty environment, 1999—. Contbr. articles to profl. jours. Mem. Czech Chem. Soc. (com. mem. 1974). Office: JE Purkyne U Fac Environmen, Na okraji 1001, 400-01 Usti n.L. Czech Republic

LOUCKS, TERRY LEE, writer, retired biosystems executive; b. Loveland, Colo., Feb. 10, 1936. BS in Petroleum Engring., U. Tulsa, 1960, MS in Petroleum Engring., 1961; PhD in Physics, Pa. State U., 1963. Prof. physics I.S.U., 1963-68; dir. Rockwell Sci. Ctr., 1975-79; pres., CEO, Compuchem, Raleigh, N.C., 1980-82, ETCC, Inc., Raritan, N.J., 1982-83; dir. Vitesse (Calif.) Electronics, 1987-88; v.p. tech. Norton Co., Worcester, Mass., 1983-88; pres., CEO, chmn. PerSeptive Biosystems, Cambridge, Mass., 1988-90, ret., 1991; cons. Rothschild Ventures, N.Y.C., 1988. Author: Burning Words, 1998. Recipient Disting. Alumni award U. Tulsa, 1990, Alumni Fellow award Pa. State U., 1992. Home: 13611 Mc Queens Ct Jacksonville FL 32225-4912

LOUCKS, VERNON R., JR., retired medical technologies executive; b. Evanston, Ill., Oct. 24, 1934; s. Vernon Reece and Sue (Burton) L.; m. Linda Kay Olson, May 12, 1972; 6 children. B.A. in History, Yale U., 1957; M.B.A., Harvard U., 1963. Sr. mgmt. cons. George Fry & Assos., Chgo., 1963-65; with Baxter Travenol Labs., Inc. (now Baxter Internat. Inc.), Deerfield, Ill., 1966-98, exec. v.p., 1976, also bd. dirs., chmn., 1980, CEO, 1980-98; bd. dirs. Dun & Bradstreet Corp., Emerson Electric Co., Quaker Oats Co., Anheuser-Busch Cos.; bd. advisors Nestlé U.S.A. Trustee Rush-Presbyn.-St. Luke's Med. Ctr.; assoc. Northwestern U. 1st lt. USMC, 1957-60. Recipient Citizen Fellowship award Chgo. Inst. Medicine, 1982, Nat. Health Care award B'nai B'rith Youth Svcs., 1986, William McCormick Blair award Yale U., 1989, Yale medal, 1997, Semper Fidelis award USMC, 1989, Disting. Humanitarian award St. Barnabas Found., 1992, Alexis de Tocqueville award for community svc. United Way Lake County, 1993, Industrialist of Yr. award Am. Israel C. of C., 1996; named 1983's Outstanding Exec. Officer in the healthcare industry Fin. World; elected to Chgo.'s Bus. Hall of Fame, Jr. Achievement, 1987. Mem. Health Industry Mfrs. Assn. (chmn. 1983), Bus. Roundtable (conf. bd., mem. policy com.), Bus. Coun. Clubs: Chgo. Commonwealth, Commercial, Mid-America.

LOUËR, DANIEL, research scientist; b. Nantes, France, Sept. 4, 1942; s. Charles and Joséphine (Robert) L.; m. Michèle Gaudin, Sept. 5, 1964; children: Christophe, Olivier, Anne-Sophie. Degree in scis., U. Rennes, 1964, D degree, 1967; D degree, U. Rennes, 1969. Attaché de recherche Centre Nat. de la Recherche Scientifique (CNRS), Rennes, 1965-69, chargé de recherche, 1970-85, dir. de recherche 2d class, 1986-94, dir. de recherche 1st class, 1995—. Contbr. more than 200 articles to profl. jours. Mem. Internat. Union of Crystallography (sec. commn. on powder diffraction 1993-96), Internat. Ctr. for Diffraction Data (cons. 1992-98, Hanawalt award 1992), Am. Crystallographic Assn., British Crystallographic Assn., Royal Acad. Scis. & Arts Barcelona (fgn. hon.), Assn. Francaise de Cristallographie. Avocations: hiking, jogging. Office: U Rennes I/Solid Chemistry, Ave Général Leclerc, 35042 Rennes France

LOUFAS, ALEXANDER CHRISTOS, mechanical engineer, writer; b. Athens, Greece, Dec. 6, 1967; s. Loufas A. and Polyxeni (Giannopoulou) Christos. MME, Nat. Tech. U. Athens, 1993; MBA, Cardiff (Wales) Bus. Sch., 1994. Writer Aeronautics of Def., Athens, 1989-94; mech. engr. Engring. Constrn., Athens, 1992-93; plant mgr. Baklis Bros.S.A., Athens. Contbr. articles to profl. jours. and mags. 2nd lt. Greek Armed Forces Res., 1994-96. Mem. Tech. Chamber of Greece. Home: Harilaou Trikoupi 7, 14565 Athens Dionysos, Greece

LOUGHEED, ALAN LESLIE, economics educator; b. Nanango, Queensland, Australia, Apr. 13, 1927; s. Leslie Francis and Lucy Ada (Wells) L.; m. Jill Carmel Blackmore; children: Brett Robert, Damon Leslie, Kirstin Carmel. BA, U. Queensland, Brisbane, 1955, B Comm., 1960, B Econ., 1965, PhD, 1974. Tchr. Queensland H.S., Australia, 1947-64; lectr. in econs. U. Queensland, Brisbane, 1964-68, sr. lectr., 1968-83, assoc. prof., 1983-92, hon. rsch. fellow, 1992—; vis. rsch. fellow U. Kent, Canterbury, Eng., 1971, 76, 83; vis. lectr. U. New Eng., Armidale, 1980, 81; vis. scholar U. Kent, Canterbury, 1988; vis. rsch. fellow U. Glasgow, Scotland, 1996. Co-author: Australian Banking, 1966, The Growth of the International Economy, 1820-1960, 1971, 4th edit. 1999, Towards New Policies for Foreign Aid and Development, 1979, Technological Diffusion and Industrialization Before 1914, 1982, others; author: The Brisbane Stock Exchange 1884-1984, 1984, Australia in the World Economy in the Twentieth Century, 1988, others. Vice-chancellors rep. Secondary Sch. Studies, Brisbane, 1975-87. Recipient Univ. medal for Outstanding Achievement, U. Queensland, 1965; vis. fellow grantee U. Glasgow, 1996; recipient Archibald scholarship, 1962. Mem. Australian Econ. Soc. (v.p. Brisbane br. 1973, 74, 76, pres. 1975, treas. 1967-70). Avocations: tennis, walking, surfing, golf. Home: 2 Titan Lane Buderim, 4556 Sunshine Coast Australia Office: Dept Econs, U Queensland/St Lucia, 4072 Brisbane Australia

LOUGHEED, THOMAS ROBERT, solar energy construction company executive; b. Detroit, July 8, 1941; s. Aloysius V. and Ruth S. (Stait) L.; m. Nancy E. Godt, Mar. 28, 1970; children—Thomas S., Patrick R. Student Wayne State U., 1961, postgrad., 1969-74; student Welch Sch. Acctg., Detroit, 1962; B.S., Central Mich. U., 1964, M.B.A., 1966, M.A., 1967; postgrad., Wayne State Univ., 1968-72. Cost auditor Fisher Body div. Gen. Office: 6449 Bristol Rd Swartz Creek MI 48473-7933

LOUGHMAN, BARBARA ELLEN, immunologist researcher; b. Frankfurt, Ind., Oct. 26, 1940; d. Jimmie Jewel and Ruth Eileen (Hoyer) Evers; m. Terry B. Loughman, June 28, 1962 (dec.); children: Lance Evers Loughman, Chad Elliott Loughman. BS, U. Ill., 1962; PhD, Notre Dame U., 1972. Rsch. scientist Ames Rsch. Labs., Elkhart, Ind., 1962-72; staff fellow NIH, Balt., 1972-74; from rsch. assoc. to rsch. mgr. The Upjohn Co., Kalamazoo, Mich., 1974-84; dir. immunology rsch. Monsanto Co., St. Louis, 1984-85; sr. dir. immunology diseases rsch. G.D. Searle/Monsanto Co., St. Louis, 1986-88; dir. project mgmt. Rorer Ctrl. Rsch., Horsham, Pa., 1988-91; dir. internat. drug regulating affairs Marion Merrell Dow, Kansas City, Mo., 1991-95; v.p. devel. svcs. Internat. Med. Tech. Cons., Inc., Lenexa, Kans., 1995-97, Pharm. Rsch. Assoc., Inc., Lenexa, Kans./Ohio, 1997-98; assoc. rsch. prof. medicine Loma Linda (Calif.) U., 1998—; v.p., drug devel. and medical affairs Encore Pharmaceuticals, Inc., Loma Linda, Calif., 1998—. Contbr. over 20 articles to profl. jours. Mem. AAAS, Am. Acad. Asthma Allergy and Immunology, Am. Assn. Immunology. Avocations: singing, golf. Home and Office: 7153 Champions Ln West Chester OH 45069-4635

LOUGHNEY, VINCENT J., JR., electric utility educator; b. Syracuse, N.Y., July 19, 1949; s. Leo M. and Mary A. (Buchols) L.; m. GayTonne Marie Loughney, Dec. 29, 1973; children: Abby, Vince Jr. BA in Polit. Sci., SUNY, Oswego, 1971. Cert. sr. reactor operator, USNRC. Control rm. reactor operator N.Y. Power Authority, Oswego, 1977-81; simulator test engr. Electronics Associated, West Long Branch, N.J., 1981-84; sr. reactor operator, instr. Ark. Power and Light, Russellville, 1984-89; insp., lic. examiner USNRC, Glen Ellyn, Ill., 1989-90; asst. mgr. Midwest, S-3 Techs., Channahon, Ill., 1990-91; program/project analyst So. Calif. Edison, San Onofre, 1991—. Sec./treas. Kiwanis, Oswego, N.Y., 1975-80. Avocations: computers, photography. E-mail: Loughnuj@songs.sce.com. Home: 1930 Comanche St Oceanside CA 92056-2955 Office: SCE Nuclear Tng Divsn PO Box E-50 San Clemente CA 92674-0128

LOUGHRIDGE, FREDERICK BRENDAN, information science educator; b. Belfast, Northern Ireland, Apr. 18, 1943; s. Frederick and Sarah Emma (McKeague) L.;m. Janet Isobel Hamilton, Dec. 14, 1973; children: Clare, Richard. BA, U. Oxford, Eng., 1964, MA, 1974. Asst. keeper Nat. Libr. Scotland, Edinburgh, 1964-70; sub-libr. U. Ulster, Coleraine, Eng., 1970-78; lectr. U. Sheffield, Eng., 1978—. Author: Which Dictionary?, 1990; contbr. articles to profl. jours. Fellow Inst. Info. Scientists, U.K. ONline User Group (treas. 1992—), Brit. Assn. Info. and Edn. and Rsch. (treas. 1998—). Avocations: birdwatching, music, travel, cricket. Office: U Sheffield Dept Info Stud, Western Bank, Sheffield S10 2TN, England

LOUGHRIDGE, JOHN HALSTED, JR., lawyer; b. Chestnut Hill, Pa., Oct. 30, 1945; s. John Halsted Sr. and Martha Margaret (Boyd) L.; m. Amy Claire Booe, Aug. 3, 1980 (div. Apr. 1995); 1 child, Emily Halsted. AB, Davidson Coll., 1967; JD, Wake Forest U., 1970. Bar: N.C. 1970, U.S. Dist. Ct. 1970, U.S. Ct. Mil. Appeals 1986. Divsn. head, v.p., counsel Wachovia Mortgage Co., Winston-Salem, N.C., 1971-79; sr. v.p., counsel Wachovia Bank, Winston-Salem, N.C., 1980—; mem. UCC Article V drafting com. N.C. Gen. Statutes Commn., 1999. Mem. cabinet, chair profl. divsn. United Way Forsyth County, 1994. Col. JAGC, USAR, 1970-2000. Mem. ABA (corp., banking and bus. law sect. 1970—, internat. law and practice sect. 1999—), N.C. Bar Assn. (internat. law sect. 1984—, fin. instns. com. 1985—, real property sect. 1971—, governing coun. 1988-91, bus. law sect. 1971—, corp. counsel sect. 1989—, governing coun. 1992-98, treas., 1999-00, sec. 2000-2001, real property curriculum com. 1990-93, bus. law curriculum com. 1999—), N.C. State Bar, N.C. Coll. of Advocacy, Forsyth County Bar Assn., Am. Corp. Counsel Assn. (v.p., bd. dirs. N.C. chpt. 1988-98, comml. law com. 1996—), Mortgage Bankers Assn. of Am. (legal issues com. 1982—, fin. affiliates com. 1988—), Res. Officers Assn. (chpt. pres. 1996-97, sec. 1997—), Union League (Phila.), Twin City Club (sec. 1990-97, gov. 1994—, pres. 1997-00), Forsyth Country Club, Phi Delta Phi, Phi Delta Theta. Republican. Presbyterian. Avocations: golf, tennis. Home: 615 Arbor Rd Winston Salem NC 27104-2331 Office: Wachovia Bank 100 N Main St Winston Salem NC 27101-4047

LOUGHRIN, JAY RICHARDSON, mass communications educator, consultant; b. Mankato, Minn., Oct. 21, 1943; s. J. Richardson and Jane Aileen (Smith) L.; m. Helen Marie Struyk, Aug. 8, 1964 (div. Sept. 1985); children: Jennifer, Amy; m. Yolanda Christina Ramos, July 17, 1986; children: Tawny, Heather. BA in Drama, Calif. State U., Los Angeles, 1968; postgrad., San Diego State U., 1968-69, UCLA, 1970-71, U. Redlands, Calif., 1983-84, Fla. State U., 1990; MA, Whittier (Calif.) Coll., 1992. Prodn. asst. Andrews-Yagemann Prodns., Hollywood, Calif., 1961-63; with merchandising, sales Sta. KTTV-TV, Hollywood, 1963-64; assoc. producer Born Losers Am. Internat. Pictures, Hollywood, 1964; assoc. producer V.P.I. Prodns., Hollywood, 1964, Ralph Andrews Prodns., North Hollywood, Calif., 1965; producer Stein Erikson Ski Films, North Hollywood, 1965, F.K. Rocket Films, North Hollywood, 1966-68; dir. promotion and publicity Sta. KCST-TV, San Diego, 1968-69; prof. mass communication Rio Hondo Coll., Whittier, 1969—; sales mgr. Warren Miller Films, Hermosa Beach, Calif., 1984-85, cons., 1985-86; exec. producer Echo Prodns., Hollywood, 1985-87; cons. Radio Concepts, Los Angeles, 1978-80, Tom Cole Prodns., Los Angeles, 1985-87, Chuck Richards Whitewater, Lake Isabella, Calif., 1984-86; media relations cons. Police Officers Standards and Training, Sacramento, 1986—; venue mgr. Los Angeles Olympic Organizing Com., Long Beach, Calif., 1984. Winter sports writer Kern Valley Sun; contbr. articles to Review Publs., Orange Coast mag., Jet Am. mag., Ted Randall Report. Pres. Rue Le Charlene Homeowners Assn., Palos Verdes, Calif., 1984, Hilltop Homeowners Assn., Walnut, Calif., 1989-90; v.p. West Walnut Homeowners Assn., 1988-89. Recipient Pub. Service Programming award Advt. Council, N.Y.C., 1982; named Adviser of Yr., U. So. Calif.'s 50th Annual Journalism Awards, Los Angeles, 1985. Mem. Acad. TV Arts and Scis., Rio Hondo Coll. Faculty Assn. (pres. 1978), So. Calif. Broadcasters Assn. (Pub. Service award 1978), N.Am. Snowsport Journalists Assn. Republican. Avocations: sailing, skiing, whitewater rafting, motorcycling, bicycling. Office: Rio Hondo Coll 3600 Workman Mill Rd Whittier CA 90601-1616

LOUIE, DAVID A., television journalist; b. Lakewood, Ohio, June 19, 1950; s. Troy and May (Chan) L. BS in Journalism, Northwestern U., 1972. Reporter KGO-TV, San Francisco, 1972-77, reporter, bur. chief, 1979-95, bus. editor and anchor, 1995—; asst. news dir. WXYZ-TV, Detroit, 1977-79. Contbr. articles to profl. jours. Bd. dirs. United Way of Bay Area, San Francisco, 1980-82, Peninsula Humane Soc., San Mateo, Calif., 1981. Mem. NATAS (exec. com., vice chmn. bd. dirs. 1990-94, chmn. bd. dirs. 1994-96, trustee 1986-90, Emmy award 1980, 88, Silver Circle award 1995), Asian Am. Journalists Assn. (nat. pres. 1990-92, Lifetime Achievement award 1996), Radio TV News Dirs. Assn. (trustee, ex-officio bd. dirs.), Medill Alumni Hall of Achievement (charter), Orgn. Chinese Ams. (Nat. Outstanding Citizen Achievement award 1999). Office: Sta KGO-TV 900 Front St San Francisco CA 94111-1427

LOUIS, WILLIAM JOSEPH, theater educator, actor, director, artist; b. Castorland, N.Y., Mar. 5, 1928; s. Loren A. and Laura Ruth Louis. BA in English, Boston Coll., 1957, MA in Comparative Dramatic Lit., 1959; PhD in Speech and Theatre and Humanities, Stanford U., 1969; postdoctoral U. Nice, France, 1967-68, 69, Lee Strasberg Acting Inst., Hollywood, Calif., summer 1976, BA in Studio Art, Avila Coll., 1990. Instr., LeMoyne Coll., Syracuse, N.Y., 1958-60; asst. prof. theatre U. B.C., Vancouver, Can., 1968-70; coord. drama Western N.Mex. U., Silver City, 1971-73; chmn. performing and visual arts dept. Avila Coll., Kansas City, Mo., 1973-87, prof. humanities, 1987-91, ret., 1991; actor; originator dept. comm. Avila Coll., 1976, artist-in-residence, 1991—. Mem. screening com. Mo. Arts Coun., 1975. With U.S. Army, 1943-47. Named Hon. Citizen of Silver City, 1971. Mem. Actors Equity, Kansas City Artists Coalition, Kansas City Clay Guild, Friends of Art, VFW, Alpha Sigma Nu. Democrat. Roman Catholic. Avocations: painting, sculpting, poetry, aerobics. Home: 109 Glen Arbor Rd Kansas City MO 64114-5163 Office: 11901 Wornall Rd Kansas City MO 64145-1007

LOUIS-DREYFUS, ROBERT, advertising executive; b. June 14, 1946; s. Jean and Jeanne (Depierre) L.; m. Sarah Oberholzer. MBA, Harvard U. Chmn. JIMS Internat., until 1989; CEO Saatchi & Saatchi Plc, London, 1989—; chmn. mgmt. bd. Adidas AG. Office: Adidas AG, Adi-Dassier-Strasse 1-2, Herzongenaurach Bavaria 91072, Germany*

LOUISON, NELSON AUGUSTUS, manufacturing company executive, consultant; b. Grenada, Jan. 18, 1960; s. Garvey Thomas and Alberta Marion (Nelson) L.; m. Jennelyn M. Charles, Sept. 10, 1994 (div. Mar. 1998); 1 child, Taylor. Diploma, London Sch. Mktg., 1979; grad., Dale Carnegie Pub. Speaking, 1985; diploma, Screen Printing Tech., 1987; diploma in Bus. Mgmt., 1991, Broomers Coll., 1990. Councillor Caribbean Ecumenical Youth Movement, 1975-79; attache Grenada Embassy, Cuba, 1979-81; head internat. rels. Ministry of Mobilization, 1981-83; mng. dir. Vanel's Enterprise Ltd., 1986—, Dove Internat., 1996—; mgr. Vantage Mfg. Export Co., 1985-89; chmn. Grenada Mfrs. Coun., 1994-96; dir. Transport Bd., 1994—; chmn. Nat. Carnival and Cultural Devel. Com., 1995; cons. Consolidated Contractors Co., U.K., 1997—; spkr. in field. Chmn. Anglican Youth Coun. Grenada, 1976-79, Windward Islands Anglican Dioscean Youth Coun., 1977-79; 1st v.p. Bank and Gen. Workers Union, Grenada, 1979-81; head internat. rels. Ministry of Mobilization, Grenada, 1982-83. Named Bus. Man of Yr., Grenada Chamber of Judistry, 1995. Mem. Inter-Am. Inst. Conf. on Water for Caribbean and the Americas, Ea. Caribbean Export Devel. Agy. (dep. chmn. bd. dirs. 1995-97), Nat. Water and Sewerage Authority (chmn. 1996—), Caribbean Mfrs. Coun., C. of C. (dir. 1990-94), Grenada Chamber of Industry and Commerce (v.p. 1994-96). Home: PO Box 49, Mount Parnassus, Saint George's Grenada West Indies Office: Vanels Enterprises Ltd, PO Box 49, Saint George's Grenada West Indies

LOUISY, FRANCIS, physician; b. La Courneuve, France, Mar. 18, 1956; s. George and Colette (Patterso) L.; m. Annick Fassion, Sept. 27, 1975; children: David, Jeremie, Benjamin. MD, Claude Bernard U., Lyon, France, 1981; DS, Rene Descartes U., Paris, 1992. Asst. rschr. IMASSA, Paris, 1986-92; rsch. specialist IMASSA, Bretigny, France, 1992—; cons. in field. Author: Angiologie, 1988, Medecine du Sport, 1991, Medecine et Armies, 1990, Aviation Space and Environmental Medicine, 1995; contbr. articles to profl. jours. Lt. French Defense Health Svc., 1995. Mem. Soc. French Medicine Aerospace, Internat. Soc. Gravitational Physiology, Aerospace Med. Assn. Avocations: flying, running, swimming. Office: IMASSA/CERMA, BP 73, 91223 Bretigny Sur Orge France

LOUISY, PEARLETTE, governor general of Saint Lucia; b. June 8, 1946. BA in English and French, U. West Indies, 1969; MA in Linguistics, Laval U., Quebec, Can., 1975; PhD in Higher Edn., U. Bristol (U.K.), 1994, LLD (hon.), 1999. Secondary sch. tchr., tutor, 1969-72, 75-81; prin. St. Lucia A Level Coll., Castries, 1981-86; dean divsn. arts, sci. and gen. studies, vice prin., prin. Sir Arthur Lewis C.C., Castries, 1985-97; gov. gen. Govt. of Saint Lucia, 1997—. Awards title Dame Grand Cross of the Order of St. Lucia bestowed by her Majesty Queen Elizabeth II, 1997, Order of St. Michael and St. George, 1999. Office: Office of Gov Gen, Govt House, The Morne Castries Saint Lucia

LOUIT, CHRISTIAN GEORGES, law educator, solicitor; b. Saint Cyprien Les Attafs, Algeria, Nov. 19, 1943; s. Gaston Marcel Louit and Clotilde Bouer; m. Christiane Pheline; children: Jean François, Jerome. BS, Inst. Polit. Studies, 1963; LLM, Aix en Provence U., 1964, PhD, 1971. Prof. Reunion U., 1974-78, Aix Marseille III U., France, 1978—; dir. Tax Studies Ctr., Aix en Provence, 1979—, European Asian Rsch. Ctr., 1999; lectr. Montreal U., York U., Peking U. Author: Finances of Public Enterprises, 1976; contbr. articles to profl. jours. Recipient Chevalier award Palmes Academiques, 1987, Order of Merit France, 1997, Legion d'honneur, France, 1998; cmdr. Order of Merit Italy, 1990. Mem. Internat. Fiscal Assn., Internat. Bus. Law Assn. (v.p.), Nat. Coun. Univs. Avocations: cycling, photography. Home: L'Eperon Saint Jacques, 13100 Le Tholonet France Office: Aix Marseille Univ, 3 Avenue R Shuman, 13100 Aix-en-Provence France

LOULMET, DIDIER FELIX, cardiac surgeon; b. Cahors, France, July 21, 1960; s. Jacques and Odette Marguerite (Pechberty) L.; 1 child, Emmanuel-

le. MD, Paris U., 1990, MSc, 1991. Resident hosps., Paris, 1985-90; fellow in surgery Brigham & Women's Hosp., Boston, 1991-92; chief resident, then staff surgeon Broussais Hosp., Paris, 1993-99; staff surgeon Lenox Hill Hosp., N.Y.C., 2000—; cons. Genzyne Corp., Boston, 1997-99, Intuitive Surg. Inc., Mountain View, Calif., 1998-99. Mem. Internat. Soc. Miminally Invasive Cardiac Surgery. Avocations: history, art history, sports, art collecting, gastronomy.

LOUNGUINE, PAVEL, film director; b. Moscow. Dir. Taxi Blues, 1990 (Best Dir. award Cannes Internat. Film Festival 1990), Luna Park, 1992; dir., writer: The Life in Red; writer Vostochnij roman, 1992, Liniya zhizni, 1996. Office: Afra-Film Enterprises 137 S Robertson Blvd # 254 Beverly Hills CA 90211-2832 also: Confedration of Film Makers Union, Vasilyevskaya St 13, 123 85 Moscow Russia Mailing: Confedn Film Makesumon, Maly Kozikhinsky Per 11, 103001 Moscow Russia*

LOUPASIS, STYLIANOS, mechanical engineer; b. Chania, Greece, Feb. 22, 1970; s. Evangelos and Ourania (Barbopoulou) L. Diploma, U. Fridericiana, 1992; diploma in mech. engring., Aristotelian U., 1992; M in Environ. Mmgt., European Assn. Environ. Mgmt., 1996. Rsch. engr. Sulzer Brothers, Winterthur, Switzerland, 1990; prodn. engr. Metsa Serla, Nokia, Finland, 1991; rsch. engr. Daimler Benz, Stuttgart, Germany, 1992; planning officer Club Meditarranee, Kos, Greece, 1994; salesman Rodi, Chania, 1994-95; rschr. European Commn., Ispra, Italy, 1996-97; project mgr. ICLEI, Freiburg, Germany, 1998-99, TNO, Apeldoorn, The Netherlands, 1999—. Mem. Greek Assn. Mech. Engrs., Tech. Ch. Greece.

LOURANTOS, XENOPHON-SPYROS, textiles executive; b. Athens, Greece, Apr. 10, 1954; s. Panagiotis Gerassimos Lourantos and Sofia Maria Milonakos; m. Kalliopi Despina Aslanidou; children: Panagiotis, Ioanna. BSc, Nat. U. Athens (Greece), 1977; MSc, U. Leeds (UK), 1978; diploma, Inst. Textile France, Lille, 1988. Resident engr. Gematex, Wad Medani, Sudan, 1979-81; project mgr. KTZ, Kafue, Zambia, 1981-85; asst. gen. mgr. Sotexka, Dakar, Senegal, 1985-89; gen. mgr./CEO NTM, Lagos, Nigeria, 1990-93, KTZ, Kafue, 1993-95; dir. Maurer Textiles, Geneva, 1995-98; gen. mgr., CEO Ktimato Logio S.A., Athens, Greece, 1998—. Greek State scholar, 1972-77. Fellow Textile Inst.; mem. Inst. Civil Engrs., Hwy. Engrs., Textile Engrs. E-mail: xslourau@ctimatologio.gr. Fax: 30-1-6537 726. Office: Maurer Textiles SA, 288 Mesogiou Ave, 15562 Athens Greece

LOURDUSAMY, D. SIMON CARDINAL, archbishop; b. Kalleri, Pondicherry, India, Feb. 5, 1924. ordained Roman Cath. Ch., 1951. Consecrated bishop Titular Ch. Sozusa, Libya, 1962; titular archbishop Philippi, 1964; archbishop Bangalore, 1968-71; proclaimed cardinal, 1985; sec. Congregation for the Evangelization of Peoples, 1973-85; pres. Pontifical Missionary Work. Home: Palazzo dei Convertendi, 64 Via dei Corridori, 00193 Rome Italy Office: Congregation for Ea Chs, Via della Conciliazione 34, 00193 Rome Italy*

LOUVARD, DANIEL FRANÇOIS, cell biologist, researcher; b. Abbeville, France, Feb. 20, 1948; s. Guy and Françoise (DeLattre) L.; m. Marie Noëlle Jeanine Marier, Apr. 23, 1973; children: Nathalie, Bertrand, Jean-Frédéric. PhD in Biochemistry, U. Marseille, 1973, PhD in Phys. Chemistry, 1976. Head of group EMBL, Heidelberg, Germany, 1978-82; head Lab. Membrane Biology Institut Pasteur, Paris, 1982-95; dir. rsch. CNRS, Paris, 1987—; prof. molecular biology Institut Pasteur, Paris, 1990—; dir. biology divsn. Inst. Curie, Paris, 1993-95, dir. rsch. divsn., 1995—, dir. dept. biology, 1996—; expert Human Capital Mobility Program, European Union, 1992-94; mem. sci. couns. and ad hoc coms. in various labs. in France, in Europe, in U.S. and in Singapore, 1995—; cons. mem. sci. coun. pharm. co. Rhone Poulenc Rorer, 1990—. Editor Jour. Cell Sci., 1992—; mem. several editorial bds. of internat. sci. jours.; contbr. more than 100 articles to cell and molecular boilogy internat. jours. Recipient prize Fedn. European Biochem. Socs., 1983, A. Johannides prize French Acad. Sci., 1987, R. Lounsbery prize, 1996. Mem. European Cell Biology Orgn. (pres. 1990—), Academia Europea, French Acad. Scis. (corr.). Avocations: scuba diving, fishing, jogging, theater. Office: Institut Curie, 26 rue d'Ulm, 75248 Paris Cedex 05, France

LOUX, GORDON DALE, religious organization administrator; b. Souderton, Pa., June 21, 1938; s. Curtis L. and Ruth (Derstine) L.; m. Elizabeth Ann Nordland, June 18, 1960; children: Mark, Alan, Jonathan. Diploma, Moody Bible Inst., Chgo., 1960; BA, Gordon Coll., Wenham, Mass., 1962; BD, No. Bapt. Sem., Oak Brook, Ill., 1965, MDiv, 1971; MS, Nat. Coll. Edn., Evanston,Ill., 1984; LHD (hon.), Sioux Falls Coll., 1985. Ordained to ministry, Bapt. Ch., 1965. Assoc. pastor Forest Park (Ill.) Bapt. Ch., 1962-65; alumni field dir. Moody Bible Inst., Chgo., 1965-66, dir. pub. rels., 1972-76; dir. devel. Phila. Coll. Bible, 1966-69; pres. Stewardship Svcs., Wheaton, Ill., 1969-72; exec. v.p. Prison Fellowship Ministries, Washington, 1976-84, pres., CEO, 1984-88; pres., CEO Prison Fellowship Internat., Washington, 1979-87; pres. Internat. Students, Inc., Colorado Springs, Colo., 1988-93, Gordon D. Loux & Co., LLC, Colorado Springs, 1994—, Trinity Cmty. Found., 1996—. Author: Uncommon Courage, 1987, You Can Be a Point of Light, 1991; contbg. author: Money for Ministries, 1989, Dictionary of Christianity in America, 1989. Bd. dirs. Evang. Coun. for Fin. Accountability, Washington, 1979-92, vice chmn., 1981-84, 86-87, chmn., 1987-89; vice chmn. Billy Graham Greater Washington Crusade, 1985-85; bd. dirs. Evang. Fellowship of Mission Agys., 1991-94, Ctr. for Christian Jewish Dialogue, Colorado Springs, 1996—, Hope and Home, Colorado Springs, 1998—, C2ure, Mechanicsburg, Pa., 1999—, Global Leaders Initiative. Named Alumnus of Yr., Gordon Coll., 1986. Mem. Broadmoor Golf Club (Colo. Springs). Republican. Home: 740 Bear Paw Ln N Colorado Springs CO 80906-3215 Office: PO Box 38898 Colorado Springs CO 80937-8898

LOUX, JONATHAN DALE, business development consultant; b. Oak Park, Ill., Mar. 23, 1966; s. Gordon Dale and Elizabeth (Nordland) L.; m. Jan Mary Peters, July 22, 1989; children: Kara Leigh, Kurtis Dale, Kenton Stanley, Kourtney Grayce. BS, Eastern Coll., St. Davids, Pa., 1988. CPA, Ill. Acctg. supr. Capin, Crouse, LLP, Wheaton, Ill., 1989-93; supr. internal audit Select Beverages, Ind., Darien, Ill., 1993-94; exec. v.p. Gordon D. Loux & Co., LLC, Colorado Springs, Colo., 1994—; pres. Loux Group, LLC, Colorado Springs, 1996—; trustee Eastern Coll., St. Davids, Pa., 2000—. Republican. Presbyterian. Home and Office: 6335 Moccasin Pass Ct Colorado Springs CO 80919-4452

LOVBORG, UFFE, project manager; b. Kolding, Denmark, June 2, 1954; came to the U.S., 1999; s. Carl and Inge Louise (Christiansen) L. Degree in Zoology, Aarhus (Denmark) U., 1976; Degree in Biochemistry, Copenhagen U., 1978, PhD in Immunology, 1981. R&D scientist NUNC, Denmark, 1981-85, Novo Nordisk, Denmark, 1985-93; core scientist Novo Nordisk Symbion, Denmark, 1993-95; rsch. fellow Sydney (Australia) U., 1995-99; mgr. Borg-Biomed. & Diagnostic Consulting, Australia, 1998-99; sr. exptl. scientist CSIRO, Australia, 1999; project mgr. Dako Corp., Carpinteria, Calif., 1999—; external tchr. Copenhagen U., 1987-95; referee Australian Asthma Fund, 1998-99. Author: Monoclonal Antibodies, 1982, Guide to Solid Phase Immunoassay, 1984; contbr. articles to profl. jours. Achievements include patents for rendering proteins non-allergenic through changing their molecular structure. Avocations: walking, nature, travels. Office: Dako Corp 6392 Via Real Carpinteria CA 93013-2921

LOVDEN, LARS ERIK, Swedish government official; b. 1950. Mem. Malmö (Sweden) City Coun.; now dep. min. fin. Swedish Ministry Fin., Stockholm; Mem. parliament war delegation. E-mail: regeringen@regeringen.se. Address: Ministry Fin, Rödbodgatan 6, S-103 33 Stockholm Sweden*

LOVE, DANIEL JOSEPH, consulting engineer; b. Fall River, Mass., Sept. 27, 1926; s. Henry Aloysius and Mary Ellen (Harrington) L.; m. Henrietta Maurisse Popper, June 10, 1950 (dec. Mar. 1986); children: Amy, Timothy (dec.), Terence, Kevin; m. Adeline Aponte Esquivel, Feb. 11, 1989; stepchildren: Eric, Brian, Jason. BSEE, Ill. Inst. Tech., 1951, MSEE, 1956; MBA, Calif. State U., Long Beach, 1973. registered profl. engr., Calif., Ariz., Ill., La.; cert. fire protection, Calif. Test engr. Internat. Harvester Co., Chgo., 1951-52; designer Pioneer Svc. & Engring. Co., Chgo., 1952-53; project engr., ops. mgr. Panellit Co., Skokie, Ill., 1953-60; mktg. mgr. Control Data Co., Mpls., 1961-62; mktg. mgr., asst. to pres. Emerson Electric Co., Pasadena, Calif., 1963-65; pres., gen. mgr. McKee Automation Co., North Hollywood, Calif., 1965-68; engring. specialist Bechtel Co., Vernon and Norwalk, Calif., 1968-80; chief elec. engr. Bechtel Co., Madrid, 1980-83; engring. specialist Bechtel Co., Norwalk, Calif., 1983-87; cons. engr. Hacienda Heights, Calif., 1987—. Contbr. articles to jours. in field. Pres. Wilson High Sch. Band Boosters, Hacienda Heights, 1971-73. With USN, 1944-46. Named Outstanding Engr., Inst. for Advancement Engring., 1986; recipient 3d place prize paper award Industry Application Soc., 1995. Fellow IEEE (disting. lectr., chmn. Met. L.A. sect. 1973-74, chmn. L.A. coun. 1977-78, chmn. protection com. 1990-91, Richard Harold Kaufmann award 1994, Ralph H. Lee prize paper award 1995); mem. NSPE, Nat. Acad. Forensic Engrs., Instrument Soc. Am. (sr.), Soc. Fire Protection Engrs. Republican. Roman Catholic. Avocations: duplicate bridge, travel, walking, writing. Home: 16300 Soriano Dr Hacienda Hgts CA 91745-4863

LOVE, DAVIS MILTON, III, professional golfer; b. Charlotte, Apr. 13, 1964; m. Robin; children: Alexia, Davis IV. Student, U. N.C. Profl. golfer PGA, 1985—; mem. Ryder Cup Team, 1993; winner Buick Invitational Calif., 1996. Winner The Internat., 1990, MCI Heritage Classic Champion, 1987,,91 & 92; The Players Championship, 1992; KMart Greater Greensboro Open, 1992; Infiniti Tournament of Champions, 1993; Las Vegas Invitational, 1993; Freeport-McMoran Classic, 1995; Buick Invitational, 1996; PGA Championship, 1997; Buick Challenge, 1997; MCI Classic, 1998. Office: c/o PGA 100 Ave of Champions PO Box 109601 Palm Bch Gdns FL 33410-9601

LOVE, ERIC RUSSELL, retired mathematics educator, researcher; b. London, Mar. 31, 1912; arrived in Australia, 1922; s. Robert Russell and Lilla May Reeves (Scott) L.; m. Elvie Cadle, Aug. 20, 1938; children: Antony Russell, Solway Elvie Nutting, Bernard Robert William. BA with honours, U. Melbourne, Australia, 1933, DSc, 1992; BA with honours, Cambridge (Eng.) U., 1935, PhD, 1938, ScD, 1978. Chartered mathematician Inst. Math. and Its Applications, Eng. Asst. lectr. U. London Queen Mary Coll., 1938-39, Durham (Eng.) U., 1939-40; math. cons. Munitions Supply Labs., Melbourne, 1942-43, Aero. Lab., CSIR, Melbourne, 1943-45; sr. lectr. math. U. Melbourne, 1940-41, 45-48, assoc. prof., 1948-52, prof., 1953-77, emeritus and hon. prof., 1978—; referee math. jours.; speaker over 20 math. confs., Europe, U.S., Japan.; rschr. in math. analysis. Referee Jour. Math. Analysis and Applications, 1980-91, assoc. editor, 1991-96; contbr. over 80 articles to math. jours. Mem. Cambridge Scientists' Anti-War Group, 1935-38.

LOVE, JAMES SANFORD, III, communications executive; b. Jackson, Miss., Aug. 4, 1944; s. James Sanford Jr. and Jo Ellis (Buie) L.; m. Barbara Ann Harris, June 11, 1966 (div. Oct. 1981); children: James S. IV, Caroline E., Gillian M. BBA in Bus. and Govt., U. Miss., 1966; MBA, U. Va., 1968. Acct. exec. J. Walter Thompson, N.Y.C., 1968-70; rsch. analyst, asst. v.p. Dean Witter Co., N.Y.C., 1970-73; chmn., CEO Love Broadcasting Co., Biloxi, Miss., 1972-91, Lakewood Meml. Pk., Jackson, Miss., 1972-91; rsch. analyst Baker Weeks & Co., N.Y.C., 1973-75; rsch. analyst, v.p. Paine Webber & Co., N.Y.C., 1975-77; chmn., CEO Love Comm. Co., Jackson, 1991—; cosn. Norberg Capital, N.Y.C., 1979-97; co-founder Millsaps Buie House Bed and Breakfast Inn, 1987—; owner White House Hotel, Biloxi, Miss., 1989—. Exec. prodr.: Miss. News Tonight, 1991-92. Trustee Millsaps Coll., Jackson, 1989—; chmn. bd. trustees Miss. chpt. Nature Conservan cy, 1996-97; chmn. leadership bd. Boys and Girls Club of Miss. Gulf Cost, 1994-96; mem. adv. bd. Salvation Army, 1997. Named to All-Am. Rsch. Team, Instl. Investor Mag., 1974-75; recipient George Foster Peabody award U. Ga., 1989, regional Emmy award, 1990. Mem. Boston Club (New Orleans), Windance Country Club (Gulfport, Miss.), Univ. Club (Jackson), Biloxi Yacht Club. Episcopalian. Avocations: gardening, photography, salt water fishing, history. Home: 12137 Hickman Rd Biloxi MS 39532-9429 Office: Love Comm Co 240 Eisenhower Dr Bldg C Biloxi MS 39531-3601

LOVE, JAMIE L., clinical therapist; b. Wichita, Kans., Feb. 29, 1952; d. Richard James and Maxine Elliott Vulgamore; m. Donny Carroll Love; children: Jimmy, Donna. BA in Behavioral Sci., Southwest Tex. State U., 1974; MSSW, U. Tex., Austin, 1987. Worker, supr. Child Protective Svcs., Dept. Human Svcs., Belton, Tex., 1975-86; intern, therapist Austin State Hosp., Belton, Tex., 1986-87; resident svcs. Belle Oakes Apt., Belton, 1987-88; worker, supervising Dept. of Human Svcs., Temple, Tex., 1988-91; clin. therapist Woods Psychiat., Killeen, Tex., 1991-96; pvt. practice, clin. therapist Killeen, 1996—. Recipient Social Worker of Yr. Bell County Child Welfare Bd., 1976-77, commendation for Outstanding Support and Development of Volunteer Svcs., 1977-84. Mem. NASW (treas. 1992), Am. Assn. Marriage and Family Therapy.

LOVE, JEFFREY BENTON, lawyer; b. Houston, Oct. 4, 1949; s. Benton Fooshee and Margaret (McKean) L.; m. Katherine Brownlee, Dec. 30, 1972; children: Benton Fooshee III, Elizabeth Houston. BA, Vanderbilt U., 1971; JD, U. Tex., 1976. Bar: Tex. 1976. Assoc. Liddell, Sapp, Zivley, Hill & LaBoon, L.L.P., Houston, 1976-81, ptnr., 1982—, adv. dir., 1990—, vice chmn. bd. dirs. nominating com. 1992—; dir. Tex. Commerce Bank-Houston regional adv. bd., Kinark Corp., 1985-88, St. Luke's Episc. Hosp., 1989-96; hon. consul gen. Sweden in Tex., 1983-89, U. Tex. Devel. Bd., 1991—; mem. com. for Tex. campaign U. Tex., 1992—; assoc. mem. bd. visitors U. Tex. M. D. Anderson Cancer Ctr., 1991—; chmn. Harris County Fin. Com. Re-Election Campaign, Tex. Supreme Ct. Justice Tom Phillips, 1995-96; dir. exec. com. Houston Grand Opera. Pres. Sunrisers Houston Breakfast Assn., Houston, 1979; dir. exec. com. Houston Grand Opera Assn., Houston, 1979-86; dir., chmn. Children's Fund, Inc., Houston, 1981-82; bd. dirs. Tex. Bus. Hall of Fame Found., 1985—, chmn. bd. dirs., 1987, awards com. 1992—; bd. dirs. March of Dimes, Houston, 1989—, chmn. 1989, bd. nominations com. 1992—; adv. dir. Eileen McMillin Blood Ctr., Meth. Hosp.; bd. govs., exec. com., sec. The Forum Club, 1987-92, The Hospice Tex. Med. Ctr. Cap. Campaign, 1991, St. John Divine Episcopal Ch. Cap. Campaign, 1992; bd. dirs., exec. com. Nat. Conf. Christians and Jews, Inc., 1987-90; mem. devel. council Tex. Children's Hosp., 1987—; mem. adv. bd. Covenant House Tex., 1988—; Houston Internat. Festival: co-chmn., Mayor's Gala, 1993, mem. underwriters com. Houston Ballet Ball, 1992; bd. dirs., mem. exec. com. Houston Youth Symphony & Ballet, 1990—, pres., 1992-93, chmn., emcee 1993 Cultural Leader of Yr. Dinner; hon. chair Lupus Disease Benefit, 1992. Recipient Outstanding Young Texas Ex award U. Tex. Ex Students Assn., 1988, 5 Outstanding Young Houstonian awards Houston Jr. C. of C., 1988, 5 Outstanding Young Texan awards Tex. Jaycees, 1988; named one of Outstanding Young Men in Am., U.S. Jaycees, 1980, 81; decorated Knighthood of Royal Order of North Star King Carl XVI Gustaf of Sweden, 1989, Hon. Family of Yr., Child Advocates, Inc., 1991. Mem. ABA, Houston C. of C., Houston Bar Assn., Tex. Bar Assn., Swedish Am. Trade Assn. (bd. dirs. 1983—), Swedish Am. C. of C., U. Tex. Law Alumni Assn. (bd. dirs. 1981—, nat. pres., chmn. exec. com. 1986-87), Phi Delta Theta Alumni Assn. Episcopalian. Clubs: River Oaks, Allegro, Houston. Home: 3744 Inwood Dr Houston TX 77019-3002 Office: Liddell Sapp Zivley Hill & LaBoon LLP 600 Travis St 3400 Chase Tower Houston TX 77002-3095*

LOVE, MILDRED ALLISON, retired secondary school educator, historian, writer, volunteer; b. Moultrie, Ga., Mar. 12, 1915; d. Ulysees Simpson Sr. and Susie Marie (Dukes) Allison; m. George Alsobrook Love, Aug. 24, 1956 (dec. 1978). BSEd, U. Tampa (Fla.), 1941; MS in Home Econs., Fla. State U., 1953; MA in History, U. Miami, Coral Gables, Fla., 1969. Cert. tchr., Fla. Vocat. home econs. tchr. Hamilton County Pub. Schs., Jasper, Fla., 1941-43, Pinellas County Pub. Schs., Tarpon Springs, Fla., 1946-51; vocat. home econs. tchr. Dade County Pub. Schs., Miami, Fla., 1951-61, history tchr., 1961-73; supr. food svcs. Ft. Jackson (S.C.), 1944-46. Chmn. subcoun. for crime prevention Brickell Area, City of Miami, 1983-87; mem. Crisis Response Team, Miami Police Dept., 1983—; vol. VA Hosp., Miami, 1987—; historian, vol. vets affairs VFW Aux., Miami, 1988-89; precinct worker presdl. election, 1976, 80; sponsor history honor soc. Miami Edison Sr. H.S., 1961-73; mem. Mus. of Sci., St. Stephen's Episc. Ch., Coconut Grove, Fla.; mem. Dade Heritage Trust; charter mem. Libr. Congress Assocs.; mem. Arthritis Found., Consumer Union. Mem. AAUW, VFW (aux. post 471 Miami, Fla.), Am. Assn. Ret. Persons, Hist. Assn. S. Fla., U. Miami Alumni Assn., Fla. Ret. Educators Assn., Nat. Wildlife Fedn., Am. Legion (aux. post 29 Miami, Fla.), Nat. Trust Hist. Preservation, Coll. of Arts and Scis. Assn. U. Miami, Fla. Vocat. Home Econs. Tchrs. (pres. 1947), Fla. Vocat. Home Econs. Assn. (pres. 1948-49), Dade Heritage Trust, Woman's Club of Miami Beach, Sierra Club, Phi Alpha Theta. Democrat. Episcopalian. Avocation: foreign languages. Home: 2411 S Miami Ave Miami FL 33129-1527

LOVE, PHILIP NOEL, university administrator; b. Aberdeen, Scotland, Dec. 25, 1939; s. Thomas Isaac and Ethel Violet Love; m. Isabel Leah Mearns, 1963 (dec. 1993); 3 children; m. Isobel Pardey, 1995. MA, Aberdeen U., 1961, LLB, 1963, LLD (hon.), 1997; LLD (hon.), Abertay U., Dundee, 1996. Bar: Scotland, 1963; CIMgt. Ptnr. Campbell Connon, Solicitors, Aberdeen, 1963-74; cons., 1974—; dean Faculty of Law U. Aberdeen, 1979-82, 91-92, vice-prin., 1986-90; vice-chancellor U. Liverpool, Eng., 1992—; chmn. Scottish Conveyancing and Executry Svcs. Bd., 1991-96; commr. Scottish Law Commn., 1986-95; local chmn. Rent Assessment Panel for Scotland, 1972-92; chmn. Sec. of State for Scotland's expert com. on house purchase, 1982-84; chmn. Standing Com. on Legal Edn. in Scotland, 1976-80; mem. rules coun. Ct. of Session, 1968-92; chmn. Mersey Partnership, 1995-98, Univs. and Colls. Employers Assn., 1995—. Chmn. Customer Adv. Group, Registers of Scotland, 1990-92, Aberdeen Home for Widowers' Children, 1971-92; pres. Aberdeen Grammar Sch. Former Pupils' Club, 1987-88; hon. Sheriff of Grampian, Highland and Islands, 1978—; trustee Grampian and Islands Family Trust, 1988-92; gov. Inst. Occupational Medicine, Ltd., 1990—; trustee St. George's Hall Trust, 1996—; mem. coun. Com. of Vice-Chancellors and Prins. of Univs. of U.K., 1996—. Fellow RSA, Acad. Learned Societies Soc. Scis.; mem. Law Soc. Scotland (pres. 1981-82), Scottish Law Agts. Soc. (v.p. 1970), Internat. Bar Assn. (coun. 1983-87), New Club (Edinburgh), Athenaeum (London), Royal Aberdeen Golf Club, Formby Golf Club. Home: Vice-Chancellor's Lodge, 12 Sefton Park Rd, Liverpool L8 3SL, England

LOVEJOY, GEORGE MONTGOMERY, JR., real estate executive; b. Newton, Mass., Apr. 15, 1930; s. George Montgomery and Margaret (King) L.; m. Ellen West Childs, June 30, 1956; children: George Montgomery III, Edward R., Philip W., Henry W. BA, Harvard U., 1951. V.p. Minot, DeBlois & Maddison, Boston, 1955-72; exec. v.p. Meredith & Grew, Inc., Boston, 1972-78, pres., 1978-88, chmn., 1988-95; chmn. Fifty Assocs., Boston, 1988-94, pres., 1994—; trustee various Scudder Kemper Inc. mut. funds, 1975-2000; bd. dirs. MGI Properties, Scudder Global High Income Fund, Cabot Indsl. Trust. Mem. Weston (Mass.) Planning Bd., 1961-68, chmn., 1965-67; mem. Bd. Selectmen, 1968-71, chmn., 1970-71; bd. dirs. Boston Mcpl. Rsch. Bur., 1966—, chmn., 1982-84; mem. com. Fund for Preservation Wildlife and Natural Areas, 1985-94, chmn., 1992-94; trustee New Eng. Aquarium, 1969—, pres. 1992-94, chmn. 1994; trustee Radcliffe Coll., 1987-95; mem. Corp. Northeastern U. Mem. Counselors of Real Estate (past pres., bd. dirs.), Greater Boston Bldg. Owners and Mgrs. Assn. (past pres.), Internat. Coun. Shopping Ctrs., Inst. Real Estate Mgmt. (past pres. New Eng. chpt.), Greater Boston Real Estate Bd. (past pres.), Mass. Assn. Realtors, Nat. Assn. Realtors, Nature Conservancy (mem. Mass. adv. bd., chmn. 1994-97), Harvard Club Boston (past pres.). Avocations: outdoor activities, land conservation. Home: 54 Beacon St Boston MA 02108-3531 Office: Fifty Assoc 50 Congress St Boston MA 02109-4002

LOVEJOY, LEE HAROLD, investment company executive; b. July 19, 1936; s. Harold B. and Lorene E. (Spangler) L.; m. Carol L. Nellis, Feb. 14, 1976; children by previous marriage: Steven Lee, Kristin Ann. BS, Drake U., 1958. With Paine Webber Jackson & Curtis, St. Paul, 1965-68; mgr. Twin Cities instnl. dept. Paine Webber Jackson & Curtis, Mpls., 1968-72; v.p., mgr. New Eng. Paine Webber Jackson & Curtis, Boston, 1972-74; sr. v.p., mgr. nat. instnl. equity dept. Paine Webber Jackson & Curtis, 1974-77; sr. v.p., dir., chief adminstrv. officer, dir. mktg. Paine Webber Mitchell Hutchins Inc., N.Y.C., 1977-83; sr. v.p. consumer products group Paine Webber Mitchell Hutchins Inc., Phila., 1983-88; sr. v.p., resident mgr. Tucker Anthony & R.L. Day, Inc., Phila., 1988-97, exec. v.p., prin., 1997-2000; pres. Lovejoy & Assocs. Fin. Cons., Hampton, N.J., 2000—, ret., 2000. Mem. St. Paul Mayor's Legal and Fin. Adv. Com.; bd. dirs. Presbyn. Homes Found.; trustee Drake U. Capt. USAF, 1958-65. Mem. Internat. Golf Sponsors Assn., Security Industry Assn., Boston Security Traders, Union League of Phila., Boston Investment Club, Security Traders N.Y., Sigma Alpha Epsilon, Omicron Delta Kappa, Arnold Air Soc. Republican. Home and Office: Hideaway Farm 170 Bryans Rd Hampton NJ 08827-4508

LOVELACE, DOROTHY LOUISE, volunteer; b. Birmingham, Ala., Dec. 24, 1921; d. Walter Louis and Dorothea Christina (Sayers) Howard; m. Larry Clark Lovelac, Dec. 23, 1941; children: Larry C. (dec.), Susan Lovelace Weaver, Claude Thomas II. Student, Birmingham So. Coll., 1938-40. extra (HBO movies) From the Earth to the Moon, 1997. Girl scout leader, den mother Keesler AFB, Biloxi, Miss., 1950-52; Sunday sch. tchr., choir.; mem. Orlando Civic Theatre Guild, publicity chmn. 1973-80; mem. Protestant Women of the Chapel, 1972-97, pres. 1992-96, v.p. 1987-91, hospitality chmn., 1980-87; guitar instr. Lakemont Presbn. Ch., 1992; pres. Top of the Hill Drama Club, 1989-93, Roadside Theatre Co. of Orlando, 1988-89; vol. ARC, Keesler AFB, Miss., South Ruislip AFB, London, Scott AFB, Ill., Patrick AFB, Fla., 1953-71; vol. Orlando Tng. Ctr. Chapel, 1971-98, Libr., 1980-82; vol. tchr. Head Start at Patrick AFB, Fla., 1971-72. Recipient 2d pl. award Smucker's Strawberry Festival Recipe Contest, 1998. Mem. Fla. Assn. for Family and Cmty. Edn. (treas. 1984-92, v.p. 1992-97, Best of Show 1990, First Pl. of Collection of Christmas Songs, 1991, Best of Show for Quilt, 1992, First Pl. for Song, 1992, Best of Show for Indian Beading, 1993, Best of Show children's Poetry book, 1994, Best of Show Dried Flower Art, 1995). Avocations: writing, music, needle work, drama, gardening. Home: 2518 Sweetwater Trail Maitland FL 32751-5017

LOVELL, SIR (ALFRED CHARLES) BERNARD, astronomer, educator; b. Oldland Common. Gloucestershire, Eng., Aug. 31, 1913; s. Gilbert and Emily Laura (Adams) L.; student U. Bristol; LL.D. (hon.), univs. Edinburgh, 1961, Calgary, 1966; D.Sc. (hon.), univs. Leicester, 1961, Leeds, 1966, Bath, 1967, London, 1967, Bristol, 1970; D.Univ., U. Stirling, 1974, U. Surrey, 1975; m. Mary Joyce Chesterman, Sept. 14, 1937. Asst. lectr. physics U. Manchester, 1936-39, with telecommunications research establishment, 1939-45. lectr., sr. lectr., reader physics, 1945-51, prof. radio-astronomy, dir. Nuffield Radio Astronomy Labs., Jodrell Bank, 1951-81; Reith lectr. Brit. Broadcasting System. 1958. Decorated officer Order Brit. Empire, 1946; Comdr.'s Order of Merit (Poland); recipient Duddell medal Phys. Soc., 1954; Royal medal Royal Soc., 1960, Daniel and Florence Guggenheim Internat. Astronautics award, 1961; Order du Merite pour la Recherche et l'Invention, 1962; Churchill gold medal Soc. Engrs., 1964; Benjamin Franklin medal Royal Soc. Arts, 1980. Hon. fellow Instn. Elec. Engrs., Royal Swedish Acad., Inst. Physics; fellow Royal Soc.; mem. Am. Acad. Arts and Scis. (hon. fgn.), Royal Astron. Soc. (pres. 1970-71; Gold medal 1981), N.Y. Acad. Scis. (hon. life). Author: Science and Civilization, 1939; World Power Resources and Social Development, 1945; Radio Astronomy, 1952; Meteor Astronomy, 1954; The Exploration of Space by Radio, 1957; The Individual and the Universe (The Reith Lectures), 1958; The Exploration of Outer Space, 1962; Discovering the Universe, 1963; Our Present Knowledge of the Universe, 1967; editor: (with T. Morgerison) The Explosion of Science: The Physical Universe, 1967; The Story of Jodrell Bank, 1968; The Origins and International Economics of Space Exploration, 1973; Out of the Zenith: Jodrell Bank 1957-70, 1973; Man's Relation to the Universe, 1975; P.M.S. Blackett —a Biographical Memoir, 1976; In the Center of Immensities, 1978; Emerging Cosmology, 1980; The Jodrell Bank Telescopes, 1984, Voice of the Universe, 1987; (with Sir Frances Graham Smith) Pathways to the Universe, 1988, (autobiography) Astronomer by Chance, 1990, Echoes of War, 1991; contbr. articles to phys. and astron. jours. Home: Quinta Swettenham, NR Congleton, Cheshire England Office: Nuffield Radio Astronomy Labs, Jodrell Bank, Macclesfield Cheshire, England also: care Royal Soc, 6 Carlton House Terr, London SW1Y 5AG, England

LOVELL, CARL ERWIN, JR., lawyer; b. Riverside, Calif., Apr. 12, 1945; s. Carl Erwin and Hazel (Brown) L.; m. Danna I. Wale; children: Carl Erwin III, Timothy C., Tishia R., Ashley P., Garrett T. BA, Vanderbilt U., 1966, JD, 1969. Bar: Nev. 1969, D.C. 1971, U.S. Supreme Ct. 1973. Jr. editor Land and Water Law Rev., 1973-89; instr. bus. law U. Nev., Las Vegas, Clark County C.C.; city atty. City of N. Las Vegas, 1970-73; elected city atty. City of Las Vegas, 1973-77; v.p., sec.-treas., legal counsel Circus Circus Hotels, Inc., Las Vegas, 1977-83; sr. ptnr. Lovell, Bilbray & Potter, Las

Vegas, 1984-89; pvt. practice Las Vegas, 1989—; v.p., dir. Air Nev. Airlines, Inc.; chmn. Nat. Inst. Mcpl. Law Officers Consumer Protection Adv. Com., 1973-77, Nev. Crime Commn. Bd., 1974-77; U.S. rep. to China Internat. Trade and Law Talks, 1987; arbitrator, AAA, 1989—. Bd. dirs., v.p. BBB, 1983-91; chmn. NCCJ; pres. Clark County Young Dems., 1971-72; bd. dirs. Nat. Kidney Found.; pres., trustee Nev. Donor Network, Inc., 1992-96. With USAF, 1966-68. Mem. ABA, ATLA, Nev. State Bar, Nev. Trial Lawyers Assn., Elks (justice Las Vegas chpt. 1985-88). Office: 2801 S Valley View Blvd Ste 1B Las Vegas NV 89102-0116

LOVELL, EMILY KALLED, journalist; b. Grand Rapids, Mich., Feb. 25, 1920; d. Abdo Rham and Louise (Claussen) Kalled; student Grand Rapids Jr. Coll., 1937-39; BA, Mich. State U., 1944; MA, U. Ariz., 1971; m. Robert Edmund Lovell, July 4, 1947. Copywriter, asst. traffic mgr. Sta. WOOD, Grand Rapids, 1944-46; traffic mgr. KOPO, Tucson, 1946-47; reporter, city editor Alamogordo (N.Mex.) News, 1948-51; Alamogordo corr., feature writer Internat. News Service, Denver, 1950-54; Alamogordo corr., feature writer El Paso Herald-Post, 1954-65; Alamogordo news dir., feature writer Tularosa (N.Mex.) Basin Times, 1957-59; co-founder, editor, pub. Otero County Star, Alamogordo, 1961-65; newscaster KALG, Alamogordo, 1964-65; free lance feature writer Denver Post, N.Mex. Mag., 1949-69; corr. Electronics News, N.Y.C., 1959-63, 65-69; Sierra Vista (Ariz.) corr. Ariz. Republic, 1966; free lance editor N.Mex. Pioneer Interviews, 1967-69; asst. dir. English skills program Ariz. State U., 1976; free-lance editor, writer, 1977—; part-time tchr., lectr. U. Pacific, 1981-86; part-time interpreter Calif., 1983-91, Interpreters Unlimited, Oakland, 1985-91; sec., dir. Star Pub. Co., Inc., 1961-64, pres., 1964-65. 3d v.p., publicity chmn. Otero County Community Concert Assn., 1950-65; mem. Alamogordo Zoning Commn., 1955-57; mem. founding com. Alamogordo Central Youth Activities Com., 1957; vice chmn. Otero County chpt. Nat. Found. Infantile Paralysis, 1958-61; charter mem. N.M. Citizens Council for Traffic Safety, 1959-61; pres. Sierra Vista Hosp. Aux., 1966; pub. rels. chmn. Ft. Huachuca chpt. ARC, 1966. Mem. nat. bd. Hospitalized Vets. Writing Project, 1972-99; vol. instr. autobiography & creative writing, 1991—. Recipient 1st Pl. awards N.Mex. Press Assn., 1961, 62. Pub. Interest award Nat. Safety Council, 1962. 1st Pl. award Nat. Fedn. Press Women, 1960, 62; named Woman of Year Alamogordo, 1960. Editor of Week Pubs. Aux., 1962, adm. N.Mex. Navy, 1962, col. a.d.c. Staff Gov. N.Mex., 1963, Woman of Yr., Ariz. Press Women, 1973. Mem. N.Mex. (past sec.), Ariz. (past pres.) press women, N.Mex. Fedn. Womens Clubs (past dist. pub. rels. chmn., hon. life Alamogordo), N.Mex. Hist. Soc. (life), N.Mex. Fedn. Bus. and Profl. Womens Clubs (past pres., hon. life Alamogordo), Pan Am. Round Table Alamogordo, Theta Sigma Phi (past nat. 3d v.p.), Phi Kappa Phi. Democrat. Moslem. Author: A Personalized History of Otero County, New Mexico, 1963; Weekend Away, 1964; Lebanese Cooking, Streamlined, 1972; A Reference Handbook for Arabic Grammar, 1974, 77; contbg. author: The Muslim Community in North America, 1983. Home: 3400 Wagner Heights Rd Apt 226 Stockton CA 95209-4855

LOVELL, FRANCIS JOSEPH, investment company executive; b. Mar. 21, 1949; s. Frank J. and Patricia Anna (Donnellan) L. BBA, Nichols Coll., 1971. With Brown Bros. Harriman & Co., Boston, 1971-90, v.p., 1990—. Alumni dir. St. Columbkille Sch., Brighton, Mass. Mem. New Eng. Hist. Gen. Soc., Union Club of Boston. Republican. Home: 25 Pomfret St West Roxbury MA 02132-1809 also (summer): 48 Hidden Village Rd West Falmouth MA 02574 Office: 40 Water St Boston MA 02109-3604

LOVELL, TERRY JEFFRY, business educator; b. Sacramento, Mar. 26, 1953; s. Charles C. and Maxine (Carter) L.; m. Shannon Lynn Pribble, Mar. 17, 1992; children: Jared Cameron, Terry Jessica. BA in Sociology, U. Mont., 1975; MBA, Ariz. State U., 1985; PhD in Bus., Greenwich U., 1993. Tchr./rsch. asst. Ariz. State U., Tempe, 1983-88; asst. prof. bus. U. Alaska, Anchorage, 1988-90; prof. bus. Yavapai Coll., Prescott, Ariz., 1990—; presenter, rschr. in field. Contbr. articles, rsch. papers in field. Home constrn. vol. Habitat for Humanity, Prescott, 1995—; pres. faculty senate Yavapai Coll., 1995. Mem. APA, Acad. Mgmt., Am. Sociol. Assn. Avocation: woodworking. Fax: (520) 776-2160. E-mail: bc terry@yavapai.cc.az.us. Office: Yavapai Coll 1100 E Sheldon St Prescott AZ 86301-3220

LOVELL, WALTER BENJAMIN, secondary education educator; b. Cottonwood, Ariz., Jan. 7, 1947; s. Walter William Lovell and Mary Katherine (MacDonald) Bruce; m. Patsy Nichols, July 16, 1965 (div. Nov. 1986); children: Katherine Vi, Walter Kenneth, Karen Jennifer, Kristin Diane; m. Karen Lynn Bird, Mar. 3, 1990. AA, Ea. Ariz. Coll., 1966; B of Music Edn., No. Ariz. U., 1969, MusM, 1975. Dir. of bands Kingman (Ariz.) High Sch., 1968-70; asst. dir. bands Phoenix Union High Sch., 1970-71; dir. bands Carl Hayden High Sch., Phoenix, 1971-73, Mohave High Sch., Bullhead City, Ariz., 1973-78, Elko (Nev.) High Sch., 1978—; condr. numerous winning, competitive performances with Elko H.S. Band, including Grand Champions Holiday Bowl Parade, Field and Jazz competition, 1994, pregame performance and field show, Nat. Freedom Bowl, Anaheim, Calif., 1988, 90, Disneyland Parade, Anaheim, 1990, pre-game and half-time performances Weber State U., Ogden, Utah, 1990-97, U. Utah, 1995, Concert Band Festival, Boise (Idaho) State U., 1990-97, U. Nev.-Las Vegas Band Competition, 1988, Fiesta Bowl Parade, Phoenix, 1985, Tournament of Roses Parade, Pasadena, 1983, 95, 99, Presdl. Inaugural Parade, Washington, 1981, No. Nev. Youth Band Tour of Great Britain, 1982, Macy's Thanksgiving Day Parade, 1979, 2000, Performances in Washington, 1981, 2000; assoc. dir. All-Ariz. Bi-Centennial Band, 1976. Composer: (concert band compositions) Suite For Band, 1975, Tranquility, 1988, (jazz band compositions) Maybe Tuesday, 1974, Sunday Afternoon, 1987. Recipient Gubernatorial Proclamation for Elko H.S. Band, 1981, 83, 86, 88, 90, 92, 94, 96, 98, Proclaimed The Pride of Nev., 1995, 96, 2000, Proclaimed Nev.'s Mus. Amb., 1998, 2000; Gubernatorial Proclamation No. Nev. Youth Band, 1982, Nat. Sch. Band Achievement awards, 1981, 82; recipient Disting. Svc. award U. Nev.-Reno Bands, 1986, Citation of Excellence Nat. Band Assn., Nev. State Bd. Edn., 1983, Disting. Bandmaster of Am. award, 1981, Nev. State Marching Band Champion award, 1983-86, 92-94, 97, 99, Holiday Bowl Jazz Festival Grand Champion award, 1992, Nev. Music Educator of Yr., 1999. Mem. Nat. Band Assn. (citation of Excellence 1987), Am. Sch. Band Dirs. Assn., Nev. Music Educators Assn., Music Educators Nat. Conf., Ariz. Band and Orchestra Dir.'s Assn., Nat. Assn. Jazz Educators, Ariz. Music Educators Assn. Office: Elko High Sch 987 College Ave Elko NV 89801-3419

LOVELOCK, ANDREA GEORGE, editor; b. Rome, Mar. 17, 1956; s. John Frederich Lovelock and M. Antonietta Simeoni; m. Patrizia Mencarelli; children: David, Nicholas, Thomas. Degree in polit. sci., U. Rome, 1980. Editorial cons. Turismo Attualita, Rome, 1981-89, editorial chief, 1990—; cons. Ediman, Milan, 1988, Sigma/ Alitalia, Rome, 1990. With Italian Army, 1980. Avocations: soccer, tennis, skiing. Office: Turismo & Attualita, Turismo Attualita, Via S Prisca n 16, 00153 Rome Italy

LOVENBACH, THIERRY JACQUES, company executive; b. Boulogne, S/ Seine, France, Aug. 19, 1946; s. Jan and Juliette Myriam (Philippson) L.; m. Cecelene Cover, Nov. 10, 1974. Baccalaureat Maths, Lycee Janson, 1964; BBA, Ecole Supèrieure de Commerce, Le Havre, 1969; MBA, Harvard Grad. Sch., 1971. Asst. gen. mgr. Rhone Poulenc Agrl. Div., New Brunswick, N.J., 1976-78, dir. chemicals div., 1978-79; chmn. bd. Lautier (Rhone Poulenc Group), Grasse, France, 1979-81; dir. mktg. Rhone Poulenc Specialites Chimiques, Paris, 1981; chmn. bd., chief exec. officer Prolabo (Rhone Poulenc Group), Paris, 1982-88; ptnr. Apax Ptnrs. & Co., 1988-93; mng. dir., ptnr. Fenway Group, France, 1993—; chmn. bd. Pixley Richards Inc., Plymouth, Mass., 1994—, Altor Industrie, Nantes,nce, 1997—, E.P.S., Maidstone, England. Office: Fenway Group France, 29 Rue du Colisee, 75008 Paris France

LOVERIDGE-SANBONMATSU, JOAN MEREDITH, communication studies and women's studies educator; b. Hartford, Conn., July 5, 1938; d. Gilbert Thomas and Rosabel Frances (Nowry) Loveridge; m. Akira Sanbonmatsu, Aug. 29, 1964; children: James Michael, Kevin Yosh. BA, U. Vt., 1960; MA, Ohio U., 1963; PhD, Pa. State U., 1971. Writer, programming radio/tv WRUV, WCAX, Burlington, Vt., 1956-60, WOUB, Athens, Ohio, 1962-63, AFKN, Korea, 1960-61; unit head ARC, Japan, Korea, 1960-61; asst. prof. SUNY, Brockport, 1963-77; prof. comm. studies and women's studies SUNY, Oswego, 1977-98, prof. emerita, 1999—, instr. intensive English summer program, 1992—, co-coord. women's studies program, 1978-80, 82, instr. internat. studies infusion program, 1985-91; vis. prof. Rochester (N.Y.) Inst. Tech., 1971; assoc. adj. prof. Monroe C.C., Rochester, 1972-76; instr. Pa. State, State College, 1966-67; cons. for oral history project ARC Overseas Assn., 1994—; cons. Cazenovia Coll., N.Y., 1988-89; pres. bd. dirs. Woman's Career Ctr. Inc., Rochester, 1975-76; invited Japan Lecture Tour, 1997. Co-author: Feminism and Woman's Life, 1995; contbg. author: Public Speakers in the US, 1925-1993, Vol. 2, 1994; contbr. poetry to publs., 1986—; poetry editor/editl. bd.: Lake Effect, 1985-92; contbr. articles to profl. jours. including Howard Jour. Comms., Comm. Edn., Phoebe and Feminist Jour. Religious edn. team tchr. May Meml. Unitarian Soc., Syracuse, 1979-81; mem. adv. parent com., Oswego H.S., 1986-87. Recipient Unsung Heroine award Ctrl. N.Y. NOW, Syracuse, 1987, presdl. citation for social change ARC Overseas Assn., 1998; rsch. grantee Pa. State U., 1970, SUNY, Oswego, 1978, 91, 92, 94, 95, 96, N.Y. State United Univ. Professions Profl. Devel. and Quality of Working Life grantee, 1985, 87, 93, 94, 98; fellow U. Ill., Chgo., 1983. Mem. N.Y. Asian Studies Assn., Nat. Comm. Assn. (women's caucus job placement dir., exec. bd. 1977-78), Ea. Comm. Assn., N.Y. Speech Comm. Assn., Soc. for Intercultural Edn., Tng. and Rsch., Nat. Women's Studies Assn., Speech Comm. P.R. Assn., N.Y. State Women's Studies Assn., ARC Overseas Assn. (v.p. 1999-2001). Avocations: poetry, walking. Home: 23 McCracken Dr Oswego NY 13126-6011

LOVERN, TERRANCE LEE, production manager; b. Spokane, Oct. 8, 1945; s. Theodore and Tressa Clar (Adams) L. Grad. high sch., N.Y.C. Prin. understudy Ice Capades, 1963-64; prin. skater, dancer Casa Carioca Ice Revue, Garmisch, Germany, 1964-66; prin. skater Holiday on Ice, U.S. & South Am., 1966; prin. skater, dancer Conrad Hilton Hotel Ice Revue, Chgo., 1966-68; dancer Tropicana Hotel, Las Vegas, 1968-72, Lido de Paris, Las Vegas, 1972-74; dancer, singer Bobbie Gentry Show, Las Vegas, 1974-76; prin. skater, dancer Flamingo Hilton, Las Vegas, 1976-81; dancer, singer Lido deParis Show, Stardust Hotel, Las Vegas, 1976-81; instr. ice skating Ice Land Ice Arena, Las Vegas, 1983-88; skater, dancer Flamingo Hilton, Las Vegas, 1986-89; co. mgr. Stardust Hotel, Las Vegas, 1989-91, prodn. mgr., 1991-2000; prodn. stage mgr. Wayne Newton Show, Stardust Resort & Casino, 2000—. Artistic dir. Civil Ballet, Las Vegas, 1988-95. Bd. dirs. Golden Rainbow Las Vegas, 1997. Recipient Can. Figure Skating Gold medal, Vancouver, B.C., 1963. Home: 6113 Edgewood Cir Las Vegas NV 89107-2596 Office: Stardust Resort & Casino 3000 Las Vegas Blvd S Las Vegas NV 89109-1932

LOVETT, JOHN MICHAEL, education and training service executive; b. Melbourne, Australia, July 10, 1943; s. Mark and Pola (Braun) L.; m. Jill Diana Marr, June 3, 1967; children: Craig David, Ewan James. Clerk Australian Gov., Melbourne, 1967-80, project officer, 1980-82, training & staff devel. officer, 1982-84; coord. Disability Employment Action Ctr., Melbourne, 1984-86; mgr. cmty. svcs. Victorian Deaf Soc., Melbourne, 1986-97; coord. Victorian Coun. of Deaf People, 1997; mem. disability adv. coun. of Australia, 1985-90, deputy chair, 1987-88. Author: Australian Deaf Sports Federation, 1970, 73, International Com. of Deaf Sports Hand Book, 1985, World Games for the Deaf Hand book, 1993. Pres. Com. Internat. des Sports des Sourds, 1995—, v.p., 1981-95; pres. Australian Deaf Sports Fedn., 1985-95, gen. sec., 1967-85; chmn. World Fedn. of the Deaf Asia/Pacific Deaf Sport Championship Region Conf., 1987-89. Recipient Silver medal Com. Internat. des Sports des Sourds, 1985, Gold medal, 1993, F.J. Rose Oration Australian Assn. of Worker with the Deaf, 1991, Edward Miner Gallaudet award, 1999. Mem. Jolimont Square Social Club, Australian Deaf Sports Fedn. (life), Order of Australia (awarded). Avocations: reading, walking, following all codes of football. Home: 5/42 Wright St, McKinnon VIC 3204, Australia

LOVETT, LAURENCE DOW, retired real estate and steamship executive; b. Jacksonville, Fla., Apr. 13, 1930; s. William Radford and Agnes Nisbet (Dow) L. B.A., Harvard U., 1951, LL.B., 1954. Vice pres. Eric Boulton, Inc., N.Y.C., 1958-60; vice pres. Eastern Steamship Lines, Miami, Fla., 1960-65, Suwanee Steamship Co., N.Y.C., Jacksonville, 1965-78; pres. Burgoyne Properties, 1978-85; v.p. Piggly Wiggly Corp., 1965-82. Chmn. bd. dirs. Met. Opera Guild, 1979-86; chmn. Save Venice Inc., 1987-98, Venetian Heritage, Inc., 1998—; chmn. bd. dirs. Chamber Music Soc. of Lincoln Ctr., 1989-93. Served with AUS, 1955-57. Clubs: Knickerbocker, The Brook. Address: Palazzo Sernagiotto, Canareggio 5723 Venice Italy also: 11 Ave Princess Grace, Monte Carlo 98000, Monaco

LOVETT, RADFORD DOW, real estate and investment company executive; b. Jacksonville, Fla., Sept. 6, 1933; s. William Radford And Agnes (Dow) L.; m. Katharine R. Howe, June 25, 1955 (dec. Jan. 1991); children: Katharine, William Radford, Philip, Lauren; m. Susan Wylie Rogers, June 15, 1995; children: Nick, Peter, Teddy Rogers. With Merrill Lynch, Pierce, Fenner & Smith Inc., N.Y.C., 1958-78; mng. dir. Capital Markets Group, 1975-78; pres. Piggly Wiggly Corp., Jacksonville, Fla., 1978-82; chmn. bd. Commodores Pt. Terminal Corp., Jacksonville, 1995—; chmn. Southcoast Capital Mgmt. Corp., Jacksonville, 19955; dir. First Union Corp., Fla. Rock Industries Inc., Patriot Transp., Inc., Winn-Dixie Stores, Inc. Trustee Drew U., 1976-79, St. Vincent's Found., Jacksonville Zool. Soc. Lt. F.A. U.S. Army, 1955-57. Mem. Coastal Conservation Fla. (bd. dirs.). Episcopalian. Office: Ste 1600 One Independent Dr Jacksonville FL 32202-5009

LOVIAGIN, ANDREY YEVGENYEVICH, legislative assembly member; b. Leningrad, Russia, Feb. 21, 1955; s. Evgeniy Loviagin and Olimpiada Ivanova; m. Tatiyana Borisouna Chumakova, Aug. 9, 1983 (div. Nov. 1997); 1 child, Innokentiy; m. Anna Matyeeva; 1 child, Andrey. Magister, Leningrad Poly. Inst., 1977. Programmist State Bank, Leningrad, 1977-81; chief dept. automatic systems mgmt. Trust Orgtechstroy, Leningrad, 1981-86; instr. Dist. Com. Communist Party, Leningrad, 1986-89; chmn. bd. Baltiyskiy Bank, St. Petersburg, Russia, 1989-96, chmn. bd. dirs., 1996-98; dep. Legis. Assembly, St. Petersburg, 1994—; dir. JSC Inko, St. Petersburg, 1997—. Pres. Ann. Internat. Theatre Festival Baltic House, St. Petersburg, 1996—; founder Ann. Easter Festival Symphonic Music, St. Petersburg, 1996—. Lt. Russian Air Def. Res. Mem. Internat. Info. Acad., World-Wide Club Petersburgers. Avocations: music, tennis, mountain skiing. Home: nab Martynova 6, 197110 Saint Petersburg Russia Office: St Petersburg Legis Assembl, St Isaak Sq 6, 190000 Saint Petersburg Russia

LOVINGER, ANDREW JOSEPH, polymer scientist; b. Athens, Greece, May 15, 1948; s. Joseph and Berta (Gross) L.; m. Eleanor Saul, Feb. 29, 1976; children: Michael Joseph, Daniel Abraham. BSChemE and Applied Chemistry, Columbia U., 1970, MSChemE and Applied Chemistry, 1971, ScDChemE and Applied Chemistry, 1977. Mem. tech. staff Bell Labs. Lucent Tech. (formerly AT&T Bell Labs.), Murray Hill, N.J., 1977-85, disting. mem. tech. staff, 1985—, head polymer chemistry rsch. dept., 1985-94; sr. staff scientist, dir. polymers program divsn. materials rsch. NSF, Arlington, Va., 1995—; adj. assoc. prof. dept. chem. engring. Columbia U., N.Y.C., 1980-83. Assoc. editor Macromolecules, 1988—; contbr. over 140 articles to profl. publs., chpts. to books. Welch Found. lectr. in chemistry, Houston, 1987, Waldo Semon Lectr., U. Akron, 1996; recipient Frazer Price award U. Mass., 1993. Fellow AAAS, Am. Phys. Soc. (Dillon medal 1985); mem. Am. Chem. Soc., Materials Rsch. Soc.. Achievements include research on structures and properties of polymeric materials, morphology and phase transitions, ferroelectric polymers, high-performance polymers, silicon-based polymers, organic and polymeric thin-film transistors.

LOVINGOOD, VIVIAN ANN, religious organization executive; b. Columbia, S.C., Jan. 10, 1965; d. Paul Evans and Sara Kate (Davis) L. BA, Mars Hill Coll., 1986; MDiv, Pitts. Sem., 1990; MSW, U. Pitts., 1990. Exec. dir. Wilkinsburg Cmty. Ministry, Pitts., 1992—. Democrat. Presbyterian. Avocations: needlework, music, spectator sports. Office: Wilkinsburg Cmty Ministry 710 Mulberry St Pittsburgh PA 15221-2914

LOVREN, ROBERT, mechanical engineer, educator; b. Croatia, Dec. 9, 1942; arrived in Australia, 1971; Diploma of Engring., W. Univ. Polytechnic, Zagreb, 1961; Licentiate, Inst. of Quality Assurance, London, 1976; Diploma in automotive Mech. Engring., Inst. Automotive Engrs., 1995; Grad. Diploma of Engring., Royal Melbourne Inst Tech., 1988; postgrad., LaTrobe U., Bundoora, Melbourne, 1995; PhD in Religious Edn., Am. Coll. Metaphys. Theology, 2000. Registered engr., London. Various engring. design positions various mfg. cos., 1961-71; quality control inspector Leyland Motor Corp.-Australia, Ltd., Sydney, 1971-74; engring. inspector Bradford Kendall Foundries Pty., Ltd., Sydney, 1974-78, Pongrass Industries Pty. Ltd., Mascot, 1978-79; tech. officer Vickers Cockatoo Dockyards Pty. Ltd., Sydney, 1979-81; self-employed engr. Sydney, 1982-96; faculty of vocat., access, remote studies, hon. home tutor No. territory Univ., Darwin, 1997—. Contbr. articles to profl. jours. Mem. No. Territory Univ. Found., 1999; tutor UN Mission East Timor, 1999. Mem. APA (internat.), Am. Soc. Quality Control (inspection and nuclear divsns.), Australian Inst. for Non-Destructive Testing, Psychologists Assn. of Australia (assoc.), Inst. of automotive Mech. Engrs. (No. Territory of Australia br. exec. com. 1998-99), Australian Internat. UFO-Flying Saucer Rsch. Soc. Inc. (offcl. rep.). Home and Office: 3/12 Hazell Ct, Coconut Grove NT 0810, Australia

LOVRIĆ, MILIVOJ, electrochemist, researcher; b. Zagreb, Croatia, June 17, 1951; s. Ivo and Milka (Podrebarac) L.; m. Šebojka Komorsky, Sept. 27, 1975; 1 child, Damir. Grad. in Chemistry, U. Zagreb, 1974, grad. in Oceanology, 1977, DSc, 1983. Rschr. Ruder Bosković Inst., Zagreb, 1974-77, 80-98; analyst Misurata, Libya, 1977-79; rschr. U. Buffalo, N.Y., 1980-81, U. N.C., Chapel Hill, 1985-86, Atomic Inst., Julich, Germany, 1986-87, U. Geelong, Australia, 1989-90; rsch. advisor R. Bosković Inst., 1998—; sci. collaborator U. Berlin, 1993-97, U. Greifswald, Germany, 1998-2000. Mem. editl. bd. Croatica Chemica Acta, 1995—, Jour. Solid State Electrochem., 1997—; contbr. more than 100 articles to profl. jours. Mem. Croatian Chem. Soc. Office: Ruder Boskovic Inst, PO Box 180, 10 002 Zagreb Croatia

LOVVIK, GUNNAR JOHAN, business executive; b. Havgesund, Norway, Jan. 21, 1947; s. Magne and Dagmar Lovvik; m. Margit Helen Aase, July 10, 1970; children: Kjilil, Espen, Linn. BBA, The Norgwegian Sch. of Mgmt., Norway, 1972. Mktg. dir. Haug-Data, Haugesund, 1972-74; cinema dir. Haugesund, 1974-82, culture dir., 1982—; fiscal and cultural dir. Norwegian Internat. Film Festival, Haugesund, 1986—; exec. dir. Norwegian Internat. Film Festival, Oslo, 1993. Bd. dirs. Norsk Film AS, Oslo, 1987-92, Norwegian Opera, Oslo, 1991—; chmn. bd. dirs. Norwegian Film Inst., Oslo. Mem. Rotary. Office: Norwegian Intnl Film Fest, 15 24 August, 5001 Haugesund Norway

LOW, ARNOLD KINMAN, systems executive; b. San Francisco, Feb. 22, 1942; s. Howard Y. and Patricia M. (Lee) L.; m. Junko Nerio; 1 child, Sara. AB, Dartmouth Coll., 1963; MBA, San Francisco State U., 1976; Mng. Info. Svcs. Resource, Harvard Bus. Sch., 1984. Sys. assoc. So. Pacific Co., San Francisco, 1965-67; sys. analyst Applied Data Sys. Inc., San Francisco, 1967-68; mgr. data processing I. Magnin & Co., San Francisco, 1968-77; sr. v.p. 1st Nationwide Bank, San Francisco, 1977-86; pres. Low & Assocs., San Francisco, 1986—; mem. internat. bd. advisors U.S. China Ednl. Inst., San Francisco, 1989—. Mem. adv. bd. San Francisco C.C. Dist., 1974-78; pres. Urban Crossroads Sch., San Francisco, 1975-89; pres. Big Bros.-Big Sisters, San Francisco, 1989-90; foreman San Francisco Civil Grand Jury, 1993-94; trustee Ft. Mason Found., San Francisco, 1996-99. Mem. Data Processing Mgmt. Assn. (pres. 1973-74), Olympic Club. Office: 2915 Baker St San Francisco CA 94123-3209

LOW, BAK KONG, civil engineer, educator; b. Kuala Lumpur, Malaysia, Sept. 27, 1955; s. Choong H. Low and Siew T. Tan; m. Lay C. Tan, 1991; children: Yi-Hua, Pei-Hua. BSCE, MIT, 1979, MSCE, 1979; PhD in Engring., U. Calif. Berkeley, 1985. Profl. engr., Malaysia. Civil engr. Pub. Works Dept., Malaysia, 1980-82; lectr. Nanyang Technol. U., Singapore, 1985—, assoc. prof. Contbr. articles to profl. jours. Fellow ASCE. Avocations: reading, nature, squash, badminton, travel. Office: Nanyang Technol Univ, Nanyang Ave, 639798 Singapore Singapore

LOW, DAVID J., mathematician; b. Scotland, July 12, 1967. BSc in Math., U. Edinburgh, Scotland, 1989; MSc in Math. Biology, U. Dundee, Scotland, 1991; PhD in Math., U. Aberdeen, Scotland, 1994. Chartered mathematician. Rsch. fellow Napier U., Edinburgh, 1995-99; lectr. Heriot-Watt Univ. Edinburgh, 1999—. Mem. Am. Math. Soc., Edinburgh Math. Soc., Inst. Maths. and Its Applications. Avocations: track athletics, flying helicopters. Office: Dept Civil/Offshore Engring, Heriot-Watt U Riccarton, Campus Edinburgh EH14 4AS, Scotland

LOW, DONALD, diplomat, financial investor; b. San Francisco, Sept. 25, 1927; s. Alvin Grant and Annette Violet Low; m. Marion Berman Low, Apr. 7, 1982 (dec. Jan. 1998); children: Mitch, Phillip, Mindy. BA, U. San Francisco, 1952; hon. degree, Chas. Simmons Sch. Human Rels., San Francisco, 1955. Lic. realtor; lic. stock broker. Gen. mgr., developer Villa Roma Hotel, San Francisco, 1972-80; owner Fountain Hotel, Palm Springs, Calif., 1962-72, Hotel Cons., San Francisco, 1980-86; diplomat Republic of Cameroon, San Francisco, 1986—; vice dean San Francisco Consular Corps; chief fin. officer Am. Arts Soc., San Francisco, 1990—; cons. Internat. Rels. Inc., San Francisco, 1985—. Participant 7 world tennis tours. Lt. USAAC, 1952-54. Mem. World Trade Club, Bankers Club, Commonwealth Club, World Affairs Coun. San Francisco. Avocations: music, opera, tennis, collecting fine watches, symphony. Office: Republic of Cameroon Consulate 147 Terra Vista Ave San Francisco CA 94115-3876

LOW, FREDERICK EMERSON, English educator; b. Oct. 25, 1943. AA, Am. Coll., Paris, France, 1967; BA, Queens Coll., 1969, MLS, 1976; MA, CUNY, 1972. Prof. La Guardia Comm. Coll., CUNY, Long Island City, N.Y., 1978-95; dir. Asia World Learning Ctr., Inc., Flushing, N.Y., 1996—, Asian-Am. Ctr. for Edn. of N.Y., Inc., Flushing, 1998—. E-mail: hsueh04@banet.net. Home: 221-47 59th Ave Bayside NY 11364-1929 Office: Asia-Am Ctr for Edn of NY Inc 13438 35th Ave Flushing NY 11354-2817

LOW, GEORGE SOLON, business educator, consultant; b. Edmonton, Alta., Can., June 7, 1957; (parents Am. citizens); s. LeRon Franklin Low and Elna Jeanne Bagley; m. Colleen Davidson, Aug. 14, 1982; children: Jesse Hinman, Shannon Colleen, Allen George, Margaret Jeanne. BA, Brigham Young U., 1982; MBA, U. Western Ont., London, Can., 1988; PhD, U. Colo., 1994. Media dir. Foster Advt., Winnipeg, Man., Can., 1984-85, MacLaren-McCann Advt., Calgary, Alta., Can., 1984-86; group mgr. media planning MacLaren-McCann Advt., Toronto, Alta., Can., 1987; lectr. mktg. U. Lethbridge, Alta., Can., 1988-94, asst. prof., 1994-96; asst. prof. Tex. Christian U., Ft. Worth, 1996-2000, assoc. prof., 2000—, mem. faculty senate, 1999—; cons. Exxon Corp., Irving, Tex., 1986-87, Cadillac Fairview Corp., Toronto, Ont., Can., 1988-90, PepsiCo Inc., Purchase, N.Y., 1999-2000. Reviewr Jour. Mktg., 1996—; contbr. articles to profl. jours. Chartered orgn. rep. Boy Scouts Am., Arlington, Tex., 1997—. Rsch. grantee Mktg. Sci. Inst., 1991, 93, 96, 98, Pease Found., 2000; Doctoral fellow Social Sci. and Humanities Rsch. Coun., 1992. Mem. Am. Mktg. Assn. Office: Tex Christian Univ M J Neeley Sch Bus 2800 S University Dr Fort Worth TX 76129-0001

LOW, HARRY WILLIAM, judge; b. Oakdale, Calif., Mar. 12, 1931; s. Tong J. and Ying G. (Gong) L.; m. May Ling, Aug. 24, 1952; children: Larry, Kathy, Allan. AA, Modesto Jr. Coll., 1950; AB Polit. Sci. with honors, U. Calif., Berkeley, 1952, JD, 1955. Bar: Calif. 1955, U.S. Ct. Appeals (9th cir.) 1955. Commr. Workmen's Compensation Commn., 1966; teaching assoc. Boalt Hall, 1955-56; dep. atty. gen. Calif. Dept. Justice, 1956-66; judge Mcpl. Ct., San Francisco, 1966-74; presiding judge Mcpl. Ct., 1972-73; judge Superior Ct., San Francisco, 1974-82; presiding justice Calif. Ct. Appeals, 1st dist., 1982-92; pres. San Francisco Police Commn., 1992-96; pres. San Francisco Human Rights Commn., 1999-2000; mem. Jud. Arbitration and Mediation Svcs., 1992—, Commn. on Future of Cts., 1991-94, Commn. on Future of Legal Profession, 1993-95; Calif. Ins. commr. designate, 2000. Contbr. articles to profl. jours. Chmn. bd. Edn. Ctr. for Chinese, 1969—, Chinese-Am. Bilingual Sch.; bd. visitors U.S. Mil. Acad., 1980-83; bd. dirs. Friends of Recreation and Parks, Salesian Boys Club, World Affairs Coun., 1979-85, NCCJ, San Francisco chpt. St. Vincent's Boys Home, Coro Found., 1970-76, San Francisco Zool. Trust, 1987, Union Bank Calif., 1993—; pres. San Francisco City Coll. Found., 1977-87, Inst. Chinese Western History U. San Francisco, 1987-89. Mem. ABA (chmn. appellate judges conf. 1990-91, commr. on minorities), San Francisco Bar Assn., Chinese Am. Citizens Alliance (pres. San Francisco chpt. 1976-77, nat. pres. 1989-93), Calif. Judges Assn. (pres. 1978-79), Calif. Jud. Coun., State Bar

Calif. (rsch. editor publs. 1958-76, pub. affairs com. 1987-90, exec. bd. 1992-94), Calif. Conf. Judges (editor jour. cts. commentary 1973-76), Calif. Judges Assn. (exec. bd. 1976-79), Asian Bus. League (dir. 1986-93), Nat. Ctr. State Cts. (bd. dirs. 1986-91), San Francisco Bench Bar Media Commn. (chmn. bd. dirs. 1987-92), Boalt Hall Alumni Assn. (Distinguished Svc. award 1992, Judge Lowell Jensen award 2000), Phi Alpha Delta.

LOW, MARY LOUISE (MOLLY LOW), documentary photographer; b. Quakertown, Pa., Jan. 3, 1926; d. James Harry and Dorothy Collyer (Krewson) Thomas; m. Antoine Francois Gagné, Nov. 3, 1945 (div.); children: James L., David W., Stephen J., Jeannie Wolff-Gagné; m. Paul Low, July 11, 1969 (dec. July 1991). Student, Oberlin Conservatory of Music, 1943-44, Oberlin Coll., 1944; cert., Katharine Gibbs Sec. Sch., 1945; degree in psychiat. rehab. work, Einstein Coll. Medicine, 1968-70. Sec. Dept. Store, N.Y.C., 1945; sec., treas. Gagné Assocs., Consulting Engrs., Binghamton, N.Y., 1951-66; psychiat. rsch. asst. Jacobi Hosp., Bronx, 1969-70; asst. to head of sch. Brearley Sch., N.Y.C., 1976-78; pvt. practice documentary photographer San Diego, 1984—. Contbr. articles to profl. jours. Pres., bd. trustees Unitarian-Universalist Ch., 1996-97. Recipient Dir.'s award for excellence Area Agy. on Aging, San Diego, 1993, Citizen Recognition award County of San Diego, Calif., 1993. Avocations: singing, directing church choir, traveling. Office: Molly Low Photography 5576 Caminito Herminia La Jolla CA 92037-7222

LOW, MORRIS FRASER, foreign language and history educator; b. Brisbane, Queensland, Australia, Apr. 30, 1960; s. Philip and Eileen (Lee Chin) L. BSc with Japanese Lang., Griffith U., Brisbane, 1983, BSc with 1st class honors, 1985; PhD in History, U. Sydney, Australia, 1993. Lectr. Monash U., Melbourne, Australia, 1989-93, sr. lectr., 1993-95; rsch. fellow Australian Nat. U., Canberra, 1995-98; sr. lectr. U. Queensland, 1998—; curator art collection Griffith U., Brisbane, 1981-84, 86; Sakata Archival Libr., Nagoya, Japan, 1984-86; dep. dir. Japanese Studies Ctr., Melbourne, Australia, 1993-95; mgr. Australia-Japan Rsch. Project Australian War Meml., Canberra, 1997-98, trustee, Queensland Art Gallery, 1999—. Co-author: Science, Technology and Society in Contemporary Japan, 1999; editor: Beyond Joseph Needham: Science, Technology and Medicine in East and Southeast Asia, 1999; co-editor: Japanese Science, Technology and Economic Growth Down Under, 1996; editor Bull. Internat. Soc. for History of East Asian Sci., Tech. and Medicine, 1995-99; co-editor (monograph series) Working Papers in Japanese Studies, 1991-95, Papers of Japanese Studies Ctr., 1993-95, ASAA East Asia Series, 1995—. Recipient Rsch. scholarship Japanese Govt., Nagoya, Japan, 1984-86, Postgrad. Rsch. award Austalian Commonwealth Govt., Sydney, 1987-89; grantee John Treloar Grant-in-aid, Australian War Memorial, Canberra, 1996. Mem. Japanese Studies Assn. of Australia (sec.-treas. 1989-91, pres., 1995-97). Avocations: art collecting, reading. Office: U Queensland, Dept Asian Langs and Studies, Brisbane QLD 4072, Australia

LOW, VICTOR N., historian; b. N.Y.C., Aug. 25, 1931; s. Sol and Rosamond (Trilling) L.; m. Helga Lore Brigitta Paula Frentzel-Beyme, May 10, 1962; children: Joshua David, Gideon Samson. BA, U. Chgo., 1951; MA, Columbia U., 1962; PhD, UCLA, 1967. Edn. officer No. Region Nigera, 1960-61; lectr. Addis Ababa (Ethiopia) U., Addis Ababa, Ethiopia, 1967-69; vis. asst. prof. Mich. State U., East Lansing, 1969-72, acting dir. African Studies Ctr., 1970-71; vis. sr. lectr. The Hebrew U. Jerusalem, 1972-73; sr. lectr. Tel Aviv. U., 1979-80; sr. lectr. The Hebrew U. Jerusalem, 1978-80, sr. rsch. fellow, 1978-80; sr. lectr. Ahmadu Bello U., Zaria, Nigeria, 1973-75; chair history divsn. Ahmadu Bello U., 1973-75; sr. lectr., chair history divsn. U. Ibadan, Jos, Nigeria, 1975-76; vis. assoc. prof. Dartmouth Coll., Hanover, N.H., 1990-91; chmn. Nigerian Univs. Matriculation Bd. in History, 1974-75; edn. officer no. region Nigeria, 1960-61. Author: (monograph) Three Nigerian Emirates: A Study in Oral History. 1972, (trade book) Lyme Road Letters, 1994; co-editor: (reader) History of Modern Israel, Part I: Zionism, 1979, Part 2: Israel, 1982; tech. editor U.S. Army Corps Engrs., Alexandria, Va., 1985-86; contbr. articles to profl. jours. Chmn. N.Y.C. Students for Stevenson, 1952. With U.S. Army, 1952-54. Fgn. Area Rsch. fellow The Ford Found., England and Nigeria, 1963-65, Nat. Defense Fgn. Lang. fellow, Harvard, 1966, UCLA, 1967. Jewish. Avocations: writing, tennis, classical music, jazz. Home: 171 Lyme Rd Hanover NH 03755-6608

LOWBURY, EDWARD JOSEPH LISTER, microbiologist, writer; b. London, Dec. 6, 1913; s. Benjamin William and Alice Sarah (Hallé) L.; m. Ruth Alison Young, June 12, 1954; children: Ruth, Pauline, Miriam. BA with honors, Oxford U., 1936, MA, 1940, BM, BCh, 1939, DM, 1957; DSc (hon.), Aston U., Birmingham, Eng., 1977; LLD (hon.), Birmingham U., 1980. Bacteriologist trainee Emergency Pub. Health Lab. Svc., Cambridge, 1941-43; microbiologist common cold and air hygiene unit Med. Rsch. Coun., Salisbury, Eng., 1947-49; head microbiology dept., burns unit Med. Rsch. Coun., Birmingham, 1949-79; founder, dir. Hosp. Infection Rsch. Lab., 1964-79; hon. vis. prof. U. Aston, 1979-89; chmn. operating theatre hygiene com. Med. Rsch. Coun., 1960-62, mem. antibiotics trials com., 1950-59; chmn. control of infection com. West Midlands Regional Health Authority, 1970-75. Contbr. over 220 sci. articles to profl. jours.; co-author: Control of Hospital Infection, 1975, 3rd edit., 1992, Drug Resistance in Antimicrobial therapy, 1974; author 26 collections of poetry including: Collected Poems, 1993, Selected and New Poems, 1990, Time for Sale, 1961, Mystic Bridge, 1997, Hallmarks of Poetry: Reflections on a Theme, essays, 1995; co-author: Thomas Campion: Poet, Composer, Physician, 1970, To Shirk No Idleness, 1998, A Critical Biography of the Poet, Andrew Young; co-editor The Poetical Works of Andrew Young, 1985, (with Alison Young) Selected Poems of Andrew Young, 1999. Founder mem. Birmingham Chamber Music Soc., 1952—; mem. lit. panel West Midlands Arts Assn., 1970-71; pres. Smethwick Arts Assn., 1975. Maj. RAMC, 1944-47. Recipient Newdigate, Matthew Arnold Meml. prizes. Fellow Royal Coll. Pathologists, Royal Soc. Lit., Royal Coll. Physicians (hon.), Royal Coll. Surgeons (hon.); mem. Pathol. Soc., Soc. for Gen. Microbiology, Brit. Med. Assn., Royal Soc. Medicine, N.Y. Acad. Scis., Poetry Soc., Soc. Authors, Hosp. Infection Soc. (1st pres.). Avocations: playing piano, listening to music, travel, reading. Home: 79 Vernon Rd, Birmingham BI6 9SQ, England

LOWDER, CHARLES LYNN, lawyer; b. Decatur, Ill., Dec. 19, 1945; s. Edwin Harry and Etha Fern L.; children: Kathleen Ann, Lisa Ann, Daniel Lynn. BA, U. Ill., 1976; JD, DePaul U., 1980. Commd. ensign USMC, 1967, advanced through grades to major; assoc. atty. Bullaro, Carton & Stone, Chgo., 1986-96; ptnr. Lowder & Crowley, Chgo., 1996-98; gen. counsel, exec. v.p. Mail Boxes Etc., San Diego, 1998—; bd. dir. MBE Found. for Children's Initiative, San Diego, Goad Internat., Orlando. Decorated Silver Star, Bronze Star with combat V, Purple Heart. Mem. ABA, U.S. Marine Corps. Force Recon Assn., Assn. Trial Lawyers Am., Internat. Franchise Assn., Am. Corp. Counsel Assn., Veterans of Foreign Wars, Spl. Forces Assn., Military Order of Purple Heart, Million Dollar Advocates Forum. E-mail: clowder@mbe.com. Office: Mail Boxes Etc 6060 Cornerstone Ct W San Diego CA 92121-3762

LOWE, ALAN VAUGHAN, legal educator, barrister; b. Smethwick, Midlands, Eng., Aug. 13, 1952. LLB, U. Wales, 1973, LLM, 1978, PhD, 1980; MA, U. Cambridge, 1991. Barrister, 1993. Lectr. in law U. Wales, Cardiff, 1973-78; lectr. to sr. lectr. Manchester U., Eng., 1978-88; lectr., then reader in internat. law Cambridge U., Eng., 1988-99; fellow Corpus Christi Coll., Cambridge, 1988-99; Chichele prof. pub. internat. law, fellow All Souls Coll., Oxford, Eng., 1999—; vis. prof. Duke Law Sch., 1990; barrister Essex Ct. Chambers, London. Co-author: (books) The Law of the Sea, 1982, 88, 99, The Settlement of International Disputes, 1999; editor: (books) Extraterritorial Jurisdiction, 1982, UN and the Principles of International Law: Fifty Years of the International Court of Justice, 1996. Mem. African Soc. of Internat. and Comparative Law, Am. Soc. Internat. Law, Internat. Bar Assn., Brit. Inst. of Internat. and Comparative Law, Internat. Law Assn. Office: All Souls Coll, Oxford OX1 4AL, England

LOWE, CAMERON ANDERSON, dentist, endodontist, educator; b. Alcester, S.D., Dec. 19, 1932; s. Richard Barrett and Emma Louise (Anderson) L.; m. Doris Teresita Franquez, Dec. 23, 1957; children: Barrett, Steven, Leslie. Student, George Washington U., 1951-53, U. Va., 1955-56; DDS, Georgetown U., 1956-60; cert. residency in endodontics, U.S. Naval Dental Sch., 1967-69. Commd. lt. (j.g.) U.S. Navy Dental Corps, 1960, advanced through grades to capt., 1976, ret., 1978; pvt. practice endodontist Newport News, Va., 1978-81; assoc. prof. dentistry emeritus Old Dominion U., Norfolk, Va., 1991, asst. chair Sch. Dental Hygiene, 1985-89; adj. asst. prof. Med. Coll. Va.-Va. Commonwealth U. Sch. Dentistry, Richmond, 1979-81. Contbr. articles to profl. jours. and to book: Oral Pathology, 3d edit., 1989. Tutor adult literacy, 1994-99; coord. Neighborhood Watch, 1994-98; pack and troop chmn. Boy Scouts Am., Guam, 1969-72, Virginia Beach, Va., 1972-78. With USN, 1953-55. Mem. Assn. Mil. Surgeons of U.S., Am. Assn. Endodontists, Am. Acad. Oral Medicine, Am. Dental Assn., Va. Acad. Endodontics, USN Assn. Endodontists, Peninsula Dental Soc., Sigma Alpha Epsilon, Delta Sigma Delta, Sigma Phi Alpha (Dental Hygiene Honor Soc.). Methodist. Avocations: tennis, drawing, carving, reading, sculpting. Home: 1497 Wakefield Dr Virginia Beach VA 23455-4541

LOWE, DOUGLAS HOWARD, architect; b. Akron, Ohio, Nov. 1, 1952; s. Howard Bernard and Dorothy Rachael (Nowag) L.; m. Mary Louise Folk, Jan. 1, 1975; children: Ashley Marie, Austin Douglas, Andrea Catherine. BA in Pre Architecture with honors, Clemson U., 1974, MArch, 1976. Registered profl. architect, Tex., Va., interior designer, Tex. Archtl. programmer Lockwood, Andrews, Newnam, Houston, 1978-80; sr. assoc. Planning Design Research Corp., Houston, 1980-82; v.p., head interior architecture and programming 3D/Internat., San Antonio, 1982-88, exec. v.p., chief ops. officer 3D/M subs., 1988-92; founder, pres. Facility Programming and Consulting, San Antonio, 1992—; co-founder, v.p. Facility Consulting Group, San Antonio, 1994-95. Mem., elder First Presbyn. Ch., San Antonio; mem. legis. com. Alamo Heights Ind. Sch. Dist.; mem. Design-Build Inst. of Am. Mem. AIA, Tex. Soc. Archs., Internat. Facility Mgmt. Assn., Nat. Coun. Archtl. Registration Bds., Nat. Trust Hist. Preservation, Soc. for Coll. and Univ. Planning, Rotary Club San Antonio, Soc. Coll. & Univ. Planning, Town Club San Antonio, Phi Kappa Phi, Tau Sigma Delta. Republican. Presbyterian. Avocations: remodeling homes, golf. Office: Facility Programming & Cons 100 W Houston St Ste 1170 San Antonio TX 78205-1457

LOWE, FLORENCE SEGAL, retired public relations executive; b. N.Y.C.; d. Samuel I. and Rose (Cantor) Segal; BS in Edn., U. Pa., 1930; postgrad. Sch. Social Svc., 1935-36; m. Herman Albert Lowe, June 27, 1935; children: Lesley Ellen Lowe Israel, Roger Bernard. Guidance counsellor Phila. Pub. Schs., 1935-41; Washington corr. Variety and Daily Variety, Phila. Daily News, Manchester Union Leader, TV Guide, 1942-58; spl. pub. rels. Radio Sta. WIP, Phila. and Metromedia, 1958-60; coord. spl. projects Metromedia, 1960-70; spl. asst. to chmn. pub. affairs NEA, Washington, 1970-86; sr. cons. arts and cultural comm. Kamber Group, 1986-93, ret., 1994. Mem. pub. rels. and advt. com. Nat. Symphony, 1952-56; mem. Sec. State's Commn. on Travel, 1970-71; mem. Coordinating Com. for Ellis Island, 1982-87; bd. dirs. Women of the Year award banquet, 1994-95; mem. Com. for Nancy Hanks Endowment for Arts, Duke U. Recipient All-Army Entertainment Contest award, 1958; spl. achievement award Nat. Endowment for Arts Chmn., 1983; Spl. Merit award Fed. Govt., 1981, Spl. Achievement award, 1983, Disting. Svc. award, 1985. Mem. Am. Women in Radio and TV (founder, pres. 1954-55), Am. News Women's Club (Woman of Yr. com.), Coun. Jewish Women, Women in Communications (citation for meritorious reporting 1962), Nat. Press Club, Women's Nat. Press Club (treas. 1954, v.p. 1956), Washington Press Club (bd. dirs. 1968-71, 83-84), Am. News Women's Club (v.p. 1969-70), Washington Press Club Found. Home: 2512 Que St NW Apt 305 Washington DC 20007-4310

LOWE, GERALD SCOTT, former university athletic administrator, entrepreneur; b. Silver Spring, Md., Dec. 4, 1969; s. Robert Vernon and Cheryl Ann (Easton) L.; m. Robin S. Cardin, July 3, 1997. BS in Journalism summa cum laude, U. Md., 1991. Sports editor Prince George's Post, Landover, Md., 1990-91; athletic comm. asst. Princeton (N.J.) U., 1991-93; asst. dir. sports info., dir. athletic mktg. and promotions Drexel U., Phila., 1993-95; asst. dir. athletic media rels. Loyola Coll., Balt., 1995-97, dir. athletic publs., media rels. & comms., 1997-98; rschr. Internat. Lacrosse Fedn., 1996-97; basketball coach The Park Sch., Balt., 1998—, baseball coach, 1999—; co-founder "X"tra Bases Sports Camp; dir. baseball opers. Cal Ripken Baseball, 1999—. Contbr. sports articles to Prince George's Journal, Prince George's Post, Trentonian, Washington County Observer-Reporter, NBA News, Princeton Packet, Princeton Alumni Weekly, Princeton Athletic News, College Hockey Weekly, Loyola Coll. Alumni mag., Princeton Varsity Club News, also others. Vol. baseball coach Bowie (Md.) Babe Ruth Jr. League, 1989-90, Princeton (N.J.) Am. Legion, 1992-93, Bowie H.S., 1988; radio broadcaster Princeton Ice Hockey, 1991-92; Loyola basektball and lacrosse, 1995-98; dir. hockey Md. Youth Hockey Found., 1999—. Winner several nat. and regional coll. sports info. publs. and writing awards. Mem. Soc. Profl. Journalists, Golden Key Nat. Honor Soc., Coll. Sports Info. Dirs. Am., Kappa Tau Alpha, Phi Kappa Phi. Avocations: reading, running/biking, computers/desktop publishing, travel, music. Home and Office: 11805 Greenspring Ave Owings Mills MD 21117-1603

LOWE, HAROLD GLADSTONE, JR., photojournalist, small business owner, farmer; b. Nashville, Aug. 3, 1933; s. Harold Gladstone and Kathrine (Rice) L.; m. Anne Poteat, Feb. 26, 1957 (div. 1962); 1 child, Harold Guy; m. Linda Susan Brown, Mar. 14, 1976. Student, Vanderbilt U., 1951-52, 53-54, U. of the South, 1952-53. Pres., owner Campus Cameras, Inc., Nashville, 1953-55; photographer Nashville Tennessean Newspaper, 1960-65; photo corr. UP Internat., Nashville, 1961-65; photographer, reporter Sta. WSM TV News, Nashville, 1965-71; staff photographer, editor Senator Howard Baker, Nashville, 1971-72; freelance photographer and reporter Nashville, 1973-76; photographer, reporter Sta. WTVF-TV News, Nashville, 1976-78; photograhic supr. State of Tenn., Nashville, 1978-81; photographer, owner CHSS Newspix-Capitol Press, Nashville, 1981—; pres. Campbell-Brown Farms, Inc., Dyersburg, Tenn., 1969—. Photographer Spot News, 1962 (1st Pl. award 1962); photographer, editor (documentary) United Givers Fund, 1970 (Diamond award 1970). Photographer Gov. Lamar Alexander, Nashville, 1979-80, col. aide de camp, 1979, Gov. Ned Ray McWherter, 1986. Mem. Nat. Press Photographers Assn., Tenn. Capitol Press Corps, SDX Soc. Profl. Journalists, Sports Car Club Am., Masons, Sigma Nu. Democrat. Anglican. Avocations: Music, electronics. Home: 1113 Lipscomb Dr Nashville TN 37204-4121 Office: CHSS Newspix Capitol Press 28 Legislative Pla Nashville TN 37219

LOWE, J. ALLEN, minister; b. Midland, Tex., Dec. 20, 1945; s. Homer Allen and Theresa (Lowry) L.; m. Shirley Christy, Apr. 9, 1965; children: Robert Allen, John David, Steven Scott. BS, Howard Payne U., 1968; MDiv, Tex. Christian U., 1976; postgrad, Princeton Theol., 1990. Cert. secondary tchr.; ordained to the ministry Christian Ch., 1976. Tchr. Bible history Midland (Tex.) Ind. Sch. Dist., 1968-74; assoc. min. First Christian Ch., Denison, Tex., 1974-76; campus min. United Campus Ministries, Warrensburg, Mo., 1976-78; nurture min. Meml. Christian Ch., Midland, Tex., 1978-84; assoc. min. 1st Christian Ch., Corpus Christi, Tex., 1984-91; sr. min. South Shore Christian Ch., Corpus Christi, 1991-2000, First Christian Ch., Richardson, Tex., 2000—; chmn. Cen. Area Youth Coun., Tex., 1980-84; moderator Youth Ministry Coun. S.W., 1984-87, Bluebonnet Area Youth Coun., 1988-92; advisor Gen. Youth Coun., U.S. and Can., 1985-87; vice moderator Bluebonnet Area of Christian Ch. in S.W., 1994-95. Mem. IMPACT, 1974-82, Nat. Peace Acad., 1973-78; coach YMCA basketball, 1980-81, Little League, Youth Flag Football teams, Denison and Midland, 1967-68, 70, 74; mem. ethics commn. City of Corpus Christi, 1994-2000; active City League Youth Basketball, Corpus Christi, 1995-97; mem. com. on the ministry Christian Ch. in the S.W., 1997-2000. Recipient Friend of Youth City award, 1989; O.H. Karr Ministerial scholar Tex. Christian U., 1975-76. Mem. Youth Ministry Coun. (moderator 1989-93), Ministerial Alliance. Home: 2722 Laurel Oaks Dr Garland TX 75044 Office: First Christian Ch 601 E Main St Richardson TX 75081-3521

LÖWE, JÜRGEN, economist; b. Hanover, Germany, Apr. 14, 1961; s. Wenzel and Ursula W. (Klemm) L. Diploma in banking, IHK, Hanover, 1980; M in Econs., U. St. Gallen, Switzerland, 1988, PhD, 1992. Lectr. U. St. Gallen, 1992-94, 96; vis. scholar Mich. State U., East Lansing, 1994-95; vis. faculty U. Notre Dame, Ind., 1996-97; appointed tenured lectr. of econs. U. St. Gallen, 1999; cons. in field. Author: Kontextuale Theorie der Volkswirtschaft, 1998, Staatsverschuldung in der Währungsunion, 1999. Swiss Nat. Sci. Found. fellow, Bern, 1994-98. Mem. Assn. Evolutionary Econs., Deutscher Hochschulverband, Verein für Socialpolitik. Home: Brussels 4, BP 195, B-1040 Brussels Belgium

LOWE, MALCOLM FREDERICK, religious studies educator; b. Haverfordwest, Wales, U.K., May 14, 1939; arrived in Israel, 1970; s. Eric Edward and Vera Kathleen (Gibbon) L.; m. Petra Heldt, Jan. 1, 1985. BA in Physics, Oxford (Eng.) U., 1962, MA in Physics, BPhil in Philosophy, 1965. Lectr. in philosophy Chelsea Coll., London U., Eng., 1965-70; lectr. in history of sci. Hebrew U., Jerusalem, 1970-74; editor Inst. Contemporary Judaism, Jerusalem, 1975-80; editor, fellow Shalom Hartman Inst., Jerusalem, 1980-92; lectr. in New Testament Hebrew U., Jerusalem, 1985-86, Ratisbonne Ctr., Jerusalem, 1988—; mem. Ecumenical Theol. Rsch. Fraternity in Israel, 1980—, mem. steering com., 1982-87; mem. Jerusalem Rainbow Group, Israel, 1984—. Editor: Immanuel, Israel, 1988—, People, Land and State of Israel: Jewish and Christian Perspectives, 1989, The New Testament and Christian-Jewish Dialogue, 1990, Orthodox Christians and Jews on Continuity and Renewal, 1994; assoc. editor: The Holocaust as Historical Experience, 1981; contbr. chpts. to books and articles to profl. jours. of philosophy and religion. Vice chmn. Interreligious Coordinating Coun. in Israel, 1991, chmn., 1992, ad personam mem., 1993—. Office: Ecumenical Fraternity, PO Box 249, 91002 Jerusalem Israel

LOWE, RODNEY, historian, educator; b. Epsom, England, Jan. 26, 1946. BA, U. Bristol, 1967; PhD, London Sch. Econs., 1975. Lectr. in history U. Leeds, Eng., 1971-72; lectr. in econ. history Heriot-Watt U., Scotland, 1972-78; sr. lectr, reader U. Bristol, Eng., 1979-96, prof. contemporary history, 1996—. Author: Adjusting to Democracy, 1986, The Welfare State in Britian Since 1945, 1993, 98, Welfare Policy under the Conservatives, 1998. Office: U Bristol, 13 Woodland Rd, Bristol BS8 1TB, England

LOWELL, STANLEY HERBERT, lawyer; b. Apr. 13, 1919; s. Isadore and Mildred (Cohen) Lowenbraun; m. Vivian Abrams, Mar. 29, 1947 (div. 1973); children: Jeffrey, Darcy, Lauri; m. Leona Schaevitz, June 20, 1974; stepchildren: Barry S., Scott S. BS in Social Sci., CCNY, 1939; LLB, Harvard U., 1942; LLD (hon.), CUNY, 1981. Bar: N.Y. 1942. Asst. U.S. atty. N.Y., 1943-47; ptnr. Lowenbraun & Lowell, N.Y.C., 1947-58, Lowell & Karassik and predecessors, N.Y.C., 1966-78, Fink, Weinberger, Fredman, Berman & Lowell, 1978-93; of counsel Goodkind, Labaton, Rudoff & Sucharow, 1994-99; former lectr. CCNY; vis. prof. Grad. Sch., CUNY; adj. prof. Fordham U. Sch. Social Svcs. Asst. to borough pres., Manhattan, 1950-53; exec. asst. to mayor, N.Y.C., 1954-58, dep. mayor, 1958; chmn. N.Y.C. Commn. Human Rights, 1960-65; U.S. pub. del. Madrid Conf. Helsinki Final Act, 1979; chmn. N.Y.C. com. Am. Jewish Tercentenary; past chmn. divsn. lawyers; trustee United Jewish Appeal-Fedn. Jewish Philanthropies, bd. dirs., 1962-94; chmn. Nat. Conf. on Soviet Jewry, 1974-76; past chmn. Greater N.Y. Conf. on Soviet Jewry; mem. praesidium Brussels World Conf. on Soviet Jewry; past chmn. Com. for Pub. Higher Edn.; past pres., chmn. Citizens Com. for Children of N.Y.; past vice chmn. Nat. Jewish Coun. Pub. Affairs Del. Dem. Nat. Conv., 1960, 64, 68; exec. com. Dem. State Com., 1960-68; trustee Jewish Communal Fund N.Y., 1981-91; trustee-at-large, v.p. Jewish Cmty. Rels. Coun., N.Y., 1982-94; hon. trustee, past pres. N.Y. Shakespeare Festival; spl. counsel pro bono Kings County Hosp. investigation; mem. Mayor's Commn. on Health & Hosp. Corp., 1991; co-chair Friends of City Univ., 1998—. Recipient medal City N.Y., 1965, John F. Kennedy Peace award Jewish Nat. Fund, 1996, Judge Joseph Proskauer award Lawyers United Jewish Appeal-Fedn., John H. Finley medal CCNY Alumni Assn., 1980, Pres.'s medal, 1980; Establishment of Stanley H. Lowell Ann. Humanitarian award N.Y.C. Commn. on Human Rights, 1988. Mem. N.Y. State Bar Assn., Assn. Bar City of N.Y., Harvard Law Sch. Assn. N.Y. (past trustee), Coll. City N.Y. Alumni Assn. (past pres.). Home: 30 Agnew Farm Rd Armonk NY 10504-1371 Office: 700 White Plains Post Rd Scarsdale NY 10504

LOWE-MCCONNELL, ROSEMARY HELEN, biologist; b. Liverpool, Eng., June 24, 1921; d. Harold Newton and Mary Birditt (Bradford) L.; m. Richard Bradford McConnell, Dec. 31, 1953. BS in Zoology, U. Liverpool, England, 1942, MS in Zoology, 1945, DS in Zoology, 1959. Biologist Freshwater Biol. Assn., Ambleside, England, 1942-45; fisheries rsch. officer U.K. Col. Svc., Lake Nyasa, Malawi, 1945-47, East African Fisheries Rsch. Orgn., Jinja, Uganda, 1948-54, Dept. Fisheries, Georgetown, Guyana, 1957-63; assoc. Brit. Mus. Natural History, London, 1963-87; convenor African lakes group Internat. Limnological Soc., 1987-90. Author: Fish Communities in Tropical Freshwaters, 1975, Ecological Studies in Tropical Fish Communities, 1987, 91; contbr. articles to profl. jours. Recipient Founders medal Internat. Limnological Soc. Mem. Linnean Soc. (v.p. 1976-79, Gold medal 1997). Avocations: snorkling, walking, birdwatching. E-mail: romcconnell@compuserve.com. Home and Office: Streatwick, Streat nr Hassocks, Sussex BN6 8RT, England

LOWENFELS, LEWIS DAVID, lawyer; b. N.Y.C., June 9, 1935; s. Seymour and Jane (Phillips) L.; m. Fern Gelford, Aug. 15, 1965; children: Joshua, Jacqueline. BA magna cum laude, Harvard U., 1957, LLB, 1961. Bar: N.Y. 1961; lic. corp. and securities atty. Ptnr. Tolins & Lowenfels, N.Y.C., 1967—; adj. prof. Seton Hall U. Law Sch; lectr. Practicing Law Inst., Southwestern Legal Found., U. Minn. Fed. Bar Assn., 1972; pub. gov. Am. Stock Exch., 1993-96. Co-author: Bromberg and Lowenfels on Securities Fraud and Commodities Fraud, 6 vols., 1999; contbr. articles to profl. jours. With USAR, 1957-63. Mem. ABA (fed. regulation of securities com. 1978—, lectr.), N.Y. County Lawyers Assn. (securities and exchanges com. 1974—), Phi Beta Kappa, Harvard Club. Avocations: reading, writing, athletics. Office: Tolins & Lowenfels 12 E 49th St New York NY 10017-1028

LOWENHAUPT, CHARLES ABRAHAM, lawyer; b. St. Louis, May 19, 1947; s. Henry Cronbach and Cecile (Koven) L.; m. Rosalyn Lee Sussman, Dec. 28, 1969; children: Elizabeth Anne, Rebecca Jane. BA cum laude, Harvard U., 1969; JD magna cum laude, U. Mich., 1973. Bar: Mo. 1973, U.S. Dist. Ct. (ea. dist.) Mo. 1975, U.S. Ct. Appeals (8th cir.) 1975, U.S. Tax Ct. 1975, U.S. Ct. Claims 1975, U.S. Supreme Ct. 1987. Law clk. to presiding justice U.S. Tax Ct., Washington, 1973-75; ptnr. Lowenhaupt, Chasnoff, Armstrong & Mellitz, St. Louis, 1977-94; mem. adv. faculty Inst. for Pvt. Investors, 1991-93; mem. Lowenhaupt & Chasnoff, LLC, St. Louis, 1994—; emeritus mem. adv. faculty Inst. for Pvt. Investors, St. Louis, 1995—; spkr. Nat. Assn. Ind. Schs., St. Louis Assn. Legal Assts., Washington U. Bus. Sch., Inst. for Pvt. Investors, numerous others; mem. adv. bd. dirs. Textile Mus., Washington; cmty. outreach adv. coun. St. Louis Coll. Pharmacy, 1998—; lectr. law dept. Fudan U., Shanghai, 1999. Bd. dirs. Ctrl. West End Assn., Inc., St. Louis, 1976-80, Temple Emanuel, St. Louis, 1982-89, Butterfly Ho., St. Louis, sec., 1995—; bd. dirs. Craft Alliance St. Louis, 1987-90, Helicon Found., San Diego, St. Louis Met. Assn. for Philanthropy, St. Louis Regional Med. Ctr. Found., 1993-98, chmn. bd. dirs., 1995-98; bd. dirs. Crown Ctr. St. Louis sect., Nat. Coun. Jewish Women, 1994-96, St. Louis Zoo Found., 1993-99, sec., 1995-98; mem. St. Louis Zool. Subdist. commn., 1989-92; bd. govs. Clements Libr. Assocs., U. Mich., 1997—; mem. St. Louis Cmty. Sch. Assn., 1981-89; pres. Assn. St. Louis U. Librs., Inc., 1982-83; mem. exec. com. U.S.-China C. of C. Midwestern Regional Office; mem. George W. Warren Brown Sch. Social Work nat. coun. Washington U., 2000—. Recipient Cmty. Svc. award Young Dems. of St. Louis, 1996. Mem. ABA (tax section, estate and gift section, real property section, probate and trust law, task force legal financial planning, chmn. generation-skipping transfer tax subcom., estate and gift tax com. tax sect. 1995—), Mo. Bar Assn. (tax section, probate and trust section), Bar Assn. of Met. St. Louis (tax section, real property and development sect.), Order of the Coif, St. Louis Estate Planning Coun., Mo. Athletic Club, Harvard Club of N.Y.C., Noonday Club, Harvard Club of St. Louis (pres. 1991-92, chmn. schs. and scholarship com. 1989-91). Home: 801 S Skinker Blvd Saint Louis MO 63105-3269 Office: Lowenhaupt & Chasnoff LLC 10 S Broadway Ste 600 Saint Louis MO 63102-1712

LOWENSTEIN, PEDRO RICARDO, gene therapy scientist; b. Buenos Aires; arrived in U.K., 1987; s. Karl Heinz Lowenstein and Eva Sofia Isakowitz; m. Maria Graciela Castro, Jan. 12, 1988; 1 child, Elijah David. BSc, Pestalozzi Schule, Buenos Aires, 1975; MD cum laude, U. Buenos Aires, 1981, PhD summa cum laude, 1984. Postgrad. rsch. fellow neuroendocrine pharmacology divsn. Nat. Rsch. Coun., Buenos Aires, 1982-

84; postdoctoral rsch. fellow dept. psychiatry Johns Hopkins Med. Instn., Johns Hopkins U. Sch. Medicine, Balt., 1984-86; vis. fellow lab. neurochemistry NINCDS/NIH, Bethesda, Md., 1987; grade 1 rsch. scientist anat. neuropharmacology unit Dept. Pharmacology, Med. Rsch. Coun., Oxford, Eng., 1987-90; lectr. anatomy dept. anatomy and physiology U. Dundee, Scotland, 1990-92; from lectr. neurosci. dept. physiology to sr. lectr. U. Wales, Coll. Cardiff, 1992-94; Lister Inst. prof. molecular medicine and gene therapy U. Manchester Sch. Medicine, Eng., 1995—; mem. biols. sub-com. Medicines Control Agy., U.K., 1999—; advisor, reviewer Gene Therapy Adv. Com., U.K., 1996—. Editor-in-chief Current Gene Therapy; contbr. more than 100 articles to profl. jours. Recipient Sir Henry Wellcome Commemorative award for innovative rsch. Wellcome Trust, 1998; rsch. fellow Lister Inst. Preventive Medicine, 1993-2000 rsch. grantee Med. Rsch. Coun., 1998, Biotech. and Biol. Rsch. Coun., 1998. Mem. Neural Disorders Gene Therapy Sci. Com., Am. Soc. Gene Therapy, Soc. for Neurosci., U.S.A., Brit. Neurosci. Assn., Internat. Soc. for NeuroVirology (founding mem.). Jewish. Avocations: human experimentation during the Holocaust, ethics of science, history of science, reading. Fax: 44 (0) 161 275 5672. E-mail: lowenstein@man.ac.uk. Office: U Manch Sch Med Rm 1.302, Stopford Bldg Oxford Rd, Manchester M13 9PT, England

LOWENTHAL, DAVID, historian, geographer; b. N.Y.C., Apr. 26, 1923; s. Max and Eleanor (Mack) L.; m. Mary A. Lamberty, Oct. 16, 1970. BA, Harvard U., 1943; MA, U. Calif., Berkeley, 1950; PhD, U. Wis., 1953. Rsch. analyst U.S. State Dept., Washington, 1945-46; asst. prof. history Vassar Coll., Poughkeepsie, N.Y., 1952-56; rsch. assoc. Am. Geog. Soc., N.Y.C., 1956-72; with U. of the West Indies, Jamaica, 1956-70, history lectr., rsch. assoc., cons. to vice chancellor; with Inst. of Race Rels., London, 1961-72; prof. geography U. Coll., London, 1972-85; hon. rsch. fellow U. Coll., 1986—; vis. prof. heritage studies St. Mary's U. Coll. Stawberry Hill, U.K., 1995—; mem. bd., contbg. editor Internat. Ency. Social Scis., 1964-68; U.S., U.K. del. Internat. Coun. on Monuments and Sites, mem. gen. assembly, 1981, 87, cons. hist. landscapes and site authenticity, 1994—. Author: George Perkins Marsh: Versatile Vermonter, 1958, West Indian Societies, 1972, The Past is a Foreign Country, 1985 (Univ. and Profl. Pub. award 1986), The Heritage Crusade and the Spoils of History, 1996, George Perkins Marsh, of Prophet Conservation, 2000. Georgian group del. Harrow Conservation Area Adv. Com., 1987-97; sec., dir. Crown St. and Area Residents Assn., Harrow, 1974—. With U.S. Army, 1943-45. Leverhulme emeritus fellowship, 1992-93, Landes Sr. fellowship Rsch. Inst. for the Study of Man, 1992-93, Guggenheim fellowship John Simon Guggenheim Found., 1965-66, recipient Victoria medal Royal Geog. Soc., 1997, Cullum Geog. medal Am. Geog. Soc., 1999. Mem. AAAS (councilor 1964-71), Soc. for Caribbean Studies (founding chair 1977-79), Landscape Rsch. Group (vice chair 1979-84, chair 1984-89), Internat. Cultural Property Soc. (editl. bd. 1989—). Home: Harrow on the Hill, 56 Crown St, Harrow HA2 0HR, England

LOWENTHAL, F. JULIO, retired automobile dealer; b. N.Y.C., Sept. 30, 1927; arrived in Guatemala, 1929; s. Julio and Elvira (Foncea) L.; m. Alicia Arceyuz, Sept. 30, 1951; children: Marialys, Enrique, Julio (dec.), Maryan. BArch, U. Calif., Berkeley, 1951. Pvt. practice architecture San Diego, 1951-57; franchised automobile dealer Guatemala City, Guatemala, 1957-99; pres., gen. mgr. dealership Guatemala City, 1972-99, dealer Komatsu, Clark, Ingersoll-Rand products, 1975-99; Hon. Consul-Gen. Republic South Africa from Guatemala, 1974-85; pres. Guatemalan Light and Power Co., 1975; bd. dirs. CICA Fin., Banco Internacional, Guatemala. Pres. bd. trustees Francisco Marroquin U., 1978, bd. dirs., 1970-90; asst. mayor Guatemala City, 1969-71; state councellor, 1970-74. Decorated Order of Good Hope (Republic South Africa), 1979, Order St. Fortunat (Austria) 1988. Mem. Caribbean and Cen. Am. GM Dealers Assn. (pres. 1971-72), Guatemala Mgmt. Assn., Guatemala C. of C. (pres. 1969-70). Roman Catholic. Club: Country of Guatemala. Lodge: Rotary. E-mail: cideamngr@intelnet.net.gt. Office: 30-57 10 Ave, Guatemala City 5, Guatemala

LOWENTHAL, NORMAN DROR, stockbroker, financial consultant; b. Johannesburg, South Africa, Sept. 24, 1937; s. William and Anita (Berchin) L.; m. Florence Pamela rosenberg, Apr. 20, 1959; children: Howard, Martin. BA in Law, U. Cape Town, South Africa, 1956; cert. stockbroker, Johannesburg Stock Exch., South Africa, 1972. Sr. ptnr. Lowenthal Co., South Africa, 1972-99; chmn. Incentive Lowenthal (Pty) Ltd., Johannesburg, 1972—, Consol. Mining Corp. Ltd., South Africa, 1988-96, Johannesburg Stock Exch., 1997-99. Office: Incentive Holdings Ltd, 170 Oxford Rd Rosebank, Johannesburg 2196, South Africa

LOWENTHAL, SUSAN, artist, designer, retired finance executive; b. Munich, Nov. 30, 1946; came to U.S., 1949; d. Jerry and Gertrude (Wiestreich) L.; m. Alex J. Stolitzka, Oct. ll, 1987. BA, Bklyn. Coll., 1969. Exec. dir. Manhattan Girls Club, N.Y.C., 1969-73; conf. coord. Orton Soc., N.Y.C., 1973-77; v.p. Gemtique, N.Y.C., 1977-81; broker Prudential Bache, N.Y.C., 1981-83, Smith Barney, N.Y.C., 1983-85; pres., chief exec. officer Lowenthal Fin. Svcs., Inc., N.Y.C., 1985-89, fin. cons., money mgr., 1990-98; realtor, exclusive buyer agt. March Buyers Realty, 1995—; designer/artist works sold in museum gift shops and pub. in nat. mags.; guest appearances on cable TV shows; pres. AcScents! Naturally. Artist, designer; designs published in maj. nat. mags. Jewish. Avocations: skiing, reading, bridge.

LOWENTROUT, PETER MURRAY, religious studies educator; b. Salinas, Calif., Mar. 14, 1948; m. Christine Ione, Sept. 30, 1980; children: Mary, Brandon. AB, U. Calif., Riverside, 1973; PhD, U. So. Calif., L.A., 1983. Prof. religious studies Calif. State U., Long Beach, 1981—, chair dept. religious studies, 1999—. Contbr. articles to profl. jours. Capt. Orange County Fire Dept., Orange, Calif., 1977-94. Mem. Am. Acad. Religion (regional pres. 1989-90), Ctr. for Theology and Lit. U. Durham (Eng.), Sci. Fi. Rsch. Assoc. (pres. 1991, 92). Office: Calif State U Dept Religious Studies 1250 N Bellflower Blvd Dept Long Beach CA 90840-0001

LOWERY, WILLIAM HERBERT, lawyer; b. Toledo, June 8, 1925; s. Kenneth Alden and Drusilla (Pfanner) L.; m. Carolyn Broadwell, June 27, 1947; children: Kenneth Latham, Marcia Mitchell. PhB, U. Chgo., 1947; JD, U. Mich., 1950. Bar: Pa. 1951, U.S. Supreme Ct. 1955. Assoc. Dechert Price & Rhoads, Phila., 1950-58, ptnr., 1958-89, mng. ptnr., 1970-72; mem. policy com., chmn. litigation dept., 1962-68, 81-84; of counsel Dechert Price & Rhoads, Phila., 1989—; counsel S.S. Huebner Found. Ins. Edn., Phila., 1970-89; faculty Am. Conf. of Legal Execs., Pa. Bar Inst.; permanent mem. com. of visitors U. Mich. Law Sch. Author: Insurance Litigation Problems, 1972, Insurance Litigation Disputes, 1977. Pres. Stafford Civic Assn., 1958; chmn. Tredyffrin Twp. Zoning Bd., Chester County, Pa., 1959-75; bd. dirs. Paoli (Pa.) Meml. Hosp., 1964-89, chmn., 1972-75; bd. dirs. Main Line Health, Radnor, Pa., 1984-89; permanent mem. Jud. Conf. 3d Cir. Ct. Served to 2d lt. USAF, 1943-46. Mem. ABA (chmn. life ins. com. 1984-85, chmn. Nat. Conf. Lawyers and Life Ins. Cos. 1984-88), Order of the Coif, Royal Poinciana Golf Club (bd. dirs. 1997—, sec. 1997—), Phi Gamma Delta, Phi Delta Phi. Home: 2777 Gulf Shore Blvd N Apt 4-s Naples FL 34103-4360 Office: Dechert Price & Rhoads 4000 Bell Atlantic Tower 1717 Arch St Lbby 3 Philadelphia PA 19103-2713

LOWERY, WILLIAM ODELL, protective services executive; b. Winston-Salem, Aug. 3, 1935; m. Lucienne Lowery, Mar. 5, 1962. BS in Polit. Sci., Trenton State Coll., 1987. Commd. 2d lt. U.S. Army, advanced through SGM, 1966; pers. action specialist hdqrs. 24th divsn. U.S. Army, Augsburg, Germany, 1962-65, 1961-65; instr. eng OCS U.S. Army, Ft. Belvoir, Va., 1966-73; pers. mgmt. specialist hdqrs. U.S. Army, Washington, 1967-70; pers. SGM hdqrs. DA U.S. Army, Heidelberg, Germany, 1971-74; pers. SGM U.S. Army, Ft. Ben Harrison, Ind., 1974-79; mail carrier U.S. Postal Svc., New Hope, N.J., 1979-80; pers. specialist Civilian Pers. Office, Ft. Dix, 1980-94; FECA program adminstr. Dept. of Def. Police, Ft. Dix, N.J., 1996—; pers. staff NCO to set up operation to deactivate 4th Inf. Divsn., An Khe, Vietnam. Decorated Army Commendation medal (2), Meritorious Svc. medal (2), Bronze Star medal. Home: 37 E Chestnut St Bordentown NJ 08505-2063 Office: Dept of Defense Police Bldg 6049 8th St Fort Dix NJ 08610

LOWI, ALVIN, JR., mechanical engineer, consultant; b. Gadsden, Ala., July 21, 1929; s. Alvin R. and Janice (Haas) L.; m. Guillermina Gerardo Alverez, May 9, 1953; children: David Arthur, Rosamina, Edna Vivian, Alvin III. BME, Ga. Inst. Tech., 1951, MSME, 1955; PhD in Engring., UCLA, 1956-61. Registered prof. engr., Calif. Design engr. Garrett Corp., Los Angeles, 1956-58; mem. tech. staff TRW, El Segundo, Calif., 1958-60, Aerospace Corp., El Segundo, 1960-66; prin. Alvin Lowi and Assocs., San Pedro, 1966—; pres. Terraqua Inc., San Pedro, Calif., 1968-76; v.p. Daeco Fuels and Engring. Co., Wilmington, Calif., 1978—; also bd. dirs. Daeco Fuels and Engring. Co.; pres. Lion Engring., Inc.; vis. research prof. U. Pa., Phila., 1972-74; sr. lectr. Free Enterprise Inst., Monterey Park, Calif., 1961-71; bd. dirs. So. Calif. Tissue Bank; research fellow Heather Found., San Pedro, 1966--. Contbr. articles to profl. jours.; patentee in field. Served to lt. USN, 1951-54, Korea. Fellow Inst. Humane Studies; mem. ASME, NSPE, Soc. Automotive Engrs., Soc. Am. Inventors, So. Bay Chamber Music Soc., Scabbard and Blade, Pi Tau Sigma. Jewish. Avocations: chamber music, jazz, photography, classic automobiles, motor sports, philosophy of science. Home and Office: 2146 W Toscanini Dr Palos Verdes Peninsula CA 90275-1420

LOWNDES, JEFFREY DENNIS, auto mechanic; b. Lake Syranac, N.Y., May 8, 1970; s. George and Joan (Hyde) L.; m. Janine M. Herbert, Mar. 26, 1996; children: Jeffrey (dec.), Nicholas, Grant, Victoria. Mechanic, owner Lowndes Engine Repair, Orr's Island, Maine, 1987—; investigative asst. Lowndes Investigations, Cundy's Harbor, 1997-98. Avocations: fourwheeling, dirt bikes, snowmobiling, hunting, fishing.

LOWNDES, JOHN FOY, lawyer; b. Jan. 1, 1931; s. Charles L. B. and Dorothy (Foy) L.; m. Rita Davies, Aug. 18, 1983; children: Elizabeth Anne, Amy Scott, John Patrick, Joseph Edward, Jennifer Susanne. BA, Duke U., 1953, LLB, 1958. Bar: Fla. 1958. Pvt. practice Daytona Beach, Fla., 1958, Orlando, Fla., 1959-69; sr. ptnr., chmn. bd. dirs. Lowndes, Drosdick, Doster, Kantor & Reed, P.A., Orlando, 1969—; treas. U. Ctrl. Fla. Found.; bd. dirs. First Union Nat. Bank Fla.; mem. Fla. Constl. Rev. Commn., 1998. Former chmn. bd. trustees Orlando Mus. Art, Winter Park Meml. Hosp., Mennello Mus. Am. Folk Art; bd. visitors Duke U. Capt. USMCR, 1953-55. Republican. Home: 1308 Green Cove Rd Winter Park FL 32789-2549 Office: Lowndes Drosdick Doster Kantor & Reed 215 N Eola Dr Orlando FL 32801-2095

LOWRANCE, MURIEL EDWARDS, program specialist; b. Ada, Okla., Dec. 28, 1922; d. Warren E. and Mayme E. (Barrick) Edwards; B.S. in Edn., East Central State U., Ada, 1954; 1 dau., Kathy Lynn Lowrance Gutierrez. Accountant, adminstrv. asst. to bus. mgr. East Central State U., 1950-68; grants and contracts specialist U. N.Mex. Sch. Medicine, Albuquerque, 1968-72, program specialist IV, dept. orthopaedics, 1975-86; asst. adminstrv. officer N.Mex. Regional Med. Program, 1972-75. Bd. dirs. Vocat. Rehab. Center, 1980-84. Cert. profl. contract mgr. Nat. Contract Assn. Mem. Am. Bus. Women's Assn. (past pres. El Segundo chpt., Woman of Yr. 1974), AAUW, Amigos de las Americas (dir.). Democrat. Methodist. Club: Pilot (Albuquerque) (pres. 1979-80, dir. 1983-84, dist. treas. 1984-86, treas. S.W. dist., 1984-86, gov.-elect S.W. dist. 1986-87, gov. S.W. dist. 1987-88). Home: 3028 Mackland Ave NE Albuquerque NM 87106-2018

LOWRY, DAVID BURTON, lawyer; b. Bronxville, N.Y., Nov. 6, 1943; s. Burton S. and Virginia Evelyn (Ford) L. BA, U. Ariz., 1966, JD, 1969. Bar: Ariz. 1969, Oreg. 1973. Legal aid atty. Tucson and Coolidge, Ariz. and Hillsboro, Oreg.; asst. atty. gen. Oreg.; dep. dist. atty. Marion County, Oreg.; dep. pub. defender Mohave County, Ariz.; pvt. practice Portland, Oreg., 1989—. Mem. Oreg. State Bar Assn., Ariz. State Bar Assn., Am. Mgmt. Assn., Assn. Trial Lawyers Am., Alpha Delta Sigma, Phi Alpha Delta, Alpha Sigma Phi. Republican. Home: 13490 SW Genesis Loop Tigard OR 97223-3959

LOWRY, DICK M., director; b. Oklahoma City. Student, U. Okla., Am. Film Inst. Dir.: (TV films and miniseries) Ohms, Buck Rogers in the 25th Century, Kenny Rogers as the Gambler, Jayne Mansfield: A Symbol of Fifties, Off Sides, Angel Dusted, Coward of the County, A Few Days in Weasel Creek, Rascals and Robbers: The Future Adventures of Tom Sawyer and Huck Finn, Stolen Children: A Mother's Story, Living Proof: The Hank Williams Jr. Story, Kenny Rogers as the Gambler: The Adventure Continues, Wet Gold, Agatha Christie's Murder with Mirrors, Wild Horses, Dream West, American Harvest, Case Closed, In the Line of Duty: The FBI Murders, Unconquered, Howard Beach: Making the Case for Murder, Island Son, Miracle Landing, Archie: To Riverdale and Back Again, In the Line of Duty: A Cop for the Killing, In the Line of Duty: Manhunt in the Dakotas (Best Fgn. TV Movie, Umbria, Italy), Gambler IV: Where Legends Meet, A Woman Scorned: The Betty Broderick Story, 1992 (Best TV Movie, Monte Carlo Film Festival), In the Line of Duty: Street of Wars, 1992, Her Final Fury: Betty Broderick The Last Chapter, In the Line of Duty: Ambush in Waco, 1993, One More Mountain, 1993 (Christopher award), Texas Justice, 1994 (Best Mini-Series, Banff TV Festival), Horse for Danny, 1994, In the Line of Duty: Hunt for Justice, 1995, Forgotten Sins, 1995, Project Alf, Smoke Jumpers, 1996, Blaze of Glory, 1997, Last Stand at Saber River, 1997, In the Line of Duty: Jeff & Jill, Dean Koontz's Mr. Murder, 1998, Atomic Train, Y2K, 1999. Mem. Dirs. Guild Am. Office: c/o Jil Holwager ICM 8942 Wilshire Blvd Beverly Hills CA 90211-1934*

LOWRY, MARILYN JEAN, horticultural retail company executive; b. Greensburg, Pa., Oct. 19, 1932; d. Clifford Henry and Martha McCune (Whitehead) Bushyager; m. John Cathcart Lowry, June 14, 1958; children: Martha Kim Hultberg, John Ryan, Nancy Lynn. BS, Ind. U. of Pa., 1954; MEd, Pa. State U., 1958. Tchr. Jeannette (Pa.) pub. schs., 1954-57; grad. asst. Pa. State U., University Park, 1957-58; demonstration sch. tchr. Towson (Md.) U., 1958-59; sec.-treas. Lowry & Co., Inc., Phoenix, Md., 1964—, 1987—; master flower show judge Nat. Council State Garden Clubs, Inc., St. Louis, 1987—, landscape design critic, 1985—; master gardener U. Md. Extension Svc., 1984—. Mem. Lutherville Garden Club (pres. 1979—), Am. Assn. Nurserymen Aux. (pres. 1972), Federated Garden Clubs Md. (dir. dist. III 1981-83), Am. Nursery and Landscape Assn. (chmn. wholesale plant sales profls. 1999—). Republican. Presbyterian.

LOWRY, MONTECUE JUDSON, military historian; b. Ft. Worth, Tex., Feb. 23, 1930; s. Mark and Susan (Hall) L.; m. Jo Gail Tuttle, June 4, 1955 (div. Mar. 1985); 1 child, Mary; m. Jennifer Lynn Gunlock, Dec. 27, 1985; children: Jeremy, Montecue J. II. BS, U.S. Mil. Acad., West Point, N.Y., 1953; BA, U. So. Miss., 1958; MS, U.S. Naval Postgrad. Sch., Monterey, Calif., 1965; MA, U. So. Miss., 1967; PhD in Physics, Tex. Christian U., 1977; PhD in History, U. North Tex., 1988. Officer U.S. Army, 1953-73; chief quality control Vinnell Corp., Riyadh, Saudi Arabia, 1982-83; instr. history U. North Tex., Denton, 1983-86; mil. analyst CIA, Washington, 1986-88; assoc. prof. history Liberty U., Lynchburg, Va., 1988-89; assoc. prof. physics Houston Bapt. U., 1990-96; mil. historian, 1996—. Author: Forge of West German Rearmament, 1990, Glasnost, 1991; contbr. articles to profl. jours. Neighborhood commr. Boy Scouts Am., Fulda, Germany, 1960-62; pres. PTA, Fulda, 1961-62. Mem. Am. Hist. Assn., Soc. Mil. History. Avocations: cycling, weight training, classical music, reading. Home: 7402 Redding Rd Houston TX 77036-5542

LOWSETH, LISA ANNE, veterinarian; b. Rock Springs, Wyo., May 6, 1958; d. Ernest James and Frances Margaret Lowseth. BS with honors, U. Wyo., 1980; DVM, Kans. State U., 1985. Assoc. veterinarian Good Shepherd Animal Clin., Albuquerque, N.M., 1986-87; rsch. fellow Lovelace Inhalation Toxicology Rsch. Inst., Albuquerque, 1987-89; relief veterinarian, 1990-92; study dir. Internat. Rsch. and Devel. Corp., Mattawan, Mich., 1992-98; sr. toxicologist Alcon Rsch. Ltd., Ft. Worth, Tex., 1998—. Contbr. articles and abstracts to profl. jours. Mem. adv. bd. Rock Springs (Wyo.) Humane Soc., 1990-92. Mem. Am. Vet. Med. Assn., Vet. Cancer Soc., Wyo. Vet. Med. Assn., Phi Zeta, Gamma Sigma Delta, Alpha Zeta. Achievements include discovery that serum alpha fetoprotein can be used as a diagnostic tool for canine hepatic tumors. Home: 3720 Lawndale Ave Fort Worth TX 76133-2938 Office: Alcon Rsch 6201 South Fwy Fort Worth TX 76134-2001

LOWTHER, FRANK EUGENE, research physicist; b. Orrville, Ohio, Feb. 3, 1929; s. John Finger and Mary Elizabeth (Mackey) L.; m. Elizabeth E. Koons, April 21, 1951; children: Cynthia E., Victoria J., James A., Frank Eugene. Grad., Ohio State U., Columbus, 1952. Scientist missile divsn. Raytheon Corp., Boston, 1952-57, GE, Syracuse, N.Y.,, Fla., Daytona Beach, Fla., 1957-65; chief sci. Purification Sci., Inc., 1965-72; mgr. ozone R & D W.R. Grace Co., Curtis Bay, Md., 1972-75; sr. engring. assoc. Linde divsn. Union Carbide Corp., Tonawanda, N.Y., 1975-80; scientist Atlantic Richfield-Energy Conversion and Materials Lab., L.A., 1980-93; prin. scientist Atlantic Richfield-Corp. Tech., L.A., 1983-85, sci. advisor, 1985-88; rsch. advisor Atlantic Richfield-Corp. Tech., Plano, Tex., 1988-93, cons. tech. advisor, 1993—; advisor Energy Sci., Inc., Canandaigua, N.Y., 1993—, Custom Tech. Creations, Inc., Canandaigua, 1993—, World Ecolog, Inc., Geneva, N.Y., 1999—. Recipient Inventor of Yr. award Patent Law Assn. and Tech. Socs. Coun., 1976. Fellow AIAA; mem. IEEE (life), AAAS, N.Y. Acad. Scis., Masons. Achievements include patent in field of ozone tech., plasma generators, solid state power devices, internal combustion engines, electro-desorption, thermoelectrics, virus and bacteria disinfection systems, oil field technology, electric power distribution, nuclear fusion, chemical and physical reactors, exploding bridge wires, weapons. Home and Office: 4965 Adams Dr Canandaigua NY 14424-4200

LÖWY, MICHAEL, sociologist, researcher, educator; b. São Paulo, Brazil, May 6, 1938; s. Kurt and Hedwig (Löwinger) L. Degree, U. São Paulo, 1961; PhD, U. Paris, 1974. Lectr. U. Manchester, Eng., 1968-69, U. Paris, 1969-77; researcher Nat. Ctr. for Sci. Rsch. (CNRS), Paris, 1977—; lectr. Ecole des Hautes Etudes, Paris, 1990—; guest lectr. numerous univs. including U. Mich., Harvard U.,Princeton U., Stanford U., U. Calif., Portland (Oreg.) State U., U. Fed. Mexico, others. Author: George Lukacs, From Romanticism to Bolchevism, 1980, Redemption and Utopia-Libertarian Judaism in Central Europe, 1989, On Changing the World-Essays in Political Philosophy from K. Marx to W. Benjamin, 1993, The War of Gods. Religion and Politics in Latin America, 1996, Fatherland or Mother Earth? Essays on the National Question, 1998, others; contbr. articles to jours. Office: CEIFR-EHESS, 54 Bd Raspail, 75006 Paris France

LOY, MICHAEL MING-TAK, physics educator; b. Nanjing, China, Jan. 12, 1945; s. Hing and Kam (Wang) L.; m. Ivy Y. Tung, Jan. 12, 1970; children: Michelle, Sharon. BS, U. Calif., Berkeley, 1966, PhD, 1971. Rsch. staff IBM Rsch., Yorktown Heights, N.Y., 1971-78, mgr., 1978-86, tech. planning staff, 1986-87, sr. mgr., 1987-93; prof. physics Hong Kong U. Sci. and Tech., 1993—, head. physics dept., 1997-98, dean sci., 1998—. Topical editor: Jour. Optical Soc., 1994-2000. Fellow Am. Phys. Soc. Office: Hong Kong U Sci and Tech, Dept Physics, Clear Water Bay Clear Water Bay Hong Kong

LOYE, AJIBOLA, radiologist, consultant; b. Ibadan, Oyo, Nigeria, Nov. 27, 1959; arrived in Saudi Arabia, 1996; s. Dare Joseph and Mojisola Loye; m. Bolanle Mabel Igbaroola, Mar. 3, 1990; children: Ayomide, Ayomiposi, Ayomikun. MB, BChir, U. Ibadan, 1984; Fellow Radiology, Lagos U. Tchg. Hosp., 1995. Med. officer Ministry of Health, Oyo, 1985-89; resident radiology Lagos U. Tchg. Hosp., 1990-95; specialist radiologist Ministry Health, Riyadh, Saudi Arabia, 1997—. Fellow W. African Coll. Surgeons. Avocations: reading, politics, table tennis, football. Office: Gen Hosp, Al-Quwayyah, Riyadh 11971, Saudi Arabia

LOYKE, HUBERT FRANK, internist, cardiologist; b. Cleve., Sept. 9, 1923; s. Frank Alex and Casimer Marie (Malczewski) L.; m. Ellen Marie Eynon, June 16, 1951; children: Thomas F., Christopher J. BS, John Carroll U., 1944; MD, St. Louis U., 1948; postgrad., U. Mich., 1952. Intern St. Alexis Hosp., Cleve., 1948-49; resident St. John Hosp., Cleve., 1949-51; fellow in hypertension U. Mich., 1951-52; sch. physician Pub. Health Dept., Cleve., 1952-54; chief Hypertension Clinic, Cleve., 1957-95; dir. Hypertension Lab., Cleve., 1957-95; internist, cardiologist St. Vincent Charity Hosp., Cleve., 1957-95; med. examiner FAA, Washington, 1961-63; chief cardiology St. John Hosp., Cleve., 1962-65; chief of staff St. Augustine Manor, Cleve., 1971-72; med. advisor ARC, Cleve., 1982-92; physician mem. Sr. Friendship Ctr., Ft. Myers, Fla., 1997-2000. Reviewer 6 med. jours., 1972-95; contbr. over 50 articles to profl. jours. Vol. ARC, Ft. Myers, Fla., 1997—. Capt. USAF, 1955-57. Grantee NIH, 1959-71, Kidney Found., 1977-78, Morison Found., 1980-81. Mem. AMA, Internat. Soc. Hypertension, Coun. High Blood Pressure Rsch. Democrat. Roman Catholic. Achievements include identification of effect of altitude on Sickle Cell disease, liver blood pressure effect, diseases which lower blood pressure, elements which affect blood pressure; demonstrated lowering blood pressure by animal ACE blockade. Avocations: gardening, stamps. Home: 11209 Naomi Dr Parma OH 44130-1557 Office: St Vincent Charity Hosp 2351 E 22d St Cleveland OH 44115-3111

LOZA, NASSER FATHY, psychiatrist; b. Cairo, Feb. 2, 1958; s. Fathy Nassif Loza and Francine Benjamin Behman; m. Nadine Mounir Bibawy, May 6, 1991; 1 child, Francine. MBChB, Cairo U., 1982, MSc, 1986; DPM, Inst. Psychiatry London, 1986. House officer, registrar Maudlsey Hosp., London, 1982-87; registrar, cons. psychiatry Behman Hosp., Cairo, 1987-93, med. dir., 1993—; cons. Nile Badrawy Hosp., Cairo, 1987-90, Befrienders Internat., 1994, Assn. for Relief of Children of Psychiatrists Prisoners, Cairo, 1989-96. Author: Psychiatry in the Global Village, 1992. Fellow Royal Soc. Medicine, Royal Coll. Psychiatrists; mem. Egyptian Psychiat. Assn., Arab Psychiat. Assn. Avocations: sailing, tennis, classical music. Home: 23 rd 83, Maadi Egypt Office: Behman Hosp, 32 El-Marsad St Helwan, Cairo Egypt

LOZADA, SALVADOR MARIA, lawyer, educator; b. Buenos Aires, Jan. 7, 1932; s. Eduardo Lozada Chaves and Marta (Hechart) de Lozada; m. Maria Helena Garcia Hamilton, May 11, 1954; children: Juan Cruz, Maria Helena, Ezequiel, Guillermo, Martin. JD, U. Cordoba, 1954, PhD, 1965. Cert. lawyer, Pub. Coll. Lawyers, Buenos Aires1955. Dist. atty. Judicial Power, Buenos Aires, 1959-63; judge Buenos Aires, 1963-74; pres. Latin-Am. Assn. Constitutional Law, Buenos Aires, 1972—; founder, 1st. v.p. Internat. Assn. constitutional Law, Buenos Aires, 1981—; prof. law Buenos Aires U., 1962-76; sec. gen. Latin-Am. Orgn. Catholic Univs., 1967-76. Author: Institution of Public Law, 1966, Constitutional Law, 1972, Multinational Enterprises, 1973, Human Rights in Argentina, 1999. Recipient Gral Moscony award Argentine Inst. Econ. Devel., 1972, Scalabrini Ortiz award Buenos Aires U. Pub. House, 1974. Mem. Argentine League Human Rights (co-pres. 1981—), Inst. of Constitutional Law (dep. dir., hon. pres. 1995). Home: Ave Santa Fe 2108 4A, 1123 Buenos Aires Argentina

LOZANO ESCRIBANO, TOMÁS, diplomat; b. Madrid, Jan. 26, 1927; s. Fermin Lozano Contra and Isabel Escribano Reol; m. Blanca Cutanda Sánchez de Cogolludo, Nov. 21, 1959; children: Blanca, Cristina, Inés, Alvaro. Degree in law, Ctrl. U., Madrid, 1950; diploma, Spanish Diplomatic Acad.; univ. diploma, La Paz (Bolivia) U., 1985. Sec. Embassy of Spain, Tegucigalpa, Honduras, 1959-62, Rome, 1962-69; counsellor Embassy of Spain, Montevideo, Uruguay, 1969-72; min. for econ. affairs Embassy of Spain, Lisboa, Portugal, 1974-79; amb. Embassy of Spain, La Paz, Bolivia, 1980-86, Panamá, 1986-92; Spanish rep. Indigenous People Fund, La Paz, 1992—; cons. Indigenous Peoples Affairs, Fgn. Aff. Ministry, Spain, 1992—; guest prof. U. Carlos III Getafe, Madrid. Contbr. articles to profl. jours. V.p. Latin Am. and Caribbean Fund for Indigenous Peoples, La Paz, 1995—. Lt. infantry, Spanish Army, 1946-51. Recipient Merit Order Crosses, Govts. of Italy, Argentina, Chile and Portugal, 1969-79, Great Cross-Order, Condor de Los Andej Govt., Bolivia, 1986, Great Cross Civil Merit, Govt. Spain, 1990, Great Cross V.N. Balboa, Govt. Panama, 1992, Gold Medal of the Red Cross, Spain, 1991-92. Mem. Club Financiero Genoa-Madrid. Roman Catholic. Avocations: reading, classical music, stamp collecting, jogging. Home: Calle Peñalba 4, 28223 Madrid Spain Office: Ministerio Asuntos Exterior, Plaza Provincia 1, 28071 Madrid Spain

LOZINSKII, ELIEZER LEONID, computer scientist; b. Kiev, Ukraine, USSR, Sept. 16, 1934; s. Shalom and Ida (Pearlman) L.; m. Rosa Plotkin, Sept. 29, 1959; children: Khagith, Baruch. Engr., Polytechnic Inst., Kiev, 1956, Inst. of Comms., Odessa, 1963; Doctorate, Inst. Cybernetics, Kiev, 1968. Leading engr. Computer Ctr., Kiev, 1956-63; head dept. Inst. Cybernetics, Kiev, 1963-72; assoc. prof. Hebrew U., Jerusalem, 1974-87, prof. computer sci., 1987—; vis. prof. Rutgers U., N.J., 1978-79, SUNY Stony Brook, N.Y., 1985-86, City Univ., Hong Kong, 1995-96; head computer sci. dept. Hebrew U., 1980-83. Co-author: (book) File Processing, 1970; contbr. articles to profl. jours. Mem. ACM, IEEE. Office: The Hebrew Univ, Givat Ram, 91904 Jerusalem Israel

LU, CHAN-NAN, electrical engineering educator, consultant; b. Chiayi, Taiwan, Aug. 23, 1958; s. Tien-Pi Lu and Su-Mei Yu; m. Jau-Rong Lai, Aug. 3, 1983; 1 child, Julia. BSc, Nat. Taiwan U., Taipei, 1981; M in Engring.,

Renssalaer Poly. Inst., 1983; PhD, Purdue U., 1987. Devel. engr. GE Co., Pittsfield, Mass., 1983-84; lead engr. Harris Corp., Melbourne, Fla., 1987-89; assoc. prof. Nat. Sun Yat-Sen U., Kaohsiung, Taiwan, 1989-93; prof. Nat. Sun Yat-Sen U., 1993—, chmn. dept. elec. engring., 1997-2000; cons. Taiwan Power Co., Taipei, 1994-96. Contbr. articles to profl. jours.; editor Transactions of Chinese Inst. Engrs., Taipei, 1996—. Vol. Hosp. Kaohsiung Med. Coll., 1994-2000, Libr. Sun Yat-Sen U., 1994-97. Recipient Rsch. award Nat. Sci. Coun., Taiwan, 1991-2000. Mem. IEEE (sr., chmn. Taipei chpt. 1997-98), Chinese Inst. Elec. Engring. (Young Engr. award 1997). Office: Dept Elec Engring, Nat Sun Yat-Sen U, Kaohsiung 804, Taiwan

LU, DALIAN, physics educator; b. Shanghai, China, Dec. 27, 1944; s. Ciyun and Yunji (Ye) L.; m. Xinhua Jiang, Dec. 23, 1970; 1 child, Min. BS, Shanghai Normal U., 1965; PhD, Meml. U. Nfld., St. John's, Can., 1995. Assoc. prof. Shanghai Normal U., 1987—; rsch. scientist U. Lethbridge, Alta., Can., 1995-97, ExxonMobil Rsch. and Engring. Co., Annandale, N.J., 1997—; dep. dir. semicondr. sect. Shanghai Normal U., 1970-80, Univ. Lab. Ctr., 1988-90. Mem. Am. Phys. Soc. Achievements include discovery of chain order scaling property for phospholipids; the second plateau of order parameter profile for chain mismatched bilayer membranes measurement of multiple distances in uniformly C-13 labled macromolecules; pore level network modeling of two-phase flow and predict oil/water and permeability; shaped and composite pulse sequences for nuclear magnetic resonances. Office: ExxonMobil Rsch & Engring Co Rte 22 E Annandale NJ 08801

LU, DAN, systems analyst, mathematician, consultant; b. Beijing, Jan. 22, 1960; came to U.S., 1981; s. Yingzhong Lu and Huaiqing Chen; m. Hong Lou, Sept. 28, 1994; children: Katherine H, Isabel. BS in Physics, Beijing U., 1981; MS in Physics, U. Wash., 1983, PhD in Theoretical Physics, 1986. Tchg., rsch. asst. U. Wash., Seattle, 1981-86; postdoctoral rsch. assoc. Washington U., St. Louis, 1986-88; R&D mgr. Yu Feng Internat. Ltd., Hong Kong, 1988-90; sys. cons. Summit Computer Svcs., Charlotte, N.C., 1991-93; sr. sys. cons. Criterion Group, Charlotte, 1993-94; bus. sys. analyst, mathematician INMAR Enterprise, Inc. Info. Tech. (formerly CMS, Inc.), Winston-Salem, N.C., 1994—, sr. technical architect, 1999—. Contbr. articles to profl. publs. China-U.S. Physics Examination and Application fellow, 1981. Mem. Am. Phys. Soc. Achievements include development of model for market promotion, forecasting system for coupon redemption, set of subroutines to calculate EXAFS electron energy losses. Home: 325 Craver Pointe Dr Clemmons NC 27012-8926 Office: INMAR Enterprises Inc Info Tech 2650 Pilgrim Ct Winston Salem NC 27106-5238

LU, GUIYANG, electrical engineer; b. Guiyang, China, May 10, 1946; came to U.S., 1982; s. Wen and Yunqiu Deng; m. Jing Du; 1 child, Jia. Degree in elec. engring., Tsing Hua U., Beijing, 1970; postgrad., South China U. Tech., Guangzhou, 1980-81; MA in Math., Calif. State U., Fresno, 1984; MSEE, Poly. U., N.Y.C., 1986. Instr. in elec. engring. South China U. Tech., Guangzhou, 1973-80; v.p. engring. Kawahara Corp., N.Y.C., 1986-88; H.S. math. tchr. N.Y.C. Bd. Edn., 1988-90; sr. R&D engr. Avid Inc., Norco, Calif., 1991-98; sr. RF engr. Securay Key, Chatsworth, Calif., 1998—. Mem. IEEE. Home: 1718 Eastgate Ave Upland CA 91784-9210 Office: 20447 Nordhoff St Chatsworth CA 91311-6112

LU, HSUEH-I, mathematician, computer scientist, educator; b. I-Lan, Taiwan, Jan. 12, 1965; s. Li-Hsiang Lu and Ming-Aye Lin; m. Chih-Hui Chiang, May 26, 1990; children: Jessica, Aaron. PhD, Brown U., 1997. Assoc. prof. Nat. Chung-Cheng U., Chia-Yi, Taiwan, 1997-99; dir. computer labs. Nat. Chung-Cheng U., 1997-99; asst. rsch. fellow Inst. Info. Sci., Academia Sinica. Author: Pascal in Details, 1990; contbr. articles to profl. jours. Lt. Taiwanese Army, 1988-90. Taiwan Min. Edn. fellow, 1990-93. Avocation: table tennis. Office: Academia Sinica, Inst of Information Sci, Taipei Taiwan 115

LU, JIAN, computer science educator; b. Nanjing, China, Mar. 31, 1960; s. Xing Hua and Chun Xiu (Ju) L.; m. Zhen Zhu Feng, Oct. 22, 1988; 1 child, Yun. BS, Nanjing U., China, 1982, MS, 1985, PhD, 1988. Lectr. dept. computer sci. Nanjing U., China, 1988-90, assoc. prof. Inst. Computer Software, 1990-95, prof. Inst. Computer Software, 1995—, vice dean dept. computer sci. & tech., 1995—, vice dir. Inst. Computer Software, 1995—, dir. state key lab. novel software tech., 1995—. Contbr. articles to profl. jours. Mem. Assn. Computing Machinery, China's Computer Fedn. Assn. Avocations: table tennis, basketball, reading, walking. Home: 7-303, 7 Nan Xiu Chun Shanghai Rd, Nanjing 210008, China Office: Inst Computer Software, 22 Hankou Rd, Nanjing 210093, China

LU, JIN-QIN, electrical engineer; b. July 9, 1957; s. Hanyao Lu and Fengshian Chen; m. Weiqing Wang, Apr. 22, 1985; children: Yijia, Yiyao. MSEE, Yokohama (Japan) Nat. U., 1988, PhD in Elec. Engring., 1991. Rsch. fellow Sony Corp., Tokyo, 1991-95; mgr. Sony Am., San Jose, 1995-97, NEC Electronics, Santa Clara, Calif., 1997—. Contbr. articles to profl. jours. Mem. IEEE (sr.). Achievements include 6 software patents pending. Avocations: traveling, skiing, fishing. E-mail: jin-qin lu@el.nec.com. Home: 1707 Clovis Ave San Jose CA 95124-6303

LU, LIHJENG MAURICE, finance company executive, consultant; b. Taipei, Taiwan, Apr. 1, 1958; s. Hsing-Chuang Lu and Mei-Tze Huang; m. Tien-Yi Tammy Peng, Sept. 26, 1988; children: Luo-Ying, Cheng-Kai. BS in Bus. Mgmt., Tatung U., 1981; MBA, U. Dallas, 1985. Lic. secs. broker, futures broker, branch mgr., U.S., Taiwan, lic. secs. mgr., futures mgr., Taiwan. Fin. planner First Investors Svc., U.S., 1986; personnel mgr. Taiwan br. May Dept. Stores, 1986-89; fin. cons. Taiwan br. Merrill Lynch, 1989-92; gen. mgr. Taiwan br. Cargill Investor Svcs., 1992-96, Fimat Futures, 1996-97; pres. CS Futures Co., Taipei, Taiwan, 1997—, also bd. dirs.; instr. Republic of China Secs. and Futures Inst., 1995—; master of ceremony award ceremony Jr. Chamber Internat. Asia Conf., 1993, China Night, 1993; chmn. clearing com. Taiwan Futures Exchange, 1998—. Guardian Taipei (Taiwan) Local Ct., 1997—. Ensign Republic of China Navy Mil. Svc., 1981-83. Named Champion English Speech Contest Republic of China Jr. C. of C., 1993, Outstanding Bus. Leader in Securities and Futures Industry Republic of China, 2000. Mem. Taiwan Futures Assn. (dir. 1995—, chmn. fin. com. 1995-98, chmn. mktg. promotions com. 1998—), Taiwan Bus. Arbitration Assn. (arbitrator 1997—), Taipei Secs. Assn. (cons. internat. com. 1995-98). Avocations: travel, drama, music, gourmet food. E-mail: maurice@chinasec.com.tw. Fax: 886-2-253-10309. Office: CS Futures Co Ltd Rm 1002, 10th Fl #96 Chung Shan N Rd, Sec 2 Taipei 114, Taiwan

LU, LUO, psychologist, researcher; b. Shanghai, July 29, 1964; d. Bo Bin Lu and Jin Xian Qiu; m. Jyh Horng Lin, Sept. 10, 1991. BEd, East China Normal U., 1985; D Psychology, Oxford (Eng.) U., 1989. Postdoctoral rschr. Oxford U., 1989-91; assoc. prof. psychology Kaohsiung (Taiwan) Med. Coll., 1992—. Contbr. articles to profl. jours. Mem. Chinese Psychol. Assn., Chinese Mental Health Assn., Brit. Psychol. Soc. (fgn. affiliate). Office: Kaohsiung Med Coll, 100 Shih Chuan 1st Rd, Kaohsiung 807, Taiwan

LU, MI, computer engineer, educator; b. Chong Qing, Si Chuan, China, July 22, 1949; d. Chong Pu Lu and Shu Sheng Fan. MS, Rice U., 1984, PhD, 1987. Registered profl. engr. From asst. prof. to assoc. prof. Tex. A&M U., Coll. Sta., 1987-98, prof., 1998—; stream chmn. 7th Internat. Conf. Computing and Info., Peterborough, Ont., Can., 1995; conf. chmn. 5th Internat. Conf. Computer Sci. and Informatics, 2000. Assoc. editor Jour. Computing and Info., 1995—, Info. Sci., 1996-97; contbr. articles to profl. jours. Mem. Computer Soc. of IEEE (sr.). Office: Tex A&M U Dept Elec Engring College Station TX 77843

LU, MICHAEL (HSIANG-CHENG), sales executive; b. Changhwa, Taiwan, Dec. 12, 1959; s. Huo-Neng and Yueh-Nu (Zai) L.; m. Daphane Yeh, 1986; chidren: Mary, Keny. B Engring., Nat. Taiwan U., Taipei, 1982, M, 1984. Field application engr. HP Taiwan Ltd., Tapei, 1987-89; sales rep. Hewlett Packard Taiwan Ltd., Tapei, 1989-91, field sales mgr., 1991-93; Taiwan country mgr. Synopsys, Taipei, 1993-95, Great China country mgr., 1995-96, CBA regional sales mgr., 1996-97, Asia Pacific regional mgr., 1997-98, dir. Asia Pacific region, 1998—. With Taiwan Combined Svc. Force, 1985-87. Office: Synopsys Inc Rm 2908 29/F, No 333 Keelung Rd Sec 1, Taipei 110, Taiwan

LU, MING LIANG, software company executive, educator; b. Xinbin, Liaoning, China, May 13, 1960; s. Chun Jiu and Shang Qing (Wu) L.; m. Wei Lin, Nov. 21, 1985; 1 child, Si. B of Engring., Dalian (China) U. Tech., 1982, M of Engring., 1985, D of Engring, 1989. Asst. lectr. Dalian U. Tech., 1985-86, lectr., 1989-91; rschr. Leeds (Eng.) U., 1991-94; sr. rschr. Tokyo Inst. Tech., 1994-95, assoc. prof., 1995-97; v.p. Aigis Sys., Inc., Newark, Calif., 1997-99; product integration mgr. ABB Automation Inc. Intelligent Solution Products, Bloomfield, N.J., 1999-2000; sr. advisor Aspen Tech., Inc., Boston, 2000—; cons. Japan Energy Corp., Okayama, 1994-97; presenter in field. Contbr. 70 articles to profl. jours., chpts. to books. Mem. Am. Inst. Chem. Engrs., Internat. Soc. Productivity Enhancement, Internat. Soc. for Measurement and Control. Avocations: music, swimming, mountain hiking. E-mail: mingllu@hotmail.com.

LU, NINGPING, environmental chemist; b. Sichuan, China, June 18, 1941; d. Yiungdi and Jinghua (Liu) L.; m. Li Pin-Fun, July 23, 1964 (div. 1990); children: Ying, Nin. BS in Biophysics, Sichuan U., 1964; MS of Soil Chemistry, Auburn U., 1990, PhD in Environtl. Soil Chemistry, 1993. Dir. Atomic Agrl. Ins., Sichuan, 1983; rsch. assoc. Fertilizer Ins., Sichuan, 1985-86; postdoctoral rsch. assoc. Auburn U., 1993-94; postdoctoral rsch. assoc. Los Alamos Nat. Lab., 1994-97, tech. staff mem., 1997—; vis. scientist Purdue U., West Lafayette, Ind., 1983-84, Auburn U., 1984-85; cons. UN Devel. Program in China, Beijing, 1997—. Contbr. over 55 articles to profl. publs. Mem. Agronomy Soc. of Am., Soil Sci. Soc. of Am., Am. Chem. Soc., N.Y. Acad. of Sci., Phi Kappa Phi. Achievements include development of remedial processes of radionuclide (e.g. uranium-238, cesium-137, plutonium-239) contaminated soils; research include remediation of radionuclide contaminated soil, formation and transport of radio-colloids in groundwater and on the utilization of municipal solid wastes on agricultural land. Office: E-ET Los Alamos Nat Lab Ms J514 Los Alamos NM 87545-0001

LU, QI KENG, mathematics educator; b. Fushan, Guangdong, China, May 17, 1927; s. Zi Ji Lu and Zhi Ya Liang; m. Mulan Zhang, July 15, 1962; children: Guoguang, Ying. BS, Zongshan U., Guangzhou, China, 1950. Asst. Zhongshan U., 1950-51; rsch. asst. Academia Sinica, Beijing, 1951-54, rsch. asst. prof., 1954-62, rsch. assoc. prof., 1962-78, rsch. prof. Inst. Math., 1978—, vice dir. Inst. Math., 1980-83; rsch. prof. Shantou (China) U., 1994-98. Author: The Classical Manifolds and Classical Domians, 1963 (Hua Loo-Keng prize 1993), New Results of Classical Manifolds and Classical Domains, 1997. Mem. Am. Math. Soc., Chinese Acad. Scis., Chinese Math. Soc. Avocations: classical music, swimming. Home: 812-101 Zhong Quan Cun, Beijing 100080, China Office: Inst of Math, Academia Sinica, Beijing 100080, China

LU, SHAU-ZOU, research and development manager; b. Chi-Tran, Peoples Republic of China, Feb. 10, 1943; s. Fu-Ten and Sheng-Yuan (Wang) L.; m. Mou-ying Fu, Nov. 22, 1968; children: Linda Enn, Eva. BS, Nat. Cheng-Kung U., Tainan, Republic of China, 1966; MS, Clarkson U., 1972, PhD, 1973. Process engr. GAF Corp., Binghamton, N.Y., 1973-75, pilot plant supr., 1975-77; staff scientist, materials research and devel. Celanese Corp., Summit, N.J., 1977-81, group leader polymer devel., 1981-84; mgr. materials, phys. tech. HPD, Abbott Labs., North Chicago, Ill., 1984-93, mgr. infusion therapy and renal care, 1993—; bd. dirs. E&R Enterprises, Ill.; v.p. Atomic Engring. Inc.; pres. AEC Internat., Inc. Contbr. articles to profl. jours.; patentee in field. Advisor Young's Club-North Shore, Ill., 1985-86; pres. Lake County Chinese-Am. Assn., 1987-88. NSF scholar, 1967-73. Mem. Am. Inst. Chem. Engrs., Soc. Plastics Engrs., Tri-State Chinese/Am. Assn. (bd. dirs. 1982-84). Club: Tennis (officer 1984-86). Avocations: tennis, birdwatching, golf. Home: 195 Grafton Ct Lake Bluff IL 60044-1916 Office: Abbott Labs D 44B Ap4 Abbott Park IL 60064

LU, SHIH-PENG, history educator; b. Kao-Yu, Chiang-Su, China, Sept. 16, 1928; s. Ch'un-Tai and Chu-Yin (Chia) L.; m. Wei-Chun Julia Lee; children: Ting Ting, Shin. BA, Nat. Taiwan U., Taipei, 1952. Cert. full prof., Ministry of Edn., Taiwan. Tchg. asst. Taiwan U., Taipei, 1953-55; rsch. asst. Acad. Sinica, Taipei, 1955-58; lectr. Tunghai U., Taichung, Taiwan, 1958-63, assoc. prof., 1963-67, prof., 1967—; vis. scholar Harvard U., Cambridge, Mass., 1961-63; rsch. fellow Yale U., New Haven, 1980-81; dir. evening divsn. Tunghai U., 1972-81, chmn. dept. history, 1981-87, dean Coll. Arts, 1988-94; dir. Chinese Culture Monthly, Taichung, 1988—. Author: Vietnam During the Period of Chinese Rule, 1964 (Nat. Sci. Coun. Publ. award 1965), The Modern History of China, 1979 (World Books Co. Authors award 1979), The Contemporary History of China, 1991 (Ministry of Edn. Outstanding Textbook award 1992); editor Chinese Culture Monthly, 1979—(Ministry of Edn. Best Jour. award 1991). 2nd lt. ROTC, Chinese Mil., 1952-53. Named Outstanding Youth, China Youth Corps, Taiwan, 1952, Outstanding Prof., Ministry of Edn., 1992. Mem. Assn. Modern History (chairperson bd. overseers 1994-96), Chinese Hist. Assn. (bd. dirs. 1983-94), Taiwan U. Alumni Assn. (chmn. 1987-89), Assn. for Ming Studies (exec. dir. 1995-97). Avocations: reading, classical music, table tennis, jogging, Chinese opera. Home: 19-8A Tunghai Rd, 407 T'aichung Taiwan Office: Tunghai Univ, Dept History, 407 Taichung Taiwan

LU, SHIQIANG, aeronautical educator, researcher; b. Jiangxi, Jiujiang, China, Feb. 13, 1962; parents Shengjin Lu and Yuzhi Tao; m. Yunxia Li, June 1 1988; 1 child, Cuiyuan. BS, Wuhan U., China, 1985; MS, Xi'an Jiaotong U., China, 1991; PhD, Northwestern Polytech. U., Xi'an, 1999. Assoc. engr. Jiangxi Bearing Factory, Yichun, China, 1985-91; lectr. Nanchang (China) Inst. Aeronautical Tech., 1993-96, assoc. prof., 1997—. Contbr. articles to profl. jours. Office: Nanchang Inst Aero Tech, no 173 Shanghai Rd, 330034 Nanchang China Address: Nanchang Inst Aero Tech, Dept Mat Eng, 330034 Nanchang China

LU, TSAN FEI, artist; b. Nankang, Kiangsi, China, Mar. 7, 1936; s. Chung Kuan and Ho Yin (Shi) L.; m. Yun Yu Lin, Jan. 1, 1966; children: Chi Lu, San Lu, Bin Lu. BA in Fine Arts, Nat. Normal U., Taipei, Taiwan, 1961; cert. in performing arts, Nat. Motion Picture Inst., Taipei, 1969. Art design mgr. Ocean Advt. Co., Taipei, 1963-69; prodr., actor, asst. dir., playwright Cathay Motion Pictures, Hong Kong, 1969-74; architect designer, v.p. Chevron Asphalt Co., Taipei, 1974-77; chief art dir. Gem Advt. Co., Taipei, 1979-83; cons., art dir., playwright Sun Motion Pictures, Taipei and Hong Kong, 1984-88; v.p. Fortune Holding Co., Hong Kong, Tailand and, Macau, 1989-92; artist Lu Art Studio, Northport, Ala., 1992—; chief engr. stadium complex in south east Asia, 1975 (Best Engring. award 1976). Playwright: Uneasy Days, Run for Love, Cobbles; exhbns. at Ferguson Gallery, U. Ala., 1997. Recipient contbr. award Info. Bur. China, 1977, Best Playwright award, 1986, Excellence award NAT Edn. Ctr., 1997. Fellow World Cultural Celebrity Dictionary; mem. West. Ala. Artist Assn., World Chinese Artist Almanac. Avocations: classical music, motion pictures, book reading. E-mail: slu100@hotmail.com.

LU, WEI, medical researcher; b. Guiyang, Guizhou, China, Apr. 23, 1962; arrived in France, 1988; s. Guo Liang and Le Jia (Xu) L. MD, West China U. Med. Scis., Chengdu, 1984; PhD, René Descartes U., Paris, 1995. Intern U Affiliated Hosps., Chengdu, 1983-84; asst. prof. Peking Union Med. Coll., Beijing, 1984-88, chinese Acad. med. scis., Beijing, 1984-88; vis. rsch. Inst. Nat. de la Sante et de La Recherche Med., Paris, 1988-89; rschr. Lab. D'Immunologie Tumeurs Laënnec Hosp., Paris, 1989-96; chief rschr. lab. d'oncologie et virologie moléculaire René Descartes U., Paris, 1996—; head lab. virologie Laennec Hosp., Paris, 1996-2000; dir. discovery rsch. Gene-Quant Biomed. High Techs., Paris, 1996—; co-organizer workshops and symposiums, Paris. Co-author and co-editor: Viral Quantitation in HIV Infection, 1993, Cell Activation and Apoptosis in HIV Infection, 1995; patentee in field; contbr. articles to profl. jours. Vis. rsch. fellow Foud. Pour la Recherche Medicale, Paris, 1988-89; grantee Assn. Pour La Recherce et L'etude des Maladies du Sang, Paris, 1989-93, Assn. de Recherche pour le Traitement des Serpositifes, Paris, 1993, 95, Agence Nationale Recherches sur SIDA, 1996-98. Mem. Am. Soc. Microbiology, Internat. AIDS Soc. Avocations: philosophy, music, literature, British football. Office: U René Descartes Paris V, 45 rue des Saints Péres, 75006 Paris France

LU, WEIBO, physician; b. Shanghai, China, Oct. 18, 1928; s. Ziqing Lu and Xiuying Zhu; m. Pingqing Lin, Jan. 29, 1957; 1 child, Lu Qing. Student, Tongji Med. U., Wuhan, China, 1948-55, Trad. Chinese Medicine Tng., Beijing, 1955-58. Internist, dept. internal medicine and inf. diseases Xiyuan Hosp./China Acad. of TCM, Beijing, 1958-80; dep. dir. Ctr. Lab. China Acad. of TCM, Beijing, 1980-83, dir., dept. sci. rsch., 1983-85; secret-gen. Chinese Assn. Integration of Tradition and West Medicine, Beijing, 1985-87; leader Chin-Tanz Coord. Group in Treatment of AIDS China Acad. of TCM, Salaam/Tanzania, 1988-91; dir. AIDS rsch. dept. China Acad. of TCM, Beijing, 1992—, dir. AIDS clin. rsch., 1988-96. Author/editor: Treatment and Research on AIDS and TCM, 1992, Traditional and Western Appr on Prevention and Treatment of AIDS, 1994; vice editor-in-chief Chinese Jour. Integrated Traditional and Western Medicine. Recipient Konichi award China Universal AIDS Found., Beijing, 1992. Mem. Expert Comm. of State Prevention and Control on AIDS, China Assn. of STD and AIDS Control and Prevention. Office: China Acad of TCM, 18 Beixincang Dongzhimennei, 100 700 Beijing China

LU, WEIXIN, medical researcher; b. Lanxi, People Republic China, Feb. 27, 1965; s. Donggui and EE (Fang) L.; m. Yumei Yao, Oct. 20, 1995; 1 child, Grace. MD, Shanghai Medical Univ., Shanghai, 1989; PhD, Shanghai Medical Univ., 1994. Asst. prof. Shanghai Inst. Cell Biology Chinese Acad. Sci., Shanghai, People Republic China, 1994-97; fellow Univ. Tex. M.D. Anderson Cancer Ctr., Houston, 1997-99, rsch. assoc., 1999—. Contbr. articles to profl. jours. E-mail: weixinl@notes.mdacc.tmc.edu. Fax: 713 792 8747. Home: 5606 Bissonnet St Apt 132 Houston TX 77081-6132 Office: Univ Tex MD Anderson Cancer Ctr Cell Biology 173 1515 Holcombe Blvd Houston TX 77030-4009

LU, WILLIE, communications executive; b. Haining, China; s. X. Lu; m. Janny Hu, June 6, 1992. Postgrad., GMD, Berlin, 1996; PhD, Tech. U. Malaysia, 1995; MSc, Zhejiang Tech.U., 1991, BSc, 1989. Lectr. ZJU, Zhejiang, China, 1989-91; sr. engr. MPT, Zhejiang, 1991-93; sr. rschr. UTM, Kuala Lumpur, Malaysia, 1993-95; guest scientist German Nat. Ctr. Info. Tech., Berlin, 1995-96; sr. cons. Nortel, N.J., 1996-97; dir. UTStar, Alameda, Calif., 1997-98; prin. wireless architect Siemens, San Jose, Calif., 1998—. Mem. IEEE (sr.). Home: 1960 Linden Ln Milpitas CA 95035-2504

LU, XIAOHU, chemist; b. Jintan, China, Nov. 30, 1962; s. Sourong Lu and Xiufong Pan; m. Haiyan Tang; children: Zhen, Billy. BSc, U. Sci. and Tech. China, Hefei, 1986, MSc, 1989; PhD, Royal Inst. Tech., Stockholm, 1997. From asst. lectr. to lectr., rschr. U. Sci. and Tech. China, 1989-92; from rsch. engr. to asst. prof. Royal Inst. Tech., 1997—. Author: Introduction to Molecular Spectroscopy, 1992; contbr. articles to profl. jours. Mem. AAAS, Chinese Chem. Soc. Avocations: music, fishing. Office: Royal Inst Technology Hwy Engring, Brinellvagen 34, 100 44 Stockholm Sweden

LU, XIAO-YUN, mathematician, researcher, control engineer; b. Mianyang, China, June 24, 1955; s. Guang-Yun and Hui-Fang (Liu) L.; m. Liu-Yan Tang, Jan. 8, 1993; 1 child, Si-Wei. BS, Chengdu U. Sci. and Tech., 1982; MSc, Inst. Sys. Sci./Chinese Acad., Beijing, 1986; PhD, U. Manchester Inst. Sci./Tech., Eng., 1993. Tchr. Mianyang Normal Sch., Mianyang County, China, 1976-77; head fundamental math. group, dept. applied math. Chengdu U. Sci. and Tech., 1985-89; rsch. assoc. control systems rsch., dept. engring. U. Leicester, Eng., 1994-97, rschr. control sys. rsch., dept. engring., 1997-99; rsch. asst. engr. PATH HQ, U. Calif., Berkeley, 1999-2000, assoc. rsch. engr., 2000—. Reviewer, Math. Rev., 1991—. Chinese Edn. Commn. rsch. grantee, 1984-86; Sino-Brit. Friendship scholar, 1989-93; Overseas Rsch. grantee, 1989-92. Mem. IEEE Control Sys. Soc., ASME (assoc.), Am. Math. Soc. Avocations: classical music, table tennis, hiking, Tai-Ji-Quan, car and electrical appliance maintenance. Office: PATH HQ U Calif Inst Trans 1357 S 46th St Richmond CA 94804-4648

LU, XINGZE, physics educator; b. Shanghai, China, Aug. 17, 1945; s. Depei and Yufang (Shi) L.; m. Huina Zhang. BS, U. Sci. and Tech. of China, 1967; MA, CCNY, 1984, MPhil, 1984, PhD, 1985. Lectr. Fudan U., Shanghai, China, 1988-91, assoc. prof., 1991-95, prof., 1995—; doctoral student advisor Fudan U., 1996—. Contbr. articles to profl. jours. Mem. Chinese Phys. Soc. Office: Dept Physics Fudan Univ, 220 Handan Rd, Shanghai 200433, China

LU, XUANHUI, physics educator; b. Hangzhou, Zhejian, China, Mar. 6, 1957; s. J. Lu and Qianyin (Li) L.; m. Xiaoqi Jiang, Feb. 14, 1985; 1 child. BS, Zhejiang U., Hangshou, China, 1982, MS, 1988. Asst. prof. Hangzhou U., 1988-90; assoc. prof. Zhejiang U. (formerly Hangzhou U.), Hangzhou, 1991-95, prof., 1995-99; rsch. scientist Columbia U., N.Y.C., 1999, Nev. U., Reno, 1999; vis. scholar Kiel U., Germany, 1991; v.p. R&D Ctr. for Optics and Laser, Hangzhou, 1995-99; cons. CrystaLaser, LLC., Reno, 1999. Author/inventor: (book/invention) On the Nature of Diffraction and Newbeam Laser, 1997 (Invention prize of China 1997); author: The Modes of Solid State Lasers, 1991 (Invention prize of China 1991). Mem. AAAS. Avocations: collections, photography.

LU, YADONG, physics educator, consultant; b. Baoji, Shaanxi, China, Oct. 31, 1964; parents Weijun Lu and Guohua Wen; m. Hongmei Fu, Sept. 29, 1993. BSc, Xi'an (China) Jiaotong U., 1985, MSc, 1990; DSc, Beijing U. Aero. and Astronautics, 1993. Asst. engr. Wuxi (China) Compressor Co., 1985-87; postdoctoral rsch. fellow Inst. Engring. Thermophysics Chinese Acad. Scis., Beijing, 1993-95, assoc. prof. Inst. Acoustics, 1995-98, prof., 1998—; dep. sec.-gen. TC 17: Acoustics of China State Bur. of Tech. Supervision, Beijing, 1997—; chief dir. Acoustical Lab., Beijing, 1999—. Contbr. articles to profl. jours.; patentee in field. Recipient 1st class prize of sci. and tech. for youth Scientist Dezhao Wang's Found., Beijing, 1998. Mem. Acoustical Soc. China, Acoustical Soc. Am., Environ. Physics Soc. China. Avocations: music, swimming, table tennis. Home: Zhongguancun South St, Zhongguancun Bldg 88-1-503, Beijing 100080, China Office: Inst Acoustics Chinese Acad, 17 Zhongguancun St PO Box 2712, Beijing 100080, China

LU, YUH-YIH, electrical engineer, educator, researcher; b. Taipei, Taiwan, Dec. 2, 1962; s. Deng-Tsair Lu and Shiow-Fenq Liaw; m. Heng-Hong Xiao, May 19, 1991; children: Yueh-Torng, En-Shyang. BS, Chung-Yuan Christian U., Chung-Li, Taiwan, 1985; MSEE, Chiao Tung U., 1987, PhD in Elec. Engring., 1998. Instr. St. John's and St. Mary's Inst. Tech., Taipei, Taiwan, 1989-90; instr. Ming Hsin Inst. Tech. and Commerce, Hsin-Fong, Taiwan, 1990-94, assoc. prof., 1994-98, chmn. dept. elec. engring., 1998—; cons. TXC, Ping-Cheng, Taiwan, 1998-99. Contbr. articles to profl. jours. With Chinese Naval Acad., 1987-89. Scholar Sampo Co., Taipei, 1983. Mem. IEEE, Phi Tau Phi. Avocations: swimming, running, mountain climbing, reading. Home: No 5 Alley 16 Lane 354, Kuang-Fu Rd Section 1, Hsin-Chu 300, Taiwan Office: Ming Hsin Inst Tech, No 1 Hsin-Hsing Rd, Hsin-Fong, Hsin-Chu 304, Taiwan

LU, ZHIKANG, mathematics educator, researcher; b. Huzhou, Zhejiang, China, Jan. 7, 1943; s. Hsinshan Lu and Tsailing Chin; m. Jiemin Jin, Sept. 21, 1973; 1 child, Zhengyu. Degree, Hangzhou (China) U., 1964, Hangzhou (China) U., 1967. Tchr. Yuhang (China) Sr. H.S., 1968-78; lectr. Hangzhou Tchr.'s Coll., 1978-86, assoc. prof., 1986-94, prof. math., 1994—; dir. Analysis Tchg. and Rsch. Sect., Hangzhou, 1984—. Contbr. articles to profl. jours. Recipient 3d award for natural sci. rsch. Provincial Edn. Commn., Zhejiang, 1988, 3d award for advancement of sci. and tech. Provincial Edn. Commn., 1994, 2d award for excellent paper on natural sci. Zhejiang Evaluation Commn., 1995. Mem. Am. Math. Soc., Chinese Math. Soc. Avocation: playing go. Home: 3-308 Shiyuan Xincun, 27 Wen Zr Rd, Hangzhou Zhejiang 310012, China Office: Hangzhou Tchrs Coll Dept Mt, 96 Wen Yi Rd, Hangzhou Zhejiang 310012, China

LU, ZHONG-LIN, cognitive psychologist; b. Jingzhou, China, Nov. 19, 1967; came to U.S., 1989; s. Dao-De Zhong and Hong-Chun Lu; m Wei Sun, June 26, 1990; children: James, Mae. BS, U. Sci. and Tech. of China, 1989; MS, NYU, 1991, PhD, 1992. Postdoctoral fellow NYU, 1992; asst. rschr. U. Calif., Irvine, 1992-96; asst. prof. U. So. Calif., L.A., 1996-2000, assoc. prof., 2000—. Referee Air Force Office of Scientific Rsch., 1995, Vision Rsch., 1994—, Procs. of Nat. Acad. of Sci., 1997; contbr. articles to profl. jours. Fellowship Nat. Edn. Com., 1988, Meyer fellowship NYU, 1989-90. Mem. Am. Physics Soc., Assn. for Rsch. in Vision and Ophthalmology, Soc. for Math. Psychology, Psychonomics Soc. Achievements include establishment of the functional architecture of human visual motion perception and a theoretical framework and experimental paradigm to distinguish mechanisms of attention and perceptual learning. Avocations: table tennis, hiking, cross

country skiing. Office: Dept Psychology U So Calif Seeley G Mudd Bldg 501 Los Angeles CA 90089-0001

LUAN, BEN LI, electrochemist, researcher; b. Wendeng, Shandong, China, Nov. 6, 1963; arrived in Can., 1995; s. Yun Fu Luan and Ze Ying Huang; m. Wen Juan Chen, Apr. 1, 1988; 1 child, Bo. B in Engring., Beijing U. Sci. and Tech., 1984, M in Engring., 1987; PhD in Engring., U. Wollongong, Australia, 1996. From asst. prof. to assoc. prof. Tianjin (China) U., 1987-92; rsch. fellow U. Wollongong, 1993-96; rsch. fellow Nat. Rsch. Coun., Ottawa, Ont., Can., 1997-98, rsch. officer, 1998—; guest investigator U. Sherbrooke, Can., 1997; cons. Australian Batteries Tech. Pty. Ltd., Wollongong, 1994-96; assoc. dir. Ctr. Energy Storage, Inst. Materials Manu., U. Wollongong, 1995-96. Contbr. papers to profl. jours.; inventor in field. Recipient John Crawford award, 1993, Merit Young Scientist award Sci. and Tech. Acad. China, 1992; NSERC fellow, 1997. Mem. Electrochem. Soc. Avocations: music, sports, bridge. Office: Nat Rsch Coun Canada, 800 Collip Cir, London, ON Canada N6G 4X8

LUBAR, CHARLES GORDON, lawyer; b. Washington, May 20, 1941; s. Nathan Marvin and Lenora (Abrams) L.; m. Nancy Kaplan, Apr. 23, 1966 (div. 1977); 1 child, Katherine Nicole; m. Dominique Grierson, Oct. 2, 1977; 1 child, Alexander Nathan. BA magna cum laude, Yale U., 1963; JD, Harvard U., 1966; LLM in Taxation, Georgetown U., 1967. Bar: D.C., Md. Atty.-advisor Chief Counsel's Office IRS, Washington, 1967-69; legal counsel East African Devel. Bank, Kampala, Uganda, 1970; ptnr. Margulies & Sterling, London, 1971-74; founder, ptnr. Lubar & Youngstein, London, 1974-81; ptnr. Morgan Lewis & Bockius, London, 1981—, mng. ptnr., 1981-96, chmn. internat. sect., 1995-98, vice chmn tax sect., 1998—; speaker on internat. tax issues at numerous confs. Contbr. articles to profl. jours. Am. sec. Prince of Wales Youth Bus. Trust, London, 1989-90; mem. devel. bd. Am. sect. Nat. Gallery, London, 1990-92; mem., chair several coms. Fulbright Commn. U.K., London, 1986-96. Mem. ABA, Internat. Fiscal Assn., Yale Alumni Assn. (treas., bd. govs. 1986-90), Yale Club of London (pres. 1990—). Avocations: guitar, tennis, running, golf. Office: Morgan Lewis & Bockius, 2 Gresham St, London EC2V 7PE, England

LUBART, TODD IRA, education educator, researcher; b. Poughkeepsie, N.Y., July 10, 1965; s. Barry P. and Eileen R. (Krakower) L.; m. Sylvie A. Tordjman Lubart, Aug. 28, 1994; children: Allan, Elsa. BA, Brandeis U., Waltham, Mass., 1987; MS, Yale U., New Haven, Conn., 1990, MPhil, 1991, PhD, 1994. Rsch. scholar Paris Sch. Mgmt., 1994-95; asst. prof. U. Paris, 1995—. Author: Defying the Crowd: Cultivating Creativity in a Culture of Conformity, 1995; contbr. articles for profl. jours. Grantee: U.S. Dept. Edn., 1987-91, French Sci. Min., 1999. Mem. French Psychology Soc., Am. Psychol. Assn. Office: U Rene Descartes Paris V, 71 Ave Edouard Vaillant, 92100 Boulogne-Billancourt France

LUBASH, DAN, financial executive; b. Tel Aviv, Oct. 7, 1960; s. Marcel and Jaffa (Kuciuk) L.; m. Michelle Norris. BS in Engring., U. Calif., Berkeley, 1986; MBA, Dartmouth Coll., 1988. Registered civil engr. Assoc. Kidder Peabody, N.Y.C., 1989-91; prin. banker EBRD, London, 1991-93, sr. banker, 1993-94; mng. dir. Merrill Lynch, London, 1994—. With Israeli Armed Forces, 1979-82. Avocations: music, long-distance running. Office: Merrill Lynch, 20 Farringdon Rd POB 293, London EC1M 3NH, England

LUBBE, SAMUEL IZAK, information science educator; b. Bloemfontein, South Africa, Apr. 17, 1952; s. Jan Bartholomeus and Cornelia Roelofina (Myburgh) L. BCom., U. Free State, Bloemfontein, 1974, BCom. with honors, 1982; MCom, U. Cape Town, South Africa, 1994; PhD, U. Witwatersrand, Johannesburg, 1996. Dep. sports officer U. Free State, Bloemfontein, 1980-84; fgn. affairs officer Pretoria, South AFrica, 1984-89; sr. lectr. Technikon Namibia, Windhoek, 1989-92; lectr. Rhodes U., Grahamstown, 1992-94; sr. lectr. Vista U., Bloemfontein; cons. Sam Lubbe Cons. Bloemfontein. Mem. Assn. Info. Systems. Christian. Avocations: collecting stamps, playing field hockey. E-mail: lubbe-s@blenny.vista.ac.za. Office: Vista U, Church St, Bloemfontein 9311, South Africa

LÜBCKE, POUL, philosopher; b. Copenhagen, July 22, 1951; s. Poul and Ebba (Dilling) L.; m. Pia Rasmussen, Feb. 7, 1976. MA in Art, U. Copenhagen, 1978. Scholar U. Copenhagen, 1978-87, U. Aarhus (Denmark), 1989-92, Copenhagen Bus. Sch., 1993-95; rsch. libr. The Royal Library, Denmark, 1995-96; prof. U. Roskilde (Denmark), 1996-98, U. Copenhagen, 1998—. Author: The Concept of Time, 1981, Political Ideas: On Liberalism and Socialism, 1995; editor, author: The Philosophy of Our Time, 1992, The Philosophy Dictionary, 2000. Home: Hjemmevej 47, 2860 Søborg Denmark Office: U Copenhagen, Njalsgade 80, 2860 Copenhagen Denmark

LUBENSKY, EARL HENRY, diplomat, anthropologist; b. Marshall, Mo., Mar. 31, 1921; s. Henry Carl and Adele Gertrud (Biesemeyer) L.; m. Anita Ruth Price, June 27, 1942 (dec. July 1992); children: Tom, Gerald, John Christopher; m. Margot Truman Patterson, Mar. 26, 1994. BA, Mo. Valley Coll., 1948, LLD (hon.), 1968; BS, Georgetown U., 1949; MS, George Washington U., 1967; diploma, Nat. War Coll., 1967; MA, U. Mo., 1983, PhD, 1991. Mgr. Tavern Supply Co., Marshall, Mo., 1938-42; real estate salesman Mitchell Quick Realtor, Silver Spring, Md., 1948; rsch. analyst Georgetown U., Washington, 1949; reference asst. Libr. of Congress, Washington, 1949; fgn. svc. officer Dept. of State, Washington, 1949-79, inter-Am. reg. polit. affairs officer, 1956-61, officer-in-chg. Antarctic affairs, 1958-59; officer Fgn. Svc., Germany, Philippines, Spain, Ecuador, Colombia and El Salvador; diplomat-in-residence, Olivet, Albion and Adrian Colls., Mich., 1973-74; sr. staff mem. internat. affairs Coun. on Environ. Quality, Washington, 1974-76; adj. rsch. assoc. anthropology U. Mo., 1992—. Contbr. articles to profl. jours. Mem. bd. dirs. Columbia Entertainment Co., 1993-99; treas. The Theatre Soc., 1993-99. With Mo. N.G. 1937-40, 48, 2d lt. AUS, 1942-44, U.S. Army, 1944-45, lt. col. USAR, 1948-81. Eagle Scout Boy Scouts Am., 1939. Mem. Mo. Archaeol. Soc. (charter, trustee, v.p.-treas. 1981-90, Appreciation award 1991), Soc. for Am. Archaeology (Presdl. Recognition award 1991), Inst. Andean Studies, Fgn. Svc. Assn., Diplomatic and Consular Officrs Retired, Boone County Hist. Soc., The Theatre Soc. (treas. 1993-99), others. Democrat. Avocations: genealogy, gardening, music, ham radio, philately. E-mail: lubenskye@missouri.edu. Home: 1408 Bradford Dr Columbia MO 65203-2302 Office: Dept Anthropology Univ Mo Columbia MO 65211-0001

LUBIC, ROBERT BENNETT, lawyer, arbitrator, law educator; b. Pitts., Mar. 9, 1929; s. H. Murray and Rose M. (Schwartz) L.; m. Benita Joan Alk, May 18, 1959; children: Wendy, Bret, Robin. AB, U. Pitts., 1950, JD, 1953; LLM in Patent Law, Georgetown U., 1959. Bar: Pa. 1953, U.S. Ct. Appeals (D.C.) cir. 1958, U.S. Supreme Ct. 1958, U.S. Patent Office, 1959, U.S. Dist. Ct. D.C. 1964. Atty., advisor FCC, Washington, 1957-59; pvt. practice, Pitts., 1959-63; asst. prof. law Duquesne U. Law Sch., Pitts., 1963-65; prof. law Am. U. Law Sch., Washington, 1965-2000, prof. emeritus, 2000—, assoc. dean, 1970-71; cons. to Embassy Republic of Georgia; pres. Stas. WRGI-AM-FM, Naples and Marco Island, Fla., 1974-77; vis. prof. U. P.R. Law Sch., 1993, Internat. Christian U., Tokyo, 1988-89, East China U. Politics and Law, 1994, U. Warsaw, Poland, 1995, U. Turin, Italy, 1997; gen. counsel, chief knowledge officer GlobalMedArb.com, LLC, 2000—; mem. panel conciliators and arbitrators of Internat. Ctr. of Investment Settlement Disputes of World Bank; permanent panel arbitrator U.S. Postal Sys., Washington, 1978—, U.S. Dept. Labor, Washington, 1982-87; arbitrator Pub. Employee Rels. Bd. D.C., Washington, 1984—, Pub. Employee Rels. Bd. V.I., 1982—; dir. Labor Disputes Resolution Seminar, Hamilton, Bermuda, 1982, 83, Nassau, Bahamas, 1983; labor cons. Govt. of Bermuda, 1985; creator, dir. Ea. European Summer Law Program, Moscow and Warsaw, 1979-81, Chinese Am. Summer Law Program, Beijing, Shanghai and Hong Kong, 1984-86; co-dir. Mid. East Summer Law Program, Jerusalem, 1976, 78. Author short story. With U.S. Army, 1953-55. Recipient Outstanding Tchr. award Am. U. Student Bar Assn., 1981. Mem. ABA, Fed. Comm. Bar Assn., D.C. Bar Assn., Am. Arbitration Assn. Democrat. Jewish. Home: 2813 Mckinley Pl NW Washington DC 20015-1104 Office: 2813 McKinley Pl NW Washington DC 20015-1104

LUBIN, CAROL RIEGELMAN, political scientist; b. Montclair, N.J., Sept. 23, 1909; d. Charles A. and Lilian (Ehrich) Riegelman; m. Isador Lubin, Jan. 30, 1952 (dec. July 1978); 1 child, Ann L. Buttenwieser. BA, Smith Coll., 1930; MA, Columbia U., 1933, PhD, 1950. Rschr. Carnegie Endowment for Internat. Peace, N.Y.C., 1930-35; internat. staff Internat. Labour Office, Geneva, Switzerland, 1935-52; asst. to dir. Urban Studies Ctr. Rutgers U., 1960-64; cmty. planner City of Reston, Va., 1964-67; housing assoc., N.Y. Urban Coalition, 1968-70; social policy dir. United Neighborhood Houses, N.Y.C., 1970-80; editl. bd. Unemployment Compensation Commn., Washington, 1979-81; rep. Internat. Fedn. Settlements and Neighborhood Ctrs. at UN, 1982—, also bd. dirs. Co-author: Social Justice for Women: The International Labour Orgn. and Women, 1991. Bd. dirs. Franklin and Eleanor Roosevelt Inst., 1990—; bd. dirs., sec. William Hodson Cmty. Ctr., 1960—. Mem. Nat. Women's Dem. Club, Cosmopolitan Club, Women's City Club, Smith Coll. Club N.Y., Phi Beta Kappa. Democrat. Home and Office: 1095 Park Ave New York NY 10128-1154

LUBKE, GITTA HILDEGARD, psychologist; b. Hannover, Germany, Jan. 26, 1958; arrived in The Netherlands, 1980; d. Helmut Fritz and Irmgard Gisela (Kieckebusch) L. Candidate med. sch., Frankfurt, 1979; MA, U. Amsterdam, 1997; grad., Free U., Amsterdam, 1997—. Trainer Ctr. Youth Support, Amsterdam, 1990-96; asst. prof. U. Amsterdam, 1995-96; rsch. assoc. Emory U., Atlanta, 1996-97. Contbr. articles to med. jours. Grantee Emory Care Found., 1996. Avocations: squash, hiking, ice skating. Office: Free U, VD Boechorstraat 1, 1081 BT Amsterdam The Netherlands

LUBKIN, VIRGINIA LEILA, ophthalmologist; b. N.Y.C., Oct. 26, 1914; d. Joseph and Anna Fredericka (Stern) L.; m. Arnold Malkan, June 6, 1944 (div. 1949); m. Martin Bernstein, Aug. 28, 1949; children: Ellen Henrietta, James Ernst, Roger Joel, John Conrad. BS summa cum laude, NYU, 1933; MD, Columbia Coll. Physicans & Surgeons, 1937. Diplomate Am. Bd. Ophthalmology. Intern Harlem Hosp., N.Y.C., 1938-40; asst. resident neurology Montefiore Hosp., N.Y.C., 1940, asst. resident pathology, 1940-41, fellow in ophthalmology, 1941-42; resident ophthalmology Kings County Hosp., Bklyn., 1942-43, Mt. Sinai Hosp., N.Y.C., 1943-44; attending ophthalmologist, assoc. clin. prof. emeritus Mt. Sinai Sch. Medicine, 1944—; also sr. attending surgeon N.Y. Eye and Ear Infirmary, Mt. Sinai Sch. Medicine; pvt. practice N.Y.C., 1945-90; surgeon, now sr. surgeon N.Y. Eye and Ear Infirmary, 1945—; rsch. prof. N.Y. Med. Coll., 1986—; co-creator, now chief of rsch. bioengineering lab. N.Y. Eye and Ear Infirmary (name now The Aborn), N.Y.C., 1978—; rschr. piezoelectric aspects of ocular tissues; creator first grad. course in oculoplastics and bi-yearly symposia in devel. dyslexia Mt. Sinai Sch. Medicine; educator courses in psychosomatic ophthalmology Am. Acad. Ophthalmology, 1950-60, educator course in complications of blepharoplasty, 1980-90; bd. dirs. Jewish Guild for the Blind; tchr. surg. ophthalmology in French Cameroon, Presbyn. Mission, 1951; lectr. in numerous countries including India, 1976, 92, Pakistan, 1976, 84, China, 1978, Sri Lanka, 1979, South Africa, 1982, Singapore, 1984, Thailand, 1984, Argentina, 1986, Peru, 1987. Author: (with others) Ophthalmic Plastic and Reconstructive Surgery, 1989, 2d edit., 1997; patentee topical estrogen for postmenopausal dry eye; contbr. articles to profl. jours. Bd. dirs. Ctr. fo Environ. Therapeutics, 1995. Grantee Intraocular Lens Implant Mfrs., 1989. Fellow AMA, AAAS, Am. Soc. Ophthalmic Plastic and Reconstructive Surgery (founding), Am. Coll. Surgeons, N.Y. Acad. Medicine, N.Y. Acad. Scis., Am. Acad. Ophthalmology, Am. Soc. Cataract and Refractive Surgery, PanAm. Soc. Ophthalmology, N.Y. Soc. Clin. Ophthalmology (pres. 1975), Soc. Light Treatment and Biol. Rhythms, Phi Beta Kappa, Alpha Omega Alpha. Fax: 718-549-6848; 212-979-4574. E-mail: drvlubkin@aol.com. Home: 1 Blackstone Pl Bronx NY 10471-3607 Office: NY Eye and Ear Infirmary 310 E 14th St New York NY 10003-4201

LUBUŚKA, ADAM ZBIGNIEW, metal science educator, researcher; b. Lwów, Poland, Dec. 14, 1925; s. Stanisław Andrzej and Zofia Eleonora (Ludera) L.; m. Elżbieta Ewa Wieczorek, June 9, 1984; 1 child, Ewa Maria. MSc, Silesian Poly., Gliwice, Poland, 1952, DSc, 1962. Head divsn. Inst. Ferrous Metallurgy, Gliwice, 1951-78; chmn. metal sci. Politechnika Swigtokrzyska, Kielce, Poland, 1979-2000; state expert ISO, IACS, Poland, 1966, 67. Author: Entwicklung und Anwendung Hoherfester Stable in Polen, 1975, Production and Use of HSLA Steels, 1976, Atlas of Structures of Iron and Steel, 1996; contbr. articles to profl. jours. Lt. Polish Forces, 1942-44. Recipient medal Lotnicy, War medal Polich Air Force, Ztoty Kryzzastugi, State Rep., Warsaw, 1974, 75, Kryz Kawalerski Polonia Restituta, State Rep., Warsaw, 1989. Mem. NSZZ Solidarność, Zwigzek Sybiraków, Confedn. European des Ancient Combate. Roman Catholic. Avocations: studies of world history. Office: Polytechnic Hotel, ul Jangbinova 6/72, 25-539 Kielce Poland

LUC, DINH THE, mathematician, researcher; b. Ninh Binh, Vietnam, May 28, 1952; s. Dinh The Phan and Vu Thi Tieu; m. La Dieu Huyen; children: Dinh Liuli, Dinh The Duc. MS, Moscow State U., 1974; PhD, Hungarian Acad. Scis., Budapest, Hungary, 1983; DSc, Inst. Math., Hanoi, Vietnam, 1991. Rsch. fellow Inst. Math., Hanoi, 1974—, dep. dir., 1995-99; sr. researcher Computer and Automation Inst., Budapest, 1984-86; prof. U. Avignon, France, 1993-95, 99—, dir. dept. math., 1999—; vis. prof. Centro de Investigation Estudios Avanzados del Instituto Politecnico Nacional, Mexico-City, 1988-89, U. Autonoma de Barcelona, Spain, 1992-93. Author: Theory of Vector Optimization, 1989, Introduction to Nonlinear Optimization, 1989, Nonlinear Programming, Theory and Methods, 1992; dep. editor-in-chief Acta Math. Vietnamica, Hanoi, 1990-95, editor, 1995—. Recipient Rsch. award Alexander von Humboldt-Stiftung, Germany, 1987. Mem. Working Group on Generalized Convexity (internat. scientific com. 1996—), Hanoi Math. Soc. (v.p. 1996—). Office: Inst Math PO Box 631, Blvd Hoang Quoc Viet, Hanoi Vietnam also: Univ Avignon, 33 rue L Pasteur, Avignon France

LUCÀ-MORETTI, MAURIZIO, research scientist, nutrition researcher; b. Rome, June 2, 1945; came to U.S., 1995; s. Giuseppe and Elena (Moretti) L.; m. Anna Grandi, Jan. 2, 1974; 1 child, Elena. BS, Ministry of Edn., Caracas, Venezuela, 1969; PhD in Allied Health Scis., Pacific Western U., 1990, DSc in Human Nutrition, 1990; MD (hon.), Universidad Santo Tomas, La Paz, Bolivia, 1994; MPH (hon.), Inst. Superiore di Studi Sanitari, Rome, 1995. Rschr. Inst. Italiano di Terapia Fisica e Medicina Interna, Rome, 1974-76, sr. rschr., 1976-78, dir. rsch., 1978-80; dir. rsch. Inst. Italiano di Terapia Fisica e Medicina Interna, Caracas, Venezuela, 1980-88; dir. human nutrition rsch. program and AIDS rsch. program InterAm. Med. and Health Assn., Boca Raton, Fla., 1989—, pres., 1989—; gen. sec. World Acad. Medicine, 1992—; prof. emeritus Pacific Western U., New Orleans, 1992; dir. rsch. Internat. Nutrition Rsch. Ctr., 1995—; invited prof. Univ. di Chiete, Italy, 1991, Univ. de Asuncion, Paraguay, 1992, Univ. di Roma, Rome, 1995; hon. prof. Univ. de Granada, Spain, 1994, Univ. Nacional Pedro Enrique Ureña, Santo Domingo, Dominican Rep., 1994, Inst. Superiore di Studi Sanitari, 1996, Univ. Catolica Santo Domingo, Dominican Rep., 1996, St. Thomas U., Miami, 1998. Recipient medal Univ. Asuncion, Paraguay, 1992, medal Univ. Granada, Spain, 1993; decorated Cruz de Alfonso X el Sabio, Spani, 1997. Fellow NAS (Dominican Rep.), Royal Nat. Acad. Medicine Spain, Royal Acad. Scis. Spain, Royal Acad. Medicine Salamanca, Royal Acad. Medicine Granada, Royal Acad. Medicine Valencia, Royal Acad. Medicine of Zaragoza, Nat. Acad. Medicine Bolivia, Nat. Acad. Medicine Ecuador, Nat. Acad. Medicine Paraguay, Nat. Acad. Medicine Dominican Rep., Acad. Medicine Maracaibo, Reial Acad. Medicina Catalunya. Achievements: discovery of the Master Amino Pattern (MAP); discovery of the Dietary Protein Engring. (DPE); also patents in nutritional amino acids formulations with extremely high human Net Nitrogen Utilization (NNU). Home: 3025 Saint James Dr Boca Raton FL 33434-3370 Office: Internat Nutrition Rsch Ctr 401 Linton Blvd Delray Beach FL 33444-8157

LUCAS, DEAN, electronics company executive; b. Cheltenham, Pa., Aug. 7, 1961; s. David and Ruth Edna Lucas; m. Sandra J. Lucas, Feb. 20, 1998; children: Wayne, Paige. Student, Pa. State U., 1984. Owner First Commonwealth Corp., North Miami Beach, Fla., 1989-94, Wireless Tech. Corp., Coral Springs, Fla., 1995—; owner, operator Wireless Tech. Corp., Coral Springs; cons. Z20 Smr Alliance, West Coast, Pub. Co. Mktg., Coral Springs, Fla. Fund raiser Rep. Party, Coral Springs, 1992—. Mem. Midvak Country Club, Lemas Santa Fe Golf Club. Republican. Jewish. Home: 2657 NW 27th Ave Boca Raton FL 33434-3693 Office: 9690 W Sample Rd Ste 103 Coral Springs FL 33065-4031

LUCAS, DONALD LEO, private investor; b. Upland, Calif., Mar. 18, 1930; s. Leo J. and Mary G. (Schwamm) L.; m. Lygia de Soto Harrison, July 15, 1961; children: Nancy Maria Lucas Thibodeau, Alexandra Maria Lucas Ertola, Donald Alexandra Lucas. BA, Stanford U., 1951, MBA, 1953. Assoc. corp. fin. dept. Smith, Barney & Co., N.Y.C., 1956-59; gen., ltd. ptnr. Draper, Gaither & Anderson, Palo Alto, Calif., 1959-66; pvt. investor Menlo Park, Calif., 1966—; bd. dirs. Cadence Design Systems, San Jose, Calif., Coulter Pharm., Inc., Palo Alto, Oracle Corp., Redwood Shores, Calif., Macromedia, San Francisco, TriCord Systems, Inc., Plymouth, Minn., Transcend Svcs., Inc., Atlanta, Preview Sys., Inc., Cupertino, Calif. Mem. bd. regents Bellarmine Coll. Prep., 1977—; regent emeritus U. Santa Clara, 1980—. 1st lt. AUS, 1953-55. Mem. Am. Coun. Capital Formation (dir.), Stanford U. Alumni Assn., Stanford Grad. Sch. Bus. Alumni Assn., Order of Malta, Stanford Buck Club, Vintage Club (Indian Wells, Calif.), Menlo Circus Club (Atherton, Calif.), Jackson Hole Golf and Tennis Club, Sand Hills Golf Club, Teton Pines Club, Bighorn Country Club, Calif., Zeta Psi. Home: 224 Park Ln Atherton CA 94027-5411 Office: 3000 Sand Hill Rd Ste 3-210 Menlo Park CA 94025-7119

LUCAS, GEORGE RAMSDELL, JR., philosophy educator; b. San Angelo, Tex., Sept. 8, 1949; s. George Ramsdell and Clare Elizabeth (Baldwin) L.; m. Patricia Cook; children: Jessica, Kimberly, Theresa. BS summa cum laude, Coll. William and Mary, 1971; PhD, Northwestern U., 1978. Asst. prof., chmn. dept. philosophy Randolph-Macon Coll., Ashland, Va., 1978-82; assoc. prof., chmn. dept. philosophy Santa Clara (Calif.) U., 1982-86; assoc. prof. Emory U., Atlanta, 1986-87; prof. philosophy Clemson (S.C.) U., 1987-91; asst. dir. rsch. div. NEH, Washington, 1991-95; prof. bus. Georgetown U., Washington, 1996—; prof. ethics U.S. Naval Acad., 1996—; exec. dir. Am. Acad. for Liberal Edn., 1998—. Author: The Genesis of Modern Process Thought, 1983, The Rehabilitation of Whitehead, 1989; editor: Lifeboat Ethics: Moral Dilemmas of World Hunger, 1976, Poverty, Justice and the Law, 1986; philosophy editor SUNY Press, Albany, 1989—, Ency. Americana; also articles. Am. Coun. Learned Socs. fellow, 1982; Fulbright rsch. fellow, 1989. Mem. Am. Philos. Assn., Metaphys. Soc. Am., Hegel Soc. Am., Omicron Delta Kappa, Phi Beta Kappa. Office: Dept Leadership Ethics & Law MS 7-B US Naval Acad Annapolis MD 21402

LUCAS, GEORGE W., JR., film director, producer, screenwriter; b. Modesto, Calif., May 14, 1944. Student, Modesto Jr. Coll.; BA, U. So. Calif., 1966. Chmn. Lucasfilm Ltd., San Rafael, Calif. Creator short film THX-1138 (Grand prize Nat. Student Film Festival, 1967); asst. to Francis Ford Coppola on The Rain People; dir. Filmmaker (documentary on making of The Rain People); dir., co-writer THX-1138, 1970, American Graffiti, 1973; dir., author screenplay Star Wars, 1977; exec. prodr. More American Graffiti, 1979, The Empire Strikes Back, 1980, Raiders of the Lost Ark, 1981, Indiana Jones and the Temple of Doom, 1984, Labyrinth, 1986, Howard the Duck, 1986, Willow, 1988, Tucker, 1988, Radioland Murders, 1994; exec. prodr., co-author screenplay Return of the Jedi, 1983; co-exec. prodr. Mishima, 1985; co-author, co-exec. prodr. Indiana Jones and the Last Crusade, 1989; exec. prodr. (TV series) The Young Indiana Jones Chronicles, 1992-93; writer, dir., exec. prodr.: Star Wars: Episode I The Phantom Menace, 1999. Office: Lucasfilm Ltd PO Box 2009 San Rafael CA 94912-2009

LUCAS, GEORGES, physicist, researcher; b. Marosvasarhely, Transylvania, Rumania, Dec. 11, 1914; arrived in France, 1933; s. Emeric and Hermine (Grun) Lukacs; m. Irene Weingrow, Jan. 10, 1948. Degree in Chem. Engring., U. Strasbourg, France, 1938; postgrad., Ecole Normale Superieure, Paris, 1938-40; PhD, U. Paris, Sorbonne, 1955. Rsch. assoc. astrophysics Centre Nat. de la Recherche Scientifique Observatory, Meudon, France, 1953-55; with rsch. dept. Tidewater Oil Co., Avon, Calif., 1956-65; with rsch. dept. Elf-Aquitaine, Paris, 1965-77, ret., 1977. Author: Transfer Theory for Trapped Electromagnetic Energy, 1983; contbr. articles to profl. jours., abstracts to profl. proceedings; patentee in field. Mem. Am. Phys. Soc., Am. Soc. Photobiology, European Photochemistry Assn., European Soc. Photobiology, N.Y. Acad. Scis. Avocation: drawing. Home: 83-85 rue Saint Charles, 75015 Paris France

LUCAS, HELEN AGNES ANNIE, retired educational administrator; b. Brisbane, Queensland, Australia, Sept. 21, 1935; d. Michael Harris Butterfield and Isabell Anne Walker; m. Donald Norman Lucas, June 5, 1965 (div. Sept. 1979); 1 child, Trevor Norman. BEd, U. So. Queensland, Toowoomba, Australia, 1980; M Ednl. Adminstrn., U. Queensland, Brisbane, Australia, 1986. Tchr. Queensland and NSW Edn. Depts., 1954-61, Strathcona Bapt. Girls' Grammar Sch., Melbourne, Australia, 1962-63, Papua New Guinea Dept. Edn., 1964-70, Queensland Dept. Edn., Brisbane, 1972-84; prin. Glamorganvale State Sch., Queensland, 1984-86, Hope Vale (Aborginal) State Sch., Queensland, 1987-89, New Farm State Sch., Brisbane, 1990, Everton Park State Sch., Brisbane, 1990-93; ret., 1993. Contbr. articles to profl. jours. Bd. govs. The Friends Sch., Hobart, Tasmania, 1999—, Co. of the Sch., 1999—. Fellow Queensland Inst. Ednl. Adminstrn., 1987. Mem. Lyceum Club Briane Inc. (pres. 1996-98). Mem. Soc. of Friends. Avocations: bush walking, travel, reading, family history. Home: 2/15 Eliza St, Clayfield QLD 4011, Australia

LUCAS, LOUIS M., former intergovernmental organization executive; b. Lorient, France, June 11, 1939; s. Gabriel and Renee (Le Pipe) L.; m. Patricia A. Descamps, Feb. 27, 1971; children: Claire, Herve, Marie, Vincent, Anne, Gildas. Diploma in Engring., Ecole Poly. and U. Paris, 1964. Food prodn. and processing engr. various orgns., Paris, France and Africa, 1964-80; dep. dir. tech. Dept. Food Industry Ministry Agr., Paris, 1980-89, project head adv. coun., 1989-91; dir. Internat. Inst. Refrigeration, Paris, 1991-99, hon. dir., 1999—; counselor Ministry Agr., 1999—; pres. AFF (French Assn. Refrigeration), 1999—; rapporteur cour comptes, 1999—. Office: CGGREF, 251 rue de Vaugirard, 75732 Paris Cedex 15, France

LUCAS, MARILYN DOREEN, psychologist, educator, researcher; b. Ilford, Essex, Eng., Oct. 31, 1949; arrived in South Africa, 1969; d. Arthur Evelyn and Muriel Ellen (Grimshaw) Smith; m. Terence Stanley Lucas, Aug. 31, 1968 (div. 1989); children: Kristen, Andrew; m. John Victor Weinkove, Aug. 8, 1997. BA, U. South Africa, Pretoria, 1989; BA with hons., Witwatersrand U., Johannesburg, South Africa, 1990, MA, 1992, PhD, 1999. Mature student Witwatersrand U., Johannesburg, South Africa, 1992-94; lectr. Witwatersrand U., Johannesburg, 1993-94; psychologist Johannesburg Gen. Hosp., 1994-96; prin. psychologist Sterkfontein Hosp., Krugersdorp, South Africa, 1996—; cons. Neuropsychologist, Chamber of Mines, Johannesburg, 1994-96; dep. chmn. U. Witwatersrand Ethics Com.: Rsch. on Human Subjects, 1995—. Mem. Psychology Assn. South Africa (Best Local Presentation 1994), South African Clin. Neuropsychol. Assn. Office: Sterkfontein Hosp, PO Box 2010, Krugersdorp 1740, South Africa

LUCAS, PETER CHARLES, investment company executive; b. Melbourne, Vic, Australia, July 9, 1934; s. Percy William and Ruth Mary (Patterson) L.; m. Norma Barbara McBrien, May 3, 1958; children: Prudence M., Geoffrey P., David J., Alison R., Jane E. Solicitor, Univ. Law Sch., Sydney, NSW, Australia, 1960. Bar: New Supreme Ct. 1960. Legal officer Western Mining Corp., WA, 1969-70; exec. dir. Bond Group, 1970-92; mng. dir. Bond Corp. Internat., Hong Kong, 1987-89; exec. chmn. Bond Corp. Holdings Ltd., NSW, 1990-91; chmn. St. Malo Australia, Ltd., 1994—; chmn. Cabonne Ltd., 1997—; chmn. Aust. Innovation, Ltd. Roman Catholic. Avocations: tennis, golf. E-mail: plc@stmalo.com.au. Fax: 61-2-9223-9755. Home: 10/39 Sutherland Crescent, Darling Point NSW 2025, Australia Office: St Malo Australia Ltd, Level 6, 9 Hunter St, Sydney NSW 2000, Australia

LUCAS, RHETT ROY, mediator, arbitrator, lawyer, chemical engineer, artist, photographer; b. Columbia, S.C., Nov. 27, 1941; s. Spurgeon LeRoy and Elizabeth (Wells) L.; m. Uta Henkel, Apr. 12, 1967 (div. 1973). B-SChemE, U. S.C., 1963; JD, NYU, 1967; postgrad., U. Glasgow, Scotland, 1965-66. Bar: U.S. Supreme Ct., D.C. Rsch. assoc. Twentieth Century Fund, N.Y.C., 1968-69; gen. counsel James Madison Inst., N.Y.C., 1969-72, Population Law Ctr., San Francisco, 1972-75; prin. Lucas & Assocs., Washington, 1972-84; artist Beverly Hills (Calif.) Fine Arts, 1984-86, The Rhett Lucas Collection, Santa Fe, and Scottsdale, Ariz., 1988-94; founder The Mediation Practice, 1997. Prin. author U.S. Supreme Ct. briefs in Roe v. Wade, 1972, U.S. vs. Vuitch, 1971, Doe vs. Bolton, 1972 (ACOG amicus), Reno v. Condon, 1999 (amicus), Hill v. Colo., 2000 (amicus), others; contbr.

articles to profl jours.; painter approx. 200 nat. and state parks; exhbns. include Oxford U., 1988, Banff Ctr., 1989, Grand Canyon Nat. Park, Ariz., 1991, 92, Capital Reef Nat. Park, Canyonlands Nat. Park, Cumberland Gap Hist. Nat. Park, Death Valley Nat. Pk., John Wesley Powell Meml. Mus., 1992, Powell River History Mus., 1992-93, O'Laurie (Canyonlands) Mus.; also exhbns. in Santa Fe, New Masters Gallery, Taos, N.M., Scottsdale, Fuller Lodge, Los Alamos, N. Mex., Petroglyph Nat. Monument, Casa Grande Art Mus., Hubbell's Trading Post Nat. Hist. Pk. Co-founder NARAL, N.Y.C., 1969; founder PRIVATE CITIZEN, 1998, Acad. Population Reproductive Health Counsel, 1998. Root-Tilden scholar NYU Law Sch., 1963-67; Rotary Found. fellow U. Glasgow, 1965-66; population rsch. grantee Rockefeller Found., 1972-74. Mem. ABA (litigation sect.), AIChE, Am. Soc. Marine Artists, Am. Inst. Conservation, Coll. Art Assn., Scottsdale Artist's League, Rockport (Mass.) Art Assn. (life), Wilderness Soc., Can. Alpine Club, Zero Population Growth, Sierra Club (life), Nat. Geog. Soc. (life), Rotary, Order of Coif, Mensa, Nat. Health Lawyers Assn., Am. Trial Lawyers Assn., Materials Info. Soc., Soc. Plastics Industry, Am. Chem. Soc., Order Supreme Ct. Advs. (founder), Acad. Million Dollar Counsel, Mensa, Phi Beta Kappa, Tau Beta Pi, Blue Key (pres.). Avocations: travel, photography, art collecting, golf. E-mail: owllawyer@aol.com or privacycounsel@aol.com.

LUCAS, ROBERT EMERSON, JR., economist, educator; b. Yakima, Wash., 1937. BA, U. Chgo., 1959, PhD, 1964. Lectr. U. Chgo., 1962-63; asst. prof., economics Carnegie-Mellon U., Pittsburgh, 1963-67; assoc. prof., 1967-70, prof., 1970-75; prof., economics U. Chicago, 1975-80, John Dewey Disting. Svc. prof., 1980—; Ford Found. vis. rsch. prof. U. Chgo., 1974-75; vis. prof. econ. Northwestern U., Chgo., 1981-82. Author: Studies in Business-Cycle Theory, 1981, Models of Business Cycles, 1987; co-editor: Rational Expectations and Econometric Practice, 1981; assoc. editor Jour. Econ. Theory, 1972-78, Jour. Monetary Econs., 1977—; editor Jour. Polit. Theory, 1978-81; contbr. articles to profl. jours. Woodrow Wilson fellow, 1959-60, Brookings fellow, 1961-62, Woodrow Wilson Dissertation fellow, 1963, Ford Found. Faculty fellow, 1966-67, Guggenheim Found. fellow, 1981-82; Proctor and Gamble scholar, 1955-59; recipient Nobel Prize in Econ., 1995. Fellow AAAS; mem. NAS, Econometric Soc. (2nd v.p.). Office: U Chgo Dept Econs 1126 E 59th St Chicago IL 60637-1580

LUCAS, SALVADOR, information systems educator; b. Paris, Oct. 31, 1963; s. Salvador Lucas and Amparo Alba; m. Sandra Zapata, Nov. 9, 1996; children: Paula, Anna Maria. MSc in Computer Sci., U. Politechnica, Valencia, Spain, 1994, PhD in Computer Sci., 1998. Asst. prof. U. Politecnica, 1994-98, assoc. prof. tech. studies, 1998—. Tech. reviewer Introduccion a ca Programacion Funcional Utilizando Haskell, 1999; contbr. articles to profl. publs. Roman Catholic. Avocations: music, reading, traveling, cinema. Office: U Politecnica de Valencia, Carino de Vera S/U, 46022 Valencia Spain

LUCAS, STEVEN MITCHELL, lawyer; b. Ada, Okla., Jan. 19, 1948; s. John Dalton and Cherrye (Smith) L.; m. Lori E. Seeberger; children: Steven Turner, Brooke Elizabeth, Sarah Grace. BA, Yale U., 1970; JD, Vanderbilt U., 1973. Bar: D.C. 1973, U.S. Ct. Mil. Appeals 1974, U.S. Dist. Ct. D.C. 1979, U.S. Ct. Appeals (D.C.) 1979, U.S. Supreme Ct. 1979. Assoc. Shaw, Pittman, Potts & Trowbridge, Washington, 1978-82, ptnr., 1983-92; ptnr., head fin. instns. practice Wiley, Rein & Fielding, Washington, 1992-93, Winston & Strawn, Washington, 1993-97; pvt. practice Washington, 1997—; cons. on internat. rels., Rockefeller Found., N.Y.C., 1978, mem. negotiating team Panama Canal Treaty, Washington, 1975-77, legal adviser Dept. Def. Panama Canal negotiations working group. Editor in chief Vanderbilt U. Jour. Transnational Law, 1972-73. Treas., mem. exec. com. St. Anne's Episcopal Ch., Annapolis, Md., 1999—. Capt. JAGC, U.S. Army, 1974-77. Mem. ABA, FBA (chmn. internat. law com. 1978-80, Outstanding Com. Chmn. award 1979), Inter-Am. Bar Assn., Am. Soc. Internat. Law, Army-Navy Country Club (Arlington, Va.), Yale Club (N.Y.C.), Army and Navy Club (Washington). Republican. Episcopalian. Home: 1696 Dunstable Green Annapolis MD 21401-6424 Office: 1730 K St NW Ste 304 Washington DC 20006-3839

LUCASSEN, EMY MARIAN, biochemist, educator; b. Ames, Iowa, Sept. 5, 1964; arrived in Eng., 1969; d. Jaap Lucassen and Emmie Helena Reijnders; m. John Justin Hsuan; children: Timothy, James. BA with hons., Cambridge (Eng.) U., 1985, MA, 1988; PhD, Ludwig Inst. Cancer Rsch., Switzerland, 1990; MA, Kings Coll., London, 1995. Postdoc. rschr. Inst. Virology Environ. Microbiology, Oxford, 1990-91; lectr. U. Greenwich, Eng., 1991—. Editor Ethics and Medicine, 1995—; contbr. chpts. to books and articles to profl. jours. Cambridge U. scholar, 1984, 85; Ctr. Bioethics Pub. Policy fellow, 1992—. Mem. Biochem. Soc., Soc. Applied Philosophy. Avocations: squash, choral singing. Office: Astrazeneca, 48 Curzon St, London W1Y 7RE, England

LUCCHETTI, LYNN L., career officer; b. San Francisco, Aug. 21, 1939; d. Dante and Lillian (Bergeron) L. AB, San Jose State U., 1961; MS, San Francisco State U., 1967; grad., U.S. Army Basic Officer Course, 1971, U.S. Army Advanced Officer Course, 1976, U.S. Air Force War Coll., 1983, Sr. Pub. Affairs Officer Course, 1984. Media buyer Batten, Barton, Durstine & Osborn, Inc., San Francisco, 1961-67; producer-dir. Sta. KTVA-TV, Anchorage, 1967-68; media supr. Bennett, Luke and Teawell Advt., Phoenix, 1968-71; commd. 1st lt. U.S. Army, 1971, advanced through grades to lt. col., 1985, col., 1989, brig. gen. nom., 1993, officer, 1971-74; officer D.C. N.G., 1974-78, U.S. Air Force Res., 1978-99; program advt. mgr. U.S. Navy Recruiting Command, 1974-76; exec. coordinator Joint Advt. Dirs. of Recruiting (JADOR), 1976-79; dir. U.S. Armed Forces Joint Recruiting Advt. Program (JRAP) Dept. Def., Washington, 1979-91, resources mgr. Exec. Leadership Devel. Program, 1991-94. Author: Broadcasting in Alaska, 1942-1966. Active Vols. of ARC. Decorated U.S. Army Meritorious Svc. medal, Nat. Def. medal, U.S. Air Force Longevity Ribbon, U.S. Navy Meritorious Unit Commentation, Dept. Def. Joint Achievement medal, 1984, Legion of Merit, 1999; Sigma Delta Chi journalism scholar, 1960. Mem. Women's Affairs Assn., Pub. Affairs Alumni Assn. Home: 11401 Malaguena Ln NE Albuquerque NM 87111-6899

LUCCHINI, LUIGI, business executive; b. Casto, Brescia, Italy, 1919; m. Emilia Rota. Pres. Confindustria (Italian Confedn. Industry), 1984-88; mng. dir. S.A. Eredi Gnutti Metalli SpA; v.p. Birra Wührer SpA, Credito Agrario Bresciano; pres., mng. dir. Lucchini SpA and Lucchini Siderurgica SpA, Brescia; chmn. bd. dirs. Montedison SpA, Milan; bd. dirs. Olivetti, SMI, Snia Viscosa, La Centrale, Consortium and Kronenburg; mem. exec. com., bd. dirs. Generali. Mem. internat. strategic com. BSN-Gervais Danone. Recipient Medaglia d'Acciaio Federico Giolitti, Italian Metalworking Assn., 1988; decorated knight Order of Labour Merit, Italian Republic. Mem. Industrialists Assn. Brescia (pres. 1978-83), Assn. for Pro Deo Internat. U. Social Studies, Italo-German C. of C. Home: Fasano GR, Via Zanardelli 204, I-25080 Brescia Italy Office: Montedison SpA, 3 Piazzetta Maurillo Bossi, 20121 Milan Italy*

LUCE, HENRY, III, foundation executive; b. N.Y.C., Apr. 28, 1925; s. Henry Robinson and Lila Hotz (Tyng) L.; m. Patricia Potter, June 27, 1947 (div. 1954); children: Lila Frances, Henry Christopher; m. Claire McGill, Aug. 6, 1960 (dec. June 1971); stepchildren: Kenneth, William, James; m. Nancy Bryan Cassiday, Aug. 15, 1975 (dec. Mar. 1987); stepchildren: Richard, Bryan (dec.); m. Leila Eliott Burton Hadley, Jan. 5, 1990; stepchildren: Arthur T. Hadley III, Victoria Smitter Barlow, Matthew Smitter Eliott, Caroline Smitter Nicholson. BA, Yale U., 1945; L.H.D. (hon.), St. Michael's Coll., 1973, L.I. U., 1986, Pratt Inst., 1991; LLD (hon.), Coll. of Wooster, 1994, Mapua Inst. of Tech., 2000. Commr.'s asst. Hoover Commn. on Orgn. Exec. Br. of Govt., 1948-49; reporter Cleve. Press, 1949-51; Washington corr. Time Inc., 1951-53, Time writer, 1953-55, head new bldg. dept., 1956-60, asst. to pub., 1960-61; circulation dir. Fortune and Archtl. Forum, 1961-64, House & Home, 1962-64; v.p. Time Inc., 1964-80, chief London bur., 1966-68; pub. Fortune, 1968-69; pub. Time, 1969-72, dir. corp. planning, 1972-80; dir. Time, Inc., 1967-89, Time Warner Inc., 1989-96; pres., chmn., CEO Henry Luce Found., Inc., 1958—; pres. The New Mus. Contemporary Art, 1977-98; chmn. Am. Security Systems Inc. Trustee Eisenhower Exch. Fellowships, Ctr. Theol. Inquiry, Christian Ministry in Nat. Pks., N.Y. Hist. Soc., Bklyn. Mus. Art; mem. Am. coun. UN Univ.; pres. Assn. Am. Corrs. in London, 1968; dir. Fishers Island Devel. Co., Nat. Com. on U.S.-China Rels.; chmn. Am. Russian Young Artists Orch.; chmn. pres.'s coun. Gen. Theol. Union; commr. Nat. Mus. Am. Art; mem. adv. bd. Nat. Acad. Design; mem. adv. coun. Newark Mus. Lt. (j.g.) USNR, 1943-46. 2nd Ann. recipient medal for disting. philanthropy Am. Assn. Museums, 1994, Am. award Assn. N.Y. State Arts Coun., 1995, Frederick Law Olmstead medal Central Park Conservancy, 1996, medal N.Y. Hist. Soc., 1997, St. Nicholas Soc. medal, 1998, Augustine Graham medal Bklyn. Mus. Art, 2000, Conrado Benitez medal Philippine U. for Women, 2000. Mem. Fgn. Policy Assn. (dir., gov., medal 1997), Pilgrims U.S. (pres.), Explorers Club, Fishers Island Club, Hay Harbor Club, Univ. Club, The Brook. Presbyterian (elder). Office: 720 Fifth Ave Ste 1500 New York NY 10019-4107 also: Mill Hill Rd Mill Neck NY 11765

LUCE, MRS. HENRY, III See HADLEY, LEILA ELIOTT-BURTON

LUCE, PRISCILLA MARK, public relations executive; b. N.Y.C., Feb. 4, 1947; d. S. Carl and Patricia (Greenfield) Mark; m. Robert Warren Luce, July 19, 1969; children: James Warren, David Mark. BA, U. Pa., 1968. Adminstrv. asst. Phila. Mus. Art, 1968-69; asst. dir. pub. info. Mt. Holyoke Coll., South Hadley, Mass., 1969-71; v.p. Barnes & Roche, Inc., Phila., 1971-82; mgr. civic programs TRW Inc., Cleve., 1982-85; mgr. community relations TRW Inc., 1985-88, mgr. external communications, 1988-90, dir., pub. affairs and advt., 1990-92, v.p. TRW info. sys. and svcs. comms., 1992-94, v.p. mktg. and orgn. comms., 1994—. Trustee New Orgn. for the Visual Arts, Cleve., 1983-97, Cmty. Info. Vol. Action Ctr., Cleve., 1984-86, Albert M. Greenfield Found., Phila., 1989—, pres., 1999—; trustee Cleve. State U. Found., 1996—, chmn. devel. com. 1998—, vice-chmn. 1999; trustee Bus. Vols. Unltd., Cleve., 1998—; trustee WCPN Radio, 1997—, also chmn. pub. rels. com., 1998—, chmn. media and mktg. com. Cleve. Today, 1999—; trustee Ohio Chamber Orch., Cleve., 1986-92, chmn. devel. com. 1987-88, chmn., trustee, 1991-92, exec. v.p., 1990-91; pres. New Orgn. for the Visual Arts, Cleve., 1984-86; mem. steering com. Cleve. Art Festival, 1983-84, Mayor's Cultural Arts Planning Task Force, Cleve., 1985-87; trustee Ret. Sr. Vol. Prog., 1991, Western Res. Hist. Soc., 1999—; leadership devel. prog. participant United Way Svcs., Cleve., 1983, cons., 1983-85; mem. steering com. Bus. Volunteerism Coun. of Cleve., 1984-92; comm. adv. com. Work in NE Ohio Coun., 1991-94. Recipient Woman of Profl. Excellence award YWCA of Cleve., 1990. Mem. Pub. Rels. Soc. Am., Cleve. Advt. Club. Republican. Office: TRW Inc 1900 Richmond Rd Cleveland OH 44124-3760

LUCEÑO, ALBERTO, engineering educator; b. Membrio, Caceres, Spain, Aug. 7, 1951; s. Pedro Luceño and Manuela M. Vazquez; m. Maria A. Ros, July 9, 1980; children: Alberto J., Maria A. Degree in engring., Superiour Sch. Tech. Engring., Caminos, Santander, 1976, PhD, 1979; degree in math., U. Nat. Edn. a Distancia, Madrid, 1980. Rschr. U. Cantabria (Spain), 1976-79, asst. prof., 1979-82, assoc. prof., 1982-84, prof., 1984—; cons. Nuclenor S.A., Santander, 1984-90, EAT S.A., Santander, 1993. Contbr. articles to profl. jours. Mem. Am. Statis. Assn., Royal Statis. Soc., European Network for Bus. and Indsl. Statistics, Internat. Assn. Statistical Computing. Avocation: photography.

LUCERO, DANIEL WILLIAM, educator, researcher, missionary; b. Norfolk, Va., June 8, 1962; s. C. Herbert and Joan Marie (Mantin) L.; m. Martine Pena; children: Jeremiah Daniel, Melissa, Julia, Marc Daniel. BSc, Va. Tech. U., 1990, MSc, 1994; BTh, Life East, Christiansburg, Va., 1994; PhD, INPL, Nancy, France, 1999. Rschr. Ensaia, Nancy, 1994-99; missionary Fousquare, Nancy, 1996-99; translator Nancy, 1997-99; tchr., prof. U. Nancy, France, 1995—; pres., dir. Shining Star Co., 1995-99. Contbr. articles to profl. jours. Humanitarian worker, West Africa, 1990-91; dir. Drug Rehab. Program, Spain, 1984-88. Fulbright scholar U.S. State Dept., 1994-99. Mem. Agronomy Soc. Am., Gamma Sigma Delta, Phi Kappa Phi, Phi Sigma Soc. Mem. Internat. Ch. of the Foursquare Gospel. Home: 713 W Spring St Woodstock VA 22664-1223

LUCERO, SCOTT ALAN, special education educator; b. Denver, Mar. 23, 1968; s. Raymond Lucero and Barbara Jean (McElliott) Gonzales; m. Deborah Ann Cole, Nov. 24, 1989; children: Lori Lynn, Kimberly Ann. Cert. welding, Warren Occupational, Golden, Colo., 1986; student, Arapahoe C.C., Littleton, Colo., 1992-94; grad., U. Denver, 1997. Cert. nurse, Colo. Self-employed welder Denver, 1986-88; care mgr. for developmentally disabled Arvada, Colo., 1988-94; dir. Dungaruin Inc.; guest lectr. physics and chemistry to elem. schs. Vol. Polit.-Wyo. Gov., 1985; CPR, first aid instr. Honors scholar Denver U. Mem. Honors Inst., Phi Theta Kappa (officer), Alpha Epsilon Delta, Theta Chi (Gamma Lambda chpt.). Democrat. Avocations: fishing, coaching disabled and planning activities for developmentally disabled, car restoration, motorcycles, snowboarding. Home: 11469 W Fair Ave Littleton CO 80127-2706

LUCHETTE, FREDERICK ALBERT, surgeon; b. Sharon, Pa., Aug. 9, 1954; s. Albert and Rosemary (Songer) L.; m. Barbara Ann O'Brien, Aug. 31, 1985; children: Richard, Matthew, Claire, Katherine. BA, Thiel Coll., 1976; MS, U. Louisville, 1978, MD, 1981. Diplomate Am. Bd. Surgery. From clin. instr. to asst. prof. surgery SUNY, Buffalo, 1981-93; assoc. prof. surgery U. Cin., 1994—. Fellow Am. Coll. Surgeons; mem. Am. Assn. Surgery of Trauma, Am. Trauma Soc., Eastern Assn. Surgery of Trauma, Soc. Critical Care Medicine, Surgical Infection Soc., Soc. Univ. Surgeons. Roman Catholic.9. Avocations: jogging, reading, traveling. Office: U Cin Med Ctr 231 Bethesda Ave # 558 Cincinnati OH 45229-2827

LUCHINI, UMBERTO ANDREA, marketing manager; b. Milan, Mar. 12, 1973; s. Rino Luchini and Giuliana Castellani. BSc in Econs., U. Coll., London, 1994. Sales mgr. asst. Carnaudmetalbox, Paris, 1994-95; jr. brand mgr. Philip Morris EU, Lausanne, Switzerland, 1995-97; brand mgr. Philip Morris France, Paris, 1997-98; trademark exec. Philip Morris EU, Lausanne, 1998-99; mktg. and internet mgr. ISL Worldwide, Lucerne, Switzerland, 1999—. Avocations: triathlon, contemporary history, photography. Fax: 41 41 228 97 97. E-mail: umberto.luchini@islworld.com. Home: Ave du Cour 36, 1007 Lausanne VD, Switzerland Office: ISL Worldwide, PO Box 3339 Zentralstrasse1, 6002 Lucerne VD, Switzerland

LUCHINS, DANIEL JONATHAN, psychiatrist; b. N.Y.C., July 1, 1948; s. Abraham Samuel and Edith (Hirsch) L.; children: Kerith, Matthew. BSc, McGill U., Montreal, Que., Can., 1971, MD, 1973. Diplomate Am. Bd. Psychiatry and Neurology; cert. geriatric psychiatry. Vis. scientist NIMH, Washington, 1977-81; assoc. prof. U. Chgo., 1981—; med. coord. mental health Ill. Dept. Mental Health, Chgo., 1989-91; chief of adult psychiatry U. Chgo., 1991-93; chief for clin. svcs. Office of Mental Health, Ill. Dept. Human Svcs., Chgo., 1995—; chief pub. psychiatry U. Chgo., 1996. Contbr. articles to profl. publs. Recipient A.E. Bennett award Soc. Biol. Psychiatry, Geriatric Mental Health acad. award NIMH, 1984-87, Exemplary Psychiatrist award NAMI, 1998. Fellow Am. Psychiat. Assn.; mem. Ill. Psychiat. Assn. (councillor 1989-91, pres. 1995). Jewish. Achievements include development of means for seizure prevention for polydipsic, hyponatremic schizophrenics. Office: Dept Psychiatry Univ Chgo 5841 S Maryland Ave Chicago IL 60637-1463

LUCHKOV, BORIS IVANOVICH, physicist; b. Ivanovo, Russia, Apr. 2, 1932; s. Ivan Ivanovich and Anna Nikolaevna (Savanova) L.; m. Oksana Fiodorovna Klimenko, June 6, 1933; children: Andrei, Tatyana, Aleksandr. Candidate of Phys. Sci., Moscow Engring. Physics Inst., 1965, Doctor, 1992. Engr. Lebedev Phys. Inst., Moscow, 1956-65; sr. scientist, rschr. Engring. Phys. Inst., Moscow, 1965-68, assoc. prof., 1968-92, prof., 1992—; mem. sci. group Phys. Inst., Moscow, 1956-65; asst. group leader Moscow Engring. Physics Inst., 1965-92, leader sci. group, 1992—. Mem. editl. staff (newspaper) Engr.-Physicist, Engring. Phys. Inst., 1994—; contbr. articles to profl. jours. Recipient Lenin prize, Russia, 1970, 4 medals, Russia, 1970—. Mem. Moscow Phys. Soc. (govt. mem. 1990—). Avocations: poetry, water tourism, modern skiing. Home: Lyapidevsky 6 kor 1 fl 56, 125581 Moscow Russia Office: Moscow Engring Phys Inst, Kashirskaya Rd, 115409 Moscow Russia

LUCHT, ERIK DAN TOMMY, dentist; b. Strängnäs, Sweden, Oct. 24, 1952; s. Heinrich and Irene Ottilie (Bartel) L. DDS, Karolinska Inst., Stockholm, 1978, PhD, 1994. Dentist Pub. Dental Health Svc., Stockholm, 1979—, clinic chief, 1992—; rschr. Swedish Inst. for Infectious Disease Control and Karolinska Inst., Stockholm, 1990-94, lectr., 1994—; chmn. com. for infectious disease control Pub. Dental Health Svc., Stockholm County Coun. Fellow Swedish Soc. Medicine; mem. Swedish Dental Assn., Dental Assn. for AIDS Care (adv. bd. 1993—), Swedish Soc. for Hosp. Dentistry (vice-chmn.). Home: Kungsholms Strand 113, S-112 33 Stockholm Sweden Office: Huddinge U Hosp, Dental Clin Inf Dis I 48, S-141 86 Stockholm Sweden

LUCIA, MARILYN REED, physician; b. Boston; m. Salvatore P. Lucia, 1959 (dec. 1984); m. C. Robert Russell; children: Elizabeth, Walter, Salvatore, Darryl. MD, U. Calif., San Francisco, 1956. Intern Stanford U. Hosps., 1956-57; NIMH fellow, resident in psychiatry Langley Porter, U. Calif., San Francisco, 1957-60; NIMH fellow, resident in child psychiatry Mt. Zion Hosp., San Francisco, 1964-66; NIMH fellow, resident in community psychiatry U. Calif., San Francisco, 1966-68, clin. prof. psychiatry, 1982—; founder, cons. Marilyn Reed Lucia Child Care Study Ctr., U. Calif., San Francisco; cons. Cranio-facial Ctr., U. Calif., San Francisco, No. Calif. Diagnostic Sch. for Neurologically Handicapped Children; dir. children's psychiat. svcs. Contra Costa County Hosp., Martinez. Fellow Am. Psychiat. Assn., Am. Acad. Child Psychiatry; mem. Am. Cleft Palate Assn., San Francisco Med. Soc. Office: 350 Parnassus Ave Ste 602 San Francisco CA 94117-3608

LUCIA, UMBERTO, physics research manager; b. Alessandria, Italy, Apr. 25, 1966; s. Canio and Carla (Colombo) L. M in Physics, U. Torino, Italy, 1991; M in Physics of Matter, U. Ferrara, 1998; PhD in Energetics, U. Firenze, 1995. Tchr. Secondary Sch., Alessandria, 1992; fellow in nuclear physics Nat. Lab. Gran Sasso, 1992; rschr. in thermodynamics and applied physics U. Firenze, 1992-95; rschr. in thermoelasticity and math. physics U. Torino, 1995-97; postdoctoral rschr. thermophys. props. materials/chem. phys. U. Ferrara, 1997-98; rschr. mgr. in applied physics Nat. Inst. Physics of Matter, Genoa, Italy, 1998—; coord. applied/pure and industry physics Nat. Inst. Physics of Matter, Genoa, 1998; collaborator in physics rsch. Nat. Agy. for New Techs., Energy and Ambient, collaborator of GNFM-CNR, Bologna, 1995-98; sci. coord. Centro Studi "F. Faa di Bruno," Alessandria; conf. reporter Unitre, Alessandria; conf. reporter in physics and chemistry in art conservation U. Bologna, Ravenna; cons. in physics to various jours. Contbr. numerous articles to profl. jours. With Fanteria, 1991. Mem. Italian Soc. Physics, N.Y. Acad. Scis. Roman Catholic. Avocations: philosophy, history of science, gymnastics, art, music. E-mail: ulucia@infm.it. Home: Via S G Bosco 43, I-15100 Alessandria Italy Office: Inst Nazionale Fisica Della, Materia, Corso Perrone 24, I-16152 Genoa Italy

LUCIC, DAVOR, biologist, researcher; b. Dubrovnik, Croatia, Aug. 15, 1959; s. Petar and Jasna (Schipioni) L.; m. Ivana Moretti, Aug. 20, 1988; children: Petra, Dario. BSc, U. Zagreb, Croatia, 1982, MSc, 1985, PhD, 1996. Asst. Inst. Oceangraphy Fish, Dubirvnik, 1983-85, scientist asst., 1986-96, sr. scientist, 1997—; cons. Inst. Oceanography Fish, Spit-Dubirvnik, 1997—; prof. U. Split, 1999—. Contbr. articles to profl. jours. Mem. Croatian Biological Soc., Commn. Internat. pour L'exploration Scientifique de la mer Méditerranée. Avocations: scuba diving, folk dance, football. Home: Setaliste Kralja Zvpmimira, 20000 Dubrovnik Croatia Office: Inst Oceanography & Fishery, Damjana Jude 12, 20001 Dubrovnik Croatia

LUCIER, GREGORY THOMAS, medical technology executive; b. Plainfield, N.J., May 9, 1964; s. Thomas Edward and Ann (Rivinius) L.; m. Marilena Cieri, June 4, 1988; children: Ross Edward, Grant Michael, Allana Marie. BS in Indsl. Engring., Pa. State U., 1986; MBA, Harvard U., 1990. Product mgr. Internat. Paper Co., Memphis, 1986-88; v.p. opers. Morrison Knudsen Corp., Boise, Idaho, 1990-95; gen. mgr. bus. devel. GE, 1995; pres., CEO GE-Harris Rlwy. Electronics, 1996-99; cons. in field. Fundraising organizer Arthritis Found., Boise, 1992; instr. Jr. Achievement, Memphis, 1986-88; vol. Project Outreach, Boston, 1989-90. Mem. Inst. Indsl. Engrs., Railway Suppliers Assn., Idaho Total Quality Mgmt. Inst., Harvard Club of Idaho, Tau Beta Pi. Republican. Roman Catholic. Avocations: golf, tennis, skiing. Home: 1022 N Fieldstone Ln Oconomowoc WI 53066-9229 Office: GE Harris Rlwy Electronics GE Co 3000 N Grandview Blvd Waukesha WI 53188-1615

LUCINSCHI, PETRU, president of Moldova; b. Floresti, Moldova, Jan. 27, 1940; s. Chiril and Parascovia L.; m. Antonina Georgievna, 1965; 2 children. Student, Kishinev U., CPSU Ctrl. Com. Higher Party Sch. With ctrl. com. Moldavian CP, 1963-71; mem. CPSU, 1964-91; 1st sec. Balti City Komsomol Com., 1964-65; head sect., 2nd sec., 1st sec. Ctrl. Com. Moldavian Komsomol, 1965-71; sec. ctrl. com. Moldavian CP, 1971-76; first sec. Nov, 1989-91; 1st sec. Kishinev City Com., 1976-78; dep. head propaganda dept. CPSU Ctrl. Com., 1978-86; 2nd sec. Ctrl. Com. Tadzhik CP, 1986-89; candidate mem. CPSU Ctrl. Com., 1986-89, mem., 1989-91, sec., 1990-91; dep. U.S.S.R. Supreme Soviet, 1986-89; U.S.S.R. people's dep., 1989-91; mem. CPSU Politburo, 1990-91; Moldovan amb. to Russia, 1992-93; leader Agrarian Dem. Party; chair Moldovan Parliament, 1993—; pres. Govt. of Moldova, 1996—. With Soviet Army, 1962-63. Avocations: sports, travelling, reading, theatre. Office: Office of the Pres, Stefencel Mare bld, 154, MD 2073 Chisinau Moldova*

LUCKEY, ALWYN HALL, lawyer; b. Biloxi, Miss., Oct. 3, 1960; s. Toxie Hall and Joy Evelyn (Smith) L.; m. Jeanne Elaine Carter, Aug. 4, 1984; children: Laurel McKay, Taylor Leah. BA in Zoology, U. Miss., 1982, JD, 1985. Bar: Miss. 1985, U.S. Dist. Ct. (so. and no. dist.) Miss. 1985, U.S. Ct. Appeals (5th cir.) 1985. Assoc. Richard F. Scruggs, Pascagoula, Miss., 1985-88; shareholder Richard F. Scruggs, Pascagoula, 1988—, Asbestos Group PA, 1988-93; prin. Alwyn H. Luckey, Atty. at Law, Ocean Springs, Miss., 1993—; v.p., bd. dirs. Marine Mgmt., Inc., Ocean Springs, Miss., 1987—. Author: Mississippi Landlord Tenant Law, 1985. Deacon First Presbyn. Ch., Ocean Springs, 1989; chmn. Dole for Pres. com., Jackson County, 1988. Mem. Am. Trial Lawyers Assn., Miss. Bar Assn., Miss. Trial Lawyers Assn., Jackson County Bar Assn., Jackson County Young Lawyers Assn. (v.p.), Ocean Springs Yacht Club, Bienville Club, Treasure Oak Country Club. Avocations: tennis, boating, traveling. Office: PO Box 724 Ocean Springs MS 39566-0724

LUCKEY, DORIS WARING, civic volunteer; b. Union City, N.J., Sept. 17, 1929; d. Jay Deloss and Edna May (Ware) Waring; m. George William Luckey, Mar. 29, 1958; children: G. Robert, Jana Elizabeth, John Andrew. AB, U. Rochester, 1950; CLU, Am. Coll., Bryn Mawr, Pa., 1957. With pers. dept., supr. life dept. Travelers Ins. Co., Rochester, N.Y., 1952-58; agt. asst. life underwriting Mass. Mut. Ins. Co., Rochester, 1958. Chair, various past offices Bd. Coop. Ednl. Svcs. and State Edn. Dept., Vocat. Tech. Adv. Com., Rochester and Albany, 1975—, pres. Rochester, 1975-85, Monroe County Sch. Bds. Assn., Rochester, 1980-81; v.p. Penfield (N.Y.) Schs., 1978-81; various fin. ednl. and speaking engagements LWV, 1983—, chair spkrs. bur. Rochester Metro chpt.; pres. ch. coun., chair ch. and min. com., co-chair United Ch. Christ denomination, Genesee Valley; pres. William Warfield Scholarship Fund Bd.; coord. Young Artist Competition, Penfield Symphony Orch.; former adv. to bd. St. John's Home for Aging, now mem. fin. and pension and pers. com., bd. dirs., exec. com. home for aging bd.; vol. numerous other civic, cultural, ch. and artistic orgns.; property trustee So. Emanuel United Ch. Christ, chair pastoral search com., 1999-2000. Mem. AAUW (past pres. Greater Rochester br., past bd. dirs., dist. 1 state rep., Greater Rochester br. pub. rels. chair), Genesee Valley Assn. (response team sexual harrassment in clergy N.Y. conf. United Ch. of Christ). Republican.

LUCKEY, GEORGE WILLIAM, research chemist; b. Dayton, Apr. 17, 1925; s. George Paul and Olive (Lehmer) L.; m. Doris Waring, Mar. 29, 1958; children: Robert, Jana, John. BA in Chemistry, Oberlin Coll., 1947; PhD in Chemistry, U. Rochester, 1950. Rsch. and staff asst. Eastman Kodak Co., Rochester, N.Y., 1950-59, rsch. assoc., 1959-69, lab. mgr., rsch. fellow, 1969-86. Contbr. articles to profl. jours. Mem. Am. Chem. Soc., Am. Phys. Soc., The Electrochem. Soc., Royal Soc. Chemistry, Sigma Xi, Phi Beta Kappa. Achievements include U.S. and fgn. patents; participation in improvements in diagnostic imaging with x-rays by improvements in intensifying screens, films and processing systems; improvement of performance of systems for mammography, other diagnostic uses. Home: 240 Weymouth Dr Rochester NY 14625-1917

LUCKHURST, GEOFFREY ROGER, chemistry educator; b. Gillingham, Kent, Eng., Jan. 21, 1939; s. William Thomas and Hilda Mary (Flood) L.; m. Janice Rita Flanagan, July 3, 1965; children: Nicola Jane, Caroline. BSc, U. Hull, Eng., 1962; PhD, U. Cambridge, Eng., 1965. Scientist Varian Rsch., Zurich, 1965-67; lectr. U. Southampton, Eng., 1967-70, reader in chemistry, 1970-77, prof. chemistry, 1977—, sr. curator univ. libr., 1998-2000. Editor: The Molecular Physics of Liquid Crystals, 1979, The Molecular Dynamics of Liquid Crystals, 1994; assoc. editor Molecular Physics, 1976-77, editor, 1977-81; founding editor Liquid Crystals, 1986-92. Recipient Meldola medal Royal Inst. Chemistry, 1969, Marlow medal Faraday Soc., 1971, Corday-Morgan medal Chem. Soc., 1975. Fellow Royal Soc. Chemistry; mem. Internat. Liquid Crystal Soc. (pres. 1992-96), Brit. Liquid Crystal Soc. (chmn. 1994-2000). Office: U Southampton, Dept Chemistry, Southampton Hamps SO17 1BJ, England

LUCKNER, HERMAN RICHARD, III, interior designer; b. Newark, Ohio, Mar. 14, 1933; s. Herman Richard and Helen (Friednour) L. BS, U. Cin., 1957. Cert. interior designer and appraiser. Interior designer Greiwe Inc., Cin., 1957-64; owner, internat. designer Designers Loft Interiors, Cin., 1964—; owner Designer Accents, Cin., 1991—. Mem. bd. adv. Ohio Valley Organ Procurement Ctr., Cin., 1987—, U. Cin. Fine Arts Collection and Hist. Southwest Ohio, 1987-97; bd. dirs. Cin. Club Travelers, 1997—. Mem. Am. Soc. Interior Designers, Appraisers Assn. Am., Metropolitan Club. Republican. Avocations: needlepoint, collecting 18th century Chinese porcelain. Home and Office: 555 Compton Rd Cincinnati OH 45231-5005

LUCORE, CHARLES LEE, cardiologist; b. Southington, Conn., Apr. 30, 1957; s. Charles Earl and Eleanor Christina Lucore; m. Paula F. Sorensen, Sept. 25, 1982; children: Alexander Charles, Jordan Mari, Christopher James. AB, Colgate U., 1979; MD, Duke U., 1983. Diplomate Am. Bd. Internal Medicine, Am. Bd. Cardiovasc. Diseases. Intern N.Y. Hosp.-Cornell Med. Ctr., N.Y.C., 1983-84, resident, 1984-86; cardiovasc. postdoctoral rsch. fellow Sch. Medicine Wash. U., St. Louis, 1986-88, clin. cardiology fellow, 1988-89, invasive cardiology fellow, 1989-90, asst. prof. medicine and interventional cardiology, 1990-92; interventional cardiologist Prairie Cardiovasc. Cons., Ltd., Springfield, Ill., 1992—; co-dir. cardiac catherization lab. St. John's Hosp., Springfield, Ill., 1992—, chmn. dept. cardiology, 1994—, mem. exec. com. Prairie Cardiovasc. Consultants, Ltd., 1995-96, 99—; asst. clin. prof. medicine So. Ill. U., Springfield, Ill., 1992—; exec. com. St. Johns Hosp., Springfield, 1996—, prairie edn. and rsch. coop. coord., 1995-96. Recipient Rsch. award Corvas Internat., 1991. Fellow Am. Coll. Cardiology, ACP, Soc. Angiography and Coronary Intervention, Am. Heart Assn. (thrombosis coun. 1989-97, coun. on cardiology 1994—, grantee 1992-93), Atherosclerosis, Thrombosis and Vascular Biology; mem. Phi Beta Kappa, Beta Beta Beta. Avocation: golf. Office: Prairie Cardiovasc Cons Ltd 619 E Mason St Springfield IL 62701-1034

LUCYSZYN, STEPAN EUGENE, electronics educator, research engineer; b. Bradford, Eng., Aug. 28, 1965; s. Petro and Anna (Kushnir) L. BSc, Polytechnic North London, 1987; MSc, U. Surrey, Guildford, Eng., 1988; PhD, King's Coll. U. London, 1993. Registered charter engr. Satellite sys. rsch. engr. Alcatel Espace, Toulouse, France, 1988; comms. sys. engr. Vega Space Sys. Engring., Harpenden, Eng., 1989; rsch. fellow King's Coll., London, 1992-95; lectr. electronics U. Surrey, 1995-2000, sr. lectr., 2000—. Editl. bd. Internat. Jour. Electronics, 1997—; contbr. articles to profl. jours., chpts. to books. Mem. IEEE (tech. session chairperson internat. conf. telecomms. 1995, internat. symposium on MMICS in comm. 1992, tech. session organizer 1994, editl. bd. Transactions on Microwave Theory Tech. 1995-97), IEE (vis. lectr. 1996—, referee Electronics Letters 1993—, mem. profl. group com. E12), Engring. and Phys. Scis. Rsch. Coun. Peer Rev. Coll. 9 (Eng.), Mensa. Achievements include demonstration of ultra-wide-band high performance reflection-type phase shifters for MMIC applications; demonstration of ultra-miniature millimeter-wave rectangular waveguides in monolithic technology with first ever measurements. Office: U Surrey, Sch Electronic Engring Info Tech & Math, Guildford GU2 7XH, England

LUDDEN, JOHN FRANKLIN, retired financial economist; b. Michigan City, Ind., May 6, 1930. BS in Econs., U. Wis., 1952, MS in Econs., 1955; postgrad., U. Mich., 1955-59. Wage and hour investigator U.S. Dept. Labor, 1960, mgmt. intern, 1960-61, labor economist, 1963; economist, instr. U.S. Bur. of Labor Statis., 1961-63; economist Office of Internat. Ops. IRS, 1963-68, fin. economist Audit div., 1968-86, fin. economist Office of the Asst. Commr. Internat., 1986-95; ret. Office of the Asst. Commr. Internat., 1995. With U.S. Army, 1952-54. Recipient spl. svc. award U.S. Dept. Treasury, 1967, 68, 87, spl. achievement award, 1984, Spl. Act award, 1990, Albert Gallatin award, 1995.

LÜDECKE, DIETER KONRAD, neurosurgeon; b. Kassel, Germany, Mar. 11, 1943; s. Hans and Lucia (Dux) L.; 3 children. MD, U. Hamburg, Germany, 1975. Researcher U. Hamburg, 1972-84, neurosurgeon, 1984—; chief neuro endocrine lab. and pituitary surgery unit U. Hamburg, 1980; cons. neurosurgeon Marien Krankenhaus, Hamburg, 1988. Author, editor: Progress Endocrine Research, 1988, 90; contbr. over 150 articles to profl. jours.; patentee microsurgical pressure irrigation suction system. Mem. Internat. Soc. Pituitary Surgeons, Internat. Skull Base Soc., European Neuro Endocrine Assn., German Soc. Endocrinology, German Soc. Neurosurgery, German Skull Base Soc. E-mail: Luedecke@uke.uni-hamburg.de. Fax: 0049-42803-5982. Office: Univ Hamburg, Dept Neurosurgery, 20246 Hamburg Germany

LUDIK, PAUL STEFAN, clinical pharmacologist, consultant; b. Cape Town, South Africa, Aug. 30, 1960; s. Jan Lodewyk and Hugolina Amos (Basson) L.; m. Susan Johanna Lambert, Sept. 27, 1980; children: Stefan, Hugo. BPharmacy, BSc in Chemistry, U. Potchefstroom, South Africa, 1982, PharmD, 1984. Registered specialist clin. pharmacologist; registered pathologist (toxicology and clin. pharmacokinetics); registered forensic toxicologist; diplomate Am. Bd. Forensic Examiners, Am. Coll. Forensic Examiners. Rsch. asst. Unit for Catechol Aminergic Studies, Potchefstroom, 1982-84; pharmacy mgr. Potchefstroom, 1982-84; hosp. pharmacist Keetmanshoop, namibia, 1984-86; sr. hosp. pharmacist Windhoek, namibia, 1986-90; chief Clin. and Specialized Svcs., Windhoek, namibia, 1990-95; dir. Nat. Forensic Sci. Inst., namibia, 1995—; cons. lectr. U. Namibia, 1987—; cons. toxicologist Med. Rescue Internat., Namibia, 1994—; cons. pharmacologist Dietrich, Street & Ptnrs. Labs., 1989—; specialist dir. Nat. Health Plan, Namibia, 1995—; founder, pres. DUNRAVEN Group of Cos. Contbr. articles to profl. jours. Mem. Nat. Drug Control Commn. Namibia, 1995—; chmn. So. and East frican Medicines Regulatory Authorities Conv., Sadac Countries, 1995—. Recipient Medal for Excellence, Sam Silber Found., 1978, 79, 80, 81, 82, Internat. Postgrad. Rsch. fellowship Rio Tinto, Rössing, Namibia, 1987, Postgrad. fellowship Belgian Found., 1991. Fellow Namibian Pharmacy Bd., Medicines Control Coun., African Drug Regulatory Authorities Conv. (chmn. classification com. 1994—); mem. South African Pharmacy Coun., Internat. Assn. Forensic Toxicologists (registered toxicologist). Achievements include patent in sterile intra-ocular lense stabilizing solution. Home: PO Box 50136 Bachbrecht, 9000 Windhoek Namibia

LUDING, STEFAN, physics computer science educator; b. Selbitz, Franken, Germany, Aug. 16, 1964; s. Werner and Hildegard (Geisser) L.; m. Gerlinde Gessert, Apr. 7, 1995. Diploma, U. Bayreuth, Germany, 1990; Dr.rer.nat., U. Freiburg, Germany, 1994; Habilitation, U. Stuttgart, Germany, 1998. Software developer Selbitz, Germany, 1987-97; grad. asst. U. Freiburg, 1991-94; postdoctoral rschr. U. Paris VI, 1994-95; asst. U. Stuttgart, 1995-2000, hochschuldozent, 2000—; referee various jours. and pubs. in field, 1992—; mng. editor Granular Matter, Springer Verlag, Germany, 1998—. Editor conf. procs. Granular Gases, Springer Verlag LNP; Physics of Dry Granular Media. European Union grantee, 1995. Avocations: drawing, cycling, dancing. Office: Inst Computer Applicats One, Pfaffenwaldring 27, D-70569 Stuttgart Germany

LÜDTKE, HARTWIG, archaeologist; b. Hamburg, Germany, Sept. 23, 1954. PhD, U. Hamburg, 1982; BA, Open U., 1996. Referent, asst. Archaologisches Landesmus., Schleswig, Germany, 1982-90; head Wikinger Mus. Haithabu, Schleswig, Germany, 1987-88; referent, asst. Rheinisches Landesmus., Bonn, Germany, 1990, dir., 1991-95; curator, head Museumstiftung Post und Telekommunikation, 1995—; mem. several archaeol. and museological orgns. Author, editor several publs. medieval archaeology. Office: Museumsstiftung Post und Telekommunikation, Heinrich-von-Stephan-Str 1, 53175 Bonn Germany

LUDVIG, LÁSZLÓ, manufacturing executive; b. Budapest, Hungary, July 10, 1968; s. László and Lászlóné (Czinege) L.; m. Márta Marosvári, July 4, 1992; children: Katalin, András. MS, Tech. U. Budapest, 1992, Budapest U. Economy, 1994; PhD, Tech. U. Budapest, 1997. Cert. in mech. engring. Trainee Valmet Rlwy. Divsn., Tampere, Finland, 1990; project mgr. Ganz-Hunslet Ltd., Budapest, 1992; rschr. Tech. U. Budapest, 1992-95; dep. comm. dir. Ganz-Hunslet, Budapest, 1995-97; comm. dir. ABB Daimler Benz Transp., Dunakeszi, Hungary, 1998-99; sales mgr. Daimler Chrysler Rail Sys. Gmbh, Berlin, 1999—; demonstrator Tech. U. Budapest, 1988-89. Contbr. articles and papers to profl. jours.; inventor in field. Recipient Ganz Ábrahám award, 1994. Roman Catholic. Avocations: tennis, sailing, climbing. Office: Daimler Chrysler Rail Sys, Am Rathenaupark, 13595 Hennigsdorf Germany

LUDVIGSSON, PETUR, pediatric neurologist; b. Reykjavik, Iceland, Oct. 5, 1945; s. Ludwig Hjalmtyssow and Kristjana Petursdottir; m. Nina Kristin Birgisdottir, May 8, 1971; children: Birgir, Hildur. Baccalaureate, Menntaskolinni Reykjavik, 1966; Candidate in Medicine and Surgery, U. Iceland, 1973. Resident pediat. U. Conn., 1976-79; resient child neurology Temple U., 1979-82; pediat. neurologist U. Hosp. Iceland, 1982—; cons. pediat. neurologist various hosps., Iceland, 1982—. Mem. Icelandic Med. Assn., Child Neurology Soc., Am. Epilepsy Soc. Office: Dept Pediat, Landspitalinn, 101 Reykjavik Iceland

LUDVIK, BERNHARD HEINRICH, medical educator, endocrinologist; b. Vienna, June 21; s. Walter Heinrich and Lilian Maria (Peltzer) L.; m. Gerda Maria Meyer, April 22, 1988; children: Christoph, Maximilian, Elisabeth. MD, U. Vienna, 1985. Fellow in internal medicine U. Vienna, 1985-91, specialist in internal medicine, 1991—, asst. prof., 1995-97, assoc. prof., 1997—, specialist in endocrinology and metabolism, 1996—, attendant in internal medicine, 1991—; rsch. fellow U. Calif., San Diego, 1992-94. Asst. editor: Diabetologia; contbr. articles to profl. jours. Recipient Max Kade fellow Max Kade Found., 1992, Hoechst Preis Hoechst AG, 1995. Mem. Am. Diabetes Assn., European Assn. for the Study of Diabetes, Austrian Obesity Soc. Roman Catholic. Avocations: reading, classical music, tennis. Home: Bartensteingasse 14/11, A-1010 Vienna Austria Office: Kinik Innere Medizine III, Waehringer Guertel 18-20, A-1090 Vienna Austria

LUDVÍK, JIŘÍ, electrochemist, research scientist, educator; b. Prague, Czech Republic, Apr. 17, 1953; s. Jiří and Marie (Dvořáková) L.; m. Ludmila Zajíčková, June 19, 1980; children: Kristyna, Veronika, Lucie, Matěj. MSc, Charles U., Prague, 1977, D of Natural Scis., 1978; PhD, J. Heyrovsky Inst., Prague, 1985. Rsch. asst. J. Heyrovsky Inst., Prague, 1978-81, rsch. scientist, 1985-90, head of group, 1990—; vis. lectr. Prague Inst. Chem. Tech., 1990—. Contbr. chpts. to books and articles to profl. jours. Head, pres. YMCA-Zivá Rodina, Prague, 1995—. Grantee in field, 1991-96. Mem. European Photochemistry Assn., Electrochem. Soc. Roman Catholic. Avocations: music, skiing. Office: J Heyrovsky Inst Phys Chem, Dolejskova 3, 182 23 Prague 8, Czech Republic

LUDWIG, CHRISTA, mezzo-soprano; b. Berlin; d. Anton and Eugenie (Besalla) L.; m. Walter Berry, Sept. 29, 1957 (div. 1970); 1 son, Wolfgang; m. Paul-Emile Deiber, Mar. 3, 1972. Ed. German schs. Prof. H.C. Senat, Berlin, 1995; hon. mem. Vienna Philharm., 1995. Appeared at Staedtische Buehnenm, Frankfurt, W. Ger., 1946-52, Landestheatre, Darmstadt, W. Ger., 1952-54, Hannover, W. Ger., 1954-55, Vienna (Austria) State Opera, 1955—, Medaille, Ville de Paris, 1993, Shibuya-Price, Japan, 1993, others, U.S. appearances include Avery Fisher Hall, N.Y.C., 1978, Lyric Opera, Chgo., 1959-60, 70-71, 73-74, Philharmonic Hall, N.Y.C., 1968, 69, 72, 74, Goldene Ehrennadel Landstadt, Vienna, 1997, others; guest artist London, Buenos Aires, Munich, Berlin, Tokyo, Salzburg Festival, Athens Festival, Saratoga Festival, Hunter Coll., Met. Mus., Scala Milano, Expo 67, Montreal, and others; rec. artist; author: (biography) In My Own Voice. Decorated Commdr. des Arts et des Lettres, France, 1988, Goldenes Ehren Zeichen Stadt, Salzburg, 1988, Goldene Ehrennadel Stadt und Land, Wien, Austria, 1988, Ordre Pour le Merit, France, 1997; chevalier Legion d'Honneur, France, 1989 ; recipient Mozart medal, Mahler medal, Hugo Wolf medal, Fidelio medal Opera Wien, 1991, Shibuya prize Japan, 1993, Medaille ville Paris, 1993, Medaille Ville de Dijon, 1993, Echo Deutscher Preis, 1994, Karajan preis, Berliner Bär, 1994, Grosses Ehrenzeichen Osterreich, 1994, Ehrenmitglied der Wiener Philharm., Silver Rose, Vienna Philharm., Golden Ring, Vienna Staatsoper, Musician of Yr. award Musical Am., 1994, Cordandeur Pour le Merit France, 1997; named Kammersaengerin, Govt. of Austria, 1962. Mem. NARAS.

LUDWIG, GREGORY BRIAN, editor, writer; b. Long Branch, N.J., Dec. 6, 1961; s. Howard Paul and Dorothy Olive (Trehou) L. BA, George Washington U., 1984; postgrad., Washington U., 1987. Cert. subs. tchr., N.J. Asst. mgr. Cloyd Heck Marvin Ctr., Washington, 1984-85; proofreader, editl. asst. All Am. Crafts, Inc., Newton, N.J., 1990-91; proofreader AB Bookman's Weekly, Clifton, N.J., 1992-93; proofreader, asst. editor Clinicians Pub. Group, Clifton, 1993-94; editl. asst. Reed Reference Pub., New Providence, N.J., 1995-96; now freelance writer and copy editor. Copy editor A Primer of Kleinian Therapy, 1995; contbr. articles to profl. jours. Project dir. VISTA/Food Bank Somerset County, Bridgewater, N.J., 1986-87; sec., trustee Vernon Twp. Dem. Club, Vernon, N.J., 1995—; candidate Charter Study Commn., Vernon Twp., 1995; mem. Vernon Twp. Postal Customer Adv. Coun., Vernon, 1994-96; mem. Vernon Twp. Environ. Commn., 1996-98; mem. Vernon Twp. Bd. Health, 1997. Mem. Nat. Writer's Assn., Soc. Philosophy in Contemporary World, N.Y.-N.J. Trail Conf. Avocations: reading, music. Home: PO Box 289 Highland Lakes NJ 07422-0289

LUDWIG, HARALD, educator; b. Cologne, Rhineland, Germany, Apr. 5, 1940; s. Werner and Grete (Clemens) L.; m. Christa Hettich, Mar. 3, 1978; children: Carsten, Corinna. Grad., U. Bonn, Germany, 1966, habilitation, 1991; PhD, U. Cologne, 1975. Cert. in tchr. in philosophy, pedagogics, Latin and religion; cert. rschr. in ednl. sci. Tchr. Gymnasium, Cologne, 1967-75; asst. prof. Tchrs. Coll., Bonn, 1975-80, U. Bonn, 1980-91; prof. U. Koblenz, Germany, 1991-93; full prof. ednl. sci. U. Muenster, Germany, 1993—. Author: Materialism and Metaphysics, 1975, Comprehensive Schools in Discussion, 1981, Development of Whole-Day Schools in Germany, Vol. 2, 1993, Education with Maria Montessori, 1997, others. Mem. Goerres Soc., Montessori Assn. (mng. dir. 1980—). Roman Catholic. Avocations: track and field athletics, soccer, chess, traveling. Office: U Münster, Bispinghof 5/6, 48143 Münster Germany

LUDWIG, MIROSLAV, chemistry educator; b. Litomerice, Czech Republic, Apr. 7, 1956; s. Miroslav and Lydie (Vacatova) L.; m. Hana Viskova, July 1, 1978; children: Martina, Petr. PhD, U. Chem. Tech., Pardubice, Czech Republic, 1985. Rschr. Czech Acad. Scis., Pardubice, 1984-87; asst. prof. U. Chem. Tech., Pardubice, 1987-92; assoc. prof. U. Pardubice, 1992—, vice rector, 1997-2000, rector, 2000—; mem. Internat. Union Pure & Applied Chemistry Commn. 111.2. Contbr. articles to profl. jours. Mem. Internat. Group Correlation Analysis in Chemistry. Avocation: sports. Office: U Pardubice, nam Cs legii 565, CZ-53210 Pardubice Czech Republic

LUEDERS, CARL L., finance executive; b. Apr. 15, 1950. BA in econs., Univ. Mass., 1972; MBA, Babason Coll., 1981. Sr. auditor Arthur Andersen & Co., Boston, 1974-78; v.p., controller Polariod Corp., Cambridge, Mass., 1979—. Home: 22 Brewster Rd Newton MA 02461-1302

LUEDKE, FREDERICK LEE, manufacturing company executive; b. Milw., Jan. 19, 1938; s. Frederick William and Martha Marie (Widiger) L.; m. Wilma Jeanne Seacat, July 3, 1960; children: Tracy Jeanne, Frederick William II. BSIE, Wichita State U., 1960; MBA, Harvard U., 1966. Mfg. tng. program GE, 1960-64; prodn. gen. supr. Polaroid Corp., Waltham, Mass., 1966-70; mgr. mfg. Millipore Corp., Bedford, Mass., 1970-76; dir. mfg. Berol Corp., Danbury, Conn., 1976-87; exec. v.p. Neoperl Inc., Waterbury, Conn., 1987-92; pres. Neoperl Inc., Waterbury, Conn., 1992—; bd. dirs. Nangatuck Valley Devel. Corp., 1994—, v.p. 1996-98; bd. dirs. Platt Bros. and Co., 1996—, Waterbury Partnership 2000, 1999—; mem. Gov.'s coun. for Econ. Competitiveness and Tech., 1999—; with Inner City Bus. Strategy Initiative-Waterbury City Champion, 1999. Pres. Luth. Ch. of Newtons, Mass., 1974-75, 1st Luth. Ch., Waterbury, 1988-89; bd. dirs. Danbury ARC, 1982-84, Easter Seals, bd. dirs. 1993-2000, vice chmn. 1994-96, chmn., 1996-98; pres. bd. trustees East Hill Woods Retirement Ctr., Southbury, Conn., 1989-97; mem. Waterbury Found., 1991—; chmn. Incorporators of Waterbury Hosp., 1995-97; trustee Waterbury Hosp., 1997—, sec., 1999—; founder Waterbury Neighborhood Coun. 1994; bd. dirs. Greater Waterbury Health Network, 1999—. Mem. ASME, Am. Soc. Plumbing Engrs., Plumbing Mfrs. Inst. (pres. 1999-2000, bd. dirs. 1995-2000), Am. Soc. Sanitary Engring., Greater Waterbury C. of C. (bd. dirs. 2000—), Rotary (bd. dirs.), Waterbury Club (pres. 1996-98). Republican. Lutheran. Avocations: tennis, mountain hiking. Home: 98 Woodlawn Ter Waterbury CT 06710-1929 Office: Neoperl Inc 171 Mattatuck Heights Rd Waterbury CT 06705-3832

LUEHRS-KAISER, KAI, writer, scholar, educator; b. Bremen, Germany, July 27, 1961; s. Rudolf and Ute (Kaiser) L. MA, Free U., Berlin, 1992. Lectr. Free Univ., Berlin, 1992-96, Various Study Groups, Clubs, 1996—. Author: (book) Excentrische Einsätze, 1998, Flungel und Extreme, 1999, Traditionen und Trabanten, 1999; ; contbr. articles to literary mags. and newspapers. Grantee: Free U., Berlin, 1992-94. Mem. Heimito von Doderer Gesellschaft (co-founder, pres. 1995—), Gesellschaft deutsche Sprache, Theodor Fontane Gesellschaft. Avocation: organizing literary events. Home: Roennebergstr 4, 12161 Berlin Germany

LUEKE, DONNA MAE, yoga instructor, Reiki practitioner, instructor; b. Toledo, Sept. 18, 1946; d. Herbert Henry and Margery Alberta (Welsh) L. BA, Adrian Coll., 1968. Tchr. Anchor Bay Schs., New Baltimore, Mich., 1968-74; salesperson Jacobson's, Birmingham, Mich., 1974-76; sales rep. Stark & Co., Detroit, 1976-80; regional retail supr. Norwich-Eaton Consumer Pharms., Louisville, 1980-83; territory rep. Procter & Gamble, Louisville, 1983-84; dir. Progressive Retail, Raleigh, N.C., 1984-89; nat. retail mgr. CIBA Consumer Pharms. and CIBA Vision Corp., Wayne, Pa., 1989-92; mem. apprentice program Holistic Options, 1997-98. Student govt. v.p. Adrian Coll., 1966, 67. Mem. Nature Conservancy. Avocations: creative writing, gardening, fishing.

LUEPKER, RUSSELL VINCENT, epidemiology educator; b. Chgo., Oct. 1, 1942; s. Fred Joeseph and Anita Louise (Thornton) L.; m. Ellen Louise Thompson, Dec. 22, 1966; children: Ian, Carl. BA, Grinnell Coll., 1964; MD with distinction, U. Rochester, 1969; MS, Harvard U., 1976; PhD (hon.), U. Lund, Sweden, 1996. Intern U. Calif., San Diego, 1969-70; resident Peter Bent Brigham Hosp., Boston, 1973-74; cardiology fellow Peter Bent Brigham Hosp./Med., Boston, 1974-76; asst. prof. divsn. epidemiology med. lab. physiol. hygiene U. Minn., Mpls., 1976-80, assoc. prof., 1980-87, prof. divsn. epidemiology and medicine, 1987—, dir. divsn. epidemiology, 1991—; cons. NIH, Bethesda, Md., 1980—, U. So. Calif., L.A., 1985—, Armed Forces Epidemiology Bd., 1993-97; vis. prof. U. Goteborg, Sweden, 1986, Ninewells Med. Sch., Dundee, Scotland, 1995. With USPHS, 1970-73. Harvard U. fellow, 1974-76, Bush Leadership fellow, 1990; recipient Prize for Med. Rsch. Am. Coll. Chest Physicians, 1970, Nat. Rsch. Svc. award Nat. Heart, Lung and Blood Inst., Bethesda, 1975-77, Disting. Alumni award Grinnell Coll., 1989. Fellow ACP, Am. Coll. Cardiology, Am. Heart Assn. (chmn. coun. on epidemiology 1992-94, chair program com. sci. sessions 1995-97, award of merit 1997), Am. Coll. Epidemiology; mem. Am. Epidemiol. Soc., Am. Soc. Preventive Cardiology (Joseph Stokes award 1999), Delta Omega Soc. (Nat. Merit award 1988). Office: Univ Minn Sch Pub Health Div Epidemiology 1300 S 2nd St Ste 300 Minneapolis MN 55454-1087

LUEPNITZ, ROY ROBERT, psychologist, consultant, small business owner, entrepreneur; b. Ft. McClellan, Ala., June 3, 1955; s. Carl A. and Helen Elizabeth (Brown) L.; m. Mary Kinloch Bush, Dec. 18, 1981; children: Mary, George, Noel. BA cum laude, Southwestern U., 1979; MS in Counseling Psychology, U. So. Miss., 1981; PhD in Counseling Psychology, Tex. A & M U., 1985. Fellow Am. Bd. Forensic Examiners; cert. health svc. provider in psychology; Internat. Airlines Travel Agt. Network cert. travel agt.; registered treatment provider of sex offenders; bd. cert. forensic examiner; lic. marital and family therapist; lic. psychologist. Intern, vol. Austin (Tex.) State Hosp., 1978-79; counselor Univ. Counseling Psychology Clinic, Hattiesburg, Miss., 1980; master level psychologist Pine Belt Mental Health Ctr., Hattiesburg, 1981, Tex. Rehab. Commn., Bryan, 1981-82; grad. tchr. Tex. A & M Univ., College Station, 1982-83; psychologist Brazos Valley MHMR Authority, Bryan, 1983-84; mental health dir. Brazos Valley MHMR Authority, Bryan, 1984-86; pvt. practice psychologist College Station, 1987—; chmn. bd. for sex abuse Am. Bd. Forensic Psychol. Spltys; cons. Dept. Human Svcs., Bryan, 1987—, Brazos Valley MHRA, Bryan, 1987—, St. Joseph's Hosp., Bryan, The Med. Ctr., College Station, 1991—, various chs., schs., govt. agys.; co-owner Noel's Wonderful World of Travel. Sec. Miss. APGA, 1979-81; active sex offender's assessment/treatment program. Mem. Assn. Treatment of Sexual Abuses, Am. Assn. Christian Counselors, Nat. Register Health Svc. Providers in Psychology, Tex. Psychol. Assn., Nat. Criminal Justice Assn. Republican. Methodist. Avocations: teaching Sunday school, travel cruises, fine dining. Home: 1200 Noel Ct College Station TX 77845-8756 Office: Brazos Valley Christian Counseling 2748 Longmire Dr College Station TX 77845-5424

LÜER, GERD, psychology educator; b. Egestorf, Harburg, Germany, Apr. 4, 1938; s. Rudolf and Elisabeth (Kiel) L.; m. Sigrid Dudek, Feb. 15, 1964; children: Nina, Jan Ole. Diploma Psychology, U. Hamburg, Germany, 1963; D Natural Scis., U. Kiel, Germany, 1966, Habilitation, 1972. Prof. psychology U. Kiel, 1973, Tech. U. Aachen, Germany, 1973-74; prof., chmn. psychology U. Düsseldorf, Germany, 1974-78, U. Aachen, 1978-82; prof. psychology U. Göttingen, 1982—, v.p., 1999—. Editor German Jour. Psychology, 1982-94, Zeitschrift für Experimentelle Psychologie, 1984-96; cons. European Psychologist, 1996—. Mem. German Assn. Psychology (v.p. 1990-92, pres. 1980-92), Academia Europaea, Acad. of Sci. Göttingen. E-mail: gluer@uni-goettingen.de. Home: F-V-Bodelschwingh-Str 13, D-37075 Göttingen Germany Office: Georg-Elias-Müller Inst, Gossler-Str 14, D-37073 Göttingen Germany

LUERS, WENDY WILSON WOODS, non-profit foundation executive; b. Ann Arbor, July 16, 1940; d. Ward Wilson and Patricia (Fay) Woods; m. William Turnbull, Jr., Apr. 1, 1967, (div. 1979); children: Connor, Ramsay; m. William Henry, Oct. 18, 1979. Student, U. Madrid, 1961; BA, Stanford U., 1962. Asst. editor San Francisco Mag., 1965-67; asst. producer Film Bullett, San Francisco, 1970; stringer Time Mag., San Francisco, 1964-71; commentator KOED TV, San Francisco, 1974-79; dir., special project Amnesty Internat., San Francisco; cultural correspondent Venevision TV, Caracas, 1982-83; dir. special projects Human Rights Watch, 1987-89; lectr. Nancy Nelson (Agent), N.Y., 1987-89; pres., founder, dir., cons. The Found. for a Civil Soc., N.Y.C., 1990-92; founder Project Justice in Times Transition Harvard U., 1999—, adv. bd., 1999—; bd. dirs. The Ind. Journalism Found., Civic Edn. Project, Fund for Arts and Culture in East and Ctrl. Europe, Olga Havel Found., Vaclav Havel Found.; chair White House Fellows N.Y. Regional Selection Panel, Washington, 1993-95; U.S. Delegate to Orgn. Security & Coop. in Europe Review Conf., Budapest, Hungary, 1994; cons. NBC White Paper Series on Urban Crises. Contbr. articles to mags., newspapers and profl. jours. Founder/Pres. Friends of Art & Preservation Embassies, Wash.; bd. dirs. Nat. Council on Children & TV, L.A., Ind. Com. on Arts Policy; presdl. apptd. Nat. Coun. on the Arts; mem. Luce Scholars Program, Coun. on Fgn. Rels., Leadership Coun. Internat. Rescue, The Childhood Found.; dir. Municipal Advantage Fund Inc. Recipient Gratias Agit award Czech Foreign Ministry, 1997, State Order of the Dual White Cross award Pres. Kovac, Slovakia, 1998. Democrat. Roman Catholic. Avocation: tennis. Home: 254 E 68th St Apt 15A New York NY 10021-6015

LUESCHEN, GUENTHER, sociologist; b. Oldenburg, Germany, Jan. 21, 1930; s. Gustav and Elsa (Magnus) L.; m. Klara Mertens, Dec. 1958 (div. 1989); children: Birgit, Gerhard; m. Leila Sfeir, Nov. 1989; 1 child, Gerline. PhD, Graz U., Austria, 1959; D (hon.), Jyvaskyla U., Finland, 1990. State exam. Bonn U., 1960. Rsch. assoc. Univ. Cologne, 1961-64; dozent, prof. Univ. Bremen, 1965-72; prof. Tech. U., Aachen, 1982-90, Univ.

Düsseldorf, 1990-95, U. Ala., Birmingham, 1995—; prof. emeritus U. Ill., Champaign, 1966—. Author 18 books in sociology. Office: U Ala Birmingham AL 35294-0001

LUESSENHOP, ALFRED JOHN, neurosurgeon, educator; b. Chgo., Feb. 6, 1926; s. Alfred Lewis and Gertrude L.; m. Frances Matthews; children: Cynthis, Constance, John, Charles, Suzanne, Laura. B.S., Yale U., 1949; M.D., Harvard U., 1952. Intern U. Chgo. Hosps., 1952-53; resident in neurosurgery Mass. Gen. Hosp., Boston, 1953-59; research fellow in surgery Harvard U., Cambridge, Mass., 1959; vis. scientist NIH, Bethesda, Md., 1960; prof. surgery Georgetown U. Med. Sch., Washington, 1963—; chief neurosurgery div. Gerogetown U. Med. Sch., Washington. Contbr. numerous articles to profl. jours. Served with AUS, 1943-46. Mem. Am. Assn. Neurol. Surgery, Congress Neurosurgery, Am. Acad. Neurosurgery, Soc. Neurosurgery. Republican. Presbyterian. Home: 4524 Foxhall Cres NW Washington DC 20007-1055

LUFT, ERIC V.D., librarian, educator; b. Woodbury, N.J., Dec. 5, 1952; s. Alexander v.d. and Barbara Elaine (Meeker) L.; m. Jennifer Hamlin, June 23, 1979 (div. Nov. 1993); children: Sarah, Mary Grace. AB magna cum laude, Bowdoin Coll., 1974; MA, Bryn Mawr Coll., 1977, PhD, 1985; student, Columbia U. Rare Book Sch., 1988-89; MLS, Syracuse U., 1993; student, U. Va. Rare Book Sch., 1997. Cataloging asst., libr. asst. Bryn Mawr (Pa.) Coll., 1976-80, 81-82; hist. collections asst. Coll. Physicians Phila., 1980-81; instr. philosophy Villanova (Pa.) U., 1983-85; curator hist. collections SUNY Upstate Med. U. Health Scis. Libr., Syracuse, 1987—; manuscript cataloger, Coll. Environ. Science & Forestry SUNY, 1993; list owner ALHHS-L, 1999—; adj. instr. Humanistic Studies Ctr., Syracuse U., 1986-96, cons. rare book cataloging, 1994-96; proprietor Gegensatz Press, North Syracuse, N.Y., 1996—; participant internat. confs., Belgium, Can., Germany, Iceland; vis. lectr. U. Iceland, U. Copenhagen; freelance photographer specializing in rare books, 1981-90; facilities planning cons. St. Lawrence County Hist. Assn., N.Y., 1999-2000. Author: Hegel, Hinrichs and Schleiermacher on Feeling and Reason in Religion, 1987; editor: Schopenhauer: New Essays, 1988; contbg. editor: Biographical Dictionary of Literary Influences, the Nineteenth Century, 1800-1914, 2000; assoc. editor: The Owl of Minerva, 1983-96; pronunciation editor: Biographical Encycl. of 20th Century World Leaders, 1998-99; contbr. Young Hegelians, 1983, History and System, 1984, Hegel's Philosophy of Spirit, 1987, Existence of God, 1988, Hegel and his Critics, 1989, Dictionary Am. Biography, 1992-96, Scribner Ency. Am. Lives, 1997—, also articles to profl. jours.; contbr. to Magill's Guide to Military History, 2000, International Dictionary of Library Histories, 1999-2000, Science and Its Times, 1999—; contbr.: Ency. of N.Y. State, 1999—, Ency. of N.J., 2000—, Interdisciplinary Biographical Dictionaries of the Western World's Great Cultural Ideas, 2000—, Ency. of the Ancient World, 2000—, Ency. of Land Warfare, 2000—. Recipient Prologue prize, 1972, Brown Composition prize, 1974, Adèle Mellen prize for excellence in scholarship, 1985, Pres.'s award for excellence in L.S., SUNY Health Sci. Ctr., Syracuse, 1997, Murray Gottlieb prize Med. Libr. Assn., 1999, Links2Go Key Resource award, 2000; Surdna Rsch. fellow, 1973, Whiting fellow in humanities, 1982-83, Francis C. Wood Inst. for History of Medicine fellow, 1984, 99, U.S. Dept. Edn. fellow, 1992-93. Mem. N.Am. Nietzsche Soc., Hume Soc., AM. Philos. Assn. (life mem.), Metaphysical Soc. Am., Hist. Soc. (charter), Hegel Soc. Am. (councillor 1988-92, sec. 1992-94), N.Y. State Assn. European Historians, Interdisciplinary 19th Century Studies, Friends of Book Arts Press, Documentary Heritage Com. Ctrl. N.Y., Internat. Soc. Intellectual History, Soc. for Bioethics and Classical Philosophy, Librs. in History of Health Scis., Am. Phil. Assn. (life), Bowdoin Alumni Club Ctrl. N.Y. (pres. 1985-92). Democrat. Avocations: bridge (life master Am. Contract Bridge League), chess, genealogy, fishing, carpentry. Home: 108 Deborah Ln N Syracuse NY 13212-1931 Office: SUNY Upstate Med Univ Health Scis Libr 766 Irving Ave Syracuse NY 13210-1602

LUFTGLASS, MURRAY ARNOLD, manufacturing company executive; b. Bklyn., Jan. 2, 1931; s. Harry and Pauline (Yaged) L.; children by previous marriage: Paula Jean, Bryan Keith, Robert Andrew, Richard Eric; 1 child from 2d marriage: Andrew William. BS, Ill. Inst. Tech., 1952; MS, U. So. Calif., 1959; MBA, U. Conn., 1972. With Shell Chem. Co., Torrance, Calif., 1955-60, 64-66, N.Y.C., 1960-61, 66-69, Wallingford, Conn., 1961-64; asst. gen. mgr. Westchester Plastics div. Ametek, Inc., Mamaroneck, N.Y., 1969-75; dir. corp. devel. Ametek, Inc., N.Y.C., 1975-76, v.p., 1976-83, sr. v.p. corp. devel., 1984-96; mng. dir. M&A London, LLC, N.Y.C., 1996—. Contbr. articles to profl. jours., publs.; patentee in field. Lt. (j.g.) USN, 1952-55. Mem. NAM, Soc. Plastics Industry, Assn. Corp. Growth, Soc. Plastics Engrs., Tau Beta Pi, Beta Gamma Sigma, Phi Lambda Upsilon, Univ. Club (N.Y.C.). Office: M&A London LLC 99 Park Ave New York NY 10016-1601 also: M&A London LLC PO Box 150 Montclair NJ 07042-0150

LUGEZ, CATHERINE LOUISE, chemist, researcher; b. Lille, Nord, France, Feb. 14, 1966; came to U.S., 1995; s. Patrick and Annie (Barell) L. PhD in Chemistry, U. Piere and Marie Curie, Paris, 1994. Chemist, guest rschr. NIST, Gaithersburg, Md., 1995-98; chemist Nat. Inst. Stds. and Tech., Savage, Md., 1998—. Home: 106 Lauren Ct Frederick MD 21703-1371

LUGG, MARLENE MARTHA, health information systems specialist, health planner; b. Wauwatosa, Wis., Mar. 6, 1938; d. Armand Werner and Elise (Kuehni) Heinrich; m. Richard S.W. Lugg, June 11, 1966 (div. Dec. 1976); children: Jennifer Elsie, William Thomas Armand. BS, U. Wis., 1960; MPH, U. Pitts., 1966, DrPH, 1981. Dep. chair Nat. Com. on Health and Vital Stats., Canberra, Australia, 1973-83; dir. State Ctr. for Health Stats. and Planning Health Dept. Western Australia, Perth, 1966-83; dir. health info. systems program UCLA, 1983-88; vis. prof. pub. health Calif. State U., Northridge, 1987—; health info. systems specialist Kaiser-Permanente-So. Calif., Pasadena, 1988-98; immunization coord./sr. rschr. Kaiser Permanente, Panorama City, Calif., 1998—; cons. software applications, L.A., 1987—; examiner L.A. Civil Svc. Commn., 1986-88; vis. prof. Pasadena City Coll., 1992—; mem. Calif. State Health Info. Policy Interagy. Com., 1992-94; mem. Calif. Health Data Coordinating Coun., 1995—; bd. dirs. Pub. Health Found. Enterprises, L.A., sec., 1995—/. Author: Medical Manpower in Western Australia, 1978; contbg. editor Australian Health Rev., 1998—; contbr. articles on injury, health data systems, immunization, air quality and illness, injury control and Pub. Health Conf. stats./records to profl. jours. Leave No Trace Master Educator, 1998—; Leader, trainer Girl Scouts U.S.A., Milw., Pitts., L.A., 1956—, Australian Girl Guides, Perth, Australia, 1966-82; explorer leader, trainer Boy Scouts Am., Western L.A. and Verdugo Hills, 1983-99; venturer leader/trnr. Boy Scouts Am., Verdugo Hills, 1999—; del. Girl Scouts Nat. Coun., 1996—. Recipient Broughton award Izaak Walton League Am., Wis., 1966, Fisher award Am. Med. Technologists, 1971, Outstanding Young Person award Jaycees, Perth, Australia, 1977, Take Pride in Am. award U.S. Govt., Washington, 1990, Wm. T. Hornaday Gold medal Boy Scouts Am., 1991, Silver Beaver Boy Scouts Am., 1999, Venturer Adult Leadership award, 1999, Thanks Badge Girl Scouts U.S.A., 1990, Outstanding Family award Girl Scouts San Fernando Valley, 1992, UN Environ. Conservation award, 1992, Wm. Spurgeon award, 1995, Nat. Vohs Quality award Kaiser Permanente, 1995, Spotlight on Leadership award Kaiser Permanente, 1999; named Career Woman of Yr., Daily News, 1983, Woman of the Year San Fernando Valley Girl Scouts, 1995; Nat. Health and Med. Rsch. Coun. pub. health fellow, Australia, 1978, Outstanding Cmty. Svc. Alumni award U. Wis., Milw., 1997. Fellow APHA, Australian Coll. Health Execs. (state bd. dirs. 1977-82), Royal Soc. Health, London; mem. Internat. Epidmiological Assn., So. Calif. Pub. Health Assn. (bd. dirs. 1987-95), N.Y. Acad. Scis. Lutheran. Achievements include research in development of serial section microcinematography, large linked databases, and vaccine safety studies. Office: Kaiser-Permanente So Calif 13652 Cantara St Panorama City CA 91402-5423

LUGLIO, MICHELE, engineering researcher; b. Civitavecchia, Italy, May 16, 1964; s. Giovanni Luglio and Giuseppa Lombardo; m. Cecilia Giacobbe, Oct. 16, 1993; children: Francesca, Agnese. Laurea in electronics engineering., U. Rome "Tor Vergata", 1990, PhD in Telecomm., 1994. Cons. Selenia Spazio, Rome, 1991, Telespazio, Rome, 1992-93; rschr. U. Rome "Tor Vergata", 1995—. Contbr. articles to profl. jours. Mem. inst. bd. Pitagora Sch., Rome, 1981; mem. adminstrn. bd. U. Rome "Tor Vergata," 1983-91, mem. acad. senate, 1999; mem. adminstrn. bd. ADISU, Rome, 1997. Recipient Thesis award Consorzio Roma Ricerche, Rome, 1990, Young Scientist award Internat. Symposium on Signals Systems and Electronics, 1995. Mem. IEEE. Office: U Rome Tor Vergata, Via di Tor Vergata 110, 00133 Rome Italy

LUGO, OCTAVIO A., architect, executive; b. Chihuahua, Mex., Oct. 4, 1970; s. Octavio Ramon Lugo and Norma Soledad Aguirre; m. Fala Maria Varela, Mar. 21, 1998; 1 child, Ana Cristina. BArch, Archtl. & Design Inst. State U, Chihuahua, 1995. Design leader Constrn. Dept. Monterrey Superior Studies Tech., Chihuahua, 1990-94; constrn. site rep. ARKHO Archs., Chihuahua, 1995, constrn. mgr., 1995-96; project dir. new campus constrn. dept. Chihuahua State U., 1996-97; archtl. design leader Ingenieria Internacional Punto Alto, Chihuahua, 1997, archtl. dept. mgr., 1997-99, quality and mktg., 1999, mktg. and comml. area dir., 1999—; quality control advisor Ingenieria Internacional Punto Alto, Chihuahua; standardization process cons. Copachisa Constructors, Chihuahua. Author, editor: CADD Standards Manual, 1997, Quality Control and Quality Assurance Manual, 1997. Design winner New Fairfield and Nat. Pk. Design Competition, 1995. Mem. AIA (honored). Roman Catholic. Avocations: bowling, music, traveling. Office: Ingenieria Internacional Punto Alto, Valle Excondido 5700, 31125 Chihuahua Mexico

LUGOVSKOI, YURI FEDOROVICH, mechanical engineer; b. Gomel, Belorussia, Aug. 10, 1951; s. Fedor Evdokimovich and Noiabrina Aleksandrovna (Garvardt) L.; m. Irina Michailovna Kosheleva, Oct. 4, 1980; children: Ecaterina, Andrey. Mech. engr., Kiev Politech. Inst., 1975; cand. tech. sci., Inst. Material Sci. Ukraine, 1989. Design engr. Design Bur., Kiev, Ukraine, 1977-79; rsch. engr. Inst. Problems of Strength Ukrainian Nat. Acad. Sci., Kiev, 1979-86, sci. collaborator Inst. Material Sci., 1986—. Inventor in field; contbr. articles to profl. jours. Socialist. Avocations: politics, economics, medicine. Office: Nat Acad Sci Inst Mat Sci, Str Krjijanovski 3, 252180 Kiev Ukraine

LUGOVY, MYKOLA IVANOVICH, scientist, consultant; b. Novoahtyrka, Ukraine, Mar. 29, 1963; s. Ivan Yegorovich Lugovy and Lidia Mihailovna Panova; m. Irina Vladimirovna Malevanchenko, Sept. 3, 1988 (div. Jan. 1995); m. Svitlana Yaroslavivna Boychuk, Nov. 1, 1996; 1 child, Diana. MSc, Nat. Tech. U. Ukraine, Kiev, 1986; PhD, Inst. Problem Materials Sci., Kiev, 1995. Cert. in engring. Engr. IPMS, Kiev, 1988-92, jr. rsch. assoc., 1992-96, rsch. assoc., 1996-98, sr. rsch. assoc., 1998-99; sr. rsch. assoc. Nat. Tech. U. Ukraine, Kiev, 1999—; cons. IPMS, Kiev, 1999—. Contbr. articles to profl. jours. Recipient award for young scientists Nat. Acad. Scis. of Ukraine, 1994, award for young scientists Pres. of Ukraine, 1996. Mem. Internat. Cmty. for Composites Engring. Fax: 444 2131. E-mail: lugovoj@materials.kiev.ua. Home: Stetsenko 9, Kiev 252128, Ukraine Office: Inst Problems Materials Sci, Krzhizhanovskii Str 3, Kiev 252180, Ukraine

LUH, PETER BAO-SEN, engineering educator; b. Taipei, Taiwan, Republic of China, Dec. 21, 1950; came to U.S., 1975; s. Chi-Lin and Nai-Kang (Fu) L.; m. Chwen-hwa Tsai, May 28, 1977; children: Adrian C., Corene C. BSEE, Nat. Taiwan U., 1973; MS in Aeronautics, Astronautics, MIT, 1977; PhD in Applied Math., Harvard U., 1980. Asst. prof. U. Conn., Storrs, 1980-86, assoc. prof. dept. elec. and systems engring., 1986-91, prof., 1991—; vis. prof. Nat. Taiwan U., Taipei, 1987; vis. rschr. Toshiba Corp., 1994; dir. Taylor L. Booth Ctr. Computer Application and Rsch., 1997—. Contbr. articles to profl. jours., chpts. to books; author conf. papers, tech. reports. Grantee NSF, 1981-83, 85—, State of Conn. and Pratt and Whitney, 1989-92, N.E. Utilities, 1990—. Fellow IEEE (assoc. editor Transactions on Automatic Control 1989-91, tech. editor, editor, editor-in-chief Transactions on Robotics and Automation 1990—); mem. Inst. Opers. Rsch. and Mgmt. Scis., Inst. Industrial Engrs., Sigma Xi. Democrat. Avocation: swimming. Fax: (860) 486-1273. E-mail: luh@engr.uconn.edu. Office: U Conn Dept Elec & Comput Engring Storrs Mansfield CT 06269-2157

LÜHDER, KONRAD, retired chemist, educator, researcher; b. Stralsund, Germany, Oct. 17, 1931; s. Erich and Katharina (Caesar) L.; m. Eleonore Zingler, Aug. 18, 1961; 1 child, Fred. Diploma, U. Greifswald, Germany, 1959, D, 1964, docent, 1973, D, 1982. Sci. asst. Inst. Inorganic Chemistry, Greifswald, 1959-91, prof., 1992-96. Contbr. articles to profl. jours.; patentee in field. Home: Franz-Mehring Str 54, 17489 Greifswald Germany Office: Inst Chemie und Biochemie, Soldtmannstr 16, 17487 Greifswald Germany

LUHMAN, WILLIAM SIMON, community development administrator; b. Belvidere, Ill., May 15, 1934; s. Donald R. and H. Elizabeth (Rudberg) L. AB, Park Coll., 1956; MA, Fla. State U., 1957. City planner City of Moline, Ill., 1959-64; planning dir. Rock Island County, Ill., 1964-66; exec. dir. Bi-State Met. Planning Commn., Rock Island, 1966-71; dir. regional devel. Northeastern Ill. Planning Commn., Chgo., 1971-74, assoc. dir., 1975-76, dep. dir., 1977-79, acting exec. dir., 1979-80, asst. dir., 1980-81; v.p. Pub. Mgmt. Info. Svc., Chgo., 1981; asst. dir. No. Ill. U. Ctr. Govt. Studies, DeKalb, 1981-91, program coord., 1991; exec. dir. Growth Dimensions for Belvidere-Boone County, Ill., 1991—, pres., 1982-86; vis. instr. Augustana Coll., Rock Island, 1967, 69. Bd. dirs. Rockford Area Coun. of 100, 1983-86; Boone County Regional Planning Commn., 1986—, chmn., 1986-90; mem. Belvidere-Boone County Regional Planning Commn., 1986—, chmn., 1990-92; bd. dirs. Sch. Dist. 100 Found. for Excellence in Edn., 1992-99; mem. Sch. Dist. 100 Citizens Adv. Coun., 1999—, Sch. Dist. 100 Com. Strat. Planning, 1999; bd. dirs. Boone County United Way, 1999—; active Boone County Arts Coun., Friends of Ida Pub. Libr., Belvidere Sister Cities Assn.; Ill. Regional Pub. Libr. Svc. Planning Panelist, 1996. Mem. Am. Soc. Pub. Adminstrn., Am. Planning Assn., Internat. City Mgmt. Assn., Ill. Devel. Coun. Home: 1538 Fremont St Belvidere IL 61008-5939 Office: 200 S State St Belvidere IL 61008-3687

LUHOVYI, VOLODYMYR ILLARYONOVYCH, rector, educator, researcher; b. Baltiysk, Kaliningrad, Russia, May 17, 1950; s. Illaryon Havrylovych and Valentyna Semenivna (Dudkynska) L.; m. Tamara Ivanivna Drozhzhanova, Dec. 31, 1971; children: Olexiy, Olha, Olena. Grad. degree in Physics, Kiev State U., Ukraine, 1972; Candidate of Scis. in Physics and Math., Kharkiv State U., Ukraine, 1976; DSc in Pedagogics and Psychology, Inst. Profl. Pedagogics, Ukraine, 1995. Inspector, head dept. univs. Ministry of High and Secondary Specialized Edn., Ukraine, 1975-78; instr., cons., head subdivsn. dept. sci. and ednl. insts. Ctrl. Com. Communist Party, Ukraine, 1978-88; dep. min. pub. edn. Ministry of Edn., Ukraine, 1988-92; doctorant Inst. Pedagogics of Acad. Pedagogical Scis., Ukraine, 1992-94; vice rector Kyiv State U. of Trade and Economy, Ukraine, 1994-95; rector Ukrainian Acad. Pub. Adminstrn., Ukraine, 1995—; chmn. acad. coun. Doctor of Scis. candidate selection; co-chmn. expert coun. State Accreditation Commn., Ukraine; mem. State Commn. Adminstrv. Reform Implementation, Ukraine, Coord. Coun. on Issues of Pub. Svc., Office of Pres. of Ukraine; academician Acad. Scis. of High Schs. of Ukraine, 1995—; head Kiev Dept. Acad. Scis., 1995—. Author: Development of Education in Ukraine, 1991, Pedagogical Education in Ukraine, 1994, Administration in Education, 1997; co-author Draft Law of Ukraine: On Education, 1991; editor Herald of Ukrainian Acad. Pub. Adminstrn.; contbr. articles to profl. pubs. Recipient medal In the Memory of 1500th Anniversary of Kyiv, 1982, award for Public Service, Ukraine, 1998, Yaroslav the Wise award in Sci. and Tech. Acad. Scis. of High Schs. Ukraine, 1997. Mem. Acad. Scis. N.Y.C., Internat. Acad. Pedagogies and Social Scis., Ukrainian Mcpl. Acad., Acad. Pedagogical Scis. (corr. mem.). Avocations: painting, chess. Home: 6 Kutuzova St Apt 50, 01011 Kiev Ukraine Office: UAPA, 20 Eugene Pottier St, 03057 Kiev Ukraine

LUHR, OWE ROBERT, physician, consultant; b. Stockholm, Nov. 4, 1958; s. Robert O. and Gunnel A. (Holmberg) L.; m. Maria Helena Burvall, Aug. 6, 1988; children: Malin, Johanna. MD, Karolinska Inst., Stockholm, 1987, PhD in Anesthesia and Intensive Care, 1999. Diplomate European Acad. Anesthesia and Intensive Care. Resident divsn. anesthesia and intensive care Danderyd Hosp., Stockholm, 1987-94, jr. staff, 1994-96, cons., 1996-98; med. adviser Parke-Davis, Stockholm, 1999-2000, Pfizer Inc., Sweden, 2000—. Named Swedish Sailing champion Swedish Nat. Sailing Assn., 1982; scholar Rotary, 1976-77. Avocation: sailing.

LUHRS, H. RIC, toy manufacturing company executive; b. Chambersburg, Pa., Mar. 22, 1931; s. Henry E. and Pearl (Beistle) L.; m. Grace B. Walke, June 12, 1973; children by previous marriage: Stephen Frederick, Christine Michelle, Terriann, Patricia Denise. BA, Gettysburg Coll., 1953. With The Beistle Co., Shippensburg, Pa., 1948-53, 1959—; pres., gen. mgr. Beistle Co., 1962-90, chmn. bd., 1962—, pres, CEO, 1998—; pres. Lakeside Holding Co. Inc., Boca Raton, Fla., 1996—, A-1 Holdings, Inc., Boca Raton, 1998—; bd. dirs. The Beistle Co., 1960—, First Nat. Bank of Shippensburg, 1964-80, Commonwealth Nat. Bank, 1980-91, Mellon Bank Commonwealth region, 1991-99, Boca Rsch. Inc., Boca Raton, 1998—; vice chmn. CompuPix Tech. Inc.; pres., 1986-88, gemologist, 1977—; owner Luhrs Gem Testing Lab., 1977—, Luhrs Jewelry, 1976—, Allied Leasing Co., Shippensburg, 1968; pres. South Lac Devel. Co., Boca Raton, Fla., 1986-92; owner Gun Depot, Shippensburg, 1992; chmn. The Walking Quail Sporting Goods Store, Shippensburg, 1994—; chmn. The Meadowlands Mall, Inc., Shippensburg, 1994—, pres., 1998—. Chmn. Pub. Libr., 1964-66, 1970-72, 76-78, bd. dirs., 1963-82; pres. Community Chest, 1965, bd. dir., 1963-72; pres. Shippensburg Area Devel. Corp., 1966-72; bd. dirs., trustee Carlisle (Pa.) Hosp., 1967-71, Chambersburg Hosp., 1969-75; mem. consumer adv. coun. Capital Blue Cross, 1976-78; bd. dirs. Fla. Atlantic U. Found., 1988-91, Shippensburg U. Found., 1991—. Capt. USAF, 1953-59. Mem. SAR (life), Shippensburg Hist. Soc. (life, bd. dirs. 1968), Shippensburg C. of C. (pres. 1965, bd. dirs. 1964-65), Toy Mfrs. Assn. (bd. dirs. 1969-71), Nat. Sml. Businessmen's Assn., NRA (life, benefactor), NRA Whittington Ctr. Founder's Club, NRA Golden Eagles, Shippensburg Fish and Game Assn. (life, pres. 1963), Carlisle Fish and Game Assn. (life), Pa. Flyers Assn., Am. Legion, VFW (life), Cumberland Valley Indsl. Mgmt. Club, York Printing House Craftsmen, Masons (32 deg.), Shriners, Tall Cedars of Lebanon, Green Jacket Club. Lutheran. Office: 1 Beistle Plz Shippensburg PA 17257

LUHTA, CAROLINE NAUMANN, airport manager, flight educator; b. Cleve., Mar. 26, 1930; d. Karl Henry and Fannie Arletta (Harlan) Naumann; m. Fred Harlan Jones, July 2, 1955 (div. 1961); m. Adolph Jalmer Luhta, Dec. 12, 1968 (dec. 1993); 1 child, Katherine Louise. BA, Ohio Wesleyan U., 1952; BS magna cum laude, Lake Erie Coll., Painesville, Ohio, 1977. Rsch. chemist Standard Oil Co. Ohio, Cleve., 1952-68; office mgr. Adolph J. Luhta Constrn. Co., Painesville, 1968-83; acct. Thomas Y. Ellis, CPA, Painesville, 1978; bd. dirs. Painesville Flying Svc., Inc., 1968—, flight instr., 1970—, pres., 1993—; bd. dirs. Concord Air Park, Inc., Painesville, 1968—, pres. 1993—; accident prevention counselor FAA, Cleve., 1975-85. Contbr. articles to profl. jours. Trustee Northeastern Ohio Gen. Hosp., Madison, 1973-83, chmn. bd. 1980-82; trustee Internat. Women's Air and Space Mus., Cleve., 1989—, treas. 1991-95, pres., 1997—; trustee Concord Twp., 1992—. Recipient Aerospace award Cleve. Squadron, Air Force Assn., 1966, Woman of Achievement award Lakeland C.C., 1999. Mem. Nat. Assn. Flight Instrs., Exptl. Aircraft Assn., Aircraft Owners and Pilots Assn., Ninety-Nines (life, chmn. All-Ohio chpt. 1969-70, Achievement award 1965, Amelia Earhart Meml. scholar 1970), Silver Wings (life), Order Ea. Star, Alpha Delta Pi (life). Avocations: air racing (Powder Puff Derby, All Women's Internat. Air Race). Office: Painesville Flying Svc Inc 12253 Concord Hambden Rd Painesville OH 44077-9566

LUI, ANTHONY TAT YIN, physicist; b. Hong Kong, Dec. 29, 1945; s. Siu Wai and Choi Dai (Chow) L.; m. Theresa Susan Szabo, Nov. 10, 1973; children: Jennifer, Michael, Victoria. BS, Hong Kong U., 1969; MS, U. Calgary, 1971, PhD, 1974. Postdoctoral fellow U. Calgary, 1974-75, U. Alaska, Fairbanks, 1975-76; rsch. assoc. NRC of Can., Ottawa, Ont., 1977-79; rsch. assoc. The Johns Hopkins U./Applied Physics Lab., Laurel, Md., 1979-83, sr. staff, 1984-85, prin. prof. staff, 1986—; mem. steering com. of CDAW, NASA, Greenbelt, Md., 1984-90; mem. Grand Tour Cluster SDT, NASA Hdqts., Washington, D.C., 1990-92, mem. Mercury Orbiter SDT, 1996-99; mem. inter-agy. cons. group, NASA, 1993—; cons. Los Alamos Nat. Lab., N.Mex., 1990-95; external examiner for PhD degree, U. Calgary, Can., 1992. Editor: (book) Magnetotail Physics, 1987 (JHU/APL Outstanding Publ. 1987); assoc. editor Geophys. Rsch. Letters, 1997—; contbr. (book) Amazing Mysteries of the World, 1983; contbr. articles to profl. jours. Recipient Linkage grant, NATO, 1993-96. Mem. Am. Geophys. Union (chair student awards com. 1996-98). Home: 10809 Beech Creek Way Columbia MD 21044-1031 Office: Johns Hopkins U/Applied Phy 11100 Johns Hopkins Rd Laurel MD 20723-6005

LUI, DENNIS POK-MAN, telecommunications executive; b. Hong Kong, Mar. 2, 1951; s. Hon-Yuen and Grace (Lee) L.; m. Eva Cheung Lui; children: Jeffrey, Jason. BS, U. Oreg., 1974. Mgr. Alrick Ltd. Group Cos HK subs. Italy In-Vest Group, Hong Kong, 1975-82, Universal Internat. Holdings Ltd., Match Box Trading Ltd., Hong Kong, 1982-85; gen. mgr. Lanard Toys Ltd., Hong Kong, 1985-86; group mng. dir. Greater China Hutchison Telecomm., Hong Kong, 1986-2000; pres., CEO AsiaNet Corp. Ltd., Hong Kong, 2000, Littauer Techs. Co. Ltd., 2000—; chmn. Hong Kong Radio Paging Assn., 1991—; appointee Vocat. Tng. Coun., 1992; apptd. mem. Telecom Bd., 1992-95; mem. info. infrastructure adv. com. Hong Kong Govt., 1997-2000. Govt. appointed rep. Competitive Telecommunications Svc. Provider to the Telecom Authority, Hong Kong, 1991—. Mem. Hong Kong Govt. Info. Infrastructure (adv. com.). E-mail: dennislui@littauer-tech.com. Office: Littauer Techs Co Ltd, 1702 Cheung Kong Ctr Ctrl, Hong Kong China

LUI, KUNG-JONG, educator; b. Taipei, Republic of China, June 22, 1953; came to the U.S., 1976; s. Shung-Wu Lu and Li-Chin Chen; m. Jen-Mei Tung; children: Chen-Hwa, Chen-Hsiang. BS, Fu-Jen U., Taiwan, 1975; MA, UCLA, 1977, MS, 1979, PhD, 1982. Tchg. asst. UCLA, 1979-82, postdoctoral scholar, 1982-83; statistician Ctrs. for Disease Control, Atlanta, 1983-90; assoc. prof. San Diego State U., 1990-93, prof., 1993—. Inventor in field. Mem. Am. Statis. Assn. Republican. Avocations: swimming, table tennis. Home: 12197 Brickellia St San Diego CA 92129-4149 Office: Dept Math and Computer Scis San Diego State University San Diego CA 92182-0001

LUI, SUN-WING, mechanical engineer, consultant; b. Hong Kong, Hong Kong, Aug. 20, 1950; s. Kai and Yee Lui (Kwan) L.; m. Chek-Nior Cheong, June 16, 1979; children: Steven Yee Ming, Debra Man-Yee. BEng, Feng Chia U., Taiwan, 1973; PhD, U. Birmingham, England, 1979. Grad. engr. HLK Svc. Ltd., Hong Kong, 1973-74; rsch. fellow Dept. Mech. Engring., U. Birmingham, Birmingham, 1978-81; assoc. cons., cons. Hong Kong Proucitivity Coun., 1981-85, sr. cons., prin. cons., divsn. head, 1985-92, dir. materials and process branch, 1992-2000; v.p. Hong Kong Poly. U., 2000—; exec. com. mem. Hong Kong Mould and Die Coun., Hong Kong, 1989-2000; dir. Productive Heat Treatment Co. Ltd., Hong Kong, 1992-95, Hong Kong Plastic Technology Ctr. Ltd., Hong Kong, 1992—, Design Innovation (HK) Ltd., Hong Kong, 1998-2000; hon. advisor Hong Kong Plastic Machinery Assn., Hong Kong, 1993—; chmn. mgmt. steering com. Hong Kong Rapid Prototyping Technology Ctr., Hong Kong, 1994-2000; hon. chmn. Hong Kong Auto Parts Ind. Assn., 1999—; dir. Hong Kong Product Devel. and Innovation Inst. Editor: (books) Injection Moulding of Thermoplastics Handbook, 1994, 3D Advanced Surface Design Technique on AutoCAD, 1995, Quality Moulding Handbook, 1995, Application of Moulding Machine Handbook, 1996, Industrial Standards for Mould and Die Industry, 1996, Industrial Standards Handbook for Precision Sheet Metal Components, 1997, Industrial Standards Handbook on Precision Plastic Components, 1998; editor of numerous jours. in field; patentee light and non-contact type of 3-dimension data scanner, also method of making a model. Fellow Hong Kong Assn. Advancement Sci. and Tech. (sr. v.p.); mem. Internat. Mgmt. Assn. (hon. chmn. 1998—), Asia Innovation Soc. (pres. 1998—), Soc. Mfg. Engrs. (sr.), Instn. Mech. Engrs., Hong Kong Instn. of Engrs., Hong Kong Metals Mfrs. Assn. (hon. chmn. 1995—), Inst. Mgmt. Info. Sys., Soc. Automative Engrs. Hong Kong (chmn. 1999—, CMA Design award, Gov.'s award for industry 1991). Address: The Hong Kong Polytechnic U, Hung Hom Kowloon Hong Kong

LUICK, BARBARA JEAN, physical therapist assistant; b. Alton, Ill., Feb. 18, 1952; d. Louis Elroy and Laverne Estelle (Guile) Fensterman; m. Richard Mark Luick, May 19, 1979. AAS, Ill. Ctrl. Coll., 1990. Phys. therapist asst. Profl. Therapy Svcs., East Peoria, Ill., 1990-91, Ctrl. Ill. Rehab. Assn., Peoria, 1992-99; owner Barb's Therapeutic Massage, 1999—. Author: Yesterday's Mountain, Tomorrow's Rainbow, 1989, Poetic Birth, 1991; author (gospel song) His Healing Touch; co-author (gospel songs) 24 Hours for Jesus, He is my Strength, I Bow Before Thee. Republican. Avocations: deer

hunting, tennis, writing, birdwatching, gardening. Home: 410 E Walnut St Tremont IL 61568-8624

LUIJENDIJK, TEUS, scientist; b. Leiden, The Netherlands, Dec. 14, 1960; s. Willem Luijendijk and Antonie Maria Elshout. Degree in pharmacy, Leiden U., 1988, PhD, 1995. Scientist divsn. pharmacognosy Leiden U., 1989-90, scientist-in-tng. divsn. pharmacognosy, 1990-94; scientist divsn. pharmacognosy Uppsala (Sweden) U., 1995-97; scientist Phytoconsult, Leiden, 1998—. Recipient Prof. Dr. van Os award Nederlandse Vereniging voor Genelskruiden Onderzoek, 1997. Avocations: birding, sports. Fax: 31 71 527 4511. E-mail: t.luijendijk@chem.leidenuniv.nl. Office: Phytoconsult Gorlaeus Labs, Einsteinweg 55 PO Box 9502, 2300 RA Leiden The Netherlands

LUIK, ANTINUS JOHAN, internist, nephrologist; b. Steenwyk, The Netherlands, Aug. 6, 1959; s. Antinus Johan and Albertina (vander Laan) L.; m. Maria Sophia Koop, Aug. 11, 1989; children: Lucas Olivier, Sophia Anastasia Maria, Philine Maria Josephine. MD, U. Sroninjen, The Netherlands, 1985; internist, Hosp. of the Free U., Amsterdam, 1990; nephrologist, U. Maastricht, The Netherlands, 1991, PhD, 1998. Staff mem. dept. nephrology Univ. Hosp. Maastricht, 1990-95; internist, nephrologist dept. internal medicine Ziekenhuizen Noord, Limburg, The Netherlands, 1995—. Author: (book) Blood Pressure Control in Hemodialysis Patients, 1998; contbr. numerous articles to profl. publs. Office: St Maartens Gasthus, Tegelseweg 210, 5912 BL Venlo The Netherlands

LUINE, JEROME ARTHUR, research physicist; b. San Diego, May 6, 1952; s. Arthur and Martha Belle (Bybee) L.; m. Mary Spear, May 28, 1977; children: Carynn Alice, Evan Arthur. BS in physics, Univ. Calif., 1974; PhD in physics, Univ. Colo., 1981. Lectr. Calif. State Univ., Carson, Calif., 1985—; sr. scientist TRW Space & Electronics, Redondo Beach, Calif., 1981—. Author: Science Mysteries, 1995; contbr. articles to profl. jours. Mem. com. to choose elem. sch. sci. texts Torrance Unified Sch. Dist., Torrance, Calif., 1993. Avocations: ancient numismatics, astronomy. E-mail: jerome.luine@trw.com Fax number: 310 812 0542. Office: TRW MS 1075 One Space Park Redondo Beach CA 90278

LUINI, ALBERTO, medical administrator, surgeon; b. Como, Italy, Mar. 10, 1947; s. Fernando Luini and Maria Collina; m. Giovanna Gatti. Grad. medicine, U. Degli Studi, Milan, 1973; specialist in oncology, U. Degli Studi, Genoa, Italy, 1976. Asst. in surgery Nat. Inst. for Study and Cure of Tumors, Milan, 1975-94; dep. dir. senology European Inst. Oncology, Milan, 1994-98, dir. senology, 1998—; assoc. prof. Sch. Specialization in Oncology, U. Tor Vergata, Rome, 1997—, Sch. Specialization in Gen. Surgery, U. Perugia, Italy, 1998—. Author, co-editor: (book) Manuale di Senologia Oncologica, 1993-99; co-author: (book) Conservative Management of Breast Cancer, 1983. Mem. Italian Soc. Senology (bd. dirs. 1997—). Avocations: sailing, traveling, movies. Office: European Inst Oncology, Via Ripamonti 635, 20141 Milan Italy

LUIS, ALVARINHO JOAOZINHO, oceanographer, researcher; b. Panaji, Goa, India, June 26, 1967; arrived in Japan, 1994; s. Hilario F. Luis and Maria A. Fernandes. MS in Phys. Oceanography, Goa U., 1990; MS in Marine Sci., Ryukyu U., Okinawa, Japan, 1996; PhD in Geophysics, Tohoku U., Sendai, Japan. Project scientist Nat. Inst. Oceanography, Dona Paula, Goa, 1990-94. Monbusho scholar Govt. Japan, 1994-96, Tokyu Gairai scholar, 1998-00. Avocations: sports, computer games, painting, playing guitar. E-mail: luis@ocean.caos.tohoku.ac.jp. Home: Luis Apts Caranzalem, Goa Ilhas 403002, India Office: Tohoku U, Aobayama Sendai, Miyagi Aobaku Aramaki 980-8578, Japan

LUIS, BERENGUER FUSTER, member of European parliament; b. Alicante, Spain, Jan. 19, 1946. mem. Party of European Socialists, European Parliament, com. on econ. and monetary affairs, com. on legal affairs and the internal market; mem. delegations for rels. with mem. states of ASEAN, Southeast Asia and Republic of Korea. Mem. Spanish Socialist Workers' Party. Office: European Parliament, Virgen del Socorro 35, E-03002 Alicante Spain*

LUIS, JOSÉ ANTOINE, science educator, researcher; b. Sobradillo, Salamanca, Spain, May 18, 1959; arrived in France, 1965; s. Nicanor Luis Lopez and Vicenta Lopez Blanco; m. Danielle Monique Perez, Sept. 3, 1983; children: Damien, Doriane. PhD, U. Provence, Marseilles, France, 1987, habil. diriger les recherches, 1993. Asst. prof. Faculty Pharm., U. Provence, 1987-88, prof., 1990—; rschr. Nat. Ctr. Sci. Rsch. Unité de Propre de Recherche de l'Enseignement Supérieur Associé, 1995—; rsch. instr. VA Hosp., U.S., 1988-89; rschr. Nat. Ctr. Sci. Rsch.-URA 202, France, 1989-90. Contbr. over 40 articles to sci. jours. Mem. Comm. de Specialists. Avocations: archeology, paleontology. Office: CNRS-UPRESA 6032, 27 Bd Jean Moulin, 13 385 Marseilles France

LUK, JAMES KA HAY, geriatrician; b. Hong Kong, Feb. 8, 1965; s. Siu Kon and Agnes Lai Chu (Cheung) L.; m. Noble Po Ka Law, Sept. 21, 1991; children: Brian Kai Fung, Carmen Kai Yan. B Medicine B Surgery, U. Hong Kong, 1989; MSc, U. B.C., Can., 1993. Med. officer med. unit U. Hong Kong, 1990-91; rsch. fellow U. B.C., Vancouver, 1991-94; med. officer Chinese U. Hong Kong, 1994—; sr. med. officer Fung Yiu King Hosp., Hong Kong, 1999—. Contbr. articles to profl. jours. Mem. Royal Coll. Physicians, Hong Kong Med. Assn. Avocations: photography, model making, travel. Office: Fung Yiu King Hosp, 9 Sandy Bay Rd, Shatin New Territories Hong Kong China

LUK, JOHN WANG KWONG, development executive; b. Macau, Sept. 16, 1944; s. William and Pui Ha (Lam) L.; m. Andy Kit Ying, Apr. 20, 1975; children: Johnson Hoy Cheung, Lawrence Hoy Fu. BSc in Engr., U. Hong Kong, 1966, MSc in Engr., 1968; profl. degree in civil engring., Columbia U., 1976; MBA, Chinese U. of Hong Kong, 1980; PhD, U. Hong Kong, 1982; LLB, U. London, 1987. Bar: U.K., Hong Kong, 1988. Tutor U. Hong Kong, 1966-68; consulting engr. Spencer White & Prentis, N.Y.C., 1969-77; engring. cons. Way & Sun & Assocs., Hong Kong, 1972-77; project mgr. Cheung Kong Holdings Ltd., Hong Kong, 1977-79; property & devel. mgr. Sino Realty Ltd., Hong Kong, 1979-82; asst. to chmn. Sun Hung Kai Properties Ltd., Hong Kong, 1982—. Contbr. articles to profl. jours. Fellow Institution of Civil Engrs., Institution of Structural Engrs., Hong Kong Institution ofEngrs., Chartered Institution of Arbitrators Profession Engr.; mem. Am. Club, Royal Hong Kong Jockey Club, Rotary. Home: 15 Deer Path Holmdel NJ 07733-2028 Office: Sun Hung Kai Properties Ltd, 30 Harbour Rd, Hong Kong Hong Kong

LUK, KWAI MAN, electronic engineering educator; b. Hong Kong, June 7, 1958; s. Ying Kwong Luk and Ling Ho; m. Chuen Wah Wu, Jan. 8, 1990; children: Yin Pok Alec, Yin Ki. BSc in Engring., U. Hong Kong, 1981, PhD, 1985. Lectr. dept. electronic engring. City U. Hong Kong, 1985-87, prof. dept. electronic engring., 1992—; lectr. dept. electronic engring. Chinese U. Hong Kong, 1987-92. Contbr. more than 128 articles to profl. jours. Recipient Japan Microwave prize 1994 Asia-Pacific Microwave Conf., Chiba, Japan, 1994. Fellow IEEE (sr.), Instn. Elec. Engrs. (U.K.), Engring. Coun. (U.K., charter engr.). Avocations: table tennis, swimming. Office: City U Hong Kong Elec Engring, 83 Tat Chee Ave, Kowloon Hong Kong China

LUKAC, JOSIP, biologist; b. Zagreb, Croatia, Nov. 2, 1948; s. Josip and Karolina (Arlavi) L.; m. Blazenka Paldi, Mar. 16, 1974; children: Katarina, Maja. BS, U. Zagreb, Coratia, 1973, PhD, 1976. Rsch. asst. Lab. Exptl. Medicine, Zagreb, Croatia, 1972-78; head immunology dept. U. Hosp., Zagreb, Croatia, 1978-94, 96—; assoc. prof. sch. dentistry U. Zagreb, 1995—. Contbr. articles to profl. jours. Mem. Croatian Acad. Med. Sci., Coratian Immunology Soc., Internat. Soc. Interferon Cytokine Rsch. Roman Catholic. Office: U Hosp, Vinogradska c 29, Zagreb 10000, Croatia

LUKÁČOVÁ, MÁRIA MEDVIDOVÁ, mathematician, researcher; b. Košice, Slovakia, Sept. 21, 1968; d. Ivan and Anna (Mochnáčová) Medvidová; m. Luboslav Lukáč, July 30, 1994; 1 child, Jana. MS, U. Kosice (Slovakia), 1991; PhD, U. Prague, 1995. Researcher U. Magdeburg (Germany), 1995-99; tchr., researcher U. Brno (Czech Republic), 1995-98, assoc. prof., 1998—; cons. Tech. U. Brno, 1998—. Author: Numerical Solution of Compressible Flows, 1999 (Prize of Prof. Babuska 1995); contbr. articles to profl. jours. Grantee German Acad. Exch. Agy., 1995, Grant Agy. Czech Rep., 1997-99, Deutsche Forschungs-gemeinschaft, 1995—. Greek Catholic. Avocations: music, books, aerobics, swimming, skiing. Home: Zahrebska 7, 616 00 Brno Czech Republic Office: Tech U Brno Dept Maths, Technick 2, 61600 Brno Czech Republic

LUKACS, ANDREAS, dermatologist; b. Freiburg, Germany, Feb. 15, 1961; s. Stefan and Renate Lukacs. Med. diplomate, U. Munich, 1987. Rsch. and clin. fellow U. Munich, 1990—; pvt. practice, Munich, 1997—. Grantee Deutsche Forschungsgemeinschaft, Germany, 1988-90. Address: Graefelfinger Strasse 61, D-81375 Munich Germany

LUKÁCS, GÉZA LÁSZLÓ, surgery educator; b. Mezőkövesd, Hungary, Mar. 2, 1941; s. Gáspár and Erzsébet (Buzás) L.; m. Éva Maria Belsø, Dec. 12, 1971; 1 child, Levente. MD, U. Debrecen, Hungary, 1966; PhD, Hungarian Acad. Scis., Budapest, 1984, DMS, 1992. Diplomate Hungarian Bd. Surgery. Resident 2d dept. surgery U. Debrecen Med. Sch., 1966-70, asst. lectr. 1st dept. surgery, 1971-80, sr. lectr., 1981-85, assoc. prof., 1986-91, prof., 1992—, dep. head dept., 1992-99, head dept., 1999—. Author: Surgery of Thyroid and Parathyroid Glands, 1989, Struma Maligna, 1993; contbr. articles to Jour. Cancer Rsch. and Clin. Oncology, European Jour. Surgery, Diagnostic Molecular Pathology. Grantee Ministry Nat. Edn. and Dutch Culture, Ghent, Belgium, 1978, Nat. Bd. Health and Welfare, Stockholm, 1990, German Acad. Exch. Svc., 1990. Mem. Internat. Assn. Surgeons Gastroenterologists, World Fedn. Surg. Oncology Soc. (Hungarian rep. 1997—), Hungarian Surg. Soc. (gen. sec. 1993-97), European Soc. Surg. Oncology (mem. exec. com. 1996—), German Soc. for Surgery, N.Y. Acad. Scis., Austrian Soc. Surgery, Internat. Soc. for Endocrinology. Avocations: painting, swimming, tennis, skiing, travel. Office: U Debrecen Med Sch, 1st Dept Surgery, PO Box 27, H-4012 Debrecen Hungary

LUKACS, JANOS, mechanical engineering educator; b. Pecs, Baranya, Hungary, May 23, 1958; s. Janos Lukacs and Jusztina Lang; m. Monika Huszti, Aug. 1, 1958; children: Flora Eva, Fanni Viktoria. MSc, Tech. U. for Heavy Industry, Miskolc, 1981, Tech. U. for Heavy Industry, Miskolc, 1984; Dr. Univ., Tech. U. for Heavy Industry, Miskolc, 1985; PhD, U. Miskolc, 1994, Habilitation, 1999. Rschr. Tech. U. for Heavy Industry, Miskolc, 1981-83, instr., 1983-85, asst. prof., 1985-95; assoc. prof. U. Miskolc, 1995-99, prof., 1999—; dep. dean Faculty of Mech. Engring., U. Miskolc, 1994—. Contbr. articles to profl. jours. Recipient 2nd prize Hungarian Acad. of Scis., Budapest, 1991, 1997. Mem. Hungarian Engring. Scientific Soc., ASM. Avocations: travel, books. Office: Dept Mech Engring, Univ Miskolc, H-3515 Miskolc-Egyetemvaros Hungary

LUKACS, MICHAEL EDWARD, communications researcher; b. N.Y.C., Mar. 25, 1946; s. William and Hannah (LeWitter-Wolf) L.; m. Diane Harriet Katz, Oct. 29, 1967. Student, CUNY, Queens, 1965-68; T-3, Radio Corp. Am. Inst. now Tech Careers Inst., N.Y.C., 1968-69. Tech. aide Bell Telephone Labs., Holmdel, N.J., 1969-72, sr. tech. aide, 1972-77, assoc. mem. tech. staff, 1977-81, mem. tech. staff, 1981-83; mem. tech. staff Bell Communications Rsch., Red Bank, N.J., 1983-00, rsch. scientist, 1994-99; rsch. scientist Telcordia Techs. (formerly Bell Comms. Rsch.), Red Bank, N.J., 1999—. Patentee cathode ray tube dynamic focus apparatus, cathode ray tube electro-optic linearization device, infinitely expandable video conferencing sys., video conf. sys. with multilayer keying of multi video images; (co-inventor) pel recursive motion compensated video coder; (inventor) "Lukacs" coding, disparity corrected predictive coding for 3-D video, "Personal Presence System" advanced multimedia video bridge, multilayer priority video keying, infinitely extensible video conferencing. Recipient Notable Achievement award Bell Labs Research Lab. 113, 1983; R&D 100 award, 1996. Mem. IEEE, Assn. Computing Machinery (Best Paper award 1994), Soc. Motion Picture TV Engrs. Avocations: science fiction, autocross, antique belt buckles. Office: Telcordia Techs 331 Newman Springs Rd Red Bank NJ 07701-5657

LUKÁCS, PETER, sociology and education educator; b. Budapest, Hungary, Apr. 23, 1948; s. György and Zsuzsanna (Wolf) L.; m. Ágnes Kristóf; 1 child, Gábor; m. Julia Knoll, 1994. MA in History, Elte, Hungary, 1972, MA in Russian, 1972; MA in Sociology, Mlee, Hungary, 1977; PhD in Edn., Acad. Scis., Hungary, 1991. Tchr. secondary sch. Budapest, Hungary, 1972-74; rsch. fellow Hungarian Inst. for Career Guidance, Budapest, 1974-77; sr. rsch. fellow Hungarian Inst. for Higher Edn., Budapest, 1977-80; head rsch. dept. Hungarian Inst. for Ednl. Rsch., Budapest, 1981, vice-dir., 1990-98; head of dept. Kodolányi Coll., Székesfehérár, Hungary, 1992—; dep. gen. dir. Kodolányi Coll., Szekesfehérár, 1997—; gen. dir. Nat. Bd. Pub. Edn., Hungary, 1998—. Author: The Cooperation of Secondary Schools and Higher Education Institutions, 1980, Standards and Selection, 1991; co-author, co-editor: Just to Reform, 1989, Free or Mandatory, 1992. Czéchenyi Professors' scholarship, Ministry of Culture, Hungary, 1998. Mem. Hungarian Acad. Sci. (pedagogical com. 1994—, Rsch. award 1985, 89), Pedagogical Assn. (bd. dirs. 1993—), Hungarian Sociol. Assn. (chair ednl. sect. 1996-99), Hungarian Pvt. Higher Edn. Inst. (chmn. rectors assn. 1999—). E-mail: lukacsp@mail.kodolanyi.hu. Office: Kodolányi U Coll, Szabadságharcos 59, H-8000 Székehsférvár Hungary

LUKAS, ELSA VICTORIA, radiobiologist, radiobiochemist; b. Baden nr. Vienna, Austria, Feb. 28, 1927; d. Johann and Victoria (Hauer) L.; Degree for High Sch. Tchrs., U. Vienna, 1952, Ph.D., 1955; DSc in Physics, Biology and Physiology (hon.) Marquis Giuseppe Scicluna Internat. U., 1987; PhD in Physics (hon.), Albert Einstein Internat. Acad. Found., 1990. Researcher, Max Planck Inst. Biophysics, Frankfurt/Main, Federal Republic Germany, 1959-64, Path. Inst. Justus Liebig U., Giessen, Fed. Republic Germany, 1961-64, Oak Ridge Nat. Lab., U. Radiation Biology, U. Tenn., Knoxville, 1964-67; high sch. tchr., country insp. schs., Vienna, 1967—; research. Author numerous publs. on biochem. effects of ionizing radiation in living cells, especially in their nucleic acids. Recipient Dr. J. Kowarschick award, 1957, Dr. Karl Luick award 1957, Theodor Kö rner prize 1960, Alexander von Humboldt award, 1961, Vibert Douglas award Internat. Fedn. Univ. Women, 1962, medal of honor Am. Biog. Inst., 1987, Golden Acad. award, 1991, Profl. of Yr. nomination, 1991, Cert. of Merit as Foremost Woman of the 20th Century Internat. Biog. Centre, Cambridge, Eng., 1987; named hon. citizen State of Tenn., 1965, Woman of Yr. Am. Biog. Inst., 1990; Fulbright Hays scholar, 1964; inducted to Am. Biog. Inst's. 5,000 Personalities of the World Hall of Fame, N.C., 1989. Mem. Biophys. Soc., Radiation Research Soc., Soc. German Scientists and Physicians, Austrian Biochem. Soc., Am. Inst. Biol. Scis., Soc. Parapsychology, German Bot. Soc., Soc. German Biologists, Gregor Mendel Soc., Soc. Austrian Chemists, Univ. Assn. Alma Mater Rudolphina. Roman Catholic. Home: 60 Elisabethstrasse, Baden 2500, Austria

LUKAS, MAYA, art manager; d. Slavko and Sonja (Perčin) L. Diploma in engring., Chemistry U., Zagreb, 1973; ass. mus., Music Acad., 1978. Sec. Dubrovnik Festival, Dubrovnik, Yugoslavia, 1973-76; music journalist Radio Zagreb, Yugoslavia, 1977-78; opera singer Nat. Theatre, Osijek, Yugoslavia, 1978-82; singer Vienna, 1982-84; mem. Vienna Volksopera, Vienna, 1984-86; art mgr. EPD, Prague, 1996—. Exhibited art, Prague, 1996. Mem. bd. For Peace in Yugoslavia Yugoslav Peaceful Orgn., Vienna, 1991-96. Recipient award Masaryk's Acad. Arts, 1997. Office: European Property Devel, Klimentska 46, C2-11002 Prague Czech Republic

LUKASHENKO, ALEKSANDR GRIGORYEVICH, president of Belarus; b. Kopys, Vitebsk, Aug. 30, 1954; married; 2 children. Grad., Mogilev Pedagogical Inst., 1975, Belarusian Agricultural Acad., 1985. Tchr. history, pub. scis., econs., polit. worker with border guard, 1975-77; with Communist Youth League and local govt., Mogilev Region, 1975-80; polit. officer with motorized infantry unit, 1980-82; dep. chmn. collective farm; dep. mgr. bldg. materials factory, Shklov, 1982-87; head Harazdiec State Farm, Mogilev region, 1987-94; dep. Supreme Coun. of Belarus, 1990-94; pres. Republic of Belarus, 1994—; founder Communists for Democracy; head Parliamentary Anti-Corruption Commn., 1993. Active Soviet Army, 1977-78, 80-82. Decorated Cross St. Euphrosinia of Polotsk; recipient M.A. Sholokhov Internat. prize, 1997. Office: Office of President, Ulsita Karl Marxa 38, 220016 Minsk Belarus*

LUKASHOU, ALYAKSANDR VASILJEVICH, minister of transportation of Belarus; b. Altaiskii krai, Russia, Jan. 1, 1950; married; 3 children. Degree, Altaiskii Poly. Inst. Dep. Supreme Soviet Rep. Belarus, 1990-94; sec. subcommn. pub. svc. Supreme Soviet Commn. Industry Pub. Svc., 1993-94; min. Transportation and Comm. of Republic of Belarus, 1994—. Office: Min Transport Comm, Chicherin Str 21, 220029 Minsk Belarus

LUKASIEWICZ, ANDRZEJ, chemist, researcher; b. Opinogora, Mazaowsze, Poland, May 15, 1927; s. Antoni and Maria (Szymanska) L.; m. Cecylia Dabrowska, Apr. 30, 1994,. BSc, Inst. Tech., Leningrad, USSR, 1952; PhD, Inst. Nuclear Rsch., Warsaw, Poland, 1962, assoc. prof., 1965, prof., 1974. Rsch. asst. U. Tech., Warsaw, Poland, 1952-56; rsch. asst. Inst. Nuclear Rsch., Warsaw, Poland, 1956-62, head rsch. group, 1962-65, assoc prof., 1965-74, prof., 1974-92; prof. Inst. Nuclear Chemistry and Tech., Warsaw, Poland, 1992—. Contbr. articles to profl. jours. Grantee State Commn. for Sci. Rsch., Warsaw, 1993. Mem. Polish Nucleonic Soc. Avocations: travel, non-fiction reading. Home: Tana Pawla II 72m60, 00-175 Warsaw Poland Office: Inst Nuclear Chem & Tech, Dorodna 16, 03195 Warsaw Poland

LUKASZEWSKI, ZENON, chemistry educator; b. Poznan, Poland, Dec. 1, 1940; s. Wojciech and Franciszka Hanna (Ciesiolkiewicz) L.; m. Swietlana Bielousova, Sept. 5, 1963; children: Natalia, Anna. Student, Tech. U., Gdansk, Poland, 1958-61; MSc, Mendeleyev Inst. Chem. Engring., Moscow, 1963; PhD, Adam Mickiewicz U., Poznan, 1969; Habilitation, Tech. U., Lodz, Poland, 1978. Lectr. Tech. U., Poznan, 1963-74, asst. prof., 1974-88, assoc. prof., 1988-93, prof., 1993—; dean faculty chem. engring. Tech. U., 1987-90. Contbr. articles to sci. publs. Named Honored Citizen of Poznan, Pres. of City of Poznan, 1979, Honored Citizen of Poznan Province, Govt. Provincial Rep., 1988. Mem. Polish Chem. Soc., Internat. Union Pure and Applied Chemistry (affiliate), Poznan Soc. Friends of Sci., Internat. Assn. Water Quality. Avocations: classical music, mushroom gathering. Office: Tech U Poznan Ins Chemistry, Ul Piotrowo 3, PL 60965 Poznan Poland

LUKAUSKAS, ALGIRDAS, industrial hygiene researcher, educator; b. Klaipeda, Lithuania, Mar. 8, 1937; s. Stasys and Aleksandra (Puzinaite) L.; m. Rita Viliunaite, Aug. 5, 1961; 1 child, Kristina. Physician, Med. Inst., Kaunas, Lithuania, 1960, MD, 1969. Physician Rural hosp., Vashkai, Lithuania, 1960-61, Kazlu-Ruda, Lithuania, 1961-64; lectr. Med. Inst., Kaunas, 1966-70, chief lectr., 1971-91, assoc. prof., 1991—; adj. faculty Teach the Tchrs. Uppsala (Sweden) U., 1993-95; tutor students rsch. group Med. Acad., Kaunas, 1974—; mem. Acad. Bd., Kaunas, 1990-94; mem. Internat. Commn. on Occup. Health, Singapore, 1993—. Co-author: (handbook) Higiena, 1982; contbr. articles to profl. jours. Mem. coun. Baltic U. Program, Uppsala, 1992—; mem. Saludis movement, Kaunas, 1988-90. Recipient awards. Mem. Lithuanian Assn. Hygienists (coun. 1995-97), Lithuanian Occup. Safety Assn. (coun. 1997—). Mem. Conservators Party. Roman Catholic. Avocations: travel, philately, gardening, dance. Home: Eiveniu St 31 ap 57, LT 3005 Kaunas Lithuania Office: Med Univ, MickevicIaus St 9, LT 3000 Kaunas Lithuania

LUKE, TAN KIM SIANG, otolaryngologist, educator; b. Singapore, Dec. 26, 1964; m. Carol Muen Nun Chan, Mar. 8, 1992; 1 child, Elliot Tan Tzen. B Medicine B Surgery, Nat. U. Singapore, 1988; M Med. Sci., U. Dundee, Scotland, 1997. House officer U. M.K., Singapore, 1988-89, Nat. U. Hosp., Singapore, 1992-94; registrar Nat. Health Svc., Dundee, 1994-96; fellow U. Tex. Med. Br., Galvaston, 1986-89; asst. prof. Nat. U. Singapore, 1999—; mem. reconstruction and mucovascular surgeon team NMH, Singapore, 1998-99; head and neck cons. Univ. Cancer Program, Singapore, 1998-99. Capt. Singapore Armed Forces, 1990-92. Head and neck fellow Am. Soc. Head and Neck Surgery, Soc. Head and Neck Surgeons. Fellow Royal Coll. Surgeons Eng., Royal Coll. Surgeons Glasgow. Avocations: running, dancing. Home: 14 Jalan Limau Bali, Singapore 468469, Republic of Singapore Office: Nat U Singapore Hosp, Lower Kent Ridge Rd, Singapore 119074, Republic of Singapore.

LUKIĆ, IRENA, chemical engineer, researcher; b. Zagreb, Croatia, Apr. 13, 1941; d. Danijel and Julijana (Čavlović) Esih; m. Velimir Lukić, Sept. 9, 1967; children: Silvije, Martina. Engr. of chemistry, U. Zagreb, Croatia, 1964, M of Chem. Sci., 1980. Registered chem. engr. Rsch. engr. Pliva Rsch. Inst., Zagreb, 1964—. Patentee in field; contbr. articles to profl. jours. Recipient Golden medals Rast-Yu, Yugoslav Exhbn. of Innovation, 1979, Inova '86, Exhbn. of Innovation, 1986. Mem. N.Y. Acad. Scis.; mem. Amaciz. Avocations: painting, photography. Home: Veslaćka 6, 10000 Zagreb Croatia Office: Pliva Rsch Inst, Prilaz Baruna Filipovića 25, 10000 Zagreb Croatia

LUKMAN, RILWANU, petroleum exporting executive; b. Zaria, Nigeria, Aug. 26, 1938; s. Qadi and Ramatu Lukman; m. Amina Abdullahi, Dec. 1965; children: Ramatu, Ahmed, Salihu. Gen. cert. of edn., Nigerian Coll. Art/Sci./Tech., Zaria, 1958; BSc in Engring./Mining, Imperial Coll. Sci. & Tech., London, 1962; postgrad. cert., U. Mining & Metallurgy, Leoben, Austria, 1968; postgrad., McGill U., Can., 1977-78; PhD in Chem. Engring. (hon.), U. Bologna, Italy, 1988; DSc (hon.), U. Maiduguri, Nigeria, 1989, Ahmadu Bello U., Zaria, 1991; PhD (hon.), Moore House Coll., Atlanta, 1992. Registered profl. engr. Asst. mining engr. AB Statsgruvor, Sweden, 1962-64; inspector, sr. inspector of mines Mines divsn. Ministry of Mines and Power, Jos, Nigeria, 1964-67, acting asst. chief inspector of mines, 1968-70; gen. mgr. Cement Co. No. Nigeria, Sokoto, 1970-74; gen. mgr., CEO Nigerian Mining Corp., Jos, 1974-84; minister of mines, power, and steel Nigeria, 1984-85, minister of petroleum resources, 1986-89; pres. Orgn. of Petroleum Exporting Countries, Vienna, Austria, 1986-89; minister of fgn. affairs Nigeria, 1989-90; chmn., bd. dirs. Nat. Elec. Power Authority, Lagos, Nigeria, 1993-94; sec. gen. Orgn. of Petroleum Exporting Countries, Vienna, Austria, 1995—; presdl. adv. on petroleum and energy, Nigeria, 1999—. Fellow Imperial Coll. London, 1987; decorated Knight of the British Empire, British Monarch, London, 1989, Officer of the Legion d'Honneur of France, Govt. of France, Paris, 1990, Order of the Liberator 1st Class, Govt. of Venezuela, Caracas, 1990; proclamation of Dr. Rilwanu Lukman Day, Gov. of Ga., 1989. Fellow Inst. Mining and Metallurgy (hon., London), Nigerian Mining and Geosci. Soc., Nigerian Metallurgical Soc.; mem. Chartered Engring. Inst. Avocations: reading, walking. Office: OPEC, Obere Donaustrasse 93, 1020 Vienna Austria

LUKOVIĆ, MLADEN, electrical engineer; b. Zagreb, Croatia, Oct. 21, 1964; s. Novak and Senka (Karaman) L. BA, Faculty Elec. Engring., Mech. Engring. and Naval Architecture, Split, Croatia, 1990. Engr. Energoinvest-Kibernetika, Livno, Bosnia and Herzegovina, 1990-92; svc. engr. ENEL-Computers, Split, 1992—. Mem. AIAA. Home: AB šimića 1, 21000 Split Croatia Office: Poljudrleo Setaliste 66, 21000 Split Croatia

LUKYANCHIKOVA, NATALIA BORISOVNA, physicist; b. Kiev, Ukraine, July 21, 1937; d. Boris Grigorievich and Galina Aleksejevna (Nikolaenko) Levin; m. Artem Stepanovich Lukyanchikov, Mar. 19, 1960 (div. Oct. 1983); 1 child, Dmitrii Artemovich; m. Grigorii Solomonovich Pekar, Sept. 11, 1992. Diploma in engring., Poly. Inst., Kiev, 1960; PhD, Inst. Semicondrs., Kiev, 1966, DSc, 1977, prof. diploma, 1991. Engr. Inst. Semicondrs., 1960-62, postgrad. rschr., 1962-65, jr. rschr., then sr. rschr., 1965-86, leading rschr., 1986-90, head lab., 1990-96; head dept. Inst. Semicondr. Physics, Kiev, 1997—. Author: Fluctuation Phenomena in Semiconductor Materials and Devices, 1990, Noise Research in Semiconductor Physics, 1996. Internat. Sci. Found. grantee, 1993, 94; recipient State of Ukraine award in Sci., 1995. Mem. Am. Phys. Soc., Ukrainian Phys. Soc., N.Y. Acad. Scis. Russian Orthodox. Avocations: piano playing, theater, classical music, travel, reading. Home: 8 Muzeini Pereulok Apt 23, 01001 Kiev Ukraine Office: Inst Semicondr Physics, 45 Prospect Nauki, 03650 Kiev Ukraine

LULAT, MOHAMED GORA SULEMAN, financial executive; b. Vereeniging, Gauteng, Republic of South Africa, Aug. 20, 1960; s. Suleman Mohamed and Aminabibi (Gathoo) L.; m. Farzana-Dom, Jan. 22, 2000. Diploma in acctg., Wits U., 1993. Group fin. mgr. Carpet & Decor Ctr Hld P/L, Johannesburg, Republic of South Africa, 1990-98; cost clk. Nampak Keartland Press, Johannesburg, Republic of South Africa, 1980-82; fin. acct. Star Foods P/L, Johannesburg, Republic of South Africa, 1983-86; cost contr. SA Oil Mills, Randfontein, Republic of South Africa, 1986-88;

group fin. acct. Fastfax P/L, Johannesburg, Republic of South Africa, 1988-89; with Ephron Body Parts P/L, 1998—; acctg. officer, tax cons. to various orgns., Republic of South Africa, 1994—. Fellow Chartered Inst. Bus. Mgmt.; mem. South African Inst. Mgmt., Chartered Inst. Secs. and Adminstrs. (assoc.), Inst. Chartered Accts. (assoc. gen. acct.). Mem. Nat. Party. Islam. Avocations: ten pin bowling, jogging, collecting stamps, motor racing. Home: 5 High Rd Fordsburg Flat 3, 2092 Johannesburg South Africa Office: PO Box 786353, 2146 Sandton Gauteng, South Africa

LUMBARD, ELIOT HOWLAND, lawyer, educator; b. Fairhaven, Mass., May 6, 1925; s. Ralph E. and Constance Y. L.; m. Jean Ashmore, June 21, 1947 (div.); m. Kirsten Dehner, June 28, 1981 (div.); children: Susan, John, Ann, Joshua Abel, Marah Abel. BS in Marine Transp., U.S. Mcht. Marine Acad., 1943-45; BS in Econs., U. Pa., 1949; JD, Columbia U., 1952. Bar: N.Y. 1953, U.S. Supreme Ct. 1959, Pa. 1983. Assoc. Breed, Abbott and Morgan, N.Y.C., 1952-53; asst. U.S. atty. So. Dist. N.Y., 1953-56; assoc. Chadbourne, Parke, Whiteside & Wolff, N.Y.C., 1956-58; ptnr. Townsend & Lewis, N.Y.C., 1961-70, Spear and Hill, N.Y.C., 1970-75, Lumbard and Phelan, P.C., N.Y.C., 1977-82, Saul, Ewing, Remick & Saul, N.Y.C., 1982-84; pvt. practice law N.Y.C., 1984-86; ptnr. Haight, Gardner, Poor & Havens, N.Y.C., 1986-88; pvt. practice law N.Y.C., 1988-92; ret.; chief counsel N.Y. State Commn. Investigation, 1958-61; spl. asst. counsel for law enforcement to Gov. N.Y., 1961-67; organizer N.Y. State Identification and Intelligence Sys., 1963-67; chair Oyster Bay Conf. on Organized Crime, 1962-67; criminal justice cons. to Gov. Fla. and other states, 1967; chief criminal justice cons. to N.H. Legis., 1968-69; chmn. com. on organized crime N.Y.C. Criminal Justice Coordinating Coun., 1971-74; organizer schs. of criminal justice at SUNY Albany and Rutgers, Newark; mem. departmental disciplinary com. First Dept., N.Y. Supreme Ct., 1982-88; trustee bankruptcy Universal Money Order Co., Inc., 1977-82, Meritum Corp., 1983-89; spl. master in admiralty Hellenic Lines Ltd., 1984-86; chmn. Palisades Life Ins. Co. (former Equity Funding subs. 1974-75); bd. dir. RMC Industries Corp.; chair Am. Maritime History Project, Inc., Kings Point, N.Y., 1996—; lectr. trial practice NYU Law Sch., 1963-65; mem. vis. com. Sch. Criminal Justice, SUNY-Albany, 1968-75; adj. prof. law and criminal justice John Jay Coll. Criminal Justice, CUNY, 1975-86; arbitrator Am. Arbitration Assn. and N.Y. Civil Ct.-Small Claims Part, N.Y. County; mem. Vol. Master Program U.S. Dist. Ct. (so. dist.) N.Y. Contbr. articles to profl. jours. Bd. dirs. Citizens Crime Commn. N.Y.C., Inc., Big Bros. Movement, Citizens Union; trustee Trinity Sch., 1964-78, N.Y.C. Police Found., Inc., 1971-92, chmn., 1971-74, emeritus. Lt. j.g. USNR, 1943-52. Mem. Assn. Bar City N.Y., N.Y. County Lawyers Assn., ABA, N.Y. State Bar Assn., Maritime Law Assn., Down Town Assn. Club. Republican. Home: 39B Apple Ln Hollis NH 03049-6311

LUMBROSO, HENRI RAPHAEL, chemist, educator; b. Alexandria, Egypt, Apr. 7, 1921; arrived in France, 1924; s. Albert and Georgette (Carasso) L.; m. Nicole Bader, June 30, 1947 (div. 1960); children: Claude, Gerard; m. Ruth Urbainczyk, Aug. 10, 1967; children: Anne, Marc. BS, U. Paris, 1939, BS in Phys. and Natural Scis., 1946; Engr., Ecole Nat. Superieure Chimie, Paris, 1942; DS in Phys. Chemistry, U. Paris, 1950. With ENSCP, 1940-42, CNRS, 1946-88; phys. chemist, rsch. dir. Paris, 1957-88; prof. postgrad. course Sorbonne/Paris, 1960-70; retired, 1988; referee in various scientific jours., 1950—; lectr. in field. Author: (books) Le Selenium, Le Tellure, 1977, others; contbr. articles to profl. jours. and publs. Recipient Marguerite de la Charlonie award French Acad. Sci., 1967. Office: Lab Chimie Generale, U Paris VI/4 Place Jussieu, F-75252 Paris France

LUMEIJ, JOHANNES THOMAS, veterinarian; b. London, Dec. 19, 1951; s. Lambert Lumeij and Mary Fraser; m. Johanna Smit, Dec. 10, 1987; children: Thomas, Maisie. BS, Ignatius Coll., Amsterdam, The Netherlands, 1967, Bischoppelijk Coll., Weert, 1970; DVM, U. Utrecht, The Netherlands, 1979, PhD, 1987. Diplomate Am. Bd. Veterinary Practitioners, European Coll. Avian Medicine & Surgery. Resident in internal medicine Faculty Veterinary Medicine U. Utrecht, The Netherlands, 1979-83, residen in avian & exotic animal medicine, 1983-85, asst. prof. avian & exotic animal medicine, 1985—; pres. European Coll. Avian Medicine and Surgery, 1993—. Avocations: sailing, hunting. Office: Divsn Avian & Exotic Med, Utrecht U Yalelaan 8, 3584 CM Utrecht The Netherlands

LUMME, KARI ANTERO, astronomy educator; b. Oulu, Finland, July 19, 1942; s. Antero and Synnöve (Sauso) L.; m. Ulla Maija Hammar, June 18, 1966; children: Kaisu, Sonja. MS, U. Oulu, 1966; PhD, U. Helsinki, 1973. Rsch. asst. Acad. of Finland, Helsinki, 1968-73; lectr. U. Helsinki, 1974-84, prof., 1985—; dir. dept. of astronomy, U. Helsinki, 1992—. Contbr. about 120 scientific articles to profl. jours. Mem. Internat. Astron. Union. Home: Aallokko 16 B 5, Espoo 02320, Finland Office: Observatory, U Helsinki, Helsinki 00140, Finland

LUMPKIN, NANCY ELLEN, physicist; b. Ridgewood, N.J., Oct. 26, 1956; d. Gustav Elmer and Elise Ruth (Linde) Johnson; m. Gregory Randolph Lumpkin, Mar. 18, 1978; 1 child, Jennifer Katherine. BS, Va. Poly. Inst., 1978; PhD, Macquarie U., 1998. Process engring. tech. Intel Corp., Rio Rancho, N.Mex., 1983-89; sr. tech. officer CSIRO, Marsfield, NSW, Australia, 1989-96; nanofrabrication process mgr. U. New South Wales, Sydney, 1996—; mgr. Ctr. Quantum Computer Tech. U. New South Wales. Avocations: gardening, hiking, dancing. Office: UNSW Physics Dept, Anzac Ave, Sydney NSW, Australia 2052

LUMSDEN, ANDREW GINO, neurobiologist, researcher; b. Beaconsfield, Berkshire, Eng., Jan. 22, 1947; s. Edward Gilbert and Stella Pirie (Lumsden) Sita; m. Anne Farrington Roberg, Nov. 20, 1970 (div. 1997); children: Ailsa, Isobel. BA with hons., Cambridge (Eng.) U., 1968, MA, 1972; PhD, London U., 1978. Lectr. in anatomy Guy's Hosp. Med. Sch., London, 1972-78, sr. lectr., 1978-86; reader in craniofacial development United Med. Dental Sch. Guy's and St. Thomas Hosps., London, 1986-89, prof. devel. neurobiology, 1989—; chmn. dept. devel. neurobiology Kings Coll., London, 1995—; mem. neurosci. bd. Med. Rsch. Coun., 1994-98, neurosci. panel Wellcome Trust Med. Rsch. Coun., 1997-2000; mem. Human Frontier Sci. Program Brain Functions rev. com., 1998-2001. Author: Essential Neural Development, 1997; contbr. articles to profl. jours. Grantee Wellcome Trust Med. Rsch. Coun., 1978—; Internat. Rsch. scholar Howard Hughes Med. Inst., 1992-98. Fellow Royal Soc.; mem. London Devel. Neurobiology Club (pres. 1989—). Avocations: natural history, mechanical engineering, bridge, Lotus 7s. Home: 16 Elephant Ln, London SE16 4JD, England Office: King's Coll London, Guy's Hosp/Devel Neurobiol, London SE1 1UL, England

LUNA, BARBARA CAROLE, financial analyst, accountant, appraiser; b. N.Y.C., July 23, 1950; d. Edwin A. and Irma S. (Schub) Schlang; m. Dennis Rex Luna, Sept. 1, 1974; children: John S., Katherine E. BA, Wellesley Coll., 1971; MS in Applied Math. and Fin. Analysis, Harvard U., 1973, PhD in Applied Math. and Fin. Analysis, 1975. CPA; cert. gen. real estate appraiser Calif. Office Real Estate Appraisers; cert. valuation analyst Nat. Assn. Cert. Valuation Analysts; cert. fraud examiner Assn. Cert. Fraud Examiners, mgmt. cons. Inst. Mgmt. Consultants; accredited sr. appraiser Am. Soc. Appraisers; accredited bus. valuation Am. Inst. CPAs. Investment banker Warburg Paribas Becker, L.A., 1975-77; cons., sr. mgr. Price Waterhouse, L.A., 1977-83; sr. mgr. litigation Pannell Kerr Forster, L.A., 1983-86; nat. dir. litigation cons. Kenneth Leventhal & Co., L.A., 1986-88; ptnr. litigation svcs. Coopers & Lybrand, L.A., 1988-93; sr. ptnr. litigation svcs. White, Zuckerman, Warsavsky, Luna & Wolf, Sherman Oaks, Calif., 1993—. Wellesley scholar, 1971. Mem. AICPA, Assn. Bus. Trial Lawyers (com. on experts), Am. Soc. Appraisers, Assn. Cert. Valuation Analysts, Calif. Office Real Estate Appraisers, Assn. Cert. Real Estate Appraisers, Appraisal Inst., Assn. Cert. Fraud Examiners, Inst. Mgmt. Cons., Calif. Soc. CPAs (econ. damages common interest mem. svcs. com., fraud common interest mem. svcs. com., bus. valuation common interest mem. svcs. com.), Am. Bd. Forensic Accts. and Examiners. Avocations: golf, swimming. Home: 18026 Rodarte Way Encino CA 91316-4370

LUNA, FLORENCIA, humanities educator bioethics, researcher; b. Berne, Switzerland, May 16, 1960; arrived in Argentina, 1962; d. Félix Cesar Luna and Raquel Felisa De La Fuente; m. Aldo Marcelo Agustoni, Aug. 4, 1984; children: Lucio Agustoni, Marco Agustoni. License, U. Buenos Aires, 1987, PhD, 1996; MA, Columbia U., 1992. Tchg. asst. U. Buenos Aires, 1985-95, adj. prof. dept. philosophy, 1998—, prof. bioethics, 1997-99, dir. rsch. grant, 1998—; dir. Flacso, Argentina, 1995—; vis. scholar Hastings Ctr., 1996; external referee Conicet, Buenos Aires, 1997-98; temporary adviser WHO, Geneva, 1997; fellow XXI Century Trust, Eng., 1998; cons. Cioms, Geneva, 1999. Co-author: Life and Death Decisions and Bioethics, 1995; editor Bioethic Perspectives in the Ams., 1996—, Philosophical Analysis: Bioethics, 1997; editl. cons. Dictionary of World Philosophy, 1997-99; contbr. articles to profl. jours. Career grantee Antorchas, 1999—. Mem. Internat. Assn. Bioethics (bd. dirs. 1999), Argentine Soc. Philos. Analysis, Argentine Assn. Philosophy. Home: Ugarteche 3050 4o 87, 1425 Capital Federal Argentina

LUNA, MARIA DAS GRAÇAS, microbiologist; b. Rio de Janeiro, May 17, 1963; d. Mansel Soares and Josefa Guedes L.; m. Ulisses Leite Gomes, Aug. 17, 1985; 1 child, Ugo de Luna Gomes. PhD, U. Fed., Rio de Janeiro, 1996. Tchr. U. Estado, Rio de Janeiro, 1997—. Contbr. articles to profl. jours. Mem. Am. Soc. Microbiology. Office: Univ Estado, Av 28 de Setembro 87 Jundos, 20551030 Rio de Janeiro Brazil

LUND, JAMES LOUIS, lawyer; b. Long Beach, Calif., Oct. 4, 1926; s. G. Louis and Hazel Eunice (Cochran) L.; m. Jo Alvarez, Aug. 5, 1950; 1 son, Eric James. Student, Stanford U., 1943; postgrad., Grad. Sch. Annapolis, 1949; JD, Southwestern U., 1955; postgrad. Sch. Law, U. So. Calif., 1956. Bar: Calif. 1955, U.S. Dist. Ct. (cen. dist.) Calif. 1955, U.S. Ct. Appeals (9th cir.) 1955, U.S. Tax Ct. 1955, U.S. Supreme Ct. Spl. agt. U.S. Govt., 1950-52; gen. mgr. Pacific ops., gen. counsel Holmes & Narver, Inc., L.A., 1952-66; exec. v.p. Calif. Fabricators, Oakland and Honolulu, 1966-67; sr. ptnr. James Lund Law Firm, Beverly Hills, Tehran, London and Tokyo, 1967-83; pres., founder Fortres Mgmt. Co.; ptnr. Lund & Lund, 1983—. Lt. comdr. USNR, 1943-46, 48-50. Mem. ABA, SAR, L.A. County Bar Assn., Internat. Bar Assn., Inter-Am. Bar Assn., Asia Pacific Lawyers Assn., Les Ambassadeurs Club (London). Office: Ste 1555 1901 Avenue Of The Stars Los Angeles CA 90067-6052

LUND, PEERE CAROE, anesthesiologist; b. Dickson, Alta., Can., Mar. 17, 1915; arrived in Mex., 1981; s. Johannes and Ellen (Caroe) L.; m. Ana Fernanda Hernandez, Apr. 6, 1989; m. Eileen Northcott, 1941 (div. Aug. 1988); children: John Gary, Gregory Northcott, Ingrid Richardson. MD, U. Alta., Edmonton, Can., 1940. Diplomate Am. Bd. Anesthesiologists. Chief anesthetist Deer Lodge Mil. Hosp., Winnipeg, Can., 1944-47; dir. dept. anesthesiology Meml. Hosp., Johnstown, 1947-76, dir. anesthesia residency program, 1956-81; dir. Meml. Hosp. Pain Clinic, 1955-81; cons. P.C. Lund-Pain Mgmt. Ctr., 1982—; clin. prof. anesthesiology U. Pitts., 1961-81. Author of 2 anesthesia textbooks and numersous sci. articles. Named Physician of Yr., Cambria County Med. Soc., 1978. Fellow Royal Coll. Physicians (Can.), Am. Coll. Anesthesiologists, Internat. Coll. Anesthesiology, Royal Soc. Health, Royal Soc. Medicine; mem. Am. Soc. Regional Anesthesia (Gaston Labat award 1983), Coun. of Can. (licentiate), Guadalajara Shrine Club (pres. 1997—). Avocations: golf, reading, gardening, educational traveling, writing. Home: Apdo # 550, Brisas del Lago # 8, Chapala Jalisco, Mexico Office: PO Box 550, Chapal Jalisco, Mexico

LUND, TORBEN, educator; b. Aarhus, Denmark, Oct. 7, 1949; arrived in England, 1987; s. Arnt and Rigmor Cecilie Wisman (Lorenzen) L. MS, Tech. U., Denmark, 1973; PhD, Aarhus U., Denmark, 1978. Rsch. scientist Rugshops., Copenhagen, 1983-86; lectr. U. Coll. London, sr. lectr., reader; cons. in field. Postdoctoral fellow EMBO, Heidelberg, Germany, 1980. Mem. Danish Soc. Engrs., Brit. Soc. Immunology. Avocations: literature, films. Office: Dept Immunology, 46 Cleveland St, London W1P 6PD, England

LUND, VICTOR L., retail food company executive; b. Salt Lake City, 1947; married. BA, U. Utah, 1969, MBA, 1972. Audit mgr. Ernst and Whinney, Salt Lake City, 1972-77; sr. v.p. Skaggs Cos. Inc., from 1977; v.p., contr. Am. Stores Co., 1980-83, sr. v.p., contr., from 1983, exec. v.p., co-chief exec. officer, vice-chmn., chief fin. and adminstrv. officer, pres., CEO, dir., 1992-95, chmn., CEO, dir., 1995-99; vice chmn. bd. dirs. Albertsons Inc., Boise. Office: Albertsons Inc 250 Park Ctr Blvd Boise ID 83726-0001 also: Am Stores Co 709 E South Temple Salt Lake City UT 84102-1205

LUND, WILLIAM BOYCE, computer analyst, project leader; b. Indpls., Nov. 27, 1959; s. Ralph Emerson Jr. and Madge Etta (Major) L.; m. Kathleen L. Faust, May 15, 1985; children: William Koss, Lorraine Kathleen, Kelly Marie, Kevin James. BA in Math. and Computer Sci., Ind. U., 1982; MS in Info. and Comms. Scis., Ball State U., 1988. Programmer, analyst RCA Consumer Electronics, Indpls., 1983-85; analyst, programmer Boehringer Mannheim, Indpls., 1985-87; mgmt. assoc. Citibank (S.D.) N.A., Sioux Falls, S.D., 1988-95, Citicorp, Hagerstown, Md., 1995-96, 98—; product mgr. Paysys Internat., Norcross, Ga., 1996-98; cons. Marsh Supermarkets, Ball State U. Vol. Pan Am. Games/PAX I, Indpls., 1987; United Way coord. Citibank Info. Svcs., 1988, Citibank S.D., 1990-91; fgn. exch. student host parent, 1990-92. Ind. Bell fellow, 1986; Internat. Comms. Assn. scholar, 1986. Mem. IEEE (computer & comms. socs.). Avocations: basketball, computers, home improvement, gardening, audio visual production. Office: Citicorp CCSI Fl 2 14700 Citicorp Dr Bldg 3 Hagerstown MD 21742-6000

LUND-ADAMS, MARGARET GRACE, nutritionist, researcher; b. Rockhampton, Australia, June 24, 1960; d. Charles Harold and Grace Edith (Howland) L.; m. Lawrence Mark Adams, July 27, 1991; children: Miranda Sue, Taylor Howard. BS, U. Queensland, Australia, 1981; postgrad. diploma nutrition, dietetics, Queensland U. Tech., 1983; MPH, U. Hawaii, 1989. Dietitian Greenslopes Repatriation Hosp., Brisbane, Australia, 1983-84; nutritionist Save the Children Fund Australia, Port Vila Vanuatu, 1984-87; assoc. lectr. nutrition program U. Queensland, Brisbane, 1989-94, casual cons. nutrition program, 1995—. Contbr. articles to profl. jours. Recipient East-West Ctr. scholarship, Hawaii, 1987-89, Save the Children Fund UK scholarship, 1987. Mem. Dietitians Assn. Australia.

LUNDAHL, STEVEN MARK, musician, consultant; b. Bloomington, Minn., Aug. 19, 1955; s. John Miles and Zita Marguerite (Otto) L.; m. Genevieve Catherine Munoz, May 24, 1980 (div.); children: Alexandra Maia, Anders Braeden; m. Kathryn Rose Southworth, Aug. 12, 1995; 1 child, Malia Rose. MusB in Edn., Coll. of St. Scholastica, 1979. Music dir. Utah Shakespearean Festival, Cedar City, Utah, 1979-81; pres. Boston Early Music Ctr., 1980-84; mem. New Eng. Baroque Ensemble, Boston, 1981-86, Waverly Consort, N.Y.C., 1985—; pres. Lundahl Assocs., 1990-97, Lundahl Corp., 1997—; founding mem. Boston Shawm and Sackbut Ensemble, Boston, 1981—; computer cons., 1984—. Performer, interpreter of medieval, Renaissance and Baroque instruments; rec. artist Smithsonian Chamber Players, Musical Heritage Soc., Nat. Pub. Radio, Angel/EMI, Harmonia Mundi, Telarc, Erato; guest artist Boston Camerata, 1984—, Calliope: A Renaissance Band, 1985—. Mem. Am. Fedn. Musicians 1974—. Avocation: computer cons. Home and Office: 33 Layton Dr Canterbury NH 03224-2017

LUNDBERG, PER OLOV MAGNUS, neurology educator; b. Vänersborg, Sweden, Apr. 12, 1931; s. Ernst Magnus and Lilly (Wallgren) L.; m. Kerstie Sjöberg, Dec. 4, 1960; children: Ann Charlotte, Eva Maria. MD, Uppsala (Sweden) U., 1957, PhD in Anatomy, 1960. Lic. physician. Rsch. asst. anatomy U. Uppsala, 1950-58, jr. physician, asst. prof. neurology, 1958-74, prof., head neurology dept., 1974-96, med. dir. univ. hosp., 1978-83; med. adviser Nat. Bd. Health and Welfare, Sweden, 1975—; mem. adv. bd. Med. Products Agy., Uppsala, 1981-98. Editor: Sexology, 1994; editor in chief Scandinavian Jour. Sexology, 1997—. Mem. Uppsala County Coun., 1974-85. Recipient Dr. Herman Musaph prize Med. Sexology, 1997. Mem. Scandinavian Migraine Soc. (founder, former pres.), Internat. Acad. Sex Rsch. (charter mem.; pres. 1991-93), Nordic Assn. Clin. Sexology (founder, pres. 1997—), Acad. Sci. Sexologicae Polonia (hon.), Soc. Sexuologica Bohemica (hon.), Swedish Migraine Soc. (hon.), European Fedn. Neurol. Socs. (chmn. task force for neurosexology), Albert Schweitzer World Acad. Medicine. Mem. Moderata Samlings Partiet. Avocation: ornitology. Home: Tallbacksvägen 19, S 756 45 Uppsala Sweden Office: U Hosp, Dept Neurology, S 751 85 Uppsala Sweden

LUNDBERG, ULF INGVAR, biological psychology educator; b. Stockholm, June 21, 1943; s. Gustav Hilding and Alva Ingegerd (Liljedahl) L.; m. Agneta Lagerhed, Apr. 15, 1969; children: Nina Maria, Anna Kristin. BA, Stockholm U., 1965, PhD, 1972. Rsch. Karolinska Inst., Stockholm, 1972-88, acting prof. psychology, 1983-90; rsch. asst. dept. psychology Stockholm U., 1965-72, assoc. prof., 1976-90, prof. biol. psychology, 1990—; head divsn. biol. psychology Stockholm U., 1990—, co-chairperson dept. psychology, 1992-96; vis. assoc. prof. Uniformed Svcs. U. of Health Scis., Bethesda, Md., 1981. Editor-in-Chief Internat. Jour. Behavioral Medicine; contbr. numerous articles on stress, health and behavior to sci. publs. Mem. AAAS, Internat. Soc. Behavior Medicine, N.Y. Acad. Scis. Fax: 46 8 16 78 47. E-mail: ul@psychology.su.se. Home: Lönnvägen 17A, S-135 52 Tyresö Sweden Office: Stockholm U Dept Psychology, Frescati Hagväg 14, S-106 91 Stockholm Sweden

LUNDBERGH, PER RUNO, physician; b. Sundsvall, Sweden, Mar. 2, 1938; s. Runo T. and Ingrid M. (Nyberg) L.; m. Inger M. Lundstam, May 2, 1964; children: Fredrik, Elisabet. MD, Uppsala (Sweden) U., 1964; PhD, Karolinska Inst., Stockholm, 1974. Diploma Tropical Medicine and Hygiene. Physician Infectious Diseases Hosp., Stockholm, 1964-74; head dept., 1984-89; assoc. prof. Karolinska Inst., Stockholm, 1974—; head dept. Commn. Disease Control, 1989—. Fellow Swedish Med. Soc., Swedish Med. Assn., Infectious Disease Soc. (sec. 1973-75). Home: Lärkväg 16A, 183 51 Täby Sweden Office: Karolinska Hosp, 171 76 Stockholm Sweden

LUNDBLAD, ERIC ROY, finance executive; b. Mpls., Sept. 23, 1959; arrived in Hong Kong, 1993; s. Rodger Roy and Joanna Cloud (Spooner) L. BA, Middlebury Coll., 1982; MBA, U. Pa., 1988. Internat. banking officer Norwest Banks, Mpls., 1982-86; mgmt. cons. Bain & Co., Boston, 1988-91; planning cons. Frito-Lay, Inc., Plano, Tex., 1991-93; mgr. corp. fin. Hong Kong br. PepsiCo, Inc., 1993-97; sr. dir. Treasury Asia Pacific Tricon Restaurants, Internat., Causeway Bay, Hong Kong, 1997—. Avocations: traveling, scuba diving, study of Mandarin Chinese language. Office: Tricon Restaurants Internat, 1 Harbour View St Ste 607-8 6/F, Central Hong Kong

LUNDBLAD, ROGER LAUREN, biotechnology consultant; b. San Francisco, Oct. 31, 1939; s. Lauren Alfred and Doris Ruth (Peterson) L.; m. Susan Hawly Taylor, Oct. 15, 1966 (div. 1985); children: Christina Susan, Cynthia Karin. BSc, Pacific Luth. U., 1961; PhD, U. Wash., 1965. Rsch. assoc. U. Wash., Seattle, 1965-66, Rockefeller U., N.Y.C., 1966-68; asst. prof. U. N.C., Chapel Hill, 1968-71, assoc. prof., 1971-77, prof. pathology and biochemistry, 1977-91; adj. prof., 1991—; dir. sci. tech. devel. Baxter-Hyland/Immuno, Duarte, Calif., 1991-99; biotech. cons., 2000—; vis. scientist Hyland div. Baxter Healthcare, Glendale, Calif., 1988-89. Author: Chemical Reagents for Protein Modification, 1984, 2d edit., 1990; editor: Chemistry and Biology of Thrombin, 1977, Chemistry and Biology of Heparin, 1980, Techniques in Protein Modification, 1994; editor-in-chief: Biotechnology and Applied Biochemistry, 1996—; contbr. articles to profl. jours. Recipient Career Achievement award U. N.C., 1986. Mem. Am. Soc. Biochem. Molecular Biology, Am. Soc. Microbiology, Am. Heart Assn., Sigma Xi. Office: 102 Weatherstone Dr Apt C Chapel Hill NC 27514-1587

LUNDBURG, FRANK LEONARD, conservationist; b. Lakeland, Fla., June 18, 1944; s. Kenneth Gordon and Harriet Leonard L. BA in Govt., Idaho State U., 1967; MA in Polit. Sci., U. Oreg., 1969. Asst. tng. officer Idaho Dept. Health & Welfare, Boise, 1976-77; asst. to gov. Office of Gov., Boise, 1977-80; pvt. practice pub. policy cons. Boise, 1980-94; info. officer Idaho Dept. Fish and Game, Boise, 1994-95; natural resources cons., wildlife educator Reptile Conservation Resources, Boise, 1995—. Editor Idaho Dem., 1987-90; contbr. articles to profl. jours. Pres. North End Neighborhood Assn., Boise, 1987, Idaho Herpetolog. Soc., 1990-94; legis. cons. Idaho Wildlife Fedn., 1997-2000. With U.S. Army, 1969-71. Recipient Outstanding Contbn. to Herpetology award Idaho Herpetol. Soc., 1994; named one of Outstanding Young Men in Am., 1977, 80. Mem. Idaho Acad. Sci., Idaho Herpetol. Soc., Idaho Wildlife Fedn., Pi Sigma Alpha, Pi Kappa Delta. Democrat. E-mail: repconres@aol.com. Office: Reptile Conservation Resources PO Box 6329 Boise ID 83707-6329

LUNDE, ASBJORN RUDOLPH, lawyer; b. S.I., N.Y., July 17, 1927; s. Karl and Elisa (Andenes) L. AB, Columbia U., 1947, LLB, 1949. Bar: N.Y. 1949. Pvt. practice N.Y.C., 1950-91; with Kramer, Marx, Greenlee & Backus and predecessors, 1950-68, mem., 1958-68; pvt. practice Columbia County, N.Y., 1991—. Bd. dirs., v.p. Orch. da Camera, Inc., 1964—, Sara Roby Found., 1971—; bd. dirs. Clarion Concerts in Columbia County, 1999—; mem. vis. com. dept. European paintings Met. Mus. Art. Fellow Met. Mus. Art (life); mem. ABA, N.Y. State Bar Assn., Assn. Bar City N.Y., Met. Opera Club, East India Club (London). Avocation: art collecting (donor paintings and sculptures to Met. Mus. Art, N.Y.C., Nat. Gallery Art, Washington, Mus. Fine Arts, Boston, Clark Art Inst., Williamstown, Mass., others). Home and Office: 135 LaBranche Rd Hillsdale NY 12529-5713

LUNDE, DOLORES BENITEZ, retired secondary education educator; b. Honolulu, Apr. 12, 1929; d. Frank Molero and Matilda (Francisco) Benitez; m. Nuell Carlton Lunde, July 6, 1957; 1 child, Laurelle. BA, U. Oreg., 1951, postgrad., 1951-52; postgrad., U. So. Calif., L.A., 1953-54, Colo. State U., 1957-58, Calif. State U., Fullerton, 1967-68. Cert. gen. secondary tchr., Calif.; cert. lang. devel. specialist. Tchr. Brawley (Calif.) Union High Sch., 1952-55; tchr. Fullerton (Calif.) Union High Sch. Dist., 1955-73; tchrs. aide Placentia (Calif.) Unified Sch. Dist., 1983-85; tchr. continuing edn. Fullerton Union High Sch. Dist., 1985-91; tchr. Fullerton Sch. Dist., 1988, Fullerton Union H.S. Dist., 1989-94; presenter regional and state convs., so. Calif., 1986-88. Innovator tests, teaching tools, audio-visual aids. Vol. Luth. Social Svcs., Fullerton, 1981-82, Messiah Luth., Yorba Linda, Calif., 1981-88, 91—. Recipient Tchr. of Yr. award Fullerton Union High Sch. Dist., 1989. Mem. NEA, AAUW (life, bull. editor 1979-80, corr. sec. 1981-83, program v.p. 1983-84, gift honoree Fullerton br. 1985), Calif. State Tchrs. Assn., Fullerton Secondary Tchrs. Assn., Internat. Club/Spanish Club (advisor La Habra, Calif. 1965-72), Tchrs. English to Speakers Other Langs., Calif. Assn. Tchrs. English to Speakers Other Langs. Avocations: singing, folk and interpretive dance, guitar, reading, travel. Home: 4872 Ohio St Yorba Linda CA 92886-2713

LUNDESTAD, GEIR, historian, educator; b. Sulitjelma, Nordland, Norway, Jan. 17, 1945; s. Bjarne and Anny Elvine (Nilsen-Nygaard) L.; m. Aase Synnøve Liland, July 29, 1967; children: Erik, Helge. MA, U. Oslo, 1970; PhD, U. Tromsø, Norway, 1976. Asst. prof. history U. Tromsø, 1974-79; fellow Warren Ctr., Harvard U., Cambridge, Mass., 1978-79; prof. U. Tromsø, 1979-90; fellow Woodrow Wilson Ctr., Washington, 1988-89; dir. Norwegian Nobel Inst., Oslo, 1990—; sec. Nobel Peace Prize Com., 1990—; vis. scholar Ctr. for Internat. Affairs, Harvard U., Cambridge, Mass., 1983; v.p. U. Tromsø, 1981-83. Author: The American Non-Policy Towards Eastern Europe 1943-47, 1976, America, Scandinavia and the Cold War, 1980, East, West, North, South, 1987, 4th edit., 1999, The American "Empire", 1990, The Fall of Great Powers: Peace, Stability and Legitimacy, 1994, "Empire" by Integration The United States and European Integration, 1945-1997, 1998, No End to Alliance, 1998; TV and radio commentator Norwegian Broadcasting; contbr. articles to profl. jours. Chmn. coun. Norwegian Inst. Internat. Affairs, Oslo, 1977-91; active Norwegian Arms Control and Disarmament Adv. Coun., 1986—. Mem. Soc. for Historians Am. Fgn. Rels., Nordic Assn. for Am. Studies, Norwegian Acad. Scis. and Letters, Royal Hist. Soc. (U.K.). Mem. Labor Party. Lutheran. Avocations: sports, soccer. Home: Thomas Heftyesgt 56, 0267 Oslo Norway Office: Norwegian Nobel Inst, Drammensveien 19, Oslo 2, Norway

LUNDGREN, RICHARD JOHN, real estate executive, city planner; b. N.Y.C., Dec. 13, 1940; s. John H. and Helen C. (Vetter) L.; m. Nancy Whitin Truslow, Apr. 1, 1972; children: Andrew Auchincloss, Elizabeth Whitin. BS, Rensselaer Poly. Inst., 1964; MS, Pratt Inst., 1968; MPA, Harvard U., 1990. Sr. planner Herr Assocs., Boston, 1968-69; project dir. Boston Redevel. Authority, 1969-72; dir. planning Hilgenhurst & Assocs., Boston, 1972-77; v.p. Hunneman Comml. Co., Boston, 1977-82, sr. v.p., 1982-94, pres., 1994—. Trustee The Trustees of Reservations, 1985—, Emerald Necklace Conservancy, 1997—, Mass. Farm and Conservation Lands Trust, 1985-92, Boston Local Devel. Corp., 1986-91; dir. Boston Advisors Initiative for a Competitive Inner City, 1999—, Vis. Nurse Assn. of Boston, 1972-82; mem. Met. Area Planning Coun., 1978-80, Boston Coord.

Com., 1983, Mass. Gov.'s Com. on Pvt. Rental Housing Prodn., 1983-84, Boston Mayor's Com. on Linkage, 1983-84, Center City Task Force, 1983-87, Boston Mayor's Jobs Liaison Com., 1984-90, Park Plz. Citic Ctr. Adv. Com., 1985-86; Boston Employment Com., 1986-88; chmn. Mass. Realtors Pub. Policy Com., 1989; mem. adv. com. Boston U. Sch. for Real Estate Studies, 1986-91. Served with USCGR, 1968-72. Named Greater Boston Realtor of Yr., 1984. Mem. Am. Planning Assn., Nat. Assn. Realtors, Mass. Assn. Realtors, Greater Boston Real Estate Bd. (bd. dirs. 1982-89, pres. 1983), Greater Boston Bldg. Owners and Mgrs. Assn. (bd. dirs. 1979-88, pres. 1982), Somerset Club (Boston), Harvard Club (N.Y.C., Boston), The Country Club (Brookline, Mass.), Mass. Hist. Soc., Boston Athenaeum. Episcopalian. Home: 48 Centre St Dover MA 02030-2207 Office: Hunneman Comml Co 70-80 Lincoln St Boston MA 02111-2611

LUNDIN, LENA GUNHILD MARGARETA, science educator, researcher; b. Stockholm, July 18, 1940; d. Albert and Agnes (Ekholm) Bergh; m. 1964 (div. 1981); children: (twins) Peter, Pia. BSc, Stockholm U., 1987, PhD in Environ. Psychology, 1993. Occupl. therapist Flen, Sweden, 1962-66; tchr. art ABF, Flen, 1969-76; rsch. asst. Karolinska Inst. and Stockholm U., 1985-91; rschr., owner Luftkvalitotskonsulten, Stockholm, 1992—; lectr. pub. health BIH, Karlskrona, Sweden, 1994-95; sr. lectr. Kristianstad (Sweden) U., 1996—; reviewer Swedish Coun. Bldg. Rsch., 1994—. Author: On Building Related Causes of the Sick Building Syndrome, 1991; editor report Swedish Nat. Bd. Housing; contbr. over 25 articles to sci. jours., including Indoor Air. Mem. ASHRAE, Swedish Soc. Physicians, Internat. Soc. Indoor Air Quality (mem. task force II 1993-96, task force VII 1996—). E-mail: lundin.lena@telia.com.

LUNDMAN, ULF PETER MICHAEL, lawyer, composer, writer; b. Helsingborg, Sweden, Sept. 1, 1953; s. Bruno Gottfried and Carla Helena Theresa (Olsson) L.; m. Marion Bast, May 25, 1985; children: Isabella, Mariella. Grad., U. Lund, Sweden, 1978, diploma cum laude, 1979. Notary Alingsas Ct., Sweden, 1978, Sjuharadsbygdens Ct., Boras, Sweden, 1979-80, Lansratten, Gothenburg, 1980-81; atty. Dist. Atty. Gothenburg, Sweden, 1979—; pvt. practice Gothenburg, 1982—; with SKF, Gothenburg, 1971-75. Author, composer: (record album) I Farsens drömmar, 1987. Elected controller City Gothenburg, 1982-90. With spl. svcs. Swedish Airforce, 1973-74. Mem. Swedish Bar Assn. Folkpartiet. Office: Advokathuset Gamlestaden, Saveans Strandgata, 41505 Göteborg Sweden

LUND-OLESEN, KNUD, physician, retired; b. Horsens, Denmark, Aug. 12, 1920; s. Anton and Valborg (Jørgensen) Olesen; m. Inger Merete Scheel Nissen, Sept. 3, 1960; children: Lisbet, Henrik, Pia, Susanne, Solveig. MD, U. Aarhus, 1957. Diplomate Rheumatology and Internal Medicine. Reader Aarhus (Denmark) U., 1959-61; gen. practitioner Spørring, Denmark, 1961-64; cons. Assens (Denmark) Hosp., 1965, Odense (Denmark) U. Hosp., 1965-70; chief physician Ringe (Denmark) Hosp., 1970-90; ret., 1990. Author articles on oxygen tension, orgotein sod, fibromyalgia and multiple sclerosis. Mem. Danish Soc. Rheumatology, Danish Soc. Internal Medicine. Lutheran. Avocations: gardening. Home: Holkebjergvej 10, 5250 Odense SV, Denmark

LUNDQUIST, KNUT OLOF, wood chemistry educator; b. Lund, Sweden, Aug. 26, 1933; s. Arthur and Hertha (Hansson) L.; m. Gunilla Björkman; children: Margareta, Jan. D Tech., Chalmers U. Tech., Göteborg, Sweden, 1973. Docent in organic chemistry Chalmers U. Tech., Göteborg, 1973-95, prof., 1995—. Fellow Internat. Acad. Wood Sci. Office: Chalmers U Tech, Sch Chem Engring, S-41296 Göteborg Sweden

LUNDQUIST, STEFAN HELGE, industrial engineering company executive; b. Solefteå, Sweden, June 26, 1950; s. Helge and Inga-Britt (Fjellstrom) L.; m. Elisabet K. Lundquist, Oct. 20, 1984; children: Charlotte, Joakim. MS in Elec. Engring., Charles U., Göteborg, Sweden, 1976; PhD in Elec. Engring., Chalmers U., Götteborg, 1981. Rsch. asst. dept. optoelectronics and elec. measurements Chalmers U., Göteborg, 1976-80, sr. scientist, 1981-84, asst. prof., acting head dept., 1984-85; staff scientist Saab Dynamics AB, Göteborg, 1985-95; devel. mgr. AltOptronic AB, Göteborg, 1995—. Patentee in field. Mem. SPIE. Office: AltOptronic AB, Box 8910, S-402 73 Göteborg Sweden

LUNDQVIST, MONS, laboratory manager; b. Malmö, Sweden, June 7, 1967; arrived in Denmark, 1993; s. Leif and Agneta (Berg) L.; m. Eva Nielsen, May 31, 1997. MS in Chem. Engring., Lund (Sweden) U., 1991; univ. diploma in bus. adminstrn., Copenhagen Bus. Sch., 1997. Cert. European engr. European Fedn. Nat. Engring. Assns., 1994. Lab. engr. devel. analytical chemistry Astra Draco, Lund, 1991-92; rsch. chemist and lab. supr. Heparin Rsch. Lab., Leo Pharm. Products, Copenhagen, 1992-98; lab. mgr. analytical lab. DuPont Chemoswed, Malmö, Sweden, 1998—. With Signal Corps Swedish mil., 1986-87. Mem. Swedish Soc. Chem. Engrs., Danish Chem. Soc., Swedish Chem. Soc., Am. Chem. Soc. Home: Mariedalsvågen 48A, S-217 45 Malmö Sweden Office: DuPont Chemoswed, PO Box 839, S-20180 Malmö Sweden

LUNDSTEN, RALPH, composer, film director, artist, writer; b. Ersnäs, Sweden, Oct. 6, 1936. Owner picture and elec. music studio, Sweden, 1959—. Composer numerous recs. including Nordic Nature Symphony No. 1, The Water Sprite, No. 2 Johannes and the Lady of the Woods, No. 3 A Midwinter Saga, No. 4 A Summer Saga, No. 5 Bewitched, No. 6 Landscape of Dreams, No. 7 The Seasons, Erik XIV and Gustav III, Cosmic Love, Ourfather, Nightmare, Horrorscope, Shangri-La, Universe, Discophrenia, Alpha Ralpha Boulevard, Paradise Symphony, Cosmic Phantazy, The Dream Master, The Gate of Time, The Ages of Man, Sea Symphony, Mindscape Music, Nordic Light, The Symphony of Joy (decicated to UN 50th anniversary), The Symphony of Light, The Symphony of Love, In Time and Space, Andromedian Tales, Happy Earthday; also filmmaker 12 short films, exhibited art work; author: (book and CD) Lustbarheter. Recipient Grand Prix Biennale, Paris, 1967, Swedish Film Inst. prize, 1964-67, Schwingungen prize, 1997, numerous other awards for music and filmmaking. Mem. London Diplomatic Acad. E-mail: ralph.lundsten@andromeda.se. Office: Frankenburgs väg 1, SE-13242 Saltsjö-Boo Sweden

LUNDY, ANSTIS BURWELL, artist; b. Plainfield, N.J., Aug. 28, 1924; d. William Russell and Aubrey (Eaton) Burwell; m. William Ames Atchley, Apr. 14, 1945 (div. 1955); 1 child Mark Ames Atchley; m. Victor Alfred Lundy, Sept. 19, 1960; 1 child, Nicholas Burwell Lundy. Student, Cours Fenelon, Paris, 1938, Cleve. Inst. Art, 1940-42, Boston Mus. Sch. Fine Arts, 1942-43, Glassell Sch. Art, 1977-81. Draftmans Harvard U., Cambridge, Mass., 1943-46, various archtl. and engring. cos., 1946-58, Fritz Benedict, Architect, FAIA, Aspen, Colo., 1958-59; art tchr. Anderson Ranch Art Ctr., Aspen, 1984-88, 90-93, Southwest Craft Ctr., San Antonio, 1985, Beaumont (Tex.) Art League, 1981, Spring Island, S.C., 1998; and yrly. workshops Aspen, 1993-2000. One-woman shows include Patricia Moore Gallery, Aspen, 1970, 82, 85, 90, 94, 96, Silvermine Guild Artists, New Canaan, Conn., 1972, Moody Gallery, Houston, 1984, 87, 92, Katharina Rich Perlow Gallery, N.Y.C., 1988, Evelyn Siegel Gallery, Ft. Worth, 1992, 95, Adelson Gallery, Aspen, 1996; exhibited in group shows at Silvermine Guild Artists, 1969, Guilford Art League, 1969, Creative Arts Workshop, New Haven, Conn., 1969, Moody Gallery, 1980, 85, Houston Art League, 1980, 81, Glassell Sch., Houston, 1981, Springfield Art Mus., Mo., 1981, Watercolor Art Soc., Houston, 1981, 82, 83, 84, 85, Art Ctr., Waco, Tex., 1982, Houston Festival, 1982, McNay Mus., San Antonio, 1983, Toni Jones Gallery, Houston, 1984, Transco Tower Gallery, Houston, 1985, 87, 88, Perception Gallery, Houston, 1986, Cullen Ctr., Houston, 1986, Sheraton Gallery, Dallas, 1986, 1401 W. Gray Gallery, Houston, 1988, Zan's, 1990, Aries Gallery, 1990, Butera's Cafe, Houston, 1991, Galveston Arts Ctr., Tex., 1991, Barney Wykoff Gallery, Aspen, 1995, Lobby Gallery, Houston, 1996, Cloister Gallery, Houston, 1997; represented in permanent collections Transco Energy, Tex. Commerce Banks, U. Houston, 1010 Lamar Restaurant, Moody-Rambin, Baylor Coll. Medicine, Wilson Industries, CBS, Gerald Hines Galleria, Enron, Continental Airlines, St. Luke's Tower, The Little Nell Hotel. Nat. coun. bd. Anderson Ranch Arts Ctr., Aspen, 1997-2000; sponsor Mus. Fine Arts, Houston, 1997-2000, Contemporary Arts Mus., Houston, 1997-2000; donor Aspen Art Mus., 1990-2000. Studio: Anstis Lundy Studio 701 Mulberry Ln Bellaire TX 77401-3805

LUNDY, JACKELYN RUTH, consulting firm owner, economist, researcher; b. Palo Alto, Calif., Nov. 8, 1951; d. Jack E. and Ruthe A. (Rose) L.; 1 child, Maia Rose. BA, U. Calif., Davis, 1973, MS, 1976, PhD, 1987. Staff rsch. assoc. U. Calif., Davis, 1976-80; tech. assistance officer Nat. Consumer Coop. Bank, Washington, 1980-82; assoc. analyst Calif. Office Econ. Opportunity, Sacramento, 1982-87; assoc. dir. agroecology program U. Calif., Santa Cruz, 1987-93, acting dir. Ctr. for Agroecology, 1993-97; owner Lundy and Assocs., Palo Alto, Calif., 1997—. Contbr. numerous articles to profl. jours. Bd. dirs. Internat. Tree Crops Inst., Davis, 1983—, Assoc. Coops., Richmond, Calif., 1994-96; mem. supervisory com. Santa Cruz Cmty. Credit Union, 1987-97. Fellow Resources for Future, 1988, leadership fellow Kellogg Found., 1991-94. Avocations: breeding and training golden retrievers, storytelling, tennis, piano. Office: Lundy and Assocs 598 Loma Verde Ave Palo Alto CA 94306-3032

LUNDY, J(OSEPH) EDWARD, retired automobile company executive; b. Iowa, Jan. 6, 1915; s. Vern E. and Mary L. (Chambers) L. B.A., U. Iowa, 1936. Fellow Princeton U., 1936-39, mem. econs. faculty, 1940-42, beginning as planning ofcl.; with Ford Motor Co., Dearborn, Mich., 1946-85, successively dir. fin. planning and analysis, gen. asst. contr., 1946-57, treas., 1957-61, v.p., contr., 1961-62, v.p. fin., 1962-67, exec. v.p., 1967-79, dir. and vice-chmn. fin. com., 1979-85; dir. research and analysis Office Statis. Control, Hdqrs. USAAF, 1945. Served from pvt. to maj. USAAF, 1943-45. Decorated Legion of Merit. Mem. Phi Beta Kappa, Delta Upsilon. Roman Catholic. Clubs: Detroit Princeton. Home: 7 Brookwood Ln Dearborn MI 48120-1302

LUNDY, ROBERT FIELDEN, minister; b. Stilesboro, Georgia, Mar. 29, 1920; s. Clyde Enoch and Elisabeth Marion (Teilmann) L.; m. Elizabeth Frances Hall, June 15, 1944; children: Robert Fielden, Jr., Allen Francis, Carolyn Elisa Lundy Crowe. BA cum laude, Emory and Henry Coll., 1941, DD, 1961; MDiv, Emory U., 1944; postgrad. Chinese lang., Yale U., 1948-50. Ordained to ministry The Meth. Ch., 1946. Pastor First Meth. Ch., Oak Ridge, Tenn., 1944-48; missionary The Meth. Ch., Malaysia and Singapore, 1950-64, bishop, 1964-68; mem. staff world divsn. bd. of missions United Meth. Ch., N.Y.C., 1968-71; exec. sec. southeastern jurisdiction United Meth. Ch., Atlanta, 1971-76; sr. pastor Broad St. Ch., Cleveland, Tenn., 1976-81; dist. supt. Knoxville (Tenn.) Dist., 1981-85; pastor Norris, Tenn., 1985-90; pres. Coun. of Chs., Malaysia and Singapore, 1966-67; chmn. Laymen Abroad Nat. Coun. Chs., N.Y.C., 1970-71; chmn. Appalachian devel. com. Commn. on Religion in Appalachia, 1974-77. Editor: Malaysia Message, 1952-55, 58-60, 62-64, World Divsn. Newsletter, 1968-71, Forward, 1991-97; contbr. to biography Prophetic Evangelist, 1993. Chmn. Haywood County Craft Coop., Waynesville, N.C., 1991, Haywood County Com. for Peace, Waynesville, 1995; chmn. com. on religious life Hiwassee Coll., 1996—; chmn. commn. on congrl. care Long's Chapel UMC, 1998-2000; mem. adv. coun. Found. for Evangelism, 1994—; trustee Paine Coll., 1976-81, Hiwassee Coll., 1996—. Mem. Kiwanis (chmn. internat. understanding Waynesville, N.C. 1993-96, 98—). Democrat. Avocations: biographical trivia on U.S. Presidents, yard and garden care. Home: 97 Lundy Ln Waynesville NC 28786-6686

LUNDY, SADIE ALLEN, small business owner; b. Milton, Fla., Mar. 29, 1918; d. Stephen Grover and Martha Ellen (Harter) Allen; m. Wilson Tate Lundy, May 17, 1939 (dec. 1962); children: Wilson Tate Jr., Houston Allen, Michael David, Robert Douglas, Martha Jo-Ellen. Degree in acctg., Graceland Coll., 1938. Acct. Powers Furniture Co., Milton, Fla., 1939-40, Lundy Oil Co., Milton, 1941-52; controller First Fed. Savs. & Loan, Kansas City, Mo., 1953-55, Herald Pub. Co., Indepenence, Mo., 1956-58; mgr. Baird & Son Toy Co., Kansas City, Mo., 1959-62; regional mgr. Emmons Jewelers of N.Y., Kansas City, 1963-65; owner, pres. Lundy Tax Service, Independence, 1965-85; corporate sec. and treas., purchasing mgr. Optimation, Inc., Independence, 1974-85, mgr., 1985—; v.p. Lundy Oil Co., Milton, 1941-52. Contbr. articles to profl. jours. Mem. com. Neighborhood Council, Independence, 1985. Mem. Am. Bus. Women's Assn., Independence C. of C. (mem. com. 1965-85). Republican. Mem. Reorganized Ch. of Jesus Christ of Latter Day Saints. Club: Independence Women's. Avocations: counseling, swimming, bicycling. Home: PO Box 520238 Independence MO 64052-0238 Office: Optimation Inc 300 N Osage St Independence MO 64050-2705

LUNGU, ANGELA MARIA, career officer; b. Harvey, Ill., Mar. 14, 1965; d. Ronald Raymond Saunders (stepfather) and Claudia Giovanna (Camilli) Pound; m. Sorin Lungu, Sept. 13, 1998. BS, U.S. Mil. Acad., 1987; MS in Def. Analysis, Naval Postgrad. Sch., 1997; MBA, Webster U., 2000; postgrad., Naval War Coll., 2000—. Commd. 2d lt. U.S. Army, 1987, advanced through grades to maj., 1991; terrain analysis platoon leader 63d engr. airborne co. U.S. Army, Ft. Bragg, N.C., 1988-89, co. exec. officer 175th engr. airborne co., 1989, bn. S-1 adjutant 30th engr. airborne bn., 1989-90, co. exec. officer 1st psychol. ops. airborne bn., 1990, team chief Latin Am. 1st psychol. ops. airborne bn., 1991-92; asst. S-3 constrn. officer 555th Combat Engr. Group, Ft. Lewis, Wash., 1992-93, ops. officer, 1993-94; co. comdr. Hdqs. and Hdqs. Co., 14th Combat Engr. Bn. (Corps), Ft. Lewis, Wash., 1994-96; PSYOP detachment comdr. U.S. Army, Ft. Bragg, NC, 1998; chief PSYOP Doctrine br. US Army John F. Kennedy Special Warfare Ctr., Ft. Bragg, NC, 1998—. Author, editor (Spanish handbook): Psychological Operations, 1991; author: Study of a Storm: An Analysis of Zapatista Propaganda, 1998. Decorated Joint Svc. Army Achievement medal, Army Commendation medal, 2 Army Achievement medals, 3 Meritorious Svc. medals. Mem. AAUW, NAFE, Internat. Platform Assn., Am. Mensa, Soc. Am. Mil. Engrs., Assn. Grads. U.S. Mil. Acad. Republican. Roman Catholic. Avocations: waterskiing, sky diving, languages, distance running, snow skiing. Home: 2A Summer St Newport RI 02840-1727

LUNINE, JONATHAN IRVING, planetary scientist, educator; b. N.Y.C., June 26, 1959. BS magna cum laude, U. Rochester, 1980; MS, Calif. Inst. Tech., 1983, PhD, 1985. Rsch. assoc. U. Ariz., Tucson, 1984-86, asst. prof. planetary scis., 1986-90; vis. asst. prof. UCLA, 1986, assoc. prof., 1990-95, prof., 1995—, faculty mem. program in applied math., 1992—, chair theoretical astrophys. program, 2000; interdisciplinary scientist on joint U.S.-European Cassini mission to Saturn; mem. com. planetary and lunar exploration space sci. bd. NAS, 1986-90; chmn. NASA Solar Sys. Exploration subcom., 1990-95; chmn. Pluto Express Sci. Definition Team, 1995; disting. vis. scientist Jet Propulsion Lab., 1997—; mem. exec. com. space studies bd. NRC, 1998—, chmn. com. on origin and evolution of life in the universe of space studies bd., 2000—. Author: Earth: Evolution of, 1999; contbr. articles to profl. jours.; co-editor: Protostars and Planets III, 1993. Mem. Internat. Mars Exploration Adv. Panel NASA, 1993-94, space sci. adv. com., 1990-95; exec. com. NRC Space Studies bd., 1998—. Recipient Cospar Zeldovich prize Soviet Intercosmos and Inst. for Space Rsch., 1990. 1 of the 50 emerging leaders Time Mag., 1994, Arthur Adel award Scientific Achievement No. Ariz. U., 2000; Co-Recipient James B. Macelwane Young Investigator medal Am. Geophysical Union, 1995. Fellow Am. Geophys. Union (Macelwane medal 1995); mem. Am. Astron. Soc. (Harold C. Urey prize 1988), Internat. Acad. Astronautics (corr. mem.), Internat. Coun. Sci. Unions, European Geophys. Soc., Sigma Xi. Avocation: hiking. Office: U Ariz Dept Planetary Scis PO Box 210092 Tucson AZ 85721-0092

LÜNING, FREDRIK N SON, transportation executive; b. Stockholm, Sweden, Aug. 7, 1936; s. Nils Gustav Adolf and Anna Maria (Wolke) L. Master Mariner, Stockholm Acad. Navigation, 1960; 2d engring. cert., Härnösand Acad. Navigation, 1968; MBA, Stockholm Sch. Econs., 1973. Cert. competency as master mariner, Nat. Swedish Adminstrn. Shipping and Navigation. Apprentice, mcht. navy officer Swedish Mcht. Navy, Stockholm, 1952-60; cadet, officer Royal Swedish Navy, Stockholm, 1960-64; merchant navy officer Johnson Line, Stockholm, 1964-70; marine supt. Johnson Line, Yokohama, Japan, 1973-75; area rep. Mid. East Johnson Line, Khorramshahr, Iran, 1975-77; gen. mgr. Gulf Agy. Co. Ltd., Khorramshahr, 1978-81, Lagos, Nigeria, 1981, United Arab Emirates, 1981-83; mng. dir. Algosaibi Shipping Agy. Group/Gulf Agy. Co., Dammam, Saudi Arabia, 1983-93; dir. Lüning Shipping Inc., Berkeley Heights, N.J., 1993-2000; mng. dir. Gulf Agy. Co. Pte. Ltd., Singapore, 1994-95; consul of Sweden Swedish Fgn. Ministry, United Arab Emirates, 1981-84. Author: The Gulf War As I Experienced It, 1994. Lt. comdr. Royal Swedish Navy Res. Recipient medal of merit Swedish Ministry Fgn. Affairs, Riyadh, Saudi Arabi, 1991. Mem. Royal Inst. Navigation (London), Nautical Inst. London, Inst. Marine Engrs. (consociate), Royal Nat. Lifeboat Instn. (gov. life 1990), Royal Swedish Motorboat Club (life), Swedish Tall/Deep Sea Sailing Ship Assn., Swedish Shipping and Navy League (life), Swedish Assn. Economists, Swedish Assn. for Saving of Lives at Sea (life), Royal Swedish Navy Officers Club, Royal Swedish Res. Officers Assn., Swedish Royal Navy Old Comrades Assn. (life), Stockholm Anti-Aircraft Artillery Assn. (life), Royal Swedish Cavalry Forces Old Comrades Assn. (life), Assn. for Preservation of The Royal Horse Guards (life). Avocations: historical and political studies, travel. Office: Leopoldstraat 39/41 bus 4, B-2000 Antwerp Belgium

LÜNING, ULRICH ERNST GEORG, chemistry educator; b. Dortmund, Germany, May 25, 1956; s. Richard and Ilse (Migge) Richard; m. Susanne Beate Lüning, Jan. 11, 1991; 1 child, Robert Willi Richard. PhD, Tech. Hochschule Darmstadt, 1984; habilitation, U. Freiburg, 1991. Postdoctoral rsch. Pa. State U., State College, 1984-85; asst. prof. U. Freiburg, Germany, 1985-93; assoc. prof. U. zu Kiel, Germany, 1994—; dir. Inst. for Organische Chemie, Kiel. Author: (book) Reaktivität, Reaktionswege, Mechanismen, 1997. Recipient stipend Studienstiftung des Deutschen Volkes, Bonn, 1989-82, Feodor-Lynen stipend Alexander von Humboldt-Stiftung, Bonn, 1984-85, Liebig stipend Fonds der Chemischen Industrie, Frankfurt, 1985-87. Mem. Am. Chem. Soc., Gesellschaft Deutscher Chemiker, Dechema. Office: Inst Organische Chemie, Olshausenstr 40, Kiel D-24098, Germany

LUNN, KITTY ELIZABETH, actress; b. New Orleans, Aug. 5, 1950; d. Hugh I. Morrison and Beatrice (McClung) Farrell; m. Andrew Macmillan, Dec. 21, 1989. Student, Washington Sch. Ballet, 1965-68, Neighborhood Playhouse Sch., 1968-70; degree summa cum laude, CUNY, 1995. Dancer Washington Ballet, 1965-68; radio producer WOR Radio, N.Y.C., 1983-85, WABC Talk Radio, N.Y.C., 1985-87; performer CBS TV, N.Y.C., 1990-93; founder, artistic dir. Infinity Dance Theatre, 1995. Prin. works include Agnes of God, 1992-95, Edinburgh Festival, Fan's False Face Soc., 1990, The Waiting, 1990, Sand Dragons, 1990, As the World Turns, 1990-92, Awakenings, 1990, Eyes of a Stranger, 1979, Loving, 1995, Monograms, 1996-97, numerous TV appearances, 1978-86; dancer Cleve. Ballet, Dancing Wheels. Bd. dirs. Hosp. Audiences, Inc., N.Y.C., 1990—; dir. svcs. people with disabilities Actors' Work Program, N.Y.C., 1991—; mentor networking project YWCA, N.Y.C., 1991-95; mem. White House Conf. on Libr. and Info. Svcs., Washington, 1991; N.Y. State Libr. regent advisor; del. Dem. Nat. Conv., 1992. Named Belle Zeller scholar, CUNY, 1993, Woman of Excellence, 1994. Mem. SAG, AFTRA (nat. bd. dirs.), Nat. Alliance Broadcast Engrs. and Technicians, Actor's Equity Assn. (councillor Eastern Regional adv. bd. 1990—, chair performers with disabilities com. 1990—). Roman Catholic. Office: Actors' Equity Assn 165 W 46th St Fl 15 New York NY 10036-2500

LUNSFORD, ELIZABETH MARSHALL, nurse; b. Greensboro, N.C., Mar. 30, 1963; d. Lewis and Charlotte Jackson (Berry) L.; m. Aquiles Jacob Leal, Sept. 21, 1990 (div. Sept. 1993); children: Jacob Lewis, Christian Alexander. BSN, Brenau U., Gainesville, Ga., 1998. RN, Ga. Owner, mgr. Isla Mujeres (Mex.) Travel, 1988-90; flexible nurse, Spanish translator Lanier Park Hosp., Gainesville, 1998—, cmty. nurse, 1999—; nurse educator Mt. Vernon Elem. Sch., Gainesville, 1999—. Recipient Outstanding Parent award Hall County Edn., Gainesville, 1996. Democrat. Episcopalian. Avocation: travel, sailing, snow skiing. E-mail: marchita@aol.com. Home: 3414 Mill Creek Rd Gainesville GA 30506-1220 Office: Lanier Park Hosp 675 White Sulphur Rd Gainesville GA 30501-2599

LUNT, JENNIFER LEE, lawyer; b. Big Springs, Tex., July 18, 1965; d. John Daleton and Karen Adele (Olsen) L. BS, Auburn U., 1986; JD, U. Ala., 1989, MLS, 1990. Bar: Ala. 1989, U.S. Ct. Appeals (11th cir.) 1990, U.S. Dist. Ct. (mid. dist.) Ala. 1991, U.S. Dist. Ct. (no. dist.) Ala. 1993, U.S. Supreme Ct. 1997. Rsch. asst. Supreme Ct. Ala., Tuscaloosa, 1988-90; cons. Gorham, Waldrep, Stewart, Kendrick & Bryant P.C., Birmingham, 1990; pvt. practice Montgomery, Ala., 1991—; legal asst. adv. bd. Auburn U., Montgomery, 1994—. Rsch. editor: Law and Psychology Rev., 1988-89. Mem. ABA (mem. planning bd. young lawyers divsn. com. on women in the profession 1997-99), Ala. State Bar (mem. com. on small firms and solo practitioners 1995—), Montgomery County Bar Assn. (law libr. com. 1997—). Office: 207 Montgomery St Ste 224 Montgomery AL 36104-3528

LUNTZ, MAURICE HAROLD, ophthalmologist; b. Capetown, South Africa, July 27, 1930; came to U.S., 1978; s. Montague Bernard and Sarah Miriam (Friedman) L.; m. Angela June Myerson, June 21, 1956; children: Melvyn Howard, Caryn Susan, David Sean. B Medicine B Surgery, Capetown U., 1952; MD, U. Witwatersrand, Johannesburg, South Africa, 1974. Diplomate Am. Bd. Ophthalmology. Lectr. ophthalmology Oxford (Eng.) U., 1960-62; prof., chmn. ophthalmology U. Witwatersrand, 1964-78; dir. ophthalmology Beth Israel Med. Ctr., N.Y.C., 1978-88; chief glaucoma svc. Manhattan Eye, Ear & Throat Hosp., 1992—, pres., bd. surgeon dirs., 1992-95; prof. Mt. Sinai Sch. Medicine, N.Y.C., 1978—; cons. Merck, Sharp & Dohme, N.J., 1980-82; chmn. Internat. Com. Ophthalmic Edn., 1974-90. Author: Uveitis, 1983, Glaucoma Surgery, 1984, 2d edit., 1995; mem. editl. bd. Highlights Ophthalmology, Panama, 1970—; contbr. articles to profl. jours.; prodr. film Glaucoma Surveys, 1970. Fellow Royal Coll. Surgeons (Edinburgh), Coll. Surgeons South Africa (hon.); mem. Academia Ophthalmologica Internationalis. Office: 121 E 60th St New York NY 10022-1102

LUO, GWO-HUEI, electrical engineer, research scientist; b. Taiwan, Republic of China, Oct. 28, 1959; s. Bin-Ku and Son-Mei (Lai) L.; m. Chiou-Yueh Lin Luo, Dec. 2, 1984; children: Howard, Wylie. BS, Nat. Taiwan Normal U., Taipei, Republic of China, 1982; MSEE, U. Wis., Madison, 1987, PhD, 1992. Teaching asst. Nat. Taiwan Normal U., Taipei, Republic of China, 1982-85; rsch. asst. U. Wis., Madison, 1986-92; assoc. rsch. scientist SRRC, Hsin-Chu, Republic of China, 1992—, divsn. head, 1994-95, group leader, 1994—; chmn. personnel com, 1994-95, chmn. ops. meeting, 1997—, mem. editl. com., 1994-96, SRRC, Hsin-Chu, Republic of China. Contbr. papers in field. Mem. IEEE, Chinese Engr. Assn., Sigma Xi. Achievements include mem. of construction team to build, commission, and operate the first third-generation synchrotron facility in Asia. Lead a team to increase the beam energy from 1.3 Gev to 1.5 Gev for Taiwan Light Source. Office: SRRC, No 1 R&D Rd VI, Hsin-Chu 30077, Taiwan

LUO, HONG YUAN, biomedical scientist, educator; b. Shengyang, Liaoning, China, June 29, 1951; d. Xin Luo and Rong K. Ren; children: Patrick Yj, Michael Yl. MD, Zhongshan Med. Sch., Guangzhou, China, 1976; M Medicine, Chinese Acad. Med. Scis., Beijing, 1982; PhD, McMaster U., 1993. Tchg. asst. Zhongshan Med. U., 1976-78; rsch. assoc. Beijing Nutrition, 1982-85; vis. scholar McMaster U., Hamilton, Ont., Can., 1985-87; postdoctoral fellow U. Tex. Med. Br., Galveston, 1993-95, instr. biomed. scis., 1995-99; prin. scientist StemCell Therapeutics, Phila., 1999-2000; rsch. specialist U. Pa., Phila., 2000—. Mem. Am. Soc. Hematology. Achievements include development of 2 monoclonal antibodies for human embryonic hemoglobin zeta chain, which have been used for identifying Alpha-thalassemia (Southeast Asian deletion) carriers in population; this deletion causes hydrops fetalis syndrome that leads to fetal death; these antibodies have also been used to identify the fetal cells in maternal blood for non-invasive prenatal diagnosis. Avocations: swimming, movies, music, photography. Home: 8480 Limekiln Pike # 1212 Wyncote PA 19095-2801

LUO, HONG-GANG, physicist; b. Chongqing, China, Jan. 29, 1970; s. Zheng-Yin and Zheng-Ying (Li) L.; m. Hong-Yan Chen, Mar. 27, 1997. BSc, Lanzhou (China) U., 1992, MSc, 1995, DSc, 1999. Asst. Lanzhou U., 1993-95, asst. prof. physics, 1999—; visitor Giessen (Germany) U., 1997-99. Contbr. articles to profl. jours. DAAD fellow, 1997-99. E-mail: luohg@lzu.edu.cn. Office: Lanzhou U, Tianshuilu 298, Lanzhou 730000, China

LUO, JESSICA CHAOYING, actuary; b. Guangzhou, China, Jan. 31, 1958; came to U.S., 1984; d. Xiang-Guang Luo and Xiu-Juan Qi; m. Michael Yu Wang, Aug. 21, 1991; children: Amanda Mei, Lauren Shuyan, Alexander Shufeng. BS in Mechanics, Zhongshan U., 1982; MS in Stats., U. Toledo, 1986. Actuarial analyst Towers Perrin, Denver, 1986-91; dir. actuarial support Lynchval Systems Inc., Reston, Va., 1991; chief actuary DCP Adminstrs., Inc., Bethesda, Md., 1991-95; actuarial cons. Towers Perrin, Rosslyn, Md., 1995-99; prin. cons. Watson Wyatt Ltd., Hong Kong, 1999—.

Mem. Am. Acad. Actuaries, Soc. Actuaries. Avocations: reading, music, travel. Home: 9153 Windflower Dr Ellicott City MD 21042-5629

LUO, JUN, electronic engineer; b. Wuhang, Hubei, China, Aug. 4, 1960; arrived in Germany, 1990; s. Zhiming Luo and Cuizhu Hu; m. Xiaoning Zhu, Oct. 1, 1985; 1 child, Na. Diploma, Nanjing (China) U. Sci. and Te, 1981, MSc, 1989; cert., U. Oldenburg, Germany, 1991; diploma in engring., U. Dortmund, Germany, 1993; D of Engring., U. Duisburg, Germany, 1999. Rsch. asst. East China Inst. Tech., Nanjing, 1981-84; rschr., project leader Nanjing U. Sci. and Tech., 1984-88; engr., project leader Ministry for Electronic and Mech. Industry, Beijing, 1988-90; rschr. U. Dortmund, 1991-94; sr. rschr., engr., project leader Gerhard-Mercator U. Duisburg, 1994-99; engr., project leader German Sci. Found., Bonn, 1995-97, German Found. for Environment/TSI Inc. (USA), Duisburg, 1997-98, Reinnoldus-Transport and Robortertechnik GmbH, Dortmund, 1998-99; initiator, gen. mgr. IS-Intelligent Systems GmbH, Bottrop, Germany, 1999—. Inventor, patentee in field. Recipient sci. and tech. 3d prize Ministry for Electronic and Mech. Industry, China, 1987, 2d prize China Ministry for Aviation, 1988. Office: Divsn Proc and Aerosol Measurement Tech, U Duisburg, 47048 Duisburg Germany also: IS-Intelligent Systems GmbH, Walter-Hoefer-Weg 9, 46242 Bottrop Germany

LUO, KUANG TSO, engineer; b. Kao Hsiung, Taiwan, July 22, 1958. BS, Chung Cheng Inst. Tech., Tao Yuan, Taiwan, 1981; exch. scholar, Northwestern U., 1987; MS, Poly. U., N.Y., 1995. Electronic engr. Chung Shan Inst. Sci. and Tech., Lung Tan, Taiwan, 1981-92; group leader, 1992—; cons. Tze Chiang Found. Sci. and Tech., Hsin Chu, Taiwan, 1998—; founder Consolidated Svcs. for Vehicle Engring. (CONSERVE), Hsin Chu, 1998—. Editor: Def. Tech. Monthly, 1984-85; patent for multiple triggering control circuits, method and apparatus for determining vehicle frontal collision; inventor control unit for occupant restraint system, vehicle crash severity discrimination device. Recipient Outstanding Achievement award Ministry Econ. Affairs, Taipei, 1999; winer Nat. Sci. Competition Ministry Edn., 1975; Disting. Acad. Rsch. award CCIT. Mem. Am. Orchid Soc. Harvard U., Nat. Geographic Soc. Avocations: hiking, fishing, reading. Home: 82-2 Chung She Rd Sec 1, Shih Lin 111, Taipei Taiwan Office: Chung Shan Inst Sci & Tech, PO Box 90008-16-32, Lung Tan Tao Yuan Taiwan

LUO, NIANZHU, mechanical engineer; b. Chengdu, China, Aug. 1, 1951; s. Qianhe and Jiqin (Feng) L.; m. Shufang Ye, Jan. 1, 1979; two children. BS, Southwest Jiaotong U., 1976; MS, U. Wis., 1986, PhD, 1989. Lectr. Southwest Jiaotong U., Sichuan, China, 1977-82; rsch. fellow U. Wis., Madison, 1983-85; from sr. engr. to tech. specialist Case Corp., Chgo., 1990-95; fluid power specialist Sauer-Sundstrand, Newtown, Pa., 1995-99; engring. mgr. Sauer-Danfoss Inc., 2000—. Mem. Soc. Automotive Engrs., Assn. Chinese Scientists & Engrs. Home: 261 Sassafras Dr Easley SC 29642-8264

LUO, RUOSHAN, automotive company executive; b. Guangzhou, Guangdong, China, Apr. 30, 1963; parents Longkai and Ruilian (Yang) L.; 1 child, Alexandra. BSc, Beijin U., Peking, China, 1984; Licenciate, Chalmers U. Tech., Göteborg, Sweden, 1991, PhD, 1995. Assoc. engr. Bldg. Design and rsch. Inst., Guangzhou, China, 1984-88; rsch. asst. Chalmers U. Tech., Göteborg, 1988-95; engr. Volvo, Göteborg, 1996—. Contbr. articles to profl. jours. Avocations: badminton, opera, travel. Office: AB Volvo Technol Devel, Dept 6500 PVH 34, 405 08 Göteborg Sweden

LUO, XIZHANG, physician, educator; b. Ganzhou, Jiangxi, China, Jan. 1, 1945; s. Lizhen and Yazhu (Guan) L.; m. Yinnuo Huang, Aug. 2, 1971; 1 child, Jiancong. BSc, Peking U., Beijing, China, 1969; MSc, Zhongshan U., Guangzhou, 1981. Mem. faculty Sihui (China) Sch., 1969-79; assoc. prof. dept. electronics Zhongshan U., Guangzhou, 1979-89, prof. dept. electronics, 1989—. Contbr. articles to profl. jours. Recipient award of Progress in Sci. and Tech. 2d class edn. dept., China, 1993, award of Natural Sci. 1st class Edn. Dept. Guangdong Province, 1999, award of Natural Sci. 1st class Govt. of Guangdong Province, 1999. Mem. Chinese Inst. Electronics (sr.). Avocations: reading, listening to music. Office: Zhongshan U, Dept Electronics, 501275 Ghangzhou, Guangdong China

LUO, YIXIAO, physicist; b. Zigong, China, May 28, 1944; s. Qiliang Luo and Muqing Li; m. Lanying Wu; 1 child, Xuejiao Luo. Grad., U. Sci. and Tech. China, Beijing, 1967. Head installation team Baiin (China) Nonferrous Co., 1968-77; assoc. prof. Inst. Modern Physics, Lanzhou, China, 1987-90, prof. physics, dep. dir., 1990-94, prof. physics, dir., 1994-99; vice dir. Nat. Lab. Heavy Ion Accelerator, Lanzhou, China, 1991—; vis. scientist Istituto Nazionale di Fisica Nucleare, Italy, Laboratorio Nazionale del Sud, Catania, Italy, 1982-84, Daresbury Lab., Eng., 1987; rev. panel mem. Nat. Scis. Funds., Beijing, 1992-96. Assoc. editor High Energy Physics and Nuc. Physics, China, 1994—; contbr. articles to profl. jours. Recipient awards for sci. achievement in natural sci. Chinese Acad. Scis., 1994-99, nat. award for natural sci., 1999. Mem. Chinese Nuclear Phys. Soc. (pres. 1997—). Home: 824 Nanchang Rd, Lanzhou 730000, China Office: CAS Inst Modern Physics, 363 Nanchang Rd, Lanzhou 730000, China

LUO, ZHENG-HUA, technology educator; b. Hubei, China, Feb. 14, 1962; arrived in Japan, 1984; s. Chunpin Luo and Meixiang Liu; m. Baiping Wan; 1 child, Tianhe. Bachelor's degree, East China U. Chem. Tech., 1983; Master's degree, Kyushu Inst. Tech., 1987; PhD, Osaka (Japan) U., 1990. Asst. prof. Osaka U., 1990-94; assoc. prof. Nagaoka (Japan) U. Tech., 1994—. Contbr. articles to profl. jours. Recipient Tateishi Rsch. prize, 1992, Suzuki Rsch. prize, 1995, Mikiya Rsch. prize, 1996. Mem. IEEE, Japan Soc. Robotics, Soc. Sys., Control and Info. Home: Fukasawa-cho 1769-1-503, Nagaoka Niigata Japan

LUO, ZHI-SHAN, mechanics educator; b. Da-pu, China, Aug. 20, 1936; s. Mu Luo and Ming-qing Lan; m. Xiu-Yin Wang, May 1, 1968; children: Xiao-jun, Xiao-yong. B of Engring., Tianjin (China) U., 1958. Asst. Tianjin U., 1958-79, lectr., 1979-85, assoc. prof., 1986-93, dir. lab. of mechanics, 1984-85, dir. tchg. and rsch. sect., 1985-86, prof. mechanics, 1993—; vis. prof. mech. engring. U. Hong Kong, 1992; tech. cons. Shantou Jingyi Machinery Co., Shantou, China, 1992-94, Hong Kong Press Publ., 1996-97, Hong Kong Sun Wah Publ. Co., 1996-97; chief engr., dir. rsch. room Tianjin Xingu Intelligent Optical Measuring Technique Co., 2000—. Fellow China Mechanics Soc., Soc. Exptl. Mechanics Inc. Achievements include patentee with moiré interferometry of sticking film for measurement displacement of object surface, moiré interferometer controlled and processed by computer, ultra-high sensitivity moiré interferometry by the aid of electronic-liquid phase-shifter and computer. Fax: 86-022-27404862. E-mail: lzstju@public.tpt.tj.cn. Home: Tianjin Univ, 29-5-401 Four Season Vill, Tianjin 300072, China Office: Dept Mechanics Tianjin U, 92 Weijin Rd, Tianjin 300072, China

LUOMA, JUKKA SAKARI, physician, health facility administrator; b. Tampere, Finland, Feb. 17, 1965; s. Alpo Veikko and Ritva Seija Sinikka Luoma; m. Leena Marjatta Ovaska, Feb. 27, 1993; children: Arvi, Maija. MD, U. Tampere, Finland, 1989. Asst. U. Tampere, 1991-94; rschr. A. I. Virtanen Inst. U. Kuopio, Finland, 1995-98; asst. physician Kuopio Univ. Hosp., 1998—; CEO Oy Quattrogene Ltd., Kuopio, 1993-2000, CSO, 2000—. Contbr. articles to profl. jours. With Finnish Army, 1990-91. Recipient Young Investigator award Internat. Atherosclerosis Soc., 1994. Mem. Finnish Med. Assn., Finnish Med. Soc. Duodecin, Finnish Cardiac Soc. Fax: 358-17-240876. Office: Oy Quattrogene Ltd, Neulaniementie 2 L 9, 70210 Kuopio Finland

LUONG, KHANH VINH QUOC, nephrologist, researcher; b. Cantho, Vietnam, Oct. 20, 1952; s. Hien Vinh Luong and Lieu Thi Huynh; m. Lan Thi Hoang Nguyen, Oct. 15, 1981. MD, U. Kans., 1981. Diplomate Am. Bd. Internal Medicine, Am. Bd. Nephrology, Nat. Bd. Med. Examiners. Intern in internal medicine St. Elizabeth Med. Ctr., Northeastern Ohio U., Youngstown, 1981; resident internal medicine Tulane U. Hosp. Program, New Orleans, 1982-83, City of Faith Med. and Rsch. Ctr., Oral Roberts U., Tulsa, Okla., 1986-87; fellow in nephrology Cedars-Sinai Med. Ctr., UCLA Program in Nephrology, L.A., 1987-90; pvt. practice Westminster, Calif., 1990—; vis. asst. prof. medicine UCLA Sch. Medicine, 1989-90; presenter at nat. and internat. meetings; contbr. articles to profl. jours. Contbr. articles to profl. jours. Nat. Kidney Found. So. Calif. fellow, 1989-90. Fellow ACP, Am. Coll. Endocrinology, Am. Coll. Allergy, Asthma and Immunology; mem. Am. Soc. Nephrology, Internat. Soc. Nephrology, Am. Assn. Clin. Endocrinologists, Endocrine Soc., Am. Soc. Bone and Mineral Rsch., Assn. Vietnamese Physicians of the Free World, Vietnamese Med. Assn. in U.S., Vietnamese Am. Med. Rsch. Found. (pres.). Office: 9188 Bolsa Ave Westminster CA 92683-5556

LUONG, TRAN DUC, president national assembly of Vietnam; b. Pho Khanh, Quang Ngai, Vietnam, May 5, 1937. Student, Mining and Geology Coll., USSR Acad. Econs., 1981. Geology technician League of Geol. Groups, 1954-59, leader geol. group 4, 1959-64, dep. leader, 1964-66; dep. dir. Geol. Map Dept., 1970-77; dep., dir., dir. League of Geol. Map Groups, 1977-79; gen. dir. Gen. Dept. Geology, 1979—; mem. Nat. Assembly, Vietnam, 1981—, dep. prime minister, 1992-97, president, 1997—; dep. chmn., chmn. Nat. Assembly Sci. and Tech. Commn.; Communist Party cell sec. League of Geology Groups # 20, mem. exec. Party Com. for Vietnam geol. sector; mem. party com., sec. Labour Youth Union for Mining and Geol. Coll., 1966-69, exec. mem. Party Com. for Geol. Map Dept., 1970-76, sec., 1979, alt. mem. ctrl. com., 1982-91, full mem., 1991—, mem. polit. bur., 1996—; vice chmn. Coun. Ministers, 1987, permanent rep. to Coun. for Mut. Econ. Assistance for Socialist Countries. Office: Office of Pres, Hoang Hoa Tham, Hanoi Vietnam*

LUPER, CLARA MAE, educator; b. Okfuskee County, Okla.; d. Ezell and Isabell Sheppard; m. C. P. Wilson; children: Calvin, Marilyn, Chelle. BA, Langston U.; MA, U. Okla. Tchr. Lincoln H.S., Pawnee, Okla., Douglass H.S., Oklahoma City, Dungee H.S., Spencer, Okla., N.W. Classen H.S., Oklahoma City, John Marshall H.S., Oklahoma City; cons. Oklahoma City Bd. of Educator's Adv. Com. on Sch. Desegregation, Oklahoma City Human Rels., Mayor's Cons. on Youth Opportunities, Okla. History TV Series, Freedom Ctr.'s Personal Incentive Program, also h.s.'s, colls., and univs.; adv. cons. Fed. Inter-Agy. Bd.; state dir. Miss Black Okla., Mr. Talent; co-founder Soul Bazaar; marriage cons.; pub. rels. profl. Abram Ross Advt.; co-owner CP's Catfish Cafe; spkr. in field. Author: (book) Behold the Walls; founder Black Voices Mag., Facts About the Black History Monument and Walls; dir.: A Visit with Clara Luper, Stas. KFJL, KTLV, KAEZ; dir. A Clara Luper Special, Sta. KBYE; writer, prodr., dir.: (movie) Brother President. Rebuilder, founder, pres. Freedom Ctr.; founder Black History Monument and Wall; co-founder Miss Merry Christmas Pageant; founder Miss NAACP USA Membership Pageant. Recipient Phi Beta Sigma Svc. award, Oklahoma City Beautician's award for svc., Okla. Federated Women's Club Svc. award, Ysabel Stricklin Adv. award, Carverdale Club Svc. award, Omega Psi Phi Svc. award, NAACP Nat. Advisor of Yr. award, NAACP Regional Voter Registration award, Emancipation Proclamation Centennial award, NAACP Nat. Svc. citation, NAACP State award for svc., Cmty. Outstanding Svc. award, Nat. Svc. award, NAACP Regional Svc. award, Delta Sigma Theta citation, award Sigma Gamma Rho, Alpha Kappa Alpha; named to Pioneer Hall of Fame, Ponca City, Okla.; Robert A. Taft scholar. Mem. Oklahoma City Social Sci. Tchr.'s Assn. (v.p.), Oklahoma County Tchr.'s Assn. (v.p.), Amigos Club (Svc. award, Founders award), Zeta Phi Beta (Sorority Woman of Yr., Finer Womanhood award). Fax: (610) 918-8442. Office: Lenfest Group PO Box 2660 1332 Enterprise Dr West Chester PA 19380-5970

LUPERT, LESLIE ALLAN, lawyer; b. Syracuse, N.Y., May 24, 1946; s. Reuben and Miriam (Kaufman) L.; m. Roberta Gail Fellner, May 19, 1968; children: Jocelyn, Rachel, Susannah. BA, U. Buffalo, 1967; JD, Columbia U., 1971. Bar: N.Y. 1971. Ptnr. Orans Elsen & Lupert, N.Y.C., 1971—. Contbr. articles to profl. jours. Mem. ABA, N.Y. State Bar Assn. (trial lawyers sect.), Assn. of Bar of City of N.Y. (com. fed. legislation 1977-80, profl. and jud. ethics com. 1983-86, com. on fed. cts. 1986-89, 95-96), Phi Beta Kappa. Office: Orans Elsen & Lupert 1 Rockefeller Plz New York NY 10020-2102

LUPESCU, GRIGORE, cardiologist; b. Tg-Jiu, Romania, Aug. 30, 1931; s. Grigore and Marina (Dobrescu) L.; m. Iuliana Popescu, Dec. 2, 1962; children: Grigore, Roxana. BS, Faculty Medicine Bucharest, Romania, 1960; MD, PhD, Faculty Medicine Cluj-Napoca, Romania, 1983. Internist, then cardiologist Medgidia, Tg-Jiu, Romania, 1964—; head dept. cardiology Tg-Jiu Hosp., 1997—. Mem. N.Y. Acad. Scis., Mediterranean Assn. Cardiology & Cardiac Surgery, Balkan Med. Union. Office: Tg-Jiu Hosp Dept Cardiology, 18 Progresului, 1400 Tg-Jiu Gorj, Romania

LUPESCU, MIHAI BOGDAN, chemical engineer, quality control specialist; b. Bucharest, Romania, Dec. 31, 1954; s. Cezar and Angela Cornelia (Cismarescu) L.; m. Ioana Maria Popescu, Oct. 23, 1986 (div. 1995); children: Mihai Christian, Marius Alexander Cezar. MSc in Chem. Engring., U. Politechnica, Bucharest, 1979; PhD, Inst. Phys. Chemistry, Romanian Acad., Bucharest, 1997. Chem. engr. Fiber Glass Plant, Bucharest, 1979-82, Nat. Glass Inst., Bucharest, 1983-86; chem. engr. Inst. Phys. Chemistry, Bucharest, 1986-98, rschr., 1990—, sr. rschr., 1998—; quality control mgr. Hobas Tub Romania SA, Clinceni, 1998—; vis. acad. staff Faculty Indsl. Chemistry, U. Politechnica, 1995-2000. Contbr. articles to profl. jours.; patentee in field. Mem. Romanian Journalists Assn., Romanian Tennis Fedn. (referee), Romanian Glass Assn., Gen. Assn. Engrs. Romania. Avocations: tennis, music, paradigms. Fax: 004014932151. E-mail: lupescu@hobas.ro. Home: 100 Matei Basarab, Bucharest 3, Romania Office: Hobas Tub Romania SA, 37 Sos de Centura com, Jud ilfov Clinceni Romania Address: ScC Et 2 Ap 92, 29-39 Cernisoara St Bl 61, Bucharest 6, Romania

LUPIANI, DONALD ANTHONY, psychologist; b. N.Y.C., June 7, 1946; s. Louis and Josephine (Boccia) L.; m. Linda Moyik, June 20, 1970; 1 child, Jennifer. BA, Iona Coll., 1968; MA, Columbia U., 1971, PhD, 1973; postdoctoral, Behavior Therapy Inst., White Plains, N.Y., 1976. Lic. psychologist, N.Y.; diplomat Am. Bd. Profl. Psychology, Am. Bd. Psychotherapy, Am. Acad. Behavioral Medicine, Intenat. Acad. Behavioral Medicine, Internat. Acad. Behavioral Medicine. Clin. assoc. Columbia U., N.Y.C., 1974-85, Fordham U., Bronx, N.Y., 1979-81; dir. psychology and spl. edn. svcs. Riverdale Country Sch., Bronx, 1973-87; chief psychologist Franciscan Order of Priests, N.Y.C., 1983—; pvt. practice Yonkers, N.Y., 1975—; dir. spl. svcs. Riverdale Country Sch., Bronx, 1973-87; bd. dirs. St. Ursula Learning Ctr., Mt. Vernon, N.Y. Contbr. articles to profl. jours. Bd. dirs., mem. The St. Ursula Learning Ctr. Fellow Am. Orthopsychiat. Assn., Am. Coll. Psychology, Am. Acad. Sch. Psychology; mem. APA, N.Y. State Psychol. Assn., Westchester County Psychol. Assn. (chmn. ethics com. 1980-87). Roman Catholic. Avocations: woodworking, painting, drawing. Home and Office: 227 Mile Square Rd Yonkers NY 10701-5369

LUPINI, CHRISTOPHER ALBERT, computer engineer, consultant; b. Dearborn, Mich., Apr. 22, 1965; s. Albert Dante and Cynthia Grace (Zyla) L.; m. Carrie Melissa-Olivia Toler, June 6, 1987; children: Anthony Christopher, Olivia Maria, Gabriel Albert, Nicholas James Wallace, Joseph Dominic. BS in Computer Engring., U. Mich., 1987; student, U. Colo., 1988; MSEE, Purdue U., 1992. Registered profl. engr., Ind.; cert. master technician Automotive Svc. Excellence. Assoc. software engr. Martin Marietta I&CS, Denver, 1987-88; elec. engr. Martin Marietta I&CS, Washington, 1988-89; sr. project engr. Delphi Delco Electronics Sys., Kokomo, Ind., 1989—; gen. mgr. Lupini Engring. Co., Kokomo, 1992—; educator Univ. Consortium Continuing Edn., L.A., 1993—. Author: Vehicle Multiplex Communication; contbr. articles to Automotive Engring., IEE Automotive Electronics, SAE Transactions. Recipient quality performance awards GM, 1991, 92, 93, 95, 97. Mem. Soc. Automotive Engrs. and Svc. Technicians Soc. (Excellence in Oral Presentation 1992). Republican. Roman Catholic. Achievements include discovery of equations relating clock tolerance, propagation delay, and wire length for the CAN data bus; co-development of GM' J1850 class 2 serial data bus; rsch. in future transp. tech. E-mail: christopher.a.lupini@delphiauto.com. Home: 390 S Hickory Ln Kokomo IN 46901-3995 Office: Delphi Automotive Sys One Corporate Ctr Kokomo IN 46904

LUPINI, PAOLO, manufacturing company executive; b. Senigallia, Italy, Apr. 3, 1964; s. Furio and Marina (Antonangeli) L.; m. Georgia Annamaria Spaccapietra, Mar. 28, 1993; children: Lorenza, Leonardo. Grad. in Law, U. Macerata, Italy, 1988; M in Mktg. and Comm, Milano, Italy, 1990, Expert degree in Electronic Commerce, 1993. Asst. account exec. Centro Europeo di Comunicazione, Milano, 1993; account exec. TBWA Advt. Agy., Milano, 1993-94; mktg. mgr. Clementoni S.P.A., Recanati, Italy, 1994-98; CEO Best Raffaello S.r.l., Jesi, Italy, 1998—. CEO Club of 4 Wheeler Drivers, Jesi, 1989-90. With Italian Army, 1989-90. Recipient award Nat. Mus. Pasta, Rome, 1999. Mem. Am. Mktg. Assn. N.Y., Direct Mktg. Assn. Avocations: tennis, sailing. Home: Via Coste 34, 60038 San Paolo de Jesi Italy Office: Best Raffaello Srl, Viale Papa Giovanni 23, 12, 60035 Jesi Italy

LUPO, DAVID EMORY, computer scientist; b. Charleston, S.C., Dec. 17, 1953; s. Clinton Jones, Jr. and Vera Gwendolyn (Canaday) L.; m. Terry Bean, Apr. 7, 1979; children: Nathan Andrew, Timothy David. BS in Computer Scis./Math., Duke U., 1976, MDiv, 1983. Ordained deacon and elder S.C. Conf. The United Meth. Ch. Computer programmer Duke U. Med. Ctr., Durham, N.C., 1976-80; pastor The United Meth. Ch., S.C., 1983-94; computer programmer Automated Trading Desk, Mt. Pleasant, S.C., 1994-98, v.p. of rsch. and devel., 1999—; part-time instr. in computer sci. Duke U., 1979-81. Pres. Beaufort Ministerial Assn., 1987-88. Mem. Assn. for Computing Machinery, Phi Beta Kappa. Democrat. Avocations: Boys Scouts of Am., walk to Emmaus. Office: Automated Trading Desk Inc 389 Johnnie Dodds Blvd Ste 200 Mount Pleasant SC 29464-2969

LUPO, ROBERT EDWARD SMITH, real estate developer and investor; b. New Orleans, May 27, 1953; s. Thomas Joseph and Alvena Florence (Smith) L.; m. Mary Lynn Puissegur, June 16, 1980; children: Robert Thomas Smith, Francesca Marfese Smith. BArch, Tulane U., 1977. Owner Robert Edward Smith Lupo Properties, New Orleans, 1976—; cons. various firms, New Orleans, 1977—; COO Commodore Thomas J. Lupo Enterprises, Williams-Lupo, Smith-Lupo, New Orleans, 1981—; pres. Hedwig, Inc., Zephyr, Inc., Noroaltom Devel. Co., Inc., New Orleans, 1981—; cons. Mrs. Thomas J. Lupo properties. Grad. Met. Area Leadership Forum, New Orleans, 1980; bd. dirs., pres. New Orleans Mcpl. Yacht Harbor, 1989-93; life mem. Friends Audubon Zoo, 1983—; bd. dirs. New Orleans Met. Area Com., 1985-90, Orleans Levee Dist. Commn.; guardian mem. Boy Scouts Am., 1991—; mem. capital projects oversight com. Orleans Parish Sch. Bd., 1995—; mem. bd. commrs. Orleans Levee Dist., 1996—. Recipient Gov.'s award State of La., 1980, Tulane Assocs. award Tulane U., 1986; named One of 10 Best Dress Men, Men of Fashion, 1983, named to Hall of Fame, 1991. Mem. Aquarium Ams. (life), Assn. Naval Aviation (charter), Sigma Alpha Epsilon (founding). Republican. Roman Catholic. Club: Semreh. Office: 145 Robert E Lee Blvd New Orleans LA 70124-2552

LUPTON, MARY HOSMER, retired small business owner; b. Olympia, Wash., Jan. 2, 1914; d. Kenneth Winthrop and Mary Louise (Wheeler) Hosmer; m. Keith Brahe-Wiley, Oct. 12, 1940 (dec. Apr. 1955); children: Sarah Hosmer, Wiley Guise, Victoria Brahe-Wiley; m. Thomas George Lupton, Nov. 27, 1965 (dec. Feb. 1989); 1 stepson, Andrew Henshaw Lupton. Student, Gunston Hall Jr. Coll., 1932-33; BS in Edn., U. Va., 1940. Ptnr. Wakefield Press, Earlysville, Va., 1940-55; owner, operator Wakefield Forest Bookshop, Earlysville, 1955-65, Forest Bookshop, Charlottesville, 1965-85, Wakefield Forest Tree Farm, 1955-85. Contbr. articles to profl. mags. Corr. sec. Charlottesville-Albemarle Civic League, 1963-64; sec. Instructive Vis. Nurses Assn., Charlottesville, 1961-62; chmn. pub. info. Charlottesville chpt. Va. Mus. Fine Arts, 1970-77; mem. Albemarle County Forestry Com., 1961-62; bd. dirs. Charlottesville-Albemarle Mental Health Assn., 1980-82, 89-91. Mem. AAUW, DAR (Am. Heritage com. chmn. 1983-85, 89-91), Assns. of U. Va. Libr., New Eng. Hist. Geneal. Soc., Conn. Soc. Genealogists, Geneal. Soc. Va. Hist. Soc., Albemarle County Hist. Soc., Va. Soc. Mayflower Descs. (asst. state historian 1979-82), LWV, Soc. Mayflower Descs., Am. Soc. Psychical Rsch., Brit. Soc. Psychical Rsch., Nature Conservancy, Charlottesville Soc. of Friends, Jefferson Soc., Cornerstone Soc. (charter), Lawn Soc. (charter), Chi Omega. Address: 2610 Barracks Rd Rm H252 Charlottesville VA 22901-2121

LUPU, AMCA ROXANA ILIE, physician, haematology educator; b. Bucharest, Romania, Oct. 29, 1954; d. Ilie Maria and Ana Sofia Mihail (Famasescu) Diculescu; m. Cristian Serbam Lupu, June 20, 1980; children: Raluca, Alexandru. MD, Med. Sch., Bucharest, Romania, 1979; PhD, Carol Davila U., Bucharest, Romania, 1996. Asst. internal medicine Bucharest U. Hosp., 1980; lectr. internal medicine, 1985; sr. lectr. hematology Coltea U. Hosp., 1990; asst. prof. hematology Bucharest U. Medicine, 1998—; cons. internal medicine Mcpl. U. Hosp., Bucharest, 1980, sr. cons., 1985; cons. hematologist, Coltea U. Hosp., 1990. Author: Algorith Diagnostic Therapeutic Gastrointestinal Diseases, 1995, Algorith Diagnostic Therapeutic Hematologic Diseases, 1996, Clasic, Modern in Multiple Mieloma, 1988; contbr. articles to profl. publs. Founding mem. Hematology Found., Bucharest, 1994. Mem. N.Y. Acad. Sci., European Hematology Assn., Romanian Hematology Soc., French Hematology Soc., Romanian Genetic Med. Soc. Avocation: gardening. Home: Sect 1, Bd Banu Manta 1 1B B50, Bucharest Romania Office: Coltea Hosp U Medicine, Bic Bratiamo Sect 3, Bucharest Romania

LUPU, RADU, pianist; b. Galati, Romania, Nov. 30, 1945; s. Meyer and Ana (Gabor) L. Attended Conservatoire, Moscow, USSR, 1961-69. London debut, 1969, Berlin, 1972, U.S. debut with Cleve. Orch. in N.Y.C., appearances with worldwide maj. orchs., including Berlin Philharmonic, Vienna Philharmonic, Israel Philharmonic, Orch. de Paris, Concertgebouw, N.Y. Philharmonic, Phila. Symphony Orch., Chgo. Symphony Orch., Cleve. Symphony Orch.; recs. include Beethoven cycle with Israel Philharmonic and Zubin Mehta, Schubert Sonatas, Beethoven Sonatas, Mozart Sonatas for Violin and Piano with Szymon Goldberg, Schubert Lieder with Barbara Hendricks, Mozart and Schubert duets and Mozart Concerto for 2 pianos, both with Murray Perahia, Brahms Piano Concerto #1 Mozart and Beethoven Quintets in E Flat, Schubert Piano Duets with Daniel Barenboim. Recipient 1st prize Van Cliburn Internat. Piano Competition, 1966, Enescu Competition, 1967, Leeds Internat. Piano Competition, 1969, Edison award for Schumann Kinderszenen, Kreisleriana, 1995, Grammy award for Schubert D960 and D664 record, 1995. E-mail: artists@terryharrison.force9.co.uk.

LUPULESCU, AUREL PETER, medical educator, researcher, physician; b. Manastiur, Banat, Romania, Jan. 1, 1923; came to U.S., 1967, naturalized, 1973; s. Peter Vichentie and Maria Ann (Dragan) L. MD magna cum laude, Sch. Medicine, Bucharest, Romania, 1950; MS in Endocrinology, U. Bucharest, 1965; PhD in Biology, U. Windsor, Ont., Can. Diplomate Am. Bd. Internal Medicine. Chief lab. investigations Inst. Endocrinology, Bucharest, 1950-67; rsch. asst. SUNY Downstate Med. Ctr., 1968-69; asst. prof. medicine Wayne State U., 1969-72, assoc. prof., 1973—; vis. prof. Inst. Med. Pathology, Rome, 1967; cons. VA Hosp., Allen Park, Mich., 1971-73. Author: Steroid Hormones, 1958, Advances in Endocrinology and Metabolism, 1962, Experimental Pathophysiology of Thyroid Gland, 1963, Ultrastructure of Thyroid Gland, 1968, Effect of Calcitonin on Epidermal Cells and Collagen Synthesis in Experimental Wounds As Revealed by Electron Microscopy Autoradiography and Scanning Electron Microscopy, 1976, Hormones and Carcinogenesis, 1983, Hormones and Vitamins in Cancer Treatment, 1990, Cancer Cell Metabolism and Cancer Treatment, 2000; reviewer various sci. jours.; contbr. chpts., numerous articles to profl. publs. Fellow Fedn. Am. Socs. for Exptl. Biology; mem. AMA, AAAS, Electron Microscopy Soc. Am., Soc. for Investigative Dermatology, N.Y. Acad. Scis., Am. Soc. Cell Biology, Soc. Exptl. Biology and Medicine. Republican. Achievements include research on hormones and tumor biology; studies regarding role of hormones and vitamins in carcinogenesis. Home: 21480 Mahon Dr Southfield MI 48075-7525 Office: Wayne State U Sch Medicine 540 E Canfield St Detroit MI 48201-1928

LUQUE, EMILIO EUGENIO, computer science educator; b. Madrid, Spain, Aug. 14, 1946; s. Emilio and Amelia (Fadon) L.; m. Julia M. Larena, July 29, 1972; children: Juan Jose, Pablo, Carlos, Maria. M in Physics, U. Complutense, Madrid, 1968; M in Computer Sci., Computer Sci. Inst., Madrid, 1971; PhD in Physics, U. Complutense, Madrid, 1973. Asst. prof. U. Complutense, Madrid, 1968-71, assoc. prof., 1971-76; computer sci. and automation rschr. Electric & Automation Lab., U. Complutense, Madrid, 1968-76; prof. U. Autonoma, Barcelona, Spain, 1976—, elec. and electronics dept. chmn., 1979-86, computer sci. dept. chmn., 1986-93, 97-00, computer architect and ops. system group leader, 1986—; indsl. cons. AUTRON, ALCATEL, Control and Applications, FLEXILINE, COMELTA, Spain, 1984—; vis. prof. various countries including U.S., China, Ireland, Italy,

Poland, Hungary, Cuba, Brazil, Argentina, 1985—; rsch. dir. CYTED, Coop. Rsch. Program with S.Am., 1989—, EU Rsch. Projects Copernicus; EU Cooperation projects TEMPUS#; EU IST Programme Projects; invited prof. Villanova (Pa.) U., 1991-95. Editor, co-author: Microprocessor Advanced Architectures, 1986, Mini and Microcomputers and Their Applications, 1988, Education and Application of Computer Technology, 1990, Parallel and Distributed Computing and Systems, 1996, Recent Advances in PVM and MPI, 1999; referee various sci. jours.; contbr. over 110 articles to profl. jours. and internat. confs. Tech. Studies grant March Found., Madrid, 1970, Rsch. grant Adv. Comm. for Sci. and Tech., Spain, 1981, 84, 89, 92, 95, 98. Mem. IEEE, IEEE Computer Soc., ACM. Avocations: reading, swimming, classical music, theatre. Office: Univ Autonoma Barcelona, Dept Informatica, 08193 Bellaterra Spain

LUQUET, GERARD LOUIS, paper company executive, consultant; b. France, Sept. 15, 1931. Degree in Engring., French Paper Sch., France, 1954. Prodn. engr. La Chapelle, Rouen, France, 1957-60; engr. SICA, Alizay, France, 1960-64; tech. mgr. Mougeot, Laval, France, 1964-68; engr. Papeteries de France, France, 1968-70; prodn. mgr. Chapelle Darblay, France, 1971-80, tech. mgr., 1981-89; cons. Bonsecours, France, 1990—; mem. co. of experts French Com. of the Internat. C. of C. Lt. Air Force, France, 1954-57. Home: Allee du Chant Olseaux, F76240 Bonsecours France

LURIA, GLORIA, art gallery executive, art consultant; b. N.Y.C.; d. Henry and Frances (Saul) Biren; m. Leonard Luria; children: Peter, Henry, Nancy. BS, Skidmore Coll., 1947. Art dir. Gloria Luria Gallery, Bay Harbor Island, Fla., 1966-94; art cons. Gloria Luria Fine Art, Fisher Island, Fla., 1995—; sec. L. Luna & Son, Inc., Miami Fla., 1961-71. Chmn. Am. affairs Hadassah, Miami, 1965-65; active Greater Miami Fedn. Jewish Philanthropies, 1968—; bd. dirs. Concert Assn. Fla., Miami, 1988-96. Mem. Art Dealers Assn. South Fla. (pres. 1985-88), Fifty Over Fifty. Avocations: tennis, golf, bridge, music, theatre. Office: 7774 Fisher Island Dr Miami Beach FL 33109-0956

LURIE, KONSTANTIN ANATOLY, mathematician, educator; b. St. Petersburg, Russia, Nov. 15, 1935; came to U.S., 1989, naturalized, 1994; s. Anatoly Isakovich and Berta Yakovlevna Lurie; m. Ella Sergeevna Zhuravleva, Dec. 27, 1967 (dec. Feb. 1986); 1 child, Dmitri; m. Sofya Yankelevna Fedorovich, Aug. 22, 1989; 1 child, Aleksandra Fedorovich. Engr.-rschr., Leningrad (USSR) Poly. Inst., 1959; PhD in Physics and Math., A.F. Ioffe Phys.-Tech. Inst., Leningrad, 1964; DSc in Physics and Math., Acad. of Sci. USSR, 1972. Sr. rsch. scientist A.F. Ioffe Phys.-Tech. Inst., Leningrad, 1953-88; rsch. scientist, leading rsch. scientist Acad. Sci. USSR, 1988; prof. Leningrad Shipbuilding Inst., 1986-87; Goebel vis. prof. U. Mich., Ann Arbor, 1989; prof. math. Worcester (Mass.) Poly. Inst., 1989—; vis. prof. Tech. U. Denmark, Lyngby, 1981, vis. prof. math., 1999; vis. prof.-lectr. U. Yerevan, Armenia, 1984. Author: (books) Optimal Control in Problems of Mathematical Physics, 1975, Applied Optimal Control of Distributed Systems, 1993, (book chpts.) Topics in Optimization, 1967, Recent Trends in Optimization Theory and Applications, 1995, Homogenization, 1999, (with. A. V. Cherkaev) Material Instabilities in Continuum Mechanics and Related Math. Problems, 1988, Topics in the Mathematical Modelling of Composite Materials, 1997; editor: (books) Applications of the Theory of Optimal Control to Structural Optimization, 1977, (with A. V. Cherkaev) Optimal Design of Elastic Contstruction Elements, 1981; contbr. papers in field to profl. jours. Rsch. grantee Dept. of Def., 1990-92, NSF, 1993-96, 98-2001; Fulbright fellow, 1999. E-mail: klurie@wpi.edu. Office: Worcester Poly Inst 100 Institute Rd Worcester MA 01609-2247

LURIE, MICHAEL, chemist, researcher, environmental consultant; b. Burshtin, Russia, Sept. 20, 1950; arrived in Israel, 1990; s. Vladimir and Liza (Tubman) L.; m. Marina Mittelman, Nov. 17, 1971; children: Elena, Anna. MS with honors, Perm State U., Russia, 1973; PhD, Inst. Solid Mineral Fuels Preparation, Moscow, 1982. Jr., sr. rschr. Coal Rsch. Inst., Perm, 1973-83; lab. mgr. Inst. Environment, Perm, 1983-90; rschr. Techion, Haifa, Israel, 1991-95; engr., sect. head Tower Semiconductor Ltd., Migdal Haemek, Israel, 1995—; cons. Regional Environ. Com., Perm, 1989-90; cons. field of water treatment and environment. Inventor in field; contbr. articles to profl. jours. Sgt. Soviet Army, 1973-75. Office: Tower Semicond Ltd, POB 619, 10556 Migdal Haemeq Israel

LURIE, RANAN RAYMOND, political cartoonist, political analyst, artist, lecturer; b. Port Said, Egypt, May 26, 1932; came to U.S., 1968, naturalized, 1974; s. Joseph and Rose (Sam) L. (parents Israeli citizens); m. Tamar Fletcher, Feb. 25, 1959; children: Rod, Barak, Daphne, Danielle. Student, Herzelia High Sch., Tel Aviv, Israel, 1949; student, Jerusalem Art Coll., 1951. Corr. Maariv Daily, 1950-52; features editor Hador Daily, 1953-54; editor-in-chief Tevel mag., 1954-55; staff polit. cartoonist Yedioth Aharonot Daily, 1955-66, Honolulu Advertiser, 1979; lectr. polit. cartooning U. Hawaii; univ. lectr. in fine arts, polit. cartoon and polit. analysis Am. Program Bur., Boston.; polit. cartoonist Time Internat. mag., 1994-97; inventor 1st electronically syndicated bus.-news cartoon Lurie's Business World; 101 million readers of 1105 newspapers in 102 countries; 1999 Guiness Book of World Records; chief judge Internat. Cartoon Comp., Seoul, Korea, 1996, 97. Author: Among the Suns, 1952, Lurie's Best Cartoons, 1961, Nixon Rated Cartoons, 1973, Pardon Me, Mr. President, 1974, Lurie's Worlds, 1980, So sieht es Lurie, 1981, Fed. Republic Germany, Lurie's Almanac (U.K.), 1982, (U.S.A.), 1983, Taro's International Politics, Japan, 1984, Lurie's Middle East, Israel, 1986; creator: The Expandable Painting, 1969; Cartoons used as guidelines in several encys., polit. sci. books.; 22 shows, Israel, Can., U.S., 1960-75, including, Expo 67, Can., Dominion Gallery, Montreal, Que., Can., Lim Gallery, Tel Aviv, 1965, Overseas Press Club, N.Y.C., 1962, 64, 75, U.S. Senate, Washington, Honolulu Acad. Fine Arts, 1979; represented by Circle Gallery, 1988-93; exhibited numerous group shows including, Smithsonian Instn., 1972, Circle Gallery, Washington, 1989; creator Japan's nat. cartoon symbol Taro-San, Taiwan's nat. cartoon symbol Cousin Lee; polit. cartoonist, Life Mag., N.Y.C., 1968-73, polit. cartoonist, interviewer, Die Welt, Bonn, W. Ger., 1980-81; contbr.: N.Y. Times, 1952—; contbg. editor, polit. cartoonist, Newsweek Internat., 1973-76, editor, polit. cartoonist, Vision Mag. of South Am., 1974-76, syndicated, United Features Syndicate, 1971-73; syndicated nationally by Los Angeles Times, also internationally by, N.Y. Times to over 260 newspapers, 1973-75, internationally by Editors Press Syndicate (345 newspapers), King Features Syndicate, 1975-83; syndicated in U.S. by Universal Press Syndicate, 1982-86, Cartoonews Internat. Syndicat, 1986—; polit. cartoonist, The Times of London, 1981-83, ABC's Nightline, 1991—, World News Show, 1993; sr. polit. analyst, editorial cartoonist Asahi Shimbun, Japan's largest daily newspaper, 1983-84; sr. analyst and polit. cartoonist U.S. News & World Report, 1984-85; chief editorial dir. Editors Press Service, 1985; joined staff MacNeil/Lehrer News Hour (PBS) as daily polit. cartoonist, analyst; editl. bd. Mid. East Quarterly, 1994—; creator, editor-in-chief Cartoon News, The Current Events Ednl. Mag., 1996—; polit. cartoonist Fgn. Affairs Mag., 2000—. Chief judge Seoul (Republic of Korea) Internat. Cartoon Competition, 1996, 97. Served as maj. Combat Paratroop, Israeli Army Res., 1950-67. Recipient highest Israeli journalism award, 1954; U.S. Headliners award, 1972; named Outstanding Editorial Cartoonist of Nat. Cartoonist Soc., 1971-78; Salon award Montreal Cartoon, 1971; N.Y. Front Page award, 1972, 74, 77; cert. merit U.S. Publ. Designers, 1974; award Overseas Press Club, 1979; John Fischetti polit. cartoon award, 1982, 86; sr. adj. fellow Ctr. Strategic Internat. Studies, Washington; Ranan R. Lurie Internat. Polit. Cartoon ann. award created in his honor by Nat. Fedn. Hispanic Owned Newspapers, 1994, Ranan R. Lurie Internat. award for Polit. Cartooning created by U.N. Soc. of Writers, 1995, Annual Ranan Lurie Polit. Cartoon award created in his honor by U.N., 2000; recip. 1996 Hubert Humphrey 1st Amendment and Freedom of the Press Award, 1996; UN Corrs. Assn. ranan Lurie Polit. Cartoon award created in his honor, 1999. Mem. Soc. Profl. Journalists, Nat. Cartoonists Soc. Am., Assn. Editorial Cartoonists, Mensa, Overseas Press Club, Friars Club. Inventor 1st electronically animated TV news cartoon; creator 1st syndicated bus.-news cartoon Lurie's Business World; 104 million readers of 1,105 newspapers in 104 countries; 1999 Guiness Book of World Records. Office: Cartoonews Internat 375 Park Ave Ste 1301 New York NY 10152-1399

LURTON, HORACE VANDEVENTER, brokerage house executive; b. Washington, Oct. 16, 1941; s. Horace Harmon III and Eleaner (Pentz) L.; m. Nancy Taylor Mackall, Aug. 30, 1964 (dec. 1992); children: Bowie VanDeventer, Sallie Taylor. Student, Gettysburg U., 1962; BS, Am. U., 1965. Registered prin. SEC. Stockbroker Thomson, McKinnon & Auchincloss, Washington, 1966-76, Dean Witter Reynolds, Chevy Chase, Md., 1977-79; stockbroker, branch mgr., dir. Johnston, Lemon & Co., Inc., Bethesda, Md., 1979-89; stockbroker, br. mgr., dir. Johnston, Lemon & Co., Inc., Washington, 1989-90; v.p., branch mgr. Janney, Montgomery, Scott, Washington, 1990—. Active various orgns. and charities, Washington, Md. Episcopalian. Avocation: biking. Home: 5004 Scarsdale Rd Bethesda MD 20816-2438 Office: Janney Montgomery Scott 1225 23rd St NW Washington DC 20037-1102

LÜST, REIMAR, foundation president; b. Wuppertal, Germany, 1923. B.S. Physics, U. Frankfurt, Germany, 1949; Ph. D., Max-Planck Inst., Göttingen, Germany, 1955; Fulbright fellow, Enrico Fermi Inst. U. Chgo., Germany, 1955-56; Habilitation, U. Munich TH, Germany, 1959. Vis. prof. NYU, N.Y.C., 1959-60; mem. Max-Planck-Inst. f. Physik u. Astrophysik, Munich, Germany, 1960; vis. prof. MIT, Cambridge, 1961, Cal. Tech., Pasadena, 1962; dir. ESRO (European Space Research Organization), 1962-64, Inst. f. Extraterrestr. Physik, Max-Planck-Inst. f. Physik u. Astrophysik, Garching b. Munich, Germany, 1963; aus. ord. prof. U. Munich, Germany, 1963-72; hon. prof. U. Munich TH, Germany, 1963-72; v.p. ESRO, Germany, 1968-70; chmn. Wissenschaftsrat, Germany, 1969-72; pres. Max-Planck-Gesellschaft zur Förderung der Wissenschaften, 1972-84; gen. dir. Europäische Weltraumorganisation, Paris, France, 1984-90; pres. Alexander von Humboldt-Stiftung, Bonn, Germany, 1989-99, hon. pres., 1999—; prof. U. Hamburg, Germany, 1992; Max-Planck-Inst., Göttingen, Physics, 1951-55, Fulbright Fellow, Enrico Fermi Inst., U. Chicago, 1955-56; chmn. bd. Internat. U. Bremen, 1999—. Office: Humboldt Found, Max Planck Inst, Bundesstrasse 55, D-20146 Hamburg Germany

LUSCH, CHARLES JACK, oncologist; b. Lehighton, Pa., Feb. 15, 1936; s. Charles Norman and Loretta (Gaumer) L.; m. Carole Faye Eckart, Aug. 17, 1957; children: Marjorie, Susan, Stephen, Robert. AB in Biology magna cum laude, Lafayette Coll., Easton, Pa., 1957; MD, Temple U., 1961. Diplomate in med. oncology, hematology, internal medicine, forensic medicine; diplomate Am. Bd. Forensic Medicine. Pres. Berks Hematology-Oncology Assocs., Reading, Pa., 1968—; chief sect. of med. oncology & hematology Reading Hosp. & Med. Ctr., Reading, 1970—; dir. Pa. State Hemophilia Ctr., Reading Hosp. & Med. Ctr., 1973—; v.p. Lusch Motor Parts, Lehighton, Pa., 1975—; chief sect. med. oncology & hematology Community Gen. Hosp., Reading, 1980—; asst. chief medicine Reading Hosp. and Med. Ctr., 1986—; med. dir. Pocono Internat. Raceway, 1980-85; chmn. institutional rev. bd. Reading Hosp. and Med. Ctr., 1986—, dir. continuing med. edn., 1987—; med. dir. Berks County Hospice, Berks County Vis. Nurse Assn., Reading, 1987—; dir. oncology svcs. Reading Hosp. and Med. Ctr., 1990—; med. adv. com. Pa. Blue Shield, Camp Hill, Pa., 1987—; bd. dirs. Berks Home Health Car, Reading Cancer Ctr., Reading Hosp.; malpractice cons. Med. Protective Ins. Co., Ft. Wayne, Ind., 1985—; cons. in hematology and oncology Pottsville (Pa.) Hosp. and Good Samaritan Hosp., 1975—; clin. asst. prof. medicine Pa. Med. Sch., 1984—, Pa. State Med. Sch., 1981—, Temple U. Med. Sch., clin. assoc. prof. 1990; sr. clin. instr. Mahnemann U. Med. Sch., 1968—; prin. investigator Ea. Coop Oncology Group, 1975-90, Nat. Surg. Adj. & Breast Project, 1986—. Contbr. articles to profl. jours.; editor The Med. Record (regional med. jour.), 1970-71. Advisor Future Physicians Am., Reading, 1965; bd. dirs. Berks County unit Am. Cancer Soc., Reading, 1968-78, Keystone Cmty. Blood Bank, Reading, 1970-80; adv. com. The Women's Ctr., Reading Hosp., 1987-88; mem. bd. divsn. ch. soc. Evang. Luth. Ch. Am., Chgo.; pres. ch. coun. Atonement Luth. Ch., Wyomissing, Pa. Lt. comdr. USPHS, 1965-67. Fellow ACP; mem. Pa. Soc. Hematology-Oncology (sec.-treas. 1986-87), Am. Soc. Clin. Oncology, Am. Soc. Hematology, Am. Fedn. Clin. Rsch., Acad. Hospice Physicians (publs. com. 1989—), U.S. Amateur Ballroom Dance Assn. (past pres. Reading chpt.), Sports Car Club Am., Phi Beta Kappa, Alpha Omega Alpha. Republican. Lutheran. Avocations: competition ballroom dancing, tennis, motor racing. Home: 1617 Meadowlark Rd Wyomissing PA 19610-2820 Office: Berks Hematology Oncology Assoc 301 S 7th Ave Reading PA 19611-1410

LUSCHIN, SERGEY PETROVICH, physicist; b. Zaporozhye, Ukraine, Sept. 27, 1958; s. Peter Gavrilovich Luschin and Olga Efremovna Vidisheva. Student, Machinebuilding Inst., Zaporozhye, Ukraine, 1975-81, postgrad. student, 1983-87; student, Ednl. Svcs. Internat., Zaporozhye, Ukraine, 1993. Engr./rschr. Machinebuilding Inst., Zaporozhye, 1981-83, postgrad. student, 1983-87, scientific rschr., 1987-89, reader of physics, 1989-90; prof. asst. U. State Tech., Zaporozhye, 1990—; rsch. Inst. ELPA, Moscow, 1987-89, Chem. Inst., Moscow, 1985-86; gen. mgr. Ukraine-Bulgarian Joint Venture, Zaporozhye, 1995-96. Inventor in field. Avocations: music, sports. Office: State Tech Univ, Zhukovsky str 64, 69063 Zaporozhye Ukraine

LUSHCHAK, VOLODYMYR IVANOVYCH, biochemistry educator; b. Ivano-Frankivsk, Ukraine, Sept. 18, 1956; s. Ivan Kostevych and Adelya Ivanivna Lushchak; m. Ludmyla Pavlivna Tsymbaljuk, July 31, 1982; children: Oleg, Julia, Oksana. MS in Biochemistry, Moscow State U., 1982, PhD in Biochemistry, 1986. Sci. sec. to dir. Karadag br. Inst. So. Seas Biology of Nat. Acad. Scis. Ukraine, Kurortne, Feodosia, 1987-89, rsch. fellow, 1989-91, head Fish Biochemistry Lab., 1991-99; prof. biochemistry Vassyl Stefanyk Precarpathian U., Ivano-Frankivsk, 1999—; vis. prof. Nat. Sci. and Ednl. Rsch. Coun. Can., Ottawa, Ont., 1993; vis. scientist CNPq, Brasilia, Brazil, 1996-97; rschr. Found. Apoiio a Pesquisa Distrito Federal, Brasilia, 1996-97; conf. participant Internat. Sci. Found., Washington, 1993. Contbr. articles to sci. jours., including Ukrainian Biochem. Jour., Biochemistry, Hydrobiol. Jour., Biol. Scis., Comparative Biochemistry and Physiology, Biochemistry and Molecular Biology Internat. Mem. Communist Party USSR, 1981-89. Sgt. Soviet Army, 1974-76. Avocations: hunting, gardening, aquarium fish. Fax: (380-0322) 31574. E-mail: lushchak@pu.if.ua. Home: 16 Stefanyka St, Lysets, 285021 Ivano-Frankivsk Ukraine Office: Vassyl Stefanyk U Natural, Scis Dept, 57 Shevchenka St, 76000 Ivano-Frankivsk Ukraine

LUSHER, NICHOLAS CROSSON, art dealer; b. Paget, Bermuda, Nov. 30, 1962; s. William Nicholas Pike and Joy (Forsdike) L.; m. Jamie Beth Flon, Oct. 14, 1989; children: Benjamin James, Chloé Helena. Student, Kings Coll., London, 1982-85, Sothebys Inst., Eng., 1981. Owner, dir. Nicholas Lusher Fine Art, Hamilton, Bermuda, 1981—; curator Bermuda Nat. Gallery, 1994, dir. circle, 1994—, trustee, 1997-2000. Mem. Coral Beach Club, Bermuda Soc. Arts. Avocations: reading, travel, art, community.

LUSHNIKOVA, OKSANA YURIEVNA, educator; b. Severouralsk, Russia, June 14, 1944; arrived in Russia, 1987; d. Yuriy Ivanovich Haber and Yekaterina Pavlovna Murzina; 1 child, Lev L'vovich. Mining engr., Sverdlovsk Mining Inst., Russia, 1969; D in Tech. Sci., Moscow Mining Inst., 1987. Engr. Geol. Expedition, Antrazit, Ukraine, 1969-74; engr.-in-chief sci. dept. Spetstamponazhgeologia, Antrazit, 1974-80, Grouting Enterprise of Spetstamponazhgeologia, Antrazit, 1980-87; prof. Urals State Mining Geol. Acad., Yekaterinburg, Russia, 1987—; rschr., design cons. Urals Mining Geol. Acad., Yekaterinburg, 1987—. Co-author: Grouting of Aquifer Rocks, 1989, Integrated Grouting and Hydrogeology of Fractured Rocks in the Former USSR, 1993, Control and Processing of Grouting, 1995; contbr. articles to profl. jours. Recipient USSR state prize for the creation of new technology of integrated grouting method The Soviet Govt., Moscow, 1983. Mem. N.Y. Acad. Scis., Russian Ecology Acad. (assoc.). Avocations: painting, music, traveling. Home: Flat 51, 31 Krestinskiy St, 620003 Yekaterinburg Russia

LUST, HERBERT COHNFELDT, III, securities trader; b. Chgo., Jan. 15, 1957; s. Herbert Cohnfeldt Lust II and Frances Ratcliffe Hutchins; m. Melani D'amore Espinosa, May 17, 1997; 1 child, Terry Grosvenor Hutchins. BA, NYU, 1976, MBA, 1986. Account rep., ltd. ptnr. Herzfeld & Stern, N.Y.C., 1978-88; portfolio mgr. distressed investments Halcyon Investments, N.Y.C., 1988-89; head distressed rsch. Bear Stearns & Co., N.Y.C., 1990-94; co-head high yield dept. Furman Selz, N.Y.C., 1994-95; head distressed rsch. Lehman Bros., N.Y.C., 1995-97; bus. mgr. distressed securities Smith Barney, N.Y.C., 1997-98, J.P. Morgan, N.Y.C., 1998—. Author: Alexandera Finds Out. Home: 613 Hudson St New York NY 10014-1813

LUSTIG, SUSAN GARDNER, occupational therapist; b. Beloit, Wis., Apr. 27, 1942; d. James and Sally Howell; m. Karl Anton Lustig, Aug. 16, 1969 (div. 1997); children: Kurt, Daniel, Benjamin, David, Amy, Richard, Lauren. BS with distinction, U. Minn., 1965. Cert. occupl. therapist. Occupl. therapist Minn. State Hosp., Hastings, 1965-66; occupl. therapy cons. Hawaii Divsn. Vocat. Rehab., Honolulu, 1966-67; occupl. therapist Kaneohe (Hawaii) State Hosp., 1967; occupl. therapist Minn. VA Hosp., Mpls., 1967-68, unit supervisor, 1968-70; chief occupl. therapist, occupl. therapy dept. mgr. Avery Health Care Sys., Newland, N.C., 1997-2000. Bd. dirs. Harrison County Sheltered Workshop, 1971-72, Ottawa (Ill.) Pub. Health Nursing, 1976-78, Diversified Industries, 1970-72, Cooking for Christ, 1998—; pres. LaSalle (Ill.) Co. Med. Aux., 1976-78; bd. dirs. Heartland Christian Acad. Sch., 1986-88; organist Crossnore 1st Bapt. Mem. Am. Occupl. Therapy Assn., World Fedn. Occupl. Therapists, Minn. Occupl. Therapy Assn., N.C. Occupl. Therapy Assn. Republican. Baptist. Avocations: organ, antiques, woodcarving, ice skating, reading. Home: 15 Little Cow Camp Rd Newland NC 28657-8704

LUSTIGER, JEAN-MARIE CARDINAL, archbishop; b. Paris, Sept. 17, 1926; s. Charles and Gisèle Lustiger. Ed., U. Paris, Sorbonne and Caremlite Sem., Inst. Catholique de Paris. Ordained priest Roman Cath. Ch., 1954, consecrated bishop, 1979. Chaplain to students Sorbonne, 1954-69; dir. Centre Richelieu, 1959-69; pastor Sainte-Jeanne-de-Chantal Parish, Paris, 1969-79; bishop of Orléans, 1979-81, archbishop of Paris, 1981—, elevated to cardinal, 1983. Author: Sermons d'un curé de Paris, 1978, Pain de vie, Peuple de Dieu, 1981, Osez croire/Osez vivre, 1985, Premiers pas dans la prière, 1986, Six sermons aux élus de la Nation, 1987, Le Choix de Dieu, 1987, La Messe, 1988, Le sacrement de l'Onction des malades, 1990, Dieu merci, les droits de l'homme, 1990, Nous avons rendez-vous avec l'Europe, 1991, Petites paroles de nuit de Noël, 1992, Devenez Dignes de la Condition Humaine, 1995, Le Bapteme de votre enfant, 1997, Soyez heureux, 1997, Pour l'Europe, un nouvel art de vivre, 1999, Les Pretres que Dieu donne, 2000. Mem. Acad. Francaise. Address: Maison diocésaine, 8 rue de la Ville-l'Évêque, 75384 Paris Cedex 08, France

LUTHANS, FRED, management educator, writer, consultant; b. Clinton, Iowa, June 28, 1939; s. Carl H. and Leona D. L.; m. Katharine L., June 9, 1963; children: Kristin, Brett, Kyle, Paige. BA, U. Iowa, 1961, MBA, 1962, PhD, 1965. Prof. mgmt. U. Nebr., Lincoln, 1967—; trainer, cons. Nat. Rural Electric Coop. Assn., Washington, 1970—; sr. scientist Gallup Orgn., Lincoln, 1998—. Author: Organizational Behavior, 1973, International Management, 1991; cons. editor Mc Graw-Hill Inc., N.Y.C., 1975-98, editor Orgnl. Dynamics Jour, 1989, Jour. of World Bus, 1996. Capt. U.S. Army, 1965-67. Fellow Acad. Mgmt. (pres. 1986, Disting. Mgmt. Educator 1997, Hall of Fame 2000), Decision Scis. Inst., Pan Pacific Bus. Assn. Avocations: golf, physical exercise. E-mail: fluthans1@unl.edu. Office: U Nebr Dept Mgmt Lincoln NE 68588

LUTHJE, JURGEN, academic administrator; b. Dievenow, Germany, Sept. 30, 1941. Mem. scientific staff U. Bochum, Germany, 1968-73, legal office, 1973; scientific staff mem. Fed. Min. Edn. & Sci., 1973-91; pres. U. Hamburg, Germany, 1991—. Co-author: Der numerus clausus oder Wer darf studieren?, 1973. Office: U Hamburg, Edmund-Siemers-Allee 1, 20146 Hamburg Germany

LUTHRA, RAJESH, biochemist, researcher; b. Ferozepur, Punjab, India, Nov. 15, 1957; s. Romesh Chander and Sanyogita (Gulati) L.; m. Pratibha Mehta, June 1, 1990; 1 child, Prerna. BSc, Punjabi U., Patiala, India, 1976; MSc in Biochemistry, Punjab Agrl. U., Ludhiana, India, 1979, PhD in Biochemistry, 1982. Scientist B biochemistry and molecular biology divsn. Ctrl. Inst. Medicinal & Aromatic Plants, Coun. Sci. and Indsl. Rsch., New Delhi, 1982-87; scientist C Ctrl. Inst. Medicinal & Aromatic Plants, CSIR, New Delhi, 1987-90, scientist EI, 1990-95, scientist EII, 1995—; vis. scientist Plant Biochemistry Inst., Halle, Germany, 1987; postdoctoral rsch. assoc. U. Nebr. Med. Ctr., Omaha, 1991-93. Author: (with others) Skin Cancer: Mechanisms and Human Relevance, 1994, Recent Advances in Biosynthesis of Alkaloids, 1999; contbr. articles to profl. jours. Grantee Dept. Biotechnology, 1996. Mem. Soc. Biol. Chemists (life). Home: CIMAP Colony Sector 7, Vikas Nagar, Lucknow 226015, India Office: CIMAP, PO CIMAP, Lucknow 226015, India

LUTHRA, RITA, obstetrician/gynecologist, consultant; b. Bikaner, India, July 9, 1951; came to U.S., 1979; d. Balmokand R. and Santosh B. Luthra. MB, BChir with honors, U. Rajasthan, India, 1973; MD, Postgrad. Inst. Edn. & Rsch., India, 1977; diploma in ob-gyn., Nat. Health Svcs., Esquintala, Guatemala, 1992. Diplomate Am. Bd. Ob-gyn. Assoc. in ob-gyn. U. Mass., Worcester, 1983-96; chmn. Women's Health and Edn. Orgn., Worcester, 1993-96; chief of dept. Johnson Meml. Hosp., Stafford Spring, Conn., 1995-99; chmn. Holyoke (Mass.) Hosp., 1999—; dir. devel. Woman'sHealthChannel.com for www.HealthCommunities.com; cons. midwifery program Peace Corps, Coban, Guatemala, 1993-94. Contbr. articles to profl. jours. Corporator Worcester Art Mus., 1991-95; bd. dirs. Day Break, Worcester, 1988-9; rep. to UN Internat. Year of Family, Women's Health and Edn. Orgn., Malta, 1994; mem. Internat. Affairs Coun., Yale U., 1996—. Fellow Am. Coll. Ob-Gyn. (internat. affairs com. 1996—). Avocations: travel, music, fine dining. Home: 31 Ely Way Longmeadow MA 01106-1867

LUTHY, ISABEL ALICIA, chemist, researcher; b. Buenos Aires, Argentina, Aug. 13, 1954; d. Wolfram and Orodina Isabel (Finardi) L.; m. Joseph Charles Marc Thibeault, July 6, 1989; 1 child, Gabriel Thibeault. Lic. in chemistry, U. Buenos Aires, 1978, PhD in Chemistry, 1983. Postdoctoral fellow CONICET (Argentina), Can., 1984-88; staff rschr. CONICET (Argentina), Buenos Aires, 1988—. Contbr. more than 25 articles to profl. jours. Grantee CONICET, 1998—, Fundacion Roemmers, 1993, 96, 99. Mem. Soc. Argentina de Investigacion Clinica (sec. 1999), Soc. Argentina Biologia (dir. com. 1984—, v.p. 2000-2002). Avocations: literature, music, playing with my child. Office: Inst Biol y Med Exptl, Obligado 2490, 1428 Buenos Aires Argentina

LUTJEHARMS, JOHANN REINDER ERLERS, oceanographer, educator; b. Bloemfonein, South Africa, Apr. 13, 1944; s. Wilhelm Jan and Antje Marijtje (Bloemendaal) L.; m. Ronel Vogel, July 2, 1972; children: Maria, Wilhelm. BSc, U Cape Town, South Africa, 1968, BSc (Hons), 1969; MSc cum laude, U. Cape Town, 1971, DSc, 1992; PhD, U. Wash., 1977. Rschr. CSIR, Stellenbosch, South Africa, 1972-90; prof. U. Cape Town, Rondebosch, 1990—; hon. prof. Rand Afrikaans U., Johannesburg, 1992—; dir. Ctr. Marine Studies, Cape Town, 1993-97. Tech. editor: False Bay 21 Years On, 1991; co-editor: The J.L.B. Smith Institute of Ichthyology-50 Years, 1997; contbr. articles to profl. jours. With South African Navy Res., 1966—. Rhodes U. fellow, 1989—, Nat. Environ. Rsch. Coun. fellow, 1990, U. Cape Town fellow, 1995—; recipient Alexander von Humbold Found. prize, 1993, John D. Gilchrist Gold medal South African Network for Coastal and Oceanic Rsch., 1996. Fellow Royal Soc. South Africa (v.p. 1992-94), South African Acad.; mem. Am. Geophys. Union. Mem. Dutch Reformed Ch. Avocations: jogging, gardening. Office: Dept Oceanography, U Cape Town, Rondebosch 7700, South Africa

LÜTKEPOHL, HELMUT, econometrics educator, researcher; b. Bad Oeynhausen, Germany, July 26, 1951; m. Sabine Dornbusch. Diploma (masters) in math., U. Bielefeld, Germany, 1977, PhD in Econs., 1981; Habilitation, U. Osnabrück, Germany, 1984. Lectr. U. Osnabrück, 1981-83; vis. asst. prof. U. Calif., San Diego, 1984-85; prof. stats. U. Hamburg, Germany, 1985-87, U. Kiel, Germany, 1987-92; prof. econometrics Humboldt U., Berlin, 1992—. Co-author: The Theory and Practice of Econometrics, 1985; author: Introduction to Multiple Time Series Analysis, 1991, Handbook of Matrices, 1996. Fellow Jour. Econometrics, 1989—. Mem. Internat. Statis. Inst. Office: Humboldt U Econs Faculty, Spandauer Strasse 1, 10178 Berlin Germany

LUTKIC, ALEKSANDAR, biochemistry educator; b. Zagreb, Croatia, Oct. 16, 1934; s. Nenad and Etelka (Stimac) L.; m. Zlata Samec, Aug. 4, 1962 (div. 1969); 1 child, Miroslav. Degree in chemistry, Faculty of Scis., Zagreb, 1958; DSc, Faculty of Medicine, Zagreb, 1969, habilitation, 1974. Asst. Inst. Med. Rsch., Zagreb, 1959-63; from asst. to assoc. prof. dept. physiology faculty medicine U. Zagreb, Croatia, 1964-78, prof., head dept. chemistry and biochemistry faculty vet. medicine, 1978—; guest prof. med. faculty, Rijeka, Croatia, 1975-77, vet. faculty, Leipzig, Germany, 1989, 90. Author: Biokemija, 5th edit., 1992, Medical Lexikon, 1992; contbr. chpts. to books. Alexander von Humboldt scholar, 1971, 72, 83, 84. Mem. Croatian Chem. Soc., Croatian Physiol. Soc. (v.p. 1981-85, acknowledgement 1963), Croatian Biochem. Soc. (acknowledgement 1996). Roman Catholic. Avocations: ceramics, scouting. E-mail: aleksandar.lutkic@zg.tel.hr. Home: Aleja pomoraca 5/X, HR10020 Zagreb Croatia Office: Fac Vet Med U Zagreb, Heinzelova 55 PO Box 466, HR10002 Zagreb Croatia

LUTON, JEAN MARIE, space agency administrator; b. Chamalières, Puy-de Dome, France, Aug. 4, 1942; s. Pierre Luton and Marie Piatot; m. Cécile Robine, 1967; children: Grégoire, Augustin, Clément. Lycée Blaise Pascal, France; Clermont Ferrand, ClermontúFerrand, Saint Louis, Paris; Faculty of Science, Paris; Engineer Diploma in Math. and Physics, Ecole Polytechnique, France. Researcher Centre National de la Recherche Scientifique, 1964-70; dir. of programs Ministry for Indsl. and Scientific Devel., 1971-74; with program and indsl. policy directorate Centre National d'Etudes Spatiales, 1974; head of rsch. program divsn. Centre National d Etudes Spatiales, 1974-75, head of planning and projections divsn., 1975-78, dir. programs and planning, 1978-84, dep. dir. gen., 1984-87, dir. gen., 1989-90; dir. space programs Aérospatiale, 1987-89; dir. gen. European Space Agency, 1990-97, Arianespace, 1997—. Decorated officier Order National du Mérite, chevalier Ordre National de la Légion d'Honneur; recipient Astronautics prize French Assn. for Aeronautics and Astronautics, 1985. Mem. Internat. Acad. Astronautics. Office: Arianespace, Blvd de l'Europe BP 177, 91006 Evry-Courcouronnes Cedex, France*

LÜTTGE, ULRICH ERNST, botany educator; b. Berlin, July 16, 1936; m. Ursula Zimmermann, Oct. 6, 1962; children: Christoph, Katharina, Eva Ulrike. Dr.rer.nat., U. Tech., Darmstadt, Germany, 1960, Habilitation, 1964. Asst. U. Tech., Darmstadt, Germany, 1960-65; dozent U. Tech., Darmstadt, 1965, 66-68, assoc. prof., 1970, prof., 1970—; dean dept. biology, 1971-72; postdoct. fellow U. Calif., L.A., 1965-66; vis. fellow Australian Nat. U., Canberra, Australia, 1968-69. Author: Botanik - Ein grundlegendes Lehrbuch, 3d edit., 1999, Psysiological Ecology of Tropical Plants, 1997; editor: Transport in Plants II, Part B Tissues and Organs, 1976; editor-in-chief Plant Biology; mng. editor Trees: Structure and Function; contbr. 400 articles to profl. jours. Recipient Körber prize European Sci. Körber Found., 1996. Fellow Deutsche Akademie Naturforscher Leopoldina, Academia Europaea; mem. German Bot. Soc., Bavarian Bot. Soc. Lutheran. Avocations: music, gardening, mountaineering, long distance running. Office: U Technology Inst Botany, Schnittspahnstr 3-5, D-64287 Darmstadt Germany

LUTTINGER, AMY LORE, secondary education educator, researcher; b. Stamford, Conn.; d. Lionel and Lenore Luttinger; m. Philip Kaaret, June 7, 1992; children: Alexander Kaaret, Maija-Liisa Luttinger. BS in Physics, MIT, 1981; PhD in Molecular Biology, Princeton U., 1992. Post-doctorate Pub. Health Rsch. Inst., N.Y.C., 1992-96; prof. N.Y. Inst. Tech., N.Y.C., 1996-98, Salem (Mass.) State Coll., 1998—. Contbr. articles to profl. jours. Office: Salem State Coll Dept Biology 352 Lafayette St Salem MA 01970-5348

LUTTNER, EDWARD F., consulting company executive; b. Cleve., Feb. 16, 1942; s. John J. and Angela (Haberbosch) L.; m. Nancy E., July 15, 1977; children: Amy, Mark. BA, Loyola U., 1966, MDiv, 1974; MA, U. Detroit, 1970. Cert. NASD. Dir. standards-devel. Bernard Haldane Assocs., Boston, Internat. Career Consulting Corp., Waltham, Mass.; v.p. career mgmt. svcs. Bernard Haldane Assocs., Cleve.; dir. profl. svcs. Right Assocs., Phila.; pres. Elby Career Group, Inc., Cleve. V.p. Rotary, Fairview Park, 1988-89. Mem. AACD, Nat. Career Devel. Assn.

LUTZ, ERICH, communication engineer; b. Augsburg, Germany, Apr. 2, 1950. Degree in engring., Poly. Augsburg, 1972; diploma in engring., Tech. U. Munich, 1977; D in Engring., U. Armed Forces, Munich, 1983. Sect. head German Aerospace Rsch. Establishment, Oberpfaffenhofen, Germany, 1986—. Author: System Theorie, 1983, Satellite Communication, 2000; contbr. over 100 articles to profl. jours. Informationstechnische Gesellschaft prize, 1984. Mem. IEEE (sr.).

LUTZ, HANS RUDOLF, electric power industry executive; b. Bern, Jan. 13, 1933; s. Eugen and Ida (Kämpf) L.; m. Susanna Hanna Schmid, Dec. 6, 1958 (div. 1984); children: Johannes, Simon, Julia, Viola; m. Margrit Müller, May 17, 1985. Lic. phil.nat., U. Bern, 1959, PhD in Physics, 1961, lectr., 1969. Cert. physicist. Rsch. asst. Eidg. Inst. Reaktorforschung, Wurenlingen, Switzerland, 1959-61; rsch. scientist EIR, Wurenlingen, Switzerland, 1961-66; dir. Muhleberg Nuclear Power Sta. Bernische Kraftwerke AG, Bern, Switzerland, 1967-79; dir. planning Brown Boveri Co., Baden, Switzerland, 1979-85; v.p. Atel, Olten, Switzerland, 1986-92; CEO Zwilag/NOK, Baden, 1992-99; owner, CEO, Swiss Sakura Travel GmbH, 2000—; cons. Zwilag AG, others, 1999—. Author: Zum Beispiel Wylerau, 1974. Mem. Parliament, Köniz, 1973-78, dep., Kanton Bern, 1978-87; pres. Ch. Coun., Schönenwerd, Switzerland, 1992—; dep., Kanton Solothurn, 1997—. Capt. Swiss Artillery, 1967-84. Mem. Kettenreaktion Grassroot Orgn. Nuclear Energy (pres. 1978—), Rotary (pres. 1978-79, 97-98). Mem. Swiss Peoples Party. Avocations: playing violin, skiing, skating, learning Japanese. Home: Mattenstr 1, CH-4654 Lostorf Switzerland Office: Zwilag/Nok, Parkstrasse 23, 5401 Baden Switzerland

LUTZ, JOHN SHAFROTH, lawyer; b. San Francisco, Sept. 10, 1943; s. Frederick Henry and Helena Morrison (Shafroth) L.; m. Elizabeth Boschen, Dec. 14, 1968; children: John Shafroth, Victoria. BA, Brown U., 1965; JD, U. Denver, 1971. Bar: Colo. 1971, U.S. Dist. Ct. Colo. 1971, U.S. Ct. Appeals (2d cir.) 1975, D.C. 1976, U.S. Supreme Ct. 1976, U.S. Dist. Ct. (so. dist.) N.Y. 1977, U.S. Tax Ct. 1977, U.S. Ct. Appeals (10th cir.) 1979, N.Y. 1984, U.S. Ct. Appeals (9th cir.) 1990, U.S. Dist. Ct. (no. dist.) Calif. 1993. Trial atty. Denver regional office U.S. SEC, 1971-74; spl. atty. organized crime, racketeering sect. U.S. Dept. Justice (so. dist.) N.Y., 1974-77; atty. Kelly, Stansfield and O'Donnell, Denver, 1977-78; gen. counsel Boettcher & Co., Denver, 1987, spl. counsel, 1987-88, ptnr., 1988-93; of counsel LeBoeuf, Lamb, Greene and MacRae, LLP, Denver, 1993-94, ptnr., 1995—; spkr. on broker, dealer, securities law and arbitration issues to various profl. orgns. Contbr. articles to profl. jours. Bd. dirs. Cherry Creek Improvement Assn., 1980-84, Spalding Rehab. Hosp., 1986-89; chmn., vice-chmn. securities sub sect. Bus. Law Sect. of Colo. Bar, 1990, chmn., 1990-91. Lt. (j.g.) USNR, 1965-67. Mem. ABA, Colo. Bar Assn., Denver Bar Assn., Am. Law Inst., Securities Industry Assn. (state regulation com. 1982-86), Nat. Assn. Securities Dealers, Inc. (nat. arbitration com. 1987-91), St. Nicholas Soc. N.Y.C., Denver Law Club, Denver Country Club, Denver Athletic Club (dir. 1990-93), Univ. Club (Denver), Rocky Mountain Brown Club (founder, past pres.), Racquet and Tennis Club. Republican. Episcopalian. Office: LeBoeuf Lamb Greene MacRae LLP 633 17th St Ste 2000 Denver CO 80202-3620

LUTZ, JOHN THOMAS, author; b. Dallas, Sept. 11, 1939; s. John Peter and Esther Jane (Gundelfinger) L.; m. Barbara Jean Bradley, Mar. 15, 1958; children: Steven, Jennifer, Wendy. Student, Meramec C.C., 1965. Author: The Truth of the Matter, 1971, Buyer Beware, 1976, Bonegrinder, 1977, Lazarus Man, 1979, Jericho Man, 1980, The Shadow Man, 1981; (with Steven Greene) Exiled, 1982; (with Bill Pronzini) The Eye, 1984, Nightlines, 1984, The Right to Sing the Blues, 1986, Tropical Heat, 1986, Ride the Lightning, 1987, Scorcher, 1987, Dancers Debt, 1988, Shadowtown, 1988, Kiss, 1988, Better Mousetraps (short story collection), 1988, Time Exposure, 1989, Flame, 1990, Diamond Eyes, 1990, SWF Seeks Same (Single White Female), 1990, Bloodfire, 1991, Hot, 1992, Dancing with the Dead, 1992, Spark, 1993, Thicker than Blood, 1993, (short story collection) Shadows Everywhere, 1994, Torch, 1994, Death by Jury, 1995, Burn, 1995, Lightning, 1996; (novel and screenplay) The Ex, 1996, Oops!, 1998; (with David August) Final Seconds, 1998; (short stories) Until You Are Dead, 1998; contbr. short stories and articles to mystery and private-eye mags. Mem. Mystery Writers Am. (Scroll 1981, Edgar award 1986), Pvt.-Eye Writers Am. (shamus award 1982, 88, Life Achievement award 1995). Democrat. Home and Office: 880 Providence Ave Saint Louis MO 63119-2072

LUTZ, MYRON HOWARD, obstetrician, gynecologist, surgeon, educator; b. N.Y.C., June 26, 1938; s. Morris David and Rose (Greenblatt) L.; m. Judy Cohen, Aug. 6, 1963; children: Mark Steven, Sheri Lutz Barnett, Kenneth Ian. BA, Columbia U., 1960; MD, NYU, 1964. Diplomate Am. Bd. Ob-Gyn., Am. Bd. Gynecologic Oncology. Intern Phila., Gen. Hosp., 1964-65; resident in ob-gyn. Albert Einstein Coll. Medicine, Bronx, N.Y., 1965-69; fellow M.D. Anderson Hosp., Houston, 1971-72, U. Miami (Fla.) Sch. Medicine, 1972-73; asst. prof. ob-gyn. Med. U. S.C., Charleston, 1973-76, co-dir. gynecology oncology, 1973-77, clin. assoc. prof. ob-gyn., 1977—, clin. assoc. prof. surgery, 1986—; pvt. practice, Charleston, 1973—; mem. cancer adv. bd. Roper Hosp., Charleston, 1993—; star TV mid-day talk show, 1990—. Author pub. svc. ednl. tapes on gynec. problems; mem. edtl. bd. House Calls mag., 1992—. Bd. dirs. Am. Cancer Soc., Charleston, 1974-75, v.p., 1975-76, pres., 1976-78; bd. dirs. Trident Acad., Charleston, 1982-86, Hospice, Charleston, 1984-86. Maj. M.C., U.S. Army, 1969-71. Fellow ACOG, ACS; mem. AMA, Am. Radium Soc., Am. Soc. Clin. Oncology, Soc. Gynecologic Oncologists, Felix Rutledge Soc., S.C. Med. Soc., S.C. Oncology Soc., Charleston Med. Soc. Avocations: water and snow skiing, archery, biking. Home: 55 Chadwick Dr Charleston SC 29407-7450 Office: 1606 Ashley River Rd Charleston SC 29407-5902

LUTZ, RAYMOND PRICE, industrial engineer, educator; b. Oak Park, Ill., Feb. 27, 1935; s. Raymond Price and Sibyl Elizabeth (Haralson) L.; m. Nancy Marie Cole, Aug. 23, 1958. BSME, U. N.Mex., 1958, MBA, 1962; PhD, Iowa State U., 1964. Registered profl. engr., N.Mex., Okla. With Sandia Corp., Albuquerque, summers 1958-63; instr. mech. engring. U. N.Mex., 1958-62; from asst. to assoc. prof. indsl. engring. N.Mex. State U., 1964-68; prof. head indsl. engring. U. Okla., 1968-73; prof., acting dean U. Tex. Sch. Mgmt., Dallas, 1973-76, dean, 1976-78, exec. dean grad. studies and rsch., 1979-92, prof. ops. mgmt., 1992—; cons. Bell Telephone Labs., Tex. Instruments, Kennecott Corp., Bath Iron Works, City of Dallas, Oklahoma City; cons. U.S. Army, USAF, U.S. Dept. Transp., Los Angeles and Seattle public schs.; mem. shipbldg. productivity panel NRC. Editor: The Engring. Economist, 1973-77, Indsl. Mgmt., 1983-87. Pres., bd. dirs. United Cerebral Palsy, Dallas, 1978, treas., 1984-88; bd. dirs., treas. Amigos Bibliographic Network, Dallas, 1984-90; chmn., bd. dirs. S.W. Police Inst., Dallas, 1980—; v.p., bd. dirs. Santa Fe Opera, 1988—; bdl dirs. Dallas Opera, 1989—, Santa Fe Opera Found., 1993—. Fellow AAAS, Am. Inst. Indsl. Engrs. (v.p. industry and mgmt. divsns., trustee, dir. engring. economy divsn., systems engring. group); mem. Am. Soc. Engring. Edn. (chmn. engring. economy divsn., Eugene L. Grant award 1972), INFORMS, Dallas Classic Guitar Soc. (bd. dirs. 1993-96, v.p. 1994-96), Ops. Mgmt. Assn. (bd. dirs. 1994-98), Sigma Xi (bd. dirs. 1990-98, 99—, chmn. capital campaign 1992—, exec. com. 1992-95). Avocation: jogging. Home: 1230 Turquoise Trl Cerrillos NM 87010-9716 Office: U Tex at Dallas PO Box 830688 Richardson TX 75083-0688

LUTZ, ROBERT ANTHONY, automotive company executive; b. Zurich, Switzerland, Feb. 12, 1932; came to U.S., 1939; s. Robert H. and Marguerite (Schmid) L.; m. Betty D. Lutz, Dec. 12, 1956 (div. 1979); children: Jacqueline, Carolyn, Catherine, Alexandra; m. Heide Marie Schmid, Mar. 3, 1980 (div. Dec. 1992); m. Denise Ford, Apr. 17, 1994; 2 stepchildren. BS in Prodn. Mgmt., U. Calif., Berkeley, 1961, MBA in Mktg. with highest honors, 1962; LLD, Boston U., 1985. Research assoc., sr. analyst IMEDE, Lausanne, Switzerland, 1962-63; sr. analyst forward planning GM, N.Y.C., 1963-65; mgr. vehicle div. GM, Paris, 1966-69; staff asst., mng. dir. Adam Opel, Russelsheim, Germany, 1965-66, asst. mgr. domestic sales, 1969, dir. sales Vorstand, 1969-70; v.p. Vorstand BMW, Munich, 1972-74; gen. mgr. Ford of Germany, Cologne, Germany, 1974-76; v.p. truck ops. Ford of Europe, Brentwood, Eng., 1976-77, pres., 1977-79, chmn., 1979-82, also bd. dirs.; exec. v.p. Ford Internat., Dearborn, Mich., 1982-84, Chrysler Motors Corp., Highland Park, Mich., 1986-88; pres. ops., pres., COO Chrysler Corp., Highland Park, Mich., 1988-96; vice chmn. Chrysler Corp.; chmn., ceo, pres. Exide Corp., 1998—; bd. dirs. Northrop-Grumman, Kepner-Tregoe, Silicon Graphics, Northrop-Grumman, ASCOM, Switzerland; mem., former chmn. Hwy. Users Fedn. for Safety and Mobility. Trustee Mich. Cancer Found.; bd. dirs. United Way of Southeastern Mich., USMC Command and Staff Coll. Found.; mem. adv. bd. Walter A. Haas Sch. Bus., U. Calif., Berkeley, 1979—. Capt. USMC, 1954-59. Named Alumnus of Yr., Sch. Bus., U. Calif., 1983; Kaiser Found. grantee, 1962. Mem. NAM (exec. com.), Phi Beta Kappa. Republican. Avocations: skiing, motorcycling, bicycling, helicopter flying, vintage cars, fixed-wing flying. Office: Exide Corp 2901 Hubbard St Ann Arbor MI 48105-2435 also: Exide Corp 645 Penn St Reading PA 19601*

LUTZ, SAMANTHA JUDITH, industrial engineering manager; b. Trenton, N.J., Jan. 1, 1970; d. Edward R. and Carolyn M. (Yurcho) Kramarz; m. Douglas B. Lutz, July 3, 1993. BS in Indsl. Engring., Rutgers U., 1992; postgrad. in Adminstrn., Ctrl. Mich. U., 1997-00. Registered profl. engr., Mich. Acad. counselor Rutgers U. Coll. Engring., Piscataway, N.J., 1990; indsl. engring. student GM, Saginaw, Mich., 1991; application engr. Lamb Technicon, Divsn. of UNOVA, Warren, Mich., 1993-97, mgr. mfg. systems analysis, 1998—. Instr. Jr. Achievement, Detroit, 1994-95; vol. sci. fair judge Detroit Elem. Sch. Mem. NSPE, Inst. Indsl. Engrs. (sr.), Am. Soc. Quality (sr.), Soc. Mfg. Engrs. (sr.), UNOVA (dep chair rsch. and mktg. coun.), Rutgers U. Alumni Assn. Republican. Roman Catholic. Avocations: travel, scuba diving, Neapolitan Mastiffs, rollerblading, waterskiing. Home: 53689 Applewood Dr Shelby Township MI 48315-1343 Office: Lamb Technicon Divsn of UNOVA 5663 E 9 Mile Rd Warren MI 48091-2562

LUTZE, RUTH LOUISE, retired textbook editor, public relations executive; b. Boston, Apr. 19, 1917; d. Frederick Clemons and Louise (Rausch) L. BA with honors, Radcliffe Coll., 1938; postgrad., Boston U., 1938-39. Tchr. Winthrop (Mass.) Pub. Schs., 1938-39; with pub. rels. dept. Boston City Club, 1939-42; sr. projects editor D.C. Heath & Co., Lexington, Mass., 1942-82; book reviewer, lectr., cons. on pub. rels., lectr. textbook publ. Bd. dirs. Winthrop Improvement and Hist. Assn., 1980—; vol. tchr. Boston Pub. Schs., 1967-77; mem. Winthrop Rep. Town Com., 1970—; v.p. 1st Luth. Ch. Boston, 1986, deacon, 1980—. Recipient cert. appreciation for vol. in edn., Kiwanis Club of East Boston, 1972. Mem. Radcliffe Club Boston. Avocations: volunteer work, theatre, birdwatching, reading, art exhibits. Home: 110 Circuit Rd Winthrop MA 02152-2819

LUU, JAMES CUONG PHU, correctional services educator; b. Vinh-Binh, Tra-Vinh, Vietnam, Apr. 29, 1972; s. Phuoc Thu and Thuong Thi-Nguyet (Vo) L. BA in Australian Cultural Studies, Victoria (Australia) U. Tech., 1995, MA in Asian and Internat. Studies, 1997, grad. diploma in Edn., 2000. Cmty. correctional svcs. educator Dept. of Justice, Office of Corrections, Melbourne, 1998—. Fellow Alumni Assn. Melbourne (student). Avocations: talk radio, playing soccer, martial arts, reading, movies. Home: 19 Hilgay St, Coolaroo, Victoria Melbourne VIC 3048, Australia Office: Dept Justice Of Corrections, City of Carlton, Melbourne Australia

LUUS, GEORGE AARNE, physician; b. Estonia, Apr. 23, 1937; s. Edgar and Aili (Poldmaa) L.; MD, U. Toronto (Ont., Can.), 1962; m. Margit Jaanusson, Sept. 14, 1962 (div. 1983); children—Caroline Anna Elizabeth, Clyde Gregory Edgar, Lia Esther Isabelle; m. 2d, Donna Gervais Martell, Oct. 1, 1983. Intern Toronto East Gen. and Orthopaedic Hosp.; practice medicine specializing in family medicine, Sault Sainte Marie, Ont., 1963—; mem. Algoma Dist. Med. Group, 1966—; sec. med. staff Gen. Hosp., 1972—, v.p., bd. dirs., 1973. Adv. bd. Can. Scholarship Trust Found., 1976-77. Mem. Algoma West Med. Acad., Rotary. Home: 42 Linstedt St, Sault Sainte Marie, ON Canada P6B 3H9 Office: 240 McNabb St, Sault Sainte Marie, ON Canada P6B 1Y5

LUUTONEN, JORMA KALERVO, linguist; b. Haukipudas, Finland, May 22, 1956; s. Reino Kalervo and Anna-Liisa (Sinervo) L.; m. Helena Sinikka Rintala, Aug. 15, 1981; children: Antti, Saara. MA, U. Turku, Finland, 1984, Licentiate of Philosophy, 1994, PhD, 1997, docent, 1999. Asst. dept. Finno-Ugric langs. U. Turku, 1983-98, rsch. officer, 1999—; project leader Rsch. Unit Volgaic Langs., Turku, 1993—. Author: (book) The Variation of Morpheme Order in Mari Declension, 1997 (Sci. award Soc. Uralo-Altaica 1997); contbr. articles to sci. jours. Mem. Soc. Finno-Ugrian Soc. (grantee 1993), Assn. of Finnish Lang., Linguistic Assn. of Finland (treas. 1986-87). Orthodox. Avocations: drama, bridge. Home: Kaskenkatu 1 A 15, FIN20700 Turku Finland Office: U Turku Dept Finno-Ugric, Henrikinkatu 3, FIN20014 Turku Finland

LUWEI, YANG, engineer; b. Pingdingshan, Henan, China, Mar. 20, 1970; s. Yang and Sun (Qingrong) Hongye; m. Li Jianpei. BS, Xian Jiaotong U., Xi'an, China, 1991, PhD, 1996. Asst. rschr. Chinese Acad. Scis., Beijing, 1996-98, assoc. rschr., 1998—. Contbr. articles to profl. jours.; patentee in field. Recipient Sci. & Tech. Progress award Chinese Edn. Com., 1997, 98. Avocations: basketball, chess. Office: Chinese Acad of Scis, Crogenics Lab PO Box 2711, Beijing 100080, Republic of China

LUX, WOLFGANG, corporate executive; b. Remscheid, Germany, Oct. 10, 1956; s. Emil and Marianne (Hoolmann) L.; m. Yumi Furui, July 15, 1959; children: Lux, Kai. BSc, Drexel U., Phila., 1980; MA, Sophia U., Tokyo, 1986; D in Econs., U. Adminstrn., Moscow, 1994. Cert. tchr. shorthand. Rep. Far East OBI, Tokyo, Beijing, China, 1981-86; acct. mgr. Beiersdorf AG, Hamburg, Germany, 1988-90; program dir. MCE, Brussels, 1990-93; head programs AMA Internat. Mgmt. Ctr., Tokyo, 1993-94, gen. mgr., 1994—. Co-author: Interkulturelles Management, 1994; contbr. articles to profl. jours. Mem. Tokyo Am. Club, Am. C. of C., Fgn. Corrs. Club. Avocations: sailing, literature, travel, horseback riding. Office: AMA Internat Japan, Shuwa Kioicho TBR Bldg 7F, Chiyoda 102-0083, Japan

LUXTON, JANE C(HARLOTTE), lawyer; b. Phila., June 25, 1951; d. Elvin L. and Charoltte M. (Herring) Luxton; m. Charles Matz Horn, May 29, 1976; children: Andrew Luxton Horn, Caroline Charlotte Horn. BA, Harvard U., 1973; JD, Cornell U., 1976. Bar: D.C. 1976. Atty. advisor Commr. FTC, Washington, 1976-78; trial atty. Dept. Justice, Washington, 1978-81; assoc. Steptoe & Johnson, Washington, 1981-86, Bell Atlantic, Washington, 1986-89; assoc., then ptnr. Prather Seeger Doolittle & Farmer, Washington, 1989-94; ptnr. Vedder Price, Kammholz, Washington, 1994-95, Seeger Potter Richardson Luxton Joselow & Brooks, Washington, 1995-99, King & Spalding, Washington, 1999—; lawyer; b. Phila., June 25, 1951; d. Elvin L. and Charlotte M. (Herring) Luxton; m. Charles Matz Horn, May 29, 1976; children: Andrew Luxton Horn, Caroline Charlotte Horn. A.B., Radcliffe Coll.-Harvard U., 1973; J.D., Cornell U., 1976. Bar D.C. 1976. Atty. advisor Commr. FTC, Washington, 1976-78; trial atty. Dept. Justice, Washington, 1978-81; assoc. Steptoe & Johnson, Washington, 1981-86, Bell Atlantic, Washington, 1986-89; assoc., then ptnr. Prather Seeger Doolittle & Farmer, Washington, 1989-94; ptnr. Vedder Price, Kammholz, Washington, 1994-95, Seeger Potter Richardson Luxton Joselow & Brooks, Washington, 1995-99, King & Spalding, Washington, 1999—. Mem. ABA, D.C. Bar Assn. Democrat. Mem. ABA, D.C. Bar Assn. Democrat. Office: King & Spalding Ste 1100 1730 Pennsylvania Ave NW Washington DC 20006-4795

LUYBEN, JOHANNA (ANS) GERARDA, midwife, educator, researcher; b. Aarlanderveen, The Netherlands, June 10, 1961; d. Johannes Hendrikus and Cornelia Gerarda M. (Kempen) Luyben. Matura, Ashram Coll., 1979. Midwife St. Elizabeth Clinic, 1983, Lindenhof Hosp., Berne, 1989, Cantonal Hosp., Lucerne, 1990, Univ. Hosp., Berne, 1991; tchr. in midwifery Midwifery Sch., 1997; midwifery research Swiss Midwifery Assn., 1994—; translator German Translation Svc. for Midwives, 1994—. Author: Breech Delivery, CTG discussed, Support in Labor, Midwifery Textbook; contbr. numerous numerous articles to profl. jours. Mem. Swiss Midwifery Assn., Dutch Midwife Assn., Royal Coll. Midwives. Roman Catholic. Avocations: sports, reading, drawing, writing, travelling. E-mail: luyben@swissonline.ch. Home: Lagerstrasse 9, 7000 Chur Switzerland Office: Berufsschule Gesundheits, Krankenpflege Loestrasse117, 7000 Chur Switzerland

LUZ, VIRGINIA OLIVAR, dietitian, nutritionist; b. Antique, Philippines, May 21, 1934; came to U.S., 1960; d. Adriano and Expectacion Xavier (Salazar) Olivar; m. Zosimo Umali Luz, 1965; children: Cecilia Luz-Cariaga, Patricia Ann Luz-Holgado, Melinda M. Luz-Royall. BS in Nutrition, U. Philippines, 1957. Registered dietitian, Am. Dietetic Assn. Dietetic intern Brigham Women's Hosp., 1961-62; clin. dietitian Lemuell Shattuck Hosp., Jamaica Plain, Mass., 1962-63, Temple U. Hosp., Phila., 1963-65, Santa Cabrini Hosp., Montreal, Can., 1966-67, Roxborough Meml. Hosp., Phila., 1966; chief dietitian Nazareth Hosp., Phila., 1967-77; clin. dietitian Temple U. Hosp., Phila., 1977-87, Nazareth Hosp., Phila., 1994—; gen. renal nutritionist Biomed. Applications (name now Fresenius Med. Care), Phila., 1987—; historian Mutya Philippine Dance Co., 1990—. Founder Mutya Philippine Dance Co., St. Augustine, Church Hall, Phila., 1990—; lectr., historian Pub. Grade Schs., Phila., 1963; pres. Filipino Am. Assn. Phila., Girard Avenue, 1980-82, Phila. Philippine Lions Club, 1982-84. Named Mother of Yr., Filipino Am. Assn. Phila., 1981; recipient Cultural Appreciation award Gov.'s Commn. on Heritage, Pa., 1995. Mem. Am. Dietetic Assn., Coun. on Renal Nutrition Network, Mutya Philippine Dance Co. Roman Catholic. Avocations: folklorist, modeling ethnic, drama, singing. Home: 706 Sunflower Ave Langhorne PA 19047-3748 Office: Nazareth Hosp & Fresnius Med Care 6201 Holme Ave Philadelphia PA 19152

LUZARRAGA, JOSE LUIS, sales executive; b. Bermeo, Vizcaya, Spain, Jan. 8, 1951; s. Jose Luzarraga and Dolores Goitia; m. Ana Isabel Iturrioz, May 28, 1983; children: Arantzazu, Josebaitor. Lic. ciencias econs. empresariales, U. Comml. Deusto, Bilbao, Spain, 1975; MS, MIT, 1995. Auditor Coopers & Lybrand, Bilbao, 1975-78; mgr. internal auditing Bridgestone Firestone Hispania S.A., Bilbao, 1978-84, mgr. bus. planning, dep. dir., 1984-89, dir. adminstrn., asst. controller, 1990-93, gen. dir. fin. sales divsn., 1993-96, gen. dir. subsidiaries fin. sales divsn., 1996—; inst. Coopers & Lybrand, Madrid, 1980-82. Contbr. articles to newspapers. Founder Sustraiak Basque Olimpic Sports, Bilbao, 1977-78. Min. Edn./C. of C. scholar, 1969-75. Mem. Censor Jurado Cuentas. Home: Heliodoro Torre N 1-3 dcha, 48014 Bilbao Spain

LUZEAUX, DOMINIQUE, computer engineer, researcher; b. Clichy, France, Mar. 23, 1965; m. Ghislaine Luzeaux, Apr. 23, 1994; 1 child, Yvain. Degree in engring., Poly. U., France, 1987; Master of Theoretical Computer Sci., U. Paris, 1989, PhD, 1991. Rsch. engr. Gen. Del. Armament, Arcueil, France, 1989-91, head dept., 1995—, dir. optoelectronics, 1998—. Contbr. over 50 articles to profl. jours., also chpts. to books. Col. Armament Corps., France, 1999. Mem. IEEE, N.Y. Acad. Scis. Avocations: violin, karate, culinary tasting. Office: DGA/CTA/GIP, 16 bis Ave Prieur Cote d'Or, 94114 Arcueil France

LUZIER, AILEEN BOWN, pharmacist, educator, researcher; b. Vegreville, Can., Aug. 16, 1956; came to U.S., 1989; d. Jerry Robert Bown and Stella Loraine Ziegler; m. Mark Anthony McNamee, Aug. 22, 1981 (div. 1986); children: Arlita Christina, Ryan Anthony; m. John Charles Luzier, Oct. 8, 1988. BS in Pharmacy, U. Alberta, 1978; PharmD, U. Buffalo, 1992. Licensed pharmacist. Clin. pharmacist Millard Fillmore Hosp., Buffalo, N.Y., 1989-98; asst. prof. U. Buffalo, N.Y., 1998—. E-mail: luzier@acsu.buffalo.edu. Office: Univ Buffalo 313 Cooke Hall Buffalo NY 14260-1300

LUZSA, GEORGE, radiologist, educator; b. Budapest, Hungary, Oct. 1, 1929; s. Bela and Erzsebet (Bartos) L.; m. Maria Istvánffy, Aug., 1955; 1 child, George. MD, Semmelweis U., Budapest, 1954; PhD, Hungarian Acad. Scis., Budapest, 1973; docent, Semmelweis U., Budapest, 1991, habilitation, 1995. Asst. dir. County Hosp., Györ, Hungary, 1954-61; head physician City Hosp., Mosonmagyaróvár, Hungary, 1961-77, Nat. Inst. Pulmonology, Budapest, 1977-82, Nat. Inst. Rheumatology, Budapest, 1982—; lectr. Semmelweis U., 1986—. Author: X-Ray Anatomy of the Vascular System, (in German, Russian, English) 1972-75; contbr. more than 85 articles to med. jours. Named Honored Physician, Hungarian Ministry Sanitation, 1974; recipient honor Hungarian Nat. Mus., Budapest, 1991, A. Petz County Hosp., Györ, 1974. Mem. Hungarian Radiol. Soc., Hungarian Gastroenterol. Soc., Hungarian Rheumatol. Soc., Internat. Skeletal Soc. (Chgo.). Evangelical. Avocation: gardening. Home: Petőfi S. str 10 III/2, H-1052 Budapest Hungary

LUZZATTO, EDGAR, lawyer; b. Milan, Italy, Nov. 25, 1914; s. Enrico and Maria (Norsa) L.; m. Mirella Del Monte, Apr. 4, 1948; children—Diana,

Ariel, Kfir, Marco, Rossana. Dr. Chem. Engring., Polytechnic, Milan, 1935; Dr.Law, U. Milan, 1957. Patent agt. David Moscovitz, Atty., N.Y.C., 1946-48; sole practice, Milan, 1949-75, Ashkelon, Israel, 1976-81; sr. ptnr. Luzzatto & Luzzatto, Beer-Sheva, Israel, 1982—; lectr. Polytechnic, Milan, 1958-62; mem. Italian delegation to Lisbon Conf. for revision of Paris Conv., 1958. Author: Il Consulente Tecnico, 1954; Teoria e Tecnica Brevetti, 1960; The Industrial Property Factor in Industrial Research, 1978. Contbr. articles to profl. jours. Served with U.S. Army, 1941-46. Mem. Internat. Assn. for Protection Indsl. Property, Internat. Fedn. Indsl. Property Attys. Office: Omer Indsl Park 84965, PO Box 5352, Beersheba 84152, Israel

LVSSL, ANDREAS G., geneticist, philosopher; b. Traunstein, Bavaria, Germany, Feb. 17, 1965; s. Bruno and Anita Lvssl. Degree in Agr. engring., Justus-Liebig U., Giessen, Germany, 1991; PhD, U. Tech., Munich, 1995. Engr. agr. Inst. for Resistance Genetics, Grünbach, Germany, 1991-95; sci. asst. U. Tech. Munich, Freising, Germany, 1995—. Contbr. articles to profl. jours. Rep. Regenaissance, Germany, 1998-99; coord. for release of transgenic plants U. Tech., Munich, Fürstenfeldbruck-Roggenstein, Germany, 1998-99. Avocations: meditation, fitness, jogging, classical wrestling. E-mail: Genomion@gmx.net and loessl@mm.pbz.agrar.tu-muenchen.de. Fax: 49 89 2443 24540. Office: U Tech, Alte Akademie 12, 85350 Freising Bavaria, Germany

LYAKAS, MICHAEL, physicist; b. Vilnius, Lithuania, July 31, 1946; s. Aron and Leja-Gena (Shapiro) L.; m. Liudmila Legat, Aug. 10, 1949; children: Alexander, Igor. BSc, Polytech. Inst., St. Petersburg, Russia, 1967, MSc, 1970; PhD, U. Vilmus, 1990. Lab. head Inst. for Radio Measuring Devices, Vilnius, 1985-90; rsch. assoc. Technion-Israel Inst. of Tech., 1991-95; sr. engr. Tower Semiconductor Ltd., Migdal HaEmec, Israel, 1995-2000, Intel Design Ctr., Haifa, Israel, 2000—; cons. Tech.-Israel Inst. of Tech., 1995-00. Contbr. articles to profl. jours.; inventor in field. Mem. IEEE (sr.). Avocations: sports, music, books. Home: Einstein 99a-2, 34601 Haifa Israel Office: Intel Israel 74 Ltd, PO Box 1659, 31015 Haifa Israel

LYAKH, IVAN A., minister of anti-monopoly policy of Belarus; b. Nesvizh, July 15, 1944; married; 2 children. Grad., Poly. Inst., Minsk, 1966. Engr. Minsk Mech. Enterprise, 1973; sr. engr. Inst. Economy, Acad. Sci., 1974; mem. staff scientific inst. Inst. Economy, 1986; dep. gen. dir. Byelorussian Optic-Mech. Assn., 1990; dep. chmn. State Com. of State Property, 1992; chmn. Com. Antimonopoly Policy, 1994; min. Antimonopoly Policy, Minsk, 1994—; min. of labor Ministry of Labor, 1996—. Office: Min Anti-Monopoly Policy and Labor, Pr Masherova 23 Bld 2, 220050 Minsk Belarus*

LYAKH, VIKTOR ALEKSEEVICH, biologist, researcher; b. Zaporozhye, Ukraine, Mar. 11, 1955. Candidate in Biol. Scis., Minsk, 1985; Dr in Biol. Scis., St. Petersburg, 1992. Head lab. Inst. Oilseed Crops, Zaporozhye, 1993—, dep. dir. on sci., 1995—. Author: Methods of Gamete and Zygote Selection in Tomato, 1988, Sex Plant Reproduction, 1992, Maydica, 1993, Plant Breeding, 1998, Methods of Selection of Valuable Genotypes at the Level of Pollen, 2000. Office: Inst Oilseed Crops, Vesenniaya St 1 Solnechny, 70417 Zaporozhye Ukraine

LYAKHOVITSKY, YURI MIKHAILOVICH, historian, researcher; b. Kharkov, Ukraine, July 24, 1940; arrived in Israel, 1996; s. Mikhail Mikhailovich Lyakhovitsky and Mariya Moiseevna Tiraspolskaya; M. Nonna Konstantinovna Parmakyan, 1966 (div. 1972); m. Ludmila Anatolievna Mirgorod, June 30, 1996. MSc, Kharkov Mining Acad., 1962; PhD, Kharkov Pedagogical Acad., 1969, docent, 1972. Asst. prof. pedagogics Kharkov Pedagogical Acad., 1962-95; prof. history Israel Open U., Kharkov br., 1992-96; dir. Inst. Jewish Rsch., Nat. Acad. Sci. Ukraine, Kharkov, Holocaust Ctr. Drobitsky Yar, Kharkov and Bat Yam, Israel, 1989—, Inst. Eastern Ukrainian Jewry Rsch., Bat Yam, 1996—. Author: Trampled Mezuzah (The Book of Drobitsky Yar), 1991, The Yellow Book, Part 1, 1992, The Yellow Book, Part 2, 1994, Survivors of the Holocaust, 1996, Into Holocaust Flame in Ukraine, 1999; editor: Holocaust in Ukraine and Anti-Semitism in Perspective, 1992, (with A. Kruglov and Y. Subocheva-Shulman) Genocide of the Ukrainian Jews in the Occupation Period to German Documentation, 1941-44, 1995, Holocaust, "Jewish Question" and Modern Ukrainian Society, 1996; editor-in-chief (monthly Jewish rev.) Bensiah, 1989—, (monthly newspaper) Kol Ole, 2000—. Dep. Bat Yam Municipality. Rsch. grantee Meml. Found. for Jewish Culture, 1995, Global Jewish Assistance and Relief Network, 1996, Memorial Foundation for Jewish Culture, 1997. Mem. N.Y. Acad. Scis., Ukrainian Union Journalists, Union Writers Israel, Nat. Geographic Soc. Mem. Merets Party. Fax: (03) 555 8666. Office: PO Box 7055, Bat Yam 59170, Israel

LYAKHOVSKAYA, IRINA, physicist, researcher; b. Dzherzhinsk, USSR, Mar. 25, 1941; d. Ivan Trofimovich and Klavdiya Ivanovna (Tomilina) Zhukov; m. Vladimir Dmitrievich Lyakhovsky, June 16, 1968; 1 child, Anna. Degree in physics with honors, State U. Leningrad, Russia, 1964, PhD, 1974. Jr. rschr. State U. Leningrad, 1965-85, sr. rschr., 1985—; sr. rschr. State U. St. Petersburg, 1985—. Contbr. articles to profl. jours. Avocations: music, swimming.

LYAKHOVSKY, VLADIMIR DMITRIEVICH, physicist; b. Sverdlovsk, Russia, July 15, 1942; s. Dmitry Nikitich and Zinaida Philippovna (Ivanova) L.; m. Irina Ivanovna Zhukova, June 16, 1968; 1 child, Anna. PhD, State U., Leningrad, Russia, 1969; DS, State U., St. Petersburg, Russia, 1994. Jr. rschr. State U., Leningrad, Russia, 1968-71, asst. prof., 1971-78, sr. rschr., 1978-91; leading rschr. State U., St. Petersburg, Russia, 1991-97, prof., 1997—. Author: Symmetry Groups and Elementary Particles, 1983. Grantee Russian Found. Fundamental Rsch., Moscow, 1994, 95, 97, Internat. Sci. Found., N.Y.C., 1994, Ministerio de Edn. Cultura, Madrid, 1997. Avocations: music, literature. Office: St Petersburg U Dept Phys, Ulianovskaya 1, 198 904 Saint Petersburg Russia

LYALIKOVA, NATALIA, microbiologist, researcher; b. Mitishi, Russia, Mar. 11, 1932; d. Nikolai and Natalia (Ogarkova) L.; m. Anatoli Medvedev, Mar. 30, 1962; children: Elena, Alexei. Candidate of Sci., Inst. Microbiology, Moscow, 1959, DSc, 1980. Jr. rsch. worker Inst. Microbiology of Russian Acad. Sci., Moscow, 1959-70, sr. rsch. worker, 1970-85, lead rsch. worker, 1985—. Co-author: Introduction to Geological Microbiology, 1963; contbr. articles to profl. jours. Russian Orthodox. Avocation: travel. Home: Pljushicka 9a Flat 13, 119121 Moscow Russia Office: Russian Acad Sci Inst Micro, biology 60 Oktjabja 7 Korp2, 117811 Moscow Russia

LYAPUSTIN, ALEXEI IVANOVICH, research scientist; b. Miyaki Olsheevskogo Raion, Russia, Jan. 19, 1964; came to U.S., 1997; s. Ivan Grigorievich Lyapustin and Anastasia Mikhailovna Komarova; m. Svetlana Anatolievna Suchkova, Apr. 13, 1985; children: Alex, Dmitry, Tanya. BS, MS, Moscow State U., 1987; PhD, Space Rsch. Inst., Moscow, 1991. Rsch. scientist divsn. aerospace remote sensing Rsch. Inst. Physics, Rostov-on-Don, Russia, 1991-96; head remote sensing divsn. Sci. Prodn. Co. KOFTEK, Ltd., Rostov-on-Don, 1992-96; prin. investigator Russian Space Agy., Moscow, 1993-96; sci. rschr. Space Rsch. Inst. Kazakhstan Acad. Scis., Alma-Aty, 1994-95; rsch. fellow Univs. Space Rsch. Assn., NASA Goddard Space Flight Ctr., Greenbelt, Md., 1997-99; asst. rsch. scientist U. Md. Baltimore County, NASA Goddard Space Flight Ctr., Greenbelt, 1999—. Contbr. articles to profl. jours. E-mail: alyapust@pop900.gsfc.nasa.gov. Office: NASA Goddard Space Flight Ctr Mailcode 920 Greenbelt MD 20771-0001

LYBECKER, MARTIN EARL, lawyer; b. Lincoln, Nebr., Feb. 11, 1945; s. Earl Edward and Jeanette Frances (Kiefer) L.; m. Andrea Kristine Tollefson, Dec. 27, 1969; children: Carl Martin, Neil Anders. BBA, U. Wash., 1967, JD, 1970; LLM in Taxation, NYU, 1971; LLM, U. Pa., 1973. Bar: Wash. 1970, D.C. 1972, Pa. 1982. Atty. investment mgmt. div. SEC, Washington, 1972-75, assoc. dir. div., 1978-81; assoc. prof. SUNY, Buffalo, 1975-78; ptnr. Drinker Biddle & Reath, Washington, 1981-87, Ropes & Gray, Washington, 1987—; adj. prof. Georgetown U., Washington, 1974-75, 80-81; vis. assoc. prof. Duke U., Durham, N.C., 1977-78, sr. lecturing fellow in law, 2000—. Contbr. articles to law revs. Fellow U. Pa. Ctr. for Study of Fin. Instns., 1971-72. Mem. ABA (mem. subcom. on investment cos. and investment advisers, mem. subcom. on securities activities of banks, mem. com. on fed. regulation of securities bus. law sect., chairperson com. on devels. in investment svcs. bus. law sect., co-chair com. on long-range planning, mem. subcom. on bank holding co. activities and subcom. on trust and investment svcs. of com. of banking bus. law sect.), Am. Law Inst., Univ. Club Washington. Home: 2806 Daniel Rd Bethesda MD 20815-3149 Office: Ropes & Gray 1301 K St NW Ste 800E Washington DC 20005-7008

LYBEERT, MARNIX LODEWIJK MARIA, radiotherapist; b. St Jansteen, The Netherlands, Nov. 16, 1954; s. Maurice Lybeert and Marguerite de Potter; m. Sabine Agnes Cornelia Valcke, Sept. 4, 1982; children: David, Samuel, Thimothy. Diploma, U. Edn., Gent, Belgium, 1980; Radiotherapist, Daniel den Hoed Kliniek, Rotterdam, The Netherlands, 1984. Sr. radiotherapist A.Z. - V.U.B., Brussels, 1984-87, Catharina Hosp., Eindhoven, The Netherlands, 1987—; mem. med. bd. Catherina Hosp., Eindhoven, 1992-95; com. of profl. affairs Dutch Soc. Therapeutic Radiologists, 1993-99. Contbr. articles to profl. jours. Grantee Internat. Union Against Cancer, Geneva, 1983. Mem. European Soc. Therapeutic Radiology and Oncology. Avocations: tennis, squash, skiing. Home: Sporkehout 4, 5667 JG Geldrop The Netherlands Office: Catharina Hosp, Postbus 1350, 5602 ZA Eindhoven The Netherlands

LYDEN, JOHN MICHAEL ERNEST, arbitrator, surveyor; b. Galway, Ireland, May 5, 1952. Grad., Mungret Coll., 1970. Various positions James Sheehan & Assocs., Cork, Ireland, 1970-87; prin. Lyden Assocs., Cork, Ireland, 1987—. Editor: Irish building and Engineering Casebook, 1989. Fellow Royal Inst. Chartered Surveyors, Soc. Chartered Surveyors; mem. Chartered Inst. Arbitrators (assoc.), Soc. Constrn. Law, Royal Inst. for Navigation, Inst. of Navigation, Royal Cork Yacht Club. Avocations: navigation, sailing, hill walking, bird watching. Office: 3 Castle Ct, Currabinny Rd, Carrigaline Cork, Ireland

LYDEN, PATRICK DONOVAN, neurologist, neuroscientist; b. Burbank, Calif., Sept. 15, 1956; s. Donald P. and Kathleen C. L.; m. Christy M. Jackson, July 6, 1996; children: Hannah, Hillary, Jessica. BS in Biochemistry, UCLA, 1978; MD, Baylor U., 1981; cert. in Neurology, U. Calif., San Diego, 1985. Diplomate Am. Bd. Psychiatry and Neurology. Rsch. fellow U. Calif., San Diego, 1985-87, asst. prof. neurology, 1988-93, assoc. prof., 1994-99, prof., 1999—, dir. Stroke Ctr., 1995—; chief neurology U. Calif. Med Ctr., San Diego, 1997—; staff neurologist VA Med. Ctr., San Diego, 1987—; cons. various Pharm. Cos. in CNS Rsch., 1985—. Contbr. numerous articles on strokes and stroke therapy to profl. jours. Grantee: NIH, VA Rsch., Am. Heart Assn. (numerous). Fellow Am. Acad. Neurology; mem. AMA (several offices), Calif. Med. Assn. (several offices), San Diego Med. Soc. (several offices), San Diego Stroke Coun. (co-founder). Achievements include: pioneer of new treatments for stroke; built first codestroke team, now standard model in modern medical centers. Fax: (619) 543-7771. Office: UCSD Stroke Ctr OPC 3d Fl #3 200 W Arbor Dr 8466 San Diego CA 92103-8466

LYDON, MARY ELIZABETH, artist, poet; b. Sacramento, Nov. 9, 1954; d. Richard Martin and Mary (Dokimos) L. AA in Photography with honors, Sacramento City Coll., 1975; BA in English, Calif. State U., Sacramento, 1980. Cert. desktop pub., Calif. Surgery technician Dr.'s Hosp., Carmichael, Calif., 1972-82; photographer/printer Kodak Films, Sacramento, 1975-87; assembly/ad specialist ABK Enterprises, Sacramento, 1997—; photographer Calif. Arts League, 1993. Author: Anthology of World's Famous Poets, 1982, Anthology of 19th Century Poets, 1985, Book of Am. Folklore, 1987, The Sound of Poetry, 1992; photographer Photographers Forum mag., 1992, The National Libr. of Poetry, 1998. Mem. Internat. Soc. Poets (Editor's Choice award). Democrat. Greek Orthodox. Avocations: music (piano and guitar), songwriting, underwater photography, scuba diving. Home and Office: 806 48th St Sacramento CA 95819-3512

LYERLA, BRADFORD PETER, lawyer; b. Savanna, Ill., Aug. 2, 1954; s. Ralph Herbert and Nancy Lee (Nelson) L.; m. Marilyn Wyse, Aug. 18, 1979; 3 children. BA, U. Ill., 1976, JD, 1980. Bar: Ill. 1980, U.S. Dist. Ct. (no. dist.) Ill. 1980, U.S. Dist. Ct. (no. dist.) Ind. 1982, U.S. Dist. Ct. (no. dist.) Calif. 1991, U.S. Dist. Ct. (ctrl. dist.) Ill. 1991, U.S. Dist. Ct. Neb. 1998, U.S. Ct. Appeals (7th cir.) 1983, U.S. Ct. Appeals (fed. cir.) 1991, U.S. Supreme Ct. 1995. Ptnr. Ryndak & Lyerla, Chgo.; lectr. on litigation and intellectual property law. Author publications in field; editor U. Ill. Law Rev., 1978-80. Bd. dirs. North Suburban Bd. of the Heartland Alliance, Wilmette, Ill., 1987-96, pres. 1993-94; bd. dirs. Traveler's and Immigrant's Aid, Chgo., 1991-95; bd. dirs., sec. Youth Svcs. Project, Inc., Chgo., 1987-91; mem. U. Ill. Pres.'s Coun.; founding mem. Cribbett Soc., U. Ill. Coll. Law; mem. Saints Faith Hope and Charity, Winnetka, Ill. Recipient John Powers Crowley Justice award People's Uptown Law Ctr., 1989. Fellow Am. Bar Found.; mem. ABA (editor litigation sect. intellectual properties litigation newsletter 1990—, intellectual property sect. com. on unfair competition litigation), Ill. Bar Assn. (sect. coun. gen. practice sect. 1984-85, intellectual property sect. 1989—, co-editor intellectual property newsletter 1989-95, chair 1996-97), Am. Intellectual Property Law Assn. (antitrust and fed. lit. com.), Intellectual Property Law Assn. Chgo. (trade & internat coms.), Michigan Shores Club, Wilmette Club, Phi Beta Kappa, Phi Kappa Phi. Office: Ryndak & Lyerla 30 N Lasalle St Ste 2630 Chicago IL 60602-2506

LYKES, THERON MARTEL, actor; b. Chgo., June 23, 1963; p. Archie and Mildred Lykes. Assocs., Bishop Coll. Computer operator GTE, Naperville, Ill. Author: A Collection of Poems by Touché,, 1997. Mem. Phi Beta Sigma (squire). Office: Designs by Touché PO Box 2655 Country Club Hills IL 60478-8655

LYKKETOFT, MOGENS, Danish federal official; b. Jan. 9, 1946. Mem. staff econ. bd. Danish Labour Movement, 1966-81; social dem. mem. from Glostrup constituency Danish Parliament, 1981, chmn. various coms., 1984-90; min. inland revenue Denmark, 1981-82, min. fin., 1993—; mem. governing body Social Dem. Party, 1968-70, 75-81, mem. platform com., 1974-77, chmn. standing com. nat. economy, 1977-81, spokesman econ. and budget policy, 1991—; mem. Income Tax Com., 1975-77; mem. Assessment Coun., 1976-81, 84—; polit. spokesman, 1991—. Author: Tax Reform 78, 2001, 1986; editor: Power Game and Security, 1968, The Demand for Equality, 1973, Sans og Samling, 1994; contbr. articles to profl. jours. Office: Ministry Fin, Christiansborg Slotsplads 1, DK-1218 Copenhagen Denmark

LYLE-WILSON, TREVOR, clinical physiotherapist; b. Melbourne, Australia, May 4, 1958; s. Geoffrey Lloyd and Yvonne Eva (Smith); m. Fiona Christine McKelvey, Dec. 21, 1991; children: Tarrant, Alexander. BSc (hons.), Sci. Faculty Melbourne U., Australia, 1980; B in Applied Sci. (Physiotherapy), Latrobi U., Melbourne, Australia, 1990; postgrad. diploma, Melbourne U., 1995; Cert. of Hydrotherapy, Transport Accident Commn. Comml. pilot Flight Facilities, Merimbula, 1981-82; lectr. Bruce T.A.F.E., Canberra, Australia, 1982-83; comml. pilot, navigation instr. Fairburn Aviations, Canberra, Australia, 1982-83; physiotherapist St. Vincent's Hosp., Melbourne, Australia, 1990-93, Freemasons Hosp., Melbourne, Australia, 1993-95; chief physiotherapist Junction Physiotherapy Clinic, Noosa, Australia, 1995—; dir. Transay Pty. Ltd., Melbourne, Canamarka Pty. Ltd., Melbourne. Author:'Moondusters'", 1996, The Trace, 1999. Cons. physiotherapist St. Vincent's Nursing Home and Care Facility, Noosa, 1997-99. Mem. Australian. Physiotherapy Assn., The Queensland Writers Ctr. Roman Catholic. Avocations: flying writing, gardening, collecting Australian contemporary art, Hillary Jackman's works of arts, paintings. Office: Junction Physiotherapy Clin, PO Box 2008, Noosa Heads 4567, Australia

LYLISTON, WILLIAM PHILLIP, writer, poet; b. Hampton, Va., Apr. 14, 1955; s. William D. and Aurelia M. LyL. Student, U. Richmond, 1973, Christopher Newport U., 1977-79, 84-86. Dept. store, grocery store clk., shipyard laborer, freelance writer, 1975—. Author: (sci. fiction) All Living Things, 1982, Live Wires, 1985, A Time for Caring, 1986, A Voyage to the Stars and Beyond, 1989, A World United in Endeavor, 1990, Writing Poetry for the Fun of It, 1990, Concert on a Far Planet, 1991, The Example of Jesus Christ, 1992, Scenes From the American Blue Ridge, 1992, Lament of an Artificial Intelligence, 1994, Reflections, 1996. Mem. Va. Democratic Orgn., poll-worker, office worker, poll-organizer, state conv. del., 1992;. Mem. Internat. Soc. Poets. Methodist. Avocations: walking, guitar, playing games, computers.

LYMAN, CHARLES EDSON, materials scientist, educator; b. Willimantic, Conn., Mar. 7, 1946; s. Edson Hunt and Sylvia (Hill) L.; m. Valerie Ann Livingston, Aug. 30, 1984. BS, Cornell U., 1968; PhD, MIT, 1974. Postdoctoral fellow dept. metallurgy Oxford (England) U., 1974-76; asst. prof. Rensselaer Poly. Inst., Troy, N.Y., 1976-80; staff scientist E.I. DuPont de Nemours, Wilmington, Del., 1980-84; assoc. prof. Lehigh U., Bethlehem, Pa., 1984-90, prof., 1990—; electron microscopy steering com. Argonne (Ill.) Nat. Lab., 1984—. Author, editor: Scanning Electron Microscopy, X-Ray Microanalysis, and Analytical Electron Microscopy: A Laboratory Workbook, 1990; editor-in-chief: Microscopy and Microanalysis; contbr. articles to profl. jours. Pres. Historic Bethlehem, Inc., 1996-98. Mem. Microscopy Soc. Am. (pres. 1991), Microbeam Analysis Soc. (bd. dirs. 1993-95, pres. 2000), Am. Soc. Materials Internat., Am. Chem. Soc., Burnside Plantation Inc. (pres. 1993). Home: 444 N New St Bethlehem PA 18018-5814 Office: Lehigh U Whitaker Lab 5 E Packer Ave Bethlehem PA 18015-3102

LYMAN, DAVID, lawyer; b. Washington, Sept. 25, 1936; s. Albert Moses and Freda (Ring) L. BSEE, Duke U., 1958; cert., U.S. Naval Officers Submarine, Sch., 1960; JD, U. Calif., San Francisco, 1965; postgrad. in fgn./comparative law, Columbia U., 1974. Bar: Calif. 1966. Active minesweepers and submarine force USN, 1958-62; assoc. Fitzsimmons & Petris, Oakland, Calif., 1965-66, Lempres & Seyranian, Oakland, 1966-67, Tilleke & Gibbins, Internat. Ltd.; assoc. Advocates and Solicitors, Bangkok, assoc. ptnr., 1967-84, sr. ptnr., 1984—; dir. Goodyear (Thailand) Ltd., Triumph Internat. (Thailand) Ltd.; founding mem. Prime Min. Thailand's Fgn. Investment Adv. Coun., 1975, chmn. Fgn. C. of C. in Thailand Law Change lProj. for the Prime Min., 1992; mem. USAID Adv. Com. on U.S. - Thai Trade and Investment, 1988; founder, mem. steering com. tech. cooperation office U.S. Asian Environ. Partnership Program, 1994. Contbr. articles to profl. publs. Chmn. King Bhumiphol Rama IX Park U.S. Geodesic Dome Pavillion Com., 1987; founding mem. Thailand Bus. Coun. Sustainable Devel., 1993—; founder Davos Group World Econ. Forum on Anti-Corruption Stds. for Global Bus., 1995—, co-founder, advisor Cmty. Svcs. Bangkok, 1985; mem. Internat. C. of C. Standing Com. Extortion and Bribery, 1997; founder, mem. exec. bd. nat. chpt. Thailand, 1999; sec.-gen. Thailand Soc. Prevention of Cruelty to Animals, 1996—. With USN, 1958-68; lt. comdr. Res. Recipient U.S. Naval Inst. prize, 1958, Am. Jurisprudence prize, 1965, U.S. Dept. Commerce cert., 1987; Paul Harris fellow, 1987, Thai Prime Minister's Cert. of Achievement 1990, 92, Am. C. of C. Disting. Svc. award, 1990; named Boss of Yr., Women Secs' Assn. Thailand, 1997. Mem. Am. C. of C. in Thailand (bd. govs. 1973—, v.p. 1974, 83-85, pres. 1975, 86), Asia-Pacific Coun. of Am. C. of C. (vice-chmn. 1975-77, 85-89, 92-93, bd. dirs. 1975, 86), AmCham Environ. Coun. (founder 1992), Environ. Bus. Exch. (creator 1993), Thai Bd. Trade (bd. dirs. 1975, 86), Fgn. Chambers of Commerce Working Group (sec. 1982-87, chmn. 1987-90), Thailand bd. of Investment Environ. Study Adv. Com., 1993, World Econ. Forum (program fellow Europe/East Asia Econ. Forum 1992-94), Lex Mundi (bd. dirs. 1989-91), ABA, Calif. Bar Assn., LAWAISA, U.S. Naval Inst. (life), Naval Submarine League (life), Internat. Oceanographic Found. (life), Thailand Bus. Coalition AIDS Assn. (founder 1994), 999 Wildlife Trust, Wildlife Fund Thailand, Chaines Des Rotisseurs (charge de mission 2000), Jewish Assn., Thailand, Tau Epsilon Phi, Phi Alpha Delta, Beta Gamma Sigma (hon.), Royal Bangkok Sports Club, Heritage Club (founder Gov. 1985-98), Fgn. Corrs. of Thailand (life), Siam Soc. (life), Rotary (1969-89, sec. 1982-83, v.p. Bangkok 1984-85), Cmty Svcs. of Bangkok (founder, acting pres. 1986, v.p. 1986-87, bd. dirs. 1985-88). E-mail: apple@tillekeandgibbins.com. Home: 39/221 Moo 3 Nichada Thani Soi 11, Tambol Bangtalad Amphur Pakkred, Nonthaburi 11120, Thailand Office: Tilleke and Gibbons Internt Ltd, 64/1 Soi Tonson Ploenchit, Bangkok 10330, Thailand

LYMAN, DONALD OWEN, preventive medicine physician; b. Phila., Nov. 14, 1942; s. Harold Oakley Lyman and Sarah Elizabeth Brenz; m. Elisabeth Hall, Mar. 26, 1977; children: Sarah, Richard. BA, U. Pa., 1964; MD, Yale U., 1968; diploma in tropical pub. health, U. London, 1974. Intern in medicine U. Miami, Fla., 1968-69, resident in medicine, 1969-70; resident in medicine U. Calif., San Diego, 1972-73; med. epidemiologist U.S. Ctrs. for Disease Control, Berkeley, Calif., 1970-74; disease control officer N.Y. State Health Dept., Albany, 1974-78; mgr. disease control Calif. Dept. Health, Sacramento, 1978—. Lt. comdr. USPHS, 1970-76. Office: Calif Health Dept Svcs MS # 504 PO Box 942732 Sacramento CA 94234-7320

LYMBEROPOULOS, ELIAS L., diplomat, researcher; b. Athens, Greece, Jan. 23, 1940; s. Lymberis E. and Pipitsa G. (Gyftakis) L.; m. Calliope V. Kottis, Mar. 26, 1948; 2 children. LLB, U. Athens, 1961, B in Econs. and Polit. Sci., 1965; MSc, U. Wales, Cardiff, 1975; MFA, U. Athens, 1995. Lawyer Athens, 1963-65; attaché MFA, Athens, 1965-67; sec. of embassy MFA, Prague, Czech Republic, 1967-70; consul gen. MFA, Melbourne, Australia, 1976-80; dep. permanent rep. of Greece to EEC MFA, Brussels, 1986-89; Greek amb. MFA, Montivideo, Uruguay, 1989-94; sec. of embassy MFA, Prague, Czech Republic, 1967-70; lawyer Mobil Oil Hellas SA, Athens, 1971-74. Avocations: music, reading, skiing, swimming. Home: Filadelfeos 32A, 145 62 Kifisia Greece

LYMBURNER, JAMES RICHARD WILLIAM, financial services executive, economic financial adviser; b. Toronto, July 31, 1947; s. James and Joyce LymBurner; divorced. BA, U. Guelph, Toronto, 1973; student, U. London. Economist Draper Dobie, Toronto, 1974-76; sr. economist McCleod Young Wier, Toronto, 1977; pres. James R. LymBurner & Sons, Toronto, 1978—; bd. dirs. Perpetuity Inc., Toronto. Mem. Ctr. for Study of Presidency, N.Y.C. and Washington, 1990. Mem. Nat. Club (Toronto), Econs. Club of N.Y., Univ. Club (N.Y.C.), Inst. Corp. Dirs. (London). Office: James R LymBurner & Sons, 21 New St, Toronto, ON Canada M5R 1P7 also: 900 3rd Ave New York NY 10022-4728

LYNCH, BOB DAVID, retired business agent; b. Columbus, Mo., Apr. 4, 1931; s. Henry David and Opal Blanche (Horn) L.; m. Bertha Louise Kassner, Jan. 13, 1952 (dec. Sept. 29, 1977); children: Ronnie David, Michael Alan, Steven Leroy; m. Muriel Nadine Hale, June 18, 1979. Student, Ctrl. Mo. State U., 1950-51. Cert. bus. agt., Kans. Coach Am. Jr. Bowling Congress, Kansas City, Mo., 1965-75; commr. Boy Scouts of Am., Kansas City, Mo., 1966-74; bd. dirs. Inst. Labor Studies, Kansas City, Mo., 1983-93; v.p. Allied Svcs. divsn. Transp. Comm. Union, Kansas City, Mo., 1980-93, regional rep., 1975-80; sr. vice chmn. Brotherhood Railway and Airline Clks., Kansas City, Mo., 1970-75, local chmn. Lodge 26, 1968-93; ret., 1993. Bd. dirs. Barry Harbor Homes Assoc., Kansas City, 1995—, treas., 1995—. Corp. U.S. Army, 1952-54, Korea. Named to Bowling Hall of Fame, Kans. City Bowling Assn., 1972, Mo. State Hall of Fame, State Mo. Bowling, 1992, All City Bowling Team, Ind. Examiner Paper, 1968-77. Mem. Tribe of Mic-o-say, Boy Scouts of Am. Democrat. Assembly of God. Avocations: genealogy, travel, camping, model railroading and computers. Home: 2220 NW 82nd St Kansas City MO 64151-3713

LYNCH, CHARLES THEODORE, SR., materials science engineering researcher, consultant, educator; b. Lima, Ohio, May 17, 1932; s. John Richard and Helen (Dunn) L.; m. Betty Ann Korkolis, Feb. 3, 1956; children: Karen Elaine Ostdiek, Charles Theodore Jr., Richard Anthony, Thomas Edward. BS, George Washington U., 1955; MS, U. Ill., 1957, PhD in Analytical Chemistry, 1960. Group leader ceramics div. Air Force Materials Lab., Wright-Patterson AFB, Ohio, 1962-66; lectr. in chemistry Wright State U., Dayton, Ohio, 1964-66; chief advanced metall. studies br. Air Force Materials Lab., Wright-Patterson AFB, Ohio, 1966-74, sr. scientist, 1974-81; head materials div. Office of Naval Rsch., Arlington, Va., 1981-85; pvt. practice cons. Washington, 1985-88; sr. engr. space ops. Vitro Corp., Washington, 1988-95, 96-98; cons. Burke, Va., 1996—; sr. cons. space ops. Marconi Systems Techs., Washington, 1998-99; v.p. RSC&L,Inc., Grayling, Mich., 1996—; USAF liaison mem. NMAB Panels on Solids Processing, Ion Implantation and Environ. Cracking, Washington, 1965-68, 78, 81; U.S. rep. AGARD structures and materials panel NATO, 1983-85. Co-author: Metal Matrix Composites, 1972; editor, author: Practical Handbook of Materials Science, 1989; editor: (series) Handbook of Materials Science, vol. I, 1974, vol. II, 1975, vol. III, 1975; vice chmn. editorial bd. Vitro Corp. Tech. Jour., 1989-92, chmn., 1993; contbr. articles to profl. jours. including Jour. Am. Ceramics Soc., Analytical Chemistry, Sci., Transactions AIME, Corr. Jour., Jour. Inorganic Chemistry, SAMPE, Jour. Less

Common Metals. Mem., soloist George Washington U. Traveling Troubadours, Washington, 1950-55; choir dir. Trinity United Ch. of Christ, Fairborn, Ohio, 1966-81, Univ. Bapt. Ch., Champaign, Ill., 1957-60, Chapel II, Wright-Patterson AFB, Ohio, 1960-64; pres. Pub. Sch. PTO, 1967-69. 1st lt. USAF, 1960-62. Bailey scholar U. Ill., 1958-60; recipient Commendation medal USAF, 1962, Outstanding Achievement cert. NASA, 1992, award Soc. for Tech. Comm. Publ., 1993. Mem. Am. Chem. Soc. (treas. 1966-67, chmn. audit sect. 1967-68), ASM Internat. (sec. oxidation and corrosion com. 1980-81, chmn. 1981-82). Presbyterian. Achievements include patents for new corrosion inhibitors including encapsulated types, and for alkoxides and oxides; co-development of the refractory ceramic Zyttrite, the first high density translucent zirconia made from thermal or hydrolytic decomposition of mixed alkoxides followed by hot pressing; pioneered general approach of organometallic compounds as precursors of high purity, fine particulate, materials. Office: 5629 Kemp Ln Burke VA 22015-2041

LYNCH, CHARLOTTE ANDREWS, retired communications executive; b. Fall River, Mass., Mar. 25, 1928; d. Alan Hall and Florence (Worthen) Andrews; m. Francis Bradley Lynch, June 7, 1952; children: Sarah, Richard, Stephen, William. AB in Philosophy, Radcliffe Coll., 1950; postgrad., U. Bridgeport, 1969-71. Adminstrv. asst. Mass. Congl. Confs. and Missionary Soc., Boston, 1951-52; journalist Town Crier newspaper, Westport, Conn., 1968; asst. dir. devel. Cape Cod Hosp., Hyannis, Mass., 1975-76; parish adminstr. S. Congl. Ch., Centerville, Mass., 1976-83; cons. to ethnic advt. agy. Loiminchay, Inc., N.Y.C., 1992-98; ret. Mem. Radcliffe Club Cape Cod (v.p. 1990-97, pres. 1997-2000, exec. com. 1990-2000), Harvard Club of Boston. Republican. Roman Catholic. Avocation: travel. Fax: 508-771-0275.

LYNCH, DENIS PATRICK, dentist, educator; b. Kansas City, Kans., Oct. 5, 1951; s. Patrick Edward and Helen Mary Lynch; m. Monica Colosimo, June 29, 1973; children: Sydney Alexis, Shannon Meredith. DDS, U. Calif., San Francisco, 1976; PhD, U. Ala., Birmingham, 1985. Asst. prof. U. Tex. Dental Br., Houston, 1981-88, assoc. dean acad. affairs, 1987-89, assoc. prof., 1989-93, exec. assoc. dean, 1988-92; exec. assoc. dean U. Tenn., Memphis, 1993-97, prof. medicine, 1994—, prof. grad. health scis., 1998—, prof. biologic and diagnostic scis., 1993—; cons. Commn. on Dental Accreditation, Chgo., 1990—. Author: The Mouth: Diagnosis and Treatment, 1998; author (chpt.): Development of a Houston Community-Based Dental Health Care Clinic for Indigent HIV-Positive Patients, 1994, Diseases of the Mouth, 1996, Stomatitis: Diagnosis and Treatment, 1998; reviewer Jour. Am. Dental Assn., 1988—. Instr. Confraternity of Christian Doctrine, Our Lady of Sorrow Ch., Birmingham, 1976-81; cons. Bering Dental Clinic, Houston, 1988-93; chair expert review panel for HIV/Hepatitis B Infected Dental Health Care Workers, Tex. State Bd. Dental Examiners, Houston, 1992-93; HIV/AIDS educator ARC, Houston, 1991-93. Fellow Am. Acad. Oral and Maxillofacial Pathology (chair parameters of care com. 1995-98); mem. ADA (spkr.'s bur. 1991-94), Internat. Assn. Dental Rsch. (pres. exptl. pathology group 1992-93), Am. Assn. Dental Schs. (del. exec. com. 1977-79). Roman Catholic. Avocations: golf, bridge, reading, travel. E-mail: dlynch-home@dental.utmem.edu and dlynch@utmem.edu. FAX: 901-448-2671. Home: 1924 Kilbirnie Dr Germantown TN 38139-3420 Office: Univ Tenn 875 Union Ave Memphis TN 38163-0001

LYNCH, DOUGLAS SIR, lawyer; b. Bridgetown, Barbados, July 13, 1927; s. Cyril Aubrey and Frances Louise (Webster) L.; m. Amanda Shephard, Feb. 21, 1948; children: Jimmy, Gillian Lynch DeVerteuil, Richard, Suzanne Lynch Hayes, Andrew. Student, Harrison Coll., Barbados. Ptnr. Carrington & Sealy, Barbados, 1954-70; co. dir. Barbados Shipping & Trading Co. Ltd., Bridgetown, 1961-74, dep. chmn., 1974-80, chmn., 1980-92; pvt. practice law, 1992—; bd. dirs., Barbados Mut. Life Assurance; gov. Securities Exch. Barbados, 1987—. Author: Income Tax Act 1921 of Barbados as amended, with Annotations, 1958. Pres. Barbados Boy Scouts Assn., 1987-97. Served with Brit./Indian Army, 1945-48. Named Queen's Counsel, Gov.-Gen. Barbados, 1976, Privy Councillor, 1986; Companion of most excellent order of St. Michael and St. George, Queen's Birthday Honors, 1987, Knight of St. Andrew, Barbados Independence Honors, 1990. Avocations: bridge, squash, reading, computer enthusiast. Office: Heritage House, Pinfold St, Bridgetown Barbados

LYNCH, GEAROID, retired surgeon, consultant; b. Dublin, Feb. 17, 1932; s. Fionan and Bridget (Slattery) L.; m. Fredericka Patricia Dempsey, Feb. 5, 1966; children: Patricia, John, Michelle, Martin, Paul. Surgeon Richmond Hosp., Dublin, 1968-87, James Connolly Meml. Hosp., Dublin, 1972-92, Lourdes Hosp., Drogheda, Ireland, 1966-79, Beaumont Hosp., Dublin, 1987-97. Contbr. papers to profl. jours. Fellow ACS (gov. Irish chpt. 1992-98), Royal Coll. Surgeons Eng., Royal Coll. Surgeons Ireland (dean postgrad. 1966-86, councilor 1996-2000), Royal Soc. Medicine (hon. mem. surg. sect.), Brit. Assn. Plastic Surgeons. Fine Gael. Roman Catholic. Avocations: golf, gardening, travel, music. Home: San Mateo Lispopple, Swords Dublin Ireland

LYNCH, JACQUELYN, environmental planner; b. Seattle, June 30, 1954; d. Sprague Norman and Elizabeth Scott Lynch. BA in Environ. Planning, Huxley U., 1976; M Urban and Regional Planning, U. Pitts., 1978. Cert. Am. Inst. Cert. Planners. Utilities and environ. planner King County, Bellevue, Wash., 1984-89; environ. planner City of Bellingham, Wash., 1989—. Author Puget Neighborhood Plan, 1996; editor webpage Historic Landmarks of Bellingham, 1998. Avocations: medieval history, organic gardening. E-mail: jlynch@cob.org. Office: City of Bellingham 210 Lottie St Bellingham WA 98225-4089

LYNCH, JAMES WALTER, mathematician, educator; b. Cornelia, Ga., Mar. 28, 1930; s. Ulysses Samuel and Ida Dell (Woodall) L.; m. Monika Antonie Fehrmann, May 2, 1959; children: Steve, David, Judith. AB, U. Ga., 1952, MA, 1956. Math. statistician Proving Ground, Aberdeen, Md., 1956-61; asst. prof. math. Ga. So. U., Statesboro, 1961-92, prof. emeritus math., 1992—. Contbr. articles to profl. jours.; author/contbr.: Crux Mathematicorum, 1982-92. NSF grantee, 1964. Mem. Ga. Coun. Tchrs. Math. (life), Ga. Coalition for Excellence in Teaching Math., Can. Math. Soc., Math. Assn. Am., Sigma Xi. Lutheran. Achievements include discovery that American Indians designed their projectile points to conform to the golden section ratio. Avocations: coin collecting, gardening, shooting. Home and Office: 172 Thornhill Dr Athens GA 30607-1743

LYNCH, JOHN JAMES, lawyer; b. Evergreen Park, Ill., Aug. 22, 1945; s. John J. and Agnes (Daly) L.; m. Kathleen Russell, Aug. 15, 1970; children: Kerry, Elizabeth, Erin. BA, St. Mary of the Lake Sem., 1967; MA in Philosophy, DePaul U., 1970, JD, 1973. Bar: Ill. 1973, U.S. Dist. Ct. (no. dist.) Ill. 1973, U.S. Ct. Appeals (7th cir.) 1976. Assoc. McKenna, Storer, Rowe, White & Haskell, Chgo., 1973-75; ptnr. Haskell & Perrin, Chgo., 1975—. Mem. ABA, Ill. State Bar Assn., Chgo. Bar Assn., Fedn. Ins. & Corp. Counsel. Office: Haskell & Perrin 200 W Adams St Ste 2005 Chicago IL 60606-5230

LYNCH, PAUL PATRICK, corporate lawyer; b. New Castle, Pa., Oct. 6, 1951; s. Francis Joseph and Josephine Ann (Peluso) L.; m. Marcia Lee Magno, May 21, 1982; children: Jessica Ann, Jennifer Marie. BA, Washington & Jefferson Coll., 1973; JD, U. Pitts., 1991. Bar: Pa. 1991, U.S. Dist. Ct. (we. dist.) Pa. 1991, U.S. Ct. Appeals (3d and 4th cirs.) 1996. Spl. agt. IRS, Detroit, 1973-80; pres. Paul Lynch Investments, Inc., New Castle, 1980—; bd. dirs. First Nat. Bank Pa., Hermitage, FNB Corp., Hermitage, St. Francis Hosp. New Castle, Westfield Behavior Health Sys., New Castle. Mem. Greater New Castle C. of C. (dir.), Lawrence County Hist. Soc. (dir. 1996—), Wolves Club, Scottish Rite Freemasons. Democrat. Roman Catholic. Avocations: golf, tennis, travel. Home: 11 Victoria Dr Neshannock PA 16105-1229 Office: Lynch & Gallito 2625 Wilmington Rd New Castle PA 16105-1529

LYNCH, STEPHEN VINCENT, transplant surgeon, hepatobiliary surgeon; b. Sydney, Australia, Jan. 4, 1954; s. Vincent Hiliary and Shirley Leila (Graham) L.; m. Genni Anne Danesi, Sept. 1, 1979; children: Kathleen, Angelica, Lydia. MB BS with honors, U. New South Wales, Sydney1, 1978. Diplomate in gen. surgery. Resident St. Vincents Hosp., Sydney, 1978-80, surg. registrar, 1980-84; lectr. in surgery U. New South Wales, Sydney, 1984; fellow in transplantation U. Pitts., 1984-85; staff transplant surgeon Princess Alexandra Hosp., Brisbane, Australia, 1986-90; assoc. prof. surgery U. Queensland, Brisbane, 1990—; dir. Queensland Liver Transplant Svc., 1998—. Assoc. editor Liver Transplantation and Surgery, 1993—, Hepatogastroenterology, 1995—; mem. edtl. bd. Transplantation, 1993—, Transplantation Revs., 1996—; author more than 100 publs. in field of liver transplantation. Fellow Royal Australian Coll. Surgery (Inaugural award for excellence 1994); mem. Transplantation Soc. Australia and New Zealand (councillor transplant sect. 1997—), Am. Assn. Study Liver Diseases, Gastroenterological Soc. Australia, Internat. Assn. for Study of Liver Diseases, Internat. Liver Transplant Soc. Achievements include performing first successful living related liver transplantation; development of various reduction hepatectomy techniques for pediatric liver transplant. Office: Queensland Liver Transplant Svc, Princess Alexandra Hosp, Brisbane 4102, Australia

LYNCH, WILLIAM WRIGHT, JR., investment executive, engineer; b. Dallas, Aug. 26, 1936; s. William Wright Sr. and Alma Martha (Hirsch) L.; m. June 11, 1960; children: Mary Margaret, Katherine. BSEE, U. Ariz., 1959; MBA, Stanford U., 1962. Pres. Ins. Bldg. Corp., Dallas, 1965-84; ptnr. Estacado Ptnrs., Dallas, 1985—, Encino Co., Dallas, 1970—, Cimarron Properties Co., Tucson, 1972-83; pres., bd. dirs. Argus Realty Corp., Dallas, 1972—; bd. dirs. Lynch Properties Inc., Dallas, Lynch Investment Co., Dallas, Fleetwood Transp. Svcs., Inc., Dallas; adv. dir. Sun Valley Fruit Co., Albuquerque, LTD Enersyst Devel. Ctr., Inc., Dallas, 1995-98, TEWA Mouldings, Albuquerque, Hacienda Packing, Albuquerque, Belle Vista Homes, Dallas, 1998—. Bd. dirs. Dallas Symphony Orch., 1966-74, Dallas Civic Music, 1970-77, Ednl. Opportunities Inc., Dallas, 1973-90, Dallas Coun. World Affairs, 1990-96; trustee W. W. Lynch Found., Dallas, 1968—. Capt. U.S. Army, 1959-60. Mem. Brook Hollow Club, Verandah Club, M.O. Club (Tuscon). Republican. Episcopalian. Office: Lynch Investment Co Ste 1600 1845 Woodall Rodgers Fwy Dallas TX 75201-2295

LYNDEN-BELL, DONALD, astronomer; b. Dover, Kent, Eng., Apr. 5, 1935; s. Lachlan Arthur and Monica Rose (Thring) L.; m. Ruth Marion Truscott, July 1, 1961; children: Marion, Edward. BA, U. Cambridge, Eng., 1956; PhD, U. Cambridge, 1960; DSc (hon.), U Sussex, Eng., 1987. Asst. lectr. math. Clare Coll., Cambridge, 1962-65; prin. sci. officer Royal Greenwich Obs., Sussex, 1965-72; prof. astrophysics U. Cambridge and Clare Coll., 1972—; dir. Inst. Astronomy, U. Cambridge, 1972-77, 82-87, 92-94; vis. prof. U. Sussex, 1970-72; vis. Oort prof. Leiden U., Netherlands, 1992. Harkness fellow Calif. Inst. Tech., Pasadena, 1960-62, rsch. fellow Clare Coll., 1960-65; recipient Schwarzsch medal Astronomy Assn., Fed. Republic of Germany, Dirk Brouwer prize Am. Astron. Soc., 1990; Einstein fellow Israeli Acad., 1990; Catherine Wolf Bruce Medal, Astron. Soc. of the Pacific, 1998. Fellow Royal Soc., Royal Astron. Soc. (pres., Eddington medal 1984, Gold medal 1993), Cambridge Philos. Soc. (pres.); mem. U.S. Nat. Acad. Scis. (fgn. assoc.). Mem. Ch. of Eng. Avocation: hill walking. Office: Cambridge U Astronomy Obs, Madingley Rd Rm 0 13, Cambridge CB3 0HA, England also: Queen's U, Physics Dept, Belfast BT7 1NN, Northern Ireland*

LYNDEN-BELL, RUTH MARION, chemist, physicist; b. Welwyn, Herts, U.K., Dec. 7, 1937; d. David Netherclift and Priscilla Margaret (Skinner) Truscott; m. Donald Lynden-Bell, July 1, 1961; children: Marion, Edward. BA, Cambridge U., 1959, PhD, 1962, ScD. Fellow New Hall, U. Cambridge, 1962-65, fellow, lectr. in chemistry, 1972-95; lectr. chemistry U. Sussex, Brighton, 1965-72, St. John's Coll., U. Cambridge, 1975-95; Newton Trust lectr. U. Cambridge, 1993-95; prof. condensed matter simulation Queen's U. of Belfast, 1995—. Editor Molecular Physics, 1998—; author: Nuclear Magnetic Resonance Spectroscopy, 1969; contbr. numerous articles to profl. jours. Mem. Faraday divsn. coun. R.S.C., London, 1996-99. Fellow Royal Soc. Chemistry, Inst. of Physics. Avocations: walking, gardening. Office: Queen's University, Sch Math and Physics, Belfast BT7 1NN, Northern Ireland

LYND-STEVENSON, ROBERT MACKAY, psychology educator, clinical psychologist; b. Perth, Australia, Feb. 14, 1956; s. John and Shirley Flora (Anderson) L.-S. BA in Psychology with honors, U. Western Australia, 1981; PhD in Clin. Psychology, Australian Nat. U., 1992. Cert. lectr. in clin. psychology. Part-time tutor Australian Nat. U., Canberra, 1988-89, U. Canberra, 1990-91; lectr. James Cook U. of North Queensland, Townsville, Australia, 1992-96, Flinders U., Adelaide, Australia, 1996—. Contbr. articles to profl. jours. Mem. Clin. Coll. Australian Psychol. Soc., Australian Assn. for Cognitive and Behaviour Therapy, Soc. Australasian Social Psychologists. Office: Flinders U Sch Psychology, PO Box 2100, Adelaide 5001, Australia

LYNE, DOROTHY-ARDEN, educator; b. Orangeburg, N.Y., Mar. 9, 1928; d. William Henry and Janet More (Freston) Dean; m. Thomas Delmar Lyne, Aug. 16, 1952 (div. June 1982); children: James Delmar, Peter Freston, Jennifer Dean. BA, Ursinus Coll., 1949; MA, Fletcher Sch. Law and Diplomacy, 1950. Assoc. editor World Peace Found., Boston, 1950-51; editorial assoc. Carnegie Endowment Internat. Peace, N.Y.C., 1951-52; dir. Assoc. of Internat. Rels. Clubs, N.Y.C., 1952-53; editor The Town Crier, Westport, Conn., 1966-68; editorial assoc. Machinery Allied Products Inst., Wash., 1959-63; tchr. Helen Keller Mid. Sch., Easton, Conn., 1967-89; vice chmn. Cooperative Ednl. Svcs., Fairfield, 1983-85. Editor: Documents in American Foreign Rels., 1950, Current Rsch. in Internat. Affairs, 1951. Chmn. Westport Zoning Bd. of Appeals, 1976-80, Westport Bd. of Edn., 1985-87; vice chmn. Westport Bd. of Edn., 1980-85; mem. Westport Charter Revision Commn., 1966-67. Republican. Episcopalian.

LYNGÅ, GÖSTA LARS, astronomer, researcher; b. Malmö, Sweden, Aug. 9, 1930; arrived in Australia, 1991; s. Knut Wilhelm and Astrid Ulrika (Bergendahl) L.; m. Pauline Mary Hiscox, Aug. 11, 1962; children: Ann, Ellen, Claire. MSc, Lund (Sweden) U., 1953, PhD, 1959, DSc, 1965. Amanuenis Lund U., 1955-65, docent, 1965-76, sr. lectr., 1976-88; astronomer Mt. Stromlo Obs, Canberra, Australia, 1961-63, 66-69; pres. Iau Commn. for Clusters, 1982-85. Author, editor: (computer based catalog) Open Cluster Data, 5 edits., 1982-88; contbr. articles to profl. jours. Mem. local coun. Kävlinge, Sweden, 1985-88; mem. Parliament for the Green Party of Sweden, Stockholm, 1988-91. Recipient vis. fellowship Australian Nat. U., Canberra, 1991-99. Mem. Australian Greens (sec. 1996-98). Avocations: bushwalking, bridge, parkcare, international aid, alternative economics. Home: 89 Warragamba Ave, Duffy ACT 2611, Australia

LYNGE, LISE, counselor, director; b. Copenhagen, Jan. 25; d. Karl Johan and Nancy Mariane (Pedersen) L. Student, U. Paris Sorbonne, U. Oxford; MA in Philosophy, U. Copenhagen, 1966; MSc, Royal Vet. and Agrl. U., Copenhagen, 1979; PhD in Biotech., Oxford/Wageningen, 1988; MB, Copenhagen U. Internat. Econs., 1985; MBA in Internat. Bus., Paris Sch. Econs., 1987; postgrad., Danish univs., 1993—. EDP programmer IBM, Copenhagen, 1964-68; rschr. Co-op, Aarhus, Denmark, 1979-80; head internat. application lab., internat. product mgr. Chr. Hansen's Lab., Copenhagen, 1980-87; internat. mktg. dir. Montedison-Merck-Novo Nordisk, Copenhagen, 1987-93; dir. Biotech Mktg., Copenhagen, 1993—, counselor, 1995—; asst. prof. Royal Vet. and Agrl. U., Copenhagen, 1985-87; exec. mem. Think Tank Europe. Author: Authenticity and Integrity in Leadership/Democracy; contbr. 20th Century Journey; mem. edtl. bd. The International Activities of the Company, 1996-99. Internat. operational staff Naval Res., 1963—, press officer, editor, chmn. bd. Women's Naval Res., 1974-80. Decorated KNLBO for deed & courage (Netherlands), John F. Kennedy decoration for outstanding performance (Switzerland), Soc. of the Danish Marine decoration of honor. Mem. Soc. Internat. Bus. (pres. 1993-98), Internat. Soc. Philos. Enquiry (spl. projects coord. 1995-98, diplomate, mem. Whiting Meml. Fund com., pub. rels. dir. 1998—). Avocations: thinking, books, couture. E-mail: liselyn@hotmail.com. Home: PO Box 101, DK 2610 Rødovre Denmark

LYNN, JAMES THOMAS, insurance company executive, government executive, lawyer, investment banker; b. Cleve., Feb. 27, 1927. BA, Western Res. U., 1948; LLB, Harvard U., 1951. Bar: Ohio 1951, D.C. 1977. Gen. counsel U.S. Dept. Commerce, 1969-71, under sec., 1971-73; sec. HUD, 1973-75; dir. Office Mgmt. and Budget, 1975-77; asst. Pres. U.S., 1975-77; with Jones Day Reavis & Pogue, Cleve., 1951-69; with Jones Day Reavis & Pogue, Washington, 1977-84, ptnr., 1960-69, mng. ptnr., 1977-84; with Aetna Life & Casualty Co., Hartford, Conn., 1984, vice chmn., 1984, chmn., CEO, 1984-92, also bd. dirs.; sr. advisor Lazard Frères & Co., L.L.C., N.Y.C., 1992-96. Case editor Harvard Law Rev., 1950-51. Served with USNR, 1945-46. Mem. Phi Beta Kappa. Office: 5335 Wisconsin Ave NW Ste 440 Washington DC 20015-2052

LYNN, LEONARD HARVEY, business educator; b. Portland, Oreg., Sept. 28, 1942; s. Roy Leonard and Eunice Evelyn Lynn; m. Kuniko Yamada, Oct. 25, 1969; children: Kenneth Roy, Clifford Masami. MA, U. Oreg., 1967, U. Mich., 1976; PhD, U. Mich., 1980. Advt. copy supr. Asia Advt., Tokyo, 1968-73; asst. prof. Carnegie-Mellon U., Pitts., 1979-87; assoc. prof. mgmt. policy Case Western Res. U., Cleve., 1987-95, prof. mgmt. policy, chair dept. mktg. and policy, 1995—; mem. Am. adv. com. Japan Found., N.Y.C., 1999—. Author: How Japan Innovates, 1982, Organizing Business, 1988. With U.S. Army, 1961-64. Mem. IEEE, Acad. Mgmt., Acad. Internat. Bus., Assn. Japanese Bus. Studies (treas. 1988-96, pres. 1995-97). E-mail: lhl@po.cwru.edu. Fax: 216-368-4785. Home: 23220 Shaker Blvd Shaker Hts OH 44122-2660 Office: Case Western Res Univ 10900 Euclid Ave Cleveland OH 44106-4901

LYNN, MIDGE, artist; b. N.Y.C., Dec. 4, 1945; d. Seymour and Lillian Dribben; m. Laurence L. Lynn, Feb. 18, 1989; 1 child, Kelly. BA, Calif. State U., Northridge, 1982; MFA, Otis Art Inst., 1984. Pres. L.A. Art Assn., 1998—; also bd. dirs. Editor: (newsletter) Artline, 1998-99; exhbns. include Brand Libr. Gallery, Pasadena, Glendale 1996 (Brand Assocs. award), San Bernardino County Mus. 1997 (1st Place). Mem. World Affairs Coun., Group Nine, Artist Conf. Network. E-mail: lynnlm@earthlink.net. Home: 940 E 2d St Studio 10 Los Angeles CA 90012

LYNN, PATRICIA ANNE, student services representative; b. Newton, Iowa, Sept. 9, 1950; d. Harold Clifford (dec.) and Alice Marie (Uhlig) Johnson; divorced. AA in Psychology, Trinidad (Colo.) Jr. Coll., 1970; BS in Psychology, Ft. Lewis Coll., Durango, Colo., 1972; AA in Vet. Tech., Internat. Sch., Scranton, Pa., 1980. Customer svc. agt. Waco Scaffolding & Equipment, Denver, 1980-83; leasing agt. Look Ltd. Realty, Federal Heights, Colo., 1983-84; sales assoc. Lynn & Assocs., Aurora, Colo., 1991—; customer svc. team leader EBSCO Industries, Golden, Colo., 1984-96; student svcs. rep. Coll. for Fin. Planning, Denver, 1997—. Political aide Dem. Party, Denver; docent Denver Zoo; vol. ARC, Aurora. Mem. Rocky Mountain Midget Racing Assn., Vintage Motor Racing Assn. Jehovah's Witness. Avocations: auto racing, restoring antique cars. Home: 19013 E Carmel Cir Aurora CO 80011-3621 Office: Coll for Fin Planning 4695 S Monaco St Denver CO 80237-3403

LYON, BRUCE ARNOLD, lawyer, educator; b. Sacramento, Sept. 24, 1951; s. Arnold E. and Arlene R. (Cox) L.; m. Patricia J. Gibson, Dec. 14, 1974; children: Barrett, Andrew. AB with honors, U. Pacific, 1974; JD, U. Calif.-Hastings Coll. Law, 1977. Bar: Calif. 1977, U.S. Dist. Ct. (ea. and no. dists.) Calif. 1977. Ptnr. Ingoglia, Marskey, Kearney & Lyon, Sacramento, 1977-84; sole practice Auburn, Calif., 1984-91; ptnr. Robinson, Robinson & Lyon, Auburn, 1991-98, Robinson, Lyon & Springford LLP, Auburn, 1999—; counsel Placer Sierra Bank, Auburn, 1987-99; instr. in law Sierra Coll., Rocklin, Calif., 1983-98. Mng. editor Comment, A Jour. of Comm. and Entertainment Law, 1974; contbr. articles to trade publs. Dir. Auburn Cmty. Found.; mem. Placer County Rep. Ctrl. Com., 1997—. Mem. ABA (liaison student divsn. 1974), State Bar Calif., Placer County Bar Assn., Sacramento County Bar Assn., Thurston Soc., Mensa, Internat. Platform Assn., Order of Coif, Native Sons of the Golden West. Office: Robinson Lyon & Springford LLP One California St Auburn CA 95603

LYON, GORDON WILLIAM, philosophy educator; b. Durban, South Africa, Nov. 9, 1966; s. William and Jean Margaret (Colinese) L.; m. Eileen Lesley Groth, July 26, 1997. BA, U. Natal, Durban, 1988, BA Hons., 1989; MPh, U. Cambridge, Eng., 1991, PhD, 1994. Lectr. in philosophy Rhodes U., Grahamstown, South Africa, 1994-97; vis. asst. prof. philosophy Fla. State U., Tallahassee, 1997—; chmn. Natal U. Film Soc., Durban, S. Africa, 1986-87. Mem. editl. com. Jour. Social Theory and Practice; contbr. articles to profl. jours. Pres. Cambridge U. Ramblers Hiking Club, 1992-93. Recipient U. Natal scholarships, Durban, South Africa, 1986, 87, 88, 89, South African Nat. Scholarship, 1989, Doctoral Merit scholarship Human Scis. Rsch. Coun., Ctr. for Sci. Devel., 1991-93, Overseas Rsch. Students Scheme award, Com. Vice Chancellors and Prins., London, 1989-92. Cambridge Overseas Trust, 1989-92, Trinity Coll. Overseas Students award, 1989-92. Mem. Am. Philos. Assn., So. Soc. for Philosophy and Psychology, Fla. Philos. Assn. Office: Fla State U Dept Philosophy Dodd Hall Tallahassee FL 32306-1500

LYON, JAMES BURROUGHS, lawyer; b. N.Y.C., May 11, 1930; s. Francis Murray and Edith May (Strong) L. BA, Amherst Coll., 1952; LLB, Yale U., 1955. Bar: Conn. 1955, U.S. Tax Ct. 1970. Asst. football coach Yale U., 1953-55; assoc. Murtha, Cullina LLP (and predecessor), Hartford, Conn., 1956-61, ptnr., 1961-96, counsel, 1996—; mem. adv. com., lectr. and session leader NYU Inst. on Fed. Taxation, 1973-86; mem. IRS Northeast Key Dist.'s Exempt Orgns. Liaison Group, Bklyn., 1993—. Mem. editl. bd. Conn. Law Tribune, 1988—. Chmn. 13th Conf. Charitable Orgn. NYU Inst. on Fed. Taxation, 1982; trustee Kingswood-Oxford Sch., West Hartford, Conn., 1961-91, hon. trustee, 1991—, chmn. bd. trustees, 1975-78; mem. exec. com., chmn. Amherst Coll. Alumni Coun., 1963-69; trustee Old Sturbridge Village, Mass., 1974—, chmn. bd. trustees, 1991-93; trustee Ella Burr McManus Trust, Hartford, 1980-99, Ellen Battell Stoeckel Trust, Norfolk, Conn., 1994—, Hartford YMCA, 1985—, St. Francis Hosp. Found., 1991—, Watkinson Libr., 1990—, Wadsworth Atheneum, Hartford, 1968-93, pres., 1981-84, hon. trustee, 1993—; sec. bd. trustees Horace Bushnell Meml. Hall, Hartford, 1993—, trustee, 1994—, sec. 1996—; corporator Inst. Living, 1981—, Hartford Hosp., 1975—, St. Francis Hosp., Hartford, 1976—, Hartford Pub. Libr., 1979—; bd. dirs. Conn. Policy and Econ. Com., Inc., 1991-98; mem. Conn. adv. com. New Eng. Legal Found., 1991—; bd. vis. Hartford Art Sch., 1995—; trustee Conn. Hist. Soc., 2000—, Conn. Jr. Republic, Litchfield, 2000—. Recipient Eminent Svc. medal Amherst Coll., 1967, Nathan Hale award Yale Club Hartford, 1982, Disting. Am. award No. Conn. chpt. Nat. Football Found. Hall of Fame, 1983, Community Svc. award United Way of the Capital Area, 1986; honored as a direct descendant of its founder May Lyon, Mt. Holyoke Coll., 1997. Fellow ABA (mem. exempt orgn. com., co-chairperson subcom. on mus. and other cultural orgns. sect. of taxation 1988—), Am. Coll. Tax Counsel; mem. Am. Law Inst., Connecticut State Srs. Golf Assn., Hartford Golf Club, Yale Club, Union Club N.Y.C., Dauntless Club (Essex, Conn.), Wianno Club (Osterville, Mass.), Mory's Assn. (New Haven), Yale Golf Club, Univ. Club Hartford (pres. 1976-77), Limestone Trout Club (East Canaan, Conn.), Phi Beta Kappa. Office: 185 Asylum St Hartford CT 06103-3408

LYON, JERRY D., school psychologist; b. Seattle, Nov. 29, 1944; s. John D. and Estelle G. Lyon; m. Kathleen A. L., Sept. 30, 1967 (div. 1994). BS in Psychology and Sociology, U. Wis., Superior, 1969, MS in Edn., 1970. Cert. sch. psychologist, Wash. School psychologist Coop. Ednl. Svc. Agy., Gillette, Wis., 1970-73, Ednl. Svc. Dist., Bremerton, Wash., 1973-77, Quillayute Valley Sch. Dist., Forks, Wash., 1977-86, Port Angeles (Wash.) Sch. Dist., 1986—; adv. bd. West End Outreach Svcs. Mental Health Bd., Forks, 1974-82. Vista vol. Phila., 1966; vocalist Logos Musical, Port Angeles, 1995-96. Mem. Nat. Assn. Sch. Psychologists, Wash. State Assn. Sch. Psychologists (adv. bd. 1995-97). Avocations: fly fishing, music, reading, photography. jerry-d-lyon@pasd.wednet.edu. Office: Port Angeles Sch Dist 216 E 4th St Port Angeles WA 98362-3200

LYON, TERRY SHERILL, artist, retired engineer; b. Roanoke, Va., Sept. 23, 1944; s. Worley Sherill and Margaret R. Lyon; m. Linda Hardy, Aug. 3, 1968; children: Amy, Jimmy. BS in Bldg. Constrn., Va. Tech., 1968. Engr. Hercules, Inc., Radford, Va., 1968-95; artist Studios on the Square, Roanoke, 1986—. Juried exhbns. include: Roanoke City Art Show, Va., 1988, 91, Roanoke Coll. Biannual Exhbn., Salem, Va., 1990, New Waves Exhbn., Va. Beach Ctr. for the Arts, Va., 1992, New River Valley Art Exhbn., Radford Coll., Va., 1994, Va. Tech Art Show, Blacksburg, Va., 1993; exhibitor numerous outdoor art festivals, 1985-99; numerous corp. purchases, 1986-99. Sgt. U.S. Army, 1968-74. Recipient 1st pl. award Our Lady of Nazareth Religious Art Show, Roanoke, 1987, 1st pl. award Bath County Va. Art Show, Hot Springs, 1988, 2nd pl. and merit awards Smith Mountain Lake Art Show, Bedford County, Va., 1997-98. Avocations: art, history, building.

E-mail: Jimiejimie@aol.com. Home: 2115 Beagle Club Rd Vinton VA 24179-5525 Office: Studios on the Square 206 Market Sq SE Roanoke VA 24011-1432

LYONS, DECLAN, physician, educator; b. Limerick, Ireland, Mar. 6, 1963; s. John Lyons and Terry Bugler; m. Gemma Looney, May 11, 1992; children: Sorcha, Oscar, Pierce. MB BCh BAO, U. Coll., Dublin, 1987; MSc in Clin. Pharmacology, U. Aberdeen, 1989, MD, 1995. Intern Mater Hosp., Dublin, 1987-88; sr. house officer U. Aberdeen, 1989-91; registrar Aberdeen Royal Infirmary, 1991-94; sr. registrar King's Coll., London, 1994-95, sr. lectr., cons., 1995-97; prof. med. sci., cons. U. Limerick, 1997—, Limerick Regional Hosp., 1997—. Contbr. articles to profl. publs. Fellow Coll. of Physicians (London and Ireland); mem. Royal Coll. of Physicians (U.K.). Home: Cloneen, Ennis Rd, Limerick Ireland Office: Limerick Regional Hosp, Dooradoyle, Limerick Ireland

LYONS, HARVEY ISAAC, mechanical engineering educator; b. N.Y.C., Sept. 26, 1931; s. Joseph and Betty L.; m. Rebecca Anne Szeman, June 10, 1978; children: Neal Joshua, Leslie Eve. Cert. in indsl. design, Pratt Inst., 1952; BSME, The Cooper Union, 1962, MS in Mech. Engring., 1971; PhD in Mech. Engring., Ohio State U., 1978. Registered profl. engr., N.Y., Ohio, Wis., Wash., Mont., N.H., Mich. From design engr. to sr. mech. engr. various orgns., N.Y.C., 1954-72; assoc. prof. mech. engring. Mont. State U., Bozeman, 1978-79, U. Wis.-Parkside, Kenosha, 1979-81, U. N.H., Durham, 1981-84, Seattle U., 1984-85; chmn. dept. mech. engring. Alfred (N.Y.) U., 1985-88; assoc. prof. mech. engring. Union Coll., Schenectady, 1988-92, Ind. Inst. Tech., Ft. Wayne, 1992-95; cons. engr. in pvt. practice Ft. Wayne, Ind., 1995-98; assoc. prof. mech. engring. Ea. Mich. U., 1998—. Contbr. articles to profl. jours. Sgt. U.S. Army, 1952-54, Korea. Mem. ASME, NSPE, Nat. Assn. Indsl. Tech., Am. Soc. Engring. Edn., Soc. Mfg. Engrs. Achievements include development of methods to investigate tribological phenomenon of Fretting-Wear in-situ, towards development of failure prediction criteria, development of mechanical engineering departments in industry and academe. Avocations: skiing, flying, karate, tennis, backpacking. Home: 1330 W Stadium Blvd Apt 5 Ann Arbor MI 48103-5363

LYONS, JERRY LEE, mechanical engineer; b. St. Louis, Apr. 2, 1939; s. Ferd H. and Edna T. Lyons. Diploma in Mech. Engring., Okla. Inst. Tech., 1964; MSME, S.W. U., 1983; PhD in Engring. Mgmt., Southwest U., 1984. Registered profl. engr., Calif.; diplomate Am. Bd. Forensic Engring. and Tech., Am. Coll. Forensic Examiners in forensic engring. and tech. (life). Project engr. Harris Mfg. Co., St. Louis, 1965-70, Essex Cryogenics Industries, St. Louis, 1963-65, 70-73; mgr. engring. rsch. Chemetron Corp., St. Louis, 1973-77; cons. fluid controls Wis. U., 1977—; pres., chief exec. Yankee Ingenuity, Inc., St. Louis, 1974—; v.p., gen. mgr. engring. R & D Essex Fluid Controls divsn. Essex Industries, Inc., St. Louis, 1977-90; pres. Lyons Pub. Co., St. Louis, 1983—; pres., CEO Innovative Controls subs. Yankee Ingenuity, Inc., Ft. Wayne, Ind., 1991—; chmn. exec. bd. continuing engring. edn. in St. Louis for U. Mo., Columbia, 1980-81; bd. dirs. Intertech., Inc., Houston; cons. fluid power dept. Bradley U., Peoria, 1977-84. Author: Home Study Series Course on Actuators and Accessories, 1977, The Valve Designers Handbook, 1983, The Lyons' Encyclopedia of Valves, 1975, 93, The Designers Handbook of Pressure Sensing Devices, 1980, Special Process Applications, 1980; co-author: Handbook of Product Liability, 1991; contbr. articles to profl. jours.; patentee in field. With USAF, 1957-62. Recipient Winston Churchill medal, 1988, Dwight D. Eisenhower Achievement award of honor, 1990; named Businessman of Week (KEZK radio), Eminent Churchill fellow Winston Churchill Wisdom Soc. Fellow ASME; mem. N.Y. Acad. Scis., Soc. Mfg. Engrs. (life mem., cert. product design, chmn. Mo. registration com. 1975-90, chmn. St. Louis chpt. 1979-80, internat. dir. 1982-84, 85-87, engr. of yr. 1984, internat. award of merit 1985), Nat. Soc. Profl. Engrs., Mo. Soc. Profl. Engrs., St. Louis Soc. Mfg. Engrs. (chmn. profl. devel., registration and cert. com. 1975-79), Instrument Soc. Am. (sr. life mem., control valve stability com. 1978-84), Computer and Automated Sys. Assn. (1st chmn. St. Louis chpt. 1980-81), St. Louis Engrs. Club (award of merit 1977, wisdom award of honor 1987, Wisdom Hall of Fame 1987), Am. Security Coun. (committeeman 1976—), Nat. Fluid Power Assn. (com. on pressure ratings 1975-77), Am. Legion. Lutheran. Achievements include patentee in field. Home and Office: 2607 Northgate Blvd Fort Wayne IN 46835-2986

LYONS, JOHN MATTHEW, telecommunications executive, broadcasting executive; b. N.Y.C., Nov. 5, 1948; s. Matthew Joseph and anna (Coroneos) D.; m. Natalia Astakhova, Apr. 12, ž1992; 1 child, Matthew. BSEE, Roosevelt U., Chgo., 1970; MSEE, 1976; BSE, Century U., L.A., 1981; MBA in Engring. Mgmt., 1982; PhD in Comms., Loyola U., Chgo., 1979; PhD in Broadcasting (hon.), Sicluna U. Found., 1987. Registered profl. engr. Engr., prodr. Sta. WRFM, N.Y.C., 1965-69; sr. facilities planning and project engr. Sta. WWRL-Radio, N.Y.C., 1969-76; sr. facilities planning project engr. Sta. WWRL/WRVR, N.Y.C., 1976-78; asst. chief engr. Sta. WOR, Inc., N.Y.C., 1978-80; chief engr. Sta. WRKS-FM, N.Y.C., 1980-90; sr. project mgr. DSI Comms. (now. DSI RF Sys. Inc. Somerset, N.J.), Kenilworth, N.J., 1990-94; sr. project mgr. Vista Engring. Corp., N.Y.C., 1994—; pvt. cons. 1994—; dir. Raritan Ctr. Internat. Teleport, N.J., 1992-94, 94-96; chef engr. WLTW/WAXQ, 1996—; ind. broadcasting cons., 1994—; mem. World Dance and Dancesport Coun., 1997—; pres. Lyon Records, N.Y., 1971—, Short Lines Co., N.Y., 1980—; chmn. master antenna com. Empire State Bldg., N.Y., 1980-88, exec. com., 1998—; bd. dirs. The Document Ctr., N.Y.; cons. broadcasting and telecomms.; ofcl. photographer U.S. Imperial Soc. Tchrs. of Dance, 1991—, Blackpool Dance Festival, 1992—. Prodr.: (radio broadcast) The Cuban Missile Crisis, 1962 (Peabody award 1963); exec. prodr. (broadcast series) Radio: The First 50 Years, 1970, Sta. WOR 60th Anniversary Program, 1982 (Armstrong award 1983, Internat. Radio Festival award 1983), Sta. WOR 65th Anniversary Program, 1987; photography editor Ameteur Dancers mag., Ability Mag.; contbg. photographer to Dance Scene mag., Dance News, Eng.; photographer Dance Beat, U.S.A., Australian Dance Rev., Dance Action, U.S.A., Japan Dance News, U.S. Imperial Soc. Tchrs. Dance, 1991—. Chmn. media curriculum com. Westchester Cmty. Coll., N.Y., 1987—. With USAF, 1967-70. Fellow Soc. Broadcast Engrs. (sr., life cert., bd. dirs. 1974-78), Internat. Biog. Assn.; mem. IEEE, ASCAP, Nat. Assn. Radio and Telecoms. Engrs. (cert.), Broadcast Music, Inc., Audio Engring. Soc., Internat. Radio and TV Soc., VA Hosp. Radio and TV Guild (v.p. 1976-82, 84—, pres. 1982-84, chmn. exec. com. 1984—, Bennie award 1981), Broadcast Pioneers, Broadcast Music, Am. Inst. Plant Engrs., U.S. Amateur Ballroom Dancers Assn. (regional v.p. 1987-89, dir. for internat. liaison 1989—), Knights of Malta, 1986. Avocations: competitive ballroom dancing, photography. Home: 305 E 86th St New York NY 10028-4702 Office: WLTW/WAXQ 1180 Ave of Americas New York NY 10036

LYONS, J(OHN) ROLLAND, civil engineer; b. Cedar Rapids, Iowa, Apr. 27, 1909; s. Neen T. and Goldie N. (Hill) L.; m. Mary Jane Doht, June 10, 1924; children: Marlene R. Lyons Sparks, Sharon K. Lyons Hutson, Mary Lynn. BS, U. Iowa, 1933. Registered profl. engr., Ill; register land surveyor, Ill. Field engr. Dept. Transp., State of Ill., Peoria, 1930-31; civil engr. I-IV Ctrl. Office, Springfield, Ill., 1934-53, civil engr. V, 1953-66, mcpl. sect. chief, civil engr. VI, 1966-72. Radio officer Civil Def. Agy., Springfield and Sangamon County, Ill., 1952—. Recipient Cert. of Appreciation, Ill. Mcpl. League, 1971. Mem. NSPE, NSPE, Am. Pub. Works Assn., Am. Assn. State Hwy. Ofcls. (Meritorious Svc. award 1968), Ill. Soc. Profl. Engrs., Ill. Assn. State Hwy. Engrs., State Ill. Employees Assn., Amateur Trapshooters Assn., Sangamon Valley Radio Club, Lakewood Golf and Country Club, KC, Abe Lincoln Gun Club, South Fork Conservation Club (Ill.). Address: 1278 Glenneyre St # 171 Laguna Beach CA 92651-3103

LYONS, MAUREEN ANN, banker; b. Salem, Mass., July 12, 1974; d. James A. and Ellen M. Lyons; m. Mauricio Gonzalez. BBA, U. Miami, 1996, MBA, 1997. Portfolio mgr. SunTrust Bank, Miami, Fla., 1997—. Roman Catholic. Avocation: aerobics. Office: SunTrust Bank Miami 777 Brickell Ave Ste 400 Miami FL 33131-2803

LYONS, STUART RANDOLPH, porcelain company executive; b. Oct. 24, 1943; s. Bernard L.; m. Ellen Harriet Zion, 1969; 3 children. BA, Kings Coll., U. Cambridge, U.K., 1965, MA, 1969. Mng. dir. John Collier Tailoring Ltd., 1969-74, chmn., 1974-83; dir. UDS Group plc, 1974-83, mng. dir., 1979-83; chmn. William Timpson, 1976-83, Richard Shops, 1982-83; dir. Brit. Ceramic Res. Ltd., 1987—, Royal Doulton Dodwell KK (Japan), 1988—; chief exec. Royal Doulton and subs., 1985—; now pres., CEO Royal Doulton, Ltd., Stoke-on-Trent, Staffordshire, Eng., 1996-98; mem. bd. dirs. Hogg Robinson, 1999S; pres. BCMF, 1989-90; chmn. Brit. Ceramic Confedn., 1989—; active Nat. Mfg. Coun., 1992—. Founder Sir. Henry Doulton Sch. Sculpture, 1986, trustee, 1987—; active Yorkshire and Humberside Econ. Planning Coun., 1972-75, Clothing EDC, 1976-79, Ordinance Survey Rev. Com., 1978-79, Monopolies and Mergers Commn., 1981-85; mem. coun. CBI, 1991—, Keel U., 1989; gov. Staffs U., 1991—. Office: Hogg Robinson, Abbey House 282 Farnborough Road, Farnborough Hampshire GU14 7NJ, England*

LYONS, TERRENCE ALLAN, merchant banking, investment company executive; b. Grand Prairie, Alta., Can., Aug. 1, 1949; s. Allan Lynnwood and Mildred Helen (Smith) L. B in Applied Sci., U. B.C., 1972; MBA, U. Western Ont., 1974. Registered profl. engr., B.C. Gen. mgr. Southwestern Drug Co., Vancouver, B.C., Can., 1975-76; mgr. planning Versatile Corp., Vancouver, 1976-83, asst. v.p., 1983-86, v.p., dir., 1986-88; pres., mng. ptnr. B.C. Pacific Capital Corp., 1988—; bd. dirs. Internat. Utility Structures, Ariz. Goldfields Inc., Regional Cable TV, Inc., Battle Mountain Gold Co.; pres., chief exec. officer FT Capital Ltd., 1990—; chmn., CEO Northgate Exploration Ltd. Author articles on mfg. tech. Office: BC Pacific Capital Corp Royal Ctr, PO Box 11179 1632 1055 W Georgia St, Vancouver, BC Canada V6E 3R5

LYONS, THOMAS JOHN, meteorologist, educator; b. Melbourne, Victoria, Australia, Feb. 21, 1949; s. Norbert William and Lilian Mary (Tuohey) L.; m. Margot Marie durack, Jan. 4, 1980; children: Suzannah Catherine, Elizabeth Marie. BSc with honors, U. Melbourne, 1971; PhD, Flinders U. South Australia, 1976. Vis. prof. U. B.C., Vancouver, Can., 1981-82; vis. rsch. fellow Riso Nat. Lab., Roskilde, Denmark, 1989-90; sr. lectr. Murdoch U., Perth, Australia, 1982-89, assoc. prof. atmospheric sci., 1990-94, prof. environ. sci., 1994—, exec. dean divsn. sci. and engring., 1997-99, dean biolog. and environ. sci., 1994-97. Author: (book) Principles of Air Pollution Meteorology, 1990; contbr. articles to profl. jours. Fellow Royal Meteorol. Soc.; mem. Am. Meteorol. Soc., Australian Meteorol. and Oceanographic Soc. (pres. 2000—). Roman Catholic. Avocations: family, riding, tennis. Office: Murdoch U, Divsn Sci, 6150 Murdoch Australia

LYONS, VERONICA MARGARET, senior software engineer; b. Framingham, Mass., July 4, 1955; d. John Joseph and Mary Theresa (McCarthy) L. BA in English, Framingham State, 1981; diploma in software engring., Northeastern U., 1994. Prin. instr. Digital Equipment Corp., Bedford, Mass., 1979-92; mgr. software devel. Internat. Data Group, Framingham, 1992-93; sr. software engr. Ross Sys., Waltham, Mass., 1993-97; sr. softwarer engr. Genetics Inst., Andover, MA, 1997—. Mem. IEEE, Am. Prodn. & Inventory Control Soc. Home: 21 Cedar Sq Millis MA 02054-1280 Office: Genetics Inst 1 Burtt Rd Andover MA 01810-5901

LYSAK, VALERY VLADIMIROVICH, welding technologist, educator; b. Kirov, Russia, June 20, 1951; s. Vladimir Yakovlevich and Tatyana Andreevna (Meshkova) L.; m. Irina Yurievna Smirnova, July 17, 1974; children: Vladimir, Ekaterina. DiplEngr, Kyiv (Ukraine) Poly. Inst., 1974, CandSci, 1984. Engr. Kyiv Poly. Inst., 1974-75, rschr., 1975-76, lectr., 1976-86, prof., 1986—, dep. dean, 1984-89; lectr. UNIDO Program, Kyiv, 1978-96; cons. Kirov Plant, Tlmache, Slovakia, 1989-91; dean Peoples U., Kyiv, 1980-84. Author: Thermal and Deformational Processes in the Weld and in the Weld-Adjusted Zone, 1984; contbr. articles to profl. jours.; patentee in field. Recipient State medal 1500 Yr. of Kyiv, 1983; EuroAsia Found. grantee, 1995. Mem. Ukrainian Assn. Welding Specialists, Quality Assn. Home: L Gavro 9-D kv 20, Kyiv Ukraine 254211 Office: NTUU KPI, Pobedy Ave 37, Kyiv Ukraine 252056

LYSHEDE, OLE BIRGER, plant anatomist, educator; b. Århus, Denmark, Feb. 9, 1940; s. Jens Martinus and Victoria Ottilia (Larsen) L.; m. Bodil Munk Østergaard; children: Kristine, Mikael, Bjarne. MSc, U. Copenhagen, 1971, PhD, 1974. Substitute asst. prof. plant biology U. Copenhagen, 1971, jr. rsch. fellow, 1971-74; postdoctoral fellow The Hebrew U., Jerusalem, 1975; substitute assoc. prof. Royal Vet. and Agrl. U., Copenhagen, 1975-76, sr. rsch. fellow, 1976-78; scientific asst., dep. purity dept. Danish State Seed Testing Sta., Lyngby, 1979-87; assoc. prof. plant biology Royal Vet. and Agrl. U., 1987—, head of dept., 1989-91. Referee Nordic Jour. Botany, 1982—, Annals Botany, 1997—, Acta Botanica Neerlandica, 1997—, Seed Sci. and Tech., 1999—, Am. Jour. Botany, 2000—. Sgt./cadet, Royal Danish Navy, 1959-62, Copenhagen. Mem. Danish Botanical Soc. (vice chancellor 1990—). Avocations: field excursions, choir, stamps. Office: RVAU Dept Plant Biology, Thorvaldsensvej 40, DK-1871 Frederiksberg C, Denmark

LYSNE, ALLEN BRUCE, laboratory director; b. Owen, Wis.; s. Almond P. and Helen A. (Childs) L.; children: Michael, Bruce, Brooke. BS, U. N.D., 1960. Lic. med. technologist, N.D. Bd. Clin. Lab. Practice; cert. clin. lab. scientist, Nat. Cert. Agy. Clin. lab. dir USPHS Indian Hosp., Fort Yates, N.D., 1961-62; asst. dir. biochemistry Dr. Salsbury's Lab., Charles City, Iowa, 1962-63; clin. lab. dir Lake Region Clinic, Devils Lake, N.D., 1963-69; CEO Meml. Hosp. Assn., Maddock, N.D., 1969-75; asst. exec. dir. ops. N.D. Health Care Rev., Minot, 1976-80; regional mgr. Colo. Found. Med. Care, Pueblo, Denver, Colo., 1980-87; dir. diagnositc svcs. Cmty. Hosp., Hillsboro, N.D., 1988-92; clin. lab. dir. Carroll County Meml. Hosp., Carrollton, Mo., 1992—; chmn. Coun. on Aging, Pueblo, 1980-87. Mem. Am. Chem. Soc., Am. Assn. Clin. Lab. Sci., Am. Assn. Clin. Chemistry, Sci. Pub. Interest, Mo. Assn. Clin. Lab. Sci., N.Y. Acad. Scis. Achievements include research in effectiveness, toxicity and safety of 2 new drugs for coccidioidomycosis. Office: Carroll County Meml Hosp 1502 N Jefferson St Carrollton MO 64633-1948

LYSONS, ARTHUR F., management educator; b. Vermilion, Alta., Can., Feb. 19, 1946; s. Brooks Earl Lysons and Margaret Williamson; m. Elaine Emily Waters, Aug. 29, 1969; children: Jodi Nicole, Kimberley Dawn. B in Commerce, U. Alta., Edmonton, 1973, MBA, 1974; PhD, U. Queensland, Brisbane, Australia, 1985. Tchg. asst./grad. tchg. asst. U. Atla., Edmonton, 1972-74; lectr. U. Tasmania, Australia, 1974-79; assoc. lectr. U. Queensland, Brisbane, 1980-84; assoc. prof. James Cook U., Queensland, 1985—; vis. prof., fellow U. Edinburgh, Scotland, 1988, 90, U. Twente, Enchede, The Netherlands, 1990, Queens U., Kingston, Can., 1990; consulting dir. Mgmt. Effectiveness Resource Ctr., Queensland, 1988—; cons. Commonwealth Higher Edn. Mgmt. Consulting, London, 1990—. Contbr. articles to profl. jours. Fellow Australian Mktg. Inst., Australian Inst. Mgmt. (assoc.); mem. Australian Human Resources Inst. (charter), Australia New Zealand Acad. Mgmt. (found. mem.), Am. Acctg. Assn., Inst. Chartered Secs. and Adminstrs., Inst. Corp. Mgrs., Secs. and Adminstrs. Avocations: fitness, genealogy. E-mail: Arthur.Lysons@jcu.edu.au. Fax: 61-07-47815444. Office: Sch Bus, James Cook Univ, Queensland 4811, Australia

LYTKIN, VLADIMIR VLADIMIROVICH, space history museum administrator; b. Kaluga, Russia, June 22, 1959; s. Vladimir Alekseevitch and Piama Sergeevna (Merushkina) L.; m. Olga Alekseevna Bakaeva, Feb. 28, 1981; children: Mariya, Aleksey. Grad., Pedagogical U., Kaluga, 1981; postgrad., Mus. Religious History, Leningrad, Russia, 1987; Candidate of Philosophy, State U., Leningrad, Russia, 1989. Tchr. City Sch. # 36, Kaluga, 1981-82; rschr. Space History Mus., Kaluga, 1982-84; postgrad. State U., 1984-87; sci. dir. Space History Mus., Kaluga, 1988—; asst. prof., 2000—; chair dept. social anthropology svc. Kaluga State Pedagogical U., 2000—; faculty Moscow Tech. U., Kaluga, 1994—, Internat. Space U., Strasbourg, 1994—. Inventor in field. Mem. Regional Election Cm., Kaluga, 1996—. Fellow Internat. Acad. Astronautics; mem. Tsiolkovsky Ann. Conf. (organizing com. 1992—), Acad. Social Edn. (Moscow). Avocations: traveling other countries, books, country-side walks, car driving, spending free time with family. Home: General Popov 18, block 3 flat 21, 248033 Kaluga Russia Office: Kaluga State Pedagogical U Inst Social Rels, St Rasin str 26, 248025 Kaluga Russia

LYTLE, MICHAEL ALLEN, criminologist, consultant; b. Salina, Kansas, Oct. 22, 1946; s. Milton Earl and Geraldine Faye (Young) L.; div.; 1 child, Eric Alexander. BA, Ind. U., 1973; grad. cert., Sam Houston State U., Huntsville, Tex., 1977; MEd, Tex. A&M U., 1978; postgrad., 1978-80; student, Nat. Def. U., 1988. Substitute high sch. tchr. Butler Cty., KS, 1969; instr. criminal justice Cleaveland State C.C., Tenn., 1974-77; adj. instr. criminal justice U. Tenn., Chattanooga, 1975-76; tchg. asst. Tex. A&M U. Sys., 1977-80, intern adminstrv. asst. Office Vice Chancellor Legal Affairs and Gen. Counsel, 1980, staff assoc. Office Chancellor, 1980-81, asst. to chancellor, 1981-83, asst. dir. govt. rels., 1983-84, spl. asst. to chancellor for fed. rels., 1984-87; dir. rsch. devel. and spl. asst. to v.p. for rsch. and grad. studies Syracuse U., N.Y., 1987, exec. dir. govt. rels., 1987-89, sr. rsch. assoc. tech. and info. policy prog. Maxwell Sch. Citizenship and Pub. Affairs, 1987-92, dir. fed. rels., 1989-92; adj. prof. internatl. bus. studies Syracuse U., NY, 1990-92; prin. and sr. couns. The Erik Alexander Group, 1992-93; exec. dir. instl. devel. U. Tex., Brownsville, 1993-95, sr. lectr. criminal justice, 1995-97; rsch. fellow Office Undersec. Def., 1997; sr. rsch. assoc. Sci. Applications Internat. Corp., 1997-99; adj. prof. criminal justice Marymount U. and Lutheran Colls., Wash. Consortiums, 1999—; -ep. mgr. tech. svcs. divsn. Sci. Applications Internat. Corp., 2000—; rep., Coun. on Fed. Rels., Assn. Am. Univs.; instl. rep. Rsch. Univs. Network; exec. dir. Tex. Com. for Employer Support of the Guard and Res., 1982-86; mem. US Mexico Com. Philanthropy and the Border, 1994-95, militarily critical techs. adv. com. US Internat. Bus. Studies, Tex. A&M Univ., 1986-87; res. asst. army attache to Rep. of Ireland, 1986-87; mem. exec. com. N.E. Parallel Architectures Ctr.; mem. Sec. of Army's adv. panel in ROTC affairs, 1988-92. Mem. editl. bd., Jour. Tech. Transfer, 1987-95, contbr. articles to profl. jours. Served with USAR, Vietnam and Bosnia. Trustee, Brownsville Hist. Mus. Assn., 1994-96. Decorated Legion of Merit, Bronze Star, Purple Heart, Meritorious Svc. medal with 2 oak leaf clusters, Joint Svc. Commendation medal, Army Commendation medal with 4 oak leaf clusters. Inter-Univ. Seminar Armed Forces and Soc. fellow, 1979; assoc. Ctr. NATO Studies, Kent State Univ. Fellow Am. Coll. Forensic Examiners (life); mem. AAAS (bd. advs. nat. security and sci. comm. proj. mem. awd. sel. panel. sci. freedom and responsibilty), Nat. Assn. State Univs. and Land-Grant Colls. (vet. affairs and nat. svc. com.), Am. Soc. for Pub. Adminstrn. (exec. com. sect., past chair on Nat. Security and Def. Analysis), Atlantic Counc. U.S. (councilor), Forensic Sci. Soc., Acad. Criminal Justice Scis., Internatl. Assn. Law Enforcement Intelligence Analysts, Internatl. Assn. Chief's Police, mem., US Attorney's Law Enforcement Coordinating Com., southern dist., Tex., 1995-97. Mem. Army and Navy Club, Capitol Hill Club, Sigma Xi, Phi Delta Kappa. Republican. Episcopalian. Address: 260 S Reynolds St Apt 403 Alexandria VA 22304-4430

LYTTON, LINDA ROUNTREE, marriage and family therapist, test consultant; b. Suffolk, Va., Mar. 30, 1951; d. John Thomas and Anne Carolyn (Edwards) Rountree; m. Daniel Michael Lytton, June 23, 1973; 1 child, Seth Daniel. BS, Radford U., 1973; MS, Va. Poly. Inst. and State U., 1992. Collegiate profl. cert.; lic. profl. counselor, Va., 1995; cert. employee assistance profl., 1997; lic. marriage and family therapist, 1997. Tchr., cons. Fauquier County Pub. Schs., Warrenton, Va., 1973-74, Chesterfield County Pub. Schs., Richmond, Va., 1974-78, Williamsburg (Va.)-James City Pub. Schs., 1979-83, Prince William County Pub. Schs., Manassas, Va., 1983-89; hist. area interpreter Colonial Williamsburg Found., 1978-79; outpatient therapist Prince William County Community Svcs. Bd., 1989-91, emergency svcs. therapist, therapist cons., 1991-93; marriage and family therapist Menninger Care Sys., Inc., Manassas, 1993-99; pvt. practice Ashton Profl. Ctr., 1996—; cons. Horizons for Learning, Inc., Richmond, 1989—. Great Books Leader, 1993—. Mem. Am. Assn. Marriage and Family Therapy, Va. Assn. Marriage and Family Therapy, Internat. Assn., Marriage and Family Counselors, Sigma Kappa (life). Avocations: tennis, biking, boating, water skiing. Home: 12046 Market Square Ct Manassas VA 20112-3214 also: Fairfield Office Pk 12890 Harbor Dr Woodbridge VA 22192-2921

LYTTON, ROBERT LEONARD, civil engineer, educator; b. Port Arthur, Tex., Oct. 23, 1937; m. Robert Odell and Nora Mae (Verrett) L.; m. Eleanor Marilyn Anderson, Sept. 9, 1961; children: Lynn Elizabeth, Robert Douglas, John Kirby. BSCE, U. Tex., 1960, MSCE, 1961, PhD, 1967. Registered profl. engr., Tex., La.; registered land surveyor, La. Assoc. Dannenbaum and Assocs., Cons. Engrs., Houston, 1963-65; U.S. NSF fellow U. Tex., Austin, 1965-67, asst. prof., 1967-68; NSF postdoctoral fellow Australian Commonwealth Sci. & Indsl. Rsch. Orgn., Melbourne, Australia, 1969-70; assoc. prof. Tex. A&M U., College Station, 1971-76, prof., 1976-90, Wiley chair prof., 1990-95, dir. ctr. for infrastructure engring., 1991—, Benson chair prof., 1995—; divsn. head Tex. Transp. Inst., 1982-91, head infrastructure and transp. divsn. civil engring. dept., 1993-95; bd. dirs. MLA Labs., Inc., Austin, Austin, Lyric Tech., Llc., Houston; v.p. bd. dirs. MLAW Cons., Inc., Austin, 1980—, ERES Cons., Inc., Champaign, Ill., 1981-95; prin. investigator strategic hwy. rsch. program A005 rsch. project, 1990-93; Disting. lectr. Transp. Rsch. Bd., 2000. Patentee for sys. identification and analysis of subsurface radar signals. Mem. St. Vincent de Paul Soc., Houston, 1963-65, Redemptorist Lay Mission Soc., Melbourne, Australia, 1969-70. Capt. U.S. Army, 1961-63. Recipient SAR medal of honor St. Mary's U., 1957, Soc. Am. Mil. Engrs. Outstanding Sr. cadet U. Tex., 1959, Disting. Mil. grad. award, 1960, Hamilton Watch award Coll. Engring., 1960, Everite Bursary award Coun. for Sci. and Indsl. Rsch., South Africa, 1984, Disting. Achievement award Tex. A&M U. Assn. Former Students, 1996, Zachry sr. rschr. award Tex. Transp. Inst., 1996. Fellow ASCE (John B. Hawley award Tex. sect. 1966); mem. NSPE, Transp. Rsch. Bd. (chmn. com. A2LO6 1987-93), Internat. Soc. for Soil Mechanics & Found. Engring. (U.S. rep. tech. com. TC-6 1987—, keynote address 7th internat. conf. on expansive soils 1992, keynote address 1st internat. conf. on unsaturated soils 1995), Assn. Asphalt Paving Technologists, Post-Tensioning Inst. (adv. bd.), Tex. Soc. Profl. Engrs., Internat. Soc. Asphalt Pavements, Sigma Xi, Phi Kappa Delta, Chi Epsilon, Tau Beta Pi, Phi Kappa Phi. Roman Catholic. Office: Tex A&M U 508G CE Tex Transp Inst Bldg College Station TX 77843-0001

LYUBCHIK, LEONID MICHAILOVITCH, engineering educator, researcher; b. Kharkov, Ukraine, USSR, Jan. 1, 1951; s. Michael Abramovitsh Lyubchik and Sulamif Iosifovna Shulman; m. Galina Leonidovna Grinberg, Nov. 17, 1984; children: Mariya, Evgeniy. Diploma in Engring., Kharkov Poly. Inst., 1973, DSc, 1995; PhD, Inst. Sys. Researches, Moscow, 1979. Sr. rsch. scientist Inst. Elec. Machine, Kharkov, 1977-80; sr. rsch. scientist Kharkov State Poly. U., 1980—, sr. lectr., 1980-85, assoc. prof., 1985-96, prof., 1996—; vice chmn. Ukrainian Nat. Com. Automatic Control, Kiev, 1999. Author: Model-Based Control Systems, 1996; contbr. articles to profl. jours. Recipient Ukrainian State prize, 1998. Mem. IEEE, N.Y. Acad. Scis. Office: Kharkov Poly U, 21 Frunze Str, 61002 Kharkov Ukraine

LYUBICH, MIKHAIL, mathematician; b. Kharkov, Ukraine, Feb. 25, 1959; s. Yui I. and Lidia L. (Finkelstein) L.; m. Lilia I. Gandelsman, Feb. 25, 1984; m. Sonya I. Ostrovskaya, 1979 (div. 1983); 1 child, Eva. MS, Kharkov State U., 1980; PhD, Tashkent State U., 1984. Tchr. Shipbuilding Tech. Sch., Leningrad, 1984-85; rschr. Inst. of Med. Devices, Leningrad, 1985-87, Arctic & Antarctic Inst., Leningrad, 1987-89; prof. SUNY, Stony Brook, 1990—. Contbr. articles to profl. jours. Recipient prize of Leningrad Math. Soc., 1987, Sloan Rsch. fellowship 1991-95; NSF grantee, 1991—. Mem. Am. Math. Soc., St. Petersburg Math. Soc. Achievements include rsch. with the complete picture of dynamics in the real quadratic family; renormalization theory; measure of maximal entropy in holomorphic dynamics; construction of a hyperbolic 3-dimensional lamination associated to a rational map. Avocation: tennis. Office: Suny At Stony Brk Stony Brook NY 11794-0001

LYUBICH, YURI ILLICH, mathematics educator; b. Krasnoyarsk, Siberia, Russia, Apr. 22, 1931; s. Ilya Yakovlev and Eugeniya Lyubich; m. Lidiya Finkelstein, Nov. 4, 1951; children: Genie, Mikhail. Diploma in math. with honors, Kharkov State U., 1952; DSc, Inst. Low Temperature, Kharkov, Ukraine, 1964; PhD, Kharkov (Ukraine) State U., 1957. Tchr. H.S. N36, Kharkov, 1952-56; asst. prof. math. Kharkov State U., 1956-59, assoc. prof., 1960-64, prof., 1965-89; disting. vis. prof. SUNY, Stony Brook, 1990-92; prof. Technion, Haifa, Israel, 1993—; head cathedra Kharkov State U., 1966-89. Author: (with I.M. Glazman) Finite-Dimensional Linear Analysis, 1969, Mathematical Structures in Population Genetics, 1983 (Ministry of High Edn. USSR award 1988), Norms of Matrices and Their Applications, 1984, (with G.R. Belitskii) Introduction to the Theory of Banach Representation of Groups, 1985; contbr. numerous articles to profl. publs. Recipient badge of excellent educator Ukraine, 1975. Mem. Am. Math. Soc., Israel Math. Soc.,

Moscow Math. Soc., Kharkov Math. Soc. (mem. coun. 1980-89). Office: Technion, Dept Math, 32000 Haifa Israel

LYUBOSHITZ, VLADIMIR L'VOVICH, physicist; b. Moscow, Mar. 19, 1937; s. Lev Ilyich and Ida Iosifovna (Roshal) L.; m. Galina Konstantinovna Ustinova, July 23, 1960; 1 child, Valery Vladimirovich. Physicist, rschr., Voronezh U., 1959; cand. physics and math. (hon.), Inst. Physics and Engring., 1964; D of Physics and Math. (hon.), Lebedev Inst. Physics, 1983; postgrad., Kurchatov Inst. Atomic Energy, 1959-62. Sci. worker Joint Inst. Nuclear Rsch., Dubna, Russia, 1963-87; leading sci. worker Joint Inst. Nuclear Rsch., Dubna, 1987—; cons. Inst. Phys. and Tech. Problems, Dubna, 1992-95. Author: Gibbs Paradox and Identity of Particles in Quantum Mechanics, 1975; contbr. numerous articles to profl. jours. Grantee Internat. Sci. Found., 1994-95, Russian Found. Fundamental Investigations, 1997. Avocations: classical music, literature. Office: Lab of High Energies, Joint Inst Nuclear Rsch, 141980 Dubna Moscow, Russia

LYUBUSHIN, ALEXEY ALEXANDROVICH, geophysics researcher; b. Belogorsk, Russia, Jan. 6, 1954; s. Alexander Alecandrovich and Praskovya Borisovna (Kazakova) L.; m. Zinaida Nestorovna Kremenskaya, Sept. 6, 1980; 1 child, Ekaterina. B, Phys. Tech. Inst., Moscow, 1977; DPhil, Inst. Problems Mechanics, Moscow, 1981; DS, Inst. Physics Earth, Moscow, 1996. Jr. rsch. scientist Inst. Problems Mechanics, Moscow, 1977-84; sr. rsch. scientist Inst. Physics Earth, Moscow, 1984-97, leading rsch. scientist, 1997—; assoc. prof. Geological Prospecting Acad., Moscow, 1997—; sr. rsch. scientist Internat. Inst. Earthquake Prediction, Moscow, 1994—. Contbr. articles to profl. jours. Avocations: history, religion, philosophy, walking, swimming, classical music. Home: Dudinka 2 Bldg 1 Apt 17, 129 337 Moscow Russia Office: Joint Inst Physics Earth, Bolshaya Grnzinskaya 10, 123 810 Moscow Russia

LYZ, SERGEI ALEXANDROVICH, computer operator; b. Moscow, Russia, Nov. 4, 1963; s. Alexander Ivanovich and Luydmila Alexeyevna (Burtseva) L. Engr., Moscow Railway Transport Engring. Inst., 1985. Cert. internat. financier, 1996. Probationer, researcher MIIT, Moscow, 1985-89; engr. ASUS, Moscow, 1989-90, Sodeistvie, Moscow, 1990-94; mgr. Gavan, Moscow, 1994-96; engr., chief computer opr. Belimex Ltd., Moscow, 1996—. Deputy Internat. Parliament for Safety and Peace, Palermo, Italy, 1997—; rep. Gov. of Oceanus, Puerto Rico, 1996—. Mem. Internat. Soc. Financiers. Avocations: literature, programming, tourism, classical movies. Home: Dom 26 Korp 1 Kv 87, Ul 800 Years of Moscow, 127237 Moscow Russia

MA, ALAN WAI-CHUEN, lawyer; b. Hong Kong, Apr. 20, 1951; s. Pak Ping and Oi Quon (Hung) M.; m. Carrie Pak, Mar. 17, 1993. BBA, U. Hawaii, 1975; MBA, Chaminade U., 1981; JD, Golden Gate U., 1983. Bar: Hawaii 1984, U.S. Dist. Ct. Hawaii 1984, U.S. Ct. Appeals (9th cir.) 1986, U.S. Supreme Ct. 1989. Ptnr. Oldenberg & Ma, Honolulu, 1984-90; prin. Law Offices Alan W.C. Ma, Honolulu, 1990-95; counsel Goodsill Anderson Quinn & Stifel, Honolulu, 1995—; adj. prof. law U. Hawaii, Honolulu, 1988—. Co-editor: New Waves for Foreign Investors, 1990. Recipient Outstanding Vol. award Hawaii Cmty. Svc. Coun., 1990. Mem. ABA, Am. Immigration Lawyers Assn. (chpt. chair 1993-94), Internat. Bar Assn., Inter-Pacific Bar Assn., U.S. Japan Vols. Assn. (bd. dirs. 1989—), Overseas Chinese Am. Assn. (bd. dirs. 1993-94). Avocation: tennis. Office: Goodsill Anderson et al 1800 Alii Pl 1099 Alakea St Honolulu HI 96813-4511

MA, CHUNSHENG, electronic engineer researcher; b. Changchun, Jilin, China, Oct. 8, 1945; s. Fu and Wenjie (Zhang) M.; m. Xiuying Chen, Aug. 9, 1970; children: Qian, Jun. BSc, Jilin U., 1969, MSc, 1982. Tchr. Jilin U., Changchun, 1982-87, assoc. prof., 1987-96, prof., 1996—. Contbr. articles to profl. jours. Recipient Sci. and Tech. Progress awards Chinese Ednl. Coun., 1990, 98. Avocations: painting, swimming, table tennis. Home: South Region Jilin Univ, Rome 102 Dormitory 10d, Changchun 130023, China Office: Dept Elec Engring Jilin U, 119 Jiefang Rd, Changchun 130023, China

MA, DEFU, chemistry educator; b. Shanghai, China, Sept. 17, 1943; s. Ditai and Yuexian (Shao) M.; m. Shuyi Yang, June 12, 1969; 1 child, Xingjian. Grad., East China U. Sci. & Tech., 1965. Engr. Shanghai Solvents Factory, China, 1970-78; lectr., assoc. prof., prof. Shanghai U. Engring. Sci., China, 1979—; dept. chmn. Shanghai U. Engring. Sci., 1989-94, dean studies, 1995—. Contbr. articles to profl. jours. With Chinese Navy, 1966-69. Recipient Sci. and Tech. Progress awards Shanghai Mcpl. Govt., 1992, Teaching Merits awards of Shanghai, 1997, Advanced Dir. in Practice Edn., 1989. Mem. China Chem. Engring. Soc., Shanghai Chemistry & Chem. Engring. Soc. Avocations: travel, music, recreational activities. Home: 1476-301 Xie-Tu Rd, Shanghai 200032, China Office: U Engring Sci, 350 Xian-Xia Rd, Shanghai 200 336, China

MA, DONGPING, physics educator, researcher; b. Chengdu, Sichuan, China, Oct. 24, 1937; s. Bochang Ma and Shuhua Li; m. Jurong Chen, Sept. 5, 1974; 1 child, Ma Ning. Grad. in physics, Peking U., Beijing. Asst. physics dept. Peking U., 1959-60; T U. Engring. and Tech., Xian, China, 1960-62; instr. physics Sichuan Inst. Tech., Chengdu, 1962-83, assoc. prof., 1983-85; assoc. prof. Sichuan Union U. (Chengdu U. Sci. and Tech.), 1985-86, prof., 1986—, dir. rsch. dept. solid state physics, 1986—, doctoral adviser, 1997—; vis. scholar dept. physics and astronomy Northwestern U., Evanston, Ill., 1993-94. Editor Comm. in Theoretical Physics, 1996—; contbr. over 60 articles to sci. jours., including Phys. Rev. B, Jour. Physics: Condens. Matter, Phys. Letters. Recipient excellent publ. prize City of Chengdu, 1993, Sichuan Province, 1996; sci. and tech. achievement prize Nat. Edn. Commn. China, 1997. Fellow Internat. Ctr. for Materials Physics; mem. Chinese Phys. Soc., Am. Phys. Soc. Avocations: violin, swimming. Office: Sichuan U Apl Phys Dt, Wongjiang Rd, Chengdu 610065, China

MA, HAI-FEI, research scientist; b. Qingdao, Shandong, China, May 7, 1957; came to U.S., 1997; BS, Ocean U. Qingdao, 1982; PhD, Hokkaido (Japan) U., 1989. Postdoctoral fellow Mitsubishi Kasei Inst. Life Scis., Tokyo, 1989-91; rsch. asst. prof. Inst. Devel. Biology Chinese Acad. Scis., Beijing, 1991-92, rsch. assoc. prof. Inst. Devel. Biology, 1992-97; postdoctoral fellow Baylor Coll. Medicine, Houston, 1997-99, rsch. assoc., 1999—. Editor: Advances in Developmental Biology, 1994; contbr. articles to profl. jours. Honored Grad. Student fellow Ministry Edn., 1982-89; rsch. grantee Presdl. Fund Chinese Acad. Scis., 1993-95, Nat. Natural Sci. Found. China, 1996-99. Fax: 713-798-3175. Office: Baylor Coll Medicine T719 1 Baylor Plz # T719 Houston TX 77030-3411

MA, HON MING, pulmonologist; b. Hong Kong, July 11, 1964; s. Chou Kong Ma and Ying Suk Chan; m. Yee Wai Grace Kam, Dec. 26, 1994; children: Sze King Jonathan, Sze Yee Christopher. MB, BChir, Chinese U. Hong Kong, 1988; diploma in epidemiology & applied stats., Chinese U., Hong Kong, 1993; MSc in Respiratory Med. with honors, Royal Brompoton Nat. Inst., U.K., 1994; diploma in Tropical Med., Royal Coll. Physicians, London, 1994, diploma in Geriatric Med., 1994, diploma in Child Health, 1994; dipl. in med. rehabilitation, 1996; diploma in palliative medicine, U. Wales, 1997. Med. officer The Grantham Hosp., Hong Kong, 1989-90, 91-92, Prince of Wales Hosp., Hong Kong, 1990-91; acting sr. med. officer Hong Kong Govt. TB and Chest Svcs., 1992-95; sr. med. officer Wong Tai Sin Hosp., Hong Kong, 1995-98, Tai Po Hosp., Hong Kong, 1998—; hon. hospice cons. Wong Tai Sin Hosp., 1999—; profl. advisor Cmty. Rehab. Network, Hong Kong, 1997—; chmn. HA Hospice Quality Assurance Subcom., Hong Kong, 1998; hon. palliative med. cons. First Affiliated Hosp. of Shantow U. Med. Coll., 1999—. Contbr. articles to profl. jours. Recipient Young Investigator award 3rd Hong Kong Internat. Cancer Congress, 1996, Bernard Moran award U. Wales Coll. Medicine, Hong Kong, 1997. Fellow Am. Coll. Chest Physicians, Hong Kong Coll. Physicians, Hong Kong Acad. Medicine, Royal Coll. Physicians Ireland. Avocations: reading, swimming, basketball, music, travel.

MA, JIANG-HONG, mathematician, statistician; b. Hami, China, Jan. 7, 1963; s. Jun and Zi (Chang) M.; m. Shu-Hong Liu, Oct. 24, 1993; 1 child, Bocheng. BS, Tchr.'s Coll., Baoji, China, 1982; MSc, Northwestern Poly. U., Xi'an, China, 1988; doctoral studies, Xian Jiaotong U., 1997—. Tchr. #5702 Sch., Xianyang, China, 1982-85; from asst. to lectr. Xi'an Hwy. U., China, 1988-97; assoc. dir. sect. math. Xi'an Hwy. U., 1993—, assoc. prof., 1997—; vis. rsch. assoc. Chinese U. Hong Kong, 1998-99, 2000. Author: Probability and Statistics, 1996; contbr. articles to profl. jours. Mem. Chinese Maths. Soc., Am. Maths. Soc. Avocations: computers, books, TV, movies, music. Home: Hwy U Sect Maths, 710064 Xian China Office: Xian Hwy U Sect Maths, Nan Er Huan Rd, 710064 Xian China

MA, JIAN-GUO, electrical engineer; b. Jiaocheng, Shanxi, China, Mar. 27, 1961; arrived in Can., 1996; s. Fu Ma and Cuiyang Zhang; m. Lanping Li, Feb. 20, 1986; 1 child, Chenrui. BSc, Lanzhou (China) U., 1982, MSc, 1988; D in Elec. Engring., Gerhard Mercator U., Duisburg, Germany, 1996. Lectr., engr. Lanzhou U., 1982-91; rschr. Gerhard Mercator U., Duisburg, 1991-96, Tech. U. Nova Scotia, Halifax, Can., 1996-97; asst. prof. Nanyang Tech. U., Singapore, 1997—. Author: Engineering of Electromagnetic Fields in High-Tc Superconductors, 1996; contbr. over 80 articles to profl. jours. Recipient Award Scientific Progress, 1990. Mem. IEEE (sr.). Avocations: bridge, volleyball, badminton. Office: Sch EEE Nanyang Technol U, Nanyang Ave, Singapore 639 798, Singapore

MA, JIANZHONG, science educator; b. Qinshui, Shanxi, China, May 15, 1960; parents Ma Keyao and Zhao Xiuqing; m. Yan Liping, Jan. 6, 1988; children: Ma, Yanxiao. B in Engring., N.W. Inst. Light Industry, Xianyang, 1983, M in Engring., 1989; PhD in Sci., Zhejiang U., Hangzhou, 1998. Cert. tchr. Asst. prof. N.W. Inst. Light Industry, Xianyang, 1983-91, lectr., 1991-96, assoc. prof., 1996—; vis. scientist USDA, Ea. Regional Rsch. Ctr., Wyndmoor, Pa., 1999-00. Author: (book) Chemistry of Leather Chemicals, 1998; inventor in field (1st grade prize of sci. and tech. Progressing in Light Industry Agy. 1998, 3d grade prize sci. and tech. 1999); mem. editl. bd. Chinese Leather Info. Ctr., Beijing, 1995-99. Fax: 86 910 3579700. E-mail: majzh@xa-public.sn.cninfo.net. Office: N W Inst of Light Industry, 45 Renmin Rd, 712081 Xianyang Shaanxi, China

MA, LIJUN, endocrinologist, molecular biologist; b. Nanjing, Jiangsu, China, May 16, 1968; p. Huangzheng Lee and Ningjuan Ma. MD, Nanjing Med. U., 1991, PhD, 1995. Resident Nanjing U. Sci. and Tech. Med. Ctr., 1991-94, The First Affiliated Hosp., Nanjing Med. U., 1996-99; attending physician Jiangsu Province Ofcl. Hosp., Nanjing, 1999—; rschr. Nanjing U., 1998—. Scholar Sino-Swed Pharm. Corp., 1998. Avocations: computers, reading, music. E-mail: ljma@jlonline.com. Fax: 1-413-215-9544. Office: Jiangsu Province Ofcl Hosp, 30 Luojia Rd, Nanjing 210024, China

MA, WEI, engineering executive; b. Weifang, China, July 10, 1956; came to U.S., 1997; s. Dawei Ma and Xuzhi Li; m. Shihua Wang, May 15, 1984 (div. 1990); m. Yan Cao, Jan. 9, 1991; children: Yue, Yun. BSc with honors, Xidian U., Xian, China, 1982, MSc with honors, 1984; PhD, U. Surrey, Eng., 1994. Chartered engr., British Engring. Coun. Radio technician, engr. Radio Workshop, Jilin, China, 1972-78; tchg. asst. Xidian U., Xian, 1985-88, lectr., 1988-89; rsch. asst. U. Surrey, England, 1990-94; sr. rsch. and devel. engr. Goldtron Telecom., Singapore, 1994-95; sect. mgr. TriTech Microelectronics, Singapore, 1995-97; dir. engring. ALGOREX, Inc., San Francisco, 1997-99; sr. sys. devel. mgr. Nat. Semicondr. Co., 2000—; vis. scholar U. Calif., Santa Barbara, 1986-87; rsch. asst. Queen's U., Belfast, Ireland, 1989-90; tech. rev. com. ICSPAT, 1997—. Contbr. articles to profl. jours. Mem. IEEE, IEE, Audio Engring. Soc. Avocations: traveling, swimming, basketball, table tennis. Office: Nat Semiconductor Advanced Wireless Comm 447 Battery St San Francisco CA 94111-3202

MA, WEI CHUN WIM, environmental scientist; b. Amsterdam, The Netherlands, Aug. 17, 1941; s. Ma Wen San and Liu Sho Chin; m. Sun Yuet Wah, Dec. 22, 1970; children: Sue Wen, Ili. MSc, Wageningen U., The Netherlands, 1967, PhD, 1972; rsch. prof. (hon.), Yantai (China) Normal U., 1991. Cert. Edn. (biology). Rsch. scientist UN Devel. Programme, Nairobi, Kenya, 1972-75; vis. scientist Oxford (Eng.) U., 1975-76; rsch. fellow U. Queensland, Brisbane, Australia, 1976-77; rsch. scientist Wageningen U., 1977-78, Utrecht (The Netherlands) U., 1978-79; head ecotoxicology, Alterra Inst. Wageningen U. and Rsch. Ctr., 1979—; cons. Nat. Health Coun., The Netherlands, Netherlands govt., UN Environ. Programme, European Commn., Orgn. for Econ. Coop. and Devel., com. mem. Contbr. chpts. to books, articles to profl. jours. Sec. Hua Yi Xie Shang Hui, The Netherlands. Mem. N.Y. Acad. Scis., Soc. Environ. Toxicology and Chemistry, Internat. Assn. Ecology. Avocation: study of Chinese art and history.

MA, WEN-XIU, mathematician, educator; b. Shanghai, June 20, 1962; s. Xiang-Fa Ma and Lan-Xian Zhao; m. Jian-Hong Hua, Mar. 12, 1992; 1 child, Tian-Xing. BSc in Math., U. Sci. and Tech. China, Hefei, 1982; MSc, Computer Ctr. Academia Sinica, Beijing, 1985, PhD, 1990. Asst. prof. dept. applied math. Shanghai Jiaotong U., 1985-87; postdoctoral fellow dept. math. Fudan U., Shanghai, 1990-92, assoc. prof. math., 1993-94; Humboldt Rsch. fellow dept. math. and computer scis. U. Paderborn, Germany, 1994-96; vis. scholar, dept. math. City U. Hong Kong, 1997—; vis. scholar dept. math. U. Manchester Inst. Sci. and Tech.; reviewer mathematical reviews; mem. work com. Shanghai Ctr. for Nonlinear Sci., 1993—. Editor Jour. Nonlinear Mathematical Physics; contbr. articles to profl. jours. Mem. Am. Math. Soc., Chinese Ctr. for Advanced Sci. and Tech. (assoc.), Chinese Soc. Indsl. and Applied Math., Chinese Mech Soc. (vice head youth work com. 1991—), Hong Kong Math. Soc. Avocations: table tennis, badminton, swimming. Home: 3A, Tower 7, Parc Oasis, Tat Chee Ave, Kowloon Hong Kong Office: City U Hong Kong, Dept Math, Tat Chee Ave, 83, Kowloon Hong Kong

MA, XUN, optical engineer, researcher; b. Hai Cheng, China, Mar. 20, 1925; s. You Lin Ma and Jin Lan Li; m. Mu Jie Cheng, Apr. 28, 1956; children: Ma Li, Ma Da. BSc, Chang Chun U., China, 1948; postgrad., Coll. Fgn. Langs., Beijing, 1949. Designer Exptl. Factory, Tianjin, China, 1950-60, 64-78; sect. leader, tchr. Technol. Sch., Tianjin, 1960-64; rschr. Guilin (China) Inst. Optical Comms., 1978-81, vice chief engr., 1981-91; cons. Shanghai Jiao Tong U., China, 1983-85; projector optical fiber comms. Nat. Sci. and Tech. Commn., Beijing, 1982-83; tech. leader Engring. Divsn. Comms., Tianjin, 1982-84; sci. and tech. com. Ctrl. Bur. Comms. and Broadcast, Beijing, 1985-89. Contbr. articles to profl. jours. Recipient 2d prize cert. Ctrl. Organ Govt., Tianjin, 1958, 1st prize cert. Ministry Electronics Industries, Beijing, 1983. Fellow Chinese Inst. Electronics (profl. committeeman comm. com., sr., honor cert. 1990), Chinese Optical Soc. Avocations: foreign languages, playing bridge, classical music, stamp collecting, bicycling. Home: PO Box 5, Guilin 541004, China Office: Guilin Inst Optical Comms, PO Box 5, Guilin 541004, China

MA, YING-JEOU, mayor; b. Hong Kong, July 13, 1950. SJD, Harvard U. Dep. dir. 1st Bureau of Presdl. Office, 1981-88; dep. sec.-gen. Kuomintang Ctrl. Com., 1984-88; sr. sec. Presdl. Office, 1988; chmn. Rsch. Devel. and Evaluation Commn., 1988-91; exec. sec. Mainland Affairs Commn., 1988-91; sr. vice chmn. Mainland Affairs Coun., 1991-93; min. justice Govt. of Taiwan, Taipei, 1993-96; min. state Exec. Yuan (Cabinet), Govt. of Taiwan, Taipei, 1996-97; assoc. prof. law Nat. Chengchi U., 1981—; mayor Taipei; mem. Nat. Assembly, 1992-96. *

MAA, DAH-YOU, physicist, educator; b. Beijing, China, Mar. 1, 1915; s. Youlue Ma and Chi Gao; m. Youghe Wang, Aug. 1, 1947; children: Xiaofe, Xiaobin. BS, Peking U., Beijing, 1936; MA, Harvard U., 1939, PhD, 1940. Prof. Nat. Southwest U., Kumming, 1940-46; prof., dean engring. Nat. U. Peking, Beijing, 1946-52; prof., dean Harbin Polytech. Inst., Harbin, 1952-55; rsch. prof. Acad. Sinica, Beijing, 1955—; assoc. dir. Inst. Electronics, 1956-64, Inst. Acoustics, 1964-86; prof. China U. Sci. and Tech., 1958-66, assoc. pres., grad sch., 1980-86. Author: Environmental Acoustics, 1984, Speech Communications, 1987, Selected Scientific Works of Maa Dah-You, 1990, Study of Modern Acoustics, 1995; co-author: Handbook of Acoustics, 1983. Acoustical Soc. Am. fellow, 1945. Fellow Acoustical Soc. China (hon. pres. 1985); mem. Academia Sinica, Chinese Electronics. Soc. Home: 810 Zhongguancun, Apt 403, Beijing 100080, China Office: Inst Acoustics, 17 Zhongguancun St, Beijing 100080, China

MAACHE, ABDELHALIM, endocrinologist; b. Algiers, Algeria, Dec. 26, 1964; s. Cherif and Djoher (Abid) M. MD, U. Louis Pasteur, Strasbourg, France. Resident Civil Hosp. Strasbourg, 1989-93; pvt. practice endocrinology Strasbourg, 1993—, Algiers, 1994—; rschr. in endocrinology and diabetes, 1998—. Author: Encyclopedie Medico-Churigicole, 1993. Mem. N.Y. Acad. Scis., The Endocrine Soc. Home: 3 rue des trois Gâteaux, 67000 Strasbourg France Office: Centre Europeen d'Etude du Diabete, 1 Place de l Hospital BP40, 67065 Strasbourg cedex France

MAAK, BERNHARD RUDI, physician, pediatrician, professor; b. Krolpa, Thuringia, Germany, Oct. 27, 1940; s. Rudi Werner and Nelly Frieda (Zille) M.; m. Doris Margarete Volkl, Aug. 22, 1970; children: Thomas, Susanne. MD, Friedrich-Schiller U., Jena, Germany, 1967, DSc, 1980. Intern Dist. Hosp., Saalfeld, Germany, 1965-66; asst. med. practitioner Children's Hosp., Friedrich-Schiller U., Jena, 1967-76, sr. physician, 1967-91; head Children's Hosp., Thuringen-Klinik, Saalfeld, 1991—; presenter in field. Co-author: The Premature Ward, 1972; author: Coagulation Disorders in Children, 2d. edit., 1985; contbr. articles to jours. Mem. German Pediatric Soc., German Soc. Thrombosis and Haemostasis Rsch. Home: Wiesenweg 35, 07387 Krolpa, Thuringia Germany Office: Georgius Agricola gGMBH, Rainweg 68, 07318 Saalfeld, Thuringia Germany

MAAREK, RENÉ YGAL, industry executive; b. Tunis, Tunisia, July 24, 1954; s. Armand Maarek and Claire Allouche; m. Frédérique Azan, July 13, 1986; children: Neriel, Kenan. Degree in Engring., Sch. Nat. Supr. Tech. Advances, Paris, 1977. V.p. engring. Scan Group Internat. Ltd., Israel, 1984-89; mgr. mgmt. engring. Ormat Industries, Ltd., Israel, 1989—. Enseign de vaisseau le classe, French Fleet Air Arm (svc. ctrl. aeronautique navale), 1977-78; maj. I.D.F. Armor Corps, 1980-84, Israel. Mem. IEEE, ASME, Am. Soc. for Quality, Soc. Mfg. Engrs., Assn. for Computing Machinery, Israel Internet Assn. Home: 16/2 Ben Sira St POB 32265, 61321 Tel Aviv Israel Office: Ormat Industries Ltd, Industrial Area POB 68, Yavne 81100, Israel

MAAS, ANTHONY ERNST, pathologist; b. Utrecht, The Netherlands, May 6, 1926; came to U.S., 1959; s. Willem A. and Tono Clara (Bonebakker) M.; m. Julia Margaret Lampley, July 7, 1962; children: Willem Fulton, Julie Estelle, Anthony Ernst Jr. BS, U. Utrecht, 1948, MD, 1953. MD, Pa.; cert. anatomical and clin. pathologist. Asst. pathologist United Hosp., Port Chester, N.Y., 1965-66; assoc. pathologist Polyclinic Hosp., Harrisburg, Pa., 1966-74; assoc. pathologist Holy Spirit Hosp., Camp Hill, Pa., 1974-90, dir. labs., 1990-96; dir. labs. Harrisburg State Hosp., Harrisburg, 1990-96. Contbr. articles to profl. jours. Fellow Coll. Am. Pathologists, Am. Soc. Clin. Pathologists; mem. AMA, Pa. Med. Soc., Dauphin County Med. Soc., Torch Club of Harrisburg (pres. 1983). Republican. Presbyn. Avocations: reading, traveling, gardening, walking.

MAAYOUF, REFAAT MAHMOUD ALI, nuclear scientist, educator; b. Cairo, Egypt, Nov. 26, 1938; s. Mahmoud Ali Maayouf and Zeinab Mohammed Hassan; m. Sohad Hammed Ibrahim; children: Youssef R.M., Nourhan R.M. MSc, Moscow State U., 1964, Cairo U., 1966; PhD, Edinburgh U., 1973. From asst. lectr. to prof. Atomic Energy Authority, Cairo, 1964-84; prof. Om-durman (Sudan) U., 1984-87, Atomic Energy Authority, Cairo, 1987—; prof., head Condensed Matter Rsch. Lab. NRC, AEA, Cairo, 1992—. Rschr. in field; contbr. articles to profl. jours. Mem. Syndicate Sci. Professions, Syndicate Atomic Energy Employees, Egyptian Soc. Nuclear Scis. and Applications, Egyptian Physics Soc. Home: 19 Abu-Rafeh St Shubra-Misr, Cairo Egypt Office: Atomic Energy Authority, Nuclear Rsch Ctr, Cairo Egypt

MABILANGAN, FELIPE HUGO, JR., Philippine diplomat; b. Manila, Feb. 15, 1936; s. Felipe and Felisa (Hugo) M.; m. Ada Ledesma, Dec. 8, 1943; children: Jose Antonio, Anne Marie, Lisa. BA, Balliol Coll., U. Oxford, Eng., 1959, MA, 1964; diploma in internat. relations U. Geneva, 1965. Fgn. service officer Philippines Ministry Fgn. Affairs, 1962-75, dir. gen., 1975-79, permanent del. to UNESCO, 1980-82, 85—, became ambassador to France and Portugal, Paris, 1979; amb. People's Republic of China, 1990-94; now perm. rep. of The Philippines to the UN, New York, 1994—; Carnegie fellow U. Geneva, 1964-65; recipient Outstanding Young Men award for govt. service Manila Jaycees, 1975; Order Diplomatic Merit, Govt. Republic of Korea, 1976, Nat. Order Merit, France, 1987. Clubs: Manila Polo; Racing Club France (Paris). Office: Perm Mission of Philippines to UN 556 5th Ave Fl 5 New York NY 10036-5002

MABRO, ROBERT EMILE, energy studies educator; b. Alexandria, Egypt, Dec. 26, 1934; s. Emile Mabro and Tatiana Bittar; m. Judith Howey, May 20, 1967; children: Nevine, Nyla. BSc in Engring., Alexandria U., 1956; diploma in philosophy, Sch. of Theology, Chantilly, France, 1964; MSc in Econ., London U., 1966; MA, Oxford (Eng.) U., 1969. Cert. civil engr., economist. Civil engr. Sani Ismail & Co., Alexandria, 1956-58, Egyco, Alexandria, 1958-60; sr. rsch. officer Oxford U., 1969—, fellow St. Anthony's Coll., 1971—, dir. energy seminar, 1978—; dir. Oxford Inst. for Energy Studies, 1983—; cons. in field, 1969—. Co-author: The Market for North Sea Crude Oil, 1986, OPEC's Production Policies, 1989, Energy Taxation and Economic Growth, 1994, others; editor 5 books; contbr. over 120 articles to profl. publs. Decorated comdr. Order Brit. Empire; recipient medal Pres. of Republic of Italy, 1985, award for outstanding contbns. to profession of energy econs. and its literature IAEE, 1990. Mem. Econ. Rsch. Forum (vice chmn. 1993-96), Oxford Energy Policy Club (hon. sec.), Internat. Assn. for Energy Econs. Mem. Labour Party. Avocations: cooking, travel, collecting Alexandrianas, reading, philosophy. Home: 52 Lonsdale Rd, Oxford OX2 7EP, England Office: Oxford Inst Energy Studies, 57 Woodstock Rd, Oxford OX2 6FA, England

MACAFEE, SUSAN DIANE, reporter; b. Feb. 1944. Attended, Foothill Coll. Disc jockey with news, pub. affairs; engr., editor, prodr. Sta. KZSU-Stanford U., Calif., 1975-80; freelance reporter, broadcast journalist, 1975—. Writer, prodr., engr. editor, narrator 25 original nationwide news stories and furnished story material for numerous radio stas. and networks, TV stas. including NPR, Pacifica, ABC, NBC and CBS networks, BBC radio and TV, Channel 9 Australia, numerous newspapers and magazines; rschr., documentor and author: Agent Orange Pilot Nutritional Detox Program, 1986, (5-part series) Food-Diet-Crime, Behavior and Learning Disability Connection, 1986; author, prodr., engr., editor and narrator: Treatment of Refractory Eosinophilia Myalgia Syndrome Associated with the Injestion of L-Tryptophan Containing Products, Parts I and II, 1990; interviewer, recorder, transcriber: A Historical Prospective of Vitamin C With Linus Pauling, 1991; researcher, documentor, writer Postscipt: Interactions of Glutathione, Ascorbic Acid HIV and AIDS, 1992, Neural Tube Defects and Folic Acid, 1995, Chromium - A New Treatment for Adult Type II (Maturity Onset) Diabetes, 1996. The Legality and Use of Bone Wax, 1997, 1999. V.p. Calif. Coll. Young Reps., 1967; sec., asst. to Nat. Field Dir. Coll. Young Reps., Rep. Nat. Com., Washington, 1968; dir. precinct orgn. Calif. State Assembly Campaign, San Francisco Rep. Ctrl. Com., 1968. Recipient 3 Nat. awards Young Rep. Nat. Com., 1967-68. Home and Office: 334 Paseo De Golf Green Valley AZ 85614-3319

MACAKU, ELENI IOANNOU, language educator; b. Istanbul, Turkey, July 22, 1942; arrived in Greece, 1975; d. Ioannis and Aspasia (Sirmaidu) M. Student French Lit. and Lang., U. Istanbul, Turkey, 1965; student, U. Mich., 1976, U. Cambridge, 1976. Clk. IS Bankasi, Istanbul, 1965-70; educator private school Private Sch. of Langs., Polykastro, Greece, 1978—. Avocations: cinema, fine arts, performing arts, architecture, travel. Home: Ethnikis Antistaseos 42, 56625 Thessaloniki Greece Office: Private Sch of Lang, Perikleus 5, 61200 Polykastro Greece

MACALISTER, ROBERT STUART, oil company executive; b. L.A., May 22, 1924; s. Robert Stuart and Iris Grace (Doman) MacA.; m. Catherine Vera Willby, Nov. 15, 1947 (dec. 1994); children: Rodney James, Sara Marjorie Pfirrmann; m. Grace V. LeClerc, Dec. 2, 1995. Student, Brighton Coll., Sussex, Eng., 1945; BSME, Calif. Inst. Tech., 1947. Registered profl. engr., Tex. Petroleum engr. Shell Oil Co., 1947-56; mgmt. trainee Royal Dutch Shell, The Hague, Netherlands, 1956-57; with exec. staff, mgr. Shell Oil Co., U.S.A., 1957-68; v.p., ops. mgr. Occidental Petroleum Corp., Tripoli, Libya, 1968-71; mng. dir.various subs. London, 1971-76; mng. dir., pres. Occidental Internat. Oil, Inc., London, 1976-78; pres., chmn. bd. Can. Occidental Petroleum Ltd., Calgary Alberta, 1978-81; mng. dir. Australian Occidental Petroleum Ltd., Sydney, 1982-83, Hamilton Bros. Oil & Gas Ltd., London, 1983-86; petroleum cons. Camarillo, Calif., 1986—; exec. U.K. Offshore Operators, London, 1972-78, 83-86. Cubmaster Boy Scouts Am., Larchmont, N.Y., 1964-65, scoutmaster, Houston, 1965-68. Sgt. U.S. Army, 1944-45, ETO. Mem. Am. Assn. Petroleum Geologists, Soc. Petroleum

Engrs., Can. Petroleum Assn. (bd. govs. 1978-81), Las Posas Country Club, Gold Coast Srs., Caltech Torchbearer. Republican. Episcopalian. Avocations: carpentry, crafts, watercolor painting, golfing, gardening. Home and Office: 78 Lopaco Ct Camarillo CA 93010-8846

MACAPAGAL-ARROYO, GLORIA, federal official, economist, educator, journalist; d. former President Diosdado Macapagal and Evangelina Macaraeg-Macapagal; m. Jose Miguel Tuason Arroyo; 3 children. Student, Georgetown U.; BS in Commerce magna cum laude, Assumption Coll.; M in Econs., Ateneo Manila U.; PhD in Econs., U. The Philippines. Past tchr. Assumption Coll.; past asst. prof. Ateneo Manila U.; past sr. lectr. Sch. Econs. UP; past asst. sec. Dept. Trade and Industry, The Philippines, past exec. dir. Garments and Textile Bd., past undersec.; senator Govt. of The Philippines, 1992 thru 1995, v.p.; economist introduced over 400 bills and resolutions with 37 signed into law. Journalist Balita; host (TV) Dighay Bayan. Named Woman of Yr. Cath. Edn. Assn. The Philippines, Outstanding Senator numerous assns. and pubs. Office: Office of VP 2/F Rm 210 PICC Bldg, Roxas Blvd Pasayar Metro, Manila The Philippines*

MACAR, FRANCOISE JEANNE, research scientist; b. Liege, Belgium, Mar. 30, 1946; d. Paul Francois and Suzanne (Fontenelle) M.; 1 child, Mael. Degree in psychology, U. Liege, Belgium, 1969; degree in physiology, U. Provence, France, 1970. Stagiaire rsch. FNRS, Belgium, 1969-70, aspirante rsch., 1970-73; attachee rsch. CNRS, Marseille, France, 1973-79, chargee rsch., 1979-88, dir. rsch., 1988—; tchr. U. Provence, Marseille, France, 1971-97, U. Provence, 1971-97; organizer sci. workshops, France, 1983-97; cons. Jour. Cognitive Processing, Italy, 1999. Contbr. articles to profl. jours.; author Le Temps: Perspectives Psychophysiologiques, 1980; editor: Time, Action & Cognition, 1992; editor of several spl. issues of sci. jours. Office: CRNC-CNRS, 31 Chemin Joseph-Aiguier, 13402 Marseille cedex 20, France

MACARA, ALEXANDER WISEMAN (SIR), public health physician, educator; b. Irvine, Ayrshire, Scotland, May 4, 1932; s. Alexander and Marion Wiseman (MacKay) MacA.; m. Sylvia May Williams, Apr. 2, 1964; children: Alexandra Sarah, James William. MB, ChB, U. Glasgow, Scotland, 1958; diploma in pub. health, U. London, 1960; Dr PH (hon.), U. Athens, 1992, DSc (hon.), 1998. House physician and surgeon Glasgow Tchg. Hosps., 1958-60; gen. practice, London and Glasgow, 1959-60; asst. med. health officer City and County of Bristol, Eng., 1960-63; lectr., then sr. lectr. pub. health U. Bristol, 1963-74, head dept., 1974-76, cons., sr. lectr. epidemiology and pub. health medicine, 1976-97; vis. cons. Bristol Royal Infirmary, 1976-97; cons., adviser WHO, 1970—; sec.-gen. Assn. Schs. Pub. Health in Europe, 1976-89, World Fedn. for Edn. and Rsch. in Pub. Health, 1988-97; treas. Faculty Pub. Health Medicine, U.K., 1979-84; mem. Gen. Med. Coun. U.K., 1979—. Author-co-editor: Personal Data Protection in Health and Social Services, 1988; contbr. numerous articles on Epidemiology, pub. health, environ. health, health care, internat. health., ethics to nat. and internat. med. jours., chpts. to books. Elder United Ref. Presbyn. Ch. Recipient gold medal Italian Soc. Hygiene, Preventive Medicine and Pub. Health, 1991. Fellow Royal Coll. Physicians Edinburgh, Royal Coll. Physicians London, Faculty Pub. Health Medicine, Royal Coll. Gen. Practitioners, Faculty Occupl. Medicine; mem. Brit. Med. Assn. (chmn. rep. body 1988-92, chmn. coun. 1993-98, James Preston Meml. award 1993), Soc. Pub. Health (Pub. Health award 1992, John Kershaw award 1994, BMA Gold medal 1999), Athenaeum Club. Avocations: gardening, music, reading, neglected golf and tennis. Fax: 011 796 84602. Home: Stoke Bishop, 10 Cheyne Rd, Bristol BS9 2DH, England

MACARTHUR, DONALD ROSS, pharmaceutical business reporter, consultant; b. Johnstone, Strathclyde, Scotland, Feb. 22, 1946; s. Donald and Mary (Ross) M.; m. Jacqueline Ann Crawford, Mar. 8, 1969 (div. June, 1986); children: Zoe Louise, Wendy Ann; m. Kazuko Kameyama, Nov. 29, 1986. B Pharm, U. London, Eng., 1968. Med. info. mgr. Parke-Davis & Co., Pontypool, Gwent, Wales, 1972-75; sr. info. pharmacist Roche Products Ltd., London, 1975-78; head of sci. svcs. Serono Labs. Ltd., Welwyn, Eng., 1978-80; clin. trials officer Lundbeck Ltd., Luton, Bedfordshire, Eng., 1978-80; pharm. inst. Internat. Edn. Svcs., Tokyo, 1985-86; mgr. issues reporting and analysis PJB Publs., London, 1986-90; freelance pharm. writer, cons. DM Pharma Issues Analysis, Ltd, Dorking, Surrey, Eng., 1990—; cons. to more than 25 internat. firms in the pharm. field; speaker, presenter at confs., seminars, and sci. meetings, worldwide. Editor Pharma Pricing Rev., 1997-99; contbr. numerous articles to jours., reports in pharm. field. Fellow Royal Soc. Medicine. Avocations: reading, gardening, badminton. Home and Office: 4 Boytons Acre Borough Ln, Saffron Walden Essex CB11-4FS, England

MAC AULAY, THOMAS GORDON, economics educator; b. Yarram, Australia, Dec. 16, 1941; s. William and Mary Isobel (MacKenzie) MacA.; m. Kerry Ann Jasper; children: Alexander, Catriona, Isobel, Stuart. BSc in Agrl., U. Melbourne, 1965, MSc in Agrl., 1970; PhD, U. Guelph, 1976. Rsch. economist Agrl. Can., Ottawa, 1973-80, chief poultry unit, 1980; lectr. to sr. lectr. U. New England, Armidale, Australia, 1980-90; chief rsch. economist ABARE, Canberra, Australia, 1990-92; prof. agrl. econs. U. Sydney, 1992—, head dept. agrl. econs., 1992-97, head. dept. agrl. econs., 2000—; mem. Wheat Report Authority, 1999—. Contbr. articles to profl. jours. Mem. Australian Agrl. and Resource Econs. Soc. (pres. 1994), Econometrics Soc., Australian Computer Soc., Can. Agrl. Econs. and Farm Mgmt. Soc., Am. Agrl. Econs. Assn. Avocations: woodwork, travel, microcomputers. Office: Dept Agrl Econs, U Sydney, Sydney NSW 2071, Australia

MACAULEY, WARD, dean, retired career officer; b. Richmond Hill, N.Y., Dec. 30, 1923; s. James Oliver and Jocelyn (Ward) M.; m. Sallie Wells (dec. Oct. 5, 1987); children: Ward Henson, Wesley Adams; m. Lydia Sargent. BS in Acctg., San Diego State Y., 1969, MS in Acctg., 1974. Commd. 2d. lt. U.S. Army, 1942, advanced throught grades to col., 1947-74, retired, 1974; prof. acctg. Mesa Coll., San Diego, 1974-79, assoc. dean, 1979-81, dean sch. bus., 1988-90; dean sch. bus. San Diego City Coll., 1982-87; pres. Darwell Co., San Diego, 1967-74; forensic auditor U.S. Atty., So. Calif., 1980-82. Recipient D.F.C. with 3 clusters. Mem. Dist. Flying Cross Soc. (treas. 1996-2000). Republican. Episcopalian. E-mail: Lydward@aol.com. Home: 1721 Calle De Cinco La Jolla CA 92037-7115

MACAYA, JOSE M., strategy consultant; b. Madrid, Mar. 24, 1952; arrived in Argentina, 1982; BA in Bus. Adminstrn., Inst. Cath. Adminstr. Empresas, Madrid, 1974; MBA, Harvard U., 1978. Asst. mgr. Citicorp, New York, 1978-80; planning mgr. Banco Urquijo, Madrid, 1980-82; mng. dir. Banco Quilmes, Buenos Aires, 1982-85; sr. adviser Lazard Bros., London, 1985-87; pres., owner Estudio Jose Macaya, Buenos Aires, 1987—; co-chmn. Harvard Bus. Sch. Global Conf. 2002. Author: Provocaciones Sobre Estrategia, Editorial Temas, 2000; contbr. 28 articles on strategy and investment in Latin Am. to profl. jours. V.p. Northlands Sch., Buenos Aires, 1992-95. Mem. Harvard Club (bd. dirs. Buenos Aires 1995-97, pres. 1997-99). Avocations: music, tennis, ski, golf. Office: Estudio Jose Macaya, Alicia Moreau de Justo 750, 1107 Buenos Aires Argentina

MACCALLAN, JAMES MICHAEL FERGUSON, corporate treasurer; b. Belfast, No. Ireland, Nov. 29, 1947; s. Douglas Ferguson and Patricia Traill (O'Neill) M.; m. Nicole Guilyardi, Aug. 1975; children: Georgina, Danielle. BA in Bus. Studies (hons.), Portsmouth (Eng.) U., 1970. Trainee acct. Price Waterhouse Ltd., London, 1971-74; various sr. fin. roles Gulf Oil Corp., London, 1974-83; various sr. fin. Engelhard Corp., London, 1983-86; dep. group treas. Cookson Group plc, London, 1986-88, group treas., 1988-97; gp. treas. Del Monte Internat., London, 1997-99; v.p., treas. Esselte AB, 1999—. Author: (book) Re-Engineering Corporate Treasury, 1995, Managing Banking Relationships, 1997; contbr. articles to profl. jours. Fellow Inst. Chartered Accts. in Eng. and Wales, Assn. Corp. Treasurers; m. Marylebone Cricket Club, Cavalry & Guards Club. Avocations: long distance running (marathon), tennis, wine appreciation. Home: 15 Queens Gate Gardens, London SW7 5LY, England Office: c/o Esselte Ltd, High St Cowley, Urbridge UB8 2HR, England

MACCANICO, ANTONIO, Italian government official; m. Maria Ciuci; 1 child. JD, U. Pisa. Mem. parliamentary profl. staff, 1947; head legis. office Ministry State Enterprise, 1962-63; head commns. dept. Chamber Deps., 1964, drafter minutes, 1969, dep. sec.-gen., 1972; pres. ad hoc com. direct election European Parliament, Brussels, 1975; sec.-gen. European Parliament, 1976, Presidency of Italian Republic, 1978-87; chmn. Mediobanca, 1987-88; min. regional affairs and instl. reforms Govt. of Italy, Rome, 1988-91; senator Italian Republican Party, 1992—; undersec. Presidency Coun. Mins. Govt. of Italy, 1993—, min. post and telecom., 1996-99, min. instnl. reform, 1999—. Contbr. articles to profl. jours. Decorated Knight Grand Cross Order Merit Italian Republic. Mem. Circolo Montecitorio, Circolo Tevere Remo. Avocations: tennis, swimming, sailing. Office: Ministry Instnl Reformm, Via XX Settembre 8, Palazzo Baracchini Rome 00187, Italy*

MACCHI, JEAN-DANIEL, Old Testament and Biblical Hebrew educator; b. Geneva, Dec. 10, 1963; s. Gérald and Gilberte (Fiaux) M.; m. Claire Porchet, July 14, 1989; children: Matthieu and Jérémie. Grad. in architecture, Engring. Sch. Geneva, 1983; grad. in theology, U. Geneva, 1989, diploma of specialization in theology, 1993, D Theology, 1998. Probationary pastor Ref. Ch., Vaud, Switzerland, 1989-90; asst. U. Geneva, 1990-94, U. Lausanne, Switzerland, 1994-96; lectr. U. Geneva, 1996—. Author: Les Samaritains histoire d'une légende, 1994; (with Th. Römer) Guide de la Bible hébraique, 1994, Israël el ses tribus selon Genèse 49, 1999; editor: (with A. de Pury and Th. Römer) Israel construit son histoire, 1996. Mem. Reformed Ch. Avocations: jogging, snowboarding, scuba diving. Home: Ch du Marais 2, CH-1134 Vufflens le Chateau Switzerland Office: Univ Geneva Dept Theology, 3 pl de l'Universite, CH-1211 Geneva 4, Switzerland

MACCHIAROLI, ROBERTO, industrial engineer, educator, consultant; b. Bari, Italy, Aug. 14, 1964; s. Bruno and Liliana (Boscotrecase) M.; m. Francesca Ocuana Marra Bjonocore; 1 child, Luca. Grad., U. Naples, 1984, PhD, 1994. Sys. analyst Procter & Gamble Co., Rome, 1984-91; cons. Studio Maconiaroli, Naples, 1991-94; asst. prof. U. Naples, 1994—. Contbr. articles to profl. jours. including Internat. Jour. Project Mgmt., Internat. Jour. Prodn. Rsch., IEEE Transactions. Mem. IEEE, INFORMS. Avocations: computers, sailing. Office: U Naples Dept Indsl Engring, Piazzale Tecchio 80, 80125 Naples Italy

MACCORMACK, GEOFFREY DENNIS, lawyer, researcher; b. Canterbury, England, Apr. 15, 1937; s. Douglas Muns MacCormack and Kathleen Edith (Peacock) O'Neill; m. Sabine Gabrielle Oswalt, June 22, 1965,; 1 child, Catherine. BA, U. Sydney, Australia, 1957, LLB, 1960; MA, U. Oxford, 1964, DPhil, 1966. Lectr. in law Merton Coll., Oxford, 1962-63, M. & W. Coll., Oxford, 1963-65; sr. lectr. in law U. Sydney, Australia, 1966-67; lectr. in civil law U. Glasgow, 1967-68; sr. lectr. in jurdisprudence U. Aberdeen, 1968-71, prof. jurisprudence, 1971-96; ret. 1997—; dean of faculty U. Aberdeen, 1973-76, 85-88. Author: (book) Traditional Chinese P. Law, 1990, The Spirit of Traditional Chinese Law, 1990; contbr. articles to profl. jours. Avocations: walking, classical detective fiction. Office: Faculty of Law, Univ Aberdeen, AB24 3UB Aberdeen Scotland

MACCULLAGH, BRUCE SCOTT, fund raiser, software designer; b. Zumbrota, Minn.. BA, Marietta Coll., 1984. Software trainer Deaconess Health Sys., St. Louis, 1994-96; database mgr., grants rschr. Deaconess Found., St. Louis, 1996-97; fund analyst Quodata Corp., Hartford, Conn., 1997—. Corp. bd. dirs. United Ch. Bd. World Ministries, Cleve., 1994-2000; mem. fin. com. Silver Lake Conf. Ctr. Conn. Conf. United Ch. of Christ, Hartford, 1999—; treas. Litchfield N. Assn. Conn. Conf. United Ch. of Christ, Norfolk, 2000—; vol. Conn. Pub. TV, Hartford, 1997—. Mem. Assn. Fund Raising Profls.

MACDIARMID, ALAN GRAHAM, metallurgist, educator; b. Masterton, New Zealand, Apr. 14, 1927; married 1954; 4 children. BSc, U. New Zealand, 1948, MSc, 1950; MS, U. Wis., 1952, PhD in Chemistry, 1953; PhD in Chemistry, Cambridge U., 1955. Asst. lectr. in chemistry St. Andrews U., 1955; from instr. to assoc. prof. U. Pa., Phila., 1955-64, Sloan fellowship, 1959-63, prof. chemistry, 1964—, Blanchard prof. chemistry. Recipient Francis J. Clamer medal Franklin Inst., 1993, Nobel Prize in Chemistry, 2000. Mem. Am. Chem. Soc., Royal Soc. Chemistry. Achievements include preparation and characterization of organosilicon compounds, derivatives of sulfur nitrides and quasi one-dimensional semiconducting and metallic covalent polymers such as polyacetylene and its derivatives. Office: U Pa Dept Chemistry 231 S 34th St Philadelphia PA 19104-3803

MACDONALD, ALAN HUGH, librarian, university administrator; b. Ottawa, Ont., Can., Mar. 3, 1943; s. Vincent C. and Hilda C. (Durney) MacD.; children—Eric Paul Henry, Nigel Alan Christopher. B.A., Dalhousie U., Halifax N.S., 1963; B.L.S., U. Toronto, Ont., 1964. With Dalhousie U., 1964-78, law librarian, 1965-67, 69-71, asst. univ. librarian, 1970-72, health sci. librarian, 1972-78; lectr. Sch. Library Services, 1969-78, sr. advisor Info. Resources, 1999—, asst. to v.p. (acad.), provost, 1999—; dir. info. svcs. U. Calgary, Alta., 1988-99; dir. libraries U. Calgary, Alta., Can., 1979-92, univ. orator, 1989—; dir. U. Calgary Press, 1984-90; chmn. Alta. Library Network, 1981-89; librarian N.S. Barristers Soc., 1969-74; mem. adv. bd. Nat. Libr. Can., 1972-76, Health Scis. Resource Ctr., Can. Inst. Sci. and Tech. Info., 1977-79; mem. Coun. of Prairie Univ. Librs., 1979-92, 97-98, chair, 1984-85, 89, 91; Bassam lectr. U. Toronto Faculty Info. Studies, 1994, Lorne MacRae lectr. Libr. Assn. Alta., 1996; mem. steering com. Alta. Knowledge Network, 1999—, steering. com. Can. Digital Libr. Rsch. Inst. Initiative, 1999-2000. Mem. editorial bd. America: History and Life (ABC-CLIO), 1985-93. Pres. TELED Cmty. Media Access Orgn., Halifax, N.S., 1972-74; mem. Minister's Com. on Univ. Affairs, Alta., 1979-83; bd. dirs. Alta. Found. for Can. Music Ctr., 1985-92, Can. Inst. for Hist. Microreprodn., 1990-98, pres., 1996-97, Calgary Learning Ctr., 1997—. Council Library Resources fellow, 1975; exec. fellow Univ. Microfilms Internat., 1986; recipient Disting. Acad. Librarian award Can. Assn. of Coll. and Univ. Libraries, 1988, U. Toronto Faculty of Info. Studies Alumni Jubilee award, 1999. Mem. Can. Libr. Assn. (treas. 1977-79, pres. 1980-81, Award for Outstanding Svc. to Librarianship 1997), Atlantic Provinces Libr. Assn. (pres. 1977-78), Libr. Assn. Alta. (v.p. 1988-89, Pres.' award 1992), Can. Health Libr. Assn. (treas. 1977-79), Australian Libr. and Info. Assn. (assoc. 1977), Libr. and Info. Assn. New Zealand, Soc. Can., Foothills Libr. Assn., Can. Assn. Info. Sci. (pres. 1979-80), Can. Assn. Rsch. Librs. (bd. dirs. 1981-86, v.p. 1985-86), Calgary Cmty. Network Assn. (bd. dirs. 1994-99, chair 1996-99), Order of U. Calgary. Office: U Calgary MLT812, 2500 University Dr NW, Calgary, AB Canada T2N 1N4

MACDONALD, BRIAN ALEXANDER, aquarium administrator; b. Balt., Apr. 13, 1954; s. Robert Alexander and Sheila Golleen (Moore) M.; m. Kathleen Marie Ambrose, Jan. 8, 1977; children: Brian Jr., Kaitlin, Bridget, Brett A. BA, U. Vt., 1976; postgrad., Fla. Inst. Tech., 1976-77; MBA, Boston Coll., 1985. Northeast regional sales mgr. O.I. Corp., College Station, Tex., 1978-83; sr. dir. sales and revenue New Eng. Aquarium, Boston, 1983—; pres. Danvers (Mass.) Cons. Group, 1988—; environ. cons. BKM Labs., Hathorne, Mass., 1980-83. Mem. Advt. Club Greater Boston, Am. Bus. Assn., Am. Mktg. Assn., Am. Mgmt. Assn. Democrat. Episcopalian. Avocations: racquet sports, hiking, skiing. Office: New Eng Aquarium Corp Central Wharf Boston MA 02110

MACDONALD, FERGUS, religious organization executive; b. Evanton, Ross-Shire, Scotland, Mar. 2, 1936; m. Dolina M. Mackay; 5 children. MA, U. Edinburgh, U.K., 1957; BDiv, Free Ch. Coll./U. Edinburgh, 1960. Ordained to ministry Free Ch. of Scotland, 1960. Asst. minister Hope St. free Ch., Glasgow, 1960-62; minister St. Andrew's Evang. Presbyn. Ch., Lima, 1962-67, Cumbernauld Free Ch. of Scotland, 1968-81; moderator Gen. Assembly of Free Ch. Scotland, 1987-88; former sec. Lausanne Com. for World Evangelization, Edinburgh, exec. chmn., 1994—; chmn. European Prodn. Fund Bd. of United Bible Socs., 1987-94, chmn. Middle East com., 1996-97, mem. exec. com., 1996-97; gen. sec. UBS, 1998—. Editor The Instr., 1973-81; author/co-author: Prospects for scotland, 1985, Word Evangelism, 1990, Bible Societies, in New 20th-century Ency. of Religious Knowledge, Prospects for Scotland 2000. Mem. Nat. Bible Soc. of Scotland (sec.-gen. 1981-97), ANGLOSEC - Major English-Speaking Bible Socs. (chmn. 1987-93). Avocations: gardening, walking. Home: 113 St Alban's Rd, Edinburgh EH9 2PQ, Scotland Office: United Bible Socs Gen Sec, Reading Bridge House 7th Fl, World Svc Ctr Reading RG1 8PJ, England

MACDONALD, GARY BRUCE, communications executive; b. Spokane, Wash., Apr. 17, 1950; s. William and Thelma (Wilhelm) MacD.; m. Joy Bea Fukumoto, June 1973 (div. Dec. 1980). BA, Fairhaven Coll., 1973. Fgn. svc. officer U.S. Info. Agy., Washington, 1976-84; asst. cultural attache U.S. Embassy, Rabat, Morocco, 1977-78; dir. Am. Cultural Ctr., Damascus, Syria, 1978-82; planning officer Office Acad. Programs, Washington, 1982-83; country affairs officer Office of N. African Near Eastern and South Asian Affairs, Washington, 1983-84; exec. dir. AIDS Action Coun., Washington, 1984-87; coord. Asia/Near East programs AIDSCOM Acad. Ednl. Devel., Washington, 1987-91; dep. dir. Acad. Ednl. Devel. AIDS Communication Support, Washington, 1991-93; sr. program officer social devel. programs Acad. Ednl. Devel., Washington, 1993-95; Midwest rep. Acad. Ednl. Devel., Indpls., 1995—; cons. World Bank, India, 1992—, U.S. Agy. for Internat. Devel., Washington, 1987-89, WHO, Geneva, 1987, Pan Am. Health Orgn., Mexico City, 1987, govts. of Philippines, Thailand, Indonesia, 1987-89. Editor: Five Experimental Colleges, 1973; contbr. articles to profl. jours. Clark county coord. Youth for McCarthy, Vancouver, Washington, 1968; v.p. Gay Activists Alliance, Washington, 1983-84; chmn. com. on human rels. Met. Police, Washington, 1985; pres. Indiana Youth Group, 1997-2000. Recipient Pub. Svc. award Franklin E. Kameny, 1985, Cert. of Honor City and County of San Francisco, 1986, Harvey Milk Pub. Svc. award Nat. Gay and Lesbian Health Found., 1987, Alumni Fellow award Fairhaven Coll., 1991. Office: Acad Ednl Devel 902 N Meridian St Apt 314 Indianapolis IN 46204-4047

MACDONALD, IAN ROBERT, Spanish educator, university administrator; b. The Hague, The Netherlands, May 4, 1939; s. Robert Harold and Jannette Wilhelmina (Marang) M.; m. Frances Mary Alexander, Apr. 21, 1962; children: Bruce, Andrew, Graeme. MA, U. St. Andrews, Scotland, 1961; PhD, U. Aberdeen, Scotland, 1970. Jr. mgr. United Steel Cos., Sheffield, U.K., 1961-64; lectr. U. Aberdeen, 1965-84, sr. lectr., 1984-91, prof., 1991—, dean of arts, 1992-96, sr. vice prin., 1996—; dir. Auris Ltd., Aberdeen, 1997—; dir., chmn. KCCC Ltd., Aberdeen, 1997—. Author: Gabriel Miro His Library, 1975; editor: T.E. May: Wit of the Golden Age, 1982, Gabriel Miró: El Obispo Leproso, 1995. Chmn. Cults Acad. Sch. Bd., Aberdeen, 1979-84; mem. Arts and Humanities Rsch. Bd., London, 1999—; gov. No. Coll. of Edn., Aberdeen, 1999—; mem. adv. com. U. Highlands and Islands, Inverness, Scotland, 1999—. Rsch. convener Assn. of Hispanists of Great Britain and Ireland, Soc. for Latin-Am. Studies. Avocations: walking, digging, carpentry. Home: 47 N Deeside Rd, Peterculter AB14 0QL, United Kingdom Office: U Aberdeen, King's Coll, Aberdeen AB24 3FX, United Kingdom

MACDONALD, JACQUELINE ANNE, environmental scientist; b. Palo Alto, Calif., July 25, 1964; d. John Robert and Marylee Patricia (Benham) MacD.; children: Elliott, Jonathan. BA in Maths., Bryn Mawr Coll., 1986; MS in Environ. Sci. in Civil Engring., U. Ill., 1990. Exceptions and appeals analyst U.S. Dept. of Energy, Washington, 1986-87; rsch. asst. U. Ill., Urbana, 1988-90; rsch. assoc. Nat. Rsch. Coun., Washington, 1990-92, staff officer, 1992-94, sr. staff officer, 1994-94; assoc. dir. water sci. & tech. bd. Nat. Rsch. Coun., 1997-99; engr. Rand Corp., 1999—; editor Software Pubs. Assoc., Washington, 1987-88. Contbr. articles to jours. Environ. Sci. and Tech., Indsl. Wastewater, Water Environment and Tech., Water Rsch., Jour. Am. Water Works Assn. U. Ill. faculty fellow, 1988-90. Achievements include research in water. Office: Rand Corp 201 N Craig St Ste 102 Pittsburgh PA 15213-1516

MACDONALD, JANE CRONIN, elementary school educator, supervisor; b. Bklyn., June 12, 1950; d. Joseph Victor and Edith Rita (Ferrari) Cronin; m. Kenneth Francis MacDonald, Dec. 22, 1973; 1 child, Amanda Jane. BA, Georgian Ct. Coll., 1971; MA, Kean Coll. N.J., 1975; EdD, Nova Southeastern U., 1984. Cert. elem. tchr., reading tchr., reading specialist, nursery sch. tchr., adminstr./supr., N.J. Elem. sch. tchr. Toms River (N.J.) Regional Schs., 1971—; instr. reading Brookdale C.C., Lincroft, N.J., 1994; instr. humanities Ocean County Coll., Toms River, 1992—; cons. DJ Mac Assocs., Island Heights, N.J., 1984—; internat. cons. Creative Publs.; N.E. regional mgr. Creative Publ./Chgo. Tribune. Prodr., host Going Strong! Growing Straight! series, Toms River, 1982-85, Parent Express TV show, Toms River, 1994; rschr. in field. Bd. dirs. Parent Kid Tips, South Toms River, 1992-94; mem. com. N.J. Edn. Assn., 1984-86; assembly del. NEA, Washington, 1980-85. Hilda Maehling fellow NEA, 1984. Mem. AAUW, ASCD, Assn. for Childhood Edn. Internat., Nat. Assn. for Edn. of Young Children, Georgian Ct. Coll. Alumni Assn. (v.p. of clubs 1981-87), Phi Delta Kappa, Alpha Delta Kappa. Republican. Roman Catholic. Avocations: reading, baking, travel, creating rainbows. E-mail: djmacassoc@aol.com. Home: 720 Dunedin St Toms River NJ 08753-4514 Office: DJ Mac Assocs PO Box 908 Island Heights NJ 08732-0908

MACDONALD, JEROME EDWARD, school psychologist, consultant; b. Newark, Aug. 16, 1925; s. Jerome A. and Olvinia Regina (McKenna) MacD.; m. Nan Elizabeth Kennington, June 2, 1951 (dec. Sept. 1998); children: Jerome C., Mary Jane, Charles, Blanche Kohler, Ruth, Gregory, Paul, Robert, Carol Arbing. BS, Niagara U., 1947, MA (grad. fellow), 1950; MA in Ednl. Psychology (experienced tchr. fellow), profl. diploma in sch. psychology, Jersey City State Coll., 1970; postgrad., Fordham U., 1950-55. Asst. prof. philosophy Seton Hall U., South Orange, N.J., 1948-55; lectr. in philosophy, edn. Seton Hall U., South Orange, 1955-61; tchr. English Newark Pub. Schs., 1955-60, guidance counselor, 1960-62, chmn. dept., 1963-69, psychologist, 1969-71; psychologist Metuchen (N.J.) Pub. Schs., 1971-86; vis. tchr. NDEA Reading Inst. Bowling Green (Ohio) U., 1966-67; extern psychologist N.J. Diagnostic Ctr., Menlo Park, 1969; consulting psychologist Dept. Health and Social Svcs., P.E.I., Can., 1987—. Editor: (with Eli Levinson) The English Curriculum in Secondary Schools: Ninth Grade, 1964. Troop treas. Boy Scouts Am., 1967-69. With inf., AUS, 1943-46. Decorated Bronze Star medal. Mem. Nat. Assn. Sch. Psychologists, Internat. Reading Assn., NEA, Am. Psychol. Assn., N.J. Psychol. Assn., N.J. Assn. Sch. Psychologists, Middlesex County Sch. Psychologists Assn. (pres. 1976-77, 81-82), Psychol. Assn. Prince Edward Island, N.J. Catholic Tchrs. Guild (pres. 1966), VFW, Am. Legion, DAV, Holy Name Soc., Can. Legion, Combat Infantrymen's Assn., Mensa, Phi Delta Kappa, Lions. Roman Catholic. Home: PO Box 71, 1 MacDonald Rd Cavendish, North Rustico, PE Canada C0A 1X0

MACDONALD, KAREN CRANE, occupational therapist, geriatric counselor; b. Denville, N.J., Feb. 24, 1955; d. Robert William and Jeanette Wilcox (Crane) M.; m. Geno Piacentini, Oct. 22, 1993. BS, Quinnipiac Coll., 1977; MS, U. Bridgeport, 1982; PhD, NYU, 1998. Cert. occupational therapist. Occupational therapist, coord. of spl. care unit Jewish Home for the Elderly, Conn., 1987-93, N.Y. Inst., N.Y.C., 1984-86; pvt. practice Fairfield County, Conn., 1977-88; occupl. therapist Rehab. Assocs., Fairfield, Conn., 1993-96; instr. NYU, 1985-89, Quinnipiac Coll., 1986-92; lectr., cons. in field. Contbr. articles to profl. jours. Youth leader, deacon Union Meml. Ch., Stamford, Conn., 1980-88; deacon Southport Congl. Ch., 1992-94; chair consumer com. Alzheimer's Coalition of Conn., 1991-92. Teaching fellow NYU, 1983-86. Mem. World Fedn. Occupl. Therapy, Am. Occupl. Therapy Assn. (scholar 1985, coun. edn.), Conn. Occupl. Therapy Assn. (gerontology liaison 1980-83), NY Acad. Scis., Amer. Assn. for Advancement of Scis., Pi Lambda Theta. Avocations: poetry writing, quilting. Home: 1 Davenport St Norwalk CT 06851-4601

MACDONALD, KENNETH R., JR., author; b. N.Y.C., Apr. 14, 1944; s. Kenneth R. and Wilma Christine (Lange) M. BA, Lehigh U., 1967; MA, W.Va. U., 1970, PhD, 1976. Instr. W.Va. U., Morgantown, 1980-81. Author: (books) The Destiny of Man, 1978, The Gods, 1993, The Palace of Time: The Proof of God and Immortality, 1999. Home and Office: PO Box 1027 Middlebury VT 05753-5027

MACDONALD, KIRK STEWART, lawyer; b. Glendale, Calif., Oct. 24, 1948; s. Bruce Mace and Phyllis Jeanne MacDonald. BSCE, U. So. Calif., 1970; JD, Western State U., 1982. Bar: Calif. 1982, U.S. Dist. Ct. (cen. dist.) Calif. 1982, U.S. Ct. Appeals (9th cir.) 1982, U.S. Dist. Ct. (no. dist.) Calif. 1984, U.S. Dist. Ct. (so. dist.) Calif. 1985, U.S. Dist. Ct. (ea. dist.) Calif. 1987. Dist. engr. Pacific Clay Products, Corona, Calif., 1971-76, Nat. Clay Pipe Inst., La Mirada, Calif., 1976-82; ptnr. Gill and Baldwin, Glendale, Calif., 1982—. Mem. ABA, L.A. County Bar Assn., Water Environ. Assn., Calif. Water Environ. Assn. Avocations: travel, woodworking. Office: Gill & Baldwin 130 N Brand Blvd Fl 4 Glendale CA 91203-2646

MACDONALD, LENNA RUTH, lawyer; b. Providence, July 16, 1962; d. Arthur Robert and Laina Ruth (Weake) M.; m. Robert Christopher Carew, Sept. 18, 1993. BA, Brown U., 1984; postgrad., London Sch. Econs., 1984-85; JD, Emory U., 1988. Bar: Ohio 1988, R.I., 1989, Mass. 1992, Ky. 1996. Assoc. Smith & Schnacke, Dayton, Ohio, 1988-89, Edwards & Angell, Providence, 1989-91, McDermott, Will & Emery, Boston, 1991-93; asst. gen. counsel, group mgr. BANC ONE N.H. Asset Mgmt. Corp., Manchester, 1993-96, BANK ONE CORP., Louisville, 1996-98; real estate counsel Vencor, Inc., Louisville, Ky., 1998-99; prin. legal counsel Commonwealth Industries, Inc., Louisville, 1999-2000, v.p., gen. counsel, 2000—. mem. Mass. Bar Assn., R.I. Bar Assn., Ky. Bar Assn., Am. Friends London Sch. Econs., Phi Alpha Delta. Republican. Episcopalian. Avocations: sailing, pottery. Home: 1802 Devondale Dr Louisville KY 40222-4128 Office: Commonwealth Industries Inc Citizens Plz 19th Fl 500 W Jefferson St Louisville KY 40202-2823

MAC DONALD, MARGARET CLARK, retired real estate agent; b. Lewiston, Maine, Dec. 20, 1929; d. Arthur Bailey and Blanche (Plummer) Clark; m. John Edward Mac Donald, June 16, 1951 (dec. July 1988); children: Cornelia Ann Roberts (dec.), Edward Clark, Susan Mac Donald Moynahan. BS, Skidmore Coll., 1951. Bus. rep. N.Y. Bell Co., N.Y.C., 1951-52; show room mgr. Bonnie Doone, N.Y.C., 1952-53; interior decorator Susan Wang, N.Y.C., 1953-54; designer Maggie Mac Donald Interiors, Miami, Fla., 1960-64; owner, sec. Atlantic Millwork, Inc., Miami, 1964-88; assoc. realtor Keyes Co. Realtors, Miami, 1995-98. Pres. Homemaker Svc. Dade County, Cmty. Vol. Svc. Bur., 1967-68; pres. Jr. League Miami, Inc., 1969-70, chmn. sustaining mems., 1982; pres. Vis. Nurse Assn. Dade County, Fla., Inc., 1975-77; pres., past treas. Metropolitans, 1983-84; second v.p., spl. events chmn. The Vizcayans, 1984-85; pres. Dade County Nat. Soc. Colonial Dame Am., 1988-89; pres. Colonial Dame of Am. XVII, 1989-90, rec. sec., 1998-99. Mem. Nat. DAR (Biscayne chpt., del. conf. Washington, corr. 1998-99), Daus. Colonial Wars, Founders and Patriots (v.p. 2000). Avocations: reading, tennis. Home: 123 Lakeshore Dr Apt 1145 No Palm Beach FL 33408-3603

MACDONALD, R. FULTON, venture developer, business educator; b. Monmouth County, N.J., Dec. 24, 1940; s. James Fleming Smith Macdonald and Jane Macfarlane Barnes Abbott; m. Carol Jean Archer (div.); 1 child, Paige Brubaker Smith; m. Laura Boswell; children: George Dewey Boswell, James Fleming Smith Macdonald II. AB, U. Pa., 1963, MBA, 1969; postgrad. sr. mktg. mgmt., Stanford U., 1979. Systems mgr., mcht. John Wanamaker, Inc., Phila., 1969-74; prin. Booz, Allen & Hamilton, N.Y.C., 1974-79; pres. Irwill Industries, N.Y.C., 1979-82, Internat. Bus. Devel. Corp., N.Y.C., 1982—; chmn. IBEX Mktg. Corp., N.Y.C., 1988—; pres. Simfer Operational Internat., Inc., N.Y.C., 1984; vice chmn. Neusteter Co., Denver, 1984-85; dir. Fragrances Selective, Inc., 1985-87; mng. dir. Stuyvesant Group Internat., Dutch Am. Bus. Advisors, N.Y.C. and Amsterdam, 1987-88; chmn. Am. Bus. Media, Inc., 1989-90, One Ams., Inc., Washington, 1990—; mng. dir. Synoptics Devel. Corp., N.Y.C., 1992—; dir. C4SI, Inc., Ill., 1998—, First Fin. M&A, Fla., 1998—; vice chmn., dir. CloseOutNow.com, N.Y., 1999—; adj. prof. Grad. Bus. Sch., Columbia U., N.Y.C., 1984-85, Mgmt. Inst. NYU, 1992-98, chmn. Globalization Adv. Bd., 1993-94. Designer Manpower Mgmt. Concepts computer system, 1972—; author, pub. The IBD Quarterly Report, 1996—; contbr. articles to bus. publs. Capt. inf. U.S. Army, 1963-67, Vietnam. Decorated Bronze Star. Mem. Inst. Mgmt. Consultants (cert. mgmt. cons. 1989), Global Econ. Action Inst., Soc. Mayflower Descendants, Soc. Coll. Alumni U. Pa. (pres. 1973-74, bd. mgrs. 1975—), Ripon Soc. (Washington), Penn Club (N.Y.). Republican. Christian Scientist. Avocation: squash. Home: 40 Central Park S Ph A New York NY 10019-1633 Office: Internat Bus Devel Corp 730 5th Ave Ste 900 New York NY 10019-4105

MACDONALD, RONALD FRANCIS, financial services company executive; b. Detroit, July 23, 1946; s. Alfred and Marianne Dorothy (Paddock) Mac.; m. Harriet Pratt Higgins, Dec. 18, 1982 (div. 1997); children: John Higgins, Peter Brewer. BS, U. Detroit, 1968; MBA, Mich. State U., 1970. V.p. Northern Trust Co., Chgo., 1970-84, Bankers Trust Co., N.Y.C., 1984-89; mng. dir. CapMAC Holdings, Inc., N.Y.C., 1989-97, MBIA Ins. Corp., Armonk, N.Y., 1998—. Mem. Ins. Industry Planning Forum, N.Y. Athletic Club, Royal Oak Soc. Roman Catholic. Avocations: skiing, running, art history, reading. Home: 64 E 94th St New York NY 10128-0773

MACDONELL, HERBERT LEON, criminalist, consultant, educator; b. Wellsville, N.Y., July 23, 1928; s. Leon John Duncan MacDonell and Catherine Winifred Williams; m. Phyllis Barbara Austin, Aug. 19, 1950; adopted children: Candy, Cindy, Wendie, Wendy, Cathy, Joanne, Mark, David, Debra, John, Karen, Paul. BA in Chemistry, Alfred U., 1950; MS in Chemistry, U. R.I., 1956. Cert. sr. crime scene analyst. Prof. Milton (Wis.) Coll., 1951-54, Corning (N.Y.) C.C., 1960-92; cons. Lab. Forensic Sci., Corning, 1970—; prof. Elmira (N.Y.) Coll., 1972-83. Fellow Am. Acad. Forensic Sci. (chmn. 1969-70); mem. Internat. Assn. for Identification (various coms., Dondaro award 1974), Internat. Assn. Bloodstain Analysts (dist. mem., historian 1983—), Can. and English Forensic Sci. Socs., Rotary. Democrat. Episcopalian. Achievements include inventor/patentee for MAGNA Brush for fingerprints. Avocations: model trains, stamps, glass, woodworking, firearms. E-mail: forensic@servtech.com. Home and Office: PO Box 1111 Corning NY 14830-0911

MACDONOUGH, ROBERT HOWARD, retired consulting engineer, tax consultant; b. Chgo., Jan. 24, 1941; s. John Haaf and Helen Margaret (McWilliams) MacD.; m. Joan Carol Rosecrants, Dec. 28, 1963 (div. Nov. 1975); children: John Haaf, Thomas William, Mark Peter. BS in Engring. Ops., Iowa State U., 1962; MA in Econ., Drake U., 1966. Registered profl. engr., Iowa; enrolled agent. Assoc. Mgmt. Sci. Am., Palo Alto, Calif., 1969; mng. assoc. Theo. Barry & Assocs., Los Angeles, 1970-72; mgr. indsl. engring. Advanced Memory Systems, Sunnyvale, Calif., 1972-73; mgr. planning and engring. Signetics, Sunnyvale, 1973-75; pres. Facilities Cons., Mountain View, Calif., 1976-96; instr. H&R Block; cons. assoc. Shumaker Tax Cons. Mem. Phi Gamma Delta. Mem. Nat. Assn. Enrolled Agts., Calif. Soc. Enrolled Agts., Mission Soc. Enrolled Agts. Republican.

MACDORMAN, KARL FREDRIC, robotics professor; b. Carlsbad, Calif., Feb. 25, 1966; s. Carroll Frederic and Claudia Frances (Lightner) MacD. AB, U. Calif., Berkeley, 1988; PhD in computer sci., Cambridge U., Eng., 1996. Software engr. Sun Microsystems, Zurich, 1989-90; pres. Marco Sales, Encinitas, Calif., 1991; supr. Trinity Hall Coll., Cambridge, 1992-96; fellow, sr. mem. Hughes Hall, Cambridge, 1996-97; asst. prof. Osaka U., Toyonaka, Japan, 1997—; vis. prof. Meiji U., Tokyo, 1997. Recipient Overseas Rsch. Student's award Cambridge U., 1992-95, scholarship Am. Friends of Cambridge U., 1992-94. Fellow Cambridge Philos. Soc.; mem. Toho Inst. (rsch. fellow 1996—), IEEE. Office: Osaka Univ Fac Engring Sci, Machikaneyama 1-3 Toyonaka, Osaka 560-8531, Japan

MACDOUGALL, SIR (GEORGE) DONALD (ALASTAIR), economist; b. Glasgow, Scotland, Oct. 26, 1912; s. Daniel Douglas and Beatrice Amy (Miller) MacD.; MA (George Webb Medley jr. and sr. scholarships in polit. economy), Balliol Coll., Oxford U., 1938; LLD (hon.), U. Strathclye, 1968; LittD (hon.), U. Leeds, 1971; DSc (hon.), U. Aston, 1979; m. Bridget Christabel Bartrum, 1937 (dissolved 1977); children: John Douglas, Mary Jean; m. Laura Margaret Hall, 1977 (dec. 1995). Asst. lectr., then lectr. econs. U. Leeds, 1936-39; with statis. br. Office First Lord Admiralty, 1939-40, Office Prime Minister, 1940-45; offcl. fellow Wadham Coll., Oxford U., 1945-50, domestic bursar, 1946-48, hon. fellow, 1964—, faculty fellow Nuffield Coll., 1947-50, professorial fellow, 1950-52, ofcl. fellow, 1952-64, first bursar, 1958-64, hon. fellow, 1967—, univ. Nuffield reader internat. econs., 1950-52; hon. fellow Balliol Coll., Oxford U., 1992—; econ. dir. Orgn. European Econ. Cooperation, Paris, 1948-49; chief adv. statis. br. Office Prime Minister, 1951-53; vis. prof. Australian Nat. U., Canberra, 1959, M.I.T. Center Internat. Studies, New Delhi, 1961; econ. dir. Nat. Econ. Devel. Office, 1962-64; mem. Turnover Tax Com., 1963-64; dir. gen. Dept. Econ. Affairs, 1964-68; head govt. econ. service, chief econ. adv. Treasury, 1969-73; chief econ. adv. Confedn. Brit. Industry, 1973-84. Decorated knight, 1953, officer Order Brit. Empire, 1942, comdr., 1945. Fellow Brit. Acad.; mem. Council Royal Econ. Soc. (pres. 1972-74), Nat. Inst. Econ. and Social Research (chmn. exec. com. 1974-87), Soc. Strategic and Long-Range Planning (pres. 1977-85), Soc. Bus. Economists (v.p. 1978—). Club: Reform (London). Author: The World Dollar Problem, 1957; The Dollar Problem: A Reappraisal, 1960; Studies in Political Economy, 2 vols., 1975; Don and Mandarin: Memoirs of an Economist, 1987; co-author: Measures for International Economic Stability, 1951; The Fiscal System of Venezuela, 1959; chmn. EEC Report of Study Group on Role of Public Finance in European Integration, 1977; contbr. articles to profl. publs.

MACDOUGALL, JOHN DUNCAN, surgeon; b. Indpls., Mar. 4, 1925; s. Duncan Campbell and Beulah Stewart (Ward) MacD.; m. Inga Margaretha Tranberg, Oct. 6, 1951 (div. 1980); children: Duncan Campbell, Stewart Andrew, Eric Matthew, Victoria Suzanne MacDougall Korb; m. Barbara Lee Mayse, Nov. 1, 1980; children: Katherine Jane, James William. BS, Ind. U., 1948; MD, Ind. U., Indpl., 1951. Diplomate Am. Bd. Surgery, Am. Bd. Thoracic Surgery. Pvt. practice Indpls., 1957-93; pres. med. staff St. Francis Hosp., Beech Grove, Ind., 1975, pres. adv. bd., 1993-95, chmn. governing bd. trustees, 1995—; chmn. bd. dirs. Med. Assurance of Ind., Indpls., 1987—. Exec. com. dean's coun. Ind. U. Sch. Medicine, Indpls., 1988—, mem. adv. com., 1989-96, pres. dean's coun., 1992-95; mem. Ind. Govs. Task Force on Organ Transplantation, Indpls., 1986-89; pres. Ind. Med. Polit. Action Com., Indpls., 1992-98; bd. dirs. Ind. Med. History Mus., 1989—; mem. Ind. Hist. Soc., Indpls. Mus. Art; pres. Indpls. English Speaking Union, 1997—. With U.S. Army, 1943-46, ETO. Decorated Bronze Star medal. Fellow ACS; mem. AMA (del., chmn. Ind. delegation), Ind. State Med. Assn. (pres. 1987-88), Indpls. Med. Soc. (pres. 1978-79), Orgn. State Med. Assn. Pres. (pres. 1994-95), Nat. Med. Vets. Assn. (bd. dirs. 1992—), Am. Legion (comdr. Paul Coble Post # 26 1999—), Masons, Indpls. Lit. Club, Contemporary Club, Meridian Hills Country Club. Republican. Episcopalian. Avocations: woodworking, golf, fishing. Home: 7202 Dean Rd Indianapolis IN 46240-3628 Office: Med Assurance of Ind Ste 300 8425 Woodfield Crossing Blvd Indianapolis IN 46240-2495

MACE, ADRIENNE, music educator; b. Tidworth, Hampshire, Eng., June 2, 1935; d. Arthur and Anne (Lloyd) Russell; m. John Edward Ronald Mace (dec. Feb. 1961). Student, U. Vienna, 1968. Singer, actor Piccadilly & New Theatres, London, 1966-68; singer Glyndebourne Opera, Sussex, 1968-69, Royal Opera House, London, 1969-70; tutor voice and singing London, 1970—; dir., founder Voices Theatre Co., London, 1983—, Voices Chamber Ensemble, London, 1986—; actor, dir., condr. Author: From Autumn to Summer, 2000; dir. Richard II, 1989, 94, Mother's Love, London Fringe (award); contbr. poetry to Expression, 12 vols. Recipient Shakespeare award Poetry Soc., 1963, Southall Arts, 1963. Avocations: playing piano, reading.

MACE, STEPHEN ALAN, investment advisor; b. Springfield, Mo., Dec. 30, 1957; s. Leslie Jasper and Virginia Sue (Dunaway) M.; m. Deborah Marie Smith, Dec. 3, 1983; children: Andrew Stephen, Ashley Marie, Alexander Edward. BA, William Jewell Coll., 1979; JD, U. Mo., 1982. Bar: Mo. 1982; CPA, Mo., 1991; CFA Assn. Investment Mgmt. and Rsch., 1998. Tax specialist Coopers & Lybrand, St. Louis, 1982-85; atty. Blumenfeld, Sandweiss, et al, St. Louis, 1985-86; sr. trust officer Boatmen's Nat. Bank, St. Louis, 1986-89; prin. Moneta Group, Inc., St. Louis, 1989-94; portfolio cons. Templeton Portfolio Adv., Carmel, Calif., 1994—. Mem. Mo. Bar, Bar Assn. Met. St. Louis, Internat. Assn. Fin. Planning (nat. bd. dirs., chair audit com. 1993, mem. practitioner adv. coun. 1991-93), Kiwanis Internat. (charter pres. chpt. 1982-83, Disting. Club Pres. 1983). Republican. Baptist. Avocations: scuba diving, big-game hunting, fly fishing, skiing, tae kwon do (black belt).

MACEK, KAREL, retired analytical chemistry educator; b. Prague, Czechoslovakia, Oct. 31, 1928; s. Karel Macek and Pavla (Kotaskova) Mackova; m. Olga Haaszova, June 17, 1950; children: Jiri, Jan. Dr rerum naturalium, Charles U., Prague, 1951; Dr. Sc., Tech. U., Prague, 1983. Head of labs. Rsch. Inst. for Pharmacy and Biochemistry, Prague, 1950-68, head of labs. internal dept., 1970-71; head of labs. 3rd Internal Clinic Charles U., Prague, 1971-77; leading scientist Inst. of Physiology, Czechoslovak Acad. of Scis., Prague, 1977-91; assoc. editor Jour. of Chromatography, Amsterdam, 1968-88; editor Jour. of Chromatography, Biomed. Applications, 1977-95; ret., 1996; chmn. 18 Internat. Symposia on Chromatography, 1961-93. Author, editor 18 books on chromatography; contbr. chpts. to books and 197 articles to profl. jours. Recipient 6 awards for chromatography. Mem. Czechoslovak Chem. Soc. (hon. mem.; chmn. chromatography sect. 1961-91), Gesellschaft f. Toxikologie (hon. mem.), Soc. Rsch. and Application of Connective Tissue (vice-chmn. 1997—). Achievements include two patents in field. Home: Lukesova 16, 14200 Prague Czech Republic

MACEK, MILAN, JR., molecular geneticist; b. Prague, Czechoslovakia, Dec. 24, 1961; s. Milan and Věra (Mackova) M. MD, Charles U., Prague, 1986. Rsch. fellow, 1st Sch. Medicine Charles U., 1986-89; rsch. fellow, Inst. Human Genetics Free U., Berlin, 1989-92; postdoctoral fellow, Ctr. Med. Genetics Johns Hopkins U. Sch. Medicine, Balt., 1992-95; rschr. dept. med. genetics II Univ. Hosp. Prague Motol, 1995—, assoc. prof. med. genetics, 2000—; head molecular genetic sect. Nat. Ctr. Diagnosis and Treatment of Cystic Fibrosis, U. Hosp. Prague Motol, 1997—; reviewer Internat. Granting Agy. of Czech Min. Health, Prague, 1995—; cons. State Med. Inst., Prague, 1996—. Editor (jour.) Czecho-Slovak Pediat., 1996—; contbr. numerous articles to internat. med. and scientific jours.; reviewer (jours.) Human Mutation, Human Genetics, 1992—. Recipient Ann. Czech Med. Soc. J.E. Purkyne award, 1991, Ann. Czech Min. Health Rsch. award, 1995. Mem. Am. Soc. Human Genetics, Human Genome Orgn., Cystic Fibrosis Genetic Analysis Consorium (Toronto), Johns Hopkins Med./Surg. Assn. Avocations: classical music, visual art, photography, travel. Office: Univ Hosp Motol Dept Hum Gen, V Uvalu 84, CZ 15006 Prague 5, Czech Republic

MACEK, PETR, psychologist, educator; b. Moravia, Czech Republic, July 2, 1956; s. Jiří and Jiřina (Ježková) M.; m. Hana Sedláková, June 21, 1980; children: David, Kristina. Student, U. J.E. Purkyně, Brno, Czech Republic, 1980. Rschr. Czech Acad. Sci., 1984-87; asst. prof. U. J.E. Purkyně, 1987-90; asst. prof. Masaryk U., Brno, 1990-97, assoc. prof., 1997—. Author: (book chpt.) International Handbook of Adolescence, 1995; contbr. articles to profl. jours. With Czech mil., 1980-81. Mem. Internat. Soc. Study Behavioral Devel., Soc. Rsch. on Adolescence, European Assn. Rsch. on Adolescence. Avocations: basketball, biking. Home: Domašov u Brna, 664 83 Moravia Czech Republic Office: Masaryk U Sch Soc Studies, Gorkého 7, 602 00 Brno Czech Republic

MACER, DARRYL RAYMUND JOHNSON, biology educator; b. Christchurch, New Zealand, July 22, 1962; s. John Owen and Eileen Rose (Johnson) M.; m. Nobuko Yasuhara, Nov. 23, 1987. BS with honors, U. Canterbury-Lincoln Coll., Christchurch, 1983; PhD, U. Cambridge, Eng., 1987. Sr. Rouse Ball scholar Trinity Coll., Cambridge, 1987-89; scientist Dept. Sci. Indsl. Rsch., Lincoln, New Zealand, 1990; fgn. prof. U. Tsukuba, Japan, 1990-95, assoc. prof., 1995—; dir. Eubios Ethics Inst., New Zealand, 1990—. Author: Shaping Genes, 1990, Attitudes to Genetic Engineering: Japanese and International Comparisons, 1992, Bioethics for the People by the People, 1994, Bioethics is Love of Life, 1998. Recipient Cambridge Commonwealth Prince of Wales award, 1984-87. Mem. UNESCO (internat. bioethics com. 1993-98), Human Genome Orgn. (ethics com. 1995—), Internat Union Biological Sci. Bioethics (program dir. 1997—), Internat. Assn. Bioethics (bd. dirs. 1999—). Avocations: gardening, music. Office: Univ Tsukuba, Biological Sciences, Tsukuba Ibaraki 305, Japan

MACER-STORY, EUGENIA ANN, writer, artist; b. Mpls., Jan. 20, 1945; d. Dan Johnstone and Eugenia Loretta (Andrews) Macer; divorced; 1 child, Ezra Arthur Story. BS in Speech, Northwestern U., 1965; MFA, Columbia U., 1968. Writing instr. Polyarts, Boston, 1970-72; theater instr. Joy of Movement, Boston, 1972-75; artistic dir. Magik Mirror, Salem, Mass., 1975-76, Magick Mirror Comm., 1977—. Author: Congratulations: The UFO Reality, 1978, Angels of Time, 1982, Project Midas, 1986, Dr. Fu Man Chu Meets the Lonesome Cowboy: Sorcery and the UFO Experience, 1991, 3d edit., 1994, Gypsy Fair, 1991, The Strawberry Man, 1991, Sea Condor/Dusty Sun, 1994, Awakening to the Light-After the Longest Night, 1995, (short stories) Battles with Dragons: Certain Tales of Political Yoga, 1993, 2d edit., 1994, Legacy of Daedulus, 1995, The Dark Frontier, 1997, Troll and Other Interdimensional Invasions (short stories), 1999, Vanishing Questions (poetry), 2000, Crossing Jungle River, 1998; (plays) Fetching the Archaeological Politics, Strange Inquiries, Divine Appliance, 1989, The Zig Zag Wall, 1990, The Only Qualified Huntress, 1990, Telephone Taps Written Up for Tabloids, 1991, Wars with Pigeons, 1992, Conquest of the Asteroids, 1993, Commander Galacticon, 1993, Meister Hemmelin, 1994, Six Way Time Play, 1994, Radish, 1996, Setting Up for the World Trade Centaur, 1996, Mister Shooting Star, 1998, Wild Dog Casino, 1999, The Old Gaffer From Boise (at Gallery 113), 2000, others; philosophy writer; contbr. articles to profl. jours.; author poetry in Woodstock Times, Lamia Ink!, Manhattan Poetry Rev., Sensations, Kore, The Rift mag., Poet's House, Poetry.com Anthology, 2000, Poetry Publ. Showcase, Theatre for the New City Festivals, 1997—, others; feature writer Newspeak Pubs., 1995; editor Yankee Oracle Gazette, 1999; personal appearance as profl. clairvoyant (TV documentary) Haunted Houses, 1996, UFO Desk, Sta. WBAI radio shows, 1996-97, Star People Confs., 1998—; interviewer Interview and Occult Investigations, Magonia Mag. Online, 1998, Paranoia Mag., 2000, Infinity Factory; exhbn. paintings Barcelona, Spain, 1999, 2000, 515 Greenwich Gallery, 1999, City Art Gallery, Stockholm, 2000. Shubert fellow, 1968. Mem. Am. Soc. Dowsers, Dramatists Guild (spkr., interviewer on radio shows and internet confs.), Theosophical Soc. Democrat. Avocations: swimming, outdoor activities, hiking. Office: Magick Mirror Comm PO Box 741 New York NY 10116-0741

MACESICH, GEORGE, econmomics professor; b. Cleve., May 27, 1927; m. Susana Sonja Svorkovich, Feb. 16, 1955; children: Maja, Milena, George M.P. AA, George Washington U., 1951, BA, 1953, MA, 1954; PhD, U. Chgo., 1958. Tchg. and rsch. positions while completing graduate study, 1953-58; rsch. economist U.S. C. of C., Washington, 1958-59; asst. prof. Econs. Fla. State U., Tallahassee, Fla., 1959-61; assoc. prof. Econs. Fla. State U., Tallahassee, 1961-63; prof. Econs. Fla. State U., Tallhassee, 1963—, U. Belgrade, Yugoslavia, 1972—; mem. Editorial Bd. So. Econ. Jour., 1961-63; cons. U.S. Dept. Commerce, 1961-65; vis. economist Nat. Bank of Yugoslavia, 1965; founding dir. Ctr. for Yugoslav-Am. Studies, Rsch. and Exchanges, Fla. State U., 1961—, Inst. Comparative Policy Studies Rsch. and Exchanges, 1992—; cons. Jour. of Political Economy, U. Chgo., 1968-81, The Coun. of Grad. Schs. in U.S., Washington, 1971-82, Jour. of Money, Credit and Banking, 1977-89; editorial bd. Foreign Trade and Cycles, 1970-76, So. Economic Jour., 1972-76; and numerous other roles related to economics. Author, co-author or editor of 30 published books and over 100 articles including The International Monetary Economy and the Third World, 1981, Politics of Monetarism: Its Historical and Institutional Development, 1984, Monetary Reform and Cooperation Theory, 1989, Money and Democracy, 1990, (with D. Dimitrijevic) The Money Supply Process: A Comparative Analysis, 1990, World Debt and Stability, 1990, Reform and Market Democracy, 1991, Yugoslavia in the Age of Democracy: Essays on Economic and Political Reform, 1992, Monetary Policy and Politics: RulesVersus Discretion, 1992, Successor States and Cooperation Theory, 1994, Monetary Reform in Former Socialist Countries, 1995, Integration and Stabilization: A Monetary View, 1995, Transformation and Emerging Markets, 1996, The U.S. in a Changing Global Economy: Policy Implications and Issues, 1997, World Economy at the Cross Roads, 1997, Money, Systems and Growth, 1998, Political Economy of Money: The Emerging Fiat Monetary Regime, 1999, Issues in Money and Banking, 2000; contbr. numerous articles to profl. jours. Bd. dirs. Coun. Econ. Devel., Tallahassee, Fla., 1961-63, Nikola Tesla Meml. Soc., 1980-81; mem. U.S. - Yugoslav Economic Coun., 1987—, Inst. for Internat. Edn. Screening Com. 1984-87. With U.S. Navy 1944-53. Recipient Ford Found. fellowship, 1959-60, Fulbright fellowship, 1965, Order of Yugoslav Star with Gold Wreath, Yugoslav Govt., 1983, award of Merit, U. Zagreb, 1989. Mem. Am. Acad. Polit. and Social Sci., Am. Econ. Assn., Am. Foreign Svc. Assn., Am. Statis. Assn., So. Economic Assn., U.S. Naval Inst., Pi Gamma Mu. Home: 2401 Delgado Dr Tallahassee FL 32304-1303 Office: Inst Comparative Policy and Dept Economics Fla State U Tallahassee FL 32306

MACEY, DAVID JOHN, animal physiologist; b. Cardiff, Glamorgan, Wales, Nov. 15, 1953; arrived in Australia, 1976; s. John Oliver and Joan (Leonard) M.; m. Marilyn Ann Perry; children: Huw, Sarah. BSc with honors, Bath (Eng.) U., 1976; PhD, Murdoch U., Perth, Australia, 1982. Tutor in biology Murdoch U., Perth, 1980-82, lectr. in animal physiology, 1982-90, sr. lectr. in animal physiology, 1990-98, asst. prof. in animal physiology, 1998—. Contbr. chpts. to books and articles to profl. jours. Mem. Australian Inst. Biology. Avocations: research, coaching rugby union, kids sports. Office: Biol Scis, Murdoch Univ, Perth WA 6150, Australia

MACFARLANE, ALISON JILL, statistician; b. Watford, Eng., Mar. 29, 1942; d. William Angus and Joan Morton (Perkins) M. BA, Oxford (Eng.) U., 1964; diploma in stats., Univ. Coll., London, 1965. Chartered statistician. Statistician Rothamsted Exptl. Sta., Herpenden, Eng., 1965-67, Hertfordshire County Coun. Planning Dept., Hertford, Eng., 1967-70; computer programmer Royal Coll. Art Exptl. Cartography Unit, London, 1971-72; statistician MRC Air Pollution Unit, London, 1972-75; rsch. fellow in stats. London Sch. Hygiene and Tropical Medicine, 1975-78; med. statistician Nat. Perinatal Epidemiology Unit, Oxford, Eng., 1978—; reader perinatal and pub. health stats. Oxford Univ., 1997—; mem. mgmt. com. Maternity Alliance; mem. nat. adv. body Confidential Enquiry into Stillbirths and Death in Infancy, 1993-96, mem. profl. steering group, 1996-99. Co-author: (with Miranda Mugford) Birth counts: Statistics of Pregnancy and Childbirth, 1984, 2d edition, 2000, (with Rona Campbell) Where to be Born? The Debate and the Evidence, 1st edit., 1987, 2d edit., 1994, (with Beverley Botting and Frances Price) Three Four and More: A Study of Triplet and Higher Order Births, 1990; contbr. numerous articles to med., midwifery, and statis. jours.; mem. editl. bd. Rev. d'Epidemiologie et de Santé Publique, France, 1993—. Mem. Radical Stats. Health Group, U.K., 1976—; musician and organizer folk music events in St. Albans. Fellow Royal Statis. Soc. (med. stats. sect. com. 1986-90, official stats. sect. com. 1989-98, coun. mem. 1993-98), Faculty Pub. Health Medicine (hon.). Mem. Labour Party. Avocations: playing traditional folk music, politics, history, hill walking. Office: Nat Perinatal Epidem Unit, Inst Health Sci Old Rd, Oxford OX3 7LF, England

MACFARLANE, ANNE BRIDGET, retired court master; b. London, Jan. 26, 1930; d. David Williams and Grace Mary Griffith; m. James Macfarlane (dec. 1999); children: Jessica, Deborah Frances. LLB, Bristol (Eng.) U., 1952. Pvt. practice as solicitor, London, 1954-66; asst. land registrr Her Majesty's Land Registry, London, 1966-75; registrar Bromley County Ct., London, 1975-82; master Ct. Protection, London, 1982-95; ret., 1995. Contbg. author: Atkin's Court Forms, 1982. Mem. Law Soc. (hon. life). Avocations: grandchildren, collecting and cataloguing ceramic tiles.

MACFARLANE, CAMPBELL, surgeon, emergency physician; b. Forfar, Angus, Scotland, Oct. 16, 1941; s. George Henry and Emily Ann (Low) MacF.; m. Jane Mary Fretwell, July 1966 (div. 1986); children: Catriona, Alexina, Robert. MBChB, U. St. Andrews, Scotland, 1965; MMed in Surgery, U. Singapore, 1971; PhD, Knightsbridge U., Eng., 1992; BA (hon.), U. South Africa, 1994; BS (hon.), U. Pretoria (South Africa), 1997. Med. practitioner and gen. surgery registration Gen. Med. Coun., Health Professions Coun. South Africa. Commd. regular officer Royal Army Med. Corps., worldwide, 1965-81; advanced through grades to lt. col., 1979; chief surgery Al Zahra hsop., Sharjah, United Arab Emirates, 1981-83; med. dir. Al Huwaylat Hosp., Jubayl, Saudi Arabia, 1984-86; trauma surgeon Johannesburg (South Africa) Hosp., 1986-93; tng. prin. Med. Rescue Internat., Johannesburg, 1993-96, head emergency med. svcs. tng., 1996—; prin. Ambulance Tng. Coll., Johannesburg, 1986-93; sr. lectr. dept. surgery U. Witwatersrand, Johannesburg, 1986-93; surg. cons. Ingwe Mines, Johannesburg, 1998. Contbr. articles to profl. jours., chpts. to books. Decorated officer of the Venerable Order of the Hosp. St. John of Jerusalem, 1998. Fellow Royal Coll. Surgeons Edinburgh, Am. Coll. Surgeons, Australasian Coll. Emergency Medicine, Royal Coll. Surgeons of Eng., Royal Colls., Royal Soc. Medicine; mem. Assn. Mil. Surgeons U.S., So. African Undersea dn Hyperbaric Med. Assn. (past pres.). Mem. Ch. of Scotland. Avocations: sailing, scuba diving, French language studies, strategic studies. Home: White Gables, 29 Athlone Rd, 2193 Johannesburg Gauteng, South Africa

MACFARLANE, I. J. (IAN MACFARLANE), banker; b. Sydney, June 22, 1946. M in Econs., Monash U., 1969. Former tchr. Monash U.; with Inst. Econs. and Stats. Oxford U., 1970s; econ. forecaster, economic surveyor mem. countries OECD, 1973-79; with rsch. dept. Res. Bank Australia, 1979-85, various sr. positions econ. and fin. mkt., til 1988, asst. econ. gov., 1990-

92, dep. gov., 1992-96, gov., 1996—. Office: Reserve Bank Australia, 65 Martin Pl, Sydney NSW 2000, Australia*

MACGREGOR, IAN JAMES DOUGLAS, physicist, educator; b. Glasgow, Scotland, Apr. 4, 1957; s. Ian James and Myra Richford (Macluskie) MacG.; m. Christine Margaret Lowe, Aug. 6, 1982; children: Fiona Dorothy, Ian Ross. BSc with hons., Glasgow U., 1978, PhD, 1982. Chartered physicist. Rsch. assoc. Manchester (Eng.) U., 1982-83; lectr. Glasgow U., 1983-94, sr. lectr., 1994—; guest lectr. U.K. Sci. and Engring. Rsch. Coun. Summer Sch., Guildford, 1991, Internat. Ctr. Theoretical Physics, Trieste, 1995; dir. Jordanhill Sch., Glasgow, 1996—, chair, 2000—; external examiner Scottish Qualifications Authority, 1997—; spkr. in field. Co-editor: Nuclear and Particle Physics, 1993; contbr. over 50 articles to profl. jours. Vol. cons. Children's Charities, 1995—. Grantee British Coun., 1993-97, UK Engring. and Phys. Scis. Rsch. Coun., 1996—. Fellow Inst. Physics (mem. com. Inst. Physics nuclear and particle divsn. 1986-93, West Scotland physics edn. group 1984-90); mem. Assn. Univ. Tchrs. Avocations: swimming, chess. Office: U Glasgow Dept Physics, Univ Ave, Glasgow G12 8QQ, Scotland

MACGREGOR, JOHN RUSSELL RODDICK, British government minister, businessman; b. Glasgow, Scotland, Feb. 14, 1937; s. Norman S. R. and Mary (Roddick) MacG.; m. Jean Mary Elizabeth Dungey, Sept. 22, 1962; children: Fiona, Ian, Catriona. MA, St. Andrew's U., Scotland, 1959; LLB, King's Coll., London, 1960; LLD (hon.), U. Westminster, 1995. Univ. adminstr. London U., 1961-62; mem. editorial staff New Soc., 1962-63; spl. asst. to prime min., Sir. Alec Douglas-Home, 1963-64; with Conservative Rsch. Dept., 1964-65; head of pvt. office Hon. Edward Heath, 1965-68; Conservative M.P. for South Norfolk Ho. of Commons, London, 1974—; opposition whip Ho. of Commons, 1977-79; lord commr. Her Majesty Treasury, 1979-81; parliament under-sec. of state Dept. of Industry, 1981-83; min. of state, min. of agr., fisheries and food, 1983-85, chief sec. to treasury, 1985-87, min. for agriculture, fisheries and food, 1987-89, sec. of state for edn. and sci., 1989-90; lord pres. of coun., leader Ho. of Commons, 1990-92; sec. of state for transport, 1992-94; dep. chmn. Hill Samuel Bank, 1994-96; mem. Neil Com. (Com. Standards in Pub. Life), 1998—; mem. Ho. of Commons; with Hill Samuel & Co., Ltd., 1968-79, also bd. dirs.; chair Fedn. of Univ. Conservative and Unionist Assns., 1959, Bow Group, 1963-64; non-exec. dirs. Assoc. Brit. Foods PLC, 1994—, Slough Estates PLC, 1995—, Unigate PLC, 1996—, London & Manchester PLC, 1996-98, Friends Provident, 1998—; mem. coun. King's Coll., London, 1996—. 1st pres. Conservative and Christian Dem. Youth Community, 1963-65; chmn. trustees Parliamentary Contributory Pension Fund, 1998—; trustee Found. for Bus. Responsibilities, 1998—, Conservative and Unionist Agts. Superannuation Fund, 2000—. Decorated Order Brit. Empire; fellow King's Coll. Mem. Inst. of Dirs. (coun.), Assn. County Couns. (v.p.), Assn. Inner Magic Circle with Silver Star (assoc.). Conservative Party. Avocations: music, reading, travel, gardening, conjuring. Address: House of Commons, London SW1, England

MACH, PAVEL JAROSLAV, engineering educator; b. Prague, Czech Republic, Feb. 20, 1947; s. Alois and Antonie (Kulhánková) M.; m. Alexandra Sázavská, Dec. 14, 1971; children: Pavel, Tereza, Kateřina; m. Petra Jankovská, June 14, 1986; 1 child, Antonie. MSc, Czech Tech. U., Prague, 1971, PhD, 1980. Registered profl. engr. Asst. prof. Czech Tech. U., Prague, 1971-74, asst. prof., lectr., 1976-90, assoc. prof., head dept., 1991—; rsch. worker Tesla Elstroj, Prague, 1975-76; rsch. worker Rsch. Inst. Protection, Prague, 1985-89; cons. Czech Inst. Stds., Prague, 1994—. 1st author: Analysis and Synthesis of Technological Processes, 1987 (award of chancelor of Tech. U. 1987); author: Analysis and Synthesis of Technological Processes, 1988, 2d edit., 1990, Reliability of Hybrid Integrated Circuits, 1983; 2d author: Properties and Technology of Materials, 1995, Technological Processes, 1995. Recipient award Czech Sci.-Tech. Soc.-Electronics, Prague, 1987. Mem. IEEE, IEE. Avocations: classical music, soccer. Office: CVUT-FEL Prague Dept Electrotech, Technická 2, 166 27 Prague 6, Czech Republic

MACHAC, JAN, engineering educator, researcher; b. Hranice, Moravia, Czech Republic, Apr. 1, 1953; s. Josef and Helena (Svobodova) Machac; m. Renata Savlova, Feb. 6, 1981; children: Katerina, Jan. MS in Engring., Czech Tech. U., Prague, 1977, DSc, 1996. Rschr. Czech Acad. Sci., Prague, 1982-84; asst. prof. Czech Tech. U., Prague, 1982-91, assoc. prof., 1991—. Contbr. articles to profl. jours. Recipient rsch. prize Siemens, 1998. Mem. IEEE, Czech Elec. Soc. Avocation: gardening. Office: Czech Tech U, Technická 2, 166 27 Prague Czech Republic

MACHACZKA, MACIEJ JAROSLAW, medical educator, hematologist, researcher; b. Cracow, Poland, Feb. 24, 1969; s. Jozef and Krystyna (Wnek) M.; m. Malgorzata Maria Rucinska, 1999; children: Malgorzata, Bartlomiej, Aleksandra. MD, Jagiellonian U., Cracow, 1993. Resident Pvt. Cath. Hosp., Cracow, 1993-95; fellow in internal disease Pvt. Cath. Hosp.-Regional Postgrad. Ctr., Cracow, 1995-97; asst. prof. dept. hematology Jagiellonian U., 1996—, head rsch. program, 1998—; vis. physician bone marrow transplantation Fred Hutchinson Cancer Rsch. Ctr., Seattle, 1999, vis. physician dept. hematology Salamanca's U., Spain, 2000. Contbr. articles to med. jours., including Am. Jour. Hematology, Blood. Mem. Polish Hematological Soc., European Hematology Assn., Am. Soc. Hematology, Internat. Soc. Exptl. Hematology. Avocations: art, music, sport. Home: ul Klonowica 17E, 30-654 Cracow Malopol, Poland Office: Jagiellonian U Coll Med, Kopernika str 17, 31-501 Cracow Poland

MACHALSKI, JERZY, astronomer, educator; b. Tarnopol, Poland, July 31, 1935; s. Franciszek and Maria (Skulska) M.; m. Elzbieta Honkisz, June 11, 1964; 1 child, Pawel. BS in Astronomy, Jagellonian U., Cracow, Poland, 1962, PhD in Physics, 1971, D habilitatus, 1981. Rsch. asst. Astron. Obs. Jagellonian U., Poland, 1962-70, adj. rsch. asst., 1971-80, assoc. prof., 1981-91, prof., 1992—; rsch. specialist Nat. Radio Astron Obs., USA, 1974-75; head extra galactic astron. divsn. Astron. Obs. Jagellon U., Cracow, 1989—. Contbr. articles to Astronomy and Astrophysics, Astron. Jour., 1978—. Recipient 1st prize award Polish Acad. Scis., 1980. Mem. Polish Astron. Soc., Internat. Astron. Union, European Astron. Union (founding mem.). Avocations: travel, cycling, skiing. Office: Jagellonian U Astron Obs, 171 Orla Str, 30244 Cracow Poland

MACHANIC, MINDY ROBIN, psychologist, horticulturist, educator, consultant, writer; b. N.Y.C., June 21, 1950; d. Harmon Jack Machanic and Helen Jewel (Wolf) Mamolen; m. Bradley K. Shearer, Mar. 18, 1990. BFA, San Francisco Art Inst., 1973; BS, U. State N.Y., 1983; M Planning, U. So. Calif., 1980; MA, Calif. State U., L.A., 1984; PhD, The Union Insts., 1995. Exec. dir. YWCA of U. So. Calif., L.A., 1980-81; instr. UCLA Extension, 1980, Calif. State U., Northridge, 1982, Otis Art Inst. of Parsons Sch., L.A., 1979-82, Maricopa Co. C.C., 1993-95; facility planner-analyst Steinmann, Grayson, Smylie, L.A., 1981-82; asst. prof., program coord. environ. design program Sch. of Art, E. Carolina U., Greenville, N.C., 1984-86, psychology intern TASC Inc., Phoenix, Ariz., 1994-95, assoc. faculty Goddard Coll., 1995-97, prof. Walden U., 1996—; mem. faculty Union Inst. Ctr. for Distant Learning, 1993-99; project mgr. ednl. tech. and learning Tech. U. BC, 1998; psychologist Napa (Calif.) State Hosp., 1997-98; writer Fannie Mae, Washington, 1988; field editor Area Devel. mag., 1989-92; rsch. asst. HUD, San Francisco, 1975; pres., prin. City Arts, L.A., 1978-84, Greenville, N.C., 1984-86, Washington, 1986-90, Machanic & Co., Phoenix, 1992-95, mindymac.com/Embracing Change, Portland, Oreg., 1998—, Growing Places/growing-places.com, Newberg, Oreg., 2000—; computer software trainer Forhan & Wakefield Group, Vienna, Va., 1989-90; instrnl. writer, project mgr. ComputerPrep, Phoenix, 1990-91; quality cons., instrnl. developer AG Comm. Systems, 1992; mental health therapist Salt River Indian Cmty. Mental Health Svc., 1993-94; instructional designer/developer U. Phoenix, 1993-95. Movie reviewer Daily Reflector, Greenville, N.C., 1985, Dissertation: Waiting for Cancer Test Results: Impacts on the Patient & Family, 1996; contbr. articles and book revs. to profl. jours.; one-man shows include Lycoming Coll., Pa., 1974; exhibited in group shows So. Exposure Gallery, San Francisco, 1974, 75, Barnsdall Park Mcpl. Gallery, L.A., 1981, Gray Gallery, East Carolina U., 1984, 85, 86, Cmty. Coun. for Arts, Kinston, N.C., 1985, Art League Gallery, Alexandria, Va., 1986, Gallerie Triangle, Washington, 1987, Western Eye, Phoenix Coll., 1991; patentee Stay-Dry Toilet Seat. Peer counselor Bosom Buddies Breast Cancer Hotline, 1993-95; mem. Maricopa County South Area Behavioral Health Adv. Coun., Phoenix, 1993-94; spkr., facilitator Parents Anonymous, Phoenix, 1992. Mem. Am. Psychol. Assn., Oreg. Assn. Nurseryman. Democrat. Jewish. Avocations: science, gardening, travel, drawing, photography. E-mail: (home) mindy@mindymac.com, (office) mindy@growing-places.com.

MACHARSKI, FRANCISZEK CARDINAL, archbishop; b. Kraków, Poland, May 20, 1927. D.Theology. Ordained priest Roman Cath. Ch., 1950; engaged in pastoral work, 1950-56; theol. studies, Fribourg, Switzerland, 1956-60; tchr. pastoral theology Faculty Theology, Kraków, 1963; rector Archdiocesan Sem., Kraków, 1970; archbishop of Kraków, 1979—; elevated to Sacred Coll. of Cardinals, 1979; titular ch., St. John at the Latin Gate; mem. Congregation of Clergy, 1979, Congregation of Cath. Edn., 1981, Congregation for Bishops, 1983, Coun. of Cardinals and Bishops, 1988; mem. Congregation for Insts. of Consecrated Life and for Socs. of Apostolic Life, 1989; vice chair Sci. Coun. Polish Episcopate, 1981, Episcopate Com. for Gen. Ministry, 1979; chair Episcopate Com. for Cath. Sci., 1983; mem. Episcopate Com. for Emigration Ministry, 1988. Address: ul Franciszkanska 3, 31-004 Krakow Poland

MACHAVE, YESHAVANT VASUDEO, hematologist; b. Yawal, India, Sept. 11, 1942; s. Vasudeo Amrit and Manorama Vasuedeo (Kaware) M.; m. Rohini Yeshavant Basarkar, June 24, 1967; children: Manish, Mukul. MB, BChir, BJ Med. Coll., Pune, India, 1966; diploma in clin. pathology, Armed Forces Med. Coll., Pune, India, 1976, MD, 1979. Graded specialist Def., Pune, 1976-82, reader, 1987-92; classified specialist Def., Firozpur, India, 1982-87; sr. adv. Def., Calcutta, India, 1992-95, dep. dir. med. svcs., 1999—; prof., dept. head Armed Forces Med. Coll., Pune, 1995-99. Brigadier India Army M.C., 1999. Mem. Indian Assn. Pathologists Microbiologists (life, gov. body 1990, treas., office bearer 1996), Indian Soc. Blood Transfusion and Immunohaematology. Avocations: music, singing, reading. Home: Poudroad, 8 Ananta Kripa Socy, 411038 Pune India Office: DDMS HQ Bengal Area, 246 AJC Bose Rd, 700027 Calcutta India

MACHE, DETLEF HAUKE, mathematician, educator; b. Kamen/Unna, Germany, June 11, 1960; s. Hugo R. and AnneLiese (Mork) M.; m. Petra Theiss, June 18, 1962; 1 child, Marina. Diploma in math., 1988; D. of Natural Scis., U. Dortmund, Germany, 1991. Asst. prof. Montan Tech. (TFH Bochum), 1991-95; sci. asst. U. Dortmund, Germany, 1988—; vis. prof. U. Sibiu, Romania, 1991, U. Witwatersrand, Johannesburg, South Africa, 1998; prof. Ludwig-Maximilians U., Munich, 1998-99. Contbr. articles to profl. jours. Avocations: collecting art, rowing, sailing, traveling with family. Office: U Dortmund Dept Math, Vogelpothsweg 87, D-44221 Dortmund Germany

MACHEJ, KAROL FRANCISZEK, chemical engineering educator; b. Stonawa, Silesia, Czechoslovakia, July 23, 1931; s. Karol Jan and Julia (Konieczna) M.; m. Janina Pabis, Nov. 24, 1955; 1 child, Joanna. MSc in Engring., Silesian Tech. U., Gliwice, Poland, 1955, PhD in Engring., 1960, DSc in Engring., 1976, prof., 1981. Reader Polish Acad. Scis., Gliwice, 1955-70; head of lab. Inst. Refractory Materials, Gliwice, 1959-69; vice dean dept. chem. tech. and engring. Silesian Tech. U., Gliwice, 1971-75, dean dept. chem. tech. and engring., 1978-81; vice head Inst. Chem. Engring. and Apparatus Constrn., Gliwice, 1975-77, 81, 88-90; head Inst. Chem. and Process Engring. Silesian Tech. U., Gliwice, 1990-91, 94—; mem. rsch. sect. Ministry of Sci., Warsaw, Poland, 1983-89; mem. awards com. Ministry Higher Edn., Warsaw, 1984-90; mem. Main Coun. Sci. and Higher Edn., Warsaw, 1988-90. Author: (books) Selected Mathematical Methods for Treatment of Experimental Data in Chemical Engineering, 1965, Simultaneous Transfer of Heat and Mass in Direct Contact Heat Exchangers, 1976; co-author: (book) Handbook of Ceramics, 1963; editor-in-chief: Inżynieria i Aparatura Chemiczna, 1981—. Lt. Polish Army, 1967. Recipient Polonia Restituta award Pres. Poland, 1984, award Min. Higher Edn., 1984-89. Mem. Polish Acad. Scis. (mem. ceramic com. 1970-95, mem. com. chem. engring. 1984—). Avocations: tinkering, carpentry, photography, reading. Office: Silesian Tech U, ul Ks M Strzody 7, 44-101 Gliwice Silesia, Poland

MACHELL, IAIN HUGH, artist educator; b. Dundee, Scotland, Feb. 2, 1954; s. Roger Keys and Elizabeth Margaret M. Diploma in Art, Grays Sch. of Art, Aberdeen, Scotland, 1977, postgrad. diploma in Art, 1978; MFA, U. Albany, N.Y., 1988. Sculpture instr. Newark Tech. Coll., Nottingham, Eng., 1982-84; adjunct faculty in sculpture Mansfield Coll. of Art., Eng., 1983; sculpture instr. Ulster County C.C., Stone Ridge, N.Y., 1984-86; instr., teaching asst. in sculpture and 3D design U. Albany, N.Y., 1986-88; adjunct faculty in sculpture Rensselaer Polytech. Inst., Troy, N.Y., 1988; adjunct faculty in 3D design/drawing Berkshire C.C., Pittsfield, Mass., 1989-90; faculty in drawing Bennington (Vt.) Coll., 1989—, sculpture studio mgr., teaching asst., 1988-90; adjunct faculty in drawing and painting C.C. of Vt., Bennington, 1989; vis. artist and lectr. Ind. U. Pa., 1991, Shepherd Coll., Shepherdstown, W.Va., 1993; faculty in 3D media and concepts, sculpture & installation Carnegie-Mellon U., Pitts., 1993; vis. asst. prof. in 3D foundations W.Va. U., Morgantown, 1990-92, asst. prof. in 3D foundations and sculpture, 1992-98; vis. artist, lectr. U. Mass., Amherst, 1999; chair, assoc. prof. sculpture Montserrat Coll. Art, 1998—; vis. lectr. Ind. U. Pa., 1996; curator and panelist Laura Mesaros Gallery, Morgantown, W.Va., 1994; panelist CAA Conf., St. Louis, 1995, Toronto, Can., 1998; panel chair FATE Conf., Richmond, Va., 1997. Recipient numerous grants in art. Mem. Coll. Art Assn., U.S. Scotland Consotrium. E-mail: imachell@earthlink.net. Office: Montserrat Coll Art 23 Essex St Beverly MA 01915-4508

MACHICADO SARAVIA, FLAVIO, government agency administrator; b. La Paz, Bolivia, June 21, 1938; s. Flavio Machicado Viscarra and Cristina Saravia Noriega; m. Gloria Georgette Teran Parrilla, Aug. 16, 1962 (div.); children: Flavo, María Alejandra, Moira Andrea; m. Susana Sanz-Guerrero, Apr. 28, 1998. BS in Comml. Engring., U. Chile, Santiago; MS in Econ. Devel. Planning, Ilpes-NN U. Cons. Inter-Am. Devel. Bank, Dominican Bank, 1967-68; min. planning Bolivian Govt., La Paz, 1970-71, min. of fin., 1983, 84; project mgr. Food Agrl. Orgn./UN, Santiago, 1972-73, Santo Domingo, Dominican Republic, 1974-78; chief of mission Food Agrl. Orgn./UN, Bogota, Colombia, 1981-83; dir. pub. sector devel. program UN, La Paz, 1992-94; supt. hierarchical recourses SIREFI, La Paz, 1998—; congressman Bolivian Parliament, La Paz, 1982-85; econ. cons. Ctrl. Obrera Boliviana, La Paz, 1978-80; chair U. Católica Boliviana, La Paz, 1990-96; pres. Mut. de Ahorros La Primera, La Paz, 1986-88. Author: Attitudes in Political Economy, 1990, The financial System and Economic Reactivation in Bolivia, 1993, Public Finance and Investment, 1998; editor: Dialogue for Democracy, 1987. Recipient Medal of Honor, Yugoslavian Govt., 1984, Medal of Honor, St. Silvestre, The Pope, The Vatican, 1985, Merit of Total Quality award Cochabamba Indsl. Chamber, 1991. Avocations: walking, music, reading, travel, teaching. Office: Supt Hierarchical Recourses, 4745 La Paz Bolivia

MACHIDA, YOSHIHARU, pharmaceutical educator; b. Yamanashi, Japan, Mar. 22, 1945; s. Hiroyoshi and Tamiko (Kobayashi) M.; m. Than Than Win, July 7, 1983. BS, Hoshi U., Tokyo, 1967; PhD, Hoshi U., 1980. Rsch. assoc. Hoshi U., Tokyo, 1967-81, asst. prof., 1981-85, assoc. prof., 1985-93, prof., 1993—; expert team leader Japan Internat. Cooperation Agy./Devel. Ctr. for Pharm. Tech., Rangoon, Burma, 1981-83. Co-author: (books) Transdermal Controlled Systemic Medications, 1987, Bioadhesive Drug Delivery Systems, 1989, Topics in Pharmaceutical Sciences 1989, 1989, Peptide and Protein Drug Delivery, 1991, Chitin World, 1995, Chitin Handbook, 1997, Applications of Chitin and Chitosan, 1997, Bioadhesive Drug Delivery Systems, 1999. Recipient Japan Nat. Invention prize The Invention Assn., Tokyo, 1984; rsch. grantee The Rsch. Found. for Pharm. Scis., Tokyo, 1987, Mochida Meml. Found. for Med. and Pharm. Rsch., 1989. Mem. Internat. Pharm. Fedn., The Japan Soc. of Drug Delivery System (councilor 1988—), Japanese Soc. for Chitin and Chitosan (councilor 1995-97), The Acad. of Pharmaceutical Sci. and Tech., Japan (councilor 1995—). Office: Hoshi U Dept Drug Del Rsch, Ebara 2-4-41, Shinagawa Tokyo 142-8501, Japan

MACHIELS, GUILLAUME HENRI, retired electrical engineer, researcher; b. Hasselt, Limburg, Belgium, Mar. 8, 1924; s. Martin Machiels and Gerardine Martens; m. Lucia Jeunen, May 12, 1951; children: Lucia, Godelieve, Boudewijn, Lutgart, Maria, Koenraad, Jan, Karel, Filip, Beatrijs, Reinhilde. Oude Humangora, Coll. Hasselt, 1943; engr., Inst. Gramme, Belgium, 1947; Kan. Biologie, LUC, Belgium, 1974. Chief Elec. Power Sta., Waterschei, 1947-53; R&D engr. NIR/BRT, 1954-89; asst., counselor Congulese Gt, 1965-70; schepen Dlepenbeek, 1971-76, 83-94. Author: (books) Refutation of Theory of Reality, 1968, Mathematical and Philosophical Refutation of All Science of 20th Century, 1999. Named Master of the Leopard, Congo, 1981, Ridder in De Leupolds Ordre, Belgium, 1967. CVP. Roman Catholic. Avocations: astronomy, nature, environment, gardening. Home: Steenweg 175, B3590 Diepenbeek Limburg, Belgium

MACHIN, BARRIE MICHAEL, anthropologist, filmmaker; b. Pitsea, Essex, Britain, Dec. 18, 1939; s. Albert Sidney and Sylvia Gertrude M.; m. Chikako Nishi, July 27, 1998; children: Jacob, Emily; m. Janet Wheeler, Nov. 23, 1963 (div. June 1984); children: Jessica, Daniel, Rebecca. LDS, Royal Coll. Surgeons, Eng., 1962; MLitt, Inst. of Social Anthropology, Oxford, 1992; PhD, Pacific We. U., 1997. Gen. dentistry Eng., 1963-72; lectr. in social anthropology U. Newcastle upon Tyne, Northumberland, Eng., 1972-75; sr. lectr. in anthropology U. Western Australia, Perth, 1975-89; freelance filmmaker Australia, 1989-99; anthropologist/rschr. Perth, Wash., 1989-99. Dir./author: (film) Passing Shadows, 1984 (major prize Parnu Film Festival estonia 1988); dir./author: (film/videos) Iramudun, 1984 (Blue Ribbon Am. Film Festival N.Y., 1984), Warriors and Maidens, 1988. Chmn. Campaign Against Nuclear Energy, Perth, Wash., 1975-77; dir. Environmentalists for Full Employment, Perth, 1978; commr. Commn. on Visual Anthropology, 1988-90. Grantee Sir Charles Strong Meml. Trust, Australia, 1985; recipient Anthropos Omega award, Florence, 1988. Fellow Royal Anthropol. Inst., Australian Anthropol. Soc.; mem. Assn. Commonwealth Anthropologists. Avocations: drawing, sculpture, writing rev. sketches. E-mail: barrien@primus.com.au. Office: Tamora Pty Ltd, 59 Darley Cir, Perth 6149, Australia

MACHINEA, JOSÉ LUIS, minister of economy; b. Argentina, Oct. 5, 1946. Degree in econs., U. Católica Argentina, 1968; MA in Econs., U. Minn., 1974, PhD in Econs., 1983. Min. economy, econ. policy dir. Argentina, 1980, adviser to sec. hydric resources, 1970; advisor to sec. Nat. Devel. Coun., 1971; tech. advisor Econ. Rsch. Ctr. U. Católica Argentina, 1970-71; chief analyst Banking and Monetary Rsch. Ctr. Argentine Ctrl. Bank, 1979-80, pub. fin. 2d mgr., 1979-80, pub. fin. mgr., 1980-81, rsch. and econ. stats. mgr., 1983, pres., 1986-89; undersec. for devel. programs Secretariat of Planning of Pres., 1983-85; undersec. polit. economy Ministry of Economy, 1985-86; rsch. dir. Indsl. Devel. Inst. Union Indsl. Argentina Found., 1992-97; pres. Fundación Argentina para del Desarrollo con Equidad, 1998-99; min. of economy Argentina, 1999—; cons. World Bank, Inter-Am. Devel. Bank; asst. prof. social sci. and econs. U. Católica Argentina, 1970-71, prof., 1970-71; fin. sector economy prof. U. Buenos Aires, 1996-97; macroecons. prof. grad. program Argentine Ctrl. Bank, 1976-77; spkr. in field. Co-author: Stopping Hyperinflation: The Case of the Austral Plan in Argentina, 1985-87, 1988; author: Recent Economic Performance of Argentina: Major Issues and Policy Implicationsx, 1990, (in Spanish) Structural Reforms in the Financial Sector, The Argentine Financial Crisis of 1995: Causes, Characteristics and Lessons, 1996, Argentine 1996-2010: Financing Necessities of the Public Sector; contbr. articles to profl. jours. Mem. Argentine Polit. Economy Assn. (econ. devel. editl. com. 1977-81, mem. econ. essays edit. com. 1978-83), Fin. Rsch. Forum (founder). Office: Ministry of Economy, Mipolito Vrigoyen 250, 1310 Buenos Aires Argentina*

MACHLEIDT, WIELANT, psychiatrist, psychotherapist; b. Kiel, Germany, Aug. 2, 1942; s. Dietrich and Erika (Eber) M.; m. Gilta Herma Schaefer, Aug. 7, 1976; children: Felix, Anna. MD, Free U., Berlin, 1970. Rschr., asst. Med. Sch. Hanover, Germany, 1971-82, sr. doctor, cons., 1983-88, prof., chmn., dir. dept. social psychiatry and psychotherapy, 1994—; prof. U. Cologne, Germany, 1988-94; head. sect. transcultural psychiatry German Soc. Psychiatry, Psychotherapy and Nervous Diseases, 1994—; pres. Internat. Study Group Soteria, Hanover, 1997—. Author: Basic Emotions, 1989, Father and Daughter, 3d edit., 1995; editor: Psychiatry in a Transcultural Perspective, 1997, Schizophrenia—An Affective Disorder?, 1999, Psychiatry, Psychosomatics and Psychotherapy, 1999. Pres. Recreation for Disabled People, Hanover, 1998. Lt. German Navy, 1962-64. Hans Lugwitz Found. study grantee, 1967-70. Mem. German Soc. Psychiatry, Psychotherapy and Nervous Diseases, German Psychoanalytical Soc., German Soc. Psychoanalysis, Psychotherapy, Psychosomatics and Analytical Psychology, German Soc. for Social Psychiatry. Lutheran. Avocations: transcultural traveling, tennis, swimming, sailing. Office: Social Psych/Psychotherapy, Carl Neuberg Str 1, 30625 Hannover Germany

MACHONIN, PAVEL, sociologist; b. Prostejov, Moravia, Czech Republic, June 6, 1927; s. Konstantin and Jindra Vera (Horakova) M.; m. Olga Skalska, Oct. 29, 1949; children: Jitka Hribkova, Alena Potuchkova. Degree in social studies, Charles U., Prague, Czechoslovakia, 1949, CSc, 1958, DSc, 1969. Chief dept. edn. CKD Praha, Prague, 1949-50; social scis. tchr. Czechoslovak Army, Roudnice, Prague, 1952-58; sci. worker Inst. Social and Polit. Scis. Charles U., Prague, 1958-70, vice dir., dir., rsch. team leader, 1962-69, chief dept. social structure rsch., 1990-92; rschr., analyst sport orgn. Poultry Industry, Prague, 1970-87; rsch. team leader Inst. Sociology Acad. Scis., Prague, 1993—; v.p. sci. bd. for philosophy and sociology Czechoslovak Acad. Scis., Prague, 1964-68, external mem. acad. assembly, 1995-98. Editor, co-author: Ceskoslovenska Spolecnost, 1969, Ceska Spolecnost v Transformaci, 1996, Czechoslovakia 1918-92: A Laboratory for Social Change, 1996, System Change and Modernization East-West in Comparative Perspective, 1999; author: Social Transformation and Modernization: On Building Theory or Societal Changes in the Post-Communist European Countries, 1997, Theory of Modernisation and the Czech Experience, 2000. Mem., functionary Communist Party of Czechoslovakia, 1945-70. Col. Czechoslovak Army, 1951-58. Recipient K. Engliss hon. award Acad. Scis., 1997. Mem. Masaryk's Czech Sociol. Assn., Internat. Sociol. Assn. (hon. 1991). Avocations: caring for invalid grandson, gardening. Home: Zeleny pruh 24, 14700 Praha 4, Czech Republic Office: Inst Sociology, Jilska 1, 11000 Praha 1, Czech Republic

MACHOVER, CARL, computer graphics consultant; b. Bklyn., Mar. 26, 1927; s. John Herman and Rose (Alter) M.; m. Wilma Doris Simon, June 18, 1950; children: Tod, Julie, Linda. BEE, Rensselaer Poly. Inst., 1951; postgrad., NYU, 1953-56. Mgr. applied engring. Norden div. United A/C Corp., 1951-59; mgr. sales Skiatron Electronics & TV, N.Y.C., 1959-60; v.p. mktg., dir. Info. Displays, Inc., Mount Kisco, N.Y., 1960-73; v.p., gen. mgr., Info. Displays, Inc., Mount Kisco, 1973-76; pres. Machover Assocs. Corp., White Plains, N.Y., 1976—; adj. prof. Rensselaer Poly. Inst.; mem. RPI H&SS adv. bd. Bradford EIMC Indsl. Adv. Bd. Author: Gyro Primer, 1957, Basics of Gyroscopes, 1958; mem. editl. bd. IEEE Computer Graphics and Applications, Computers and Graphics, Spectrum; editor C4 Handbook, 1989, 2d edit., 1995, The CAD/CAM Handbook, 1996; co-editor Computer Graphics Rev.; co-exec. prodr. The Story of Computer Graphics, 1999; contbr. articles to profl. jours. Mem. adv. bd. Pratt Ctr. for Computer Graphics in Design. With USNR, 1945-46. Recipient Frank Oppenheimer award Am. Soc. for Engring. Edn., 1971, Orthagonal award N.C. State U., 1988, Vanguard award Nat. Comp. Graphics Assn., 1993; named to Computer Graphics Hall of Fame Fine Arts Mus. of L.I., Hempstead, N.Y., 1988. Fellow Soc. for Info. Display (pres. 1968-70), Eurographics Assn.; mem. IEEE, Assn. for Computing Machinery, Am. Inst. Design and Drafting, Nat. Soc. Profl. Engrs., Nat. Computer Graphics Assn. (bd. dir., pres. 1989-90), Computer Graphics Pioneer, Art and Sci. Collaborators Inc. (pres. 1995—), Sigma Xi, Tau Beta Pi, Eta Kappa Nu. Home: 152 Longview Ave White Plains NY 10605-2314 Office: Machover Assocs Corp PO Box 308 152A Longview Ave White Plains NY 10605-2314

MACHOVICH, RAYMUND, biochemistry educator, medicine consultant; b. Budapest, Hungary, Nov. 3, 1936; s. Raymund Machovich and Erzsébet Dányi; m. Ildikó Szabolcs, July 25, 1968. MD, Semmelweis U., Budapest, 1961; PhD, Hungarian Acad. Scis., Budapest, 1974, DSc, 1981. Resident in internal medicine Mcpl. Hosp., Szolnok, Hungary, 1961-63; asst. prof. biochemistry Semmelweis U., 1963-73; sci. advisor Postgrad. Med. Sch., Budapest, 1973-80; assoc. prof. Semmelweis U., 1981-90, prof., 1991—; cons. in internal medicine; fellow Harvard Med. Sch., Boston, 1970-71; vis. assoc. prof. McMaster U., Hamilton, Ont., Can., 1978-79; rsch. assoc. Mayo Clinic, Rochester, Minn., 1986—; dir. Internat. Thrombosis Tng. Ctr., Budapest, 1993—; lectr. in Europe, Can., U.S. Editor, author: The Thrombin, Vols. I-II, 1984, Blood Vessel Walls and Thrombosis, Vols. I-II, 1988, Medical Biochemistry, 1996; editor, mem. editl. bd. Thrombosis Rsch., 1981-85, Excerpta Medica, 1986—; contbr. over 100 articles to internat. med. jours.;

patentee in field. Recipient award Can. Heart Found., 1978; grantee U.S.-Hungarian Joint Fund, 1993—. Mem. Internat. Soc. on Thrombosis and Hemostasis, N.Y. Acad. Scis., Hungarian Pathobiochem. Soc. (pres.). Avocations: classical music, writing, tennis, travel, photography. Office: Semmelweis U, Dept Med Biochem Puskin St 9, Budapest H-1088, Hungary also: Mayo Clinic Hematology Rsch PL5 Rochester MN 55905-0001

MACHTOU, PIERRE E., endodontist; b. Alger, France, Aug. 26, 1943; s. Williams B. and Suzanne S. (Zemmour) M.; m. Josiane Friedmann, Nov. 30, 1972; children: Julie, Charlotte. DDS, U. Paris, 1967, DCD, 1973. Docteur En Sciences Odontolo, 1980. Instr. Paris Dental Sch., 1968-75, asst. prof., 1975-83, maitre de conferences, 1983-97, prof., 1997-99, vice-dean, 1999—; sci. dir. French Endodontic Soc., Paris, 1981-83, gen. sec. 1983-84. Author: (book) Guide Pratique du Controle de Infection au Cabinet Dentaire, 1991, Endodontie Clinique, 1993; contbr. articles to profl. jours. Recipient award Soc. Francaise d'Endodontie. Fellow Pierre Fauchard Acad.; mem. Cercle Parisien d'Endodontologie Appliquée, European Soc. Endodontology, Internat. Fedn. Endodontic Assn., Am. Assn. Endodontists, Internat. Coll. Dentists, Paris Soc. Odontology. Avocations: computers. Office: Fac Chirurgie Dent Paris 7, 5 Rue Garanciere, 75006 Paris France

MACIÁ, ENRIQUE BARBER, research institute executive, educator, researcher; b. Sabadell, Barcelona, Spain, May 13, 1962; s. Juan Mercadé Maciá and Pepita Girbau Barber; m. Victoria Rodero Hernández;. BS in Physics, U. Granada, Spain, 1984; MS in Physics, U. Complutense, Madrid, 1986, PhD in Physics, 1996. Pres. Inst. Interdisciplinary Studies, Madrid, 1989—; tchg. assoc. U. Complutense, 1992-98, assoc. prof., 1998—; cons. Agrupacio Astronomica Sabadell, 1986—. Author: The Origin of Life at the Light of Stars, 1996, Electrons, Phonons and Excitons in Low Dimensional Aperiodic Systems, 2000; contbr. articles to sci. jours., including Phys. Rev., Phys. Rev. Letters, Jour. Physics A, Semicondr. Sci. and Tech. Rsch. grantee Amics Gaspar de Portolá, 1996, Astrophysics Inst. Canaries, Tenerife, Spain, 1988. Mem. Internat. Soc. for Study Origin of Life, Colegio Oficial Fisicos (advisor 1990—), Real Sociedad Española de Fisica (advisor 1997—), N.Y. Acad. Scis. Office: Inst Interdisciplinary Stud, Apdo 104, 28700 San Sebastian Reyes Madrid, Spain

MACIA SANTAMARIA, JAVIER, physics educator and researcher; b. Tarragona, Catalunya, Spain, Oct. 3, 1967; s. Jose Macia and Rosa Santamaria. PhD in Physics, U. Barcelona, 1990. Rschr. Barcelona U., 1990-95, 1995-97, 1996—; tchr. Gereralitat Catalunya, Spain, 1991—. Author, designer hardware; author software; rschr. autoconfigurable electronic circuits design. Office: GAMA SD, Cronista Sesse 11-4-2, 43005 Tarragona Spain

MACIAS-VIRGOS, ENRIQUE, mathematician, educator, researcher; b. Vigo, Galicia, Spain, Jan. 23, 1956. Lic., U. Santiago de Compostela, Spain, 1979, D degree, 1983. Asst. prof. U. Santiago de Compostela, 1979-86, prof., 1986—, dean faculty math., 1994—; postdoctoral fellow U. Lille, France, 1985-87. Editor: Analysis & Geometry in Foliations, 1995; contbr. articles to profl. jours. including Topology, Geometriae Dedicata, Trans. Am. Math. Soc. and Ill. Jour. Math. Mem. Real Sociedad Matematica Espanola, Am. Math. Soc. Office: U Santiago de Compostela, Dept Geometry and Topology, 15706 Santiago de Compostela Spain

MACIEJEWSKI, RYSZARD ROMUALD, anatomist; b. STaszow, Poland, Feb. 7, 1954; s. Tadeusz and Celina (Cwiklo) M.; m. Teresa Greniuk, Apr. 12, 1980; 1 child, Marcin. MD, U. Sch. Medicine, Lublin, Poland, 1979. Asst. U. Sch. Medicine, Lublin, Poland, 1979-88, tutor, 1988-95, prof., 1996—; chmn. Lublin Dept. Anatomical Soc., 1997—. Author: Atlas of the Broncho-Vascular Ramifications of the Lung, 1995. Mem. Ind. Workers Orgn. "Solidarnosc", Poland, 1980. Mem. Polish Anatomu Soc., Assn. Polish Surgeons. Roman Catholic. Avocations: travel, stamp collecting. Office: Dept Human Anatomy, Spokojna 1, 20-074 Lublin Poland

MACÍK, KAREL, economist, educator, researcher; b. Hamburg, Germany, Mar. 29, 1935; s. Karel and Margarete Frieda (Vocke) M.; m. Jana Zahálková, Aug. 4, 1962; children: Lenka, Jan. MSc, Czech Tech. U., Prague, 1960, PhD, 1973. Asst. prof. Czech Tech. U., Prague, 1960-88, assoc. prof., 1988-97, prof., 1997, head of dept., 1992; cons. ISQ Ltd., Prague, 1993; directing bd. Czech Made Award, Prague, 1994; bd. dirs. European Bus. Sch., Prague, 1994. Author (with J. Vysušil) Costing and Input-Output Analysis, 1985, How to Calculate Enterprise Costs, 1994, Accounting for Managers, 1995, Cost Calculation-Basis for Enterprise Controlling, 1999, Accounting for Managerial Practice, 2000. Mem. Europa Inst. Schweiz, Soc. for Organizational Consultancy (cons.). Avocations: classical music, traveling, history, painting. Office: Fac of Machinery, Czech Tech U Horská 3, 128 00 Prague Czech Republic

MACINNIS, PETER ANDREW, science writer; b. Ipswich, Australia, Apr. 22, 1944; s. Ian Dumaresq and Veronica Fay Macinnis; m. Christine Dorothea Clarke, May 19, 1969; children: Angus, Catriona, Duncan. BSc, U. Sydney, NSW, Australia, 1969, diploma in edn., 1970, MEd, 1982. Cert. M.A.C.E. Sci. subject officer NSW Dept. Edn., Sydney, 1976-79; sr. edn. officer NSW Dept. TAFE, Sydney, 1980-81; sr. edn. officer NSW Dept. Edn., Sydney, 1982-85, prin. edn. officer, 1985-87; cmty. svcs. mgr. Powerhouse Mus., Sydney, 1987-90; mus. educator Australian Mus., Sydney, 1991-93; tchr. St. Pauls Coll., Manly, Sydney, 1994-99; sci. writer Webster Pub., Sydney, 1999—; cons. assessment and rsch. Secondary Schs. Bd., NSW, 1982-87, Bd. Sr. Sch. Studies, NSW, 1986-87. Author: (sci. book) Exploring the Environment, 1986, (nonfiction) Applied Studies in Science, Mathematics and Technology, 1993; co-author: (illustrated children's book) The Rainforest, 1999; contbr., sci. content provider: (CD-ROM) Webster's World Encyclopedia, 1997—. Recipient Michael Daley award for sci. and tech. journalism Australian Govt., 1991, 93. Avocations: wilderness walking, reading, writing, arguing. Fax: 61 2 9939 8355. E-mail: macinnis@websterpublishing.com. Home: 22 Heathcliff Crescent, Balgowlah Heights NSW 2093, Australia Office: Webster Pub, Upper Level 36-38 Wattle Rd, Brookvale NSW 2100, Australia

MACINTYRE, IAIN, scientist, research institute administrator; b. Glasgow, Scotland, Aug. 30, 1924; s. John and Margaret Fraser (Shaw) MacI.; m. Mabs Wilson Jamieson, July 14, 1947; 1 child, Fiona Bell. MB, ChB, U. Glasgow, 1947; PhD, U. London, 1960, DSc, 1970; MD (hon.), U. Turin, Italy, 1985. Med. diplomate. Hon. demonstrator in biochemistry U. Sheffield, Eng., 1948-52; registrar in chem. pathology Royal Postgrad. Med. Sch., London, 1952-54, meml. rsch. fell. Sir Jack Drummond, 1954-56, asst. lectr., then lectr. and reader in chem. pathology, 1956-67, dir. endocrine unit, prof. endocrine chemistry, chem. pathology, 1967-90, chmn. acad. bd., 1985-90; assoc. dir. William Harvey Rsch. Inst., London, 1990-95, rsch. dir., 1995—; dir. svc., mem. spl. health authority, cons. chem. pathologist Hammersmith Hosp., London, 1983-90; dir. svc., mem. spl. health authority Queen Charlotte's Hosp., London, 1983-90; dir. svc. Chelsea Hosp. for Women, London, 1983-90; vis. prof. NIH, 1960-61, U. Calif., 1964, U. Melbourne, 1979-80, USSR Acad. Scis., 1978; examiner U. London, 1974-85; mem. Med. Rsch. Coun., U.K., 1972, 74-76; mem. com. Soc. Endocrinology, 1977-80; chmn. organizing com. Hammersmith Internat. Endocrine Mtgs., 1967, 69, 71, 73, 77, 79, 81. Contbr. more than 500 articles to profl. jours. Fellow Royal Coll. Physicians, Royal Coll. Pathologists, Royal Soc., Acad. Med. Scis.; mem. Brit. Med. Soc., Queens Club, Athenaeum, Hurlingham Club, Eng. Chess Assn. (v.p.), Assn. Am. Physicians (hon.). Avocations: tennis, computing sci., graphics, music. Home: Great Broadhurst Farm, Broad Oak, Heathfield East Sussex TN21 8UX, England Office: William Harvey Rsch Inst, Charterhouse Square, London EC1M6BQ, England

MACIONIS, JOHN JOHNSTON, professor, writer; b. Phila., Oct. 19, 1947; s. John Joseph and May (Johnston) M.; m. Amy Marsh Macionis, June 6, 1987; children: McLean, Whitney. BA, Cornell U., 1970; MA, U. Penn., 1971, PhD, 1975. Prof., Prentice Hall disting. scholar sociology Kenyon Col., Gambier, Ohio, 1978—. Author: Sociology, 1987, Sociology, Can. edit., 1994, Hebrew edit., 1999, Asian edit., 1998, Spanish translation, 1999, Internat. English edit., 1998, Society: The Basics, 1992, Can. edit., 1999, Cities and Urban Life, 1998, (with others) Seeing Ourselves: Classic, Contemporary and Cross-Cultural Readings in Sociology, 1989, Sociology: A Global Introduction, 1998, Sociology, 1998, Hebrew transl., 1999, Sociology: International English Edit., 1998, Sociologia, 1999. Recipient award for Disting. Contbn. to Tchg., North Ctrl. Sociol. Assn., 1998. Home: 1300 Park Rd Mount Vernon OH 43050-3855 Office: Kenyon Col Dept Sociology Gambier OH 43022

MACK, ALAN WAYNE, interior designer; b. Cleve., Oct. 30, 1947; s. Edmund B. and Florence I. (Oleksa) M. BS in Interior Design, Case Western Res. U., 1969. Designer interior design dept. Halle's, Cleve., 1969, 71-73; designer Nahan Co., New Orleans, 1973-75, Hemenway's Contract Design, New Orleans, 1975-76; ptnr. Hewlett-Mack Design Assocs., New Orleans, 1976-85; prin., dir. interior design HLM Design, Inc., 1985—; mem. adv. com. interior design dept. Delgado Jr. Coll., New Orlean s; mktg./merchandising adv. coun. St. Mary's Dominican Coll., New Orleans; mem. friends devel. coun. U. Iowa Mus. Art, 1986-91, chair, 1990-91; chmn. adv. com. interior design program Iowa State U., 1991-96; mem. design review com., City of Iowa City, 1992-93. Co-author: audiovisual presentation Nat. Home Improvement COun. Conf., 1981. Bd. dirs. Johnson County United Way, 1991-96. Served with U.S. Army, 1969-71. Mem. ASID (profl. mem., presdl. citation 1980, treas. La. dist. chpt. 1984), Vis. Nurses Assn. (bd. dirs. 1991-96), Found. for Interior Design Edn. Rsch. (standards com. 1972-76, bd. visitors 1977-80, accreditation com. 1981-95, trustee 1996-99, chmn. bd. dirs. 1998, pres. 1999). Home: 3800 N Lake Shore Dr Ste 2G Chicago IL 60613-3313

MACK, DORIS MARGARETHE, urologist, researcher, educator; b. Salzburg, Austria, Feb. 16, 1958; d. Helmut and Ruth (Rothwangl) Trummer; 1 child, Lukas. MD, U. Austria, 1983, Docent, 1987. Univ. asst. U. Innsbruck, Austria, 1984-88; jr. resident U. Salzburg, Austria, 1988-90, sr. resident, 1990-92, staff mem., 1992-97; prof. U. Vienna, Austria, 1997—; health mgmt. cons. Govt. Salzburg, 1995—; health consulting group mem. Govt. IDG, 1996—. Author book and contbr. articles to profl. jours. Fellow European Bd. Urology, European Orgn. of Rsch. and Treatment of Cancer, European Assn. Urology (1st Poster prize 1988), German Soc. Urology, Austrian Assn. Urology (1st prize 1987), Am. Urologists' Assn., Women in Urology, Soroptimist Internat. Avocations: music, painting, cooking, literature. Office: LKA Salzburg, Dept Urology, A-5020 Salzburg Austria

MACK, DOUGLAS STUART, librarian, educator; b. Bellshill, Scotland, Jan. 30, 1943; s. James and Kathleen Dunwoodie Proudfoot (McGlashan) M.; m. Wilma Stewart Grant; children: John Douglas Johnson, Gordon James Grant. MA, U. Glasgow, 1964; PhD, U. Stirling, 1985. Rsch. asst. Nat. Libr. Scotland, Edinburgh, 1965-66; asst. libr. U. St. Andrews, Scotland, 1966-70; asst. libr., lectr. U. Stirling, Scotland, 1970-94; reader U. Stirling, 1994-2000, prof., 2000—. Editor: Selected Poems of James Hogg, 1970, J. Hogg, The Brownie of Bodsbeck, 1976, W. Scott, The Tale of Old Mortality, 1993, J. Hogg, The Shepherd's Calendar, 1995; gen. editor Stirling/S.C. Rsch. Edit. James Hogg, 1990—. Fellow Royal Soc. Edinburgh; mem. James Hogg Soc. (pres. 1982—), Assn. Scottish Literary Studies. Scottish Nat. Party. Scottish Episc. Ch. Avocations: soccer, theatre, sailing. Home: 2 Law Hill Rd, Dollar FK14 7BG, Scotland Office: Dept English Studies, Univ Stirling, Stirling FK9 4LA, Scotland

MACK, FRANK RAINER, physicist, development engineer; b. Stuttgart, Baden-W., Germany, Jan. 20, 1971; s. Hans Ernst and Anneliese Lina (Steichele) M. Diploma in physics, U. Stuttgart, 1996, PhD in Natural Scis., 1999. Rschr. Max-Planck-Inst. Solid State Rsch, Stuttgart, 1996-99; devel. engr. Transfer Ctr. Microelectronics, Göppingen, Germany, 1999—. Contbr. articles to sci. jours., including Phys. Rev. Letters, Physics of Manganites, others. Mem. German Phys. Soc. Home: Elbestr 43, 70376 Stuttgart Baden W, Germany

MACK, HANANEL, researcher; b. Jerusalem, Apr. 27, 1941; s. Emmanuel and Miriam (Halperin) M.; m. Offira Kirson; children: J. Haggith, Tamar, Yair, Efrat. BSc, Hebrew U., Jerusalem, 1965, MSc, 1971, PhD, 1981, 91. From lectr. to sr. lectr. Hebrew U., Jerusalem, 1991-97; lectr. Bar-Ilan U., Ramat-Gan, Israel, 1993-97, sr. lectr., 1997—. Author: (books) The Aggadic Midrash Literature, Hebrew edit., 1989, English edit., 1992, The Ancient Jewish Commentary to the Bible, 1991. Sgt. Israeli Def. Forces-Paratrooper Forces, 1960-61, res., 1961-73. Home: 30 Hidda St, 96464 Jerusalem Israel Office: Bar-Ilan U, Ramat-Gan Israel

MACK, JANE BARNES, English and American studies educator; b. L.A., Dec. 1, 1942; d. Walthew Turner and Venus (Day) Barnes; m. Gerhard Mack, Apr. 15, 1967 (div. 1985); m. Joseph Cozzo, Dec. 6, 1998. BA, U. Calif., Berkeley, 1963; MA cum laude, Calif. State U., 1965; postgrad., Claremont Grad. Sch., 1965-69. Dir. publicity Constructive Action, Inc., La Jolla, Calif., 1966; rsch. assoc. Pepperdine Rsch. Inst., L.A., 1967-69; instr. Modesto (Calif.) Jr. Coll., 1976-78; lectr. Calif. State U., Turlock, Calif., 1981-83; instr. Stanislaus Dept. Edn., Modesto, 1983-85, Merced (Calif.) High Sch., 1985-86, Time-Life, Ltd., Tokyo, 1986-87, Simul Acad. Internat. Communication, Tokyo, 1987-88; lectr. Keio U., Hiyoshi, Japan, 1988-90, Japan Women's U., 1990-93; assoc. prof. Hitotsubashi U., Tokyo, 1993-96; prof. Reitaku U., Kashiwa, Japan, 1996-99; freelance writer; rep. Sacramento (Calif.) Conf. on Edn., 1964; announcer Mainichi Weekly, Tokyo, 1988; freelance writer. Author: Great Western Composers, 1990, Famous Western Women, The Penguin Book of Unique Short Stories (annotation), 1991; (published under name Samantha Day) A Gaijin's Portrait of Young Japanese, 1991, The Mosaic of Modern English, 1992, Westerners: Their Character and Cuisine, 1993, Well Written, Well Spoken, 1993, Postmodern Culture in America, 1993, Fact or Fiction?, 1994, Feminism: For and Against, 1994, Controversial Issues in Modern Society, 1995, Political Correctness on College Campuses, 1998; contbr. articles to profl. jours. Scholar Claremont Grad. Sch., 1966-67. Mem. Assn. Literary Scholars and Critics, Intercollegiate Studies Inst. (scholar 1963-65, Richard Weaver fellow 1965-66). Republican. Anglican. Avocations: classical pianist, actress. Home: 816 Nostrand Dr San Gabriel CA 91775-2118

MACK, JOHN J., investment company executive; b. 1944. Mng. dir. Morgan Stanley & Co., N.Y.C., 1979-87; mng. dir. Morgan Stanley Group, N.Y.C., 1987-92, mem. exec. com., 1987-97, chmn. operating com., 1992-97, pres., 1993-97; pres., COO Morgan Stanley Dean Witter & Co., N.Y.C., 1997—, also bd. dirs. Office: Morgan Stanley/Dean Witter 1585 Broadway New York NY 10036-8200

MACK, JUDITH COLE SCHRIM, political science educator; b. Cin., Aug. 9, 1938; d. James Douglass and Cathleen (Cole) Schrim; m. Thomas H. Mack, Jan. 3, 1968; children: Robert Michael, Cathleen Cole. AB with high distinction, U. Ky., 1960; AM, Radcliffe Grad. Sch., 1962; MPhil, Columbia U., 1988, postgrad., 1986—. Tchr. The Lexington (Ky.) Sch., 1962-63; instr. Russian Emory U., Atlanta, 1963-64, Kent (Ohio) State U., 1964-65; instr. Hunter Coll., N.Y.C., 1988-90; adj. lectr. Barnard Coll., N.Y.C., spring 1991, 92; instr. Douglass Coll. Rutgers U., 1992-93; rsch. asst. sociology dept. U. Ky., summer 1961; rsch. asst. Russian and East European Studies Ctr., UCLA, 1965-67; rsch. asst. security studies ctr. UCLA, 1967-68; adj. lectr. Hunter Coll., N.Y.C., spring 1988; presenter in field. Chmn. State Pub. Affairs Com., N.J. Jr. Leagues, 1979-80; bd. dirs. Children's Aide Adoption Soc., Hackensack, N.J., 1979-90, v.p. 1985-90; bd. dirs. Assn. for Children N.J., Newark, 1982—, v.p. 1983-88, chair special events 1999; trustee Divsn. Youth and Family Svcs., Trenton, 1982-91, v.p. 1983-88, others; mem. Millburn-Short Hills County Com. Rep. Party, 1994—, corr. sec., 1994-96, chmn. 1996-98. Recipient Woodrow Wilson fellowship Radcliffe Coll., 1960-61, Nat. Def. fellowship Radcliffe Coll., 1961-62. Mem. Nat. Soc. Colonial Dames Am. (N.J. treas. 1995—), Mortar Board, Phi Beta Kappa, Phi Sigma Iota. Episcopalian. Avocations: bridge, cooking, ballet, theater, movies. Home: 47 Knollwood Rd Short Hills NJ 07078-2821

MACK, RONALD BRAND, pediatric dentist, clinician, educator, writer, lecturer; b. San Francisco, Feb. 20, 1948; s. Edward Semmel and Susan Tabor (Brand) M.; m. Janet Berringer, July 12, 1986; children by previous marriage: Joshua Hamilton, Aaron Edward. Diplomate Am. Bd. Pediatric Dentistry. BS, U. Calif., Davis, 1969; DDS, U. Pacific, 1973; cert. pediatric dentistry Ind. U., 1975. Practice dentistry specializing in pediatric dentistry, San Francisco, 1975—; instr., mem. staff, Oakland (Calif.) Children's Hosp., 1976—; instr. gen. practice residency Mt. Zion Hosp., San Francisco, 1978-84; adj. assoc. prof. pediatric dentistry, U. Pacific Sch. Dentistry, 1983—, Ind. U. Sch. Dentistry, 1995—. United Cerebral Palsy clinical fellow, 1973, 74; G.R. Baker fellow, 1975. Master and fellow Am. Soc. Dentistry for Children; fellow Internat. Coll. Dentists, Am. Coll. Dentists, Am. Acad. Pediatric Dentistry, Acad. Dentistry for Persons with Disabilities, Am. Soc. Dentistry for Children, Acad. Dentistry Internat., Pierre Fauchard Acad., Master Am. Soc. of Dentistry for Children; mem. San Francisco Dental Soc., Bay Area Dental Guidance Council for the Disabled (co-founder, 1977), U. Pacific Sch. Dentistry Alumni Assn. (life mem.), Calif. Dental Assn., Coll. Diplomates of Am. Bd. Pediatric Dentistry (bd. dirs. 1994-97), Calif. Soc. Pediatric Dentists (charter mem., bd. dirs. 1979-81), No. Calif. Soc. Dentistry for Children (pres. 1981-82, 94-95), ADA, Am. Soc. Dentistry for Children (bd. trustees, 1988-94), Ind. U. Pediatric Dentistry Alumni Assn. (bd. dirs. 1981-95, pres. 1991-93), Bay Area Pediatric Dentistry Study Club (pres. 1983-84), Internat. Assn. Dentistry for Children, Internat. Assn. Dentistry for the Handicapped, Fédération Dentaire Internationale, San Francisco Dolphin South End Runners, Roadrunners Club Am., Tau Kappa Omega, Alpha Omega Internat. (pres. San Francisco alumni chpt. 1977-78). Contbr. numerous articles to profl. jours., chpts. to books. Office: 632 Taraval St San Francisco CA 94116-2512

MACKALL, HENRY CLINTON, lawyer; b. Ft. Lauderdale, Fla., Apr. 6, 1927; s. Douglass Sorrel and Mildred (Parker) M.; m. Mary Margaret Sullivan, June 21, 1952; children: Caroline Clark, Nancy Sorrel, Lucy Parker. BA, U. Va., 1950, LLB 1952. Bar: Va. 1951. Ptnr. Mackall, Mackall, & Gibb, P.C. and predecessors, Fairfax, Va., 1952—; asst. commr. accounts Fairfax County (Va.), 1963—; spl. commr. in chancery for audit functions for Cir. Ct. Fairfax County, 1976—; substitute judge Fairfax County Ct., Juvenile and Domestic Relations Ct. Fairfax County, 1964-69. Trustee, Fairfax Hosp. Assn., 1966-75; with Va. State Bar Client Security Fund Bd., 1976-88, chmn., 1977-78; bd. dirs. F & M Bank, No. Va. Served with AUS, 1945-46. Fellow Am. Coll. Trusts & Estate Counsel, Am. Coll. Real Estate Lawyers, Va. Law Found.; mem. ABA, Va. Bar Assn. (regional v.p. 1963-64), Fairfax County Bar Assn. (pres. 1966-67), Hist. Soc. Fairfax County (pres. 1970-72), Jamestowne Soc. (gov. 1995-97). Democrat. Episcopalian. Clubs: River Bend Country (pres. 1967-68) (Gt. Falls, Va.); Georgetown Assembly (Washington). Home: 1032 Towlston Rd Mc Lean VA 22102-1111 Office: 4031 Chain Bridge Rd Fairfax VA 22030-4103

MACKAY, EDWARD, engineer; b. Kilmarnock, Ayrshire, Scotland, Feb. 29, 1936; s. Edward and Gertrude (Black) M.; widowed. Higher Nat. Cert., Glasgow Tech. Coll., Scotland, 1957. Layout engr. Stanley Works, New Britain, Conn., 1957-58; project engr. Grumman Olson, Athens, N.Y., 1961-69, asst. chief engr., 1969-74; chief engr. Grumman Olson, Sturgis, Mich., 1974-78, v.p. engring., 1978-95; cons. engr. Dundonald Enterprise, Three Rivers, Mich., 1995—. With U.S. Army, 1959-61. Presbyterian. Avocation: sheep highland cattle farming, manufacturing of livestock handling equipment. Office: Dundonald Enterprise 19085 Hoshel Rd Three Rivers MI 49093-9316

MACKAY, ERIC VINCENT, medical practitioner; b. Melbourne, Australia, Nov. 2, 1924; s. Eric Reay and Ethel Maude (Carney) M.; m. Gaenor Mae Gregory Mackay, July 7, 1956; children: Andrea, Reay. MBBS, U. Melbourne, Australia, 1948. Medical diplomate. Resident/registrar Prince Henry's Hosp., Melbourne, Australia, 1949-50; registrar Royal Women's Hosp., Melbourne, Australia, 1951-52; second asst. U. Melbourne, Australia, 1953-54; house officer Queen Charlottes Hosp., London, 1954; registrar of surgery Edinburgh Royal Infirmary, 1955; registrar of ob/gyn Mill Rd. Maternity, Liverpool, 1955; cons. Welsh Regional Hosp. Bd., 1956; rsch. fellow UCLA, 1956; first asst. ob/gyn U. Melbourne, 1957-64; prof., chmn. ob/gyn U. Queensland, Brisbane, 1964-89. Co-author: 4 Medical Text Books; Editor: ANZ J Obstetrics & Gynaecology, 1961-82; contbr. 160 pubs. for med. rsch. Recipient Order of Australia. Fellow Royal Coll. Ob-Gyn., Royal Australian Coll. Ob-Gyn., Royal Australian Coll. Surgeons, Royal Coll. Surgeons Edinburgh, Am. Coll. Ob-Gyn. (hon.). Avocations: medical authorship, native forestation, horse breeding. Office: Dept Ob/Gyn Clinical Scis, Royal Brisbane Hospital, Queensland 4029, Australia

MACKAY, GEORGES WILLIAM, III, communications company executive, writer; b. Warwick, N.Y., Feb. 28, 1961; s. George William Jr. and Helen Margot Bower M. BA summa cum laude, Hunter Coll., 1995. Exec. prodr. Gedeon Comms., France, 1995—; judge Promax Europe, U.K., 1998-99. Author: (screenplay) Illusion of Beauty, 1998, Flash, 1999, In Search of Normal, 1999. Fellow Promax/Broadcast Design Awards Internat. (judge 1998-99); mem. Phi Beta Kappa. Home: 9 BD St Denis, 75003 Paris France Office: Gedeon Comms, 44-50 Ave Capitain Glarner, 93585 St Duen France

MACKAY, JAMES PETER HYMERS (LORD MACKAY OF CLASHFERN), university official; b. July 2, 1927; s. James Mackay and Janet Hymers; m. Elizabeth Gunn Hymers; 3 children. BA, Cambridge U., 1952; MA in Math. and Natural Philosophy with honors, Edinburgh U., 1948, LLB with distinction, 1955, LLD (hon.), 1983; LLD (hon.), Dundee U., 1983, Strathclyde U., 1985, Aberdeen U., 1987, St. Andrews U., 1989, Cambridge U., 1989; DCL (hon.), William and Mary Coll., 1989; LLD (hon.), Birmingham U., 1990, Newcastle U., 1990. Admitted to Faculty of Advocates, 1955; QC (Scot.), 1965. Sheriff prin. Renfrew and Argyll, 1972-74; vice-dean Faculty of Advocates, 1973-76, dean, 1976-79, Lord Advocate Scotland, 1979-84; Lord Appeal in Ordinary, 1985-87; senator Coll. of Justice Scotland, 1984-85; Lord Chancellor London, 1987-97; chancellor Heriot-Watt U.; standing jr. counsel to Queen's and Lord Treas.'s Remembrancer, Scottish Home and Health Dept., Commrs. Inland Revenue Scotland; mem. Scottish Law Commn., 1976-79 (part-time), Ins. Brokers' Registration Council, 1977-79. Named Hon. Master of the Bench, Inner Temple, 1979. Fellow Royal Soc. Edinburgh, Internat. Acad. Trial Lawyers, Inst. Taxation (hon.), trinity Coll. (hon.), Girton Coll. Cambridge U. (hon.), Am. Coll. Trial Lawyers (hon.); mem. Royal Coll. Physicians (hon.), Royal Coll. Surgeons (hon. fello w), Royal Coll. Ob-Gyns. (hon. fellow), Soc. Pub. Tchrs. Law (hon.), Law Soc. Scotland (hon.). Club: New (Edinburgh). Avocation: walking. Address: Office of the Chancellor, Heriot-Watt U, Edinburgh EH14 4AS, Scotland

MACKELLAR, KEITH ROBERT, hospital administrator; b. Chgo., Dec. 26, 1943; s. Duncan Harvey and Julie Marie MacK.; m. Deborah Marie Boone, Aug. 26, 1967; children: Andrea Kathleen, Bethany Kristine. AA, Morton Coll., 1969; B in Orgnl. Behavior, Northwestern U., 1978; M in Human Resources, Loyola U. Chgo., 1987. Dir. Ill. Masonic Med. Ctr., Chgo., 1967-74, Northwestern Meml. Hosp., Chgo., 1974-80; div. dir. AMA, Chgo., 1980-89; dir. human resources Physicians & Surgeons Hosp., Shreveport, La., 1989-91; v.p. resource mgmt. Eastern N.Mex. Med. Ctr., Roswell, 1991-98; chief human resources officer Houston N.W. Med. Ctr., Houston, 1998—; past chmn. N.Mex. Hosp. Workers Compensation Bd. Sec. Sch. Bd. Dist. #88, Bellwood, Ill., 1980-83. Sgt. USMC, 1962-66, Vietnam. Mem. Am. Coll. Healthcare Execs., Am. Soc. Healthcare Human Resources Assn., Am. Mgmt. Assn., Soc. Human Resources Mgmt., N.Mex. Healthcare Human Resources Assn. (pres. 1997-98), Rotary Internat., Leadership Roswell Alumni Assn. (past pres.), Tex. Health Care Human Resources Assn. (bd. dirs. 1998—), Houston Soc. for Healthcare Human Resources Adminstrn. (pres. 2000-01). Baptist. Avocations: hiking, camping, softball. Home: 22414 Willow Branch Dr Tomball TX 77375-5492 Office: Houston NW Med Ctr 710 FM 1960 W Houston TX 77090-3402

MACKEN, FIDELMA O'KELLY, federal justice; b. 1945. Mem. Bar of Ireland, 1972; legal advisor, patent and trade mark agts. Ireland, 1973-79, barrister, 1979-95; sr. counsel Bar of Ireland, 1995-98; mem. Bar of Eng. and Wales; judge High Ct. In Ireland, 1998; lectr. in legal sys. and methods, Averil Deverell lectr. Trinity Coll., Dublin; justice Ct. of Justice of the European Cmtys., Luxembourg, 1999—. Office: Ct Justice European Cmtys, Palais de Cour de justice, Kirchberg L-2925, Luxembourg*

MACKENZIE, ANN HALEY, science educator; b. Centerville, Ind., Jan. 29, 1957; d. William Howard and Shirley Anne (Wilson) Haley; children: Kristen Rae, Matthew Adler. MEd, U. Cin., 1987, EdD, 1989. Sci. tchr. Hazelwood (Mo.) West Jr.-Sr. H.S., 1979-81, Kings Mills (Ohio) schs., 1987-92; instnl. coord. Mo. Botanical Garden, St. Louis, 1981-82; grad. rsch. asst. U. Cin., 1983-87, adj. instr., 1986; adj. instr. Miami U., Oxford, Ohio, 1986,

vis. asst. prof., 1992-95; project dir. Miami U., Ohio's NSF State Systemic Inst. in Math. and Sci., 1993-94; asst. prof. Miami U., Oxford, Ohio, 1995—; chair secondary sci. Nat. Bd. Profl. Tchg. Stds., 1991—; evaluator, cons. GE Aircraft Engines, Evendale, Ohio, 1987-91; cons. Biol. Sci. Curriculum Study, Colorado Springs, 1990—; cons. Am. Physiol. Soc., 1994—, Nat. Geog., 1997—; internat. rschr., Australia; instr./leader Dragonfly Workshops, 2000—; evaluator NSTA Sci-Links Project, 2000—. Recipient Ohio Tchr. of Yr. award Chief State Bd. Supts., 1990, Presdl. award for excellence in math. and sci. teaching NSF/NSTA, 1991. Mem. AAAS (evaluator, author), Nat. Assn. Rsch. in Sci. Teaching, Am. Edn. Rsch. Assn., Nat. Sci. Tchrs. Assn., Nat. Assn. Biology Tchrs. Home: 8397 Sailboat Ln Maineville OH 45039-8858 Office: Miami U 467 McGuffey Hall Oxford OH 45056-2076

MACKENZIE, CHARLES SHERRARD, academic administrator; b. Quincy, Mass., Aug. 21, 1924; s. Charles Sherrard and Dorothy (Eaton) MacK.; m. Florence Evelyn Phelps Meyer, Aug. 28, 1964 (dec. 1981); 1 child, Robert Walter Meyer; m. Lavonne Rudolph Gaiser, Mar. 30, 1985. Student, Boston U., 1942-43; B.A., Gordon Coll., 1946; M.Div., Princeton Theol. Sem., 1949, Th.D., 1955, PhD, 1957, LHD, 1997; post-grad., U. Paris, 1953. Ordained to ministry Congl. Christian Ch., 1949. Pastor Carversville (Pa.) Christian Ch., 1948-51; fellow faculty Princeton Theol. Sem., 1949-51, 53-54, Princeton U., 1954-64; pastor First Presbyn. Ch., Avenel, N.J., 1954-64, Broadway Presbyn. Ch., Columbia U., N.Y.C., 1964-67, First Presbyn. Ch., Stanford U., San Mateo, Calif., 1967-71; pres. Grove City (Pa.) Coll., 1971-91, chancellor, 1991-92; advisor to pres., prof. philosphy Reformed Seminary, Orlando, Fla., 1992—; sr. min. Eastminster Presbyn. Ch., Wichita, Kans., 1993; bd. dirs. Covenant Life Ins. Co., C.S. Lewis Inst.; cons. Oxford Project, 1992—, Provident Mutual Ins. Co.; lectr. Oxford U., 1965, U. Hamburg, 1968, Columbia U., 1964-67, Stanford U., 1967-71, U. Pitts., 1990-93; adv. Provident Mutual Ins. Co. Author: The Anguish and Joy of Pascal, 1973, Freedom, Equality, Justice, 1980, The Trinity and Culture, 1985. Bd. dirs. Knox Fellowship, Frontline, Orlando; mem. Human Relations Commn., San Mateo, 1968-70; mem. Indsl. Devel. Council, Grove City, 1972-75. Served with USAF, 1951-53. Mem. Presbyn. Coll. Union, Am. Assn. Pres.'s Ind. Colls. and Univs. (dir., pres.), Nat. Assn. Ind. Colls. and Univs. (mem. secretariat 1985-91), Freedoms Found. (nat. jury), Soc. Christian Philosphers, Duquesne Club (Pitts.), Univ. Club Boston, Citrus Club (Orlando), Evangelical initiative Notre Dame U., Rockford Inst. Main St. com. (De Toqueville award 1998). Republican. Address: 1231 Reformation Dr Oviedo FL 32765-7197

MACKENZIE, CRAIG HUGH, English language educator; b. Durban, Natal, South Africa, Aug. 9, 1960; s. Brian Hugh and Ali (Brandse) MacK.; m. Susan Mary Jenkins; children: Daniel, Matthew, Jessica. BA, U. Natal, Durban, South Africa, 1982, BA in English with honors, 1983, MA in English, 1985; PhD in English, Rhodes U., Grahamstown, South Africa, 1997. Curator, rschr. Nat. English Literary Mus., Grahamstown, South Africa, 1987-91; lectr. Rand Afrikaans U., Johannesburg, South Africa, 1991—. Author: Bessie Head: An Introduction, 1989, Bessie Head, 1999, The Oral-Style South African Short Story in English, 1999; editor: A Woman Alone: Autobiographical Writings (Bessie Head), 1990, English in Africa, 1994—. Avocations: surfing, piano and guitar playing. Office: Rand Afrikaans U, Kingsway, Auckland Park 2006 Johannesburg Gauteng, South Africa

MACKENZIE, DONALD ANGUS, sociology educator; b. Inverness, Scotland, May 3, 1950; s. Angus Donald and Anne (Paterson) MacK.; children: Alice MacKenzie Bamford, Iain Angus MacKenzie Bamford. BSc, U. Edinburgh, 1972, PhD, 1978. Lectr. in sociology U. Edinburgh, 1975-88, reader in sociology, 1988-92, prof. sociology, 1992—; vis. prof. Harvard U., 1997. Author: Statistics in Britain, 1981, Inventing Accuracy, 1990 (Ludwik Fleck prize 1993, co-winner Merton award 1993), Knowing Machines, 1996. Recipient Usher prize Soc. for History of Tech., 1986, U.S. Navy prize in Naval History, 1989, Life Mems. prize in Elec. History IEEE, 1992. Avocations: cycling, walking, chess. Office: U Edinburgh, 18 Buccleuch Pl, Edinburgh EH8 9LN, Scotland

MACKENZIE, DONALD MATTHEW, JR., minister; b. Chgo., Mar. 25, 1944; s. Donald Matthew Sr. and Ruth Vicory (Yoakum) M.; m. Judith Joy Petterson, May 31, 1966; children: Mary Hye Won, Alice Eun Ah. AB, Macalester Coll., 1966; MDiv, Princeton (N.J.) Sem., 1970, ThM, 1971; PhD, NYU, 1978. Assoc. dir. field edn. Princeton Sem., 1971-80; assoc. pastor Nassau Presbyn. Ch., Princeton, 1980-83; pastor The Ch. of Christ at Dartmouth Coll., Hanover, N.H., 1983-95; examiner D in Ministry program Princeton Sem., 1980—; min. and head of staff U. Congl. United Ch. of Christ, Seattle, 1995—; adj. prof. practical theology Bangor (Maine) Theol. Sem., 1991-95. Contbr. articles to profl. jours. Bd. dirs. Trenton (N.J.) Ecumenical Area Ministry, 1977-83, Wesley-Westminster Found., Princeton U., 1981-83; trustee N.H. Conf., United Ch. of Christ, 1990-92. Mem. Assn. Profs. and Researchers in Religious Edn., United Ch. of Christ, Washington, North Idaho, Conf. United Ch. of Christ, Phi Delta Kappa. Democrat. Home: 16011 36th Ave NE Seattle WA 98155-6623 Office: U Congl United Ch of Christ 16th Ave NE Seattle WA 98105

MACKENZIE, FRED T., geochemist, educator; b. Garwood, N.J., Mar. 17, 1934; s. Fred E. and Bessie V. Mackenzie; m. Mary L. Mackenzie, June 4, 1960; children: Scott D., Michele L. Bonke; m. Judith A. Mackenzie, Dec. 20, 1987. BS, Upsala Coll., East Orange, N.J., 1955; MS, Lehigh U., 1959, PhD, 1962. Geologist Shell Oil Co., Houston, 1962-63; staff geochemist, asst. dir. Bermuda Biol. Sta. for Rsch., Bermuda, 1963-67; prof. Northwestern U., Evanston, Ill., 1967-81; prof. dept. oceanography U. Hawaii, Honolulu, 1981—; life trustee Bermuda Biol. Sta. for rsch., 1996—. Contbr. more than 200 articles to profl. jours.; author 7 books; editor 7 volumes. With U.S. Army, 1956-58. Recipient Regents Medal of Excellence for rsch., U. Hawaii, 1991, Regents Medal for Excellence in Tchg., 1994. Fellow AAAS, Geol. Soc. Am., The Geochem. Soc., Mineral. Soc. Am. Avocations: mountaineering, running. Home: 415 Koko Isle Cir Honolulu HI 96825-1818 Office: Univ of Hawaii Dept Oceanography Honolulu HI 96822

MACKENZIE, IAN DONALD, actuary; b. Paisley, Scotland, Aug. 19, 1971; s. John and Johan White (McCarren) MacK.; m. Janet Melanie Anderson, June 25, 1994. Student, Robert Gordon's Coll., Aberdeen, Scotland, 1983-86, George Watson's Coll., Edinburgh, Scotland, 1986-89; BSc in Math. with 1st class honors, U. Edinburgh, 1993. Actuary Scottish Provident Instn., Edinburgh, 1993-96, Nat. Westminster Life Assurance, Bristol, Eng., 1997-98, J. Rothschild Assurance Group, Cirencester, Eng., 1999—. Fellow Faculty of Actuaries in Scotland. Avocations: scouting, swimming, walking.

MAC KENZIE, JAMES DONALD, clergyman; b. Detroit, Nov. 17, 1924; s. James and Ida Catherine (Conklin) M.; m. Elsie Joan Kerr, May 7, 1960; children: Janet Eileen, Kayly Kathleen, Christy Carol, Kenneth Kerr. Student, Moody Bible Inst., 1946-49, Union Theol. Sem., 1952. Ordained to ministry Presbyn. Ch., 1953. Pastor Calvary Ch., Swan Quarter, N.C., Edenton (N.C.) Presbyn. Ch., 1952-60, Kirkwood Ch., Kannapolis, N.C., 1960-64, Barbecue and Olivia Ch., Olivia, N.C., 1964-71, Elise Ch., Robbins, N.C., 1971-92, Horseshoe Presbyn. Ch., Carbonton, N.C., 1971—; Co-founder, Rehoboth Gospel Fellowship, Chicago, 1949. Columnist The Chowan Herald, Edenton, N.C., 1952-60, The Robbins (N.C.) Record, 1971-86, The Pilot, Southern Pines, N.C., 1987—. Historian Fayetteville Presbytery, 1975—, chmn. hist. com., 1983—, moderator, 1978. Founder Conf. on Celtic Studies, Campbell Coll. (now Campbell U.), Buies Creek, N.C., 1972—; councillor Conf. on Scottish Studies (Can.), 1968-75; co-funder Rehoboth Gospel Fellowship, Chgo., 1949. With AUS, 1943-45, ETO. Decorated Purple Heart, Bronze Star, Combat Inf. Badge; recipient Disting. Citizen award, Robbins, 1983, Disting. Pastor award, 1988, Scottish Heritage Ctr. award St. Andrews Presbyn. Coll., Laurinburg, N.C., 1999. Fellow Soc. Antiquaries Scotland; mem. N.C. Presbyn. Hist. Soc. (pres. 1972-74, Author's award 1970, 75, Cert. Merit 1975), Harnett Hist. Soc. (pres. 1968-71, Distinguished Service award 1970, Scottish Heritage award 1999), Irish Uillean Pipers Soc., Gaelic Soc. of Inverness, An Comunn Gaidhelach (life). Author: Colorful Heritage, 1970; editor: The Uilleann Piper, 1974—; contbr. articles to profl. jours. Home and Office: PO Box 867 Robbins NC 27325-0867

MACKENZIE, JAMES FREDERICK, career military officer; b. Pembury, Kent, U.K., Sept. 5, 1948; s. James Charles and Hila Winnifred (Fowler) M.; m. Jennifer Anne Breakwell, Mar. 29, 1975; 1 child, Sarah Anne. BS, Royal Mil. Coll. of Sci., 1975, MS, 1975. Mem. Instn. Engrs. Australia; chartered profl. engr., Australia. U.K. exch. officer SME, Australia, 1987-89; U.K. liaison officer USAF AFCESA, 1994; rsch. scientist USACE WES, 1994-96, DERA, U.K., 1996—. Contbg. author books on terrorism and related subjects; contbr. numerous publs. in field. Maj. Brit. Army, 1970—. Mem. Am. Soc. Civil Engring., Inst. Engrs./Australia. Mem. Ch. of England. Office: Fortifications Bldg 138, Chobham Ln, Chertsey/Surrey KT16 OEE, United Kingdom

MACKENZIE, J(OHN) LACHLAN, English language educator, researcher; b. Aberdeen, Scotland, May 28, 1950; arrived in The Netherlands, 1977; s. Niven St. Clair and Marjorie Kathleen (Taylor) M.; children: Iona, Joanne. MA with honors, U. Aberdeen, 1973; PhD, Edinburgh (Scotland) U., 1978. Lectr. Free U., Amsterdam, The Netherlands, 1977-87, prof. English lang., 1987—; chmn. Inst. Functional Rsch. into Lang. and Lang. Use, Amsterdam, 1993-99. Author: Principles and Pitfalls of English Grammar, 1997; co-author: (with M. Hannay) Effective Writing in English, 1996; contbr. Atlas of the World's Languages, 1993; editor (scholarly jour.) Working Papers in Functional Grammar, 1988—. Mem. European Soc. Study of English, Netherlands Soc. English Studies (chmn. 1996—). Avocations: music-making, cycling, reading. Office: Free U Amsterdam Dept Eng, De Boelelaan 1105, 1081 HV Amsterdam The Netherlands

MACKENZIE, MALCOLM ROBERT, personnel management consultant; b. Revere, Mass., Oct. 12, 1924; s. Malcolm John and Helen Margaret (Pelrine) Mack.; m. Chieko Yoshida, Nov. 4, 1954; 1 child, Kenneth Andrew. BA, Tufts U., 1945; Japanese Lang. cert., Sophia U., Tokyo, 1951; Advanced Mgmt. Program, U. Hawaii, 1966. Dep. civilian pers. dir. U.S. Army, Camp Zama, Japan, 1959-63; civilian pers. dir. Fort Shafter U.S. Army, Honolulu, 1963-65; chief employee mgmt. U.S. Army Pacific Headquarters, 1965-69; civilian pers. dir. electronics command Fort Monmouth, N.J., 1969-76; command civilian pers. mgr. Naval Edn. and Tng., Naval Air sta. Pensacola, Fla., 1976-81; pers. mgmt. cons. Gulf Breeze, Fla., 1981—. Mem. Human Rights Advocacy Com., Dist. 1, Pensacola, 1982-84; asst. dist. dir. Fla. Spl. Olympics, Pensacola, 1982-86; bd. dirs. Pensacola Penwheels, Employ the Handicapped, Pensacola, 1983—; pres. Pensacola Spl. Steppers retarded dancers, 1983; mem. Fla. gov.'s Com. on Employment of Handicapped, 1983; co-chmn. com. for handicapable dancers United Square Dancers Am., 1984-2000; active Handicapped Boy Scouts, Pensacola; pres. Assn. retarded Citizens-Escambia, Pensacola, 1985-87, Fla. State Assn. for Retarded Citizens, 1987-90; mem. Fla. Developmental Disbility Coun., 1992-2000; state bd. dirs. Fla. Blueprint for Sch. To Community Transitions, 1993-96, Aging & Devel. Disabilities Effort, 1994-2000. With USNR, 1943-45, PTO. Recipient Commemorative medallion Tokyo Met. Govt., 1963, cert. appreciation, Chief of Staff, Ground Office, Defense Agy., Japan, 1963, dir. fgn. affairs. Kanagawa Prefecture, Japan, 1963, dir. fgn. affairs, Saitama Prefecture, Japan, 1963. Mem. Internat. Pers. Mgmt. Assn. (pres. far east chpt. 1960-63, Honolulu chpt. 1964-65, N.J. chpt. 1973-74), Am. Soc. Pub. Adminstrn., Fed. Pers. Coun. Pacific (chmn. 1965-66), Fed. Pers. Coun. N.J. (chmn. 1972-73), Gulf State Fed. Pers. Coun. (vice-chmn. 1980-81), Indsl. Rels. Rsch. Assn., Am. Soc. Tng. and Devel., Fla. Pub. Pers. Assn., Eastern Regional Orgn. for Pub. Adminstrn., Am. Arbitration Assn. (mem. comml. and trade panels), Northwest Fla. Area Agy. on Aging (adv. coun. 1990-92), Parent Edn. Network (cert. trainer 1989-92). Republican. Roman Catholic. Avocations: bowling, golf. Home and Office: 2652 Venetian Way Gulf Breeze FL 32561-3038

MAC KENZIE, NORMAN HUGH, retired English educator, writer; b. Salisbury, Rhodesia, Mar. 8, 1915; s. Thomas Hugh and Ruth Blanche (Huskisson) MacK.; m. Rita Mavis Hofmann, Aug. 14, 1948; children: Catherine, Ronald. B.A., Rhodes U., South Africa, 1934, M.A., 1935, Diploma in Edn., 1936; Ph.D. (Union scholar), U. London, 1940; DLitt (hon.), St. Joseph's U., Phila., 1989. Lectr. in English Rhodes U., South Africa, 1937, U. Hong Kong, 1940-41, U. Melbourne, Australia, 1946-48; sr. lectr.-in-charge U. Natal, Durban, 1949-55; prof., head English dept. U. Coll., Rhodesia, 1955-65; dean Faculty Arts and Edn. U. Coll., 1957-60, 63-64; prof., head English dept. Laurentian U., Ont., Can., 1965-66; prof. English Queen's U., Kingston, Ont., 1966-80; emeritus prof. Queen's U., 1980—, dir. grad. studies in English, 1967-73, chmn. council grad. studies, 1971-73, chmn. editorial bd. Yeats Studies, 1972-74; Exec. Central Africa Drama League, 1959-65; mem. exec. com. Can. Assn. Irish Studies, 1968-73. Author: South African Travel Literature in the 17th Century, 1955, The Outlook for English in Central Africa, 1960, Hopkins, 1968, A Reader's Guide to G.M. Hopkins, 1981; editor: (with W.H. Gardner) The Poems of Gerard Manley Hopkins, 1967, rev. edit., 1970; Poems by Hopkins, 1974, U. Natal Gazette, 1954-55, The Early Poetic Manuscripts and Notebooks of Gerard Manley Hopkins in Facsimile, 1989, The Poetical Works of Gerard Manley Hopkins, 1990, rev. 1992, The Later Poetic Manuscripts of G.M. Hopkins in Facsimile, 1991; contbr.: chpts. to Testing the English Proficiency of Foreign Students, 1961, English Studies Today-Third Series, 1963, Sphere History of English Literature, Vol. VI, 1970, rev. edit., 1987, Readings of the Wreck of the Deutschland, 1976, Festschrift for E.R. Seary, 1975, British and American Literature 1880-1920, 1976, Myth and Reality in Irish Literature, 1977, Dispersal and Renewal: Hong Kong University during the War Years, 1998; articles to Internat. Rev. Edn., Bull. Inst. Hist. Research, Times Lit. Supplement, Modern Lang. Quar., Queen's Quar., others. Served with Hong Kong Vol. Def. Corps, 1940-45; prisoner of war, China and Japan 1941-45. Brit. Council scholar, 1954; Killam sr. fellow, 1979-81; Martin D'Arcy lectr. Oxford U., 1988-89. Fellow Royal Soc. Can.; mem. English Assn. Rhodesia (pres. 1957-65), So. Rhodesia Drama Assn. (vice chmn. 1957-65), Hopkins Soc. (pres. 1972-75), Yeats Soc. (life), MLA (life), Internat. Hopkins Assn. (bd. scholars 1979—), Queen's U. Saturday Club (sec. 1977-97). Home: 416 Windward Pl, Kingston, ON Canada K7M 4E4

MACKENZIE-SMITH, SYDNEY (LORD WHITFORD), marketing and financial executive; b. Sheffield, Eng., June 25, 1937; s. Sydney and Amy Laura (Brown) Mac: m. Jutta Von Zitzewitz, Apr. 19, 1963; children: Sigrid, Oliver. FCA, Brit. Inst. of Chartered Accts., London, 1958; ATII, Brit. Inst. of Taxation, London, 1959; F. Inst. SMM, Brit. Inst. of Sales, Mktg. and Mgmt., London, 1982; PhD, U. London, 1998. Dep. mng. dir. S. Casket, P.L.C., Manchester, Eng., 1963-85; dir. Eltec Svcs., Ltd., Bradford, Eng., 1984-89; chmn. Pathfinder Mktg., Chester, Eng., 1982—; cons. to Can. Govt.; underwriting mem. Lloyds of London, 1977—. Author: How to Stop Smoking the American Way, 1984, The Profit Program, 1994, Kitchens of the World, 1995. treas. various charities. Mem. Mensa. Avocations: bridge, golf, travel, writing financial articles for Canadian mags.

MACKEOWN, PATRICK KEVIN, physicist, educator; b. Dublin, Ireland, Feb. 9, 1940; s. Michael and Mary Ann (Byrne) M.; m. Kitty K. Woo, Apr. 3, 1993. BSc, Nat. U., Ireland, 1962; PhD, U. Durham, Eng., 1966. Postdoctoral fellow Tata Inst. Fundamental Rsch., Bombay, 1966; rsch. asst. prof. La. State U., Baton Rouge, 1967-68; rsch. assoc. U. Md., 1969-70; lectr. U. Hong Kong, 1970-93, reader, prof., 1993—; vis. scholar U. Maoyr de San Andres, La Paz, Bolivia, 1969. Author: (with D.J. Newman) Computational Techniques in Physics, 1987, Stochastic Simulation in Physics, 1997. Fellow Inst. Physics. Avocation: philately. Office: U Hong Kong Dept Physics, Pokfulam, Hong Kong China

MACKERRAS, SIR (ALAN) CHARLES (MACLAURIN), conductor; b. Schenectady, N.Y., Nov. 17, 1925; s. Alan Patrick and Catherine Mackerras; m. Helena Judith Wilkins, 1947; 2 children. Student, Sydney Conservatorium Music, Australia, 1938-42; student with Vaclav Talich, Prague Acad. Music, 1947-48; DMus (hon.), U. Hull, 1990, U. Nottingham, 1991, U. Brno, Czech Republic, 1994, York (Eng.) U., 1994, Griffith U., Brisbane, Australia, 1994, Oxford (Eng.) U., 1997, Prague Acad. Music, 1999, Napier U., Scotland, 2000. Prin. oboist Sydney (Australia) Symphony Orch., 1943-46; staff condr. English Nat. Opera (formerly Sadler's Wells Opera), London, 1948-54, musical dir., 1970-77; prin. condr. BBC Concert Orch., 1954-56; first condr. Hamburg Opera, 1966-69; chief guest condr. BBC Symphony Orch., 1976-79; chief condr. Sydney Symphony Orch., Australian Broadcasting Commn., 1982-85; prin. guest condr. Royal Liverpool Philharm. Orch., 1986-88; prin. guest condr. Scottish Chamber Orch., 1992-95, condr. laureate, 1995—; music dir. Orch. of St. Luke's, 1998—; freelance condr. with most Brit. and many continental orchs., concert tours USSR, South Africa, N.Am., Australia, 1957-66, U.S. coast-to-coast, 1983; prin. guest condr. San Francisco Opera, 1993-96, Royal Philharm. Orch., 1993-96; prin. guest condr. Czech Philharm. Orch., 1997—; mus. dir. Welsh Nat. Opera, 1987-92, condr. emeritus, 1993—; appearances at internat. festivals and opera houses; frequent radio and TV broadcasts; comml. recordings, notably Handel, Mozart operas and symphonies, Janácek, Brahms, Beethoven and Schubert. Published ballet arrangements Pineapple Poll (Sullivan), Lady and the Fool (Verdi), reconstrn. Sullivan's lost Cello Concerto; contbr. appendices to book: A Musicians' Musician, articles to Opera Mag., Music and Musicians, other jours. Hon. fellow Royal Coll. Music, Royal Acad. Music, Trinity Coll. Music (London), Royal No. Coll. Music, St. Peter's Coll., Oxford, 1999; recipient Evening Standard award for opera, 1977, Janáček medal, 1978, Gramophone Record of Yr. award, 1977, 80, 1999, Grammy award for best opera recording, 1981, Gramophone Best Opera Recording awad, 1983, 84, 94, 99, prix Fondation Jacques Ibert, 1983, Record of Yr. award Stereo Rev., 1983, Chocs de l'Année award, 1998, Edison award, Preis der Deutschen Schallplattenkritik, Prix Caecilia, 1999, Royal Philharmonic Soc. Conducting award, 1999; Chopin prize and lifetime achievement award, Cannes Classical, awards at Midem, 2000; decorated comdr. Order Brit. Empire, 1974; decorated knight, 1979, Companion, Order of Australia, 1997, Medal of Merit Czech Republic, 1996. Office: Askonas Holt Ltd Lonsdale Chambers, 27 Chancery Ln, London WC2A 1PF, England

MACKEVIČIUS, VIGIRDAS, mathematician, researcher; b. Kaunas, Lithuania, Jan. 1, 1950; s. Jonas and Liudmila (Kazanaite) M.; m. Eugenija Kačenaite, Apr. 24, 1971; children: Jogaila, Aiste, Mažvydas. Diploma, Vilnius (Lithuania) U., 1972, D of Math., 1973, D habilitatus of math., 1987. Rsch. fellow Vilnius U., 1972-73, asst., 1973-78, docent, 1978-88, prof., 1988—. Author: Integral and Measure, 1998; contbr. articles to profl. jours. E-mail: vigirdas.mackevicius@maf.vu.lt. Office: Dept Math & Info Vilnius U, Naugarduko 24, 2600 Vilnius Lithuania

MACKEY, LEONARD BRUCE, lawyer, former diversified manufacturing corporation executive; b. Washington, Aug. 31, 1925; s. Stuart J. and Margaret B. (Browne) M.; m. Britta Beckhaus, Mar. 2, 1974; children—Leonard B., Cathleen C., Wendy F. B.E.E., Rensselaer Poly. Inst., 1945; J.D., George Washington U., 1950. Bar: D.C. 1951, N.Y. 1954. Instr. elec. engring. Rensselaer Poly. Inst., Troy, N.Y., 1946-47; patent examiner U.S. Patent Office, Washington, 1947-50; atty. Gen. Electric Co., Schenectady and N.Y.C., 1953-60; dir. licensing, asst. sec. ITT, N.Y.C., 1960-73; v.p., gen. patent counsel, dir. licensing ITT, 1973-90; of counsel Davis Hoxie Faithfull & Hapgood, N.Y.C., 1990-93; cons. licensing and tech. transfer Sarasota, Fla., 1994—. Mem. Recreation Commn., Rye, N.Y., 1966-67; mem. Planning Commn., 1967-70, 72-75, city councilman, 1970-71. Served with USNR, 1943-45; to lt. 1951-53. Mem. ABA (coun. mem., intellectual property law sect. 1989-93), Am. Intellectual Property Law Assn. (bd. mgrs. 1968-70, pres. 1982-83), Licensing Execs. Soc. U.S.A. (pres. 1978), Licensing Execs. Soc. Internat. (pres. 1986), Eta Kappa Nu, Am. Yacht Club (sec. 1968-70), N.Y. Yacht Club, Masons, Apawamis. Republican. Presbyterian. Office: 219 S Orange Ave Sarasota FL 34236-6801

MACKEY, RICK, dog musher; b. N.H., 1953; s. Dick Mackey; married; 1 child, Brenda. Kennel owner; 13th pl. finisher Iditarod, 1975, 23d pl. finisher, 1977, 8th pl. finisher, 1979, 9th pl. finisher, 1981, 11th pl. finisher, 1982, 1st pl. finisher, 1983, 29th pl. finisher, 1984, 5th pl. finisher, 1985, 7th pl. finisher, 1988, 8th pl. finisher, 1989, 12th pl. finisher, 1990, 9th pl. finisher, 1991, 8th pl. finisher, 1992, 3d pl. finisher, 1993; winner Coldfoot Classic, Kusko 300, SuValley 300. Recipient Fastest Time Safety to Nome award, 1981, 88, 89, 91, Humanitarian award, 1983, Gold Coast award, 1993; mem. of 1st father-son pair to win Iditarod race championships; Named winner Yukon Quest Race, 1997. *

MACKINNON, JOHN KENNETH, film and television studies educator; b. Inverness, Scotland, Dec. 11, 1942; s. John and Agnes Frances (MacKay) M. MA with 1st class honors, U. Edinburgh, Scotland, 1965; BLitt, U. Oxford, Eng., 1969; Diploma in Film Studies, U. London, 1979. Lectr. Greek U. London, 1968-69; lectr. classics Poly. of North London, 1972-84; lectr. film studies U. North London, 1984—, prof., 1991—. Author: Hollywood's Small Towns, 1984, Greek Tragedy Into Film, 1986, Misogyny in the Movies: The De Palma Question, 1990, The Politics of Popular Representation: Reagan, Thatcher, Aids and the Movies, 1992, Uneasy Pleasures: The Male as Erotic Object, 1997. Avocation: playing the piano. Office: University of North London, 166-220 Holloway Rd, London N7 8DB, England

MACKINTOSH, FREDERICK ROY, oncologist; b. Miami, Fla., Oct. 4, 1943; s. John Harris and Mary Carlotta (King) MacK.; m. Judith Jane Parnell, Oct. 2, 1961 (div. Aug. 1977); children: Lisa Lynn, Wendy Sue; m. Claudia Lizanne Flournoy, Jan. 7, 1984; 1 child, Gregory Warren. BS, MIT, 1964, PhD, 1968; MD, U. Miami, 1976. Intern then resident in gen. medicine Stanford (Calif.) U., 1976-78, fellow in oncology, 1978-81; asst. prof. med. U. Nev., Reno, 1981-85, assoc. prof., 1985-92, prof. medicine, 1992—. Contbr. articles to profl. jours. Fellow ACP; mem. Am. Soc. Clin. Oncology, Am. Cancer Soc. (pres. Nev. chpt. 1987-89, Washoe chpt. 1988-90), No. Nev. Cancer Coun. (bd. dirs. 1981-92), No. Calif. Cancer Program (bd. dirs. alt. 1983-87, bd. dirs. 1987-91). Avocation: bicycling. Office: Nev Med Group 781 Mill St Reno NV 89502-1320

MACKLIS, ROGER MITON, physician, educator, researcher; b. Stratford, Conn., Mar. 12, 1956; m. Carol Clark, July 25, 1987; children: Andrew Clark, Paul Clark Macklis. BS, MS, Yale U., 1978; MD, Harvard U., 1983. Diplomate Am. Bd. Radiation Oncology. Instr. Harvard Med. Sch., Boston, 1988-89, asst. prof. radiation oncology, 1989-93; dep. div. chief Children's Hosp., Boston, 1990-93; chmn. dept. radiation oncology Cleve. Clinic Found., 1993—; biomed. cons., Boston, 1989—; prof. radiology/radiation oncology Ohio State U., 1995—; assoc. prof. history of medicine Case Western Res. U., 1995—. Author: Manual of Introductory Clinical Medicine, 1984; contbr. articles to profl. jours. Recipient Resident Rsch. award ASTRO, 1988, Jr. Faculty Rsch. award Am. Cancer Soc., 1990. Mem. Radiation Rsch. Soc., Am. Soc. Clin. Oncology (Young Investigator award 1987), Am. Soc. Therapeutic Radiology and Oncology, Soc. of Chairs of Acad. Radiation Oncology Programs (treas., v.p., pres.). Achievements include research on new approaches to cancer treatment involving radioactively labeled molecules and novel technologies for minimizing medical errors in oncology. Office: Cleve Clinic Found Dept Radiation Oncology 9500 Euclid Ave Cleveland OH 44195-0001

MAĆKOWIAK, JAN MAREK, physicist, educator; b. Jaffa, Israel, Dec. 1, 1943; arrived in Poland, 1956; s. Alojzy and Helena (Haręża) M.; m. Ewa Maria Gryglewicz, Oct. 10, 1968 (div. Mar. 1992); children: Helena Nasierowska, Anna. MSc, Nicholas Copernicus U., Toruń, Poland, 1969, PhD, 1973, D habilitation, 1986. Asst. N. Copernicus U., Toruń, 1969-74, adj., 1974—. Contbr. articles to profl. jours. Scholar Brit. Coun., Queen Mary Coll., London, 1976; rsch. grantee State Coun. for Rsch., Toruń, 1995, 97. Avocations: skiing, tourism. Home: 87-100 Toruń Poland Office: N Copernicus U Inst Physics, Grudziadzka 5/7, 87-100 Toruń Poland

MAC LAREN, DAVID SERGEANT, manufacturing corporation executive, inventor; b. Cleve., Jan. 4, 1941; s. Albert Sergeant and Theadora Beidler (Potter) MacL.; children: Alison, Catherine, Carolyn. AB in Econs., Miami U., Oxford, Ohio, 1964. Chmn. bd., pres., Jet Inc., Cleve., 1967—; founder, chmn. bd., pres. Air Injector Corp., Cleve., 1966-78; founder, pres., chmn. bd. Fluid Equipment, Inc., Cleve., 1966-72; founder, chmn. bd., pres. T&M Co., Cleve., 1966-71, Alison Realty Co., Cleve., 1966—; chmn. bd., pres. Sergeant Realty, Inc., 1979-86; bd. dirs. Gilmore Industries, Cleve., 1975-77, MWL Systems, L.A., 1979-85; mem. tech. com. Nat. Sanitation Found., Ann Arbor, Mich., 1967-90. Patentee in field. Mem. Rep. State Cen. Com., 1968-72; bd. dirs. Cleve. State U. Found., 1986-90. Served with arty. AUS, 1964-66. Fellow Royal Soc. Health (London); mem. Nat. Environ. Health Assn., Am. Pub. Health Assn., Nat. Water Pollution Control Fedn., Cen. Taekwondo Assn. (2d Dan), Jiu-Jitsu/Karati Black Belt Fedn. (black belt instr.), Mercedes Benz Club N.Am. (pres. 1968), H.B. Leadership Soc. (sch. headmaster soc., devel. com. 1976-78), SAR, Soc. Mayflower Descendants, Delta Kappa Epsilon (nat. bd. dirs. 1974-86, dir. Kappa chpt. 1969—),

Mentor Harbor Yachting Club, The Country Club, Cotillion Soc., Union League Club (N.Y.C.), Yale Club (N.Y.C.), Deke Club (N.Y.C.), N.Y. Acad. Scis. Office: Jet Inc 750 Alpha Dr Cleveland OH 44143-2167

MACLAREN, WILLIAM GEORGE, JR., engineering executive; b. Chgo., May 6, 1928; s. William George Sr. and Dorothy Pauline (Costello) MacL.; m. Marie Lorraine Logan, Sept. 15, 1951 (div. Dec. 1977); children: Vanessa Ann MacLaren-Wray, Jon Mark, Scott William; m. Mary Patricia Loftus, Dec. 22, 1977 (div. Oct. 1995); m. Brigitte Hildegard Krakau, Apr. 19, 1997. BS in Indsl. Engring., U. Pitts., 1951; MS in Indsl. Engring., Syracuse U., 1958; PhD in Indsl. Mgmt., Columbia Pacific U., 1989. Commd. 2nd lt. USAF, 1951, advanced through grades to major gen., 1974; comdr. 5BW Minot AFB, N.D., 1972-74; chief of staff 15 AF, 1975; comdr. Pacific Comm. Area, 1975-78; vice comdr. Air Force Comm. Command, 1978-79; dir. Command Control and Comm. Hdqs. USAF, 1979-81; dir. Comm. and Info. Sys. NATO, 1981-84; ret. USAF, 1984; v.p. Gia, Inc., Arlington, Va., 1984-90, 93-95; dir. gen. NATO/NATO Air Command and Control Mgmt. Agy., Brussels, 1990-93; v.p. BEI, Inc., Alexandria, Va., 1995—. Contbr. articles to profl. jours. Regional bd. dirs. Boy Scout Am., Minot, N.D., 1972-74. Named Disting. Engring. Alumnus U. Pitts., 1986. Mem. AIAA, Inst. Indsl. Engrs., Air Force Assn., Armed Forces Comm. and Electronics Assn. (regional v.p. 1975-78, Gold medal 1983), Am. Def. Preparedness Assn., Order of Daedalians (chpt. pres. 1976-78, merit award 1979), Rotary. Republican. Avocations: golf, long distance bicycling, private flying. Home: 438 N Park Dr Arlington VA 22203-2344 Office: BEI Inc 1800 Diagonal Rd Ste 510 Alexandria VA 22314-2840

MACLEAN, BABCOCK, lawyer; b. N.Y.C., Jan. 26, 1946; s. Charles Chalmers and Lee Selden (Howe) MacL.; m. Cynthia Gannon, Feb. 15, 1983. BA, Yale U., 1967; MA, Columbia U., 1970; JD, Case Western Res. U., 1975; LLM in Taxation, NYU, 1987. Bar: Ohio 1975, N.Y. 1983. Assoc. Hadley, Matia, Mills & MacLean, Cleve., 1976-77, mem., 1977-83; tax editor Rsch. Inst. Am., N.Y.C., 1983-85; assoc. Robinson Borg, N.Y.C., 1985-86, mem., 1987—; adj. asst. prof. taxation Pace U., N.Y.C., 1983-84; adv. bd. Rsch. Inst. Am., 1992-97. Mem. ABA (sect. taxation), N.Y. State Bar Assn. (sect. taxation), Assn. Bar City N.Y., Yale Club, St. Anthony Club, N.Y. Yacht Club, Seawanhaka Corinthian Yacht Club, St. Andrew's Soc. N.Y., Pilgrims of the U.S. Republican. Episcopalian. Home: 77 W 55th St New York NY 10019-4910 Office: Robinson Brog 1345 Avenue Of The Americas New York NY 10105-0144

MACLEOD, SIR (NATHANIEL WILLIAM) HAMISH, former Hong Kong government official; b. Jan. 6, 1940; arrived in Scotland, 1995; s. George Henry Torquil Macleod and Ruth Natalie Wade; m. Fionna Mary Campbell, 1970; 2 children. MA in Social Sci. with Honors, U. St. Andrews; diploma of Social Sci. in Sociology, U. Bristol, Eng. Comml. trainee Stewarts & Lloyds, Birmingham, 1958-62; adminstrv. officer Govt. Hong Kong, 1966-83, dir. trade, chief trade negotiator, 1983-87, sec. trade and industry, 1987-89, sec. treasury, 1989-91, justice of peace, fin. sec., 1991-95; ret., 1995; non-exec. dir. bd. Scottish Oriental Smaller Co., Fleming Asia Trust, Scottish Cmty. Found. Decorated knight Order of Brit. Empire. Fellow Chartered Inst. Secs.; mem. Hong Kong Club, Hong Kong Yacht Club, Kilspindie Golf Club. Avocations: golf, walking. Home: 20 York Rd, Edinburgh EH5 3EH, Scotland

MACLEOD, JAMES L., minister, finance executive, gallery owner; b. Oakdale, La., Apr. 27, 1937; s. William Lasater and Sara Louise (Macaulay) MacL. BA, Washington and Lee U., 1959; MA, BD, Emory U., 1968; D. Miss. State U., 1972. Minister U.S.-So. Presbyn. Ch., 1963-85, minister assoc. reform synod, 1985—; educator Ga. State Schs., 1972-91; pres. Brunswick (Ga.) Fin., 1991—, Brunswick Gallery, 1993—; min. First Assoc. Reformed Pres. Ch., Augusta, Ga., 1988-2000. Author: Great Dr. Waddel, 1985, A Season of Grace, 1974, Presbyterian Tradition in the South, 1978. Mem. Soc. of the Cin., Washington, 1970; councilman City of Brunswick, 1994—, mayor pro tem, 1996—. Scholar Fulbright Commn., Calcutta, India, 1980, NEH, Sarasota, Fla., 1986. Fellow Soc. of Antiquaries Scotland; mem. NEA, Ga. Assn. Edn., Pinnacle Club, Phi Delta Kappa. Democrat. Presbyterian. Home: Centennial House 304 Singleton Ave Sylvania GA 30467-1847 Office: Centennial House 508 Walke Augusta GA 30901-2316

MACLEOD, JEAN SUTHERLAND (CATHERINE AIRLIE), writer; b. Glasgow, Scotland, Jan. 20, 1908; d. John and Elizabeth (Allen) Mac Leod; m. Lionel Walton, Jan. 1, 1935; 1 child, David. Sec. British Ministry of Labor, Newcastle upon Tyne, England, 1930-35; writer, 1935—. Author: Life for Two, 1936 Human Sympathy 1937, Summer Rain, 1938, Sequel to Youth, 1938, Mist Across the Hills, 1938, Dangerous Obsession, 1939, The Whim of Fate, 1940, Lonely Furrow, 1940, Heatherbloom, 1940, Reckless Pilgrim, 1941, Shadow of a Vow, 1941, One Way Out, 1941, Forbidden Rapture, 1941, Penalty for Living, 1942, Blind Journey, 1942, Bleak Heritage, 1942, Reluctant Folly, 1942, Unseen Tomorrow, 1943, The Rowan Tree, 1943, Flower O' the Bloom, 1943, Circle of Doubt, 1943, Lamont of Ardgoyne, 1944, Two Paths, 1944, Brief Fulfillment, 1945, This Much to Give, 1945, One Love, 1945, Tranquil Haven, 1946, Sown in the Wind, 1946, House of Oliver, 1947, And We in Dreams, 1947, Chalet in the Sun, 1948, Ravenscrag, 1948, Above the Lattice, 1949, Tomorrow's Bargain, 1949, Katherine, 1950, The Valley of Palms, 1950, Roadway to the Past, 1951, Once to Every Heart, 1951, Cameron of Gare, 1952, Music at Midnight, 1952, The Silent Valley, 1953, The Stranger in their Mist, 1953, Dear Doctor Everett, 1954, The Man in Authority, 1954, After Long Journeying, 1955, Master of Glenkeith, 1955, The Prisoner of Love, 1958, Gated Road, 1959, Air Ambulance, 1959, The Little Doctor, 1960, The White Cockade, 1960, The Silver Dragon, 1961, The Country of the Heart, 1961, Slave of the Wind, 1962, The Dark Fortune (Cartland Hist. Novel award 1962), Sugar Island, 1964, The Black Cameron, 1965, Crane Castle, 1965, The Wolf of Heimra, 1965, The Drummer of Corrae, 1966, The Tender Glory, 1967, Lament for a Lover, 1967, The Master of Keills, 1967, The Bride of Mingulay, 1967, The Moonflower, 1967, Summer Island, 1968, The Joshua Tree, 1970, The Way through the Valley, 1970, The Fortress, 1970, The Scent of Juniper, 1971, Light in the Tower, 1971, Moment of Decision, 1972, Adam's Wife, 1972, Time Suspended, 1973, Rainbow Days, 1973, Over the Castle Wall, 1974, The Phantom Pipes, 1975, Island Stranger, 1977, Viking Song, 1977, The Ruag Inheritance, 1978, Search for Yesterday, 1978, Meeting in Madrid, 1979, Brief Enchantment, 1979, Black Sand, White Sand, 1980, Moreton's Kingdom, 1981, Cruel Deception, 1982, Zamora, 1982, A Distant Paradise, 1983, Beyond the Reef, 1983, Valley of the Snows, 1985, The Olive Grove, 1985, The Apollo Man, 1986, After the Hurricane, 1986, Call Back the Past, 1988, Legacy of Doubt, 1989, Shadow on the Hills, 1989, Tidal Wave, 1990, Flame of Avila, 1990, Home to the Hills, 1991, A Handful of Shells, 1993, The Jade Pagoda, 1993, Keeper of the Trees, 1995, Lovesome Hill, 1996; (as Catherine Airlie) The Wild Macraes, 1948, From Such a Seed, 1949, The Restless Years, 1950, Fabric of Dreams, 1951, Strange Recompense, 1952, The Green Rushes, 1953, Hidden in the Wind, 1953, Wind Sighing, 1954, Nobody's Child, 1954, The Valley of Desire, 1955, The Ways of Love, 1955, The Mountain of Stars, 1956, Unguarded Hour, 1956, Land of Heart's Desire, 1957, Red Lotus, 1958, The Last of the Kintyres, 1959, Shadow on the Sun, 1960, One Summer's Day, 1961, In the Country of the Heart, 1961, The Unlived Year, 1962, Passing Strangers, 1963, The Wheels of Chance, 1964, The Sea Change, 1965, Lonesome Hill, 1996, others. Pres. Nat. Soc. for Prevention of Cruelty to Children (Alne Tollerton br.). Mem. Romantic Novelists Assn., Soc. Yorkshire Bookmen, Women of Scotland, Clan MacLeod Soc., St. Andrew Soc. Presbyterian. Office: Rose Garth, Thornton-Le-Beans, North Yorkshire England*

MACLEOD, JOHN AMEND, lawyer; b. Manila, June 5, 1942; s. Anthony Macaulay and Dorothy Lillian (Amend) M.; m. Ann Klee; children: Kerry, Jack. BBS, U. Notre Dame, 1963, JD, 1969. Bar: D.C. 1969, U.S. Supreme Ct. 1980. Assoc. Jones, Day, Reavis & Pogue, Washington, 1969-73, ptnr., 1974-79; ptnr. Crowell & Moring, Washington, 1979—; mem. mgmt. com., 1979-82, 83-86, 91-94, 99-2000, chmn., 1984-85, 93-94. mem. mgmt. bd. and exec. com., 2000—, chmn. of the firm, 2000—. Editor-in-chief Notre Dame Law Rev., 1968-69; contbr. articles to profl. jours. Trustee, exec. com. Estn. Mineral Law Found.; bd. dirs. St. Francis Ctr., 1982-91, C&M Internat., 1991-94, 99—. Served to lt. U.S. Army, 1963-65. Recipient disting. mining lawyer award Nat. Mining Assn., 1995, forest industry victory of yr. award Am. Forest and Paper Assn., 1994. Mem. ABA, D.C. Bar Assn., Notre Dame Law Assn. (dir., exec. bd.), Ptnrs. Leadership Forum, Metro. Club (Washington). Home: 4040 Swartz Rd Maurertown VA 22644-2320 Office: Crowell & Moring 1001 Pennsylvania Ave NW Fl 10 Washington DC 20004-2595

MACLEOD, SANDRA DAWN CATHERINE, communications research executive; b. Montreal, Can., Sept. 13, 1959; d. Patrick Hugh Henderson Macleod and Francoise Willemhe Donny Andreej; m. Michael Stuart Arnold, May 16, 1987; children: Felicity, Christopher. BA in Pub. Rels. with honors, Mt. St. Vincent U., Montreal, 1981. Pub. rels. exec. Northern Telecom, Montreal, 1979-80; acct. exec. Info. et Enterprise, Paris, 1981-83; acct. group mgr. Edelman Pub. Rels., London, 1983-88; head of pub. rels. PA Mgmt. Cons., London, 1985-88; mng. dir. Hays Macleod, London, 1988-90; mng. dir. Europe CARMA Internat., London, 1990—; chief exec. Echo Rsch., London, 1999—; trustee IPRF, 1996-98; bd. adv. U. Sterling, 1997—. Author: How Far Will You Go for Total Quality. Non exec. dir. Bus. Links Surrey, Eng., 1998-99. Fellow Inst. Pub. Rels.; mem. Internat. Pub. Rels. Assn., Inst. Pub. Rels. Found., London Sch. Econs. Comm. Rsch. Forum (founder 1997). Avocations: skiing, tennis. Office: Echo Research, Friary Station Rd, Godalming GU7 1EX, England

MAC LOUGHLIN, ERNESTO SANTIAGO, internist, intensivist; b. Buenos Aires, Jan. 1, 1943; s. Ernesto Eduardo and Elena Irma (Alustiza) Mc L.; m. Marta Amalia Ceballos, Oct. 14, 1967; children: Ernesto Marcos, German Horacio, Sebastian, Jacqueline, Evelin, Fernando. Bachelor's, Nat. Coll., Rio Cuarto, Argentina, 1960. Med. diplomate, Argentina. Med. resident in internal medicine Jewish Hosp. and Med. Ctr., Bklyn., N.Y., 1977-79; chief intensive care unit Hosp. del Valle, Cordoba, Argentina, 1972-76, Hosp. Aeronautico, Cordoba, 1974—; asst. prof. medicine Cath. U. Cordoba, 1980-82; chief intensive care unit Hosp. Rawson, Cordoba, 1992—. Author (chpts. in books) Avances en Medicina 94, 1994, Program of Actualization, 1997; co-author (chpt. in book) Medical Emergencies, 1996, 98, Avances en Medicina, 2000; dir. El Vocero newspaper, 1960-61; contbr. articles to La Voz del Interior; contbr. articles to profl. jours. Vice-rector Jose Manuel Estrada U. Major Coll., Cordoba, 1966-68. Mem. Córdoba Intensive Care Soc. (pres. 1989-90), Hemodialysis and Transplantation Assn. (pres. 1995-97), Internat. Critical Care Update (hon. pres. 1995), Am. Soc. Enteral and Parenteral Nutrition, Argentine Intensive Care Therapy, Argentine Nephroloy Soc. Roman Catholic. Avocations: swimming, shooting, tennis. FAX: 54-351-4814745.

MACMAHON, MICHAEL KENNETH COWAN, phonetics educator; b. Winchester, Eng., Aug. 7, 1943; s. Kenneth Austin and Alice (Cowan) MacM.; m. Janet Phillips Hotchkies Gallacher, Sept. 4, 1968; children: Caroline, Kenneth. BA, U. Durham, Eng., 1965; diploma in linguistics, U. Reading, Eng., 1966; PhD, U. Glasgow, Scotland, 1982. Lectr. in phonetics and linguistics Jordanhill Coll. Edn., Glasgow, 1966-72; lectr. in phonetics and linguistics U. Glasgow, 1972-83, lectr. in English lang., 1983-86, sr. lectr. in English lang., 1986-97, prof. phonetics, 1997—. Author: Basic Phonetics, 1988; contbr. articles to profl. jours. Elder Ch. of Scotland. Mem. Philol. Soc., Internat. Phonetic Assn., Linguistics Assn. Great Britain, Brit. Assn. Acad. Phoneticians, Yorkshire Dialect Soc., Henry Sweet Soc., Royal Sch. Church Music, Elgar Soc. Avocations: singing, flute. Home: 6 Jubilee Gardens, Bearsden Glasgow G61 2RT, Scotland Office: U Glasgow, Dept English Language, Strathcl Glasgow G12 8QQ, Scotland

MACMANUS, SUSAN ANN, political science educator, researcher; b. Tampa, Fla., Aug. 22, 1947; d. Harold Cameron and Elizabeth (Riegler) MacM. BA cum laude, Fla. State U., 1968, PhD, 1975; MA, U. Mich., 1969. Instr. Valencia C.C., Orlando, Fla., 1969-73; rsch. asst. Fla. State U., 1973-75; asst. prof. U. Houston, 1975-79, assoc. prof., 1979-85, dir. MPA program, 1983-85; rsch. assoc. Ctr. Pub. Policy, 1982-85; prof., dir. PhD progam Cleve. State U., 1985-87; prof. pub. adminstrn. and polit. sci. U. South Fla., Tampa, 1987—, chair dept. govt. and internat. affairs, 1987-93, disting. univ. prof., 1999; vis. prof. U. Okla., Norman, 1981—; field rsch. assoc. Brookings Inst., Washington, 1977-82, Columbia U., summer, 1979, Princeton (N.J.) U., 1979—, Nat. Acad. Pub. Adminstrn., Washington, summer, 1980, Cleve. State U., 1982-83, Westat, Inc., Washington, 1983—. Author: Revenue Patters in U.S. Cities and Suburbs: A Comparative Analysis, 1978, Federal Aid to Houston, 1983, (with others) Governing A Changing America, 1984, (with Francis T. Borkowski) Visions for the Future: Creating New Institutional Relationships Among Academia, Busines, Government, and Community, 1989, Reapportionment and Representation in Florida: A Historical Collection, 1991, Doing Business with Government: Federal, State, Local and Foreign Government Purchasing Practices for Every Business and Public Institution, 1992, Young v. Old: Generational Combat in the 21st Century, 1996, (with Elizabeth R. McManus) Citurs, Sawmills, Critters & Crackers: Life in Early Lutz and Central Pasco County, 1998, Targeting Senior Voters, 2000, The Lutz Depot (with Elizabeth R. McManus), 2000; writer manuals in field; mem. editl. bds. various jours.; contbr. articles to jours., chpts. to books. Bd. dirs. Houston Area Women's Ctr., 1977, past pres., v.p. fin., treas.; mem. LWV, Gov.'s Coun. Econ. Advisers, 1988-90, Harris County (Tex.) Women's Polit. Caucus, Houston; bd. dirs. USF Rsch. Found., Inc.; chair Fla. Elections Commn., 1999—. Recipient U. Houston Coll. Social Scis. Tchg. Excellence award, 1977, Herbert J. Simon award for best article in 3d vol., Internat. Jour. Pub. Adminstrn., 1981, Theodore & Venette Askounes-Ashford Disting Scholar award U. South Fla., 1991, Disting. Rsch. Scholar award, 1991, Tchg. Excellence award, 1999; Ford Found. fellow, 1967-68; grantee Valencia C. C. Faculty, 1972, U. Houston, 1976-77, 79, 83; Fulbright Rsch. scholar, Korea, 1989; Choice mag. award, 1996; named Disting. Univ. Prof., 1999; rsch. fellow Fla. Inst. of Govt., 2000—. Mem. Am. Polit. Sci. Assn. (program com. 1983-84, chair sect. intergovtl. rels., award 1989, mem. exec. coun. 1994—, pres.-elect sec. urban politics 1994-95, pres. sect. urban politics 1995-96), So. Polit. Sci. Assn. (v.p. 1990-91), pres.-elect 1992-93, pres. 1993-94, V.O. key award com. 1983-84, best paper on women and politics 1988), Midwest Polit. Sci. Assn., Western Polit. Sci. Assn., Southwestern Polit. Sci. Assn. (local arrangements com. 1982-83, profession com. 1977-80), ASPA (nominating com. Houston chpt. 1983, bd. mem. Suncoast chpt., pres.-elect 1991, Lilly award 1992), Policy Studies Orgn. (mem. editl. bd. jour. 1981—, exec. coun. 1983-85), Women's Caucus Polit. Sci. (portfolio pre-decision rev. com. 1982-83, prjects and programs com. 1981, fin.-budget com. 1980-81), Fla. Polit. Sci. Assn. (pres. 1997-98), Acad. Polit. Sci., Mcpl. Fin. Officers Assn., Phi Kappa Phi (Artist/Scholar award U. South Fla. 1997), Phi Beta Kappa, Pi Sigma Alpha (mem. exec. oun. 1994-96, pres. 2000—), Pi Alpha Alpha. Methodist. Home: 2506 Collier Pky Land O'Lakes FL 34639-5228 Office: U South Fla Dept Polit Sci Tampa FL 33620

MACMILLAN, ANGUS CAMPBELL, English military officer; b. Glasgow, Scotland, July 21, 1962; s. Angus Campbell and Margaret Curran (McHenry) MacM.; m. Fiona Kathleen London, Dec. 17, 1989 (div. Sept. 1989); 1 child, Scott Angus; m. Hayley Amanda Paterson, Dec. 12, 1992; children: Megan Louise, Shannon Marie. Pvt. English Army, Dover, Eng., 1979-80; cpl. English Army, Plymouth, Eng., 1980-88; sgt. Rochester, Eng., 1988-92; staff sgt. Wimbish, Eng., 1992-97; WOZ Def. Sch., Rochester, Eng., 1997-99, Nat. Search Ctr., Rochester, 1999—. Mem. IMCE. Roman Catholic. Avocations: running, skiing, climbing, weight training. Office: Nat Search Ctr, Lodge Hill Camp, Kent Rochester ME3 8NZ, England

MACMILLAN, DAVID PAUL, retired oil company executive; b. East Orange, N.J., Nov. 16, 1943; s. Hugh Dame and Marie Ann (Hahn) MacM.; m. Rosemary Longo, Nov. 16, 1969; children: Melanie, Hugh. With Exxon Rsch. and Engring. Co., various locations, 1969-85; sect. head Exxon Rsch. and Engring. Co., Florham Park, N.J., 1978-80; project mgr. Exxon Rsch. and Engring. Co., Denver, 1980-82; spl. assignment to sr. gen. mgr. Exxon Rsch. and Engring. Co., Florham Park, 1982-83; project mgr.-Belgium Exxon Rsch. and Engring. Co., 1983-85; engring. mgr. Exxon Rsch. and Engring. Co., U.K., 1993-95, mgr. spl. projects divsn., 1996-97, mgr. project mgmt. divsn., 1996-97; project dir. Japan Exxon Rsch. and Engring. Co., 1997-99; staff advisor controllers dept., Exxon Co. Internat., Florham Park, N.J., 1986-88, sr. advisor materials dept., 1991-93; materials mgr. Exxon Cen. Svcs., Florham Park, 1989-91. Served with USMC, 1961-65. Mem. Nat. Assn. Purchasing Mgrs., Am. Soc. Quality Control, Tokyo Am. Club, Kyokawa Country Club, Tau Beta Pi, Pi Tau Sigma. Republican. Presbyterian. Home: PO Box 101 Florham Park NJ 07932-0101

MACNALLY, ROBERT FALCONER, II, retired sports equipment company executive; b. Evanston, Ill., Apr. 28, 1932; s. Maxwell Falconer and Dorothy Hosmer (Nelson) MacN.; m. Elizabeth Weeks, June 30, 1956; children: Robert F. III, Susan E., Anne M. Goto, William N. AB in Chemistry, Dartmouth Coll., 1953; MBA, Harvard Bus. Sch., 1958. With W.R. Grace & Co., Cambridge, Mass., 1958-69; with Ideal Roller Co., Chgo., 1969-73, pres., 1973-74; v.p., gen. mgr. Sta-Hi Sys., Nashua, N.H., 1974-76; pres. chem. group Kinark Corp., Hinsdale, Ill., 1976-79; pres., CEO Tommy Armour Golf Co., Morton Grove, Ill., 1979-95, chmn., 1995-97; ret., 1997; bd. dirs. Adams Golf Co., Plano, Tex., C.O. Tools, Inc., Elkhart, Ind. Patentee weight-balanced golf clubs. Bd. dirs. emeritus, chmn. Nat. Golf Found., Jupiter, Fla., 1979—; chmn. The Cmty. House, Hinsdale, 1985-86, Midwest Indsl. Mgmt. Assn., Westchester, 1988-89; bd. dirs., treas. Chgo. Boys & Girls Clubs, 1971—; sr. warden Grace Episcopal Ch., Hinsdale, 1996-99. Lt. (j.g.) USN, 1953-56, Korea. Recipient Herb Graffis award Nat. Golf Found., 1992, John F. Atkinson award Chgo. Boys & Girls Clubs, 1989, Ernie Sabayrac award PGA of Am., Palm Beach Gardens, Fla., 1997; named to Ill. PGA Hall of Fame, 1991, Golf Father of Yr., Golfweek Mag., Orlando, 1992. Mem. Hinsdale Golf Club (bd. dirs. 1977—). Republican. Episcopalian. Avocations: golf, travel, photography. E-mail: rfmacnally@aol.com. Home: 750 Wilson Ln Hinsdale IL 60521-4842

MACNAMARA, THEREZA MARIA, engineer; b. Bombay, India; d. Crescencio and Aurea (Dias) L.; m. Thomas Edmund, Oct. 8, 1966; children: David, John, Louise Marie. BS, U. Surrey, U.K., 1963; MS, U. London, 1971. Microwave engr. Wayne-Kerr Labs., Tolworth, U.K., 1969-71, Bradley Electronics, London, 1971-72; patents examiner U.K. Patent Office, London, 1974-77; lectr. S. Thames Coll., Putney, 1978-84; sr. microwve engr. ERA, Leatherhead, U.K., 1984-90; electromagnetics specialist sys. engr. British Aerospace, Farnborough, U.K., 1990—. Author: (book) Antennas for EMC, 1995; contbr. articles to profl. jours. Avocations: antiques, theatre, walking, reading. Office: BAE Systems, Farnborough Aerospace Cen, GU14 6YU Farnborough United Kingdom

MACNAUGHTON, JIMMY NORMAN, physicist, educator; b. Ann Arbor, Mich., Feb. 6, 1942; arrived in Austria, 1974; s. William Norman and Caroline Esther (Curtis) MacN.; m. Yumiko Takashima, Feb. 21, 1981. BS, Duke U., 1963; MA, U. Calif., Berkeley, 1965, PhD, 1971; postgrad., Monterey Inst. Fgn. Studies, 1965-67. Rschr. Cath. U., Nijmegen, The Netherlands, 1971-74; staff sci. Inst. for High Energy Physics Austrian Acad. Scis., Vienna, 1974—; fellow Japanese Soc. for Promotion Sci., Nat. Lab. for High Energy Physics, Tsukuba, Japan, 1981, vis. prof., Monbusho, 1990-91; spl. vis. prof. Tohoku U., Sendai, Japan, 1990, vis. prof., 1991-92. Contbr. articles to profl. jours. Mem. Austrian Phys. Soc., Japanese Phys. Soc., Austrian-Japanese Soc. Vienna, Phi Beta Kappa. Avocation: learning foreign languages. Office: Inst High Energy Physics, Nikolsdorfergasse 18, A-1050 Vienna Austria

MACNEILL, JOHN HARMON, mechanical engineer; b. Honolulu, Oct. 27, 1919; s. John Pehrson and Harriett Thelma (Harmon) MacN.; m. Margaret Elizabeth Benedict, Sept. 16, 1947; children: Jean Benedict, John Benedict. BS, U. Calif., Berkeley, 1942. Registered profl. engr., Calif. Mech. engr. Fairchild Engine & Airplane Corp., Oak Ridge, 1947-48, Raytheon Mfg. Co., Waltham, Mass., 1948-50; sr. engr. Air Force Missile Test Ctr., Patrick AFB, Fla., 1950-54; v.p. engring. Soroban Engring., Inc., Melbourne and Palm Bay, Fla., 1954-70, Optical Bus. Machines, Melbourne, 1970-82; sr. engr. Fla. Data Corp., Melbourne, 1982-88, Technoogy Svc. Group Inc., Melbourne, 1988-93; owner MacNeill Engring., 1995—; Careers Day presenter various schs., 1980-94; judge state sci. and engring. fairs Fla. Found. Future Scientists, 1980-00. Sponsor, organizer internat. sailing regatta, 1969-94. 1st lt. Ordnance, U.S. Army, 1942-46, PTO. Mem. ASME, Space Coast Personal Computer Users Group, Phi Beta Kappa, Sigma Xi, Tau Beta Pi. Republican. Achievements include patents for rack and pinion differential printer, high speed tape punch, high speed dot matrix printer, optical character reader. Avocations: restoring and repairing autos, sailing, listening to music. Home: 1320 S Riverside Dr Indialantic FL 32903-3553

MACNICOL, JOHN SIMSON, social policy educator, researcher; b. Madras, India, Nov. 13, 1947; (parents Brit. citizens); s. Robert Simson and Eona Kathleen (Fraser) M. MA, U. Edinburgh, Scotland, 1970, PhD, 1978. Lectr. social policy Bedford Coll., U. London, 1978-90, reader Royal Holloway Coll., 1990-99, prof., 1999—; adj. prof. London program Boston U., 1987—. Author: The Movement for Family Allowances, 1918-45, 1980, The Politics of Retirement, 1878-1948, 1998; co-editor: Aspects of Ageing, 1990; editor: Paying for Old Age, 1880s-1940s, 6 vols., 2000. Recipient award Econ. and Social Rsch. Coun., 1985, 89; Leverhulme fellow, 1997-98. Mem. Social Policy Assn., Social History Soc. Avocation: jazz trumpeter. Home: 90 Brondesbury Rd, London NW6 6RX, England Office: U London Royal Holloway Col, Dept Social Policy, Egham Surrey TW20 0EX, England

MACON, CAROL ANN GLOECKLER, micro-computer data base management company executive; b. Milw., Mar. 25, 1942; d. William Theodore and Gwendolyn Martha (Rice) Gloeckler; m. Jerry Lyn Macon, Aug. 28, 1981; children: Christian, Marie. BS in Edn. cum laude, U. Wis., Milw., 1969; postgrad., Midwestern State U., Wichita Falls, Tex., 1977, U. Tex., San Antonio, 1978, U. Colo., Colorado Springs. Tchr. Lubbock, Tex.; patient affairs coord. Cardiac Assocs., Colorado Springs; co-founder, CFO Macon Systems, Inc., Colorado Springs. Artist, Australia, Tex., Colo. Founding mem. Pikes Peak Botanic Gardens. Mem. Ikebana Internat. (chpt. 95), Colorado Springs Fine Arts Ctr., Pikes Peak Rose Soc. (v.p.), Colo. Mountain Club, Kissing Camels Garden Club, Phi Kappa Phi, Kappa Delta Pi, Sigma Tau Delta, Psi Chi.

MACOSKO, PAUL JOHN, II, psychotherapist; b. Erie, Pa., May 15, 1952; s. Paul Sr. and Susan Ann (Miraldi) M.; m. Marsha Gail Blystone, July 1, 1978; children: Paul John III, Benjamin Jamison. BA in Psychology, Mercyhurst Coll., 1976; postgrad., Grand Rapids Bapt. Bible Sem., and Edinboro U., 1976-78; MA in Bibl. Counseling, Grace Theol. Sem., Winona Lake, Ind., 1983; DPhil, Oxford U., 1992. Protective svc. caseworker I Trumbull County Children's Svcs. Bd., Warren, Ohio, 1976-77; counselor Regular Bapt. Children's Agy., St. Louis, 1978-81; coord. devel. dual diagnosis program Dr. Gertrude A. Barber Ctr., Erie, 1987-92; pvt. practice Erie, 1984-94; dir. Christian Care Ministry Grace Bapt. Ch., Erie, 1992-94; outpatient therapist The Achievement Ctr., Erie, 1994-97; supr., therapist Sarah A. Reed Children's Ctr., 1997—. Mem. ACA, Am. Assn. Christian Counselors, Assn. Religious and Value Issues in Counseling, Pa. Counseling Assn., Nat. Disting. Svc. Registry. Baptist. Avocations: reading, biking, hiking, fishing, camping. Office: 3933 Oxer Rd Erie PA 16505-3345

MACPHAIL, SIR BRUCE (DUGALD), navigation company executive; b. May 1, 1939; s. Dugald Ronald and Winifred Marjorie MacPhail; m. Susan Mary Gregory, 1963 (dec. 1975); 3 children; m. Caroline Ruth Grimston Curtis-Bennett Hubbard. MA, U. Oxford, Eng., 1969; MBA, Harvard U., 1967. With Price Waterhouse, 1961-65, Hill Samuel & Co. Ltd., 1967-69; fin. dir. Sterling Guarantee Trust Ltd., 1969-74; mng. dir. Town & City Properties Ltd., 1974-83, Sterling Guarantee Trust PLC, 1983-85, The Peninsular and Oriental Steam Navigation Co., London, 1985—. Gov. Royal Ballet Sch., 1982—; life gov., mem. coun. Haileybury Coll., 1992—, chmn. coun. Templeton Coll., Oxford, 1993-95; chmn. coun. Sch. Mgmt. Studies, U. Oxford, 1995—; trustee Sir Jules Thorn Charitable Trust, 1994—. Barclay fellow Templeton Coll., 1995—. Fellow Inst. Chartered Accts. Avocations: reading, wine, scuba diving. Office: Peninsular & Oriental Steam Navigation Co, 79 Pall Mall, London SW1Y 5EJ, England*

MACPHERSON, ELLE, model; b. Sydney, Australia, Mar. 29, 1964; m. Gilles Bensimon, May 24, 1986 (div.). Appeared on covers of Sports Illustrated swimsuit edit., 1986, 87, 88, 94, Elle, Cosmopolitan, Self; film appearences include Husbands and Wives, 1992, Sirens, 1994, If Lucy Fell, 1996, The Mirror Has Two Faces, 1996, The Edge, 1997, Batman and Robin, 1997, Beautopia, 1998, With Friends Like These, 1998; TV appearancein Friends, 1994. Office: Artist Mgmt Penn House B 414 E 52d St New York NY 10022

MACPHERSON, MARTIN DOUGLAS, defence consultancy company executive; b. London, July 27, 1945; s. Alexander Douglas and Norah (Watson) M.; m. Virginia Constance Edgar, Feb. 28, 1970; children: Nicholas

Douglas, Toby David. Grad., Britannia Royal Naval Coll., 1964. Cert. U.K. Bd. Trade. With Brit. Royal Navy, 1980-83, capt. HMS Trafalgar, 1980-84; capt. submarine sea tng. Brit. Royal Navy, Faslane, Scotland, 1988-90; dir. Def. Intelligence Svc. Brit. Royal Navy, London, 1990-93, dep. flag officer submarines, 1993-96; dir. naval ops. Royal Navy/Min. Def., 1996-98; CEO, mng. dir. Landair Internat. Ltd., Salisbury, Eng., 1998—, also bd. dirs. Nat. coord. Submarine Centennial Appeal, Portsmouth, Eng., 1999. Named Officer of Brit. Empire, Queen of Eng., 1984. Mem. Nautical Inst., Inst. Dirs. Mem. Ch. of Eng. Avocations: golf, military history, sports. Home: Springfield Cottage, Bedfield Ln, Winchester Hants SO23 7JQ, England Office: Landair Internat Ltd, Brickworth Ln Whiteparish, Salisbury Wiltshire SP5 2QE, England

MACPHERSON, SHIRLEY, clinical therapist; b. Bayonne, N.J., June 16, 1934; d. Alexander Phillip and Milldred (Gurstelle) Gottlieb; m. Duncan MacPherson, Jan. 2, 1981; children from previous marriage: Suzanne Pugsley, Brett Barber. BS, Columbia U., NYU, 1951; MS, Juilliard Sch. Music, 1955; MEd, Calif. State U., Northridge, 1967; MA in Psychology, Pepperdine U., 1992; PhD in Psychology, Pacific Western U., 1998. Concert pianist Norman Seman Prodns., N.Y.C., 1952-61; indsl. health educator Am. Med. Internat., L.A., 1968-70; cons., lectr. Hosp. Mgmt. Corp., L.A., 1970-80; regional dir. Control Data Corp., L.A., 1980-86; outplacement specialist Ind. Cons., L.A., 1986-90; psychologist, intern Airport Marina Counseling Svcs., L.A., 1990-93; staff psychologist Forensic Psychology Assocs., Sherman Oaks, Calif., 1993-94; staff clin. psychologist Pacific Psychologist Assocs., L.A., 1992-94; clin. therapist employee profiling and crisis intervention MacPherson Relationship Counseling, L.A., 1993—. Author: Rx for Brides, 1990, Understanding Your Man, 1998. Vol. Cmty. Alliance to Support and Empower, L.A., 1994-96, South Bay Free Clinic, L.A., 1995-97; mem. Town and Gown Scholarship program, U. So. Calif., L.A. Mem. AAUW, APA, Calif. Psychol. Assn., L.A. Psychol. Assn., L.A. World Affairs Coun., Am. Bd. Hypnotherapy, Am. Assn. Humanistic Psychology, Am. Assn. Suidiology, Juilliard Alumni Assn., Pepperdine Allumni Assn., Internat. Wound Ballistics Assn. Avocations: French and Italian, piano, studies.

MACQUEEN, CHER, retired newscaster, sportscaster; b. Kansas City, Mo., Mar. 20, 1952; d. Ira Raymond and Peggy Estelle (Turner) Milks. AA in Liberal Arts, L.A. Valley Coll., 1982; BS in Broadcasting, U. New York, Albany, 1993; grad., Barbizon Sch. Modeling, 1996; postgrad., Calif. State U., San Bernardino, 1998—, U. Calif., Riverside, 1999. Lic. radio-TV operator. Personnel specialist U.S. Army, Honolulu, Hawaii, 1973-75; adminstrv. specialist U.S. Army, San Francisco, Calif., 1975-77; broadcast journalist U.S. Army, Vicenza, Italy, 1977-80; radio traffic specialist Armed Forces Radio and TV, L.A., 1980-84, radio prodn. specialist, 1984-86; supr. broadcast support specialist Armed Forces Radio and TV, Sun Valley, Calif., 1986-90; broadcast support mgr, Armed Forces Radio and TV, Sun Valley, 1990-91, internal info. mgr., 1991-94, news and sports specialist, 1994-99. Mem. DAV (life), Armed Forces Broadcasters Assn. (v.p. L.A., 1991-93), Women in Mil. Svc. for Am. (charter mem.), Pacific Pioneer Broadcasters. Avocations: handcrafts especially crochet. Home: PO Box 276 Highland CA 92346-0276

MACQUIBAN, TIMOTHY STUART ALEXANDER, Methodist minister, educator; b. Chester, Eng., Jan. 11, 1952; s. Gordon and Beryl (Davies) M.; m. Angela Spencer, July 26, 1975. Diploma in adminstrn. of archives, Liverpool (Eng.) U., 1974; MA, Cambridge (Eng.) U., 1977, Bristol (Eng.) U., 1986; PhD, Birmingham (Eng.) U., 2000. Ordained to ministry Methodist Ch., 1987. Borough archivist Doncaster, Eng., 1977-84; Meth. circuit min. Halifax, Eng., 1987-90; tutor in history Wesley Coll., Bristol, 1990-93; dir. Wesley and Meth. Studies Ctr. Westminster Inst., Oxford, Eng., 1993—, head of ch. and internat. rels., 1993-99; convenor archives and history com., Brit. Meth. Ch., 1986-96; sec. Oxford Inst. Meth. Theol. Studies, 1992—. Author: Methodist Prison Chaplains, 1994, Pure Universal Love: Reflections on the Wesleys and Inter-Faith Dialogue, 1995; editor: Methodism in Its Cultural Milieu, 1994, Issues in Education: Some Methodist Perspectives, 1996. Mem. World Meth. Hist. Soc. (v.p. 1996—). Liberal Democrat. Avocation: choral singing. E-mail: t.macquiban@ox-west.ac.uk. Home and Office: Wesley and Meth Stud Ctr, Westminster Inst Edn, Oxford OX2 9AT, England

MACRAE, CAMERON FARQUHAR, III, lawyer; b. N.Y.C., Mar. 21, 1942; s. Cameron F. and Jane B. (Miller) MacR.; m. Ann Wooster Bedell, Nov. 30, 1974; children: Catherine Fairfax, Ann Cameron. AB, Princeton U., 1963; LLB, Yale U., 1966. Bar: N.Y. 1966, D.C. 1967, U.S. Dist. Ct. (so. dist.) N.Y. 1975. Atty.-advisor Office of Gen. Counsel to Sec. Air Force, Washington, 1966-69; assoc. Davis, Polk & Wardwell, N.Y.C., 1970-72; dep. supt. and counsel N.Y. State Banking Dept., N.Y.C., 1972-74; sr. ptnr. LeBoeuf, Lamb, Greene & MacRae, N.Y.C., 1975—. Trustee, sec. St. Andrew's Dune Ch., 1982—; hon. chmn. Clear Pool Inc., 1990-94. Capt. USAF, 1966-69. Mem. Assn. of Bar of City of N.Y. (past mem. securities regulation com., banking law com.), D.C. Bar Assn. Republican. Episcopalian. Clubs: Racquet and Tennis, Union (N.Y.C.), Meadow (v.p., bd. govs.), Bathing Corp., Shinnecock Hills Golf (Southampton), Cottage (Princeton, N.J.). Note and comment editor Yale Law Jour., 1965-66. Office: LeBoeuf Lamb Greene & MacRae 125 W 55th St New York NY 10019-5369

MACREADIE, IAN GEOFFREY, biochemist; b. Richmond, Victoria, Australia, June 17, 1954; s. Geoffrey Thomas Macreadie and Reanie Tonkin Frith; m. Johann Louise Schriver, Mar. 20, 1976; children: Matthew, Peter, Rachel, Rebekah. BSc with honors, Monash U., Clayton, Australia, 1975, PhD, 1983. Postdoctoral fellow U. Tex. Health Sci. Ctr., Dallas, 1983-85; sr. rsch. scientist Commonwealth Sci. and Indsl. Rsch. Orgn., Parkville, Australia, 1985-90; prin. rsch. scientist Biomolecular Rsch. Inst., Parkville, Australia, 1990—; adj. prof. R.M.I.T. U., 1999;mem. course adv. com. Royal Melbourne (Australia) Inst. Tech. U., 1999; mem. sci. adv. com. Ctr. Molecular Biology and Medicine, Melbourne, 1999. Cub scout leader Australian Scouts, 1987-92; discussion leader Bible Study Fellowship Internat., Melbourne, 1996—. Recipient Brit. Coun. Travel award, 1991, Ramaciotti Travel award, 1998, Commonwealth Scientific and Indsl. Rsch. Org. Chmn.'s Medal, 1997; Fulbright Sr. scholar Fulbright Found., 1990. Mem. Australian Soc. Biochemistry and Molecular Biology (hon. sec. 1997—), Australian Soc. Microbiology (Frank Fenner Rsch. award 1995). Avocations: bushwalking, travel, skiing. Fax: 9662-7266. Office: Biomolecular Rsch Inst, 343 Royal Parade, Parkville Australia

MACRORIE, RODERICK ANDREW, physician; b. N.Y.C., June 5, 1960; arrived in Nepal, 1993; s. Norman Dallas and Ellen Mary (McLean) MacR.; m. Claire Elizabeth Kennerley, Dec. 28, 1962; children: Brian James, Daniel Owen, Matthew Henry. BA, Hertford Coll., Oxford, Eng., 1982; MB BCh, Oxford U., 1985. Cert. in tropical medicine and hygiene, child health, obgyn. House physician Royal Sussex County Hosp., Brighton, Eng., 1985; sr. house officer, accident and emergency St. James U. Hosp., Leeds, Eng., 1988, Royal Liverpool (Eng.) Children's Hosp., 1989; programme head Myagdi Dist. Hosp. Devel. Project, Nepal, 1994; project dir. Tb Leprosy Project, Surkhet, Nepal, 1997—; Contbr. articles to profl. jours. including Leprosy Revs., Brit. Med. Jour., Tropical Doctor. Macmillan scholar, 1979-82. Mem. Brit. Med. Assn., Christian Med. Fellowship, Royal Coll. Gen. Practitioners. Christian. Avocations: choral singing, cricket, Biblical hermeneutics. Office: Internat Nepal Fellowship, PO Box 1230, Kathmandu Nepal

MACRURY, KING, management counselor; b. Manchester, N.H., Oct. 14, 1915; s. Colin H. and Lauretta C. (Shea) MacR.; 1 son, Colin C. A.B., Rollins Coll., 1938; postgrad., St. Anselms Coll., L.I. Coll. Medicine, Princeton. Asst. personnel dir. Lily-Tulip Cup Corp., 1939; asst. dir. market research Ward Baking Co., 1940-41; staff mem. Nat. Indsl. Conf. Bd., 1941-43; cons. indsl. relations and orgn. planning McKinsey & Co., 1946-48; internal cons. Oxford Paper Co., 1949-50; installer, dir. indsl. relations Champion Internat. Co., 1950-51; pvt. practice mgmt. counselor, 1951—; lectr. Indsl. Edn. Inst., 1962-68, Mgmt. Center, Cambridge, 1968-71, Dun & Bradstreet, 1979—; extension div. U. N.H., 1968—; extension program U. Maine, 1978—; also U. Bridgeport, extension program U. Conn.; coordinator mgmt. edn. extension div. U. Conn., 1964-68, Philippine Council Mgmt., 1969—, Econ. Devel. Found. Philippines, 1969—, Am. Metal Stamping Assn., 1969—; condr. mgmt. seminars for Asian Assn. Mgmt. Orgns. C.I.O.S., 1972; Mem. Indsl. Devel. Commn. Andover, 1957-58; manpower com. U.S. Dept. Labor Bus. Adv. Council, 1958-61. Author: Developing Your People Potential; Contbr. numerous articles in field to profl. jours. Served to lt. USNR, 1943-46. Mem. N.H. Dental Soc. (hon.), Smaller Bus. Assn. N.E., Res. Officers Assn. Office: PO Box 215 Rye NH 03870-0215

MACURA, ANNA BARBARA, mycologist researcher, dermatologist; b. Kraków, Poland, Mar. 26, 1942; d. Piotr and Izabella (Kłosowska) Z.; m. Cezary Macura, Sept. 8, 1969; 2 children. MD, Med. Acad., Poland, 1965, PhD, 1977. Cert. hygiene and epidemiology, dermatology and venerology. Intern Hosp., Katowice, Poland, 1966-68; asst. dept. hygiene Med. Acad., Kraków, Poland, 1968-69, sr. asst. dept. hygiene, 1969-74, sr. asst. dept. mycology, 1974-77, lectr. dept. mycology, 1978-91, assoc. prof., 1992—; coord. candidaemia monitoring Poland, European Confedn. Med. Mycology, Kraków, 1997—. Author: Textbook of Medical Mycology, 1997; contbr. articles to profl. jours. Mem. ISHAM, ECMM (coord. 1993—), EADV, Polish Soc. Microbiology (bd. dirs.), Polish Soc. Dermatology (bd. dirs.). Avocations: painting, history of art and tourism. Office: Dept Mycology Inst Microbio, CM UJ 18 Czysta St, 31-121 Kraków Poland

MACURA, JIŘÍ, avionics engineer, pilot; b. Knínice, Czech Republic, July 27, 1940; s. František and Vlasta (Mrka'çkova') M.; m. Helena Nejezova', Apr. 29, 1962; children: Michal, Monika. Degree in engring., Transport U., Žilina, Slovakia, 1973. Pilot Czech Air Force, Mošnov, 1961-67, Olomouc, 1967-68, Prostějov, 1968-95; avionics engr. Tech. Inst., Prague, Czech Republic, 1996—. Mem. Czech Assn. Airmen (dep. chmn. 1990). Home: Dbrovske'ho 12, 79601 Prostejov Czech Republic Office: Air Force Tech Inst, Mladsboleslavska', 17906 Praha Czech Republic

MAC WHINNIE, JOHN VINCENT, artist; b. Rockville Centre, N.Y., Apr. 22, 1945; s. Milton Joseph and Inez Genevieve (LaFlamme) Mac W.; m. Virginia Gail Gettling, June, 1985; children: Milton John, Emma Katherine. B.A. magna cum laude, Southampton Coll., 1972. Artist, painter Water Mill, N.Y. Exhibited in group shows: Met. Mus. Art, 1979, Guggenheim Mus., 1979, Lehigh U., 1979, Bklyn. Mus., 1981, Am. Acad. and Inst. Arts and Letters, 1981, New Orleans Mus. Contemporary Art, Guild Hall, Easthampton, N.Y.; one-man shows include: Marlborough Gallery, N.Y., Andre Emmerich Gallery, N.Y.; represented in permanent collections: Guggenheim Mus., Bklyn. Mus., Phillips Collection, Walker Art Ctr., Parrish Art Mus., Guild Hall, numerous others. Recipient First prize in painting Parrish Art Mus., 1971, Excellence in Painting award Heckscher Mus., 1974. Avocations: metaphysics, gardening, antique collecting. Home and Studio: Deerfield Rd Water Mill NY 11976

MADABHUSHI, RANGARAJ, technology company executive; b. Visakhapatnam, India, Nov. 28, 1954; s. Krishnamachari and Ranganayaki Madbhushi; m. Hitomi Madbhushi, Apr. 19, 1986. BS, Andhara U., Visakhapayanam, 1974, MS in Tech., 1977; D Electronics Engring., Tohoku U., Sendai, Japan, 1989. Project assoc. Indian Inst. Tech., Madras, 1977-80; sr. sci. officer Govt. of India R&D Labs., Dehradun, India, 1980-84; rschr. NEC Corp., Kawasaki, Japan, 1989-91, asst. mgr., 1991-96, mgr. rsch., 1996-99; tech. mgr. Lucent Techs., Breinigsville, Pa., 1999—. Contbr. articles to profl. jours.; holder over 13 Japanese patents, 8 U.S. patents in field. Mem. IEEE (sr.), OSA, IEICE. Office: Lucent Tech 9999 Hamilton Blvd Breinigsville PA 18031-9304

MADALINSKI, KAZIMIERZ Z., immunologist, researcher; b. Warsaw, Poland, July 23, 1936; s. Stanislaw and Maria (Makólska) M.; m. Monika Jadwiga Chróścicka, Mar. 2, 1968 (div. May 1982); children: Madaliński Maciej, Piotr; m. Danuta Daniela Dzierzanowska, Jan. 21, 1984. MSc in Biology, U. Warsaw, 1958, MD, 1964; PhD, Nat. Inst. Hygiene, Warsaw, 1967, Habil. Degree, 1976. Asst. Inst. Hematology, Warsaw, 1960; sr. asst. Warsaw Med. Sch., Warsaw, 1961-65; asst. prof. Nat. Inst. Hygiene, Warsaw, 1965-77; asst. prof., head dept. clin. immunology Child Health Ctr. (Inst.), Warsaw, 1978-91, prof. and head, 1991—. Chief editor Polish Jour. Immunology, 1991—, Ctrl. European Jour. Immunology, 1996—; contbr. over 200 articles to profl. jours., 14 chpts. to books. Vice chmn. Solidarity, Child Health Ctr., 1992-95. Capt. Polish Res. Mem. Polish Soc. Immunology (mem. coun. 1983-95, Best Pub. in Polish Immunology Jour. award 1992-95), Polish Soc. for Clin. and Exptl. Immunology (v. chmn. 1998—), Polish Soc. Cytometry (mem. coun. 1996—), Polish Acad. Scis. (sec. com. for immunology 1990-95, chmn. 1996-98), N.Y. Acad. Sci. Roman Catholic. Avocations: tourism, skiing. Fax: 815-71-59. E-mail: kmadal@czd.waw.pl. Home: Pozaryskiego 23 Apt 21, 04-703 Warsaw Poland Office: Child Health Meml Inst, Child Health Meml Inst, 20 Al Dzieci Polskich, 04-730 Warsaw Poland

MADAN, IRA, occupational physician, consultant; b. London, Nov. 7, 1961; d. Satya Paul and Kanchan (Sethi) M.; m. David Bruce Muiry, Aug. 5, 1989; children: Rupert Muiry, Piers Muiry, Gabriella Muiry. MB, BS with honors, U. London, 1985. Sr. house officer Good Hope Hosp., Sutton, Coldfield, Eng., 1987-88, med. registrar, 1988-89; med. registrar Southmead Hosp., Bristol, Eng., 1989-90; lectr. occupl. health United Med. and Dental Schs. Guy's and St. Thomas' Hosps., U. London, 1990-93; cons. Southmead Hosp., Bristol, 1993-97; hon. sr. clin. lectr. U. Bristol, 1993-99; cons. United Bristol Healthcare Trust, Bristol, 1997-99; cons. med. advisor Houses of Parliament, 1999—; cons. Guy's, St. Thomas's NHS Trust, 2000—. Contbr. articles to profl. jours. Fellow Royal Coll. Physicians, Faculty Occupl. Medicine, Soc. Occupl. Medicine, Brit. Med. Assn. Avocations: horse riding, skiing, tennis, enjoying my children. Home: 20A Broadwater Down, Tunbridge Wells TN2 5NR, England Office: Occupatl Health Dept, Houses of Parliament, SWI OAA Westminster SW1 0AA, England

MADAN, KEWAL KRISHAN, civil engineer; b. Jammu-Tawi, India, Dec. 4, 1938; s. Raghunath Rai and Rajwanti Madan; m. Sneh Sethi, May 7, 1966; children: Alok, Niti Bajaj. BE in civil Engring., Engring. Coll., Poona, India, 1958; postgrad., Internat. Inst. Seismology and Earthquake Engring., Tokyo, 1969-70, U. Coll. London, 1980. Registered civil engr. Project dir. Nat. Bldg. Constrn. Corp., Libya, 1981-84; dir. consultancy svcs. Ctrl. Pub. Wks. Dept., Delhi, 1984-86, chief engr., 1987, chief engr. environment and forests, 1987-92, addl. dir. gen., 1992-93, dir. gen. works, 1994-96; apptd. mem. Union Pub. Svc. Commn., 1996—; cons. Asian Devel. Bank, Manila; expert UN/World Bank, Washington, ILO, Geneva, UN Ctr. for Human Settlement, Nairobi, UNDP, Common Wealth Fund for tech. Corp., London. Contbr. articles to profl. jours. Recipient Nat. Citizen's award Nat. Citizen's Com., Delhi, 1993, India Internat. Gold award NRI Inst., 1994, Rajiv Gandhi Excellence award Shiromani Inst., Delhi, 1994. Fellow Instn. of Engrs.; mem. Internat. Coun. Cons. (found. mem.), Indian Bldgs. Congress (life, pres. 1995-96), Indian Rds. Congress (life, pres. 1994-95), Internat. Assn. Bridge and Structural Engrs. (India chpt.), Indian Coun. Arbitration (life), Internat. Coun. for Bldg., Working Commn., Indian Inst. Bridge Engrs. Avocations: reading, music, badminton, swimming, lawn tennis. Home: AB-9 Pandara Rd, New Delhi 110003, India Office: Union Pub Svc Commn, Shahjahan Rd, New Delhi 110011, India

MADAN, MIRA, science educator, technology administrator; b. Lahore, Pakistan, Aug. 1, 1934; d. L.B.B. and R.B. Madan. MSc with honors in Biology, Chandigarh U., Panjab, India, 1963, MSc in Botany with honors, 1965, cert. in German, 1969, PhD in Botany, 1972. Sr. rsch. fellow U. Chandigarh, 1970-72; lectr. U. G.N.D.U., Amritsar, Panjab, India, 1972-80; lectr. ctr. RDT Indian Inst. Tech., New Delhi, sr. sci. officer, 1981-90, prin. sci. officer, 1990-94, prof., 1994-95, prof. emeritus, 1995—, head Ctr. Rural Devel. and Tech., 1993-94; mem. internat. confs. and programs, North Palmerston, New Zealand, FAO, Nepal, West Bengal, Gujarat, India, Al Ain, United Arab Emirates, Perth, Australia, Copenhagen, Geneva; visitor labs. Singapore, U.K., U.S.; cons. in chief water project Rajiv Gandhi Water Mission Found., Ministry of Rural Devel.; cons. in field; mem. and chairperson rsch. adv. com. Nat. Ctr. Mushroom Rsch. and Tng., Solan, India; mem. adv. coun. World Resource Found. U.K.; v.p. Social Forestry and Rural Orgn., Ranichauri, Tehri Garhwal, India; expert mem. for development of vocational course of extension, Nat. Edn. of India Gandhi/Open Univ., Delhi, organizer various confs., workshops, seminars, exhbns., etc. Mem. editl. bd. Internat. Jour. Resource, Conservation and Recycling; editor-in-chief jour. Gram Praudyogiki; editor, writer, compiler books, booklets, monographs, brochures, procs.; contbr. articles to profl. publs., more than 400 rsch. paprs in field. Mem. adv. coun. World Resource Found. UK. Fellow Nat. Acad. Scis., Phytopathol. Soc. India, Soc. Mycology and Plant Pathology, Linnean Soc. London; mem. N.Y. Acad. Scis., Internat. Assn. Water, Pollution Rsch. and Control (mgmt. com., specialist group on alternative waste mgmt. techs. for developing countries), life, hon. and founder mem. over 35 nat. and internat. socs. Avocations: watching the natural environment, gardening, mushroom cultivation, reading, writing. E-mail: mmadam@netearth.ittdernet.in. Office: Indian Inst Tech Ctr RDT, Hauz Khas, New Delhi 110016, India

MADANI, GHAZIO, academic administrator; b. Medina, Saudi Arabia, 1939. BA in Bus. Adminstrn., MBA, PhD in Bus. and Fin. Pres. King Abdul Aziz U., Jeddah, Saudi Arabia. Office: King Abdul Aziz U, POB 1026, 21441 Jeddah Saudi Arabia*

MADARIAGA, LOURDES MERCEDES, accountant; b. Sagua La Grande, Cuba, July 10, 1959; came to U.s., 1967; d. Jose I. and Mercedes (Estrada) M. AA with honors, Miami Dade C.C., 1978; BBA, Fla. Internat. U., 1981. Staff/audit mgr. Pub. Svc. Commn., Miami, Fla., 1981-89; sr. acct. Price Waterhouse, Miami, 1990-92; staff analyst Regulated Industries, Miami, 1992; CFO, YWCA, Miami, 1993-96; chief fiscal dir. Little Havana Activities and Nutrition Ctrs. of Dade County, Miami, 1996-97; CFO, N.W. Dade Ctr., Miami, 1997-99; cons., sole practitioner acctg. and tax svcs., Miami, 1997-99; pres. Madariaga & Assocs., Inc., acctg. and tax svcs., Miami, 1999—. Vol. League Against Cancer, Miami, 1991—; co-chair GESU Centennial Alumni Reunion, Miami, 1996; treas., mem. host com. Willy Chirino Found., 1999—. Mem. Am. Soc. Woman Accts. Democrat. Roman Catholic.

MADATHIL, SAHADEVAN GOVINDAN, retired medical educator, neurology consultant; b. Tellicherry, Kerala State, India, Sept. 4, 1929; s. Govindan Madathil and Madhavi Govindan; m. Suneethi Kammangat, Dec. 24, 1956; children: Renjith Sahadevan, Duleep Sahadevan. MBBS, Madras (India) Med. Coll., 1952. With Indian Govt., Kuthuparamba, Kerala, 1953-59, Hammersmith Hosp., London, 1959-63, Calicut Med. Coll., Kozhikode, India, 1963-65; prof. medicine Calicut Med. Coll., Kerala, 1971-84, supt., 1984-85; prof. medicine emeritus Trivandrum Med. Coll., Kozhikode, 1985—; with Trivandrum Med. Coll., Kerala, India, 1969, Alleppey Med. Coll., Kerala, 1970-71; cons. physician, neurologist P.V.S. Hosp., Kozhikode, 1985—, Baby Meml. Hosp., Kozhikode, 1985—; mem. PAI Com.-Health Reform, Kerala, 1973. Past editor Kerala Med. Jour.; contbr. articles to profl. jours. Major Indian Army, 1965-69. Named Best Dr., State Govt. of Kerala, 1996. Fellow Royal Coll. Physicians London, Indian Med. Assn. (past pres., Best Dr. 1996), Kerala Govt. Med. Coll. Tchrs. Assn. (past pres.), Rotary Club Calicut (past pres.), Freemason. Home: Camelot, Cannanore Rd, Kozhikode Kerala, India 673 001

MADAULE, PHILIPPE MARCEL, oil and gas industry executive; b. Cagnes Sur Mer, France, June 26, 1949; s. Pierre Felix and Augusta Marie-Paule (Estable) M.; m. Brita Elisabeth Hellström, Mar. 22, 1975; children: Natacha, Katia. MSc in Math. and Physics, U. Pierre & Marie Curie, Paris, 1968; D in Engring., Ecole Superieure Physique, Paris, 1972; D in Chem. Engring., French Oil Inst., Rueil, 1973. Process engr. Heurtey Industries, Paris, 1974-77; head dept. early prodn. facilities Schlumberger, Melun, France, 1977-82; oil and gas engring. mgr. Soc. Parisienne Industrie Electrique Batignoles, Paris, 1982-85; mgr. offshore production sys. Blue Water, Fribourg, Switzerland, 1985-91; oil and gas project mgr. Sofresid, Paris, 1991-92; oil and gas project mng. dir. Total S.A., Paris, 1992—. Contbr. articles to jours. in field. Bd. dirs. Ecole Superieure de Physique et Chimie Industrielles de Paris, 1984; mem. France-Finland Assn., Paris, 1975, Dalian (China) U. Tech. Friends Assn., 1993—. Served with French Air Force/French Nuc. Agy., 1973-74. Mem. Soc. Petroleum Engrs., French Environ. Commn. Avocations: history, film, rugby, skiing, golf. Home: 23 Rue Fantin Latour, 75016 Paris France Office: Total SA, 24 Cours Michelet, 92069 Paris France

MADAY, CLIFFORD RONALD, insurance professional; b. Cin., Mar. 15, 1947; s. John J. and Betty (Kucha) M.; m. Ellen Doolittle, Aug. 31, 1968; children: Michael, Brian, Christina, Andrew. BS, Northeastern U., 1976. Cert. protection profl. With The Hartford Ins., 1977—; loss control mgr. The Hartford Ins., Manchester, N.H., 1981-83, Charlotte, N.C., 1983—. Bd. dirs., soccer commr. and coach Matthews (N.C.) Athletic and Recreation Assn., 1983-91; select coach Charlotte United Soccer, 1991-95. 1st lt. U.S. Army, 1965-69, Vietnam. Decorated Bronze Star. Mem. Am. Soc. for Indsl. Security, Am. Soc. Safety Engrs. Avocations: soccer coach, gourmet cooking. Home: 321 W 7th St Charlotte NC 28202-1607 Office: Hartford Ins Co 8711 University East Dr Charlotte NC 28213-4204

MADDEN, BARTLEY JOSEPH, economist; b. N.Y.C., Nov. 3, 1943; s. Bartley Joseph and Genevieve Helen (Ghehan) M.; m. Maricela Elizondo, 1995; children: Lucinda, Miranda, Jeffrey, Gregory. BS in Mech. Engring., U. So. Calif., Los Angeles, 1965; MBA, U. Calif., Berkeley, 1970. V.p. Callard, Madden & Assocs., Chgo., 1970-83; sr. v.p. Harbor Capital Advisors, Chgo., 1983-92; ptnr. Holt Value Assocs., Chgo., 1993—. Author: CFROI Valuation: A Total System Approach to Valuing the Firm, 1999. With U.S. Army, 1966-68. Mem. Tau Beta Pi, Beta Gamma Sigma. Office: Holt Value Assocs 300 S Riverside Plz Ste 1400N Chicago IL 60606-6737 Address: 28 S Loomis St Naperville IL 60540-4937

MADDEN, BRENDAN PATRICK, cardiothoracic and transplant physician, educator; b. Dublin, Ireland, June 29, 1961; arrived in Eng., 1988; s. Denis J. and Joan M. (Redmond) M.; m. Aileen Peake, 1998; 1 child, Aisling. MB, BCh and BAO, all with honors, Univ. Coll., Dublin, 1984, MD, 1991; MSc, Brunel U., London, 1992. Cert. cons. cardiothoracic and transplant physician, instr. advanced life support and advanced trauma life support. Sr. house officer Dublin, 1985-87; registrar Meath Hosp., Dublin, 1987-88; cardiothoracic registrar Harefield Hosp., Middlesex, 1988-90; sr. registrar Harefield and Brompton Hosps., London, 1990-93; sr. registrar, tutor Brompton Hosp., London, 1993-94; cons. thoracic, intensive care and transplant physician St. Georges Hosp., London, 1994—; med. advisor USA Cystic Fibrosis Trust, Washington, 1996, French Transplant and Cystic Fibrosis Soc., 1992—, Transplant Ctrs. in Brazil and Argentina, 1992—, U.K. Cystic Fibrosis Trust, 1992—; lectr. in field; examiner Royal Coll. Surgeons Eng., 2000—. Author book chpts. on thoracic surgery, ARDS, intensive care, cystic fibrosis, pulmonary rehab., lung transplantation; contbr. numerous articles and sci. papers to profl. jours. Dir. Med. Students Overseas Relief, Kenya, 1983. Scholar Univ. Coll., 1980, 82; grantee Brit. Heart Found., 1996, 97, 99. Fellow Royal Coll. Physicians Ireland, Royal Acad. Medicine of Ireland, Royal Coll. Physicians London; mem. Brit. Thoracic Soc. Roman Catholic. Avocations: French, snow skiing, scuba diving, music, foreign travel. Office: St Georges Hosp Cardiothoracic Unit, Blackshaw Rd, Tooting London SW17 OQT, England

MADDEN, IAN BERESFORD, lawyer, historian; b. Auckland, New Zealand, Feb. 27, 1931; s. Charles Beresford and Elsie Madge (Masefield) M. BA, U. New Zealand, 1954; MA, Auckland Tchrs. Coll., 1956; LLB, U. Otago, Dunedin, New Zealand, 1969. Bar: Supreme Ct. Dunedin, 1971. Staff mem. Alfred Buckland & Sons Ltd. and successors, Auckland and Dunedin, 1949-56, 68-73; tchr. Otahuhu Coll., Auckland, 1956-57; legal officer State Advances Corp., Auckland, 1958-66; staff mem. Earl, Kent, Massey, Auckland, 1967-68, Dyer & Dowd, Auckland, 1973-74, Peak, London & Co., Auckland, 1975; property mgr. Auckland, 1975-92; cons., 1993—. Author: Riverhead, The Kaipara Gateway, 1966; Antique Fair and Exhibition Handbook, 1965; contbr. articles on history, genealogy, heraldry, antiques, art, architecture to jours. and texts. Mem. Auckland Libr. Heritage Trust, 1992—, Monarchist League of New Zealand, 1996—, councillor, 2000—; found. mem. Mus. of Transport and Tech., Auckland, 1960—; mem. Cornwall br. com., del. to Remuera exec. Nat. Party, 1993-95, asst. treas. Cornwall br., 1996, N.Z. Nat. Party No. divsn. Conf. Auckland, 1999; mem. Northern Divsnl. Parliamentarian List Selection Com., 1999; mem. Epsom Election Campaign Com., Nat. Party, 1999; mem. N.Z. Nat. Party No. Region policy com., 2000—. Mem. Soc. Genealogists (London, life mem.), Soc. Genealogists (Australia, life mem.), Soc. N.Z. Genealogists, Heraldry Soc. (New Zealand br. found. mem. 1962—, councilor 1962-68, 94-96), N.Z. Founders Soc. (life mem., Auckland br. com., dept. chmn. 1990-94), Auckland Hist. Soc. (v.p. 1962-65, pres. 1966), Nat. Hist. Places Trust, Auckland

Inst. and Mus. (life mem.), Auckland Patriotic Socs. (cen. comm. 1989-94), Navy League New Zealand, Inc., N.Z. Mil. Hist. Soc., N.Z. Book Coun., Royal Australian Hist. Soc. Mem. Ch. of Eng. Home and Office: Rosslea, 15 Belvedere St, Epsom Auckland 1003 Auckland 3, New Zealand

MADDEN, JAMES COOPER, V, management consultant; b. Glen Cove, N.Y., June 18, 1961; s. James Cooper IV and Linda Marie (Lizza) M.; m. Heather Madden; 1 child, Jennifer Louise. Student, Webb Inst. Naval Architecture, Glen Cove, 1979-80; BA cum laude, So. Meth. U., 1983, BBA magna cum laude, 1983. Cert. Soc. Naval Architects and Marine Engrs. Cons. Andersen Cons./Arthur Andersen, Houston, 1983-85, sr. cons., 1985-87; mgr. Andersen Cons./Arthur Andersen, L.A., 1987-90, sr. mgr., 1990-91; prin. Booz-Allen & Hamilton, L.A., 1991-93; v.p. mng. dir. MCI Systemhouse, L.A., 1993-95, pres. U.S. and Mexico ops., 1995-97, CFO, 1997-98; chmn., pres. Exult, Inc., Irvine, Calif., 1998—. Contbr. articles to profl. jours. Bd. dirs. Exolt. Webb Inst. Naval Architecture scholar, 1979-80. Avocations: sailing, snow skiing, travel, reading. Office: Exult Inc 4 Park Plz Ste 1000 Irvine CA 92614-2552

MADDEN, JAMES DESMOND, forensic engineer; b. Jersey City; s. Louis A. and Ann Madden. BSChemE, U. S.C., 1963, ME, 1966. Lic. profl. engr., Ohio; cert. diplomate forensic engr. Process engr. Monsanto Co., Alvin, Tex., 1966-67; process and project engr. Union Carbide Corp., Houston, 1967-70; systems engr. M.W. Kellogg Co., Houston, 1970-73, prin. systems engr., 1974-77; sr. process engr. Litwin Co., Houston, 1973-74; sr. project engr. Davy Powergas, Houston, 1977-78, supervising project engr., 1978-79; mgr. equipment engring. DM Internat., Houston, 1979-80, project engring. mgr., 1980-83; owner, forensic engr. Madden Forensic Engring., Parma, Parma Heights and Brecksville, Ohio, 1983—. Pres. Houston Young Adult Rep. Club, 1970-73; chmn. Tex. Young Adult Rep. Clubs, 1973. NSF rsch. grantee, 1963; NASA fellow, 1963-65. Mem. ASME, NSPE, AIChE, Soc. Automotive Engrs., Nat. Fire Protection Assn., Inst. Transp. Engrs., Am. Soc. Agrl. Engrs., Bldg. Ofcls. and Code Adminstrs. Internat., Nat. Acad. Forensic Engrs., Sigma Xi, Sigma Pi Sigma, Tau Beta Pi, Omicron Delta Kappa. Office: 10175 Brecksville Rd Cleveland OH 44141-3205

MADDEN, WANDA LOIS, nurse; b. Augusta, Kans., Apr. 26, 1929; d. George W. and Lillian B. (Dobyns) Provost; m. Laurence R. Madden, June 3, 1947 (div. 1961); children: Matthew, Mark, Luke, John, Michele. ADN, Pasadena City Coll., 1970; postgrad., Calif. State U. Consortium, 1986. RN, Calif.; ordained to ministry Am. Fellowship Ch., 1995. CCU nurse Huntington Meml. Hosp., Pasadena, Calif., 1970-71; ICU Community Hosp., Pico Rivera, Calif., 1971-72; CCU nurse Queen of the Valley Hosp., West Covina, Calif., 1973-74; ICU supr. Visalia (Calif.) Community Hosp., 1974-77, 89-90, ICU nurse, 1978; ICU nurse San Miguel Hosp. Assn., San Diego, 1978-79; supr. Casa Blanca Corp., San Diego, 1979-80; dir. nursing Visalia Convalescence Hosp., 1981-89, Westgate Gardens Convalescent Ctr., Visalia, 1990; psychiat. staff nurse Mill Creek Hosp., Visalia, 1990-91; AIDS case mgr. Tulare County Health Svcs., 1993-95; assoc. lay pastor Met. Cmty. Ch. of Sequoias, Visalia, 1994-95; pastor Tulare County Rainbow Cmty. Ch., 1995—; mem. Tulare County HIV Care Consortium, Tulare County HIV-AIDS Edn. and Prevention Planning Com.; gay and AIDS activist, Tulare County; mem. AIDS Outreach Ministry in Home & Hosp. and Outreach to Gay/Lesbian and Transgender Cmty. Home and Office: 2725 N Canary Dr Visalia CA 93291-1719

MADDOCK, LAWRENCE HILL, retired language educator; b. Ogden, Utah, July 14, 1923; s. Lawrence J. and Nellie (Hill) M. Student, U. Fla., 1941-42; BA, George Peabody Coll., 1946, PhD, 1965; MA, U. So. Calif., 1949. Tchr. pub. schs. Jacksonville, Fla., 1949-52; instr. U. Fla., Gainesville, 1952-53; asst. prof. California (Pa.) State Coll., 1955-56, assoc. prof., 1956-64; assoc. prof. N.E. La. State Coll., Monroe, 1964-67, U. West Fla., Pensacola, 1967-90. Author: The Door of Memory, 1974, John Maddock: Mormon Pioneer, 1996; contbr. chpts. to books and articles to profl. jours. Mem. MLA (bibliographer 1978-93), Thomas Wolfe Soc., Mormon History Assn. Republican. Mormon. Home: 1012 Gerhardt Dr Pensacola FL 32503-3222

MADDOCKS, DAVID CHARLES, medical company executive; b. Bath, Avon, Eng., June 11, 1965; s. Glyn Athol and Carla Elizabeth (Stella) M.; m. Krystyna Elzbieta Scott; children: Jake, Alisha. BA in European Bus. Studies with honors, Trent Poly. Inst., Nottingham, Eng., 1988. Mktg. dir. Glyn Maddocks Travel, Bath, 1988-91; sales rep. Johnson & Johnson Med., Ascot, Berkshire, Eng., 1991-93, asst. product mgr., 1993-95, product mgr., 1995-96, European bus. mgr., 1995-97, European mktg. dir., 1997-99; gen. mgr. U.K. and Ireland Ansell Healthcare, 2000—.

MADDOCKS, JEREMY CHRISTOPHER C., marketing director; b. Wigan, Lancashire, Eng., Dec. 8, 1965; s. Bertram Catterall Maddocks and Angela Vergette (Forster) M.; m. Nicola Jayne Humphreys, Sept. 7, 1996; children: Lottie Emily Bruckshaw Maddocks, Hamish William Catterall Maddocks. Diploma, Sorbonne, Paris, 1985; BDiv, King's Coll., London, 1988. Mktg. dir. Home Sec., Dorking, Eng., 1991-94, Conservative Ctrl. Office, London, 1994-95; comm. cons. Countrywide, 1995-96; comm. and mktg. dir., sec. Buffalo Comm., London, 1996; product mktg. dir. QAS Systems Ltd., London, 1996-98; product mktg. dir. land based satellite comm. Nera Telecomm. Ltd., London, 1998-99; mktg. dir. NDS Group PLC, 1999—; dir. Ranmore Park Mgmt., Surrey, 642 Fulham Rd. Ltd., London, dir. Global Fax Ltd., London. Editor The Bladder mag., 1983, The Bladder Lit. Supplement, 1983, The Sheriffian, 1984; dep. editor The Meteor, 1983. Polit. agt. to Kenneth Baker, Home Sec., 1991-94; chmn. King's Coll. London Conservatives, 1987; treas. London Conservatives, 1987, chmn., Sands End, 1996; gove. Lady Margaret's, Parsons Green, 1996. 2d lt. Royal Marines, 1988-91. Mem. Manchester Tennis and Racquet Club. Conservative Party. Ch. of Eng. Avocations: photography, travel. Home: 642 Fulham Rd, London SW6 5RT, England Office: NDS Ltd, 190 Munster Rd, Fulham London SW6 6AU, England

MADDOX, JOHN ROYDEN, retired journal editor; b. Penllergaer, Swansea, Wales, Nov. 27, 1925; s. Arthur John Maddox and Mary Elizabeth Davies; m. Nancy Fanning, Mar. 12, 1949 (dec. 1960); 2 children; m. Brenda Power Murphy, Nov. 11, 1960; 2 children. BA in Chemistry, Oxford (Eng.) U., 1947, MA, 1952; D Univ. (hon.), U. Surrey, 1988; DLitt (hon.), U. East Anglia, 1993, U. Liverpool, Eng., 1995; PhD (hon.), Nottingham Trent U., 1996; DSc (hon.), U. Glamorgan, Wales, 1997. Lectr. theoretical physics U. Manchester, Eng., 1949-55; sci. editor Manchester Guardian, 1955-64; asst. dir., coord. Nuffield sci. tchg. project Nuffield Found., London, 1964-66, dir., 1975-80; chmn. Maddox Editl. Ltd., London, 1973-75; editor Nature, London, 1966-73, 80-95, editor emeritus, 1995—; mem. Royal Commn. on Environ. Pollution, 1976-81, Genetic Manipulation Adv. Group, 1977-82; chmn. European Union Conf. on Growth Promoters, 1985. Author: Revolution in Biology, 1963, The Doomsday Syndrome, 1972, Beyond the Energy Crisis, 1974, What Remains To Be Discovered, 1998. Chmn. Queen Elizabeth Coll., U. London, 1980-85; mem. Erwood Cmty. Coun., 1987—, chmn., 1999—. Created knight Order of Brit. Empire. Recipient cultural award Eduard Rhein Found., Germany, 1997. Fellow Am. Acad. Arts and Scis. (hon. fgn.), Royal Soc.; mem. Am. Inst. Physics. Mem. Liberal Democratic Party. Home and Office: 9 Pitt St, London W8 4NX, England

MADDOX, MARILYN COLEMAN, literature and composition educator; b. Eupora, Miss., Feb. 18, 1948; d. Ernest Edgar and Nannie Mae (Springer) Coleman; m. Jimmy Dale Maddox, Dec. 27, 1970; children: Kristen Brooke, Mallory Hope. AA, N.W. C.C., Senatobia, Miss., 1967; BS, Miss. State U., 1969, MS, 1970. Cert. English edn., guidance and counseling. Counselor SPATS (Spl. Program for Academically Talented Students) Miss. State U., Starkville, summer 1970; English tchr. Long Beach (Miss.) H.S., 1970-71; guidance counselor Eupora Middle Sch., 1972-73; tchr. Eupora H.S., 1974-77; owner, mgr. personal rental property Eupora, 1978—; asst. prof. Wood Coll., Mathiston, Miss., 1991—. Mem. Eupora Twentieth Century Club, 1986-93, Jr. Miss Com., Eupora, 1988, chmn., 1989. Mem. ASCD, Nat. Coun. Tchrs. English, Miss. Coun. Tchrs. English. Office: PO Box 289 Mathiston MS 39752-0289

MADDUX, GREGORY (ALAN), professional baseball player; b. San Angelo, Tex., Apr. 14, 1966. Grad. high sch., Las Vegas. Baseball player Chicago Cubs, 1984-92, Atlanta Braves, 1992—. Recipient Cy Young award Baseball Writers' Assn. Am., 1992, 93, 94, 95; named to All-Star team, 1988, 92, 94-5; recipient Gold Glove Award, 1990-96; Sporting News All-Star Team, 1992-94; named Nat. League Pitcher of Yr., Sporting News, 1993; Nat. League Innings Pitched Leader, 1991-92, earned run avg., 1995, fielding percentage, 1990-95. Achievements include being a mem. World Series championship team, 1995. Office: Atlanta Braves Turner Field PO Box 4064 Atlanta GA 30302-4064

MADDY, DUANE KEITH, management consultant; b. Washington, Oct. 6, 1964; s. Keith Thomas and Colleen Jo-Anne (Barlow) M.; m. Valerie Ann Dawley, Mar. 17, 1990. BS in Bus. Adminstrn., U. Phoenix, San Jose, 1987; MBA in Mgmt., Southwest U., Kenner, La., 1989, PhD in Venture Mgmt., 1994. Equities analyst Dean Witter Reynolds, Sacramento, Calif., 1985-87; separate acct. analyst Am. Gen. Life Ins. Co., Sacramento, Calif., 1987-88; corp. trust analyst Tex. Commerce Bank, Houston, 1988-90; tax compliance analyst IRS, Seattle, 1991-93; acct. compliance analyst Western Wireless, Bellevue, Wash., 1994; sr. sales cons. Princess Cruises, Seattle, 1994-97; sr. merger cons. David Stone & Assocs., San Francisco, 1997-99; chmn. bd. Maddy Consulting, Milford, Ohio, 1986—; pub. spking. Readers Digest Assn., Fair Oaks, Calif., 1980. Author: The Maddy Report, 1986-91, Finite Stock Selection, 1987. Life Scout Boy Scouts, Davis, Calif., 1980; reserve Police Officer Davis (Calif.) Police Dept., 1982. Mem. Am. Mgmt. Assn., Am. Heart Assn. Republican. Methodist. Avocations: photography, travel, model railroading, car restoration. E-mail address: maddyconsulting@yahoo.com. Fax: 513-722-0074. Office: Maddy Consulting 590 Lodgepole Dr Milford OH 45150-6546

MADDY-WEITZMAN, BRUCE ALAN, historian, political analyst; b. Syracuse, N.Y., Mar. 4, 1953; arrived in Israel, 1979; s. Bernard A. and Harriet R. (Hordies) Maddy; m. Edie Weitzman, Aug. 15, 1976. BA, Brandeis U., 1975; MA, Harvard U., 1977; PhD, Tel Aviv U., 1988. Jr. rsch. fellow, Shiloah Inst., Dayan Ctr. Tel Aviv U., 1979-88, rsch. fellow, Dayan Ctr., 1989-92; vis. asst. prof. Emory U., Atlanta, 1990-91; vis. Middle East fellow Carter Ctr., Atlanta, 1990-91; sr. rsch. fellow, Dayan Ctr. Tel Aviv U., 1993—, editor, Dayan Ctr., 1995—; vis. fellow Leonard Davis Inst., The Hebrew U., Jerusalem, 1995-96; vis. prof. Middle East Tech. U., Ankara, 1998, Brandeis U., 2000; Dayar Ctr. acad. amb. Brandeis U., 2000. Author: The Crystallization of the Arab State System, 1993; co-editor: Middle East Contemporary Survey (annual), 1994, editor, 1995-99; co-editor: Religious Radicalism in the Greater Middle East, 1997. Bd. mem. Israel Assn. Baseball, 1995—; baseball coach Israel Little League, Ra'anana, 1994—. with Israel Def. Forces, 1983. Recipient rsch. grants Haifa (Israel) U., 1988-89, U.S. Inst. Peace, Washington, 1989-90, 91-93, Israel Founds. Trustees, Tel Aviv, 1992-94, Leonard Davis Inst. Hebrew U., 1995-96, Tami Steinmetz Ctr. for Peace Rsch. Tel Aviv U., 1998. Mem. Am. Hist. Assn., Israel Oriental Soc., Middle East Studies Assn. N.Am., Am. Inst. for Maghribi Studies. Avocations: baseball, jazz. Office: Tel Aviv U, Moshe Dayan Ctr, 69978 Ramat Aviv Israel

MADEBO, TESFAYE, physician, researcher; b. Awassa, Ethiopia, Aug. 25, 1965; arrived in Norway, 1994; m. Madebo Haidebo and Belaynesh Medefo; m. Annlaug Mugas; 1 child, Dawit. MD, Addis Ababa U., Ethiopia, 1990; postgrad., U. Bergen, Norway, 1994—. MD Yirga alim (Ethiopia) Hosp., 1990-94; rsch. fellow U. Bergen, Norway, 1994-97; MD Haukeland U. Hosp., Bergen, Norway, 1997-98, Stord (Norway) Hosp., 1998—. Contbr. articles to profl. jours. Mem. Norwegian Drs. Assn. Avocations: football, indoor games, swimming, visiting historical places. Home: Furulyvn 52, 5416 Stord Norway Office: Stord Hosp, P Box 4000, 5409 Stord Norway Address: U Bergen Ctr Int Hlth, Armauer Hansen Bldg, 5021 Bergen Norway

MADEI, WERNER FERDINAND, anesthesiologist, researcher, pharmacologist; b. Würzburg, Bavaria, Germany, July 20, 1954; s. Werner K. and Anna M. (Kreisl) M.; m. Johanna Hörner, July 30, 1979; children: Stefanie, Manuel, Jasmin, Sebastian. MD, Ludwig-Maximilians U., Munich, 1984, PhD magna cum laude, 1985. Rschr. in pharmacology Ludwig-Maximilians U., 1984-85, rschr. in gen. medicine, 1985-88, resident in anesthesiology, 1989-93; staff anesthesiologist Army Hosp., Munich, 1993-94, Amberg, Germany, 1995—. Contbr. articles to profl. jours. Lt. col. German Army, 1995—. Recipient Honor medal NATO, 1996, Honor medal German Forces, 1996. Mem. German Soc. Anesthesiologists, Internat. Anesthesia Rsch. Soc. Avocations: swimming, golf, running, biking. Office: Army Hosp, Köferingerstr 1, D-92224 Amberg Bavaria, Germany

MADELIN, ALAIN, French government official; b. Paris, Mar. 26, 1946; children: Gaëlle, Armelle, Brian-Stefan. Law degree. Bar: Paris. Atty. Nat. Fedn. Ind. Republicans, Paris, 1968—, nat. secretariat, 1977; mem. mission Cabinet of Sec. of State Ministry of Industry, Commerce and Artisans, 1977-78; minister of post Dept. Telecomms. and Tourism, 1986-88; dep. UDF, Ille-et-Vilaine, 1988—; minister of enterprise, indsl. devel. Govt. of France, 1994-95, minister econs. and fin., 1995—; mem. European Parliament, Brussels, Belgium; mem. Commn. for Cultural, Family and Social Affairs, Regional Coun., Bretagne, 1978—; nat. del. Parti républicain, 1977-85; gen. del. PR, 1988-89; mem. European Parliament, 1989. Author: Pour libérer l'école, l'enseignement à la carte, 1984. Mem. France-Czechoslovakia Friendship Group (pres.), Inst. Euro 92 (pres. 1988—). Mem. Union for French Democracy. Office: 113 rue de l'Universite, F-75007 Paris France*

MADER, CHARLES LAVERN, chemist; b. Dewey, Okla., Aug. 8, 1930; s. George Edgar and Naomia Jane (Harer) M.; m. Emma Jean Sinclair, June 12, 1960; 1 child, Charles L. II. BS, Okla. State U., 1952, MS, 1954; PhD, Pacific Western U., 1980. Fellow Los Alamos (N.Mex.) Nat. Lab., 1955—; JIMAR sr. fellow U. Hawaii, Honolulu, 1985-94; pres. Mader Cons. Co., Honolulu, 1985—. Author: Numerical Modeling of Detonation, 1979, Numerical Modeling of Water Waves, 1988, Numerical Modeling of Explosives and Propellants, 1997; editor: Los Alamos Explosives Performance Data, 1982, LASL Phermex Data, vol. 1, 1980, vol. 2, 1980, vol. 3, 1981; contbr. numerous articles to profl. jours.; author 70 reports. Scoutmaster Boys Scouts Am., Los Alamos, 1971-85. Fellow Am. Inst. Chemists; mem. Am. Chem. Soc., Combustion Inst., Tsunami Soc. (editor 1985—), Marine Tech. Soc., Sigma Xi, Pi Mu Epsilon, Phi Lambda Upsilon. Methodist. Achievements include development and definition of field of numerical modeling of explosives and water waves. Office: Mader Cons Co 1049 Kamehame Dr Honolulu HI 96825-2860 also: 214 Barranca Rd Los Alamos NM 87544-2410 also: PO Box 5930 Avon CO 81620-5930

MADES MILGRAM, ROBERTA, psychology educator, researcher; b. Everett, Mass., Aug. 17, 1931; d. Abram and Esther (Landsman) M.; m. Norman (Noach) Alvin Milgram, Feb. 21, 1951; children: Shoshana Milgram Knapp, Jonathan Rimon. BA, Boston U., 1952, MA, 1957; B.J. Ed., Boston Hebrew Coll., 1953; EdD, Am. U., 1969. Assoc. prof. dept. psychology West Chester (Pa.) State U., 1969-71; lectr. in ednl. psychology Tchrs.' Colls. Israel Ministry Edn., 1971; from lectr. to prof. emeritus in ednl. psychology Sch. Edn. Tel Aviv U., 1972—; prof. ednl. psychology Coll. Judea and Samaria, Ariel, 1986—; vis. scholar Sch. Edn. Stanford U., Calif.; vis. prof. Va. Poly. Inst. and State U., Blacksburg, Radford (Va.) U., U. Nev., Las Vegas, Rhodes Coll., Memphis; mem. nat. adv. com. on identification of gifted Israel Ministry Edn.; presenter, lectr. in field. Editor: Teaching Gifted and Talented Learners in Regular Classrooms, 1989, Counseling Gifted and Talented Children: A Guide for Teachers, Counselors, and Parents, 1991, Teaching and Counseling Gifted and Talented Adolescents: An Internationl Learning Style Perspective, 1993; cons. editor: The Creativity Rsch. Jour.; ad hoc reviewer psychol. reports Jour. Ednl. Psychology, Child Devel., Gifted Child Quarterly, Megamot, European Jour. High Ability, Jour. Creative Behavior, World Psychology; guest editor spl. global issue Roeper Rev.: A Jour. on Gifted Edn. on the Topic of Talent Devel.; contbr. more than 85 articles to profl. jours. Active Profs. for a Strong Israel; mem. nat. adv. com. Nat. Authorithy on Rd. Safety Ministry Transp.; mem. Likud Party. Mem. Am. Psychol. Assn. (fgn. affil.), Internat. Coun. Psychologists, Gifted and Talented Internat. Coun. Psychologists (mem. editl. rev. bd.). Jewish. Avocations: hiking, foreign travel, collecting Israeli stamps and coins. Fax: 97297493186. E-mail: milgram@post.tau.ac.il. Home: PO Box 157 Baram 15, 44864 Kochav Yair Israel Office: Coll Judea & Samaria, Dept Behavioral Scis, Ariel Israel also: Tel-Aviv U, Sch Edn, Ramat-Aviv Israel

MADHOK, VINOD, management consultant; b. Sailkot, Pakistan, Feb. 12, 1941; s. Dev Raj and Kamala M.; m. Jyoti Puri. BA hons, Delhi U., 1964, diploma in Advanced Credit, Fin. Analysis & Corp. Law. Banking asst. Am. Express Bank, New Delhi, India, 1965-69; credit officer Bank of Am., Bombay, India, 1970; treasury mgr. Zuariagro Chems. Ltd., Goa, India, 1971-89, gen. mgr., 1989-90; mng. dir. World Growth Fund, New Delhi, 1992-93; dir. Dalmia Bros. Pltd, DSS Mobile Comm. Ltd., Sri Meenakshi Mills Ltd., New Delhi, 1993—. Avocations: reading, listening to music, golf.

MADHYASTHA, NAGAPPAYYA MATTU, bioscience educator; b. Mattu, Karnataka, India, June 23, 1942; s. Haridas Mattu and Jalajakshi Mattu Madhyastha; m. Vathsala Madhyastha, Mar. 17, 1976; 1 child, Vinay. BSc, Mahatma Gandhi Meml. Coll., Udipi, India, 1962; MSC, Inst. Sci., Bombay, 1965, PhD, 1970. Lectr. bioscis. Mangalore (India) U., 1970-78, reader bioscis., 1978-83, prof. dept. bioscis., 1983—, dean sci. and tech., 1990-92, chmn., prof. dept. bioscis., 1994—; vis. prof. Sch. Environment and Life Scis., Salford U., U.K.; coord. West Coast region Nat. Biodiversity Strategy Action Plan; mem. biodiversity com. Karnataka State. Contbr. articles to profl. jours. Active Dist. Com. on Sci. and Tech., 1990—, Dist. EPA, 1996-99; chmn. Village Adoption Com., 1990-96. Mem. Asian Fisheries Soc. (life), Indian Sci. Congress Assn. (life), Nat. Environ. Sci. Acad. (life, v.p. 1999—). Avocations: swimming, reading. Home: 2 Vinyas Prashanth Nagar, Mangalore 575006, India Office: Dept Biosciences, Mangalore Univ, Mangalore 574199, India

MADIAN, ALAN LEONARD, economist; b. N.Y.C., May 25, 1938; s. Sydney and Anna (Lieber) M.; m. Susan R. Kneller, Apr. 20, 1986; children: Nicolas James Kneller, Antonia Chloe Kneller. AB, U. Calif., Berkeley, 1959; MA, Yale U., 1961; postgrad. New Coll., Oxford (Eng.) U., 1963-65. Sr. rsch. scientist econs. Columbia U., 1963; asst. prof. U. Rochester, N.Y., 1964-65; asst. prof., then assoc. prof. London Sch. Econs., 1965-70; sr. economist Inst. Pub. Adminstrn., N.Y.C., 1971-74; pres. Econ. Strategies, Inc., N.Y.C., 1975, 78; econ. advisor to gov. State of N.Y., 1976-77; prin. assoc. Robert R. Nathan Assocs., Washington, 1979-80; cons. U.S. Senate Antitrust Subcom., 1980; dir. econ. studies Hamilton, Rabinovitz & Szanton, Inc., Washington, 1981; pres. Madian Econ. Assocs., 1981-97; mng. dir. Erb & Madian, Inc., 1984-97; CEO Lafayette Capital Corp., 1987—; prin. Hagler Bailly Inc., 1997, v.p., 1997-99, sr. v.p., 1999—; cons. World Bank, Goldman Sachs, others. Contbr. to books and profl. jours. Mem. exec. com. Young Dems. Calif., 1958-59; dir. Children's Found., 1985-96; No.-Calif./gov. campaign mgr. Edmund G. Brown, 1962. Served with AUS, 1955. Woodrow Wilson fellow, 1959-60; Falk Found. fellow, 1960. Mem. Am. Econ. Assn., Royal Econ. Soc., Internat. Assn. Energy Economists, Nat. Assn. Bus. Economists, Phi Beta Kappa. Home: 2910 Garfield St NW Washington DC 20008-3536 Office: 1776 Eye St NW Washington DC 20006-3700

MADIANOS, MICHAEL GEORGE, psychiatry educator; b. Athens, Greece, Oct. 29, 1941; s. George Michael and Maria Eva (Costaragloy) M.; m. Dimitra Anna Gefou, July 3, 1972; children: Maria, George. MD, U. Athens, 1968; MPH, Columbia U., 1976; Doctorate in Medicine, U. Athens, 1980. Cert. in neurology and psychiatry, Greece. Rsch. fellow dept. psychiatry St. Vincent's Hosp., N.Y.C., 1976; rsch. scientist biometrics rsch. N.Y. Psychiat. Inst./Columbia U., N.Y.C., 1977; clin. assoc. dept. psychiatry Med. Sch., U. Athens/Eginition Hosp., 1978-82, asst. prof. psychiatry, 1982-88, assoc. prof. psychiatry, 1989-97; prof. psychiatry Sch. Social Scis., Faculty of Nursing, U. Athens, 1998—; head Byron Kessariani Cmty. Mental Health Ctr./Eginition Hosp., U. Athens, 1978-79; cons./temporary advisor WHO, Geneva, 1978—; chief monitoring and evaluation of psychiat. svcs. unit Univ. Mental Health Rsch., 1994—. Author 5 textbooks on social psychiatry and rehab.; contbr. articles to profl. jours. Gen. coord. exec. com. on psychiat. reform program Ministry of Health, 1990-92, pres. com. on sectorization of psychiat. care, 1999; mem. nat. mental health com. Ctrl. Health Coun. of Greece, 1996-98. Gulbright fellow, 1975-77; WHO fellow, 1978; Biomed. grantee Social Fund DG V European Commn., 1984-89, 92-97, Ministry of Health and Welfare, 1984—. Mem. World Assn. Psychosocial Rehab. (v.p. 1998—), Am. Psychiat. Assn., European Assn. Psychiatrists. Avocations: swimming, jazz, folk music, model car collecting. Home: 23 Kanari, 145-63 Kifissia, Athens Greece Office: U Athens Sch Hlth Scis, 123 Papadiamantopoulou, 115-27 Athens Greece

MADIEVSKI, ANTON, applied mathematician, researcher; b. Moscow, Apr. 4, 1965; arrived in Australia, 1991, naturalized, 1993; s. Gregory and Taissa (Roschina) M.; m. Tania Brown, July 28, 1998. MS in Applied Math., Moscow State U., 1987; PhD in Automatic Control, Australian Nat. U., Canberra, 1995. Rschr. Geophysics R&D, Moscow, 1987, sr. rschr., 1987-88, team leader, 1988-91; rschr. Coop. Rsch. Ctr. for Robust and Adaptive Systems, Canberra, 1995; rschr. Motorola, Sydney, Australia, 1995-98, sr. rsch. scientist, 1998—; guest rschr. Delft (The Netherlands) U. Tech., 1994, Cath. U. Louvain, Louvain-la-Neuve, Belgium, 1994, Swiss Fed. Inst. Tech., Lausanne, Switzerland, 1994, Lab. D'automatique de Grenoble, France, 1994. Contbr. articles to profl. jours.; reviewer profl. jours. Mem. IEEE (sr.), NY Acad. Scis. Avocations: travel, hiking, reading, swimming, skiing. Office: Motorola Rsch Ctr, 12 Lord St Botany, NSW Sydney 2019, Australia

MADISON, ANDREA PLESHETTE, health educator; b. Franklin, La., Sept. 8, 1967; d. Morris, Sr. and Mildred Mae M. AD in Gen. Studies, Northwestern State U., 1989, BA in Social Scis., 1990; MPH, Tulane U. Sch. Pub. Health, 1998. Sec. St. Mary Parish Coun., Franklin, La., 1984-90; exec. sec. La. Youth Outreach Coalition, Couchatta, La., 1987-94; legal sec. Law Offices of David Fine, New Orleans, 1994-95; adminstrv. asst. Tulane U. Sch. Medicine, New Orleans, 1995-98; pub. health intern La. Office Pub. Health, New Orleans, 1998; cons. La. Youth Outreach Coalition, Coushatta, 1996—; hosp. liaison So. Eye Bank, New Orleans, 1998—. Deaconness Spl. Providence Bapt. Ch., Franklin, La. Mem. APHA, New Orleans Track Club, AAUW, Am. Soc. for the Prevention of Cruelty to Animals. Democrat. Baptist. Avocations: running, kickboxing, nature walks. Home: 5501 Tullis Dr Apt 11-108 New Orleans LA 70131-8840

MADISON, EDDIE LAWRENCE, JR., public relations consultant, editor, writer; b. Tulsa, Sept. 8, 1930; s. Eddie Lawrence Sr. and Laverta (Pyle) M.; m. Davetta Jayn Cooksey, Nov. 17, 1956; children: Eddie Lawrence III, Karyn Devette, David Cooksey. B in Journalism, Lincoln U., Jefferson City, Mo., 1952; MA, U. Tulsa, 1959. Editor-in-chief Okla. Eagle, Tulsa, 1954-59; assoc. editor Chgo. Daily Defender, 1959-61; dep. editor Assoc. Negro Press, Chgo., 1961-63; sect. editor Chgo. Tribune, 1963-65; dep. dir. pubs. divsn. Domestic and Internat. Bus., U.S. Dept. Commerce, Washington, 1965-69; mgr. cmty. svcs. Evening Star Broadcasting Co., Washington, 1969-78; asst. editor Bus. Am. Mag., Washington, 1978-81; press asst. Ho. of Reps., Washington, 1981-82; pub. affairs specialist U.S. Dept. HHS, Washington, 1982-92, mgr. HHS radio, 1991-92; asst. prof., chmn. dept. comm. Lincoln U., 1992-99; editorspecial pubs. Okla. Eagle, Tulsa, 1999—; founder Nat. Broadcast Assn. for Cmty. Affairs, Washington, 1974, 1st pres., 1974-77. Pres. Brightwood Civic Assn., Washington, 1969-72; mem. media adv. com. Mo. Arts Coun., 1996-99; mem. tobacco coalition and assist coms. Am. Cancer Soc., 1993-99; Hist. Preservation Commn., 1997-99; bd. dirs. Opportunities Industrialization Ctr., Washington, 1971-77, D.C. United Way, 1972-77, Boy Scouts Am., Washington, 1972-77. With U.S. Army, 1952-54. Mem. Alpha Phi Alpha (pres. Washington chpt. 1969-72, nat. dir. pub. rels. 1985-91, v.p. Montgomery County chpt. 1987-89, pres. Jefferson City Beta Zeta Lambda chpt. 1993, assoc. editor Sphinx mag.). Methodist. Avocations: photography, aerobics, jogging. Home: 4355 S Braden Ave Tulsa OK 74135-6337 Office: The Okla Eagle 624 E Archer St Tulsa OK 74120-1000

MADISON-COLMORE, OCTAVIA DIANNE, adult education educator; b. Lynchburg, Va., Mar. 28, 1960; d. Raymond Barlow Sr. Madison and Doreatha Madison Anderson. BA, Hampton U., 1982; MEd, Lynchburg Coll., 1983; postgrad., George Mason U., Fairfax, Va., 1989-94; EdD, Va. Poly. Inst. and State U., 1997. Lic. profl. counselor, addiction counselor, lic. marriage and fam. therapist; cert. sports counselor. Resource counselor Lynchburg Community Action Group, 1983, placement specialist, 1984; program mgr. Lynchburg 70001 Program, 1985; therapist, case mgr. Cen. Va. Community Svcs., Lynchburg, 1985-88; substance abuse counselor II Fairfax County Govt., 1988-94; therapist Women's Ctr. No. Va., Vienna, 1990-93; psychotherapist Dr. Carolyn Jackson-Sahni-Assocs., 1993; mental

health therapist Arlington County Dept. Human Svcs., 1994-97; grad. asst. Va. Poly. Inst. and State U., 1994-97; asst. prof. Va. Tech., 1997—. Asst. sec. So. Christian Leadership Conf., Lynchburg, 1983-84; mem. single ministry, asst. chair youth adv. bd. Mt. Pleasant Bapt. Ch., Alexandria, Va., 1991—; bd. examiners Profl. Counselors, 1991—; sec.-treaas. Va. Counselors' Assn. Multucultural and Devel. Divsn., 1999. Recipient 2-Star award United Way (coord.), 1989. Mem. Am. Assn. for Counseling and Devel., Women's Ctr. Career Network, Advs. for Infants and Mothers, Inc., Nat. Black Alcoholism Coun., Va. Counselor's Assn. (sec.-treas. multicultural devel. divsn. 1999), Washington Met. Area Addictions Counselors, Nat. Bd. Cert. Counselors, Psi Chi, Beta Kappa Chi. Avocations: reading, swimming, sports, viewing mountains. Home: 6341 Mary Todd Ct Centreville VA 20121-3547

MADJIROVA, NADEJDA PETROVA, psychiatrist, educator; b. Plovdiv, Bulgaria, Nov. 7, 1945; d. Peter Todorov and Ivanka Nikolova (Kostova) M.; m. Petko Tanev Valkov, Oct. 31, 1940; 1 child, Stoyanka. MD, Higher Med. Inst., Plovdiv, 1971; PhD, Med. Acad., Sofia, Bulgaria, 1985. Psychiatrist Psychiat. Hosp., Radnevo, Bulgaria, 1971-76; asst. prof. Higher Med. Inst., Plovdiv, 1976-85, chief asst. prof., 1985-89, assoc. prof., 1989—. Contbr. articles to profl. jours. Mem. N.Y. Acad. Sci., Psychiat. Soc. in Bulgaria, Assn. for Child Psychiatry, Chronobiol. Soc., Internat. Soc. Chronobiology, Bulgarian Chronobiology and Biometeorology Soc. (pres. 1998—). Avocations: pen and ink drawing, wood carving. Home: Peter Stoev 123, 4004 Plovdiv Bulgaria Office: High Med Inst, Vassil Aprilov 15-A, 4002 Plovdiv Bulgaria

MADLANG, RODOLFO MOJICA, retired urologic surgeon; b. Indang, Cavite, The Philippines, Apr. 9, 1918; came to U.S., 1953; s. Simeon Fajardo and Eugenia R. (Mojica) Madlangsacay; m. Lourdes Recto Gregorio, Dec. 8, 1946; children: Cesar, Rodolfo G., Mercy Lynn. AA, U. Philippines, Manila, 1939, MD, 1945. Diplomate Am. Bd. Urology. Resident in gen. surgery Philippine Gen. Hosp., Manila, 1946-49; resident in urology St. Francis Hosp., Peoria, Ill., 1953-55; asst. prof. physiology Far Ea. U. Inst. Medicine, Manila, 1956-58, cons. in urology, 1956-58; attending urologist St. Catherine Hosp., East Chicago, Ind., 1958-81, chief surgery, 1977-79; attending urologist St. Margaret Hosp., Hammond, Ind., 1960-81; chief urology U.S. VA Outpatient Clinic, L.A., 1982-98. Fellow ACS; mem. AMA, Am. Urol. Assn., Pan Pacific Surg. Assn., Assn. Mil. Surgeons of the U.S., Ind. State Med. Assn., N.Y. Acad. Scis. Republican. Roman Catholic.

MADNI, ASAD MOHAMED, engineering executive; b. Bombay, Sept. 8, 1947; came to U.S., 1966; s. Mohamed Taher and Sara Taher (Wadiwalla) M.; Gowhartaj Shahnawaz, Nov. 11, 1976; 1 child, Jamal Asad. Gen. cert. edn., U. Cambridge, Eng., 1964; AAS in Electronics, RCA Insts., Inc., 1968; BS in Engring., UCLA, 1969, MS in Engring., 1972; postgrad. exec. inst., Stanford U., 1984; cert. in engring. mgmt., Calif. Inst. Tech., 1987; PhD in Engring., Calif. Coast U., 1987; sr. exec. program, MIT, 1990. Chartered elec. engr., U.K.; chartered engr. Engring. Coun., U.K. Sr. instr. Pacific States U., L.A., 1969-71; sr. electronics auditor Pertec Corp., Chatsworth, Calif., 1973-75; project engr., sr. engr., prog. mgr., dir. advanced programs Microwave div. Systron Donner, Van Nuys, Calif., 1975-82, dir. engring., 1982-92; gen. mgr. Microwave and Instrument div. Systron Donner, Van Nuys, Calif., 1985-90; chmn., pres., chief exec. officer Systron Donner Corp., 1990-92; pres., CEO Sensors and Controls Group BEI Electronics, Inc., 1992-93, BEI Motion Sys. Co., 1993-94, BEI Sensors & Sys. Co., 1994—; pres., COO BEI Techs. Inc., 2000—; vice-chmn. IEEE-MTTS, San Fernando Valley chpt., 1991-92, chmn., 1992-94; tech. advisor Test and Measurement World, Boston, 1982-90; adv. Calif. State U. Northridge. Mem. editorial rev. bd., West coast chmn. Microwave Systems News and Communications Tech., 1982-90; contbr. more than 60 articles to numerous tech. publs.; patentee in field. Fellow IEEE (3d Millennium medal), Instn. Elec. Engrs. (U.K.), Inst. for Advancement of Engring., N.Y. Acad. Scis.; mem. AIAA (life sr.), AAAS, NRA (life), Soc. Automotive Engrs., Assn. Old Crows (life, gold cert. of merit 1992), Calif. Rifle and Pistol Assn. (life), MIT Soc. Sr. Execs. (life), UCLA Alumni Assn. (life), MIT Alumni Assn. (life). Home: 3281 Woodbine St Los Angeles CA 90064-4836 Office: BEI Sensors & Systems Co 13100 Telfair Ave Sylmar CA 91342-3576

MADONNA (MADONNA LOUISE VERONICA CICCONE), singer, actress; b. Bay City, Mich., Aug. 16, 1958; d. Sylvio and Madonna Ciccone; m. Sean Penn, Aug. 16, 1985 (div. 1989); 1 child, Lourdes. Student, U. Mich., 1976-78. Dancer Alvin Ailey Dance Co., N.Y.C., 1979; CEO Maverick Records, L.A. Albums include Madonna, 1983, Like a Virgin, 1985, True Blue, 1986, (soundtrack)Who's That Girl, 1987, (with others) Vision Quest Soundtrack, 1983, You Can Dance, 1987, Like a Prayer, 1989, I'm Breathless: Music From and Inspired by the Film Dick Tracy, 1990, The Immaculate Collection, 1990, Erotica, 1992, Bedtime Stories, 1994, Something to Remember, 1995, Ray of Light, 1998 (Grammy award for Best Pop Album 1999), (with others) Austin Powers, The Spy Who Shagged Me soundtrack, 1999; film appearances include A Certain Sacrifice, 1980, Vision Quest, 1985, Desperately Seeking Susan, 1985, Shanghai Surprise, 1986, Who's That Girl, 1987, Bloodhounds of Broadway, 1989, Dick Tracy, 1990, Truth or Dare, 1991, Madonna, 1992, Body of Evidence, 1992, A League of Their Own, 1992, Dangerous Game, 1993, Blue in the Face, 1995, Four Rooms, 1996, Girl 6, 1996, Evita, 1996 (Golden Globe, 1997); Broadway theater debut in Speed-the-Plow, 1987; TV Happy Birthday Elizabeth: A Celebration of a Life, 1997, The Next Best Thing, 2000; author: Sex, 1992. Roman Catholic. Office: 8491 W Sunset Blvd Ste 485 West Hollywood CA 90069-1911 Address: Maverick Recording Co 9348 Civic Center Dr Ste 100 Beverly Hills CA 90210-3606

MÁDR, OTO, theologian, researcher, editor; b. Prague, Czech Republic, Feb. 15, 1917; s. František and Anna (Marková) M. ThD, Charles U., Prague, 1950; ThD (hon.), Friedrich-Wilhelm U., Bonn, Germany, 1991. Ordained priest Roman Cath. Ch., 1942. Priest Archdiocese of Prague, 1942-51, 70-78; state prisoner Czech Socialist Republic, 1951-66; worker hosp., Prague, 1966-69; prof. Faculty of Theology, Prague-Litoměřice, 1969-70; editor-in-chief Teologické texty, Prague, 1978—; cons. Cardinal Tomášek, Prague, 1968-90; prof. theology underground univ., Prague, 1978-89; sec. theol. commn. Czech Bishop Conf., Prague, 1969-70, mem. theol. commn., 1990—. Author: The Church's Modus Moriendi, 1977, Tolerance Within the Context of Ethics, 1982, How the Church Does Not Perish, 1986, A Word About This Time, 1992; editor Czech Cath. samizdat, Prague, 1978-89. Bd. dirs. Living Theology, Prague, 1969-70; leader underground student movement, Prague, 1950-51. Named Monsignore-Prelate, Pope John Paul II, Rome, 1991; named to Masaryk Order, Pres. of Czech Republic, Prague, 1997. Mem. Czech Dept. of European Assn. for Cath. Theology (chmn. 1990-97). Home: Marie Cibulkové 5, 140 00 Prague Czech Republic Office: Teologické texty, Londynská 44, 120 00 Prague Czech Republic

MADRAZO CUELLAR, JORGE LUIS, Mexican government official. Atty. gen. Govt. of Mex., 1996—. Office: Office of Attorney General, Reforma Norte y Violeta 2o Col, Guerrero 06300, Mexico*

MADRICK, JEFFREY G., writer, economic consultant; b. N.Y.C., July 15, 1947; s. Milton and Corazon (De Arego) M.; m. Gloria Jean Adrian, June 29, 1969 (div. 1975); 1 child, Matina. BS salutatorian, NYU, 1969; MBA, Harvard U., 1971. Writer, columnist Money Mag., N.Y.C., 1972-75; fin. editor, columnist Bus. Week, N.Y.C., 1975-78; exec. asst. to pres. Columbia Pictures, N.Y.C., 1979-80; writer, cons. N.Y.C., 1980-82; TV corr., commentator ESPN, N.Y.C., 1982-85, NBC News, N.Y.C., 1985-93; writer N.Y.C., 1993—; adj. prof. social sci. Cooper Union, N.Y.; sr. fellow World Policy Inst., N.Y. Author: Taking America, 1987 (Bus. Week award 1987), The End of Affluence, 1995 (N.Y. Times Notable Book award); editor Challenge Mag., 1995—. Recipient Emmy award, 1986, Page One award Newspaper Guild, 1979. Mem. Beta Gamma Sigma.

MADRID, OLGA HILDA GONZALEZ, retired elementary education educator, association executive; b. San Antonio, May 4, 1928; d. Victor A. and Elvira Ardilla Gonzalez; m. Sam Madrid, Jr., June 29, 1952; children: Ninette Marie, Samuel James. Student, U. Mex., San Antonio, St. Mary's U., San Antonio; BA, Our Lady of Lake U., 1956, MEd, 1963. Cert. bilingual tchr., adminstr., Tex. Sec. Lanier High Sch. San Antonio Ind. Sch. Dist., 1945-52, tchr. Collins Garden Elem. Sch., Storm Elem. Sch., 1963-92; tutor Dayton, Ohio, 1952-54; bd. dirs., sch. rep. San Antonio Tchr.'s Coun., 1970-90; chair various coms. Collins Garden Elem., 1970-92. Elected dep. precinct, senatorial and state Dem. Convs., San Antonio, 1968—; apptd. commr. Keep San Antonio Beautiful, 1985; life mem., past pres. San Antonio YWCA; bd. dirs. Luth. Gen. Hosp., Nat. Conf. Christians and Jews, Cath. Family and Children's Svcs., St. Luke's Luth. Hosp.; nat. bd. dirs. YWCA, 1985-96, also mem. exec. com.; mem. edn. commn. Holy Rosary Parish, 1994—; mem. bus. assocs. com. Our Lady of the Lake U., 1995—. Recipient Outstanding Our Lady Lake Alumni award Our Lady Lake U., 1975, Guadalupana medal San Antonio Cath. Archdiocese, 1975, Yellow Rose Tex. citation Gov. Briscoe, 1977; Olga H. Madrid Ctr. named in her honor, YWCA San Antonio and San Antonio City Coun., 1983; Lo Mejor De Lo Nuestro honoree San Antonio Light, 1991, honoree San Antonio Women's History Month Coalition, 1996; named Our Lady of Lake Outstanding Alumna, 1999. Mem. San Antonio Bus. and Profl. Women, Inc. (mem. exec. com.), Salute Quality Edn. (honoree 1993), Delta Kappa Gamma (Theta Beta chpt., mem. exec. com.). Avocations: reading, gardening. Home: 2726 Benrus Blvd San Antonio TX 78228-2319

MADRIGAL, JOSE ALEJANDRO, hematology, educator, researcher; b. Mexico City, Nov. 4, 1953; arrived in Eng., 1993; s. Luis Madrigal and Aurora Fernandez; m. Maria Elena Macarty, June 1977. BS, U. de Valle de Mexico, 1973; MD, U. Nacional Autonoma, Mexico, 1978; PhD, U. London, 1989. Specialist internal medicine U. Nacional Autonoma, Mexico, 1979-83; clin. rsch. fellow Harvard U., Dana-Farber Cancer Inst., Boston, 1983-85; hon. sr. registrar St. Bartholomew's Hosp., London, 1985-88; clin. rsch. fellow Imperial Cancer Rsch. Fund, London, 1985-88; postdoctoral rsch. fellow Stanford U. Sch. Medicine, 1989-93; hon. lectr. dept. immunology Royal Postgrad. Med. Sch., 1993—, hon. sr. lectr. dept. hematology, 1993—; rsch. dir. The Anthony Nolan Rsch. Inst., 1995—; prof. hematology Royal Free Hosp. Sch. Medicine, U. London, 1997—; vis. fellow Meml. Sloan-Kettering Cancer Ctr., N.Y., 1985;. Contbr. articles to profl. jours. Fellow Royal Coll. Physicians London; mem. European Fedn. for Immunogenetics, Am. Soc. Hematology, Am. Soc. Histocompatibility and Immunogetics, Brit. Soc. Immunology, Royal Coll. Pathologists London, Harvard Med. Alumni Assn. Avocations: tennis, marathon running. E-mail: madrigal@rfhsm.ac.uk. Fax: 44 20 7284 8331. Office: Anthony Nolan Rsch Inst, Royal Free U Pond St, Hampstead NW3 2QG, England

MADRON, FRANTIŠEK, management consultant; b. Brno, Czechoslovakia, May 6, 1948; s. František and Božena (Vaigl) M.; m. Libuše Veverka; children: Miloš, Vit. MS, Tech. U., Pardubice, Czech Republic, 1971; PhD, Czech Acad. Sci., Prague, Czech Republic, 1975. Rschr. Vuanch, Ústi n L, Czech Republic, 1975-92; pres. Chemplant Tech., Ústi n L, Czech Republic, 1993—. Author: (books) Process Plant Performance, 1992, Balancing in Process Industries, 1997. Avocation: gardening. Office: Chemplant Tech SRO, Hrncirska 4, 40001 Ústi n L Czech Republic

MADSEN, BJØRN LINDEGAARD, orthopaedist; b. Nykøbing, S.J., Denmark, Sept. 9, 1958. MD, Copenhagen U., 1986. Orthopaedist CS Slagelse Hosp., Denmark, 1988-89, Bispebjerg Hosp., Denmark, 1991-93, Rask Koege Hosp., Denmark, 1993-96, Kas Glostrup Hosp., Denmark, 1996-98. Mem. Danish Orthop. Soc.

MADSEN, H(ENRY) STEPHEN, retired lawyer; b. Momence, Ill., Feb. 5, 1924; s. Frederick and Christine (Landgren) M.; m. Carol Ruth Olmstead, Dec. 30, 1967; children: Stephen Stewart, Christie Morgan, Kelly Ann. MBA, U. Chgo., 1948; LLB, Yale U., 1951. Bar: Wash. 1951, Ohio 1953, U.S. Supreme Ct. 1975. Research asst. Wash. Water Power Co., Spokane, 1951; assoc. Baker, Hostetler & Paterson, Cleve., 1952-59, ptnr., 1960-88, sr. ptnr., 1989-92; ret., 1992; chmn. bd. trustees Blue Cross Northeastern, Ohio, 1972-81; Danish consul for Ohio, 1973-98, bd. dirs. Compradore Ltd. Active Bus. Advisers Cleve.; trustee Breckenridge Ret. Cmty., Ohio Presbyn. Ret. Cmty. Served with AC U.S. Army, 1943-46. Decorated Knight Queen of Denmark, 1982. Fellow ABA (life); mem. Am. Coll. Trial Lawyers (life), Am. Law Inst., Cleve. Bar Assn., The Country Club of Cleve., The Club at Soc. Ctr. Office: Baker & Hostetler 3200 National City Ctr 17409 Wildoak Pl Chagrin Falls OH 44023-1414

MADSEN, KNUD VESTERGAARD, quality assurance engineer; b. Denmark, Jan. 18, 1945; s. Christian Ole and Kristine M. Student, Aarhus Acad., Denmark, 1969; MSc in Engring., Danish Tech. U., Denmark, 1975. Quality assurance engr. Corp. Danfoss, Denmark, 1976-78; quality coord. Storno Inc., Copenhagen, 1979-83; pvt. practice internat. mgmt. cons., 1983-87; quality assurance EDP Statis. and OR, 1987-91, cons., 1992—. Served with Danish mil., 1963-64. Mem. Soc. Danish Engrs. Liberal. Avocations: classical music, literature, art, sports. Home: Stengaardsvaenge 66, DK-2800 Lyngby Denmark Office: Stengaards Vaenge 66, DK-2800 Lyngby Denmark

MADSEN, KRISTEN BENT, retired psychologist, educator; b. Kalundborg, Denmark, June 5, 1922; s. Ambrosius and Kirstine (Kristensen) M.; m. Ellen Stjernholm Larson, Aug. 3, 1946; children: Birger, Arne. Degree in Psychology, U. Copenhagen, 1950, PhD, 1959. Tchr. Copenhagen, 1944-51, sch. psychologist, 1951-55; lectr. Tchr. Training Coll., Copenhagen, 1955-62; prof. psychology U. of Edn., Copenhagen, 1962-89; retired U. Copenhagen, 1989. Author: Psychology, 1949, Theories of Motivation, 1959, 4th edit. 1968, Modern Theories of Motivation, 1974, A History of Psychology in Metascientific Perspective, 1988, 22 others; contbr. articles to profl. jours. Mem. The Danish Psychol. Assn. (hon.). Home: Kaerdals Alle 14, 2610 Rødovre Denmark

MADU, LEONARD EKWUGHA, lawyer, human rights officer, newspaper columnist, politician, business executive; b. Ibadan, Nigeria, Mar. 17, 1953; came to U.S., 1977; s. Luke E. and Grace (Dureke) M.; m. Jaculine Stephanie Turner, June 4, 1980; children: Christine, Oscar. BA, Marshall U., 1980; JD, U. Tenn., 1988; MA, Am. U. Rsch. assoc. Lamberts Publs., Washington, 1980-82; data specialist Govt. Employees Ins. Co., Washington, 1982-85; law intern Knoxville (Tenn.) Urban League, 1986-88; cons. Morris Brown Coll., Atlanta, 1988; staff atty. East Carolina Legal Svc., Wilson, N.C., 1989-90; cons. youth devel. Nat. Crime Prevention Coun., Washington, 1990; contract compliance officer Walters State C.C., Morristown, Tenn., 1990; examiner Dept. of Human Svc., Nashville, 1990-93; human rights officer Human Rights Commn., Nashville, 1993—; pres. Panafrica, Nashville, 1994—; CEO Madu and Assoc. Internat. Bus. Cons., 1996—; with Bus. Forum & Banquet, 1994—; polit. cons. Embassy of Nigeria, Washington, 1995; cons. Embassy of Sierra Leone, Washington, 1995, Healthcare Internat. Mgmt. Co., 1996—; bd. dirs. Peace and Justice Ctr., Nashville. Editor: African Nations Handbook, 1994, Directory of African Universities and Colleges, 1994; editor-in-chief Panafrican Digest, 1994, Panafrican Jour. of World Affairs, 1994; columnist Met. Times, Nashville, 1991—, The African Herald, Dallas, 1995—, U.S./African Voice, Balt., 1995—, African Sun Times, 1995—, The Nigerian and African, 1995—, The African Press, N.Y. Co-chmn. Clergy and Laity Concerned, Nashville, 1992-95; mem. curriculum and character com. Met. Sch. Bd., Nashville, 1994-97; co-coordinator The Haitian Project, 1991-94; vice-chmn. Nigerian Network Leadership awards N.Y., 1996; chmn. Internat. Women's Expo, Knoxville, 1996; co-chair Miss Nigeria Internat. Beauty Pageant, Washington, 1995, Miss Africa Internat. Beauty Pageant, Nashville, 1996, Igbo Union Chieftaincy Coronation Ceremony, Nashville, 1995; chmn. Nigerian Patriotic Front, 1997—; coord. United Nigeria Congress Party, 1997—, Southeast U.S.; recruiter internat. students Tenn. State U., 1998—. Recipient World Hunger Devel. Program award Marshall U., 1978-79, Hall of Nations scholar Am. U., 1980, 82, Mary Strohbel award United Way, 1994-95, Nonprofit Vol. award Nat. Conf. of Christians and Jews, 1994. Mem. NAACP, U.S. Com. on Fgn. Rels., Soc. Profl. Journalists, UN Assn., Orgn. African Natonals (pres. 1994), African C. of C. (pres. 2000—). Avocations: reading, travel, soccer, ping-pong, tennis. Office: Panafrica 1016 18th Ave S Nashville TN 37212-2105

MADUNA, PENUELL, federal official; b. Johannesburg, South Africa, Dec. 29, 1952; 3 children. LLB, LLM. Atty., notary, conveyancer; establisher dept. legal constl. affairs African Nat. Congress; dep. min. Ministry of Home Affairs, 1994-96; min. Ministry of Mineral and Energy Affairs, Pretoria, South Africa, 1996—, Ministry of Justice and Constnl. Devel., Pretoria. Office: Pvt Bag X 646 Synodical Ctr, Corner Andries and Visagie, Pretoria 0001, South Africa Address: Paul Kruger & Pretorias St, Pvt Bag X276 8th Fl, Pretoria 0001, South Africa*

MADUREIRA, OMAR MOORE DE, mechanical engineering educator; b. São Paulo, Oct. 24, 1935; s. Olyntho and Giannina (Moore) M.; m. Marina Mesquita Sampaio, Jan. 20, 1965; children: Miriam, Mauricio, Flavia. Degree in mech. engring., U. São Paulo, 1960; MSME, Purdue U., 1963. Registered profl. engr., Brazil. Engr. Willys, São Paulo, 1964-68; engr. Ford Brazil, São Paulo, 1968-73, engring. supr., 1973-76, engring. mgr.; supt. Promec SC Ltd., São Paulo, 1978-80, dir., 1980—; pvt. cons., São Paulo, 1985—; prof. Escola Politecnica Univ. Sao Paulo, São Paulo, 1961-96, Fund. Vanzolini, São Paulo, 1991—, Assn. Brasileira de Engenharia Automotiva, São Paulo, 1990—. Contbr. articles to profl. publs. Oswaldo Aranha scholar, 1961. Mem. Assn. Brasileira de Ciencias Mecanicas, Soc. Automotive Engrs.- Brazil, Inst. Engring. Sao Paulo. E-mail: promec@sti.com.br. Office: Promec SC Ltda, Rua Pinheiros 1405 4oA, 05422012 São Paulo SP, Brazil

MADŽAR, LJUBOMIR, economics educator; b. Budačka Rijeka, Karlovac, Croatia, Sept. 30, 1938; arrived in Serbia, 1949; s. Djuro Grudič and Dragana M.; m. Marta Bazler, Oct. 14, 1967; children: Aleksandar, Lidija. BA in Econs., U. Beograd, Yugoslavia, 1961; MA Ctr. for Devel. Econs., Williams Coll., Williamstown, Mass., 1964; PhD in Econs., U. Beograd, 1968. Rsch. asst. Fed. Planning Bur., Beograd, Yugoslavia, 1961-62; rsch. asst. Inst. Econ. Scis., Beograd, 1963-68, rsch. assoc., 1969-73, sr. rsch. assoc., 1974-84, sci. advisor, 1984—; asst. prof. Faculty Econs., Univ. Beograd, 1970-75, assoc. prof., 1976-82, prof. econs., 1982—. Author: (books) Essentials of the Theory of Production, 1972, Optimization Methods in the Theory of Production and Growth, 1973, 3d rev. edit., 1979, Twilight of Socialist Economies, 1990, Ownership and Reform (2 vols.), 1995.; editor-in-chief Ekomomska Misao, Beograd, 1987-91; staff Econ. Anals. Mem. Coun. Econ. Advisors, Federal Govt., Beograd, Yugoslavia, 1989-90. Served with Yugoslav People's Army, 1961-62. Recipient award Inst. Econ. Scis., Beograd, 1965, Charter of Honor, Serbian Econ. Assn., Beograd, 1987. Mem. Civic Assn. (Econ. Coun.). Home: Arsenija Čarnojevica 126, 11070 Novi Beograd Serbia, Yugoslavia Office: Econ Faculty U Beograd, Kamenička 6, 11000 Beograd Serbia, Yugoslavia

MAE, TADAHIKO, plant physiologist; b. Tokyo, May 14, 1943; s. Minori and Kimiko (Takagi) M.; m. Michiko Yamazaki, May 30, 1976; three children. BS, Chiba U., 1966; MS, Tohoku U., 1968, PhD, 1971. From rsch. assoc. to prof. Tohoku U., Sendai, Japan, 1971—; postdoctoral fellow Ctr. Plant Physiol. Rsch., Wageningen, The Netherlands, 1972-73, U. Ill., Urbana, 1976-77; vis. prof. Inst. Grassland & Environ. Rsch., Aherstwyth, U.K., 1990-91. Mem. Japanese Soc. Soil Sci. & Plant Nutrition (award 1991), Japan Soc. Promotion of Sci. (grantee 1997—). Avocation: fishing. Office: Gras Sch Agrl Sci Tohoku U, 1-1 Tsutsumidori Amamiyamachi, Sendai 981-8555, Japan

MAEDA, HISATOSHI, medical technology educator; b. Shizuoka, Japan, Nov. 26, 1944; s. Shin-ichi and Hana Maeda; m. Noriko Suzuki; children: Masao, Ryoko, Shigekazu. MSEE, Calif. Inst. Tech., 1970, PhD, 1972; DSc, Tokyo U., 1977; MD in Radiology, Kyoto (Japan) U., 1978. Asst. dept. radiology Kyoto U., 1980-83; lectr. dept. radiology Fukui (Japan) Med. Sch., 1983-88; dir. dept. radiology Okazaki (Japan) Mcpl. Hosp., 1988-93, Nagoya (Japan) Red Cross Hosp., 1993-95; assoc. prof. med. tech. Nagoya U., 1995-99, prof. med. sci., 1999—. Avocations: tennis, skiing, yachting. Home: 4-5-7 Kibougaoka Chikusa-ku, Nagoya 464, Japan

MAEDA, KATSUNOSUKE, chemical company executive; b. Feb. 5, 1931. Pres., CEO Toray Industries, Inc., Tokyo, chmn. bd.; CEO Katsuhiko Hirai. Office: Toray Industries Inc, 2-1 Nihonbasahi-Muromachi 2-chome, Chuo-ku Tokyo 103-8666, Japan*

MAEDA, KENJI, medical educator; b. Tsu-City, Japan, Apr. 1, 1939; s. Tamotsu and Sumi (Kubo) M.; m. Mayuko Matsunaga, Mar. 30, 1975; children: Kayaho, Mayuho. MD, Nagoya U., 1965, PhD, 1978. Intern Nagoya U. Br. Hosp., 1965-66, asst., 1973-79, assoc. prof., 1979-91, prof., 1991—, dir., 1992-96. Editor: Contributions to Nephrology, 1993, 94; contbr. articles to profl. jours. Recipient Jinkenkyukai award Japan Kidney Found., Tokyo, 1993. Mem. N.Y. Acad. Sci., AAAS, Am. Soc. Nephrology. Home: 20-1 5 chome Fujimidai, Chikusa-ku, Nagoya Aichi 464-0015, Japan Office: Nagoya U Daiko Med Ctr, 20-1-1 Daiko Higashi-Ku, Nagoya 461-0047, Japan

MAEDA, MASANOBU, physiology educator, researcher; b. Osaka, Japan, Aug. 24, 1952; s. Shunichirou and Misao Maeda; m. Eiko Ikeuchi, June 12, 1982; children: Akiko, Ayako, Satoko, Eiichi. MD, Osaka City U., 1979, PhD, 1985. Resident Osaka City U. Hosp., 1979-81; instr. Osaka City U. Med. Sch., 1985-91, asst. prof., 1991-92; assoc. prof. sys. physiology U. Occupl. Environ. Health, Kitakyushu, Japan, 1993-2000; prof. physiology Med. U., Wakayama, Japan, 2000—; vis. prof. U. Medicine and Dentistry of N.J., N.J. Med. Sch., Newark, 1989-91. Contbr. articles to profl. jours. Grantee Ministry of Edn., Sci., Sports and Culture of Japan, 2000. Fellow Physiol. Soc. Japan; mem. Am. Physiol. Soc., Soc. for Neurosci., Internat. Soc. for Autonomic Neurosci., Am. Heart Assn. (circulation coun.). Avocations: music, mountaineering. Office: Wakayama Med U Dept Physiol, 811-1 Kimiidera, Wakayama City 641-8509, Japan

MAEDA, NOBUAKI, biochemist, educator; b. Yokohama, Kanagawa, Japan, Mar. 12, 1959; s. Masayoshi and Sumie (Murayama) M. BS, Nagoya (Japan) U., 1981, MS, 1983; PhD, Osaka (Japan) U., 1988. Postdoctoral fellow Inst. for Protein Rsch., Osaka, 1988-90; rsch. assoc. Inst. Devel. Rsch., Aichi, Japan, 1990-92, Nat. Inst. Basic Biology, Aichi, 1992-97; asst. prof. Grad. U. Advanced Studies, Aichi, 1993-97; assoc. prof. Nat. Inst. for Basic Biology, Aichi, 1997—, Grad. U. for Advanced Studies, Kanagawa, 1999—. Contbr. articles to profl. jours. Recipient postdoctoral fellowship Japan Soc. for Promotion of Sci., 1988-90. Mem. Japanese Biochem. Soc., Japanese Soc. Neurosci. Office: Nat Inst Basic Biology, 38 Nishigonaka, Myodaijicho, Okazaki 444-8585, Japan

MAEDA, NOBUO, health economist; b. Kazuno-shi, Japan, Dec. 25, 1932; s. Enzo and Asa Maeda; m. Naoko Abe, Nov. 30, 1958; children: Jun, Michiko. B of Econs., Tohoku U., 1955; PhD, Med. Sch., 1963. Asst. Tohoku U., Sendai, Japan, 1955-61, lectr., 1961-64, asst. prof., 1964-68; researcher Nat. Inst. Pub. Health, Tokyo, 1968-88; prof. Sapporo (Japan) Med. U., 1988-95, Seigaku-In U., Ageo, Japan, 1995—. Author: Book of Health Care and Social Policy. Fellow WHO, 1973, Fulbright Commn., 1981, 93. Mem. Am. Pub. Health Assn. (founder Nobuo Maeda's award). Avocations: Go, Japanese chess, photography, trips. Home: 4-1302 6-1 Hikarigaoka, Nerima-ku Tokyo 179-0072, Japan Office: Seigaku-In U, Ageo-shi Saitama 362-0053, Japan

MAEDA, YASUO, biologist, educator; b. Nagoya, Aichi-ken, Japan, Dec. 12, 1942; s. Toyotaro and Kiyoko Maeda; m. Mineko Kibata, June 4, 1966; 1 child, Miwako. BS, Nagoya U., 1965; MS, Osaka (Japan) U., 1967; DSc, Kyoto (Japan) U., 1971. Asst. prof. Kyoto U., 1967-82; assoc. prof. Tohoku U., Sendai, Japan, 1982-92, prof., 1992—; organizer 46th Yamada Conf. on Dictyostelium, 1996. Editor: (book) Dictyostelium: A Model System for Cell and Developmental Biology, 1997. Recipient Zool. Sci. award Zool. Soc. Japan, 1996. Avocations: tennis, fishing, hiking, classical music. Home: Kawauchi-jutaku 1-101, Motohasekura 35, Aoba-ku 980-0861, Japan Office: Tohoku U, Biol Inst Grad Sch of Sci, Aoba 980-8578, Japan

MAEDA, YOSHINOBU, physicist, educator; b. Yokkaichi, Mie, Japan, May 1, 1959; s. Kuranoshuke and Toshiko (Murayama) M.; m. Sumiko Yamamoto, Nov. 18, 1984; children: Daiki, Yoshiki. BS, Nihon U., Tokyo, Japan, 1982; MS, Mie U., Tsu, Japan, 1984; PhD, Nagoya (Japan) Inst. Tech., 1989. Rschr. Mitsubishi Electric Corp., Tokyo, 1984-85; rsch. asst. Toyota Tech. Inst., Nagoya, 1989-92, lectr., 1992—; Precursory Rsch. for Embryonic Sci. and Tech. rschr. Rsch. Devel. Corp. Japan, Tokyo, 1992-94; vis. scholar U. Pitts., 1994. Contbr. articles to profl. jours. Mem. Japan Soc. Applied Physics, Physics Soc. Japan, Laser Soc. Japan, Inst. Elec. Info. and Comm. Engr. Achievements include discovery of negative nonlinear absorption effect (Maeda effect) and all-optical operational amplifier. Home:

2220 Kawarada, Yokkaichi 510, Japan Office: Toyota Tech Inst, 2-12-1 Hisakata Tempaku, Nagoya 468, Japan

MAEGAKI, YOSHIHIRO, pediatric neurologist; b. Mikata-chyo, Hyogo, Japan, Apr. 10, 1962; s. Bentaro and Sumiko (Kishi) M.; m. Junko Nakamura, May, 1992; 3 children. MD, Tottori U., Yonago, Japan, 1988. Resident in pediat. Tottori U., Yonago, 1988-89, from rsch. fellow to asst. prof., 1993-97; pediatrician Tottori Prefectural Hosp., Tottori, 1989-90, Nishi-Tottori Nat. Hosp., Tottori, 1990-91; rsch. fellow Cleve. Clinic Found., Cleve., 1997-98; chief dr. inpatient Tottori U., Yonago, 1993-96, chief dr. outpatient, 1994-95. Contbr. articles to profl. jours. Mem. Japanese Soc. Child Neurology, Japanese Soc. Neurology, Japanese Soc. Clin. Neurophysiology. Avocations: sports, music, movies, sight-seeing. Office: Tottori U Divsn Child Neur, 36-1 Nishi-Machi, 683-8504 Yonago Japan

MAEKAWA, KATSUHIRO, manufacturing educator, machinist, researcher; b. Furano, Hokkaido, Japan, Feb. 6, 1950; s. Toyomi and Ryoko (Kawamura) M.; m. Yoko Takahashi, Sept. 21, 1985; 1 child, Kotaro. BEng, Muroran Inst. Tech., 1973, MEng, 1975; PhD, Tokyo Inst. Tech., 1979. Rsch. assoc. Tokyo Inst. Tech., 1979-80; asst. prof. Kitami (Japan) Inst. Tech., 1980-88; assoc. prof. Ibaraki U., Hitachi, Japan, 1988-00, prof., Superplasticity Rsch. Ctr., 2000—; cons. Hitachi Koki Engring, 1990—; advisor Japan Key-TEC Ctr., Tokyo, 1993-95. Recipient Sci. Rsch. grant Japanese Ministry Edn., 1989-90, 93-94, 96-97, Rsch. fellowship Leeds U., Engring. and Phys. Scis. Rsch. Coun., U.K., 1995-96. Mem. Japan Soc. Precision Engring. (jour. referee 1992—), Precision Engring., Japan Soc. Precision Engring., Inst. Materials Japan Soc. Mech. Engrs., Am. Soc. Precision Engring., Inst. Materials (U.K.). Fax: (81) 294 385047. E-mail: mae@mech.ibaraki.ac.jp. Home: 3064-1 Sawa, 312-0001 Hitachinaka Japan Office: Ibaraki U Superpl Rsch Ctr, 4-12-1 Nakanarusawa, 316-8511 Hitachi Japan

MAEKAWA, YASUNARI, chemist, researcher; b. Kumamoto, Japan, May 29, 1963; s. Tokunari and Kazuko M. BS, Sci. U. Tokyo, 1986; MS, U. Tokyo, 1988, PhD, 1991. Vis. scientist IBM Almaden Rsch. Ctr., San Jose, Calif., 1991-92; rsch. assoc. U. Wis., Madison, 1992-93; rschr. Hitachi (Japan) Rsch. Lab., 1994-98; sr. rschr. Japan Atomic Energy Rsch. Inst., Takasaki, 1998—. Contbr. articles to sci. jours., including Jour. Am. Chem. Soc., Macromolecules, others. Mem. AAAS, Am. Chem. Soc., Chem. Soc. Japan, Soc. Polymer Sci. Japan. Fax: 03081-27-346-9687. E-mail: yasum@taka.jaeri.go.jp. Office: Japan Atomic Energy Rsch In, 1233 Watanuki, Gunma Takasaki 370-1292, Japan

MAELAND, JOHAN ANDREAS, microbiologist, researcher; b. Hordaland, Norway, Feb. 22, 1934; s. Nils and Hilda Maeland; divorced; children: Frode, Njall, Dag. MD, U. Bergen, Norway, 1959, PhD, 1969. Cert. specialist in med. microbiology. Intern Haugesund (Norway) Hosp., 1959-60; intern U. Hosp., Bergen, Norway, 1961-63, resident, 1963-74; asst. prof. U. Buffalo, 1971-72; head dept. microbiology Regional Hosp., Trondheim, Norway, 1975—; prof. U. Trondheim, 1975—, dean med. faculty, 1978-80; bd. dirs. Norwegian Rsch.Counsel, 1980-86. Contbr. 100 articles to profl. jours. Lt. Norwegian Air Force, 1961. Recipient Schering Corp. prize, 1984. Mem. ESCMID, Am. Soc. Microbiology, Scandinavian and Nat. Med. Socs. Mem. Conservative Party. Lutheran. Avocations: traveling, music, literature. Home: Havstadv 15A, Trondheim N 7021, Norway Office: Regional Hosp, Olav Kyrresg 17, N 7006 Trondheim Norway

MAENG, SUNG-JAE, microwave engineer, researcher; b. Yesan, Korea, May 2, 1960; s. Sang-Kuk Maeng and Kyu-Hwan Kim; m. Young-Se Lee, Nov. 5, 1988; children: Ji-Ye, Ji-Yoon. BS, Seoul Nat. U., Republic of Korea, 1984; MS, Korea Adv. Inst. Sci. & Tech., Taejon, Republic of Korea, 1986, PhD in Materials and Sci. Engring., 1996. Engr. ETRI, Taejon, 1986-90, sr. and prin. engr., 1991-2000; pres. Genstech Inc., Daejon, 2000—. Contbr. articles to Jour. Applied Physics, IEEE Transactions Microwave Theory and Technique, IEE Electronics Letters. Mem. IEEE, KITE. Achievements include phase shifters and power amplifiers for CDMA cellular phones and LMDS. Home: Hanbit Apt 130-204 Yusong, Daejon 305-755, Republic of Korea Office: Genstech Inc ICU, Chungbu Leasing Bld 3F 1305, Yusong-Gu Seo-Gu Daejon 302-830, Republic of Korea

MAENNIG, WOLFGANG GEORG CHRISTOPH, economics educator; b. Berlin, Feb. 12, 1960; s. Wolfgang and Barbara (Wassenberg) M. Dr.rer., U. Tech., Berlin, 1985. Prof. econs. European Sch. Mgmt., Berlin, 1991-92, U. Hamburg, Germany, 1992—; cons. in field. Contbr. articles to profl. jours. Mem. German Rowing Fedn. (prs. 1995—, Olympic champion 1988). Office: U Hamburg, von Melle Park 5, D-14052 Berlin Germany

MAERFELD, CHARLES, technology company executive; b. Paris, Apr. 29, 1940; s. Benjamin and Necha (Kirenberg) M.; m. Emma Benoit, July 12, 1965; children: Agnès, Karine, Julien. Group leader Thomson ASM, France; CEO CGR Ultrasonics, France, 1982-84; dir. dept. Thomson Sintra ASM, France, 1985-89; mng. dir. airborne sonars Thomas Sintra, France, 1989-92; dir. internal ops. Thomson Sintra ASM, France, 1992-93; chmn., CEO Thomson Microsonics, Sophia Antipolis, France, 1994—. Office: Thomson Microsonics, 399 Rte Des Cretes, 06904 Sophia Antipolis France

MAES, MICHAEL, psychiatrist, researcher; b. Ghent, Belgium, Mar. 10, 1954; came to U.S., 1991; s. Leo and Jeanne (Delfosse) M.; m. Steyaert Carine, Mar. 3, 1981; 2 children: Annabel, Eveline. MD, RUG Univ., Ghent, 1979, Psychiatrist, 1986; PhD, U. Antwerp, Belgium, 1991. Asst. U. Antwerp, 1986-91; asst. prof. psychiatry Case Western Res. U.-Univ. Hosp. Cleve., 1991—; asst. dir. Mental Health Clin. Rsch. Ctr.-Univ. Hosp. Cleve., 1992-95; dir. Clin. Rsch. Ctr. Mental Health, Antwerp, Belgium, 1995—; adj. prof. psychiatry Vanderbilt U., Nashville, 1996—; prof., chmn. dept. psychiatry U. Maastricht (The Netherlands), 1999—. Contbr. numerous articles to profl. jours. Mem. AAAS, Soc. Biol. Psychiatry, Internat. Brain Rsch. Assn., World Psychiat. Assn. (sec. sects.), European Coll. Neuropsychopharmacology, Internat. Soc. Psychoneuroendocrinology, European Assn. Psychiatrists, N.Y. Acad. Scis. Achievements include research in psychoneuroendocrinology and immunology of severe depression in man. Office: U Maastricht Dept Psyciatry, Postbus 5800, 6202 AZ Maastricht 6229, The Netherlands

MAETANI, IRURU, medical educator; b. Tokyo, Mar. 10, 1958; s. Teruji and Sadako (Saeki) M.; m. Haruko Hayashi, Jan. 11, 1961. M of Med. Sci., Toho U., Tokyo, 1982, MD, 1990. Resident 3d dept. internal medicine Toho U., Tokyo, 1982-87, resident, 1987-96, instr. then asst. prof., 1996—. Contbr. articles to profl. jours. Office: Toho U Ohashi Hosp, 2-17-6 Ohashi Meguro-ku, 153-8515 Tokyo Japan

MAEV, ROMAN GRIGORIEVICH, physicist, educator; b. Moscow, May 23, 1945; arrived in Can., 1993; s. Grigorii Romanovich and Miriam Benetelievna (Kompaneetz) M.; m. Elena Yuryevna Topchieva, Sept. 23, 1994. BSc, MSc, Moscow Phys. Engring. Inst., 1969; PhD, USSR Acad. Scis., Moscow, 1973. Asst. prof., assoc. prof. applied Physics and Biophysics Moscow Phys. Tech. U., 1983-94; head lab. biophys. introscopy Inst. Chem. Physics, USSR Acad. Scis., Russia, 1984-87; dir. Acoustic Microscopy Ctr. Russian Acad. Scis., 1987-97, dir. Internat. Advanced Material Study Ctr., 1997—; prof. physics, dir. Ultrasonic Rsch. Lab. U. Windsor, Ont., Can., 1996—; dir. Daimler Chrysler-U. Windsor Ctr. Imaging Rsch. and Advanced Materials Characterization, Can., 1997—; guest rschr. Nat. Inst. Stds. and Tech., Washington, 1993; vis. prof. U. Munich, 1990, Oxford U., 1988; sci. cons. Daimler-Benz AG, Siemens AG, German-Russian Non-Profit Mktg. Venture Project, 1991-94, Can.-Russia Intergovtl. Advanced Tech. Working Group, 1995—. Co-author: Sound and Light: Interaction in the Media, 1981 (award 1984); co-editor, author: Microscope Photometry and Acoustic Microscopy in Science, 1985 (award Leitz Corp. Germany 1986); co-inventor method of investigation of internal structure of objects in transmission acoustic, 1986 (gold medal Russian Nat. Exhbn. 1987). Fellow gen. counsel All Soviet Union Orgn. Young Scientists and Specialists, 1975-84; mem. UNESCO Commn. Men and the Biosphere, 1980-96; chief commn. Young Scientists in Nat. Russian Chem. Soc., 1988—; mem. program com. All Soviet Union Regular Sch. Actual Problems of Physics, 1974-84. Recipient Pioneer award World Fedn. Ultrasound in Medicine and Biology, 1988, Internat. Sci. Found. award Am. Inst. Ultrasound in Medicine, 1988, Centenary Ernst Abbe medal World Microscopical Soc., 1987. Fellow Can. Phys. Soc., Russian Acad. Scis. (sci. acoustic coun. 1982—); mem. IEEE (sr.). Avocations: skiing, music, art. Office: U Windsor Dept Physics, 401 Sunset Ave, Windsor, ON Canada

MAFFEI, ROCCO JOHN, lawyer; b. Portland, Maine, Nov. 23, 1949; s. Rocco and Grace Marie (Bartlett) M; m. Susan Marie Farrell, June 23, 1973; children: Rocco Francis, Christopher Matthew. BA in History, Trinity Coll., 1972; JD, U. Maine, 1975. Bar: Maine 1975, Mass. 1975, U.S. Dist. Ct. Maine 1975, Ohio 1977, U.S. Ct. Claim 1980, U.S. Supreme Ct. 1980, Minn. 1981, U.S. Dist. Ct. Minn. 1981. Ptnr. Briggs & Morgan Law Firm, St. Paul, 1980-83, Hart & Bruner Law Firm, Mpls., 1983-85; v.p. gen. counsel Computing Devices Internat., Bloomington, Minn., 1985-98; assoc. gen. counsel Lockheed Martin Tactical Def. Sys., Eagan, Minn., 1999—; adj. prof. law William Mitchell Sch. Law, St. Paul, 1982—, Air Force Inst. Tech., 1983—. Contbr. articles to profl. jours. Capt. USAF, 1975-80; col. USAFR. Fellow Nat. Contract Mgmt. Assn. (bd. advisors, pres. Twin Cities chpt. 1985-86, regional v.p. 1990-91, Charles J. Delaney award 1986); mem. ABA (chmn. com. pub. contract law sect. 1984-88, 93—), Fed. Bar Assn., Minn. Bar Assn., Huber Hts. Jaycees (Jaycee of Yr. 1978). Republican. Roman Catholic. Avocation: long distance running. Home: 1161 Tiffany Cir N Saint Paul MN 55123-1871 Office: Lockheed Martin Tactical Defense Sys PO Box 64525 Saint Paul MN 55164-0525

MAFFEI FACCIOLI, CARLO FRANCESCO, financial executive; b. Verona, Italy, Oct. 22, 1960; s. Scipione and Annalisa (Casella) Maffei F.; m. Paola Arcangeli; children: Nicolo, Federico. Degree in Bus. Econs., Bocconi U., Milan, 1985. Sr. Arthur Andersen-Audit, Milan, 1985-87, Arthur Andersen Cons., Milan, 1987-88; group contr. Blugroup, Verona, Italy, 1988-90; CEO, contr. Interaction, Milan, 1990-94; gen. mgr. Medicenter, Florence, Italy, 1994-95; CFO Cia Medianetwork Italia, Milan, 1995-2000, Inferentia SpA, Milan, 2000—. With Italian mil., 1984. Avocations: skiing, sailing, savate, cars. Home: Via Ippolito Nievo 1, 20145 Milan Italy Office: Inferentia SpA, Via Tacito 6, 20137 Milan Italy

MAGA, OTHMAR, conductor; b. Bruenn, June 30, 1929; m. Gisela Dennig, 1954; children: Alexander, Jorge. Grad. in musicology, Univ. Tuebingen, Germany, 1956. Chief condr. Goettingen (Germany) Symphony Orch., 1962-67, Nuernberg (Germany) Symphony Orch., 1967-70; gen. music dir. Bochum (Germany) Symphony Orch., 1970-82; chief condr. Odense (Denmark) Symphony Orch., 1984-88, Orch. I Pomeriggi Musicali Di Milano, Italy, 1984-88, KBS Symphony Orch., Seoul, Korea, 1992-96; prof. Folkwang H.S. for Music, Essen, Germany, 1974-79. Office: E Zinner, Kirchenalle 22, D-20099 Hamburg Germany

MAGALHAES, DUARTE RAPOSO, company executive, consultant; b. Lisbon, Feb. 13, 1956; s. José Raposo and Maria Raposo (Guerra) M.; m. Isabel Raposo Farrusco, Feb. 9, 1980; children: Francisco, Goncalo, Diogo, Bernardo. Lic. economy, Lyon II, France, 1978, ISCTE, Lisbon, 1979. Dir. fin. Ravafe, Lisbon, 1980-81; dir. Teixeira Duarte, Lisbon, 1981-92; bd. adminstrn. Neovidrosa, M Grande, Portugal, 1996—; vice chmn. Gesvitrisa, Alcobaca, Portugal, 1998—; exec. chmn. Vitrocristalsa, Leiria, Portugal, 1997—; vice chmn. Atlantis S.A., Alcobaca, 1992—; pres. Novovidro ACE, Leiria, 1996—; cons. HLC S.A., Lisbon, 1999—, Arte da Mesa, Lisbon, 1996-98. Dir. DIP, Lisbon, 1998; sec. AESE, Lisbon, 1998. Mem. Glass Industry Assn. (pres. 1997—). Roman Catholic. Office: Atlantis SA, Casal da Areia co's, 2460 Alcobaca Portugal

MAGANG, DAVID NTSIMELE, government official; b. Molepolole, Botswana, Oct. 11, 1938; married; 3 children. LLB, Univ. Coll. London, 1968. Barrister, Botswana. State counsel and registrar of cos., 1969-72; pvt. legal practitioner Magang & Co., 1972—; legal cons. Minchin and Kelly, attys.; Mem. Parliament for Kweneng East Govt. Botswana, 1979; chmn. Parliamentary Law Reform Com., 1984-92; asst. min. Fin. and Devel. Planning, 1985-86, 89-92, Min. Works, Transport and Comm., 1992-94, Min. Minerals Energy & Water Affairs, 1994-98, Min. SADC Affairs, leader of del., 1994-2000, Min. Works, Transport and Comm., 1998—. Mem. Botswana Dem. Party. Office: Ministry Mineral Resources, Min Works Transp and Comm, Pvt Bag 007, Gaborone Botswana*

MAGANTO, CARMEN, psychotherapist, educator, clinical psychologist; b. Pamplona, Spain, Sept. 22, 1944; d. Daniel and Victoria (Mateo) M. Degree in Psychology, U. Barcelona, Spain, 1974, Honors Degree in Psychology, 1977, PhD in Psychology, 1987. Cert. psychotherapist. Lectr. asst. U. San Sebastian, Spain, 1980-81, lectr., 1982-90, lectr. for state, 1991—, dir. dept. psychology, 1988-89, sec. dept. psychology, 1987-89, 95-96; mem. directive com. Fedn. Psychologists, Basque Country, Spain, 1992—. Author: The Animal Drawing Test. Mental and Emotional Assessment, 1988, Childhood Psychological Assessment, 1996; contbr. chpt. to book, articles to profl. jours. Univ. of the Basque Country doctoral thesis grantee, 1984-86; U. Reno grantee, 1997. Mem. Spanish Soc. Psychiatry and Psychotherapy, European Assn. Psychol. Assessment, European Coun. for High Ability. Roman Catholic. Avocations: swimming, reading, walking, gardening. Home: Uribegela 18-1o, 01013 Vitoria Spain Office: U of Psychology, Avenida Tolosa 70, 20018 San Sebastian Spain

MAGARELLI, NICOLA, radiologist, researcher; b. Molfetta, Bari, Italy, Aug. 3, 1965; s. Vincenzo R.L. Magarelli and Grazia P. Maggialetti. MD, G. D'Annunzio U., Chieti, Italy, 1991. Diplomate in radiology, Italy. Tng. in radiology G. D'Annunzio U., 1991-95, rschr., 1992—; radiologist Richerche Radiologiche, Molfetta, 1996—, Hosp. S.S. Annunziata, Chieti, 1998—. Author: Manuale Teorico Pratico di Angiografia con Risonanza Magnetica, 1996; contbr. articles to med. jours., including European Radiology, Neuroradiology, Jour. Neuroradiology. Mem. Radiol. Soc. N.Am. Avocations: sports cars, fishing. Office: Hosp SS Annunziata, Via PA Valignani 1, 66100 Chieti Italy

MAGAZINER, ELLIOT ALBERT, musician, conductor, educator; b. Springfield, Mass., Dec. 25, 1921; m. Sari Fromkin; 2 children. Student, Nat. Orch. Assn., 1937-40, Princeton U., 1943, Juilliard School of Music, 1946-50. Music dir., prof. music Manhattanville Coll., Purchase, N.Y., 1970—; faculty Westchester Conservatory Music. Debut: Town Hall, N.Y.C., 1952; staff artist, concertmaster CBS-TV and Radio; Networks: condrs. Reiner, Ansermet, Beecham, Stokowski; condr. and sr. violin instr. Westchester Conservatory of Music; vis. condr. Dubuque Symphony; soloist N.Y. Philharm. Symphony, Symphony of the Air, Kol Visrael, symphonies in Chgo., Ft. Myers, Dubuque, York, St. Petersburg; recitals in N.Y.C., Washington, Detroit, Amsterdam, Paris, Jerusalem; star of CBS-TV, The Violin. Recs.: Charles Ives Sonata #2, Charles Ives Trio (with Frank Glazer and David Weber); Vivaldi Concerto in C and Concerto in B (with orchestre Symphonique de Paris); conductor Westchester All County Festival Orch. Mem. AAUP, N.Y. TV Musicians (pres.), CBS Musicians Fund (sec.). Avocations: collecting unique and ancient instruments. Home: 250 Garth Rd Apt 2b3 Scarsdale NY 10583-3954 Office: Manhattanville Coll 2900 Purchase St Purchase NY 10577-2131

MAGEE, BRYAN JOHN, materials engineer, educator; b. Larne, Northern Ireland, July 1, 1971; came to U.S., 1998; s. William and Marielle Magee; m. Alyson Louise Magee, June 25, 1997. BEngCE, U. Dundee, Scotland, 1993, PhDCE, 1997. Rsch. asst. U. Dundee, 1993-97; postdoctoral rsch. engr. U. Cape Town, South Africa, 1997-98; postdoctoral rsch. assoc. Purdue U., West Lafayette, Ind., 1998-99; asst. rsch. prof. U. N.H., Durham, 1999—; dir. outreach project program Recycled Materials Rsch. Ctr., 1999—. Contbr. articles to profl. publs., including Cement and Concrete Rsch., Materials and Structures, others. Rsch. grantee Nat. Coop. Hwy. Rsch. Program, 1999, others. Mem. Am. Concrete Inst., Instn. Civil Engrs., Concrete Soc., Transp. Rsch. Bd. Avocations: reading, hill walking, sailing, golf. E-mail: bryan.magee@rmrc.unh.edu. Office: U NH 122 Nesmith Hall Durham NH

MAGEE, CHARLES THOMAS, international consultant, retired diplomat; b. Clifton Forge, Va., Mar. 6, 1932; s. Charles Thomas and Dorothy Elizabeth (McPherson) M.; m. Maideh Mazda, May 30, 1959; 1 child, Maya. BA, Harvard U., 1953. Vice consul Am. Consulate, Windsor, Can., 1961-63; polit.-mil. affairs officer Am. Emb., Paris, 1964-66; polit. officer Soviet desk Dept. State, 1966-68; polit. officer Am. Embassy, Moscow, 1969-71; dep. dir. for ops. Exec. Secretariat Dept. State, Washington, 1971-72, officer-in-charge French desk, 1972-74; polit. officer, exec. asst. to amb. Am. Embassy, Paris, 1974-77; dep. chief mission Am. Embassy, Sofia, Bulgaria, 1977-80; chief jr. officer div. Bur. Pers. Dept. State, 1980-82, fgn. svc. insp., 1982-83; cons. gen. U.S. Consulate Gen., Leningrad, USSR, 1984-86; spl. asst. to mayor City of San Francisco, 1986-87; dir. Russian lang. ops. U.S. Del. to Negotiations on Nuclear and Space Arms with USSR, Geneva, 1988-91; sr. program officer Citizens Democracy Corps, Washington, 1992-93; amb. mission to Latvia Orgn. Security and Coop. Europe, 1994-97, amb. mission to Ukraine, 1998-99; ofcl. election observer, Ukraine, 1998, Russia, 2000; head election observation mission to Former Yugoslav Republic of Macedonia, 2000; cons. Acad. Arrangements Abroad, N.Y.C., 1987—, Dept. of State, 1989—, Seabourn Cruise Line, San Francisco, 1989-92, Acad. Travel Abroad, Washington, 1995; asst. prof. Dept Navy, 1959-61. Lt. USN, 1953-59. Mem. Am. Fgn. Svc. Assn., Harvard Club. Home and Office: 4518 Albemarle St NW Washington DC 20016-2016

MAGEE, JOHN FRANCIS, research company executive; b. Bangor, Maine, Dec. 3, 1926; s. John Henry and Marie (Frawley) M.; m. Dorothy Elma Hundley, Nov. 19, 1949; children: Catherine Anne, John Hundley, Andrew Stephen. AB, Bowdoin Coll., 1947; MS, U. Maine, 1952; MBA, Harvard U., 1948; LLD, Bowdoin Coll., 1996. With Arthur D. Little, Inc., Cambridge, Mass., 1950-98, v.p., 1961-72, pres., 1972-86, chief exec. officer, 1974-88, chmn., 1986-98, also dir., 1968-98. Author: Physical Distribution Systems, 1967, Industrial Logistics: Analysis and Management of Physical Supply and Distribution Systems, 1968, (with D. M. Boodman) Production Planning and Inventory Control, 1968; (with W. Capacino and W. Rosenfield) Modern Logistics Management, 1985. Trustee New Eng. Aquarium, Emerson Hosp., Thompson Island Outward Bound Edn. Ct.; emeritus trustee Bowdoin Coll.; hon. trustee Woods Hole Oceanographic Instn.; mem. dean's coun. Harvard U. Grad. Sch. Edn. Mem. Ops. Research Soc. Am. (pres. 1966-67), Inst. Mgmt. Scis. (pres. 1971-72), Phi Beta Kappa, Phi Kappa Psi. Clubs: Concord (Mass.) Country (gov. 1971-74); The Country (Brookline, Mass.); Somerset (Boston). Comml. (pres.). Office: Arthur D Little Inc 25 Acorn Park Cambridge MA 02140-2301

MAGER, PETER PAUL, pharmacologist, toxicologist, educator; b. Gerings Walde, Germany, June 18, 1946; s. Paul and Gertrud (Thamm) M.; m. Christine Gollmann, Mar. 23, 1968; children: Andrea, Angelika. MD, U. Leipzig, Germany, 1973, DSc, 1982, Dr. med. habilitation, 1991. Med. asst. U. Greifswald, Germany, 1973-76; sr. rschr. U. Halle, Germany, 1976-80; head rsch. group of pharmcochemistry U. Leipzig, Germany, 1980-93; mng. dir. Inst. Pharmacology and Toxicology U. Leipzig, 1993-95, prof. pharmacology and toxicology, 1996—; cons. FMC Co., Princeton, N.J., 1985-90, Biostructure Co., Illkirch, France, 1991—; lectr. in field. Author: Pharmacochemistry, 1984, Chemometrics, 1988, Design Statistics, 1991; contbr. articles to profl. jours. Mem. Ludwig-Erhard-Stiftung, Bonn, Germany, 1990. Fellow N.Y. Acad. Scis.; mem. Internat. Union Pure and Applied Chemistry (affiliate), Internat. Med. Chem. Divsn., Corp. Chem. Divsn., German Chem. Soc. Home: Am Wohnpark 3, D-04828 Neuweissenborn Germany

MAGGERT, JEFFREY ALLAN, professional golfer; b. Columbia, Mo., Feb. 20, 1964; m. Michelle. Tex. A&M U. Profl. golfer, 1986—; winner Malaysian Open, 1989, Vines Classic, Australia, 1990, Knoxville (Tenn.) Open (NIKE Tour), 1990, Buffalo (N.Y.) Open (NIKE Tour), 1990; mem. PGA Tour, 1991—; winner Walt Disney World/Oldsmobile Classic, 1993, WGC Andersen Cons. Match Play, 1999; mem. Pres. Cup Nat. Team, 1994, Ryder Cup Nat. Team, 1995, 97, PGA Tour Charity Team, Buick Open, 1999. Avocations: fishing, hunting, camping, sporting events. Office: c/o PGA Box 109601 100 Ave of Champions Palm Beach Gardens FL 33410

MAGGIORE, MAURIZIO, aeronautic company executive; b. Como, Italy, Feb. 15, 1959; s. Michele and Silvana (Bentivoglio) M.; m. Emanuela Moro, July 20, 1987; children: Manfredi, Eleonora. Degree in Aero. Engring., Politecnico, Milan, 1985. Mission analysis staff Agusta, Cascina Costa, Italy, 1986-91; rsch. coord. Agusta, Cascina Costa, 1991—; dep. Agusta rep. Euromart, 1992—; sec. 25th European Rotorcraft Forum, Rome, 1999. Translator, editor: Mondadori Informatica, 1984-92; contbr. articles to profl. jours. With Italian Air Force, 1985-86. Roman Catholic. Avocations: photography, computing, languages. Home: Via B Oriani 54, 20156 Milan Italy Office: Agusta, Via G Agusta 520, 21017 Samarate Italy

MAGID, ERIK JAKOB, clinical chemist; b. Copenhagen, Aug. 11, 1935; s. Efim and Eugenie (Ginsberg) M. MD, U. Copenhagen, 1961, DMS, 1970. Intern med. and surg. depts. Diakonissestiftelsen, Frederiksberg, 1961-63; rsch. fellow U. Copenhagen, 1963-66; resident dept. clin. chemistry Kommunehospitalet, Copenhagen, 1966-69; rsch. fellow U. Ann Arbor, Mich., 1969-70; head dept. Copenhagen Mcpl. Hosp. System, 1971—; head dept. clin. chemistry Amager Hosp., Copenhagen, 1987—; bd. dirs. NORDKEM. Editor: Standardizations books, 1991-93, Clinical Test Evaluation, 1992, Laboratory Cost Managment, 1993. Mem. Internat. Fedn. Clin. Chemistry (chmn. sci. div. 1983-88, chmn. steering com. of Bergmeyer Confs. 1988-92, chmn. edn. and mgmt. div. 1992-98), Danish Soc. Clin. Chemistry (chmn. 1979-83). Avocations: skiing, swimming, winterbathing. Home: Vilvordevej 68, DK-2920 Charlottenlund Denmark Office: Amager Hosp, Italiensvej 1, DK-2300 Copenhagen Denmark

MAGID, PER, lawyer; b. Copenhagen, Feb. 20, 1943; s. Efim and Eugenie (Ginsberg) M.; m. Nonni Suenson, May 18, 1968; children: Samuel, Tobias, Camilla. Candidatus Juris, U. Copenhagen, 1967. Bar: Danish Ct. Appeals 1972, Danish Supreme Ct. 1978. Sec. The Danish Ombudsmand, 1967-68; asst. atty. Danish Ministry Justice, 1968-72; asst. Govt. Atty., 1972-74; assoc. White & Case, N.Y.C., 1977-78, Jonas Bruun, Copenhagen, 1974-76; ptnr. Jonas Brunn, Copenhagen, 1976—; agt. Danish Govt. before Internat. Ct. Justice, 1988-93; external asst. prof. internat. and EEC law U. Copenhagen, 1970-79; mem. panels of conciliators and arbitrators under Internat. Ctr. for Settlement of Investment Disputes. Co-author: Alf Ross: Folkeret, 6th edit., 1984. Mem. Danish Bar Assn., Oriental Club London. Office: Law Firm of Jonas Bruun, Bredgade 38, 1260 Copenhagen Denmark

MAGIDOR, MENACHEM, mathematics educator, academic administrator; b. Petah Tikva, 1946. Assoc. prof. math. Hebrew U., Jerusalem, 1978-81; prof. Hebrew U., 1981—; pres. Hebrew U., Jerusalem; asst. prof., U. Colo., 1972-73; lectr., U. Calif., Berkeley, 1973-75; sr. lectr. Ben-Grion U. Negev, 1975-78; vis. prof., UCLA, Calif. Inst. Tech. Office: Mount Scopus, 91905 Jerusalem Israel

MAGIDSON, JAY, statistician; b. Chgo., Mar. 18, 1947; s. Samuel and Shirley Arlene (Weininger) M.; m. Elizabeth Katherine Morgan, Oct. 26, 1976; children: Jeremy, Jenna. BA, U. Ill., 1969; MS in Bus., U. Wis., 1971; PhD in Mgmt., Northwestern U., 1976. Sr. analyst Ill. Bell Telephone Co., Chgo., 1971-72; sr. statistician Abt Assocs., Inc., Cambridge, Mass., 1976-81; founder, pres. Statis. Innovations, Inc., Belmont, Mass., 1981—; presenter seminars; cons. A.C. Nielsen Co., Chgo., Nat. Geographic Soc., Washington, 1984—, Beneficial Mgmt. Corp., Peapack, N.J., 1989—; instr. Boston U., Tufts U.; mem. govt. adv. panel USDA, 1984; expert reviewer govt. panel NIH, Washington, 1989, 91, NSF, Washington, 1982, 87. Author: Reforming Schools, 1980, SPSS PC+ CHAID version 5.0 for DOS and 6.0 for Windows Computer Manual; editor: Analyzing Qualitative/Categorical Data, 1978, Advances in Factor Analysis and Structural Equation Models, 1979; designer CHAID market segmentation computer package, GOLDMINER (graphical ordinal logit displays based on monotonic regression) computer package, latent gold program for latent class modeling, TYPE-O-GRAPHIC profiler statistical modeling program; contbr. articles to profl jours.; mem. editl. rev. bd. Jour. Direct Mktg., Evanston, Ill., 1988—, Jour. Targeting, Measurement and Analysis for Mktg.; computer sect. editor Jour. Mktg. Rsch., 1983-85. Coach youth basketball, baseball and soccer teams. Mem. Am. Statis. Assn., Assn. for Psychol. Type. Achievements include patent for Apparatus and Method for Graphical Display of Statistical Effects in Categorical and Continuous Outcome Data. Office: Statis Innovations Inc 375 Concord Ave Belmont MA 02478-3048

MAGLARAS, CONSTANTINOS, electrical engineer, educator; b. Athens, Creece, Dec. 18, 1969; s. Dimos and Chrysoula M.; m. Niki Kouri. BS in Elec. Engring., Imperial Coll., London, 1990; MS in Elec. Engring., Stanford

U., 1991, PhD in Elec. Engring., 1998. Rsch. scientist Canon Rsch. Ctr. Am., Palo Alto, Calif., 1991-93; asst. prof. Columbia U. Grad. Sch. Bus., New York, 1998—. Mem. IEEE, Inst. Ops. Rsch. and Mgmt. Sci. (Nicholson prize 1999). E-mail: c.maglaras@columiba.edu. Office: Columbia U 409 Uris Hall 3022 Broadway New York NY 10027

MAGLIOCCA, LARRY ANTHONY, education educator; b. New Castle, Pa., Sept. 3, 1943; s. Anthony Norman Magliocca and Madeline Rose Ross; m. Judie Alene Kerr, Sept. 1, 1964 (div.); children: Jeannine Marie, Seth Bryan; m. Phyllis Marion Gentry, May 9, 1981 (div.); 1 child, Nicholas Rossi; m. Karen Elizabeth Sanders, Jan. 23, 1996. BSEd, Slippery Rock State Coll., 1967; MEd, U. Pitts., 1970; PhD, Ohio State U., 1978. Dir. Youth Devel. Ctr. of Pa., New Castle, 1967-70; state cons. S.D. Dept. Pub. Inst., Pierre, S.D., 1970-73; coord. Balt. City Pub. Schs., 1973-76; exec. dir. Ctr. for Spl. Needs Population, Columbus, Ohio, 1979—; assoc. prof. Ohio State U., Columbus, 1988—; vis. lectr. Melbourne (Australia) State Coll., 1978-79; adj. faculty Johns Hopkins U., Balt., 1974-76; blue ribbon task force, Chgo. City Pub. Schs., 1985; sr. ptnr. The Compact. Author three books in spl. edn. field, 1978-92; contbr. articles to profl. jours.; editor: The Directive Teacher jour., 1976-84; author/designer instructional materials in math. problem solving, 1992. Founder Young Scientists Club, Westerville, Ohio, 1990-92; rsch. fellow Internat. Sys. Inst., 1994-96. Mem. Soc. for Gen. Systems Rsch., Am. Assn. for Artificial Intelligence, Coun. for Exceptional Children. Democrat. Unitarian-Universalist. Avocations: poetry, travel, fly fishing. Office: Ctr Spl Needs Populations 700 Ackerman Rd Ste 440 Columbus OH 43202-1559

MAGLIOCCHINO, ANNA, secondary education educator, poet, artist; b. San Mauro Forte, Matera, Italy, June 4, 1938; d. Joseph Magliocchino and Caroline Filardi. French cert., U. Naples, Italy, 1959; English cert., English Inst., Naples, 1959; tchg. cert., Tng. Coll., Matera, 11964. Tchr. state schs., San Mauro Forte, 1966-92, tchr. French and English, 1992—; state trainer fgn. lang. tchrs., Matera, 1992-96, state glottodidactic trainer, 1992-97. Contbr. poetry to various publs.; exhibited in group shows Art Expo, L.A., 1988, Euro Art Expo, Rome, 1989, Verona, Italy, 1995. Avocations: reading, writing, painting, travel. Home: Via Piave 26, 75010 San Mauro Forte MT, Italy

MAGLIONE, LILI, fine artist, art consultant; b. Manhasset, N.Y., Jan. 30, 1929; d. Angelo and Mary (Marciano) M.; m. Bernhart H. Rumphorst, June 1, 1957; children: Catherine, Douglas. AD, Traphagen Sch., N.Y.C., 1950; student, Art Students League, N.Y.C., 1950-52. Fashion artist Butterick Pattern Co., N.Y.C., 1952-53; fashion art cons. Miss. America Inc., N.Y.C., 1953-54; dept. head fashion art office Simplicity Pattern Co., N.Y.C., 1953-58, fashion art cons., 1958-62; art dept. cons. Nassau County Mus., Roslyn, N.Y., 1984-86; dir. decorative affairs Harbor Acres Assn., Port Washington, N.Y., 1987-89, Sands Point (N.Y.) Mus., 1989-91; art cons. Horst Design Assocs., Huntington, N.Y., 1992—. Exhibited paintings in one-woman shows at Palm Gallery, Southampton, N.Y., 1980, Art Internat., Chgo., 1985, Isis Gallery, Port Washington, 1987, Gallery 84, N.Y.C., 1989, 91, 93; one woman retrospective shows include Harkness Gallery, 1978, James Hunt Barker Gallery, 1984, Sands Point Mus., 1988, Fairfield U., 1995, exhibited at Nat. Arts Club, N.Y.C., 1997; contbr. poetry to Nat. Libr. of Poets, 1997, Artists Mag., 1998, Am. Artist Mag., 1999. Hon. trustee Parents TV Coun., 2000—. Winner Art Expo 98, B.J. Spoke Gallery, N.Y.C., 1998; recipient Manhattan Arts Internat. Critics Choice award, 1998, Liquetex Purchase award, 1998, Amsterdam award of excellence, 1998, award for acrylic painting Nat. Arts Club, N.Y.C., 1998, Art Calendar Centerfold award, 1998, award of merit Allied Artists of Am., 1999, cert. of merit Art Calendar mag., 1999, Award of Excellence, Manhattan Arts Internat., 2000, award Nat. Assn. Women Artists, 2000. Mem. Nat. Assn. Women Artists, Nat. Mus. Women in the Arts, Internat. Soc. of Poets, Portrait Soc. Am. Inc. Roman Catholic. Avocations: horticulture, flower arrangement, nutrition, music, child care. Home: 7 Harmony Rd Huntington NY 11743-2315

MAGNAGA, MARTIN-FIDELE, government official. Pvt. sec. Ministry Pub. Health and Population, Libreville, Gabon, 1966-68; cabinet dir. rels. with nat. assembly, dep. spkr. nat. assembly Ministry State Pub. Works, Transport, Posts and Telecomm., Libreville, Gabon, 1968-70, min., 1994-97; 2d counselor Embassy Gabon, Tokyo, 1970-71; gov. Ogoou-Lolo Province, 1975-79, Ogue-Maritime Province, 1979-81; min. nat. def. Ministry Vet.'s Affairs, Pub. Security and Immgration, 1990-94; min. Ministry Transports, Tourism and Nat. Pks., Libreville, 1994; mem. cabinet Gabon, Libreville, 1998—. Mem. Gabonese Dem. Party. Office: Min Commerce Industry, BP 3096, Libreville Gabon*

MAGNANI, LORENZO, philosopher, educator; b. Sannazzaro de'Burgondi, Pavia, Italy, July 14, 1952; s. Angelo and Giovanna (Carpani) M.; married, Sept. 30, 1974; children: Lorenza, Giovanna. Grad., U. Pavia, Italy, 1976, PhD, 1980. Prof. logic and epistemology, sr. rsch. scientist U. Pavia, 1980-88, dir. Computational Philosophy Lab., 1994—; vis. rschr. Carnegie Mellon U., Pitts., 1992, Waterloo (Ont.), U., 1993, McGill U., Montreal, 1993, Ga. Inst. Tech., Atlanta, 1995, 98, vis. prof., 1999—; cons. Kluwer Acad Pub., Dordrecht, The Netherlands, 1999. Author: Knowledge Engineering, 1997, Abduction, Reason, and Science: Processes of Discovery and Explanation, 2000, Philosophy and Geometry: Theoretical and Historical Issues, 2000; editor: (with N.J. Nersessian and P. Thagard) Model-Based Reasoning in Scientific Discovery; author chpts. in books; contbr. articles to profl. jours. Grantee Premio Cerini, 1980, Murst Rsch., 1998. Fellow Associazione Italiana di Intelligenza Artificiale; mem. Societa Italiana de Logica e di Filosofia della Scienza, Am. Philos. Assn., Am. Assn. Artificial Intelligence. Avocations: swimming, gym activities. E-mail: lorenzo@philos.unipv.it. Office: U Pavia/Dept Philosophy, Piazza Botta 6, 27100 Pavia Italy

MAGNES, HARRY ALAN, physician; b. Orange, N.J., Dec. 3, 1948; s. Sam and Shirley (Daniels) M.; m. Patricia Bruce, Mar. 25, 1989; 1 child, Carlos Fontiveros. AB in Biology magna cum laude, Brown U., 1970; MD, Yale U., 1974; M in Med. Mgmt., Tulane U., 1998; cert. in med. mgmt., Am. Coll. Physician Execs., 1997. Diplomate Am. Bd. Internal Medicine, Am. Bd. Med. Mgmt. Intern, resident internal medicine U. Iowa Hosps. and Clinics, 1974-77; ptnr., med. dir., pres., CEO Gallatin Med. Clinic, Downey, Calif., 1977—; pres., CEO Gallatin Med. Corp., Downey, Calif., 1992-94; med. dir., bd. dirs. Gallatin Med. Found., Downey, Calif., 1993—; staff physician Downey Cmty. Hosp., 1977-96, Presbyn. Intercmty. Hosp., 1992—; clin. instr. Rancho Los Amigos Hosp., Downey, 1981-83; chairperson bd. dirs. Primehealth of So. Calif., 1997-99; bd. dirs. Calif. Health Network, sec.-treas., 1998-99; project adv. bd. VA/UCLA/RAND Calif. Med. Group, IPA Governance Project, 1997-98. Author: Rheumatic Fever in Connecticut, 1974. James Manning scholar Brown U., 1968. Mem. Am. Coll. Physician Execs., Healthcare Assn. So. Calif. (chmn. med. dirs. forum 1997-98), Am. Med. Group Assn. (policy com. 1994-98, legis. com. 1997—), Med. Group Mgmt. Assn., Phi Beta Kappa, Sigma Xi, Delta Omega. Avocation: racquetball. Office: Gallatin Med Found 10720 Paramount Blvd Downey CA 90241-3306

MAGNIN, GEORGE ERNEST, physician; b. Oconto Falls, Wis., Apr. 14, 1922; s. Ernest Emil and Martha Helen Magnin; m. Anna Delores Magnin, June 23, 1947; children: George Ernest II, David Robert Daniel Ovid. BS, U. Wis., 1943, MD, 1946. Diplomate Am. Bd. Internal Medicine. Intern Christ Hosp., Cin., 1946-47; resident in internal medicine U. Wis. (Madison), 1949-52; mem. Marshfield (Wis.) Clinic, 1952-92; active staff St. Joseph's Hosp., Marshfield, 1952-92; preceptor U. Wis., Marshfield, 1953-68; dir. U. Wis. Tchg. Svc., Marshfield, 1968-77; clin. prof. medicine U. Wis., Madison, 1969-92; dir. internal medicine residency program U. Wis., Marshfield, 1974-90, ret., 1992. Recipient George E. Magnin Internal Med. Residents Tchr. of Yr. award Marshfield Clinic, St. Joseph's Hosp., 1974—, Addis Costello Internis of Yr. award Wis. Soc. Internal Medicine, 1981, Disting. Svc. award State Med. Soc. Wis., 1982, Guest Lectr. award Ben and Ruth Lawton Lecture, 1990, Spl. Recognition award Wis. Soc. Internal Medicine, 1991, Wis. Laureate award ACP, 1990, Citation award Wis. Med. Alumni, 1994; bronze bust in his honor George E. Magnin Med. Libr., Laird Bldg., 1997. Fellow ACP (Wis. gov. 1974-78, med. practice com. 1977-79); mem. Am. Soc. Internal Medicine (mini oral examiner 1970-71), Phi Eta Sigma, Alpha Omega Alpha. Avocations: fly-fishing, hunting, golf, reading, music appreciation. Home: 301 Columbus Dr Marshfield WI 54449-2545

MAGNISSALIS, KOSTAS GEORGES, author, public relations consultant, educator; b. Chios, Greece, Feb. 18, 1934; s. Georg and Evangelia Magnissalis; m. Ioannidou Smaro, Sept. 1, 1963; m. 2d, Patzika Timi, Dec. 29., 1974; m. 3d, Petraki Vassiliki, June 20, 1985. BA in Polit. Sci., Pantios U. Polit.-Social Scis., Athens, Greece, 1961, PhD, 1963. Head tng. and rsch. div. Greek Atomic Energy Commn., Athens, 1960-64; dir. community devel. programs Royal Nat. Found., Athens, 1965-67; dir. Devel. Studies Soc., 1967—; cons. to Greek and fgn. cos., Athens, 1967—. Author more than 30 books, among them Public Relations Handbook, 8th edit., 2000, translated into English and Russian; Creativies, Theory and and Techniques of Creativity Development, 4th edit., 1996; Consumer Behavior Handbook, 2d edit., 1998, Mechanisms of Idea Production, 2d edit., 1998, Positive Thinking, 1999, Lessons of Creative Thinking Development, 2d edit., 2000. Recipient Laurel awrd of CAM Found., 1984, Laurel of Enosis Andrion, 1998. Mem. Greek Assn. Pub. Rels. (pres. tng. com. 1987, lst prize 1984), European Cultural Found. (nat. gen. sec. 1988), Inst. Mgmt. and Comm., Greek Mgmt. Assn., European Assn. for Creativity and Innovation, Alumni Assn. Pantios U. (pres. 1964). Office: Devel Studies Soc, Devel Studies Soc, 45 Levidiou, 10442 Athens Greece

MAGNUSON, ROY WILLIAM, secondary school educator; b. St. Paul, July 30, 1954; s. Osgood Teofil and Ethel Sylvia Magnuson; m. Mary Patricia Drew, July 15, 1989. BA in History, Augsberg Coll., 1991. Cert. tchr. social studies, grades 7-12, Minn. Dir. recreation ctr. St. Paul Pks. and Recreation, 1974-78; youth worker Wilder Found., St. Paul, 1985-91; ednl. asst. St. Paul Pub. Schs., 1980-85, coach football, wrestling, track Como Sr. H.S., 1979—, tchr. U.S., African Am., Asian history Como. Sr. H.S., 1992—. Mem. exec. bd. St. Paul Trades and Labor Assembly, 1997—. Mem. St. Paul Fedn. Tchrs. (chair COPE com. 1996—, mem. exec. bd. 1996—). Democrat. Avocations: reading, golf, horseshoes, travel. E-mail: rmagnuson@mail.como.st.paul.K12.mn.us. Home: 727 Wheelock Pkwy W Saint Paul MN 55117-4110 Office: Como Pk Sr HS 740 Rose Ave W Saint Paul MN 55117-4042

MAGNUSSEN, JAN, Danish county administrator; b. Copenhagen, Jan. 8, 1943; s. Gudmund and Ruth Magnussen; children: Christian, Magnus, Mikkel; m. Birte Magnussen June 25, 1994. MS, U. Copenhagen, 1969. Assoc. prof. U. Copenhagen, 1970-85; prof., head of inst. South Jutland U. Ctr., Esbjerg, Denmark, 1985-88, rector, 1988-98; chmn. Danish Bd. Tech., Copenhagen, 1991-95; dir. edn. industry and culture Frederiksborg County, Hillerød, Denmark, 1998—; chmn. Social Sci. Rsch. Coun., Copenhagen, 1980-84; bd. dirs. Nordic Inst. Planner, Stockholm, Scanex A/S, 1998-99, Innovationcenter, Horsholm, 1998—, Scan East Gresund, 1999—; chmn. Danish Bd. Tech., Copenhagen, 1991-95, Interprimo A/S, Tistrup, 1994—, Sydinvest A/S, Aabenraa, 1993-2000, Global Resource Info. Database (GRID)-Denmark, UN, UN Environ. Program, Dansk Biomasse A/S, 1995-98, Sydinvest, 1999, Medicon Valley Acad., 2000—; mem. editl. bd. Scandinavian Housing & Planning Rsch., 1980-96. Chmn. sch. bd. Vittenberg, Ribe, Denmark, 1990-94; planner Masterplan for Met. Copenhagen, 1978. Sgt. Danish Civil Def., 1962-63. Office: Frederiksborg County, Amtsgarden Kongens Vaenge 2, 3400 Hillerød Denmark

MAGNUSSON, BERNT ERLAND, forestry executive; b. Örgryte, Gothenburg, Sweden, Aug. 28, 1941; s. Erland and Helfrid M.; m. Anna Charlotte Wikström, June 17, 1967; children: Cecilia, Catharina, Christina. MA, U. Uppsala, Sweden, 1964. Various asst. positions Swedish Cellulose Co., Sundsvall, 1965-69; cons. econs. R.N. Herbert, San Francisco, 1967-68; mgr. adminstrn. and mktg. Alfa-Laval, Tumba, Sweden, 1970-72; dep. MD Alfa-Laval South Africa, Johannesburg, Africa, 1972-74, Alfa-Laval Agrar, Hamburg, Germany, 1975-76; gen. mgr. Uddeholm (Sweden) Forest Div., 1976-79; exec. v.p. Swedish Match Group, Stockholm, 1979-85, Match Group/Swedish Match, Nyon, Switzerland, 1981-85; pres., chief exec. officer Nordstjernan AB, Stockholm, 1985-91; chief exec. officer NCC AB, Solna, Sweden, 1991-92, chmn. bd. dirs., 1991-99; chmn. bd. dirs. AssiDomän AB, Swedish Match AB; vice chmn. Avesta Sheffield AB; bd. dirs. Volvo Car Corp., Höganäs AB, Merita Corp. Fin., MeritaNordbanken AB, Net Insight AB, Emtunga Int. AB; adviser European Bank for Reconstrn. and Devel. Office: Hovslagargatan 5 B, 111 48 Stockholm Sweden

MAGNUSSON, GUDMAR E., import company executive; b. Reykjavik, Iceland, May 14, 1941; s. Magnus Loftsson and Jonina Asbjornsdottir; m. Ragna Bjarnadottir, June 3, 1961; children: Bjarni, Sigridur, Magnus, Sveinn, Runa Vigdis. Diploma in bus. edn., Coop. Sch., Iceland, 1961; diploma in mktg. mgmt., U. Iceland, 1998. Mng. dir. Bjarni Th. Halldorsson Heildverslun, Reykjavik, 1982—; security dealer re-edn. divsn. U. Iceland, 2000—. Mem. Seltjarnarnes (Iceland) Town Coun., 1974-90, pres., 1986-90; bd. dirs. EAN Iceland, 1992—; mem. gen. assembly EAN Internat., 1993—. Mem. Iceland Wholesalers Assn. (bd. dirs. 1991-99), Masons. Mem. Conservative Party. Office: Bjarni Th Halldorsson Heil, PO Box 1136, 121 Reykjavik Iceland

MAGNÚSSON, HALLGRIMUR, physician; b. Reykjavik, Iceland, Jan. 17, 1949; s. Magnús Gudmundsson and Anna Hallgrímsdóttir; m. Sesselja Arthúrsdóttir, Aug. 26, 1983 (div. 1992); 1 child, Einar. Degree, U. Oslo, Norway, 1971, U. Iceland, 1977; MD, U. Iceland, 1989. Chief physician Health Ctr., Patreksfjördur, Iceland, 1978-81; psychiatrist Nat. U. Hosp., Iceland, 1983-89; chief physician Health Ctr., Grundarfjördur, Iceland, 1990—. Author: The Epidemiology of Octogeniarians in Iceland, 1989; contbr. articles to profl. jours. Organist, Patreksfjördur, Iceland, 1978-81. Recipient Rsch. award Nordic Psychiatric Assn.; Rsch. grantee Icelandic Rsch. Fund Reykjavik, 1984-86. Mem. Internat. Psychogeriactic Assn., British Geriatric Soc., Nordic Soc. Rsch. in Brain Aging (pres. 1994-96), Coun. of the Icelandic Nat. Ch., Internat. Psychogeriatric Assn., Brit. Geriatric Soc., Assn. Rural Physicians in Iceland, Assn. Health Care Ctrs. in Iceland. Avocations: organ and piano. Home: Fossahlid 3, 350 Grundarfirdi Iceland Office: Heilsugaeslustöd, Grundarfjardar, 350 Grundarfirdi Iceland

MAGNUSSON, THOR ASTTHOR, cultural association administrator; b. Reykjavik, Iceland, Aug. 4, 1953; s. Magnus K. Jonsson and Unnur H. Larusdottir; 1 child, Alma Bjork Astthorsdottir. Diploma in English, Oxford U., Eng., 1971; Diploma in Mktg. and Photography, Medway Coll. Design, 1974. Founder Eurocard Iceland, Peace 2000 Inst., 1995—; mem. Coun. Conflict Prevention, 1996—. Author: Virkjum Bessastadir, 1996. Presdl. candidate, Iceland, 1996. Recipient Holy Cross of the Greek Orthodox Ch., 1998. Avocations: private pilot, citation jet racing. Office: Peace 2000 Inst, PO Box 190, 121 Reykjavik Iceland

MAGNUSSON, TOMAS HERBERT, dentist, researcher; b. Linköping, Sweden, Apr. 1, 1949; s. Herbert Gustav and Iris Viola (Wetterström) M.; m. Annica Birgitta Hedmo, Oct. 11, 1969; children: Malin, Jenny, Cecilia. LDS, Faculty Odontology, Göteborg, Sweden, 1974, D of Odontology, 1981, docent/reader, 1986. Dentist Pub. Dental Svc., Jokkmokk, Sweden, 1974-80; head of dept. of stomatognathic physiology Pub. Dental Svc., Luleå, Sweden, 1980-88; sr. cons. dept. stomatognathic physiology Pub. Dental Svc., Jönköping, Sweden, 1988—. Co-author (with Gunnar E. Carlsson) Klinisk Bettfysiologi for Allmäntandläkaren, 1982, 2nd edit., 1983, Greek edit., 1984, (with Gunnar E. Carlsson & Inger Nordberg) Bettskenor i Kliniken och pa Laboratoriet, 1987, (with Gunnar E. Carlsson) Bettskenor, 1987, Management of Temporomandibular Disorder in the General Dental Practice, 1999, German edit., 2000, Italian edit., 2000, Korean edit., 2000; contbr. articles to profl. jours. Mem. Soc. Oral Physiology (adv. bd., past pres.), Swedish Soc. Stomatognathic Physiology. E-mail: tomas.magnusson@odont.ltjkpg.se. Home: Swedenborgsgatan 66 B, SE-55448 Jönköping Sweden Office: Inst Postgrad Dental Edn, SE-55111 Jönköping Sweden

MAGOHA, GEORGE ALBERT, medical educator, consultant; b. Kisuma, Kenya, July 2, 1952; s. Bernard Bonaface Magoha and Sarah Joan Aloo; m. Odudu Barbara Essien, May 15, 1982; 1 child, Michael Agustus. MBBS, U. Lagos, Nigeria, 1978; MD, Nigerian Postgrad. Med. Coll., 1985. Intern Lagos U. Tchg. Hosp., Nigeria, resident; resident Hammersmith Hosp., London; lectr. anatomy U. Lagos, 1981-85; cons. urologist Duro Soleye Hosps., Lagos, 1985-87; lectr. surgery U. Nairobi, Kenya, 1988-89, sr. lectr., 1989-96, assoc. prof., 1996-2000, chmn. dept. surgery, 1999-2000, prof. surgery, dean Faculty of Medicine, 2000—; mem. Erectile Dysfunction Adv. Coun., 1998—. Contbr. articles to profl. jours. Fellow W. African Coll. Surgeons; mem. Internat. Soc. Urology, Brit. Assn. Urol. Surgeons, Pan African Urol. Surgeons Assn. (treas. 1995—), Kenya Assn. Urol. Surgeons (treas.). Avocations: walking, jogging, basketball, classical music, reading. Home: PO Box 19868, Nairobi Kenya Office: U Nairobi, PO Box 19676, 19676 Nairobi Kenya

MAGOMETSCHNIGG, HEINRICH, vascular surgeon; b. Klagenfurt, Karnten, Austria, Nov. 5, 1952; s. Anton and Kreszentia (Libiseller) M.; m. Eva Maria Gottschligg, Oct. 28, 1988 (div.); children: Abelina Carissima, Julian David Desiderius. MD, U. Vienna, 1980. Asst. Inst. Pathol. Anatomy U. Vienna, Austria, 1980-81; physician med. dept. U. Vienna Hosp., 1981-82, med. specialist surgery, 1982-87, head physician, head surgery dept., 1988-94; dir., head vascular surgery dept. Landeskrankenhaus Salzburg, Austria, 1994—; lectr. U. Vienna, 1994—. Home: Oberplainfeld 196, 5322 Hof Austria Office: Landeskrankenhaus Salzburg, Mullner Hauptstr 48, 5020 Salzburg Austria

MAGONI, DESPO, artist; b. Feb. 17, 1943. MFA, Polytechnion of Athens, 1967. One-person shows include Henry-Hicks Gallery, Bklyn., 1976, Nonson Gallery, N.Y.C., 1976, 78, Ora Gallery, Athens, 1978, 81, 83, Kouros GAllery, N.Y.C., 1984, Alternative Mus., N.Y.C., 1986, New Forms Gallery, Athens, 1988, 99, Bklyn. Coll. Art Gallery, 1994, Robeson Gallery, Rutgers U., Newark, 1994, André Zarre Gallery, N.Y.C., 1997, Parsons Sch. of Design, N.Y.C., 1999, John Jay Coll. Art Gallery, N.Y.C., 1999; exhibited in group shows at Kouros Gallery, 1983, Mint Mus., Charlotte, N.C., 1989, Mitchell Mus., Mt. Vernon, Ill., 1989, Haggerty Mus. Art, Marquette U., Milw., 1990, Pratt Inst. Gallery, N.Y.C., 1990, André Zarre Gallery, 1997, Islip Mus., Oakdale, N.Y., 1997; pub. collections include Vorres Mus., Paiania, Greece, Mus. Modern Art, Guadalajara, Mexico, Mint Mus., Charlotte, N.C., Alternative Mus., N.Y.C., Pratt Inst. Libr., N.Y.C.

MAGOON, DONALD W., retired business educator; b. Big Rapids, Mich., Mar. 1, 1910; s. Elbert Elvin Magoon and Edith Marie Whitsey; widowed, 1994; children: Elbert, Louise, Carol Feakins. BSME, U. Mich., 1932, MS, 1934, MBA, 1941. Grad. gemologist Gemological Inst. Am. Instr. Findlay (Ohio) Coll., 1932-33, asst. prof., 1934-37; rschr. L.A. Examiner, 1938-39; asst. prof. bus. La. State U., Baton Rouge, 1940-41; treas. Meijer Supermkts., Grand Rapids, Mich., 1946-60; cons. U.S. State Dept., Israel, Mex., 1961-64; prof. bus. Ea. Mich. U., Ypsilanti, 1965-80; prof. emeritus, 1980—. Tutor, Canton (Ohio) City Schs., 1996—. Capt., U.S. Army Signal Corps, 1941-46. Mem. Rotary Club Canton (various coms. 1985-95). Avocation: gemology.

MAGOON, NANCY AMELIA, art association administrator, philanthropist; b. N.Y.C., Apr. 19, 1941; d. Jack and Norma Harriet (Hirschl) Parker; m. Robert Cornelius Magoon, Mar. 16, 1978; children: Adam Glick, Peri Curnin. Student, Cornell U., 1958-59. Gallerist Hokin Gallery, Miami, 1986-89; sec. Nat. Found. Advancement in Arts, 1989-94; nat. coun. mem. Aspen Art Mus., 1985—, Aspen Ballet, 1985—; v.p. Ctr. for Fine Arts, Miami, 1984-94, Miami City Ballet, 1990-94. bd. dirs. Cmty. Alliance Against AIDS, 1990-92; coun. mem. Susan Komen Breast Cancer, Aspen, 1994—; hon. trustee Ctr. for Fine Arts, Miami Beach, 1996; trustee Site Santa Fe, 1996; mem. nat. coun. Jazz Aspen, 1999—. Named one of Outstanding Women in Miami, 1992; NEA grantee, 1995. Avocations: skiing, golf, fly fishing, skeet and clay target shooting.

MAGOS, LÁSZLÓ PAUL, toxicologist, consultant; b. Rákoskeresztur, Pest, Hungary, Feb. 4, 1921; arrived in Eng., 1963.; s. Pál and Mária (Kandikó) Fleischhacker; m. Éva Mary Benjamin, Apr. 9, 1952; 1 child, Adam László. MD, U. Szeged, Hungary, 1948; diploma in clin. pathology, Bd. Med. Specialization, Budapest, Hungary, 1954; Cadidature, Bd. Sci. Grades, Budapest, 1958. Demonstrator to asst. prof. Szeged U., 1946-50; from sci. officer to sr. sci. officer Inst. Occupl. Health, Budapest, 1950-63; sci. officer to spl. appt. MRC Toxicology Unit, Carshalton, Eng., 1963-86, hon. cons., 1986-93; freelance cons., 1986—; temporary cons. WHO, Geneva, Switzerland, 1972-92, Commn. of EC, Luxembourg, 1977, Mediterranean UNEP, Athens, Greece, 1987, 90, Internat. Atomic Energy Agy., Vienna, Austria, 1993; WHO sponsored mem. Group of Experts on Sci. Aspects of Marine Pollution, 1978-86; vis. prof. Dept. Radiation Biology and Biophysics, Rochester, 1971, 75. Asst. editor: Brit. Jour. Indsl. Medicine, 1978-93; European editor: Jour. Applied Toxicology, 1980-97. Recipient medal and diploma for work in field of toxicology U. Pavia, Italy, 1979. Fellow Royal Coll. Pathologists; mem. Internat. Commn. on Occupl. Health (hon.). Avocations: bridge, pottery. Home: 107 Boundary Rd, Surrey Wallington SM6 OTE, England

MAGOSHI, EMIKO, educator; b. Tokyo, Apr. 16, 1952; d. Yoshio and Kunie (Takahashi) Sakurai; m. Kentaro Magoshi, Mar. 2, 1977; children: Taro, Shiro. B in French, Internat. Rels., Sophia U., Tokyo, 1976; M in Econs., Keio U., Tokyo, 1994; PhD in Internat. Mgmt., U. East Asia, Yamaguchi, Japan, 1999. Pres. Inter Link Corp., Tokyo, 1989—; lectr. Sophia U., 1991-96; assoc. prof. Tokyo Junshin Women's Coll., 1996—; rschr. Inst. Labor, Tokyo, 1992-95. Author: The White Collar Re-Styling, 1995, Foreigners in Kaisha, 1996, Transcultural Management, 2000, Heartfelt Management for Equidistant Companies, 2000. Mem. Suginami Mcpl. Govt. Coun., Tokyo, 1999—.

MAGOSHI, JUN, polymer engineer, researcher, educator; b. Takefu, Fuki, Japan, Oct. 11, 1942; s. Yuichi and Sadako Magoshi; m. Yashiko Koike; children: Masayuki, Tomoko. B in Engring., Fukui U., 1965; M in Engring., Guma U., Ki Ryu, Japan, 1967; DSc (hon.), Osaka U., 1975. Rschr. Ministry of Agr., Forestry, and Fisheries, Tokyo, 1967-78; chief rschr. Ministry of Agr., Forestry, and Fisheries, Tsukuba, 1978-80; chief lab. Nat. Inst. Agrobiol. Resources, Tsukuba, 1980—. Author: Polymeric Materials Encyclopedia, 1996; contbr. articles to profl. jours. including Jour. Polymer Scis., Polymer. Recipient award Soc. Fiber Sci. and Tech., 1994, Fiber and Textiles, 1998, Internat. Conf. Advance Fiber Materials, 1999. Avocations: tennis, fishing. Office: Nat Inst Agrobiol Resources, 2-1-2 Kannondei, Tsukuba Ibaraki 305-8602, Japan

MAGOWAN, ARTHUR KENNETH TRAIN, retired dentist; b. Glasgow, Scotland, May 13, 1926; s. William John and Prudence Christian (Hodge) M.; m. Marjory Fraser Ames, Nov. 19, 1958; children: William Arthur, Raymond Fraser. B Dental Surgery, U. Glasgow, 1953. Pvt. practice, Glasgow, 1953-88; ret., 1988; charity worker Oxfam, Glasgow, 1989-91. Sub-lt. Royal Navy, 1944-47. Mem. Parklands Country Club. Avocations: private pilot, motoring activities, aviation projects, rugby.

MAGOWAN, PETER ALDEN, professional baseball team executive, grocery chain executive; b. N.Y.C., Apr. 5, 1942; s. Robert Anderson and Doris (Merrill) M.; m. Jill Tarlau (div. July 1982; children: Kimberley, Margot, Hilary; m. Deborah Johnston, Aug. 14, 1982. BA, Stanford U., 1964; MA, Oxford U., Eng., 1966; postgrad., Johns Hopkins U., 1967-68. Store mgr. Safeway Stores Inc., Washington, 1968-70; dist. mgr. Safeway Stores Inc., Houston, 1970-71; retail ops. mgr. Safeway Stores Inc., Phoenix, 1971-72; divsn. mgr. Safeway Stores Inc., Tulsa, 1973-76; mgr. internat. divsn. Safeway Stores Inc., Toronto, Ont., Can., 1976-78; mgr. western region Safeway Stores Inc., San Francisco, 1978-79; CEO Safeway Stores Inc., Oakland, Calif., 1980-93, chmn. bd. dirs., 1980-98; pres., mng. gen. ptnr. San Francisco Giants, 1993—; bd. dirs. Daimler Chrysler Corp., Caterpillar, Safeway Inc. Office: San Francisco Giants 24 Willie Mays Plz San Francisco CA 94107-2199

MAGPAYO, JOSE MARI SANTO TOMAS, communications educator, communications executive; b. Manila, The Philippines, May 15, 1959; s. Armando Tempongko Sr. and Lourdes (Santo Tomas) M.; m. Marie Veronica Ongkeko, Sept. 7, 1996. BA, De La Salle U., Manila, The Philippines, 1984; MA, U. Tex., 1989. Asst. prof. De La Salle U., Manila, The Philippines, 1983-97; mng. creative dir. Creasia, Inc., Manila, The Philippines, 1996—; cons. Megascopegraphics, Inc., Manila, 1993-96, Mass Transit Railway Corp., Hong Kong, 1995. Writer, dir. approx. 100 videos; author: (tv drama) Selfish Heaven, 1984 (Cath. Mass Media awards), tv comedies, dramas, variety shows; dir. (children's tv show) The Gongs, 1996 (Cert. of Excellence Chgo. Internat. Children's Film Festival 1996). Mem. Cory

Aquino for Pres. Movement, Manila, The Philippines, 1985. Nat. Citizen's Movement for Free Elections, Manila, 1986. Recipient Anvil Pub. Rels. award of excellence, 2000; Fulbright-Hays scholar U. Tex., 1987-89. Mem. Phi Kappa Phi. Roman Catholic. Avocations: scuba diving, tennis, reading, trekking, swimming. Office: Creasia Inc, 3869-B Bermeo St, Palanan Makati The Philippines

MAGRASSI, PAOLO, technology industry executive; b. Broni, Italy, July 13, 1954; s. Dino and Amelia (Contardi) M.; m. Mirella Piccinini, Dec. 28, 1985. Maturita Classica, Loceo Grattoni, Voghera, Italy, 1973; lic. in physics, U. Pavia, Italy, 1979. Sys. engr. Siemens, Milan, Italy, 1981-82; sr. cons. GE, Amsterdam, The Netherlands, 1982-86; R&D mgr. Nixdorf, Milan, 1987-91; v.p., rsch. dir. Gartner Group, Stamford, Conn., 1991—; cons. European Union, Brussels, 1988-92; mem. Esprit Indsl. Working Group, Brussels, 1989-92. Developer mgmt. systems in field; author: Applications Development in Europe, 1993, Architecture: A Foundation for Durable Applications, 1995. With Italian Army, 1980-81. Mem. IEEE, Assn. Computing Machinery, N.Y. Acad. Scis.

MAGRATH, C. PETER, educational association executive; b. N.Y.C., Apr. 23, 1933; s. Laurence Wilfrid and Giulia Maria (Dentice) M.; m. Deborah C. Howell, 1988; children: Valerie Ruth, Monette Fay. BA summa cum laude, U. N.H., 1955; PhD, Cornell U., 1962. Mem. faculty Brown U., Providence, 1961-68, prof. polit. sci., 1967-68, assoc. dean grad. sch., 1965-66; dean Coll. Arts and Scis. U. Nebr., Lincoln, 1968-69, dean faculties Coll. Arts and Scis., 1969-72, interim chancellor univ., 1971-72, prof. polit. sci., 1968-72, vice chancellor for acad. affairs, 1972; pres. SUNY, Binghamton, 1972-74, prof. polit. sci., 1972-74; pres. U. Minn., Mpls., 1974-84, U. Mo. System, 1985-91, Nat. Assn. State Univs. and Land Grant Colls., Washington, 1991—. Author: The Triumph of Character, 1963, Yazoo: Law and Politics in the New Republic, The Case of Fletcher v. Peck, 1966, Constitutionalism and Politics: Conflict and Consensus, 1968, Issues and Perspectives in American Government, 1971, (with others) The American Democracy, 2d edit., 1973, (with Robert L. Egbert) Strengthening Teacher Education, 1987; Served with AUS, 1955-57. Mem. Assn. Am. contbr. articles to profl. jours. Served with AUS, 1955-57. Mem. Assn. Am. Univs. (chmn. 1985-86), Phi Beta Kappa, Phi Kappa Phi, Pi Gamma Mu, Pi Sigma Alpha, Kappa Tau Alpha. Office: Nat Assn State U and Land Grant Colls 1307 New York Ave NW Ste 400 Washington DC 20005-4722

MAGRINI, ANNA ANGIOLA, engineering educator; b. Genoa, Italy, Oct. 13, 1962; d. Ugo Enrico Magrini and Elena Iandelli; m. Marco Roveta, June 25, 1995. DME, U. Genoa, 1986; PhD, U. Pisa, Italy, 1992. With Ansaldo SpA, Genoa, 1987-88; tchr. 2d Degree Sch., Genoa, 1991-92; rschr. U. Genoa, 1992-98; prof. engring. U. Pavia, 1998—; mem. European Normalization Com.; coord. working group Italian Normalization Com. Mem. Italian Assn. Air Conditioning Heating and Refrigeration. Office: Faculty of Engineering, Univ of Pavia Via Ferrata 1, 27100 Pavia Italy

MAGRISSO, MONI YEUDA, physics educator, researcher; b. Pleven, Bulgaria, July 13, 1956; s. Yeuda Nisim and Lussie Solomon (Kadmonova) M.; m. Valentina Lubenova Tsvetanova, July 10, 1977; children: Yuri, Oleg, Emil. Grad. phys. engring., K. Ochridsky U., Sofia, Bulgaria, 1981; grad. in med. physics, Med. Acad., Sofia, 1986, PhD, 1997. Technologist nuclear tools factory, Pleven, 1981-82; asst. prof. physics K. Ochridsky Higher Med. Sch., Pleven, 1983-99; rschr. Ben-Gurion U., 1999—. Contbr. articles to sci. jours., including Anal. Chim. Acta, Jour. Biochem. Biophys. Methods, Nephron, Luminescence, Jour. Biolum. Chemilum. Avocation: swimming. Office: Dept Clin Biochemistry, Ben-Gurion Univ, 84105 Beer Sheva Israel

MAGRIZOS, MOISSIS, textile engineer; b. Larissa, Greece, Aug. 15, 1950; s. Zacharias and Zouli Magrizos; m. Mazaltov Giousouroum; children: Zacharias, Noah, David. Grad. in Textile Engring., Bolton Tech. Coll., Eng., 1978. Mng. dir. Magrizos Bros. S.A., Larissa, 1980-90; pres. IRIS S.A., Larissa, 1990; vice chmn. Koroatex S.A., Ala., 1990-92; pres. Real Estate S.A. Iris, 1992. Hon. consul Samoa for Greece. Sgt. Greek Mil., 1970-75. Mem. Greek C. of C. and Industry, Textile Orgn. Avocations: social life, tennis, travels around the world. Fax: 041-536494. Home: Patroklov 14, Larissa Greece Office: PO Box 1194, Larissa Greece

MAGRO, EMANUEL PAUL, cataloger, priest. Diploma in philosophy and theology, Sacred Heart Sem., Victoria-Gozo, Malta, 1979; MSLS, Cath. U. Am., 1988, MA, 1989, postgrad., 1989—. Lectr. Cath. U. Am., Washington, 1991-93, St. Mary's Sem. and U., Balt., 1994, Georgetown U., Washington, 1995-97; sr. subject cataloger Libr. of Congress, Washington, 1998—; cons. Our Lady of Victory Parish, Washington, 1996—. Contbr. articles to religious pubs. tchr. German Cathedral Parish Ctr., Victoria-Gozo, Malta, 1985-86, Hotel Ta-Cenc, Sannat-Gozo, Malta, 1985, Sacred Heart Sem., Victoria-Gozo, 1985-86. Scholar Cath. U. Am., Washington, 1989-91, 88-89, 89-91. Mem. ALA, Cath. Theol. Soc. Am., Am. Acad. Religion, Assn. Profs. and Rschrs. in Religious Edn., Coll. Theology Soc., Lions, Beta Phi Mu. Office: 4835 MacArthur Blvd NW Washington DC 20007-1564

MAGUIRE, CHARLOTTE EDWARDS, retired physician; b. Richmond, Ind., Sept. 1, 1918; d. Joel Blaine and Lydia (Betscher) Edwards; m. Raymer Francis Maguire, Sept. 1, 1948 (dec.); children: Barbara, Thomas Clair II (dec.). Student, Stetson U., 1936-38, U. Wichita, 1938-39; BS, Memphis Tchrs. Coll., 1940; MD, U. Ark., 1944. Intern, resident Orange Meml. Hosp., Orlando, Fla., 1944-46; resident Bellevue Hosp. and Med. Ctr., NYU, N.Y.C., 1954, 55; instr. nurses Orange Meml. Hosp., 1947-57, staff mem., 1946-68; staff mem. Fla. Santarium and Hosp., Orlando, 1946-56, Holiday House and Hosp., Orlando, 1950-62; mem. courtesy and cons. staff West Orange Meml. Hosp., Winter Garden, Fla., 1952-67; active staff, chief dept. pediat. Mercy Hosp., Orlando, 1965-68; med. dir. med. svcs. and basic care Fla. Dept. Health and Rehab. Svcs., 1975-84; med. exec. dir., med. svcs. divsn. worker's compensation Fla. Dept. Labor, Tallahassee, 1984-87; chief of staff physicians and dentists Ctrl. Fla. divsn. Children's Home Soc. Fla., 1947-56; dir. Orlando Child Health Clinic, 1949-58; pvt. practice medicine Orlando, 1946-68; asst. regional dir. HEW, 1970-72; pediat. cons. Fla. Crippled Children's Commn., 1952-70, dir., 1968-70; med. dir. Office Med. Svcs. and Basic Care, sr. physician Office of Asst. Sec. Ops., Fla. Dept. Health and Rehab. Svcs.; clin. prof. dept. pediat. U. Fla. Coll. Medicine, Gainesville, 1980-87; mem. Fla. Drug Utilization Rev., 1983-87; real estate salesperson Investors Realty, 1982—; bd. dirs. Stavros Econ. Ctr. Fla. State U., Tallahassee; mem. pres.'s coun. Fla. State U., U. Fla., Gainesville; Charlotte Edwards Maguire eminent scholar chair and scholarships for qualified students, 1999. Recipient adv. com. Fla. Center for Clin. Services at U. Fla., 1952-60; del. to Mid-century White House Conf. on Children and Youth, 1950; U.S. del from Nat. Soc. for Crippled Children to World Congress for Welfare of Cripples, Inc., London, 1957; pres of corp. Eccleston-Callahan Hosp. for Colored Crippled Children, 1956-58; sec. Fla. chpt. Nat. Doctor's Com. for Improved Med. Svcs., 1951-52; med. adv. com. Gateway Sch. for Mentally Retarded, 1959-62; bd. dirs. Forest Park Sch. for Spl. Edn. Crippled Children, 1949-54, mem. med. adv. com., 1955-68, chmn., 1957-68; mem. Fla. Adv. Coun. for Mentally Retarded, 1965-70; dir. Fla. poison control Orange Meml. Hosp.; mem. orgn. com., chmn. com. for admissions and selection policies Camp Challenge; participant 12th session Fed. Exec. Inst., 1971; del. White House Conf. on Aging, 1980; dir. Stavros Econ. Ctr. Fla. State U. Charlotte Edwards Maguire Eminent Scholarship named in hon. Fla. State U. Mem. AMA (life), Nat. Rehab. Assn., Am. Congress Phys. Medicine and Rehab., Fla. Soc. Crippled Children and Adults, Ctrl. Fla. Soc. Crippled Children and Adults (dir. 1949-58, pres. 1956-57), Am. Assn. Cleft Palate, Fla. Soc. Crippled Children (trustee 1951-57, v.p. 1956-57, profl. adv. com. 1957-68), Mental Health Assn. Orange County (charter mem.; pres. 1949-50, dir. 1947-52, chmn. exec. com. 1950-52, dir. 1963-65), Fla. Orange County Heart Assn., Am. Med. Women's Assn., Am. Acad. Med. Dirs., Fla. Med. Assn. (life, chmn. com. on mental retardation), Orange County Med. Assn., Orange Med. Soc. (life), Fla. Pediat. Soc. (pres. 1952-53), Fla. Cleft Palate Assn. (counselor-at-large, sec.), Nat. Inst. Geneal. Rschr., Nat. Geneal. Soc., Assn. Profl. Genealogists, Tallahassee Geneal. Soc., Fla. State U. Found. Inc. (bd. dirs. Stavoris Ctr. for Econ. Edn.), Capital City Tiger Bay Club, Fla. Econs. Club, Eppes Soc. Fla. State U., Fla. State U. Found. Club: Governors. Home: 4158 Covenant Ln Tallahassee FL 32308-5765

MAGUIRE, KEVIN JEROME, lawyer; b. Amarillo, Tex., Jan. 14, 1963; s. Michael Francis and Rhea Marie (Crane) M.; m. Kerry Lucille Sowden, Apr.

6, 1991; children: Morgan Kimberly, Patrick McCoy, Mary Rhea, Sean McCann. BA, U. Okla., 1985; JD, So. Meth. U., 1988. Bar: Tex. 1988, U.S. Dist. Ct. (no., so. ea. and we. dists.) Tex. 1989, U.S. Ct. Appeals (5th cir.) 1989. Assoc. Strasburger & Price, L.L.P., Dallas, 1988-96, ptnr., 1996—; mem. Jesuit Alumni Exec. Bd., Dallas, 1996—. Mem. ABA, Dallas Bar Assn. (legal ethics com. 1990-93), Lawyers Alliance for Justice in Ireland, Defense Rsch. Inst. Roman Catholic. Home: 4229 Bryn Mawr Dr Dallas TX 75225-6739 Office: Strasburger & Price LLP 901 Main St Ste 4300 Dallas TX 75202-3724

MAGUIRE, PETER JAMES, family physician, medical educator; b. Sheffield, Eng., Sept. 13, 1953; arrived in Australia, 1962; s. Peter Francis and Mary Margaret (Gilvarry) M.; m. Rita Joan Thain, July 7, 1979; children: Alana, Brendan. MB, BS, U. Western Australia, 1977. Family physician Royal Perth Hosp., Perth, Australia, 1982-91; med. educator Royal Australian Coll. Gen. Practitioners, Perth, Australia, 1991—; family physician Claremont, Australia, 1996—; med. educator Royal Australian Coll. Gen. Practitioners, Perth, Australia, 1991—; family physician Claremont, Australia, 1996—. Fellow Royal Australian Coll. Gen. Practitioners (nat. chmn. QA/CE program 1996-99); mem. Australian Med. Assn., Australian Assn. Med. Edn. (treas. 1996-99). Office: Royal Australian Coll, 328 Stirling Hwy, Claremont 6010, Australia

MAGUIRE, RAYMER F., JR., lawyer; b. Orlando, Fla., Oct. 20, 1921; s. Raymer F. Sr. and Ruth (McCullough) M.; m. Sara Corry, Aug. 13, 1951; children: Craig Corry, Raymer F. III, Sara Maguire LeMone, Edmund Corry. BA, U. Fla., 1943, JD, 1948. Bar: Fla. 1948, U.S. Dist. Ct. (so. dist.) 1948, U.S. Supreme Ct. 1969. Assoc. Maguire, Voorhis & Wells, P.A., Orlando, 1948-53, mem., 1953—; bd. dirs. Sun Bank, N.A.; bd. dirs. and trustee various corps. and trusts. Elder First Presbyn. Ch., 1961—; mem., chmn. community coll. coun. State of Fla., 1976-79, mem. community coll. coordinating bd., 1979-83, vice chmn. 1979-81, chmn. 1981-82; trustee Valencia Community Coll., 1967-86, chmn. 1967-72; bd. dirs. Orange County Hist. Soc., 1982—, pres., 1987-88; chmn. bd. Cen. Fla. chpt. Am. Heart Assn., 1966-67; bd. dirs. Valencia Community Coll. Found., pres., 1974-75; chmn. citizens com. Orange County Sch. Bd. Referendum, 1964. Named in honor of Raymer F. Maguire Jr. Learning Resource Ctr., Valencia Community Coll., 1977. Mem. ABA, Fla. Bar Assn. U. Fla. Alumni Assn. (bd. dirs. 1954—, pres. 1959-60, Disting. Alumnus award 1975), Kiwanis (pres. 1962), U. Fla. Found. Republican.

MAGURA, IGOR SILVESTROVITCH, neurophysiologist, educator; b. Kiev, Ukraine, Nov. 22, 1928; s. Silvestr Silvestrovitch and Tatiana Andrejevna (Mechkovskaja) M.; m. Anna Aleksandrovna Rudenko, June 4, 1952; children: Tatiana, Elena. Student, Med. Inst., Kiev, 1947-52; PhD, Bogomoletz Inst. Physiology, Kiev, 1963, DSc, 1973. Intern Navy Faculty of Med. Inst., Leningrad, Russia, 1952-53; physician hosp. of tng. detachment of North Navy, Solovky Is, Russia, 1953-55; physician, specialist in underwater physiology and medicine Black See Navy, Sevastopol, Russia, 1955-57; rsch. scientist Bogomoletz Inst. Physiology, Kiev, 1958-63, sr. scientist, 1963-86, leading scientist, 1986—; cons. prof. Shevchenko Nat. U., Kiev, 1982-96; prof. Kiev br. Moscow Phys.-Tech. Inst., 1982—. Author: Problems of Electrical Excitability of Neuronal Membrane, 1981; (with others) Biophysics, 1988. Recipient USSR State prize in sci. and tech. Investigation on Problem of Neuronal Excitability, 1983, Ukraine State prize in sci. and tech., 1992, Soros prof. grant, 1994. Mem. Nat. Acad. Scis. Ukraine, Ukrainian Biophys. Soc. Avocation: travel. Home: Lomonosova Str 24 Apt 139, 252022 Kiev Ukraine Office: Bogomoletz Inst Physiology, Bogomoletz Str 4, 252024 Kiev Ukraine

MAG WALZ, GÜNTHER, artist; b. Graz, Styria, Austria, Feb. 19, 1939; s. Rudolf and Anna (Arnsek) W.; m. Elisabeth Walz-Babor, Oct. 9, 1979. Diploma in Painting and Graphics, U. of Applied Art Vienna, 1961. Cert. graphic artist. Artist numerous exhibition. Individual exhbns.: Kleine Galerie, Vienna, 1986, Gallery at Fliederlich, Nuremberg, Germany, 1996, Magnus Hirschfeld Ctr., Hamburg, Germany, 1997, Limner Gallery, N.Y., 1994, Galerie Im Sonntags-Club, Berlin, 1996, Gallery "Y", Johannesburg, South Africa, 1983, Gallery Prisma, Vienna, 1993. Home: Sedlitzkygasse 20, A-1110 Vienna Austria

MAGYAR, LÁSZLÓ ANDRÁS, historian; b. Budapest, Hungary, Jan. 26, 1956; s. Imre and Éva (Fodor) M.; m. Ágnes Éva Bolla, Feb. 23, 1980; children: András, Mihály, Borbála. MA, Eötvös L. U., 1981, PhD, 1985. Libr. Semmelweis Libr., Budapest, 1981-84, rsch. fellow, 1985-99, dept. dir., 1999—; editor Comms. Hist. Art. Med., Budapest, 1987. Author: Idyllium, 1989, Introduction into Ghostology, 1989, History of Artifical Man, 1992, The Lie, 1998. With Hungarian Army, 1974-75. Mem. Hungarian Soc. of Med. History (sec. 1985). Home: Torok u 4, H-1023 Budapest Hungary Office: Semmelweis Libr, Török u 12, H-1023 Budapest Hungary

MAHADEVAPPA, MADAPPA, rice breeder, university vice chancellor; b. Madapura, Karnataka, India, Apr. 8, 1937; s. Madappa and Puttabasamma Madappa; m. Sudha Mahadevappa, May 21, 1964; children: Mamatha, Rajendra. BS in Agr., Mysore (India) U., 1960; MSc, Madras U., 1962, PhD, 1965. Sr. rsch. fellow CFTRI, Mysore, 1966-68; asst. maize breeder U. Agrl. Sics., Bangalore, India, 1968-69; plant scientist U. Agrl. Sics., Bangalore, 1969-81; sr. rsch. fellow IRRI, Manila, 1977-80; prof., head U. Agrl. Scis., Bangalore, 1981-92, dir. instrn., 1992-94, vice chancellor, 1994—; vis. scientist IRRI, Manila, 1977-80; UGC vis. prof. U. Havana, Cuba, 1989-90; mem. tech. com. Water Resource Devel. Orgn. GOK, Bangalore, 1990. Author: Sudharita Beejotpadane in Kannada, 1985 (Best Book prize); inventions in field. Recipient K.K. Murthy award U. Agrl. Sics., 1973, Nagamma Dattatreya Rao Desai award, 1989, Syndicate Agrl. Found. award 1981, Sir Chotu Ram award 1996, Bharatha Rathna Sir M. Visvesvaraya Meml. Nat. Parisara Rathna award, 1999. Mem. Indian Agrl. Univs. Assn. (pres.), Karnataka Jour. of Agrl. Sci. (pres. 1994—), Seed Tech. and Plant Breeding Assn. (pres.), Assn. of Rice Rsch. Workers of India Cuttack (v.p.). Avocations: singing, playing instruments, writing articles. Home: Samarasa MH-2 8th Main, Saraswathipuram, Mysore 570 009, India Office: U Agrl Scis, Dharwad, Office of Vice Chancellor, Krishnagar Dharwad 580 005, India

MAHAJAN, JASWANT RAI, chemistry educator; b. Gurdas Nangal, India, Oct. 25, 1930; s. Chuni Lal and Indra Devi Mahajan; m. Wanda Polewacz, July 15, 1977; 1 child, Indra Maria. BSc with honors, Panjab U., 1953, MSc with honors, 1955; DPhil, Calcutta U., 1959. Postdoctoral fellow Johns Hopskins U., Balt., 1960, Ind. U., Bloomington, Ind., 1961-64; vis. prof. Ctrl. Inst. of Chemistry U. of Brasilia, Brazil, 1965; prof. postgrad. studies IQ-UFMG, Belohorizonte, 1966-68; prof. titular chemistry U. Brasilia, 1968-96; assoc. rschr. Quimica U. Brasilia, 1996-98; coord. U. Brasilia, 1968-70, head of dept. chemistry, 1970-72. Editl. bd. Jour. Brazilian Chem. Soc., 1990-94, ad. bd., 1994—; author: (with others) Organic Synthesis in Brazil: An Overview, 1994, Quimica Organica Sintetica-Brazil, 1987; patentee chem. process. Recipient Honorable Mention State Govt. Prize, 1983. Mem. Congress Club. Avocations: tennis, gardening, walking. Office: Quimica-IE-UnB, 70910900 Brasilia DF, Brazil

MAHAKUTESHWAR, HEBBALLI YALLAPPA, information scientist, educator; b. Navalgund, India, Aug. 18, 1950; s. Yallappa Magundappa and Siddalingamma Yallappa (Kuratti) Ganiger; m. Sumangala Patil, May 25, 1981; children: Anand M. Kuteshwar, Rashmi M. Kuteshwar. BSc, Karnataka U., India, 1971, MSc in Physics, 1974; ADISc, Indian Statis. Inst., Calcutta, 1978. Quality control supr. Shakti Insulated Wires Pvt. Ltd., Bombay, 1971-72; jr. rsch. fellow dept. physics, Karnatak U., Dharwad, 1974-76; sr. documentation asst. Indian Nat. Sci. Documentation Ctr., New Delhi, 1977-80; computer scientist, Ctrl. Drug Rsch. Inst., Lucknow, India, 1980-81; scientist, Ctrl. Food Technol. Rsch. Inst., Mysore, 1981—, head dept. libr., computer, printing and pubs., 1998—; hon. joint sec. Acad. Info. Sci., CFTRI Libr., Mysore, 1998—; treas. CFTRI Info. Soc. Mysore, 1990-91. Mem. Soc. for Info. Sci. (life), Karnataka State Libr. Assn. (life). Avocations: reading and discussion, watching TV and movies, internet and computers, listening to music. E-mail: maha@cscftri.ren.nic.in. Office: Ctrl Food Tech Rsch Inst, Chaluvamba Mansion, Mysore 570 013, India

MAHANTY, RUPA, management consultant, educator; b. Bombay, Jan. 18, 1956; d. Deba Priya and Reba (Bannerjee) Mukherjee; m. Niroop Kumar Mahanty, Nov. 16, 1977; 1 child, Neel. BS with honors, Elphinstone Coll.,

Bombay, 1975; GI and GII, Max Mueller Inst., Pune, India, 1976; M in Bus. Mgmt., Indian Inst. Mgmt., Calcutta, 1978. Cert. Reiki I and II, Usui Shiki Ryoho, 1996, 97, cert. Reiki Master, 1999. Sr. mgmt. devel. officer Tata Steel, Jamshedpur, India, 1986-89; dep. mgr. career planning, 1989-91, divsnl. mgr., staff, 1991-92; administr. Ctr. for Excellence, Jamshedpur, India, 1992-95; mgmt. cons., founder R.M. Assocs., Jamshedpur, India, 1996—; vis. faculty Xavier Labour Rels. Inst., Jamshedpur, 1996—, Tata Mgmt. Tng. Ctr., 1998—, Nat. Inst. Direct Taxation, Nagpur, India, 1995, Indian Mine & Metal Workers' Fedn., Puri, India, 1995—, Bhubaneshwar (India) Mgmt. Forum, 1995; dir., organizer seminar Empowering Women Managers to Succeed, 1995. Co-author: Changing Management — Now or Never, 2000. Founding mem. Safety Awareness for Everyone, Jamshedpur, 1998—; gov. com. Bal Vihar Group of Charities, Jamshedpur, 1998—; hosp. adv. com. Tata Steel, 1995—; founder, pres. Jamshedpur Youth for Tomorrow's India, 1970-71. Mem. All India Mgmt. Assn., Jamshedpur Mgmt. Assn., Computer Soc. India (sec. organizing coun. 1981-86), Soc. Promotion of Profl. Excellence (sec. 1993-97), Jamshedpur Rifle Club (life), Indian Women Pilots Assn. (life), Ninetynines Inc. (life), Jamshedpur Flying Club (mng. com. 1985-91). Avocations: flying (licensed pilot), yoga (instructor), shooting, cooking, music. Fax: 91 (657) 223415. E-mail: Kvma@satyam.net.in. Home: 3 Hesal Rd, Kaiser Bungalows, Jamshedpur 831 005, India Office: RM Assocs, 3 Hesal Rd, Jamshedpur 831 005, India

MAHAPATRA, RAJAT KANTI, medical administrator; b. Sautia, India, Aug. 6, 1943; s. Naba Kumar and Mohamaya (Bhattachariya) M.; m. Dipta Panda, May 19, 1973; children: Anirban, Rita. MBBS, Govt. Med. Coll., Burla, India, 1966; MD, Postgrad. Inst. Med. Edn. and Rsch., Chandigarh, India, 1971; DM in Cardiology, All India Inst. Med. Scis., New Delhi, 1976. Diplomate Am. Bd. Internal Medicine. Registrar All India Inst. Med. Scis., New Delhi, 1973-76; cardiologist Saf Darjang Hosp., New Delhi, 1976; rsch. assoc. Maimonides Hosp., 1977-78; staff cardiologist USAF, Ft. Worth, Tex., 1980-87; assoc. prof. U. Health Sci. Ctr., 1985-91; asst. prof. Meharry Med. Coll., Nashville, 1987-89; dir. N.K. Cardiac Ctr., Midnapur, India, 1989—; dir. Hunter Rsch., 1989-95. Author: Systemic Thromboembolism in RHD, 1979 (Benjamin Castleman award 1977), Ace Efficacy and Safety, 1986 (Squibb grantee 1987), Beta Blocker in Arrhythmia and Hypertension, 1976, 87 (Ciba grantee 1987), Ramipril in Hypertension LVH Regression, 1999 (Astra grantee 1997). Mem. sch. bd. R.K. Mission, India, 1958; rural health educator, South Bengal, India, 1989-99; med. ethics Indian Med. Assn., South Bengal, India, 1989-99; educator individual rights, South Bengal, 1999. Maj. USAF, 1980-82. Hunter Rsch. grantee, 1997, Upjohn grantee, 1977. Fellow Internat. Coll. Angiology, Am. Coll. Angiology, Assn. Physicians India (v.p. 1999). Republican. Buddhist. Avocations: reading, writing, fishing.

MAHAR, ELLEN PATRICIA, law librarian; b. Washington, Jan. 15, 1938; d. Richard A. and Lina Mahar. BA, St. Joseph Coll., Emmitsburg, Md., 1959; MLS, U. Md., 1968. Asst. librarian Covington & Burling, Washington, 1971-73, libr. dir., 1978-92; librarian Shea & Gardner, Washington, 1974-78; mgr. info. ctr. Assn. Comml. Real Estate, Herndon, Va., 1992-94; head libr. Caplin & Drysdale Chtd., Washington, 1994—. Co-editor: Legislative History of the Securities Act of 1933 and the Securities Act of 1934, 11 vols., 1973. Mem. Am. Assn. Law Libraries, Spl. Libraries Assn., Law Librarians' Soc. Washington. Office: Caplin & Drysdale Chtd 1 Thomas Cir NW Fl 11 Washington DC 20005-5802

MAHARAJ, RUSSELL, JR., research engineering geologist, consultant; b. San Fernando, Trinidad and Tobago, July 15, 1965; s. Seepersad and Joyce (Ramdhan) M.; m. Penella Corine Ghouralal, Oct. 1, 1991; children: Pierce Rossi, Chloé Michiko. BSc with honors, Univ. of W.I., Jamaica, 1988, MPhil, 1991; postgrad. cert. engring. geology, Kyoto (Japan) U., 1996. Engr. EXLOG S.A., Trinidad and Tobago 1988; asst. lectr., mus. curator The Univ. W.I., Jamaica, 1990-91; sr. engring. geologist The Inst. of Marine Affairs, Trinidad and Tobago, 1991-94; rsch. fellow Kyoto (Japan) U., 1994-96; engring. geologist The Inst. Marine Affairs, Trinidad and Tobago, 1996-97; cons. geotech. engr. Trinidad and Tobago, 1997-98; petroleum geologist Petrotrin, Trinidad and Tobago, 1997-98; commonwealth secretariat/CFTC expert Coastal Geosci. & Engring., South Pacific Applied Geosci. Commn., Suva, Fiji, 1998—; cons. engring. geologist The Univ. W.I., Jamaica, 1990-91, The Inst. of Marine Affairs, Trinidad, 1991-94, UNFCCC, 1999, Internat. Global Change Inst./U. Waikato, New Zealand, 1999, 2000, World Bank/Internat. Global Change Inst., 1999; tech. advisor Govt. of Trinidad and Tobago, 1991-93; program cons., sr. lectr. BSc degree program U. London, Inst. Tertiary Tutors, Trinidad and Tobago; cons. UN Framework Convention on Climate Change, 1999; adj. lectr. U. of the South Pacific, 1999—; referee several internat. jours.; project advisor various internat. projects, Europe, Caribbean, South Pacific, N.Am., Japan, Brazil; cons. in field. Mem. editorial bd. The Inst. of Marine Affairs, Trinidad, 1991-93; contbr. articles to profl. jours. and books. Presbyterian. Commonwealth Found. grantee, 1992, rsch. grantee People's Republic China, 2000; Monbusho fellow Japan Govt., 1994; scholar U. W.I., 1989. Fellow Geol. Soc. London; mem. ASCE (Geoinstitute), Internat. Assn. Engring. Geology, Internat. Assn. for Impact Assessment, Assn. of Engring. Geologists, Internat. Soc. for Soil Mechanics and Geotechnical Engrs. (U.S. nat. com.), IUGS Commn. on Environ. Planning, Coastal Edn. and Rsch. Found., N.Y. Acad. Scis., IUGS Project 425 Landslides and Cultural Heritage. Avocations: swimming, hiking, fishing, cycling, listening to music. E-mail: rossi@sopac.org.fj. Fax: 679 370040. Home: 27 Ecclesville Rd, Rio Claro Trinidad and Tobago

MAHATHIR BIN MOHAMAD, prime minister of Malaysia; b. Alor Setar, Kedah, Malaysia, Dec. 20, 1925; m. Siti Hasmah, 1956; 5 children. Student, Sultan Abdul Hamid Coll., Alor Setar, Malaysia; MBBS, U. Malaya, Singapore, 1947, King Edwar VII Coll. Medicine, Singapore, 1952; postgrad., Harvard U., MA, 1967. Med. officer malaysian Govt. Svc., Alor Star, Langkawi and Perlis, Malaysia, 1953-57; pvt. practice Malaysia, 1957-72; Malaysian rep. to UN New York, 1963; mem. parliament for Kota Setar Selatan Govt. of Malaysia, 1964-69; mem. supreme coun. United Malays Nat. Orgn., 1965-69, v.p., 1975-78, pres., 1978-81; senator Govt. of Malasia, 1973-76; mem. parliament for Kubang Pasu Govt. of Malaysia, 1974-90, min. edn. 1974-76, dep. prime min. of malaysia and ministry, 1976-81, prime min., 1981—, minister of def., 1981-86; min. of home affairs, 1986—; chmn. FIMA (Food Industry of Malaysia), 1973; chmn. 1st Higher Edn. Coun., 1968; mem. Higher Edn. Adv. Coun., 1972; chmn. Univ. Kebangsaan Coun., 1974. Author: The Malay Dilemma, 1969. Former chmn. Kedah Anti Tb Assn., chmn. Kedah Child Welfare Coun. Office: Jabatan Perdani Menteri, Jalan Dato Onn, 50502 Kuala Lumpur Malaysia*

MAHATUMARAT, CHARAN, plastic surgery educator, consultant; b. Ayudhya, Thailand, Jan. 25, 1949; s. Muay and Louis (Tang) M.; m. Korapin Kasemsant Mahatumarat, Apr. 20, 1991; children: Padcha, Passorn, Warat, Natcha. BS, Chulalongkorn U., Bangkok, Thailand, 1971, MD, 1973. Cert. bd. gen. and plastic surgery, Thai Med. Coun, 1978, craniofacial, Australian CFU, 1985. Fellow Australian Craniofacial Unit, Adelaide, Australia, 1985, Nassau County Med. Ctr., N.Y.C., 1986; vis. fellow Innsbruck (Austria) U., 1989; founder Chulalongkorn Craniofacial Fund, Bangkok, Thailand, 1987—; head, founder Chulalongkorn Craniofacial Team, Bangkok, Thailand, 1986—; assoc. prof. in plastic surgery Chulalongorn U., Bangkok, Thailand, 1992—; sec. gen. The Soc. of Plastic Surgery of Thailand, 1997-99; coun. mem. Asian Pacific Craniofacial Assn., Adelaide, Australia, 1995—; edtl. bd. The Jour. of Craniofacial Surgery, Fla., 1998—; v.p. The Soc. of Plastic Surgery of Thailand, 1999—. Recipient Mahidol U. B.Braun prize, Thailand, 1999, King's scholarship, Thailand, 1985, Best V.D.O. presentation, Royal Coll. Surgeons, 1997. Fellow Internat. Soc. Craniofacial, Asian-Pacific Craniofacial Assn., Soc. of Plastic Surgeons of Thailand. Democrat. Buddhist. Avocations: travel, golf, swimming, volunteer plastic surgeon for the poor. Home: Sukhumvit Rd 39, 33/8 Soi Promjai, Bangkok 10110, Thailand Office: Plastic & Recon Surgery, Chulalongkorn Univ, Bangkok 10330, Thailand

MAHAYNI, RIAD GHALEB, urban planning educator; b. Damascus, Syrian Arab Republic, May 6, 1942; came to U.S., 1961; s. Ghaleb and Rushdiah M.; m. Fatina Mahayni, July 28, 1981; children: Basil, Tamim. BS in Civil Engring, Oreg. State U., 1966; M of Urban Planning, U. Oreg., 1969; PhD, U. Wash., 1972. Civil engr. Eugene (Oreg.) Water and Electric Bd., 1966-69; asst. prof. urban planning U. R.I., Kingston, 1973-77, assoc. prof.,

1977-79; tech. coordinator Makkah (Saudi Arabia) Region Planning Project, 1983-86; prof., chairperson Iowa State U., Ames, 1979-83, 96—, prof., 1979—; cons. R.I. Dept. Health, Providence, 1975, R.I. dept. Social Svcs., Providence, 1976, Brookhaven Nat. Lab, N.Y.C., 1977, Oak Ridge (Tenn.) Nat. Lab., 1993-94, Ames (Iowa) Nat. Lab., 1993. Contbr. articles to profl. publs. Chmn. R.I. Festival of the Arts, Kingston, 1977, Hist. Preservation Commn., Ames, 1988-92; mem. Ames Planning and Zoning Commn., 1998—. Fellow Am. Inst. Cert. Planners; mem. Am. Planning Assn., Phi Beta Delta. Home: 1617 Amherst Dr Ames IA 50014-3925

MAHDAVI, KAMAL B., writer, researcher; b. Esfahan, Iran, Sept. 1, 1933; came to U.S., 1958, naturalized.; s. Ebrahim B. and Ghamar (Jalilian) M. BA, U. Calif., Berkeley, 1964; MA, U Toronto, 1965; postgrad., U. Cambridge, Eng., 1965-69. Cert. coll. tchr., Calif. R&D rschr. U. Stockholm, 1969-71; freelance rschr., writer self-employed, San Francisco, San Diego, 1972—; ind. legal rschr. San Francisco, San Diego, 1980—. Author (as K.M.B. Writer): Technological Innovation: An Efficiency Investigation, 1972; contbr. articles to profl. jours. Civil rights litigant. Avocations: swimming, chess. Office: PO Box 121164 San Diego CA 92112-1164

MAHDI, SALAH EL, musician, composer, artist; b. Tunis, Feb. 9, 1925. Student of Aly Derwish and Khemaïs Ternane, Rashidia Inst.; student, Zituna U.; D in Musicology, Poitiers U., France. Tchr. music Rashidia Inst., dir., 1949; dir. dept. fine arts Ministry of Edn., Tunisia; appointed judge Law Cts. Tunis; organizer Nat. Acad. Music, Dance and Dramatic Art.; head Direction of Music and Fold Art, Ministry of Culture, 191; pres. Nat. Cultural Com.; pres. Nat. Com. of Music; founder Nat. Troup of Popular Arts, 1962, Tunisian Symphonic Orch., 1969, Tunisian Symphonic Orch., 1969, Nat. Soc. for Preservation of Coran, Nat. Sch. Coranic Intoned Psalms; mem. exec. com. Islamic Orgn. History, Culture and Art, Istanbul, Turkey, Internat. Counsel of Music; high com. Islamic Civilisation, Istanbul; v.p. Internat. Inst. Music, Dance and Dramatic Art, Internat. Inst. Counsel Folk Music; founding mem. Internat. Inst. Comparative Music, Berlin; pres. World Orgn. Folk Arts and Traditions; contbr. numerous articles on mus., hist. and lit. works. Composer under pseudonym of Ziryab; writer mus. criticism (newspapers) Essabah, Essarih, El Amal; author plays for radio and on stage; performed with El-Kawakab Assn. Tunis; author over 700 compositions in classical and folk songs and instrumental music; symphonic works performed at Moscow Festival, Leningrad Festival. Decorated Order of Republic meda , 2d class, Order of Labour medal, Order of Culture medal 1st class (Tunis); recipient Grand Prize del la Ville de Tunis, League Arab States, 1999. Mem. Internat. Soc. Mus. Edn. (v.p., com. dir.), French Assn. Writers, Composers and Pubs. Office: c/o Club Ziriab, 71 Bis Rue de Palestine, Tunis Tunisia

MAHECHA GÓMEZ, JORGE EDUARDO, physics educator, researcher; b. La Palma, Colombia, Aug. 8, 1948; s. Anibal and Isabel (Gómez) Mahecha; m. Clara Inés Botero, Sept. 9, 1977; children: Eduardo, Andrés. BSc in Physics, U. Antioquia, Medellin, Colombia, 1973; MSc in Physics, U. u Beogradu, Yugoslavia, 1979, PhD in Physics, 1993. Prof. physics U. Antioquia, 1971—, head atomic physics group, 2000—. Author: Mecánica Clásica Avanzada, 1987; contbr. articles to sci. jours. Rsch. grantee Colciencias, 1993-95. Mem. Internat. Ctr. Theoretical Physics (assoc.), Soc. Colombiana de Física, Soc. Mex. de Física, Am. Phys. Soc. Avocations: jogging, reading. Office: U de Antioquia, Depto de Fisica, AA 1226, Medellín Antioquia, Colombia

MAHENDRA, ALLA RAMACHANDRA, geologist, consultant; b. Madras, India, Mar. 7, 1935; s. Alla Ramachandra Naido and Varadarajulu Naidu Leelavathi; m. Mahendra Sukrutha, Nov. 23, 1962; children: Smitha, Praveen Kumar. BSc with honors, Cen. Coll., Bangalore, India, 1954, MSc, 1955. Cert. in engring. geology and geohydrology. Asst. geologist Geol. Survey of India, 1956-63, geologist, 1964-70, sr. geologist, 1971-81; chief geologist Gulf Mining & Exploration Co., Tanzania, 1983-84, Nat. Rsch. Devel. Soc., India, 1985-86; dir. Geo. Engring. Svcs., Hyderabad, India, 1987—; chief cons. Natural Resources Devel. Co., India, 1984; cons. Intg. GeoInsts. and Svcs. (p) Ltd., 1990, 97, Wat & Powe Contancy, Govt. India, 1995-96; approved cons. Indian Bur. Mines, Govt. India, 1994-95. Contbr. articles to profl. jours. Mem. Mining Engrs. Assn. India (life), Indian Soc. Engring. Geology (life), N.Y. Acad. Scis. Hindu. Avocations: animal welfare, traveling, writing, reading. Home: 4-1-2/1 Eden Bagh, Hyderabad 500 001, India

MAHENDRA, SOM NATH, electrical engineer, educator; b. U.P., India, July 10, 1949; s. Bhola Nath and Sushila Devi (Mehrotra) M.; m. Chhaya Tandon; children: Ankur, Pallav. BSc in Engring., Banaras Hindu U., Varanasi, India; diploma in music, Banaras Hindu U., Varanesi, India, 1970; MSc in Engring., Banaras Hindu U., 1972; PhD, The City U., London, 1977. Devel. engr. Tullu Motors Pvt. Ltd., Varanesi, 1972-73; lectr. in elec. engring. Banaras Hindu U., Varanasi, 1973, 1977-79, reader in elec. engring., 1979-93, prof. elec. engring., 1993—; demonstrator The City U., London, 1973-77; cons. Bharat Heavy Elec. Ltd., Bhopal, India, 1984-96, Indian Railways, Lucknow, India, 1985-91, Ministry of Textiles, Varanasi, 1988-91; prin. investigator projects on linear induction motor and its application to underground transport sys. Ministry Human Resource Devel. Govt. of India, New Delhi, 1994—, All India Coun. for Tech. Edn. projects. Co-author: Electric Traction, 2000. Recipient Republic Day award Nat. Rsch. Devel. Coun., 1993. Fellow IEE; mem. IEEE (sr., vice-chmn. U.P. sect. 1993), Inst. Engrs. (exec. com. 1992), Indian Soc. Tech. Edn. (awards 1996, 97). Achievements include inventing an attachment for handloom for the visually handicapped. Avocations: reading books, watching TV. Home: 53/4 Kabir Nagar Coloney, Durgakund, Varanasi 221 005, India Office: Dept Elec Engring Inst Tech, Banaras Hindu U, Vanarasi 221 005, India

MAHENDRA RAJ, S., gastroenterologist; b. Kuala Lumpur, Malaysia, June 22, 1958; s. Sundramoorthy and Annalakshmi (Thillainathan) Sundramoorthy; m. Gurjeet Kaur Chatar Singh, June 3, 1990; children: Jayanand, Suresh. B Medicine B Surgery, U. Glasgow, Scotland, 1982. House officer Greater Glasgow Health Bd., 1982-83, registrar in gastroenterology, 1986-88; sr. house officer Lanarkshire Health Bd., Airdrie, U.K., 1983-84, registrar in medicine, 1984-86; lectr. U. Sci. Malaysia, Kota Bharu, Malaysia, 1988-92; assoc. prof. U. Sci. Malaysia, Kota Bharu, 1993—; chmn., coord. clin. undergrad. program U. Sci. Malaysia, 1995-98; mem. Nat. Concensus Expert Panels on Med. Mgmt., 1995-2000. Contbr. numerous articles to profl. publs.; mem. editl. bd. Med. Jour. Malaysia, 1996—. Rsch. grantee U. Sci. Malaysia, 1992-97, Govt. of Malaysia, 1994-97. Fellow Royal Coll. Physicians U.K., Royal Coll. Physicians and Surgeons Glasgow, Royal Soc. Tropical Medicine and Hygiene; mem. Malaysian Soc. Gastroenterology/Hepatology (pres.-elect 1997-98), pres., 1998-99, Acad. Medicine Malaysia. Home: 2445 Taman Kenangan, Cherang Jalan Hosp, 15200 Kota Bharu Kelantan Malaysia Office: U Sci Malaysia Sch Med Scis, Dept Medicine, 16150 Kota Bharu Kelantan Malaysia

MAHENTHIRAN, JOTHIHARAN, physician, cardiologist, consultant; b. Colombo, Sri Lanka, Aug. 19, 1966; came to U.S., 1994; s. Canapathipillai and Somavathy Mahenthiran; m. Rathipriya Mahendran, Nov. 24, 1993; 1 child, Ashorne Krithiesh. MB, BS, U. Madras, India, 1989. Diplomate Am. Bd. Internal Medicine. Intern G. Stanley Hosp./Med. Sch., Madras, 1990-91; sr. house officer Victoria Hosp., Blackpool, U.K., 1992-94; resident in internal medicine Coney Island Hosp., Bklyn., N.Y., 1994-97, fellow in cardiovascular diseases, 1997-2000; fellow in cardiovascular diseases Cornell Med. Ctr., N.Y.C., 1997-2000; fellow in nuclear cardiology St. Lukes Hosp., Columbia Presbyn. Med. Ctr., N.Y.C., 2000—; chief resident in medicine Coney Island Hosp., 1996-97, chief fellow in cardiology. Fellow Royal Coll. Physicians of Can.; mem. ACP, Royal Coll. Physicians U.K., Am. Coll. Cardiology (assoc.). Avocations: sports, travel. E-mail: rajoe@hotmail.com. Home: 788A S Gannon Ave Staten Island NY 10314-4322 Office: Coney Island Hosp 2601 Ocean Pkwy Brooklyn NY 11235-7791

MAHENTHIRAN, SAKTHI, accounting educator, consultant; b. Colombo, Sri Lanka, July 8, 1959; came to U.S., 1986; s. Canadathipillai and Somavathy Mahenthiran; m. Shivanthi Selvaratnam, June 22, 1986; 1 child, Arjuna. MBA, Temple U., 1989, PhD, 1991. Acct. W.J. Wisenberg & Co., Ndola, Zambia, 1984-86; prof. acctg. Pa. State U., Erie, 1991-95, Butler U., Indpls., 1995—; sec./treas. R.J. Berg & Co., Indpls., 1998—. Contbr. articles to profl. jours. Fellow Assn. Chartered Cert. Accts. U.K.; mem. Assn. Chartered Mgmt. Accts. U.K. (assoc.), Am. Acctg. Assn., Inst. Mgmt. Accts. Hindu. Avocations: travel, tennis, golf. E-mail: Amahenth@butler.edu. Office: Butler Univ 4600 Sunset Ave Indianapolis IN 46208-3487

MAHENTHRAN, LAKSHMANAN VEERABADRAN, immunologist, immunogeneticist; b. Madurai, India, Feb. 21, 1960; s. Lakshmanan Veerabadran and Veerabadran Saraswathy M.; m. Mahenthran Jegadeeswari, Feb. 10, 1992; 2 children. BSc, Madura Coll., Madurai, India, 1982; MSc, Thiuagarajar Coll., Madurai, 1984; PhD, M.K. U., Madurai, 1992. Sr. technician M.K. U., Madurai, 1984-86, sr. sci. officer, 1992-94; cons. immunologist M.M.H.R.C., Madurai, 1996-97; sr. rsch. fellow CSIR, New Delhi, 1990; propr. M/S Majestic Immunodiagnostic Centre, Madurai, 1997—. Mng. trustee Matha Trust, Madurai, 1997—. Recipient Best Immunologist award City Cultural Assn., 1994, Best Clin. Lab. awrd, 1995, Great Win awrds TN Cultural Acad., 1998. Avocations: reading, sports, drawing, swimming, photography, rangoli. Home: No 1 Karugappillaikara St, 625 001 Madurai India Office: M/S Majestic Immunodiag Ctr, 30A Arappalayam Main Rd, Padithurai, Madurai 625 016, India

MAHER, CORNELIUS CREEDON, III, neurologist, toxicologist, army officer; b. N.Y.C., Jan. 30, 1949; s. Cornelius Creedon Jr. and Hester (Sullivan) M.; m. Lynn Marie Elliott, July 15, 1972; children: Christa, Cornelius IV, Kimberley. BS in Chemistry, Boston Coll., 1969; MS in Chemistry, U. Mich., 1973, PhD in Chemistry and Environ. Health, 1976; MD, St. Louis U., 1986. Diplomate Am. Bd. Psychiatry and Neurology. Rsch. fellow Brookhaven Nat. Lab., Upton, N.Y., 1969; rsch. fellow then lectr. U. Mich., Ann Arbor, 1969-76; rsch. assoc. Children's Hosp. Med. Ctr., Boston, 1976-77; indsl. toxicologist West Allis (Wis.) Meml. Hosp., 1977-82; commd. 2d lt. U.S. Army, 1982, advanced through grades to lt. col., 1995; intern in neurology Letterman Army Med. Ctr., San Francisco, 1986-87, resident in neurology, 1987-90; staff neurologist William Beaumont Army Med. Ctr., El Paso, 1990-94; asst. chief neurology dept. Walter Reed Army Med. Ctr., Washington, 1994-98; chief operational neurology Madigan Army Med. Ctr., Tacoma, 1999—; mem. neurology faculty Tex. Tech. U., 1991—, Uniformed Svcs. U. of Health Scis., 1995—, U. Wash., 1999—. Contbr. articles to profl. jours. Mem. AMA, Am. Acad. Neurology, Am. Chem. Soc., Assn. Mil. Surgeons, N.Y. Acad. Scis., Sigma Xi, Phi Lambda Upsilon, Alpha Chi Sigma. Office: Neurology Dept Madigan Army Med Ctr Fort Lewis WA 98431

MAHER, DANA FITZGERALD, composer, musician; b. Tulsa, Okla., Aug. 8, 1969; d. Michael Thomas and Judith Welham Fitzgerald; m. Brian William Maher, Nov. 21, 1992; 1 child, Quinn Christopher. BA, U. Tulsa, 1991, MusM, 1996. Accompanist, choir dir. Trinity Presbyn. Ch., Tulsa, 1991-97; accompanist Tulsa Pub. Schs., 1995-98; pianist Goodwin/Maher Duo, Tulsa, 1995—; artistic dir. Amadeus Piano Festival, Tulsa, 1995—. Composer A Dwelling Place, 1997, Four Fables for Piano, 1999, Nocturne, 1999, An Artists Palette, 1999. Mem. Music Tchrs. Nat. Assn. (profl. cert. piano and theory), Okla. Music Tchrs. Assn. (adjudicator 1997—, jr. audition chair 1998—), Tulsa Music Tchrs. Assn. (bd. mem. 1996—), Hyechka Club (bd. mem. 1998—), Piano Study Club (pres. 1997-98). Avocations: reading, cooking. E-mail: fitzgeraldsales@webzone.net.

MAHER, GRAEME ANDREW, hydropower development company executive; b. Longford, Tasmania, Australia, Mar. 11, 1960; s. John and Alice Maud (James) M.; m. Susan Maree Scarafiotti, Jan. 13, 1990. BE, U. Tasmania, Hobart, Australia, 1981. Cert. practicing engr. Engr. Commonwealth Govt., Canberra, Australia, 1981-83; constrn. engr. Hydro Electric Commn., Queenstown, Australia, 1983-87; dam design engr. Hydro Electric Commn., Hobart, 1987-93; project coord. HECECAUST Pty Ltd., Vientiane, Laos, 1993-96; dep. gen. mgr. design and constrn. ALP Mgmt. Pty. Ltd., Vientiane, Laos, 1996-98, Xe Kaman Hydroelectric and Southern Laos Transmission Sys. Project; sr. engr. Hydroelectric Corp., Tasmania, Australia, 1999—. Mem. Instn. Engrs. Australia (sec. Tasmania divsn. 1989-93).

MAHER, MICHAELEEN CONSTANCE, parapsychologist; b. Maywood, Calif., Apr. 16, 1939; d. Eugene Hugh Maher and Constance Loveland; m. Donald Roger Snyder, Apr. 17, 1967; children: Degan Ocean, Ariel Quetzalcoatl. BA magna cum laude, CUNY, 1974, MA in Psychology, 1981, PhD in Basic and Applied Neurocognition, 1983. Rsch. assoc. psychology dept. CUNY, N.Y.C., 1972-82; cons. Am. Soc. for Psychical Rsch., N.Y.C., 1983-85; freelance editl. cons. N.Y. Mag., N.Y.C., 1986-88; rsch. cons. Thirteen.WNET, N.Y.C., 1989-92; adj. prof. New Sch. U., N.Y.C., 1986—; freelance editl. cons. The New Yorker, N.Y.C., 1996—; instr. CUNY, 1976-77, SUNY, Purchase, 1978-79, Hunter Coll. CUNY, 1979-80, Pace U., 1981-82. Film maker Riff '65, 1966, Para 1000, 1967, (with Sheldon Rochlin) Tibetan Medicine: A Buddhist Approach to Healing, 1979; contbr. articles to profl. jours. Recipient Rsch. award Soc. for Phsychial. Rsch., 1976, Rsch. award Parapsychol., 1985, 92, 97. Mem. Parapsychol. Assn. (Rsch. award 1985, 92, 97), N.Y. Neuropsychology Group. Avocations: film making, videography, poetry, mountain climbing, experimental research.

MAHER, STEPHEN FRANCIS, advertising executive; b. London, Feb. 19, 1961; s. Francis John and Bridget Rita (Dillon) M.; m. Sarah Jane Beckett, Sept. 23, 1989; children: Sophie Elizabeth, Edward Archie Francis, Frederick George. MA in Modern History, Balliol Coll., Oxford, Eng., 1983. Acct. exec. ABM, London, 1983-86; acct. exec. AMV-BBDO, London, 1986-87, acct. dir., 1987-89; bd. dirs. Simons Palmer, London, 1989-92, head acct. mgmt., 1992-94; CEO Maher Bird Assocs., London, 1994—. Mem. I.P.A., Mktg. Soc., Mktg. Coun. Avocations: soccer, music, travel. Office: Maher Bird Assocs, Academy House 161-167 Oxford St, London W1R 1TA, England

MAHER, STEPHEN TRIVETT, lawyer, educator; b. N.Y.C., Nov. 21, 1949; s. William John and Jean Dorothy (Trivett) M.; m. Sharon Leslie Wolfe, Nov. 22, 1981; children: Meaghan Wolfe, Caitlin Wolfe. BA, NYU, 1971; JD, U. Miami, Coral Gables, Fla., 1975. Bar: Fla. 1975, U.S. Dist. Ct. (so. dist.) Fla. 1976, D.C. 1979, U.S. Dist. Ct. (no. dist.) Fla. 1979, U.S. Supreme Ct. 1980, U.S. Ct. Appeals (5th and 11th cirs.) 1981, U.S. Dist. Ct. (so. dist.) Fla. 1982, U.S. Dist. Ct. (mid. dist.) Fla. 1983. Assoc. Chonin & Levey, Miami, 1975; staff atty. Legal Svcs. of Greater Miami, Inc., 1975-81; assoc. Finley, Kumble, Wagner et al, Miami, 1981-84; dir. clin. program Sch. of Law U. Miami, Coral Gables, 1984-90, assoc. prof. law Sch. of Law, 1984-92; pvt. practice Stephen T. Maher, P.A., Miami, Fla., 1992—; mem. Fla. Bar/Fla. Bar Found. Joint Commn. on Delivery Legal Svcs. to the Indigent, Tallahassee, 1990-91, chair, organizer Seventh Adminstrv. Law Conf., Tallahassee, 1990, Conf. on the Fla. Constn., 1995; cons. on in-house legal edn. Contbr. articles to profl. jours. Fellow Fla. Bar Found. (life, bd. dirs. 1984-91); mem. ABA, Fla. Bar (chair adminstrv. law sect. 1993-94, chair coun. of sects. 1996-97), Dade County Bar Assn. Home: 1015 Sevilla Ave Miami FL 33134-6328 Office: 1500 Miami Ctr 201 S Biscayne Blvd Miami FL 33131-4332

MAHER, THOMAS GEORGE, producer, media educator; b. St. Louis, Feb. 18, 1947; s. Dale Russel and Dorothy Leone (Levzow) M.; m. (div.). BA, St. Louis U., 1969, AM, 1971; PhD, U. So. Calif., 1985. Cert. C.C. tchr. and supr., Calif. Tchg. fellow St. Louis U., 1969-71; assoc. prof. Chaffey Coll., Rancho Cucamonga, Calif., 1974-79, media dir., 1980-84; assoc. producer Corp. for C.C. TV, Orange, Calif., 1979-80; assoc. dir. instrnl. tech. Calif. State Poly. U., Pomona, 1984-89; dir. office media svcs. U. Ill., Chgo., 1989-94; dir. office instrnl. svcs. Colo. State U., Ft. Collins, 1994—, interim v.p. divsn. ednl. outreach, 2000—; cons. Rsch. Comm., Ltd., Boston, 1984—; book reviewer Focal Press, Inc., Boston, 1985—. Writer: (TV series) Project: Universe, 1978 (Emmy award nomination 1979), The Business of Management, 1981; assoc. producer, dir., writer (TV series) Oceanus: The Marine Environment, 1979 (Emmy award 1980); exec. producer (TV program) For the People: Local Gov. Budget Making, 1992 (Cert. Merit, Chgo. Internat. Film/Video Festival 1992); producer, dir. numerous ednl. TV shows, 1974—. 1st lt. USAF, 1971-74. Mary Clemens scholar St. Louis U., 1965-67, Educare scholar U. So. Calif., 1983-84. Mem. Acad. TV Arts and Scis., Am. Ednl. Research Assn., Assn. for Ednl. Comm. and Tech. Democrat. Roman Catholic. Avocations: reading spy novels, computers, running, theatre. Office: Colo State U A 71 Clark Bldg Fort Collins CO 80523-0001

MAHER, VINCENT MARY GERARD, cardiologist; b. Tippeary Town, Ireland, Apr. 26, 1958; s. Daniel Maher and Carmel Owens; m. Majella G. sammon, Sept. 7, 1985; children: Ciana, Lewena, Edana, Alaina. MB, U. Coll. Galway, Ireland, 1981; MD, Trinity Coll., Dublin, Ireland, 1991. Med. Doctor. Lectr. Trinity Coll., Dublin, 1986-87; hon. sr. registrar cardiology Hammersmith Hosp., London, 1988-92; attending physician U. Wash., Seattle, 1992-98; cardiologist Adelaide Meath Hosp., Dublin, 1998—; med. dir. Irish Heart Found., Dublin, 1998—; chmn. Health Promoting Hosp. Network, Ireland, 1999—; bd. mem. Achion Smoking and Health, Ireland. Author numerous book chpts.; contbr. articles to profl. jours. Grantee NIH, 1994-97. Fellow Royal Coll. Physicians; mem. Irish Cardiac Soc. Roman Cath. Avocations: guitar, golf, jogging, family activities.

MAHESH, SHRIPRIYA, internet company executive; b. Madras, India, Aug. 28, 1973; came to U.S., 1995; d. K. and Shrimathi (Iyengar) Mahesh. Diploma, Nat. Inst. Info. Tech., Madras, 1993; BA in Econs., Madras U., 1993; MBA, Harvard U., 1997. Exec. asst. to CEO Lucas-TVS, Madras, 1993-94; mgr. new products Sundaram Brake Linings, Madras, 1994-95; summer assoc. Citibank N.Am., N.Y.C., 1996; assoc. Mitchell Madison Group, Cambridge, Mass., 1997-99; dir. E-Commerce NextCard Inc., San Francisco, 1999—; bd. dirs. TVS Global, Madras. Founder, trustee Values Art Found., Madras, 1995—. Hindu. Avocations: karate, photography, tennis, bicycling, music. Office: NexCard Inc 595 Market St Ste 1800 San Francisco CA 94105-2827

MAHESH, VIRENDRA BHUSHAN, endocrinologist; b. India, Apr. 25, 1932; came to U.S., 1958, naturalized, 1968; s. Narinjan Prasad and Sobhagyawati; m. Sushila Kumari Aggarwal, June 29, 1955; children: Anita Rani, Vinit Kumar. BSc with honors, Patna U., India, 1951; MSc in Chemistry, Delhi U., India, 1953, PhD, 1955; DPhil in Biol. Sci, Oxford U., 1958. James Hudson Brown Meml. fellow Yale U., 1958-59; asst. rsch. prof. endocrinology Med. Coll. Ga., Augusta, 1959-63, assoc. rsch. prof., 1963-66, prof., 1966-70, Regents prof., 1970-86, Robert B. Greenblatt prof., 1979-99, chmn. endocrinology, 1972-86, chmn., Regents prof. physiology and endocrinology, 1986-99, chmn. physiology and endocrinology, 1986-99, regents prof., chmn. emeritus physiology and endocrinology, 1999—, Robert B. Greenblatt prof. emeritus endocrinology, 1999—; dir. Ctr. for Population Studies, 1971-99; mem. reproductive biology study sect. NIH, 1977-81, mem. human embryology and devel. study sect. NIH, 1982-86, 90-93, chmn., 1991-93. Contbr. articles to profl. jours., chpts. to books; editor: The Pituitary, a Current Review, Functional Correlates of Hormone Receptors in Reproduction, Recent Advances in Fertility Research, Hirsutism and Virilism, Regulation of Ovarian and Testicular Function, Excitatory Amino Acids: Their Role in Neuroendocrine Function; mem. editl. bd. Steroids, 1963—, Jour. of Clin. Endocrinology and Metabolism, 1976-81, Jour. Steroid Biochemistry and Molecular Biology, 1991—, Assisted Reproductive Tech./Andrology, 1993—, Endocrinology, 1999—; mem. adv. bd. Maturitas, 1977-81; editor-in-chief Biology of Reprodn., 1999—. Recipient Rubin award Am. Soc. Study Sterility, 1962, Billings Silver medal, 1965, Best Tchr. award freshman class Sch. Medicine, Med. Coll. Ga., 1969, Outstanding Faculty award Sch. Medicine, 1992, Outstanding Faculty award Sch. Grad. Studies, 1981, 94, Disting. Teaching award, 1988, Excellence in Rsch. award Grad. Faculty Assembly, 1987-91, 93-95, Disting. Scientist award Assn. Scientist Indian Origin in Am., 1989, Lifetime Achievement award Sch. Medicine, 1997; rsch. grantee NIH, 1960—. Mem. Chem. Soc. (Eng.), Soc. Biochem. and Molecular Biol., Soc. Neurosci., Endocrine Soc., Soc. for Gynecologic Investigation, Internat. Soc. Neuroendocrinology, Soc. for Study Reproduction (Carl G. Hartman award 1996), Am. Physiol. Soc., Internat. Soc. Reproductive Medicine (pres. 1980-82), Soc. Exptl. Biology and Medicine, Am. Fertility Soc., Am. Assn. Lab. Animal Sci., N.Y. Acad. Scis., AAUP, Sigma Xi. Office: Med Coll of Ga Dept Physiology & Endocrinology Augusta GA 30912-3000

MAHESHWARI, HARI KRISHNA, palaeobotanist, researcher; b. Aligarh, India, Nov. 13, 1938; s. Moti Lal and Ganga Devi (Bhatter) M.; m. Sarojini Kumari Malu, Feb. 28, 1960; children: Praveen, Pankaj. BS, Muslim U., Aligarh, 1956, MS, 1958; PhD, Lucknow (India) U., 1964. Lectr. Maharani coll., Balrampur, India, 1958-59; rsch. scholar BS Inst. Palaeobotany, Lucknow, 1959-62, sci. asst., 1962-72, sci. officer, 1972-82, asst. dir., 1982-94, dep. dir., 1994-99; vis. assoc. prof. Ohio State U., Columbus, 1969-70; head dept. palaeophytic evolutionary botany, BS Inst. Palaeobotany, 1982-97, project leader ultrastructure of plants, 1997-99; cons. Gondwana Palaeobotany and Palynostratigraphy. Editor: (with B.S. Venkatachala) Indian Gondwana, 1991; contbr. articles to profl. jours. Fellow Palaeobotanical soc. (editor 1971-74), Indian Assn. Palynostratigraphers (editor 1978—); mem. Internat. Assn. Plant Taxonomy (fossil plants com. 1974—). E-mail: hkmaheshwari@satyam.net.in. Home: D-2228 Indiranagar, 226 016 Lucknow India Office: Ganga-Moti D Block, Indiranagar, Lucknow 226 016, India

MAHFOUZ, ILHAM BADREDDINE, artist; b. Damascus, Syria, Jan. 2, 1956; came to U.S., 1972; d. Abdul Rahman Badreddine and Zabia Zebian Keilani; m. Abdul Razak Mahfouz, Aug. 27, 1972; children: Ruba, Rodwan. BFA in Painting, Ea. Mich. U., 1992; cert. interior design, La Salle U., 1979. Mem. Student Artist Gallery/Ea. Mich. U., Ypsilanti, 1991-92, Access, Dearborn, Mich., 1990-93; tchr. ceramic, painting, mixed media Pontiac (Mich.) Art Ctr., 1997-99; tchr. ceramic, mixed media Birmingham Bloomfield (Mich.) Art Ctr., 1999—; ceramics and mixed media tchr. Pontiac Creative Art Ctr., Mich., 1997-2000; tchr. art Internat. Sch., Farmington Hill, Mich., 1997; co-founder Alternative Artiss Group, 1994—; tchr. Lake Orion Sch. Author poetry; one-woman shows include Pontiac Creative Art Ctr., 2000, Trapper Alley Gallery, Detroit, 1998, Alternative Artist Space Gallery, Southfield, Mich., 1997, M.Y.N.A. Art Show, Franklin, Mich., 1991-92, The Cultural Assn., Franklin, 1989, Islamic Cultural Inst., Auburn Hills, Mich., 1989, Urban Park Gallery, Detroit, 1998; exhibited in group shows at Pontiace Creative Art Ctr., 1999-2000, Contemporary Mus., 1999-2000, Oak Park Libr., Mich., 1997, Pontiac Art Ctr., 1997, Am. Friendship Fedn., El-Cajon, Calif., 1997, Pontiac Artists Studio Tour, Pontiac, 1996, Arab/Latino Art Show, Detroit, 1996, Mich. Sci. and Rsch. Devel., Dearborn, 1995, Arab World Festival, Detroit, 1994, Agora Gallery, N.Y.C., 1994, 98, Common Ground Gallery, Windor, Ont., Can., 1994, numerous others; contbr. articles to profl. jours. Recipient Merit award Manhattan Arts Internat., N.Y., 1993, 1st prize McKenny Union's Art Show, Ea. Mich. U., 1991, Earth and Art Gallery, Milford, Mich., 1990. Mem. Internat. Muslimah Women Artists Group (pres. 1997-98), Golden Key. Islamic. Avocations: Arabic and conversational Spanish languages.

MAHFOUZ, NAGUIB (NAGĪB MAHFŪZ), author; b. Gamaliya, Cairo, Dec. 11, 1911; s. Abdel Aziz Ibrahim and Fatma Mostapha Mahfouz; m. Attiyat Allah, 1954; children: Om Kolthoum, Fatima. Grad. in philosophy, Secular U., Cairo, 1930. Civil servant, 1934; sec. U. Cairo, 1936-38; with Ministry of Waqfs, 1939-54, Dept. Arts and Censorship Bd., 1954-59; dir. Found. for Support of Cinema State Cinema Orgn., Cairo, 1959-69; cons. cinema affairs Ministry of Culture, Cairo, 1969-71; staff mem. Ar-Risāla; contbr. Al-Hilāl, Al-Ahrām. Author: (fiction) Hams al-junun, 1938, 'Abath al aqdār, 1939, Radubis, 1943, Kifah Tība, 1944, Al-Qāhira al-jadida, 1945, Khān al-Khalīlī, 1946, Zuqāq al-Midaqq, 1947 (pub. as Midaq Alley, 1966), Al-sarāb, 1948, Bidāya wa-nihāya, 1949 (pub. as The Beginning and the End, 1985), Al-thulāthiya: Vol. I: Bayn al-Qasrayn, 1956 (pub. as Palace Walk, 1989; Egyptian State prize 1956), Vol. II: Qasr al-shawq, 1957 (pub. as Palace of Desire, 1991), Vol. III: Al-Sukkariya, 1957 (pub. as Sugar Street, 1992), Awlād hāratina, 1959 (pub. as Children of Gebelawi, 1981, Children of our Alley, 1996), Al-lis wa-l-kilāb, 1961 (pub. as The Thief and the Dogs, 1984), Al-sammān wa-l-kharif, 1962 (pub. as Autumn Quail, 1985), Dunya Allah, 1962 (pub. as God's World, 1988), Al-Tariq, 1964 (pub. as The Search, 1987), Al-shahhāz, 1965 (pub. as The Beggar, 1986), Bayt sayyi' al-sum'a, 1965, Tharthara fawq al Nil, 1966 (pub. as Adrift on the Nile, 1993), Mirāmār, 1967 (pub. as Miramar, 1978), Khammārat al-qitt al-aswad, 1969, Taht al-midhalla, 1969, Hikāya a bi-la bidāya wa-la nihāya, 1971, Shahr al-'asal, 1971, Al-marāya, 1972 (pub. as Mirrors, 1977), Al-hubb tahta al-matar, 1973, Al-jarīma, 1973, Al-Karnak, 1974 , Hikāyāt hāratina, 1975 (pub. as Fountain and Tomb, 1988), Qalb al-layl, 1975, Hadrat al-muhtaram, 1975 (pub. as Respected Sir, 1986), Malhamat al harāfish, 1977 (pub. as The Harafish, 1994), Al-hubb fawqa Hadabat al-Haram, 1979, Al-shaytān ya'iz, 1979, 'Asr al-hubb, 1980, Afrā al-qubbah, 1981 (pub. as Wedding Song, 1984), Layāli alf laylah, 1982 (pub. as Arabian Nights and Days, 1995), Ra'aytu fima yara al-na'im, 1982, Al-bāqi min al-zaman sā'ah, 1982, Amāma

al'arsh, 1982, Rihlat Ibn Fattumah, 1983 (pub. as The Journey of Ibn Fattouma, 1992), Al-tandhim al-sirri, 1984, Al-a'ish fi al-haqiqah, 1985 (pub. as Akhenaton: Dweller in Truth, 1998), Yawm qutila al-za'im, 1985 (pub. as The Day the Leader was Killed, 1997), Hadith al sabah wa-al-masa, 1987, Sabah al-ward, 1987, Qushtumor, 1988, Al-Fajr al-Kadhib, 1988, Asda' al-Sira al-dhatiya, 1996 (pub. as Echoes of an Autobiography, 1997). Recipient Nat. prize for Letters (Egypt), 1970, Collar of the Republic, 1972, Nobel prize for lit., 1988; named to Egyptian Order of Ind., Order of the Republic. Mem. Am. Acad. and Inst. Arts and Letters (hon.). Agent: The Am U in Cairo Press, 113 Sharia Kasr El Aini, Cairo Egypt

MAHFUZ, NAGĪB See MAHFOUZ, NAGUIB

MAHIEU, CLAUDE THEODORE, chemist, researcher; b. Romainville, France, July 31, 1941; s. Theodore Auguste and Suzanne (Deroche) M.; m. Helene Kaspar Mahieu, May 16, 1969; children: Emmanuel, Alexis. PhD, Lycee J.B. Say Univ. Paris XI, Paris, 1967. Chemist rschr. L'Oreal, Aulnay, France, 1969—. Patentee: Organic Chemistry, Polymer and Lipid Chemistry. Office: L'Oreal, Avenue E Schueller, 93601 Aulnay-sous-Bois France

MAHLA, MICHAEL E., anesthesiologist, educator; b. Wilmington, Del., Mar. 8, 1953; s. Elbert Myron and Mary Pauline (Tice) M.; m. Sno Ellen White, June 8, 1979; 1 child, Melody Joy. BS in Chemistry, Davidson Coll., 1975; MD, Jefferson Med. Coll., 1979. Diplomate Am. Bd. Anesthesiology. Intern Walter Reed AMC, Washington, 1979-80, resident in anesthesiology, 1980-83; fellow in neuroanesthesiology Johns Hopkins Med. Inst., Balt., 1983; mem. staff Shands Teaching Hosp., Gainesville, Fla.; assoc. prof. anesthesiology/neurosurgery U. Fla. Coll. Medicine; program dir. anesthesiology residency Walter Reed AMC, Washington, 1986-88; assoc. prof., assoc. chair edn. dept. anesthesiology U. Fla. Coll. Medicine, Gainesville, 1995—. Author: (with others) Clinical Anesthesiology Practice, 1994, Clinical Neuroanesthesia, 1997. Fellow Am. Soc. Neurologic Monitoring; mem. AMA, Am. Soc. Anesthesiologists, Soc. Neurosurg. Anesthesia and Critical Care. Office: Box 100254 Dept Anesthesiology Gainesville FL 32610-0254

MAHLER, GÜNTER, physicist, educator; b. Freudenstadt, Baden, Germany, Feb. 9, 1945; s. Emil and Paula (Springmann) M.; m. Anneliese Schneeweis, June 1972; children: Anja, Maike, Nils. Diploma in physics, U. Frankfurt, Germany, 1969; PhD, U Regensburg, Germany, 1972. Asst. rschr. U. Frankfurt, 1967-69, U. Munich, 1969-70, U. Regensburg, 1970-77; prof U. Stuttgart, 1978—; vis. prof. U. Strasbourg, France, 1983, Ariz. State U., Tempe, 1987, Santa Fe Inst., 1991, U. Oreg., Eugene, 1997. Author: Quantum Networks, 1995, rev. edit., 1998; editor: Molecular Electronics, 1996; contbr. more than 140 articles to profl. jours. Mem. Deutsche Physikalische Gesellschaft. Office: Inst fur Theoretische Phys, Pfaffenwaldring 57, 70550 Stuttgart Germany

MAHLERS, YURI PETROVICH, physicist, educator; b. Leninsk-Kuznetski, Russia, Oct. 1, 1961; s. Yan Valdemar and Zinaida Anatolivna (Ryabukha) M.; m. Olena Anatolivna Rokitska, Mar. 29, 1997; 1 child, Anatoli. BS, Moscow Engring. Physics Inst., 1984, PhD, 1990. Engr. Inst. Nuc. Rsch., Kiev, Ukraine, 1984-94, divsn. head., 1994—; lectr. Kiev U., 1989, 96. Contbr. articles to profl. jours. Grantee for Young Scientists, Ministry of Sci., Kiev, 1994, grantee Internat. Atomic Energy Agy., Vienna, 1995. Avocations: music, travel. E-mail: mahlers@gluk.org. Fax: 38044-265-5105. Office: Inst Nuc Rsch, 47 Prospect Nauki, 252022 Kiev Ukraine

MAHLKNECHT, ULRICH RUDOLPH, physician, researcher; b. Ravensburg, Germany, Apr. 29, 1967; s. Edmund and Maria (Dreher) M.; m. Susanne Friederike Völter, Mar. 23, 1996. MD, U. Tübingen, Germany, 1994; cert., Ednl. Commn. Fgn. Med. Grad., 1997; PhD, SUNY, 1998. Resident in internal medicine U. Freiburg, Germany, 1995-96; postdoctoral The Picower Inst. for Med. Rsch., Manhasset, N.Y., 1996-98, sr. scientist, 1998-99; sr. scientist U. Frankfurt, Germany, 1999—. Co-author: Handbook of Hematology, 1998, The Acid-Base Status: The Red Book, Hematology and Medical Oncology, 1998; translator: Instant Anatomy of Whitaker and Borley, 1997; contbr. over 40 Raetoroman poems to profl. publs. and articles to profl. jours. German Nat. Merit Found. fellow, 1988-94; German Nat. Sci. Found. grantee, 1997-99. Fellow The German Nat. Merit Found. (selection com., 1995); mem. AAAS, N.Y. Acad. Scis., N.Y. Soc. for the Study of Blood, German Soc. of Biochemistry and Molecular Biology, German Soc. of Heamtology/Oncology, German Red Cross, Molecular Medicine Soc. Roman Catholic. Avocation: classical music. Home: Schwarzwaldstr 15, D-60528 Frankfurt Am Main, Germany Office: U Frankfurt Med Ctr, Theodor-Stern-Kai 7, D-60590 Frankfurt Germany

MAHLMAN, JERRY DAVID, research meteorologist; b. Crawford, Nebr., Feb. 21, 1940; s. Earl Lewis and Ruth Margaret (Callendar) M.; m. Janet Kay Hilgenberg, June 10, 1962; children—Gary Martin, Julie Kay. A.B., Chadron State Coll., Nebr., 1962; M.S., Colo. State U., 1964, Ph.D., 1967; LHD (hon.), Chadron State Coll., 2000. Instr. Colo. State U., Fort Collins, 1964-67; from asst. prof. to assoc. prof. Naval Postgrad. Sch., Monterey, Calif., 1967-70; rsch. meteorologist NOAA Geophys. Fluid Dynamics Lab., Princeton, N.J., 1970-84, lab. dir., 1984—; lectr. with rank of prof. Princeton U., 1980—; chmn. panel on mid-atmosphere program NAS-NRC, 1982-84, mem. climate rsch. com., 1986-89, mem. panel on dynamic extended range forecasting, 1987-90; mem. U.S.-USSR Commn. on Global Ecology, 1989-92; mem. Bd. on Global Change, 1991-95, Bd. on Sustainable Devel., 1995—; U.S. rep. world climate rsch. program Joint Sci. Commn., 1991-96. Contbr. over 100 articles to profl. jours. Elder Monterey Presbyterian Ch., 1968-70, Lawrence Road Presbyn. Ch., Lawrenceville, N.J., 1972-75; bd. dirs. Lawrence Non-Profit Housing Inc., 1978-88. Recipient Disting. Authorship award Dept. Commerce, 1980, 81, Gold medal, 1986, Disting. Svc. award Chadron State Coll., 1984, Presdl. Rank award disting. exec. 1994, Honor Alumnus award Colo. State U. 1995. Fellow Am. Geophys. Union (Jule Charney lectr. 1993), Am. Meterol. Soc. (awards com. 1984, 95, chmn. upper atmosphere com. 1979, assoc. editor Jour. Atmospheric Sci. 1979-86, councilor 1991-94, Editor's award 1978, Carl-Gustaf Rossby Rsch. medal 1994, disting. lectr. 1999). Democrat. Home: 9 Camelia Ct Lawrenceville NJ 08648-3201 Office: Princeton U Geophys Fluid Dynamics Lab PO Box 308/NOAA Princeton NJ 08542-0308

MAHMOOD, ADNAN BAQUAR, lawyer; b. Secunderabad, Andhra Pradesh, India, May 17, 1955; s. Baquar Mohiuddin and Aleemunissa Baquar Mahmood; m. Asma Adnan Asma Azam, July 18, 1985; children: Fatima Adnan, Zeeshan Adnan, Farhan Adnan, Nabhan Adnan, Aman Adnan. BCom, Osmania U., Hyderabad, India, 1974, LLM, 1977. Bar: State of Andhra Pradesh, 1977. Advocate Mahood & Co. Advocates, Secunderabad, 1977—; chmn., mng. dir. Mahmood Builders Pvt. Ltd. Mem. Secunderabad Club. Avocations: cricket, reading books, gardening. Home: Adnan Mahmood 143-A, Prenderghast Rd, Secunderabad 500 003, India Office: Mahmood & Co Advocates, 1-7-201 to 205 PG Road, 500 003 Secunderabad India

MAHMOOD, AKHTAR HASAN, physicist, educator, researcher; b. Dhaka, Bangladesh, Mar. 26, 1969; s. Mohammad Ahsan Ali and Selima Akhtar; m. Sitara Swati Zaman, Jan. 12, 1997. BSc with honors, Edinboro U. Pa., 1992; MSc, SUNY, Albany, 1994, PhD, 1998. Rsch. asst. SUNY, Albany, 1994-98, lab. instr., 1994-97, rsch. scientist high energy physics lab., 1998-99; lectr. U. Tex. Pan Am., Edinburg, 1998-99, asst. prof., dir. Ctr. High Energy Physics, 1999—; grant reviewer NASA, 1999. Contbr. articles to profl. jours. Rsch. grantee Tex. Higher Edn. Coord. Bd., 1999, Rsch. grantee U. Tex. Pan Am., 1999, Faculty Rsch. grantee, 1999. Mem. AAAS, CLEO, Am. Phys. Soc., N.Y. Acad. Scis., Sigma Xi, Pi Mu Epsilon. Muslim. Achievements include discovery of several new subatomic particles. Home: 917 Stonehaven Blvd Apt 3 Edinburg TX 78539-7576 Office: U Tex Pan Am Dept Physics 1201 W University Dr Edinburg TX 78539-2909

MAHMOOD, M. F., research scientist, educator; s. Abdul Wahab and Mehrun Nisa (Begum) M.; m. Ghazala Mahmood; children: Fahad, Zafar, Asad and Sara. MS in mathematics, Allahabad Univ., Allahabad, India, 1966; MS in physics, Aligarh Univ., Aligarh, India, 1968; PhD in physics, Howard Univ., Wash., D.C., 1988. Tchr. in physics & mathematics Schs./Colls./Univs., India and Abroad, 1970-82; adj. prof. in mathematics & physics Univ. of Dist. of Columbia, Wash., D.C., 1983-88; rsch. scientist Howard Univ., Wash., D.C., 1988—; adj. assoc. prof. Div. of Theoretical Physics, Molise, Italy, 1995—; asst. prof. of mathematics Howard Univ., Wash., D.C., 1999—. contbr. articles to profl. jours., contbr. rsch. papers in field, contbr. in scientific experimentation. Recipient rsch. grants, Air Force Office of Scientific rsch. and Dept. of Army, Wash. D.C., 1994-97, 1995-00. Mem. Am. Physical Soc., Optical Soc. of Amer., Inst. of Elec. and Electronics Engrs., SPIE (The Internat. Soc. for Optical Engrg.), Optical Soc. of Amer., Hon. Soc., Sigma Pi Sigma Physics. E-mail: mmahmood@howard.edu. Avocations: reading, listening to classical music, drawing, badminton, chess. Office: Howard U 2400 6th St NW MSC 590048 Washington DC 20059

MAHMOOD, TARIQ, engineering company executive, social worker; b. Bahawalpur, Punjab, Pakistan, Jan. 1, 1954; s. Mahmood Khan and Saeeda Akbar; m. Rubina Akram, Dec. 17, 1981; children: Hamza, Zainab, Hajra. BSc in Engring., U. Engring., Lahore, Pakistan, 1976. Trainee engr. Dawood Hercules Chems., Lahore, 1976-77; project engr. Pakarab Refinery Ltd., Karachi, Pakistan, 1977-79; project mgr. ICI-Polyester, Lahore, 1979-80; mng. dir. Khan Yama Industries, Lahore, 1980-87; CEO HAQ Group of Cos., Lahore, 1988—; dir. Vocat. Tng. Inst., 1998—. Dir. Childcare Found., Lahore, 1977—; convenor Child Labor Com., Lahore, 1995—; mem. Lahore Gymkhana, 1981—. Paul Harris fellow Rotary Club, 1994. Mem. Composites Fabricators Assn., Pakistan Engring. Coun., Lahore C. of C. and Industry. Avocations: swimming, cricket, traveling. Office: Bhaq Group, 24 Habib Ullah Rd, Lahore Pakistan

MAHMOUD, HOSAM M., statistics educator, academic administrator; b. Cairo, Apr. 16, 1954; came to U.S., 1979; s. M. Mahmoud and M. Shafi; m. Fatemeh Rahnavard, Sept. 14, 1984. BS, Cairo U., 1976; MS, Ohio State U., 1981, PhD, 1983. Prof. George Washington U., 1983—, chmn. stats. dept., 1998—; vis. prof. Waterloo U., Ont., Can., 1990, Princeton (N.J.) U., 1998; vis. scholar Ctr. Math. Rsch., Spain, 1996, Int. Nat. Rsch., France, 1997. Contbr. articles to profl. jours. Office: George Washington U Dept Stats 2201 G St # 315 Washington DC 20052-0001

MAHMOUD, YEHIA ABDEL-GALELE, microbial biochemistry educator, researcher; b. Tanta, Egypt, Dec. 18, 1962; s. Abdel-Galele Abdel-Kahlik and Essmat El-Sayed M.; m. Narges Talat Mahmoud, Dec. 4, 1974; children: Ahmed, Amgad, Aeyh, Yehia. BSc, Tanta U., 1986, MSc, 1992, PhD in Biochemistry, 1996. Rsch. scientist Va. Poly. Inst. and State U., Blacksburg, 1993-96; lectr. in biochemistry Tanta U., 1996—. Contbr. articles to World Jour. Microbiology and Biotechnology and Archives of Biochemistry and Biophysics; contbr. poster to ASM Conf., 1995. Mem. Home Dem. Party, Tanta, 1996. With Egyptian Army, 1987. Recipient ASM travel grant, 1995; postdoctoral fellow Japan Soc. for Promotion Sci. Achievements include inhibition of cryptococcus neoformans malate dehydrogenase by heparin, inhibition of C. neoformans fatty acid synthetase by heparin and dextransulfate; research on relationship between mouse urea cycle enzyme m-RNA and fungal infection. Office: Tanta U Faculty Sci, Botany Dept, Tanta Egypt

MAHMOUDIAN, MAHMOUD, biotechnology microbial physiologist, biotechnologist; b. Tabriz, Iran, Sept. 8, 1962. BSc in Biochemistry/Physiology, Newcastle U., Newcastle-Upon-Tyne, U.K., 1984; MSc in Biotechnology, Imperial Coll., London, 1985, PhD in Biotechnology, 1989. Prin. rsch. scientist Glaxo Wellcome Medicines Rsch. Ctr., U.K., 1989—; cons. 5th Eu-Programe, 2000. Author: Progress in Biotechnology No. 8, 1992, No. 9, 1994, Biotechnology of Industrial Antibiotics, 1996, Focus on Biotechnology, 2000; mem. editl bd.: Enzyme Technol. Jour., Organic Process R & D; contbr. articles to profl. jours.; patentee in field. Recipient MSC sponsorship Imperial Chem. Industries, Billingham, U.K., 1984-85; Rsch. assoc. Imperial Chem. Industries, 1988. Mem. Soc. for Gen. Microbiology, Soc. Chem. Industry, Am. Soc. Microbiology, Soc. Indsl. Microbiology, Am. Chem. Soc., Royal Soc. of Chemistry. Avocations: swimming, basketball, karate, tennis. Office: Glaxo Wellcome, Gunnels Wood Rd, Stevenage SG1 2NY, England

MAHMUD, SHIREEN DIANNE, photographer; b. Chittagong, Pakistan, Oct. 4, 1949; came to U.S., 1974; d. Mohammed Mazhurul Qudus and Mumtaz Mahal Begum; m. Abdul Wazed Mahmud, Apr. 10, 1966 (div. 1996); children: Sharmin, Anita. BA in Mass Comm., U. Hartford, 1982. Part-time med. sec. Middletown, Conn., 1979-82; freelance photographer Middletown, 1985—; typist Aetna Ins. Co., Middletown, 1991; freelance photographer Conn. Post; prodr. feature program Storer Cable Comm., Clinton, Conn., 1991-95; freelance photojournalist Middletown Press, Durham Gazette, Middletown, 1991-95; mem. Bridgeport Regional Bus. Coun., 1997. Literacy vol. Russell Libr., Middletown, Conn. Mem. AAUW, Nat. League Am. Pen Women, Internat. Soc. Poets (Hall of Fame award 1997), Conn. Soc. Poets, Conn. Songwriter's Assn., Internat. Platform Assn. Home: 2612 North Ave Unit G-4 Bridgeport CT 06604-2324

MAHMUD, SULTAN, television news editor. BA, Govt. Coll., Lahore, 1956. Free-lance journalist, 1953-76; news prodr., reporter, editor, and sr. news editor Pakistan TV, 1976-91, ret., 1991; sports reporter BBC World Svc., Lahore, 1992—; former univ. cricket player; mem. selection com. for Punjab U. Cricket team, 1961-64, chmn., 1978-82. Author: Cricket After Midnight 1947-77, 1992, Cricket After Midnight 1947-98, 1998. Mem. Punjab Sports Writers Assn. (founder), Punjab Cricket Assn. (hon. sec. 1976-80). Office: Iqbal Rd, 8 Aziz Park Sardar St, Lahore Pakistan

MAHNCKE, DIETER MARTIN, political scientist, educator; b. Tsumeb, Namibia, Apr. 24, 1941; s. Martin and Hildegard Elisabeth (Huber) M.; m. Monika Elisabeth Knorr, July 2, 1968; children: Tim Hendrik, Severin Martin, Jacob Christian. BA, U. N.C., 1962; MA, Johns Hopkins U., 1964, PhD, 1968; Habilitation, U. Bonn, Germany, 1974. Rsch. fellow German Soc. Fgn. Affairs, Bonn, 1968-73; prof. U. Armed Forces, Munich, 1974, Hamburg, Germany, 1975-80; spl. advisor Office of the German Pres., Bonn, Germany, 1980-87; dep. chief planning staff Ministry of Def., Govt. of Germany, Bonn, 1988-96; prof. Coll. of Europe, Bruges, Belgium, 1996—, dir. dept. polit. and adminstrv. studies, 1996—; v.p. Univ. of Armed Forces, Hamburg, 1977-79; vis. prof. Dartmouth Coll., N.H., 1990, 94, Duke U., Durham, N.C., 1991; mem. selection bd. German students, Coll. of Europe, 1982—; bd. dirs. Bibliothek für Zeitgeschichte, Stuttgart, 1987—; chmn. Hochschulgruppe des Deutschen Hochschulverbandes, Univ. Bundeswehr, Hamburg, 1978-79. Author: Nukleare Mitwirkung Die Brep. Dtl. in der atlantischen Allianz 1954-1970, 1972, Berlin im geteilten Deutschland, 1973, Vertrauensbildende Massnahmen als Instrument der Sicherheitspolitik, 1987; author, editor: Amerikaner in Deutschland, Grundlagen und Bedingungen der transatlantischen Sicherheit, 1991; editor: Europe 2020: Adapting to a Changing World, 1999. Bd. dirs. Dartmouth Coll. German Vis. Professorship, 1993—. Mem. German Soc. Fgn. Affairs. Office: College of Europe, Dyver 11, 8000 Brugge Belgium

MAHNER, MARTIN, biologist; b. Althuette, Germany, May 9, 1958. MS, Free U., Berlin, Germany, 1985, PhD, 1992. Rsch. assoc. McGill U., Montreal, Can., 1993-96; freelance lectr. Berlin, Germany, 1996-98; exec. dir. Ctr. for Inquiry-Germany, Rossdorf, 1999—. Author: Creationism-Content and Structure of Antievolutionary Argumentation, 1986, Systema Cryptoceratorum Phylogeneticum, 1993, Foundations of Biophilosophy, 1997, Philosophische Grundlagen der Biologie, 2000; contbr. articles to profl. jours. Recipient Rsch. grant Deutsche Forschungsgemeinschaft, Bonn, Germany, 1992, 94. Mem. GWUP, German Soc. for History and Theory of Biology. Office: Ctr for Inquiry-Germany, Arheilger Weg 11, D-64380 Rossdorf Germany

MAHOMED, ISMAIL, judge. Chief justice Supreme Ct. Namibia, Windhoek. Office: care Namibian Perm Mission UN 135 E 36th St New York NY 10016-3404 also: PO Box 258, Bloemfontein 9300, South Africa also: Supreme Ct, Private Bag 13179, Windhoek Namibia*

MAHON, MARGARET M., advanced practice nurse; b. Chgo., June 6, 1958; d. William G. and Anna Marie (McGough) M. BSN, Loyola U., 1980; MSN, U. Pa., 1982, PhD, 1992, postgrad., 1993. Cert. pediat. nurse practitioner. Staff nurse Children's Meml. Hosp., Chgo., 1979-82, Thomas Jefferson U., Phila., 1982-85; faculty Sch. Nursing U. Pa., Phila., 1982-99; staff nurse Children's Hosp. of Phila., 1986-89; fellow U. Pa. Ctr. for Bioethics, Phila., 1997—; advanced practice nurse ethics and end of life care Hosp. of U. of Pa., Phila., 1999—; facilitator sibling bereavement program Children's Hosp. of Phila., 1992-97; facilitator When a Parent Has Cancer, Wellness Cmty., Phila., 1998-99; regular guest Kids Corner Radio, Sta. WXPN, Phila., 1988—. Contbr. articles to med. jours. NEH fellow; recipient multiple rsch. grants on child bereavement and family adaptation Lyndsay Victoria Cummings Meml. Fund, Am. Nurses Found., Nurses Ednl. Fund, Assn. for Death Edn. and Counseling. Mem. Soc. Pediat. Nursing, Assn. for Death Edn. and Counseling, Sigma Theta Tau.

MAHONEY, ANN DICKINSON, fundraiser; b. Topeka, Sept. 12, 1961; d. Jacob Alan II and Ruth (Curd) Dickinson; m. Michael James Mahoney, May 29, 1993; children: James Junius Castle, Catherine Lane. AB in History, Grinnell Coll., 1983; postgrad., McGill U., Montreal, Quebec, Can., 1985. Analyst, corp. fin. dept. E.F. Hutton & Co., Inc., N.Y.C., 1983-85; pres., owner The Dark Side, N.Y.C., 1985-87; asst. dir. individual giving Meml. Sloan-Kettering Cancer Ctr., N.Y.C., 1987-88, dir. spl. gifts, 1988-91; assoc. dir. devel. Sch. Humanities and Scis. Stanford (Calif.) U., 1991-96; ind. fundraising cons., 1996—; devel. asst. regional office Brandeis U., N.Y.C., 1987. Vol. interviewer Grinnell Coll., N.Y.C., San Francisco, 1983—. Mem. Nat. Soc. Fund Raising Execs., Jr. League San Francisco (com. chmn. 1996-98), Pacific Rsch. Inst. for Pub. Policy, Hist. Topeka (Kans.) Assn., Friends of Filoli (Woodside, Calif.), Peninsula Assn. Retarded Children & Adults Aux. (San Mateo, Calif.; bd. dirs. 1998—, pres. 2000—), Spokane Club (Wash.). Republican. Episcopalian. Avocations: photography, dressage, literature. Office: PO Box 332 Burlingame CA 94011-0332

MAHONEY, JOËLLE KATHERINE, astrological consultant, communications educator; b. Amiens, France, Jan. 6, 1948; came to U.S., 1953; d. Louis James and Regine (LeClercq) Dennis; m. John William Christopher Mahoney, Aug. 14, 1971. AA, Boro Manhattan C.C., 1971; BA, Adelphi U., 1982; postgrad., Hofstra U., 1989—. Profl. cert. in astrology; cert. master practitioner neurolinguistic programming; cert. neurolinguistics programming. Tri-lingual translator N.A. Bogdan Co., N.Y.C., 1967-71; practicing astrologer Long Island, N.Y., 1971-74; founding pres. Astrological Rsch. Centre and Tng. Inst. Ltd., Mineola, N.Y., 1974-84; internat. astrological cons. Brewster, N.Y., 1984—; pres. French Regional Alliance for Nat. Costume Edn., 1999—. Author: Concept I, II and III, 1974, In Search of Time, 1989. Vol. fund raiser Americares, New Canaan, Conn., 1991-94, Silver Hill Hosp., New Canaan, 1992-94, City Harvest, N.Y.C., 1995-97; amb. All Nations Universal Pageant Orgn., 1998-99. Named Mrs. France, 1996, Mrs. All Nations Universal, 1997; named amb.-at-large All Nations Universal Orgn., 1998. Mem. Astrologers Guild Am. (pres. 1980-83), Congress of Astrological Orgns. (v.p. 1981-84). Avocations: equitation, oil painting, writing, fitness, animal welfare. Home: 5 Fair Meadow Dr Brewster NY 10509-4617

MAHONEY, KATHLEEN MARY, lawyer; b. Methuen, Mass., Oct. 24, 1954; d. Joseph Patrick and Beatrice Evelyn (Blackington) M.; m. Mark Dennis Schmitt, May 26, 1979; children: Alexis Anne Schmitt, Brynne Elizabeth Schmitt. BA, Keene (N.H.) State Coll., 1976; JD, Syracuse (N.Y.) U., 1979. Bar: Minn. 1979, U.S. Dist. Ct. Minn. 1980, U.S. Ct. Appeals (8th cir.) 1985, U.S. Supreme Ct. 1988. Instr. Sch. of Law Hamline U., St. Paul, 1979-80; law clk. to hon. justice Douglas K. Amdahl Minn. Supreme Ct., St. Paul, 1980-81; law clk. to hon. judge Neal P. McCurn U.S. Dist. Ct. (no. dist.) N.Y., Syracuse, 1981-83; spl. asst. atty. gen. Atty. Gen.'s Office State of Minn., St. Paul, 1983-89; assoc. Oppenheimer, Wolff & Donnelly, St. Paul, 1989-91, sr. assoc., 1991-93; ptnr., 1994—, chair labor and employment practice group, 1995-97; mng. ptnr. St. Paul, 1997-2000; cons. George Banzhaf Co., Milw., 1979-80; adj. prof. Hamline U. Sch. of Law, 1987-89. Mem. Dist. 621 Study Adv. Com., Shoreview, Minn., 1989-91, chair, 1991-93; mem. Turtle Lake Sch. Adv. Com., Shoreview, 1988-96; mem. exec. com., bd. dirs. Voyageurs Regional Nat. Park Assn., 1993-95; mem. Class of '93; bd. dirs. St. Paul Vol. Ctr., 1994-99; leader Girl Scouts Am., 1993-99; mem. Leadership St. Paul. Mem. ABA, Minn. Bar Assn., Ramsey County Bar Assn. Office: Oppenheimer Wolff & Donnelly Plz VII 45 S 7th St Ste 3300 Minneapolis MN 55402

MAHONEY, THOMAS HENRY, IV, finance executive; b. Cambridge, Mass., May 27, 1952; s. Thomas Henry Donald and Kathrine Phyllis (Norton) M.; m. Emily A. Chien, Nov. 11, 1989. AB, Harvard Coll., 1973; MBA, U. Pa., 1976. Assoc. corp. fin. Dillon, Read & Co. Inc., N.Y.C., 1976-80, v.p. corp. fin., 1981-84; v.p. corp. fin. Oppenheimer & Co., Inc., N.Y.C., 1984-86; v.p. debt fin. Merrill Lynch Capital Markets, N.Y.C., 1986-87, dir. product devel., 1988-89, mng. dir., 1989-96; mng. dir. global pvt. capital Deutsche Morgan Grenfell, N.Y.C., 1996-98; mng. dir., group head Pvt. Equity Group, PaineWebber Inc., N.Y.C., 1998-2000; v.p. fin., CFO Molecular OptoElectronics Corp., Watervliet, N.Y., 2000—; bd. dirs. Molecular Optoelectronics Corp., Notifact Corp. Bd. dirs. New Eng. Soc. in City N.Y., N.Y.C. Opera. Mem. Coun. Fgn. Rels., Doubles Club, Harvard Club (N.Y.C.), Harvard Club (Boston), Univ. Club, Meadow Club Southampton. Republican. Home: 21 E 87th St Apt 8C New York NY 10128-0506 Office: Molecular OptoElectronics Corp 877 25th St Watervliet NY 12189

MAHONY, CARDINAL ROGER MICHAEL, archbishop; b. Hollywood, Calif., Feb. 27, 1936; s. Victor James and Loretta Marie (Baron) M. AA, Our Lady Queen of Angels Sem., 1956; BA, St. John's Sem. Coll., 1958, BST, 1962; MSW, Cath. U. Am., 1964. Ordained priest Roman Cath. Ch., 1962, ordained bishop, 1975, created cardinal priest, 1991. Asst. pastor St. John's Cathedral, Fresno, Calif., 1962, 68-73, rector, 1973-80; residence St. Genevieve's Parish, Fresno, Calif., 1964—, adminstr., 1964-67, pastor, 1967-68; titular bishop of Tamascani, aux. bishop of Fresno, 1975-80; chancellor Diocese of Fresno, 1970-77, vicar gen., 1975-80; bishop Diocese of Stockton (Calif.), 1980-85; archbishop Archdiocese of L.A., 1985—, cardinal priest, 1991—; diocesan dir. Cath. Charities and Social Svc. Fresno, 1964-70; exec. dir. Infant of Prague Adoption Svc., Cath. Welfare Bur., Fresno, 1964-70; chaplain St. Vincent de Paul Soc., Fresno, 1964-70; named chaplain to Pope Paul VI, 1967; mem. faculty extension div. Fresno State U., 1965-67; sec. U.S. Cath. bishops ad hoc com. on farm labor Nat. Conf. Bishops, 1970-75; chmn. com. on pub. welfare and income maintenance Nat. Conf. Cath. Charities, 1969-70; bd. dirs. West Coast Regional Office Bishops Com. for Spanish-Speaking, 1967-70; chmn. Calif. Assn. Cath. Charities Dirs., 1965-69; trustee St. Patrick's Sem., Archdiocese of San Francisco, 1974-75; mem. adminstrv. com. Nat. conf. Cath. Bishops, 1976-79, 82-85, 87-90, 92-95, 98—, com. migration and refugees, 1976-95, chmn. com. farm labor, 1981-92, com. moral evaluation of deterrence, 1986-88; cons. com., chmn. for ProLife Activities, 1990-95; mem. com. social devel. and world peace U.S. Cath. Conf., 1985-93, chmn. internat. policy sect., 1987-93; com. justice and peace, Pontifical Couns., 1984-89, 90-98, chmn. com. domestic policy, 1998—, pastoral care of migrants and itinerant people, 1986-91, social comms., 1989—. Mem. Urban Coalition of Fresno, 1968-72, Fresno County Econ. Opportunities Commn., 1964-65, Fresno County Alcoholic Rehab. Com., 1966-67, Fresno City Charter Rev. Com., 1968-70, Mexican-Am. Council for Better Housing, 1968-72, Fresno Redevel. Agy., 1970-75, L.A. 2000 Com., 1985-88, Fed. Commn. Agrl. Workers, 1987-93, Blue Ribbon Com. Affordable Housing City of L.A., 1988; mem. commn. to Draft an Ethics Code for L.A. City Govt., 1989-90; bd. dirs. Fresno Cmty. Workshop, 1965-67, Rebuild L.A., 1992-95; trustee St. Agnes Hosp., Fresno, 1969-73, Cath. U. Am., 1984-88, 98—. Named Young Man of Yr. Fresno Jr. C. of C., 1967. Mem. Canon Law Soc. Home: 114 E 2nd St Los Angeles CA 90012-3711 Office: Archdiocese LA 3424 Wilshire Blvd Los Angeles CA 90010-2241

MAHOUAST, MAHMOUD, educator; b. Cap-Aokas, Béjaia, Algeria, Mar. 10, 1948; arrived in France, 1954; s. Mohand and Ourida (Bouakeur) M.; m. Safia Toumi, Apr. 7, 1980; children: Amel, Yacin. Engr., Ecole Nat. Superior Mech. Aero, Poitiers, France, 1973; PhD in Mechanics and Energetics, Inst. Nat. Poly. Lorraine, Nancy, France, 1988. Lectr. Ecole Nat. Engrs. Tech. d'Algérie, Cap-Matifou, Algeria, 1974-77, Inst. Algérien du Pétrole, Boumerdes, Algeria, 1977-83, Ecol. Nat. Superior Elec. & Mech.-Inst. Nat. Poly. Lorraine, Nancy, 1987-88; asst. prof. U. Franche-Comté, Belfort, France, 1988—; head gas dept. IAP, Boumerdes, 1980-81; head dept. Génie Thermique et Energie IUT, Belfort, 2000—. Contbr. articles to profl.

jours. Mem. Assn. U. Mécanique, European Mechanics Soc. Office: Inst Univ Tech De Belfort, Rue Engel Gros, 90000 Belfort France

MAHRAN, GAMAL EL-DIN HUSSEIN, pharmacognosy and pharmacology educator; b. Naji Zuriche, Egypt, Aug. 1, 1928; s. Hussein Mahran and Zohra Dahia; m. Sofia Ingeborg Schuster, Sept. 5, 1955; children: Ahmed, Laila. BPharm, Faculty of Pharmacy, Cairo, 1949; PhD of Pharmacy, Sch. of Pharmacy, London, 1954. Demonstrator Cairo U. Faculty of Pharmacy, 1949-54, lectr., 1955-60, assoc. prof., 1960-67, prof., 1968-69, chair, 1969—, vice dean, 1970-73; pres. African U., Lagos, Nigeria, 1960-80; cons. Chem. Industries Co., Cairo, 1960—. Author: Medicinal Plants, 1967, Principles of General Pharmacognosy, 1978, Practical Pharmacognosy and Medicinal Plants, 1978, Alcoholics and Narcotics, 1991, Scientific Miraculousness of Holy Koran, 1991, Nutrition in the Holy Koran, 1995, Plants in the Holy Koran, 1996. Recipient Order of merit, 1959, Order of Sci. and Art, 1981. Mem Pharmaceutical Soc. Egypt (pres. 1970), Egyptian Pharmacopoeia Assn. (v.p.), Syndicate of Pharmacy of Egypt (v.p. 1971). Home: 10 Str 150 Maadi-Cairo, Cairo Egypt Office: Cairo U Fac Pharm Dept Med, Plants Kasr-El-Aini Str, Cairo Egypt

MAHRAN, MAHER AHMED, obstetrician, gynecologist, consultant; b. Cairo, Mar. 22, 1930; s. Ahmed Omar Mahran and Effat Mohamed Mustafa; m. Luise Hartmut Sportmann; children: Ahmed, Reem. MD, Ain Shams U., Cairo, 1953. Lectr. ob-gyn. Ain Shams U., Cairo, 1958-63, asst. prof., 1964-70, prof., 1970—, chmn. dept., 1980—; sec.-gen. Nat. Population Coun., Egypt, 1985; v.p. ICPD, UN, Cairo, 1994. Author: Text Book of Ob-Gyn, 1978; editor: Recent Advances in Ultrasound, 1980. Mem. Parliament, Govt. of Egypt, 1990, chmn. of health com., 1992—, Minister of Population, 1993-96; vis. prof. WHO, Mid. and Far East, 1966, Queen's U., Belfast, 1969. Fellow Royal Coll. Surgeons, Royal Coll. Ob-Gyn; mem. Royal Coll. Ob-Gyn. (master), Heliopolis Rotary, Heliopolis Sporting Club. Moslem. Avocations: photography, history, education. Home: 63 El Horreya St, Cairo Egypt Office: Ain Shams U Dept Ob-Gyn, 6 Adly St, Cairo Egypt

MAHTO, C. B., chemistry educator; b. Muzaffarpur, India, Mar. 13, 1943; s. Rameshwar and Fulkumari (Devi) M.; m. Meena Kajali Devi, Mar. 10, 1966; children: Neelam, Dazy, Rosy, Sharad Chandra, Shrawan Kumar Pinki, Ladocli. BS in Chemistry with honors, L.S. Coll., Muzaffapur, India, 1964, MS in Chemistry, 1966, PhD, 1980. Lectr. J.J. Coll., Assah, India, 1966-67; lectr. Gopalganj Coll., India, 1967-80, reader, head, 1980-92, prof., head, 1992—; supr. Rsch. Faculty, Gopalganj, 1980—. Author of 6 books; contbr. 44 articles to profl. jours. Fellow Indian Chem. Soc.; mem ABI (adv. bd., Mem. Yr. 1998). Hindu. Avocations: astrology, palmistry, poetry, religious songs. Home: East Tov M Field, Gopalganj 841428, India Office: Gopalganj Coll, Gopalganj 841428, India

MAHUNKA, SÁNDOR, acarologist, researcher, museum official; b. Budapest, Hungary, Oct. 17, 1937; s. Sándor and Margit (Závodszky) M.; m. Lujza Papp, Sept. 1, 1966; 1 child, Ágnes. BSc, Eötvös Loránd U., 1961, PhD, 1974; DSc, Hungarian Acad. Sci., 1983. Cert. secondary sch. tchr., zoologist. Hydrobiologist Nat. Hygiene Inst., Budapest, 1961-63; museologist Hungarian Natural History Mus., Budapest, 1963—, dep. dir. gen., 1989—. Author: Primitive Oribatids of the Palaearctic Region, 1983, Oribatid Species Described by Berlese (Acari), 1995; editor: Batorliget Nature Reserves After Forty Years, 1991, Fauna of the Hungarian National Parks I-VIII, 1983-99; mem. editl. bd. Internat. Jour. Acarology, 1980—. Recipient Pro Natura award Hungarian Ministry Environ., 1990, Hermann Otto award Hungarian Biol. Soc., 1991, acad. award Hungarian Acad. Sci., 1998. Mem. Hungarian Entomol. Soc. (editor 1975—, Frivaldszky gold medal 1992), Internat. Soc. for Entomofaunistics Mid. Europe (sec. 1985—), Hungarian Acad. Sci. (corr. mem.). Avocations: numismatics, collecting evergreens. E-mail: mahunka@zoo.zoo.nhmus.hu. Home: Dózsa György ut 9, H-1224 Budapest Hungary Office: Hungarian Natural Hist Mus, Baross utca 13, H-1088 Budapest Hungary

MAHY, MARCUS JOHN, trust and estate practitioner; b. Southampton, Hampshire, Eng., Feb. 8, 1961; s. William John and Irene Hilda-May (Ferbrache) M. BSc in Aerospace Engring., Royal Air Force Coll., Halton, Eng., 1981; MBA, Century U., N.Mex., 1990. Registered trust and estate practitioner, Eng. Acct. Ernst & Young, Guernsey, Channel Islands, 1981-82; aviation underwriter Transglobe Underwriters, Guernsey, 1982-83; fund mgr. Hambros Bank Ltd., Guernsey, 1983-84; trust officer Saffery Champness, Guernsey, 1984-86, Bank of Bermuda Ltd., 1986-92; mgr. Coutts & Co., Bermuda, 1992-95; gen. mgr. State House Trust Co. Ltd., Hamilton, Bermuda, 1995-99; CEO Landmark Trust (Bermuda) Ltd., Hamilton, Bermuda, 1999—; com. mem. Bermuda Govt.'s Investment Svcs. Adv. Com., 1994; mem. exec. com. Chartered Inst. Bankers, Bermuda, 1994; guest spkr. various internat. trust confs. Author: (books) Speed and Safety, 1995, Inside the Mig 29, 1997; contbr. articles to profl. jours. Com. mem. Bermuda Govt.'s Proceeds of Crime Rev. Com., 1997; mem. Big Bros. and Big Sisters Bermuda, 1995—. Flight lt. Royal Air Force, 1978-81. Mem. Offshore Inst., Soc. Trust and Estate Practitioners (chmn. 1996, 97), Newcomen Soc., Royal Airforce H.A.A. and Mensa. Avocations: aviation, soccer, vintage cars, travel. Home: Terra Nova, 9 Trimingham Hill, Paget PG05, Bermuda Office: Landmark Trust (Bermuda) Ltd, 52 Reid St, HM12 Hamilton Bermuda

MAI, JOHN DZUNG, aerospace engineer, researcher; b. Saigon, South Vietnam, Aug. 12, 1971; came to U.S., 1975; s. Peter and Anh Loan (Nguyen) M.; BS in Aerospace Engring., UCLA, 1993, MS in Aerospace Engring., 1995, PhD in Aerospace Engring., 2000. Tech. staff assoc. Jet Propulsion Lab., Pasadena, Calif., 1996—. Patentee: low pressure and low temperature hermetic wafer bonding using microwave heating. UCLA rschr., 1997-2000; rsch. assistanceship AFOSR, Wrigh-Patt. AFB, 1995-96. Mem. AIAA, Am. Phys. Soc. Designed MEMS (micro-electro-mech-systems) impinging jet heat enhancer, MEMS seismometer. Office: Microwave Bonding Instruments Inc 3360 E Foothill Blvd Pasadena CA 91107-6023

MAI, YIU-WING, educator; b. Hong Kong, Jan. 5, 1946; s. Lam and Yuet-Yau (Tsui) M.; m. Louisa Kit-Ling Lui, Mar. 12, 1980. BS, Hong Kong U., 1969, PhD, 1972, DSc, 1999; DEng., U. Sydney, 1999. Sr. rsch. asst. Hong Kong U., 1972-73; lectr. U. Sydney, NSW, Australia, 1977-78, sr. lectr., 1979-82, assoc. prof., 1983-87, assoc. dean, 1990-93, prof., 1987—, dir. Ctr. Advanced Materials Tech., 1988—, assoc. dean R&D, 1995-97, dir. Grad. Sch. Engring., 1995-97; pro-dean engring. U. Sydney, 1998—; vis. prof. Hong Kong Poly., 1989-90, 91, Nanyang Tech. U., Singapore, 1991-92, City U. of Hong Kong, 1997; guest scientist Nat. Bur. Stats., Gaithersburg, Md., 1985, 88-89. Author: Elastic and Plastic Fracture, 1985, Fracture Mechanics of Cementitious Materials, 1996, Engineered Interfaces in Fibre Reinforced Composites, 1998; editor (proceedings): Advances in Inorganic Fibre Technology, 1992. Pres. Chinese Australian Acad. Assn., Sydney U., 1991-93. Rsch. scholar U. Mich., Ann Arbor, 1974-75, Fulbright Sr. scholar U.S. Edn. Found., Nat. Bur. Stats., 1988, Rsch. fellow Imperial Coll., London, 1975-76, Sr. Vis. fellow U.K. Sci. Rsch. Coun. Imperial Coll., 1980, Australian Acad. Tech. Scis. and Engring. fellow, 1992; recipient RILEM award and Robert L'Hermite medal Internat. Union Testing and Rsch. Labs. for Materials and Structures, 1981. Fellow Inst. Engrs. Australia, Hong Kong Inst. Engrs., ASME. Avocations: reading, walking, music. Office: U Sydney Dept Mech Engring, Parramatta Rd, Sydney NSW 2006, Australia

MAIA, ALMIR DE SOUZA, university president; b. Pirapetinga, Brazil, Sept. 15, 1945; s. Braulino de Souza and Alcides de Souza Maia; m. Susana Fernandes Ribeiro Maia, Jan. 17, 1973; children: André, Samuel, Filipe, Tiago. DDS, U. Fed. de Juiz de Fora, Brazil, 1972; M, U. Estadual de Campinas, Piracicaba, Brazil, 1981, PhD, 1990. Lic. dentist. Dentist Secretaria de Estado da Saúde/MG, Juiz de Fora, 1976-77; dir. Biology and Health Ctr. U. Meth. Piracicaba, 1978-79, adminstrv. v.p., 1979-86, pres., 1986—; v.p. Orgn. Brazilian Univs. Pres., Brasília, 1992-93, mem. exec. directory, 1988-96; pres. Gen. Coun. Meth. Instns. Edn., Piracicaba, 1996—; mem. Latin Am. Univs. Union, Mexico City, 1986—. Named Citizen of Piracicaba City Hall, 1994. Mem. Brazilian Assn. Univ. Pres. (v.p. 1986-88), Inter-Am. Orgn. Univs. Edn., Internat. Assn. Meth. Schs., Colls. and Univs, Nat. Coun. Edn. Mem. Methodist Ch. Avocations: reading, travel, music, sports. Office: U Meth de Piracicaba, Rua Rangel Pestana 762, 13400901 Piracicaba Sao Paulo, Brazil

MAICKEL, ROGER PHILIP, pharmacologist, educator; b. Floral Park, N.Y., Sept. 8, 1933; s. Philip Vincent and Margaret Mary (Rose) M.; m. Lois Louise Pivonka, Sept. 8, 1956; children: Nancy Ellen Maickel Ward, Carolyn Sue Maickel Anderson. B.S., Manhattan (N.Y.) Coll., 1954; postgrad., Poly. Inst. Bklyn., 1954-55; M.S., Georgetown U., 1957, Ph.D., 1960. Biochemist Nat. Heart Inst., Bethesda, Md., 1955-65; asso. prof. pharmacology Ind. U., 1965-69, prof., 1969—, head sect. pharmacology med. scis. program, 1971-77; prof. pharmacology and toxicology, head dept. Sch. Pharmacy and Pharmacal Scis. Purdue U., West Lafayette, Ind., 1977-83; dir. lab. animal program Purdue U., West Lafayette, 1988-98, emeritus prof., 1999—; acting v.p. product acquisition and devel. BetaMED Pharms., Inc., Indpls., 1983-84. Adv. editor: Pergamon Press, 1970-88; adv. editorial bd.: Neuropharmacology, 1974-88. Bd. dirs. TEAMS, Inc., 1981-87, Am. Coun. on Sci. and Health, 1993—; trustee AAALAC, 1992—. Recipient Alumni award in medicine Manhattan Coll., 1972. Fellow AAAS, Am. Coll. Neuropsychopharmacology, Am. Inst. Chemists (bd. dirs. 1989-92, pres.-elect 1992-94, pres. 1994-96, chmn. 1996-98), Royal Soc. Chemistry, Collegium Internat. de Neuro-Psychopharmacologicum; mem. ASTM, Am. Chem. Soc., Am. Soc. Pharmacology and Exptl. Therapeutics, Am. Soc. Clin. Pharmacology and Therapeutics, Soc. Forensic Toxicologists, Internat. Assn. Chiefs Police, Internat. Soc. Psychoneuroendocrinology, N.Y. Acad. Scis., Soc. Neurosci., Soc. Toxicology, Sigma Xi, Rho Chi. Home: 3567 Canterbury Dr Lafayette IN 47909-3714

MAIDA, CARDINAL ADAM JOSEPH, cardinal; b. East Vandergrift, Pa., Mar. 18, 1930. Student, St. Vincent Coll., Latrobe, Pa., St. Mary's U., Balt., Lateran U., Rome, Duquesne U. Ordained priest Roman Cath. Ch., 1956, consecrated bishop, 1984. Bishop Green Bay, Wis., 1984-89; archbishop Detroit, 1990—; elevated to Cardinal, 1994—. Home: 75 E Boston Blvd Detroit MI 48202-1318 Office: Archdiocese of Detroit 1234 Washington Blvd Ste 1 Detroit MI 48226-1800

MAIDL, BERNHARD ROBERT, engineering educator; b. Bukschoja, Romania, Aug. 15, 1938; s. Anton and Christina (Kübeck) M.; m. Ulrike Ruhland, Dec. 23, 1963; children: Julia, Ulrich, Nadine. Diploma in engring., U. Munich, 1963, PhD, 1967, pvt. dozent, 1969; prof., Ruhr (Germany) U., 1974. Site mgr. Leonard Moll KG, Munich, 1963-64, Roual State Ry., Thailand, 1966; acad. asst. U. Munich, 1967, lectr. in tunneling, 1967-69; project mgr., divsn. mgr. Hochtief AG, Essen, Germany, 1969-75; prof. in constrn. methods and mgt. Ruhr U., Bochum, Germany, 1974—; vis. prof., lectr. U. Calif., Berkeley, 1978, U. New South Wales, Kensington, 1984, 85-86, Tongji U., Shanghai, 1979, 80, 86, 88, James Cook U., Townsville, Australia, 1981, Tunnelbau im Sprengvortrieb. Author: Handbuch d. Tunnel-u. Stollenbaus I & II, 1984, 88, Steel Fiber Reinforced Concrete, 1994, Handbuch für Spritzbeton, 1992, Mechanized Shield Tunneling, 1995, Tunnelbau im Sprengvortrieb, 1997. Mem. Verein Deutscher Ingenieure, Internat. Soc. for Rock Mechanics, Deutscher Ausschuss für unterirdisches Bauen. Roman Catholic. Avocations: golf, hiking, tennis. E-mail: Bernhard.Maidl@ruhr-uni-bochum.de. Office: Ruhr U Bochum, Universitätsstr 150, 44780 Bochum Germany

MAIELLO, DOMENICO MIMMO, coal trade consultant, economist; b. Naples, Italy, Feb. 10, 1933; s. Salvatore Maiello and Cristina De Luca; m. Roberta Kailer, June 11, 1966; children: Cristina, Salvatore. D in Maritime Scis. and Econ., Univ. Naval Inst., Naples, 1960. With sales and pub. rels. dept. Gastaldi & C., Naples, 1950-60; economist Sidermar, Genoa, Italy, 1960-70; coal and fuel buyer Italsider, Genoa, 1970-88, ILVA, Genoa, 1988-89; spl. rep. Island Creek, Italy, Algeria, 1990-93, Westmoreland, U.S., 1990-93, Consol Coal, Algiers, Algeria, 1994—; cons. Norfolk So., Genoa, Italy, 1990—; sales rep. Mitsubishi, Dusseldorf, Germany, 1995—; rep. Mout Isa Mine, Brisbane, Australia, 1990—; sales rep. P.T. Adaro, Indonesia, 1997—; asst. prof. transp. and econ. Genoa U., 1963-70.$Der, Genoa, 1970-88; economist Sidermar, Genoa, 1960-70; sales organizer Gastaldi, Naples, 1950-60; chmn. UN Draught Survey Code taskforce, 1992. Contbr. over 200 articles to profl. pubs. Avocation: swimming. E-mail: dmaiello@tin.it. Office: Norfolk So Corp, Piazza R Rossetti 2/19d, 1-16129 Genoa Italy

MAIENSCHEIN, JANE ANN, historian, philosopher, educator; b. Oak Ridge, Tenn., Sept. 23, 1950; d. Fred Conrad and Joyce Evelyn (Kylander) M.; m. J. Richard Creath, Mar. 13, 1982. BA, Yale U., 1972; MA, Ind. U., 1975, PhD, 1978. Asst. prof. Dickinson Coll., Carlisle, Pa., 1978-80; vis. scholar Harvard U., Cambridge, Mass., 1983-84; vis. assoc. prof. Stanford (Calif.) U., 1987; asst. prof. Ariz. State U., Tempe, 1981-86, assoc. prof. philosophy, 1986-90, prof. philosophy and bioogy, 1990—. Author: Transforming Traditions, 1991, 100 Years Exploring Life, 1989; editor: Defining Biology, 1986; co-editor: Biology and the Foundations of Ethics, 1999, Biology and Epistenology, 2000. Recipient various grants NSF; fellowship Josiah Macy Jr. Found., 1974-78, Congl. fellow, Ariz. Congressman Matt Salmon, 1998-99. Fellow AAAS (various coms.); mem. History of Sci. Soc. (various coms.), Internat. Soc. for History, Philosophy and Social Studies of Sci. (pres. 1989-91), Sigma Xi. Office: Ariz State U Philosophy Dept Tempe AZ 85287-2004

MAIER, BURKHARD, data processing consultant; b. St. Valentin, Austria, Sept. 20, 1949; m. Ingetraut Schlager, June 27, 1978; children: Florentine, Liane. D, Econ. U., 1975. Asst. prof. Econ. U., Vienna, Austria, 1974-81; ele. data processing mgr. Glanzstoff Austria AG, St. Polten, 1981-90; cons. pvt. practice, Wilhelmsburg, Austria, 1990—. Author: Fundamentals of Data Processing and Application Program Development, 1980. Mem. IEEE.

MAIER, HERMANN, skier; b. Flachau, Austria, Dec. 7, 1972. Bricklayer, ski instr., alpine skier, 1979—; mem. Austrian nat. skiing team, 1996—. Recipient Gold medal men's alpine skiing giant slalom Olympic Games, Nagano, Japan, 1998, Gold medal men's alpine skiing super-G, 1998. Avocations: motorbiking, soccer, mountain climbing. Address: Austrian Olympic Com, Rennweg 44, 1030 Vienna Austria*

MAIER, MICHAEL, network executive; b. Salzburg, Austria, Nov. 21, 1965; s. Gunther and Anneliese (Bugelnig) M.; 1 child, Maximilian. Exec. MBA, Calif. State U., San Francisco, 1997. Chief tech. officer ZUV, 1990-99; pres. Access Networking, Salzburg, 1995—. Mem. IEEE. Office: Access Networking, Rotwegg 66, Salzburg 5020, Austria

MAIER, PETER KLAUS, lawyer, business executive; b. Wurzburg, Germany, Nov. 20, 1929; came to U.S., 1939, naturalized, 1945; s. Bernard and Joan (Sonder) M.; m. Melanie L. Stoff, Dec. 15, 1963; children: Michele Margaret, Diana Lynn. BA cum laude, Claremont McKenna Coll., 1949; JD, U. Calif., Berkeley, 1952; LLM in Taxation, NYU, 1953. Bar: Calif. 1953, U.S. Supreme Ct. 1957; cert. specialist in taxation law, Calif. Atty. tax div. U.S. Dept Justice, Washington, 1956-59; pvt. practice tax law San Francisco, 1959-81; prof. law Hastings Coll. Law, U. Calif., San Francisco, 1967-95; vis. prof. U. Calif. Boalt Sch. Law, Berkeley, 1988-98, Stanford U. Sch. Law, 1996-98; chmn. Maier & Siebel, Inc., Larkspur, Calif., 1981—; mng. dir. U.S. Trust Co. NA, San Francisco, 1998—; chmn. Fromm Inst. for Lifelong Learning, U. San Francisco, 1997—; pres. John B. Huntington Found., 1996—. Author books on taxation; contbr. articles to profl. jours. Chmn. Property Resources Inc., San Jose, Calif., 1968-77; pres. Calif. Property Devel. Corp., San Francisco, 1974-81. Capt. USAF, 1953-56. Mem. San Francisco Bar Assn. (chmn. sect. taxation 1970-71), Order of Coif. Home: PO Box 1245 Belvedere CA 94920-4245 Office: Maier & Siebel Inc 80 E Sir Francis Drake Blvd Larkspur CA 94939-1709

MAIESE, KENNETH, neurologist; b. Audubon, N.J., Dec. 5, 1958; s. Charles and Margaret (Fioretti) M. BA summa cum laude, U. Pa., 1981; MD, Cornell U., 1985. Intern N.Y. Hosp., 1985-86, resident in neurology, 1986-89, asst. attending physician, 1989-94; asst. prof. Cornell U. Med. Coll., N.Y.C., 1989-94; assoc. prof. dept. neurology, anatomy and cell biology Wayne State U. Ctr. for Molecular Toxicology & Medicine, Detroit, 1994—; dir. lab. molecular and cellular cerebral ischemia Wayne State U. Ctr. for Molecular Toxicology, Detroit, 1994—, prof. dept. neurology, anatomy, cell biology, 1999—; dir. neurol. diagnosis N.Y. Hosp., 1991-94. Author: Neurology and General Medicine, 1989, Neurological and Neurosurgical ICU Medicine, 1988; contbr. articles to Neurology, Jour. Cerebral Blood Flow and Metabolism, Jour. Intensive Care Medicine, Jour. Neurosci., Jour. Neurosci. Rsch., Neurosci. Lett., Jour. Brain Rsch., Jour. Neurochem. Joseph Collins scholar, 1981-85, Grupe Found. scholar, 1985; grantee NIH, 1990—, Nat. Stroke Assn., 1992-94, Alzheimer's Assn., 1994—, Am. Heart Assn., 1995—, United Cerebral Palsy Found., 1995—, Janssen Found., 1995—; recipient Young Scientist award Jours. Cerebral Blood Flow, 1991, Hoechst Investigator award, 1993, Robert G. Siekert award in stroke, 1994, Johnson and Johnson Disting. Investigator award, 1996-98, Maiese Lab. Neurosci. Tng. award J & J/Janssen, 1998, Boehringer Investigator award, 1999. Mem. Am. Acad. Neurology, N.Y. Acad. Scis., Assn. for Rsch. in Nervous and Mental Diseases, Am. Neurol. Assn. (elected), Soc. Neurosci. Roman Catholic. Achievements include rsch. in imidazole receptors, cerebral ischemia, nitric oxide toxicity, growth factor neuroprotection, signal cellular transduction mechanisms, metabotropic glutamate receptors, gene regulation, and gene therapy. Office: Wayne State U Sch Medicine 8C-1 U Health Ctr Dept Neur 4201 Saint Antoine St Detroit MI 48201-2153

MAILACHALAM, BABU, research scientist; b. Nellikuppam, Tamlnadu, India, July 27, 1966; s. Rangasamy and Chandra) Mailachalam; m. Priya Natarajan, Dec. 6, 1998. BE, Annamalai U., Chidambaram, India, 1987; ME, Birla Inst. Tech. & Sci., Pilani, India, 1989; PhD, Indian Inst. Tech., Madras, 1997. Customer engr. HCL Ltd., New Delhi, 1987-88; project assoc. Indian Inst. Tech., Madras, 1989-90, 95-97; cons. Sigma Tech Electronics, India, 1994-95; sr. systems analyst Ramco Systems, India, 1997-99; rsch. fellow Ctr. High Performance Embdded Systems, Nanyang Tech. U., Singapore, 1999—; cons. Micro Time Systems, Madras, 1990-94. Contbr. articles to profl. jours. Sec. Brahmaputra Hostel Coun., Indian Inst. Tech., Madras, 1992-93, mem. bd. adad. rsch., 1993-94. Mem. IEEE. Avocations: reading, amateur radio. Home: Block 926 Jurong West St 92, # 10-131, Singapore 640926, Singapore Office: Nanyang Tech U CHIPES, Sch Applied Sci, Singapore 639798, Singapore

MAILANDER, WILLIAM STEPHEN, lawyer; b. Dover, N.J., July 25, 1958; s. William Stephen and Doris Elizabeth (Post) M.; m. Judith Gay Burrows, May 20, 1989 (div. 1993); m. Rosalind Eager, Dec. 15, 1999. BA, NYU, 1984; JD, Temple U., 1988. Bar: Pa. 1988, N.J. 1991, D.C. 1996; U.S. Ct. Vets. Appeals 1991, U.S. Ct. Appeals (fed. cir.) 1993, U.S. Supreme Ct. 1994. Staff atty. Bd. Vets. Appeals, Washington, 1988-90, Coast Guard Chief Counsel, Washington, 1990-91, VA Gen. Counsel, Washington, 1991-93; asst. gen. counsel Paralyzed Vets. Am., Washington, 1993—; faculty continuing legal edn. seminars, various cities, 1993—. Contbr. articles to profl. jours. With USMC, 1976-79. Decorated Navy Achievement medal. Mem. FBA (chair membership vets. law sect. 1993-94, editor newsletter 1996—). Avocations: reading, running. Office: Paralyzed Vets Am 801 18th St NW Washington DC 20006-3517

MAILER, NORMAN, author; b. Long Branch, N.J., Jan. 31, 1923; s. Issac Barnett and Fanny (Schneider) M.; m. Beatrice Silverman, 1944 (div. 1952); 1 dau., Susan; m. Adele Morales, 1954 (div. 1962); children: Danielle, Elizabeth; m. Jeanne Campbell, 1962 (div. 1963); 1 dau., Kate; m. Beverly Bentley, 1963 (div. 1980); children: Michael, Steven; m. Carol Stevens, 1980 (div. 1980); 1 dau., Maggie; m. Norris Church, 1980; 1 son, John Buffalo. SB cum laude, Harvard U., 1943; postgrad., Sorbonne, Paris, France, 1947-48. columnist Village Voice, 1946, Commentary, 1962-63, Esquire, 1962-63; contbg. editor Dissent, 1953-69; co-founding editor Village Voice, 1955. Author: No Percentage, 1941, The Naked and the Dead, 1948, Barbary Shore, 1951, The Deer Park, 1955, The White Negro: Superficial Reflections on the Hipster, 1957, Advertisements for Myself, 1959, Deaths for the Ladies and Other Disasters, 1962, The Presidential Papers, 1963, An American Dream, 1965, Cannibals and Christians, 1966, Why Are We in Vietnam?, 1967 (Nat. Book award nomination 1967), The Short Fiction of Norman Mailer, 1967, The Bullfight, 1967, The Armies of the Night, 1968 (Pulitzer prize for non-fiction 1969, George Polk award 1969), Miami and the Siege of Chicago, 1968 (Nat. Book award for non-fiction 1968), The Idol and the Octopus, 1968, Of a Fire On The Moon, 1970, King of the Hill, 1971, The Prisoner of Sex, 1971, The Long Patrol, 1971, Existential Errands, 1972, St. George and the Godfather, 1972, Marilyn, 1973, The Faith of Graffiti, 1974, The Fight, 1975, Some Honorable Men, 1975, Genius and Lust, 1976, A Transit to Narcissus, 1978, The Executioner's Song, 1979 (Pulitzer Prize for fiction 1980, Nat. Book Critics Circle award nomination 1979, Am. Book award nomination 1980), Of a Small and Modest Malignancy, Wicked and Bristling with Dots, 1980, Of Women and Their Elegance, 1980, Pieces and Pontifications, 1982, Ancient Evenings, 1983, Tough Guys Don't Dance, 1984, The Last Night, 1984, Harlot's Ghost, 1991, How the Wimp Won the War, 1991, Oswald's Tale, 1995, Portrait of Picasso as a Young Man, 1995, The Gospel According to the Song, 1997; (plays) The Deer Park: A Play, 1967, Strawhead, 1985; editor: Genius and Lust: A Journey Through the Major Writings of Henry Miller, 1976; screenwriter: (films) The Executioner's Song, 1982 (Emmy award nomination outstanding adapted screenplay 1983); screenwriter, prodr., dir., actor: (films) Wild 90, 1967, Maidstone: A Mystery, 1971; screenwriter, prodr.: (films) Beyond the Law, 1968; screenwriter, dir.: (films) Tough Guys Don't Dance, 1987; actor: (films) Ragtime, 1981. Served with AUS, 1944-46. Recipient Edward MacDowell medal MacDowell Colony, 1973, Nat. Arts Club Gold medal, 1976, Emerson-Thoreau Medal for lifetime of literary achievement, 1989; Nat. Inst. and Am. Acad. grantee, 1960; Pappas fellow U. Pa., 1983. Mem. PEN Am. Ctr. (pres. 1984-86), Nat. Inst. Arts and Letters. Office: care Random House Author's Mail 299 Park Ave New York NY 10171-0002

MAIMINAS, EFREM ZALMANOVITSH, economist, educator; b. Kaunas, Lithuania, June 18, 1932; arrived in Russia, 1965; s. Zalman Shliomo and Tauba Solomono (Walt) M.; m. Julija Viktoro Andriushaityte, Feb. 12, 1955; children: Andrius, Alexander. BS in Econs., Vilnius (Lithuania) U., 1951, MA in Fin., 1953, PhD in Econs., 1958; DSc in Econs., Moscow U., 1968. Asst. prof. econs. Vilnius U., 1956-59, assoc. prof., 1959-65; assoc. prof. Moscow U., 1965-69, prof., 1969—; head lab. Ctrl. Econ. Math. Inst., Russian Acad. Sci., 1970-86, head. dept. Inst. Econ. Forecasting, 1986-95, fellow, 1995—; vis. prof. Humboldt U., Berlin, 1970, 85, Bulgarian H.S. Econs., Swishtow, 1973, Warsaw (Poland) U., 1977. Author: Planning Processes in Economy: Informational Aspect, 1967, 2d edit., 1971; co-author: Decisions, 1981, Economic Cybernetics, 1982, Memoirs Criculum Vitae, 2000; contbr. articles to profl. jours. Named Honoured Sci. Worker of Russian Fedn. Mem. Russian Econ. Soc. Home: Michurinsky Prospect, 54 b 2 apt 116, 117192 Moscow Russia Office: Inst Econ Forecasting, 47 Nakhimovsky Prospect, 117418 Moscow Russia

MAIMISTOV, ANDREI IVANOVICH, physicist, educator, researcher; b. Ulbeiay, Okhotski, Russia, Jan. 27, 1951; s. Ivan Andreevich and Janna Mikhailovna (Dubik) M.; m. Marina Stanislavovna Fetisova, Oct. 11, 1975; children: Kirill Andreevich, Natalia Andreevna. Engr., Moscow Engring. Physics Inst., 1974, PhD, 1980, Dr Phys Sci, 1996. Engr. Moscow Engring. Physics Inst., 1974-76, 79-80, jr. sci. rschr., 1980-86, asst. prof., 1986, assoc. prof., 1986-99, prof., 1999—. Contbr. articles to profl. jours. Open Soc. Inst. grantee, 1995, 97, 98, 99, Soros Assoc. Prof., 1995. Mem. Moscow Phys. Soc. Avocation: reading. Home: Anokhina 6-1-45, 117602 Moscow Russia Office: Moscow Engring Physics Inst, Kashirskoe Sh 31, 115 409 Moscow Russia

MAIMUSOV, DMITRY FEDOSOVICH, soil scientist, educator; b. Monastirschina, Russia, Apr. 3, 1924; s. Fedos Arkhipovich and Lidiya Dmitriyevna (Stanovskaya) M.; m. Lidiya Iosifovna Zapalskaya, Aug. 7, 1953; 1 child, Galina. Cert. geography tchr., Smolensk Tchr.'s Tng. Coll., Russia, 1953; M of Geog. Scis., Belorussian U., Minsk, 1965; D of Agrl. Scis., Belorussian Inst. Soil Sci., Minsk, 1992. Asst. dept. phys. geography Smolensk Tchr.'s Tng. Coll., 1954-65, sr. lectr., 1965-71, head dept., 1971-76, sr. lectr., 1976-92, prof., 1993—; dir. regional dept. Acad. Natural Sci., Russia, 1996—, full mem., 1997—. Author: Natural Systems of the Smolensk Region, 1987, Soils of the Smolensk Region, 1992; author, editor: Dokuchaev's Heritage in Science and Practice, 1996; contbr. articles to profl. jours. Sgt. maj. inf., 1943-49, Ukraine. Named Exemplary Educator of Russia, Ministry of Edn., 1961, 87. Mem. Trade Union of Educators. Avocations: fiction, classical music, photography. Office: Pedagogical U, Przhevalsky str 4, 214000 Smolensk Russia

MAIN, EDNA (JUNE) DEWEY, education educator; b. Hyannis, Mass., Sept. 1, 1940; d. Seth Bradford and Edna Wilhelmina (Wright) Dewey; m. Donald John Main, Sept. 9, 1961 (div. Dec. 1989); children: Alison Teresa Main Ronzon, Susan Christine Main Leddy, Steven Donald Main. Degree in merchandising, Tobe-Coburn Sch., 1960; BA in Edn., U. North Fla., 1974,

MA in Edn., 1979, M in Adminstrn. and Supervision, 1983; PhD in Curriculum and Instrn., U. Fla., 1990. Asst. buyer Abraham & Straus, Bklyn., 1960-61; asst. mdse. mgr. Interstate Dept. Stores, N.Y.C., 1962-63; tchr. Holiday Hill Elem. Sch., Jacksonville, Fla., 1974-86; instr. summer sci. inst., 1984-92; prof. edn. Jacksonville U., 1992—; also coord. masters program in integrated learning and ednl. tech.; instr. U. Fla., 1987-90; cons. Assn. Internat. Schs. in Africa, 1994-97. Co-author: Developing Critical Thinking Through Science, 1990. Rep. United Way, 1981-86; tchr. rep., chpt. leader White House Young Astronaut Program, 1984-85; team leader NSF Shells Elem. Sci. Project. Mem. ASCD, ISTE, Nat. Sci. Tchrs. Assn. (sci. tchrs. achievement recognition award 1983), Phi Kappa Phi, Phi Delta Kappa, Delta Kappa Gamma, Kappa Delta Pi. Republican. Episcopalian. Office: Jacksonville U 2800 University Blvd N Jacksonville FL 32211-3394

MAIN, PATRICIA ENGLANDER, investor; b. London, Apr. 8, 1931; d. Harry Norman and Eve (Roth) Englander; m. Frank Graham Main, Apr. 30, 1966 (div. Apr. 1981); m. Franklin Walter Mohney, Aug. 10, 1981 (dec. May 2, 1991); children: Lisa Nicole Kelly, Susan Jennifer Kerschner, Jacqueline Eve Singer. Student, Mt. Holyoke Coll., 1948-50. Dir. pub. rels. Contemporary Arts Mus., Houston, 1962-64; relocation sales assoc. Paul Reinke Corp., Cherry Hill, N.J., 1964-69; account exec. Relocation Realty Svc. Corp., N.Y.C., 1972-76, v.p. ops., 1976-79; owner Patricia Mohney Gallery, Reading, Pa., 1981-84; v.p. Venture Components Corp., N.Y.C., 1984-92; pvt. investor N.Y.C., 1992—. Trustee, bd. mem. Reading Art Mus., 1980-83; mem. bus. and profl. com. N.Y.C. Ballet, 1985-95; mem. com. denominational affairs All Souls Ch., N.Y.C., 1998—. Mem. Mt. Holyoke Coll. Alumnae Club (bd. dirs. 1969-77, pres. 1977-79). Office: 65 E 76th St Ste 3B New York NY 10021-1844

MAIN, PAUL GRAEME NEILSON, general practice physician, educator; b. Cambridge, Eng., Feb. 25, 1947; s. Alexander Morrice and Ethel Annie (Page) M.; m. Joy Annette Perkins, Oct. 4, 1975; children: Rebecca, James, Thomas, Bethany. BA, U. Cambridge, 1969, MB BChir, 1973, MA, 1974; diploma, Royal Coll. Ob-Gyn., London. Assoc. Chartered Inst. of Pers. and Devel. (CIPD). Surgeon King's Coll. Hosp., London, 1973-74; house physician Joyce Green Hosp., Dartford, Kent, Eng., 1974; registrar in gen. practice U. Bristol, 1975-77; prin. in gen. practice Bristol, 1977—; tchr. gen. practice Bristol U., 1978—, trainer gen. practice, 1984—; course organizer Bristol U. Gen. Practice Vocat. Tng. Scheme, 1986—; regional assoc. advisor in gen. practice for trainer assessment, 1996—; primary healthcare cons. Know How Fund, Kazakstan, 1996—; primary health care cons., Brit. Coun., Egypt, 2000—. Contbr. articles and editls. to profl. publs. Mem. Bishop of Bristol Health and Healing Adv. Group, 1985-95; mem. Coun. Mgmt., Network Counseling, Bristol, 1985-92; mem. Bristol and Dist. Gen. Practice Adv. Com., 1985-91; mem. Avon Local Med. Com., Bristol, 1988-93. Mem. Royal Coll. Gen. Practitioners (joint hosp. visitor for Royal Coll. Physicians gen. profl. tng. 1996—, joint com. for postgrad. tng. in gen. practice visitor 1999—), Brit. Med. Assn., Bristol Medico-Chirurgical Soc. (hon. treas. 1995—). Avocations: family, literature and writing, audio-visual arts, traveling, hill walking. Office: Hartcliffe Health Ctr, Hartcliffe, Bristol BS13 0JP, England

MAIN, ROBERT GAIL, communications educator, training consultant, television and film producer, former army officer; b. Bucklin, Mo., Sept. 30, 1932; s. Raymond M. and Inez L. (Olinger) M.; m. Anita Sue Thoroughman, Jan. 31, 1955; children: Robert Bruce, David Keith, Leslie Lorraine. BS magna cum laude, U. Mo., 1954; grad. with honors, Army Commd. Gen. Staff Coll., 1967; MA magna cum laude in Comm., Stanford U., 1968; PhD, U. Md., 1978. Commd. 2d lt. U.S. Army, 1954, advanced through grades to lt. col., 1968; mem. faculty Army Commd. Gen. Staff Coll., 1968-70; chief speechwriting and info. materials divsn. U.S. Army Info. Office, 1971, chief broadcast and film divsn., 1972-73; dir. def. audiovisual activities Office of Info. for Armed Forces, 1973-76; ret., 1976; prof. instrnl. tech. Calif. State U., Chico, 1976—, dept. chair, 1993-98; cons. in field. Author: Rogues, Saints and Ordinary People, 1988; prodr. (TV documentary) Walking Wounded, 1983, Army Info. Films, Army Radio Series, 1972-73; contbr. articles on computer based tng. and telecoms. to scientific and profl. jours. Decorated Legion of Merit, Meritorious Svc. medal, Commendation medal with oak leaf cluster, combat Inf. Badge; Vietnamese Cross of Gallantry; recipient Freedom Found. awards, 1972, 73, 74; Bronze medal Atlanta Film Festival, 1972; Best of Show award Balt. Film Festival, 1973; Creativity award Chgo. Indsl. Film Festival, 1973; Cine gold award Internat. Film Prodrs. Assn., 1974; named an Outstanding Prof. Calif. State U., 1987-88. Mem. Phi Eta Sigma, Alpha Zeta, Phi Delta Gamma, Omicron Delta Kappa, Alpha Gamma Rho.

MAINGUET, MONIQUE MICHEL, environmentalist, educator; b. Sarrebourg, France, Feb. 13, 1937; d. Roger and Henriette (Wahl) Michel; m. Serge Mainguet, May 18, 1964; children: Judith, Pierre. Diploma in history, Geographie U., Strasbourg, France, 1961, cert. in mineralogy, 1962, Doctorate 3 cycle, 1963; PhD, Paris-Sorbonne, 1972. Attaché rsch. Nat. Ctr. Sci. Rsch. U. Paris The Sorbonne, 1964-66; asst., chief asst. geography U. Parix X, 1966-70; conf. leader U. Reims (France), 1970-75, prof. geography, 1975-85, 88—; dep. dir. desertifiction control UNEP, Nairobi, Kenya, 1985-88; cons. numerous UN orgns. Author: Le Modelé des Grès, 2 vols., 1972, L'Erg de Fachi-Bilma, 1978, l'Homme et La Sécheresse, 1995 (Prix Soc. Geographie 1996), Aridity, Droughts and Human Development, 1999. Mem. Gesellschaft Erd und Völkerkunde zu Stuttgart (hon.), Third World Assn. Remote Sensing, Com. Des Travaux Historiques et Scientifiques, Internat. Geographic Union, Geog. Soc. Paris, Univ. Inst. France, N.Y. Acad. Scis. Avocation: renovating interiors of historical houses. Home: 2 Rue Quinault, 78100 St Germain En Laye France Office: Lab Geog Zonal Devel Reims, 57 Rue Pierre Taittinger, 51100 Reims France

MAINIERI, MIKE, vibraphonist, producer, arranger, composer; b. Bronx, N.Y., July 4, 1938. Student, Juilliard Sch. Music. Jazz vibraphonist, 1964—. Performed with Paul Whiteman Band; mem. Buddy Rich Band; also worked with Billie Holliday, and numerous other artists including Charlie Shavers, Roy Eldridge, Paul Simon, Linda Ronstadt, Billy Joel, Aerosmith, George Benson, Don McClean, Dire Straits, Coleman Hawkins, Eddie Vinson, Paul Simon, Benny Goodman, Chico Hamilton, Philly Joe Jones, Elvin Jones, Paul Desmond, Bob James, Laura Nyro, Carly Simon; producer Carly Simon albums including Torch, Hello, Big Man, Come Upstairs, Andy Summers World Gone Strange, Bendik album 9, David Spinozza, Nick Holmes, Kazumi Watanabe, Stephen Bishop, Ben Sidran; arranger Dire Straits albums including Brothers in Arms, Love Over Gold, others; formed big band White Elephant with Steve Gadd, Tony Levin and Warren Bernhardt, albums include Blues on the Other Side, White Elephant, Love Play, Journey Through an Electric Tube, Insight, Wanderlust; now performing with Steps Ahead with Mike Mainieri, Jeff Andrews, Steve Smith, Bendik, Rachel Z., Jimi Tunnell, albums include Smokin' in the Pit, Step by Step, Paradox, Steps Ahead, Modern Times, Magnetic, N.Y.C. Office: NYC/Exit 9 Records PO Box 877 New York NY 10023*

MAINO, GIUSEPPE, physicist; b. Bologna, Italy, Dec. 28, 1953; s. Arturo and Laura (Castel Bolognesi) M.; m. Donatella Biagi, Sept. 16, 1984. Diploma maturita, Classical Studies, Bologna, 1972; PhD in physics, U. Bologna, 1977. Lectr. U. Bologna, 1977-79; grant holder Italian Nat. Agy for New Tech., Energy & Environ., Bologna, 1980-84, rschr., 1984-93, asst. dir. applied physics divsn., 1994—; prof. nuc. physics U. Bologna, 1986-96; prof. computer sci. U. Bologna-Ravenna, 1997—; coord. rsch. on complex sys. ENEA, 1990—; assoc. rschr. Italian Nat. Inst. Nuc. Physics, Florence, 1990—; mem. commn. applied math. Italian Nat. Rsch. Coun., CNR, Rome, 1995—; dir. internat. rsch. project, GIANO. Editor: Dynamical Symmetries and Chaos, 1989, Nonlinear Systems in Physics, 1990, Nonlinear Problems in Engineering, 1991, Perspectives for the Interacting Boston Model, 1994, Dynamics of Transport in Plasmas and Charged Beams, 1996; editor Incontri, 1976-84. Journalist Order of Italian Press, Rome, 1981—. Recipient grant European Physical Soc., 1980, Found. A Della Riccia, 1981, Competition award European Cmty. Directories XII, 1986. Fellow European Sci. Found. (mem. steering com. 1993-98); mem. Internat. Atomic Energy (cons., rsch. program on activation gross sect. 1991-95), Italian Nat. Rsch. Coun. (mem. com. on applied math. 1994—), Internat. Radiation Physics Soc., Am. Phys. Soc., N.Y. Acad. of Sci., Inst. Physics, Am. Assn. Advancement Sci. Avocations: history of art, music. Home: Roncati 17, Bologna 40134 Italy Office: ENEA, Fiammelli 2, Bologna 40129, Italy

MAINWARING, SCOTT PATTERSON, political scientist, educator; b. July 18, 1954; s. William Thomas and Camille Brent Mainwaring; m. Susan M. Elfin, Aug. 9, 1986; children: Benjamin E., Grace E. BA in Polit. Sci., MA in Polit. Sci. magna cum laude, Yale U., 1976; PhD in Polit. Sci., Stanford U., 1983. Asst. prof. govt. U. Notre Dame, Ind., 1983-88, assoc. prof. govt., 1988-93, prof. govt., 1993-96, chair dept. govt., Eugene Conley Prof. of Govt., 1996-97; dir. Kellogg Inst. Internat. Studies, Notre Dame, 1998—; mem. Coun. on Fgn. Rels., 1986-91; mem. rsch. coun. Internat. Fourm for Dem. Studies, Nat. Endowment for Democracy, Washington, 1994—; cons. The Ford Found., N.Y., Inter-Am. Dialogue, Washington, MacArthur Found., Chgo., Woodrow Wilson Ctr. for Scholars, Washington. Author: The Catholic Church and Politics in Brazil, 1916-1985, 1986, Rethinking Party Systems in the Third Wave of Democratization: The Case of Brazil, 1999; co-editor: Building Democratic Institutions: Party Systems in Latin America, 1995, Presidentialism and Democracy in Latin America, 1997. Recipient Hubert Herring prize Pacific Coast Coun. on Lat. Am. Studies, 1983-84. Mem. Am. Polit. Sci. Assn., Latin Am. Studies Assn. (treas. 1997—), Phi Beta Kappa. E-mail: Mainwaring.1@nd.edu. Office: Kellogg Inst 205 Hesburgh Ctr Notre Dame IN 46556-5677

MAINZER, FRANCIS KIRKWOOD, neurosurgeon, health facility consultant; b. Clearfield, Pa., May 16, 1930; s. Francis Stanislaus and Dorothy (Kirkwood) M.; m. Joan Elizabeth Heydon, Sept. 19, 1964; children: Karen Elizabeth, Kristen Ann Mainzer Gillespie, Kathleen Patricia Mainzer Neumuller, Carole Jenifer Mainzer Bower. BA in Biology and Psychology, Amherst Coll., 1952; MD, George Washington U., 1959. Cert. Am. Bd. Neurol. Surgery. Attending neurosurgeon St. Vincent Health Ctr., Erie, Pa., 1965-92, chief of neurosurgery, 1992, asst. chief surgery, 1992; attending neurosurgeon Hamot Med. Ctr., Erie, 1965-84, chief neurosurgery, 1974; cons. neurosurgery VA Med. Ctr., Erie, 1965-80, Metro Health Ctr., Erie, 1965-92; physician surveyor Joint Commn. on Accreditation of Healthcare Orgns., Oakbrook Terrace, Ill., 1992-98; survey team leader J.C.A.H.O., Oakbrook Terrace, Ill., 1994-98; cons. in hosp. quality improvement, 1998—; mem. spinal cord injury adv. com. Pa. Dept. Health, Harrisburg, 1973-78; mem. stds. com. Pa. Trauma Systems Found., Harrisburg, 1985-92; reviewer Keystone Peer Rev., Harrisburg, 1986-89. Mem. Erie Philharm. Bd., 1967-71. Capt. USMCR, 1952-63, Korea. Mem. Am. Assn. Neurol. Surgeons, Congress Neurol. Surgeons, Pa. Neurosurg. Soc. (sec.-treas. 1981-84, pres. 1985, dir. 1975—), Mid-Atlantic Neurosurg. Soc. (dir. 1980—). Episcopalian. Avocations: radio-controlled model aeronautics, woodworking, skiing. Office: 1149 Spring Valley Dr Erie PA 16509-2950

MAIOR, OVIDIU CORNEL, chemist, educator; b. Dej, Cluj, Romania, Oct. 4, 1930; s. Gheorghe Corneliu and Terezia (Coroianu) M.; m. Elisabeta Mihalache, Mar. 26, 1962. Grad., Cluj-Napoca (Romania) U., 1953; PhD, U. Bucharest, Romania, 1966. Rsch. scientist Rsch. Carbon Inst., Bucharest, 1953-54; chief lab. U. Medicine and Pharmacy, Bucharest, 1954-61; asst. faculty chemistry U. Bucharest, 1962-67, lectr. faculty chemistry, 1967-72, reader, 1972-90, prof., 1990—. Author: (with others) Name Reactions in Organic Synthesis, 1996; contbr. numerous sci. papers to profl. jours.; patentee in field. Recipient Award of Edn., Ministry for Sci. Activity, 1969. Mem. Nat. Geog. Soc., Romanian Chem. Soc., N.Y. Acad. Scis. Avocation: traveling. Home: Instr Buturugeni #2 Bl P1, Sc C ap 12 Sect 5, 77362 Bucharest Romania Office: U Bucharest Fac Chemistry, Sos Panduri 90-92 Sect 5, 76233 Bucharest Romania

MAIORIELLO, RICHARD PATRICK, otolaryngologist; b. Mar. 17, 1936; s. Gesumino Theodore and Angelina (Del Rossi) M.; m. Susan Hemenway, Mar. 6, 1979; children: Gabriel, Angela, Richard. *Wife Susan, registered OR nurse. She has won many national dressage awards USDF Gold, Silver, and Bronze medals, 3 reserve and 4 Champion Horse of the Year awards. Competed in Amateur Ballroom Dancing at the National Championship level with Richard. The family warmblood horsebreeding farm, Valhalla's Pride is internationally recognized. Father Gesumino, Philadelphia Attorney. Brother Joseph, JD from Harvard, Justice Department Trial Attorney and Commander USNR. Brother Monsignor Gabriel, PhD, President Pre-Senate, Pastor-Director of Education Arlington Diocese, Principal Norfolk, O'Connell, John Vianney. Sister Jaqueline, MD Women's Medical Board of Pathology Dermatology, founder of Cryogenics. Sister Rosemarie AB, Registered Physical Therapist, Lt. USAR, Husband William, General Counsel SBA.* AB, U. Pa., 1960; MD, Jefferson Med. Coll., 1964; MS, Thomas Jefferson U., 1972. Diplomate Nat. Bd. Med. Examiners, Am. Bd. Otolaryngology. Commd. 2d lt. USAF, 1963, advanced through grades to col., 1977, ret., 1979; intern Keesler Hosp., 1965-67; chief flight medicine USAF Base, Bitburg, Fed. Republic Germany, 1965-68; resident in otolaryngology Thomas Jefferson Hosp., Phila., 1968-71, 72-73; dir. med. edn. Andrews AFB, 1974-78; assoc. prof. uniformed svcs. Univ. Health Scis., 1978-79; assoc. prof. Northeastern Ohio U. of Medicine, 1983—; mem. staff Aultman Hosp., 1979—; assoc. staff Timken Mercy Med. Ctr., 1981—, Union Hosp., 1988—; cons. otolaryngology to Surgeon Gen., 1977—; pres. Mid-Ohio Dressage Assn. *Richard Maioriello was a naval aviator at age twenty; he flew photo-fighter jets with over 150 carrier landings. After medical school he joined the USAF pilot-physician program as a designated flight surgeon. He spent three years flying phantom jets, and conducting aeromedical consultation and research. Richard finished his military career at Andrews AFB in clinical practice and as medical director of education. He then became a private practitioner, well published in medical literature. He has over twenty-years experience in German warmblood horse breeding, producing grand prix horses, approved stallions, elite mares, champions, one top performance test stallion and his horse is a USDF central states breeders champion. He is a noted equestrian and with his wife Susan, who is first whip, were awarded Colors with gully ridge hunt.* With USNR, 1954-58. Decorated Air Force Commendation medal. Fellow ACS, Am. Soc. Head and Neck Surgery; mem. Am. Acad. Otolaryngology, Am. Acad. Facial Plastic and Reconstructive Surgery, Am. Assn. Cosmetic Surgery, Vail Cosmetic Surg. Soc., Hanoverian Soc. (exec. v.p.), U.S. Dressage Fedn. (chmn. all-breeds coun.), Centurion Club. Republican. Roman Catholic. Office: 1445 Harrison Ave NW Canton OH 44708-2620

MAIR, BRUCE LOGAN, interior designer, company executive; b. Chgo., June 5, 1951; s. William Logan and Josephine (Lee) M. BFA, Drake U., 1973; postgrad., Ind. Wesleyan U., 1990—. Mgr., head designer Reifers of Indpls., 1973-79; pres. Interiors Internat., Indpls., 1979-87; sr. designer Kasler Group, Indpls., 1987-89; dir. devel. Tillery Interiors and Imports, Greenwood, Ind., 1990; v.p. Tillery Interiors and Imports, Indpls., 1990-92; owner Mair Interior Design Group, Indpls., 1992—; pres. Tokens Inc., Indpls., 1982-88, Meg-A-Wat Enterprises Inc., Indpls., 1985-87, Luxury Ice Creams Inc., Indpls., 1986-87. Cover designer Indpls. Home and Garden mag., 1978, feature designer 1980; feature designer Builder mag., 1979; co-designer feature Indpls. At Home mag., 1979. Campaigner Anderson for Pres., 1980. Mem. Am. Soc. Interior Designers (profl; treas. Ind. chpt. 1982-83, Pres. awards 1981-82), U.S. Rowing Assn. (master 1987—), St. Joseph Hist. Neighborhood Assn., Columbia Club (rowing crew coxswain 1986—), Highland Model A Club, Tower Harbor Yacht Club (Douglas, Mich.), Alpha Epsilon Pi. Avocations: sculling, historic preservation, model A Ford restoration, fishing, farming. Office: Mair Interior Design Group 2047 SE 29th Ln Cape Coral FL 33904-3011

MAIRANOWSKI, VIKTOR, chemist, consultant; b. Moscow, July 26, 1936; arrived in Germany, 1993; s. Hirsh Moses and Dvoira Josef (Rabinowitch) M.; m. Bella Benzion Lurik, July 9, 1962; children: Gregory (dec.), Elena. Engr., Dipl. Chem., Lomonosow Coll. Fine Chem Tech, Moscow, 1961; PhD, Acad. Sci. USSR, 1965; DSc in Chemistry, Moscow Lomonosow State U., 1980; prof. chemistry, Ministry of the Higher Edn., USSR, 1985. Rsch. scientist All Union Vitamin Rsch. Inst., Moscow, 1961-69, head analytical methods lab., 1969-71, head phys. chem. lab., 1972-93; cons. Interdisciplinary Rsch. Ctr. Thin Organic and Biochem. Films, Potsdam, Germany, 1994—. Contbr. chpts. to books and articles to profl. jours.; patentee in field. Recipient Gold and Silver medals All Union Exhbn. Achievement, Nat. Economy of the USSR, 1985. Mem. Electrochem. Soc., N.Y. Acad. Sci. Avocations: music, history. E-mail: vmairan@freenet.de.

MAIRE, JEAN-CLAUDE, science educator, consultant; b. Saint-Maixent l'Ecole, France, Apr. 9, 1934; s. Henri and Madeleine (Renaud) M.; m. Christiane Piepenbring (div.); children: Catherine, Thierry; m. Yolande Limouzin, Apr. 19, 1977; 1 child, Olivier. MS, Faculty of Scis., Strasbourg, France, 1956; grad. in Chem. Engring., Ecole Nat. Superior Chemistry, Strasbourg, France, 1956; grad. in Phys. Sci., Faculty of Scis., Strasbourg, France, 1959, DSc, 1961. Prof. U. Marseille, France, 1963-77; dean Faculty of Scis., Marseille, 1977-85; del. rsch. and tech. Region Provence Alpes Cote d'Azur, Marseille, 1985-94; del. indsl. rels. U. Marseille, 1994—; sci. advisor Cybernetix, Marseille, 1994—. Author: Gmelin Series-Gallium, 1993. Served to comdr. French Air Force. Mem. Conf. European Mycology Mediterranean (pres.). Avocations: fishing, mycology, gliding. Home: Traverse des Marronniers, Marseille 13012, France Office: Faculty de Scis, Rue Normandie-Niemen, 13397 Marseille Cedex 20, France

MAIRE, THIERRY, theologian, educator; b. Payerne, Vaud, Switzerland, Apr. 11, 1963; s. Philippe and Ginette (Kraft) M.; m. Myriam Nydegger, Aug. 7, 1993. Master's degree, Lausanne (Switzerland) U., 1987, bib. theology spec. postgrad. diploma, 1992; pedagogical diploma, Sém. Pédagogique Sec., Lausanne, 1993. Asst. Lausanne U., 1989-91; tchr. Ecole Normale, Lausanne, 1991-96, computer dept. mgr., 1996—; collaborator Séminaire Culture Théologique, Lausanne, 1990-92. Author: (book) Ainsi Parle La Sagesse, 1992, (software) Lexique HIB (Biblical History), 1995; contbr. articles to profl. jours. Mem. Soc. Suisse Etude Proche-Orient ancien, Computer and Theology Soc., Assn. Française Bible-informatique et multimedia. Mem. Evangel. Reformed Ch. Avocations: video production, shareware programming, cinema. Office: Ecole Normale de Lausanne, Av de Cour 33, CH-1007 Lausanne Switzerland

MAISIN, JEAN RENÉ SIMON, medical researcher, educator; b. Leuven, Belgium, May 25, 1928; m. Claudine Derrider, Sept. 18, 1958; 3 children. MD, Cath. U. Louvain, 1954, dipl. Electro-Radiology, 1958, specialist in Pathology, 1959. Head radiobiology dept. CEN/SCK, Mol, Belgium, 1960-87; lectr., prof. Cath. U. Louvain, 1973-93, prof. emeritus, 1993—; spkr. in field. Contbr. over 300 articles to sci. publs. Sec.-gen. European Late Effects Project Group, 1970-85, chmn. 1985-95, hon. mem., 1996—; mem. governing bd., v.p. Internat. Coun. Lab. Animal Sci., 1991, acting chmn., 1994-95, chmn. 1995-99, hon. mem., 1999—; rep. UN Sci. Com. on Effects Atomic Radiation, 1985—, pres. sessions, 1991-92; chmn. European Soc. Radiation Biology, 1986-88, hon. chmn., 1996—. Decorated gt. officer Order of Crown, comdr. Order of Leopold II, and officer Order of Leopold, Hanns-Langendorff Medaille, 1994; recipient Bacq and Alexander award, 1997. Mem. European Soc. Lab. Animal Sci. (mem. governing bd.) European Assn. Late Effects (chmn. 1983-95), Internat. Assn. Late Effects., Belgian Soc. Lab. Animal Sci. (former sec. and chmn.), Belgian Soc. Radiation Biology (former chmn.). Roman Catholic. Home: Ave du Manoir 55, B-1410 Waterloo Belgium Office: Unite Radiobiol Radioprotec, 54 Ave Hippocrate, B-1200 Brussels Belgium

MAÏSTERRENA, BERNARD, biochemist, researcher, educator; b. Lyon, France, June 6, 1948; s. Jules and Camille (Siredey) M.; m. Christiane Claron, July 22, 1972; children: Carine, Thierry. BS, UCB Lyon I, 1971, Dr. in Chemistry, 1974, PhD, 1989. Tchr. high sch. Lyon, 1975-85; asst. prof. U. Lyon I, 1986-93, prof. biochemistry, 1993—, head biol. dept. IUTA, 1990-95, dir. Applied Biochemistry Lab., 1995—. Contbr. articles to profl. jours.; patentee in field. With French Army, 1974-75. Mem. AAAS, N.Y. Acad. Scis., ACS. Roman Catholic. Avocations: salmon fishing, music. Office: UCB Lyon I, Lab Biochem Appl IUTA, 69622 Villeurbanne France

MAITI, CHINMAY KUMAR, electrical engineering educator; b. Contai, W. Bengal, India, Aug. 8, 1949; s. Rakhal Chandra and Santi Lata (Bakshi) M.; m. Bhaswati Das, July 26, 1962; children: Ananda, Anindya. B Tech, Calcutta U., 1972, M Tech., 1974; MSc, Loughborough U., U.K., 1976; PhD, Indian Inst. Tech., India, 1984. Sr. rsch. asst. Indian Inst. Technology, 1976-80, lectr., 1980-83; cons. Haris 'Al Afaq, United Arab Emirates, 1983-84; asst. prof. Indian Inst. Tech., 1984-90, assoc. prof., 1990-99, prof., 1999—. Contbg. author: (book) Ferrite Materials: Science and Technology, 1990. Recipient Internat. Scientific Collaboration award European Union, Brussels, 1995, Acad. Vis. award Queen's U., Belfast, U.K., 1995-98. Mem. IEEE (sr., chmn. Kharagpur sect. 1992). Avocation: stamp collecting. Office: Indian Inst Tech, Dep Electronics, 721302 Kharagpur India

MAITI, MOTILAL, biophysicist, researcher; b. Midnapur, India, Sept. 11, 1944; s. Raikishore and Kadmbini (Datta) M.; m. Swapna Baguli, Mar. 4, 1971; children: Sharmistha, Sharmila, Sirshendu. BSc with honors, Calcutta U., 1965, MSc, 1967, PhD in Biophysics, 1972. Sr. scientific officer Sch. Tropical Medicine, Calcutta, 1972-74; scientist B Indian Inst. Chem. Biology, Calcutta, 1974-79, scientist C, 1979-85, scientist EI, 1985-88, scientist EII, 1988-93, scientist F, 1993—. Fellow West Bengal Acad. Sci. & Tech., 1994. Mem. Internat. Union Pure & Applied Biophysics, Indian Biophys. Soc. (convener Calcultta chpt. 1991—, treas., 1992—). Avocations: writing scientific articles, reading novels, playing cards. Office: Indian Inst Chem Biol, 4 Raja SC Mullick Rd, Calcutta 700 032, India

MAITI, RATIKANTA, botanist, research scientist; b. Midnapore, W. Bengal, India, Aug. 1, 1938; arrived in Mex., 1992; s. Girish and Josodha Maiti; m. Sila Bera, Jan. 5, 1963; children: Sandip, Madhumita, Sanjay. BSc with honors, Calcutta U., 1960, MSc in Botany, 1962, PhD, 1968, DSc, 1974. Rsch. scholar Calcutta U., 1963-65; botanist Jute Agrl. Rsch. Inst., 1965-75; crop physiologist Internat. Crops Icrisat Rsch. Inst., 1975-85; prof. agronomy U. Autonoma de Nuevo Leon, 1985-86, prof. botany, 1986-98; prof. rsch. sci. Univ. De Las Americas, Puebla, Mexico, 2000—; vis. scientist Icrisat, India, 1975-85; project evaluator Connacyt, Mex., 1992-96; mem. evaluation com. Fulbrights Awards, Mex., 1994; pres. ann. meeting Econ. Botany, Mex., 1994. Author of 12 books, including Fibras Vegetales del Mundo, 1995, Sorghum Science, 1996, Pearl Millet Science, 1997, Bean Science, 1997, World Fibre Crops, 1997, Maize Science, 1998, Adventure, Homeland and Abroad: One Autobiography, 2000; contbr. more than 180 articles to profl. jours. Recipient Best Nat. Sci. award U. Autonoma de Nuevo Leon, 1992, rsch. award, 1993, Sr. Nat. Rsch. Scientist award Nat. Rsch. Com., 1988-2000. Home: Ave del Mueseo 1118, CP 66430 Monterrey Nuevo Leon, Mexico

MAITLAND, GEOFFREY DOUGLAS, manipulative physiotherapist, consultant, educator, author; b. Adelaide, Australia, Aug. 27, 1924; s. Douglas Bertram and Laurel Gladys (Wait) M.; m. Elizabeth Ann Bird Thacker, Oct. 2, 1945; children: John Douglas, Wendy Anne. Assoc., U. Adelaide, 1949; M in Applied Sci., South Australian Inst. Tech., 1986. Mem. physiotherapy dept. Royal Adelaide Hosp., 1950-52; with Adelaide Children's Hosp., 1951; clin. tutor physiotherapy U. Adelaide, 1952; pvt. practice, 1952-98; convenor 2 physiotherapy congresses for Australian physiotherapy assns.; internat. lectr.; cons. in field; part-time sr. lectr. and clin. tutor for grad. diploma in advanced manipulative therapy Sch. of Physiotherapy, U. South Australia, Adelaide. Author: Vertebral Manipulation, 6 edits., 1964-2000, Peripheral Manipulation, 3 edits., 1973—, Examination and Recording Guide, 6 edits.; co-author: Practical Orthopedic Medicine, 1983, Musculoskeletal and Sports Injuries, 1994, Vertebral Neuro-Musculoskeletal Disorders, 1998; pub. 14 video tapes of Maitland Concept, 2000. Server Anglican Ch. of Australia, Plympton, 1956, server and coun., 1959, server and sidesman, lay asst., Glen Osmond, 1965. Served with Royal Australian Air Force, 1942-45; mem. Australian Examining Coun. Overseas Physiotherapy Immigration Dept., 1982-86; mem. South Australian Registration Bd., 1960-82; hon. pres. Internat. Maitland Tchrs. Assn., Switzerland, 1978—. Awarded Most Excellent Order by the Brit. Empire; recipient award for internat. leadership in phys. therapy World Confedn. Phys. Therapy, 1995. Fellow Australian Coll. Physiotherapists, Australian Coll. Manipulative Physiotherapists (hon.), Chartered Soc. Physiotherapy (Eng.) (fellowship); mem. Australian Physiotherapy Assn. (South Australia br. com. 1950-78, hon. sec. 1955-59, pres. 1959-78, fed. del. 1956-68, founding mem. coll. 1957—), Am. Phys. Therapy Assn. (hon. life, Mildred Elson award), South African Soc. Physiotherapists (hon. life, manipulative study group), Schwericher Verband für Manipulative Physiotherapie (hon. life), World Fedn. for Phys. Therapy, Nederlandse Vereniging Manipulatieve Therapie, Deutscher Verband Manuelle Therapie, South Australian Cricket Assn. Avocations: tennis, golf, writing, art work, reading. Home and Office: Maitland GMI, 7 Warburton Ct, Beaumont 5066, Australia

MAITLAND, GUY EDISON CLAY, lawyer; b. London, Dec. 28, 1942; (mother Am. citizen); s. Paul and Virginia Francesca (Carver) M. BA,

Columbia U., 1964; JD, N.Y. Law Sch., 1968. Bar: N.Y. 1969, U.S. Dist. Ct. (so. and ea. dists.) N.Y. 1969, U.S. Ct. Appeals (2d and D.C. cirs.) 1969. Assoc. Burlingham, Underwood & Lord, N.Y.C., 1969-74; admiralty counsel Union Carbide Corp., N.Y.C., 1974-76; exec. v.p., gen. counsel, dir. Liberian Svcs., Inc., N.Y.C. and Reston, Va., 1976-89, pres., 1990—; del. UN Conf. on Trade and Devel., Manila, 1979, Belgrade, 1983; participant London Conf. on Limitation of Maritime Liability, 1976; mem. legal com. Internat. Maritime Orgn. (UN) London, 1980—; del. UN Conf. on Law of the Sea, 1976-82, London UN Maritime Law Conf., 1984; co-founder The Admiralty-Fin. Forum, N.Y.C., 1986; exec. v.p. Internat. Registries, Inc. Contbr. articles on maritime law, U.S. shipping policy. Del. Rep. Nat. Conv., Kansas City, 1976; sec. N.Y. Rep. County Com., 1976-87, vice chmn., 1988—; co-chmn. Citizens for Reagan, N.Y. State, 1979-80; trustee Am. Mcht. Mariine Mus. Found. at U.S. Mcht. Marine Acad., King's Point, Nat. Maritime Hist. Soc., N.Y. Maritime Coll. at Ft. Schuyler Found., Inc.; bd. dirs. Coast Guard Found.; del. Un Geneva Conf. on Arrest of Vessels, 1999; mem. Ctr. for Seafarers Rights; mem. adv. com. Am. Maritime History Project. Named Outstanding Young Man of Am. U.S. Jaycees, 1975; hon. del Rep. Nat. Conv., Dallas, 1984. Mem. ABA, Assn. of Bar of City of N.Y. (chmn. admiralty com. 1982-85), Maritime Law Assn. U.S. (chmn. com. on intergovtl. orgns. 1987-95), Ctr. for Seafarer's Rights Seamen's Ch. Inst. (bd. dirs. 1995—), Maritime Assn. Port of N.Y. (dir. 1984-87, 98—). Office: Internat Registries Inc Exec Vice Pres 12 E 49th St New York NY 10017-1028

MAITRA, ARINDAM, molecular biologist; b. Calcutta, Dec. 7, 1970; s. Arunabha and Sudarshana Maitra. BS, Presidency Coll., West Bengal, India, 1991; MS, U. Calcutta, 1993; PhD, All India Inst. Med. Scis., New Delhi, 1999. Rsch. fellow All India Inst. Med. Scis., New Delhi, 1994-99; field application specialist applied biosystems LABINDIA Instruments Pvt. Ltd., New Delhi, 1999—. Contbr. articles to profl. jours. Coun. Sci. and Indsl. Rsch. fellow, 1993, Fgn. Travel grantee, 1999. Avocations: molecular biology, genetics, reading. Home: 605 Asia House Gandhi Marg, New Delhi 110001, India Office: LABINDIA Instruments Ltd A8, Qutub Instnl Area Vaitalik, USO Rd New Delhi 110067, India

MAITRA, PRADEEP, electronics company executive; b. Nov. 27, 1947; s. Sudhansu Sobhan and Hena (Sanyal) M.; m. Anita Mukharji, Jan. 15, 1974; children: Smita, Sushmit. B. Tech., Indian Inst. Tech., Delhi, 1969; MS, U. Calif., Berkeley, 1970. Devel. engr. Gulf Energy and Environ. systems, San Diego, 1971-73; v.p. engring. Continental Device India Ltd., New Delhi, 1973—. Patentee electronic devices. Recipient silver medal Indian Inst. Tech., 1969. Mem. IEEE, IMAPS, Electronic Component Industries Assn. Hindu. Avocations: reading. Home: D-39 Sujan Singh Park, All/12 Vasant Vihar, New Delhi 110057, India Office: Continental Device India Ltd, C-120 Naraina Indsl Area, New Delhi 110028, India

MAITZ, MANFRED FRANZ, physician, researcher; b. Munich, Germany, July 6, 1968; s. Franz and Anita (Scherer) M. MD, Univ. Würzburg, Germany, 1994. Acad. freelance dept. history of medicine Univ. Würzburg, 1991—, rsch. fellow, 1995—; fellow European Project Umwelt-Campus, Birkenfeld, Germany, 1996-99, TNO Inst. Indsl. Tech., Eindhoven, The Netherlands, 1996—. Fellow Würzburger medizinhistorische Gesellschaft; mem. AAAS, N.Y. Acad. Scis., Soc. Biomaterials. Roman Catholic. Home: Föhrenstr 123, W 83052 Bruckmühl Germany Office: Forschungszentr Rossendorf, Ionenstrahlphysik, D-01314 Dresden Germany

MAITZ, PETER KARL-MARIA, surgeon; b. Vienna, Austria, Sept. 6, 1963; s. Peter Karl and Renate (Isper) M. MD, U. Vienna, Austria, 1991. Resident U. Vienna, Austria, 1994-97; rsch. fellow Harvard U., Boston, 1992-94, MIT, Cambridge, 1993-94, Macquarie U., Sydney, Australia, 1997-98, U. Vienna, 1998-99; dir. burns unit Sydney U. Concord Hosp., 1999—. Contbr. articles to profl. jours. Mem. Austrian Nat. Ski Team, 1987-91. Rsch. grantee Brigham Surg. Group, Boston, 1992; grantee Schroedinger Found., Austria, 1997-98, Microsearch Found. Australia, 1998, grantee, Ministry of Sci., 1993, Univ. of Vienna, 1997, Austrian Soc. of Surg., 1997. Mem. Austrian Soc. Plastic Surgery, Austrian Soc. Surgery, Internat. Microsurg. Soc., Austrian Soc. Surgical Rsch., NY Acad. Scis., German Speaking Soc. of Microsurgery, Australian & New Zealand Burn Assn., Internat. Soc. Burn Injuries. Home: 2/6 Loftus Rd Darling Point, Sydney 2027 NSW, Australia Office: U Sydney Concord Hosp, Hosp Rd Concord Burns Unit, Sydney NSW 2139, Australia

MAIWA, HIROSHI, engineering educator; b. Nyuzen, Toyama, Japan, July 20, 1964; s. Toshiko and Ryouji (Okuda) M.; m. Tomoko Shimidzu, Oct. 13, 1991; children: Tetsushi, Kouko. B in Engring., Waseda U., Tokyo, 1987, M in Engring., 1989, DEng, 1995. Rsch. assoc. Shonan Inst. Tech., Fujisawa, Japan, 1989-96, asst. prof., 1996—. Author, editor: All About Ceramics, 1996; contbr. articles to profl. jours. Kanagawa Acad. Sci. and Tech. Found. grantee, 1993, Murata Sci. Found., 1994, Ministry of Edn., Sci. and Culture, 1995, 96, 97, 99, 00; vis. scholar N.C. State U., 1998-99. Mem. Japan Soc. Applied Physics, Ceramin Soc. Japan. Avocations: tennis, skiing, piano. Home: 3-12-5 Katasekaigan, Kanagawa Fujisawa 251-0035, Japan Office: Shonan Inst Tech, 1-1-25 Tsujidou-Nishikaigan, Kanagawa Fujisawa 251-8511, Japan

MAJAMAA, TERO PENTTI UOLEVI, laboratory engineer, research secretary; b. Jamijarvi, Finland, Dec. 8, 1967; s. Pentti Erland and Anja Kyllikki (Rajala) M. MSc, U. Tech., Espoo, 1994; lic. in tech., Helsinki U. Tech., 1996. Rsch. asst. Electron Physics Lab. Helsinki U. Tech., Espoo, 1990-94, rsch. scientist, 1994—, lab. mgr., 1997—, student advisor dept. elec. and comms. engring., 1994-97, program mgr. nat. rsch. program, 1998—; sci. sec. Acad. Finland, 1998—; spkr. conf. presentation 3d Internat. Conf. on Atomically Controlled Interfaces and Surfaces, 1996, 17th Nordic Semiconductor Meeting, 1996, 18th Nordic Semiconductor Meeting, 1998, 9th Internat. Conf. on Solid Films and Surfaces, 1998; mem. strategy group eu info. soc. tech. Contbr. articles to profl. jours. including Applied Surface Sci. and Physica Scripta. 2d lt. Finnish Army, 1986-87. Grantee Helsinki U. Tech., 1996. Mem. Finnish Phys. Soc., European Phys. Soc. Office: Acad Finland, Vilhovuorenkatu 6 PO Box 99, FIN-00501 Helsinki Finland

MAJANI, BERNARD PAUL, communications company executive; b. Paris, Nov. 24, 1952; s. Dominique and Denyoe (d'Inguimbert) M.; m. Sophie Tabakoff, Dec. 31, 1990; children: Manon, Margaux. DEA in Polit. Sci., U. Paris, 1977; MS in Econ., U. Pantheon, Paris, 1977. Ind. film broker Paris, 1978-79; sales exec. Patné Cinéma, Paris, 1980-84; owner Long Island Intenrat., Paris, 1985-93; dir. MG Droits Audiovisuels, Paris, 1993—; gen. mgr. T.C.M., Paris, 1996—; bd. dirs. T.V.F.I., Paris. Mcpl. councillor St.-Antonin, France, 1995—. Lt. French armed forces res., 1975. Avocations: hunting, fishing, jogging, skiing. Office: M6 DA, 89 Ave Charles de Gaulle, 92575 Neuilly Sur Seine France

MAJDALI, KAMEEL AMEEN, college principal, minister; b. Los Angeles, Oct. 5, 1954; arrived in Australia, 1987; s. Frank and Louise (Haddad) M.; m. Leanne Vicky Sayle, Apr. 25, 1980; children: Haifa, Ania. BA, Evergreen State Coll., Olympia, Wash., 1975; MA, Inst. Holy Land Studies, Jerusalem, 1979; PhD, U. Melbourne, Australia, 1997. Cert. polit. scientist; ordained to ministry Assemblies of God Australia. Headmaster Shiloh Christian Sch., Ft. Wayne, Ind., 1983-84; missionary evangelist Europe, Africa, Australia, 1984-86; assoc. pastor Westside Christian Ctr., Melbourne, Australia, 1987—; acad. dean Harvest Bible Coll., Melbourne, Australia, 1990-95, prin., 1995—; tour dir. Land of the Bible Tours, Middle East, China, 1995; chmn. Pentecostal & Charismatic Bible Colls. Australasia; bd. dirs. Flinders Christian C.C. Author: Salt: Biblical Integrity Today, 2000; author (world trends column) Evangel Now and Alive Mag., 1993—; contbr. articles to profl. jours.; lectr., designer in field. Mem. Australians for Constl. Monarchy, 1994—. Named Boys' State Rep., Vancover, Wash., 1971; Schauer Meml. scholar, Vancover, Wash., 1972. Mem. Asia Pacific Theol. Assn. (accreditation commr., exec. bd. dirs.). Mem. Assemblies of God Ch. Avocations: reading, bicycling, cooking. Office: Harvest Bible Coll, PO Box 7, Mulgrave East VIC 3170, Australia

MAJEED, GULNAZ SYED, gynecologist; b. Karachi, Pakistan, Sept. 4, 1962; arrived in Eng., 1995; d. Syed Shah Mohammed Abul and Akbari-Un-Nisa (Hakim) M. BSc, Punjab U., Pakistan, 1983; MB, BChir, King Edward Med. Coll., Pakistan, 1987; test of profl. knowledge and proficiency, Gen. Med. Coun., Eng., 1989; diploma in anesthetics, Royal Coll. Anesthetists, Eng., 1991. With Rawalpindi Gen. Hosp., Pakistan, 1987-88, Crowley Hosp., Eng., 1990-92; sr. ho. officer in ob-gyn. Farnborough Hosp., Eng., 1992-93; specialist registrar in ob-gyn. Maidstone Hosp., Eng., 1994, All Saints Hosp., Eng., 1995; clin. rsch. fellow U. Bristol., Eng., 1996-98. Fellow Royal Coll. Surgeons (U.K.); mem. Royal Coll. Ob-Gyn., Royal Coll. Physicians (Ireland). Avocations: reading, cinema, aerobics. E-mail: gmajeed@hotmail.com. Address: Maidstone Hosp Dept Ob-gyn, Hermitage Lang, Maidstone Kent ME16 9QQ, England

MAJEED-SAIDAN, MUHAMMAD ALI, pediatrician; b. Baghdad, July 1, 1944; s. Majeed and Aylia (Sultan) Saidan; m. Fawziyah Abdullah Al-Tassan, Oct. 3, 1988; children: Abdullah, Ahmed, Maryam. MbChB, Baghdad Med. Sch., 1969, DCH, 1975. Resident, sr. resident Med. City Teaching Hosp., Baghdad, 1971-75; cons. pediatrician Diwaniyah (Iraq) Hosp., 1976-77; registrar in pediatrics various hosps., London, 1978-83; sr. registrar, locum cons. various hosps., 1983-85; sr. registrar in pediatrics Riyadh (Saudi Arabia) Armed Forces Hosp., 1985-87, cons. pediatrician, cons. neonatologist, 1988—. Contbr. articles to profl. jours. and chpts. to books. Med. officer Iraqi Army, 1970-71. Muslim. Avocations: Arabic literature, photography, sports. Office: Riyadh Armed Forces Hosp, W932 PO Box 7897, Riyadh 11159, Saudi Arabia

MAJER, JOZSEF MIHALY, ecologist, educator; b. Martonvasar, Hungary, Apr. 15, 1944; s. Jozsef and Jozsefne (Horvath Borbala) M.; m. Margit Bordacs, Aug. 13, 1968; 3 children. PhD, Sci. Acad. Hungary, 1988; Dr. hab., Janus Pannonius U., 1994. Secondary sch. tchr. Simontornya, Hungary, 1968-75; jr. lectr. Coll. Pécs, Hungary, 1975-82; sr. lectr. U. Pécs, 1982-88; asst. prof. JP U., Pécs, 1988-94, prof., 1994—; prof. zoology U. Pécs, 1978-82; chief ecology group JP U., 1982-92, head ecology dept., 1992—. Author: Rhagionidae-Athericidae, 1977, Tabanidae, 1987, How Do the Animals Behave, 1982, Introduction into Ecology, 1995. Pres. Nature Conservation Orgn., Baranya, Hungary, 1972—. mem. Hungarian Acad. Sci. (zool. com. 1988—, ecol. com. 1992—), Pannonian Ecologists Club (pres. 1992—). Avocations: birdwatching, gardening, nature photography, nature. Office: JPTE TTK Ecology Dept, U Pecs Ecology Dept, Ifjusag u 6, 7601 Pécs Hungary

MAJER, VLADIMIR, chemistry researcher, educator; b. Prague, Czechoslavakia, Nov. 17, 1948; arrive in France, 1990; s. Vladimir and Milada (Hendl) M.; m. Françoise Vignon, Apr. 28, 1984; children: Martin, Alice. Diploma in chem. engring., Inst. Chem. Tech., Prague, 1972, PhD, 1977. Asst. tchr. Inst. Chem. Tech., 1972-77, asst. prof., 1977-86; sr. scientist U. Del., Newark, 1986-89; scientist French Nat. Ctr. Sci. Rsch., Clermont-Ferrand, 1989-95, rsch. dir., 1996—; vis. prof. Inst. Chem. Tech., 1993—; dir. lab. of solutions and polymers Blaise Pascal U., Clermont-Ferraud, France. Author: Enthalpies of Vaporization of Organic Compounds, 1985, Heats of Vaporization of Fluids, 1989, Heat Capacities of Liquids, 1996; contbr. over 70 articles to profl. jours. Mem. IUPAC, Internat. Assn. Properties Water & Steam, Calorimetry Conf. (counselor 1996—, bd. dirs. 1994—, pres. French nat. com.). Avocations: skiing, hiking, mountaineering. Home: rue des Reservoirs, 63170 Aubiere France Office: Lab Thermodynamics, Ave des Landais, 63177 Aubiere Cedex, France

MAJJI, AJIT BABU, ophthalmologist, consultant; b. Srikakulam, India, July 8, 1962; s. Laxman Rao and Kannamma (Dumpala) M.; m. Shahikala Devi Dumpala, May 17, 1987; children: Swetha, Arpitha, Siva Teja. MBBS, Andhra Med. Coll., Visakhapatnam, India, 1985; MD in Ophthalmology, A.I.I.M.S., New Delhi, 1990. Diplomate Nat. Bd. Ophthalmology, 1991. Ho. surgeon Andhra Med. Coll., 1985-86; jr. resident All India Inst. Med. Scis., 1988-90, sr. resident, 1991-93; cons. L.V. Prasad Eye Inst., Hyderabad, India, 1993—, jr. ophthalmologist, 1993-95, asst. ophthalmologist, 1995—; rsch. fellow Wilmer Eye Inst., Johns Hopkins U., Balt., 1997-98. Contbr. 7 chpts. to textbook; contbr. articles to profl. jours. Mem. Am. Acad. Ophthalmology, Vitreous Soc. (internat.), Assn. Rsch. & Vision in Ophthalmology (internat.). Avocations: sports, music, swimming. Office: L V Prasad Eye Inst, Road No 2 Banjara Hills, Hyderabad 500 034, India

MAJOLI, IVA, tennis player; b. Zagreb, Croatia, Aug. 12, 1977. Profl. tennis player, 1993—. 7 singles titles WTA Tour, 1 singles Grand Slam titles. Avocations: ice skating, in-line skating, snow skiing, jet-skiing. Office: c/o WTA Tour 133 1st St NE Saint Petersburg FL 33701*

MAJOR, BOGUSŁAW JAN, materials science educator; b. Wieliczka, Poland, July 30, 1945; s. Franciszek and Aniela (Klimczyk) M.; m. Jolanta Maria Podlipska, Aug. 7, 1976; children: Łukasz, Roman. MS, U. Mining and Metallurgy, Cracow, Poland, 1970; PhD, Polish Acad. Scis., Cracow, Poland, 1976, DSc, 1989. Rsch. scientist Polish Acad. Scis. Inst. Metallurgy and Materials Sci., Cracow, 1970-90, assoc. prof., 1990—; sci. dir. Inst. Metallurgy and Materials Sci., 1999—. Contbr. articles to profl. jours. Scholar Danish Ministry Edn., 1983, Deutsche Akademischer Austausch, 1990, Republik Österreich Ministerium fur Wissenschaft und Forschung, 1993. Mem. Found. for Promoting Devel. of Materials Sci. (v.p. 1993-99). Roman Catholic. Avocations: swimming, skiing. Home: Aleksandry 25/176, 30-837 Cracow Poland Office: Polish Acad Scis Inst Metal, & Materials Sci Reymonta 25, 30-059 Cracow Poland

MAJOR, JOHN, former prime minister of United Kingdom; b. Mar. 29, 1943; s. Thomas and Gwendolyn Minny (Coates) M.; m. Norma Christina Elizabeth Johnson, 1970; 2 children. Ed., Rutlish Sch., Merton, Am. Inst. Banking. Former banker Standard Chartered Bank; various exec. posts, Eng. and fgn. countries, 1965-79; PPS to ministers state Home Office, 1981-83; asst. govt. whip, 1983-84; lord commr. Her Majesty's Treasury, 1984-85, chief sec., 1987-89; parliamentary under sec. state for social security Dept. Health and Social Security, 1985-86, minister state for social security, 1986-87; sec. state for fgn. and Commonwealth affairs, 1989; chancellor of Exchequer, 1989-90; prime minister, 1st lord of treasury, 1990-97; M.P. for Huntingdonshire, 1979-83, for Huntingdon, 1983—; chmn. European adv. coun. Emerson Electric Co.; mem. European adv. bd. The Carlyle Group; bd. advisors Baker Inst., Houston; mem. InterAction Coun., Tokyo; bd. govs. Peres Ctr. for Peace, Israel; chmn. Westminster Woodland; non-exec. dir. Mayflower Corp. plc, 2000—; mem. InterAction Coun., Tokyo, 1998—; bd. advisors Baker Inst., Houston, 1998—; chmn. European adv. coun. Emerson Elec. Co., 1999—. Mem. Lambeth Borough Coun., 1968-71, chmn. housing com., 1970-71; joint sec. environ. com. Conservative Parliamentary Party, 1979-81; parliamentary cons. Guild Glass Engravers, 1979-83; mem. bd. Warden Housing Assn., 1975-83; pres. Ea. Area Young Conservatives, 1983-85; pres. Nat. Asthma Campaign, 1998—; chmn. The Westminster Woodland, 1998—; internat. bd. govs. Peres Ctr. for Peace, Israel, 1997—. Recipient Companion of Honor, 1999. Mem. Surrey County Cricket Club (v.p., pres. 2000). Avocations: opera, cricket, football. Office: House of Commons, London SWIA OAA, England

MAJOR, ROY COLEMAN, language educator; b. Wyandotte, Mich., June 29, 1945; s. Coleman Joseph and Marjorie Lois (Shenk) M.; m. Elza Arientie de Magalhães, June 12, 1970 (div. Jan. 1993); children: Sylvia Magalhães, Alexander Christopher. BA, U. Akron, 1967; MA, U. Ariz., 1970, Ohio State U., 1976; PhD, Ohio State U., 1979. Instr. English Curso Oxford, Rio de Janeiro, 1971-73, Inst. Brasil-Estados Unidos, Rio de Janeiro, 1971-74; instr. linguistics, English Tchr.'s Tng. Course, Rio de Janeiro, 1971-74; instr. linguistics Pontifícia U. Cath., Rio de Janeiro, 1972-73; instr. English U. Gama Filho, Rio de Janeiro, 1973-74; grad. tchg. asst. Ohio State U., Columbus, 1975-79; lectr. San Diego State U., 1979-81; asst. prof. Wash. State U., Pullman, 1981-87, assoc. prof., 1987-92, dir. TESOL, 1981-92; assoc. prof. Ariz. State U., Tempe, 1992-99, prof., 1999—; dir. programs in linguistics and TESL, Ariz. State U., Tempe, 1997—; 1st acad. coord. Intensive Am. Lang. Ctr., Wash. State U., 1983-85, acting dir. undergrad. program linguistics, 1989-90; vis. assoc. prof. U. Hawaii, Honolulu, 1990; vis. assoc. prof. No. Ariz. U., Flagstaff, 1993; lectr. in field. Guest editor: Studies in Second Language Acquisition, 1998; reviewer numerous jours.; rschr. second lang. phonology Ontogeny Model, The Similarity Differential Rate Hypothesis; contbr. chpts. to books and articles to profl. jours. Doris Duke Found. grant, 1969; Fulbright Found. scholar, 1982-83; Postdoctoral fellow NIH, 1985, Travel grant Am. Coun. Learned Socs., 1990. Mem. Linguistics Soc. Am., Am. Assn. Applied Linguistics, TESOL, Ariz. TESOL. Democrat. Avocations: hiking, camping, running, concerts, plays. Office: Ariz State Univ Dept English Tempe AZ 85287-0302

MAJOR, SUZETTE, management sciences educator; b. Hamilton, New Zealand, Oct. 12, 1971. B Mgmt. Studies with Honors, U. Waikato, New Zealand, 1993, M Mgmt. Studies, 1996. Doctoral asst. U. Waikato, 1994-98, lectr., 1998—. Scholar U. Waikato, 1998; postgrad. fellow New Zealand Fedn. Univ. Women, 1997. Office: U Waikato, Pvt Bag 3105, Hamilton New Zealand

MAJORANA, CARMELO ERNESTO, engineer, researcher; b. Caltanissetta, Italy, Apr. 28, 1954; s. Emanuele Luigi and Maria Teresa (Lo Trovato) M.; m. Antonella Giulia Nicastro, Nov. 22, 1953; children: Emanuele, Alberto, Francesco. Degree in Civil Engring., U. Padua, Italy, 1978. Rschr. U. Padua, 1983—, lectr., 1992-98, assoc. prof., 1998—; cons. Astrophysics Obs. Arcetri/U. Ariz., Florence, Tucson, 1985-87, Nat. Galileo Telescope, Padua, 1993-96, Nat. Bur. Altern. Energy/Commissariat Energie Atomique, Rome and Paris, 1994-95, Padua Rsch./European Cmty., Padua, 1995-98. Contbr. articles to profl. jours. Pres. Italian Assn. Families for Def. and Ear Deafness Children, Padua, 1993-98; mem. coun. Valmarana Found., Padua, 1995-98. Grantee Dynamic of Giotto Halley Multicolor Camera, Padua, 1983-84, Dynamic of Columbus Telescope, Florence, 1985-87, Brite Euram III-High Temperature Concrete, Brussels, 1996. Mem. Internat. Union Testing and Rsch. Labs. for Materials and Structures (tech. com. 1989-92), Internat. Assn. for Bridge and Structural Engring., Italian Assn. Theoretical and Applied Mechanics, Italian Group Computational Mechanics, European Mechanics Soc. Roman Catholic. Avocations: music. E-mail: majorana@caronte.dic.unipd.it. Home: P le S Croce 20/2, 35123 Padua Italy Office: Univ Padua Faculty Engring, Via Marzolo 9, 35100 Padua Italy

MAJORKOWSKA-KNAP, KRYSTYNA, engineering educator; b. Plock, Poland, Feb. 17, 1941; d. Franciszek and Maria (Zlobecka) Majorkowski; m. Andrzej Knap; children: Małgorzata, Marek. MS in Civil Engring., Warsaw (Poland) U. Tech., 1965, PhD in Tech. Sci., 1973; DSc in Applied Mechanics, Tech. U., Poznań, Poland, 1986. Cert. civil engr. Engr., sr. engr. Bldg. Investment and Project Office, Plock, 1965-68; asst. lectr., asst. prof. Warsaw (Poland) U. Tech., 1968-87, assoc. prof., 1987-88, 89, 1991-96, prof., 1996—, assoc. dir. inst., dean for student matters, 1975-78; mem. sect. mechanics com. Polish Acad. Sci., Warsaw, 1987-89, 94—; mem. The Senate Com. for Internat. Cooperation, Warsaw U. Tech., Poland, 1987-89, 93-99; vis. prof. U. Karlsruhe, Germany, 1989; vis. scholar Mich. State U., East Lansing, 1989-90, Northwestern U., Evanston, Ill., 1990-91. Contbr. articles to profl. jours. Mem. AIAA, ASME, European Mechanics Soc., Nat. Tech. Orgn., Polish Soc. Theoretical and Applied Mechanics, Gesellschaft fur Angewandte Mathematik und Mechanik, Soc. Engring. Sci., Inc., Am. Ceramic Soc., Polish Soc. Applied Electromagnetics. Roman Catholic. Home: Al Jana Pawla II 74/12, 00-175 Warsaw Poland Office: Warsaw U Tech Fac Power and Aero Engring, Inst A&AM str Nowowiejska 24, 00-665 Warsaw Poland

MAJOROS, ISTVAN JOZSEF, chemist, researcher; b. Felsötelekes, Jan. 1, 1948; came to the U.S., 1990; s. Istvan Majoros and Istvanne (Margit) Molna'r; m. Csilla Blaskovits, June 17, 1972 (dec. July 1982); children: Istvan-Ajtony, Peter (dec. Aug. 1982); m. Timea Marsalko, Mar. 8, 1986; 1 child, David. MSChemE, Tech. U. Chemistry, Prague, Czechoslovakia, 1971; PhD in Chemistry and Chem. Engring., Kossuth L. U., Debrecen, Hungary, 1979. Dept. engr. Coll. Karincbarcika, Hungary, 1971-74; asst. prof. Kossuth L. U., Debrecen, 1974-80, assoc. prof., 1982-93; chief engr. High Fructose Corn Syrup and Alcohol Corp., Szabadegyhaza, Hungary, 1980-82; polymer scientist, vis. prof. U. Akron, Ohio, 1990-98; sr. rsch. assoc. U. Mich., Ann Arbor, 1998—; presenter in field. Co-author: Chemical Processes, 1988, Advances in Polymer Science, 1994; contbr. 64 articles to profl. jours. Mem. Am. Chem. Soc., Hungarian Chem. Engring. Soc., N.Y. Acad. Scis. Achievements include 14 patents in fiels; novel well-defined star-shaped polymer. Avocations: TV, reading, soccer, computer. Office: Univ Mich IntMed-Allergy Kresge Res II 200 Zina Pitcher Pl Ann Arbor MI 48109-2205

MAJORS, RICHARD GEORGE, psychology educator; b. Ithaca, N.Y.; s. Richard G. II and Fannie Sue Majors; legal guardian: Lillian A. McGill. AA, Auburn (N.Y.) Community Coll., 1974; BA in History, Plattsburgh State Coll., 1977; PhD in Ednl. Psychology, U. Ill., 1987. Various social svc. positions, 1976-79; probation officer, ct. investigator Plattsburgh, 1979; clin. intern McKinley Health Ctr., Urbana, Ill., 1981; rsch. asst. U. Minn., Mpls., 1981, U. Ill., Urbana, 1981-84; instr. Parkland C.C., Champaign, Ill., 1985; rsch. asst. U. Ill., Champaign, 1985-86; postdoctoral fellow U. Kans., Lawrence, 1987-89; postdoctoral fellow, clin. fellow Harvard Med. Sch., Boston, 1989-90; asst. prof. psychology U. Wis. Sys., 1990-93; sr. rsch. assoc. The Urban Inst., Washington, 1993-95; sr. fellow David Walker Rsch. Inst., Mich. State U., East Lansing, 1995—; vis. scholar Georgetown U., 1996-97; Leverhulme vis. fellow for rsch. in Eng., 1996-97; sr. fellow Manchester U., England, 1997—. Co-author: Coolpose: The Dilemmas of Black Manhood in America, 1992, The American Black Male: His Present Status and Future, 1994; founder Jour. of African Am. Men. Named one of Outstanding Young Men of Am., 1987; Canterbury fellow U. Christchurch, New Zealand, 2000. Fellow APA (predoctoral minority fellow 1984, Minority Achievement award for Rsch. in Psychology 1995); mem. Nat. Coun. African Am. Men (chmn., co-founder), Soc. for Psychol. Study of Ethnic Minority Issues, Am. Orthopsychiat. Assn., Greenpeace, Kappa Delta Pi, Phi Delta Kappa. Avocations: reading, traveling, cycling. Office: 17 Regency Wharf, Hooten Ln, Leigh, Lancashire WN7 3BF, England

MAJTA, JANUSZ, materials engineer, educator; b. Swidnica, Poland, Nov. 10, 1955; s. Franciszek and Genowefa (Turkas) M.; m. Dobroslawa Muszynska, Apr. 16, 1976; 1 child, Milosz. MSc, U. Mining and Metallurgy, Cracow, Poland, 1980; PhD, U. Mining and Metallurgy, 1991. Prodn. engr. Metal Industry, Cracow, 1980-86; lectr. U. Mining Metallurgy, Cracow, 1986-87, sr. lectr., 1987-92, assoc. prof., 1992—; vis. staff mem. Los Alamos Natl. Lab., N.Mex. Contbr. articles to Jour. Materials Processing Tech., Materials Sci. Engring. U. Waterloo fellow, 1993-94. Mem. Iron Steel Soc., Nat. Geog. Soc., Polish Assn. Metall. Engrs. Technicians, Minerals, Metals and Materials Soc., Deutsche Gesellschaft Materialkunde, European Sci. Assn. for Material Forming. Office: U Mining and Metallurgy, Al Mickiewicza 30, 30-059 Cracow Poland

MAJTENYI, CATHERINE, neuropathologist; b. Budapest, June 3, 1929; d. Victor Majtenyi and Jella Fulop; m. Kornel Lukacs, Apr. 7, 1951 (wid. 1984); children: Kornel, Adrienne. Diploma, U. Medicine, Debrecen, 1953; Cert. Neurology Bd., U. Medicine, Budapest, 1963, Cert. Psychiatry Bd., 1957, Cert. Neuropathology Bd., 1976. Medical diplomate. Psychiatrist Inst. of Psychiatry, Budapest, 1953-57; neurologist Inst. of Psychiatry and Neurology, Budapest, 1957-62, neuropathologist, 1962—, head dept. neuropathology, 1982—. Contbg. author: Gerontopsychiatry, 1992. Recipient Santha Kalman award Santha Found., Debrecen, 1991, Schaffer Karoly award Hungarian Assn. of Neurologists and Psychiatrists, Budapest, 1993. Mem. Hungarian Assn. Neuropathology (councillor 1992—), Internat. Soc. Neuropathology, Am. Assn. of Neuropathologists. Avocation: gardening. Home: Szephalom str 1, 1021 Budapest Hungary Office: Nat Inst Psychiatry/Neurol, Huvosvolgyi str 116, 1281 Budapest Hungary

MAJTENYI, STEVEN ISTVAN, civil engineer, consultant; b. Elek, Hungary, Jan. 20, 1936; came to U.S., 1962; s. Vilmos Gyorgy and Edit (Laczo) M.; m. Joan E. Zimmerman, Jan. 21, 1972; children: Vivian Claire, Juliet Eve. Student, U. Poitiers, France, 1962; MSc, Cornell U., 1965, PhD, 1969. Registered profl. engr., Va., Ohio. Tchg. and rsch. asst. Cornell U., Ithaca, N.Y., 1964-68; soils engr. TAMS, N.Y.C., 1968-71; hwy. rsch. engr. U.S. Dept. Transp./FHWA, Washington, 1971-76; hwy. engr. The World Bank, Washington, 1976-81; sr. cons. The World Bank, U.S. Dept. Transp./FHWA, Washington, 1981-95; procurement expert UN, N.Y.C., 1995-98; civil engring. cons. Gahanna, Ohio, 1998—; speaker in field. Contbr. articles to profl. jours. Josephine de Karman scholar, 1962-64. Fellow ASCE. Roman Catholic. Achievements include participation in the development of numerous technical ideas in the U.S. Government and private industry; improvement of procurement documents in numerous countries worldwide. Avocations: culinary arts, travel. Home and Office: 167 Highmeadow Dr Gahanna OH 43230-1791

MAJUMDAR, RAMANATH, biochemist, molecular biologist; b. Asansol, India, Mar. 3, 1957; arrived in Saudi Arabia, 1996.; s. Matilal and Dolly (Guha) M.; m. Radha Chanda; children: Abir, Manjari. BSc in Chemistry with honors, Calcutta U., 1976, MSc in Biochemistry, 1978, PhD in Biochemistry, 1986. Postdoctoral fellow U. Alta., Edmonton, 1986-90, lectr., 1990-91, asst. prof., 1992-96; rsch. scientist King Fahad Nat. Guard Hosp., Riyadh, Saudi Arabia, 1996—; lab. dir. U. Alta., Edmonton, 1992-96, Neurogenetics Lab.-King Fahad Nat. Guard Hosp., Riyadh, 1996—. Contbr. articles to profl. jours. Alberta Heritage Found. for Med. Rsch. Postdoctoral fellow U. Alta., Edmonton, 1986-90. Mem. AAAS, Am. Soc. for Biochemistry and Molecular Biology, Am. Soc. Human Genetics, Can. Soc. for Biochemistry and Molecular Biology. Avocation: traveling. Office: King Fahad Nat Guard Hosp, PO Box 22490, Riyadh 11426, Saudi Arabia

MAJUMDER, PARIMAL, researcher; b. Comilla, Bangladesh; s. Harendra Kumar and Shandana (Prova) M.; m. Dimple Rani Bosu, Nov. 26, 1996; 1 child, Rusha Yuki. BS with honours, Dhaka (Bangladesh) U., 1992, MS, 1995; M of Agr., Shinshu U., Ueda, Nagano, Japan, 1998. Rschr. dept. applied biology Sinshu U., Tokida, Ueda, Nagano, Japan. Hindu. Avocation: chess. E-mail: parimal@bs.shinshu-u.ac.jp. Office: Sinshu U Dept Appl Biology, Tokida 3-15-1, Ueda, Nagano 386-8567, Japan

MAJUMDER, SABIR AHMED, process engineer; b. Chandpur, Bangladesh, July 15, 1957; came to U.S., 1986; s. Quashem Majumder and Momtaz Begum; m. Hamida Khanam, Dec. 15, 1985; children: Faryha, Nabilah, Abir. BS in Chemistry with honors, U. Dhaka, Bangladesh, 1981, MS, 1983; MS, Duquesne U., 1988; PhD, U. N.Mex., 1994. Corr. The Daily Janapad, Dhaka, Bangladesh, 1973-74; rsch. fellow U. Dhaka, 1983-84, lectr. in Chemistry, 1984-86; teaching asst. Duquesne U., Pitts., 1986-88, U. N.Mex., Albuquerque, 1988-90; Assoc. Western Univs. grad. lab. fellow Sandia Nat. Labs., Albuquerque, 1991-93, postdoctoral fellow, 1994-96; postdoctoral fellow U. Minn., Mpls., 1997-98; sr. process engr. Aplex Inc., Sunnyvale, Calif., 1998—; rsch. scientist Strasbaugh, San Luis Obispo, Calif., 1999—; sr. process engr. Lam Rsch. Corp., Fremont, Calif., 2000. Contbr. articles to profl. jours. Gen. Sec. Bangladesh Youth Coun., Dhaka, 1982; mem. Nat. Student League Ctrl., Dhaka, 1983. Trainee Youth Leadership Tng. Inst., Singapore, 1981; recipient Link Energy Fellowship Link Found., Rochester, N.Y., 1987. Mem. Am. Chem. Soc., Bangladesh Chem. and Biol. Soc. N.Am. (elected gen. sec. 1993-94, pres. 1997-98, advisor 1999—), Electrochem. Soc. Democrat. Muslim. Achievements include patent disclosure: photocatalytic degradation of aromatic compounds by metalloporhyrins adsorbed into alumina using visible light. Home: 342 Washington Blvd Fremont CA 94539-5215 Office: Aplex Inc 830 Stewart Dr Sunnyvale CA 94085-4513

MAK, KAN HING, orthopedist; b. Kwangchow, Kwangtung, China, Aug. 2, 1951; s. Cheung Wai Mak and Yiu Tai Lee; m. Pansy Yee Ping Tsang, May 18, 1980; children: Hayley, Hester, Herrick. MBBS, U. Hong Kong, 1976. Cons. United Christian Hosp., Hong Kong, 1985-88; chief svc. Kwong Wah Hosp., Hong Kong, 1988—; chmn. Doctors Assn., Hong Kong, 1987. Contbr. articles to profl. jours. Mem. HKSSH, HKCOS. Avocations: swimming, reading. Office: Dept Ortho & Traumatology, Kwong Wah Hosp, Kowloon Hong Kong

MAK, KEN PING, brokerage executive; b. Stamford, Conn., June 20, 1972; s. Ty Tse-Fai and Susan Pui-San Mak. AB, Brown U., 1994; MBA, Columbia U., 1999. Fin. analyst Kidder, Peabody & Co., N.Y.C., 1994; sr. analyst TD Securities (USA) Inc., N.Y.C., 1995-97; equity rsch. analyst Putnam Investments, Boston, 1998; v.p. product devel. DLJ Direct, Inc., Jersey City, 1999—. Avocations: reading, investing, cooking, playing tennis, traveling. E-mail: kenpmak@hotmail.com. Home: 310 Riverside Dr Apt 1101 New York NY 10025-4124 Office: DLJ Direct Inc Harborside Fin Ctr 501 Plaza II Jersey City NJ 07311

MAKABE, TOSHIAKI, physical electronics educator; b. Yamato, Kanagawa, Japan, May 8, 1947; s. Rihichi and Teru Makabe; m. Shigeko Nakazato, Jan. 1977; children: Hideaki, Akira. B in Plasma Physics, Keio U., Yokohama, Japan, 1970, PhD, 1975. Instr. Keio U., Yokohama, 1975-80, lectr., 1980-84, assoc. prof., 1984-91, prof., 1991—, head dept., 1996—; exec. com. Gaseous Electronics Conf., Am. Phys. Soc., N.Y., 1993-95. Author: Gaseous Electronics and its Applications, 1991, Plasma Electronics, 1999; editor Japanese Jour. Applied Physics, 1992-97, Plasma Processing (Japan), 1993, 97, 99, Gaseous Electronics (Austria), 1997, Basic Aspects of Non Equilibrium Plasma Interacting with Surfaces, 1998, JVST, Low Tem. Plasma Modelling (IEEE), 1999. Mem. Japanese Soc. Applied Physics (sec. gen. plasma electronics 1993-95, divsn. rep. 1998-2000). Office: Keio Univ, 3-14-1 Hiyoshi, Yokohama Kanagawa 223-8522, Japan

MAKADOK, STANLEY, management consultant; b. N.Y.C., Mar. 30, 1941; s. Jack and Pauline (Speciner) M.; BME, CCNY, 1962; MS in Mgmt. Sci., Rutgers U., 1964; m. Neilia A. David, Nov. 12, 1989; 1 child from previous marriage, Richard. Bus. systems analyst Westinghouse Electric Corp., Balt., 1964-65; project engr., corp. cons. Am. Cyanamid Corp., Pearl River, N.Y., Wayne, N.J., 1965-68; v.p., bus. devel. and planning Pepsico Inc. and affiliates, Purchase, N.Y., Miami, Fla., 1968-75; mgr. fin. and planning cons. Coopers & Lybrand, N.Y.C., 1975-77; pres. Century Mgmt. Cons., Inc., Princeton, N.J., 1977—. Contbr. articles to profl. jours. Office: Century Mgmt Cons Inc 32 Nassau St Princeton NJ 08542-4503

MAKAMORI, YOSHHIKO, dean, law educator. Dean grad. sch. law, faculty law Kyoto U., Japan. Office: Kyoto U, Yoshida-Hanmachi, Kyoto 606-8501, Japan*

MAKAREM, ESSAM FAYEZ, manufacturing company executive; b. Lagos, Nigeria, Aug. 20, 1936; s. Fayez Mahmoud and Jamal Mohammed Makarem; m. Ghada Mahmoud Aawar; children: Hitaf, Wael, Joumana, Nader, May, Ussama. Diploma in English and Arabic, Nat. Coll., Aley, Lebanon, 1953; BSBA, U. Beverly Hills, 1989; D in Bus. Adminstrn. (hon.), Internat. U. Found., 1989. Dir., gen. mgr. Faiz Moukarim & Sons Ltd., Majia and Kano, Nigeria, 1954-91; also dir., mng. dir. Moukarim Metalwood Factory Ltd., Kano, Ikeja, Katsina, Maidugri and Jos, Nigeria, 1959-91; bd. dirs. Borno Engring. and Steel Mfrs. Ltd., Nigeria Gas Industries Ltd., Moukarim Bros. Ltd.; chmn. Mouka Ltd., Ikeja, Nigeria, 1993—; chmn., gen. mgr. Mada Holding S.A.L., Beirut, DAR Altijara S.A.L., Beirut, 1992—; dir Mgmt. and Fin. Internat. Ltd., Beirut, United Devel. Corp. (Holding) S.A.L., Beirut, Dar Al Kalimah S.A.R.L., Majia Co. S.A.R.L., Beirut, Faiz Holding S.A.L., Beirut. Chmn. Nat. Hosp. Healthcare EST, S.A.L., Aley, Lebanon; founder, shareholder Solidere S.A.L., Beirut, 1994; chmn. and CEO Berytus Parks S.A.L., Beirut, 1998—; pres. Nat. Coun. Nigeria, World Lebanese Cultural Union, 1972-73, v.p. world coun., 1976-83; sec. gen. Druze Found. for Soc. Welfare, Beirut, 1983-91, 93—; pres., founder Kamal Jumblatt Soc. Found., Beirut, 1981-92; trustee, bd. mem. Sheik Muhammed Abu Shakra Hosp. and Aged Home, The Health Establishment of Druze Cmty., Ain Wazein Al Shouf, Lebanon, 1981—; trustee, bd. mem. Iman Hosp., Aley, Lebanon, 1999—; trustee, founder, pres. Jabal Hosp., Falouga, Lebanon, 1982-92; bd. dirs. Lebanese Econ. Forum; trustee Directorate of Druze Endowments, 1999—; activemem. St. Jude Children's Rsch. Hosp., Beirut, 2000—. Decorated commandeur de l'Ordere du Merit, Societe Francaise d'Encouragement; recipient Nat. medal Lebanese Child Welfare Found., 1985, Albert Einstein medal, 1990. Mem. C. of C. and Industry of Kano, Nigeria Assn. Steel Tube Mfrs. (chmn. 1979-80), Assn. Foam Mfrs., Safa Sporting Club Beirut, Social Work League (Druze Graduates), Beirut, Kano Lebanon Club (pres. 1973-76), Assn. Makarem Family, Ras El Metn Lebanon (pres. 1992—), Odd Fellows, Rotary (pres. Kano, Nigeria club 1971-72, founder, mem. Aley club 1997), Alkhaa Alahley Sporting Club, Masons. Avocations: reading, theater, cinema. Home: Ramlat AlBaida Rafic Hariri Blvd, Ali Arab Bldg PO Box 145336, Beirut Lebanon Office: La Mode Bldg PO Box 145336, Berlin St, Off Shouran, Beirut Lebanon

MAKARENKO, VICTOR, philosopher, political scientist, educator; b. Polonnoje, Ukraine, Apr. 1, 1944; s. Pavel Makarenko and Sophia Kozyr; m. Tatiana Marchenko, Mar. 26, 1994; children: Nadezhda, Sophia. PhD, Rostov (Russia) U., 1979; PhD habilitation, Inst. Philosophy Acad. Scis., Moscow, 1988; D in Polit. Scis. habilitation, St. Petersburg (Russia) U., 1996; DSc (hon.), Tomsk (Russia) U., 1991, Moscow U., 1992. Asst. Rostov U., 1975-80, assoc. prof., 1981-84, sr. rschr., 1984-86, prof. philosophy, 1987-90, prof. polit. scis., 1991—; prof. philosophy Pedagogical U., Rzeszow, Poland, 1997—; vis. prof. U. Maria Sklodovskaja-Curie, Lublin, 1988-89, Tomsk (Russia) U., 1991, Moscow U., 1992; sr. rschr. Inst. Philosophy and Sociology, Acad. Scis., Warsaw, Poland, 1997. Author: Faith, Power and Bureacracy, 1988, Legitimation of Political Power, 1996, Russia Power, 1998, Political Philosophy, 1999; contbr. articles to profl. jours. Named Honored Scientist of Russia, Pres. of Russia, 1998, Ordinary prof. Pres. of Poland, 1999; grantee State Com. Edn. Russia, 1993, Found. Soros, 1994, Humanities Scis. Found. Russia, 1995, Found. Stephan Bátory, Poland, 1999. Mem. Acad. Social Scis. Russia, Acad. Polit. Scis. Russia, Acad. Humanities Scis. Russia. Office: Rostov State U, B Sadovaya 106, 344006 Rostov-na-Donu Russia

MAKAREVICH, VLADISLV ANATOLIEVICH, geophysicist; b. Omsk, USSR, May 28, 1939; s. Anatoly Lukich and Valerij Antonovna (Rakovska) M.; m. Naumenko Nina Igroreva (div. 1979); 1 child, Anna. Degree in Engring., Instrument Making U., Sevastopol, Crimea, 1966. Engr., programmer Computer Ctr., Sevastopol, Crimea, 1966-69; postgrad. fellow The Mariner of Hidrophys. Inst. Ukrain Acad. Scis., Sevastopol, Crimea, 1969-72, rsch. worker, 1972-80; rsch. worker Sevastopol Dept. State Oceanog. Inst., Crimea, 1980-81. Author: The Black Book of the USSR, 1998; contbr. papers in field. Home: Burjaka 9-5, Sevastopol 335002, Ukraine

MAKAREWICZ, RUFIN JOZEF, acoustics educator, consultant; b. Bydgoszcz, Poland, July 30, 1947; s. Mikolaj and Melania (Buda) M.; m. Maria Ewa Purzycka, Dec. 17, 1974; 1 child, Katarzyna. MS, Adam Mickiewicz U., Poznań, Poland, 1970; PhD, Adam Mickiewicz U., Poznań, 1974, Habilitation, 1980. Prof. Adam Mickiewicz U., Poznań, 1974-78, 79-85; prof., 1986-95, full prof., 1998—, vice dean dept., 1981-85, dean dept., 1987-93, head inst., 1999—; prof. Fla. State U., Gainesville, 1978-79, Max Planck Inst., Goettingen, 1985-86; full prof. Kyushu Inst. Design, Fukuoka, Japan, 1995-98'; named to univ. chair, Poznan, 1980-85; cons. WHO, Geneva, 1992. Author: Sound, 1994, Noise, 1996; contbr. over 67 articles to profl. jours. Mgr. univ. chair, Poznań, 1980-85. Recipient award for scientific edn. Ministry Edn., 1982, 86. Roman Catholic. E-mail: makaaku@amu.edu.pl. Home: Muchomorowa 16, 62-002 Zlotniki Poland Office: Adam Mickiewicz U, Umultowska 85, 61-614 Poznań Poland

MAKARIUS, ROMAN, mining engineer; b. Brno, S. Moravia, Czech Republic, Aug. 6, 1938; s. Alois and Ludmila (Spiskova) M.; m. Jana Bednarova; children: Lucie, Milan. D in Law, Charles U., 1974; CSc, Czechoslovak Acad. Scis., Prague, 1990. Dep. dir. prodn. Mine Tuchlovice, Kladno, 1961-77; dir. dept. Czech Mining Authority, Prague, 1977-90, vice chmn., 1990-97, chmn., 1997—; chmn. supr. bd. Severoceske doly a.s., Chomutov, 1992-97, Revirini Banska Zachranna Stanice, Ostrava, 1995-97; mem. supr. bd. OKD Joint Stock Co., Ostrava, 1995-97; mem. acad. coun. dean Faculty of Mining and Geology, Mining U., 1991-97; mem. acad. coun. rector Mining U. Ostrava, 1997, lectr., 1996. Author: Elimination of Fire in Underground Mines, 1984, Safety at Work, 1990, Forming Inert Atmosphere in Underground Fires, 1993, Historical Development of the Safety Regulations, 1997, Czech Mining Law, 1999. Magister Knight Sovereign Order of the Knights of St. John, 1990, Malteser Order. Avocation: music. Home: Josefska 2, 118 00 Praha 1 Czech Republic Office: Czech Mining Authority, Kozi 4, 11001 Praha 1 Czech Republic

MAKAROV, LEV LVOVITCH, chemistry educator; b. St. Petersburg, Russia, June 20, 1925; s. Lev Romanovitch and Marija Michailovna (Egorova) Makarov; m. Tatjana Petrovna (Merkurjeva) Makarova, Sept. 25, 1929; children: Alexander, Bladimir. PhD in Chemistry, U. St. Petersburg, Russia, 1958, D in Chemistry, 1972. Post-grad. U. St. Petersburg, Russia, 1953-56; from jr. to sr. rschr. U. St. Petersburg, 1956-76, prof. Radiochemistry, 1976—. Author: Course of Applied Radiochemistry, 1966, (with others) Radiochemistry and Chemistry of Nuclear Processes, 1964; contbr. articles to profl. jours. Jr. Lt. with Soviet Army, 1943-47. Avocations: chess, billiards, hunting. Home: Bolotnaja St 14 Apt 15, 194021 St Petersburg Russia Office: St Petersburg St U, U Naber 7/9, 199164 St Petersburg Russia

MAKAROVA, MARINA, chemist, researcher; b. Novosibirsk, Russia, Mar. 17, 1960; arrived in The Netherlands, 1995; d. Arnold Fleer and Alla Makarova; m. Andreas De Winter; 1 child, Natasha. BSc, U. Novisibirsk, 1982; PhD, Semenov Inst. Chem. Physics, Moscow, 1987. Rsch. scientist Boreskov Inst. Catalysis, Novosibirsk, 1987-91; rsch fellow U. Manchester (Eng.) Inst. Sci. Tech., 1991-95; rsch. chemist Shell Rsch. and Tech. Ctr., Amsterdam, The Netherlands, 1995—; vis. scientist Royal Instn. Great Britain, London, 1989. Contbr. over 30 articles to profl. jours. Mem. Brit. Zeolite Assn., N.Y. Acad. Scis. Office: Shell Rsch & Tech Ctr, Badhuisweg 3 PO Box 38000, 1030 BN Amsterdam The Netherlands

MAKAROVA, TATIANA L., physicist, educator; b. Leningrad, USSR, Feb. 22, 1959; d. Ludvig V. Belyakov and Tamara I. Zubkova; m. Aleksandr Makarov (div. Aug. 1999); 1 child, Anna Makarova. MS, State Tech. U., St. Petersburg, Russia, 1982; diploma cum laude (hon.), Tech. U., 1983; postgrad., Electron Rsch. Inst., St. Petersburg; PhD, Ioffe Physico-Tech. Inst., St. Petersburg, 1993. Rschr. Electron Rsch. Inst.; sr. rschr. Ioffe Physico-Tech. Inst., 1993—; tchr. Tech. U., St. Petersburg, 1993-98. Contbr. numerous articles to profl. jours.; author student manuals. Alexander von Humboldt Found. fellow. Mem. Electrochem. Soc., Carbon Soc. Home: 40 Vernosti Apt 2, 195273 Saint Petersburg Russia Office: Ioffe PTI, 26 Polytechnicheskaya, 194021 Saint Petersburg Russia

MAKAROVS, VLADIMIRS, Latvian government official; b. Rezekne, Latvia, 1957; married; 2 children. Degree in History, U. Latvia, 1982. Locksmith, installer, tchr.; head splst. Chief Social Ins. Divsn., Vidzeme; dir. Social Asst. Dept., 1991-94; min. public affairs Govt. of Latvia, 1994, min. social welfare, 1995—, min. environment protection and regional devel. Mem. For Fatherland and Freedom. Office: Ministry Social Welfare, Skolas iela 28, LV-1331 Riga Latvia Address: Peldu iela 25, LV-1494 Riga Latvia*

MAKARUK, HANNA EWA, theoretical physicist; b. Warsaw, Poland; d. Leszek Henryk and Halina (Wojnowska) M.; m. Robert Michal Owczarek. MSc, U. Warsaw, 1989; PhD summa cum laude, Polish Acad. Scis., 1994. Rsch. asst. Polish Acad. of Scis. Inst. of Fundamental Technol. Rsch., Warsaw, 1989-94, assoc. prof., 1994—; postdoctoral fellow Los Alamos Nat. Lab., 1996-98, tech. staff mem., 1999—; lecturing prof. Polish Acad. of Scis., 1995-96. Referee Classical and Quantum Gravity, Jour. of Physics, Jour. of Tech. Physics, Reports on Math. Physics; reviewer Math. Revs.; contbr. articles to profl. jours. Fellowship Kosciuszko Found., N.Y.C., 1996, Japanese Soc. for the Promotion of Sci., 1995; rsch. grant Polish State Com. for Sci., Warsaw, 1995. Mem. Internat. Soc. for Interaction between Math. and Mechanics, Polish Soc. for Applied Electromagnetics, Soc. for Indsl. and Applied Math., Polish Phys. Soc., Am. Math. Soc., Inst. of Physics U.K. Roman Catholic. Achievements include research in the description of conductivity in conducting polymers by multidimensional Dirac equation, spinor structure methods; new algebraic methods in strongly nonlinear problems and field theory; math. methods in theory of neural networks. Office: Los Alamos Nat Lab E 517 Los Alamos NM 87545-0001

MÄKELÄ, JIRKI TAPANI, gastroenterological surgeon, educator, consultant; b. Helsinki, Finland, Jan. 2, 1953; s. Jouko Vihiori and Sirkka Ilia (Aniika) M.; m. Pirjo Kaarina Piikkö, Julky 28, 1975; children: Johanna, Janne, Juho. Lic. in medicine, Oulu (Finland) U., 1977, MD, 1987, docent in gastroenterol. surgery, 1992. Med. diplomate. Gen. practitioner Sikalatva Health Svc. Ctr., 1977-80; resident in surgery Oulu U. Hosp., 1980-84, resident in gastroenterol. surgery, 1984-87, gastroenterol. surgeon, 1987-89; asst. prof. Oulu U., 1989-99, prof., 1999—; consulting surgeon Oulu U. Hosp., 1989—. Author: Acute Abdomen, 1999. Served with Finnish mil., 1996. Recipient thesis award Pres. Paasikivi Found., Helsinki, 1977. Fellow Finnish Surg. Soc. (Best Lecture award 1997), Finnish Gastroenterol. Soc., Finnish Digestive Surgeons. Lutheran. Avocations: fishing, basketball, sports medicine. Office: Dept Surgery Divsn Gastroen, Kajaanintie 50 PO Box 22, 90220 Oulu Finland

MAKER, CAROL JUNE, gifted and talented education educator; b. Caneyville, Ky., Aug. 7, 1948; d. Arnold David and Bernice (Smith) Shartzer. BS, Western Ky. U., 1970; MS, So. Ill. U., 1971; PhD, U. Va., 1978. Cert. elem. edn. tchr. Tchr. Caneyville (Ky.) Pub. Schs., 1970; tchr. of gifted Edwardsville (Ill.) Pub. Sch., 1971; regional supr. Ill. Office Edn., Springfield, 1971-74; adminstrv. intern U.S. Office Edn., Washington, 1974-75; grad. instr. U. Va., Charlottesville, 1976-77, off-campus instr., 1977-78; asst. prof. U. N.Mex., Albuquerque, 1978-81; asst. prof. U. Ariz., Tucson, 1981-83, assoc. prof., 1983-96, prof., 1996—; keynote spkr. World Coun. for Gifted, Oporto, Portugal, 1986, Sydney, Australia, 1989, Victorian Assn for the Gifted, Melbourne, 1996, 7th Nat. Conf. on Gifted & Talented Edn. for Native People, Hilo, Hawaii, 2000; conf. on Creation and Success, China Inst. Promoting Eminent Tchrs. Experience, Beijing, 2000; 6th Asia-Pacific Conf. on Giftedness, divsn. World Coun. on Gifted & Talented, Beijing, 2000. Author: Teaching Models in Education of Gifted, 1982, 2d edit., 1995, Curriculum Development for the Gifted, 1982, Curriculum Development and Teaching Strategies for Gifted Learners, 2d edit., 1996; co-author: Intellectual Giftedness in Disabled Persons, 1985, Nurturing Giftedness in Young Children, 1996; editor: (book series) Critical Issues in Education of Gifted, Vol. I, 1986, Vol. II, 1989, Vol. III, 1994; mem. editl. bd. Jour. for Edn. of Gifted, 1977—, Gifted Edn. Internat., 1985—. Mem. H.S. task force Tucson (Ariz.) Unified Sch. Dist., 1983, 85; mem. task force gifted concerns Ariz. State Bd. Edn., Phoenix, 1985-87; steering com. China-U.S. Conf. Edn., 1996-97; bd. dirs. Arts Genesis, Inc., Tucson, 1994-97, Am. Logos Found., 1997—; coord. U.S.-China Interactive Learning Ctr., 1996—. Fulbright scholar U. de las Ams., Mexico City, 1987; Rsch. grantee U.S. Dept. Edn., Office of Bilingual Edn., 1987-89, 93-96, U.S. Dept. Edn., Javits Gifted Edn. Program, 1993—, Shonto Prep. Acad., 1996-2000. Mem. Nat. Assn. for Gifted (bd. dirs., sec. 1972-89), Ariz. Assn. for Gifted and Talented (bd. dirs., sec. 1981-87), World Coun. for Gifted and Talented (com. chair 1986-93), Coun. for Exceptional Children (com. chair 1975-94). Democrat. Avocations: photography, yoga, hiking, gardening. Home: 503 E 2nd St Tucson AZ 85705-7870 Office: Univ Ariz Dept Special Edn & Rehab Tucson AZ 85721-0001

MAKHADMI, JAMIL ABDULLAH, academic director; b. Makkah, Saudi Arabia, Oct. 8, 1956; s. Abdullah A. Makhadmi and Khadijah A. Faiead; m. Tracey J. Murphy, May. 11, 1985; children: Mohammed, Mashael, Ibrahim, Sulman, Khadijah. AS in Aerospace Engring., Pima C.C., Tucson, 1982; BS in Mech. Engring., U. Miami, 1986; MS in Mech. Engring., San Jose State U., 1987; PhD in Mech. Engring., U. Leeds (Eng.), 1995. Maintenance engr. Petromin Mobile Refinery, Pemr-Ef, Yanbu Al, Saudi Arabia, 1988-89; maintenance engr. internat. airport project Ministry Def. and Aviation, Jeddah, Saudi Arabia, 1989-90; asst. prof. dept. mech. engring. Umm Al-Qura U., Makkah, Saudi Arabia, 1990-99; chmn. mech. engring. dept. Umm Al-Qura U., Makkah, 1990-99, dir. registration com. 5th Saudi Engring. Conf., 1998, dir. acad. suprs. and registration dept. students; grad. student advisor, cons. Saudi Arabia Cutlural Attache, Washington, DC, 2000—. Contbr. articles to profl. jours. Home: PO Box 15898, Jeddah Saudi Arabia 34470 Office: Umm Al-Qura U Mech Engring, PO Box 715, Makkah Saudi Arabia

MAKHANYA, EDWARD MBUYISELO, geographer; b. Brakpan, South Africa, Apr. 14, 1937; s. Richard and Beauty (Ndimande) M.; m. Victoria Lekhanya, Aug. 20, 1965; children: Geraldine, Faith, Jacqueline, Richard. BA, Ft. Hare U., 1962, U. South Africa, 1964; MA, U. South Africa, 1970; PhD, London U.; diploma in rural surveys, ITC, Enschede, 1974. Lectr. U. Ft. Hare, Alice, South Africa, 1965-71, U. Botswana, Lesotho, Swaziland, 1971-74; sr. lectr. U. Lesotho, 1974-80; prof. U. Zululand, Umlazi, South Africa, 1980—; extramural dean U. Zululand, 1993—. Author: The Use of Land Resources for Agriculture in Lesotho, 1977, Plight of the Rural Population in Lesotho, 1980. Fulbright fellow, 1981. Mem. South African Geographical Assn., Br. Remote Sensing Soc., South African Soc. for Photogrammetry and Geographic Info., Farmer Found., Internat. Geog. Union. Methodist. Avocations: golf, tennis, soccer, boxing. Home: 12 Cuckoo Cir Yellowwood Pk, 4004 Durban South Africa Office: U Zululand, Pvt Bag X10 Isipingo, 4110 Durban South Africa

MAKHIJA, SUSHIL KUMAR, medical microbiologist, researcher; b. New Delhi, Nov. 8, 1956; s. Fatehchand Dayaram and Kamla Fatehchand (Rajani) M. MB, BChir, Govt. Med. Coll., Nagpur, India, 1979, MD in Microbiology, 1988; BA in English Lit., Nagpur U., 1985. Rsch. asst. microbiology Govt. Med. Coll., Nagpur, 1987-89, lectr. microbiology, 1989-97; lectr. microbiology V.N. Govt. Med. Coll., Yavatmal, India, 1997—; tech. expert Microbiological Techniques, lab. manual. Prin. author: (manual) A Guide to Laboratory Diagnostic Techniques in STDs and AIDS, 1993; co-author: (manual) Reference Manual for Laboratory Workers Diagnosis of Sexually Transmitted Diseases, 1994; contbr. articles to profl. jours. Mem. Indian Assn. Med. Microbiologists (life), N.Y. Acad. Scis. Hindu. Avocations: yoga, western classical music, public speaking, painting, playing keyboard. Office: Shri VN Govt Med Coll, Dept Microbiology, Mahar St Yavatmaltra 445 001, India

MAKHNACH, ALEXANDER V., psychologist; b. Slavgorod, Altay, USSR, Dec. 21, 1959; s. Valentin M. and Valentina M. (Ryabova) M.; m. Marina M. Moutchnik, Mar. 11, 1983 (div. Dec. 1988); m. Natalia V. Gladysheva, Apr. 23, 1997. BA, Tomsk State U., 1983; cert. clin. psychologist, Bekhterev Inst., Leningrad, 1984; PhD, Russian Acad. Scis., Moscow, 1992. Clin. psychologist Mental Hosp., Tomsk, 1983-84; asst. Tomsk State U., 1984-85; rschr. Rsch. Inst. Biology and Biophysics, Tomsk, 1985-89; sr. rschr. Inst. Psychology Russian Acad. Scis., Moscow, 1989—; counsellor RHR Internat., Moscow, 1996; dir. Moscow Ctr. Psychology and Psychotherapy, Moscow, 1993—; lectr. Tomsk State Pedagogical Inst., 1984-85, Psychol. Coll., Moscow, 1995-96, Internat. Slavic U., Moscow, 1997, Psychol. U., Moscow, 1997. Editor: Psychology and Christianity: A Way of Integration, 1995; contbr. articles to profl. jours. Grantee Russian Humanities Sci. Fund, 1995, Russian Fund Fundamental Studies, 1996. Mem. APA, European Assn. Personality, European Assn. Personality Assessment. Orthodox. Avocations: reading books, theater, classical music. Office: Russian Acad Scis Inst Psyc, 13 Yaroslavskaya St, 129366 Moscow Russia

MAKHOUS, MONZER MOHAM, geochemist; b. Lattaquia, Syria, Nov. 9, 1943; s. Moham and Fatima Makhous. MS in Engring., Geochemistry, Lomonosov Moscow State U., 1969, PhD in Geology, Mineralogy, 1974, DSc in Petroleum Exploration Prodn., 1993; DSc in Geology, Geochemistry, U. Strasbourg, 1996. Head dept. devel. Syrian Min. Petroleum Mineral Resources, Damascus, 1969-70; expert, head dept. geochemistry Sonatrach, Algiers, Algeria, 1975-91; rsch. prof. Russian Acad. Sci., Moscow State U., 1991-93; rschr. Nat. Ctr. Scientific Rsch., Strasbourg, 1993-96; rsch. prof. Lomonosov Moscow State U., 1996-97; cons. rschr. Paris U., 1997—; energy econ. rschr. Sorbonne U., Paris, 1999—. Author: The Formation of Hydrocarbon Deposits in the North African Basins: Geological and Geochemical Conditions, 2000; co-author: (chpt.) Geology of Petroleum Deposits, 1975, Petroleum History in Sedimentary Basins, 1994, Evolution of Sedimentary Basins and Petroleum Formation, 1996; contbr. articles to profl. jours. Recipient Oil Discovery award Syrian Min. Energy Mines and Algerian Min. Energy Mines, 1970, 82. Mem. European Union Geosci., Am. Assn. Petroleum Geologists, Russian Soc. Earth Explorers, N.Y. Acad. Sci. Avocations: theater, music, painting. Fax: 33 1 45 61 94 92. Office: T and O Casprini, 76 Ave Champs Elysees, 75008 Paris France

MAKHOVER, MIKHAIL SERGEEVICH, mathematician, educator; b. St. Petersburg, Russia, Nov. 12, 1946; s. Sergey Mikhailovich and Eugenia Vladimirovna Makhover; m. Tatiana Georgievna Maraeva, Mar. 30, 1974 (div. Sept. 1985); 1 child, Vitaliy; m. Galina Leonidovna Kelner, Oct. 20, 1985; children: Kormakova Ekaterina, Boyarinova Ksenia. Diploma, A. Hertsen State Pedagog Inst., Leningrad. Tchr. math. Russia, 1970-71, Leningrad, 1971-75; tchr. math. and English Mwehse Secondary Sch., Zambia, 1975-76; tchr. math. Gimnazija 11, St. Petersburg, 1979—; tchr. Methodist in math. of Vasilevskii Island, St. Ptersburg, 1998—. Author: (textbooks) Exponencial and logarithmetical equations, 1992, Some aspects of school course of algebra, 1993, It's possible to learn trigonometry, 1997, Geometry in Plane (definitions and properties), 1998. Recipient Merit Badge of Pub. Edn., 1990, others; grantee in field. Mem. N.Y. Acad. Scis. Avocations: travel, soccer. Home: 6 line, 199004 Saint Petersburg Russia Office:

Gymanitarnaja Gimnazija, 16 line Vasilevskij Ostrov, 11917B Saint Petersburg Russia

MAKHZOUMI, FOUAD MUSTAPHA SULTANI, marketing executive; b. Lebanon, 1952; s. Mustapha F.S. and Ayesha I. (Zeidan) M.; m. May Naamani, Dec. 13, 1975; 1 son, Rami F.; 2 daus., Tamara, Camellia. BSc, Mich. Tech. U., 1973, MSc in Chem. Engring., 1975; postgrad. in exec. mgmt., Columbia U., 1978. Dir. mktg. and bus. devel. Saudi Arabian Amiantit Group Cos., Riyadh, Saudi Arabia, 1975—; chmn. Gulf Eternit Industries-Dubai, 1984; cons. bus. promotion, 1975—; internat. bd. dirs. Coun. on Fgn. Rels. US/Mid. East Project; vice chmn. Inst. Social and Econ. Policy in Mid. East Harvard U. Mem. Am. Inst. Chem. Engrs., Order Engrs. Lebanon, Internat. Desalination Assn. (pres.), US-Arab C. of C. (bd. dirs.), Lebanese Engring. Assn. Moslem. Home: PO Box 13-5009, Ras Beirut Lebanon

MAKHZOUMI, ZIAD, management consultant; b. Beirut, Jan. 20, 1955; s. Mustapha and Aicha (Zeidan) M.; m. Zeina Takieddine; children: Hala, Tarek. BS in Engring., U. Manchester, 1978, MBA, 1981. Assoc. Booz Allen & Hamilton, N.Y.C., 1981-85; founder, dir. City of London Investment Group PLC, London, 1987—; sr. v.p. Future Pipe Industries BV, London, 1997—; master practitioner Neuro-Linguistic Programming, Switzerland, 1987—. Contbr. Am.-Arab Affairs Council, Washington, 1987. Moslem. Avocations: marathon running, tennis, music. Office: Future Pipe Ltd, 6 Earls Ct Rd Whitlock Ho, London W8 6EA, England

MAKI, ATSUSHI, economics educator; b. Kanagawa, Japan, Jan. 14, 1948; s. Sadao and Eiko (Yamaguchi) M.; m. Michie Yabu, Feb. 28, 1975; children: Chiori, Hisashi. BA, Keio U., 1971, MA, 1973, PhD, 1993. Asst. prof. Keio U., Tokyo, 1973-79, assoc. prof., 1979-87, prof., 1987—; guest rsch. officer Ministry Posts and Telecom., 1988-90; vis. scholar Harvard U., Cambridge, Mass., 1982-84; vis. prof. Osaka (Japan) U., 1989, Ecole Superieure des Scis. Econs. et Cmmls., France, 1994; vis. fellow Australian Nat. U., Canberra, 1990, Massey U., New Zealand, 1991, U. Western Australia, Perth, 1993, Victoria U., Wellington, New Zealand, 1997. Author: Consumer Preferences and Measurement of Demand, 1983, Japanese Consumer Behavior, 1998. Reciient award Japan Found., 1996; grantee Inamori Rsch. Promotion Found., 1990, Zengin Found. for Studies on Econs. and Fin., 1994; Nomura travel grantee, 1998. Mem. Am. Econ. Assn., Econometric Soc., Japanese Econ. Assn., Japan Assn. Stats., Japan Soc. Household Econs., Royal Econ. Soc. Home: 107-8 Terao Kawagoe-shi, Saitama 350-1141, Japan Office: Keio U, 2-15-45 Mita Minato-ku, Tokyo 108-8345, Japan

MAKIHARA, MINORU, diversified corporation executive; b. London, Jan. 12, 1930. BA, Harvard U., 1954. With Mitsubishi Corp., Tokyo, 1956-59, London, 1959-67; with Marine Products dept. Mitsubishi Corp., Tokyo, 1967-70, dep. gen. mgr., 1976-80, gen. mgr. Marine Products dept., 1980-83, gen. mgr. mktg. and coordination dept., 1983-85, bd. dirs., 1986-88, mng. dir., 1988-90, sr. mng. dir., 1990-92, pres., chmn., 1992-98, 1998—; with, then gen. mgr. Mitsubishi Internat. Corp., Seattle, 1970-71, v.p., gen. mgr., 1980-83; gen. mgr. Mitsubishi Internat. Corp., Washington, 1971-76, exec. v.p., gen. mgr., 1985-86; pres. Mitsubishi Internat. Corp., N.Y.C., 1987-90, chmn., 1990-92; chmn. Mitsubishi Group, Tokyo, 2000. Chmn. Com. on Trade and Investment; pres. Japan-Columbia Com., pres. Japan-Venezuela Com. for the Keidanren (Japan Fedn. of Econ. Orgns.); mem. exec. com. Trilateral Comm. (Japan, NAm., Europe); chmn. Japan U.S. Bus. Coun. Office: Office of the Chmn, 2-6-3 Marunouchi, Chiyoda Tokyo 100 8086, Japan*

MAKIMOTO, TSUGIO, electrical engineer; b. Nakatane, Kagoshima, Japan, May 15, 1937; s. Genshichi and Haru (Hidaka) M.; m. Yuko Tanimoto, June 1, 1959; children: Toshiki, Yoshiko, Nobuo, Akio. BA, U. Tokyo, 1959, PhD, 1971; MS, Stanford U., Palo Alto, Calif., 1966. Registered semiconductor engr. With Hitachi Ltd., 1959—, gen. mgr. semiconductor and integrated cirs. divsn., 1992-95, exec. mng. dir., 1993-97, sr. exec. mng. dir., 1997-98, corp. chief technologist, 1998—; bd. dirs. Hitachi Ltd., 1991-99; bd. dirs., exec. dir. Semiconductor Industry Rsch. Inst. Japan, 1996-98; mem. adv. bd. Nara Inst. Sci. and Tech., 1998—; prof. Toyo U., 1999—; adv. bd. Nat. Sci. Tech. Bd. Singapore, 1999—. Author: Living With The Chip, 1994, Digital Nomad, 1997; patentee in field. Recipient Ichimura award The New Tech. Devel. Found., 1973. Fellow IEEE (mem. edtl. bd. IEEE Spectrum 1997—); mem. Tokyo Inst. Elec. Info. and Comm. Avocations: golfing, reading, photography. Office: New Marunouchi Bldg, 5-1 Marunouchi 1-chome, Tokyo 100-8220, Japan

MAKIN, ANTHONY JOHN, economist; b. Toowoomba, Australia, June 7, 1955; s. Thomas Gerrard and Lorinda Fay (McAuliffe) M.; m. Brenda Majella Marshall, Dec. 17, 1994. BA, U. Queensland, 1975; B in Econ., 1980; M in Econ., Australian Nat. U., 1986; PhD, 1992. Econ. Dept. Trade, Canberra, 1980, Dept. Fin., Canberra, 1981-84; sr. econ. The Australian Treasury, Canberra, 1984-86; sr. econ. adviser Dept. Prime Minister and Cabinet, Canberra, 1987; lectr. Mgmt. Sch., U. Canberra, 1987-89; reader Econ. Dept., U. Queensland, 1989; cons. Bus. Coun. Australia, Melbourne, 1994, Australian Competition and Consumer Commn., 1996; Australia's ofcl. internat. finance specialist Pacific Econ. Cooperation Coun., 1996—. Author: International Capital Mobility and External Account Determination, 1994, Open Economy Macroeconomics, 1996, Global Finance and the Macroeconomy, 2000; contbr. many articles to profl. jours. Recipient G.S.L. Tucker award Australian Nat. U., Canberra, 1986, C.R. Kelly award Soc. mem. Parliament, Canberra, 1993. Mem. Australian Econ. Soc., Am. Econ. Assn., Royal Econ. Soc., Internat. Trade and Fin. Assn. Avocations: music, literature. Office: U Queensland, Dept Econs, Brisbane 4072, Australia

MAKINDE, MARTIN OLADIRAN, veterinary physiologist; b. Ilesa, Nigeria, Aug. 25, 1950; s. Gabriel and Arinola Alice M.; m. Yetunde Abiose, Apr. 28, 1979; children: Oludare, Olamide, Olumide, Kolade. DVM, U. Ibadan, Nigeria, 1976; diploma in neurophysiology, U. Edinburgh, Scotland, 1981; PhD, U. Ibadan, 1986. Lectr., sr. lectr. U. Ibadan, Nigeria, 1978-90; sr. lectr. U. Zimbabwe, Harare, 1989-94, assoc. prof., 1995-96; prof. U. Venda, Thohoyandou, South Africa, 1996—. Mem. Physiological Soc. So. Africa, Am. Soc. Animal Sci., N.Y. Acad. Scis. Home: 9 Barnard St, Louis Trichardt 0920, South Africa Office: U Venda, Pvt Bag X5050, Thohoyandou 0950, South Africa

MAKINS, CHRISTOPHER JAMES, foreign policy institute administrator; b. Southampton, N.Y., July 23, 1942; s. Roger Mellor and Alice Brooks (Davis) M.; m. Wendy Whitney, July 26, 1975; 1 child, Marian Whitney. BA, Oxford U., Eng., 1963; MA, Oxford U., 1971. From 3rd to 1st sec. Her Majesty Diplomatic Svc., London, Paris, Washington, 1964-75; dep. dir. Trilateral Commn., N.Y.C., 1975-76; sr. assoc. Carnegie Endowment for Internat. Peace, Washington, 1977-79; sr. scientist, asst. v.p. Sci. Applications Internat. Corp., Washington, 1979-89; dir. internat. security programs Roosevelt Ctr. Am. Policy Studies, Washington, 1985-89; v.p., sr. v.p. Aspen Inst., Washington, 1989-97; pres. Atlantic Coun. U.S., Washington, 1999—; sr. adviser German Marshall Fund U.S., Washington, 1997-99; mem. internat. adv. bd. ICL Ltd., London, 1999—. Author: (monograph) The Study of Europe in the United States, 1998; contbr. articles to profl. jours. Dir. Washington Concert Opera, 1987—, chmn., 1993-97; coun. mem. Non-Profit Sector Rsch. Fund, Washington, 1997—; trustee The Phillips Collection, Washington, 1991-98, Greater Washington Ednl. Telecomms. Assn., 1980-88. Fellow All Souls Coll., Oxford, 1963-70; mem. Coun. Fgn. Rels., Internat. Inst. Strategic Studies, Pratts Club, Met. Club. Avocations: tennis, squash, boating, opera. Home: 3034 P St NW Washington DC 20007-3052 Office: 1024 29th St NW Washington DC 20007-3831

MAKKAR, HARINDER PAUL SINGH, nutritional biochemist, researcher, consultant; b. Ranchi, Bihar, India, June 16, 1955; s. Mehtab Singh and Ram Kaur M.; m. Surinder Kaur Arora, Mar. 1, 1981; 2 children (twins). BSc, M.L.N. Coll., Yamunagagar, India, 1974; MSc, N.D.R.I., Karnal, India, 1976; PhD, U. Nottingham, Eng., 1985; habilitation, U. Hohenheim, Germany, 1999. Sr. rsch. fellow Nat. Dairy Rsch. Inst., Karnal, 1976-77; scientist Indian Vet. Rsch. Inst., Palampur, India, 1977-86, sr. scientist, 1986-91, 94-98; Alexander von Humboldt fellow, vis. scientist U. Hohenheim, Stuttgart, 1991-94; cons. in field; tech. officer Internat. Atomic Energy Agy., Vienna, 1999—. Contbr. articles to profl. jours. Mem. AAAS, Royal Soc. Chemistry, N.Y. Acd. Scis., Soc. Biol. Chemists (life), Animal Nutrition Soc. (life). Avocations: reading, playing cricket, badminton and table tennis. Home: Hofzeile 15/2/4, 1190 Vienna Austria Office: IAEA Animal Prodn & Health Sect, Wagramerstr 5 PO Box 100, A-1400 Vienna Austria

MAKKONEN, LASSE JUHANI, geophysicist; b. Helsinki, July 18, 1953; s. Olli Juhani and Aira Maritta (Niemi) M.; m. Anna-Maija Lallukka, July 8, 1983; children: Tuomas, Satu. BS, U. Helsinki, 1975, MS, 1977, Lic. Sci., 1981, PhD, 1985. Scientist Inst. Marine Rsch., Helsinki, 1977-83; vis. scientist Nat. Rsch. Coun., Ottawa, Ont., Can., 1983-84; sr. rsch. scientist Tech. Rsch. Ctr. Finland, Espoo, 1985—; vis. prof. U. Alta., Edmonton, 1984, Hokkaido U., Sapporo, Japan, 1998; vis. scientist Hokkaido U., Sapporo, Japan, 1989; docent U. Helsinki, 1993—; lectr. Helsinki U. Tech., 1992-95; postgrad. advisor Luleå U. Tech., 1990-95; evaluator European Union, Brussels, 1996, 97. Editor: Ice and Construction, 1994; sci. editor Jour. Glaciology, 1992—; contbr. articles to profl. jours. Rsch. grantee Vaisala Found., 1983, 96, Acad. Finland, 1983, 96, 98; Nat. Sci. and Engring. Coun. Can. vis. fellow, 1983. Mem. Internat. Glaciological Soc. (coun. 1988-95), Finnish Ice Rsch. Soc. (pres. 1995—), The Adhesion Soc., Geophys. Soc. Finland. Avocations: golf, flyfishing, travel, gastronomy. Home: Yläkalliontie 27, 02760 Espoo Finland Office: Tech Rsch Ctr Finland, PO Box 18071, 02044VTT Espoo Finland

MAKO, WILLIAM LAWRENCE, manufacturing executive; b. Cleve., June 16, 1958; s. Lawrence M. and Margret E. (Borchard) M.; m. Bonnie M. Schultz, Mar. 19, 1994; children: Brooke A., Bethany M., Brenna M. BA in Bus., Wittenberg U., 1981; MBA, Cleveland State U., 1989. V.p. Conmak, Inc., Conneaut, Ohio, 1981-82; pres. Le Bears' Inc., Moreland Hills, Ohio, 1982-83; mgr. Wendy's Old-Fashioned Hamburgers, Bozeman, Mont., 1984; exec. v.p. Great Lakes Properties Corp., Conneaut, 1984-88; v.p. Conneaut Harbor Devel. Co., Ohio, 1988-90; exec. v.p. Def-Tec Corp., Rock Creek, Ohio, 1990-95; pres., gen mgr. MFG Justin Tanks Inc., Georgetown, Del., 1995-96; plant mgr. Molded Fiberglass Co., Ashtabula, Ohio, 1996-97; gen. mgr. Metal Sales Mfg. Corp., Jefferson, Ohio, 1997—. Mem. Safari Club Internat., N.Am. Hunting Club (life). Republican. Roman Catholic. Avocations: hunting, fishing, outdoor sports. Home: 222 Elliott Ave Jefferson OH 44047-1230 Office: Metal Sales Mfg Corp PO Box 675 352 E Erie St Jefferson OH 44047-1406

MAKOVETSKY, KIRYLL LVOVICH, chemist, researcher; b. Ekaterinburg, Russia, Dec. 22, 1930; s. Lev Alexandrovich and Elizabeta Georgievna (Time) M.; m. Kira Nikolayevna Karpova, Mar. 8, 1952 (div. Sept. 1963); 1 child, Vladimir; m. Kira Georgievna Yankovskaya, Oct. 19, 1963; 1 child, Anna. Chemistry technologist, Technol. Inst. Leningrad, 1953, PhD, 1964; DS, Inst. Petrochem. Synthesis, 1979. Rschr. Inst. Synthetic Rubber, Leningrad, Russia, 1953-58; engr. Technol. Inst. Leningrad, 1959-64; rsch. fellow Inst. Elementoorganic Compounds, Moscow, 1964-66, Inst. Petrochem. Synthesis, Moscow, 1966—; cons. Monsanto Co., Springfield, 1991-93, B.F. Goodrich Co., Brecksville, 1994—. Editl. bd. mem. Polymer Sci. Jour., 1988—; patentee in field; contbr. articles to profl. jours. Grantee Russian Govt., 1995-97, 98—, Russian Fund Fundamental Rsch., 1993-95. Mem. Mendeleev Russian Chem. Soc., N.Y. Acad. Scis. Avocations: general history, history of art, skiing. Home: Profsoyuznaya 142 4/25, 117321 Moscow Russia Office: Inst Petrochem Synthesis, Leninsky pr 29, 117912 Moscow Russia

MAKOVICKA, DANIEL, civil engineer, educator; b. Prague, Czech Republic, May 10, 1941; s. Vojtech and Anna (Subrtova) M.; m. Marie Diatkova, Jan. 9, 1942; children: Daniel, Petr. Degree in civil engring., Coll. Transport Engring., Zilina, Czechoslovakia, 1963; PhD, Tech. U. Prague, 1968, DSc, 1983. Works foreman Transport Constrns., Olomouc, Czech Republic, 1963-64; from rschr. to chief rsch. scientist Klokner Inst., Prague, Czech Republic, 1965—; assoc. prof. Tech. U. Prague, 1998. Co-author: Calculation of Building Structures Loaded by Dynamic Effect of Machines, 1977; contbr. articles to profl. jours., chpts. to books. Mem. Czech Assn. Civil Engring., Czech Assn. Connoisseurs. Avocation: beekeeping. Home: K Jasankam 895, CZ-15500 Prague 5, Czech Republic Office: Klokner Inst, Solinova 7, CZ-16608 Prague 6, Czech Republic

MAKRIS, ANDREAS, composer; b. Salonica, Greece, Mar. 7, 1930; came to U.S., 1950, naturalized, 1962; s. Christos and Kallitza (Andreou) M.; m. Margaret Lubbe, June 12, 1959; children: Christos, Myron. Grad. with highest honors, Nat. Conservatory, Salonica, 1950; postgrad., Kansas City (Mo.) Conservatory, 1953, Mannes Coll. Music, 1956, Aspen Music Festival, 1956-57, Fontainbleau (France) Sch., 1958; pupil of Nadia Boulanger. adv. to Maestro Rostropovich for new music, 1979-90. Compositions premiered and performed in U.S., Can., S.Am., Europe, Japan, USSR; composer-in-residence Nat. Symphony Orch., 1979-90; prin. works include Scherzo for Violins, 1966, Concerto for Strings, 1966, Aegean Festival, 1967, Anamnesis, 1970, Viola Concerto, 1970, Concertino for Trombone, 1970, Efthymia, 1972, Five Miniatures, 1972, Mediterranean Holiday, 1974, Fantasy and Dance for Saxaphone and Piano, 1974, Saxaphone and Concert Band or Saxaphone Strings and Harp, 1974, Chromatokinesis, 1978, In Memory, 1979, Variations and Song for Orchestra, 1979, Fanfare Alexander 1980, Fourth of July March, 1982, Violin Concerto, 1983, Nature-Life Symphonic Poem, 1983, Caprice "Tonatonal", 1986, Intrigues for Solo Clarinet and Wind Ensemble, 1987, Concertante for Violin, Cello, Clarinet, French Horn, Percussion and Orchestra, 1988, Sonata for Cello and Piano, 1989, Symphony to Youth for Full Orchestra, 1989, Trilogy for Orchestra, 1990, Polychornion Chorus and Orchestra, 1990, Procession Chorus and Brass Quintet, 1990, Intrigues for Solo Clarinet, Strings, Brass and Percussion, 1991, Concertino for Organ, Flute and Strings, 1992, A Symphony for Soprano and Strings, 1992, Woodwind Quintet, 1993, Decalog (ten songs for young students), 1995, Antithesis for Orch., 1995, J.F.K. Commemorative Fanfare for Strings and Snare Drum, 1995, Concerto for Violin and Strings, 1996, Introduction and Kalamatianos for solo trumpet, strings, snare and bass drums, 1997, Sonatina for Solo Violin, 1997, Sextet for Woodwind Quintet and Piano in 3 Movements, 1999, Concertino for Flute or Violin and Piano, 1999; also works for violin, string quartets, voice quintets, duets and arrangements of Paganini, Bach, Corelli and Fiorillo. Recipient citation Greek Govt., 1980; Student Program grantee Phillips U., Enid, Okla., 1950, grantee Nat. Endowment Arts, 1967, grantee Martha Baird Rockefeller Fund, 1970, grantee Damrosh Found., 1958. Mem. ASCAP (ann. awards 1980-99), Internat. Platform Assn. Greek Orthodox. Home: 11204 Oak Leaf Dr Silver Spring MD 20901-1313 Office: Nat Symphony Orch Kennedy Ctr Washington DC 20566-0001

MAKRIS, JOHN P., physics and electronics educator, geophysics researcher; b. Athens, Greece, June 10, 1966; s. Panayiotis John and Malamo Emmanouil (Petroulaki) M.; m. Joanna Emmanouil Poulaka, July 26, 1998. BS in Physics, Nat. and Capodistrian U., Athens, 1990, PhD in Physics, 1997; cert. in microcontrollers, Hellenic Ctr. of Productivity, Athens, 1992. Earthquake prediction rschr. Faculty Exact Scis. Nat. and Capodistrian U. of Athens, 1992-94; tchr. physics pvt. sch., Athens, 1991-94; scientist, rschr. geophysics, earthquake prediction Solid Earth Physics Rsch. Inst., Athens, 1995-98; prof. physics and electronics earthquake prediction rsch. Faculty of Technol. Applications, Tech. Ednl. Inst., Chania, Crete, Greece, 1998—; prof. physics, electronics, geoelectromagnetism, geophysics, earthquake prediction rsch. Tech. Ednl. Inst. of Crete, Occupatl. Tutoring Inst. of Crete, Chania Br. Contbr. articles to sci. publs.; presenter confs. Mem. Am. Geophys. Union, Greek Physicists' Union. Social democrat. Orthodox. E-mail: jmakris@chania.teiher.gr or jpmakris@otenet.gr. Home: 28 Solomou St, CreteIsl Chania 731 34, Greece Office: Tech Ednl Inst Crete Dept Electronics, 3 Romanou St, CreteIsl Chania 731 33, Greece

MAKRIS, NIKOLAOS DIMITRIOS, obstetrician-gynecologist, educator; b. Santa Anna, Greece, Dec. 6, 1946; s. Dimitrios Nikolaos and Alexandra George (Afendra) M.; m. Paraskevi Dimitrios Mexi; children: Dimitrios, Alexandros. MD, Athens (Greece) U., 1971. House officer Athens U. Med. Sch., 1974-77, registrar, 1980-86, sr. registrar, 1978-80, specialist in diagnostic and surg. hysteroscopy, 1989—, lectr., 1988-98, asst. prof., 1998—; dir. Ob-gyn. Clinic, Cefallinia Gen. Hosp., Argostolion, Greece, 1977-78; hon. fellow U. Pa., Phila., 1979-80, Jefferson Med. Coll., Phila., 1979-80. Author: (textbooks) Obstetrics, 1989, Gynecology, 1999; contbr. over 100 articles to profl. jours. Rsch. grantee Athens U., 1995, Athens U./Hammersmith Hosp., 1998. Mem. EAGO, European Sterilty Soc., Internat. Soc. for Gynecol. Endoscopy, European Soc. for Gynecol. Endoscopy, Soc. for Study of Reproduction. Greek Orthodox. Avocations: model shipbuilding, sports. Home: 31 G Seferi St, 154 51 Athens Greece Office: 6 Semitelou St, 115 28 Athens Greece

MAKSIMOV, ROBERT D., materials scientist; b. Kraslava dist., Latvia, July 2, 1938; s. Dmitri J. and Proskovi M. (Osipova) M.; m. Valentina-Maria Pavlovich, Mar. 3, 1977; 1 child, Sofia. Engring. Degree cum laude, Riga Poly. Inst., Latvia, 1960; Dr.Sci.Engring., Latvian Acad. Scis., 1969; Dr.Habil.Sci.Eng., Inst. Polymer Mechanics, 1986. Engr. Inst. Polymer Mechanics of Latvian Acad. Scis., 1963-64, chief engr., 1964-68, sr. rschr., 1969, sci. sec. of inst., 1970-74, dep. dir., 1979-84, dir. inst., 1986-88, head of lab., 1975—, mem. habil. and promotion coun., 1992—; mem. sci. com. of regular internat. con. on polymer characterization U. North Tex., Denton, 1993, 95-2000; prof. polymer physics and mechanics USSR Supreme Cert. Commn., Moscow, 1991. Author: Prediction of Deformability of Polymer Materials, 1975; edit. bd. Jour. .Mechanics of Composite Materials, 1969—; contbr. over 160 articles to profl. jours. Recipient Prize of USSR Coun. of Mins. for Achievements in Sci. and Engring., 1983, Latvian State Prize for Achievements in Sci. and Tech., 1982, Honour Diploma, Presidium of Supreme Coun. of Latvian SSR, 1981, 88. Fellow Latvian Nat. Com. for Mechanics, Latvian Materials Rschrs. Soc.; mem. Latvian Acad. Scis. (corr., F. Cander prize 1976, Presidium First award 1974). Avocation: fishing. Home: Bikernieku 81-53, LV-1039 Riga Latvia Office: Inst Polymer Mechanics, Aizkraukles 23, LV-1006 Riga Latvia

MAKSYMIUK, JERZY, conductor; b. Grodno, Poland, Apr. 9, 1936. Student, Warsaw Conservatory; LittD (hon.), Strathclyde U., 1990. Former condr. Warsaw Orch.; founder, prin. condr. Polish Chamber Warsaw; prin. condr. Polish Nat. Radio Orch., 1975-77; past prin. condr. Polish Radio and TV Orch.; prin. condr. BBC Scottish Symphony Orch., Glasgow, 1983—, condr. laureate, 1993—; guest condr. English Chamber, Scottish Chamber, L.A. Chamber, London Symphony Orch., London Philharm., Philharmonia, City of Birmingham Symphony, Tokyo Met. Symphony, Orchestre National de France, Sydney Symphony, Ensemble Orch. de Paris, Rotterdam Philharm., Hong Kong Philharm., Royal Liverpool Philharm., Toyko Metropolitan Symphony, English Nat. Opera, Ulster Orch. Waterfront, Halle, New Zealand Symphony, Winterthur Orch., Bournemouth Sinfonietta, others; founder, condr. Sinfonia Varsovia (formerly Polish Chamber Orch.), 1971—; worldwide tours include European festivals Aix-en-Provence, Vienna, Proms, USA, Can., Japan, Australia, Israel, others; debut with English Nat. Opera, 1991. Recordings include (with BBC Scottish Symphony Orch.) Macmillan's The Confession of Isobel Gowdie (Gramophone award in contemporary music 1993), works by Greig, Medtner's Piano Concertos Nos. 2 & 3 for Hyperion (Gramophone award for Best Concerto of Yr. 1992), (with Nat. Symphony Orch.) works by Rachmaninov, others. Recipient First prize Paderewski Piano Competition, 1964, (2) Wiener Floten Uhr reward for the Best Mozart's record; named condr. laureate, BBC, 1993. Address: IMG Artists Lowell House, 616 Chiswick High Rd, Chiswick W4 5RY, England also: care BBC Scottish Symphony Orch, BBC Brdcast Ho Queen Margaret Dr, Glasgow G12 8DG, Scotland

MAKTOUF, SAMIR, education company executive; b. Sousse, Tunisia, June 25, 1957; s. Salem Bechir and Douja (Zaabouri) M.; m. Raja Khabcheche, Apr. 3, 1995 (div. Feb. 1997); 1 child, Ameen. Grad., Tunisian Air Force Acad., pilot cert. Pilot Tunisian Air Force, Bizerta, 1979-83; sales mgr. Sorena, Tunis, Tunisia, 1983-84; pilot Aeroclub Herault, Montpellier, France, 1984-86; asst. chief flight instr. Pro-flite, Vero Beach, Fla., 1986-89; pres., owner Fla. Pilot Sch. Inc., Fort Pierce, Fla., 1990—; tchr. Indian River Cmty. Coll., Fort Pierce, Fla., 1992—; cons. aviation degree Palm Beach Cmty. Coll., 1997-99; cons. Training Piper Aircraft Corp., Pratt & Whitney and Sikorsky Aircraft; aviation safety counsellor, FAA, 1997—. Author: Radio Communication, 1989, Economic Growth of General Aviation in South Fla., 1989. Mem. Aircraft Owner & Pilot Assn., Nat. Assn. Flight Instr. Avocations: reading, boating, traveling. Home: 1045 Admirals Walk Vero Beach FL 32963-2424 Office: Florida Pilot Sch Inc PO Box 258 Stuart FL 34995-0258

MAL, BIMAL CHANDRA, irrigation and water management specialist; b. Khamarbarh, India, July 11, 1950; s. Satish and Magan (Kasundi) M.; m. Champa Khan, Mar. 12, 1972; children: Sonali, Barnali, Monali. B in Technology, Indian Inst. Technology, Kharagpur, 1971, M in Technology, 1973, PhD, 1984. Asst. engr. Govt. West Bengal, India, 1973-75; from rsch. officer to prof. Indian Inst. Technology, Kharagpur, 1976—; cons. Agrl. Fin. Corp., India, 1988-89, Jalpaiguri Zilla Parishad, India, 1995-97, SPWD, New Delhi, 1998-99, Indo-British Rainfed Farming Project, U.K., 1999-2000. Author: Introduction to Soil and Water Conservation Engineering, 1995; contbr. articles to profl. jours. Mem. Inst. Engrs. India, Indian Soc. Agrl. Engrs., Indian Assn. Soil & Water Conservations. Avocations: reading, badminton, volleyball, social service. Home: Qr No A-21, 721 302 Kharagpur India Office: IIT Kharagpur, Agrl & Food Engring Dept, 721 302 Kharagpur India

MALA, THEODORE ANTHONY, physician, consultant; b. Santa Monica, Calif., Feb. 3, 1946; s. Ray and Galina (Liss) M.; children: Theodore S., Galina T. BA in Philosophy, DePaul U., 1972; MD, Autonomous U., Guadalajara, Mex., 1976; MPH, Harvard U., 1980. Spl. asst. for health affairs Alaska Fedn. Natives, Anchorage, 1977-78; chief health svcs. Alaska State Divsn. Corrections, Anchorage, 1978-79; assoc. prof., founder, dir. Inst. for Circumpolar Health Studies, U. Alaska, Anchorage, 1982-90; founder Siberian med. rsch. program U. Alaska, Anchorage, 1982, founder Magadan (USSR) med. rsch. program, 1988; commr. Health and Social Svcs. State of Alaska, Juneau, 1990-93; pres., CEO Ted Mala, Inc., Anchorage, 1993-97; pres., ptnr. Mexican-Siberian Trading Co., Monterrey, Mex., 1994-96; CEO, Confederated Tribes of Grand Ronde, Oreg., 1998-99; dir. tribal rels. Southcentral Found., Anchorage, 1999—, 2000—; traditional healing coord. Southcentral Found., Anchorage, 2000—; Alaska rsch. and publs. com. Indian Health Svc., USPHS, 1987-90; advisor Nordic Coun. Meeting, WHO, Greenland, 1985; mem. Internat. Organizing Com., Circumpolar Health Congress, Iceland, 1992-93; chmn. bd. govs. Alaska Psychiat. Inst., Anchorage, 1990-93; cabinet mem. Gov. Walter J. Hickel, Juneau, 1990-93; advisor humanitarian aid to Russian Far East U.S. Dept. State, 1992—; cons. USAID on U.S.-Russian Health Programs, 1994. Past columnist Tundra Times; contbr. articles to profl. jours. Trustee United Way Anchorage, 1978-79; chmn. bd. trustees Alaska Native Coll., 1993-96. Recipient Gov.'s award, 1988, Outstanding Svc. award Alaska Commr. Health, 1979, Ministry of Health citation USSR Govt., 1989, Citation award Alaska State Legislature, 1989-90, 94, Commendation award State of Alaska, 1990, Alaska State Legislature, 1994, Honor Kempton Svc. to Humanity award, 1989, citation Med. Comty. of Magadan region, USSR, 1989; Nat. Indian fellow U.S. Dept. Edn., 1979. Mem. Assn. Am. Indian Physicians (pres. elect), N.Y. Acad. Scis., Internat. Union for Circumpolar Health (permanent sec.-gen. 1987-90, organizing com. 8th Internat. Congress on Circumpolar Health 1987-90), Russian Acad. Polar Medicine. Avocations: cross-country skiing, hiking, photography, travel. E-mail: tmala@post.harvard.edu.

MALACH, ANTONIN, education educator, researcher; b. Kunicky, Blansko, Czech Republic, Nov. 11, 1926; s. Antonin and Emilie (Sedlakova) M.; m. Jindriska Buchtova, 1949; children: Jaroslava Kolencikova-Malachova, Antonin, Josef, Jindrich. Diploma in Engring., Tech. Mil. U., Brno, Czech Republic, 1960; CS, Polit. U., Bratislava, 1973; Docent, Polit. Univ., Bratislava, 1980. Tchr. sch. com. Boskovice, Czech Republic, 1945-50; schoolmaster sch. com. Boskovice, 1950-55; head of dept. Army Edn. Establishment, Nitra/Slovak Rep., 1961-68; head Rsch. Ctr. of Edn. Methods Means, Brno, 1969-86; sr. rschr. Masaryk U., Brno, 1987—. Co-author: (book) Simulator Training, 1976; author: (monograph) The Czech SchoolSystem Development Analysis, 1996, State of Schoolreform and Developmental Trends in Czech Educational System, 1997, Situation and Perspectives in the Regulation of the Czech Educational System, 1997, Der Bietritt zur Europaischen Union und die Auswirkungen auf das Unterrichtswesen, 1997, European Integration and Czech Education, 1999, Education in the Czech Republic-Legislation and the Future, 1999; patentee in field;

editor: Inovations in Edn. jour., 1970-86. Chmn. of culture com. local bd., Kunicky, 1945-48; mem. com. Regional Assn. of Youth, Blansko, 1948-50; examinator Assn. for Army Cooperation, Bratislava, 1959-67; mem. coun. Czech Pedagogical Assn., Brno, 1979-88. Col. Rsch. Ctr. of Edn., 1980-86, Brno. Grantee Phare Com., 1994, OECD Commn., Praha, 1995, Ministry of Edn., 1996, 97. Mem. Ednl. Leadership Internat. U. Oslo, Assn. of Programmed Learning (U. Glasgow), Pedagogical Assn. Acad. of Scis. Avocations: music, poetry, gardening, skiing. Office: Fac Econs/Adminstrn, Masaryk U/Lipova 41a, 602 00 Brno Czech Republic

MALACH, MONTE, physician; b. Jersey City, Aug. 15, 1926; s. Charles and Yetta (Pascher) M.; m. Ann Elaine Glazer, June 15, 1952 (dec. June 1989); children: Barbara Sandra, Cathie Tara, Matthew David; m. Barbara Meryl Lipstein, Dec. 24, 1994; stepchildren: Heather Ilene, Jennifer Beth, Matthew Howard. BA, U. Mich., 1949, MD, 1949. Diplomate Am. Bd. Internal Medicine, Nat. Bd. Med. Examiners. Intern Beth Israel Hosp., Boston, 1949-50; resident Beth Israel Hosp., 1950-51, chief resident, 1951-52; chief resident Kings County Hosp., Bklyn., 1954-55; practice medicine specializing in internal medicine and cardiology Bklyn., 1955-97; dir. CCU Bklyn. Hosp., 1965-91, dir. emeritus CCU, 1991—; med. dir., clin. coord. Medicare IPRO Downstate N.Y., 1990—; pres. profl. staff Bklyn. Hosp., 1966-69, chmn. med. bd., 1971-72; attending staff Caledonian Hosp., pres. profl. staff, 1984-85; pres. profl. staff Bklyn. Hosp.-Caledonian Hosp., 1987-89, chmn. med. bd., 1988-89; cons. Kings County Hosp.; tchg. fellow Tufts U. Med. Sch., 1951-52; instr. medicine Downstate Med. Ctr., Bklyn., 1955-59, clin. asst. prof. medicine, 1959-68, clin. assoc. prof., 1969-76, clin. prof., 1976—; clin. prof. medicine NYU Med. Ctr., 1994—; bd. dirs. Bay St. Landing One Owners Corp., 1985-87; v.p. Ocean View Condos, 1989-90, pres., 1990-95; med. dir. IPRO Medicare Rev., N.Y. State, 1990—, IPRO N.Y. State Peer Rev., 1990—. Kings County committeeman Democratic Party, 1964, 65. Served with USNR, 1944-46, to 1st lt. M.C. U.S. Army, 1952-54. Recipient 1st Prize for Crisis Mgmt. Habitat Mag., 1987. Fellow Am. Coll. Chest Physicians, ACP (master, Laureate award 2000), Am. Coll. Cardiology (task force Health Care Quality Improvement Initiative 1996—); mem. AMA (chmn. sect. coun. internal medicine 1980), N.Y. Heart Assn., Am. Soc. Internal Medicine (master, trustee 1975-79, sec.-treas. 1979—, pres. elect 1981, pres. 1982-83, chmn. investment com. 1985-93), N.Y. State Soc. Internal Medicine (pres. 1973-74, dir. 1966-84, chmn. Bklyn. chpt., v.p. 1971, award of merit 1978), Bklyn. Soc. Internal Medicine (mem. council 1965, pres. 1969-72), Med. Soc. State of N.Y. (chmn. sect. internal medicine 1976, chmn. med. care ins. com. 1988-93), Federated Council for Internal Medicine (chmn. 1979-80), Med. Soc. County Kings (censor 1985-91).

MALADRY, DAVID HENRI, plastic surgeon, hand surgeon; b. Toulouse, France, Apr. 11, 1960; s. Francis Victor and Claudine Huguette (Tourne) M.; m. Patricia Yvonne Muller, Oct. 24, 1987; children: Eline, Louis, Claire-Lise. Degree in Medicine, Faculty of Lille, France, 1984; MD, Saintantoine U., Paris, 1990; MSc in Cosmetology, Dermatology, Faculty of Chatenay-Malabry, France, 1986. Resident Assistance Publique Paris, 1985-90; sr. resident, asst. Saint Antoine Faculty, Paris, 1990-91, Necker Faculty, Paris, 1991-93; asst., plastic surgeon S.O.S. Main Hosp. Boucicaut, Paris, 1993—; dir. Lab. Microsurgery and Reconstructive Surgery, S.O.S. Mains Hosp. Boucicaut, 1993—. Rep. of residents Hosp. Broussais, paris, 1985-86. Lt. French Health Svc., 1986-87. Recipient medal D'Argent Des Hopitaux DeParis, 1990. Mem. French Soc. Plastic Reconstructive Esthetic Surgery, French Hand Surgery Soc. (assoc.), French Plastic Reconstructive and Esthetic Surgery Coll. Office: 12 Villa Dufresne, Paris 75016, France

MALAFEYEV, OLEG ALEXEYEVICH, mathematician; b. Ulijanovsk, Russia, May 19, 1944; s. Alexey Nikolaevitch and Raisa Dmitrievna (Veretennikova) M.; m. N.V. Proshko, June 30, 1944 (div. 1983); 1 child, Anna Olegobna. MS, U. Leningrad, 1967, PhD, 1971, PhD in math. and physic, 1989; hon. diploma, Russian Ministry of High Edn., 1999. Researcher U. Leningrad, 1970-72, asst. prof., 1972-89, prof., 1989—, head socioecon. systems modeling chair, 1991—, dir. competitive and synergistic systems lab., 1991-97; head Scientific Rsch. programs on applied math., Gov. USSR, 1969-89; co-pres. Nevskaya Acad., Leningrad, 1988—; co-dir. All-Russian Republic Program Revival of Russian Peoples U. Leningrad, 1990—; co-founder Dept. Natural Scis., 1992—. Author: Solutions' Stability of Multicriteria Optimization Problems and Competitive Controlled Dynamical Processes, 1990, Dynamical Systems of Conflict, 1993; co-author: Synergetics of Technological Progress and Ethics of Competition, 1996, Conflict Situations Modeling in Socioeconomical Systems, 1998, Stability and Numerical Methods in Control Systems of Conflict, 1998, Fundamentals of Conflict Systems Theory, 2000, Mathematical Modeling of Processes in Agroindustrial Complex, 2000; contbr. numerous articles to profl. jours. Mem. Am. Math. Soc. Home: 6 Frunze str Flat 225, 196070 Saint Petersburg Russia Office: SPB U Faculty of Applied Math, 2 Bibliotechnaya Sq, 198904 Saint Petersburg Russia

MALAKA, BERNWARD, publishing executive; b. Dusseldorf, Germany, Aug. 31, 1962; s. Peter and Ursula (Goerigk) M.; m. Marion Pieper; children: Sophia, David. Dipl., U. Cologne, 1987, PhD, 1991. Asst. U. Cologne, Germany, 1987-90; asst. to pub., mktg. dir. VGS Verlagsgesellschaft, Cologne, 1991-94, dir. mktg. and bus., 1994-99, mng. dir., 2000—. Musician (record with Die Krupps) Wahre Arbeit, wahrer Lohn, 1982, Stahlwerk-symphonie, 1981, Zensur & Zensur, 1980. Mem. GEMA, GVL, Foerdergesellschaft Produkt-mktg., Koelnischer Kunstverein, Verein der Freunde der Kunsthochschule f. Medien. Avocations: fine arts, music, gardening. Office: VGS Verlagsgesellschaft, Gertrudenstrasse 30-36, D-50667 Cologne Germany

MALAKA, RAINER, research scientist, project manager; b. Esslingen, Germany, June 7, 1965; s. Norbert and Ingeborg H. (Bartsch) M. Diploma, U. Karlsruhe, Germany, 1992, Dr.rer.nat., 1996. Cert. computer scientist; cert. rschr. in computational neurosci. Rschr. U. Karlsruhe, 1992—; guest scientist U. Calif., Berkeley, 1994, 96. Author: Praktikum Neuronale Netze, 1996, Neural Information Processing in Insect Olfactory Systems, 1997; contbr. articles to profl. jours. Active Social Dem. Party, State of Baden Württemberg, Germany, 1982—. With German Mil., 1985-86. Recipient Scheffel prize Sheffel-Gesellschaft, 1984, Klaus-Tschira prize U. Karlsruhe, 1997; grantee Deutscher Akademischer Auslandsdienst, 1994. Mem. Assn. Computing Machinery; Gesellschaft für Informatik. Office: European Media Lab, Schloss-Wolfsbrunnenweg 33, D-69118 Heidelberg Germany

MALAKAR, BIMAN, dairy engineering educator; b. Calcutta, India, Jan. 3, 1949; s. Girindranath and Binapani Malakar; m. Sumita Sarkar, Dec. 10, 1972; children: Sushmita, Ranajoy. B Tech. with honors, Indian Inst. Tech., Kharagpur, 1970, DIIT in Dairy Engring., 1971, PhD in Engring., 1984. Chartered engr. Asst. engr. Govt. Gujarat, India, 1971-72, Govt. West Bengal, India, 1972-78; technical expert Govt. Montserrat, West Indies, 1977-78; lectr. Bidhan Chandra Agrl. U., India, 1982-84, reader, 1984-94; prof. Bighan Chandra Agrl. U., India, 1994-95; prof. West Bengal U. Animal and Fishery Scis., Mohanpur, India, 1995—, head dept. dairy engring., 1982-87, 92-97, mem. faculty coun., 1997—; tech. expert Commonwealth Secretariat, Commonwealth Fund Technical Cooperation, London, 1977-78, UN Indsl. Devel. Orgn., Vienna, 1980-87, FAO, Rome, 1978-88, Asian Devel. Bank, Manila, 1978-88; prin. investigator Indian Coun. Agrl. Rsch., 1993-98; external mem. undergrad. and postgrad. faculty coun. Bidhan Chandra Agrl. U., 1997—. Author: Milk Handling Equipment, 1997, Handbook of Animal Husbandry Sciences; contbr. articles to profl. jours. Gen. sec. Resident Welfare Forum, Kalyani, India, 1993-95. Named Best Musician Indian Inst. Tech., Kharagpur, 1969. Mem. Instn. Engrs. (India), Indian Dairy Assn. (life), Rotary Internat. Home: B-8/40, Kalyani 741235, India Office: West Bengal U Animal &, Fishery Scis, Mohanpur 741252, India

MALAKHOV, VLADIMIR, dancer; b. Krivoy Rog, Ukraine, USSR, Jan. 7, 1968; arrived in Can., 1994; s. Anatoly and Elena Malakhov. Grad., Bolshoi Ballet Acad., Moscow, 1986. Prin. dancer Vienna State Opera, 1992-94; prin. dancer Nat. Ballet Can., 1994-97, guest artist, 1997-98; prin. dancer Am. Ballet Theatre, N.Y.C., 1995—; guest artist Am. Ballet Theatre, 1994. Appeared in Giselle, Swan Lake, Nutcracker, Manon, Romeo and Juliette, others; performed in major opera houses worldwide. Recipient Gold medal Varna Ballet Competition, 1986, Gold medal Moscow Ballet Competition, 1986, Serge Lifar prize, 1991. Address: Am Ballet Theatre 890 Broadway New York NY 10003-1211*

MALAKHOV, VLADIMIR VASIL'EVITCH, zoology educator; b. Sverdlovsk, Russia, Mar. 13, 1951; s. Vassily Yakovlevitch and Svetlana Georgiyevna (Goryunova) M.; m. Elena Antonovna Zamyshlyak, Aug. 11, 1973 (div. Feb. 1988); 1 child, Boris; m. Lioubov Andreevna Medvedeva, Aug. 26, 1988. MSc, Moscow State U., 1973, PhD, 1976, DSc, 1980. Asst. rschr. Moscow State U., 1976-80, prof., 1985—; sr. rschr. Koltsoff Instn. Developmental Biology, Moscow, 1980-82; head lab. Instn. Marine Biology, Vladivostok, Russia, 1982-85. Author: Nematodes, 1994, Cephalorhyncha, A New Phylum of Animal Kingdom, 1995, Vestimentifera, Gutless Invertebrates of Sea Floor, 1998. Mem. Russian Soc. Nematologists (pres. 1995-98), Russian Acad. Sci. (corr.). Home: Skulptora Muhinoy 10-128, 119634 Moscow Russia Office: Moscow State Univ, Leninsky gory, 119899 Moscow Russia

MALAKHOVSKII, ALEXANDER VALENTIN, physicist, researcher; b. Kemerovo, USSR, Jan. 6, 1937; arrived in Israel, 1992; s. Valentin Fabian Malakhovskii and Evgeniya Aron Rishes; m. Dolores Dmitrii Chernikova, 1961 (div. 1981); 1 child, Ekaterina; m. Lyubov Mihail Demidenko, July 9, 1982; children: Denis, Mariya. Degree in electronic engring., V.I. Uliyanov Leningrad Inst., 1960; PhD in Physics, USSR Acad., Krasnoyarsk, 1974, postgrad., 1983. Sr. engr. Machine Works, Krasnoyarsk, 1960-65; sr. engr. Inst. Physics, Krasnoyarsk, 1965-69, sci. worker, 1969-80, sr. sci. worker, 1980-92; sr. rschr. Bar-Ilan U., Ramat-Gan, Israel, 1994—. Author: Selected Problems of Optics and Magneto-optics of Transition Elements Compounds, 1992; contbr. articles to profl. jours.; patentee in field. Avocations: photography, travel. E-mail: malakha@mail.biu.ac.il. Office: Bar-Ilan U, Dept Chemistry, 52900 Ramat-Gan Israel

MALAMUD, BRUCE D., scientist; b. Geneva, Switzerland, July 19, 1963; s. Ernest I. and Jean (Goldstein) M. BA, Reed Coll., 1986; PhD, Cornell U., 1998. H.s. physics and chemistry tchr. Peace Corps, Niger, 1986-88; accelerator operator, ops. engr. Stanford Linear Accelerator, Menlo Park, Calif., 1988-91; tchg. asst., grad. rsch. asst. Cornell U., Ithaca, N.Y., 1991-97, vis. lectr., postdoctoral rsch. assoc., 1997-98, postdoctoral rsch. assoc., 1999-2000; lectr. Kings Coll., London, 2000—; Fulbright fellow Inst. for Study of Snow, Glaciers and the Environment, Mendoza, Argentina, 1998-99. Contbr. articles to profl. jours.

MALAN, DANIEL FRANÇOIS, rock mechanics engineer, researcher; b. Bethlehem, South Africa, Nov. 4, 1968; s. Mathys Michiel and Cecilie (Long) M.; m. Maria Petronella Claasen, Jan. 9, 1993. BIng in Electronics cum laude, Rand Afrikaans U., Johannesburg, South Africa, 1991, MIng in Electronics cum laude, 1993; PhD in Mining Engring., U. the Witwatersrand, Johannesburg, 1998. Rsch. engr. CSIR Miningtek, Johannesburg, 1993-97, project mgr., 1997-2000, rsch. area mgr., 2000—. Contbr. articles to sci. jours., including Tectonophysics, Internat. Jour. Rock Mechanics, others. Mem. South African Inst. Mining and Metallurgy, South African Inst. Rock Engring. Democrat. Avocations: coin and banknote collecting, model aircraft building. Home: 857 Quail West Sr, Roodepoort 1724 GT, South Africa Office: CSIR Miningtek, Carlow Rd POB 91230, Johannesburg 2006 AP, South Africa

MALAN, JACQUES DANIEL, actuary; b. Montagu, South Africa, Nov. 2, 1948; s. Daniel and Susanna (duToit) M.; m. Johanna Elizabeth Loubser, July 7, 1973; three children. Bsc, U. Stellenbosch, 1970. Sr. mgr. Sanlam, South Africa, 1971-83; sr. dir. Alexander Forbes, South Africa, 1983-95; mng. dir. Jacques Malan & Assocs., South Africa, 1995—. Office: PO box 3950, 7536 Tyger Valley South Africa

MALAN, PEDRO, Brazilian government official; b. Rio de Janeiro, 1943. Pres. Econ. Inst., Rio de Janeiro; founder Inst. Rio Economists, 1979; prof. econs. Pontifical Catholic U., Rio de Janeiro, 1979—; expert Applied Econ. Rsch. Inst.; dir. Center on Transnat. Corps., 1983, World Bank, 1985, 92, Internat. Devel. Bank; fgn. debt negotiator Ministry of Finance, 1990-91; pres. Ctrl. Bank Brazil, 1993-94; min. finance Govt. of Brazil, 1994—. Office: Esplanada dos Ministérios, Bloco P 5o andar, 70048-900 Brasilia Brazil*

MALANDRAKI, OLGA EVARESTOS, physicist, researcher; b. Ilisia, Greece, July 15, 1969; d. Evarestos Manousos Malandrakis and Konstadina Pandelis Marouga. Diploma, Hellenic-Am. Union, Athens, 1992; diploma d'etudes superieures, Inst. Français D'Athenes, Athens, 1988; degree in physics, Kapodistrian U. Athens, 1993; postgrad., Demokritos U. Trace, Xanthi, Greece, 1994—. Young rschr. nuclear physics divsn. Kapodistrian U. of Athens, 1992-93; young rschr. Inst. Ionospheric and Space Rsch. Nat. Obs. Athens, 1996-98, rep. space physics and elec. engring. dept., 1994—; mem. Ulysses/Hi-Scale Experiment Internat. Sci. Team, Lucent Tech., Murray Hill, N.J., 1994—. Contbr. articles to profl. jours. Grantee EEC, Greece, 1996-98, Obs. Paris, 1998, 2000. Greek Orthodox. Avocations: playing dulcimer, traditional Greek music, athletics, cinema, theater. Fax: 003016138343. Home: Aggelou Gini 25A, 11525 New Phychiko Athens, Greece Office: Nat Obs Athens, Metaxa & Vas Pavlou St, 15236 Athens Greece

MALASSENET, FRANCOIS JACQUES, electrical engineering educator, researcher; b. Nimes, Gard, France, May 19, 1964. Diploma in engring., Supelec, Gif, France, 1986; MS, Ga. Tech., 1986, PhD, 1991. Acad. profl., dir. Ga. Tech., 1992—; treas. SEE, Est, France, 1995—. Mem. IEEE. Office: Ga Tech Lorraine, 2-3 rue Marconi, 57070 Metz France

MALATERRE, HENRI ROMAIN, cardiologist; b. Marseille, France, Mar. 7, 1963; s. Henri and Regine (Vitou) M.; m. Laurence Marie Daver, Dec. 28, 1965; children: Lea, Timothee. MD, U. Marseille, 1992. From intern to hosp. practitioner Univ. Hosp. Marseille, 1988—. Mem. French Soc. Cardiology, Am. Soc. Echocardiography. Roman Catholic. Avocations: tennis, skiing, windsurfing. Home: 34 rue Marx Dormoy, 13004 Marseille France Office: Univ Hosp Marseille, Hopital la Conception, 13385 Marseille Cedex 5, France

MALAVOLTA, EURIPEDES, agriculture educator, consultant; b. Araraquara, Brazil, Aug. 13, 1926; s. Antonio and Lucia Canassa Malavolta; m. Leila Machado Brito (div.); children: Lucia, Ligia, Fernanda, Marcelo, Giampaolo. BS in Agr., U. São Paula, Piracicaba, Brazil, 1948. Asst. prof. Escola Superior de Agricultura Luiz de Queinoz U. São Paulo, 1949-51, assoc. prof., 1951-54; rsch. assoc. U. Calif., Berkeley, 1952-53; prof. Escola Superior de Agricultura Luiz de Queinoz U. São Paulo, 1954-84, dean, 1964-70; rschr. Centro de Energia Nuclear Agricultura U. São Paulo, Piracicaba, 1984—; cons. Petrofertil, São Paulo, Brazil, 1964-85. Author: On the Mineral Nutrition of Tropical Crops, 1962, Elements of Plant Nutrition (in Portuguese), 1980, Fertilizing for High Yield Sugar Cane, 1994 Evaluation of Nutritional Status (in Portuguese), 1997. Recipient prize Moinho Santista, São Paulo, 1982, Sci. Merit award Govt. of Brazil, 1998. Roman Catholic. Avocations: reading, stamp collecting, watching Formula One racing. E-Mail: mala@cena.usp.br.

MALAWSKI, ANDRZEJ JERZY, mathematical economist, researcher; b. Cracow, Poland, May 10, 1948; s. Tadeusz and Anna (Haydukiewicz) M.; m. Barbara Antonina Sopicka, Nov. 17, 1973; children: Maciej, Maria. MS in Math., Jagiellonian U., Cracow, 1971, MA in Philosophy, 1975; PhD in Econs., Cracow U. Econs., 1979. Asst. dept. math. Cracow U. Econs., 1972-79, asst. prof. dept. math., 1979-93, assoc. prof. dept. math., 1993—; dep. dir. core studium Cracow U. Econs., 1993-96, vice dean faculty of mgmt., 1996-99. Author: Relatively Isolated Systems and Their Models in Economics, 1992, Introduction to Mathematical Economics, 1995, Axiematic Method in Economics, 1999. Mem. Polish Math. Soc. Avocations: gardening, hiking, skiing. Home: Sabaly 53/10, 31-479 Cracow Poland Office: Cracow Univ Econs, Rakowicka 27, 31-500 Cracow Poland

MALBIN, SAM, administrator; b. Johannesburg, South Africa, Aug. 11, 1933; s. Max Mottel and Hinda Sarah (Rosowsky) M.; m. Nita Rabinowitz, Aug.12, 1956; children: Heather Miller, Karen Horwitz. Diploma mktg. mgmt., Damelin Mgmt. Sch., 1972. Refrideration engr. H. Polliack & Co., Johannesburg, South Africa, 1948-53, Modern Appliances, Johannesburg, South Africa, 1953-55; sales & svc. E. Papert & Co., Johannesburg, South Africa, 1955-59; regional sales mgr. S.A. Philips, Johannesburg, South Africa, 1960-68; sales dir. Lewis Appliance Corp., Johannesburg, South Africa, 1969-78; ret. TEK Corp. Defy Appliances Ltd., Johannesburg, 1998; sales dir. Pioneer Electronics S.A., 1969-74, Jarome Sewing and Knitting Co. S.A., 1969-78; mdse. mgr. Morkels Ltd., Cape Town, South Africa, 1979-81; dir. TEK Corp. Defy Appliances Ltd., Johannesburg, 1981-98. Jewish. Avocations: classical music, literature, lawn bowls, martial arts. Fax: 2711-6210399. Home: 403 Upper Houghton, 16 St Peters Rd, Johannesburg 2198, South Africa Office: Defy Appliances Ltd, PO Box 27150, Benrose 2011, South Africa

MALBRAN, ENRIQUE S., ophthalmologist, consultant; b. Buenos Aires, Argentina, May 8, 1930; s. Jorge L. and Mercedes (Madero) M.; m. Ana M. Echague Malbran, Sept. 19, 1953; children: Ana, Enrique, Mercedes, Francisco, Marcos, Nicolas, Jorge, Tomas. Med. sch., U. Buenos Aires, 1952. Med. diplomate. Eye surgeon Hosp. Italiano, Buenos Aires, 1955-69; dir. medicine Fund. Talmologica Argentina, 1964-72, pres., 1972—; mem. Internat. Coun. Opathalmology, 1978-86; chmn. Alademia Ophthalmologist Internat., 1983—; pres. Pan Am. Assn. Ophthalmology, 1989-91; chair mem. Acad. Nat. Medicine. Buenos Aires, 1981—. Author: Modern Problems in Ophthalmology, 1964; contbr. clinical rsch. in field. Recipient Gold medal Inst. Barraquer, Carcelona, 1993, Paul Kayser Internat. award Retina Rsch. Found., Houston, 1995. Mem. Club Jules Gonin, Internat. Ophthalmology Microsurgery Group. Roman Catholic. Avocations: tennis, wind surfing, soccer. Office: Centro Oftalmolo Gico, Clin Optolmologia Malbran, Parera 164, 1014 Buenos Aires Argentina

MALCA, SAMUEL ALBERT, neurosurgeon; b. Casablanca, Morocco, June 2, 1954; arrived in France, 1973; s. Aaron Henri and Esther (Soussan) M.; m. Maryline El Beze, Aug. 13, 1984; children: Nathaniel Aaron, Davy Joseph, Kéren Esther. MD, Faculty Medicine, Marseille, France, 1985. Intern Pub. Assistance, Marseille, France, 1980-85; clin. chief Faculty Medicine, Marseille, France, 1985-90; neurosurgeon hosp. practitioner Ste. Marguerite Hosp., Marseille, France, 1990—; cons. in field. Contbr. articles to profl. jours. Mem. Soc. France Neurosci., Soc. Neurosurgery France, Club France Neurosurgery. Avocations: squash, French boxing. Office: Ste Marguerite Hosp, 270 Blvd de Ste Marguerite, 13009 Marseille France

MALCATA, FRANCISCO XAVIER, science educator; b. Malange, Angola, May 23, 1963; arrived in Portugal, 1964; s. Antonio Malcata and Maria Engracia (Domingos) Julião; m. Angela Carvalho Macedo, Aug. 17, 1988; 1 child, Filipa. BSChemE, U. Oporto, Portugal, 1988; PhDChemE, U. Wis., 1991; D in Biotechnology, Portuguese Cath. U., 1991. Cert. engr. Tchg. asst. Portuguese Cath. U., Porto, 1987-91, asst. prof., 1991-97, assoc. prof., 1997—; coord. dairy R&D Portuguese Cath. U. Porto, 1991—, dir. biotech. grad. sch., 1996-97, dir. Coll. Biotech., 1998—; cons. Regional Directorate of Agr., Braga, Portugal, 1992—; dir. NATO Advanced Study Inst., Povoa de Varzim, Portugal, 1995; adminstr.-in-chief Assn. Trustee Cos. for Coll. Biotechnology, 1998—; lectr. in field. Author: Hydrolysis of Butterfat with Immobilized Lipase, 1991, Contingence and Utopy: Reports and Thoughts, 2000, Socio-economic and Scientific-technological Evolution of the Northern Region in food Biotechnology: Perspectives for Internationalization, 2000, The Green Book of Cooperation University/Industry-Agrofood Sector, 2000, others; editor: Engineering of/with Lipases, 1996, Iberian Traditional Cheeses: Contributions for Their Scientific and Technological Knowledge, 1999; contbr. articles to profl. jours. Recipient C.P. Sprately award and Centennial award Coll. Engring. Oporto, 1986, J.V. Luck award Inst. Food Technologists, 1990, R.H. Potts Meml. award Am. Oil Chemists Soc., 1991; Internat. Sci. Exch. Program fellow NATO, 1987, 1988-91, CANDIA Inst. fellow Ctr. Internat. Rsch. André Gaillard, 1993-94. Mem. AAAS, AIChE, Internat. Union Food Sci. and Tech., Internat. Assn. Food Protection, Am. Oil Chemists Soc., Am. Chem. Soc., N.Y. Acad. Sci., Am. Dairy Sci. Assn. (Founders award 1998), European Alliance Dairy Tchrs., Knights of the Order Acad. Palms French Govt., Inst. Food Technologists, Portuguese Soc. Biochemistry, Portuguese Soc. Chemistry, Sigma Xi, Tau Beta Pi, Phi Tau Sigma. Roman Catholic. Avocations: reading, collecting. Fax: (351) 2-5090351. Office: Escola Superior Biotech, Rua Dr Antonio Bernardino Almeida, P-4200-072 Porto Portugal

MALCHOW, TOM, Olympic athlete; b. Aug. 18, 1976. Student, U. Mich. Winner Silver medal Pan Am. Games, 1995, 200 meter butterfly swimming Atlanta Olympics, 1996, Gold medal World Univ. Games, 1995. Office: US Swimming Inc One Olympic Plz Colorado Springs CO 80909

MALCURIA, SHERRY JOANNE, real estate company executive, interior designer; b. Wendall, Idaho, Apr. 16, 1942; d. John Donald and Vera Ella (Frost) Kingery; children: Artist Roxanne, Buddy (George II), Kami JoAnne, Launi JoElla; m. Samuel Ross Malcuria, June 12, 1999. Student, Ariz. State U., 1960. Corp. sec., treas. Karbel Metals Co., Phoenix, 1963-67; sec. to pub. Scottsdale (Ariz.) Daily Progress, 1969-72; with D-Velco Mfg. of Ariz., Phoenix, 1959-62, dir., exec. v.p., sec., treas., 1972-87; mng. ptnr., financial and real estate investment Karitage, Ltd., Scottsdale, 1987—.

MALDINI, CESARE, professional soccer coach, former player; b. Trieste, Italy, Feb. 5, 1932; m. Maria Luisa; children: Valentina, Donatella, Monica, Alessandro, Pier, Cesare, Paolo. Player, capt. AC Milan Football Club, Italy; winner European Cup, 1963; player Torino Football Club, Italy; coach Parma Football Club, Italy, Foggia Football Club, Italy, Terni Football Club, Italy; dep. coach Italian Nat. Team, coach; coach Italian Nat. Team (under-21); chief scout AC Milan, 1999. Office: AC Milan, Via Turati 3, IT-20121 Milan Italy*

MALDINI, PAOLO, professional soccer player; b. Milan, Italy, June 26, 1968; s. Cesare Maldini; m. Adriana Fossa, 1994. Defender, capt. AC Milan, Italy, 1984—, Italian Nat. Team, 1998; winner Italian Championship, 1988, 92-94, European Champions' Cup, 1989, 90, 94, European Super Cup, 1989, 90, 95; winner World Club Cup, 1989, 90, defender, 1998. Named World Player of Yr., World Soccer, 1994. Office: Milan Assn Calcio SpA, Via Turati 3, 20121 Milan Italy*

MALDONADO, JAIME J., mechanical engineer; b. Ponce, P.R., July 26, 1967; s. Jaime and Haydeé (Bravo) M.; m. Marisol Juarbe, Dec. 25, 1998. BS in Mech. Engring., U. P.R., Mayaguez, 1990; MS in Indsl. Engring., Cleve. State U., 1996; MS in Mech. Engring., Case Western Res. U., 1997. Aerospace engr. NASA, Cleve., 1990-98; sr. fusion process engr. Corning Inc., Harrodsburg, Ky., 1998—. Contbr. articles to profl. jours. Avocations: hiking, biking, inline skating. Home: 412 Whitfield Dr Lexington KY 40515-4771 Office: Corning Inc 680 E Office St Harrodsburg KY 40330-1300

MALDONADO-LOPEZ, RAFAEL, life sciences researcher; b. Cadiz, Spain, Dec. 2, 1961; s. Juan and Isabel (Lopez-Siloniz) Maldonado-Selvatico; m. Olga Valverde-Granados. MD, U. Cadiz, 1985, PhD in Neuropsychopharmacology, 1988; PhD in Molecular Pharmacochemistry, U. René Descartes, Paris, 1990, diploma Life Scis. Rsch. Dir., 1993. Predoctoral fellow U. Cadiz, 1986-87; postdoctoral fellow Inst. Nat. de la Santé et de la Recherche Med., Paris, 1988-89; postdoctoral Rsch. Inst. Scripps Clinic, San Diego, 1990-91; assoc. rsch. INSERM U266, Paris, 1991-92, sci. rschr., 1992—; cons. rschr. Rsch. Inst. Scripps Clinic, San Diego, 1992, Addiction Rsch. Ctr., Balt. 1992, German Cancer Rsch. Ctr., 1995; project leader biomed. and health rsch. program Commn. of European Cmtys., 1994—, project leader of PECO programme of the Commn. of European Cmtys. for Coop. in Sci. and Tech. with Ctrl. and Ea. European Countries and with new independent states of former USSR. Author chpts. in books; contbr. articles to profl. jours. Recipient Roussel prize U. René Descartes, 1991, Almirall prize, Spain, 1992, Upjohn prize, Spain, 1994. Mem. Spanish Soc. Pharmacology (Young Rsch. award 1995), Am. Soc. Neurosci., N.Y. Acad. Scis. Avocations: photography, trekking, chess. Office: Health & Life Scis Sch Universitat Pompeu Fabra, Aiguader 80, 08003 Barcelona Spain Address: c/Ausias March 124 5-2, Barcelona 08013, Spain

MALECKA-PANAS, EWA IZABELA, gastroenterologist, educator; b. Lodz, Poland, Mar. 3, 1956; d. Ignacy Malecki and Izabela Wiktoria Planeta-Malecka; 1 child, Maciej. MD, Med. Sch. Lodz, 1980, PhD, 1988.

Bd. cert. in gastroenterology and internal medicine. Lectr., rsch. assoc. dept. med. biology and parasitology Med. Sch. Lodz, 1980-81, lectr., rsch. assoc. dept. gastroenterology, 1981-84, sr. lectr., rsch. assoc. dept. digestive tract diseases, 1984-89, asst. prof. dept. digestive tract diseases, 1990-92, 93-97, assoc. prof. dept. digestive tract diseases, 1997—; vis. scholar sect. gastroenterology U. Calif., Davis, Martinez, 1989-90; rsch. scholar dept. medicine Wayne State U., Allen Park, Mich., 1992-93. Contbr. numerous articles to med. jours. Mem. Citizen of the World, 1978. Mem. Internat. Gastro-Surg. Club, Am. Pancreatic Assn., Am. Coll. Gastroenterology (internat. mem.), Am. Gastroenterol. Assn. (internat. mem.). Avocations: documental literature, skiing, swimming, scuba diving. Fax: 48 42 6786480. E-mail: ewuncia@poczta.onet.pl. Home: Nastrojowa 41/4, Lodz 91-496, Poland Office: Med Sch Lodz, Kopcinskiego 22, Lodz 90-153, Poland

MALEEV, VLADIMIR YAKOVLEVICH, biophysicist; b. Rostov na Donu, Russia, Mar. 30, 1930; s. Yakov Fedorovich and Sofia Georgievna (Bezmelnitsina) M.; m. Tamara Alexandrovna Vinogradova, Mar. 22, 1963; children: Alexey, Olga. Physicist, Kharkov State U., 1953, cand. sci., 1961, DS of Physics, 1975. Rschr. Inst. Radiophysics and Electronics Nat. Acad. Sci. Ukraine, Kharkov, 1956-63, head biophysics dept., 1964—; prof. Kharkov State U., 1978—. Contbr. articles to profl. jours. Mem. Ukrainian Biophys. Soc. (v.p.). Home: AC 8711, 61085 Kharkov Ukraine Office: Nat Acad Sci Ukraine, 12 Acad Proscury Str, 61085 Kharkov Ukraine

MALEIANE, ADRIANO AFONSO, banker. Gov. Ctrl. Bank Mozambique. Office: Banco de Mocambique, 1695 Ave 25 de Septembro, Maputo Mozambique*

MALEIKA-RABE, ANNETTE, obstetrician, gynecologist, researcher; b. Hildesheim, Germany, June 4, 1965; d. Hans-Ludwig and Linde (Waidelich) M.; m. Thomas Rabe, June 16, 1995; children: Leonie, Antonia, Maximilian. Grad., U. Saarland, Germany, 1991, postgrad., 1992. Med. diplomate. Resident Univ. Women's Hosp., Heidelberg, Germany, 1991—. Contbr. articles to profl. jours., chpt. to book. Avocations: music, piano and violin playing, horseback riding. Home: Mittelgewann 11a, 68723 Schwetzingen Germany Office: Univ Women's Hosp, Voss Str 9, 69115 Heidelberg Germany

MALEK, FREDERIC VINCENT, finance company executive; b. Oak Park, Ill., Dec. 22, 1936; s. Fred W. and Martha (Smickilas) M.; m. Marlene A. McArthur, Aug. 5, 1961; children: Fred W., Michelle A. BS, U.S. Mil. Acad., 1959; MBA, Harvard U., 1964; D of Humanities (hon.), St. Leo Coll., St. Petersburg, Fla., 1970. Assoc. McKinsey & Co., Inc., L.A., 1964-67; chmn. exec. com. Triangle Corp., Columbia, S.C., 1967-69; dep. under sec. HEW, Washington, 1969-70; spl. asst. to Pres. U.S., Washington, 1970-73; dep. dir. U.S. Office of Mgmt. and Budget, Washington, 1973-75; with Marriott Corp., Washington, 1975-88, sr. v.p., 1975-77, exec. v.p., 1978-88; pres. Marriott Hotels and Resorts, 1981-88; pres. Northwest Airlines, Mpls., 1989-90, vice chmn., 1990-91, also bd. dirs.; campaign mgr. Bush-Quayle '92, 1991-92; co-chmn. CB Comml. Real Estate Group, 1989-96; chmn. Lodging Opportunities Fund, 1991—, Thayer Capital Ptnrs., 1992—, Thayer Hotel Investors, 1994—; chmn. 1996 Rep. Presdl. Trust, 1995-96; bd. dirs. Automated Data Processing Corp., Am. Mgmt. Sys. Inc., N.W. Airlines, FPL Group Inc., Paine Webber Funds, Manor Care Inc.; dir. with rank of amb., 1990 Econ. Summit, 1989—; adj. prof. U. S.C., 1986-89; lectr. Kennedy Sch. Govt., Harvard U., 1976. Mem. Pres.'s Commn. on White House Fellows, 1971-75, White House Domestic Coun., 1974-75, Pres.'s Commn. on Pers. Interchange, 1974-76; dep. dir. com. for Re-election of Pres., 1972; Pres.'s Commn. on Pvt. Sector Initiatives, 1982-85, dir. conv. Bush for Pres., 1988; mem. Nat. Coun. on Surface Transp. Rsch., 1993-95; nat. adv. bd. Nat. Ctr. Econ. Edn. of Children, 1980-82; mem. Pres.'s Coun. on Phys. Fitness and Sports, 1986-91. Mem. Am.-Israel Friendship League (bd. trustees 1991—), Aspen Inst. (bd. trustees 1996—). Episcopalian. Avocations: biking, skiing. Office: 1455 Pennsylvania Ave NW Washington DC 20004-1008

MÁLEK, JIŘÍ, inorganic chemistry researcher; b. Polička, Czech Republic, Sept. 7, 1959; s. Jiří and Věra (Málková); m. Naděžda Málková, Nov. 27, 1982; 1 child, Magdalena. MS, U. Chem. Tech., Pardubice, Czech Republic, 1982, PhD, 1986; DSc, U. Chem. Tech., 2000. Rsch. scientist U. Chem. Tech., Pardubice, Czech Republic, 1985-87, Joint Lab. Solid State Chemistry, Pardubice, Czech Republic, 1987—; assoc. prof. Pardubice U., 1996—, rector, 2000—; sci. bd. chmn. Joint Lab. Solid State Chemistry, Pardubice, 1994-2000. Mem. editl. bd. Thermochimica Acta; contbr. over 70 articles to profl. jours. Recipient Young Scientist award Internat. Confederation for Thermal Analysis and Calonimetry, 1992. Mem. Czech Chem. Soc. Avocations: photography, lit., art. Home: Pernstynská 43, 530-03 Pardubice Czech Republic Office: Joint Lab Solid State Chem, Studentská 84, 53210 Pardubice Czech Republic

MALEK, MARLENE ANNE, cultural organization, foundation executive; b. Oakland, Calif., June 22, 1939; d. William Alexander and Yolanda Katherine (Stella) McArthur; m. Frederic Vincent Malek, Aug. 5, 1961; children: Frederic William, Michelle Anne. Student, Armstrong U., 1959, Marymount U., 1979. Mem. women's bd. Am. Heart Assn., 1973—; bd. dirs., mem. exec. com. Marymount U., Arlington, Va., 19745; mem. cmty. bd. and nat. com. for the performing arts Kennedy Ctr.; chmn. Eisenhower Meml. Found., Washington, 1972-74; mem. adv. bd. Second Genesis Drug Rehab. Program, Bethesda, Md., 19835; bd. dirs. Nat. Mus. Women in Arts, 1987, Friends of Cancer Rsch.; presdl. appointment to Nat. Cancer Adv. Bd., 1991-96; mem. bd. overseers Duke U. Cancer Ctr. Episcopalian. Avocations: cross country skiing, mountain and cross country biking.

MALEK, MOHAMMED ABDUL, scientist; b. Mymensingh, Bangladesh, Oct. 1, 1951; s. Mohammed Abdul Gafur and Rahatan Nessa; m. Syeda Kaniz Amina, Dec. 24, 1983; children: Ashik, Omar. DVM, BD Agrivarsity, Mymensingh, 1977, MSC in Vet. Sci., 1979; PhD in Radiobiology, CSRIRR, Leningrad, Russia, 1989. Instr. DYD, Dhaka, Bangladesh, 1980-82; sci. officer BAEC, Bangladesh, 1982-87, sr. sci. officer, 1987-95, prin. sci. officer, 1995—; STA fellow JAERI, Takasaki, Japan, 1993-94. Contbr. articles to profl. jours. Mem. Bangladesh Atomic Energy Scientist Assn., Bangladesh Assn. Advancement of Scis., Bangladesh Microbiology Soc. Home: House 5 Rd 1/A Sector 4, Uttara Dhaka 1230, Bangladesh Office: Atomic Energy Rsch, PO Box 3787, Dhaka 1000, Bangladesh

MALEK-MOHAMMADI, EHSANOLAH, engineer, researcher; b. Tehran, Iran, Feb. 4, 1949; s. Esmail and Maasoomeh (Sharifi) Malek-M.; m. Fatemah Rezaii-Zanjani, Aug. 11, 1997 (div. 1998). BSc in Agriculture, U. Tehran, 1971; diploma in stats., London Sch. Econs. and Polit. Sci., 1976; MSc in Stats., Birkbeck Coll., London, 1979. Lectr. U. Abourayhan, Tehran, 1979, Inst. Stats., Tehran, 1980; head dept. stats. Iran Cancer Orgn., Tehran, 1980-82; cons. Yecom Consulting Engrs., Tehran, 1990, Tehran Urban and Suburbs Rlwy. Co., 1991-92; rschrs. Mahab Godss Consulting Engrs., Tehran, 1993-99; cons. Ministry Power and Energy, Iran, 1995-99, Ministry Agr., Iran, 1996-99. Polit. prisoner, Tehran and Karaj, Iran, 1982-89. Lt. Ext. Corp., Iran, 1971-73. Grantee U. Isfehan, Iran, 1976. Avocations: mountain climbing, swimming. Home: No 30 Negarestan Yecom, Pasdaran Ave, 16619 Tehran Iran Office: Mahab Ghodss Cons Engrs, 17 Takharestan Ally, Shahid Dastgerdy Av Tehran Iran

MALEKZADEH, REZA, medical educator; b. Kazerun, Fars, Iran, June 14, 1952; s. Javad and Ozra M.; m. Azam Saddat Lari, June 11, 1978; children: Fatemh, Zinab, Massud, Muna. MD, Pahlavi U., Iran, 1979. Cert. in internal medicine; cert. in gastroenterology. Asst. prof. med. dept. Shiraz (Iran) U., 1983-87, assoc. prof., 1988-92, prof., 1992; prof., chmn. dept. Gastroenterology Shariati Hosp. Tehran (Iran) U., 1993—; vice chancellor Shiraz U., 1983-84, chancellor Shiraz U., 1984-87. Assoc. Ed. Iranian Jour. of Med. Scis.; mem. editorial bd. Med. Jour. of Islamic Republic of Iran; chmn. editorial consultants bd. Nabz Jour. Dep. min. for education Ministry of Health, Tehran, 1984-91, min. of health and med. edn., Tehran, 1991-93; councilor The High Council for Cultural Revolution of Iran, 1991-93; chmn. bd. trustees Med. Scis. Univ. and Iranian Acad. of Med. Scis. Disting Achievement award by President Rafsanjani, 1993. Mem. Amer. Gastroenterology Assoc. Moslem. Avocation: mountain climbing. Home: Borj #10 Hormozan Complex, Hormozan St Ghods City phs2, 14666 Tehran Iran Office: Shariati Hospt Tehran Univ, Kargar Shomali St, 14114 Tehran Iran

MALENDOWICZ, LUDWIK KAZIMIERZ, medical educator; b. Swarzedz, Poznan, Poland, Feb. 21, 1942; s. Bernard and Helena Malendowicz; m. Janina Kazimiera Klinska, Dec. 4, 1965; children: Slawomir Ludwik, Witold Jan, Bogna Maria. MD, Sch. Medicine, Poznan, 1966, PhD, 1969, Dr.habil., 1975; postgrad., U. Va., Charlottesville, 1971-72. Rschr. Sch. Medicine, Poznan, 1963-75, prof., 1975—, dean faculty, 1984-90; vis. prof. U. Padua, Italy, 1983-84. Contbr. over 330 articles to sci. jours. Pres. orgn. com. World Philatelic Exhibit, 1993. Recipient Sci. I, Polish Acad. Scis., 1975, Ministry of Health, 1979, 84, 89, 93; grantee NIH, 1971-72, NATO, 1992-93. Mem. Polish Histochem. and Cytochem. Soc., Polish Anatomical Soc., Polish Philatelic Fedn. (v.p. 1977—, pres. 1994—), Internat. Fedn. Philately (juror 1992—), Poznan Soc. Friends of Scis. (sec. 1982—). Roman Catholic. Avocations: philately, gardening, touring. Home: 5 Krancowa, PL62 020 Swarzedz Poznan, Poland Office: Sch Medicine Dept Histology, 6 Swiecicki St, PL60 781 Poznan Poland

MALERBA, LUIGI, author; b. Berceto, Parma, Italy, Nov. 11, 1927; s. Pietro and Maria Olari; m. Anna Lapenna, 1962; 2 children. Ed., Liceo Classico Romagnosi di Parma, Faculty Law, U. Parma. Dir. rev. Sequenze, 1948-51; advt. mgr. rev. Discoteca, 1956-60, editor, 1960-65. Author: La scoperta dell'alfabeto, 1963, Il Serpente (premio Selezione Campiello), 1966, Salto mortale (Premio Sila, French prix Médicis for best non-French novel), 1968, (with Tonino Guerra, illus. by Adriano Zannino) Storie dell'Anno Mille, 1969-71, Il Protagonista, 1973, Le rose imperiali, 1974, Mozziconi, 1975, Storiette, 1977, Le parole abbandonate, 1977, Pinocchio con gli stivali, 1977, Il pataffio, 1978, C'era una volta la città di Luni, 1978, La storia e la gloria, 1979, Dopo il pescecane, 1979, Le galline pensierose, 1980, Diario di un sognatore, 1981, Storiette tascabili, 1984, Cina Cina, 1985, Il pianeta azzurro, 1986 (Premio Mondello 1987), Testa d'argento, 1988, Il Fuoco greco, 1990, le Pietre Volanti, 1992, Premio Viareggio, 1992, Premio Selezione Campiello, 1992, Il viaggiatore sedentario, 1993, Le maschere, 1995, Che vergogna scrivere, 1996, Itaca per sempre, 1997, Interviste impossibili, 1997, Avventure, 1997, La superficie di Eliane, 1999, (TV film) Ai poeti non si spara (Internat. TV Festival of Monte Carlo Golden Nymph award 1966); writer, narrator, on-film commentator New North, 1989, Sea of Slaughter, 1990.

MALEUVRE, JEAN-YVES, educator; b. Corps-Nuds, Bretagne, France, Aug. 3, 1943; s. Francis and Thérèse (Cottais) M.; m. Pascale Meudec, Apr. 4, 1975 (div. Dec. 1989); children: Lavinie, Elise. BA, Faculty of Arts, Rennes, France, 1964; Agrégation, Sorbonne, Paris, 1969; D, Paris X Nanterre, France, 1992. Tchr. Lycée Kompong-Thom, Cambodge, 1967-69, Lycée Hammam-Lif, Tunisia, 1969-71, Lycée P. Gauguin, Papeete, 1971-74, Lycée J. Jaurès, Montreuil, 1975-79, Lycée B. Diagne, Dakar, Senegal, 1979-82, Lycée J. Prévert, Longjumeau, 1989-90, Coll. M Cochin, Blanc-Mesnil, 1990-91, Coll. République, Bobigny, 1992-95, Coll. J. Macé, Fontenay, 1995—. Author: La Mort de Virgile d'apres Horace et Ovide, 1993, 2d edit., 1999, Petite Stéréoscopie des Odes et Epodes d'Horace, 1995-97, Jeux de Masques dans l'élégie latine, 1998, Catulle ou l'anti-César, 1998, Violence et Ironie dans les Bucoliques de Virgile, 2000; contbr. articles to profl. jours. Home: 13 Rue Fabre d'Eglantine, 94120 Fontenay-Sous-Bois France

MALEWEZI, JUSTIN, Malawian government official; b. Ntchisi, Malawi, Dec. 23, 1944; married; 4 children. BA in Biology, Columbia U., 1967; cert. in edn., Econ. Devel. Inst., Washington, 1978. Tchr., headmaster, 1967-74, edn. adminstr., 1974-81; permanent sec. Ministry of Health, Malawi, 1981-83, Ministry of Edn., Malawi, 1984, Ministry of Treasury, Malawi, 1985-89; head civil svc. Govt. of Malawi, 1989-91; dir. planning and programs United Dem. Party, 1992-93, 2nd v.p., 1993—; 1st v.p. Govt. of Malawi, Lilongwe, 1994—. Office: Office of 1st VP, Private Bag 301, Capital City, Lilongwe 3, Malawi*

MALFATTI, VALERIANO, company executive; b. Trento, Italy, Aug. 7, 1937; s. Cesare and Camilla (Salvadori) M.; m. Fedorka Orebic, Nov. 25, 1970. D Econs., U. Torino, Italy, 1965. Cons. Soris Spa, Torino, 1968; asst. U. Torino, 1968-69; funzionario Doxa Spa, Milan, 1969, Tekne Spa, Milan, 1970-74, Provincia Autonoma, Trento, 1975-88; mng. dir. Sinco S.r.l, Milan, 1990—; asst. U. Trento, 1986—; mng. dir. SAD-Trasporto Locale Spa, Bolzano, Italy, 1992—. Author: Il Trasporto Pubblico Locale, 1993, Trasporti, 1998; contbr. articles to profl. jours. Mem. Internat. Union Pub. Transport. Home: Via Castelbarco, 38068 Rovereto Trento, Italy Office: SAD Spa, 60 via conciapelli, 39100 Bolzano Italy

MALHOTRA, DINA NATH, publisher; b. Lahore, Pakistan, Feb. 22, 1923; s. Rajpal and Saraswati M.; m. Sayta Sikri Malhotra, Jan. 17, 1950; children: Madhvi, Shekhar. Student in Econ. honours, Dayanand Anglo Vedic (D.A.V.) Coll., Lahore, Pakistan, 1942; MA in Polit. Sci., Punjab U., Lahore, Pakistan, 1944. Lectr. polit. sci. Dayananad Anglo Vedic (D.A.V.) Coll., Srinagar, India, 1944-45; mng. dir. Indian Book Co. Ltd., Lahore, Pakistan, 1945-47; dir. Tej Printing Press, Delhi, India, 1948-50, Rajpal and Sons Pubs., Delhi, India, 1950-58; mng. dir. Hind Pocket Books Ltd., Delhi, India, 1958-88, chmn., 1988—; pres. Fedn. Pubs. and Book Sellers, Delhi, India, 1960-63, Fedn. Indian Publishers, Delhi, India, 1980-82, 84, 90-92; cons. UNESCO Book, 1966; chmn. joint com. World Intellectual Property Orgn., and UNESCO, 1972-74; chmn. Copyright Coun., Delhi, India, 1993-97. Editor: Book Publishing in India, 1984. Recipient Internat. Book award UNESCO, Paris, 1988, Padma-Shri, Pres. India, 2000. Mem. India Internat. Ctr., Chelmsford Club. Arya Samaj. Avocations: reading, writing, music, travel. Home: 30 Jor Bagh, New Delhi 110003, India Office: Hind Pocket Books Ltd, 18-19 Dilshad Garden GT Rd, Delhi 110095, India

MALHOTRA, VINAY, cardiologist; b. Bhubaneshwar, India, Oct. 3, 1968. MBBS, Armed Forces Med. Coll., Pune, India, 1990. Diplomate Am. Bd. Internal Medicine. Rotary clk. Safdarjung Hosp., New Delhi, 1991; resident in internal medicine Sitaram Bharatiya Inst. Sci. and Rsch., New Delhi, 1992-93; resident in internal medicine U. Ill., Chgo., 1994-97, fellow in cardiology, 1997-99, chief fellow dept. cardiology, 1999—. Mem. Am. Coll. Cardiology, Am. Heart Assn. (mem. various couns. including arteriosclerosis, thrombosis and vascular biology). Office: Sect Cardiology 840 S Wood St # Mc787 Chicago IL 60612-7317

MALHOTRA, YOGINDER NATH., finance company executive; b. Rukanpur, Punjab, India, Aug. 7, 1937; s. Shanker Dass and Parkash Wati (Khanna) M.; m. Urmila Chawla, Nov. 20, 1964; children: Shikha, Surbhi. BS in Engring., Muslim U., Aligarh, India, 1960; MS in Engring., Glasgow U., 1979, MBA, 1981. Cert. fin. planner. Sr. exec. engr. Pub. Works, India, 1960-75; sr. engr. NEI Clarke Chapman-Mossend, Scotland, 1976-82; exec. Malikks of Bellshill, Uddingston, Scotland, 1982-88, Property and Investment Ctr., Glasgow, Scotland, 1988—. Avocations: painting, reading, swimming, travel. Office: Property and Investment Ctr, 251 Great Western Rd, 649EG Glasgow Scotland

MALIETOA TANUMAFILI, II, Western Samoan government official; b. Jan. 4, 1913; married; 5 children. Ed., Wesley Coll., Pukehohe, New Zealand. Adv. Samoan Govt., 1940; now pres. Govt. of Ind. State of Samoa, Apia; mem. New Zealand del. to UN, 1958; former mem. Council of State; joint head of state of Western Samoa, 1962-63, sole head of state, 1963—; Fautua of Maliena. Decorated comdr. Order Brit. Empire. Office: Govt House, Motoolua, Apia Samoa*

MALIK, GUNWANTSINGH JASWANTSINGH, diplomat, physical chemist; b. Karachi, Sind, India, May 29, 1921; s. Jaswant Singh and Balwant Kaur (Bhagat) M.; m. Gurkirat Kaur Singh, Sept. 15, 1948 (div. 1982); children: Kiran Bir Singh, Arunpal Singh. BS, U. Bombay, 1938; BA, Cambridge (Eng.) U., 1941, MA, 1943. Physicist Brit. Indsl. Plastics, Oldbury, 1941; 2d sec. Embassy of India, Brussels, 1948-50; 1st sec. Embassy of India, Buenos Aires, 1952-56, Tokyo; counsellor Commn. of India, Singapore, 1960-63; amb. Embassy of India, Manila, 1965-68, Dakar, Santiago, Chile, 1970-74, Bangkok, 1974-77, Madrid, 1977-79; chmn. Maharani Voyage, New Delhi, 1995—. Flight lt. RAF, 1943-46. Mem. Assn. Indian Diplomats (pres. 1986-87), Soc. for Internat. Devel. (v.p. Delhi chpt. 1985-89), Alliance Francaise de Delhi (pres. 2000—). Avocations: photography, motoring, writing humorous and nonserious articles. Home: C-224 Defence Colony, 110024 New Delhi India

MALIK, IFTIKHAR HUSSAIN, pathologist; b. Quetta, Bawchistan, Pakistan, Feb. 26, 1956; s. Sadiq Hussain and Khurshid Begum Malik; m. Nasreem Gul Taran; children: Talal Hussain, Ijlal Hussain. MB, BChir, Bolaw Med. Coll., Quetta, 1982; DCP, PGMI, Lahore, Pakistan, 1986; MCPS, CSP, Karachi, Pakistan, 1989. MO M.O.H. Baluchistan, Queeta, 1982-85; demonstrator B.M.C., Quetta, 1986-89; pathologist M.O.H., Turbet, Pakistan, 1989; lab. specialist M.O.H. Saudi Arabia, Maznab, 1990—. Avocations: history, watching movies, reading books. Home: HNO 620-X/B-3 Bouuchistan, Quetta Pakistan Office: Ministry Health, Gen Hosp, Midnas Al Qassem Saudi Arabia

MALIK, MAQBOOL AHMED, business executive; b. Sialkot, Punjab, Pakistan, Jan. 30, 1930; s. Lal Din and Hussain (Bibi) M.; m. Khurshid Maqbool; children: Zafar, Arshed, Shahnila. BA, Punjab U., 1950. Chief exec. Monthly Bisween Saadi, Lahore, 1954—, Khurshid Maqbool Press, Lahore, 1996—, Maqbool Acad., Lahore, Pakistan, 1954—. Editor 3 books. Mem. Lahore C. of C. Office: Maqbool Acad, 199 Circular Rd, Lahore Pakistan

MALIK, MUMTAZ, media consultant; b. Tapah, Perak, Malaysia, Sept. 3, 1957; d. H.J. Fakir Mohamad Malik and Kursid Bibi Sher Mohd; m. Ali Mokhtar; 2 children. Student, Inst. of Counseling/Health Studies, 1995, diploma in child devel. and psychology, diploma in bus. devel. and effective English. Mng. dir. Cat Eye Pte Ltd., Singapore, 1989-94; bus. cons. Creative Media, Malaysia, 1996-99; mng. dir. Mumtaz-MS, 1999—; seminar spkr. Contbr. articles to profl. jours. Chairperson Women Affair, Johor, 1995-98; sec. Resident Com., Johor Malaysia, 1995-98; spokesperson S.P.C.A., 1998, vice chairperson, 1997-98; mem. com. RC; town coun. rep. Johor. Avocations: prevention of cruelty on stray animals. Office: Creative Media, No 51 Jalan Bukit Kempas 43, Johor Bahru 81200, Malaysia

MALIK, MUNAWAR IQBAL, economist; b. Faisalabad, Pakistan, Aug. 14, 1950; arrived in Saudi Arabia, 1989; s. Nisar Ahmed and Ghulam Fatima M.; m. Tehseen Suleiman; children: Ayesha, Ahmed, Rabia, Yahya. BA, Punjab. U., Lahore, Pakistan, 1970, MA in Econs., 1972; MA in Econs., McMaster U., Hamilton, Can., 1976; PhD in Econs., Simon Fraser U., Vancouver, Can., 1979. Staff economist, sr. rsch. economist Pakistan Inst. Devel. Econs., Islamabad, 1973-81; dean inst. social scis. Internat. Islamic U., Islamabad, 1981-83, dir., 1983-84, prof. econs., dir. rsch., 1984-89; econ. advisor Al-Rajhi Banking & Investment Corp., Riyadh, Saudi Arabia, 1989-91; sr. economist, head spl. assignments unit Islamic Rsch. & Tng. Inst., Jeddah, Saudi Arabia, 1991-97; chief of rsch. Islamic Banking and Finance Divsn., 1997—. Editor: Money and Banking in Islam, 1983, Distributive Justice and Need Fulfillment in an Islamic Economy, 1988; editor Rev. Islamic Econs., 1985-87, editor, Islamic Econ. Studies, 1993—. Sec. gen. 2d Internat. Conf. Islamic Econs., Islamabad, 1983, sec. steering com. 3d Conf., 1992. Merit scholar Ministry Edn., Lahore, 1970. Mem. Internat. Assn. Islamic Econs. (sec. gen. 1983-87). Avocations: reading, social lectures, walking. Office: Islamic Rsch & Tng Inst, PO Box 9201, Jeddah 21413, Saudi Arabia

MALIK, NAZAR-MUHAMMAD, mathematics educator; b. Rawalpindi, Punjab, Pakistan, Apr. 5, 1935; s. Hayat-Muhammad and Gule (Bano) M.; m. Azra Zamir, Dec. 25, 1960; children: Khurram, Shahana, Romana. BA, Govt. Coll., Rawalpindi, 1954; MA in Maths., Punjab U., Lahore, Pakistan, 1957. Lectr. Pakistan Air Force Coll., Lower Topa, Pakistan, 1958-67, P-A-F Coll., Sargodha, Pakistan, 1967-77; sr. edn. officer Ministry Edn., Owerri, Nigeria, 1977-80; prin. edn. officer State Edn. Bd., Owerri, 1980-86; prof. Aitchison Coll., Lahore, 1988-95, Lahore Coll. Arts and Scis., 1995—. Sec. All Pakistan Social Svc. Orgn., 1954-56. Mem. Mathemat. Soc. (Punjab U. joint sec. 1954-55), Pakistan Air Force Staff Club (sec. Lower Topa 1959-62, sec. Sargodha 1973-75), Resort Club Internat., Def. Club Lahore, Cmty. Ctr. Def. Lahore. Avocations: writing, gardening, tennis, hiking. Office: Lahore Coll Arts & Scis, 68/A-E-I Gulberg, Lahore Punjab, Pakistan

MALIK, RAKESH KUMAR, veterinary and animal science educator, researcher; b. Bidhal, Haryana, India, Feb. 9, 1963; s. Nr ain Singh and Ved Kaur (Kundu) M.; m. Kusum Sahrawat, May 5, 1985; children: Kamal Deep, Rakshit. B of Vet. Sci. and Animal Husbandry, Chaudhary Charan Singh Haryana Agrl. U., Hisar, India, 1984, M of Vet. Sci., 1995. Vet. officer Milk Plant, Haryana Dairy Devel. Cooperative Fedn., Sirsa, India, 1986-87, Nat. Dairy Rsch. Inst., Karnal, India, 1987-90, Nat. Bur. Animal Genetic Resources (ICAR), Karnal, 1990-96; asst. prof. Haryana Agrl. U., Hisar, 1996—. Co-author: Advances in Human and Animal Reproduction, 1996; contbr. articles to profl. jours. Leading mem. Mountaineering and Trekking Course, Dharmshala, 1982; judge Dairy Mela, Nat. Dairy Rsch. Inst., Karnal, 1988-93; capt. volleyball, table tennis Nat. Bur. Animal Genetic Resources, 1993, mem. ctrl. joint staff coun., 1992. Univ. merit fellowship Haryana Agrl. U., 1993-94. Mem. Soc. of Animal Physiologists of India (life), Indian Assn. for the Advancement of Vet. Rsch. (life), Indian Soc. for Buffalo Devel. (life). Prajapita Brahma Kumaris Ishwariya Vishwa Vidyalaya. Avocations: attending pray meetings, visiting historical site. Home: House No 49 Chander Ln, Kaimry Rd, Hisar 125001, India Office: Haryana Agrl U, Dept Animal Prod Physiology, Hisar 125004, India

MALIK, RAMESH CHANDER, geneticist, researcher, veterinarian, educator; b. Punjab, India, Feb. 24, 1942; s. Sobh Raj and Jai Devi M.; m. Santosh Kumari Soni, Mar. 13, 1972; children: Sushma, Sameer. B in Vet. Scis., Punjab Agrl. U., Hisar, India, 1965; MS in Animal Breeding, Haryana Agrl. U., Hisar, India, 1970; PhD in Animal Genetics, U. New Eng., Armidale, New South Wales, Australia, 1986. Vet. Vet. Dept., Punjab, Haryana, India, 1965-71; geneticist Indian Coun. Agrl. Rsch., New Delhi, 1971-77; sr. lectr. U. Tech., Lae, Papua New Guinea, 1982-89; rsch. scientist Kuwait Inst. Scientific Rsch., 1989-90, 91—, project leader, prin. investigator, 1991-99. Editor: symposium proceedings; author 85 rsch. articles. Mem. Australian Soc. Animal Prodn., Australian Assn. Animal Breeding and Genetics, Assn. Indian Profls. Avocations: reading, music, cricket, table tennis. Office: Kuwait Inst Scietific Rsch, PO Box 24885, 13109 Safat Kuwait

MALIK, SHAHID, magician; b. Karachi, Pakistan, Mar. 8, 1954; s. Bashir and Naema Malik; m. Lisa Fraser, Apr. 24, 1982. Diploma in interior design, Bradford Coll. Art & Tech. magic advisor for films and TV. Named Magician of the Yr., Internat. Brotherhood of Magicians, U.K., 1985-86. Avocations: magic, illusions, designing, computing. E-mail: shahid@shahidmalik.co.uk. Fax: 44 0 1274 490179.

MALIK, SHAKTI KUMAR, publishing executive; b. Udhampur, India, Mar. 4, 1937; s. Chaman Lal and Kamlawati (Sikka) M.; m. Raj Sikka; children: Ateev, Abhinav. BA, Camp Coll., Delhi, 1963. Investigator Indian Inst. Pub. Opinion, Delhi, 1964-70; proprietor Abhinav Publs., Delhi, 1970—. Fax: 91-11-6857009. E-mail: shakti@nde.vsnl.net.in. Office: Abhinav Publs, E-37 Hauz Khas, New Delhi 110016, India

MALIKIOSI-LOIZOS, MARIA, psychologist, educator, researcher; b. Athens, Attika, Greece, Oct. 29, 1947; d. Xenophon A. and Dorothy F. (Franzen) Malikiosi; m. Nicolas D. Loizos, June 6, 1979; children: Dimitris, Fotini, Dorothy. MA, U. Maine, 1974, EdD, 1978. Rsch. asst. Nat. Ctr. Social Rsch., Athens, 1971-72, rschr., 1974-83; rsch. collaborator Nat. Ctr. Sci. Rsch./U. Paris VII, 1983-85; collaborator UNESCO Internat. Inst. for Ednl. Planning, Paris, 1984; lectr. in psychology dept. early childhood edn. U. Athens, 1987-90, asst. prof., 1990-94, assoc. prof., 1994—; cons. in counseling programs Rsch. Ctrs., Athens, 1994-96; dir. tng. in counseling U. Athens European Program, 1996-99; dir. tchr. tng. program in career guidance and counseling, 1999—. Author: Counseling Psychology, 1994, Education, Communication, and Counseling, 1999, Counseling Psychology in Education, 2000; mem. editl. bd. Jour. Mind and Behavior, 1980—. Rsch. grantee French Govt., Paris, 1983. Mem. APA, Hellenic Psychol. Soc., European Assn. for Counseling, European Forum for Student Guidance, European Fedn. for Welfare of the Elderly. Avocations: painting, gardening, cinema. Home: 21 Vassileos Alexandrou St, 145 61 Kifissia Greece Office: U Athens Dp Early Child Edn, 13a Navarinou St, 106 80 Athens Greece

MALIN, HOWARD GERALD, podiatrist; b. Providence, Dec. 2, 1941; s. Leon Nathan and Rena Rose (Shapiro) M. AB, U. R.I., 1964; MA,

Brigham Young U., 1969; BSc, Calif. Coll. Podiatric Medicine, 1969, DPM, 1972; MSC, Pepperdine U., 1978; postgrad. in classic, U. So. Calif., 1983—. Diplomate Am. Bd. Podiatric Pub. Health, Am. Bd. Podiatric Orthopedics, Am. Acad. of Wound Care Mgmt. Extern in podiatry VA Med. Ctr., Wadsworth, Kans., 1971-72, Marine Corps Res. Dept., San Diego, 1972; resident in podiatric medicine and surgery N.Y. Coll. Podiatric-Medicine, N.Y.C., 1972-73; resident in podiatric surgery, instr. in podiatric surgery N.Y. Coll. Podiatric Medicine, N.Y.C., 1973-74; pvt. practitioner in podiatric medicine and surgery Bklyn., 1974-77; mem. staff Prospect Hosp., Bronx, N.Y., 1974-77; chief podiatry service, mem. staff, cons. sports medicine David Grant U.S. Air Force Med. Ctr., Travis AFB, Calif., 1977-80; chief podiatric sect., mem. staff VA Med. Ctr., Martinsburg, W.Va., 1980—; instr. ednl. devel. program VA Med. Ctr., Martinsburg, W.Va., 1980—; clin. prof. med. sci. Alderson-Broaddus Coll., U. Osteopathic Medicine and Health Scis.; adj. prof. Barry U. Sch. Podiatric Medicine; dir. extern program Pa. Coll. Podiatric Medicine. Editorial rev. bd. Jour. Contemporary Podiatric Physician, 1991—. Lt. Col. USAFR, 1977—. Fellow Am. Soc. Podiatric Dermatology, Am. Coll. Foot Orthopedics, Am. Coll. Podiatric Physicians, Am. Coll. Podiatric Radiology (archivist, past pres.), Am. Soc. Podiatric Medicine (past pres., archivist), Am. Coll. Foot and Ankle Pediatrics (archivist/historian), Royal Soc. Health; mem. Am. Acad. Podiatric Sports Medicine (assoc.), Assn. Mil. Surgeons U.S. (life), Am. Coll. Podiatric Surgery (assoc.), Am. Assn. Podiatric Med. Writers (archivist), Phi Kappa Theta, Phi Kappa Psi. Home: 210 Shenandoah Rd Apt 2D Martinsburg WV 25401-3723 Office: VA Med Ctr Dept Podiatry Martinsburg WV 25401

MALINA, JAN RUDOLF, surgeon; b. Ostrava, Czech Republic, Sept. 6, 1929; s. Jan and Olga (Lederer) M.; m. Irmgritt Maria Laszlo, Dec. 31, 1953; 1 child, Martin. Doctorate, Masaryk U., Brno, Czech Republic, 1953; PhD, Palacky U., Olomouc, Czech Republic, 1963. Asst. surgeon Mcpl. Hosp., Ostrava, Czech Republic, 1953-57; chief surgeon Teaching Hosp., Ostrava, 1958-68; chief surgeon, cons. Teaching Hosp., Orebro, Sweden, 1969-85; head surgeon Divsn. Thoracic Surgery Lund U. - Univ. Hosp., Malmo, Sweden, 1986-96; ret., 1997; assoc. prof. Lund U., 1984, sr. lectr., 1985—, cons., 1985, 97—, rschr., 1997—. Author: Carcinoid and Carcinoid Syndrome, 1963, Thrombendarterectomy in Segmental Sclerotic Occlusion, 1963, Acute Thoracic Surgery, 1996; co-author: Textbook of Traumatology, 1972; contbr. articles to profl. jours. Mem. Asian Assn. Thoracic and Cardiovascular Surgeons (hon.), Swedish Thoracic Soc., Swedish Med. Assn., Rotary. Avocations: music, nuclear physics, mathematics. Office: Univ Hosp MAS, S-205 02 Malmö Sweden

MALINA, MARTIN, surgeon; b. May 4, 1962; s. Jan Rudolf M.; m. Janne Sydnes; children: Madeleine, Alexandra. MD, U. Linkoping, Sweden, 1986, Surgeon, 1992; PhD, U. Lund, Sweden, 1998. Vascular surgeon Malmoe U. Hosp., 1994—. Contbr. articles to profl. jours., chpts. to books in field. Office: Dept Vascular Surgery, Malmoe Univ Hosp, S-20502 Malmö Sweden

MALINAUSKAS, ALBERTAS, chemist; b. Vilnius, Lithuania, Nov. 24, 1952; s. Albertas and Irena M.; m. Jule Vasiulyte, Dec. 23, 1977; children: Tomas, Rasa. MSc, U. Vilnius, 1975; PhD, U. Moscow, 1979; D Habilitation, Inst. Chemistry, Vilnius, Lithuania, 1994. From engr. to jr. scientist Inst. Biochemistry, Vilnius, Lithuania, 1975-80; from jr. scientist to head dept. Inst. Chemistry, Vilnius, 1980—. Office: Inst Chemistry, Gostauto Str 9, LT-2600 Vilnius Lithuania

MALININ, THEODORE, medical educator, researcher; b. Krasnodar, Russia, Sept. 13, 1933; came to U.S., 1949; s. Ivan M. and Olga A. (Senitzkaya) M.; m. Dorothy Rearick, Sept. 4, 1960; children: Ellen T., Alexander T., Catherine T., Michael T. BS, Concord Coll., 1955; MS, U. Va., 1958, MD, 1960; DSc (hon.), U. Scranton, 1990. Asst. prof. Georgetown U., Washington, 1964-68, assoc. prof., 1968-70; prof. surgery U. Miami, Fla., 1970-79; prof. orthopaedics U. Miami, 1979—. Author: Surgery and Life, 1978; editor 3 books; contbr. over 200 articles to profl. jours. Active Nat. Rep. Com., Washington, 1964—. Surgeon USPHS, 1962-64. Recipient Orden, U. Javeriana, 1992. Mem. AMA, Am. Acad. Orthopaedic Surgeons, Am. Soc. Invest. Pathology, Royal Soc. Medicine, Rotary (Disting. Rotarian 1994). Achievements include patents in field; research on latent injury in cryopreservation of cartilage, cartilage structure, and tissue banking; definition of behavior of transplanted cartilage and bone. Office: U Miami Dept Orthopaedics R-12 PO Box 16960 Miami FL 33101-6960

MALININ, VLADIMIR VIKTOROVICH, scientist; b. Pskov, Russia, Nov. 28, 1961; s. Viktor Pavlovich and Tamara Ivanovna (Guseva) M.; m. Elena Vladimirovna Brodskaya, Feb. 27, 1997; children: Audrey, Elizaveta. Student, S.M. Kirov Mil. Med. Acad., Leningrad, USSR (now St. Petersburg, Russia), 1985, PhD in Med. Scis., 1992. Dr. Baikal Dept. Army, Mongolia, 1985-89; rschr. Rsch. Lab. Peptide Bioregulators Kirov Mil. Med. Acad., 1992-93, sr. rschr., 1993-94; sr. rschr. Rsch. Lab. Extreme States, St. Petersburg, 1994-96; head methodol. dept., sr. rschr. Rsch Lab. AIDS & Infectious Diseases, Armed Forces Russia, St. Petersburg, 1996-97; head rsch. dept., acad. sec. Inst. Bioregulation and Gerontology, St. Petersburg, 1997—. Patentee substance revealing immunomodulating effect, substance stimulating repari processes and method of its application; contbr. chpt. to book Immunology, 1999, also article to jour. Maj. Russian Med. Corps Res., 1985-97. Russian Orthodox. Avocations: literature, reading, swimming, skiing, fishing. Office: Inst Bioregulation/Gerontol, 3 Dynamo Pr, 197110 Saint Petersburg Russia

MALINKOVSKAJA, SOFIJA SERGEJ, library director; b. Volodarsk, Ukraine, Russia, Feb. 10, 1930; d. Sergej and Lidija (Lutchko) Titov; m. Albert Malinkovskij, 1952 (div. Sept. 1972); children: Sergej, Vladimir. Logic lectr. Riga State Pedagogical Inst., 1953-58; sch. prin. Riga H.S., 1958-62; dir. libr., pensioner U. Latvia, Riga, 1992—. Contbr. articles to profl. jours. Dep. Regional Soviet, Riga, 1959-62. Recipient three medals for Disting. Govt. Labor, Ministry of Edn., 1967-90, achievement medals, 1992; hon. Culture Figure of Latvia, 1979. Mem. Coun. Rsch. Librs., Coun. Librs. Latvia Ministry of Edn. (chairwoman 1962-92). Avocations: reading, music, philosophy of religion. Office: Latvian State U Libr, Bul'var Rajnisa 19, Riga Latvia

MALINOVSKY, MILAN, linguistics educator, researcher, musician; b. Prague, Czech Republic, Sept. 3, 1938; s. Alois and Anna (Cihlarova) M.; m. Eva Cerovska, Dec. 14, 1978; children: Vit, Jan. MusB, Conservatory Music, Prague, 1959; PhD, Charles U., Prague, 1980, 90. Music master Sch Arts, Prague, 1962-65; instr. lang. Cultural Inst., Prague, 1973-79; asst. prof. comparative and gen. linguistics Czech Tech. U., Prague, 1979-95, assoc. prof., 1995—, mem. sci. bd. and collegium of dean Coll. Civil Engring., 1990-92, chmn. dept. fgn. langs. Coll. Civil Engring., 1990-92, chmn. Czech studies, 1990—. Co-author: Pimsleur International Speak and Read Essential Czech, 1993; contbr. articles to profl. jours., including Jour. Modrn Philology, Moderne Sprachen, Fgn. Langs. Active Velvet Revolution, Prague, 1989-90, Chech chpt. Amnesty Internat., Prague, 1996—, Children of Earth, Prague, 1996—; chmn. Nat. Voting Precinct, Prague, 1990; bd. dirs. Restoration Prague Old Town Square, Marian Column Soc., 1990—. Recipient Prague 5th Symphony Orch. 75th Anniversary award, 1984; grantee Brit. Coun., summers 1983, 87; Fulbright Fellow, 1991. Mem. Circle Modern Philologists, J. William Fulbright Alumni Assn. Mem. Christian-Democratic Party. Roman Catholic. Avocations: playing bassoon in wind quintet, writing to newspapers, travel to English-speaking countries. Home: Raisova 4, 160 00 Prague 6, Czech Republic Office: CVUT Coll Civil Engring, Thakurova 7, 166 29 Prague 6, Czech Republic

MALINOWSKI, ARTHUR ANTHONY, lawyer, labor arbitrator; b. Chgo., Apr. 4, 1929; s. Ignatius and Sophie (Data) M. BS in Econs., DePaul U., 1956, JD, 1960; MS in Indsl. Rels., Loyola U., 1958; PhD, Ill. Inst. Tech., 1972; LLM in Labor Law, Chgo. Kent Coll. Law, 1981. Bar: Ill. 1960. Instr. indsl. rels. Loyola U., Chgo., 1963-69, prof., 1969-94; prof. emeritus, 1994—; mem. Ill. Office Collective Bargaining, Chgo., 1973-83; lectr. dept. econs. Ill. Inst. Tech., Chgo., 1965-68. Mem. Ill. Bar Assn., Indsl. Rels. Rsch. Assn., Nat. Acad. Arbitrators, Knights Malta, Phi Alpha Delta, Alpha Sigma Nu, Pi Gamma Mu, Iota Sigma Epsilon, Beta Gamma Epsilon. Home: 9240 Major Ave Morton Grove IL 60053-1552 Office: Loyola U of Chgo 820 N Michigan Ave Chicago IL 60611-2147

MALINSKI, MIROSŁAW ANDRZEJ, physicist, researcher; b. Koszalin, Poland, May 17, 1955; s. Henryk and Janina (Walczak) M.; m. Teresa Głocko, Oct. 23, 1982; children: Aleksandra, Radosław. MS, Nicholas Copernicus U., Toruń, 1979, PhD, 1988. Quality specialist Semiconductor & Rsch. Prodn. Ctr., Koszalin, 1988-93; tutor faculty electronics Tech. U. Koszalin, 1993-99, press agt. faculty electronics, 1998-99. Contbr. articles to sci. jours. Roman Catholic. Avocations: sports, touring. Home: 30/10 Krzyzanowskiego St, 75-328 Koszalin Poland Office: Tech U Koszalin Fac Elec, 17 Partyzantów St, 75-411 Koszalin Poland

MALISHENKO, TIMOTHY PETER, military; b. Reading, England, Nov. 4, 1944; s. John and Myra Phills (Morris) M.; m. Jane Ann Baxter, Mar. 17, 1968; 1 child, Andrew Peter. BS in bus. adminstrn., Ohio State Univ., 1968; MBA in supply chain mgmt., Mich. State Univ., 1969; MS in systems mgmt., Univ. Southern Calif., 1972. Chief contract support Deputy Asst. Sec. of Air Force, Washington, 1987-88, chief systems contracting, 1988-89; deputy DAS of the Air Force Asst. Sec. of Air Force, Washington, 1989-90; dir. of contracting Electronic Systems Ctr., Hanscom AFB, Mass., 1990-93, HQ Air Force Material Command, Wright-Patterson AFB, Ohio, 1993-95; deputy asst. sec. of Air Force asst. sec. of the Air Force for Acquisition, Washington, 1995-97; dir. Defense Contract Mgmt. Agy., Ft. Belvior, Va., 1997—; major gen. U.S. Air Force, 1969—; chmn. bd. adv. Nat. Contract Mgmt. Assn., Vienna, Va., 1994-96, chmn. coun. of fellows, 1985-87. Contbr. articles to profl. jours. Fellow Nat. Contract Mgmt. Assn.; mem. Air Force Assn (life), Appalacian Trail Conf. (life). Avocations: cycling, hiking, golfing, sking. Home: 4416 S Pershing Ct Arlington VA 22204-1379 Office: Defense Contract Mgmt Command 8725 Kingman Rd Fort Belvior VA 22204

MALK, RAUL, diplomat; b. Parnu, Estonia, May 14, 1952; s. August and Linda Malk. Student, Tartu (Estonia) U., 1970-75; studies in journalism, St. Petersburg, Russia, 1983-85. Jr. rsch. fellow, economist Acad. Scis., Inst. Economy, Estonia, 1975-77; sr. editor, then dep. editor in chief Estonian Radio, 1977-83; editor-in-chief Polit. Observer, Estonian Radio, 1985-90; dep. head, councellor chmn.'s office Supreme Coun., 1990-92; councellor to min., head min.'s office, dep. undersec. Ministry Fgn. Affairs, Estonia, 1992-96; amb. Estonian Embassy, U.K. and Ireland, 1996—, min. fgn. affairs, 1998-99; amb Estonian Embassy, Portugal, 2000; mem. bd. State News Agy., 1995-96, Estonian Sch. Diplomacy, 1995—; head govtl. dels. for border negotiations with Russia, Latvia, Finland, 1995-99; Estonian rep. for negotiation of Russian troop withdrawal, 1994. Contbr. commentary on fgn. policy to various newspapers, 1978—. Recipient Estonian Journalist Union award, 1990. Mem. Scottish Club (Tallinn, Estonia), Farmers Club (London). Avocations: foreign policy theory, theatre, attending basketball, football, track and field events. Office: Estonian Embassy, 16 Hyde Park Gate, London SW7 5DG, England

MALKIN, MOSES MONTEFIORE, employee benefits administration company executive; b. Revere, Mass., Sept. 18, 1919; s. Irving and Annie (Helfant) M.; m. Hannah Lacob, Oct. 11, 1941. AB, U. N.C., 1941; BSME, Columbia U., 1948. Enrolled actuary; CLU. Engr. GE, Schenectady, N.Y., 1948-50; engr. Gen. Bronze, Inc., Jersey City, 1950-51; v.p. Malkin Warehouse, Inc., New Haven, 1951-57; pvt. practice actuary New Haven, 1957-72; chmn., actuary Profl. Pensions, Inc., East Haven, Conn., 1972-99; ret., 1999; presenter pension issues at numerous confs., 1970-80. Pres., founder Milford, Conn., 1962, Milford Child Guidance Clinic, 1966; pres. Clifford Beers Child Guidance, New Haven, 1971, Jewish Family Svc., New Haven, 1973. With U.S. Army, 1941-45, ETO. Mem. Am. Acad. Actuaries, Am. Soc. Pension Actuaries (instr. 1984), Am. Soc. CLUs, Phi Beta Kappa, Tau Beta Pi. Jewish. Office: Profl Pensions Inc 444 Foxon Rd New Haven CT 06513-2098 Address: 22 Lighthouse Rd Aquinnah MA 02535-1352

MALKOV, SERGEJ VIKTOROVICH, geneticist, researcher; b. Samara, Russia, Jan. 11, 1957; s. Viktor Pavlovitch and Tatjana Ivanovna (Beljakova) M.; m. Vitalina Vladimirovna Ermoljeva, Aug. 25, 1995. Degree in Biology, Kazan State U., 1979; postgrad., Inst. Gen. Genetics, Moscow, 1979-82. Asst. Kazan State U., 1982-90, docent, 1990—. Author: Genetic Transformation and the Genome Juvenilization Hypothesis, 1998; contbr. articles to profl. jours. Recipient Lenin Komsomol award in sci., 1983. Mem. N.Y. Acad. Sci. Muslim. Office: Kazan State U, Kremljovskaya 18, 420008 Kazan, Tatarstan Russia

MALKOV, VICTOR PANTELEEVICH, mechanical engineer; b. Novaya Polyanka, Udmurtia, Russia, Oct. 1, 1936; s. Panteley Dmitrievich Malkov and Nadegda Romanovna Malkova; m. Nina Ivanovna Kritskaya, Aug. 6, 1960; 1 child, Markina Marina Victorovna. Student, Nizhni Nougorod Fac., 1962, Dr Tech Scis., 1976. Asst. prof. Nizhhegorodsy Arch and Civil Engring. Inst., 1962-64; sr. lectr. Nizhny Nougorod State U., 1968-76, profl., 1978, head chair elasticity and plasticity, 1977—; expert Maths and Mechs. of High Attestation com., 1987. Author: Optimization of the Elastic System, 1981, Hook's Law Analyses: Lectures on Anesotropic Elasticity, 1992, Power Content of Mechanical Systems, 1995, Step-by Step Parametrical Optimization, 1998. State sci. grantee Russian Acad. Scis., 1994. Mem. Russian Nat. Com. on Theoretical and Applied Mechanics, Internat. Soc. Structural and Multidsciplinary Optimization, Internat. Engring. Acad., Russian Acad. Natural Sci., N.Y. Acad. Sci., Acad. of People of the Word Elite. Avocations: painting, tourism. Office: Nizhy Novgorod State U, Gagarin av 23, 603600 Nizhny Novgorod Russia

MALKUSCH, WOLF PETER, biologist; b. Schoeningen, Germany, Feb. 12, 1949; s. Horst Ado and Hildegard (Haufe) M.; m. Hedwig Grosse Niesse, Apr. 2, 1976; 1 child, Sebastian. BS in Biology, U. Cologne, Germany, 1975; PhD in Sci. Medicine, U. Essen, Germany, 1998. Sci. asst. Zool. Inst., Cologne, 1973-75; application asst. IMANCO, Offenbach, Germany, 1975-76; application mgr. Cambridge Instruments, Dortmund, Germany, 1976-87; mktg. mgr. Analytic & Svc., Dortmund, 1987-90; gen. mgr. DAISY GmbH, Wetter, 1990-92; rsch. scientist Hygiene Inst., Essen, 1992-94; product mgr. Kontron Elektronik, Eching, 1995-97, Carl Zeiss Vision, Eching, 1997—. Contbr. articles to profl. jours. Sgt. Germany Army, 1968-69. Mem. German Soc. Metallurgy, German Zool. Soc., N.Y. Acad. Scis. Avocations: hiking, cycling, swimming. Fax: 49-8165-77-575. Email: malkusch@zeiss.de. Home: Suitbertstr 50, D 44287 Dortmund Germany Office: Carl Zeiss Vision GmbH, Zeppelinstr 4, D 85399 Hallbergmoos Bavaria, Germany

MALLACH, ALAN, writer, consultant; b. Pitts., Oct. 15, 1944; S. Aubrey and Esther (Dingol) M. BA cum laude, Yale U., 1966. Lic. profl. planner, N.J. Evaluation coord. Community Progress, Inc., New Haven, 1965-67; dir. program devel. N.J. Dept. Community Affairs, Trenton, 1967-71; asst. dean Livingston Coll., Rutgers U., New Brunswick, N.J., 1971-73; asst. prof. Stockton State Coll., Pomona, N.J., 1973-74; research dir. N.J. Govt. Study Commn., Trenton, 1973-75; pres. Alan Mallach Assocs., Inc., Phila., 1975-80; exec. dir. Atlantic Co. Improvement Authority, Atlantic City, 1980-83; city planning and housing con. Roosevelt, N.J., 1983-90; dir. dept. housing and devel. City of Trenton, N.J., 1990-99; pvt. practice Roosevelt, N.J., 1999—; adj. lectr. Rutgers U., Newark, 1988-90; exec. com. Housing and Cmty. Devel. Network N.J., 1998—; bd. dirs. Rowan U. Inst. for Pub. Policy. Author: Inclusionary Housing Programs, 1984; contbr. articles to profl. jours. V.p. Bedminster Hills Housing Corp., Pluckemin, N.J., 1985-91; chmn. Roosevelt Borough Planning Bd., 1986-90; pres. Abrams Hebrew Acad., Yardley, Pa., 1984-87; sec. Roosevelt Arts Project, 1987—; commr. Delaware Valley Regional Planning Commn., 1990-99; N.J. adv. bd. Local Initiatives Support Corp., 1997—; bd. dirs. Preservation N.J. Named Citizen of Yr. N.J. Soc. Arch., 1998; recipient Environ. Quality award U.S. Environ. Protection Agy., 1997. Mem. AIA (R/UDAT task group 1995—), Am. Inst. Cert. Planners, Am. Planning Assn. (Paul Davidoff award N.J. chpt. 1998). Office: PO Box 623 Roosevelt NJ 08555-0623

MALLARY, MICHAEL LEIGH, engineering researcher; b. Berkeley, Calif., May 6, 1945; s. Robert W. and Margot Mallary; m. Helen Owen (div. Sept. 1994); children: Elaine, Caroline, Dominic; m. Cindy Lee; 1 child, Joanna Lee. BSc, MIT, 1966; PhD, Calif. Inst. Tech., 1972. Rsch. assoc. Rutherford Lab, Chilton, Eng., 1972-76; assoc. prof. Northeastern U., Boston, 1976-79; engr. Magnetic Corp. Am., Mass., 1979-81; sr. cons. Digital Equipment Corp., Maynard, Mass., 1981-94; fellow Quantum Corp., Milpitas, Calif., 1994—. Achievements include 40 patents in magnetic recording. Home: 4 Matthew Ln Sterling MA 01564-1541

MALLET, JACQUES ROBERT, art dealer; b. Paris, Feb. 19, 1945; came to U.S., 1972; s. Jean-Pierre Theodore and Christiane Claire (De Watteville-Berckheim) M.; m. Laurie Helene Belhassen, May 30, 1973 (div. 1985); children: Clementine, Arthur. B in Maths., Lycee Louis-Le-Grand, Paris, 1966; M in Econs., U. Paris, 1971; MBA, Columbia U., 1973. Salesman mut. funds Banque De Neuflize, Schlumberger, Mallet, Paris, 1969; asst. v.p. Kuhn Loeb & Co. Inc., N.Y.C., 1973-78; sr. assoc. corp. fin. ABD Securities Corp., N.Y.C., 1978-80; pres. Mallet Fine Art Ltd., N.Y.C., 1982—. Clubs: Nat. Arts (N.Y.C.); Brooks's (London). Office: Mallet Fine Art Ltd 220 Park Ave S Apt 9B New York NY 10003-1519

MALLET, MICHEL MARIE-JOSEPH, ophthalmologist; b. Bayonne, France, Dec. 12, 1934; s. Jacques Alfred and Marguerite Jeanne (Barbeau) M.; divorced. MD, U. Paris, 1961. Intern, then resident in opthalmology Hosp. Saint-Louis, Paris, 1959-64; practice medicine specializing in opthalmology Levallois Perret, France, 1964-92. Served to lt. Medical Service French mil., 1962-63. Recipient Medaille Commemorative des operations de Maintien de l'ordre en AFN. Roman Catholic.

MALLET, VICTOR JOHN, journalist, writer; b. Bonn, Germany, May 14, 1960; s. Philip Louis Victor and Mary Moyle Grenfell Borlase Mallet; m. Michele Marie Weldon, May 27, 1995; children: Natasha, Genevieve. Student, Winchester (Eng.) Coll., 1973-78; BA with honors, Oxford (Eng.) U., 1981. Corr. Reuters, London, Paris,, Johannesburg, Cape Town, 1981-86; Africa corr. Fin. Times, Lusaka, Zambia, 1986-88; Mid. East corr. Fin. Times, London, 1988-91; S.E. Asia corr. Fin. Times, Bangkok, 1992-94; dep. features editor Fin. Times, London, 1994-96; So. Africa corr. Fin. Times, Johannesburg, 1998—. Author: (book) The Trouble with Tigers: The Rise and Fall of Southeast Asia, 1999. Avocation: sailing. Office: Fin Times, 1 Southwark Bridge, SE1 9HL London England

MALLEY, JAMES HENRY MICHAEL, industrial engineer; b. Providence, Oct. 15, 1940; s. Leo Henry and Gladys Elizabeth (Canning) M.; children: James Michael, Julie Michele; m. Joyce Sue Marie Greenwell, Aug. 28, 1993. BS in Engring., U.S. Mil. Acad., 1962; MS in Indsl. Engring., U. R.I., 1977. Commd. U.S. Army, 1962-84, advanced through grades to lt. col., ret., 1984; milt. advisor U.S. Army, Rep. of Vietnam, 1964-65; co. comdr. Army Tng. Ctr., Ft. Benning, Ga., 1965-67; ops. and exec. officer First Air Cavalry Divsn., Vietnam, 1968-69; asst. prof. U. R.I., Kingston, 1969-73; asst. inspector gen. U.S. Army Criminal Investigation Command, Washington, 1973-76; ops. rsch. analyst and study dir. U.S. Army Concepts Analysis Agy., Bethesda, Md., 1977-80; dir. tng. U.S. 7th Army Combined Arms Tng. Ctr., Vilseck, Germany, 1980-81; chief of ops. rsch. and sys. analysis U.S. Army Europe, Heidelberg, Germany, 1981-84; mgr. engring. svcs. Orion Internat. Tech., Inc., Albuquerque, 1985-90; temp. recall, Ops. Desert Shield/Desert Storm U.S. Army, 1991; army after action report integrator ODCSOPS-HQDA, Washington, 1991; prin. analyst Gen. Rsch. Corp., Washington, 1992; ops. rsch. and analysis exec. Lockheed-Sanders, Merrimack, N.H., 1992-98; ops. rsch. exec. Textron Sys., Wilmington, Mass., 1998—; mgmt. advisor to chmn./CEO PC Support, Inc., Albuquerque, 1986—; presenter numerous symposia, U.S. and Europe. Decorated Silver Stars (2), Legion of Merit, Bronze Stars (3), Air medals (4), Purple Heart, Vietnamese Cross of Gallantry with Gold Star (1) with Palm (2). Mem. Ops. Rsch. Soc. Am., Assn. of U.S. Army, U.S. Naval Inst., Internat. Test & Evaluation Assn. Home: PO Box 746 Merrimack NH 03054-0746

MALLEY, RAYMOND CHARLES, retired foreign service officer, industrial executive; b. Cambridge, Mass., Dec. 22, 1930; s. William and Evangeline (Vautour) M.; m. Rita Ann Masse, May 26, 1951 (dec. June 1989); children: Keith, Bruce, Gregory; m. Josette Lucile Vidril Murphy, Aug. 11, 1995. AA, Boston U., 1950, BS, 1952; MA Equivalent, U. Geneva, Switzerland, 1955; MA and PhD A.B.D., Fletcher Sch. Law & Diplomacy (Tufts U. and Harvard U.), Mass., 1956. Economist, fin. analyst Texaco, Inc., N.Y.C., 1957-61; fgn. svc. officer U.S. Dept. State/A.I.D., Washington & fgn. posts, 1961-82; dir. U.S. Trade and Devel. Program, Washington, 1980; v.p. Silopress, Inc., Sioux City, Iowa, 1982-87; cons., advisor Labat-Anderson Internat., Arlington, Va., 1988-93; sr. group advisor, N. Am. rep. Halla Bus. Group, Seoul (Korea), N.Y.C., Washington, 1991—; chmn. Halla Am. Inc., 1996—. Mem. exec. bd. Coll. of Mgmt., Long Island U., Brookville, N.Y., 1994—. 2nd Lt., 1st Lt., Capt. then Major U.S. Air Force Res. Recipient Nat. Def. Svc. medal during Korean War. Mem. Acadian Cultural Soc., Am. Fgn. Svc. Assn., U.S. Profl. Tennis Registry, Harvard Club. Roman Catholic. Avocation: tennis (ranked sr. player, cert. tennis instr.). Home: 10 Berrill Farms Ln Hanover NH 03755-3205 also: 6224 Loch Raven Dr Mc Lean VA 22101-3133 Office: Halla Am 60 Oxford Dr Moonachie NJ 07074-1022

MALLIAS, ALEXIUS JOHN, physician; b. Volos, Greece, Sept. 7, 1936; s. John Alexios and Stuliani Nicolaos (Sieanox) M.; m. Haido John Papagellon; children: Despina, John. MD, U. Athens, 1961. Diplomate Am. Bd. Pediats. Dir. pediats. Bastaniou Hosp., Nyline, 1983-85. Asst. surgeon Greece Army, 1961-63. Mem. Rotary Club. Home and Office: 10 Kavetsoy, 81100 Myline Greece

MALLINCKRODT, GEORGE W., bank executive; b. Eichholz, Germany, Aug. 19, 1930; s. Arnold Wilhelm and Valentine (von Joest) von M.; m. Charmaine Brenda Schroder, July 31, 1958; children: Claire, Philip, Edward, Sophie. Student, various bus. schs.; DCL (hon.), Bishops U., Lennoxville, Can., 1994. With AGFA A.G., Munich, 1948-51, Munchmeyer and Co., Hamburg, 1951-53, Kleinwort Sons and Co., London, 1953-54, J. Henry Schroder Banking Corp., N.Y.C., 1954-55, 57-60, Union Bank Switzerland, 1956; with J. Henry Schroder & Co. Ltd., London, 1960—, also bd. dirs.; chmn. Schroders PLC, London, 1984-95, pres., 1995—; chmn. bd. dirs. J. Henry Schroder Bank A.G., Zurich, 1967; chmn., pres. Schroders Inc., N.Y.C., 1985; bd. dirs. Schroders Australia Ltd., Sydney, 1984—, Schroder Wertheim and Co. Inc., N.Y.C., 1986—, Schroders Ltd., Bermuda, 1991, British Invisibles, 1995—; bd. dirs. Euris S.A., Paris, Siemens plc., London, Schroder Internat. Mcht. Bankers Ltd., Singapore, Fgn. and Colonial German Investment Trust plc.; mem. Brit. N.Am. com., 1988—; trustee Kurt Hahn Trust, 1991—. V.p. German Brit. C. of C., London, 1992-95; chmn. Coun. World Econ. Forum, Davos, 1992—; mem. CBI City Adv. Group, London; mem. Brit. Mus. Devel. Trust, 1995—, Nat. Art Collection Devel. Coun., 1995—. Recipient Verdienstkreuz Am. Bande Des Verdienstordens Der Bundesrepublik Deutschland, 1986, Verdienstkeuz 1 Klasse Verdienstordens, 1990; apptd. Hon. Knight Comdr. of the Most Excellent Order of Brit. Empire, 1997. Fellow Royal Soc. Arts; mem. Inst. Mgmt. (companion 1986—). Office: Schroders PLC, 120 Cheapside, London EC2V 6DS, England also: Schroders Inc 787 7th Ave New York NY 10019-6018 also: 31 Greslam St, London EC2V7QA, England*

MALLING, HEINRICH VALDEMAR, geneticist; b. Copenhagen, Apr. 21, 1931; came to U.S., 1963; s. Henry August Valdemar and Jenny Bolette (Hansen) M.; m. Bodil Jensen, June 15, 1955 (div. June 1968); children: Tove, Soren, Jakob, Mikael; m. Martha Hale Shackford, July 18, 1969; children: Richard, Kevin, Kirsten. PhD, U. Copenhagen, 1957, Lic. Sci., 1962. Rsch. staff Leo Pharm., Copenhagen, 1957-58; postdoctoral fellow Inst. Genetics U. Copenhagen, 1958-61, assoc. prof., 1961-63; rsch. staff mem. Oak Ridge (Tenn.) Nat. Lab., 1963-72; sect. head Nat. Inst. Environ. Health Sci., Research Triangle Park, N.C., 1972-76, 82—, lab. chief, 1976-82; adj. prof. N.C. State U., Raleigh, 1972-78, U. N.C., Chapel Hill, 1976—; dir. Environ. Mutagen Info. Ctr., Oak Ridge, 1968-72. Editorial bd. Environ. and Molecular Mutagenesis, 1989—, Mutation Rsch., 1971—; contbr. articles to profl. jours. Nation chief YMCA Indian Guides, Knoxville, Tenn, 1970, Raleigh, 1974. Recipient Sci. award Environ. Mut. Soc., Washington, 1980; Grad. fellow U. Copenhagen, 1953-57, postdoctoral fellow NSF, 1958-61. Mem. Environ. Mutagen Soc. (com. 1989—), Med. Rsch. Coun. (Can., grant revs. 1987—). Democrat. Lutheran. Achievements include patent in transgenic mice for study of mammalian mutagenesis; first to demonstrate mammalian liver microsomes can active non-mutagenic carcinogens to mutagens, others achievements. Home: 3200 Winged Elm Ln Chapel Hill NC 27514-9530 Office: Nat Inst Environ Health Sci PO Box 12233 Durham NC 27709-2233

MALLING, JOACHIM STOLTZE, publishing company executive; b. Copenhagen, July 1, 1949; s. Hubert Ryan and Ulla (Hansen) M.; children: Karen Shin, Andreas. Grad., pub. sch., Sorø, Denmark. With Forlaget Rhodos, Copenhagen, 1968-72, Fremads Forlag, Copenhagen, 1972-75; co-founder Mallings Forlag, Copenhagen, 1975—; pres. Hans Reitzels Forlag, Copenhagen, 1984-87, chmn. bd., 1993-99, also bd. dirs.; pres. Høst & Sø Forlag, Copenhagen, 1986-87; pres., CEO Munksgaard Internat. Pubs., Copenhagen, 1987-99; bd. dirs. Andreas Fred. Høst & Søns Forlag, 1987-99, chmn. bd., 1993-99, Blackwell Pub. Cos., Oxford, Eng., DBK Bogdistbn., Bogklubben 12 Bøger, Interaktiv Distbn. A/S, 1994; chmn. bd. Scientia, 1992, Compact Data, 1993-99, Mondo A/S; CEO Det Berlingske Officin, 1999—. Mem. Danish Pubs. Assn. (bd. dirs. 1988-92). Home: Niels Hemmingsgen Gade 20 5, 1153 Copenhagen K, Denmark Office: Pilestraede 34, 1147 Copenhagen Denmark

MALLINSON, RICHARD GREGORY, chemical engineering educator; b. Indpls., Apr. 9, 1954; s. Harry and Susan Louise (Keckler) M. BSChemE, BS in Biomed. Engring., Tulane U., 1977; MSChemE, Purdue U., 1979, PhD, 1983. Rsch. asst. Purdue U., West Lafayette, Ind., 1977-83, Argonne Nat. Lab., Chgo., 1978; asst. prof. chem. engring. U. Okla., Norman, 1983-89, assoc. prof., 1989-99, dir. Inst. for Gas Utilization Techs., 1995—, prof., 1999—; faculty fellow Lawrence Livermore Nat. Lab., Livermore, Calif., 1990; vis. prof. Tianjin (China) U., 1994—, Chulalongkorn U., Bangkok, 1994—; ptnr. OKKINETICS, Norman, 1996—; prin. investigator Univ. Technologists, Inc., Norman, 1988-91; Kerr McGee Disting. lectr. Kerr-McGee Found./U. Okla., 1989-94. Author: (book chpt.) Methane and Alkane Conversion Chemistry, 1995; contbr. articles to Energy and Fuels, Indsl. and Engring. Chemistry Rsch. Bd. dirs. C.D. Mallory Found., Inc., Ala., 1994-99, Heartland Found., Inc., Okla., 1995—; mem. Okla. Found. for Excellence, 1993—. 1st lt. USAR, 1977-85. Mem. AIChE (dir. local sect. 1989, symposia organizer 1986-89), Am. Chem. Soc. (symposia organizer 1985-91), Am. Soc. Engring. Edn., Sigma Xi. Achievements include patents pending and patents in field for high density natural gas storage at high temperature, patent pending for chemical conversion of natural gas at low temperatures, natural gas utilization, clean production of N204, emulsion polymerization modeling, alkane cracking modeling, coal conversion modeling. Avocations: competitive sailing, sailing race management, sail cruising, scuba, swimming. Home: 4631 Ridgeline Dr Norman OK 73072-1700 Office: U Okla 100 E Boyd St Rm T335 Norman OK 73019-1028

MALLON, MEG, professional golfer; b. Natick, Mass., Apr. 14, 1963. Student, Ohio State U., 1983-87. Winner Oldsmobile LPGA Classic, 1991, Mazda LPGA Championship, 1991, Women's U.S. Open, 1991, Daikyo World Championship, 1991; 4th ranked woman LPGA Tour, 1992; winner PING/Welch's Championship, 1993, Sara Lee Classic, 1993, Cup Noodles Hawaiian Ladies Open, 1996, Sara Lee Classic, 1996, Star Bank LPGA Classic, 1998, Sara Lee Classic, 1999, Subaru Meml. Naples, 1999; 2nd major LPGA championship, 1991; winner 6 LPGA titles; mem. Solheim Cup Team, 1992, 94, 96, 98. Office: care LPGA 100 International Golf Dr Daytona Beach FL 32124-1082

MALLON, THOMAS, writer; b. Glen Cove, N.Y., Nov. 2, 1951; s. Arthur Vincent and Caroline (Moruzzi) M. AB, Brown U., 1973; AM, Harvard U., 1974, PhD, 1978. Asst. prof. English Vassar Coll., Poughkeepsie, N.Y., 1979-85, assoc. prof., 1985-89, lectr. in English, 1989-91; lit. editor Gentlemen's Quar., N.Y.C., 1991-95, writer-at-large, 1995—. Author: Edmund Blunden, 1983, A Book of One's Own, 1984, Arts and Sciences, 1988, Stolen Words, 1989, Aurora 7, 1991, Rockets and Rodeos, 1993, Henry and Clara, 1994, Dewey Defeats Truman, 1997, Two Moons, 2000. Recipient Ingram Merrill award, 1994, Nat. Book Critics Cir. award for excellence in reviewing, 1998, Great Lakes Book award for fiction, 1998; Rockefeller Found. fellow, 1986-87, Guggenheim fellow, 2000-2001. Mem. PEN Am., Phi Beta Kappa. Home: 230 Saugatuck Ave Westport CT 06880-6401

MALLOUH, AHMAD ABDELLATIF, pediatric hematologist, oncologist; b. Abukishk, Palestine, Jan. 10, 1945; s. Abdellatif Saleh and Ayisha Ibrahim M.; m. Alia Ibrahim, May 9, 1973; children: Manal, Areej, Amany, Amjad, Mohammad. MB BCH, Cairo U., 1969. Intern Cairo U. Hosp., 1969-70; gen. practitioner As Salamam Hosp., Saudi Arabia, 1970-72; resident D.C. Gen. Hosp., Washington, 1972-75; pediatrician ARAMCO, Dhahran, Saudi Arabia, 1976, As Salamam Hosp., 1976-77; pediatric hematologist/oncologist Dhahran Health Ctr.-ARAMCO, 1979-92, chief gen. pediat. divsn., 1992-96, chief speciality pediat. divsn., 1996-98, sr. cons. pediat. hematology/oncology, 1998—. Contbr. articles to profl. jours. Pediatric fellow U. Ala., Birmingham, 1977-79. Fellow ASCO, Am. Acad. Pediatrics, Am. Acad. Pediatric Hematology/Oncology, Am. Soc. Hematology. Muslem. Home: PO Box 8250, Dhahran 31311, Saudi Arabia Office: ARAMCO, PO Box 76 Dhahran Health Ct, Dhahran 31311, Saudi Arabia

MALLOY, EDWARD ALOYSIUS, priest, university administrator, educator; b. Washington, May 3, 1941; s. Edward Aloysius and Elizabeth (Clark) M. BA, U. Notre Dame, 1963, MA, 1967, ThM, 1969; PhD, Vanderbilt U., 1975. Joine Congregation Holy Cross, 1963, ordained priest Roman Cath. Ch., 1970. Instr. U. Notre Dame, Ind., 1974-75, asst. prof., 1975-81, assoc. prof., 1981-88, prof. theology, 1988—, assoc. provost, 1982-86, pres. elect, 1986, pres., 1987—; bd. regents U. Portland, Oreg., 1985—. Author: Homosexuality and the Christian Way of Life, 1981, The Ethics of Law Enforcement and Criminal Punishment, 1982, Culture and Commitment: The Challenge of Today's University, 1992, Monk's Reflections: A View from the Dome, 1999; co-author: Colleges and Universities as Citizens, 1999; contbr. articles to profl. jours. Chmn. Am. Coun. on Edn.; bd. dirs. NCAA Found., 1989—; mem. Bishops and Pres.' com. Assn. Cath. Colls. and Univs., 1988—; bd. dirs. Internat. Fedn. Cath. Univs., 1988—; mem. Pres.'s Adv. Coun. on Drugs, 1989—; mem. adv. bd. AmeriCorps and Nat. Civilian Community Corps, 1994-97; interim chmn. Ind. Commn. on Community Svc., 1994-97; mem. Boys and Girls Clubs Am., 1997—; trustee St. Thomas U., 1997—, Vanderbilt U., 1999; bd. advisors Bernardin Ctr., 1997—; bd. dirs. Points of Light; past chmn. Campus Compact. Established chair Cath. Studies in the name of Edward A. Malloy, Vanderbilt U., 1997. Mem. Cath. Theol. Soc., Am. Soc. Christian Ethics, Bus.-Higher Edn. Forum, Assn. Governing Bds. of Univs. and Colls. (vice chair 1996—), The Conf. Bd., Nat. Assn. of Ind. Colls. and Univs. (bd. dirs. 1997). Office: U Notre Dame Office Pres Notre Dame IN 46556

MALLUCHE, HARTMUT HORST, nephrologist, medical educator; b. Breslau, Fed. Republic Germany, Jan. 1, 1943; came to U.S., 1975, naturalized, 1985; s. Harald E. and Renate (Muenzberg) M.; m. Gisela Gleich, Dec. 19, 1975; children: Nadine, Danielle, Tiffany. Abitur, Albertus Magnus Coll., Koenigstein, Germany, 1963; postgrad. Phillips U., Marburg/Lahn, Fed. Republic of Germany, 1963-65, U. Innsbruck, Austria, 1965-66, U. Vienna, Austria, 1966; MD, J. W. Goethe U., Frankfurt, Fed. Republic of Germany, 1969. Diplomate German Bd. Internal Medicine. Intern, County Hosp., Aichach, Fed. Republic of Germany, 1969-70; resident in internal medicine and fellow in nephrology Ctr. Internal Medicine, Univ. Hosp., Frankfurt am. Main, 1970-75, asst. prof. medicine U. So. Calif., Los Angeles, 1975-78, assoc. prof., 1978-81; prof., dir. Div. Nephrology, Bone and Mineral Metabolism U. Ky. Med. Ctr., Lexington, 1981—; cons. NIH, FDA; Va. merit Rev. bd. nephrology. Author (monograph) Atlas of Mineralized Bone Histology, 1986; editor: Clinical Nephrology; contbr. articles to profl. jours. and books. Grantee NIH, 1982—, Shriner's Hosp. for Crippled Children, Lexington, 1982—. Fellow ACP; mem. Am. Soc. Nephrology, Am. Soc. Clin. Investigation, Am. Soc. Bone and Mineral Research, Am. Soc. Physiol. Endocrinology, European Dialysis and Transplantation Assn., Am. Fedn. Clin. Research, Internat. Soc. Nephrology, AAAS, Internat. Soc. of Bone Morphometry (founder).

MALM, RITA H., securities executive; d. George Peter and Helen Marie (Woodward) Pellegrini; m. Robert J. Malm, Apr. 19, 1970. Student, Packard Jr. Coll., 1950-52, N.Y. Inst. Fin., 1954, Wagner Coll., 1955. Sales asst. Dean Witter & Co., N.Y.C., 1959-63, asst. v.p., compliance dir., 1964-74; v.p., dir. Securities Ind. Assocs., N.Y.C., 1969-72; CEO Muriel Siebert & Co., Inc., N.Y.C., 1981-83; pres., founder Madison-Chapin Assocs., N.Y.C., 1984-89; pres. Hayward Malm Securities, Ltd., 1989-93; pres., founder Concord Stuart, Inc., 1993—; art mktg. cons. Author: Dying On Wall Street, 1996; author NASD Series 63 Blue Sky Uniform Securities Agent State Law Exam for Potential Stock Brokers, NASD Stockbroker Examination, NASD Series 6 primer. Bd. dirs. Head Start, 1996—. Mem. NAFE (bd. dirs.), Am. Caner Soc. (bd. dirs. Jupiter/Tequesta chpt. 1992-95), Profl. Women's Network (founder Palm Beach and Martin Counties 1991), Women's Bond Club N.Y. (dir., v.p. program chmn., pres. 1980-82), Cornell U. Club Ea. Fla. (bd. dirs. 1995). Address: PO Box 8603 Jupiter FL 33468-8603

MALM, ROGER CHARLES, lawyer; b. Hot Springs, S.D., July 8, 1949; s. Harry Milton and Angeline Mae (Johnson) M.; m. Sandra M. Metz, July 15, 1972; children: Andrew, Elliott, Nicholas. BA, St. Olaf Coll., 1971; JD, U. N.D., 1974. Bar: N.D. 1974, Ariz. 1975, Minn. 1980, U.S. Dist. Ct. N.D. 1974, U.S. Dist. Ct. Ariz. 1976, U.S. Ct. Appeals (9th cir.) 1981, U.S. Supreme Ct. 1981, U.S. Ct. Appeals (8th cir) 1982, U.S. Dist. Ct. Minn. 1985, U.S. Claims Ct. 1985, U.S. Tax Ct. 1988. Ptnr. Brink, Sobolik, Severson, Malm & Albrecht, P.A., Hallock, Minn., 1980—; county atty. Kittson County, Minn., 1995—; pres. N.W. Minn. County Atty.'s Coun. Hospice dir. Kittson County Hospice, Inc., 1984—; bd. dirs. Cmty. Theatre, Hallock, 1987—, Greater Grand Forks Cmty. Theater, 1991-95. Mem. ABA, Ariz. Bar Assn., N.D. Bar Assn., Minn. Bar Assn. (mem. bd. govs. 1993-2000), Am. Acad. Hosp. Attys., Norwest Minn. Atty.'s Coun. (pres.). Lutheran. Avocations: skiing, sailing. Office: Brink Sobolik Severson Malm & Albrecht PO Box 790 Hallock MN 56728-0790

MALMANGER, MAGNE, art educator; b. Bergen, Norway, May 10, 1932; s. Erling and Britta (Nerhus) M.; m. Marit Ingeborg Lange, July 27, 1968; children: Anna, Mathias, Johan Erling. MA in Art History, Oslo U., 1958, PhD, 1982. Asst. prof. Oslo U., 1967-68; rsch. sec. Norwegian Inst. Rome, 1968-74; keeper of paintings Nat. Gallery, Oslo, 1974-86; prof. Oslo U., 1986-90; dir. Norwegian Inst. Rome, 1990-96; prof. Oslo U., 1996—. Author: David Hume: Ethical Texts, 1968, Nowegian Painting from Classicism and Early Realism, 1981, Form and Concept Essays, 1982, August Cappelen, 1997, Olivier Debré in Norway, 1998; Art and Beauty. Western Aesthetics and Art Theory from Homer to Hegel (pub. in Norwegian); editor: ACTA of Norwegian Inst. Rome, 1968-74, The World of the Baroque, 1998. Home: Schultz Gt 12, 0365 Oslo Norway Office: Oslo U, Pb 1019 Blindern, 0315 Oslo Norway

MALMBERG, PETER, electrical engineer; b. Helsingor, Denmark, June 23, 1946; s. Sven Peter and Else (Jensen) M.; m. Arunee Dhipkomut, Nov. 19, 1983; children: Josephine, Steffen. MS, Tech. U., Copenhagen, 1972. Supt. Danish Arctic Contractors, Thule, Greenland, 1972-74; svc. engr. Mohawk Data Scis., Copenhagen, 1974-76; site engr. European Space Agy., Darmstadt, Germany and, Madrid, 1976-78; instrumentation engr. Risoe Rsch. Ctr., Roskilde, Denmark, 1979-81; sect. mgr. Danish PTT, Copenhagen, 1981-92; devel. mgr. Tele Greenland, Copenhagen, 1992-2000; radar specialist Danish Navy, 2000—; Danish rep. Eutelsat ACT, Paris, 1983-89; Nordic rep. Intelsat BG/T, Washington, 1989-91, vice-chmn. 1991-92; chmn. ICDSC-9, Copenhagen, 1992. Contbr. articles to profl. jours. Sgt. Royal Danish Navy, 1964-66. Mem. AIAA. Achievements include system design of satellite station for European Broadcasting Orgn., system design of satellite station for Greenlandic settlements. Office: Tele Greenland, Thoravej 4, 2400 Copenhagen Denmark

MALMGREN, HARALD BERNARD, economist; b. Boston, July 13, 1935; s. Berndt Birger and Magda Helena (Nilsson) M.; m. Patricia A. Malmgren, 1959 (div. 1975); children: Karen Philippa, Britt Patricia, Erika Nina; m. Linda V. Einberg, Oct. 3, 1987; children: Markus Harald, Liivia Linda, Viivianne Vaike. BA summa cum laude, Yale U., 1957; postgrad., Harvard U., 1959; PhD, Oxford U., 1961. Asst. prof. dept. engring. and econs. Cornell U., Ithaca, N.Y., 1961-62; head, econ. group Inst. for Def. Analyses, Washington, 1962-64; asst. U.S. trade rep. Exec. Office Pres. The White House, Washington, 1964-69; sr. fellow Overseas Devel. Coun., 1969-71; ambassador, dep. U.S. trade rep., 1972-75; sr. fellow Woodrow Wilson Internat. Ctr. for Scholars, Washington, 1975-76; prof. George Washington U., Washington, 1976-77; pres. Malmgren, Inc., Washington, 1977—; mng. dir. Malmgren, Golt, Kingston, Ltd., London, 1979-99; chmn. Malmgren O'Donnell, London, 1998—; vice chmn. Cordell Hull Inst., Washington; mem. adv. coun. Ctr. Strategic and Internat. Studies, Washington, 1987-97; adv. Senate Fin. Com., Washington, 1970-71, 75-76, Interaction Coun., 1985—; chmn. exec. com. Cordell Hull Inst., Washington. Author: International Economic Peace Keeping, 1972; co-author: Assisting Developing Countries, 1972; editor: Pacific Basin Development, 1972; bd. editors: The International Economy, 1987—, The Washington Quarterly, 1987-95, The World Economy, 1980-90; contbr. articles to profl. jours. Mem. Am. Econ. Assn. Met. Club, Reform Club. Home: Summerfield Farm 7620 Cannonball Gate Rd Warrenton VA 20186-7304

MALMINIEMI, KIMMO HEIKKI, pharmaceutical company executive, researcher; b. Tampere, Finland, July 2, 1957; s. Matti Henrik and Kaija Hillevi Nieminen; m. Outi Irmeli, Jan. 23, 1988; children: Sini, Satu. MD, Tampere U., 1983; MSc, U. Tampere, 1985, Specialist in Clin. Pharmacology, 1998; PhD, Tampere U., 1999. Lic. physician. Lectr. U. Tampere, 1982-85; internist U. Hosp. Tampere, 1983-85; vis. scientist NIH Inst. Aging, Bethesda, Md., 1985-86; scientist Alko Inc., Helsinki, 1986-87; clin. coord. Leiras Pharms. Inc., Tampere, 1987-96; cons. physician Star Pharms. Inc., 1996—, Santen Inc., Tampere, Finland, 1997-2000; resident physician Tampere U. Hosp., 1997—; lectr. U. Tampere, 1987—; sr. med. officer Nat. Agy. Medicine, Finland, 2000—. 2d lt. Finnish mil., 1976-77. Mem. Finnish Med. Assn., European Assn. of Study on Diabetes, Nordic Pharmacology Soc., Soc. for Rsch. in Vision and Ophthalmology. Avocation: amateur radio. Office: Santen, PO Box 33, FIN33721 Tampere Finland

MALMROS, LARS, automotive industry executive, mechanical engineer; b. Stockholm, Apr. 11, 1927; s. Folke and Ester (Ohlsson) M.; m. Vicky Karlsson, Mar. 30, 1953. MME, Royal Tech. U., Stockholm, 1951; Techn. D. (hon.), State U. Ghent (Belgium), 1985. Engr. AB Volvo, Skovde, Sweden, 1951-55; mgr. mfg. engring. Ford Motor Co., Detroit and Sao Paulo, Brazil, 1955-59; mgr. purchasing engring. AB Volvo, Göteborg, Sweden, 1959-63; mng. dir. Volvo Europa NV, Ghent, 1964-69, Volvo Truck Div., Göteborg, 1969-76; exec. v.p. AB Volvo, Göteborg, 1975-84; pres. Volvo Europe Car & Truck, Ghent, 1985-88, Techman NV, Ghent, 1988—. Decorated comdr. Order of Crown (Belgium); recipient prize Flemish Region, Belgium, 1988, City of Gothenburg gold medal, 1990. Mem. Swedish Acad. Engring. Scis., Belgian Acad. Sci. (assoc. engring. com.), Soc. Automotive Engrs. Home and Office: Lindenpark 6, B-9831 Sint Martens-Latem Belgium

MALMUTH, NORMAN DAVID, research scientist, program manager; b. Brooklyn, N.Y., Jan. 22, 1931; s. Jacob and Selma Malmuth; m. Constance Nelson, 1970; children: Kenneth, Jill. AE, U. Cin., 1953; MA in Aero. Engring., Polytech. Inst. of N.Y., 1956; PhD in Aeronautics, Calif. Inst. Tech., 1962. Rsch. engr. Grumman Aircraft Engring. Corp., 1953-56; preliminary design engr. N.A. Aviation Div., L.A., 1956-68; teaching asst. Calif. Inst. Tech., L.A., 1961; mem. maths. sci. group Rockwell Internat. Sci. Ctr., 1968-75, project mgr. fluid dynamics rsch., 1975-80, mgr. fluid dynamics group, 1980-82, sr. scientist, project mgr., 1982—; cons. Aeroject Gen., 1986-89; lectr. UCLA, 1971-72; mem. adv. group for aerospace R&D Fluid Dynamics Panel, 1995; vis. scientist Rensselaer Poly. Inst. Referee AIAA Jour.; bd. editors Jour. Aircraft; contbr. articles to Jour. of Heat Transfer, Internat. Jour. Heat Mass Transfer, and others. Named Calif. Inst. Tech. fellow; recipient Outstanding Alumnus award Univ. Cin., 1990. Fellow AIAA (Aerodynamics award 1991), Am. Phys. Soc.; mem. Am. Acad. Mechanics, Am. Inst. Physics (fluid dynamics divsn.), Soc. Indsl. and Applied Math. Achievements include patent in Methods and Apparatus for Controlling Laser Welding, hypersonic transition delay; pioneering development of high aerodynamic efficiency of hypersonic delta wing body combinations, hypersonic boundary layer stability, transonic wind tunnel interference, plasma aerodynamics, flow control web dynamics, combined asymptotic and numerical methods in fluid dynamics and aerodynamics. Home: 182 Maple Rd Newbury Park CA 91320-4718 Office: Rockwell Sci Ctr PO Box 1085 1049 Camino Dos Rios Thousand Oaks CA 91360-2362

MALONE, KARL, professional basketball player; b. Summerfield, La., July 24, 1963. Student, La. Tech. U., 1981-85. Basketball player Utah Jazz, 1985—; mem. U.S. Olympic Basketball Team (received Gold medal), 1992. Mem. NBA All-Star team, 1988-94; recipient NBA All-Star Game MVP award, 1989, co-recipient, 1993; mem. All-NBA first team, 1989-94; mem. All-NBA second team, 1988; mem. NBA All-Defensive second team, 1988; mem. NBA All-Rookie Team, 1986; co-leader most seasons (8) with 2000 points, 1987-95; NBA Most Valuable Player, 1997. Office: Utah Jazz Delta Ctr 301 W South Temple Salt Lake City UT 84101-1216

MALONE, LAURENCE ADAMS, economist, consultant; b. Cleve., Dec. 4, 1911; s. Cornelius Fitzgerald and Grace Adams (True) M.; m. Ethel Whatley, Jan. 2, 1962 (dec. 1987); m. Nettie Allen, July 24, 1987. LLB, Chgo. U., 1962; PhD, Columbia Pacific U., 1967. Contracting officer USN Sea Systems Command, Washington, 1941-79; economist Direct Answer Publishing Inc, Chagrin Falls, Ohio. Author: An Evolving World, 1972, Restoration, 1972, Our Debt Money Systems, 1985, How to Stop Foreclosure, 1982; patentee in field. Decorated Order of St. John, Knights of Malta. Roman Catholic. Avocations: research, writing, poetry. Home: 16779 Chillicothe Rd Chagrin Falls OH 44023-4519

MALONE, LISA R., accountant, scheduler; b. Baytown, Tex., Aug. 14, 1964; d. Bob R. Allen and H. Ruth (Reeder) Allen; m. Terry K. Quick, Oct. 5, 1991 (div. July 1997); 1 child, Valerie Ann Watkins. AA in Bus. Adminstrn., Lee Coll., 1985; BBA in Gen. Bus., U. Houston, Clear Lake, 1987, BS in Finance, 1994, MS in Fin., 1998. Accounts receivable supr. D.E. Harvey Builders, Inc., Houston, 1988-89; document controller Halliburton, Houston, 1989-90, cost engr., 1990-94, internal auditor, 1994-95; acct., scheduler Brown & Root, Inc., Houston, 1996-2000; earned value analyst Lockheed Martin Corp., Houston, 2000—. Methodist. Avocation: cross stitch. Office: Lockheed Martin Corp 595 Gemini Mail Code L1D Houston TX 77058

MALONE, NICHOLAS SHERLON, systems analyst, consultant; b. Huntington, W.Va., Aug. 6, 1958; s. Clarence Edward Malone and Ernestine (Queen) Vaughn; m. Julie Stratton, Mar. 4, 1985 (div. Dec. 3, 1990); m. Tracy Lynne Prunty, Dec. 21, 1991; 1 child, Nicolle Morgynne Malone. BA in Political Science, Marshall U., Huntington, W.Va., 1981. Owner Mgmt. Resources, Mount Claire, W.Va., 1977-; dir. W.Va. Science Fiction Assn., Charleston, 1980-86; mem. bd. dirs. UN Ednl. Orgn., N.Y., 1979-82, MARCON, 1983-90. Author: (book) Social Alternatives in Rsch., 1982, Comp. Security Program, 1990; contbr. articles to profl. jours. Rsch. analyst W.Va. Code Reform Orgn., Charleston, 1979, W.Va. GOP, Huntington, 1980; NORML, Huntington, 1985-86; project mgr. U.N. Edn. Org./NGO Soc., N.Y., 1981-82. Served With USMC, 1979-92. Recipient Gold Star award Michelien du France, 1981, award Rikido-USA, 1981, Nat. Top 10 award RPGA, 1978, 79, 80, 81, Nat. Top 100 Rating UFFA, 1975, 76, 77, 78; inducted into Naidh Nasc, 1999. Mem. NRA, Am. Soc. Tran. & Devel., Assn. Computing Machines, Am. Soc. Industry Security, Millennium Soc., Boy Scouts of Am., Soc. Noble Celts. Republican. Mem. Daoist Ch. Avocations: martial arts, gourmet coking, SCA, chess, hunting. Office: Mgmt Resources Int 3160 Meadowdale Blvd Richmond VA 23234-6348

MALONEY, MILFORD CHARLES, retired internal medicine educator; b. Buffalo, Mar. 15, 1927; s. John Angelus Maloney and Winifred Hill; m. Dione Ethyl Sheppard. BS, Canisius Coll., 1947, postgrad., 1947-49; MD, U. Buffalo, 1953. Diplomate Am. Bd. Internal Medicine. Rsch. chemist Buffalo Electrochem. Co., 1947-49; intership Mercy Hosp./Georgetown U., 1953-54; med. residency Buffalo VA Hosp., 1954-56; cardiology fellow Buffalo Gen. Hosp., 1956-57; chmn. dept. medicine Mercy Hosp., 1969-94; program dir., internal medicine residency Mercy Hosp., Buffalo, 1972-89; with steering com. Assn. Program Dirs. in Internal Medicine, 1976, coun. mem., 1977-80; clin. prof. medicine SUNY, Buffalo, 1981-94; trustee Am. Soc. Internal Medicine, 1984-90; edn. leader med. seminar Am. Soc. Internal Medicine, Austria, Switzerland, France, 1987, Argentina, Brazil, Paraguay, 1988; faculty instr. Christopher Wren Assn. Coll. William and Mary, Williamsburg, Va., 1997—; bd. dirs. Internal Medicine Ctr. for Advancement and Rsch. Edn.; pres. Heart Assn. Western N.Y., Buffalo, 1969; sr. cancer rsch. physician Roswell Park Meml. Cancer Inst., 1959-62; mem. internal medicine liaison com. N.Y. State, 1980-90; faculty instr., mem. curriculum com. Christopher Wren Assn. Coll. William & Mary, Williamsburg, Va., 1997-99. Editor (newsletter) N.Y. State Soc. Internal Medicine, 1972-78. Bd. dirs. Health Sys. Agy. Western N.Y., Buffalo, 1981; mem. exec. com., bd. dirs. Blue Cross Western N.Y., Buffalo, 1987; mem. bd. regents Canisius Coll., Buffalo, 1987—; mem. pres. assocs. SUNY, Buffalo; founding mem. Greater Williamsburg Va. Symphony Soc., 1998. Capt. M.C., U.S. Army, 1957-59. Recipient merit award N.Y. State Soc. Internal Medicine, 1980, Man of Yr. award Heart Assn. Western N.Y., 1982, ann. honoree award Trocaire Coll., 1986, Disting. Alumni award Canisius Coll., 1991, Berkson Excellence award in tchg. and art of medicine, SUNY at Buffalo, 1992, Outstanding Med. Tchg. Attending award Mercy Hosp./SUNY Med. Residents, 1994, Lifetime Career Achievement award Med. Alumni Assn. SUNY, Buffalo, 1998; named to Sports Hall of Fame, Canisius Coll., 1978. Fellow ACP (Upstate Physician Recognition award 1989), Am. Coll. Cardiology; mem. AMA (SUNY rep. 1986-94, rep. to sect. med. schs. at ann. meetings 1984-94, chmn. sect. on internal medicine 1990-91), Am. Soc. Internal Medicine (bd. dirs. Internal Medicine Ctr. for Advancement of Rsch. Edn. 1988-91, trustee 1984-90, pres. 1990-91, chmn. long range planning com., rep. to Federated Coun. on Internal Medicine 1990-91, rep. to AMA nat. practice parameters and guidelines com. 1989-91), N.Y. State Soc. Internal Medicine (pres. 1974-75), Alumni Assn. SUNY (pres. 1975), Med. Soc. County Erie (pres. 1991-82), Va. Soc. Internal Medicine (hon.), Greater Williamsburg Va. Symphony Soc. (founding mem. 1998). Home: 116 Cove Point Ln Williamsburg VA 23185-8613

MALONEY, PAT, SR., lawyer; b. Dallas, Tex., Aug. 9, 1924; s. James Edward and Flora Agnes (Kessler) M.; m. Olive Boger, May 20, 1950; children: Patricia, Pat Jr., Michael, Janice, Tim. BJ, U. Tex., 1948, LLB, 1950. Bar: Tex. 1950, U.S. Dist. Ct. (we. dist.) Tex. 1955, U.S. Supreme Ct. 1951; cert. civil law and personal injury trial law, Tex. Bd. Legal Specialization, civil trial advocacy Nat. Bd. Trial Advocacy. 1st asst. trial chief Dist. Atty.'s Office, San Antonio, Tex., 1950-53; pvt. practice Law Offices of Pat Maloney P.C., San Antonio, 1953—; moderator, founder annual seminar Anatomy of a Lawsuit, St. Mary's U., San Antonio; frequent lectr. throughout U.S. in areas of product liability and personal injury law. Author: Winning the Million Dollar Law Suit, 1980; co-author: Trials and Deliberations: Inside the Jury Room, 1992. With USMC, 1942-45, PTO. Recipient Warhorse award So. Trial Lawyers Assn., 1992. Fellow Law Sci. Acad. Am., Am. Bd. Trial Advocates (pres. inner circle of trial advocates) mem. ATLA, Internat. Soc. Barristers, Internat. Acad. Trial Lawyers, San Antonio Trial Lawyers Assn. (co-founder, pres. 1967, 72, bd. dirs. 1967-73,) San Antonio Bar Assn., State Bar of Tex., Tex. Trial Lawyers Assn. (director emeritus). Democrat. Roman Catholic. Achievements include 1977 personal injury verdict awarding his client $26,510,800.00. At that time the largest personal injury verdict in the history of the U.S. He has obtained verdicts and settlements in excess of a million dollars more than fifty times. Office: 239 E Commerce St San Antonio TX 78205-2931

MALOOF, JOAN E., biologist, educator; b. Wilmington, Del., July 31, 1956; d. John B. and Elizabeth (Cooper) Lukas; m. Richard D. Maloof, Aug. 12, 1978; 1 child, Alyssa. BS, U. Del., 1978; MS, U. Md., 1991, PhD, 1999. Dir. horticulture Salisbury (Md.) State U., 1981-83; instr. Wor-Wic C.C., 1984-89; tchg. asst. life scis. U. Md., Princess Anne, 1989-91; instr. biol. scis. Salisbury State U., 1993—. Home: 4701 Whitehaven Rd Quantico MD 21856-2129

MALOON, JERRY L., trial lawyer, physician, medicolegal consultant; b. Union City, Ind., June 23, 1938; s. Charles Elias and Bertha Lucille (Crevistin) M.; children: Jeffrey Lee, Jerry Lee II. BS, Ohio State U., 1960, MD, 1964; JD, Capital U. Law Sch., 1974. Intern Santa Monica (Calif.) Hosp., 1964-65; tng. psychiatry Ctrl. Ohio Psychiat. HOsp., 1969, Menninger Clinic, Topeka, 1970; clin. dir. Orient (Ohio) Devel. Ctr., 1967-69, med. dir., 1971-83; assoc. med. dir. Western Electric, Inc., Columbus, 1969-71; cons. State Med. Bd. Ohio, 1974-80; pvt. practice law Columbus, 1978—; pres. Jerry L. Maloon Co., L.P.A., 1981—; medicolegal cons., 1972—; pres. Maloon, Maloon & Barclay Co., L.P.A., 1990-95; guest lectr. law and medicine Orient Devel. Ctr. and Columbus Devel. Ctr., 1969-71; dep. coroner Franklin County (Ohio), 1978-84. Dean's coun. Capital U. Law Sch. Capt. M.C., AUS, 1965-67. Fellow Am. Coll. Legal Medicine, Columbus Bar Found.; mem. AMA, ABA, ATLA, Ohio Bar Assn., Columbus Bar Assn., Ohio Trial Lawyers Assn., Columbus Trial Lawyers Assn., Ohio State U. Alumni Assn., U.S. Trotting Assn., Am. Profl. Practice Assn., Ohio State U. Pres.'s

Buckeye Club. Home: 2140 Cambridge Blvd Upper Arlngtn OH 43221-4104 Office: 1335 Dublin Rd Ste 100A Columbus OH 43215-7007

MALORZO, THOMAS VINCENT, lawyer; b. Rome, N.Y., Jan. 10, 1947; s. Vincent T. and Helen Adeline (Grande) M.; m. Catherine Marie Healy, Dec. 28, 1968; children: Amy, Craig, Mary, Thomas Jr. BA, Walsh U., Canton, Ohio, 1969; JD, Cleve. State U., 1979. Bar: Ohio 1979, U.S. Dist. Ct. (no. dist.) Ohio 1980, U.S. Patent Office 1980, Tex. 1981, U.S. Dist. Ct. (no. dist.) Tex. 1981, U.S. Ct. Appeals (7th cir.) 1994, U.S. Dist. Ct. (ea. dist.) Tex., 1998, U.S. Dist. Ct. (so. dist.) Tex., 2000. Environ. regulations analyst Diamond Shamrock Corp., Dallas, 1979-81; ind. counsel, agt. Southwestern Life Ins. Co., Dallas, 1981-83; staff atty. NCH Corp., Irving, Tex., 1983-89; gen. counsel Wormald US, Inc., Dallas, 1989-90; patent atty. Otis Engring. Corp., Carrollton, Tex., 1990-93; pvt. practice Addison, Tex., 1993-95; ptnr. Falk, Vestal & Fish LLP, 1995; pvt. practice Dallas, Tex., 1996-97; of counsel Bennett & Weston P.C., 1997—; asst. prof. law Dallas/Ft. Worth Sch. Law, Irving, Tex., 1990-92. Dist. com. Circle 10 Boy Scouts Am., Dallas, 1985—; first aid team ARC, Cleve., 1972-80. Recipient Dist. Award of Merit, Boy Scouts Am., 1990, Silver Beaver award Boy Scouts Am., 1997. Mem. State Bar Tex. (chmn. trademark com. intellectual property sect. 1989). Office: Bennett & Weston PC 10670 N Central Expy Ste 200 Dallas TX 75231-2100

MALOTT, JOHN RAYMOND, consultant; b. Kankakee, Ill., Nov. 5, 1946; s. Raymond Roderick and Ruth Pearl (Jacobs) M.; m. Hiroko Iwami, Nov. 23, 1971; children: David Iwami, Rumi Justine. BA, Northwestern U., 1967; grad., Nat. War Coll., 1983. Civilian advisor U.S. Dept. State, Vietnam, 1969-70; China desk officer U.S. Dept. State, Washington, 1970-71; Am. consul U.S. Dept. State, Kobe, Japan, 1971-73; 1st sec. Am. Embassy U.S. Dept. State, Tokyo, Japan, 1974-77; Sri Lanka desk officer U.S. Dept. State, Washington, 1977-78, India desk officer, 1978-80; Am. consul &, Bombay, India, 1980-82; with Nat. War Coll. &, Washington, 1982-83, dep. dir. Japan Affairs, 1983-85, spl. asst. to Under Sec. State Econ. Affairs, 1985-86; Am. consul gen. &, Osaka, Japan, 1986-89; dir. Japan Affairs &, Washington, 1989-91, sr. seminar, 1991-92, dep. asst. sec. state South Asian Affairs, 1992-93; sr. advisor to Undersec. State for Econ. Affairs, Washington, 1993-95; U.S. amb. to Malaysia Dept. State, 1995-98; exec. chmn. Malott & Assocs., 1999—. Author: Partners, 1992. Recipient Vietnam Svc. award, 1970, Meritorious Honor award Dept. State, 1982, Superior honor award, 1991. Presbyterian. Home: 25211 Via Piedra Roja Laguna Niguel CA 92677-1822

MALOUF, (GEORGE JOSEPH) DAVID, poet, novelist; b. Brisbane, Queensland, Australia, Mar. 20, 1934; s. George and Welcome (Mendoza) Malouf. BA with honors, U. Queensland, 1954. Asst. lectr. English U. Queensland, Brisbane, Australia, 1955-57; schoolmaster St. Anselm's Coll., Birkenhead, England, 1962-68; lectr. in English U. Sydney, Australia, 1968-77; writer, 1977—; mem. Literature Bd. of the Australia Coun., 1972-74. Author: (poetry) Bicycle and Other Poems, 1970, Neighbours in a Thicket: Poems, 1974 (Grace Leven prize 1974, Australian Literature Society Gold medal, 1974, James Cook U. North Queensland award Found. for Australian Lit. Studies, 1975), Poems 1975-76, 1976, Wild Lemons, 1980, First Things Last, 1981, Selected Poems, 1981, Poems, 1959-89, 1992; (novels) Johnno, 1975, An Imaginary Life, 1978 (New South Wales Premier's Fiction award, 1979), Fly Away Peter, 1981 (Age Book of the Year award, 1982, Age Fiction award, 1982), Child's Play with Eustace and the Prowler, 1981 (Fly Away Peter and Child's Play pub. in U.S. edit. as The Bread of Time to Come, 1981), Harland's Half Acre, 1984, The Great World, 1990 (Commonwealth Fiction prize, Prix Femina Etranger), Remembering Babylon, 1993 (L.A. Times Fiction prize, Internat. Inpac Dublin Lit. award), The Conversations at Curlow Creek, 1996; (short stories) Antipodes, 1985 (Victorian Premier's award 1985), Dream Stuff, 2000; (plays) Blood Relations, 1988 (New South Wales Premier's Drama award, 1987); (opera libretto) Baa Baa Black Sheep: A Jungle Tale, 1993, Jane Eyre, 2000; (nonfiction) (with Katharine Brisbane and R.F. Brissenden) New Currents in Australian Writing, 1978, Tewlve Edmondstone Street, 1985; editor: We Took Their Orders and are Dead: An Anti-War Anthology, 1971, Gesture of a Hand, 1975. Australian Coun. fellow Australian Acad. Humanities, 1978. Office: c/o Rogers Coleridge White, 20 Powis Mews, London W11 1JN, England

MALPAS, JAMES SPENCER, oncology consultant; b. Wolverhampton, Eng., Sept. 15, 1931; s. Tom Spencer and Hilda (Chalstrey) M.; m. Joyce May Cathcart, May 25, 1957; children: James Julian, Timothy John. BSc (hons.), London U., Eng., 1952, MB, BS, 1955; PhD, Oxford (Eng.) U., 1965. House physician St. Bartholomew's Hosp., London, 1955-57, Aylwen clin. rsch. bursar, 1960-61, sr. registrar and sr. lectr., 1965-73, cons. in oncology, prof. med. oncology, 1973-95, emeritus prof. med. oncology, 1995—; house physician Royal Postgrad. Med. Sch., Hammersmith, Eng., 1960-61; lectr. in medicine Oxford (Eng.) U., 1962-65; master The London Charterhouse, 1996—; dean of med. coll. St Bartholomew's Hosp., London, 1969-72, treas., v.p., 1986-93, chmn. med. coun., 1985-87; dep. dir. (clin.), Imperial Cancer Rsch. Fund, London, 1985-90; gov. St. Dunstan's Coll., Catford, London, 1985-93. Editor Brit. Jour. Cancer, 1992-94; contbr. numerous articles on investigation and treatment of cancer to profl. jours. Founder, mem. Sick Children's Trust, London, 1978; pres. Leukemia Care Soc., Exeter, Devon, Eng., 1980-81; Freeman City of London, 1988; trustee St. Bartholomew's Hosp., 1997—, spl. trustee, 1999—. Flight lt. RAF, 1957-60. Named Cooper & Conventon scholar St. Bartholomew's Hosp., London, 1966-68, Dorothy Platt Meml. Lectr., King's Coll. Hosp., London, 1976, Subhod Mitra Orator & Medalist All India Inst., Delhi, 1991. Fellow Royal Coll. Physicians (Lockyer lectr. 1978), Royal Coll. Radiologists (Skinner lectr. and medal 1986, Medicus Hippocraticus prize 1996), Royal Soc. Medicine, Royal Coll. Paediatrics and Child Health; mem. Fellowship Postgrad. Medicine (treas., v.p. 1985—), Assn. Cancer Physicians (pres. 1995-99). Episcopalian. Avocations: sailing, painting, travel, avoiding gardening, amateur molecular biologist. Office: St Bartholomew's Hosp-Dept Med Oncology, West Smithfield, London EC1A 7BE, England

MALPASSI, MAURO, dentist; b. Rome, Nov. 9, 1965; s. Andrea and Elena (Panosetti) M.; m. Gabriella Tiranti, June 19, 1993; 1 child, Chiara. Cert. dental technician, Inst. Rome, 1984; grad. in dentistry, U. Rome Tor Vergata, 1990. Pvt. practice dentistry Rome, 1994—; presenter in field. Contbr. articles to profl. publs. Vol. cons. U. Rome, Tor Vergata, 1990—. Mem. Italian Soc. Endodontics, Italian Soc. Restorative Dentistry. Roman Catholic. Avocation: family. Office: Piazza Pontelungo 4, 00181 Rome Italy

MALPHURS, ROGER EDWARD, biomedical marketing executive; b. Lake Worth, Fla., Dec. 15, 1933; s. Cecil Edward and Muriel Thelma (Ward) M.; m. Carolyn Sue Calapp, Feb. 2, 1963(div. 1993); children: Steven, Brian, Darren, Regina, Victoria. BS, U. Utah, 1961; D of Chiropractic, Palmer Coll. Chiropractic West, 1990. Cert. med. technologist; lic. chiropractor, Calif., Ariz. Supr. spl. chemistry Cen. Pathology Lab., Santa Rosa, Calif., 1968-73; mgr. lab. Cmty. Hosp., Santa Rosa, 1973-76; supr. chem., staff asst. Meml. Hosp., Santa Rosa, 1976-85; pres., CEO R.E. Malphurs Co., Sunnyvale, Calif., 1972—; owner, developer REMCO Mktg. Assocs., Santa Rosa, 1970-71; pvt. commodity trader, 1974—; owner Better Bus. Forms and Typeset, Santa Rosa, 1977-81, commodity pool operator, 1979-80; dept. mgr. immunochemistry Spectra Labs., Fremont, Calif., 1990-95; clin. trials cons. hematology, tech. writer Abbott Diagnostics, Santa Clara, Calif., 1995-2000; tech. writer Healtheon/WebMD, Santa Clara, Calif., 2000—. Author: A New, Simple Way to Win at Blackjack, 1972. Served as squadron commdr. CAP USAF Aux., 1982-84. Mem. APHA, Am. Chiropractic Assn., Calif. Chiropractic Assn., Optimists Internat. (youth awards chmn. 1969-74), Toastmasters (sec./treas. 1988-89), Rep. Senatorial Inner Circle. Republican. Avocations: flying, computers, pistol shooting, oil painting, writing.

MALROUX, CLAIRE, poet, translator; b. Albi, France, Sept. 3, 1935; d. Augustin and Paule (Mauries) M.; m. Saxon MacLean Poole; children: Julian, Marina. Author of poems; translator Emily Dickinson: Poems 1989, 90, 98, D. Walcott: Poems and Plays. Recipient Grand Prix Nat. de la Traduction, 1995, Légion d'honneur. Home: 6 rue Dulac, 75015 Paris France

MALSCH, REINHARD PETER, pharmacist; b. Bretten, Germany, Sept. 5, 1961; s. Reinhard Friedrich and Wilhelmine Elisabeth (Schober) Reinhard; m. Doris Nagy, Dec. 13, 1989; children: Laura-Esther, Richard, Melissa. PhD, U. Heidelberg, Germany, 1994. Asst. rschr. 1st Dept. Medicine, Mannheim, Germany, 1990-93, rschr., 1993-97; pharmacist Markt-Pharmacy, Neustadt, Germany, 1997—; cons. in field. Inventor in field. Rsch. grantee Deutsche Forschungsgemeinschaft, Bonn, Germany, 1993, Faculty Clin. Medicine, Mannheim, 1995. Mem. Gesellschaft Thrombose & Heaemostasis, N.Y. Acad. Scis. Avocations: reading, sports, music. Office: Markt-Apotheke, Markstrasse 2, D-31535 Neustadt Germany

MALTBY, FLORENCE HELEN, library science educator; b. Sumner, Iowa, Mar. 2, 1933; d. Harold George and Blanche Theresa (Gritzner) Garland; m. George Robert Maltby, June 3, 1964 (dec. Oct. 1985); 1 child, Patricia Garland. BA, U. No. Iowa, Cedar Falls, 1954; MS in Libr. Sci., U. Ill., 1960, cert. advanced study librarianship, 1967. Elem. sch. libr. Barrington (Ill.) Pub. Sch., 1954-57; elem. sch. libr. USAF Dependent Sch. Europe, Sculthorpe, Eng., 1957-58, Ramstein, Fed. Republic of Germany, 1958-59, Wiesbaden, Fed. Republic of Germany, 1960-61; grad. asst. U. Ill., Champaign, 1959-60; reference asst., instr. Libr. Cen. Mich. U., Mt. Pleasant, 1961-63; asst. prof. libr. sci. Southwest Mo. State U., Springfield, 1963-66, 67-80, assoc. prof. libr. sci., 1980-97; instr. libr. sci. U. Ill., Champaign, 1966-67; evaluator North Cen. Assn., Springfield, 1989, Dept. Elem. and Secondary Edn., Mo. Sch. Improvement, 1989; com. mem. Children's Lit. Festival, Springfield, 1990, treas., 1991. Contbr. to Masterplots II: Juvenile and Young Adult Fiction, 1991, 97. Mem. AAUP, ALA, Assn. Libr. and Info. Sci. Edn., Mo. Assn. Sch. Librs. (mem. standards rev. com. for state sch. libr. media standards 1994), Beta Phi Mu, Alpha Beta Alpha, Kappa Delta Pi. Roman Catholic. Avocations: reading, playing organ and piano, cert. literary braille transcriber.

MALTBY, LARS PETTER, chemical company executive; b. Oslo, Aug. 30, 1961; s. Per Eugen and Elisabet (Ruud) M.; m. Tone Merete Winther, Sept. 1, 1997; children: Mats, Tage. MS, Tech. U. Trondheim, Norway, 1988, D Engring., 1993. Cert. chem. engr. Rsch. asst. Postec Rsch., Porsgrunn, Norway, 1989-93; sr. R&D engr. Norton AS, Lillesand, Norway, 1993-96, tech. mgr., 1996, plant mgr., 1996-97, tech. dir., 1997—. Contbr. articles to profl. jours.; patentee in field. Office: Norton AS, Nordheim, 4971 Lillesand Norway

MALTESE, DOMINIQUE, engineer; b. Paris, May 2, 1965; s. Joseph and Josephine (Castiglione) M.; m. NAthalie Albouy, Aug. 23, 1998; children: Adrien. Degree in phys. engring., ENPSM, Marseilles, France, 1989. Engr. SAT/DOD, Paris, 1990-96, SAGEM/DDS, Argenteuil. contbr. articles to profl. jours. Mem. SPIE. Avocation: violin, swimming. Office: SAGEM SA, 72-74 rue de la Tour Prilly, 95101 Argenteuil Cedex France

MALTESE, GIULIO, information technology company professional, historian of science; b. Palermo, Sicily, Italy, Apr. 4, 1956; s. Paolo and Antonina (Baviera) M.; m. Dory Caretto, Sept. 27, 1986; 1 child, Claudio. Degree in physics with honors, U. La Sapienza, Rome, 1981. Rschr. in physics Montedison, Ferrara, Italy, 1983; rschr. in automatic speech recognition IBM, Rome, 1986—, responsible for product devel., 1992—; contract prof. history of sci. U. Genoa, Italy, 1996-97, U. La Sapienza, Rome, 1997; contbr. Istituto Della Enciclopedia Italiana, Rome, 1995-98. Author: (books) La Storia Di F=ma, 1992, Climate and Computers, 1992, An Introduction to the History of Dynamics in the Seventeenth and Eighteenth Centuries, 1996; contbr. articles to profl. jours. With Italian Air Force, 1982. Mem. Italian Phys. Soc., Italian Soc. History of Sci. E-mail: 75821816@it.ibm.com.

MALTSEV, ANATOLIY ANDREEVICH, radiophysicist, researcher; b. Solikamsk City, Perm, USSR, Sept. 29, 1941; s. Andrey Vasilevich and Anna Konstantinovna (Gusarova) M.; m. Svetlana Mikhailovna Lustova, Aug. 26, 1966 (div. Jan. 1976); 1 child, Mikhail. MSc in Radiophysics and Electronics, Gorky State U., 1968; PhD in Info. Measurement Sys., All-Union Sci.-Rsch. Inst. Opt.-Phys. Measuring, Moscow, 1989; DSc in Physics, Joint Inst. Nuc. Rsch., Dubna, USSR, 1996. Miner Solikamsk Kali Kombinat, 1959-60; sr. sgt. Soviet Army, Germany, 1960-63; sr. lt. Soviet Navy, 1968-70; prof., scientific leader Joint Inst. Nuc. Rsch., Dubna, 1970—. Contbr. over 70 articles to profl. jours.; inventor in field. Leader trade union, hunter union Joint Inst. Nuc. Rsch., Dubna, 1973-84. Served with USSR mil., 1950-63, 68-70. Avocations: books, photography, tourism, fishing, hunting. Home: Pontekorvo 9-111, RU141980 Dubna Russia Office: Joint Inst Nuc Rsch, Joliot Curie 6, RU141980 Dubna Russia

MALTSEV, YURI, geophysicist; b. Murmansk, Russia, Oct. 12, 1945; s. Pavel and Lidia (Popova) M.; m. Irene Golovchanskaya, Feb. 17, 1993; 1 child, Elena. Candidate of Physics, St. Petersburg U., Russia, 1973, D Physics, 1985. Sr. collaborator Polar Geophys. Inst., Apatity, Russia, 1968-73, jr. rschr., 1973-85, sr. rschr., 1985-90, chief of lab., 1990—. Author: Magnetosphere-Ionosphere Interactions, 1983; editor: Matnetosphere-Ionosphere Physics, 1993; contbr. articles to profl. jours. Mem. Dem. Union, Russia, 1988—; mem. Anti-War Ctr., Apatity, 1995-96. Russian Basic Rsch. Found. grantee, 1994—. Avocations: fishing, travel, writing, politics, economics. E-mail: maltsev@pgi.kolasc.net.ru. Home: Fersman St 35 Apt 27, 184209 Apatity Russia Office: Polar Geophys Inst, Fersman St 14, 184200 Apatity Russia

MALUF, MIGUEL ANGEL, surgeon, educator; b. Cordoba, Argentina, May 9, 1950; arrived in Brazil, 1977; s. Hermesther Rene and Luisa Silvana (Casazza) M.; m. Virginia Cecilia Ordonez, July 27, 1973; m. Pablo Sebastian, Carolina, Stephanie. B, Gen. Paz Mil. Sch., Cordoba, 1967; physician degree, Cordoba Nat. U., 1972. Gen. surgeon Cordoba Hosp., 1973-75, thoracic surgeon, 1975-77; adult cardiac surgeon Heart Inst., San Paulo, Brazil, 1977-85; pediatric cardiac surgeon Sao Paulo Fed. U., 1986—, Albert Einstein Hosp., Sao Paulo, 1994—, Sao Luiz Hosp., Sao Paulo, 1996—; duzoliar prof. Sao Paulo Fed. U., 1986-88, asst. prof., 1988-91, assoc. prof., 1991-98, pvt. docent, 1998—. Inventor in field; contbr. articles to profl. jours. Lt. Argentinian Army. Recipient Hon. Prof. award Peruvian Soc. Cardiology, 1998. Mem. Brazilian Soc. Cardiology (50 yrs. to celebrate 1993), Brazilian Soc. Cardiovasc. Surgery, Argentina Soc. Cardiology (hon. prof. award 1996), Internat. Soc. Cardiovasc. Surgery. Avocations: swimming, tennis, aerobic exercises. Office: Sao Paulo U, 740 Rua Botucato Vila Clem, 04023900 Sao Paulo Brazil Address: Rua Apeninos 930, CJ 182 Paraiso, 04104020 Sao Paulo Brazil

MALUNGO, ALBINO, government official; b. Huambo, Angola, Dec. 13, 1954. Student, U. Geneva, 1988-90; LLM, Cuba, 1985; postgrad., Agostinho Neto U., Luanda, Angola, 1978-80; Diploma Multilateral Diplomacy, U. Geneva, 1990. Emergency assistance jud. advisor, sec. of state of cooperat Govt. of Angola, 1985-87, advisor Ministry of Exterior Affairs, coord. inter-ministeri, 1986-89, sec. gen. Angolan Action for Devel., 1989-92, minister of assistance and social reintegration, 1994—; dir.-gen. Naval Dockyards of Luanda, Min. of Fisheries, 1976-77, dir. gen. UNIPESCA, Cacuaco, 1978, dir. gen. EMPROMAR, 1980-79; asst. lectr. law faculty Agostinho Neto U., Luanda, 1985; pres. Gen. Assembly Fedn. Sailing Boars of Angola, Angolan Assn. Against Drugs. Pres. Angola Red Cross. Recipient Medal of Merit of the Region of Lille France; named Commdr. and Cavalier of the Order Priors of St. John of Jerusalem, Mem. of the Legion of Honour. Avocations: reading and writing portuguese, french, spanish, german,italian and umbundu. Office: Ministry Assistance & Socia, Avenida dos Massacres 117, CP 102 Luanda Angola

MALVERN, LAWRENCE EARL, engineering educator, researcher; b. Sterling, Okla., Sept. 14, 1916; s. George Michael and Anna Francesca (Elsass) M.; m. Marjorie Malene McCarther, Aug. 8, 1939 (dec. Jan. 1985); 1 dau., Maureen; m. Myra Louise Engelhardt, Sept. 18, 1987. Sc.B., Southwestern Okla. State Coll., 1937; M.A., U. Okla., 1939; Ph.D., Brown U., 1949. High sch. tchr. Marlow, Clinton, El Reno, Okla., 1937-38, 39-40, 40-42; asst. prof. math and mechanics Carnegie-Mellon U., Pitts., 1949-53; assoc. prof. applied mechanics Mich. State U., East Lansing, 1953-58, prof., 1958-69; prof. engring. scis. U. Fla., Gainesville, 1969-93; prof. emeritus. Assoc. editor: Jour. Applied Mechanics, 1978-85; author: Introduction to the Mechanics of a Continuous Medium, 1969, Engineering Mechanics-Statics and Dynamics, 2 vols., 1976. Served to lt. (j.g.) USNR, 1944-46. Guggenheim fellow, 1959. Fellow ASME (Worcester Reed Warner medal 1989), Am. Acad. Mechanics; mem. Soc. Engring. Sci. (dir. 1967-70), Sigma Xi. Home: 5620 NW 45th Ln Gainesville FL 32606-4367 Office: U Fla 231 Aerospace Bldg Gainesville FL 32611

MALY, MILAN, educator; b. Komarov, Czech Republic, Mar. 11, 1936; s. Vaclav and Milada (Hartmannova) M.; m. Jaroslava Horrova, June 30, 1972; children: Simona, Milan. M, Tech. U., Ostrava, Czech Republic, 1959, PhD, 1968. Rschr. Tevuh, Prague, Czech Republic, 1959-68; lectr. UEP, Prague, Czech Republic, 1969-85, vice-rector, 1991-92; vice-dean PIBS, Prague, Czech Republic, 1992—; vis. prof. Tex. A&M U., 1994, Johannes Kepler U., Austria, 1996. Author: MIS in Industry, 1985, Management and Organiation, 1986, Organizational Architecture, 1997. 1st lt. Czech Republic Mil., 1960-61. Rsch. grantee AKTION, Austria, 1996; rsch. fellow ITASA, Laxenburg, Austria, 1986-89. Mem. IABS. Roman Catholic. Avocations: opera, science fiction, tennis, skiing. Office: U Econs Prague, W Churchill Sqr 4, 130 67 Prague 3, Czech Republic

MALY, PETR, physicist; b. Prague, Czechoslavakia, Jan. 3, 1955; s. Karel andJirina (Vrabcova) M.; m. Marketa Munclingerova, Feb. 13, 1987; children: Pavel, Lucie. First degree, Charles U., Prague, 1979, RNDr., 1982, CSc., 1985. Rschr. Charles U., 1983-86, lctr., 1986-92, assoc. prof., 1992-94, divsn. head, 1994—. Contbr. articles to profl. jours. Mem. Czech Union Physicists. Avocations: skiing, literature. Office: Charles U, Ke Karlovu 3, CZ-12116 Prague Czech Republic

MALYGIN, VLADIMIR IVANOVICH, radiophysicist, researcher; b. Gorky, USSR, Nov. 16, 1957; s. Ivan Andreevich and Nina Jakovlevna Malygin' m. Ekaterina Vladimirovna Lutova, Aug. 1, 1981; children: Maxim, Anton. MPhSc, State U., Gorky, 1979; PhD, Inst. Applied Physics/Acad., Nizhny Novrogod, Russia, 1999. Engr. Radiophys. Rsch. Inst., Gorky, 1979-83; sci. rschr. Ins. Applied Physics/Russian Acad. Scis., Nizhny Novgorod, 1983—. Contbr. articles to profl. jours. Avocations: soccer, ice hockey. Office: Inst Applied Physics, Russian Acad Sci/46 Ulyanov, Nizhny Novgorod 603600, Russia

MALYSHEV, CYRIL, physicist; b. Leningrad, Russia, Jan. 26, 1962. Grad., Leningrad State U., 1984; PhD, Math. Inst., St. Petersburg, Russia, 1993. Jr. sci. rschr. A.F. Ioffe Phys.-Tech. Inst., Leningrad, 1984-89; sci. rschr. Math. Inst., St. Petersburg, 1992-99, sr. sci. rschr., 1999—. Internat. Sci. Found. grantee, 1995-96. Avocations: reading, sports. Office: VA Steklov Math Inst, Fontanka 27, 191011 Saint Petersburg Russia

MALYSHEV, IGOR YURJEVICH, pathophysiologist; b. Novokuznetzk, Siberia, Russia, Jan. 17, 1959; s. Yurij Nikolaevich and Alexandra Iljinichna (Loginova) M.; m. Elena Vasiljevna Shabunina, Sept. 11, 1987; children: Yurij, Vasilij. Student, Tomsk (Russia) Med. U., 1977-83; MD, PhD, Inst. Gen. Path. & Pathophys., Moscow, 1989, DSc, 1992. Jr. scientist Cardiol. Ctr., Tomsk, 1983-86; researcher Inst. Gen. Pathology and Pathophysiology, Moscow, 1986-89, sr. scientist, 1989-92, leading scientist, 1992-93, head of lab., 1993—. Author: Phenomenon of Adaptive Stabilization of Structures and Protection of the Heat, 1993; contbr. articles to profl. jours. Recipient award of Pres. of Russia, 1993-95, 95-99; grantee Russian Found. Basic Investigations, 1993-95, 97-99. Mem. Acad. Informatization, Internat. Soc. Heart Rsch., Internat. Soc. Adaptive Medicine. Avocations: sports, music, driving. Office: Inst Gen Pathol & Pathophys, Baltijskaya 8, 125315 Moscow Russia

MALZBENDER, JÜRGEN, scientist; b. Düren, Germany, Jan. 2, 1966; s. Peter and Elfriede M.; m. Monika Gorges, May 28, 1999. Diplom Ingenieur of Physics Tech., Fachhochschule Aachen, Germany, 1991; BSc in Applied Physics, Coventry Polytech., U.K., 1991, Cert. Mgmt., 1993, PhD, 1994. Technician Rsch. Ctr. Jülich, Germany, 1982-85; sgt. Germany Air Force, 1986-87; scientist Coventry U., U.K., 1992-95, Max-Planck-Inst. for Microstructural Physics, Germany, 1995-97, Tech. U. Eindhoven, The Netherlands, 1998—. Contbr. over 40 articles to sci. publs. Recipient Physics Prize Coventry U., 1991. Avocations: sports, travel, music. E-mail: J.Malzbender@Tue.nl. Fax: 0031403445619. Office: Tech Univ Eindhoven, Postbus 513, 5600 MB Eindhoven The Netherlands

MAMADOU, MICHEL KOUI, supreme court president. Pres. Supreme Ct., Ivory Coast. Office: Le Cour Supreme, rue Gourgas, BP V30 Abidjan Côte d'Ivoire*

MAMALAKIS, GEORGE, psychologist, researcher; b. Rethymnon, Crete, Greece, Apr. 18, 1958; s. Dimitrios and Eleni (Christonaki) M. BA in Psychology, Deree Coll., Athens, Greece, 1981; MA in Psychology, Austin Peay State U., 1986. Educator Nele, Rethymnon, Greece, 1988-89; rschr. U. Crete, Iraklion, Greece, 1989—. Contbr. articles to profl. jours. including Internat. Jour. of Addictions, Jour. Social Psychology, European Jour. Clin. Nutrition, Jour. Am. Coll. Nutrition, Am. Jour. Clin. Nutrition, Internat. Jour. of Obesity and Hlth. Edn. Rsch. Mem. N.Y. Acad. Scis, Greek Psychol. Assn. Avocations: electronics, martial arts. E-mail: geor40@yahoo.com. Home: Zambeliou 36, Rethymnon Crete, Greece

MAMBO, ESTÊVÃO DA CRUZ, economist; b. Cabinda, Angola, Nov. 1, 1965; s. António Francisco and Maria de Fátima (Cumba) M.; m. Fátima Fita da Cruz, Aug. 19, 1994; children: Genivaldo Eufrates da Cruz Mambo, Donaldo da Cruz Mambo, Joyce da Cruz. BSBA in Econs. and Internat. Bus., U. Tulsa, 1993. Acctg. trainee Chevron Overseas Corp., Cabinda, 1985-87, accounts payable acct., 1987-88, scholar, 1989-93, supr. work in progress acctg., 1994-96, bus. devel. coord., 1996—; cons. small and med. pvt. businesses, Cabinda, 1996—; bus. advisor Provincial Govt., Cabinda, 1996—. Mem. Assn. Angola Economists - Nuc. Cabinda (sci. officer 1999—). Roman Catholic. Avocations: soccer, listening to music, reading. E-mail: abdev6@chevron.com. Home: PO Box 2950, Luanda Angola Office: Chevron Overseas Petroleum Inc Cabinda Pouch Mail PO Box 5046 San Ramon CA 94583-0946

MAMCARZ, ANDRZEJ, ichthyologist; b. Szczecin, Pomerania, Poland, May 26, 1950; s. Henryk and Janina (Glowacka) M.; m. Bozenna Gadomska, May 17, 1980. MSc, Olsztyn U. Agr. and Tech., Poland, 1974, PhD, 1983; DSc, Agr. U., Szczecin, 1991. Registered profl. engr. Instr. Inland Fisheries Inst., Olsztyn, 1974-75; instr. dept. fisheries Olsztyn U. Agr. and Tech., 1975-83, asst. prof., 1983-93, prof., 1993—, head dept., 1991-93, dean faculty Water Protection and Inland Fisheries, 1993-96. Mem. European Union Ichthyologists, Polish Hydrobiol. Soc., Internat. Working Group on Larviculture. Avocations: genealogy, history, geographical discoveries, aquarium, music. Office: Olsztyn U Agr & Tech, Oczapowskigeo 5, 10-957 Olsztyn Kortowo, Poland

MAMCHENKO, GALENA FYODOROVNA, medical educator; b. Korostyshev, Kievsky, Ukraine, Mar. 21, 1942; d. Fyodor Vasilyevich and Varvara Petrovina (Chorba) M.; m. Vlademyr Nikolaevich Savchenko, Sept. 6, 1970 (div. oct. 1980); 1 child, Valery Vladimirovich. MD, Odessa Med. U., 1968, PhD in Med. Sci., 1980. Therapeutist Dist. Hosp., Ivanovka, 1968-69, chief therapeutic dept., 1969-70; intern Cardiology Ctr. Cardiology Ctr., Odessa, 1970-73; internal diseases lectr. Odessa Med. U., 1973-98, lectr., chair family and folk medicine, 1998—; dir., cons. Ctr. Biol. Therapeutics, Odessa, 1998—. Author: Clinical Homeopathy, 1996, Life and Treatment According to Laws of Nature, 1999; sec.-in-chief Jour. Ukrainian Homeopathic Annual, 1998—; contbr. articles to profl. jours. Mem. Internat. Homeopathic League, N.Y. Acad. Scis. Avocations: literature, sports, music. Home: 4 Osipova Str Apt 17, 65011 Odessa Ukraine Office: Odessa Med U, 2 Valehovsky By-St, 270100 Odessa Ukraine

MAMED OGLY, ATAKISHIYEV NATIG, physicist, researcher; b. Baku, Azerbaijan, Feb. 15, 1939; s. Atakishiyev Mamed Agakishi Ogly and Mehdiyeva Nargiz Abdul Halyg Gyzy; m. Mesuma Kyazim Gyzy Kyazim-Zade, Feb. 15, 1964; children: Sevinj Natig Gyzy, Mamed Natig Ogly. MSc in Phys. and Math. Scis., Azerbaijan State U., 1961; PhD, Inst. High Energy Physics, Serpukhov, Russia, 1971; D in Phys. and Math. Scis., Inst. Theoretical Physics, Kiev, Ukraine, 1987. Jr. rschr. Physics Inst., Baku, Azerbaijan, 1961-72; sr. rschr. Physics Inst., Baku, 1972-83, head Lab. for Elem. Particles, 1983-94; rschr. Inst. de Investigaciones en Matematicas Aplicadas Y en Sistemas, Cuernavaca, 1994-96, Inst. de Matem, U. Nat. Autonoma Mex., Cuernavaca, 1996—. Co-editor: The IV Wigner Symposium, 1996; contbr.

articles to profl. jours. Mem. Mexican Acad. Scis. Avocation: reading. Home: Santa Fe 45 Col Maravillas, CP 62230 Cuernavaca Morelos, Mexico Office: Inst Matem UNAM, Av Universidad Apdo 273-3, CP 62210 Cuernavaca Morelos, Mexico

MAMEDOV, EDOUARD AKHMED, chemist, researcher; b. Gyandja, Azerbaijan, Nov. 1, 1941; s. Akhmed and Vera (Belokoz) M.; m. Irada Akhoundova, Mar. 3, 1979; 1 child, Narmina Mamedova. BSc, State U., Baku, Azerbaijan, 1964; PhD, Inst. Catalysis, Novosibirsk, Russia, 1971; DSc, Inst. Petrochemistry, Baku, 1986. Jr. staff scientist Inst. Catalysis, Novosibirsk, Russia, 1970-71; sr. staff scientist Inst. Petrochemistry, Baku, 1971-86; head of lab. Inst. Phys. Chemistry, Baku, 1986-93; sabbatical leave Inst. Catalysis, Madrid, 1993-95; catalyst advisor Saudi Basic Industries Corp., Riyadh, 1995-97; sr. rschr. Sabic Tech. Ctr., Houston, 1997—; internat. expert UN Indsl. Devel. Orgn., Vienna, Austria, 1982-91; lectr. State U., Baku, 1986-93; expert Cert. Commn., Baku, 1991-93. Co-author: Oxidative Coupling of Hydrocarbons, 1992, Ammoxidation of Alkylaromatics, 1992; contbr. over 100 articles to profl. jours.; patentee in field. Mem. N.Y. Acad. Scis. Muslim. Office: Sabic Tech Ctr 16200 Park Row # A Houston TX 77084-5108

MAMEDOV, MAHIR DJAFAR OGLU, biochemist; b. Baku, Azerbaijan, May 1, 1958; s. Djafar Abbas oglu Mamedov and Gullu Tahir Djakhangirova; m. Sevda Adalyat Guseinova, June 20, 1993; 1 child, Adalyat. MS, Azerbaijan State U., Baku, 1980; PhD, Moscow State U., 1987, DSc, 1995. Cert. biologist. Sci. rschr. Inst. Botany Acad. Scis., Baku, 1980-83; postdoctoral fellow A. N. Belozersky Inst. Moscow State U., 1988-92, sr. sci. rschr. A. N. Belozersky Inst., 1992-95, prin. sci. rschr. A. N. Belozersky Inst., 1995—. Contbr. articles to profl. jours. Grantee Pres. of Russia for Young Drs. of Scis., 1997-99, INTAS, 1997-99, Internat. Sci.-Engring. Found., 1998-99. Avocation: playing football. Fax: 7 095 939 3181. E-mail: mahir@electro.genebee.msu.su. Office: Moscow State U, Vorob'evy Gory, Moscow Russia

MAMET, DAVID ALAN, playwright, director, essayist; b. Chgo., Nov. 30, 1947; s. Bernard Morris and Lenore June (Silver) M.; m. Lindsay Crouse, Dec. 1977 (div.), m. Rebecca Pidgeon, Sept. 22, 1991. B.A., Goddard Coll., Plainfield, Vt., 1969; DLitt (hon.), Dartmouth Coll., 1996. Artist-in-residence Goddard Coll., 1971-73; artistic dir. St. Nicholas Theatre Co., Chgo., 1973-75; guest lectr. U. Chgo., 1975, 79, NYU, 1981; assoc. artistic dir. Goodman Theater, Chgo., 1978; assoc. prof. film Columbia U., 1988; chmn. bd. Atlantic Theater Co. Author: (plays) The Duck Variations, 1971, Sexual Perversity in Chicago, 1973 (Village Voice Obie award 1976), Reunion, 1973, Squirrels, 1974, American Buffalo, 1976 (Village Voice Obie award, N.Y. Drama Critics Circle award), A Life in the Theatre, 1976, The Water Engine, 1976, The Woods, 1977, Lone Canoe, 1978, Prairie du Chien, 1978, Lakeboat, 1980, Donny March, 1981, Edmond, 1982 (Village Voice Obie award 1983), The Disappearance of the Jews, 1983, The Shawl, 1985, Glengarry Glen Ross, 1984 (Pulitzer prize for drama, N.Y. Drama Critics Circle award), Speed-The-Plow, 1987, Bobby Gould in Hell, 1989, The Old Neighborhood, 1991, Oleanna, 1992, The Cryptogram, 1994 (Obie award 1995), (dir. only) Ricky Jay and His 52 Assistants, 1994, (one act) Death Defying Acts, 1995, Boston Marriage, 1999; screenplays: The Postman Always Rings Twice, 1979, The Verdict, 1980, The Untouchables, 1986, House of Games, 1986, (with Shel Silverstein) Things Change, 1987, We're No Angels, 1987, Homicide, 1991 (also dir.), Hoffa, 1991, Oleanna, 1994, The Edge, 1996, The Spanish Prisoner, 1996, Wag The Dog, 1997, Ronin, 1998, The Winslow Boy, 1999; (children's books) Warm and Cold with drawings by Donald Sultan, 1985, The Duck and the Goat, Jafsie & John Henry, 1999, Bar Mitzvah, 1999; (essays) Writing In Restaurants, 1986, SomeFreaks, 1989, on Directing Film, 1990, The Cabin, 1992, Make-Believe-Town, 1996; (novels) The Village, 1994, The Old Religion, 1996, True and False, 1996, 3 Uses of the Knife, 1996, (books) Passover, The Duck and the Goat, 1996, Henrietta, 1999, The Hero Pony, 1990 (poetry), The China Man, 1999 (book), Wilson, 2000 (book); dir. (films) House of Games, 1986, Things Change, 1987, Homicide, 1991, Oleanna, 1994, the Spanish Prisoner, 1996, The Winslow Boy, 1998, (play) Dangerous Corner (J.B. Priestly), 1995, (film) State and Main, 2000. Recipient Outer Critics Circle award for contbn. to Am. theater, 1978; Acad. award nominee for best screenplay adaptation, 1983, 98; Rockefeller grantee, 1977; CBS Creative Writing fellow Yale U. Drama Sch., 1976-77.

MAMIANETTI, ARNALDO, medical educator; b. Capital Federal, Argentina, Jan. 23, 1936; s. Arnaldo Jose and Mercedes (Gonzalez) M.; m. Maria Del Carmen Blas, June 5, 1960 (div. June 1967); children: Andrea Claudia, Arnaldo Gustavo, Marcelo Gabriel; m. Nelvy Verónica Del Ciampo, May 28, 1988; 1 child, Adrian. MD, U. Buenos Aires, 1963. Resident in internal medicine Alvarez Hosp., Buenos Aires, 1963-64; chief health dept. Antartida Argentina, 1965-67; asst. physician Air Force Ctrl. Hosp., Buenos Aires, 1967-72; chief gastroenterology unit Air Force Hosp., Buenos Aires, 1973-81, chief dept. internal medicine, 1982—, mem., investigator edn. dept., 1972—; assoc. dir. tchg. dept. Air Force Hosp., 1998—; assoc. prof. internal medicine Salvador U., Buenos Aires, 1992-95, U. Buenos Aires, 1995; co-dir. rsch. dept. Sch. Pharmacy and Biochemistry, Buenos Aires, 1982-95. Contbr. articles to profl. jours. With Argentine Air Force, 1964-95. Recipient Carlos Bonorino Udaono Nat. Acad. Medicine, Buenos Aires, 1975, award Fundacion de Farmacia y Bioquimica, Buenos Aires, 1989, award Acad. Pharmacy and Biochemistry, Buenos Aires, 1994, Hosp. Aeronautico Ctrl., Air Force Ctrl. Hosp., Buenos Aires, 1994. Mem. AAAS, Argentine Med. Assn., Argentine Assn. Gastroenterology, Argentine Assn. Hepatology. Avocations: soccer, jogging, literature. Home: 448 Gelly y Obes St, 1706 Haedo Argentina Office: Hosp Aeronautiico Ctrl, 3697 Ventura de la Vega St, 1437 Capital Federal Argentina

MAMIYA, KIKYO, physician; b. Kochi, Japan, Sept. 21, 1965; s. Yoshimochi and Shizuko Mamiya. MD, Kochi U., Nankoku, Japan, 1991, PhD, 1995. Resident Hosp. of Kochi Med. Sch., Nankoku, 1991-92, mem. jr. staff, 1996-97, mem. sr. staff, 1997-99; mem. staff Saitama Children's Med. Ctr., Nankoku, 1995-96. Contbr. articles to profl. jours. including Anesthesiology, Can. Jour. Anaesthesia, Acta Anaesthesiologica Scandinavica. Mem. Japan Soc. Anesthesiologists, Japan Med. Assn.

MAMMONE, RICHARD JAMES, engineering educator; b. N.Y.C., Sept. 3, 1953; s. Americo Anth and Helen (Kowalski) M.; m. Christine Podilchuk, Aug. 19, 1989; children: Robert, Jason, Richard, James Jr. BE, CCNY, 1975, ME, 1977; PhD, CUNY, 1981. Computer systems analyst Picatinny Arsenal, Dover, N.J., 1975-77; rsch. fellow CCNY, 1977-81; asst. prof. Manhattan Coll., Riverdale, N.Y., 1981-82; assoc. prof. engring. Rutgers U., Piscataway, N.J., 1981-93, prof., 1993—; co-founder Computed Anatonomy Inc., N.Y.C., 1982; founder SpeakEZ, Inc., N.J., 1992, chmn. of bd., 1995—; chief tech. advisor, bd. dirs T-NETIX, Inc., Colo., 1995—; founder, CEO Visionary Systems Inc. (VSI), 1999; cons. in field. Co-author: Image Recovery: Theory and Applications, Acad. Press Pubs., 1987, Computational Methods of Signal Recovery and Recognition, 1992; co-editor: Neural Networks: Theory and Applications, 1991; editor: Artificial Neural Networks for Speech and Vision, 1993; editor Pattern Recognition Jour., 1989—; series editor Chapman-Hall on Neural Networks, 1991—; editor artificial neural networks speech and vision Chapman-Hall Pubs., 1993—; asst. editor IEEE Transactions on Speech and Audio Processing, IEEE Transactions on Neural Networks; contbr. articles to profl. jours.; patentee in filed. Assoc. Whitaker Found. grant, 1982, NSF grant, 1992; Internat. Tel. & Tel. grant, 1984; CAIP Rsch. Ctr. grant, 1985; Henry Rutgers fellow, 1985-87; U.S. Nat. Security Agy. grant, 1986—, USAF grant, 1986—, Temeplex grant, 1986—. Mem. IEEE (sr., editor Comms. Jour. 1983-89), N.Y. Acad. Scis. Office: Rutgers U Dept Elec Engring Piscataway NJ 08854

MAMUN, KAZI ZULFIQUER, physician; b. Dhaka, Bangladesh, June 30, 1954; s. Kazi Abdul and Shams Talat (Begum) Khaleque; m. Shahina Tabassum, Sept. 7, 1980; children: Kazi Taib, Kazi Andelib. MBBS, Dhaka Med. Coll., 1978; M in Tropical Medicine, Liverpool U., England, 1988, PhD, 1992. Med. officer Ministry of Health, Dhaka, 1978-80, registrar, 1980-86, asst. prof., 1992-99, assoc. prof., 1999—; hon. fellow Liverpool Sch. Tropical Medicine, 1993—. Commonwealth scholar England, 1987-92. Mem. Path. Soc., Hepatology Soc. Avocations: reading, stamp collecting. Home: 36 Dhanmondi Rd 2, Dhaka 1205, Bangladesh Office: Nat Inst Cardiovas Disease, Dhaka 1000, Bangladesh

MAMUT, MARY CATHERINE, retired entrepreneur; b. Calabria, Italy, Oct. 17, 1923; came to U.S., 1928; d. Carmelo Charles and Caterina (Tripodi) Cogliandro; m. Michael Matthew Mamut, May 15, 1954; children: Anthony Carl, Charles Terrance. Student, Stenotype Comml. Coll., 1946-50. Sec. to pres. Thomas Goodfellow, Inc., Detroit, 1942-50; asst. to v.p. R.G. Moeller Co., Detroit, 1951-52; sec. to pres. United Steel Supply Co., Detroit, 1952-54; sec. to libr. Farmington (Mich.) Schs., 1962-68; real estate agt., 1969; owner, mgr. Crystal Fair, Birmingham, Mich., 1969-88; ret. Crystal Fair, Mich.; tchr. Stenotype Comml. Coll., Detroit, 1952-54. Vol. Henry Ford Mus., Dearborn, Mich., 1989-90, Greenfield Village, 1989-90, West Bloomfield Libr., 1993-95. Recipient World Lifetime Achievement award Am. Biog. Inst. U.S.A., 1993. Mem. Am. Bus. Women's Assn., Birmingham-Bloomfield C. of C., Profl. Secs. Internat, NAFE. Roman Catholic. Avocations: reading, music, art, theater. Home: 7423 Coach Ln West Bloomfield MI 48322-4022

MAMUZIĆ, ILIJA, metallurgy educator; b. Zagreb, Croatia, Feb. 18, 1940; s. Slavko and Jelena (Marković) M.; m. Gordana Eržen, Aug. 15, 1963; children: Boško, Martina. BSc, U. Belgrade, Yugoslavia, 1961, DSc, 1975; MA in Sci., U. Zagreb, 1971; Academician, Acad. Engring. Scis. Ukraine, Kyiv, 1993. Registered metall. engr. Chief rolling mill Steelworks, Sisak, Croatia, 1961-63; asst. tech. faculty U. Zagreb, 1964-71, lectr., 1972-74, asst. prof., 1975-77; prof. metall. faculty U. Sisak, Croatia, 1978-81, full prof., 1982—, dir. metall. faculty, 1978-79, vice-dean, 1984-86, dean, 1990-97; v.p. com. econs. U. Zagreb, 1984-87; pres. chair of plastic deformation of Metall. Faculty, Belgrade, 1986-89. Co-author: Plastic Deformation of Metals, 1971 (cert. 1972), Theory, Materials and Technology for Steel Tubes, 1996 (state reward for sci. 1996); editor Metallurgy, 1982— (cert. 1986). Recipient Cert. Inst. Metallurgy, Sisak, 1974, 84, Berg Acad. Freiberg, 1977, Gold medal Soc. Metal Testing, Zagreb, 1976. Mem. Croatian Engring. Soc. (cert. 1984), Slovakian Metall. Soc. (cert. 1995), Assn. Engrs., Miners, Metallurgists and Geologists Croatia (pres. 1982-86), Assn. Engrs., Miners, Metallurgists and Geologists Yugoslavia (v.p. 1988-90), Croatian Metall. Soc. (pres. 1992—). Avocations: jogging, chess. Home: Lavoslava Ružičke 46, 1000 Zagreb Croatia Office: Faculty Metallurgy, Aleja Narodnih Heroja 3, 44000 Sisak Croatia

MAMYRIN, BORIS ALEXANDROVICH, physicist; b. Lipteck, Russia, May 25, 1919; s. Alexandr Ivanovich Mamyrin and Anna Sergeevna Zvyagina; m. Maria Iosephovna Ginzburg, Jan. 23, 1942. Diploma, Poly. Inst. St. Petersburg, Russia, 1941, Poly. Inst. St. Petersburg, Russia, 1952; D Phys. Mat. Sci., Poly. Inst. St. Petersburg, Russia, 1966. Sci. collaborator, chief Lab. Mass Spectrometry A.F. Ioffe Phys.-Tech. Inst., St. Petersburg, 1948—; prof. dept. radio-physics Poly. Inst. St. Petersburg, 1956-80; head rschr. Bur. Acad. Sci., St. Petersburg, 1969—; mem. editl. bd. Jour. Tech. Phys., 1970—; mem. Task Group on Fundamental Constants Physics, 1972—, Senate Inst. Commn. Russian Acad. Sci., 1950—. Author: Helium Isotopes, 1981, Energoizdat, 1981, Helium Isotopes in Nature, 1984; contbr. numerous articles to profl. jours.; 35 inventions and 7 patents in field. Lt. Soviet Army, 1941-47. Recipient 1 mil. order and 8 medals, Govt. of Russia, 1948—, 2 Gold medals for devices, award Russian Acad. Sci., 1982, Phys. Soc. St. Petersburg, 1992, award for disting. contbn. in mass spectrometry Am. Soc. for Mass Spectrometry, 2000. Mem. Russian Acad. Scis. (diploma), Russian Acad. Natural Scis. (diploma). Avocations: music, piano, travel, collecting cast-iron statues, reading history and memoirs. E-mail: mamyrin.mass@pop.ioffe.rssi.ru. Home: M Toreza 9 89, 194021 Saint Petersburg Russia Office: A F Ioffe Phys-Tech Inst, Polytekhnicheskaya 26, 195021 Saint Petersburg Russia

MAN, KIM FUNG, engineering educator; b. Hong Kong, Hong Kong, May 9, 1951; arrived in Eng., 1967; s. Tang Kwai and Kwan Lan (Yeung) M.; m. Yuet Ho Wong, Aug. 21, 1982; children: Haw-Yan, Yu-Hin. PhD, Cranfield (Eng.) Inst. Tech., 1983. Chartered engr., Eng. Flight control engr. Marconi Avionics, Rochester, Eng., 1978-79; sys. engr. Hunting Engring., Bedford, Eng., 1979-80; rsch. assoc. Cranfield Inst. Tech., 1981-83; prin. engr. Marconi Def. Sys., Stanmore, Eng., 1984-88; sr. lectr. City U. Hong Kong, 1988—; rsch. prof. South China U. Tech., Guangzhou, 1996—. Author: Genetic Algorithms for Control and Signal Processing, 1997, Genetic Algorithms: Concepts and Designs, 1998; editor-in-chief Jour. Real-Time Systems, 1998—; track editor IEEE Transactions on Indsl. Electronics, 1999—, guest editor, 1996; guest editor IFAC (Internat. Fedn. Automatic Control) Control Engring. Practice, 1996. Mem. IEEE (sr.), Indsl. Electronics Soc. of IEEE (fin. chmn. 1996—, mem. adminstrv. com. 1995—), Internat. Fedn. Automatic Control (tech.). Office: City Univ Hong Kong, Dept Elec Eng, Tat Chee Ave, Kowloon Hong Kong China

MANABE, TAKASHI, biochemist, educator; b. Imabari City, Japan, Aug. 11, 1944; s. Kazuo and Yutaka (Shibata) M.; m. Nobuko Kajiwara, Nov. 9, 1969 (dec. May 1992); children: Akiko, Hiroshi; m. Hideko Yamamoto, Jan. 8, 1995; children: Takahito, Haruhito. BS, Kyoto U., Japan, 1967, MS, 1969, PhD, 1973. Rsch. assoc. Wayne State U., Detroit, 1973-74; instr. Tokyo Met. U., 1975-90; assoc. prof. Himeji Inst. Tech., Japan, 1990-94; prof. Ehime U., Matsuyama, Japan, 1994—, dean, 2000—. Author: Proteins Separation Purification Analysis, 1990, Gel Elctrophoresis of Proteins, 1991, Instrumental Analysis, 1993, Capillary Electrophoresis, 1995. Mem. Japanese Electrophoresis Soc. (Kodama award 1983, dir. 1996—), Japanese Biochem. Soc., Japan Soc. for analytical Chemistry. Office: Ehime U, Faculty Sci Bunkyo-Cho, Matsuyama 790-8577, Japan

MANAFI, ALI, plastic surgeon; b. Ardebil, Iran, Sept. 27, 1960; s. Avaz and Maasoomeh M.; m. Farideh Dezham, Aug. 6, 1987; children: Amir, Farzad, Navid. MD, Shiraz Med. Sch., Iran, 1987, Gen. Surgical Speciality, 1993; Plastic Surgical Subspeciality, Iran Med. Sch., Tehran, 1997. Cert. Iranian Nat. Bd. Gen. and Plastic Surgery. Asst. prof. gen. surgery Shiraz U. Med. Sci., Iran, 1993-95; asst. prof. plastic surgery Shiraz U. Med. Sci., 1997-99; cons. attending Shiraz Med. Sch., 1993-99. Contbr. articles to profl. jours. Recipient certificate of first rank, Minister of Health, Tehran, 1997. Fellow Iranian Plastic Surgery Assn., N.Y. Acad. Sci. Avocations: football, caligraphy. Office: PO Box 71935, Shiraz 1445, Iran

MANAM, THOMPSON JOHN, electrical engineer; b. Ndian, Cameroon, Apr. 9, 1965; s. John Urua and Arit John Manam; m. Evelyn Thompson Manam, June 10, 1995; 1 child, Daniel Thompson. Nat. diploma, Polytechnic Calabar, 1985; higher nat. diploma, Yaba Tech, 1990; mgmt. diploma, U. Calabar, 1996, MBA, 1999; postgrad., U. Uyo, 1998—. Computer engr. Ebita Nig. Ltd., Calabar, Nigeria, 1990-91; materials man E.T. Anidi Ltd., Eket, Nigeria, 1991-92; instrument technologist Mobil Producing Nigeria, Eket, 1992-97, instrument group team lead, 1997-2000, instrument supr., 2000—; exec. dir. Manet Sys. Ltd., Calabar, 1996—; cons. Manet Ltd., Calabar, 1996—; assoc. mem. Nigeria Inst. Mgmt. Mem. Bishop Lartey A.M.E. Zion Ch. Mem. Mobil Pegasus Club, Nigerian Soc. Engrs. Avocation: reading. Office: Mobil Producing Nigeria, Qua Iboe Terminal, PMB 1001 Eket Nigeria

MANARA, JAMES ANTHONY, software executive, consultant; b. Westfield, Mass., Sept. 17, 1945; s. James Anthony and Genevieve Sophia (Chlastawa) M.; m. Sheila Aileen Barry, Sept. 6, 1970; children: Gregory James, Beth Ann. BA, Rutgers U., 1973; MBA, Fairleigh Dickenson U., 1977. Cert. data processing; project mgmt. profl. Programmer AT&T, Bedminster, N.J., 1973-80; v.p. Security Pacific Nat. Bank, Glendale, Calif., 1980-86; mgr. Candle Corp., L.A., 1985-94; with New Dimension Software, 1994-98; cons. ESQ Bus. Sys., 1998-99; dir. OAO Corp., Actadena, Calif., 2000—; dir. 4th Dimension Software, 1994—; sr. instr. UCLA, 1980-93; cons. Sigma Delta Group, Thousand Oaks, Calif., 1986—; speaker in field. Bd. dirs. Hart Pony League Baseball, 1986-89. Sgt. USMC, 1966-70, Vietnam. Republican. Roman Catholic. Avocations: model railroads, youth sports. Office: OAO Corp 11th Fl 464 W Woodbury Altadena CA 91001

MANAS, MIROSLAV, economics educator, researcher; b. Prague, Czech Republic, July 10, 1935; s. Jan and Bozena (Berankova) M.; m. Vera Hlucha, Dec. 20, 1960; children: Jan, Petr. CSc, Charles U., Prague, 1965, RNDr, 1966; DSc in Quantitative Econs., U. Econs., Prague, 1988. Lectr. quantitative econs. U. Econs., Prague, 1961-62, sr. lectr., 1962-78, asst. prof., 1978-84, prof., 1984—, dir. Ctrl. and East European Studies Program, 1993—, vice rector sci. and rsch., 1998-2000. Author: Theory of Games and Optimal Decisions, 1974, Theory of Games and Its Applications, 1991; co-author: Mathematical Models in Economics, 1989. Mem. Czech Soc. for Ops. Rsch., Czech Econometrical Soc. Avocation: gardening. Office: U Econs, Nam W Churchilla 4, 13067 Prague 3, Czech Republic

MANASSON, VLADIMIR ALEXANDROVICH, physicist; b. Chernovtsy, Ukraine, Mar. 4, 1952; came to U.S., 1991; s. Alexander and Chaya (Finkelsteyn) M.; m. Katrine Kokhanovskaya, Aug. 2, 1975; children: Alexander, Julia. BSEE, Moscow Inst. Electronic Mfg., 1973, MSEE, 1974; PhD in Physics, Chernovtsy U., 1984. Entr. Acad. of Scis. of the Ukraine Material Sci. Inst., 1975-78, sr. engr., 1978-80, jr. rsch. assoc., 1980-85, sr. rsch. assoc., 1985-90; rsch. scientist Phys. Optics Corp., Torrance, Calif., 1991-94, sr. scientist, 1994-95; leader antenna devel. WaveBand Corp., Torrance, Calif., 1996-98, dir. rsch., 1999-2000, v.p. R&D, 2000—. Patentee several photosensitive devices and antennae. Grantee NSF, 1993-94, 97, 98, Dept. Def., 1994, 95, 96, 97, 98, 99, Dept. Transp., 1994, 97, 98, U.S. Dept. Commerce, 1997, Nat. Rsch. Coun./Nat. Acad. of Sci., 1995, 98, L.A. Regional Tech. Alliance, 1999. Mem. IEEE, Optical Soc. Am., Assn. of Old Crows. Avocations: playing piano, reading, children, cooking. Office: 375 Van Ness Ave Torrance CA 90501-1497

MANCA, ENRICO, media executive; b. Rome, Nov. 27, 1931. Degree in Law honoris causa, U. La Sapienza, Rome, 1956; Degree in Comm. Scis., U. Siena, Italy, 1990. Editor in chief Radio Televisione Italiana, Rome, 1961-72, pres., 1986-92; min. fgn. trade Parliament, Rome, 1980-82, pres. industry com., 1982; pres. Inst. for Study of Innovation in the Media and Multimedia, Rome, 1993—; pres. Permanent Forum of Comms., Rome, 2000—. Author: Information and Democracy, 1989, Information Age, 1992; editor Another Italy, 1970. Vice sec. Partito Socialista Italiano, Rome, 1976, head econ. dept., 1983-86, directive mem., 1986. Mem. In and Out Naval and Mil. Club. Avocation: horses. Office: ISIMM, Via Del Tritone 61/D, 00187 Rome Italy

MANCEL, CLAUDE PAUL, household product company executive; b. Paris, Oct. 27, 1942; s. Pierre Mancel and Marcelle E. (Grimaud) Mirowicz; m. Annie Simon, Sept., 1967; children: Pacome, Elodie, Sebastien. Diploma in engring., E.N.S.C., Bordeaux, France, 1966, ENSIC, Nancy, France, 1967; MS in Chem. Engring., Worcester (Mass.) Poly. Inst., 1971, PhD in Chem. Engring., 1974; hon. doctorate, Worcester Poly Inst., 1990. Mem. R & D staff Procter & Gamble European Tech. Ctr., Brussels, 1973-80; dir. R & D Procter & Gamble European Tech. Ctr., 1981-85, Procter & Gamble U.S., Cin., 1986-87; mgr. R & D Procter & Gamble European Tech. Ctr., Brussels, 1987-88; v.p. R & D Procter & Gamble Europe and Middle East, 1989-99, Global Home Care, 2000—; v.p. bd. trustees ENSIC, 2000—; chmn., bd. dirs. Assn. Internat. Savonnerie, 1990; bd. dirs., vice chmn., treas. European Ctr. Ecotoxicology and Toxicology of Chems.; pres. bd. trustees ENSCPB, 2000—. Fulbright Found. grantee, 1969. Mem. Sigma Xi. Home: 115 Ave Bellevue, 1410 Waterloo Belgium Office: Procter & Gamble, Temselaan 100, 1853 Strombeek Bever Belgium

MANCERA AGUAYO, MIGUEL, retired central banker; b. Mexico, Dec. 18, 1932; s. Rafael and Luisa (Aguayo) Mancera; m. Sonia Corcuera, July 18, 1959; children: Miguel, Carlos, Jaime, Alvaro, Gonzalo. Licenciado en Economía, Inst. Tecnilogico Autónomo, 1956; M in Econs., Yale U., 1960. With Banco De Comercio, S.A., 1953-56; economist Pub. Investment Commn., Presidency of the Rep., Mex., 1957-58; economist Banco De Mex., 1958-62, adminstr. export fin. and export credit guarantee fund, 1962-67, mgr. internat. affairs, 1967-71, dep. dir., 1971-73, gen. dep. dir., 1973-82, dir. gen., 1982-94, gov., 1994-97; tchr. Free Sch. Law, 1957, L.Am. Ctr. Econ. Studies, 1962-64; mem. bd. govs.Instituto Tecnológico autónomo México, tchr. 1958-64. Bd. govs. Soc. Friends Nat. Mus. Art, Nat. History Mus., Tesorero Fundación Octavio Paz; pres. hon. bd. dirs. Fundacion Mexicana para el Desarrollo Rural; bd. dirs. Fondo Mexicano para la Conservación de la Naturaleza, Centro Mexicano para la Filantropía; mem. econ. adv. com. Inst. Mex. Ejecutivos Finanzas; chmn. Grupo Siemens, S.A. de C.V. Recipient Gran Oficial De La Orden De Rio Branco, Brasil, 1983; officer de la Legion de Honneur, France, 1990; recipient prize in econs., Rey Juan Carlos, Madrid, 1992, medal Ciudad de Mexico, 1993. Mem. Colegio Nacional de Economistas, Asociación Nacional de Ex-Alumnos del Inst. Tecnologico Autónomo de Méx, Yale U. Alumni Assn. Roman Catholic. Avocations: reading, classical music, riding.

MANCHANDA, DEV PARKASH, physician, consultant; b. Burham, Punjab, Pakistan, June 24, 1926; s. Faqir Chand and Durga (Devi) M.; m. Sudershan Gulati; children: Mukul, Vipul, Subina. MB BS, Madras Med. Coll., Madras, India, 1949; MD, King George Med. Coll., Lucknow, India, 1959; diploma in hosp. adminstrn., Madras U., 1997. House officer Gen. Hosp., Madras, 1950-51; provincial svcs. physician Uttar Pradesh Govt., Lucknow, 1951-73, cons. physician, 1963-70, civil surgeon, 1970-73; physician to the Dalai Lama Mussoorie, 1959-60; hon. cons. cardiology North Railway Hosp., Moradabad, 1975-80; hon. cons. Lions Health Ctr., India, 1971-80, Viveranand Hosp., Moradabad, 1985—; examiner Nat. Bd. Exams., New Delhi, 1989-95. Author: Know Your Diabetes, 1982, rev. edit., 1988; contbr. articles to profl. jours. Named Best Citizen award Punjabi Sabha, 1999, Pub. Hon. award Punjab Nat. Bank, 1997. Mem. Indian Med. Assn. (sec., pres.), Assn. Physicians India, Cardiol. Soc. India, Lions, Rotary (award 1995), Giants Internat. Avocations: jogging, badminton, carrom, chess, table tennis. Home: 2 Faqir Niwas, Civil Lines, Moradabad 244001, India

MANCILLAS-PEREZ, EDUARDO JOSÉ, business educator, consultant; b. Ensenada, Mex., May 8, 1949; s. Eduardo and Elia (Pérez) M.; m. Gloria Arcelia Tripp, July 26, 1968; children: Dafny, Eduina. Bachelor, U. Nacional Autonoma Mex., Mexico City, 1974; Master, Nat. U. San Diego, 1982; Doctor, U. Autonoma Guadalajara, Mex., 1992. Gen. mgr. Supermercado EME, S.A., Ensenada, 1973-74; assoc. Law and Mgmt. Firm, Ensenada, 1975-77; pvt. practice bus. cons. Ensenada, 1980—; prof. CETYS, Ensenada, 1982-89; prof. bus. mgmt. U. Autonoma de Baja Calif., Ensenada, 1989—. Contbr. articles to profl. jours. Mem. Colegio Nacional de Licenciados en Admón, Pro Musica AC, Sem. Hist. Baja Calif. (treas.). Avocations: history, music, tennis, camping, dancing.

MANCINI, MARCELLO, banker; b. Florence, Italy, May 14, 1951; s. Silvano and Nella (Cecchini) M.; m. Antonella Niccoli, Sept. 24, 1977; children: Francesco, Isabella, Letizia. Degree in Polit. Sci., C. Alfieri U., Florence, 1977; Degree in Corp. Fin., London Bus. Sch., 1989. Credit analyst Credito Italiano, Florence, 1976-79; mgr., chief mgr. Credito Italiano, Asti, Venice, others, 1980-87; dep. chief mgr. Credito Italiano, London, 1988-90, chief mgr., 1991-95; dep. head internat. network Credito Italiano, Milan, 1995, head internat. network, 1996-98; head internat. network Unicredito Italiano, Milan, 1998—; chmn. CIFCO, Nassau, The Bahamas, 1996—. With Italian Air Force, 1975-76. Fellow London Bus. Sch. Alumni; mem. Bankers Club (London). Avocations: golf, travel, reading, music. Office: Unicredito Italiano, Piazza Cordusio, 20100 Milan Italy

MANCINI, MARY CATHERINE, cardiothoracic surgeon, researcher; b. Scranton, Pa., Dec. 15, 1953; d. Peter Louis and Ferminia Teresa (Massi) M. BS in Chemistry, U. Pitts., 1974, MD, 1978; PhD in Anatomy and Cellular Biology, La. State U. Med. Ctr., 2000; M in Med. Mgmt., U. Tex. Southwestern, 2000. Diplomate Am. Bd. Surgery (speciality cert. critical care medicine), Am. Bd. Thoracic Surgery. Intern in surgery U. Pitts., 1978-79, resident in surgery, 1979-87; fellow pediatric cardiac surgery Mayo Clinic, 1987-88; asst. prof. surgery, dir. cardiothoracic transplantation Med. Coll. Ohio, Toledo, 1988-91; assoc. prof. surgery, dir. cardiothoracic transplantation La. State U. Health Scis. Ctr., Shreveport, 1991-98, prof. surgery, chief cardiothoracic surgery, 1999—; dir. cardiovascular rsch. Willis Knighton Med. Ctr.; med. advisor Total Artificial Heart Devel., ABIOMED Corp. Author: Operative Techniques for Medical Students, 1983; contbr. articles to profl. jours. Recipient Pres. award Internat. Soc. Heart Transplantation, 1983, Charles C. Moore Tchg. award U. Pitts., 1985, Internat. Woman of Yr. award Internat. Biog. Inst., Eng., 1992-93, Internat. Order of Merit award, 1995, Nina S. Braunwald Career Devel. award Thoracic Surgery Found., 1996-98; Am. Heart Assn. grantee, 1988; Whittaker grantee, 1998, grantee NIH, 2000. Fellow ACS, Am. Coll. Chest Physicians, Internat. Coll. Surgeons (councillor 1991—); mem. Assn. Women Surgeons, Am. Assn. Thoracic Surgery, Am. Physiol. Soc., So. Surg. Assn., Rotary (gift

of life program 1991). Roman Catholic. Achievements include first multiple organ transplant in La., first pediatric heart transplant in La., 1993. Office: La State U Med Ctr 1501 Kings Hwy Shreveport LA 71103-4228

MANCUSO, EVA-MARIE, lawyer; b. Providence, Oct. 4, 1960; d. Anthony J. and Marie C. M.; m. Sean P. Feeney, Dec. 3, 1988; children: William, Ryan, Emily Marie. BA, U. R.I., 1982; JD, Suffolk U., Boston, 1985. Bar: R.I., Mass. Asst. dist. atty. Bristol County, New Bedford, Mass., 1985-88; asst. atty. gen. R.I., Providence, 1988-89; mng. ptnr./trial atty. Hamel, Waxler, Allen & Collins, Providence, 1989—; mem. R.I. Domestic Violence Task Force, 1988-93. Dem. candidate for R.I. atty. gen., 1998. Cheerleading coach North Kingstown Jaguars, 1998—. 8th grade religious edn. tchr., lector Christ the King parish, Kingston, R.I. Mem. ATLA (bd. govs. 1998—, state del. 1997-98), R.I. Trial Lawyers Assn. (pres. 1996-97, bd. dirs., mem. exec. com. 1994—), Bus. & Profl. Women (R.I. Woman of Achievement 1997). Roman Catholic. E-mail: Mancuso98@aol.com. Office: Hamel Waxler Allen & Collins 387 Atwells Ave Providence RI 02909-1026

MANDABACH, KEITH H., chef, educator; b. Evanston, Ill., Aug. 30, 1951; s. Paul J. Jr. and Claudia (White) M.; 1 child, Irene Davoll Mandabach. BS, St. Edward's U., Austin, Tex., 1989; M in Hospitality Mgmt., U. Houston, 1991, EdD, 1998. Cert. exec. chef Am. Culinary Fedn. Sous chef Rockresorts Jackson Lake Lodge, Moran, Wyo., 1974-79; exec. chef Kiawah Island Resort, Charleston, S.C., 1980-82, Holiday Corp., 1982-89; exec. chef, catering svcs. dir. Meml. Healthcare Sys., Houston, 1989-96; asst. prof. Purdue U., Westville, Ind., 1996-97, U. Mo., Columbia, 1997-98; assoc. prof. N.Mex. State U., Las Cruces, 1998—; cons. N.Mex. Restaurant Assn., 1998—. Author: The History of American Professional Culinary Education Prior to WWII: The Washume Trade School, 1998; columnist Keith's Kitchen, 1998-99. Named Chef of the Yr. S.C. Chefs Assn., 1984, Outstanding Chef of the S.E. Pace Mag., 1985; recipient Meritorious Achievement award U.S. Dept. Labor, 1985. Fax: 505-646-8100. Office: NMex State U Box 80003 HRTM 3 msc Las Cruces NM 88003-8003

MANDACHE, CIPRIANA-CORINA, physicist, researcher; b. Bucharest, Romania, July 19, 1949; d. Mircea and Elena (Coman) Tomescu; 1 child, Mircea. MSc, U. Bucharest, 1972, PhD in Physics, 1982. Sr. scientist Inst. Atomic Physics, Bucharest, 1990—, leader cesium frequency standards, 1990-97, dep. head plasma lab., 1996-97. Contbr. articles to profl. jours. Recipient D. Hurmuzescu prize Romanian Acad., 1985. Mem. Romanian Soc. Physics. Avocations: painting. Office: Inst Atomic Physics, INFLPR Lab 22 PO Box M 9-36, Bucharest Romania

MANDAI, SHIGEMI, mechanical engineer, researcher; b. Kobe City, Hogo, Japan, Feb. 24, 1947; s. Shigeo and Fusae (Yamamoto) M.; m. Mikiko Yoshinaka, Mar. 9, 1974; children: Yumi, Kumiko, Takao. BS, Doshisha U., Kyoto, Japan, 1969; PhD, Osaka U., Suita, Japan, 1996. Cert. mech. engr., Japan. Engr. Mitsubishi Heavy Industries, Takasago, Japan, 1969-81, sr. engr., 1981-87, asst. chief engr., 1987-94, dep. chief engr., 1994-97, sr. rsch. engring. mgr., 1998—; part-time lectr. Doshisha U., Kyoto, 1996-2000. Author: High Temperature Gasification of Coal and Its Utilization, 1994, Combustion Engineering Handbook, 1995, Energy New Engineering Book, 1996, Catalysis series vol. 12, 1996. Recipient J.P. Davis best Application Paper award ASME, 1986. Mem. Combustion Soc. Japan (v.p. 1997—, dir. 1995-96), Japan Soc. Mech. Engrs. (steering com. thermal engring. 1993-95, chmn. com. combustion tech. and the relating issues 1990-92, Engring. award 1994, Hatakeyama award 1969), Japanese Gas Turbine Soc., Japan Inst. Energy (Best Paper award 1999). Home: Nishi ward, 1-3-5806 Mikatadai, Kobe 651-2277, Japan Office: Mitsubishi Heavy Industries Ltd, 2-1-1 Shinhama Arai-cho, Takasago 676-8686, Japan

MANDAK, JOSEF, engineering educator; b. Zlín, Czechoslovakia, Sept. 25, 1952; s. Josef and Marie (Malinakova) M.; m. Vlasta Andrlikova, July 22, 1977; 1 child, Lenka. MSc in Engring., Tech. U., 1977, PhD, 1983. Asst. Tech. U., L. Mikuláš, 1977-91, head of dept., 1991-93; dep. dir. fgn. student inst. Tech. U., Brno, Czech Republic, 1993-95; prof. engring. Tech. U. Kosice, 1994—; FEM specialist Královopolská a.s., Brno, 1996-99; bus. mgr. Bomar Co. Ltd., Brno, 2000—; cons. ZTS, Dubnica, 1980-93. Editor: Mechanical-Engineering, 1993; contbr. articles to profl. publs.; patentee in field. Mem. N.Y. Acad. Scis., Slovak Metrol. Soc. Czech Metrol. Soc. Avocations: hiking, travelling, swimming, music, book reading. Fax: 00420545152581. E-mail: josefmandak@volny.cz. Home: Mikulaskovo namesti 17, CZ62500 Brno Czech Republic Office: Bomar Co Ltd, Lazaretni 7, CZ 61500 Brno Czech Republic

MANDAL, ABUL, agriculture educator; b. Dinajpur, Bangladesh, Jan. 2, 1952; s. Tamiz and Nesa Mandal; m. Barbara Tutejska, Mar. 19, 1978 (div. June 1991); children: Rafael, Patrick; m. Shaila Matin, Nov. 11, 1992; 1 child, Linda. BSc, Bangladesh Agrl. U., 1972; MSc, U. Agr., Cracow, Poland, 1977, PhD, 1983; postgrad., Swedish U. Agrl. Scis., Uppsala, 1991-96. Rsch. asst. U. Agr., Cracow, 1983, staff scientist, 1984; postdoctoral rschr. U. Stockholm, 1985-86; guest scientist Genetic Ctr., Uppsala, Sweden, 1987, rsch. assoc., 1988; sr. scientist Swedish U. Agrl. Scis., Uppsala, 1989-96; sr. lectr., assoc. prof. U. Skövde, Sweden, 1997—; project supr. INTAS, European Union, Brussels, 1994-96; examiner European Commn., 1995. Contbr. articles to profl. jours.; patentee in field. Active mem. Solidarity Movement in Poland, 1981-83, Social Dem. Party, Stockholm, 1985-87; chief advisor Bengals Assn., Uppsala, 1992-95, pres., 1996-97. UNO scholar, Cracow, 973-78; grantee Swedish Coun. for Forestry and Agrl. Rsch., 1988-93, INTAS, 1994-96, UNESCO Biotech. Action Coun., 1995-96. Mem. Internat. Soc. for Plant Molecular Biology, Internat. Plant Growth Substances ASsn., Scandinavian Soc. for Plant Physiology, Soc. for In Vitro Biology. Avocations: fishing, badminton, tennis, movies. E-mail: abul.mandal@inv.his.se. Office: U Skovde Dept Natural Scis, Box 408, SE-54128 Skovde, Skaraborg Sweden

MANDAL, ASHIS K., cardiothoracic surgeon; b. Burdwan Town, India, Sept. 1, 1931; came to U.S., 1959; s. Mrigendra N. and Sarala Bala Mandal; m. Bina Bhatacharjee, July 14, 1957 (dec. June 1978); 1 child, Aloke; m. Mina R. Mandal, Apr. 24, 1987. MB BChir, Calcutta Nat. Med. Coll., 1957. Civil asst. surgeon Govt. India, Nefa, 1957-59; resident in gen. surgery Howard U., Washington, 1958-65; fellow in cardiovasc. surgery U. Minn., Mpls., 1965-66; resident in cardiothoracic U. Alta., Edmonton, Can., 1966-67, in-charge cardiovasc. rsch. lab., 1967-69; cons. surgeon Ft. St. John (B.C., Can.) Med. Clinic, 1969-73; from asst. prof. surgery to assoc. prof. surgery Drew-UCLA Med. Ctr., L.A., 1973-84, prof. surgery, 1984-98, prof. surgery emeritus, 1999—. Author: Anatomical Basis of Infectious Disease, 1985 (Assam Govt. award 1958), Antimicrobial Therapy in Abdominal Surgery, 1991 (Commendation cert.). Fellow ACS, Royal Coll. Surgeons, Am. Coll. Chest Physicians; mem. Am. Assn. Thoracic Surgeons, Soc. Thoracic Surgeons. Office: King-Drew Med Ctr 12021 Wilmington Ave Los Angeles CA 90059-3019

MANDAL, JNANENDRA NATH, civil engineering educator, consultant; b. Calcutta, India, Apr. 19, 1951; s. Bishnu Pada and Shetbarani (Bera) M.; m. Mausumi Das, Feb. 9, 1988; 1 child. B in Civil Engring., Bengal Engring. Coll., India, 1974; M in Tech., Indian Inst. Tech., Kharagpur, India, 1977, PhD, 1982; DSc, Musashi Inst. Tech., Japan, 1984. Lectr. Regional Inst. Tech., India, 1980-82; asst. prof. Indian Inst. Tech., Mumbai, 1984-90, prof., 1990—; cons. in field. Editor: Geotextiles and Reinforced Soil, 1988, Geosynthetics World, 1994, Soil Testing in Civil Engineering, 1994, Indian Geotechnical Jour.; editl. bd. mem. Elsevier Sci. Ltd., 1984—, editl. adv. mem., 1992—; contbr. articles to profl. jours.; contbr. chpts to books. Fell., Instn. of Engrs., India. Recipient prize for outstanding paper Indian Geotech. Soc., New Delhi, 1988, 94, Shamsher Prakash Prestigous Rsch. Awd. in Geotech. Engrg. for Recognition of his Disting. Contbrns. and Promise of Excellence, 1997, Vijaya Shree Awd., Internat. Friendship Assn. for Outstanding Tech. Contbrn. in Engrg., 1998. Avocations: sports, music. Home: C-160 Hill Side IIT Powai, Block A-3rd Fl, Maharashtra India Office: Dept Civil Engring, IIT Powai, Mumbai 400076, India

MANDALAKI-YIANNITSIOTI, TITICA EMMANUEL, hematologist; b. Athens, Greece, July 29, 1929; d. Emanuel G. and Lina E. (Papakyriakou) M.; m. Anastasios Yiannitsiotis; children: Emi, George. Diploma in medicine, U. Athens, Greece, 1953, MD, 1957. Asst. U. Clin. Internal Medicine, Athens, Greece, 1956-60; chief lab. 1st Region Transfusion Ctr., Athens, Greece, 1960-71; dir. 2d regional Transfusion Ctr., Laikon Hosp., Athens, Greece, 1971-97; assoc. prof. U. Athens, 1971-97; mem. scientific com. European Sch. Transfusion Medicine, 1990; vice chmn. Nat. Com. Blood Transfusion, 1991-96; nat. rep. Com. Experts on Blood Transfusion, Coun. Europe, 1982-94, Com. Blood Products Sufficency, European Union, 1992-95. Author: Contribution to the Study of Haemophilia, 1956, Experimental Study on Faxtor XIII, 1967; contbr. articles to profl. jours. Pres. Hellenic Com. on Thromboembolism, AIDS Com. Mem. World Fedn. Haemophilia, Internat. Soc. Thrombosis Haemostasis, Internat. Soc. Blood Transfusion (councelor), Hellenic Haemophilia Soc. (elected med. advissor), Hellenic Soc. Haematology (founding), Mediterranean League Thromboemobolism (founding, councelor), Cyprus Haemophilia Soc. (hon. pres.), Turkish Soc. Haematology (hon.).

MANDEL, ANDREA SUE, packaging engineer; b. N.Y.C., Mar. 25, 1951; d. Louis and Sylvia Polovsky; m. Richard Gordon Mandel, Aug. 30, 1970; 1 child, Lauren Rachel. BSME, CUNY, 1973; MS, Rutgers U., 1977. Cert. packaging profl. Scientist Johnson & Johnson, North Brunswick, N.J., 1973-78; chief packaging engr. Howmedica-Pfizer, Rutherford, N.J., 1978-80; mgr. packaging Drake Bakeries-Borden, Wayne, N.J., 1980-86; mgr. packaging engring. Lehn and Fink, Sterling Drug, Kodak, Montvale, N.J., 1986-88; sr. mgr. packaging devel. Church & Dwight, Inc., Princeton, N.J., 1988-93; pres. Andrea S. Mandel Assocs. Packaging Tech. Cons. Firm, Princeton Jct., N.J., 1993—; chmn. Nat. Tamper Evidence Conf., 1983. Active Middlesex County Rep. Party, East Brunswick, N.J., 1977. Recipient Svc. award, Packaging Inst. N.J., 1985. Mem. ASME (assoc.), Inst. Packaging Profls. (N.J. chpt. chmn. 1984-85, editorial adv. bd. Jour. Packaging Tech. 1988—, vice chairperson 1999—), Packaging Execs. Club, Soc. Plastics Engrs. Jewish. Achievements include pioneering use of personal computers in the packaging engineering field. Home and Office: 46 Ellsworth Dr Princeton Junction NJ 08550-3516

MANDEL, CAROLA PANERAI (MRS. LEON MANDEL), foundation trustee; b. Havana, Cuba; d. Camilo and Elvira (Bertini) Panerai; ed. pvt. schs., Havana and Europe; m. Leon Mandel, Apr. 9, 1938. Mem. women's bd. Northwestern Meml. Hosp., Chgo. Trustee Carola and Leon Mandel Fund Loyola U., Chgo. Life mem. Chgo. Hist. Soc., Guild of Chgo. Hist. Soc., Smithsonian Assos., Nat. Skeet Shooting Assn. Frequently named among Ten Best Dressed Women in U.S.; chevalier Confrerie des Chevaliers du Tastevin. Capt. All-Am. Women's Skeet Team, 1952, 53, 54, 55, 56; only woman to win a men's nat. championship, 20 gauge, 1954, also high average in world over men, 1956, in 12 gauge with 99.4 per cent; European women's live bird shooting championship, Venice, Italy, 1957, Porto, Portugal, 1961; European woman's target championship, Torino, Italy, 1958; woman's world champion live-bird shooting, Sevilla, Spain, 1959, Am. Contract Bridge League Life Master, 1987. Named to Nat. Skeet Shooting Assn. Hall of Fame, 1970; inducted in U.S. Pigeon shooting Fedn. Hall of Fame, 1992. Mem. Soc. Four Arts. Club: Everglades (Palm Beach, Fla.), The Beach. Home: 324 Barton Ave Palm Beach FL 33480-6116

MANDEL, MAURICE, II, lawyer, educator; b. Hollywood, Calif.; s. Maurice and Wynne Mary Mandel. BSBA, U. So. Calif., 1971, MEd, 1972; JD, Western State U., 1979. Bar: Calif. 1980, U.S. Dist. Ct. (ctrl. dist.) Calif. 1982, U.S. Ct. Appeals (fed. and 9th cirs.) 1983, U.S. Dist. Ct. (we. dist.) Tenn. 1987, U.S. Dist. Ct. Ariz. 1990, U.S. Dist. Ct. (so. dist.) Calif. 1991, U.S. Supreme Ct. 1991, U.S. Ct. Appeals (5th cir.) 1995; cert. level I ski instr. PSIA Nat. Acad. 1998, child specialist 1999, settlement officer, USDC-CDCa. Tchr. Orange County (Calif.) Sch. Dist., 1972-82; pvt. practice law Newport Beach, Calif., 1982—; fed. settlement officer CDCA, 1998—; instr. Coastline C.C., 1987-95, prof., 1995—, Coastline C.C. Acad. Senate, Coastline C.C. Parlimentarian 1996-99; prof. law Irvine (Calif.) U. Coll. of Law, 1994-98; instr. Orange County Bar Assn. Coll. of Trial Advocacy, 1994—; instr. Orange County Bar Assn. Mandatory Continuing Legal Edn., 1992—, Bear Mountain Calif. Ski Sch., 1996—, Ziet Maros, 1998—; FBA/OCC Mandatory Continuing Legal Edn. provider, 1994—, COURSE Vail Co. Alpine World Cup Finals, 1997, Alpine World Championships, 1999, World Cup, 1999. Counselor Troy Camp, 1969-72; chmn. Legal Edn. for Youth, 1984-86; active Ctr. Dance Alliance, Orange County, 1986—; JOC racing dir. So. Cal, 1998—; mem. Friends Am. Ballet Theatre, Opera Pacific Guild, Opera Pacific Bohemians, Calypso Soc., World Wildlife Found., L.A. County Mus. Art, Newport Beach Art Mus., Met. Mus. Art, Laguna Beach Mus. Art, Smithsonian Instn., Friend of Ballet Pacifica, Friends of Joffrey Ballet; assoc. U.S. Ski Team, 1975—; com. assoc. U.S. Olympics, 1988—; 100th Olympics vols., 1996; F.I.S. vol., 1997—, COURSE Alpine World Cup Finals, Vail, Colo., 1997, Alpine World Championships, 1999; mem. alumni and scholarship com. Beverly Hills H.S.; Opera Pacific Bohemians, Friends of Ballet Pacifica. Recipient cert. of appreciation U.S. Dist. Ct., L.A., 1985, Thwarted Thwart award Newport Harbor C. of C., 1989, Tovarich award Kirov Ballet, 1989, 92, Perostroika award Moscow Classical Ballet, 1988-89, 94, Skrisivi Nogi award Bolshoi Ballet, 1990, Marinskii Dance award St. Petersburg, 1993; ABT Romeo & Juliet, 1996, Thwarted Thwart award Newport Harbor, 1996; Ziet Maros award Moscow Classical Ballet, 1998, 99, 2nd Place award JOC Slalom, 1998, 1st place award JOC Slalom, 2000, 2d place award Big Bear Instrs. Giant Slalom, 2000, 1st place award JOC Concourse, 2000. Mem. ABA, ATLA, Assn. Bus. Trial Lawyers, Federal Bar Assn., (founding pres. Orange Country chpt. 1986, nat. del. 1988-90, founder criminal indigent def. panel 1986, mem. numerous other coms., nat. chpt. activity award 1987, nat. membership award 1987, chpt. svc. award 1989, nat. regional membership chmn. 1990, spl. appointee nat. membership com. 1991), Calif. Bar Assn. (Pro Bono awards 1985-89), Pres.'s Coun. (founder 1996—), Orange County Bar Assn. (legal edn. for youth com. 1982-90, chmn, 1985, fed. practice com., sports com., mandatory fee arbitration com. 1985—, lawyer's referral svc. com. 1984—, Merit award 1986), Orange County Bar Found. (trustee 1984-87), Women Lawyers of Orange County, U.S. Supreme Ct. Hist. Soc., 9th Jud. Cir. Hist. Soc., Am. Inns of Ct., Calif. Trial Lawyers Assn., Calif. Employee Lawyers Assn., Plaintiff Employee Lawyers Assn., Employees Rights Coun., Bar Leaders Coun. Dist. 8, Amicus Publico, U. So. Calif. Alumni Assn., Mensa, Cougar Club of Am., So. Calif. Cougar Club, San Diego Cougar Club, So. Calif. Jaguar Owners Assn. Club: Balboa Yacht. Avocations: skiing, yachting, tennis. Home: PO Box 411 Newport Beach CA 92662-0411 Office: 160 Newport Center Dr Ste 260 Newport Beach CA 92660-6969

MANDELA, NELSON ROLIHLAHLA, South African government official, lawyer; b. Transkei, 1918; m. Evelyn Ntoko (div. 1958); 2 children: Makgatho, Makaziwe; m. Winnie Mandela (separated 1992); children: Zeni, Zindzi. Ed., Univ. Coll. of Ft. Hare, U. Witwatersrand; LLD (hon.), Nat. U. Lesotho, 1979, CCNY, 1983; DLitt (hon.), Calcutta U., 1986; LLB, U. South Africa, 1989. Pvt. practice law Johannesburg, Republic of South Africa, 1952; pres. Republic of South Africa, 1994-99; nat. organizer African Nat. Congress (A.N.C.), dep. pres., 1990; on trial for treason 1956-61 (acquitted 1961); arrested 1962, sentenced to five years' imprisonment Nov. 1962; on trial for further charges Nov. 1963-June 1964, sentenced to life imprisonment June 1964, released Feb. 1990. Author: No Easy Walk to Freedom, 1965, I Am Prepared to Die, 1979, The Struggle Is My Life, 1986, The Long Walk to Freedom, 1994. Recipient Jawaharlal Nehru award, India, 1979, Bruno Kreisky prize for Human Rights, 1981, Freedom of City of Glasgow, 1981, Simon Bolivar Internat. prize UNESCO, 1983, Third World prize, 1986, Gaddafi Internat. Prize for Human Rights, 1989, Human Rights prize European Parliament, 1988; named Hon. Citizen of Rome, 1983, Nobel Peace Prize, Nobel Foundation, 1993. Address: African Nat Congress, 51 Plein St, Johannesburg 2001, South Africa also: Office of the President, Union Bldgs W Wing Gov Ave Private Bag, Pretoria 0001, South Africa*

MANDELA, NOMZAMO WINNIE, South African politician; b. Bizana, Pondoland, Transkei, 1934; d. Columbus Madikizela; m. Nelson Mandela, 1958 (separated 1992). Social worker Child Welfare Soc., 1962; med. social worker Baragwanath Hosp.; founder Black Parents Assn., 1976; dep. min. arts, culture, sci. and tech. Govt. Nat. Unity, South Africa, 1994-95; head Aoril, 1997—. Author: Part of My Soul Went with Him, 1985. First social worker in Republic of South Africa; banned under Suppression Communism Act 1962-75; twice charged for contravening banning order 1967; detained under Sec. 6 Terrorism Act 1969 and held in solitary confinement for 17 mos.; acquitted 1970; banned and placed under house arrest 1970; charged a number of times for breaking banning orders and received suspended sentence for communicating with another banned person 1971; detained under preventive detention clause of Internal Security Act., 1976; banished to Phatakahle, Brandfort, Orange Free State, 1977; subsequently served with banning orders, 1982-83; banning orders under rev., 1986. Recipient Third World prize, 1985. Mem. Nat. Exec. Fedn. of Republic of South Africa, Congress of Traditional Leaders in South Africa (nat. exec. mem.), Congress South African Students (hon. pres.), Pan African Women's Orgn. Mem. African Nat. Congress, chmn. bd. Orlando br., 1960, head social welfare ops., 1990-92, pres. women's league, 1993, mem. nat. exec. com., 1994. Office: Keppler Assocs Inc 4350 N Fairfax Dr Ste 700 Arlington VA 22203*

MANDELKER, DANIEL ROBERT, law educator. BA, U. Wis., 1947, LLB, 1949; JD, Yale U., 1956. Asst. prof. law Drake U., Des Moines, 1949-51; atty. Housing and Home Fin. Agy., Washington, 1952-53; asst. to assoc. prof. law Ind. U., Bloomington, 1953-62; assoc. prof. law Washington U., St. Louis, 1962-63, prof. law, 1963-74, Howard A. Stamper prof. law, 1974—; vis. prof. dept. urban planning, U. Washington, 1968-69; Walter E. Meyer vis. rsch. prof. law and social problems, Columbia U. Sch. Law, N.Y.C., 1971-72; invited lectr. in field, including Inaugural Robert E. Boden lectr., Marquette U. Law Sch., Milw., 1997, Inaugural Norman Williams Jr. Ann. Symposium on Law and Pub. Policy, Rutgers U. Law Sch., Newark, 1997, Disting. Vis. lectr., Seton Hall U. Coll. Law, 1998, numerous others; mem. Pres.'s commn. risk assessment and risk mgmt., St. Louis, 1994; spkrs. numerous nat. confs. and workshops, frequently on land use and environ. law.; sr. fellow Urban Land Inst., 1989-95, vis. fellow faculty of laws Univ. Coll., London, 1989, U. Copenhagen, 1989; vis. scholar Dept. Urban Planning, Technion, Haifa, Israel, 1983, Inst. State and Law, Moscow, 1978; mem. Urban Seminar faculty Salzburg (Austria) Seminar in Am. Studies, 1977; mem. urban program faculty Brookings Instn., 1965-73; cons. in field, including State of Hawaii Office State Planning, legis. program devel., 1993-9, Am. Planning Assn., 1996-98, 98—, Hamilton, Ohio sign ordinance, 1999—, others; expert witness and cons. numerous litigations; presenter testimony U.S. Ho. of Reps. and Sen. judiciary coms., 1998, Ho. of Rep. subcoms. on banking, fin. and urban affairs, 1990, 91, others. Author 21 books, including: (with G. Feder and M. Collins) Reviving Cities Through Tax Abatement, 1980, Environment and Equity: A Regulatory Challenge, 1981, (with J. Gerard and T. Sullivan) Federal Land Use Law, 1986, Supplement 1999, (with W. Ewald) Street Graphics and the Law, 1988, (with others) Housing and Community Development: Cases and Materials, 3d edit., 1999, (with F. Anderson and D. Tarlock) Environmental Protection: Law and Policy, 3d edit., 1999, NEPA Law and Litigation, 2d edit., 1992, Supplement, 2000, Land Use Law, 4th edit., 1997, (with R. Cunningham & J. Payne) Planning and Control of Land Development, 4th edit., 1995), Supplement, 2000, (with D. Netsch et al) State and Local Government in a Federal System, 4th edit., 1996, (with G. Hylton et al) Property Law and the Public Interest, 1998, others; author, editor monographs; contbr. numerous chpts. to books and monographs; contbr. numerous articles to profl. jours. (John C. Vance award Transp. Rsch. Bd. 1988); bd. consulting editors Ency. Housing, 1991-96; editl. adv. bd. Lexis-Nexis/Michie Casebook Series, 1989-98; mem. editl. bd. Fla. State U. Jour. Land Use and Environ. Law, 1985—, Jour. Planning Lit., 1984—, Urban Affairs Quar., 1985-89, Urban Law and Policy, 1977-92, Sage Urban Studies Abstracts, 1973—, Real Estate Law Jour., 1972-93, Jour. Am. Planning Assn., 1975-85, Land Econs., 1972-75. Adv. bd. Nat. Ctr. Revitalization Ctrl. Cities, 1997—; adv. coms. numerous instns., including U.S. Coun. Environ. quality, 1994-95, Rocky Mt. Land Use Inst., 1992—, Transp. Rsch. Bd., 1991-92, 90-94, U.S. Ho. of Reps. com. banking and urban affairs, 1989-91, others. Ford Found. fellow, Yale U., 1951-55, Ford Found. Law Faculty fellow, London, 1959-60, rsch. fellow Urban Land Inst., 1976-89, sr. fellow, 1989-95. Mem. Am. Planning Assn. (amicus curiae com. 1997—, property rights task force 1995-96, task force on affordable housing legis., 1992-93, task force on model state enabling legis., 1991-94, various coms.; bd. dirs. 1981-84), ABA (spl. com. housing and urban devel. law, 1980-82, adv. commn. housing and urban growth, 1976-77, Assn. Am. Law Schs. (chair sect. local govt. law 1969-70, program chair 1975-76, 81-83), NAS (com. social and behavioral urban rsch. 1967-68), Internat. Union Conservation of Nature (commn. on environ. law 1997—), Order of Coif, Phi Kappa Phi, Phi Beta Kappa. Office: Washington U Campus Box 1120 Saint Louis MO 63130

MANDELKER, LESTER, veterinarian; b. Memphis, July 31, 1945; s. Maurice and Alice (Herman) M.; m. Brenda Conger, Oct. 21, 1989; children: Zev and Blakelee (twins). BS, Mich. State U., 1968, DVM, 1969. Diplomate Am. Bd. Vet. Practitioners. Assoc. veterinarian Yarbrough Animal Hosp., Miami, Fla., 1969-71, Gulf Bay Animal Hosp., Clearwater, Fla., 1971-72; owner, dir. Cmty. Vet. Hosp., Largo, Fla., 1972—; mem. Am. Bd. Vet. Practitioners; mem. adv. bd. Vet. Forum, N.Y.C., 1980—, Vetoquinol USA, Inc., Tampa, Fla., 1996—; computer specialist, pharmacology moderator Network of Animal Health, Chgo., 1995—; pharmacology cons. Vet. Info. Network. Author: Veterinary Practice Tips I, 1980, II, 1985, Pharmaceutical Index, 1994. Founder, past pres. Class Inc., Clearwater, 1973-80. Mem. AVMA, Am. Animal Hosp. Assn., Pinellas County Vet. Med. Soc. (past pres.). Jewish. Avocations: tennis, cooking, dancing, computers. Office: Cmty Vet Hosp 1631 W Bay Dr Largo FL 33770-3001

MANDELL, GORDON KEITH, aerospace engineer; b. N.Y.C., Mar. 6, 1947; s. Bertram Herman and Maria Catherine (O'Hagan) M. BS, MIT, 1969, MS, 1970. Research aerospace engr. MIT, Cambridge, Mass., 1970-72; aero. cons. Eagle River, Alaska, 1972-76, designated engring. rep., 1976-82; aerospace engr. FAA, Anchorage, 1982—. Author/editor: Topics in Advanced Model Rocketry, 1973; mng. editor Model Rocketry mag., Cambridge, 1968-72; contbr. articles to profl. jours. NSF fellow, MIT, 1969; scholar Grumman Aerospace Corp., MIT, 1965. Mem. Nat. Assn. Rocketry, Planetary Soc., Nat. Space Soc., Sigma Xi, Sigma Gamma Tau, Tau Beta Pi. Buddhist. Avocations: rural living, model building, home computing. Home: PO Box 671388 Chugiak AK 99567-1388 Office: FAA Aircraft Cert Office ACE-115N 222 W 7th Ave Unit 14 Anchorage AK 99513-7587

MANDELL, ROSS H., investment banker, stockbroker; b. Bklyn., Mar. 18, 1957; s. David Mandell and Cynthia Lois Adler; m. Stephanie Ann Sarno, June 14, 1998; 1 child, Skylar Rose. BA, U. Md., 1978. Licensed stockbroker. Ptnr., founder Roan Capital, N.Y.C., 1997—; ptnr. Thornwater Co., N.Y.C., 1997—; cons. RSM Advisors Co., Atlantic Beach, N.Y., 1994—. Avocation: two puppies. Home: 1233 Beech St Atlantic Beach NY 11509-1600

MANDELSTAM, STANLEY, physicist; b. Johannesburg, South Africa, Dec. 12, 1928; came to U.S., 1963; s. Boris and Beatrice (Liknaitzky) M. BSc, U. Witwatersrand, Johannesburg, 1952; BA, Cambridge U., Eng., 1954; PhD, Birmingham U., Eng., 1956. Boese postdoctoral fellow Columbia U., N.Y.C., 1957-58; prof. math. physics U. Birmingham, 1960-63; asst. rsch. physicist U. Calif., Berkeley, 1958-60, prof. physics, 1963-94; prof. emeritus U. Calif., 1994—; vis. prof. physics Harvard U., Cambridge, Mass., 1965-66, Univ. de Paris, Paris Sud, 1979-80, 84-85. Editorial bd. The Phys. Rev. jour., 1978-81, 85-88; contbr. articles to profl. jours. Recipient Dirac medal and prize Internat. Ctr. for Theoretical Physics, 1991. Fellow AAAS, Royal Soc. London, Am. Phys. Soc. (Dannie N. Heineman Math. Physics prize 1992). Jewish. Office: U Calif Dept Physics Berkeley CA 94720-0001

MANDERS, KARL LEE, neurosurgeon; b. Rochester, N.Y., Jan. 21, 1927; s. David Bert and Frances Edna (Cohan) Mendelson; m. Ann Laprell, July 28, 1969; children: Karlanna, Maidena; children by previous marriage: Karl, Kerry, Kristine. Student, Cornell U., 1946; MD, U. Buffalo, 1950. Diplomate Am. Bd. Neurol. Surgery, Am. Bd. Clin. Biofeedback, Am. Bd. Hyperbaric Medicine, Am. Bd. Pain Medicine, Nat. Bd. Med. Examiners. Intern U. Va. Hosp., Charlottesville, 1950-51, resident in neurol. surgery, 1951-52; resident in neurol. surgery Henry Ford Hosp., Detroit, 1954-56; pvt. practice Indpls., 1956—; med. dir. Cmty. Hosp. Rehab. Ctr. for Pain, 1973—; chief hosp. med. and surg. neurology Cmty. Hosp., 1983, 93; coroner Marion County, Ind., 1977-85, 92-96. With USN, 1952-54, Korea. Recipient Cert. achievement Dept. Army, 1969, Disting. Physician award Comm. Hosp., 1997. Fellow ACS, Internat. Coll Surgeons, Am. Acad. Neurology; mem. Congress Neurol. Surgery, Internat. Assn. Study of Pain, Am. Assn. Study of Headache, N.Y. Acad. Sci., Am. Coll. Angiology, Am. Soc. Contemporary Medicine and Surgery, Am. Holistic Med. Assn. (co-founder), Undersea Med. Soc., Am. Acad. Forensic Sci., Am. Asssn. Biofeedback Clinicians, Soc. Cryosurgery, Pan Pacific Surg. Assn., Biofeedback

Soc. Am., Acad. Psychosomatic Medicine, Pan Am. Med. Assn., Internat. Back Pain Soc., North Am. Spine Soc., Am. Soc. Stereotaxic and Functional Neurosurgery, Soc. for Computerized Tomography and Neuroimaging, Ind. Coroners Assn. (pres. 1979), Royal Soc. Medicine, Nat. Assn. Med. Examiners, Am. Pain Soc., Midwest Pain Soc. (pres. 1988), Am. Acad. Pain Medicine, Cen. Neurol. Soc., Interurban Neurosurg. Soc., Internat. Soc. Aquatic Medicine, James A. Gibson Anat. Soc., Am. Bd. Med. Psychotherapists (mem. profl. adv. council), James McClure Surg. Soc., Brendonwood Country Club, Highland Country Club. Home: 5845 High Fall Rd Indianapolis IN 46226-1017 Office: 7369 Shadeland Sta Ste 100 Indianapolis IN 46256-3958

MANDERSON, LENORE HILDA, medical educator, medical anthropologist; b. Melbourne, Victoria, Australia, June 21, 1951; d. Alexander and Marjorie Hannah (Hogarth) M.; m. Patrick John Galvin, Nov. 6, 1980; children: Tobias, Kerith. BA in Asian Studies with honors, Australian Nat. U., Canberra, 1973, PhD, 1978. Rsch. dir. Secretariat for Internat. Women's Yr., Canberra, 1974-75, prin. exec. officer, 1975-76; rsch. fellow U. Sydney, Australia, 1978-80; from lectr. to sr. lectr. U. NSW, Sydney, 1980-87; prof. tropical health U. Queensland, Brisbane, 1988-98; prof. women's health, dir. Key Ctr. Women's Health, U. Melbourne, 1999—; vis. fellow Rsch. Sch. Pacific Studies Australian Nat. U., Canberra, 1983-86; mem. ministerial adv. com. on ethnic health Govt. Queensland, 1993-95; mem. adv. group on internat. health Commonwealth of Australia, 1991-93; mem. steering com. on social and econ. rsch. WHO Tropical Disease Rsch., Geneva, 1989-93, mem. steering com. applied field rsch., 1994-96. Author: Women, Politics and Change, 1980, Sickness and the State, 1996; co-author: (with M. Crouch) New Motherhood, 1993; co-editor: (with M. Jolly) Sites of Desire/Economies and Pleasure, 1997. Numerous rsch. grants. Fellow Acad. Social Scis. of Australia (exec.), Royal Anthrop. Inst., Soc. for Applied Anthropology. Avocations: theater, postcolonial literature. Office: Univ Melbourne, Parkville 3052, Australia

MANDEVILLE, HUBERT TURNER, JR., oil company executive; b. N.Y.C., Apr. 24, 1974; s. Hubert Turner Mandeville and Judith Knudsen. BBA, So. Meth. U., 1994, JD, 1998. Fin. analyst Amerada Hess Corp., Houston, 1994-95; sr. fin. analyst Santa Fe Energy, Houston, 1995-96; v.p. Mandeville Oil Co., Houston, 1996—; pres. Mandeville Corp., Houston, 1997—, EncrypTech Corp., Miami, 1999—; cons. Oracle Software, Houston, 1996-97. Mem. Dallas Symphony, Houston Symphony. Mem. Dallas Hall Soc., Houstonian Club, Houston Livestock Show and Rodeo, One Hundred Club, River Oaks Country Club, Petroleum Club, Met. Racquet Club. Republican. Presbyterian. Avocations: financial markets, golf, tennis, snow skiing, fundraising. Summer home: 111 N Post Oak Ln Houston TX 77024-7703 Office: Mandeville Oil Corp 2323 N Field St Apt 2500 Dallas TX 75201-1761 also: EncrypTech Corp 1101 Brickell Ave Fl 5 Miami FL 33131-3105 Address: 1111 Brickell Bay Dr Ph 2 Miami FL 33131-2950

MANDIC, ZLATKO ANTUN, pediatrician; b. Osijek, Slavonija, Croatia, July 15, 1947; s. Vinko and Margareta M.; m. Milena Lela, Sept. 15, 1973; 1 child, Mirna. MD, Med. Sch., Zagreb, Croatia, 1973, pediatrician, 1980, PhD, 1994. Head pediat. ICU Clin. Hosp., Osijek, Croatia, 1977—; head pediats. Clin. Hosp., Osijek, 1992—; asst. Med. Sch., Zagreb, 1988; asst. prof. Med. Sch., Osijek, 1997. Mem. Croatian Med. Assn. (Povelia -HLZ award 1992), Croatian Pediat. Soc., Croatian Soc. Allergy Clin. Immunology. Avocation: horseback riding. Office: Klinicka Bolnica Osijek, Huttlerova 4, HR 31000 Osijek Slavonia, Croatia

MANDL, JOZSEF DAVID, biochemist, educator; b. Budapest, Hungary, June 29, 1947; s.Leo and Edit (Lichtman) M.; m. Zsuzsa Molnár, Aug. 29, 1973; children: Judit, Peter. MD, Semmelweis U., Budapest, 1973, PhD, 1983, DSc, 1991. Prof.'s asst. Semmelweis U., Budapest, 1973-83, adjoin prof., 1983-89, dozent, 1989-92, prof., dir. dept. biochemistry, 1992—; gen. dir. Ministry of Welfare, Budapest, 1989—. Co-author: book chpts.; contbr. articles to profl. jours. Mem. Med. Rsch. Coun. of Hungary (sec.). Office: Semmelweis U Dept Med Chem, PO Box 260, 1444 Budapest Hungary

MANDRAVEL, CRISTINA LUCIA MARIA, education educator; b. Blaj, Alba, Romania, Sept. 21, 1936; d. Iacob and Victoria Pia (Popescu) Borcea; m. Ioan Mandravel, Aug. 8, 1961; children: Iana, Andreea. BSc, Faculty Chemistry, Bucharest, Romania, 1958; PhD, St. Petersburg (Russia) U., 1964. Asst. Bucharest U., 1958-60; asst. fellow St. Petersburg U., 1960-64; from lectr. to attending prof. Pedagogical Inst., Bucharest, 1964-73; attending prof. Poly. Inst., Bucharest, 1974-90; prof. U. Bucharest, 1991—; adv. doctoral studies U. Bucharest, 1991—, chair dept. physical chemistry, 1992-96; vis. prof. U. Colo., Boulder, 1997; assoc. prof. U. Pitesti, Romania, 1996-99. Author: The Electronic Structure of Atoms, 1986 (Gh. Spacu prize 1987); editor Annals Bucharest Univ., 1991-99. Pres. Union Tchrs. from H.S., 1982-86. Merit award Romanian Min. Edn., 1998. Mem. AAAS, Romanian Soc. Chemistry, N.Y. Acad. Scis. Roman Catholic. Avocations: reading, decorating, travel. Office: Bucharest Univ Dept Phys Ch, Bd Elizabeta 4-12, 70346 Bucharest Romania

MANDYSOVÁ, EVA, cardiologist, researcher; b. Prague, Czech Republic, Mar. 6, 1951; d. Karel and Helena (Hanusová) Časar; m. Václav Mandys; children: Michaela, Zuzana. MD, Charles U., Prague, 1975; PhD, Czechoslovak Acad. Scis., 1991. Lectr. Med. Faculty Charles U., Prague, 1975-80; physician Rsch. Inst. of Tuberculosis, Prague, 1980-84; rschr. Czechoslovak Acad. Scis., Prague, 1984-92; chief non-invasive dept. cardiology Hosp. Na Homolce, Prague, 1992—. Contbr. articles to profl. jours. Mem. N.Y. Acad. Scis., Czech Cardiology Soc. (chmn. working group for echocardiography 1997—). Avocations: literature, skiing, family life. Home: Kolínská 17, 130 00 Prague 3, Czech Republic Office: Hospital Na Homolce, Roentgenova 2, 150 30 Prague 5, Czech Republic

MANETSCH, DOMINIC CLAUDIUS, economist, bank executive, consultant; b. Lucerne, Switzerland, Dec. 14, 1945; s. Claudius D. and Elisabeth (Aeschbacher) M.; m. Dim S. Viennia, Oct. 1, 1987; children: Oh, Justine, Colette, Claudio. Lic. Dec., Basel (Switzerland) U., 1969. Asst. dir. ELENA Securities A, Geneva, 1970-76; mktg. mgr. TAMIC, N.Y.C., 1977-79; mktg. dir. Bank in Liechtenstein, London, 1980-85; dep. dir. DG Bank (Suisse), Geneva, 1986-89; mgmt. CREDIT Suisse, Manama-Bahrain, Switzerland, 1989-92; mng. dir. M.D. Bahrain Forum, Manama-Bahrain, Switzerland, 1992-97. Sgt. Maj. Swiss Army, 1969-89. Mem. Planetary Soc., City-Swiss-Club London. Avocations: tennis, skiing, art history, astronomy.

MANEV, EMIL DEYANOV, chemistry educator, researcher; b. Sofia, Bulgaria, June 12, 1939; s. Deyan Petrov and Efrosia Petrova (Zlatanova) M.; m. Svetla Vassileva Sazdanova; 1 child, Yana. MSc, Sofia U., 1961, PhD, 1973. Chemist Ctrl. Dept. Geology Rsch., Sofia, 1961-62; asst. prof. Sofia U., 1962-77, assoc. prof., 1977—; vis. scientist Cambridge (Eng.) U., 1968-69, Paris U., 1976, Columbia U., N.Y., 1978-80, Ill. Inst. Tech., Chgo., 1980-81, Wageningen (The Netherlands) Agrl. U., 1989, Inst. for Surface Chem., Stockholm, 1989-91; cons. Shoumen (Bulgaria) U., 1996—. Contbr. articles to profl. jours. Mem. Union Bulgarian Scientists, Internat. Assn. of Colloid and Interface Scientists. Avocations: classical music, tennis, languages. Home: Bl 69 Ent 4 Apt 90, Mladost 1, 1784 Sofia Bulgaria Office: Sofia U Faculty Chem, J Bourchier Ave 1, 1126 Sofia Bulgaria

MANEVAL, DAVID RICHARD, mineral engineering consultant; b. Williamsport, Pa., Dec. 18, 1928; s. Paul David and Julia May (Heisler) M.; m. Lyne Page Heisley, Feb. 25, 1951 (dec.); children: David R. Jr., Michael W. (dec.), Holly M. McDonough, Laurie M. Zellers. BS, Pa. State U., 1950, MS, 1957, PhD, 1961. Asst. prof. Pa. State U., State College, 1961-63, dir. rsch. Pa. dept. of mines, 1963-69, dep. sec. Pa. dept. environment, 1969-70; sci. advisor Appalachian Regional Com., Washington, 1971-78; asst. dir. Office of Surface Mining, Washington, 1979-81; prof. U. Alaska, Fairbanks, 1981-89; mineral engring. cons. State College, 1989—; cons. in field, 1961—; extramural reviewer Alaska Sci. and Engring. Found., Anchorage, Alaska, 1989—; lectr. Pa. State U., 1992—. Author: (book chpts.) Mining Engineering Handbook, 1973, Coal Preparation, 1979; contbr. articles to profl. jours. Mem. College Area Sch. Bd., State College, 1957-63; mem. adv. com. Bur. Land Mgmt., Fairbanks, 1983-89; exec. bd. dirs. Juniata Valley Boy Scout Coun., 1993—. With U.S. Army, 1950-52. Recipient Superior Svc. award U.S. Dept. of Interior, 1979, Silver Beaver award Juniata Valley Boy Scout Coun., 1962. Mem. Am. Inst. Mining, Metallurg. and Petroleum Engrs. (disting. mem. 1990, Distin. Svc. award for environ. conservation 1980), Rotary Club State College (sr. active mem., bd. dirs. 1995-97, Paul Harris fellow 1988), Pa. State Ret. Faculty Club (treas. 1995-98). Republican. Presbyterian. Avocations: gardening, travel, photography. Home: 126 W Lytle Ave State College PA 16801-5925

MANEVICH, MICHAEL, physicist, researcher; b. Novosibirsk, Russia, July 19, 1946; arrived in Israel, 1992; s. Lev and Chana (Pischin) M.; m. Lyubov Belonosov, June 20, 1966; 1 child, Ylia. MS, Novosibirsk Inst. Elec. Engrs., 1971, PhD, 1988. Engr. Novosibirsk (Russia) Inst. Semiconductor Devices, 1971-75; rschr., head lab. Novosibirsk Inst. Electrovacuum Devices, 1975-81; head lab., head dept. Novosibirsk Inst. Applied Microelectronics, 1981-92; sr. rschr. Jerusalem (Israel) Coll. Tech., 1993—; lectr., assoc. prof. Novosibirsk Inst. Electrotech. Engring., 1986-92. Inventor in field of microoptics and microelectronics; contbr. articles to profl. jours. Jewish. Office: Jerusalem Coll Tech, 21 Havaad Haleumi St #16031, 91160 Jerusalem Israel

MANFREDINI, ROBERTO, internist, educator; b. Ferrara, Italy, Oct. 13, 1957; s. Gherardo and Renata (Balboni) M.; m. Raffaella Salmi, May 18, 1991. Diploma in Medicine and Surgery, U. Ferrara, 1982; specialty diploma in Endocrinology, U. Modena, Italy, 1985; specialty diploma in Internal Medicine, U. Parma, Italy, 1990. Med. diplomate. Internal fellow Inst. Med. Semeiotics, U. Ferrara, 1979-82, vol. asst., 1982-88; med. asst. 2nd Med. Divsn. St. Anna Hosp., Ferrara, 1988, med. asst. emergency dept., 1988-90; asst. prof. Inst. Internal Medicine, U. Ferrara, 1990-95, sect. head, 1995—; prof. emergency medicine Sch. Dentistry, U. Ferrara Med. Sch., 1988-90, prof. emergency medicine, 1994—, prof. internal medicine univ. diploma in nursing, 1994—; prof. med. pathology Nursing Sch., St. Anna Hosp., Ferrara, 1988—. Author: Cronobiologia Dell'Apparato Cardiovascolare, 1995, Disturbi d'ansia in medicina interna, 1998; contbr. articles to profl. jours. Lt. Italian Army Health Svc., 1983-84. Rsch. grantee Italian Ministry Sci. and Tech. Rsch., 1994, 1995, 96, 97, 98, 99. Mem. N.Y. Acad. Scis., Italian Nat. Soc. Internal Medicine (bd. dirs.), Italian Soc. Chronobiology (bd. dirs.), European Assn. Internal Medicine, European Soc. Chronobiology, Internat. Soc. Chronobiology. Roman Catholic. Home: Viale Cavour 5, I-44100 Ferrara Italy Office: U Ferrara Inst Internal Medicine, Via Savonarola 9, I-44100 Ferrara Italy

MANGALVEDEKAR, HARIVITTAL APPURAO, electrical engineering educator, researcher; b. Tiruchirapalli, India, May 29, 1957; s. Appu Vadirajarao and Sharada (Appurao) M.; m. Arundhathi Harivittal, Jan. 21, 1991; 1 child, H. Sindhuja. BE in Elec. Engring., S.P. Coll. Engring., Mumbai, India, 1979; ME in Elec. Engring., V.J. Tech. Inst., Mumbai, 1984, PhD, 1995. Trainee engr. Gen. Electric Ltd., India, 1979-80; jr. engr. Asian Paints (I) Ltd., India, 1981-82; application engr. Voltas Switchgear Ltd., India, 1984-86; lectr. V.J. Tech. Inst., 1986-88, asst. prof., 1988—. Contbr. articles to Elec. Machines and Power Systems, IEEE Transactions Automatic Control. Recipient grants, 1988, 96, 97. Mem. IEEE, ISTE (life). Avocations: music, yoga. Office: V J Tech Inst, HR Mahajani Marg, 400 019 Matunga/Mumbai India

MANGANELLO, JAMES ANGELO, psychologist; b. Cambridge, Mass., Nov. 30, 1944; s. Almando and Carmella (Spera) M.; m. Rosemarie Bombara, Dec. 26, 1965; children: Jason, Jennifer. BA, Eastern Nazarene Coll., 1966; MA, Boston U., 1970; EdM, Suffolk U., 1969; EdD, Boston U., 1977; M in Pub. Health, Harvard U., 1980. Instr. biology N.Y. Christian Acad., Bklyn., 1966-67; minister youth, edn. St. Paul Ch., Somerville, Mass., 1967-69; dir., founder Community Nursery Sch., Somerville, 1967-69; resident dir., instr. Malone Coll., Canton, Ohio, 1969-70; clin., research fellow dept. psychiatry Mass. Gen. Hosp., Boston, 1973-75; psychologist North Shore Counseling Ctr., Beverly, Mass., 1975-79; instr. North Shore Community Coll., Beverly, 1975-78; pres. Health Integration Services, Peabody, Mass., 1978-83; clin. fellow dept. psychiatry Harvard U. Med. Sch., Boston, 1983-84; pres. Dr. Manganello & Assocs., Danvers, Mass., 1983—, The Charis Inst., Lexington, Mass., 1994—; cons. psychologist Erich Lindemann Mental Health Ctr., Boston, 1971-75, Westwood Lodge, 1973-74. Contbr. articles to profl. jours. Chpt. mem. Rep. Presdl. Task Force, Washington, 1983—; mem. guidance adv. bd., bd. trustees Lexington Christian Acad., Mass., 1977—; mem. pres.'s council Gordon-Conwell Theol. Sem., Hamilton, Mass., 1983—. Mem. AAAS, Am. Orthopsychiat. Assn., Am. Pub. Health Assn., Am. Coll. Health Care Execs., Am. Sci. Affiliation, Soc. for Sci. Study of Religion, MIT Enterprise Forum, Pi Lambda Theta. Avocations: tennis, basketball, music. Home: 2 Crest Cir Lexington MA 02421-7144 Office: 3 Militia Dr Lexington MA 02421-4739

MANGAPIT, CONRADO, JR., manufacturing company executive; b. Cavite, Philippines, Oct. 17, 1946; s. Conrado Lebang Sr. and Amparo Ajuste (Odion) M.; m. Rosalinda Martinez Travis, Dec. 19, 1970; 1 child, Regina. BEE, U. So. Calif., Los Angeles, 1969; MA in Human Resource Mgmt., Pepperdine U., 1978. Commd. ensign USN, 1969, advanced through grades to lt. comdr., resigned, 1979; project engr. Continental Can Co., Houston, 1979-80; applications engr. Toshiba Houston Internat. Corp., 1980-83, asst. mktg. mgr., asst. product mgr., 1983, mgr. mktg., products, 1983-89, mgr. power apparatus div., 1989-96, mktg. mgr. packaging group, 1995-96, dir. ops.-contract, 1995-96, mktg. mgr. switchgear products group, 1996-97, sr. sales exec., 1997-98; sales mgr. Power Conversion Divsn., Liteon, Houston, 1998-99; dir. engring. Factory Automation Sys., College Park, Ga., 1999—. Advisor Filipino-U.S. Mil. Assn., Guam, 1977-78; co. rep. Japan-Am. Soc., Houston, 1985—, Houston Minority Bus. Coun., 1997—. Recipient Humanitarian Service medal U.S. Dept. Def., 1978; named Outstanding Young Man of Am. U.S. Jaycees, 1980. Mem. IEEE, Am. Mgmt. Assn. Republican. Roman Catholic. Clubs: Mission Bend Homeowners Assn. (Houston). Avocations: reading, guitar, electronics, camping, college recruiting for the University of Southern California. Office: Factory Automation Sys 5139 Southridge Pkwy Atlanta GA 30349-5966

MANGAZE, MARIO, judge. Justice Supreme Ct. Mozambique. *

MANGELL, CHARLES PETER, physician, colorectal surgeon, researcher; b. Malmo, Sweden, Apr. 13, 1958; s. Jacob and Suse (Grünewald) M.; m. Ann Kersti Salomonsson, Sept. 3, 1989; children: Victor Natanel, Gabriel Eli. MD, U. Lund, Sweden, 1985. Cons. surgeon County Hosp., Halmstad, Sweden, 1990-92, U. Hosp. MAS, Malmo, Sweden, 1992—; sr. cons. surgeon County Hosp., Helsingborg, Sweden, 1996. Recipient Swedish Soc. Vascular Surgery award, Kristianstad, Sweden, 1997, European Soc. for Vascular Surgery award, Antwerpen, Belgium, 1995. Mem. Swedish Med. Assn., Swedish Surg. Soc., Swedish Soc. Colo-Rectal Surgery, Nordic Surg. Soc. Jewish. Office: U Hosp MAS, Dept Surgery, S-205 02 Malmö Sweden

MANGER, GERALD H., real estate broker; b. Jersey City, Feb. 10, 1948; s. Henry C. and Irene M. Manger; children: Christopher, Paul. BFA, Pratt Inst., 1970; postgrad., Rutgers U., 1970-73. Real estate salesperson Max E. Spann Realtors, Bernardsville, N.J., 1976-82; adminstrv. broker Weichert Referrals, Morris Plains, N.J., 1982-95; pres. Wyndemere Real Estate Co., Inc., Blairstown, N.J., 1996—. Co-chmn. Main St. & Village Assn., Blairstown, 1997-99. Mem. Nat. Assn. Realtors, N.J. Assn. Realtors, Warren County Bd. Realtors (sec. 1998—), Blairstown Bus. Assn. (pres. 2000). E-mail: wyndemere@goes.com. Office: Wyndemere Real Estate Co Inc PO Box 669 3 Main St Blairstown NJ 07825-2601

MANGER, MATTHIAS MANFRED, chemist, consultant; b. Werneck, Germany, Aug. 5, 1971; s. Erich Ernst and Regina Rosa (Göbel) M. Diploma, U. Würzburg, Germany, 1995, PhD, 1997. Student supr. U. Würzburg, 1995-98; rschr. SFB347, Würzburg, 1997-98, F.A. Hoffman-LaRoche AG, Basel, Switzerland, 1998; postdoctoral scholar Calif. Inst. Tech., Pasadena, 1998-99; cons. Wassermann AG, Munich, 1999—; postdoctoral scholar Calif. Inst. Tech. Contbr. articles to profl. jours. Alexander von Humboldt Found. grantee, 1998-99, Fonds der Chemischen Industrie grantee, 1995-97, Studienstiftung des Deutschen Volkes grantee, 1993-95; recipeint Unterfr. Gedenkjaherstift award, 1999. Mem. Gesellschaft Deutscher Chemiker, Humboldtiana Schweinfurt. Roman Catholic. Avocations: sports, business.

MANGER, WILLIAM MUIR, internist; b. Greenwich, Conn., Aug. 13, 1920; s. Julius and Lilian (Weissinger) M.; m. Lynn Seymour Sheppard, May 30, 1964; children: William Muir, Jr., Lilian Wade (Mrs. Porter Fleming), Stewart Sheppard, Charles Seymour. BS, Yale U., 1944; MD, Columbia U., 1946; PhD, Mayo Found., U. Minn., 1958. Diplomate Nat. Bd. Med. Examiners, Am. Bd. Internal Medicine. Intern Presbyn. Hosp., N.Y.C., 1946-47, resident, 1949-50; fellow internal medicine Mayo Found., 1950-55; asst. physician Presbyn. Hosp., 1957—; dir. Manger Rsch. Found., 1961-77, clin. asst., vis. physician Columbia divsn. Bellevue Hosp., 1964-68; asst. attending physician NYU Bellevue Hosp., 1969-77, assoc. attending physician, 1977-83, attending physician, 1983—; instr. medicine Columbia U. Coll. Phys. and Surg., 1957-66, assoc. medicine, 1966-70, lectr., 1981—; asst. attending physician Presbyn. Hosp., 1966-68; asst. clin. prof. medicine N.Y.U. Med. Ctr., 1968-75, assoc. clin. prof. medicine, 1975-83, prof. clin. medicine, 1983—; mem. devel. com. Mayo clinic, 1981-87; vice chmn. bd. Manger Hotels, Inc., 1957-73. Co-author: Chemical Quantitation of Epinephrine and Norepinephrine in Plasma, 1959, Pheochromocytoma, 1977, Clinical and Experimental Pheochromocytoma, 1996; author: Catecholamines in Normal and Abnormal Cardiac Function, 1982; editor, contbr. Hormones and Hypertension, 1966; editor: Am. Lecture Series in Endocrinology, 1962-75; guest editor First Irvine H. Page Internat. Hypertension Rsch. Symposium, 1990; contbr. articles to profl. and lay jours. Mem. bd. govs. St. Albans Sch., Washington, 1958-64, 67-73, 83-89, chmn., 1967-69; trustee Found. Rsch. in Medicine and Biology, 1971-77, Buckley Sch., 1975-85, Lycee Francais, N.Y., 1996-98, Found. for Advancement Internat. Rsch. in Microbiology, 1977-82, Thyroid Found., 1980-85; mem. bd. visitors Boston U. Med. Sch., 1992—; trustee Found. for Depression and Manic Depression, 1978-89, pres., 1980-89; elder Presbyn. Ch., 1968-70, 92-93, trustee, 1962-67, 80-84, deacon, 1959-61. Lt. (j.g.) M.C., USNR, 1947-49. Recipient Mayo Found. Alumni award for Meritorious Rsch., 1955, Disting. Alumnus award, 1992. Fellow ACP, Acad. Psychosomatic Medicine, Am. Geriatric Soc., Coun. on Geriatric Cardiology, N.Y. Acad. Medicine (admission com. 1976-78, edn. com. 1979-92) Am. Coll. Cardiology, Am. Coll. Clin. Pharmacology, Royal Soc. Health, Am. Inst. Chemists; trustee Nat. Hypertension Assn. (chmn. 1977—), AMA, Am. Soc. Internal Medicine, N.Y. State Med. Soc., N.Y. County med. Soc., Am. Heart Assn. (fellow coun. on circulation and coun. for high blood pressure rsch.), Nat. High Blood Pressure Edn. Program (mem. Coord. Com.), Inter-Am. Soc. Hypertension, Internat. Soc. Hypertension, Am. Soc. Hypertension (designated hypertension specialist), Am. Thoracic Soc., N.Y. Acad. Sci., AAAS, Am. Physiol. Soc., Am. Chem. Soc., Am. Soc. Pharmacology and Exptl. Therapeutics, Am. Soc. for Clin. Pharmacology and Therapeutics, Clin. Autonomic Rsch. Soc., Am. Autonomic Soc., Med. Strollers, N.Y.C., Endocrine Soc., Pan Am. Med. Assn., Harvey Soc., Soc. Exptl. Biology and Medicine, Rsch. Discussion Group (founding mem., sec.-treas. 1958-80), Am. Fedn. Clin. Rsch. Am. Soc. Nephrology, Royal Soc. Medicine (affiliate), Fellows Assn. Mayo Found. (v.p., pres. 1953), Mayo Alumni Assn. (v.p. 1981-82, exec. com. 1981-89, pres. elect 1982-85, pres. 1985-87), Chatecholamine Club (founder, sec.-treas. 1967-80, pres. 1981-82), Doctors Mayo Soc., Albert Gallatin Assocs., New Eng. Soc., S.R. (chmn. admissions com. 1959-67, bd. mgrs. 1959-67, 69-70), Soc. Colonial Wars, Soc. of the Cin., Sigma Xi, Nu Sigma Nu, Phi Delta Theta, Explorers, Meadow (L.I., N.Y.), Univ.; Yale; N.Y. Athletic Club (N.Y.C.), Southampton Bathing. Achievements include research on the mechanism of salt-induced hypertension on the mechanism whereby potassium lowers blood pressure and prevents stroke, and on pheochromocytoma. Home: 8 E 81st St New York NY 10028-0201

MANGERUD, JAN, geologist, researcher; b. Oslo, Norway, Nov. 29, 1937; s. Kaare and Ruth (Hansen) M.; m. Bjørg Myhr, July 2, 1960; children: Gunn, Asbjørn, Vemund. Grad., U. Oslo, 1961, U. Bergen, 1962; PhD, U. Bergen, 1973. Prof. U. Bergen, 1967—, head dept. geology, 1981-83; vis. scientist Stockholm U., 1965, U. Minn., 1972; vis. prof. U. Colo., 1982-84, 90-91, 97; mem. Coun. for Natural Sci. Rsch., Norway, 1976-79; mem. internat. steering com. European Sci. Found., France, 1989-95; chmn. Nat. Radiocarbon Lab., Trondheim, 1994—. Contbr. more than 200 articles to profl. jours. including Nature, Boreas, Quaternary Rsch., Global and Planetary Change, among others. Recipient Nansen award for polar rsch. U. Oslo. Fellow Royal Norwegian Soc. Scis. and Letters, Academia Europeae (London), Norwegian Acad. Sci., Royal Acad. Scis. Lund Sweden; mem. Norwegian Geol. Soc. (pres. 1986-88), Geol. Soc. Am. Achievements include discovering many sites and described climatic variations during the last ice age in the Arctic and in Norway. Office: U Bergen Dept Geology, Allegt 41, N-5007 Bergen Norway

MANGES, JAMES HORACE, investment banker; b. N.Y.C., Oct. 8, 1927; s. Horace S. and Natalie (Bloch) M.; m. Joan Brownell, Oct., 1969 (div.); m. Mary Seymour, Mar. 28, 1974; children: Alison, James H. Jr. Grad., Phillips Exeter Acad., 1945; BA, Yale U., 1950; MBA, Harvard U., 1953. With Kuhn, Loeb & Co., N.Y.C., 1954-77, ptnr., 1967-77; mng. dir. Lehman Bros., Kuhn Loeb Inc., N.Y.C., 1977-84, Shearson Lehman Hutton, Inc., N.Y.C., 1984-90; adv. dir. Lehman Bros., N.Y.C., 1990-96; dir. Baker Industries, 1967-77, Proudfoot PLC, 1996-98; dir., exec. com. Metromedia, Inc. 1970-86. Trustee The Episcopal Sch., 1978-92, St. Bernard's Sch., 1985-2000, Phillips Exeter Acad., 1985-89, mem. trustee coun., 1989-95. Mem. Bond Club, Yale Club (N.Y.C.), Century Country Club (Purchase, N.Y.). Home: 875 Park Ave New York NY 10021-0341 Office: 45 Rockefeller Plz Ste 2016 New York NY 10111-0100

MANGETE, ERIC OTORUDIGIYO, surgeon, health facility executive; b. Nembe, Rivers St., Nigeria, Nov. 9, 1939; s. Samuel Ayerite and Grace Enemimienyo (Nee Ockiya) M.; m. Florence Ayebbatoyeseigha, Nov. 24, 1973; children: Otonyo, Biobelemo. MD, Med. Sch., Bonn, Fed. Republic of Germany, 1968; specialist degree in gen. surgery, U. Dusseldorf, Federal Republic of Germany, 1974; specialist degree in thoracic surgery, U. Hannover, Federal Republic of Germany, 1978. Cert. med. doctor. Intern U. Bonn Tchg. Hosp., 1968-69; resident in chest surgery Hannover, Fed. Republic of Germany, 1968-74; resident in gen. surgery Dusseldorf, Fed. Republic of Germany, 1969-74; fellow in surgery Nigerian Med. Coll., Lagos, Nigeria, 1982, West African Coll. of Surgeons, Ibadan, Nigeria, 1982; sr. lectr., head dept. surgery U. Port Harcourt, Nigeria, 1980-85; dir. clin. svcs., tng. U. Port Harcourt Tchg. Hosp., Nigeria, 1985-94, chief med. dir., chief exec., 1994—. Dir. Risonpalm, Ltd., Port Harcourt, Nigeria, 1983-85; chmn. Rivers St. Sports Coun., Port Harcourt, 1985-87. Fellow Am. Assoc. Advancement of Sci., N.Y. Acad. Scis. Avocations: reading, music, sports. Home: Rivers St, Amarara-Polo, Nembe Nigeria Office: U Port Harcourt Tchg Hosp, PMB 6173, Port Harcourt Nigeria

MANGIN, CHARLES-HENRI, electronics company executive; b. Riom, France, Apr. 16, 1942; s. Louis Eugene and Monique (Mathivon) M.; m. Marguerite Stern, Nov. 27, 1974; children: Charlotte, Louis-David, Maxence. MBA, Ecole Superieure de Commerce, Reims, France, 1965. Computer salesman IBM, Paris, 1967-68; asst. to pres. EDC, Rome, 1969-71; gen. mgr. CEGI, Paris, 1971-77; pres. CEERIS, Paris, 1977-81, CEERIS Internat., Inc., Old Lyme, Conn., 1982—; cons. The Mitre Corp., Washington, 1973-78, Coyne & Bellier, Paris, 1973-76, IITRI, Chgo., 1979-81, PRC, London, 1980-81. Author: Lebanon, 1965, The Atlantic Facade, 1973, Flights Over Europe, 1974, Surface Mount Technology, 1986, Managing the SMT Challenge, 1990; contbg. editor Electronic Packaging and Prodn., 1988-91; contbr. articles to profl. jours. Mem. Surface Mount Tech. Assn., N.Y. Yacht Club, Ocean Cruising Club, Cruising Club Am., Ski Club (Les Arcs, France). Roman Catholic. Avocations: sailing, skiing, opera. Office: Ceeris Internat Inc PO Box 939 Old Lyme CT 06371-0939

MANGLICK, ASHOK, engineering executive; b. Meerut City, India, June 10, 1951; arrived in Australia, 1975; B Tech., Indian Inst. Tech., Kanpur, 1972, M Tech., 1975; PhD, U. Sydney, Australia, 1985; MBA, Australian Grad. Sch. Mgmt., 1999. Engr. Electricity Commn. NSW, Australia, 1981-95; mgr. sys. planning Transgrid, Sydney, 1995-99, group mgr. project devel., 1999—; presenter in field. Contbr. numerous articles to profl. jours. Nat. merit scholar Govt. of India, 1965-74; W.G. Watson fellow U. Sydney, 1975-79. Fellow Inst. Engrs. Australia; mem. IEEE. Home: 55 Whelan Ave, Chipping Norton NSW 2170, Australia

MANGOAELA, PERCY METSING, diplomat; b. Teyateyaneng, Lesotho, Aug. 26, 1942; s. Maphike Samuel and Matšeliso Theresa (Malebo) M.; m. Flesba Winnifred Boyce, Aug. 19, 1967; children: Tabita, Natasha. BSc, Meml. U., St. John's, Newfoundland, Can., 1966, B in Edn., B in Sci., 1966; LLB, Dalhousie U., Halifax, Nova Scotia, Can., 1973; D of Laws, Meml. U.

St. Johns, Newfoundland, Can., 1999. Head programs Radio Lesotho, Maseru, 1966-68; fgn. svc. officer Ministry of Fgn. Affairs, Maseru, 1968-70; dir. civil aviation Dept. Civil Aviation, Maseru, 1973-76; prin. sec. Ministry of Transport & Comm., Maseru, 1976-79; dep. coord. UN Econ. Commn. for Africa, Addis Ababa, Ethiopia, 1979-89; prin. sec. Ministry of Transport & Comm., Maseru, 1990-91, Ministry of Trade & Industry, Maseru, 1991-92; dir. So. African Transport & Comm. Commn., Maputo, Mozambique, from 1992; permanent rep. from Lesotho to UN N.Y.C.; dir. Lesotho Bank, Maseru, 1976-79, Sun Hotels Internat., Maseru, 1991-92; chmn. Lesotho Airways, Maseru, 1976-79; dir. Norsad Fund, Lusaka, Zambia, 1991-92. Sec. Lesotho Civil Servants Assn., Maseru, 1969; mem. U.N.E.C.A. Staff Coun., Addis Ababa, 1985. Mem. Am. Soc. Internat. Law, Rotary Club of Maputo. Avocations: collecting African art, photography, cooking. Office: Permanent Mission of Kingdom of Lesotho to UN 204 E 39th St New York NY 10016-2754

MANGOLA, BRUNO CHARLES, emergency physician; b. Lyon, France, July 14, 1951; s. Victor Gustave and Jane (Sigrist) M.; m. Agnes Laputte, Nov. 13, 1976 (dec. 1996). MD, U. Lyon, 1982. Resident Centre Hospitalier Gen. Les Chanaux, France, 1978-81, asst., 1985, practitioner, 1985—; dir. ER and EMS, Macon, 1990. Physician Fire Dept. Macon, 1984; v.p. The Bridge, Macon, 1998, Adams, Saone Et Loire, 1997. Mem. Trade Emergency Medicine (sec. 1994). Avocations: skiing, swimming. Home: Rue de L'Ancienne Gare, 71960 Prisse France Office: Centre Hosp Gen Les Chanaux, Boulevard De L'Hopital, 71018 Macon France

MANGOLD, ARCHIE WAYNE II, insurance agent; b. Pekin, Ill., Dec. 8, 1973; s. Archie Wayne Sr. and Rebecca Ann Mangold. BA in English, The U. of No. Iowa, 1996. Bean walker Arthur Milikins Farm, Hedrick, Iowa, 1991; telephone sales rep. APAC Customer Svcs., 1995; telephone sales rep., ins. agt. APAC Customer Svcs., Oskaloosa, Iowa, 1996—. Editor Literary: The Magazine of Writing, 1990—. Mem. Reform Party of Am. Lutheran. Home: 4684 145th St Hedrick IA 52563-8049 Office: APAC Customer Svcs 200 High Ave E Oskaloosa IA 52577

MANGOLD, ROBERT L., sculptor, retired educator; b. Huntingburg, Ind., Nov. 28, 1930; s. Ernest and Mazo Opal (Cato) M.; m. Peggy Denney Burks, Sept. 30, 1955; children: Lisa Mangold-White, Michelle Mangold-Herb. BA, Ind. U., 1958, MFA, 1960. Tchg. asst. Ind. U., Bloomington, 1958-60; asst. prof. U. Denver, 1960-64; prof. sculpture Met. State Coll., Denver, 1964-95, prof. emeritus, 1995—; mem. adv. com. arts and multimedia Red Rocks C.C.; advisor Rocky Mountain Coll. Art and Design, Denver, 1995—; condr. sculpture symposia Denver Sculpture Symposium, 1968, Art in Cities, Denver, 1973, Internat. Metals Workshop, Mexico City, 1990. One-man shows, 1960, including Expositvm Galleria Arte, Mexico City, 1990, Artyard, Gallery Outdoor Sculpture, Denver, 1992, 97, Loveland (Colo.) Mus., 1995, Lumina Gallery, Taos, N.Mex., 1998; exhibited in numerous group shows, 1960—, including Hakone Open-Air Mus., Tokyo, 1989, Sculpture in Park, Loveland, 1991-92, Henderson Mus. Gallery Fine Arts, U. Colo., Boulder, 1964, Denver Art Mus., 1969, 88, 95, Joslyn Mus., Omaha, 1970, Elaine Horwitch Gallery, Palm Springs, Calif., 1989, City of Palm Desert, 1995, Lumina Gallery, 1997,98, Navy Pier, Chgo., 1997-98, 2000, Pyramid Hill, Sculpture Park and Mus., Hamilton, Ohio, 1998, Mus. Outdoor Arts, Littleton, Colo., 1999, OCA Gallery, Ft. Collins, Colo., 1999, White House, Washington, 1999, 2000, 20th Century Am. Sculpture, White House, 2000; represented in permanent collections, Mus. Contemporary Art, Juarez, Mex., Hakone Open Air Mus., Mus. Outdoor Arts, Denver, Vangard Art 1930-1975 in Colo., Boulder Mus. Contemporary Art, Walker Airport, Grand Junction, Colo., City of Loveland, Denver Pub. Libr., Ind. U., U. Denver, Denver Parks and Recreation Found., VA Hosp. Chapel, Denver, Denver Art Mus., also pvt. and corp. collections; work represented in numerous publs. Active Friends Contemporary Art, Art in City, Denver, 1960-69, bd. dirs., 1970-72; bd. dirs. Denvar Parks Found., 1970-80, cons., 1980, trustee, 1975-80; b. dirs. Modern Contemporary Art Dept./Denver Art Mus.; mem. Denver Area Coun. Arts and Humanities, 1970, Colo. Coun. Arts and Humanities, 1971-72; trustee Internat. Sculpture Ctr., Washington, 1995—, Mus. Contemporary Art Denver, 1996—, Denver Art Mus., 1998—; mem. Denver Art Comm., 1978-79, 81-83; mem. acquisition com. Denver Bot. Gardens, 1983, numerous others. Recipient Superior award-6th Henry Moore grand prize Hakone Open Air Mus., Tokyo, 1989, AFKEY award for outstanding cmty. svc. Denver Art Mus., 1990; grantee Colo. Coun. on Arts and Humanities, 1966, Mus. Outdoor Art, John Madden Co., Englewood, Colo., 1989. Home: 1184 S Williams St Denver CO 80210-1822 Office: Artyard 1251 S Pearl St Denver CO 80210-1537

MANGUM, GARRY ROWLAND, retired entertainer; b. Monahans, Tex., Aug. 15, 1949; s. Joseph Soloman Mangum and Isabell Grace Klinger. BA in Journalism, Tex. Tech. U., 1971. Entertainer Tanner Prodns., Phoenix, Ariz., 1972—; ret.; advisor Miss Gay Phoenix-Am. Pageant Sys., Phoenix, 1985-91. Actor: (play) The Ritz, 1982; asst. dir.: (play) Widows and Children First, 1981; dir.: (mus. revue) Crackers, 1980-81; columnist: Fairy Tales, 1982-86. Regional rep. Gay People of West Tex., Lubbock, 1971-73; del. Tex. Gay Task Force, Austin, 1974; bd. dirs. Gay Bar and Bus. Employees Soc., Phoenix, 1981-82, Valley of the Sun Comty. Ctr., 1995-98; fundraiser Ariz. AIDS Project, Phoenix, 1983-97. Named Entertainer of Yr., Western Express Newspaper, 1982, 83, 84, 88, Humanitarian of Yr., Echo Mag., 1994, Humanitarian of Yr., Raven/Parker Prodns. & Miss Gay Am.-Ariz. Pageant Sys., 1998; recipient Founder's award Aunt Rita's Found., 1998, Pres. award of merit Ariz. Ctrl. Pride Bd. Dirs., 1999, Male Disting. Svc. award Echo Mag., 1999. Mem. Ariz. Cen. Lesbian, Gay, Bisexual and Transgendered Pride (bd. dirs., v.p. 1993-98). Democrat. Methodist. Avocations: reading, live theater, painting, writing. Fax: (602) 200-9117. E-mail: info@azpride.org. Office: Ariz Cen Lesbian Gay Bisexual and Transgendered Pride Com PO Box 16847 Phoenix AZ 85011-6847

MANGUM, JOHN K., lawyer; b. Phoenix, Mar. 7, 1942; s. Otto K. and Catherine F. Mangum; m. Deidre Jansen, Jan. 10, 1969; children: John Jansen, Jeffery Jansen. Student, Phoenix Coll. 1960-62; BS, U. Ariz., 1965, JD, 1969. Bar: Ariz. 1969. Sr. trial atty. criminal div. Maricopa County Atty.'s Office, Phoenix, 1969-71; ptnr. Carmichael, McClue and Stephens, P.C., Phoenix, 1972-74; sr. ptnr. O'Connor, Cavanagh, 1992-94, Phoenix; pvt. practice, Phoenix, 1994—; ct. commr., judge pro tem Maricopa County super. ct., Phoenix, 1974-78, spl. commr., 1979-82; legal csl. to speaker of Ariz. Ho. of Reps., Phoenix, 1975-86; mem. John K. Mangum and Assocs., P.C., Phoenix, 1974-92; sr. mem. O'Connor & Cavanaugh, 1992-94; pvt. practice, 1994—. Mem. Maricopa County Bd. Health, 1974-79, Ariz. State Commn. on Elected Ofcls. Salaries, 1987-93; chmn. curriculum com., mem. legal asst. adv. com. Phoenix Coll., 1973-75; legal counsel Maricopa County Rep. Com., 1986-90; mem. task force com. on career edn. Phoenix Mayor's Youth Commn., 1972-73; v.p. The Samaritans, 1984-87. Mem. State Bar Ariz. (exec. bd. young lawyers sect. 1974-76), Maricopa County Bar Assn. (pres. young lawyers sect. 1974-75, dir. 1973-75), Ariz. C. of C. (dir. 1974-79), Phoenix Country Club, Ariz. Club, Rotary. Republican. Office: 340 E Palm Ln Ste 100 Phoenix AZ 85004-4529

MANI, RAMASWAMY, chemist, researcher; b. Namakkal, India, May 19, 1964; came to U.S., 1996; s. Vellaiya Gounder and Ramaswamy (Ramayee) R.; m. Gandhi Kavitha, June 9, 1997. PhD in Chemistry, Nat. Chem. Lab., Pune, India, 1995. Rsch. assoc. Nat. Chem. Lab., Pune, 1995-96, U. Minn., St. Paul, 1996—; rsch. assoc. Coun. Sci. and Indsl Rsch., Govt. India, 1995. Reviewer Macromolecules, Jour. Am. Chem. Soc., Washington, 1998—, European Polymer Jour, Leis, Eng., 1999—; contbr. articles to profl. jours., chpts. to books. Mem. AAAS, Am. Chem. Soc., Bio/Environmentallly Degradable Polymer Soc., Soc. Plastics Engrs. Avocations: reading, music. E-Mail: manix002@tc.umn.edu. Office: U Minn 1390 Eckles Ave Saint Paul MN 55108-1038

MANIADAKI, KATERINA, clinical child psychologist, researcher; b. Peristeri, Athens, Greece, July 24, 1972; d. Nikolaos and Styliani (Hinoporou) M.; m. Ioannis Bralios, Mar. 25, 1998. Grad., Anavrita Coll., Athens, 1990; diploma in Pedagogy, Philosophy, Psychology, U. Athens, 1994; M in Psychology, U. Strasbourg, France, 1995; grad. in Psychology, U. Paris VIII, 1996; postgrad., U. Southampton, 2000—. Clin. child psychologist Psychol. Ctr. Learning Difficulties, Athens, 1996—. Co-author: Attention Deficit/Hyperactivity Disorder, 2000. Mem. APA, Am. Acad. Child and Adolescent Psychiatry, Hellenic Psychol. Assn. Avocations: traditional music, theatre. Home: 52 Karatasou St, Thrakomakedones, 136 76 Athens Greece

MANIATIS, GEORGE MARINOS, medical educator, researcher; b. Athens, Greece, Dec. 25, 1934; s. Marinos D. and Kalliopi Maniatis; m. Alice Kallinikos, Nov. 16, 1961; children: Lydia M., Marinos-Alexis, Gregory-Aristotle. MD, U. Athens, 1959, Dr. Med. Sci., 1963; PhD in Biochemistry, MIT, 1969. Rsch. assoc. MIT, Cambridge, Mass., 1967-71; asst. prof. Columbia U., N.Y.C., 1971-77, sr. rsch. assoc., 1977-78; prof., dir. lab. biology U. Patras Med. Sch., Greece, 1978—; rector U. Patras, 1981-82; vis. prof. MIT, Cambridge, 1984; chmn. sci. coun. Nat. Hellenic Rsch. Found., Athens, 1993-94; dep. chmn. Nat. Bioethics Com., Greece, 1999—; mem. Nat. Adv. Com. for Rsch., 1993-98. Contbr. articles to profl. jours. Pres. MIT Club of Greece, Athens, 1988-93. Fellow Med. Found., Boston, 1970; recipient Career Scientist award J.T. Hirschl Found., N.Y.C., 1973-78. Mem. Am. Soc. Hematology, Human Genome Orgn., Hellenic Soc. for Human Genetics. E-mail: gmm@med.upatras.gr. Home: 6A Sofocleous, GR-26442 Patras Greece Office: University of Patras, Univ Patras, Medical School, GR-26504 Patras Greece

MANIMTIM, WINSTON MENDOZA, pediatrician; b. The Philippines, July 1, 1961; s. Florencio Sabalvaro and Suprema (Mendoza) M. BS in Zoology, U. St. Tomas, The Philippines, 1981, MD, 1985. Diplomate Am. Bd. Pediatrics. Pediatric resident Philippine Children's Med. Ctr., 1987-90; registrar neonatology Mercy Hosp. Women, Melbourne, Australia, 1992-94; pediatric resident Albert Einsten Coll. Medicine, Bronx, N.Y., 1995-97; fellow in neonatology U. Md., Balt., 1997—, clin. instr.; instr. Neonatal Resucitation Program, Balt. Capt. Philippine Med. Corps., 1986. Resident scholar Philippine Pediatric Soc., 1987; Internat. fellow Am. Respiratory Care Found., 1991. Fellow Am. Acad. Pediat.; mem. AMA, Ea. Soc. Pediatric Rsch. Avocations: reading, Russian art. Home: 415 E 37th St Apt 23C New York NY 10016-3243 Office: U Md Sch Medicine 22 S Greene St # N5w68 Baltimore MD 21201-1544

MAN IN'T VELD, WILLEM ARIE, biochemist; b. Gendringen, The Netherlands, Aug. 17, 1948; s. Herman and Johanna (Kortbeek) M. Diploma, Free U., Amsterdam, The Netherlands, 1979. Scientist State U., Leiden, The Netherlands, 1980-85, Plant Protection Svc., Wageningen Gelderland, The Netherlands, 1993-99; traveling Asia, 1985-93. Contbr. articles to profl. jours. Avocations: traveling, writing. Fax: 31-317-421701. Home: Rembrandtlaan 302, 6717 NV Ede The Netherlands Office: Plant Protection Svc, 15 Geertjesweg, 6700 HC Wageningen The Netherlands

MANIRE, JAMES MCDONNELL, lawyer; b. Memphis, Feb. 22, 1918; s. Clarence Herbert and Elizabeth (McDonnell) M.; m. Nathalie Davant Latham, Nov. 21, 1951 (div. 1979); children: James McDonnell, Michael Latham, Nathalie Manire Willard; m. Nancy Whitman Colbert, Dec. 30, 1995. LL.B., U. Va., 1948. Bar: Tenn. 1948, U.S. Supreme Ct. 1957. Pvt. practice Memphis, 1948—, city atty., 1968-71; of counsel Waring Cox, Memphis, 1986—. Editor in chief Va. Law Rev., 1947-48. Served to lt. comdr. USNR, 1941-46. Fellow Am. Coll. Trial Lawyers, Am. Bar Found. (life); mem. Tenn. Bar Assn. (pres. 1966-67), Memphis and Shelby County Bar Assn. (pres. 1963-64, Lawyer's Lawyer award 1995), Tenn. Bar Found. (charter), 6th Circuit Jud. Conf. (life), Raven Soc. Clubs: Memphis Country, Memphis Hunt and Polo. Home: 2927 Frances Pl Memphis TN 38111-2401 Office: Waring Cox PLC 1300 Morgan Keegan Twr 50 N Front St Memphis TN 38103-2126

MANJUNATH, THITENAMANE RAJAPPA, economics educator; b. Malladihalli, Karnataka, India, July 13, 1956; s. Thitenamane Rajappa and Nadiga Gowaramma; m. Sundramani R. Madyal, May 3, 1989; children: Spoorthi T.M., Abhishree T.M. BA, U. Mysore, India, 1976; MA in Econs., U. Mysore, 1978, PhD in Econs., 1995. Lectr. in econs. Nat. Coll. Commerce, Shimoga, India, 1978-79, U. Mysore, 1979-87; chmn. postgrad. dept. econs. Kuvempu U., Shimoga, 1988-94, reader in econs., 1995—. Mem. Indian Econ. Assn. (life), Kuvempu Univ. Econs. Tchr. Assn. (life). Avocations: yoga, meditation, travel. Home: Prathipala 6th Cross Bhovi, Colony Vidyanagara 577, Shimoga Karnataka 203, India Office: Kuvempu U Dept Econs, Shankaraghatta 577, Shimogo Karnataka 451, India

MANK, EDWARD WARREN, marketing professional; b. Boothbay Harbor, Maine, Oct. 2, 1962; s. Edward Raymond Jr. and Sandra Gail (Strahan) M. Assoc. in Liberal Arts, C.C. Vt., 1985; cert. ophthalmic technician, Nat. Edn. Ctr., San Francisco, 1992; cert. real estate broker, Am. Sch. Mortgage Banking, Walnut Creek, Calif., 1994. Lic. real estate salesman, Calif.; cert. Am. Bd. Optometry Dispensing. Tng. coord. Burger King Corp., South Burlington, Vt., 1985-87, San Francisco, 1988-89; asst. mgr. Bonanza Family Restaurant, South Burlington, 1987-88; supr. U.S. Census Bur., San Francisco, 1990; sales rep. Viacom Cablevision, San Francisco, 1991; programming researcher NBC, San Francisco, 1992; mktg. cons. Calyx & Corolla, San Francisco, 1993; mktg. rep. Alliance Bancorp, Millbrae, Calif., 1993—. Sustaining mem. Rep. Nat. Com., Washington, 1989—; sponsor Heritage Found., Washington, Cato Inst., Washington. Mem. Acad. Polit. Sci., Coun. Fgn. Rels., World Affairs Coun., Nat. Rifle Assn. (life), Reason Found. Republican. Episcopalian. Home: 3401 E 18th St Apt 3 Oakland CA 94601-3003 Office: Alliance Bancorp 800 El Camino Real Millbrae CA 94030-2010

MANKARIOUS, RAMSEY N., hotel developer; b. Alexandria, Egypt, Mar. 14, 1968; came to U.S., 1978; s. Neal and Narguis (Mikhail) M.; m. Jennifer Lyn Kubanek, Aug. 22, 1992. BA, Mich. State U., 1990; MA in Property Valuation and Law, City U., London, 1998. Sr. assoc. HVS Internat., Mineola, N.Y., 1990-92; assoc. dir. HVS Internat., London, 1992-96; exec. v.p. devel. Kingdom Holding Co., Riyadh, Saudi Arabia, 1996—; bd. dirs. Hotel George V, Paris, Four Seasons Hotel, Cairo, Four Seasons Hotel, Amman, Jordan, Movenpick Hotel, Beirut. Contbr. articles to profl. jours. Coptic Religion. Office: Kingdom Holding Co, PO Box 2, Riyadh 11321, Saudi Arabia

MANKELEVICH, YURII ALEKSANDROVICH, physicist, researcher; b. Grodno, USSR, Feb. 13, 1963; s. Aleksandr Aleksandrovich and Yanina Iosifovna (Shostak) M.; m. Galina Vladimirovna Yudina, May 18, 1991. BS with honors, Moscow Phys. Tech. Inst., 1986, PhD, 1990. Rschr. Nuclear Physics Inst. Moscow State U., 1990-93, sr. rschr., 1993—. Contbr. articles to profl. jours. Cand. in Chess Master, 1979. Avocations: tennis, chess. Office: Moscow State U Nuclear Phys, Vorob'evy Gory, 119899 Moscow Russia

MANKERTZ, ANNETTE, virologist, biochemist; b. Berlin, Germany, May 20, 1962; d. Guenther Heinz Herbert and Rotraut Emma Elisabeth (Richter) Gielow; m. Joachim Mankertz, Feb. 5, 1993; children: Lukas, Fiona. Diploma in Biochemistry, Freie U., Berlin, 1988. Grad. student Max Planck Inst., Berlin, Germany, 1988-90; scientific asst. Robert Koch Inst., Berlin, Germany, 1991—; mem. circovirus study group Internat. Com. on Taxonomy of Viruses, 1997—. Contbr. articles to profl. jours. Mem. German Virology Soc. Avocation: choir. Office: Robert Koch Inst, Nordufer 20, D-13353 Berlin Germany

MANKIN, ROBERT STEPHEN, financial executive; b. N.Y.C., Mar. 26, 1939; s. Samuel Harry Mankin and Dorothy (Rosenblum) Goldstein; m. Joyce Marie Cabel, June 13, 1971 (div.); children: Seth Howard, Laura Nicole, Gina Danielle. BA cum laude, Bklyn. Coll., 1961; MBA, Bernard Baruch Coll., 1970; Dr. Profl. Studies with distinction, Pace U., 1982. Mgr. ABC, N.Y.C., 1969-71, Babcock and Wilcox, N.Y.C., 1971-74; v.p. Chase Manhattan Bank, N.Y.C., 1974-84; sr. v.p. 1st Interstate Bank, N.Y.C., 1984-87; mng. dir., sr. v.p., co-head fixed income, mem. mgmt. com. Nomura Securities Internat., N.Y.C., 1987-94; mng. dir. Paine Webber, N.Y.C., 1994-95; pres., CEO Lakeside Fin. Svcs., Hoboken, N.J., 1995—; COO Thomson Fin. Electronic Settlements Group, Boston, 1997-98; acting pres. Ocwen Tech. Exch., West Palm Beach, Fla., 1999; bd. dirs., sec. Nomura Mortgage Capital Corp., N.Y.C.; bd. dirs., pres., CEO Nomura Asset Capital Corp., N.Y.C., 1988-94; bd. dirs. PaineWebber Real Estate, 1994-95. Contbr. articles to profl. jours. Mem. Planning Forum, Assn. for Computing Machinery, Assn. Computer Programmers and Analysts (chmn. bd. 1971). Home and Office: 422 Grand St Hoboken NJ 07030-2727

MANKO, THOMAS JOSEPH, school superintendant; b. Cuba, N.Y., May 8, 1954; s. George James and Mary Leonarda M.; m. Janet Marie, Aug. 12, 1978; children: Stephen, Daniel, Michael. MA, Colgate U., 1979; MPA, Syracuse U., 1980, postgrad., 2000. Cert. sch. adminstr./supr., N.Y., sch. dist. adminstr., N.Y., pub. sch. tchr., N.Y. Social studies tchr. Greenwich (Conn.) H.S., 1977-79; adminstrv. intern East Syracuse (N.Y.) Minoa Ctrl. Sch., 1980-81; asst. prin. Oswego County BOCES, Mexico, N.Y., 1981-85; mid. sch. prin. Cato (N.Y.)-Meridian Ctrl. Sch., 1985-93; supt. New York Mills (N.Y.) Union Free Sch. Dist., 1993-00, York Ctrl. Sch., Retsof, N.Y., 2000—. Bd. dirs. Boy Scouts Am., Utica, N.Y., 1996-2000; edn. com. United Way Greater Utica, 1998-2000; bd. dirs. New York Mills Little League, 1998, Kiwanis, 2000—. Mem. Am. Assn. Sch. Adminstr., ASCD, Nat. Assn. Secondary Sch. Prin., N.Y. State Coun. Sch. Supts., N.Y. State Mid. Sch. Assn. (v.p. 1993-99, regional dir. 1990-93). Avocations: biking, gardening. Home: 21 Cedar Ln New York Mills NY 13417-1205 Office: York Ctrl Sch PO Box 102 Retsof NY 14539-0102

MANKOFF, ALBERT WILLIAM, cultural organization administrator, consultant; b. Newark, Aug. 24, 1926; s. Albert and Dorothy M.; m. Audrey Emery, Mar. 18, 1972; 1 child, Robert Morgan. BLS, U. Okla., 1967. With Am. Airlines, Inc., 1947-69; mgr. mgmt. tng. and devel. Am. Airlines Inc., 1957-67; mgr. orgn. devel. Am. Airlines, Inc., Tulsa, 1968-69; dir. personnel Peat, Marwick, Mitchell & Co., Chgo., 1969-72; ptnr. Lexicon, Inc. Cons., Raleigh, N.C., 1972-77; Pacific area mgr. safety and tng. Trailways, Inc., L.A., 1978-80; tng. cons. State of Calif., Sacramento, 1980-91; pres. Inst. Am. Hist. Tech., Hendersonville, N.C., 1987—. Author: Trolley Treasures, 4 vols., 1986-87, The Glory Days, 1989, Tracks of Triumph, 1993, Tarnished Triumph, The Edison Paradigm, 1994, Sacramento's Shining Rails, 1995, Trolleys in America: The Long Road Back, 1995; contbr. articles to profl. jours. Bd. dirs., v.p. OASIS; Midwest Centre for Human Potential, Chgo., 1970-72, Tulsa Urban League, 1962-69; v.p., bd. dirs. Meditation Groups Inc., Ojai, Calif., Psychosynthesis Internat., Ojai Internat. Assn. Managerial and Orgnl. Psychosynthesis, Thousand Oaks, Calif., Ctr. World Servers, Asheville, N.C. Avocations: street car and light rail technology, historical trolley photographs, cat humor. E-mail: awmank@bellsouth.net. Home and Office: 1300 Brevard Rd Apt 18 Hendersonville NC 28791-2503

MANKOV, YURIY INNOKENTEVICH, physicist; b. Pskov region, Russia, Sept. 15, 1946; s. Innokentiy Aleksandrovich and Aleksandra Ivanovna (Chernaya) M.; m. Tamara Leonidovna Zamolotskaya, Nov. 1, 1974; 1 child, Svetlana. Grad., Novosibirsk (Russia) State U., 1968; postgrad., Kirensky Inst. Physics, Krasnoyarsk, Russia, 1975; docent, Krasnoyarsk State U., 1997. Rsch. scientist Kirensky Inst. Physics, Krasnoyarsk, 1971-81, sr. rsch. scientist, 1981—; assoc. prof. Krasnoyarsk State U., 1990—. Contbr. articles to profl. jours. Sr. lt. Soviet Army, 1969-70. Grantee Internat. Sci. Found. and Russian Govt., Moscow, 1995, NATO, Brussels, 1997, 99. Office: Kirensky Inst Physics, SB RAS Academgorodok, 660036 Krasnoyarsk Russia

MANLEY, DAVID BOTT, III, lawyer; b. Jacksonville, Fla., June 19, 1953; s. David Bott and Bernadette Claire Manley; m. Gayle Aileen Whitney, Nov. 1, 1978; children: David Jeremiah, Alexandra Ina Claire. BA with honors magna cum laude, U. Ga., 1975, JD, 1982. Bar: Ga. 1983, U.S. Dist. Ct. (no. dist.) Ga. 1983, U.S. Ct. Appeals (11th cir.) 1986. Auditor So. Hostess Sys., Inc., Augusta, Ga., 1975-76; prosecutorial asst. fraud investigator State Ga., Atlanta, 1976-79; assoc. Gadrix & Green, P.C., Atlanta, 1982-83, Lowe, Barham, Eubanks & Lowe, Atlanta, 1983-85; mem. Barham & Manley, Atlanta, 1985-89; dir., ptnr. Campbell Martin & Manley, LLP, Atlanta, 1989—; corp. counsel Highland Homes, Inc., Dallas, 1990—, Mast Advt. and Pub. Inc., Nashville, 1991—; corp. sec., counsel Agrisel USA, Inc., Atlanta and Hong Kong, 1998—. Pres. U.S. Jaycees, Mt. Park/Lilburn, 1985; cert. coach Lucky Shoals Youth Athletic Assn., Norcross, Ga., 1992-98; bd. dirs Fulton County, Ga. Dept. Family and Children's Svcs. (commendation, bd. resolution for bravery, 1978). Named Jaycee of Yr., U.S. Jaycees-Mt. Park/Lilburn, Ga., 1984. Mem. ABA, State Bar Ga. (legis. com. corp. and banking law sect. 1987-88, mem. corp. and banking law sect. 1987—, adv. mem. law revision com. 1989-90, mem. real property sect. 1996—, advocate for spl. needs children 1996—), Nat. Youth Sports Coaches Assn. (continuing mem.), Sandy Springs Bar Assn. (treas. 1987-88, pres. 1988-89, dir. 1989-90), Omicron Delta Kappa. Avocations: coaching youth sports, model railroading, photography, collecting, travel. Home: 4390 Flippen Trl Norcross GA 30092-3902 Office: Campbell Martin & Manley LLP 990 Hammond Dr NE Ste 800 Atlanta GA 30328-5510

MANLEY, JOHN, Canadian government official; b. Ottawa, Ontario, Canada, Jan. 5, 1950; s. John Joseph Manley and Mildred Charlotte (Scharf) M.; m. Judith Mary Rae, April 21, 1973; children: Rebecca Jane, David John, Sarah Kathleen. Attended, Carleton U., U. Ottawa. Law clerk for Rt. Hon. Bora Laskin Chief Justice Can., 1976-77; chair Ottawa-Carleton Bd. Trade, 1985-86; min. Industry Govt. of Can., 1993, min. Western Econ. Diversification, min. Atlantic Can. Opportunities Agy., min. Can. Econ. Devel. Quebec Region, 1996; min. for Can. Econ. Devel. for Que. Regions Can., 1996—. Elected to H. of C. g.e., 1988. Office: Industry Can, 235 Queen St 11th Fl East, Ottawa, ON Canada K1A 0H5 also: 1883 Bank St, Ottawa, ON Canada K1V 0W3

MANLOVE, COLIN (NICHOLAS), literary critic; b. Falkirk, Scotland, May 4, 1942; s. Denis and Winifred Ann (Wardrop) M.; m. Evelyn Mary Schuftan, Sept. 2, 1967; children: John Derek, David Francis. MA with first class honors, U. Edinburgh, 1964; BLitt, Pembroke Coll., Oxford, 1968; DLitt, U. Edinburgh, Scotland, 1990. Lectr. U. Edinburgh, Scotland, 1967-84, reader in English lit., 1984-93. Author: Modern Fantasy: Five Studies, 1975, Literature and Reality, 1600-1800, 1978, The Gap in Shakespeare: The Motif of Division from "Richard II" to "The Tempest," 1981, The Impulse of Fantasy Literature, 1983, Science Fiction: Ten Explorations, 1986, C.S. Lewis: His Literary Achievement, 1987, Critical Thinking: A Guide to Interpreting Literary Texts, 1989, Christian Fantasy: From 1200 to the Present, 1992, The Chronicles of Narnia: The Patterning of a Fantastic World, 1993, Scottish Fantasy Literature: A Critical Survey, 1994, The Fantasy Literature of England, 1999; editor: An Anthology of Scottish Fantasy Literature, 1996; contbr. numerous books and jours. Recipient Dist. Scholarship award Internat. Assn. for the Fantastic in the Arts, 1989. Home: 92 Polwarth Terr, Edinburgh EH11 1NN, Scotland

MANN, ALAN GEORGE, company executive; b. Worthing, Eng., Aug. 22, 1936; m. Sharon A. Mann, Feb. 28, 1973; children: Thomas J., Henry J. Brighton (Eng.) Coll. Chmn., CEO Alan Mann Racing Ltd., U.K., 1963-74, Alan Mann Group, U.K., 1970—, Wester Ross Salmon Ltd., U.K., 1978—. Fellow Game Conservancy Trust. Mem. Sunningdale Golf Club, Brora Golf Club, Key Largo Anglers Club. Avocations: fly fishing, golf, shooting, aviation. Office: Fairoaks Airport, Chobham, Woking, Surrey GUL4 3HX, England

MANN, BARLOW TREADWELL, financial consultant, lawyer; b. Mobile, Ala., Sept. 5, 1953; s. Cameron Mann and Jane Snowden (Treadwell) Mann Martin; m. Roma Joyce Crockett, Apr. 23, 1981; children: Arthur Barlow Treadwell, Jr., Lawson Henderson. B.A. with honors, Tulane U., 1975; J.D., Memphis State U., 1978. Bar: Tenn. 1978, U.S. Dist. Ct. (we. dist.) Tenn. 1979. Assoc. Memphis Area Legal Clinic, Memphis State U. Clinic, 1977-78; asst. dir. devel. Memphis State U., 1978-82; dir. devel. U. Tenn., Memphis, 1982-84; COO, v.p., legal counsel Robert F. Sharpe and Co., Memphis, 1984—. Contbr. articles to profl. jours. Mem. ABA, Tenn. Bar Assn., Memphis Bar Assn., Shelby County Bar Assn., Council for Advancement and Support of Edn., Nat. Soc. Fundraising Execs., Phi Alpha Delta (pres. 1977-78), Delta Kappa Epsilon (pres. 1974-75). Clubs: Memphis Country, University (Memphis). Home: 4581 Normandy Ave Memphis TN 38117-2421

MANN, BRUCE QUINTIN, biologist; b. Eshowe, South Africa, May 2, 1964; s. Quintin Vaughan and Annette Elizabeth (Conradie) M.; m. Judy Brenda Lang, Apr. 24, 1993. Matric, Weston Agrl. Coll., Mooi River, South Africa, 1981; BSc, U. Natal, South Africa, 1987; BSc with honors, Rhodes U., Grahamstown, South Africa, 1988, MSc, 1992. Fisheries biologist Oceanographic Rsch. Inst., Durban, South Africa, 1992-98, 98—; marine ecologist KwaZulu-Natal Nature Conseration Svc., 1998; chmn. Marine Linefish Rsch. Group. Contbr. articles to profl. jours. Served with South

African mil., 1982-84. Recipient Margaret Smith Bursary award Rhodes U., 1990. Mem. Wildlife Soc., Zool. Soc. Southern Africa, South African Network for Coastal and Oceanic Rsch. Avocations: scuba diving, marine and freshwater angling, spearfishing, hiking, canoeing. Office: Oceanographic Rsch Inst, PO Box 10712, 4056 Durban South Africa

MANN, CATHERINE L., economist. Asst. dir., spl. asst. to staff dir. internat. fin. divsn. Fed. Res. Bd. Govs., 1984-87, 89-97; prin. staff mem. for chief economist World Bank, 1988-89; sr. economist Pres.'s Coun. Econ. Advisors, 1991-92; adj. prof. Vanderbilt U.; lectr. U. Chgo., Princeton U., U. Md., Georgetown U., Boston Coll., MIT. Contbr. articles to profl. jours. Sr. fellow Inst. Internat. Econs., Ford Found. fellow Nat. Bur. Econ. Rsch., 1987. Office: Inst Internat Econs 11 Dupont Cir NW Washington DC 20036-1207*

MANN, CHRISTOPHER JOHN, publishing company executive; b. Bushey, Eng., July 10, 1948; s. Charles William and Elizabeth Mary (Haas) M.; m. Liselotte Margaretha Ljunghorn, Oct. 22, 1975 (div. 1982); m. Gillian Elizabeth Kilner, Apr. 1, 1986; 1 child, Jonathan; stepchildren: Emily Russell, James Russell. Diploma, U. Kingston, 1969. Acad. mgr. Cornarket Press, Ltd., London, 1969-72; group advertisement mgr. Kogan Page, Ltd., London, 1972-77; mng. dir. Swallow Pub., Ltd., London, 1977-88; chmn. Plenham, Ltd., Berkhamsted, 1988—. Author: (book) Where the Famous Lived in London, 1976; pub. (mag.): Bodyshop Mag., 1987— (Ben Trade Mag. of Yr. 1996); compiler: Shell Commercial Vehicle Buyers Guide, 1976-84. Mem. Ferrari O.C., Vintage Sports Car Club. Avocations: motor racing, antiques, food and wine. Office: Plenham Ltd, Castle Mill Lower Kings Rd, Berkhamsted England

MANN, DELBERT, film, theater, television director and producer; b. Lawrence, Kans., Jan. 30, 1920; s. Delbert Martin and Ora (Patton) M.; m. Ann Caroline Gillespie, Jan. 13, 1942; children: David Martin, Frederick G., Barbara Susan, Steven P. BA, Vanderbilt U., 1941; MFA, Yale U.; LLD (hon.), Northland Coll. Dir. Town Theatre, Columbia, S.C., 1947-49; stage mgr. Wellesley Summer Theater, 1947-48; floor mgr., asst. dir. NBC-TV, N.Y.C., 1949, dir., 1949-55; freelance film and TV dir., 1954—; former bd. govs. Acad. TV Arts and Scis.; former co-chmn. Tenn. Film, Tape and Music Commn.; former pres. Dirs. Guild, Ednl. and Benevolent Found., Cinema Circulus; former lectr. Claremont (Calif.) McKenna Coll. Dir., Philco-Goodyear TV Playhouse, 1949-55, also Omnibus, Ford Star Jubilee, Playwrights 56, Producers Showcase, DuPont Show of the Month, Playhouse 90; films Marty, 1954 (Palme d'Or, Cannes Internat. Film Festival, Acad. Award), The Bachelor Party, 1956, Desire Under the Elms, 1957, Separate Tables, 1958, Middle of the Night, 1959, The Dark at the Top of the Stairs, 1960, The Outsider, 1960, Lover Come Back, 1961, That Touch of Mink, 1962, A Gathering of Eagles, 1962, Dear Heart, 1963, Mister Buddwing, 1965, Fitzwilly, 1967, Kidnapped, 1972, Birch Interval, 1976, Night Crossing, 1982; TV spl. Heidi, 1968, David Copperfield, 1970, Jane Eyre, 1971, The Man Without a Country, 1973, A Girl Named Sooner, 1975, Breaking Up, 1977, Tell Me My Name, 1977, Home To Stay, 1978, All Quiet on the Western Front, 1979, To Find My Son, 1980, All the Way Home, 1981, Bronte, 1982, The Member of the Wedding, 1982, The Gift of Love, 1983, Love Leads the Way, 1984, A Death in California, 1985, The Last Days of Patton, 1986, The Ted Kennedy Jr. Story, 1986, April Morning, 1987, Ironclads, 1991, Against Her Will: An Incident in Baltimore, 1992, Incident in a Small Town, 1993, Lily in Winter, 1994, The Memoirs of Abraham Lincoln, 1996; plays include A Quiet Place, 1956, Speaking of Murder, 1957, Zelda, 1969, The Memoirs of Abraham Lincoln, 1996,; opera Wuthering Heights, N.Y.C. Ctr., 1959; author: Looking Back...At Live Television and Other Matters, 1998. Bd. trustees Vanderbilt U., 1962—. 1st lt. USAAF, WWII; B-24 pilot and squadron intelligence officer, 1944-45. Recipient Acad. Award for dir. Marty, 1955. Mem. Dirs. Guild Am. (past pres. 1967-71) (Dirs. Guild award, 1955), Kappa Alpha. Democrat. Presbyterian. Avocation: reading history. Home and Office: Caroline Prodns Inc 401 S Burnside Ave Apt 11D Los Angeles CA 90036-5376

MANN, FRANK BERT, visual artist, painter; b. Washington, D.C., Apr. 22, 1950; s. Frank Bert and Wilda Vendetta Kaufman. BS, High Point Univ., 1972; BA, George Washington Univ., 1978; MFA, Pratt Inst., 1981. Guest lectr. Corcoran Sch. of Art, Washington, D.C., 1979, Pennsylvanina State U., Reading, 1986-87, Pratt Inst., Bklyn., 1987-88, Parsons Sch. Art & Design, N.Y.C., 1996-97; exec. dir. Colaborative Projects, Inc., N.Y., 1987-88, Basicarts Network, N.Y., 1989-90; vis. artist Coalition for the Homeless Camp, 1997, Children's Friends for Life, N.Y., 1997, Project for St. Cyrils Ch., N.Y., 1992. Author: Eye of the Painter, 1997; illustrator (book) Nerves, 1993; exhibits in numerous public and private collections. U.S. rep. Biennale Internazionale, Florence, Italy, 1999. Recipient Mabel Sanger Webb award Ford Found., 1980, artist grant N.Y. State Coun. Arts, 1988, N.Y. City Dept. of Cultural Affairs, 1989. Mem. Drawing Soc., Am. Soc. Contemporary Artists, Am. for the Arts. Lutheran. Home and Office: 212 E 34th St Apt 3E New York NY 10016-4846

MANN, JACK MATTHEWSON, bottling company executive; b. Marshall, Tex., Apr. 14, 1932; s. Jack Slater and Mary (Matthewson) M.; m. True Sandlin, Sept. 4, 1954 (div. 1989); children: Jack, Robert, Daniel, Nathaniel. Student, N.Mex. Mil. Inst., 1952; BBA, U. Tex., 1954; MBA, Harvard U., 1960. Credit analyst Republic Nat. Bank, Dallas, 1959; chem. coord. Humble Oil and Refining Co., Baytown, Tex., 1960-61; asst. sales mgr. The Made-Rite Co., Marshall, Tex., 1957-58; asst. gen. mgr. The Made Rite Co., Marshall, Tex., 1961-63; gen. mgr. The Made Rite Co., Longview, Tex., 1963-92, pres., 1972—, owner, chmn., 1982—; v.p. Longview Econ. Devel. Corp., 1994—, treas., 1995-96, pres., 1996-97; bd. dirs. Longview Nat. Bank, Region's Bank; mem. pres.'s adv. coun. Le Tourneau U., 1994-97. Exec. com. Rep. Party Tex., 1962-65; mem. exec. bd. Episcopal Diocese Tex., Houston, 1974-76; mem. small bus. adv. com. Tex. Dept. Commerce, 1988-91. Mem. Tex. Soft Drink Assn. (pres. 1972), Nat. Dr. Pepper Bottlers Assn. (pres. 1983-85), Longview C. of C. (dir. 1965-68, 84-86). Club: Summit (Longview) (gov. 1982-94). Avocation: University of Texas athletics. Home: 45 Stonegate Dr Longview TX 75601-3600 Office: The Made Rite Co PO Box 3283 Longview TX 75606-3283

MANN, JOSEPHINE See **PULLEIN-THOMPSON, JOSEPHINE MARY WEDDERBURN**

MANN, KENNY, writer, educator; b. Nairobi, Kenya, May 1, 1946; came to U.S., 1982; d. Igor and Erica Mann; 1 child, Sophie. BSc, U. Nairobi, 1968; diploma in film & theatre, U. Bristol, Eng., 1969; MEd, Bank St. Coll. Edn., 1992. Editor, writer, journalist Ho. Hamptons, N.Y., 1989-2000, Inst. Children's Lit., Conn., 1996-99. Author: African Kingdoms of the Past, 1993-97, The Ancient Hebrews, 1998, I am not Afraid, 1993, Yellow Dog Dreaming, 1995, Isabel and Ferdinand, 2000; writer, dir., prodr.: (film) Surrender, 1999. Mem. Assn. Independent Video and Filmmakers, Author's Guild, Independent Feature Project. Avocations: theater, film. Home and Office: 29 Henry St Sag Harbor NY 11963-4449

MANN, NANCY LOUISE (NANCY LOUISE ROBBINS), entrepreneur; b. Chillicothe, Ohio, May 6, 1925; d. Everett Chaney and Pauline Elizabeth R.; m. Kenneth Douglas Mann, June 19, 1949 (div. June 1979); children: Bryan Wilkinson, Laura Elizabeth. BA in Math., UCLA, 1948, MA in Math., 1949, PhD in Biostatistics, 1965. Sr. scientist Rocketdyne Divsn. Rockwell Internat., Canoga Park, Calif., 1962-75; tech. staff Rockwell Sci. Ctr., Thousand Oaks, Calif., 1975-78; rsch. prof. UCLA Biomath., L.A., 1978-87; pres., CEO, owner Quality Enhancement Seminars, Inc., L.A., 1982—; pres., CEO Quality and Productivity, Inc., L.A., 1987—; curriculum adv. UCLA Ext. Dept. of Bus. and Mgmt., L.A., 1991—; mem. com. on Nat. Statistics, Nat. Acad. Scis., Washington, 1978-82; mem adv. bd. to supt. U.S. Naval Posgrad. Sch., Monterey, Calif., 1979-82. Co-author: Methods for Analysis of Reliability and Life Data, 1974; author: Keys to Excellence, 1985, The Story of the Deming Philosophy, 2d edit., 1987, 3d edit., 1989; contbr. articles to profl. jours. Recipient award IEEE Reliability Soc., 1982, ASQC Reliability Divsn., 1986. Fellow Am. Statis. Assn. (v.p. 1982-84); mem. Internat. Statis. Inst. Office: Quality Productivity Inc 10724 Wilshire Blvd # 711 Los Angeles CA 90024-4463

MANN, OSCAR, physician, internist, educator; b. Paris, Oct. 13, 1934; came to U.S., 1953; s. Aron and Helen (Biegun) M.; m. Amy S. Mann, July 19, 1964; children: Adriana, Karen. AA with distinction, George Washington U., 1958; MD cum laude, Georgetown U., 1962. Diplomate Am. Bd. Med. Examiners, Am. Bd. Internal Medicine, Am. Bd. Internal Medicine subspecialty Cardiovascular Disease; cert. advanced achievement in internal medicine; re-cert. in internal medicine. Intern Georgetown U. Med. Ctr., Washington, 1962-63, jr. asst. med. resident, 1963-64, clin. fellow in cardiology with Proctor Harvey program, 1965-66; sr. asst. resident in medicine Georgetown svc. D.C. Gen. Hosp., Washington, 1964-65; clin. prof. medicine Georgetown U. Sch. Medicine, 1985—; nat. chmn. med. alumi fund Georgetown U. Med. Sch., Washington, 1993-95; pvt. practice internal medicine and cardiology, Washington, 1966—; mem. Med.-Nursing Audit Com., CME adv. com., teaching. adv. com., Opthamology dept. rev. com., surgery dept. rev. com., faculty com., search com. for a new dean for acad. affairs Georgetown U. Med. Ctr.; appointed coun. to the dean Georgetown U. Sch. Medicine, 1977—; mem. Instnl. Self Study Task Force. Contbr. articles to profl. jours. Served with the U.S. Army, 1953-55. Recipient Mead Johnson Postgrad. Scholar ACP, 1964-65, Physicians Recognition award AMA, 1987-96, Advanced Achievement in Internal Medicine, 1987. Fellow ACP, Am. Coll. Cardiology, Am. Coll. Chest Physicians; mem. AMA, Am. Soc. Internal Medicine, Am. Heart Assn. (coun. clin. cardiology), Med. Soc. D.C., Cosmos Club, Georgetown U. Alumni Assn. (bd. govs. 1993—, chair med. alumni bd. 1995—), Alpha Omega Alpha, Phi Delta Epsilon. Home: 4925 Weaver Ter NW Washington DC 20016-2660 Office: Foxhall Internists PC 3301 New Mexico Ave NW Ste 331 Washington DC 20016-3622

MANN, SIMRANJIT SINGH, political party official; b. Simla, Panjab, India, May 20, 1945; s. Jogindar Singh and Gurbachan Kaur (Shergill) M.; m. Geetinder Kaur Kahlon, Oct. 16, 1970; children: Emaan Singh, Pavit Kaur, Nanki Kaur. BA with honors, Govt. Coll. for Men, Chandigarh, India, 1966; Indian Police Svc., Union Pub. Svc. Commn., Delhi, 1967. Sr. supt. Indian Police Svc., Ferozepore, 1977-78, Faridkot, 1978-80; asst. inspector gen. Govt. Railway Police, Patiala, India, 1980-82; sr. supt. Criminal Investigation Dept., Chandigarh, India, 1982; group commandant Indsl. Security Force, Bombay, 1983-84; pres. Shiromani Akali Dal, Amritsar, India, 1987—; mem. com. fgn. afairs & comm. Ho. of Reps.; MP House of Reps., 1989-91, 99—; mem. Shiromani Gurdwara Prabandak Com., Amritsar, India, 1996—. Polit. prisoner, 1984-89, 90, 92, 95. Recipient Gold Medal in History U. Panjab, 1996. Mem. Chandigarh Golf Club, Gymn Khana Club. Sikh. Avocations: golf, mountaineering, reading, gardening. Home: Quilla S Harnam Singh, PO Tallaniah, 140406 Dist Fatehgarh Sahib Panjab, India Office: Shiromani Akali Dal, Quilla S Harnam Sing P O Tallania, 140406 Dist Fatehgarh Sahib Panjab, India

MANN, STEFAN MARTIN, surgeon; b. Munich, July 30, 1963; s. Gerhard Rudolf and Ingeborg Anna (Becker) M.; m. Ute Margarete Bloss, June 25, 1994; 1 child, Alexandra. Diploma, Friedrich Alexander U., 1991, MD, 1991. Scientific asst. U. Hosp., Regensburg, Germany, 1991—. Civil svc. FRG, Erlangen, 1981-83. Mem. German Soc. of Clin. Data Mgmt. and Computing (scientific bd. 1996—), German Surg. Soc., European Soc. of Tech. Computing in Anaes/Intensive Care. Avocations: diving, traveling, swimming. Home: AM Dachsberg 4C, D-90607 Rueckersdorf Germany Office: Dept Surgery, F Josef Strauss Allee 11, D-93042 Regensburg Germany

MANN, ZANE BOYD, editor, publisher; b. St. Paul, Jan. 28, 1924; s. Michael M. and Rose Lee (Reuben) M.; m. Esther Zeesman, Mar. 25, 1945; children: Michael L., Eric F. Personal Fin. Planning, U. Calif., Riverside, 1986. Registered investment advisor Securities and Exch. Commn. Mcpl. fin. cons. Ehlers Mann & Assoc., Mpls., 1956-64; v.p. mcpl. bond underwriter Ebin Robertson, Mpls., 1964-70; v.p. mcpl. dept. Piper Jaffrey & Co., Mpls., 1970-72; ret., 1972; editor, pub. monthly investment newsletter Calif. Mcpl. Bond Advisor, Palm Springs, Calif., 1984—. Author: Fair Winds and Far Places, 1978; contbr. articles to profl. jours. Mem. Twin City Met. Planning Commn., St. Paul, 1958-70; bd. dirs. CORAL, Riverside County, Calif., 1984-91. Staff sgt. U.S. Army, 1942-45. Decorated DFC with cluster, Air medal with cluster, Soldier's medal, Purple Heart U.S. Army Air Corp. Mem. Nat. Fedn. Mcpl. Analysts, Calif. Soc. Mcpl. Analysts, Internat. Combat Camera Assn., Writers Guild Am. (ret.), Com. for the Sci. Investigation of Claims of the Paranormal (assoc.), Royal Corinthian Yacht Club (life, Cowles, Eng.), Mensa., Sports Car Club Am. Avocations: sailing, racing and cruising, scuba, SCCA competition driver, pilot. Home: 1300 E Verbena Dr Palm Springs CA 92262-5873 Office: Calif Mcpl Bond Advisor 1037 S Palm Canyon Dr Palm Springs CA 92264-8378

MANNA, INDRANIL, metallurgical engineering educator; b. Calcutta, India, Jan. 22, 1961; s. Gobinda Kishore and Latika (Das) M.; m. Snigdha Bala, Dec. 14, 1985; children: Oindrila, Rudroneel. B in Engring., Calcutta (India) U., 1983; M in Tech., Indian Inst. Tech., Kanpur, India, 1984; PhD, Indian Inst. Tech., Kharagpur, India, 1990. Engr. Midhani, Hyderabad, India, 1984-85; lectr. Indian Inst. Tech., Kharagpur, 1985-90, asst. prof., 1990-97, assoc. prof., 1997—; guest scientist Max-Planck-Inst., Stuttgart, Germany, 1988-90; vis. fellow U. Liverpool, U.K., 1995. Referee/reviewer for several sci. jours.; contbr. articles to profl. jours. Recipient Young Metallurgist award Ministry of Steel, New Delhi, 1991, Young Scientist medal Indian Nat. Sci. Acad., New Delhi, 1992, Career award All India Coun. Tech. Edn., New Delhi, 1995; Premchand Roychand studentship Calcutta U., 1992. Mem. Indian Inst. Metals (life), Indian Sci. Congress Assn. (life), Indian Laser Assn. (life). Hindu. Avocations: reading, traveling. Office: Indian Inst Tech, Metal & Mater Engring Dept, Kharagpur 721302, India

MANNA, VINCENZO, psychiatrist; b. Troia, Italy, June 8, 1956; s. Giovanni and Maria Ausiliatrice (Gentile) M. MD, U. L'Aquila, 1980, splty. in neurology, 1984, trained psychotherapist, 1983-91. Internal practitioner neurologic clinic U. L'Aquila, Italy, 1980-84; guard practitioner Nat. Health Svc., Troia, 1981-87, psychiat. asst. dept. mental health, 1987-96; dir. Servizio Tossicodipendenze ASL FG3, Foggia, Italy, 1996—; vis. practitioner neurologic clinic U. La Sapienza, Rome, 1984-85; dir. Gruppo Operativo Tossico Dipendenze Sociosanitary Unit Foggia, Troia, 1988—; asst. prof. istituto Superiore Educazione Fisica, L'Aquila, 1983-85, Scuola Superiore Servizio Sociale, Urbino, Italy, 1985-87; cons. neurologist Istituto Neuro-Traumat. Ital. Grottaferrata, Rome, 1984-87, Nat. Health Svc., Torremaggiore, Italy, 1989-93. Author: L'Assordante Silenzio Della Liberta, 1992. Active World Goodwill, 1987. Recipient Ercole D'oro Academia Int. Studi Economici e Sociali, 1989, Gran Croce al Merito per la Sanitá, 1991, Magister Preclarae Vitae, 1994. Mem. Internat. Headache Soc., AAAS, N.Y. Acad. Scis., Amnesty Internat., Touring Club, Automobil Club. Avocations: Oriental philosophies and meditative activities. Home: Piazza Marconi N 12, 71029 Troia Italy Office: Nat Health Svc Servizio Tossicodipendenz, Socio-Sanitary Unit 3, 71100 Foggia Italy

MANNATH, JOE, philosopher; b. Palai, Kerala, India, July 31, 1944; s. Thomas and Mary (Polachira) M. BPh, Salesian U., Rome, 1965, MPh, 1966, PhD, 1969; BTh, Pontifical Athenaeum, Pune, India, 1974; Postdoctoral Cert., Boston Theol. Inst., 1986. Ordained priest, Roman Cath. Ch. Prof. philosophy Salesian Coll., Yercaud, India, 1969-70, 72-73, Salesian U., Rome, 1979-80; prof. philosophy Sacred Heart Coll., Madras, India, 1975-78, prof., chair, 1981-84, 86-93; assoc. prof. U. Madras, 1993—; vis. prof. U. Valencia, Spain, 1997, Cath. Theol. Union, Chgo., 1998, 99, 2000, Fordham U., N.Y., 1999; dir. spirituality workshops Boston, Osaka, Ballygowan, U.K., 1987-2000. Author: You Surprised Me, 1987, 5th edit., 1999, Harvey of Nedellec's Proofs for the Existence of God, 1969; co-author: Youth Workers' Resource Book, 1985; editor spl. issue Jour. of Dharma, 1997. Vice rector Sacred Heart Sem., Madras, 1991-92; dir. Salesian Provincial House, Madras, 1994-95; resource person Anna Inst. Mgmt., Madras, 1984, Internat. Movement of Cath. Students, Hong Kong, 1988. Mem. Assn. Christian Philosophers of India (sec. 1981-84, pres. 1994-97, 97—), Indian Philos. Congress (life), Indian theol. Assn., Mensa. Roman Catholic. Avocations: cartooning, lecturing, counseling. Home: St Marys Church, 63 Armenian St, Chennai 600001, India Office: Univ of Madras, Dept Christian Studies, Chennai 600005, India

MANNDORFF, HANS, museum director, educator; b. Hinterbrühl, Austria, Apr. 26, 1928; s. Max and Albertine (Mannlicher) M.; m. Gertrude Graf, Sept. 28, 1955 (div.); children: Wolfgang, Rudolf; m. Elisabeth Bauer, Mar. 10, 1984; 1 child, Hemma. PhD, U. Vienna, Austria, 1953; postgrad., Sch. Oriental and African Studies, London, 1955-56, 59. Anthrop. researcher UNESCO, India, 1953-54, 56-57; head Southern Asia Dept. Mus. Ethnology, Vienna, 1950-59, dir., 1976-94; field researcher UN Asia Found., Northern Thailand, 1961-62, 63-65; researcher Mus. Ethnology Vienna in India, 1973-75, 80, 82; docent U. Vienna, 1965, prof., 1971-99. Author of numerous books, handbooks; contbr. articles to sci. jours. Decorated Austrian Cross of Honour for Sci. and Rsch., 1st class, Grand Decoration of Honour for Svc. to the Republic of Austria, Comtur Cross for Merit, Lower Austria, Cross of Honour for Merit for Sci. and Rsch., Burgenland, So. Cross in Officer's rank, Brazil, two mil. decorations, Germany. Mem. Nat. Assn. Ethnology, Anthropology and Prehistory, Internat. Assn. Ethnology, Anthropology and Prehistory. Avocations: mountain climbing, skiing, classical music. Home: Johannesstrasse 3, A-2371 Hinterbrühl Austria Office: Mus of Ethnology, Neue Hofburg, A-1014 Vienna Austria

MANNE, DEBORAH SUE, oncology nurse, consultant, dental hygienist; b. Vincennes, Ind., Nov. 20, 1954; d. Charles Kenneth and Susan Jane (Fox) Thornberry; m. Marshall Stanley Manne, Dec. 21, 1985. AA, Maplewoods C.C., Kansas City, Mo., 1973; BS in Dental Hygiene, U. Mo., 1975; BSN, St. Louis U., 1991, MSN in Oncology Nursing, 1998. RN, reg. dental hygienist, Mo. Dental hygienist Dr. Marshall S. Manne, St. Louis, 1978—, office nurse, 1991—; oncology nurse CIRCLE Barnes-Jewish Hosp., St. Louis, 1993-98; staff nurse Radiation Oncology Ctr. Barnes-Jewish Hosp. North, 1997; nurse educator Cancer Family Care, St. Louis, 1998; clin. asst. prof. divsn. dental hygiene Sch. Dentistry U. Mo., Kansas City, 1999—; instr. dental hygiene dept. St. Louis C.C., Forest Park, 1999—; clin. instr. So. Ill. U., Carbondale, 2000—; coord., cons. Oncology Dental Support Svcs., St. Louis, 1992—; mem. curriculum rev. com. dental hygiene program St. Louis C.C., 1993; mem. adv. bd. ACCESS Dental Hygiene Jour., 1994—. Contbr. articles to profl. jours. Bd. dirs., v.p. Am. Cancer Soc., St. Louis, 1992-93, chair Gt. Am. Smokeout, 1992, mem. Breast Cancer task force, 1994-98; mem. profl. adv. com. Wellness Cmty., St. Louis, 1994—; chmn. Tobacco-Free Mo. Super Coalition, St. Louis, 2000—. Recipient Vol. Recognition award Am. Cancer Soc., 1992, Mo. Dental Hygienist of Yr. award, 1995, Irene Newman award, 1997, Susan Brockman-Bell Humanitarian award U. Mo. Kansas City Dental Hygiene Alumni Assn., 2000. Mem. Am. Dental Hygienists Assn. (council on pub. rels., coun. on edn., Susan Brockmann-Bell Humanitarian award 2000), Oncology Nursing Soc. (chair oral care focus group, pres.-elect St. Louis chpt. 1998, pres. 1999, editor patient edn. sig newsletter 1999-2000), Mo. Dental Hygienists' Assn. (pres.), Greater St. Louis Hygienists' Assn. (pres.), Sigma Phi Alpha, Sigma Theta Tau. Avocations: walking, raising golden retrievers and cats. Home: 11617 Larkmont Dr Creve Coeur MO 63141-6907 Office: Oncology Dental Support Svc 3009 N Ballas Rd Ste 211 Saint Louis MO 63131-2323

MANNERS, RONALD BROWN, mining executive; b. Kalgoorlie, Australia, Jan. 8, 1936; s. Charles Brown and Nancy Jean (Stevens) M.; m. Jenny Marie MacDonald; children: Ian Bruce, Scott James, Craig William, Sarah Jane. Degree in elec. engring., Western Australian Sch. Mines, 1962. Mng. ptnr. W.G. Manners & Co., 1962-82; exploration dir. Mistral Mines NL, 1982-86; dir. Gt. Ctrl. Mines NL, 1984--86, King Mining NL, 1984-86; mng. dir., chmn. Croesus Mining NL, 1985—; dir. Eldorado Gold Corp., 1995-98, Mannkal Econ. Edn. Found., Australia, 1998—. Editor: So I Headed West, 1992, Kanowna's Barrowman, 1993; editor, author: Never A Dull Moment, 2000. Patron Golden Mile Art Axhbn. Group, 1993—; chmn. Australian Prospectors & Miners Hall of Fame, Ltd., 1996—; exec. councillor Assn. Mining & Exploration Cos., 1987—. Mem. The Duke of Edinburgh Study Group, 1968. Fellow Australasian Inst. Mining & Metallurgy, Australian Inst. Co. Dirs. Office: 19 Richardson St, West Perth 6005, Australia

MANNERVIK, BENGT, biochemistry educator, researcher; b. Stockholm, Aug. 19, 1943; s. Tage and Lisbeth (Johansson) Eriksson; m. Anne-Charlotte Österberg, June 19, 1965; children: Mattias, Jonatan, Johanna. MSc, Stockholm U., 1964, Fil. Lic., 1967, PhD, 1969. From sr. lectr. to assoc. prof. Stockholm U., 1970-88; prof. biochemistry Uppsala (Sweden) U., 1988—, Karin and Herbert Jacobsson chair biochemistry, 1988—; sec. Swedish Nat. Com. on Biochemistry 1985-87, chmn., 1988-90; chmn. Nordic Com. on Biochemistry, 1979-80. Mem. editorial bd. Biochem. Jour., 1986-93. Mem AAAS, Swedish Biochem. Soc. (sec. 1976-82), Swedish Chem. Soc., Swedish Soc. Biochemistry and Molecular Biology, Biochem. Soc. U.K., Am. Assn. Cancer Rsch., Am. Soc. for Biochemistry and Molecular Biology (hon.), Royal Soc. Scis. at Uppsala, N.Y. Acad. Scis. Office: Uppsala U Dept Biochem, Biomed Ctr, S-75123 Uppsala Sweden

MANNHEIM, ADIE, dairy products researcher, food engineer; b. Tel-Aviv, Israel, Jan. 13, 1959; s. Chaim and Bilha (Friedman) M.; m. Edna Stiller, Oct. 21, 1981; children: Ittay, Ron, Shai. BS in Food Engring., Technion Inst. Tech., Israel, 1985; MS in Food Sci., U. Ill., 1988, PhD in Food Sci., 1991. Cert. food engr. Mgr. milk powder plants TNUVA Dairy Products, Israel, 1985-87; rsch. asst. U. Ill., Urbana, 1987-90; mgr. protein applications rsch. ADM Co., Decatur, Ill., 1990-93; food technologist OSEM Food Co., Petah Tikva, 1993-94; mgr. Tagad Food Ltd., Tel Aviv, 1994-97; head R&D TNUVA Dairy Products, Tel Aviv, 1997—; cons. U. Ill., Urbana, 1989-90; vis. lectr. dept. food engring. Technion U., Haifa, Israel, 1998. Contbr. articles to sci. jours., including Jour. Food Sci., Cereal Chemistry. With Israel Def. Force, 1977-80. Mem. Am. Assn. Cereal Chemists, Inst. Food Sci. (profl.), Israel Assn. Engrs. Avocations: skiing, scuba diving, gardening, carpentry, reading. E-mail: madi@tnuva-com.co.il. Home: PO Box 80532, 90805 Mevasseret Zion Israel Office: TNUVA R&D Ctr, PO Box 2525, 76123 Rehovot Israel

MANNING, MARTINA MELITTA, urologist; b. Heidelberg, Germany, Sept. 12, 1966; d. Ehrenfried and Ilse (Hauptvogel) M. Doctorate, U. Heidelberg, Germany, 1994. Resident in tng. dept. Surgery, Mannheim, Germany, 1993-94; resident in tng. dept. urology Klinikum Mannheim, 1995-98; rsch. fellow Ctr. Reproductive Medicine and Med. Genetics, Brussels, 1998-99; urologist U. Hosp., Giessen, Germany, 1999—. Contbr.: (books) Urologie für die Praxis, 1996, Male Sexual Dysfunction, 1997, Male Infertility and Sexual Dysfunction, 1997, Erectile Dysfunction, 1997; contbr. articles to med. jours. including Lancet, Am. Jour. Urology, European Jour. Urology. Smith-Kline-Beecham scholar European Urol. Scholarship Program, 1997; rsch. grantee U. Heidelberg, 1995, 96. Mem. European Urol. Assn. (jr.), German Soc. Urology (jr.). Office: Dept Urology, Klinikstr 29, D-35385 Giessen Germany

MANNING, PETER KIRBY, sociology educator; b. Salem, Oreg., Sept. 27, 1940; s. Kenneth Gilbert and Esther Amelia (Gibbard) M.; m. Victoria Francis Shaughnessy, Sept. 1, 1961 (div. 1981); children—Kerry Patricia, Sean Peter, Merry Kathleen; m. Betsy Cullum-Swan, Aug. 4, 1991 (div. 1997). BA, Willamette U., 1961; MA, Duke U., 1963, PhD, 1966; MA (hon.), Oxford U., Eng., 1983. Instr. sociology Duke U., 1964-65; asst. prof. sociology U. Mo., 1965-66, Mich. State U., East Lansing, 1966-70; assoc. prof. sociology and psychiatry Mich. State U., 1970-74, prof., 1974—; prof. criminal justice, 1993—; Beto chair lectr. Sam Houston State U., 1990; Ameritech lectr. E. Ky. U., 1993; vis. prof. U. Victoria, 1968, MIT, 1982, SUNY, Albany, 1982, U. Mich. 1990-91, York U., Toronto, 1999; cons. Nat. Inst. Law Enforcement and Criminal Justice (now Nat. Inst. Justice), U.S. Dept. Justice, Rsch. Triangle Inst., NSF, Nat. Health and Med. Rsch. Coun., Australia, 1980—, Social Sci. Rsch. Coun. Eng., AID (Jamaica), 1991, Sheehy com. Police Pay and Performance, Eng., 1993. Author: Sociology of Mental Health and Illness, 1975, Police Work, 1977, 2d edit., 1997, The Narcs' Game, 1980, Semiotics and Fieldwork, 1987, Symbolic Communication, 1988, Organizational Communication, 1992, Private Policing, 1999, other books; also book chpts., articles in profl. jours.; cons. editor series: Principal Themes in Sociology; co-editor Sage Series in Qualitative Methods; mem. editorial bd. numerous jours. in social scis. Recipient Bruce Smith Sr. award Acad. Criminal Justice Scis., 1993, O.W. Wilson award, 1997, Charles H. Cooley award Mich. Sociol. Assn., 1994; NDEA fellow, 1962-64, NSF fellow, 1965, fellow Balliol Coll., Oxford U., 1982-83, vis. fellow Wolfson Coll., Oxford U., 1981, 82-83, fellow, 1984-86; Am. Bar Found. rsch. fellow, 1998; Rockefeller resident, Bellagio, Italy, 2000. Mem. Am. Soc. Criminology, Am. Sociol. Assn., Brit. Soc. Criminology, Internat. Sociol. Assn., Midwest Sociol. Soc., Soc. Study of Social Problems, Soc. for the Study of Symbolic Interaction (spl. recognition award 1990, v.p. 1992-93, program chair 1993), Internat. Soc. for Semiotics and Law. Office: Mich State U 516 Baker Hall East Lansing MI 48824-1118

MANNING, ROBERTA THOMPSON, historian, educator; b. Austin, Tex., Jan. 24, 1940; d. Robert Bennet and Lucille Luby Thompson; m. Gerald Stuart Manning, Mar. 24, 1964; children: Innessa Anne, Rebecca Emily. BA, Rice U., 1962; MA, Columbia U., 1967, PhD, 1975. Acting asst. prof. U. Calif., San Diego, 1975; asst. prof. Boston Coll., Chestnut Hill, Mass., 1975-81; assoc. prof. Boston Coll., Chestnut Hill, 1981—; pres. The Tragedy of the Soviet Village Inc., Newton, Mass., 1998—. Author: The Crisis of the Old Order in Russia: Gentry and Government, 1982 (Herbert Baxter Adams prize Am. Hist. Assn. 1983), Bel'skii Raion 1937g, 1998; editor: Stalinist Terror, 1993, Tragediia Sovietskoi Derevni: Kollektivization, 1999; mng. editor Russian History, 1975-88; editor Sci. and Soc., 1981-96. Guggenheim fellow, N.Y.C., 1989; Collaborative Projects fellow NEH, Washington, 1997, 99. Fellow Davis Ctr. for Russian Studies; mem. Am. Hist. Assn., Am. Assn. for the Advancement Slavic Studies. Democrat. E-mail: manning@bc.edu. Office: Boston Coll Dept History Commonwealth Ave Chestnut Hill MA 02467

MANNING-WEBER, CLAUDIA JOY, medical radiography administrator, consultant; b. Oak Park, Ill., Mar. 17, 1950; d. Charles Lawrence and Carrie Joy (Lund) Manning. AAS, Coll. of DuPage, 1980; BA with honors, Nat. Coll. of Edn., 1986, MS, 1989. Registered med. radiography technologist, Am. Registry of Radiologic Technologists; cert. med. radiography technologist, Ariz.; cert. adult and continuing edn. tchr., Ariz. State Cmty. Coll. Bd. Faculty Coll. of DuPage, Glen Ellyn, Ill., 1987-90, South Suburban Coll., South Holland, Ill., 1989-91; mentor tchr. Prescott (Ariz.) Coll., 1992—; dir. Ariz. Continuing Edn. Svcs., Avondale, 1992—; clin. instr. Phoenix Bapt. Hosp., 1992-93; program dir. PTR Bryman Sch., 1993-95; program dir. med. radiography Apollo Coll., 1995-96; now writer, edn. cons. Avondale, Ariz.; contbr., cons. EDUMED Co., Minnetonka, Minn., 1995—; treas. ASSRT, Mesa, Ariz., 1993-94; cons. Coll. of DuPage, 1988-91. Author: Distance Delivered Education in Nuclear Medicine Technology, 1989, Multiskilling: Radiography for Health Care Providers. Mem. ASCD, AAUW, Internat. Soc. Radiographers and Radiologic Technicians, Assn. for Educators in Radiologic Sci., Am. Soc. Radiologic Technologists, Ariz. State Soc. Radiologic Technologists (ednl. dir. 1992-93, treas. 1993-94, seminar presenter 1991, 92), Delta Kappa Gamma. Avocations: reading, writing, hiking, horseback riding. Home: 10938 W Bermuda Dr Avondale AZ 85323-4304

MANNINO, EDWARD FRANCIS, lawyer; b. Abington, Pa., Dec. 5, 1941; s. Sante Francis and Martha Anne (Hines) M.; m. Mary Ann Vigilante, July 17, 1965 (div. 1990); m. Antoinette K. O'Connell, June 25, 1993; children: Robert John, Jennifer Elaine. BA with distinction, U. Pa., 1963, LLB magna cum laude, 1966. Bar: Pa. 1967. Law clk. 3d cir. U.S. Ct. Appeals, 1966-67; assoc. Dilworth, Paxson, Kalish & Kauffman, Phila., 1967-71, ptnr., 1972-86, co-chmn. litigation dept., 1980-86, sr. ptnr., 1982-86; sr. prin. Elliott, Mannino & Flaherty, PC, Phila., 1986-90; chmn. Mannino Griffith PC, Phila., 1990-95; sr. ptnr. Wolf, Block, Schorr & Solis-Cohen, Phila., 1995-98; ptnr. Akin, Gump, Strauss, Hauer & Feld LLP, Phila., 1998—; hearing examiner disciplinary bd. Supreme Ct. Pa., 1986-89; lectr. Temple U. Law Sch., 1968-69, 71-72; mem. Phila. Mayor's Sci. and Tech. Adv. Com., 1976-79; mem. adv. com. on appellate ct. rules Supreme Ct. Pa., 1989-95; project mgr. Pa. Environ. Master Plan, 1973; chmn. Pa. Land Use Policy Study Adv. Com., 1973-75; chmn. adv. com., hon. faculty history dept. U. Pa., 1980-85. Author: Lender Liability and Banking Litigation, 1989, Business and Commercial Litigation: A Trial Lawyer's Handbook, 1995, The Civil RICO Primer, 1996; mem. editl. bd. Litigation mag., 1985-87, Comm. Lending Litigation News, 1988—, Bank Bailout Litigation News, 1989-93, Bus. Torts Reporter, 1988-99, Practical Litigator, 1989—, Civil RICO Report, 1991—; contbr. articles to profl. jours. Pres. parish coun. Our Mother of Consolation Ch., 1977-79; bd. overseers U. Pa. Sch. Arts and Scis., 1985-89, chmn. recruitment and retention of faculty com.; commonwealth trustee Temple U., 1987-90, mem. audit, bus. and fin. coms. Named one of Nation's Top Litigators Nat. Law Jour., 1990, Pa.'s Top Ten Trial Lawyers, 1999. Fellow Am. Bar Found., ABA (chmn. various coms.), Am. Law Inst., Hist. Soc. U.S. Dist. Ct. Ea. Dist. Pa. (bd. dirs.), Pa. Bar Assn., Phila. Bar Assn. (gov. 1975), Pa. Soc., Order of Coif, Phi Beta Kappa, Phi Beta Kappa Assocs. Democrat. Office: Akin Gump Strauss Hauer & Feld LLP One Commerce Sq 2005 Market St Ste 2200 Philadelphia PA 19103-7014

MANNINO, ROBERT, lawyer; b. Phila., July 20, 1968; s. Edward Francis and Mary Ann Mannino. BA, U. Pa., 1991; JD cum laude, Am. U., 1995. Bar: Pa. 1995, N.J. 1995, U.S. Dist. Ct. N.J. 1995, U.S. Dist. Ct. (ea. dist.) Pa. 1996. Intern U.S. Dept. Justice, Washington, summers 1993-94, U.S. Senate Com. on the Judiciary, Washington, 1994; student atty. D.C. Law Students in Ct., Washington, 1994-95; assoc. Lavin, Coleman, et al, Phila., 1995-97, Gollatz, Griffin & Ewing, Phila., 1997—. Com. person Rep. Party, Phila., 1989-91; rsch. asst. Ref. Manual Chpts., U.S. Atty's Manual Criminal Tax Sects., summer 1993. Mem. Penn Club N.Y.C., Penn A.C. Rowing Assn. Roman Catholic. Office: Gollatz Griffin & Ewing 16th Fl Two Penn Center Philadelphia PA 19102

MANNION, PHILIP THOMAS, medical microbiology consultant, disease control consultant; b. Warrington, Cheshire, Eng., Apr. 21, 1957; s. Kenneth and Audrey (Smith) M.; m. Ann Marie Linnane, July 26, 1980; 3 children. MB, BChir, Manchester (Eng.) U., 1980; MSc in Med. Microbiology, London U., 1985. Sr. house officer in pathology Wythenshawe (Eng.) Dist. Gen. Hosp., 1982-83, sr. house officer in orthop., 1983-84; trainee med. microbiologist Pub. Health Lab. Svc., Brighton, Eng., 1984-86; asst. med. microbiologist Pub. Health Lab. Svc., Brighton, 1986-88, Liverpool, Eng., 1988-89; cons. med. microbiologist Pub. Health Lab. Svc., Chester, Eng., 1989—; bd. dirs., sec. Deva Consulting Ltd., Chester, 1994—; cons. communicable disease control South Cheshire Health Authority, Chester, 1992—. Fellow Royal Coll. Pathologists. Office: Chester Pub Health Lab Countess Health P, Liverpool Rd, Chester CH2 1UL, England

MANNIX, CHARLES RAYMOND, law educator; b. Elizabeth, N.J., Aug. 2, 1950; s. Charles Raymond and Helen Joan (French) M. BA, Duquesne U., 1972, MA, 1976, JD, 1976; MPA, Harvard U., 1998. Bar: Iowa 1976, N.Y. 1996, Va. 1980, D.C. 1980, U.S. Ct. Claims 1976, U.S. Tax Ct. 1976, U.S. Ct. Mil. Appeals 1976, U.S. Ct. Internat. Trade 1976, U.S. Ct. Appeals (4th and 5th cirs.) 1977, U.S. Ct. Appeals (D.C. cir.) 1977, U.S. Dist. Ct. Va. 1980, U.S. Supreme Ct. 1980, U.S. Ct. Appeals (D.C. cir.) 1980, U.S. Ct. Appeals (fed. cir.) 1982, N.Y. 1996. Commd. 2d lt. USAF, 1973, advanced through grade to lt. col., 1982; intern UN Office of Legal Affairs, N.Y.C., 1975; various legal assignments; lectr. USAF Med. Law Cons. Program, 1981-99; adj. faculty Georgetown U., Washington, 1984-99; assoc. prof. and chmn. dept. med. jurisprudence, asst. prof. mil. medicine, v.p. and gen. counsel Uniformed Svcs. U. Health Scis. Decorated Meritorious Svc. medal with Oak Leaf Cluster, Air Force Commendation medal with Oak Leaf Clusters. Mem. ABA, FBA, ATLA, D.C. Bar Assn., Va. State Bar Assn., Am. Soc. Internat. Law, Am. Soc. Law and Medicine, Am. Arbitration Assn. (arbitrator), Am. Acad. Hosp. Attys., Nat. Assn. Coll. and Univ. Attys., N.Y. State Bar Assn., Bar Assn. of the City of N.Y., Assn. Mil. Surgeons U.S., Harvard Club of N.Y. Home: 10205 Walker Lake Dr Great Falls VA 22066-3558 Office: Uniformed Svcs U Health Scis Gen Coun Jones Bridge Rd Bethesda MD 20815-5737

MANNS, MICHAEL PETER, physician; b. Koblenz, Germany, Nov. 16, 1951; s. Heinrich and Gertrud Manns; m. Cornelia Goebel, Sept. 29, 1976; children: Hanna, Lisa, Clara, Anna-Sophia. Student, U. Vienna, Austria, U. Mainz, Germany; MD, U. Mainz, Germany, 1976. Lic. physician, specialist internal medicine, subspecialist hepatology and gastroenterology. Med. intern pharmacology, internal medicine, surgery, 1976-77; resident, rsch. asst. internal medicine Free U. Berlin, 1977-81; resident, rsch. asst. internal medicine U. Mainz, 1981-85, staff physician dept. medicine, 1986-87, staff physician, prof., 1988-91; rsch. assoc. Scripps Clinic and Rsch. Found., LaJolla, Calif., 1987-88; prof., chmn. dept. gastroenterology and hepatology Zentrum Innere Medizin Med. Sch. Hannover, Germany, 1991—; gen. med. dir. Med. Sch. Hannover, Germany, 1997-99. Contbr. articles to profl. jours., chpts. to books. Recipient Boehringer Ingelheim prize U. Mainz, 1985, Asche prize Deutsche Gesellschaft für Verdauungs-und Stoffwechselkrankheiten, 1987, Collaboration Rsch.award NATO, 1990, Clin. Rsch. prize Smith Kline Beecham Found., U. Göttingen, 1990, Clemens van Pirquet award U. Calif., Davis, 1991, Internat. Hans Popper award, 1995. Mem. German Soc. Gastroenterology (mem. sci. bd. 1989—, sec. 1991—), European Assn. for Study of Liver (sci. com. 1992-94), Internat. Assn. for Study of Liver, German Soc. Internal Medicine, German Soc. Immunology, German Assn. for Study of Liver (mem. sci. com. 1985-88, sec. 1988-91), Am. Assn. for Study Liver Diseases. Office: Medizinische Hochschule Hannover, Carl-Neuberg Str 1, 30625 Hannover Germany

MANNWEILER, MARY-ELIZABETH, painter; b. Norwood, Ohio, June 23, 1916; d. Wilbur Lawrence Young and Augusta Minnis (Newman) Davis; m. Robert Mays Lang, Sr., May 25, 1940 (dec. July 1981); children: Robert Mays Lang, Jr., Gary Davis Lang, Julianna Elizabeth Lang Crawford; m. Gordon Bannatyne Mannweiler, Apr. 17, 1982. Student, Miami U., Oxford, Ohio, 1935-37. Portrait painter; permanent collections in colls., high schs. and pvt. homes; donated (with husband) stained glass window to Congl. Ch., Naugatuck, Conn. Past pres. Athena Club, Freeport, N.Y., Woodbury (Conn.) Women's Club, 1977-78, Watertown (Conn.) Art League; past dir. Waterbury (Conn.) Symphony Orch.; sec./treas. Mannweiler Found., Naugatuck, Conn. Recipient numerous blue ribbons for artwork; music room named in honor of Mr. and Mrs. Mannweiler at Conn. Jr. Republic, Litchfield, 1997. Mem. DAR (regent Ruth Floyd Woodhull chpt. 1966-67). Home: 435 Hillside Ave Naugatuck CT 06770-2727

MANO, YUKIO, medical educator, physician; b. Nagoya, Aichi-ken, Japan, Aug. 26, 1943; s. Yutaka and Takeko Ml m. Kiyoko Takeuchi; children: Tomoo, Yukiko. MD, Nagoya (Japan) U., 1968, PhD, 1979. Intern Nagoya Univ. Hosp., 1968-69; resident Nagoya 1st Red Cross Hosp., 1969-71; resident Nagoya U., 1972, cons., 1976-78; resident NYU, 1972-74; resident, asst. instr. Baylor Coll. Medicine, 1974-75; rsch. fellow U. Md., 1975-76; chief of rsch. Nat. Inst. Nervous, Mental and Muscular Disorder, Tokyo, 1978-80; assoc. prof. Nara Med. U., Koshihara, Japan, 1981-95; prof., chmn. dept. rehabilitative medicine Hokkaido U., Sopporo, Japan, 1995—; Editor: Jour. Neurol. Therapeutics, 1995—' mem. editl. bd. Jour. Electromyography and Kinesiology, 1990—. Mem. Japanese Soc. Rehabilitative Medicine (mem. coun. 1997—), Japanese Soc. Electrophysiology and Kinesiology (pres. 1997—), Japanese Soc. Neurol. Therapy (mem. coun. 1997—), Japanese Soc. Clin. Environ. Medicine (1994—). Home: 648 Sue Saya-cho, Ama-gun Aichi-ken 496-0902, Japan Office: Hokkaido U Rehab Medicine, N-15 W-7, Sapporo 060-8638, Japan

MANOFF, SAWA SLAVTCHEV, physicist, educator, researcher; b. Pleven, Bulgaria, June 7, 1943; s. Slavtcho Bankov and Janka Nikolova (Kazakhova) M.; m. Ivanka Dimitrova Tomova, Aug. 16, 1970. MSc in Physics, Friedrich Schiller U., Jena, Germany, 1968, PhD, 1973; Habilitation, Inst. Nuclear Rsch. and Nuclear Energy, Sofia, Bulgaria, 1985; DSc, Sofia, Bulgaria, 2000. Physicist Inst. Physics, Sofia, 1968-70; asst. prof. 2d degree Inst. Nuclear Rsch. Nuclear Energy, Sofia, 1974-80, asst. prof. 1st degree, 1980-85, sr. scientific rschr., assoc. prof., 1985—; invited lectr. Kliment Ochridski U., Sofia, 1979-81, 89, 91-96. Contbr. articles to profl. jours. Friedrich Schiller U. fellow, 1967; recipient First prize Conf. Young Physicists Bulgaria, 1975. Mem. Union Physicists Bulgaria, Union Scientists Bulgaria. Office: Inst Nuc Rsch & Nuc Energy, Blvd Tzarigradsko Chaussee 72, 1784 Sofia Bulgaria

MANOJLOVIC, NENAD, physicist; b. Belgrade, Yugoslavia, June 23, 1962; s. Dusan and Olga (Bokonjic) M.; m. Tatjana Stojicic, Apr. 20, 1996. MS, U. Belgrade, 1987; PhD, Imperial Coll., London, 1991. Assoc. prof. physics U. Algarve, Faro, Portugal, 1993-2000. Mem. Am. Phys. Soc.

MANOLESCU, NICOLAE MANOLACHE, veterinary science researcher; b. Romania, July 21, 1936; s. Manolache and Olga (Budachievici) M.; grad. in Vet. Surgery, Vet. Acad. Bucharest, 1966, DSc, 1969; m. Ioana Badescu, Mar. 1, 1973; children: Manuela, Bogdan. Vet. surgeon, Agrl. Sta., Rusetu, Romania, 1966-67; asst. to prof. Vet. Acad., Bucharest, Romania, 1967-69; chief lab. morphopathology and electronic microscopy Pasteur Inst. for Vet. Rsch. and Biol. Prodn., Bucharest, 1969-87; sci. researcher Oncol. Inst. Bucharest, 1987—; head of dept., 1987—; prof. pathological and comparative oncology, Faculty of Veterinary Medicine, Bucharest, 1992—; head of dept. postgrad. edn., 2000—; gen. dir., councillor, min. rsch. and tech., dir. Dept. Univ. Scientific Rsch. Ministry of Nat. Edn., Romania, 1991-95, 97-98. Author 350 sci. papers and 23 books in field including: Normal and Pathological Cytology of Animals, 1980; Leukemic Cells, Comparative Cytopathology, 1981; Comparative Histology in SEM, 1982; Hematologic Guide for Animals in Industrial Breeding, 1978; The Ultrastructure of Some Sanguine Cells in SEM, 1979; Comparative Black/White and Colours Images for Electronic Microscopy, 1984; Comparative Hematologie, 1985; Comparative General Histopathology in SEM, 1985, Veterinary Oncology, Vol. I, II, 1991, 93, Aspects of Comparative Cell Pathology, Vol. I, II, III, 1997-99, Animal Hematology Treaty, Vol. I, II, 1999, Compendium of Clinic Pathology Anatomy, 2000, Introduction in Comparative Oncology, 2000. Mem. Acad. Med. Scis. (Romania), Romanian Acad., Comparative Pathology Soc. (sec. 1980—), Romanian Acad. (Ion Ionescu Dela Brad prize). Home: Bd T Vladimirescu no 82, bl 133 sc 1 ap 1 sect 5, 50335 Bucharest 76350, Romania Office: Faculty Vet Med, Splaiul Independentei 105 sect 5, 76201 Bucharest Romania also: Tudor Vladimirescert, 82 bl 133 Sc 1 ap 1 sect 5, Bucharest Romania

MANOLIS, ANTONIS S., cardiologist, electrophysiologist; b. Kastania, Nafpaktos, Greece, Dec. 7, 1954; came to the U.S., 1981; s. Stavros A. and Kondylo Manolis; m. Helen Melita, Sept. 22, 1984; children: Stavros, Theodora, Anthony. MD magna cum laude, Athens U., 1978, DSc magna cum laude, 1989. Resident in internal medicine N.Y. Med. Coll., Cabrini Med. Ctr., N.Y.C., 1981-84, chief resident in medicine, 1983-84; fellow in cardiology N.Y. Med. Coll., Cabrini Med. Ctr. & St. Vincent's Hosp., N.Y.C., 1984-86; fellow in electrophysiology Tufts U., Boston, 1986-88, instr. in medicine, 1986-87, asst. prof., 1987-93, assoc. prof., 1993-95; prof. cardiology Patras (Greece) U., 1995—; chief of cardiology Patras U. Hosp., 1995—; dir. Electrophysiology Lab. Onassis Hosp., Athens, Greece, 1994—; assoc. in electrophysiology Tufts U., 1987-91, assoc. dir. electrophysiology lab., 1991-93, co-dir., 1993-95. Co-editor: ICDs: A Comprehensive Textbook, 1994; co-editor: Interventional Cardiology, 1995; contbr. more than 100 articles to profl. jours. 2d lt. Greek Air Force, 1978-80. Recipient Young Investigator's award Am. Coll. Chest Physicians, 1987. Fellow Am. Coll. Cardiology, European Soc. Cardiology; mem. North Am. Soc. Pacing and Electrophysiology. Avocations: racquetball, swimming. Home: 41 Kourempana St, 17343 Aghios Dimitrios Athens, Greece Office: Patras U Hosp, Rio, Patras Greece

MANOOGIAN, WILLIAM, lawyer; b. Fresno, Calif., Mar. 29, 1946; s. Morris Anthony and Doris Eunice (Parigian) M.; m. Margaret Ann Solt, Oct. 18, 1975; children: Nicole-Helene, Claire-Louise. BA, Stanford U., 1968; postgrad., U. Paris, 1968-70; JD, Am. U., Washington, 1973. Legis. atty. Rep. Nat. Com., Washington, 1973-75; minority counsel Civil Svc. com. Civic Svc. com. Ho. of Reps., Washington, 1975-83; spl. counsel Dept. of Edn., Washington, 1983-84; counsel to Amb. John Gavin Dept. of State, Mexico City, 1984-86; cons. to Dr. Armand Hammer Occidental Petroleum, L.A., 1986-87; gen. atty. Criminal divsn., Dept. of Justice, Washington, 1987-89, Immigration and Naturalization Svc., San Diego, 1989—; advisor to William Saroyan, Paris, 1969-70. Contbr. articles to profl. jours. Legal advisor to Rep. campaigns, Washington, 1974. Mem. D.C. Bar Assn., Chi Psi. Armenian Orthodox. Avocations: swimming, foreign languages. Home: 12992 Carmel Creek Rd San Diego CA 92130-2132 Office: Justice Dept 880 Front St Ste 1234 San Diego CA 92101-8834

MANORIK, PETRO ANDRIJOVITCH, chemist, educator; b. Kyiv, Ukraine, Apr. 8, 1953; s. Andrew Vasiljovitch and Lubov Petrivna (Torgalo) M.; m. Olga Vasilivna Mocharnik, Oct. 10, 1978 (div. 1992); 1 child, Andrew; m. Maya Albertivna Phedorenko, Sept. 24, 1992; 1 child, Elizabeth. MSD, Kyiv State U., 1975; PhD, Inst. Phys. Chemist, NASU, Kyiv, 1980, Dr. habilitation, 1995. Engr. Inst. Phys. Chemistry NASU, Kyiv, 1974-80, jr. rsch. scientist, 1980-83, head lab. bioinorganic chemistry of ternary complexes, 1988-96, head dept. physico-inorganic chemistry, 1996—; sci. sec. sci. orgn. dept. Presidium Nat. Acad. Scis. Ukraine, Kyiv, 1983-88; lectr. dept. biophysics and bioinorganic chemistry Bauman's Moscow Physicotechnical Inst., Kyiv, 1998—. Author: Mixed-ligand Complexes of Biometals in Chemistry, Biology, Medicine, 1991; contbr. articles to profl. jours. Mem. Communist Party USSR, Kyiv, 1982-91. Avocations: reading, fishing, basketball, football, philately. Home: 4 Bulvar Lychatcheva ap 74, 252133 Kyiv Ukraine Office: Nat Acad Scis Ukraine, 31 Prospect Nauki, 252039 Kyiv Ukraine

MANSFELD, FREDRIK NILS, software developer; b. Stockholm, Apr. 3, 1965; s. Jan Hugo and Ulla Kristina (Berg) M. Filosofie Kandidat, U. Stockholm, 1988. Cert. database designer. Mgr. tech. support Idé-Data, Danderyd, Sweden, 1989-93; sys. devel. Af-Data, Stockholm, 1993-94, S-E-Banken, Kista, Sweden, 1994-95; sys. designer and devel. Abaris, Stockholm, 1996-2000; software engr. Oz.com, 2000—. Author: Technical Reference for Graph-in-the-Box, 1991; programmer (software) Graph-in-the-Box Executive, 1990, Graph-in-the-Box Windows, 1991-93. Mem. SVS, Mensa (bd. dirs. 1995—, treas. 1995-97). Avocation: mountain climbing. Home: Frejgatan 6, S-11420 Stockholm Sweden

MANSFIELD, LOIS EDNA, mathematics educator, researcher; b. Portland, Maine, Jan. 2, 1941; d. R. Carleton and Mary Bowdish) M. BS, U. Mich., 1962; MS, U. Utah, 1966, PhD, 1969. Asst. prof. computer sci. U. Kans., Lawrence, 1970-74, assoc. prof., 1974-78; assoc. prof. math. N.C. State U., Raleigh, 1978-79; assoc. prof. applied math. U. Va., Charlottesville, 1979-83, prof., 1983—; vis. asst. prof. computer sci. Purdue U., 1969-70; mem. adv. panel computer sci. NSF, 1975-78; cons., vis. scientist Inst. Computer Applications in Sci. & Engring., Hampton, Va., 1976-78. Consbr. articles to profl. jours. Grantee NSF and DOE, 1976-91. Mem. Am. Math. Soc., Soc. Indsl. and Applied Math. (mem. editl. bd. Jour. Sci. Statis. Computing 1979-88), Assn. Computing Mathinery (bd. dirs. SIGNUM 1980-83). Office: U Va Dept Computer Sci Thornton Hall Charlottesville VA 22903

MANSI, MOSTAFA KAMAL, urologist, educator; b. Tanta, Gharbia, Egypt, Oct. 10, 1951; s. Abdulfatah Mahmoud Mansi and Fayza Abdelrahman Elsharkawy; m. Nahed Ismail Ali, Aug. 11, 1981; children: Sherief, Amr, Tarek, Ahmed. MBChB, Tanta Sch. Medicine, 1975, MS in Urology, 1980, PhD in Urology, 1988. Diplomate in Urol. Surgery. Intern, then resident Tanta U. Hosps., 1976-80; demonstrator Tanta U., 1980-82, lectr., 1988-90, assoc. prof. urology, 1990-96; prof. urology, 1996—; sr. registrar King Faisal Hosp., Taif, Saudi Arabia, 1982-85; assoc. cons. urologist King Faisal Splty. Hosp., Riyadh, Saudi Arabia, 1990-93, cons. urologist, 1996-2000; dir. urodynamic unit King Faisal Splty. Hosp., 1990-93; dir. male infertility unit King Fahad Nat. Guard, Riyadh, 1994—. Author: Impotence, Causes & Treatment, 1994; contbr. articles to profl. jours. Mem. AMA, ACS, Am. Urol. Assn., EAU, Urodynamic Soc. Islam. Avocations: reading, swimming, tennis. Office: King Fahad Nat Guard Hosp, PO Box 22490, Riyadh 11426, Saudi Arabia

MANSON, KEITH ALAN MICHAEL, lawyer; b. Warwick, RI, Oct. 26, 1962; s. Ronald Frederick and Joan Patricia (Reardon) M.; m. Jennifer Annette Stearns; children: Kristin Elizabeth, Michelle Nicole. BA, R.I. Coll., 1985; cert. computer info. systems, Bryant Coll., 1988; cert. law, U. Notre Dame, London, 1990; JD, Thomas M. Cooley Law Sch., 1991. Bar: Ind. 1991, U.S. Dist. Ct. (no. dist.) Ind. 1991, U.S. Dist. Ct. (so. dist.) Ind. 1991, U.S. Dist. Ct. (so. dist.) Ga. 1992, U.S. Ct. Mil. Appeals 1991. Spl. asst. U.S. atty. U.S. Dist. Ct. Ga., Brunswick, 1992-93; pvt. practice Fernandina Beach, Fla., 1994—; atty., securities compliance divsn. Prudential Ins. Co., 1997-98; counsel Stonier Transportation Group, Jacksonville Beach, Fla., 1998-99; cons. The Law Store Ltd. Paralegal Svcs., Fernandina Beach., 1994—, Barnett Bank, Nations Bank, 1998. Contbr. articles to profl. jours. Dist. fin. and mem. chmn. North Fla. coun. Boy Scouts Am., Jacksonville, 1993—; com. mem. sea scout ship 660 St. Peter's Ch., Fernandina Beach, 1994-96; chmn. Scouting for Food Dr., Nassau County, Fla., 1994—. Lt. USN, 1985-86, 90-96. Recipient Nassau Dist. award of merit Boy Scouts Am., 1999, God and Svc. award, 2000; F.C. Tanner Trust, Fed. Products Inc. scholar, Providence, 1981-85, Esterline Corp. scholar, Providence, 1986. Mem. ABA, Ind. Bar Assn., Judge Advocate Assn., Jacksonville Bar Assn., Navy League U.S., Rotary (project mgr. Webster-Dudley Mass. chpt. 1986-88), Am. Legion, Phi Alpha Delta. Avocations: gardening, rugby, sports history, military history, collecting historical items. Home and Office: 1908 Reatta Ln Fernandina Beach FL 32034-8937

MANSON, ROBERTO RAMON, surgeon, educator; b. Santa Fe, Argentina, Feb. 21, 1941; s. Roberto E. and Valentina C. (Troiani) M.; m. Amalia Buffo, June 11, 1966; children: Roberto Jose, Pablo Andres, Carolina Amalia, Sebastian, Ana Amelia. MD, Facultad Medicina, Tucuman, Argentina, 1965. Diplomate Am. Bd. Surgery, Am. Bd. Colon and Rectal Surgery. Intern St. John Hosp., Detroit, 1966-67; resident Mayo Grad. Sch., Rochester, Minn., 1967-72; staff mem. Carle Clinic, Urbana, Ill., 1972-81; staff mem. Sanatorio Modelo, Tucuman, 1981—, dir., 1990—; asst. prof. U. Ill., 1973-81, U. Tucuman, 1983—. Mem. Argentina Soc. Surgery, Argentina Acad. Surgery. Republican. Roman Catholic. Avocation: sky diving. Office: Sanatorio Modelo, Laprida 544, 4000 San Miguel Tucuman, Argentina

MANSOUR, ALI, electrical engineer; b. Tripoli, Lebanon, Oct. 19, 1969; s. Hassan and Leila (Mohamed) M.; m. Houwaida Elfawal, Aug. 1, 1997; 1 child, Taha. Degree in elect. engring., Libanese U., Lebanon, 1992; diploma D'Etudes Approfondies, Inst. Nat. Poly., Grenoble, France, 1993, DEng, 1997. With Traitement D'Images et Reconnaissance de Formes, Grenoble, 1996-97; rschr. Bio-Memetic Riken, Nagoya, Japan, 1997—; tchr. 3I-U. Joseph Fourier, Grenoble, 1993-97, Geotech-U. Joseph Fourier, France, 1993-96, Inst. U. de Tech., France, 1996-97; lectr. Nagoya U., 2000. Contbr. articles to profl. jours. Mem. IEEE, N.Y. Acad. Scis., IEICE. Avocations: travel, reading, swimming, biking, jogging. Home: 501 Residence Ohshimizu, 487-0025 Kasugai Japan Office: Bio-Mimetic Control Rsch, Moriyama-ku, Nagoya 463-0003, Japan

MANSOUR, MOHAMED MAGDY FAHIM, botany educator; b. Banha, Kalubia, Egypt, Jan. 1, 1955; s. Fahim Ahmed Mansour and Zakia Omar Salem; m. Hala Mohamed Bazaraa, May 4, 1962. BS, Ain Shams U., Cairo, Egypt, 1978, MS, 1983; PhD, U. Minn., 1990. Tchg. asst. Ain Shans U., Cairo, 1978-82, asst. lectr., 1983-89, asst. prof., 1990-95, assoc. prof., 1996—; editor sci. bull. Ain Shams U., 1999—. Author: (with others) Strategies for Improving Salt Tolerance in Higher Plants, 1997; contbr. articles to profl. jours. Mem. Scientific Affairs Syndicate, Cairo, 1978—. PhD scholarship US AID, 1985; postdoctoral rsch. grant Netherlands Univs., 1992, competitive rsch. grant King Abdul Aziz City for Sci. and Tech., 1998. Mem. Am. Soc. for Plant Physiology, Scandinavian Soc. for Plant Physiology. Avocation: reading. Office: Ain Shams U Fac Sci, Dept of Botany, Cairo 11566, Egypt

MANSTAVIČIUS, EUGENIJUS, mathematics educator; b. Stulgiai, Lithuania, Sept. 22, 1947; s. Antanas and Stase (Garalevičiute) M.; m. Zita Adomenaite, June 21, 1974; children: Martynas, Kristupas. Grad., Vilnius (Lithuania) U., 1972, PhD, 1973. Asst. prof. Vilnius U., 1972-74, sr. lectr., 1974-76, assoc. prof., 1976-94, head prof. dept. probability theory and number theory, 1994—; vice dean faculty math. Vilnius U., 1976-77; vis. prof. Paderborn U.-GH, Germany, 1989-90, Witwatersrand U., Johannesburg, South Africa, 1995, U. Bretagne Occidentale, Brest, 1997, U. Provence, Marseille, France, 1999; mem. Sci. Coun. Lithuania, 1996-99. Recipient Gold medal Ministry Edn., Lithuania, 1964, prize Lithuanian Com., 1976. Mem. Lithuanian Math. Soc., Am. Math. Soc. Avocations: reading, chess, gardening. Home: Dukstu str 12-86, 2010 Vilnius Lithuania Office: Vilnius Univ, Naugarduko str 24, 2600 Vilnius Lithuania

MANSUR, MIGUEL JOSÉ, holding and investment company executive; b. Oranjestad, Aruba, Mar. 19, 1946; s. Elias Mansur and Damia Mawad; m. Madeline Arends, Aug. 14, 1971; children: Miguel, Mirzah, Melina. BS, Spring Hill Coll., 1968. Mng. dir. Superior Tobacco Co. Inc., Aruba, 1968-84, Mansur Trading Co. Inc., Aruba, 1985—, Trac-Rent-A-Car, Aruba, 1989-94; mem. Com. of 30 Experts, Aruba, 1986-87. Adviser Min. of Econ. Affairs, Aruba, 1986; pres. Aruba C. of C., 1984, 87-88; pres. bd. trustees Internat. Sch. Aruba, 1988. Recipient Loyal Svc. award Aruba C. of C., 1979-85, 86-88, Loyal Support award richmond Baseball Orgn., 1981, Valuable Svc. award Internat. Sch. Aruba. Mem. Aruba Nautical Club, Aruba Tivoli Club. Roman Catholic. Avocations: shooting sports, fishing, tennis.

MANSUR, WEBE JOÃO, civil engineering educator; b. Conselheiro Pena, Brazil, Sept. 9, 1948; s. João José and Ayde (Jorio) M.; m. Alzira Machado

Taquetti; children: Samantha Taquetti, Juliana Taquetti. Civil Engr., Fed. U. Rio de Janeiro, 1971, MSc, 1975; PhD, Southampton (Eng.) U., 1983. Lic. engr. Asst. prof. Fed. U. Rio de Janeiro, 1976-83, adj. prof., 1983-91, prof. civil engring. dept., 1991—; cons. Petrobras, Rio de Janeiro, 1983-2000, Furnas, Rio de Janeiro, 1992-94. Home: care Rua Prof Gastão Bahiana 496/808, 22071030 Rio de Janeiro Brazil Office: COPPE/Fed U Rio de Janeiro, Ilha do Fundão CXP 68506, 21945970 Rio de Janeiro Brazil

MANTARAKIS, NICOLAS Z., educational administrator; b. N.Y.C., July 21, 1957; s. Zanis and Anna (Nikidis) M.; m. Jane Thomas, Aug. 14, 1982. Diploma in theatre arts, Drama Sch. of Vafias, Athens, Greece, 1977; BA, Nat. U. of Athens, 1980; MA, Western Mich. U., 1981; EdD, No. Ill. U., 1994. Tchr. English as fgn. lang. Am. Cmty. Schs., Athens, 1979-80; instr. English as fgn. lang. Tchr. Tng. Inst. for Vocat. and Tech. Edn., Athens, 1980-81; program coord. Lesley Coll. Grad Sch./Epimorphosi, Athens, 1987-90, No. Ill. U./Epimorphosi, Athens, 1990-95; dep. prin. H.S., coord. English dept. elem., mid. and high sch. Psychico Coll., Athens, 1980—; grad. tchg. asst. No. Ill U., DeKalb, 1992-93; spl. programs coord. Epimorphosi: Ctr. of Liberal Studies, 1987-97; lectr., cons. Pangrition Ednl. Instn., Crete, Greece, 1995-96; lectr. Edge Hill Coll., Eng., 1989, USA Embassy, Athens, 1980-81; cons. ednl. activities spl. programs DIAN Publs., 1997—. Contbr. articles to profl. publs. Mem. TESOL, ASCD, Assn. Profls. in Spl. Edn. (mem. exec. coun. 1991—), Am. Cmty. Schs. Alumni Assn. (pres. 1999—), Eleftherios Deliyianis (acad. chmn. Athens Coll.), Phi Delta Kappa, Kappa Delta Pi. Avocations: travel, reading, theater. Office: Psychico Coll English Dept, PO Box 65005, 15410 Psychico Athens Greece

MANTEGAZZA, PAOLO, pharmacology educator; b. Oct. 2, 1923. Rector U Degli Studi di Milano, Italy. Fax: 58320279. Office: U Degli Studi di Milano, Via Festa del Perdono 7, 20122 Milan Italy

MANTEGAZZA, SERGIO, executive; b. Mendrisio, Switzerland, Oct. 31, 1927; s. Antonio and Angela (Ribolzi) M.; m. Sebastiana Hernandez, Feb. 25, 1955; children: Fabio, Dolores, Paolo. D of Bus. Adminstrn., Gademann Handelschule, 1945. With Globus Gateway Tours, Lugano, Switzerland, 1945-48, mgr., 1948-52, gen. mgr., 1952-56, dir., 1956-60; mng. dir. Globus and Cosmos Groups, Lugano, Switzerland, 1960-75, pres., 1975—; main shareholder Monarch Airlines Ltd., 1967. Named Knight of the Order of St. Gregorio Magno and Hon. Consul of Mexico. Mem. Lyford Cay, Maxims Bus. Club, Mark's Club. Avocations: tennis, yachting, golf, jogging, rowing. Office: Globus Travel Svcs, Via alla Roggia, CH-6916 Grancia Switzerland

MANTEL, DIRK GUSTAV, retired chemical engineer; b. Bandung, Java, Indonesia, Nov. 22, 1923; s. Peter Gustav and Justine (Willems) M.; m. Vera Edna Shaw, June 6, 1932; children: Jennifer, Peter, Leigh, Andrew. Grad., Lyceum, Hilversum, The Netherlands, 1943; MIChemE, Inst. Chem. Engrs., U.K., 1955. Chartered engr. Chem. engr. African Explosives and Chem. Industries, South Africa, 1952-60; tech. dir. White's S.A. Portland Cement Co., South Africa, 1960-72, Salisbury Portland Cement Co., Rhodesia, 1965-72; group tech. mgr. Pretoria (South Africa) Portland Cement Co., 1973-92; ret., 1992; cons. in cement tech., 1992—. Contbr. articles to profl. jours.; patentee in field. Mem. Inst. Chem. Engring., N.Y. Acad. Scis. Methodist. Home and Office: PO Box 133 Strathavon, 2031 Sandton Gauteng, South Africa

MANTHEY, MERRILY RUTH, psychotherapist, educator, consultant, author, producer, natural medicine integration; b. Seattle, Mar. 25, 1943. BA, Evergreen State Coll., 1976; MS, Ea. Washington U. Lic. therapist, Washington. Rsch. publs. supr. Stanford Rsch. Inst., Huntsville, Ala., 1965-67; communications dir. Marine Constrn. & Design Co., Seattle, 1967-71; pvt. practice therapy, 1971—; instr., public affairs dir. Seattle Acad., 1971-72; owner, dir., tchr. Kent (Wash.) Montessori Sch., 1972-76; instr. Green River Coll., 1974—; dir., therapist Inst. Exec. Stress Mgmt., Inc., Kent, 1976—; cons. human rels.; legis aide to Wash. senator Kent Pullen, 1977-79, lic. cons., 1977—; bd. dirs., trustee Harborview Med. Ctr., 1992, trustee, Bastyr U., 1993—; mem. bd. King Cty. Natural Medicine Clin., 1996—; dir. Found. for Excellence in Health Care, 1995—. Ednl. div. chmn., comm. dir. Wash. Taxpayers Assn., Citizens Taxpayers Assn.; supr. King Tut Exhbn., Seattle Art Museum, 1978; mem. Kent Arts Commn., 1985-89; bd. dirs., trustee Bastyr U., Kent, Wash., 1992; singer The Rainier Chorale. Recipient Torch award Nat. Honor Soc., 1961, cert. Internat. Found. Human Rels., Amsterdam, Holland, 1980, Outstanding Svc. award Citizens for Health, 1995, Telly award for video A Message Of Hope, Found. Excellence in Health Care; named Disting. Alumnus, Green River Coll., 1994. Mem. Am. Soc. Group Psychotherapy and Psychodrama, Internat. Stress and Tension Control Assn., Assn. Transpersonal Psychology, Internat. Assn. Progressive Montessorians (cert. 1971), Am. Assn. Counseling and Devel., Am. Running and Fitness Assn., Women in Music Internat. (pres. 1989—), Psychodrama of Wash. Club. Author: Editorial Standards Guide, 1965; How to Promote Your Cause, 1975; Natural Medicine Handbook for People Over 50, 1998; editor: The Sou'Wester, 1961; research on stress, human sexuality. Nov. 10, 1986 proclaimed Merrily Manthey Day, Mayor, City of Kent, Wash. Home: PO Box 873 Kent WA 98035-0873 Office: 317 W Meeker St # E Kent WA 98032-6005

MANTO, MARIO UBALDO, neurologist, researcher; b. Charleroi, Hainaut, Belgium, May 20, 1967; s. Leopoldo and Flora (D'Avella) M.; m. Ana Roman; 1 child, Valentin. MD, Free U. Brussels, 1992, PhD, 1996. Neurologist Free U. Brussels, 1998—, charge de recherches, 1998—; rsch. fellow Neuromuscular Rsch. Ctr., Boston, 1999. Contbr. articles to profl. jours. Sec. Fondation De L'Ataxie Cerebelleuse, Belgium, 1998. Recipient award Fifty-One Club Internat., 1992; David and Alice Van Buuren fellow, 1999. Avocations: soccer, music. Office: Fonds Nat Recherche Sci, Lab Ataxies Cerebelleuses, Charleroi Belgium

MANTON, EDWIN ALFRED GRENVILLE, insurance company executive; b. Earls Colne, Essex, Eng., Jan. 22, 1909; came to U.S., 1933; s. John Horace and Emily Clara (Denton) M.; m. Florence V. Brewer, Feb. 1, 1936; 1 child, Diana H. Manton Morton. Student, London (Eng.) U., 1925-27, N.Y. Ins. Soc., 1933-35; DHL (hon.), Coll. of Ins., 1994. With B.W. Noble Ltd., Paris, 1927-33; casualty underwriter Am. Internat. Underwriters Corp., N.Y.C., 1933-37, sec., 1937-38, v.p., 1938-42, pres., 1942-69, chmn., 1969-75; sr. advisor Am. Internat. Group, Inc.; hon. dir. C.V. Starr & Co., Inc. Trustee St. Luke's-Roosevelt Hosp., N.Y.C. Mem. Salmagundi Club, Mendelssohn Glee Club, Williams Club, St. George's Soc., Downtown Assn. Episcopalian. Office: Am Internat Group Inc 70 Pine St New York NY 10270-0002

MANTRAVADI, MURTY V., retired optics scientist; b. Perakalapudi, India, Oct. 4, 1929; came to U.S., 1956, 84; s. Gangadhara Sastry and Venkatalakshmi (Upadrasta) Mantravadi; m. Suryaprabhadevi Upadrasta, Mar. 12, 1952; children: Sandhyarani, Gangadhar, Lakshmi, Ravikumar, Suryanarayana, Padma. BSc, Andhra Christian Coll. (India), 1949; DMIT, Madras Inst. Tech. (India), 1952; PhD, Inst. Optics, U. Rochester (N.Y.), 1959. Lectr., Madras Inst. Tech., 1952-55; asst. Inst. Optics, U. Rochester, 1956-59, asst. prof., 1959-64; prof. Madras Inst. Tech., 1964-66; scientist, engr. Bhabha Atomic Rsch. Ctr., Bombay, India, 1966-82; prof. Centro de Inv en Optica, Leon, Guanajuato, Mex., 1982-84; chief scientist Halo Technologies, Costa Mesa, Calif., 1984-86; prof. Ala. A&M U., Huntsville, 1986-87; rsch. engr./scientist Northrop Grumman Corp., Hawthorne, Calif., 1987-94, ret.; cons. Contbr. chpts. to books, articles to profl. jours.; patentee in field. Fellow Indian Acad. Scis., Optical Soc. India, Optical Soc. Am., Internat. Soc. Optical Engring. Home: 21610 Villa Pacifica Cir Carson CA 90745-1737

MANTYLA, KAREN, distance learning consultant; b. Bronx, N.Y., Dec. 31, 1944; d. Milton and Sylvia (Diamond) Fischer; m. John A Mantyla, May 30, 1970 (div. 1980); 1 child, Michael Alan. Student, Rockland Community Coll., Suffern, N.Y., 1962, NYU, 1967, Mercer U., 1981. Mktg. coordinator Credit Bur., Inc., Miami, Fla., 1973-79; dist. mgr. The Research Inst. Am., N.Y.C., 1979-80, regional dir., 1980-85, field sales mgr., 1985-86, nat. sales mgr., 1986-87; nat. accounts mgr. The Rsch. Inst. Am., N.Y.C., 1989; v.p. sales Bur. Bus. Practice/Paramount Comm., Inc., Waterford, Conn., 1989-93; pres. Quiet Power, Inc., Washington, 1993—. Author: Consultative Sales Power, 1995, Interactive Distance Learning Exercises That Really Work, 1999, The 200/2001 ASTD Distance Learning Yearbook, 2000; co-author: Distance Learning: A Step-By-Step Guide for Trainers, 1997. Mem. ASTD, Sales and Mktg. Execs. (past bd. dirs. N.Y. chpt., v.p. Ft. Lauderdale chpt. 1979), U.S. Distance Learning Assn. (editor Distance Learning News, mem. tech. and comm. com. Fla. chpt.), Nat. Assn. Women Bus. Owners, U.S. C. of C., Women Entrepreneurs. Avocations: antiques, tennis, writing, swimming. Home: 8246 Silver Run Ct Pasadena MD 21122-4637 Office: Quiet Power Inc 1201 Pennsylvania Ave NW Washington DC 20004-2401

MÄNTYNIEMI, PÄIVI BIRGITTA, seismologist; b. Helsinki, Finland, Apr. 29, 1963; s. Pertti and Pirkko (Hilvonen) M. MS, U. Helsinki, 1991. Rsch. asst. U. Helsinki, 1985-91, seismologist, 1992—. Contbr. articles to profl. jours. Office: U Helsinki Inst Seismology, PO Box 26, FIN00014 Helsinki Finland

MANU, FRANKLYN ACHAMPONG, business educator, consultant; b. Kumasi, Ghana, Sept. 4, 1956; s. Joseph E. A. and Comfort Manu; m. Margaret Manu; children: Kwame, Nana. BSc in Adminstrn., U. Ghana, Legon, 1977; MBA, NYU, 1981, PhD, 1989. Mgmt. trainee Volta River Authority, Accra, Ghana, 1977-78; instr. Sch. Adminstrn. U. Ghana, Legon, 1978-79; instr. Coll. Bus. and Pub. Adminstrn. NYU, 1986-88; asst. prof. Sch. Bus. Loyola Coll., Balt., 1988-93; prof. Sch. Bus. Morgan State U., Balt., 1993—; cons. CDH Group, Accra. Mem. editl. bd. Jour. African Bus. Mem. Acad. Internat. Bus., Assn. Global Bus., Acad. Mktg. Sci., Soc. Mktg. Advances. Avocations: African history, African literature, music, travel. Fax: 410-319-4034. Office: Morgan State U Sch Bus 1700 E Cold Spring Ln Baltimore MD 21251-0002

MANUEL, ABIOBUA KIO STEPHEN, chemistry educator; b. Abonnema, Degema, Nigeria, July 17, 1952; s. Kio Oruambo Awoloye and Warigbani Josephine (Ejike) M.; m. Bernadette Jennifer Obata, Dec. 15, 1984 (dec. Sept. 1992); children: Abiye Mason, Bala Stephanie. NCE in Physics and Chemistry, U. Ibadan, Nigeria, 1975, EdB with honors, 1979. Cert. chemistry edn. and guidance counseling. Sci. tutor Nyemoni Grammar Sch., Abonnema, 1971-72; sci. master Fed. Govt. Tchr. Tng. Coll., Degema, Nigeria, 1975-76; vice prin. Govt. Secondary Sch., Degema, 1980-81; prin. Cmty. Secondary Sch., Onuebum, Nigeria, 1981-82; lectr. Sch. Basic Studies, Port Harcourt, Nigeria, 1982-83; sr. asst. registrar Coll. Edn., Port Harcourt, 1983—; guidance counselor Steve Manuel & Co., Nigeria, 1982-90, counseling dir., 1990-96; facilitator Ednl. Opportunities Programme, Nigeria, 1996-97; mng. ptnr. Dear Steve Partnership, Nigeria, 1998. Contbg. writer (newspaper) The Tide, 1997—. Founder, pres. The Mercysiders, Nigeria, 1994—; deliverance min. Ministry of Perfection, 1994, elder, usher leader, 1998, pastor Choba br., 1999; disciple of Christ, The Body of Christ, 1994. Mem. Internat. Coun. Psychologists, Nigerian Psychol. Assn., Sci. Tchrs. Assn. Nigeria. Avocations: traveling, reading, choral music, swimming, current affairs. Home: 32 Captain Amangala St, Port Harcourt Nigeria Office: Dear Steve Partnership, PO Box 2296, Port Harcourt Nigeria

MANUEL, TREVOR ANDREW, South African government official; b. Cape Town, South Africa, Jan. 31, 1956; m. Lynne Matthews; children: Govan, Pallo, Jamie. Student, Peninsula Technikon. Civil engring. technician, 1973-81; field worker Ednl. Resource and Info. Ctr., Cape Town, 1982-84; mixed-race head econ. planning dept. African Nat. Congress, policy mgr. devel., 1989—, mem. nat. exec. com., 1991—; min. trade and industry Govt. of South Africa, 1994—, min. fin.; publicity sec. African Nat. Congress, West Cape, South Africa. Cmty. organizer Cape Areas Housing Action Com., 1980-83; sec. Kensington Civic Assn., 1977-82; supporter migrant workers' rights, organizer bus boycotts and rent strikes; sec. United Dem. Front in Western Cape, 1983; mem. nat. exec. com. United Dem. Party, 1983-86, 89-90. Office: 240 Vermeulen St 26th Fl, Pvt Bag X115, Pretoria 0001, South Africa

MANUEL, VIVIAN, public relations executive; b. Queens County, N.Y., May 6, 1941; d. George Thomas and Vivian (Anderson) M. BA, Wells Coll., 1963; MA, U. Wyo., Laramie, 1965. Mgmt. analyst Dept. Navy, 1966-68; account supr. GE Co., N.Y.C., 1968-72, corp. rep. bus. and fin., 1972-76; dir. corp. comm. Std. Brands Co., N.Y.C., 1976-78; pvt. cons. N.Y.C., 1978-80; pres. V M Comm. Inc., N.Y.C., 1980-97; pub. info. officer Mont. Dept. Commerce, Helena, 1997—. Bd. dirs. Am. Lung Assn. of No. Rockies, 1999—; mem. com. Girls Club N.Y., 1983-84; trustee Wells Coll., 1983-90; mem. adv. bd. Glenholme Sch., 1991-92; mem. audit com.-disaster relief agys. and youth orgns. United Way Mont., 1998—. Mem. AAUW, N.Y. Women in Comms. (bd. v.p. 1983-85, chair Matrix awards 1985), Women Execs. in Pub. Rels. (bd. dirs. 1985-88), Women's Econ. Roundtable. Address: 1400 Flowerree St Helena MT 59601-6024 Office: 1424 9th Ave Helena MT 59601-4503

MANUSAMA, ERIC ROBERT, surgeon, researcher; b. The Hague, The Netherlands, Apr. 8, 1965; s. Hendrik Stephanus and Yan Frouwina (De Korte) M. MD, State U. of Utrecht, The Netherlands, 1990; PhD, Erasmus U., Rotterdam, 1998. Naval dr. Royal Dutch Navy, 1991-92; rschr. Erasmus U., Rotterdam, The Netherlands, 1992-95; surgeon-in-tng. Delft (The Netherlands) Gen. Hosp., 1996-99, Rotterdam Acad. Hosp., 1999—. Contbr. articles to profl. jours. Mem. Am. Assn. Cancer Rsch. (assoc.). Avocations: skating, chess. Home: Voorstraat 31, 2611 Delft The Netherlands Office: Acad HospRotterdam, U Hosp Rotterdam, DIJK216T Rotterdam The Netherlands

MANUTA, DAVID MARK, research chemist, consultant; b. Bklyn., June 10, 1957; s. Gerald and Vivian Bernice (Chartoff) M.; m. Ruth Pauline Krog, Mar. 27, 1988 (dec. Dec. 1993). BS in Chemistry, SUNY, Oneonta, 1979; PhD in Chemistry, SUNY, Binghamton, 1985. Lab. tech. Sci. Process & Rsch., Somerset, N.J., 1980-81; from tchg. asst. to postdoctoral fellow SUNY, Binghamton, 1981-86; asst. prof. Upper Iowa U., Fayette, 1986-88; asst. prof. II Shawnee State U., Portsmouth, Ohio, 1989-90; rsch. staff U.S. Enrichment Corp., Piketon, Ohio, 1990—; founder Manuta Chem. Consulting Inc., 1998; tchr. Christ the King Regional H.S., N.Y.C., 1986; instr. Stanley Kaplan Exam. Prep. Svcs., Garden City, N.Y., 1986; cons. City of Portsmouth, 1989; mem. strategic planning com. Ohio Acad. Sci., 1996. Sec. Big Bros./Big Sisters of South Ctrl. Ohio, 1996; pres. Waverly Heights Crime Watch, 1995; treas. Pike County Humane Soc., Ohio, 1997; fin. chair Portsmouth employees chpt. Nat. Mgmt. Assn., 1997. With USN, 1978-79. IBM Corp. grad. fellow, 1984-85. Fellow Am. Inst. of Chemistry; mem. AAAS, ASTM, Am. Chem. Soc., Assn. Consulting Chemists Chem. Engrs. Avocations: chess, reading, running, bicycling, traveling. E-mail: dmanuta@dmanta.com., dmanuta@zoomnet.net. Home: 431 Gordon Ave Waverly OH 45690-1208 Office: US Enrichment Corp 3930 US Rte 23 S PO Box 628 MS/2224 Piketon OH 45661-0628

MANVELOV, LEV SERGEEVICH, neurologist; b. Moscow, Sept. 5, 1938; s. Manvelov Sergey Stepanovich and Antonina Kuzminichna Manvelova; m. Tatyana Vasilievna Bychkova, Feb. 20, 1999. MD, Med. Acad., Moscow, 1966; MA, Russian Acad. Sci., Moscow, 1992. Physician's asst. Sanitary & Epimeiologic Sta., Moscow, 1960-64; physician on duty Moscow Clin. Hosp. 940, 1964-66; physician Moscow Emergency, 1966-70, dept. dir., 1970-71; neurologist Rsch. Inst. Neurology Russian Acad. Sci., Moscow, 1971—, Moscow Clin. Hosp. 912, 1978—; instr. Moscow Med. Sch. 98, 1970; examiner-neurologist Med. Labor Examination, Moscow, 1982-90. Contbr. articles to profl. jours. People's assessor People's Ct., Moscow, 1980-90; mem. com. popularisation med. sci., Moscow, 1988—. Mem. Znanie (dep. chmn. 1975—). Avocations: reading, painting, gardening. Office: Russian Acad Sci, Volokolamskoye Rd, 80, 123367 Moscow Russia

MANVILLE, STEWART ROEBLING, archivist; b. White Plains, N.Y., Jan. 15, 1927; s. Leo and Margaret (Roebling) M.; m. Ella V. Grainger, Jan. 19, 1972 (dec.). Student, U. Wyo., 1944-46; BS, Columbia U., 1962. Various office positions N.Y.C., 1947-51, 56-58; asst. stage dir. several European opera houses, 1951-55; editor Jas. T. White & Co., N.Y.C., 1959-63; archivist, curator Percy Grainger Library, White Plains, 1963—. Author: The Manville/Manvel Families in America; contbr. articles and revs. on music to mags. and newspapers. Mem. SAR, Nat. Trust Hist. Preservation, Victorian Soc. in Am. (past dir. N.Y. chpt.), Société des Antiquaires de Picardie, Brit. Music Soc., Westchester Trails Assn. (past dir.), St. Nicholas Soc. N.Y. Quaker. Office: 7 Cromwell Pl White Plains NY 10601-5005

MANZ, JOHANNES JAKOB, Swiss diplomat; b. Zurich, Switzerland, Dec. 15, 1938; s. Jakob J. and Margaret (Ruegg) M.; m. Marie-Antoinette Kunz, May 26, 1966; children: Alexander Cyril, Isabel Carmela. Student, Oreg. State U., 1958-59; LLD, U. Zurich, 1969. Sec. Mission of Switzerland, N.Y.C., 1971-75; counselor Swiss Embassy, Vienna, Austria, 1975-81; min., dep. head mission Mission of Switzerland, Geneva, 1981-84; amb., chief protocol Swiss Confedn., Bern, 1984-88; amb., dir. adminstrn. and pers. Swiss Dept. for Fgn. Affairs, Bern, 1988-91; under sec. gen., spl. rep. to sec. gen. for Western Sahara, UN, N.Y.C., 1990-91; amb., head of mission, permanent observer to UN, Mission of Switzerland, N.Y.C., 1992-97; amb. to Japan, Swiss Embassy, Tokyo, 1997—. Contbg. author: Manual of Swiss Foreign Policy, 1991. Pres. Platform for Young Citizens, Zollikon, Switzerland, 1967-68. Mem. Delta Upsilon (hon. Oreg. State U. chpt.). Avocations: cross-country skiing, golf, swimming, classical music. Address: Embassy of Switzerland, 5-9-12 Minami Azabu, Minato-ku Tokyo 106-8589, Japan

MANZAR, SYED MUHAMMAD, manufacturing company executive; b. Sadatpur (Siwan), India, Sept. 1, 1933; arrived in Pakistan, 1952; s. Syed Abdul Shakoor and Syeda Quraisha Khatoon; m. Syeda Safia Khatoon, Dec. 21, 1957; children: Nasreen, Parween, Nazneen, Mumshad, Shireen, Shamshad, Rishad. Ordained priest, Khanquah-e-Rashidia, Joanpur, India, 1996; cert. naval arch. UN Food and Agr. Orgn. for designing mechanized fishing boats, 1960. Propr. Manzar & Co., Chittagong, Bangladesh, 1956-71; mng. dir. Manzar & Co. (Shipyard) Ltd., Chittagong, Bangladesh, 1962-71; propr. EPAID Co., Dhaka, Bangladesh, Karachi, Pakistan, 1969-92; chmn. Bengal Constrn. Ltd., Chittagong, 1967-71; mng. dir. Bengal Motors Ltd., Chittagong, 1968-71; chmn./CEO Manzar Marine Products (Pvt.) Ltd., Karachi, 1976—, EPAIDCO (Pvt.) Ltd., Karachi, 1992—; chmn. Manzar Ceramics (Pvt.) Ltd., Karachi, 1996—; chmn./CEO Manzar Power Generation Corp. Ltd., Karachi, 1992—; chmn. Chittagong Mechanized Fishing Assn., 1969-71, patron East Pakistan Anglers Assn., Dhaka, 1965-71; chmn. for province of Sindh, Rural Devel. Found. Pakistan, Karachi, 1983-90. Editor book of Urdu poetry by Muhammad Abdul Alim'Asi', 1988. Active mem. Indian Muslim League, Sadatpur, 1945-47; v.p., sec. Muslim Student Unit, Gangtok, Sikkim State, 1945-50; trustee Noria Rizvia Darululoom (Arabic Coll.), Karachi, 1978—; pres. Trade Tower Owner sAssn., Karachi, 1998—; pres. Islamic Rsch. & Adv. Bur., Karachi, 1989—. Recipient 5th Arab trophy The East Trade/Madrid, Geneva, Switzerland, 1988. Mem. Karachi Chamber of Commerce & Industry, Trade Leaders' Club, Quetta Club Ltd., Karachi Lions Club. Mem. Pakistan Muslim League. Moslem (Hanfi sect). Avocations: football, angling, squash, swimming, travel. Office: Manzar 111-113 Trade Tower, Abdullah Haroon Rd, Karachi 75530, Pakistan

MANZHELII, ELENA VADIMOVNA, physicist; b. Kharkov, USSR, Mar. 28, 1961; d. Vadim Grigorievich and Ludmila Smenovna Manzhelii. MS, Kharkov State U., 1983; PhD, Inst. Low Temperature Physics & Engring., Kharkov, 1983. Engr. Inst. Low Temperature Physics & Engring., Kharkov, 1983-89, jr. rsch. fellow, 1989-99, rsch. fellow, 1999—. Contbr. articles to profl. jours. Rsch. grantee Internat. Sci. Found., 1993; fellow Nat. Acad. Scis. Ukraine, 1994-95. Fax: 0572-335593. Home: Lenin ave 67 Apt 10, 61164 Kharkov Ukraine Office: Inst Low Temperature Physics & Engring, 47 Lenin Ave, 61164 Kharkov Ukraine

MANZHIROV, ALEXANDER VLADIMIROVICH, mathematician; b. Rostov on Don, Russia, May 24, 1957; s. Vladimir Michailovich and Tamara Semenovna (Afanacieva) M.; m. Tatiana Victorovna Larina, Oct. 27, 1984 (div. Jan. 1998); 1 child, Marina Alexandrovna. MSc, Rostov State U., Russia, 1979; PhD, Moscow Inst. Elec. Engring., 1983; DSc, Inst. Problems in Mechanics, 1993. Engr. Inst. Problems in Mechanics, Russian Acad. Sci., Moscow, 1983-84, jr. rschr., 1984-89, rschr., 1989-92, sr. rschr., 1992-95, prof., 1995—; prof. math. Bauman Moscow State Tech. U., Moscow, 1997—, Moscow State Acad. Engring. and Computer Sci., Moscow, 1994—; editl. bd. jour. Mechs. of Solids, Moscow, 1995—; expert in math. and mechs. Higher Cert. Com. of Russian Fedn., Moscow, 1999—. Author: (with N.Kh. Arutyunyan and V.E. Naumov) Contact Problems in Mechanics of Growing Solids, 1991; (with A.D. Polyanin) Handbook of Integral Equations, 1998, Handbuch der Integralgleichungen: Exakte Lösungen, 1999; (with N.Kh. Arutyunyan) Contact Problems in the Theory of Creep, 1999, others; contbr. over 60 articles to profl. jours.; patentee in field. Mem. European Mechs. Soc. Avocations: driving, movies, basketball, volleyball, table tennis. E-mail: manzh@ipmnet.ru. Office: Inst Problems in Mechs, Vernadsky Ave 101 Bldg 1, 117526 Moscow Russia

MANZONI, GIACOMO, composer, educator; b. Milan, Sept. 26, 1932; s. Lino Manzoni and Wanda Gisuti; m. Eugenia Tretti, 1960; 1 child, Nicola. Diploma in piano, Verdi Conservatory, Milan, 1954, diploma in composition, 1956; degree in fgn. langs., U. Bocconi, Milan, 1955; Dr. (h.c.), U. Udine. Tchr. composition Verdi Conservatory, Milan, 1962-64, 74-91, Martini Conservatory, Bologna, Italy, 1965-74; tchr. spl. courses Music Sch. Fiesole, Italy, 1988—, Acad. Musicale, Pescara, Italy, 1993-96. Author: Tradizione e Utopia, 1994; (opera) Dr. Faustus, 1989, Per M. Robespierre, 1975, Atomtod, 1965, (symphonic music) Insiemi, 1967, Parole da Beckett, 1971, Ode, 1982, Dedica, 1985, Scene Sinfoniche per Il Dr. Faustus, 1984, 10 Versi di E. Dickinson, 1988, Il Deserto Cresce, 1992, Moi, Antonin A., 1997, Trame d'ombre, 1998, others. Recipient Ambrogino d'Oro Municipality of Milan, 1979. Mem. Accademia Santa Cecilia. Home: viale Papiniano 31, 20123 Milan Italy

MAO, I-FANG, environmental scientist; b. Tainan, Taiwan, Dec. 22, 1947; s. Fu-shine and Lan-Shin (Chen) M.; m. Lee-En Wang, May 21, 1974; children: Chin-Ting, Chin-Chi, Chun-Chieh. BS, Taipei Med. Sch., 1970; MPH, Nat. Taiwan U., 1973, Dr. P.H., 1990. Cert. pharmacist. Mgr. Tatung Coop., Taipei, 1974-83; lectr. Nat. Taiwan U., Taipei, 1974-83; lectr. Nat. Yang-Ming U., Taipei, 1983-87, assoc., 1987-96, prof., 1996—, dir. dept. pub. health, 1994-98, dir. Inst. Environ. Health Sci., 1998—; cons. Tatung Coop., Taipei, 1974—. Contbr. articles to Sci. of Total Environment, Am. Indsl. Health Assn. Jour., others. Lt. Air Force, Taiwan, 1970-71. Recipient Acad. award Nat. Sci. Coun., Republic of China, 1990-91, 93, 95-97. Mem. Nat. Pub. Health Assn. Republic of China, Chinese Occup. Health Assn. Taiwan, Formosan Med. Assn. Avocation: mountain climbing. Office: Nat Yang-Ming U, 155 Li-Long St, Pei-Tou, Taipei Taiwan

MAO, JIANHUA, pediatrician, researcher; b. YuYao, ZheJiang, China, Apr. 26, 1969; s. RenYang and HaiQing (Chen) M.; m. Zhang Yang, July 10, 1996. MMed, KunMing (China) Med. Coll., 1996. Diplomate in medicine. Tng. Pediatric Hosp., NingBo, China, 1987-93; rschr. Coll. KunMing, China, 1993-96; mem. staff Pediatric Hosp, HangZhou, China, 1996—. Recipient Advancement of Sci. prize YunNan, China, 1996. Office: Childrens Hosp Dept Med, ZheJiang Med U, HangZhou 310003, China

MAO, JIFANG, biologist, researcher; b. Shanghai, People's Republic of China, Mar. 16, 1950; s. Xingran and Zhimei (Yan) M.; m. Baoying Liu, Feb. 2, 1973. BS, Shanghai Med. U., 1970; MS, Fourth Mil. Med. U., Xi'an, China, 1982, PhD, 1989. Surgeon County People's Hosp., Wuwei City, 1970-79; biochemistry lectr. Fourth Mil. Med. U., Xi'an, 1979-86, assoc. prof. biochemistry, 1989-91; prof. biochemistry Shanghai Inst. Med. Biotech. and Molecular Genetics, 1995-98, prof., chmn. dept., 1995—; vis. scientist physiology U. Ill., Chgo., 1991-95, vis. scientist physiology and biophysics, 1998-99. Contbr. articles to profl. jours. including Biochem. and Biophys. Rsch. Comm., Endocrinology. Grantee Chinese Natural Sci. Found. Mem. Chinese Soc. Biochemistry and Molecular Biology. Office: Shanghai Inst Med Tech, 800 Xiangyin Rd, Shanghai 200433, Peoples Republic of China

MAO, JUNFA, electronic engineering educator, researcher; b. Hunan, China, Aug. 8, 1965; s. Kanggui Mao and Jinmei Wu; m. Jing Yang, Nov. 1, 1993. BS, Nat. U. Def. Tech., Changsha, China, 1985; MS, Shanghai Inst. Nuclear Rsch., 1988; PhD, Shanghai Jiao Tong U., 1992. Asst. engr. Shanghai Corp. Nuclear Tech., 1988-89; lectr. Shanghai Jiao tong U., 1992-93; rsch. assoc. Chinese U. Hong Kong, 1994-95; postdoctoral researcher U. Calif., Berkeley, 1995-96; assoc. prof. Shanghai Jiao Tong U., 1996-97, prof., 1997—, assoc. dean, 1999—. Contbr. articles to profl. jours. Mem. IEEE (sr.), N.Y. Acad. Sci. Office: Shanghai Jiao Tong U, Dept Elec Engring, Shanghai 200030, China

MAO, ZAI-SHA, chemical engineer, researcher; b. Chengdu, Sichuan, China, July 3, 1943; s. Ji-Ren Mao and Bao-Shie Xie; m. Junxian Zhou, Feb. 24, 1975; children: Yu, Xiang. Student, Tsinghua U., Beijing, 1960-66; MS, Academia Sinica, Beijing, 1981; PhD, U. Houston, 1988. Prof. Inst. Chem. Metallurgy, Academia Sinica, 1994—, PhD candidate supr., 1995—. Contbr. articles to profl. jours. including Chem. Engring. Sci., others; patentee in chem. engring. Recipient Best Fundamental Paper award AIChE, South Tex. sect., 1992. Office: Acadamia Sinica Inst Chem, Metallurgy PO Box 353, Beijing 100080, China

MAO, ZHENG, systems control engineer; b. Xianyang, Shaanxi, China, Jan. 25, 1959; m. Xiao Jun Qu, Sept. 28, 1987; 1 child, Yu-Xin Mao. BS of Engring., Beijing Inst. Tech., 1982, MS of Engring., 1987. Asst. engr. Shaanxi Mech. and Elec. Inst., China, 1982-89, engr., 1989-94, sr. engr., 1994-98, rsch. fellow, vice dir. tech. dept., 1998—. Pres. The Sci. and Tech. Assn. for Youth, China, 1996—. Recipient Sci. and Tech. Advance award Norinco, 3d class, 1989, 1st class, 1996, 2d class, 1996. Mem. China Ordnance Soc., Shaanxi Computer Soc. Avocations: basketball, classical music. Office: Shaanxi Mech & Elec Inst, #5 Eastern Biyuan Rd, Xianyang 712099, China

MAOPE, KELEBONE ALBERT, Lesotho government official; b. Ha Maope, Sept. 15, 1945. Public prosecutor, 1972-75; lectr. Nat. Univ. Lesotho, 1979-84, sr. lectr., 1984-86; atty. gen. Govt. Lesotho, Maseru, 1986-93, min. justice and human rights, 1993—, min. law and constl. affairs, 1993-95, min. fgn. affairs, 1995-99, dep. prime minister, 1999—, min. fin. devel. planning; editor Lesotho Law Journal, 1985—. Office: Ministry Fgn Affairs, Office of Prime Minister, PO Box 527, Maseru 100, Lesotho*

MAOZHONG, YI, science educator, engineering educator; b. Lixian, Hunan, China, Feb. 12, 1962; s. Changfu Yi and Liu Shuying; m. Ran Liping, Oct. 1, 1987; 1 child, Zi. Ph.B., Ctrl. South U. Tech., Changsha, China, 1981; Ph.M., Xi'an (China) U. Tech., 1988, PhD, 1996. Asst. Xi'an U. Tech., 1982-88, lectr., 1988-94, assoc. prof., 1994-97, 1994-97; assoc. prof. Ctrl. South U. Tech., Changsha, China, 1997-98; prof. Ctrl. South U. Tech., Changsha, 1998—. Contbr. articles to profl. jours.; patentee in field. Mem. Human Tribology Soc., Hunan Aeronautics Soc. Office: Ctrl South U Tech, State Key Lab Powder Metallurgy, 410083 Changsha Hunan, China

MAPEL, PATRICIA JOLENE, farmer, consultant; b. Lake City, Iowa, June 24, 1933; d. John Gilbert and Blanche Evelyn (Taylor) Sharkey; m. J.R. Mapel, Sept. 1, 1952 (dec. 1992); children: Pati Jo, Mark L., Grant L., Penelope R., Kay Collene. Student, Wesley Meml. Hosp. Sch. of Nursing, 1951-52. Ptnr. farming Lake City, Iowa, 1953-92; ptnr., pres. Mapel Farms Ethanol, Inc., Lake City, Iowa, 1984-92; house dir. Delta Delta Delta Simpson Coll., Indianola, Iowa, 1993—; cons. Dept. of Energy, Kansas City, 1981; demonstrator, educator Iowa Cen. Community Coll., Ft. Dodge, Iowa. Contbr. articles to profl. jours. Bd. dirs. Cen. Sch. Preservation, Inc., Lake City, 1984-90. Mem. Entre Nous Music Club, Eastern Star. Democrat. Mem. Ch. of Christ. Avocations: sewing, leathercraft. Home: 705 N C St Indianola IA 50125-1274

MAPES, GLYNN DEMPSEY, newspaper editor; b. N.Y.C., July 15, 1939; s. John George and Dorothy (Glynn) M.; m. Elizabeth Adlum, Apr. 13, 1963; children—Timothy Glynn, Susannah Glynn. B.A., Williams Coll., 1961. Reporter Wall St. Jour., San Francisco, 1965-67; bur. chief Wall St. Jour., Phila., 1967-70; fgn. editor Wall St. Jour., N.Y.C., 1970-71, bur. chief, 1971-75, Page One editor, 1975-88, Reports editor, 1988-89; bur. chief Wall St. Jour., London, 1989-93; money and investing editor Wall St. Jour., N.Y.C., 1993-99, asst. mgn. editor, 1999—. Served to lt. (j.g.) USN, 1961-65. Mem. Collegiate Chorale Club, London Concert Choir Club. Democrat. Club: Collegiate Chorale, London Concert Choir. Home: 37 W 12th St Apt 2H New York NY 10011-8503 Office: Wall St Jour 200 Liberty St New York NY 10281-1003

MAPES, WILLIAM RODGERS, JR., lawyer; b. Cleve., Nov. 29, 1952; s. William R. and Marian (Atkins) M.; m. Patricia Soochan, Sept. 3, 1984. BS in Bus. Adminstrn., Miami U., Oxford, Ohio, 1974; JD, Am. U., 1977. Bar: D.C. 1978, U.S. Ct. Appeals (D.C. cir.) 1979, U.S. Ct. Appeals (fed. cir.) 1980, U.S. Ct. Appeals (5th cir.) 1981, U.S. Supreme Ct. 1982, U.S. Ct. Appeals (3d cir.) 1985, U.S. Ct. Appeals (4th cir.) 1987, U.S. Ct. Appeals (6th cir.) 1988. Ptnr. Ross, Marsh & Foster, Washington, 1978—. Treas., bd. dirs. Holy Land Christian Ecumenical Found. Mem. ABA (editor nat. resources sect. newsletter 1984-89), Fed. Energy Bar Assn., Univ. Club Washington. Avocations: boating, tennis, cycling. Home: 6916 Greenvale St NW Washington DC 20015-1437 Office: Ross Marsh & Foster 2001 L St NW Ste 400 Washington DC 20036-4946

MAPOTHER, TOM CRUISE, IV See CRUISE, TOM

MAPP, ALF JOHNSON, JR., writer, historian; b. Portsmouth, Va., Feb. 17; s. Alf Johnson and Lorraine (Carney) M.; m. Hartley Lockhart, Mar. 28, 1953; 1 son, Alf Johnson III; m. Ramona Hartley Hamby, Aug. 1, 1971. A.A., Coll. William and Mary, 1945, A.B. summa cum laude, 1961. Editorial writer Portsmouth Star, 1945-46, assoc. editor, 1946-48, editorial chief, 1948-54; news editor, editorial writer Virginian-Pilot, Norfolk, 1954-58; free-lance writer, 1958—; lectr. Old Dominion U., 1961-62, instr., 1962-67, asst. prof. English and history, 1967-73, asso prof. English, journalism, creative writing, history, 1973-79, prof., 1979-82, eminent prof., 1982-89, eminent scholar, 1989-92, eminent scholar emeritus, 1992—, Louis I. Jaffe prof. English, 1990-92; Louis I. Jaffe prof. emeritus, 1992—; radio commentator WSAP, Portsmouth, Va., 1947-48; profl. lectr., 1984—; frequent analyst or guest on radio and TV including individual stas. and Universal Studio and BBC radio networks, CBS-TV, 1985—, C-SPAN, 1998—. Host TV series Jamestown to Yorktown, 1975-77; author: The Virginia Experiment, 1975, 3d edit., 1987, Frock Coats and Epaulets, 1963, 5th edit., 1996, America Creates Its Own Literature, 1965, Just One Man, 1968, The Golden Dragon: Alfred the Great and His Times, 1974, 4th edit., 1990, Thomas Jefferson: A Strange Case of Mistaken Identity, 1987, 3d edit., 1989 (Book-of-Month Club feature selection 1987), Thomas Jefferson: Passionate Pilgrim, 1991, 3d edit., 1993 (Book-of-Month Club feature selection 1991), (novel) Bed of Honor, 1995, 2d edit., 2000, Three Golden Ages: Discovering the Creative Secrets of Renaissance Florence, Elizabethan England, and America's Founding, 1998; co-author: Chesapeake Bay in the Revolution, 1981, Portsmouth: A Pictorial History, 1989, Constitutionalism: Founding and Future, 1989, Constitutionalism and Human Rights, 1991, Great American Presidents, 1995; mem. editl. bd. Jamestown Found., 1967—; author lyrics for symphonic composition, world debut with Va. Symphony; author nationally distributed AP editl., 1998; contbr. to N.Y. Times, Wall St. Jour., other newspapers and mags. Mem. Portsmouth-Norfolk County Savs. Bond Com, 1948-51, Va. Com. on Libr. Devel., 1949-50; mem. publs. com. 350th Anniversary of Rep. Govt. in the Western World, 1966-69, War of Independence Commn., 1967-83; chmn. Portsmouth Revolutionary Bicentennial Com., 1968-81; chmn. awards jury Baruch award United Daus. Confederacy-Columbia U., 1976, mem., 1980; chmn. Portsmouth Mus. and Fine Arts Commn., 1983-85, Southeastern Va. Anglo-Am. Friendship Day, 1976, Bicentennial Commemoration of Cornwallis' Embarkation for Yorktown, 1981, World Premiere of Mary Rose Marine Archeol. Exhibit, 1985; mem. grant rev. com. Va. Commn. for the Arts, 1986-87; bd. dirs. Portsmouth Pub. Libr., 1948-58, v.p., 1954-56; bd. dirs. Va. Symphony, 1986-87, trustee, 1987—; mem. taxes and mandates com. City of Portsmouth, 1982-86; mem. adv. com. City Mgr. of Norfolk, 1988-94; bd. dirs. Portsmouth Area Cmty Chest, 1948-52, Va. YMCA Youth and Govt. Found., 1950-52; mem. All-Am. cities com. for award-winning city Nat. League Municipalities, 1976; bd. advisors Ctr. Study Interactive Learning, Pasadena, Calif., 1993—; mem. steering com. Old Dominion U. Friends of the Libr., 1994-95, dir., 1995—; trustee Coun. for Am.'s First Freedom, 1994—. Named Portsmouth Young Man of Year, 1951; recipient honor medal Freedoms Found., 1951, Disting. Rsch. award Old Dominion U., 1987, Great Citizen award Hampton Roads 8 Cities, 1987, Notable Citizen award Portsmouth, Va., 1987; English award Old Dominion Coll., 1961; Troubadour, Great Tchrs. award, 1969; Outstanding Am. Educator award, 1972, 74; Nat. Bicentennial medal Am. Revolution Bicentennial Adminstrn., 1976; medal Comité Francais du Bicentenaire de l'Independence des Etats-Unis, France, 1976; (with Ramona Mapp) Nat. Family Svc. award Family Found. Am., 1980; Laureate award Commonwealth of Va., 1981; Disting. Alumnus award Old Dominion U., 1982; Liberty Bell award Portsmouth Bar Assn., 1985; Old Dominion U. Triennial Phi Kappa Phi Scholar award, 1986, 91; History medal Nat. Soc. Daus. Am. Revolution; Portsmouth Downtown Merchants award, 1984, 85, Nat. Founders and Patriots award, 1995; Old Dominion U. Outstanding Achievement award, 1995; Gladstone Hill Friend of the Arts award (with Ramona H. Mapp), 1995, Richard Hakluyt award for Am. history, 1996; named to Order of the Crown of Charlemagne, 1993. Mem. Am. Hist. Assn., Va. Hist. Soc., Portsmouth Hist. Soc. (historiographer 1975-82, v.p. 1982-84, pres. 1985), Norfolk Hist. Soc. (dir. 1965-72), No. Neck Hist. Soc., Hist. Socs. Eastern Va. (dir. 1971—), SAR, Am. Assn. U. Profs., Authors Guild, Va. Library Assn. (legislative com. 1950-51), Poetry Soc. Va. (pres. 1974-75, adv. com. 1976—), Va. Writers Club, Assn. Preservation of Va. Antiquities, Order of Cape Henry (dir. 1970—, nat. pres. 1975-76), Jamestowne Soc. (chief historian 1975-77, internat. sec. state 1978-79), English Speaking Union (dir. 1976-77), Modern Lang. Assn., Order of First Families Va. 1607-1624 (councillor 1996-99), Nat. Historians Circle, Phi Theta Kappa, Delta Phi Omega (chpt. pres. 1961), Phi Kappa Phi. Baptist. Home: Willow Oaks 2901 Tanbark Ln Portsmouth VA 23703-4828

MAPPS, DESMOND JAMES, information science educator, researcher; b. Pontypridd, Wales, July 23, 1944; s. Cyril and Florence Gertrude (Beese) M.; m. Margaret Elizabeth Gazard, May 28, 1971; children: David, Catherine, Michael. BSEE, U. Wales, Cardiff, 1966, PhD, 1969. Rsch. engr. Data Recording Instruments, Staines, U.K., 1969-70, sr. rsch. engr., 1970-72, prin. rsch. engr., 1972-73; lectr. U. Plymouth, Eng., 1973-80, reader, 1980-86, prof., 1986—, head Ctr. for Rsch. in Info. Storage Tech.,; Sony prof. electronic info. engring. Sony Corp., Yokohama, Japan, 1993—; holder Sony sabbatical chair Sony Rsch. Ctr., 1991-92. Contbr. over 100 articles to rsch. jours.; patentee in field; presenter in field. Chmn. C.R.A.C., Plymouth, 1990-93. Rsch. grantee U.K. Govt., 1973—. Fellow Instn. Elec. Engrs. (chartered engr.), Inst. Physics (chartered physicist). Avocations: chess, travel, music. Office: U Plymouth, Drake Circus, Plymouth PL4 8AA, England

MAR, EUGENE, lawyer, financial consultant; b. Hong Kong, July 5, 1940; s. Timothy T. and Shuh Yin Mar; m. Sara C. Mar, Aug. 5, 1965; children: Christopher E., Jonathan. BS in Metall. Engring., U. Md., 1964; JD, Cath. U. Am., 1969. Bar: Va. 1970, U.S. Ct. Mil. Appeals, U.S. Supreme Ct., U.S. Tax Ct., U.S. Ct. Appeals D.C. Assoc. Philpitt, Steininger & Priddy, 1964-65; examiner U.S. Patent Office, 1965-68; assoc. Arthur Schwartz, Arlington, Va., 1968-72; ptnr. Bacon & Thomas, Arlington, 1978—, mng. ptnr., 1981—, bus./fin. cons., 1978—. Mem. ABA, Am. Intellectual Property Law Assn., Licensing Execs. Soc., Phi Alpha Delta, Phi Kappa Sigma. E-mail: gmar@baconthomas.com. Home: 4304 Victoria Ln Alexandria VA 22304-7400 Office: 625 Slaters Ln Fl 4 Alexandria VA 22314-1176

MARABLE, SIMEON-DAVID, artist; b. Phila., May 10, 1948; s. Daniel Berry and Marsima (Maddela) M.; m. Pamela Joyce Sorenson, June 1, 1969; children: Simeon-David dePaul, Daniel-Dale Christopher, Jason-Andrew Bartley, Jo Anna Lee, Benjamin Arthur Kurtis. BA in Art and English, Lea Coll., Minn., 1970; postgrad., Tyler Sch. Art, Phila. Tchr. 7th and 8th grade art Pennsbury (Pa.) Sch. Sys., 1970-88; tchr. 9th and 10th grade art Charles H. Boehm H.S., Pennsbury, 1988—, Medill Bair H.S., Pennsbury, 1990—; tchr. Neshaminy Adult Edn., 1972-82; resident artist Middletown Hist. Assn., 1976, Three Arches Corp., 1975, also treas.; founder, creator Rivulet Art 2000. Sculptures represented in Albert Lea (Minn.) Libr.; painting in chapel Ft. Dix, N.J.; portraits of Mr. Mike Schmidt, 1986, Mr. Lee Elia, 1986; creator Phila. City of Champs logo; creator children's ednl. programs Falls Twp. 300th Pa. statehood; artwork represented in Middletown Twp. 300th ann. calendar, 1992, Falls Twp. 300th ann. calendar, 1992; creator Olde Phila. Ednl. Program, 1999. Vol. Rep. Nat. Convention, Phila., 2000; mgr. Boys Soccer League, Boys Little League, Middletown Twp.; sr. Babe Ruth coach, mgr. Langhorne Athletic Assn., 1988-89; sr. coach Babe Ruth League, 1989; J.V. baseball coach, 1989; mem. Presdl. Task Force; elected to Nat. Trust for Historic Preservation, 1995; involved with ednl. program Honoring the 200th Anniversary U.S. Constn. Commemorative Olde Phila. Constn. Atty. Served with USAR, 1970. Named Artist of Yr. award Albert Lea Lions Club, 1970. Mem. Buck County Art Educators (pres. 1973-74), Levittown Artists Assn., Nat. Soc. Arts and Lit., Internat. Platform Assn. Roman Catholic. Home: 18 Spindletree Rd Levittown PA 19056-2215 Office: 600 S Olds Blvd Fairless Hills PA 19030-2441

MARACLE, DAVID EARL, electrical engineer; b. Everett, Mass., Mar. 18, 1948; s. Lorne Hilton and Ida Lillian (Davis) M.; B.S.E.E., Lowell Tech. Inst., 1969, M.S.E.E., 1974; m. Linda Elaine Griffin, June 21, 1969; children: Tabitha, Matthew, Timothy. Design engr. Tactical Ground Def. Systems, Raytheon Corp., 1969-71, design engr. Bedford Labs. (Mass.), 1971-75, lead engr., 1975-78, sect. mgr. fire control hardware Tactical Ground Def. Systems, 1978-81, sect. mgr., project engr. for product improvement, 1981-84; tech. dir. Hawk Ground Support Equipment, 1985, radar programs mgr., 1986-95, project engring. mgr., 1986-95, tech. dir. phase three pip program mgr. Saudi Arabian Hawk, 1995—; cons., ptnr. Wheeler & Maracle, Topsfield, Mass., 1974-84; expert witness Fed. Ct., Boston, Isleworth Crown Ct., London. Contbr. articles to profl. publs. Mem. IEEE. Republican. Mem. Protestant Assemblies of God Ch. Home: 4 Apollo Cir Andover MA 01810-2414 Office: Hartwell Rd Bedford MA 01730

MARADIS, SOTIRIS G., telecommunications professional; b. Athens, June 23, 1963; s. Georgios and Aspasia Lazarou M. Diploma in Physics, U. Athens, 1988, MS in Telecomms., 1993. Rsch. engr. Pan-Drive S.A., Athens, 1993-94; telecomms. systems designer Telmaco S.A., Athens, 1995-97; tech. edn. prof., 1997—; cons. SGM Electronics, Athens, 1987-97; translator SGM Graphics, Athens, 1990-97. Sgt. Greek Air Force, 1991-92, Athens. Mem. AAAS, IEEE, Union of Greek Physicists, N.Y. Acad. Scis. Avocation: photography.

MARAI, IBRAHIM FAYEZ MAHMOUD, agronomist, educator, researcher, consultant; b. El-Saff, Gieza, Egypt, Jan. 10, 1930; s. Mahmoud Sayed and Eisha Mohamed Rageb (Abu-Senna) M.; m. Wafaa Mohamed Amin Salama, Feb. 3, 1966; children: Tamer, Rehan, Mohamed. BSc in Agr., U. Cairo, 1950, PhD in Animal Prodn., 1964. Tchr. Agr. Secondary Sch., Moushtohor, 1950-58; demonstrator High Inst. Agr., Moushtohor, 1958-60; lectr. High Inst. Agr., Zagazig, 1960-64, asst. prof., 1964-67, asst. prof. Faculty of Agr., 1967-76, prof. Faculty of Agr., 1976—, head dept. animal prodn., 1972-82, vice dean Faculty of Agr., 1982-85; head Bldgs. Constrn. Coop. Zagazig Univ., Zagazig, 1985-92; cons. Sharkeya Governorate, Zagazig, 1968-92. Editor, author: New Techniques in Sheep Production, 1987, Pollution in Livestock Production Systems, 1994, Nuevas Tecnicas de Produccion Ovina, 1994, 10 books in Arabic lang. on animal prodn., 1965-99; author: Sodium in Agriculture, 1995; gen. sec. Egyptian Jour. Rabbit Sci., 1990—. Head of City Coun., Husseneya, Sharkeya Govt., Egypt, 1968-72; bd. dirs. Omar Abdel-Aziz Bldgs. Coop., Helwan, 1995—, Diarb-Negm Poulty Com., Egypt, 1992—. Mem. Egyptian Assn. Animal Prodn., Zagazig U. Staff Mems. Club, Egyptian Rabbit Sci. Assn. (pres. 1998—), N.Y. Acad. Sci. Moslem. Avocations: swimming, riding horses, fishing, hunting, travel. Home: Khalid Ben Walid St Villa, Prof Fayez Marai U Bldgs, Zagazig Sharkeya Egypt Office: Zagazig U Faculty Agr, Dept Animal Prodn, Zagazig Sharkeya Egypt

MARAIS, ERNST LOUIS, electronic engineer; b. Pretoria, South Africa, Mar. 24, 1968; s. Ernst Louis Henry and Engela Petronella (Germishuizen) M.; m. Karen Alice Opperman, Nov. 6, 1993; children: Marissa, Marius. B of Engring., U. Pretoria, South Africa, 1991. Lab. head time and frequency Nat. Metrology Lab., Pretoria, South Africa, 1992—. With South African Mil., 1986-87. Mem. IEEE, South African Inst. Elec. Engring. Avocation: motorcycling. Home: 377 Grootfontein Country Estates, Pretoria South Africa Office: CSIR-NML, PO Box 395, 0001 Pretoria South Africa

MARAJ, RALPH, Trinidadian government official; b. Jan. 21, 1949; married; 1 son. Grad., Point Fortin Coll., Waparima Coll.; BA, U. W.I., St. Augustine. M.P. from San Fernando West Trinidad and Tobago; min. of fgn. affairs Trinidad and Tobago, 1992—. Host (TV series) Feedback, Book Talk, Cross Country. Bd. dirs. TTT TV, Trinidad and Tobago, 1987-91. Mem. Nat. Drama Assn. (pres.). Hindu. Avocations: arts, theatre. Office: Knowsley Bldg, 11 Queen's Park West, Port of Spain Trinidad and Tobago*

MARAMBIO NÚÑEZ, ALEJANDRO OCTAVIO, lawyer, consultant; b. Las Condes, Chile, July 19, 1963; s. Ramon Orlando Marambio Salinas and Edith De Las Mercedes Núñez Salfate. Baccalaureate, Lycée Carnot, Paris, 1983; Licenciado en Derecho, U. Complutense Madrid, 1989; postgrad. in European law, 1992-93; PhD in Internat. Commerce, Camara de Comercio Madrid, 1990; M of European Economy, U. de Alcala de Henares, Madrid, 1992; lawyer, U. Chile, 1995. Cert. atty. at law. Lawyer Agencia de Aduanas Transiberica, Madrid, 1990-91; lawyer, cons. Estudio Juridico Muñoz Perea, Madrid, 1991-92; cons. fidae Feria Internat. Del Aire, Fuerza Aerea, Chile, 1993; lawyer estudio Juridico Fidel Reyes Castillo, Santiago, Chile, 1994-96; lawyer Chuquicamata Mine Copper, 1997, Estudio Juridico Ulises Aburto Spitzer, Santiago, 1998—; prof. U. Santo Tomas, Santiago, 1995, U. Adolfo Ibañez, Santiago, 1996, U. Las Condes, Santiago, 1998, cons., 1997. Active mem., cons., dir. European Law Student's Assn., 1989-92. With Chilean Res., 1996-98. Mem. Amnesty Internat. (mem. Paris 1981-83, Madrid 1985-88, comision Chilena derechos humanos 1983-85), Colegio de Abogados Chile, Asociacion Gremial de Abogados LAboralistas de Chile, Circulo de Profesionales Hispanicos de Chile (dir. 1994-99), Asociacion Franco-Chilena de Profesionales. Renovacion Nacional. Roman Catholic. Avocations: martial arts, Alpinist, stamp collecting, fencing. Home: Calle Las Hualtatas 9399, 668 1149 Comuna de Vitacura Santiago, Chile Office: Casilla 275 Correo 30, Vitacura Santiago, Chile

MARAN, STEPHEN PAUL, astronomer; b. Bklyn., Dec. 25, 1938; s. Alexander P. and Clara F. (Schoenfeld) M.; m. Sally Ann Scott, Feb. 14, 1971; children: Michael Scott, Enid Rebecca, Elissa Jean. BS, Bklyn. Coll., 1959; MA, U. Mich., 1961, PhD, 1964. Astronomer Kitt Peak Nat. Obs., Tucson, 1964-69; project scientist for orbiting solar observatories NASA-Goddard Space Flight Center, Greenbelt, Md., 1969-75; head advanced systems and ground observations br. NASA-Goddard Space Flight Ctr., 1970-77, mgr. Operation Kohoutek, 1973-74, sr. staff scientist Lab. for Astronomy and Solar Physics, 1977-95; asst. dir. Space Scis. for Info. and Outreach, 1995—; Cons. Westinghouse Rsch. Labs., 1966; vis. lectr. U. Md., College Park, 1969-70; sr. lectr. UCLA, 1976; press officer Am. Astron. Soc., 1985—; A. Dixon Johnson lectr. in sci. comm., Pa. State U., 1990; vis. scholar Univ. Ctr. Ga., 1997; lectr. on astronomy cruises and eclipse tours. Author: (with John C. Brandt) New Horizons in Astronomy, 1972, 2d edit., 1979, Arabic edit., 1979, (with Jacqueline Mitton) Gems of Hubble-Superb Images fm the Hubble Telescope, 1996, Astronomy for Dummies, 1999; editor: Physics of Nonthermal Radio Sources, 1964, The Gum Nebula and Related Problems, 1971, Possible Relations Between Solar Activity and Meteorological Phenomena, 1975, New Astronomy and Space Science Reader, 1977, A Meeting with the Universe, 1981, Astrophysics of Brown Dwarfs, 1986, The Astronomy and Astrophysics Encyclopedia, 1991; assoc. editor: Earth, Extraterrestrial Scis, 1969-79; editor: Astrophys. Letters, 1974-77, assoc. editor, 1977-85; contbg. editor Air & Space/Smithsonian, 1990—; mem. editl. adv. bd. Astronomy Mag., 1997—, Astronomy and Geophysics, 1997—; contbr. articles on astronomy, space to popular mags. Named Disting. Visitor Boston U., 1970; recipient Group Achievement awards NASA, 1969, 74, Exceptional Achievement medal, 1991, Klumpke-Roberts award Astron. Soc. of Pacific, 1999. Fellow AAAS; mem. Internat. Astron. Union (editor daily newspaper 1988, minor planet 9768 named Stephenmaran in honor 2000), Am. Astron. Soc. (Harlow Shapley vis. lectr. 1981—), press. officer 1985—), Royal Astron. Soc., Am. Phys. Soc., Am. Geophys. Union. Office: Code 600 Nasa Goddard Space Flight Ctr Greenbelt MD 20771-0001

MARANDJIAN, HRANT BABKENI, mathematician and researcher; b. Arzni, Armenia, Oct. 12, 1939; s. Babken Karapeti and Antonina Theodor (Timofeeva) M.; m. Julietta Artavazdi Sarkissian, June 6, 1966; children: Anna Hranti, Serge Hranti. MS, Poly. Inst., Yerevan, Armenia, 1963; PhD, Acad. Scis. of Russia, Moscow, 1971; DSc in Math., Acad. Scis. of Armenia, Yerevan, 1999. Engr. Yerevan Poly. Inst., 1963-65; sr. engr. Computing Ctr. Acad. of Sci., Yerevan, 1966-70, sr. rschr., 1971-73, head dept., 1973-85; sr. rschr. Acad. of Scis. Russia, Moscow, 1983; dep. dir. and head of dept. Inst. for Informatics and Automation Problems, Acad. of Sci., Yerevan, 1986—; prof. Yerevan State U., 1974—. Author: Algorithm Theory and Its Applications, 1989, Selected Topics in Recursive Function Theory in Computer Science, 1990; co-editor workshop proceedings: Hungarian-Armenian Workshop, 1987. Head Sci. Experts Commn. of Armenia, 1992-93. Recipient Honor Cert., Armenian Acad. Scis., 1975, Gitelik (Knowledge), 1985. Mem. ACM, Am. Math. Union (v.p. 1994—), European Assn. Computer Sci. Logic, European Assn. for Theoretical Computer Sci., Russian Acad. of Natural Scis. (Armenian br.). Avocations: photography, watch-making, mountain tourism. Home: Babayan 36/20, Yerevan 375037, Armenia Office: Inst for Info & Auto Prob, P Sevak 1, Yerevan 375044, Armenia

MARANO, ANTHONY JOSEPH, cardiologist; b. White Plains, N.Y., Apr. 14, 1934; s. Anthony Joseph and Mary Antoinette (Perrotta) M.; m. Mary Regina Marbach, Aug. 23, 1958; children—Thomas, Kathryn, Michele. B.A., Williams Coll., 1956; M.D., Cornell Med. Coll., 1960. Diplomate Am. Bd. Internal Medicine, Am. Bd. Cardiovascular Disease. Intern Bellevue Hosp., N.Y.C., 1960-61; resident St. Luke's Hosp., N.Y.C., 1961-63; NIH fellow in cardiology Mt. Sinai Hosp., N.Y.C., 1963-64, research assoc., 1964-75; clin. assoc. in medicine Coll. Physicians and Surgeons, N.Y.C., 1970-86; pres. med. staff White Plains Hosp., 1984-86, chief cardiology, 1985-91, chief cardiology emeritus, 1991—, bd. dirs., 1983-88; cons. in cardiology Burke Rehab. Ctr.; med. dir., founder Paramedic Ambulance, White Plains, 1976-82. Contbr. articles to med. jours. Trustee Pace U., N.Y.C., 1975—, Home Savs. Bank, White Plains, 1973-90; bd. dirs. YMCA, White Plains, 1978-82 ; team physician White Plains High Sch., 1967—; cons. physician Dept. Pub. Safety, White Plains, 1968—; cons. physician City of White Plains Sch. System, 1994—; bd. dirs. Westchester County Sports Hall of Fame, 1993—; alumni trustee Tyng Found., Williams Coll., 1994—. Tyng scholar Williams Coll., 1952-59; recipient Outstanding Achievement award Emergency Med. Services Council, 1982; named to White Plains High Sch. Hall of Fame, 1998. Fellow ACP, Am. Coll. Cardiology; mem. AMA, Am. Coll. Sports Medicine, Am. Heart Assn., N.Y. State Heart Assn. (bd. dirs. 1982-85), Westchester Heart Assn. (v.p. 1983-86, pres. 1987-90), Phi Beta Kappa. Clubs: University (White Plains) (pres. 1970-71); Westchester Country (Harrison, N.Y.). Avocations: tennis, skiing, gardening. Home: 46 Eagle Ct White Plains NY 10605-5116 Office: 20 Old Mamaroneck Rd White Plains NY 10605-2060

MARANTA, CHRISTIAN ARTURO, otolaryngologist; b. Geneva, Sept. 1, 1961; s. Arturo and Augusta Theresia (Szabo) M.; m. Ester Mottolini, Oct. 13, 1990; children: Laura Medea, Gian Andrea, Olivia Noemi. MD, U. Zurich, 1986; specialist in Ear, Nose and Throat, Swiss Med. Fedn., 1995. Resident in anesthesia Univ. Hosp., Zurich, 1988, rsch. fellow ear, nose and throat dept., 1989, resident dept. surgery, 1990, resident Ear Nose and Throat dept., 1991-93; resident Ear Nose and Throat Clinic, Lucerne, Switzerland, 1994; ear nose and throat dept. Univ. Zurich, 1995-96; chief resident Ear Nose and Throat Clinic, Aarau, Switzerland, 1996, physician, otolaryngologist, 1996-98; pres. Pro Audito SV, Zurich, 1999; docent med. faculty U. Zurich, 1995-96, resident rep. med. faculty, 1991-93; mem. med. direction Clinic St. Raphael, Kuesnacht, 2000. Contbr. articles to profl. jours. Maj. Swiss Army, 2000. Mem. Med. Soc. Zurich (del. 1994-97), Ear Nose and Throat Soc. Switzerland, Swiss Soc. Immunology and Allergy, N.Y. Acad. Sci. Avocations: sailing, piano, philosophy. E-mail: Christian.Maranta@hin.ch. Office: Goldbacherhof Seestr 29, CH-8700 Kuesnacht Switzerland

MARATHE, BHASKAR, development engineer; b. Mumbai, India, Dec. 31, 1964; s. Vishnu R. and Neela V. Marathe; m. Ashwini B. Dandekar, June 9, 1991. B in Tech., Banaras Hindu U., Varanasi, India, 1986; M in Tech., Indian Inst. Tech., Mumbai, 1989; PhD, Pa. State U., 1998. Exec. engr. Bharat Electronics Ltd., Taloja, India, 1986-87; sr. engr. Bombardier Motor Corp. Am., Grant, Fla., 1995-98; devel. engr. Luk Inc., Wooster, Ohio, 1999—. Reviewer Jour. Fluid Engring, 1998—; contbr. articles to profl. jours. Organizer, vol. India-Fest India Assn., Melbourne, Fla., 1996-98. Mem. ASME, Soc. Automotive Engrs. Fax: 330-287-7299. Home: 2750 Winchester Woods Apt K Wooster OH 44691-2594 Office: Luk Inc 3401 Old Airport Rd Wooster OH 44691-9544

MARAVELIAS, CHRISTOS, marine and fisheries biologist, educator; b. Sparta, Lakonia, Greece, May 7, 1967; s. Dimitrios and Aikaterini (Kaneli)

M. BSc in Biology, Aristotle U., Thessaloniki, Greece, 1992; MS in Fisheries Biology and Mgmt., U. Wales, Bangor, 1993; PhD in Marine Biology, U. Aberdeen, Scotland, 1997. Diplomate on acoustical oceanography; cert. ichthyologist; cert. SCUBA diver. Rsch. asst. Inst. Marine Biology Crete, Iraklio, Greece, 1993-94, U. Aberdeen, 1994-96, 97; doctoral rsch. fellow Commn. European Cmtys., Aberdeen, Scotland, 1994-96; postdoctoral rsch. fellow Commn. European Cmtys., Aberdeen, 1996-97; lectr. in fisheries dept. Agr. U. Thessaly, Volos, Greece, 1999—; fisheries expert scientist Nat. Ctr. Marine Rsch., Athens, 1999—; cons. Inst. Marine Biology, Heraklion, Greece, 1997—; geostatistician U. Crete, Heraklion, 1996. Contbr. articles to profl. jours. Maj. sgt. Greek Army, 1998-99. PhD grantee Commn. of European Cmtys., 1993. Mem. European Soc. Ichthyologists, Fisheries Soc. of Brit. Isles (rsch. travel grantee 1996), Greek Soc. Biologists. Avocations: diving, sports, hiking, music. Home: 45 Kaftajoglou St, GR-11144 Athens Greece Office: Inst Marine Biol Resources, Nat Ctr Marine Rsch, Agios Kosmas 166 04 Hellinikon, Greece

MARAVIGLIA, BRUNO, physicist, educator; b. Pescia/Pistoia, Tuscany, Italy, Apr. 29, 1938; s. Narciso and Nada (Guidi) M.; m. Maria Antonietta Macri, Jan. 31, 1992; 1 child, Beatrice. Master's degree, U. Florence, Italy, 1962; postgrad., La Sapienza U., Rome, 1964. Researcher Nat. Inst. Nuclear Physics, Rome, 1962-68; asst. prof. dept. physics Duke U., Durham, N.C., 1969-70; assoc. prof. Inst. Physics La Sapienza U., Rome, 1970-79, prof. physics, 1980—, dir. Postgrad. Sch. Med. Physics, 1986—, dir. dept. physics, 1992-95; vis. prof. dept. physics U. B.C., Vancouver, Can., 1977-78; dir. magnetic resonance and brain function E. Fermi Sch. Physics., 1998. Editor: Physics of NMR Spectroscopy, 1988, Nuclear Magnetic Double Resonance, 1992, (book procs.) XXIII Congress Ampere, 1986; contbr. over 140 sci. papers to profl. jours.; mem. editorial bd. Jour. Magnetic Resonance, 1992—, Magnetic Resonance in Medicine, 1986—, Applied Magnetic Resonance, 1990—, Solid State Nuclear Magnetic Resonance, 1995—. Mem. Internat. Soc. Magnetic Resonance (com. mem. 1985—), Soc. Magnetic Resonance in Medicine, Italian Phys. Soc., Groupement Ampere (v.p. 1986-94, pres. 1994—). Avocations: skiing, hiking, archeology. E-mail: bruno.maraviglia@romal.infn.it. Home: Via Jacopo Sannazzaro 82, 00141 Rome Italy Office: La Sapienza U Dept Physics, P le Aldo Moro 2, 00185 Rome Italy

MARAVIGNA, ROSARIO CLAUDIO, medical products company executive; b. Catania, Sicily, Italy, Dec. 8, 1947; s. Arturo and Clara (Pennisi) M.; m. Rosaria Marcoccio, Dec. 28, 1983; 1 child, Arturo. Student, S. Caterina, Pisa, Italy, 1958; Classic Degree, St. Gabriel, Catania, Italy, 1966; LLD, Catania U., 1970. Mktg. dir. Arturo Maravigna, Catania, 1970-78; pres. Iniziativa Sicilia, Catania, 1978-90, Gama Sanitas Soc. Responsabilita Limitata, Catania, 1989—, Rhosemberg & Assoc., Catania, 1988—, Phoenix Pharma Soc. Accomandita Semplice, Catania, 1995—; cons. Glaxo, Verona, Italy, 1989—, Esportex, Milan, 1992-94, Lachifarma, Lecce, Italy, 1991-92, Iris Biomedia, Senise, Italy, 1996—; sales ptnr. Baxter, Rome, 1991—. Author: Management Implant in Thalassemia, 1996; contbr. articles to profl. jours.; inventor in field. Pres. Fnaarc Confcommercio, Italy, 1980, Victims of Pub. Adminstrn., Italy, 1995, Sindacato Regionale Fornitor Ospedaliere, Catania, 1996; v.p. Confcommercio, Catania, 1983. Recipient Gold Mercury award Min. Commerce, Como, Italy, 1979. Mem. AAAS, N.Y. Acad. Scis. Mem. Liberty Pole. Roman Catholic. Avocations: big game, swimming, music, golfing. Office: Gama Sanitas SRL, via Aldo Moro No 7, 95030 Catania Sicily, Italy

MARAYE, MITRAJEET D., bank executive. Gov. Ctrl. Bank of Mauritus. Office: Governor Bank of Mauritus, Sir William Newton St PO Box 29, Port Louis Mauritius*

MARAZZITI, DONATELLA, psychiatrist, researcher; b. Baschi, Italy, Dec. 12, 1956; s. Francesco and Maria (Carletti) M.; m. Giancarlo Gambinotti, June 22, 1986. Degree in Medicine and Surgery, Sch. Medicine, Pisa, Italy, 1981. Resident Dept. Psychiatry U. Pisa, Italy, 1981-85; fellow Norwegian Govt., Oslo, Norway, 1983; gen. practitioner Italian Health Svc., Pescia, Italy, 1983-92; asst. prof. Dept. Psychiatry Splty. Sch. Psychiatry U. Pisa, Italy, 1987—. Contbr. over 300 publications in internat. jours. and 4 monographs; author: current Insights in OCD, 1994. Recipient Nat. award Formenti, 1989, Ole Rafaelsen award CINP, Kyoto, Japan, 1990, Internat. award ECNP, Montecarlo, 1991. Mem. Italian Soc. Psychiatry, Itlaian Soc. Neuroscience, European Neuroscience Assn., European Coll. Neuropharmacology, Internat. Soc. for Neurochemistry, Internat. Soc. Psychoneuroendocrinology, European Assn. for Psychiatry, Am. Soc. for Biol. Psychiatry, N.Y. Acad. Sci. Roman Catholic. Home: via 27 Aprile 91, 51017 Pescia Italy Office: Univ of Pisa Dept Psychiatry, via Roma 67, 56100 Pisa Italy

MARBACH, JOSEPH R., political science educator, consultant; b. Phila.; s. Joseph John and Florence Marbach; m. Paula Ann Marbach, June 24, 1989; children: Joseph, Jillian. BA, LaSalle Coll., Phila., 1983; MA, Temple U., 1986, PhD, 1993. Asst. dir. Ctr. for Study of Federalism, Phila., 1990-94; assoc. prof. Seton Hall U., South Orange, N.J., 1994—; co-dir. Inst. for Svc. Learning, South Orange, 1998—; cons. USIA, Novosibirsk, 1993-94, Seoul, Korea, 1999, mem. faculty, Steamboat Springs, Colo., 1995-99. Contbr. articles to profl. jours. Advisor Coll. Reps., 1995—, Seton Hall UN Assn., 1995—. Fellow Earhart Found., 1985-87. Mem. Am. Polit. Sci. Assn., Acad. Polit. Sci., Northea. Polit. Sci. Assn., Turners Orgn. Roman Catholic. Office: Seton Hall U 400 S Orange Ave South Orange NJ 07079-2697

MARBURY, RITCHEY MCGUIRE, III, engineering executive, surveyor; b. Albany, Ga., May 18, 1938; s. Ritchey McGuire and Shirley Kathryn (VanHouten) M.; m. Fonda Gayle Starnes, June 16, 1962; children: Mary Kathryn, Ritchey McGuire IV. BCE, Ga. Tech. Inst., 1960, M in City Planning, 1966. Registered profl. engr., Ga., Fla., Idaho, Ala.; land surveyor, Ga. V.p. Marbury Engrng. Co., Albany, Ga., 1965-78, pres., chmn. bd., 1981—; pres. Marbury, Ritter, Scott & Turner, Inc., Albany, 1970-78, 81-92, Marbury Assocs., Inc., 1991—, Idaho Boise Mission of Latter-day Saints Ch., 1978-81; presenter seminars on total quality mgmt. to nat. convs. of Am. Cons. Engrs. Coun., Design Constrn. Quality Inst., Sml. Firm Coalition of Cons. Engrs., Assn. for Project Mgrs. Exec. bd. Boy Scouts Am., Southwest Ga., 1982—. Served to 1st lt. U.S. Army, 1963-65. Mem. NSPE (Southwest Ga. chpt. pres. 1993-95), Am. Cons. Engrs. Coun., Surveying and Mapping Soc. of Ga. (bd. dirs. 1966-78), Ga. Planning Assn., Home Builders Assn. (bd. dirs. 1985-86), Rotary. Mem. LDS Ch. Avocations: fishing, writing, music, computer, golf. Home: 1824 Green Valley Dr Albany GA 31707-3116 Office: 2334 Lake Park Dr Albany GA 31707-3132

MARC, BERNARD ROBERT, physician, emergency medicine physician; b. Paris, Mar. 14, 1961; s. Maurice and Mireille (Le Careux) M.; m. Brigitte Marie Jouault, May 16, 1992; 1 child, Marie-Agnès. Student, St. Louis U., Paris, 1979-85; MD, Rennes (France) I U., 1990, MPH, 1991; postgrad., Paris XII U., 1989; PhD, Paris Sorbonne U., 1999. Diplomate forensic medicine and scis.; cert. hosp. physician. Asst. prof. Paris V U., 1990-92; sr. physician, specialist Assistance Publique-Hopitaux, Paris, 1992-97, univ. tchg. hosp. physician, 1997—; cons. Masson Editor, Paris, 1999—. Author: Medecine Légale et Toxicologie, 1992, L'internet pour l'infirmiere, 1999, Guide des conduites Medico-Legales, 1999; co-editor: (with O. Diamant-Berger and M. Garnier) Urgences Medico-Judiciaires, 1992, 95; mem. internat. editl. bd. Jour. Clin. Forensic Medicine, 1996—. Capt. Mil. Health Svc., Paris, 1992—. Mem. AAAS, N.Y. Acad. Scis. Roman Catholic. Avocations: tennis, oneology, history, choral singing. E-mail: bmarc@cybercable.fr. Home: 67 bd Serurier, 75019 Paris France Office: CHU Jean Verdier, Avenue 14 Juillet, 93140 Bondy France

MARCAK, HENRYK, geophysicist; b. Las-Zywiec, Beskid, Poland, Dec. 1, 1939; s. Franciszek and Emilia (Skrypek) M.; m. Teresa Furmanska, Sept. 14, 1971. MSc in Geophysics, Acad. Mining and Metallurgy, Cracow, 1964; MSc in Physics, U. Poznan, 1966; D in Physics, Acad. Scis., Warsaw, 1971. Asst. Acad. Mining and Metallurgy, Cracow, 1964-67, chief lab., 1971-74, chief dept. geophysics, 1974—, dir. Geophysics Inst., 1990-96, prof. Geophysics Inst., 1996—; chief lab. Petroleum Inst., Cracow, 1967-71; chief dept. Inst. Geophysics U. Mining and Metallurgy, Cracow, 1973-90, vice dean faculty geol. prospecting, 1983-87, dir. Geophys. Inst., 1991-95, prof. geophysics, 1990—. Co-author: Geophysics in Mines, 1994; contbr. more than 90 articles to profl. jours. Mem. Com. Surface Protection in Mining, Katowice, 1996; country rep. Environ. and Engrng. Geophysics, 1994—. Recipient numerous grants. Mem. Polish Acad. Scis. (geophys. com. 1991—). Home: Strzelcow 21/65, 31-422 Cracow Poland Office: U Mining and Metallurgy, Al Mickierwicza 30, 30-059 Cracow Poland

MARCALI, JEAN GREGORY, chemist, retired; b. Jermyn, Pa., May 29, 1926; d. John Robert and Anna Marie Gregory; m. Kalman Marcali, Oct. 6, 1956; children: Coleman, Frederick. Student, U. Pa., 1948-52, U. Del., 1971-72. Microanalyst E.I. du Pont de Nemours & Co., Deepwater, N.J., 1943-60; tech. info. analyst Jackson Lab., Deepwater, 1960-64; tech. info. analyst Jackson Lab., Wilmington, Del., 1964-67, sr. adviser tech. info., 1967-70, supr. tech. info., 1970-82, 85-89, supr. adminstrv. svcs., 1982-85, cons., 1989-92; retired Jackson Lab., Wilmington, 1992. Sec. Alfred I. Dupont Elem. PTA, 1971, pres. 1972; pres. PTA Brandywine Sch. Dist., 1973; mem. Wilmington Dist. Rep. Com., 1976—. Mem. Am. Chem. Soc. (treas. div. chem. info. 1976-81, chmn.-elect 1981, chmn. 1982, 83, div. councilor 1983-90), Am. Chem. Soc. (com. on chem. abstracts svc. 1983-85, 87-93, mem. joint bd. coun. com. on chem. abstracts svc. 1994-96, 98, 99, 2000, Del. sec. chem. vets chmn.-elect 1999—), Order Ea. Star, Du Pont Country. Lutheran. Home: 312 Waycross Rd Wilmington DE 19803-2950

MARCELLAN, OLGA NOEMI, geneticist, researcher; b. Balcarce, Argentina, Sept. 12, 1964; d. Agustin and Beatriz Irene (Marcos) M. Engr., Nat. U. Mar del Plata, Balcarce, 1988, Magister Scientiae, 1994, PhD, 1998. Rschr./faculty Nat. U. Mar del Plata, Balcarce, 1989—. Contbr. articles to profl. jours. Recipient medal Santa Rosa de Lima Inst., 1982. Fellow Agronomic Engr. Soc., Argentinian Genetic Soc., FIMU. Roman Catholic. Avocations: biking, walking, travel, reading. home: 11-260, 7620 Balcarce Argentina Office: Univ Nac Mar Del Plata, Fac Ciencias Agrarias CC276, 7620 Buenos Aires Argentina

MARCH, JACQUELINE FRONT, retired chemist; b. Wheeling, W.Va., 1914; m. A.W. March (dec.); children: Wayne Front, Gail March Cohen. BS, Case Western Res. U., 1937, MA, 1939; postgrad., U. Chgo.; PhD, U. Pitts., 1945. Clin. chemist U. Chgo.; rsch. analyst Koppers Co.; info. scientist Union Carbide Corp., Carnegie-Mellon U., Pitts.; propr. March Med. Rsch. Lab. etiology of diabetes, Dayton, Ohio; guest scientist Kettering Found., Yellow Springs, Ohio; Dayton Found. fellow Miami Valley Hosp. Rsch. Inst.; chemistry faculty U. Dayton, computer/chem. info. scientist Rsch. Inst. U. Dayton; on-base prin. investigator Air Force Info. Ctr. Wright-Patterson AFB, 1969-79; chem. info. specialist Nat. Inst. Occupl. Safety and Health, Cin., 1979-90; propr. JFM Cons., Ft. Myers, Fla., 1990-93; ret., 1993; designer info. sys., spkr. in field. Contbr. articles to profl. publs. Active Retired and Sr. Vol. Program Lee County Sch. Dist., 1992-93, Lee County Hosp. Med. Libr., Rutenberg County Libr. Wyeth Gastrointestinal fellow Med. rsch. U. Chgo., 1940-42. Mem. AAUP (exec. bd. 1978-79), Am. Soc. Info. Sci. (treas. South Ohio 1973-75), Am. Chem. Soc. (emeritus, Fla. chpt., pres. Dayton 1977), Dayton Engrng. Soc. (hon.), Sampe Soc. Advancement Materials and Process Engrng. (Fla. chpt., pres. Midwest chpt. 1977-78), 60 Dayton Affiliated Tech. Socs. (Outstanding Scientist and Engr. award 1978), Alumni Assn. of Carnegie-Mellon U. (hon.), Sigma Xi (emeritus Fla. chpt., pres. Cin. fed. environ. chpt. 1986-87).

MARCHAL, PHILIPPE, chemical process engineer, educator; b. Villerupt, France, Sept. 19, 1962; s. Marc and Genevieve (Hanry) M.; m. Sylvie Brassely: 1 child, Elise. Degree in engrng., Ecole Nat. Superieure des Industries Chimiques, Nancy, France, 1985; DEA, Inst Nat. Poly. de Lorraine, Nancy, 1985, PhD, 1989. Rschr. Rhone Poulenc, Decines, France, 1988-93, sci. group leader, 1993-96, technol. assoc., 1996—; process and pilot devel. engr. Rhodia Silicones SA, St. Fons Cedex, France, 1998—; tchr. chem. engring. U. Claude Bernard, Lyon, France, 1989—. Contbr. articles to profl. jours. Recipient Moulton medal Instn. Chem. Engrs., 1997. Mem. Group Français de Croissance Cristalline. Office: Rhodia Silicones/USSIL, 55 rue des Freres Perret, BP 22 F 69191 Saint-Fons Cedex, France

MARCHAND-TONEL, MAURICE JOHN, business executive; b. Lyon, France, Feb. 14, 1944; s. Gabriel J. and Juliette M. (Bourganel) M.-T.; m. Claude Jeanne Jeandeau, July 1, 1970; children: Xavier, Aude, Isabelle. BA, U. Paris Sorbonne, 1966; MS, H.E.C., Paris, 1966; MBA, Harvard U., 1970. With Boston Cons. Group, Boston, Paris, Munich, 1970-79; CEO Olivier Cie, Paris, 1979-83, Sommer, Paris, 1983-87, Givenchy, Paris, 1987-91, Ciment Français Europe, Paris, 1991-94, Transalliance, Paris, 1994-97; sr. v.p. Monitor Co., Paris, 1997-2000; ptnr. Arthur Andersen & Co., 2000—; bd. dirs. Souchier Group, Marnes-la-Vallee, France, 1989—. Contbr. articles to profl. jours. Lt. French Navy, 1966-67. Mem. French-Am. C. of C. (pres.). Home: 14 Pl Etienne Pernet, 75015 Paris France Office: Arthur Andersen, 41 Rue Ybry, 92200 Neuilly-sur-Seine France

MARCHANT, FRANK RICHARD, database administrator, state official; b. Waukesha, Wis., Apr. 4, 1952; s. Frank Lockyer and Marcella Virginia (Loescher) M. Student, Springfield (Ill.) High Sch., 1971. Various position main computer facility State of Ill., Springfield, 1977-80, tape media supr., 1980-89, database mgr., 1989-00; lectr. Frank Lloyd Wright's life and work. Performer in one man shows as Mark Twain. Docent Dana-Thomas House Frank Lloyd Wright Historic Site, 1991-00; mem. Dana House Found. Avocations: designing and constructing art glass windows and lamps in Prairie and Usonian styles. Home: 2000 Stanhope Rd Springfield IL 62702-2045

MARCHEIX, FRANCOIS PHILIPPE NOEL, aerospace engineer, industry consultant; b. Paris, Dec. 15, 1967; s. Robert Noel and Madeleine Jeanne (Vialette) M.; m. Norma Resendiz Valero, May 29, 1999, 1 child, Ariane. MS in Aerospace Engring., Ecole Centrale Paris, 1991. Engr. Internat. Nuclear divsn. SGN (Cogema Group), Paris, 1992—; proj. mgr. internat. engring. div. Air Liquide, Champigny-Sur-Marne, 1996-98, product mgr., 1998-2000; industry cons. Societe Generale, 2000—. Contbr. articles to Spent Fuel Mgmt. Seminar, Washington. Lt. French Army, 1991-92. Mem. Assn. des Anciens ECP, Assn. des Techniques de L'energie et de L'environmment, Assn. Francaise des Ingenieurs et Techniciens de L'environnement, Assn. des Economistes de L'energie, Societe Francaise de L'energie Nucleaire, Auvergne Bus. Club. Home: 152 Rue Marcadet, F-75018 Paris France Office: Soc Generale/Tour Risq/Pil, Sec F-92, Paris-La-Defense France

MARCHESE, RONALD THOMAS, ancient history and archaeology educator; b. Fresno, Calif., Mar. 17, 1947; s. John Anthony and Julie Rita (Ferrarese) M.; m. Marcia Lynn Schneider, Apr. 6, 1974 (div. Apr. 1980); 1 child, Stephanie Jo; m. K. Werdin, 1988; children: Alexander Joseph, Kayla Marie. BA summa cum laude, Calif. State U., Fresno, 1970; MA, N.Y.U., 1972, PhD with distinction, 1976; postgrad., Columbia U., 1972-73. Asst. prof. Va. Poly. Inst., Blacksburg, 1976-77; asst. to assoc. prof. ancient history and archaeology U. Minn., Duluth, 1977-87, prof., 1987—; rsch. assoc. dept. classics NYU, 1972-74; evaluator grant proposals NEH, HSF; excavator numerous sites in Israel, Turkey, and Greece; lectr. in field. Author, editor 5 books; contbr. articles to profl. jours. Recipient Fulbright-Hays Sr. Research fellowship, Turkey, 1984-85, 91-92, The Am. Council Learned Socs. fellowship, 1977-78, NDEA Title VI Fgn. Languages fellowship, 1972-75, Spl. Commendation for Excellence award Phi Alpha Theta, 1979; grantee NEH, 1978, 80, nat. Geographic Soc., 1974, Andrew Mellon Found., NSF, Ford Found., 1971-72, U. Minn., others. Mem. NEH, Nat. Assn. Scholars, Coun. for Internat. Exchange, Am. Coun. Learned Socs., Fulbright Alumni Assn., Phi Alpha Theta, Sigma Xi, Alpha Phi Omega. Roman Catholic. Avocations: tennis, golf, dressage. Home: 5789 220th St N Forest Lake MN 55025-9677

MARCHESSOU, HELENE DAISY, English and American literature educator; b. Antwerp, Belgium, Mar. 20, 1939; arrived in France, 1940; d. Norbert and Anna (Schaechter) Bronner; m. François Jean Laurent Marchessou, Sept. 11, 1965; a child, Anne. Master's degree, U. Poitiers, France, 1961, PhD, 1964; doctorat d'etat, U. Paris VII, 1975. Asst. Faculty Arts, U. Poitiers, Poitiers, 1964-69, head dept. am. studies, 1970-84; maître de confs. U. Poitiers, 1975, prof. Am. and English lit., 1977—; instr. Hebrew to Jewish and non-Jewish adults; instr. Biblical Hebrew to Benedictines. Freelance journalist editor Sources, 1980-84, Mires, 1985-94; author poems under name Hélène Bronner, 1998; author: Le Jour dans la Nuit, Hélu Twin Sister's Painting, Le Renouveau du Lyrisme dans la Poésie americaine on William Carlos William, 1967; translator Louis Muhlstock's poems, bilingual edit., 2000; contbr. articles on Am. fiction writers from 1976-87 to profl. jours. Pres. Enquête sur la Tragique Histoire des Internements dans les Camps en France. Jewish. Avocation: sculpturing. Home: 199 rue de la Grève, 86130 Dissay France

MARCHETTI, CRISTINA, medical physicist, hospital department director; b. Venezia, Italy, Mar. 4, 1950; d. Gianfranco and Mariarosa (Morabito) M. PhD, U. Phys. Inst., Padova, Italy, 1975; specialist, U. Politecnico, Milano, Italy, 1976. Physicist Hosp. Med. Phys. Dept., Padova, 1977-78; physicist Hosp. Med. Phys. Dept., Vicenza, Italy, 1979-86, vice head, 1987-89; dir. Hosp. Med. Phys. Dept., Mestre Venezia, Italy, 1990—; expert cons. Internat. Electrotechnical Commn., 1982—; reviewer Radiotherapy and Oncology Jour., Europe, 1989—; instr. Radiographers Hosp. Sch., Vicenza, 1979-89; regional coord. Quality Assurance in Mammography, Italian Nat. Program, 1987—. Contbr. numerous sci. articles to profl. jours. Cons. Civil Group for Nuclear Emergency, Vicenza, 1986-89, Air Pollution Control network of Adminstrn. of Met. area Venice, 1984—, Regional Adminstrn. for Radioprotection, 1996—; mem. councillors Nat. Bd. AIFM (Italian Soc. Physics in Medicine), 1999—. Recipient award European Soc. for Therapeutic Radiol. Oncology, Montecatini, Italy, 1990. Mem. European Soc. Therapeutic Radiol. Oncology, Am. Soc. Therapeutic Radiol. Oncology, Am. Assn. Physics in Medicine, Internat. Orgn. Med. Physics, Third World Assn. Med. Physics. Roman Catholic. Avocations: lectures, music, arts, travelling, animals. Home: S Croce 598, I-30135 Venezia Italy Office: Med Physics Dept Hospital, Via Circonvallazione 50, I-30170 Mestre-Venezia Italy

MARCHI, MARCELLO, plastic surgeon, microsurgeon; b. Rome, Jan. 25, 1956; s. Carlo and Jolanda Marchi; m. Catherine Crowley, May 15, 1988; children: Grace, Michelle, Vincent, Martine. MD, U. Rome, 1981; Plastic Surgery Diploma, U. Catania, Italy, 1988. Diplomate Am. Bd. Plastic and Reconstructive Surgery. Resident in plastic surgery U. Catania, 1982-86; resident in gen. surgery St. Vincent's Hosp. and Med. Ctr., N.Y.C., 1986-88; resident in plastic surgery Baylor Coll. Medicine, Houston, 1989-91; fellow in reconstructive surgery M.D. Anderson Cancer Ctr., Houston, 1991-92; dir. microsurgery unit U. Catania, 1993-95; attending plastic surgeon U.S. Naval Hosp., Sigonella, Italy, 1993—; cons. microsurgeon dept. orthopedics U. Catania, 1995—; attending plastic surgeon Rome Am. Hosp., 1992—; clin. instr. plastic surgery Baylor Coll. Medicine, 1993—. Contbr. articles to profl. jours. Flight surgeon Italian Air Force, 1981-82. Mem. European Assn. Plastic Surgeons, Italian Assn. Plastic Surgeons (Best Reconstructive paper 43d Nat. Meeting, 1994), U. Tex. M.D. Anderson Cancer Ctr. Alumni ASsn. Avocations: fishing, outdoor sports, farming. E-mail: mmplsurg@tin.it. Office: Via Agrigento 17, 00160 Rome Italy

MARCHI, SERGIO SISTO, Canadian government official; b. Buenos Aires, May 12, 1956; s. Ottavio and Luisa (D'Agostinis) M.; m. Laureen Storozuk, Oct. 1, 1983. BA with honors, York U., Toronto, 1979. Exec. asst. to Ron Irwin and Hon. Jim Flemming, 1980-82; alderman City of North York, 1982-84; M.P. for York West dist. Ho. of Commons, Ottawa, 1984—, min. citizenship and immigration, 1993-96; min. of environment, 1996-97; min. internat. trade Govt. Canada, 1997-99; mem. permanent mission amb. of UN and WTO Permanent Missions of Can. to Office of UN, Geneva, 2000—; mem. cabinet coms. on treasury bd., social policy and program review. Mem. Cabinet Com. on Treas. bd., Social Policy and Program Review; vice chmn. North York Planning Bd., Toronto, 1982-84, Standing Com. on Transport, Ottawa, 1990-93; chmn. Nat. Liberal Caucus, Ottawa, 1990-93. Mem. Liberal Party. Roman Catholic. Avocations: reading, walking, fishing, skiing. Home: 50 Westward Way, Rockcliffe, ON Canada K1L 5A7 Office: Perm Mission Amb of Can, #5 Ave de L'Arina, Geneva 1202, Switzerland

MARCHIONE, WILLIAM PHILIP, historian, writer; b. Boston, Jan. 12, 1942; s. William F. and Maria (Salvucci) M.; m. Mary Ann Cuggino, Jan. 21, 1967; children: David, Karen. BA, Boston U., 1964; MA, George Washington U., 1969; PhD, Boston Coll., 1994. Asst. to pres. Boston City Coun., 1970; tchr. U.S. history Norwell (Mass.) Pub. Schs., 1970-98; assoc. prof. history Art Inst. Boston, 1997—. Author: The Bull in the Garden: A History of Allston-Brighton, 1986, The Charles: A River Transformed, 1998, The Italian-Americans of Greater Boston: A Proud Tradition, 1999. Pres. Brighton-Allston Hist. Soc., 1977-79, 85-87; treas. Friends of Boston City Archives; bd. dirs. Bostonian Soc., 1991-92; mem. Boston Sch. Com., 1984-86, commr. Boston U.S. Constn. Bicentennial Commn., 1986-91, Boston Landmarks Commn., 1995—. Recipient Outstanding History Tchr. in Mass. award DAR, 1993, Boston History award Bostonian Soc., 1998. Home and Office: 30 Kenrick St Brighton MA 02135-3804

MARCHIONNA, MARIO, chemist; b. Milan, May 18, 1959; s. Ermanno and Cesarina (Tibiletti) M.; m. Cristina Ferrari, Oct. 31, 1992. Chemistry Laurea, U. Milan, 1982, PhD, 1986. Jr. rschr. Snamprogetti S.p.A., San Donato Milanese, Italy, 1986-88, sr. rschr., 1988-89, rsch. group mgr., 1989-92, rsch. dept. mgr., 1992—. Author: Oxygenates by Homologation, 1994; contbr. articles to sci. jours.; patentee in field. With Italian Army, 1982-83. Fellow Am. Chem. Soc.; mem. Italian Chem. Soc. (v.p. indsl. chems. divsn.). Avocations: music, soccer, reading, skiing. Home: Viale Abruzzi 44, I-20131 Milan Italy Office: Snamprogetti Spa, Via Maritano 26, 20097 San Donato Milanese, Italy

MARCHIONNI, MARK ANDREW, neurobiologist, researcher; b. Yonkers, N.Y., Mar. 6, 1952; s. Andrew James and Carmel Christine (Camise) M.; m. Kazumi Kobayashi, Aug. 4, 1990; 1 child, Kentaro Michael. BS, Cornell U., 1974; PhD, Kans. State U., 1980. Postdoctoral fellow Harvard U., Cambridge, Mass., 1981-84; rsch. assoc. Harvard U., Cambridge, 1985-87; molecular biology scientist Biogen, Inc., Cambridge, 1984-85; molecular biology group leader Cambridge NeuroSci., Cambridge, 1987-96; sr. scientist Cambridge NeuroSci., 1996-98, dir. molecular neurobiology, 1998—; vis. scientist Dana Farber Cancer Inst., Boston, 1998-99; radiation safety officer Cambridge Neurosci., 1987-91, mgr. info. systems, 1987-90; conf. organizer Banbury Ctr., Cold Spring Harbor, N.Y., 1997. Contbr. 45 articles to profl. jours.; holder 15 patents. Recipient NIH tng. grants, 1977-80, postdoctoral fellowship Nat. Cancer Inst., 1981-84, small bus. innovation rsch. grants Nat. Inst. Gen. Medicine, 1979-84, Nat. Cancer Inst., 1997, Nat. Inst. Neurological Disorders and Stroke, 2000. Mem. Soc. for Neurosci., N.Y. Acad. Scis. Democrat. Roman Catholic. Achievements including cloning and molecular analysis of neurotransmitter receptors, cell death genes, neural growth factors and glycolytic enzymes; discovery research program leader on potential therapies for multiple sclerosis. Avocations: sailing (racing and cruising), alpine skiing, gardening, woodworking. Office: Cambridge Neuro Sci Inc 1 Kendall Sq Cambridge MA 02139-1562

MARCHIORO, CARLA, health facility administrator; b. Schio, Vicenza, Italy, Apr. 24, 1960; d. Francesco and Linda (Reghellin) M.; m. Tino Rossi, Oct. 9, 1993. Laurea in Chemistry, U. Padua, Italy, 1984; D in Nuc. Chemistry, U. Padua, 1986. Fellow Glaxo Spa, Verona, Italy, 1985-86; jr. rsch. scientist Glaxo Spa, Verona, 1986-87, rsch. scientist, 1987-88, sr. rsch. scientist, 1988-90, head spectroscopy lab., 1990-95; head spectroscopy lab. Glaxo Wellcome Spa, Verona, 1996-2000, head analytical chemistry, 2000—. Author: Topics in Pharmacological Sciences, 1985; contbr. articles to profl. jours. Dinamite Spa fellow U. Padua, 1984-85. Mem. Gruppo Italiano di Risonanze Magnetiche (bd. dirs. 1996—), Gruppo Italianao Risonanze Magnetiche (bd. dirs. 1997—), Società Chimica Italiana, Associazione Farmaceutica Italiana Gruppo NMR (pres. 1997—), Am. Chem. Soc. Office: Glaxo Wellcome Spa, Via Fleming 4, 37135 Verona Italy

MARCINIAK, JAN JÓZEF, mechanical engineer, educator; b. Tarnowskie Góry, Silesian, Poland, Mar. 10, 1943; s. Jan Antoni and Anastazja Anna (Langer) M.; m. Marianna Joanna Melcer, Apr. 18, 1970; children: Anna, Barbara, Maria. MA, Silesian Tech. U., Gliwice, Poland, 1968, PhD, 1972, DSc, 1982, prof., 1990. Master of the metal physics team Silesian Tech. U. Inst. Engring./Biomed. Materials, Gliwice, 1975-80, dir. sci., 1982-85, master metal sci. dept., 1984-88, dir. inst., 1985-93, master spl. materials and techs., 1991—; pres. Assn. Faculty Mechanics, Gliwice, 1983-88; chmn. bd. sci. Silesian Tech. U., Gliwice, 1985. Author: Biomaterials in Surgery, 1992 (Ministry of Nat. Edn. award 1993), Menace of Electromagnetic Environment, 1995; co-author: Metal Science and Heat Treatment of Tool Materials

(Ministry of Edn. award 1991); inventor in field. Recipient Hon. award in gold Chief Tech. Orgn., Katowice, 1980, Order of Merits for Devel. in the Province of Katowice, Voivode of Katowice, 1986, Order of Merits for the Province of Leszno, Voivode of Leszno, 1988, Gold Medal INPEX XIII, Pittsburgh, 1997, Golden Key Award, London Intern Inventione Fair, 1997. Mem. Assn. Polish Mech. Engrs. (chmn. metal sci. sect. 1971-94, Hon. award in gold 1980), Polish Soc. Biomechanics, Polish Soc. Applied Electromagnetics, Sci. Sect. Polish Acad. Sci., Polish Club Ecology. Roman Catholic. Avocations: music, history, medicine of the East, religion. Home: Staszica 8, 42-600 Tarnowskie Góry Poland Office: Silesian Tech U Inst Engr & Biomed, Konarskiego 18a, 44-100 Gliwice Poland

MARCINIAK, MARIAN, physicist; b. Czarkowka, Poland, Oct. 6, 1949; d. Marian and Janina (Moczulska) M.; m. Halina Janowicz, Feb. 5, 1978; 1 child, Dorota. MSc, U. Marie Curie Sklodowska, 1977; PhD, Polish Acad. Scis., Warsaw, 1989; DSc, Warsaw U. Technology, 1997. Assoc. prof. Acad. Telecomms., Zegrze, Poland, 1978-97; dept. head Nat. Inst. Telecomms., Warsaw, 1996—; chmn. Nat. Commn. Fibre Standards, Warsaw, 1998—; rsch. project evaluator European Commn., Brussels, Belgium, 1999. Author: BPM Modelling of Optical Waveguides, 1995, Optical Fibre Communications, 1998. Mem. IEEE, N.Y. Acad. Scis., Optical Soc. Am. Roman Catholic. Office: Nat Inst Telecomms, Szachowa 1, 04-894 Warsaw Poland

MARCINIAK, TOMASZ, sociologist; b. Chełmno, Poland, Apr. 5, 1966; s. Włodzimierz Jerzy Marciniak and Ingrid Cichowicz. MA in Social Pedagogy, Nicolas Copernicus U., Toruń, Poland, 1991, MA in Sociology, 1994. Sociologist Polish Acad. Scis., Toruń, 1991; rsch. asst. Nicolas Copernicus U., Toruń, 1993. Contbr. numerous articles to profl. jours. Grantee Rotary Found., 1993, Inst. Psychiatry and Neurology, 1996. Mem. Polish Sociol. Assn. Roman Catholic. Avocations: traveling, comics. E-mail: tomk@cc.uni.torun.pl. Home: SW Józefa Str 60/21, 87-100 Toruń Poland Office: Inst Sociology Dept Cultural Studies, Fosa Staromiejska Str 1A, 87-100 Toruń Poland

MARCINIAK, WITOLD LUKASZ, orthopaedic surgeon; b. Poznan, Poland, Oct. 18, 1929; s. Justyn and Jadwiga (Kubanek) M.; m. Zofia Fedorczyk, Jan. 4, 1955 (div. 1973); 1 child, Wojciech; m. Krystyna Bogumila Alwin, Aug. 18, 1980. MD, K. Marcinkowski Med. Sch., Poznan, 1954. Intern, resident, fellow dept. orthopaedics Poznan, 1954-60, adj., 1960-75, docent, 1975-89, prof., 1989-90, prof. dept. pediatric orthopaedics, 1990-00; dir. Inst. Orthopaedics and Rehab., Poznan, 1988-97; head dept. orthopaedics, Poznan, 1988-89, head dept. pediatric orthopaedics, 1989-00; regional cons. Ministry of Health, Poland, 1995-98. Author: Club Foot, 1976; editor: Early Conservative Treatment of Club Foot, 1993; co-author: Dega's Orthopaedics and Rehabilitation, 1996. Mem. Polish Soc. Orthopaedics and Traumatology (pres. pediatric orthopaedics divsn. 1997-00). Roman Catholic. Avocations: sightseeing, recreational activities, gardening. Home: Grunwaldzka 29a/18, 60-783 Poznan Poland Office: Inst Orthopaedics Rehab, ul 28 Czerwca 1956, 61-545 Poznan Poland

MARCINKOWSKI, TADEUSZ, physician, retired educator; b. Wilno, Poland, Oct. 16, 1917; s. Stanisław and Rozalia (Miakisz) M.; m. Maria Aleksandra Rzewuska, Apr., 1944 (dec. May 1975); children: Ewa, Jerzy Tadeusz, Stanisław Janusz Sławomir; m. Wiesława Bortel, July 11, 1981. Cert. physician, U. Poznań, Poland, 1945; MD, Jagellonian U., Cracow, Poland, 1949, MPhil, 1952. Orderly Mil. Hosp., Sochaczew, Poland, 1939; physician, tchr. Ujazdowski Hosp., Warsaw, Poland, 1940-44; physician Country Army/underground, Warsaw, 1942-44; bn. physician Polish Army, Tarnow and Brzeg, 1945-46; regional physician Social Welfare, Inowrocław Bydgoszcz, Poland, 1946-52; head of ward Country Hosp., Poland, 1952-53; head of dept. Pomeranian Med. Acad., Szczecin, Poland, 1953-88; ret., 1988. Author books in field; contbr. articles to profl. jours. Served with Polish Army, 1945—. Mem. Polish Forensic Medicine Soc., Polish Soc. History of Medicine, Polish Soc. Pharmacology, Disabled Soldiers Union. Office: Pomeranian Med Acad, ul Powstańów Wlkp 72, 70-111 Szczecin Poland

MARCO, GUY ANTHONY, librarian, educator, musicologist; b. N.Y.C., Oct. 4, 1927; s. Gaetano Mongelluzzo and Evelyn Capobianco; m. Karen Csontos, July 23, 1949; 1 son, Howard William. Student, DePaul U., 1947-50; B.Mus., Am. Conservatory Music, Chgo., 1951; M.A. in Music, U. Chgo., 1952, M.L.S., 1955, Ph.D. in Musicology, 1956. Librarian, instr. musicology Chgo. Mus. Coll., 1953-54; asst. classics library U. Chgo., 1954; asst. librarian, instr. music Wright Jr. Coll., Chgo., 1954-56; librarian, instr. music Amundsen Jr. Coll., Chgo., 1957-60; asso. prof. library sci., chmn. dept. Kent State U., 1960-66; prof., dean Kent State U. (Sch. Library Sci.), 1966-77; chief gen. reference and bibliography div. Library of Congress, Washington, 1977-78; dir. for N.Am., Library Devel. Cons.'s, London, 1979-81; prof., dir. div. library sci. San Jose State U., 1981-83; exec. dir. Global Research Services, Washington, 1984-85; chief libr. activities U.S. Army, Ft. Dix, N.J., 1985-89; sr. fellow, adj. prof. libr. sci., editor Third World Librs. Rosary Coll., River Forest, Ill., 1989-96; pres. Global Rsch. Svcs., Chgo., 1996—; vis. lectr. library sci. U. Wis., summer 1955; reference librarian Chgo. Tchrs. Coll., summer 1957; vis. prof. library sci. N.Y. State Coll. Tchrs., Albany, summer 1956, 58; guest lectr. library sci. U. Denver, summer 1959; vis. prof. U. Okla., summer 1960, Coll. Librarianship, Wales, summer 1974, 76, 77, U. Md., summer 1978. Author: The Earliest Music Printers of Continental Europe, 1962, An Appraisal of Favorability in Current Book Reviewing, 1959, (with Claude Palisca) The Art of Counterpoint, 1968, Information on Music, vol. I, 1975, vol. II, 1977, vol. III, 1984, Opera: A Research and Information Guide, 1984, 2d edit., 2000, Ency. of Recorded Sound in the United States, 1993, Literature of American Music, 1997; contbr. 150 articles to profl. jours., also book revs.; contbr. Ency. Americana, Collier's Ency. Encarta; music adviser Ency. Britannica. Served with AUS, 1946-47. Mem. ALA, Am. Musicological Soc. Home: 3450 N Lake Shore Dr Apt 3508 Chicago IL 60657-2864

MARCO, MARK CHARLES, safety engineer, industrial engineer; b. Elmont, N.Y., Dec. 11, 1951; s. Peter and Josephine Marco; m. Kathryn Theresa Marco, Aug. 2, 1980. BS, Hofstra U., 1975, MBA, 1977. Cert. safety profl., N.Y. Indsl. engr. Rosco Tools, Inc., Smithtown, N.Y., 1976-84; engring. mgr. Raytheon Corp., Melville, N.Y., 1984-87, safety engr. mgr., 1987-93; safety engr. Pall Corp., East Hills, N.Y., 1993—. Mem. Am. Soc. Safety Engrs. Avocations: tennis, fishing, chess, gardening. Home: 177 Irving Ave North Babylon NY 11703-3911 Office: Pall Corp 2200 Northern Blvd Greenvale NY 11548-1289

MARCO, OLIVIER MANUEL, astronomer, researcher; b. Paris, Sept. 21, 1968; s. Michel and Jocelyne (Donzeaud) M. M in Astrophysics, U. Paris 6, 1992, PhD in Astrophysics, 1997. Researcher Paris-Meudon Observatory, France, 1993-97; mem. adminstrv. coun., scientific coun., 1994-97; tchr. U. Paris, France, 1993-97; astronomer European Southern Observatory, Chile, 1998—; mem. scientific coun. U. Paris 6, 1994-96; mem. French Ednl. Ministry Coun. (CNESER), 1995-97. Contbr. articles to profl. jours. Mem. Soc. Française des Specialistes en Astronomie. Office: ESO Alonso de Cordova 3107, Casilla 19001, Vitacura Santiago 19, Chile

MARCOMBES, ERIC FRANÇOIS, finance company executive; b. Lyon, France, Oct. 31, 1957; s. Michel and Gaetane Marcombes; m. Frederique Labossiere; children: Gabrielle, Amelie, Severin, Paul, Clarisse. Ancien Eleve, Ecole Polytech., Paris, 1981; Civil Engr., Des Mines, Paris, 1983; diplome etudes approfondies, U. Paris, Dauphine, 1983. Assets liabilities mgmt. exec. Compagnie Bancaire, Paris, 1983-86; head derivatives dept., stockbroker J-P Pinatton, Paris, 1987-91; dir., head mktg. making Compagnie Parisienne de Reescompte, Paris, 1991-96; chief investment officer, dir. gen. C.P.R. Gestion, Paris, 1996—. Office: CPR Gestion, 30 rue Saint Georges, 75009 Paris France

MARCONI, PETER PAUL, JR., financial analyst; b. Worcester, Mass., Aug. 26, 1963; s. Peter Paul and Sally Ann Marconi; m. Gail Ann Marconi, Apr. 30, 1994; 1 child, Nicholas Peter. BS, Worcester State Coll., 1985; MBA, Nichols Coll., 1999. Bus. analyst Gulf Oil Co., Canton, Mass., 1986-91; internal auditor Fallon Cmty. Health Plan, Worcester, 1991-97; fin. analyst U. Mass. Med. Ctr., Worcester, 1997-98; sr. fin. analyst Southboro (Mass.) Med. Group, 1998—. Mem. Delta Mu Delta. Avocations: sports, music, travel. E-mail: SkipSMG@aol.com.

MARCOS BARRADO, ANDRES, food science educator; b. La Fuente de San Esteban, Salamanca, Spain, Jan. 20, 1934; s. Heraclio Marcos-Regalado and Avelina Barrado-García; m. María de la Asunción Esteban-Quílez; children: Ana, Andrés, Begoña. Bachelor degree, Colegio M. Auxiliadora, Salamanca, Spain, 1953; Lic. Vet., U. Zaragoza, Spain, 1960, PhD in Vet. Sci., 1964; Catedrático, Facultad de Vet., Córdoba, Spain, 1968. Asst. prof. Facultad de Vet., Zaragoza, 1960-65; assoc. prof. U. Complutense de Madrid, Spain, 1965-68; full prof. Facultad Vet., Córdoba, 1968-2000; prof., rschr. food sci. and tech. U. Córdoba, Spain, 1968-2000; adv. bd. Am. Bibliographical Inst. Contbg. author: Elsevier Applied Science Publisher, Ltd., 1987, Chapman & Hall, 1993; books in field; contbr. articles to profl. jours. Recipient Gold Star award Internat. Ctr., Cambridge, Eng., 1999. Mem. AAAS, N.Y. Acad. Scis., Inst. Food Technologists (Chgo. chpt.). Office: Facultad de Vet Campus U Rabanales, Carretera Nat IV Módulo C 1, 14014 Córdoba Spain

MARCOS SANCHEZ, OSCAR, physician, surgeon; b. Salamanca, Spain, May 31, 1969; s. Nicolas Marcos and Maria Teresa Sanchez; m. Sonia Maria Vazquez, May 31, 1997. Licenciate medicine, U. Salamanca, Spain, 1993, D in Neurosics., 1995. Resident Ramon y Cajal Hsop., Madrid, 1995-99; dir. Maxillofacial Surgery Ctr., Salamanca, 1999—; cons. Sleep Apnea Unit, Madrid, 1998-99, Maxillofacial Dept. San Carlos Ctr., Alicante, Spain, 1999. Author: Autoevaluation in Maxillofacial Surgery, 1999, Manual de Urgencias Quirurgicas, 1997. Recipient Photo Finish award in med. photography, 1997, Ethicon award in maxillofacial surgery, 1999, award Spanish Soc. Implantology, 1999. Mem. Spanish Soc. Oral & Maxillofacial Surgery, Alpha Club for Implantology Rsch. Avocations: martial arts, literature, cinema. Home: Cuesta del Carmen 11-6oA, 37002 Salamanca Spain

MARCOTT, CURTIS ALLEN, chemist, researcher; b. Mpls., Apr. 8, 1952; s. Allen Henry and Marion Lorraine (Grahl) M.; m. Susan Frances Marshall, Apr. 28, 1984; children: Steven, Pamela. BA, Concordia Coll., 1974; PhD, U. Minn., 1975. Rsch. fellow Procter & Gamble, Cin., 1979—. Mem. editl. adv. bd. Vibrational Spectroscopy, 1990-99, Analytical Chemistry, 1995-97, Applied Spectroscopy, 1998—. Mem. Coblentz Soc. (bd. mgrs. 1990-94, Williams-Wright award 1993). Home: 10125 Cliffwood Ct Cincinnati OH 45241-1086 Office: Procter & Gamble Co Miami Valley Labs Cincinnati OH 45253-8707

MARCOTTE, PAUL JOHN, neurosurgeon, educator; b. Ottawa, Ont., Can., Oct. 15, 1958; (parents Can. and Am. citizens); s. Paul John and Elinor Ann (Simeone) M. BSc, U. Ottawa, 1980, MD, 1984. Intern Ottawa Civic Hosp., 1984-85; resident U. Ottawa, 1985-90, asst. prof., 1990-92; fellow in spinal surgery Barrow Neurol. Inst., Phoenix, 1991-92; asst. prof. U. Pa., Phila., 1993—. Contbr. articles to profl. jours., chpts. to books. Fellow ACS, Royal Coll. Physicians and Surgeons (Can.); mem. Congress Neurol. Surgeons, Can. Congress Neurol. Surgeons. Roman Catholic. Avocations: hockey, model railroading, automobiles. Office: Hosp U Pa 3400 Spruce St Philadelphia PA 19104-4206

MARCOVITCH, JACQUES, rector. Rector U. de Sao Paulo. *

MARCOVITCH, MYLES JOSEPH, human resources executive; b. Phila., July 30, 1945; s. I. William and Esther Marcovitch; m. Michele Diane M., Apr. 7, 1968; children: Beth Alyson Salamon, Adam Jason. BS, Mich. State U., 1968; MEd, Temple U., 1971. Indsl. educator Sch. Dist. Phila., Ctrl. Bucks H.S. East, Buckingham, Pa.; mgr., tech. tng. Fischer & Porter Co., Warminster, Pa.; tng. cons. Arco Chem. Co., Newtown Square, Pa.; dir. edn. and tng. Engelhard Corp., Menlo Park, N.J.; dir. workforce devel. Henkel Corp., Gulph Mills, Pa.; chief learning officer Henkel Group, Dusseldorf, Germany. Contbr. articles to profl. jours. Mem. Am. Soc. Tng. and Devel., Deutsche Gesellschaft für Personalführung. Avocations: model railroading, computer graphics, golf, guitar, photography. E-mail: myles.marcovitch@henkel.de. Office: Henkel KGaA, Henkelstrasse 67, D-40191 Dusseldorf Germany

MARCOVITZ, LEONARD EDWARD, retail executive; b. Bismarck, N.D., Sept. 6, 1934; s. Jacob and Frieda Marcovitz. Asst. mgr. Greengard's Clothing, Mandan, N.D., 1955-58; mgr. K-G Men's Stores, Inc., Bismarck, 1958-61, Billings, Mont., 1961-69; v.p. store ops. K-G Men's Stores, Inc., 1969-73; pres. Leonard's Men's Stores, Yakima, Wash. and Billings, Mont., 1973-77; chief exec. officer K-G Retail div. Chromalloy Am. Corp., Englewood, Colo., 1977-81; pres. DeMarcos Men's Clothing, Casper, Wyo., 1982—, Idaho Falls, Idaho, 1984—, Billings, Mont., 1986-96, Twin Falls, Idaho, 1996—, Ft. Collins, Colo., 1999—. Mem. Menswear Retailers Am. (past dir.), Order of Demolay (Degree of Chevalier 1952, Internat. Master Councilor 1953, Demolay Dad 1959), Elks. Home: PO Box 95124 Las Vegas NV 89193-5124

MARCSTRÖM, ARNE OSCAR EMANUEL, physiology educator, researcher; b. Älvsbyn, Norrbotten, Sweden, Oct. 30, 1925; s. Emil and Lydia Anna (Jonsson) M.; m. Ann-Mari Huhtasaari, July 13, 1957; children: Stefan, Peter, Andreas. MSc, U. Uppsala, Sweden, 1953, Lic. of Sci., 1958; PhD, Faculty Math. and Natural Sci. U. Uppsala, Sweden, 1967. Docent, 1967; rschr. in sensory physiology principles dept. zoophysiology Uppsala U., 1953—, dep. lectr. dept. zoophysiology, 1962-72, prof. depts. zoophysiology and biology Edn. Ctr., 1972-91, rschr. in events in insulin secretion, dept. med. cell biol., 1988—; head dept. Zoophysiology, U. Uppsala, 1972-73; mem. bd. Depts. Zoophysiology and Biology Edn. Ctr., U. Uppsala, 1973-89, dir. studies, 1973-87; cons. media resource svc. Ciba Found., 1985-97. Author: Studies on the Connection between Physico-chemical Properties and Stimulating Abilities of some Sweet and Bitter Compounds, 1967, Pedagogical Projects in Physiology for H.S. and Univs. in Sweden, 1972 -87; coord. A New Method for Measuring the Ability of Fish to Orient in Chemical Gradients, 1982; contbr. articles to newspapers and periodicals. Contbr. media resource svc. Novartis Found. Recipient Disting. Svc. Gold medal Govt. Sweden, 1985. Mem. Acad. Soc., Soc. Arts and Scis., Motor Hist. Soc. Sweden. Lutheran. Avocations: hunting, fishing, painting. Home: Höstrångsvägen 20, S-756 47 Uppsala Sweden

MARCU, DĂNUT ION, mathematician, researcher; b. Bucharest, Romania, Jan. 11, 1952; s. Ion Gheorghe and Marta (Hotima) M.; m. Sanda Marilena Borza, Nov. 7, 1986. BS in Math., U. Bucharest, 1974, MS in Computer Sci., 1975, PhD in Math., 1986. Programmer Romtelecom, Bucharest, 1975-79, sys. analyst, 1979-84, sr. programmer, 1984-93, rsch. leader, 1993—. Contbr. over 275 articles to profl. jours. Mem. Decus-Europe, Romanian Math. Soc., Romanian Assn. Artist Photographers, Nat. Geog. Soc., N.Y. Acad. Scis. Avocations: recreational mathematics, music, photography, literature.

MARCUS, BERNARD, retail executive; b. 1929; married. BS, Rutgers U., 1954. V.p. Vornado Inc., 1952-68; pres. Odell Inc., 1968-70; v.p. Daylin Inc., 1970-73; with Handy Dan Home Improvement, Los Angeles, 1972-78; with Home Depot Inc., Atlanta, 1978—, chmn., chief exec. officer, sec., to 1997, also bd. dirs., chmn. bd. Office: Home Depot Inc 2455 Paces Ferry Rd SE Atlanta GA 30339-4024

MARCUS, ERIC COLTON, social psychologist, organizational consultant; b. N.Y.C., July 18, 1957; s. Peter and Esther (Falkenstein) M.; m. Amy L. Glantzman, Sept. 9, 1987; children: Elli Caroline, Lucy Elizabeth. BA, SUNY, Binghamton, 1979; MA, Columbia U., 1982, PhD, 1985. Mgr. bus. rsch. AT&T, 1985-86; internal cons. Avon Products, 1986-87; mng. dir. The Marcus Group, N.Y.C., 1985—; orgn. devel. specialist NASA, 1987-88; pres. Orgn. Devel. Network Greater N.Y. Inc., 1999—. Mem. Acad. Mgmt., Am. Psychol. Assn., Orgn. Devel. Network, Human Resource Planning Soc., Internat. Assn. Conflict Mgmt., Soc. Indsl. and Orgnl. Psychology, Met. N.Y. Assn. Applied Psychology, Sigma Xi. Home: 220 W 93rd St Apt 10D New York NY 10025-7494

MARCUS, KENNETH HEARNE, historian, educator; b. N.Y.C., Jan. 21, 1961; s. Rudolph Arthur and Laura Hearne M.; m. Christine Ersig-Marcus, Dec. 23, 1997. BA, U. Calif., Berkeley, 1984; MBA, Ecole Superieure de Commerce, Paris, 1987; PhD, Cambridge U., Eng., 1992. Lectr. Boston Coll., 1992; tutor Harvard U., Cambridge, Mass., 1992-93, rsch. asst., 1992-93; lectr. Calif. State Polytech. U., Pomona, 1994—, Woodbury U., Burbank, Calif., 1995-99. Author: The Politics of Power: Elites of an Early Modern State in Germany, 2000; composer, musician: (CD) Some American Music, 1999. Scholar Am. Friends of Cambridge U., 1989, fellowship Inst. for European History, Mainz, Germany, 1995. Mem. Clare Coll. Assn., Am. Hist. Assn., Am. Musicol. Soc. Avocations: music, skiing, tennis, gardening, fluent in German and French. Home: 1111 Blanche St Apt 110 Pasadena CA 91106-3018 Office: Calif State Polytechnic U Pomona/3801 W Temple Ave Pomona CA 91768

MARCUS, LAURA KAY, literature educator; b. London, Mar. 7, 1956; d. Norman Geoffrey and Joyce Ruth (Kreeger) M.; m. Richard William Outhwaite, Oct. 28, 1994; 1 child, Daniel. BA in English with honors, U. Warwick, U.K., 1978; MA, U. Kent, U.K., 1980, PhD, 1989. Lectr. U. Southampton, U.K., 1984-86; lectr. U. Sussex, U.K., 1986-87, reader, 1999—; sr. lectr. U. Westminster, U.K., 1987-90; lectr. Birkbeck Coll., U. London, 1990-99. Author: Autobiographical Discourses, 1994, Virginia Woolf: Writers and Their Work, 1997; editor: Close Up 1927-33: Cinema and Modernism, 1998; author, editor: Sigmund Freud's The Interpretation of Dreams, 1999. Humanities rsch. grantee Brit. Acad., 1997-98; recipient Humanities Rsch. award Leverhulme, 1998; Beinecke vis. fellow Yale U., 1998. Avocations: film, theater. Office: U Sussex, Arts B, Brighton BN1 9QN, United Kingdom

MARCUS, RUDOLPH ARTHUR, chemist, educator; b. Montreal, July 21, 1923; came to U.S., 1949, naturalized, 1958; s. Myer and Esther (Cohen) M.; m. Laura Hearne, Aug. 27, 1949; children: Alan Rudolph, Kenneth Hearne, Raymond Arthur. BS in Chemistry, McGill U., 1943, PhD in Chemistry, 1946, DSc (hon.), 1988; DSc (hon.), U. Chgo., 1983, Poly. U., 1986, U. Göteborg, Sweden, 1987, U. N.B., Can., 1993, Queens U., Can., 1993, U. Oxford, Eng., 1995, Yokohama Nat. U., 1996, U. N.C., 1996, U. Ill., 1997, Technion-Israel Inst. Tech., 1998, Polytechnic U. Valencia, 1999, Northwestern U., 2000. Rsch. staff mem. RDX Project, Montreal, 1944-46; postdoctoral rsch. assoc. NRC of Can., Ottawa, Ont., 1946-49, U. N.C., 1949-51; asst. prof. Poly. Inst. Bklyn., 1951-54, assoc. prof., 1954-58, prof., 1958-64; prof. U. Ill., Urbana, 1964-78; Arthur Amos Noyes prof. chemistry Calif. Inst. Tech., Pasadena, 1978—; vis. prof. theoretical chemistry U. Oxford, 1975-76; Baker lectr. Cornell U., Ithaca, N.Y., 1991; Linnett vis. prof. chemistry Cambridge (Eng.) U., 1996; hon. prof. Fudan U., Shanghai, 1994—; hon prof. Inst. Chemistry Chinese Acad. Scis., Beijing, 1995—; hon. fellow Univ. Coll., Oxford, 1995—; professorial fellow Univ. Coll., Oxford, 1975-76; mem. Courant Inst. Math. Scis., NYU, 1960-61; trustee Gordon Rsch. Confs., 1966-69, chmn. bd. dirs., 1968-69, mem. coun., 1965-68; mem. rev. panel Argonne Nat. Lab., 1966-72, chmn., 1967-68; mem. rev. panel Brookhaven Nat. Lab., 1971-74; mem. rev. com. Radiation Lab., U. Notre Dame, 1975-80; mem. panel on atmospheric chemistry climatic impact com. NAS-NRC, 1975-78, mem. com. kinetics of chem. reactions, 1973-77, chmn., 1975-77, mem. com. chem. scis., 1977-79, mem. com. to survey opportunities in chem. scis., 1982-86; mem. math. panel Internat. Benchmarking of U.S. Rsch. Fields, 1996-97; adv. com. for chemistry NSF, 1977-80, external adv. bd. NSF ctr. Photoinduced Charge Transfer, 1990—, mem. presdl. chairs com., Chile, 1994-96; advisor Ctr. for Molecular Scis., Chinese Acad. Scis. and State Key Lab. for Structural Chemistry of Unstable and Stable Species, Beijing, 1995—; co-hon. pres. 29th Internat. Chemistry Olympiad, 1997; hon. visitor Nat. Sci. Coun., Republic of China, 1999; mem. panel on accountability of federally funded rsch. Com. on Sci., Engring. and Pub. Policy, 2000—. Former mem. editl. bd. Jour. Chem. Physics, Ann. Rev. Phys. Chemistry, Jour. Phys. Chemistry, Accounts Chem. Rsch., Internat. Jour. Chem. Kinetics Molecular Physics, Theoretica Chimica Acta, Chem. Physics Letters, Faraday Trans., Jour. Chem. Soc.; mem. editl. bd. Laser Chemistry, 1982—, Advances in Chem. Physics, 1984—, World Sci. Pub., 1987—, Internat. Revs. in Phys. Chemistry, 1988—, Progress in Physics, Chemistry and Mechanics (China), 1989—, Perkins Transactions 2, Jour. Chem. Soc., 1992—, Chem. Physics Rsch. (India), 1992—, Trends in Chem. Physics Rsch. (India), 1992—; hon. editor Internat. Jour. Quantum Chemistry, 1996—. Alfred P. Sloan fellow, 1960-61, sr. postdoctoral fellow NSF, 1960-61; sr. Fulbright-Hays scholar, 1972; recipient Sr. U.S. Scientist award Alexander von Humboldt-Stiftung, 1976, Electrochem. Soc. Lecture award Electrochem. Soc., 1979, 96, Robinson medal Faraday divsn. Royal Soc. Chemistry, 1982, Centenary medal Faraday divsn., 1988, Chandler medal, Columbia U., 1983, Wolf prize in Chemistry, 1985, Nat. Medal of Sci., 1989, Evans award Ohio State U., 1990, Nobel prize in Chemistry, 1992, Hirshfelder prize in Theoretical Chemistry, U. Wis., 1993, Golden Plate award Am. Acad. Achievement, 1993, Lavoisier medal French Chem. Soc., 1994; named Hon. Citizen, City of Winnipeg, 1994, Treasure of L.A., Ctrl. City Assn., 1995, Oesper award U. Cin., 1997, Key to City of Taipei, Taiwan, 1999. Fellow AAAS, Am. Acad. Arts and Scis. (hon., exec. com. western sect., co-chmn. 1981-84, rsch. and planning com. 1989-91), Internat. Soc. Electrochemistry (hon.), Royal Soc. Chemistry (hon.), Royal Soc. London (hon.), Chinese Acad. Scis. (hon.), Internat. Acad. Quantum Molecular Sci. (hon.), Royal Soc. Can. (hon.); mem. NAS (hon.), Am. Philos. Soc. (hon., mem. coun. 1999—), Korean Chem. Soc. (hon.), Am. Phys. Soc., Am. Chem. Soc. (past divsn. chmn., mem. exec. com., mem. adv. bd. petroleum rsch. fund, Irving Langmuir award in chem. physics 1978, Pter Debye award in phys. chemistry 1988, Willard Gibbs medal Chgo. sect. 1988, S.C. Lind Lecture, East Tenn. sect. 1988, Theodore William Richards medal Northwestern sect. 1990, Edgar Fahs Smith award Phila. sect. 1991, Ira Remsen Meml. award Md. sect. 1991, Pauling medal Portland, Oreg., and Puget Sound sect. 1991, Auburn-Kosolapoff award 1996, Theoretical Chemistry award 1997, Top 75 Chem. & Engring. News award 1998). Achievements include responsibility for the Marcus Theory of electron transfer reactions in chemical systems and RRKM theory of unimolecular reactions. Home: 331 S Hill Ave Pasadena CA 91106-3405

MARCUSA, FRED HAYE, lawyer; b. Paterson, N.J., Jan. 31, 1946; s. Harry and Alice Marcusa; m. Andrea Disario, June 28, 1986; children: Michael, Daniel. AB, Dartmouth Coll., 1967; JD, U. Pa., 1970. Bar: N.Y. 1971. Assoc. Davis, Polk & Wardwell, N.Y.C., 1970-79; v.p., gen. counsel The Coca-Cola Bottling Co. of N.Y., Inc., N.Y.C., 1979-81; ptnr. Kaye, Scholer, Fierman, Hays & Handler, N.Y.C., 1981—. Office: Kaye Scholer Fierman Hays & Handler 425 Park Ave New York NY 10022-3506

MARCUSSON, JAN ANDERS, dermatologist, researcher; b. Asele, Sweden, Feb. 14, 1942; s. Anders Eugen and Hjordis Aina (Svensson) M.; m. Margareta Gerd Hanna Hakansson, Sept. 21, 1972; children: Anders, Karin. MD, Umea, 1970; PhD, Karolinska Inst., Stockholm, 1979. Resident Dermato Venereology, Stockholm, 1973-81; mgr. Dept. Dermatology, St. Gorans Hosp., 1982-84, Dept. Dermatology, Hudding Hosp., 1984-99; mgr. dept. dermatology Haukelandsykehus, Bergen, Norway, 1999—. Mem. Am. Acad. Dermatology, Internat. Soc. Dermatol. Surgery, Swedish Soc. Dermatology. Avocations: music, literature, cookig, traveling. Office: Dept Dermatology, Dept Dermatology, haukeland Sykehus, 5021 Bergen Norway

MARCZYNSKI, BOLESLAW, biochemist; b. Andrychow, Poland, July 9, 1947; s. Boleslaw and Agnieszka (Kisiala) M.; m. Christine Pietrek, Mar. 8, 1975; 1 child, Anna. MSc, U. Silesia, Katowice, Poland, 1970, PhD, 1976. Rsch. worker U. Silesia, Katowice, 1970-82; Carnegie trust fellow, rsch. worker U. Stirling, Scotland, 1981-82; rsch. worker U. Dortmund, Germany, 1988-90, U. Bochum, Germany, 1990—. Contbr. articles to profl. jours. Mem. German Soc. for Pharmacology and Toxicology, Soc. for Lung and Respiration Rsch. Roman Catholic. Office: Occupat Med Rsch Inst, Bürkle-de-la-Camp Platz, 44789 Bochum Germany

MARDARE, CRISTINEL, mathematician, researcher; b. Murgeni, Vaslui, Romania, Sept. 26, 1970; s. Lazar and Elena (Purcel) M. PhD, U. Paris VI, 1997. Maitre de conferences U. Paris VI, 1998—. Contbr. articles to profl. jours. Sgt. Artillery, 1988-89. Avocations: reading, dance, travel. Office: U Paris VI Analyse Num Lab, 4 Place Jussieu, 75005 Paris France

MARDER, ABRAM PAVLOVICH, architect, researcher, educator; b. Kyiv, Ukraine, Russia, Sept. 12, 1931; s. Pavel Abramovich and Vera Samoylovna (Fliter) M.; m. Diamara Froimovna Dubinska, Mar. 20, 1955. BS in Architecture, Kyiv Inst. Engrs. & Constructors, Ukraine, 1955; postgrad. studies, Scientific & Rsch. Inst. Theory & Hist. of Architecture, Ukraine, 1964-67; PhD in Architecture, Kharkiv Inst. Engrs. & Constructors, Ukraine, 1971; HabDC in Architecture, Kyiv Tech. U. Building & Architecture, Ukraine, 1996. Arch., chief arch. Design Insts., Kyiv, Ukraine,

1955-64; scientific rschr. Scientific & Rsch. Inst. of Theory and Hist. of Arch. and Town Planning, Ukraine, 1968-77, learned sec., 1977-95, dep. dir. sci., 1995—; asst. prof., Kyiv Nat. U. Building & Arch., Kyiv, Ukraine, 1990-96, prof., 1997—. Prin. works include dwelling houses in Ashkhabad, power stations in Gorodiwche, Andrushivka, Luka, Olexandria, Mala Viska, others, garage parking in Kyiv, bus stations in Sevastopol, Donetsk, Shakhtarsk, Yevpatoria, Yenakiyevo, others; author: Aesthetical Problems of Increase of the Quality of Architecture, 1978, Metal in Architecture, 1980, Aesthetics of Architecture: The Theoretical Problems of Architectural Creation, 1988, Kóv v Architectúre, 1989; co-author, editor: Architecture: Short Dictionary, 1995; contbr. over 60 articles to profl. jours. Recipient First Degree diploma World Archl. Biennial Interarch-83, Sofia, 1983, Gold medal, 1985. Corr. mem. Ukrainian Acad. Architecture; mem. Nat. Union of Architects of Ukraine. Avocations: traveling, drawing, painting. Home: Apt 107 Bl 1 126, 40-Riccha Zhovtnia Av, 127 Kyiv 03127, Ukraine Office: NDITIAM, 9 Velyka Zhytomyrska St, 01025 Kyiv Ukraine

MARDER, CAROL, advertising specialist and premium firm executive; b. Bklyn., Sept. 20, 1941; d. Simon and Sylvia (Rothstein) Cohen; m. Edwin Marder, Apr. 15, 1961; children: Elisa, Steven Alan, Susan. Prin. owner Boys Ego Retail Clothing, Englishtown, N.J., 1974-76; pres. Motivators, Inc., Old Bridge, N.J., 1976-83, Inkwell Promotions Corp., Morganville, N.J., 1983—; cons. Specialty Advt. of N.Y., 1988—. Recipient citation Monmouth County Bd. Recreation Commrs., Lincroft, N.J., 1987. Mem. East Flatbush League Retarded Children (bd. dirs. 1965-69), Marlboro Chpt. Retarded Children (founder, pres. 1969-71, 73-74, bd. dirs. 1971-76), Marlboro Jewish Ctr. Sisterhood (bd. dirs. 1971-73), N.J. Women in Bus., Middlesex County C. of C., Western Monmouth C. of C. Democrat. Jewish. Avocations: golf, cooking, travel. Office: Inkwell Promotions 1020 Campus Dr W Morganville NJ 07751-1260

MARDER, SETH HAUHART, small business owner; b. Oil City, Pa., Apr. 15, 1970; s. Matt Howard and Emilia (Earhart) M. BSEE, Ohio State U., 1992. Engr. Metcalf & Eddy, Columbus, Ohio, 1993-95; CEO Marder Demolition, Columbus, 1995—. Author: (novel) On the Road, 1962. Bd. dirs. Columbus Coalition for the Homeless, 1996-98. Recipient Medal of Honor, Pres. of U.S., 1997.

MARDIS, RICHARD LYLE, television producer and director, production manager; b. Ponca City, Okla., Dec. 30, 1963; s. Richard Leon and Geneva Louise (Peterson) M.; m. Donna Shaw. BA, Cen. State U., 1986; AA, No. Okla. Coll., 1984. Prodr. Sta. KCSC-TV, Edmond, Okla., 1985-86; prodr., dir., prodn. mgr. Sta. KAUT-TV, Oklahoma City, 1986-91; sr. prodr., dir., prodn.mgr. Sta. KOKH-TV, Oklahoma City, 1991—; freelance dir., slo-mo dir. Sooner Vision, 1996—. Freelance photographer John Crowe Prodns., 1988-89, 91, Home Sports Entertainment, 1988-90, Challenger Prodns., 1989, ESPN, 1988-89, Cox Cable, 1989, Sports Comm. Inc., 1985; prodr.-dir. (TV comml.) All Asian Auto Parts, 1989 (Telly award 1990), Cimarron Pottery, 1992-96, Alzheimer's Couch Potato Gala, 1992-99, Muscular Dystrophy Assn., 1992—, OKC Blazers, 1996-98, OKC Cavalry, 1996-97, Tulsa Ice Oilers, 1996-98, IGA Tennis Classic, 1997-99, Salvation Army, 1998-99 (Telly award 1999), Sprint PCS It's Clearly Christmas, 1997-99, (TV shows) Colorado Dreamer, 1985, Snake Charmer, 1986; dir. (TV show series) Around Campus, 1985-86, Camp Kids Club, 1987-98 (Telly award 1997, 98), Spotlight on Oklahoma, 1990-92, Oklahoma Football, 1991-98, The Gary Gibbs Show, 1991-94, OU Sooners Football, 1991—, The Billy Tubbs Show, 1991-94, Discover Oklahoma, 1992-2000, Dance Magic, 1989-99, Carpenters Children, 1994-97, The Magic Forest, 1994-98, Revival for Christ, 1994-98, The Howard Schnellenberger Show, 1995, The John Blake Show, 1996-98, The Kelvin Sampson Show, 1995—, Oklahoma Medical News, 1996, Easter Comedy Show, 1998, (made-for-TV play) Weird Ducks, 1986; launched Fox 25 News, 1996. Democrat. Baptist. Avocations: music, playing drums, aviculture. Office: Sta KOKH-TV 2301 Gladstone Terr Oklahoma City OK 73120-3616

MARDON, AUSTIN ALBERT, geographer, writer, researcher; b. Edmonton, Alta., Can., June 25, 1962; came to U.S. 1985; s. Ernest George and May Gertrude (Knowler) m. Stephanie Ngar Ling Liu, 1996. BA in Geography, U. Lethbridge, Alta., 1985; MSc in Geography, S.D. State U., 1988; MEd Edn. Curriculum and Instruction, Tex. A&M U., 1990; grad. work in space sci., U. N.D., 1990; PhD in Geography, Greenwich U., 2000; postgrad., U. Alberta; student, U. Calgary, U. Grenoble. Research scientist NASA/NSF, Antarctica, 1986-87; freelance writer, 1991—; dir. pres. Antarctic Inst. Canada, Edmonton, 1985—; mem. meteorite recovery expedition, Antarctic, 1986-87; mem. Com. Space Rsch. Internat. Com. Sci. Unions; geophys. con. Stargate Rsch. Lab., Calif., 1999—; self-help network coord., 1999—; adj. faculty mem. Greenwhich U., 2000—. Author/co-author 18 books in areas of space sci., meteorite sci., astronomy, Alberta history, space exploration tech., polar sci., Medieval English history, and geography; contbr. more than 90 articles to profl. jours. With Can. Army, 1981, 85, hist. rschr. and cons., Alberta Culture and Multiculturalism, 1989-91. Recipient Antarctic Svc. medal, U.S. Navy, 1987; Duke of Edinburgh award, Can., 1987; Tex. State Proclamation, 1989; Polar Continental Shelf Proj. Arctic Research grantee, 1988, personal audience with Pope in Rome, 1996, Gov. Generals Caring Canadian Award, 1998, Nadine Stirling award Can. Mental Health Assn., 1999. Mem. Anta. Progressive Conservative. Roman Catholic. E-mail: mardon@freenet.edmonton.ab.ca. Office: Main Post Office, PO Box 1223, Edmonton, AB Canada T5J 2M4

MARECEK, VLADIMIR, chemist; b. Tursko, Czech Republic, Nov. 30, 1944; s. Vladimir and Jarmila (Vrana) M.; m. Blanka Jilkova, Mar. 10, 1978; children: Kristyna, Vladimir, Vendula. PhD, Acad. Scis. Czech Republic, Prague, 1972, DS, 1989. Rschr. J. Heyrovsky Inst. Phys. Chemistry, Prague, Czech Republic, 1972-79, sr. rschr., 1979—, dept. head, 1988-91, vice dir., 1993, dir., 1993—; assoc. prof. Prague Inst. Chem. Tech., 1992—; mem. scientific bd. U. Pardubice, Czech Republic, 1995—; mem. scientific bd. Prague Inst. Chem. Tech., 1991-2000, Charles U., Prague, 2000—. Contbr. articles to profl. jours. Recipient Acad. Scis. Czech Republic award, 1992. Mem. Czech Chem. Soc., Internat. Soc. Electrochemistry. Avocations: sports, music. Office: J Heyrovsky Inst Phys Chemistry, Dolejskova 3, 182 23 Prague Czech Republic

MARECOS, EDGARDO MIGUEL, physician, researcher; b. Corrientes, Argentina, Oct. 13, 1968; came to U.S., 1994; s. Eduardo Amado and Blanca Beatriz (Martinez) M. MD, U. Nacional Nordeste, Corrientes, 1994. Cert. ECFMG. rsch. fellow in radiology Mass. Gen. Hosp., Boston, 1996—. Ctr. Innovative Minimally Invasive Therapy fellow, Boston, 1996-97. Roman Catholic. Avocations: water skiing, skiing, playing piano. Office: Mass Gen Hosp Bldg 149 Rm 5406 Boston MA 02114

MAREE, JACOBUS GIDEON, educational psychology educator; b. Koekenaap, South Africa, Dec. 7, 1951; s. Jacobus Gideon and Maude (Hauser) M.; 1 child, Anton. MEd, Career Counseling, Pretoria, South Africa, 1979, DEd, 1986; PhD, Didactics of Math., Pretoria, 1992; DPhil in Psychology, U. Pretoria, Pretoria, 1997. Tchr. Dept. Edn., Kemdorp, 1975, head of dept., 1984-85; from lectr. to sr. lectr. to assoc. prof. U. Pretoria, 1985-95, prof., 1996—; cons. Human Scis. Rsch. Coun., Pretoria, 1993-97; part-time psychologist, Pretoria, 1990—. Author: (books) Make Your Child Brighter, 1991, Become an Ace at Maths, 1992, Trial Match, 1998; editor: Jour. of Edn. and Tng., 1996—; columnist: (mag.) Keu, 1994-96; radio announcer Sta. SABC and Punt Radio. Maj. South African Nat. Def. Force, 1982. Recipient 2d Afrikaans Lang. and Culture Soc. Book award, 1995. Mem. Edn. Assn. South Africa, Psychol. Soc. South Africa. African Nat. Congress. Dutch Reformed Ch. Avocations: tennis, country music, reading, walking. Home: 1300 Arcadia St, 0083 Hatfield Gauteng, South Africa Office: U Pretoria, Brooklyn, 0002 Pretoria Gauteng, South Africa

MAREE, WENDY, painter, sculptor; b. Windsor, Eng., Feb. 10, 1938. Student, Windsor & Maidenhead Coll., 1959; studied with Vasco Lazzlo, London, 1959-62. Exhibited in group shows at Windsor Arts Festival, San Bernardino (Calif.) Mus.; one-woman shows include Lake Arrowhead (Calif.) Libr., 1989, Amnesty Internat., Washington, 1990, Phyllis Morris Gallery, Many Horses Gallery, L.A., 1990, Nelson Rockefeller, Palm Springs, Calif., 1992, 94, Stewart Gallery, Rancho Palos Verdes, Calif., Petropavlovsk (Russia) Cultural Mus., Kamchatka, Russia, 1993, Coyle-Coyle Gallery, Blue Jay, Calif., 1995, La Quinta Sculpture Park, Calif., 1995, Avante-Garde Gallery, Palm Springs, 1996, Avante-Garden Gallery, La Jolla, Calif., 1996, Avante Garde Gallery, La Jolla, 1996, Carmichael Gallery, Rancho Mirage, Calif., 1998, Art in the Courtyard, Palm Springs, Calif., 1997, L.G.O. Internat. Galerie des Arts Palm Springs, 1998, others; represented in pvt. collections His Royal Highness Prince Faisal, Saudi Arabia, Gena Rowlands, L.A., John Cassavetes, L.A., Nicky Blairs, L.A., Guilford Glazer, Beverly Hills, Calif., June Allyson, Ojai, Calif., Amnesty Internat., Washington, L.G.O. Internat. Gallery, Palm Springs; commd. Ingleside Inn, Palm Springs. Recipient award San Bernardino County Mus., 1988, Gov. Kamchatka of Russia, 1993. Mem. Artist Guild of Lake Arrowhead. Address: 246 Saturmino Dr Palm Springs CA 92262

MAREHALAU, JESSE B., ambassador; b. Dec. 25, 1948; m. Martha Lorerang; 1 child. Student, Chaminade U., Honolulu, U. Hawaii, U. Guam. Asst. fisheries officer, chief marine resources Yap State Govt., until 1980; officer fgn. svc. Govt. of Federated States of Micronesia, 1980—; formerly with dept. external affairs Govt. of Federated States of Micronesia, Kolonia, Pohnpei; former 1st permanent rep. to UN Govt. of Federated States of Micronesia, former dep. rep., then rep. to U.S., until 1990; amb. to U.S.A. Govt. of Federated States of Micronesia, Washington, 1990—. Office: Embassy Fed States Micronesia 1725 N St NW Washington DC 20036-2801*

MAREK, IVO KAREL, mathematics educator; b. Praha, Bohemia, Czechoslovakia, Jan. 24, 1933; s. Marie (Hašková) Markova; m. Eva T. Trnkova; 1 child, Ivo. MSc, Charles U., Prague, Czech Republic, 1956, PhD, 1962; DSc, Acad of Sci., Prague, Czech Republic, 1968. Rsch. fellow Nuclear Rsch. Inst., Prague, 1956-63; rsch. fellow Charles Univ., Prague, 1963-68, prof., 1970—; chmn. dept. numerical math. Charles U., Prague, 1968-94; vis. prof. Case Western Res. U., Cleve., 1968-70, U. Wis., Madison, 1970, U. Hamburg, Germany, 1995. Author: (2 vol. book) Matrix Analysis for Applied Sciences, Vol. I., 1983, Vol. II, 1986.; co-author: (monograph) Mathematical Problems of Kinetic Neutron Transport, 1986. Recipient Nat. prize Govt. of Czech Republic, Prague, 1982; named Honorary Prof., U. Politecnica de Madrid, 1985. Mem. Acad. Europea Scientarium et Artium (Salzburg, Austria), N.Y. Acad. Scis. Home: Vestinska 815, 153 00 Prague 5, Czech Republic Office: MFF Karlovy U, Sokolovska 83, 183 00 Prague 8, Czech Republic

MARELIUS, ANDERS, physics educator, researcher; b. Örebro, Sweden, Oct. 14, 1938; m. Ingrid Magnusson; 1 child, John. PhD, Uppsala U., 1968. From lectr. to asst. prof. Uppsala (Sweden) U., 1968—, head dept. physics, 1990-95; rector Dalarna U. Coll., 1995-97. Office: Uppsala U Dept Physics, Box 530, S-75121 Uppsala Sweden

MARELLA, PHILIP DANIEL, broadcasting company executive; b. Italy, Sept. 9, 1929; came to U.S., 1930; s. T. Joseph and Julia (Santolina) M.; m. Lucinda Minor, Dec. 30, 1955; children: Philip Daniel, Laura Ann, William Scott. BS, Calif. State U., 1955; MS, Syracuse U., 1956. Account exec. WGR-TV, Buffalo, 1956-57; account exec., sales mgr. WIIC-TV, Pitts., 1957-66; gen. mgr. WCHS-TV, Charleston, W.Va., 1966-68; v.p. radio and television Rollins, Inc., Atlanta, 1968-70; pres. WAVY-TV, Inc., Tidewater, Va., 1970—; v.p. ops. Lin Broadcasting, Inc., N.Y.C.; also dir.; pres., owner WMGC-TV, Binghamton, N.Y., 1978-86; CEO, pres. Pinnacle Comm., Inc., 1987—; CEO Pinnacle Broadcasting Co., 1987; owner radio stas. WFXC-FM, WDUR, WFXK, Raleigh, N.C., WRNS-AM-FM, WANG-FM, WMSQ-AM, WERO-FM, WCPQ, WDLX-AM, Coastal, N.C., WKOO-FM, WKJA-FM, Jacksonville, N.C., WYAV-FM, WRNN-FM, WMYB-FM, WYAK-FM, Myrtle Beach, S.C., KLLL-AM-FM, KONE-FM, KMMX-FM, Lubbock, Tex., WYNG-FM, Evansville, Ind., WSOY-AM-FM, WDZQ-FM, WDZ-AM, WCZQ-FM, Decatur, Ill., WPXX-FM, Danville, Va.; bd. dirs. Radio Advt. Bur., N.C. Assn. Broadcasters. Bd. dirs. Salvation Army, 1966-68; bd. dirs., v.p. United Fund; bd. dirs. Portsmouth chpt. ARC, Tidewater Regional Health and Planning Commn.; bd. dirs., v.p. Binghamton Symphony. Served with USMC, 1948-49, 50-52. Mem. Nat. Assn. Broadcasters (v.p., radio advt. bd. dirs.), Va. Assn. Broadcasters, N.C. Assn. Broadcasters (bd. dirs.), Nat. Adv. Bur. (bd. dirs.), Variety Club Pitts., Radio and TV Club, Portsmouth C. of C. (pres.-elect), Norfolk C. of C., Newport News C. of C., Cavalier Golf and Yacht Club (Virginia Beach, Va.), N.Y. Athletic Club, Binghamton Country Club. Home: 2073 Cheshire Rd Binghamton NY 13903-3199 also: Central Pk Pl 301 W 57th St Apt 43C New York NY 10019-3180

MARENGHI, ALBERTO, business executive; b. Rome, Dec. 22, 1976; s. Franco and Cristina (Merciai) M. PhD, U. Florence, 1990. Mng. dir. Cartiera Mantovana Srl, Mantova, Italy, 1996—, Marenghi 1690 Srl, Mantova, 1998, La Pila, Mantova, 1996; sport car journalist ACI, Mantova, 1996—; mem. exec. bd. Assocarta, Milan, 1998, Gruppo Giovani Industriali, Mantova, 1997, Comitato Piccola Industria, Mantova, 1996, Costituente Giovani UCID, Rome, 1997, Economy Commn. of Giovani Industriali di Confidustria, Rome, 1997, Gruppo Giovani Industria di Federlombardia, Milan, 1997. Mem. Round Table. Avocations: skiing, tennis, sports cars. Home: Via Principe Amedeo 17, 46100 Mantovana Italy

MARENGO, MARC MICHAEL ROGERS, diplomat, United Nations ambassador; b. Anse Royale, Seychelles, Aug. 9, 1955; s. Marie Marengo. BA in Polit. Sci., Marymount Manhattan Coll., N.Y.C., 1993; MS in Social Scis., L.I U., 1994. Protocol officer Seychelles Ministry Fgn. Affairs, 1977-80, sr. protocol officer, 1980-82; desk officer consular, Am. and commonwealth affairs Seychelles Ministry Planning and External Rels., 1982-86; chargé d'affaires ad interim Seychelles Embassy, Paris, 1986-87; chargé d'affaires ad interim Seychelles Mission to UN, N.Y.C., 1987-93, permanent rep.; chargé d'affaires ad interim Seychelles Embassy, Washington, 1987-93, amb. to U.S., 1993—; acting high commr. Seychelles High Commn. to Can., 1989-93, high commr., 1993—; Seychelles rep. at numerous internat. confs. and meetings; Seychelles vice chmn. 9 regular sessions UN Gen. Assembly, 1987-95; del. UN Conf. on Environ. and Devel., 1992. Office: 235 E 40th St Apt 24A New York NY 10016-1752

MAREŠ, STANISLAV, geophysics educator, researcher; b. Poříčí, Czech Republic, Nov. 1, 1932; s. Antonín and Anna (Smejkal) M.; m. Marie Hulík, May 20, 1962; children: Pavel, Tomáš, Jan, Marie. MS, Charles U., Prague, Czech Republic, 1956, PhD, 1968. Cert. geophysicist. Lectr., sr. lectr. Charles U., Prague, 1956-60; rschr. Geoindustria Co., Prague, 1962-67; rschr. Charles U., Prague, 1967-69, scientist, 1969-75, sr. scientist, 1975-91, prof., 1991—; dir. Inst. Geol. Scis., Charles U., Prague, 1991-94. Editor: Geophysical Methods in Hydrogeology and Engineering Geology, 1983 (Rector's award 1983), Introduction to Applied Geophysics, 1984, Applied Geophysics in Environmental Engineering and Science, 1997. Named Meritorious Rschr. of Czech Geol. Svc., Czech Geol. Office, 1982. Mem. Mineral and Geotech. Logging Soc., Near-surface Geophysics (now named Soc. Exploration Geophysicists), Environ. and Engring. Geophys. Soc. Roman Catholic. Avocations: hiking, gardening, skiing. Home: Ouholická 453/35, CZ181 00 Prague 8, Czech Republic Office: Charles U Faculty Sci, Albertov 6, CZ128 43 Prague 2, Czech Republic

MARESCA, ESTEBAN MIGUEL, construction company executive, consultant; b. Buenos Aires, Jan. 29, 1940; s. Antonino Rafael and Maria Juana (Ditone) M.; m. Adriana Eva Zecca, Apr. 15, 1971; children: Flavia L., Marina G., Maximiliano E., Gabriel G., Leonardo V., Fabricio D. Diploma in civil engring., U. Buenos Aires, 1968; M in internat. rels., UNA, Buenos Aires, 1988. Gen. ops. dir. Ing. A.H. Spinazzola, Buenos Aires, 1979-83; prodn. dir. Sitra S.A., Buenos Aires, 1983-88; gen. dir. Ferrovias, Buenos Aires, 1994; mng. dir., CEO Roman Ingenieria, Buenos Aires, 1995, A.H.S. Group, 1995-97; mng. dir., CEO railway concessions CNRT, 1997—; spl. commn. mem. Ctrl. Bd. Engring. Architecture and Surveying Profl. Couns., Buenos Aires, 1966-70. Contbr. articles to profl. jours. Pres. Assn. Exalumnos En/De IV Buenos Aires, 1963-71, Club Social de la Boca, Buenos Aires, 1992—. Soldier EMGE, 1961-62. Fellow CPIC; mem. CABJ (hon.), Union de La Boca (hon.), Argentine Med. Assn. (hon.), Argentine Constrn. Assn. (dir. 1964-70), Nat. Registry Constrn. Industry (dep. advisor 1966-68), Builders Assn. (v.p. 1962-75), Assn. Ligure Argentina, Centro Naval. Roman Catholic. Avocations: classical music, opera, jogging, golf. Home: Juan M Aranguren 1326, 1405 Buenos Aires Argentina Office: CNRT, Maipú 88 Piso 5, 1084 Buenos Aires Argentina

MARES-GUIA, MARCOS LUIZ, biochemist, consultant; b. Santa Barbara, Brazil, June 3, 1935; came to U.S., 1994; s. Jose Maria and Judith (Coelho) M-G.; m. Henriqueta Martins, May 22, 1959; children: Frederico, Christiana, Juliana, Luciana, Tatiana, Fabiana. MD, Fed. U. Minas Gerais, Belo Horizonte, Brazil, 1958; PhD, Tulane U., 1964. Prof. Biochemistry Fed. U. Minas Gerais, Belo Horizonte, 1958-93; emeritus prof., 2000—; v.p. rsch. Biobras S.A., Belo Horizonte, 1971-93; pres. Biomm, Inc., Miami, Fla., 1993—; cons. Diabetes Rsch. Inst., U. Miami, 1994—; bd. dirs. Biobras S.A., 1994—. Patentee in field. Recipient Order of Scientific Merit Ministry of Sci., Brasilia, 1992. Mem. Am. Chem. Soc., N.Y. Acad. Scis., Brazilian Acad. Scis. Achievements: founder of Biobras S.A., 1971; co-founder Pythagoras Ednl. Sys. in Brazil, 1966; founder of Biomm, Inc., 1993; work on active ctr. chemistry of proteolytic enzymes. Office: Biomm Inc 14775 SW 132nd Pl Miami FL 33186-7685

MARET, KARL HELMUTH, medical research corporation executive, consultant; b. Hamburg, Germany, Apr. 14, 1948; came to U.S., 1961; s. Erich Paul and Margot Kathe Frida (Eckert) M.; m. Ann Sauer, Feb. 23, 1978 (div. Jan. 1980). Diploma in engring., Meml. U. Newfoundland, St. John's, Can., 1967; BScEE, Queens U., Kingston, Ont., Can., 1969; M Engring., U. Toronto, Ont., 1974, MD, 1977. Registered profl. engr., Ont. Postdoctoral fellow U. Calif., San Diego, 1978-82; pres. Maret Cons. Svcs., San Diego, 1982—, Eukroisis Aesentis, San Diego, 1985-97; pres., CEO Fashioners of Manas, Inc., San Diego, 1983-94, Dove Health Alliance, Inc., Aptos, Calif., 1995—; biomed. engring. cons. St. Michael's Hosp., Toronto, 1974-76; biomed. engring. dir., mem. Am. Med. Rsch. Expdn. to Mt. Everest, 1978-81; lectr. Pacific Coll. Oriental Medicine, San Diego, 1986-87; instr. Inst. for Psychostructural Balancing, San Diego, 1989-92. Contbr. articles to profl. publs. Bd. dirs. City Moves Dance Found., San Diego, 1996. Capt. Can. Air Force, 1965-73. Francis B. Parker fellow U. Calif., San Diego, 1978-82. Mem. Internat. Soc. for Study of Subtle Energy and Energy Medicine. Avocations: musical composition, astrology, teaching, nutritional consulting, anthroposophy. Fax: (831) 688-8898. Office: Dove Health Alliance 430 Cliff Dr Aptos CA 95003-5121

MARETH, PAUL DAVID, communications consultant; b. N.Y.C., Nov. 16, 1945; s. Josef Gleicher and Elisabeth Gay; m. Evelyn Heineman, Dec. 26, 1968 (div. 1980); children: Leda J., Joanna R. BA, Brandeis U., 1967; MFA, UCLA, 1969. Lectr. U. Pitts., 1976-77; asst. prof. communications Temple U., Phila., 1977-81; vis. faculty fellow in history of sci. Princeton (N.J.) U., 1981-82; founder, owner Projections Co., White Plains, N.Y., 1982—; cons. IBM, RCA, Bell Labs., Ednl. Testing Svc., Children's TV Workshop, Prodigy. Contbr. to Acad. Am. Ency., 1985—, Channels of Communications, 1983-85; editorial advisor IEEE Jour., IEEE Spectrum, 1983-84; contbr. numerous articles to profl. jours. Bd. dirs. Westchester Choral Soc., 1991-95. Grantee WGBH Pub. TV, Boston, 1974, Swedish Film Inst./Swedish Broadcasting Corp., 1973, Pa. Coun. on the Arts, 1976, 79. Mem. Soc. Motion Picture and TV Engrs., Internat. Interactive Communications Soc. (chmn. program com. 1987-90), Univ. Film/Video Assn. Avocation: choral singing. Office: Projections Co 45 S Clover St Poughkeepsie NY 12601-3004

MARFIL, SILVINA ANDREA, geology educator; b. Buenos Aires, June 7, 1963; d. Fidelio Rubén and Hilda Berta (Fabiani) M.; m. Rodolfo Claudio Salomón, Dec. 29, 1988; children: Salomón, Frederico José. Lic. in geology, South Nat. U., Bahía Blanca, Argentina, 1985, D Geology, 1990. Lectr. South Nat. U., 1985—; fellow Commn. Sci. Rsch., Bahía Blanca, 1986-88, CIC, Bahía Blanca, 1988-91; asst. rschr. CIC, 1991-94, rschr., 1994—. Mem. N.Y. Acad. Scis. Home: Almafuerte 1330, 8000 Bahia Blanca Argentina Office: U Nat del Sur Dept Geology, San Juan 670, 8000 Bahia Blanca Argentina

MARGALLO, AGNES ATUTUBO, biology educator; b. Legaspi City, Philippines, Apr. 10, 1945; d. Vicente Padilla and Natividad Garcia (Rendon) A.; m. Edgar Loria Margallo, Dec. 16, 1972 (dec. Apr. 1998); children: Christine, Edgar Jr., Raymund Adrian. MA in Teaching, U. Philippines, 1972; EdD, Bicol U., Philippines, 1997. Asst. prof. Bicol U. Coll. Edn., Philippines, 1975-82, assoc. prof., 1982-91, prof., 1991—; tng. & curriculum devel. officer Civol U. Regional Sci. Teaching Ctr., Philippines, 1993—; prof. Bicol U. Grad. Sch., Philippines, 1994—. Author: Growth of Cassava Cuttings of Different Morphological Ages in Relation to the Teaching of Vegetative Propagation in Secondary School Biology, 1988, The Bicol University Regional Science Teaching Center: Its Status and Prospects, 1997; contbr. articles to profl. jours. Mem. Philippine Assn. Sci. & Math. (life), Sci Club Advisors Assn. Philippines, Nat. Biology Tchrs. Assn., Regional Biology Tchrs. Assn., U. Philippines Alumni Assn (life). Avocations: collecting coins, music, reading, gardening, hiking. Home: 1521 Banag Daraga Albay, Region 5 4501, Philippines Office: Bicol U, Regional Sci Teaching Ctr, Legaspi City 4500, Philippines

MARGARET, PRINCESS (ROSE MARGARET), Countess of Snowdon; b. Glamis Castle, Scotland, Aug. 21, 1930; d. King George VI of Eng. and Queen Elizabeth; m. Anthony Charles Robert Armstrong-Jones, 1st Earl Snowdon, May 6, 1960 (div. 1978); children: David Albert Charles (Viscount Linley), Lady Sarah Frances Elizabeth. DMus, U. London, 1957; LLD, U. Keele, 1962, U. Cambridge. Pres., Friends of the Elderly, Invalid Children's Aid Nationwide (chmn. of the council), also Royal Ballet, National Society for the Prevention Cruelty to Children, The Guide Assn., Scottish Children's League, Victoria League, Horder Centres for Arthritis, English Folk Dance and Song Soc.; hon. pres. Brit. Mus. Devel. Trust; joint pres. of Lowland Brigade Club; patron of Brit. and Internat. Sailor's Soc. Ladies' Guild, English Harbour Repair Fund (patron-in-chief), Queen Alexandra's Royal Army Nursing Corps Assn., Bristol Royal Soc. for the Blind, Friends of St. John's, also the patron of the Friends of Southwark Cathedral, Light Inf. Club, St. Margaret's Chapel (Edinburgh Castle) Guild, Olave Baden-Powell Soc., Mustique Edn. Trust, Tenovus (Inst. for Cancer Rsch.), Royal Coll. Nursing, Assn. Anaesthetists of Gt. Britain and Ireland, Friends of Iveagh Bequest, Kenwood, Heart Disease and Diabetes Rsch. Trust, London Lighthouse, Purine Rsch. Lab., Migraine Trust Nat. Pony Soc., Princess Margaret Rose Hosp. (Edinburgh), Svcs. Sound and Vision Corp., Barrister's Benevolent Assn. Mary Hare Grammer Sch. for the Deaf, Suffolk Regimental Assn., Youth Clubs Scotland, Scottish Community Drama Assn., Peckham Settlement, Zebra trust U. London; grand pres. St. John Ambulance;dep. col.-in-chief Royal Anglian Regt.; col.-in-chief Queen Alexandra's Royal Army Nursing Corps, Highland Fusiliers Can., Princess Louise Fusilers, Royal Highland Fusiliers; liveryman Haberdashers' Co.; freeman City London; hon. pres. British Mus. Devel. Trust; patron London Lighthouse, Purine Rsch. Lab., Zebra Trust. Decorated Gold Chain and Grand Cross of Royal Victorian Order, Order Crown India, Dame Grand Cross Order of St. John of Jerusalem, Order of Crown, Lion and spears Toro Kingdon, Grand Cross Order of Lion (Netherlands); Order Brilliant Star of Zanzibar 1st class, grand cross Order of Crown of Belgium, Grand Cross 1st class Order of Merit (Republic of Germany); Order of Precious Crown 1st class (Japan); named hon. air comdr. Royal Air Force Coningsby. Hon. fellow Royal Soc. London (life); fellow Royal Coll. Surgeons Eng., Royal College Obstetricians and Gynecologists; hon. mem. Automobile Assn., Order of Inst. Brit. Architects. Royal Soc. Medicine, Soc. London Road, Royal Automobile Club, Air Force Club (life); life mem. Brit. Legion (women's sect.); hon. mem., patron Grand Antiquity Assn. of Glasgow; mem. Royal Scottish Soc. for the Prevention of Cruelty to Children (pres.), Order of Road.

MARGARÉTHA, HERBERT MORIZ PAUL MARIA, chemical consultant; b. Vienna, Austria, Oct. 29, 1911; s. Eugen and Katharina (Seidel) M.; m. Christine Veronica Mauthner, Sept. 14, 1940; children: Elisabeth, Pavl. LLD, U. Vienna. Dir. Magyar Textil Festogyar, Budapest, 1938-40; supt. Magyar Poszto Gyar, Budapest, 1940-44; tech. svc. rep. Ciba Ag, Rio de Janeiro, 1948-58; mem. bd. Danubia Petrochemie, Schwechat, 1958-63; dir. Gebrueder Schoeller, Vienna, 1963-65; mem. bd. Montana Ag, Vienna, 1965-75, Jungbunzlauer Ag, Vienna, 1967-70; ret. Jung Bunzlauer Ag, Vienna, 1970. Contbr. articles to profl. jours. Mem. Am. Chem. Soc., Alt-Hietzinger (v.p. 1965—), Techniker Cercle (pres. 1982-88, honor pres. 1988). Home and Office: 97 Hietzinger Hauptstr, A-1130 Vienna Austria

MARGARITONDO, GIORGIO, physics educator; b. Rome, Aug. 24, 1946; arrived in Switzerland, 1990; s. Giuseppe and Maria Luisa (Averardi) M.; m. Marina Savalli, Sept. 1, 1971; children: Laura, Francesca. PhD in Physics,

U. Rome, 1969. Staff scientist Italian Nat. Rsch. Coun., Rome, 1971-78; resident visitor Bell Labs., Murray Hill, N.J., 1975-77; from asst. prof. to assoc. to prof. physics U. Wis., Madison, 1978-90, assoc. dir. Synchrotron Radiation Ctr., 1984-90; prof. physics Swiss Fed. Poly., Lausanne, 1990-96, dir. Inst. Applied Physics, 1990-96, 2000—; vis. prof. physics Vanderbilt U., Nashville, 1990—; sci. dir. Sincrotrone Trieste, Italy, 1995-98; coord. European Round Table for Synchrotron Radiation, 1997—. Contbr. articles to profl. jours. Served to 2nd lt. Italian Army, 1972-73. Recipient Yarwood meml. Brit. Vacuum Coun., 1995; Romnes Found. fellow, 1983, McMinn Found. fellow, 1994. Fellow Am. Phys. Soc., Am. Vacuum Soc., Inst. Physics; mem. AAAS, European Phys. Soc., Swiss Phys. Soc., Italian Phys. Soc. Roman Catholic. Avocations: classical music, antiques, art, watches. Home: Rt du Signal 21, CH-1018 Lausanne Switzerland Office: Ecole Poly Fédérale, Institut de Physique Appliquée, CH-1015 Lausanne Switzerland

MARGÉOT, JEAN CARDINAL, bishop; b. Quatre-Bornes, Mauritius, Feb. 3, 1916. Student, Royal Coll. Curepipe, Mauritius, B in Philosophy, 1935; Licentiate in Theology, Gregorian U., Rome, 1939. Ordained priest Roman Cath. Ch., 1938. Priest, 1938—, vicar gen., 1956, bishop, 1969, nominated cardinal, 1988. Decorated Chevalier de l'Ordre Nat. de la Légion d'Honneur, 1988; named Hon. Citizen Town of Quatre-Bornes, 1986, Hon. Citzen Town of Beau-Bassin/Rose-Hill, 1986, Hon. Citizen Dist. of Grand Port/Savanne, 1989. Home and Office: Bonne Terre, Vacoas Mauritius

MARGER, EDWIN, lawyer; b. N.Y.C., Mar. 18, 1928; s. William and Fannie (Cohen) M.; m. Kaye Sanderson, Oct. 1, 1951; children: Shari Ann, Diane Elaine, Sandy Ben; m. L. Suzanne Smyth, July 5, 1968; 1 child, George Phinney; m. Mary Susan Hamel, May 6, 1987; 1 child, Charleston Faye. BA, U. Miami, 1951, JD, 1953. Bar: Fla. 1953, Ga. 1971, D.C. 1978. Sole practice Miami Beach, Fla., 1953-67, Atlanta, 1971—; gen. counsel Physicians Nat. Risk Retention Group, 1988-91, Physicians Reliance Assn., 1988-91, Physicians Nat. Legal Def. Corp., 1988-91; spl. asst. atty. gen. Fla., 1960-61; of counsel Richard Burns, Miami, 1967—. Contbr. articles to legal jours. Tchr. Nat. Inst. Trial Advocacy; mem. Miami Beach Social Svc. Commn., 1957; chmn. Fulton County Aviation Adv. Com., 1980—; trustee Forensic Scis. Found., 1984-88; v.p., 1986-88; lt. col., a.d.c. Gov. Ga., 1971-74, 80-84; col., a.d.c. Gov. La., 1977-87; Khan Bahador and mem. exiled King of Afghanistan Privy Council, 1980—. With USAAF, 1946-47. Fellow Am. Acad. Forensic Scis. (chmn. jurisprudence sect. 1977-78, sec. 1976-77, bd. dirs. 1978-79, exec. com. 1983-86); mem. ABA, Fla. Bar Assn. (aerospace com. 1971-83, bd. govs. 1983-87, 90-94, exec. com. 1993-94), State Bar Ga. (chmn. sect. environ. law 1974-75, aviation law sect. 1978, bd. govs. 1999—), Ga. Trial Lawyers Assn., Nat. Assn. Criminal Def. Lawyers, Ga. Assn. Criminal Def. Lawyers, Assn. Trial Lawyers Am., Am. Judicature Soc., Am. Arbitration Assn. (commn. panel 1978), Inter-Am. Bar Assn. (sr.), World Assn. Lawyers (founding), Lawyer-Pilots Bar Assn. (founding, v.p. 1959-62), VFW, Rotary, Advocates Club. Office: 44 N Main St Jasper GA 30143-1501

MARGETA, JURE, engineering educator; b. Osijek, Croatia, June 6, 1950; s. Andrija and Mara (Glavinic) M.; m. Silvana Kirhner, Dec. 3, 1983; children: Tomislau, Dunja, Irena. BSc, Faculty Civil Engring., Zagreb, Croatia, 1974, MSc, 1980, PhD, 1983; postgrad., Colo. State U., 1982. Cert. profl. engr. Asst. prof. Faculty Civil Engring., Split, Croatia, 1985-87, assoc. prof., 1987-91, prof., 1991—; assoc. dean Faculty Civil Engring., Split, 1996-98; coord. water resources activity UN Environ. Program-Mediterranean Action Plan/Priority Action Programme, 1986—. Author, editor: (book) Integrated Approach to Water Resources Developments, Management and Use, 1998 (Best Hydrotech. Book of Yr. 1998). Fulbright postdoctoral scholar, 1981. Mem. Internat. Water Resources Assn., Am. Water Works Assn., Am. Water Resources Assn. Avocations: skiing, tennis, sailing, hunting. Home: Obala K Branimyra 3, 21000 Split Croatia Office: Faculty Civil Engring, Matice Hrvatske 15, 21000 Split Croatia

MARGHERITI, LUCIA, geologist, researcher; b. Terni, Italy, May 13, 1967; d. Gabriele and Anna Luisa (Amati) M.; m. Francesco Pio Lucente, July 29, 1999; 1 child, Diana Lucente. BS in Earth Sci., U. La Sapienza, Rome, 1991. Cons. Ente Nazionale Energie Alternative Disp., Rome, 1992; grantee USGS, Menlo Pk., Calif., 1993; cons. U. L'Aquila, Italy, 1994; grantee Istituto Nazionale di Geofisica, Rome, 1996—; rschr. Inst. Nat. Geofisica. Contbr. articles to profl. jours. Mem. Am. Geophys. Union. Roman Catholic. Avocations: tennis, travel. E-mail: margheriti@ingrm.it. Office: Inst Nazionale di Geofisica, Via di Vigna Murata 605, Roma 00143, Italy

MARGHESCU, ION, radio and mobile communications educator; b. Iablanita, Romania, Oct. 20, 1944; s. Traian and Lenuta (Bojinovici) M.; m. Georgeta Ploesteanu, July 26, 1978; children: Cristina-Ioana. MS, Politehnica U., Bucharest, Romania, 1967, PhD, 1979. Cert. engring. Asst. prof. telecom. dept. Politehnica U., Bucharest, 1968-79, lectr. telecom. dept., 1979-90, assoc. prof. telecom. dept., 1990-95, prof. telecom. dept., 1995—. Author or co-author: Discrete Transmission of Signals, 1978, Radioreceivers, 1982, Analog and Digital Communications, 1995, Land Mobile Communications, 1997, 99, GSM-Systems and Networks, 1999. Recipient Tech. Scis. award Romanian Acad., Bucharest, 1981. Mem. IEEE, Audio Engring. Soc., Gen. Assn. Engrs. from Romania. Orthodox. Avocations: mountain trips, fiction, movies, tennis. E-mail: marion@comm.pub.ro. Office: Politehnica Univ, Spl Independentei 313, 77206 Bucharest 6, Romania

MARGINEDA, JOSE, physics educator, researcher; b. Balaguer, Lleida, Spain, Aug. 10, 1948; s. Isidro Margineda and Ana Puigpelat; m. Ana Maria de Godos, Dec. 21, 1975; children: Jorge, Miguel, Daniel, Julia. DSc, U. Valladolid, Spain, 1977. Cert. in physics. Tchg. asst. U. Valladolid, 1974-77, asst. prof., 1977-79; lectr. U. Murcia, Spain, 1979-82, prof., 1983—, head of dept. of physics, 1988-96. Author: (book) Physics and Chemistry, 1997; contbr. articles to profl. jours. including Measurement Sci. and Tech., Jour. of Physics E: Sci. and Instrumentation. Mem. IEEE, Spanish Royal Soc. Physics, European Phys. Soc. Fax: 34 968 364148. Office: U Murcia, Dept Physics, 30071 Murcia Spain

MARGOLIN, ABRAHAM EUGENE, lawyer; b. St. Joseph, Mo., Oct. 16, 1907; s. Jacob and Rebecca (Cohn) M.; m. Florence Solow, Feb. 1, 1931 (dec. Feb. 1998); children: Robert J., Judith (Mrs. Goodman), James S. BA, Dartmouth Coll.; LLB, Mich. U., Ann Arbor, JD, 1929. Pvt. practice Kans. City; bd. mem. Tension Envelope Corp., UMB Mortgage Co.; pres. ctrl. governing bd. Children's Mercy Hosp., 1972-76, life mem.; dir. life Truman Med. Ctr., Menorah Med. Ctr.; mem. bd. govs. City Trust Kansas City, Rsch. Mental Health Found.; dir., v.p. Jewish Fedn. Greater Kanas City. Bd. govs. Hebrew Acad. Kans. City; gov. Am. Royal Assn.; pres. coun., fellow Brandeis U.; trustee B'nai B'rith Found.; mem. adv. bd. Anti-Defamation League; mem. nat. exec. coun. Am. Jewish Com., Am. Joint Distbn. Com. Named Disting. Law Alumnus, Washington U.; recipient Man of Yr. award Congregations Beth Shalom. Mem. ABA, ATLA, Am. Judicature Soc., Fed. Bar Assn., Mo. Bar Assn., Met. Kans. City Bar Assn., U.S. Supreme Ct. Hist. Soc., Heritage Found., Cato Inst., World Jewish Congress, Am. Jewish Congress, Kans. City Club, Oakwood Golf and Country Club, Nat. Lawyers Club, Order of Coif, Delta Sigma Rho. Home: 221 W 48th St Apt 606 Kansas City MO 64112-3139 Office: 2345 Grand Blvd Ste 2500 Kansas City MO 64108-2603

MARGOLIN, JEAN SPIELBERG, artist; b. N.Y.C., Oct. 12, 1926; d. Jack and Ida (Grossman) Spielberg and Bess Liebowitz Spielberg (stepmother); m. Paul Margolin, May 19, 1946 (dec. Mar. 1989). Student, Ind. U., 1951-55, Skowhegan Sch. Painting/Sculp., 1954. tchr. painting and drawing Ind. U., Bloomington, 1954-55; curator group show Pace U. Gallery, N.Y.C., 1984. Paintings exhibited John Herron Art Mus., Indpls., 1952-55, J.B. Speed Art Mus., Louisville, 1953, Cin. Mus. Art, 1955, L.A. County Mus. Art, 1956, A.C.A. Gallery, N.Y.C., 1959-60, Pa. Acad. Fine Arts, Phila., 1962, Heckscher Mus., Huntington, N.Y., 1964, Skowhegan Benefit Exbhn., Nat. Arts Club, N.Y.C., 1974, Arthouse, Storrs, Conn., 1979, Landmark Gallery, N.Y.C., 1980-82, Pace U. Gallery, N.Y.C., 1980, 84, The Artists Choice Mus., Alex Rosenberg Gallery, N.Y.C., 1983; paintings exhibited by appointment only, N.Y.C., 1985—. Recipient 1st prize purchase award for painting Skowhegan Sch. Painting and Sculpture, 1954, scholar, 1954. Home: 4 Washington Square Vlg Apt 12S New York NY 10012-1908

MARGOLIN, SOLOMON BEGELFOR, pharmacologist; b. Phila., May 16, 1920; s. Nathan and Fannie (Begelfor) M.; m. Gerda Levy, Jan. 17, 1947 (div. Feb. 1985); children: David, Bernard, Daniel; m. Nancy A. Cox, Apr. 30, 1987. BSc, Rutgers U., 1941, MSc, 1943, PhD, 1945. Asst. Rutgers U., New Brunswick, N.J., 1943-45; rsch. biologist Silmo Chem. Co., Vineland, N.J., 1947-48; rsch. pharmacologist Schering Corp., Bloomfield, N.J., 1948-52, dir. pharmacology dept., 1952-54; chief pharmacologist Maltbie Labs., Belleville, N.J., 1954-56; chief pharmacologist Wallace Labs, Carter-Wallace, Inc., Cranbury, N.J., 1956-60, dir. pharmacology dept., 1960-64, v.p. biol. rsch., 1964-68; pres. AMR Biol. Rsch., Inc., Princeton, N.J., 1968-78; from prof., chmn. pharmacology dept. to emeritus prof. St. George's (Grenada) U. Sch. Medicine, 1978—; pres. MARNAC, Inc., Dallas, 1990—. Author: Harper's Handbook Therapeutic Pharmacology, 1981; author: (with others) Physiological Pharmacology, 1963, World Review, Nutrition & Dietetics, 1980; contbr. numerous articles to profl. jours. including Annals of Allergy, Proc. Soc. Exptl. Biol. & Med., Nature. Mem. AAAS, Endocrino Soc., Am. Chem. Soc., Soc. Exptl. Biology and Medicine, Am. Soc. Pharmacology and Exptl. Therapeutics, N.Y. Acad. Scis., Drug Information Assn. Achievements include U.S., European, and Japanese patents for Prevention and Treatment of Fibrotic Lesions also, multiple sclerosis and other neurodegenerative disorders; research in anti-histamines anti-cholinergics, endorphins, sedative-hypnotics, tranquilizers, muscle relaxants, glucocorticoids, cardiovascular agents, anti-inflammatory drugs, anti-fibrotic agents, multiple sclerosis agents. Home: PO Box 12186 Dallas TX 75225-0186

MARGOLIS, HOWARD, public policy studies educator; b. Boston, Mar. 20, 1932; s. Abraham and Ann Margolis; m. Joan Olva Thuma, Jan. 17, 1962; children: Peter, Jenny, Sarah. BA, Harvard U., 1953; PhD, MIT, 1979. Speechwriter Sec. of Def., Washington, 1962-64; journalist Sci. Mag., Washington Post, Washington, 1960-62, 64-65; rsch. staff Inst. Def. Analyses, Arlington, Va., 1965-72; rsch. fellow MIT, Cambridge, 1972-81; vis. scholar Inst. Advanced Study & Russell Sage Found., N.Y.C. and Princeton, 1981-83; lectr. U. Calif., Irvine, 1983-85; prof. U. Chgo., 1985—. Author: Selfishness, Altruism and Rationality, 1982, Patterns, Thinking and Cognition, 1987, Paradigms and Barriers, 1993, Dealing With Risk, 1996. Avocations: skiing, hiking, windsurfing. Office: U Chgo Harris Sch Chicago IL 60637

MARGRABE, MARY VIRGINIA, retired secondary education educator, librarian; b. Brunswick, Md., May 21, 1923; d. John Anthony and Lula Brunswick (Darr) McMurry; m. Carl William Henry Margrabe Sr., Dec. 10, 1943 (dec. 1988); 1 child, Carl William Henry Jr. BA, Hood Coll., 1943; postgrad., Cath. U. Cert. tchr., Md. Tchr. Brunswick (Md.) H.S., 1943; libr. Linganore H.S., Frederick County, Md., Waverley Elem., Frederick County. Author: Now Library, 1973, Media Magic, 1979; co-author: Pre-1800 Houses of Frederick County, 1990; co-author, editor: Brunswick: 100 Years of Memories, 1990. Co-founder, charter mem. Brunswick Pub. Libr., 1962; co-founder Brunswick Railroad Mus., 1969, Brunswick Potomac Found., 1969, Brunswick Hist. Commn., 1976, pres., 1987-92. Mem. Hood Club of Frederick County. Libertarian. Episcopal. Avocations: writing, research. Home and Office: 31 Priory Ln Pelham NY 10803-3603

MARGRETHE, HER MAJESTY II (MARGRETHE ALEXANDRINE THORHILDUR INGRID), Queen of Denmark; b. Copenhagen, Apr. 16, 1940; d. King Frederik IX and Queen Ingrid; m. Henri-Marie-Jean-André Count de Laborde de Monpezat (now Prince Henrik of Denmark), June 10, 1967; children: Crown Prince Frederik André Henrik Christian, Prince Joachim Holger Waldemar Christian. Baccalaureate, U. Copenhagen, U. Aarhus; student in prehistoric archaeology, Cambridge U., 1960-61, LLD (hon.), 1975; student, U. Sorbonne, Paris, London Sch. Econs.; hon. fellow, London Sch. Econs., 1975; LL.D. (hon.), U. London, 1980; D (hon.), U. Iceland, 1986, Oxford (Eng.) U., 1992; Hon. Bencher, The Middle Temple, 1992; D (hon.), Edinburgh Univ., 2000. Succeeded to throne of Denmark in Jan., 1972 on death of King Frederik IX. Hon. freeman City of London, 2000. Decorated Order of the Elephant; decorated Knight of Garter; recipient medal of headmaster Paris U., 1987. Royal fellow Soc. Antiquaries London. Address: Amalienborg, DK-1257 Copenhagen Denmark

MARGULIS, BORIS Y., chemist in oil industry, researcher; b. Soroky, Moldavia, USSR, Sept. 16, 1949; s. Yakov A. and Phenya A. Margulis; m. Lidiya G. Rogulina, Aug. 17, 1979; children: Anna, Jane. Degree as Engr., Kazan (Russia) State U., 1966-71, PhD in Chemistry, 1975. Lead engr. JSC Tatneft, Geol. Exploration Bd., Kazan, 1975—. Contbr. more than 50 articles to profl. jours.; holder 15 patents. Mem. N.Y. Acad. Scis., Engring. Acad. Udmurtian Republic. Avocations: chess, sauna. E-mail: borism@mi.ru. Office: Tatar Geol Expl/JCS Tatneft, K Marks Str 49/13, Kazan, Tatarstan Russia 420015

MARI, DANIELE, engineering executive, researcher; b. Milan, June 2, 1961; arrived in Switzerland, 1993; s. Loris and Angela (Procicchiani) M.; m. Georgette Marie Vincent, Sept. 3, 1994; children: Luca, Alessandro, Sofia. Degree in Physics Engring., Ecole Poly. Fédérale, Lausanne, Switzerland, 1986; PhD, Inst. de Génie Atomique, Lausanne, 1991. Postdoctoral staff MIT, Cambridge, 1992-93; R&D dir. Ateliers Mécaniques Yverdon (Switzerland) SA, 1993-99; CEO, Advanced Composite and Microwave Engring., Versoix, 1993-98; sci. dir. Advanced Composite and Microwave Engring., 2000—; rschr. Inst. de Génie Atomique Ecole Polytech Fédérale Lausanne, 1997—. Office: EPFL-IGA, 1015 Lausanne VD, Switzerland

MARIA, GHEORGHE, chemical engineer, educator; b. Fundeni, Romania, Oct. 2, 1955; arrived in Switzerland, 1992; s. Constantin and Angela (Burghel) M.; m. Cristina Popovici, Aug. 16, 1985. MSc in Chem. Engring., Poly. U. Bucharest, 1979, PhD in Chem. Engring., 1987. In-stage chem. engr. Chem. Enterprises, Bucharest, 1979-82; rsch. engr. Chem. & Biochem. Energetics Inst., Bucharest, 1982-90; asst. prof. Poly. U. Bucharest, 1990-91, assoc. prof., 1997-99, prof., 1999—; asst. prof. Swiss Federal Inst. Tech., Zurich, 1992-96; reviewer Computers & Chem. Engring. Contbr. articles to profl. jours., chpts. to books. Recipient N Teclu prize Romanian Acad. Sci., 1985. Greek Orthodox. Avocation: travel. Office: Polytech U Bucharest, Polizu 1, 78126 Bucharest Romania

MARIA DOS SANTOS, ALEXANDRE JOSÉ, archbishop; b. Inhambane, Mozambique, Mar. 18, 1924. Ordained bishop Roman Cath. Ch., 1953. Elected to Ch. in Lourenço Marques (now Maputo), 1974; consecrated bishop, 1975, created cardinal, 1988. Office: Paço Arquiepiscopal, Avda Eduardo Mondlane 1448, CP 258 Maputo Mozambique*

MARIAN, CZAUDERNA, chemist, educator; b. Piaseczno near Warsaw, Poland, Sept. 8, 1952; s. Stanislaw Antoni and Zofia (Chuszcz) C.; m. Julia Elzbieta Wagner, Dec. 25, 1978; children: Maciej, Krzysztof. MSc, Warsaw U., 1976, PhD, 1980. Asst., doctoral fellow faculty chemistry Warsaw U., 1976-79, asst. lectr., 1980-82, lectr., 1982-94, instr. radiochemistry lab., 1987-94, lectr. methods of activation analysis, 1985-94; lectr. Inst. Animal Physiology and Nutrition Polish Acad. Sci., Jablonna near Warsaw, 1994—. Contbr. articles to internat. jours. Mem. Trade Union Solidarnosc, 1981—. Roman Catholic. Home: 9/28 Biatostocka Street, 03-741 Warsaw Poland Office: Instytucka St 3, 05-110 Jablonna near Warsaw Poland

MARIAN, IULIU OVIDIU, physicist, educator; b. Cluj, Romania, July 12, 1946; s. Victor and Cecilia Marian; m. Ana Cădan, July 11, 1972; 1 child, Călin Ovidiu. Undergrad. degree, G. Baritiu U., Cluj, 1964; grad. degree, Babes-Bolyai U., Cluj, 1969, PhD, 1998. Tchr. G. Baritiu, Cluj, 1969-71; asst. Babes-Bolyai U., 1971-91, lectr., 1991—. Co-author: Electronics for Chemists, 1978; contbr. articles to profl. jours. Mem. ISE. Greek Orthodox. Avocations: fencing, fishing. Home: Rahovei 34, 3400 Cluj-Napoca Romania Office: Faculty Chemistry/Chem Engr, Arany Janos 11, 3400 Cluj-Napoca Romania

MARIANI, JEAN, neurobiologist, psychiatrist; b. Venaco, Corsica, France, July 4, 1949; s. Francois and Marianne (Guerrini) M.; m. Emmanuelle Elizabeth Wollman, Nov. 14, 1978; children: Louise-Laure, Simon. M in Biochemistry, U. Pierre & Marie Curie, Paris, 1974, MD, 1978, Scis. Doctorate, 1987. Resident in medicine Assistance Publique Paris, 1973-78; chargé de recherche INSERM, Paris, 1978-89, dir. de recherche, 1989—; clin. neurophysiologist Hopital Lariboisiere, Paris, 1997-99; scientist Institut Pasteur, Paris, 1978-85; lab. directorship U. Paris, 1985—. Contbr. articles to profl. jours. Mem. Initiative for European Citizens, Paris, 1990—, Union Rationaliste, Paris, 1993—. Lt. Health Svc., 1972-73, Paris. Recipient Silver medal U. Paris V, 1978, prize Scis. Acad., Paris, 1982. Mem. Soc. of Neuroscis., European Neurosci. Assn., Soc. Française Neurosciences. Avocations: theater, sports (running, skiing, tennis), screen play writing. Office: U Pierre & Marie Curie, 9 Quai Saint Bernard Box 14, 75005 Paris France

MARIAS, ANTAL, economist, educator; b. Budapest, Hungary, Sept. 17, 1925; s. Antal and Margit (Muller) M.; m. Irma Kapitany, Dec. 23, 1951; children: Andras, Agnes, Gyorgy. MS, U. Econs. Scis., Hungary, 1950; PhD, Acad. Scis. Hungary, Budapest, 1963. Asst. Tech. U., Budapest, 1951-63, asst. prof., 1964-66, prof., 1967-68; prof. U. Econs. Scis., Budapest, 1968-69, prof. emeritus, 1969—. Contbr. articles to profl. jours. Recipient Order of Merit Hungary Rep. Small Cross, Pres. Rep., 1996, Pazmany Peter prize Pro Renovanoa Cultura Hungariae, 1997. Mem. Hungarian Acad. Scis. (mgmt. and orgn. com. 1978), Hungarian Economists Assn. Avocations: music, minibooks. Home: 85 Bartok Bela UT, 1115 Budapest Hungary Office: BUES Dept Mgmt and Orgn, Fovam Ter 8, 1093 Budapest Hungary

MARIĆ, JASMINA, oenologist, researcher; b. London, Mar. 6, 1951; d. Velimar Vulić; m. Davor Marić, Oct. 2, 1976; children: Marina, Dubravko. Grad. in agrl. engring., U. Zagreb, Croatia, 1976; MSc in Viticulture, U. Zagreb, 1991, Dsc in Oenology, 1999. Sci. asst. U. Zagreb Faculty Agr., 1976—; cons. Croatian Ministry Agr., 1978-95, to all wineries, Croatia, 1983—, Croatia Dept. Oenology, 1996-97; sec. wine tasting Zelina Wine Exhbn., 1998, Zagreb Fair, 1998. Co-author: (exhbn. catalogue) Slavko Marć, 1998. Recipient recognition, Agri-Corp., Djakovo, Croatia, 1996, Kutjevo, Croatia, 1997, 98. Fellow Assn. Oenologists Croatia (sec. 1996, recognition 1998), Assn. Wine Prodrs. Croatia (recognition 1998, 99). Avocations: painting, music, swimming, water polo, ecology. Home: Labudovac 2, 10 000 Zagreb Croatia Office: U Zagreb Faculty Agr, Dept, Oenology, Svetosimunska 25, 10 000 Zagreb Croatia

MARIČIC, ANDRIJA, computer science educator; b. Belgrade, Yugoslavia, Dec. 8, 1946; arrived in New Zealand, 1995; s. Andrija and Anka (Radelic) M.; m. Rada Lazic, July 20, 1975; children: Aleksandar, Vladimir. BSc, U. Zagreb, Croatia, 1969, MSc, 1973, PhD, 1992. Engr., rschr. Rade Koncar Co., Zagreb, 1969-77; asst. prof., rschr. Faculty Elec. Engring. and Computing, U. Zagreb, 1977-95; instrumentation engr. specialist Sirte Oil Co., Marsa el Brega, Libya, 1988-89; lectr. Auckland (New Zealand) Inst. Tech., 1995-96; sr. lectr. Northland Poly., Whangarei, New Zealand, 1996—. Author: Modeling and Simulation of Continuous Systems, 1988; contbr. articles to profl. publs. Maj. Yugoslav Army, 1973-74. Mem. IEEE. Avocations: photography, swimming, woodworking. E-mail: amaricic@extra.co.nz. Home: 16 Ridgeway Dr, Whangarei Kamo 0121, New Zealand Office: Northland Poly Sch Bus, Raumanga Valley Rd PB 9019, Whangarei New Zealand

MARIE, JEAN-PIERRE, hematologist; b. Aug. 4, 1948; s. Rene and Jacqueline M.; m. Francoise Russo, Sept. 6, 1973; children: Helene, Olivier. MD, U. Paris VII, 1976. Intern Hôpitaux de Paris, 1974-78, chief of clinic, 1978-82, prof. agrègè, 1982—; staff Hematology Svc., Hôpitaux Hotel Dieu, Paris, 1982—. Mem. Am. Assn. Cancer Rsch. (corr.), Soc. Française d'Hematologie. Home: Rue des Bruyeres, Sevres Paris 92310, France Office: Dept Hematologie d'Oncologie Med, Notre Dame 1 place du Parvis, Paris 75181, France

MARIETTI, PIERO MASSIMO, electronics educator; b. Cagliari, Sardinia, Italy, Apr. 7, 1941; s. Mario and Biancamaria (Angeletti) M.; m. Rosamaria Loretelli, Jan. 18, 1943; children: Susanna, Mario. MA in Electronic Engring., U. La Sapienza, Rome, 1964, MA in Indsl. Orgn., 1964. Asst. prof. U. La Sapienza, Rome, 1964-80, assoc. prof., 1980-86, prof. electronics, 1986—, lectr. applied electronics, 1974-80; lectr. physics U. L'Aquila, Italy, 1968-76; mem. Nat. Microelectronics Programme, Ministry of U. Italy, 1982-86; dir. Nat. Sch. PhD Students, Italy, 1994—; cons. Ministry of Industry, Italy, 1989—; sec. gen. Red de Universidades Latinoamericans y Europeas, 1995—; organizer series of confs. on energy, environ, tech. innovation, 1989, 92, 95, 99. Author: Encyclopedia Italiana Treccani, 1990; editor, author: (book series) Applied Electronics, 1994; patentee in field. Nat. sec. Conf. Generale Italiana Lavoratori, U. Br., Rome, 1974-84; rep. Nat. U. Coun., Italy, 1979-86; mem. Parliament's Com. for Tech. Innovation, Italy, 1993—; vice-coord. internat. rels. U. La Sapienza, Rome, 1995. Recipient Spl. prize U.S. Trade Ctr., Milan, 1971. Roman Catholic. Avocations: guitar playing, songwriting, short story writing, basketball. Office: U Rome Dept Elec Engring, Via Eudossiana 18, 00184 Rome Italy

MARIGHETTI, LUCA P., business executive; b. Milan, Apr. 25, 1961; arrived in Germany, 1980; s. Rolando and Zenaide (Arpili) M. Magister Artium, U. Costance (Germany), 1985, PhD, 1988. U. fellow U. Costance (Germany), 1985-87; asst. brand mgr. Procter & Gamble, Frankfurt am Main, Germany, 1988-91; brand mgr. Procter & Gamble, Mainz, Germany, 1991-92; EuroBrand mgr. Procter & Gamble, London, 1993; comml. dir. S.C. Johnson Wax, Düsseldorf, Germany, 1993-95; cons. McKinsey & Co., Frankfurt, Germany, 1996—. Office: McKinsey and Co, Tamuustor 2, Frankfurt Germany

MARIJUAN, PEDRO CLEMENTE, information scientist, educator; b. San Martin, La Rioja, Spain, July 28, 1952; s. Pedro Jose Marijuan and Luisa Fernandez; m. Isabel Muñoz, Oct. 18, 1989; 1 child, Alicia. Grad. engr., U. Poly. Catalonia, Barcelona, Spain, 1976; Doctorate, U. Barcelona, 1989. Various indsl. and comml. positions Barcelona, 1976-86; collaborator U. Barcelona, 1986-89; rsch. assoc. Australian Nat. U., Canberra, 1989-90, U. Chgo., 1990-91; investigator U. Zaragoza, Spain, 1992-2000; cons. engr. Barcelona Municipality, 1983-85; organizer Cajal on Consciousness Conf., 1999. Author: (with K.P. Collins) El Cerebro Dual, 1997; guest editor (spl. issue) Foundations of Information Science Biosystems, vol. 38, 1996, Fundementals of Info. Sci. Cybernetics and Human Knowledge, vol. 5, 4, 1998, (with K. Matsuno) (spl. issue) Symmetry: Culture and Science, 1996, (with K. Kirby) (spl. issue) Found. of Info. Sci., 2nd Conf., Biosystems, 1998, (spl. issue) Fundamentals of Information Science Cybernetics of Human Knowledge, 1998; mem. editl. bd. Biosystems, 1996, Symmetry: Culture and Science, 1996. Collaborator Anti-Franco Orgns., Barcelona, 1970-78. Avocations: reading, writing, music, gastronomy, walking. Home: Gran via 19 1st Der, 50006 Zaragoza Aragon, Spain Office: CPS Univ Zaragoza, Maria de Luna 3, 50015 Zaragoza Aragon, Spain

MAŘÍK, IVO ANTONÍN, health facility administrator, physician; b. Prague, Czech Republic, Feb. 6, 1950; s. Antonín and Olga (Kuncová) M.; children: Olga, Radka, Helena; m. Alena Korinková, Nov. 26, 1994; children: Antonín, Jan. MD, Charles U., Prague, 1975; PhD, Charles. U., Prague, 1987; specialization in pediat., 1979, specialization in orthop., 1982. Resident in pediat. Beroun (Czech Republic) Hosp., 1976-80; resident in orthop. surgery Orthop. Clin. 2d Med. Faculty, Charles U., 1980-82, rsch. fellow, 1982-86, sr. rsch. worker, 1988-91, asst. prof., 1991-94; head Ambulant Ctr. Defects Locomotor Apparatus, Prague, 1994—; lectr. dept. anthropology and human genetics Charles U., 1998—; cons. dept. rehab. Kostelec Hosp., 1991-96, dept. orthop. Pribram Hosp., 1994—. Founder, editor, editor-in-chief Locomotor Sys.-Advances in Rsch., Diagnostics and Therapy, 1994—; conbtr. over 50 articles to profl. jours. Founder The Mařík Fdn., 1992-94. Capt. Czech Air Force Res., 1975-76. Mem. Czech Soc. Surgery of Hand and Rehab. (founding mem.), Czech Soc. Connective Tissue Rsch. and Biol. Use (founding mem.), Czech Soc. Prosthetics and Orthotics, Czech Med. Soc. J.E. Purkyně (founding mem.), Czech Soc. Accidental Surgery, Czech Pediat. Soc., Czech Soc. Orthopaedics and Traumatology. Avocations: rowing, cycling. Home: Žitomírská 39, 101 00 Prague Czech Republic Office: Ambulant Ctr Locomotor Def, Olšanská 7, 130 00 Prague 3, Czech Republic

MAŘÍK, VLADIMÍR, control engineering educator; b. Prague, Czech Republic, June 25, 1952; s. Vladimír and Milada (Šenfelderová) M.; m. Taťána Kvasilová, July 15, 1977; children: Vladimír, Jakub. MSc, Czech Tech. U., Prague, 1975, PhD, 1979. Cert. elec. engr. Asst. prof. Czech Tech. U., Prague, 1979-84, assoc. prof., 1984-90, prof. control engring., 1990—, head dept. control engring., 1997-99, head dept. cybernetics, 1999—; mng.

dir. Rockwell Automation Ltd., Rsch. Ctr. Prague, 1993—; mem. bd. Czech Soc. Cybernetics and Informatics, Prague, 1992-96; mem. bd. Internat. Inst. Advanced Studies in Systems Rsch. and Cybernetics, Windsor, Can., 1994—. Co-editor: Advanced Topics in Artifical Intelligence, 1992, Database and Expert Systems Applications, 1993, Information Management in CIM, 1995, Intelligent Systems for Manufacturing, 1998. Recipient Czechoslovak state prize Govt. of Czech Republic, Prague, 1989. Mem. IEEE, N.Y. Acad. Scis., European Coordinating Com. on Artificial Intelligence. Home: Na Kremínku 664, 154 00 Prague 5, Czech Republic Office: Czech Tech U K 333, Technická 2, CZ 16627 Prague 6, Czech Republic

MARIN, EMILIO, archaeologist; b. Split, Croatia, Feb. 6, 1951; s. Ante and Nevis (Orlandini) M.; m. Hajdi Vidic, June 9, 1984. MA, U. Zagreb, Croatia, 1977; PhD, U. Zagreb, 1990. Asst. keeper Archaeol. Mus., Split, 1973-79, sr. keeper, 1980-85, prin. keeper, 1986-87, dir., 1988—; external rschr. Centre A. Merlin-CNRS, Paris, 1980—; asst. prof. Inst. Art and Archaeology, U. Sorbonne, Paris, 1981-83; co-dir. Croatian-French archaeol. project for researching early Christian artifacts, Split, Paris, Rome, 1983—; vis. fellow All Souls Coll., Oxford, Eng., 1985; vis. prof. U. Sorbonne, 1990-91; prof. U. Split, 1997—; sec. gen. com. for 13th Internat. Congress Early Christian Archaeology, 1988-94; vis. mem. Found. Hardt, Geneve, 1996. Author: Muzej Imaginacije, 1982, Starokrscanska Salona, 1988, Pro Salona, 1994, Ave Narona, 1997, Salona Narona-Razgovori, Sarajevo-Sinj, 1998; editor: Don Frane Bulic, 1984, Disputationes Salonitanae III, 1986, IV, 1993, Po Rusevinama Stare Salone, 1986, Acta Primi Congressus Internationalis Archaeologiae Christianae, 1993, Acta XIII CIAC Split-Poreč, 1994, Città del Vaticano—Split, 1998, Salona I, 1994, Salona II, 1995, Salona III, 2000, Salona Christiana, 1994, Salona Christiana Vista Dall'Urbe, 1995, Corpus Inscriptionum Naronitanorum-Eresova Kula-Vid, Macerata-Split, 1999, Narona I.-Sv. Vid, Split, 1999, Narona, Zagreb-Opuzen, 1999, Hello Narona, Metkovic, 1999; contbr. articles to profl. jours. Bd. dirs. Retrats Antics a Iugoslavia, 1989, Retratos Antiguos en Yugoslavia, 1989, Doba Francuske Uprave u Dalmaciji, 1989, Starohrvatski Solin, 1992, Der Attische Jagdsarkophag Budapest-Split, 1992, Latina et Graeca, 1973-74, Vjesnik za Arheologiju i Historiju Dalmatinsku, 1988—. Grantee Govt. of France, 1980-81, 86, 92, Brit. Coun., 1983, 85, Govt. of Bulgaria, 1987, Govt. of Germany DAAD, 1996-97; recipient prize of Town Split, 1996; Ordre for Culture of Croatia, 1996. Fellow Ancient Monuments Sco. London; mem. French Soc. for Classical Archaeology, Assn. L'Antiquite Tardive France, Croatian Soc. for Classical Philology, Assn. Internat. d'Epigraphie Grecque et Latine, Pontificia Accademia Romana di Archeologia, 1996, Soc. Nat. Antiquaires France (Paris), Real Academia Buenas Letras (Barcelona), Comitato promotore dei congressi Internat. di Archeologia Cristiana, Académie des Inscriptions et Belles Lettres. Office: Arheoloski Muzej, Zrinsko-Frankopanska 25, 21000 Split Croatia

MARIN, GILLES WILFRED, healing practitioner; b. Toulon, France, July 14, 1956; came to U.S., 1980; s. Richard and Sylvette (Perrone) M.; m. Emily Ashworth (div.); children: Jessy Ashworth-Marin. Diplome d'Edn., U. Grenoble, France, 1979. Cert. CNT practitioner, 1982. Pvt. practice massage therapist San Francisco, 1982-90; dir., sr. instr. San Francisco Chi Nei Tsang Tng. Ctr., 1990-95, The Chi Nei Tsang Inst.-Healing From Within, Berkeley, Calif., 1995—; practitioner The Tao Found., San Francisco, 1982. Author: (book) Healing From Within, 1999, (audiotape) Bone Breathing Meditation, 1996; tech. editor: (book) Chi Nei Tsang, 1990. Mem. Healing Tao Instrs. Assn. Avocations: Chi-king, music, poetry, martial arts, Taoist scholar.

MARIN-ANTUNA, JOSE MIGUEL, physics educator; b. Havana, Cuba, Nov. 7, 1942; s. José Miguel Marin-Hernández and Nemesia Antuna-Tavío; children from previous marriage, Raysa, Ulises; m. Teresa de Jesus Tamayo-Prieto, Oct. 21, 1994; 1 child, Wanda. BS, Edison Inst., Havana, 1960; MS, Moscow U., 1967, PhD, 1986. Asst. prof. physics U. Havana, 1967-76, prof. physics, 1976—, dir. theoretical physics, 1968-76, pres. tribunal prof. categories, 1983—; cons. U. Angola, Luanda, 1981-83; mem. permanent tribunal for PhD degrees Ministry of Higher Edn., Havana, 1993—. Author: Theory of Functions of Complex Variable, 1977, 2d edit., 1990, Mathematical Methods of Physics, 1992; contbr. articles to profl. jours. Recipient Order For the Cuban Edn., Ministry of Higher Edn. Cuba, 1989, Order Rafael Maria-Mendive, Nat. Trade Union Educators Cuba, 1992, Jose Tey medal Coun. of State of The Rupbulic of Cuba, 1994, Alma Mater award U. Har, 1998, 99, Postgrad. Activity Spl. award Min. of Higher Edn., 1998; named Best Prof. in MSc Advising Wk., U. Hav, 1998, Republic of Cuba's Relevant Worker, Nat. Trade Union Educators, 1999. Mem. Am. Phys. Soc., Cuban Phys. Soc. (founder). Avocations: reading, playing guitar, traveling, riding bicycle. Home: Stos Suárez, Santa Catalina 682 Bajos, 10500 Havana Cuba

MARINE, SUSAN SONCHIK, analytical chemist, educator; b. Maple Heights, Ohio, Mar. 10, 1954; d. Stephen Robert and Gloria Ann (Hach) Sonchik; m. Michael D. Marine; 1 child, Matthew Robert Marine. BS in Chemistry magna cum laude, John Carroll U., 1975; MS in Analytical Chemistry, Case Western Res. U., 1978, PhD in Phys. Chemistry, 1980. Asst. chemist Horizons Research Inc., Beachwood, Ohio, 1974-75; chemist specialist Standard Oil of Ohio, Warrensville Heights, Ohio, 1975-79; organic chemistry br. mgr. Versar, Inc., Springfield, Va., 1980-83; mgr. gas chromatography program IBM Instruments Inc., Danbury, Conn., 1983-87, radiation safety officer, 1985-87; expert witness, cons. Martin, Craig, Chester & Sonnenschein, Chgo., 1981-83; adv. engr. in advanced lithography IBM Corp., Essex Junction, Vt., 1987-95; vis. assoc. prof. chemistry Centre Coll., Danville, Ky., 1995-98; asst. prof. chemistry and biochemistry Miami U., Middletown, Ohio, 1998—; vis. asst. prof. chemistry and math. Heritage Coll., 1991-92; spkr. in field. Author: African Walking Safari, 1985; editorial adv. bd. Jour. Chromatographic Sci., 1977-93, guest editor, 1987. Mem. Danbury Conservation Commn., 1986-87, tchr. and tutor chemistry, 1985-89, 91-92, 94; troop leader Lake Erie coun. Girl Scouts U.S.A., 1971-80, Southwestern Conn., 1983-87; leader explorer post Cleve. coun. Boy Scouts Am., 1977-78; managerial advisor Jr. Achievement, Warrensville Heights, Ohio, 1977-78; judge State or Regional Sci. Fair, 1977, 80, 89-91, 99, 2000, Odyssey of the Mind, 1994; asst. leader Internat. Folk Dancers, Newtown, Conn., 1985-87; tchr. religion, 1981-84, 87-90, 93-94. Recipient Overall Best Paper award Eastern Analytical Symposium, 1984, First Gas Chromatograph award IBM Instruments Inc., 1985, contbn. award (tech. paper) 10th Internat. Congress of Essential Oils, Flavors, Fragrances, Washington, 1986. Mem. ASTM (exec. com. E-19 1985-2000, chmn. subcom. 1986-2000, vice chmn. arrangements 1994-98), Am. Chem. Soc. (chmn. membership com. Green Mountain sect. 1988-89, chair elect 1989-90, chmn. 1990-91, local coord. Nat. Chemistry Week 1991, 93-98, Phoenix award 1994, 97), Iota Sigma Pi (pres. N.E. Ohio chpt. 1978-79, mem.-at-large fin. mgr. 1993-97, nat. v.p. 1996-99, nat. pres. 1999—), No. Vt. Canoe Cruisers (treas. 1990-92), Green Mountain Steppers (sec. 1993-95), Centre Coll. Outdoors Club (faculty liaison 1996-98). Roman Catholic. Avocations: camping, dancing, travel. Home: 4667 Sebald Dr Franklin OH 45005-5328 Office: Miami U Middletown 4200 E University Blvd Middletown OH 45042-3458

MARINELLI, JOSEPH MARCELLO, aerospace advisor; b. Phila., Aug. 15, 1948; s. William Marinelli and Lillian (Nicolena) Navarro. Grad. high sch., Phila. Aerospace advisor Rissler Sci. Orgn., Phila., 1982—. Mem. Air Force Assn. (life), U.S. Naval Inst. (life), Navy League (life), Am. Def. Preparedness Orgn. (life), World Future Soc. (life), Tailhook Assn. (life), Assn. Am. Politics (life), Assn. Naval Aviation (life), Cruiser Olympia Assn. Inc. (life), F-4 Phantom 2 Soc. (life), Am. Aviation Hist. Soc. (life), Nat. Space Soc., Planetary Soc., Nat. Air and Space Soc. Democrat. Roman Catholic. Home: 2141 S 21st St Philadelphia PA 19145-3502

MARINER, WILLIAM MARTIN, chiropractor; b. Balt., Jan. 2, 1949; s. William Joseph and Ellen (Dexter) M. AA, Phoenix Coll., 1976; BS in Biology, L.A. Coll. of Chiropractic, 1980, D Chiropractic summa cum laude, 1980; DD (hon.), Universal Life Ch., Modesto, Calif., 1986. Health food restaurant mgr. Golden Temple of Conscious Cookery, Tempe, Ariz., 1974-75; health food store mgr. Guru's Grainery, Phoenix, 1975; physical therapist A.R.E. Clinic, Phoenix, 1975-76; research dir., founder G.R.D. Healing Arts Ctr., Phoenix, 1974-77; aminstrv. asst., acad. dean L.A. Coll. Chiropractic, Whittier, Calif., 1977-80; faculty Calif. Acupuncture Coll., L.A., 1978-80; ednl. cons. Avanti Inst., San Francisco, 1985-91; found. dir., head clinician Pacific Healing Arts Ctr., Del Mar, Calif., 1980-93, Mt. Shasta, Calif., 1993—; ednl. cons. John Panama Cons., San Francisco, 1991-99. Patentee in field. Co-dir. "We Care We Share" Charitable Orgn., San Diego, 1985-86. Named Outstanding Sr., L.A. Coll. Chiropractic, 1980. Mem. Calif. Chiropractic Assn., Am. Chiropractic Assn., Internat. Coll. Applied Kinesiology, Holistic Dental Assn., Brit. Homopathic Assn. Avocations: Yoga, meditation, personal growth, natural healing methods, cooking. Office: Pacific Healing Arts Ctr PO Box 192 Mount Shasta CA 96067-0192

MARINESCU, ALEXE, aeronautical engineer; b. Cuza-Voda, Romania, Aug. 2, 1925; s. Ivanciu and Maria (Ionescu) M.; m. Veronica Lihaciov, Mar. 15, 1957 (dec. 1967); 1 child, Doina. Degree in engring., Politech. Inst., Bucharest, Romania, 1950; PhD, Romanian Acad., Bucharest, 1958. Head lab. Romanian Acad., Bucharest, 1950-69; sr. scientist Inst. Aerospace Constrn., Bucharest, 1968-92; cons. Nat. Inst. Aerospace Rsch., Bucharest, 1992-99; cons. in field. Author: Introduction in Rocket Dynamics Experimental Aeromechanics, 1967, Calculus and Construction of Rocket Optimal Problem in Space Flights Dynamics, 1967, Helicopter Aerodynamics and Dynamics Space Flight Mechanics, 1992; contbr. articles to profl. jours. Recipient Romanian Acad. prize, Bucharest, 1965. Mem. AIAA. Avocation: tourism. Office: Nat Inst Aerospace Rsch, Iuliu Maniu no 220 sector 6, 77538 Bucharest Romania

MARINESCU, ANDREI VICTOR, electrical engineer, educator; b. Craiova, Dolj, Romania, May 14, 1940; s. Mihail and Gabriella Ileana (Rosenfeld) M.; m. Ecaterina Constanta Grama, July 13, 1968; children: Andreea-Adina, Raluca-Ileana. Diploma in elec. engring., Poly. U., Bucharest, Romania, 1961, PhD in Engring., 1977. Test engr. Electroputere Works, Craiova, 1961-68; head of high voltage lab. Romanian Nat. Rsch./Test Inst. ICMET, Craiova, 1968-90, sci. mgr. R&D Inst., 1990—; part-time prof. U. Craiova, 1966—, condr. PhD students, 1991—; guest scientist Technische U., Karlsruhe, Germany, 1992, 96, NATO fellshp. prog., Greece, 1999. Author: (books) Power Transformer Switching Impulse Behaviour, 1988 (Traian Vuia prize Romanian Acad. 1988), (with B. Mathe and D. Costina) Insulation Test of Power Transformers, 1966, (with E. Marinescu) Introduction in Magnetoelasticity, 1997; patentee in field (Gold medal 1994). Mem. Romanian Acad. Tech. Sci., Internat. Conf. on Large High Volt Electric Sys., Romanian Electromagnetic Compatibility Assn. (founder, chmn.), IEEE. Home: Valea Rosie Bl 3-C-11, 1100 Craiova Dolj, Romania Office: ICMET, Calea Bucuresti, 1100 Craiova Dolj, Romania

MARIN-GARCIA, JOSE, researcher; b. Lorqui, Spain; s. Jose and Facunda Marin; m. Daniele M. Marin, July 1, 1967; 1 child, Melanie. MD, Granada, Spain, 1960. Dir. The Molecular Cardiology Inst., Highland Park, N.J., 1993—. E-mail: tmci@worldnet.att.net. Office: The Molecular Cardiology Inst 75 Raritan Ave Highland Park NJ 08904-2442

MARINHO DE BASTOS, JOAQUIM L.F., air transport policy administrator; b. Lisbon, Portugal, Feb. 28, 1947; s. Joaquim and Maria Portugal (Ferreira) Marinho De B.; m. Isabel De Mesquita Alves, Aug. 7, 1971; children: Sofia, Sandra, Vanessa. Min Fin., Tech. U. Lisbon, 1971; diploma in internat. monetary rels., U. Hong Kong, 1973. Chartered acct., Belgium. Dep. dir. State Econ. Dept., Macau, 1971-73; commr. State Banking Authority, Macau, 1973-77; dir. State Dept. Fin. and Treasury, Macau, 1977-81; chmn. State Tourism Authority, Macau, 1981-86; chmn., mng. dir. World Trade Ctr., Macau, 1986-88; prin. adminstr., air transport policy Coun. of European Union, Brussels, 1988—. Mem. Exec. Coun. Govt. Macau, 1977-81; vice chmn. Boy Scout Orgn., Macau, 1983-88. 1st lt., Portuguese Army (acctg. and treasury), 1974, Lisbon. Recipient commendation Govt. Macau, 1978, Portuguese Authorities, Lisbon and Brussels, 1992. Mem. Geography Soc. Lisbon, World Trade Ctr. Macau (hon.). Avocations: Portuguese history in the Far East, opera. Office: Coun of European Union, 175 Rue de la Loi, B-1048 Brussels Belgium

MARINI, DOMINIC, JR., secondary education educator; b. Niagara Falls, N.Y., Nov. 18, 1950; s. Dominic and Maria M.; m. Patricia S. Plunkett, Mar. 23, 1974; children: Dawn Davina, Dominic III. BA, Roberts Wesleyan Coll., 1972; M in Tchg., Niagara U., 1976. Tchr. Niagara Wheatfield Sch., Sanborn, N.Y., 1974-80, Fairport (N.Y.) Ctrl. Sch., 1982—. Mem. Am. Fedn. Tchrs., N.Y. State Tchrs. Assn. Roman Catholic. Avocations: little league baseball, pony league baseball, club volleyball.

MARINICH, MIKHAIL AFANASYEVICH, diplomat; b. Gomel, Jan. 13, 1940; married; 2 children. Grad., Byelorussian Poly. Inst., 1964, PhD in Econs., 1996. Vice-mayor Minsk, 1984-90; mayor Minsk, 1990-91; people's dep. Republic Belarus, 1990-91; vice-min. fgn. econ. rels. Belarus Czech Republic, 1991-94; amb. E. and P. Slovak Republic, Hungary, 1994; min. fgn. econ. rels. Belarus, 1994-98, amb. to Latvia, Estonia, Finland, 1999—. Office: Embassy of Rep of Belarus, 12 Jezus Bazaznicas, Riga LV 1050, Latvia

MARINIS, THOMAS PAUL, JR., lawyer; b. Jacksonville, Tex., May 31, 1943; s. Thomas Paul and Betty Sue (Garner) M.; m. Lucinda Cruse, June 25, 1969; children: Courtney, Kathryn, Megan. BA, Yale U., 1965; LLB, U. Tex., 1968. Bar: Tex. 1968. Assoc. Vinson & Elkins, Houston, 1969-76, ptnr., 1977—. Bd. dirs. Phoenix House of Tex., Inc. Fellow Tex. Bar Found.; mem. ABA (sec. taxation sect. 1986-87), Houston Country Club, Houston Ctr. Club, Coronado Club.

MARINO, ADRIAN, author, literary critic; b. Iasi, Romania, Sept. 5, 1921; s. Neculai and Ecaterina Marino; m. Lidia Bote. Student, U. Iasi, Romania, 1940-43, U. Bucharest, Romania, 1943-44; PhD specialisation, Faculty Letters, Geneva, 1946. Asst. U. Bucharest Faculty Philology, 1944-47; polit. prisioner, 1949-57, deported,, 1957-63; freelance writer, Cluj, Romania. Author over 25 books, including The Criticism of Literary Ideas, 1974, The Hermeneutics of Mircea Eliade, 1980, Romanian Literature, West Literature, 1981, Etiemble or the Militant Comparatism, 1982, Romanian: Hermeneutica ideii de Literature, 1987, Pro Europa, 1995, Culture and Politics, 1996, Theory of Literature, 1994, The Biography of "The Idea of Literature" From Antiquity to the Baroque, 1996 (in Romanian 6 vols.). Former supporter Nat. Peasant Party; co-founder Anti-Totalitarian Front Romania, 1990-91. Recipient Herder prize, Vienna, Austria, 1985. Mem. MLA (hon.), Internat. Comparative Lit. Assn. (com. coordination 1977-83). Home: Eremia Grigorescu 72, 3400 Cluj Romania

MARINO, FRANCESCOMARIA, engineering educator, researcher; b. Bari, Italy, Feb. 24, 1968; d. Diomede Marino and Rachele de Bonis; m. Paola Leonetti, Dec. 14, 1996; 1 child, Davide. Laurea cum laude, Poly. di Bari, 1991, PhD, 1995. Cert. in engring. Rschr. Poly. di Bari, 1995-96, Istituto di Elaborazine del Segnale e Delle Immagini, Bari, 1996-97; vis. rschr. U. Tex., Austin, 1997; faculty rsch. assoc. Ariz. State U., Tempe, 1997-98; prof., rschr. Poly. di Bari, 1998—; invited vis. rschr. Tampere (Finland) U. Tech., 1999; rsch. cooperator Intel Co., Chandler, Ariz., 1997-98. Patentee in field; contbr. sci. articles to profl. jours. Mem. Italian Profl. Engr.'s Assn. Avocations: family, soccer, trips, trekking. Fax: 390805460410. E-mail: marino@ercole.iesi.ba.cnr.it. Office: Poly di Bari, Via Orabona 4, 70125 Bari Italy

MARINO, IGNAZIO ROBERTO, transplant surgeon, educator, researcher; b. Genoa, Italy, Mar. 10, 1955; s. Pietro Rosario and Valeria (Mazzanti) M.; m. Rossana Parisen-Toldin, Sept. 15, 1990; 1 child, Stefania Valeria. Maturità-Classica, Coll. of Merode, Rome, 1973; MD, Cath. U., Rome, 1979. Diplomate Nat. Bd. Gen. Surgery, Nat. Bd. Vascular Surgery. Intern, then resident Gemelli U. Hosp., Rome, 1979-84; temp. asst. dept. surgery Cath. U., Rome, 1981, asst. prof. surgery, 1983-92; asst. prof. surgery Transplantation Inst. U. Pitts., 1991-95, assoc. prof. surgery Transplantation Inst./, 1995-99, prof. surgery, 1999—; prof. surgery postgrad. Sch. Microsurgery, Exptl. Surgery U. Milan, 1994—; prof.surgery Sch. Medicine U. Perugia, 1994—; attending surgeon U. Pitts. Med. Ctr., Pitts., 1991—; assoc. dir. transplant divsn. VA Med. Ctr., Pitts., 1992—; attending surgeon Children's Hosp. Pitts., 1993—; prof. surgery Transplantation Inst., U. Pitts., 1999—; mem. surg. team 1st and 2d baboon to human liver transplants U. Pitts. Med. Ctr., 1992, 93, dir. European med. divsn., 1995—; sci. journalist Agenzia Nazionale Stampa Associata, 1992—; mem. nat. ad hoc donations com. United Network for Organ Sharing, 1995—; dir. Ist. Mediterraneo per i Trapianti e Terapie ad Alta Specializzazione, 1997—; cons. Nat. Transplant Com. Italy, 1999—; mem. regional com. Organ Procurement Orgn. for Sicily, 1999—; mem. Nat. Tech. Commn. for Informative Campaign on Organ Donation of Italy, 1999—, Nat. Ctr. for Transplantation of Italy, 2000—. Author: New Technique to Avoid the Revascularization Syndrome in Liver Transplantation, 1985 (Ann. prize Italian Soc. Surgery 1986), New Technique in Liver Transplantation, 1986 (De Angelis award 1986); mem. editl. bd. Clin. Transplantation, Leadership Medica, Transplantation, Jour. Investigative Surgery; contbr. 452 articles to profl. jours. Grantee Italian Nat. Coun. Rsch., 1979, 86, 87, 88, 89-93, Gastroenterology Soc., 1988; recipient award Instituto Nazionale Previdenza Dirigenti Aziende Industriali, 1982. Mem. ACS, Am. Soc. Transplantation Surgeons, Am. Soc. Transplant Physicians, Italian Soc. Surgery, Transplantation Soc. (grant 1988), European Soc. for Organ Transplantation, Soc. Surgeons Under 40 (ann. prize 1986), Cell Transplant Soc. (founding mem.), Acad. Surg. Rsch., Soc. Critical Care Medicine, Internat. Liver Transplantation Soc., Italian Order Journalists, Assn. Italian Corrs. in N.Am. (assoc.), Xenotransplantation Club (founding mem.), Internat. Coll. Surgeons, Assn. for Acad. Surgery, Nat. Assn. VA Physicians, Univ. Physician Practice Assn., Xenotransplantation Assn., Am. Assn. for the Study of Liver Diseases. Avocations: reading (history books), sailing, Annibale (pet cat). Home: Corso Italia 29, Rome 00198, Italy Office: U Pitts Transplantation Inst European Med Divsn 200 Lothrop St Ste 10097 Pittsburgh PA 15213-2546

MARINO, LOUIS J(OHN), mathematics educator; b. Whitestone, N.Y., May 3, 1949; s. Lewis F. and Lillian (Sheilds) M.; m. Sheila Burris, Dec. 19, 1969; children: Sheila Noelle, Heather Michelle. BS, U. Tenn., 1971, MS, 1975; MA in Teaching, U. S.C., 1977; AS in Engring., Piedmont Tech. Coll., 1981. Cert. tchr., S.C. Salesman Harper Bros., Inc., Greenwood, S.C., 1971-72; tchr. Orangeburg County (S.C.) Sch. Dist. 5, 1975-76, Greenwood County (S.C.) Sch. Dist. 50, 1976-77; mgr. Burger King, Greenwood, 1977-79; tchr. Laurens County (S.C.) Sch. Dist. 55, 1980-94; math. tchr. Long Cane Acad., McCormick, S.C., 1994-95; entrepreneur, 1995-98; security agent Omnisec, Greenville, S.C., 1998-99; math tchr. Long Care Acad., McCormick, S.C., 2000—; adj. prof. Limestone Coll., Spartanburg, S.C., 1978-79, Piedmont Tech. Coll., Greenwood, 1979-81. S.C. Dept. Edn. grantee, 1986. Mem. Laurens County Edn. Assn. (pres. 1991-92, sec. 1980-83, 90-91, assn. rep. 1984-94, mem. svcs. 1984-86, chmn. membership com. 1988-89), Carollina Classic Cruisers, Phi Delta Kappa. Democrat. Presbyterian. Avocations: astronomy. Home: 103 Essex Ct Greenwood SC 29649-9561

MARINO, MIGUEL ANGEL, engineering educator; b. Cienfuegos, Cuba, Nov. 10, 1940; s. Ramon and Julia Marino; m. Irma Padovani, July 27, 1968; 1 child, Raquel Christina. AA, Andrew Coll., 1959; BS, N.Mex. Inst. of Mining and, Tech., Socorro, 1962, MS, 1965; PhD, UCLA, 1972. Cert. profl. hydrologist, Am. Inst. Hydrology. Asst. geohydrologist N.Mex. State Engrs. Office, Santa Fe, 1964; asst. hydrologist Ill. State Water Survey, Champaign, 1965-69; asst. prof. U. Calif., Davis, 1972-76, assoc. prof., 1976-80, prof., 1980-99, dir. hydrology program, 1996-98, prof., 1999—. Author: (book) Groundwater and Seepage, 1982; editor: (monograph) Subsurface Flow and Contamination, 1987, (jour.) Jour. of Water Resources Planning and Mgmt., 1984-88; contbr. articles to profl. jours. Bd. dirs. Univs. Coun. on Water Resources. Recipient Richard R. Torrens award Am. Soc. Civil Engrs., 1986. Fellow Am. Water Resources Assn.; mem. N.Y. Acad. Scis., Am. Geophys. Union, Am. Soc. Civil Engrs. (hon. mem. 1999, Outstanding Jour. Paper awards 1986, 90, Julian Hinds award 1996), Am. Water Resources Assn., Am. Inst. Hydrology, Internat. Assn. Hydrol. Scis., Tau Beta Pi, Sigma Xi. Home: 813 Harrier Pl Davis CA 95616-0173 Office: Univ Calif 139 Veihmeyer Hall Davis CA 95616

MARINO, RAUL, JR., neurosurgeon; b. São Paulo, Brazil, Mar. 22, 1936; s. Raul and Brigida Quartim (de Albuquerque) M.; m. Angela Zacarelli; children: Ricardo, Rodolfo. MD, U. São Paulo Med. Sch., 1961. Medical Diplomate. Resident Lahey Clinic, Boston, 1964-65; rsch. fellow Harvard Med. Sch., Boston, 1965-66; resident McGill U., Can., 1966-67; vis. scientist NIH, Bethesda, 1967-68; neurosurgeon, founder functional neurosurgery divsn. U. São Paulo, 1970-90; prof., chmn. divsn. neurosurgery Hosp. das Clínicas/U. São Paulo Med. Sch., 1990—. Author: The Japanese Brain, 1990; editor: Functional Neurosurgery, 1979. Med. lt. Brazilian Army, 1961. Mem. São Paulo Acad. Medicine (pres. 1993-95). Avocations: philosophy, theology, history of medicine. Office: S Paulo Neurol Inst, Rua Maestro Cardim 808, 01323001 São Paulo Brazil

MARINO, RUCHE JOSEPH, retired district court judge; b. New Orleans, Jan. 22, 1936; s. Ruche and Amy L. M.; m. Juanita Duplantis, Jan. 25, 1958; children: Mark, Yvette, Mollie, Justin, Ruche, Juanita R. LLB, JD, La. State U., 1962. Bar: La. 1962. Dist. ct. judge State of La., 1971-96; ret., 1996; ad hoc for state ct. jurisdiction La. Supreme Ct., Juvenile Ct., Parish of Jefferson. Guitar player with Memory Lane. Minister, lector, choir mem., guitar and bass player Sacred Heart Ch. With USMC, 1956. Mem. ABA, Les Judges, Am. Judges Assn., La. Bar Assn., 4th and 5th Cir. Judges Assn., So. Assn. Juvenile Judges, La. Juvenile Judges. Democrat. Roman Catholic. Office: PO Box 129 Norco LA 70079-0129

MARINOS, LOUIS, software engineer; b. Athens, Greece, June 20, 1961; s. George and Vasiliki M. BSc, Tech. U. Patras, Greece, 1985; PhD, U. Koblenz, Germany, 1991; postdoc., Erasmus (The Netherlands) U., 1991-93. Rschr. Gesellschaft für Mathematik und Datenverarbeitung, Sankt Augustin, Germany, 1986-91; vice area leader info. security Sparkaessenn Informatik-Zentrum, Bonn, Germany, 1993-97; sr. cons., area leader security Integrated Info. and Comm. Sys. GmbH, Bonn, 1997—; rschr. U. Patras, 1984-85; cons. GTE-Labs, 1988. Author: Knowledge ENG Shells, 1993, The Impact of CASE on Software Process, 1994; contbr. articles to profl. jours. Mem. IEEE (Best Student Paper). Office: Sparkassen Info, Koenigswinterersrt 552, 53227 Bonn Germany

MARINOS, YANNIS, journalist, government official; b. Hermoupolis, Greece, July 20, 1930; s. Paul and Elisabeth (Patiniotou) M. MA in Law, Athens U., 1956; PhD (hon.), Aristotelian U., Salonica, 1999. Journalist To Vima, Athens, Greece, 1953-65; editor-in-chief Economicos Tachydromos, Athens, Greece, 1954-65, editor, dir., 1964-96; dep. Greek Polit. Party Nea Democratia and The European Popular Party, 1999—; mem. European Parliament, 1999—; polit. commentator Ta Nea, Athens, 1972-75. Author: The Palestinian Problem and Cyprus, 1975, For a Change Towards Better, 1983, Greece in Crisis, 1987, Common Sense, 1993; columnist To Vima, 1992—; mem. editl. bd. Economicos Tachydromos, 1996—. Active Red Cross Internat. Amnesty, 1976—. Named the Best European Journalist, Commn. the European Cmty./Assn. the European Journalists, 1989. Mem. Union European Econ. /Fin. Press (exec. com. 1974-91, 95), Athens Music Hall Orgn. (bd. dirs.). Greek Orthodox. Avocations: literature, history, classical music, fishing. Home: 9 Merlin St, 106 71 Athens Greece Office: 9 Merlin St, 106 71 Athens Greece

MARINOSCHI, GABRIELA, mathematician; b. Bucharest, Jan. 30, 1957; d. Gabriel and Georgeta Marinoschi; m. Dinu Bratosin, Aug. 13, 1983. Bachelors degree in math., U. Bucharest, 1979, specialization in fluid mechanics, 1980. Hydrologist Inst. Meteorology and Hydrology, Bucharest, 1980-85, rschr., 1985-90; sr. rschr. Inst. Applied Math. Caius Iacob, Bucharest, 1991—; sci. sec. dept. math. Romanian Acad., Bucharest, 1990—. Contbr. articles to profl. publs. Mem. Romanian Nat. Com. Math., Geselschaft Angewandte Math., Mechanics. Avocations: reading, travel. Fax: 40 1 2116608. E-mail: gmarino@acad.ro. Office: Romanian Acad, Calea Victoriei 125, RO71102 Bucharest Romania

MARINOV, MILKO TODOROV, software engineering educator; b. Nedan, Bulgaria, June 9, 1958; s. Todor Marinov and Sadbina Dimitrova (Alexieva) T.; m. Svetlana Trifonova Koceva, June 5, 1988; 1 child, Tihomir. MSc in Computer Engring., U. Rousse, Bulgaria, 1983, PhD in Knowledge-Managed Computer Aided Instrn. Sys., 1985. Sys. programmer Computer Ctr., Rousse, 1983-85; prin. lectr. software engring. dept. computer sys. U. Rousse, 1985—. Contbr. articles to profl. publs. Mem. N.Y. Acad. Scis. Avocations: soccer, skiing, mountain climbing, movies. Home: 11 Bitolya Str, 7004 Rousse Bulgaria Office: U Rousse Dept Computer Sys, 8 Studentska Str, 7017 Rousse Bulgaria

MARINOVIĆ, NENAD JOSIP JURAJ, electrical engineering educator, researcher; b. Šibenik, Croatia, Aug. 11, 1929; s. Vinko Vicko and Marija (Posinković) M.; m. Tamara Pintarić, Oct. 7, 1943; children: Marina, Morana. Diploma in engring., U. Zagreb, Yugoslavia, 1955; DSc, Tech. U. Berlin, 1976; prof., U. Zagreb, 1980. Engr. RAŠA Coal Mine, Labin, Croatia, 1950-60; dept. mgr. Inst. KONČar, Zagreb, 1960-90; prof. U. Zagreb, 1990—; sec. IEC/SC 31J Internat. Elec. Commn., Geneva, 1980—; hon. lectr. U. Zagreb, 1961-90; head cert. svc. S-Komisija, Zagreb, 1963. Editor KONČ-Stručne informacije, Zagreb, 1970-90, S-BILTEN, Zagreb, 1972—; author: Electrotechnology in Mining, 1990, Electrotechnology for Explosive Atmospheres, 1986, Electrical Installations for Explosive Atmospheres, 5th edit., 1999, General Electricity and Electronics, 1993, 2d edit., 1996. Recipient N. Tesla award Croatian Com. Sci., 1966. Avocations: sailing, skiing. Home: Alagovićeva 22, 10000 Zagreb Croatia Office: 5 Komisija Dznm A, Bastjanova b b, 10000 Zagreb Croatia

MARIN-ROJAS, RAFAEL ANGEL, immunohematologist, educator; b. San Carlos, Alajuela, Costa Rica, Nov. 7, 1944; s. Marco Antides Marin and Emérita Rojas; m. Eligia Irene Chaves (July 9, 1982 (div. Feb. 1990); 1 child, Hilda; m. Olga Igorevna Muraviova, Feb. 5, 1994; 1 child, Alfonso. Licenciate in Microbiology, U. Costa Rica, San Pedro, 1969, MS in Microbiology, 1980. Instr. U. Costa Rica, 1969-74, prof., 1974—; immunohematologist Forensic Lab., San José, Costa Rica, 1972-93; dir. med. lab. San Juan de Dios Hosp., San José, 1993-96. Contbr. articles to profl. jours. Mem. Microbiologist Coll., Am. Assn. Blood Banks, N.Y. Acad. Scis. Roman Catholic. Avocations: climbing, hiking. Home: Residential Cedral #122, 489-2050 San Pedro San Jose, Costa Rica

MARION, ANDRÉ, research engineer; b. La Seyne, France, July 14, 1942; s. Jean and Jeanne (Lepigeon) M.; m. Colette Bats, Sept. 30, 1967; 1 child, Rodolphe. Lic. in Physics, U. Orsay, France, 1959, D Nuclear Physics, 1966, Maitre Electronics, 1973. Electronics engr. Ctr. Spectrometrie, Ctr. Nat. de la Rsch. Sci., France, 1967-77; mgr. image acquisition ctr. Inst. d'Optique, Ctr. Nat. de la Rsch. Sci., France, 1977-96, computer engr., 1987-96, mgr. image processing ctr., 1996—; instr. Conservatoire Nat. des Arts et Metiers, 1973-83, Supoptique, 1988—, Sup Elec., 1992—; tech. reviewer Anvar, France, 1996—; mem. sci. com. image processing ctr. INAG, France, 1977-79; mem. sci. com. Ctr. Internat. d'Etudes sur le Linceul de Turin, 1996—. Author: Introduction to Digital Image Processing, 1987, New Discoveries on the Shroud of Turin, 1997, Image Acquisition and Visualization, 1997 (Prix Roberval 1998), Jesus and the Science, 2000. Roman Catholic. Avocations: animal protection, travel, swimming, classical music. Office: CNRS Inst d'Optique, Bt 503 Ctr U BP 147, 91403 Orsay France

MARION, FABIENNE, emergency medicine physician, researcher; b. Tours, France, May 26, 1968; d. André and Christiane (Jaugey) M.; m. Frederic Joye; 1 child, Clément Joye-Marion. MD, Tours U., 1997; emergency medicine specialization, 1999. Physician Tours Hosp., 1997-98; emergency physician Chateauroux Hosp., France, 1998—, Carcassonne Hosp., France, 1998. Contbr. articles to profl. jours. Mem. SFUM, SRLF. Avocations: photography, sports. Office: Samu 77 CHG Antoine, Gayraud Rte St Hilaire, 11890 Carcassonne Cedex 9, France

MARIOTTE, FRÉDÉRIC PIERRE, physicist; b. Pantin, France, Sept. 21, 1960; s. Pierre C. and Denise L. (Denis) M.; m. Anne M. Grenouillet, July 20, 1991; 2 children: Charles, Thibault. Engring. Diploma, Ecole Sup. de Chimie, Ind. de Lyon, 1984; PhD, U. Bordeaux, 1994. Mil. rschr. CEA-CENG, Grenoble, France, 1984-85; nuclear engr. COGEMA, La Hague, France, 1985-88; R&D rschr. CEA-CESTA, Le Barp, France, 1988-91, project mgr., 1992-95; vis. scientist U. Pa., Phila., 1991-92; chief inspector Internat. Atomic Energy Agy., Vienna, Austria, 1996—. Editor: Procs. of Chiral '94, 1994; contbr. articles to profl. jours. Mem. IEEE (sr. mem.), SEE, N.Y. Acad. Scis. Avocations: scuba diving, skiing, travel, judo. E-mail: f.mariotte@iaea.org. Office: Internat Atomic Energy Agy, Wagramer Strasse 5 POB 200, A-1400 Vienna Austria

MARIOTTI, EGIDIO, cardiologist, researcher; b. Arcevia, Ancona, Italy, Sept. 17, 1953; s. Emiliano Mariotti and Elda Lorenzini; m. Luciana Fortunati; children: Giacomo, Giorgio. MD, U. Rome, 1978, postgrad., 1981. Asst. physician Policlinico, U. Rome, 1978-79; intern Policlinico Rome I Clinica Medica, 1979-80; asst. physician Mil. Hosp., Udine, Italy, 1981, intern cardiology, 1981-82; asst. physician Ospedale San Salvatore, Pesaro, Italy, 1982-93, asst. head, dir. cardiac divsn., 1993—, cons. cardiologist hematol. divsn., 1988—, chief cardiovascular rsch. bone marrow transplantation, 1992—; co-organizer European Bone Marrow Transplantation Register, 1993—. Contbr. articles to profl. jours. Lt. Med. Corps Italian Armed Forces, 1980-81. Recipient medal and good svc. cert. for earthquake assistance Med. Corps., 1980. Mem. European Soc. Cardiology, Italian Soc. Echochardiogrphy, Assn. Hosp. Cardiologists (regional exec. bd.). Office: Ospedale San Salvatore, Piazzale Cinelli 4, 61100 Pesaro Marche Italy

MARIS, CHARLES ROBERT, surgeon, otolaryngologist; b. Champaign, Ill., Nov. 24, 1948; s. Harold Franklin and Marjorie Ellen (Beermann) M.; m. Karen Lynne Richardson, Dec. 27, 1970; children: Katherine, Emily, Charles Jr. BS, Eastern Ill. U., 1971; MD, U. Ill., 1975. Diplomate Am. Bd. Surgery, Am. Bd. Otolaryngology. Resident in otolaryngology U. Nebr. Med. Ctr., Omaha, 1982; chief of surgery Sarah Bush Lincoln Health Ctr., Mattoon, Ill., 1984-85, chmn. exec. com., 1985, 89, 94, chief of staff, 1986, 90, 95; br. med. dir. Carle Clinic, Mattoon/Charleston, Ill., 1998—; bd. dirs. 1st Mid-Ill. Bank & Trust. Mem. Charleston Community Unit Dist. #1 Sch. Bd., 1984-88; v.p. fin., pres.-elect Lincoln Trails coun. Boy Scouts Am. Lt. Col. U.S. Army Reserve, 159th Mash (Operation Desert Storm) 1990-91. Named one of Outstanding Young Men in Am., 1985. Fellow Am. Coll. Surgeons, Am. Acad. Otolaryngology-Head and Neck Surgery, Am. Acad. Facial Plastic and Reconstructive Surgery. Republican. Methodist. Office: 200 Lerna Rd S Mattoon IL 61938-9388

MARISCOTTI, MARIO ALBERTO JUAN, nuclear physicist, consultant; b. Buenos Aires, Nov. 12, 1939; s. Ventura and Elda Victorina (De Lorenzi) M.; m. Amalia Lina Boselli, Apr. 24, 1962; children: Alberto Juan, Patricia Inés, Fernando Mario, Maria Eugenia. Lic. in Physics, U. Buenos Aires, 1962, D in Physics, 1967. Physicist Brookhaven Nat. Lab., 1965-70; scientist, chmn. dept. physics, dir. R&D AEC, Argentina, 1970-88; prof. physics U. Buenos Aires, 1971—; pres. Nat. Acad. Exact, Phys. and Natural Scis., Argentina, 1994-98, Nat. Agy. for Promotion of Sci. and Tech., Argentina, 1997-99; bd. dirs. Sci. Rsch. Coun., Buenos Aires; vis. rschr. KFA, Julich, Germany, 1974; vis. prof. U. Manchester, U.K., 1975; vis. sr. scientist Brookhaven Nat. Lab., N.Y., 1986-89; cons. UN Indsl. Devel. Orgn., Geneva, 1980; dir. Reinforced Concrete Tomography Inc., Buenos Aires, 1992—, Higher Edn. Quality Improvement Fund, Buenos Aires, 1993—. Author: The Secret of Huemul Island, 1985; editor: Basis for a Discussion of Science and Technology Policies, 1996; contbr. articles to profl. jours. Mem. Fgn. Affairs Argentine Coun., 1995—. Recipient grants Conicet and others, Argentina, 1965—, Konex prize Konex Found., Buenos Aires, 1983, award UN Indsl. Devel. Orgn., 1994. Mem. IEEE (sr.), Argentine Phys. Soc. Roman Catholic. Avocations: tennis, golf, skiing. Home: 2017 Reclus, 1609 Boulogne BA, Argentina Office: Nat Acad Exact Phys Nat Sci, 1711 Ave Alvear, 1014 Buenos Aires Argentina

MARIX EVANS, MARTIN FORBES, book producer, writer, photographer; b. Southport, U.K., Dec. 25, 1939; s. Jean-Paul Robert and Margaret (Smith) Marix Evans; m. Gillian Mary Haselwood, Apr. 2, 1966; children: Louise Mary, Polly Harriet. Student, Wesleyan U., Middletown, Conn., 1959; BA, U. Cambridge, U.K., 1963, MA, 1985. Various editl. and mktg. posts Longman Group, Harlow, U.K., 1963-74; editl. dir., mktg. dir. Pitman Pub., London, 1974-79, 79-81; editl. dir. Frederick Warne Ltd., London, 1981-82, Thames Head Ltd., Avening, 1982-87; editl. dir., COO BLA Pub., East Grinstead, 1987-89; proprieter Book Packaging and Mktg., Silverstone, 1989—; mem. com. Ind. Pubs. Guild, London, 1984-90, chmn., 1988-90. Author, photographer: The Battles of the Somme, 1996, Passchendaele and the Battles of Ypres, 1997, Retreat Hell! We Just Got Here! -- The American Expeditionary Force in France 1917-1918, 1998, The Boer War: South Africa 1988-1902, 1999, The Fall of France: Act With Daring!, 2000, Encyclopedia of the Boer War, 2000; exec. editor: Contemporary Photographers, 3d edit., 1995. Avocations: painting, old Aston Martin cars, rebuilding old walls. Office: Book Packaging and Mktg, 3 Murswell Ln Silverstone, Towcester NN12 8UT, United Kingdom

MARJANCZYK, JOSEPH ANICETUS, priest; b. Elizabeth, N.J., Apr. 17, 1921; s. Joseph John and Catherine Frances (Cwik) M. BA, Seton Hall U., 1941; MDiv, Darlington Sem., 1975. Ordained priest Roman Cath. Ch., 1945; named monsignor, 1979. Asst. pastor St. Valentine's Ch., Bloomfield, N.J., 1945-72; pastor St. Adalbert's Ch., Elizabeth, 1972-83, Our Lady of Mt. Carmel Ch., Bayonne, N.J., 1983-96; named protonotary apostolic, 1988; vicar Episcopal South Hudson Vicariate, 1991-96; prof. Polish Master Sch. Fgn. Langs., Seton Hall U., 1948-60; pastor emeritus Our Lady of Mt. Carmel Ch., Bayonne, 1996—; chmn. pers. bd. Archdiocese of Newark, 1972-74, mem. pastoral coun., 1972-83, archdiocesan trustee 1975-86; chmn. adminstrv. com., mem. exec. bd. Archdiocesan Pastoral Coun., 1972-84; dean Union County East Deanery, 1975-83; Polish Apostolate rep. Nat. Conf. Cath. Bishops Com. on Migration, 1989-96, chmn. Polish adv. bd. to conf. office for pastoral care of migrants and refugees, 1989-96. Chmn. bd. dirs. Polish Cultural Found., 1974-90, 92-97, 98—; trustee Seton Hall U., 1978-96, Immaculate Conception Sem., South Orange, N.J., 1979-86; commr. bd. edn. City of Elizabeth, 1979-83; nat. chaplain Polish Army Vets. Assn. Am., 1980-98; founder, pres. N.J. chpt. John Paul II Found., 1986—; chmn. exec. bd. Polish chapel renovation and rededication Nat. Shrine of Immaculate Conception, Washington, 1986-89. Decorated Gold Order of Merit (Republic of Poland); recipient Polish Apostolate Pride of Polonia award, 1996; named Canon of Cathedral chpt. Archdiocese Warsaw, Poland, 1995. Mem. Archdiocesan Polish Clergy Soc. (hon. pres. 1979—), Polish Am. Priests Assn. (exec. com. 1991—), Polish Am. Congress, Polish Am. Hist. Assn., N.J. Hist. Soc., Polish Am. Numis. Assn., Polonians Club, KC. Home: PO Box 456 Point Pleasant NJ 08742-0456

MARK, ALAN FRANCIS, plant ecologist, educator; b. Dunedin, Otago, New Zealand, June 19, 1932; s. Cyril Lionel and Frances Evelyn (Marshall) M.; m. Patricia Kaye Davie, June 28, 1957; children: Jenifer Kaye, Stephen Dwight, Alastair John, Bridget Caroline. BSc, U. New Zealand, Dunedin, 1953, MSc, 1955; PhD, Duke U., 1958. Ecologist Otago Catchment Bd., Dunedin, 1959-60; rsch. fellow Hellaby Indigenous Grasslands Rsch. Trust, Dunedin, 1960-64; lectr. U. Otago, Dunedin, 1964-66, assoc. prof., 1966-75, prof. dept. botany, 1975-98, prof. emeritus, 1998—; rsch. advisor Hellaby Indigenous Grasslands Rsch. Trust, 1965-2000; chmn. Guardians of Lakes Manapouri, Monowai and Te Anau, New Zealand, 1973-98; mem. New Zealand Nat. Parks and Res. Auth., 1981-90. Author: New Zealand Alpine Plants, 1973; contbr. over 140 articles to sci. publs. Mem. Otago Catchment Bd., 1974-86, Otago Conservation Bd., Dunedin, 1990—. Named Comdr. of Brit. Empire, Govt. of New Zealand, 1989; recipient Commemorative medal Govt. of New Zealand, 1990, Hutton medal, 1998, Conservation and Environ. award, 1997. Fellow Royal Soc. New Zealand; mem. Ecol. Soc. Am., New Zealand Ecol. Soc. (v.p. 1975), Royal Forest and Bird Protection Soc. (pres. 1986-90), Phi Beta Kappa. Home: 205 Wakari Rd, Dunedin Otago, New Zealand Office: U Otago, Box 56, Dunedin Otago, New Zealand

MARK, HANS MICHAEL, physicist, government official; b. Mannheim, Germany, June 17, 1929; came to U.S., 1940, naturalized, 1945; s. Herman Francis and Maria (Schramek) M.; m. Marion G. Thorpe, Jan. 28, 1951; children: Jane H., James P. A.B. in Physics, U. Calif. at Berkeley, 1951; Ph.D., MIT, 1954; Sc.D. (hon.), Fla. Inst. Tech., 1978; D. Eng. (hon.), Poly. U. N.Y., 1982; DEng (hon.), Milw. Sch. Engring., 1991; LHD (hon.), St. Edward's U., 1993. Rsch. assoc. MIT, Cambridge, 1954-55, asst. prof., 1958-60; rsch. physicist Lawrence Radiation Lab., U. Calif., Livermore, 1955-58, 60-69, exptl. physics div. leader, 1960-64; assoc. prof. nuclear engring. U. Calif., Berkeley, 1960-66, prof., 1966-69, chmn. dept. nuclear engring., 1964-69; lectr. dept. applied sci. U. Calif., Davis, 1969-73; cons. prof. engring. Stanford U., 1973-84; dir. NASA-Ames Rsch. Ctr., 1969-77; under-sec., dir. Nat. Reconnaissance Office USAF, Washington, 1977-79, sec., 1979-81; dep. adminstr. NASA, Washington, 1981-84; chancellor U. Tex. System, Austin, 1984-92; prof. aerospace engring. and engring. mechanics U. Tex., Austin, 1988—; dir. defense rsch. and engring. Dept. Defense, Washington, 1998—; mem. Pres.'s Adv. Group Sci. and Tech., 1975-76; bd. dirs. Astronautics Corp. Am.; trustee Poly. U., 1984—. Author: (with N.T. Olson) Experiments in Modern Physics, 1966 (with E. Teller and J.S. Foster, Jr.) Power and Security, 1976, (with A. Levine) The Management of Research Institutions, 1983, The Space Station-A Personal Journey, 1987, (with Victor G. Szebehely) Adventures in Celestial Mechanics, 1998; also numerous articles.; Editor: (with S. Fernbach) Properties of Matter Under Unusual Conditions, 1969, (with Lowell Wood) Energy in Physics, War and Peace, 1988. Recipient Disting. Svc. medal NASA, 1972, 77, medal for exceptional engring. achievement, 1984, Exceptional Civilian Svc. award USAF, 1979, Disting. Pub. Svc, medal, Dept. Def., 1981. Fellow AIAA (Von Karman lectr. astronautics 1992), Am. Phys. Soc.; mem. Nat. Acad. Engring., Am. Nuclear Soc., Am. Geophys. Union, Coun. Fgn. Rels., Cosmos Club. Achievements include research on nuclear energy levels, nuclear reactions, applications, nuclear energy for practical purposes, atomic flourescence yields, measurement X-rays above atmosphere, spacecraft and experimental aircraft design. Office: Dir Def Rsch-Engring 3030 Defense Pentagon Washington DC 20301-3030

MARK, HAROLD WAYNE, industrial chemist; b. Chanute, Kans., May 2, 1949; s. Earl James and Wilma Ruth (Roberts) M. BS, U. Kans., 1971; PhD, Northwestern U., 1975. Rsch. chemist Phillips Petroleum Co., Bartlesville, Okla., 1975-80, sr. rsch. chemist, 1980-88; rsch. chemist Westvaco Corp., Charleston, S.C., 1988-90; analytical and assurance mgr. Westvaco Corp., DeRidder, La., 1990—. Inventor in field. Mem. ASTM, AAAS, ASQC, Am. Chem. Soc., Sigma Xi. Avocations: cyclist. Office: Westvaco Corp PO Box 836 Deridder LA 70634-0836

MARK, JAN(ET MAJORIE), children's writer; b. Welwyn, Hertfordshire, England, June 22, 1943; d. Colin Denis and Marjorie Brisland; m. Neil Mark, March 1, 1969 (div. 1989); children: Isobel, Alexander. NDD, Canterbury Coll. Art, 1965. Writer; tchr. art and engl. Southfields Sch., Gravesend, Kent, England, 1965-71; writer fellow arts coun. Oxford Polytechnic, 1982-84. Author: Thunder and Lightnings, 1976 (Penguin/Guardian award, 1975, Carnegie medal Libr. Assn., 1976, Guardian commendation, 1977, Notable Book Citation ALA), Under the Autumn Garden, 1977, The Ennead, 1978 (Notable Children's Trade Book citation in the field of Social Studies Nat. Coun. Social Studies and Children's Book Coun., 1978), Divide and Rule, 1979, The Short Voyage of the Albert Ross, 1980, The Dead Letter Box, 1982, Aquarius, 1982 (Young Observer/Rank Teenage Fiction prize, 1982), Handles, 1983 (Carnegie medal, 1983), Trouble Halfway, 1985, At the Sign of the Dog and Rocket, 1985, Dream House, 1987, The Twig Thing, 1988, Presents From Gran, 1988, Man in Motion, 1989, Finders, Losers, 1990, The Hillingdon Fox, 1991, Great Frog and Mighty Moose, 1992, The Snow Maze, 1992, All the King and Queens, 1993, Taking the Cat's Way Home, 1994, Worm's Eye View, 1994, They Do Things Differently There, 1994, A Fine Summer Knight, 1995, The Coconut Quins, 1997, Under the Red Elephant, 1995, The Sighting, 1997, God's Story, 1997, My Frog and I, 1997, Lady Long-Legs, 1999, (juvenile story collections) Nothing to Be Afraid Of, 1980, Hairs in the Palm of the Hand, 1981, Feet and Other Stories, 1983 (Angel Lit. award for Fiction, 1983), Frankie's Hat, 1986, Enough is Too Much Already and Other Stories, 1988, A Can of Worms, 1990, In Black and White, 1991, (picture books) The Long Distance Poet, Out of the Oven, 1986, Fur, 1986, Fun, 1987, Strat and Chatto, 1989, Carrot Tops and Cotton Tails, 1993, Fun with Mrs. Thumb, 1993, This Bowl of Earth, 1993, Haddock, 1994, The Tale of Tobias, 1995, Mr. Dickens Hits Town, 1999, The Midas Touch, 1999 (plays) Izzy, 1985, The Weathermonger, 1985, Interference, 1987, (with Stephen Cockett) Captain Courage and the Rose Street Gang, 1987, Time and the Hour; and, Nothing To Be Afraid Of, 1990, (adult fiction) Two Stories, 1984, Zeno Was Here, The Eclipse of The Century, 1999; editor: School Stories, 1989, A Book of Song and Dance, 1992, The Oxford Book of Children's Stories, 1993. Home: 98 Howard St, Oxford OX4 3BG, England Office: David Highams Assocs Ltd, 5-8 Lower John St Golden Sq, London W1R 4HA, England

MARK, JORGEN, agronomist; b. Rudberjggaard, Denmark, Mar. 13, 1938; s. Carl and Grete (Maegaard-Nielsen) M.; m. Asta Hansigne Tjernlund, Oct. 1, 1970; 1 child, Eva Christina. MSc in Agriculture, Agrl. & Veterinary Univ., Copenhagen, 1962; B in Commerce, Copenhagen Sch. Commerce, 1965. Sec. Agrl. Coun., Copenhagen, 1962-65; mktg. mgr. Dronninborg Maskinfabrik, Randers, Denmark, 1966-73; ind. landowner Denmark, Scotland, 1973—. Mem. city coun. Purhus, Jutland, 1982-92; chmn. Conservative Party, Purhus, 1975-82. Lt. Danish army, 1957-59. Fellow Rotary of Randers (pres. 1992-93); mem. Regional Forestry Assn. (chmn. 199-89), Nat. Fedn. Lage Farmers (vice chmn. 1982-93), Danish Soc. Mgmt. Mem. Evang.-Lutheran Ch. Avocations: hunting, golf, skiing. E-mail: jmark@post3.tele.dk.

MARK, MARION THORPE, writing educator; b. Hayward, Calif., Sept. 28, 1930; d. Milton William and Johanna Altgelt (Schwab) Thorpe; m. Hans Michael Mark, Jan. 28, 1951; children: Jane, Rufus. BS in Edn., Boston U., 1952, MS in Edn., 1953; EdD, George Washington U., 1982. Diagnostician, tchr. Boston U. Reading Clinic, 1951-53; tchr. remedial reading, dir. ednl. testing and diagnosis Natick (Mass.) Pub. Schs., 1953-55; pvt. tutor of adults and children in reading Livermore, Calif., 1955-61; pvt. turor, home tchr. Berkeley, Calif, 1961-68; instr. reading McKinley Continuation H.S., Berkeley, 1968-69; chmn. dept. English Ravenswood H.S., Redwood City, Calif., 1969-71; honors English tchr. San Mateo Sch. Dist., Redwood City, 1971-76; instr. George Washington U., Washington, 1981-82; reading specialist Prince Georges County, Camp Springs, Md., 1971-76; curriculum specialist Austin (Tex.) Ind. Sch. Dist., 1984-91; tchr. advanced placement English St. Michael's Acad., Austin, 1993-97; instr. writing St. Edward's U., Austin, 1995—; mentor handicapped students St. Edward's U., 1997—, mentor migrant students, 1995—. Author: (lession series) Teaching Literary Appreciation, 1953, The Pious Tiger, 1964, The Scientific Grammarian, 1985, The Mathematical Historian, 1986; author diagnostic test: Mathematics Skills, 1975. Bd. dirs. ARC, Austin, 1989, Camp Fire Boys and Girls, Austin, 1984-92, U. Tex. Migrant Edn., Austin, 1984-92, Ballet Austin; leader Camp Fire Boys and Girls, Berkeley, Calif., 1961-69; adv. coun. U. tex. Migrant Edn.; vol. adv. com. Austin Ind. Sch. Dist. Named Tchr. of the Yr., Menlo-Atherton Student Coun., 1975; recipient Leadership award Camp Fire Boys and Girls, 1991. Mem. The English Speaking Union, PEO, Pan Am. Round Table, Austin Women's Club, Am. History Club, Univ. Ladies Club, Tuesday Club, Tex. Phios. Soc. Democrat. Episcopalian. Avocations: piano, reading, needlepoint, antique dolls, family history. Home: 1710-III Rockmoor Pl Austin TX 78703 Office: 1715 Scenic Dr Austin TX 78703-2000

MARK, MICHAEL DAVID, lawyer; b. Bklyn., Sept. 16, 1944; s. Irving and Mildred Mark; children: Dana Lynne, Stephanie Lauren. BA, Rutgers U., 1966; JD, U. Tenn., 1969. Bar: Tenn. 1969, N.J. 1970, U.S. Dist. Ct. N.J. 1970, U.S. Supreme Ct. 1973; cert. civil trial atty., N.J. Supreme Ct. 1992. House counsel Liberty Mut. Ins. Co., East Orange, N.J., 1969-71; assoc. Skoloff & Wolfe, Newark, 1971-73; pvt. practice, Union, N.J., 1973—; past assoc. bd. dirs. United Jersey Bank, Union; Police Benevolent Assn. lawyer City of Linden, N.J., 1980—, Clark Twp., Clark, N.J., 1986; mem. Union-Essex County Early Settlement Panels, Elizabeth and Newark. Mem. Am. Acad. Matrimonial Lawyers (bd. mgrs. 1982—), N.J. Bar Assn., Union County Bar Assn., Union Lawyers Club (past pub. defender). Republican. Avocation: private pilot. Office: 2444 Morris Ave Union NJ 07083-5711

MARK, REUBEN, consumer products company executive; b. Jersey City, N.J., Jan. 21, 1939; s. Edward and Libbie (Berman) M.; m. Arlene Slobzian, Jan. 10, 1964; children: Lisa, Peter, Stephen. AB, Middlebury Coll., 1960; MBA, Harvard U., 1963. With Colgate-Palmolive Co., N.Y.C., 1963—; pres., gen. mgr. Colgate-Palmolive Co., Venezuela, 1972-73, Can., 1973-74; v.p., gen. mgr. Far East div. Colgate-Palmolive Co., 1974-75, v.p., gen. mgr. household products div., 1975-79, group v.p. domestic ops., 1979-81, exec. v.p., 1981-83, chief operating officer, 1983-84, pres., 1983-86, chief exec. officer, 1984—, chmn. bd., 1986—; lectr. Sch. Bus. Adminstrn., U. Conn., 1977. Served with U.S. Army, 1961. Mem. Soap and Detergent Assn. (bd. dirs.), Grocery Mfrs. Am. (dir.), Nat. Exec. Service Corp. Office: Colgate-Palmolive Co 300 Park Ave Fl 8 New York NY 10022-7499

MARK, RICHARD KUSHAKOW, internist; b. N.Y.C., Feb. 11, 1951; s. Eugene and Gertrude (Kushakow) M.; m. Harriet Bass, Sept. 17, 1989; children: Sabrina, Ari, Etan. BS, Hofstra U., 1972; MD, U. Autonomous Guadalajara, 1976, SUNY, Bklyn., 1977. Diplomate Am. Bd. Internal Medicine. Resident in medicine Maimonides Med. Ctr., Bklyn., 1977-82; clin. instr. medicine Downstate Med. Ctr., Bklyn., 1982-90, asst. prof. medicine, 1990-93; prof. clin. medicine CUNY, 1993—; pvt. practice internal medicine Bklyn., 1982—; dept. attending emergency Cabrini Med. Ctr., N.Y.C., 1982-84; med. cons. The Lighthouse. Author: Consumer's Guide to Preventive Medicine, 1996. Mem. N.Y.C. Coalition for the Homeless, 1986—, The Children's Fund., N.Y.C., 1990—. Recipient Cmty. Svc. award Borough of Bklyn., 1986, Physicians Recognition award AMA, 1993-97, Preceptorship award ACP, 1996, Tchr. of Yr. Maimonides Clin. Tchg. award CUNY, 1995, 96, 97, 98, 99; recipient Tchr. of the Yr. 1982, 83. Fellow ACP; mem. Acad. Medicine, Inter-Am. Coll. Medicine, King's County Med. Soc. Democrat. Jewish. Avocations: sailing, photography, skiing. Office: 8023 19th Ave Brooklyn NY 11214-1753

MARK, TIMOTHY IVAN, lawyer; b. Hershey, Pa., Oct. 8, 1951; s. Howard Behm and Ethel Mae Beam Mark; m. Janice Leigh Evans, Jan. 5, 1974; children: Andrew James, Amy Elizabeth. BA cum laude, East Stroudsburg U., 1973; JD cum laude, Temple U., 1978. Bar: Pa. 1978, U.S. Dist. Ct. (mid. dist.) Pa. 1978, U.S. Supreme Ct. 1983, U.S. Ct. Appeals (3d cir.) 1983. Law clk. intern U.S. Dist. Ct. (ea. dist.) Pa., Phila., 1978; asst. atty. gen. Com. of Pa., Harrisburg, 1978-79; shareholder Goldberg, Evans and Katzman, Harrisburg, 1979-85; ptnr. Evans, Stone and Mark, Harrisburg, 1985-87; shareholder Mette, Evans and Woodside, Harrisburg, 1987-92, Caldwell & Kearns, Harrisburg, 1992-97; of counsel Thomas Thomas and Hafer, Harrisburg, 1997-99; pvt. practice, Hummelstown, Pa., 1999—; lectr. Pa. Bar Assn., Harrisburg, 1992—. Mem. Pa. Def. Inst. (bd. dirs. 1990-96), Def. Rsch. Inst., Pa. Trial Lawyers Assn., Pa. Bar Assn. Avocations: golfing, reading, computer research. Home and Office: 811 Providence Cir Hummelstown PA 17036-9753

MARKATOS, EVANGELOS PAVLOS, computer engineer, educator; b. Argostoli, Cephalonia, Greece, Feb. 22, 1966; s. Pavlos and Evangelia (Melisinou) M.; m. Catherine Chronaki, Aug. 8, 1966. BS in Computer Engring., U. Patras, Greece, 1988; MS in Computer Sci., U. Rochester, 1990, PhD in Computer Sci., 1993. Programmer GTE, Waltham, Mass., 1990; rschr. ICS Forth, Herakleion, Greece, 1992—; vis. asst. prof. Tech. U. Crete, Chania, Greece, 1992—; asst. prof. U. Crete, 1996—. Mem. IEEE, Assn. for Computing Machinery, Greek C. of C. Home: 43 Vrioulon St, 71306 Herakleion Greece Office: ICS Forth, PO Box 1385, 71306 Herakleion Greece

MARKEN, WILLIAM RILEY, magazine editor; b. San Jose, Calif., Sept. 2, 1942; s. Harry L. and Emma Catherine (Kraus) M.; m. Marilyn Tonascia, Aug. 30, 1964; children—Catherine, Elizabeth, Michael, Paul. Student, Occidental Coll., 1960-62; BA, U. Calif., Berkeley, 1964. Editor-in-chief Sunset Mag., Menlo Park, Calif., 1981-96, eHow.com, 1999—. Bd. dirs. Calif. Tomorrow, 1979-83; pres. League to Save Lake Tahoe, 1994-97. Avocations: tennis; skiing; basketball.

MARKHAM, CHARLES HENRY, neurologist; b. Pasadena, Calif., Dec. 24, 1923; s. Fred Smith and Maziebelle Valeta (Glover) M.; m. Kathleen Tiernan, Sept. 29, 1945 (div. 1971); children: Charles H., Arthur Tiernan, Daphne, James Daniel; m. Lisa Wells Overly, July 10, 1971; children: John Wells, Sara Brennan. Student, Colo. Sch. Mines, 1941-43; AB, Stanford U., 1947, MD, 1951. Intern, med. asst. resident Lane Hosp., San Francisco, 1950-52; fellow in neurology Children's Med. Ctr., Boston, 1952-53; asst. resident Boston City Hosp., 1953-54, chief resident, 1954-55; asst. prof. neurology UCLA Sch. Medicine, 1958-65, assoc. prof., 1965-70, assoc. prof. neurology, 1970-71, prof. neurology, 1971-94, prof. emeritus, 1994—; sci. dir. Dystonia Med. Rsch. Found., Chgo., 1985-94, mem. bd. trustees, 1994—; sci. dir. Hereditary Disease Found., L.A., 1979-81; mem. adv. bd. Am. Parkinson Disease Assn., N.Y.C., 1976-83; attending physician UCLA Sch. Medicine, 1957—, cons. in neurology St. John's Hosp., Santa Monica, Calif., 1960-94. Contbr. articles to profl. jours.; author numerous books and abstracts. Trustee Westlake Sch. for Girls, L.A., 1965-74, St. Matthews Parish Sch., L.A., 1985-87; bd. dirs. Jubilee Christian Acad., 1996-99, Wildling Mus., 1997—, Las Positas Park Found., 1998-2000. With U.S. Army, 1943-45, ETO. Grantee NIH, NASA. Mem. Am. Acad. Neurology, AAAS, Am.

Bd. Psychiatry and Neurology, Am. Epilepsy Soc., Am. Neurol. Assn., Am. Pain Soc., Am. Soc. for Gravitational and Space Biology, Bárány Soc. (Hallpike-Nylen prize 1990), Internat. Brain Rsch. Orgn., Internat. League Against Epilepsy, L.A. Soc. Neurology and Psychiatry, N.Y. Acad. Scis., Soc. for Neurosci., Western Inst. on Epilepsy, Rsch. Soc. for Parkinson Disease and Movement Disorders (pres. 1984-2000). Republican. Achievements include research in L-dopa and other therapy for Parkinson's disease, dystonia, brain stem mechanisms for vestibular and quick and slow eye movements, long-term exposure to microgravity, space motion sickness. Office: UCLA Sch Medicine Dept Neurology Los Angeles CA 90095-0001

MARKHAM, CLAIRE AGNES (M. CLARE MARKHAM), retired chemistry educator, consultant; b. New Haven, Conn., Aug. 12, 1919; d. James J. and Agnes V. (Manning) M. BA, St. Joseph Coll., West Hartford, Conn., 1940; PhD, Cath. U. Am., 1952. Joined Sisters of Mercy, Roman Cath. Ch., 1940. Tchr. chemistry and math. Sacred Heart H.S., Waterbury, Conn., 1945-49; mem. faculty chemistry St. Joseph Coll., West Hartford, 1952-97, cons. instl. advancement, 1996—; dept. chair St. Joseph Coll., 1959-70, dean grad. sch., 1979-87, asst. to pres. acad. affairs, 1987-95; dir. numerous tchr. insts., 1959-89; mem. vis. faculty Calvin's Lab., NSF, U. Calif., Berkeley, 1967-68. Contbr. articles to profl. jours.; editor sci. series McGraw Hill, 1956-60. Undersec. for energy Office of Policy and Mgmt., State of Conn., Hartford, 1977-79; mem. adv. com. Permanent Commn. Status of Women, Hartford, 1995—; mem. adv. coun. Dept. Higher Edn., State of Conn., Hartford, 1970-80; energy advisor Nat. Gov.'s Assn., 1977-79. Faculty fellow NSF, Trondheim, Norway, 1967, travel grantee, cons., Madras, India, 1974-77; recipient Equity award AAUW, 1992. Fellow Conn. Acad. for Edn.; mem. AAAS, Am. Chem. Soc. (councilor 1968-88, chair Conn. Valley sect. 1955-67, 20 Yr. award 1988), Conn. Acad. Sci. and Engrng. (chair tech. bd. 1994-98), Sigma Xi (sect. chair). Democrat. Avocations: photography, music, literature. Home: 1678 Asylum Ave West Hartford CT 06117-2764 Office: St Joseph Coll West Hartford CT 06117

MARKHAM, CLARENCE MATTHEW, III, city administrator; b. Toledo, Apr. 26, 1937; s. Clarence Matthew Jr. and Olga Frances (Hughes) M.; m. Katherine Kirwan, Nov. 26, 1960; children: Juliet Kristina, Christopher Matthew, Allan Kirwan. BS, No. Ill. U., 1960; postgrad., Calif. State U., 1962-66, Claremont U., 1969-71, Yale U., 1970; MA in Urban Studies, Occidental Coll., 1972. V.p. Safety Savs. & Loan Assn., L.A., 1966-67; auditor, contr. Pasadena Commn. on Human Needs and Opportunity, 1967-68; exec. dir. Claremont (Calif.) U. Ctr., 1968-69, asst. dir. admissions, 1969-70; exec. dir. Job Resources & Educational Ctr., Monrovia, Calif., 1971-73; adminstr. human svcs. City of West Covina, Calif., 1973—; ptnr. Wilson-Markham & Assocs., L.A., 1986-92; owner C.M. Markham & Assocs., Irwindale, Calif., 1989—. Active YMCA Indian Guides, 1970-74; bd. dirs. La Verne-San Dimas Reachout, 1973-76, East San Gabriel Valley Hotline, Glendora, 1973-76; spl. olympics Del Haven Community Ctr., 1986-92. Mem. Nat. Assn. Housing and Devel. Ofcls. and Regional Bd. (v.p. 1980-81, pres. 1981-82, bd. dirs., 1982-83), West Covina Kiwanis (treas. 1988-89, v.p. 1989-91, pres. 1991-92). Roman Catholic. Avocations: snow skiing, fishing, hiking, golf, swimming. Office: City of West Covina 1444 W Garvey Ave S West Covina CA 91790-2716 ADDRESS: 147 Evergreen Rd Jonesborough TN 37659-6208

MARKHAM, J. DAVID, educator, writer, historical consultant; b. Austin, Tex., Dec. 26, 1945; s. James Walter and Myrtle (Sturges) M.; m. Barbara Ann Munson, May 14, 1983. BS, U. Iowa, 1971; MA, U. No. Iowa, 1972; postgrad., So. Ill. U., 1972-74, U. Wis., 1981-82; MEd, Ariz. State U., 1991; postgrad., Fla. STate U., 1996, 97, Oxford (Eng.) U., 1996. Instr. sociology U. Wis., Fond du Lac/Stevens Point, 1974-76; dir. Vietnam edn. grants Wis. Dept. Vet. Affairs, Madison, 1979-83; coordinator internat. edn. AFSCME, Phoenix, 1983-84; vets. svcs. officer Ariz. Vets. Service Commn., Phoenix, 1984-86; asst. to dir. Commn. on Ariz. Environ., Phoenix, 1986-88; div. supr. Ariz. Dept. Liquor Lics. and Control, Phoenix, 1988-89; world history and English tchr. Tolleson Union H.S. Dist., 1990-92; world history tchr. Lake Worth H.S., Palm Beach, Fla., 1992-2000; history tchr. Tumwater H.S., 2000—; instr. sociology and polit. sci., Maricopa C.C. Dist., Phoenix, 1985-91; instr. Palm Beach C.C., 1993-95. Bd. dirs. World Affairs Coun. Ariz., 1987-90; v.p. Ariz. Com. for Bicentennial of the French Revolution, 1988-89; exec. v.p. Napoleonic Alliance, 1996—. With U.S. Army, 1968-69, Vietnam. Decorated Bronze Star; recipient medal of Landtag of Badden-Württenberg, Germany, 1987, Spl. Svc. award Alliance Francaise of Phoenix, 1992, Marengo medal Province of Alessandria, Italy, 1997, medal City of Ajaccio, Corsica, France, 1997. Mem. Internat. Napoleonic Soc. (exec. v.p. and editor-in-chief 1995—, Legion of Merit 1996), Napoleonic Alliance (bd. dirs. 1992—, editor conf. procs., asst. editor bull., Pres. medal 1998), Inst. on Napolean and the French Revolution (hon.), Western Soc. for French History (hon.), Internat. Byron Soc. (hon.), Sierra Club, Zero Population Growth, Alpha Kappa Delta, Phi Kappa Phi, Phi Alpha Theta. Democrat. Avocations: collecting Napoleonic items, outdoor activities, travel, music, writing history. E-mail: imperialglory@home.com. Home: 1841 52nd Way SE Olympia WA 98501-8000

MARKHAM, JESSE WILLIAM, JR., lawyer; b. Nashville, Apr. 13, 1951; s. Jesse William and Penelope M.; m. Darcy Hartmann, Aug. 22, 1981; children: Elizabeth, Blakely. BA, Harvard U., 1974; MA in Philosophy, U. Mass., 1976; JD, Vanderbilt U., 1979. Dep. atty. gen. State of Calif., San Francisco, 1988-93; ptnr. Markham & Oshiro, San Francisco, 1993-97, Jackson, Tufts, San Francisco, 1997-99, Orrick, Herrington & Sutcliffe, San Francisco, 1999—; adj. prof. antitrust law U. San Francisco Law Sch., 1990—; chmn. antitrust sect. Calif. State Bar, 1998. Author, editor: (law treatise) Calif. Antitrust Law, 1992. Dir. East Bay Agy. for Children, Oakland, Calif., 1998—. Avocations: skiing, hiking, mountain biking. Office: Orrick Herrington & Sutcliffe 400 Sansome St San Francisco CA 94111-3143

MARKHAM, REED B., education educator, consultant; b. Alhambra, Calif., Feb. 14, 1957; s. John F. and Reeda (Bjarason) M. BA, Brigham Young U., 1982, MA, 1982; BS, Regents Coll., 1981, MA, 1982; MPA, U. So. Calif., 1983; MA, UCLA, 1989; PhD, Columbia Pacific U., 1991. Mem. faculty Brigham Young U., Provo, Utah, 1984; mem. faculty Calif. State U., Fullerton and Long Beach, 1984, Northridge, 1985; mem. faculty El Camino Coll., Torrance, Calif., 1986, Orange Coast Coll., Costa Mesa, Calif., 1986, Pasadena (Calif.) Coll., 1986, Fullerton (Calif.) Community Coll., 1986; instr., mem. pub. rels. com. Chaffey (Calif.) Coll., 1986-87; prof., CARES dir. Calif. State Poly. U., Pomona, 1987-98; adj. prof. Calif. State U., L.A., 1992-93, dir. Ctr. for Student Retention, 1995—; prof. East L.A. Coll., 1996-98, Salt Lake C.C., 1998—; rsch. asst. to pres. Ctr. for the Study of Cmty. Coll., 1985; mem. faculty Riverside (Calif.) Coll., 1989-90, Rio Hondo (Calif.) Coll., 1989-90, English Lang. Inst., 1994, Calif. Poly Summer Bridge, 1989-95, East L.A. Coll.; adj. prof. Citrus Coll., 1998—; speechwriter U.S. Supreme Ct., Washington, 1980; cons. gifted children program Johns Hopkins U./Scripps Coll., Claremont, Calif., 1987-88; mem. faculty PACE Program East L.A., 1995-96; faculty East L.A. Coll., 1996-97; adj. prof. U. So. Calif., 1998—; prof. Salt Lake C. C., 1998-99; mem. Pres.'s Coalition for Am. Reads Challenge, 1999. Author: Power Speechwriting, 1983, Power Speaking, 1990, Public Opinion, 1990, Advances in Public Speaking, 1991, Leadership 2000: Success Skills for University Students, 1995, Excellence in Public Speaking, 1997; co-author: Student Retention: Success Models in Higher Education, 1996, Upward Bound Program Grant Proposal, 1996, Making Marriage Magnificent, 1998; editor Trojan in Govt., U. So. Calif., 1983; editl. bd. mem. Edn. Digest, Speaker and Gavel, Innovative Higher Edn., Pub. Rels. Rev., Nat. Forensic Jour., The Forensic Educator, Clearinghouse for the Contemporary Educator, Hispanic Am. Family Mag.; writer N.Y. times, Christian Sci. Monitor; ednl. columnist San Bernardino (Calif.) Sun., 1992-98. Pres. bd. trustees Regents Coll., 1986; aapointed to Pres.'s Coalition for Am. Reads Challenge. Mem. Doctorate Assn. N.Y. Scholars, Nat. Assn. Pvt. Nontraditional Colls. (accrediting com. 1989—), Pub. Rels. Soc. Am. (dir.-at-large inland empire 1992-93, faculty advisor). LDS. Office: Salt Lake CC Comm Dept PO Box 30808 Salt Lake City UT 84130-0808

MARKHAM, STEPHEN KEITH, management consultant, educator; b. Lancaster, Calif., Sept. 26, 1959; s. Keith George and Lela Ruth M.; m. Allyson Rae, Aug. 17, 1984; children: Emily, Jillian, Keith, Ashley. MS in Psychology, Brigham Young U., 1986; PhD, Purdue U., 1993; MBA, U. Calif., Irvine, 1988; PhD, Purdue U., 1993. Cert. new product devel. prof. Prof. N.C. State U., Raleigh, N.C., 1992-2000; chief fin. officer Lipomed, Inc., Raleigh, 1995-2000, bd. dirs., 1995-2000; chief fin. officer Lips, Inc., Cary, N.C., 1996-2000, bd. dirs., 1996-2000; chief fin. officer Kyma Technologies, Inc., Raleigh, 1999-2000, bd. dirs., 1999-2000; dir. technology, edn. and commercialization program, Raleigh, 1993-2000. Contbr. articles to profl. jours. Scoutmaster Boy Scouts of Am., West Lafayette, Inc., 1988-92, Raleigh, 1993-99. Rsch. grantee NSF, 1994-99. Mem. Product Devel. and Mgmt. Assn. (v.p. 1994-95, Internat. Dissertation winner 1992), Acad. of Mgmt., IEEE, ORSA/TIMS. Mem. LDS Ch. Office: NC State Univ PO Box 7229 Raleigh NC 27695-0001

MARKI, HANS PETER, chemist, researcher; b. Zuerich, Switzerland, July 26, 1952; s. Hans and Verena (Frey) M.; m. Anna Danzig, July 16, 1976; children: Yvonne C., Sarah A. Diploma in chemistry, U. Zurich, 1976, D in Chemistry, 1980. Rsch. chemist F. Hoffmann La Roche Ltd., Basel, Switzerland, 1982-87, group leader, 1987-92, area head, 1992—. Patentee renin inhibitors, calcium antagonists, pancreatic lipase inhibitors, heparin mimetics; contbr. articles to profl. jours. Office: F Hoffmann La Roche Ltd, Pharm Rsch Dept, CH 4070 Basel Switzerland

MARKING, T(HEODORE) JOSEPH, JR., transportation and urban planner; b. June 28, 1945; s. Theodore Joseph and Alvena Cecilia (Thieman) M.; m. Kathy K. Hagerman, Nov. 25, 1969. BA, So. Ill. U., 1967, M City and Regional Planning, 1972. Intelligence rsch. specialist Def. Intelligence Agy., Washington, 1967-68; planner I St. Louis City Plan Commn., 1970; transp. planner Alan M. Voorhees & Assocs., St. Louis, 1970-74, sr. transp. planner, 1974-78, assoc., 1978; sr. transp. planner Booker Assocs, Inc., St. Louis, 1978-80; chief traffic and transp. sect. PB Booker Assocs, Inc., St. Louis, 1980-85; mgr. transit planning East-West Gateway Coord. Coun., St. Louis, 1985-88; mgr. planning dept. Harland Bartholomew & Assocs., St. Louis, 1988-91; sr. transp. planner Burns & Mcdonnell Engrng. Co., St. Louis, 1992-95, PB Booker Assoc. Inc., St. Louis, 1996-98, Parsons Brinckerhoff, St. Louis, 1998—; planner-in-charge, Mo.; guest lectr. St. Louis C.C. Dist., Webster U., St. Louis U. Mem. am. Inst. Cert. Planners (charter), Am. Planning Assn. (charter, treas. transp. planning divsn., past pres., pres., sec., bd. dirs. St. Louis sect.), Inst. Transp. Engrs., Traffic Engrs. Assn. Met. St. Louis (past pres.), Transp. Rsch. Bd. Office: 1831 Chestnut St Ste 700 Saint Louis MO 63103-2231

MARKL, HUBERT, zoology educator; b. Regensburg, Germany, Aug. 17, 1938. Phd. Zool., U. Munich, Germany, 1962; Habilitation, U. Frankfurt, Germany, 1967; Dr.rer.nat. (hon.), U. Saarland, 1992, U. Dublin, 1997, U. Potsdam, 1999; DHL (hon.), Jewish Theol. Sem., 2000. Prof., dir. Zool. Inst. TH Darmstadt, Darmstadt, Germany, 1968-74; prof. biol. U. Konstanz, Germany, 1974—; v.p. Deutsche Forschungsgemeinschaft, Bonn, Germany, 1977-83, pres., 1986-91; Heinrich Hertz visiting prof. U Karlsruhe, 1994-1995; pres. Max Planck Soc., 1996—; v.p. Alexander von Humboldt-Stiftung, Bonn, 1986-91; pres. Berlin-Brandenburgische Akademie der Wissenschaften, 1993-95, Gesellschaft Deutscher Naturforscher & Ärzte, 1993-94. Author: Natur als Kulturaufgabe, 1986, Evolution, Genetik u. menschl. Verhalten, 1986, Wissenschaft: Zur Rede gestellt, 1989, Wissenschaft im Widerstreit, 1990, Die Fortschrittsdroge, 1992, Wissenschaft gegen Zukunftsangst, 1998; editor: Evolution of Social Behavior, 1980; co-editor: Biophysik, 1977, 82; mng. editor Behavioral Ecol. Sociobiology, 1976-88. Recipient Lorenz Oken Medaille Ges. Dt. Naturforscher u. Ärzte, 1984; Karl Vossler prize Bayer. Staatsmin. f. Unterricht u. Kultus, 1985, Arthur-Burkhardt-Preis, 1989, Karl-Winnacker-Preis, 1991, Ernst-Robert-Curtius-Preis, 1995, Prognos-Preis, 1997, Leibniz-Ring, 1999. Mem. Heidelberger Akademie der Wissenschaften, Berlin-Brandenburgische Akademie der Wissenschaften, Dt. Akademie d. Naturforscher Leopoldina, Bayer, Akademie der Wissenschaften, Nordrhein-Westfalia Akademie der Wissenschaften, Akademie der Wissenschaften zu Göttingen, Academia Europaea, Am. Acad. Arts And Scis. (fgn. hon. mem.), Indian Acad. Scis., Am. Philosophical Soc. (fgn. mem.), Ges. Dt. Chem. (hon.). Office: Max-Planck-Gesellschaft, Postfach 101062, D-80084 Munich Germany

MARKLUND, STELLAN, environmental chemistry educator; b. Skellefteå, Sweden, May 6, 1949; s. Bertil Karl and Iris (Åhman) M.; m. Christina Marklund, 1973 (div. 1986); 1 child, Johanna; m. Inga-Lill Bonnedahl. MSc, Umeå (Sweden) U., 1973, PhD, 1990. Tchg. asst. Umeå U., 1974-79; rsch. scientist Nat. Def. Rsch. Inst., Sweden, 1979-81; rsch. engr. Umeå U., 1981-91, rsch. assoc., 1992-93, assoc. prof. environ. chemistry, 1994—, lectr., 1997—; acting prof. environ. chemistry, Umeå U., 1994, chmn. Inst. Environ. Chemistry, 1997. Mem. Swedish Chem. Soc., Air Waste Mgmt. Assn. E-mail: suid@chem.umu.se. Home: Björnvägen 120, S-906 43 Umeå Sweden Office: Umeå U, Dept Environ Chemistry, S-901 87 Umeå Sweden

MARKMAN, ARTHUR BRIAN, psychology educator; b. Plainfield, N.J., Feb. 28, 1966; s. Edward Steven and Sondra Rae (Gold) M.; m. Betsy Gail Guinzburg, June 24, 1991; 1 child, Lucas Gabriel. BS, Brown U., 1988; MA, U. Ill., 1990, PhD, 1992. Vis. asst. prof. Northwestern U., Evanston, Ill., 1991-93; asst. prof. psychology Columbia U., N.Y.C., 1993-98; assoc. prof. U. Tex., Austin, 1998—. Author: (book) Knowledge Representation and Cognitive Psychology; co-editor: Cognitive Dynamics; contbr. articles to profl. jours.; mem. editl. bd. Jour. Exptl. Psychology, Learning, Memory and Cognition, 1995-2000, Memory and Cognition, 1998—, Cognitive Science, 2000—. Mem. APA, Am. Psychol. Soc., Cognitive Sci. Soc., Am. Assn. for Artificial Intelligence, Psychonomic Soc., Sigma Xi, Phi Kappa Phi. Achievements include seminal research on parallels between analogy and similarity; research on the role of comparison in decision-making. Avocation: ham radio. Office: U Texas Dept Psychology Mezes Hall 330 Austin TX 78712

MARKMAN, SHERMAN, investment banker, venture capitalist, corporate financier; b. Denver, Aug. 21, 1920; s. Abe and Julia (Rosen) M.; m. Paula Elaine Henderson; children: S. Michael, Joan, Lori. Student, So. Meth. U., 1962-64. V.p. Lester's Inc., Oklahoma City, 1940-59; exec. v.p. Besco Enterprises, San Francisco, 1960-61; sr. v.p. Zale Corp., Dallas, 1962-69; pres., CEO Leased Jewelry divsn., 1965-69, Designcraft Industries, N.Y.C., 1969-75; pres. Tex. Internat. Export Co., Dallas, 1975—, CAC Fin. Group (Tex.), Dallas, 1975—; fin. advisor Vocational Video, Huntington, N.Y., Consolidated Transplant Network, Metairie, La., Thera-Test Diagnostic Labs., Chgo., Kemper Mil. Acad., Boonville, Mo., Soft-Trac Info. Systems, Jasper, Ala., client referal arrangement The Dai-Ichi Kangyo Bank, Ltd.; former bd. dir. Pipelife Svc. Corp., Chem. Applicators, Lafayette, La., Coverage Cons., N.Y.C., Transworld Ins. Intermediaries, Ltd.; former cons. Homecare Mgmt., Ronkonkoma, N.Y., Credicorp, Chgo., The Windy City Group, Chgo.; charter mem. N.Y. Ins. Exch.; guest lectr. fin. risk confs., 1982—, spkr. Am. Real Estate Investment Conf., London, 1986; pres., CEO The Markman Fin. Orgn., Dallas, 1975—. Contbr. articles to profl. jours. Vol. social worker Presbyn. Hosp., Dallas; mem. Dallas Coun. World Affairs, 1962—; active NCCJ. With USMCR, 1942-45, PTO. Mem. Press Club, City Club (Dallas), India Temple Club (Oklahoma City), L.A. Athletic Club, Columbian Golf and Country Club, Young Men's Philanthropic League (N.Y.C.). Address: 6600 Rolling Rd Richmond VA 23226-3421

MARKO, KURT JOHANNES, historian, educator; b. Scheibbs, Austria, July 20, 1928; s. Johann and Emilie (Herbst) M.; m. Ingeborg Schubert, June 22, 1970. PhD, U. Vienna, 1953. Asst. Seminar on Slavic Philology and Archeology U. Vienna, 1952-56, asst. Inst. East European History and S.E. European Rsch., 1956-62, prof., 1973—; rschr. Fed. Inst. for Internat. and East European Studies, Cologne, W. Ger., 1962-73; lectr. polit. philosophy and ideological studies U. Vienna, 1969—. Author: Sic et Non. Kritisches Wörterbuch des sowjetrussischen Marxismus-Leninismus der Gegenwart, 1962, also others. Recipient Cardinal Innitzer prize, Vienna, 1965. Mem. PEN, Deutsche Gesellschaft für Osteuropakunde. Home: Johannesgasse 22,, Vienna, Austria A-1010 Office: Inst E & SE Euro Rsch, Spitalgasse 2-4 Hof 3, Vienna Austria A-1090

MARKOPOLOS, HARRY M., investment professional; b. Erie, Pa., Oct. 22, 1956; s. Louis Harry and Georgia Ann (Pappas) M. BBA, Loyola Coll., Balt., 1981; MS in Fin., Boston Coll., 1997. Chartered Fin. Analyst. Dist. mgr. ATFC Fin. Corp., Towson, Md., 1981-87; trader Makefield Securities Corp., Washington Crossing, Pa., 1987-88; asst. portfolio mgr. Darien Capital Mgmt., Greenwich, Conn., 1988-91; portfolio mgr. Rampart Investment Mgmt., Boston, 1991—; v.p. edn. Boston Security Analysts Soc., 2000—; bd. dirs. Boston Security Analysts, QWAFAFEW, Boston, Boston GARP; derivatives instr. Boston Security Analysts. Maj. U.S. Army Res., 1978-95. Decorated U.S. Army Achievement medal, 1990, Nat. Def. Svc. medal, 1990. Mem. Internat. Assn. Fin. Engrs., Am. Fin. Assn., Fin. Mgmt. Assn., Assn. for Investment Mgmt. and Rsch., Boston Security Analysts Soc. (v.p. edn. 2000—), U.S. Army Command and Gen. Staff Coll. Alumni (life mem.). Avocations: trout fishing, hunting. Office: Rampart Investment Mgmt 1 International Pl Boston MA 02110-2602

MARKOPOULOS, JOHN S., economist; b. Athens, Greece, Aug. 14, 1951; s. Spiridon M.; m. Mary Koffa, 1974; children: Yolanda, Demosthenis. BA in Econs., Aristotle U., Thessaloniki, Greece, 1974; MBA, INSEAD, France, 1978. Fin. analyst Steyer Daimler Puc AG, Vienna, 1982; credit officer Chase Manhattan Bank, London and Athens, 1982-85; mgr. Interzact S.A., Athens, 1986-90; chmn., mng. dir. Sigma Securities S.A., Athens, 1990—; chmn. Sigma Money Brokers S.A., Athens, Space Imaging Europe S.A., Athens. Mem. U.S. Greece Bus. Coun. (bd. dirs.), Assn. Mem. A.S.G. (bd. dirs.), Fedn. Industries Greece. Office: Sigma Securities SA, 10 Stadiou Str, GR-10564 Athens Greece

MARKOPOULOS, PETROS, retired career officer, consultant; b. Volax, Greece, Aug. 14, 1941; s. Angelos A. and Maria P. Markopoulos; m. Laskaritsa I. Koumeli, Apr. 25, 1971; 1 child, Angelos. Degree, Mil. Cadet Sch., Athens, Greece, 1965; diploma, War and Staff Coll., Thessaloniki, Greece, 1980; M, Nat. Def. Coll., Athens, 1990. Enlisted Greek Army, 1965, advanced through grades to maj. gen.; various positions Arty. and Army Aviation Units, Greece, 1965-81; staff duty Divsn. Arty. Command, Kozani, Greece, 1981-82, 4th Staff Office/Divsn., Kozani, 1982-83; comdr., lt. col. Field Arty. Bn., Soufli, Greece, 1984-87; comdr., col. Divsn. Arty. Command, Mytilini, Greece, 1991-93; dir., brig. gen. Directorate Logistic/Nat. Def. Staff, Athens, 1994-95; comdr., brig. gen. 1st Support Brigade, Konzani, 1994-95; dir., maj. gen. Army Aviation Directorate, Athens, 1995-96; ret., 1996; cons. armament sys., 1997. Gen. sec. Coord. Com. Cultural Orgns., Athens, 1998. Christian Orthodox. Avocations: culture, reading, sports, music. Fax: 01-30-2112767. Home and Office: Kitheronos 41-43, 11255 Athens Greece

MARKOU, DEMETRIOS, accountant; b. Nicosia, Cyprus, July 2, 1944; arrived in Eng., 1962; s. Marcus Demetriou and Maria Demetriou (Nicola) M.; m. Christalla Loizou, June 16, 1968; children: Marcus, Andrew, Constantine. Grad., Handsworth Tech. Coll., Birmingham, Eng., 1964, Aston Coll., Birmingham, Eng., 1968, Aston Coll., Birmingham, Eng., 1970. Articled clk. Farmiloes, Birmingham, 1966-70; prin., owner Marcus & Co., Birmingham, 1970—; mng. dir. Dynamis Ltd., Birmingham, 1979—; bd. dirs. numerous cos.; cons. in field. Owner, editor (mag) Businesses and Premises for Sale, 1996. Trustee, advisor Greek Orthodox Ch., London and Birmingham, 1964—; treas. Small Heath Conservative Assn., Birmingham, 1982-94; chmn. One Nation Forum, London and Birmingham, 1989-94; mem. Conservative Nat. Union Exec. Com., London, 1993-96; pres. Sparkbrook Conservative Assn., Birmingham, 1995—. Named Mem. of the Brit. Empire, Her Majesty the Queen, 1992. Fellow Inst. Chartered Accts.; mem. Inst. Dirs., Carlton Club. Avocations: skiing, backgammon, political philosophy, letter/subject writing. Office: Marcus & Co Ryland House, 44/48 Bristol St, Birmingham B57AA, England

MARKOULIDAKIS, JOHN GEORGE, electrical engineer, mobile communications consultant; b. Athens, Greece, Dec. 14, 1966; s. George John and Aggeliki Eleni (Mikrouli) M. Diploma in Elec. Engrng., Nat. Tech. U. Athens, 1995, PhD in Elec. Engrng. Rsch. assoc. Orgn. of Telecomms. of Ellas, Athens, 1990-94; sr. rsch. engr. Nat. Tech. U. Athens, 1994—. Contbr. articles to profl. jours. Mem. IEEE, Tech. Chamber of Greece. Avocations: volleyball, swimming, photography. Home: Analipseos 36-38, Athens Greece 16231 Office: NTUA, Heroon Polytechniou 9, Athens Greece 15773

MARKOV, GERMAN SERGEEVICH, radiochemist, researcher; b. Yaroslavl, Russia, Nov. 19, 1931; s. Sergey Georgievich and Lidiya Pavlovna (Vinogradova) M.; m. Lidiya Nikolaevna Stepanova, Feb. 4, 1970. Degree in Chemistry, Lenigrad U., Russia, 1955; Candiate Chemistry Scis., Radium Inst., Leningrad, Russia, 1968; postgrad., Siberian Chem. Enterprise, Seversk, Russia, 1971-78. Cert. chemist. Sr. lab. worker V.G. Khlopin Radium Inst., Leningrad, Russia, 1958-60, postgrad., 1960-62, jr. scientist, 1962-72, sr. scientist, 1972-90, leading scientist, 1990—. Contbr. articles to profl. jours.; author papers. Mem. Russian Nuclear Soc. Office: V G Khlopin Radium Inst, 2d Murinsky Ave 28, 194021 Saint Petersburg Russia

MARKOV, PETER JORDANOV, chemistry educator; b. Harmanli, Bulgaria, June 20, 1933; s. Jordan Petrov and Vera Yakimova (Stojanova) M.; m. Jordanka Borisova Berkovska Markova, Aug. 25, 1957; children: Markov, Juri, Petrov. Engr., chemist, High Poly. Inst., Sofia, Bulgaria, 1957; PhD, Sofia U., Bulgaria, 1967; DSc, 1983. Asst. Dept. Organic Chemistry Sofia U., Bulgaria, 1958-70; vis. lectr. Oslo (Norway) U., 1968-69; docent Dept. Organic Chemistry Sofia U., Bulgaria, 1970-85; prof. $, 1985—. Contbr. articles to profl. jours. Mem. Bulgarian Parliament, 1991-94. Recipient Invention No 3 of Bulgaria, Bulgarian State, 1983, Nat. Award for Chemistry and Biology, Bulgarian Acad. Scis., 1978. Office: Sofia University Dept Organic Chemistry, 1 James Baucher Ave, 1126 Sofia Bulgaria

MARKOVA, KALINKA IVANOVA, chemistry educator; b. Varna, Bulgaria, May 7, 1940; d. Ivan Nikolov Zhechev and Julia Ivanova Kuncheva; m. Marko Nikolov Markov, July 9, 1961; 1 child, Nikolai Markov. Cert. chemists' technician, Tech. Sch. Chemistry, Varna, Bulgaria, 1959; degree in engrng., Higher Inst. Chem. Engrng., Sofia, 1967, PhD, 1975. Chemist MK Kremikovtsi, Sofia, 1967-70; specialist and sci. rschr. in chemistry St. Kliment Ohridski U. of Sofia, 1975-78, assoc. prof., 1978—. Co-author: (in Russian) Oxidation and Autocombustion of Solid Fuels, 1994; contbr. over 100 articles to profl. jours. Recipient First prize for sci. Nat. Scientific Rsch. Fund, 1997. Mem. Union Bulgarian Scientists (achievement award 1994), Bulgarian Geol. Soc., N.Y. Acad. Scis. Avocation: flower cultivation. Home: Zh K Mladost 3 Bl 318, 1712 Sofia Bulgaria Office: U Sofia St Kliment Ohridski, Blvd Tsar Osvoboditel 15, 1000 Sofia Bulgaria

MARKOVIC, NENAD S., internist, hematologist, oncologist, educator; b. Skopje, Macedonia, Jan. 24, 1938; came to the U.S., 1993; s. Svetomir K. and Olga R. Markovic; m. Olivera T. Markovic, 1961; 2 children. MD, Med. Faculty, Skopje, 1962, specialist internist, 1968, primarius, 1981; DSc, Med. Faculty, Belgrade, Yugoslavia, 1975. Prof. internal medicine Med. Faculty, Skopje, 1978-85; sci. dir. Clinic of Hematology, Skopje, 1981-85; vis. prof. dept. pathology U. Pa., Phila., 1985-88; prof. oncology Inst. Oncology, Novi Sad, Yugoslavia, 1988-93; med. officer FDA Ctr. for Drug Evaluation and Rsch., Rockville, Md., 1994-98; vis. prof. pharmacology Med. Coll. Pa., Phila., 1988-94; chmn. oncology Med. Faculty, Novi Sad, 1991-94, dir. English speaking med. program, 1991-94; expert cons. ProSciCon., Rockville, Marcons Cons., Rockville, 1999—; adj. prof. Am. U., Washington, 2000—. Author: Quantitative Cytochemistry of Enzymes, 1986, Manual on Bone Marrow Morphology Screening, 1989; editor: UICC Manual of Cancer Chemotherapy, 1982; contbr. articles to profl. jours. Mem. Fed. Physicians Assn., Am. Assn. for Clin. Rsch., Am. Soc. Hematology, Yugoslav Cancer Soc. (pres. 1979-83). Avocation: chess.

MARKOVITS, ANDREI STEVEN, political science educator; b. Timisoara, Romania, Oct. 6, 1948; came to U.S., 1960, naturalized, 1971; s. Ludwig and Ida (Ritter) M. BA, Columbia U., 1969, MBA, 1971, MA, 1973, MPhil, 1974, PhD, 1976. Mem. faculty NYU, 1974, John Jay Coll. Criminal Justice, CUNY, 1974, Columbia U., 1975; rsch. assoc. Inst. Advanced Studies, Vienna, Austria, 1973-74, Wirtschafts und Sozialwissenschaftliches Inst., German Trade U. Fedn., Düsseldorf, Germany, 1979, Internat. Inst. Comparative Social Rsch., Sci. Ctr. Berlin, 1980; asst. prof. govt. Wesleyan U., Middletown, Conn., 1977-83; assoc. prof. polit. sci. Boston U., 1983-92; prof., chair dept. politics U. Calif., Santa Cruz, 1992-99; prof. dept. Germanic langs. and lit. U. Mich., Ann Arbor, 1999—; Fulbright prof. U. Innsbruck, Austria, 1996; vis. prof. Tel Aviv U., 1986, Osnabruck U., 1987, Bochum U., 1991; sr. rsch. assoc. Ctr. for European Studies, Harvard U., 1975-99. Author, editor books and papers in field; TV and radio commentator. Univ. Pres.'s fellow Columbia U., 1969, B'nai B'rith Found.

fellow, 1976-77, Kalmus Found. fellow, 1976-77, Ford Found. fellow, 1979, Hans Boeckler Found. fellow, 1982 Inst. for Advanced Study Berlin fellow, 1998-99; N.Y. State scholar Columbia U., 1969. Mem. N.Y. Acad. Scis., Am. Polit. Sci. Assn., Internat. Polit. Sci. Assn., AAUP. Home: 718 Onondaga St Ann Arbor MI 48104-2611 Office: Univ Mich 3110 Modern Lang Bldg 812 E Washington St Ann Arbor MI 48109-1275 also: Harvard U Ctr European Studies 27 Kirkland St Cambridge MA 02138-2043

MARKOWITSCH, HANS JOACHIM, neuropsychologist, researcher; b. Singen Htwl, Germany, Mar. 26, 1949; s. Erich G. and Lisbeth (Sawatzki) M. Degree, U. Konstanz, Germany, 1977, D in Habilitation, 1980. Cert. clinical neuropsychologist. Asst. prof. U. Konstanz, Germany, 1977-80, assoc. prof., 1980-84; scholar German Rsch. Council, Bonn, Germany, 1985-89; assoc. prof. U. Bochum, Germany, 1989-91; prof. U. Bielefeld, Germany, 1991—; vis. prof. Rotman Rsch. Inst., Toronto, 1993, U. Calif., Davis, 1994. Author: Information Processing by the Brain, 1988, Intellectual Functions of the Brain, 1992; editor: Transient Global Amnesia, 1990; editor Neurocase, 1999. First Lt. German Army, 1967-70. Fellow APA, Am. Psychology Soc. Avocations: mountain climbing, cycling, chess. Home: Butenkamp 25, 33739 Bielefeld Germany Office: Univ Bielefeld, Universitaetstr 25, 33615 Bielefeld Germany

MARKOWITZ, FRAN, anthropologist, educator; b. N.Y.C., Feb. 23, 1952; arrived in Israel, 1992; d. Alan Markowitz and Fay C. (Shoham) Miskin. BA, SUNY, Binghamton, 1975; MS, Ga. State U., 1978; PhD, U. Mich., 1987. Adj. asst. prof. De Paul U., Chgo., 1990-92; lectr. Ben-Gurion U. Negev, Beersheva, Israel, 1992-95; sr. lectr. Ben-Gurion U. Negev, Beersheva, 1995—; cons. Naale Min. Edn./Fgn. Affairs, State of Israel, 1993-94. Author: A Community in Spite of Itself: Soviet Jewish Emigres in New York, 1993 (Choice Book award 1993); co-editor: Sex, Sexuality, and the Anthropologist, 1999; contbr. articles to profl. jours. Grantee NIMH, 1984-86; Hebrew U. fellow, 1987-88, Internat. Rsch. Exchange Bd. award, 1995-96; recipient award U.S.-Israel Nat. Sci. Found., 1997-2000. Fellow Am. Anthrop. Assn.; mem. Israel Anthrop. Assn. (bd. dirs. 1993-96). Avocations: walking, singing, needlework, classical music. Home: Rehov Mamshit 28, PO Box 1237, 85025 Meitar Israel Office: Dept Behavioral Scis, Ben-Gurion U PO Box 635, 84105 Beer-Sheva Israel

MARKOWITZ, HARRY M., finance and economics educator; b. Chicago, Ill., Aug. 24, 1927; s. Morris and Mildred (Gruber) M.; m. Barbara Gay. PhB, U. Chgo., 1947, MA, 1950, PhD, 1954. With research staff Rand Corp., Santa Monica, Calif., 1952-60, 61-63; tech. dir. Consol. Analysis Ctrs., Inc., Santa Monica, 1963-68; prof. UCLA, Westwood, 1968-69; pres. Arbitrage Mgmt. Co., N.Y.C., 1969-72; pvt. practice cons. N.Y.C., 1972-74; with research staff T.J. Watson Research Ctr. IBM, Yorktown Hills, N.Y., 1974-83; Speiser prof. fin. Baruch Coll. CUNY, N.Y.C., 1982-93; dir. rsch. Daiwa Securities Trust Co, Jersey City, N.J., 1990-2000; v.p. Inst. Mgmt. Sci., 1960-62. Author: Portfolio Selection: Efficient Diversification of Investments, 1959, Mean-Variance Analysis in Portfolio Choice, 1987; co-author: SIMSCRIPT Simulation Programming Language, 1963; co-editor: Process Analysis of Economic Capabilities, 1963. Recipient John von Neumann Theory prize Ops. Rsch. Soc. Am. and Inst. Mgmt. Sci., 1989, Nobel Prize in Econs., 1990. Fellow Econometric Soc., Am. Acad. Arts and Scis.; mem. Am. Fin. Assn. (pres. 1982—). Office: 1 Evertrust Plz Jersey City NJ 07302-3051

MARKOYANNIS, NIKI, psychiatrist; b. Athens, Greece, Oct. 12, 1951; d. Constantine and Cathrin (Koymoytsakis) M.; 1 child, Danai Marneris. DDS, U. Athens, 1974, MD, 1977, specialization in psychiatry-neurology, 1982. Med. diplomate specialized in neurology and psychiatry; lic. family therapist. Tchr. psychosomatic medicine Assn. for Psychosomatic Studies, Athens, 1980-85; tchr. Coll. for Social & Psychology Studies, Athens, 1980-84; pvt. practice Athens, 1982—; rsch. fellow Arnica Researchiantes, Sweden, 1987-92. Contbr. articles to newspapers and mags.; guest spkr. TV shows for family therapy and psychosomatic medicine, 1980—. Mem. Assn. for Study of Psychosomatic Medicine (sec. 1982-84), Soroptimist Internat. (govt. 1987-89, pres. 19889-91, union health coord. 1998-2000). Avocations: horseback riding, painting. Home: Kokkonis 13 P PSychico, 15452 Athens Greece

MARKS, ANDREW ROBERT, molecular biologist; b. N.Y.C., Feb. 22, 1955; s. Paul Alan and Joan Harriet (Rosen) M.; m. Margaret Foster, Jan. 14, 1984; children: Joshua, Daniel, Sarah. BA (magna cum laude), Amherst Coll., 1976; MD, Harvard Med. Sch., 1980. Diplomate Am. Bd. Internal Medicine; cert. in cardiovascular diseases. Intern, resident Mass. Gen. Hosp., Boston, 1980-83, cardiology fellow, 1985-87; fellow genetics Harvard Med. Sch., Boston, 1983-85, instr. medicine, 1987-90; asst. prof. molecular biology Mt. Sinai Sch. Medicine, N.Y.C., 1990-93; assoc. prof. molecular biology and medicine, 1993-97; Fishberg prof. medicine in cardiology Mt. Sinai Sch. Medicine, N.Y.C., 1995-97; Wu prof. medicine, prof. pharmacology Coll. Physicians and Surgeons Columbia U., 1997—, dir. molecular cardiology, 1997—; Contbr. articles to profl. jours. Mem. editl. bd. Jour. Biol. Chemistry. Established investigatorship, Am. Heart Assn., 1993. Recipient Clinician-Scientist award Am. Heart Assn., 1986, Excellence in Rsch. award Am. Fedn. for Clin. Rsch., 1990, Syntex Scholars award, 1991. Mem. Am. Assn. Biol. Chemistry and Molecular Biology, Am. Assn. Cell Biology, Am. Soc. Clin. Investigation (nat. coun. 1997-2000), Biophys. Soc., Harvey Soc., Sierra Club. Achievements include research on the calcium release channel in cardiac and skeletal muscle; characterization of smooth muscle calcium release channel. Office: Columbia U PYS Bldg 630 W 168th St Bldg 9-401 New York NY 10032-3795

MARKS, DAVID FRANCIS, psychologist, consultant, writer; b. Liphook, Hamphire, Eng., Feb. 12, 1945; s. Victor William and Mary Dorothy (Goodman) Francis; children: Jessica Mary, Michael Andres Francis; m. Yoriko Taniguchi. BSc, Reading U., Eng., 1966; PhD, Sheffield U., Eng., 1970. Lectr U. Otago, New Zealand, 1970-74, sr. lectr., 1974-86; prof., head Sch. Psychology Middlesex U., Enfield, Eng., 1986-94, head Health Rsch. Ctr., 1989-00; prof. health psychology City U., London, 2000—; chmn. Spl. Group on Health Psychology, U.K., 1992-94; convenor European Fedn. Profl. Psychologists' Assns. Task Force on Health Psychology Europe, 1992-97; sci. com. on tobacco and health Dept. Health, Eng., 1993-2000; adv. group European Commn. Alzheimer's, 1996—; vis. prof. U. Oreg., U. Wash., Hamamatsu U., Fukuoka U. Japan, U. Rome; hon. rsch. fellow U. Coll., London; founding chmn. New Zealand Skeptics, 1986. Author: (with P. Sulzberger, I. Hodgson) The Isis Smoking Cessation Programme, 1979, The Quit for Life Programme: An Easier Way to Stop Smoking and Not Start Again, 1993; (with R. Kammann) The Psychology of the Psychic, 1980, 2nd rev. edit., 2000; (with C. Francome) Improving the Health of the Nation, 1996, (with M. Murray, B. Evans, C. Willig) Health Psychology. Theory, Research & Practice, 2000; (with C.M. Sykes) Dealing With Dementia, 2000; editor: (book) Theories of Image Formation, 1985; (with P. Hampson, J.T.E. Richardson) Imagery: Current Developments, 1990; editor Jour. Health Psychology, 1996—; contbr. chpts. to books, articles to profl. jours. Recipient Gold Disc for music therapy rec., New Zealand, 1979. Fellow Brit. Psychol. Soc. (chartered health psychologist), Com. for Sci. Investigation of Claims of the Paranormal; mem. European Movement (life), Tottenham Hotspur Football Club. Avocations: travel, soccer, visual arts, music. E-mail: d.marks@city.ac.uk. Office: Ctr Health & Counseling, City Univ Northampton Sq, London EC1V 0HB, England

MARKS, DENNIS MICHAEL, arts and media executive; b. London, July 2, 1948; s. Samuel Marks and Kitty Ostrovsky; married; 2 children. Student, Trinity Coll. Dir., prodr. BBC TV Music and Arts, 1972-78; cofounder Bristol Arts Unit, 1978-81; founder 3d Eye Prodns., 1981-85; editor Music Features BBC TV, 1985-88, asst. head of music and arts, 1988-91; head of music BBC TV, 1991-93; gen. dir. English Nat. Opera, 1993-97; founder & mng. dir. Director's Cut, 1999—; pres. Internat. Music Ctr., Vienna, 1989-92. Author: Great Railway Journeys, 1981, Repercussions, 1985; radio shows include Fault Line, 2000. Recipient Italia prize, 1989, Royal Philharm. Soc. award, 1990. Avocations: cooking, travel. *

MARKS, ISAAC MEYER, psychiatrist; b. Cape Town, South Africa, Feb. 16, 1935; arrived in the U.K., 1960; s. Morris N. and Anna (Janowsky) M.; m. Shula E. Winokur, Mar. 31, 1957; children: Lara V., Raphael C. MD, U. Cape Town, 1973, DPM, 1973. Intern, resident Grooke Schuur Hosp., Cape Town, 1957-59; prof. Inst. Psychiatry Bethlehem-Maudsley Hosp., London, 1978-2000; with Charing Cross Campus Imperial Coll., 2000—. Contbr. 12 books and 400 articles to profl. jours. Med. advisor to self-help charities; active local transport subcoms. Fellow Royal Coll. Psychiatrists. Office: Inst Psychiatry, London SE5 8AF, England

MARKS, JON OWEN, physician; b. Bklyn., Dec. 28, 1946; s. Peter J. and Lily I. (Fagelson) M.; m. Ellen A. Zimmerman, June 10, 1967 (div.); m. Eileen M. Rich; children: Ian, Lana, Laura. BS in Aerospace Engring., NYU, 1967, MS in Aerospace Engring., 1969; MD, N.Y. Med. Coll., 1976. Diplomate Am. Bd. Urology. Rsch. engr. Grumman Aerospace, Bethpage, N.Y., 1969-72; resident Lenox Hill Hosp., N.Y.C., 1976-78, 78-81; staff urologist Beth Israel Med. Ctr., N.Y.C., 1981-84; physician pvt. practice, N.Y.C., 1984—; med. dir. Met. Lithotriptor Assocs., N.Y.C., 1987—, Repro Lab, N.Y.C., 1994—. Mem. AMA, Am. Urologic Assn., Am. Soc. Reproductive Medicine, Am. Lithotripsy Soc., Endourology Soc., Soc. Urology and Engring., Tau Beta Pi, Sigma Gamma Tau. Avocation: piano. Home: 27 Walden Rd Tarrytown NY 10591-3016 Office: Urologic Assocs 55 E 9th St New York NY 10003-6311

MARKS, LILLIAN SHAPIRO, secretarial studies educator, author; b. Bklyn., Mar. 16, 1907; d. Hayman and Celia (Merowitz) Shapiro; m. Joseph Marks, Feb. 21, 1932; children: Daniel, Sheila Blake, Jonathan. BS, NYU, 1928. High sch. tchr., N.Y.C., 1929-30; tchr. Evalina de Rothschild Sch., Jerusalem, Palestine, 1930-31; social worker United Jewish Aid, Bklyn., 1931-32; tchr. Richmond Hill High Sch., 1932-40, Andrew Jackson High Sch., Cambria Heights, N.Y., 1940-71; mem. faculty New Sch. Social Rsch., N.Y.C., 1977-87; staff Vassar Summer Inst., 1946; vol. tchr. English Israel schs., 1987—. Am. editor: Teeline, A System of Fast Writing, 1970; author: College Teeline, 1977, College Teeline Self-Taught, 1983, Touch Typing Made Simple, 1985; contbr. articles to profl jours. Mem. Am. Fedn. Tchrs. Democrat. Home and Office: 11716 Park Ln S Kew Gardens NY 11418-1021

MARKS, SHIRLEY I., artist; b. N.Y.C., July 12, 1928; d. Hyman Max and Rose (Rosen) Isaacson; m. Herman Marks, June 8, 1947; children: Paulette Marks Lebowitz, Jeffrey I. dir. Diana Kan Workshops, Panama City Beach, Fla., 1996—. One-person shows include Phyliss Powers Art Gallery, 1984-86, Radisson Hotel, 1987, Biscayne Bay Marriot Hotel, 1988, Contemporary Art Ctr., Kingston, Jamaica, 1989, Pen and Brush, N.Y.C., 1992, A.E. Bean Backus Gallery, 1993, Elliot Mus., Stuart, Fla., 1996; group shows include Suntrust Gallery, 1995, Heim/Am. Gallery, Fisher Island, 1995, Wetz Gallery, 1996, Am. Artists Profl. League Allied Artists Am., N.Y., 1996, Jupiter Town Hall Gallery Art, 1997, Ga. Watercolor Soc., 1998, numerous others; represented in permanent collections So. Exposure Gallery, W. Palm Beach, Fla., Coconut Grove Gallery, Miami. Fundraiser, newsletter chmn. Theater Art League, Miami, Fla., 1977-98; bd. dirs., arts and crafts dir. Nat. Children's Cardiac Hosp., Miami, 1960-63; youth coord. Coral Gables B'nai B'rith, Miami, 1960-64. Numerous awards, incl. many best in shows. Mem. Am. Artist Profl. League (pres. 1993-95), Nat. Arts Club, Sumi Soc. Am., Fla. Profl. Artist Guild, Miami Watercolor Soc., Fla. Watercolor Soc., Ga. Watercolor Soc., Salmagundi Club. Democrat. Jewish. Avocations: photography, travel. Fax: 305-666-1946. Home: 9603 SW 69th Pl Pinecrest FL 33156-3071

MARKS, WILLIAM H., organ transplant program director, pharmacognosist, director for laboratory transplantation biology; b. Chgo., Aug. 16, 1948; s. Louis M. and Bertha M. (Michaelson) M.; m. Christine M. Marks, Nov. 1971; children: Annika, Daniel, Susie, Julia. BS, Loyola U., Chgo., 1970; MS, U. Ill., Chgo., 1973; MD, Loyola U., 1977; PhD, Lund U., 1983. Instr. U. Mich., Ann Arbor, 1973-85; asst. prof. surgery and biochemistry Loyola U., Maywood, Ill., 1985-87; assoc. prof. surgery Yale U., New Haven, Conn., 1987-93; adj. assoc. prof. pharmacology Nat. Products Chemistry U. Ill., Chgo., 1987—; dir. organ transplantation Swedish Med. Ctr., Seattle, 1994—, dir. lab. for transplant biology; med. dir. Life Ctr. N.W. Donor Network, Seattle, 1998—; med. dir. Life Ctr. N.W. Organ Procurement Agcy., 1997—; USMLE surg. step II Nat. Bd. Med. Examiners, Phila., 1992—. Editor Phytomedicine, 1994; contbr. articles to profl. jours.; patentee in field. Exec. com. N.W. Kidney Ctrs., Seattle, 1993; sec. bd. dirs. Life Ctr. NW, 1996—; bd. dirs. CenterSpan, Inc., 1996—. Fellow ACS (SK&F fellowship 1985, 86); mem. Am. Soc. Transplant Surgeons, Am. Soc. Transplant Physicians, Soc. Univ. Surgeons, The Transplant Soc., Soc. Surgery of the Alimentary Tract. Avocations: writing, skiing, mountaineering. Office: Organ Transplant Program 1120 Cherry St Ste 400 Seattle WA 98104-2023

MARKTL, WOLFGANG, physiologist, medical educator; b. Waiern, Austria, May 14, 1944; s. Kurt and Maria (Fruehauf) M.; m. Erika Gantner, Mar. 7, 1970; 1 child, Sabine. Dr.univ.med., Univ., Innsbruck, 1968. Univ. asst. U. Vienna, 1968-94, asst. prof., 1994—; head L. Boltzmann Inst., Bad Tatzmannsdorf, Austria, 1986—. Contbr. articles to profl. jours. Mem. Codex Alimentarius Austriacus, Vienna, 1995—. Mem. Österr. Ges. fur Ernahrung, European Soc. Chronobiology, Internat. Soc. Chronobiology, European Acad. Nutrition Sci., Deutsche Physiol. Gesellschaft, European Soc. Classical Natural Medicine, others. Office: Inst fur Physiologie U Wien, Schwarzspanierstr 17, A-1090 Wien Austria

MARKUS, MANFRED WILHELM, English language and literature educator; b. Hagen, Westphalia, Germany, Feb. 15, 1941; arrived in Austria, 1981; s. Erich and Lilly (Heckeler) M.; m. Ingrid Müller, Apr. 19, 1968; children: Dirk, Ronald. Grad., U. Göttingen, Fed. Republic Germany, 1967; PhD, U. Regensburg, Fed. Republic Germany, 1970, habilitation, 1980. Asst. prof. U. Regensburg, 1968-81; ordinary prof. U. Innsbruck, Austria, 1981—, dir. dept. English, 1985-95; vis. prof. U. Mass., Amherst, 1974-75. Author: Moderne Erzählperspektive in den Werken des Gawain-Autors, 1971, Tempus und Aspekt, 1977, Point of View im Erzähltext, 1985, Mittelenglisches Studienbuch, 1990, Icamet Manual, 1999; editor 8 books; contbr. articles to profl. jours. Mem. Anglistentag, Mediävistenverband, Soc. Linguistica Europea. Avocations: sports, working in home and garden, music. Home: Knappenweg 9, A-6020 Innsbruck Austria Office: U Innsbruck, Innrain 52, A-6020 Innsbruck Austria

MARKUS, MILES BERKELEY, parasitologist, researcher; b. Pretoria, South Africa, Jan. 26, 1942; s. August Frederick and Lorna Mary Ruth (Hook) M.; m. Jane Louise Markus, Sept. 21, 1977; 1 child, Victoria. BSc, U. Pretoria, 1963, MSc cum laude, 1970; MSc, U. London, 1970, PhD, diploma of Imperial Coll., 1975; BA with honors, U. Witwatersrand, 1999. Registered med. scientist, South Africa. Lectr. U. Pretoria, 1967-69, vis. scientist, 1971; demonstrator, tutor Imperial Coll., U. London, 1971-74; lectr., sr. lectr., assoc. prof., then prof. U. Witwatersrand, Johannesburg, South Africa, 1975—, dir. parasitology rsch. program, 1989—; advisor, com. chmn. South African Med. Rsch. Coun., 1992—; cons. South African Dept. Water Affairs and Forestry, 1995—, South African Dept. Arts, Culture, Sci. and Tech., 1996—; dir. Cons. Svcs. Internat., South Africa, 1996—; cons. univ. edn. in U.K., 1997—; freelance editor and translator, 1997—. Contbr. over 200 articles to internat. med. and sci. jours., chpts. to books. Recipient Llewellyn Andersson prize So. African Ornithol. Soc., 1966; overseas scholar Brit. Coun., 1971-74; overseas study grantee South African Med. Rsch. Coun., 1974-75. Fellow Royal Soc. Tropical Med. and Hygiene (life, local sec. 1994—); mem. South African Assn. for Med. Scientists, Parasitol. Soc. So. Africa, South African Translators' Inst., South African Assn. for the Advancement of Sci. (life), So. African Orthithol. Soc. (life), So. African Sci. Commn. Network, Royal Soc. South Africa (life), Microscopy Soc. So. Afria, Wildlife Mgmt. Soc. So. Africa (life), Zool. Soc. So. Africa (life), English Acad. So. Africa, Am. Soc. Tropical Medicine and Hygiene (life), Am. Soc. Parasitologists, Am. Ornithologists Union (life), Am. Med. Writers Assn., European Med. Writers Assn., European Assn. Sci. Editors, Brit. Soc. for Parasitology, Brit. Ornithologists' Union (life), Soc. Freelance Editors and Proofreaders, Wildlife Disease Assn., Profl. Editors' Group, Australian Soc. for Parasitology, Adler Mus. of the History of Medicine (life). Avocations: applied linguistics, science writing, music, ornithology. Office: Cons Svcs Internat, PO Box 853, Pinegowrie 2123, South Africa

MARKUSOVYCH, MYKHALEVYCH VOLODYMYR, mechanics researcher, mathematics educator; b. Vinnytsia, Ukraine, Apr. 11, 1953; s. Marquss Lvovich Ziydler and Maja Averkievna Mykhalevych; m. Tetyana Vadimovna Kyrylenko, June 20, 1989; 1 child, Oleksiy. Mech. Engr., Machine-Bldg. Faculty, Vinnytsia, 1975; CandSci, Technology Inst., Moscow, 1986; DSc, Inst. for Problems of Strength, Kiev, Ukraine, 1996. Jr. mem. tchg. staff Vinnytsia State Tech. U., 1976-80; postgrad. fellow Ctr. Inst. Tech./Mech. Engring., Moscow, 1980-83; rsch. fellow Ctr. Inst. Tech./Mech. Engring., Volgodonsk, Russia, 1983-86; lectr. Vinnytsia State Tech. U., 1986-96, prof., 1996-98, chair mgr., 1998—. Author: Tensor Models of Damage Accumulation, 1998; contbr. articles to profl. jours. Mem. N.Y. Acad. Scis., Nat. Com. of Ukraine on Theoretical and Applied Mechanics. Avocation: computer. Home: 15/9 Kwyateka Str, 286029 Vinnytsia Ukraine

MARLAS, JAMES CONSTANTINE, holding company executive; b. Chgo., Aug. 22, 1937; s. Constantine J. and Helen (Cotsirilos) M.; m. Kendra S. Graham, 1968 (div. 1971); m. Glenn Close, 1984 (div. 1987); m. Marie Nugent-Head, 1993. A.B. cum laude, Harvard U., 1959; M.A. in Jurisprudence, Oxford (Eng.) U., 1961; J.D., U. Chgo., 1963. Bar: Ill. 1963, N.Y. 1966. Assoc. firm Baker & McKenzie, London and N.Y.C., 1963-66; exec. v.p. South East Commodity Corp., N.Y.C., 1967-68; chmn. bd. Union Capital Corp., N.Y.C., 1968—; vice chmn. bd. Mickelberry's Food Products Co., N.Y.C., 1970-71; pres., dir. Mickelberry Comm. Corp., N.Y.C., 1972—; chief exec. officer Mickelberry Comm. Corp., 1973—; chmn. bd. Mickleberry Commn. Corp., 1984—; chmn. bd., CEO Newcourt Industries, Inc., 1976—; chmn. bd. dirs. Bowmar Instrument Corp., chmn. exec. com., 1983-92. Coeditor: Univ. Chgo. Law Rev, 1962-63; Contbr. articles to profl. jours. Bd. dirs. N.Y.C. Opera, Commanderie de Bordeaux, Brasenose Coll. Charitable Found. Mem. Am. Fgn. Law Assn., Young Pres.'s Orgn. Clubs: Boodle's (London); Racquet and Tennis (N.Y.C.). Office: Mickelberry Comm Corp 405 Park Ave New York NY 10022-4405

MARLATT, TOM OWEN, artist; b. San Jose, Calif., Sept. 4, 1946; s. Clarence Jack and Florence Lexie Marlatt. BA, San Jose State U., 1972. Profl. artist, 1973—. Exhbitied in numerous shows; represented in permanent collections Hoover Meml. Bldg., Stanford U., 1980. Avocations: archaeology, traveling, collecting, antiquities. Home: 21465 Summit Rd Los Gatos CA 95033-8400

MARLEAU, DIANE, Canadian government official; b. Kirkland Lake, Ont., Can., June 21, 1943; d. Jean-Paul and Yvonne (Desjardins) LeBel; m. Paul C. Marleau, Aug. 3, 1963; children: Brigitte, Donald, Stéphane. Student, U. Ottawa, Ont., 1960-63; BA in Econs., Laurentian U., Sudbury, Ont., 1976. With Donald Jean Acctg. Svcs., Sudbury, 1971-75; receiver mgr. Thorne Riddell, Sudbury, 1975-76; treas. No. Regional Residential Treatment Program for Women, Sudbury, 1976-80, Com. for the Industry and Labour Adjustment Program, Sudbury, 1983; mem. transition team Ont. Premier's Office, Toronto, 1985; firm adminstr. Collins Barrow-Maheu Noiseux, Sudbury, 1985-88; M.P. from Sudbury House of Commons, Ottawa, 1988—; min. of health for Can., 1993-96; min. of public works Canada, 1996-97; min. for internat. cooperation, min. responsible for La Francophonie, 1997-99; councilor Regional Municipality of Sudbury, 1980-85, chair fin. com., 1981; alderman City of Sudbury, 1980-85; mem. No. Devel. Coun., Sudbury, 1986-88; vice chair Nat. Liberal Standing Com. on Policy, 1989; chair Ont. Liberal Caucus, 1990; apptd. nat. exec. Liberal Party Can., 1990, assoc. critic Govt. Ops., 1990, Dep. Opposition Whip, 1991, assoc. critic Fin., 1992; vice chair standing com. fin., 1992. Chmn. fund-raising Canadian Cancer Soc., Sudbury, 1987-88; co-chmn. Laurentian Hosp. Cancer Care Svcs. fund-raising campaign, Sudbury, 1988; chair bd. govs. Cambrian Coll., 1987-88, bd. govs., 1983-88; mem. Sudbury and Dist. Health Unit Bd., 1981-82; mem. fin. com., bd. dirs. Laurentian Hosp., 1981-85; chair Can. Games for the Physically Disabled, 1983; apptd. Ont. Adv. Coun. Women's Issues, 1984. Recipient Paul Harris award, 1996. Mem. Sudbury Bus. and Profl. Women Club. Avocations: playing piano, gardening, cooking. Office: House of Commons, Parliament Bldgs, Ottawa, ON Canada K1A 0A6 also: 36 Elgin St, Sudbury, ON Canada P3C 5B4*

MARLETTA, GIOVANNI, physical chemistry educator, researcher; b. Augusta, Italy, June 8, 1953; s. Salvatore and Irene (Caramagno) M.; m. Elisabeth De Felice, June 2, 1988; 1 child, Stéphanie. Laurea, U. Catania, Italy, 1980. Rsch. fellow U. Catania, 1980-84, asst. prof., 1984-92; prof. U. Catania, Italy, 1996—; assoc. prof. U. Cosenza, Italy, 1992-94; prof. U. Potenza, Italy, 1994-96; mem. chemistry nat. bd. CNR, Rome, 1988-94, mem. informatics nat. bd., 1988-94, bd. dirs. nat. project spl. materials, 1997—; mem. Italian del. for energetics com. EEC, 1998; invited lectr. Gordon Conf., U.S., 1990; mem. scientific coms. of numerous Italian and European Labs.; mem. various confs. on ion-solid interactions, various others. Co-editor: Materials for Photonics, 1992, Nanometric Phenomena, 1997. Mem. Divsn. Phys. Chemistry (bd. dirs. 1992—), European Materials Rsch. Soc. (exec. com. 1999—, v.p. 1999-2000, pres. 2000—), Am. Chem. Soc., Bömische Phys. Soc. Avocations: linguistics, poetry, literary theory, philosophy. Office: U. Catania Dept Chemistry, Viale A Doria 6, 95125 Catania Italy

MARLICZ, KRZYSZTOF, gastroenterologist, educator; b. Aleksandrów Kujawski, Pomerania, Poland, Dec. 12, 1935; s. Adam and Marta (Sarnowska) M.; m. Maria Iljaszewicz, Jan. 22, 1969; 1 child, Wojciech. MD, Pomeranian Acad. Medicine, Szczecin, Poland, 1966. Asst. Pomeranian Med. Acad., Szczecin, 1958-75, assoc. prof., 1975-87, prof., 1987—, rector, 1996—. Contbr. articles to profl. jours. advisor to Pres. of Poland, 1993-95. Recipient I prize of Polish Soc. Physicians, 1966. Mem. Lions. Roman Catholic. Avocations: sports, tourism, history. Home: Pogodna 34 B, 71-376 Szczecin Poland Office: Pomeranian Medical Academy, Rybacka 1, 70-204 Szczecin Poland

MARLIN, RICHARD, lawyer; b. N.Y.C., June 1, 1933; s. Edward and Lillian (Milstein) M.; m. Merrel Pincus, June 12, 1955 (div. 1972); children: John F., Elizabeth; m. Jenesta Rutherford, July 29, 1974 (div. 1981); m. Caroline Mary Hirsch Magnus, Nov. 1, 1981. BA magna cum laude, Yale U., 1955, LLB, 1958; LLM, NYU, 1964. Bar: N.Y. 1959, Fla. 1978. Law clk. to presiding justice U.S. Dist. Ct. Conn., New Haven, 1958-59; assoc. Cleary, Gottlieb, Steen & Hamilton, N.Y.C., 1959-62, Wien Lane & Klein, N.Y.C., 1962-64; ptnr. Mnuchin Moss & Marlin, N.Y.C., 1964-66, Marshall, Bratter, Greene, Allison & Tucker, N.Y.C., 1966-79; sr. ptnr. Kramer, Levin, Naftalis & Frankel LLC, N.Y.C., 1979—; bd. dirs. FAB Industies, N.Y.C. Bd. editors Yale Law Jour. Mem. ABA, N.Y. State Bar Assn., Assn. Bar City N.Y., N.Y. County Lawyers' Assn. (corp. law com., chmn. subcom.), Glen Oaks Club (Old Westbury, N.Y.) (bd. govs. 1979-85, 92-94), Phi Beta Kappa. Office: Kramer Levin Naftalis & Frankel LLC 919 3rd Ave New York NY 10022-3902

MARLIN, ROBERT MATTHEW, secondary school educator; b. Buffalo, N.Y., June 11, 1940; s. Clarence Lewis and LaVerna (Haentgus) M.; m. Margaret Mary Steve, July, 1962 (div. July 1970); 1 child, Wendy. BEd, U. Alaska, 1967; postgrad., Alaska Pacific U., 1967-71, U. Ga., 1970, U. Salamanca, Spain, 1987, Calif State U., 1984-87. Cert. tchr., Calif. Radio traffic analyst USAF Security Svc., Anchorage, 1958-63; copywriter Anchorage Daily Times, 1963-67; tchr. Anchorage Sch. Dist., 1967-72; mgr. Transamerica Corp., L.A., 1972-84; tchr. L.A. Unified Sch. Dist., 1984—; participant sci. seminar on quality of edn., Pinar de Rio, Cuba, 1995, Matanzas, Cuba, 1996, Manzanillo, Cuba, 1997, Cienfuegos, Cuba, 1998. Bd. dirs. Upward Bound, Alaska Meth. Univ., Anchorage, 1969; vol. counselor Gay and Lesbian Cmty. Svcs. Ctr., L.A., 1975-76; cons. Constl. Rights Found., L.A., 1994—; gay and lesbian edn. commn. site liason L.A. Bd. Edn., 1996—. With USAF, 1958-63. Grantee Dept. Commerce, 1969, NSF, 1970, 71, L.A. Unified Sch. Dist., 1988. Mem. NEA, Gay, Lesbian, Straight Edn. Network, Calif. Tchrs. Assn., United Tchrs. L.A. (gay lesbian issues com.), Calif. Coun. for Social Studies. Democrat. Home: 531 W Avenue 46 Los Angeles CA 90065-5007 Office: Berendo Middle Sch 1157 S Berendo St Los Angeles CA 90006-3301

MARLOW, AUDREY SWANSON, artist, designer; b. N.Y.C.; d. Sven and Rita (Porter) Swanson; student (scholarships) Art Students League, 1950-55; spl. courses SUNY (Stony Brook), L'Alliance Française m. Roy Marlow, Nov. 30, 1968. With Cohn-Hall-Marx Textile Studio, 1961-65, R.S. Assocs. Textile Studio, 1965-73; freelance designer, illustrator Prince Matchabelli, Lester Harrison Agy., J. Walter Thompson Agy., 1957-78; portrait and fine artist, Wading River, N.Y., 1973—; instr. Phoenix Sch. Design (N.Y.C.); illustrator children's books: Breads of Many Lands and 4H Club Bakes Bread, 1966, Anna Smith Strong and the Setauket Spy Ring, 1991, Timothy and the Acrobat, 1992; exhibits include: Nat. Arts Club, NAD, Parish Art Mus., South Hampton, N.Y., Guild Hall, East Hampton, N.Y., Portraits Inc., Lincoln Ctr., Chung-Cheng Art Gallery, St. John's U., Mystic (Conn.)

Art Assn., Harbour Gallery, St. Thomas, V.I., Palais Rameau, Lisle, France, 1988, Sumner Mus., Washington, 1992, East End Arts & Humanities Coun., L.I., N.Y., 1996; one-person shows: Salmagundi Club, 1982, Rockefeller Gallery, N.Y.C., 1992; portrait commns. include: Millicent Fenwick, Harrison J. Goldin, Thomas R. Bayles, Mons. John Fagan, others. Trustee, Middle Island Public Library, 1972-76. Recipient John W. Alexander medal, 1976, award Council on Arts, 1978, award of excellence Cork Gallery, Lincoln Center, 1982; Grumbacher Bronze medal, 1983; Grumbacher Silver medal 1986; Best in Show award N.Y. Arts Council, 1986, Suburban Art League, 1993, Excellence award Town of Oyster Bay, 1995, Brookhaven Arts & Humanities Coun., 1996. Mem. Pastel Soc. Am. (award 1977, 80, 90), Am. Artists Profl. League (2 1st prize awards), Hudson Valley Art Assn. (award), Knickerbocker Artists (2 awards), Catharine Lorillard Wolfe Art Club (award 1982), Salmagundi Club (5 awards), Nat. League Am. Pen Women (Gold award, Gold medal of Honor, Best in Show 1990). Works represented at NYU, Longwood Pub. Libr., Sr. Citizen's Complex, Newark, St. Theresa of the Child Jesus Convent, Wading River Congl. Ch., L.I., pvt. collections. Home: 147 N Side Rd Wading River NY 11792-1112

MARLOW, EDWARD A., former army officer; b. Cleve., Nov. 22, 1946; m. Gari Ann Dill, Sept. 20, 1975. AA, Long Beach City Coll., 1971; cert., Officer Candidate Sch., Ft. Benning, 1974, Basic Infantry Officer Course, Ft. Benning, 1976; student, Am. Law Inst., N.Y., 1979-80; cert., Advance Armor Officer Course, Ft. Knox, 1982, U.S. Army Command and Gen. Staff Coll., 1986; BS in Bus. Mgmt. and Polit. Sci., SUNY, 1987; MPA, U. So. Calif., 1990; cert., Advance Intelligence Officer Course, Ft. Huachuca, 1991. Registered investment adv. with SEC, 1978-90. Commd. 2d lt. inf. U.S. Army, 1974, advanced through grades to maj., 1988; chief real property br. Mil. Dept., Sacramento, 1968—; pres. and dir. TEAM Mgmt. Corp., 1978—; pres. Western Res. Corp., Goldfield, Nev., 2000—, also bd. dirs. Mng. sr. ptnr. Caribbean Basin Latin Am. Devel. Orgn., Sacramento, 1988-98; trustee Hosp. Relief Fund Caribbean, Inc., Washington, 1989-92; mem. Caribbean Pvt. Sector Disaster Coord. subcom. White House Internat. Disaster Adv. Com., 1991-92; sr. ptnr. Caribbean Basin Latin Am. Devel. Orgn. Endowment Group, Sacramento, 1992—; chair bd. trustees CABALADO Relief Fund, Inc., 1993-99; provided disaster assistance and med. equipment to Glendon Hosp., Plymouth, Montserrat, West Indies, 1994-95. Mem. DAV (life), NRA, Am. Assn. Retired Persons. Avocations: sailing, fishing.

MARLOW, IAN MICHAEL, insurance company executive; b. Bklyn., Jan. 18, 1975; s. David Zachary and Ann Marlow. BSChemE, Rensselaer Poly. Inst., 1996. Environ. engr. Dept. Def., N.Y., 1993-96; nuc. engr. Dept. Energy, N.Y., 1996-97; v.p., dir., actuarial analyst Homestead Ins. Co., Florham Park, N.J., 1997-99; v.p., corp. devel., dir. IS & actuarial analyst Signet Star Reinsurance Co., Florham Park, 1999—. Mem. Datawarehousing Inst., Phi Lambda Phi (Nat. Engring. award). Avocations: sailing, automobiles, travel. Home: 11 Champion Blvd Livingston NJ 07039-8240

MARLOW, JAMES ALLEN, lawyer; b. Crossville, Tenn., May 23, 1955; s. Dewey Harold and Anna Marie (Hinch) M.; m. Sabine Klein, June 9, 1987; children: Lucas Allen, Eric Justin. BA, U. Tenn., 1976, JD, 1979; postgrad., Air War Coll., Maxwell AFB, Ala., 1990-91, Internat. Studienzentrum, Heidelberg, Germany, 1985-86. Bar: Ga. 1979, D.C. 1980, Tenn. 1980, U.S. Dist. Ct. (mid. dist.) Tenn. 1984, U.S. Ct. Fed. Claims 1987, U.S. Ct. Internat. Trade 1988, U.S. Tax Ct. 1987, U.S. Ct. Mil. Appeals 1980, U.S. Ct. Appeals (fed. cir.) 1987, U.S. Supreme Ct. 1987. Assoc. Carter & Assocs., Frankfurt, Fed. Republic Germany, 1984-85; chief internat. law USAF, Sembach AFB, Germany, 1986-96; pvt. practice Crossville, 1997—; instr. Ctrl. Tex. Coll., 1997—; asst. prof. Embry-Riddle Aero. U., Kaiserslautern, Fed. Republic Germany, 1985—. Capt. USAF, 1980-84, Lt. Col. USAFR. Mem. Phi Beta Kappa. Avocations: genealogy, basketball, chess, German and Spanish languages. Home and Office: 5746 Highway 127 S Crossville TN 38555-1137

MARLOW, NEIL, neonatology educator; b. Market Harboro, Eng., Nov. 10, 1951; m. Elaine Susan Floyd, 1973; children: Rebecca, Simon, Thomas, Oliver. BA with honors, U. Oxford, 1973, MA, 1981, DM, 1985; MBBS, U. London, 1976. Rsch. fellow St. Mary's Hosp., Manchester, Eng., 1981-83; lectr. U. Liverpool (Eng.), 1985-89; sr. lectr. U. Bristol (Eng.), 1989-96; prof. neonatology U. Nottingham (Eng.), 1997—, dir. rsch. Sch. Human Devel., 1997—. Author: A Neonatal Vade Mecum, 3d edit., 1998; contbr. articles to med. jours. Interventions for prematurity rsch. grantee Action Rsch., 1995, extreme prematurity grantee BLISS, 1997, high frequency vench ventilation rsch. grantee MRC, 1997. Fellow Royal Coll. Physicians, Royal Coll. Pediats. and Child Health; mem. Brit. Med. Assn. Office: Queens Med Ctr, Dept Child Health, Nottingham NG7 2VH, England

MARLOW, ORVAL LEE, II, lawyer; b. Denver, May 1, 1956; s. Jack Conger and Barbara A. (Stolzenburg) M.; m. Paige Wood, June 8, 1985; children: Lorri Wood, Orval Lee III. BA, U. Nebr., 1978, JD, 1981. Bar: Tex. 1981, U.S. Dist. Ct. (so. dist.) Tex. 1984, U.S. Ct. Appeals (5th cir.) 1984. Assoc. Krist & Scott, Houston, 1981-82; prin. Marlow & Assocs., Houston, 1982-83; ptnr. Lendais & Assocs., Houston, 1983-91; dir. Morris, Lendais, Hollrah & Snowden, 1992—. Mem. ABA, Internat. Bar Assn., Tex. Bar Assn., Houston Bar Assn., Phi Delta Phi. Lutheran. Avocations: golf, snow skiing, chess. Office: Morris Lendais Hollrah & Snowden 1980 Post Oak Blvd Ste 700 Houston TX 77056-3881

MARLOWE, WILLIE, artist, fine arts educator; b. Whiteville, N.C., Jan. 17, 1943; d. John David and Tessie Ernestine (McLawhorn) M.; m. Thomas Blakeslee Speight, July 11, 1980. BS, East Carolina U., 1965; MFA, U. Idaho, 1969; postgrad., Peace Coll., 1993. Instr. dept. art Skidmore Coll., Saratoga Springs, N.Y., 1970-74, mentor univ. without walls, 1972-74; instr. dept. art Columbia-Greene C.C., Hudson, N.Y., 1973-74; instr. Empire State Coll. SUNY, Albany, 1974; prof. divsn. fine arts The Sage Colls., Albany, 1977—, chairperson, 1979-81; co-founder, tchr., bd. dirs. Saratoga Arts Workshop, Saratoga Springs, N.Y., 1970-74; tchr. Somerville Coll., Oxford U., Eng.; vis. artist U. Ga. studies abroad program, Cortona, Italy; vis. artist, Wexford Arts Ctr., Ireland, artist-in-residence for Ptnrs. of the Americas, Barbados, W.I., The Millay Colony for the Arts, Austerlitz, N.Y., 1999; bd. dirs. Albany Ctr. Gallery, 1996-2000, artist selection com., 1998; guest lectr. in field. One-woman shows include The Mint Mus. Art, Charlotte, N.C., 1971, Schenectady Mus., N.Y., 1975, Marist Coll., Poughkeepsie, N.Y., 1976, Stockton State Coll., Pomono, N.J., 1977, The Coll. of St. Rose, Albany, 1979, The Greenville Mus. Art, N.C., 1982, 97, Ann Grey Gallery The Casino, Saratoga Springs, N.Y., 1985, The Barrett Art Gallery Utica Coll. of Syracuse U., N.Y., 1986, The Atrium Gen. Electric Corp. R&D Ctr., Schenectady, N.Y., 1988, The Lake George Arts Project, N.Y., 1988,The Old Forge Arts Ctr., N.Y., 1989, The Forum Gallery, Gütersloh, Germany, 1992, Albany Ctr. Gallery, 1992, 97, McHenry County Coll., Chrystal Lake, Ill., Dobbs Ferry (N.Y.) Arts Workshop, 1995, The Wexford Arts Ctr., Ireland (10 yr. retrospective 1988-98) 1998, numerous others; exhibited in group shows at Artemisia Gallery, Chgo., 2000, Nexus Gallery, N.Y.C., 1997, 98, 99, The Gang Gallery, N.Y.C., Eng. & Co., London, 1993, Steinbaum-Krauss Gallery, N.Y.C., 1990, Stux Gallery, Boston, 1987, Nat. Mus. Women Arts, Washington, 1987, Westbeth Gallery, N.Y.C., 1994, Clocktower, N.Y.C., 1986, The Rice Gallery The Albany Inst. of History & Art, 1986, numerous others; represented in pvt. collections in the U.S., Germany, England, Swedan, Ireland; represented in collections at Legis. Offices Empire State Plz., Albany, First Albany Corp., The Md. Dept. Econ. & Cmty. Devel., Balt., Quad Graphics, Boston, SUNY Albany, N.C. Nat. Bank, Charlotte, The Greenville Mus. Art, N.C., East Carolina U., Greenville, N.C., Boston Pub. Libr., The Budapest Gallery, Russell Sage Coll., Troy, N.Y., The Mint Mus. Art, Charlotte, N.C., Four Winds Ctr., Saratoga Springs, The Univ. Mus. SUNY Albany; co-curator and curator for mail art shows. Recipient of numerous awards including Purchase award in painting Hudson Mohawk Regional Ann., SUNY Albany, 1977, 95, 97, honorable mention in watercolor The Oswego Art Guild, N.Y., 1986, medal Internat. Art Competition Metro Arts, Inc., Scarsdale, N.Y., 1986, honorable mention in painting Third Ann. Nat. C.C. Miniature Painting Show, Lexington, 1987, Sywer award, 1995, and numerous others; N.Y. State Coun. on the Arts grantee Barrett Art Gallery Syracuse U., 1986, grantee Artists' Space, 1988. Mem. Nat. Assn. Women Artists, Albany Inst. History and Art, Fulton St. Gallery, Albany Ctr. Gallery, Woman's Caucus For Art. Avocations: painting, visual poetry, mail art.

MARMOLEJO, FRANCISCO J., educational association administrator; b. Ojuelos, Jalisco, Mex., Apr. 15. B in Bus. Adminstrn., U. San Luis Potosi, Mex., 1981, MBA, 1986. Mgr. exptl. station U. San Luis Potosi, 1981-84, assoc. dean. sch. agrl., 1984-97; prof. Nat. Autonomous U. Mex., Mex. City, 1987-90; v.p. acad. affairs U. of Ams., Mex. City, 1990-92, v.p. adminstrn. and fin., 1992-94; ACE fellow U. Mass., Amherst, 1994-95; dir. U.S.-Mex. Ednl. Interchange Project Western Interstate Comm. for Higher Edn., Tucson, 1995-97; exec. dir. Consortium for N.Am. Higher Edn. Collaboration, Tucson, 1997—; bd. dirs. Mex. Assn. Internat. Edn.; mem. external adv. bd. Autonomous U. Nuevo Leon, Monterrey, Mex., 1998—. Councilman County Ojuelos, Jalisco, Mex., 1980-82, 85-87. Fellow First Mex. Am. Coun. on Edn., Am. Coun. Edn., Washington, 1994; named Outstanding Alumnus, U. San Luis Potosi, 1990, Outstanding Citizen of Los Altos de Jalisco, State Govt. Jalisco, San Juan de los Lagos, 1999; received founder recognition Mex. Soc. Agribus., Torreon, 1998. Roman Catholic. Avocations: computers, reading. Fax: 520-626-2675. E-mail: fmarmole@u.arizona. Office: U Ariz Usb Rm 414E Tucson AZ 85721-0001

MAROHN, ANN ELIZABETH, health information professional; b. Grand Rapids, Mich., Feb. 26, 1946; d. Luther Alfonse and Mary Inez (Pinkstaff) M. BS, Ind. U., 1968; MS, SUNY, Buffalo, 1978. Asst. med. record dir. Highland Park (Mich.) Gen. Hosp., 1968-70; asst. dir. med. record svcs. Meml. Hosp., Elmhurst, Ill., 1970-73; dir. med. record tech. program Alfred (N.Y.) State Coll., 1974-76; mem. faculty med. record adminstrn. dept. Lincoln Coll., Melbourne, Australia, 1977-78, Kean Coll., Union, N.J., 1984-85, Med. U. S.C., Charleston, 1985-87; mem. faculty health record dept. Ferris State Coll., Big Rapids, Mich., 1979-80; dir. health info. mgmt. Armstrong State Coll., Savannah, Ga., 1980-84; dir. med. record dept. Tucson Gen. Hosp., 1988-89, N.D. State Hosp., Jamestown, 1990-92; cons. Prospective Payment Specialists, Tucson, 1992-93; health info. mgr. Sierra Med. Ctr., El Paso, Tex., 1993-94; dir. health info. mgmt. program Southern U., Shreveport, La., 1994-97; dir. health info. mgmt. N. VA Mental Health Inst., Falls Church, Va., 1997; dir. health info. tech. program Molloy Coll., Rockville Centre, N.Y., 1997-99; coord. health info. mgmt. program Santa Fe C.C., Gainesville, Fla., 1999—; cons. Oglethorpe Ctr., Savannah, 1983-84. Columnist Australian Med. Record Jour., 1981-87, Communique, 1981-84, Palmetto Breeze, 1985-87, Progress Notes, 1984-85. Recipient disting. mem. award Ga. Med. Record Assn., 1984; fellow Aspen Inst., 1988. Mem. Assembly on Edn., Am. Health Info. Mgmt. Assn., Ariz. Health Info. Mgmt. Assn. (program chmn. 1988-89, sec. 1989—), Tex. Health Info. Mgmt. Assn. (dist. III v.p.), L.I. Health Info. Mgmt. Assn., Fla. Health Info. Mgmt. Assn., N.E. Fla. Health Info. Mgmt. Assn. (del. 2000 state house dels.; incoming pres.-elect, 2000—), Alachua County Vocat. Edn. Assn., Internat. Fedn. Health Record Orgns. Episcopalian. Avocations: swimming, reading, travel, photography, cooking. Home: 4000 NW 51st St Apt C60 Gainesville FL 32606-4349 Office: 3000 NW 83d St CO2 Gainesville FL 32606

MARON, IAN HOWARD, insurance company executive, actuary; b. Johannesburg, South Africa, Aug. 1, 1965; s. Lionel and Shirley (Uran) M.; m. Gayle Rubin; 1 child, Raziel. BSc with honors, U. Witwatersrand, Johannesburg, South Africa, 1992. Actuarial trainee Liberty Life, Johannesburg, 1987-88, actuarial asst., 1988-89, actuary-model office, 1989-92, actuary-product devel., 1992-99, CEO employee benefits, 1999—; dir. Integral Quantitative Asset Mgmt., Capetown, South Africa, 1989—. Fellowship Faculty of Actuaries, 1989. Fellow Actuarial Soc. of South Africa, Faculty of Actuaries. Avocation: running. Office: Liberty Life Assn, PO Box 10499, Johannesburg 2000, South Africa

MARONDE, ROBERT FRANCIS, internist, clinical pharmacologist, educator; b. Monterey Park, Calif., Jan. 13, 1920; s. John August and Emma Florence (Palmer) M.; m. Yolanda Cerda, Apr. 15, 1970; children—Robert George, Donna F. Maronde Varnau, James Augustus, Craig DeWald. B.A., U. So. Calif., 1941, M.D., 1944. Diplomate: Am. Bd. Internal Medicine. Intern L.A. County-U. So. Calif. Med. Ctr., 1943-44, resident, 1944-45, 47-48; asst. prof. physiology U. So. Calif., L.A., 1948-49, asst. clin. prof. medicine, 1949-60, assoc. clin. prof. medicine, 1960-65, assoc. prof. medicine and pharmacology, 1965-67, prof. medicine and pharmacology, 1968-90, emeritus, 1990—, prof. emeritus, 1990—; spl. asst. v.p. for health affairs, 1990—; cons. FDA, 1973, Medco Containment Co. Inc., 1991-97, State of Calif. Dept. Health Svcs., 1993; mem. adv. panel State of Calif., 1997—. Served to lt. (j.g.) USNR, 1945-47. Fellow ACP; mem. Am. Soc. Clin. Pharmacology and Therapeutics, Alpha Omega Alpha. Home: 785 Ridgecrest St Monterey Park CA 91754-3759 Office: U So Calif 2025 Zonal Ave Los Angeles CA 90033-1034

MARONEY, SUSIE JEAN, swimmer; b. Sydney, NSW, Australia, Nov. 15, 1974; d. Norman William and Pauline Frances (Odgers) M. Amb. Australia Day, 1993—, Leukemia Found., 1997—, Asthma Found., 1989—, Rivercare 2000, 1990—, Spl. Olympics, 1991—, World Vision, 1999; bd. dirs. Police Clubs; patron Rett Syndrome Med. Rsch. Team, Starlight Found., Handicapped Childrens Ctr. Sylvanvale, Bonny Babes Found., Young at Heart Victor Chang Rsch.; mem. steering com. NSW Women of Excellence Com. Inducted into Internat. Swimming Hall of Fame, Ft. Lauderdale, Fla.; recipient Order of Australia, 1993, Young Achiever Sports award Channel 10, 1991, Paul Harris award Rotary Club, Outstanding Contbn. to Sports award Advance Australia, Jr. Sports award Toyota, 1989, 90, 91, Sr. Sports award Toyota, 1992, 93; named Sportswoman of Yr. Variety Club, 1998, NSW, 1993, Achiever of Yr. for NSW Asthma Found., 1996, 97, Young Achiever of Yr., 1990, 91. Holds several world records including double crossing of English Channel, longest swim recorded (Mexico to Cuba). First person to swim from Cuba to Key West. Avocations: reading, movies. Home: PO Box 693, NSW Miranda 1490, Australia

MAROO, VIJAY, publishing executive; b. Ranchi, Bihar, India, Nov. 29, 1947; s. Sitaram and Gita Maroo; m. Suman Bhuraria, Mar. 9, 1970; children: Sonia, Manish. BSc in Engring., Birla Inst. Tech., Mesra, India, 1969. Dir. Ranchi Prakashan Pvt. Ltd., 1970-74, exec. dir., 1975—. Mem. Ranchi Jr. Chamber (pres. 1975), Indian Jr. Chamber (v.p. 1976), Media Rsch. Users Coun. (exec. com. 1994—), Maheshwary Club (sec. 1996-98). Office: Ranchi Prakashan Pvt Ltd, 5/14 INS Bldg Rafi Marg, 110001 New Delhi India

MAROSI, CHRISTINE, oncologist, cytogeneticist; b. Regensburg, Germany, May 6, 1956; d. Friedrich and Elisabeth (Glaser) Pollak; m. Leo Marosi, May 9, 1986; 1 child, Ilja. MD, U. Vienna, Austria, 1980. Cert. med. oncologist and cytogeneticist. Lectr. U. Vienna, Austria, 1981-94, asst. prof., 1994—, neuro-oncologist, 1994—. Contbr. articles to profl. jours. Office: U Vienna Dept Internal Med Div Oncology, Wahringer Gurtel 18-20, 1090 Vienna Austria

MAROTO, BEATRIZ GRACIELA, chemistry educator; b. Cordoba, Argentina, Dec. 4, 1960; d. Francisco and Maria M.; m. Jorge Pereyra; children: Maria Celina, Jorgelina. B of Chem. Engring., U. Tech., Cordoba, Argentina, 1985; PhD in Engring., U. Nat. Plata, Argentina, 1998. Asst. U. Tech., Cordoba, Argentina, 1981-87, U. Nat. Cordoba, Argentina, 1986-92; prof. unit operations U. Techs., 1986-87, prof. organic chemistry, 1993—. Contbr. articles to profl. jours. Argentine-Brazil Biotech. Com. fellow, 1996, Funds Improvement Teaching, World Bank fellow, 1996; recipient Dr. Pedro N. Arata prize Argentine Chem. Assn., 1999. Avocations: swimming, tennis. E-mail: bmaroto@agro.uncor.edu. Home: Tristan Narvaja 1640, 5006 Cordoba Argentina Office: Facutad de Agropecuarias, CC509, 5000 Cordoba Argentina

MAROTO, FEDERICO GARCIA, molecular biology educator, researcher; b. Granada, Spain, June 16, 1961; s. Manuel Garcia Serrano and Rosario Maroto Camacho; m. Rosa Marin Morales, Sept. 21, 1991; 2 children: Jesus, Javier. MSc in Chemistry, U. Autonoma Madrid, 1986, PhD in Chemistry, 1988. Cert. chemist. Permanent prof. U. Politecnica de Madrid, 1993-96, U. de Almeria, Spain, 1996—. Contbr. articles to profl. jours. European Molecular Biology Orgn. fellow Max-Planck-Inst. für Züchtungsforschung, Cologne, Germany, 1991-93. Mem. Spanish Biochemistry and Molecular Biology Soc. Avocations: botany, photography. E-mail: fgmaroto@ualm.es. Fax: 34-950-215800. Home: Amazonas n 15, 04120 Almeria Spain Office: Univ de Almeria, La Canada de san Urbano sn, 04120 Almeria Spain

MAROTO-VALER, MARIA MERCEDES, chemist, researcher, educator; b. Vitoria, Spain, Nov. 30, 1971; d. Avelino Maroto and Consuelo Valer. BSc in Applied Chemistry with honours, U. Strathclyde, Glasgow, Scotland, 1993, PhD in Applied Chemistry, 1997; BSc in Indsl. Chemistry, U. Basque Country, Bilbao, Spain, 1994, DChE, 1998. Tchg. asst. U. Strathclyde, 1993-96, rsch. sicentist, 1997; rsch. scholar U. Ky., Lexington, 1997-98; rsch. assoc. Pa. State U., University Park, 1998-2000, asst. prof. energy and geo-environ. engring., 2000—; cons. in industry; conf. chair and conf. symposium organizer. Contbg. author: Encuclopedia of Separation Science, 2000; contbr. articles to profl. jours.; author conf. procs. Recipient Bellahouston award, Glasgow, 1996, Ritchie prize U. Strathclyde, 1997, prize Coal Rsch. Forum, U.K., 1995, 97, NMR Discussion Group award, U.K., 1997. Mem. Am. Chem. Soc. (R.A. Glenn award, fuel divsn. 1996). Avocations: hill-walking, cinema, travel, sports, foreign cultures. E-mail: mmm23@psu.edu. Office: Pa State U 405 Acad Activities Bldg University Park PA 16802

MAROTTA, FRANCESCO, gastroenterologist; b. Augusta, Siracusa, Italy, Jan. 15, 1957; s. Giuseppe and Anna (Maltese) M.; m. Antonella Galizia, May 23, 1992; children: Katherine, Carole. MD, Catania (Italy) U., 1981, Gastroenterology Bd., 1986. Rsch. fellow gastroenterology dept. U. Catania, 1981-82; registrar gastroenterology dept. U. Cape Town, South Africa, 1983-86; PhD rsch. fellow surg. gastroenterolgoy dept. U. Hirosaki, Japan, 1986-89; Japan Ministry of Sci. fellow Nat. Cancer Ctr., Tokyo, 1989-90; gastroenterology cons. Liver unit Niguarda Hosp., Milan, 1990-93; chief cons. Gastroenterology Svc. St. Anna Hosp., Como, Italy, 1993—; chief endoscopy unit S. Giuseppe Hosp., Milan; rsch. cons. ECONUM Lab., Villeneuve d'Ascq, France, 1988, Osato Found., Gifu, Japan, 1993, Shianxi Hosp-Gastroenterology Dept., Xian, China, 1995, Japan/China Corp., Tokyo, 1995; sci. dir. Noguchi Meml. Rsch. Inst., Nagoya, Japan; spl. guest Digestive Disease Week, Japan, 1999, v.p. MediWeb Co., 2000. Contbr. articles to profl. jours. Recipient Best Paper award Japan Surgery Soc. Assn., Nagoya, 1995; named Silver Medal Vis. Prof., Shinshu U., Matsumoto, Japan, 1994; travel grantee Asian/Pacific Gastroenterol. Assn., Yokohama, Japan, 1996, Internatl Assn. Study of Liver, Japan, 2000. Mem. Am. Coll. Gastroenterology, N.Y. Acad. Sci. Roman Catholic. Avocations: running, karate, music, art, history. Home: via Pisanello 4, 20146 Milan Italy

MAROULIS, KONSTANTINOS EFTHIMIOS, gas company executive, electrical engineer; b. Volos, Magnissia, Greece, May 11, 1962; s. Efthimios D. and Victoria K. (Georgiades) M.; m. Filitsa N. Pitsios, Aug. 21, 1993; children: Victoria, Efthimios. Cert. English, Spring Hill Coll., Mobile, Ala., 1982; BSEE, U. South Ala., 1988; MSEE, Aristotle U., 1999. Project engr. CCA Electronics Inc., Atlanta, 1988-89, dir. testing & quality assurance, 1989-91; engring. supr., inspector Asprofos S.A., Athens, Greece, 1992-95; dist. mgr. Pub. Gas Corp. of Greece, Farsala, 1995—; tchg. cons. Continuing Edn. Ctr., Volos, Greece, 1995—. Contbr. articles to Thessalia newspaper on topics related to natural gas industry. Sgt. maj. Spl. Forces of Greece-Marines, 1991-92. Mem. IEEE. Avocations: music, athletics, reading. Home: 1 Kartali 12B, 38221 Volos M/T, Greece Office: Pub Gas Corp Greece SA, 40300 Ampelia Farsala F/L, Greece

MAROVITZ, SANFORD E., English language and literature educator; b. Chgo., May 10, 1933; s. Harold and Gertrude (Luster) M.; m. Eleonora Dimitsa, Sept. 1, 1964. BA with honors, Lake Forest Coll., 1960; MA, Duke U., 1961, PhD, 1968. Instr. English Temple U., 1963-65; Fulbright instr. U. Athens, Greece, 1965-67; from asst. prof. English to prof. Kent State U., Ohio, 1967-96, prof. emeritus, 1996—; vis. prof. English, Shimane U., Matsue, Japan, 1976-77, chair, 1987-92; co-dir. Melville Among the Nations, Greece, 1997. Co-editor: Artful Thunder: Versions of Romanticism in American Literature in Honor of Howard P. Vincent, 1975; co-author: Bibliographical Guide to the Study of the Literature of the U.S.A., 5th edit. 1984, Abraham Cahan, 1996; contbr. articles to profl. jours. Nat. trustee Lake Forest Coll., 1990-98. With USAF, 1953-57. Woodrow Wilson fellow, 1960-61; recipient Disting. Svc. Citation Lake Forest Coll., 1985, Disting. Tchg. award Kent State U., 1985, Presdl. Citation Shimane U., 1998. Mem. MLA, Am. Studies Assn., Melville Soc. (sec. 1994-96, pres. 1998), Hawthorne Soc., Western Lit. Assn., Henry James Soc., Aldous Huxley Soc. (curator 1998—), W.D. Howells Soc., Saul Bellow Soc., R.W. Emerson Soc., Phi Beta Kappa, Omicron Delta Kappa, Phi Beta Delta. Democrat. Jewish. E-mail: smarovit@kent.edu. Home: 1155 Norwood St Kent OH 44240-3342 Office: Kent State U Dept English Kent OH 44242-0001

MAROY, MICHEL, European affairs consultant; b. Uccle, Belgium, Dec. 18, 1952; s. Pierre Maroy and Nicole Janssen; m. Jacqueline de Dorlodot; 1 child, Gabriel. Law candidate, Facultes U. St. Louis, Brussels, 1973; grad. in law, Cath. U. Louvain, Belgium, 1976. Bar: Brussels 1977. Attaché Cabinet Min. Edn., Brussels, 1977-80; dir. Bie Press Agy., Brussels, 1981-83; attaché Cabinet Min. Pres., Brussels, 1985-86; v.p. Imterel, S.A., Brussels, 1987-88; sr. cons. G.J.W., Ltd., London, 1988-89; dir. 2M Pub. Affairs, Brussels, 1990—; spkr., Team Europe, Brussels, 1992—; dir. Telex Africa, 1981-87, Telex Mediterranean. Roman Catholic. Home: Manypré, B-1325 Corroy LeGrand Belgium Office: 2M Public Affairs, Square Vergote 39, B-1030 Brussels Belgium

MARQUARDT, OTFRIED HELLMUT, molecular biologist; b. Vikhammer/Trontheim, Norway, May 28, 1946; arrived in Germany, 1947; s. Rudolf Zollner and Hedwig Marquardt; m. Karin Maria Henning; children: Andreas Sebastian, Johanna Christine. Student, Georg-August U., Göttingen, Germany, 1968-70, Freie U., Berlin, 1970-74; Phys. Dr., Freie U., Berlin, 1976; Habilitation in Biochemistry, Eberhard-Karls U., Tübingen, 1993. Sci. asst. Max-Planck Inst., Berlin, 1976-77, Martinsried, Germany, 1979-85; sci. asst. U. Hamburg, Germany, 1977-78; sci. dir. Fed. Rsch. Ctr. for Virus Diseases of Animals, Tübingen, Germany, 1985—. Contbr. articles to profl. jours. Office: Fed Rsch Ctr Virus Diseases, Paul-Ehrlich-Strasse 28, Tübingen 72076, Germany

MARQUARDT, STEVE ROBERT, library director; b. St. Paul, Sept. 7, 1943; s. Robert Thomas and Dorothy Jean (Kane) M.; m. Judy G. Brown, Aug. 4, 1968; 1 child, Sarah. BA in History, Macalester Coll., 1966; MA in History, U. Minn., 1970, MLS, 1973, PhD in History, 1978. History instr. Macalester Coll., St. Paul, 1968-69; cataloger N.Mex. State U. Libr., Las Cruces, 1973-75; acting univ. archivist, acting dir. Rio Grande Hist. Collections N. Mex. State U. Libr., Las Cruces, 1973-74; acquisitions librarian Western Ill. U. Libr., Macomb, 1976-77, head cataloger, Online Computer Libr. Ctr. coord., 1977-79; asst. dir. resources & tech. svcs. Ohio U. Libr., Athens, 1979-81; dir. librs. U. Wis., Eau Claire, 1981-89; dir. univ. librs. No. Ill. U., DeKalb, 1989-90; dir. librs. U. Wis., Eau Claire, 1990-96; dean of librs. S.D. State U., Brookings, 1996—. Editor Jour. Rio Grande History, 1974; contbg. editor: Library Issues, 1994-99; contbr. articles to profl. jours. Coord. Amnesty Internat. Adoption Group 275, Eau Claire, 1985-88; pres. Chippewa Valley Free-net, 1994-96. Mem. ALA, Assn. Coll. and Rsch. Librs. (chmn. performance measures in acad. librs. com. 1985-89). Lutheran. Avocations: tennis, bicycling. Office: SD State U Briggs Libr PO Box 2115 Brookings SD 57007-0001

MARQUES, HECTOR NESTOR, lawyer; b. Pehuajó, Argentina, Nov. 3, 1949; s. Teodoro Pedro Marqués-Arrieu and Mena Volpe; m. María Elena Peterson, Dec. 10, 1978; children: Catriel Agustín, Santiago Agustín. Lawyer, Cath. U., La Plata, Argentina, 1973. Ptnr. Marqués, Migliore & Assoc., Buenos Aires, 1974-77, Marqueés & Ale Iturralde Internat. Cons., Buenos Aires, 1987-94, Marqués & Assocs., Buenos Aires, 1977—; asst. registrar Nat. Registry of Vital Stats., San Fernando, Argentina, 1981-83; adherent Coun. for Internat. Rels., Buenos Aires, 1995-96. Past pres. Argentine-Baltic Assn. Friendship and Interchange, Buenos Aires, 1991-95; past v.p. Argentine-Chinese Ctr. Friendship and Interchange, Buenos Aires, 1993-95. Mem. Internat. Bar Assn. S.E. Asia, Bar Assn. for Migration in Argentina, Adminstrv. Law Inst., Universitarian Club Buenos Aires. Avocations: swimming, tennis, horsing. Office: Marqués & Assoc, Viamonte 1454 3p H, 1055 Buenos Aires Argentina

MARQUES, JOSÉ FERREIRA, psychology educator; b. Dec. 23, 1936; s. Josè Marques and Carmelina Borba Costa; m. Olga Maria Henzler, July 25, 1965; children: Jose Frederico, Tomas, Luis. MA, U. Lisbon, 1959, PhD, 1970. Asst. faculty arts U. Lisbon, 1959-60, 63-69, aux. prof., 1970-72, extraordinary prof., 1972-78, prof., 1979-80, prof. psychology Faculty

Psychology and Edn., 1981—, pres. bd. dirs., 1981-92. Author: Estudos Sobre e WISC, 1969, Guidance and the School Curriculum, 1978, Educational and Vocational Guidance Services in Portugal, 1993; editor: Guidance in 1975 and Its Perspectives on the Near Future, 1976-77, Career Guidance Services for the 90's, 1995; contbr. sci. articles to profl. jours. Mem. Portuguese Psychol. Soc. (pres. 1988-90), Internat. Assn. Ednl. and Vocat. Guidance (bd. dirs. 1979-83, 83-87, v.p. 1987-91, pres. 1991-99), Internat. Assn. Applied Psychology (exec. com. 1990-98), Assn. Psychologie Scientifique de Langue Française (exec. com. 1981-95, pres. 1987-89). Home: Rua S Felix 37 R/C D, 1200 Lisbon Portugal Office: Faculty of Psychology & Edn, Alameda da Universidade, 1600 Lisbon Portugal

MARQUES, OTAVIO AUGUSTO VUOLO, biologist, researcher; b. Sao Paulo, Sao Paulo, Brazil, Apr. 13, 1964; s. Euclydes Fontegno and Maria Nilda (Vuolo) M.; m. Wânia Duleba, March 20, 1993; 1 child, Isabela. Diploma in Biology, U. Sao Paulo, 1987, Masters, 1992, PhD, 1998. Rschr. Butantan Inst., Sao Paulo, 1993—. Avocations: photography, jogging, swimming. Office: Butantan Inst., Av Vital Brazil 1500, 05503900 Sao Paulo Brazil

MARQUES CARDOSO, ANTÓNIO JOÃO, electrical engineering educator, researcher; b. Coimbra, Portugal, Aug. 21, 1962; s. Silvino Baptista and Maria Adélia (Marques) C.; m. Deolinda Dos Santos Pessoa, July 20, 1986; children: Diogo, Rodrigo. Elec. engr. diploma, U. Coimbra, Coimbra, Portugal, 1985, PhD, 1995. Asst. U. Coimbra, 1985-89, sr. asst., 1989-95, asst. prof., 1995—, dir. elec. machines lab., 1996—; coun. mem. of elec. engr. dept. U. Coimbra, 1987-90, 95—, security coun., 1999—; mem. Internat. Orgn. for Stds., Switzerland, 1991—, convenor, 1994—, tech. com. mem. Portuguese Inst. Quality, Lisbon, Portugal, 1992—, convenor, 1995—; mem. overseas adv. panel Condition Monitoring & Diagnostic Tech., 1990-93; active European Com. Standardization Brussels, 1995—. Author: Fault Diagnosis in 3-Phase Induction Motors, 1991; mem. editl. bd. Internat. Jour. Condition Monitoring & Diagnostic Engring. Mgmt., 1998—. Founding mem. Rsch. European Consortium, 1993. Recipient Rsch. scholarship Nat. Inst. Scientific Rsch., 1990-94. Mem. IEEE (sr. mem., elec. machines com., indsl. drs. com.), Portuguese Fedn. Indsl. Maintenance, Portuguese Engr. Assn. (Sr. Mem. award 1996), European Power Elec. and Drs. Assn., N.Y. Acad. Scis. Avocations: jogging, reading, fishing. Office: U Coimbra Dept Elec Engring, Pólo II-Pinhal Marrocos, P-3030 Coimbra Portugal

MARQUEZ CAMPOS, ALFREDO, surgeon, editor; b. Lagos de Moreno, Jalisco, Mex., May 26, 1923; s. Jose Marquez and Herminia Muñoz; m. Estela del Consuelo Barriga Lopez, June 17, 1948; children: Estela, Alfredo, Consuelo, Juan Jose, Magdalena, Alejandro, Graciela, Jaime Antonio, Ana Cecilia. Medicine, U. Autonoma Mex., Mexico City, 1947. Med. dir. Ciba de Mex. Owner, editor Revista de Medicina y Ciencias Afines, 1942-85, Semana Medica de Centroamerica y Panama, 1959-79, Semana Medica de México, 1954-85, Noticias Medicas, 1974—. Recipient Gold medals Presea Ignacio L. Vallarta Grant Govt. of the State of Jalisco, 1958, Presea Mariano Azuela Grant of the Govt. of the State of Jalisco, 1981. Mem. Mexican Soc. Geography and Statistics (academician), Mex. Acad. Bioethics (academician), Nat. Acad. History and Geography (academician). Roman Catholic. Avocation: writing. Home: Sofocles 353, 11530 Mexico City Mexico Office: Homero 109-105B, 11540 Mexico City Mexico

MARQUIS, RONALD JAMES, sales executive; b. Perth, U.K., Feb. 19, 1946; s. James and Sarah Nellie Brewster (MacDonald) M.; m. Linda Margaret Mary Greig, Mar. 27, 1976; children: Christopher Alexander, Jonathan James, Michael Ronald. BS, U. Dundee, Scotland, 1972. Flight trials engr. Ferranti, Edinburgh, Scotland, 1973-75, Dunsfold, U.K., 1975-76; trials mgr. Ferranti, Stranrear, U.K., 1976-80; sr. trials/devel. Ferranti, Edinburgh, 1980-83, sales exec., 1983-87, product sales mgr., 1987-88; mktg. mgr. Middleeast GEC-Ferranti, Edinburgh, 1988-93; sales mgr. GEC-Marconi, Edinburgh, 1993-95, mktg. mgr. Asia Pacific, 1995-99; regional sales dir. Asia Pacific Alenia Marconi Sys., Edinburgh, 1990—. Author: (book) TIALD in the Gulf, 1992. Home: 23 Carfrae Rd, Edinburgh EHG 3QG, Scotland

MARRA, ANTHONY TULLIO, audio visual specialist; b. Newark, N.J., June 26, 1947; s. John and Christine (Sapparito) M.; m. Erica Jane Curci, Nov. 25, 1987; children: Becky Michelle George, Antonio Tullio, Becky Lynn George, Crystal Marra, Heather Leigh Marra, Megan Marra. Advisor Govt. Liason for Ednl. Insts., Washington, 1978-91; media specialist, advisor Washington & Lee U., Lexington, Va., 1978-91; media specialist Longwood Coll., Farmville, Va., 1978-91, Hollins Coll., Salem, Va., 1978-91, Lynchburg (Va.) Coll., 1978-91, Randolph Macon Women's Coll., Lynchburg, Va., 1978-91; dir. audio-visual Sweet Briar (Va.) Coll., 1978-91; media cons. Africa Global Perspectives, 1994—; pres., owner Audio/Visual Advisors, 1997—; agt. bus. comms. sys. divsn. Lucent Techs./Bell Labs, 1997—; acoustic expert rsch. and devel. NASA Langley Field, Hampton, Va., 1971-78. Author: (books) Poetry in LIfe To Be in Death I Am, 1972, The Holy Quran-The Hereafter, 1989; inventor: overhead copy stand for ch.-sch. system, 1991, marking device for NASA Test Flights, 1972; designer TV studio and control room, 1994. Bd. dirs. S.W. Va. Free Clinic. With USMC, 1964-68, Vietnam. Recipient cert. appreciation NASA fors rsch. 1976, 78. Avocations: photgraphy, videography, working with bldg. computers, cmty. work. Home: PO Box 575 Madison Heights VA 24572-0575 Office: 3421 Plymouth Pl Lynchburg VA 24503-1300

MARRANGHELLO, NORIAN, computer science educator; b. Porto Alegre, Brazil, Oct. 22, 1957; s. Italo and Nadyr Marranghello; m. Sandra Maria Prado, Apr. 22, 1987. Degree in electronic engring, PUC-RS, Porto Alegre, Brazil, 1982; MEE, U. Campinas, Brazil, 1987, PhD in Elec. Engring., 1992; Livre-Docente in Digital Sys., São Paulo State U., 1998. Asst. programmer Ormesa S/A, Porto Alegre, 1979; owner NPI Ltd., Porto Alegre, 1980-84; asst. engr. Polymax S/A, Porto Alegre, 1982; asst. prof. São Paulo State U., S.J. Rio Preto, Brazil, 1992-98; assoc. prof. São Paulo State U., S.J. Rio Preto, 1998—; vice head dept. computer sci. Inst. Humanities Biol. and Exact Scis., São Paulo State U., S.J. Rio Predo, 1994-96, chmn. rsch. com., 1998—; cons. Interlocalizer, S.J. Rio Preto, 1996; postdoctoral vis. rschr. U. Aahrus, Denmark, 1997-98. Contbr. articles to profl. jours. Scholar Brazilian Nat. Higher Edn. Com., Brazilian Nat. Rsch. Coun., São Paulo State Rsch. Found., 1984-92; São Paulo State Rsch. Found. rsch. grantee, 1993-98. Mem. IEEE (sr.), Brazilian Soc. Microelectronics (founder), Brazilian Soc. Computing. Office: DCCE/IBILCE/UNESP, Rua Cristovao Colombo 2265, 15054000 SJ Rio Preto Brazil

MARRÈ, ERASMO, plant physiologist, researcher; b. Genova, Italy, Feb. 6; s. Carlo and Giuseppina Marrè; m. Coda Eugenia, Aug. 16, 1945; children: Carlo, Maria Teresa, Valentino. D of Natural Scis., 1946. From assoc. prof. to prof. plant physiology U. Genoa and U. Milan, 1951-59; prof. emeritus plant physiology U. Milan, 1996; vis. prof. horticulture, Columbia, Mo., 1950-51; dir. Ctr. Italian Nat. Rsch. Coun. for Oxidation-reductions in Plants, 1971-77; mem. com. for biology and medicine Italian Nat. Rsch. Coun., 1976-81. Contbr. numerous articles to sci. jours. Recipient award Italian Ministry of Edn., 1973, Gold medal, 1978. Mem. Italian Plant Growth Substances Assn. (v.p. 1982-85), Italian Soc. Plant Physiology (pres. 1961, 68, 72, Am. Soc. Plant Physiologists (hon. life, Charles Reid Barnes award 1983), Italian Soc. Plant Physiology (hon. life), Italian Acad. of XL, Nat. Acad. Lincei, Lombard Acad. for Scis. and Letters. Office: U Milan Dept Biology, Via Celoria 26, 20133 Milan Italy

MARRETT, MICHAEL MCFARLENE, chaplain; b. Greenwich Town, Surrey, Jamaica, Oct. 7, 1935; s. Kenneth Louis and Ivy Lynmae (McFarlane) M.; m. Margery Eva Mugford, Jan. 29, 1984. Cert. gen. ordination, Oxford (Eng.) U., 1961; cert. edn. in English lang., London U., 1967; MDiv, Gen. Theol. Sem., 1969, STM, 1970; STM, N.Y. Theol. Sem., 1972; postgrad., Princeton Theol. Sem., 1972-73, Columbia U., 1973-75; BA, Fordham U., 1974; postgrad., The Coll. of Preachers, 1979, Yale U., 1979-81; PhD, NYU, 1980; MS, So. Conn. State U., 1982. Lic. pastoral counselor, Md.; cert. profl. mental health clergy, chaplain and fellow of Coll. Chaplains; nat. cert. bereavement facilitator Am. Acad. Bereavement; diplomate Am. Psychotherapy Assn. Staff chaplain St. Elizabeths Hosp., Washington, 1986-99; ret., 1999. Author: The Lambeth Conferences and Women Priests, 1981. Appointed commissary Diocese of Akoko, West Africa, 1984, appointed hon. canon St. Stephens Cathedral, 1987. Mem. Assn. Clin. Pastoral Edn. (clin.), Am. Assn. Christian Counselors, Am. Assn. Family Counselors. Home: PO Box 48232 1902 C St NE Washington DC 20002-6714

MARRIAN, IAN FREDERIC YOUNG, professional society administrator; b. Kilwinning, Ayrshire, Scotland, Nov. 15, 1943; s. Stanley Frederic and Ellen McLeish (Sherry) M.; m. Moira Selina McSwan, Dec. 22, 1967; children: Kirsten, Kerr, Kate. MA, U. Edinburgh, Scotland, 1965. Chartered acct., Scotland. Trainee acct. Delotte Haskins, Sells, Edinburgh, 1965-69; sr. acct. Delotte Haskins, Sells, Rome, 1969-72; ptnr. Delotte Haskins, Sells, London and Edinburgh, 1972-81; dir. edn. Inst. Chartered Accts. Scotland, 1981-94, dep. chief exec., 1994—; vis. prof. U. Edinburgh, 1990—; cons. European Commn., Czech Repubic, 1994-98. Author: Audit Committees, 1988. Chmn. Spott Cmty. Assn., East Lothian. Fellow Royal Soc. Arts Industry; mem. Inst. Chartered Accts. Scotland. Avocation: gardening. Home: Bowerhouse, Dunbar EH42 IRE, Scotland Office: Inst Chartered Accts, CA House 21 Haymarket Yards, Edinburgh EH12 5BH, Scotland

MARRIOTT, JOHN WILLARD, JR., lodging and senior living executive; b. Washington, Mar. 25, 1932; s. John Willard and Alice (Sheets) M.; m. Donna Garff, June 29, 1955; children: Deborah, Stephen Garff, John Willard, David Sheets. BS in Banking and Fin., U. Utah, 1954. V.p. Marriott Hot Shoppes Inc., 1959-64, exec. v.p., bd. dirs., 1964; pres. Marriott Corp., 1964—, chief exec. officer, 1972—; chmn. bd. Marriott Internat., Inc. (formerly Marriott Corp.), 1985—; bd. dirs. GM, U.S.-Russia Bus. Coun., Host Marriott Svcs. Corp., Naval Acad. Endowment Trust. Trustee Nat. Geog. Soc.; mem. nat. adv. bd. Boy Scouts Am.; mem. Bus. Coun., Bus. Roundtable.; exec. com. World Travel and Tourism Coun. Lt. USNR, 1954-56. Recipient Bus. Leader of Yr. award, Georgetown U. Sch. Bus. Adminstrn., 1984, Svc. Above Self award, Rotary Club at JFK Internat. Airport, 1985, Am. Mgr. of Yr. award, Nat. Mgmt. Assn., 1985, Golden Chain award, Nations's Restaurant News, 1985, Hall of Fame award, Consumer Digest Mag., 1985, Citizen of Yr. award, Boy Scouts of Am., 1986, Restaurant Bus. Leadership award, Restaurant Bus. Mag., 1986, Gold Plate award, Am. Acad. Achievement, 1986, Hall of Fame, Am. Hotel and Motel Assn., 1986, Hall of Fame award, Culinary Inst. of Am., 1987, Hospitality Exec. of Yr. award, Pa. State U., 1987, Bronze winner in Fin. World's Chief Exec. Officers award, 1988, Silver Plate award Lodging Hospitality Mag., 1988, Chief Exec. Officer of Yr. Chief Exec. Officer Mag., 1988, Signature award CA chpt. Nat. Multiple Scelerosis, 1988, Excellence Cmty. award Suburban Hosp., 1993, Silver Plate award Internat. Foodsvc. Mfrs. Assn., 1993, Good Scout award Boy Scouts Am. Greater N.Y. Coun., 1990, Trendsetter award Foodsvc. Cons. Soc., 1989. Mem. Conf. Bd., U.S. C. of C., Bald Peak C.C. (N.J.), Avenel Golf Club, Sigma Chi. Mem. LDS Ch. Clubs: Burning Tree (Washington), Met. (Washington). Office: Marriott Intl Inc 1 Marriott Dr Washington DC 20058-0001

MARRO, ANTHONY JAMES, newspaper editor; b. Middlebury, Vt., Feb. 10, 1942; s. Francis James and Esther Martha (Butterfield) M.; m. Jacqueline Helen Cleary, June 5, 1965; 1 child, Alexandria. B.A. in History, U. Vt., 1965; M.S. in Journalism, Columbia U., 1968. Reporter Rutland (Vt.) Herald, 1964-67; Reporter Newsday, L.I., N.Y., 1968-74, chief Washington bur., 1979-81, mng. editor, 1981-86, exec. editor, 1986-87, editor, 1987—; reporter Newsweek, Washington, 1974-76, N.Y. Times, Washington, 1976-79. Co-recipient Pulitzer prizes for Pub. Service Reporting, 1970, 74. Office: Newsday 235 Pinelawn Rd Melville NY 11747-4250

MARROCCO, THOMAS MICHAEL, software engineer; b. Rochester, N.Y., Nov. 16, 1951; s. Joseph William and Amelia Antoinette Marrocco; m. Audrey Catherine Fragassi, June 7, 1975; children: Melissa, Dina. Assocs. in Graphic Arts, Rochester (N.Y.) Inst. Tech., 1977. Software engr. Eastman Kodak Co., Rochester, N.Y. With USMC, 1969-71, Vietnam. Mem. Marine Corps League (jr. vice commandant). Roman Catholic.

MARRON, DONALD BAIRD, investment banker; b. Goshen, N.Y., July 21, 1934; m. Catherine D. Calligar. Student, Baruch Sch. Bus., 1949-51, 55-57. Investment analyst N.Y. Trust Co., N.Y.C., 1951-56, Lionel D. Edie Co., N.Y.C., 1956-58; mgr. research dept. George O'Neill & Co., 1958-59; pres. D.B. Marron & Co. Inc., N.Y.C., 1959-65; pres. Mitchell Hutchins & Co. Inc. (merger with D.B. Marron & Co. Inc. 1965), N.Y.C., 1965-69, pres., chief exec. officer, 1969-77; pres. PaineWebber Inc. (merger with Mitchell Hutchins & Co. Inc. 1977), N.Y.C., 1977-88, chief exec. officer, 1980—, chmn. bd., 1981—, also bd. dirs.; co-founder, former chmn. Data Resources, Inc.; former dir. N.Y. Stock Exchange. Vice chmn. bd. trustees Mus. of Modern Art; bd. overseers and mgrs. Meml. Sloan-Kettering; trustee for cultural resources N.Y.C., trustee Dana Found.; bd. dirs. N.Y.C. Partnership; bd. dirs. Bus. Com. for the Arts, Inc.; mem. Govs.'s Sch. and Bus. Alliance Task Force, N.Y.; mem. Coun. on Fgn. Rels., Inc.; mem. pres.'s com. on The Arts and The Humanities, Inc. Office: Paine Webber Group Inc 14th Fl 1285 Avenue of the Americas New York NY 10019 also: Mus Modern Art 11 W 53rd St New York NY 10019-5401

MARSALEK, JAROSLAV, microbiologist; b. Jablonne, Czech Republic, Aug. 28, 1947; s. Miroslav and Vera (Suchoparova) M.; m. Jana Choderova, July 16, 1976; children: Linda, Lukas. Degree in biology, Charles U. of Prague, Czech Republic, 1970, Rer.Nat.Doctoris, 1975, candidate of sci., 1985; grad., U. Mark-Len., 1982. Rsch. scientist Rsch. Inst. Ores, Prague, Czech Republic, 1971-73, mgr. microbiology lab., 1973-77; microbiologist, genetics scientist Rsch. Inst. for Feed Supply Vet. Drugs, Kourim, Czech Republic, 1977-85, rsch. program mgr., 1980-92, rsch. dept. mgr., 1985-88, mgr. genetics, ferment. labs., 1988-92; plant mgr. Lonza Biotec, Kourim, 1992—, investment project mgr., 1994-96; bd. dirs. LONZA Biotec; cons. biotech. Charles U. of Prague, 1989. Author: Thiobacillus Ferrooxidans and its Role in Bacteriological Leaching of Ores, 1979; contbr. articles to profl. jours.; patentee in field. Second basketball coach Slavia PV UK, Prague, 1968-70, 71-77; chmn. co. com. Trade Union Rsch. Inst. Feed Supply Vet. Drugs, Kourim, 1978-88; trainer children's basketball, baseball and volleyball Sport Club, Kourim, 1978-87. Lance cpl. Min. Interior, Czech Republic, 1970-71. Fellow Czech Microbiol. Soc.; mem. Biotech. Soc. Roman Catholic. Avocations: basketball, baseball, volleyball, gardening, cycling. Home: Spojovaci 561, 281 61 Kourim Czech Republic Office: Lonza Biotec sro, Okruzni 134, 281 61 Kourim Czech Republic

MARSALIS, SHERRY H., municipal official; b. Charleston, Miss., June 15, 1948; d. Paul F. and Irene (Woolbright) Hall; m. John C. Marsalis, June 20, 1968; children: Susan Denise Marsalis, John Thomas Marsalis. Cert. mcpl. recorder. Sec. St. Francis, Vicksburg, Miss., 1983-85, Executone, Jackson, Miss., 1989-91; computer operator IHSS, Jackson, Miss., 1991-93; nurse technician Smyrna (Tenn.) Nursing Home, 1993-94, NHC, Murfreesboro, Tenn., 1994-95; city recorder City of Eagleville, Tenn., 1995—. Author: Journeys of the Heart, 1997, Sacred Gift Given to Me by Eagle Eye, 1998. Mem. Profl. Secs. Assn., Cert. Mcpl. Recorders Assn., Tenn. Govt. Fin. Assn. Avocations: reading, writing. E-mail: marsalissherri@home.com. Home: 1506 Amberwood Cir Murfreesboro TN 37128-6757 Office: City of Eagleville 126 S Main St Eagleville TN 37060-4507

MARSCHALL, MARIANNA, biologist, educator; b. Sátoraljaújhely, Zemplén, Hungary, Mar. 13, 1968; d. István and Jolán (Nagyházi) M. BSc, Kossuth U., Debrecen, Hungary, 1986, MSc, 1991, PhD, 1999. Asst. rschr. Kossuth U., Debrecen, 1991-92; asst. lectr. Eszterházy Coll., Eger, Hungary, 1994-98, lectr., 1998—. Rsch. grantee World Wide Bank, U. Exeter, 1995, Hungarian Govt., U. Exeter, 1998. Mem. Internat. Assn. Bryologists, Hungarian Assn. Plant Physiologists. Avocations: swimming, dancing, gardening, mountain-climbing, playing piano. Office: Eszterházy Coll, 6-8 Leányka Út, H-3301 Eger Heves, Hungary

MARSCHALL, MIKLÓS, civic organization executive, economist; b. Rajka, Hungary, Mar. 22, 1953; s. Lajos Marschall and Márta Marosi; m. Csilla Bálint, Sept. 22, 1979; children: Márton, Lívia. PhD, Karl Marx U. Econs., Budapest, Hungary, 1984. Rsch. fellow Inst. for Culture, Budapest, 1980-90; dep. mayor City of Budapest, 1991-94; exec. dir. Civicus, Washington, 1994-98, Transparency Internat., Berlin, 1999—; pub. Citizens: Strengthening Global Civil Society, 1994. Contbg. author: The Third Sector: Comparative Studies, 1990. Chmn. Pro Cultura Urbis Found., Budapest, 1991-94; bd. dirs. Budapest Festival Orch., 1992—. Fulbright scholar Yale U., 1988-89. Mem. Univ. Club. Home: 73/B Pasareti Ut, Budapest 1026, Hungary Office: Transparency Internat, Otto-Suhr-Allee 97-99, D-10585 Berlin Germany

MARSDEN, ANDREW CHARLES, marketing professional; b. Sheffield, England, Nov. 9, 1956; s. Willis Charles and Mary Florence (Johnson) M.; m. Karen Julie Fewkes, May 23, 1981. BS with honors, Bradford U., England, 1978. Sr. mktg. mgr. Unilever, England, 1978-92; jr. mng. dir. Vileda L.P., England, 1992-94; mktg. dir. MP Foods, England, 1994-96, Britvic Soft Drinks, England, 1996—. Contbr. articles to profl. jours. Dir. Inst. Sales Promotion, England, 1999, chmn., 1993. Mem. Carlton Club. Avocations: travel, wine, sailing, golf. Office: Britvic Soft Drinks, Broomfield Rd, Chelmsford CM1 1TN, England

MARSDEN, JERROLD ELDON, mathematician, educator, engineer; b. Ocean Falls, British Columbia, Aug. 17, 1942; married 1965; 1 child. BSc, U. Toronto, Canada, 1965; PhD in Math., Princeton U., 1968. Instr. math. Princeton U., N.J., 1968; lectr. U. Calif., Berkeley, 1968-69, asst. prof., 1969-72, assoc. prof., 1972-77, prof. math., 1977—; asst. prof. U. Toronto, Canada, 1970-71; prof. Calif. Tech., Pasadena, 1995—. Recipient Norbert Weiner Applied Math. prize Am. Math. Soc., 1990. Mem. IEEE, Am. Phys. Soc. Achievements include research in mathematical physics, global analysis, hydrodynamics, quantum mechanics, nonlinear Hamiltonian systems. Office: Control Dynamical Sys MS 107 81 Pasadena CA 91125-0001*

MARSH, CARLA A., document control group leader; b. Star Lake, N.Y., June 29, 1964; d. Lyle Henry Marsh and Agnes Diane Malady. AAS, Canton (N.Y.) Agrl. & Tech. Coll., 1985; BA, U. No. Iowa, 1995. Lab. technician bio-products divsn. Eastman Kodak, Rochester, N.Y., 1986-90; small scale fermentation technician Genencor Internat., Rochester, 1990-91; lab. technician Genencor Internat., Cedar Rapids, Iowa, 1991-94; validation technologist Diamond Animal Health, Des Moines, 1996-97; document specialist Centeon, Bradley, Ill., 1997-98; group leader document control Aventis Behring, Kankakee, Ill., 1998—. Mem. Am. Soc. Quality, Soc. for Indsl. Microbiology. Avocations: water aerobics instruction, photography, cycling, kayaking, skiing. Office: Aventis Behring 1201 Kinzie N Bradley IL 60915-1238 also: PO Box 511 Kankakee IL 60901-0511

MARSH, CAROL K., adult community administrator; b. Elloree, S.C., Sept. 15, 1933; d. William Conrad and Allie (Ulmer) Kemmerlin; m. Edward A. Peeples, Sept. 20, 1963 (div. Dec. 1988); 1 child, William E. Kemmerlin Peeples; m. Charles Marsh, March 15, 1953 (div. Sept. 1961), remarried May. 27, 1989; children: Shera Marsh Jones, Mickee Brown. Operator So. Bell Telephone, Allendale, S.C., 1951-54; bookkeeper Colonial Stores, Chamblis, Ga., 1955-57, Florence, S.C., 1957-58; retail acct. Piggly Wiggly Carolina, Charleston, S.C., 1958-65; ptnr. Southern Inventory Svc., Charleston, S.C., 1976-85; substitute tchr./trainer Charleston County Schs., 1979-88; gen. mgr. Beachwood at the Heritage, Myrtle Beach, S.C., 1988—; ptnr. Marsh Contractors Ltd., 1990—. Contbr. poetry to Internat. Libr. Poetry. Bd. dirs. Mfrd. Housing Inst. S.C., Columbia, 1996—; life mem. Luth. Sem. Aux./So. Sem., Columbia; pres. WELCA St. Matthews Luth. Ch., 1984-86. Named Vol. of the Yr., Charleston County Schs., 1984. Mem. NAFE, Myrtle Beach C. of C., Am. Bus. Women's Assn. (pres. 1996-98, Woman of Yr. 1998), PTA (life, hon.), S.C. PTA (hon. life), Am. Soc. Notaries. Lutheran. Home: PO Box 3111 Myrtle Beach SC 29578-3111 Office: Beachwood at the Heritage 1712 Club House Dr Myrtle Beach SC 29577-5090

MARSH, DWIGHT CHANEY, English educator, editor; b. Hall County, Nebr., Oct. 2, 1932; s. Howard Lawson Marsh and Mary May Chaney; m. Martha Jane Murray, Dec. 30, 1955; children: Thomas, John, Anne, Margaret. BA, Hastings Coll., 1954, LHD (hon.), 1998; MA, U. Nebr., 1956, PhD, 1968. Tchg. asst. Ind. U., Bloomington, 1956-58; asst. prof. Nebr. Wesleyan, Lincoln, 1958-62; instr. U. Nebr., Lincoln, 1962-65; asst. prof. Wartburg Coll., Waverley, Iowa, 1965-66; prof. Hastings (Nebr.) Coll., 1966-1998. Editor Nebr. Coun. English Tchrs., 1978-82, Plainsongs, 1983—; actor cmty. theatre, 1973-99; freelance poet, 1978-99. Bd. dirs. Nebr. Civil Liberties Union, 1973-77, Nebr. Assn. Cmty. Theatres, 1977-79. Fellow Nat. Def. Edn. Act, 1967-68. Presbyterian. Avocations: wine making, gardening, writing, reading. Office: Hastings Coll 7th and Turner Hastings NE 68902

MARSH, ELLA JEAN, pediatrician; b. Chgo., Dec. 16, 1941; d. Charles and Eleanor (Canfield) M. BA, St. Mary of Woods (Ind.) Coll., 1963; DO, Chgo. Coll. Osteo. Medicine, 1971. Diplomate Am. Coll. Osteo. Pediatricians (chmn. evaluating com. 1981-89), Nat. Osteo. Bds. Intern Doctor's Hosp., Columbus, Ohio, 1971-72; resident in pediatrics Chgo. Coll. Osteo. Medicine, 1972-74, asst. prof., 1974-78, assoc. prof. pediatrics, 1978-82; assoc. prof. W.Va. Coll. Osteo. Medicine, 1975-86; clin. assoc. prof. pediatrics South Eastern Osteo. Sch. Medicine, 1984-96, chmn. pediatric and newborn nursery, 1982-94; assoc. dir. med. edn. Orlando (Fla.) Gen. Hosp., 1985-88; mem. staff Arnold Palmer Children's Hosp., Fla. Hosp., Health Ctr.; pediatric cons. Nat. Bd. Osteo. Examiners; lectr., cons. in field. Bd. dirs. St. Mary of Woods Coll., 1992-95, Ctrl. Fla. Primary Care, 1994-97. Donald Bucknar Moore scholar, 1963. Fellow Am. Coll. Osteo. Pediatricians (v.p. 1986, pres. 1988), Am. Acad. Pediat.; mem. AMA, Am. Osteo. Assn., Fla. Osteo. Assn., Fla. Med. Soc., Orange County Med. Soc., Osteo. Acad., Cen. Fla. Pediatric Soc., Chgo. Coll. Osteo. Medicine Alumni Assn., Am. Coll. Osteo. Pediatricians, Am. Acad. Pediatricians, Irish Am. Pediatric Soc., Am. Acad. of Osteopathy. Roman Catholic. Home and Office: 8210 Imber St Orlando FL 32825-8233

MARSH, HAROLD MICHAEL, anesthesiologist; b. Sydney, Australia, Mar. 7, 1939; came to U.S., 1974; m. Elizabeth Eleanor. BSc in Medicine, U. Sydney, 1956, MBBS, 1963. Intern Royal Prince Alfred Hosp., Sydney, Australia, 1964, resident, 1965-68; resident Mayo Grad. Sch. Medicine, Rochester, Minn., 1969-71; clin. assoc. dept. anesthesiology Toronto Western Hosp., 1971; dir. dept. intensive care Royal Prince Alfred Hosp., 1972-74; instr. anesthesiology Mayo Med. Sch., Rochester, 1975-76, asst. prof. anesthesiology, 1976-83; asst. prof. anesthesiology Mayo Grad. Sch., Rochester, Minn., 1981-89, prof. anesthesiology, 1989; chmn. dept. anesthesiology Henry Ford Hosp., Detroit, 1989-98; prof. chmn. dept. anesthesiology Wayne State U., 1998—; spec.-in-chief anesthesiology Detroit Med. Ctr., 1998—; part-time lectr., tutor faculty medicine U. Sydney, 1972-74; cons. anesthesiology Mayo Clinic, 1974-89, med. dir. surg. and respiratory intensive care units, 1977-81, dir. critical care svcs., 1981-83, 87-89, assoc. dir. critical care svcs., 1984-87, chmn. divsn. intensive care & respiratory therapy, 1985-89; vis. prof. dept. anesthesia U. Pa., 1976, Nat. Naval Med. Sch., 1981, Northwestern U., 1982, 89, Royal Prince Alfred Hosp., 1983, Sir Charles Gairdner Hosp., 1984, U. Md., 1987, Sloan-Kettering Inst., 1990, Rush-Presbyn.-St. Luke's Med. Ctr., Chgo., 1991, U. Hosp., London, Ont., 1993; invited lectr. dept. anesthetics IV Pan Am. Congress of Diseases of Chest, Caracus, Venezuela, 1987, Uniformes Svcs. U. Health Scis. Med. Sch., Bethesda, Md., 1987, Walter Reed Amry Med. Ctr., 1987, Naval Hosp., 1987, Bethesda, World Congress Intensive Care, Kyoto, Japan, 1989, Uddevalla (Sweden) Hosp., 1993, Karolinska Hosp., Stockholm, Sweden, 1993, Nat. Inst. Cardiology, Mexico City, Mexico, 1993; presenter in field. Contbr. chpts. to books and articles to profl. jours. With Australian Mil., 1958-61. Faculty of Anaesthetists, Royal Australasian Coll. Surgeons fellow, 1968. Fellow Am. Coll. Chest Physicians; mem. AAAS, Am. Bd. Anesthesiology, Am. Coll. Anesthesiologists. Achievements include research on general anesthesia and the lung, acute lung injury, metabolism, epidemiology in critical care. Office: Detroit Med Ctr DHR/UHC Dept Anesthesiolog 4201 Saint Antoine St Detroit MI 48201-2153

MARSH, JOHN HAIG, electronics educator, researcher; b. Edinburgh, Scotland, Apr. 15, 1956; s. Arthur Hireson and Christine Wilkie (Haig) M.; m. Anabel Christine Mitchell, Mar. 21, 1981. BA in Engring., Cambridge (Eng.) U., 1977; M in Electronic and Elec. Engring., U. Liverpool, 1978; PhD in Electronic and Elec. Engring., U. Sheffield, 1982. Chartered elec. engr., Eng. Rsch. assoc. U. Sheffield, 1980-83, univ. rsch. scientist, 1983-86; lectr. U. Glasgow, 1986-90, sr. lectr., 1990-94, reader, 1994-96, prof. optoelectronics sys., 1996—; dir., founder Intense Photonics Ltd., 2000—; dir. NATO Advanced Study Inst., Glasgow, 1990. Editor: Waveguide Optoelectronics, 1992; mem. editl. bd. Internat. Jour. Optoelectronics, 1995-98; contbr. more than 300 articles to profl. jours. Sch. gov. Balby Carr Sch., Woodfield Middle, Nightingale First, Doncaster, 1984-86. Fellow Royal

Soc. Arts, Instn. Elec. Engrs. (U.K.), Royal Soc. Edinburgh, IEEE; mem. IEEE Lasers and Electro-Optics Soc. (sr., founding chmn. Scottish chpt.), IEEE Electron Devices Soc., Optical Soc. Am. Avocations: hill walking, music, cooking, malt whisky. Home: 1 Bellshaugh Gardens, Glasgow G12 0SA, Scotland Office: U Glasgow, Dept Electron-Elec Engring, Glasgow G12 8QQ, Scotland

MARSH, MARY ELIZABETH TAYLOR, recreation administrator, dietician, nutritionist; b. Medina, N.Y., Dec. 10, 1933; d. Glenn Aaron and Viola Hazel (Lansill) Grimes; m. Wilbur Alvin Fredlund, Apr. 12, 1952 (div. Jan. 1980); 1 child, Wilbur Jr.; m. Frederick Herbert Taylor, Mar. 15, 1981 (dec. Dec. 1996); children: Martha Dayton, Jean Grout, Beth Stern, Cindy Hey, Carol McLellan, Cheryl Dearborn, Robert, Marilyn Ridens, Janice Emory, Gordon Marsh, Margaret Hana; m. Earl R. Marsh, Apr. 4, 1998. BS in Food and Nutrition, SUCB, Buffalo, 1973; MEd in Health Sci. Edn. and Evaluation, SUNY, 1978. Registered dietitian, 1977. Diet cook Niagara Sanitorium, Lockport, N.Y., 1953-56; cook Mount View Hosp., Lockport, N.Y., 1956-60, asst. dietician, 1960-73, dietician, food svc. dir., 1973-79, cons. dietician, 1979-81; instr. Erie Community Coll., Williamsville, N.Y., 1979-81; sch. lunch coord. Nye County Sch. Dist., Tonopah, Nev., 1982-93; retired Nye County Sch. Dist., 1993; food svc. mgmt. cons., fin. mgmt. advisor pvt. practice, 1994—; activity dir. Preferred Equity Corp. Recreation Vehicle Resort, Pahrump, Nev., 1993-95; tchr. maturing body and nutrition Nev. Cmty. Coll., Pahrump, Fall 1997; nutritionist Equal Opportunity Bd. Clark County, Las Vegas, 1997-2000; cons. dietitian Nye Gen. Hosp., Tonopah, 1983-88; adj. instr. Erie C.C., Williamsville, 1978-79, So. Nev. C.C., 1997; nutrition instr. for coop. extension Clark County C.C., 1990—; cons. Group Purchasing Western N.Y. Hosp. Adminstr., Buffalo, 1975-79, vice-chmn. adv. com., 1976-78; cons. BOCES, Lockport, 1979-81. Nutrition counselor Migrant Workers Clinic, Lockports, 1974-80; mem. Western N.Y. Soc. for Hosp. Food Svc. Adminstrn., 1974-81; nutritionist Niagara County Nutrition Adv. Com., 1977-81; mem. Helping Hands, Pahrump, 1997—; nutritionist Equal Opportunity Bd. Clark Conty, 1997-2000. Recipient Outstanding Woman of the Yr., YWCA-UAW Lockport, 1981, Disting. Health Care Food Adminstrn. Recognition award Am. Soc. for Hosp. Food Svc. Adminstrs., 1979, USDA award Outstanding Lunch Program in Nev. and Western Region, 1986, 91. Mem. Am. Assn. Ret. Persons, Am. Sch. Food Svc. Assn. (bd. dirs. 1987, 92-93, cert. dir. II 1987, 5-yr. planning com. 1990, mem. ann. confs. 1988-93), Am. Dietetic Assn. (nat. referral system for registered dietitians 1992-93), So. Nev. Dietetic Assn. (pres. 1985-86), Nev. Food Svc. Assn. (participant ann. meetings 1990-93), Nutrition Today Soc., Nev. Sch. Food Svcs. Assn. (dietary guidelines com. 1991-93), Pahrump Kawians. Republican. Lutheran. Avocations: travel, knitting, crocheting, sewing. Home: 481 N Murphy St Pahrump NV 89060-3851

MARSH, ROBERT CHARLES, writer, music critic; b. Columbus, Ohio, Aug. 5, 1924; s. Charles L. and Jane A. (Beckett) M.; m. Kathleen C. Moscrop, July 4, 1956 (div. 1985); m. Ann Noren, Feb. 25, 1987; 1 child, James MacArtain. BS, Northwestern U., 1945, AM, 1946; postgrad., U. Chgo., 1948; EdD, Harvard U., 1951; postgrad., Oxford U., 1952-53, Cambridge U., 1953-56. Instr. social sci. U. Ill., 1947-49; lectr. humanities Chgo. City Jr. Coll., 1950-51; asst. prof. edn. U. Kansas City, 1951-52; vis. prof. edn. SUNY, 1953-54; humanities staff U. Chgo., 1956-58, lectr. in social thought, 1976; music critic Chgo. Sun-Times, 1956-91; dir. Chgo. Opera Project, Newberry Libr., 1983—; pres. Zerbinetta Corp., 1996. Author: Toscanini and the Art of Orchestral Performance, 1956, rev. edit., 1962, The Cleveland Orchestra, 1967, Ravinia, 1985, James Levine at Ravinia, 1993, Dialogues and Discoveries, 1998, James Levine, Sein Leben, Sein Musik, 1999; editor: Logic and Knowledge, 1956. Co-recipient Peabody award for ednl. broadcasting, 1976; Ford Found. fellow, 1965-66. Mem. Harvard U. Faculty Club. Roman Catholic. Home and Office: 1001 7th St New Glarus WI 53574-9516

MARSH, SUE ANN, special education educator; b. Marshall, Tex., Dec. 5, 1949; d. Orman and Della Florence (Floyd) M. BS in Edn., Stephen F. Austin State U., Nacogdoches, Tex., 1971, MEd, 1975. Cert. elem. tchr., reading tchr., spl. edn. in mental retardation, Tex. Tchr. Title 45 Dickinson (Tex.) Ind. Sch. Dist., 1971, tchr. Title I, 1971-72; tchr. trainable mentally retarded Conroe (Tex.) Ind. Sch. Dist., 1972-85, tchr. Option III, 1985—; coach, asst. coach Vol. Spl. Olympics, Conroe, 1973—, advt. chmn for golf tournament, 1989-90. Editor: Almost Reader Series. Leader for mentally retarded boys and girls Boy Scouts Am., Conroe, 1990—; chmn. Crockett Cougars Year Book Advertisement 50th Anniversary Edit. Named Crockett Intermediate Tchr. of Yr., 1992; recipient Sam Houston Disting. Scouting award of merit, 1993, Sam Houston Disting. Scouting award of Merit, 1996; co-recipient State Centennial Farm award, Career Ladder, 1984-93. Mem. Assn. Tex. Profl. Educators (bldg. rep. 1983—), Classroom Tchrs. Assn. (bldg. rep. 1975-78), Floyd Family Assn. (sec.-treas. Plantersville, Tex.), River Plantation Lions (camp chmn. 1990-94, chmn. attendance 1990-91, bd. dirs. 1990-96, 3rd v.p. 1992-93, 2nd v.p. 1993-94, v.p. 1994-95, pres. 1995-96, treas. 1996). Democrat. Baptist. Avocations: travel, needlecrafts, plays, concerts. Office: Wash Intermediate Sch 507 Avenue K Conroe TX 77301-3881

MARSHALL, ALAN GEORGE, chemistry and biochemistry educator; b. Bluffton, Ohio, May 26, 1944; s. Herbert Boyer Marshall Jr. and Cecile (Mogil) Rosser; m. Marilyn Gard, June 13, 1965; children: Gwendolyn Scott, Brian George. BA in Chemistry with honors, Northwestern U., 1965; PhD in Phys. Chemistry, Stanford U., 1970. Instr. II U. B.C., Vancouver, Can., 1969-71, asst. prof., 1971-76, assoc. prof., 1976-80; prof. chemistry and biochemistry Ohio State U., Columbus, 1980-93; from prof. chemistry to Kasha prof. Fla. State U., Tallahassee, 1993-2000, Kasha prof., 2000—; Kasha prof. Fla. State U., 2000—; cons. Extrel FTMS, Madison, Wis., 1989-92, Oak Ridge (Tenn.) Nat. Lab., 1990—; dir. Ion Cyclotron Resonance Program Nat. High Magnetic Field Lab., 1993—. Author: Biophysical Chemistry, 1978, Fourier Transforms in Spectroscopy, 1990; editor ICR/ION Trap newsletter, 1986—; editor Rapid Comm. on Mass Spectrometry, 1988—; mem. editorial bd. Analytical Chemistry, 1990-92, Internat. Jour. Mass Ion Procs., 1987—, Jour. Am. Soc. Mass Spectrometry, 1989-97, Mass Spectrometry Rev., 1994—, Jour. Magnetic Resonance, 1995-98; contbr. 300 articles to profl. jours. Recipient Disting. Scholar award Ohio State U., 1988, Maurice F. Hasler award Spectroscopy Soc. Pitts., 1997, gold medal N.Y. Soc. Applied Spectroscopy, 1998. Fellow AAAS, Internat. Mass Spectrum Soc. (Thomson medal 2000), Am. Phys. Soc.; mem. Am. Chem. Soc. (award in chem. instrumentation, Akron sect. award, award in analytical chemistry Ea. Analytical Symposium 1991, Frank H. Field and Joe L. Franklin award 1995), Soc. Applied Spectroscopy (chmn. local sect. 1990-91), Am. Soc. Mass Spectroscopy (bd. dirs. 1991-92, Disting. Contbn. award 1999), Internat. Mass Spectroscopy Soc. (Thomson medal 2000). Office: Fla State Univ Nat High Magnetic Field Lab 1800 E Paul Dirac Dr Tallahassee FL 32310-3748

MARSHALL, ALLEN WRIGHT, III, communications executive, financial consultant; b. Griffin, Ga., Dec. 4, 1941; s. Allen Wright, Jr. and Evelyn Louise (Halliburton) M.; m. Carole Anne Moore, Dec. 24, 1964; 1 child, Allen Wright IV. BA in Journalism, U. Ga., 1964; diploma Elkins Inst. Radio, Atlanta, 1964; postgrad. Ga. State U., 1968, MBA Ga. State U., 1988; cert. Coll. Fin. Planning, Denver, 1991. 1st class radio telephone lic. FCC; cert. fin. planner. Pres., Sta. WKEU-AM-FM, Griffin, Ga., 1954-86; co-founder, v.p. Griffin Cable TV, 1971-74; co-founder, pres. Custom Services, Inc. (now Marshall Plans, Inc.), Griffin, 1974—; co-founder, v.p. Cobbwells Marshall, Inc., Griffin, 1982-87, Page One, Griffin, 1983-87; co-founder, pres. Toolware, Inc., Griffin, 1993-97; co-founder, sec./treas. Magnolia Broadcasting, Inc., LaGrange, Ga., 1993-95; founder, mng. mem. Spalding Speculators LLC, Griffin, 1995—; dir. First Union Nat. Bank, Griffin, Face Internat. Corp., Norfolk, QualityClick.com, Newport News, Va.; bd. dirs. Goals for Griffin and Spalding Counties, Inc., 1981-92, pres., 1991. Author radio programs, editorials (Ga. AP awards 1969-84); also articles; speaker in field. Mem. adv. com. Griffin Vocat.-Tech. Sch., 1982-87; bd. dirs. Jr. Achievement, Griffin, 1977-87; chmn. Griffin-Spalding Indsl. authority, 1984; mem. Gov.'s Adv. Com. on Area Planning and Devel. Commns., 1971-72; bd. dirs. McIntosh Trail Area Planning and Devel. Commn., Ga., 1971-73; founding trustee, vice chair, dir. St. George's Episc. Sch., 1995—; trustee, treas., trustee Nat. Episc. Radio/TV Found., 1986-93. Sgt. U.S. Army, 1966-68. Named Man of Yr., Exchange Club of Griffin, 1984. Mem. Ga. Assn. Broadcasters (bd. dirs. 1970-74, Radio Sta. of Yr. 1977), Griffin Area C. of C. (bd. dirs. 1980, chmn. indsl. com. 1980, 81). Episcopalian. Clubs: Country (charter mem. 1966). Lodge: Rotary (pres. 1976-77). Avocations: photography, landscape design, archtl. renovation. Home and Office: 1800 Maple Dr Griffin GA 30224-7405

MARSHALL, ANDREW P., writer, producer; b. Lowestoft, Suffolk, United Kingdon, Aug. 27, 1954; s. Michael D. and Doris C. (Greaves) M. EdB with honors, U. London, 1977. Writer, prodr.: 2 Point 4 Children, Agatha Christie's Poirot, Health and Efficiency, DAD; (with David Renwick) The Burkiss Way, End of Part One, 1978-78 (Rediffusion award), Whoops Apocalypse, 1980 (N.Y. Internat. TV Festival silver award), (TV vers.) Whoops Apocalypse, Hot Metal, 1982-83, Wilt, Alexei Sayle's Stuff (BPG award, Internat. Emmy), If You See God, Tell Him. Mem. Writers' Guild, British Acad. Film & TV Arts, Royal TV Society.

MARSHALL, BARRY STEWART, communication studies educator, researcher; b. Sheffield, Yorkshire, Eng., Jan. 26, 1946; arrived in Australia, 1990; s. Robert and Alice (Jenkinson) M.; m. Elizabeth Harper, May 27, 1968 (div. Dec. 1987); 1 child, Lorna Elizabeth; m. Margaret Momo Mase, Apr. 11, 1990; 1 child, Desmond. BA with 1st class honors, U. York, Eng., 1971; MPhil, U. Leeds, Eng., 1973; postgrad. diploma in edn. tech., Sheffield (Eng.) Poly., 1981. Inc. engr. Engring. Registration Bd., U.K. Trainee elec. engr. Ctrl. Electricity Generating Bd., Eng., 1962-68; lectr. Sunderland Poly., Eng., 1973-75; prin. lectr. Sheffield City Poly., 1976-85; prof. comm. U. Tech., Papua New Guinea, 1985-90; head of comty. studies Bachelor Coll., N.T., Australia, 1990-93; prof. of comm. Monash U., Churchill, Victoria, Australia, 1993-98; prof., dean faculty informatics and communication Ctrl. Queensland U., Rockhampton, Australia, 1999—; chief examiner for comm. Inst. Chartered Secs. and Adminstrs., 1980-85; cons. on comm. Inst. Mech. Engring., U.K., 1981-85, Ramu Sugar, Papua New Guinea, 1985-90; reader Methuen Pubs., U.K., 1982-85; coord. acad. studies Inst. Distance Edn., U. Swaziland, 1996-98. Author: Exercises in Teaching Communication, 1986, (book chpts.) Communication and Simulation, 1988, Perspectives on Academic Gaming and Simulation, 1981. Mem. Inst. Elec. and Electronic Inc. Engrs. (U.K.), Open and Distance Learning Asn. of Australia, Asian Mass Comm. Rsch. and Info. Ctr. Avocations: cycling, walking, reading. Office: Ctrl Queensland U, Faculty Informatics & Comm, Rockhmptn Queensland QLD 4702, Australia

MARSHALL, BRIAN LAURENCE, trade association executive; b. Kingston-on-Thames, England, Apr. 6, 1941; came to U.S., 1949; s. John and Marguerite Elizabeth (Sandele) M. BA in European History, U. N.C., 1963; MS in Internat. Mgmt., Am. Grad. Sch. Internat. Mgmt., Glendale, Ariz., 1973. Commd. 2d lt. USAF, 1964, advanced through grades to capt., 1972; instr. Armed Forces Air Intelligence Tng. Ctr., Denver, 1965-68; intelligence analyst Task Force Alpha, Nakhon Phanom, Thailand, 1968-69; intelligence systems analyst Headquarters Tactical Air Command, Langley AFB, Va., 1969-72, resigned, 1972; sr. analyst Computer Scis. Corp., Falls Ch., Va., 1974-87; dir. U.S. membership and pubs. U.S.-Mexico C. of C., Washington, 1987-91; v.p. pub. affairs, bd. dirs. N.Am. Free Trade Assn., Washington, 1991-96; v.p. N.Am. Trade and Investment Group, Washington, 1991-97, also bd. dirs.; contract team leader, strategic planning studies and analyses U.S. Dept. Defense, Joint Chiefs of Staff, Washington, 1976-82; regional ops. supr. for elections in Bosnia, Orgn. for Security and Cooperation in Europe, 1997 (OSCE), election supr. Bosnia and Kosovo, 1997-98, 2000; internat. trade cons., 1998—. Contbr. articles to booklets and newsletters. Vol. Pres. Ford Com., Washington, 1976; bd. dirs. Columbia Plaza Tenants Assn., Washington, 1981-84. Mem. VFW, Assn. Former Intelligence Officers, World Affairs Coun., Fgn. Policy Assn. (group leader discussion program), Thunderbird Alumni Assn. (pres. Washington chpt. 1980-87), Washington Mgmt. and Bus. Assn. (vice chmn. 1981-83, treas. 1987-91). Republican. Lodge: D.C. Hash House Harriers. Avocations: jogging, tennis, travel, discussion groups, reading. Home: 5304 Albemarle St Bethesda MD 20816-1827 Office: American Acad for Liberal Edn Ste 901 1700 K St NW Washington DC 20006-3814

MARSHALL, CHRISTOPHER JOHN, molecular cell biologist; b. Birmingham, U.K., Jan. 19, 1949; s. James and Lillian (Thornton) M.; m. Vivien Morrall, (div. 1996); children: Joseph, Lucy, Francis. MA in Natural Scis., U. Cambridge, 1970; DPhil, U. Oxford, 1973. Postgrad. fellow Imperial Cancer Rsch. Fund, London, 1973-78, Sidney Farber Cancer Inst., Boston, 1978-80; scientific staff Inst. of Cancer Rsch., London, 1980—; dir. CRC Ctr. for cell and molecular biology ICR, London, 1994—. Contbr. articles to profl. jours. Gibb Life fellowship Cancer Rsch. Campaign, 1992. Fellow Royal Soc.; mem. European Molecular Biology Orgn. Office: Inst of Cancer Rsch, 237 Fulham Rd, London SW3 6JB, England

MARSHALL, SIR COLIN, airline executive; b. Edgware, Middlesex, Eng., Nov. 16, 1933; s. Edward Leslie and Florence Mary Marshall; m. Janet Winifred Cracknell, May 10, 1958; 1 child. Student, U. Coll. Sch., Hampstead, Eng., 1946-51. From cadet purser to dep. purser Orient Steam Navigation Co., 1951-58; mgmt. trainee Hertz Corp., Chgo. and Toronto, Ont., Can., 1958-59; gen. mgr. Hertz Corp., Mexico City, 1959-60; asst. to pres. Hertz Corp., N.Y.C., 1960; gen. mgr. U.K. divsn. Hertz Corp., London, 1961-62; gen. mgr. U.K. The Netherlands and Belgium divsn. Hertz Corp., 1962-64; regional mgr., v.p. Avis Co., London, 1964-66; gen. mgr. Europe and Middle East divsn. Avis Co., 1966-69, v.p. gen. mgr. Internat. divsn., 1969-71; exec. v.p., chief operating officer Avis Co., N.Y.C., 1971-75; pres., chief operating officer Avis Co., 1975-76, pres., chief exec. officer, 1976-79; exec. v.p., sector exec. Norton Simon Inc., N.Y.C., 1979-81; dir. dep. chief exec. Sears Holdings Plc, London, 1981-83; CEO Brit. Airways, London, 1983-95, apptd. dep. chmn. bd. dirs., 1989-93, exec. chmn. bd. dirs., 1993-95; chmn. bd. dirs. Brit. Airways, 1996—; now chmn. bd. dirs. Invensys Plc, London; bd. dirs. Brit. Airways, Brit. Tourist Authority, Midland Bank Plc., Grand Met. Plc., IBM United Kingdom Holdings Ltd., Panel 2000, Midland Group, HSBC Holdings, brit. Telecomm.; chair internat. adv. bd. Brit. Am. Bus. Coun., 1994—. Awarded Knight Bachelor, Her Majesty the Queen, 1987. Club: Queens. Avocations: tennis, cross country skiing. Office: Comp Invensys Plc, Carlisle Pl, London SW1P 1BX, England*

MARSHALL, CONRAD JOSEPH, entrepreneur; b. Detroit, Dec. 23, 1934; s. Edward Louis Fedak and Maria Magdalena Berzsenyi; m. Dorothy Genieve Karnafil, Dec. 1, 1956 (div. 1963); children: Conrad Joseph Jr., Kevin Conrad, Lisa Marie; m. Beryle Elizabeth Callahan, June 15, 1965 (div. 1972); children: Brent Jasmer, Farah Elizabeth. Diploma, Naval Air Tech. Tng. Ctr., Norman, Okla., 1952; student, Wayne State U., 1956-59; Diploma, L.A. Police Acad., 1961. Dir. mktg. Gulf Devel., Torrance, Calif., 1980-83; sales mgr. Baldwin Piano Co., Santa Monica, Calif., 1977-80; dir. mktg., v.p. Western Hose, Inc., L.A., 1971-76; city letter carrier U.S. Post Office, L.A., 1969-71; writer freelance L.A., 1966—; police officer L.A. Police Dept., 1961-66; asst. sales mgr. Wesson Oil Co., Detroit, 1958-60; agt. Life Ins. Co. of Va., Wayne, Mich., 1956-58; pres. Am. Vision Mktg., L.A., 1990—, Con-Mar Prodns., L.A., 1983—; sr. v.p. Pacific Acquisition Group, 1992—, Invest. Admin. HealthCom., Inr., 1993—; pres. Midway TV Co., 1994—; tech. advisor Lion's Gate Films, Westwood, Calif., 1970-74, Medicine Wheel Prodns., Hollywood, Calif., 1965-75; mng. gen. ptnr. Encino Wireless #1, 1994—; CEO Midway TV Inc., 1995; v.p. nat. bus. affairs MMA Internat., 1997; v.p. mktg. Kidkritter, Inc., 1998; sr. prodn. exec. Alpine Pictures Inc., 1999. Author: (series) "Dial Hot Line", 1967, (screenplay) "Heads Across the Border", 1968, "The Fool Card", 1970, "Probable Cause", 1972; co-author: The Fedak File, 1995; albums include Song Shark, 1992, Conrad Marshall Quintet, 1991. Campaign vol. Dem. Ctrl. Com., L.A., 1976, Rep. Ctrl. Com., 1994. Mem. Screen Actors Guild, Internat. Platform Assn. Avocations: poetry, song writing, club singing, philosophy, theology. Home: 11853 Kling St Valley Vlg CA 91607-4073 Office: Con Mar Prodns 2026 Holly Hill Ter Hollywood CA 90068-3812

MARSHALL, CRAIG TYLER, urban planner; b. St. Louis, May 10, 1956; s. John Waldron and Marilyn Jane Marshall; m. Betty Sue Wooten, Dec. 30, 1983; children: Melanie Jane, Cynthia Rose. BS in Phys. Geography, U. Md., 1979; M in Planning, U. Va., 1984. Cert. urban planner Am. Inst. Cert. Planners; lic. profl. planner N.J. Bd. Profl. Planners. Asst. planner Town of Union, N.Y., 1984-87; prin. planner Mercer County Govt., Trenton, N.J., 1987-89, MARC Assocs., Hainesport, N.J., 1989-90; asst. planner Twp. of S. Brunswick, Monmouth Junction, N.J., 1990-98, dir. planning and cmty. devel., 1998—; pres. Marshallplan, Burlington, N.J., 1992—. Mem. Am. Planning Assn., Sons Am. Legion. Episcopalian. Avocations: fishing, camping, canoeing, home brewing. Fax: 732-274-2084. Office: Twp of S Brunswick PO Box 190 Monmouth Junction NJ 08852-0190

MARSHALL, DAVID WILLIAM, materials engineer; b. Stoneham, Mass., Oct. 5, 1938; s. David and Eileen Marjorie (Baker) M.; m. Bette Bruce Clark, Aug. 31, 1963; children: David Scott, James Clark, Laura Elizabeth. B-SChemE, MIT, 1960, MS in Materials Engring., 1961, MED in Materials Engring., 1965. Engr. Avco Corp., Lowell, Mass., 1963-69; project leader Amicon Corp., Lexington, Mass., 1969-70; dept. mgr. Kennecott Copper, Lexington, 1970-79; co-owner Marshall and Pike, Salem, N.H., 1979-81; v.p. Key Polymer, Lawrence, Mass., 1981-85; owner Marshall Assocs., North Reading, Mass., 1985—; engring. cons. Textron System, Wilmington, Mass., 1989—. Author: (with others) The Science of Adhesive Joints, 1963, Filiment Winding, 1964. Mem. Forestry com., North Reading, 1988—, mosquito control, 1995-98, charter commn., 1996-97. Mem. Am. Chem. Soc. (sr.), Soc. of Plastics Engrs., Soc. for the Advancement of Materials and Process Engring. Achievements include 9 patents for flame-sprayed roofing material, copper filled conductive epoxy, heating panel, multiple track cathodes for electroformation of metallic filaments, method of making a flexible electrical conductor, fabrication of cathodes for electrodeposition, antifouling and anti-sliming coating material, methods for achieving particle to particle contact in an antifouling coating, antifouling and anti-sliming gel coat. Avocations: squash, tennis. Home: 21 Country Club Rd North Reading MA 01864-3109 Office: Textron Systems Corp 201 Lowell St Wilmington MA 01887-4113

MARSHALL, DONALD THOMAS, medical technologist; b. Omaha, June 9, 1955; s. William A. and Alma J. Marshall; m. Beverly Ann Everett, Sept. 22, 1990. Med. tech., Pikes Peak Inst. Med. Tech., 1977; EMT, Pikes Peak C.C., Colorado Springs, 1979; PhD of Religion, Universal Life Ch., 1995, D of Metaphysics (hon.), 1995. Registered med. technologist; cert. clin. lab. technologist. X-ray and med. lab. technician St. Joseph Hosp. of Plains, Cheyenne Wells, Colo., 1977-79; med. lab. technician Conejos County Hosp., La Jara, Colo., 1979-84; med. technologist Nat. Health Lab., Englewood, Colo., 1984-91; med. technologist, tech. cons., quality assurance officer Cmty. Health Svcs. Denver Health, Denver, 1996—, med. technologist, 1996—. EMT, fireman La Jara Vol. Fire Dept., 1979-84, Meritorious Svc. Citation, 1983. Mem. Am. Assn. Bio-Analysts, Am. Med. Technologists, Mason (worshipful master 1994), York Rite, Scottish Rite, Shriners (drummer in Pipe Band). Republican.

MARSHALL, ENID ANN, law educator; b. Boyndie, Scotland, July 10, 1932; d. John and Lizzie (Gilchrist) M. MA with honors, U. St. Andrews, Scotland, 1955, LLB with distinction, 1958, PhD, 1966. Law apprentice Pagan & Osborne, Cupar, Scotland, 1956-59; lectr. law Dundee Coll. Tech., 1959-72; lectr. bus. law U. Stirling, Scotland, 1972-74, sr. lectr. bus. law, 1974-77, reader in bus. law, 1977-94, reader in Scots law rsch., 1994-99; external examiner U. Scotland, 1973-79, Colls. in Scotland, 1974-83; moderator Scotvec, Scotland, 1972-90; external lectr. Coll. Estate Mgmt., Reading, Eng., 1989-94. Author: General Principles of Scots Law, 7 edits., 1971-99, Scots Mercantile Law, 3 edits., 1983-97, Scottish Cases on Contract, 2 edits., 1978-93, Oliver and Marshall's Company Law, 10th to 12th edits., 1987-94; editor Scottish Law Gazette, 1983—. Chmn. Social Security Appeal Tribunals, Stirling & Falkirk, Scotland. Fellow Royal Soc. Arts; mem. Chartered Inst. Arbitrators (assoc.), Royal Instn. Chartered Surveyors (hon. assoc.), Law Soc. Scotland (solicitor). Avocations: animal welfare, veganism. Home: 24 Easter Cornton Rd, Stirling FK9 5ES, Scotland

MARSHALL, JOHN, ophthalmology educator, consultant, executive; b. Woking, Eng., Dec. 21, 1943; s. Henry Thomas George and Ellen Emily Martha (Bishop) M.; m. Judith Anne Meadows, Mar. 18, 1972. BSc in Zoology with honors, Sir John Cass U., London, 1965; PhD in Anatomy Medicin, Inst. Ophthalmology, London, 1968. Lectr., anatomy Inst. Ophthalmology, 1968-73, sr. lectr., visual sci., 1973-80, reader, exptl. pathology, 1980-83, Sembal Prof. Ophthalmology, 1983-91; Frost Prof. Ophthalmology St. Thomas' Hosp., U. London, 1991—; laser safety advisor to WHO, UN Environment Program, European Union, Internat. Com. Red Cross, Geneva, 1974—, also to non-ionizing radiation com. Internat. Radiol. Protection Assn., Internat. Electro-Tech. Commn., and Brit. Stds. Instn.; med. adv. bd. Summit Tech., Boston, 1985—; dir. Diomed, Cambridge, Eng., 1991—;. Author: Hazards of Light, 1986, Laser Technology of Ophthalmology, 1988, others; contbr. over 350 articles on lasers in ophthalmology to profl. jours. and conf. procs., 1967—; inventor and patentee in field of photorefractive keratectomy; editor 10 peer rev. jours. Bd. govs. Moorfields Eye Hosp., London, 1988-90; mem. Prevention of Blindness Com., Royal Nat. Inst. for the Blind, London, 1988—. Recipient Ashton medal Royal Coll. Ophthalmology, London, 1993, Ridley medal European Soc. Refractive Surgery, 1990, other awards. Fellow Royal Soc. Medicine, Royal Soc. Art, Coll. Optometry, London (hon.); mem. Brit. Retinitis Pigmentosa Soc. (trustee 1976-97), Internat. Retinitis Pigmentosa Assn. (co-chmn. med. adv. bd. 1979-95, Athenaeum. Avocations: reading, work. Home: Wildacre, 27 Cedar Rd, Farnborough, Hampshire GU14 7AU, England Office: St Thomas Hosp Dept Ophthal, Rayne Inst Lambeth Palace R, London SE1 7EH, England

MARSHALL, JOHN A., building materials retailer; b. Barbados, June 25, 1945; s. John B. and Florence May (Farmer) M.; m. Betty M. Hutson, Jan. 11, 1969; children: Anthony Paul, John Allan. Student, Barbados, 1955-63. Chmn. Marshall Trading Ltd., Wildey St. Michael, Barbados, 1975—. Anglican. Avocations: fishing, hunting. Office: Marshall Trading Ltd, Lot 14 Wildey Indsl Estate, Bridgetown Barbados

MARSHALL, LINDA MURPHY, linguist, government official; b. St. Louis, Aug. 6, 1950; d. Samuel Baldwin and Barbara Anne (Chivvis) Murphy; m. Joseph A. Kelley, Aug. 31, 1974 (div. Sept. 1987); children: Alex, Mia; m. William Peyton Marshall, July 8, 1989. BA, U. Denver, 1972; MA, St. Louis U., 1974, PhD, 1978; postgrad., Washington U., 1981-85, Georgetown U., 1997-98. Translator Aerospace Ctr., Def. Mapping Agy., St. Louis, 1978-81; multi-linguist U.S. Fed. Govt., Washington, 1985—. Cons.: Sotho Newspaper Reader, Reference Grammar and Lexicon, 1998; contbr. articles to profl. jour. Mem. Phi Beta Kappa. Episcopalian. Avocations: classical piano, poetry, travel, foreign languages. Home: 10391 Green Mountain Cir Columbia MD 21044-2455

MARSHALL, LOUISE JANE, education educator; b. Melbourne, Australia, Nov. 8, 1958; d. Vernon Charles and Patricia (Warren) M.; m. Peter Maxwell Kohane; children: Elsa Louise, Felix Vernon. BA (hon.), U. Melbourne, Australia, 1980; MA (hon.), 1982; PhD, U. Pa., Phila., 1989. Lectr. Dept. Fine Arts U. Melbourne, Australia, 1989, U. Sydney, Australia, 1990—. Contbr. articles to profl. jours. Grantee U. Rsch. U. Sydney, 1992; Kress fellowship U. Pa., 1986-87; Chester Dale fellowship Ctr. for Advanced Study in the Visual Arts, Nat. Gallery Art, Washington, 1985-86. Mem. Australian Art Assn., Coll. Art Assn., Renaissance Soc. Am. Office: Dept Art History & Theory, U Sydney, New South Wales 2006, Australia

MARSHALL, M. H. SHEN, educational institution executive; b. Tainan, Taiwan, Sept. 29, 1946; s. Kwan San and Chu (Wu) Shen; m. Sue Lin, July 29, 1973; children: Maisie, Maggie, Marlene. BS, Chang Yuan U., 1970; MS, Ctrl. Mo. State U., 1990; EdS, St. Mary's U., 2000. Pres. Cheer Kindergarten, Tainan, 1980—, Cheer Infant Sch., Tainan, 1980—; lectr. Chia Nan U., 1990-98; pres. Cheer English Computer Music Sch., 1997—, Cheer Orch., 1998; assoc. prof. Da Yeh U., 2000—. Editor: Parenthood Awareness Education, 1983, Parent Relationship, 1985, Sprout Series I, II, III, IV, 1997-99. With Taiwanese Armed Forces, 1970. Recipient Outstanding Tchr. of Nation award, 1994, Outstanding Career Developing Youth Exemplar of Nations award, 1984, Outstanding Social Welfare of Nation award, 1997, Outstanding Alumni award of elem. sch.; named Outstanding Parenthood Awareness Edn. of Nation award, 1983. Mem. Early Childhood Edn. Assn. (pres. Tainan 1988—), Jaycees Internat. (senator N.Y. chpt. 1985, pres. Tainan chpt. 1979), Rotary (pres. Tainan Ctrl. Club, 1990, dir. Early Childhood Found. 1990—, Far Chen Humanity Found. 1994, exec. dir. Rotary Social Welfare Found. 1995—), Tainan Music Assn. (pres. 2000—). Avocations: photography, philately, touring. Office: Cheer Ednl Instn, 36 Yu-Ho Rd, Tainan 701, Taiwan

MARSHALL, MARY JONES, civic worker; b. Billings, Mont.; d. Leroy Nathaniel and Janet (Currie) Dailey; m. Harvey Bradley Jones, Nov. 15, 1952 (dec. 1989); children: Dailey, Janet Currie, Ellis Bradley; m. Boyd T. Marshall, June 27, 1990. Student, Carleton Coll., 1943-44, U. Mont., 1944-46, UCLA, 1959. Owner Mary Jones Interiors. Founder, treas. Jr. Art Council, L.A. County Mus., 1953-55, v.p., 1955-56; mem. costume council Pasadena (Calif.) Philharm.; co-founder Art Rental Gallery, 1953, chmn. art and architecture tour, 1955; founding mem., sec. Art Alliance, Pasadena Art Mus., 1955-56; benefit chmn. Pasadena Girls Club, 1959, bd. dirs., 1958-60; chmn. L.A. Tennis Patron's Assn. Benefit, 1965; sustaining Jr. League Pasadena; mem. docent council L.A. County Mus.; mem. costume council L.A. County Mus. Art., program chmn. 20th Century Greatest Designers; mem. blue ribbon com. L.A. Music Ctr.; benefit chmn. Venice com. Internat. Fund for Monuments, 1971; bd. dirs. Art Ctr. 100, Pasadena, 1988—; pres. The Pres.'s L.A. Children's Bur., 1989; co-chmn. benefit Harvard Coll. Scholarship Fund, 1974, steering com. benefit, 1987, Otis Art Inst., 1975, 90th Anniversary of Children's Bureau of L.A., 1994; mem. Harvard-Radcliffe scholarship dinner com., 1985; mem. adv. bd. Estelle Doheny Eye Found., 1976, chmn. benefit, 1980; adv. bd. Loyola U. Sch. Fine Arts, L.A., Art Ctr. Sch. Design, Pasadena, Calif., 1987—; patron chmn. Benefit Achievement Rewards for Coll. Scientists, 1988; chmn. com. Sch. Am. Ballet Benefit, 1988, N.Y.C.; bd. dirs. Founders Music Ctr., L.A., 1977-81; mem. nat. adv. council Sch. Am. Ballet, N.Y.C., nat. co-chmn. gala, 1980; adv. council on fine arts Loyola-Marymount U.; mem. L.A. Olympic Com., 1984, The Colleagues; founding mem. Mus. Contemporary Art, 1986; chmn. The Pres.'s Benefit L.A. Children's Bur., 1990; exec. com. L.A. Alive for L.A. Music Ctr., 1992; mem. exec. com. Children's Bur. of L.A. Found., 1992; chmn. award dinner Phoenix House, 1994, 96; bd. dirs. Andrews Sch. Gerontology, U. So. Calif., 1996—, Leakey Found., 1996—; bd. regents Children's Hosp. L.A., 1996—. Mem. Am. Parkinson Disease Assn. (steering com. 1991), Valley Hunt Club (Pasadena), Calif. Club (L.A.), Kappa Alpha Theta. Home: 10375 Wilshire Blvd Ste 8B Los Angeles CA 90024-4712

MARSHALL, MERYL C(ORINBLIT), telecommunications executive, lawyer; b. L.A., Oct. 16, 1949; d. Jack and Nita Corinblit. BA, UCLA, 1971; JD, Loyola Marymount U., L.A., 1974. Bar: Calif. 1974. Dep. pub. defender County of L.A., 1975-77; sole practice L.A., 1977-78; ptnr. Markman and Marshall, L.A., 1978-79; sr. atty. NBC, Burbank, Calif., 1979-80, dir. programs, talent contracts bus. affairs, 1980; asst. gen. atty. NBC, N.Y.C., 1980-82; v.p., compliance and practices NBC, Burbank, 1982; v.p. program affairs Group W Prodns., 1987-89, sr. v.p. future images, 1989-91, TV producer, Meryl Marshall Prodns., 1991-93; pres. Two Oceans Entertainment Group, 1991—. Chmn., Nat. Women's Polit. Caucus, Westside, Calif., 1978-80; mem. Calif. Dem. Ctrl. Com., 1978-79; mem. Hollywood Women's Polit. Com., 1988. Mem. Acad. of TV Arts and Scis. (treas. 1985, 93-97, bd. govs. 1989—, pres. 1997-99, chmn. bd., CEO 1999—), Women in Film. Democrat. Jewish. Office: Two Oceans Entertainment Group 4528 Camellia Ave North Hollywood CA 91602-1908

MARSHALL, NATHALIE, artist, writer, educator; b. Pitts., Nov. 10, 1932; d. Clifford Benjamin and Clarice (Stille) Marshall; m. Robert Alfred Van Buren, May 1, 1952 (div. June 1965); children: Christine Van Buren Popovic, Clifford Marshall Van Buren, Jennifer Van Buren Lake; m. David Arthur Nadal, Dec. 30, 1976 (div. Oct. 1995). ABA, Silvermine Coll. Art, New Canaan, Conn., 1967; BFA, U. Miami, Coral Gables, 1977; MA, U. Miami, 1982, PhD in English and Fine Arts, 1982. Instr. in humanities Miami Ednl. Consortium, Miami Shores, Fla., 1977-79, Barry U., Miami Shores, 1979-81, U. Miami, 1977-81; sr. lectr. Nova U., Ft. Lauderdale, Fla., 1981-84, assoc. prof. humanities, 1985-86; prof. art, chair dept. art Old Coll., Reno, Nev., 1986-88; asst. registrar Lowe Art Mus., Coral Gables, 1976-78; co-founder, dir. The Bakehouse Art Complex, Miami, 1984-86; advisor, bd. mem. NAH YAH EE (Indian children's art exhibits), Weimar, Calif., 1984—; mem. adv. bd. New World Sch. Arts, Miami, 1985-86. One-woman shows include Silvermine Coll. Art, New Canann, Conn., 1968, Ingber Gallery, Greenwich, 1969, Capricorn Gallery, N.Y.C., 1969, Pierson Coll. at Yale U., New Haven, 1970, The Art Barn, Greenwich, 1972, Art Unltd., N.Y.C., 1973, Benevy Gallery, N.Y.C., 1974, Richter Libr., U. Miami, 1985, 97, 98, Nova U., Ft. Lauderdale, 1985, Ward Nasse Gallery, N.Y.C., 1985, Old Coll., Reno, 1986, Washoe County Libr., Reno, 1987, Sabal Palms Gallery, Gulfport, Fla., 1992, Ambiance Gallery, St. Petersburg, 1995, 96, Gulfport Libr., 1996, Thresholds Studio, Gulfport, 1998, 99; group shows include: Capricorn Gallery, N.Y.C., 1968, Ingber Gallery, 1968, Compass Gallery, N.Y.C., 1970, Finch Coll. Mus., N.Y.C., 1971, Town Hall Art Gallery, Stamford, Conn., 1973, 74, Jewish Cmty. Ctr., Miami Beach, 1981, Continuum Gallery, Miami Beach, 1982, South Fla. Art Inst., Hollywood, Fla., 1984, Met. Mus., Coral Gables, 1985, Ward Nasse Gallery, N.Y.C., 1985, Brunnier Mus., Iowa State U., Ames, 1986, Nat. Mus. of Women in The Arts Libr., Washington, 1987, 89, U.S. Art in Embassies Program, 1987-88, UN World Conf. Women, Nairobi, 1987, Raymond James Invitational, St. Petersburg, 1989-92, Arts Ctr., St. Petersburg, 1990, 91, 92, Global Gallery, Tampa, Fla., 1990, 91, Sabal Palms Gallery, 1992, No. Nat. Nicolet Coll., Rhineland, Wis., 1992, Internat. Biennale, Bordeaux, France, 1993, Salon de Vieux Colombier, Paris, 1993, Synchronicity Space, N.Y.C., 1993, Women's 1st Internat. Biennal of Women Artist, Stockholm, 1994-95 (gold medal), Tampa Arts Forum, Fla., 1995, 96,. Recipient Sponsor's award for Painting Greenwich Art Soc., 1967; Steven Buffton Meml. award Am. Bus. Women's Assn., 1980; grantee Poets & Writers, 1993; one of 300 global artists in Internat. Hope and Optimism Portfolio, Oxford. Mem. MLA, Coll. Art Assn., Nat. Women's Studies Assn., Women's Caucus for Art (nat. adv. bd. 1983-88, pres. Miami chpt. 1984-86, southeast regional v.p. 1986), Gulfport Arts Coun. (pres. 2000). Address: 52271/2 27th Ave S Gulfport FL 33707

MARSHALL, PENNY (C. MARSHALL), director, actress; b. N.Y.C., Oct. 15, 1943; d. Anthony W. and Marjorie Irene (Ward) M.; m. Michael Henry (div.); 1 child, Tracy Lee; m. Robert Reiner, Apr. 10, 1971 (div. 1979). Student, U. N.Mex., 1961-64. Appeared on numerous television shows, including The Odd Couple, 1972-74, Friends and Lovers (co-star), 1974, Let's Switch, 1974, Wives (pilot), 1975, Chico and the Man, 1975, Mary Tyler Moore, 1975, Heaven Help Us, 1975, Saturday Night Live, 1975-77, Happy Days, 1975, Battle of Network Stars (ABC special), 1976, Barry Manilow special, 1976, The Tonight Show, 1976-77, Dinah, 1976-77, Mike Douglas Show, 1975-77, Merv Griffin Show, 1976-77, Blansky's Beauties, 1977, Network Battle of the Sexes, 1977, Laverne and Shirley (co-star), 1976-83; TV films More Than Friends, 1978, Love Thy Neighbor, 1984, Challenge of a Lifetime, 1985, The Odd Couple: Together Again, 1993; appeared in motion pictures How Sweet It Is, 1967, The Savage Seven, 1968, The Grasshopper, 1970, 1941, 1979, Movers and Shakers, 1985, She's Having a Baby, 1988, The Hard Way, 1991, Hocus Pocus, 1993, Get Shorty, 1995; dir. films: Jumpin' Jack Flash, 1986, Big, 1988, Awakenings, 1990, A League of Their Own, 1992, Renaissance Man, 1994, The Preacher's Wife, 1996; co-exec. prodr. TV series A League of Their Own, 1993 (also dir. pilot); prodr. Getting Away With Murder, 1995, With Friends Like These, 1998, Saving Grace, 1998; dir: The Time Tunnel: The Movie, 1999, Get Shorty, 1995, Special Delivery, 1999, (TV movie) Jackie's Back, 1999. Office: Parkway Productions 10202 Washington Blvd Culver City CA 90232-3119*

MARSHALL, SUSAN LOCKWOOD, civic worker; b. Orange, N.J., Dec. 2, 1939; d. Richard Rouglas and Helen Lockwood (Stratford) Nelson; m. William Pendleton Marshall, Aug. 20, 1960; children: Jill, James. BE, Wheelock Coll., 1961. Vol. Newton-Wellesley (Mass.) Hosp., 1962-63, New Eyes for Needy, Inc., 1963-64; vol. amblyopia screening program, Short Hills, N.J., 1969-71; bd. dirs. Jr. League Oranges and Short Hills, Inc., 1967-72, corr. sect., 1970-72; fund raising vol. Children's Aid and Adoption Soc. N.J., 1969-73, dir., 1970-73, asst. sec., 1970-72, 1st v.p., 1972-73; bd. dirs. Jr. League Stamford-Norwalk (Conn.), 1974-78, asst. treas., 1976-77, treas., 1977-78; bd. dirs. Program One to One, Inc., 1975-76, treas.; vol. Voluntary Action Ctr., 1975-76; bd. dirs. Episcopal Churchwomen St. Luke's Parish, 1974-81, 2d v.p., 1976-77, asst. treas., 1977-78, treas., 1978-80, pres., 1980-81; bd. dirs. Lockwood Mathews Mansion Mus., 1979-95, vol., 1979-2000, treas., 1979-95, v.p., 1983-88; mem. coun. parent bd. Darien Sch., 1978-83, rec. sec., 1981-83; bd. dirs. Middlesex Jr. H.S. Parents Assn., 1979-83, treas., 1982-83; mem. Vol. Ctr., 1984—; mem. vol. mgmt. assistance program adv. com. Darien chpt. Am. Field Svc., 1984-87; chmn. Darien H.S. Parents Assn., 1984-85; bd. dirs. Darien United Way, 1984—, asst. treas., 1988-95, treas., 1995-98, 1st v.p. 1998-99, pres., 1999—. Address: 358 Hollow Tree Ridge Rd Darien CT 06820-3218

MARSHALL, WAYNE KEITH, anesthesiology educator; b. Richmond, Va., Feb. 9, 1948; s. Chester Truman and Lois Ann (Tiller) M.; m. Dale Claire Reynolds, June 18, 1977; children: Meredith Reynolds, Catherine Truman, Whitney Wood. BS in Biology, Va. Poly. Inst. and State U., 1970; MD, Va. Commonwealth U., 1974. Diplomate Am. Bd. Anesthesiology, Nat. Bd. Med. Examiners; bd. cert. in pain mgmt. Surg. intern U. Cin., 1974-75, resident in surgery, 1975-77; resident in anesthesiology U. Va. Coll. Medicine, Charlottesville, 1977-79, rsch. fellow, 1979-80; asst. prof. anesthesia Pa. State U. Coll. Medicine, Hershey, 1980-86, assoc. prof., 1986-95, assoc. clin. dir. oper. rm., 1982-95, dir. pain mgmt. svc., 1984-95, chief divsn. pain mgmt., 1992-95; prof., chmn. dept. anesthesiology Med. Coll. Va., Richmond, 1995-99; med. dir. operating rms. MCV Hosp., 1995-99; prof. anesthesiology Coll. Medicine Pa. State U., Hershey, 1999—; moderator nat. meetings. Mem. editorial bd. Am. Jour. Anesthesiology, 1987-99, Jour. Neurosurg. Anesthesiology, 1988—; contbr. articles and abstracts to med. jours. Recipient Antarctic Svc. medal NSF, 1980. Mem. AMA, Soc. Neurosurg. Anesthesia and Critical Care (sec.-treas. 1985-87, v.p. 1987-88, pres. 1989-90, bd. dirs. 1985-91), Assn. Univ. Anesthetists, Am. Soc. Anesthesiologists (del. ASA ho. of dels. 1990-92), Internat. Anesthesia Rsch. Soc., Pa. Soc. Anesthesiology. Republican. Baptist. Office: Dept Anesthesiology Penn St Univ Coll of Med PO Box H-187 Hershey PA 17033-2360

MARSHALL, WILLIAM TAYLOR, lawyer; b. Dallas; s. Willis A. and Jane T. Marshall; m. Peggy Taylor, May 18, 1973; 1 child, Taylor. BSPA with honors, U. Ark., 1973, MBA with honors, 1975; JD with honors, U. Ark., Little Rock, 1981. Bar: Ark. 1981, U.S. Dist. Ct. (fed. dist.) 1982, U.S. Ct. Appeals (8th cir.) 1982, U.S. Supreme Ct. 1984; CPA, Ark. Fin. analyst Hosp. Affiliates Internat., Nashville, 1975-76, sr. fin. analyst, 1976-78; CFO Hosp. Affiliates Internat./Doctor's Hosp., Little Rock, 1978-81; assoc. House Holmes & Jewell, Little Rock, 1981-83, ptnr., 1983-85; ptnr. Robinson, Staley, Marshall & Duke, Little Rock, 1985—; lectr. in field. Contbr. articles to profl. jours. Mem. ABA, AICPAs, Ark. Bar Assn. (cert. tax specialist, health law sect. 1985—), Am. Health Lawyers Assn. Home: 1900 Beechwood St Little Rock AR 72207-2004 Office: Robinson Staley Marshall & Duke PA 400 W Capitol Ave Ste 2891 Little Rock AR 72201-3463

MARSHALL, WILLIS HENRY, psychiatrist; s. Willis Henry Sr. and Pauline Elizabeth (Murphy) M.; m. Carolyn Mae Kowalski; children: Louann Lorinda Marshall Johnson, John Willis. AB cum laude, U. Evansville, 1957; MD, Ind. U., 1961. Intern Detroit Meml. Hosp., 1961-62; resident psychiatry Mental Health Inst., Cherokee, Iowa, 1965-67, 69-70, staff psychiatrist, 1967-69; staff psychiatrist Mental Health Ctr., Muskegon, Mich., 1970-71; pvt. practice psychiatry Madison, Tenn., 1974-85, Bowling Green, Ky., 1987—; staff psychiatrist chief admission svc., staff psychiatrist treatment unit Mid. Tenn. Mental Health Inst., Nashville, 1984-85, staff psychiatrist evaluation unit forensic svcs. div., 1985-87, chief of staff, 1986-87; forensic psychiatrist State of Tenn., 1985-87; part-time staff psychiatrist Ottawa County Mental Health Ctr., Grand Haven, Mich., 1971-73, Tenn. Dept. Mental Health and Mental Retardation Mid. Tenn. Mental Health Inst., Nashville, 1981-83, Lifeskills, Inc., Glasgow, Ky., Franklin, Ky., 1987-89; psychiat. cons. Allegan County Mental Health Ctr., Allegen, Mich., 1973; med. svcs.. cons. dept. of forensic svcs. Mid. Tenn. Mental Health Inst., Nashville, 1983-84; clin. asst. prof. psychiatry dept. allied health Trevecca Nazareene Coll., Nashville, 1985-87; part-time pvt. practice psychiatry, Muskegon, Mich., 1970-74, Madison, Tenn., 1986-87; assoc. clin. dir. mental health unit Med. Ctr., Bowling Green, Ky., 1987-91; preceptor, asst. clin. prof. physician asst. program U. Ky., 1988-91; acting med. dir. Rivendell Children's Psychiat. Hosp., Bowling Green, 1989; med. dir. adult mental health unit Rivendell of Ky., 1992-94. Commd. officer, surgeon USPHS, 1962-65. Recipient AMA Physicians Recognition award, 1969, 79, 83, 86, 89, 92, Exemplary Psychiatrist award Nat. Alliance for Mentally Ill, 1993. Mem. Am. Psychiat. Assn. (art assn. 1976—), Ky. Med. Assn., Warren County Med. Soc., Am. Profl. Practice Assn., Am. Acad. Clin. Psychiatrists, Am. Physicians Art Assn., NRA, Nat. Geog. Soc., AAA Automobile Club, Gallatin Gun Club, Alpha Omega Alpha. Avocations: sculpture, photography, painting, hunting, fixing old guns. Home: 100 Moccasin Bend Rd Chattanooga TN 37405-4415 Office: 5115 Silver Ln Apison TN 37302-9594

MARSOT-DUPUCH, KATHLYN, physician; b. Antony, France, Jan. 17, 1949; d. Jacques and Jeanne (Cavargini) M.; m. GiPbert DuPuch, Feb. 13, 1976 (div. 1989); children: Sonia, Samantha. Intern and resident Hopitaux de Paris, 1974-80; fellowship Hopitaux de Paris, Paris, 1980-83, medean, 1983—; MD, 1983—; co-dir. Head and Neck Imaging Tchrs., U. Bicetre and St. AnFoine, 1992—; founda tor CIREOL, Paris, 1989. Author: Head and Neck Imaging, 1995, Scrotal Ultrasonography, 1985; contbr. articles to profl. jours. Mem. Nat. Cmty. of Hosp. Drs., Paris, 1994. Recipient Cert. of Merit Chgo. RSNA, 1991, First prize of the scientific exhibit Pais SFR, 1991. Avocations: tennis, biking, skiing. Home: 123 Rue de Reuibly, 75012 Paris France Office: Hopital St Antoine, 184 Rue de Faubourg St, 75012 Paris France

MARSTON, NICHOLAS JOHN, musicologist; b. Penzance, Cornwall, England, Dec. 27, 1958; s. Joseph and Livonia Priscilla (Williams) M. BA, Corpus Christi Coll., Cambridge, Eng., 1980, MA, 1984, PhD, 1986. Lectr. U. Exeter, 1989-94; lectr. to sr. lectr. U. Bristol, 1994-95; lectr., reader U. Oxford, 1995—; fellow St. Peter's Coll., Oxford, 1995—; lectr. St. Edmund Hall, Oxford, 1995—. Editl. bd. Music Analysis, 1998—, Beethoven Forum, 1997—, JRMA, 1997—; editor SMA Newsletter, 1994—; author: Beethoven's Piano Sonata in E Op. 109, 1995, Schumann: Fantasie, Op. 17, 1992; co-author: The Beethoven Compendium, 1991. Sr. scholarship DAAD, 1996; postdoctoral rsch. fellowship British Acad., 1986-89, Trevelyan Rsch. fellowship Selwyn Coll., 1984-86. Mem. Royal Musical Assn. (coun. mem.), Soc. for Music Analysis, Am. Musicol. Soc. Avocations: wine, cooking, walking. Office: St Peters Coll, New Inn Hall St, Oxford OX1 2DL, United Kingdom

MARSTRAND-JORGENSEN, MADS, lawyer; b. Copenhagen, Denmark, Dec. 12, 1947; s. Bent and Gerda (Marstrand) Jorgensen; children: Kristine, Annelise, Niels Jacob, Mette. LLM, U. Copenhagen, 1972. Pvt. practice, Copenhagen, 1972-92; ptnr. Norsker & Jacoby, Copenhagen, 1992—; asst. prof. U. Copenhagen, 1973-78; chmn. Coca-Cola Denmark A/S, 1983-91, Schenker Internat. A/S, Denmark, 1985-97, 2-M Security System A/S, Denmark, 1984—; vice chmn. G&S Internat. A/S, Denmark, 1981—, Tokai U., 1995—. Hon. gen. consul Republic of Costa Rica, Denmark, 1977—. Fellow McGeorge U. Law; mem. Assn. Fgn. Countries' Consuls in Denmark (v.p. 1997—), Internat. Trademark Assn. (mem. internat. com.), European Cmtys. Trademark Assn., Assn. Internat. pour Protection Internat., Licensing Execs. Assn., Internat. Bar Assn. Office: Norsker & Jacoby, 3 Kvaesthusgade, 1261 Copenhagen Denmark

MARTA, ELENA, psychologist, researcher; b. Legnano, Italy, Nov. 3, 1963; d. Egidio and Paola (Molinari) M.; m. Sergio Luca Rizzi, May 18, 1991; 1 child, Valentina. M in Philosphy, Cath. U., Milan, 1986, PhD in Psychology, 1989, PhD in Social and Devel. Psychology, 1994. Rschr. Cath. U., Milan, 1995-99, prof., 1999—. Editor: (book) Family Relationships and Adolescence, 1995, Social Cognitions and Family Relationships, 2000; (CD) Informati, Orientati, Apprendi, 1998. Mem. European Assn. Rsch. on Adolescence, Soc. Rsch. on Adolescence, Internat. Acad. Family Psychology. Avocations: reading, film, gardening, knitting. Home: Via Carducci, 8, 20015 Parabiago Italy Office: Cath U, L Go Gemelli, 20123 Milan Italy

MARTELET, CLAUDE MARIE GEORGES, chemical engineering educator; b. Lyon, Rhône, France, Nov. 26, 1945; s. Jean and Louise (Voisin) M.; m. Bernadete Giuliani, Oct. 17, 1973; children: Caroline, Raphaele, Alix, Helene. Lic. Physics, Lyon U., 1967; Doctorat d'Etat, U. Lyon I, 1973; Engr. Chemist, ICPI, Lyon, 1968. Cert. engr. chemist. Asst. Ecole Centrale de Lyon, Ecully, France, 1967-73, master asst., 1973-84, master confs., 1985-91, prof. univ., 1992—. Contbr. articles to profl. jours.; patentee in field. Mem. Micro Chem. Sensors Club (editor info. letter French Club 1989—). Avocations: treking in mountains, philately, illusionism, photo-video. E-mail: claude.martelet@ec-lyon.fr. Home: Morateur 1, 18 Chemin des Combes, F69370 Saint Didier France Office: Ecole Centrale de Lyon BP163, 36 Av Guy de Colongues, F69131 Ecully France

MARTELLA, RONALD CHARLES, psychology educator, consultant; b. El Centro, Calif., Dec. 30, 1961; s. Ronald C. and Arlene C. Martella; m. Nancy E. Marchand, Apr. 25, 1987; children: Amédee Marchand Martella, Dominic Marchand Martella. BA in Psychology and Bus. Adminstrn., Ft. Lewis Coll., 1985; MS in Behavior Analysis and Therapy, So. Ill. U., 1987; MBA in Bus. Adminstrn., Utah State U., 1991, PhD in Spl. Edn., 1991. Spl. projects coord. U. Mont., Missoula, 1993-95; asst. prof. psychology Ea. Wash. U., Cheney, 1995-97; family intervention specialist U.S. Dept. Edn., Cheney, 1996-97; co-dir. Ctr. for Social Policy and Rsch., Cheney, 1997—; co-project dir. U.S. Dept. Edn., Cheney, 1997—; assoc. prof. psychology Ea. Wash. U., Cheney, 1997—; vis. assoc. prof. U. Mont., Missoula, 1993-95; ednl. cons. Head Start, Des Moines, 1993, mental health cons., Spokane, Wash., 1997-98; transition cons. ECHO Svcs., Spokane, 1998—. Author: (book) Research Methods, 1999; editor: (book) Promoting Health and Safety, 1993; mem. editl. bd. various profl. jours.; jour. reviewer; contbr. numerous articles to profl. jours. and conf. presentations. Bd. dirs. Artisans Ark, Spokane, 1996; IDEA mem. PTA, Missoula, 1995; mem. adv. coun. Family Care Program, Missoula, 1995. Mem. APA, CEC, Assn. for Behavior Analysis (edn. rep. 1987-98). Office: Eastern Wash U MS-92 Cheney WA 99004

MARTELLI, CLAUDIO, Italian government official; b. Gessate, Italy, Sept. 24, 1943. Grad. in philosophy. Former instr. polit. philosophy Milan U.; mem. Mcpl. Coun., Milan; active Italian Socialist Party, dep. sec., 1981, sole dep. sec., 1984; mem. Italian Parliament, Rome, 1979—, mem. edn. and fine arts com., 1979, mem. fgn. affairs and emigration com., 1983; dep. prime min. Govt. of Italy, Rome, 1989-92; min. justice Govt. of Italy, 1991-94; mem. European Parliament, Brussels, Belgium, 1994—. Address: Via Corso Vittorio Emanuele 173, I-00100 Roma Italy*

MARTEN, LUTZ, information management specialist; b. Bremen, Germany, June 23, 1961; s. Dietrich F.O. and Ilse B.L. (Kruempel) M. MS, Rheinisch-Westfalisch Tech., Germany, 1988, PhD, 1994. Info. mgmt. mgr. Fraunhofer-Gesellschaft Inst. für Lasertechnik, Aachen, 1988-96, Wuerzburg (Germany) U., 1996-2000, IBM Global Svcs., 2000—. Author: Informations Management, 1994. Pvt. 2d class Germany Mil., 1980-81. Mem. Assn. for Computing Machinery, Gesellschaft für Informatik, Gesellschaft von Freunden der Aachener Hochschule. Avocations: cycling, skiing, jazz music, reading, country cooking. E-mail: marten@acm.org. Home: Bentheimstrasse 13, D-97072 Würzburg Germany Office: IBM Global Svcs, Virchowstr 22, 97072 Würzburg Germany

MARTENS, GERD, transportation executive, consultant; b. Schleswig-Holstein, Germany, Dec. 27, 1945; s. Hans and Dorothea (Jensen) M.; m. Gabriele Maria Köper, Apr. 18, 1983; 1 child, Kai Yanto. Grad., Tech. U. Aachen, 1969; diploma in engring., Tech. U. Berlin, 1974, D in Engring., 1982; postgrad., Northwestern U., 1974-75. Group mgr. Pub. Transport, Nürnberg, 1975-76; project mgr. Tech. U. Berlin, 1976-83, Consulting, Berlin, 1983-84, 88-89; sr. adviser BPP Teknologi, Jakarta, Indonesia, 1984-88; cons. Berlin, 1989—; expert European Commn., Brussels, 1992. Co-author (with H. Verron): Advances in Economic Psychology, 1978, World Conference on Transport Research, 1983, Behavioral Research for Transport Policy, 1986. Rep. in univ. bodies, Berlin, 1971-78. Lt. German Mil. Fed. Army, 1965-67. Mem. Transp. Rsch. Bd., German Soc. Transport Sci. Avocations: sailing, jogging, literature, arts, politics. Office: Martens Internat, Friedrichshaller Str 7, D-14199 Berlin Germany

MARTENS, HARALD AAGAARD, data analysis researcher; b. Kristiansand, Norway, Oct. 16, 1946; s. Hans Ditlef and Ellen (Aagaard) M.; m. Magni Martens, Jan. 8, 1972; children: Silje, Johannes. MSc, Norwegian U. Sci. and Tech., 1971, Dr. of Tech., 1985. Registered engr., chemistry. Rschr. Norwegian Food Rsch. Inst., Aas, Norway, 1973-86, Norwegian Computing Ctr., Oslo, 1986-89; pres. Consensus Analysis AS, Ski, Norway, 1989—; rsch. group leader Internat. Digital Technologies GmbH, Munich, 1994-97; prof. II dept. phys. chemistry (chemometrics) Norwegian U. Sci. and Tech., Trondheim, Norway, 1996—; guest prof. Tech. U. Denmark, Inst. Biotech., Copenhagen, 1996—; vis. scientist Makerere U., Uganda, 1972, Kyoto U., 1972-73, Lund U., 1975-76; vis. statistician U. Calif., Davis, 1988-89; vis. prof. Royal Vet. & Agrl. U., Denmark, 1999—; data analysis cons. in U.S. and Europe, 1981-94. Editor, author: Food Research and Data Analysis, 1983; author Multivariate Calibration, 1989; initiator, designer (software) Unscrambler; contbr. articles to profl. jours.; patentee in field. Rsch. scholarship Rotary Found., 1972, Kellogg Found., 1975, Perstrop Found., 1988, Award in Chemometrics Ea. Analytical Symposium, 1999. Mem. AAAS, Norwegian Chem. Soc. (hon. mem., group for chemometrics, Chemometrics award 1993, Galactic Industries award for Achievement in Chemometrics 1999), Soc. for Applied Spectroscopy, Norwegian Soc. of Chartered Engrs., Norwegian Acad. of Tech. Scis. Avocations: cooking, interdisciplinary reading, hiking. Office: Consensus Analysis AS, Skt Peders Straede 25, DK-1453 Copenhagen Denmark Address: Sankt Peders Strede 25, DK-1453 Kobenhavn Danmark

MARTENS, JOHN DALE, telecommunications company executive; b. Wayne, Nebr., Nov. 12, 1943; s. Leonard William and Irma Bertha (Von Seggern) M.; m. Laura Elizabeth Price, Dec. 28, 1966 (div. 1996). BSBA, U. Colo., 1966; MS, Thunderbird Grad. Sch. Internat. Mgmt., 1972; postgrad., Queen Mary Coll., U. London, 1976. Analyst overseas ops. Ford Motor Co., Dearborn, Mich., 1972-73; internat. mktg. ofcl. Agrico Chem. Co., Tulsa, 1973-76; tech. and comml. devel. ofcl. Resource Scis. Co., Tulsa, 1976-78, planning and corp. devel. ofcl., 1978-80; chief exec. officer, pres., treas., dir. Sterling Oil of Okla., Inc., Tulsa, 1980-82; dir. strategic devel. MCI Communications Corp., Washington, 1983-84, v.p. corp. devel., 1984-86; v.p. mktg. So. New Eng. Telecommunications Co. Inc., New Haven, 1986-92; sr. v.p. comml. sales Williams Telecom. Group, Inc., Tulsa, 1992-93; founder, pres. Corp. Devel. Co., Tulsa, 1993—; founder, dir., pres., CEO Global Advanced Tech. Co., 1997, CDC Gen. Boot Co., 1998; bd. dirs. Thermoplastic Pultrusions, Inc. Capt. USAF, 1967-70. Roman Catholic.

MARTENS, MAXIMILIAAN PIETER JAN, art history educator; b. Ghent, Flanders, Belgium, Sept. 26, 1960; s. Roger Adolf and Imelda Maria (Pyfferoen) M.; m. Geertrui Anna Witdouck, May 14, 1986; children: Raphael, Romeo. MA, U. Ghent, 1983; PhD, U. Calif., Santa Barbara, 1992. Tchg. asst. U. Calif., Santa Barbara, 1987-88; rsch. asst. J.P. Getty Mus., Malibu, Calif., 1988-89; asst. prof. ad interim Royal Acad. Fine Arts, Ghent, 1990; assoc. prof. medieval art history U. Groningen, The Netherlands, 1992—, sec. dept. art history, 1993-95, mem. com. arts faculty libr., 1994—; Co-author: Petrus Christus/Metropolitan Museum of Art, 1994; editor/author: Bruges and the Renaissance (2 vols.) Municipal Museums Bruges, 1998; Lodewyk Van Gruuthuse/Municipal Museums Bruges, 1992; author: De Muurschilderkunst te Gent, 1989. Theodore Rousseau fellow Met. Mus. Art, N.Y., 1989, Fulbright fellow, Comm. Edn. Exch., Brussels, 1986. Mem. Royal Assn. Friends Mus. Fine Arts (pres. 1996—). Office: Univ Groningen Dpt Art Hist, Oude Boteringestraat 34, 9700 AS Groningen The Netherlands

MARTENS, S.K., legal administrator, retired. Pres. Supreme Ct. of The Netherlands, The Hague, ret., 2000. Office: Supreme Ct Netherlands, POB 20303, 2500 EH The Hague Tne Netherlands

MARTENS, VLADIMIR YAKOVLEVICH, physics educator; b. Zhigansk, Yakutia, Russia, Jan. 9, 1950; s. Yakov Abramovich Martens and Maria Ivanovna Kalitina; m. Larissa Yakovlevna Borovskaya, Aug. 15, 1975; children: Olga, Oleg. Engr., Tomsk Inst. Automatic Control Sys. and Radioelectronics, Russia, 1972, PhD, 1985. Lectr. Tomsk Inst. of Autom. Control Systems and Radioelectronics, Russia, 1974-79, 82-86, assoc. prof., 1986-92; dep.-dir. North-Caucasus Ecol. Coll., Stavropol, Russia, 1992-94; assoc. prof. North-Caucasus State Tech. U., Stavropol, Russia, 1994—; rsch. scholar Tomsk Inst. of Autom. Control Systems and Radioelectronics, 1974-85, sci. rsch. group leader, 1985-92. Co-author: Charged-particle beam sources with a plasma emitter, 1993; contbr. articles to profl. jours.; inventor in field. Grantee Internat. Soros Sci. Edn. Program, 1997. Mem. N.Y. Acad. Scis. Avocations: gardening, football. Home: Flat 47, 10 Botanichesky Proezd, 355038 Stavropol Russia Office: North-Caucasus State Tech U, 2 Kulakov Prospekt, 355038 Stavropol Russia

MARTENSEN-LARSEN, BRITTA TANJA, art historian, researcher; b. Copenhagen, Mar. 14, 1944; d. Oluf and Else (Paludan-Müller) M. MA in Art History, U. Copenhagen, 1977. Asst. prof. Copenhagen U., Inst. Art History, 1979, 82; registrar The Øregaard Mus., Copenhagen, 1980, 85-86; curator Ordrupgaard Collection, Copenhagen, 1982-83; dir. Gallery A Gruppen, Copenhagen, 1981-87; sec. Min. Culture, Copenhagen, 1988-89, Min. Fgn. Affairs, Copenhagen, 1991-92; curator The Danish Filmmus., Copenhagen, 1996; dep. gov. Rsch. and Advice Bd. ABI. Contbr. articles to profl. jours. Lay assessor City Ct. Copenhagen, 1996—. Grantee Ny Carlsberg Found., Copenhagen, 1990, 96, The Ingwersenske Found., Copenhagen, 1995. Fellow Internat. Biographical Assn.; mem. Danish Art Historian Soc., Danish Fedn. U. Women, Order of Internat. Amb. USA. Avocations: photography, painting, designing knit-wear. Home: Lundsgade 3, 2100 Copenhagen Denmark

MÅRTENSSON, ARNE EDWARD GEORG, bank executive; b. Vanersborg, Sweden, Oct. 10, 1951; s. Aldo and Ingrid Mårtensson; m. Jonas O Oscar. MBA, Stockholm Sch. Econs., 1973; PMD, Harvard U., 1983. With Svenska Handelsbanken, Stockholm, 1974—, exec. v.p., gen. mgr. regional unit Western Sweden, 1984-89, pres. elect, 1989-90, group chief exec., 1991—; bd. mem., vice chmn. Svenska Bankföreningen; bd. mem. Holmen AB, Svenska Handelsbanken, V&S Vin & Sprit AB, Sandvik AB, Svenska ICC, Näringslivets Börskommitté, Teleoptimering i Sverige AB; mem. Coun. of World Econ. Forum. Mem. Royal Swedish Acad. Engring. Scis. (indsl. coun.), Royal Swedish Yacht Club. Office: Svenska Handelsbanken, Kungstradgardsgatan 2, SE-10670 Stockholm Sweden

MARTENSSON, LENA, pharmaceutical executive; b. Mälmo, Sweden, Feb. 9, 1954; d. Sven and Ingaberit (Kindberg) M.; children from previous marriage: Karl, Sara; m. Christer Wernrud, Apr. 30, 1999. BSc, U. Lund, Sweden, 1977, PhD, 1983. Asst. rsch. fellow U. Lund, 1976-83; postdoctoral fellow Erasmus U., Rotterdam, The Netherlands, 1982-84; head preclin. Gambro AB, Lund, 1984-92; assoc. prof. U. Lund, 1991—; med. dir. Perstorp Pharma, Lund, 1992-95; dir. project mgmt. Pharm. Corp., Helsingborg, Sweden, 1995—. Contbr. articles to profl. jours. Home: Drottninggatan 244, 25433 Helsingborg 25433, Sweden Office: Pharmacia Corp, Norrbo Plats 2, Helsingborg 25109, Sweden

MARTH, FRITZ LUDWIG, sports association executive; b. Essen, Germany, Feb. 23, 1935; s. Fritz and Elizabeth (Dietrich) M.; came to U.S., 1952, naturalized, 1959; student pub. schs. Essen; m. Sonja Wiehl, June 17, 1964; children: Fritz Thomas, William Robert. Stock clk. Hamilton Art Metal Co., N.Y.C., 1952-55; with Keystone Metal Finishers, Inc., Secaucus, N.J., 1955—, asst. plant mgr., 1962-66, plant mgr., 1966-83; adminstr. amateur div. U.S. Soccer Fedn., N.J. 1983—. Pres. N.J. State Soccer Assn., 1965-70; sec. So. N.Y. State Soccer Assn., 1972-83; gen. sec. Cosmopolitan Soccer League, 1961—; mem. div. soccer U.S. Olympic Com. With U.S. Army, 1958-59, Korea. Lutheran. Mem. Hoboken (N.J.) Soccer Football. Home: 121 W Passaic Ave Bloomfield NJ 07003-4528 Office: 7800 River Rd North Bergen NJ 07047-6245

MARTH, MARY ELLEN (KIM MARTIN), entertainer; b. Atkinson, Minn., July 15, 1936; d. Sigvard B. Kanikkeberg and Beatrice M. (Lundberg) Wangen; m. T.A. Martinez (div.); m. Luther H. Marth (div.); children: Mitzie, Leslie, Tina, Allen. Entertainer The Kim Martin Show, 1960—; band leader Kim Martin Show, 1960—; real estate owner Marth Properties, Mpls., 1972—. Author of poems, songs, articles, short stories, childrens books, historian, humanitarian. Sec. Hennepin County Adult Foster Care, Mpls, 1983—; mem. Summit Ministries, Colo, 1995, Columbia Heights Owners Assn., 1990—, Multi-Housing Assn., Mpls, 1993—, Vesterheim Geneal. Mus., 1990, Norwegian Am. Mus., 1988—. Named Queen of Country Music, Country Entertainers Assn., Mpls., 1977, Entertainer of Yr. 1978, Female Vocalist of Yr., 1978, Best Band of Yr., 1979, Songwriter of Yr., 1980. Mem. Winnesheik Geneal. Soc., Filmore County Hist. Soc., Vesterheim Geneal. Soc., Minn. Historical Soc. Lutheran.

MARTHAK, KIRAN VITHAL, physician, researcher; b. Bombay; s. Vithaldas Ramji and Daya (Vithaldas) M.; m. Ketkj Kiran; 1 child, Vidhi. MBBS, U. Bombay, 1972, MD, 1978; DBM, Indian Mchts. Chamber, Mumbai, 1988; FFPP, U. London, 1992; diploma in Tb Diseases, Coll. Physicians & Surgeons, Bombay, 1972. Sr. med. advisor Hindustan Ciba-Geigy, Bombay, 1978-91; med. dir. German Remedies, Bombay, 1991-94, Tata Pharma, Bombay, 1994-95; v.p. clin. rsch. divsn. Pfizer Ltd., Bombay, 1995-97; v.p. med. clin. rsch. Ranbaxy Rsch. Lab., Delhi, India, 1998—; cons. BARC, Belgium, Genetica Ltd., Bombay, 1997-98, Orchid Healthcare Ltd., 1998-99. Editor Cepilepsy Jour. Recipient awards Am. Biog. Soc., 1998, 99. Fellow Coll. Chest Physicians, Internat. Coll. Angiology; mem. Natural History Soc. (life), AMAPI (pres. 1993-95), OPPI (med. com. 1999, rsch. and devel. com. 1999). Avocations: cricket, bird watching, reading. Home: A-603 Sejal Apts, New Link Rd, Andhery, Mumbai India Office: Ranbaxy Rsch Labs, Plgt # 20 Sector 18, Lidyoc Vihar Inds 122001, India

MARTI, ANDREAS, church musician, hymnology educator; b. Berne, Switzerland, Nov. 5, 1949; s. Walter and Katharina (Weber) M.; m. Rosmarie Dubach, Jan. 3, 1975; children: Benjamin D., Sophie K., Hanna J., Sara E., Eva D. Organ educator, Berne Conservatory, Switzerland, 1974, harpsichord educator, 1975; Verbi Divini Minister, U. Berne, Switzerland, 1976, ThD, 1981, titular prof., 1991. Organist, choir dir. Reformed Ch., Koeniz, Switzerland, 1974—; rector Kirchlich-Theologische Sch., Berne, Switzerland, 1977-89; hymnology and church music tchr. U. Berne, 1982—; hymnology and liturgy tchr. Musikhochschule, Berne, 1983—, Zürich, Switzerland, 1993—; dozent evangel. hymnologie U. Musik, Graz, Austria; mem. Swiss Reformed Hymnal Com., 1981-98; commr. on liturgy and hymnology Reformed Chs. of German Speaking Switzerland, 1989—, pres. liturgical commn., 1990—; pres. Internat. Fellowship for Rsch. on Hymnology, 1989-93. Author: (book) Cantatas of J.S. Bach (in German), 1981; musician: (compact disc) Johann Sebastian Bach: Die Choräle der Neumeister-Handschrift; contbr. numerous articles in religious music periodicals; harpsichord player: many discs. Mem. Ambassador Club Berne 1980. Mem. Social Dem. Party. Reformed Ch. of Switzerland. E-mail: andreas.marti@swissonline.ch. Home and Office: Koenizstrasse 252, CH-3097 Liebefeld Berne, Switzerland

MARTIKAINEN, A(UNE) HELEN, retired health education specialist; b. Harrison, Maine, May 11, 1916; d. Sylvester and Emma (Heikkinen) M. AB, Bates Coll., 1939, DSc (hon.), 1957; MPH, Yale U., 1941; DSc, Harvard U., 1964; DSc (hon.), Smith Coll., 1969. Health edn. sec. Hartford Tb and Pub. Health Assn., 1941-42; cons. USPHS, 1942-49; chief health edn. WHO, GEneva, 1949-74; chair intrenat. affairs N.C. divsn. AAUW, 1986-94. Hon. trustee Bridgton Acad., North Bridgton, Maine; mem. N.C. Women's Forum, 1984—; bd. dirs. N.C. Ctr. of Laws Affecting Women, Inc.; bd. dirs. West Triangle chpt. UNA-USA; chair resident's health and social svcs. com., mem. resident's coun. Carver Woods. Recipient Delta Omega award Yale U., Nat. Adminstrv. award Am. Acad. Phys. Edn., Key award Bates Coll., Internat. Svc. award, France, 1953, Prentiss medal, 1956, Spl. medal, cert. for internat. health edn. svc. Nat. Acad. Medicine for France, 1959, Profl. award Soc. Pub. Health Educators, 1963, Benjamin Elijah Mays award Bates Coll. Alumni Assn., 1989. Fellow APHA (chmn. health edn. sect., Excellence award 1969); mem. AAUW, LWV, Women's Internat. League for Peace and Freedom, U.S. Soc. Pub. Health Educators, Internat. Union Health Edn. (Parisot medal, tech. adviser), Acad. Phys. Edn. (assoc.), N.C. Coun. Women's Orgns. (mem. coun. assembly 1988-92, Women of Distinction award 1989), Phi Beta Kappa. Home: 3113 Carol Woods 750 Weaver Dairy Rd Chapel Hill NC 27514-1438

MARTIN, AGNES, artist; b. Maklin, Sask., Can., 1912; came to U.S., 1932, naturalized, 1950; Student, Western Wash. State Coll., 1935-38; BS, Columbia U., 1942, MFA, 1952. One-woman shows include Betty Parsons Gallery, N.Y.C., 1958, 59, 61, Robert Elkon Gallery, N.Y.C., 1961, 63, 72, 76, Nicolas Wilder Gallery, Los Angeles, 1963-66, 67, Visual Arts Ctr., N.Y.C., 1971, Kunstraum, Munich, 1973, Inst. Contemporary Art U. Pa., Phila., 1973, Pace Gallery, N.Y.C., 1975, 76, 77, 78, 79, 80-81, 81, 83, 84, 85, 86, 89, 91, 92, 94, 95, Mayor Gallery, London, 1978, 84, Galerie Rudolf Zwirner, Cologne, Fed. Republic Germany, 1978, Harcus/Krakow Gallery, Boston, 1978, Margo Leavin Gallery, Los Angeles, 1979, 85, Mus. N.Mex., Santa Fe, 1979, Richard Gray Gallery, Chgo., 1981, Garry Anderson Gallery, Sydney, Australia, 1986, Waddington Galleries Ltd., London, 1986, Stedelijk Mus., Amsterdam, 1991, Whitney Mus. Am. Art, N.Y.C., 1992; exhibited in group shows at Carnegie Inst., Pitts., 1961, Whitney Mus. Am. Art, N.Y.C., 1962, 66, 67, 74, 77, 92, Tooth Gallery, London, 1962, Gallery Modern Art, Washington, 1963, Wadsworth Atheneum, Hartford, Conn., 1963, Solomon R. Guggenheim Mus., N.Y.C., 1965, 66, 76, Mead Corp., 1965-67, Mus. Modern Art, N.Y.C., 1967, 76, 85, Inst. Contemporary Art, Phila., 1967, Detroit Inst. Art, 1967, Corcoran Gallery Art, Washington, 1967, 81, Finch Mus., N.Y., 1968, Phila. Mus., 1968, Zurich Art Mus., Switzerland, 1969, Ill. Bell Telephone Co., Chgo., 1970, Mus. Contemporary Art, Chgo., 1971, Inst. Contemporary Art U. Pa., Phila., 1972, Randolph-Macon Coll., N.C., 1972, Kassel, Fed. Republic Germany, 1972, Stedelijk Mus., Amsterdam, 1975, U. Mass., Amherst, 1976, Venice Biennale, Italy, 1976, 80, Cleve. Mus. Art, 1978, Albright-Knox Gallery, Buffalo, 1978, Inst. Contemporary Art, Boston, 1979, Art Inst. Chgo., 1979, San Francisco Mus. Modern Art, 1980, ROSC Internat. Art Exhbn., Dublin, Ireland, 1980, Marilyn Pearl Gallery, N.Y.C., 1983, Kemper Gallery, Kansas City Art Inst., 1985, Am. Acad. and Inst. Arts and Letters, N.Y.C., 1985, Charles Cowles Gallery, N.Y.C., 1986, Moody Gallery Art U. Ala., Birmingham, 1986, Butler Inst. Am. Art, 1986, Art Gallery Western Australia, Perth, 1986, Mus. Contemporary Art, Los Angeles, 1986, Boston Fine Arts Mus., 1989; represented in permanent collections Mus. of Modern Art, N.Y.C., Albright-Knox Gallery, Aldrich Mus., Ridgefield, Conn., Art Gallery Ont., Can., Australian Nat. Gallery, Canberra, Grey Art Gallery and Study Ctr., N.Y.C., Solomon R. Guggenheim Mus., High Mus. Art, Atlanta, Hirshhorn Mus. and Sculpture Garden, Washington, Israel Mus., Jerusalem, La Jolla (Calif.) Mus. Contemporary Art, Los Angeles County Mus. Art, Mus. Art R.I. Sch. Design, Providence, Mus. Modern Art, Neuegalerie der Stadt, Aachen, Fed. Republic Germany, Norton Simon Mus. Art at Pasadena, Calif., Stedelijk Mus., Amsterdam, The Netherlands, 1992, Mus. Modern Art, paris, 1992, Tate Gallery, London, Wadsworth Atheneum, Walker Art Ctr., Mpls., Whitney Mus. Am. Art, 1993, Sofia, Madrid, 1993, Huosten, 1993, Worcester (Mass.) Art Mus., Yale U. Art Gallery, New Haven; subject of various articles. Office: 414 Placitas Rd # 37 Taos NM 87571-2513

MARTIN, ALDEN JEFFREY, petrophysicist, geologist; b. Houston, Oct. 13, 1948; s. A.J. and Jessie Mae (Whittaker) M.; m. Marie Patricia Martin, Mar. 17, 1979. BS in Geology, Lamar U., 1970. Geologist Texaco, Inc., New Orleans, 1970-76; sr. staff engr. Conoco, Inc., Houston, 1976—. With U.S. Army, 1970-72. Mem. Soc. Profl. Well Log Analysts, Soc. Petroleum Engrs., Am. Assn. Petroleum Geologists. Methodist. Avocations: unpublished sci-fi author, golf, sailing, antique autos. E-mail: a-j-jeff.martin@usa.conoco.com and martimj@nstci.com. Home: PO Box 480 Fulshear TX 77441-0480

MARTIN, ALVARO, engineering company executive; b. Guadalajara, Mex., Feb. 9, 1967; s. Jose Martin and Cecilia Hernandez; m. Laura Garza. BS in Elec. Engring., ITESO, Guadalajara, 1989, MBA, 1998. Buyer Hewlett Packard, Guadalajara, 1989-91; buyer AT&T, Guadalajara, 1991-93, sr. buyer, 1993-95; purchasing mgr. Lucent Techs., Guadalajara, 1995-98; mgr., global purchasing Lucent Techs., Eatontown, N.J., 1998-2000, VTech Innovations, L.P., Eatontown, 2000—. E-mail: amartin@aatphones.com. Office: VTech Innovations LP 246 Industrial Way W Eatontown NJ 07724-2206

MARTIN, ANDREW AYERS, lawyer, physician, educator; b. Toccoa, Ga., Aug. 18, 1958; s. Wallace Ford and Dorothy LaTranquil (Ayers) M.; children: William Ayers, Malorie Ayers. BA, Emory U., Atlanta, 1980, MD, 1984; JD, Duke U., 1988. Bar: Calif. 1989, La. 1990, D.C. 1991; diplomate Am. Bd. Pathology, Nat. Bd. Med. Examiners; lic. physician, La., Miss., Ark. Intern in pediatrics Emory U./Grady Meml. Hosp., Atlanta, 1984; intern Tulane U./Charity Hosp., New Orleans, 1989-90, resident in anatomic and clin. pathology, 1990-94; surg. pathology fellow Baylor Coll. Medicine, Houston, 1994-95; law clk. Ogletree, Deakins, Smoak, Stewart, Greenville, S.C., summer 1986, Thelen Marrin Johnson Bridges, L.A., summer 1987, Duke Hosp. Risk Mgmt., 1987-88; assoc. Haight Brown Bonesteel, Santa Monica, Calif., 1988; pvt. practice L.A., 1989; physician/atty. Tulane Med. Ctr./Charity Hosp., New Orleans, 1989-94, Baylor Coll. Medicine/Tex. Med. Ctr., Houston, 1994-95; lab. dir. King's Daus. Hosp., Greenville, Miss., 1995—; asst. clin. prof. pathology Tulane U.; lab. dir., owner Vicksburg Pathology Lab., Bolivar Med. Ctr., Cleveland, Miss.; staff pathologist Delta Regional Ctr., Greenville, Miss., N.W. Miss. Regional Medical Ctr., Clarksdale, Miss., No. Sunflower County Hosp., Ruteville, Miss., Tallahatchie County Hosp., Charleston, Miss.; sr. ptnr. Mid-South Pathology Assocs.; med. dir. of labs. Vicksburg Pathology Lab., N.W. Miss. Regional Med. Ctr., Bolivar Med. Ctr., Delta Regional Med. Ctr., North Sunflower County Hosp., 1997—, Tallahatchie (Miss.) County Hosp., N.W. Miss. Regional Med. Ctr., Clarksdale, Lab Corp., Southaven, Miss., Tallahatchie County Hosp.; adj. faculty Moorhead U.; bd. dirs. Martin Bldrs., Inc., Toccoa; mem. AIDS Legis. Task Force for La.; case cons. Office of Tech. Assessment, Washington; tech. cons. and autopsy extra Oliver Stone's "JFK"; adj. clin. faculty Moorhead Coll. Contbr. articles to profl. jours.; author: Reflections on Rusted Chrome (book of poetry). Fellow Coll. Am. Pathologists, Coll. Legal Medicine, La. State Med. Soc. (del. meeting 1992-93). Home: 935 Lakehall Rd Lake Village AR 71653-6096 also: 4104 Alabama Ave Kenner LA 70065-5603 also: 3850 Old Highway 27 Vicksburg MS 39180-8829 Office: Mid-South Pathology Assocs PO Box 5880 Greenville MS 38704-5880

MARTIN, ANDREW READ, paper company researcher; b. Manhasset, N.Y., Nov. 27, 1968; s. Lawrence Thomas and Elizabeth (Read) M.; m. Eva Viktoria Oberg, May 4, 1996. BSME, U. Fla., 1991, MSME, 1993, PhD, 1997. Engr.-in-tng. Gen. Dynamics/Elec. Boat Divsn., Groton, Conn., 1988-90; rsch. & tng. asst. U. Fla. Dept. Mech. Engring., Gainesville, 1991-97; rsch. assoc. Royal Inst. Tech., Stockholm, 1999, Swedish Pulp & Paper Rsch. Inst., Stockholm, 1999—; guest rschr. Royal Inst. Tech., 1998. Contbr. articles to profl. jours. Postdoctoral fellow Wenner-Gren Found. Scientific Rsch., Stockholm, 1998; grad. fellow GE Corp., 1995. Mem. ASME, Sigma Xi. Office: Swedish Pulp & Paper Rsch, PO Box 5604, S-114 86 Stockholm Sweden

MARTIN, ARCHER JOHN PORTER, retired chemistry educator; b. London, Mar. 1, 1910; s. William Archer Porter and Lilian Kate (Brown) M.; m. Judith Bagenal, Jan. 9, 1943; 5 children. Student, Peterhouse, Cambridge, Eng., 1929-32, MA, 1936; PhD, DSc, Leeds U., 1968; LLD (hon.), U. Glasgow, Scotland, 1973; laurea honoris causa, U. Urbino, Italy, 1985. Chemist Nutritional Lab., Cambridge, 1933-38, Wool Industries Rsch. Assn., Leeds, 1938-46; mem. rsch. dept. Boots Pure Drug Co., Nottingham, Eng., 1946-48; mem. staff Med. Rsch. Coun., 1948-52; head phys. chemistry div. Nat. Inst. Med. Rsch., Mill Hill, 1952-56; chem. cons., 1956-59; dir. Abbotsbury (Eng.) Labs. Ltd., 1959-73; profl. fellow U. Sussex, Eng., 1973-77; Robert A. Welch prof. chemistry U. Houston, 1974-78; guest prof. Ecole Polytechnique Fed. de Lausanne, Switzerland, 1980-85; cons. Wellcome Rsch. Labs., Beckenham, Eng., 1970-73; Extraordinary prof. Tech. U., Eindhoven, The Netherlands, 1965-74. Decorated comdr. Brit. Empire; Order of Rising Sun Japan; recipient Berzelius Gold medal Swedish Med. Soc., 1951, Nobel prize chemistry (with R.L.M. Synge) for invention of partition chromatography, 1952, John Scott award, 1958, John Price Wetherill medal, 1959, Franklin Inst. medal, 1959, Koltoff medal Acad. Pharm. Sci., 1969, Callendar medal Inst. Measurement & Control, 1971, Fritz-Pregl medal Austrian Chemical Soc., 1985. Fellow Royal Soc. (Leverhulme medal 1964). Club: Chemist's (N.Y.C.) (hon.). *

MARTIN, BETTY I., materials manager; b. Carmel, Calif., July 26, 1946; d. Carl Franklin and Evelyn Pearl Knapp; m. Thomas C. Baxter, Aug. 1986 (dec. Oct. 1997); children: Evelyn Lenore Coffee, Diana Jean Martin. BS, U. Tex., 1979. Cert. purchasing mgr. From buyer to sr. buyer Occidental Chem., Houston, 1973-79; materials mgr. L.R. Williams, Inc., Stockton, Calif., 1980-82, Anicom, Inc., Corona, Calif., 1998—; with B&H Mfg., Ceres, Calif., 1982-86; purchasing mgr. C.S.T. Autoweigh, Modesto, Calif., 1986-95; purchasing agt. Youngs Market Co., Orange, Calif., 1995-98. Mem. Nat. Assn. Purchasing Mgrs. (bd. dirs. 1986, founding newsletter editor 1988-89). Home: PO Box 7072 Riverside CA 92513-7072

MARTIN, CLAUDE RAYMOND, JR., marketing consultant, educator; b. Harrisburg, Pa., May 11, 1932; s. Claude R. and Marie Teresa (Stapf) M.; m. Marie Frances Culkin, Nov. 16, 1957; children: Elizabeth Ann, David Jude, Nancy Marie, William Jude, Patrick Jude, Cecelia Marie. B.S., U. Scranton, 1954, M.B.A, 1963; Ph.D., Columbia U., 1969. Newsman Sta. WILK-TV, Wilkes-Barre, Pa., 1953-55; news dir. Sta. WNEP-TV, Scranton, Pa., 1955-60; dir. systems Blue Cross & Blue Shield Ins., Wilkes-Barre, 1960-63; lectr. mktg. St. Francis Coll., Bklyn., 1964, U. Mich., Ann Arbor, 1965-68; asst. prof. U. Mich., 1968-73, asso. prof., 1973-77, prof., 1977-80, Isadore and Leon Winkelman prof. retail mktg., 1980—, chmn. mktg. dept., 1986-90; bd. dirs. Perry Drug Stores, cons. mktg., 1983-89; spl. cons. on rsch. changes in U.S. currency Fed. Res. Sys., 1978—; pub. mem. Nat. Advt. Rev. Bd., 1989-94. Contbr. articles on mktg. analysis, consumer research to profl. publs. Trustee U. Scranton, 1996—. Served with USNR, 1955-57. Mem. Acad. Mktg. Sci., Am. Mktg. Assn., S.W. Mktg. Assn., Bank Mktg. Assn., Assn. Consumer Research, Am. Collegiate Retailing Assn., Am. Acad. Advt. Roman Catholic. Home: 1116 Aberdeen Dr Ann Arbor MI 48104-2812

MARTIN, CLYDE VERNE, psychiatrist; b. Coffeyville, Kans., Apr. 7, 1933; s. Howard Verne and Elfrieda Louise (Moehn) M.; m. Barbara Jean McNeilly, June 24, 1956; children: Kent Clyde, Kristin Claire, Kerry Constance, Kyle Curtis. Student Coffeyville Coll., 1951-52; AB, U. Kans., 1955; MD, 1958; MA, Webster Coll., St. Louis, 1977; JD, Thomas Jefferson Coll. Law, Los Angeles, 1985. Diplomate Am. Bd. Psychiatry and Neurology. Intern, Lewis Gale Hosp., Roanoke, Va., 1958-59; resident in psychiatry U. Kans. Med. Ctr., Kansas City, 1959-62, Fresno br. U. Calif.-San Francisco, 1978; staff psychiatrist Neurol. Hosp., Kansas City, 1962; practice medicine specializing in psychiatry, Kansas City, Mo., 1964-84; founder, med. dir., pres. bd. dirs. Mid-Continent Psychiat. Hosp., Olathe, Kans., 1972-84; adj. prof. psychology Baker U., Baldwin City, Kans., 1969-84; staff psychiatrist Atascadero State Hosp., Calif., 1984-85; clin. prof. psychiatry U. Calif., San Francisco, 1985—; chief psychiatrist Calif. Med. Facility, Vacaville, 1985-87; pres., editor Corrective and Social Psychiatry, Olathe, 1970-84, Atascadero, 1984-85, Fairfield, 1985-97. Contbr. articles to profl. jours. Bd. dirs. Meth. Youthville, Newton, Kans. 1965-75, Spofford Home, Kansas City, 1974-78. Served to capt. USAF, 1962-64, ret. col. USAFR. Oxford Law & Soc. scholar, 1993. Fellow Am. Psychiat. Assn. (life), Royal Soc. Health (London), Am. Assn. Mental Health Profls. in Corrections, World Assn. Social Psychiatry, Am. Orthopsychiat. Assn.; mem. AMA, Assn. for Advancement Psychotherapy, Am. Assn. Sex Educators, Counselors and Therapists (cert.), Assn. Mental Health Adminstrs. (cert.), Marines Meml. Club, San Francisco, Capitol Hill Club, Washington D.C., St. James Club, London, Phi Beta Pi, Pi Kappa Alpha. Methodist (del. Kans. East Conf. 1972-80, bd. global ministries 1974-80). Office: PO Box 3365 Fairfield CA 94533-0587

MARTIN, DALLAS REA, lawyer; b. Kansas City, Kans., Aug. 3, 1954; s. H. Thayne and Frances Colleen Martin; m. Lianne Marie Taylor, June 2, 1979; 1 child, Elise Taylor. BA in Philosophy with distinction, U. Kans., Lawrence, 1976, JD, 1979. Bar: Kans. 1979, U.S. Dist. Ct. Kans., 1979, U.S. Ct. Appeals (10th cir.) 1979, Colo. 1985, U.S. Dist. Ct. Colo. 1985. Pvt. practice Olathe, Kans., 1979-81; contracts counsel Midwest Rsch. Inst., Kansas City, Mo., 1981-84; counsel and contracts mgr. Precision Visuals, Inc., Boulder, Colo., 1984-90; mgr. tech. transfer Nat. Renewable Energy Lab., Golden, Colo., 1990-94; dir. intellectual property U.S. West Advt. Tech., Inc., Boulder, 1994-97; sr. counsel intellectual property First Data Corp., Englewood, Colo., 1997—. Contbr. articles to profl. jours. Bd. dirs. Blue Knights, Inc., Denver, 1997—. Mem. ABA (intellectual property sect. 1991—), Tech. Transfer Soc. (bd. dirs. 1996-98), Licensing Execs. Soc. (symposium com. 1998—). Office: First Data Corp 6200 S Quebec St Englewood CO 80111-4729

MARTIN, DANIEL C., surgeon, gynecologist, educator; b. St. Louis, Apr. 7, 1946; s. Dan Allen and Ruth Keel (Fields) M.; m. Glenn Ann Blakemore, July 7, 1970; children: Josh, Adam. BS in Physics, Emory U., 1968, MD, 1972. Diplomate Am. Bd. Ob-Gyn. Rsch. asst. physics and radiology Emory U., Atlanta, 1968-69; intern, resident, fellow, instr. The Johns Hopkins Med. Instns., Balt., 1972-77; from asst. prof. to clin. asst. prof. U. Tenn., Memphis, 1977-90, clin. assoc. prof., 1990—; surgeon Reproductive Surgery, P.C., Memphis, 1977—; gynecologist, reproductive surgeon Bapt. Meml. Hosp., 1977—; Axel Munthe presenter, Naples, Italy, 1992; guest spkr. 15th Annual Japanese Endometrosis Symposium, Osaka, 1994; dir. gynecologic laser and endoscopy workshops, 1982-93. Editor: (textbooks) Lasers in Endoscopy, 1990, Laparoscopic Appearance of Endometriosis, 1990, Manual of Endoscopy, 1990, Atlas of Endometriosis, 1993, Endoscopic Management of Gynecologic Disease, 1996. Basketball coach Grace St. Luke's Ch., Memphis, 1992-95. Picker Found. fellow Emory U., 1969; Tex. Assn. Ob-Gyn. hon. fellow, 1989; recipient Bridges trophy for athletics Emory U., 1968, Codman surg. award, 1982, 83, Video award Am. Fertility Soc., 1992, Physician Recognition awrd Endometriosis Assn., 1995; named one of Best Drs. Am. Woodward and White Inc., 1992, 94, 96, 98, Hon. mem. Australian Gynecol. Endoscopy Soc., 1993. Mem. ACOG (sect. chair jr. fellows Md.), Tenn. Med. Assn., Memphis and Shelby County Med. Soc. (comm. com.), Am. Nat. Std. Inst. (subcom. on laser safety in med. facility), Am. Assn. Gynecol. Laparoscopists (pres. 1990-91, Videoendoscopy award 1993), Gynecologic Surgery Soc. (pres. 1994-96, chmn. bd. 1996-98), Australian Gynecol. Endoscopy Soc. (hon.), Argentinian Ob-Gyn. Soc. (hon.). Office: Reproductive Surgery PC 1717 Kirby Pkwy Ste 100 Memphis TN 38120-4331

MARTIN, DARRYL JAMES, audio-visual specialist; b. St. Albans, N.Y., Sept. 4, 1950; s. Sydney and Helen Martin; m. Theresa McCarthy, July 29, 1978 (div. 1986); children: Jamielynn, Kristina Marie. Student in bus. adminstrn., Nassau C.C., 1971-73; assoc. in fire Svc. Acad., 1971-78; paramedic tng. in advanced cardiac care, St. Francis Hosp., Roslyn, N.Y., 1973-77; BA in Audio Visual Tech., N.Y. Inst. Tech., 1975; M in Computer Sci. and Tech., U. Berkeley, 1999. Audio-visual coord. Farmingdale (N.Y.) Pub. Schs., 1971-79; dir. audio-visual svcs. Bethpage (N.Y.) Pub. Schs., 1979—; audio-visual coord. evening classes C.W. Post Coll., L.I.U., Green Vale, N.Y., 1982-85, lead call ctr. ops. Cablevision L.I., 1996—. Author: Security Procedures for An Educational Institution, 19981, Poems of the Heart, 1990, Class of 68, 1991, Suffer In Silence, 1999. Engine capt. Bethpage Fire Dept., 1972-82. With U.S. Army, 1968-71. Mem. Nat. Assn. Ednl. Radio, N.Y. State Ednl. Comm. Assn., Nat. Audio Visual Assn. Home: 36 Acme Ave Bethpage NY 11714-4610 Office: Bethpage Pub Schs Adminstrn Bldg Cherry Ave Bethpage NY 11714

MARTIN, DIDIER HERMAN, neurosurgeon, researcher; b. Verviers, Liège, Belgium, Sept. 19, 1961; s. Eugene Rodolphe and Edith Maria (Lecoq) M.; m. Mireille Justine Delacollette, Sept. 12, 1987; children: François, Guillaume, Renaud. MD, U. Liège, Belgium, 1986; Neurosurgeon, U. Liège, 1992, PhD, 1992. Aspirant splst. U. Liège, 1986-90; cons. rsch. on spinal cord injury, 1990—; splst. adj. U. Liège, 1994-96, chef de clinique assoc., 1996—, maitre conf., 1997—; aspirant FNRS, Belgium, 1990-92, chargé de recherche, 1992-94. Author: La Paraplegie Traumatique, 1992; contbr. articles to profl. jours. Recipient prize Fondation Van Goethem Brichant, 1989, annual prize Fondation Paul et Philippe Martin, 1993, FNRS prize Pharmacia & Upjohn Co., 1996. Mem. Belgium Neurosurg. Soc., French Speaking Neurosug. Soc. Office: U Liége Univ Hosp, B35 Neurosurgery, B-4000 Liége Liége, Belgium

MARTIN, DONALD JAMES, marketing professional; b. Brantford, Ont., Can., May 2, 1928; s. Norman Wilfred and Leeta Maude (Woodley) M.; m. Annette Roselyn Mills, Aug. 25, 1952; children: Paul Stuart, Cheryl Anne. PhB, Northwestern U., 1964; postgrad., U. Chgo., 1965-66. Account rep. J. Walter Thompson, Toronto, Can., 1951-56; supr. mgmt. J. Walter Thompson, Sao Paulo, Brazil, 1956-60; v.p. J. Walter Thompson, Chgo., 1960-66; dir. corp. rels. Kraft, Inc., N.Y.C., Chgo., 1966-73; v.p. external affairs Scott Paper, Phila., 1973-76; v.p. com.. Conrail, Phila., 1976-79; pres. Rennoc Corp., Vineland, N.J., 1979-84, Martin Broadcasting Inc., Vineland, 1979-84; v.p. internat. paper real estate Hilton Head Island, S.C., 1979-84; pres. Marcom Inc., S.C., 1989—; talk show host Sta. WHHI-TV, 1992—; instr. internat. mktg. Northwestern U., Evanston, Ill., 1964-66; prof. broadcast mgmt. Mercer (N.J.) Coll., 1980-83; dir. Broadcast Pioneers Am.. Mgr. Hilton Head Concert Orch., 1985-89; exec. prodr. summer festival Hilton Head Eastman Sch. Music, 1986-89; bd. dirs. Hilton Head Dance Theater,

1986, 87, Cultural Coun. Hilton Head Island, 1987-90; mem. cmty. adv. bd. Hilton Head Med. Ctr. Clinics, 1995—; actor Hilton Head Playhouse. Recipient Svc. Appreciation award Sunshine Found., 1979, Outstanding Media award United Way, 1998. Mem. Rotary (Svc. Above Self award 1992-93), S. C. Yacht Club. Avocations: tennis, sailing, acting. Office: WHHI-TV Courtyard Building Ste 103 Hilton Head Island SC 29928-4637

MARTIN, DONALD WALTER, author, publisher; b. Grants Pass, Oreg., Apr. 22, 1934; s. George E. and Irma Ann (Dallas) M.; m. Kathleen Elizabeth Murphy, July, 1970 (div. May 1979); children: Daniel Clayton, Kimberly Ann; m. Betty Woo, Mar. 18, 1985. Enlisted USMC, 1952; advanced through grades to staff sgt. USMC, Japan, Republic of Korea, Republic of China, 1956-61; reporter Blade-Tribune, Oceanside, Calif., 1961-65; entertainment editor Press-Courier, Oxnard, Calif., 1965-69; mng. editor Argus-Courier, Petaluma, Calif., 1969-70; assoc. editor Motorland mag., San Francisco, 1970-88; founder, prin., CEO Pine Cone Press, Inc., Columbia, Calif., 1988—. Author: Best of San Francisco, 1986, 90, 94, Best of the Gold Country, 1987, 92, San Francisco's Ultimate Dining Guide, 1988, Inside Francisco, 1991, Best of the Wine Country, 1991, 95, 00, Oregon Discovery Guide, 1993, 95, 96, Northern California Discovery Guide, 1993, The Ultimate Wine Book, 1993, 00, Washington Discovery Guide, 1994, Utah Discovery Guide, 1995, Adventure Cruising, 1996, Arizona Discovery Guide, 1996, Arizona in Your Future, 1991, 93, 97, The Toll-Free Traveler, 1997, Las Vegas: The Best of Glitter City, 1997, 98, 00, New Mexico Discovery Guide, 1998, California-Nevada Roads Less Traveled, 1999, San Diego: The Best of Sunshine City, 1999, Nevada in Your Future, 2000, Seattle: The Best of Emerald City, 2000. Recipient Diane Seely award Ventura County Theatre Council, 1968. Mem. Soc. Am. Travel Writers. Republican. Avocations: traveling, hiking, white water rafting, biking. Home: 631 Stephanie St PMB 138 Henderson NV 89014-2633

MARTIN, DONALD WILLIAM, psychiatrist; b. Columbus, Ohio, Aug. 13, 1921; s. Olin R. and Clara (Jahraus) M.; m. Clara Jane Jones, June 23, 1951; children: Jennifer Christine, David Lawrence. B.A., Ohio State U., 1942, M.D., 1944. Diplomate: Am. Bd. Psychiatry and Neurology. Intern Met. Hosp., N.Y.C., 1944-45; resident psychiatrist Kings Park (N.Y.) State Hosp., 1945-46, sr. psychiatrist, 1948-49; supervising psychiatrist Central Islip (N.Y.) State Hosp., 1950-56; staff psychiatrist Summit County Receiving Hosp. (name now Fallsview Psy. Hosp.), Cuyahoga Falls, Ohio, 1956-59; supt. Summit County Receiving Hosp. (name now Fallsview Psy. Hosp.), 1959-63; dir. Pontiac (Mich.) State Hosp. (name now Clinton Valley Center), 1963-79; pvt. practice cons. psychiatry, 1979-90, ret., 1990. Served from 1st lt. to capt. M.C., U.S. Army, 1946-48. Fellow Am. Psychiat. Assn. (life). Home: care David L Martin 12216 11th Dr SE Everett WA 98208-5919

MARTIN, EARIN MILLER, grant administrator, program director, educator, trainer; b. Austin, Tex., July 6, 1952; d. Alse Edward Jr. and Wilma Nell (Maufrais) Ethridge; m. Paul Chapman Goggan, Jan. 11, 1975 (div. Nov. 1982); m. Bobby Lee Martin, May 24, 1986. BA, S.W. Tex. State U., 1974; MA, U. Tex., 1987, EdD, 1996. Cert. English and sociology tchr., Tex. Tchr. aide, tchr. English Irving (Tex.) Ind. Sch. Dist., 1976-78; tchr. English Frenship Ind. Sch. Dist., Wolfforth, Tex., 1978-79; staff asst. Farm Credit Banks Tex., Austin, 1982-85, tng. specialist, 1985-87; fiscal program specialist II Tex. Edn. Agy., Austin, 1987-90, ednl. program dir., 1990, dir. programs II, 1990-98, assoc. sr. dir., 1998-99, sr. dir., 1999—; strategic planning com. Tex. Edn. Agy., 1994—, bus. reingineering task force, 1995—, coord. funding adv. com., 1997—; chairperson Title VI Nat. Steering Com., 1996-98. Recipient fellowship Alexander Caswell Ellis, 1986-87. Mem. ASCD, Phi Kappa Phi, Kappa Delta Pi, Phi Delta Kappa. Methodist. Avocations: water sports, gardening, reading, writing. Home: 5301 Waterbrook Dr Austin TX 78723-4042

MARTIN, EDWARD BRIAN, electrical engineer; b. Lawrence, Kans., Feb. 9, 1936; s. Edward Brian and Dorothy Irene (Dowers) M.; m. Sharon Anne Zimmerman, Dec. 21, 1955; children: Terry Brian, Ricky Lynn, Mindy Anne, Timothy Alan. BSEE, U. Kans., 1958; MSEE, St. Louis U., 1969. Registered profl. engr., Mo. Program mgr. McDonnell Douglas, St. Louis, 1980-85, mgr. avionics, 1985-86, dir. engring., 1986-88, dir. electronics, 1988-89, sr. dir. tech. processes, 1989-91, sr. dir. avionics tech., 1991-92, dir. advanced missile systems, 1992-95, dir. advanced weapon systems, 1995-97; dir. advanced tactical missiles The Boeing Co., 1997—; chmn. bd. dirs. Martin Internat., Ltd. Contbr. numerous articles to profl. jours. Pres. PTA, St. Louis, 1972; founder Martin Family Found. Mem. AIAA. Avocations: running, mountain climbing, writing. Home: 5335 Lancelot Dr Saint Charles MO 63304-5742

MARTIN, ERNEST LEE, academic administrator, historian, theologian, writer; b. Meeker, Okla., Apr. 20, 1932; s. Joel Chester and Lula Mae (Quinn) M.; m. Helen Rose Smith, Aug. 26, 1957 (div. 1980); children: Kathryn, Phyllis, Samuel; m. Ramona Jean Kinsey, June 27, 1987. BA, Ambassador U., 1958, MA, 1960, PhD, 1966. Dean faculty Ambassador U., St. Albans, Eng., 1965-72; chmn. dept. theology Ambassador U., Pasadena, Calif., 1972-74; dir. Found. for Bibl. Rsch., Pasadena, 1974-84, Acad. for Scriptural Knowledge, Portland, 1985—; dir. 450 coll. students with Prof. Benjamin Mazar Herodian Western Wall archaeol. excavations, Jerusalem, 1969-74. Author: Birth of Christ Recalculated, 1978, 2d edit., 1980, The Original Bible Restored, 1984, Secrets of Golgotha, 1987, 2d edit., 1996, The Star That Astonished the World, 1996, 101 Bible Secrets That Christians Do Not Know, 1993, The People That History Forgot, 1993, The Place of the New Third Temple, 1994, Restoring the Original Bible, 1994, The Biblical Manual, 1995, ABC's of the Gospel, 1997, The Essentials of New Testament Doctrine, 1999, The Temples that Jerusalem Forgot, 1999, Angels-The Fictions and the Facts, 2000. Tech. sgt. USAF, 1950-54, USAR, 1950. Mem. Soc. Bibl. Lit. (advisor to Original Bible Project), Planetarium Soc. E-mail: doctor@askelm.com. Home: PO Box 25000 Portland OR 97298-0990 Office: Assocs Scriptural Knowledge 4804 SW Scholls Ferry Rd Portland OR 97225-1668

MARTIN, EVA VIKTORIA, research scientist; b. Luleå, Sweden, June 13, 1968; d. Karl Yngve and Hulda Ingegerd (Karlsson) Öberg; m. Andrew Read Martin, May 4, 1996. MS, Royal Inst. Tech., Stockholm, 1993; PhD, U. Fla., 1998. Rsch. and tchg. asst. U. Fla., Gainesville, 1993-98; rsch. assoc. Royal Inst. Tech., Stockholm, Sweden, 1998—. Contbr. articles to profl. jours. Recipient John and Barbara Yellott award, Am. Solar Energy Soc., Washington, 1997. Mem. ASME, Internat. Solar Energy Soc., Sigma Xi. Office: Royal Inst Tech, Teknikringen 50, SE100-44 Stockholm Sweden

MARTIN, GARY J., retired business executive, mayor; b. Des Moines, Feb. 8, 1937; s. William Carl Martin and Mary Louise (Festner) Sweeney; m. Carolyn J. Karau, July 28, 1956; children: Victoria, Cheryl, Dennis. BBA, Marquette U., 1972. CPA Wis., 1973. Mfr. GM, Milw., 1957-68, engring. mgr., 1968-73; CFO Miller Brewing Co., Milw., 1974-76, dir. corp. planning, 1977-78; pres. Better Brands of N.Y., N.Y.C., 1978-79; exec. v.p. Seven Up Co., St. Louis, 1979-85; v.p. mktg. Schenley Industries, Dallas, 1985-86; cons. Martin & Assocs., Dallas, 1986-89; mayor Osage Beach, Mo., 1992-95. Bd. dirs. Family Hosp., Milw., 1976-78; mem. lay bd. St. Mary Health Ctr., St. Louis, 1980-85. With USN, 1954-57. Avocations: computers, boating, golfing, travel. Home: 2349 Fairskies Dr Spring Hill FL 34606-7257

MARTIN, GUNTHER, writer, translator; b. Rodaun, Austria, Dec. 12, 1928; s. Hans and Marie (Schretter) M.; m. Otti Haltrich, Mar. 4, 1960; children: Ruediger, Gudrun. Diplome, Sem. Sch. Photography, 1951. Journalist various profl. papers, Vienna, Austria, 1953-59; freelance writer Vienna, Salzburg, Austria, 1961—. Author: Das Silberne Viles, 1970, 78, Als Victorianer in Wien, 1984, Hietzinger Geschichten, 1989, Loden-Brevier, 1993, Prominent in Salzburg, 1998, Boging, Chanel & Co., 2000, others; translator: circa 40 books; editor 5 books. Recipient medal of Merit for preservation cultural monuments Fed. Min. Culture, 1976, ofcl. hon. title Prof., 1984, Golden Cross of Merit, Lower Austria, 1985, Silver Star Hon., Vienna, 1998. Conservative. Roman Catholic. Home: Altmannsdorfer Strasse 164/12/17, A-1230 Vienna Austria Other: Hoeglwoerthweg 55, A-5020, Salzburg, Austria

MARTIN, GUY, chemist, educator; b. Combourg, France, Sept. 5, 1934; s. René Martin; m. Marie José Le Louer, Aug. 8, 1960; 1 child, Nathalie. Grad., U. Rennes (France), 1960, Doctorate, 1966. Prof. chemistry U. Rennes, 1968-94; ind. cons., 1994—; cons. Inst. Tech. Gaz et Air, 1965. Author: Azote, 1979, Point sur Epuration, 1-2-3, 1982—, Odeurs et desodorisation, 1991, Odors and Deodorization, 1994; contbr. articles to profl. jours. Mem. Internat. Ozone Assn. (hon.). Avocation: painting. Home: 34 rue des Lauriers, 35510 Cesson-Sévigné France

MARTIN, JAMES GRUBBS, medical executive, former governor; b. Savannah, Ga., Dec. 11, 1935; s. Arthur Morrison and Mary Julia (Grubbs) M.; m. Dorothy Ann McAulay, June 1, 1957; children: James Grubbs, Emily Wood, Arthur Benson. BS, Davidson Coll., 1957; PhD, Princeton U., 1960. Assoc. prof. chemistry Davidson (N.C.) Coll., 1960-72; mem. 93d to 98th Congresses from N.C., 1973-85; gov. State of N.C., 1985-92; v.p. Carolinas HealthCare System, Charlotte, N.C., 1993—; mem. Mecklenburg (N.C.) Bd. County Commrs., 1966-72, chmn., 1967-68, 70-71; pres. N.C. Assn. County Commrs., 1970-71; mem., tuba player Charlotte Symphony, 1961-66; dir. J.A. Jones Constrn., Family Dollar Stores, Inc., Duke Energy Co., Applied Analytical Industries, Inc., Palomar Med. Technologies, Inc. Chmn. Global TransPark Found., 1993—; trustee Davidson Coll., 1998—. Danforth fellow, 1957-60. Mem. Beta Theta Pi (v.p., trustee 1966-69, pres. 1975-78), Masons (33 deg.), Shriners. Presbyterian. Office: Carolinas Med Ctr PO Box 32861 Charlotte NC 28232-2861

MARTIN, JAMES VICTOR, JR., foreign service officer, writer; b. Tokyo, Nov. 15, 1916; (parents Am. citizens); s. James Victor Sr. and Esther Belle (Ludwig) M.; m. Elizabeth Shaler Smith, June 28, 1941; children: Sarah Martin Brown, Susan P. Martin, David Ludwig Martin. BA, DePauw U., 1938; MA, Tufts U., 1939, PhD, 1948; postgrad. in Japanese lang., Harvard U., 1941-42, Yale U., 1948-49. Vice consul U.S. Consulate Gen., Bombay, 1946-48; polit. officer, head transl. sect. Office of Polit. Adviser, Tokyo, 1949-50; econ. officer U.S. Consulate Gen., Kobe-Osaka, Japan, 1951-53; prin. officer U.S. Consulate, Fukuoka, Japan, 1953-56; officer-in-charge Japanese Affairs U.S. Dept. State, Washington, 1956-58, personnel planning staff, 1958-61; chief polit. sect. U.S. Embassy, Rangoon, Burma, 1962-64; U.S. polit. adviser Office of U.S. High Commn. to the Ryukyu Islands, Okinawa, 1964-67; polit. counselor U.S. Embassy, Canberra, Australia, 1968-70; country dir. for Australia, N.Z. and Pacific Islands, U.S. Dept. State, Washington, 1970-73; lectr. Far East internat. rels. Am. U., Washington, summer 1961; occasional lectr. U.S. Asian policy U. Md. Extension, Okinawa, 1965-67; cons. Pacific Islands, U.S. Dept. of Interior, Washington, 1973-74. Contbr. articles to profl. jours. Trustee Japan-Am. Soc. Washington, Inc., 1982-89; bd. dirs. Com. for Community Democracies-U.S.A., Washington, 1983-92, v.p., 1986-87; sec., treas. Com. for Community of Democracies (D.C.), Washington, 1985-88. Lt. USN, 1941-46, PTO. Mem. Assn. for Asian Studies, Mid-Atlantic Region Chpt. Assn. for Asian Studies (treas. 1972-76), Washington and Southeast Region Seminar on Japan, Diplomatic and Consular Officers Ret. Methodist. Avocations: painting, woodblock printing, photography.

MARTIN, JAY GRIFFITH, lawyer; b. Washington, Oct. 13, 1951; s. Drexel Reese and Joyce (Towne) M.; 1 child, Trevor. BBA, So. Meth. U., 1973, MPA, 1976, JD, 1976. Bar: Tex., D.C., U.S. Ct. Appeals (5th cir.), U.S. Dist. Ct. (so. dist.) Tex., U.S. Dist. Ct. D.C., U.S. Supreme Ct. Counsel Pennzoil Co., Houston, 1976-78, sr. counsel, 1978-81; divsn. counsel The Superior Oil Co., Houston, 1981-85; sr. counsel Mobil Natural Gas, Houston, 1985-87, gen. counsel, 1987-91; asst. gen. counsel Mobil Oil Corp., Fairfax, Va., 1991-96; ptnr. Andrews & Kurth LLP, Washington, 1996-2000, Phelps Dunbar LLP, Houston, 2000—; mem. sr. adv. bd. Bus. Laws Inc., Chesterland, Ohio, 1997—; mem. adv. bd. Inst. Transnat. Arbitration, Southwestern Legal Found., 1996—. Author: International Arbitration, 1998; contbr. articles to profl. law jours.; mem. adv. bd. Natural Gas Contracts, 1991—. Chair fundraising com. So. Meth. U., Washington, 1996-97, mem. dean's adv. coun. So. Meth. U. Sch. Law, 1995—. Named one of World's Leading Energy and Natural Resources Lawyers, Euromoney, 1997-99. Fellow Tex. Bar Found.; mem. Tex. Bar Assn., State Bar of Tex. (chmn. corp. counsel sect. 1990-91, adv. bd. 1985—), State Bar Coll. of Tex., D.C. Bar Assn. (internat. sect.), Internat. Bar Assn. (sect. energy and natural resources 1994—), Fed. Energy Bar Assn. (chmn. antitrust sect. 1986-87, chmn. internat. energy com. 1998-99), ABA (exec. coun., budget chmn. sect. on environment, energy and law 1996—, chmn. natural resources, energy and environ. law internat. energy com. 1996-98, sr. liaison oversight responsibility for all energy and resource coms. 1998—, liaison to Federal Energy Bar Assn. 1997—, sect. pub. utility law 1991—, vice chmn. sect. on environment, energy and resources' natural gas and electric mktg. and transp. subcom. 1997-98, litig. sect. rep. on Am. Bar Assn. Coordinating Com. on Energy Law 1991-97, ad hoc mem. of com. 1997—), Houston Bar Assn., Fed. Bar Assn. (bd. dirs. 1990-92, chmn. internat. energy com. 1997—, antitrust sect. 1991-98, chmn. 1986-87), Assn. Internat. Petroleum Negotiators, Am. Soc. Internat. Law, Rocky Mountain Law Inst. (trustee 1991—), Delta Theta Phi. Avocations: reading history, current events and politics, tennis, golf, jogging. Home: 3133 Buffalo Speedway Apt 7207 Houston TX 77098-1828 Office: Phelps Dunbar 3040 Post Oak Blvd Houston TX 77056-6500

MARTIN, JEAN F., physician, consultant; b. Lausanne, Vaud, Switzerland, Nov. 18, 1940; s. Paul and Helene D. (Moinat) M.; m. Laurence C. Monod, June 22, 1966; children: Antoine, Alexandre, David. MD, U. Lausanne, Switzerland, 1965; diploma in tropical medicine, Swiss Tropical Inst., Basle, Switzerland, 1967; MS in Pub. Health, U. N.C., 1971. Cert. prevention and pub. health. Intern, resident St. Loup Hosp., Pompaples, Switzerland, 1965-68; acting med. dir. Hosp. Amazonico, Pucallpa, Peru, 1968-70; med. officer WHO, South East Asia Region Office, New Delhi, 1972-74; field dir. U. N.C. Population Ctr., Yaounde, Camaroon, 1974-76; dep. chief cantonal med. officer Pub. Health Svc. Canton of Vaud, Lausanne, 1976-85, chief cantonal med. officer, 1986—; lectr. U. N.C., Yaounde, 1974-76, U. Lausanne, 1985—; cons. WHO; jury mem. of PhD theses various Swiss and French Univs. Author: Pour la Sante Publique, 1987, La Consultation Medicale, 1990, Enjeux Ethiques en Sante Publique, 1991, Medecine pour la Medecine ou Medecine pour la Sante, 1996, L' Actuel et le Durable, 1999; co-author: Les Cancers de A à Z-Histoire Science, Médicine, Société, 1995; editor: High Risk Mothers and Newborns-Detection, Management and Prevention, 1987, Faire Face au SIDA, 1988, Le SIDA en Suisse-L'épidémie, ses Conséquences et les Mesures Prises, 1989, Maternal and Child Care in Developing Countries- Assessment, Promotion, Implementation, 1989, Santé et Pollution de L'air, 1989, L'Amour Préservé-Les Jeunes et le SIDA, 1989, L'Expérience Vaudoise des Médiateurs Scolaires, 1992, Les Familles Face au SIDA, 1995; contbr. articles to profl. jours. Mem. Swiss Fed. AIDS Commn., 1988—, Swiss Fed. Commn. for Reform of Med. Edn., 1997-99, Sci. Coun. French Nat. Health Ins. Agency, Paris, 1999—, Echandens Legis. Coun., Switzerland, 1978—, Constituent Assembly of Canton of Vaud, Switzerland; exec. bd. Swiss Devel. Found., Bern, 1985—; bd. dirs. AIDS Documentation Found., Switzerland, 1990—. Recipient several Grants Swiss Nat. Sci. Found. for studies of ambulatory med. care. Mem. Swiss Acad. Med. Sci. (various commns.) Montpellier, France, Acad. Sci. and Humanities (corr. mem.), Swiss Soc. Health Policy (v.p. 1980—), Swiss Soc. Pub. Health (bd. dirs. 1978—). Avocations: long distance running, trekking, reading, wine tasting. Office: Svc de la Sante Pub, Cite Devant 11, CH 1014 Lausanne Vaud Switzerland

MARTÍN, JOAN, botanist, educator; b. Figueres, Catalonia, Spain, May 14, 1949; s. Ricard Martín and Adela Villodre; m. Clara Valentí, Nov. 7, 1981 (div. 1989). Lic. in pharmacy, U. Barcelona, Spain, 1975, PhD, 1988. Aux. prof. Faculty of Pharmacy U. Barcelona, 1977-95, assoc. prof., 1995-2000, titular prof., 2000—; tutor Faculty of Pharmacy, U. Barcelona, 1989—, mem. faculty coun., 1983-87, 89-98, mem. acad. staff, 1978-97. Contbr. articles to profl. jours. Mem. Inst. for Def. & Study Nature, Orgn. Phytotaxonomic Investigation Mediterranean Area, N.Y. Acad. Scis. Avocations: reading, travel, cinema, philology. Home: Moline 1 1e 2a, 08006 Barcelona Spain Office: Faculty of Pharmacy, U Barcelona, 08028 Barcelona Spain

MARTIN, JOHN DRISCOLL, school administrator; b. Chgo., July 28, 1954; s. Walter Roy and Constance Kathleen (Driscoll) M.; children: Patrick, Kelsey; m. Caroline J. Martin, Mar. 28, 1996. BA, Augustana Coll., 1976; MA, Northwestern U., 1982. Cert. tchr., Ill. Tchr. J.D. Darnall High Sch., Geneseo, Ill., 1976-77, St. Viator High Sch., Arlington Heights, Ill., 1977-79; tchr. Hoffman Estates (Ill.) High Sch., 1979-88, athletic dir., 1988-90; athletic dir. Adlai E. Stevenson High Sch., Lincolnshire, Ill., 1990—; adv. com. Ill. High Sch. Assn., Bloomington, 1989-92; master tchr. Gov.'s Master Tchr. Program, 1984—. Mem. AAHPERD, Ill. Assn. Health, Phys. Edn., Recreation and Dance, Nat. Athletic Adminstrs. Assn., Ill. Athletic Dirs. Assn. (conf. chair 1995, cert. athletic adminstr.). Avocations: golf, reading. E-mail: jmartin@district125.k12.il.us. Office: 1 Stevenson Dr Lincolnshire IL 60069-2824

MARTIN, JOHN RANDOLPH, judge; b. Lexington, Ky., May 26, 1948; s. Harry and Geraldine (Gray) M.; m. Jacqueline Lauren Snyder, Apr. 24, 1976; 1 child, Lauren Elizabeth. BA, U. Okla., 1973, MA, 1976, JD, 1980. Bar: Okla. 1981, U.S. Ct. Mil. Appeals 1981, U.S. Dist. Ct. (we. dist.) Okla. 1982, S.C. 1983, U.S. Ct. Appeals (10th cir.) 1983, U.S. Dist. Ct. S.C. 1984, U.S. Ct. Appeals (4th cir.) 1984, U.S. Supreme Ct. 1995. Assoc. Finkel, Georgaklis et al, Columbia, S.C., 1984-86; ptnr. Mumford, Wishart & Martin, North Myrtle Beach, S.C., 1986-87, Gertz, Kastanes, Moore & Martin, North Myrtle Beach, S.C., 1987-91; with Office of Hearings and Appeals, Social Security Adminstrn., Houston, 1991—. Lt. col. U.S. Army, 1967-70, Vietnam, with Res. 1975-78, 84-96, Desert Storm, JAGC, 1981-84. Mem. NRA, Masons, Shriners, Elks, Phi Delta Phi, Pi Kappa Alpha. Republican. Episcopalian. Avocations: singing, shooting. Office: Office of Hearing and Appeals 6800 West Loop S Ste 300 Bellaire TX 77401-4522

MARTIN, JOHN THOMAS, physician, author, educator; b. Cleve., June 8, 1924; s. Clarence Henry and Clara May (Feeney) M.; m. Marion Elizabeth George, Feb. 18, 1946; children: Thomas R., David B., Richard G., Janet E., Patricia L., Robert W. MD, U. Cin., 1948. Commd. 1st lt. USAF, 1949, advanced through grades to maj., 1953; resident in anesthesiology Lackland AFB Hosp., San Antonio, 1953-55; asst. chief USAF Sch. Anesthesiology, Lackland AFB, 1955-57; attending anesthesiologist Baylor U. Hosp., Dallas, 1957-58; cons. dept. anesthesiology Mayo Clinic, Rochester, Minn., 1958-72; head Meth sect. anesthesiology Mayo Clinic, 1966-72; assoc. clin. prof. anesthesiology, 1968-72; chmn. dept. anesthesiology Ochsner Med. Ctr., New Orleans, 1972-74; clin. assoc. prof. anesthesiology Tulane U. Sch. Medicine, New Orleans, 1972-74; prof. anesthesiology Med. Coll. Ohio, Toledo, 1974-90; chmn. dept. anesthesiology Med. Coll. Ohio, 1980-89, emeritus prof. anesthesiology, 1990—. Editor, author: Positioning Patients Anesthesia/Surgery, 1978, 2d edit., 1987, 3d edit., 1997; editor ASA Handbook of Hosp. Facilities for Anesthesia, 1972, 2d edit., 1974; contbr. articles to profl. jours. Chmn. conductor selection com. Rochester Symphony Orch., 1963-66; pres. Rochester Civic Music, 1965. Mem. Internat. Anesthesia Rsch. Soc. (chmn. 1979-81, trustee 1965-90), Minn. Soc. Anesthesiologists (pres. 1966-67), Ohio Soc. Anesthesiologists (pres. 1988-89), Am. Med. Writers Assn. (pres. Minn. chpt. 1970-71), Assoc. Physicians Med. Coll. Ohio (bd. dirs. 1974-89), Am. Soc. Anesthesiology, Sigma Xi, Alpha Omega Alpha, Sigma Chi, Phi Chi. Republican. Avocations: medical writing, computers, music, fishing. Home: 4605 Woodland Ln Sylvania OH 43560-3221 Office: Med Coll of Ohio PO Box 10008 Toledo OH 43699-0008

MARTIN, JOHN WILSON, metallurgist, researcher, consultant; b. Peterborough, Eng., Oct. 14, 1926; s. Gilbert Algernon and Gladys (Wilson) M.; m. Carol Marion Thompson, Oct. 1, 1951; children: Janet Virginia, Philip John. MA in Metallurgy, Cambridge (Eng.) U., 1951, PhD in Metallurgy, 1953, ScD in Metallurgy, 1978. Chartered engr., Eng. Fellow St. John's Coll., Cambridge, 1954-57; lectr. Oxford (Eng.) U., 1957-89, reader in phys. metallurgy, 1990-94, emeritus reader in phys. metallurgy, 1994—; fellow St. Catherine's Coll., Oxford, 1960—. Author: Micromechanisms in Particle-Hardened Alloys, 1980, Materials for engineering, 1996; co-author: Stability of Microstructure in Metallic Systems, 1997; mem. editl. adv. bd. Materials Characterization, 1967—, Precipitation Hardening, 1998. Lt. comdr. Royal Naval Res., 1958-71. Recipient Vol. Res. Decoration, Royal Navy, 1960, Clasp, 1971; numerous rsch. grants U.K. Rsch. Coun. Fellow Inst. of Materials (cons. editor 1995—, S.G. Thomas medal and prize 1986). Mem. Ch. of England. Avocations: madrigals, piano, organ. E-mail: john.martin@materials.ux.ac.uk. Office: Oxford University, Dept Materials Parks Rd, Oxford OX1 3PH, England

MARTIN, JOSEPH BOYD, neurologist, educator; b. Bassano, Alta., Can., Oct. 20, 1938; s. Joseph Bruce and Ruth Elizabeth (Ramer) M.; m. Rachel Ann Wenger, June 18, 1960; children: Bradley, Melanie, Douglas, Neil. BSc, Eastern Mennonite Coll., Harrisonburg, Va., 1959; MD, U. Alta., 1962; PhD, U. Rochester, N.Y., 1971; MA (hon.), Harvard U., 1978; ScD (hon.), McGill U., 1994, U. Rochester, 1996, U. Wis., 1997, U. Alta., 1998. Resident in internal medicine Univ. Hosp., Edmonton, Alta., 1962-64; resident in neurology Case-Western Res. U. Hosps., 1964-67; rsch. fellow U. Rochester, N.Y., 1967-70; mem. faculty McGill U. Faculty Medicine, Montreal, Que., Can., 1970-78; prof. medicine and neurology, neurologist-in-chief Montreal Neurol. Inst., 1976-78; chmn. dept. neurology Mass. Gen. Hosp., Boston, also Dorn prof. neurology Harvard U. Med. Sch., 1978-89; dean Sch. Medicine U. Calif., San Francisco, 1989-93; chancellor U. Calif., San Francisco, 1993-97; dean faculty medicine Harvard U., Boston, 1997—; mem. med. adv. bd. Gairdner Found., Toronto, 1978-83, 97—; adv. council neurol. disorders program Nat. Inst. Neurol., Communicative Disorders and Stroke, 1979-82. Co-author: Clinical Neuroendocrinology, 1977, The Hypothalmamus, 1978, Clinical Neuroendocrinology: A Pathophysiological Approach, 1979, Neurosecretion and Brain Peptides: Implications for Brain Functions and Neurological Disease, 1981, Brain Peptides, 1983; editor Harrison's Principles of Internal Medicine, 1980—, Molecular Neurology, 1998—. Recipient Moshier Meml. gold medal U. Alta. Faculty Medicine, 1962, John W. Scott gold med. award, 1962, Abraham Flexner award AAMC, 1999; Med. Rsch. Coun. Can. scholar, 1970-75. Mem. NAS, Am. Neurol. Assn. (pres. 1990), Am. Physiol. Soc. (Bowditch lectr. 1978), Royal Coll. Phys. and Surg. Can., Endocrine Soc., Soc. Neurosci., Am. Soc. Clin. Investigation, Assn. Am. Physicians, Am. Acad. Arts and Scis., Inst. of Medicine, Nat. Adv. Coun., Nat. Inst. Aging. Office: Dean of the Faculty of Medicine Harvard Med Sch 25 Shattuck St Boston MA 02115-6027

MARTIN, KARINE ALINE, quality assurance professional; b. Les Lilas, France, June 25, 1971; d. Jean-Louis Henri and Michele Paule Louise (Ayme) M. Diploma in biology, U. Bobigny, 1995; brevet de technicien, Acad. Internat. Mgmt., Paris, 1996. Tchr. adults Villemomble, France, 1998-99; quality mgr. Societe Louis Martin, Romainville, France, 1996—. Mem. Assn. Nat. de tie de la Police. Avocations: music, painting, writing, sports, motorbiking. Office: Societe Louis Martin, 1 Rue de la Pointe, 93230 Romainville France

MARTIN, KIM See MARTH, MARY ELLEN

MARTIN, LEONARDO S.J., urologist, surgeon; b. Macati, Rizal, The Philippines, Nov. 26, 1926; came to U.S., 1953; s. Nemesio Martin and Felicidad San Juan; m. Helen Mary Dougherty, May 24, 1958; children: Leonard, John and David (twins), Mark, Regina Mary, Daniel. AA, U. The Philippines, 1947; MD, U. Santo Tomas, Manila, The Philippines, 1952. Diplomate Am. Bd. Urology; cert. physician and surgeon, Calif. Resident in urology Phila. Gen. Hosp., 1954-57; fellow in urology Mass. Gen. Hosp., Boston, 1957-59; urologist Manila Specialists Med. Ctr., 1959-63; instr. urology U. Santo Tomas, 1959-63; assoc. cancer urologist Roswell Pk. Meml. Hosp., Buffalo, 1963-65; urologist Sunnyvale (Calif.) Med. Ctr., 1965-94; mem. clin. tchg. staff Stanford (Calif.) Med. Ctr., 1965-94; cons. urology Los Altos, 1994—; commr., med. expert Calif. Med. Bd. Licensure, Sacramento, 1987—. Contbr. some 40 articles to profl. jours. Bd. dirs. Flint Cultural Ctr., Cupertino, Calif., 1970-80; mem adv. bd. Santa Clara County unit Boys and Girls Club Am. Named one of 10 Outstanding Young Men, Jaycees, The Philippines, 1960, Disting. Men of Medicine, U. The Philippines Coll. Medicine, 1960. Fellow ACS (cert. merit 1964); mem. AMA (cert. Inc. merit 1964), Am. Urol. Assn. (AUA, Inc. cert. merit 1964), Am. Assn. Clin. Urologists, Philippine-Am. Urol. Soc. (founding pres. 1972), U. Santo Tomas Med. Alumni Assn. in Am. (pres. 1996-97). Republican. Roman Catholic. Avocations: oil painting, piano and organ, stained glass, tennis, golf. Home and Office: 1931 Deodora Dr Los Altos CA 94024-7055

MARTIN, L(ESLIE) JOHN, retired journalism educator and dean; b. Budapest, Hungary, Jan. 5, 1921; came to U.S., 1948; s. Joseph and Elizabeth Caroline Martin; m. Lois Ann Henze, Mar. 22, 1951; children: Keith Douglas, Brian John. BA, Am. U., Cairo, 1947; postgrad. U. Oreg., 1948-49; MA, U. Minn., 1951, PhD, 1955. Corr., reporter, editor various newspapers, London, Paris, others, 1941-47; asst. prof. comm. U. Nebr., Lincoln, 1954-57; copy editor, night editor Detroit Free Press, 1957-58; prof.

comm. U. Fla., Gainesville, 1958-61; divsn. chief, overseas rsch. dir. USIA, Washington, 1961-69; prof. internat. and cross-cultural comm., rsch. methods in mass communication, public opinion and propaganda U. Md., College Park, 1969-89, prof. emeritus, 1989—, dir. grad. studies, 1974-79, 82-89, dean Coll. Journalism, 1975, 79-80, assoc. dean, 1988-89, dir. PhD program in pub. comm., 1983-85, faculty ombuds officer, 1999—. Author: International Propaganda: Its Legal and Diplomatic Control, 1969 (Sigma Delta Chi nat. award 1959), 1969; editor: (with A. Chaudhury) Comparative Mass Media Systems, 1983, 1991 (in Arabic), 1997 (in Malaysian), (with R. Hiebert) Current Issues in International Communication, 1990, 3 other books; contbr. 20 chpts. to books; contbr. 3 encys.; contbr. numerous articles to profl. jours. and conf. procs. Recipient Disting. Svc. to Internat. Comm. award, Assn. Edn. in Journalism and Mass Comm., Washington, 1989. Mem. Kappa Tau Alpha. Avocations: reading, writing, travel, walking, computers. E-mail: ljmartin@wam.umd.edu. Home: 5313 Iroquois Rd Bethesda MD 20816-3104 Office: U Md Office Of Pres College Park MD 20742-0001

MARTIN, LORI YVONNE, secondary education educator; b. Dayton, Ohio, Jan. 30, 1965; d. Jesse Willard Moore Jr. and Susan Diane Martin Berry; 1 child, Sara. Nursing cert., Ohio Hi-Point Sch. Nursing, Bellefontaine, 1991; BA, Wright State U., 1996, MEd, 2000. Nurse Mercy Meml. Hosp., Urbana, Ohio, 1991-94; tchr. Hillsboro (Ohio) City Schs., 1997-98, Calvary Christian Sch., Bellefontaine, 1999-2000, Ohio Hi Point Joint Vocat. Sch., Bellefontaine, 2000—. Author: An Angel for Sara, 1993. Mem. Am. Cancer Soc., Va. Hist. Soc., Smithsonian Instn., Kappa Delta Phi. Republican. Avocations: cooking, travel, reading, puzzles, history. E-mail: snlmartin@hotmail.com.

MARTIN, LORNA JEAN, forensic pathologist, specialist, consultant; b. Jarrow, Eng., Aug. 17, 1965; arrived in South Africa, 1973; d. David and Rosalind (Reeve) M. MB.BCh., U. Witwatersrand, Johannesburg, South Africa, 1989; MD, Coll. Medicine, Johannesburg, 1992; M.Med.Path, U. Cape Town, South Africa, 1999. Forensic medicine diplomate. Intern Baragwanath Hosp., Soweto, South Africa, 1990; dist. surgeon Dept. of Health, Johannesburg, 1991-95; registrar dept. forensic pathology WITS, Johannesburg, 1995-96, U. Cape Town, 1996—; presenter in field. Founding mem. Rape Forum, Johannesburg, 1993-95; cons. Network on Violence Against Women, Johannesburg, 1995-96; ongoing activist women's orgns. Mem. POWA (hon.). Avocations: reading, walking, hiking, golf. Office: U Cape Town Dept Forensic Medicine Med Sch, Anzio Road Observatory PO Box 668, Cape Town South Africa

MARTIN, LOUIS FRANK, surgery and healthcare outcomes analyst; b. Troy, N.Y., Nov. 7, 1951; s. Eugene Lavern and Lois Jane (Perkins) Martin; m. Deborah Lynn Tjarnberg, Mar. 12, 1977; children: Jesse Tjarnberg, James Casey, Tyler Gene. BA, Brown U., 1973, MD, 1976; MS in Health Administrn., U. Louisville, 1993. Diplomate Am. Bd. Surgery, Am. Bd. Med. Mgmt. Resident in gen. surgery U. Wash. Affiliated Hosps., Seattle, 1977-78; resident in gen. surgery U. Louisville, 1978-83, rsch. fellow trauma rsch. and health care ednl. adminstrn., 1980-82; asst. prof. surgery Pa. State U., Hershey, 1983-88, asst. prof. physiology, 1986-88, assoc. prof. surgery and cellular and molecular physiology, 1988-92; prof. surgery La. State U., New Orleans, 1992—, prof. preventative medicine and pub. health, 1994—; prof. neurosci., 1995—; med. dir. St. Charles Weight Mgmt. Ctr. La. State U., New Orleans, 1995—; vis. scientist INSERM, Poste Orange, France, 1990-91; cons. TENET Health Care Corp. Med. Affairs Dept., 1995—, Ethicon Endo-Surgery, Inc., 2000—. Mem. editl. bd., Shock, 1994-97, Obesity Surgery, 1997—, Jour. Surgical Outcomes, 1997-99; author med. books; contbr. articles to newspapers and profl. jours. Recipient Loyal Davis Traveling Surg. scholar ACS, 1990, Clin. Investigator award NIH, 1985-90. Mem. ACS, Am. Soc. Bariatric surgery (program chmn. 1997, 98, mem. exec. coun. 1997—), Am. Coll. Critical Care Medicine, Am. Physiol. Soc., Assn. for Acad. Surgery (councilman 1988-90), Collegium Internat. Chirurgiae Digestivae, Soc. Internat. Chirurgie, Soc. Univ. Surgeons, New Orleans Surg. Soc. (pres. 1999), Shape Up Am. Home: 3005 Palm Vista Dr Kenner LA 70065-1560 Office: La State U Dept Surgery 1542 Tulane Ave New Orleans LA 70112-2825

MARTIN, LUAN, accountant, payroll and timekeeping supervisor; b. Dimmitt, Tex., Dec. 9, 1952; d. Walter Johnnie and Nellie Beth (Connell) Martin; 1 child, Dani D'Ann; m. Richard Cordi, Feb. 2000. Grad., Amarillo Jr. Coll., 1986; BS Occupational Edn., Wayland Bapt. U., 1997. Credit mgr. Castro County Credit Bur., Dimmitt, 1978-79; parts mgr. Case Power and Equipment, Dimmitt, 1979-82; bookkeeper Dimmitt Agri Industries, Inc., 1982; personnel dir. Deaf Smith Gen. Hosp., Hereford, Tex., 1983-84; payroll acct. Mason & Hanger-Silas Mason Co., Inc., Amarillo, Tex., 1984—; owner, pres. Dugan Mgmt., Amarillo, 1987-94, Martin Enterprises, Amarillo, 1997—. Vol. local sch.; spkr. in behalf of blood, bone marrow and organ donations. Mem. Toastmasters Internat. (Pantex Lunch Bunch chpt.). Methodist. Avocations: reading, computers, sports, helping teenagers, bowling. Home: 7505 Countryside Dr Amarillo TX 79119-6488 Office: Mason Hanger Silas Mason Co PO Box 30020 Amarillo TX 79120-0020

MARTIN, MARILYN MANN, library media specialist; b. Greencastle, Ind., July 14, 1939; d. Emil Albert and Edith Costa Mann; m. Max Lee Martin; children: Michael Lee, Melanie Sue Martin Boesen. BS, Ind. State U., 1960, MS, 1970, 88. Tchr. Latin, sch. libr. Danville (Ind.) H.S., 1960; libr., media specialist Greencastle (Ind.) H.S., 1971—; mem. tech. connections com. Greencastle H.S., 1997-98; mem. exec. bd. Stone Hills Libr. Svcs., Bloomington, Ind., 1990-96. Mem. NEA, Ind. Tchrs. Assn., Ind. Libr. Found., Ind. Coop. Libr. Svcs., Assn. Ind. Media Educators (dist. advocacy chmn. 1998), Greencastle Classroom Tchrs. (scholarship chmn. 1985-2000), Phi Kappa Phi. Avocations: gardening, reading, volunteering. Office: Greencastle High Sch 910 E Washington St Greencastle IN 46135-1898

MARTIN, MARY COATES, genealogist, writer, volunteer; b. Gloucester County, N.J.; d. Raymond and Emily (Johnson) Coates; m. Lawrence O. Kupillas (dec.); m. Clyde Davis Martin (dec.); 1 child, William Raymond. Contbg. editor Md. & Del. Genealogist, St. Michaels, Md., 1985—. Author: The House of John Johnson (1731-1802) Salem County, N.J. and His Descendants, 1979, Fifty Year History of Daughters of Colonial Wars in the State of New York, 1980, 350 Years of American Ancestors: 38 Families: 1630-1989, 1989, Colonial Families: Martin and Bell Families and Their Kin: 1657-1992, Clifton--Coates Kinfolk and 316 Allied Families, 1995. Pres. Washington Hdqrs. Assn., 1970-73, bd. dirs., 1962—; Centennial pres. Sorosis, Inc., 1966-68; bd. dirs. Soldiers Sailors Airmen's Club, N.Y.C., 1976-81, Yorkville Youth Coun., N.Y.C., 1954-60; co-chmn. Colonial Ball, N.Y.C., 1965-67; rec. sec. Parents League of N.Y., Inc., 1954-57; mem. com. Internat. Debutante Ball, N.Y.C., 1977-81; mem. Am. Flag Inst., N.Y.C., 1963-72. Mem. Hereditary Order of Descendants of Colonial Govs. (gov. gen. 1981-83), Nat. Soc. Colonial Dames of Seventeenth Century (N.Y. State pres. 1977-79, parlimentarian 1979-81), Nat. Soc. Daus. of Colonial Wars (N.Y. State pres. 1977-80), Nat. Soc. DAR (regent 1962-65, pres. roundtable 1964-65, N.Y. State chaplain 1968-71, parliamentarian 1980-83, nat. platform com. 1970-76, certificate of award 1971, nat. vice chmn. lineage rsch. com. 1977-80, geneal. com. 1980-83), Nat. Soc. New Eng. Women (dir. gen. 1972-77, nat. vice chmn. helping hand disbursing fund 1968-71), Order of Crown of Charlemagne U.S.A. (corr. sec. gen. 1985-88, 3rd v.p. 1988-89, 2nd v.p. 1989-91), Nat. Soc. Children Am. Revolution, Nicasius de Sille Soc. (pres. 1960-62), Order Ams. of Armorial Ancestry (1st v.p. gen. 1985-88, councillor gen. 1988—), Nat. Gavel Soc., Nat. Soc. Magna Carta Dames, Descendants of Soc. of Colonial Clergy, Huguenot Soc. Am., Descendants of a Knight of Most Noble Order Garter, Nat. Soc. Daus. Am. Colonists, Nat. Soc. U.S. Daus. 1812, Order of Descendants of Colonial Physicians and Chirurgiens, Plantagenet Soc., Vt. Soc. Colonial Dames, Del. Geneal. Soc., Huguenot Hist. Soc., DuBois Family Assn. (1st v.p.), Cumberland County N.J. Hist. Soc., Gloucester County N.J. Hist. Soc., Md. Hist. Soc., Hist. Soc. Del., Salem County N.J. Hist. Soc., Woodstown-Pilesgrove N.J. Hist. Soc., Hereditary Order First Families of Mass., Inc. Avocation: travel. Home: Hague Towers # 1815 330 W Brambleton Ave Norfolk VA 23510-1325

MARTIN, MARY LAURA, language educator, literature educator; b. Atlanta, Mar. 23, 1961; d. David Willis and Carol Ann (Strauss) M. BA, Eckerd Coll., St. Petersburg, Fla., 1984; MA, Emory U., 1988, PhD, 1996. Instr. lang. U. Regensburg, Germany, 1991-95; lectr. U. Glasgow, Scotland, 1995—, dep. dir. Ctr. for European Romanticism, 1997-98. Contbr. articles to profl. jours. Rotary fellow, 1984-85, grad. fellow Emory U., 1987-91; Presdl. scholar Eckerd Coll., 1979-83. Mem. MLA, Conf. of Univ. Tchrs. of German. Avocation: singing semi-professional soprano.

MARTIN, MICHAEL, government official; b. Cork, Ireland, Aug. 16, 1960. BA in Polit. History, U. Coll., Dublin; MA, U. Coll. Elected to Cork Corp., Ireland, 1985; alderman Cork Corp., 1991; mem. FF Nat. Exec., 1988—; elected to Dail, 1989; lord mayor Cork, 1992-93; min. Dept. Edn., Dublin, 1997—; min. health and children Govt. Ireland, Dublin. Office: Dept Health, Hawkins Houset, Dublin 2, Ireland*

MARTIN, MICHAEL TOWNSEND, racing horse stable executive, sports marketing executive; b. N.Y.C., Nov. 21, 1941; s. Townsend Bradley and Irene (Redmond) M.; m. Jennifer Johnston, Nov. 7, 1964 (div. Jan. 1977); children: Ryan Bradley, Christopher Townsend; m. Jean Kathleen Meyer, Mar. 1, 1980. Grad., The Choate Sch., 1960; student, Rutgers U., 1961-62. Asst. gen. mgr. N.Y. Jets Football Club, N.Y.C., 1968-74; v.p. NAMANCO Prodns., N.Y.C., 1975-76; v.p., gen. mgr. Cosmos Soccer Club, N.Y.C., 1976-77; exec. asst. Warner Communications, N.Y.C., 1978-84; owner, operator Martin Racing Stable, N.Y.C., 1983—; pres. Sports Mark, Inc., N.Y.C., 1990—; ptnr. Halstead Property Co., N.Y.C., 1987—; bd. dirs. Night Kitchen, N.Y. Bd. dirs. Mote Marine Lab., Sarasota, Fla., Phipps Houses, VZV Rsch. Found., Inc., Juilliard Sch., Coun. of Visitors, Woods Hole Marine Biol. Lab., Nat. Lighthouse Ctr. and Mus.; bd. advisors The Pennington Sch. Mem. Athletics Congress (life, cert. official 1984—), U.S. Tennis Assn. (life), Internat. Oceanographic Found. (Miami life mem.), Fla. Thoroughbred Breeders Assn., Quogue Field Club, The Union Club. Republican. Episcopalian. Avocation: collecting Inuit (Eskimo) art. Home: 131 E 69th St Apt 11A New York NY 10021-5158 Office: 575 Madison Ave Ste 1006 New York NY 10022-2511

MARTIN, MIRCEA AURELIAN, literary critic, educator; b. Resita, Romania, Apr. 12, 1940; s. Ion and Aurelia (Pop) M.; m. Angela Teodorescu, Aug. 1, 1975; children: Matei, Iunia. MA, Faculty Arts, Bucharest, 1962, PhD, 1980. From asst. to prof. Faculty Arts, Bucharest, 1962-90, prof., 1990—; gen. dir. Univers Pub. House, Bucharest, 1990—. Author: Generation and Creation, 1969, Criticism and Profoundity, 1974 (Romanian Writers' Union Literary Criticism prize 1974), Identifications, 1977, George Călinescu and the Complexes of Romanian literature, 1981 (Romanian Writers' Union Literary Criticism prize 1981), Introduction to Benjamin Fundoianu's Work, 1984, The Sole Criticism, 1986, The Diction of Ideas, 1991; co-author: Les Actes du Colloque International Béguin-Raymond, Cartigny, 1977, 1980. Grantee Fulbright Found., 1995. Mem. PEN (v.p. 1990—), Romanian Writers' Union (bd. dirs. 1990-95), Romanian Publishers' Assn (pres. 1991—). Office: Univers Pub House, 1 Piata Presei Libere, 79739 Bucharest Romania

MARTIN, NED HAROLD, chemistry educator; b. New Brunswick, N.J., May 18, 1945; s. Harold and Gertrude (Link) M.; m. Lynda Susan Blackadar, June 14, 1980; 1 child, Tara Elizabeth. BA, Denison U., 1967; PhD, Duke U., 1972. NDEA trainee Duke U., Durham, N.C., 1967-69; rsch. chemist Research Triangle Inst., Research Triangle Park, N.C., 1969-70; rsch. asst. Duke U., Durham, 1970-72, lectr., 1971-72; asst. prof. U. N.C., Wilmington, 1972-77, assoc. prof., 1977-82, prof., 1982—, chair chemistry dept., 1992-97, Will S. DeLoach prof. chemistry, 1996—; cons. Corning Glass, Wilmington, 1979-80, LaQue Ctr. for Corrosion Tech., Wrightsville Beach, N.C., 1983-87, Condux, Inc., Newark, Del., 1989-90, Trinity Mfg., Inc., 1991; postdoctorate researcher U. Geneva, 1980-81. Co-author: Organic Chemistry Lab Manual with Waste Management and Molecular Modeling, 1993, Chemistry 211/212 Lab Manual, 1987. Mem. N.C. Acad. Sci. (v.p. 1988-90, pres.-elect 1989-90, pres. 1990-91, past pres. 1991-92), Am. Chem. Soc., Sigma Xi (assoc.; chpt. pres.-elect 1998-99, pres. 1999-2000, past pres. 2000—), Phi Beta Kappa, Omicron Delta Kappa, Phi Soc., Phi Eta Sigma, Phi Lambda Upsilon. Office: UNCW Dept Chemistry 601 S College Rd Wilmington NC 28403-3201

MARTIN, PAUL, Canadian government official; b. Windsor, Ont., Can., Aug. 28, 1938; s. Paul Joseph and Eleanor (Adams) M.; m. Sheila Ann Cowan, Sept. 11, 1965; children—Paul William James, Robert James Edward, David Patrick Anthony. BA in Philosophy and History, U. Toronto, Can., 1962, LLB, 1965; LLB, U. Toronto, Can., 1965. Bar: Ont. 1966. Exec. asst. to pres. Power Corp. Can. Ltd., 1966-69, v.p., 1969-71; v.p. spl. projects Consol.-Bathurst Ltd., 1971-73; v.p. planning and devel. Power Corp., Can., 1973-74; pres. Can. S.S. Lines Ltd., Montreal, 1974-80, chief exec. officer, 1976-80; pres., chief exec. officer CSL Group Inc., 1980-88; M.P. Ho. of Commons, 1988-93; min. of fin. Dept. of Fin. Can., 1993—; former min. for fed. office of regional devel. Can. Govt., 1993-95; co-chair Nat. Platform Com. of Liberal Party of Can. Co-author (with Chaviva Hosek): Creating Opportunity: The Liberal Plan for Canada. Former mem. C.D. Howe Inst. Policy Analysis Com., Birt, N.Am. Com., Ctr. Rsch. Action on Race Rels.; former bd. dirs. Can. Coun. Christians and Jews; founding dir. emeritus North-South Inst., Can., Coun. Native Bus.; bd. govs. Concordia U., coun., v.p., past mem. bd. advisors; inaugural chair G-20, 1999. Liberal. Avocations: sports, reading. Office: Dept of Finance Can, 140 O'Connor St, Ottawa, ON Canada K1A 0G5

MARTIN, PAUL EDWARD, lawyer; b. Atchison, Kans., Feb. 5, 1928; s. Harres Crawford and Thelma Fay (Wilson) M.; m. Betty Lou Crawford, Aug. 28, 1954; children: Cherry Gayle Martin Luna, Paul Alexander, Mary Lou Martin Brieger. BBA, Baylor U., 1955, LLB, JD, 1956; LLM, Harvard U., 1957. Bar: Tex. 1956, Pa. 1958; cert. in estate planning and probate law Tex. Bd. Legal Specialization. Assoc. Ballard, Spahr, Andrews & Ingersoll, Phila., 1957-59; ptnr. Fulbright & Jaworski, Houston, 1959-77; ptnr. Chamberlain, Hardlicka, White, Williams & Martin, Houston, 1977-90, shareholder, 1990—; former instr. estate planning U. Houston. Co-author: How To Live and Die with Texas Probate, 1968, 7th edit., 1995. Pres. devel. coun. Baylor U., Waco, Tex., 1973-74; past chmn. bd. deacons West Meml. Bapt. Ch., Houston; past trustee fgn. missions bd. So. Bapt. Conv.; past trustee Baylor U., Meml. Hosp. Sys., Houston. Lt. comdr. USN, 1947-53, Korea. Fellow Am. Coll. Trust and Estate Counsel; mem. State Bar Tex., Houston Bar Assn., Houston Estate and Fin. Forum (pres. 1965-66), Houston Bus. and Estate Planning Coun. Republican. Home: 2111 Welch St Apt B315 Houston TX 77019-5654 Office: Chamberlin Hrdlicka Et Al 1200 Smith St Ste 1400 Houston TX 77002-4401

MARTIN, PAUL RUSSELL, clinical psychologist, educator; b. Weymouth, Dorset, Eng., Feb. 22, 1951; arrived in Australia, 1979; s. William Frederick Charles and Lorna Mildred Edith (Machar) M.; m. Fiona Margaret Hay, May 12, 1979; children: Kathryn Alison, Richard Charles. BS with honors, U. Bristol (Eng.), 1972; PhD in Clin. Psychology, U. Oxford (Eng.), 1977. Rsch. clin. psychologist U. Oxford, 1976-79; lectr. Monash U., Melbourne, Australia, 1979-81; assoc. prof. clin. psychology U. Western Australia, Perth, 1981-95; prof., head dept. psychology U. New Eng., Armidale, Australia, 1996—; hon. clin. psychologist Oxfordshire Health Authority, Oxford, 1976-79, Prince Henry's Hosp., Melbourne, 1979-81; dir. clin. psychology unit U. Western Australia, Perth, 1985-91. Author: Psychological Management of Chronic Headaches, 1993, Treating Postnatal Depression, 1999; editor: Behavioural Medicine, 1981, Handbook of Behavior Therapy and Psychological Science, 1991, Clinical Psychology, 1996. Nat. Health and Med. Rsch. Coun. grantee, 1985-86, 94-95, 95-96. Fellow Australian Psychol. Soc. (conf. chair 1994-95, dir. sci. affairs 1997—), British Psychol. Soc. (assoc.); mem. Australian Behaviour Modification Assn. (nat. pres. 1984-85). Avocations: tennis, jogging, history, reading, viticulture. Home: Winsford Hill Boorolong Rd, Armidale NSW 2350, Australia Office: Sch Psychology, U New Eng, Armidale NSW 2351, Australia

MARTIN, PETER, psychology educator; b. Bochum, Germany, Oct. 14, 1955; came to U.S., 1978; s. Wolfgang Karl and Antonie Elisabeth (Volkmann) M.; m. Beth Ann Martin, Sept. 27, 1980; children: Nora, Kai, Glenn. BA in Psychology, Wartburg Coll., 1979; diploma in psychology, U. Bonn, Fed. Republic Germany, 1982, PhD in Psychology, 1985; PhD in Human Devel., Family Studies, Pa. State U., 1985. Asst. prof. dept. child and family devel. U. Ga., Athens, 1985-90, assoc. prof., 1990-91; assoc. prof. dept. human devel. and family studies Iowa State U., Ames, 1991-95, prof. dept. human devel. and families studies, 1995—; dir. German Ctr. for Rsch. on Aging U. Heidelberg, 1998-2000; dir. gerontology program Iowa State U., 2000—; workshop presenter. Contbr. articles to profl. publs. Grantee NIMH, 1988—, 90—, HHS, 1990—; Lilly fellow, 1986-87. Mem. APA, Nat. Coun. Family Rels., German Psychol. Assn., German Gerontology Soc., Internat. Soc. for Study Behavioral Devel., Gerontol. Soc. Am., Gamma Sigma Delta. Office: Iowa State U 1100 Elm Hall Ames IA 50010

MARTIN, PHILIPPE MARIE JEAN, geography and physical geography educator; b. Paris, May 1, 1957; s. Gabriel Marie and Jeannine (Malick) M.; m. Christine Germaine Brousse; children: Thomas, Benoit. PhD, U. Aix-Marseille II, Aix en Provence, 1991. Tchr. U. Poitiers, 1992-93; tchr., rschr. U. Artois, Arras, 1993—; pres. Dept. Com. of Speleology, 1986-87. 2d class Chasseur.Alpin, 1980-81. Prix duc de villars Acad. Scis. Lettres et Arts, De Marseille, 1991. Mem. French Speleology Fedn. Agnostic. Avocation: speleology. E-mail: phmartin@club-internet.fa. Home: Les Criquets Bat B, 52 Rue de Montaury, 30900 Nimes France Office: U d'Artois UFR Histoire, Geographie Rue du Temple, 62030 Arras France

MARTIN, QUINN WILLIAM, lawyer; b. Fond du Lac, Wis., Mar. 12, 1948; s. Quinn W. and Marcia E. Martin; m. Jane E. Nehmer; children: Quinn W., William J. BSME, Purdue U., 1969; postgrad., U. Santa Clara, 1969-70; JD, U. Mich., 1973. Bar: Wis. 1973, U.S. Dist. Ct. (ea. dist.) Wis. 1973, U.S. Ct. Appeals (7th cir.) 1973. Sales support mgr. Hewlett-Packard, Palo Alto, Calif., 1969-70; assoc. Quarles & Brady, Milw., 1973-80, ptnr., 1980—; bd. dirs. Associated Bank Milw., U-Line Corp., Gen. Timber and Land, Inc., Fond du Lac. Active McCallum for Lt. Gov., Wis., U. Mich. Law Sch. Fund; chmn. bd. dirs. Milw. Zool. Soc., Found. for Wildlife Conservation. Mem. ABA, Wis. Bar Assn., Milw. Bar Assn., Milw. Club, Ozaukee Country Club, Chaine des Rottiseurs, Delta Upsilon (sec.), Milw. Alumni Club, Rotary. Office: Quarles & Brady 411 E Wisconsin Ave Ste 2550 Milwaukee WI 53202-4497

MARTIN, RAYMOND EDWARD, management consultant; b. N.Y.C., Sept. 17, 1957; m. Denise Marie Martin. BBA, Cleve. State U., 1980, MBA, 1995. Cons. Ernst & Young, Cleve., 1980-82, Scott Fetzer, Cleve., 1982-83; bus. analyst Am. Consumer Products, Cleve., 1983-87; bus. mgr. APCOA, Inc., Cleve., 1988-92; prin. Martin Mgmt. Svcs., Cleve., 1992—. bd. dirs. United Way, Cleve., 1981. Roman Catholic.

MARTIN, ROGER HARRY, college president; b. N.Y.C., June 26, 1943; s. Edwin Diller and Emma (Neuenburg) M.; m. Susan Bradford, Aug. 29, 1970; children: Katherine R., Emily G. BA, Drew U., 1965; BD, Yale U., 1968, STM, 1969; DPhil, Oxford (Eng.) U., 1974. Program officer Edn. Incentive Program, N.Y.C., 1969-70; devel. officer NYU, 1970-71, 75-76; asst. dir. devel. Rensselaer Polytech Inst., Troy, N.Y., 1974-75; asst. prof. history, exec. asst. to pres. Middlebury (Vt.) Coll., 1976-80; assoc. dean Harvard Div. Sch., Cambridge, Mass., 1980-86; prof. history, pres. Moravian Coll., Bethlehem, Pa., 1986-97; pres. Randolph-Macon Coll., 1997—. Author: Evangelicals United: Ecumenical Stirrings in Pre-Victorian Britain, 1795-1830, 1983. Mem. Greater Richmond C. of C. (bd. 1999—), Harvard Club (N.Y.C.), Commonwealth Club (Richmond). Mem. Soc. of Friends. Avocations: skiing, running. Home: 305 Caroline St Ashland VA 23005-1602 Office: Randolph-Macon Coll Office of Pres PO Box 5005 Ashland VA 23005-5505

MARTIN, SHANE PATRICK, education educator, consultant; b. L.A., Aug. 1958; s. Robert Curtis and Lucille Catherine (Koch) M. BA in History, Loyola Marymount U., 1980; MDiv, Jesuit Sch. Theology, Berkeley, Calif., 1991, ThM, 1992; PhD, U. So. Calif., 1995. Clear secondary tchg. credential, Calif.; joined Soc. of Jesus, 1981, ordained priest, 1992. Mem. faculty Bellarmine Coll. Prep. Sch., San Jose, Calif., 1984, 85-88, dir. campus ministry, 1987-88; grad. tchg. asst. Jesuit Sch. Theology, 1990-92; lectr. Loyola Marymount U., L.A., 1994-95, asst. prof. edn., 1995—, coord. secondary edn., 1996—, acting coord. bilingual and multicultural edn. programs, 1999—; adj. prof. U. San Francisco, 1996—; cons., sr. assoc. Karadenes & Assocs., L.A., 1998—. Author: Cultural Diversity in Catholic Schools, 1996. Trustee Loyola H.S., L.A., 1997-98. Grantee Loyola Marymount U., 1996, 98, 99. Mem. Am. Anthrop. Assn., Am. Ednl. Rsch. Assn., Am. Assn. for Colls. Tchr. Edn., Assn. Tchr. Educators, Nat. Assn. for Multicultural Edn., Nat. Cath. Edn. Assn. (McGivney Meml. Fund grantee 1993). Avocations: travel, cultural events, music, technology, mentoring. E-mail: smartin@lmu.edu. Office: Loyola Marymount U Sch Edn 7900 Loyola Blvd Los Angeles CA 90045-2659

MARTIN, SUSAN KATHERINE, librarian; b. Cambridge, Eng., Nov. 14, 1942; came to U.S., 1950, naturalized, 1961; d. Egon and Jolan (Schonfeld) Orowan; m. David S. Martin, June 30, 1962. BA with honors, Tufts U., 1963; MS, Simmons Coll., 1965; PhD, U. Calif., Berkeley, 1983. Intern libr. Harvard U., Cambridge, Mass., 1963-65, systems libr., 1965-73; head systems office gen. libr. U. Calif., Berkeley, 1973-79; dir. Milton S. Eisenhower Libr. Johns Hopkins U., Balt., 1979-88, exec. dir. Nat. Commn. on Libraries and Info. Sci., 1988-90; univ. libr. Georgetown U., Washington, 1990—; mem. libr. adv. com. Princeton (N.J.) U., 1987-95; mem. vis. com. Harvard U. Libr., 1987-93, 94-2000; bd. overseers for univ. libr. Tufts U., 1986—; mem. libr. adv. com. Hong Kong U. Sci. Tech., 1988-95; mem. acad. libr. adv. group U. Md. Sch. Librs. and Info. Sci., 1994-96; cons. to various librs. and info. cos., 1975—; mem. adv. bd. ERIC, 1990-92, History Assocs., Inc., 1990-92; mem. Chadwyck-Healey North Am. Adv. Com. on Lit. Online, 1997-99; vice chair, chair Chesapeake Info. and Rsch. Libr. Alliance, 1996-98; cons. libr. devel. & fundraising, 1998—; spkr. in field. Author: Library Networks; Libraries in Partnership, 1986-87; editor; Jour. Libr. Automation, 1972-77; co-editor: Portal: Libraries and Academia, 2000—; mem. editl. bd. Advanced Tech./Librs., 1973-93, Jour. Libr. Adminstrn., 1986—, Libr. Hi-Tech., 1989-93, Jour. Acad. Librarianship, 1994-99; contbr. articles to profl. jours. Trustee Phila. Area Libr. Network, 1980-81; bd. dirs. Universal Serials and Book Exch., 1981-82, v.p., 1983, pres., 1984; trustee Capital Consortium, 1992-95; mem. bd. Potomac Internet, 1995-96. Recipient Simmons Coll. Disting. Alumni award, 1977; Council on Library Resources fellow, 1973. Mem. ALA (coun. 1988-92, structure revision TF, 1995-97, chair task force on ind. accrediting body 1999—), Internat. Fedn. Libr. Assns. Commn. on Access to Info. and Freedom of Expression, Rsch. Librs. Group (gov., exec. com. 1985-87), Libr. and Info. Tech. Assn. (pres. 1978-79), Assn. Rsch. Librs. (info. policy com. 1995-97, stats. com. 1998—), Libr. of Congress (optical disk pilot project adv. com. 1985-89), Assn. Jesuit Colls. and Univ. Librs. (chair 1997-98), Coalition for Networked Info. (leader working group 1990-92), Assn. Coll. and Rsch. Librs. (pres. 1994-95), Cosmos Club (libr. com. 1989-96), Georgetown Club, Phi Beta Kappa (chair Georgetown U. chpt. 2000—). Home: 4709 Blagden Ter NW Washington DC 20011-3719 Office: Georgetown U Lauinger Libr Washington DC 20057-0001

MARTIN, THOMAS GEOFFREY, government official; b. Newry, Northern Ireland, July 26, 1940; s. Thomas and Saidee Adelaide (Day) M.; m. Gay Madeleine Annesley Brownrigg, July 6, 1968; chldren: Bluebell, Poppy, Thomas, Gabriella. BSc with honors, Queen's U., Belfast, Northern Ireland, 1966. Pres. NUS, U.K., 1966-68; dir. Shelter, London, 1973-74; mem. diplomatic staff Commonwealth Secretariat, London, 1974-79; head office European Commn., Belfast, 1979-85; head press and info. svcs. S.E. Asia European Commn., Bangkok, Thailand, 1985-87; head external rels. European Commn., London, 1987-93, head representation in U.K., 1993—. Avocation: running. Office: European Commn, 8 Storey's Gate, London SW1P 3AT, England

MARTIN, TODD, professional tennis player; b. Hinsdale, Ill., July 8, 1970. Student, Northwestern U. Profl. tennis player, 1990—; mem. U.S. Davis Cup Team, 1994-98. Moved into world's top ten in tennis 1994; 3 pro singles titles 1993, 94 (2); winner Rolex Nat. Indoor Collegiate Championship award, 1990; champion RCA/U.S. Men's Hardcourt Championships, 1993, USTA Men's Clay Courts of Tampa, Fla., 1993, America's Red Clay Tennis Championship, Coral Springs, Fla., 1993, Stella Artois Grass Ct. Championships, London, 1994, Kroger/St. Jude Internat., 1994, 95, Peters NSW Open, Sydney, Australia, 1996; named rookie of Yr., Tennis Mag., 1991, Most Improved Player, Tennis Mag., 1993; recipient Sportsmanship award Adidas/ATP Tour, 1993, 94. Office: Advantage Internat 1751 Pinnacle Dr Ste 1500 Mc Lean VA 22102-3833*

MARTIN, TONY, geographer, educator; b. Blackhill, Durham, England, Apr. 22, 1942; s. William Carson and Stella (Browell) M.; m. Jette Bojsen Hansen, Aug. 15, 1964; children: Lars Andrew and Birgitte Alison. BA in Geography, U. Liverpool, 1963; postgrad., U. Copenhagen, 1963-64. Asst. lectr. U. Strathclyde, Glasgow, Scotland, 1966-68; lectr. U. Strathclyde, Glasgow, 1968-94, sr. lectr., 1994-98; coord. Nat. Inventory War Memls., Scotland, 1997—; freelance writer, lectr. & cons., 1998—; dir. Skill, London, 1993-96, Ochil Tower Sch., Auchterarder, Perthshire, Scotland, 1984-96. Scottish trustee Friends of War Memls., 1999—. Mem. Royal Scottish Geog. Soc., Inst. Brit. Geographers. Avocations: genealogy, philately, outdoor activities, gardening. Home: Birchgrove Harviestoun Rd Dollar FK14 7PT, Scotland

MARTIN, VIRVE PAUL, licensed professional counselor; b. Tallinn, Estonia, Nov. 19, 1928; came to U.S., 1949; d. Walter Gerhard and Alice (Haas) Paul; m. Albert Lynn Martin Jr., May 31, 1952; children: Lynda Lee, Elaine Lynne, Monique Louise. Student, U. Heidelberg, Germany, 1948-49; BA, Wesleyan Coll., Macon, Ga., 1952; MA, U. Minn., 1970. Cert. profl. counselor, Ga.; diplomate Am. Psychotherapy Assn. Interpreter Internat. Refugee Orgn., Nuremberg, Frankfurt, Heidelberg, Fed. Republic of Germany, 1947-49; rsch. asst. Kenny Inst., Mpls., 1966-67; vocat. evaluator Dept. Human Resources, Atlanta, 1970-73, rehab. counselor, 1973-96; interpreter Mpls. C. of C., 1963-65, Dem. Nat. Conv., Atlanta, 1988; attaché Estonian Olympic Com. 1996 Olympics, Atlanta. Writer, editor World Pen Pals, 1964-66. V.p., bd. dirs. Ms. JCs, Minn., 1959-62; pres. Valley View Mothers' Club, Bloomington, Minn., 1961-62. Mem. AAUW, Nat. Rehab. Assn., Ga. Rehab. Assn. (membership chair 1988, 1970-97), Lic. Profl. Counselors Assn., Am. Mental Health Counselors Assn. Avocations: travel, reading, metaphysics, dancing, knitting. Home: 1106 Norwich Cir NE Atlanta GA 30324-2908

MARTIN, WALTER, retired lawyer; b. Crookston, Minn., Nov. 7, 1912; s. Frederick and Rosalie (Mertz) M.; m. Catherine Mary Severin, May 1, 1942 (dec. May 1979); children: Frederick H., Jacqueline K., Patricia, Priscilla, Walter Jr., John E. BA, Albion Coll., 1937; JD, U. Mich., 1939. Bar: Mich. 1939, U.S. Dist. Ct. (fed. dist.) 1939, U.S. Ct. Appeals (6th cir.) 1947, U.S. Supreme Ct. 1958. Ptnr. Martin & Martin, Saginaw, Mich., 1939-94; ret., 1994. Fellow Mich. Bar Assn., Saginaw County Bar Assn. (pres. 1958). Lutheran. Avocations: hunting, fishing. Office: 803 Court St Saginaw MI 48602-4223

MARTIN, WESLEY GEORGE, electrical engineer; b. Chgo., Apr. 15, 1946; s. Chester W. and Marie L. (Seifarth) M.; m. Margaret Rose Kowach, Aug. 17, 1968; children: Patrick, Christopher. BS, Milw. Sch. Engring., 1969; Cert., Alexander Hamilton Inst., N.Y.C., 1976. Registered profl. engr., Ill., Ind., Wis. Elec. engr., estimator The Austin Co., Des Plaines, Ill., 1969-78; elec. estimator Skidmore, Owings & Merrill, Chgo., 1978-83; elec. engr. Holabird & Root, Chgo., 1983-95, assoc. ptnr., 1986-95, dir. elec. engring., 1988-89, project engr., 1989-95; owner W.G. Martin & Assocs., Cons., Palatine, Ill., 1978—; sr. elec. engr. Consoer Townsend Envirodyne Engrs., Chgo., 1995—, assoc., 1996—, project mgr., 1996—. Contbr. articles to profl. jours. Dem. precinct capt., Palatine, 1979-82; cubmaster pack # 91 Boy Scouts Am., 1986-88. Recipient Award of Merit, Chgo. Lighting Inst., 1981-83, 90-92, 97-98. Mem. NSPE, Illuminating Engring. Soc. N.Am. (Internat. Illumination Design award 1992), Ill. Soc. Profl. Engrs., Nat. Eagle Scout Assn. Roman Catholic. Home: 918 W Colfax St Palatine IL 60067-2316 Office: Consoer Townsend Envirodyne Engrs 303 W Wacker Dr Chicago IL 60606-1204

MARTIN, WILLIAM ALLEN, sociology educator; b. Galveston, Tex.; s. James F. and Myra F. (Lide) M.; m. Debra J. Taylor; children: Zachary, Michelle. BA, So. Meth. U., 1970; MA, Tex. Christian U., 1971; PhD, U. Tex., 1976. Rsch. assoc. II U. Tex., Austin, 1970-74; part-time instr. U. Tex., 1974-75; instr. Ark. State U., State University, 1975-77; asst., assoc. prof. U. Tex. at Tyler, 1977-89, prof., 1989—; faculty adv. coun. U. Tex. Sys., 1994-99; pres. faculty senate U. Tex. at Tyler, 1994-98; rsch. cons. Nat. Pk. Svc., 1984; mem. spl. com. AAUP, 1998-99. Author: (book) Race & Ethnic Relations, 1999; contbr. articles to profl. jours. Mem. Phys. Environment Com. Tex. Coun. of Govts., 1995—. Recipient Tex. Higher Edn. Coordinating Bd. fellowship, 1992. Mem. Am. Sociol. Assn., Population Assn. Am., Assn. Am. Geographers, Southwestern Sociol. Assn. (v.p.), Tex. Assn. Coll. Tchrs. (pres. 1999-2001). E-mail: Amartin@mail.uttyl.edu. Office: U Tex 3900 University Blvd Tyler TX 75799-0001

MARTIN, WILLIAM EDWARD, economist; b. Ilford, Essex, Eng., Mar. 10, 1951; s. Joseph Edward and Pamela Maude (Ruse) M.; m. Yvette Mary McBrearty; children: Samuel, Anna. BA in Social Studies, Exeter U., 1972; MSc in Econs., Cardiff U., Wales, 1974. Economist Dept. Trade & Industry, 1973-81; adviser Ctrl. Policy Rev. Staff, 1981-83; economist, chief economist Phillips Drew/UBS Ltd., 1983-96; co-dir. econ. rsch. UBS Ltd., London, 1996-98; chief economist Phillips & Drew, London, 1998—; spl. adviser Treas. Select Com., 1986-96. Editor, author: The Economics of the Profits Crisis, 1981; contbr. articles to profl. jours. including Jour. Indsl. Econs. Avocations: music, reading, visual arts. Office: Phillips & Drew, Triton Ct., 14 Finsbury Sq, London EC2A 1PD, England

MARTIN ALONSO, OLGA, auditor; b. Madrid, Spain, Nov. 13, 1959; d. Miguel Martin and Encarnacion Alonso de Martin; m. Angel Ogueta-Fernandez, Oct. 15, 1986. M. Econs., U. Autonoma, Madrid, 1981; M. Laws, U. Complutense, Madrid, 1982; M in Acctg. and Auditing, INAE, Madrid, 1986; M. Math., U. Complutense, Madrid, 1983; M in Fin. Auditing, Gen. Coun. Econ. Colls. Spain, 1988. CPA 1988; cert. fin. auditor Censor Jurado de Cuentas 1988; registered acctg. auditor 1989. Prof. pub. econs. U. Autonoma, Madrid, 1981-85; lectr. Anglo-Spanish Seminar on EEC, Loughborough U., Eng. and Buitrago, Spain, 1981, Lawyer Coll. Lawyers of Madrid, 1982—; pvt. practice auditing Madrid, 1988—; prof. pub. econs. U. Autonoma, Madrid, 1981-85; cons. and lectr. various firms, Madrid, 1981—; lectr. on software BMD-BMP, Madrid, 1981; lectr. internat. rels. and polit. power, Madrid, 1982; lectr. on EEC and pub. firms Coll. Economists of Madrid-INI-IEF, Madrid, 1983; lectr. on auditing Econ. Sch., Alicante, 1988, lectr. on auditing stardards, 1991; lectr. on auditing info., Madrid, 1991. Author: Urban Development in Spain, 1982, State Monopolies and Legality in the EEC, 1983, Spanish Public Firms in the EEC, 1984, EEC Laws and Public Firms, 1984. Recipient End of Career award in econs. Spanish Ministry of Edn., 1981, Law, 1982; grantee Spanish Ministry of Edn., 1981, 82. Mem. Coll. Economists of Madrid, Coll. Lawyers of Madrid, Coll. Mathematicians Madrid, Registered Economists Auditors, Spanish Assn. Acctg. and Fin. Adminstrs., Inst. of Auditors, Inst. of Contabilidad y Auditoria de Cuentas, Internat. Acctg. Standard Com. Internat. Fed. Accts., European Union of Econ. Acctg. and Fin. Experts. Avocations: golf, tennis, horseback riding, yachting. Home: Mirasierra, C/Nuria 80, 28034 Madrid Spain Office: C/Gen Kirkpatrick 34, 28027 Madrid Spain

MARTINDALE, CARLA JOY, librarian; b. Ladysmith, Wis., Sept. 9, 1947; d. Howard Walter and Audrey Elizabeth (Stanton) M. BA, Mt. Senario Coll., 1970; MLIS, U. South Fla., 1990. Libr. Blackhawk Schs., South Wayne, Ind., 1975-79, Osceola County Libr., Kissimee, Fla., 1989-90, Fla. Tech. Coll., Orlando, 1991-92, Orlando Coll. South, 1993-98; ret., 1998; vis. prof. distance learning libr. St. Leo (Fla.) U., 1999—; chair for libr. 21st curriculum Phillips Coll., Orlando, 1995, acad. com., 1993-98, accreditation steering com., 1996. Library named in her honor Orlando Coll. South, 1995. Mem. ALA, Fla. Libr. Assn. Avocations: reading, pets, stock investing. Home: 39637 Otis Allen Rd Zephyrhills FL 33540-6801

MARTIN-DUVERNEUIL, NADINE, neuroradiologist; b. Vincennes, Paris, France, Oct. 15, 1955; d. Maurice and Raymonde (Faynel) Martin; m. Pascal Duverneuil, June 19, 1992; children: Audrey, Lorraine. Bachelor, Creteil, 1972; MD, 1980. Diplomate Radiology. Intern Hosp. de Paris, 1978-82; asst. Hospitalier, Paris, 1982-86, mem. staff, 1987-99. Author: Imagerie du Sida, 1991, A Propos du Nerf Facial, 1994, Imagerie Maxillo-Faciale, 1998; contbr. 236 articles to profl. jours. Mem. European Soc. Head Neck Radiology (faculty com. French chpt.), European Soc. Neuroradiology, French Soc. Neuroradiology, French Soc. Head Neck Radiology, French Soc. Radiology. Roman Catholic. Avocations: photography, bonsaiis, tennis, skiing. Office: Sve Neuroradiology Charcot, 75013 Paris France

MARTÍNEK, JAN, physician; b. Prague, Czech Republic, May 16, 1969; s. Antonín Martínek and Zuzana Zachová Machácková; 1 child, Simon. MD, Charles U., Prague, 1994, U. Lausanne, Switzerland, 1999. Tchg. fellow Anatomy Inst. Charles U., Prague, 1993-94; med. asst. Hosp. Motol, Prague, 1994-95; rsch. fellow Ctr. Hosp. Univ. Vandois-Gastroenterology, Lausanne, 1995-97, med. assoc., 1997-98; med. assoc. Inst. Clin. and Exptl. Medicine, Prague, 1998—. Co-author: Medizinische Publizistik, 1997, Proton Pump Inhibitors, 1999; contbr. articles to profl. jours. Active Civics Forum, Prague, 1989. Mem. Am. Gastroenterol. Assn. Avocations: sports, nature. Office: IKEM Clinic Hepato-Gastro, Videnská 1958, 140 21 Prague Czech Republic

MARTINELLI, ALBERTO PIERO, research scientist; b. Lucca, Italy, Aug. 31, 1932; s. Guglielmo Omero and Maria Giuseppa (Astore) M. D in Elec. Engring., U. Pisa, Italy, 1958; MSc in Elec. Engring., MIT, 1964. Rsch. asst. U. Pisa, Italy, 1957-59; elec. and safety engr. The Nuclear Power Group, Knutsford, Cheshire, Eng., 1960-62; rsch. asst. MIT Energy Conversion Lab., Cambridge, Mass., 1962-63, MIT Nat. Magnet Lab., Cambridge, 1963-64; rsch. scientist EURATOM/Max Planck Inst. for Plasmaphysics, Garching/Munich, Germany, 1965-75; sr. rsch. scientist EURATOM/Max Planck Inst. for Plasmaphysics, Garching/Munich, 1977-94, Commissariat Energie Atomique, Saclay/Paris, France, 1975-77; R&D internat. mgr. Internat. Thermonuclear Exptl. Reactor, Garching/Munich, 1994—; Euratom cons. Applied Superconductivity, European Cmty., Brussels, 1967-77; prof. dir. energy conversion U. Pisa, Italy, 1972-78; internat. mgr. Nuclear Energy Agy., Paris, 1975-77. Contbr. articles to profl. jours. Fulbright grantee USIS, 1961. Avocations: architecture, antiques and art, oldtime cars, swimming. Office: NET-ITER/Max Planck Inst, Boltzmannstr 2, D-85748 Garching Germany

MARTINELLI, LUCIA, biologist, researcher, laboratory manager; b. Trento, Italy, Nov. 5, 1957; d. Vittorio and Elsa (Carloni) M. D Biol. Sci., U. Bologna, Italy, 1982; PhD in Agrl. Environ. Sci., U. Wageningen, The Netherlands, 1997. Postdoctoral fellow Inst. Genetics, U. Bologna, 1982-85; rschr. Inst. Genetics, U. Wageningen, The Netherlands, 1985-86; rschr., project leader Agrimont R&S (Montedison Group), Milan and Massa Carrara, Italy, 1987-88; head Lab. Biotech., Inst. Agrario, San Michele all'Adige, Italy, 1988—; vis. scientist Plant Cell Rsch. Inst., Dublin, Calif., 1987-88. Mem. editl. bd. Jour. Vitis; contbr. articles to sci. jours. Mem. Com. Equal Opportun. of Aut. Province of Trento. Rudolf Hermanns Found. prize, 1994. Mem. Ordine Nat. Biologi Italiani (prov. del. 1987—), Italian Soc. Agrarian Genetics (dir. border), I.A.P.T.C., Assn. Prospettive. Avocations: playing piano and guitar, singing, scuba diving. Home: Passaggio Peterlongo 8, 38100 Trento Italy Office: Istituto Agrario, Via E Mach 1, 38010 San Michele A/Adige, Italy

MARTINEN, JOHN A., travel company executive; b. Sault Ste Marie, Mich., Mar. 26, 1938; s. John Albert and Ina Helia (Jarvi) M. BS with highest honors, Mich. State U., 1960; LLB, NYU, 1963. With Grace Line, N.Y.C., 1963-69; cons. Empresa Turistica Internat., Galapagos Cruises, Quito, Ecuador, 1969-70; regional mgr. Globus & Cosmos (Group Voyagers Inc.), N.Y.C., 1970-73, v.p., 1974-76, exec. v.p., 1977-78, pres., CEO, 1979-92; pres., CEO Globus & Cosmos (Group Voyagers Inc.), Littleton, Colo., 1993-98, chmn., 1998; pres., CEO Vista Travel Ventures, Inc., Denver, 1999—. Pres., bd. dirs. Edbrooke Condominium Assn. Mem. U.S. Tour Operators Assn., Am. Soc. Travel Agts., Tour Operator Plan, Denver Acad. Travel and Tourism (bd. dirs.) Lotus, Sky and Wings Club (N.Y.), Columbine Country Club, Denver Athletic Club. Democrat. Home: 1450 Wynkoop St Denver CO 80202-1116 Office: Vista Travel Ventures 370 17th St Ste 4060 Denver CO 80202-5642

MARTINEX-PADILLA, LAURA PATRICIA, food scientist, educator, researcher; b. Mexico City, Mar. 14, 1959; d. Manuel Martinez-Vargas and Gloria Padilla-de-Martinez. Diploma in food engring., Nat. Autonomous U. Mex., 1983; DEA food sci., Nat. Poly. Inst. Lorraine, Vandoeuvre les Nancy, France, 1985, PhD in Biotechnology and Food Industry, 1988. Asst. prof. Nat. Autonomous U. Mex., 1980-83, subject prof., 1983-92, titular prof., 1992—, dir. rheological and functional properties lab., 1990-00, chief engring. and tech. dept., 1995-98; invited assoc. prof. Wash. State U., Pullman, 1996; invited prof. U. Paris VII, 1999-00. Contbr. articles to profl. jours. Scholar CONACYT, 1984, 96, 99, grantee, 1996; grantee Nat. Autonomous U. Mex., 1993. Mem. AIChE, Food Tech. Mex. Assn., Mex. Assn. Chem. Rsch. and Edn. Avocations: art films, travel. Fax: 52 58 73 01 42. Office: UNAM FESC, Av. Primero de Mayo S. N., Cuautitlan Izcalli 54740, Mexico

MARTINEZ, ANDRE GEORGES JOSEPH, corporate officer; b. Toulouse, France, Jan. 10, 1953; s. Rufin and Yvonne (Thibaut) M.; m. Odile de la Grange, May 17, 1990; children: Olivia, Victor. MBA, Hautes Etudes Commerciales, Paris, 1975; postgrad., Inst. d'Etudes Politiques, Paris, 1977; M. in Econs., U. Paris, 1977. Contract negotiator Airbus Industrie, Toulouse, 1979-82; regional v.p. devel. Meridien Gestion S.A., Paris, 1982-84, corp. sr. v.p. devel., 1984-86; pres., CEO Meridien Hotels Inc., N.Y., 1986-92, vice chmn., 1993-94; pres., CEO, Meridien Can. Ltd., Montreal, 1986-92; pres. Meridien SA (formerly Meridien Gestion SA), Paris, 1989-94, Soc. des Hotels Meridien, Paris, 1991-94; chmn. Meridien Hotels Investment Group, 1993-94; mng. ptnr. André Martinez Conseil Sarl, Paris, 1995—; pres., CEO, Compagnie des Wagons-Lits, Paris, 1997—; chief devel. and strategy officer Accor Tour Maime Montparnesse, Paris, 1999—. Office: Accor Tour Maime, 33 Ave du Maime, 75015 Paris France

MARTINEZ, ANTHONY JOSEPH, real estate appraiser; b. San Pedro, Calif., Nov. 2, 1947; s. Antonio Jose and Frances (Gonzales) M.; m. Judith Lyn Miller, July 24, 1971; children: Ronda Adrienne, Amanda Elizabeth, Melanie Melissa. AA, Cerritos Coll., 1968; BA, U. Americas, Mexico City, 1970. Cert. secondary tchr., Calif.; cert. gen. real estate appraiser, Ariz. Corp. officer Canyon Savs. & Loan, Prescott, Ariz., 1976-80; Ariz. dir. Nat. Assn. Ind. Fee Appraisers, Phoenix, 1989-91; with bd. dirs. Ariz. State Bd. Appraisal, Phoenix, 1990-96, chmn., 1990-94; owner RAM Enterprises, Prescott, 1980-86, A.J. Martinez & Assocs., Prescott, 1986—; instr. Yavapai Coll., Prescott, 1973—; chmn. Bus. Adv. Coun. Yavapai Coll., 1988-89; with accredited residential sq. footage stds. com. Am. Nat. Stds. Instn., 1995-96. Tech. editor: Principios De La De Bienes Raicdes Residenciales, 1983. Charter mem. Prescott Town Hall. Mem. Nat. Assn. Ind. Fee Appraisers (sr., cert. instr. 1984—), Assn. Regulatory Ofcls. (nat. pres. 1994-95), Outward Bound-Prescott (bd. dirs. 1976-80), West Yavapai Guidance Clinic (bd. dirs. 1978-84), Prescott Sister Cities Assn. (pres. 1975-78), Lions (pres. Prescott Sunrise club 1979-80). Republican. Lutheran. Avocations: reading, camping, hunting. Office: Anthony J Martinez & Assocs PO Box 4195 Prescott AZ 86302-4195

MARTINEZ, ARTHUR C., retail company executive; b. N.Y.C., Sept. 25, 1939; s. Arthur F. and Agnes (Caulfield) M.; m. Elizabeth Rusch, July 30, 1966; children: Lauren, Gregory. BSME, Polytech. U., 1960; MBA, Harvard U., 1965; JD (hon.), U. Notre Dame, 1997. Dir. planning Internat. Paper Co., N.Y.C., 1967-69; asst. to pres. Talley Industries, Mesa, Ariz., 1969-70; dir. fin. RCA Corp., N.Y.C., 1970-73, v.p., 1973-80; sr. v.p., CFO Saks Fifth Ave., N.Y.C., 1980-84, exec. v.p., 1984-87, vice chmn., dir., 1990-92; sr. v.p. and group chief exec. Batus Inc., Louisville, 1987-90; vice chmn., dir. Saks Fifth Ave., 1990-92; chmn., CEO Sears Merchandise Group, Chgo., 1992-95; chmn., ceo Sears, Roebuck and Co., 1995—; bd. dirs. Sears, Roebuck and Co., Ameritech, Pepsico, Inc.; dep. chmn. Fed. Res. Bank, Chgo.; former chmn. Nat. Minority Supplier Devel. Coun., Inc. Bd. dirs. Defenders of Wildlife, 1992—, Nat. Urban League; chmn. bd. trustees Polytech. U., 1990—; trustee Art Inst., Orch. Assn. Chgo. Symphony Orch.; bd. dirs. Northestern Meml. Hosp., Chgo. 1st lt. U.S. Army, 1961-63. Named CEO of Yr., Fin. World Mag., 1996; recipient T.C. and Elizabeth Clarke medallion Sch. of Bus., Coll. William and Mary, 1997, Olin Sch. of Bus. Excellence in Bus. award, Washington U., St. Louis, 1997. Mem. Nat. Retail Fedn. (chmn. bd. dirs.). Avocations: tennis, golf, gardening. Office: Sears Roebuck and Co 3333 Beverly Rd Hoffman Est IL 60179-0001

MARTINEZ, CONCHITA, tennis player; b. Monzon, Spain, Apr. 16, 1972. Profl. tennis player, 1994—. Named WTA Player of Yr., 1995, Most Impressive Newcomer award, 1989, 32 singles titles WTA Tour, 9 double titles; nominated Most Improved Player award WTA Tour, 1993. Avocations: horseback riding, playing golf, soccer, shopping, music. Office: Sanex c/o WTA Tour 133 1st St NE Saint Petersburg FL 33701-3352*

MARTINEZ, FERNANDO V., civil engineer; b. Blewett, Tex., July 2, 1927; s. Catarino G. and Refugia V. M.; m. Dora Garza, Sept. 27, 1953; children: Fernando G., Karen Martinez Solano, Edward A. BS in Civil Engring., Tex A&M U., 1951. Registered profl. engr., Tex. Field engr. Farnsworth & Chambers Co, Houston, Tex., 1953-54; design engr. Link Belt Co., Houston, 1954, Anderson Clayton & Co., Houston, 1954-59; project engr. Olin Mathieson Chem. Corp., Pasadena, Tex., 1959-80; project mgr. Mobil Oil Corp., Pasadena, 1980—. 1st lt. U.S. Army, 1951-53, Korea. Republican. Roman Catholic. Home: 710 Skylark Rd Pasadena TX 77502-4560 Office: Mobil Oil Corp 2001 Jackson Rd Pasadena TX 77501

MARTINEZ, GINEZ, economist, consultant, educator; b. Castelnau de Guers, France, Nov. 25, 1936; s. Isidore Pierre and Catherine (Rodriguez) M.; m. Claudine Salanon, Oct. 25, 1962; children: Ginez-Louis, Gwendoline. BA in Econs., Paris and Oxford U., 1962; MBA, French Inst. Mgmt., Paris, 1975; PhD in Rsch., Pacific Western U., 1993; postgrad., Oxford U., 1995. CPA, Paris; cert. French Inst. Bus. Adminstrn. and Bus. Strategy, Paris, Coll. Social and Econ. Scis., Paris; cert. economist and internat. cons. Dep. mng. dir. cosmetic divsn. Coty Fragrance, 1962-71; gen. mgr. European countries Hunter Douglas, Rotterdam, The Netherlands, 1971-75; pres. MS 2000, 1974-81, Rouzee SA, 1981-85; cons., 1985—; prof., pres. NSED Inst.; CEO, pres., mng. dir. various cos.; prof. internat. bus. mgmt. European Mgmt. Inst., Bus. Schs. of Amiens, Reims, and Grenoble, France. Patentee muffler noise reducer, 1978 (Gold medal), antiscaling water device, 1978. Consul spl. affairs (hon.), Philippines. Officer French Army, 1958-60. Recipient Prestige de la France award for contbn. to devel. of SMEs and innovation in corp. governance Ministry of Industry, 1978. Mem. Am. Mgmt. Assn., Fed. Res. Assn., Oxford Club. Mem. Party of Jacques Chirac. Fax: 33-3-23-83-42-22. Office: La Baronerie BP 4, 02310 Charly sur Marne France

MARTINEZ, HERMINIA S., economist, banker; b. Havana, Cuba; came to U.S., 1960, naturalized, 1972; d. Carlos and Amelia (Santana) Martinez Sanchez; m. Mario Aguilar, 1982; children: Mario Aguilar, Carlos Aguilar. BA in Econs. cum laude, Am. U., 1965; MS in Fgn. Svc. (Univ. fellow); MS in Econs., Georgetown U., 1967, PhD in Econs., 1969; postgrad., Nat. U. Mex. Instr. econs. George Mason Coll., U. Va., Fairfax, 1967-68; researcher World Bank, 1967-69, indsl. economist, devel. econs. dept., 1969-71; economist World Bank Latin Am. (Ctrl. Am., Mex., Venezuala, Equador, Panama and Dominican Republic, Washington, 1971-79; sr. loan officer for Middle East and North Africa World Bank, 1977-81, sr. loan officer for Western Africa region, 1981-84, sr. economist Africa Region, 1988-91, prin. ops. officer pvt. sector fin. group Africa region, 1992-97, portfolio mgr. lead specialist, pvt. sector fin. group Africa region, 1997—. Contbg. author: The Economic Growth of Colombia: Problems and Prospects, 1973, Central American Financial Integration, 1975. Mid-Career fellow Princeton U., 1988-89. Mem. Am. Econ. Assn., Soc. Internat. Devel., Brookings Inst. Latin Am. Study Group. Roman Catholic. Home: 5145 Yuma St NW Washington DC 20016-4336 Office: World Bank 1818 H St NW Washington DC 20433-0001

MARTINEZ, J. ALFREDO, nutritionist, educator; b. Soria, Spain, Mar. 1, 1957; s. Alfredo and Nieves (Hernandez) M.; m. Maria Dolores Urbistondo; children: Diego, Maria. BPharm, U. Navarra, 1979, PhD, 1982. Postdoctoral fellow U. Nottingham, U.K., 1982-84; asst. lectr. U. Navarra, Spain, 1984-86, lectr., 1987-88, prof. food scis. and nutrition, 1992—; lectr. U. Santiago, Spain, 1986-87, 88-90; prof. U. Pais Vasco, Spain, 1987-88, 90-92; mem. steering com. IEFS, Ireland, 1993. Author 40 books; contbr. over 240 articles to profl. jours. Mem. Soc. Espanola Nutricion (pres. 1999), Soc. Espanola Obesidad, Real Acad. Farmacia, Colegio Oficial de Farmaceuticos, Inst. European Food Studies. Office: U Navarra, c/ Irunlarrea s/n, 31008 Pamplona Navarra, Spain

MARTINEZ, JOE LOUIS, JR., neurobiologist, educator; b. Albuquerque, Aug. 1, 1944; s. Joe Louis and Maria Elena (Werner) M.; m. Janice Susanna Hepner, Sept. 17, 1967 (div. Oct. 1987); children: Adan, Adria, Aric; m. Kimberly Smith, Dec. 2, 1990; 1 child, Ariel. BA, U. San Diego, 1966; MS, N.Mex. Highlands U., 1968; PhD, U. Del., 1971. From asst. to assoc. prof. Calif. State U., San Bernardino, 1971-75; assoc. researcher U. Calif., Irvine, 1975-82; prof. U. Calif., Berkeley, 1982-94; prof. neurobiology, dir. divsn. life scis. U. Tex., San Antonio, 1994—. Mem. AAAS (lifetime mentor award 1994), APA (pubs. and comm. bd. 1993-99). Office: U Tex 6900 N Loop 1604 W San Antonio TX 78249-1130

MARTINEZ, JOHN STANLEY, entrepreneur; b. Phila., Apr. 14, 1930; s. Joseph Vincent and Helen Leeds (Simpson) M.; m. Britta K. Ponder, Dec. 29, 1987; children: John Jr., Joseph G., Mary Lynn. BChemE, Rensselaer Poly. Inst., 1951; diploma, Oak Ridge Sch. Reactor Tech., 1957; PhD, U. Calif., Berkeley, 1962. Rsch. engr. N.Am. Aviation Co., Santa Susanna, Calif., 1954-55, Jet Propulsion Lab., Calif. Inst. Tech., Pasadena, Calif., 1955-61; rsch. assoc. Livermore (Calif.) Nat. Lab., 1959-61; with TRW Systems Group, Redondo Beach, Calif., 1961-76, mgr. high energy laser bus. area, 1970-76; pres. Physics Internat. Co., San Leandro, Calif., 1976-84, Jamar Enterprises, Moraga, Calif., 1970—, HLX Laser Inc., San Diego, 1986-87, Air-Sea Comm. Corp., San Diego, 1988-89; pres., CEO Jamar Tech. Co., San Diego, 1987-89, Calif. Jamar, Inc., 1989-92; chmn. Surgilase, Inc., Warwick, R.I., 1991-94; CEO, chmn. Jmar Industries, San Diego, 1993-98; chmn. Jmar Precision Sys., Inc., Chatsworth, Calif., 1993—, Jmar Semiconductor Inc., Irvine, Calif., 1997—; CEO, chmn. Jmar Technols., Inc., San Diego, 1998—; supervisory dir. Pisces Internat., Netherlands, 1982-84; pres., chmn. Hermosa Entertainment Corp., Hermosa Beach, Calif., 1969-72;. Contbr. articles to profl. publs.; patentee in field. Chmn. Hermosa Beach City Improvement Commn., 1968-70. Capt. USMC, 1951-54, Korea. AEC fellow, 1958, Ford Found. fellow, 1960. Mem. IEEE, Sigma Xi, Tau Beta Pi. Avocations: skiing, bicycling. Home: PO Box 1030 Del Mar CA 92014-1030 Office: 3956 Sorrento Valley Blvd San Diego CA 92121-1427

MARTINEZ, JOSE MARIA, business executive; b. Madrid, Sept. 8, 1950; s. Jose and Maria G.; m. Ana Maria Miron, Dec. 2, 1977; children: Ana Maria, Jose Maria. Diploma in Econ. and Bus., U. Autonoma, Spain, 1973; MBA in Bus., London Bus. Sch., 1981; MS in Mktg., Inst. Empresa, Madrid, 1980. Mktg. planning mgr. Abello, S.A., Madrid, 1973-78; mktg. and bus. devel. dir. Juste, S.A., Madrid, 1978-84; mktg. dir. Allergan, S.A., Madrid, 1984-87, bus. devel. dir., 1987-90, regulatory affairs dir., 1991-93, sci., regulatory and external affairs dir., 1994-95, European partnership and spl. projects dir., 1995-96; mng. dir. Inst. Oftalmologico de Alicante, Spain, 1996—, Cienciaoftal S.L., Madrid, 1999—, Hosp. Oftalmologico Internat., 1999—; founder AIMFA, Madrid, 1980; chmn. OPHTA Group, Barcelona-Madrid, 1990-96; assoc. de Empresas Sanitarias Provincia de Alicante. Author: Pharmaceutical Marketing in Spain and Its Inclusion in the EEC, 1982; inventor: Marketing/R&D An Inseparable Pair in the Pharmaceutical Industry, 1985, New Products Demand Forecast in the Pharmaceutical Field, 1978, Pharmaceutical marketing and New Medicines Production, 1982. Named Mktg. Man of Yr. Actualidad Economica Mag., Madrid, 1982, Internat. Hon. Citizen, New Orleans; recipient recognition for outstanding contbns. in ophthalmology La. State U., New Orleans, commemorative 270 Anniversary of La Havana U. Mem. Economist Acad., Farmaindustria, APharma Group. Roman Catholic. Avocations: theatre, travel, literature. E-mail: funioa@interbook.net. Fax: 34-6-516 38 06. Office: Inst Oftalmologico, Avenida de Denia 111, 03015 Alicante Spain

MARTÍNEZ, LUÍS OSVALDO, radiologist, educator; b. Havana, Cuba, Nov. 27, 1927; came to U.S., 1962, naturalized, 1967; s. Osvaldo and Felicita (Farinas) M.; children Maria Elena, Luis Osvaldo, Alberto Luis; m. Nydia M. Ceballos. MD, U. Havana, 1954. Cert. in diagnostic radiology. Intern Calixto Garcia Hosp., Havana, 1954-55; resident in radiology Jackson Meml. Hosp., Miami, Fla., 1963-65, fellow in cardiovascular radiology, 1965-67; instr. radiology U. Miami, 1965-68, asst. prof., 1968, clin. asst. prof., 1968-70, assoc. prof., 1970-76, prof., 1976-91, clin. prof., 1991-94; chief radiol. svcs. VA Med. Ctr., 1991—; assoc. dir. dept. radiology Mt. Siai Med. Ctr., Miami Beach, Fla., 1969-91, chief divsn. diagnostic radiology, 1970-91, dir. residency program in diagnostic radiology; dir. Spanish Radiology Seminar. Reviewer Am. Jour. Radiology, Radium Therapy and Nuclear Medicine,

1978; contbr. articles to profl. jours. Former pres. League Against Cancer. Recipient Gold medal Interam. Coll. Radiology, 1975, Antoine Bèclere medal Internat. Congress Radiology, 1989, Carlos J. Finlay Gold medal Cuban Med. Convb., 1990, Honors Achievement award, Cert. of Merit Mallinckrodt Pharms., 1972-74; Luis O. Martinez M.D. Lecture named in his honor, Interam. Coll. Radiology. Mem. AMA (Physician's Recognition award 1971, 74-83), AAUP, Radiol. Soc. France (hon. 1991), Internat. Soc. Lymphology, Interam. Coll. Radiology (pres.), Internat. Coll. Surgeons, Internat. Coll. Angiology, Internat. Soc. Radiology, Cuban Med. Assn. in Exile, Am. Coll. Chest Physicians (assoc.), Radiol. Soc. N. Am., Am. Coll. Radiology, Am. Roentgen Ray Soc., Am. Assn. Fgn. Med. Grads., Am. Profl. Practice Assn., Am. Thoracic Soc., Pan Am. Med. Assn., Am. Assn. Univ. Radiologists, Brit. Inst. Radiology, Am. Heart Assn. (mem. council cardiovascular radiology), Faculty Radiologists, Soc. Gastrointestinal Radiologists, Am. Geriatrics Soc., Am. Coll. Angiology, Royal Coll. Radiologists, Am. Soic. Therapeutic Radiologists, Assn. Hosp. Med. Edn., Cuban Radiology Soc. in exile (founder, pres.), Cuban chpt. Inter Am. Coll. Radiology (founder, pres.), Am. Coll. Med. Imaging, Interasma, So. Med. Assn., N.Y. Acad. Scis., Fla. Thoracis Soc., Fla. Radiol. Soc., Dade County Med. Assn., Greater Miami Radiol. Soc., cuban Radiol. Soc. (sec.), Can. Assn. Radiologists, Soc. Thoracic Radiologists (founding mem.), Emeritus mem. Am. Coll. Angiology, 1989, Emeritus mem. Am. Heart Assn., 1992; hon. mem. numerous med. socs. of Mex., Cen. and S. Am. Roman Catholic. Office: 1201 NW 16th St Miami FL 33125-1624

MARTINEZ, MANUELA, physician, psychobiologist, educator, researcher; b. Buñol, Valencia, Spain, July 12, 1958; d. Amador Martinez and Manuela Ortiz; 1 child, Ana Isla Garcia-Martinez. Degree in medicine, U. Valencia, 1983, PhD, 1987. Lectr. U. Valencia, 1986-87, temporary prof., 1988-89, titular prof., 1990—; vis. scholar U. Cambridge, U.K., 1995, 98. Guest editor: Aggressive Behavior, 1998; contbr. articles to profl. jours. By-fellow Churchill Coll., U. Cambridge, Eng., 1998. Mem. Internat. Soc. for Rsch. on Aggression, N.Y. Acad. Sci. Avocations: travelling, art. Office: Fac Psych U Valencia, Avda Blasco Ibañez No 21, 46010 Valencia Spain

MARTINEZ, MIGUEL ACEVEDO, urologist, consultant, lecturer; b. Chihuahua, Mex., Aug. 18, 1953; came to U.S., 1956; s. Miguel Nuñez and Velia (Acevedo) M. AB, Stanford U., 1976; MD, Yale U., 1983. Diplomate Am. Bd. Urology. Intern U. S.C. Med. Ctr., 1983-84; resident in urology White Meml. Med. Ctr., L.A., 1984-89, urologist, 1989—; cons., lectr. physician asst. program U. So. Calif., L.A., 1990—, clin. instr.; patient edn. cons. ICI Pharm., Del., 1991—, Zeneca's Speaker Forum; patient edn. and med. cons., lectr. Abbott Labs., 1991—; mem. edn.cons. several radio/TV stas., 1991—; mem. subcom. for diseases on kidney and transplantation NIH, Washington, 1991. Author: Intercellular Pathways, 1981. Polit. cons. Xavier Becerra, U.S. Congress, 1992, Martin Gallegos, Gil Cedillo, Calif. State Assembly, 1993, others; bd. dirs. Latino Ctr. for Prevention and Action in Health, Orange County, calif.; bd. govs., sec., rep. Zeneca Urology Econ. Summit, Washington, 1993; mem. Pfizer Nat. Hispanic Adv. Bd. Named one of Outstanding Young Men of Am., 1981. Mem. AMA, Am. Urological Assn., Calif. Med. Assn. (polit. action com. bd. dirs. 1997—, del.), L.A. Med. Assn. (polit. action com. 1992—), L.A. County Med. Assn., Yale Alumni Assn., Stanford Alumni Assn., L.A. Athletic Club. Office: White Meml Med Ctr Rm 500 1701 Cesar Chavez Ave Los Angeles CA 90033-2438

MARTÍNEZ, MIGUEL-ANGEL, international organization executive; b. Madrid, Spain, Jan. 30, 1940; married Carmen Gómez; 2 children. Degree in French Philology. Internat. civil servant, 1967-73; sec. gen. Socialist Internat. Orgn. Edn., 1970-73; pres. European Coordinating Office Internat. Youth Orgns., 1973-75; head svc. Gen. Secretariat Internat. Confdn. Free Trade-Union Orgns., 1977—; PSOE mem. Spanish Parliament Ciudad Real, mem. com. fgn. affairs, pres. com. I on polit. affairs, internat. security, and disarmament PSOE, France, 1977—; PSOE sec. gen. Castilla-La Mancha, mem. Interparliamentary Union, chmn. Spanish del., v.p. parliamentary assembly of Western European Union France, chmn. Spanish del., pres. parliamentary assembly Coun. Europe; mem. European Parliament, Brussels, Belgium. Recipient Legion of Honor award Govt. France, 1995. Office: Urb Montepríncipe, parcela A/4 Chalet n 41, E-28660 Boadilla Del Monte Spain*

MARTINEZ, PETER, astronomer; b. Cape Town, South Africa, Apr. 26, 1966; s. Pedro and Maria Tereza (Germano) M.; m. Esther Roux van den Berg, Dec. 19, 1992. BS, U. Cape Town, South Africa, 1986, BS with honors in Materials Enginring., 1987, MS with distinction, 1990, PhD, 1993. Tech. officer U. Cape Town, 1989-94, sr. scientific officer, 1995-96; rsch. fellow South African Astron. Obs., 1997-98, divsn. head, sci. edn. liaison, 1999—; mem. Boyden Obs. com. U. Orange Free State, Bloemfontein, South Africa, 1995—; coord. Working Group Basic Space Sci. in Africa, 1996—; cons. Arthur Clarke Ctr. Modern Techs., Colombo, Sri Lanka, 1996-98. Contbr. articles to profl. jours. Mem. Friends of South African Mus., 1994—. Grantee Found. Rsch. Devel., South Africa, 1993, 94, 96, 97, 99, Internat. Astron. Union, 1994, 96, UN, 1995, 96; recipient FRD postdoctoral award Found. Rsch. Devel., South Africa, 1994. Fellow Royal Astron. Soc.; mem. Royal Soc. South Africa, Astron. Soc. South Africa, South African Vexillological Assn., South African Heraldry Soc., Internat. Astronomical Union. Avocations: walking, reading, cinema. Home: SAAO House 8, PO Box 9, Observatory 7935, South Africa Office: South African Astron Obs, PO Box 9 Obs 7935, Cape Town 7935, South Africa

MARTINEZ, RICHARD ISAAC, science administrator; b. Havana, Cuba, Aug. 16, 1944; came to U.S., 1950; s. Joseph Louis and Susana (Nardea) M.; children: David B.J., Robyn S.M. BSc, McGill U., 1964; PhD in Chemistry, UCLA, 1976. Lab. asst. DuPont of Can. Ltd., Maitland, Ont., Can., 1962; teaching asst. McGill U., Montreal, Que., Can., 1964-65; teaching and rsch. asst. San Diego State U., 1965-67; chemist Shell Chem. Co., Torrance, Calif., 1967-70; rsch. chemist UCLA, 1971-76, Dept. Commerce Nat. Inst. Standards and Tech., Gaithersburg, Md., 1976-92; sci. rev. adminstr. Office Sci. Rev., Nat. Inst. Gen. Med. Scis., NIH, Bethesda, Md., 1992—; apptd. mem. City of Gaithersburg's Tech. and Innovation Com., 1998—. Contbr. over 40 articles to profl. publs., chpts. to books. Pres., chmn. bd. dirs. Bethesda-Chevy Chase Jewish Cmty. Group, 1991-93. Recipient I-R 100 award, 1983, Bronze medal U.S. Dept. Commerce, 1981; postdoctoral rsch. assoc. Nat. Acad. Scis., 1976-78; doctoral fellow UCLA, 1970-73. Sr. Fellow Coun. for Excellence in Govt., 1996—; mem. Am. Chem. Soc., Soc. Advancement of Chicanos and Native Ams. in Sci. Achievements include patents in methods for producing carbocyclic compounds, flue-gas desulfurization (I-R 100 award 1983); discovered dioxiranes (Ency. Brit. Yearbook of Sci. and the Future, 1979), metastable excited sulfur dioxide, vicinal hydroxy-substituted alkyl and oxoalkyl nitrates, peroxynitrates; research in development, standardization and application of MS/MS Tandem Mass Spectrometry for the study of the kinetics and mechanisms of complex ion-molecule reactions; rsch. on the kinetics and mechanims of complex organic reaction systems relevant to oxidation and atmospheric chemistry (including the oxidation chemistry of olefins and sulfur compounds; free-radical reactions; ozone-olefin and ozone-sulfide reactions); developed cutting-edge rsch. methodologies. E-mail: rm63f@nih.gov. Office: Nat Inst Gen Med 45 Center Dr Bethesda MD 20892-0001

MARTINEZ-CALATAYUD, JOSÉ, analytical chemistry educator; b. Onteniente, Valencia, Spain, Mar. 23, 1945; s. José Maria and Encarnacion (Calatayud) Martinez; m. Remedios Ferrero-Mico, July 29, 1972; children: Eugenia Martinez, Alberto Martinez. BSc in Chemistry, U. Valencia, 1968, PhD, 1972. Asst. tchr. U. Valencia, 1968-70, adj. tchr., 1970-80, prof. analytical chemistry, 1990—; prof. titular Centro Estudios Universitarios, Valencia, 1974—, dir. Sch. Pharmacy, 1992-98; vice-rector rsch. U. Cardenal Herrera, 1999—. Author: Alchemists: mystics, savants, rascals..., 1992, Flow Injection Analysis of Pharmaceuticals. Automation in the Laboratory, 1996, Pharmaceutical Sciences, From Amulet to the Computer, 1999; contbr. to ency. Comprehensive Analytical Chemistry, 1995; contbr. over 200 articles to profl. jours. Recipient Nat. Rsch. award Cardenal Herrera, Madrid, 1998. Mem. Royal Soc. Chemistry, Soc. Espanola Quimica Analitica, F.C. Quimicas (sec.). Roman Catholic. Avocations: history of sciences, cycling, bricolage, social activities.

MARTINEZ DE HURTADO, ELADIO, oil industry executive; b. Madrid, Feb. 18, 1958; s. Eladio Martinez de Hurtado and Rosario Martin; m. Cristina Diaz Perez, Dec. 9, 1989; 1 child, Lucia. BS in Civil Engring., Madrid Poly. U., MS in Civil Engring., PhD in Civil Engring., 1983. Retail fuels engr. Mobil Canaries, Gran Canaria, 1988-91; retail investment mgr., Spain and Portugal Mobil Grupo Iberico, Madrid, Lisbon, 1992-95; retail investment mgr. Mobil Europe Ltd., London, 1995-96; bus. support dir. Mobil Oil Spain, Madrid, 1996-97; mng. dir., pres. Mobil Oil Portuguesa, Lisbon, 1997-98; bus. devel. dir. Mobil Europe Ltd., London, 1999—. Lt., Army Engring. Corps, 1983-84, Madrid. Mem. Club Tenis Chamartin, Health Ctr. Mariott Hotels, Real Club Nautico Tenerife. Avocations: tennis, swimming, family. Office: Mobil Europe Lubricants Ltd, 3 Clements Inn Mobil Ct, London WC2A 2EB, London

MARTINEZ-DE-TODA, FERNANDO, agricultural studies educator; b. Badaran, La Rioja, Spain, Feb. 16, 1955; s. Crispin and Aurora (Fernandez) Martinez-de-toda; m. Rosa Maria Cabeza, July 10, 1987; children: Cristina, Irene. Ingeniero Agronomo, Escuela Tecnica Superior, Madrid, 1978, D Ingeniero Agronomo, 1982. Prof. asociado U. Politecnica, Madrid, 1979-83, prof. titular, 1983-87; prof. titular U. La Rioja, Logrono, Spain, 1988—; assesor Gobierno de la Rioja, Logrono, 1988-89; cons. Bodegas Berberana, Cenicero, Spain, 1989-91. Author: Bologia de La Vid, 1991, Mecanizacion Integral Vinedo, 1995. Office: U de la Rioja, Avda de la Paz 105, 26004 Logrono La Rioja, Spain

MARTÍNEZ DOMÍNGUEZ, GUILLERMO, economist, financial executive; b. Monterry, N.L., Mex., Aug. 1, 1923; s. Alfonso and Rafaela Martinez Donimquez; m. Mina Benavides, July 1, 1953; children: Rose Laura, Ana Silvia, Paula Daniela. Degree in Econs., Nat. Faculty of Econs., Mexico City, 1947. Prices dir. Mexico, 1947-48; dir. small commerce Nat. Bank, Mexico City, 1952-55; chief budgetary control and ofcl. mayor Fed. Power Commn., Mexico City, 1955-59, dir. gen., 1964-70; counselor Mexican Coffee Inst., 1960-64; tech. coord. Sugar Industry Planning Fund, 1960-64; dir. gen. Nacional Funanciera S.A., Mexico City, 1970-74; dir. equity investment Interam Devel. Bank, Washington, 1978-80; econ. columnist Excelsior, 1995-97; tchr. Nat. Sch. Econs., 1948-64; bd. dirs. Comision Federalde Electricidad, Banco de Mexico, Petróleos Mexicanos,, Teléfonos de México; bus./fin. counselor, Mexico City, 1970-74. Author: Los Braceros, 1946, Mexican Social Security Financial Crisis, 1947, Attempts for Price Control in Mexico, 1951, Mexican Electric Industrial Integration, 1971, 50 Years of Mexican Development Bank, 1980, Nacional Financiera Ante el Siglo XXI, 1994. Pres. Liga de Economistas Revolucionarios, 1952-54. Recipient Nat. Prize Journalism, Assn. Mexicana de Periodistas, 1953, Nat. Gold medal prize Lazaro Cardenas, 1995; others. Mem. Colegio Nacional de Economistas (pres. 1954-56), Am. Econs. Assn. Home: Cerrada de Presa Escolta 24, 10200 Mexico City Mexico Office: Privada Trini 10, San Jeronimo 10200 D F, Mexico

MARTINEZ FINKELSHTEIN, ANDREI, mathematician, educator, researcher; b. Moscow, Jan. 13, 1963; arrived in Cuba, 1973, Spain, 1994; s. Francisco Martinez Soler and Lidia Efimovna Finkelshtein. BS, Havana (Cuba) U., 1986; PhD, Moscow State U., 1991. Prof. Havana U., 1986-94; asst. prof. U. Almeria, Spain, 1994-99, prof., 1999—; vis. prof. U. Autonoma, Madrid, 1993, U. Carlos III, Madrid, 1994, U. South Fla., Tampa, 2000. Contbr. articles to profl. jours. Mem. nat. bd. dirs. Univ. Students Fedn., Havana, 1983-86. Recipient Jose Antonio Echevarria medal Cuban State Coun., 1985. Mem. Am. Math. Soc., Cuban Math. Soc., Spanish Math. Soc., Soc. Indsl. and Applied Math. Avocations: music, sports. Office: U Almeria Dept Stats and Applied Math, La Canada, 04120 Almeria Spain

MARTINEZ FRIAS, JESUS, mineralogist, researcher; b. Madrid, Oct. 3, 1960; s. Jesus Martinez Rodriguez and Concepcion Frias Mas; m. Joaquina Martin Hernandez, Apr. 15, 1988; 1 child, Jesus Enrique. Degree in geology, U. Complutense, Madrid, 1982, PhD in Mineral Deposits, 1986. Fellow U. Complutense, 1983-86; lectr. U. San Pablo, Madrid, 1983-88; postdoctoral fellow Spanish Sci. Rsch. Coun., Madrid, 1987-88; geol. rschr. Spanish Sci. Rsch. Coun., Granada, 1989-94, Madrid, 1994—; dir. rsch. projects Interministry Commn. of Sci. and Tech., Spanish Sci. Rsch. Coun., NATO, 1989—; Spanish rep. Internat. Geol. Correlation Program 318, Internat. Union Geol. Scis./UNESCO, Granada and Madrid, 1991—; Western Europe rep. UN Com. of Natural Resources, 1998; Spanish rep. UN Commn. on Sci. and Tech. for Devel., 1999—. Editor: Mineral Resources of Spain, 1992; contbr. articles to profl. publs. Grantee Spanish Ministry of Sci. and Edn., 1983, CSIC, 1987, 89. Mem. Spanish Soc. Mineralogy (com. 1988-92), Spanish Mineral Deposit Assn. (com. 1992-96), Spanish Assn. Scientists, CSIC (sci. com.). Avocations: choral singing, science fiction, movies. Office: Museo Nat Cie Natural, Jose Gutierrez Abascal 2, 28006 Madrid Spain

MARTÍNEZ NEGRETE, EDUARDO, university program director; b. Irapuato, Mex., Aug. 18, 1971; s. Alvaro Martínez Vaca and Elena Negrete. Lic. in info. systems, Tech. Inst. of Monterrey, Irapuato, 1993, M in Mktg., 1998. Mem. adminstrv. staff CABASA Constrns. Inc., Irapuato, 1993; mgr. Burger King restaurant, Irapuato, 1994-96; chair prof. Tech. Inst. of Monterrey, Irapuato, 1996-97, prof., 1996-97, coord. program to qualify tchrs. at virtual univ., 1997-98, gen. corrd. virtual univ., prof., 1998—; cons. info. systems Integral Support in Info. Sys., Irapuato, 1995-96; prof mktg. seminarium, ethics, internat. mktg., franchises. Named Best Student of Mex., Diario de Mex., Mexico City, 1994. Mem. IEEE, Planetary Soc., Nat. Geog. Soc., Polaris Astron. Soc. (founder 1998). Mem. Nat. Action Party. Roman Catholic. Avocations: basketball, reading scientific magazines, TV, science fiction movies. Home: Ramón Corona # 387, 36500 Irapuato Mexico Office: Inst Tech & Superior Study, Paseo Mirador del Valle # 445, 36670 Irapuato Mexico

MARTINEZ-PONS, MANUEL, psychology educator; b. Dominican Republic, Apr. 19, 1940; s. Manuel and Alsacia (Gorsd) Martinez. AA, U. State of N.Y., 1973, BS, 1975; BGS, U. Nebr., Omaha, 1973, MS, 1975; PhD, U. Nebr., Lincoln, 1977; MPh, CUNY, 1985, PhD, 1988. Rsch. assoc. CUNY, 1982-85, instr. computer programing, 1985-86; assoc. prof. Sch. Edn., Bklyn. Coll., CUNY, 1986—; adj. instr. U. Nebr., Lincoln, 1975-77, U. Nebr., Omaha, 1978, City Coll., CUNY, 1980-81; adj. asst. prof. Medgar Evers Coll., CUNY, 1985, Queens Coll., CUNY, 1986. Author: Research in the Social Sciences and Education: Principles and Process, 1997, Statistics in Modern Research: Applications in the Social Sciences and Education, 1999; (with others) Student Perceptions in the Classroom: Causes and Consequences, 1992; contbr. articles to profl. jours.; cons. editor Jour. Experimental Edn., 1997—. Recipient numerous grants. Mem. Am. Edn. Rsch. Assn., Am. Psychol. Soc., Am. Mensa. Home: 453 Beach 138th St Belle Harbor NY 11694-1341 Office: Brooklyn Coll Sch of Edn Brooklyn NY 11210

MARTINEZ-RACINES, CESAR P., agricultural products researcher; b. Cienaga, Magdalena, Colombia, Sept. 2, 1943; s. Numa P. Martinez and Elsa Racines; m. Myriam Marulanda, June 9, 1972; children: Isabel Cristina, Claudia Patricia, Paulo Cesar, Carolina. B in Agriculture, Nat. U. Palmira, 1966; M in Plant Breeding, U. Philipines, Los Baños, 1971; PhD in Plant Breeding, Oreg. State U., 1976. Asst. rice breeder Colombian Agrl. Inst., Palmira, 1967-81; rice breeder Internat. Ctr. Tropical Agriculture, Cali, Colombia, 1981-98, Monsanto Co., 1999, Internat. Ctr. Tropical Agrl., 2000—; cons. Empresa Brasilera de Pesquisas/Centro Nacional de Pesquisas Arroz y Feijao, Goiania, Brazil, 1981; with Cornell U., Ithaca, N.Y., 1990-91. Contbr. articles to profl. jours. Scholar Internat. Rice Rsch. Inst., 1969-71; fellow Rockefeller Found., 1973-76. Mem. Crop Sci. Soc. Am., Asiava Asosiacion Colombiana Ingenieros Agronomos, Sigma Xi. Roman Catholic. Avocations: soccer, jogging, swimming, classical music, reading. Home: Arboledas, Kra 2A Oeste 7-121, Cali Valle Valle, Colombia Office: CIAT, AA 67-13, Cali Valle, Colombia

MARTINEZ-RAMIREZ, SAGRARIO, chemist; b. Palencia, Spain, Sept. 19, 1963; s. Francisco Martinez and Julia Ramirez; married. BSc in Chemistry, U. Complutense Madrid, 1988, PhD, 1995. Postdoctoral fellow CSIC, Madrid, 1990-95; % UMIST, Manchester, England, 1995-98; grantee CSIC, Madrid, 1998—. Office: Inst Scis, C/Serrano Galvache s/n, 28033 Madrid Spain

MARTINEZ SOMALO, EDUARDO CARDINAL, archbishop; b. Banos de Rios Tobia, Spain, Mar. 31, 1927. Ordained priest Roman Cath. Ch., 1950. Elected bishop of Tagara, later archbishop, 1975, created cardinal,, 1988; prefect Congregation for Insts. of Consecrated Life and Socs. Apostolic Life; protodeacon SS Nome de Gesu, 1996. Office: 00120 Vatican City State Vatican City State*

MARTIN-GULLON, IGNACIO, chemical engineer, researcher, educator; b. Alicante, Spain, June 26, 1966; s. Isidro and Maria Teresa (Gullon-Fernandez) Martin-Roldan; m. Maria Teresa Aldana-Felix, 1997. Degree in chemistry, U. Alicante, Spain, 1989, PhDChemE, 1995. Asst. rschr. U. Alicante, 1991-95, asst. prof., 1998—; postdoctoral scholar U. Ky., Lexington, 1996-97; R&D scientist Norit N.V., Amersfoort, The Netherlands, 1997-98. 2d lt. Spanish Army, 1987-90. Roman Catholic. Office: U Alicante Dept Chem Engrng, PO Box 99, 03080 Alicante Spain

MARTINI, CARLO MARIA CARDINAL, archbishop; b. Turin, Italy, Feb. 15, 1927. Joined Soc. of Jesus, Roman Cath. Ch., 1944, ordained priest, 1952; biblical scholar; sem. prof., Chieri, Italy, 1958-61; prof., rector Pontifical Biblical Inst., 1969-78; rector Pontifical Gregorian U., 1978-79; archbishop of Milan, 1980; elevated to Sacred Coll. of Cardinals, 1983. Author: theological, biblical and spiritual works. Mem. Council for Pub. Affairs of the Ch. Address: Palazzo Arcivescovile, Piazza Fontana 2, 20122 Milan Italy

MARTINI, RICHARD K., theatrical producer; b. Bergenfield, N.J., Mar. 11, 1952; s. John F. and June L. (Fenton) M.; m. Susan C. Weaving, Aug. 1, 1981. BA, St. Francis Coll., Loretto, Pa., 1974; MEd, U. S.C., 1975. V.p. Am. Theatre Prodns., N.Y.C., 1975-81; pres. Edgewood Orgn., N.Y.C., 1981-86; pres., owner KL Mgmt., N.Y.C., 1986—; owner, operator Martini Entertainment, Inc., N.Y.C., 1991—. Home: 201 E 37th St New York NY 10016-3159 Office: Martini Entertainment Co 1501 Broadway Ste 1401 New York NY 10036-5601

MARTINIERE, GERARD DE LA, holding companies executive; b. Sept. 12, 1943; married; 4 children. Grad., Ecole Poly., 1965, Ecole Nat. d'Adminstrn., 1969. With French Ministry of Fin., 1969-84; gen. sec. French Securities and Exch. Regulatory Body, 1984-86; chmn. Paris Derivatives Clearing House, 1986-88; CEO Paris Stock Exch., 1988-89; chmn., CEO Meeschaert Rousselle Brokerage unit AXA Group, 1989-91, exec. v.p. investment and fin. svcs. ops., 1991-93, 1993—, CFO; mem. AXA mgmt. bd., 1997—; chmn. econ. and fin. commn. French Fedn. Ins. Cos., 1993—. Office: AXA Group, 25 Ave Matignon, Paris 75008, France

MARTIN-MARTINEZ, JOSE MIGUEL, chemistry educator; b. Granada, Spain, Apr. 3, 1956; s. José Martín-Navarro and Isabel Martínez-Fernández; m. María Del Mar Torres-Ubago, Dec. 15, 1989; children: María Del Mar, Elvira, José Miguel. PhD, U. Granada, 1981. Asst. prof. U. Granada, 1979-81; assoc. prof. U. Alicante, Spain, 1981-93, prof., 1993—, dir. internal affairs dept., 1996-98, rschr. dept. inorganic chemistry, 1981-93, head rsch. Adhesion and Adhesives Lab., 1990—; internat. coord. cyted network VIII D, Sci. and Tech. Program for the Sci. Devel. L.Am., 1997—; chmn. Mittal award com. Jour. Adhesion Sci. and Tech., 1999; mem. com. plasma treatment of polymers EC Cost 527, 2000—; head new campus project U. Alicante, 1999—. Author: Adhesion of Elastomers, 1993; mem. editl. bd. Jour. Adhesion, 1995, Jour. Adhesion Sci. and Tech., 1993—, Internat. Jour. Adhesion and Adhesives, 1992—. Recipient 1st prize Footwear Fair Instn., 1990, 1st prize for adhesives presentation EUROCOAT 98, Barcelona, Spain, 1998. Mem. Inst. Materials, Adhesion Soc. USA, Am. Chem. Soc., Soc. Rheology, French Soc. Adhesion, Spanish Chemistry Soc. Roman Catholic. Avocations: classical music, swimming, collecting stickers and trading cards, classical theatre. Office: U Alicante, Adhesion and Adhesives Lab, 03080 Alicante Spain

MARTIN-NETO, LADISLAU, physicst, researcher; b. Duartina, Brazil, June 4, 1960; s. Egydio and Therezinha M.; m. Mitze Fatima Zanin Bricks, Jan. 21, 1989; 1 child, Ana Flavia. Degree in physics, UNESP, Bauru, Brazil, 1981; M in Physics, USP, São Carlos, Brazil, 1985; D in physics, USP, 1988; postdoctoral student, U. Calif., Berkeley, 1994. Rschr. FIPAI/EMBRAPA, São Carlos, 1986—; asst. rschr. EMBRAPA-CNPDIA, São Carlos, 1990-92, head rsch. and devel., 1994-97; exec. sec. automation EMBRAPA, São Carlos, 1997—; cons. Soil Sci. Soc. Am. Jour., Madison, Wis., 1996, Brazilian Jour. Soil Sci., Vicosa, 1996—. Contbr. articles to profl. jours. CNPq fellow USP, 1982-84, FAPESP fellow, 1984-86; grantee EMBRAPA, 1997. Mem. Internat. Humic Substance Soc. (chpt. coord. 1997—), Internat. Union Soil Sci. (v.p. soil chemistry 1998—), Soil Sci. Brazilian Soc., Physics Brazilian Soc. Home: Alameda Jaboticabeiras 305, 13561260 Sao Carlos Brazil Office: EMBRAPA CNPDIA, Rua XV Novembro 1452, 13560970 Sao Carlos Brazil

MARTINO, DONNA FRANCES, newspaper sales administrator; b. N.Y.C., May 8, 1947; d. Samuel Edward and Angelina (Scudieri) M. BA, Coll. Mt. St. Vincent, 1969; MA, Columbia U., 1972. Cert. early childhood tchr., N.Y., N.J. Acct. mgr. Contra Costa Times, Walnut Creek, Calif., 1980-83; nat. acct. mgr. San Francisco Chronicle/Examiner, 1983-85; retail acct. exec. The N.Y. Times, N.Y.C., 1986-94, nat. acct. mgr. pharm. advt., 1994-96; nat. sales mgr. pharms. Newspaper Nat. Network, N.Y.C., 1997—. Project leader spl. advertorials to The N.Y. Times, 1994—. Mem. Columbia U. Alumni Club Bergen/Passaic Counties (pres. 1998—), Healthcare Mktg. and Comm. Coun. Avocations: sailing, rock climbing, antiques, art. Office: Newspaper Nat Network 711 3rd Ave New York NY 10017-4014

MARTINO, JOAO ANTONIO, electronics engineer, educator; b. Sao Paulo, Apr. 17, 1959; s. Nicola and Ottilia (Coti) M.; m. Marines Dalla Valle, Feb. 3, 1984; children: Fernanda Dalla Valle, Marcio Dalla Valle. Degree in engring., Faculdade de Engenharia Industrial/Fundagao de Ciências Aplicadas, 1981; MS, U. São Paulo, 1984, PhD, 1988. Mem. faculty Faculdade de Engenharia Indsl./Fundacao de Scis. Aplicadas, Brazil, 1984—, prof. microelectronics, 1995—, head dept. electronic engring., 1996—; vice dir. Faculdade de Info., Fundacao de Scis. Aplicadas, Brazil, 1998—; rschr. head CMOS/LSI/USP, Brazil, 1989—; guest rschr. IMEC/KUL, Leuven, Belgium, 1989-94; assoc. prof. dept. sys. electronics U. São Paulo, 1992—. Contbr. articles to profl. jours. Mem. SBMicro (coun. 1995-99). Avocation: astronomy. Home: Rua Dom Armando Lombardi, 701 Apt 82, 05616011 São Paulo Brazil Office: U Sao Paulo Av Prof Luciano Gualberto, Trav 3 158, São Paulo 05508900, Brazil also: FEI/FCA, Av Humberto AC Branco, 3970 São Paulo Brazil

MARTINO, JOSEPH PAUL, research scientist; b. Warren, Ohio, July 16, 1931; s. Joseph and Anna Elizabeth (Kubina) M.; m. Mary Lou Bouquot, May 18, 1957; children: Theresa, Anthony, Michael. A.B., Miami U., Ohio, 1953; M.S., Purdue U., 1955; Ph.D., Ohio State U., 1961. Commd. 2d lt. USAF, 1953, advanced through grades to col., 1973; project engr. armament lab. USAF, Wright-Patterson AFB, Ohio, 1955-58; mathematician Office Sci. Rsch. USAF, Washington, 1961-62; staff scientist Avionics Lab. USAF, Wright-Patterson AFB, 1972-73; dir. engring. standardization Def. Electronics Supply Ctr. USAF, Dayton, Ohio, 1973-75; ret. USAF, 1975; sr. scientist, rsch. inst. U. Dayton, 1975-93. Author: Technological Forecasting for Decisionmaking, 1972, rev. edit., 1983, 3d edit., 1992, A Fighting Chance-The Moral Use of Nuclear Weapons, 1988, Science Funding: Politics and Porkbarrel, 1992, Research and Development Project Selection, 1995; assoc. editor: Tech. Forecasting and Social Change Jour., 1968—. Fellow IEEE, AAAS, AIAA (assoc.); mem. Inst. for Ops. Rsch. and Mgmt. Sci., Am. Soc. Engring. Mgmt., Engrs. Club of Dayton. Roman Catholic.

MARTINO, MICHAEL CHARLES, entertainer, musician, actor; b. Philadelphia, Pa., Sept. 10, 1950; s. Salvatore Joseph and Marie Angela (Langone) M. Grad. high sch., Upper Darby, Pa. Spokesperson/rep. Petosa Accordion Co., Seattle, 1979—; featured TV entertainer Mike Martino Show, Delaware County, Pa., 1987-89; accordion tchr. Drexel Hill, Pa., 1989—; entertainer/host/producer St. Jude's Children's Hosp. Marathon, King of Prussia, Pa., 1973; opening act comedian Morty Gunty Downingtown, Pa., 1973, opening act comedian Morty Gunty, 1973, Pat Cooper, Phila., 1981; guest artist/entertainer Internat. Platform Assn. Conv., Washington, 1979; nite club performer Glen Mills, Pa., 1989; actor TV commls., Elkton, Md.,

1979, Halloween Spl. KYW-TV, Phila., 1986; performed radio contest jingle Sta. KISS 100 radio, Media, Pa., 1992. Author: (movie script) Forever Fiftys, 1990; composer popular songs; directed, produced, starred video Forever Fiftys; composed theme song Forever Fiftys, (movie theme) That First September; creator, performer Suspended Triple Bellows Shake Technique for the Accordion, 1994; composer (ballad) Through the Music, Through the Words I Sing, 1995, Through the Music Through the Words I sing, (sung by Donna Theodore) 1998; actor: (movie) Jesus' Son, 1999. Recipient citation U.S. Ho. Reps., 1989, Proclamation Mike Martino Day Mayor Ward, Del. County, 1988, Danny Thomas Hon. award St. Jude's Hosp., Del. County, 1973, Mayor's Svc. award Upper Darby, Pa., 1994. Roman Catholic. Avocations: antique cars, dogs. Home: 2530 Stoneybrook Ln Drexel Hill PA 19026-1610

MARTINOVA, ELENA ALEXANDROVNA, immunologist, consultant, researcher; b. Armavir, Russia, June 13, 1957; d. Alexander Artiemovich and Svetlana Fiedorovna (Skirdina) M.; m. Andrey Eugenievich Baryshnikov, Sept. 1, 1984 (div. May 1987). MD in Internal Medicine, N. Semashko Moscow Med. Inst., 1980; MD in Immunology and Allergology, Acad. Med. Scis., Moscow, 1982; PhD in Biochemistry, Russian Acad. Med. Scis., Moscow, 1992. Postdoctoral fellow Inst. Immunology Acad. Med. Scis., Moscow, 1980-82, rschr. All Union Cancer Rsch. Ctr., 1982-84; scientist Inst. Viral Products Min. Pub. Health, Moscow, 1984-87; sr. scientist Inst. Nutrition Russian Acad. Med. Scis., Moscow, 1987-95, leader rsch. group Cardiology Sci. Ctr., 1995-96, leader rsch. group Inst. Nutrition, 1996—. Author chpts. to books; contbr. articles to profl. jours. Mem. League of Women, Moscow, 1991-92. Grantee Russian Found. for Fundamental Investigations, 1995-99. Mem. Am. Chem. Soc., Internat. Assn. Clin. Immunologists, Fedn. European Biochem. Socs., N.Y. Acad. Scis. Russian Orthodox. Avocations: poetry, short novels, drawing, dancing, swimming. Fax: (095) 298-1872. E-mail: samoilov@practica.ru. Office: Russian Acad Med Scis Inst Nutrition, 2/14 Ustinsky Proezd, 109240 Moscow Russia

MARTIN-PAREDERO, VICENTE, vascular surgeon; b. Madrid, May 31, 1954; s. Vicente Martin-Garcia and Romualda Paredero; m. Isabel Fernandez-Lopez; 1 child, Irene. MD, U. Autonoma, Madrid, 1977, PhD, 1981, Vascular Surgeon, 1981; Fellow, UCLA, 1982. Chief of residents Jimenez Diaz Found., Madrid, 1979, vascular surgeon, 1983; chief of vascular surgery Hosp. Rio Hortega, 1986, Hosp. Joan XXIII, Tarragona, 1991; assoc. prof. Rovira & Virgili U., Tarragona, 1997, dir. med. edn. in vascular surgery, 1997-98; cons. in field. Co-editor: Archivos Cir. Vascular, 1986, Angiologia, 1998; author/editor: Experimental Reno-Vascular Hypertension, 1980, (award 1983); contbr. articles to profl. jours. Mem. Internat. Soc. Cardiovascular Surgery, Spanish Soc. for Vascular Surgery, Cirujanos Vascular Habla Hispana, others. Office: Avda Roma 5-B 3/2, 43005 Tarragona Spain

MARTINS, ESTEVAO DE REZENDE, educator; b. Rio de Janeiro, Brazil, Apr. 29, 1947; s. Jose Maria De Rezende and Lucia Maria De Rezende (Chaves) M.; m. Martine De Rezende Creusot, July 8, 1976; 1 child, Francois Xavier. BA, Faculty Media, Brazil, 1969; PhD, U. Munich, Germany, 1976, 85. Asst. Faculty Media, Sao Paulo, Brazil, 1968-69, U. Gama Filho, Rio de Janeiro, 1973-74; asst. U. Brasilia, Brazil, 1977-79, prof., 1979—; cons. in field. Author: Studien zu Kants Freiheitsauffassung, 1976; co-author: Filosofia y metodologia de la ciencia, 1979, Multiculturalismo e Racismo, 1997, O estudo da politica, 1998. Recipient Dom Pedro medal, 1993; Humboldt Found. fellow, 1982—. Mem. Internat. Commn. History Parliamentary Instns. (v.p. 1999—). Roman Catholic.

MARTINS, NELSON, physics educator; b. Santos, Brazil, Oct. 18, 1930; s. Aniceto and Angelica Martins; m. Maria Lucia, Jan. 8, 1959 (div. Sept. 1983); children: Flavia, Paulo. BS in Physics, Mackenzie U., São Paulo, Brazil, 1958; D in Physics, Pontifica U., Campinas, Brazil, 1977. Cert. physicist. Dir. engring. Mackenzie U., 1971-73, dir. Exact Sci., 1983-90; gen. dir. Ednl. Found., Barretos, Brazil, 1973-76; chief physics dep. Engring. Sch., Araraquara, Brazil, 1991; chief physics dept. U. Santo Amaro, São Paulo, 1990-92; dir. CCET Ctr. Exact Scis. and Tech., São Paulo, 1992-95. Author: (with others) Electriciy and Magnetism, 1973, Dimensional Analysis, 1980, Dynamics, 1982. Mem. Am. Assn. Physics Tcrhs., Brazil Soc. Physics. Office: Sorocaba Engring Sch, Rod Sen Jose Ermirio Moraes, Sorocaba 18001970, Brazil

MARTINS, PETER, ballet master, choreographer, dancer; b. Copenhagen, Oct. 27, 1946; came to U.S., 1967, naturalized, 1970; m. Lise La Cour (div. 1973); 1 child, Nilas; m. Darci Kistler, 1991. Pupil of Vera Volkova and Stanley Williams with Royal Danish Ballet. With N.Y.C. Ballet, 1967—, tchr., 1975, ballet master, 1981-83, co-ballet master-in-chief, 1983-89; ballet master-in-chief, 1989—; Tchr. Sch. Am. Ballet, 1975; artistic adviser Pa. Ballet, 1982—. Mem. Royal Danish Ballet, 1965-67, prin. dancer (including Bournonville repertory), 1967; guest artist N.Y.C. Ballet, 1967-70, prin. dancer, 1970-83; guest artist regional ballet cos. U.S., also Nat. Ballet Can., Royal Ballet, London, Grand Theatre Geneva, Paris Opera, Vienna State Opera, Munich State Opera, London Festival Ballet, Ballet Internat., Royal Danish Ballet; TV appearance in series of Balanchine works, 1974; also has appeared on PBS Dance in America series including A Choreographer's Notebook: Stravinsky Piano Ballets by Peter Martins, 1984; choreographed Broadway musicals including Dream of the Twins (co-choreographer) 1982, On Your Toes, 1982, Song and Dance, 1985; works choreographed include Calcium Light Night, 1977, Tricolore (Pas de Basque sect.), 1978, Rossini Pas de Deux, 1978, Tango-Tango (ice ballet), 1978, Dido and Aeneas, 1979, Sonate di Scarlatti, 1979, Eight Easy Pieces, 1980, Lille Suite, 1980, Suite from Histoire du Soldat, 1981, Capricio Italien, 1981, The Magic Flute, 1981, Symphony No. 1, 1981, Delibes Divertissement, 1982, Piano-Rag-Music, 1982, Concerto for Two Solo Pianos, 1982, Waltzes, 1983, Rossini Quartets, 1983, Tango, 1983, A Schubertiad, 1984, Mozart Violin Concerto, 1984, Poulenc Sonata, 1985, La Sylphide, 1985, Valse Triste, 1985, Eight More, 1985, We Are the World, 1985, Eight Miniatures, 1985, Ecstatic Orange, Tanzspiel, 1988, Jazz, 1993, Symphonic Dances, 1994, Barber Violin Concerto, 1994, Mozart Paino Concerto (No. 17), 1994, X-Ray, 1995; author: (autobiography) Far from Denmark, 1982. Recipient Dance mag. award 1977, Cue's Golden Apple award 1977, award of merit Phila. Art Alliance, 1985, Liberty award N.Y.C., 1986, H.C. Andersen Ballet prize, Royal Danish Theatre, 1988; named Knight of Order of Danneborg, Denmark, 1983. Office: NY State Theater NYC Ballet 20 Lincoln Center Plz New York NY 10023-6913

MARTIN SANCHEZ, JUAN ANTONIO, plant breeder; b. Berganciano, Salamanca, Spain, Feb. 21, 1940; s. Julian Martin Rodriquez and Maria Bernarda Sanchez Delgado. Agrl. Engr. Superior, High Tech. Sch. Agrl. Engrs., Madrid, 1964, Dr. Agrl. Engr., 1982. Prof. Lab. Genetics and Plant Breeding High Tech. Sch. Agrl. Engrs., Madrid, 1965-70; mgr. rsch. in plant breeding MAHISSA Maices Hibridos y Semillas, CIBA Geigy, Borjas Blancas, Spain, 1970-83; tchr. genetics and plant breeding Tech. Sch. Agr. of Poly. U. Barcelona, Lerida, Spain, 1975-78; prof. Tech. Sch. Agr. Engrs., Lerida, 1977—; dir. Tech. Sch. Agr. and High Tech. Sch. Agrl. Engrs., Lerida, 1978-84, Centro U. de Lleida-Inst. Food and Agrl. Rsch. and Tech., Lerida, 1985—. Decorated comdr. Order Civil Merit in Agr. Mem. Nat. Assn. Agrl. Engrs., Spanish Assn. Genetics, Genetics Soc. Am., Eucarpia. Roman Catholic. Developer 12 varieties of wheat, 3 of Triticale. Office: Escuela Tecnica Superior Ingenieros, Dept Prduc Veg Roure, 177 Lleida 25198, Spain

MARTINSEN, ØRJAN GRØTTEM, physicist; b. Narvik, Norway, Dec. 4, 1960; s. Evald Johan and Astri-Irene (Grøttem) M.; m. Kjersti Grannes, July 11, 1981; children: Anders, Einar, Øyvind, Johan Jørgen. Cand.Sci., U. Oslo, 1990, ScD, 1995. Project engr. Siemens, Oslo, 1983-87; rsch. fellow U. Oslo, 1990-92, lectr., 1992-95, assoc. prof., 1995—. Patentee on measurement of moisture content in skin, 1996. Mem. IEEE, Internat. Soc. Bioengring. Skin, IEEE Computer Soc. Avocations: fishing, music, reading. Home: Fagerstrandv 30, N-1368 Stabekk Norway Office: Univ of Oslo Dept Physics, Box 1048 Blindern, N-0316 Oslo Norway

MARTIN-SMITH, NICHOLAS, lawyer, consultant; b. Rye, Sussex, England, Oct. 17, 1950; s. Patrick Geoffrey and Phyllis Dorothy (Brown) M. BA, Oxford (England) U., 1973, MA, 1976. Solicitor. Lawyer Clifford Chance, London, 1975-83, partner, 1983-98. Office: Clifford Chance, 200 Aldersgate St, London EC1A 4JJ, England

MARTIN-STERN, CLAUDIA MARIA, interpreter, educator; b. Lugano, Ticino, Switzerland, Nov. 26, 1946; d. Rudolf Ferdinand Stern and Clorinda Eleonora Della Croce; m. Reginald Wesley Martin, Oct. 14, 1976; children: Ryan, Cristina. BA in Polit. Sci., U. Oreg., 1969; translator's degree, U. Geneva, Switzerland, 1972; conf. interpreter, Sch. of Interpreters, Zurich, Switzerland, 1975. Conf. interpreter European Union, Brussels, 1975-76; freelance interpreter, 1976—; asst. lectr. U. Geneva, 1986-96; vis. lectr. Sch. of Interpreters, Zurich, 1987—. Sec.-gen. Local Legislative Govt. in Coinsins, Switzerland, 1989-95. Mem. Internat. Assn. Conf. Interpreters, Phi Beta Kappa.

MARTINUSSEN, MONICA, psychology educator; b. Bodo, Norway, Mar. 3, 1963; d. Svein-Erik and Astrid Lilly (Rikardsen) M.; m. Bard Fjukstad, May 16, 1988; children: Bjorn, Erik. MA, U. Oslo, 1989; PhD, U. Tromso, Norway, 1997. Registered psychologist. Mil. psychologist Norwegian Air Force, 1986-89; rsch. fellow U. Tromso, Norway, 1990-95, assoc. prof., 1996—. Contbr. articles to profl. jours. Mem. Norwegian Psychol. Assn., Assn. Aviation Psychologists. Office: Dept Psychology, U Tromso, N-9037 Tromso Norway

MARTINUSSEN, WILLY MARTIN, sociologist, educator; b. Vestvågøy, Norway, July 21, 1938; s. Johan and Solveig (Pettersen) M.; m. Brit Borchgrevink, June 17, 1966 (div. 1978); children: Benedikte, Pia Cecilie; m. Hjørdis Kaul. PhD, U. Oslo, 1965. Sch. tchr. Reine (Norway) El. Sch., 1959; traffic officer Scandinavian Airlines Sys., Oslo, 1960-61; rsch. scholar Norwegian Rsch. Coun., Oslo, 1966-68, U. Oslo, 1969-72; rsch. dir. Inst. Social Rsch., Oslo, 1973-76; prof. Norwegian U. Sci. and Tech., Trondheim, 1977—; exec. dir. Inst. Social Rsch., Oslo, 1973-76; cons. Norwegian Rsch. Coun., Oslo, 1975—. Editor: Norwegian Social Sci. Jour., 1973-76, Norwegian Jour. Sociology, 1993-96; author: Voters and Political Front Lines, 1972, The Distant Democracy, 1975, Sociological Analysis, 1984, Limits of Solidarity, 1989, Sociological Explanations, 1999. Dir., leader Nat. Coun. Sociology, Norway, 1995-96; mem. bd. dirs. Norwegian Students Union, Oslo, 1963-64. Scholar Norway-Am. Assn., Ann Arbor, Mich., 1967-68. Mem. Norwegian Rsch. Coun. (rsch. grantee 1968—, bd. sociology 1995—), Swedish Rsch. Coun. (bd. sociology and anthropology 1995—), Norwegian Found. for Profl. Lit. (bd. dirs. 1995—). Avocations: hiking, sports fishing. Home: Hauganvn 17, 7563 Malvik Norway Office: Norwegian U Sci and Tech, 7055 Dragvoll Norway

MARTIRE, MARIA CONCETTA, pharmacology educator; b. Longobardi, Cosenza, Italy, Jan. 18, 1955; d. Settimio and Francesca (Bruno) M.; m. Stefano Salvati, Oct. 1, 1988; children: Francesca, Federica. Degree pharmacy, La Sapienza State U., Rome, 1978; postgrad. degree in neurosci., Cath. U., Rome, 1988. Rschr. Cath. U., 1988-92, assoc. prof., 1992—. Contbr. articles to profl. jours. Fellowship Karolinska Inst., 1984. Mem. Italian Soc. of Pharmacology, Soc. for Neurosci. Home: Via Lorenzo Rocci, 67-00151 Rome Italy Office: Inst Pharm Cath U, L Go F Vito 1, 00168 Rome Italy

MARTIROSSIAN, RADICK M., academic dean; b. Madagis, Armenia, May 1, 1936; s. Martiross A. Martirossian and Astchick G. Harutunian; m. Renna A. Kasparova, 1965; two children. Degree, Yerevan State U., Lebedev Phys. Inst. Acad. Sci., Moscow. Dir. Inst. Radiophysics and Electronics Nat. Acad. Scis. Armenia, 1993—; rector Yerevan State U., 1993—. Mem. Armenian Acad. Scis. Avocation: chess. Office: Yerevan State U, 1 Alex Manoogian St, 375049 Yerevan Armenia*

MARTIS, LEO, healthcare researcher; b. Pangala, Karnatka, India, June 3, 1945; s. Gregory and Apolina Martis; m. Jacintha B. Castelino, June 10, 1975; children: Sameeth, Nikhil. MS, U. Wash., 1970, PhD, 1973; MBA, Northwestern U., 1980. Diplomate Am. Bd. Toxicology. Postdoctoral fellow dept. neurosci. U. Wash., Seattle, 1973-74; mgr., dir., v.p. Baxter Healthcare, Deerfield, Ill., 1974—; guest lectr. U. Ill., Chgo., 1985—. Contbr. over 200 articles and abstracts to sci. jours.; inventor in field. Pres. India Cath. Assn. Am., Chgo., 1992-93. Mem. Am. Soc. Nephrology, Fedn. Am. Socs. Exptl. Biology, Am. Soc. Pharmacology and Exptl. Therapeutics, Am. Soc. Toxicology, Am. Chem. Soc. Avocations: tennis, golf, running. E-mail: martisl@baxter.com. Home: 5524 Old Wood Ln Long Grove IL 60047-8215 Office: Baxter Healthcare 1620 Waukegan Rd Waukegan IL 60085-6730

MARTON, EVA, opera singer; b. Budapest, Hungary, June 18, 1943; m. Zoltan Marton; children: Zoltan, Diana. Student, Liszt Acad., Budapest. Debut Budapest State Opera, 1968-72; performed with Frankfurt Opera, 1972-77, Hambrug State Opera, 1977-80, Maggio Musicale Fiorentino, Vienna State Opera, La Scala Milan, Met. Opera, N.Y., Lyric Opera, Chgo., Grand Opera, Houston, San Francisco Opera, Convent Garden, London, Teatro Liceo, Barcelona, Munich State Opera, Berlin, Paris, Sydney, Teatro Colon Buenos Aires, Bayreuth Festival, Salzburg Festival, Area of Verona, others; roles include Manon Lescaut, Tosca, Turandot, Aida Elisabetta in Don Carlo, Leonora in Forza del destino and in II Trovatore, Fedora, Maddalena in A Chenior, Wally, Gioconda, Leonore in Fidelio, Salome, Ariadne, Helene in Agyptische Helene, Chrysothemis and Electra in Electra, Empress/Wife in Die Frau ohne Schatten, Vensu and Elisabeth in Tannhäuser, Elsa and Ortrud in Lohengrin, Sieglinde and Bruünnhilde in the Ring, Isolde, others; rec. include Turandot, Tosca, La Fanciulla del West, A Chenier, Fedora, La Gioconda, Violanta, Tiefland, La Wally, Semirama, Bluebeards Castle, Mefistofele, Electra, Salome, Die Walkuere, Siegfrid, Götterdämmerung, Gurrelider, Forza del destino, Puccini Arias, Wagner arias, Songs by Bartok and Liszt, others. Office: 31 Ave Princesse Grace, Monte Carlo 98, Monaco

MÁRTON, LÁSZLÓ, agriculturist, researcher; b. Karcag, Szolnok, Hungary, Mar. 1, 1951; s. László and Lászlóné (Major Mária) M.; m. Lászlóné Barasits Kinga, Aug. 30, 1975; children: Gábor, Adrienn. BS, Agrl. U., Keszthely, Hungary, 1975, D of Agrl. Chemistry Engring., 1984; postgrad., Agrl. U., Gödöllő, Hungary, 1980. Grad. asst. Agrl. U., Keszthely, 1975-77, grad. rsch. asst., 1977-85, rsch. worker, 1985-88, asst. lectr., 1988-89; rsch. cons. Agrl. U., Brasilia, 1989-96; rsch. fellow Rsch. Inst. Soil Sci. and Agrl. Chemistry, Hungarian Acad. Scis., Budapest, 1996—. Contbr. articles to sci. jours. including Plant Prodn., Agrochemistry and Soil Sci. 2d lt. Hungarian Army, 1970-94. Avocations: sports, gymnastics, swimming, yachting, reading. Home: Nyarfa ul 14, 5321 Kunmadaras Szolnok, Hungary Office: Rsch Inst Soil Sci-HAS, Herman O 15, 1022 Budapest Hungary

MARTON, SANDOR ISTVAN, ecology educator, consultant; b. Episcopia, Romania, May 22, 1942; s. Sandor and Maria (Firtea) M.; m. Rozalia Schek, June 20, 1965 (div. Sept. 1996); children: Timeea, Andrea. Diplomate in Biology and Geography, U. Babes-Bolyai, Cluj, Romania, 1964, Dr in Biology, 1977; diploma in utiliz. radioactive isotopes, U. Bucharest, Romania, 1979; Diploma in Integrated Waste Mgmt., U. Minn., Timisoara, Romania, 1994; Diploma in Environ. Curricula, U. Minn., Sinaia, Romania, 1995. Prof. Gen. Sch., Telciu, Romania, 1964-69; rschr. Biol. Rsch. Ctr., Cluj, 1969-80; biologist, head of lab. COMTIM, Timisoara, 1980-90; prof. Econ. H.S., Timisoara, 1990-93; assoc. prof. Faculty of Hydrotechnics, U. Politehnica, Timisoara, 1993-96, prof., 1996—; cons. Rigraprod SRL, Timisoara, 1996-98. Author: Ecotoxicology, 1999; co-author: Treatise of Algology, 4 vols., 1976-81 (Romanian Acad. award 1983), Natural Zeolites, 1989, The Protection of the Environment, 1997, Environmental Protection by Managing Wastes, 1998, Ecology and Tourism, 2000. Mem. Internat. Assn. Theoretical and Applied Limnology, N.Y. Acad. Scis., Soc. for Protection of Man and Environment (pres. 1990—). Avocation: travel. Home: Str Ghirodei nr 32, 1900 Timisoara Romania Office: Faculty of Hydrotechnics, Str G Enescu nr 1/A, 1900 Timisoara Romania

MARTONE, MASSIMILIANO, telecommunications consultant; b. Rome, Apr. 20, 1965; s. Giorgio and Gianna (Megone) M. Diploma in science, JFK Lyceum, 1984; D. of elecs., U. Rome, 1990. Design engr. S.P.E. Inc., Rome, 1990; staff engr. TRS X-Cons., Rome, 1990-91, Alenia (Space Divsn.), Rome, 1991-94; sr. engr. ATSI, Inc., Waltham, Mass., 1994-95, Watkins-Johnson Co., Gaithersburg, Md., 1995—; cons. Alfacons., Inc., Rome, 1991, Staer,Inc., Rome, 1993, Microlab., Inc., Rome, 1993-94; researcher Rensselaer Polytech. Inst. , Troy, N.Y., 1993-94. Contbr. articles to profl. jours. Mem. IEEE, N.Y. Acad. Scis., Electrotech. Assn. Italy. Roman Catholic. Home: 1249 Lakeside Dr Apt 3065 Sunnyvale CA 94085-1016 Office: Watkins-Johnson Co Wireless Telecomm Dept 3333 Hillview Ave Palo Alto CA 94304

MÁRTONYI, CSABA LÁSZLO, ophthalmic photographer, imager; b. Budapest, Hungary, Mar. 23, 1941; came to U.S., 1951; s. Louis Péter and Magda (Gyürky) M.; m. Elnajean Beyst, Sept. 4, 1976; 1 child, Erika Lyn. Cert. retinal angiographer. Chief photographer U. Mich. Photog. Svcs., Ann Arbor, 1967-71; dir. ophthalmic photography, dept. ophthalmology U. Mich., Ann Arbor, 1971-75, instr. dept. ophthalmic photography, 1975-80, asst. prof., 1980-83, assoc. prof., 1983—. First author: Clinical Slit-Lamp Biomicroscopy and Photo Slit-Lamp Biomicrography, 1985; author, artist exhibit of eye images Landscapes of the Eye, 1993; author sci. exhibits. With U.S. Naval Air Res., 1965-67. Recipient Disting. Tchg. award Joint Commn. on Allied Health Pers. in Ophthalmology, 1997. Fellow Ophthalmic Photographers Soc. (parliamentarion 1988—, chair hon. life membership com. 1991—, fellowship com., pres. 1978-80, chair bd. certification 1978-84, chmn. editl. com. 1987-89, awards including top award for outstanding contbns. to ophthalmic photography), Am. Acad. Ophthalmology (assoc., Honor award 1984); mem. Washtenaw Coun. for the Arts, Mich. Guild Artists and Artisans. Avocations: guitar (classical-traditional), woodsculpting, fine arts photography, tennis. Home: 1261 Laurel View Dr Ann Arbor MI 48105-9765 Office: U Mich WK Kellogg Eye Ctr 1000 Wall St Ann Arbor MI 48105-1912

MARTORANA, ARCANGELO, engineering geologist; b. Caltanissetta, Sicily, Italy, July 21, 1939; s. Alfonso and Carmela Grazia (Mirisola) M.; m. Maria Carmen Giordano, July 10, 1971; children: Luca, Alessandro. D of Geology, U. Palermo, 1967. Lic. geologist. Cons. geologist Caltanissetta, Italy, 1967—. Mem. ASTM, Internat. Assn. Engring. Geology, Internat. Assn. Soil Mechanics and Founds. Engring. Home: Via Don Minzoni 24/C, 93100 Caltanissetta Sicily, Italy Office: CP 105, 93100 Caltanissetta Sicily, Italy

MARTORI, JOSEPH PETER, lawyer; b. N.Y.C., Aug. 19, 1941; s. Joseph and Teresa Susan (Fezza) M. BS summa cum laude, NYU, 1964, MBA, 1968; JD cum laude, U. Notre Dame, 1967. Bar: D.C. 1968, U.S. Dist. Ct. D.C. 1968, U.S. Dist. Ct. Ariz. 1968, U.S. Ct. Appeals (9th cir.) 1969, U.S. Supreme Ct. 1977. Assoc. Sullivan & Cromwell, N.Y.C., 1967-68, Snell & Wilmer, Phoenix, 1968-69; pres. Goldmar Inc., Phoenix, 1969-71; ptnr. Martori, Meyer, Hendricks & Victor, P.A., Phoenix, 1971-85; ptnr. Brown & Bain, P.A., Phoenix, 1985-94, chmn. corp. banking & real estate dept., 1994—; chmn. bd. ILX Resorts, Inc., Phoenix; bd. dirs. Firstar, Met. Bank, Phoenix; chmn. ILX Inc., Varsity Clubs Am. Inc. Author: Street Fights, 1987; also articles, 1966-70. Trustee Boys' Clubs Met. Phoenix, 1974—; consul for Govt. of Italy, State of Ariz., 1987-97. Mem. ABA, State Bar Ariz., Maricopa County Bar Assn., Lawyers Com.for Civil Rights Under Law (trustee 1976—), Phoenix Country Club, Plaza Club (founding bd. govs. 1979-90). Republican. Roman Catholic. Office: ILX Inc 2111 E Highland Ave Ste 210 Phoenix AZ 85016-4786

MARTOWSKI, ADAM STANISLAW, economist; b. Warsaw, Poland, Mar. 30, 1936; s. Tadeusz and Zofia (Maciejczyk) M.; m. Hanna Waloch; children: Marzenna Jolanta, Robert Marek. MA in Econs., Sch. Econs., Warsaw, Poland, 1960; D of Econs., Am. U., Beirut, Lebanon, 1969. Comml. attache Polish Embassy, Beirut, Lebanon, 1965-69; deputy gen. mgr. Polimex Corp., Warsaw, Poland, 1969-74; comm. counsellor Polish Embassy, Vienna, 1974-78; head dept. Min. Fgn. Trade, Warsaw, 1978-87; comml. counsellor Polish Embassy, Vienna, 1987-91; pres. BRE Leasing, Warsaw, 1991—; cons. in field. Author: Monetary Policy of Lebanon, 1967, History of Economy of Saudi Arabia, 1969. Mem. Polish Assn. Leasing (vice chmn. 1994—), Mgmt. Club (chmn. 1991—). Roman Catholic. Avocations: yachting, tourism, history, music. Office: Bre Leasing, Marszalkowska 82, 00-963 Warsaw Poland

MARTRENCHAR, ARNAUD, veterinarian; b. Cenon, Aquitaine, France, Aug. 20, 1962; s. Pierre and Suzanne (Epherre) M.; m. Nadine Chevassus-A-L'Antoine, May 11, 1994; children: Fabien, Vincent, Kéli. DVM, Vet. Nat. Sch., Toulouse, France, 1985; Diploma in Tropical Path. and Livestock, Tropical Vet. Medicine, Livestock Inst., Maisons-Alfort, 1986; Diploma in Systematical Virology/Bact., Pasteur Inst., Paris, 1987; Diploma/Civil Servant Min. of Agr., Maisons-Alfort, 1988. Rschr. CIRAD-EMVT, Cayenne, France, 1987-88; rschr. Zootech. Rsch. Inst. CIRAD-EMVT, Garoua, Cameroon, 1989-90; head of Adiagnostic Unit/Nat. Vet. Lab. Ministry of French Cooperation, Garoua, 1990-94; dir.'s adviser Nat. Lab. for Support of Agrl. Devel. Ministry of French Cooperation, Abidjan, Ivory Coast, 1994-95; head unit animal welfare French Agy. for Food Safety, Ploufragan, 1995—; rsch. and devel. CIRAD, Ministry of French Cooperation and CNEVA, Cayenne, 1987-94, 95-98; instnl. advisor Ministry of French Cooperation, Abidjan, 1994-95. Author: Diagnosis of Main Bacterial Diseases of Ruminants in Africa, 1992; contbr. articles to sci. and profl. jours. Office: French Agy for Food Safety, BP 53 Zoopole Beaucemaine, 22440 Ploufragan France

MARTTILA, OLLI JUHANA, physicist; b. Helsinki, Finland, Mar. 15, 1934; s. Viljo Erkki and Kerttu Annikki (Hukka) M.; m. Anja Inkeri Nikko, Oct. 12, 1956; children: Erika, Iiu Silja, Laura, Heta. Cand. of Philosophy in Physics, U. Helsinki, 1956, Lic. of Philosophy in Nuclear Physics, 1960. Qualified for radiation protection officer in charge. Asst. in physics U. Helsinki, 1956-66, lab. mgr. neutron physics lab. and radiation protection, 1966-98, head accelerator lab., 1977-79; vis. prof. nuclear physics U. Dar es Salaam, Tanzania, 1978-79; sec. Nat. Rsch. Coun. of Scis., Finland, 1969-70; lectr. optics Instrumentarium Vocat. Sch. for Opticians, 1964-79; radiation expert High Command of Civil Def., Ministry of Interior, Finland, 1969-98; tech. coop. expert Atomic Energy Rsch. Establishment, Dhaka, Bangladesh, 1983, Inst. Nuclear Physics, Tirana, Albania, 1987; mem. Adv. Com. on Nuclear Safety, Helsinki, 1988-97, chmn. of divsn., 1991-97, vice chmn., 1994-97, mem. divsns., 1998—; part-time occupl. health and safety rep. of employees of faculty of sci. U. Helsinki, 1994-98. Author, editor: Radiation, Uses and Control, 1970; author: Fundamentals of Radiation Protection, 1982-98, Practice of Radiation Protection, 1989; contbr. articles to profl. jours. Bd. dirs. Finnish Evangelic-Luth. Sunday Sch. Assn., Helsinki, 1970-85, vice chmn. exec. com., 1980-81, 84-85, chmn., 1981-84; bd. dirs. Lasten Keskus Pub. House, Helsinki, 1974-99, chmn., 1982-87. Recipient medal 2d class Civil Def. Ministry of the Interior, Finland, 1973, 1st class, 1987, Medal for Long Svc. XXX, State of Finland, 1987, Knight of Order of White Rose of Finland, Pres. of Republic, 1990. Mem. Finnish Phys. Soc. (bd. dirs. 1964-66), Nordic Soc. for Radiation Protection, Finnish Nuclear Soc. E-mail: olli.marttila@kolumbus.fi. Home: Menninkäisentie 8H, 02110 Espoo Finland

MARTUCCI, WILLIAM CHRISTOPHER, lawyer; b. Asbury Park, N.J., Mar. 10, 1952; s. Frank and Evelyn (Gerrity) M.; children: Daniel Robert, William Sessions, John Andrew, James Christopher, Andrew Michael. AB magna cum laude, Rutgers Coll., 1974; JD with honors, U. Ark., 1977; LLM, Georgetown U., 1981. Bar: Mo. 1977. Law clk. to presiding justice Mo. Ct. Appeals, Kansas City, 1977-78; assoc. Spencer, Fane, Britt & Browne, Kansas City, 1981-86, ptnr., 1987-99; ptnr. Shook, Hardy & Bacon, Kansas City, 2000—; mem. practice and procedure com. Nat. Labor Relations Act; adj. prof. employment law U. Mo. Law Sch., Kansas City, 1988—, chair minority affairs com. 1992—. Editor-in-chief Ark. Law Rev., 1976-77; contbr. articles to profl. jours. Chmn. adv. coun. Urban League Greater Kansas City Tng. Ctr., chmn. mentor program, 1988—; mem. Kansas City Civic Coun.; mem. Kansas City Tomorrow Leadership Program, 1992-93; adv. bd. Boys and Girls Club Kansas City, Reviving Baseball in the Inner City. Served to lt. JAGC, USN, 1978-81. Mem. ABA, Mo. Bar Assn. (exec. com. continuing legal edn. 1987—, chair 1993—), Kansas City Bar Assn. (chmn. continuing legal edn. 1984-86, mem. exec. com. 1985-87, leadership award 1985, chmn. labor and employment law com. 1988-90, Pres. award 1992, 97), Lawyers Assn. Kansas City (mem. exec. com. young lawyers sect. 1981-82), Nat. Inst. Mcpl. Law Officers (vice-chmn. labor rels. and pers. law com. 1988-90), Kansas City Club, Homestead Country Club, Rotary. Republican. Roman Catholic. Club: Kansas City.

Home: 1251 W 59th St Kansas City MO 64113-1148 Office: Shook Hardy and Bacon 1 Kansas City Pl 1200 Main St Kansas City MO 64105-2118

MARTY, MARTIN EMIL, religion educator, editor; b. West Point, Nebr., Feb. 5, 1928; s. Emil A. and Anne Louise (Wuerdemann) M.; m. Elsa Schumacher, 1952 (dec. 1981); children: Frances, Joel, John, Peter, James, Micah, Ursula; m. Harriet Lindemann, 1982. MDiv, Concordia Sem., 1952; STM, Luth. Sch. Theology, Chgo., 1954; PhD in Am. Religious and Intellectual History, U. Chgo., 1956; LittD (hon.), Thiel Coll., 1964; LHD (hon.), W.Va. Wesleyan Coll., 1967, Marian Coll., 1967, Providence Coll., 1967; DD (hon.), Muhlenberg Coll., 1967; LittD (hon.), Thomas More Coll., 1968; DD (hon.), Bethany Sem., 1969; LLD (hon.), Keuka Coll., 1972; LHD (hon.), Willamette U., 1974; DD (hon.), Wabash Coll., 1977; LLD (hon.), U. So. Calif., 1977, Valparaiso U., 1978; LHD (hon.), St. Olaf Coll., 1978, De Paul U., 1979; DD (hon.), Christ Sem.-Seminex, 1979, Capital U., 1980; LHD (hon.), Colo. Coll., 1980; DD (hon.), Maryville Coll., 1980, North Park Coll. Sem., 1982; LittD (hon.), Wittenberg U., 1983; LHD, Rosary Coll., 1984; LHD (hon.), Rockford Coll., 1984; DD (hon.), Va. Theol. Sem., 1984; LHD (hon.), Hamilton Coll., 1985, Loyola U., 1986; LLD (hon.), U. Notre Dame, 1987; LHD (hon.), Roanoke Coll., 1987, Mercer U., 1987, Ill. Wesleyan Coll., 1987, Roosevelt U., 1988, Aquinas Coll., 1988; LittD (hon.), Franklin Coll., 1988, U. Nebr., 1993; LHD (hon.), No. Mich. U., 1989, Muskingum Coll., Coe Coll., Lehigh U., 1989, Hebrew Union Coll. and Governors State U., 1990, Whittier Coll., 1991; Calif. Luth. U., 1993; DD (hon.), St. Xavier Coll. and Colgate U., 1990, Mt. Union Coll., 1991, Tex. Luth. Coll., 1991, Aurora U., 1991, Baker U., 1992; LHD (hon.), Luth. U., 1993; LHD, Calif. Luth. U., 1993, Midland Luth. Coll., 1995; DD, Hope Coll., 1993, Northwestern Coll., 1993; LHD (hon.), George Fox Coll., 1994, Drake U., 1994, Centre Coll., 1994, Fontbonne Coll., 1996; DD, Yale U., 1995; LHD (hon.), Otterbein Coll., 1996; ThD (hon.), Lycoming Coll., 1997; LHD, Dana Coll., 1998; LittD (hon.), Alma Coll., 1998, Concordia U. Portland, 1998, Niagara U., 1998; LHD (hon.), Kalamazoo Coll., 1999, William Jewell Coll., 1999; LittD (hon.), U. Miami, 1999. Ordained to ministry Luth. Ch., 1952. Pastor Washington, 1950-51; asst. pastor River Forest, Ill., 1952-56; pastor Elk Grove Village, Ill., 1956-63; prof. history of modern Christianity Div. Sch. U. Chgo., 1963—, Fairfax M. Cone Disting. Service prof., 1978-98, prof. emeritus, 1998—; assoc. editor Christian Century mag., Chgo., 1956-85, sr. editor, 1985-98; co-editor Ch. History mag., 1963-97; pres. Park Ridge (Ill.) Ctr.: An Inst. for Study of Health, Faith and Ethics, 1985-89; dir. fundamentalism project Am. Acad. Arts & Scis., 1988—; dir. The Pub. Religion Project, 1996—. Author: A Short History of Christianity, 1959, The New Shape of American Religion, 1959, The Improper Opinion, 1961, The Infidel, 1961, Baptism, 1962, The Hidden Discipline, 1963, Second Chance for American Protestants, 1963, Church Unity and Church Mission, 1964, Varieties of Unbelief, 1964, The Search for a Usable Future, 1969, The Modern Schism, 1969, Righteous Empire, 1970 (Nat. Book award 1971), Protestantism, 1972, You Are Promise, 1973, The Fire We Can Light, 1973, The Pro and Con Book of Religious America, 1975, A Nation of Behavers, 1976, Religion, Awakening and Revolution, 1978, Friendship, 1980, By Way of Response, 1981, The Public Church, 1981, A Cry of Absence, 1983, Health and Medicine in the Lutheran Tradition, 1983, Pilgrims in Their Own Land, 1984, Protestantism in the United States, 1985, Modern American Religion, The Irony of it All, Vol. 1, 1986, An Invitation to American Catholic History, 1986, Religion and Republic, 1987, Modern American Religion. The Noise of Conflict, Vol. 2, 1991, (with R. Scott Appleby) The Glory and the Power, 1992; editor: (with Jerald C. Brauer) The Unrelieved Paradox: Studies in the Theology of Franz Bibfeldt, 1994 (with Micah Marty) Places Along the Way, 1994, Our Hope for Years to Come, 1995, Modern American Religion, Under God, Indivisble, Vol. 3, 1996, The One and the Many, 1997, The Promise of Winter, 1997, When true Simplicity is Gained, 1998; editor (jours.) Context, 1969—; sr. editor The Christian Century, 1956-98; contbr. articles to religious publs. Chmn. bd. regents St. Olaf Coll.; dir. The Pub. Religion Project, 1996—. Sr. scholar-in-residence The Park Ridge Ctr., 1989—; recipient Nat. Medal Humanities, 1997, Alumni medal U. Chgo., 1998. Fellow Am. Acad. Arts and Scis. (dir. fundamentalism project 1988-94), Soc. Am. Historians; mem. Am. Phil. Soc., Am. Soc. Ch. History (pres. 1971), Am. Cath. Hist. Assn. (pres. 1981), Am. Acad. Religion (pres. 1987-88), Am. Antiquarian Soc. Office: 239 Scottswood Rd Riverside IL 60546-2223

MARTY, RENÉ PIERRE, obstetrician/gynecologist; b. Paris, France, Apr. 9, 1929; s. Rémy and Simone Renée (Grousseaud) M.; m. Genoveva Elisa Dotremont, Apr. 9, 1955; children: Audrey, Sabine. 2 baccalauréats, U. Paris. Cert. Gynecologist & Obstetrician, Faculté de médecine de Paris, 1978. Attaché in gynecology U. Hosp., Avicenne-Paris, 1977-88, attaché en Premier, 1988-90, attaché cons., 1990—; attaché cons. U. Hosp., Jean Verdier-Paris, 1995—; vis. prof. Cleveland Clin. Edn. Found., 1994; vis. surgeon Mayo Clin. Med. Sch., 1969; head Fibrohysteroscopic Unit Diagnostic & Operative with Laser Surgery, Hosp Avicenne-Paris, 1987, Hosp. Jean Verdier-Paris, 1995. Author: (book) Hysteroscopy, Principles & Practice, 1984, Hysteroscopy Update, 1991, Office Hysteroscopy, 1996. Internat. spkr. in field. Mem. Internat. Soc. Gynecol. Endoscopy, European Soc. Gynecol. Endoscopy, Am. Assn. Gynecologic Laparoscopists (internat. advisor), Am. Fertility Soc., Soc. Argentina Cirugia Laparoscopica (hon.), French Club Gynecologique D' Endoscopie Flexible (founding mem., bd. dirs.), 1991. Office: 26 boulevard d'Argenson, 92200 Neuilly-Sur-Seine France

MARTYNENKO, ALEXEY IVANOVICH, agricultural executive; b. Kyiv, Ukraine, Oct. 29, 1958; s. Ivan Ivanovich Martynenko and Luiza Vasilievna Vorobieva; m. Valentina Vasilievna Trach, Mar. 15, 1986; children: Dasha, Andrey. MS in Engring., Ukrainian Agrl. Acad., 1980; MS in Biophysics, Moscow State U., 1984; PhD in Engring., Moscow Inst. of Agr., 1986; DS in Engring., Nat. Agrarian U., Kyiv, 1994; Academician (hon.), Ukrainian Acad. of Engring., Scis., 1999. Rschr. Inst. of Farm Mechanization and Electrification, Kyiv, 1980-86; sr. rschr. Inst. of Plant Physiology and Genetics Nat. Acad. of Sci., Kyiv, 1986-89, prin. scientist, 1989-96, leading scientist Inst. Agroresources, 1996-98; prof. Nat. Agrarian Univ., Kyiv, 1996—; dir. Internat. Cooperation Dept. Ukrainian Acad. of Agrarian Scis., Kyiv, 1997—; cons. of project mgmt. unit, Kyiv, 1997-99. Author: (books) Applied Physics and Biophysics, 1999, Automatization of Technological Processes in Agriculture, 1995. Lt. Russian Army, 1980. Recipient awards for biodiversity conservation in the Azov-Black Sea Ecol. Corridor, GEF/DEPA, 1998-99, saving of rare and disappearing plants in Crimea, CIDA (Can.) 1999, development of ecotourism in Crimea, Dutch Govt., 1999, reforming of agrl. rsch. system in Ukrain, 1998-99. Mem. Nat. Ecol. Ctr. of Ukraine, Russian Soc. Plant Physiologists, Ukrainian Assn. of Automatic Control. Mem. Agrarian Party, Orthodox Ch. Avocations: Alpinism, ecological tourism, computer engring. Home: 9 Dneprovskaja naber Apt 28, Kyiv 252098, Ukraine Office: Ukrainian Acad Agrarian Sci, 9 Suvorova Sr, 252010 Kyiv Ukraine

MARTYNOV, SERGUEI NIKOLAEVICH, Belarus diplomat; b. Leninakan, USSR, Feb. 22, 1953; s. Nikolai Artemievich and Anna Vassilievna (Krasikova) M.; children: Ivan, Nikita. MA, State Inst. Internat. Rels., Moscow, 1975. 3d sec. Ministry Fgn. Affairs, Minsk, Belarus, 1975-76, 2d sec., 1976-77, asst. to fgn. min., 1978-88, dep. dir., 1988-90; dep. permanent rep. Mission to UN, N.Y.C., 1991-92; chargé d'affaires Belarus Embassy, Washington, 1992-93, amb. to U.S., 1993-97; 1st dep. fgn. min. Govt. of Belarus, Minsk, 1997—; various positions UN, N.Y.C., 1985-91, chmn. nuclear disarmament group Commn. on Disarmament, 1988-90, chmn. UN Commn. on Disarmament, 1998. Contbr. articles to Belarus jours. Pres. Geneva Conf. on Disarmament, 2000. Avocations: art, history, tennis. Office: Belarus Min Fgn Affairs, 19 Lenin St, Minsk Belarus

MARTYNOVA, OLGA ISAKOVNA, power engineering educator; b. Khortitza, Ukraine, Jan. 24, 1916; arrived in Russia, 1934; d. Isak Ivanovitch and Ekaterina Andreevna (Wallmann) Thiessen; m. Vladimir Konstantinovich Martynov, May 5, 1936 (dec. Oct. 1943); m. Mikhail Adolfovich Styrikovich, Mar. 23, 1948; children: Natalia, Irina. Engring. diploma, Chem. Engring., Moscow, 1944; PhD, Moscow Energy Inst., 1952, DSc, 1963. Chemist Inst. Wodgeo, Moscow, 1934-44; educator Moscow Energy Inst., 1944-60, prof., 1960-65, head chair, 1965-90, hon. prof., 1996—; cons. Russian Fedn. Ministry of Energy, Moscow, 1970-95; bd. dirs. VGB-Engring., Essen, Germany; mem. EC, Internat. Assn. Properties of Steam, Palo Alto, Calif., 1975. Author: Steam Generation Processes, 1969 (Polzunov award 1975), Water Chemistry in Nuclear Plants, 1987 (award USSR Acad. Scis.); editor (manual) Power Plants Chemistry, 1990 (award of H.S. Ministry 1990); bd. dirs. Jour. Thermal Engring., 1978—, Desalination Jour., 1978—. Grantee Russian Found. Fundamental Studies, Moscow, 1993, 97, Sores's Found., Moscow, 1993. Fellow Assn. Corrosion Engrs.; mem. CODATA, Ho. Scientists. Avocation: classical music. Home: Apt 32, Leninskij Prospect 13, 117071 Moscow B 71, Russia Office: Moscow Energy Inst, Krasnokasarmennaja 17, 111250 Moscow Russia

MARTZEN, PHILIP D., physicist, software developer; b. Dinuba, Calif., Oct. 23, 1948; s. Dave and Vivian M.; m. Eloise Thompson, Jan. 29, 1972 (div. May 1988); Children: Natashya, Kinarii; m. Cynthia Stapp Landriz, July 1, 1995 (div. May 1997). BS, U. Calif., Santa Barbara, 1973, PhD, 1979. Staff mem. Geodynamics Corp., Santa Barbara, Calif., 1979-95; cons. Frontier Tech. Inc., Santa Barbara, Calif., 1996; cons. speech tech. lab. Panasonic, Santa Barbara, 1997; engring. splst. Aerospace Corp., El Segundo, Calif., 1997—; mem. physics patent com. Aerospace Corp., El Segundo, 1999—. Contbr. to profl. jours. V.p. REACTS, Santa Barbara, 1995-96; mem. Sci. and Engering. Coun. Santa Barbara, 1995—. Republican. Episcopalian. Avocations: golf, rock climbing, sailing, hiking. Home: 4166 San Martin Way Santa Barbara CA 93110-1429

MARUANI, ALAIN DAVID, physicist, engineering educator; b. Tunis, Tunisia, May 15, 1946; s. Félix M. and Hélene L. (Chemama) M.; m. June 27, 1969 (div. Oct. 1983); children: Sébastien, Caroline; m. Nadia Szmulewicz, Oct. 27, 1986; children: Emmanuel, Antoine. B in Math. and Philosophy, Lycee Hoche, Versailles, France, 1964; degree in engring., Ecole Superieure Electricite, Paris, 1969; Dr. es Sci., U. Paris, 1981. Engr. CNET, Bagneux, 1970-73; researcher Ecole Normale Superieure, Paris, 1973; group leader CNET, Bagneux, France, 1979-81; prof. Telecom, 1981; group leader Telecom Paris, 1983; chief engr. France Telecom., Paris, 1991—; v.p. Ecole Psychosomatique, Paris, 1985-91; mgr. France-Can./Conf. Grandes Ecoles, Paris, 1988-91, Neural Project, France, 1991—; cons. Obs. Fr. Tech. Av., Paris, 1988-90; pres. commns. réforme programmes classes préparatoires aux grandes écoles. Co-developer conoscopic holography; editor books in field; contbr. articles to profl. jours. Decorated Chevalier des Palmes Academiques. Home: 4 rue du Docteur Roux, 92330 Sceaux France Office: Télécom Paris, 46 rue Barrault, 75634 Paris Cedex 13, France

MARUF, TAHA MUHYI AL-DIN, Iraqi government official; b. Sulaimaniyah, Iraq, 1924; s. Muhyiddin and Fatima M. Attended, Coll. Law, U. Baghdad, Iraq. Practiced law; with Iraqi Diplomatic Svc., 1949, Embassy of Iraq, Cairo, 1960; civil servant Ministry Fgn. Affairs, Baghdad, 1964; min. Embassy of Iraq, London, 1968; min. state Govt. of Iraq, Baghdad, 1968-70, min. works and housing, 1968, amb. to Italy, non-resident amb. to Malta and Albania, 1970-74, v.p., 1974—; active Supreme Com. Progressive Regional and Nat. Fronts, 1975—. Mem. Arab Ba'ath Socialist Party. Office: Office of VP, Presdl Palace Karradit Mariam, Baghdad Iraq*

MARUPING, ANTHONY MOTHAE, bank executive. Gov. Ctrl. Bank of Lesotho, Maseru. Office: Ctrl Bank Lesotho, Moshoehoe Road, Maseru 100, Lesotho also: Cen Bank Lesotho, POB 1184, Maseru 100, Lesotho*

MARUSIC, ANA, anatomy educator, researcher; b. Mostar, Bosnia and Herzegovina, June 16, 1962; d. David and Bosiljka (Krvavica) Mandic; m. Matko Marusic, Sept. 15, 1984; children: Stjepan Ljudevit, Marija Franka. MD, Zagreb U., Croatia, 1985, MS, 1987, PhD, 1989. Asst. prof. anatomy Zagreb U., 1986-92, assoc. prof. anatomy, 1992-97, prof. anatomy, 1997—; postdoctoral fellow U. Conn., Farmington, 1989-90; DAAD fellow Pathology Inst., Munich, Germany, 1992-93. Founder, editor in chief Croatian Med. Jour., 1992-95; translator, editor: Lewis Thomas: The Youngest Science, 1995, Atlas of Anatomy, 2000; co-editor: Psychological Help to War Victims: Women Refugees and Their Families, 1995; contbr. chpts. to books, articles to profl. jours. Recipient various awards; U.S.-Croatian rsch. grantee, 1995. Mem. Am. Bone and Joint Soc., U.K. Bone and Tooth Soc., World Assn. Croatian Physicians, World Assn. Med. Editors. Avocations: reading, English language, sports. Home: Vinogradska 101, 10000 Zagreb Croatia Office: U Zagreb Sch Med Dept Anatomy, Salata 3, 10000 Zagreb Croatia

MARUSTE, RAIT, judge European Court; b. Pärnu, Estonia, Sept. 27, 1953; s. Albert and Lea M.; m. Mare Nurk, April 16, 1976; children: Madli, Kristjan. LLB, U. Tartu, 1977; LLM, U. Leningrad, U.S.S.R., 1984. Law educator Tartu U., 1977-92; assoc. prosecutor Pub. Prosecuting Office, Voru, Estonia, 1977; law lectr. U. Tartu, Estonia, 1977-84, assoc. law prof., 1984-91, head dept. criminal law and procedure, 1986-91; chief justice Supreme Ct. of Estonia, 1992-98; judge European Ct. Human Rights, Strasbourg, Estonia, 1998—. British Coun. Fellow Cambridge Univ., 1992. Mem. Estonian Acad. Law Soc., Soc. Estonian Judges, Criminal Law Reform Soc. E-mail: Rait.Maruste@court1.coe.fr. Office: Nat. Ct./Supreme Ct., European Ct Human Rights, F67075 Strasbourg Cedex, Estonia

MARUTHAMUTHU, PICHAI, chemistry educator, researcher; b. Sedunagar, Tamilnadu, India, Oct. 9, 1946; s. Maruthappa Pichai and Umaiyal; m. Meenakshi Ayyavu, Sept. 9, 1973; children: Jaya, Venkat. BSc, Raja Doraisingam Meml. Coll., Sivaganga, India, 1967; MSc, Indian Inst. Tech., Madras, 1969; PhD in Chemistry, Madras U., 1975. Analyst/rsch. asst. Madras U., 1970-76; reader Bharathidasan U., Tiruchirapalli, India, 1978-83; prof., head chem. energy dept. Madras U., 1983—, acad. dean, 1999—; guest rschr. Nat. Inst. Stds. and Tech., Gaithersburg, Md., 1993-94; vis. prof. Concordia U., Montreal, Que., Can., 1992-93; EEC sr. scientist Max-Planck-Inst., Mülheim, Germany, 1990, vis. scientist, 1980-82. Contbr. numerous articles to scientific jours. Recipient Tansa award Tamilnadu Sci. and Tech., Madras, 1995-96. Mem. NAS, Tamilnadu Acad. Scis. (life, sec. 1995), Indian Coun. Chemists (life); mem. European Photochemistry Assn. Avocations: sports, walking, TV, gardening. Home: A-11 RAA no 2 JR Nagar, Adyar/Madras, 600020 Tamil Nadu 600020, India Office: Madras U Energy Dept, A C College Campus, Madras 600025, India

MARUYAMA, FUMIHIRO, computer company executive, researcher; b. Tokyo, June 26, 1955; s. Takahisa and Michiko (Ogiwara) M.; m. Yuko Suzuki, May 5, 1987; 1 child, Asako. BS, U. Tokyo, 1978, D in Engring., 1991. Rschr. Fujitsu Labs. Ltd., Fukuoka, Japan, 1978-92, sr. rschr., 1992-98; rsch. fell. Fujitsu Labs. Ltd., 1998—; vis. scholar Stanford U., Palo Alto, Calif., 1981-82, 95; part-time lectr. Tsukuba U., Japan, 1990—, Shizuoka U., Japan, 1993—, vis. prof., Japan Inst. Advanced Sci. and Tech. Author: AI Technology, 1986; contbr. articles to scientific jours.; inventor and patentee in field, 1993. Recipient award Prof. Motooka Commemorative Com., 1988. Mem. IEEE, Info. Processing Soc. Japan (20th Anniversary Best Paper 1980), Inst. Electronics and Comm. Engrs. of Japan (Young Engr. award 1982). Avocations: travel, skiing, singing, jogging. Home: 52-2-502 Matsugaya, Hachioji 192-0354, Japan Office: Fujitsu Labs Ltd, 2-2-1 Momochihama Sawara-ku, Fukuoka 814-8588, Japan

MARUYAMA, HIROSHI, retired mechanical engineering educator; b. Fukushima-shi, Japan, July 15, 1924; m. Tsuneko Fukuyama; 1 child, Takashi. B of Engring., U. Tokyo, 1946, DEng, 1961. Rschr., chief of lab. Railway Tech. Rsch. Inst. Japanese Nat. Railways, Kokubunji-shi, Japan, 1946-76, dir. gen., 1977-80; dean Faculty of Sci. and Tech., Sci. U. Tokyo, 1984-88, councillor, 1987-91, prof., 1981-2000; ret.; part time lectr. Waseda U., Tokyo, 1966-76; spl. asst. to minister for sci. and tech., Agy. of Sci. & Tech., Tokyo, 1971—; mem. Japan Indsl. Standardization com., Ministry of Internat. Trade & Industry, Tokyo, 1950—; advisor Kenyu-sha Assn., Kokubunji, Japan, 1980—; councillor Japan Std. Assn., Tokyo, 1992—. Editor: (book) Railway Technology, 1980 (Award for Railway Publs. 1982); inventor of Electronic Railway Ticket Invending and Issuing Machine, 1970 (JSME medal 1971); patent Railway Vehicle Noise Reduction Method, 1977. Recipient Award of Minister of Internat. Trade and Industry for implementation of indsl. stds., 1983, Medal with Blue Ribbon, Emperor, 1990. Mem. ASME Internat., Japan Soc. Mech. Engring. (Medal for Super High Speed Vehicle Wheel Grinding Machine 1965), Am.-Japan Soc. Inc. Avocation: listening to classical music. Home: 11-18 Higashi-cho 1-chome, Koganei-shi 184-0011, Japan

MARUYAMA, ICHIRO, biologist, educator; b. Tsunan, Nigata, Japan, Nov. 8, 1952; came to U.S., 1991; s. Nihei and Iku Maruyama; m. Hiroko Iketani, Aug. 4, 1982; children: Risa, Gene. BSc, Nigata U., 1975; MS, U. Tokyo, 1977, PhD, 1981. Postdoctoral fellow Nat. Inst. Genetics, Mishima, Japan, 1981-83; mem. sci. staff MRC Lab. Molecular Biology, Cambridge, Eng., 1983-86, MRC Molecular Genetics Unit., Cambridge, 1986-91; asst. prof. cell biology Scripps Rsch. Inst., La Jolla, Calif., 1991-98, assoc. prof., 1998—. Mem. AAAS, Am. Soc. Cell Biology, N.Y. Acad. Sci. Office: The Scripps Rsch Inst 10555 N Torrey Pines Rd La Jolla CA 92037

MARUYAMA, KOSHI, pathologist, educator; b. Sapporo, Hokkaido, Japan, Feb. 19, 1932; s. Kotaro and Oe (Nakamura) M.; m. Rumy Misawa, May 6, 1961; children: Nariyuki, Narihiro, Yumie. MD, U. Hokkaido, 1957, PhD, 1962. Diplomate Japanese Bd. Pathology. Staff pathologist Nat. Inst. Leprosy Rsch., Tokyo, 1962-65, Nat. Cancer Ctr. Rsch. Inst., Tokyo, 1965-67; assoc. prof., assoc. virologist U. Tex. M.D. Anderson Hosp. and Tumor Inst., Houston, 1967-75; dir. dept. pathology Chiba (Japan) Cancer Ctr. Rsch. Inst., 1975-97; vis. prof. Dalian (China) Med. U., 1995—; dir. geriatric health svcs. facility Heart Village, Hasunuma, Japan, 2000; cons. Immunobiology Labs. Co., Guma, 1997—; dir. Geriatric Health Svcs. Facility, Hasunuma, Japan, 2000—. Mem. bd. editors Japanese Jour. Cancer Clinic, 1978—, Cancer Bull., 1978-89, The Year Book of Cancer, 1979; contbr. articles to profl. jours. Trustee Tex. Gulf Coast chpt. Leukemia Soc. Am., Houston, 1973-75. Named hon. prof. Liaoning Cancer Hosp. and Inst., Shenyang, China, 1992; recipient Culture Promotion award The Tsuchiya Found., 1995; scholar Leukemia Soc. Am., 1968. Fellow N.Y. Acad. Scis., Charles Darwin Assocs., Molecular Medicine Soc., Japanese Pathol. Soc. (coun. internat. exch. 1997-98), Japanese Cancer Assn., Japanese Soc. Lymphoreticular Tissue; mem. AAAS, Am. Assn. Cancer Rsch., Am. Soc. Microbiology (emeritus), Microscopy Soc. Am. (emeritus), Am. Assn. Investigative Pathology, Japan Assn. Hosp. Pathologists, Internat. Assn. Comparative Rsch. on Leukemia and Related Diseases (world com. 1993-99), Internat. Soc. for Preventive Oncology, Internat. Acad. Pathology (bd. dirs. Japan divsn. 1995-98), U. Tex. Japan Exes (trustee 1996—). Office: 3-26-9 Someino, Sakura, Chiba 285-0831, Japan

MARUYAMA, KOYO, marketing consultant; b. Tokyo, Dec. 10, 1945; s. Chyosaburo and Hisako (Isogai) M. MA in Jurisprudence, St. Paul's (Rikkyo) U., Tokyo, 1969. Sr. account dir. McCann-Erickson, Tokyo, 1969-83; mktg. mgr. McDonald's Japan, Tokyo, 1983-84, RCA/Columbia Pictures Video, Tokyo, 1984-91; account mgmt. dir. J. Walter Thompson Japan, Tokyo, 1992-97; mktg. cons. Brown & Williamson (Japan) Inc., Tokyo, 1998—. Avocations: movies, videos, music, automobiles, books. E-mail: koyokoyo@dion.ne.jp. Home: 2-9-26 Minami-Azabu, Minato-ku Tokyo 106-0047, Japan Office: Brown & Williamson Ind, 3-1 Toranomon 4, Minato-ku Tokyo 105-6020, Japan

MARUYAMA, TAMAMI, antenna research engineer; b. Tokyo, Nov. 21, 1962; d. Suzuki and Koizumi (Katsuko) Masao; m. Tamami Suzuki, Oct. 25, 1992. B in Engring., Tsuda Coll., Tokyo, 1985, MS, 1988. Rsch. engr. NTT Wireless Sys. Lab., Yokosuka, 1988—. Recipient Young Engr. award Tokyo chpt. IEEE, 1995. Mem. IEEE, Inst. Electronics, Info., and Comms. Engrs. (Excellent Paper award 1997). Fax: 81 468 55 1752. E-mail: tamami@wslab.ntt.co.jp. Home: Minam-ku Nakasato, Yokohama 232-0063, Japan Office: NTT Network Innovation Labs, 1-1 Hikarinooka, Yokosuka-shi 239-0847, Japan

MARVAN, PETR, phycologist, researcher; b. Brno, Moravia, Czechoslovakia, Apr. 29, 1929; s. Vladimir and Stanislava (Antosová) M. m. Ludmila Hermanská, Dec. 27, 1954; children: Petr, Michal. RNDr, Masaryk U., Brno, Czechoslovakia, 1952; CSc, Czechoslovak Acad. Scis., Prague, 1965. Asst. lectr. faculty of sci. Masaryk U., Brno, 1952-54, rschr. faculty of sci., 1991-94; engr. Water Rsch. Inst. Prague, Brno, 1954-63; scientist Microbiol. Inst. Czechoslovak Acad. Scis., Brno, 1963-71; from scientist to sr. scientist Inst. of Botany Czech Acad. Scis., Brno, 1991-94, cons. (ret.), 1994; vis. lectr. faculty of sci. Palacky U. Olomouc, Czech Republic, 1990-94. Editor: (book) Algal Assays and Monitoring Eutrophication, 1979; inventor of biological methods of water quality monitoring; contbr. about 170 articles to Algological Studies, Stuttgart and other sci. jours. Mem. Czech Bot. Soc., Czech Limnological Soc. Roman Catholic. Avocations: hiking, classical music, botany. Home: Doležalova 8, CZ 61600 Brno Moravia, Czech Republic

MARVIN, BLANCHE, drama critic, playwright, actress; b. N.Y.C., Jan. 17, 1925; m. Mark Marvin (dec. 1958); children: Nicolette, Herbert. BA, Antioch Coll., 1944. Artistic dir. Cricket Theatre and Merri-Mimes Children's Theatre, N.Y.C., 1958-68, Rock Garden Theatre, London, 1978-81; drama agent Blanche Marvin Agy.-Sweeney Todd, London, 1968-91; pub.-editor London Theatre Revs., 1991—. Writer 15 plays for children; prodr., dir. films and plays; playwright Gertrude Stein and A Companion (Emmy award 1987, Am. Video Conf. award 1987, ACE Video award 1987. Developer ednl. programs for deaf, U.S. and Eng. Recipient Cert. of Merit, NARAS, 1965. Mem. Writers Guild, Actors Equity, PMA, Brit. Acad. Film and TV Arts. Home: 21A St Johns Wood, High St, London NW8 7NG, England

MARVIN, CHARLES RODNEY, JR., lawyer; b. Elizabeth, N.J., Feb. 26, 1953; s. Charles Rodney Sr. and Doris Marie (Richards) M.; m. Carol Ann Welteroth, Aug. 30, 1975; children: Kathryn, Kristin, Cynthia, Gregory. BA in Econs., Mich. State U., 1975; JD, Boston U., 1978; LLM in Mil. Law, Judge Advocate Gen. Sch., 1987; LLM in Govt. Contracts, George Washington U., 1995. Bar: N.J. 1982, U.S. Dist. Ct. N.J. 1982, U.S. Ct. Mil. Appeals 1982, U.S. Ct. Appeals (fed. cir.) 1994, D.C. 1996, U.S. Ct. Fed. Claims 1996. Commd. 2nd lt. U.S. Army, 1975, advanced through grades to lt. comdr., 1993; nuclear missile officer U.S. Army, Schwaebisch Gmund, Germany, 1979-82; mil. prosecutor U.S. Army, Fort Sill, Okla., 1983-86; sr. def. counsel U.S. Army Trial Def. Svc., Ft. Polk, La., 1987-89; trial counsel, chief protest br. U.S. Army Contract Appeals Divsn., Arlington, Va., 1990-94; ptnr. Venable, Baetjer, Howard & Civiletti, Washington, 1994—. Mem. ABA (vice-chair, bid protest com., pub. contract law sect. 1992-93), FBA, Bd. Contract Appeals Bar Assn. (bd. govs. 1993-96), Fed. Cir. Bar Assn., John Carroll Soc., Nat. Contract Mgmt. Assn. Roman Catholic. Avocations: musical composing, adult education, golf. Office: Venable Baetjer et al 1201 New York Ave NW Ste 1000 Washington DC 20005-6197

MARVIN, FREDA MARY, art educator, nurse; b. Everett, Wash., July 3, 1930; d. Robert Laffayette and Georgeina (Mahlstedt) Pressey; m. Donald Conrad Lawrence, 1950 (div. 1966); children: Linda, Karen, Donna, Betty; m. William Hammond Marvin, July 30, 1971. AA, San Jose City Coll., 1964; BS, Calif. State U., Fresno, 1974; cert., Beartooth Sch. Wildlife, 1995, 96. RN, Calif.; cert. sch. audiometrist Calif. Head nurse II Agnew State Hosp., San Jose, Calif., 1964-71; head nurse I Med. Ctr. Fresno (Calif.), 1971-72; intern nurse St. Agnes Hosp., Fresno, 1974-75; sch. nurse Teague Sch. Dist., Fresno, 1976-78; intensive care pvt. duty nurse Fresno, 1980-94; relief dir. nursing Sierra View Convescent Hosp., Fresno, 1995; art tchr. Marvin Art Studio, Prather, Calif., 1995—. Numerous two-women and group shows including Timberline Gallery, Oakhurst, Calif., Marvin Art Gallery, Prather, Calif. Fresno State Coll. scholar, 1973, 74; recipient Art award Clovis Art Guild, Soc. Western Artists Signature Show award, 1999. Mem. Soc. Western Artists (pres. 1994, 95, degree of honor 1993), Yosemite Western Artists (exec. bd. dirs. 1980-90, exec. bd. 1995, awards). Republican. Avocations: gardening, painting, reading, computer. Fax: 209-322-0904. E-mail: Bilfrema@msn.com. Home: 14916 Garlock Ln Prather CA 93651-9731

MARVIN, MONICA LOUISE WOLF, lawyer; b. San Francisco, Feb. 3, 1947; d. Andrew John and Hazel Louise Wolf; m. Gregory Lewis Marvin, Aug. 17, 1969; children: Brett Lewis, Elizabeth Louise. Student, Pacific U., Forest Grove, Oreg., 1964-66, Sonoma State U., Rohnert Park, Calif., 1966-67; BA in Psychology, Chico (Calif.) State U., 1969; JD, Empire Coll., Santa Rosa, Calif., 1982. Bar: Calif. 1982, U.S. Dist. Ct. Calif. 1982. Assoc. Fitzgerald Fitzgerald and Gowen, Santa Rosa, Calif., 1982-83, Gowen and Marvin, Santa Rosa, 1983-85, Rodeno Robertson & Assocs., Napa, Calif., 1985-86; pvt. practice St Helena, Calif., 1986—; of counsel Hardell & Yost, LLP, 2000—; judge pro tempore Napa County Consol. Cts., Small Claims Divsn., 1991—. Bd. dirs., v.p. Cmty. Resources for Children, Napa, 1991-94; mem. Napa County Commn. on Children, Youth and Family, 1994-97; mem. Napa County Dem. Ctrl. Com., 1994-98; mem. adv. bd. Napa County

Vol. Ctr. Ombudsman Program, 1994-95; founder, chair St. Helena C. of C. Jumelage Com., Sister Chamber affiliation with Libourne C. of C. and Industry, France. Mem. State Bar Calif., Napa County Bar Assn. (bd. dirs. 1994), Napa Women Lawyers (past pres., sec. 1987-92), St. Helena C. of C. (bd. dirs. 1992-94), St. Helena Rotary Club (pres. 1999-2000). Office: PO Box 271 Saint Helena CA 94574-0271

MARVISI, MAURIZIO, internist, researcher; b. Salsomaggiore Terme, Parma, Italy, Jan. 30, 1959; s. Ennio and Carmen (Curati) M.; m. Teresa Ferri; children: Chiara, Davide. MD, U. Parma, 1987, specialist in pneumology, 1991. Asst. divsn. internal medicine Rimini, Italy, 1991; asst. emergency Unit Fiorenzvola, 1991-92; asst. divsn. internal medicine Cortemaggiore (Italy) Hosp., 1993-96, med. mgr. divsn. internal medicine, 1996—; dir. pneumology unit Cortemaggiore Hosp., 1996—. Contbr. articles to med. jours. Recipient rsch. grant in diabetology Fidenza (Italy) Hosp., 1991. Mem. European Respiratory Soc., Italian Soc. Internal Medicine, Italian Soc. Pneumology, N.Y. Acad. Scis. Office: Cortemaggiore Hospital, Liberta 25, Piacenza Cortemaggiore Italy

MARWAHA, JAY, management consultant. BCom with honors, U. Delhi; MBA, U. Chgo. Assoc. ptnr. Anderson Corp., Washington, 1997-99, 1999. Office: Viant 3102 Oak Lawn Ave Fl 2D Dallas TX 75219-4241

MARWINSKI, KONRAD FERDINAND, librarian, historian; b. Königsberg, Germany, Jan. 16, 1934; s. Kurt Ferdinand and Lisbeth (Leupold) M.; m. Felicitas E. Marwinski, Apr. 03, 1961; 1 child, Titus. Diploma in History, Humboldt U., Berlin, 1966; PhD, U. Leipzig, Germany, 1975. Diplomed libr. Regional Libr. Thuringia, Weimar, Germany, 1956-69; libr. higher svc. Univ. Libr., Jena, 1969-79, subs. dir., 1980-90; libr. Friedrich-Schiller-Univ. Jena, 1990-99, Thuringian U., Jena, 1990—. Co-editor: Bibliothek-Forschung Praxis, 1991, Zeitschrift des Vereins für Thüringische Geschichte, 1992. Mem. Commn. Thuringian History, Commn. Hessian History, Soc. Thuringian History, Rotary.

MARX, ALFRED RODOLPHE, theology educator; b. Ingwiller, Bas-Rhin, France, May 28, 1943; s. Georges and Anne (Huber) M.; m. Hélène Matter, July 11, 1986; children: Jean-Samuel, Anne-Claire. ThM, Princeton (N.J.) Theol. Sem., 1966; D. of Religious Sci., U. II Strasbourg, France, 1978, ThD, 1986. Prof. Faculty Protestant Theology, Yaounde, Cameroun, 1966-68, Kisangani, République Démocratique du Congo, 1968-69; asst. Faculty Protestant Theology, Strasbourg, 1969-74, head of conf., 1974-89, prof., 1989—. Author: Les offrandes végétales dans l'Ancien Testament, 1994, (with C. Grappe) Le Sacrifice. Vocation et subversion du sacrifice dans les deux Testaments, 1998; contbr. articles to profl. jours. Decorated Palmes académiques (Officer) Ministry of Nat. Edn., 1996. Lutheran. Office: Faculty Protestant Theology, Palais Universitaire, 67084 Strasbourg Cedex, France

MARX, GARY T., sociologist, writer; b. Hanford, Calif., Oct. 1, 1938. BA, UCLA, 1960; MA, U. Calif., Berkeley, 1962, PhD, 1966. Rsch. assoc. U. Calif., Berkeley, 1965-67, lectr. dept. sociology, 1966-67; rsch. assoc. Harvard-MIT Joint Ctr. for Urban Studies, 1967-73; asst. prof., lectr. dept. social rels. Harvard U., 1967-73; sr. rsch. assoc. Ctr. for Criminal Justice Harvard Law Sch., 1973-75; assoc. prof. MIT, 1973-79, prof., 1979-94, emeritus prof. dept. urban studies and planning, 1994; prof. U. Colo., Boulder, 1992-99, chair dept. sociology, 1992-96; vis. scholar U. Wash., 1999—; vis. prof. U. Calif., San Diego, 1977-78, SUNY, Albany, 1980, Cath. U., Louvain and Louvain La Neuve, Belgium, Tech. U., Vienna, Austria, 1993, Nankai U., China, 1995; mem. exec. com. Am. Sociol. Assn., 1973-76; mem. adv. bd. Office of Tech. Assessment, 1985-87, NAS, 1989-91, Electronic Privacy Info. Ctr., 1992; presenter testimony U.S. Congress, 1981, 91, 97. Author: Protest and Prejudice, 1967, rev. edit., 1969, Japanese edit., 1971, Undercover: Police Surveillance in America, 1988, Chinese edit., 1995; co-author: (with others) Inquiries in Sociology, 1972, (with N. Goodman) Society Today, rev. edit., 3d. edit., 1978, 4th edit., 1982, (with Doug McAdam) Collective Behavior and Collective Behavior Process, 1993; contbr. numerous articles to profl. jours.; editor: (book) Muckracking Sociology: Research as Social Criticism, 1972, (jours.) Social Problems, 1969-75, Am. Sociol. Rev., 1972-75, Ann. Rev. Sociology, 1978-84, 97-98, Jour. Conflict Resolution, 1984-91, Qualitative Sociology, Justice Quar., 1990-93, Sociol. Forum, 1991-96, Criminology, 1991-93; co-editor: (books) (with others) Confrontation: Psychology and Problems of Today, 1970, (with N. Goodman) Sociology: Classic and Popular Approaches, 1980, (with C. Fijnaut) Undercover: Police Surveillance in Comparative Perspective, 1995; mem. editl. bd. The Info. Soc., 1995—, The Am. Sociologist, 1997—, Policing and Society, 1997—, Ethics and Info. Tech., 1998—. Recipient Disting. Scholarship award Am. Sociol. Assn., 1990, named Jensen lectr., 1989; Outstanding Book award Acad. Criminal Justice Scis., 1990, Bruce Smith Lifetime Achievement award, 1999; Silver Gavel award ABA, 1991; Guggenheim fellow, 1970-71, rsch. fellow Ctr. for Advanced Study in the Behavioral Scis., 1987-88, 96-97, fellow Woodrow Wilson Internat. Ctr. for Scholars, Washington, 1997-98; rsch. grantee NSF, 1973-75, 85-86, 91-95, 20th Century Fund, 1982-87, Austauschdienst, Whiting Found., Deutscher Akademischer, 1991; named resident scholar Rockefeller Study and Conf. Ctr., Belagio, Italy, 1990, Stice Meml. lectr. in social scis. U. Wash., 1992, Appel Disting. lectr. in law and tech., Denver U., 1994. Address: 4615 New Sweden Ave Bainbridge Island WA 98110-3116

MARX, PETER A., lawyer; b. N.Y.C., June 14, 1942; s. Robert L. and Helen (Sohn) M.; m. Barbara K. Marx, Dec. 21, 1974; children: Laura, Lisa. BA, Cornell U., 1965, MBA, JD, 1968. Bar: N.Y. 1969, D.C. 1970, Mass. 1980. Atty., advisor U.S. Securites & Exch. Commn., Washington, 1968-71; assoc. Shaw, Pittman, Potts & Trowbridge, Washington, 1971-74; v.p., gen. counsel Chase Econometrics and Interactive Data Corp., Waltham, Mass., 1975-85; ptnr. Goulston & Storrs, Boston, 1985-87; prin. The Marx Group, Wellesley, Mass., 1987—; dir. Info. Industry Assn., Washington, 1980-84, hon. counsel to bd., 1993—; chmn. N.E. Computer Law Forum, 1982-89; adv. bd. CNC Interactive, 1998, LifetecNet.com, 1999—, ForPower.com, 1999—, Eye on Interactive, 1999; host Venture Capital Quest, 1998—; vice chmn. bd. dirs. Internet Alliance. Editor: Contracts in the Information Industry, 1988, II, 1990, III, 1995; mem. bd. advisors Computer Law Strategist, 1987-99; info. law editor Info. Mgmt. Rev., 1987-90; host program N.E. Bus. Forum, Sta. WCAB-TV, 1991—; coord. editor The Info. Industry Deal Making Directory, 1994. Mem. ALI-ABA Computer Law Inst. (chmn. 1980-88), New Eng. Corp. Counsel Assn. (chmn. 1981-82). E-mail: peter@marxgroup.com. Office: The Marx Group 60 Valley Rd Wellesley MA 02481-1448

MARYANTO, RUSMANTO, journalist, magazine editor; b. Sragen, Ctrl. Java, Indonesia, July 23, 1963; s. Mariyo Somaidjaja and Parinem (Kartoidjaja) M.; m. Idah Siti Zubaedah Rusmanto Emong Ediwijaya, Aug. 22, 1988; children: Faris, Nahri, Qisthi, Salwa. BSc, U. Indonesia, Jakarta, 1988; M in Mgmt., Sch. Mgmt. Sci., Jakarta, 2000. Mem. staff Nat. Atomic Energy Agy., Jakarta, 1986-89; educator Nat. Atomic Energy Agy., Yogyakarta, 1989-94; rschr. Nat. Atomic Energy Agy., Jakarta, 1994-95; journalist, editor Elektro Indonesia mag., Jakarta, 1994—; mgr. Elekro Tech. Devel. Found., Jakarta, 1995—; graphic designer, webmaster Elektro Online; tng. supr. on info. mgmt. and tech. Info Solusi, Jakarta, 1997-99; trainer, mktg. mgr. Nurul-Fikri Computer and Stats., 1999—; lectr. Tugu Polytechnic, Jakarta, 1999—. Mem. Indonesian Computer and Informatics Profl. Assn., Indonesian Electricity Soc., Jakarta Linux User Group (former v.p.), World Energy Coun. Moslem. Avocations: photography, bicycle riding, jogging. Office: Elektro Tech Devel Found, Jln Gatot Subroto 52, Jakarta 12710, Indonesia

MÄRZ, REINHARD HELLMUT, physicist, researcher; b. Milan, July 25, 1956; s. Walter and Ingrid (Krüger) M.; m. Sabine Ullmann, Mar. 15, 1985 (div. Mar. 1993). Diploma in physics, U. Frankfurt, Germany, 1980, PhD, 1983. Sci. asst. U. Frankfurt, 1981-84; scientist optical comm. tech. Siemens, Munich, 1984—; exploitation mgr. Konrad Zuse Zentrum, Berlin, 1993—; conf. chair Intenat. Soc. Optical Engring., Bellingham, Wash., and China, 1998; editor Taylor & Francis/Fiber and Integrated Optics, Wash., 1992—. Author: (book) Integrated Optics: Design and Modeling, 1994; co-author: Encyclopedia of Electrical and Electronics Engineers, 1999. Mem. German Physics Soc. Avocations: rock climbing, mountaineering. E-mail: reinhard.maerz@infineon.com. Home: Schuchstr 18, D-81477 Munich Germany

MARZETTI, SILVA, economist, educator; b. Massalombarda, Ravenna, Italy, Sept. 25, 1947; d. Enzo and Franca (Franzaroli) M.; m. Fabrizio Dall'Aste Brandolini, Oct. 6, 1973; children: Cesare, Mitzi. Degree in econs., U. Bologna, Italy, 1972. Holder U. Bologna, 1972-74, asst., 1974—, lectr., 1990—. Author: Microeconomia del Consumo e della Produzione, 1991; co-author: Guida alla Controllabilità di Modelli di Politica Economica, 1994; co-editor: A Treatise on Probability, 1994 (Italian translation), La Probabilita in Keynes: Premesse e Influenze, 1999. Mem. Univ. Women Assn. Italy, Italian Soc. Logic and Philosophy of Sci. Avocations: tennis, music, ballet. E-mail: marzett:@economia.unibo.it. Office: Dept Econ Sci, Piazza Scaravilli 2, 40126 Bologna Italy

MARZLOFF, GEORGES M., management company executive; b. Rabat, Morocco, Apr. 8, 1944; s. Jean Marzloff and Claude Richard de Soultrait; m. Rosine M. Facques, Sept. 10, 1971; children: Thibault, Alexandra. Grad., EDHEC, France, 1967; MBA, European Inst. Bus. Adminstrn., France, 1970. V.p. Rhône Poulenc Chimie, France, 1972-89; consejero delegado Grupo Salvat, Spain, 1989-91; sr. exec. v.p. Neste Oy, Espoo, Finland, 1991—; pres., CEO Neste Chems. Oy, Helsinki, 1999—; bd. dirs. various N.Am. and European cos. Lt. French Navy, 1967-69. Mem. Internat. Forum, World Econ. Forum, Order of Lion (officer 1996). Avocations: golf, sailing. Home: Ave Van Bever 5, 1180 Brussels Belgium Office: Neste Chemicals Oy, Snellmaninkatu 13, 00170 Helsinki Finland

MARZO, AMANDA LEE, immunologist, researcher; b. Auburn, NSW, Australia, Jan. 6, 1963; d. Leo Alfred Marzo and Joan Olive (Albrecht) Wilson. BSc, U. Western Australia, Perth, 1983, BSc with honors, 1984. Rsch. asst. Royal Perth Hosp., Clin. Immunology Rsch. Unit, Perth; rsch. officer Dept. Medicine of Western Australia, Perth; supr. rsch. asst. Dept. Medicine, Perth, 1994-98. Author: (book) New Techniques for Evaluating Lung Immunology and Immunopathology, 1995; contbr. articles to profl. jours. Instr., fund raiser Riding for Disabled, Claremont, Perth, 1991-93. Recipient Sandoz Young Investigators award Sandoz, 1995, Freemasons Bursary award, 1996, 97, 98; Dora Lush postgrad. scholar Nat. Health and Med. Rsch. Ctr., 1995-98; John Nott Cancer fellow Cancer Found. of Western Australia, 1995. Mem. Australian Soc. for Immunology, Australian Soc. for Biochemistry and Molecular Biology. Avocations: tennis, lacrosse, horse riding, reading. Office: Univ Dept Medicine, QEII Med Ctr Verdum St, 6008 Perth Australia

MARZO, ANTONIO PIETRO, pharmacologist; b. San Pietro in Lama, Italy, May 1, 1939; s. Salvatore Maria and Elena Grazia Marzo; m. Marisa Branca, Apr. 29, 1967; children: Paolo, Matteo. Degree in indsl. chemistry, U. Milan, Italy, 1965, degree in pharmacy, 1980, degree in pharm. chemistry and tech., 1991. Rschr. Italian Nat. Rsch. Coun., Milan, 1966-70; head biochem. lab. SIMES S.P.A., Milan, 1970-81; head biol. divsn. BTB S.P.A., Milan, 1981-85; head pharmacokinetic dept. Sigma Tau, Rome, 1985-93; head clin. pharmacology dept. IPAS S.A., Ligornetto, Switzerland, 1993—; univ. lectr. in pharmacokinetics U. Milan, 1974—, U. Parma, Italy, 1984-85, 96—. Contbr. articles to profl. jours. Avocations: music, theater, opera. Office: IPAS SA, Via Mastri, 6853 Ligornetto Switzerland

MARZOCCHI, ALFREDO, mathematician; b. Salo, Italy, Nov. 11, 1960; s. Sergio and Irma (Wemmer) M.; m. Claudia Schwarzer, Jan. 4, 1992; 1 child, Fiorenza. BS, Liceo Scientifico, Salo, 1979; MSc, Cath. U. Brescia, 1983; DSc, U. Paris, 1990. Rschr. Cath. U. Brescia, Italy, 1988—.

MASA, GEORGE JOHN, banker; b. Chgo., Apr. 29, 1947; s. George John Sr. and Barbara Ann (Kos) M.; m. Judy Ann Martin, Apr. 24, 1971; children: Kimberly Janine, Kristin Marie. BS in Commerce, De Paul U., 1969; cert. in banking, Rutgers U., 1979; cert. in mgmt., Pa. State U., 1987. Field bank examiner FDIC, Chgo., 1969-77, rev. examiner, 1977-82; asst. regional dir. FDIC, Dallas, 1982-85; asst. dir. policy FDIC, Washington, 1985-86, asst. dir. ops., 1986-89; regional dir. FDIC, Chgo., 1989-91, San Francisco, 1991—. With USAR, 1970-76.

MASADA, HIROMITSU, chemistry researcher; b. Nishinomiya, Hyogo, Japan, Feb. 3, 1938; s. Yoshio and Michiko (Kawachi) M.; m. Yoko Danno, Oct. 17, 1969; 1 child, Noriko. B of Engring., Osaka U., Japan, 1962; M of Engring., Kyoto U., Japan, 1964, D of Engring., 1967. Asst. prof. Kanazawa (Japan) U., 1967-72, assoc. prof., 1972-96, prof., 1996—. Recipient Seikyo Newspaper Culture award, Tokyo, 1986. Avocations: travel, research of Buddhism. Office: Kanazawa U, 40-20 Kodatsuno 2 chome, Kanazawa 920-8667, Japan

MASAI, YASUO, geography educator; b. Tokyo, June 1, 1929; s. Teruo and Tomi (Masui) M.; m. Emiko Hayashi, Jan. 13, 1961; children: Kazuo, Megumi. MS, Tokyo Bunrika U., 1953, DSc, 1962; PhD, Mich. State U., 1960. Lectr. Rissho U., Tokyo, 1963-64, prof. geography, 1984—; lectr. Ochanomizu U., Tokyo, 1964-65, assoc. prof., 1965-74, prof., 1974-75; prof. U. Tsukuba, Japan, 1975-84, Rissho U., Tokyo, 1984—; chmn. Nat. Com. for Pacific Sci. Assn., Sci. Coun. Japan, 1983-88. Author: A Comparative Study of Japanese and American Cities, 1977; editor: Geography of Japan (21 vols.), 1963-80, Atlas Tokyo, 1986, Grand World Atlas, 1996. Recipient Fulbright Commn. scholarship, 1957-60, award for promotion of geography edn. Japan Edn. Rsch. Union, Tokyo, 1987. Mem. Japan Cartographers Assn. (pres. 1995—, Presdl. award 1992), Internat. Cartographic Assn. (chmn. Commn. on Urban Cartography 1980-88, award com. 1993-97), Rissho Geog. Soc. (pres. 1996—), Japan Assn. Geog. Edn. (pres. 1993-95). Buddhist. Avocations: travel, sketching, gardening, nature watching. Home: 1-17-15 Fujimidai, Nerima-ku, Tokyo 177-0034, Japan Office: Rissho U, Osaki, Shinagawa-Ku, Tokyo 141, Japan

MASAKI, AKIRA, education educator, author; b. Akashi City, Hyogo, Japan, Feb. 5, 1925; s. Masuzo and Yukie (Hiwada) M.; m. Shizuko Okuda, Jan. 8, 1954. Student, Osaka Prefectural U. of Synthetic Sci., 1945; BA, Kansai U., Suita City, Japan, 1950, MA, 1955. Lectr. Kansai U., 1962-91, Nat. U. Osaka, Suita City, 1966-96; prof. edn. Ashiya (Japan) U., 1967-85, supreme prof. Grad. Sch., 1985-93; dir. Hirano Kindergarten, Kawanishi, Hyogo, 1976—; participant nat. meetings, 1952. Author: Critical Ontology of Literature, 1989, Junction on Arts and Science, 1994; also articles and treatises, others. Pres. Saturday Party, Kansai area, 1964-92; adviser Osaka Refrigeration and Air Conditioning Industries Assn., Kansai area, 1965-90. With inf. Japanese Army, 1945-46. YMCA fellow, 1971-74; recipient svc. award Ashiya U., 1984, commendation Hyogo Police Hdqrs., 1988, merit award Kansai U., 1991, Supreme commendation Hyogo Police Hdqrs., 1994. Mem. English Lit. Soc. Japan, Alumni Assn. Drs. and Masters (subpres. Suita 1985-92, adviser 1992—). Avocations: driving, singing, mountain climbing, writer, potted plants. Home: 7-27, 1-chome, Midoridai, Kawanishi City, Hyogo Kansai 666-0129, Japan

MASAKI, ISHIZAKA, physician; b. Tokyo, Sept. 5, 1957; s. Ishizaka Shigeki and Watanabe Teruko; m. Kawaziri Tomoko, May 26, 1985; children: Miki, Keisuke. BA, Niigata U. Sch. Medicine, Japan; PhD, Niigata U. Sch. Medicine. Contbr. articles to profl. jours. Home: 1-6-4 Minamidekizima, Niigata 950-0963, Japan

MASAMOTO, JUNZO, chemist, researcher; b. Tsuna, Japan, May 14, 1937; s. Kazuo and Kiyoko Masamoto; m. Noriko Masamoto, Oct. 1, 1967; children: Kyoko, Kenichi. BS, Kyoto U., 1961, MS, 1963, PhD, 1969. Rsch. chemist Asahi Chem. Industry, Japan, 1963—, mgr., 1975—, asst. gen. mgr., 1983—, gen. mgr., 1987—, rsch. fellow, 1992—; vis. prof. Kyoto (Japan) U., 1995—, Kyoto Inst. Tech., 1996—; prof. Fukui U. Tech., 2000—. Author: Poly-B-alanine Fiber, 1976, Modern Acetal Resins, 1993, Nylon-3, 1996, Polyacetals (Homopolymer, Copolymer and Block Copolymer), 1996, Polyphenylene Sulfide (Elastomer Toughened), 1996, Polyarylate, 1999; contbr. articles to profl. jours. Recipient Atsugi award Fiber Sci. and Tech. Japan, 1971, award Soc. Chem. Engrs., 1988-89, Okochi Meml. prize, 1989, Ichimura prize, 1989, Mainichi Newspaper Tech. award, 1990, award of Nat. Invention, Japan, 1994; selected among Top 10 Rschrs. in Japan in Past 10 Yrs., 1993. Mem. Japan Chem. Industry Assn. (tech. award 1991), Chem. Soc. Japan (award 1991), Soc. Polymer Sci. (v.p. Chugoku and Shikoku regional br. 1992—, award 1991), Sci. and Tech. Agy. (dir. gen., award 1991), Am. Chem. Soc., N.Y. Acad. Scis. Achievements include pioneering in development of synthetic fiber-nylon 3; new process for polyacetal resins; new formaldehyde process by methylal oxidation; new acetal homopolymer process; new acetal-copolymer process; synthesis of ultrahigh molecular weight polyoxymethylene; discovery of novel reaction between cyclic formals and ethylene oxide, and discovery of various novel cyclic compounds; development of new process for the production of bisphenol A polyarylate by melt process and solid-state polymerization process, new elastomer toughened polyphenylene sulfide, new bisphenol A polyarylate process. Home: 602 Daikan-Plaza, 2-22-28 Nikko, Fukui-shi 910-0029, Japan Office: Fukui U Technology, Gakuen, Fukui-shi 910-8505, Japan

MASARIK, JÁN, chemist; b. Male Hoste, Slovakia, Aug. 21, 1949; s. Emil and Vilma Anna (Marusincova) M.; m. Viera Slivovska, Apr. 21, 1979; children: Daniel, Veronika. Degree in engring., Slovak Tech. U., 1973; postgrad., Charles U., 1978. Rschr. Rsch. Inst. Chem. Fibres, Svit, Slovakia, 1973-90, 1995—. Patentee in field; contbr. articles to profl. jours. Active Slovak Parliament, 1990, 90-92, 92-94. Roman Catholic. Avocation: beekeeping.

MASARIK, JOZEF, nuclear, space-environmental physicist, educator; b. Jalovec, Slovakia, Oct. 5, 1959; s. Jozef and Olga (Kotianova) M.; m. Jana Janosova, Oct. 10, 1992; children: Jozef Eduard, Maria Jana. MSc, Comenius U., Bratislava, Slovakia, 1983, PhD, 1991, assoc. prof., 1996, DSc, 1997. Lectr. dept. nuclear physics Comenius U., Bratislava, 1983-96, assoc. prof., 1996—; chief dept., faculty math. and physics, Comenius U., 1992; postdoctoral fellow Los Alamos (N.Mex.) Nat. Lab., 1992-95; vis. scientist Max-Planck-Inst., Mainz, Germany, 1995-96; guest scientist Swiss Fed. Inst. for Environ. Sci. and Tech., Swiss Fed. Inst. Tech., Dübendorf, 1996-98; guest scientist Space Scis. Lab. U. Calif., Berkeley, 1998-99. Contbr. over 100 articles to internat. scientific jours. and conf. procs. Chmn. Univ. Student Soc., Comenius U., 1988-89. Capt., Czechoslovak Army, 1983-84, Strašice. Mem. European Geophys. Soc., European Phys. Soc., Meteoritical Soc. Roman Catholic. Avocations: music, skiing, modern literature.

MASATAKA, NOBUO, psychologist; b. Osaka, Japan, Dec. 10, 1954; s. Tsuneyoshi and Sawa (Mori) M.; m. Motoko Inaba, July 7, 1982; children: Yuji, Morio. BA, Osaka U., 1977, MA, 1979, PhD, 1982. Asst. prof. Kyoto U., 1988-90, assoc. prof., 1993—; asst. prof. U. Tokyo, 1990-93. Contbr. articles to profl. jours. Office: Kyoto U Primate Rsch Inst, Inuyama, Aichi 484-8506, Japan

MASAYOSHI, SON, Internet company executive; b. Aug. 11, 1957; married; 2 children. Student, Holy Name Coll., 1977; BA in Econs., U. Calif., Berkeley, 1980. Founder, pres., CEO Softbank Corp., Tokyo. Patentee hand-held electronic translator. Office: 24-1 Nihonbashi, Hakozaki-cho, Tokyo Japan

MASCARENHAS, FLAVIO CESAR BORBA, engineering educator; b. Rio de Janeiro, Dec. 4, 1952; s. Flavio Capllonch and Yvette (Borba) M.; m. Anna Elizabeth Cavalcanti Salomao, Feb. 1, 1983 (div. 1989); 1 child, Fernanda. BS in Civil Engring., Cath. U., Rio de Janeiro, 1976; MSc in Civil Engring., Fed. U., Rio de Janeiro, 1980, PhD in Civil Engring., 1990. Head tech. mechanics dept. Fed. U., Rio de Janeiro, 1990-92, coord. civil engring., 1992-94, chief computational hydraulics lab., 1996-97, head water resources program, 1998—; sr. lectr. Fed. U. Ouro Preto, Brazil, 1988; coord. consulting COPPE-UFRJ, Rio de Janeiro, 1995—; Pronex mem. Sci. and Tech. Ministry, Brasilia, Brazil, 1993—; rsch. leader COPPE-UFRJ, Rio de Janeiro, 1995; urban drainage sr. cons. UFRJ, Rio de Janeiro, 1995; sr. cons. City Mayor Office, Rio de Janeiro, 1996—; bd. dirs. Numerical Methods Commn., Rio de Janeiro. Contbr. chpt. to book and articles to profl. jours. Group leader Brazilian Rsch. Coun., Brasilia, 1991; sector mgr. Mayor Office of Joinville, Santa Catarina State, 1995; mgr. Contract Between Coppe and Itaipu, Rio de Janeiro, 1996; mgr. Rio de Janeiro Mayor Office, 1997. Grantee Brazilian Rsch. Coun., 1991, UNESCO, 1994, others. Mem. Internat. Water Resources Assn., Brazilian Assn. Groundwater (hon., sr. cons. 1995, group leader 1995), Brazilian Water Resources Assn. (founder 1977—, dir. 1992-94), N.Y. Acad. Scis. (leader 1997, sr. leader 1997). Avocations: home sound, architecture, home office planning, fishing, soccer. Home: Cosme Velho, Rua Itamonte 150, 22241260 Rio de Janeiro Brazil Office: Coppe-Program Civil Engring, PO Box 68506, 21945970 Rio de Janeiro Brazil

MASCARENHAS MONTEIRO, ANTONIO, president of Cape Verde; b. 1944. Pres. of Cape Verde, 1991—. Office: President of Republic, Palacio do Governo, POB 100, Praia Sao Tiago, Cape Verde*

MASCETTA, JOSEPH ANTHONY, principal; b. Canonsburg, Pa., Sept. 2, 1931; s. Joseph Alphonso and Amalia (Ciavarra) M.; m. Jean Verrone, June 18, 1960; children: Lisa Marie, Linda Jo, Lori Jean. BS, U. Pitts., 1954; MS, U. Pa., 1963; cert. advanced study, Harvard U., 1970. Cert. tchr. math., phys. scis., adminstr. secondary sch., Pa. Tchr. chemistry Canonsburg High Sch., 1956-59; tchr. chemistry Mt. Lebanon High Sch., Pitts., 1959-75, chair sci. dept., 1967-75; coord. secondary curriculum Mt. Lebanon Sch. Dist., Pitts., 1975-81; prin. Mt. Lebanon Sr. High Sch., Pitts., 1981-91; ret., 1991, ednl. cons., 1991—; vis. team mem. Mid. States Assn. Colls. and Schs., Phila., 1967-78, chair vis. teams, 1981-96, Pa. state adv. com., 1988-91; mem. sch. bd. and edn. commn. St. Patrick Sch., Canonsburg, 1972-85, 95—; regional dir. Pa. Jr. Acad. Sci., Pitts., 1976-82; ednl. cons. Pitts. area schs., 1992—; mem. quality edn. com. Pitts. Diocese, 1995-97. Author: Perry Como Commemorative Booklet, Modern Chemistry Review, 1968, Chemistry the Easy Way, 1989, revised, 1995, Barron's SAT II, Chemistry, 1994, rev. edit., 1998; contbg. author: (ency.) Barron's Student Concise Ency., 1988, rev. 1994, Barron's New Student's Concise Ency., 1993. Recipient Outstanding Tchr. award Spectroscopy Soc., 1973; grantee NSF, 1961, 62-63, 63, 67, 69-70, 73; sci. fellow GE, 1959. Mem. ASCD, Nat. Assn. Secondary Sch. Prins. (cert. recognition 1991), Pa. Assn. Curriculum & Supervision (exec. bd. dirs. 1985-87, regional pres. 1987), Western Pa. Assn. Curriculum & Supervision (v.p. 1983-85, pres. 1985-87, exec. bd. dirs. 1989—), Greater Canonsbury Heritage soc., Phi Delta Kappa. Roman Catholic. Avocations: painting, writing. Home: 451 Mcclelland Rd Canonsburg PA 15317-2258

MASCHEK, WERNER, physicist, researcher; b. Mautern, Austria, July 14, 1947; s. Eduard and Gertrud (Koch) M.; m. Eva Anna-Elisabeth Ilias, July 13, 1974; children: Anette, Michael. MS in Engring., Tech. U., Graz, Austria, 1972, D Tech. in Physics, 1974. Asst. prof. physics U. Graz, 1972-74; group leader Kernforschungszentrum Karlsruhe, Germany, 1975-82; guest scientist Los Alamos (N.Mex.) Nat. Lab., 1983-85; dep. sect. head Forschungszentrum Karlsruhe, 1986—; cons. Fact-Finding Commn. German Parliament, Bonn, 1979-82, Wholecore Accident Cooles Group, Brussels, 1975-82; court expert, Düsseldorf, Germany, 1984; cons. Electricite de France, Lyon, France, 1995; cons./expert Japanese Atomic Indsl. Forum Inc., Japan, 1995-96. Author: Multiphase Processes in LMFBR Analysis, 1982; contbr. numerous articles to internat. nuc. sci. jours. and confs. Lectr. Ctr. for Advanced Technol. and Environ. Tng., Leopoldshafen, Germany, 1993—. Mem. Kerntechnische Gesellschaft.

MASCI, JOSEPH RICHARD, medical educator, physician; b. New Brunswick, N.J., Nov. 27, 1950; s. Joseph Nicholas and Delfina (Musa) M.; m. Elizabeth Bass, May 21, 1993; 1 child, Jonathan Samuel. BA, Cornell U., 1972; MD, NYU, 1976. Diplomate Am. Bd. Internal Medicine, Am. Bd. Infectious Diseases. Instr. medicine Boston U. Sch. Medicine, 1979-80; instr. medicine Mt. Sinai Sch. Medicine, N.Y.C., 1982-84, asst. prof. clin. medicine, 1984-88, asst. prof. medicine, 1988-90, assoc. prof. medicine, 1990—, chief infectious diseases, 1999—; assoc. dir. medicine, cfief infectious diseases Elmhurst (N.Y.) Hosp. Ctr., 1987—; peer reviewer NIH, 1994—. Author: Primary and Ambulatory Care of the HIV-Infected Adult, 1992, Outpatient Management of HIV-Infection, 1996. Fellow Am. Coll. Chest Physicians; mem. ACP, Am. Soc. Microbiology, Assn. Program Dirs. Internal Medicine. Office: Elmhurst Hosp Ctr 79-01 Broadway Elmhurst NY 11373-1329

MASCLE, GEORGES HENRI M., geology educator; b. Dakar, Senegal, Sept. 29, 1937; s. Henri Julien and Suyanne H.Y.A. (Denisot) M.; m. Marie-Noelle Pradelle, Dec. 30, 1986. Licence es Sciences, U. Paris, 1959, Maitre es Sciences, 1960, Docteur es Sciences, 1973; Agregation, Sc. Naturelles, France, 1962. Prof. Lycee, St. Cloud, France, 1962-64; asst. U. Paris, 1966-69, maitre-asst., 1969-81; prof. Institut Des Sciences De La Terre U. J. Fourier, Grenoble, France, 1981—; v.p. Nat. Coun. Univs. France, 1985-90, pres., 1990-94; sci. councilor BRGM, Orleans, France, 1988-90; councilor Nat. Inst. Earth Scis., Nat. Ctr. Sci. Rsch., Paris, 1990-94, councilor nat. coun., 1995—. Author: Etude Geologique Des Monts Sicani Sicile, 1973, Les Grandes Structures Geologiques, 1991; contbr. articles to profl. jours. Officer French Navy, 1964-66. Fellow Geol. Ssoc. Nepal; mem. Geol. Soc. France (sec. 1973-77, v.p. 1978, councilor 1978-82, Pierre Pruvost award 1984), Geol. Soc. Am., Geol. Soc. Italy, Deutsche Geol. Vereingung. Avocations: archaeology, botanics, sailing, trekking. Office: Inst Des Scis De La Terre, Univ J Fourier BP53, 38041 Grenoble Cedex 9, France

MASDEU, JOSE CRUZ, neurologist, medical school administrator; b. Madrid, Sept. 15, 1946; came to U.S., 1972; s. Jose and Maria Luisa Masdeu. MD, U. Madrid, 1969. Diplomate Am. Bd. Psychiatry and Neurology. Resident in neurology Chgo. Med. Sch., 1972-75; fellow in neuropathology Peter Bent Brigham Hosp., 1976-77; sect. chief neurology Hines (Ill.) VA Hosp., 1978-82; asst. prof. neurology Loyola, 1978-82; head, neurology sect. North Ctrl. Bronx (N.Y.) Hosp., 1982-87; assoc. attending staff Montefiore Med. Ctr., Bronx, 1982-87; assoc. prof. neurology Einstein, 1982-87; dir. neurology St. Vincent's Hosp./Med. Ctr., N.Y.C., 1987—; attending staff, clin. prof. neurology Bellevue Hosp./NYU Med. Ctr., N.Y.C., 1987—; prof., chmn. neurology dept. N.Y. Med. Coll./West County Med. Ctr., Valhalla, 1991—; chmn. neuroimaging rsch. group World Fedn. Neurology, 1997—. Author: (with C. Gonzalez, C.B. Grossman) Head and Spine Imaging, 1985, (with P. Brazis, J. Biller) Localization in Neurology, 3 edits., 1985-96, (with L. Sudarsky L. Wolfson) Gait Distubances of Aging, 1997; editor-in-chief: The HyperTesxt Neurological Knowledgebase, 1999; contbr. over 100 scientific papers to profl. jours. Named Outstanding New Citizen of Yr., 1977, Chgo. Citizenship Coun., named amoung best neurologists in N.Y., N.Y. Mag., 1991, 96, named among 22 best neurologists in the U.S., Am. Health mag., 1996. Mem. Am. Acad. Neurology (chmn. neuroimaging sect. 1996—, chmn. subcom. practice com. 1990—), Am. Soc. Neuroimaging (pres. 1994-96), World Fedn. Neurology (chmn. neuroimaging rsch. group 1997—). Roman Catholic. Avocations: tennis, golf. Address: Neurology CUN, Avda Pio XII, 31008 Pamplona Spain

MASEFIELD, JOHN THOROLD, government official; b. Kampala, Uganda, Oct. 1, 1939; s. Geoffrey Bussell Masefield and Mildred Joy Thorold Rogers; m. Jennifer Mary Trowell, 1962; 4 children. With Commonwealth Rels. Office, 1962, pvt. sec. to perm. undersecretary, 1963-64; 2d sec. Commonwealth Rels. Office, Kuala Lampur, 1964-65, Warsaw, 1966-67; 2d sec. FCO, 1967-69, dep. head planning staff, 1974-77, asst. undersecretary state, 1992-94; 1st sec. U.K. del. Disarmament Conf., Geneva, Switzerland, 1970-74; fellow Ctr. Internat. Affairs Harvard U., 1987-88; mem. Civil Svc. Selection Bd., 1988-89; high commr. Tanzania, 1989-92, Nigeria, 1994-97; gov. Bermuda, 1997—. Office: Govt House, 11 Langton Hill, Pembroke HM13, Bermuda

MASELLI, FABIO, research scientist; b. Florence, Toscana, Italy, Dec. 8, 1961; s. Mario and Jolanda (Matteini) M. Degree in natural sci., U. Florence, 1985, degree in biol. sci., 1987. Non-permanent rschr. CNR-IATA, Florence, 1988-93, 94-96, permanent rschr., 1996—; lectr. Faculty Agriculture, U. Florence, 1989-97, lectr. Faculty Sci., 1990-97; cons. Found. for Applied Meteorology, Florence, 1996-97. Contbr. articles to sci. publs. Mem. Italian Soc. Remote Sensing. Office: CNR-IATA, P le Cascine 18, 50144 Florence Toscana, Italy

MASENG, TORLEIV, research scientist; b. Stockholm, Dec. 24, 1946; s. Torleiv and Solveig (Borge) M.; m. Else Margrethe Oeien, Dec. 18, 1971 (div. July 1992); children: Mette, Jens Andre; m. Anna Gjerstad, Dec. 31, 1993; children: Maria, Ivar Paal. Degree in elec. engring., Tech. U. Trondheim, Norway, 1970. Scientist SINTEF, Trondheim, 1972-74; sr. scientist Shape Tech. Ctr., Den Haag, The Netherlands, 1974-82; prin. rsch. scientist SINTEF, 1982-92; tech. mgr. NetCom Global Sys. Mobile, Inc., Oslo, 1992-94; prof. Lund (Sweden) U., 1994-96; dir. rsch. Norwegian Rsch. Establishment, Oslo, 1996—. Tech. editor IEEE Comm. Mag., 1986—; contbr. over 80 articles to profl. jours.; patentee in field. Recipient award for outstanding rsch. for contbn. of design of GSM radio modem specifications. Mem. IEEE. Avocation: wind surfing. Home: Kransen 3, 1165 Oslo Norway Office: Norwegian Def Rsch Est, PO Box 25, 2007 Kjeller Norway

MASER, FREDERICK ERNEST, clergyman; b. Rochester, N.Y., Feb. 26, 1908; s. Herman A. and Clara (Krumm) M.; m. Anne S. Spangeberg, Aug. 3, 1933; m. Mary L. Jarden, Dec. 25, 1959. AB, Union Coll., Schenectady, N.Y., 1930; MA, Princeton U., 1933; MDiv, Princeton Theol. Sem., 1933; DD, Dickinson Coll., 1957; LL.D. (hon.), McKendree Coll., 1964. Ordained to ministry Methodist Ch., 1933. Pastor Alice Focht Meml. Ch., Birdsboro, Pa., 1933-38, Central Ch., Frankford, Phila., 1938-45, St. James Ch., Olney, Phila., 1945-53; dist. supt. Northwest dist. Phila. Meth. Ann. Conf., 1953-58; pastor Old St. George's Ch., Phila., 1958-67; on sabbatical leave Europe, 1967-68; acting dean students Conwell Sch. Theology, 1968-69; dir. pub. relations Eastern Pa. Conf. United Meth. Ch., 1969-72; exec. sec. World Meth. Hist. Soc., 1971-74; cons. commn. on archives and history United Meth. Ch., 1974—; Tipple lectr. Drew U., Madison, N.J., 1977; spl. lectr. N.Am. sect. World Meth. Hist. Soc., Ashbury Sem., Wilmore, Ky., 1984—; rep. from Northeast Jurisdiction to TV Radio and Film Commn. Meth. Ch., 1952-60; exec. com. Am. Hist. Socs. of Meth. Ch., 1952-68; vice chmn. N.E. Jurisdictional Hist. Socs., 1948; chmn. div. evangelism Pa. Council Chs., 1953-58; mem.-at-large TV, Radio and Film Commn. Meth. Ch., 1960-64; del. Phila. Ann. Conf. to Jurisdictional Conf. of Meth. Ch., 1952; leader ministerial del. to Gen. Conf. Meth. Ch., Mpls., 1956; del. 9th World Conf. of Methodism, Lake Junaluska, 1956, 10th Conf., Oslo, 1961, 12th Conf., Denver, 1971, 13th Conf., Dublin, 1976, 14th Conf., Hawaii, 1981; dir. pub. relations Phila. Meth. ann. conf., 1961-68; exec. sec. World Meth. Hist. Soc., 1971-74. Author: The Dramatic Story of Early American Methodism, 1965, The History of Methodism in Central Pennsylvania, 1971, The Human Side of the Mother of Methodism, 1973, Challenge of Change: The Story of a City's Central Church, 1982, Robert Strawbridge, First American Methodist Circuit Rider, 1983, The Story of John Wesley's Sisters or Seven Sisters in Search of Love, 1988, The Wesley Sisters, 1990, Unfolding the Secret of History, 1991, Theories of the Atonement and the Final Solution, 1993, Sara Teasdale, A Returning Comet, 1993, John Wesley and the Indians of Georgia, 1995, The Little Known Appearances of Jesus, 1996; co-author: Proclaiming Grace and Freedom, 1984, (with Mary L. Maser) Christina Rossetti, 1991, United Methodism in America, A Compact History, 1992; editor Discovery, 1990—; mem. editorial bd. Meth. History, 1971-75; editor in chief Jour. Joseph Pilmore, 1968; mem. editorial bd., author History American Methodism, 1964, Ency. World Methodism, 1974, Second Thoughts on John Wesley, 1977, Affectionately, your Brother, 1994, The Little Known Appearences of Jesus-A Fantasy, 1996, The Story of Captain Webb, 1996, The Street Cries of London in Wesley's Day, 1997, When is the Bible the Last Word, 1998; (with Drew Simpson) If Saddlebags Could Talk, 1999; contbr. articles to religious jours. Trustee George Ruck Trust, 1958-82; mem. adv. council Wesley Theol. Sem., Washington, 1960-72. Recipient St. George's Gold medal award for disting. svc. to Meth. Ch., 1967, Citation Temple U., 1971, (with Mary L. Maser) Phyllis Goodhart award Bryn Mawr Coll. Libr., 1988, cert. appreciation for disting. contbns. to field of Meth. history Commn. on Archives and History of United Meth. Ch., honoree for life-long commitment to Wesley studies The Charles Wesley Soc., 1992. Mem. Pa. Acad. Fine Arts, Colonial Phila. Hist. Soc. (bd. dirs. 1956-64), Union League, Wesley Soc. (life, honored for disting. contbn. in field of rsch.), Philobiblon Club, Phi Beta. Home: 200 Veterans Ln Doylestown PA 18901-6716

MASER, JACK D., psychology educator; b. Balt., Dec. 15, 1937; s. Louis R. and Naomi S. Maser; m. Irma Visser, Nov. 19, 1962; 1 child, Andrea L. BS, U. Md., 1961; MA, Temple U., 1964, PhD, 1969. From asst. to assoc. prof. Tulane U., New Orleans, 1969-75; health scientist adminstr. NIMH, Rockville, Md., 1975-99; prof. psychiatry dept. U. Calif.-San Diego, La Jolla, 1999—; cons. dept. psychiatry U. Pisa, Italy, 1995—; bd. dirs. Freedom from Fear, S.I., N.Y. Editor, author: Comorbidity of Mood and Anxiety Disorder, 1990, Handbook of Antisocial Behavior, 1997; also articles. With U.S. Army, 1961-63. Recipient Disting. Friend to Behavior Therapy award Assn. for Advamcement Behavior Therapy, 1995. Fellow Am. Psychopath. Assn.; mem. Assn. for Rsch. in Personality Disorders (bd. dirs.), Soc. for Rsch. in Psychopathology. Fax: 858-6426442. E-mail: jmaser@VApop.UCSD.edu. Home: 2841 Vista Mariana Carlsbad CA 92009-7112 Office: VA Med Ctr Psychiatry Svc 116A 3350 La Jolla Village Dr San Diego CA 92161-0002

MASER, SIEGFRIED, design educator, researcher; b. Stuttgart, Germany, Nov. 30, 1938; s. Heinrich and Gertrud (Walker) M.; m. Helga Federman, Aug. 6, 1965; children: Claudia, Vera. PhD, U. Stuttgart, 1965, Habilitation, 1968; hon. doctorate, U. Kosice, Slovakia, 1991. Asst. U. Stuttgart, 1965-69; prof. U. Ulm, Germany, 1969-71; prof. Acad. Arts, Braunschweig, Germany, 1971-78, rector, 1976-78; rector U. Wuppertal, Germany, 1987-91, prof. design, 1978—; Bd. dirs. VDID, Deutscher Werkbund. Author: Numerische Aesthetik, 1970, Kommunikationstheorie, 1971, Planungstheorie, 1993. Bd. dirs. German-Polish Relationship, 1993. Mem. Evangelic Ch. Avocations: music, philately. Fax: 0202-439-4720. Office: U Wuppertal, Hofaue 35-39, D 42103 Wuppertal Germany

MASERA, RAINER STEFANO, Italian government official; b. Como, Italy, May 6, 1944; m. Giovanna Aveta; two children. Degree in Stats., La Sapienza U. of Rome, 1967; PhD Econs., U. Oxford, 1969. Rsch. fellow Linacre Coll., Oxford, 1971-75; economist Bank for Internat. Settlements, Basle, 1975; rsch. worker to head, internat. sector Bank of Italy, Rome, 1977-81; head rsch. dept. Bank of Italy, 1985-88; mem. faculty of stats. U. Rome, 1988—; Minister of Budget Govt. of Italy, 1995-96; now prof. internat. fin. Ind. Internat. U. Soc. Studies, Rome; mng. director (CEO) San Paolo IMI, Turin, Italy; alt. mem. EEC Monetary Com., mem. permament com. on Euro-currencies, G-10 Group of Deputies; al. mem. bd. dirs. Bank for Internat. Settlements; cen. mgr. for econ. rsch., others; gen. mgr. Inst. Mobiliare Italiano S.p.A. Co-editor: Europe's Money: Problems of European Monetary Coordination and Integration, 1984. Decorated Grand Officer of the Order of merit of the Italian Rep.; recipient 75th Ann. prize for article on fiscal recovery in Italy, 1987. Mem. Italian Soc. of Economists. Avocations: tennis, skiing. Office: San Paolo IMI, Piazza San Carlo 156, 10121 Turin Italy

MASH, ROBERT FRANK, biology educator; b. Weymouth, Eng., Feb. 24, 1939; s. Arthur Douglas and Doris (Davies) M.; m. Kathleen Mary Lyons, July 22, 1972; 1 child, Fabian. BA, Balliol Coll., Oxford, Eng., 1961, BSc, 1965, MA, 1968. Sr. programmer Ednl. Sys. Ltd., Harrow, Eng., 1965-68; rsch. officer Brit. Med. Assn., London, 1968-69; head biology Clayesmore Sch., Blandford Forum, Eng., 1969-99; tutor biology, psychology, zoology Oxford U., 1963-65; sci. corr. Radio France Internat., Paris, 1994-97. Author: How to Keep Dinosaurs, 1982, Clostridial Diseases of Sheep, 1967. Recipient Outstanding Tchr. award, Chgo., 1992. Avocations: music, wine. Home: Old Thatch Havelins, Stourpaine Blandford Forum DT11 8TH, England

MASHARIQA, MUHAMMAD ZUHAYR, Syrian government official. V.p. Govt. of Syrian Arab Republic, Damascus, 1984—. Office: Office of Pres, Abu Rumanch, al-Rashid St, Damascus Syria*

MASHHOUR, ZAKARIA MAGHDOUR, manufacturing company executive; b. Anzali, Gilan, Iran, Dec. 6, 1949; s. Mohamad Ali Maghdour Mashhour and Ehsan Ranandehdoost; m. Farideh Biglarbiki Ghajar, Sept. 15, 1977; 2 children. B Commerce, Tehran (Iran) Bus. Coll., 1971; MBA, Tex. A&I U., 1977. Expert Iran Civil Cervise Commn., Tehran, Iran, 1972-75; fgn. purchasing supr. Arak (Iran) Machine Bldg. Plant, 1977-82; comml. dir. Iran Siporex Co., Tehran, 1982-89, Tehran Export Devel. Co., 1993-96, Pars Appliance Mfg. Co., Tehran, 1996—; comml. dir., head ctrl. office Hamgam China Mfg. Co., Iran, 1989-93; cons. in field. Author, editor market sect. Iranian Dimensional Stone Mag., 1993-97. Avocations: books, translating from English to Persian. Home: No 85 Falamak Jonoobi, Shahrak Ghods (Gharb), 14676 Tehran Iran Office: Pars Appliance Mfg Co, Taleghani Ave 246, 15836 Tehran Iran

MASHIN, VLADIMIR ANATOLEVICH, psychophysiologist, educator; b. Ulyanovsk, Russia, Feb. 10, 1959; s. Anatole Aleksandrovich and Maria Pavlovna Mashin; m. Margarita Nikolaevna Panteleeva; children: Vadim, Anna. D in Psychology, Moscow U., Russia, 1993. Psychologist Atom Energy Tng. Ctr., Novovoronezhsk, Russia, 1985-86; head psychophysiol. lab. Atom Energy Tng. Ctr., Novovoronezhsk, 1986—. Contbr. articles to profl. jours. Sgt. USSR Army, 1977-79. Mem. N.Y. Acad. Scis. Office: Atom Energy Tng Ctr, 396072 Novovoronezh Voronezh, Russia

MASHKEVICH, STEFAN VLADIMIROVICH, physicist, researcher, computer scientist; b. Kiev, USSR, Aug. 15, 1971; s. Vladimir Stefanovich Mashkevich and Lyudmila Petrovna Godenko; m. Veronica Petrovna Kaninska, Sept. 15, 1995; 1 child, David Stefan. MS, Kiev State U., 1990; PhD in Physics and Math., Joint Inst. for Nuc. Rsch., Dubna, Russia, 1993. Jr. rschr. Inst. Theoretical Physics, Kiev, 1993-95, rschr., 1995-98; systems analyst Optimark Technologies, Jersey City, N.J., 1998-00; sr. specialist Merrill Lynch, N.Y.C., 2000—; vis. scientist Inst. de Physique Nucléaire, Orsay, France, 1995, Ctr. for Advanced Study, Oslo, 1995-96; vis. scholar U. Wash., Seattle, 1996. Contbr. articles to profl. jours. Linkage grantee NATO, 1993-94; fellow Ctr. Nat. Rsch. Sci., Paris, 1995, Norwegian Acad. Sci. and Letters, Oslo, 1995-96. Avocations: poetry, music, chess, Preference card game. Home: 1712 Madison Pl Brooklyn NY 11229-2628

MASHONGANYIKA, CHARLES, anesthesiologist, consultant; b. Charter District, Zimbabwe, Jan. 24, 1964; arrived in South Africa, 1991; s. Mavis Mashonganyika; m. Tsitsi Sabinah Zinyemba, Oct. 26, 1991; children: Godfrey Munya Radzi, Chido Lynn, Nyasha Craig. MB BChir, U. Zimbabwe, 1987. Diplomate Coll. Family Practice. Jr resident med. officer Ministry of Health, Zimbabwe, 1988, sr. resident med. officer, 1989; gen. med. officer Ministry of Def., Zimbabwe, 1990-91; med. registrar dept. medicine U. Natal, Durban, South Africa, 1992-94, locum cons. dept. medicine, 1995, anesthesiology registrar, 1996—. Mem. Adler Mus. History of Medicine, 1997—. Army capt. Zimbabwe Nat. Army, 1990-91. Fellow Coll. Physicians, Coll. Medicine, Coll. Anesthesiology; mem. Resuscitation Coun. So. Africa, Critical Care Soc. So. Africa, South African Soc. Anesthesiologists. Roman Catholic. Avocations: classical music, martial arts. Office: U Natal, PO Conlella, 4013 Durban South Africa

MASILAMANI, SUBBAIYAN, educator; b. Chidembaram, India, June 15, 1942; s. Masilamani and Valambal M.; m. Rajakumari Netarajan, May 24, 1970. BS, Govt. Coll., Kumbakonam, India, 1964; MS, U. Madras, India, 1969, PhD, 1976. Sr. lab. asst. CECRI, Karaikudi, India, 1965-66; demonstrator analytical chemistry dept. U. Madras, India, 1968-72, lectr., 1972-82, reader, 1982-88, prof., head analytical chemistry dept., 1988—. Mem. Indian Soc. Analytical Scientists (life; pres. 1999-2002), Soc. Advancement Electrochem. Sci. and Tech., Indian Sci. Contress Assn. Avocation: photography. Home: 17/3 1st St Rangarahapuram, Saidapet, 600 015 Madras India Office: U Madras, Analytical Chemistry Dept, U Madras Guindy Campus, 600 025 Madras India

MASILAMANI, SUBRAMANIAM, sericulturist, researcher; b. Chidambaram, Tamil Nadu, India, May 20, 1959; s. Rathinam Subramaniam and Subramaniam Thyanayagi; m. Masilamani Kalaivani, Sept. 14, 1988; children: Muthamizh Selvi, Mangai Meenakshi. BSc, Madras U., Tamil Nadu, 1981; MSc, Annamalai U., Tamil Nadu, 1984; BLS and Info. Sci., Annamalai U., 1985. Cert. scientist in sericulture R&D. Asst. libr. Cen. Silk Bd., Mysore, India, 1986-89; sr. rsch. officer Regional Sericultural Rsch. Sta., Coonoor, India, 1989—; documentator Cen. Sericultural Rsch. and Tng. Inst., Mysore, 1986-89; mulberry breeder Regional Sericultural Rsch. Sta., Coonoor, 1993-2000. Editor: (periodical) Seridoc, 1988-91; contbr. articles to sci. jours. including Indian Jour. Agrl. Scis., Sericologia, Jour. Breeding and Genetics. Avocations: reading biological journals, watching birds, grafting flower plants, collecting cactus and orchids, playing table tennis. Home: 7 Hospital St, 607 402 Bahour India Office: Regl Sericultural Rsch Sta, Cornwall Rd, 643 101 Coonoor India

MASINI, ELEONORA BARBIERI, futurist; b. Quirigua, Los Amates, Guatemala, Nov. 28, 1928; d. Vincenzo and Edith Frances (Fullerton) Barbieri; m. Francesco Maria Masini, Jan. 31, 1953; children: Alessandro, Andrea, Federico. LLD, U. Rome, 1952, D.Sociology, 1964. Dir. Ctr. of Forecasting Instituto Ricerche Applicate Documentazione E Studi, Rome, 1972-75; rsch. dir. UNESCO, 1972-78; rsch. dir. Centro Italiano Femminile, 1972-78; coordinator projects UN Univ., 1978, 84-90; chmn. social forecasting Pontifical Gregorian U., Rome, 1977—; sec. gen. World Future Studies Fedn., Rome, 1975-80, pres., 1980-89; Author: Space for Man, 1972, Social and Human Forecasting, 1973, Social Indicators and Forecasting, 1977, Visions of Desirable Societies, 1983, Why Futures Studies?, 1993; editor: Women, Households and Change, 1991, The Future of Asian Cultures, 1993, The Future of Cultures, 1994. Fulbright fellow, 1951, 85; Fullbright prof., 1986, U.S.A. Mem. Club of Rome, Internat. Sociol. Assn. (pres. com. on futures research 1978—), World Acad. Arts and Scis. Home and Office: Via Bertoloni 23, 00197 Rome Italy

MASIUK, STANISLAW, chemistry educator; b. Vilna, Poland, Dec. 16, 1939; s. Jan and Jadwiga (Czernichowska) M.; m. Maria Eugenia Liszewska, July 27, 1974; children: Marek, Helena. MSCE, Tech. U., Szczecin, Poland, 1963, DSc, 1969. Jr. asst. Tech. U., Szczecin, Poland, 1963-64, asst., 1964-65, asst. lectr., 1965-69, lectr., 1969-89, asst. prof., 1989-92, prof., 1992—. Author: Engineering Drawing for Chemists, 1986, Dynamics of Processes, Part I, 1989, Part II, 1990, Mechanics of Fluids, 1992; contbr. articles to profl. jours. Mem. Polish Acad. Scis., N.Y. Acad. Scis. Roman Catholic. Avocations: animal behavior, astronomy, books, films, swimming. Office: Tech U Szczecin Dept Chem Engring, Al Piastow 42, 71-065 Szczecin Poland

MAŚKA, RUDOLF, retired chemist, finance executive; b. Zabrzeg, Poland, Nov. 4, 1926; came to U.S., 1956; s. Franciszek and Anna (Puchałka) M.; m. Krystyna Maria Koziarski, June 19, 1954; children: Yvonne, Lydia. BS in Chemistry, Salford (Eng.) U., 1956; MS in Chemistry, Carnegie Mellon U., 1970. Chemist Koppers Co., Pitts., 1956-62; sr. rsch. assoc. PPG Industries, Pitts., 1962-91; registered rep. Allegheny Investment Ltd., Pitts., 1992—; vol. polymer chemist Exec. Svc. Corp., Stamford, Conn., 1992—, cons., Dokki, Egypt, 1995, Port Said, Egypt, 1999. Contbr. chpt. to book: Annual Reviews of Industrial and Engineering Chemistry, 1970; U.S. and fgn. patentee in polymer chemistry. Mem. Am. Chem. soc., Polymer Orgn. Pitts., Internat. Assn. Fin. Planning, Alcoma Golf Club. Republican. Roman Catholic. Avocations: tennis, bee keeping, travel. Home: 117 Hodil Ter Pittsburgh PA 15238-1109

MASLANSKY, CAROL JEANNE, toxicologist; b. N.Y.C., Mar. 3, 1949; d. Paul Jeremiah and Jeanne Marie (Filiatrault) Lane; m. Steven Paul Maslansky, May 28, 1973. BA, SUNY, 1971; PhD, N.Y. Med. Coll., 1983. Diplomate Am. Bd. Toxicology; cert. gen. toxicology. Asst. entomologist N.Y. State Dept. Health, White Plains, 1973-74; sr. biologist Am. Health Found., Valhalla, N.Y., 1974-76; rsch. fellow N.Y. Med. Coll., Valhalla, 1977-83, Albert Einstein Coll. Medicine, Bronx, N.Y., 1983; copr. toxicologist Texaco, Inc., Beacon, N.Y., 1984-85; prin. GeoEnviron. Cons., Inc., White Plains, N.Y., 1982-97, Maslansky GeoEnviron. Inc., Prescott, Ariz., 1997—; lectr. in entomology Westchester County Parks and Preserves, 1973-96, lectr. toxicology and hazardous materials, 1985—. Author: Air Monitoring Instrumentation, 1993, Health and Safety at Hazardous Waste Sites, 1997, (with others) Training for Hazardous Materials Team Members, 1991 (manual, video) The Poison Control Response to Chemical Emergencies, 1993. Mem. Harrison (N.Y.) Vol. Ambulance Corps., 1986-91, Westchester County (N.Y.) Hazardous Materials Response Team, 1987-96. Monsanto Fund Fellowship in Toxicology, 1988-90; grad. fellowship N.Y. Med. Coll., 1977-83. Mem. AAAS, Nat. Environ. Health Assn., N.Y. Acad. Sci., Am. Soc. Toxicology, Am. Indsl. Hygiene Assn., Environ. Mutagen Soc. Achievements include participation in development of genetic toxicity assays to identify potential carcinogens; rsch. on air monitoring instrumentation at hazardous materials sites, health and safety for hazardous waste site workers, environmental and chemical toxicology, genetic toxicology.

MASLEN, DAVID KEITH, mathematician; b. Dunedin, Otago, New Zealand, June 17, 1968; s. Keith Ian Desmond and Marjorie (Jones) M. BSc with honors, U. Otago, Dunedin, 1989; PhD, Harvard U., 1993. Rschr. Max-Planck-Inst. for Math., Bonn, Germany, 1993-95, U. Utrecht, The Netherlands, 1995-97, Centrum voor Wiskunde en Informatica, Amsterdam, The Netherlands, 1997—; vis. asst. prof. dept. math. Dartmouth Coll., 1998—; quantitative rsch. assoc. Susquehanna Investment Group, 1999—. Contbr. articles to profl. jours. Mem. Am. Math. Soc. Office: Susquehanna Investment Group 401 E City Ave Ste 200 Bala Cynwyd PA 19004-1117

MASLOG, CRISPIN C., communications educator, consultant; b. Maribojoc, Bohol, The Philippines, Dec. 5, 1931; s. Ireneo Butalid and Asuncion (Chio) M.; m. Florita Santos, Sept. 11, 1965; children: Edgar S., Juliet S. LittB in Journalism, U. Santo Tomas, Manila, 1955, PhB, 1960; MA in Journalism, U. Minn., 1962, PhD in Mass Comm., 1967. News editor Agence France Presse, Manila, 1956-60; instr. journalism S.D. State U., Brookings, 1965-66; prof., dir. Sch. Comm. Silliman U., Dumaguete, The Philippines, 1967-82, dir. info. office, 1973-82; prof. Inst. Devel. Comm. U. of The Philippines, Los Banos, 1982-98, dir. publs. office, 1984-91; sr. v.p., dean Asian Inst. Journalism and Comm., Manila, 1998—; tng. cons. Press Found. Asia, Manila, 1982-92; editl. cons. Internat. Inst. Rural Reconstruction, Silang, Cavite, The Philippines, 1983-84; comm. cons. Devel. Acad. of The Philippines, Metro Manila, 1984-91; comm. dir. Philippine Govt. Peace and Devel. Panel for Mindanao and the Cordilleras, Manila, 1987; comm. cons Internat. Rice Rsch. Inst., Los Banos, 1992-93; rsch. cons. Philippine Press Inst., Manila, 1986. Co-author: A Brief History of Asian Mass Communication, 1978; author: Five Successful Asian Community Newspapers, 1985; author, editor: Philippine Communication: An Introduction, 1988, Communication, Values and Society, 1992, Heroes of Asian Journalism, 1999, Asian Artists and Writers: Conscience of Society, 1999, others; contbr. articles to profl. jours. Pres. Leadership Initiative for Environment Found., Inc., Los Banos, 1996-97. Recipient Outstanding Filipino award Jaycees, 1995, Outstanding Boholano Around the World award; Fulbright-Smith/Mundt scholar, 1960-62. Mem. Philippine Assn. Comm. Educators (founding mem., former pres., Disting. Svc. award 1995), Nat. Rsch. Coun. of The Philippines, Asian Mass Comm. Rsch. and Info. Ctr. (founding mem.), Nat. Press Club (life). Roman Catholic. Avocations: tennis, movies, hiking, traveling, reading. E-mail: crismas@csi.com.ph. Home: 11350 Dao St, Forestry, Los Banos 4031, The Philippines Office: Inst Journalism and Comm, 11 Annapolis St, Greenhills San Juan Manila The Philippines

MASLOV, ALEXANDER K., medical researcher; b. Astrakhan, Russia, Dec. 22, 1948; s. Konstantin N. and Zinaida S. (Klimova) M.; m. Nataliya S. Zagnoyko, Mar. 24, 1973; 1 child, V.A. MD, Ctrl. Dermatol. Venereal. Inst, Moscow, 1982. Physician Leprosy Rsch. Inst., Astrakhan, 1972-74, aspirant, 1974-77, sci. rschr., 1977—. Contbr. articles to profl. jours.; inventor in field. Mem. N.Y. Acad. Scis. Home: Lenin St 23 Apt 49, 414000 Astrakhan Russia Office: Leprosy Rsch Inst, Ostrowsky Passage 3, 414057 Astrakhan Russia

MASLOV, ANDREI VICTOROVICH, geologist, researcher; b. Voronezh, Russia, May 25, 1957; s. Victor Alexeevich and Elvira Fedorovna (Gavrilenko) M.; m. Emma Evgenevna Paija, Aug. 9, 1987; 1 child, Jane. PhD, Geol. Inst., Moscow, 1986; DSc, Russian Acad. Scis. Inst. Geo., Ekaterinburg, Russia, 1997. Jr. rschr. Inst. Geology Ufa. Russian Acad. Scis., Ekaterinburg, 1979-82, rschr. Inst. Geology, 1986-88, sr. rschr., head lithology lab., vice-dir. Inst. Geology, 1989—. Author: Lithology of Upper Riphean Deposits of the Bashkirian Anticlinorium, 1988, (with M.T. Krupenin) Cross-sections of the Riphean Deposits of the Bashkirian Anticlinorium, 1991, Sedimentary Complexes in the Cross-sections of the Riftogenous Structures, 1994, Sedimentary Associations of the Riphean Stratotype Region, 1997, (with M.V. Ischerskaya) Riphean Sedimentary Associations of the Volga-Urals Region, 1998, (with E.Z. Gareev, M.T. Krupenin, I.G. Demchuk) Fine-grained Alumosiliciclastics in the Upper Precam Brian of the Bashkirian Anticlinorium, 1999; contbr. articles to profl. jours. including Tectonophysics and Lithology and Mineral Deposits. Grantee Russian Found. for Basic Rsch., 1995, 97, 2000, Internat. Assn. for the Promotion to Coop. with Scientists, 1995. Mem. Nat. Geog. Soc. Avocations: photography, walking, furniture making, shopping. Office: Russian Acad Sci/Inst Geol, 7 Pochtovy Per, 620151 Ekaterinburg Russia

MASLOV, VASYL IVANOVICH, plasma physicist, educator; b. Lisky, Russia, Jan. 13, 1955; s. Maslov Ivan Trofimovich and Polina Illinichna (Tereshchenko) M.; m. Natalia Michajlovna Maslova, Nov. 6, 1993. Master's degree, Kharkov (Ukraine) State U., 1979; PhD, Kharkov Inst. Physics & Tech., 1989, DSc, 1999. Cert. in theoretical physics. Rsch. asst. Kharkov Inst. Physics & Tech., 1979-81, rsch. assoc., 1981-86, rsch. scientist, 1986-89, sr. rsch. scientist Nat. Sci. Ctr., 1989—; assoc. prof. Kharkov State U., 1994—; mem. theoretical sci. coun. Kharkov Inst. Physics & Tech., 1987-97. Contbr. numerous sci. papers and reports to profl. jours. Travel grantee Innsbruck (Austria) U., 1992, Soros Fund, 1995, Toki (Japan) NIFS, 1998, collaborative grantee (3) Bayreuth (Germany) U. and Sci. Fund of NATO, 1992, 94, 95, project grantee Sci. and Tech. Ctr. in Ukraine, 1996. Mem. Am. Phys. Soc., Ukrainian Phys. Soc., Am. Phys. Soc. Avocations: scientific public activity, sports, theater. Fax: (0572) 351688. E-mail: vmaslov@kipt.kharkov.ua. Office: Nat Sci Ctr Kharkov Inst, 1 Academicheskaya str, Kharkov 310166, Ukraine

MASLOWSKI, ANDREW HENRY, interventional cardiologist; b. Edinburgh, Scotland, Sept. 11, 1949; arrived in New Zealand, 1976; s. Henry Alexander and Jean (Rutherford) M.; m. Rona Macbeth Thomson, 1974 (div.); children: Gareth, Grant; m. Christine Sandra Hutton, Feb. 8, 1986; children: Katherine, Alina. MB, BChir, Bristol (Eng.) U., 1973. Cardiology registrar Christchurch, New Zealand, 1978-82, Green Lane Hosp., New Zealand, 1982-84; cons. cardiologist Middlemore Hosp., Auckland, New Zealand, 1984-93; founding ptnr. Auckland Cardiology, 1992—; interventional cardiologist, med. dir. Ascot Angiography Ascot Integrated Hosp., 1999—. Contbr. articles to profl. jours. including New Eng. Jour. Medicine, The Lancet, others. Fellow Royal Australasian Coll. Physicians; mem. Cardiac Soc. Australia and New Zealand, New Zealand Interventional Cardiology Group. Avocations: sailing, flying, windsurfing, diving, chess. Office: Auckland Cardiology at Ascot Ascot Integrated Hosp, 90 Greenlane Rd E, Remuera Auckland, New Zealand

MASŁOWSKI, ANDRZEJ STANISŁAW, engineering educator; b. Warsaw, Poland, Sept. 7, 1942; s. Józef and Maria (Boncler) M.; m. Alicja Szatańska, Feb. 15, 1969; children: Damian, Małgorzata. MSc, Warsaw U. Tech., 1966, PhD, 1972, DSc, 1979. Rsch. scientist Inst. Nuclear Rsch., Warsaw, 1966-70; tchr. Warsaw U. Tech., 1970-76; head, chair Automation and Sys. Divsn., head Inst. Robotics Bialystok (Poland) U. Tech., 1976-95; prof. Mil. U. Tech., Warsaw, 1995—; cons. Rsch. Inst. Automotive Industry, Warsaw, 1983-93; dep. dir. Inst. Arms Tech., Kielce, Poland, 1984-87; dir. Intelligent Autonomous Mobile Sys. Divsn. Rsch. Inst. Automation and Measurements, Warsaw, 1993—. Grantee, IREX, 1980-81. Mem. IMEKO. Home: Sobieskiego 6-71, 02-957 Warsaw Poland Office: Mil Univ Tech, Kaliskiego 2, 01-489 Warsaw Poland

MASON, ANN DARLENE, real estate broker; b. Louisville, Mar. 2, 1934; d. James Robert and Lilly Mae (Hedgepeth) Noe; m. Dallas House, Dec. 23, 1953 (div. 1978); children: Dallas, James, Henry, Jon; m. Sidney E. Mason, Aug. 10, 1984; stepchildren: Bruce, Linda. Student, Fla. So. Coll., 1952-53, U. Ga., 1953-55, Ringling Sch. Art, Sarasota, Fla., summer 1952, Herr Krupp Art Sch., Ramstein, Germany, 1958-60, Manatee Jr. C.C., Sarasota, 1969. Lic. real estate broker. Real estate broker Harry Robbins Real Estate Office, Sarasota, 1994—; chmn. Health Effects of Lawncare Pesticides, Sarasota, 1986—; real estate broker Arvida Corp., Merril L., Boomhower. Contbr. articles to profl. jours. V.p. Facts About Alternatives to Chem. Trespassing, 2000—; vice chair Fla. Against Chem. Trespass, Sarasota, 1997, Sarasota Rally Against Malathion, Sarasota, 1997; mem. Coalition to Stop Children's Exposure to Pesticies, 1996-97, Sarasota County Environ. Pest Mgmt. Adv. Bd., Sarasota County Mosquito Control Adv. Bd.; chair Health Effects Pesticides, 1986-97; pub. affairs com. Jr. League Sarasota, Inc., 1969-97. Named Sustainer of Yr., Jr. League Sarasota, Inc., 1988-89. Mem. PEO. Republican. Baptist. Avocations: swimming, sailing, sewing, public speaking, radio and television talk shows. Fax: 941-954-0004. Home: 2290 Clematis St Sarasota FL 34239-3907 Office: Harry Robbins Real Estate Sarasota FL 34239

MASON, SIR ANTHONY FRANK, judge; b. Australia, Apr. 21, 1925; m. Patricia Mary McQueen, 1950; 2 children. LLD (hon.), Australian Nat. U., 1980, U. Sydney, 1988, U. Melbourne, 1992; DCL (hon.), Oxford (Eng.) U., 1993; LLD (hon.), Monash U., 1995, Griffith U., 1995, Deakin U., 1995. Bar: NSW, 1951, Queen's Coun., 1964. Commonwealth solicitor-gen. Govt. of Australia, 1964-69; judge Ct. of Appeal of Supreme Ct., NSW, 1969-72, justice of high ct., 1972-87, chief justice, 1987-95; mem. panel of arbitrators and advisers Intelsat, 1965-69; vice chair UN Commn. Internat. Trade Law, 1968; pro-chancellor Australian Nat. U., 1972-75; chancellor U. New South Wales, 1994-99; Australian lectr. Menzies lectr. series U. Va., 1985; mem. Permanent Ct. of Arbitration, 1987-99; Leon Ladner lectr. U. B.C. and U. Victoria, 1989; law lectr. Singapore Acad., 1995; Arthur Goodhart prof. legal sci., 1996-97; vis. fellow Gonville & Caius Coll., 1996-97; justice Supreme Ct. of Fiji, 1995-2000; pres. Solomon Islands Ct. of Appeal, 1997-99; justice Hong Kong Ct. of Final Appeal, 1997—; chmn. adv. bd. Nat. Inst. for Law, Ethics and Pub. Affairs, Griffith U., 1995-99; presiding arbitrator Internat. Ctr. for Settlement of Investment Disputes, Dispute under N.Am. Free Trade Agreement, Washington, 1999—. Chmn. Nat. Libr. Australia, 1995-98. Served Royal Australian Air Force, 1944-45. Nat. fellow Rsch. Sch. Social Scis. Australian Nat. U., 1995-99; named Comdr. of Order Brit. Empire, 1969, Knight Comdr. of Order of Brit. Empire, 1972, Companion Order of Australia, 1988. Fellow Acad. of Social Scis.; mem. Am. Law Inst. Office: Level 3, 1 Castlereagh St, Sydney NSW 2000, Australia

MASON, BARBARA ELLEN, business owner; b. Battle Creek, Mich.; d. Orville Earle and Margaret Ellen Mason; m. Myron Donald Katz, Aug. 20, 1973 (div. Sept. 1984); children: Ryan Donald, Aaron Joseph. AA, Kellogg C.c., Battle Creek, 1997; BA, Western Mich. U., 1999, postgrad., 1999—. Cert. lab. asst. Auditor office Jacobsons, Battle Creek, 1973-74; lab. asst. Leila Hosp., Battle Creek, 1974-80; mgr. lab. Oaklawn Hosp., Marshall, Mich., 1981-97; owner Mason-Raque, Inc., Marshall, 1999—; rsch. cons. Western Mich. U. Sch. Pub. Affairs, Kalamazoo, 1999. Campaign mgr. Rep. Party, Lansing, Mich., 2000. Mem. Phi Theta Kappa. Avocations: downhill skiing, gardening, biking, camping. E-mail: bba14@aol.com. Office: Mason-Racqui Inc 749 E Green St Marshall MI 49068-2018

MASON, CRAIG WATSON, corporate planning executive; b. Stamford, Conn., June 4, 1954; s. Harry Leeds and Alice Henrietta (Watson) M.; m. Lisa Ellen Boe, Aug. 30, 1980; children: Katherine Anne, Whitney Elizabeth, Lindsey Allison. BA in English, Yale U., 1976. Brand asst. Procter & Gamble Co., Cin., 1976-77; sales trainee Procter & Gamble Co., St. Louis, 1977; asst. brand mgr. Procter & Gamble Co., Cin., 1978-79, Instant Folger's brand mgr., 1979-82, Biz and Mr. Clean brand mgr., 1982-83; dir. brand mgmt. Beecham Products USA, Pitts., 1983-87, dir. bus. planning, 1987-88, dir. bus. and logistics planning, 1988-89; dir. bus. and logistics planning SmithKline Beecham Consumer Brands, 1989-93; dir. N.Am. planning Smith Kline Beecham Consumer Healthcare, 1994—. Editor: The Insiders Guide to the Colleges, 1975; contbr. articles to profl. jours. Class agt. Yale Alumni Fund, 1976—; trustee Peters Twp. (Pa.) Pub. Libr., 1986-90; vestryman St. David's Ch., 1997-2000. Mem. Rolling Hills Country Club, Yale Club of N.Y.C. Republican. Episcopalian. Avocations: photography, travel. Home: 128 Lampliter Ln Mc Murray PA 15317-3614 Office: SmithKline Beecham 100 Beecham Dr Pittsburgh PA 15205-9715

MASON, DAVID CHARLES, lawyer; b. Nashville, Mar. 12, 1956; s. Sanaoni (Reed) M. BS, Austin Peay State U., 1980; JD, Washington U., 1983. Bar: Mo. 1983, U.S. Ct. Appeals (8th cir.) 1983. Asst. atty. gen. Mo. Attys. Gen. Office, Jefferson City, 1983-85; gen. counsel Mo. Dept. Corrections, Jefferson City, 1985-88; assoc. Peper, Martin, Jensen, Maichel & Hetlage, St. Louis, 1988-90, Husch & Eppenberger, St. Louis, 1990—; vice chmn. St. Louis Regional Conv. and Sports Complex Authority, 1990—. Mem. ABA, Mo. Bar Assn., Nat. Assn. Blacks in Criminal Justice (br. pres. 1985-88), Mo. Corrections Assn. (legis. com. 1986-89), Phi Delta Phi. Republican. Roman Catholic. Avocations: reading, bowling, music. Home: 605 Clara Ave Apt 506 Saint Louis MO 63112-1935 Office: Husch & Eppenberger 100 N Broadway Fl 13 Saint Louis MO 63102-2728

MASON, DEAN TOWLE, cardiologist; b. Berkeley, Calif., Sept. 20, 1932; s. Ira Jenckes and Florence Mabel (Towle) M.; m. Maureen O'Brien, June 22, 1957; children: Kathleen, Alison. BA in Chemistry, Duke U., 1954, MD, 1958. Diplomate Am. Bd. Internal Medicine, Am. Bd. Cardiovasc. Diseases, Nat. Bd. Med. Examiners. Intern, then resident in medicine Johns Hopkins Hosp., 1958-61; clin. assoc. cardiology br., sr. asst. surgeon USPHS, Nat. Heart Inst., NIH, 1961-63, asst. sect. dir. cardiovascular diagnosis, attending physician, sr. investigator cardiology br., 1963-68; prof. medicine, prof. physiology, chief cardiovascular medicine U. Calif. Med. Sch., Davis-Sacramento Med. Center, 1968-82; dir. cardiac ctr. Cedars Med. Ctr., Miami, Fla., 1982-83; physician-in chief Western Heart Inst., San Francisco, 1983—; chmn. dept. cardiovascular medicine St. Mary's Med. Ctr., San Francisco, 1986-99, hon. med. staff, 2000—; co-chmn. cardiovascular-renal drugs U.S. Pharmacopeia Com. Revision, 1970-75; mem. life scis. com. NASA; med. rsch. rev. bd. VA, NIH; vis. prof. numerous univs., cons. in field; mem. Am. Cardiovascular Splty. Cert. Bd., 1970-78. Editor-in-chief Am. Heart Jour., 1980-96; author 25 books on cardiovasc. medicine; contbr. numerous articles to med. jours. Recipient rsch. award Am. Therapeutic Soc., 1965; Theodore and Susan B. Cummings Humanitarian award Dept. State-Am. Coll. Cardiology, 1972, 73, 75, 78; Skylab Achievement award NASA, 1974; U. Calif. Faculty Rsch. award, 1978, Award of Honor Wisdom Soc., 1997, Medal of Honor Winston Churchill Soc., 1998, Armand Hammer Creative Genius award, 1998, Dwight D. Eisenhower Admirable Am. of Achievement award, 1998, Eternal Jesus Christ award, 1998, Blessed Lord's Prayer award, 1998, Dean Towle Mason Eminent Physician of Wisdom award, 1999; named Outstanding Prof. U. Calif. Med. Sch., Davis, 1972. Master Am. Coll. Cardiology (pres. 1977-78); fellow A.C.P., Am. Heart Assn., Am. Coll. Chest Physicians, Royal Soc. Medicine; mem. Am. Soc. Clin. Investigation, Am. Physiol. Soc., Am. Soc. Pharmacology and Exptl. Therapeutics (Exptl. Therapeutics award 1973), Am. Fedn. Clin. Research, N.Y. Acad. Scis., Am. Assn. U. Cardiologists, Am. Soc. Clin. Pharmacology and Therapeutics, We. Assn. Physicians, AAUP, We. Soc. Clin. Research (past pres.), Phi Beta Kappa, Alpha Omega Alpha. Republican. Methodist. Club: El Marcero Country. Home: 44725 Country Club Dr El Macero CA 95618-1047 Office: Western Heart Inst St Marys Med Ctr 450 Stanyan St San Francisco CA 94117-1079

MASON, GREGG CLAUDE, orthopedic surgeon, researcher; b. Schenectady, N.Y., July 28, 1958; s. George and Maureen (Murphy) M.; m. Dina Marie Sokolowski, June 16, 1990. BS in Chemistry magna cum laude, Allegheny Coll., 1980; MD, U. Pitts., 1984. Diplomate Am. Bd. Orthop. Surgery, Nat. Bd. Med. Examiners. Gen. surgery intern U. Colo./U. Colo. Med. Ctrs., Denver, 1984-85; orthopaedic rsch. fellow U. Pitts., 1985-86, resident in orthopaedic surgery, 1986-89; orthopedic surgeon U.S. Naval Hosp., Okinawa, Japan, 1989-92; pvt. practice, Erie, 1992—; active staff St. Vincent Med. Ctr., St. Vincent Surgery Ctr., Hamot Med. Ctr., Union City Meml. Hosp.; lectr. in field. Contbr. articles to profl. jours. Comdr. M.C. USNR, 1980—. Recipient Outstanding Student Rsch. award U. Pitt. Sch. Medicine, 1984, Harold Henderson Sankey Orthop. award, 1984; rsch. grantee Competitive Med. Rsch. Fund., Presbyn.-Univ. Hosp. of Pitts., 1986-87, U. Pitts. Rsch. Devel. Fund, 1986-87. Disting. Alden scholar 1977, 78, 79, 80, Sandra Doane Turk scholar, 1979, Armed Svcs. Health Professions scholar, 1981-84. Fellow ACS, Internat. Coll. Surgeons, Mil. Soc. Orthop. Surgeons, Am. Acad. Orthop. Surgeons (tchg. seal 1993); mem. AMA, Pa. Orthop. Soc. (Best Rsch. Paper 1987, 88), Erie Orthop. Soc., U. Pitts. Med. Ctr. Orthop. Alumni., Am. Orthop. Soc. of Sports Medicine (Cabaud award 1988), Ea. Orthop. Assn. (Founders award 1988), Phi Beta Kappa. Office: Orthopaedic Surgeons Inc 204 W 26th St Erie PA 16508-1898

MASON, JOAN, research scientist; b. London, June 3, 1923; d. Mark and Annie (Harris) Banus; m. Stephen Finney Mason, Oct. 1, 1955; children: Oliver Neil, Andrew Lawrence, Lionel Jeremy. BA, Cambridge (Eng.) U., 1944, MA, 1947, PhD, 1950, DSc, 1982. Lectr., rsch. assoc. U. So. Calif., L.A., 1950-51; from asst. lectr. to rsch. assoc. U. Coll. London, 1951-56; rsch. fellow Ohio State U., Columbus, 1953; Sci. Rsch. Coun. fellow U. E. Anglia, Norwich, Eng., 1964-70; lectr. Open U., Milton Keynes, Eng., 1970-78, sr. lectr., 1978-82, reader, 1983-88; affiliated rsch. scholar dept. history philosophy sci. U. Cambridge, 1988—. Author, editor: Multinuclear NMR, 1987; co-author: Cambridge Women: Twelve Portraits; contbr. articles to profl. jours. Fellow Royal Soc. Chemistry; mem. Assn. Women Sci. & Engring. (founding chair). Fax: 44 1223 740775. E-mail: jm148@cam.ac.uk. Home and Office: 12 Hills Ave, Cambridge CB1 7XA, England

MASON, SIR (BASIL) JOHN, meteorologist; b. Docking, Norfolk, Aug. 18, 1923; s. John Robert and Olive Mason; m. Doreen Sheila Jones, 1948; 2 children. Ed., U. Coll., Nottingham; DSc (hon.), U. Nottingham, 1966, U. Durham, 1970, U. Strathclyde, 1975, City U., 1980, Sussex U., 1983, U. E. Anglia, 1988, Plymouth U., 1990, Heriot-Watt U., 1991, Manchester Inst. Sci. & Tech., 1994, Reading U., 1998. Shirley rsch. fellow U. Nottingham, 1947; asst. lectr. meteorology Imperial Coll., London, 1948-49, lectr., 1949; Warren rsch. fellow Royal Soc., 1957; vis. prof. meteorology U. Calif., 1959-60; prof. cloud physics Imperial Coll. Sci. and Tech., U. London, 1961-65; dir.-gen. meteorol. office, 1965-83; pres. Royal Meteorol. Soc., 1968-70; mem. exec. com. World Meteorol. Orgn., 1965-75, 77-83; chmn. coun. U. Surrey, 1971-75, pro-chancellor, 1979-85; chancellor U. Manchester Inst. Sci. and Tech., 1986-96; pres. Inst. of Physics, 1976-78; treas., sr. v.p. Royal Soc., 1976-86; dir. Fulmer Rsch. Inst., 1976-78; pres. B.A.A.S., 1982-83; dir. Royal Soc. Project on Acidification of Surface Waters, 1983-90; mem. adv. bd. Rsch. Couns., 1983-86; chmn. ICSU/WMO Sci. Com. for World Climate Rsch. Program; chmn. coordinating com. Marine Scis. and Tech., 1987-90; pres. Soc. Environ. Engrs., 1999—. Author: The Physics of Clouds, 1957, 72, Clouds, Rain and Rain-making, 1962, Acid Rain, 1992. Recipient Hugh Robert Mill medal Royal Meteorol. Soc., 1959, Charles Chree medal and prize Phys. Soc., 1965, Rumford medal Royal Soc., 1972, Glazebrook medal and prize Inst. Physics, 1974, Symons Meml. Gold medal Royal Meteorol. Soc., 1975, Royal medal Royal Soc., 1991; named Bakerian lectr. Royal Soc., 1971, Halley lectr. Oxford U., 1977; hon. fellow Imperial Coll. Sci. and Tech., 1974, UMIST, 1979. Mem. Academia Europaea, Norwegian Acad. Sci. and Letters (hon.), London Math. Soc. (Naylor prize and lectureship). Home: 64 Christchurch Rd, East Sheen London SW14 7AW, England

MASON, JOHN OLIVER, freelance journalist; b. Kingston, Pa., Aug. 1, 1957; s. Oliver B. and Dorothy Mae (Hunter) M. BA, Temple U., 1984. Editorial writer Temple News, Phila., 1983-85; writer Phila. Tribune, 1989-95, Irish Edition, Phila., 1990-95, Northeast Breeze, Rockledge, Pa., 1993—, Germantown Courier, Phila., 1996—, Phila. Sunday Sun, 1996—. Sec. Concerned Citizens of Delaware Valley, 1990; treas. A. Philip Randolph Inst., Phila., 1996; mem. Jewish Labor Com., Phila., 1985. Mem. Nat. Writers Union, Meridian Writers Collective, B'nai Brith. Avocations: philately, reading, cultural activities.

MASON, JUDITH ANN, freelance writer; b. Newark, Dec. 27, 1945; d. Richard Algie and Mary Ann (Beneck) M. Diploma in legal sci., Spencerian Bus. Coll., 1965; BA, Northeastern Ill. U., 1984. Legal sec. Harney B. Stover, Atty., Milw., 1967-69, Robert P. O'Meara, Atty., Waukegan, Ill., 1969-70; sec. to pres. First Midwest Bank, Waukegan, 1970-72, asst. cashier, 1972-76; legal sec. Eugene M. Snarski, Atty., Waukegan, 1976-81; adminstrv. aide Lake County Forest Preserve Dist., Libertyville, Ill., 1981-89; freelance writer Tucson, 1989—; legal sec., asst. Jeffrey H. Greenberg, Atty.; office mgr. Greenberg & Assocs., Tucson, 1989-96; legal asst. Leonard, Felker, Altfeld, Greenberg & Battaile, 1997—; exec. adminstr. JHG Devel. Co. LLC, 1995—, 1998—; travel rep. Antioch (Ill.) Travel Agy., 1980-89, Advance Travel Agy., Zion, Ill., 1980-89; pub. speaker for various orgns., Lake County, Ill., 1984-89. Author: Why I Remember Yesterday, 1979, Haggadah (play), 1982; editor poetry column: Bank Man Magazine, 1972-75; contbg. article writer Compendum Mag. Tchr. Confraternity Christian Doctrine St. Patrick's Ch., Wadsworth, Ill., 1980-85; lector, eucharistic min. Prince of Peace Ch., Lake Villa, Ill., 1980-89; hospice vol. St. Therese Hosp., Waukegan, 1984; speech writer Grace Mary Stern lt. gubernatorial campaign, Lake County, 1984; voter registrar County of Lake Ill., 1986-89; cons. pub. rels. Lake County Cir. Ct. Judge campaign, 1988, Presdl. Campaign Paul Simon; co-chmn., organizer Women's Exhibit, Evergreen Air Show, 1993. Recipient Brian F. Shehanhan Creative Writing award Am. Inst. Banking, 1972, 1st Place pub. speaking, 1974. Mem. AAUW (pub. rels. chair 1986, pres. Chain O'Lakes br. 1988-89, Ill. Pub. Info. award 1987, pub. rels. chair Tucson br. 1991-92), NAFE, Northeastern Ill. U. Alumni Assn., Soc. Southwestern Authors, Pi Rho Zeta (pres. 1964-65). Democrat. Roman Catholic. Home: 6231 N Montebella Rd Apt 335 Tucson AZ 85704-2889 Office: PO Box 191 Tucson AZ 85702-0191

MASON, MALCOLM DAVID, oncologist, researcher; b. London, May 31, 1956; s. Seymour and Marion (Grant) M.; m. Lee-Anne Isaacs, Mar. 27, 1983; children: Danielle Cynthia, Jenna Frances. MB, BS, U. London, 1979, MD, 1991. Registrar Royal Marsden Hosp., London, 1984-87; Bob Champion clin. rsch. fellow Inst. Cancer Rsch., Sutton, Eng., 1988-89; lectr. clin. oncology Royal Marsden Hosp., Sutton, 1989-91; cons. clin. oncologist Velindre Hosp., Cardiff, Wales, 1992-96; Cancer Rsch. Wales prof. clin. oncology U. Wales, Cardiff, 1997—; dir. rsch. Velindre Nat. Health Svc. Trust, Cardiff, 1996—; clin. trial coord. Med. Rsch. Coun., U.K., 1994—; chmn. U.K. "Coin" Prostate Cancer Working Group, 1996-99. Contbr. articles to profl. cancer jours., chpt. to Oxford Textbook of Oncology, 1994; asst. editor (jour.) Clinical Oncology, 1994—. Fellow Royal Coll. Radiologists, Royal Coll. Physicians, Royal Soc. Medicine (sec. oncology sect. 1997—, pres.-elect 1998—), Brit. Assn. Cancer Rsch., Brit. Oncol. Assn. (scientific com. 1995-96). Avocations: music, art. Office: Velindre NHS Trust, Velindre Rd Whitchurch, Cardiff CF14 2TL, Wales

MASON, MARILYN GELL, library administrator, writer, consultant; b. Chickasha, Okla., Aug. 23, 1944; d. Emmett D. and Dorothy (O'Bar) Killebrew; m. Carl L. Gell, Dec. 29 1965 (div. Oct. 1978); 1 son, Charles E.; m. Robert M. Mason, July 17, 1981. B.A., U. Dallas, 1966; M.L.S., N. Tex. State U., Denton, 1968; M.P.A., Harvard U., 1978. Libr. N.J. State Libr., Trenton, 1968-69; head dept. Arlington County Pub. Libr., Va., 1969-73; chief libr. program Metro Washington Coun. Govts., 1973-77; dir. White House Conf. on Librs. and Info. Svcs., Washington, 1979-80; exec. v.p. Metrics Rsch. Corp., Atlanta, 1981-82; dir. Atlanta-Fulton Pub. Libr., Atlanta, 1982-86, Cleve. Pub. Libr., 1986-99; writer, cons., 1999—; trustee Online Computer Library Ctr., 1984-97; Evalene Parsons Jackson lectr. div. librarianship Emory U., 1981. Author: The Federal Role in Library and Information Services, 1983, Strategic Management for Today's Libraries, 1999; editor: Survey of Library Automation in the Washington Area, 1977; project dir.: book Information for the 1980's, 1980. Bd. visitors Sch. Info. Studies, Syracuse U., 1981-85, Sch. of Libr. and Info. Sci. , U. Tenn.-Knoxville, 1983-85; trustee Coun. on Libr. Resources, Washington, 1992—. Recipient Disting. Alumna award N. Tex. State U., 1979, Herbert and Virginia White award, ALA, 1999; inducted into Ohio Libr. Coun. Hall of Fame, 1999. Mem. ALA (mem. council 1986—), Am. Assn. Info. Sci., Ohio Library Assn., D.C. Library Assn. (pres. 1976-77). Home and Office: 811 Live Oak Plantation Rd Tallahassee FL 32312-2412

MASON, PAUL ALEXANDER, astronomer; b. Lafayette, La., July 13, 1962; s. David E. and Betty (Oxford) M.; m. Denise R. Baker, May 15, 1983 (div. 1987). BS in Physics and Math., U. Ariz., 1987, BS in Astronomy, 1987; MS in Physics, La. State U., 1992; PhD in Astronomy, Case Western Res. U., 1996. Rsch. asst. U. Ariz., Tucson, 1986-88; teaching asst. La. State U., Baton Rouge, 1988-91, rsch. asst., 1991-92; postdoctoral fellow in astrophysics N.Mex. State U., Las Cruces, 1996—; dir. Picture Rocks Obs., Tilden, Tex. Contbr. articles to profl. jours. Grantee La. Space Consortium, 1992, NASA, 1996; Towson Meml. scholar, 1994-95. Mem. Am. Astron. Soc., Astron. Soc. Pacific. Achievements include discovery of many properties of the complex magnetic cataclysmic variable star BY Cam; research in magnetic cataclysmic variables, low-mass X-ray binaries, and gamma ray bursts. Home: 2208 Magnolia Dr Las Cruces NM 88001-4420 Office: NMSU Astronomy PO Box 30001 Las Cruces NM 88003-8001

MASON, PETER, visual historian, analyst; b. England, Aug. 21, 1952; arrived in The Netherlands, 1977; children: Nada, Hannah, Oliver. MA in Humanities, U. Oxford, 1978; PhD in Anthropology, U. Utrecht, 1990. Interpreter Br. Coun. Aid to Refugees, 1975-77; editl. officer CEDLA, Amsterdam, 1980-86; vis. lectr. Ctr. Archaeology, Leiden, The Netherlands, 1990-91; cons. Fundacion America, Santiago, Chile, 1997—; freelance translator and editor, 1997-80, 86-90, 91-97; internat. editl. adviser Jour. History Collections, 1999—. Author: The City of Men, 1984, Deconstructing America, 1990, Infelicities, 1998; co-author: The Mammoth and the Mouse, 1997. Avocations: opera, swimming. Office: Lauriergracht 116, 1016RR Amsterdam The Netherlands

MASON, RAYMOND E., JR., distributing company executive; b. Columbus, Ohio, Mar. 20, 1920; s. Raymond E. and Lula Estella (Potter) M.; m. Margaret E. Edwards, Feb. 6, 1942; children: Raymond E. III, Michael D., Bruce R. BS, Ohio State U., 1941; grad., U.S. Command and Gen. Staff, 1962, U.S. Army War Coll., 1965. Ops. mgr. Suburban Motor Freight, Columbus, 1946-47; pres., gen. mgr. CFL Lines, Columbus, 1947-48; pres., chmn. Columbus Truck & Equipment Co., 1949—; pres., chmn. Bode-Finn Co., Cin., 1966-99, REM Realty, Columbus, 1962—; chmn. Ford Bros. Inc., Ironton, Ohio, 1975-79; mem. distbr. adv. coun. Mack Trucks; mng. dir. J.D. Ranch, Myakka City, Fla. Active Boy Scouts Am.; chmn. bd. trustees emeritus Franklin U.; former trustee Freedoms Found. of Valley Forge, Ohio Hist. Found.; emeritus trustee New Coll. Found.; dir. Mote Marine Lab., Ohio State U. Found. With U.S. Army, 1941-45, maj. gen. Res., ret. Decorated Bronze Star medal with V for Valor, Legion of Merit, Silver Star; recipient Pres. Unit citation; Truck Dealer of Yr. award Time mag., 1972, Good Scout award Cen. Ohio Coun. Boy Scouts Am., Baden-Powell fellow World Scout Found., Silver Beaver award, Silver Antelope award, Boy Scouts Am., Centennial medal Ohio State U., Pacesetters award Coll. Bus. ISU, 1996, Virginia Steckler Internat. Svc. award ARC, 1998, Lifetime Achievement award Ohio State U., 1999, Disting. Citizen of Yr. award Boy Scouts Am., 1999, others; named State of Ohio Vet. Hall of Fame, 1997, Buckeye Boys State Hall of Fame, 1999, Ohio State U. ROTC Hall of Fame. Mem. Am. Truck Dealers, Ohio Truck Assn., U.S. Army Artillery Assn., Armor Assn., Army War Coll. Alumni Assn., Ohio State U. Alumni Assn., Columbus Club, Queen City Club, Masons, Rotary (past dist. gov., Man of Yr., Paul Harris fellow). Office: Columbus Truck Equipment Co PO Box 83250 Columbus OH 43203-0250 Home: 85 Sugar Mill Dr Osprey FL 34229-9067

MASON, ROBERT JEFFREY, geography educator; b. Schenectady, N.Y., Oct. 27, 1955; s. Frank Lloyd Mason and Concetta Helen Barbini. BA, State Univ. N.Y., 1977; MA, Univ. Toronto, 1979; PhD, Rutgers Univ., 1986. Adj. assoc. prof. Columbia Univ., New York, 1985; lectr. Ohio State Univ., 1986; assoc., asst. prof. Temple Univ., Phila., and Japan, 1986—; dir. environmental studies prog. Temple Univ., 1998—; mem., bd. editors, Ctr. for Urban Policy Rsch., Rutgers Univ., 1989-93; tech. asst. Nat. Environ. Info. Conf., U.S. Environ. Protection Agy., Phila., 1991. Author: Atlas of United States Environmental Issues, 1990, Contested Lands: Conflict and Compromise in New Jersey's Pine Barrens, 1992. Dir. Clean Air Coun. Del. Valley, Phila., 1992-94; mem. Community Adv. Com. Rohm & Glass and Allied Chem. Cos., Phila., 1988-93; dir. Contemporary Agri. & Rural Land Use Specialty Group Assn. of Am. Geographers, Washington, 1991-94; councillor Del. Valley Geographical Assn., West Chester, Pa., 1989—. Fellow Am. Geographical Soc; mem. Assn. Am. Geographers (Rsch. in pvt. land conservation 1987-88), pres. Middle States Divsn., 1996, Soc. Risk Analysis. Democrat. Avocations: travel, bicycling, hiking. Office: Temple Univ Dept Geography 309 Gladfeller Hall Philadelphia PA 11922

MASON, ROBERT MARION, mathematician, musician; b. Toledo, Ohio, May 27, 1928; s. Ernest E. and Joanna H. Mason; m. Janet E. Polich, Mar. 31, 1956. BE, U. Toledo, 1950, MA, 1951. Jazz pianist, music tchr. Am. Fedn. Musicians, Toledo, 1949-53, Bach Conservatory, Toledo, 1951; mathematician U.S. Naval Rsch. Lab., Washington, 1953-74, cons., 1961-68, mem. tactical electronic warfare divsn., lead lab staff, 1968-74; cons. Rsch. Computation Ctr., 1961-65, Applied Math. Staff, 1965-68; dir. computer ctr. divsn. U.S. Naval Oceanog. Office, Suitland, Md., 1974-76; math. statistician Dept. Commerce, Washington, 1976-79; cons. CLEF, Peterborough, N.H., 1980—; writer, pub. Schoolhouse Press, 1985—; advisor math. and info. scis. divsn. Office Naval Rsch., Washington, 1967-68; mem. panel Project LEX Task Force Engrs. Joint Coun., N.Y.C., 1968; spl. agt. U.S. Dept. Census, Suitland, 1979. Co-author: Applied Matrix and Tensor Analysis, 1970; author: Modern Methods of Music Analysis Using Computers, 1985; contbr. articles to profl. jours. Mem. Am. Math. Soc., Am. Musicological Soc., Assn. Computing Machinery (reviewer 1961-74), Math. Assn. Am. Achievements include 2 patents. Avocations: music composition, keyboard improvisation, MIDI programming. Office: CLEF 46 Mountain View Dr Peterborough NH 03458-1325

MASON, ROGER MAXWELL, molecular pathology educator; b. Hull, Yorkshire, U.K., Oct. 24, 1940; m. Margaret Anne Phillipson, Aug. 4, 1978. MB, BChir. U. Wales, U.K., 1965, PhD, 1970; MD, U. London, 1982. Vis. scientist NIH, Bethesda, Md., 1978-79; reader in biochemistry Charing Cross and Westminster Med. Sch., London, 1982-88, prof. biochemistry, 1988-92, head biochemistry, 1992-97; head molecular pathology Imperial Coll. Sch. Medicine, London, 1997—. Contbr. articles to profl. jours. Fellow Royal Soc. Arts, Royal Coll. Physicians, Med. Soc. London. Avocations: sailing, walking, theatre, reading, music. Home: 68 Mortlake Rd KEW. London TW9 4AS, England Office: Imperial Coll Sch Medicine, Exhibition Rd. London SW7 2A2, England

MASON, STEPHEN OLIN, nonprofit association administrator; b. Fresno, Calif., July 11, 1952; s. Olin James and Mary Edna (Moyer) M. BA, Bridgewater (Va.) Coll., 1974; MEd, James Madison U., 1979; PhD, Loyola U., Chgo., 1991. Asst. to the dir. student ctr. Bridgewater Coll., 1974-76; guidance counselor Woodlawn Elem. Sch., Sebring, Fla., 1976-77; asst. dean for student devel. Bridgewater Coll., 1977-81; dir. student life Roger Williams Coll., Bristol, R.I., 1981-83; assoc. dean for residential svcs. Dickinson Coll., Carlisle, Pa., 1983-84; v.p., dean student affairs Westmar Coll., LeMars, Iowa, 1984; rsch. assoc. to pres. Elmhurst (Ill.) Coll., 1986-87; v.p. student affairs Felician Coll., Chgo., 1987-88; dean students Huntingdon Coll., Montgomery, Ala., 1988-90; dir. devel. McPherson (Kans.) Coll., 1990-94, v.p. fin. svcs., 1994-97; exec. dir. Assn. of Brethren Caregivers, Elgin, Ill., 1997—. Participant ARC Blood Drive, 1978-79; mem. allocations com. United Way, Carlisle, 1984; mem. adv. bd. LeMars chpt. Siouxland Coun. for Alcoholism and Drug Abuse, 1984; site coord. for coat drive Mental Health Greater Chgo., 1985; dir-at-large Bridgewater Coll. Alumni Bd., 1987-93; v.p. McPherson Habitat for Humanity, 1993, 94, bd. dirs., 1993-96, pres., 1994; bd. dirs. McPherson Mus. and Arts Found., 1992-94, Assn. Brethren Caregivers, 1993-97. Mem. Assn. Forum Chicagoland. Avocations: calligraphy, community theatre, barbershop singing, spelunking. Home: 649 N Spring St Elgin IL 60120-3651 Office: Assn Brethren Caregivers 1451 Dundee Ave Elgin IL 60120-1674

MASOUD, MAMDOUH SAAD, chemistry educator, researcher; b. Damanhour, Bohira, Egypt, Feb. 15, 1942; m. Sohier Salem El-Sherief, Sept. 18, 1970; children: Heba, Nancy, Mohamed. BSc, Alexandria (Egypt) U., 1963, MSc, 1966, PhD, 1970; diploma, Egyptian Govt., 1999. Assoc. prof. King Abdulaziz U., Jeddah, Saudi Arabia, 1976-79; Alexandria U., 1979-81, demonstrator, 1963-66, asst. lectr. chemistry, 1966-70, lectr., 1971-76, assoc. prof., 1976-81, prof., 1981—, rschr., 1963—, dir. Cen. Lab., faculty sci.; cons. to refractories and on applied chemistry, Alexandria, 1980—; chmn. faculty sci., rschr. King Abdulaziz U., Jeddah, 1975-79; lectr. U. Beirut, 1993-95; referee numerous sci. jours.; contbr. numerous internat. confs. on structural chemistry and analytical applications of biol. active compounds and their complexes; mem. Egypt Com. for Sci. Affairs, 1970—. Contbr. numerous articles to Spectroscopy Letters, Inorganic Synthesis, Transition Metal Chemistry, Inorganica Chim. Acta, Polyhedron, Polish Jour. Chemistry, Pakistan Jour. Chemistry, Egypt Jour. Chemistry, Jour. Phys. Chemistry, Jour. Analytical Chemistry, Indian Jour. Chemistry, also others. Mem. AAAS, N.Y. Acad. Scis., World Cultural Coun (diploma), Famous Egyptian Scientists. Muslem. Avocations: chess, reading, research, attending conferences, refeering journals. Office: Alexandria U Faculty Sci, Chemistry Dept, Alexandria Egypt

MASOVER, GERALD KENNETH, microbiologist; b. Chgo., May 12, 1935; s. Morris H. and Lillian (Perelgut) M.; m. Bonnie Blumenthal, Mar. 30, 1958 (dec. 1992); children: Steven, Laurie, David; m. Lee H. Tower, Mar. 25, 1995. BS, U. Ill., Chgo., 1957, MS, 1970; PhD, Stanford U., 1973. Registered pharmacist, Calif., Ill. Owner, operator Ropert Pharmacy, Chgo., 1960-68; rsch. assoc. Stanford U. Med. Sch., Palo Alto, Calif., 1974-80; assoc. rsch. cell biologist Children's Hosp., Oakland, Calif., 1980-83; rsch. microbiologist Hana Biologics, Berkeley, Calif., 1983-86; pharmacist various locations, 1970—; quality control sect. head Genentech, Inc., South San Francisco, 1986-90, quality control sr. microbiologist, 1990—. Contbr. articles to profl. jours., chpts. to books. 1st Lt. USAR, 1957-66. NSF predoctoral fellow, 1970-73; Rsch. grant NIH, 1974-78. Mem. Soc. In Vitro Biology, Internat. Orgn. for Mycoplasmology, Parenteral Drug Assn., Am. Soc. Microbiology, Sigma Xi. Jewish. Achievements include patents on triphasic mycoplasmatales detection method, triphasic mycoplasmatales detection device. Home: 4472 24th St San Francisco CA 94114-3522 Office: Genentech Inc 1 DNA Way South San Francisco CA 94080-4990

MASPERI, LUIS, physicist; b. Spoleto, Perugia, Italy, Dec. 27, 1940; arrived in Argentina, 1948; s. Giancarlo and Graziella (Michelazzi) M.; m. Vittoria Miceli, Dec. 28, 1968; children: Lara, Alessandro, David. Chem. Engr., U. del Litoral, Santa Fe, Argentina, 1961; M.Physics, Instituto Balseiro, Bariloche, Argentina, 1964, PhD in Physics, 1969. Rsch. fellow Centro Atómico Bariloche, Argentina, 1965-66, rschr. in physics, 1968—; rsch. fellow Internat. Centre Theoretical Physics, Trieste, Italy, 1967; assoc. prof. Instituto Balseiro, Bariloche, 1969-78, full prof., 1978—, dep. dir., 1972-76; head theory divsn. Centro Atómico Bariloche, 1985-91; dir. Centro Latinoamericano de Física, Rio de Janeiro, 1997—. Contbr. chpts. to books; translator: Science, Education and Development by Abdus Salam, 1987. Mem. Mcpl. Constnl. Conv., Bariloche, 1985-86; mem. Nat. Com. Partido Intransigente, Buenos Aires, 1983-89; sec. Assembly for Human Rights, Bariloche, 1982-97. Recipient Diez Jóvenes sobresalientes 1973, Jr. Chamber, Buenos Aires, Forum award Am. Phys. Soc., 1992. Mem. Argentina Physics Assn. (chmn. 1982-84), Internat. Network of Engrs. and Scientists (exec. com. 1997—), Pugwash Conf. (coun. mem. 1999—). Avocations: classical music, swimming. Home: Onelli 148, 8400 San Carlos Bariloche Argentina Office: Centro Atómico Bariloche, 8400 San Carlos Bariloche Argentina

MASQUELET, ALAIN CHARLES, orthopaedic surgeon, educator; b. Enghien, Val d'Oise, France, May 8, 1948; s. Robert Arthur and France Adeline (Jacquin) M. MD, Med. Sch., Paris, 1981; Spl. Diploma, Univ. II, Shanghai, 1982. Resident Hosp. Bichat, Paris, 1978, Hosp. Trousseau, Paris, 1980, Ninth People's Hosp., Shanghai, 1982; orthop. surgeon Assistance Publique Hosp. of Paris, 1987-90, head dept., 1995—; prof. medicine, rschr. U. Paris, 1990—. Author: Lambeaux de couverture, 1990, Atlas of Surgical Exposures of the Upper Extremity, 1990, Atlas of Surgical Exposures of the Lower Extremity, 1993, An Atlas of Flaps in Limb Reconstruction, 1995 (Royal Soc. Medicine Med. Book award 1995). Mem. French Orthop. Soc., French Acad. Surgery, Royal Soc. Medicine (Eng.). Avocations: philosophy, old gaffers boats. Office: Avicenne Hospital, 125 Rt de Stalingrad, 93009 Bobigny France

MASRI, MERLE SID, biochemist, consultant; b. Jerusalem, Palestine, Sept. 12, 1927; came to U.S., 1947; s. Said Rajab and Fatima (Muneimné) M.; m. Maryjean Loretta Anderson, June 28, 1952 (div. 1974); children: Kristin Corinne, Allan Eric, Wendy Joan, Heather Anderson. BA in Physiology, U. Calif., Berkeley, 1950; PhD in Mammalian Physiology and Biochemistry, U. Calif. Berkeley, 1953. Rsch. asst. Dept. Physiology, Univ. Calif., Berkeley, 1950-53; predoctoral fellow Baxter Labs., Berkeley, 1952-53; rsch. assoc. hematology Med. Rsch. Inst., Michael Reese Hosp., Chgo., 1954-56; sr. rsch. biochemist Agrl. Rsch. Svc., USDA, Berkeley, 1956-87; supervisory rsch. scientist Agrl. Rsch. Svc., USDA, N.D. State U. Sta., Fargo, N.D., 1987-89; pvt. practice as cons. Emeryville, Calif., 1989—; lectr. numerous confs. Contbr. articles to profl. jours. and books. Recipient Spl. Svc. and Merit awards USDA, 1966, 76, 77, Superior Svc. award USDA, 1977. Mem. AAAS, Am. Chem. Soc., Am. Oil Chemists Soc., Am. Assn. Cereal Chemists, N.Y. Acad. Scis., Inst. Food Technologists, Commonwealth Club Calif., Internat. Platform Assn., World Affairs Coun. of No. Calif., Sigma Xi. Achievements include patents for detoxification of aflatoxins in agricultural crops and aflatoxin contaminated milk, improved dyeability of cotton fabrics and reduced dye and electrolyte discharge in plant effluent, new closed-circuit raw wool scouring technology to conserve water and energy and control pollution, synthesis and use of polymers and modification of biopolymers for wastewater treatment, and for enzyme immobilization, toxic heavy metals removal and textile finishing treatment, non-polluting new technology for scouring raw wool in a closed circuit with water recycling and re-use and waste effluent control; studied chlorination of water in food processing operations and water re-use and recycle and the generation of mutagens and means of improving disinfection efficiency and reducing mutagen formation, pharmacology and toxicology of natural and synthetic compounds, cereal and baking technology and wheat and durum quality, carbohydrate chemistry, fermentation and enology, confectionery, and ceramic chemistry; discovered new methods and reagents for protein and amino acid residue modification and analysis, new mammalian metabolic pathways; developed other non-polluting textile finishing treatments. Home: 9 Commodore Dr Emeryville CA 94608-1652

MASRI, TAHER NASHAT, Jordanian government official; b. Nablus, Jordan, Mar. 5, 1942; s. Nashat and Hadiyyah (Solh) M.; m. Samar Bitar Masri, Dec. 31, 1967; children: Nashat, Nadine. BBA in Bus. Adminstrn., North Tex. State U., Denton, 1965. Dep. chief dept. fin. Cen. Bank of Jordan, 1965-73; mem. Lower House of Parliament, Jordan, 1973-74, 84-88, 89-93, 93-97; min. of state for occupied ter. affairs, 1973-74, amb. to Spain, 1975-78, amb. to France, 1978-83; rep. UNESCO, 1978-83, EEC, 1978-80; amb. to U.K., 1983-84, min. fgn. affairs, 1984-88, 91, dep. prime min., min. econ. affairs, 1989, chmn. fgn. rels. com., 1989-91, prime min., min. def., 1991; speaker Lower House of Parliament, 1993-94; mem. Upper House of Parliament (senate), 1998—; mem., reporter Royal Com. for Drafting Nat. Chpt. Chmn., bd. trustees Japan U. Sci. and Tech., 1998—. Named Grand Cordon of the Jewelled Al-Nahda, Jordan, Al-Nahda 1st degree, Jordan, Al-Kawkab 1st degree, Jordan, Grande Officier de Légion d'Honeur, France, Commandre Legion d'Honeur, France, Grand Brit. Empire, Grande Officier de l'Order Nat. Merite, Knight of Grand Cross of The Order of the Republic if Italy, Grande Cordon de l'Ordre Nat. de Cedre, Lebanon; recipient Isabela Catolica award Spain, Merito Civil award Spain, Grand Decoration of Honour in Gold with Sash for Svcs. to Republic of Austria, Merit Gwanghawa medal Order of Diplomatic Svc., Korea; named to Grand Brit. Empire. E-mail: t.n.masri@index.com.jo. Office: PO Box 5550, Amman 11183, Jordan

MASSA, RICHARD WAYNE, retired communications educator; b. Carona, Kans., May 2, 1932; s. Columbo and Ella (Whitehead) M.; m. Mary Lou Marshall, May 29, 1960 (div. 1969); m. Teresa Rose Ramirez, Mar. 19, 1971; children: Tod, Daphne, Sara. B in Journalism, U. Mo., 1954, MA, 1955; postgrad., U. Ark., 1964-65. Instr. U. Mo., Columbia, 1955, Miss. State Coll. for Women, Columbus, 1957-58; from instr. to assoc.prof. comm. Okla. Coll. for Women/Okla. Coll. Liberal Arts, Chickasha, 1958-69; assoc. prof. Mo. So. State Coll., Joplin, 1972-87, prof., 1987-99, head dept. comm., 1980-99, dir. Inst. Internat. Studies, 1996-99, acting head dept. lang. and lit., 1979-80; v.p. Interpersonal Comm. Consultants, Oklahoma City, 1969-72. Co-author: Principal Ideas of Medieval and Renaissance Man, 1967, Contemporary Man in World Society, 1969; co-editor: Classical Readings for Contemporary Man, 1967, Inquisitive Man; His Quest for Truth, 1970. With U.S. Army, 1955-57. Recipient Gov.'s award for Excellence in Tchg., Mo. Dept. Higher Edn., Jefferson City, 1996. Home: 25399 Demott Dr Joplin MO 64801-6309 Office: Missouri So State Coll 3950 Newman Rd Joplin MO 64801-1512

MASSACANE, ARMANDO LUIS, communications company executive, consultant; b. Capital Federal, Argentina, Dec. 9, 1941; s. Armando and Emelina (Martinez Costa) M.; m. Nilda Diana Solis, Jan. 4, 1968 (div. Oct. 1992); children: Valeria, Sebastian. Prof. Colegio Pio IX, Argentina, 1968-71; tech. adminstr. Thomson-CSF, Argentina, 1971-73; programmer Fed. S.A., Argentina, 1973-76; mgr. La Papelera del Plata, Argentina, 1976-78, Video Cable Comms., Argentina, 1983-86; exec. ALMA, Argentina, 1978—; cons. in field, 1978—. Contbr. articles to mags. Avocation: amateur radio. Home: Pl Rivera 4822 8-E, 1431 Capital Federal Argentina

MASSAD, CARLOS, bank executive; married; five children. Pres., advisor Ctrl. Bank, Chile, 1996—. Office: Banco Central de Chile, Agustinas 1180 Casilla 967, Santiago Chile*

MASSAD, MALEK GEORGE, surgeon, researcher; b. Beirut, Sept. 2, 1957; came to US, 1987; s. George C. and Chamat Issa M.; m. Helene Rubeiz, Oct. 13, 1988; children: Nina, Nicole. BS in Biology-Chemistry, Am. U. Beirut, 1978, MD, 1983. Diplomate Am. Bd. Surgery, Am. Bd. Thoracic Surgery. Acad. surgeon U. Ill., Chgo., 1996—, dir. circulatory support program, 1996—, heart and lung transplant surgeon, 1996—, dir. cardiovascular rsch. labs., 1998—, head thoracic organ transplantation, 1998—; cardiovascular and thoracic surgeon U. Ill. Hosp., Chgo., 1996—; cons. thoracic surgeon Westside VA Hosp., Chgo., 1998—; mem. curriculum adv. bd. Osler Inst., Terre Haute, Ind., 1996-98; mem. thoracic organ transplant subcom. Regional Bank Ill., Chgo., 1996—. Recipient Investigator award Am. Coll. Chest Physicians, 1988, 99. Fellow ACS; mem. AAAS, AHA (mem. coun. thoracic and cardiovascular surgery 1995—), Nat. Transplant Soc. (mem. med. adv. bd. 1997—), Internat. Soc. Heart and Lung Transplantation, Ill. State Med. Soc., Soc. Thoracic Surgeons, Karl Meyer Soc., Warren Cole Soc. Avocations: tennis, reading, writing, research. Home: 110 Kraml Dr Burr Ridge IL 60521-0302 Office: U Ill Divsn Cardiothoracic Surg 840 S Wood St Ste 417 Chicago IL 60612-7317

MASSAJOLI, PIERLEONE FRANCESCO W., anthropologist, dialectologist, researcher; b. Turin, Piemonte, Italy, May 24, 1928; s. Italo and Matilde (Tabbia) M.; m. Laura Castelli, June 30, 1963; children: Matilde, Francesca. Degree in Law, U. Genoa, Italy. Prof. cultural anthropology Faculty of Sci. Formation U. Genoa, 1993—; Dir. terra Ameriga mag., 1964-72; pub., editor, dir. The Eagle's Nest, 1983—. Author: Dizionario Della Cultura Brigasca, vol. 1, 1991, Dizionario Della Cultura Brigasca II, 1996, Voices of Tradition, others; contbr. over 300 articles to profl. jours. Recipient prize for anthropology Milano-Spoleto, 1983, others. Mem. Italian Americanistic Studies Assn. (sec., v.p. 1964-72), Il Nido D'Aquila Study Ctr. (pres. 1989—), Vegia Arba Artists and Writers Assn. Avocation: writing. Home: Via F D Guerrazzi 14/14, 16146 Genoa Italy

MASSARINI, ANTONIO, nuclear engineer, researcher; b. Bolzano, Italy, May 2, 1962; s. Carlo and Niobe (Pigozzi) M.; m. Claudia Cesari, June 1, 1996; 1 child, Marco. Grad. in nuclear engring., U. Bologna, Italy, 1987, PhD in Elec. Engring., 1992. Cert. profl. engr. Rschr. engring. scis. dept. U. Modena e Reggio Emilia, Italy, 1992—; cons. AGIP, Venice, Italy, 1993. Contbr. articles to sci. jours., including IEEE Trans. on Circuits and Sys., IEEE Tras. on Power Electronics. Counselor Commune of Porto Ceresio, Italy, 1988-91. With Transmission Corps, Italian Army, 1987-88. Avocations: bicycle riding, skiing. Fax: 059 364132. E-mail: antonio.massarini@unimo.it. Home: via Guidicini 2, 40137 Bologna Italy Office: U Modena e Reggio Emilia Engring Scis Dept, via Campi 213/B, 41100 Modena Italy

MASSARO, JOSEPH JAMES, secondary school educator; b. Buffalo, Dec. 28, 1950; s. James Vincent and Mary Frances (Valentine) M.; m. Cathy Massaro, May, 1999; 1 child, Jeffrey Matthew. AS, Genesee C.C., 1975; BS in Health and Phys. Edn., SUNY, Brockport, 1976; MEd, SUNY, Buffalo, 1988. Cert. health and phys. edn. tchr., N.Y. Tchr. aide West Seneca (N.Y.) Sr. H.S., 1977-79; health instr. Royalton Hartland H.S., Middleport, N.Y., 1979—, varsity wrestling coach, 1979-98, jr. varsity softball coach, 1982-83, jr. varsity soccer coach, 1992, athletic dir., 1993-94; prin., English tchr. Brockport Migrant Edn. Program, 1986-88; health tchr. Lockport (N.Y.) Sr. H.S., 1990, 92, 94; nutrition instr. Cornell Coop. Extension, Lockport, summer 1993; real estate broker Stovroff Realty; mktg. exec. Malelenca Inc. Chmn. Cmty. Chem. Intervention Group, Middleport, 1979-83; advisor SADD, Middleport, 1986-92. Named Wrestling Coach of Yr., Channel 7, Buffalo, 1988; recipient Sportsmanship award Niagara Frontier Ofcls. Assn., 1988. Mem. ASCD, N.Y. State Tchrs. United, N.Y. State Fedn. Health Edn., Assn. for Advancement of Health Edn., Am. Youth Soccer Orgn. (bd. dirs. 1992-95). Republican. Roman Catholic. Avocations: physical fitness, camping, fishing, woodworking, gardening. Office: Royalton Hartland Ctrl Sch 54 State St Middleport NY 14105-1114

MASSARRAT, SADEGH, physician; b. Machhad, Iran, May 24, 1932; came to Fed. Republic Germany, 1952; s. Hasan and Osera (Khaniani) M.; m. Shahin Khabir-Mohsen, July 1, 19598; children: Sheherezade, Kyros, Darius. MD, U. Heidelberg, 1954. Research fellow German Research Assn., Marburg, 1961-63; research asst. dept. internal medicine U. Marburg, 1963-69, prof. medicine, 1972—, cons. physician, 1970-92; prof. Tehran (Iran) U. Med. Scis., 1993—. Contbr. articles to profl. jours. Mem. Internat. Soc. Clin. Enzymology, Deutsche Gesellschaft für Innere Medizin, Deutsche Gesellschaft für Verdaungs und Stoffwechselkrankheiten, Am. Gastroenterology Assn. (sr.). Office: Digestive Disease Ctr, Shariati Hosp, Tehran Iran also: Shariati Hosp, Digestive Disease Ctr, Tehran Iran

MASSELOS, JIM COSMAS, history educator, researcher; b. Townsville, Queensland, Australia, July 20, 1940; s. George and Fofo (Kapralos) M. BA, Sydney (Australia) U., 1961; PhD, Bombay (India) U., 1965. Lectr. Sydney U., 1965-70, sr. lectr., 1970-80, reader in history, 1980—; hon. cocurator Dancing to the Flute, Indian Art Exhbn., Art Gallery of New South Wales, Australia, 1997. Author: Towards Nationalism, 1974, Indian Nationalism, 1993, co-author: Dancing to the Flute: Music and Dance in Indian Art, 1997; editor: Struggling and Ruling: The Indian National Congress, 1885-1985, 1987, India: Creating a Modern Nation, 1990. Mem. South Asian Studies Assn. (pres. 1994—), Asian Studies Assn. of Australia (mem. coun. 1994—), Asian Arts Soc. Australia (mem. coun. 1991-96). Avocations: photography, travel, cinema, Indian art. Office: Univ Sydney, Dept History, New South Wales 2006, Australia

MASSELOS, VASSILIS, business executive; b. Athens, Greece, Mar. 19, 1968. B, Athens U. Econs., 1991; Exec. Tng. Program, Tokyo, 1994-95. Trainee Konzum RT, Pecs, Hungary, 1987; mktg. rchr. Sci-Tec Instruments, Saskatoon, Sask., Can., 1989; mgmt. trainee Okura & Co., Tokyo, 1990; info. sys. mgr. Masselos SA, Athens, 1991-94, mng. dir., 1999—; sec. gen. Hellenic Info. Sys. Inst., 1997—; chmn. Hellenic Electronic Commerce Ctr., 1993—; pres. Hellenic Somatometric Inst., 1999. Contbg. author: Contemporary Japan: Issues and Perspectives, 1998. Mem. Friends of the Athens Opera House, 1996—; mem. Athens Concert Hall, 1996—. Served with Hellenic Navy, 1997-99. Greek Orthodox. Avocations: golf, sailing, opera, reading. Office: Masselos SA, 13 Leocharous St, 105 60 Athens Greece

MASSET, JEAN-PIERRE, diplomat; b. Casablanca, Morocco, Sept. 11, 1936; s. Louis J. and Helene (Barrau) M.; m. Lassez Francoise, Apr. 23, 1959; children: Nathalie Caudron, Valerie Branche, Marion Imbert. Degree in law, U. Bordeaux, France, 1957; M in Economy, U. Paris, 1960; postgrad., Inst. for Advanced Studies, Paris; postgrad. in Russian, Arabic, Inst. Oriental Civilisation, Paris. With French Embassy, Rabat, Morocco, 1963-66, Moscow, 1966-70; personal asst. Min., Paris, 1971-73; with French Embassy, Washington, 1973-77, Bonn, Germany, 1977-80; dir. Soviet and Eastern European Affairs French Fgn. Ministry, Paris, 1980-82; min. counsellor French Embassy, Moscow, 1982-85; asst. sec. for UN affairs French Ministry, Paris, 1986-89; amb. to Pakistan French Embassy, Islamabad, 1989-93; dep. to Lord Owen Conf. Former Yugoslavia, Geneva, 1993—; amb. to Iran-French Embassy French Embassy, Teheran, 1994-98; amb. to Denmark French Embassy, Copenhagen, 1998—. Served to lt. col. Marine Reserves, 1961-63. Recipient Legion of Honour award French Govt., 1990; named Comdr. in Order of Merit, French Govt., 1997. Home: 3 Blvd Henry IV, Paris France Office: Amb France to Copenhagen, 128 bis rue de l'Universite, 75351 Paris France

MASSEY, ALLYN F., artist, educator; b. Norwood, Mass., Aug. 3, 1949; d. Gordon J. and Gwendolyn M. BFA, Corcoran Sch. Art, 1986; MFA, Md. Inst. Coll. Art, 1989. Prof. U. Md., Coll. Park, 1990-91, Corcoran Sch. Art, Washington, 1992-97, Goucher Coll., Balt., 1997—; bd. dirs., chair program adv. com. Md. Art Pl., Balt., 1998-2000; mem. adv. bd. Clipper Artists Fire Fund, Balt., 1996. Illustrator: Second Person Plural, 1980; sculptor, printmaker, installation artist. Artist, panelist Balt. Mus. Art, 1993, BWI airport commn. Md. Aviation Bd., Linthicum, 1995, 1% for art commn. Gen. Svcs. Adminstrn., Balt./Washington, 1996. Henry A. Walters fellow Md. Inst. Coll. Art, 1989; recipient award for individual new genre Md. State Arts Coun., 1992, 95, 97. Mem. Internat. Scuplture Ctr., Sculptors Inc. (sec. 1991-93, editor newsletter 1995-97), Cultural Alliance, Contemporary Mus. Avocations: astronomy, geology. Office: Goucher Coll 1021 Dulaney Valley Rd Baltimore MD 21204-2753

MASSEY, DONALD WAYNE, clergyman, small business owner; b. Durham, N.C., Mar. 7, 1938; s. Gordon Davis and Lucille Alma (Gregory) M.; m. Violet Sue McIlvain, Nov. 2, 1958; children: Kimberly Shan (dec.), Leon Dale, Donn Krichele, Anthony Donn Prestarri. Student, U. Hawaii, 1959, U. Ky., 1965, 66, U. Va., 1970, Piedmont C.C., 1982. Ordained Hookerton Christian Ch., 1999. Head microfilm sect. Ky. Hist. Soc., Frankfort, 1961; dir. microfilm ctr. U. Ky., Lexington, 1962-67; dir. photog. svcs. and graphics U. Va., Charlottesville, 1967-73; pres. Micrographics II, Charlottesville, Charleston, S.C., 1973—; min. Hookerton (N.C.) Christian Ch., 1999—, Bethel Christian Ch., Grifton, 1999—; instr. U. Va. Sch. Continuing Edn., 1971-72, Ctrl. Va. Piedmont C.C., 1976; cons. Microform Systems and Copying Ctrs.; owner Masland Farm, Shadwell, Va.; basketball coach Rock Hill Acad., 1975-77; chaplain Cedars Nursing Home, Charlottesville, 1992-94, Colonnades Charlottesville, 1992—, Our Lady Peace Charlottesville, 1996—, Manor House, 1999—. Pub.: Micropublishing Series, 18th Century Sources for Study of English Lit. and Culture, Women Authors 18th and 19th Centuries, 1993, Va. Colonial History, 1994—, Theology in the 18th and 19th Centuries, 1995; author: Episcopal Churches in the Diocese of Virginia, 1989, A Catechism for Children, 1995, A Guide to Colonial Churches in Virginia, 1996, The Christian Philosphy of Patrick Henry, In Memoriam to the Rt. Rev. William Meade, Third Bishop of Virginia, 1996, Jamestown, the Beginning of the Church in Virginia, 1996, Christ Epsicopal Church, Monticello Parish, Charlottesville, Va.. The First 100 Years, 1924-1924, 1996, Ministry in Nursing Homes and Health Care Centers, 1997, St. John's-Waldrop a Church History, 1845-1997, 1998, Jamestown and the Colonial Churches in Virginia, 1999, Twelve Gates to the Kingdom of God, Apostles of Christ, 1999; contbg. editor Va. Libr., 1970-71; contbr. articles to profl. jours. Chmn. bd. dirs. Park St. Christian Ch., 1970, 75; pres. Rock Hill Acad. Aux., 1975-76; pres. bd. Workshop V for handicapped, Charlottesville, 1972-73; bd. chmn. Park St. Christ Ch., 1969-76; mem. Emmanuel Epsic. Ch., Greenwood, Va., Grace Epsic. Ch., Cismont, Va.; pres. region XV Epsic. Diocese Va.; chalice bearer St. Luke's Chapel Simeon, Va., Christ ch., Charlottesville, 1992, lay eucharistic min., 1993—; lay reader eucharistic minister Christ Episcopal Ch., Charlottesville; chaplain Cedars Nursing Home, Charlottesville, 1991—; rep. Senatorial Inner Cir., 1990, George Bush Rep. Task Force, 1990; eucharistic min. Grace Epsic. Ch., Cismont, 1996—, Introduced and Leader of Fest. of Carols and Liturgy in Retirement and Nursing Homes, 1995-98. With USMCR, 1957-73. Named Ky. Col.; recipient Jey award Workshop V. Mem. ALA, Va. Libr. Assn., Soc. Reprodn. Engrs., Nat. Microfilm Assn. (libr. rels. com. 1973), Va. microfilm Assn. (pres. 1971-72, v.p. 1973-74, program chmn. ann. conf. 1974, Pioneer award 1973, fellow 1976), Ky. Microfilm Assn. (Oustanding award 1967, pres. 1964-67), Assn. Info. and Image Mgmt., Va. Gamebird Assn., Thoroughbred Owners and Breeders Assn., Am. Rose Soc., Thomas Jefferson Rose Soc. (charter), NRA, Nat. Trust Hist. Preservation, Va. Microfilm Assn. (contbg. editor icro-News 1983-85). Home: 3304 Keswick Rd Keswick VA 22947-2600 Office: Hookerton & Bethel Christian Chs PO Box 186 Hookerton NC 28538-0186

MASSEY, KATHLEEN MARIE OATES, lawyer; b. Chgo., Dec. 2, 1955; d. William Robert Jr. and Ethelyn Rose (Calhoun) Oates. Student, U. Claremont-Ferrand, France, 1976-77; BA cum laude, Kalamazoo Coll., 1978; JD, U. Wis., 1981. Bar: Wis. 1981, Minn. 1981, U.S. Dist. Ct. Minn. 1981, U.S. Dist. Ct. (ea. dist.) Wis. 1983. With Larkin, Hoffman, Daily & Lindgren Ltd., Mpls., 1981-87; ptnr. Habush, Habush & Davis, Milw., 1987-90; asst. gen. counsel A.O. Smith Corp., Milw., 1992-97; sr. litigation counsel Motorola Inc., Schaumburg, Ill., 1997—. Mem. ABA, Minn. Bar Assn., Wis. Bar Assn., Phi Beta Kappa, Alpha Lambda Delta, Phi Eta Sigma.

MASSEY, SAM GUERRY, financial analyst; b. Macon, Ga., Oct. 15, 1964; s. E. Guerry and Jane Claire M.; m. Dione Michelle Hubacek, Sept. 1, 1990; children: Madison, Andrew. BS in Indsl. Mgmt., Ga. Inst. Tech., 1987; MBA, State U. West Ga., 1989. Acct., ops. mgr. Real Estate West, Carrollton, Ga., 1988-89; fin. cons. A.G. Edwards & Sons, Inc., Gainesville, Ga., 1990-92; assoc. equity analyst Interstate/Johnson Lane, Atlanta, 1992-95, assoc. v.p., equity analyst, 1997-98; high yield bond sales Alex Brown & Sons Inc., Atlanta, 1995-97; fin. analyst BellSouth Small Bus. Svcs., Atlanta, 1998—. Disaster vol. ARC, Athens, Ga., 1999. Mem. Assn. for Investment Mgmt. and Rsch., Atlanta Soc. Fin. Analysts. Avocations: investing, golfing, reading. Office: BellSouth Small Bus Svcs 1057 Lenox Park Blvd NE Rm 2d16 Atlanta GA 30319-5309

MASSEY, WILLIAM WALTER, JR., sales executive; b. Lawrenceburg, Tenn., Sept. 21, 1928; s. William Walter and Bess Ann (Brian) M.; m. Virginia Claire Smith, Aug. 16, 1952; children: William Walter III, Laura Ann, Lynn Smith, Lisa Claire. BBA, U. Miami, Fla., 1949; BFA, U. Fla., 1969. Exec. v.p., dir. Massey Motors, Inc., Jacksonville, Fla., 1950—; v.p., dir. Atlantic Discount Co. Inc., Jacksonville, 1954-64; pres. Owners Surety Corp., Jacksonville, 1959—, General Svcs. Corp., Jacksonville, 1960-69, Owners Guaranty Life, Phoenix, Ariz., 1960-64, Securities Guaranty Life, Phoenix, Ariz., 1961-64, Fla. Properties, Inc., Jacksonville, 1961-66, Chi-Cha, Inc., Jacksonville, 1965-70, Univ. Square Properties, Jacksonville, 1969-80; v.p., bd. dir. Southside Country Day School, Jacksonville, 1963-68; bd. dirs. Southside Atlantic Bank, Jacksonville, 1965-93. Exhibited in group shows at Internat., N.Y., 1970, Ball State U., 1972. Lt. USAF, 1950-1952. Mem. Ponte Vedra Club, River Club, Epping Forest Club, Deerwood Club, Sigma Chi. Methodist. Avocations: music, painting, writing.

MASSEY, W(ILMET) ANNETTE, retired nurse, former educator; b. Big Chimney, W.Va., June 30, 1920; d. Robert Lee and Twila Augusta (Pringle) M. Student, Morris Harvey Coll., 1938-39; diploma, Phila. Gen. Hosp. Sch. Nursing, 1943; BS in Edn., U. Pa., 1948; MSN, Yale U., 1959. Nurse cadet instr. U.S. Cadet Nurse Corps. Huntington (W.Va.) Meml. Hosp., 1943-45; nurse instr. St. Mary's Sch. Nursing, Huntington, 1948-51; WHO nurse cons. Govt. Ceylon, 1951-55; staff nurse instr. VA Hosp., Ft. Thomas, Ky., 1955-57; asst. prof. nursing Brighan Young U., Provo, Utah, 1959-61; assoc. prof. nursing W.Va. U., Morgantown, 1961-83, chmn. dept. psychiat. nursing, 1968-72, ret., 1983; cons. Applachian Regional Hosp., Beckley, W.Va. Dept. Mental Health, Charleston, Valley Cmty. Mental Ctr., Kingwood, W.Va.; group leader med.-nursing group to India, Expt. Internat. Living, Brattleboro, Vt., 1965. Mem. Appalachian Trail, Morgantown Hospice, Rep. Nat. Com., Drummond Chapel United Meth. Ch., United Meth. Women, health adv. com. Coun. Mins., ARC, Nat. Coun. Sr. Citizens, Monongalians Srs., Rails to Trail, W.Va. Highlands Conservancy, W.Va. Citizens Action, Cooper's Rock Found. NIMH grantee, 1964-75. Mem. ANA, League Nursing, Am. Orthopsychiat. Assn., Internat. Transactional Analysis Assn., Am. Counseling Assn. (dir. 1981-82, v.p. 1982), Am. Soc. Profl. and Exec. Women, Environ. Def. Fund, Nat. Parks and Conservation Assn., Nat. Trust for Hist. Preservation, Tarrytown Group, Nat. Registry Psychiat. Nurse Specialists (edn. and resources com.), Internat. Acad. Cancer Counselors and Cons., Nat. Alliance Family Life, Inc. (founding), AAUP, Nat. Hist. Soc., Hastings Ctr., Nat. Wildlife Fedn., Smithsonian Assocs., Phila. Gen. Hosp. Sch. Nursing Alumni, U. Pa., Yale U., W.Va. U. Sch. Nursing (hon.) Alumni Assns., 20/20 Vision Winterthur Guild, Empower Am., Pub. Citizen, Friends of the Earth, W.Va. Pub. Theatre, Am. Rivers, Project Vote Smart, W.Va. Rivers Coalition, World Learning, Wash. Nat. Cathedral, So. Property Law Ctr., Am. Red Cross, Am. Farmland Trust, Sierra Club, Lakeview Resort Club, Appalachian Trail, Sigma Theta Tau. Clubs: Alpine Lake Recreation Cmty. (Terra Alta, W.Va.), Penn (N.Y.C.). Home: 432 Western Ave Morgantown WV 26505-2135

MASSIE, MAUREEN TERESA, elementary school educator; b. St. Louis, Apr. 13, 1953; d. James H. and Teresa B. Moran; m. Jim Massie, Feb. 3, 1973; 1 child, Kate. BA in Child Study, Webster Coll., 1977, MAT, 1990. Cert. tchr. K-8, Mo. 1st grade tchr. No. St. Francis County Sch. Dist., Bonne Terre, Mo., 1977-87; 4th grade tchr. Lindbergh Sch. Dist., St. Louis, 1987-89; instr. tchg. methods Ctrl. Meth. Coll. at Mineral Area Coll., Park Hills, Mo., 1991—; tchr. Farmington (Mo.) Sch. Dist., 1989—. Asst. youth group leader Teenage Ministry, 1993-2000; resource com. co-chair Habitat for Humanity of St. Francois County, Farmington, Mo., 1997—; bd. dirs. Farmington Soccer Adv. Bd., 1991-93; vol. tchr. Project Head Start, Farmington, 1975-76. Project Aiding Children's Edn. state incentive grant State of Mo., 1991, Truman Learning Ctrs. group state incentive grantee, 1994, Learn and Svc. State grantee, 1998, 99, Group State Incentive grantee, 2000. Mem. ASCD, Mo. Nat. Edn. Assn. Home: 770 Market St # 116 Farmington MO 63640-1951 Office: Jefferson Elem 9 Summit Dr Farmington MO 63640-1641

MASSIER, PAUL FERDINAND, mechanical engineer; b. Pocatello, Idaho, July 22, 1923; s. John and Kathryn (Arki) M.; m. Miriam Parks, May 1, 1948 (dec. Aug. 1975); children: Marilyn Massier Schwegler, Paulette Massier Holden; m. Dorothy Hedlund Wright, Sept. 12, 1978. Cert. engring., U. Idaho (so. br.), 1943; BSME, U. Colo., 1948; MSME, MIT, 1949. Engr. Pan-Am. Refining Corp., Texas City, Tex., 1948; design engr. Maytag Co., Newton, Iowa, 1949-50; research engr. Boeing Co., Seattle, 1951-55; sr. research engr., supr. and dep. sect. mgr. Jet Propulsion Lab. Calif. Inst. Tech., Pasadena, 1955-84, task mgr., 1984-88, mem. tech. staff, 1989-94. Contbr. articles to profl. jours. Moderator Arcadia Congl. Ch., 1996-98; mem. Arcadia High Sch. Music Club, 1966-71. With U.S. Army, 1943-46. Recipient Apollo Achievement award NASA, 1969, Basic Noise Rsch. award NASA, 1980, Life Mem. Svc. award Calif. PTA, 1970, Layman of Yr. award Arcadia Congl. Ch., 1971, Mil. Unit Citation award, 1946. Fellow AIAA (assoc., Sustained Svc. award 1980-81); mem. N.Y. Acad. Scis., Planetary Soc., Order of the Engr., Sigma Xi, Tau Beta Pi, Pi Tau Sigma, Sigma Tau. Congregationalist. Achievements include 50% reduction of cooling requirements for rocket engines, experimental evaluation of heat transfer from thermally ionized gases at temperatures up to 13,000 degrees; experimental determination of starting characteristics, shock-wave structures, heat transfer and pressure distributions in supersonic diffusers led to the development of criteria for their design and their use as a means of simulating altitude conditions at ground level for static testing of rocket engines; experimental/analytical determination of the relationships of large-scale turbulent structures, density and temperature fluctuations, inverted velocity profiles, internally generated pure tones, twin jet shielding, and aircraft flight on noise emitted from aircraft supersonic jets; understanding of the formation of cenospheres during the combustion of heavy oils by analysis of electron microscope photo images of droplets and stages of formed globules and cenospheres gathered on slides during combustion experiments. Avocations: travelog and documentary film production and presentations, genealogy and family history research, antiques, collecting sheet music. Home: 1000 N 1st Ave Arcadia CA 91006-2533

MASSIGNON, DANIEL, retired physicist, educator; b. Paris, Apr. 9, 1919; s. Louis and Marcelle (Dansaert-Testelin) M.; D.Sc., U. Paris, 1955; m. Nicole Deney, Apr. 24, 1970; 1 child, Bérengère. With Nat. Center for Sci. Research, Paris, 1945-56; dep. head phys. chemistry dept. Commissariat l'Énergie Atomique, Paris, 1956-70, head chem. physics dept., 1969—; asst. prof. statis. mechanics U. Paris, 1956-75; mem. nat. com. Nat. Ctr. for Sci. Rsch., Paris, 1966-75. Decorated officer Legion of Honor; recipient Prix La Caze, French Acad. of Sci., 1976, also Prix Doistau-Blutel, 1980. Mem. French Phys. Soc., French Chem. Soc., Am. Phys. Soc., European Phys. Soc., Am. Inst. Chem. Engrs., Internat. Union for Pure and Applied Chemistry. Roman Catholic. Author: Mécanique Statistique des Fluides, 1957; Cours de Mécanique Statistique, 1961; Uranium Enrichment by Gaseous Diffusion, 1979, Russian transl., 1983, Uranium Enrichment (tech. engring. ency.), 1992. Patentee in field. Home: 6 rue de la Source, 75016 Paris France

MASSON, JEAN PHILIPPE, radiologist; b. Paris, Mar. 30, 1957; s. Jacques Andre and Francoise (Bouvet) M.; m. Beatrice Chave, July 25, 1985; children: Veronique, Alice, Isabelle, Anne. MD, U. Paris, 1983. Cert. radiologist. Resident Pontoise Hosp., France, 1982-84, Beaujon Hosp., France, 1984-86; ptnr. Clinique Montreal, Carcassonne, France, 1988-92, sr. ptnr., 1992—; adminstr. Gie de la Voie Domimenne. Fellow Fedn. Radiologists (sr., chmn. 1994), Internat. Radiology Soc.; mem. Fedn. Physicians (sec. 1991), Rotary (Carcassonne), Havana Cite Club. Roman Catholic. Avocations: sailing, ski, hunting. Home: Rue Henri IV, 11170 Villesequelande France Office: Clinique Montreal, Dept Radiology, 11890 Carcassonne 09, France

MASSON, JEAN-YVES, translator, writer; b. Créhange, Moselle, France, Sept. 28, 1962; s. Louis and Suzanne (Roussel) M. DEA in Philosophy, U. Paris IV, 1985, PhD in Comparative Lit., 1998. Asst. U. Paris IV, 1987-90; asst. prof. U. Paris X, 1998—; translator, writer, 1990-98; editor Editions Verdier, 1990—; author: Onzains de la nuit et du desir, 1995, L'isolement, 1996; translator over 40 books; contbr. chpts. to books and articles to profl. publs. Recipient Prix Nelly Sachs, 1990, Chevalier des arts et lettres Ministere de la Culture, 1993. Home: 214 Rue Saint-Maur, 75010 Paris France Office: 234 Rue du Faubourg, Saint Antoine, 75012 Paris France

MASSON, MANJU, graphic designer, scientist, daycare administrator; b. New Delhi, May 23, 1953; came to U.S., 1972; d. Des Raj and Chandar (Kanta) M. MA, SUNY, New Paltz, 1974; BA, U. Md., 1982. Tchr. Childway, College Park, Md., 1974-79; lab. scientist U. Md., College Park, 1979—; dir., adminstr. First Steps Day Care, Wheaton, Md., 1988—. Co-author: Stereotaxic Atlas of the Chick Brain, 1988. Avocations: singing, reading, travel, exercise. E-mail: mm22@umail.umd.edu. Home: 721 Brandon Green Dr Silver Spring MD 20904-3564

MASSON, ROBERT HENRY, paper company executive; b. Boston, June 27, 1935; s. Robert Louis and Henrietta Hill (Worrell) M.; m. Virginia Lee Morton, Dec. 28, 1957; children: Linda Anne, Kenneth Morton, Robert Louis, II. BA in Econs. cum laude, Amherst Coll., 1957; MBA, Harvard U., 1964. Fin. staff Ford Motor Co., Dearborn, Mich., 1964-68; mktg. services div. controller Ford Motor Co., 1968-70; pres. Knutson Constrn. Co., Mpls., 1970-72; v.p. fin., treas. Ellerbe, Inc., Bloomington, Minn., 1972-77; fin. dir. CirTech, Inc., Mpls., 1973-77; v.p. fin. transp. div. PepsiCo., Inc., Tulsa, 1977; corp. v.p., treas. PepsiCo., Inc., Purchase, N.Y., 1978-80; v.p., treas. Combustion Engring., Inc., Stamford, Conn., 1981-86, v.p. fin. and venture devel., 1986-87, v.p. venture fin. and internat. ops., 1988-90; v.p., CFO Parsons & Whittemore, Inc., Rye Brook, N.Y., 1990—; mem. adv. bd. Fleet Bank, 1988—. Author: (with others) The Management of Racial Integration in Business, 1964. Pres. North Georgtown Homeowner's Assn., Birmingham, Mich., 1968-70, U.S. Presdl. Advance Man, 1972-76; trustee, chmn. fin. com. Naval Aviation Mus. Found., 1987—; trustee Hebron Acad., 1993-97; elder Presbyn. Ch. of Old Greenwich, 1992—. Served to lt. USN, 1957-62; lt. comdr. Res. Mem. Am. Forest and Paper Assn. (fin. com. 1991—), Fin. Execs. Inst. (com. on corp. fin. 1981—), Fairchester Treas. Group (pres. 1986), Lucas Point Homeowner's Assn. (pres. 1986-87), Theta Delta Chi. Clubs: Wayzata Yacht (dir.-treas. 1973-77), Riverside Yacht (asst. treas. 1985-87). Office: Parsons & Whittemore Inc 4 International Dr Ste 5 Rye Brook NY 10573-1064

MASSONE, RAUL ENRIQUE, pharmaceutical exporting company executive; b. Buenos Aires, July 15, 1944; s. Arnaldo and Haydee (Carena) M.; m. Maria I. Etcheverry, Dec. 18, 1968; children: Nicolas, Agustina, Francisco, Mariana. Lic. in bus. adminstrn., U. Argentina de La Empresa, Buenos Aires, 1974. Co-founder, pres. Instituto Massone S.A., Buenos Aires, 1964—. Avocations: music, literature, sailing. Home: Santa Rita 200, 1609 Boulogne BA, Argentina Office: Instituto Massone SA, Arias 4431, 1430 Buenos Aires Argentina

MASSURA, EDWARD ANTHONY, accountant; b. Chgo., July 1, 1938; s. Edward Matthew and Wilma C. (Kussy) M.; m. Carol A. Barber, June 23, 1962; children: Edward J., Beth Ann, John B. BS, St. Joseph's Coll., Rensselaer, Ind., 1960; JD, DePaul U., 1963. Bar. Ill. 1963; CPA, Mich., Ill., others. Tax acct. Arthur Andersen LLP, Chgo., 1963-98, ptnr., 1973-98; dir. tax div. Arthur Andersen LLP, Detroit, 1974-84; dep., co-dir. internat. tax Arthur Andersen & Co., Detroit, 1983-84, ptnr.-in-charge internat. trade customs practice, 1983-88. Co-author: West's Legal Forms, 2d. edit., 1984; contbr. numerous articles to bus. jours. Bd. dirs. Arts Found. of Mich., Detroit, 1982-95, treas., 1982-93; bd. dirs. Ctr. for Internat. Bus. Edn. and Rsch., Wayne State U. Mem. AICPA, Internat. Fiscal Assn. (v.p. Eastern Gt. Lakes region), Assn. for Corp. Growth, Mich. Assn. CPAs, Mich. Dist. Export Coun. (chmn. 1985-92), Detroit Internat. Tax Group (founder,co-moderator), Licensing Exec. Soc., World Trade Club of Detroit, Bus. Assn. Mexico and Mich, Inc., Orchard Lake Country Club, Butterfield Country Club, Lely Golf & Country Club. Office: Arthur Andersen LLP 500 Woodward Ave Detroit MI 48226-3416

MASTER, PETER ANTONY, educator, author, editor; b. Watford, Eng., Jan. 23, 1948; s. Antony Edward and Eva Jana Master. BA, U. Calif., Santa Barbara, 1969; MA, San Francisco State U., 1977; PhD, UCLA, 1987. EFL instr. Berlitz, Zurich, 1970-73; ESL instr., dir. courses ESL Lang. Ctr., Oakland, Calif., 1974-78; supr. U. Calif. Berkeley Extension English Lang. Program, 1980-83; ESL instr. U. Calif., Berkeley, 1978-84; tchg. fellow UCLA, 1984-87; assoc. prof. Calif. State U., Fresno, 1987-95; assoc. prof. San Jose (Calif.) State U., 1995-2000, prof., 2000—, dir. Lang. Devel. Ctr.; mem. adv. bd. Global English, Daly City, Calif. Author: (textbook) Systems in English Grammar, 1996; editor/author: Responses to English for Specific Purposes, 2000; co-editor/author: New Ways in English for Specific Purposes, 1998; co-editor: New Ways in Content-Based Instruction, 1997; co-editor English for Specific Purposes, 1994—. Recipient Daniel M. Horowitz award English for Specific Purposes, 1992, Disting. Tchg. Asst. award UCLA, 1987. Mem. TESOL (column editor, presenter), Calif. TESOL (journ. co-editor 1993-97, presenter), Am. Assn. Applied Linguistics (Strand coord., presenter). Democrat. Avocations: piano, woodworking, bicycling, rock climbing. E-mail: pmaster@sjsu.edu. Office: San Jose State U One Washington Sq San Jose CA 95192-0093

MASTERS, ARLENE ELIZABETH, singer; b. Freeport, Ill., Oct. 6, 1960; d. Elmer and Mary (Green) Masters; m. Douglas Dewayne Burck (div.); 1 child, Douglas. Singer classic rock and blues. Home: PO Box 8221 Rockford IL 61126-8221

MASTERS, JON JOSEPH, corporate governance consultant, mediator; b. N.Y.C., June 20, 1937; s. Arthur Edward and Esther (Shady) M.; m. Rosemary Dunaway Cox, June 16, 1962; children: Brooke Alison, Blake Edward. B.A., Princeton U., 1958; J.D., Harvard U., 1964. Bar: N.Y. 1965, U.S. Dist. Ct. (so. dist.) N.Y. 1965, U.S. Ct. Appeals (2d cir.) 1965. Cons. asst. to under sec. Dept. Army, 1961; mem. policy planning staff asst. sec. for internat. security affairs Dept. Def. Washington, 1962; mem. Pres. Johnson's Spl. Polit. Research Staff, Washington, 1964; assoc. Shearman & Sterling, N.Y.C., 1965-68, 69; mem. staff Bedford-Stuyvesant D & S Corp., Bklyn., 1968-69; v.p., sec., gen. counsel, dir. Baker, Weeks & Co., Inc., N.Y.C., 1969-76; ptnr. Christy & Viener, N.Y.C., 1976-96; prin. Lear, Yavitz & Assocs., N.Y.C., 1996—; mng. prin., 1998—; mem. bd. dirs. Robb, Peck, McCooey Fin. Svcs. Corp., N.Y.C., 1996-98; vice chmn. Robb, Peck, McCooey Specialist Corp., N.Y.C., 1996-98; mem. SEC adv. com. broker-dealer compliance, 1972-74; legal advisor NACD Blue Ribbon Commn. on CEO and Dir. Performance Evaluation, 1994; chmn. bd. Clear and Present Prodns., 1992-93; bd. dirs. Harris & Harris Group Inc., 1992-98. Mem. implementation com. Econ. Devel. Task Force of N.Y. Urban Coalition, 1968; mem. bd. Internat. Social Service, Am. Br., Inc., 1978-83, pres., 1979-83; bd. dirs. The Arts Connection, 1979-85; mem. steering com. N.Y. Lawyers Alliance for Nuclear Arms Control, 1983-96. Served with USN, 1958-61. Mem. ABA, Assn. Bar City N.Y. (com. mcpl. affairs 1977-80), N.Y. State Bar Assn. Home and Office: 520 E 86th St New York NY 10028-7534

MASTERSON, HAROLD THOMAS, social services administrator; b. Lisbellaw, Northern Ireland, Feb. 23, 1947; arrived in Switzerland, 1984; s. Thomas and Ida May (Martin) M.; m. Fionnuala Mary McHugh, Sept. 12, 1970 (div. 1978); 1 child, Ciara; m. Kirsten Hoe Bendixen, Apr. 12, 1981; children: (triplets) Karen, Louise, Marianne. BA in Geography, Queen's U. Belfast, 1968, diploma in edn., 1969; MS in Geography, London Sch. Econs., 1970; postgrad., Aarhus (Denmark) U., 1978-80. Tchr. Min. Edn., Zambia, 1971-75; tchr. English as fgn. lang. Aarhus Commune, Denmark, 1975-77; rep. League of Red Cross Socs., Malawi, 1981-83; head delegation League of Red Cross Socs., Turkey, 1984; from desk officer to head field personnel dept. League of Red Cross Socs., Geneva, Switzerland, 1985-93; head tng. Internat. Fedn. Red Cross and Red Crescent Socs., Geneva, 1994—. Home: 2 Rue Argand, 1201 Geneva Switzerland Office: Internat Fedn Red Cross/Red Crescent Socs, PO Box 372, 1211 Geneva 19, Switzerland

MASTERSON, PATRICK, educational administrator; b. Dublin, Ireland, Oct. 19, 1936; m. Frances Masterson; children: Rosemary, Laurence, Lucy, Naomi. BA, U. Coll., Dublin, 1958; PhD, U. Louvain, Belgium, 1962; Doctorate (hon.), U. Caen, 1987, U. Dublin, 1992, NYU, 1998. Lectr. dept. metaphysics U. Coll. Dublin, 1963-72, prof. faculties of arts, philosophy and sociology, 1972-80, dean faculty philosophy and sociology, 1980-83, registrar, 1983-86, pres., 1986-93; vice chancellor Nat. U. Ireland, Dublin, 1987-88; prin. European U. Inst., Florence, Italy, 1994—. Author: Atheism and Alienation: A Study of the Philosophical Sources of Contemporary Atheism, 1971. Mem. Fitzwilliam L.T.C., Royal Irish Acad., Lisbon Acad. Scis. Roman Catholic. Office: European U Inst Badia Fiesolana, Via del Roccettini 9 I-50016, San Domenico di Fiesole Florence Italy

MASTERSON RAINES, JUDITH AMANDA, marketing executive; b. Chgo., Aug. 18, 1952; d. Thomas Robert and Dorothy Jean Masterson; m. Stephen S. Raines, July 18, 1981; stepchildren: Jennifer, Jeffrey. BA with honors, Emory U., 1974. Dir. advt. Alex Cooley Presents, Atlanta, 1974-79; gen. mgr. Theatre League of Atlanta, 1981-94, Chesapeake Concerts, Atlanta, 1979-94; v.p. Nat. Franchise Assocs., Atlanta, 1983—; pres. M&R Advt., Atlanta, 1986—. Author/editor Franchise News, 1991—; contbr. articles to profl. jours. Mem. Ga. Com. on Music Industry, Atlanta, 1989-93; local press rep. Nat. Black Arts Festival, Atlanta, 1990, The Phantom of the Opera, Atlanta, 1991; organizer benefits NAPWA/Aid Atlanta, Zoo Atlanta, UNICEF, Atlanta Food Bank. Recipient 20th Century Award of Achievement Internat. Biog. Ctr., 1995. Mem. AAUW, NOW, NAFE, Nat. Wildlife Fund, Phi Beta Kappa. Avocations: water sports, travel, reading, gardening. Office: M&R Advertising 240 Lake View Ct Lavonia GA 30553-2018

MASTERTON, GORDON GRIER THOMSON, civil and structural engineer; b. Charlestown, Scotland, June 9, 1954; s. Alexander Bain and Mary Low Grier (Thomson) M.; m. Lynda Christine Jeffries, July 17, 1976; children: Matthew, Natalie. BS, U. Edinburgh, 1976; BA, Open U., 1981; MS, Imperial Coll., 1982. Asst. engr. Babtie Shaw & Morton, Glasgow, U.K., 1976-80, project engr., 1980-83, assoc., 1983-87; divisional dir. Babtie Group, Glasgow, 1987-93, dir., 1993—; dir. Babtie Group, Kuala Lumpur, Malaysia, 1995-96; cons. Babtie Jurutera Perunding, Kuala Lumpur, 1995-96; dir. Babtie Internat. Ltd., Glasgow, 1993—, Babtie BMT (Asia) Ltd., Hong Kong, 1995-97; vis. prof. U. Paisley, 1998—. Designer Annan River bridge, 1988 (Saltire award 1988), Buccleuch St. bridge, 1984 (Saltire award 1985); editor: Bridges and Retaining Walls-Broadening the European Horizons. Pres. Glasgow Grand Opera, 1992-94. Philip Gooding Traveling scholarship Concrete Soc., 1982, Harding Prize British Tunneling Soc., 1979. Fellow Instn. of Civil Engrs. (chmn. grads. and student sect. 1992-94, vice chmn. 1997-2000, chmn. 2000—), Fellow Instn. of Structural Engrs., Assn. of Cons. Engrs.; mem. Royal Scottish Automobile Club. Avocations: opera, engineering history, badminton. Office: Babtie Group Ltd, 95 Bothwell St, Glasgow G2 7HX, Scotland

MASTNAK, WOLFGANG, music therapist, educator; b. Salzburg, Austria, Apr. 13, 1959; s. Roland and Irene (Wildolf) M.; m. Petra Šipová, June 17, 1995; children: Marie-Thérèse, Barbara Kristyna. D of Natural Scis., U. Salzburg; PhD, U. Mozarteum, Salzburg; D of Edn., U. Potsdam, DSc. Univ. asst. U. Mozarteum, Salzburg; head of music and body oriented therapy Neuropsychiat. Hosp., Salzburg; prof., chair U. Music, Munich; lectr. U. Strasbourg, U. Prague, U. Prešov, Cons. of Music Shanghai; cons. U. London, Tokyo-Gakugei U. Author: Popper, Gebser und die Musikpädagogik, 1990, Sinne-Künste-Lebenswelten, 1994; co-author: (with Michaela Schwarzbauer) Klingende Welten-Verbindende Sinne, 1994; editor: Künste and Bildung Zwischen Ost und West, 1994. Mem. N.Y. Acad. Scis., Internat. Soc. for Polyaesthetic Edn. Office: Hochschule Musik & Theater, Arcisstrasse 12, D-80333 Munich Germany

MASTRANGELO, VICTOR, science educator; b. Castel del Monte, Italy, July 12, 1941; arrived in France, 1947; m. Michèle Dehen, Dec. 18, 1971; children: Jean-Gabriel, Jean-Pierre, Jean-François. DSc, U. Lyon, France, 1977, PhD in Nuclear Scis., 1968. Vis. scientist Commissariat l'Energie Atomique/Saclay, Paris, 1973-77, Joint Rsch. Ctr./European Commission, Ispra, Italy, 1990-91; assoc. prof. U. Paris VI, 1991-97; prof. Conservatoire National des Arts et Metiers, Paris, 1973—; cons., expert European Commn., Brussels, 1993-96, Organization de Cooperation et de Development Economiques/ Agence pour Energie Nucleaire Académiques, Paris, 1994-97. Reviewer math. jours. Decorated Palmes Académiques Chevalier, 1991. Mem. French Physical Soc. (Nuclear Physics Dvsn.), European Phys. Soc. (computational physics group), European Math. Soc., French Mechanics Univ. Assn., N.Y. Acad. Scis. Office: CNAM, 292 rue Saint Martin, 75141 Paris 03, France

MASTRANTONI, JULIO W., wholesale distributor; b. Weirton, W.Va., Apr. 1, 1935; d. Amedeo and Mary (Amorocciti) M.; m. Leanna Iren Mastrantoni, May 9, 1958; children: Amedeo, Julio, Paul, Mario, Fernando, Geno, Sherry. Grad., Weir H.S., Weirton, W.Va., 1954. Apprentice bricklayer Weirton, 1950-53; mason contr. Mastrantoni Masonry, Weirton, 1953-80; wholesale distbr. Mastrantoni Inc., Weirton, 1980—, retail mattgress and vacuum owner, 1998—. With USMC, 1957-63. Avocations: farming cows, horses (Belgians). Home and Office: 1717 Pennsylvania Ave Weirton WV 26062-3424

MASTRODIMITRIS, PANAYOTIS, literature educator; b. Mantudi, Greece, Aug. 6, 1934; s. Dimitrios and Marianthi (Karayanni) M.; m. Maria Karlatira, Dec. 27, 1959; children: Eleni, Dimitris. BA, U. Athens, 1957, PhD, 1970. Asst. The U. Athens, 1959-61; prof. Greek Secondary Edn., Chalkis, Greece, 1961-66; lectr. Modern Greek U. Athens, 1967-72; prof. Modern Greek Lit. Salonica U., Greece, 1972-75, U. Athens, 1975—; chair Faculty Arts, U. Athens, 1986-91; cons. in field. Author: Introduction to Modern Greek Letters, 1972, 96, Five Essays on Modern Greek Prose, 1987, Prospects and Intrepretations, 1991, The Poetry of modern Greeks, 1984, 99. Sgt. The Greek Army, 1957-59. IKY scholar, Athens, 1965-67, Greek Min. External Affairs, Italy, 1970-71. Mem. OMED, Soc. Etudes Helléniques, Inst. Siciliano Studi Bizantini E Neoellenici. Greek Orthodox. Home: Eleftheriou Venizelou 5, 15121 Pefki Greece Office: U Athens Faculty Arts, Panepistimioupolis, 15784 Zografou Greece

MASTROIANNI, P. FIORENZO FERDINANDO, broadcoast and communications media executive; b. July 4, 1939. Diploma, Biblioteconomia al Vaticano; degree in communications, SPICS, Rome. Journalist, 1984—; corr. ANSA; instr. Pontificio Ateneo Antonianum, Rome, Facult of Theology, Naples, Inst. Donnaregina, Naples, Studentato Cappuccini, Naples; program dir. Radio Tabor, Diocese of Naples; dir. mag. Studi e ricerche francescane, 1972—, others. Editor: Un amico di B.B. Vico nella storia dei Cappuccini di Napoli: B.M. Giacco, (1672-1744), 1972, Analisi storica socio-religiosa di un'inchiesta pontificia relativa alla Calabria Ultra del Cinque-Seicento, 1976, Stile e cultura nelle Oracioni sacre di B.M. Giacco, cappuccino (1672-1744), 1981, L'inchiesta di Innocenzo X sui conventi cappuccini italiani (1650), Analisidei dati , Rome, 1985, Qui Risponde P. Fiorenzo, 1989, Raccogliete i frammenti, 1989, Adorabile volonta. La O'bbedienza nell'epistolario di Madre Rubatto, 1990, Maria nella Civilta dell'amore, 1991, Cari figli. I Messagi di Maria a Oliveto Citra (1985-1997), 1997, Oliveto. Messaggi mariani dall'A alla Z., 1997, S. Antonio di Padova. Vita e dottrina, 1999, I Cappuccini tra riforme francescane e riforma della Chiesa, 1999, Albacina. La prima legislazione cappuccina, 1999, Communicazione socials. La dottrina ufficiale della Chiesa, 2000; contbr. numerous articles to mags., newspapers, profl. jours.; also contribued to documentary films. Address: Naples Italy

MASTROKOSTOPOULOS, IOANNIS, NATO official; b. Athanasios Diakos, Fokida, Greece, Oct. 19, 1944; m. Theodosia Soula Georgiou; 2 children: Theodoros, Alexandra. Grad., Mil. Acad. Evelpidon, 1967; BEE, Naval Postgrad. Sch., Monterey, Calif., MS in Computer Sci., 1982. Commd. 2d lt. Hellenic Armed Forces, 1967, advanced through grades to lt. gen., 1999, early mil. career svc.includes platoon leader, co. comdr., comdr. Army electronic Warfare bn.; staff officer sys. ops. br. in comm. and info. sys. Hellenic Armed Forces, Naples, Italy, 1986-89; chief of staff Hellenic First Army Signals Command Hellenic Armed Forces, 1991-92, comdr. Signals command Higher Mil. Command Interior & Island, 1992, dir. Signals Directorate Hellenic Army Gen. Staff, 1993; chief of comm. and info. sys. divsn. Hellenic Nat. Def. Gen. Staff, 1994-96; also Greek rep. to NATO Comm. and Info. Sys. Com., 1994-96, dep. dir. Sginals Directorate, 1996; chief of staff Hellenic First Army Larisa, Greece, 1997-99; Greek mil. rep. to NATO Mil. Com. Brussels, 1999—. Decorated Order of Merit, Comdr. of Order of Phoenix, Army Meritorious Command medal. Mem. Tech. C. of C.,Armed Forces Comm. and Electronics Assn. Office: NATO Hdqrs, Blvd Leopold III, 1110 Brussels Belgium*

MASTRONARDI, CORINNE MARIE, lawyer; b. Binghamton, N.Y.; d. Joseph Daniel and Frances Marie (Romano) M. BS, Liberty U., 1990; JD, Regent U ., 1993. Bar: Fla. 1994, D.C. 1996. V.p. corp. affairs Va. Metro Protective Svcs., Inc., Virginia Beach; atty., pres. corp. affairs Pro Rep., Inc., Ft. Lauderdale; pvt. practice Ft. Lauderdale. Treas. Christian Legal Soc. Republican. Office: PO Box 13176 Chesapeake VA 23325-0176

MASUD, AHMAD IJAZ, radiation oncologist; b. Sahiwal, Pakistan, Apr. 21, 1964; s. Wali Muhammad and Saeeda Wali (Mohammad) Bhatti; m. Humera Nazir, Apr. 1999. MBBS, Nishtar Med. Coll., 1988. Resident in surgery Nishtar Hosp., Multan, Pakistan, 1988-89, resident in radiotherapy, 1992-94, primary fellow in radiation oncology, 1993, postgrad. resident in radiotherapy, 1994—; demonstrator in physiology Nishtar Hosp., 1989-92; co-rschr. Nishtar Hosp., Multan, 1995, prin. rschr. head and neck cancer, 1996. Contbr. articles to profl. jours. Mem. Cancer Soc. (life, edn. promotion sec. 1996). Avocations: listening to light music, reading, fine arts. Home: 7 Lawyers Colony, Khanewal Rd, Multan 60000, Pakistan Office: Nishtar Med Coll and Hosp, Nishtar Rd, Multan 60000, Pakistan

MASUDA, SUMIKO, language and literature educator; b. Nagoya, Aichi, Japan, Aug. 11, 1930; d. Yoshio and Shun Azuma; m. Ken-ichi Masuda, Mar. 26, 1966. MA, Keio U., Tokyo, 1965. Instr. Gifu Women's U., 1970-74, assoc. prof., 1974-82, prof., 1982-91, prof. emeritus, 1991—. Author: Tsurezuregusa-no-kokoro, 1989; contbr. numerous articles to publs.; author numerous studies. Mem. Soc. Japanese Lang. and Lit., Soc. Japanese Lit. in Mid. Ages, Soc. Arts. Home: 3-4-5 Ishiodai, Kasugai 487-0006, Japan

MASUJIMA, TOSHIYUKI, public administration educator; b. Tokyo, Mar. 29, 1936; s. Kanichi and Nuiko (Kobayashi) M.; m. Sugako Nishikubo, Mar. 14, 1939; 2 children. B of Law, Tokyo U., 1959. Dir. of mins. secretariat Mgmt. and Coordination Agy., Prime Mins. Office, Tokyo, 1984-85, dep. dir. gen. adminstrv. mgmt. bur. for info. systems, 1985-88, dep. dir. gen. adminstrv. mgmt. bur., 1988-90, dir. gen. of adminstrv. mgmt. bur., 1990-93, adminstrv. vice-min., 1993-94; prof. pub. adminstrn. Faculty of Policy Studies, Chuo U., Tokyo, 1995—, dean of grad. sch. policy studies, 1999—; councilor Chuo Univ., Tokyo, 1997—. Author: Perspectives of Adminstrative Managemnt, 1981, Perspectives of Adminstrative Reform, 1996; author, editor: The Management and Reform of Japanese Government, 2d edit., 1995. Chmn. Adv. Commn. for Adminstrv. Reform, Higashimurayama City, 1996—. Mem. Japanese Soc. for Pub. Adminstrn. (bd. dirs. 1990-98), Japan Soc. for Planning Adminstrn. (bd. dirs. 1992-98, auditor 1999—), Internat. Inst. of Adminstrv. Scis. (editl. com. 1982—), Pub. Policy Studies Assn. Lutheran. Avocations: Go, golf. Office: 742-1 Higashinakano, Hachioji-shi, Tokyo 192-0351, Japan

MASUM, MOHAMMED ABDULLAH-EL, microbiologist, researcher; b. Khulna, Bangladesh, Jan. 1, 1949; s. Mohammed Abdul Matin and Zainab Musammat Begum; m. Ziaun Nahar, Feb. 27, 1977; 3 children. MB, BS, Mymenshingh Med. Coll., Bangladesh, 1973; DPH, Royal Inst. Pub. Health and Hygiene, London, 1980; D Tropical Medicine and Hygiene, London Sch. Hygiene and Tropical Medicine, 1986, MSc in Med. Parasitology, 1986; PhD, London U., 1997. In-svc. trainee Mymenshingh Med. Coll. Hosp., 1973-74; Thana health adminstr. Ghatail, Tangail, Bangladesh, 1974-79; asst. surgeon Nat. Inst. Preventive & Social Medicine, Dhaka, Bangladesh, 1980-81, asst. prof. hosp. adminstrn., 1981-82, asst. prof. parasitology, 1982-87; sr. sci. officer in parasitology Inst. Epidemiology, Disease Control and Rsch., Dhaka, 1987—, prin. sci. officer, 1997—. Contbr. articles to med. jours., including Trans. Royal Soc. Tropical Medicine and Hygiene, Jour. Preventive and Social Medicine. Mem. Bangladesh Med. Assn. Avocations: reading, gardening, photography. Home: Gourhanga, Holding 56/A PO, Rajshahi Dist Ghoramara Bangladesh Office: Inst Epidemiology Disease, Control and Rsch, Mohakhali Dhaka 1212, Bangladesh

MASUMI, AHMAD EFTEKHARI, trading company executive; b. Tehran, Iran, Dec. 11, 1944; s. Asghar Eftekhari and Iran Eftekhari (Safarian) M. B of Engring., U. Tokyo, 1968, M of Engring., 1970; PhD in Computer Sci., U. Ill., 1973. Rsch. assoc. U. Ill., Urbana, 1970-73; cons. SONY, Tehran, Iran, 1974-80, Am. Electronic Labs., N.J., 1975-78, Taichi Corp., Tokyo, 1978-82; CEO, pres. Seian Corp., Tokyo, 1982—; cons. Fujitsu Ltd., Tokyo, 1984—; advisor Ministry of Higher Edn., Tehran, 1975-78. Scholarship Japanese Govt., 1962-70, Pahlavi Found., 1963-73; fellowship U. Ill., 1970-73. Mem. N.Y. Acad. Sci., Ill. Alumni Assn., U. Tokyo Alumni Assn., Elec./Info. Processing Socs. of Japan. Avocations: internet, philosophy of existence, verses, horses, travel. Home: Yoyogi West 301 29-2, Yoyogi 4-chome Shibuya-ku, Tokyo 151-0053, Japan Office: Seian Co Lions Mansion 1103, 14 Iwato-cho Shinjuku-ku, Tokyo 162-0832, Japan

MASUMI, TAIZO, physicist, educator, researcher; b. Kyushu, Japan, Mar. 31, 1932; s. Keizo and Kame (Masuda) M.; m. Taeko Mifune, Sept. 6, 1970; 1 child, Yuri. BS, U. Tokyo, 1954, MS in Engring., 1956, D Engring., 1959. Rsch. scientist Inst. Phys. and Chem. Rsch., Tokyo, 1959-64; rsch. assoc. U. Ill., Urbana, 1959-62; assoc. prof. U. Tokyo, 1964-77, prof., 1977-92; prof. emeritus, 1992—; prof. Gunma U., Japan, 1992-97; rsch. scientist Nat. Rsch. Inst. for Metals, Tsukuba, Japan, 1997—; vis. prof. U. Alta., Edmonton, Can., 1995; head Cryogenic Ctr., U. Tokyo, 1981-82, head course of coord. scis., 1979-81, 86-89, head dept. pure and applied scis., 1983-84; mem. program com. Internat. Conf. on Physics of Semicondrs., Kyoto, 1980, San Francisco, 1984, Stockholm, 1986, Beijing, 1992; mem. reviewing com. dept. materials sci. U. Tsukuba, Japan, 1994. Author: Quasi-Particle Physics in Condensed Matters, 1986; author, editor: Physics of Condensed Matters, 1997; editor-in-chief Jour. Phys. Soc. Japan, 1988-90; mem. regional editors Gordon & Breach Sci. Pub. Phase Transitions, 1985-96; 30 patents in field of superconductive optoelectronics. Fellow Nishina Meml. Found., 1959-60; Grantee specially disting. rsch. Ministry Edn., Sci. and Culture, Japan, 1989-92. Mem. Phys. Soc. Japan, Japan Soc. Applied Physics, Am. Phys. Soc. Avocations: music, arts. Home: 4-55-10 Utsukushiga-oka, Aoba-ku, Yokohama Kanagawa 225-0002, Japan Office: Nat Rsch Inst Metals, 1-2-1 Sengen, Tsukuba Ibaraki 305-0047, Japan

MASUMOTO, YASUAKI, physicist, educator; b. Hiroshima, Japan, Dec. 16, 1948; s. Toshio and Fumiko Masumoto; m. Sumiko Sato, Apr. 8, 1979; 3 children. BS, U. Tokyo, 1972, MS, 1974, ScD, 1977. Rsch. assoc. Inst. Solid State Physics, U. Tokyo, 1977-86; assoc. prof. Inst. Physics, U. Tsukuba, 1986-92, prof., 1992—; dir. Erato project Japan Sci. and Tech. Corp., Tsukuba, 1995—. Contbr. articles to profl. jours. Recipient IBM Sci. prize, 1992. Avocation: reading. Office: Inst Physics, Univ of Tsukuba, Tsukuba 305-8571, Japan

MASUNAGA, SHIGEKI, environmental science educator; b. Fukui, Japan, Aug. 16, 1952; s. Tamio and Kazuko M.; m. Yuko, Oct. 18, 1981; children: Nozomi, Shoko, Taiju. B Engring., U. Tokyo, 1975, M Engring., 1977, D Engring., 1980. Rschr. Nat. Rsch. Inst. Pollution and Resources, Tsukuba, Japan, 1980-85, sr. rschr., 1985-90; guest investigator Environ. Rsch. Lab., Athens, Ga., 1990-91; sr. rschr. Nat. Inst. Resources and Environment, Tsukuba, 1991-96; assoc. prof. Inst. Environ. Sci. and Tech. Yokohama (Japan) Nat. U., 1996-97, prof., 1997—; sr. assoc. NRC, Wash., 1990-91. Office: Yokohama Nat U Inst Environ Sci, 79-7 Tokiwadai Hodogaya-ku, Yokohama 240-8501, Japan

MASUNAGA, SHIN-ICHIRO, radiology educator, researcher; b. Osaka, Japan, Apr. 19, 1955; s. Morio and Reiko (Sasajima) M.; m. Ritsuko Hamano, Sept. 29, 1991. MD, Kyoto (Japan) U., 1983, PhD, 1991. Postdoctoral fellowship U. Rochester, N.Y., 1993-95; asst. prof. Kyoto U., Osaka, 1991-96, assoc. prof., 1996—. Office: Kyoto U Rsch Reactor Inst, Noda Kumatori-cho, Osaka 590-0494, Japan

MATA, ELIZABETH ADAMS, English language educator, land investor; b. Raleigh, N.C., Jan. 11, 1946; d. John Quincy Adams and Beulah Honeycutt; m. Juan Mata, June 21, 1968; children: Laura, Juan, Daniel. Student, Sweet Briar Coll., Paris, 1966-67; BA in French, Randolph-Macon Women's Coll., 1968; tchr. cert. in French and Spanish, N.C. State U., 1981; postgrad., U. Salamanca, Spain, 1983-86; MA in Spanish, NYU, 1986; cert. mentor tchr., N.C. State U., 1989; postgrad., Fordham U., 1994, U. N.C., 1991. Lic. real estate agt., N.C.; cert. ESL tchr. Tchr. ESL, Am. Inst., Madrid, 1968-69; tchr. English, Ay J Garriques, Madrid, 1968-74, pvt. classes, Madrid, 1975-78; tchr. French, Wake County Schs., Cary, N.C., 1982; tchr. Spanish, Wake County Schs., Apex, N.C., 1982-2000; instr. ESL Wake Tech. Coll., Raleigh, N.C., 1999-2000; chmn. sch. improvement team Wake County Schs., Apex, 1991-93. Named Tchr. of Yr., Apex H.S., 1992-93. Mem. Am. Assn. Tchrs. Spanish and Portuguese, Univ. Coun. on Edn., Alpha Kappa Delta (Beta Omicron chpt. historian 1996-98, v.p. 1998-2000). Democrat. Avocations: sculpting, reading, gourmet cooking, restoring antiques, writing. Home: 643 Kings Fork Rd Cary NC 27511-5711

MATALON, NORMA, travel and public relations executive; b. N.Y.C., Jan. 20, 1949; d. Albert and Suzanne Matalon. BA, Skidmore Coll., 1970. Cert. market mgmt., fin. mgmt. Am. Mgmt. Assn., computer automation. Cons., regional sales mgr. Revlon, N.Y.C., 1970-76; dir. sales, mktg. Diane Von Furstenberg Inc., N.Y.C., 1976-78; pres. Norma Matalon Cosmetic Cons., N.Y.C., 1978—, Norma Matalon Internat. Ltd., N.Y.C., 1982—; cons. to overseas cosmetic and fragrance cos., 1986—. Patentee in field. Com. mem., April in Paris Charities, 1976—, Project Hope, 1986—, United World Coll. Schs., 1983—, Northwood Inst., 1978—, Internat. Debutante Found. Charities, 1976—, Princess Grace Found. for Arts U.S., 1984—, Am. Cancer Soc., 1976—, raffle chmn., 1985, 86, 87. Recipient Outstanding Performance award Revlon, N.Y.C., 1972. Mem. Foreign Policy Assn., N.Y.C. (Nat. Adv. Bd. 1985—), The Fragrance Found., Am. Mgmt. Assn., The Foragers of Am., Newport Preservation Soc., Royal Oak Found., Royal Acad. Art, Royal Acad. Music, Met. Mus. Art, Mus. Modern Art, Whitney Mus. Unitarian. Clubs: The Lansdowne (London), The American (London); Cosmopolitan (N.Y.C.), St. Anthony (N.Y.C.), New Eng. (N.Y.C.), Regency Whist (N.Y.C.), The Tuxedo of N.Y., Annabel's (London). Avocations: travel, vol. fundraising, foreign languages. Home: 445 E 77th St New York NY 10021-2318

MATANI, ASHOK GURMUKHDAS, mechanical engineering educator; b. Amravati, India, Sept. 30, 1962; s. Gurmukhdas Ganesharam and Gurabai Gurmukhdas Matani; m. Aruna Ashok Haswani, Feb. 10, 1989; 1 child, Pallavi. B in Engring., Nagpur U., India, 1985; MBA, Amravati U., 1987, PhD, 1999, postgrad., 1999. Supr. Shriniwas Laddha Co., Amravati, 1985-87; jr. engr. Maharashtra State Electricty Bd., Mumbai, India, 1988-92; lectr. Govt. Poly., Amravati, 1992—; tng. and placement officer Govt. Poly., Amravati, 1995-96, coord., 1997—, lectr. I.I.I., 1997—; workshop supt. Govt. Poly., Khamgaon, India, 1996-97; presenter in field. Author: Automobile Manufacturing Systems, 1997, Refrigeration and Air Conditioning, 1997, Industrial Organization, Supervisory Management, 1997, CNC Machines, 1998; contbr. articles to profl. jours. Active Cancer Care Trust, Indore, India, 1995, Blind Welfare Assn., Amravati, 1997, Saibaba Temple Trust, Amravati, 1998, Jawahar Nehru Sports Stadium, Amravati, 1998. Mem. Indian Soc. for Tech. Edn. (life), Operational Rsch. Soc. India (life), Nat. Found. Engrs. (life), Inst. Stds. Engrs. (life), Inst. Engrs. India (life). Avocations: reading, writing, consulting, research, training. Home: 3rd Ln Dastur Nagar, Chhatri Talav Rd, Amravati 444606, India

MATARÉ, HERBERT F., physicist, consultant; b. Aachen, Germany, Sept. 22, 1912; came to U.S., 1953; s. Josef P. and Paula (Broicher) M.; m. Ursula Krenzien, Dec. 1939; children: Felicitas, Vitus; m. Elise Walbert, Dec. 1983; 1 child, Victor B. BS in Physics, Chemistry and Math., Aachen U. Geneva, 1933; MS in Tech. Physics, U. Aachen, 1939; PhD in Electronics, Tech. U. Berlin, 1942; PhD in Solid State Physics summa cum laude, Ecole Normale Supérieure, Paris, 1950. Asst. prof. physics & electronics Tech. U. Aachen, 1936, 45; head of microwave receiver lab. Telefunken, A.G., Berlin, 1939-46; mgr. semicondr. lab. Westinghouse, Paris, 1946-52; founder, pres. Intermetall Corp., Düsseldorf, Fed. Republic Germany, 1952-56; head semincondr. R & D, corp. rsch. labs. Gen. Telephone & Electronics Co., N.Y.C., 1956-59; dir. rsch. semicondr. dept. Tekade, Nürnberg, Fed. Republic Germany, 1959-61; head quantum physics dept. rsch. labs. Bendix Corp., Southfield, Mich., 1961-64; tech. dir., acting mgr. hybrid microelectronics rsch. labs. Lear Siegler, Santa Monica, Calif., 1963-64; asst. chief engr. advance electronics dept. Douglas Aircraft Co., Santa Monica, 1964-66; tech. dir. McDonnell Douglas Missile Div., 1964-69; sci. advisor to solid state electronics group Autonetics (Rockwell Internat.), Anaheim, Calif., 1966-69; pres. Internat. Solid State Electronics Cons., L.A., 1973—; prof. electronics U. Buenos Aires, 1953-54; vis. prof. UCLA, 1968-69, Calif. State U., Fullerton, 1969-70; dir. Compound Crystals Ltd., London, 1989—; cons. UN Indsl. Devel. Orgn. to 15 Indian insts. and semiconductor cos. with conf. talks at India Inst. Tech., New Delhi and Bombay, 1978. Author: Receiver Sensitivity in the UHF, 1951, Defect Electronics in Semiconductors, 1971, Conscientious Evolution, 1978, Energy, Facts and Future, 1989, (with P. Faber) Renewable Energies, 1993, Bioethics: The Ethics of Evolution and Genetic Interference, 1999; patentee of about 60 patents including first European transistor (1948), first vacuum growth of silicon crystals with levitation, growth of bicrystals, first low temperature transistor with bicrystals, optical heterodyning with bicrystals, first crystal TV transmission link, first color TV transmission over fiber with LEDs and bicrystals, liquid phase epitaxy for LEDs and batch process for III-V-solar cells; contbr. over 100 articles to profl. jours. Fellow IEEE (life); mem. AAAS, IEEE Nuclear Plasma Scis. Soc., IEEE Power Engring. Soc., Inst. for Advancement of Man (hon.), Am. Phys. Soc. (solid state div.), Electrochem. Soc., Am. Vacuum Soc. (thin film div.), Materials Rsch. Soc., N.Y. Acad. Scis. (emeritus). Avocations: astrophysics, biology, classical music, piano. Office: ISSEC PO Box 2661 Malibu CA 90265-7661

MATARINGA, MIHAELA IRINA, physician, neuropsychiatrist; b. Constanta, Constanta, Romania, May 9, 1964; d. Stefan and Maria (Marcu) Kivu; m. Mihail Mataringa, July 28, 1984; children: Mihai Alexandru. Physician, U. Medicine, Bucharest, Romania, 1988; Child and Adolescent Neuropsychiatrist, U. Medicine, 1994, postgrad. in psychiatry, 1997—. Physician U. Hosp., Constanta, Romania, 1988-90; child and adolescent neuropsychiatrist U. Hosp., Constanta, 1994—, Hosp. G.H. Marinescu, Bucharest, 1991-94; collaborator Glaxo-Wellcome, Romania, 1998—; intern dept. child and adolescent psychiatry Sophia Children's Hosp.-U. Erasmus, Rotterdam, The Netherlands, 1999. Contbr. articles to profl. jours. Mem. Internat. League Against Epilepsy, Internat. Child Neurology Assn., European Epilepsy Acad. Avocations: travel, art, music, computers. Home: Al Stejarului Nr I Bl G4, SC A ET I AP 8, 8700 Constanta Romania Office: U Hosp Constanta, B-Dul Tomis I45, Constanta 8700, Romania

MATASA, CLAUDE GEORGE, researcher, science administrator, educator; b. Romania, Apr. 1, 1930; s. George D. and Marguerite A. (Aurand) M.; m. Eugenia Tonca (div.); m. Netty Matasa. Chem. Engr., Polytechnic U., Bucharest, Romania, 1949-54, Polytechnic U., Timisoara, Romania, 1965-70; D in Tech. Sci., Polytechnic U., Vienna, Austria, 1970-72; D in Chem. Engring. (hon.), Ecologic U., Bucharest, 1994. Rsch. engr., sr. rsch. engr., head rsch. and devel. Chem. Combine of Craiova and the Synthetic Fibers Works of Savinesti, 1954-70; cons. Chem. Construction Corp., Corpus Christi, Tex., 1970-73; rsch. scientist Unitek Corp., Monrovia, Calif., 1973-76; chief rsch. chem. dept. Consol. Aluminum Corp. Sci. Ctr., St. Louis, 1977-79; chief rsch. Imperial Coatings Corp., New Orleans, 1979-82; pres. Ortho-Cycle Co., 1982—; prof. Univ., Bucharest, Romania, 1990, U. Ill., Chgo., 1995—, Nova Southeastern U., Fla., 1998—; cons., referee Am. Journal of Orthodontics and Dentofacial Orthopedics, Chgo., 1986—; lectr. M. Richter Courses for the Austrian, German, and Swiss orthodontists, U. Innsbruck, Austria, 1990; guest lectr., rsch. cons. David B. Kriser Dental Ctr., NYU, 1991; internat. cons. Journal of Orthopedics-Orthodontics and Pediatric Dentistry, Caracas, Venezuela, 1995; vis. prof. U. Pa., Phila., 1996-97; hon. vis. prof. Valahia U., Targovista, Romania. Author: 2 books; editor: The Orthodontic Materials Insider, 1987—; contbr. over 100 articles to profl. jours. Mem. AAAS, Am. Chem. Soc., Am. Soc. for Materials, Romanian-Am. Acad., Romanian Acad. Sci., Acad. Medicine of Romania (hon.). Home: 1507 Hollywood Blvd Hollywood FL 33020-5239 Office: Ortho-Cycle Co 2026 Scott St Hollywood FL 33020-2417

MATA-SEGREDA, JULIO F.R., chemistry educator; b. San José, Costa Rica, Aug. 3, 1948; s. Julio and Zelmira (Segreda) Mata; m. Luisa M. Diaz-Sánchez; children: Julio A., Priscilla, Nicolás, Maria Fernanda, Rebeca. Licenciate in chemistry, U. Costa Rica, 1971; PhD in Chemistry, U. Kans., 1975. Prof. chemistry U. Costa Rica, 1975—; cons. CEQSA, La Uruca, Costa Rica, 1994—. Recipient Nat. Sci. award Costa Rica, 1982. Mem. Costa Rican Coll. of Chemists, Am. Chem. Soc., Costa Rican Assn. History and Philosophy of Sci., Nat. Acad. Sci. Costa Rica. Achievements include research on agrochemical products developed and trade market for CEQSA Especialidades Quimicas, S.A., and Monsanto; patent on bromelain recovery. Office: U Costa Rica, Sch Chemistry, 2060 Costa Rica

MATASSINO, DONATO, animal geneticist; b. Ariano Irpino, Italy, Apr. 17, 1934; s. Raffaele Matassino and Giiovanna Sicuranza; m. Elvira Bruni, Sept. 27, 1971. Degree in agrl. scis., U. Naples, Italy, 1957. Asst. faculty agrl. scis. U. Naples, 1959-66, dep. tchr. spl. zootechnics, 1968-71, prof. spl. zootechnics, 1971-78, prof. gen. zootechnics, 1978-82, dir. dept. animal prodn., 1981-87, prof. gen. zootechnics and genetic improvement, 1992-95, prof. genetic improvement in livestock prodn., 1995—; v.p. biotech. and molecular biology com. Nat. Rsch. Coun., 1994—, pres. biotech. and molecular biology com., 1997—; pres. action group European Union Leader II Iniative for Devel. of Rural Economy, 1995—. Editor Animal Production jour., 1987; mem. editl. bd. numerous jours.; contbr. over 400 articles to profl. jours. Recipient Effeciency Oscar, 1970. Mem. AAAS, Sci. Assn. Animal Prodn. (pres. 1980-98), Soc. for Studies of Reproduction,Italian Soc. Agrl. Genetics, N.Y. Acad. Scis., Biometric Soc., Soc. Studies of Reproduction, European Assn. Embryonic Transfer. Home: ConSDABI, Azienda Casaldianni, 82020 Circello Italy Office: Sci Zootech Federico II, U Naples Via Universita 133, 80055 Portici Italy

MATEER, DON METZ, lawyer; b. Evanston, Ill., July 29, 1945; s. Bruce DeLoss and Ann (Timson) M.; m. Dawn Rebecca Hallsten, Oct. 4, 1981; children: Andrew, Alexandra; m. Jacquelyn Susan Henkin, June 7, 1969 (div. Apr. 1981); children: Kristin, Julie. BA, U. Mich., 1967; JD, U. Ill., 1971. Bar: Ill. 1971, U.S. Dist. Ct. (no. dist.) Ill. 1972, U.S. Ct. Appeals (7th cir.) 1974, U.S. Supreme Ct. 1981. Assoc. Gilbert & Powers, Rockford, Ill., 1971-74; ptnr. Gilbert, Powers & Mateer, Rockford, 1975, Gilbert, Powers, Mateer & Erickson, 1976, Mateer & Erickson, 1978-90, Mateer & Assocs., 1990—; arbitrator 17th Jud. Cir. State of Ill., 1988—, mediator, 1992—. Precinct and ward coord. mayoral campaign, Rockford, 1980-84; campaign chmn. Rockford Park Dist. Commr., 1989; bd. dirs. Covenant Children's Home, 1987-93, v.p. 1990-91, pres. 1991-93, chair 100 Hole Golf Marathon fundraiser, 1994-98, mem. fund devel. com., 1994-99, mem. investment adv. com., 1996—; mem. Protestant Cmty. Svcs., 1986-92, chmn. pers. com. 1987-89, v.p. 1989-90, pres. 1990-92; mem. Bethesda Covenant Ch., chmn. bd. Christian edn., 1986-88, v.p. 1997-99, pres. 1999—. Mem. ABA (vice chair trial techniques com. tort and ins. practice sect., judge for final rounds of the nat. appellate adv. competition, 1991), Am. Arbitration Assn. (arbitrator), Winnebago County Bar Assn. (chmn. jud. liaison com. 1986-87), Ill. Bar Assn. (assembly mem. 1988-94), Assn. Trial Lawyers, Am. Def. Rsch. Inst., Ill. Def. Counsel, Am. Judicature Soc., Forest Hills Country Club, U. Mich. Club (bd. dirs. 1986-92, 98—, v.p. 1989-90, 98-99, pres. 1990-91, 1999-2000). Democrat. Home: 2006 Oxford St Rockford IL 61103-4833 Office: Mateer & Assocs Enterprise Bldg 401 W State St Ste 400 Rockford IL 61101-1240

MATEEV, VLADIMIR MATEEV, physicist, educator; b. Rousse, Bulgaria, Apr. 10, 1958; s. Matei Goergiev and Ivanka Marinova (Vytova) m.; m. Svetoslava Petkova Georgieva, Oct. 14, 1989; 1 child, Joana Vladimirova. MS in Physics, St. Kliment Ohridski U., 1984. Researcher dept. metal sci. Tech. Tech. U., Rousse, Bulgaria, 1985-86; rsch. scientist Ctrl. Lab. Optical Storage & Processing Info Bulgarian Acad. Scis., 1987-91; asst. prof. Dept. Physics Tech. U., Rousse, 1992—. Inventor in field; contbr. articles to profl. jours. Mem. Union Physicists in Bulgaria. Avocations: reading, running, music, cinema, mountain touring. Home: 1 Jundola St, BG 7005 Rousse Bulgaria Office: Tech Univ Rousse, 8 Studentska St, BG 7017 Rousse Bulgaria

MATEJCEK, ZDENEK, child psychologist, researcher; b. Chlumec, Czech Republic, Aug. 16, 1922; s. Jaroslav and Vlasta (Janska) M.; m. Jaroslava Zizkova, Mar. 5, 1931; children: Jarmila, Jana, Zdenek. PhD, Charles U., Prague, 1951, CSc, 1970, Doc, 1977; Dr.h.c., U Sask., Can., 1991, Prof., 1994. Clin. psychologist Sociodiagnostic Inst., Prague, 1950-53, Child Psychiatry, Prague, 1953-69; tchr./rschr. Postgrad. Med. Inst., Prague, 1969-91; rschr. Psychiat. Ctr., Prague, 1991—; lectr. Charles U., 1957—; clin. psychologist Child Ctr. Paprsek, Prague, 1994—. Contbr. articles to profl. jours. Pres. Czech Com. for UNICEF, 1990-91. Recipient First Internat. award Orton Dyslexia Soc., 1991, medal for merits Pres. of Czech Republic, 1996. Mem. Internat. Acad. for Rsch. in Learning Disabilities (sec. 1989-97), N.Y. Acad. Scis., German Pediat. Soc. (hon.), Polish Dyslexia Assn. (hon.), Czech Psychol. Soc. (hon.). Avocations: gardening, fishing, hunting, bee-keeping, travel. Fax: 420 2 22 51 22 83. Home: Kubanske nam 24, 100 00 Prague Czech Republic Office: Psychiat Ctr Prague, Londynska 45, 120 00 Prague Czech Republic

MATĚJKA, PAVEL, chemist, researcher, educator; b. Louny, Czechoslovakia, June 30, 1966; s. Josef and Ludmila (Hrodková) M.; m. Stanislava Brčáková, July 19, 1991; children: Kristina, Filip. Rerum Naturalis Doctor, Charles U., Prague, Czech Republic, 1989, PhD, 1994. Sr. lectr.-rschr. dept. analytical chemistry Inst. Chem. Tech., Prague, 1993—; mem. senate of the faculty of sci. Charles U., Prague, 1990-92; PhD fellow U. Amsterdam, The Netherlands, 1991; post-doctoral felllow Lasir CNRS, Thiais, France, 1996. Contbr. articles to profl. jours. Mem. Spectroscopic Soc. J.M. Marci (Young Spectroscopist award 1992), Czech Chem. Soc. Roman Catholic. Avocations: amateur photography, music. Home: Nad Kesnerkou 5, 150 00 Prague 5, Czech Republic Office: Inst Chem Tech, Technická 5, 166 28 Prague 6, Czech Republic

MATELAN, MATHEW NICHOLAS, software engineer; b. Stephenville, Tex., Aug. 21, 1945; s. Mathew Albert and Mary Frances (Hardwick) M.; m. Lois Margaret Waguespack, Apr. 5, 1975; children: Evelyn Nicole, Eleanor Gillian. BS in Physics, U. Tex., Arlington, 1969; MS in Computer Engring., So. Meth. U., 1973, PhD in Computer Sci., 1976. Sr. aerospace engr. Gen. Dynamics, Ft. Worth, 1969-75; sys. engr. Lawrence Livermore (Calif.) Labs., 1975-76; group mgr. Gen. Dynamics, Ft. Worth, 1976-78; computer R&D mgr. United Techs./Mostek, Carrollton, Tex., 1978-82; chief sys. arch. Honeywell Comm., Dallas, 1982-83; pres., CEO, chmn., co-founder Flexible Computer Corp., Dallas, 1983-90; chief arch. Matelan Software Sys., Dallas, 1991-94; chief engr. Expertware, Santa Clara, Calif., 1991-94; chief tech. officer Learn Techs. Interactive, N.Y.C., 1994—; cons. Bendix Flight Controls Divsn., Teterboro, N.J., 1974-75; founding dir. Picture Telephone, Boston, 1984-86, Spectrum Digital, Washington, 1984-86; adv. bd. Axavision, N.Y.C., 1993—. Contbr. articles to profl. jours. Libr. automation bd. So. Meth. U., Dallas, 1985-86. Devel. grantee U.S. Energy Dept., 1975, NASA, 1985. Mem. IEEE (sr. mem.), Assn. for Computing Machinery. Avocations: traveling, music, skiing, aviation. Home: 3969 Courtshire Dr Dallas TX 75229-2732 Office: Learn Techs Interactive 3530 Forest Ln Ste 61 Dallas TX 75234-7950

MATEO-DE-ACOSTA, OSCAR, research institute director; b. Ciudad Habana, Cuba, Aug. 19, 1927; s. Oscar and Aracely (Fernandez) M.; children: Oscar Luis, Cristina, Carlos; m. Nieves Andino; 1 child, David Antonio. MD, Havana U. Sch. Medicine, 1951, DSc, 1981. Resident U. Hosp. Calixto Garcia, Habana, 1951-55; instr. Havana U. Sch. of Medicine, Habana, 1959; dir. Lila Hidalgo Hosp., 1959; dir. Med. Edn. and Pub. Health Sch., Habana, 1959-62, dir. med. sci. edn. and postgrad. studies, 1963; dir. dept. of endocrinology Cmote Fajardo Hosp., Habana, 1964-65; dir. Nat. Inst. of Endocrinology, Habana, 1966—; sec. Scientific Coun. of MPH, Habana, 1973-83; cons. nat. rsch. dpet., 1973-80; mem. adv. coun. Min. of Pub. Health, 1977-80; mem. steering com. of task force on infertility HRP/WHO, Geneva, 1978-86; mem. steering com. on diabetes in developing countries WHO/IDF, Geneva, 1981. Author: Manual de Diagnosti Tratamiento Enfermedades Endocrinas, 1985, Lo Que Todo Diabetico Debe Saber, 1989, Diabetes Mellitus: Conceptos Fundamentales, 1968; editor: Normas de Diagnostico y Tratamiento en Endocrinologia, 1981, 2d edit., 1985; editor Revista Cubana de Endocrinologia, 1989. Recipient Carlos J. Finlay award Acad. of Scis., 1991, Paho Prize in Health Adminstrn. Paho-XXXV Directive Coun., 1991. Office: Inst Nacional Endocrinol Hosp Fajardo, Zapata y D, 10400 Habana 4 Cuba

MATERNA, JOSEPH ANTHONY, lawyer; b. Passaic, N.J., June 13, 1947; s. Anthony E. and Peggy Ann Materna; m. Dolores Corio, Dec. 14, 1975; children: Jodi, Jennifer, Janine. BA, Columbia U., 1969, JD, 1973. Bar: N.Y. 1975, Fla. 1977, U.S. Dist. Ct. (ea. and so. dists.) N.Y. 1977, U.S. Supreme Ct. 1977, U.S. Tax Ct. 1978, U.S. Ct. of Claims 1978. Trusts and

estates atty. Chadbourne Parke Whiteside & Wolff, N.Y.C., 1973-76, Dreyer & Traub, N.Y.C., 1976-80, Finley Kumble Wagner Heine Underberg & Casey, N.Y.C., 1980-85; ptnr., head trusts and estates dept. Newman Tannenbaum Helpern Syracuse & Hirschtritt, N.Y.C., 1985-90, Shapiro Beilly Rosenberg Aronowitz Levy & Fox LLP, N.Y.C., 1990—; lectr. in field; expert witness in trusts and estate field ct. litigations, N.Y., 1999—. Contbr. articles to profl. jours. Chmn. planned giving com., mem. bd. govs. Arthritis Found. N.Y. Chpt., N.Y.C., 1980—; mem. bd. trustees, corp. treas. Cath. Interracial Coun., N.Y.C., 1992—; mem. bequests and planned gifts com. Cath. Archdiocese of N.Y., N.Y.C., 1988—; corp. sec. Arthritis Found. N.Y. chpt., N.Y.C., 1997—; mem. Meml. Sloan-Kettering Nat. Trusts and Estates Assocs. Recipient Planned Giving award Arthritis Found.-N.Y. Chpt., N.Y.C., 1994, Discovery Alliance award Arthritis Found.-N.Y. Chpt., N.Y.C., 1995; named Accredited Estate Planner, Nat. Assn. Estate Planners, Marietta, Ga., 1995. Mem. ABA, Fla. Bar (trusts and estate com.), N.Y. State Bar Assn. (com. on estates and trusts), Bar Assn. of the City of N.Y. (com. on surrogate's ct.), N.Y.C. Estate Planning Coun. (lectr., author), N.Y. County Lawyers Assn. (mem. com. on trusts and estates 1979—), Queen County Bar Assn. (mem. com. trusts and estates 1990—), Am. Judges Assn. (civil ct. arbitrator N.Y.C.), Am. Arbitration Assn. (panel of arbitrators), N.Y. State Trial Lawyers Assn., Richmond County Bar Assn. (com. on surrogates ct.), Columbia Coll. Alumni Assn. of Columbia U. (class pres. 1969—). Republican. Roman Catholic. Home: 155 Johanna Ln Staten Island NY 10309-3604 Office: Shapiro Beilly Rosenberg Aronowitz Levy & Fox LLP 225 Broadway New York NY 10007-3001

MATERNA, PETR JAN, air navigation services administrator; b. Prague, Czechoslovakia, Dec. 26, 1942; s. Jaroslav and Antonie (Holečková) M.; m. Miroslava Vlasta Hrudová, Jan. 30, 1975; children: Petr, Ondřej. Grad. in Elec. Engring., Czech Tech. U., Prague, 1966; postgrad., U. Transport, Zilina, Slovak Republic, 1981-83. Field engr. Air Traffic Control Adminstrn., Prague, 1973-76, chief navaids maintenance, 1977-85, head systems dept., 1985-91; v.p. Computers-Info.-Comm., Prague, 1991-92; dir. gen. Air Traffic Control Adminstrn./Air Navigation Svc. Czech Republic, Prague, 1992—. Recipient Laurel, Aviation Week & Space Tech., 1994. Mem. Lions Club. Avocation: radio amateur (call sign-OK1DMA). Office: Air Navigation Svcs, K Letisti 1040/10 PO Box 41, 160 08 Praha 6, Czech Republic

MATERSON, RICHARD STEPHEN, physician, educator; b. Phila., Feb. 11, 1941; s. Alfred Lawrence and June Eileen (Slakoff) M.; m. Rosa Maria Navarro, Aug. 22, 1964; children: Lisa Gail, Lawrence Mark. MD, U. Miami, Coral Gables, Fla., 1965. Diplomate Am. Bd. Phys. Medicine and Rehab. Intern Walter Reed Gen. Hosp., Washington, 1965-66; resident Letterman Gen. Hosp., San Francisco, 1966-68; chief phys. medicine and rehab. Tripler Gen. Hosp., Honolulu, 1968-72; asst. prof. phys. medicine and rehab. Ohio State U., Columbus, 1972-76; assoc. clin. prof. phys. medicine and rehab. Baylor Coll. Medicine, Houston, 1976-93, prof., 1997—; pres. Materson MD, PA, Houston, 1976—; sr. v.p. for med. affairs, med. dir. Nat. Rehab. Hosp., Washington, 1990-96; prof. neurology George Washington U. Med. Ctr., Washington, 1994-97; med. v.p. Meml. Healthcare Sys., Houston, 1997—; prof. phys. medicine and rehab. U. Tex. Health Sci. Ctr., Houston, 1997—; fellow Kaiser Inst., 1999; chief med. officer Meml. Hermann Continuing Care Corp., 2000—; med. dir. Dept. Phys. Medicine and Rehab., Meml. Hosp. SE, Houston, 1978-90, Ctr. for Sports Medicine and Rehab., 1987-90, Electromyography Lab., 1978-90; faculty Kaiser Inst., 2000—. Co-author: Physical Medicine and Rehabilitation, 1977, 2d rev. edit., 1980, The Practice of Rehabilitation Medicine, 1982; co-editor: Management of Persons with Stroke, 1993; co-editor, author: The Non Surgical Management of Acute Low Back Pain, 1997, Pain Management, 1998; contbg. author: Practice of Medicine, 1978. Trustee Meml. Hosp. System, Houston, 1986-90, Nat. Rehab. Hosp., Washington, 1990-96; host family Experiment in Internat. Living, 1985, 86, 87. Served to maj. U.S. Army, 1965-72. Fellow Am. Acad. Phys. Medicine and Rehab. (pres. 1986-87, Distng. Pub. Svc. award, 1992, Walter J. Zeiter lectr., 1994), Am. Assn. Electrodiagnostic Medicine; mem. AMA (del. 1978-93), Phys. Medicine and Rehab. Edn. and Rsch. Found. (founder, pres. 1982-90, bd. dirs. 1983—), Houston Acad. Phys. Medicine and Rehab. (pres. 1979-80), Am. Acad. Pain Mgmt. (chmn. bd. advisors 1989-90, mem. bd. advisors 1990—), Internat. Wine and Food Soc., Knights of Vine (master comdr. 1982—), Confrerie des Chevaliers du Tastevin, Chaine des Rotisseurs. Jewish.

MATES, ABRAHAM, microbiologist, immunologist; b. Iasi, Moldava, Romania, July 16, 1936; arrived in Israel, 1951; s. David and Adela Mates; m. Zipora Fishler, Jan. 12, 1944; children: Mali, David, Alon. BSc, Bar Ilan U., Ramat-Gan, Israel, 1962, MSc, 1963; PhD, Queen's U., Kingston, Ont., Can., 1966; MPh, Hebrew U., Jerusalem, 1983. Lectr. Bar Ilan U., Ramat Gan, 1967-75; dir. lab. Poria Hosp., Tiberias, Israel, 1975-79; dir. lab. Pub. Health Lab., Haifa, Israel, 1979-88, Tel-Aviv, 1988-90; dir. dept. lab. Ministry of Health, Jerusalem, 1990—. Ford of Can. Postdoctoral fellow, 1966-67. Home: 15 Tabenkin St, 53202 Ramat-Gan Israel Office: Ministry Health Dept Labs, 9 Yakov Eliar St, 94467 Jerusalem Israel

MATES, ROBERT EDWARD, mechanical engineering educator; b. Buffalo, May 19, 1935; s. Cyril S. and Ruth Elizabeth (Dougan) M.; m. Gail Paxson, June 5, 1960; children: Robert E., Elisabeth, Steven,. BS, U. Rochester, 1957; MS, Cornell U., 1959, PhD, 1963. Instr. Cornell U., Ithaca, N.Y., 1958-61; asst. prof. SUNY, Buffalo, 1962-65, assoc. prof., 1965-69, chmn. mech. and aero. engring., 1967-70, 79-82, prof. mech. engring., 1969-97, dir. Ctr. Biomed. Engring., 1989-96, prof. emeritus, 1997—. Editor various symposium proceedings; contbr. articles to profl. jours. NIH spl. rsch. fellow, 1970-71, 78-79, H.R. Lissner award Am. Soc of Mechanical Engineers, 1995. Fellow ASME (chmn. winter ann. meeting com. 1989-93, mem.-at-large bd. comm. 1988-93, v.p. bd. comm. 1994-98), Am. Inst. for Med. and Biol. Engring. (founding, chmn. acad. coun. 1996-97); mem. AAUP, Biomed. Engring. Soc. (bd. dirs. 1991-94, chmn. awards com. 1991-92, mem. pub. bd. 1992-94), Am. Soc. Engring. Edn.

MATESKY, ELISABETH ANNE, international solo violinist, educator, composer; b. L.A., Oct. 1, 1946; d. Ralph and Betty (Blumberg) M.; m. Allen Leslie Odens, Feb. 18, 1973 (div. Nov. 1979). MusB in Violin Performance, U. So. Calif., 1964; pvt. study, with Nathan Milstein, London, 1969-71. Artist in residence in violin Syracuse (N.Y.) U., 1971-72; concertmaster Syracuse Symphony Orch., 1971-72; violinist Chgo. Symphony Orch., 1972-73; concertmaster Rockford Symphony Ill., 1981-86; artist tchr. violin, chmn. dept. string Am. Conservatory Music, Chgo., 1986-91; spl. lectr. in violin Chgo. Musical Coll., 1991-93; in residency artist Trinity Coll. Music, London, 1996—; mistress ceremonies Stradivari Soc. Concert Series, Chgo., 1993—; entrepreneur young artists concerts, London, 1994—; mem. bd. patrons Sascha Lasserson Meml. Trust, London, 1996—; guest tchr., performer Sibelius Acad. Music, Helsinki, 1999. Writer The Strad Mag., Asta Jour., Sun-Scandinavia Newspaper; interviewer Internat. Young Artists; guest artist Ravinia Music Festival; guest soloist Grant Park Music Festival; violinist, student (film) Heifetz Master Class: Elisabeth Matesky in Khachaturian Violin Concerto, 1963; rec. artist BBC of various concertos and recitals, 1967—; solo violinist, artist (TV London film) Grace Under Pressure, 1970-71; dedicatee (PBS TV concert) Bradshaw Violin Concerto, 1981; violinist (TV comml.) Sta. WFMT Radio, 1985 (1st prize N.Y. TV Comml. 1986); guest violinist Salte to My Teachers: Heifetz & Milstein, 1995; artist tchr. (film) Elisabeth Matesky Violin & Chamber Music Master Classes at Trinity College of Music, 1996. Guest violinist at State Dinner with Pres. Jimmy Carter, White House, Washington, 1977. Named Woman of the Yr. Syracuse Jour. Newspaper, 1971; Fulbright scholar Royal Coll. Music, London, 1964-65, 65-66; NEA grantee Sacramento Symphony Orch., 1979-80. Mem. Fulbright Alumni Assn. (honoree 1996), Am. String Tchrs. Assn., Chgo. Symphony Alumni Assn. Home: 215 E Chestnut St Apt 1803 Chicago IL 60611-6712

MATH, MILJENKO DINO, mechanical engineering educator, researcher; b. Zagreb, Croatia, Jan. 8, 1949; s. Donat and Blanka Katarina (Gottlieb) M.; m. Ana Dumbović, Apr. 1, 1978; children: Donat, Dino. BSc, Faculty Mech. Engring., Zagreb, 1974, MSc, 1981, PhD, 1990. Asst. Faculty Naval Engring. & Naval Architecture, 1974-82, sci. asst., 1982-92, asst. prof., 1992-97, assoc. prof., 1997—. Author: Theory of Metal Forming Processes, 1996, Introduction to Metal Forming, 1997. Roman Catholic. Home: Bogišićeva 4, 10000 Zagreb Croatia Office: Faculty Mech Engring, 1 Lučića 5, 10000 Zagreb Croatia

MATHAI, GEORGE K., monitoring and evaluation expert, consultant; b. Cochin, Kerala, India, Sept. 21, 1943; s. K. Varghese and Aleyamma John Mathai; m. Isabella K. George, Nov. 6, 1976. BA, Kerala U., 1967; MA, S.P. U., Gujarat, India, 1970; PhD in Econs., Ranchi U., India, 1983. Rsch. asst. Bombay U., 1970-74; economist Dairy Bd., Gujarat, 1974-78; planning officer Bank of Baroda, India, 1978-81; sr. mgr. evaluation Punjab Nat. Bank, Delhi, India, 1981-90; chief monitoring and evaluation Govt. of Papua New Guinea, 1990-92; monitoring and evaluation cons. Asian Devel. Bank, Papua New Guinea, 1992-95; dir. Agrl. Gender & Environ. Adv. Svcs., India, 1994—; dir. Cratpaw, Delhi, 1985-90. Author: An Evaluation of Rural Development Projects, 1988, Rural Development: A Story of Roots, 1994; contbr. articles to profl. jours. Active YMCA, Delhi, 1981-90. Recipient fellowships. Mem. Indian Orthodox Ch. Avocations: photography, travel, eco-tourism, medicinal plants. E-mail: ages 1999@yahoo.com. Office: AGES Dir, Melmana Ave, 686 730 Kochi Kerala, India

MATHAISEL, DENNIS F.X., aeronautical engineering educator; b. Boston; m. Clare L. Comm. BS, Northeastern U.; MS, U. Calif., Irvine; PhD, MIT. Br. mgr. ops. rsch. McDonnell Douglas, Long Beach, Calif., 1970-76; postdoctoral rschr. MIT, Cambridge, Mass., 1980-84, rsch. scientist, 1984—; prof. Babson Coll., Babson Park, Mass., 1984—. Office: Babson College Babson Hall Babson Park MA 02457

MATHENY, CHARLES WOODBURN, JR., former army officer, civil engineer, city official; b. Sarasota, Fla., Aug. 7, 1914; s. Charles Woodburn Sr. and Virginia (Yates) M.; m. Jeanne Felkel, July 12, 1942; children: Virginia Ann, Nancy Caroline, Charles Woodburn III. BSCE, U. Fla., 1936; grad., Army Command Gen. Staff Coll., 1944. Lic. comml. pilot; lic. civil engr., surveyor, Ga. Sanitary engr. Ga. State Dept. Health, 1937-39; civil engr. Fla. East Coast Ry., 1939-41; commd. 2d lt. F.A., USAR, 1936; 1st lt. FA, USAR, 1939; 2d. lt., vol. active army svc. FA, US Army, 1942; advanced through grades to col. F.A., USAR, 1955; comdr. 351st Field Arty. Bn., 1945; commr. 33rd Field Arty. Bn., 1st Infantry Divsn., 1946, artillery staff officer, 1947; gen. staff G-3 Plans Dept. Army, 1948-51; qualified Air Force liaison pilot, 1951, qualified Army aviator airplanes and helicopters, 1952; aviation officer 25th Infantry Divsn., Korea, 1952-53; sr. Army aviation advisor Korean Army, 1953; first dir. combat devel. dept. first dep. commandant Army Aviation Sch., Ft. Sill, Okla., 1954-55; dep. dir. rsch., dep. dir. dept. tactics U.S. Army Field Arty. and Missile Sch., Ft. Sill, 1955-57; aviation officer 7th U.S. Army, Germany, 1957-58; Munich sub area comdr. So. Area Command, Europe, 1958-59; qualified sr. army aviator, 1959; dep. chief of staff for info. So. Area Command, 1960; Mich. sector comdr. VI Army Corps., 1961-62, ret., 1962; asst. dir. Tampa (Fla.) Dept. Pub. Works, 1963-81, ret., 1981; During World War II, Germany Commd., 351st field artillery Battalion in combat and occupation, 1945, also 33d field artillery battalion, 1st Infantry Divsn., in occupation, 1946. Initiator and originator of tactical use of helicopters in Army, Army warrant officer helicopter aviator program and organization of first five Army Transp. Helicopter Co. 1949, army combat units equipped with helicopter mobility, 1950; initiated and prepared directive signed by Army chief of staff, Gen. J. Lawton Collins ordering first feasibility tests of Army super-mobile inf. and artillery units equipped with helicopter mobility, 1951; pilot 1st combat observation mission in army helicopter, Korea, 1952; organizer, comdr., helicopter pilot 1st Army combat ops. using helicopter mobility to support inf. and engr. front line combat units 25th Inf. Div., Korea, 1952 proving feasibility of Army helicopter mobility on the battlefield; 1st to advocate, perform and rsch., prepare orgn. plans and design of super-mobile Army combat units equipped with armed and unarmed helicopter mobility, with model designs of helicopters armed with missiles, rockets, etc. to equip proposed units, 1955-56; 1st to urge Army to develop a high performance observation and reconnaissance helicopter, 1957; pilot 100 combat observation missions, Korea, 1952-53; author 1st state legis. to establish profl. sch. civil engring. for state of Fla., 1974; mem. U.S. Army's Strategic Planning Com., 1950-51. Contbr. numerous articles on tactical use of helicopter aerial vehicles, also need for profl. shc. for civil engring. to mags., 1950-80. Mem. troop com. Boy Scouts Am., 1965-73; active various cmty. and ch. activities; patron Tampa Art Mus., 1965-83, Tampa Cmty. Concert Series, 1979-82; bd. dirs. Tampa YMCA, 1967-71, Fla. Easter Seal Soc., 1978, Easter Seal Soc. Hillsborough County, 1971-84, hon. bd. dirs., 1984-95, treas., 1973-76, pres., 1977. Decorated Bronze Star with oak leaf cluster, Air medal with three oak leaf clusters; recipient of the Eagle Scout award, 1928; named to U. Fla. Student Hall of Fame, 1936. Mem. ASCE (pres. West Coast br., dir. Fla. sect. 1973, Engr. of Yr. award West Coast br. Fla. sect. 1979, life mem. 1980), Am. Soc. Profl. Engrs., Fla. Engring. Soc., Am. Pub. Works Assn. (pres. West Coast br. Fla. chpt. 1972, exec. com. Fla. chpt. 1972-77, v.p. 1977, pres. 1978), Ret. Officers Assn., Army Aviation Assn., SAR, Fla. Blue Key, Alpha Tau Omega, Sigma Tau. Episcopalian. Home: 2519 Surf Rd Panacea FL 32346-2641 Office: VAMC 915 N Grand Blvd Saint Louis MO 63106-1621

MATHER, GEORGE ROSS, clergy member; b. Trenton, N.J., June 1, 1930; s. Samuel Wooley and Henrietta Elizabeth (Deardorff) M.; m. Doris Christine Anderson, June 28, 1958; children: Catherine Anne Mather-Grimes, Geoffrey Thomas. BA, Princeton U., 1952; MDiv, Princeton Theol. Sem., 1955; DD, Hanover Coll., 1986. Ordained to Ministry, 1955. Asst. pastor Abington (Pa.) Presbyn., 1955-58; pastor 1st Presbyn. Ch. Ewing, Trenton, 1958-71; sr. pastor 1st Presbyn. Ch. Ft. Wayne, Ind., 1971-86; pastor 3d Presbyn. Ch. Ft. Wayne, Ind., 1987-95. Author: Frontier Faith: The Story of the Pioneer Congregations, 1992; co-editor: On the Heritage Trail, 1994; contbr. articles to profl. jours. Pres. Allen County Libr. Trustees, Ft. Wayne, Allen County Libr. Found., Ft. Wayne, Clergy United for Action, Ft. Wayne; trustee Hanover (Ind.) Coll.; chmn. Bicentennial Religious Heritage Commn., 1994; bd. dirs. Smock Found., 1971-85. Mem. Ind. Religious History Assn. (bd. dirs.), Allen County Ft. Wayne Hist. Soc. (bd. dirs.), The Quest Club (pres.). Avocations: tennis, travel, hiking, canoeing. Home: 6726 Quail Ridge Ln Fort Wayne IN 46804-2874

MATHER, RUTH ELSIE, writer; b. Waverly, Wash., Feb. 14, 1934; d. James Orrin and Leona Ezthelda (Mather) Tallman; m. Mike Nicholas Dakis, Apr. 20, 1958 (div. Nov. 1971); children: Cynthia Michelle, Martin Nicholas; m. Fred Junior Morgan, Nov. 20, 1971. BA with highest honors, Brigham Young U., 1961, MA, 1965; postgrad., U. Miss., 1977-78. Cert. secondary tchr., Idaho, cert. elem. tchr. and secondary tchr. grades 7-14, Calif. English tchr. Iglesia Jesucristo Rama Roma, Mexico City, 1955-56, Lemhi County Schs., Leadore, Idaho, 1962-66; English instr. Yonsei U., Seoul, Republic of Korea, 1973-74, U. Md. Far East Divsn., Seoul, 1975-77, Boise (Idaho) State U., 1978-79, Coll. of the Redwoods, Eureka, Calif., 1980-81; writer hist. video scripts History West Pub. Co., Oklahoma City, 1990—; screenwriter Frontier Images, Canyon Country, Calif., 1994—; cons. on hist. video for PBS, A La Carte, San Francisco, 1994-95; guest expert on Secrets of the Gold Rush-PBS, 1995; cons. Western Mont. Coll. Schmittroth collection of electronically printed Western history books, Dillon, 1997—. Author: Hanging the Sheriff: A Biography of Henry Plummer, 1987, John David Borthwick: Artist of the Gold Rush, 1989, Gold Camp Desperadoes: Study of Crime & Punishment on Frontier, 1990, Vigilante Victims, 1991, Scandal of the West: Domestic Violence on the Frontier, 1998, The Bannack Gallows, 1998, The Cottonwood Murders: Unsolved, 1999; contbr. short stories, book revs., articles to encys. and profl. jours. Local campaign dir. Dem. Party, Arcata, Calif., 1969-70. Mem. Nat. Outlaw and Lawman Assn., Western Outlaw and Lawman Assn., Virginia City Preservation Alliance, People for the Ethical Treatment of Animals, Nat. Anti-Vivisection Soc., Physicians' Com. for Responsible Medicine. Avocations: reading, hiking. Office: History West Pub Co PO Box 23133 Oklahoma City OK 73123-2133

MATHES, EDWARD CONRAD, architect; b. New Orleans, Mar. 10, 1943; s. Earl L. and Margaret (Gash) M.; m. Anne M. Ergenbright, Mar. 1, 1964; children: Margaret Elizabeth Hughes, Anne Catherine. BArch, U. Southwestern La., 1968. Registered arch., La., Miss., Fla., Tex., Ala., Tenn., Ky., N.C., W.Va., Conn. Tchr. U. Southwestern La., Lafayette, 1968-69; asst. to mng. arch. Rogers, Taliaferro, Kostritsky & Lamb, Balt., 1969; pres. Mathes, Bergman & Assocs., Inc., New Orleans, 1969-82, The Mathes Group, New Orleans, 1982—. Chmn. Orleans Svc. Ctr., ARC, 1993-94; bd. dirs. City Park Improvement Assn., 1996—, pres.-elect. Recipient Am. Sch. and Univ. award 1983, 85, Honor award La. Archs. Assn., New Orleans, 1982, 86, Partnership award ARC, 1998, CEO's award S.E. La. chpt. ARC, Peoples Choice award for music, comms., theatre complex, Loyola New Orleans, 1989, People's Choice award for univ. libr., 1999, 2000. Mem. AIA (Inst. scholar 1968-69, honor award New Orleans chpt. 1982, 89, pres. 1989), Constrn. Industry Assn. (pres. 1984-85, Honor award 1993), Pickwick Club, Metairie Country Club, City Energy Club, Rotary (pres. New Orleans 1985-86). Republican. Presbyterian. Avocations: tennis, travel. Home: # 4 Park Island Dr New Orleans LA 70122 Office: The Mathes Group 201 Saint Charles Ave Fl 41 New Orleans LA 70170-1000

MATHESON, ANN, librarian, writer; b. Lochalsh, Wester Ross, Scotland, July 5, 1940; d. Alexander and Catherine (MacRae) M.; m. T. Russell Walker, Nov. 24, 1973. MA, U. St. Andrews, 1962; Diploma in Scottish Studies, U. Edinburgh, 1968, MLitt, 1970, PhD, 1979; Order of the Brit. Empire, 1998; DLitt, St. And, 1999. Asst. keeper Nat. Libr. Scotland, Edinburgh, 1975-82, keeper, 1983—; gen. sec. Ligue des Bibliothèques Européennes de Recherche, 1994—. Author: (with Mary Ferguson) The Scottish Gaelic Union Catalogue, vol. I, 1984, Theories of Rhetoric in the 18th-century Scottish Sermon, 1995; editor: (with Patrick Cadell) For the Encouragement of Learning, 1989; editor Transactions of the Edinburgh Bibliographical Society, 1973-83; contbr. articles and revs. to profl. jours. Decorated Order Brit. Empire. Home: Yewbank, 52 Liberton Brae, Edinburgh EH16 6AF, Scotland Office: Nat Libr Scotland, George IV Bridge, Edinburgh EH1 1EW, Scotland

MATHESON, LINDA, retired clinical social worker; b. Martna, Estonia, Dec. 29, 1918; came to U.S., 1962, naturalized, 1969; d. Endrek and Leena Endrekson; m. Charles McLaren Matheson, Feb. 5, 1955. Diploma, Inst. for Social Scis., Tallinn, Estonia, 1944; MS, Columbia U., 1966; D in Social Work, Columbia U., 1974. Diplomate clin. social work. Social work officer UN Rehab. and Resettlement Assn., Germany, 1946-48; social worker Victorian Mental Hygiene, Australia, 1955-62; rsch. assoc., social work project dir. Arthritis Midway Ho., N.Y.C., 1966-68; rschr. Columbia Presbyn. Med. Center, N.Y.C., 1971-75; field instr. Columbia U. Sch. Social Work, 1977-79, Columbia Presbyn. Med. Ctr., NYU Sch. Social Work, 1989-90; ret., 1992. Family Found. fellow, 1966, 89-90; NIMH grantee, 1969-72. Mem. Nat. Assn. Social Workers, Nat. Wildlife Fedn., Center for Study of Presidency, Smithsonian Assn., English Speaking Union, Alliance Francaise, Columbia U. Alumni Assn., Internat. Platform Assn., Met. Mus. of N.Y. Lutheran. Home: 30-95 29th St Astoria NY 11102-2735

MATHESON, THOMAS, neuroscientist, researcher; b. Cambridge, Waikato, New Zealand, Apr. 4, 1965; arrived in Eng., 1990; s. Noel Bruce and Edna Isabel (Crompton) M.; m. Helen Elizabeth Lloyd, June 18, 1988. BSc in Zoology with hons., U. Canterbury, Christchurch, New Zealand, 1987; PhD in Zoology, U. Canterbury, 1991. Postdoc. assoc. dept. zoology U. Cambridge, Eng., 1990-92, 96-97; postdoc. fellow dept. zoology Girton Coll., Cambridge, 1992-95; sr. rsch. assoc. dept. zoology U. Cambridge, Eng., 1998-99, advanced rsch. fellow dept. zoology, 2000—. Coeditor: Nervous Systems and Behaviour, 1995; assoc. editor New Zealand Natural Scis., 1989, editor, 1989-90; asst. editor Jour. Exptl. Biology, 1991-95; contbr. articles to profl. jours. U. Canterbury scholar, 1986-90, Charles Cook, Warwich House Meml. scholar U. Canterbury, 1987-88; Girton Coll. Rsch. fellow, 1992-95. Mem. Physiol. Soc. (U.K.), Internat. Soc. for Neuroethology, Br. Neurosci. Assn. Avocations: photography, canoeing, windsurfing. Office: Dept Zoology U Cambridge, Downing St, Cambridge CB2 3EJ, England

MATHÉUS, FRÉDÉRIC PIERRE, mathematician, educator; b. Boulogne Billancourt, France, Nov. 16, 1967; s. Jean Frédéric and Isabelle Marie (De Carmoy) M.; m. Frédérique Fanny Deshors, June 12, 1993; children: Agathe, Capucine. Degree in math., U. Grenoble I, France, 1990, PhD in Math., 1994. Tchr. math. Ecole Normale Supérieure, Lyon, France, 1995-97; sr. lectr. U. South Brittany, France, 1997—. Home: 8 rue Carnot, 56000 Vannes France Office: U Bretagne Sud Lab Math, 1 rue de la Loi, 56000 Vannes France

MATHEWS, CHARLES RACE THORSON, researcher; b. Melbourne, Victoria, Australia, Mar. 27, 1935; s. Raymond Cyril and Jean Isobel (Morse) M.; m. Geraldine McKeown, May 26, 1956 (dec. June 1970); children: Sean, Jane, Vanessa; m. Iola Lindsay Hack, Sept. 2, 1972; children: Keir, Talya. BEd, Melbourne U., 1978, MA, 1990; PhD, Monash U., 1999. Cert. primary tchr. Clk. Shell Co., Melbourne, 1952; tchr., speech therapist Dept. Edn., Melbourne, 1953-67; prin. pvt. sec., leader of opposition Australian Parliament, Canberra, 1967-72; Ho. of Reps., Canberra, 1972-75; prin. pvt. sec., leader of opposition Victorian Parliament, Melbourne, 1976-79; Victorian Legis. Assembly, Melbourne, 1979-92; sr. rsch. fellow Grad. Sch. Govt., Monash U., Melbourne, 1992-99, sr. rsch. fellow Ctr. for Mgmt. in Govt., 1999—; chmn. select com. on specific learning difficulties Ho. of Reps., Australian Parliament, 1974-75; min. for police and emergency svcs., min. for the arts Victorial Parliament, 1982-87, min. for cmty. svcs., 1987-88. Author: David Bennett: A Memoir, 1985, Australia's First Fabians, 1994, Jobs of Our Own, 1999; editor: (with others) Whitlam Revisited, 1993. Councillor City of Croydon, Melbourne, 1964-66; mem. coun. Victorian Inst. Secondary Edn., 1979-85. Mem. Australian Inst. Polit. Sci. (bd. dirs. 1976-81), Australian Fabian Soc. (sec. 1960-67, 80-87, 1998—). Avocations: theatre, film, books, music. Home: 123 Alexandra Ave, South Yarra Vic 3141, Australia Office: Monash U Ctr Pub Mgmt, 30 Collins St, Victoria Melbourne Vic 3000, Australia

MATHEWS, ELIZABETH, lawyer, healthcare administrator; b. Mpls., MS in Health Svcs. Adminstrn., Cardinal Stritch U., Milw., 1992; JD, U. Minn., 1992; postgrad., Kennedy Western U., Cheyenne, Wyo.; Dr of the Faculty (hon.), Commonwealth U., Brit. V.I., 1997. Mem. Minn., U.S. Dist. Ct. Minn., U.S. Ct. Appeals (8th cir.), U.S. Ct. Fed. Claims, U.S. Supreme Ct. Med. info. specialist Merck & Co./Purdue Fr./ICN, Mpls. and Rochester, Minn., 1982-88; intern, clk. to Hon. Kevin S. BUrke, 4th Jud. Dist., Mpls., 1990-91; healthcare program adminstr. VHA Upper Midwest, LLC, Edina, Minn., 1998-2000; litigation atty. Lambert & Boeder, Wayzata, Minn., 1993-95; corp. counsel, staff atty. West Legal Pub., St. Paul, 1995-97; founding and mng. ptnr. Mathews Law Offices, PA, Mpls., 1995—; CMO, pres. Allid Healthcare Risk Cons., LLC, Mpls., 1999—; adj. faculty Cardinal Stritch U., Edina, Minn., 1992—. Contbr. articles to profl. jours. Trustee St. Mary's Cathedral, Mpls.; pres. Spinler Homeowners Assn., Mpls. Mem. Minn. State Bar Assn., Hennepin County Bar Assn., Am. Coll. Healthcare Exe s., Project Mgmt. Inst., others. Eastern Orthodox. Avocations: registered dachsunds, bonsai, balalaika, hockey. E-mail: eamhealthlaw@netzero.net. Office: Mathews Law Offices PA 3259 Ulysses St NE Ste 300 Minneapolis MN 55418-2246

MATHEWS, GEORGE MEPRATHU, accounting executive; b. Taiping, Perak, Malaysia, Feb. 23, 1960; came to U.S., 1985; s. Mathews and Annamma Chempanal; m. Asha Henry, May 29, 1993; children: Reishma Ann, Raveen Henry. B of Commerce, U. Kerala, Trivandrum, South India, 1982; MBA, U. Dallas, 1987. Acctg. asst. AGK Acctg. & Mgmt., Butterworth, Penang, West Malaysia, 1982-83; acctg. officer Sabah Rubber Fund Bd., Kota Kinabula, Sabah, East Malaysia, 1984; acctg./LAN mgr. Karol Media, Wilkes-Barre, Pa., 1988-94; chief adminstr. Amway Corp., Ada, Mich., 1994—. Mem. Am. Mgmt. Accts., Sigma Iota Epsilon. Avocations: hiking, stamp and coin collecting, table tennis, badminton. Office: Amway Corp 7575 E Fulton St Ada MI 49301

MATHEWS, KURUVILLA, African studies educator; b. Calicut, Kerala, India, Jan. 1, 1940; s. Anekkatt John and Elikutty Mathews; m. Rosie John, Feb. 22, 1975; children: Sunil, Sujata, Priya. BA, U. Kerala, Trivandrum, India, 1962; MA, U. Delhi, 1964; PhD, J. Nehru U., New Delhi, 1973. Lectr. U. Delhi, 1964-76, prof. dept. African studies, 1991—; vis. assoc. prof. Centre Fgn. Rels., Dar Es Salaam, 1980-81; assoc. prof. U. Dar Es Salaam, Tanzania, 1976-82; sr. lectr. U. Nigeria, Nsukka, 1982-88; vis. fellow U. Oxford, Eng., 1988-89; head dept. African studies U. Delhi, 1994-97, 2000-02; provost Mansarowar Hostel Du, Delhi, 1994-97; vis. rsch. fellow Africa Inst. of South Africa, Pretoria, 1998. Co-editor: Foreign Policy of Tanzania, 1982; Africa, India and South-South Cooperation, 1996; chief editor Indian Jour. African Studies, 1992—, The African Rev., 1980-82; contbr. articles to profl. jours. Mem. India Internat. Centre, New Delhi, 1996—; mem. bd.

FICCI Group on Africa, New Delhi, 1996—; mem. governing body Delhi Coll. Arts and Commerce, Delhi, 1994-96. Senate rsch. grantee U. Nigeria, Nsukka, 1983-86; recipient rsch. fellowship Ford Found., U. Oxford, 1988-89, internship UNITAR/UN, N.Y.C., 1972; faculty rsch. fellow Indo-Canadian Shastri Inst., Carlton U., Ottawa, 1998. Mem. Indian Coun. World Affairs (life, mem. exec. com. 1971-76), Internat. Peace Rsch. Assn., African Studies Assn. Roman Catholic. Avocations: table tennis, badminton, photography, swimming, travel. Office: U Delhi Dept African Studies, 38/3 Probyn Rd, Delhi 110007, India

MATHEWS, MARTIN REGINALD, accounting educator; b. London, July 21, 1940; s. Reginald Francis and Lilian Alice (Read) M.; m. Rita Elizabeth Jenkins, Dec. 7, 1960; children: Clive, Pamela, Clare. M Social Sci., Tope U. Birmingham, U.J., 1977; PhM, Massey U., Palmerston North, New Zealand, 1984, Loughborough U., U.K., 1988; EdD, U. Mont., 1993. Tchr. Mooroolsbark Tech. Sch., Victoria, Australia, 1974; lectr. Worcester Tech. Coll., U.K., 1975-79, 1977-79; sr. lectr. Massey U., 1979-83, reader, 1984, prof., 1985—. Author: Socially Responsible Accounting, 1993; co-author: Accounting Theory and Development, 1996. Fellow Inst. Chartered Accts. New Zealand, Australian Soc. Cert. Practicing Accts. Avocations: gardening, home decoration.

MATHEWS, MARY KATHRYN, retired government official; b. Washington, Apr. 20, 1948; d. T. Odon (dec.) and Kathryn (Augustine) M. Student, Pa. State U., 1966-68; BBA, Am. U., 1970, MBA, 1975. Personnel mgmt. specialist, coordinator coll. recruitment program, GSA, Washington, 1971-75, adminstrv. officer, 1975-78; personnel mgmt. specialist Office of Personnel Mgmt., Washington, 1978; employee devel. specialist Office Sec. Transp., Washington, 1978-80, dep. chief departmental services and spl. programs div., 1980-81; asst. dir. adminstrv. div. Farm Credit Adminstrn., Washington, 1981-84; dir. adminstrv. div. Farm Credit Adminstrn., McLean, Va., 1984-86; chief adminstrv. services div. Farm Credit Adminstrn., McLean, 1987-88; dep. staff dir. for mgmt. U.S. Commn. Civil Rights, Washington, 1988-90, asst. staff dir. for mgmt., 1990-91, asst. staff dir. for congl. affairs, 1991-94, staff dir., 1994-97; ret., 1997; chief spl. programs staff and homebound handicapped employment program GSA, Washington, 1973-74; mem. task force Presdl. mgmt. intern program U.S. Office Pers. Mgmt., Washington, 1977-78; coord. mgmt. devel. program for women Office Sec. Transp., Washington, 1979-81. Vol. mentor, speaker Alexandria Commn. on Women. Mem. Exec. Women in Govt. (treas. 1993-94, v.p. 1994-95, pres. 1995-96, bd. dirs.), Small Agy. Coun. (exec. com. 1990-91, 94-96, chmn. micro agy. group 1990-91), Internat. Alliance (bd. dirs. 1996-97), Nat. Trust Hist. Preservation, Nat. Assn. Mus. Women in Arts (charter), Delta Gamma (rush advisor 1971-73, pres. bd. dirs. local chpt. house corp. 1972-73). Avocations: antiques, classical music.

MATHEWS, PETER JOHN, bank executive; b. Ashburton, New Zealand, May 21, 1951; arrived to Australia, 1990; s. John Guscott and Ella Elizabeth Doig (Gray) M.; m. Victoria Alice Mills, Dec. 28, 1972; 2 children. BA, Otago U., Dunedin, New Zealand, 1972, LLB, 1973. Lawyer; chartered sec.; notary pub. Ptnr. Gibson Sheat, Lower Hutt, New Zealand, 1976-89; cons. Corrs Chambers Weitgarth, Melbourne, Australia, 1990-93; gen. counsel Graywinter Group, Melbourne, Australia, 1993-96; gen. counsel, co. sec. Greenfields Energy, Melbourne, 1996-97, Energy 21, Melbourne, 1998; co. sec. Australia and New Zealand Banking Group Ltd., Melbourne, 1999—. Fellow Chartered Secs. Australia Ltd.; mem. Law Inst. Victoria. Avocations: reading, gardening.

MATHEWS, RITA WHITE, retired research scientist, educator; b. N.Y.C., July 6, 1922; d. Julius Augustus White and Rita Mary Kohler; m. Gerard M. Thompson, Sept. 13, 1941 (div. Jan. 1957); children: Gerard M. Jr., Molly; m. Sidney Mathews, Mar. 1957 (div. Nov. 1978); 1 child, Sarah Kohler. BS, Columbia U., 1967; MA, Hunter Coll., 1971; PhD, CUNY, 1973. V.p. 401 East 163rd St Corp., N.Y.C., 1960-65; dir., corp. sec. Kohler & Campbell, Inc., Granite Falls, N.C., 1965-84; rsch. technician Am. Nat. Red Cross Lab., N.Y.C., 1966-69; asst. prof. Hunter Coll., N.Y.C., 1974-81; investigator Marine Biol. Lab., Woods Hole, Mass., 1975-81; prof. rsch. sci. NYU Med. Ctr., N.Y.C., 1981-90; ret., 1990; cons. Hemotech, Inc., N.Y.C., 1984-89; lectr., cons. scientist M.V. Illyria, 1989-94. Contbr. chpt. to book and articles to profl. jours. Pres. New Marlborough (Mass.) Land Preservation Trust, 1993-2000; chair New Marlborough Conservation Commn., 1993-2000, Hartsville Water Com., New Marlborough, 1998-2000; judge Internat. Sci. Fair, Louisville and Toronto, Can., 1995-96. Recipient U.S. Antarctic Svc. medal, 1980; fellow NSF, N.Y., 1972-73. Fellow Royal Geog. Soc., Explorers Club (dir. 1989-99, v.p. for rsch. and edn. 1989-99, Edward C. Sweeney medal); mem. AAAS, Am. Inst. Biol. Sci., , Soc. Women Geographers, N.Y. Acad. Scis., Phi Sigma. Achievements include patentee in field. Avocations: photography, skiing, mountain climbing, golf. Fax: (413) 229-0357. E-mail: explomat@bcn.net. Home: PO Box 237 Southfield MA 01259-0237

MATHEWS, WILLIAM EDWARD, neurological surgeon, educator; b. Indpls., July 12, 1934; s. Ples Leo and Roxie Elizabeth (Allen) M.; m. Eleanor Jayne Comer, Aug. 24, 1956 (div. 1976); children: Valerie, Clarissa, Marie, Blair; m. Carol Ann Koza, Sept. 12, 1987; 1 child, William Kyle. BS, Ball State U., 1958; DO, Kirksville Coll. Osteo. Med., 1961; MD, U. Calif., Irvine, 1962; fellow, Armed Forces Trauma Sch., Ft. Sam Houston, Tex., 1967-68. Diplomate Am. Bd. Neurol. and Orthopedic Surgery, Am. Bd. Pain Mgmt., Am. Bd. Indsl. Medicine, Am. Bd. Spinal Surgeons (v.p. 1990-92), Am. Bd. Forensic Medicine, Am. Bd. Traumatic Stress, Am. Bd. Clin. Neurosurgery, Am. Bd. Spinal Surgery. Intern Kirksville (Mo.) Osteo. Hosp., 1961-62; resident neurosurgery Los Angeles County Gen. Hosp., 1962-67; resident in neurosurgery Rancho Los Amigos Spinal Rehab. Ctr., 1964-65; with Brooke Army Hosp., Ft. Sam Houston, 1967-68; with 8th field hosp. U.S. Army Neurosurgeon C.O. & 933 Med. Corp, Vietnam, 1968-69; chief neurosurgery Kaiser Med. Group, Walnut Creek, Calif., 1969-77; staff neurosurgeon Mt. Diablo Med. Ctr., Concord, Calif., 1977—; NIH student rsch. fellow/early rsch. on the clin. use of electromyography, 1959-61; chief resident neurosurgery Los Angeles County Gen. Hosp., 1962-67; asst. prof. biochemistry Kirksville Coll. Osteo. Medicine, 1958-62; asst. lecturing prof. neuroanatomy U. Calif. Coll. Medicine, 1962-65; sec. Am. Fedn. Med. Edn., 1997—; chmn. Am. Bd. Spinal Surgery, 1998, chmn. Am. Bd. Med. Accreditation, 1999—. Author: Intracerebral Missile Injuries, 1972, Intrasellar Chordoma, 1976, Intraoperative Myelography, 1982, Thin Slice Computed Tomography of the Cervical Spine, 1985, Early Return to Work Following Cervical Disc Surgery, 1991, Iatrogenic Tethering of the Spinal Cord, 1998; contbr. articles to profl. jours. Mem. adv. com. Rep. Presdl. Selection Com. Maj. U.S. Army, 1967-69, Vietnam. Recipient Disting. Svc. award Internat. Biography, 1987; scholar Psi Sigma Alpha, 1957. Fellow Congress Neurol. Surgeons (joint sect. on neurotrauma), Royal Coll. Medicine, Am. Acad. Neurologic and Orthopedic Surgeons (pres. 1981-82, bd. dirs. 1990—), Bay Area Spinal Surgery Soc., Internat. Coll. Surgeons; mem. AMA, Calif. Med. Assn., San Francisco Neurologic, Contra Costa County Med. Soc. Roman Catholic. Avocations: pen and ink art, golf, gardening.

MATHEWSON, SIR GEORGE, bank executive; b. May 14, 1940; s. George M. and Charlotte (Ross) Gordon; m. Sheila Alexandra Graham, 1966; 2 children. BSc, Perth Acad.; PhD, St. Andrews U.; MBA, Canisius Coll. Ast. lectr. St. Andrews U., 1964-67; various positions in R & D Avionics Engrng. Bell Aerospace, Buffalo, N.Y., 1967-72; joined Indsl. & Comml. Fin. Corp., Edinburgh, Scotland, 1972; area mgr. Indsl. & Comml. Fin. Corp., Aberdeen, Scotland, 1974-79, asst. gen. mgr., dir., 1979-81; ceo, mem. Scottish Devel. Agy., 1981-87; dir. strategic planning, devel. Royal Bank of Scotland Group, 1987-90, dir., 1987—, dep. group ceo, 1990-92; group ceo Royal Bank of Scotland Group, Edinburgh, 1992—; bd. dirs. Scottish Investment Trust Ltd., Citizens Fin. Group, Inc., Direct Line Group Ltd. Fellow Chartered Inst. Bankers in Scotland, Royal Soc. Edinburgh; mem. New Club; companion Inst. Mgmt. Avocations: geriatric rugby, tennis, business. Address: 29 Saxe Coburg Pl, Edinburgh EH3 5BP, Scotland Office: Royal Bank Scotland, 42 St Andrew Sq, Edinburgh EH2 2YE, United Kingdom*

MATHEWSON, HUGH SPALDING, anesthesiologist, educator; b. Washington, Sept. 20, 1921; s. William Eldridge and Jennie Lind (Jones) M.; m. Dorothy Ann Gordon, 1943 (div. 1952); 1 child, Jane Mathewson Holcombe; m. Hazel M. Jones, 1953 (div. 1978); children: Geoffrey K., Brian E., Catherine E. Brock, Jennifer A. Jehle; m. Judith Ann Mahoney, 1979 (div. 1990). Student, Washburn U., 1938-39; A.B., U. Kans., 1942, M.D., 1944. Intern Wesley Hosp., Wichita, Kans., 1944-45; resident anesthesiology U. Kans. Med. Ctr., Kansas City, 1946-48; pvt. practice specializing in anesthesiology Kansas City, Mo., 1948-69; chief anesthesiologist St. Luke's Hosp., Kansas City, 1953-69; med. dir., sect. respiratory therapy U. Kans. Med. Ctr., 1969-92, assoc. prof., 1969-75, prof., 1975-92, prof. anesthesiology emeritus, respiratory care edn., 1992—; examiner schs. respiratory therapy, 1975-95; oral examiner Nat. Bd. Respiratory Therapy; mem. Coun. Nurse Anesthesia Practice, 1974-78; prof. phys. therapy edn., 1993-98. Author: Structural Forms of Anesthetic Compounds, 1961, Respiratory Therapy in Critical Care, 1976, Pharmacology for Respiratory Therapists, 1977; contbr. articles to profl. publs.; mem. editorial bd. Anesthesia Staff News, 1975-84; assoc. editor: Respiratory Care, 1980-90, cons. editor, 1980—, editor-in-chief Respiratory Mgmt., 1989-92. Pres. Overland Park Civic Band, 1997, Overland Park Orch., 1998-2001; trustee Kansas City Mus., Kansas City Conservatory of Music, 1993—. Served to lt. comdr. USNR, 1956. Recipient Bird Lit. prize Am. Assn. Respiratory Therapists, 1976, Spl. Recognition award Am. Assn. Nurse Anesthetists, 1997. Mem. Mo. Soc. Anesthesiologists (pres. 1963), Kans. Soc. Anesthesiologists (pres. 1974-77), Kans. Med. Soc. (council), Phi Beta Kappa, Sigma Xi, Lambda Beta (hon.). Office: Kans Med Ctr 39th And Rainbow Blvd Kansas City KS 66160-0001

MATHIAS, CHRISTOPHER JOSEPH, physician, educator, researcher, consultant; b. Mangalore, India, Mar. 16, 1949; arrived in the U.K., 1972; s. Elias Salvadore and Hilda Frances (Lobo) M.; m. Rosalind Margaret Jolleys, July 31, 1977; children: Sarah, James, Timothy. MB, BChir, Bangalore U., India, 1972; PhD, U. Oxford, Eng., 1976; DSc, U. London, 1995. Hon. rsch. officer, registrar Dept. Neurology, Oxford, 1972-76; sr. house officer dept. medicine Royal Postgrad. Med. Sch., London, 1976-77; registrar dept. medicine, Portsmouth and renal unit Southampton (Eng.) U., 1977-79; Wellcome Trust sr. clin. rsch. fellow St. Mary's Hosp. and Med. Sch., London, 1979-84; Wellcome Trust sr. lectr. St. Mary's Hosp. and Med. Sch. and Nat. Hosp. Inst. Neurology, London, 1984-91; prof. neurovascular medicine St. Mary's/Imperial Coll., Sch. Medicine, Nat. Hosp., Inst. Neurology, 1991—; chmn. rsch. com. World Fedn. Neurology on Autonomic Disorders, 1993-97; chmn. sci. panel European Fedn. Neurol. Soc., 1994-99; guest lectr. Thailand Neurol. Soc., 1995; Nimmo vis. prof. U. Adelaide, Australia, 1996; mem. sci. com. Internat. Spinal Rsch. Trust, 1996; Allan Birch Meml. lectr., London, 1997, Abbie Meml. lectr. U. Adelaide, Australia, 1999; vis. prof. U. Hawaii. Co-editor (with M. Weber) Book on Mild Hypertension, 1984, (with P. Sever) Concepts in Hypertension, 1989, (with Sir Roger Bannister) Autonomic Failure: A Textbook of Clinical Disorders of the Autonomic Nervous System, 3d edit., 1992, 4th edit., 1999; contbr. chpts to books and articles to profl. jours.; found. editor-in-chief Clin. Autonomic Rsch. Official Jour. Am. Autonomic Soc., Brit. Clin. Autonomic Rsch. Soc., 1991—; mem. editl. bd. various internat. med./sci. jours. Named Rhodes scholar U. Oxford, 1972-75, Dr. J. Thomas lectr. St. Johns Med. Coll., U. Bangalore, 1988, Lord Florey Meml. lectr. U. Adelaide, 1991, Sir Hugh Cairns Meml. lectr., Adelaide, 1996; recipient Prof. Ruitinga award and vis. professorship U. Amsterdam, The Netherlands, 1988. Fellow Royal Coll. Physicians (London, Brit. Petroleum lectr. 1992), Royal Soc. Medicine; mem. Am. Antonomic Soc. (bd. dirs.), Royal Coll. Physicians and Surgeons (licentiate Glasgow and Edninburg), Assn. Physicians Gt. Britain, Physiol. Soc., Assn. Brit. Neurologists, Brit. Pharm. Soc., Clin. Antonomic Rsch. Soc. (chmn. 1987-90, found. sec. 1982-86), Brit. European and Internat. Hypertension Soc., Royal Instn. Movement Disorders Soc., European Fedn. Autonomic Socs. (pres. 1999—). Avocations: gardening, watching cricket and football, observing human and canine behavior. Home: Meadowcroft West End Ln, Stoke Poges Bucks SL2 4NE, England Office: St Marys Hosp Imperial Coll Sch Medicine, Neurovascular Medi Unit Praed St, London W2 1NY, England

MATHIAS, JULIAN ROBERT, investment manager; b. Arundel, Eng., Sept. 7, 1943; s. Anthony Robert Mathias and Cecily Mary Hughes; m. Frances Bone, May 31, 1996. MA, Oxford U., Eng., 1963. Mgr. Hill Samuel & Co. Ltd., London, 1964-71; ptnr. Buckmaster & Moore, London, 1971-81; dir. Fgn. & Colonial Mgmt. Ltd., London, 1981-95, BZW Investment Mgmt., London, 1995-96; with Rapael Asset Mgmt., 1996-97. Mem. Boodles, Berkshire Golf Club. Roman Catholic. Avocations: bridge, golf, shooting, wine tasting.

MATHIAS, MARGARET GROSSMAN, manufacturing company executive, leasing company executive; b. Detroit; d. D. Ray and Lila May (Skinner) Grossman; children: Deborah, Robert, Lesley, Jennifer, Mary. BA, Mt. Holyoke Coll.; cert., Am. Acad. Art. Artist and co-mgr. Mary Chase Marionettes, N.Y.C.; exec. v.p. Star Five Corp., Elkhart, 1975-88, pres., treas., chmn. bd., 1985-90; sec., chmn. bd. L & J Press Corp., Elkhart, Ind., 1985-91, also chmn. bd. dirs.; chmn., pres., CEO Magland Co., Elkhart, 1986—, Magco Inc., Elkhart, 186—; pres., chmn., CEO Tech Products, Inc., Elkhart, 1992—. Mem. fin. com. United Fund, Elkhart; mem. parents adv. bd. Furman U., Greenville, S.C., 1978-83, mem. art adv. bd. Mt. Holyoke Coll., South Hadley, Mass., 1982—; pres. Tri Kappa Service Orgn., Elkhart, 1965-66; trustee Stanley Clark Sch., South Bend, Ind., 1977-87; bd. dirs. Bridgework Theatre, Goshen, Ind., also Balt., 1996—; mem. adv. bd. Ruthmere 1910 House Mus. designated one of Am.'s castles, 1999—; instr., spkr. etiquette Montessori Schs., Elkhart, Ind., 1998—. Recipient Lawson Top Sculpture Purchase award Midwest Mus. Am. Art, 1990. Mem. Elkhart C. of C. Republican. Clubs: Elcona Country (Elkhart), Woman's Athletic (Chgo.), Thursday (Elkhart) (pres. 1976). Avocations: sculpting, traveling, skiing. Home: 1077 Greenleaf Blvd Apt 101 Elkhart IN 46514-3562 Office: 429 S Main St Elkhart IN 46516-3210

MATHIE, ROBERT TAYLOR, physiologist; b. Glasgow, Scotland, May 28, 1952; s. Angus and Margaret Forsyth (Taylor) M.; m. Caroline Margaret Fitzgerald; children: Hannah, Kirstie. BSc, U. Glasgow, 1974, PhD, 1978. Rsch. asst. U. Glasgow, 1974-79; lectr. U. London, 1979-91, sr. lectr., 1991—. Editor: Blood Flow Measurement in Man, 1982, Principles of Surgical Research, 1989, 95, Ischaemia-Reperfusion Injury, 1999, The Haemodynamic Effects of Nitric Oxide, 1999; contbr. articles to profl. jours. Fellow Royal Photographic Soc.; mem. British Assn. for Study of Liver, British Soc. Cardiovascular Rsch. Mem. Ch. of Scotland. Avocations: photography, lawn bowling, travel. Office: Imperial Coll Sch Med, Hammersmith Hosp/Surgery Anaesthetics, London WI2 ONN, England

MATHIESEN, LARS R., physician, researcher; b. Denmark, Feb. 20, 1950. MD, ECFMG, U. Copenhagen, 1975; diploma in hygiene and tropical medicine, London, 1985. Resident Kom Hosp., Copenhagen, 1975-76; rsch. fellow NIAID, Bethesda, Md., 1976-78, State Serum Inst., Copenhagen, 1978-79; resident Hvidovre Hosp., Copenhagen, 1979-81; asst. prof. Hvidovre Hosp., 1986—; from resident to sr. resident Rigshospitolet, Copenhagen, 1981-86. Contbr. over 100 articles to profl. jours. Office: Dept Infectious Diseases, Hvidovre Hosp, 2650 Hvidovre Denmark

MATHIEU, GEORGES VICTOR ADOLPHE, artist; b. Boulogne, France, Jan. 27, 1921; s. Adolphe Mathieu d'Escaudoeuvres and Madeleine Dupre d'Ausque. Ed., Facultés de droit et des lettres, Lille, France. Tchr. English; mgr. pub. rels. U.S. Lines. Exhbns. include Paris, 1950, N.Y.C., 1952, Japan, 1957, Scandinavia, 1958, Eng., Spain, Italy, Switzerland, Fed. Republic Germany, Austria and S.Am., 1959, Middle East, 1961-62, Can., 1963, Musée Municipal d'Art Moderne, Paris, 1963, Galerie Charpentier, Paris, 1965, Musée Nat. d'Art Moderne, Paris, 1967, Musée de la Manufacture Nat. des Gobelins, 1969, Antibes, 1976, Ostend, 1977, Grand Palais, Paris, 1978, Wildenstien Gallery, N.Y.C., Dominion Gallery, Montreal, Que., Can., 1979, Musée de la Poste, Paris, 1980, Palais des Papes, Avignon, 1985, Galerie Sapone, Nice, 1987, Galerie Protée, Paris, 1988, Abbaye de Chateautoux, France, 1990, Musée de Boulogne Sur Mer, St. Germain en Laye, 1994, Refectoize des Jacobins, Toulouse, 1995; prin. works include Hommage à la Mort, 1950, Hommage au Marechal de Turenne, 1952, Les Capetiens Partout, 1954, La Victoire de Denain, 1963, Hommage à Jean Cocteau, 1963, Paris, Capitale des Arts, 1965, Hommages aux Freres Boisseree, 1967, Hommages à Condillac, 1968, La prise de Berg op Zoom, 1969, Election de Charles Quint, 1971, Matta-Salums, 1978, La Liberation de Paris, 1980, La liberation d'Orleans par Jeanne d'Arc, 1982, Le Massacre des 269, 1985, Paradis des Orages, 1988, Les enfants de Bogota, 1989, Rumeurs de Paradis, 1991; designed gardens and bldgs. for B.C. transformer factory, Fontenay-le-comte, 1966; 16 posters for Air France; tapestries; 18 medals for Paris Mint, 1971, new 10 F coin, 1974; creater Tachism; author: Audela du Tachisme; Le privilege d'Etre; De la Revolté à Rénaissance; La Réponse de l'Abstraction lyrique; L'Abstraction Prophetique, Les Massacre de la Sensibilité, Desormais, Seul en Face de Dieu; represented in 90 museums and pub. collections. Mem. Acad. Fine Arts.

MATHIEU, HENRI-PIERRE, physician, business executive; b. Oran, Algeria, May 6, 1954; s. Guy Mathieu and Paule Perez; m. Nicole Carne, Nov. 3, 1978; children: Jean-Baptiste, Marie, Suzanne. MD, Montpellier, France, 1982. Resident Montpellier Hosps., Perpignan (France) Hosps.; asst. product mgr. Lab. Servier, Paris, 1982-83; mgr. Sante-Info, S.A.R.L., 1987-95; pvt. practice Paris, 1984-96; mgr. Info. Tech. Works, LLC, Wilmington, Del., 1998—; adminstrv. mgr. Coll. de Hautes Etudes en Medicine Generale des hauts de Jeine, Paris, 1988-92; v.p. FMC 92, Paris, 1984-91. Contbr. articles to profl. publs. Mem. N.Y. Acad. of Sci. Office: Info Tech Works LLC 3422 Old Capitol Trl Wilmington DE 19808-6124

MATHIEU, MICHELE SUZANNE, medical association administrator; b. Chgo., Mar. 24, 1950; d. Joseph Edward Mathieu and Mary Ellen Fisher; m. Robert Steven Harris, May 1, 1988 (div. Feb. 2000). BS in Mktg., Regents Coll., Albany, N.Y., 1998; cert. web site design, Columbia Coll., Chgo., 2000. Broadcast coord. Grey-North Advt., Chgo., 1967-71; head drama dept. Patricia Stevens Coll., Chgo., 1972; instr. beginning acting Ted Liss Sch. Performing Arts, Chgo., 1973-75; project coord. grants and contracts Am. Dietetic Assn., Chgo., 1974-81, adminstr. govt. affairs, 1981-86, mgr. licensure comm., 1986-90, adminstr. nutrition svcs. payment systems, 1990-94, team leader, health care fin. team, 1994-97, dir. health care fin. team, 1998-00, dir. mem. web, 2000—; grant proposal cons. various performance arts, Chgo., 1978—; med. reporter, writer various internat. clients, 1994—; PC cons., Chgo., 1994—. Editor Legis. Newsletter, 1981-86; contbg. editor Nutrition Forum, 1986, Courier, 1987—; contbr. articles to profl. jours., mags., newspapers. Ill. Arts Coun. grantee, 1981. Mem. Am. Soc. Assn. Ecs. (Excellence in Govt. award 1989). Roman Catholic. Avocations: reading, fitness walking. Office: Am Dietetic Assn 216 W Jackson Blvd Chicago IL 60606-6909

MATHIS, DONALD HILLIARD, chief operating officer, naval reserve officer; b. Ft. Lauderdale, Fla., Mar. 6, 1966; s. David Hilliard and Susan Oliver (Porter) M.; m. Jennifer Rose Carlin, Oct. 20, 1996. BA in Asian Studies with honors, Vassar Coll., 1990; MBA with honors, Harvard U., 1998. Cons. Andersen Consulting, Phila., 1990-92; analyst CS First Boston, N.Y.C., 1992-93; CFO Freedom House, N.Y.C., 1993-97; assoc. McKinsey & Co., N.Y.C., 1997-99; COO Small World, Inc., N.Y.C., 1999—. Writer, dir. (documentary film) A Measure of War, 1992, Cambodian Elections Monitor, UN, 1993, The Last Wall, 1995. Co-founder, dir. Third Millennium, N.Y.C., 1993, Leadership & Ethics Forum, Harvard Univ.; founder, chmn., Magellan Prodns.- A Human Rights Documentary Company. Lt. USNR, 1984—. Mem. Harvard Club. Avocations: pilot (commercial/instrument), documentary maker, international travel. Home: 25 Central Park W Apt 11D New York NY 10023 Office: Small World Inc 838 Broadway Fl 5 New York NY 10003

MATHIS, FRANZ, historian, educator; b. Hohenems, Vorarlberg, Austria, Nov. 27, 1946; s. Rudolf and Anna (Amann) M.; m. Christine Pankler, July 12, 1999; children: Claudia, Pia. BA, U. Innsbruck, 1971, MA, 1973, PhD, 1979. Asst. prof. U. Innsbruck, Austria, 1973-79; assoc. prof. history U. Innsbruck, 1979-93, full prof. history, 1993—. Author: Tyrol in 1703, 1975, Austrian Cities in the 17th Century, 1978, Big Business in Austria, 1987, 90, German Economy in the 16th Century, 1992; editor: Zwanowetz-Festschrift, 1984, Vorarlberg since 1945, 2000; contbr. articles to profl. jours. Mem. Gesellschaft fuer Sozial und Wirtschaftsgeschichte, Gesellschaft fuer Unternehmensgeschichte, Oesterreichisches Lateinamerika Inst., Austrian Asst. For Am.Studies, Inst. fuer Oesterreichkunde, Internat. Soc. for Alpine History, Institut fuer bankhistorische Forschung. Home: Franz-Zingerle-Weg 29, A-6094 Axams Austria Office: U Innsbruck, Innrain 52, A-6020 Innsbruck Austria

MATHIS, JACK DAVID, advertising executive; b. La Porte, Ind. Nov. 27, 1931; s. George Anthony and Bernice (Bennethum) M.; student U. Mo., 1950-52; BS, Fla. State U., 1955; m. Phyllis Dene Hoffman, Dec. 24, 1971; children: Kane Cameron, Jana Dene. With Benton & Bowles, Inc., 1955-56; owner Jack Mathis Advt., 1956—; cons. films, including That's Action!, 1977, Great Movie Stunts: Raiders of the Lost Ark, 1981, The Making of Raiders of the Lost Ark, 1981, An American Legend: The Lone Ranger, 1981; Heroes and Sidekicks: Indiana Jones and the Temple of Doom, 1984, The Republic Pictures Story, 1991, The Making of The Quiet Man, 1992, Roy Rogers: King of the Cowboys, 1992, Cliffhangers: Adventures from the Thrill Factory, 1993, The Making of Sands of Iwo Jima, 1993, Gene Autry: Melody of the West, 1994. Mem. U.S. Olympic Basketball Com. Recipient citation Mktg. Research Council N.Y., inducted Ill. Basketball Hall of Fame. Mem. Alpha Delta Sigma. Author: Valley of the Cliffhangers, Republic Confidential, Valley of the Cliffhangers Supplement. Office: PO Box 3580 Barrington IL 60011-3580

MATHIS, LAURELLE SHEEDY, executive recruiter, volunteer; b. Southampton, N.Y., Aug. 29, 1948; d. Edmund Sheedy and Tatiana (Widrin) Brooks; children: Liliana Sheedy, Bronwyn Trimble, Kane Timberlake. BA, Stephens Coll., Columbia, Mo., 1970; MBA, Harvard U., 1977. Spl. asst. Congressman Ed Foreman, Washington, 1970; staff asst. Senator James L. Buckley, Washington, 1971-72; staff asst. to Pres. of U.S. Washington, 1973-75; v.p. Blyth Eastman Paine Webber, N.Y.C., 1977-81, Merrill Lynch Capital Markets, N.Y.C., 1981-83; pres. Harris Energy Corp., Greenwich, Conn., 1988-91; CFO Diocese of Mt. Kilimanjaro, Arusha, Tanzania, 1991-93; v.p. TechnoServe, Norwalk, Conn., 1994-96, TMP Exec. Resourcing, N.Y.C., 1997—. Bd. curators Stephens Coll., 1981-83; bd. dirs. Putnam Indian Field Sch., Greenwich, 1986-91, chmn. auction, 1987; chmn. Christ Ch. Antiques Show, 1987, 88, 89; bd. dirs. Episcopal Ch., Women of Christ Ch., Greenwich Acad. Mother's Bd. Recipient Alumni Achievement award Stephens Coll., 1980. Republican. Episcopalian. Home: 62 N Sound Beach Ave Riverside CT 06878-1231 Office: 100 Park Ave Fl 15 New York NY 10017-5516

MATHIS, REMY RENE, orthodontist educator; b. Muttersholtz, Alsace, France, Feb. 3, 1949; s. Rene and Jenny (Sigwalt) M.; m. Odile Marie Grolet, Mar. 11, 1972; children: Charles-François, Juliane. D in Dentistry, Strasbourg (France) U., 1974, DSc, 1983. Prof. asst. Dental U. of Strasbourg, France, 1979-84, prof., 1984—; cons. Nat. Health Ins., Strasbourg, 1977—. Mem. European Begg Soc., North Am. Study Soc. of Orthodontics, Nat. Tchrs. Assn. (vice sec.), French Orthodontic Soc., French Begg and Tip Edge Soc. Avocations: skiing, old-timers. Office: 2 Rue du Sand, 67600 Selestat France

MATHIS, ROBERT ARTHUR, planner, rancher; b. Price, Utah, June 23, 1947; s. Wallace and Gladys Meeks Mathis; m. Barbara Ellen Lighthall, Dec. 17, 1971; children: Jason Robert, Bian Alan Lighthall, MaryAnn. AS, Coll. Easter Utah, 1969; BS, U. Utah, 1972; MPA, Brigham Young U., 1976. Cert. AICP. Planner South Ea. Idaho Cmty. Action Agy., Pocatello, 1972-73; sr. svcs. planner South Ea. Idaho Coun. Govts., Pocatello, 1973-74; county planner Wasatch County, Heber City, Utah, 1976-99; Olympic planner Wasatch County, Heber City, 1999—; exec. sec. Heber Valley Spl. Svc. Dist., 1977-82; mem. bd. USEPA Mgmt. Adv. Group to the Office on Water, Washington. Active Lion's Club Internat., 1978-98, Boy Scouts Am., 1976-98. Recipient Calvin Sudweeks award State Utah. Democrat. Mem. LDS Ch. Avocations: reading, skiing, toy trains. E-mail: bobmathis@shadowlink.net. E-mail: bmathis@co.wasatch.ut.us. Fax: 435-654-9993. Office: Wasatch County 25 N Main St Heber City UT 84032-1827

MATHIS, SAMUEL MARK, lawyer; b. Hartford, Conn., Oct. 27, 1967; s. Mark Andre Mathis and Hannah Bradeen Spencer; m. Lynn Crampton Mallory. BA, U. Vt., 1990; JD, U. Oreg., 1995. Bar: Maine 1995, U.S. Dist. Ct. Maine 1996, U.S. Ct. Appeals (1st cir.) 2000. Ptnr. Woodruff & Mathis, Auburn, Maine, 1996—. Office: Woodruff & Mathis 98 Court St Auburn ME 04210-5905

MATHIS, WOLFGANG, physicist; b. Celle, Germany, May 13, 1950; s. Max and Irmgard (Bihan) M.; m. Barbara Wessel, Apr. 17, 1985; children: Marie, Richard. Diploma in physics, Tech. U. Braunschweig, 1980, D in Engring., 1984. From rsch. asst. to asst. prof. Tech. U. Braunschweig, Germany, 1980-90; prof. U. Wuppertal, Germany, 1990-96, U. Magdeburg, Germany, 1996-2000, U. Hannover, Germany, 2000—. Author: Nonlinear Networks, 1987, Oscillators, 1994; contbr. articles to profl. jours. Fellow IEEE (sr.). Avocations: history of science, blues music, guitar, tennis. Home: Am Kurzen Holze 29, 38302 Wolfenbuttel Germany Office: U Hannover Inst Theor Elek, Appelstr 9A, 30167 Hannover Germany

MATHLOUTHI, MOHAMED, chemistry educator; b. Kalaa-Kebira, Tunisia, Nov. 14, 1940; s. Abderrahman and Khadija (Benameur) M.; m. Zahia Bentayeb, July 26, 1986; children: Jazia, Ridha. Degree in engring., Ecole Nat. Supérieure des Industries Agricoles et Alimentaires, Massy, France, 1966; DEng, U. Dijon, France, 1973, DSc, 1980. Head lab. Tunisian Sugar Co., Beja, 1967-69; asst. prof. chemistry U. Dijon, 1970-79, maitre asst., 1980-84, maitre de conf., 1985-86; prof. chemistry U. Reims, France, 1987—. Editor: Food Packaging, 1986, Sweet Taste Chemoreception, 1993, Food Packaging and Preservation, 1994, Sucrose, Properties and Applications, 1995, Le Sacchrarose, 1996, Emballage et Conditionnement de Produits Alimentaires, 1996, Sucrose Crystallization Science and Technology: Selected Papers of Andrew Van Hook, 1997; contbr. over 120 articles to sci. jours., chpts. to books. Recipient B. Delessert medal, Centre d'Etude et de Documentation du Sucre, Paris, 1981, Assn. French Food Chemists, Paris, Silver medal, 1997, Gold medal, 1997. Mem. Am. Chem. Soc., French Carbohydrate Group, Andrew Van Hook Assn. (pres.). Avocations: poetry, music, psychology, food. Office: Faculte des Sciences, BP 1039, 51687 Reims France

MATHON, STEPHANE ROGER, data processing company executive; b. Tourcoing, Nord, France, Aug. 11, 1938; s. Jean and Madeleine (Motte) M.; m. Claude Regnault de Beaucaron, May 20, 1967; children: Gwendoline, Coralie, Douglas, Héloise. Degree in physics, U. Lille, France, 1961; diploma, Inst. d'etudes Politiques, Paris, 1963. Salesman IBM France, Lille, 1965-68; internat. account mgr. IBM France, Paris, 1968-71; regional mgr. Itel France, Paris, 1972-74, mktg. mgr., 1975-76, gen. mgr., 1977-78; gen. mgr. Comdisco France, Paris, 1979-80; founder, pres. Data Budget, Paris, 1981-99, Data Syscom, Brussels, 1992—; with Mathon Motte Techs., Vanves, France, 1996—; v.p. MEDEF 92 Sud, Issy Les Moulineaux, France, 1992—. Councilor City Coun., Vernou en Sologne, France, 1990—. Lt. Air Force, 1963-65. Mem. Cercle du Bois de Boulogne. Avocations: computer collector, historical studies, tennis. Office: Mathon Motte Technologies, 7 rue du 4 Septembre, 92170 Vanves France also: OrdiWorldCom, 7 rue du 4 Septembre, 92170 Vanves France

MATHUR, PRACHEESHWAR SWAROOP, aerospace engineer; b. Shahjahanpur, India, Dec. 19, 1945; came to U.S., 1967; s. Parmeshwar Sarup and Gopal Rani M., m. Meena Mathur, Dec. 27, 1976; children: Shashank, Nishant, Priyank. BSc, Agra Coll., India, 1962; BS in Tech., I.I.T., Kanpur, India, 1967; MS, MIT, 1968, DSc, 1972. Engr. GE aircraft engines, Lynn, Mass., 1972-77; mgr. metal processing GE aircraft engines, Cin., 1977-80, mgr. customer support, 1980-86, program mgr., 1986-90; dir. Asia Pacific Lucas Aerospace, New Delhi, India, 1990-93; pres. Asia Pacific Dowty Aerospace, Singapore, 1993—; dir. Lucas Repair Ctr., Singapore, 1991-93, Dowty Aerospace Aviation Svcs., Singapore, 1993—. Author: (book chpt.) Superalloy Processing, 1981; patentee in metals processing and joining; appeared in various plays. Home: Vasant Vihar, B-54 Paschimi Marg, 110 057 New Delhi India Office: Dowty Aerospace, 21 Loyang Crescent, 1750 Singapore Singapore

MATHUR, PREMENDU PRAKASH, life sciences educator, researcher; b. Agra, U.P., India, July 2, 1955; s. Om Prakash and Shanti Devi M.; m. Anita Mathur, Nov. 21, 1983; children: Garima, Mahima. BSc, Banaras Hindu U., Varanasi, India, 1974, MSc., 1976, PhD, 1980. Lectr. Kurukshestra (India) U., 1982-88; assoc. prof. Pondicherry (India) U., 1988-97, prof., 1997—, head Sch. Life Scis., 2000—; fellow-in-residence The Population Coun., N.Y.C., 1985-87; scientist-in-charge Bioinformatics Ctr., Pondicherry U., 1991—; vis. scientist Population Coun., N.Y.C., 1990, 92-94, 97, 99, Inst. Reprodn. Med., Munster, 1998, 99. Contbr. over 55 articles to profl. jours. Abstractor (vol.) Biological Abstracts, U.S., 1979-94. Young Scientist award Indian Sci. Congress, 1985; Spl. award Rockefeller Found., N.Y.C., 1985-87, Biotech. Career award, Rockefeller Found., N.Y.C., 1992-94, INSA (India) - DFG (Germany) Exch. award, Munster, Germany, 1998. Mem. Soc. Study of Reprodn. (minority affairs com.), Indian Soc. for Study of Reprodn. and Fertility (mem. exec. comm. 1997—), Am. Soc. Andrology, Endocrine Soc. of India, Internat. Consortium on Male Contraception, Nat. Assessment and Accreditation Coun. (mem. peer teams), Population Coun. N.Y.C. (joint sec.), Nat. Task Force in Bioinformatics and Infrastructure Facilities. Avocations: writing popular sci. articles, reading, travel, internet surfing. Office: Pondicherry Univ, New Science Block, Pondicherry 605014, UT India

MATHUR, VEERENDRA SWARUP, trade unionist, educator, social scientist; b. Rajgarh, Rajasthan, India, July 27, 1920; s. Banwari Swarup and Lakshmi Devi Mathur; m. Kamlesh Rani Mathur, Dec. 10, 1954. BA, Hindu Coll., Delhi, 1939; LLB, U. Delhi, 1942. Sec. Indian Fedn. Labour, Delhi, 1941-48, Hind Mazdoor Sabha, Delhi, 1948-51; gen. sec. Indian Adult Edn. Assn., Delhi, 1948-52, 79-80; pres. Indian Adult Edn. Assn., New Delhi, 1981-83; dir. edn. for Asia Internat. Confedn. Free Trade Unions, Calcutta, 1952-65; gen. sec. Asian and Pacific Regional Orgn. Internat. Confedn. Free Trade Unions, New Delhi, 1965-89. Contbr. articles to profl. jours. Gen. sec. Radical Dem. Party Delhi Br., 1945-48; mem. Delhi Mcpl. Com., 1946-54. Recipient Labour award Mazoor Award Coun. of Pakistan, All Pakistan Fedn. Trade Unions, Lahore, 1985, Nehru Literacy award Indian Adult Edn. Assn., New Delhi, 1993, Friend of Labour award Indian Nat. Trade Union Congress, New Delhi, 1997. Mem. Labour Orgn. of the Rural Poor (pres. 1975—), Soc. for Promotion Orgns. Rural Poor (pres. 1979—), Lok Shiksha Samaj (pres. 1983—), Appropriate Tech. Devel. Assn. (chmn. 1996—). Radical Humanist. Home and Office: P-20 Green Park Extension, New Delhi 110016, India

MATHUR, VISHNU DAYAL, historian, educator, researcher; b. Ajmer, India, Aug. 28, 1939; s. Raghubar and Chandrakala M.; m. Saroj Mathur; children: Saurabh M., Gaurav. BA, Agra U., 1958; MA, U. Rajasthan, 1960; PhD, Agra U., 1982. Instr. history M.B. Coll., Udaipur, India, Govt. Coll., Banswara, India; sr. lectr., head dept. history Agrawal Coll., Jaipur, India, 1965-97, ret., 1997; cons. in field. Author: States' People's Conference, 1984; contbr. articles and book revs. to profl. jours. Mem. Indian History Congress (life). Home: Raghubar Bhawan, D-155 Bapu Nagar, Jaipur 302 015, India

MATIA, PAUL RAMON, federal judge; b. Cleve., Oct. 2, 1937; s. Leo Clemens and Irene Elizabeth (Linkert) M.; m. Nancy Arch Van Meter, Jan. 2, 1993. BA, Case Western Res. U., 1959; JD, Harvard U., 1962. Bar: Ohio 1962, U.S. Dist. Ct. (no. dist.) Ohio 1969. Law clk. Common Pleas Ct. of Cuyahoga County, Cleve., 1963-66, judge, 1985-91; asst. atty. gen. State of Ohio, Cleve., 1966-69; adminstrv. ast. to atty. gen. State of Ohio, Columbus, 1969-70; senator Ohio State Senate, Columbus, 1971-75, 79-83; ptnr. Hadley, Matia, Mills & MacLean Co., L.P.A., Cleve., 1975-84; judge U.S. Dist. Ct. (no. dist.) Ohio, 1991-99, chief dist. judge, 1999—; mem. 6th Cir. Jud. Coun., 1999—. Candidate Lt. Gov. Rep. Primary, 1982, Ohio Supreme Ct., 1988. Mem. Fed. Bar Assn., , Am. Judicature Soc., Ohio Bar Assn., Cleve. Bar Assn. (President's award 1988), Cuyahoga County Bar Assn., Club at Key Ctr. Avocations: skiing, gardening, travel. Office: US Dist Ct 201 Superior Ave E Cleveland OH 44114-1201

MATIC, TIN, lawyer, journal editor; b. Zagreb, Croatia, Jan. 30, 1961; s. Stjepan and Magdalena (Toscano) M.; m. Marina Dude; children: Tina, Stjepan, Mario. Law Degree, U. Zagreb, 1984, MSc in Law, 1998. Bar: Croatia. Atty. in pvt. practice, Zagreb, 1988—; mem. editl. bd., mem. coun. Croatian Investment Promotion Agy., Zagreb, 1997—. Author: Legal Framework for Doing Business in Croatia, 1997, 98; contbg. author: Kimes International Law Directory, 1997, 98; editor-in-chief Odujetnik Jour. of Croatian Bar Assn., 1995, 96, 97, 98; contbr. more than 20 articles to profl. jours. Mem. Croatian Bar Assn. (mem. mng. bd. 2000), Internat. Bar Assn., Croatian Arbitration Assn., Golf Club Bundek. Roman Catholic. Avocation: golf. Office: Bednjanska 14, 10000 Zagreb Croatia

MATIJASEVIC, LJUBICA, chemical engineering educator, researcher; b. Sobocani, Croatia, July 2, 1950; m. Jovan Matijasevic, Feb. 18, 1978 (dec. Dec. 1987); children: Uros, Ozren. BS, Faculty of Tech., Zagreb, Croatia, 1974; MSc, U. Zagreb, 1981, PhD, 1992. Mem. faculty chem. engring. and tech. U. Zagred, 1975-76, rsch. asst., 1976-81, asst. prof. faculty chem. engring. and tech., 1981—. Contbr. articles to profl. jours.; lectr. in field. Dancer, Folk and Dance Group, Sisak, 1970-79; mountaineer Mountaineering Assn. Croatia, Sisak, 1994—. Recipient PD cert. in environ. mgmt. and cleaner prodn. in industry World Cleaner Prodn. Soc. Mem. N.Y. Acad. Scis. Achievements include plant design, mathematical modeling, mass and heat transfer. Home: Olivera Potzla 46, 44000 Sisak Croatia Office: Fac Chem Engring and Tech, Savskac 16, 10000 Zagreb Croatia

MATIJEVIC, RATKO, gynecologist; b. Zagreb, Croatia, June 8, 1964; p. Vladeta and Nadezda (Ajdukovic) M. MD, U. Zagreb, 1989, MSc, 1992. Rsch. fellow U. Zagreb, 1989-93; intern, resident Srehi Duh Hosp., Croatia Liverpool Maternity Hosp., Arrowe Park Hosp.,Leighton Hosp., 1989-96; trainee in ob-gyn. North-West Regional Health Auth., U.K., 1993-96; clin. lectr. ob-gyn. U. Manchester, Eng., 1996-98; cons. ob-gyn. U. Zagreb, 1998—; head ultrasound dvsn. dept. Sveti Duh Hosp., Zagreb, 1998—. Contbr. articles to profl. jours. Mem. Royal Coll. Ob-Gyn. Avocations: computers, sailing, cycling. Office: U Zagreb Dept Ob-Gyn, Sveti Duh Hosp, 10000 Zagreb Croatia

MATILAINEN, ROSE BIRGITTA, chemist, educator; b. Rautalampi, Finland, Aug. 11, 1966; d. Jouko Pellervo and Eila Armiida (Keurulainen) M. MS, U. Jyväskylä, Finland, 1990, DSc, 1997. Asst. U. Jyväskylä, 1991-97, sr. asst., 1997—; vice mem. Faculty Math. and Natural Scis., Jyväskylä, 1997—. Coach women's ice hockey team, 1999—; gen. mgr. Finnish Women's Olympic Team. Mem. Chem. Industry Fedn. Finland (ICP-AES working group 1991-97). Avocation: playing womens ice hockey. Home: Pohjanaho 4B13, 40520 Jyväskylä Finland Office: U Jyväskylä, Survontie 9 PO Box 35, 40351 Jyväskylä Finland

MATILE, STEFAN, organic chemist, educator; b. Zurich, Switzerland, July 13, 1963; s. Remy and Barbara M.; m. Naomi Sakai, July 15, 1996; 1 child, Luis. Diploma, U. Zurich, 1989, degree, 1994. Postdoctoral rsch. fellow Columbia U., N.Y.C., 1994-96; asst. prof. Georgetown U., Washington, 1996-99; assoc. prof. U. Geneva, Switzerland, 1999—. Mem. AAAS, Am. Chem. Soc., New Swiss Chem. Soc., Sigma Xi. Office: U Geneva Dept Organic Chem, 30 quai Ernest-Ansermet, Geneva CH-1211, Switzerland

MATIN, AKBAR, electrical engineer; b. Lahore, Punjab, Pakistan, Dec. 25, 1965; m. Siddiqui and Rehana Matin; m. Shazia Shafiq, Feb. 2, 1998. BSEE, NED U., Karachi, Pakistan, 1989; MSEE, Polytechnic U., 1994. Sr. asst. editor TV Times, Karachi, 1985-89; elec. engr. AEG Pakistan Ltd., Karachi, 1990; tchg. asst. Polytechnic U., Bklyn., 1991-93; elec. engr. MF Electronics, New Rochelle, N.Y., 1993; prodn. engr. Pico Electronics, Inc., Pelham, N.Y., 1994—. Contbr. articles to profl. jours. Mem. IEEE, Rotaract Club (pres. 1988, Best Pres. award 1988). Avocations: reading, arts, travel, photography. E-mail: info@picoelectronics.com. Office: Pico Electronics Inc 143 Sparks Ave Pelham NY 10803-1810

MATISHOV, GENNADY GRIGORJEVITCH, geography educator; b. Preobrazhenie Bay, Russia, Jan. 1, 1945; s. Grigory Ivanovitch and Elena Vasiljevna (Kamenyar) M.; m. Ludmila Afansjevna Dumenko, Apr. 16, 1966. Degree in geography, U. Rostov, 1967, postgrad. student, 1967-72; DSc in Geography, U. Moscow, 1980. Jr. rschr. PINRO, Murmansk, Russia, 1967-73, sr. rschr., 1973-79, chief Marine Geology Lab.,, 1979-81; dir. Murmansk Marine Biol Inst., Russian Acad. Scis., 1981—, academician, 1997—; prof. geoecology Murmansk U., 1990; sci., tech. policy and ecology adviser Gov. of Murmansk region, 1998; co-chmn. subgroup 1 Russian-Finnish Offshore Tech Working Group; project leader Barents Sea State Project, 1996—. Author: Bottom of the Ocean in the Glacial Period, 1984, World Ocean and Earth Glaciation, 1987, General Ecology and Paleogeography of the Polar Oceans, 1990, Radionuclides in Ecosystem of the Barents and Kara Seas, 1994, Evolution of the Ecosystems and Biogeography of the Arctic European Seas, 1994, Marine Colonial Birds of Murman, 1995, Scientific and Methodological Approaches to the Assessment of the Oil and Gas Extraction Impact on the Arctic Seas Ecosystems (on the example of the Stockman Project), 1997, Bathymetric Map of the Barents and West Kara Seas, 1997, Ecosystems and Biological Resources of the Russian European Seas on the boundary of the XX and XXI centuries, 1999). Chmn. regional coun. of young scientists, Murmansk, 1972-82; dep. Soviet City of People's Deputies, 1982-91. With anti-aircraft def. Russian Mil., 1967-68. Recipient Vet. of Labour medal, 1985, The Badge of Honour Order, 1986, Order of Honour, 1999. Mem. N.Y. Acad. Scis. (hon.), Russian Acad. of Scis. (corrs. mem., mem. Internat. Geosphere-Biosphere Programme Nat. Com., Arctic and Antarctic Study Coun., Hydrobiology and Ichthyology Coun., World ocean Study nat. Com.), Russian Geograph. Soc. (acad. bd.),. Russian Orthodox. Avocations: running, hunting, fishing. Home: 19 Starostina St Flat 20, 183038 Murmansk Russia Office: Murmansk Marine Biol Inst, 17 VLadimirskaya St, 183010 Murmansk Russia

MATISONN, JOANNE RONA, executive secretary; b. Johannesburg, Gauteng, South Africa, Mar. 28, 1959; 1 child, Talia Haidee. Assoc. Inst. Chartered Secs., Wits/Damelin, South Africa, 1994; higher diploma in company law, U. Witwatersrand, South Africa, 1996. Asst. group sec. Premier Pharms. Ltd., Johannesburg, South Africa, 1993-95, Alpha Ltd., Johannesburg, South Africa, 1995-97; asst. group sec. Times Media Ltd., Johannesburg, South Africa, 1997, group sec., 1998—; com. mem. Finmed Med. Aid Scheme, South Africa, 1997—, Inst. of Dirs. Corp. Governance and Ethics Portfolio Com., South Africa, 2000. Named Best Student for Co. Law in South Africa, Chartered Inst. Secs. and Adminstrs., South Africa, 1990. Avocations: walking, table tennis, reading, sewing, gym. Office: Times Media Ltd, 4 Biermann Ave, Rosebank Gauteng 2192, South Africa

MATISONS, JANIS GUNARS, polymer scientist, educator; b. Adelaide, South Australia, Aug. 13, 1955; s. Gunars and Irija (Akots) M.; m. Ina Zandersons, Dec. 16, 1978; children: Simon Peter, Lidija. BS, Adelaide U., 1976, diploma in edn., 1978, PhD, 1983. Physics tutor Adelaide (Australia) U., 1977, rsch. asst., 1978; postdoctoral fellow U. Alberta, Canada, 1983-85; teaching co. fellow Sola Internat., South Australia, 1985-87; rsch. dir. polymer sci. group U. South Australia, 1987-92, rsch. dir., assoc. prof., 1993; chem. cons. Bramite/Flexichem Pty Ltd., Adelaide, 1987-93, editl. bd. Chemistry Australia, 1998—. Editor Polymer Divsn. News, 1997—; editl. bd. Jour. Adhesion Sci. Tech., 1999—; contbr. articles to profl. jours.; patentee in field. Recipient William Culross prize Adelaide U., 1983; George Murray travel scholar Adelaide U., 1983, South Australian Edn. scholar, 1972-75. Mem. AAAS, Royal Australian Chem. Inst. (organizer 20th Australian polymer symposium 1994, chmn. thermal analysis workshop 10th nat. conv. polymer divsn. 1994, mem. standing com. polymer divsn. 1994, macro 98 organizing com., Polymer citation outstanding contbns. to silicon rsch. and polymer edn.), Am. Chem. Soc., N.Y. Acad. Sci., Internat. Conv. Thermal and Calorimetry (Australian councillor), Internat. Calorimetry and Thermal Analysis Conv. Baptist. Avocations: Bible study, basketball, bushwalking. Office: U South Australia, Polymer Sci Group, Mawson Lakes SA 5095, Australia

MATKOWSKY, BERNARD JUDAH, applied mathematician, educator; b. N.Y.C., Aug. 19, 1939; s. Morris N. and Ethel H. M.; m. Florence Knobel, Apr. 11, 1965; children: David, Daniel, Devorah. B.S., CCNY, 1960; M.E.E., NYU, 1961, M.S., 1963, Ph.D., 1966. Fellow Courant Inst. Math. Scis., NYU, 1961-66; mem. faculty dept. math. Rensselaer Poly. Inst., 1966-77; John Evans prof. applied math., mech. engring. & math. Northwestern U., Evanston, Ill., 1977—, chmn. engring. sci. and applied math. dept., 1993-99; vis. prof. Tel Aviv U., 1972-73; vis. scientist Weizmann Inst. Sci., Israel, summer 1976, summer 1980, Tel Aviv U., summer 1980; cons. Argonne Nat. Lab., Sandia Labs., Lawrence Livermore Nat. Lab., Exxon Research and Engring. Co. Editor Wave Motion—An Internat. Jour., 1979-99, Applied Math. Letters, 1987—, SIAM Jour. Applied Math., 1976-95, European Jour. Applied Math., 1990-96, Random and Computational Dynamics, 1991-97, Internat. Jour. SHS, 1992—, Jour. Materials Synthesis and Processing, 1992—; mem. editl. adv. bd. Springer Verlag Applied Math. Scis. Series; contbr. chpts. to books, articles to profl. jours. Fulbright grantee, 1972-73; Guggenheim fellow, 1982-83. Fellow Am. Acad. Mechanics; mem. AAAS, Soc. Indsl. and Applied Math., Am. Math. Soc., Combustion Inst., Am. Phys. Soc., Am. Assn. Combustion Synthesis, Conf. Bd. Math. Scis. (coun., com. human rights of math. scientists), Com. Concerned Scientists, Soc. Natural Philosophy, Sigma Xi, Eta Kappa Nu. Home: 3704 Davis St Skokie IL 60076-1745 Office: Northwestern U Technological Institute Evanston IL 60208-0001

MATLOFF, GREGORY LEE, consulting environmental, space and computer scientist; b. N.Y.C., Mar. 2, 1945; s. Simon and Eudice (Strom) M.; m. Constance Bangs, 1986. BA, Queens Coll. CUNY, 1965; MS, NYU, 1969, PhD, 1976. Engr. Kollsman Inst. Corp., Elmhurst, N.Y., 1965-67, Grumman Aerospace Co., Bethpage, N.Y., 1967-69; rsch. engr. United Aircraft Research Co., East Hartford, Conn., 1969-70; rsch. assoc. Wesleyan U., Middletown, Conn., 1970-71; asst. editor Am. Inst. Physics, N.Y.C., 1971-72; rsch. asst. NYU, 1972-75, postdoctoral research scientist, 1975-77; cons. staff scientist Systems and Applied Sci. Corp., Riverdale, Md., 1978-81; cons. environ. scientist, Bklyn., 1980—; mem. faculty Pratt Inst., 1980-82, adminstr., 1983-85; mem. faculty N.Y.C. Tech. Coll., 1979—, Baruch Coll. CUNY, 1986-89, St. Hilda's and St. Hugh's Sch., 1988-90, CUNY, 1993—, N.Y.U., 1993—. Author: (with E. Mallove) Starflight Handbook, 1989, Urban Astronomer, 1991, Telescope Power, 1993; contbr. articles to profl. jours. Dir. Astronomy program N.Y.C. Dept. Parks and Recreation, 1987-91. NSF grantee, 1975. Fellow Brit. Interplanetary Soc.; mem. AAAS, Am. Meteorol. Soc., Am. Optical Soc., Internat. Acad. Astronautics, N.Y. Acad. Scis., Planetary Soc., Sigma Xi. Lodge: K.M. Home: 417 Greene Ave Brooklyn NY 11216-1111

MATOS, ARNALDO JOSÉ DUARTE, otolaryngologist; b. Porto, Portugal, Aug. 20, 1950; s. Armando Alves and Maria Natalia Governo (Duarte) M.; children: Diogo, Inês, Francisco, José Nuno. MD, F.R. Porto, 1974. Lic. medicine and surgery, specialty in otolaryngology. Intern gen. medicine H.S. Joao, Porto, 1974-79, intern ear, nose and throat, 1980-85; specialist H. Maria Pia, Porto, 1985-94, chief specialist, 1994-95; pvt. practice Porto, 1996—; monitor U. Porto Sch. Medicine, 1980-82, invited asst., 1982-90. Mem. Portuguese Soc. Otolaryngology, Spanish Soc. Otolaryngology. Home: R Molhe 604, 4150 Porto Portugal Office: Arnaldo Matos, Clinica de Otolaryngology, 4200 Porto Portugal

MATOUSEK, JOSEF, glass and ceramic chemistry educator; b. Kelcice, Czech Republic, Dec. 13, 1939; s. Karel and Jarmila (Cveckova) M.; m. Jitka Nesvadbova, June 18, 1960; 1 child, Jiri. MSc, Univ. of Tech., Prague, Czech Republic, 1961, DrTech, 1967; DrSc, Inst. Chem. Tech., Prague, 1982. Postdoctoral fellow Case Western Res. U., Cleve., 1977; rsch. fellow Inst. Chem. Tech., Prague, 1967-80, assoc. prof., 1980-83, prof. glass and ceramic chemistry and tech., 1983—, dean Faculty Chem. Tech., 1980-90, head dept. silicate tech., 1981-89. Author 4 textbooks, numerous articles; patentee; lectr. in field. Mem. Czech Glass Soc. (pres. 1993—), Assn. Glass and Ceramic Industries of Czech Republic (bd. dirs. 1993-99), Am. Ceramic Soc., European Soc. Glass Sci. and Tech. (mem. steering com. 1994—, pres. 1997-99, intern com. class 1997-2000). Avocations: classical music, history, nature, travel. Office: Inst Chem Tech Dept Glass Ceramics, Technicka 5, 166 28 Prague Czech Republic

MATOUSEK, MICHAEL, geriatrician; b. Plzen, Czechoslovakia, June 3, 1960; arrived in Sweden, 1968; s. Milos M. and Alena Lukesova Hanson; m. Louise Anna Maria Tottie, Oct. 12, 1996; 1 child; Beatrice Sophie. MD, Göteborg U., Sweden, 1984, PhD in Medicine, 1995. Cert. specialist in somatic long-term care and geriatric medicine. Physician Sahlgren's and Vasa Hosp., Göteborg, 1984-91, tutor, dept. geriatric medicine, 1991-96, physician, 1996—. Author: Movement Performance in the Elderly, 1995. Ensign, Swedish Army, 1990—. Named Hon. Citizen Upper Dublin Twp., Montgomery County, Pa., 1978. Mem. Internat. Psychogeriatric Assn., European Neurosci. Assn., Swedish Med. Soc. Avocations: art, tennis, sailing, downhill skiing, dance. Office: Vasa Hospital, Dept Geriatric Medicine, 411 33 Göteborg Sweden

MATRAS, JAN WIESŁAW, agriculture educator; b. Halinówka, Lublin, Poland, May 21, 1947; s. Stanisław and Helena (Krzewinska) M.; m. Krystyna Ewa Olesinska, June 30, 1979. MSc, Agrl. U., Lublin, 1970, PhD, 1979, habilitation, 1991. Asst. Agrl. U., Lublin, 1971-73, sr. asst., 1973-78, tutor, 1978-96, prof., 1996—, head sect. animal nutrition, 1997—; protector of choir Agrl. U., Lublin, 1990—; mem. zootechny sect. Polish Com. Sci. Rsch., 1998—. Contbr. articles to profl. jours. Recipient Bronze Order of Merit, Pres. Poland, 1979, Nat. Edn. Bd. medal Ministry Edn. Poland, 1996, Silver Order of Merit, Pres. Poland, 1997, Gold Order of Bd., Polish Soc. Choirs and Orchs., 1997. Mem. Sci. Soc. Roman Catholic. Avocations: music, foreign languages, history. Office: Agrl Univ, Akademicka 13, 20-934 Lublin Poland

MATRICARDI, MARCO, physicist, researcher; b. Ortona, Chieti, Italy, Dec. 27, 1961; s. Dino Amedeo and Giuliana Maria (Dellafrana) M.; m. Tiziana Mancini, Aug. 3, 1997; 1 child, Matteo. Degree in physics 1st class with honors, U. La Sapienza, Rome, 1990. Postgrad. rsch. asst. physics dept. Rome U., 1990-91; physics educator E. Fauser H.S., Novara, Italy, 1992-93; rschr. E.N.E.A., Rome, 1993-94; cons. ECMWF, Reading, Eng., 1994—. Contbr. articles to profl. publs. Sgt. Italian Navy, 1981-83. Mem. Royal Meteorological Soc., Optical Soc. of Am. Avocations: photography, wood working, mountain trekking, cycling. Office: ECMWF, Shinfield Bank, Reading RG2 9AX, England

MATSAS, GEORGE EMANUEL AVRAAM, physics researcher; b. Sao Paulo, Brazil, Dec. 7, 1964; s. Avraam Nisim Ilias and Helene (Patrikelis) M. B in Physics, U. Sao Paulo, 1985; MS, Inst. Fisica Teorica, Sao Paulo, 1988, DSc, 1991. Assoc. rschr. Inst. Fisica Teorica, Sao Paulo, 1993-94, rschr. I, 1995-98, rschr. II, 1999—. Author: (essay) General Relativity and Gravitation, 1994 (Hon. Mention by Gen. Relativity Found. 1994). Mem. Brazilian Soc. of Physics. Office: Inst Fisica Teorica/UNESP, Rua Pamplona 145, 01405900 São Paulo Brazil

MATSCHKE, MANFRED JUERGEN, finance educator; b. Zeyersniederkampen, Elbing, Germany, June 21, 1943; s. Heinrich and Lydia (Steffen) M.; m. Christine Buerkle, Dec. 11, 1968; 1 child, Xenia. Diploma in polit. econ., U. Cologne, Germany, 1968, D in Polit. Sci., 1973, Habil., 1977. Prof. U. Siegen, Germany, 1977-82, Tech. U. Clausthal, Germany, 1982-95; dean faculty of mining, 1985-87; prof. U. Greifswald, Germany, 1995—; dean faculty law and econ., 1999-2000. Author: Entscheidungswert der Unternehmung, 1975, Funktionale Unternehmensbewertung, 1979, Finanzierung der Unternehmung, 1991, Investitionsplanung und Investitionskontrolle, 1993, Betriebliche Umweltwirtschaft, 1996, Kommunale Finanzierung, 1998, Internationale und Aussenhandelsfinanzierung, 1999. Home: Karl-Schildener-Str 5, D17491 Greifswald Meck-Vor, Germany Office: Ernst Moritz Arndt U, Loeffler Str 70, D17 489 Greifswald Germany

MATSKIN, MIHHAIL, computer scientist; b. Odessa, Ukraine, May 14, 1956; s. Boriss and Meeri (Henzel) M.; m. Juulia Hazan, Nov. 29, 1996; 1 child, Artur. MSc, Tech. U., Tallinn, Estonia, 1978; PhD, Inst. of Cybernetics, Tallinn, Estonia, 1984. Rschr. Inst. of Cybernetics, Tallinn, 1978-85, head of dept., 1988-92, leading rschr., 1992-95; head of dept. Soviet New Generation Project, Tallinn, 1985-88; assoc. prof. Norwegian U. of Sci. and Technology, Trondheim, Norway, 1995—. Co-author: Cybernetics, 1982, Computers and Artificial Intelligence, 1986, Notes of the Academy of Science of USSR, Computer and Systems Sciences, 1988, Fundamenta Informaticae, 1997. Recipient Soviet State prize Coun. of Ministers of the USSR, 1987. Mem. ACM, IEEE. Office: Dept Computer/Info Sci, Norwegian U Sci/Tech, N-7491 Trondheim Norway

MATSUBAYASHI, GEN-ETSU, chemistry educator; b. Akashi, Hyogo, Japan, Nov. 14, 1941; s. Baiyu Ichihashi and Iyoko Matsubayashi; m. Michiko Yamanaka, Apr. 16, 1972; children: Takanori, Yoshinori. B Engring., Osaka (Japan) U., 1964, M Engring., 1966, D Engring., 1969. Asst. Osaka U., 1967-79, assoc. prof., 1979-91, prof. chemistry, 1991—. Author:

(with Y. Yamamoto and H. Ogino) Metal Complex Chemistry (Japanese), 1990; Introduction to Chemical Bonding (Japanese), 1995. Mem. Chem. Soc. Japan, Royal Soc. Chemistry, Am. Chem. Soc. Home: 2-12-6 Yuyama-dai, Kawanishi 666-0137, Japan Office: Osaka U, 1-16 Machikaneyama, Toyonaka 560-0043, Japan

MATSUDA, AKIHIKO, pharmaceutical executive, researcher; b. Ube, Yamaguchi, Japan, Sept. 25, 1959; s. Yoshiaki and Kimiko (Koizumi) M.; m. Mitsuko Tagami, June 28, 1987; children: Kent, Sala. BS, Kumamoto U., 1983, MS, 1985; PhD, Kyoto U., 1997. Pharmacology rsch. worker Morishita Pharm. Co., Ltd., Yasu, 1985-92, Roussel Morishita Co., Ltd., Yasu, 1992-96, Nippon Hoechst Marion Roussel Ltd., Yasu, 1996-97, Hoechst Marion Roussel Ltd., Kawagoe, 1998-99, Eli Lilly Japan K.K., Kobe, Japan, 1999—. Contbr. articles to profl. jours. including. Jour. Nutrition Sci. and Vitaminology, Biol. Trace Element Rsch., Clin. Chemistry, among others. Mem. Japanese Pharmacol. Soc. Avocations: playing tennis, driving a car, listening to music. Home: 554-5 Hiramatsu, Kousei-cho, Kouga-gun, Shiga 520-3232, Japan Office: Eli Lilly Japan KK, 7-1-5 Isogamidori, Chuo-ku Kobe 651-0086, Japan

MATSUDA, JUN-ICHI, planetary science educator; b. Amagasaki, Hyogo, Japan, Aug. 21, 1948; s. Takeo and Yoneko (Nishida) M.; m. Kazuyo Hasenaka, June 3, 1976; children: Yoshikazu, Michiaki, Rieko, Sayoko. BS, Tokyo U., 1972, MS, 1974, PhD, 1978. Rsch. assoc. Kobe (Japan) U., 1976-84, assoc. prof., 1984-91; assoc. prof. Osaka (Japan) U., 1991-94, prof., 1994—. Editor: Noble Gas Geochemistry and Cosmochemistry, 1994; exec. editor Geochem. Jour., 1998—. Mem. Am. Geophys. Union, Meteoritical Soc., Geochem. Soc. Japan. Office: Osaka U Grad Sch Sci, Toyonaka, Osaka 560-0043, Japan

MATSUDA, MASATAKE, rail transportation executive. CEO E. Japan Railway, Tokyo, pres. Office: 2-2 Yoyogi 2-chome, Shibuya-ku, Tokyo 151-8578, Japan also: East Japan Rlwy Co One Rockefeller Plz New York NY 10020*

MATSUDA, MICHIYUKI, health facility administrator; b. Kogoshima, Japan, Apr. 27, 1958; m. Naoko Matsuda; children: Akari, Sakino. MD, U. Tokyo, 1983, PhD, 1987. From rschr. to sr. rschr. NIH, Tokyo, 1987-96, head lab virology cell. signal dept. pathology, 1996; dir. dept. pathology Rsch. Inst. Internat. Med. Ctr. Japan, Tokyo, 1996—; assoc. Rockefeller U., N.Y., 1988-90; rschr. Presto Japan Rsch. Devel. Corp., Tokyo, 1992-94. Recipient Sugiura award Japanese Assn. Virology, 1994, Young Scientist Encouragement award Japanese Soc. Oncology, 1997. Mem. AAAS, ASM. Avocation: mountain climbing. Office: Rsch Inst Internat Med Ctr, 1-21-1 Toyama Shinjuku-ku, 162-8655 Tokyo Japan

MATSUDA, TAKAYOSHI, surgeon, educator, biomedical researcher; b. Tonan, Japan, 1937; came to U.S., 1965; MD, Keio Gijuku U., Tokyo, 1963. Diplomate Am. Bd. Surgery. Rotating intern Cook County Hosp., Chgo., 1965-66, resident in surgery, 1966-71, mem. staff, 1971—, dir. burn ctr., 1975-93; asst. prof. U. Ill., Chgo., 1977—; pres. TM & Assocs., River Forest, Ill., 1994—; cons. alternative medicine, cons. leadership devel. Editl. bd. Jour. Burn Care Rehab., 1987-93; contbr. numerous articles to profl. publs., chpts. to books. Fellow ACS; mem. Internat. Soc. Surgery, Internat. Soc. Burn Injuries, Am. Burn Assn., Am. Assn. Surgery Trauma, Soc. Critical Care Medicine, Chgo. Surg. Soc. Office: TM & Assocs Alternative Medicine Cons PO Box 5638 River Forest IL 60305-5638

MATSUEDA, REI, medicinal chemist, researcher; b. Kasaoka City, Okayama, Japan, Feb. 25, 1941; s. Hidefumi Ohnishi and Sadako Matsueda; m. Kakuko Ukita, Sept. 30, 1968; children: Miki, Ei. PhD, U. Tokyo, 1970. Diplomate pharmacist, U.S. Profl. Tennis Assn. Rschr. Sankyo Co. Ltd., Tokyo, 1964, chief rschr., 1980—; rsch. assoc. Tokyo Inst. Tech., 1967-69, U. Ill. Med. Ctr., Chgo., 1978-79; vis. prof. U. Chgo., 1979-80; CEO Japan Tennis Wellness Assn., Tokyo, 1998. nventor of 3-Nitro-2-pyridinesulfenyl (NPy's) reagent and co-inventor of oxidation-reduction condensation reaction with Dr. Teruaki Mukaiyama. Mem. com. Japan Tennis Assn., Tokyo, 1984, Japanese Peptide Soc., Osaka, 1988, Internet Tennis Japan, Tokyo, 1995. Mem. Japan Chem. Soc., Am. Chem. Soc., N.Y. Acad. Scis. Avocations: tennis, fishing. Home: 5-23-2 Matsubara Setagaya, Tokyo 156-0043, Japan Office: Sankyo Co Ltd Exp Chem, Rsch Labs 1-2-58 Hiromachi, Shinagawa 140-8710, Japan

MATSUHASHI, NOBUYUKI, physician, researcher, educator; b. Tokyo, Nov. 7, 1956; s. Kazuo and Yukiko (Yamada) M.; div.; children: Ayuko, Tomoyo; m. Mayumi Iwakiri, Feb. 13, 1994; 1 child, Megumi. BM, U. Tokyo, 1982, MD, 1991. Resident U. Tokyo, 1982-84, asst. prof., 1989—; asst. prof. Tokyo Women's Med. Coll., 1984-85; sr. resident Jichi Med. Sch., Tochigi, Japan, 1985-86. Contbr. articles to profl. jours. U. Tokyo fellow, 1986-88, Nat. Inst. Radiol. Sci. fellow, 1988-89; grantee Japanese Found. Rsch. Promotion Endoscopy, 1995, Takeda Sci. Found., 1995, Chiyoda Mutual Life Found., 1995; recipient Acad. Prize of The Japanese Gastroenterological Endoscopy Soc., 1999. Mem. Japanese Soc. Gastroenterology, Japanese Soc. Immunology, Soc. Mucosal Immunology, Am. Soc. Gastrointestinal Endoscopy, Am. Gastroenterol. Assn. Avocations: fishing. Office: U Tokyo Dept Int Medicine, 7-3-1 Hongo Bunkyo-ku, Tokyo 113, Japan

MATSUI, ROBERT TAKEO, congressman; b. Sacramento, Sept. 17, 1941; s. Yasuji and Alice (Nagata) M.; m. Doris Kazue Okada, Sept. 17, 1966; 1 child, Brian Robert. AB in Polit. Sci, U. Calif., Berkeley, 1963; JD, U. Calif., San Francisco, 1966. Bar: Calif. 1967. Practiced law Sacramento, 1967-78; mem. Sacramento City Council, 1971-78, vice mayor, 1977; mem. 96th-106th Congresses from 5th Calif. dist., 1979—; mem. ranking minority, ways and means, s.s. subcom.; dep. chair Dem. Nat. Com., 1995—; chmn. profl. bus. forum Dem. Congl. Campaign Com.; congl. liaison nat. fin. council Dem. Nat. Com.; mem. adv. council on fiscal policy Am. Enterprise Inst. chmn. Profl. Bus. Forum of the Dem. Congl. Co. and Com.; congl. liaison Nat. Fin. Council, Dem. Nat. Com.; mem. Am. Enterprise Inst. Adv. Council on Fiscal Policy. Named Young Man of Yr. Jr. C. of C., 1973; recipient Disting. Service award, 1973. Mem. Sacramento Japanese Am. Citizens League (pres. 1969), Sacramento Met. C. of C. (dir. 1976). Democrat. Clubs: 20-30 (Sacramento) (pres. 1972), Rotary (Sacramento). Office: US Ho Reps 2308 Rayburn Hob Washington DC 20515-0505

MATSUI, TAKAYOSHI, health facility administrator; b. Marugame, Kagawa, Japan, Jan. 11, 1940; s. Shigenobu and Chieko (Nishiyama) M.; m. Mihoko Fukada, June 1, 1971; children: Masaki, Yumi, Rie. Bachelor Degree, Tokyo U., 1967, Doctorate Degree, 1977. Med. diplomate; qualified specialist neurosurgery. Asst. Tokyo U., 1972-73; rsch. fellow Montefiore Med. Ctr., N.Y.C., 1973-77; assoc. prof. Teikyo U., Tokyo, 1977-83, Osaka Med. Sch., Takatsuki, Japan, 1983-84; prof. Teikyo U., Tokyo, 1984-88; pres. Matsui Neurosurg. Hosp., Kanonji, Japan, 1988-92, Japan Neurological Inst., Japan, 1988—, Matsui Hosp., Kanonji, Japan, 1992—; lectr. Osaka Med. Sch., Takatsuki, 1985—, Ehime U., Matsuyama, Japan, 1995—. Author: Atlas of Stereoscopic Neuroradiology, 1976, An Atlas of the Human Brain for Computerized Tomography, 1978 (Fgn. Min. prize 1981), Color Atlas of Pathology of the Nervous System, 1981, Atlas d'anatomie pathologue due System Nourveux, 1981. Pres. Kagawa All Japan Hosp. Assn., Tokyo, 1997, Orient Med. Rsch. Found., Kanonji, 1997; dir. Japan Brain Found., Tokyo, 1998. Mem. Japan Soc. Neurosurgery (councillor 1968—), Japan Soc. Clin. Neurosurgery (dir. 1998—), Congress Neurosurgeons. Avocations: boat cruising, playing golf, photography. Office: Matsui Hosp, Muragurocho, Kanonji Kagawa 768-0013, Japan

MATSUI, TSUNEO, engineering educator and researcher; b. Gifu, Japan, Sept. 1, 1947; s. Masao and Sanae (Tsuchiya) M.; m. Takako Toda, Jan. 20, 1974; 2 children. BEngring, Nagoya (Japan) U., 1970, MEngring, 1972, DEngring, 1975. Rsch. assoc. Northwestern U., Evanston, Ill., 1975-76, Ariz. State U., Tempe, 1976-77; engr. Hitachi (Japan) Ltd., 1977-79; rsch. assoc. Nagoya U., 1979-89, assoc. prof., 1990-94, prof. engring., 1994—. Mem. Japan Atomic Energy Soc. (dir. Chu-bu br. 1997—, award 1975), Japan Thermal Analysis and Calorimetry. Avocations: tennis, baseball. Office: Nagoya U Grad Sch Engring, Furo-Cho, Chikusa-ku, 464-8603 Nagoya, Aichi Japan

MATSUKAWA, NAOHIRO, semiconductor device reliability engineer; b. Tokyo, Oct. 4, 1952; s. Tsutomu and Noriko (Oana) M.; m. Masumi Tokuyama, Oct. 16, 1983 (div. Nov. 1998); 1 child, Mamoru. Bachelor Degree, Tokyo U. Agr. and Tech., 1975; Master Degree, Tokyo U., 1977, PhD, 1982. Rschr. Toshiba Co., Kawasaki, Japan, 1980-92; sr. rschr. Toshiba Co., Kawasaki, 1992-94, sr. specialist, 1994—; exch. engr. Hewlett Packard Lab., Palo Alto, Calif., 1987-88; com. mem. Reliability Ctr. Japan, Tokyo, 1995—. Contbr. articles to profl. jours. Mem. IEEE (assoc.). Avocations: chorus, swimming, skiing. Home: Tanabe Coopo 303 Namamugi, 4-32-14 Tsurumi-ku, Yokohama-shi 230-0052, Japan Office: Toshiba Co, Shinsugita-cho 8 Isogo-ku, Yokohama-shi 235-8522, Japan

MATSUMINE, HIROTO, neurologist, researcher, educator; b. Nagano, Japan; s. Ryuzo and Fusako M.; m. Toshiko Takanashi; children: Eri, Yuki, Takahiro. MD, Jichi Med. Sch., Tochigi, Japan, 1978; PhD, Juntendo U., Tokyo, 1999. Intern, residency Jichi Med. Sch./Univ., Tochigi, Japan, 1978-79; rsch. fellow dept. endocrinology U. Tex. Southwestern Med. Sch., Dallas, 1987-90; dir. neurology Kobayashi Neurosurg. Hosp., Nagano, Japan, 1990-92; rsch. instr. dept. neurology Juntendo U. Sch. Medicine, Tokyo, 1993-2000; chief scientist Pharmadesign, Tokyo, 2000—. Contbr. articles to profl. jours. Fax: 81-3-3523-9631. Office: Pharmadesign, 4-2-10 Hacchobori Chuo, Tokyo 104-0032, Japan

MATSUMOTO, HIROYUKI, biochemistry educator, researcher; b. Izuhara, Nagasaki, Japan, May 5, 1948; came to U.S., 1977; s. Masayuki and Yuriko (Heima) M.; m. Makiko Ohnishi; 1 child, Masaomi. BS, Kyoto U., Japan, 1972, PhD, 1977. Jr. rschr. U. Hawaii, Honolulu, 1977-79; ass. rsch. scientist Purdue U., West Lafayette, Ind., 1980-85; from asst. asst. prof. to assoc. prof. U. Okla. Health Sci. Ctr., Oklahoma City, 1985-97; prof. Health Sci. Ctr., U. Okla., Oklahoma City, 1997—; mem. study sect. NIH, 1998—; dir. Epscor Okla. biotech. network laser mass spectrometry facility NSF. Contbr. articles to profl. jours. including Nature, Science. Rsch. grantee NSF, 1980-88, NIH, 1985—. Mem. Assn. Rsch. Vision and Ophthalmology, Am. Soc. Biol. Chemists, Protein Soc., Am. Soc. for Mass Spectrometry, Am. Soc. for Photobiology, Japanese Soc. Zoology, Sigma Xi. Achievements include prediction of beta-ionone ring binding pocket in rhodopsin; discovery of phosphorylated homologs of arrestin; research in molecular mechanism of vision, biological mass spectrometry, and ocular proteomics. Home: 1525 Cinderella Ave Norman OK 73072-6030 Office: U Okla Health Sci Ctr 940 Stanton L Young Blvd Oklahoma City OK 73104-5020

MATSUMOTO, JIRO, biology educator, editor; b. Tokyo, Jan. 12, 1932; m. Akiko Cecilia Sato; children: Yoshihiko, Mina. DSc, Tokyo U. Edn., 1964. Asst. prof. cell biology Keio U., Tokyo, 1963-66, assoc. prof. cell biology, 1966-68, prof. cell biology, 1968-97, prof. emeritus cell biology, 1997—; pres. Japanese Soc. for Pigment Cell Rsch., Tokyo, 1997—. Editor Pigment Cell Rsch., 1996-99. Recipient Myron Gordon award Internat. Fedn. Pigment Cell Socs., 1996. Office: Editl Office Pigment Cell, 1-6-35 Tsurumi Tsurumi-ku, Yokohama 230-0063, Japan

MATSUMOTO, KAZUKO, linguistics and second language learning researcher; b. Osaka, Japan, Sept. 22, 1955; d. Isamu and Kiyoko Matsumoto. BA, Osaka City U., 1978; MA, So. Ill. U., 1981; PhD, UCLA, 1996. Cert. in ESL, Japanese Ministry Edn. Asst. prof. Soai U., Osaka, 1981-92; assoc. prof. Aichi U. Edn., Kariya, Japan, 1992—; jour. manuscript reviewer Japan Assn. for Lang. Tchg., 1990—, TESL Can. Fedn., 1996—. Author: Intonation Units in Japanese Conversation: Syntactic, Informational, and Functional Structures, 2000; contbr. articles to profl. jours. including Can. Modern Lang. Rev., TESL Can. Jour., English Lang. Tchg. Jour., RELC Jour., JALT Jour., Linguistics, Pragmatics, Text, Lang. Scis., Studies in Lang. Fellow Osaka-San Francisco Sister City Assn., 1977, Rotary Found., 1979; Fulbright Rsch. grantee Japan-U.S. Ednl. Commn., 1997. Mem. Linguistic Soc. Am., Internat. Pragmatics Assn., TESOL (Summer Inst. scholarship 1986), Amer. Assn. for Applied Linguistics, Rotary Found. (v.p. Dist. 266 club 1984-87, pres. 1988-91, cons., advisor 1984-91). Office: Aichi U Edn Dept English, 1 Hirosawa Igaya-cho, Kariya Aichi 448-0001, Japan

MATSUMOTO, MITSUOMI, physician, educator; b. Kobe, Japan, June 5, 1941; s. Gen-ichi and Shizu (Abe) M.; m. Junko Usui, Mar. 27, 1966; 2 children. MD, Gunma U., Maebashi, Japan, 1966, PhD, 1976. Chief radiologist Gunma Cancer Ctr., 1977-88; assoc. prof. Gunma U., Maebashi, 1988-94; prof. Tokyo Met. U. Health Scis., 1994—; cons. Maebashi Med. Assn., 1988-94, Arakawa Cancer Screening Ctr., Tokyo, 1994—; tchr. Tokyo Women's Med. U., 1994—, Gunma U., Maebashi, 1994—. Editor, author: Computer Tomography of the Body, 1983; author: Computer Tomography of the Chest, 1986, New Computer Tomography of the Chest, 1997. Recipient Koyama Med. award Tokyo Met. Govt., 1994. Office: Tokyo Met U Health Scis, 2-10, 7-chome Higashi-Ogu, Arakawa-ku, Tokyo 116-8551, Japan

MATSUMOTO, TSUKASA, orthopedic surgeon; b. Akune City, Kagoshima, Japan, Jan. 17, 1934; s. Muneo and Moku Chuman; m. Itsuko Matsumoto, Mar. 25, 1960; children: Noritsugu, Masako Nozawa, Junko Itoh, Hisako Takahashi. MB, Juntendo U. Sch. Medicine, Tokyo, Japan, 1961, MD, 1966, PhD, 1966. Diplomate in Orthopedic Surgery. Chief orthopedic surgeon Izunagaoka Juntendo Hosp., 1966-68; chief orthopedic surgery Izumi-City Hosp., Izumishi, Japan, 1968-70; dir. dept. of orthopedic surgery Rosai Hosp., Tokyo, 1970-89; hon. rsch. fellow dept. rheumatology U. Birmingham, U.K., 1990-91; owner, physician Matsumoto Orthopedic Clinic, Tokyo, 1992—; expert med. witness Tokyo High and Low Cts., 1976-90; spl. cons. Japan Supreme Ct., 1980-90. Author: What are the Blood Cells? Part 1, 1997, Part II, 1998; contbr. articles to profl. jours. Recipient Rsch. awards Ministry of Labor, 1992. Mem. AAAS, Japan Traumatology and Occupl. Medicine Assn. (exec. editl. bd. 1977-89), Japanese Soc. for Surgery of the Hand (exec. bd. 1982-95), Japan Fracture Soc. (exec. bd. 1986-99). Avocations: GO, reading, classic music, golf. Home: 1-23-11 Higashi Tamagawa, Setagayaku, Tokyo 158-0084, Japan Office: Matsumoto Living Cell, 2-1-19 Ohmorinaka Ohtaku, Tokyo 143-0014, Japan

MATSUMOTO, YOSHIHISA, metallugist, educator; b. Oita, Japan, Dec. 15, 1964; s. Takashi and Hisako (Kakisaka) M.; m. Tomoko Kuribayashi, Sept. 25, 1993; children: Shota, Takahiro. M Engring., Toyohashi (Japan) U. Tech., 1989; D Engring., Nagoya (Japan) U., 1999. Rsch. assoc. Oita Nat. Coll. Engring., 1989-93, lectr., 1993-97, assoc. prof., 1997—; rsch. fellow Nagoya U., 1997-98. Contbr. articles to profl. jours. Mem. Japan Inst. Metals, Iron and Steel Inst. Japan, Soc. Materials Sci. Avocations: tennis, fishing, skiing, amateur radio. Home: 236-5 ino, Oita 870-0134, Japan Office: Oita Nat Coll Tech, 1666 Maki, Oita 870-0152, Japan

MATSUMURA, KENDO, marine biologist, researcher; b. Hofu, Japan, Sept. 3, 1946; s. Takeo and Mitsuyo Matsumura; m. Kazuko Satoh, Oct. 13, 1974; children: Cey, Meguru, Ryou, Saiko. DVM, Yamaguchi (Japan) U., 1970; PhD, Azabu U., Kanagawa, Japan, 1979. Rschr. Yamaguchi Prefectural Rsch. Inst. of Health, 1971-79, sr. rschr., 1980—; lectr. Yamaguchi U., 1979—. Contbr. articles to Toxicon, Nature, Jour. Agr. and Food Chemistry, otjers. Grante Yamaguchi Prefectural Office, 1991, Chiyoda Found., Tokyo, 1993. Mem. Japanese Soc. Vet. Sci., Japanese Assn. Vet. Informatics. Office: Yamaguchi Pref Rsch Inst, 2-5-67 Aoi, Yamaguchi 753-0821, Japan

MATSUNAGA, KATSUYA, engineering educator; b. Mizuho, Nagasaki, Japan, Aug. 15, 1941; s. Hiraki and Fujika (Baba) M.; m. Sumie Ide, May 9, 1971; children: Sayaka, Yuko, Yujin. MA, Kyushu U., Fukuoka, Japan, 1969, PhD, 1976. Rsch. asst. Kyushu U., Fukuoka, 1972-74, assoc. prof., 1978-97, prof. dept. engring., 1997—; asst. prof. Kumamoto (Japan) U., 1974-77, assoc. prof., 1977-78; advisor Nat. Orgn. for Automobile Safety and Victim's Aid, Tokyo, 1985—. Contbr. articles to profl. jours.; patentee in field. Mem. IEEE. Office: Kyushu Univ, 6-10-1 Hakozaki, Fukuoka 812-8581, Japan

MATSUNO, KOICHIRO, biophysics educator; b. Asahikawa, Hokkaido, Japan, Mar. 14, 1940; s. Kunie and Misue (Miyatake) M.; m. Yukiko Kondoh, Mar. 23, 1964; children: Kyoko, Nahoko. BSc, U. Tokyo, 1963, MSc, 1965; PhD, MIT, 1971. Mem. tech. staff NEC Corp., Tokyo, 1965-68, 72-77; assoc. prof. Toyo U., Tokyo, 1978-79; assoc. prof. Nagaoka (Japan) U. Tech., 1980-84, prof., 1985—; vis. prof. U. Miami, Fla., 1982-84. Author: Molecular Evolution and Protobiology, 1984, Protobiology: Physical Basis of Biology, 1989, The Origin and Evolution of the Cell, 1992; editor Jour. BioSystems, 1988, Jour. Uroboros, 1991, Jour. Symmetry, 1992, Jour. Biocomputing, 1995. Recipient Internat. Inst. Adv. Studies in Sys. Rsch. Cybernet award, 1994; Nat. Found. for Cancer Rsch. grantee, 1984. Mem. Sigma Xi. Home: 606-55 Mizuno, Sayama 350-13, Japan Office: Nagaoka U Tech, 1603-1 Kamitomioka, Nagaoka 940-21, Japan

MATSUNO, TETSUYA, biochemist; b. Yokohama, Kanagawa, Japan, Nov. 26, 1942; s. Masuzoh and Ikuko (Naitoh) M.; m. Noriko Kaneko, May 3, 1969; children: Yumiko, Sayaka. PhD, DSc, U. Tokyo. Vis. researcher Keio U., Tokyo, 1973-76; researcher NIH, Tokyo, 1976-77, chief, 1977-96; vis. prof. Tokyo Med. and Dental U., 1990-96, Columbia U., 1996—. Author: Affinity Chromatography, 1977, A Manual for Virus Research, 1979, Principles and Practice of Experiments with Virus, Chlamydia and Rickettsia, 1987, Propolis-Its Pharmacology and Therapeutic Effects, 1994, rev., 1996, Why Now Propolis?, 1995. Avocations: music, driving, collecting bags and watches. Office: Columbia U Inst Cancer Rsch 701 W 168th St New York NY 10032-2704

MATSUOKA, KAZUMI, linguist, educator; b. Higashiosaka, Osaka, Japan, July 26, 1965; d. Isamu and Mitsue Matsuoka; m. John A. Helwig, Sept. 10, 1994. BA, Kyoto U. Foreign Studies, Japan, 1988; MEd, U. Tsukuba, Ibaraki, Japan, 1990; PhD, U. Conn., 1988. Lectr. U. Conn., Storrs, 1993-95; rsch. asst. U. Conn., Haskins Lab., Storrs and New Haven, 1995-96; vis. instr. Mt. Holyoke Coll., South Hadley, 1996-98; asst. prof. U. Memphis, Tenn., 1998—; vis. instr. Ea. Conn. State U., Windham, 1995; lectr. Yale U., 1996; referee 9t Japanese-Korean Linguistics Conf., Ohio State U., 1999, Studies in Language Sci., Nagoya, Japan, 1999—. Contbr. articles to profl. jours. Vol. Habitat for Humanity, Amherst, Mass., 1990-92, Am. tour de sol, Greenfield, Mass., 1994-97, Spl. Olympics World Games, New Haven, Conn., 1995; faculty advisor Japanese Cultural Orgn., Storrs, Conn., 1994-96. Scholar Rotary Found., 1990-91; fellow U. Conn., 1993. Mem. Linguistic Soc. Am., Assn. Asian Studies, Assn. Tchrs. Japanese, Tsukuba Soc. English Language Tchg. Avocations: women's basketball fan, traveling, choir, nonfictional writing. E-mail: kmatsuok@memphis.edn. Office: Univ Memphis Foreign Language & Lit PO Box 526430 Memphis TN 38152-0001

MATSUOKA, MASATO, occupational and environmental physician, researcher; b. Kitakyushu, Fukuoka, Japan, May 9, 1958; s. Yasunobu and Chizuko (Sagami) M.; m. Atsuko Mabuchi, Aug. 17, 1960; 2 children. MD, U. Occupl. & Environ. Health, Kitakyushu, Japan, 1984, DMSc, 1988. Instr. U. Occupl. and Environ. Health, Kitakyushu, 1988-90, asst. prof., 1990-93, assoc. prof., 1994—; vis. scientist Harvard Sch. Pub. Health, Boston, 1993-94. Rsch. grantee Kaibara Morikazu Med. Sci. Promotion Found., 1992, Health Sci. Ctr. Found., 1995, Sasakawa Health Sci. Found., 1996. Office: Univ Occupl/Environ Health, 1-1 Iseigaoka Yahatanishi-ku, Kitakyushu Fukuoka 807-8555, Japan

MATSUSHIMA, AKIRA PAUL, international company executive; b. Tokyo, July 7, 1937; came to U.S., 1970; s. Hiromasa and Tomiko (Watanabe) M.; m. Kathleen Sue Rowland, Aug. 18, 1968; children: John Hikaru, Karen Emi, Amy Kathryn. BS, Waseda U., Tokyo, 1961; MSME, Waseda U., 1964; M in Mgmt., Northwestern U., 1981. Registered profl. engr., Calif. Asst. mgr. R & D NOK Corp. (Nippon Oil Seal Industry), Tokyo, 1965-67, mgr. rsch. planning, 1968-70; dir. engring. NOK-USA, Inc., L.A., 1970-72, v.p., 1973-74; exec. v.p. NOK-USA, Inc., Chgo., 1975-83, sec., 1979-82, dir., 1971-85; dep. gen. mgr. engring. divsn. NOK Corp., Tokyo, 1983-85; v.p., gen. mgr. original equipment Chgo. Rawhide Mfg. Co., Elgin, Ill., 1985-87; v.p. corp. ops. and tech. Chgo. Rawhide Mfg. Co., Elgin, 1987-95, sr. v.p., 1995-98; pres. Matsushima Mgmt., Palatine, Ill., 1999—; bd. dirs. Hobson Mould Works, Inc., Shell Rock, Iowa; bd. dirs., vice chmn. ARS Mfg., Inc., Virginia Beach, Va., 1999—; bd. dirs., exec. v.p. Koyo-Chgo. Rawhide Co., Ltd., Osaka, Japan, 1986-99; bd. dirs. Chgo. Rawhide-Mexicana, S.A. de C.V., Guadalajara, Mex., 1988-91, 96-98, K.C. Engring., Ltd., Yokohama, Japan, 1989-93, rep. dir., chmn. bd. dirs., 1993—; Japanese govt. del. to Internat. Standardization Orgn., 1973-78; del. Motor Equipment Mfr. Assn./Japan Auto Mfr. Assn. Conf., 1990, 92, 94; mem. adminstrv. commn. Chgo. Presbytery, 1982-83; treas. PLACO Co., Ltd., Saitama, Japan, 2000—. Contbr. articles to tech. jours.; patentee sealing device; holder numerous Japanese patents in field. Mem. governing bd. United Way of Elgin, 1988-96, v.p. planning, 1991-92; mem. N.W. Suburban YMCA, Oak Crest Residence, Elgin, 1989-99, 1st v.p., 1990-92, pres. 1993-95; fund drive chair western divsn. Jr. Achievement, Chgo., 1988-89, mem. governing bd., 1990-98. Mem. Soc. Automotive Engrs. (adv. bd. seals com., chmn. various subcoms., Cert. Appreciation 1986), Nat. Soc. Profl. Engrs., Internat. House of Japan. Presbyterian. Office: Matsushima Mgmt 1660 Beaver Pond Rd Palatine IL 60067-4433

MATSUSHIMA, YOSHIHARU, neurosurgeon, educator; b. Shibuya-ku, Tokyo, Feb. 28, 1936; s. Kazuo and Minako (Kubota) M.; m. Eiko Johnouchi, Apr. 12, 1963; children: Shigeki, Yuko, Hideki. MD, Tokyo Med. and Dental U., 1962, D MSc, 1967. Med. cert. Japan. Intern USAF Hosp., Tachikawa, Japan, 1962-63; surg. fellow Children's Hosp. L.A., 1967-68; assoc. Bokuto Met. Hosp., Tokyo, 1971-73; chmn. dept. neurosurgery Musashino Red Cross Hosp., Tokyo, 1973-80; resident Tokyo Med. and Dental U., 1963-67, instr., 1968-71, asst. prof. dept. neurosurgery, 1980-85, assoc. prof., 1985—. Dir. English Speaking Soc., Musashino City, Tokyo, 1989-96. Grantee Ministry Edn. Japan, 1971, 83, 84, 86, 87, 88, 89, 90, 91, 92, 93, 94, 95, 96, 97, 98, 99, 2000. Fellow Japanese Soc. Neurol. Surgery, Japanese Soc. Stroke, Japanese Soc. Pediat. Neurology, Japanese Soc. Pediat. Neurosurgery. Achievements include development of the encephalo-duro-arterio-synangiosis (EDAS) procedure to treat moyamoya disease. Avocations: tennis, go, sho-gi, reading English novels. Office: Tokyo Med & Dental U, 1-5-45 Yushima, Tokyo 113-8519, Japan

MATSUSHITA, JUNICHI, chemistry educator; b. Yokosuka, Japan, July 4, 1959; s. Noburo and Asako (Suzuki) M.; m. Yuri Kato, Oct. 12, 1986; 1 child, Yuya. B of Engring., Tokai U., Hiratsuka, Japan, 1983; M of Engring., Toyota Tech. Inst., Nagoya, Japan, 1986; PhD, Tokai U., 1991. Rsch. mgr. Toshiba Ceramics Co., Ltd., Tokyo, 1983-96; asst. prof. Tokai U., Hiratsuka, Japan, 1996-98, assoc. prof., 1999—; adj. asst. prof. Pa. State U. University Park, 1998, adj. assoc. prof., 1999—. Contbr. articles to profl. jours. Grantee Tokyo Elec. Power Co. Found., 1997, Iketani Sci. & Tech. Found., 1998, Izumi Sci. & Tech. Found., 1998, Tokuyama Sci. & Tech. Found., 1998, Yazaki Sci. & Tech. Found., 1998, Japan Sheet Glass Found., 1999, Encouragement Assn. Prodn. Tech. Found., 1999, Tanigawa Thermal Tech. Found., 1999, Japan grant-in-aid for sci. rsch. Tokyo Ouka Sic. and Tech. Found., 2000. Office: Tokai U Dept Applied Chem, 1117 Kitakaname, Hiratsuka 259-1292, Japan

MATSUSHITA, KEIICHIRO, economics educator; b. Kobe, Japan, Oct. 8, 1953; s. Haruaki and Shoko (Minami) M.; m. Uyen Ton-Nu-Le, June 27, 1981; children: Kenichi, Kaoru, Megumi. BA, Kyoto (Japan) U., 1976, MA, 1978; PhD in Econs., U. Mich., 1986. Rsch. assoc. Ctr. Southeast Asian Studies Kyoto U., 1980-85; rsch. scientist Inst. Population Problems Ministry of Health and Welfare, Tokyo, 1985-88; demographer Japan Internat. Cooperation Agy., Dept. Census and Stats., Colombo, Sri Lanka, 1988-89; assoc. prof. sociology Ryukoku U., Otsu, Shiga, Japan, 1989-98, prof., 1998-2000; prof. econs. Kansai U., 2000—; vis. prof. U. Colombo, 1996-97. Mem. Population Assn. Am., Am. Econ. Assn., European Soc. Population Econs. Office: Kansai U, Dept Econ, Suita Osaka 564-8680, Japan

MATSUSHITA, YASUO, former banker; b. Jan. 1, 1926. Student, Tokyo U., 1950. Min. of fin., 1950, dep. vice min., 1978; pres. Taiyo Kobe Bank, 1987; chmn. Mitsuit Taiyo Kobe Bank, 1990, Sakura Bank, 1992; gov. Bank of Japan, 1994-98; advisor Sakura Bank Ltd. Vice-chair Tokyo C. of C., 1994. Avocations: reading, tennis. Office: Bank of Japan, 2-1-1 Nihanbashi-Hongokucho, Chuo-ku, Tokyo 103, Japan*

MATSUURA, KOICHIRO, business executive. Grad. law faculty, U. Tokyo; grad. in econs., Haverford Coll. Dir. gen. Econ. Cooperation Bus., Japan's Ministry of Fgn. Affairs, 1988; dir.-gen. N.Am. Affairs Bur.,

Ministry of Fgn. Affairs, 1990, dep. min. for fgn. affairs; chairperson UNESCO World Heritage Com., 1999. Office: 7 place de Fortenoy, 75352 Paris 07 SP, France*

MATSUURA, NAOMI, English and American poetry educator; b. Hyogo Prefecture, Japan, Apr. 27, 1931; m. S. Ishihara, 1999; 2 children. B of Edn., Kobe (Japan) U., 1954. Prof. Kyoto (Japan) Women's U., 1973-97, acad. advisor grad. course, 1982, dean dept. lit., dir., trustee, 1982-84; vis. prof. U. Coll. Swansea, United Kingdom, 1977. Author: Collections of Japanese Poetry, 1969, 82, Image and Metamorphosis, 1975, Dylan Thomas and His Welsh Background, 1979, The Green Fuse-Appreciation of Dylan Thomas' Poetry, 1980, My Long Friend Dylan - Through His Awareness of Word and Being (The Dylan Thomas Soc. Great Britain, 1995); Essays on Contemporary British Poetry, 1996. Mem. English Lit. Soc. Japan, Dylan Thomas Soc. of Great Britain (overseas com. mem.), Wales br. Dylan Thomas Soc. (hon., life). Avocations: oil painting, gardening.

MATSUURA, SHU, biophysicist; b. Fuchu City, Tokyo, Japan, July 23, 1959; s. Tomio and Kimiko (Kishimoto) M. BS, Nagoya U., 1983, MS, 1985, DSc, 1990. Rsch. assoc. Tokai U., Numazu, Japan, 1991-95, lectr., 1995-99, assoc. prof., 1999—; lectr. Aichi Prefectural U. of Fine Art and Music, Nagoya, 1990. Author: (with others) Fractals in Biology and Medicine, 1993, Formation, Dynamics and Statistics of Patterns, 1993; contbr. articles to profl. jours. Grantee The Ministry of Edn., 1993, 94, 95, 98, 99. Mem. Phys. Soc. of Japan, Biophys. Soc. of Japan, Mycol. Soc. of Japan. Avocations: photography, PC programming, plays. Office: Sch High Tech Human Welfare, Tokai U Nishino 317, Numazu Shizuoka 410-0395, Japan

MATSUURA, YUICHIRO, medical school dean; b. Kure, Hiroshima, Japan, May 12, 1936; s. Hideo and Ayako Matsuura; m. Chifumi Tsutamura, Aug. 2, 1965; children: Yuko, Kanji, Yoko. DMS, Hiroshima U., 1961, PhD, 1967. Intern Tsuyama Cent. Hosp., Okayama, Japan, 1961-62; asst. fellow Hiroshima U. Hosp., 1962-65, 66-68, instr., 1968-72; rsch. fellow Med. Coll. S.C., 1965-66; chief Hiroshima Prefectural Hosp., 1969-86; prof. Hiroshima U., 1986—; dir. Hiroshima U. Hosp., 1995-97; dean faculty medicine Hiroshima U., 1998-00. Contbr. articles to profl. jours. Mem. Internat. Coll. Surgeons, Internat. Acad. Chest Physicians and Surgeons, Soc. Thoracic Surgery, Internat. Soc. Heart-Lung Transplant, Internat. Coll. Angiology, Am. Coll. Angiology, Internat. Soc. Artificial Organs, Am. Soc. Artificial Organs, Japan Surg. Soc., Japan Soc. Thoracic Surgery, Japan Soc. Circulation, Japan Soc. Angiology, Rotary Club (Hiroshima). Home: 3-18-6 Midori, Minamiku, Hiroshima 734, Japan Office: Hiroshima U Sch Medicine, 1-2-3 Kasumi Minamiku, Hiroshima 734, Japan

MATSUYAMA, YOSHINORI, university chancellor, psychology educator; b. Kyoto, Japan, Dec. 5, 1923; m. Michiko Kinugasa, 1949; 3 children. Grad., Doshisha U., Osaka U.; LLD (hon.), Wesleyan U., Amherst U. Prof. psychology emeritus Doshisha U., Kyoto, 1959—, pres., 1973-79, 80-83, chancellor, 1985—. Author: A Study on Behaviour Disorders, 1957, A Study on Anxiety, 1961, Psychology of Motivation, 1967, Human Motivation, 1981. Office: Doshisha Univ, Karasuma Imadegawa, Kyoto Kamigyo-ku 602-8580, Japan*

MATSUZAKI, JUNJI, broadcast executive; b. Tokyo, May 19, 1941; s. Nobuo and Fujiko (Soh) M.; m. Miyukiko Hamano, May 16, 1971; children: Ryu, Gen, Shu. BEE, U. Tokyo, 1964. Staff Japan Broadcasting Corp. NHK, Tokyo, 1964, staff Tech. Rsch. Labs., 1965-81, mgr. engring. hdqrs., 1984-90, gen. mgr. HDTV divsn., 1991-92, dep. dir. gen. Engring. Adminstrn. Dept., 1994-96; sr. v.p. NHK Engring. Svcs., Inc., 1995-99, Nippon Broadcasting Corp., Takada, Japan, 2000—; vis. rsch. assoc. Stanford (Calif.) U., 1970; exec. prodr. Internat. Electronic Cinema Festival Japan Com., 1991-92; lectr. Tokai U., 1992-93. Mem. Soc. Motion Picture and TV Engrs. Avocations: skiing, calligraphy. Home: 3-24-3 Shinmei Adachiku, Tokyo 121-0051, Japan Office: Nippon Broadcasting Corp, 3-23-22, Takada 150-0042, Japan

MATTARELLA, SERGIO, minister of defense. Min. edn. Italy, 1989-91; dep. leader Christian Dem. Party, 1990-92; dep. premier, 1998; min. def. Italy. Editor Il Popolo newspaper. Office: Min Defense, Vial XX Settembre 8, 00187 Rome Italy*

MATTAS, RICHARD FRANK, nuclear energy industry executive; b. Chgo., Sept. 14, 1947; s. Charles Joseph and Lillian (Sebek) M.; m. Loretta Ann Urbaczewski, June 27, 1970. BA, Yale U., 1969; MS, U. Ill., 1971, PhD, 1974. Lab. asst. U. Ill., Champaign, 1969-74; post-doctoral appointee Argonne (Ill.) Nat. Lab., 1974-75, metallurgist, 1975-81, prin. investigator, 1981-85, mgr. fusion blanket tech., 1985-89, assoc. dir. fusion power, 1989-99, sr. scientist, 1999, dir. fusion power, 1999—; task leader liquid metals tech. Internat. Energy Agy., Vienna, 1993—; chmn. tech. program Internat. Symposium on Fusion Nuclear Tech., L.A., 1995, tech. program com., 2000; nat. coord. Advanced Limiter-Divertor Program, 1998—. Contbr. articles to sci. and profl. jours. Bd. dirs. Galena (Ill.) Territory Assn., 1997—. Recipient Cert. of Appreciation U.S. DOE, 1988, 90. Mem. Am. Soc. for Metals, Fusion Power Assocs, Driftless Area Ptnrship. Natural Resource Conservation Orgn. (vice chmn. 1997—), Sierra Club. Avocations: photography, oil painting, bird watching. Home: 1585 Stonebridge Trl Wheaton IL 60187-7112 Office: Argonne Nat Lab 9700 Cass Ave Argonne IL 60439-4803

MATTEI, MASSIMILIANO, electrical engineer; b. Napoli, Italy, Feb. 7, 1969; s. Antonio and Fausta Rosaria (Sena) M.; m. Laura Ricci, Oct. 24, 1997; 1 child, Fousto. Degree in aero. engring., U. Napoli (Italy) Federico II, 1993, PhD in Elec. Engring., 1997. On contract prof. sys. theory U. Napoli, 1996-97; asst. prof. U. Reggio Calabria, Italy, 1997—; cons. various cos., Italy, 1993—. Contbr. articles to profl. jours. Recipient Premio di Laurea award Consorzio Napoli Richerche, 1993. Mem. IEEE, AIAA. Roman Catholic. Avocations: playing piano, running, canoeing, history, philosophy. Home: II traversa croce, di Piperno 32, 80126 Napoli Italy Office: DIMET U Reggio Calabria, Via Graziella, 89100 Reggio Calabria Italy

MATTELAER, JOHAN JOZEF, urologist; b. Sept. 28, 1937. MD, Cath. U., Louvain, 1962. Chief dept. urology O.L.V. Hosp., Kortryk, Belgium, 1969-88, St. Maartens Clin., Kortryk, 1988—; lector extra muros Cath. U., Leuven, 1989-94. Editor: De Historia Urologiae Europaeae, Vol. I-VII; author: The Phallus in Art and Culture. Mem. European Assn. Urology (chmn. hist. com. 1993—), Belgian Assn. Urology (pres. 1996-98), European Bd. Urology (sec.). Avocations: tribal art, history of medicine, golf. Office: St Maartens Clin, Burgemeestr Vercruysselan 5, B-8500 Kortryk Belgium

MATTER, THEODORE SAYLOR, retired chemical engineer; b. Allentown, Pa., Nov. 25, 1917; s. Guy Earl Matter and Lilla Edna Saylor; m. Margaret Elizabeth Edwards, Oct. 11, 1947; children: Kemble S., Andrew B., Craig E. BS in Chem. Engring., U. Pa., 1939, postgrad., 1947-49. Jr. chem. engr. Am. Viscose Corp., Lewistown, Pa., 1939-42; pilot plant supr. Am. Viscose Corp., Marcus Hook, Pa., 1946-53, sr. process engr. R&D, 1954-60, 69-76; quality control materials and processes GE Missile Space Dept., Valley Forge, Pa., 1960-63; sr. engr. tech. svc. Am. Viscose (FMC), Marcus Hook, 1963-69; ret., 1976. Author: Reverend Andrew Bashore Saylor, vol. I, 1996, vol. II, 1997, vol. III, 1998, vol. IV, 1999. Vol. leader, dist. tng. chmn. Boy Scouts Am., Upper Darby, Pa., 1946-59; pres. Elder's Assn. Del. and Montgomery Counties—Presbyn. Ch., 1980-86. Capt. U.S. Army, 1942-46, PTO. Decorated Bronze Star. Republican. Presbyterian. Avocations: tennis, genealogy, ship models, church activities. Home: 510 Netherwood Rd Upper Darby PA 19082-3623

MATTES, ROBERT BRITT, civil rights advocate; b. Youngstown, Ohio, Aug. 31, 1962; s. Carl Stephen and Beatrice Anne (Gainard) M.; m. Amanda Gouws, Sept. 16, 1990 (div. June 1998); 1 child, Frances Marie. AB, Youngstown State U., 1984; MA, U. Del., 1986; PhD, U. Ill., 1992. Instr. U. Ill., Urbana, 1989; vis. lectr. U. Cape Town, S. Africa, 1993-94; program mgr. Inst. for Democracy in S. Africa, Cape Town, 1996-99. Author: (book) Judgment and Choice in South Africa: 1994 Election, 1996; contbr. articles to profl. jours. Grantee U.S. Inst. Peace, Washington, 1987; vis. scholar, Brookings Inst., 1990. Roman Catholic. Office: Inst Democracy S Africa, 6 Spin St, 8001 Cape Town S Africa

MATTESON, CLARICE CHRIS, artist, educator; b. Winnipeg, Man., Can., Sept. 2, 1918; came to U.S., 1922; d. Sergis and Nina (Balter) Alberts; m. D.C. Matteson, 1956 (dec. 1976); children: Kemmer, Gretchen. BA, Met. State U., 1976; MA in Liberal Studies, Hamline U., 1986; PhD in Humanities, LaSalle U., 1995. Mem. Orson Welles' staff, Hollywood, Calif., 1945-46; owner Hilde-Gardes Co., L.A., 1947-56; instr. art North Hennepin C.C., Brooklyn Park, Minn., 1975-81; prodr., host Accent on Art TV Program, St. Paul, 1979—; instr. art Lakewood C.C., U. Minn., Normandale C.C., Bloomington (Minn.) Sch. Dist., Mpls. Sch. Dist., St. Paul Sch. Dist., 1981—; guest artist Montserrat Gallery, Soho, N.Y.C., winter and summer 1999; appeared as guest artist WCCO-TV, 1998. One-woman shows include Decathlon Club, 1998; exhibited in group shows at Mpls. Inst. Art, 1994-98, St. Paul, 2000, Landmark Ctr. Art Show; represented in collection Gov.'s Residence; represented by Montserrat Art Gallery, N.Y.C., Gallery 416, Mpls., Jean Stephen Art Gallery, Mpls., 1999, 2000; corr. Schaumburg (Ill.) Newspapers, 1962-68; prodr., host TV series Kids Art, Mpls.-St. Paul, 1995—; prodr. series program Internat. Cafe Internet Arts, 1996—; (TV show) Accent On Art , Mpls., 1980—; patentee plastic products; composer. Active Minn. Orch. (WAMSO), Mpls., 1972—, vol. Recipient award for creative leadership Minn. Assn. for Continuing Adult Edn., 1977, Gold Cup award Bloomington Cable, 1989, Gov.'s Letter of Commendation, 1994, honored as outstanding grad. for past 25 yrs. by Met. State U., 1997; Park Cable TV grantee, 1982, Minn. Humanities Commn. grantee, 1985. Mem. ASCAP (award 1997, 98, 99, 2000), AAUW (dir. arts com. 1989-90, bd. dirs. 1990-92), Am. Pen Women (Minn. chpt. 1994—, v.p. 1998), Am. Composers Forum, Minn. Artists Assn., Minn. Territorial Pioneers (bd. dirs. 1995—, v.p. 1997, 98, 99, 1st v.p. 1999, 2000, elected Minnesotan of Yr., 2000), Internat. Alliance for Women in Music, St. Paul Neighborhood Network, N.Y. Neighborhood Network, Internat. Platform Speakers (award 1998), Mpls. Telecom. Network, Metro Cable Network, Century Cable. Avocations: tennis, dancing, writing children's books, composing liturgical music. Home and Office: 2119 Sargent Ave Saint Paul MN 55105-1126

MATTESON, WILLIAM BLEECKER, lawyer; b. N.Y.C., Oct. 20, 1928; s. Leonard Jerome and Mary Jo (Harwell) M.; m. Marilee Brill, Aug. 26, 1950; children: Lynn, Sandra, Holly. BA, Yale U., 1950; JD, Harvard U., 1953. Bar: N.Y. 1954. Clk. to judge Augustus N. Hand U.S. Ct. Appeals, 1953-54; clk. to U.S. Supreme Ct. Justice Harold H. Burton, 1954-55; assoc. firm Debevoise & Plimpton (and predecessors), N.Y.C., 1955-61; ptnr. Debevoise & Plimpton (and predecessors), 1961—, Debevoise & Plimpton (European office), Paris, 1973-78; presiding ptnr. Debevoise & Plimpton, 1988-93; lectr. Columbia U. Law Sch., 1972-73, 78-80. Trustee Peddie Sch., Hightstown, N.J., 1968-73, Kalamazoo Coll., 1972-77, Miss Porter's Sch., Farmington, Conn., 1977-83, N.Y. Inst. Spl. Edn., 1981—, Salk Inst., La Jolla, Calif., 1993-96, vice-chair, 1994-96, Statue of Liberty Ellis Island Found., 1996—, Hartford Found., 1996—; active USA Bus. and Industry Adv. Com. to the Orgn. for Econ. Coop. and Devel., Paris, 1986-2000; chmn. Worldwide Bus. and Industry Adv. Com., 1994-96; vice chmn. U.S. Coun. for Internat. Bus., 1990-2000, hon. trustee. Mem. ABA, FBA, Internat. Bar Assn., N.Y. State Bar Assn., Assn. of Bar of City of N.Y. (chmn. securities regulation com. 1968-71), Harvard U. Law Sch. Assn. N.Y.C. (trustee 1968-73), Coun. Fgn. Rels., Union Club, Sky Club, Sankaty Head Club, John's Island and Winsdor Clubs, N.Y. Yacht Club. Office: Debevoise & Plimpton 875 3rd Ave Lowr 16 New York NY 10022-6225

MATTHAU, CHARLES MARCUS, film director; b. N.Y.C., Dec. 10, 1965; s. Walter and Carol M. BA, U. So. Calif., 1986. Pres. The Matthau Co., L.A., 1987—; bd. govs. Cedar Sinai Med. Ctr., L.A. Dir. motion picture Doin' Time on Planet Earth, 1990 (Saturn award Coun. Film Orgns., Silver Scroll award Acad. Sci. Fiction); dir., prodr. TV show Mrs. Lambert Remembers Love, 1993 (Golden Angel award Best TV Spl. 1993, Golden Medal award Best Drama Prodn. 1993, Grand award The Houston Internat. Film Festival); dir., prodr. motion picture The Grass Harp, 1996 (recipient Best Dir. Family Film awards 1996); dir. The Marriage Fool, 1998; dir. over 50 feature shorts. Nat. spokesperson Am. Lung Assn., L.A., 1989—; active Action on Smoking and Health, Washington, 1986—. Recipient Cine award, Coun. Non-Theatrical Events, Washington, 1985, Golden Seal award, London Amateur Film Festival, 1986, Platinum Circle award Am. Film Inst. Mem. Dirs. Guild Am.

MATTHES, HEIDE-DÖRTE, agriculturist, researcher, educator; b. Dessau, Germany, Jan. 15, 1939; d. Karl Ferdinand and Gertrud (Kapol) Bückmann; m. Joachim Matthes, De. 1, 1961; children: Dörte, Karl, Hinrich, Hilke. Diploma in agr., U. Rostock, Germany, 1963; D of Agr., Berlin Acad., 1972; DSc, U. Rostock, 1986. 2d chmn. Farm Orgn., Lambrechshagen, Germany, 1963-69; scientist Rsch. Ctr. of Animal Prodn., Dummerstorf, Germany, 1969-92, Rsch. Inst. of Animal Breeding, Ulan Bator, Mongolia, 1992; lectr. U. Rostock, 1993—, U. Greifswald, 1998—, Alepro (Sy.), 1999; scientist U. Budapest, 1989; chmn. Orgn. of Ecol. Agr.-Bioparkmarket, Germany, 1991—, dir. orgn. of comml. ecol. products, Bioparkmarket, 1993—; bd. dirs. Found. for Environment, 1994; mem. adv. bd. Ministry of Environ., Germany, 1992-94; prof. U. Rostock, 1999—. Editor: Lenzener Gespräche, 1992—, Schriftenreihe Biopark, 1996—, Regulation of Metabolism, 1994, Cattle and Sheep Breeding Ecology, 1991, Organic Agriculture, 1991, Landscape Care, 1992, Meat Quality and Extensification, 1993, Animal Health and Welfare, 1994. E-mail: matthes@fbn-dummeislolf.de. Home: Vorweden 1, D-18069 Rostock Germany Office: Rsch Inst Biology Farm Animals, J-von-Liebig-Weg 2, D-18059 Rostock Germany

MATTHEW, LYN, sales and marketing executive consultant; b. Long Beach, Calif., Dec. 15, 1936; d. Harold G. and Beatrice (Hunt) Matthew; m. Wayne Thomas Castleberry, Aug. 12, 1961 (div. Jan. 1976); children: Melanie, Cheryl, Nicole, Matthew. BS, U. Calif., Davis, 1958; MA, Ariz. State U., 1979. Cert. hotel sales exec., meeting prof. Pres. Davlyn Cons. Found., Scottsdale, Ariz., 1979-82; cons., vis. prof. The Art Bus., Scottsdale, 1982—; pres., dir. sales and mktg. Embassy Suites, Scottsdale, 1987-98, Matthew Enterprises, Inc., Scottsdale, 1998—; trustee Hotel Sales and Mktg. Assn. Internat. Found., 1988-90, chmn., 1991-93, mem. exec. com., 1993-95; mktg. exec. HSMAI, 1998—; vis. prof. Maricopa C.C., Phoenix, 1979—, Ariz. State U., Tempe, 1980-83; cons. Women's Caucus for Art, Phoenix, 1983-88; state dir. AOBTA, 1999—. Author: The Business Aspects of Art, Book I, 1979, Book II, 1989, Marketing Strategies for the Creative Artist, 1985, Moxibustion Manual, 1999. Bd. dirs. Rossom House and Heritage Square Found., Phoenix, 1987-88. Mem. Women Image Now (Achievement and Contbn. in Visual Arts award 1983), Women in Higher Edn., Nat. Women's Caucus for Art (v.p. 1981-83), Ariz. Women's Caucus for Art (pres. 1980-82, hon. advisor 1986-87), Ariz. Vocat. Edn. Assn. (sec. 1978-80), Ariz. Visionary Artists (treas. 1987-89), Hotel Sales and Mktg. Assn. Internat. (pres. Great Phoenix chpt. 1988-89, regional dir. 1989-90, bd. dirs. 1985-90), CHME (profl. designation tng. chair 1995, cert. commr. 1998—), Meeting Planners Internat. (v.p. Ariz. Sunbelt chpt. 1989-91, pres. 1991-92, Supplier of Yr. award 1988, CMP cert. trainer 1995—), Soc. Govt. Meeting Planners (charter bd. dirs. 1987, Sam Gilmer award 1992, nat. conf. co-chair 1993-94), Ariz. Visionary Artists (treas. 1987-88), Ariz. Acad. Performing Arts (v.p. bd. dirs. 1987-88, pres. 1988-89).

MATTHEW, NEIL EDWARD, artist, educator; b. Anderson, Ind., Jan. 19, 1925; s. Mark Neil and Mary Bertha (Clifford) M.; m. Jeannette Morrow, Dec. 22, 1963. BA in Edn., Ariz. State U., 1949; MFA, Ind. U., 1955; postgrad., U. Iowa, 1957-58, State Acad. of Fine Arts, Stuttgart, Germany, 1959-60. Tchr., art Covington (Ind.) Jr. H.S., 1949-50, Clay H.S., South Bend, Ind., 1955-57; instr. art Ind. U., Kokomo, Ind., 1960-64; instr. to asst. prof. art. Ind. U., Indpls., 1964-71; asst. to assoc. prof. art Herron Sch. Art/Ind. U. Purdue U., Indpls., 1971-87, assoc. prof. emeritus, 1987—; art exhbit judge Kokomo Art Assn., Ind., 1970; rschr. for salary studies AAUP, Ind. U. Purdue U., 1970s, others. Painter oils, acrylics, and watercolors, 1945—; printmaker etching and woodcuts, 1953—; photographer; one-man shows include: Lyman-Snodgrass Gallery, Indpls., 1984, Lieber's Gallery, Indpls., 1962, 68, Purdue U. Gallery, 1962, Ind. U. Med. Ctr., Indpls., 1966, Ind. U. at Kokomo, 1967, Ind. U. Purdue U. Archives and Libr., 1996, 98, others; group shows include: Ind. Arts Competition, 1988, Purdue U., 1966, 69, Libr. of Congress, 1956, 58, 59, numerous others; work represented at Lieber's Gallery, Indpls., 1959-73, Assoc. Am. Artists, N.Y.C., 1965-72, Lyman-Snodgrass Gallery, Indpls., 1984-85, Ruschman Gallery, Indpls., 1989—; permanent collections include: U. Ariz. Mus. of Art, Tucson, Ctr. for Creative Photograhy, Tucson, Archives, Ind. U. -Purdue U. at Indpls., Indpls. Mus. Art, others. Pvt. first class U.S. Army, 1950-52. Named Outstanding Art Grad., Ariz. State U., Tempe, 1949; recipient tuition scholarship U. Iowa, Iowa City, 1957-58; Fulbright grantee, Stuttgart, 1959-60. Mem. Soc. Ind. Pioneers, Coll. Art Assn., Ctr. for Creative Photography, Assocs. of Art History (bd. dirs. 1991-97), Fulbright Assn. Republican. Presbyterian. Avocations: travel, reading, art history, fiction. Home: 5233 North Via Sempreverde Tucson AZ 85750-5967

MATTHEWS, ALLAN FREEMAN, geologist; b. Wakefield, Mass., May 27, 1916; s. Ralph Freeman Matthews and Mary (Morrill) Hill; m. Shirley Jean Spencer, Dec. 23, 1937 (div. Oct. 1955); children: David Allan, Kim; m. Doris Olive Haignere, June 26, 1962. BA, Carleton Coll., 1937; MS, Antioch Coll., 1939; postgrad., Johns Hopkins U., 1939-40. Tech. editor Ceramic Industry Jour., Chgo., 1940-41; editor, sect. chief U.S. Bur. of Mines, Washington, 1941-51; asst. dir., staff Pres.'s Materials Policy Commn., Washington, 1951-52; materials cons. Nat. Security Resources Bd., Washington, 1952-53; ops. analyst Johns Hopkins Ops. Rsch. Office, Chevy Chase, Md., 1953-54; program officer U.S. Agy. for Internat. Devel., Washington, 1954-75; editor, pub. Developing Country Courier, McLean, Va., 1978-85; del. UN Global Modeling Conf., Paris, 1982; initiated citizens transnat. constl. conv., The Hague, Netherlands, 1998; chmn. constn. action group Alliance for Democracy, Waltham, Mass., 1997-99; minerals cons. Global 2000 Project, 1978-80; drafter petition and rationale for nat. initiative and referendum sys. at www.unitedpeople.org; cons. in field. Author: Sovereigns Peacefully Take Charge, 1997; editor: Minerals Yearbook, 1947-50; contbr. articles to profl. jours. and chpts. to books. Dir., sec. Assn. to Unite the Democracies, Washington, 1957—; core planner 20/20 Vision, Washington, 1991-97; a founder The Reston Forum, 1990-92; pres. Waterford Sq. Condominium Assn., Reston, 1992. Lt. (j.g.) USN, 1944-46. Recipient Meritorious award U.S. Agy. for Internat. Devel., 1955, Commendation for Devel. Analysis, 1957; named Fellow in Geology, 1937-39. Mem. AAAS, ACLU, Democratic Socialists Am., Natural Resources Def. Coun., U N Assn., World Federalist Asssn., Unitarian Universalist Assn., Fed. Am. Scientists, Soc. for Internat. Devel. (proposer continental fed. unions at N.Am. regional conf. 2000), Sierra Club. Achievements include evaluation of mineral resources adequacy and advancement of transnational constitutions. Home: 11500 Fairway Dr Apt 503 Reston VA 20190-4457

MATTHEWS, ANDREW JULIAN MORTON, solicitor; b. Loughborough, Eng., May 20, 1958; s. Geoffrey Richard and Margaret Joan (Morton) M. BA with honors, Durham U., 1979. Bar: Law Soc. Eng. 1982, Chamber of Advocates Czech Republic, 1997. Solicitor Lovell, White & King, London, 1980-85; assoc. Allen & Overy, London, 1985-90; resident mgr. McKenna & Co., Prague and Moscow, 1990-94; resident ptnr. Clifford Chance, Prague, 1995-97, Gimaldi & Clifford Chance, Rome, 1998-99, Clifford Chance Wirot, Bangkok, 1999—. Contbr. articles to profl. jours. Mem. Czech Chamber of Advocates, Solicitors Co. Avocations: motor sports, scuba diving, travel. Home: High Trees House, Greatwood, Chislehurst BR7 5HU, England Office: Clifford Chance Wirot, 130 Wirless Rd Fl 21 Tower3, 10330 Bangkok 1, Thailand

MATTHEWS, CHARLES SEDWICK, petroleum engineering consultant, research advisor; b. Houston, Mar. 27, 1920; s. Charles James and Zadoc Coleman (Sedwick) M.; m. Miriam Loraine Ormerod, June 2, 1945; children—Joan Gail, Wendy Loraine. BSChemE, Rice U., 1941, MSChemE, 1943, PhD in Chemistry, 1944. Registered profl. engr., Tex. Engr. Shell Devel. Co., San Francisco, 1944-48; rsch. engr. Shell Devel. Co., Houston, 1948-56, dir. rsch., 1967-72; chief reservoir engr. Shell Oil Co., Houston, 1965, mgr. engring., 1972-73, sr. petroleum engring. cons., 1973-89; engring. adv. com. Rice U., Houston, 1973-77; cons. Dept. Energy, Washington, 1974-78, adv. com., 1975-79; spl. asst. Nat. Petroleum Council, Washington, 1981-83; reserves com. Am. Petroleum Inst. Author: Pressure Buildup and Flow Tests in Wells, 1967; contbr. articles to profl. jours.; patentee in field. Chmn. Tex. Engrs. for Conservation, Houston, 1973. Recipient Disting. Alumnus award Rice U., 1994. Mem. NAE, Soc. Petroleum Engrs. (hon. mem., Lester Uren award 1975, disting. author, disting. lectr. 1968, Disting. lectr. emeritus 1986), Phi Beta Kappa, Sigma Xi, Tau Beta Pi, Phi Lambda Upsilon. Republican. Methodist. Clubs: Houston, Meyerland (treas. 1982-85). Avocations: swimming; fishing. Home: 5307 S Braeswood Blvd Houston TX 77096-4149

MATTHEWS, ERIC GLASSWELL, museum curator, researcher; b. Neuilly, Seine, France, Feb. 9, 1932; arrived in Australia, 1969; s. Herbert Lionel and Edith (Crosse) M.; m. Barbara Jane Marshall, June 17, 1961; children: Elizabeth, Leslie, Christopher. BA, Columbia U., 1953; PhD, Cornell U., 1960. Prof. U. P.R., Rio Piedras, 1961-69; curator of insects South Australian Mus., Adelaide, Australia, 1970—; vis. lectr. Instituto Politécnico Nacional, Mex., 1964. Author: Insect Ecology, 1976, (with R.L. Kitching), 2d edit., 1984; author: (7 books) Guides to the Genera of Beetles of South Australia, 1980-97; contbr. articles to profl. publs. Pvt. 1st class U.S. Army Med. Corps, 1953-55. Postdoctoral fellowship NIH/Harvard U., 1960, Fulbright fellowship Australian-Am. Found., 1967, Rsch. fellowship Commonwealth Sci. and Indsl. Rsch. Orgn., 1969. Mem. Australian Entomological Soc., Sigma Xi, Phi Kappa Phi. Avocations: restoration of vintage cars. E-Mail: matthews.eric@saugov.sa.gov.au. Office: South Australian Museum, North Terrace, Adelaide SA 5000, Australia

MATTHEWS, MELVYN WILLIAM, priest; b. East Cowes, England, Sept. 29, 1940; m. June Pamela Knight; three children. BD, London U., 1967; MA, Oxford U., 1969. Ordained priest, Ch. of Eng. Asst. curate St. Andrew Eafield London Diocese, 1967-70; asst. chaplain Southampton U., 1970-73; lectr. U. Nairobi, Kenya, 1973-76; vicar All Saints Ch., London, 1976-79; sr. chaplain U. Bristol, England, 1979-87; dir. Ammerdown Ctr., Bath, England, 1987-93; canon, chancellor Wells Cathedral, England, 1997—. Author: Delighting in God, 1987, The Hidden Journey, 1989, God's Space in You, 1992, The Hidden Word, 1992, Finding Your Story, 1992, Rediscovering Holiness, 1996, Both Alike to Thee, 2000. Home: 8 The Liberty, Wells Somerset BA5 2SU, England

MATTHEWS, WYHOMME S., music educator, college administrator; b. Battle Creek, Mich., July 22, 1948; d. Woodrow R. and LouLease (Graham) Sellers; m. Edward L. Matthews, Apr. 29, 1972; children: Channing DuVall, Triston Curran, Landon Edward, Brandon Graham. AA, Kellogg C.C., 1968; MusB, Mich. State U., 1970, MA, 1972, MusM, 1972. Cert. elem. and secondary tchr., Mich. Tchr., vocal music dir. Benton Harbor (Mich.) Pub. Schs., 1971-72, dir. vocal music, 1972; dir. edn. head start program Burlington (N.J.) County, 1972-73; pvt. music tchr., 1973-89; tchr. Southeastern Jr. H.S., 1986-87, W.K. Kellogg Jr. H.S., 1987-89; chair visual and performing arts dept. Kellogg C.C., Battle Creek, Mich., 1989-99; dir. Eastern acad. Ctr. Kellogg C.C., 1999—; part-time instr. Kellogg C.C., 1973-89, dir. Eclectic Chorale, 1973—, dir., organizer Kellogg C.C. Eclectic Chorale Sacred Cultural Festival, 1979—, judge various contests; artistic dir. Battle Creek Sojourner Truth Monument Presentation Day, 1999; presenter in field. Pres. Dudley Elem. Sch., 1981-85; active Battle Creek Pub. Schs. PTA, Pennfield Pub. Schs. PTA, Mt. Zion African Meth. Episc. Ch. Mich. State U. fellow, 1971; recipient Outstanding Cmty. Svc. award, 1975, Sojourner Truth award, 2000, George award City of Battle Creek, 2000. Mem. Mich. Music Tchr. Assn., Nat. Music Tchrs. Assn., Battle Creek Music Tchrs. Assn., Battle Creek Morning Music Club (bd. dirs.), Nat. Leadership Acad., Battle Creek Cmty. Concert Assn. Home: 466 Alton Ave Battle Creek MI 49017-3212 Office: Kellogg CC 450 North Ave Battle Creek MI 49017-3306

MATTHIAS, GEORGE FRANK, retired educator; b. Aug. 22, 1934; s. George and Marguerite (Blanchard) M.; m. Mary Jo Avery, Aug. 18, 1956; children: Todd Avery, Tara Lynn. BS, SUNY, Cortland, 1957; MS, Syracuse U., 1962; MA, Conn. Wesleyan U., 1970. Tchr. secondary earth sci. Belleville (N.Y.) Acad., 1957-58, Croton-Harmon H.S., Croton-on-Hudson, N.Y., 1961-89; tchr., prin. Raquette Lake (N.Y.) Elem. Sch., 1958-61; ret., 1989; mem. N.Y. State Earth Sci. Syllabus Revision Writing Commn., 1967-70, 89-91; coord. Bur. of Sci. Edn., N.Y. State Dept. Edn., 1971-72; instr. Finger Lakes Inst., Alfred U., 1970; guest staff Coll. of St. Rose, summers 1984-85, 88-90; freelance cons. earth science edn.; item writer

Nat. Testing Service, Nat. Assessment for Ednl. Progress, 1984; cons. pub. schs. Author: (with Berey, Higham, Knabel, Maust) Observation and Interpretation in Earth Science, 1972, (with Daley and Higham) Earth Science: A Study of a Changing Planet, 1986, (with Deacon) Plate Tectonics, 1980; developer: (with Snyder) Individualized Earth Science Program, 1975-89, (with Snyderetal) Prentice-Hall General Science Series, 1986, NYS Student Performance Examination (Ed. Assessment), 1994; also articles. NSF grantee, 1963, 67-70; Shell merit fellow, 1971. Mem. Nat. Assn. Geology Tchrs., Nat. Assn. Rsch. in Sci. Tchg., Sci. Tchrs. Assn. N.Y. State, N.Y. State United Tchrs., Am. Fedn. Tchrs. Home and Office: 143 Dutch St Montrose NY 10548-1505

MATTHIASSON, THOROLFUR, economics educator; b. Iceland, Dec. 8, 1953; s. Matthias Petursson and Kristin (Thorarinsdottir) M.; m. Jona Gudmundsdottir; children: Eirny T., Vala T. Degree in Econs., U. Oslo, 1981. Researcher U. Iceland, Reykjavik, 1981-82, asst. prof., 1989-94, assoc. prof., 1994—; economist Ministry of Fin. (Iceland), 1982-88; dir. Inst. Econ. Studies, 1989-90, chair dept. econs., 1992-95. Contbr. articles to profl. jours. Mem. Union Icelandic Univ. Tchrs. (acting pres. 1999—). Office: Oddi V/ Sturlugata, U Iceland, 101 Reykjavik Iceland

MATTHIESSEN, CHRISTIAN WICHMANN, geography researcher and educator; b. Copenhagen, Denmark, Feb. 14, 1945; s. Tønnes Wichmann and Dagny (Kibak) M.; m. Eva Lundberg, Apr. 10, 1990; children: Mads Andreas, Laura Fugmann. MSc, U. Copenhagen, 1972, PhD, 1975, Habilitation, 1985. Asst. prof. U. Copenhagen, 1972-75, assoc. prof., 1975-88, prof., 1988—; v.p. Cost 332 European Union, Brussels, 1996—. Author: Innovation and Urban Population Dynamics, 1992, The European Urban Scene, 1994; mem. editl. bd. Danish Jour. Geog.; contbr. articles to profl. jours. Named Knight of the Dannebrog. Mem. Nat. Com. Geog. (gen. sec. 1990-98, pres. 1999—), Royal Danish Geog. Soc. (bd. dirs. 1988—), Inst. Geog. (dir. 1986-90, 96-99), European Network Univs. in Capital Cities. Home: Birkebakken 66 B, 3460 Birkerod Denmark Office: Inst Geog, Oster Voldgade 10, 1350 Copenhagen Denmark

MATTHYS, HEINRICH, medical educator; b. Zurich, Switzerland, Mar. 24, 1935; arrived in Germany, 1969; s. Heinrich and Anna (Aeberli) M.; m. Elisabeth Frieda Berger, Mar. 26, 1936; children: Urs, Susanne, Claudia. MD, U. Zurich, 1965; PhD, U. Basel, Switzerland, 1966; Habil, U. Ulm, Germany, 1971. Tchr. physiology U. Fribourg, 1965-67; asst. med. dept. U. Zurich, 1967-68, U. Basel, 1968-70; asst. prof. dept. medicine U. Ulm, 1970-75; prof. med. dept., med. dir., head dept. U. Freiburg, 1976—. Author: Medizinische Tauchfibel, 1971, Pneumologie, 1982, 3d edit., 1988, 2000, Schlafmedizin, 1995, 2000; contbr. articles to profl. jours. Recipient rsch. grants Deutsche Forschungs Gemeinschaft, Bundes Ministerium fur Forschung und Technologie. Mem. European Soc. Clin. Respiratory Pathophysiology (sec. gen. 1972-79), European Respiratory Soc. (pres. 1987-90), Swiss Respiratory Soc., German Respiratory Soc., Austrian Soc. Pneumology, Internat. Soc. Aerosols (pres. 1991-94, career achievement award 1994), Internat. Respiratory Care Assn. (pres. 1995—), Deutsche Gesellschaft Pneumologie (pres. 1996-97). Avocations: mountain climbing, diving, skiing, building, reading. Office: Medizinische U Klinik, Hugstetterstr 55, 79106 Freiburg Germany

MATTIE, HERMAN, internist; b. Amsterdam, May 4, 1933; s. Antonius Hermanus and Maria A.E. (De Bruin) M.; m. Lucie M. J. De Boer, Jan. 21, 1961; children: Christiaan H.F., Erik H., Roelof Th, Herbert J. MB, U. Amsterdam, 1956, MD, 1959; PhD, State U. Leiden, Netherlands, 1972. Asst. Pharmacol. Lab., Amsterdam, 1961-62; trainee internal medicine OLVG, Amsterdam, 1962-65; rsch. asst. Pharmacol. U., Leiden, 1965-73; head Div. Clin. Pharmacol., U. Leiden, 1973-85; internist Dept. Infectious Disease, U. Hosp., Leiden, 1967-98; assoc. prof. State U., Leiden, 1974-98; mem. exec. com. Internat. Therapeutic Union, Paris, 1981. Editor Pijninformatorium, 1979—. 1st lt. Meds., 1959-60. Mem. Infectious Disease Soc. Am., Brit. Pharmacol. Soc., Netherlands Soc. Clin. Pharmacology (life, founder). Roman Catholic. Avocation: piano. E-mail: h.mattie@wxs.nl. Home: Zoeterwoudsesingel 17, 2313 AZ Leiden The Netherlands Office: U Hosp, Post Box 9600, 2300 RC Leiden The Netherlands

MATTILA, PAULI TANELI, dental researcher; b. Enontekiö, Lapland, Finland, June 29, 1960; s. Vilho Ludvig and Hertta Orvokki (Välitalo) M.; m. Anne Irmeli Talvensaari, June 24, 1988; children: Jouni Miikka Matias, Maaret Miia Pauliina, Oula Miika Aleksi. Diploma in dentistry, U. Oulu, Finland, 1985, PhD, 1999. Dental practitioner Ii-Kiiminki KTTKL, 1985-89; specialist in periodontology U. Oulu, 1989-92, rschr., dental specialist, 1992—. Avocations: sports, coaching soccer, music, writing, fishing. Office: Inst Dentistry U Oulu, Aapistie 3, 90220 Oulu Finland

MATTINGLEY, CHRISTOBEL ROSEMARY, writer; b. Adelaide, Australia, Oct. 26, 1931; d. Arthur Raymond and Isabelle Margaret (Provis) Shepley; m. Cecil David Mattingley, Dec. 17, 1953; children: Rosemary, Christopher, Stephen. BA with honors, U. Tasmania, 1951; cert. proficiency, Pub. Libr. Victoria Tng. Sch., Australia, 1952; LittD (hon.), U. South Australia, 1995. Cert. assoc., Libr. Assn. Australia, 1971. Libr. Dept. Immigration, Canberra, Australia, 1951; regional libr. Latrobe Valley, Victoria, 1953; libr. Prince Alfred Coll., Adelaide, Australia, 1956-57, St. Peters Girls Sch., Adelaide, Australia, 1966-70; reader svcs. libr., acquisitions libr. Wattle Park Tchrs. Coll., Adelaide, Australia, 1971-72; reader svcs. libr. Murray Park Coll. Advanced Edn., Adelaide, Australia, 1973-74; libr. com. Burnside City Coun., Adelaide, 1971-84; chair Nat. Book Coun., South Australia, 1979-83; authors rep. Pub. Lending Right Com., Sydney, Australia, 1984-88; presenter in field. Author: The Picnic Dog, 1970, Windmill at Magpie Creek, 1971, Worm Weather, 1971, Emu Kite, 1972, Queen of the Wheat Castles, 1973, The Surprise Mouse, 1974, Tiger's Milk, 1974, The Battle of the Galah Trees, 1974, Show and Tell, 1974, Lizard Log, 1975, The Great Ballagundi Damper Bake, 1975, The Long Walk, 1976, New Patches for Old, 1977, The Special Present, 1977, The Big Swim, 1977, Hide and Seek, 1977, First Love Till Last Light, 1977, Budgerigar Blue, 1978, Katzenfell, 1978, The Jetty, 1978, Black Dog, 1979, Rummage, 1981, Brave with Ben, 1982, Lexl and the Lion Party, 1982, The Strawberry Masks, 1983, The Magic Saddle, 1983, Duck Boy, 1983, Southerly Buster, 1983, The Angel with a Mouth Organ, 1984, Ghost Sitter, 1984, The Grazier's Wife, 1984, The Miracle Tree (Notable Book award 1985), Muttaburrasaurus and the Microchip, 1986, McGruer and the Goat, 1987, Survival in Our Own Land, 1988, Initiation, 1989, The Butcher, The Beagle and the Dog Catcher, 1990, Tucker's Mob, 1992, The Sack, 1993, No Gun for Asmir, 1993 (High Commendation Human Rights award 1994, Notable Book 1994), The Race, 1995 (Crichton award 1996, High Commendation Human Rights award 1995), Asmir in Vienna, 1995, Escape from Sarajevo, 1996 (Notable Book 1996), Daniel's Secret, 1997, Ginger, 1997 (Notable Book 1998), Work Wanted, 1998, Hurry Up, Alice!, 1998, Cockawun and Cockatoo, 1999 (Notable Book 2000), First Friend, 2000; contbr. articles to profl. jours.; author numerous poems, and film scripts. Active Aboriginal Land Rights, Australia, 1983—, Australian Conservation Found., Melbourne, 1965—, The Wilderness Soc., Hobart, 1988—, World Wide Fund for Nature, Sydney, 1994—. Recipient Advance Australia award Advance Australia Found., 1990, Pheme Tanner award LaTrobe U., Bus. Profl. Women's Assn., 1999; named mem. Order of Australia, 1996. Mem. The Wilderness Soc., Australian Soc. Authors, South Australian Writers Centre, Childrens Book Coun. Australia. Anglican. Avocations: natural history, bird watching, travel, reading, classical music, swimming. Home: 10 Rosebank Terr, 5066 Stonyfell Australia

MATTIUSSI, CLAUDIO TOMASO, telecommunications industry executive, researcher; b. Elisabethville, Katanga, Zaire, Oct. 31, 1965; s. Alberto and Vittorina (Bortolotti) M. BEng, I.T.I. A. Malignani, Udine, Italy, 1984; MEng, U. Trieste (Italy), 1993. Cert. electronic engr. R & D mgr. CLAMPCO Sistemi s.r.l., Trieste, 1994—. Contbr. articles to profl. jours. Home: Piazza Italia 19, 33030 Majano UD, Italy Office: CLAMPCO Sis NIRLAB Sci Park, Padriciano 99, 34012 Trieste TS, Italy

MATTOLI, SABRINA, pharmaceutical company executive, consultant, scientist; b. Terni, Italy, Jan. 1, 1957; d. Gianfranco and Mara (Proietti) M. MD, U. Perugia, Italy, 1981; degree respiratory medicine, Cath. U., Rome, 1985. Clin. instr. dept. of medicine Cath. U., Rome, 1985-87; clin. and rsch. asst. McMaster Univ., Hamilton, Ont., Can., 1987-89; chief lab. respiratory cell and molecular biology Dept. Medicine, U. Milan, Italy, 1989-92; head diagnostic ctr. for respiratory and allergic diseases Inst. of Experimental Medicine, Milan, 1989-94; head dept. of clin. rsch. and med. affairs Ferring Srl, Pharms. subsidiary of Ferring AB, Milan, 1992-94; dir. GM snc internat. cons., Terni and Basel, Italy and Switzerland, 1995-98; owner, mng. dir. AVAIL GmbH Biomed. Rsch., Basel, Switzerland, 1998—; chair Italian Found. Exptl. Medicine, 1997-98. Ad hoc reviewer Am. Jour. of Respiratory and Critical Care Medicine, Jour. of Allergy and Clin. Immunology; contbr. numerous articles to profl. jours. Chmn. Italian Found. Exptl. Medicine, 1997-98. Recipient Top 10 Spl. Fellow in Tng. award Am. Acad. of Allergy and Immunology, 1987, Rsch. fellow award Med. Rsch. Coun. of Can., 1987, Honourable Mention for Progress in Rsch. Pharmacia Allergy Rsch. Found., 1990, Award for Rsch. in Allergy and Asthma, 1993; scholarship Nat. Rsch. Coun., 1983-86, Min. of Edn., 1983-86; grantee Nat. Rsch. Coun., 1989-91, 90-92, 93-95, Min. of Univ., Scientific and Technol. Rsch., 1991-93, Italian Assn. of Cancer Rsch., 1993-94. Mem. Italian Coll. of Physicians, Am. Thoracic Soc., Pharmacia Allergy Rsch. found., European Respiratory Soc., BioValley Switzerland. Avocations: astronomy, anthropology, opera, fiction books and movies, travelling. Home: Spalentorweg 18, 4051 Basel Switzerland Office: AVAIL GmbH, Aeschenvorstadt 71, CH-4051 Basel Switzerland

MATTOON, JAMES RICHARD, biology educator; b. Loveland, Colo., Dec. 9, 1930; s. Arthur Maxwell and Margaret (Scilley) M.; m. Martha Jean McKissick, June 16, 1953; children: Thomas Edward, Jean Ellen. BS in Chemistry, U. Ill., 1953; MS in Biochemistry, U. Wis., 1954, PhD in Biochemistry, 1957. From instr. to asst. prof. chemistry U. Nebr., Lincoln, 1957-62; rsch. assoc. physiol. chemistry Johns Hopkins U. Sch. Medicine, Balt., 1962-64, from asst. to assoc. prof. physiology and chemistry, 1964-79; prof. biology U. Colo., Colorado Springs, 1979—, dir. Biotech Ctr., 1988—; vis. prof. biochemistry Fed. U. Rio de Janeiro, 1975-77; vis. rsch. prof. Autonomous U. Mex., Mexico City, summer 1971, 74, San Marcos U., Lima, Peru, 1974, faculty of medicine U. Buenos Aires, summer 1980, 84, 93; organizing chmn. Rocky Mountain Microbrewing Symposium, Colorado Springs, 1995—. Contbr. rsch. articles to profl. jours. Fellow in chem. tchg. and rsch. Nat. Acad. Sci., U.S. and Brazil, 1975-77. Mem. Am. Chem. Soc., Am. Soc. for Biochemistry and Molecular Biology, Am. Soc. Brewing Chemists, Genetics Soc. of Am., Nat. Acad. Exact Phys. and Natural Scis. of Argentina (corr. mem.), Sigma Xi. Achievements include patent for enhancing production of hemoproteins. Avocations: gardening, reading, music. Home: 1090 Garlock Ln Colorado Springs CO 80918-3134 Office: U Colo Biotech Ctr 1470 Austin Bluffs Pkwy Colorado Springs CO 80918-3733

MATTOSO, LUIZ HENRIQUE CAPPARELLI, materials engineer, researcher; b. Sao Carlos, Sao Paulo, Brazil, Nov. 27, 1961; s. Luiz Antonio and Maria de Lourdes (Capparelli) M.; m. Valeria Duarte Benatti, Dec. 9, 1988; children: Carolina, Gabriela, Samuel Henrique, Davi Augusto. Materials Engr., Fed. U. Sao Carlos, 1986, MSc, 1988, DSc, 1993. Rschr. Physics Inst. of Sao Carlos, 1988-94; sr. rschr. Embrapa/Cnpdia, Sao Carlos, 1994—, project leader, 1996—; vis. prof. U. Sao Paulo, 1993—; mem. coun. Brazilian Inst. Natural Products, Sao Carlos, 1996—; prof. conducting polymer U. Sao Carlos, 1993—. Mem. editorial com. and coun. Polimeros: Ciencia e Tecnologia, 1995—; contbr. chpt. to book, articles to profl.jours.; patentee on a new synthesis method of a high molecular weight polyaniline. Mem. Youth and Childhood City Coun., Sao Carlos, 1994; catechist St. Elizabeth Cath. Ch., Sao Carlos, 1990—. U. Pa. fellow, 1991-92; U. Languedoc fellow, Montpellier, France, 1990; Domaine U. fellow, Grenoble, France, 1990. Mem. Brazilian Polymer Assn., Brazilian Chem. Soc., Brazilian Physics Soc. Roman Catholic. Avocations: playing the piano, teaching catechism, soccer, swimming. Home: Rua Borba Gato 525, 13564100 São Carlos Brazil Office: CNPDIA/EMBRAPA, Caixa Postal 741, 13560970 São Carlos Brazil

MATTSON, CLARENCE RUSSELL, safety engineer; b. Norwood, Mass., Nov. 3, 1924; s. Clarence R. and Jane P. (Dawson) M.; m. Constance W. Towne, June 7, 1953; children: Jennifer Lynn, Sue Ann. AA in Transp., Northeastern U., 1953, BBA, 1956. Cert. safety profl.; registered profl. engr., Calif. Ins. industry safety engr., 1953-62; mgr. accident prevention Dravo Corp., Pitts., 1962-72; corp. mgr. safety and environ. affairs Perini Corp., Framingham, Mass., 1972-84; dir. safety and tng. The Marr Co., South Boston, Mass., 1984; mng. dir. Long Beach-L.A. rail project Transit Ins. Adminstrs.-L.A. County Transp. Commn., 1984-86; v.p. tech. svcs. Fred S. James & Co., Short Hills, N.J., 1987-89; pres. Athena Assocs. Ltd., Safety Mgmt. Cons., Sunset Beach, N.C., 1990—. Deacon Scituate (Mass.) Congl. Ch. Recipient Disting. Svc. award Nat. Safety Coun., 1988. Mem. Am. Soc. Safety Engrs., Nat. Safety Coun. (hon. life, past gen. chmn. constrn. exec. com., disting. svc. award 1988), Assn. Gen. Contractors Am. (past chmn. safety and health com., safety engrs. adv. com.), Nat. Constructors Assn., Vets. of Safety, Mass. Safety Coun. (bd. dirs.), Mass. Constrn. Safety Congress (bd. dirs.), Elks. Republican. Home and Office: 655 Kings Ct Sunset Beach NC 28468-5326

MATTSSON, STIG-ARNE I., business executive; b. Angelholm, Skane, Sweden, June 4, 1942; s. Sture F. and Astrid (Troedsson) M.; m. Birgitta M. Wik, Nov. 11, 1967; 1 child, Per. MS, Lund (Sweden) U., 1973; Licentiate, Linköping (Sweden) U., 1974. Cert. in prodn. inventory mgmt. Mng. dir. Prodadm, Malmö, Sweden, 1981-89, Permatron, Malmö, 1990-92; dir. Emhart Glas, Zug, Switzerland, 1992-94, Intentia Internat., Stockholm, 1994—; adj. prof. Vaxjo (Sweden) U., 1995—. Author: Materialplaneringsmetoder, 1995, Effectvisering i supply chains, 1998, Contemporary Management, 1999. Mem. PLAN (pres. 1996—), ELA (treas. 1998—), APICS. Avocations: World War II history, sports, country and western music. Home: Beleshogsvagen 30, S-21774 Malmö Sweden Office: Intentia Internat, Stora Varvsgatan 11N, S0219 49 Malmö Sweden

MATUG, ALEXANDER PETER, lawyer; b. Chgo., May 25, 1946; s. Alexander J. and Marianne (Paszek) M.; m. Jeanne Marie Buker, Aug. 16, 1969; children: Alexander W., Krista E., Thomas E. BA, St. Mary's Coll., Minn., 1968; JD, Loyola U., Chgo., 1972. Bar: Ill. 1972, U.S. Dist. Ct. (no. dist.) Ill. 1972. Pvt. practice, Palos Heights, Ill., 1972—. Bd. dirs. Am. Heritage, Sertoma, Palos Heights, 1991—; profl. adv. bd. Sertoma Speech and Hearing Ctr., Palos Hills, Ill., 1991—. Mem. Ill. Bar Assn., S.W. Suburban Bar Assn. Roman Catholic. Office: 7110 W 127th St Ste 250 Palos Heights IL 60463-1571

MATULIS, ALGIRDAS, physicist; b. Kaunas, Lithania, Jan. 20, 1939; s. Juozas and Adele (Malelaite) M.; m. Grazina Diliute, June 3, 1967; children: Daiva, Jurgita. PhD, Vilnius U., 1967, DSc, 1982. Rschr. Inst. Physics & Maths., Vilnius, Lithuania, 1962-67; from rschr. to head lab. Inst. Semicondr. Physics, Vilnius, 1967—; prof. Vatauti Magni U., Kaunas, Lithuania, 1991-96. Author: Theory of Warm Electrons, 1990, Solid State Physics, 1994; contbr. articles to profl. jours. Mem. Acad. Scis. Lithuania. Avocations: hiking, jogging, windsurfing. Home: Zirgo 5-7, 2040 Vilnius Lithuania Office: Inst Semicondr Physics, Gostauto 11, 2600 Vilnius Lithuania

MATURO, MARIA GRACIELA, writer, educator; b. Santa Fe, Argentina, Aug. 15, 1928; d. Domingo Maturo and Maria Esther Saporiti; m. Alfonso Sola-Gonzalez, June 21, 1947 (dec.); children: Tristan, Cristobal, M. Fernanda, M. del Rosario, Laura Julieta, Graciela Mercedes; m. Eduardo Antonio Azcuy, Dec. 20, 1969. Prof. Cuyo Nat. U., Mendoza, 1954-67, Cath. U., Buenos Aires, 1988—, U. Salvador, Buenos Aires, 1968-72, U. Buenos Aires, 1970-96; dir. Biblioteca Maestros, Buenos Aires, 1990-93; bd. dirs. Centro E. Latino Americanos, Ediciones G. Cambeiro, Centro de E. Iberoamericanos. Author: Proyección del Surrealismo en la Literatura Argentina, 1965, Julio Cortazar y el Hombre Nuevo, 1967, Claves Simbolicas de Garcia Marquez, 1972, Fenomenologia, Creacion y Critica, 1989, La mirada del poeta, 1997, Marechal: el camino de la belleza, 1999, (poetry) Un viento hecho de pájards, 1958, El Rostro, 1960, EP marque en miresuena, 1965, Habita entre nosotros, 1968, El mar se llama ahora contunombre, 1995, Cantos de Orfeo y Euridice, 1995, Memoria del trasmundo, 1999. Mem. Sociedad Argentina de Escritores, Argentine Assn. Phenomenologists, Inst. Internacional Lit. Iberoamericana. Roman Catholic. Home: Aguirre 1066 1er p, 1414 Buenos Aires Argentina

MATÚŠ, FRANTIŠEK, mathematician, computer science researcher; b. Poprad, Slovak Republic, July 30, 1961; s. František and Lydia (Tauberová) M.; m. Jana Hančová, Aug. 16, 1986; 1 child, Vladislav. Degree in engring., Czech Tech. U., Prague, 1984; PhD, Czech Acad. Scis., Prague, 1989. Rsch. fellow Inst. Info. Theory and Automation, Prague, 1988—. Contbr. rsch. articles to sci. jours. Rsch. fellow Humboldt Found., Germany, 1995-97. Avocation: playing piano. Office: ÚTIA AVČR, Pod Vodárenskou Věži 4, 18208 Prague Czech Republic

MATUSCHEK, MARKUS, biologist, research scientist; b. Bad Oldesloe, Germany, Apr. 23, 1967; s. Edmund and Ruth Matuschek. MS, U. Goettingen, Germany, 1993, PhD, 1996. Rsch. scientist U. Goettingen, 1996-97; biotech. rsch. scientist Inst. Pasteur, Paris, 1997-98; chemistry rsch. scientist BASF AG, Ludwigshafen, Germany, 1998—. Contbr. articles to profl. jours. Mem. Am. Soc. for Microbiology, Marie Curie Fellowship Assn. (fellow 1997-98), Vereinigung für Allgemeine und Angewandte Mikrobiologie. Avocation: cycling. E-mail: markus.matuschek@basf.ag.de. Office: BASF AG, ZHF/D-A30, 67056 Ludwigshafen Germany

MATUSIEWICZ, RYSZARD, physician; b. Laznia, Poland, Feb. 8, 1936; s. Jan and Aniela (Cur) M.; m. Krystyna Rusiecka, Oct. 9, 1982; children: Agata, Rafal. Degree, Spec. of Internal Dis., Olsztyn, Poland, 1966, Spec. of Internal Dis., Bialystok, Poland, 1971, Spec. of Allergol Dis., Warsaw, Poland, 1980; MD, Med. Acad., Bialystok, Poland, 1973; D Biol. Sci., World Assn. Acupuncture, Malaga, 1987. Asst. physician Hosp., Morag, Poland, 1963-68; dir. medicine Hosp., Ciechanowiec, Poland, 1968-73; head of ward Hosp., Wolomin, Poland, 1973-76; cons. cardiologist Out Patient Clinic, Warsaw, 1976-81; head of ward, prof. medicine Grochow Hosp., 1981—; assoc. prof. Med. Acad., Warsaw, 1980-82, Med. Ctr., 1981-96; mem. scientific coun. Mil. Acad., Lodz, Poland, 1990-95. Editl. bd.: Biologishe Med., Baden, Germany, 1996; contbr. articles to profl. jours. Recipient Hans-Heinrich Reckeweg prize Internat. Soc. Homotoxicology Baden, 1995. Mem. Am. Acad. Allergy, Asthma, Immunology, Brit. Soc. Allergy Clin. Immunology, N.Y. Acad. Scis. Avocation: history of wars. Office: First Dept Internal Dis, Grenadierow 51/59, 04-073 Warsaw Poland

MATUSOW, NAOMI C., state legislator; b. Nashville, Oct. 31, 1938; m. Gene R. Matusow; children: Gary, Jason. BA cum laude, Vanderbilt U., 1960; MA in Counseling and Guidance, NYU, 1966; JD, Pace U., 1979. Bar: N.Y. 1981. Editl. asst. Golden Press, 1960-62; tchr. math. N.Y.C. Pub. Schs., 1962-65, guidance counselor, 1965-67; pvt. practice as lawyer Armonk, 1981-92, White Plains, 1981-90; mem. N.Y. State Assembly, 1992—, chair librs. and edn. tech. com., mem. assembly coms. Mem. econ. devel., environ. conservation, local govt., consumer affairs, tourism, arts, sports devel., spkrs. steering com.; bd. dirs. Juvenile Diabetes Found. Westchester County; chair Hudson River Valley Task Force, Women's Bus. Devel. subcom., mem. task force on auto ins. rates. Mem. NOW, Nat. Women's Polit. Caucus. Office: NY State Assembly 125-131 Main St Mount Kisco NY 10549-2316

MATUTE, DAUL J., diplomat; b. Ica, Peru, Dec. 24, 1952; s. Genaro I. Matute and Catalina D. Mejia; m. Maria G. Blanco, Nov. 26, 1994; children: Daniella I., Alexandra S. Degree in pre-law, San Luis U., Ica, 1969; law degree, Federico Villarreal U., Lima, Peru, 1974; degree in diplomacy, Academia Diplomatica, Lima, 1977, postgrad. degree in diplomacy, 1987; degree in internat. trade, Sch. Bus., Lima, 1988. 3d sec. Ministry of Fgn. Affairs, Lima, 1979, 1st sec., 1987-90; chief cabinet Presdl. Sec., Lima, 1980; 3d sec. Peruvian Embassy, Stockholm, 1981-84; 2d sec. Peruvian Embassy, Algeria, Algers, 1985-86; 1st sec. Peruvian Embassy, Washington, 1991-92; counsellor Consul in Washington Peruvian Embassy, 1993-94; chief chancellery Peruvian Embassy, Tokyo, 1994-95; ministry counselor Mission of Peru UN, N.Y.C., 1996-97, v.p. com. econ. and fin. affairs 54th Gen. Assembly, 1999—. Mem. Club Terrasas. Avocations: reading, tennis, sailing. E-mail: dmatute@hotmail.com. Home: 9604 Minstead Ct Burke VA 22015-4056 Office: Mission of Peru UN 820 2d Ave New York NY 10017

MATVEEV, VLADIMIR FIODOROVICH, aquatic ecologist, research scientist; b. Moscow, Russia, Feb. 13, 1950; s. Fiodor Matveevich and Ludmila Vasilyevna (Penkina) M.; m. Lilian Kazbekovna Tulepova, Mar. 25, 1977; children: Denis, Marya. Diploma, State Pedagogical Inst., 1972; PhD, USSR Acad. of Scis., 1978. Probation rschr. Inst. of Animal Morphology Ecology, USSR Acad. of Scis., Moscow, 1972-74, jr. rsch. scientist, 1974-86, sr. rschr. scientist, 1986-92; sr. rsch. scientist CSIRO, Albury, Brisbane, Australia, 1992-97; prin. rsch. scientist CSIRO, Brisbane, Australia, 1997—. Contbr. articles to profl. jours. Mem. Australian Soc. Limnology, Internat. Soc. Limnology. Avocations: bushwalking, photography. Office: CSIRO Land & Water, 120 Meiers Rd Indooroopilly, Queensland 4068, Australia

MATVEYEV, VALENTIN VOLODYMYROVICH, research scientist; b. Trostyanets, Ukraine, Nov. 10, 1929; s. Volodymyr Ivanovych and Anfisa Ivanivna (Shyiko) M.; m. Lesia Vasylivna Vasechko, May 16, 1952; children: Tatiana, Sergey. Diploma in Mech. Engring., Road-Transport Inst., Kiev, Ukraine, 1952, PhD in Engring., 1964, DSc in Physics and Math., 1974. Engr. Ministry of Internal Affairs, Kiev, 1952-57; asst. prof. Higher Artillery Engring. Sch., Kiev, 1958-59; asst. Poly. Inst., Kiev, 1959-63, prof., lectr., 1977-83, chmn. State Examining Bd., 1986-91; scientist Inst. Problems of Material Scis. NAS Ukraine, Kiev, 1963-64, sr. scientist Inst. Problems of Materials Sci., 1965-66, sr. scientist Inst. Problems of Strength, 1966-75, head dept. Inst. Problems of Strength, 1975—, dep. dir. Inst. Problems of Strength, 1977-88; dep. head dept. mechanics NAS Ukraine, 1983—. Author: Vibration Damping in Deformable Bodies, 1985; co-author: Strength of Materials Reference Book, 1975, 88, French edit., 1979, 85, Spanish edits. 1979, 85, 89, Portuguese edit. 1985, The Strength of Materials and Structural Elements Under Extreme Conditions, 1980; editor-in-chief: Aerdynamic Vibration Damping of Turbine Blades, 1991; mem. editl. bd. Jour. Problems of Strength, 1971—, Jour. Vibration in Engring. in Techs., 1998—; contbr. over 300 articles to profl. pubs., chpts. to books. Mem. sect. Com. State Prizes of Ukraine, Kiev, 1982—. Decorated Order of the Badge of Honour Supreme Soviet USSR, 1971; recipient State Prize USSR, 1982; named Honoured Scientist of the Ukraine, 1982. Mem. Nat. Soviet Ukraine for the Mechanics of Machines and Mechanism, Nat. Com. Theoret. and Applied Mechanics of the Ukraine and Russia, Assn. Reliability and Lifetime of Machines and Constructions (v.p. 1992—), NAS Ukraine (corr., Academician A.N. Dinnik's prize), N.Y. Acad. Scis. Avocations: chess, literture. Home: 15 Bastionna St Apt 70, Kiev Ukraine Office: Inst Problems of Strength, 2 Timiryazevska St, 01014 Kiev Ukraine

MATWEEV, LEONID VLADIMIROVICH, physician; b. Chelyabinsk, Russia, Mar. 29, 1961; s. Vladimir and Galina Grigoryeona (Krasnyanskaya) M.; m. Larisa Yuryevna Baronkina, Apr. 8, 1989; children: Olga, Aleksander. PhD, Moscow Phys.-Tech. Inst., 1993. Jr. rschr. JRINITI, Troitsk, Russia, 1984-95, rschr., 1995-99, sr. rschr., 1999—; jr. rschr. Nuclear Safety Inst. Russia, 1992-96; tchr. Moscow Phys.-Tech. Inst., 1994-95. Contbr. articles to profl. jours. Avocation: sports. Office: JRINITI, 142092 Troitsk Russia

MATWICZAK, KENNETH MATTHEW, university educator, consultant; b. Milw., Sept. 26, 1948; s. Matthew T. and Dorothy M. Matwiczak; m. Barbara A. Larsen, June 12, 1971; 1 child, Brynn E. BS, U.S. Mil. Acad., 1971; MS, Purdue U., 1979; MBA, L.I. U., 1982; PhD in Indsl. Engring., Tex. A&M U., 1990. Commd. 2d lt. U.S. Army, 1971, advanced through grades to lt. col., 1990; air def. platoon leader, exec. officer 2 Bn. 56th ADA, Pirmasens, Fed. Rep. Germany, 1971-74; air def. battery comdr. 2/5 ADA, 2nd AD, Ft. Hood, Tex., 1975-76; asst. dean acad. computing U.S. Mil. Acad., West Point, N.Y., 1979-82, assoc. prof., 1989-93; chief studies and analysis Forward Area Air Def. Joint Test Force, Ft. Bliss, Tex., 1982-85; bn. exec. officer staff and faculty battalion U.S. Army Air Def. Sch., Ft. Bliss, 1985-86; adj. assoc. prof. U. Tex., Austin, 1993-99, sr. lectr., 1999—; statis. cons., 1994-99; owner, proprietor Fare Choice Vending Svcs., Austin, 1996-99; guest lectr. Ctr. Pub. Mgmt., San Marcos, Tex., 1997-. Admissions rep. U.S. Mil. Acad.-W. Point, Austin, 1997—. Mem. ASPA, Inst. Ops. Rsch. and Mgmt. Sci., W. Point Soc. Ctrl. Tex. (pres. 1995-97, bd. dirs.), KC. Repblican. Avocations: bowling, traveling, golf, reading, softball. E-mail: kmat@mail.utexas.edu. Office: U Tex LBJ Sch Pub Affairs Drawer Y University Sta Austin TX 78713

MÁTYÁS, ANTAL, economist, educator; b. Budapest, Hungary, Sept. 27, 1923; s. Antal and Hegyessy Róza M.; m. Márta Halmos. PhD, Hungarian Econ. U., Budapest, 1958; D in Econ. Sci., Hungarian Scientific Com., Budapest, 1972. Scientific rschr. Rsch. Inst. Economic Sci., Budapest, 1950-53, from reader to prof. economic thought, 1953-66, prof., 1966-96, prof. emeritus, 1996—; founder, head dept. history economic thought Hungarian Econ. U., Budapest, 1970-96; mem. doctoral com. Hungarian Acad. Scis., 1999—. Author: Sketch History of Hungarian Economic Thought, 1962, History of Modern Economic Thought, 1985, 6th edit., 1999, History or Early Economics, 3d edit, 1992, The Development of Macro-economic Theory in the Course of the Dispute between Moetarist and Neo-keynesian Economists, Critique and Expansion of the Scope of Investigation of Traditional Economics by the Representatives of New Institutional School, 1999, also others; contbr. articles to profl. jours. With Hungarian Army, 1944-45, prisoner of war, USSR. Recipient Govt. prize Hungarian Coun. Mins., 1988, Pub. awards, 1960, 62, 79, 85. Mem. Hungarian Acad. Scis. (Acad. award 1982), Assn. U. Profs. Hungary. Avocations: music, travel. Home: Irinyi József utca 31, 1111 Budapest Hungary Office: Econ U Budapest, Fővám tér 8, 1093 Budapest Hungary

MATYAS, LASZLO, economist, educator; b. Budapest, Hungary, Aug. 24, 1957; s. Laszlo and Elisabeth (Gidaly) M.; m. Kinga Konczey, Apr. 1987; children: Melinda, Viktor. M in Econs., Budapest U. Econs., 1982, PhD, 1987. Rsch. fellow Rsch. Inst. Agrl. Econs., 1983-89; assoc. prof. Budapest U. Econs., 1989-97, prof. econometrics, 1997—; sr. lectr. Monash U., Melbourne, Australia, 1991-97. Author: Practical Econometrics, 1992; editor: The Econometrics of Panel Data, 1993, 2d edit. 95, Generalised Method of Moments Estimation, 1999. Office: Ctrl European Univ, Nador U 9, 1051 Budapest Hungary

MATYAŠ, ZDENĚK, food hygiene and technology educator; b. Brno, Czechoslovakia, Dec. 14, 1923; s. Viktor and Vojtěška (Huláková) M.; m. Zdenka Katolicka, Mar. 19, 1951 (dec. Nov. 1995); 1 child, Iva. Bacalareat, Secondary Sch., Brno, 1942; D of Vet. Medicine, Vet. U., Brno, 1950. Diplomate veterinary medicine. Asst. Vet. Univ., 1948-51, assoc. asst., 1951-60, assoc. prof., 1960-66, prof., 1966-88; food hygienist WHO, Geneva, 1966-71, chief vet. pub. health, 1977-84; chief food hygiene dept. Vet. Rsch. Inst., Brno, 1971-77; head Ctr. Food Hygiene Nat. Health Inst., Brno, 1984-92. Author, editor: Meat Hygiene, 1965 (Best Book Yr. 1965); author: Technology of Food of Animal Origin, 1973, Hygiene of Food of Animal Origin, 1974, General Food Hygiene, 1991, Hazard Analysis Critical Control Points, 1993 (Best Rsch. Results award 1994), HACCP for Meat and Meat Products, 1996, HACCP for Milk and Milk Products, 1998. Capt. Vet. Corps, 1950-52. Mem. Czechoslovak Microbiology Soc., Czechoslovak Soc. Nutrition, State Vet. Orgn. Prague (Outstanding Worker award 1993), State Vet. Orgn. Bratislava (Outstanding Worker award 1985), Am. Vet. Epidemiology Soc. (hon.). Moravian Brothers. Avocations: gardening, languages. Home: Nove Namesti, 62100 Brno Czech Republic Office: Vet & Pharm U, Palackeho 1-3, 61242 Brno Czech Republic

MATYS, VÁCLAV, communications company executive, journalist; b. Hubenov, Czech Republic, Feb. 28, 1920; s. Jan and Anežka (Zemanová) M.; m. Marie Koutná, Nov. 14, 1942; children: Václav Dipl.ing, Marie Peňázová. Student, U. Tomášov, 1938-41. Worker Bata Shoe Factory, Zlin, 1935-38; corr. Bata Export of Machines Dept., Zlin, 1940-41, supr., 1941-51; translator Rubber and Plastics Rsch. Inst., Zlin, 1951-52, mgr. of dept. info. sci. and tech. libr., 1952-53; mgr. dept. info. sci. and tech. libr. Rubber and Plastics Technology Rsch. Inst., Zlin, 1953-80; now freelance tech. journalist. Co-author: German-Czech Rubber and Plastics Technical Dictionary, 1960, Czech-German Rubber and Plastics Technical Dictionary, 1961, English-Czech Technical Dictionary, 1970, Czech-English Technical Dictionary, 1972, Russian-Czech Technical Dictionary, 1974, French-Czech Technical Dictionary, 1978. 1st lt. Sapper, 1946-47. Mem. Tennis Club. Roman Catholic. Avocations: tennis, swimming. Home: Na vyhlidce No 1605, 76001 Zlin Czech Republic

MATYUSHICHEV, VLADISLAV BORISOVICH, enzymology researcher, laboratory administrator; b. Leningrad, USSR, May 22, 1938; s. Boris Dormidontovich and Anna Mihailovna (Bernova) M.; m. Evgenia Gavrilovna Gorina, Mar. 9, 1966; 1 child, Marina Vladislavovna Matyushicheva Hernbrandt. BS, U. Leningrad, 1964, candidate of sci., 1975, PhD in Biochemistry, 1985. Jr. rsch. worker U. Leningrad, 1969-76, sr. rsch. worker, 1976-87, chief rsch. worker, 1987-92; head of lab. U. St. Petersburg, Russia, 1992—; leader postgrads., U. St. Petersburg, 1978—, prof. enzymology, 1982—; cons. Yurma, St. Petersburg, 1993-94, St. Petersburg Marine Hosp., 1987—; mem. acad. coun. Ukhtomsky Rsch. Inst., 1991—. Author: Elements of Statistical Treatment of Biochemical Experiment Results, 1990 (univ. prize 1991); contbr. over 150 articles to profl. jours. and conf. procs. Mem. Dissertational coun. U. St. Petersberg, Russia, 1986, Rsch. Inst. Grippe, St. Petersburg, 1987; grantee State Com. Higher Edn., Russia, 1992, U. St. Petersburg, 1995. Mem. N.Y. Acad. Scis., Russian Biochem. Soc. (mem. bd. St. Petersburg chpt. 1987—). Avocations: books, music, sports. Home: Botanicheskaya St 18/3, Apt 49, 198904 St Petersburg Russia Office: Ukhtomsky Rsch Inst Physiol, Universitetskaya nab 7/9, 199034 St Petersburg Russia

MATZ, DIETER RUDOLF, clinical neurologist, educator; b. Witten/Ruhr, Germany, June 9, 1946; s. Paul and Charlotte (Noetzel) M.; m. Radegundis Matz, Apr. 6, 1973; children: Ansgar, Felix. MD, U. Münster, Germany, 1973, Habilitation, 1981. With U. Münster, Münster, 1974; asst. Neurology Clinic, Münster, 1975-77; asst. in physiol. chemistry Psychiat. Clinic, Essen, Germany, 1977-78; asst. med. dir. Neurology Clinic, Münster, 1976-82; prof. neurology U. Münster, Germany, 1982—; med. dir. dept. neurology Evangelisches Krankenhaus, Lippstadt, Germany, 1983—. Author: Schwindel, 1985, 2d edit. 1992, Therapiehandbuch, 1983-92, Epilepsien u. Neurotransmission, 1985. Kreisverbandsarzt Deutsches Rotes Kreuz, 1982. Fellow German EEG Soc., N.Y. Acad. Sci., Internat. Liga gegen Epilepsie. Mem. Evangelical Ch. Avocation: golf, surrealistic art. Home: Gerhart-Hauptmann Str 9, Lippstadt D-59555, Germany Office: Neurology Ev Krankenhaus, Wiedenbrücker Str 33, Lippstadt D-59555, Germany

MATZA, JOSHUA, government official; b. Jerusalem, 1931; married; 4 children. Mem. Jerusalem City Coun., 1965-69; deputy mayor Jerusalem, 1969-79; mem. Knesset 11th, 12th, 13th, 14th, 15th, 1984—; chmn. Internal Affairs & Environ. Com.; min. Ministry Health, Jerusalem, 1996-98; acting chmn. bd. dirs. Shikun Upituach Govt. Housing & Devel. Co., 1988-92; mem. state control com., 1998—, econ. affairs com., 1998—. Capt. Israeli Army. Home: 22 Metzarey Tiran St, 93591 Jerusalem Israel

MATZNER, EGON, economics educator; b. Klagenfurt, Austria, Mar. 2, 1938; s. Heinrich and Josefine (Posautz) M.; m. Monica Siegel, Mar. 2, 1959 (div. 1983); children: Joerg, Robert; m. Gabriele Holzer, Oct. 14, 1984; 1 child, Sissela. M in Econs., U. Econs., Vienna, PhD, 1961; Docent, U. Linz, 1970. Asst. dir. Bank for Labor and Industry, Vienna, 1962-65; rsch. fellow Internat. Inst., Stockholm (Sweden) U., 1965-67; asst. prof. Linz U., 1968-70; dir. Inst. Urban Studies, Vienna, 1971; prof. econs. U. Tech., Vienna, 1972-98, dean of faculty, 1992-95; dir. Sci. Ctr., Berlin, 1984-89; dir. rsch. unit for socio-econs. Austrian Acad. Sci., Vienna, 1992-98; fellow Max Weber Coll., 1998—; cons. Fed. Min. Fin., Vienna, 1970-79, OECD, Paris, 1975; coord. Fed. Ministry Tech., Bonn, Germany, 1986-88. Author: Trade Between East and West, 1970, Monopolar World Order, 2000; co-editor: Barriers to Full Employment, 1988, Beyond Keynesianism: The Socio-Economics of Production and Full Employment, 1991, The Market Shock, 1992. Mem. German Econ. Assn., SASE, European Assn. Polit. Economy. Avocation: mountaineering. E-mail: Matzner@uni-erfurt.de or egmaj@chello.at. Office: Max Weber Ctr, U Erfurt, D99084 Erfurt Germany

MATZOURANIS, GEORGE, Greek army aviation officer; b. Pireaus, Attiki, Greece, Nov. 29, 1964; s. Nikolaos and Dimitra Matzourani; m. Irene Orfanou, Nov. 13, 1995; 1 child, Christine. Student, Hellenic Army Mil. Acad., Athens, 1983-87, Mil. Engring. Sch., Loutaki, Greece, 1987-88, Army Aviation Sch., Volos, 1991-92. 2d lt. in engring. Hellenic Army, 1987-90, 1st lt. in aviation, 1990-94, capt. in aviation, 1994—. Christian Orthodox. Avocations: skiing, scuba diving.

MÄTZSCH, THOMAS WINFRIED, surgeon; b. Hannover, Germany, Dec. 13, 1950; arrived in Sweden, 1951; s. Winfried Curt and Sonja Irma Erna (Marth) M.; m. Kerstin Thorborg Ekenstierna, May 13, 1989. MD, Med. Hochschule Hannover, 1976, D in Medicine, 1978; PhD, U. Lund, Sweden, 1990. Registrar U. Lund, 1979-84, cons., 1984-92, asst. prof., 1989-92, assoc. prof., 1992—. Contbr. over 75 articles to profl. jours., chpts. to books. With UN Forces, 1993-95, 99. Mem. Swedish Soc. Surgery, European Soc. Vascular Surgery, Internat. Soc. Surgery. Office: Malmö U Hospital, Dept Vascular Disease, SE-20502 Malmö Sweden

MAU, VLADIMIR ALEXANDROVICH, economist, government official, researcher; b. Moscow, Dec. 29, 1959; s. Alexander M. and Anna P. (Ashrafian) M.; m. Irina Stardoubrovskaia, Sept. 5, 1987; 1 child, Anton. MA, Inst. Nat. Economy, Moscow, 1981; PhD, Inst. Econs., Moscow, 1986; DSc, Acad. Nat. Economy, Moscow, 1993; PhD in Applied Econs., U. Pierre Mendese, Corendole, France, 1999. Sr. rsch. fellow Inst. Econs. USSR Acad. Scis., Moscow, 1981-90; assoc. prof. Moscow State U., 1987-91; head dept. Inst. Econ. Policy, Moscow, 1990-91; asst. to Prime Minister of Russia Govt. of Russia, Moscow, 1991-94, dir. Govt. Ctr. Econ. Reforms, 1997—; prof. Moscow Sch. Econs., 1994—; dep. dir. Inst. for the Economy in Transition, Moscow, 1994—. Mem. bd. Jour. Problems of Econs., 1994—, Jour. Econ. Transformation, 1995—; author 10 books; contbr. more than 300 articles to profl. pubns. Fowler Hamilton fellow Oxford U., Eng., 1997; grantee McArthur, 1995. Mem. polit. bd. Democratic Choice of Russia, Moscow, 1996-99. Office: Inst Economy in Transition, Gazetny 5, 103918 Moscow Russia

MAUCK, WILLIAM M., JR., executive recruiter, small business owner; b. Cleve., Mar. 30, 1938; s. William M. and Elizabeth Louise (Stone) M.; m. Paula Jean Mauck, Aug. 15, 1969 (div. Mar. 1983); children: Brian, David; m. Jeanne Lee Mauck, May 21, 1987. BS in Bus., Ind. U., 1961. Sales engr. Inland Container Corp., Louisville, 1961-69; sales mgr. Dixie Container Corp., Knoxville, Tenn., 1969-70, gen. mgr., 1970-75; v.p., ptnr. Heidrick & Struggles, Inc., Houston, 1975-81; pres. Booker & Mauck, Inc., Houston, 1981-85; ptnr. Ward Howell Internat. Inc., Houston, 1985-88; prin. William M. Mauck, Jr., Houston, 1988—; owner Pepe Engring., Inc., Houston, 1990—; mem. adv. bd. Women's Sports Found., N.Y.C., 1985-96. Mem. Plaza Club (Houston) (chmn. bd. govs. 1987-88), Sertoma Club (Knoxville 1972-75) (pres. 1974-75). Republican. Methodist. Home: 2718 N Southern Oaks Dr Houston TX 77068-2611 Office: 9950 Cypresswood Dr Ste 300 Houston TX 77070-3412

MAUDGAL, PRABHAT CHANDER, ophthalmologist; b. Tewar, India, May 15, 1948; arrived in Belgium, 1973; s. Rati Ram and Poorna Devi (Vashishth) Sharma; m. Marleen Alice Victoria De Meulemeester, Oct. 29, 1975; children: Krishan, Gayatri, Manou Mohan. MBBS, Panjab U., 1971; DSc, Cath. U., 1977. Asst. in ophthalmology Cath. U., Leuven, Belgium, 1976-81, 1st asst. ophthalmology, 1982, work leader ophthalmology, 1983-85; chief polyclinic ophthalmology Free U., Amsterdam, The Netherlands, 1986-87; prof. Cath. U., 1989—; adj. head clinic U. Hosp., 1987—. Author: Superficial Keratitis, 1979; editor: Herpetic Eye Diseases, 1985; inventor in field. Mem. Belgium Soc. Ophthalmology (mem. mgmt. bd. 1995—), Internat. Soc. Antiviral Rsch., Internat. Soc. Eye Rsch. Hindu. Avocation: gardening. Office: UZ St Rafael, Kapucijnenvoer 33, B-3000 Leuven Belgium

MAUDUIT, NICOLAS ANDRÉ, engineering executive; b. Alger, Algeria, Apr. 16, 1963; s. André George and Thérèse Germaine (Lévègue) M.; m. Hendrike Elisabeth Margarita Schmidt, Aug. 30, 1997; children: Ulysse André, Adrien Hermann. Diploma in engring., Inst. Computer Sci., Evry, France, 1987; MS, U. Paris 6, 1987; PhD, U. Paris 11, Orsay, France, 1990. Rsch. asst. U. Paris 6, 1987; rsch. scientist Lab. Electronics Philips, Limeil Brevannes, France, 1988-91; faculty mem. U. Calif., San Diego, 1991-96; rsch. cons. U. Paris 11, Orsay, 1996-97; faculty mem. U. Paris 13, Villetaneuse, France, 1997-98; founder, CEO Vision Integree, Paris, 1998—; cons. Scitex, San Diego, 1996, Aerospatiale, Magny Les Hameaux, France, 1997, Thomson, Guyancourt, France, 1998. Contbr. articles to profl. jours. Mem. IEEE, Optical Soc. Am. Office: Vision Integree, 9, Rue Berthollet, 75005 Paris France

MAUGHAN, WILLARD ZINN, dermatologist; b. Riverside, Calif., Apr. 21, 1944; s. Franklin David and Martha Charlotte (Zinn) M.; m. Rona Lee Wilcox, Aug. 20, 1968; children: Julie Anne, Kathryn Anita, Willard Wilcox, Christopher Keith. Student, Johns Hopkins U., Balt., 1962-64; BS, U. Utah, 1968, MD, 1972. Diplomate Am. Bd. Dermatology. Intern Walter Reed Army Med. Ctr., Washington, 1972-73; fellow Mayo Clinic, Rochester, Minn., 1976-79; pvt. practice Ogden, Utah, 1979—. Contbr. articles to profl. jours. Commr. Boy Scouts Am., Weber County, Utah, 1980-84, dist. chmn., 1993-94, assoc. mem. bd. dirs. Trapper Trails coun., 1995-99, v.p., mem. exec. bd., 1999—; pres. Am. Cancer Soc., Weber County, 1985-86. Maj. U.S. Army, 1971-76. Recipient Dist. award of merit Boy Scouts Am., 1985, Silver Beaver award 1994. Fellow ACP, Am. Acad. Dermatology, Royal Soc. Medicine (London); mem. N.Y. Acad. Scis., Kiwanis Club, Alpha Omega Alpha, Phi Sigma Iota. Republican. Mormon. Avocations: woodcarving, camping. Home: 2486 W 4550 S Roy UT 84067-1944 Office: 3860 Jackson Ave Ogden UT 84403-1956

MAUKSCH, MICHAEL, chemist; b. Hannover, Germany, Aug. 17, 1966; s. Harri and Monika (Herrmann) M. Diploma in chemistry, Friedrich-Alexander U., Erlangen, Germany, 1994, PhD, 1999. Sci. employee Computer Chemistry Ctr., Erlangen, 1995-99; rsch. assoc. Friedrich-Schiller U., Jena, Germany, 1999—. Contbr. articles to profl. jours. Social Democrat. Avocations: movies, travel, English literature, classical music, theatre. Home: Am Herrenberge 11, 07745 Jena Germany Office: Inst Organic/Macromolec Che, Humboldtstr 10, 07743 Jena Germany

MAUL, ARTHUR BENJAMIN, management consultant; b. Port of Spain, Trinidad and Tobago, Mar. 21, 1924; s. Arthur Theophilus and Beatrice Philomen (Williams) M.; m. Violet Adelaide Williams (wid. July 1969); children: Myrna N. Maul Thijs, Arlene V. Maul-John, Robert A.B., Lystra Ann B. Lee-Sam; m. Gloria Severine Constantine; 1 child, Craig Anthony. Cert. Systems Profl. Sect. head Shell Trinidad Ltd., 1957-62, div. head, 1962-67, mgr. Govt.-Cen. Statis. Office, Port of Spain, 1967-69; sr. cons. Peat Marwick Mitchell & Co., Port of Spain, 1969-75; adminstr. PAHO/WHO Carec, Port of Spain, 1975-84; cons. Dataskil Ltd., Port of Spain, 1984—, also bd. dirs., 1984—; cons. Bensev Ltd., Port of Spain, 1986—, also bd. dirs., 1986—. Mem. govt. teaching svc. commn., Trinidad and Tobago, 1988—. Recipient Silver Ibis award Scout Assn. of Trinidad and Tobago, 1977, Golden Poui, 1981, Silver Dolphin, The Barbados Scout Assn., West Indies, 1986, Youth of the Americas award Interam. Scout Com., Western Hemisphere, 1988. Fellow The British Computer Soc., Inst. of Mgmt.; mem. Assn. for Systems Mgmt., Assn. of Inst. for Certification of Computer Profls., Lions Club (1st v.p. Port of Spain ctrl. 1992—), REACT Internat. (bd. fin. 1992), Scouts (hon. commr.), Anglican Church Mens Soc. (chmn.). Anglican. Avocations: computer systems, lawn tennis, stamp collecting. Home and Office: 36 Petra St Woodbrook, Port of Spain Trinidad and Tobago

MAULDIN, JOHN INGLIS, public defender; b. Atlanta, Nov. 6, 1947; s. Earle and Isabel (Inglis) M.; m. Cynthia Ann Balchin, Apr. 15, 1967 (div. Dec. 1985); children: Tracy Rutherford, Abigail Inglis; m. Linda W. Farmer, Nov. 7, 1998. BA, Wofford Coll., 1970; JD, Emory U., 1973. Bar: S.C. 1974, U.S. Ct. Appeals (4th cir.) 1974, U.S. Dist. Ct. S.C. 1975, U.S. Supreme Ct. 1978. Asst. pub. def. Defender Corp. Greenville County, S.C., 1974-76; ptnr. Mauldin & Allison, Greenville, 1977-92; pub. defender Greenville County, S.C., 1992—; chair S.C. Commn. on Indigent Def., 1993-96; adj. prof. Greenville Tech. Coll., 1975-80; sec., treas. Def. Corp. Greenville County, 1979-92, bd. dirs. Bd. dirs. Speech Hearing & Learning Ctr., Greenville, 1977-90, pres., 1982; bd. dirs. Save Our Sons, 1995—. Named S.C. Atty. Yr. ACLU, S.C., 1986. Mem. Nat. Assn. Criminal Def. Attorneys, Nat. Legal Aid and Defender Assn. (defender policy bd. 1999—), S.C. Trial Lawyers Assn., S.C. Assn. Criminal Def. Lawyers (bd. dirs. 1997-99), S.C. Pub. Defender Assn. (bd. dirs. 1992—), Rotary, Sigma Delta Phi. Democrat. Methodist. Office: PO Box 10264fs Greenville SC 29603

MAULE, JAMES EDWARD, law educator, lawyer; b. Phila., Nov. 26, 1951; s. Edward Randolph George and Jennie Elisabeth (Zappone) M.; m. Susan Margaret Noonan, June 26, 1982 (div. May 1988); children: Charles Edward, Sarah Margaret; m. Susan K. Garrison, Apr. 7, 1990 (div. 1991). BS cum laude, U. Pa. Wharton Sch., 1973; JD cum laude, Villanova U., 1976; LLM with highest honors, George Washington U., 1979. Bar: Pa. 1976, U.S. Tax Ct. 1986. Atty.-adv. Office Chief Counsel to IRS Legis. and Regulations Divsn., Washington, 1976-78; atty.-adv. judge U.S. Tax Ct., Washington, 1978-80; asst. prof. law Dickinson Sch. Law, 1981-83, lectr. and tax program chmn. continuing legal edn., 1981-83; assoc. prof. Villanova Sch. Law, 1983-86, prof., 1986—; lectr. continuing legal edn. Pa. Bar Inst. Harrisburg, Continuing Legal Edn. Satellite Network, Inc., 1988—; Nat. Merit scholar, 1969-73; lectr. state and local taxes Georgetown U. Law Ctr. Inst., 1992; sr. tax and tech. ptnr. Ctr. Info. Law and Policy, 1993—. Author: Cases and Materials in Federal Income Taxation, 1981, 20th edit., 2000, Materials in Partnership Law and Taxation, 1985, 6th edit., 1991, Materials in Partnership Taxation, 1987, 18th edit., 2000, Materials in Introduction to Taxation, 1987, 2nd edit., 1988, Cases and Materials in Introduction to the Taxation of Business Entities, 1992, 8th edit., 2000, Materials in Taxation of Fundamental Wealth Transfers, 1986, 2nd edit., 1988, Materials in Tax Consequences of Disposition of Property, 1983, 3rd edit., 1985, Materials and Problems in Taxation of Property Disposition I, 1987, 2nd edit., 1989, Materials in Tax Planning for Real Estate, 1986, Materials in Estate and Gift Tax, 1983, 3rd edit., 1985, Materials in Taxation of Real Estate Transactions, 1986, 2nd edit., 1988, 3rd edit., 1992, Taxation of Residence Transactions, 1985, S Corporations: State Law and Taxation, 1989, supp. 1989, 90, 91, 92, 93, Materials and Problems in Computer Applications in the Law, 1990, 6th edit., 1995, Materials in Tax Policy, 1990, Materials in Digital Legal Practice Skills, 1996, Materials and Problems in Computer Applications in Tax Law, 1991, 8th edit., 1998, Better That 100 Witches Should Live, 1995, Materials in Decedents Estates and Trusts, 4th edit., 2000, (with A. Clay) Preparing the 1065 Return, 1992, 93; author Continuing Legal Edn. Publs., 1981—; contbg. author: Federal Tax Service, Tax Practice Series; contbr. articles to profl. jours. and monographs, chpts. to books; author and developer Computer Assisted Legal Edn. Programs in Taxation; owner, author, editor TaxJEM Inc. (computer assisted tax law instruction); owner JEMBook Pub. Co.; cons. and prin. author ABA Section of Taxation Model S Corporation Income Tax Act and Commentary, 1989; author, editor Report of the Subcommittee on Comparison of S Corporations and Partnerships, 1990, 91; case and comment editor Villanova Law Rev., 1975-76; columnist, mem. editl. adv. bd. S Corps. Jour., 1987-91; columnist, mem. editl. adv. bd. Jour. of Ltd. Liability Cos., 1994-98, BNA Tax Mgmt., 1994—. Recipient Dist. Author award BNA Tax Mgmt., 1993. Mem. ABA (chair and reporter phaseout Elimination Project, Tax Simplification and Restructuring Com., sect. of taxation, cons., ex-officio mem. subcom. on state law, S Corp. com., chmn. subcom. on comparison of partnerships, mem. task force on pass-through entities, tax sect., chmn. subcom. manuscripts and unpub. tchg. material, com. tchg. tax), Phila. Bar Assn. (lectr. tax sect. state and local tax CLE program 1991, fed. income taxes 1992—), Ctr. Info. Law and Policy, Order of Coif, Friars Sr. Soc. (Phila), Beta Alpha Psi. E-mail: maule@law.villanova.edu. Home: 219 Comrie Dr Villanova PA 19085-1402 Office: Villanova U Sch Law Villanova PA 19085

MAULION, RICHARD PETER, psychiatrist, neurolinguist; b. Rosario, Argentina, Sept. 2, 1949; s. Peter Henry and Vivien Ormsby (Gough) M.; divorced; 1 child, Maximillian. BS, Colegio Salesiano San Jose, Rosario, ARgentina, 1967; MD, U. Nacional de Rosario, 1980. Diplomate Am. Bd. Psychiatry and Neurology, Am. Acad. Psychoanalysis, Am. Acad. Addiction Medicine, Am. Acad. Pain Mgmt., Am. Bd. Forensic Examiners, Am. Bd. Quality Assurance and Utilization Rev. Physicians, Am. Bd. Disability Analysts, Am. Acad. Experts in Traumatic Stress; cert. neurolinguistic practitioner. Intern Kans. U., Kansas City, 1981-82; resident in psychiatry Tulane U., New Orleans, 1983-86, fellow in psychoanalytic medicine, 1984-87; pvt. practice gen. psychiatry Covington, La., 1986-87; pvt. practice psychiatry Ft. Lauderdale, 1987—; founder, med. dir. The Rose Inst., Ft. Lauderdale, Fla., 1988—; founder Integrative Medicine Sch. of Thought, 1999; practitioner, trainer Meurolinoustic Program, 2000—; sec. med. exec. com., chmn. quality assurance com. The Retreat Hosp., Sunrise, Fla., 1994-95; med. dir. Anxiety and Depression prog., CPC Ft. Lauderdale Hosp., 1989-90; med. dir. Acad. Medicine and Psychology, Ft. Lauderdale, 1988-89, CEPHAS Prog., HSA Greenbrier Neuropsychiat. Hosp., Covington, La., 1986-87, chief med. staff, 1987; clin. instr. psychiatry Tulane U. Med. Ctr., 1986-87; pres. med. exec. com., chief med. staff, chmn. quality assurance com. Retreat Hosp., 1992-96; workshop speaker; radio program host The Rose Institute Hour; lectr. in field; cons. in field. Host ednl.-cmty. svc. radio program The Rose Inst. Hour, 1995-97. Mem. pub. health com. for the Health and Human Svcs. Bd., Dist. 10; mem. alcohol, drugs and mental health com.. Fellow Am. Acad. Psychoanalysis, Am. Bd. Forensic Examiners, Internat. Coll. Physicians and Surgeons; mem. AMA, Am. Psychiat. Assn., Am. Acad. Psychoanalysis, Am. Soc. Clin. Hypnosis, Fla. Med. Assn. (Med. Speaker of Yr. award, 1st pl. radio, 2nd pl. t.v., 1990, del. 1993—), Fla. Psychiat. Soc. (coun. mem. 1993-94), Broward County Psychiat. Soc. (med. exec. com., pres. 1994-95), Broward County Med. Assn. (chmn. physicians recovery network com., bd. dirs.), Broward County Psychiat. Soc. (pres. 1993-96), M.I.N.D. Home and Office: 1521 Alton Rd # 332 Miami Beach FL 33139-3301

MAUMUS, OLIVIER JEAN-DOMINIQUE, investment executive; b. Tarbes, France, Feb. 18, 1946; s. Jean Maumus and Jeanne Lacaze; m. Chantal A. Wiart, Dec. 11, 1975; children: Laure, Florian. MBA, Columbia U., 1972. Dep. gen. sec. ELF, Paris, 1972-73; dep. mgr. Emerson Electric, Paris, 1973-75; dep. CFO GAN, Paris, 1975-86; CFO GMF, Paris, 1986-94; CIO CDC Asset Mgmt. Europe, Paris, 1994-99; CEO Noval Sys. Corp.-Europe, 1999—. Fulbright Found. scholar, 1970. Mem. AIMA. Avocation: piano. Home: 25 Blvd Suchet, 75016 Paris France Office: Modal Sys Corp-Europe, 7 Place des Cinq Martyrs, 75015 Paris France

MAUNDER, LEONARD, retired engineering educator, consultant; b. Swansea, Wales, May 10, 1927; s. Thomas George and Elizabeth Ann (Long) M.; m. Moira Anne Hudson, Sept. 1, 1958; children: Joanna Lynn, David Hudson. BSc, Univ. Coll. Swansea, 1947; PhD, U. Edinburgh, Scotland, 1950; ScD, MIT, 1954. Instr., asst. prof. MIT, 1950-54; sect. leader aero. rsch. lab. USAF, 1954-56; lectr. U. Edinburgh, 1956-61; prof. U. Newcastle Upon Tyne, Eng., 1961-92, dean of engring., 1973-78, head of mech engring., 1967-92; chmn. Govt. Tchg. Co. Scheme, U.K., 1981-85; mem. Cabinet Office Adv. Coun. on Sci. and Tech., U.K., 1987-93; mem. Nat. Rsch. Devel. Coun. and Brit. Tech. Group, 1976-92; lectr. Royal Instn.-BBC Christmas Lectrs., 1983. Author: (books) Machines in Motion, 1986; co-author: (with R. N. Arnold) Gyrodynamics, 1961; contbr. numerous articles and papers to profl. jours.; patentee in field. Dep. chmn. Newcastle Hosps. Mgmt. Com., 1971-73; mem. Newcastle Dist. Health Authority, 1973-91, No. Regional Health Authority, 1969-75. Decorated Officer of Order of Brit. Empire; fellow Univ. Wales Swansea, 1989. Fellow Royal Acad. Engring. (chmn. Gatsby Continuum exec. bd. 1997—), Instn. Mech. Engrs. (v.p. 1976-81); mem. Internat. Fedn. for Theory of Machines and Mechanisms (pres. 1976-79), Brit. Assn. for Advancement of Sci. (pres. engring. 1980), Polish Soc. Applied Mechanics (fgn. mem.). E-mail: Leonard.Maunder@ncl.ac.uk. Office: U Newcastle, Old Forge Bldg, Newcastle Upon Tyne NE1 7RU, England

MAUNEY, THOMAS LEE, theater designer; b. Lexington, N.C., May 29, 1967; s. Thomas Pete and Iris Elnita (Washburn) M. BFA, U. N.C., Greensboro, 1990; MFA, U. Mont., 1995. Asst. tech. dir., designer Raleigh (N.C.) Little Theatre, 1989-90; tech. dir. U. Mont., Missoula, 1990-92; designer Big Fork (Mont.) Summer Playhouse, 1994-98; prodn. supr. Raleigh Meml. Auditorium, 1998—; freelance designer theatre and spl. events.

MAURANDY, JEAN-PIERRE J., sales professional; b. Varese, Italy, May 1, 1965. Diploma, Ecoles de Hautes Études Commls. du Nord, Lille, France, 1989; diploma in acctg. and fin., London Sch. Econs., 1989; MBA, UCLA, 1991. Sr. fin. analyst Mattel Toys, El Segundo, Calif., 1991; v.p. internat. instnl. sales Compagnie Financière de CIC, Paris, 1992-94; instnl. salesman, ptnr. Sanford C. Bernstein, N.Y.C., 1994—. Brig. French Mountain Rescues, 1985-86.

MAURER, HANS HILARIUS, pharmacology educator; b. Homburg, Germany, Nov. 25, 1950; s. Hilarius Andreas and Elisabeth (Greff) M.; m. Claudia Regina Kessler, Oct. 9, 1981; children: Christine, Johannes. Lic. in pharmacy, U. Saarland, Saarbrücken, Germany, 1977, PhD, 1983, Habilitation, 1988. Asst. prof. pharmacology U. Saarland, 1983-88, univ. lectr., 1988-92; prof. pharmacology/toxicology, head dept. toxicology U. Saarland, Homburg, Germany, 1992—. Author: (with Pfleger and Weber) Mass Spectral and GC Data, 1985, 3d edit., 1999, Mass Spectral Library, 1987, 3d edit., 2000, (with De Zeeuw, Franke, and Pfleger) Gas Chromatographic Retention Indices, 1992, (with Schaefer) Diagnosis and Therapy of Intoxications, 1993, (with Niessen) Current Status of GC-MS, 2000. Capt. M.C., German Army, 1977-78. Recipient Med. Faculty Young Scientist award, 1983. Mem. German Pharm. Soc. (chpt. pres. 1990-92, 98-2000), Soc. Toxicology and Forensic Chemistry (treas. 1987—, com. chmn. 1997—), Internat. Assn. Forensic Toxicologists, Internat. Assn. Therapeutic Drug Monitoring Clin. Toxicology (com. chmn. 1997—, Outstanding Contbn. award 1997), German Soc. Pharmacology and Toxicology, Toxicol. Soc. Belgium and Luxembourg, Am. Soc. of Forensic Toxicologists, Lions Club Internat. Roman Catholic. Avocations: music, art, theater, history of toxicology. Office: U Saarland, Univ Clinics, D-66421 Homburg Germany

MAURER, KATHLEEN ANN, educator, supervisor; b. Jamaica, N.Y., Feb. 28, 1951; d. William Michael and Ann Marilyn; 1 child, Sophia Anndrina Maria Buterakos. BA in English and Edn., Queens Coll., 1972, MS in Edn., 1977; postgrad., SUNY, Albany, 1978, Brigham Young U., 1978, McPherson Coll., 1978; diploma in ednl. supervision, St. John's U., Jamaica, N.Y., 1982; postgrad., Adelphi U., 1983, U. Mont., 1986, U. N.Mex., 1999, Coll. of St. Rose, 2000. Cert. tchr., adminstr., supr., N.Y. Tchr. Elijah Clark Jr. H.S., South Bronx, N.Y., 1972-75, Intermediate Sch. 291, Bklyn., 1975; tchr., dean, asst. prin. Jean Nuzzi Jr. H.S., Queens Village, N.Y., 1975-83; asst. prin. William Cowper Intermediate Sch., Maspeth, N.Y., 1983-93; asst. prin.-in-charge I.S. 73 Annex, Elmhurst, N.Y., 1994-97; adminstr.-in-charge 51st Ave. Annex for P.S. 7 and P.S. 71, Elmhurst, N.Y., 1997-99; adminstr.-in charge 51st Ave. Annex for P.S. 7 and I.S. 5, Elmhurst, N.Y., 1999; middle sch. enrichment specialist for talented and gifted Locust Valley (N.Y.) Middle Sch., 1999—. fellow Hofstra U., 1990. Mem. Nat. Sci. Tchrs. Assn., Nat. Coun. Tchrs. English, Internat. Reading Assn. Roman Catholic. Avocations: playing piano, roller skating, ice skating, dancing, travel. Office: Locust Valley Middle Sch Horse Hollow Rd Locust Valley NY 11560

MAURER, P(AUL) REED, pharmaceutical company executive; b. Minersville, Pa., Sept. 20, 1937; s. Paul Reed and Ruth Lillian (Daniel) M.; m. Beverly Mae Seaman, June 25, 1963 (div. Feb. 1984); children: Paul Reed, Glenn Charles; m. Yuko Arai, June 30, 1984; children: Michelle Aoi, Tricia Haruna, Brett Ken. BS, Kutztown U., 1959; MS, U. Pa., 1962; cert., Stanford U., 1967-68. Fellowship U. Otago, Dunedin, New Zealand, 1961; tchr. Allentown (Pa.) H.S., 1959-60; asst. prof. Bucknell U., Lewisburg, 1963-64; v.p. Eli Lilly, Kobe, Japan, 1970-76, Merck & Co., Tokyo, 1976-86; pres. Metpac, Ltd., Honolulu, 1986-99, Nippon Pharma Promotion K.K., Tokyo, 1995—; mgr. IAL (USA) LLC, Honolulu, 1997—; dir. Colby Group Internat., Tokyo; pres., dir. Internat. Alliances Ltd., Tokyo, 1989—. Author: Competing in Japan, 1989; editl. bd. Hearing Internat., 1992—. Fellowship Rotary Found., 1961, Paul Harris fellow, 1980. Mem. Pharma Delegates. Avocations: writing, tennis, boating. Home: Arisugawa Park Hills #902, 5-6-48 Minami Azabu, Minato-ku 106, Japan Office: Internat Alliances Ltd, 1-5-12-101 Kita Aoyama, Minato-ku 107, Japan

MAURI, GIUSEPPE, retired secondary school educator; b. Monza, Italy, Jan. 1, 1943; s. Angelo and Natalina (Capra) M. Diploma, Lycée, Monza, 1962; DS, U. Milan, Italy, 1968. Sr. H.S. tchr. Carate, Italy, 1970-71, 77-84, Monza, 1971-73, Desio, Italy, 1985-92. With Italian Def. Svc., 1969-70.

MAURICE, DON, personal care industry executive; b. Peoria, Ill., Aug. 29, 1932; s. Imajean (Webster) Crayton; m. Cindalu Jackson, Aug. 31, 1990. Student, Loma Linda U., 1984-86; cert. paralegal studies, Calif. State U., San Bernardino, 1994. Lic. hair stylist, skin therapist; cert. paralegal, notary pub. Owner 2 schs. in advanced hair designs, San Diego, 1962-64, D & M Enterprises, Advt. Agy., 1964-78; now cons. D&M Enterprises Advt. Agy.; dist. mgr. AqRo Matic Co. Water Purification Systems, San Diego, 1972-75; profl. sales educator Staypower Industries, San Diego, 1972-76, 3d v.p., 1975-76; regional bus. cons. Estheticians Pharmacology Rsch., Garden Grove, Calif., 1975-81; owner, operator Don Maurice Hair Designs, Hemet, Calif., 1980-83; dir., operator Hair Sytles by Maurice, Loma Linda, Calif., 1984-88; owner, pres. Grooming Dynamics, Redlands, Calif., 1988—; bus. cons. Yogurt Place, Paradise Valley, Ariz., 1978-79, others; regular guest Channel 6/Channel 8, San Diego, 1968-78; cons. infomercial Pre-Paid Legal Svcs., Inc., 1994—; undercover criminal investigator, 1955-59, 1999—. Author: The New Look For Men, 1967, The Art of Men's Hair Styling, 1968 (accepted by Library of Congress), Baldness, To Be or Not To Be, 1989. Promoter Spl. Olympics, Hemet, 1981. Sgt. U.S. Army, 1950-53, Korea. Decorated Purple Heart, 1952; named Leading Businessman in His Profession, Union and Evening Tribune, 1969. Mem. Internat. Platform Assn., Christian Businessmen's Assn. Avocations: writing, sculpting, art, sports, music. Office: Grooming Dynamics PO Box 1279 Loma Linda CA 92354-1279

MAURY, MIREILLE, finance administrator; b. Cairo, Aug. 2, 1955. Grad., Bus. H.S. Paris, 1976. With Saint-Gobain, Paris, 1976-85, fin. mgr., 1985-90; CFO Hermès Internat., Paris, 1990-92, dep. mng. dir. fin., 1992—. Office: Hermès Internat, 24 rue du Faubourg St Honor, 75008 Paris France

MAURY, RENÉ, economics and history educator; b. Beziers, France, Jan. 29, 1928; s. Emile and Henriette (Rouanet) M.; m. Geneviève Vialet, July 2, 1951 (div. 1971); children: Maxime, Isabelle, Emmanuel; Marie-Helene Lebaud, May 21, 1981. Agréré scis. économiques, U. Paris, 1954; LittD, Montpellier (France) U., 1948, PhD in Econs., 1950; postgrad., Harvard U., 1959. Prof. econs. U. Montpellier, 1954-97; founder, mgr. Montpellier Bus. Sch., 1956-81; internat. cons., 1956—; vis. prof. Keio (Japan) Bus. Sch., 1977; adj. prof. U. Limerick, Ireland, 1983; companion of western Europe, Cambridge (Eng.) U., 1990; chmn. French-Japanese Bank, Paris, 1993; cons. Japanese Govt., numerous C. of C. in France. Author: L'intégration européenne, 1954, Manuel d'Economie Politique, 1959, L'Homme Mystifié, 1966, Pur Comprendre la Cirse, 1974, La Société d'Inflation, 1975, Marianne à l'École Japonaise, 1986, Les Patrons Japonais Parlent, 1990, L'Etat-Maquereau, 1992, L'Assassin de Napoleon, 1994, J'accuse l'impot sur le Revenu, 1996, La Libéeration des Pauvres, 1997, Albine, le Dernier Amour de Napoleon, 1998; journalist Econ. Chronicle. Chevalier/Commandant wine cos., including Languedoc, Barsac. Fellow Internat. Napoleonic Soc.; mem. N.Y. Acad. Scis. Home: 600 Chemin de Cantagrils, La Devèze, 34 980 Montferrier sur Lez France

MAUTALEN, CARLOS ALFREDO, medical researcher; b. Buenos Aires, Dec. 22, 1934; s. Juan and Maria Esther (Bianchi) M.; m. Maria Cela Somoza Bosch; children: Carlos Adolfo, Andrea, Santiago Alfredo. MD in Medicine, U. Buenos Aires, 1959, PhD in Medicine, 1984; Dr. honoris causa, Sch. Medicine, Montevideo, Uruguay, 1984. Resident in medicine Henry Ford Hosp., Detroit, 1961-63, resident in endocrinology, 1963-64; fellow in medicine Cornell U., N.Y.C., 1964-66; dir. Ctr. Bone Diseases, Buenos Aires, 1979—; prin. investigator Nat. Coun. Rsch., Argentina, 1986-95; head sect. on metabolic bone diseases Hosp. de Clínicas, U. Buenos Aires, 1992; superior investigator Nat. Coun. Rsch., Argentina, 1996—. Author: (book) Tiene Ud Osteoporosis?, 1997; contbr. numerous sci. articles to profl. jours. Recipient Dr. Boy Frame Meml. award Am. Soc. for Bone and Mineral Rsch., 1996, Dr. Brachetto Brian award Nat. Acad. Medicine, 1977, Mariano Castex award, 1982. Mem. Chilean Soc. Osteology (hon.), Nephrology Soc. of Peru (hon.), Latin Am. Soc. Osteology (v.p. 1996-98, pres.-elect 1998-2001). Avocation: soccer. Office: Ctr Bone Diseases, J E Uriburu 1267, 1114 Buenos Aires Argentina

MAUTNER, BRANCO, cardiologist, researcher; b. Zagreb, Croatia, Jan. 16, 1938; arrived in Argentina, 1948; s. Jorge and Cilly (Frenkl) M.; m. Renée Leonor Yedlin, Aug. 16, 1970; children: Vanesa, Nicolas. MD, U. Buenos Aires, 1963. Cert. cardiologist, internist. Staff physician Buenos Aires City Hosp., 1964-78; chief coronary care unit Fernandez Hosp., Buenos Aires, 1978-92; chief emergency dept. Favaloro Found., Buenos Aires, 1992-96, chief medicine dept., 1996-99, chmn. clin. rsch. and edn. dept., 1999—, acad. vice chancellor, 1999—; prof. medicine cardiology, vice chancellor Favaloro U., Buenos Aires, 1993-98; spkr. in field. Contbr. articles to profl. jours. Pres. Argentine Found. Cardiology, 1986-89, trustee, 1986-98; rep. to exec. bd. Internat. Heart Found., 1990-94. Recipient Garfunkel award Argentine Nat. Acad. Medicine, 1991. Fellow Am. Coll. Cardiology, European Soc. of Cardiology; mem. Argentine Soc. Cardiology (pres. 1985, adv. bd. 1986—), Internat. Soc. Holter and Non-Invasive Electrocardiology (pres. 1998—), Argentinian Med. Assn. (hon.), Spanish Soc. Cardiology (corr.), Santo Domingo Soc. Cardiology (hon.), Am. Heart Assn. (internat. fellow coun. clin. cardiology). Home: Av Libertador 2200, 1425 Buenos Aires Argentina Office: Favaloro Found, Belgrano 1746, 1093 Buenos Aires Argentina

MAVER, ANDREW G., optometrist; b. Melbourne, Victoria, Australia, June 2, 1957; s. Robert and Nancy (Draper) M.; m. Andrea Joan Ward, Oct. 27, 1981; children: Fiona, Katherine, Robert. BSc in Optometry, U. Melbourne, 1978, postgrad. diploma adv. clin. optometry, 2000. Cert. low vision rehab. cons. optometrist. Pvt. practice Melbourne, 1978-79; pvt. practice as locum optometrist Hobart, Australia, 1979-83; prin. optometrist Hobart, 1983-88; ptnr. Provision Total Eyecare Optometrists, Hobart, 1988—; cons. low vision optometrist Lion's Low Vision Clinic, Royal Hobart Hosp., 1989—; dir. Vision Care Optical Lab., Hobart, 1991—. Mem. Optometrist Assn. Australia (treas., sec., councillor 1982-85), Tasmanian Underwater Hockey Assn. (life), Australian Finswimming Commn. (exec. mem.), Contact Lens Soc. Australia. Avocations: finswimming, underwater hockey, tae kwon do, fly fishing. Office: Sims Knipe et al, 9 Magnet Ct Sandy Bay, 7005 Hobart Tasmania, Australia

MAVER, THOMAS WATT, educator and researcher; b. Glasgow, Scotland, Mar. 10, 1938; s. Thomas Archibald and Jean Hill (Strang) M.; m. Avril Elizabeth Cuthbertson, Mar. 27, 1963; children: Justine, Esmé. BSc, U. Glasgow, Scotland, 1960, PhD, 1965. Personal prof. U. Strathclyde, Glasgow, Scotland, 1974-80, prof. CAD, 1980—, dir. grad. sch., 1992—, vice dean, 1996—. Rsch. fellow U. Glasgow, 1961-65, U. Strathclyde, 1967-70. Fellow Inst Energy, Royal Soc. Art, Royal Inc. Architects Scotland (hon.); mem. Chartered Inst. Bldg. Svcs. Engring. Home: 8 Kew Terr, Glasgow G12 0TD, Scotland Office: U Strathclyde, George St, Glasgow G1 1XQ, Scotland

MAVLO, DMITRY P., physicist, mathematician, educator; b. Kiev, Ukraine, 1950; s. Alla Chetchovich and Panteleymon M.; m. Svetlana Alexandrovna Martyshova, Jan. 19, 1996. Degree in Physics, Kiev State U., 1972; postgrad., Moscow State U., 1972-75; PhD in Theoretical Nuclear Physics, Joint Inst. Nuclear Rsch., 1977. Tchr. theoretical physics and math. various univs. Moscow and Kiev; rsch. worker Joint Inst. Nuc. Rsch., Dubna, Russia, 1972-78; faculty Sch. Young Mathematicians and Physicists Moscow Phys.-Tech. Inst., 1979—; dep. dir. gen. Internat. Biog. Ctr. Cambridge U., England, 1997—; founder, owner DPM Press Internat. Author: Can You Do Better Than Augustin - Louis Cauchy?, 1996, Can You Do Better Than Blaise Pascal?, 1996, What You Know and What You Don't Know About Archimedean Lemma, 1996, What You Know and What You Don't Know About Excircles, 1996, Admit That You Know Nothing About Semiscribed Circles, 1996, Admit That You Know Nothing About the Remarkable Trapezoid, 1996; author numerous poems; co-author: Physics: Problem-Solving Book, 1988; contbr. articles to profl. jours. Named Internat. Man of Yr. Internat. Biog. Ctr., 1994-95; recipient 20th Century award of Achievement, 1995; mem. Order of Internat. Fellowship, 1995; Dir. Gen.'s Honours list, 1996; recipient 1995 Man of Yr. Commemorative medal Am. Biog. Inst., 1996; named Personality of Yr., 1996; inaugurated lifetime dep. gov., 1996; recipient World Lifetime Achievement award, 1996; named to Order of Internat. Ambassadors, 1996. Mem. Math. Assn. Am., Order Internat. Fellowship (dir. gen. honor list, 1996). Home: Festivalnaya 25-64, 125195 Moscow Russia also: Alma Atinskaya 36-7, 253092 Kiev 92, Ukraine

MAVRELLIS, CHRISTOS DEMOSTHENES, lawyer; b. Arsos, Cyprus, July 19, 1946; s. Demosthenes Christodoulou and Eleni Demosthenous (Patsalides) M.; m. Anastasia Georgiades, Feb. 11, 1973; children: Demosthenes, Leto, Constantinos. JD, U. Athens, 1969; diploma in shipping law, U. London, 1971. Advocate Supreme Ct. Cyprus. Practicing advocate M.M. Houry, Limassol, Cyprus, 1972-78; ptnr. Chrysses Demetriades, Limassol, 1978-82, 88—; min. communications and pub. works Republic of Cyprus, 1982-85, min. of finance, 1985-88; senator Offshore Inst., 1989—; chmn. Libra Holidays Group Ltd., Options Caosulides Ltd., Stevemos Hotels Ltd., Depro Pearl Growmush Ltd.; bd. dirs. Astarti Devel. Co. Ltd., Louis Cruise Lines Ltd., Avacom Computer Svcs. Ltd., Avacom Net Svcs. Ltd., Hawaii Hotels Ltd., Medochemie Ltd. Contbr. articles to profl. jours.; contbr. chpt. to Spitz Tax Havens Ency. Active Ctrl. Com. Dem. Party, Cyprus. With Cyprus Nat. Guard, 1969-70. Mem. Internat. Tax Planning Assn. (sec. 1992-99), Mediterranean Coun. Maritime Arbitrators, Chartered Inst. Arbitrators (assoc.), Rotary. Greek Orthodox. Avocations: shooting, hunting, swimming, boating. Office: Chrysses Demetriades & Co, 284 Arch Makarios Ave, Fortuna Ct Limassol Cyprus

MAVRIDOGLOU, NICHOLAS ISIDORE, shipping and trading company executive; b. Chios, Greece, July 17, 1947; s. Isidore and Maria (Caramaounas) M.; m. Elina D. Tangos, July 15, 1981; children: Maria, Irini. BA, U. Piraeus, Greece, 1973; MBA, Northeastern U., 1978. Mgr. Greek br. C.F.C., chems., Piraeus, 1976-80; mgr., owner Shipping & Trading, Piraeus, 1982-86; mgr. Karamaounas Leather Industry, Athens and Chios, 1961—; owner, mgr. Mavridoglou Maritime S.A., Piraeus, 1979—, D. Tangos, meat trading, Athens, 1981—. With Greek Navy, 1969-71.

MAVRIKOS, ELIAS, market analyst, investment consultant; b. Athens, Greece, Feb. 10, 1965; arrived in U.K., 1988; s. Emmanouel and Maria (Kourogeni) M. BSc in Econs., U. Athens, 1988; MBA in Fin., U. Wales, Cardiff, 1990. Fin. analyst Morgan Stanley Internat., London, 1990-93; economist, mkt. analyst Alpha Credit Bank, Athens, 1996—; fin. strategist Risk Mgmt. S.A., Athens, 1993-94. Dep. editor Greek Bus. Jour., Athens, 1995-96; contbr. numerous articles to profl. jours. With Greek Air Force, 1994-95. Mem. Assn. Greek Economists. Avocations: golf, sailing. Office: 40 Stadiou Str, 10252 Athens Greece

MAVROGORDATOS, GEORGE THEMISTOCLES, political scientist, educator; b. Athens, Greece, Mar. 27, 1945; s. Themistocles J. and Stavroula (Paraskevopoulos) M.; m. Lila E. Liapis, Sept. 20, 1989 (div. 2000); 1 child, Themistocles. Degree in politics and econs., U. Athens, 1967, degree in law, 1969; MA in polit. sci., Purdue U., 1972; PhD in polit. sci., U. Calif., Berkeley, 1979. Asst. prof. U. Athens, 1982-89, assoc. prof. polit. sci., 1989-97, prof. polit. sci., 1997—; vis. prof. U. Calif. at Berkeley, 1983, Johns Hopkins U., Bologna, Italy, 1986, U. Salzburg, Austria, 1997. Author: Stillborn Republic: Social Coalitions and Party Strategies in Greece, 1922-1936, 1983, Rise of the Green Sun: The Greek Election of 1981, 1983, Between Pityocamptes and Procrustes: Occupational Interest Groups in Contemporary Greece (in Greek), 1988, National Schism and Mass Organization (in Greek), 1996. Recipient dean's fellowship U. Calif., Berkeley, 1973, Fulbright visiting scholarship, 1983, Woodrow Wilson Found. award Am. Polit. Sci. Assn., 1984. Home: 3 Neophytou Douca St, Athens 10674, Greece Office: Dept Polit Sci U Athens, 19 Omirou St, Athens 10672, Greece

MAVROMATIS, HARRY ANTHONY, physics educator; b. N.Y.C., Jan. 19, 1941; came to Saudi Arabia, 1987; s. Anthony Mavromatis and Lefki Anthony Mavromatis-Kranidiotis; m. Vasso Themistocles Ioannides, June 9, 1968; children: Blanche, Anthony. BS with high distinction, Princeton U., 1962, PhD, 1966; grad. honoris causa, U. Patras, 1973. Prof. Am. U., Beirut, 1967-86, U. Tuebingen, Germany, 1986-87, King Fahd U. of Petroleum and Minerals, Dhahran, Saudi Arabia, 1987—; tchr., rschr. U. Sussex, Brighton, Eng., Mich. State U., East Lansing, Oxford (Eng.) U., Harwell (Eng.) Nat. Lab., Oak Ridge (Tenn.) Nat. Lab.; chmn. dept. physics Am. U., Beirut, 1977-80; summer faculty fellow NASA, 1983, 84. Mng. editor Arabian Jour. Sci. and Engring., 1992—; editor Grad. Bull. King Fahd U., 1992, 96; author 4 books, including: Exercises in Quantum Mechanics, 1992; contbr. over 95 rsch. articles to profl. jours. Active Internat. Concert Com., Saudi Arabia, 1992, 93, 94, 95. Recipient Disting. Rschr. award King Fahd U. Petroleum and Minerals, 1992, 97. Mem. AAAS, N.Y. Acad. Scis., Internat. Ctr. Theoretical Physics (sr. assoc.). Christian-Greek Orthodox. Avocations: writing prose and poetry, chess, music, foreign languages. Office: King Fahd U Petrol Minerals, PO Box 58 Dept Physics, Dhahran 31261, Saudi Arabia

MAVROMOUSTAKOS, THOMAS MICHAEL, chemist, researcher; b. Morphou, Nicosia, Cyprus, June 18, 1960; s. Michael Nicolaou and Thoma (Panagidou) M.; m. Marina Michael Efstathiou, Aug. 22, 1982; children: Elena, Michael, Nicolas, Kyriaki. BSc, U. Athens, Greece, 1985; MSc, U. Conn., 1988, PhD in Pharmacy, 1990. Tchr. Paideia, Storrs, Conn., 1987-88; postdoctoral fellow U. Conn. Sch. Pharmacy, Storrs, 1990-91; rsch. assoc. Nat. Hellenic Rsch. Found.-Inst. Organic & Pharm. Chemistry, Athens, 1991—. Author: Marihuana, 1987, Emerging Technologies on New Directions in Drug Abuse Research, 1991, Steroids and Neuronal Activim, 1991; contbr. articles to profl. pubs.; editor: Bioactive Peptides in Drug Discovery and Design: Medical Aspects, 1999. Recipient award Acad. of Athens, 1998; fellow U. Athens, 1981, U. Conn., 1985, Royal Soc., London, 1992. Mem. Union Greek Chemists. Orthodox. Avocations: chess, basketball, reading, teaching high school students. Home: Tsakalof 1, 15343 Agia Paraskevi Athens, Greece Office: Nat Hellenic Rsch Found, Vas Constantinou 48, 11635 Athens Greece

MAVROS, GEORGE S., clinical laboratory director; b. Adelaide, Australia, Oct. 14, 1957; came to U.S., 1970; s. Sotirios George and Angeliki (Korogiannis) M.; m. Renee Ann Cuddeback, June 24, 1979. BA in Microbiology, U. South Fla., 1979, MS in Microbiology, 1987; MBA, Nova U., 1991; PhD in Health Sci. Mgmt., LaSalle U., 1995. Cert. lab. dir. Nat. Certifying Agy. for Clin. Lab. Pers.; diplomate Am. Coll. Health Care Execs. Med. technologist Jackson Meml. Hosp., Dade City, Fla., 1979-81; microbiology supr. HCA Bayonet Point-Hudson Med. Ctr., Hudson, Fla., 1981-82, dir. labs., 1982-88; lab. mgr., adminstrv. and tch. dir. Citrus Meml. Hosp., Inverness, Fla., 1988—; lab. cons. HCA Oak Hill Hosp., Spring Hill, Fla., 1983-84; cons. lab. info. systems Citation Computer Systems, St. Louis, 1983—, Hosp. Corp. of Am., Nashville, 1986; instr. Microbiology Pasco Hernando Com. Coll., New Port Richey, Fla., 1986-88, Inst. Biolog. Scis. Cen. Fla. Community Coll., Lecanto, 1989—; bd. dirs. Gulf Coast chpt. Clin. Lab. Mgrs. Assn., Tampa, Fla., 1987, pres., 1987-89. Parish pres. Greek Orthodox Ch. of West Cen., Inverness, Fla.; chmn. Bayonet Point Hosp. Good Govt. Group, Hudson, 1986-88. Mem. APHA, Am. Mgmt. Assn., Am. Soc. Microbiology, Am. Soc. Clin. Pathologists (cert. in lab. mgmt.), Am. Soc. Med. Technologists (cert.), Fla. Soc. Med. Technologists, Clin. Lab. Mgmt. Assn. (pres. Gulf Coast chpt. 1988-90), Am. Assn. Clin. Chemists, Am. Acad. Microbiology (cert.), Fla. State Bd. Clin. Lab. Pers. (chmn. 1994). Democrat. Clubs: Greek Orthodox Youth Am. (Clearwater, Fla.). Lodges: Order of DeMolay, Sons of Pericles (sec.). Home: 6 Byrsonima Ct W Homosassa FL 34446-4610 Office: Citrus Meml Hosp 502 W Highland Blvd Inverness FL 34452-4754

MAVROV, VALKO STOYTCHEV, engineering educator; b. Bourgas, Bulgaria, Dec. 29, 1945; arrived in Germany, 1990; s. Stoytcho Todorov and Russa Valkova (Staleva) M.; m. Jivka Duneva Duneva, Aug. 9, 1978; 1 child, Russalina. Chem. Engr., Tech. U., Prague, Czech Republic, 1970, PhD, 1974. Asst. U. Bourgas, 1974-81, assoc. prof., 1981-90; scientist Max-Planck Inst., Frankfurt, Germany, 1990-92; scientist U. Saarland, Saarbrücken, Germany, 1992-93, lectr., assoc. prof., 1993—, vice dir. Inst. Environ. Tech., 1995—; sci. dir. Lab. Sea Water Chemistry, bulgarian Acad. Sci., Bourgas, 1983-90, Tech. Ctr. Ecology, Bourgas, 1987-90; vice rector U. Bourgas, 1989-90. Author: Membranes and Pressure Driven Membrance Processes, 1990 (Best Sci. Book in Bulgaria 1990), Water Technology-Waste Water Treatment, 1987; contbr. articles to profl. jours.; patentee in field. Mem. European Desal. Soc. Orthodox. Home: Hellwigstr 17, 66121 Saarbrücken Germany Office: U Saarland Inst Env Comp, Im Stadtwald Geb 47, 66123 Saarbrücken Germany

MAVROVIC, IVO, chemical engineer; b. Fiume, Italy, Dec. 5, 1927; came to U.S., 1959; s. Janko and Milica (Gregorina) M.; m. Erna Gallian, oct. 14, 1955; 1 child, Paul. BSChemE, U. Zagreb, Yugoslavia, 1952, MSChemE, 1955. Registered profl. engr, N.Y. Chem. engr. Dorr-Oliver, Milan, Italy, 1956-59, Chemico, N.Y.C., 1960-65; cons. N.Y.C., 1965-77; pres. UTI/UTI Constrn. Inc., Hackensack, N.J., 1977—. Patentee in field; contbr. articles to profl. jours. Mem. AICE. Roman Catholic. Office: UTI/UTI Constrn Inc 2 University Plaza Dr Hackensack NJ 07601-6202

MAWBY, COLIN JOHN, musician, composer, writer; b. Portsmouth, Eng., May 9, 1936; s. Bernard John and Enid Dorothy (Vaux) M.; m. Beverley Jane Courtney, July 15, 1987; children: Benedict John, Clement Donald. Student, Royal Coll. Music, London, 1951-54. Choirmaster Plymouth (Eng.) Cathedral, 1955-56, Sacred Heart, Wimbledon, Eng., 1978-81; organist St. Anne's Ch., London, 1957-59; asst. master music Westminster Cathedral, London, 1959-61, master of music, 1961-78; choral dir. Radio Telefis Eireann, Dublin, Ireland, 1981-95; dir. Irish Nat. Chamber Choir, 1996—; prof. Trinity Coll. Music, London, 1975-80; short term chorus master BBC, London, 1973; exec. assoc. bd., London, 1978; has conducted BBC Singers, Belgian Radio Choir, Pro Cantione Antiqua, London Mozart Players, The Nash Ensemble; regular spkr. and condr. BBC Radio 3. Composer 21 masses and more than 200 other choral pieces, also 2 operas for young people; recorded with Argo, Naxos, Unicorn, Classics for Pleasure, Oreg. Cath. Press, others. Decorated officer of merit Knights of Malta; fellow Guild Ch. Music, 1989. Roman Catholic. Home: Gerrardstown, Garlow Cross, Navan County Meath, Ireland

MAWEU, DAVID, pathologist, consultant; b. Machakos, Kenya, July 28, 1935; s. Mbai and Meli; m. Mary June Mumo Mutuku, June 16, 1966 (dec. Aug. 1998); children: Brian, Musomba, Beth Mueni, Dawn Mumbua, John Musembi. MB, BChir, Makerere U., Kampala, Uganda, 1964. Resident pathology Cleve. Met. Gen. Hosp., 1966-67; sr. house officer, registrar pathology Bolton (Eng.) Dist. Gen. Hosp., 1967-69; sr. registrar pathology Royal So. Hosp., Liverpool, Eng., 1970-74; cons. pathologist Zambia Consol. Copper Mines, Kitwe, 1974-87, King Faisal Mil. Hosp., Khamis, Saudi Arabia, 1988-89, Armed Forces Hosp., Muscat, Oman, 1991-96. Fellow Royal Soc. Tropical Medicine and Hygiene (local sec. Zambia 1978-87); mem. Am. Soc. Clin. Pathologists, Assn. Clin. Pathologists, Brit. Med. Assn., Nat. Geog. Soc., N.Y. Acad. Scis. Avocations: photography, sports, music. Home and Office: PO Box 82309, Mombasa Kenya

MAWHOOD, ARISTIDE ROSCOE, mechanical engineer; b. Darjeeling, India, Nov. 18, 1933; parents Brit. citizens; s. Charles Timothy and Thelma Quida (Hollow) M.; m. Mary Bridget McManamon, Dec. 1, 1962; children: Sean Ross, Anton Morgan. BSME, Brit. Inst. Engring. Tech., 1955; postgrad., Imperial Coll. Sci. and Tech. Registered profl. engr., U.S.; profl. engr., U.K. Apprentice engr. Cen. Electricity Generating Bd., 1951-55; dist. engr., mgr., adv. and field engr. Worthington Corp., 1956-63; sr. maintenance engr., maintenance project engr. Hess Oil Virgin Islands Corp., 1970-73; mgr. field engring. svcs. Sam P. Wallace, Internat., 1973; chief engr., chief planning engr., sr. constrn. engr. C.E. Lummus Corp., 1973-75; chief field and resident engr. Pritchard Internat., Inc., 1976-77; engr. 1 mech. (project mgmt. team) Arabian Am. Oil Co., 1977-82; sr. sys. engr. ITT-Fed. Electric Corp., 1985; sr. engr.-cum-cons. Mawhood & Assocs., 1983, 84, 86; sr. mech. engr.-cum-cons. Brown & Root Internat., Inc., 1987-88; sr. engr.-cum-cons. Allis Chalmers Compressor Corp., Appleton, Wis., 1988-89; tech. asst. specialist Corporacion Venezolana de Guayana, S.A., 1989-90, M&H Engring., Inc., Houston, 1990-91; project mgr., engr. Am. Samoa Govt., Pago Pago, American Samoa, 1991-94; sr. program officer, cons. Fed. Emergency Mgmt. Agy. (Pacific), 1994-95; mech. engr., cons. Saudi Arabian Oil Co., Dammam, Saudi Arabia, 1995-96; mech. engr. Dow Chem. Co., Houston, 1996-97; cons. electronic data processing, 1997—; mech. engr., cons. Saudi Arabian Oil Co., Damman, Saudi Arabia, 1995-96; mech. engr. tech. support unit, engring. and constrn. divsn. Dow Chem. USA, Inc., 1996-97, Engring. and Constrn. Venezuela (Petrozuata) Extra Heavy Crude Oil Engring. Project, Brown & Root USA, Inc., 1997-98; semi-ret. project mgr., engr., tech. cons., 1998—; condr. seminars and revs. Tex. Employment Commn., Houston, 1983-84. Author: Value Engineering, 1975, Role of Gas Turbines, 1978 (IGTI award 1980), Machinery Diseases, 1982 (Vibration Inst. award 1983), Saline Water Conversion, 1987 (Water Inst. award 1988). Active various ch. groups, Houston. Recipient Safety at Constrn. Sites award Constrn. Assn. Can., 1974, Tech. Transfer award Operaciones al Sur del Orinoco, Puerto Ordaz, Venezuela, Value Engring. award Refineria Isla, Curacao, 1987. Fellow Instn. Plant Engrs., India Soc. Mech Engrs., Japan

Soc. Mech. Engrs.; mem. ASME (corp.), NSPE, Am. Soc. Metals, Soc. Am. Mil. Engrs., Am. Inst. Plant Engrs., Instn. Mech. Engrs. (assoc.). Republican. Christian Scientist. Achievements include development of solutions for erosion/corrosion problems on pump casings; findings on excess stiffness characteristics in Bendex Diaphragm Couplings for high-speed gas compressors. Avocations: model engineering, photography, philately, world travel, fitness. Home: West Univ PO Box 272562 Houston TX 77277-2562

MAX, BUDDY (BORIS MAX PASTUCH), musician; b. Jan. 25; m. Freda Max; 1 child, John. Musician, performer as America's Singing Flea Market Cowboy: albums include: Many Styles and Sounds of Buddy Max, 1980, The Great Nashville Star, 1984, The Story of Freda and Bud, 1985, Cowboy Junction Stars, 1985, Tribute to Challenger's Crew of 7, 1986, With Our Friends at Cowboy Junction, 1989, Little Circle B, 1990, Together-Our Masterpiece, 1991, The Life to Fame and Fortune, 1992, Orange Blossom Special, 1996, Hall of Fame, Gold Record Award Winning Buddy Max, 1996, Hall of Fame; composer songs include When the Magnolia Tree Blooms in Lecanto, The Story of Barney Clark, Hang My Guitar on the Wall, John F. Kennedy, The Challenger, Where the Maple Syrups Flow, Little Circle B, Way Up on the Mountain, Desert Storm, When Do I Love You, The Pretty Girl on TV. Recipient World Hall of Fame award and gold medalion, 1997, numerous trophies, awards for benefit and non-profit shows Am. Heart Assn., Am. Lung Assn., Girl Scouts Am., Citizens of Citrus County Fla., Deaf Svcs. of Citrus County, Statue of Liberty trophy and coin award Cowboy Junction Opry Country Music Show, 2000 for song I Love Miss America. Address: care Cowboy Junction 3949 W Hwy & Jct 490 Lecanto FL 34461-9232

MAX, THEODORE CONRAD, surgeon; b. Langhorne, Pa., Apr. 29, 1929; s. Theodore Louis and Marian (Smith) M.; m. Melva Sholenberg, June 17, 1950; children: Christopher, Steven, Melva, Theodore, Erica. BS, Hobart Coll., 1950; MD, U. Rochester, 1954. Diplomate Am. Bd. Surgery. Resident in surgery Strong Meml. Hosp., Rochester, N.Y., 1954-60; instr. surgery U. Rochester Sch. Medicine, 1961-63; pvt. practice gen. and vascular surgery Utica, N.Y., 1963—; chief surgery, pres. med. staff St. Luke's Meml. Hosp., Utica; chief surgery, pres. med. staff St. Elizabeth Hosp., Utica, dir. surgery family practice residency program, 1976—; mem. bd. profl. conduct N.Y. State Dept. Health, 1978-86; dir. Med. Liability Ins. Co., N.Y.C., 1986—. Dir., chpt. pres. Am. Heart. Assn., 1976-78; mem. adv. coun. Inst. Tech. SUNY, 1997—. Capt. USAF, 1957-59. Fellow Am. Coll. Surgeons (pres. chpt. 1977-78, gov. 1982-88); mem. N.Y. Soc. Surgeons (pres. 1974-76), Med. Soc. State of N.Y. (del. for surgery 1974-94). Home: PO Box 238 9495 Main St Holland Patent NY 13354-3813 Office: 2206 Genesee St Utica NY 13502-5829

MAXEY, SUSAN MARIE, geology department head; b. Evansville, Ind., July 6, 1946; d. Russell H. and Irene G. (Horn) Wiberg. BS, U. Tex., 1969, postgrad., 1986—; MA, U. Tex., Dallas, 1976. Tchr. Forest Oaks Mid. Sch., Ft. Worth, Tex., 1969-71, Browne Mid. Sch., Dallas, 1971-76; lectr. U. Tex., Dallas, 1977-78; geology dept. head Brookhaven Coll., Dallas, 1978—. Mem. editl. rev. bd. Jour. Coll. Sci. Tchg., 1984-87; contbr. articles to profl. jours. Maj. gifts chmn. Sta. KERA-TV Auction, Dallas, 1985-88; grad. Leadership Lewisville, Tex., 1989-90; v.p. Lewisville Edn. Found., 1989-96; bd. dirs. Greater Lewisville Habitat for Humanity, 1995-97; del. Tex. Rep. Convention, 1996, 2000; mem. adv. bd. Lake Lewisville Environ. Learning Area, 1995—. Recipient Master Tchr. award Nat. Inst. for Staff & Organizational Devel., 1987; Kellogg Found. fellow, 1988. Mem. Geol. Soc. Am., Lions (Balloon Festival com. chair 1991—, treas. 1992-96), Delta Kappa Gamma. Avocations: underwater photography, quilt-making. Home: 20 Horseshoe Dr Highland Vill TX 75077-6714 Office: Brookhaven Coll 3939 Valley View Ln Dallas TX 75244-4906

MAXIMOS V HAKIM, patriarch; b. Tanta, Egypt, May 18, 1908; s. Salim and Gazaleh (Eugenee) H. DD in Theology, St. Anne, Jerusalem, 1930; postgrad., U. Laval, Que., Can., 1965, Notre Dame, 1972, U. Alger, 1975. Tchr. Patriarcal Sch., Beirut, 1930-31; rector Patriarcal Coll., Cairo, 1931-34, prin., 1934-43; archbishop Akka-Nazareth, Palestine, Israel, 1943-67; patriarch Antioche and All the East, Syria, 1967—. Author: (books) Life of Jesus, in Arabic, 1950, Gospel Pages, in French, English, Dutch and Spanish, 1960. Officer Legion D'Honneur Grand Croix French Govt., 1991. Home: PO Box 22249, Damascus Syria Office: Patriachate, PO Box 50076, Beirut Lebanon*

MAXWELL, DOROTHEA BOST ANDREWS, civic worker; b. Greenville, Ill., Apr. 20, 1911; d. Samuel Washington and Viola Maud (Bost) Andrews; m. Richard Wesley Maxwell, June 1, 1935; children: Andrea Judith Maxwell Platz, Anne Dorothea Maxwell Walsh. BA with honors, diploma in piano, Greenville Coll., 1933; MusM, Northwestern U., 1937. Cert. primary and secondary tchr., music tchr., Mo. Dir. sch. music spring Arbor (Mich.) Jr. Coll., 1933-34; tutor orthopedic handicapped children St. Louis Pub. Schs., 1950-56. Pres. Women's Assn., 2d Presbyn. Ch., St. Louis, 1956-58; tour guide Mo. Bot. Garden, St. Louis, 1975-87; pres. The Wednesday Club St. Louis, 1983-85, archivist, 1985-92; guide tours of distinction St. Louis Symphony Soc., 1980-85; assoc. mem. Nat. Mus. Women in Arts, Washington. Mem. Clan Maxwell Soc. U.S.A., Mo. Hist. Soc., St. Louis Genealogy Soc., Nat. Soc. DAR (Jefferson chpt. St. Louis), Piano Club St. Louis, Washington U. Faculty women's Club, Mu Phi Epsilon. Republican. Congregationalist. Home: 901 S Skinker Blvd Saint Louis MO 63105-3242

MAXWELL, ELISABETH JENNY JEANNE, educator; b. St. Alban de Roche, France, Mar. 11, 1921; arrived in England, 1945; d. Paul Louis and Colombe Marguerite (Pentel) Meynard; m. Robert Ian Maxwell, Mar. 14, 1945 (dec. 1991); children: Karine (dec.), Isabel, Christine, Philipe, Anne, Michael (dec.), Ghislaine, Kevin, Ian. BA, St. Hugh's Coll., Oxford, Eng., 1974, DPhil, 1981. Editl. rels. Pergamon Press, Eng., 1962-81, dir. editl. rels., 1985-91; freelance lectr. Europe, U.S. and Can., 1989—; chairperson Remembering for the Future, 1986-92; chairperson Remembering for the Future 2000, 1997—. Author: A Mind of My Own, 1994; contbr. articles to profl. jours. Avocations: trekking, swimming, music, reading. E-mail: drmaxwell@compuserve.com. Office: 11 Lochmore House, Cundy St, London SWIW 9JX, England

MAXWELL, FLORENCE HINSHAW, civic worker; b. Nora, Ind., July 14, 1914; d. Asa Benton and Gertrude (Randall) Hinshaw; m. John Williamson Maxwell, June 5, 1936; children: Marilyn Maxwell Grissom, William Douglas. BA cum laude, Butler U., 1935. Coord., bd. dirs. Sight Conservation and Aid to Blind, 1962-73, nat. chmn., 1969-73; active various fund drives; chmn. jamboree, hostess coms. North Ctrl. H.S., 1959, 64, Girl Scouts USA, 1937-38, 54-56; mus. chmn. Sr. Girl Scouts USA Regional Coun., 1956-57; scorekeeper Little League, 1955-57; bd. dirs. Nora Sch. Parents' Club, 1958-59, Eastwood Jr. H.S. Triangle Club, 1959-62, Ind. State Symphony Soc. Women's Com., 1965-67, 76-79, Symphoguide chmn., 1976-79; vision screening Indpls. inner city pub. sch. kindergartens, pre-schs., 1962-69, 81—, Headstart, 1967-98; asst. Glaucoma screening clinics Gen. Hosp., Glendale Shopping Ctr., City County Bldg., Am. Legion Nat. Hdqrs., Ind. Health Assn. Conf., 1962-73; chmn. sight conservation and aid to blind Nat. Delta Gamma Found., Indpls., Columbus, Ohio, 1969-73; mem. telethon team Butler U. Fund, 1964; symphoguide hostess Internat. Conf. on Cities, 1971, Nat. League of Cities, 1972; mem. health adv. com. Headstart, 1976-98, sec., 1980-98, mem. social svcs. com., 1987-98, coord. vision rescreening and referrals, assessment team of compliance steering com., 1978-79, 84, 86, 87, 88, 91, 92, 94, 96, 98 (Appreciation award 1983); founder People of Vision Aux., 1981, bd. dirs., 1981—, v.p., 1990-92, mem. coord. vision and glaucoma screenings and office svcs., 1990-92, sec. emeritus, 1997; initiated vision screening and eye safety edn. at Jameson Camp for Children, 1987; trainer vision screening, 1988—. Recipient Key to City of Indpls., 1972, Those Spl. People award Women in Comm., 1980, Jefferson award for Disting. Pub. Svc. Indpls. Star, 1991, Cmty. Action Head Start Outstanding Vol. award, 1996, Health/Social Svcs. award Family Devel. Svcs., 1998. Mem. Nat. Soc. to Prevent Blindness (now Prevent Blindness Am.), Ind. Audubon Soc., Ind. Hist. Soc., Ind. Soc. to Prevent Blindness (now Prevent Blindness Ind., dir. 1962-99, exec. com. 1971-95, v.p. 1983-86, sec. 1971-83, asst. sec.-treas. 1987-92, adv. bd. 1999—, Ind. del. to nat. 3-yr. program planning conf. 1985, internal analysis task force for svcs. 1987, Sight Saving award 1974, life hon. v.p. 1983—, Svc. Appreciation award 1999), Jameson Camp Aux., Ind. State Symphony Soc. Women's Com. (vol. Indpls. symphony orch.'s discovery concerts, vol. Indpls. noontime concerts, vol. Yuletide, coffee concerts), People of Vision, Delta Gamma (chpt. golden ann. celebration decade and comm. chmn. 1975, treas. Alpha Tau house corp. 1975-78, nat. chmn. Parent Club Study Com. 1976-77, instr. province leadership sem. workshop 1989, Cable award 1969, Outstanding Alumna award 1973, Svc. Recognition award 1977, Shield award 1981, scholarship hon. 1981, Stellar award 1986, Oxford award 1992). Republican. Address: 1502 E 80th St Indianapolis IN 46240-2706

MAXWELL, GEORGE RUSSELL, scenic designer; b. Salt Lake City, Oct. 18, 1951; s. George Henry and LaRae Greathouse Maxwell. BS, Weber State U., 1973. Property master Pioneer Theatre Co., Salt Lake City, 1974-87, resident scenic designer, 1987—; scenic designer Utah Shakespearean Festival, Cedar City, Utah, 1995-2000. Set designer of 100's of prodns., including A Funny Thing Happened on the Way to the Forum, The Count of Monte Cristo, An American Daughter, South Pacific, Evita, Cabaret, Peer Gynt, The Grapes of Wrath, Man of La Mancha, Crazy for You, Ain't Misbehavin', The Coronation of Poppea, The Winter's Tale, The Mikado, The Tempest, You Can't Take It With You, Hamlet, Romeo and Juliet, Relative Values, You Never Can Tell, The Lion in Winter, Damn Yankees. Bd. dirs. Salt Lake Arts Coun., Salt Lake City, 1989-93. Mem. United Scenic Artists. Office: Pioneer Theatre Co 300 S 1400 E Rm 205 Salt Lake City UT 84112-0660

MAXWELL, KATRINA DIANE, information scientist; b. Mpls., Nov. 24, 1961; arrived in France, 1988; d. William Hall Christie and Mary Carolyn (McLaughlin) M.; m. Herve Jacques Balloux, July 19, 1990; children: Caroline, Emilie, Olivia. BSCE, U. Ill., 1983; PhD, Brunel U., 1986. Mgmt. scientist M&M/Mars Group, Maidenhead, Eng., 1986-88; rsch. assoc. INSEAD, Fontainebleau, France, 1988-90; cons. ID Ptnrs., Paris, 1991-92; rsch. assoc., fellow INSEAD, Fontainebleau, 1992-97; ptnr. Datamax, Fontainebleau, France, 1997—. Contbr. articles to profl. jours. Episcopalian. Avocations: walking, swimming, singing, gastronomy, golf. Office: Datamax, 7 bis bld Foch, 77300 Fontainebleau France

MAXWELL, KENNETH ROBERT, historian; b. Wellington, Somerset, U.K., Feb. 3, 1941; s. Kenneth Bruce Maxwell and Jean Anderson. BA, Cambridge U., 1963, MA, 1967; MA, Princeton (N.J.) U., 1967, PhD, 1970. Prof. history Columbia U., N.Y.C., 1976-84, dir. Camoes Ctr., 1988-99; program dir. Tinker Found., N.Y.C., 1979-85; sr. fellow Latin Am. Coun. on Fgn. Rels., N.Y.C., 1989—, v.p., dir. studies, 1996, Nelson and David Rockefellor sr. fellow, 1995—; vis. prof. history and L.Am. studies Princeton U., N.J., 1985-86; vis. prof. history Yale U., New Haven, Conn., 1991-92; consultative coun. Luso-Am. Found., Lisbon, Portugal, 1996—; bd. dirs. Spanish Inst. Author: Pombal: Paradox of Enlightment, 1995, The Making of Portuguese Democracy, 1995, Conflicts and Conspiracies: Brazil and Portugal, 1973; co-author: The New Spain, 1994; book reviewer: Foreign Affairs.; contbr. articles to profl. jours. and publs.; columnist no.com.br., 2000—. Bd. trustees Latin Am. Scholarship, Cambridge, Mass., 1991-97; founding mem. Com. for Internat. Grantmakers, Washington, 1981-86; adv. com. Ams. Watch, N.Y.C., 1996—; adv. Dwight D. Eisenhower Exch. Fellowship, Phila., 1996; selection com. Hubert H. Humphery fellowship, 1985. Recipient Grand Cross Order of Merit, 1996; named Comdr. Order of Rio Branco, 1997; Herodotus fellow Inst. for Advanced Study, 1971-75, Guggenheim fellow, 1976-77, hon. fellow Romance Inst. London U., 1993—. Mem. Century Assn., Norfolk Country Club, Am. Hist. Assn., Coun. on Fgn. Rels., Instituto Historico Geografico Brasileiro. Avocations: swimming, drawing. Home: 165 Litchfield Rd Norfolk CT 06058-1279 Office: Coun on Fgn Rels 58 E 68th St New York NY 10021-5953

MAXWELL, MAKENZIE ELENA, school counselor; b. Portsmouth, Va., Jan. 17, 1967; d. Robert Peter and Kathleen (Butler) M.; children: Connor Alexander Smith-Maxwell, Lachlan. BS, Old Dominion U., 1991, MEd, 1996. Cert. elem. edn. tchr. State Bd. Edn., Va. Homebound tchr. Va. Beach Pub. Schs., 1992-93, Norfolk Pub. Schs., 1993-95; elem. sch. counselor Portsmouth Pub. Schs., 1996—. Appeared in an action movie, including Vanishing Son, 1993; industry film includes Parenting Styles, 1998. Mem. ACA, Va. Psychol. Assn. (presenter 1993), Va. Counselors Assn. (presenter 1999), Hampton Roads Counselors Assn. Democrat. Roman Catholic. Avocations: scuba diving, acting, international adoption, creative writing. E-mail: makmaxwell@aol.com. Home: 4175 Prindle Ct Apt 103 Chesapeake VA 23321-3652 Office: John Tyler Elem Sch 3649 Hartford St Portsmouth VA 23707-1205

MAXWELL, PATRICIA JOY, fund raising executive; b. Belle Plaine, Iowa, Feb. 7, 1937; d. Verne Edwin and Julia Inez (Beem) M. Student Pepperdine Coll., 1954-55; BS, Iowa State Tchrs. Coll., 1958; MPA, Roosevelt U., 1982. Cert. fund raising exec. Dir. resource devel. Boys Clubs Am., 1978-81; exec. dir. Westlake Health Svcs. Found., 1981-84; assoc. dean devel. and alumni affairs U. Ill. Coll. Medicine, 1984-91; sr. maj. gifts officer U. Ill., 1991-93; v.p. devel. Orlando (Fla.) M.D. Anderson Cancer Ctr., 1993; assoc. dir. nat. hdqrs. Alzheimer's Assn., Chgo., 1994; dir. devel. N.Y. Acad. Scis., N.Y.C., 1997, sr. dir. devel., Calif. State U., Long Beach, 1997—; cons. Ency. Britannica Ednl. Corp., Prentice Hal l Inc., U.S. State Dept. Mem. N.Y. Acad. Scis., Am. Mktg. Assn. (co-founder Acd. of Health Svcs. Mktg. 1980), Chgo. Area Pub. Affairs Group, Univ. Club (Chgo.), Balboa (Calif.) Bay Club, Lake Nona Club (Orlando). Office: Calif State U Office Devel CNSM F05-104 1250 Bellflower Rd Long Beach CA 90840-0001

MAXWELL, RICHARD ANTHONY, retail executive; b. N.Y.C., Apr. 1, 1933; s. Arthur William and Mary Ellen (Winestock) M.; m. Jacqueline Ann Creamer, Oct. 27, 1962. Student, NYU, 1957-58, Acad. Advanced Traffic, 1959. Import ops. mgr. Associated Merchandising Corp., N.Y.C., 1950-52, 56-65; v.p. Associated Dry Goods Corp., N.Y.C., 1965-86, sr. v.p. mktg., 1980-82, exec. v.p. mktg., 1982-86; pres. A.D.G. Export Mktg., Florence, Italy, 1982-86, Associated Dry Goods Ltd., Hong Kong, 1983-86, Inter Textyle Corp., 1987-89; with Matol Botanical Internat. Ltd.; exec. v.p. Matol World Corp., Montreal, Que., Can., 1992-94; dir. Matol Botanical New Zealand, New Zealand, 1994-96; v.p. internat. ops. L'Aprina Internat. Inc., 1994-96; chief internat. officer Camelot Concept Co., Montreal, 1995-96; CFO Showcase Prodns., Phoenix, Ariz., 1996; exec. v.p. Harmony House Internat., Phoenix, 1996-97, IGW Trust, Phoenix, 1997-99, Pre-Paid Legal Svcs., Inc., 1999—; pres. Team 39, Inc., Dunedin, Fla., 2000—; mem. industry sector adv. com. Dept. Commerce, 1984-93. Mem. shippers adv. com. Nat. Maritime Coun. Served with USAF, 1952-56. Recipient Silver medal for contbns. to trade expansion, Republic of China, 1980; appt. to rank of comdr. in Order of Merit in recognition of improvement of trade between Italy and U.S., Republic of Italy, 1985. Mem. Am. Assn. Exporters and Importers (past pres., dir.), Shippers Conf. Greater N.Y. (past pres., dir.), Nat. Retail Mchts. Assn. (vice chmn. fgn. trade com.), Nat. Com. Internat. Trade Documentation (past vice chmn. gen. bus. com.), Transp. Assn. Am., Italy-Am. C. of C. (past pres., dir.), Am. Soc. of Italian Legion of Merit (dir.). Home: 2408 Stag Run Blvd Clearwater FL 33765-1832

MAXWELL, RICHARD CALLENDER, lawyer, educator; b. Mpls., Oct. 7, 1919; s. Bertram Wayburn and Blossom (Callender) M.; m. Frances Lida McKay, Jan 27, 1942; children—Richard Callender, John McKay. B.S.L., U. Minn., 1941, LL.B., 1947; LL.D. (hon.), Calif. Western U., 1983; LLD (hon.), Southwestern U., 1993. Assoc. prof. U. N.D., 1947-49; assoc. prof. U. Tex., 1949-51, prof., 1951-53; counsel Amerada Petroleum Corp., 1952-53; prof. UCLA, 1953-81; dean UCLA (Sch. Law), 1959-69, Connell prof., 1979-81, Connell prof. emeritus, 1981—; Chadwick prof. Duke U. Sch. Law, 1981-89, Chadwick prof. emeritus, 1989—; vis. prof. Columbia U., 1955; vis. Alumni prof. U. Minn., 1970-71; Fulbright lectr. Queen's U., No. Ireland, 1970; vis. Ford Found. prof. U. Singapore, 1971; Thompson prof. U. Colo., 1982; vis. prof. Hastings Coll. Law, 1976, Duke U., 1979-80, U. Tex., 1985; pres. Minn. Law Rev., 1946; chmn. Council Legal Edn. Opportunity, 1971-72; pres. Assn. Am. Law Schs., 1972; chmn. adv. com. law Fulbright Program, 1971-74, chmn. adv. com. U.K., 1974-77; mem. com. on gas prodn. opportunities NRC, 1977-78; mem. law sch. editorial and adv. bd. West Pub. Co., 1971-94. Author: (with S. A. Riesenfeld) Cases and Materials on Modern Social Legislation, 1950, (with H.R. Williams and C.J. Meyers) Cases on Oil and Gas Law, 1956, 7th edit., (with Stephen F. Williams, Patrick H. Martin, Bruce M. Kramer), 2000, (with S. A. Riesenfeld) California Cases on Security Transactions, 1957, 4th edit. (with S.A. Riesenfeld, J.R. Hetland, W.D. Warren), 1991; West Coast editor Oil and Gas Reporter, 1953—. Mem. Los Angeles Employee Relations Bd., 1971-74; bd. dirs. Constl. Rights Found., 1963-81; trustee Calif. Western U., 1979-81; bd. visitors Duke U. Sch. Law, 1973-79, chmn. bd. Pvt. Adjudication Ctr., 1984-89; bd. visitors Southwestern U. Sch. Law, 1981—. Served to lt. comdr. USNR, 1941-46. Recipient Disting. Tchg. award UCLA, 1977, Duke Law Sch., 1986, UCLA medal, 1982, Clyde O. Martz Tchg. award Rocky Mountain Mineral Law Found., 1994. Mem. ABA (com. on youth edn. for citizenship 1975-79, spl. com. on public understanding about the law 1979-84), Order of Coif. (nat. exec. com. 1980-86). Office: Duke U Sch Law Durham NC 27708-0362

MAXWELL, SARA ELIZABETH, psychologist, educator, speech pathologist, director; b. DuQuoin, Ill., Jan. 23; d. Jean A. (Patterson) Green; m. David Lowell Maxwell, Dec. 27, 1960 (div. Mar. 1990); children: Lisa Marina, David Scott; m. James F. Manning, July 19, 1997 (div. Aug. 1998). BS, So. Ill. U., 1963, MS, 1964, MSEd, 1965; MEd, Boston Coll., 1982; attended, Harvard U., 1983; PhD, Boston Coll., 1992. Cert. and lic. speech.-lang. pathologist, early childhood specialist, guidance counselor, sch. adjustment counselor, behavior specialist, EMT. Clin. supr. Clin. Ctr. So. Ill. U., Carbondale, 1964-65, grad. clin. instr., 1965-66; speech/lang. pathologist, sch. adjustment counselor Westwood (Mass.) Pub. Schs., 1967-93; grad. faculty Emerson Coll., Boston, 1979-81; cons. Mass. Dept. Mental Health, Boston, 1979-82; grad. clin. supr. Robbins Speech/Hearing Ctr., Emerson Coll., Boston, 1979-82; predoctoral intern in clin. psychology South Shore Mental Health Ctr., Quincy, 1985-86; devel. and clin. staff psychologist South Shore Mental Health Ctr., Hingham and Quincy, Mass., 1989-93; emergency svcs. team and respite house manager South Shore Mental Health Ctr., Quincy, Mass., 1990-93; cons. Westwood Nursery Preschs., 1986-93; pvt. practice Twin Oaks Clin. Assocs., Westwood, Mass, 1986-88, South Coast Counseling Assocs., Quincy, 1989-93; cons. local collaboratives and preschs., Westwood, 1980-83; profl. workshops presenter Head Start, 1980; program specialist speech, lang., learning Broward County (Fla.) Schs., 1993-96, exceptional student edn. specialist, 1996-98; behavior specialist, 1999—; adj. prof. grad. sch. of psychology Nova Southeastern U., 1995—; presenter Head Start, ASHA, CEC, APSC, IALP and other profl., nat. and state confs., 1980-99; invited del. to Sino-Am. Conf. on Exceptionality, Beijing Normal U., People's Republic of China, 1995. Contbr. articles to profl. jours., chpts. to textbooks. Mem. adv. coun. Westwood (Mass.) Bd. Health, 1977-80; emergency med. technician Westwood Pub. Schs. Athletic Dept., 1981. Vocat. Rehab. fellow So. Ill. U., 1964; Merit scholar Perry County, Ill., 1959-64, Credi meml. scholar So. Ill. U., 1964. Mem. Am. Speech & Hearing Assn. (nat. schs. com., nat. chairperson Pub. Sch. Caucus 1985-87), Am. Psychol. Assn., Assn. Psychiat. Svcs. for Children, Coun. Exceptional Children, Internat. Assn. of Logopedics, Rio Vista Civic Assn., Boston Coll. Alumni Assn., Harvard Club. Episcopalian. Avocations: squash, sailing, skiing. Office: Nova Southeastern U Ctr Psychol Studies Maxwell Maltz Psych Bldg 3301 College Ave Fort Lauderdale FL 33314-7796

MAXWELL, THOMAS WILLIAM, tertiary educator; b. Cowra, Australia, May 23, 1947; s. Thomas William and Joyce Lorraine (Eddy) M.; divorced; children: Anna Alicia, Emily Eve. BSc, Univ. Sydney, 1968, Diploma in Edn., 1968; M in Edn., Univ. New England, Armidale, Australia, 1981, PhD, 1991. Secondary tchr. NSW Dept. of Edn., Australia, 1969, 72; lectr. Macquarie Univ., Australia, 1980-82; cons. Catholic Edn. Office, Armidale, Australia, 1983-87; sr. lectr. Univ. New England, 1988—. Contbr. numerous articles to profl. jours.; chpts. to books. Sec. NSW Amateur Athletic Assn., Sydney, 1968-69. Mem. Australian Coll. Edn., UNE Sports Union. Office: Univ New England, Dept of Edn Studies, Armidale 2351, Australia

MAY, ALAN ALFRED, lawyer; b. Detroit, Apr. 7, 1942; s. Alfred Albert and Sylvia (Sheer) M.; m. Elizabeth Miller; children: Stacy Ann, Julie Beth. BA, U. Mich., 1963, JD, 1966. Bar: Mich. 1967, D.C. 1976; former reg. nursing home adminstr., Mich. Ptnr. May and May, PC, Detroit, 1979—; spl. asst. atty. gen. State of Mich., 1970—; pres., instr. Med-Leg Seminars, Inc., 1978; lectr. Wayne State U., 1974; instr. Oakland U., 1969. Chmn. Rep. 18th Congressional Dist. Com., 1983-87, now chmn. emeritus; chmn. 19th Congressional Dist. Com., 1981-83; mem. Mich. Rep. Com., 1976-84; del. Rep. Nat. Conv., 1984, rules com., 1984; del. Rep. Nat. Conv., 1988, platform com., 1988; former chmn. Mich. Civil Rights Commn.; mem. Mich. Civil Svc. Commn., 1984-88; trustee NCCJ (exec. bd., vice chmn. nat conf. for cmty. and justice), Temple Beth El Birmingham, Mich., pres. exec. bd.; mem. Electoral Coll.; bd. dirs. ADL, Mich.; bd. dirs. exec. bd., pres., Detroit Region/Nat. Conf. Cmty. and Justice, Charfoos Charitable Found. Mem. Nat. Conf. Cmty. and Justice (exec. bd., vice chmn.), Detroit Bar Assn., Oakland County Bar Assn., Victors Club, Franklin Hills Country Club (past pres., bd. dirs.), President's Club (trustee). Home: 4140 Echo Rd Bloomfield Hills MI 48302-1941 Office: May & May PC 3000 Town Ctr Ste 2600 Southfield MI 48075-1375

MAY, BENJAMIN TALLMAN, securities specialist, administrator; b. N.Y.C., Dec. 22, 1957; s. Joseph Leserman and Natalie Maria (McCuaig) M.; m. Kaaren Todd Clark, Sept. 1, 1985; children: Caroline Todd, Emily Applegate, Suzannah Tallman. BA, Yale U., 1980; MBA, NYU, 1985. Corp. bond trader, v.p. Drexel Burnham Lambert, N.Y.C., 1980-84; high yield bond trader, sr. v.p. Dillon Read, Inc., N.Y.C., 1984-95; mng. dir. high yield bonds 1st Union Corp., Charlotte, N.C., 1995—. Mem. Alexis de Toqueville Soc., United Way, Charlotte, 1997; trustee Charlotte Arts and Sci. Coun. Mem. Yale Club N.Y. (Yale Alumni Recruiter). Republican. Jewish. Home: 4301 Canoebrook Rd Charlotte NC 28210-7349 Office: 1st Union Corp 301 S College St Charlotte NC 28202-6000

MAY, CARL EMIL, accountant; b. Cape Town, South Africa, Dec. 20, 1958; s. Peter Ludwig and Ethel (Harris) M.; m. Marilyn Nanette Reznik, Mar. 31, 1996. BCom, U. Cape Town, South Africa, 1982, BCom in Taxation with honors, 2000. Trainee acct. Moores Roland, Cape Town, South Africa, 1985-88; acct. Atlantic Trust Co., Cape Town, South Africa, 1989-90; prin. acct. May & Co., Cape Town, South Africa, 1990—; taxation cons. in field. Sgt. South African Police Svcs., 1978-81. Mem. South African Inst. Chartered Accts., Hebrew Order David Haifa (pres. 1999-2000). Jewish. Avocations: cycling, travel, aerobics. Home: 9 Monastery Rd Fresnaye, Cape Town 8001, South Africa Office: May & Co, 8th Fl Vogue Ho Thibault Sq, Cape Town 8001, South Africa

MAY, CAROL LEE, mechanical engineer; b. Arlington, Va., May 10, 1961; d. Ralph Waldo Jr. and Jane Brownley (Moore) M. BS, Va. Poly. Inst. and State U., 1983; postgrad., U. Göttingen, Germany, 1984-85; MS, Stanford U., 1984. Registered profl. engr., Va. Engring. technician (co-op student) Nat. Park Svc., Wyo., Colo., Alaska, 1980-82; physics instr. Fairfax County Pub. Schs., Oakton, Va., 1985; sr. engr. Cortana Corp., Falls Church, Va., 1986—. Author, co-author over 50 corp. reports on submarine tech., 1986—; contbr. articles to profl. jours. and conf. procs. Stanford U. grad. fellow, 1983-84; Deutsche Akademische Austauschdienst postgrad. fellow in fluid mechs., 1984-85. Mem. AIAA, Naval Submarine League. Achievements include coordinating transfer and documentation of fluid mechanics technology from Russian and Ukrainian institutes; providing design recommendations for U.S. and foreign submarines; investigating influence of boundary layer control techniques on drag and flow noise. Home: 7215 Janet Pl Falls Church VA 22046-3724 Office: Cortana Corp 520 N Washington St Ste 200 Falls Church VA 22046-3549

MAY, DAVID A., protective services official, public official; b. Buffalo, N.Y., May 23, 1947; s. Arthur F. M.; m. Mary E. Beer, Oct. 6, 1973; children: Jordan D., Jared R. AAS in Bus. Adminstrn., Niagara County C.C., Sanborn, N.Y., 1983; BS in Pub. Adminstrn., Empire State Coll., 1988; MA in Orgn. Mgmt., U. Phoenix, 1996; PhD in Mgmt., LaSalle U., 1997. V.p. Simpson Security, Inc., Niagara Falls, N.Y., 1973-78; lt. Niagara Falls (N.Y.) Police Dept., 1986—. Bd. mem. Nat. Conf. Christians and Jews, 1984-90, ARC, 1986-89, Music Sch. of Niagara, 1987-90, Niagara Falls Little Theatre, chmn., 1994; pres. Niagara Cmty. Ctr., Niagara Falls, 1987, Niagara Falls (N.Y.) Sch. Bd., 1988, Niagara Falls (N.Y.) Meml. Day Assn., 1990, 91, 93; lt. gov. N.Y. State Kiwanis, 1989; mem. Niagara Co. Lrgis., 1994. Recipient Svc. award Fellowship House Found., Niagara Falls, 1986; named Civic Leader of Yr., Niagara Cmty. Ctr., Niagara Falls, 1990. Mem. Kiwanis Club North Niagara Falls (pres. 1987, Kiwanian of the Yr. 1991), Lasalle Am. Legion (vice commdr. 1975), Lasalle Sportsmens Club (fin. sec.

1989). Avocations: playing tennis, golfing, amateur historian. Home: 3024 Macklem Ave Niagara Falls NY 14305-1832

MAY, DAVID IAN HICKMAN, writer; b. Hampstead, England, June 5, 1935; s. Ronald Ernest and Florence Dorothy (Hickman) M.; m. Dorothy Margaret Oaten, July 16, 1960; children: Richard Louis, Jacqueline Frances. BSEE, London U., 1961. Sr. engr. The G.E.C. Ltd., London, 1956-66; chief engr., tech. dir. Hatgield Instruments Ltd., Plymouth, 1966-73; with Plessey/Siemens, Havant, 1974-91; author, cons., free-lance journalist Waterlooville, 1991—. Com. mem. NADFAS, Portsmouth, 1997—. With Royal Air Force, 1954-56. Mem. IEEE, IEE, FEANI. Roman Catholic. Avocations: electronics, music, walking, mycology, wine making. E-Mail: Davemay@m5635809.demon.co.uk.

MAY, DONALD ROBERT LEE, ophthalmologist, retina and vitreous surgeon, educator, farmer; b. Spring Valley, Ill., Nov. 26, 1945; s. Reo Georg and Edna Antoinette (Klein) M.; m. Jane N. Sakauye, Nov. 12, 1988. BS in Liberal Arts & Scis. with high honors and distinction, U. Ill., 1968, MD, 1972. Diplomate Am. Bd. Ophthalmology, Nat. Bd. Med. Examiners. Rsch. fellow dept. ophthalmology U. Ill. Eye and Ear Infirmary, Chgo., 1971-72; intern Northwestern U. Sch. Medicine Meml. Hosps., Chgo., 1972-73; resident in ophthalmology U. Ill. Eye and Ear Infirmary, Chgo., 1973-76, instr. dept. ophthalmology, 1974-77, attending surgeon dept. ophthalmology, 1976-77, fellow in diabetic retinopathy study, diabetic retinopathy vitrectomy study, and retina and vitreous surgery, 1976-77; asst. prof. ophthalmology, founder, dir. Retina/Vitreous/Ocular Trauma Svc. U. Calif. Davis Sch. Medicine, Calif., 1979-81; assoc. prof., dir. retina, vitreous and ocular trauma svc. U. Calif. Sch. Medicine, Davis, 1981-84; prof. ophthalmology Tulane U. Sch. Medicine, New Orleans, 1984-89, dir. med. student edn. dept. ophthalmology, 1985-89; dir. ophthalmology Tulane U. Sch. Medicine, Charity Hosp., New Orleans, 1985-89; prof. Tex. Tech U. Health Scis. Ctr., Lubbock, Tex., 1989—; chmn. dept. ophthalmology and visual scis. Tex. Tech U. Health Scis. Ctr., Lubbock, 1989-94; prof. dept. health orgn. mgmt. Tex. Tech U Health Scis. Ctr., Lubbock, 1993—; assoc. dean Sch. Medicine Tex. Tech U. Health Scis. Ctr., Lubbock, 1994-96; co-investigator in the Intraocular Gentamicin Prophylaxis Study, Govt. Erskine Hosp., Madurai, So. India, 1975, Dept. Ophthalmology, Audie Murphy VA Hosp., San Antonio, 1977-79, Martinez VA Hosp., Calif., 1979-84, VA Hosp., New Orleans, 1984-89, VA Med. Ctr., Alexandria, La., 1985-89, VA Med. Ctr., Big Spring, Tex., 1989-93, 96—, VA Ctr., Lubbock, Tex., 1989-92, 96—; cons. People's Republic China, 1980, 82, 85, 96, Japan, 1982-83, 85; vis. prof. Germany, 1984, Switzerland, 1987; 1st v.p. U.S. Eye Injury Registry, 1990-92, pres.-elect, 1992-94, pres. 1994-96; founder, med. dir. Tex. Eye Injury Registry, 1991—. Contbg. editor Ocutome/Fragmatome Newsletter, 1978-81; assoc. editor Vitreoretinal Surgery and Tech., 1989-98; mem. editl. bd. Jour. Eye Trauma, 1996—; contbr. articles to profl. jours.; appeared in numerous TV and radio programs. Com. mem. Sch. Medicine, U. Calif. Davis, Tulane U. Sch. Medicine, New Orleans, Sch. Medicine Tex. Tech. U. Health Scis. Ctr., U. Med. Ctr., Lubbock; bd. dirs. Lubbock Internat. Cultural Ctr., Inc., 1997—, chmn. ways and means com., 1998-2000. Maj. USAF, 1973-80. Decorated Air Force Commendation medal. Mem. ACS, AMA, Am. Acad. Ophthalmology (bylaws and rules com. 1990-95, com. on internat. ophthalmology 1991-95, Honor award 1986, Sr. Honor award 1998), Assn. Rsch. in Vision and Ophthalmology (pub. rels. com. 1997—), Chinese Am. Ophthal. Soc. (charter mem.), Christian Med. Soc., So. Med. Assn. (vice-chmn. sec. ophthalmology 1995-96, chmn. sec. ophthalmology 1996-97), So. Retina Study Group (steering com. 1987-89), Tex. Med. Assn. (com. continuing edn. 1993-96), Tex. Ophthal. Assn. (chair edn. com. 1990-93, coun. 1990-93, nominating com. 1991-93), Tex. Tech. Rsch. Found. (bd. dirs. 1993-96), Rsch. To Prevent Blindness, Schepens Internat. Soc., Pan-Am. Assn. Ophthalmology, Retina Soc., Vitreous Soc. (charter), World Eye Found. (bd. dirs. 1982—), Soc. Med. Cons. to Armed Forces, Am. Farm Bur. Fedn., Ill. Agrl. Assn., Ill. Farm Bur., Ret. Officers Assn., Sigma Xi (sec. Tex. Tech. chpt. 1990-91, v.p., pres.-elect 1999-2000, pres. 2000—). Republican. Lutheran. Avocations: travel, photography, cycling, hiking. Home: PO Box 1678 Lubbock TX 79408-1678 Office: Tex Tech U Health Scis Ctr Sch Medicine Lubbock TX 79430-0001

MAY, ERNEST DEWEY, music executive, organist, choirmaster; b. Jersey City, May 8, 1942; s. Ernest Max and Harriet Elizabeth (Dewey) M.; m. Eileen Marie Mayhew, Jan. 29, 1963 (div. 1984); children: Ernest Jr., Beth May Goodell, Katherine May Waite, Caroline, Christopher, Abigail May Robles, Deirdre; m. Mary L. Milkey, June 29, 1985. AB, Harvard U., 1964; MFA, Princeton U., 1968, PhD, 1975. Asst. prof. music Amherst (Mass.) Coll., 1969-75; from asst. prof. to prof. music dept. music and dance U. Mass., Amherst, 1976-88, prof. music, chmn. dept. music and dance, 1988-2000, presiding officer faculty senate, 1997-2000, sec. faculty senate, 2000—; faculty rep. Bd. Trustees, U. Mass., 1988-97; organist, dir. mus. South Congl. Ch., Springfield, Mass., 1983—. Rec.: Music for Trumpet and Organ, 1979; co-editor: J.S. Bach: Neve Ausgabe Samtlicher Werke Vol. I/20, 1986, J.S. Bach as Organist, 1986; contbr. New Harvard Dictionary of Music, 1986. Mem. Nat. Assn. Schs. Music Commn. on Accreditation, Am. Guild Organists, Internat. Music Soc., Am. Musicological Soc. (pres. New Eng. chpt. 1988-90). Home: 44 Amherst Rd Pelham MA 01002-9700 Office: U Mass Faculty Senate Amherst MA 01003

MAY, GEOFFREY JOHN, engineering company executive; b. Parsons Green, London, May 7, 1948; s. James Ebrey Clare and Eleanor Isobel (Tate) M.; m. Sarah Elizabeth Felgate, Jan. 5, 1974; children: Timothy, Daniel. Student, Eltham Coll., London; MA, Fitzwilliam Coll., Cambridge, Eng., 1970; PhD, U. Cambridge, 1973. Chartered engr. Tech. mgr. Chloride Group, U.K., 1974-82; dir. Tungstone Batteries, U.K., 1982-88; gen. mgr. Brush Fusegear, U.K., 1988-90; mng. dir. Barton Abrasives, U.K., 1990-91; group dir. tech. Hawker Batteries Group (BTR Plc), Market Marborough, Eng., 1991-97, Invensys Power Sys., Market Marborough, 1997-2000; exec. dir. Fiamm SpA, Newport, Eng. Contbr. articles to tech. jours. Fellow Inst. Materials. Avocations: skiing, gardening, sailing. Home: Troutbeck House 126 Main St, Loughborough LE12 8TJ, England Office: Fiamm SpA Pky, Crumlin, Newport NP11 3EL, England

MAY, GEORGES (CLAUDE), French language and literature educator, university official; b. Paris, France, Oct. 7, 1920; came to U.S., 1942, naturalized, 1943; s. Lucien and Germaine (Samuel) M.; m. Martha Corkery, Feb. 19, 1949 (dec. Dec. 1997); children: Anne May Berwind, Catherine May Dias. BA, U. Paris, 1937; Licence es Lettres, U. Montpellier, France, 1941; Diplome, d'Etudes Superieures, 1941; PhD, U. Ill., 1947; LHD, U. New Haven, 1990, Quinnipiac Coll., 1996, Wesleyan U., 1997, Albertus Magnus Coll., 2000. Asst. U. Ill., 1942-43, 46-47; faculty Yale, 1947—, successively instr., asst. prof., assoc. prof., 1947-56, prof. French, 1956-71; dean Yale Coll., 1963-71, Sterling prof. French, 1971-91, prof. emeritus, 1991—; chmn. dept. French, 1978-79, provost, 1979-81; prof. summers U. Ill., 1946, Middlebury Coll., 1951, 54, U. Minn., 1948, U. Mich., 1952, U. Calif. at Berkeley, 1959; sec. Fourth Internat. Congress Enlightenment, 1975. Author: Tragedie cornélienne, tragedie racinienne, 1948, D'Ovide a Racine, 1949, Quatre Visages de Denis Diderot, 1951, Diderot et La Religieuse, 1954, Rousseau par lui-meme, 1961, Le Dilemme du roman au XVIIIe siecle, 1963, L'Autobiographie, 1979, Les Mille et une nuits d'Antoine Galland, ou le Chef-d'oeuvre invisible, 1986, La Perruque de Dom Juan, ou Du bon usage des énigmes dans la littérature de l'âge classique, 1995; editor: Corneille's Polyeucte and Le Menteur, 1964, Diderot's Commentary on Hemsterhuis' Lettre sur l'homme, 1964, Diderot's La Religieuse, 1975, Diderot's Sur Terence, 1980, Jean-Jacques Rousseau et Madame de LaTour/Correspondance, 1998; contbr. articles on French lit. to profl. pubs. Trustee Hopkins Grammar Day Prospect Hill Sch., 1970-78; bd. dirs. Am. Council Learned Socs., 1979-89, chmn. bd., 1982-89, chmn. emeritus, 1989-95. Served with French Army, 1939-40; Served with AUS, 1943-45. Decorated chevalier French Legion of Honor; Guggenheim Found. fellow, 1950-51, 84-85. Mem. Am. Acad. Arts and Scis., Am. Philos. Soc., Am. Soc. 18th Century Studies (pres. 1974-75), Internat. Coun. Philosophy and Humanistic Studies (v.p. 1982-84), Am. Assn. Tchrs. French, Union Academique Internationale (bd. dirs. 1983-86, v.p. 1986-89, pres. 1989-92), MLA, Assn. des Etudes Francaises, Soc. d'Etude du XVIIIe Siecle, Phi Beta Kappa. Home: 177 Everit St New Haven CT 06511-1306

MAY, JEFFREY R., business executive; b. July 21, 1951. BS, Calif. State U., Fullerton, 1973; secondary tchg. credential, C.S.U.F., 1974. Rescue boat capt., ocean lifeboard Calif. Lifeguards, Huntington Beach, 1969-80; tchr., coach Calif. State U., Fullerton, 1973-75; traffic officer Calif. Hwy. Patrol, 1980-87; owner/founder JRM Enterprises Internat., Sisters, Oreg., 1982—. Home and Office: 31402 Lovegren Ln Sisters OR 97759-9501

MAY, PHILIP ALAN, sociology educator; b. Bethesda, Md., Nov. 6, 1947; s. Everette Lee and Marie (Lee) M.; m. Doreen Ann Garcia, Sept. 5, 1972; children: Katrina Ruth, Marie Ann. BA in Sociology, Catawba Coll., 1969; MA in Sociology, Wake Forest U., 1971; PhD in Sociology, U. Mont., 1976. NIMH predoctoral fellow U. Mont., Missoula, 1973-76; dir. health stats. and rsch. Navajo Health Authority, Window Rock, Ariz., 1976-78; asst. prof. U. N.Mex., Albuquerque, 1978-82, assoc. prof., 1982-89, prof., 1989—, dir. Ctr. on Alcoholism, Substance Abuse and Addictions, 1990-99; sr. rsch. scientist Ctr. on Alcoholism, Substance Abuse and Addictions, 2000—; mem. fetal alcohol syndrome study com., Inst. of Medicine/Nat. Acad. Scis., 1994-96; cons. various govt. agys., 1976—; dir. Nat. Indian Fetal Alcohol Syndrome Prevention Program, Albuquerque, 1979-85; mem. adv. bd. Nat. Orgn. on Fetal Alcohol Syndrome, Washignton, 1990—; rsch. assoc. Nat. Ctr. for Am. Indian and Alaska Native Mental Health Rsch., 1986—; mem. U.S. Surgeon Gens. Task Force on Drunk Driving, 1988-89; prin. investigator fetal alcohol syndrome epidemiology rsch. in South Africa, 1997—. Contbr. chpts. to books and articles to profl. jours. V.p. Bd. Edn. Laguna Pueblo, N.Mex., 1998—. Lt. USPHS, 1970-73. Recipient Spl. Recognition award U.S. Indian Health Svc., 1992, award Navajo Tribe and U.S. Indian Health Svc., 1992, Human Rights Promotion award UN Assn., 1994, Program award for Contbns. to Mental Health of Am. Indians, U.S. Indian Health Svc., 1996, O.B. Michael Outstanding Alumnus award Catawba Coll., 2000. Mem. APHA, Am. Sociol. Assn., Population Ref. Bur., Coll. on Problems of Drug Dependence, Rsch. Soc. Alcoholism. Methodist. Home: 4610 Idlewilde Ln SE Albuquerque NM 87108-3422 Office: U NMex CASAA 2350 Alamo Ave SE Albuquerque NM 87106-3202

MAY, RICHARD WARREN, writer, consultant, inventor; b. Marlboro, Mass., Mar. 1, 1944; s. Richard and Lavinia (Crane) M. BS in Psychology, U. Mass., 1968; MA in Humanities and Philosophy, Calif. State U., Dominguez Hills, 1991. Lic. real estate broker. Tchr. Boston Pub. Schs., Boston, 1970-89; pres., founder The Aleph (formerly Promethean Pastimes), Boston, 1975—; adv. bd. mem. and rsch. assoc. Point One Adv. Group, Inc., Madisonville, Ky. Author: (games of strategy) Game of the Gods, 1984, Trihex, 1985, Aliens and Amazons, The Game of Tetra, 1994; contbr. (anthology) Thinking on the Edge, 1993; patentee game bd. and pieces TriHex, 1988. Mem. Assn. Advance Ethical Hypnosis, West Orange, N.J., 1974-75, Boston Tchrs. Union, 1984-89, Point One Adv. Group. Fellow Internat. Soc. Philos. Enquiry (asst. historian 1981-82, diplomate); mem. Nat. Coalition of Ind. Scholars, Prometheus Soc. (past first jour. editor, ombudsman 1984-94, pres. 1991-98), Hoeflin Rsch. Group, The Mega Soc., One-in-Million Soc., Triple Nine Soc. (membership officer 1983-84, regent 1987-90), Mensa, Intertel, Am. Acad. Religion, Internat. Acad. Philosophy (bd. dirs., founder Found.), The Jewish Geneal. Soc. Office: Point One Adv Group PO Box 1111 Madisonville KY 42431-0022

MAY, RONALD JAMES, political scientist, researcher; b. Sydney, NSW, Australia, Oct. 29, 1939; s. Henry Wilkinson and Kathleen Mitchell (McCredie) M.; m. Patricia Spicer, Dec. 4, 1967; children: Ranid Peter. BEc, U. Sydney, 1961, MEc, 1965; DPhil, Oxford U., 1967. Sr. economist Res. Bank of Australia, 1957-72; field dir. New Guinea Rsch. U., Papua, 1972-75; dir. Inst. of Applied Social and Econ. Rsch., Papua, 1976-77; sr. fellow Australian Nat. U., 1972—; cons. Oxford Analytica, U.K., 1997—; chair rsch. com. Australian Inst. of Internat. Affairs, 1995-96. Author: Federalism and Fiscal Adjustment, 1969, The Changing Role of the Military in Papua New Guinea, 1993, Kaikai Aniani, A Guide to Bush Foods, Markets & Culinary Arts in Papua New Guinea, 1984; joint editor: The Philippines after Marcos, 1985. Recipient Ind. medal Papua New Guinea, 1977. Mem. Internat. Polit. Sci. Assn., Pacific Islands Polit. Sci. Assn., Asian Studies Assn. of Australia. Home: 17 Osmand St, Wanniassa ACT 2903, Australia Office: Rsch Sch Pacific/Asian Std, Australian Nat U, Canberra ACT 0200, Australia

MAY, STEPHEN JAMES, communications educator, writer; b. Toronto, Ont., Can., Sept. 10, 1946; s. Thomas and Claire (Thompson) M.; m. Caroline Casteel, Sept. 27, 1947; 1 child, Trevor. BA, Calif. State U., Carson, 1975; MA, Calif. State U., L.A., 1977; DLitt, Internat. U., London, 1990. Prof. and chair dept. of Englist and Lit. Pikes Peak C.C., Colorado Springs, Colo., 1980-91; prof. Colo. N.W. C.C., Craig, 1992-98; chair dept. of English and Lit. Pikes Peak C.C., Colorado Springs, Colo., 1998—; advisor Internat. Biog. Ctr., Cambridge, Eng., 1989-95; vis. prof. U. Colo., 2000—. Author: Pilgrimage, 1987, Fire From the Skies, 1990, Footloose, 1993, Zane Grey, 1997, Maverick Heart, 2000; contbr. to profl. jours. including SouthWest Art, Ohio Review. Mem. Western Writers Am., Colo. Authors League, Zane Grey Soc., Soc. S.W. Authors, C.C. Humanities. Avocations: traveling, writing, drawing. E-mail: stepkm@msn.com. Home: 5546 Escondido Dr Colorado Springs CO 80918-1913

MAYA, JOSE MARIA, physician, medical educator, rector; b. Pacora, Caldas, Colombia, Mar. 10, 1953; s. Jose and Herminia (Mejia) M. MD, Juan N. Corpas, Bogotá, 1980; MPH, U. de Antioquia, Medellín, 1983; M degree, U. de los Andes, Bogotá. Rural physician Servicio Seccional de Salud, Medellín, 1980-81, chief med. attendant, 1981-82, chief spl. programs, 1984; gen. dir. Hosp. la Maria, Medellín, 1984-88; chief postgrads. Inst. de Ciencias de la Salud, Medellín, 1988-91, dean Sch. Medicine, 1993-2000, rector, 2000—; med. dir. Clinica El Rosario, Medellín, 1991-93; cons. Centro de Gestion Hospitalaria, 1992. Contbr. articles to profl. jours. Juryman Premio Nacional Gestion Hospitales, 1993, 95, 96; mem. Grupo Directores Clinicas y Hospitales, 1993-97; mem. directive coun. Hosp. Gen. de Medellín; assesor CICAD-OEA, 1997; pres. Asociacion Colombiana de Facultades de Medicina, 1998-2000. Republican. Roman Catholic. Avocations: reading, travel, music. Office: Inst de Ciencias dela Salud, Cale 10A 22-4, Medellin Colombia

MAYANJA-NKANGI, JOSHUA SIBAKYALWAYO, Ugandan government official; b. Aug. 22, 1931. Attended, Kings Coll. Budo, 1947-49; BA, Makerere U., 1953; postgrad., Keble Coll., 1954-57; degree in Law, Lincoln's Inn, 1959. Cert. barrister. Pvt. practice law Uganda, 1959, 71; M.P. for Masaka East, 1962, apptd. min. without portfolio, 1962, min. commerce and industry, 1963, prime min., 1964, exiled to Britain; rsch. fellow dept. econs. Lancaster U., 1967, head dept. monetary econ., lectr., 1968-71; min. of labour Govt. of Uganda, 1985, min. edn., 1988, min. planning and econ. devel., 1989, min. fin. & econ. planning; now min. of justice Govt. of Uganda, Kampala. co-founder Kabaka Yekka Youth Wing, 1959; founder Conservative Party, 1980. Office: Ministry of Justice, Parliamentary Bldg Box 7183, Kampala Uganda*

MAYATEPEK, ERTAN HILMI, physician, researcher; b. Aachen, Germany, May 21, 1962; s. Hakki I. and Hildegard E. (Barth) M.; m. Christina H. Mayatepek, Aug. 10, 1963; children: Leo H., Tobias A., Nico J., Corinna E. MD, U. Dusseldorf, Germany, 1989; Habil., U. Heidelberg, Germany, 1996. Intern, resident U. Children's Hosp., Heidelberg, 1989; fellowship Inst. Hygiene, Heidelberg, 1990-91; rsch. fellow Cancer Rsch. Inst., Heidelberg, 1991-92; fellowship U. Children's Hosp., Heidelberg, 1992-95, head metabolic divsn., 1996-2000, head divsn. metabolic and endocrine diseases, 2000—. Contbr. articles to profl. jours. Grantee Deutsche Forschungsgemeinschaft, Bonn, Germany, 1991-92, 94—. Mem. Am. Pediat. Soc., Soc. Study of Inborn Errors of Metabolism, Deutsche Gesellschaft Kinderheilkunde, Arbeitsgemeinschaft Pädiatrische Stoffwechselstörungen, Deutsche Gesellschaft Pädiatrische Infektiologie, Deutsche Diabetes Gesellschaft, European Soc. Clin. Investigation, European Soc. Pediat. Rsch. Roman Catholic. Office: U Children's Hosp, Im Neuenheimer Feld 150, Heidelberg 69120, Germany

MAYBERRY, DENNIS PAUL, JR., band owner; b. Creve Coer, Mo., Apr. 15; s. Dennis Paul Sr. and Sharon Lynn (Quick) M. Grad., Bismarck, Mo. Dir. Bismarck Cmty. Jazz Band, 1993—; dir. of bands St. Paul Luth. Sch., Farmington, Mo., 1995-97; dir., owner Dennis Mayberry Big Band, Cape Girardeau, Mo., 1997—; pres. Collegiate Music Educators Nat. Conf., Parkhills, Mo., 1995-97. Performing mem., pres. Golden Eagles Marching Band. Recipient Louis Armstrong award Bismarck H.S., 1994, 95, John Phillip Sousa award Bismarck H.S., 1995; named Best New Member, Golden Eagles Marching Band, S.E. Mo. State U., 1997. Mem. Bismarck C. of C. (advisor 1997-98), Phi Mu Alpha (pres. 2000—, dir. jazz festival S.E. Mo. State U. 1997—). Democrat. Baptist. Avocations: listening to music, instruments, private instruction, cars. Home: 1316 Cedar St Bismarck MO 63624-9474

MAYEKAR, GOPAL GOVIND, university administrator; b. Mumbai, Mar. 10, 1934; s. Govind Gopal and Sakhubal Govind Mayekar; m. Usha Gopal Shalini Naik, Oct. 30, 1962; children: Rajendra, Ravindhra, Shailedra, Reshma. BA, Mumbai U., 1958, MA, 1960. Tchr. Dr. Schirodkar H.S., Mumbai, 1958-62; head Marathi Sanskrit D. Dempe Coll., Panagi, Goa, India, 1962-67; min. edn. Goa Govt., 1967-70; prin. Devgad (India) Coll., 1974-82, VNS-Bandekar Coll., Mapusa, Goa, 1982-95; dir. coll. devel. coun. Goa U., 1997-2000. Contbr. poetry to anthologies. Mem. Goa Legis. Assembly, 1967-72; mem. Indian Parliament, 1989-91, mem. pub. accts. com., 1989-90; pres. Gomartak Marathi Acad., 1987-90. Avocations: reading, lecturing. Home: Ashivad Bldg Dattanadi, 403507 Mapusa Bardez, India Office: Gomartak Marathi Acad, Paraji Goa Goa, India

MAYER, CHARLES ARTHUR, management consultant, musician; b. Salt Lake City, Oct. 6, 1949; s. Robert C. and Barbara (Arthur) M.; m. Carolyn Familetti, June 21, 1975 (div. June 1989); 1 child, George. BS in Indsl. Mgmt., Purdue U., 1971; MBA, Temple U., 1978. Cert. mgmt. cons. Systems analyst Burroughs Corp., Detroit, 1972-76; cons. Pinkerton Computer Cons., Phila., 1976-79, Coopers & Lybrand, Phila., 1979-82, Deloitte Haskins & Sells, Phila., 1982-85; prin. Mayer Computer Solutions, Merion Station, Pa., 1985—. Pres. Merion Park Civic Assn., Merion Station, Pa., 1979-80; Uptown String Band, (treas., 1999—). Mem. Inst. Mgmt. Cons. (chpt. pres. 1987-89), Cynwyd Club (treas. 1986-94). Office: PO Box 368 Merion Station PA 19066-0368

MAYER, GEORGE ROY, educator; b. National City, Calif., Aug. 28, 1940; s. George Eberly and Helen Janet (Knight) M.; m. Barbara Ann Fife, Sept. 9, 1964 (div. June 1986); children: Kevin Roy, Debbie Rae Ann; m. Jocelyn Volk Finn, Aug. 3, 1986. BA, San Diego State U., 1962; MA, Ind. U., 1965, EdD, 1966. Cert. sch. psychologist; bd. cert. behavior analyst. Sch. counselor, psychologist Ind. U., Bloomington, 1964-66; asst. prof. guidance and ednl. psychology So. Ill. U., Carbondale, 1966-69; profl. edn. Calif. State U., L.A., 1966—; cons. in field; mem. adv. bd. Dept. Spl. Edn., L.A., 1986—, Alamansor Edn. Ctr., Alhambra, Calif., 1986-90, Jay Nolan Ctr. for Autism, Newhall, Calif., 1975-86; lectr. in field; mem. study group on youth violence prevention Nat. Ctr. for Injury Prevention and Control, Divsn. Violence Prevention of the Ctrs. for Disease Control and Prevention, 1998. Author: Classroom Management: A California Resource Guide; co-author: Behavior Analysis for Lasting Change, 1991; contbr. articles to profl. jours. Recipient Outstanding Prof. award Calif. State U.-L.A., 1988; U.S. Dept. Edn. grantee, 1996—. Mem. Assn. for Behavior Analysis, Nat. Assn. Sch. Psychologists, Calif. Assn. Behavior Analysis (pres., Outstanding Contbr. to Behavior Analysis award 1997, hon. life), Cambridge Ctr. for Behavioral Studies (adv. bd.), Calif. Assn. Sch. Psychologists (chmn. practitioners conf. 1994—). Avocations: horseback riding, fishing, swimming. Home: 10600 Pinyon Ave Tujunga CA 91042-1517

MAYER, GUY NOËL, business executive; b. Paris, Apr. 26, 1937; s. Julien Noël and Amelia Armandine (Leleu) M.; children: Gilles, Eric, Christian, Regis, Alexia. BS, Lycee Carnot, Paris, 1956; HEC Diplom, Ecole des Hautes Etudes Comml., Paris, 1961; postgrad., Columbia U. Cert. in internat. mgmt. Gen. mgr. Scad. France (L'Oreal), Paris, 1975-80; area mgr. for Europe L'Oreal, Paris, 1980-88; mng. dir. Laboratoires Garnier Internat. (L'Oreal), Paris, 1988-97; chmn JWI, Washington, 1998-99, Paris, 1998-99. Lt. col. French Paratroops. Mem. Ritz Club (hon.), Assn. Hautes Etudes Commerciales, Bagheera. Roman Catholic. Avocations: golf, sea diving, shooting, sailing.

MAYER, HEINZ MICHAEL, orthopedic surgeon and neurosurgeon; b. Winnweiler, Germany, Apr. 30, 1954; s. Georg Franz and Rita (Zöller) M.; m. Isabel Carolin Mayer, Aug. 14, 1986; children: Lukas Dominik, Frizzi Maria Annabel. MD, Johannes-Gutenberg U., Mainz, Germany, 1981. Resident dept. neuropathology Free Univ. of Berlin, Germany, 1982-83; resident dept. neurosurgery Free Univ. of Berlin, 1983-85, resident dept. orthopaedic surgery, 1985-87, neurosurgeon dept. neurosurgery, 1987-89, staff neurosurgeon dept. neurosurgery, 1989-92, chief staff surgeon dept. orthopaedic surgery, 1992-97; asst. prof. Free U. Berlin, Germany, 1991—; med. dir. Spine Ctr., Orthopaedic Clinic Munich-Harlaching, Munich, 1998—. Recipient award to young neurosurgeons World Fedn. of Neurosurgical Socs., 1989. Mem. European Spine Soc. (ednl. com. 1992—, mem. exec. com. 1995—, sec. 1997-98, 99-00), German Orthopedic Soc., German Neurosurg. Soc., Internat. Intradiscal Therapy Soc. (membership com. 1997-98, award for best presentation 1988), German Laser Soc., Internat. Soc. for Minimally Invasive Spine Surgery (nat. rep.), German Assn. Orthopedic Surgeons (sect. on degenerative diseases and laser medicine 1990—, Lindemann-Kuhlendahl award 1986), Internat. Soc. for the Study the Lumbar Spine. Roman Catholic. Avocations: saxophone, soccer, running. Office: Spine Ctr Munich Orth Klinik Muenchen Harlaching, Harlachinger Str 51, D-81547 Munich Germany

MAYER, HERWIG RUDOLF, physicist, material scientist; b. Austria, May 17, 1962; s. Wilfried and Helga Mayer. MS, Tech. U., Vienna, Austria, 1986, D Technics, 1989; Habilitation in Applied Physics, U. Agr., Vienna, 1999. Asst. prof. U. Vienna, 1986-89; asst. prof. U. Agr., Inst. Meteorology and Physics, Vienna, 1991-99, prof., 1999—; lectr., scientist U. Shizuoka, Japan, 1991, U. Pa., 1993. Avocations: jazz, skiing. E-mail: herwig.mayer@mail.boku.ac.at.

MAYER, JOYCE HARRIS, artist; b. N.Y.C., May 7, 1935; d. Harold and Dorothy H.; m. Bernard Charles Mayer, Mar. 15, 1969; 1 child, Robert Charles Mayer. AAS, Inst. of Applied Art & Sci., N.Y.C., 1957. Sketcher Merrylen Cartooning Studio, 1952; client contact, layout artist Haire Publs., N.Y.C., 1957-59; art dir. Real Estate Forum, N.Y.C., 1959-60, Denhard & Stewart, N.Y.C., 1960-67, self employed N.Y.C., 1967-71. Work exhbns. include N.Y. Inst. of Applied Arts and Sci., Horizon Gallery, Royal Typographers, N.Y., Nat. Arts Club, Tulane U., Dominican Coll., Robinson Gallery, Mario Villa, and Author Roger, New Orleans, TWEED Gallery, Plainfield, N.J., Barbara Gillman Gallery, Miami; co-curator New Orleans Mus. of Art, 1985; paintings and monoprints in numerous pub. and pvt. collections in Europe and U.S. Mem. Bd. Edn., Greenwich, Conn., 1978; art advisor Freeport McMoRan Art Collection, New Orleans, 1985; curator Mario Villa Gallery, New Orleans, 1989; juror Arts Coun., New Orleans, 1990. Coll. Art Assn. Avocations: reading, attending theater, ballet, bird watching. Home: 325 Audubon Blvd New Orleans LA 70125-4124

MAYER, MARILYN GOODER, steel company executive; b. Chgo.; d. Seth MacDonald and Jean (McMullen) Gooder; m. William Anthony Mayer, Nov. 14, 1959; children: William Anthony Jr., Robert MacDonald. Grad., Career Inst., Chgo., 1941; student, Lake Forest Coll., Ill., 1942. Adminstrv. asst. Needham, Louis & Brorby, Chgo., 1949-53; v.p. RMB Corp., Chgo., 1963-71, Mayer Motors, Ft. Lauderdale, Fla., 1965-74, Gooder-Henrichsen, Chicago Heights, Ill., 1975—; dir. Barnett Bank, West Palm Beach, Fla. Trustee Gulf Stream (Fla.) Sch.; trustee emeritus St. Andrew's Sch., Boca Raton, Fla.; bd. dirs. Bethesda Hosp. Assn., Boynton Beach, Fla., pres. 1981-82; bd. dirs. Gulf Stream Civic Assn. Mem. Soc. Four Arts, Little Bath and Tennis Club (gov. of Gulf Stream). Avocation: travel. Home: 2925 Polo Dr Delray Beach FL 33483-7331

MAYER, MICHAL, medical educator; b. Prague, Czech Republic, Apr. 8, 1959; s. Jiri and Marie (Prenosilova) M.; married; 2 children. MD, Palacky U., Olomouc, Czech Republic, 1984. Physician Higher Nervous Activity Rsch. Inst. Faculty Hosp., Olomouc, Czech Republic, 1984-90; assoc. prof. dept. neurology Med. Faculty Palacky U., Olomouc, Czech Republic, 1990-97; physician cons. dept. rehab. Faculty Hosp. Olomouc, Czech Republic, 1997—; assoc. prof., cons. dept. physiotherapy and algotherapy Palacky U., Olomouc, 1994—. Office: Dept Rehab, I P Pavlova 6, 77500 Olomouc Czech Republic

MAYER, NONNA, political science researcher; b. Neuilly, Seine, France, Mar. 25, 1948; d. Maurice Mayer and Marjorie Helen Galbraith; m. Samy Cohen, Mar. 14, 1987. Degree in pub. law, U. Paris, 1971; degree in polit. sci., Inst. Polit. Studies, 1973, PhD in Polit. Sci., 1984, MA in Polit. Sci., 1971; DHC in Social, Polit. and Econ. Scis., Free U. Brussels. Rsch. asst. CNRS, Paris, 1974-81, rschr., 1981-88, dir. rsch., 1988—; co-dir. PhD program Inst. for Polit. Studies, Paris, 1996—; vis. assoc. prof. Stanford program in Paris, 1991—. Author: Ces Français qui Votent FN, 1999; co-author: Les Comportements Politiques, 1992; editor: Les Modèles Explicatifs du vote, 1997; co-editor: L'Electeur a Ses Raisons, 1997, The French Voter Decides, 1993; mem. editorial bd. Patterns of Prejudice, 1994—, Revue Française de Sociologie, 1986—. Mem. French Polit. Sci. Assn. (bd. dirs. 1996—), Am. Polit. Sci. Assn. Avocations: good food, wine. Office: CEVIPOF, 10 rue de la Chaise, 75007 Paris France

MAYER, SUSAN LEE, nurse, educator; b. N.Y.C., Feb. 10, 1946; d. Hans and Frieda (Schein) Abramson; m. Steven Mayer, June 24, 1973; children: Jason, Stuart, Richard, Deborah. BSN, Hunter Coll., 1968; MA, NYU, 1974; EdD, Columbia U., 1996; postgrad., Yeshiva U., 1986, Adelphi U., 1987. RN, N.Y.; cert. in gerontology; cert. tchr., N.Y. Staff nurse ICU-CCU, Montefiore Hosp., Bronx, N.Y., 1968; organizer CCU, Jewish Meml. Hosp., N.Y.C., 1968; supr., adminstr. Morrisania City Hosp., N.Y.C., 1969-76; instr. Adelphi U., Garden City, N.Y., 1977-78; substitute nurse Great Neck (N.Y.) Pub. Schs., 1980-90; adj. instr. Queensborough C.C., 1987—; rsch. asst. to dean Sch. Nursing, Adelphi U., 1987—; part-time staff nurse Winthrop U. Hosp., Mineola, N.Y., 1987-90, per diem nurse, 1987-90; instr. dept. nursing edn. Bronx Mcpl. Hosp. Ctr. (now Jacobi Med. Ctr.), 1990-96; asst. prof. Helene Fuld Sch. Nursing, 1996—; adj. instr. Bronx C.C., 1992; adj. asst. prof. Iona Coll. Sch. Nursing; adj. assoc. prof. Tchrs. Coll./Columbia U., 1997—; per diem RN Home Care Winthrop U. Hosp., Mineola, 1996—; presenter 100th Anniv. Internat. Coun. Nursing, 1999, 17th Ann. Internat. Assn. for Human Caring Conf., 2d Internat. & Interdisciplinary Health/Rsch. Symposium, Internat. Assn. History Nursing; tchr. CPR; lectr. to PTA groups, 1981-82; lectr. and presenter in field. Contbr. articles to profl. jours. including Nursing and Health Care. Bd. dirs. Great Neck Synagogue, 1981-91, v.p. Sisterhood, 1978-79, pres., 1979-81; former bd. dirs. Russell Gardens Assn.; founder Work for Share Zedek Hosp., 1977—; pres., fin. sec. L'Chaim chpt. Hadassah Nurse Coun. N.Y. State Regents scholar, 1963. Mem. ANA, Assn. Orthodox Jewish Scientists, Nat. League for Nursing, N.Y. Counties Registered Nurses Assn., N.Y. State Nurses Assn. (chair coun. ethical practice, nurse practice com., treas. Dist. 13), Am. Assn. for History of Nursing, Nurses Edn. Alumni Assn. (historian), Sigma Theta Tau, Kappa Delta Pi. Democrat. Home: 28 Laurel Dr Great Neck NY 11021-2827

MAYER, WOLFGANG OTTO HEINRICH, aerospace engineer; b. Ellwangen, Germany, Jan. 1, 1959; s. Kurt and Gisela (Stahl) M.; m. Karin Lipp, Apr. 29, 1988; children: Elena, Edgar. Diploma in Aerospace Engr., U. Stuttgart, Germany, 1988; PhD in Chem. Engring., U. Nürnberg, Germany, 1993. Rschr. German Aerospace Rsch. Establishment, Lampoldshausen, Germany, 1988-93; vis. rsch. scientist, lectr. Nat. Aerospace Lab., Kakuda, Japan, 1993-95; head of propellant lab. German Aerospace Ctr., Lampoldshausen, 1995-96, nat. programme mgr. rocket engine tech., 1996—; cons. Lipp Inc., N.Y.C., 1988-89; project reviewer European Commn., Brussels, 1996—; dep. pres. Inst. Coun., DLR, Lampoldshaussen, 1996—; vis. prof. Pa. State U., 2000. Author: Liquid Rocket Engines, 1993; contbr. articles to profl. jours. Chmn. exec. bd. Conservation of Ellwangen (Germany) Soc., 1994—. Officer German Army, 1978-79. Recipient Sci. and Tech. award European Commn., 1994, Japanese Govt. Rsch. award, 1998, Japanese Govmt. Rsch. Awd., 1998. Mem. AIAA (liquid propulsion com.), ILass-Europe. Avocation: flying. Home: Freigasse 9, D-73479 Ellwangen Germany

MAYER-KOENIG, WOLFGANG, writer, educator, industrial director; b. Vienna, Austria, Mar. 28, 1946; s. Ernst and Hertha (Koenig) Mayer. DLitt (hon.), DFA (hon.). Apptd. univ. prof. Republic of Austria, mem. cabinet Chancellor Kreisky, 1971-77; indsl. dir. bd. dirs. Porr Co., 1978-90; chmn. Austrian Meetings of Execs., 1974-77; founder Literarische Situation, Austrian U. Cultural Cr., 1968-70; lectr. univs., France, Italy, U.S., Austria, 1978-82; pres. Mozart Co.; bd. dirs. Austrian Inst. Rsch. Conflict, Karl Renner Inst.; v.p. Pro Austria Nostra; exec. dir. Transportbeton KG; mem. adv. bd. PORR-Internat. AG; coord. Internat. Meeting on Future Sci. and Tech.; coord. negotiations between Austria and Arab States, 1975; chmn. Munich-Brenner-Verona ry. line consortium; 1st v.p. internt. consortium Asse Munich-Verone. Co-author: Austrian Civil Service Law; author: Sichtbare Pavilions, 1969, Stichmarken, 1970, Psychologie und Literatursprache, 1975, Texte und Zeicnungen, 1975, Language-Politics-Aggression, 1977, Italienreisen Goethes, 1978, Robert Musils Möglichkeitsstil, 1979, In den Armen unseres Waerters, 1980, Vorlaeufige Versagung, 1985, Chagrin non dechiffre, 1986, Colloqui nella Stanza, 1986, The Corselet of the Mighty, 1986, A hatalom bonyolult angyala, 1989, Verzögerung des Vertrauens, 1995, Colloquios nel Cuarto, 1996, Fire and Ice, 1996, Mirror Wading, 1996, Behind Desires Deficits, 1997, Confessions of an Angry Loving European, 1999; editor jour. LOG; contbr. articles to profl. jours. Chmn. Humanitarian Aid Program Indochina, Earthquake Victims Italy; permanent rep. to UN, 1992. Decorated Austrian Cross of Honor for Sci. and Arts, 1976, officer Order of Merit (Egypt), 1974, Order des Arts et des Lettres (France), 1987, Cross of Honor Lower Austria, 1982, comdr. Order of St. Agatha (San Marino), 1982, Golden medal of merit Internat. ARC, 1983, Golden cross Order of Eagle of Tyrol, 1988, Papal Lateran Cross 1st class, Grand Cross of Honor (Govt. of Carinthia), 1993, cross of merit 1st class of Lilienfeld, 1984, Cross of Merit of Greek Orthodox Papal Patriarch of Alexandria (Egypt), Star of Peace (Rome), grand master Order pour le Merite, others; recipient Theodor Körner prize, 1974, Premio Prometeo Aureo Lazio, Vienna Art Found. prize. Mem. Acad. Tibernia, Acad. Burckhardt St. Gallen, Acad. Cosentina, Acad. Europa, Austrian Writers Assn. (bd. dirs.), PEN-Club. Home: 41 Hernalser Guertel, A-1170 Vienna Austria

MAYES, ILA LAVERNE, minister; b. Eldorado, Okla., Dec. 23, 1934; d. Thomas Floyd and Irene Elizabeth (Buchanan) Jordan; m. Forrest Clay Mayes, July 2, 1954; children: Barbara, Marian, Cynthia, Janice. BA, U. Tex., El Paso, 1973; MSW, U. Mich., 1976; MDiv, Austin Presbyn. Sem., 1986. Ordained to ministry Presbyn. Ch. (U.S.A.), 1986; cert. social worker. Pastor First Presbyn. Ch., Childress, Tex., 1986-97; interim pastor Trinity Presbyn. Ch., Iowa Port, Tex., 1999—, First Presbyn. Ch., Iowa Port, 1999—; med./social worker Childress Regional Med. Ctr., 1996-97; mem. Austin Sem. Alumni Bd., 1991-94, Synod of the Sun Evangelism Com., Denton, 1990-93, Transition Coordinating Agy., 1991-97. Chmn. ARC, Childress, 1990; bd. dirs. Am. Cancer Soc., Childress, 1988-89; vice moderator, Palo Duro Presbytery, 1996-98. Mem. AAUW, Mortarboard, Rotary Internat., Alpha Chi, Alpha Lambda Delta. Home and Office: 3 Gloria Cir Wichita Falls TX 76309-3506

MAYHEW, AUBREY, music industry executive; b. Washington, Oct. 2, 1927; s. Aubrey and Verna June (Hall) M.; m. Carol de Onis, May 10, 1962 (div. 1971); children: Lawrence Aubrey, Michael Aubrey, Parris Mitchell, Casey Aran. Student, Wilson Tchs. Coll., 1948. Dir. Sta. WWVA, Wheeling, W.Va., 1947-54, Sta. WCOP, Boston, 1954-56; asst. to pres. MGM Records, N.Y.C., 1957-58; v.p. mktg. Capitol Records, Los Angeles, 1958-60; prodr., dir. Sta. KCAM-TV Prodns., Nashville, 1981—; pres., founder John F. Kennedy Meml. Ctr., 1968; authority on John F. Kennedy life and memorabilia. Author: (books) Commandants Marine Corps, 1953, World Tribute to John F. Kennedy, 1965; composer (music) Touch My Heart, 1966 (Broadcast Music, Inc. award, 1967); record producer, artist mgmt., 1947—; music pub., 1954—; developed careers numerous entertainers including Johnny Paycheck, Jeannie C. Riley, Bobby Helms. Served to cpl. U.S. Army Signal Corps, 1945-48. Named Govs. Aide, Nashville, 1978. Mem. Country Music Assn., Broadcast Music Inc., Manuscript Soc., N.Y. Numismatic Soc., Gospel Music Assn. Republican. Episcopalian. Avocations: collector, historian, author. Office: Amcorp Music Group 827 Meridian St Nashville TN 37207-5856

MAYNARD, MICHAEL, librarian; b. Yuma, Ariz., July 8, 1955; s. Ernest Ray and Refugio (Guerrero) M. AAS in Electronic Tech., Phoenix Coll., 1986; BA in German, Ariz. State U., 1989; postgrad., U. Leipzig, 1990, Eberhard-Karls U., Tubingen, Germany, 1990-91; MLS, U. Ariz., 1992. Electronics technician USN, 1977-83; asst. libr. Chapel Libr., Venice, Fla., 1983-84; security officer Anderson Agy., Phoenix, 1984-89; grad. asst. U. Ariz., Tuscon, 1989-90, libr. asst. main libr. acquisitions dept., 1992; asst. libr. Internat. Bapt. Coll., Tempe, Ariz., 1992-94; head libr. Fitch Libr., Mesa, Ariz., 1994-97; libr. II Ariz. Dept. Corrections, Douglas, 1997-2000, Goodyear, Ariz., 2000—. Author: History of the Debate Over I John 5:7-8, 1995. With USN, 1977-83. Scholar U. Ariz., 1989-90, Herman Weinel scholar, 1990. Mem. Assn. Christian Librs. Baptist. Avocations: foreign languages, long distance running, nutrition, collecting biographical sketches, New Testament textual criticism. E-mail: receptus@sprynet.com. Home and Office: Receptus Press PO Box 1625 Tempe AZ 85280-1625

MAYNARD, VIRGINIA MADDEN, charitable organization executive; b. New London, Conn., Jan. 29, 1924; d. Raymond and Edna Sarah (Madden) M. BS, U. Conn., 1945; postgrad., Am. Inst. Banking, 1964-66, Cornell U., 1975. With Nat. City Bank (now Citibank), N.Y.C., 1954-79, asst. cashier, 1965-69, asst. v.p., 1969-74, v.p. internat. banking group, 1974-76, comptroller's div., 1976-79; v.p. First Women's Bank, N.Y.C., 1979-80; Internat. Fedn. Univ. Women rep. UN, 1982—. Trustee fellowships endowment fund AAUW Ednl. Found., Washington, 1977-80, Va. Gildersleeve Internat. Fund Univ. Women, Inc., pres., 1987-93, bd. dirs., 1994-2000, rep. UN, 1997—; bd. dirs. Conf. Nongovtl. Orgns. Found., Inc., 1997—, treas., 1999—. Mem. AAUW (fin. chmn. N.Y.C. br. 1976-79, bylaws chmn. 1979-83, adminstr. Meml. Fund 1983-92, 2000—, bd. dirs. 1992-94, 96-99, Woman of Achievment 1976). Republican. Congregationalist. Home: 601 E 20th St New York NY 10010-7622

MAYNE, RICHARD JOHN, writer, broadcaster; b. London, Apr. 2, 1926; s. John William and Kate Hilda (Angus) M.; m. Margot Ellingworth Lyon (div.); m. Jocelyn Mudie Ferguson; children: Zoe, Alice. BA, Trinity Coll., Cambridge, 1950, MA, 1953, PhD, 1955. Asst. tutor Cambridge Inst. Edn., 1954-56; sr. ofcl. High Authority of the European Coal and Steel Cmty., Luxembourg, 1956-58, Commn. European Econ. Cmty., Brussels, 1958-63; personal asst. to Jean Monnet Paris, 1963-66; Paris correspondent ENCOUNTER, 1966-71; vis. prof. U. Chgo., 1971; dir. Federal Trust for Edn. and Rsch., London, 1971-73; head U.K. offices European Commn., London, 1973-79, spl. adv. 1979-80; co-editor Encounter, London, 1985-90; film critic Sunday Telegraph, London, 1986-90, The European, London, 1990-98. Author: The Community of Europe, 1962, The Recovery of Europe, 1970, The Europeans, 1972, Postwar, 1983, The Language of Sailing, 2000, (with John Pinder) Federal Union: The Pioneers, 1990; editor: The New Atlantic Challenge, 1975, Western Europe, a Handbook, 1986, Europe Tomorrow, 1972; contbr. (film) The Economist, 1996—; translator: The Memoirs of Jean Monnet, 1978, Europe: a History of its Peoples, 1990, Illustrated History of Europe, 1993, A History of Civilizations, 1994. Recipient Scott-Moncrieff prize, 1978. Avocations: travelling, sailing. Home: Albany Cottage, 24 Park Village East, London NW1 7PZ, England

MAYNE, WILEY EDWARD, lawyer; b. Sanborn, Iowa, Jan. 19, 1917; s. Earl W. and Gladys (Wiley) M.; m. Elizabeth Dodson, Jan. 5, 1942; children—Martha (Mrs. F.K. Smith), Wiley Edward, John. S.B. cum laude, Harvard, 1938; student, Law Sch., 1938-39; J.D., State U. Iowa, 1939-41. Bar: Iowa bar 1941, U.S. Supreme Ct. 1950. Practiced in Sioux City, 1946-66, 75—; mem. Shull, Marshall, Mayne, Marks & Vizintos, 1946-66, Mayne and Berenstein, 1975-87, Mayne & Mayne, 1988-99, Mayne, Marks, Madsen and Hirschbach, 1999—; spl. agt. FBI, 1941-43; Mem. 90th-93d Congresses, 6th Dist. Iowa; mem. judiciary com., agr. com. Commr. from Iowa Nat. Conf. Commrs. Uniform State Laws, 1956-60; chmn. grievance commn. Iowa Supreme Ct., 1964-66; del. FAO, 1973; chmn. Woodbury County Compensation Bd., 1975-80. Chmn. Midwest Rhodes Scholar Selection Com., 1964-66; pres. Sioux City Symphony Orch. Assn., 1947-54, Sioux City Concert Course, 1982-85; vice chmn. Young Republican Nat. Fedn., 1948-50; bd. dirs. Iowa Bar Found., 1962-68. Served to lt. (j.g.) USNR, 1943-46. Fellow Am. Coll. Trial Lawyers; mem. ABA (ho. of dels. 1966-68), Iowa Bar Assn. (pres. 1963-64), Sioux City Bar Assn., Internat. Assn. Def. Counsel (exec. com. 1961-64), Harvard Club (N.Y.C.), Sioux City Country Club, Masons (Scottish Rite/33 deg.). Fax: 712-252-1535. Home: 2728 Jackson St Sioux City IA 51104-3623 Office: Pioneer Bank Bldg 701 Pierce St Ste 300 Sioux City IA 51101-1038

MAYNES, JOHN PETER, retired trade union officer, accountant; b. Melbourne, Australia, Mar. 15, 1923; s. Peter Leo Maynes and Lily May Walworth; m. Therèse Jane Dynes, Oct. 7, 1944; children: Pamela, Brendan, Kevin, Carmel, Phillip, Lisa. AM, CPA. Nat. v.p. Federated Clks. Union of Australia, 1950-52, nat. dep. pres., 1952-54, nat. pres., 1954-91. State v.p. Victorian Br. Federated Clks. Union Australia, 1950-55, state dep. pres., 1955-60, pres., 1960-88; mem. various world sect. coms. Internat. Transport Workers Fedn., London, 1961-91; world exec. mem. Internat. Fedn. Comml. Clerical and Tech. Employees, Geneva, 1974-91, mem. found., 3d v.p. Asia, 1974-79, 1st v.p. Asia, 1980-86, pres., Singapore, 1986-89; exec. mem. Australian Coun. Trade Unions, 1981-91, exec. com., 1987-91; mem. Auto Industry Mfg. Coun., 1984-89; nat. com. Australian Overseas Disaster Response Orgn., 1982-83; tech. change com. Australian Sci. and Tech. Coun., 1984-88, mem. coun., 1986-89; chmn. CARE Occupation Superannuation Plan Australia, 1986-2000; mem. Australia Day Coun., 1974-2000, chmn., 1994-98. Named to Order of Australian (gen. divsn.), 1985. Mem. Australian Soc. Practicing Accts. (life), Royal Automobile Club of Victoria, Melbourne U. Bus. Sch. Alumni. Fax: (03) 98463568. Home: 12 Tatterson Ct, Templestowe 3106, Australia

MAYO, DANA WALKER, chemistry educator; b. Bethlehem, Pa., July 20, 1928; s. Dana Harret Nickerson and Ethel Marie (Chapman) M.; m. Odile Jeanne d'Arc Mailhiot, Jan. 12, 1962; children: Dana Lawrence, Chapman Scott, Sara Walker. BS, MIT, 1952; PhD, Ind. U., 1959. Asst. prof. chemistry Bowdoin Coll., Brunswick, Maine, 1962-65, assoc. prof. chemistry, 1965-68, prof. chemistry, 1969-70, Charles Weston Pickard prof. chemistry, 1970-91, Charles Weston Pickard rsch. prof. chemistry, 1991—; pres. Microscale Organic Lab. Co., New Castle, N.H., 1985—. Author: Microscale Organic Laboratory, 1986, 2d edit., 1989, 3d. edit., 1994, 4th edit., 2000, Microscale Techniques for the Organic Laboratory, 1991, 2d edit., 2000; patentee microscale spinning band distillation column. Capt. USAF, 1956-61. Fellow MIT, 1959-62; recipient Charles A. Dana Found. award, N.Y.C., 1986, John A. Timm award New Eng. Assn. Chemistry Tchrs., 1987, Catalyst nat. award Chem. Mfr. Assn., Washington, 1989. Fellow AAAS, mem. Nat. Inst. Chemists (cert.), Am. Chem. Soc. (health and safety award 1987, James Flack Norris award New Eng. sect. 1988, chair Maine sect. 1971-72), Soc. Applied Spectroscopy, Coblentz Soc. (bd. dirs. 1977-79). Avocations: book collecting, genealogical research, forest management, swimming.

MAYO, JAMES WATIE (JIM MAYO), publishing executive; b. Fort Smith, Ark., July 17, 1942; s. Richard Wheeler and Florence Marie (Baker) M.; m. Rebecca Ann Boen, July 17, 1965; children: John Robert, Jeffrey William. BAin Journalism, U. Okla., 1964. Assoc. pub., gen. mgr. Sequoyah County TIMES, Sallisaw, Okla., 1968-86, pub., 1986—; bd. dirs. First Nat. Bank, 1975-91; v.p. Lincoln County Pubs., Chandler, Okla., 1987-99. Author: History of Sallisaw, 1993. Mem., former pres. Sallisaw C. of C., 1968—; mem. Okla. Coun. Judicial Complaints, Okla. City, 1974-77; mem. Okla. Coun. Grand River Dam Authority, Vinita, Okla., 1980; bd. dirs. nominating com. Grand River Dam Authority, Vinita, Okla., 1980; bd. dirs. Okla. Hist. Soc., 1986-88, Higher Edn. Alumni Coun., Oklahoma City, 1993-95; dist. chairman Indian Nations Coun. Boy Scouts Am., Tulsa, 1987-90; coun. bd. Indian Nations Coun. Boy Scouts Am., 1987-90. Lt. (j.g.) USNR, 1964-67. Named to Okla. Journalism Hall Fame The Soc. Profl. Journalists U. Ctrl. Okla., 1993. Mem. Nat. Newspaper Assn., Internat. Soc. Weekly Newspaper Editors, Okla. Press Assn. (pres. 1986-87, H. Milt Phillips award for outstanding contbns. to newspaper industry and pub. svc. 1999), Okla. Newspaper Found (pres. 1993-95), Sallisaw Lions Club (pres. 1972). Democrat. Presbyn. Avocation: hiking, photography. Office: Sequoyah County TIMES 111 N Oak St Sallisaw OK 74955-4637

MAYO, LOUIS ALLEN, corporation executive; b. Durham, N.C., Nov. 27, 1928; s. Louis Allen and Amy Earl (Overton) M.; m. Emma Jean Minshew, Oct. 31, 1953 (div.); children: Louis Allen III, Robert Lawrence, Carolyn Jean; m. 2d, Myrna Ann Smith, Feb. 16, 1980 (div.). Student, Calif. State Poly. Coll., 1948-50; BA in Criminology, Calif. State Coll., Fresno, 1952; MA in Pub. Adminstrn., Am. U., 1960, PhD in Pub. Adminstrn., 1983; postgrad., U. So. Calif., 1960-62. Spl. agt. U.S. Secret Svc., Treasury Dept., L.A., 1956-58, 60-63, White House, Washington, 1958-60, 63-66; program mgr. law enforcement Office Law Enforcement Assistance, Justice Dept., 1967-68; acting chief Rsch. Ctr., rsch. program mgr. Nat. Inst. Law Enforcement and Criminal Justice, 1968-74; alternate assoc. mem. Fed. Coun. on Sci. and Tech., White House, 1973-74; dir. tng. and testing divsn. Nat. Inst. Justice, 1975-87; pres. Murphy, Mayo & Assocs., Alexandria, Va., 1987—; lectr. criminology Armed Forces Inst. Tech., 1954-55; professorial lectr. Am. U., 1974-82; adj. prof. August Vollmer U., 1990-95. 2d lt. to 1st lt. USAF, 1952-56. Mem. Police Assn. Coll. Edn. (exec. dir., founder), Internat. Assn. Chiefs of Police, Am. Soc. Pub. Adminstrn. (nat. chmn. sect. on criminal justice adminstrn. 1975-76), Acad. Criminal Justice Scis., Police Exec. Rsch. Forum, Soc. Police Futurists Internat., Pi Sigma Alpha. Methodist. Home and Office: 5200 Leeward Ln # 101 Alexandria VA 22315-3944

MAYOCK, ROBERT LEE, internist; b. Wilkes-Barre, Pa., Jan. 19, 1917; s. John F. and Mathilde M.; m. Constance M. Peruzzi, July 2, 1949; children: Robert Lee, Stephen Philip, Holly Peruzzi Luff. BS, Bucknell U., 1938; MD, U. Pa., 1942. Diplomate Am. Bd. Internal Medicine. Intern Hosp. U. Pa., Phila., 1943-44; resident in internal medicine Hosp. U. Pa., 1944-45, chief med. resident, 1945-46, attending physician, 1946—; chief pulmonary disease Phila. Gen. Hosp., 1955-72, chief pulmonary disease sect., 1959-72, sr. cons. pulmonary disease sect., 1972—; asst. prof. clin. medicine U. Pa., 1949-59, assoc. prof., 1959-70, prof. medicine, 1970-87, prof. emeritus, 1987—; med. adv. com. for Tb Commonwealth of Pa., 1965-74, med. adv. com. on chronic respiratory disease, 1974-92, chmn. adv. com., 1981-90; mem. subsplty bd. pulmonary disease Am. Bd. Internal Medicine, 1965-76; nat. bd. dirs. Am. Lung Assn., 1983-92, local bd. dirs., 1961, local pres., 1966-69, dir. at large, 1983—. Contbr. articles to profl. jours. Capt. U.S. Army, 1952-54. Robert L. Mayock-David A. Cooper Prof. of Medicine Endowed Chair named in his honor U. Pa. Sch. Medicine, 1997. Fellow ACP, Am. Coll. Chest Physicians (regent 1972-79), Phila. Coll. Physicians; mem. AMA, Am. Thoracic Soc., Am. Fedn. Clin. Rsch., Pa. Lung Assn. (dir. 1976—), N.Y. Acad. Scis., Pa. Med. Soc., Phila. County Med. Soc., Physiology Soc. Phila., Laennec Soc. Phila., Merion Cricket Club, Westmoreland Club, Swiftwater Res., Sigma Xi. Home: 244 Gypsy Ln Wynnewood PA 19096-1113 Office: U Penn Ravdin Bldg 3d Fl Ste F Philadelphia PA 19104

MAYOR OREJA, JAIME, Spanish government official; b. San Sebastian, Spain, July 12, 1951; m. Isabel Bastida; 4 children. Mem. for Guipuzcoa UCD, 1977; mem., govt. del. Basque Autonomous Parliament, 1982, spokesman Coalicion Popular, 1984-86; campaign mgr., pres. Popular Party Mgmt. in Basque Country Popular Party, 1989; mem. for Vizcaya Spanish Parliament, 1989-90, min. interior, 1996—; pres. Popular Party in Basque Country. Office: Ministry of Interior, Amador de los Rios 7, 28071 Madrid Spain*

MAYR, ERNST, retired zoologist, philosopher; b. Kempten, Germany, July 5, 1904; came to U.S., 1931; s. Otto and Helene (Pusinelli) M.; m. Margarete Simon, May 4, 1935; children: Christa E., Susanne. Cand. med., U. Greifswald, 1925; Ph.D., U. Berlin, 1926; Ph.D. (hon.), Uppsala U., Sweden, 1957; D.Sc. (hon.), Yale U., 1959, U. Melbourne, 1959, Oxford U., 1966, U. Munich, 1968, U. Paris, 1974, Harvard U., 1980, Guelph U., U. Cambridge, 1982, U. Vt., 1984; DSc (hon.), U. Mass., 1993; PhD (hon.), U. Vienna, 1994; DPhil (hon.), U. Konstanz, 1994; DSc (hon.), U. Bologna, 1995. Asst. curator zool. mus. U. Berlin, 1926-32; mem. Rothschild expdn. to Dutch New Guinea, 1928, expdn. to Mandated Ty. of New Guinea, 1928-29, Whitney Expdn., 1929-30; research asso. Am. Mus. Natural History, N.Y.C., 1931-32; asso. curator Am. Mus. Natural History, 1932-44, curator, 1944-53; Jesup lectr. Columbia U., 1941; Alexander Agassiz prof. zoology Harvard U., 1953-75, emeritus, 1975—; dir. Mus. Comparative Zoology, Harvard U., 1961-70; Messenger lectr. Cornell U., 1985; Hitchcock prof. U. Calif., 1987; hon. fellow Ctr. for Philosophy of Sci., U. Pitts. Author: List of New Guinea Birds, 1941, Systematics and the Origin of Species, 1942, Birds of the Southwest Pacific, 1945, Birds of the Philippines, (with Jean Delacour), 1946, Methods and Principles of Systematic Zoology, (with E. G. Linsley and R. L. Usinger), 1953, Animal Species and Evolution, 1963, Principles of Systematic Zoology, 1969, 2d edit., 1991, Populations, Species and Evolution, 1970, Evolution and the Diversity of Life, 1976, (with W. Provine) Evolutionary Synthesis, 1980, Biologie de l'Evolution, 1981, The Growth of Biological Thought, 1982, Toward a New Philosophy of Biology, 1988, One Long Argument, 1991, This is Biology, 1997; editor: Evolution, 1947-49. Pres. XIII Internat. Ornith. Congress, 1962. Recipient Leidy medal, 1946, Wallace Darwin medal, 1958, Brewster medal Am. Ornithologists Union, 1965, Daniel Giraud Elliot medal, 1967, Nat. Medal of Sci., 1970, Molina prize Accademia delle Sci., Bologna, Italy, 1972, Linnean medal, 1977, Gregor Mendel medal, 1980, Balzan prize, 1983, Darwin medal Royal Soc., 1987, Disting. Scientist award UCLA, 1993, Salvin Godman medal, 1994, Japan prize, 1994, Benjamin Franklin medal 1995, 96, Lewis Thomas prize, 1998, Crafoord prize, 1999; establishment of the Ernst Meyr Lectureship of the Berlin-Brandenburgische Akademie. Fellow Linnaean Soc. N.Y. (past sec. editor), Am. Ornithol. Union (pres. 1956-59), N.Y. Zool. Soc.; mem. NAS, Am. Philos. Soc., Am. Acad. Arts and Scis., Am. Soc. Zoologists, Soc. Systematic Zoology (pres. 1966), Soc. Study Evolution (sec. 1946, pres. 1950); hon. or corr. mem. Royal Soc., Royal Australian, Brit. ornithol. unions, Zool. Soc. London, Soc. Ornithol. France, Royal Soc. New Zealand, Bot. Gardens Indonesia, S. Africa Ornithol. Soc., Linnean Soc. London, Deutsche Akademie der naturforsch Leopoldina, Accad. Naz. dei Lincei, Royal Soc., Academie des Sci., Ctr. for Philosophy of Sci. (Pitts.), Russian Acad. Sci., Berlin - Brandenburgische Akademie. Office: Harvard U Mus Comparative Zoology 26 Oxford St Cambridge MA 02138-2902

MAYR, ERNST W., computer scientist, educator; b. Fürstenfeldbruck, Bavaria, Germany, May 18, 1950; s. Wilhelm and Emilie (Ott) M.; m. Christa M. Jodlbauer, Sept. 15, 1980; children: Stephanie, Alexandra. Dipl. Math., Tech. U. Munich, Germany, 1975; MS in Computer Sci. & Elec. Engring., MIT, 1977; Dr. rer. nat., Tech. U. Munich, Germany, 1980. Rsch. assoc. Tech. U. Munich, 1977-80; vis. scientist MIT, Cambridge, Mass., 1980-81; lectr. Stanford (Calif.) U., 1981-82, asst. prof., 1982-88; prof. computer sci., chair J.W. Goethe U., Frankfurt, Germany, 1988-93, Tech. U. Munich, 1993—; dir., chmn. Inst. for Computer Sci., Munich, 1993—; chmn. computer sci. dept. J.W. Goethe U., Frankfurt, 1990-91. Contbr. articles to profl. jours.; editor (jour.) Info. & Computation, Computing. Lt. German Army, 1969-71. Recipient Presdl. Young Investigator award NSF, 1983, Faculty award IBM, 1984, Rsch. award AT&T, 1985, Leibniz award German Rsch. Foun., 1997. Mem. IEEE, Assn. Computing Machinery, Soc. Indsl. & Applied Math., Gesellschaft Informatik, Sigma Xi. Roman Catholic. Office: Inst fur Informatik, Tech Univ Munchen, D-80290 Munich Germany

MAYR, GEORG WILHELM, physician, biochemist, biologist, researcher; b. Peissenberg, Germany, Sept. 18, 1951; s. Georg and Anna M. (Meyer) M.; m. Elke Seidel, 1978 (div. 1993); children: Marion, Andrea. MD, U. Munich, 1982. Sci. asst. in medicine U. Munich, 1979-80; rsch. scientist U. Bochum, 1980-83, asst. prof., 1983-89, Heisenberg prof., 1989-93; prof. physiol. chemistry U. Hamburg, 1993-98, spkr. study course of biochemistry and molecular biology, 1998—; coord. study course of biochemistry and molecular biology, U. Hamburg, 1993—, dir. dept. of cellular signal transduction, 1993-99, dir. Inst. of Med. Biochemistry and Molecular Biology, 1994—, mem. faculty bd.; mng. dir. Inst. Med. Biochemistry and Molecular Biology, 1999—; mem. med. faculty U. Hamburg, 1994—. Contbr. articles to profl. jours., chpts. to books; inventor novel microanalytical techniques in cellular signaling research; patentee on signalling therapeutics. Med. officer Air Force, 1978-79. Mem. Gesellschaft Biologische Chemie, Gesellschaft Deutscher Chemiker, Aerztekammer Hamburg. Avocations: children, skiing, software writing. Office: Inst Med Biochem & Mol Biol, U Hosp Hamburg Eppendorf, 20 246 Hamburg Germany

MAYR, HERBERT, chemistry educator; b. Weilheim, Germany, June 8, 1947; s. Alfred and Elisabeth (Huber) M.; m. Edith Durach, Apr. 4, 1975; children: Andreas, Birgit, Christine. Chemistry Diplom, U. Munich, 1971, PhD in Chemistry, 1974. Lab. asst. U. Munich, 1972-74; rsch. asst. Case Western Res. U., Cleve., 1975-76; rsch. asst. U. Erlangen-Nuernberg, 1976-81, lectr., 1981-84; prof. chemistry Medizinische Universitaet Luebeck, 1984-91, dir. chemistry inst., 1984-91; prof. organic chemistry Technische Hochschule Darmstadt, 1991-96, Ludwig-Maximilians U., Munich, 1996—; dean

of fac. of chem. and pharm.; vis. prof. Gunma U., Japan, 1991. Contbr. over 170 articles to profl. jours.; patentee in field. Recipient Dozentenpreis Fonds der Chemischen Industrie, Frankfurt, 1983; Brit. Coun. sr. fellow, 1987. Mem. Am. Chem. Soc., German Chem. Soc. Roman Catholic. Office: U Munich, Butenandtstr 5-13 (Haus F), D-81377 Munich Germany

MAYS, VICKIE M., psychology educator. BA in Psychology, Philosophy, Loyola U. Chgo., 1972, MA in Clin. Psychology, 1973; PhD in Clin. Psychology, U. Mass., 1979. Instr., dorm counselor Upward Bound program U. Mass., Amherst, 1974; lectr. devel. of Black child SW Residential Coll., U. Mass., Amherst, 1974; instr. career planning continuing edn. for women div. George Washington U., Washington, 1975-76; clin. supr. psychol. svcs. clinic U. Mass., Amherst, 1976-77, acting intake coord./clin. supr. psychol. svcs. clinic, 1977; asst. prof. clin. psychology UCLA, 1979-87, assoc. prof. clin. psychology, 1987—; fellow/vis. scholar Nat. Survey of Black Americans Program NIMH, 1981; cons. community rels. div. George Washington U., 1975-76, Everywoman's Ctr. U. Mass., Amherst, 1977-78; psychol. cons. com. for the collegiate edn. of Black students U. Mass., Amherst, 1978-79; consultation, edn. and prevention specialist Didi Hirsch Community Mental Health Ctr., Culver City, Calif., 1980-81; psychologist Calif. Heatlh news program Sta. KCBS, L.A., 1986-87; presenter in field. Assoc. editor Psychology of Women Quar., 1986-88; mem. editorial bd. Clin. Psychology of Women, AIDS Edn. and Prevention, Jour. of Homosexuality; guest editor Am. Psychologist; ad hoc reviewer Jour. Health and Social Behavior, Jour. Consulting and Clin. Psychology, Jour. Personality and Social Psychology, Milbank Quar., Profl. Psychology, Psychol. Bull. Pub. Health Reports, Sex Roles. NIMH Predoctoral fellow, 1973-74, fellow Nat. Ctr. for Health Svcs. Rsch. Award RAND/UCLA Health Studies Ctr., 1987-89; recipient NIMH New Investigator Rsch. award, 1983-85; named Outstanding Young Woman of Yr., Bd. Outstanding Young Women, Montgomery, Ala., 1984, 86. Mem. APA (chair com. on Black women's concerns div. 35 1984, coun. of reps. 1986-89, chair women's caucus sec. 1988-89, publ. and comm. bd. task force on ethnic bias in lang. in publ. 1985, edn. and tng. com. on ethnic minority human resources devel. 1985-87, task force on AIDS 1986—), APHA (Black caucus health workers program com. 1991), Western Psychol. Assn., Acad. Behavioral Medicine Rsch. Office: UCLA Dept Psych 1285 Franz Hall PO Box 951563 Los Angeles CA 90095-1563

MAYSTADT, PHILIPPE, financial executive; b. Mar. 14, 1948; married; 3 children. LLB, Cath. U., Louvain, Belgium; MA in Pub. Administrn. Asst. prof. Cath. U. of Louvain, 1970-77, prof., 1989—; counselor min. of Walloon Affairs Govt. of Belgium, Brussels, 1974; mem. Ho. of Reps. Dist. of Charleroi, Belgium, 1977; jr. min. of regional economy and planning Govt. Belgium, Walloon Region, 1979-80; min. pub. svc. and sci. policy Govt. Belgium, Brussels, 1980-81, min. budget and sci. policy, 1981-85, min. of econ. affairs, 1985-88, vice prime min., 1986-88, 95-98, min. of fin., 1988-98, min. of fgn. trade, 1995-98; pres. European Invesment Bank, Luxembourg, 2000—, chmn. bd. dirs.; chmn. interim com. Internat. Monetary Fund, 1993-98. Author: Listen and Then Decide, 1988, Market and State in a Globalized Economy, 1998; co-author: The Intervention of Pub. Authorities in the Econ. Life, 1973 (recipient spl. prize Belgian Lawyers Assn.). Office: European Investment Bank, 100 blvd K Adenauer, 2950 Luxembourg Luxembourg

MAYUMI, MAKOTO, immunology educator; b. Tokyo, Japan, Mar. 7, 1938; s. Atsushi and Yoshiko (Nagano) Mayumi. MD, U. Tokyo, 1962; D of med. sci., Univ. Tokyo, 1969. Rsch. on complement Howard Hughes Med. Inst., Miami, 1965-68. Rsch. scientist U. Kumamoto, Kumamoto-Ken, Japan, 1969-70; rsch. assoc. U. Tokyo, 1970-72; assoc. prof. Jichi Med. Sch., Tochigi-Ken, Japan, 1972-79, prof., 1979—. Contbr. articles to profl. jours. Recipient Erwin von Bälz Preis award Boeringer Sohn, 1979, Med. Sci. award Japan Med. Assn., 1998. Mem. Japan Soc. Hepatology, Am. Assn. Immunologists,. Buddhist. Achievements include establishment of method to detect hepatitis B surface antigen by immune adherence hemagglutination and the mechanism of hepatitis B virus transmission and perinatal infection; determination of genotypes of hepatitis C virus and their clinical significance; discovery of relation between genetic variation of hepatitis viruses and diseases they induce in hosts. E-mail: immundiv@jichi.ac.jp. Office: Jichi Med Sch Immunology, Minamikawachi-Machi, Tochigi 329-0498, Japan

MAZAL, PAVEL, university administrator; b. Brno, Czechoslovakia, July 7, 1955; s. Adolf and Drahomira (Žižková) M.; m. Lenka Kopřivová, Mar. 31, 1979; children: Zdeněk, Miroslav, Jane. Engring. degree, Tech. U., 1979; CSc, Czechoslovak Acad. Scis., 1985. Rschr. Inst. of Phys. Metalurgy, Brno, 1979-84; asst. prof. Tech. U., Brno, 1984-90, 92-94, E.N.S.E.T., Tunis, Tunisia, 1990-92; vice dir. Inst. of Design Faculty Mech. Engring., Brno U. Tech., Brno, 1994—; dir. D.M.V. Material Servis s.r.o., Brno, 1996—. Author: Technologie de Construction, 1991, (with others) Bases of Designing, 1994; contbr. articles to profl. jours. Grantee Grant Agy. of Czech Republic, 1996—, Tech. U. of Brno, 1994-96. Mem. N.Y. Acad. Scis., Assn. of Mech. Engrs., Assn. for Heat Treatment, European Structural Integrity Soc., Alliance Francaise. Avocations: acoustic emission, railway modelling, tourism. Office: Brno U Tech Inst Design, Technická 2, Brno CZ 61669, Czech Republic

MAZÁNEK, MILOŠ, engineering educator; b. Tanvald, Czech Republic, Nov. 22, 1950; s. Miloš and Marie (Křížková) M.; m. Eva Panschabová, June 7, 1975; children: Kateřina, Klára. Eng., Czech Tech. U., Prague, 1974, PhD, 1980. Rschr. Czech Tech. U., Prague, 1975-76, asst. prof., 1976-90, assoc. prof., 1990—; rschr. Czech Acad. Scis., Prague, 1984-91; head dept. electromagnetic field Czech Tech. U., 1997, prof., 2000—. author: Radiocommunication for Future, 1981; editor Radioengring., 1992—; contbr. articles to profl. jours. Head Soc. for Edn., Czech Republic, 1992—; mem. Univ. Senate, Prague, 1993-96. Czech Tech. U. Rsch. awardee, 1995. Mem. IEEE, Radioengring. Soc. (head 1991—), Instn. Elec. Engrs. (London), Internat. Union of Radio Sci. Avocations: youth education camps organizer, photography. Office: Czech Technical Univ, Technická 2 K317, 16627 Prague Czech Republic

MAZANKOWSKI, DONALD FRANK, Canadian government official; b. Viking, Alta., Can., July 27, 1935; s. Frank and Dora (Lonowski) M.; m. Lorraine Poleschuk, Sept. 6, 1958; children: Gregory, Roger, Donald. Student, pub. schs., 1987; PhD in Engring (hon.), N.S. Inst. Tech.; LLD (hon.), U. Alta., 1993. MP Ho. of Commons, 1968—, chmn. com. transp., 1972-74, mem. com. govt. ops., 1976-77, mem. com. trans. and communication, 1977-79; min. of transp., min. responsible for Can. Wheat Bd. Govt. of Can., 1979-80, min. of transp. (re-drafted Nat. Transp. Act), 1984-86, dep. prime min., 1986—, govt. house leader, 1986-88, pres. Privy Coun., 1986-91, pres. Treas. Bd., 1987-88, min. responsible for privatization and regulatory affairs, 1988-91, min. of agriculture, 1988-91, min. of fin., 1991-93; chmn. Inst. of Health Econs.; former mem. bd. govs. U. Alta; bd. dirs. Gulf Can. Resources, Power Corp. Can., Power Fin. Corp., Great West Life Assurance, The Investors Group, Shaw Comms. Inc., Weyerhaeuser Co., IMC Global Inc., Gulf Indonesia Resources Ltd., ATCO Ltd., London Life Ins.; chmn. Can. Genetic Diseases Network. Apptd. chmn. Premier's Adv. Coun. on Health. Apptd. Officer of Order of Can., 2000. Mem. Royal Can. Legion (life). Roman Catholic. Club: Vegreville Rotary (past dir.). Lodge: KC. Fax: 780-632-4737. E-mail: maz1@agt.net.

MAZARAKI, ANATOLIY ANTONOVICH, rector, economics educator; b. Kiev, Ukraine, July 27, 1950; s. Anton Fedorovich and Evdokiya Ivanovna (Zozulya) M.; m. Irina Nickolaevna Ivanova, Feb. 3, 1979; 1 child, Nataliya Mazaraki. Degree in pub. catering tech., Kiev Inst. Trade & Econs., Ukraine, 1972; Candidate Sci. in Productive Forces, Nat. Acad. Sci., Ukraine, 1980, PhD in Econs., 1995. Engr., sr. rschr. com. investigation of productive forces Nat. Acad. Sci., Kiev, Ukraine, 1975-84; dep. dir. Sci. & Rsch. Inst. Trade, Kiev, Ukraine, 1984-87; dep. gen. dir. Sci. Prodn. Assn. "Torgprogress", Kiev, Ukraine, 1987-88; dean trade & econs. faculty Kiev Inst. Trade & Econs., Ukraine, 1988-90, first prorector, 1990-91; rector Kiev State U. Trade & Econs., Ukraine, 1991—; chmn. sci. coun. Kiev State U. Trade & Econs., Ukraine, 1991—; adv. to pres. Ukraine, Kiev, 1998—. Author: Development of Trade in the System of Social Infrastructure Under Market Economy Conditions, 1994, (textbook) Modern Problems of Regional Development of Trade, 1994, World Market of Trade Services, 1996. mem. Vatutinsky dist. adminstrn., Kiev, Ukraine, 1994—, adv. of pres. of Ukraine, 1998. Recipient 1500 anniversary of Kiev medal Supreme Coun. Ukraine, 1982, Ukraine honored worker of sci. & tech. award Acad. Sci., Kiev, 1995, Ukraine honored worker of edn. award Ministry of Edn., Kiev, 1996. Mem. Internat. Acad. Higher Sch., N.Y. Acad. Sci., Ukrainian Acad. Sci. of Nat. Progress. Avocations: hunting, fishing, music, swimming, tennis. Office: Kiev State U Trade & Econs, 19 Kioto St, 02156 Kiev Ukraine

MAZARAKIS-BALTSAVIAS, PHÉDON, international and maritime consultant, publicist; b. Athens, Greece, Nov. 17, 1932; s. Michael Panayotou and Alexandra Gerasimou (Valentis) Mazarakis Baltsavias. Cert. in English, Poly.-Sch. Modern Langs., London, 1951; seminar cert. in polit. economy, U. Geneva, 1952, in sociology, 1954, in stats., 1957, in internat. law, 1959, internat. instns. cert., 1958; MA in Polit. and Social Sci., U. Stockholm, 1955; assiduity cert., Acad. Internat. Law, The Hague, The Netherlands, 1955; student Inst. High Internat. Studies, U. Paris, 1956-57, 76-77; cert. spl. internship course, ILO, Geneva, 1958; D. Polit. and Econ. Scis., High Studies Acad., Bari, Italy, 1959; cert. press officers program, Pub. Adminstrn's. Ednl. Ctr., Athens, 1970; student Bus. Adminstrn. Inst., High Sch. of Commercial and Econ. Scis., Athens, 1971-72. Greek govt. candidate polit. divsn. NATO Hdqrs., Paris, 1957; adviser gen. divsn. of press Prime Minister's Office, Athens, 1957; officer publicity divsn. Nat. Tourist Orgn., Athens, 1959-60; pres. and info. dir. Greek Embassy, Stockholm, Helsinki, 1967-69; chief nat. and internat. sect. Nat. Orientation divsn. Prime Minister's Office, Athens, 1969-71; adviser to gov. Greek Manpower Orgn., Athens, 1971; advisor to minister Nat. Economy, Athens, 1972-73; assoc., mgr. United Europe Mgmt. Cons., Inc., Greece, 1963-64; pres. Solymar Compania Maritima S.A., Panama, 1970—, Adymnos Mediterranean Shipping Co., S.A., Panama, 1970—; dir. Octal Fin. Ltd., London, 1988-94, Bus. Contact Office, Athens, 1988-94; European rep. Inst. Sociology, Russian Acad. Scis., 1990—; founder, mgr. Internat. Maritime Exch. E.E.I.G., 1993—, Internat. Maritime Exch. Inc., 1997—; prof. extraordinary polit. sci. High Studies Acad., Bari, Italy, 1959; lectr. pub. info. Pub. Adminstrn.'s Ednl. Ctr., Athens, 1974; bus. cons. and promoter; mem. bus. cooperation network Greece of Commn. European Union, Brussels, 1988-94, consulting orgn., UN Indsl. Devel. Orgn., Vienna, 1994. Free-lance journalist, publicist, editor, 1953—; copyright author: Geographic Codes of Greek Prehistory-Navigational Guide and Inserted Symbolisms, 1999; owner, editor Trade Mark Neos Aeon, 1999—. Capt. Greek Mcht. Marine, 1979. Recipient commemorative awards including Order Unknown Heroes. Mem. Greek Psychol. Soc. (assoc.), Greek Geog. Soc. (adminstrv. bd. 1976), Greek Publicists' Soc. (spl. adviser 1974), Greek Heraldic and Genealogy Soc. (adminstrv. bd. 1988—), Greek Nat. Heritage Protection Soc., Assn. Greek Economists, Greek Psychosomatic Medicine Soc., European Info. Industry Assn., Panathinaikos Athletic Club (Athens). Greek Orthodox. Office: PO Box 30633, GR-100-33 Athens Greece

MAZARIEGOS, GEORGE VINCENT, pediatric transplant surgeon; b. July 24, 1963. BS, Northwestern U., 1984, MD, 1986. General surgery resident Mich. State U. Butterworth Hosp., Grand Rapids, 1986-91; fellow surgical critical care, transplantation U. Pitts. Med. Ctr., 1991-93, asst. prof. surgery, 1994—; transplant surgeon Children's Hosp. of Pitts., 1997—. Fellow ACS; mem. Am. Soc. Transplantation. Office: Children's Hosp Pitts 3705 5th Ave Pittsburgh PA 15213-2524

MAZARS, MARTIAL ELIE MAURICE, physicist, educator; b. Antony, France, Jan. 26, 1967; s. Jacques and Josette (Grandjean) M. Agregation, Ecole Normale Supérieure, Cachan, France, 1991; D Theoretical Physics, U. Paris XI, 1997. Lectr. U. Versailles, France, 1994-97, lectr. Inst. U. Formation des Maitres, 1997-98, prof. agrégé, 1999—; tchr. Coll. Emile Zola, Vernouillet, France, 1999—. Contbr. articles to profl. jours. Mem. Commn. de Recherche et d'Info. Ind. sur la Radioactivity, 1992, conscientious objector, 1992-94. Mem. Groupe de Scientifiques pour l'Info. sur l'Energie Nucléaire, Assn. de controle de Radioactivity dans l'Ouest. Office: Lab Physique Theorique, U Paris XI Bat 210, 91400 Orsay France

MAZAUD, JEAN-FRANCOIS, organization executive; b. Boulogne, France, Mar. 3, 1967; s. Georges and Suzane (Parveau) M.; m. Marie-Laure Delplace, Aug. 27, 1994; children: Guillaume, Alexandre. BA, Strathclyde U., Glasgow, Scotland, 1990; ESC, Bordeaux, France, 1990; MS in Fin. Engring., EM Lyon, France, 1991. V.p. Banque Indosuez, Tokyo, 1991-93; v.p. Soc. Generale, Paris, 1993-97, dir., 1997—, head equity-linked orgn., 1998—. Avocations: tennis, skiing. Office: Soc Gen, 17 Cours Valmy, 92972 Paris La Defense Cedex, France

MAZAURIC, VINCENT GEORGES, physicist; b. Rouen, Normandy, France, Nov. 11, 1962; s. Claude Gilbert Mazauric and Annette Thérèse (Hog) Gallot; m. Isabelle Claire Napoly, July 4, 1987; children: Louise, Anne-Laure. MEE, Inst. Nat. Poly., Grenoble, France, 1986; M in Solid State Physics, U. Orsay, 1988; M in Pure Maths., U. Paris, 1989; PhD in Physics, U. Orsay, 1992. Asst. rschr. Office Nat. d'Etudes et Recherches Aerospatiales, Paris, 1987-91; asst. prof. U. Rouen, 1991-92; assoc. rschr. Osaka (Japan) U., 1992-94; mgr. electromagnetics rsch. Schneider Elec., Grenoble, 1994—; rsch. cons. U. Paris Sud, Orsay, 1987-92. Contbr. articles to profl. jours. Coord. Valentin Feldmann Club, Dieppe, France, 1988-91. Sgt. Mil. H.S. for Mountaineering, 1986-87. Fellow Japan Soc. for Promotion of Sci.; mem. IEEE, European Phys. Soc., French Soc. Physics, Am. Phys. Soc. Avocations: Alpine skiing (former competitor), mountaineering, sailing, cruise, classical music. E-mail:vincent mazauric@mail.schneider.fr. Fax: 33-0-4-76-57-98-60. Home: 7 rue de la liberté, 38000 Grenoble France Office: Schneider Elec Corp Rsch Divn, Rsch Ctr A2 rue Volta, 38050 Grenoble France

MAZEL, JOSEPH LUCAS, publications executive, consultant; b. Paterson, N.J., Oct. 1, 1939; s. Joseph Anthony and Anne (Kidon) M.; children: Joseph William, Jeanne Eileen; m. Joyce Virginia Kronenberger, Feb. 14, 1992. BME, Newark Coll. Engring., 1960. Mech. engr. Austin Co., Roselle, N.J., 1960-61; engr. Western Electric Co., Newark, Atlanta, 1961-62; asst. assoc., sr. editor Factory mag. McGraw-Hill Publs. Co., N.Y.C., 1962-71; editor-in-chief, sr. editor 33 Metal Producing mag., Newark, Summit, N.Y.C., 1971-85, chmn. editl. bd., 1980-82; pub. rels. account supr. Hammond Farrell, Inc., N.Y.C., 1985-87; mgr. corp. publs. Siemens Corp., Iselin, N.J., 1987-92; pres. Mazel Editl. Assocs., Fair Lawn, N.J., 1992—; guest lectr. Writers Conf., N.J. Inst. Tech., 1972-83; group editor Inst. Mgmt. and Adminstrn., Inc., N.Y.C., 1993—. Mem. editl. adv. com. Tech. and Soc. publ., 1981-85. Property maintenance com. Borough of Fair Lawn, N.J., 1996-97; employment assistance response network St. Catharine's Ch., Glen Rock, N.J., 1993-99. Mem. N.G., 1963-69. Recipient Apolloneer award GE Co., 1966, Jesse H. Neal cert. of merit, 1977, 79, 83, Jesse H. Neal Editl. Achievement award, 1979, Disting. Alumni award for oustanding achievement N.J. Inst. Tech., 1979, Steuben Wise Old Owl award U.S. Steel Corp., 1981. Mem. Soc. Profl. Journalists, Nat. Assn. Purchasing Mgmt., Am. Soc. Engring. Mgmt., Am. Prodn. and Inventory Control Soc., Inc., Materials Handling and Mgmt. Soc., Coun. Logistics Mgmt., Inst. Indsl. Engrs., KC (grand knight 1967-68, trustee 1968-71), Sigma Delta Chi. Home: 40-22 Tierney Pl Fair Lawn NJ 07410-5141

MAZEYRAT, ROSELINE, pediatrician; b. Leuven, Belgium, Jan. 25, 1950; d. Herve and Zita (Grade) Nelissen; m. Roseline Nelissen; children: Chloe, Loic, Fleur, Quentin, Amaury. Doctorated in medicine, U. Louvain, 1974, specialization in paediatrics, 1979, specialization in allergology, 1995. Intern in pneumology Clinic Stluc, Namur, Belgium, 1975-76; intern in pediatrics Hosp. Necker/Sick Children, Paris, 1976-79, Kingston (U.K.) Hosp., 1981-82; pvt. practice in pediatrics and allergology Herblay, France, 1984—; cons. pediatric allergology Pontoise, France, 1995—, Hopital Necker/Enfant Malades, 1995—. Contbr. articles to profl. publs. Home: 21 rue de Chantepuits, 95220 Herblay France Office: Hopital Necker, 149 rue de Sevres, 75743 Paris France

MAZIASZ, PHILIP JAMES, metallurgical engineer, research scientist; b. Dearborn, Mich., Feb. 1951; s. Chester Walter and Frances Josephine Maziasz; m. Veronica Maziasz, May 12, 1973; children: Andrew, Matthew, Jonathan, Emily. BS in Materials and Metall. Engring., U. Mich., 1973, MS in Nuclear Engring., 1974; PhD in Metall. Engrnig., U. Tenn., Knoxville, 1984. Sr. devel. engr. Oak Ridge (Tenn.) Nat. Lab., 1974—; presenter sems. at various univs., conf., and nat. labs. in U.S., Japan, Eng., and Germany; mem. rev. panel NSF, 1998. Editor: Gas Turbine Materials Technology, 1999; co-editor: Iron and Nickel Aluminides, 1997; contbr. more than 175 articles to profl. jours.; 6 patents in field. Recipient R&D 100 award R&D Mag., 1990, Significant Contbn. award Am. Nuclear Soc., 1989, Materials, Sci. and Tech. award, 1977, grand prize metallography Am. Powder Metall. Inst., 1996. Fellow ASM Internat. (chair materials sci. divsn. 1995-98, tech. programming bd. mem.-at-large 1998-2000, nominating com. 2000, chair energy and utilities indsl. sector 2000—). Republican. Avocations: skiing, golf, bicycling, walking, photography. Office: Oak Ridge Nat Lab 1 Bethel Valley Rd Bldg 4500-S Rm-B254 Oak Ridge TN 37831

MAZIERE, CÉCILE, biochemistry educator; b. Ha Dong, Vietnam, Sept. 17, 1947; arrived in France, 1963; d. Mong Bich and Thi Lan (Vu) Nguyen; m. Jean-Claude Maziere, Dec. 23, 1972; children: Jean-Yves, Sylvie. PhD, U. Paris 6, 1973. Cert. med. rsch. Sr. lectr. U. Paris 6, 1987-97, U. Picardie, Amiens, France, 1997—. Contbr. articles to profl. jours. Avocation: creating gardens. Home: 36 rue Voiture, 80000 Amiens France Office: Hosp Nord, Lab Biochemistry, 80054 Amiens Cedex 01, France

MAZILU, PETRISOR, research scientist; b. Lapusata, Romania, June 29, 1942; s. Alexandru and Irina (Bulacu) M.; m. Magda Paula Savca, Feb. 26, 1966; children: Michael, Irina. PhD, U. Bucharest, Romania, 1969; DSc, Nat. Poly. Inst., Grenoble, France, 1994. Rschr., prin. rschr. Math. Inst., Bucharest, Romania, 1969-75; prin. rschr. Inst. Machine Tools, Bucharest, Romania, 1975-78, Nat. Inst. Sci. & Tech., Bucharest, Romania, 1978-79; rsch. scientist U. Bochum, Germany, 1980-83, Tech. U., Darmstadt, Germany, 1984—; vis. prof. Nat. Polytech Inst., Grenoble, France, 1986-87, U. Metz, France, 1990, 92, 93; vis. scientist Tech. U., Darmstadt, 1979-80, Mich. Tech. U., Houghton, 1983-84. Contbr. articles to profl. jours. Grantee German Rsch. Soc., 1994, 96. Fellow Internat. Soc. Interaction of Mechanics and Math., German Soc. Rheology. Romanian Orthodox. Office: Tech U, Petersenstr 30, D-64287 Darmstadt Germany

MAZO, EVSEY BORISOVITCH, urologist; b. Borisov, Belorussia, USSR, Oct. 29, 1931; s. Boris Evseevitch and Mariya Iakovlevna (Krigman) M.; m. Edelina Michailovna Rabinovitch, July 17, 1956; 1 child, Vsevolod Evseevitch. Doctorate, 2nd Med. Inst., Moscow, 1955, Cand. of Med. Scis., 1973, MD, 1983. Diplomate in Medicine. Resident in urology 2nd Med. Inst., Moscow, 1960, sr. scientific employee, asst., sr. lectr., to prof., 1966-90; urologist City Hosp. # 1, Moscow, 1960-64; head Urol. Clinic Russian State Med. U., Moscow, 1990—. Co-author: Urology, 1977; contbr. articles to profl. jours. and monographs. Decorated Order of Chevalier, Prince Sianuk, Phnom-Pen, Cambodia, 1966, Laureate of State prize of USSR, Govt. USSR, Moscow, 1985, Star of Vernadsky award Internat. Interacademic Assn. Mem. Am. Urol. Assn. (corr.), Russian Football Club, Pub. Com. of Automobile Police. Avocations: books, automobiles, dogs, football. Fax: 095-952-4345. Home: Malaya Gruzinskaya 28-25, 123557 Moscow Russia Office: Russian State Med Univ, Ostrovitianova str 1, 117513 Moscow Russia

MAZO, MARK ELLIOTT, lawyer; b. Phila., Jan. 12, 1950; s. Earl and Rita (Vane) M.; m. Fern Rosalyn Litman, Aug. 19, 1973; children: Samantha Lauren, Dana Suzanne, Ross Elliott, Courtney Litman. AB, Princeton U., 1971; JD, Harvard U., 1974. Bar: D.C. 1975, U.S. Dist. Ct. D.C. 1975, U.S. Claims Ct. 1975, U.S. Ct. Appeals (D.C. cir.) 1976, U.S. Supreme Ct. 1979. Ptnr. Hogan & Hartson, L.L.P., Washington and Paris, 1990—. Contbr. articles to profl. jours. White House intern Exec. Office of Pres., Washington, 1972. Capt. USAR, 1971-79. Mem. ABA, Harvard Law Sch. Assn., D.C. Bar Assn., Columbia Country Club, Princeton Club (N.Y.C.), Colonial Club, City Club, Phi Beta Kappa. Republican. Home: 3719 Cardiff Rd Chevy Chase MD 20815-5943 Office: Hogan & Hartson LLP 555 13th St NW Ste 800E Washington DC 20004-1161 Office: Hogan & Hartson Cariddi Mee Rue, 12 rue de la Paix, 75002 Paris France

MAZOR, DAVID S., film distribution company executive; b. Redwood City, Calif., June 21, 1958; s. Lester J. and Sondra R. (Slipowitz) M.; m. Kathleen Michelle Mathews, Apr. 23, 1988; children: Kerry, Kacie. BA, Evergreen State Coll., 1980. Film booker Western Mass. Theatres, Springfield, Mass., 1980-82; dir. film svcs. Atlantic Releasing Corp., N.Y.C., 1983-85; pres. ASA Communications, Inc., Northampton, Mass., 1985-89, No. Arts Entertainment, Inc., Williamsburg, Mass., 1990—; pres. Buyers Assn. Group, Inc. Bd. dirs. Northampton Film Festival, 1998—, Martial Arts Buyers Assn.; Mass. state dir. Amateur Athletic Union Tae Kwon Do, 1998—. Mem. Motion Picture Bookers Club. Avocations: chess, skiing, sailing, Tae Kwon Do (black belt). Office: Northern Arts Entertainment Northern Arts Studios Williamsburg MA 01096

MAZPARROTE, ERDOCIAIN SERAFIN, biological text editor; b. Pitillas, Spain, Oct. 12, 1932; s. Constantino Mazparrote and Julia Erdociain; m. Rosa Isabelina Julia Vazquez, May 20, 1967; children: Julio Javier, Angel-Serafin, Javier Antonio, Carlos José. Lic. in biology, U. Paris, 1967-68. Chief MAC Lab., Cumaná, Venezuela, 1965-69; gerente LaSalle Found., Caracas, Venezuela, 1969-79; pres. Editorial Biosfera, Caracas, Venezuela, 1979—. Author: Textos de Biologia Para la Enseñanza, edits. 4-9, Fundamentos de Ecologia, 1985, Salvemos La Tierra, 1995. Recipient medal for meritorious work, 1987. Mem. Venezuelan Editors assn. (v.p. 1994-96). Avocation: swimming. Home: Apt 50634, Av Chulavista Qta Isamar, 1050-A Caracas Venezuela Office: Editorial Biosfera 50634, Av Chama Colinas de Bello, 1050-A Caracas Venezuela

MAZRUI, ALI AL'AMIN, political science educator, researcher; b. Mombasa, Kenya, Feb. 24, 1933; came to U.S., 1960; s. Al'Amin Ali and Safia (Suleiman) M.; m. Molly Vickerman, 1962 (div. 1982); children: Jamal, Al'Amin, Kim Abubakar; m. Pauline Uti, Oct. 1991; children: Farid Chinedu, Harith Ekenechukwu. BA with distinction, U. Manchester, Eng., 1960; MA, Columbia U., 1961; DPhil, Oxford U., 1966. Lectr. Makerere U., Kampala, Uganda, 1963-65, prof. polit. sci., head dept. polit. sci., 1965-73; dean faculty social scis. Faculty Social Scis., Makerere U., Kampala, Uganda, 1967-69; prof. polit. sci. U. Mich., Ann Arbor, 1974-91, prof. Ctr. Afroam. and African Studies, dept. polit. sci., 1974-91; Andrew D. White prof.-at-large Cornell U., Ithaca, 1986-92; research prof. polit. sci. U. Jos, Nigeria, 1981-86; Albert Schweitzer prof. humanities SUNY, Binghamton, 1989—; Albert Luthuli prof.-at-large U. Jos (Nigeria), 1991—; sr. scholar, Andrew D. White prof.-at-large emeritus Cornell U, Ithaca, 1992—; dir. Inst. Global Cultural Studies SUNY, Binghamton, 1991—; Ibn Khaldun prof.-at-large Sch. Islamic and Social Scis., Leesburg, Va., 1997—; Reith lectr. BBC, London, 1979; vis. prof. various univs. including U. London, U. Chgo., Oxford U., U. Pa., Ohio State U., Manchester U., Harvard U., Nairobi U., UCLA, Northwestern U., U. Singapore, Colgate Coll., U. Australia, Stanford U., U. Cairo, Sussex U., U. Leeds, Internat. Islamic U., Malaysia, 1965—; mem. bank's coun. African advisers, World Bank, Washington, 1988-91; Walter Rodney disting. prof. U. Guyana, Georgetown, 1997-98. Author: Towards A Pax Africana: A Study of Ideology and Ambition, 1967, The Anglo-African Commonwealth: Political Friction and Cultural Fusion, 1967, On Heroes and Uhuru-Worship: Essays on Independent Africa, 1967, Violence and Thought: Essays on Social Tensions in Africa, 1969, Cultural Engineering and Nation-Building in East Africa, 1972, World Culture and the Black Experience, 1974, The Political Sociology of the English Language: An African Perspective, 1975, Soldiers and Kinsmen in Uganda: The Making of a Military Ethnocracy, 1975; co-editor: (with Robert I. Rotberg) Protest and Power in Black Africa, 1970, (with Hasu Patel) Africa in World Affairs: The Next Thirty Years, 1973; editor: The Warrior Tradition in Modern Africa, 1978, Africa since 1935 Volume III Unesco General History of Africa, 1973-93, (with Alamin M. Mazrui) The Political Culture of Language: Swahili, Society and the State, 1996—, (with Alamin M. Mazrui) The Power of Babel: Language and Governance in Africa's Experience, 1998; sr. editor: (with T.K. Levine) The Africans: A Reader, 1986; author: The Trial of Christopher Okigbo, 1971, A World Federation of Cultures: An African Perspective, 1976; Africa's International Relations: The Diplomacy of Dependency and Change, 1977, Political Values and the Educated Class in Africa, 1978, The African Condition: A Political Diagnosis, 1980, (with Michael Tidy) Nationalism and New States in Africa, From About 1935 to the Present, 1984; narrator, presenter: The Africans: A Triple Heritage, 1986, Cultural Forces in World Politics, 1990; mem. editl. bd. various profl. jours., 1963—; contbr. articles to profl. publs. Fellow Ctr for Advanced Study in Behavioral Scis., Palo Alto, Calif., 1972-73; sr. fellow

Hoover Instn. on War, Revolution and Peace, Stanford, Calif., 1973-74, Mich. Soc. Fellows, 1978-82. Fellow Internat. Assn. Mid. Ea. Studies, Ghana Acad. Arts and Scis. (hon.); mem. African Studies Assn. (exec. bd. 1975-80, pres. 1978-79, Disting. Africans award 1995), Internat. Congress African Studies (v.p. 1978-85), Internat. Polit. Sci. Assn. (v.p. 1970-73), World Order Models Project (dir. African sect. 1968-83), Royal African Soc. (v.p.), Royal Commonwealth Soc., United Kenya Club (Nairobi), Athenaeum Club (London). Office: SUNY Inst Global Cultural Studies Off Schweitzer Chair PO Box 6000 Binghamton NY 13902-6000

MAZUMDAR, RAVI RASENDRA, engineering and mathematics educator; b. Bangalore, India, Apr. 17, 1955; naturalized Can. citizen, 1993; s. Rasendra Indulal and Yamini Kulinchandra (Majmudar) M.; m. Catherine Patricia Rosenberg; children: Claire, Eric. B in Tech., Indian Inst. Tech., Bombay, 1977; MSc, DIC, Imperial Coll., London, 1978; PhD, UCLA, 1983. Mem. tech. staff AT&T Bell Labs., Holmdel, N.J., 1983; vis. asst. prof. UCLA, 1983-84; vis. docent U. Twente, The Netherlands, 1984-85; asst. prof. elec. engring. Columbia U., N.Y.C., 1985-88; prof. Nat. Inst. Sci. Rsch., Montreal, Que., Can., 1988-97; prof. math. U. Essex, Colchester, Eng., 1996-99; prof. Sch. Elec. and Computer Engring. Purdue U., West Lafayette, Ind., 1999—; vis. prof. Indian Inst. Sci., Bangalore, 1994-95, Nat. Superior Sch. Telecom., Paris, 1995; invited prof. elec. engring. McGill U., Montreal, 1988-96; sci. counselor CNET, France Telecom., Lannion, 1994-97. Contbr. over 75 articles to profl. publs. Fellow Royal Statis. Soc; mem. IEEE (sr.), Soc. Indsl. and Applied Math., Bangalore Club. Avocations: reading, travel, squash, bridge. Office: Purdue U Sch Elec and Computer Engrg West Lafayette IN 47907

MAZUMDER, JYOTIRMOY, mechanical and industrial engineering educator; b. Calcutta, India, July 9, 1951; came to U.S., 1978; s. Jitendra Mohan and Gouri (Sen) M.; m. Aparajita, June 17, 1982; children: Debashis, Debayan. B in Engring., Calcutta U., 1973; diploma, PhD, Imperial Coll., London U., 1978. Rsch. scientist U. So. Calif., L.A., 1978-80; asst. prof. mechanical and indsl. engring. U. Ill., Urbana, 1980-84, assoc. prof., 1984-88, prof., 1988-96, co-dir. ctr. laser aided materials processing, 1990-96; Robert H. Lurie Prof. Engring. U. Mich., Ann Arbor, 1996—, dir. ctr. laser aided intelligent mfg., 1996—; co-dir. ctr. laser aided material processing U. Ill., 1990-96; dir. Quantum Laser Corp., Edison, N.J., 1982-89; pres. Laser Scis., Inc., Urbana, 1988—; dir., CEO POM Inc., Plymouth, Mich.; vis. scholar physics dept. Stanford (Calif.) U., 1990. Author: (with others) Laser Welding; editor and co-editor more than 9 books including co-editor: Laser Materials Processing, 1984, 88; more than 250 technical papers; contbr. numerous articles to profl. jours. Fellow Am. Soc. of Metals and Laser Inst. of Am. (life, sr. editor Jour. Laser Application); mem. Am. Inst. Metallurgical Engrs. (phys. mets. com. 1980—), Optical Soc. Am. Achievements include patent: weld pool visualization system for measurement of free surface deformation, apparatus and method for monitoring and controlling multi-layer cladding. Office: U Mich Dept Mech Engring & Mechs 2041 GG Brown Ann Arbor MI 48109-2125

MAZUMDER, MOTAHARUL KABIR, electrical engineer, researcher; b. Rakasherpar, Comilla, Bangladesh, Aug. 31, 1953; s. Ashraf Uddin and Ambiya (Khaton) M.; m. Hosne Jaha Ferdous Ara, June 3, 1983; children: Nabila Kabir, Yasir Kabir. BS, Jahangir Nagar U., Savar, Bangladesh, 1976, MS, 1977; M.Engring., Tohoku U., Sendai, Japan, 1988, D.Engring., 1991. Rsch. fellow Jahangir Nagar U., Savar, 1978-79; lectr. physics Chittagong (Bangladesh) U., 1979-82, asst. prof. physics, 1982-94; vis. rsch. engr. Mitsubishi, Hyogo, Japan, 1992—. Contbr. articles to profl. jours. Mem. IEEE, Japan Soc. Applied Physics. Avocations: reading, badminton, football. Home: Village Rakasher Par, 3500 Lalmai Bazar Comilla, Bangladesh Office: Mitsubishi Elec Corp, ULSI Lab 4-1 Mizuhara, Itami 664-8641, Japan

MAZUR, LEONARD L., pharmaceutical company executive; b. Ansbach, Germany, Jan. 23, 1945; came to U.S., 1949; s. Walter and Maria (Zatwarnitsky) M.; m. Helena Maria Olijnyk, Nov. 1966; children: Maria, Michael, Irene. BA, Temple U., 1968, MBA, 1975. Mktg. mgr. Cooper Labs., Inc., Fairfield, N.J. and Palo Alto, Calif., 1971-81; dir. product mgmt. Knoll Pharm. Corp. divsn. BASF, Whippany, N.J., 1981-84; v.p. ICN Pharm. Corp., Costa Mesa, Calif., 1984-88; pres., COO Chantal Pharm. Corp., L.A., 1988-89; exec. v.p. Medicis Pharm. Corp., N.Y.C., 1989-93; vice chmn. Cabot Labs., Inc., N.Y.C., 1994-96; chmn., CEO Genesis Pharm., Inc., Morristown, N.J., 1996—; ptnr. Mazier Ptnrs. LLC, Morristown, N.J., 1995—. Patentee in field. Mem. adv. bd. Manor Jr. Coll., Jenkintown, Pa., 1972-78; ind. observer Referendum for Independence, Ukraine, 1991. Roman Catholic. Office: Genesis Pharm Inc 44 Whippany Rd Morristown NJ 07960-4558

MAZUR, PETER, cell physiologist, cryobiologist; b. N.Y.C., Mar. 3, 1928; s. Paul M. and Adolphia (Kaske) M.; m. Drusilla Stevens, May 28, 1953 (dec. May 1982); 1 child, Timothy Stevens; m. Sara Jo Bolling, June 16, 1984. AB magna cum laude, Harvard U., 1949, PhD, 1953; DSc (hon.), Wilson Coll., 1998. NSF postdoctoral fellow Princeton (N.J.) U., 1957-59; rsch. staff biology divsn. Oak Ridge Nat. Lab., 1959-98; group leader fundamental and applied cryobiology Oak Ridge Nat. Lab., 1966-98, sci. dir. biophysics and cell physiology, biology div., 1974-75, corporate fellow, 1985; chmn. ORNL Corp. Fellows Coun., 1995-96; mem. vis. com. biology Harvard U. Bd. Overseers 1972-77; rsch. prof. dept. biochem. and cellular and molecular biology U. Tenn., 1998—; mem. Space Sci. Bd. of Nat. Acad., 1975-77; Sigma Xi nat. lectr., 1980. Trustee Wilson Coll., Pa., 1984-93; bd. dirs. Meth. Hosp. Found., Oak Ridge, 1997—. Served to capt. USAF, 1953-57. Recipient author of yr. awrad Martin-Marietta Energy Sys., 1985, disting. svc. award Am. Assn. Tissue Banks, 1993, rsch. & devel. 100 award R&D Mag., 1993; Lalor fellow Harvard U., 1952, John Harvard fellow, 1951. Fellow AAAS; mem. Soc. Cryobiology (pres. 1973-74, bd. govs. 1979-96), Rotary Club Oak Ridge, Phi Beta Kappa, Cosmos Club (Washington). Current work includes cryobiology and the mechanisms of freezing injury in living cells and tissues. Subspecialties are cell biology and biophysics. Home: 125 Westlook Cir Oak Ridge TN 37830-3856 Office: Dept of Biochemistry and Cellular and Molecular Biology M407 Walters Life Sci Bldg Knoxville TN 37996-0001

MAZURANIC, IVICA, physician; b. Rijeka, Croatia, Dec. 13, 1953; s. Ivan and Karmen (Franciskovic) M.; m. Marija Miloslavic, Nov. 4, 1980; children: Ana, Anton. MD, U. Zagreb, Croatia, 1979; postgrad., U. Zagreb, 1984-85. Residency in pulmoary medicine Univ. Hosp. "Jordanovac", Zagreb, 1983-87; residency in radiology Univ. Clin. Hosp. "Rebro", U. Hos. "Jordanovac", Zagreb, 1989-92. Contbr. articles to profl. jours. Mem. Croatian Med. Soc., Croatian Thoracic Soc., Croatian Radiology Soc., European Radiology Soc., N.Y. Acad. Scis. Avocations: soccer, tennis, skiing, golf.

MAZURKIEWICZ, BOLESLAW KAZIMIERZ, university educator; b. Koscierzyna, Gdansk, Poland, May 9, 1931; s. Stanislaw and Bronislawa (Wenta) M.; m. Krystyna Barbara Kamrei, Oct. 9, 1955; 1 child, Maria. MS, Tech. U. Gdansk, 1956, PhD, 1964, DS, 1968; Dr HC, Tech. U., St. Petersburg, Russia, 1989, Tech. U., Odessa, Ukraina, 1995, Navy Acad., Gdynia, Poland, 1997, U. St. Petersburg, Russia, 1998, U. Fridericiana, Karlsruhe, Germany, 1998, Technical U. Szczecin (Poland), 1999. Designer Design Offices, Gdansk, 1954-60; rschr. Tech. U., Gdansk, 1960-69, asst. prof., 1969-80, prof., 1980—, rector, 1986-90, dept. head, 1981—; cons. Polish Shipbldg. Orgn., Gdansk, 1960—; engr. Shipyard Gdynia, Poland, 1973-77. Author: (book) Design and Construction of Dry Docks, 1980 (1st prize Ministry of Edn. 1982). Pres. Polish Yachting Assn., Gdansk, 1964-92, Mus. for Ship Assn., Gdynia, 1982—; chmn. Maritime Inst., Gdansk, 1995—, Inst. Hydroengring., Polish Acad. Scis., 1999—. Decorated Polish Nat. Orders (four times), Polish Pres., Warsaw, 1973-94. Mem. Internat. Assn. of Univs. (adminstrv bd. 1990—). Avocation: sailing. Home: ul Syrokomli 7, 81-439 Gdynia Poland

MAZ'YA, VLADIMIR G., mathematician, educator; b. Leningrad, USSR, Dec. 31, 1937; arrived in Sweden, 1990; m. Tatyana Shaposhnikova. Honours diploma in Math. and Mechanics, Leningrad U., 1960; Doctor Honoris Causa, U. Rostock, Germany, 1990. Jr. rschr. Inst. Math. and Mechanics Leningrad U., 1960-64, sr. rschr., 1964-86; lectr. Leningrad Shipbuilding Inst., 1968-72, prof., 1971; with Leningrad Inst. Engring. Studies, 1986-90; prof. U. Linköping, Sweden, 1990—. Author: Sobolev Spaces, 1985, (with Gelman) Abschätzungen für Differentialoperatoren im Halbraum, 1981, (with Shaposhnikova) Theory of Multipliers in Spaces of Differentiable Functions, 1985, (with Nazarov and Plamenevski) Asymptotische Theorie Elliptischer Randwertaufgaben in Singular Gestörten Gebieten, 1991, 2000, (with Shaposhnikova) Jacques Hadamard, a Universal Mathematician, 1998, (with Kozlov) Theory of a Higher Order Sturm-Liouville Equation, 1997, (with Kozlov and Rossmann) Elliptic Boundary Value Problems in Domains with Point Singularities, 1997, Spectral Problems Connected with Corner Singularities of Solutions to Elliptic Equations, 2000, (with Poborchi) Differentiable Functions on Bad Domains, 1998, (with Kozlov) Differential Equations with Operator Coefficients, 1999, (with Kozlov and Movchan) Asymptotic Analysis of Fields in Multi-Structures, 1999. Recipient prize Leningrad Math. Soc., 1965, Alexander von Humboldt prize 2000. Office: U Linköping, Math Inst, S-58183 Linköping Sweden

MÁZZAFERO, MARTIN VICENTE ENRIQUE, public health administrator, researcher; b. Buenos Aires, May 6, 1931; s. Vicente Antonio Mazzáfero and Ana Martin. MD, U. Buenos Aires, 1958; MPH, U. Chile, 1959; PhD, U. Buenos Aires, 1971. Jefe guardia Hosp. de Infecciosas F. J. Muñiz, Buenos Aires, 1960-62, jefe servicio cuidados intensivos, 1962-70; dir. hosp. gen. J. M. Ramos Mejia, Buenos Aires, 1970-74; chmn. pub. health dept. faculty of medicine U. Buenos Aires, 1982—, dir. Sch. Pub. Health, 1988—, dir. Inst. Hygiene and Social Medicine, 1996—; prof. Escuela Nacional de Sanidad, Madrid, 1999-2000; vis. prof. faculty of medicine U. Santiago de Compostela, Spain, 1990, 91, 95, 96, 97, 98; corr. acad. Real Acad. de Cirugia y Medicina, Galicia, Spain, 1995; mem. study team EPI-AIM, Commn. of European Commtys., 1994; mem. WHO Expert Adv. Panel on Health Situation and Trend Assessment, WHO/UN, 1989-95. Author: (books) Epidemiologia Fundamental y Aplicada, 1976, Infecciones Hospitalarias, 1978, Medicina en Salud Publica, 1994; editor: Revista del Instituto de Higiene y Medicina Social, 1997—. Recipient 1st Meml. prize J. J. Montes de Oca Medicine Nat. Acad. Hosp. Infections, 1978, 79, 80. Mem. Internat. Epidemiol. Assn., Argentine Med. Assn. (pres. sociedad investigaciones epidemiologicas en salud 1997-98, 1st Meml. prize 1970-71), Asociacion Latino Americana y del Caribe de Educacion en Salud Publica (rep. regional de paises del conosur 1997—), Guyaquil Hosp. Pub. Health Ministry (hon.), Vets. Rugbiers Hindu Club. Roman Catholic. Avocations: rugby, football. Home: Juncal 2340 7oB, 1125 Buenos Aires Argentina Office: U Buenos Aires, Juncal 2340 7-B Cap Fed, 1125 Buenos Aires Argentina

MAZZARELLA, JAMES KEVIN, business administration educator; b. Phila., Sept. 22, 1955; s. Samuel Charles and Rosemary C. (Queenan) M. BA, St. Joseph's U., 1977; MBA, La Salle U., 1981; MA, Temple U., 1987; PhD, Columbia-Pacific U., 1987; DBA, Pacific-Western U., 1988; cert. in acctg., Thomas Edison State Coll., 1994; BS, SUNY, 1996. Cert. mgmt. acct.; cert. in fin. mgmt. Asst. mgr. Olney Oil & Burner Co., Phila., 1977-80; data processing Craig Fuel Co., Phila., 1980-84; supr. M. Kelley Son's Inc., Phila., 1984-86; adj. instr. Holy Family Coll., Phila., 1987-88, instr., 1989, asst. prof., 1989—; adj. instr. Phila. (Pa.) Coll. Textiles, 1984-86, La Salle U., Phila., 1985—, Rosemont (Pa.) Coll., 1988-91. Mem. Acad. Fin. Svcs., Am. Econs. Assn., Am. Fin. Assn., Am. Statis. Assn., Nat. Assn. Bus. Econs., Am. Risk and Ins. Assn., Inst. Mgmt. Accts., Math. Assn. Am., Fin. Mgmt. Assn., Prodn. and Ops. Mgmt. Soc., Midwest Fin. Assn., Western Econs. Assn. Internat., Ea. Econ. Assn., Ea. Fin. Assn., Am. Mgmt. Assn., So. Fin. Assn., Multinat. Fin. Soc., Am. Math. Soc., Am. Law and Econs. Assn., Nat. Coun. Tchrs. Math. Roman Catholic. Home: 5101 N Fairhill St Philadelphia PA 19120-3126 Office: Holy Family College Grant & Frankford Ave Philadelphia PA 19114

MAZZARELLA, ROSEMARY LOUISE, business administration executive; b. Phila., Aug. 20, 1959; d. Samuel Charles and Rosemarie Claire Mazzarella. BA, La Salle U., 1985, MS in Orgnl. Devel. & Mgmt., 1991. Materials mgmt. exec. Sun Refining & Mktg. Co., Phila., 1979-91; purchasing asst. Children's Seashore House, Phila., 1992-94; adminstr. FMC Corp., Phila., 1994-99, Aramark Corp., Phila., 2000—. Mem. Assn. Behavior Analysis (sustaining), Alpha Sigma Lambda.

MAZZEO, DANIEL PATRICK, aerospace engineer, aviation consultant; b. N.Y.C., Apr. 18, 1949; s. Gennaro and Marie Grace (Mazzei) M.; m. Belva Faye Musick, Sept. 10, 1977; children: Gennaro, Jina Marie. BS in Aerospace Engring., Poly. Inst. Bklyn., 1971; grad. in Aviation Safety, U.S. Naval Postgrad. Sch., Monterey, Calif., 1981. Commd. ensign USN, 1969, advanced through grades to comdr., 1982, aviator, 1969-91; aviation program mgr. BDI Engring., Pensacola, Fla., 1991-95; aviation project mgr. DH Engrs., Sarasota, Fla., 1995-99; pres., CEO Aerocomm Group, Pensacola, Fla., 1999—; airline transport pilot rating FAA, 1979; mem. State Aviation Planning Process, Fla., 1990—; completed over 150 major airport improvement projects. Contbr. articles to profl. jours. Tech. advisor in aviation County Govt., Escambia, Fla., 1985, Santa Rosa, Fla., 1987, Tallahassee, Fla., 1994. Decorated Navy commendation medal, Navy expdn. medal, Def. Svc. medal with one bronze star; recipient Sci. grant N.Y.C., 1965, 68, Innovative Environmental award FAA, 1997, Airport of the Year award Fla. Dept. Transp., 1997. Mem. ASCE (section pres.), AIAA, Soc. Am. Mil. Engrs., Aircraft Owners and Pilots Assn. (advisor 1997). Achievements include invention of electrophotographic imaging machine and invention of the respirograph employed in medical research. Home: PO Box 614 Gulf Breeze FL 32562-0614 Office: Aerocomm Group Pensacola FL 32502

MAZZEO, PIETRO, chemistry educator; b. Rome, Lazio, June 4, 1935; s. Benedetto and Maria Cristina (Rausa) M.; m. Anna Farina, Sept. 10, 1966; children: Marco, Fabio. Chemistry Degree, U. Rome, 1960, Pharmacy Degree, 1967. Assoc. prof. U. Rome, 1969-80; prof. U. Bari, Italy, 1980-84; prof. dept. chemistry U. L'Aquila, Coppito, Italy, 1984—; nat. coord. Pharm. Analysis Rsch. Group, 1982-96. Fellow Italian Chem. Soc. Avocations: classical music, painting, gardening. Home: Via Urbino 27, 00182 Rome Italy Office: U L'Aquila Dept Chemistry, Via Vetoio, 67010 Coppito L'Aquila, Italy

MAZZER, MAURIZIO, statistician, researcher; b. Rome, Apr. 9, 1956; s. Fulvio Mazzer and Valeria Cerroni; m. Paola Passerini, June 17, 1989. Degree in physics, "La Sapienza", Rome, 1978. Physicist Ente Nazionale Energie Alternative, Rome, 1979-80; rschr. Centro Sviluppo Materiali, Rome, 1980-89; sr. statistician Tex. Instruments, Avezzano, Italy, 1989—. Inventor in field; contbr. articles to tech. jours. and conf. procs. Office: Micron Tech Italia, Via Pacinotti 5, I-67051 Avezzano Italy

MAZZILLI, ROSLYN, sculptor; b. Bklyn., July 23, 1941; d. Sol and Minna (Heller) Krawatsky; m. Ron Mazzilli (div. 1978); children: Darrin, Andrew; m. Gregg Melvin, Dec. 3, 1988. BA in Sculpture, San Jose State U., 1977, MA in Sculpture, 1981. lectr. AAUW, Sacramento, 1984, Civic Arts Ctr., Walnut Creek, Calif., 1985, San Mateo (Calif.) Art Ctr., 1987, Mercer Island (Wash.) ARt Ctr., 1994, San Jose (Calif.) State U., 1996. Executed sculptures at Hyatt Regency, West Houston, Tex., 1983, Spectrum Ctr., Dallas, 1983, Pleasant Hill (Calif.) Cmty. Ctr., 1984, Chapman Coll., Orange, Calif., 1985, Calif. Plz., Walnut Creek, 1986, Koll Devel. Corp., San Jose, 1987, Belmont (Calif.) CalTrain Sta., 1987, Oakland (Calif.) City Ctr., 1988, Cucamonga Calif. Town Ctr., 1990, Emerson Elec. Corp., St. Louis, 1990, City of Mercer Island, 1993. others. Grantee Calif. Coun. for Arts, 1986. Mem. Pacific Rim Sculptors Group, Internat. Sculptors, Women's Caucus for Arts. Home: PO Box 609 Moss Beach CA 94038-0609

MAZZIO-MOORE, JOAN L., radiology educator, physician; b. Belmont, Mass., Oct. 26, 1935; d. Frank Joseph and Maria L. Mazzio; children: James Thomas, Edwin Stuart. BA in Chemistry and Theology, Emmanuel Coll., 1957; MA in Genetics and Physiology, Mass. Wellesley Coll., 1961; PhD in Genetics, Bryn Mawr (Pa.) Coll., 1964; MD, Phila. Coll. of Medicine, 1977, MSc in Radiology, 1981. Instr. in biochemistry Gwynedd Mercy Coll., Springhouse, Pa., 1963-65; instr. in genetics Holy Family Coll., Phila., 1965-66; instr. in anatomy Phila. Coll. of Medicine, 1971-77, tchr., 1973-77, asst. prof., 1977-84; prof. W.Va. Sch. of Medicine, 1984—; rotating intern Phila. Coll. of Medicine Hosp., 1977-78, resident in radiology, 1978-81; lt. col. USAR, 1984—; prof. W.Va. Sch. of Medicine, Lewisburg, 1984—. Author: (with Dr. DiVirgilito) Essentials of Neuropathology, 1974. Lector St. Ann's Cath. Ch., Phoenixville, Pa., 1981-84; treas. Hist. Soc. of Frankford, Phila., 1968-75, Sch. Mother's Assn., Devon (Pa.) Prep., 1980-81. Lt. col. U.S. Army Med. Corps, 1992. Mem. AAUP, Am. Acad. Family Physicians, Am. Assn. Women Radiologists, Am. Med. Women's Assn., Am. Osteo. Coll. of Radiology, Am. Soc. Clin. Oncology, Am. Soc. Therapeutic Readiologists, Hist. Soc. of Lewisburg (life), Pa. Osteo. Med. Assn., Pa. Osteo. Gen. Practitioner's Soc., Radiol. Soc. N.Am., Radiation Rsch. Soc., Res. Officers Assn. (life), W.Va. Soc. Osteo. Medicine, Greenbrier Hike and Bike Trail. Fax: 304-497-2752. E-mail: jmoore@wvsom.edu. Home: RR 1 Box 123 Frankford WV 24938 Office: WVa Sch of Medicine 400 N Lee St Lewisburg WV 24901-1128

MAZZOLENIS, DANIEL ALEJANDRO, pharmaceutical executive, hematologist; b. La Plata, Argentina, Mar. 19, 1961; s. Juan José and Mabel Libia (Martinez) M.; m. María Inés Noli, Apr. 26, 1991; 1 child, María Victoria. MD, U. La Plata (Argentina), Buenos Aires, 1984; postgrad., U. de CEMA, Buenos Aires, 1999-2000; M in Pharmacology, U. Buenos Aires, 2000. Cert. Bd. Hematology. Resident in internal medicine Sanatorio Güemes, Buenos Aires, 1985-89, staff hematologist, 1991-93; resident in hematology Hosp. Clínicas, Buenos Aires, 1989-91; staff hematologist Fundación Favaloro, Buenos Aires, 1992-95; med. advisor Chemotechnica Sintyal, Buenos Aires, 1995-96; med. dir. Sintyal Otsuka Pharm. S.A., Buenos Aires, 1996-98; cons. pharms. and biomed. devices, 1998-2000; project mgr. EBCT-GBA, Buenos Aires, 1998-2000; product mgr. Novo Nordisk Pharma Argentina S.A., Buenos Aires, 2000—. Fellow AHA, Argentine Hematol. Soc., Internat. Soc. Thrombosis and Haemostasis. E-mail: dmaz@novo.dk. Office: Nova Nordisk 4th Fl Off 402, Alicia Moreau de Justo 1960, 1107 Buenos Aires Argentina

MAZZOTTI, MASSIMO, history of science educator, consultant; b. Milan, Italy, Oct. 27, 1968. Laurea, State U., Milan, 1994; PhD, U. Edinburgh, 1999. Tchr. U. Edinburgh, 1997-99; rsch. fellow Dibner Inst. for History of Sci. and Tech., MIT, Cambridge, Mass., 1999—; cons. various librs. and publishers, 1996—. Contbr. articles to profl. jours. Mem. History of Sci. Soc., Brit. Soc. for History of Sci., Soc. for Social Study of Sci. Office: Dibner Inst/MIT, E-56-100 38 Memorial Dr Cambridge MA 02142-1347

MAZZUCCHELLI, TREVOR GORDON, psychologist; b. Kalgoorlie, WA, Australia, July 11, 1970; s. Richard Harold and Brenda Gordon (Sloane) M. BA with honors, U. Western Australia, Perth, 1992, M in Clin. Psychology, 1994. Registered clin. psychologist Registration Bd. Western Australia. Clin. psychologist Disability Svcs. Commn., Perth, 1994-96, specialist clin. psychologist, 1996—. Author (videotape) Feel Safe Video, 1998; contbr. chpt. to book. Mem. APA (fgn. affiliate), Australian Assn. Cognitive and Behavior Therapy (sec. 1997-98, pres. 1999—), Australian Psychol. Soc. Avocations: distance running, camping, hiking, art, philosophy. Office: Disability Svcs Commn, 8 Davidson Terr, Joondalup WA 6027, Australia

MBADUGHA, LORETTA NKEIRUKA AKOSA, social services administrator, consultant; b. Onitsha, Anambara, Nigeria, Dec. 10, 1957; d. James and Sylvia O. (Asika) Akosa; m. Christian Mbadugha; children: Kristen Ogechi, Kyle Kelechi, Kelsey Odinaka. Assoc., Langham Secretarial Coll., London, 1978; BS, Tex. So. U., Houston, 1981, MS, 1982; PhD, U. New Orleans, 2000. Program analyst Tex. So. U., Houston, 1982-84; sanitarian City of Houston Health Dept., 1984-85; adj. faculty So. U., New Orleans, 1981-90; asst. to exec. dir. YWCA, New Orleans, 1984-93; family rep. Jefferson Parish Human Svcs. Authority, New Orleans, 1993-94; CEO Profl. Family Support Svcs., New Orleans, 1994—; cons., founder, bd. mem. Camelot Providers, New Orleans, 1987—; bd. mem. United Svcs. AIDS Found., 1990-92; trainer Coun. for Early Childhood Profl. Recognition, 1987—; cons., trainer on child devel. State of La., 1987-89. Sec. Chapel of Praise, 1997. Recipient Mayoral Cert. of Merit, New Orleans, 1991; Grace Hodge fellow YWCA, 1992. Mem. ACA, Nigeria Ebony Club for Women (pres. 1995). Home: 7141 Westhaven Rd New Orleans LA 70126-2132 Office: 7041 Real Ln New Orleans LA 70127

MBEKI, THABO, South African government official; b. Idutywa, Transkei, June 18, 1942; s. Govan and Epainette Mbeki; m. Zanele Mbeki. Degree in econs., U. London, 1961-62; MA in Econs., U. Sussex, 1966. Youth organizer African Nat. Congress, Johannesburg, South Africa, 1961-62; ofcl. African Nat. Congress, London, 1967-70; asst. sec. revolutionary coun. African Nat. Congress, 1971-72; acting rep. African Nat. Congress, Swaziland, 1975-76; mem. nat. exec. com. African Nat. Congress, 1975—; rep. African Nat. Congress, Nigeria, 1976-78; polit. sec. office of pres. African Nat. Congress, dir. info. and publicity, sec. presdl. affairs, 1984-89, head dept. internat. affairs, 1989—; exec. dep. pres. South Africa, 1994-98; state pres., 1999—; leader African Nat. Congress delegation Dakar Talks with IDASA, 1987; African Nat. Congress del. on Talks about Talks with South African Govt., 1990; mem. polit. and mil. coun. African Nat. Congress, mem. nat. working com.; African Nat. Congress rep. Nat. Peace Com.; mem. transitional arrangements working group Conv. Dem. South Africa. Office: Office of Pres, Union Bldgs Pvt Bag X1000, Pretoria 0001, South Africa*

MBOMA, PATRICK, soccer player; b. Cameroon, Nov. 15, 1970. Formerly with Paris St. Germain, also Metz; forward Gamba Osaka, Japan, Cagliari, Italy, 1998-2000, Parma, 2000. Address: Ennio Tardini, Viale Partigiani d Italia, 43100 Parma Italy*

MBOUMBOU-MIYAKOU, ANTOINE, Gabon government official; b. Mayumba, Gabon, Mar. 12, 1924. Prefect Govt. Gabon, 1974-75, gov. Haut-Ogooue province, 1975-81; sec. of state Govt. Gabon, Libreville, 1981-84, min. of territorial adminstrn. and local orgn., 1984, third dep. prime min. for civil svc. and adminstrv. reform, 1984-90, min. of territorial adminstn. and local cmtys., 1990-94, min. of interior, collectives and mobile security, 1994, min. of transp., the merchant marine, fisheries, nat. parks, 1994—, sr. min. of interior, security and decentralization. Mem. Gabonese Dem. Party. Office: Ministry of Interior, BP 2110, Libreville Gabon*

MBOWENI, TITO T., South African government official. Dep. head African Nat. Congress; min. labor South African Govt., 1994—; with Gov. Res. Bank, Pretoria. Office: Laboria Bldg, Schoeman & Paul Kruger Sts P/Bag X499, Pretoria 0051, South Africa Address: 370 Church St, PO Box 427, Pretoria 0001, South Africa*

MBU, MATTHEW TAWO, shipping executive, legal consultant; b. Okundi, Nigeria, Nov. 20, 1929; s. Mbu and Eshan (Atim) Tawo; m. Katherine Diana Anigbo, Oct. 22, 1955. LLD (hon.), U. Ibadan, Nigeria, 1988; DLitt (hon.), U. Cross River State, Uyo, Nigeria, 1991, U. Calabar, 1992, Abia State U., Uturu, Nigeria, 1996; PhD, 1994. Barrister-at-law; adv., solicitor Supreme Ct. Nigeria. Mem. Ea. House of Assembly and Ho. of Reps., 1952-53; Fed. Min. of Labor, 1953-54; mem. Ho. of Reps., 1954-55; Acting Min. of Transport and Acting Min. Commerce, 1954-55; mem. Parliament, 1960-66; Min. Def., 1961-65, spl. asst. to Prime Min. Fgn. Affairs, 1963-66, Min. Transport and Aviation, 1966, internat. legal cons.; solicitor, adv. Supreme Ct. Nigeria, 1960—; Nigerian Pioneer diplomat; 1st High Commr. Nigeria, U.N., 1955-59; 1st Nigerian chief rep., Washington, 1959-60; 1st Nigerian chief rep. U.N., 1959-60; Nigerian chief del. and chief negotiator U.N. Disarmement Conf., Geneva, 1963-65; Nigerian chief del. Internat. Parliamentary Union Confs., 1960-66, U.N. Conf. Diplomatic Privileges and Intercourse, Vienna, Austria, 1961-63, Internat. Civil Aviation Orgn. Conf., Tokyo, 1964; v.p. Internat. Parliamentary Union, 1960-66; pres. Juridical and Parliamentary Com. IPU, 1962-66; Nigerian ambassador to Germany, 1998-99; chmn. numerous pvt. cos. including Alraine (Nigeria) Ltd., PGN Ltd., WTN Plc, Plessey Co. (Nigeria) Ltd., Intertrans (Nigeria) Ltd., Stanbic Merchant Bank Ltd., Scan Constrn. (Nigeria) Ltd., M.J. Gleeson Internat. (Nigeria) Ltd. Chmn. bd. govs. Boki Boys' Secondary Sch., Cross River State; gov. Holmewood House Sch., Kent, Eng.; chmn. Ea. Nigerian Pub. Svc. Commn., 1966-67, Investment Trust Co. Ltd. Cross River State Govt., 1971-75, Cross River State Think Tank Forum, 1984-87, Nigerian Cocoa Rsch. Inst., 1991; Biafran Fgn. Min., 1967-70; mem. Constituent Assembly, 1977-78, Transitional Coun., Nat. Def. and Security Coun., Sec. Fgn. Affairs, 1992-93, Interim Nat. Govt. Sec. Fgn. Affairs, 1993; pro-chancellor U. Ife, 1980-84; chancellor Abia State U., 1995; cons. Federal Govt., 1999—. Chieftain Otu Agrinya of Boki, Ada-Idaha-ke-Eburutu. Fellow London Inst. World Affairs, Royal Soc. Arts, Royal Econ. Soc., Nigerian Soc. Internat.

Law, Royal Yatching Club London, Royal Commonwealth Soc.; mem. Nigerian Mfr.'s Assn. (coun.), Island Club Lagos, Lagos Tennis Club, Amb. Club London and others. Home: 2A Fosbery Rd Ikoyi, Lagos Nigeria

MBUI, ARAM MUTEMA, entrepreneur, agricultural engineer; b. Embu, Kenya, Feb. 17, 1953; s. Bethuel and Tabitha (Muthoni) M.; m. Lucy Waruguru, Dec. 1, 1979; children: David, Charles, Karen. BSc in Mech. Engring. with honors, U. Nairobi, 1976; postgrad., Utah State U., 1989, Auburn (Ala.) U., 1989. Registered grad. engr., Kenya. Engr. trainee Metal Box (K) Ltd., Kenya, 1976; asst. mech. engr. Ministry Pub. Works, Nairobi, 1977-78; sales and mktg. mgr. Gailey & Roberts Ltd. (Unilever Co.), Nairobi, 1978-87; mng. dir. Rift Valley Machinery Svcs. Ltd., Nakuru, Kenya, 1987—; chmn. Rift Valley br. Fedn. Kenya Employers, 1995—, ex-officio nat. vice chair, 1995—. Mem. bd. govs. Ngiriambu Girls H.S., 1996—; mem. Tng. for Devel. NGO, Nairobi, 1989—. Recipient Cert. of Achievement U.S. AID, 1989. Mem. Am. Soc. Agrl. Engrs., Kenya Soc. Agrl. Engrs. (exec. com. 1997—), Instn. Engrs. of Kenya, Kenya Inst. Mgmt., Nat. Indsl. Tng. Coun., Kenya/U.S. Assn. Anglican. Avocations: football, rugby. E-mail: rivamac@net2000ke.com. Office: Rift Valley Machinery Svcs, PO Box 40, Nakuru Kenya

MCADAM, JAMES, retail executive; b. Dec. 10, 1930; s. John Robert and Helen (Cormack) McA.; m. Maisie Una Holmes, 1955; 2 children. Grad., Lenzie Acad. With Coats, Ltd., 1945; various positions fin. divsn. Coats, Ltd., Spain, Portugal, S.Am., India; fin. dir. Coats Chile, 1962-66, Coats India, 1966-70, Coats Patons, 1970-75; CEO Coats Patons, Plc., 1985-86, also chmn. bd. dirs.; COO Coats Viyella, Plc., U.K., 1986-91; also dep. chmn. bd. dirs. Coats Viyella, Plc., 1986-91, chmn., 2000; chmn., CEO Signet Group, Plc., London, 1992-2000, also chmn. bd. dirs., chmn., 2000—; Non-exec. chmn. Bisley Office Equipment Co., Ltd., 1991—. Chmn. bd. dirs. Brit. Clothing Industry Assn., 1991—, Brit. Knitting and Clothing Confedn., 1991—, Brit. Apparel and Textile Confedn., 1992—. Mem. Companion Inst. Mgmt., fellow of the Inst. Dirs., Royal Soc. Arts; mem. Royal Automobile Club, Farmers Club. Fax: 0 207 408 1493. Office: Signet Group plc, 66 Grosvenor St, London WIX 9DB, England

MCADAM, JAMES HENRY, environmental scientist; b. Donaghadee, U.K., Jan. 15, 1952; s. Frederick Leslie and Mary Elizabeth (Boal) McA.; m. Sally Gibson, May 3, 1975; children: Emma Jane, Thomas. BSc, Queens U., 1971, BAgr with honors, 1973, MAgr, 1975, PhD, 1987. Pasture agronomist Overseas Devel. Assn., Falkland Islands, 1976-78; high sci. officer Dept. Agl. and Rural Devel., 1979-82, sr. sci. officer, 1982-87, prin. sci. officer, 1987—; lectr. Queens U., Belfast, No. Ireland, 1982-97, reader, 1997—; chmn. AgroForestry Forum, 1993—; cons. U.K. Falkland Island Trust, London, 1983—, sc. advisor, 1989-98; trustee Falklands Conservation, London, 1985—; vis. prof. U. Magallanes, Chile. Author: The Upland Goose, 1993; editor Falkland Islands Jour., 1990—. Mem. Killyleagh Devel. Assn., No. Ireland, 1997-98; sec. East Down Yacht Club, No. Ireland, 1993, class capt. 1992-95. Brit. Coun. travelling fellow, 1989. Fellow Inst. Biology; mem. Royal Agrl. Soc., Brit. Grassland Soc., Brit. Ecol. Soc. Avocations: sailing, natural history, Falkland Islands, trees. Office: Dept Agr and Rural Devel, Newforge Ln, Belfast BT9 5PX, Northern Ireland

MCADOO, MICHAEL BRENDAN, accounting consultant, lecturer, broadcaster; b. Cork, Ireland, Oct. 29, 1945; s. John Francis and Monica Catherine (O'Donnell) McA.; m. Patrice Eileen Mary Hodgins, Sept. 4, 1971; children: Michelle, Kevin, Susan, Ian, Brian, Kieran. Leaving cert., Christian Bors. Coll., Cork, 1962. CPA, Ireland. Articled clerk Scannell McAdoo, Cork, 1962-72, mgr., 1972-79; mgr. Deloitte Touche, Cork, 1979-85; prin. McAdoo & Co., Cork, 1985-92; cons. Gordon Lane Co., Cork, 1992—; lectr. U. Coll., Cork, 1994—, Cork Vocat. Edn. Com., 1992-96; broadcaster RTE, Cork, Dublin, 1985—. Author: Bonanza or Belly Up, 1991. Irish del. Edn. COm. IFAC, 1991-94. Fellow Cert. Pub. Accts. in Ireland; mem. Munster Soc. CPA (chmn. 1985), Inst. CPA (coun. mem. 1979-92), Cork Constn. (trea. 1972-75), Munster ASSCE (sec. 1974-87, pres. 1993), Rugby Referees. Roman Catholic. Avocations: rugby, hospital radio, writing. Office: Gordon Lane Co, 19 Academy St, Cork Ireland

MCAFEE, I. PAUL, III, editor; b. Denver, Oct. 23, 1955; s. I. Paul Jr. and Shirley Naomi McAfee; m. Aimee Suzanne Kepner, Apr. 9, 1976; children: Harmony, Megan, Tessie. BA in English, Biola U., 1978. City editor S.E. News-Signal, South Gate, Calif., 1983-85; asst. city editor City News Svc., Hollywood, Calif., 1986-87, Progress Bull., Pomona, Calif., 1988-89; city editor Inland Valley Daily Bull., Ontario, Calif., 1990, bus. editor, 1991-95; editor The Business Press, Ontario, Calif., 1996—. Mem. Soc. Profl. Journalists (pres. Inland chpt. 1999-00, Best Bus. Story 1994, Best Feature Story 1996, Best Tech./Sci. Story 1998, Best Legal Affairs Story 1999), Soc. Am. Bus. Editors and Writers. Avocations: Internet research, book writing, competitive rollerskating. E-mail: paulmac@linkline.com. Office: The Business Press 3700 Inland Empire Blvd Ste 450 Ontario CA 91764-4914

MCAFEE, JOHN WILSON, SR., retired principal; b. Hallsville, Tex., May 17, 1942; s. Howard Lawrence Sr. and Julia (Hart) McA.; m. Ruby Lee Runnels, May 31, 1966 (div.); children: Veronica Michelle, Charlotte Nichelle, John Wilson Jr.; m. Karen Walker, Nov. 23, 1993; children: Christopher Walker, Derrick Walker. BS, Bishop Coll., 1963; MEd, East Tex. State U., 1970, EdD, 1977. Tchr. Terrell (Tex.) Ind. Sch. Dist., 1963-79, prin., 1979-83, head start dir., 1979-83; head start dir. Midland (Tex.) Ind. Sch. Dist., 1983-86, prin., 1986-98; now ret. Author and presenter video Coun. Minority Students, 1988; spkr. in field. Election judge City of Terrell, 1980-82; co-chairperson Census Redistricting Com., Terrell, 1981; bd. dirs. YMCA, Midland, 1983-90; rep. Dist. Tchr. Com., Midland, 1988-93; mem. distbn. panel United Way, Midland, 1990-93; speaker Achievement Day Wiley Coll., 1994, Baylor U., 1998, Multicultural Achievement Day, 1998. Recipient Helping Hands award Midland Reporter-Telegram, 1995; named Man of Distinction, Austin, Tex., 1990. Mem. NAACP (edn. chmn., chmn. dropout prevention program 1986-89), Tex. Elem. Prins. Assn. (dist. officer), Midland Prins. Assn., Renaissance Club (v.p., Achievement award 1980), Kappa Alpha Psi, Pi Lambda Theta, Phi Delta Kappa (historian 1980-81), Kappa Psi (Achievement award 1978). Mem. Ch. of Christ. Avocations: jazz music, accapella singing. Home: PO Box 9052 Midland TX 79708-9052 Office: Midland Ind Sch Dist 615 W Missouri Ave Midland TX 79701-5017

MCAFEE, WILLIAM GAGE, lawyer; b. N.Y.C., Mar. 23, 1943; arrived in Hong Kong, 1976; s. Horace J. and Kathryn (Gage) McA.; m. Linda, June 3, 1978; children: Zachary, Dallas, Matthew. AB, Harvard U., 1965; JD, Columbia U., 1968. Bar: N.Y. 1969, U.S. Supreme Ct. 1973, D.C. 1979. Legal adviser AID Dept. State, Saigon, Vietnam, 1969-71; adj. prof. Saigon U. Faculty Law, 1970-71; assoc. Davis Polk Wardwell, N.Y.C., 1971-73; with Coudert Bros., Singapore, Hong Kong, 1973-76, ptnr., 1976-94; advisor consultative com. for the basic law of Hong Kong, 1986-89, pres., 1985-86; v.p. AmCham, 1992, chmn. govt. rels. com., 1987-90, trustee Charitable Found.; mng. dir. The GE Asia Pacific Capital Tech. Fund, Asia Pacific Capital Ltd. and APC Asset Mgmt. (HK) Ltd.; dir. Lark Entertainment, UA Cinema Circuit Ltd., Cityline Ltd. and Studio City Cinemas Ltd.; mem. Hong Kong Gen. C. of C., legal com., dep. chmn. exec. com.; mem. campaign com. Cmty. Chest Hong Kong, coun. mem. Coun. Fgn. Rels.; sec. Law Assn. for Asia and the Western Pacific Energy Sect.; mem. Law Reform Commn., 1993-99; mem. Andover Devel. Bd. Andover Phillips Acad., The Fairbank Ctr. com. Harvard U.; assoc. Urban Land Inst.; comml. panel arbd Inst.; comml. panel arbitrators Am. Arbitration Assn. Editor Energy Law and Policy in Asia and the Western Pacific, 1985, Introduction to the Energy Laws of Asia, 1984; contbg. editor Oil & Gas Law & Taxation Rev.; hon. cons. Econ. & Law Rev.; adv. com. China Oil mag. Mem. ABA, Internat. Bar Assn., D.C. Bar Assn., N.Y. Bar Assn., Internat. Inst. Strategic Studies, Chartered Inst. Arbitrators (legal panel Hong Kong br.), Porcellian Club (Cambridge), Harvard U. (N.Y.C., Hong Kong), Pacific Club (bd. govs.), Fgn. Correspondents' Club. Episcopalian. Home: 47 Barker Rd, The Peak Hong Kong Office: APC Asset Mgmt (HK) Ltd, 3A Chater Rd Hong Kong Club Bldg, Central Hong Kong Hong Kong

MCALEER, JOHN JOSEPH, English literature educator; b. Cambridge, Mass., Aug. 29, 1923; s. Stephen Ambrose and Helen Louise (Collins) McA.; m. Ruth Ann Delaney, Dec. 28, 1957; children: Mary Alycia, Saragh Delaney, Seana Caithlin, John Joseph, Paul Bernard, Andrew Stephen. AB, Boston Coll., 1947, MA, 1949; PhD, Harvard U., 1955. Teaching fellow Boston Coll., 1947-48, English and Latin instr., 1948-50; Dexter fellow in Europe Harvard U., 1952, teaching fellow gen. edn., 1953-55; from asst. prof. to prof. Boston Coll., 1955—; vis. fellow Durham (Eng.) U., 1988-89. Author: Ballads and Songs Loyal to the Hanoverian Succession, 1962, Theodore Dreiser: A Biography, 1968, Artist and Citizen Thoreau, 1971; (with M. Tidjer) Notes on Life: The Philosophical Writings of Theodore Dreiser, 1974, Rex Stout: A Biography, 1977, Justice Ends at Home: The Early Crime Fiction of Rex Stout, 1977; (with others) Rex Stout: An Annotated Primary and Secondary Bibliography, 1980; (with Billy Dickson) Unit Pride, 1981, Royal Decree: Conversations with Rex Stout, 1983, Ralph Waldo Emerson: Days of Encounter, 1984, Queens Counsel: Conversations with Ruth Stout, 1986, Coign of Vantage, 1988; editor-in-chief: Rex Stout Jour., 1979—, Thorndyke File, 1981-95, Best Sellers, 1965-85, Shakespeare newsletter, 1959-71, Armchair Detective, 1978-82, The Quarterdeck: The Master Book of the Patrick O' Brian Society, 1999—; cons. editor: Dreiser Studies, 1971—; mng. editor Crimestalkers Casebook, 1998—; mng. editor: Quarterdeck: Muster Book of the Patrick O'Brian Society, 1999—. Mem. Boston Athenaeum Libr.; adv. bd. Walden Woods Project, 1990—, Parents Choice, 1980—. Sgt. U.S. Army, 1942-46. Recipient Cath. Press Assn. award, 1969, New Eng. Hist. Soc. award, 1985, Humanities award Boston Coll. Alumni Assn., 1991, Ignatian medal Boston Coll., 1995; permanent mem. Soc. of Fellows, Durham (Eng.) U., 1988—. Mem. Thoreau Soc. (pres., dir. 1971—), Mystery Writers Am. (v.p., dir. 1979-89, Edgar Allan Poe award 1978), R. Austen Freeman Soc. (pres. 1981—), Edith Wharton Soc., Jane Austen Soc. (Burke award 1991), Internat. Dreiser Soc. (founding mem. 1991—), Trollope Soc., Freeman Wills Croft Soc. (1st v.p. 1997—), Irene Adler Soc., Boston Authors Club (pres., dir. 1982-2000), Manuscript Soc., Tavern Club (Boston), Baker St. Irregulars, Patrick O'Brian Soc. (pres. 1995—). Democrat. Roman Catholic. Avocations: swimming, bibliopoly, genealogy, philately, gardening. Home: 121 Follen Rd Lexington MA 02421-5942 Office: Boston Coll Dept English McGuinn 529 Chestnut Hill MA 02167

MCALEESE, MARY PATRICIA, President of Ireland; b. Belfast, Ireland, June 27, 1951; d. Patrick Joseph and Claire (McManus) Leneghan; m. Martin Philip McAleese, Mar. 9, 1976; children: Emma Claire, Justin Charles, Sara Mai. LLB, Queen's U., Belfast, 1973; BL, Inn of Ct. No. Ireland, Belfast, 1974, Kings Inns, Dublin, 1978; MA, Trinity Coll., Dublin, 1986; LLD (hon.), NUI, U. Nottingham, Victoria U. Tech., Australia, St. Mary's U., Can., Queen's U., Belfast, Loyola Law Sch., U. of Aberdeen, U. Surrey; LHD (hon.), Rochester Inst. Tech., Trinity Coll., Dublin. Reid prof. Trinity Coll., 1975-79, 81-87; TV presenter Radio Telefis Eireann, Dublin, 1979-85; dir. Inst. Profl. Legal Studies Queens U., Belfast, 1987-97; Pres. of Ireland Dublin. Editor and dir. computer programs Criminal Procedure Indictment, 1990, Criminal Procedure Summary, 1991; contbr. articles to profl. jours. Recipient Silver Jubilee commemoration medal Charles U., Prague; hon. fellow Inst. Engrs. Ireland, Trinity Coll. Dublin. Fellow Royal Soc. Arts, Royal Coll. Surgeons (hon.), Coll. Anaesthetists (hon.), Liverpool John Moore's Univ. (hon.), Royal coll. Physicians and Surgeons Glasgow (hon.); mem. Royal Irish Acad., Bar N. Ireland, Inn of Ct. No. Ireland (hon. bencher, barrister-at-law), Internat. Bar Assn., Irish Coun. for Civil Liberties, Hon. Soc. King's Inns (hon. bencher, barrister-at-law), Inst. Linguists. Roman Catholic. Avocations: hill walking, theater, knitting, travel, theology. Home and Office: Áras an Uachtaráin, Phoenix Park, Dublin 8, Ireland

MCALHANY, TONI ANNE, lawyer; b. Decatur, Ind., May 1, 1951; d. Robert Keith and Evelyn L. (Fisher) McA. BA, Ind. U., 1973; JD, Valparaiso U., 1976. Bar: Mich. 1976, Ind. 1982, Ill. 1986, U.S. Dist. Ct. (no. dist.) Ind. 1989. Asst. prosecutor Ottawa County Prosecutor's Office, Grand Haven, Mich., 1976-81; assoc. Hann, Doss & Persinger, Holland, Mich., 1981-82, Romero & Thonert, Auburn, Ind., 1982-85; ptnr. Dahlgren & McAlhany, Berwyn, Ill., 1985-88, Colbeck, McAlhany & Stewart, Angola, Ind. & Coldwater, Mich., 1988-98; atty. Angola Housing Authority, 1989-98. Bd. dirs. Child and Family Svcs., Ft. Wayne, Ind., 1983, Fillmore Ctr., Berwyn, 1986-88, Altrusa, Coldwater, 1989-92. Mem. ATLA, State Bar Mich., State Bar Ind., State Bar Ill., Mich. Friend of the Ct. Assn., Referees Assn. Mich., Branch County Bar Assn., Steuben County Bar Assn. Avocations: traveling, horseback riding.

MCALISTER, HUGH FRANCIS, consultant cardiologist; b. Batu Gajah, Perak, Malaysia, Aug. 6, 1955; arrived in New Zealand, 1955; s. Lloyd Dawson and Beryl Weir (Lang) McA.; m. Diana Elizabeth Perry, Aug. 11, 1979; children: Cameron, Fiona, Kathryn, Andrew. BHB, U. Auckland, New Zealand, 1976, MB, BChir, 1979. Cardiology fellow Green Lane Hosp., Auckland, 1983-87; pacemaker fellow Montefiore Med. Ctr., N.Y.C., 1987-88; electrophysiology fellow Cleve. Clinic, 1988-89; cons. cardiologist Health Waikato, Hamilton, New Zealand, 1989—. Fellow Am. Coll. Cardiology (assoc.), Royal Australasian Coll. Physicians; mem. Cardiac Soc. Australia and New Zealand (regional exec.), N.Am. Soc. Pacing and Electrophysiology. Avocations: bridge, golf, cricket. Office: Waikato Hosp, Waikato Hosp, Pembroke St, Hamilton New Zealand

MCALLISTER, HECTOR GERARD, engineering educator; b. Larne, Northern Ireland, Dec. 23, 1948; s. Hector and Annie (Mulvenna) McA.; m. Patricia Margaret Fitzsimons, Apr. 1, 1978; children: John Patrick, Louise Mary, Elaine Margaret. BSc, Queens U., Belfast, No. Ireland, 1977, MSc, 1983; PhD, U. Ulster, No. Ireland, 1996. Chartered engr. Devel. engr. Bangor, No. Ireland, 1977-78; rsch. officer Queens U., Belfast, 1978-83, sr. rsch. officer, 1983-87; lectr. U. Ulster, Jordanstown, No. Ireland, 1987-93; sr. lectr. U. Ulster, Jordanstown, 1993—. Contbr. articles to profl. jours. Mem. Instn. Elec. Engrs. (Megaw Meml. award 1977, Premium award 1997). Avocations: reading, walking. Office: U Ulster, Shore Rd, Jordanstown BT37 0QB, Northern Ireland

MCALLISTER, MARIALUISA NICOSIA, mathematics educator, editor, consultant; b. Milan, Italy, Aug. 22, 1933; came to U.S., 1957; d. Emanuel Michael and Marcella (Borrini) Nicosia; m. Gregory Thomas McAllister, Dec. 3, 1961; children: Kevin Gregory, Sabina Luisa, Matthew Gregory. Grad., Albertini Lyceum, Rome, 1952; PhD in Math., U. Rome, 1957. Assoc. prof. math. Towson State U., Balt., 1963-65; adj. prof. math. Moravian Coll., Bethlehem, Pa., 1966-81; prof. math. Moravian Coll., Bethlehem, 1981—; chair math. dept., 1988-89; lectr. Elec. Power Inst., Bejing, 1984, Polish Acad. Scis., Warsaw, 1986, U. Canton, Peoples Republic of China, 1987, U. Guyang, 1987, Gregorshwyn U., Tokyo, 1987, Sogesta Inst., Urbino, Italy, 1988. Newsletter editor: N.Am. Fuzzy Info. Processes Soc., 1976-92; bull. editor: Internat. Jour. Approximate Reasoning, 1988-90. Recipient K.S. Fu award N.Am. Fuzzy Info. Processing Soc., 1990, 93; Fulbright scholar, 1988; NSF grantee, 1974-76. Mem. Math. Assn. Am. (exec. com. 1981-84, founder, chair spl. interest groups 1983-87), Computer Soc. Am. Democrat. Roman Catholic. Avocations: skiing, piano, reading, computing. E-mail: memnmol@moravian.edu. Home: 3604 Gloucester Dr Bethlehem PA 18020-7541 Office: Moravian Coll 104 Comenius Hall 1200 Main St Bethlehem PA 18018-6614

MCALPIN, KIRK MARTIN, lawyer; b. Newark, Sept. 14, 1923; s. Aaron Champion and Margaret (Martin) McA.; m. Sarah Frances Morgan, Dec. 14, 1951; children: Kirk Martin Jr., Philip Morgan, Margaret Champion Margeson. LLB, U. Ga., 1948; postgrad., Columbia U., 1949. Bar: Ga. 1949. Asst. solicitor gen. Ea. Jud. Cir. Ct. Ga., 1951; assoc. Bouhan, Lawrence, Williams, Levy & McAlpin, Savannah, Ga., 1952-53; ptnr. Bouhan, Lawrence, Williams, Levy & McAlpin, Savannah, 1954-63; sr. ptnr. King & Spalding, Atlanta, 1963-86; pvt. practice Savannah, 1987-97, Atlanta, 1998—; chmn. Inst. Continuing Legal Edn., 1980-81, Inst. Continuing Jud. Edn. in Ga., 1981-84, Jud. Council Ga., 1979-82. Pres. Atlanta Legal Aid Soc., 1971. Fellow Am. Bar Found., Am. Law Inst., Am. Coll. Trial Lawyers, Internat. Acad. Trial Lawyers, Internat. Soc. Barristers; mem. ABA (Jr. Bar Conf. chmn. 1958-59, chmn. gen. practice sect. 1972-73, chmn. sr. lawyers div. 1986-87, ho. of dels. 1960-90, state del. 1970-90, bd. govs. 1973-76), State Bar Ga. Assn. (chmn. Young Lawyers 1953-54, bd. govs. 1953-63, pres. 1979-80), Atlanta Bar Assn., Savannah Bar Assn. (v.p. 1960-61), Nat. Conf. Bar Pres. (exec. com. 1981-83), Ga. Def. Lawyers Assn., Ga. Trial Lawyers Assn., Am. Trial Lawyers Assn., Fed. Bar Assn., Am. Judicature Soc., Assn. R.R. Trial Counsel, Soc. of Cin., Sons Colonial Wars, St. Andrews Soc., Capital City Club, Piedmont Driving Club, Oglethorpe Club, Phi Delta Phi, Sigma Alpha Epsilon. Episcopalian. Fax: 404-467-0619. Office: 77 E Andrews Dr NW Apt 352 Atlanta GA 30305-1392

MCAMIS, EDWIN EARL, lawyer; b. Cape Girardeau, Mo., Aug. 8, 1934; s. Zenas Earl and Anna Louise (Miller) McA.; m. Malin Eklof, May 31, 1959 (div. 1979); 1 child, Andrew Bruce. AB magna cum laude, Harvard U., 1956, LLB, 1959. Bar: N.Y. 1960, U.S. Dist. Ct. (so. dist.) N.Y. 1962, U.S. Supreme Ct. 1965, U.S. Ct. Appeals (2d and 3d cirs.) 1964, U.S. Ct. Appeals (D.C. cir.) 1981. Assoc. law firm Webster, Sheffield & Chrystie, N.Y.C., 1959-61, Regan Goldfarb Powell & Quinn, N.Y.C., 1962-65; assoc. law firm Lovejoy, Wasson, Lundgren & Ashton, N.Y.C., 1965-69, ptnr., 1969-77; ptnr. Skadden, Arps, Slate, Meagher & Flom, N.Y.C., 1977-90, spl. ptnr., pro bono, 1990-93; adj. prof. law Fordham U., 1984-85, Benjamin N. Cardozo Sch. Law, N.Y.C., 1985-90. Bd. dirs. Aston Magna Found. for Music, Inc., 1982-93, Cmty. Rsch. Initiative N.Y., 1988-89; mem. Lambda Legal and Edn. Fund, 1991-95. With U.S. Army, 1961-62. Mem. ABA, Selden Soc. Home: 4110 Kiaora St Coconut Grove FL 33133-6350

MCANALLY, JAMES FRANCIS, nephrologist; b. Camden, N.J., May 24, 1949. BS with honors, Fairfield U., 1971; MD, N.J. Med. Sch., 1975. Diplomate Am. Bd. Internal Medicine, Am. Bd. Nephrology. Intern N.J. Med. Sch. Affiliated Hosps., Newark, 1976-77, internal medicine res., 1976-77, chief res. internal medicine, 1977-78; nephrology fellow Georgetown U. Hosp., Washington, 1978-80, chief res. internal medicine, 1979-80; attending, dir. divsn. nephrology Elizabeth (N.J.) Gen. Med. Ctr., 1980; asst. attending nephrology St. Michael's Med. Ctr., Newark, 1980; attending, chief nephrology St. Elizabeth Gen. Med. Ctr., Elizabeth, 1981; attending Union (N.J.) Hosp., 1982, Rahway (N.J.) Hosp., 1982; instr. medicine Georgetown U. Sch. Medicine, 1979-80, clin. asst. prof. medicine, divsn. nephrology, 1991; clin. asst. prof. medicine, U. Medicine and Dentistry N.J., Newark, 1982; dir. divsn. nephrology, clin. assoc. prof. medicine Seton Hall U. Grad. Sch. Med. Edn., 1988; dir. Bally Total Fitness Corp. Contbr. chpts. to books, articles to profl. jours. Med. advisor, trustee, Kidney Fund of N.J. Fellow ACP, Am. Coll. Cardiology; mem. AAAS, AMA, Am. Soc. Hypertension, Am. Med. Joggers Assn., Am. Soc. Internal Medicine, Am. Soc. Nephrology, Internat. Soc. Artificial Organs, Am. Soc. Artificial Internal Organs, Internat. Soc. Nephrology, Med. Soc. N.J., N.Y. Acad. Scis., N.Y. Soc. Nephrology, Nephrology Soc. N.J., Renal Physician Assn., Union County Med. Soc.

MCANDREW, PAUL JOSEPH, JR., lawyer; b. Kalona, Iowa, Mar. 8, 1957; s. Paul Joseph and Virginia (Krowka) McA.; m. Lola Maxine Miller, Mar. 1, 1975; children: Stephanie, Susan, Rose, Paul Joseph III, Bridget. BA with honors, U. Iowa, 1979, JD with high distinction, 1983. Bar: Iowa 1983, U.S. Dist. Ct. Iowa 1985, U.S. Claim Ct. 1985, U.S. Ct. Appeals (8th cir.) 1999, U.S. Supreme Ct. 2000. Law clk. to chief judge U.S. Dist. Ct. (so. dist.) Iowa, Des Moines, 1983-85; ptnr. Meardon, Sueppel, Downer & Hayes, Iowa City, 1985-99, Paul J. McAndrew Law Firm, Iowa City, 1999—. Claimant's counsel rep. Iowa Workers' Compensation Adv. Com., 2000—. Recipient Hancher-Finkbine award, 1979. Mem. ABA, ATLA (1st v.p. workers' compensation sect. 2000), Iowa Bar Assn. (chmn. worker's compensation sect. 1993-95), Iowa Trial Lawyers Assn. (rep. bd. govs. 1993—, workers' compensation sect. 1997—), Johnson County Bar Assn., Iowa Assn. Workers Compensation Attys. (rep. bd. govs. 1993—), Work Injury Litigation Group (Iowa rep. to nat. bd. govs. 1997—). Democrat. Roman Catholic. Avocations: jogging, biking, golf, travel. Home: 620 Scott Park Dr Iowa City IA 52245-5140 Office: Paul McAndrew Law Firm 528 S Clinton St Iowa City IA 52240-4212

MCANENA, OLIVER JAMES, general surgeon, consultant; b. Ballymote, Sligo, Ireland, Feb. 22, 1956; s. Frank and Anne Nancy (Snee) McA.; m. Eavan Jane O'Connor, June 26, 1982; children: Lisa, Katherine, Peter. B Medicine and Surgery, U. Coll. Galway, Ireland, 1979; M of Surgery, Nat. Univ. Ireland, 1985. Fellow in surg. oncology Meml. Sloan Kettering Cancer Ctr., N.Y.C., 1984-86; fellow in trauma and crit. care U. Colo. an Denver Gen. Hosp., 1988-89; sr. registrar in surgery Beaumont Hosp. Dublin and Royal Coll. Surgeons, 1989-90, Mater Hosp., Dublin, 1990-91; sr. lectr., hon. cons. surgeon Royal London Hosp., U. London, 1991-93; cons. surgeon U. Coll. Hosp., Galway Ireland, 1993—; cons. gen. surgeon, Galvia Pvt. Hosp., 1993—; regional dir. cancer svcs. Western Health Bd., Ireland, 1997—. Contbr. articles to profl. jours., publs. Fellow Royal Coll. Surgeons (Ireland), Assn. Surgeons of Gt. Britain and Ireland; mem. Soc. Surg. Oncology, Surg. Rsch. Soc. Gt. Britain and Ireland, Assn. Endoscopic Surgeons of Gt. Britain and Ireland. Avocations: swimming, golf. Office: Dept of Surgery, Univ Coll Hosp, Galway Ireland

MCARDLE, BARRY FRANCIS, dentist; b. Boston, Jan. 28, 1958; s. Joseph William and Brigitte Johanna Maria (Block) McA. BS, Boston U., 1980; DMD, Tufts U., 1985. Rsch. assoc. Naval Blood Rsch. Lab., Boston, 1980-81; dentist pvt. practice, Portsmouth, N.H., 1985—; cons. United Dental Systems, Portsmouth, 1996—; bd. dirs. Priority Dental Health, Inc., Concord, N.H.; active med. staff in dentistry, Concord (N.H.) Hosp., 1998—; spkr., lectr. in field. mem. editl. bd. Granite State Dentist newsletter, N.H. Dental Soc., 1999—; patentee in field. Mem. ADA, New England Dental Soc., N.H. Dental Soc., Seacoast Esthetic Dentistry Assn. (co-founder), Bus. Network Internat. (pres. Tri-State Seacoast chpt. 1998-99), Portsmouth C. of C., Boston U. Alumni Assn. Independent. Avocations: fine art, jazz, bodybuilding, hockey. Office: Capt Moses House 118 Maplewood Ave Ste B-7 Portsmouth NH 03801-3787

MCAULIFFE, KEITH WILLIAM, association administrator; b. Wellington, New Zealand, Dec. 26, 1954; s. John William and Doris (Pyke) McA.; m. Margaret Amanda Graham, Nov. 12, 1988; children: Blair, Scott. B in Agrl. Sci., Massey U., Palmeston, New Zealand, 1976, M in Agrl. Sci. with honors, 1978, diploma in bus. adminstrn., 1998. Cons. agronomist New Zealand Sports Turf Inst., 1979; sr. lectr. Massey U., 1980-88; CEO New Zealand Sports Turf Inst., Palmerston, 1989; president in field. Contbr. more than 170 articles to profl. jours. Mem. Internat. Turfgrass Soc. (dir. 1993—), New Zealand Sports Turf Industry Tng. Orgn. (chair 1993-96), New Zealand Land Drainage Assn., Internat. Soc. for Sports Surface Scis., New Zealand Soc. Assn. Execs. Avocations: golf, soccer, tennis. Office: New Zealand Spts Turf Inst, Box 347, Palmerston New Zealand

MC AULIFFE, MICHAEL F., retired bishop; b. Kansas City, Mo., Nov. 22, 1920. Student, St. Louis Prep. Sem., Cath. U. Ordained priest Roman Cath. Ch., 1945, consecrated bishop, 1969; bishop diocese of Jefferson City Roman Cath. Ch., Mo., 1969-97. Office: Chancery Office PO Box 417 Jefferson City MO 65102-0417*

MCAUSLAND, RANDOLPH M. N., arts administrator; b. Phila., Oct. 9, 1934; s. John Randolph and Helen (Neal) McA.; m. Marilynn Kemp, July 10, 1965 (div. 1976); children: Andrew, Sean; m. Jan E. Tribbey, May 9, 1986. AB, Princeton U., 1957. Copy editor Wall Street Journal, N.Y.C., 1960-61; editor, publisher Stowe Reporter, 1961-63; consulting editor Interpub. Group Cos., 1963-67; creative dir. The Progress Group, N.Y.C., 1967-70, gen. mgr., 1970-75; dir. mktg. Billboard Pubs., N.Y.C., 1975-77; asst. to pres. Macmillan Mag., Stamford, Conn., 1977-80; editor The New Satirist, New Canaan, Conn., 1980-82; pres. Design Pubs. Inc., N.Y.C., 1983-89; dir. Design Arts Program, NEA, Washington, 1989-90; dep. chmn. programs NEA, Washington, 1990-93; writer, arts cons. Richmond, Va., 1993-94; founder, dir. Design History Found., N.Y.C., 1988-89. Author: Supermarkets: History of an American Institution, 1980; contbr. articles to profl. jours. Bd. dirs. Hand Wodkshop, Richmond, 1993-94, Richmond Choral Soc., 1994, Worldesign Found., 1994—, Fla. Friends Librs., 1995—, Fla. Ctr. for the Book, Broward County Vision Com., 1998-99. With U.S. Army, 1957-60. Recipient Commendation N.Y.C. Police Dept., 1971, Pres. Cup Am. Comedy Club N.Y., N.Y.C., 1974, Bronze Apple award Indsl. Design Soc., 1987, Disting. Svc. award NEA, 1991-92. Mem. Am. Ctr. For Design (hon.), Coalition Ind. Scholars, Ivy Club. Home: 7405 Fair Oaks Dr Cincinnati OH 45237-2925

MCBEE, ROBERT LEVI, retired federal government official, writer, consultant; b. Braymer, Mo., Aug. 25, 1927; s. Calvin Levi and Wavah E. (Tripp) McB.; m. Lucy Armijo, June 13, 1959; children: Martin Christopher, Mark Antony Christian, Mathieu Alfonso Calvin. BA, Westminster Coll.,

Fulton, Mo., 1952. Editor Take-Off Smoky Hill AFB, Salina, Kans., 1947-48; publicity writer Westminster Coll., Fulton, Mo., 1950-52; advt. mgr. Battenfeld Grease and Oil Corp., Kansas City, Mo., 1952-53; asst. to advt. mgr. Ash Grove Lime and Cement Co., Kansas City, Mo., 1953-57; publicity dir. Am. Campaign Svcs., Kansas City, Mo., 1957; freelance writer Chelan, Wash., 1957-58; reporter Kansas City (Mo.) Times Star, 1958-61; assoc. editor Bailey Publs., Independence, Mo., 1961-63; editor Nat. Cath. Register, Denver, 1963-64; mng. editor Pleasant Hill (Mo.) Times, 1964-67; community affairs specialist Region 7 Job Corps, Kansas City, Mo., 1967-69; pub. info. officer Region 7 Office Econ. Opportunity, Community Svc. Adminstrn., Kansas City, Mo., 1969-81; pub. affairs specialist Kansas City Dist. Army C.E., 1981-85; chief community rels. Fifth U.S. Army, San Antonio, 85-88; acting dir. Chgo. Regional Office Pub. Affairs Dept. Vet. Affairs, 1989-90, asst. dir., 1988-94; acting dir. Dept. Vets. Affairs Chgo. Regional Office Pub. Affairs, 1991. Sec., asst. treas. Kansas City Area Transp. Authority, 1965-70; pres. Pleasant Hill (Mo.) C. of C., 1966-67; sec. City Planning and Zoning Commn., Pleasant Hill, 1966; bd. dirs. Cath. Info. Svcs., Kansas City, 1966-72; adv. trustee Rsch. Med. Ctr., Kansas City, 1967-82. Mem. Westminster Coll. Alumni Coun. (life), Skulls of Seven, Pi Delta Epsilon (charter pres.), Eta Sigma Phi, Kappa Alpha. Democrat. Roman Catholic. Avocations: reading, genealogy.

MCBEE, SUSANNA BARNES, journalist; b. Santa Fe, Mar. 28, 1935; d. Jess Stephen and Sybil Elizabeth (Barnes) McBee; m. Paul H. Recer, July 2, 1983. AB, U. So. Calif., 1956; MA, U. Chgo., 1962. Staff writer Washington Post, 1957-65, 73-74, 77-79, asst. nat. editor, 1974-77; asst. sec. for public affairs HEW, 1979; articles editor Washingtonian mag., 1980-81; assoc. editor U.S. News & World Report, 1981-86; news editor Washington Bur. of Hearst Newspapers, 1987-89, asst. bur. chief, 1990—; Washington corr. Life mag., 1965-69; Washington editor McCall's mag., 1970-72. Bd. dirs. Washington Press Club Found., 1992-95. Recipient Penney-Missouri mag. award, 1969, Hall of Fame award, Soc. Profl. Journalists 1996; Sigma Delta Chi Pub. Svc. award, 1969, Hearst Eagle award, 1994. Mem. Nat. Press Club, Cosmos Club. Home: 5190 Watson St NW Washington DC 20016-5329 Office: 1701 Pennsylvania Ave NW Washington DC 20006-5805

MCBRIDE, DONNA JANNEAN, publisher; b. Kansas City, Kans., July 3, 1940; d. Donald Merle and Hazel Frances (Williams) McBride; life ptnr. Barbara Grier, 1972. AB, Central Coll., 1962; MLS, U. Mo.-Columbia, 1969. Tchr., Pilot Grove (Mo.) H.S., 1961-62; corr. Bus. Men's Assurance Co., Kansas City, Mo., 1962-66; acctg. clk. Prudential of Eng., Sydney, Australia, 1966-67; head tech. processes Kansas City Pub. Library (Mo.), 1967-77; customer rep. C.L. Systems, Inc., Newtonville, Mass., 1977-80; dir. support services Leon County Pub. Library, Tallahassee, 1980-82; v.p., CFO The Naiad Press, Inc., Tallahassee, 1982—; dir. The Naiad Press, 1976—, Sappho's Libr., 1983—. Mem. ALA, Nat. Gay Task Force, Am. Booksellers Assn., Nat. Women's Studies Assn., NOW. Home: 1097 Alligator Dr Alligator Pt FL 32346-5107 Office: The Naiad Press Inc PO Box 10543 Tallahassee FL 32302-2543

MCBRIDE, KENNETH EUGENE, lawyer, title company executive; b. Abilene, Tex., June 8, 1948; s. W. Eugene and I. Jean (Wright) McB.; m. Peggy Ann Waller, Aug. 7, 1969 (div. 1980); m. Katrina Lynne Small, June 1, 1985; children: Katherine Jean, Kellie Elizabeth. BA, Central State U., 1971; JD, Oklahoma City U., 1974. Bar: Okla. 1974. Assoc. Linn, Helms & Kirk, Oklahoma City, 1974-76; city atty. City of Edmond (Okla.), 1976-77; v.p., gen. counsel Am. First Land Title Ins., Oklahoma City, 1977-81; pres. Am. First Abstract Co., Norman, Okla., 1981-90, Lawyers Title of Oklahoma City, Inc., 1990—; CEO Am. Eagle Title Ins. Co., 1994—; pres. Okla. Land Title Assn., 1987-88, LT Exch. Corp., 1996—. Bd. dirs. Norman Bd. Adjustment, 1982-85, Leadership Okla., Inc., 1986-94, pres., 1989-90, 93-94. Fellow Okla. Bar Found.; mem. ABA, Okla. Bar Assn. (bd. dirs. Real Property Sect. 1992-94), Oklahoma County Bar Assn., Oklahoma City Met. Assn. Realtors (bd. dirs. 1995-96), Oklahoma City Real Property Lawyers Assn., Leadership Norman Alumni. Democrat. Presbyterian. Avocation: sailing. Office: Lawyers Title Oklahoma City Inc 1141 N Robinson Ave Oklahoma City OK 73103-4929

MCBRIDE, MILDRED MAYLEA, retired elementary school educator; b. Bowerston, Ohio, Oct. 7, 1922; d. Harry Scott and Mary McGary (Mowl) McB.; 1 adopted child, Marjorie Mi Sang McBride. BS in Music, Baldwin-Wallace Coll., 1944; MA, Columbia U., N.Y.C., 1949. Cert. tchr., Ohio, Hawaii. Traveling music tchr. Tuscarawas County Sch., 1944-45; tchr. elem. music Parma (Ohio) Schs., 1945-48, tchr. jr. h.s. music, 1946-48; tchr. h.s. gen. music, chorus Kamehameha Sch. for Girls, Honolulu, 1949-59; tchr. elem. music Tempe (Ariz.) Schs., 1959-60; tchr. elem. music Hawaii Pub. Sch. Sys., 1960-86, ret., 1986; co-founder Elem., Intermediate, Gen. Music Interest Group, Honolulu, 1969-79. Author, editor: (biography) Meg!, 1996, 4 hist. novels; writer mus. plays. Helper Bowerston Pub. Libr., 1939, 48, 97—; bd. dirs. Hawaii Habitat for Humanity, Honolulu, 1986-93; mem. Honolulu Symphony Chorus; head soup kitchen, vol. Harris United Meth. Ch., Honolulu, 1990-96, mem. choir, 1975-96. Avocations: golf, travel, singing, cooking, enjoying daughter. Home: 2934 Espy Ave Pittsburgh PA 15216-2017

MCBRIDE, SHARON LOUISE, counselor, technical communication educator; b. Peoria, Ill., Dec. 5, 1939; d. Ralph Cannon and Joyce Eliz (Shoff) McB.; m. Armond B. Ciota, Jr., Apr. 23, 1960 (div.); children: Matthew Ciota, Eliz Faron, Thomas Ciota, Nathan Ciota. BA, Bradley U., 1960, MA, 1987. Various positions to undergrad. student adviser Bradley U., Peoria, 1972—; instr. Ill. Ctrl. Coll., East Peoria, 1987—; chmn. bd. dirs. Greater Peoria Mass Transit. Trustee West Peoria Twp., 1984-96; sec.-treas. Ill. Twp. Trustees, 1993-96; chairperson West Peoria Zoning Bd. Appeals. Mem. Am. Soc. Engring. Edn., Am. Pub. Transit Assn. (governing bds. com.), Am. Assn. Women in C.C., Lions (bd. dirs. West Peoria chpt. 1984-97, precinct com. person). Republican. Avocations: travel, community volunteer. Home: 2413 W Kellogg Ave West Peoria IL 61604-5011

MCBRIDE, THOMAS DWAYNE, management consultant; b. Brownwood, Tex., Feb. 13, 1947; s. Thomas Alfred and Eula Faye (Harvey) McB.; m. Peggy Anne Kimbrough McBride, Oct. 14, 1967; children: Jeffery Dwayne, Stacy Anne. AS, Crowder Coll., Neosho, Mo., 1967; BS in Mech. Engring., U. Mo., Rolla, 1970; MBA in Mgmt., U. Akron, 1978. Registered profl. engr., Ohio. Engring. supr. Babcock & Wilcox, Barberton, Ohio, 1972-79; mgr. engring. Bendix Corp., South Beloit, Ill., 1979-83; mgr. sales engring. Bendix/Warner & Swasey, Worcester, Mass., 1983-84, mgr. Product Engring., 1984-86; program mgr. Design Tech. Corp., Billerica, Mass., 1986-87; mgr. engring. Netco, Inc., Haverhill, Mass., 1987-88; dir. engring. The Nelmor Co., North Uxbridge, Mass., 1988-95; tech. mgr. Lawrence (Mass.) Pumps Inc., 1995-96, ops. mgr., 1996-2000; pres. Ptnrs. for Creative Solutions, Shrewsbury, Mass., 2000—; tech. and bus. cons. Micromation, Inc., Altoona, Pa., 1988-90. Inventor: Granulator Knife, 1991, 94, Bin Deflector, 1991; author: Society of Manufacturing Engineers, 1992, M&A Today, 2000. Mem. Worcester Area C. of C. 1st lt. U.S. Army, 1970-72. Recipient Curator's scholarship U. Mo., 1967. Mem. Environ. Industry Assn. (co-chair Wastec divsn. subcom. on safety standards for size reduction equipment 1995-96), Phi Theta Kappa (chpt. pres. 1966-67), Soc. Mfg. Engrs., Am. Mgmt. Assn., Turnaround Mgmt. Assn., Assn. Corp. Growth. Mem. Trinity Ch. Avocations: golf, bicycling, genealogy, religious history, hiking. Office: Ptnrs for Creative Solutions 36 Deerfield Rd Shrewsbury MA 01545-1530

MCBRIDE, WANDA LEE, psychiatric nurse; b. Dayton, Ohio, Dec. 13, 1931; d. Owen Francis Staup and Ruby Madonna (Campbell) Inscore; m. Richard H. McBride, July 28, 1951 (div. Mar. 1966); children: Kathleen Kerns, Kimberlee Haley. Diploma, Christ Hosp. Sch., Cin., 1953; student, U. Cin., 1954-55. Cert. psychiat. mental health nurse ANA. Various health-care positions, 1953-66; from supr. 4 acute male units to supr. outpatient dept. Cen. Ohio Psychiat. Hosp., Columbus, 1966-77; supr. hosp., head nurse urology and respiratory diseases flr. St. Anthony Hosp., Okla., 1977-83; shift supr. and coord. child program Willowview Hosp., Spencer, Okla., 1983-88; adminstrv. nursing supr. Grant Ctr. of Deering Hosp., Miami, 1988—, assessment specialist, 1995—; disabilities case mgr. Kemper Nat. Svcs., Plantation, Fla., 1996—; clin. nurse Savannas Hosp., Pt. St. Lucie, Fla., 1997, relief night shift supr., 1997-98; hosp. supr. New Horizons of the Treasure Coast, Ft. Pearce, Fla., 1998—. Mem. Gov.'s Com. for Mental Health and Retardation, 1963-66, Logan County Mental Health League, Ohio, 1963-66. Named Nurse of Yr., 1983-90. Mem. Nat. League for Nursing, Mental Health League (past pres.), Lioness Club (past pres.). Republican. Episcopalian. Avocations: orchid growing, classical music, cooking, fishing, camping. Home: 1 Cartagesa Port Saint Lucie FL 34952-3436

MCBROOM, THOMAS WILLIAM, SR., lawyer; b. Atlanta, Mar. 29, 1963; s. William Ralph and Ethel Irene (Bradley) McB.; m. Susan H.; 1 child, Thomas William Jr. B in Mech. Engring., Ga. Tech., 1985, MS in Mech. Engring., 1987; JD, Ga. State U., 1992, MBA, 1992. Bar: Ga. 1993, D.C. 1994, U.S. Tax Ct. 1993, U.S. Supreme Ct. 1996; registered profl. engr., Ga.; lic. comml. pilot and flight instr., registered mediator and arbitrator, Ga. Mfg. engr. AT & T Techs., Norcross, Ga., 1985-86; energy systems engr. Atlanta Gas Light Co., 1987-89, sales engr., 1989-90, dir. power systems markets, 1991-94, sr. corp. planning analyst, 1994-95, mgr. major accounts, 1995-97, dir. major accts., 1997-99; gen. counsel The Shiloh Group, Newman, Ga., 1999-2000, The Shiloh Group, LLC, 1999-2000; pres. Thomas W. McBroom, P.C., 2000—. Mem. Grad. Leadership Coweta, 1996, Grad. Coverdell Rep. Leadership Inst., 1997; vice chmn. state ho. dists. Coweta County Rep. Com., 1997-99, vice chair legis. dists., 1999; state com. Ga. Rep. Party, 1997-99. With USAR, 1997—, 1st lt. JAGC. Mem. Ga. Bar Assn., Coverdell Leadership Inst., Phi Delta Phi (exchequer 1991). Home: 15 Culpepper Way Newnan GA 30265-2217

MCBURNEY, CHARLES WALKER, JR., lawyer; b. Orlando, Fla., June 6, 1957; s. Charles Walker McBurney and Jeane (Brown) Chappell. BA, U. Fla., 1979, JD, 1982. Bar: Fla. 1982, U.S. Dist. Ct. (mid. dist.) Fla. 1983, U.S. Ct. Appeals (11th cir.) 1984. Assoc. Mathews, Osborne, McNatt, Gobelman & Cobb, Jacksonville, Fla., 1982-84; asst. state's atty. State's Atty.'s Office, Jacksonville, 1984-90, civil atty., 1987-88, sr. trial atty., 1988-90; ptnr. Fischette, Owen, Held & McBurney, Jacksonville, 1990—; dir. Serious or Habitual Juvenile Offender Program, 1986. Bd. dirs. Civic Round Table, 1988-92, treas., 1988-89, pres. 1989-90; chmn. com. congl. campaigns, Jacksonville, 1982, 84, 88; mem. Mayor's Bicentennial Constnl. Commn., 1989-91; dir. Internat. Devel. Commn. for Jacksonville, 1993—, treas., 1995-97; bd. dirs. Am. Heart Assn. N.E. Fla., 1990-92. Mem. ABA, Jacksonville Bar Assn. (chmn. bankruptcy sect. 1998-2000), Jacksonville Bankruptcy Bar Assn. (bd. dirs. 1999—), Nat. Dist. Attys. Assn., Comml. Law League (So. region exec. coun. 1998—, treas. 2000—), Fla. Jaycees (legal counsel 1987-88, most outstanding local pres. award 1987), Jacksonville Jaycees (pres. 1986, Jaycee of yr. 1984), Jacksonville C. of C. (bd. govs. 1987, govtl. affairs com. 1998—), Summit Civitan (judge adv. 1991-93, ctrl. civitan 1991—, bd. dirs.), Masons, Bull Snort Club (pres. 1995-96, 99—, chmn. bd. 1996-97, 1998-99), C. of C. (trustee 1996-98, govtl. affairs com. 1998—), N.E. Fla. Alumni Assn. (v.p. 1998-2000), James Madison Inst., Jacksonville Hist. Soc., Phi Beta Kappa. Republican. Presbyterian. Home: 6326 Christopher Creek Rd E Jacksonville FL 32217-2485 Office: Fishette Owen Held & McBurney Riverplace Tower Ste 1916 Jacksonville FL 32207

MC CABE, JOHN CHARLES, III, writer; b. Detroit, Nov. 14, 1920; s. Charles John and Rosalie (Dropiewski) McC.; m. Vija Valda Zarina, Oct. 19, 1962 (dec. 1984); children—Linard Peter, Sean Cahal and Deirdre Rose (twins); m. Rosina Lawrence, June 8, 1987 (dec. June 1997). Ph.B., U. Detroit, 1947; M.F.A. in Theatre, Fordham U., 1948; Ph.D. in English Lit, Shakespeare Inst., U. Birmingham, Eng., 1954. Instr. theatre Wayne State U., 1948-51, CCNY, 1955; mem. faculty N.Y. U., 1956-68, prof. dramatic art, chmn. dept., 1962-68; chmn. dept. drama and theatre arts Mackinac Coll., Mackinac Island, Mich., 1968-70; founder The Sons of the Desert (group devoted to works Laurel and Hardy), 1963. Profl. actor, 1928—, producer-dir., Milford (Pa.) Playhouse, summers, 1948-53, prodr., N.Y.U. Summer Theatre, Sterling Forest, N.Y., 1963-65, author-in-residence, Lake Superior State Coll., Sault Ste. Marie, Mich., 1970-86; author: Mr. Laurel and Mr. Hardy, 1961, rev. edit., 1966, George M. Cohan: The Man Who Owned Broadway, 1973, The Comedy World of Stan Laurel, 1974, Laurel & Hardy, 1975, (with G.B. Harrison) Proclaiming the Word, 1976, Charles Chaplin, 1978, Grand Hotel: Mackinac Island, 1987, Babe: The Life of Oliver Hardy, 1990, The High, 1992, Cagney, 1997; ghostwriter James Cagney's autobiography, Cagney by Cagney, 1976. Served with USAAF, 1943-45, ETO. Mem. Shakespeare Assn. Am., Actors Equity Assn., Catholic Actors Guild Am., Baker St. Irregulars. Clubs: The Players (N.Y.C.), The Lambs (N.Y.C.). Home: PO Box 363 Mackinac Island MI 49757-0363

MCCABE, ROBERT JOHN, automotive industry executive; b. Cambridge, Mass., May 28, 1943; s. Francis Thomas and Luberta Marie (Harden) McC; m. Maureen Anne Miller (div. Jan. 1985); m. Susan Lynn Morton; children: Christa A., Kasey M., Kami J., John F., Katherine L. BS, Cornell U., 1967, MBA, 1970. Small bus. owner Cambridge, 1961-63; with fin. mgmt. dept. Borg Warner Morse Chain, Ithaca, N.Y., 1965; from mid-mgmt. level to dir. treas. office GM, N.Y.C. and Detroit, 1970-81, asst. comptr., spl. asst. to group v.p. intetnat., 1981-82; asstr. comptr. assembly divsn. GM, Warren, Mich., 1982-84; asstr. comptr. Detroit Diesel Corp., Redford, Mich., 1984-86; chmn. bd. dirs., CEO Terex Equipment Ltd., Scotland, 1986-88; dir. fin. Packard Electric (now Delphi), Warren, Ohio, 1988-92; group dir. finance powertrain group GM, Pontiac, Mich., 1992-97; gen. dir. fin., svc. parts ops. GM, Grand Blanc, Mich., 1997—. Bd. dirs. Flint-Genesee Econ. Growth Alliance, 1998—, Flint Area Conv. and Visitors Bur., 1998—. Mem. Flint-Genesee C. of C. (bd. dirs. 1998—). Roman Catholic. Avocations: SCUBA diving, ice skating, skiing, sky diving. Office: GM PO Box 6020 6200 Grand Pointe Dr Grand Blanc MI 48439-5501

MCCAFFER, RONALD, construction management educator, consultant; b. Glasgow, Scotland, Dec. 8, 1943; s. John Gegg and Catherine Turner (Gourlay) McC.; m. Margaret Elizabeth Warner McCaffer, Aug. 13, 1966; 1 child, Malcolm Andrew. BSc, U. Strathclyde, Scotland, 1965; DSc, U. Strathclyde, 1998; PhD, Loughborough U., U.K., 1978. Sr. lectr. Loughborough U., Leics, U.K., 1978-83, reader dept. civil engring., 1983-86, prof. constrn. mgmt., 1986—, head dept. civil engring., 1987-93, dean of engring., 1992-97, dep. vice-chancellor, 1997—. Author: Modern Construction Management, 1995, 5th edit., 2000, Estimating and Tendering for Civil Engineering Works, 1991, Management of Construction Equipment, 1991; editor Engr. Constrn. and Architectural Mgmt.; contbr. articles to profl. jours. Fellow Royal Acad. Engring.; mem. ECITB. Office: Loughborough U, Ashby Rd, Loughborough LE113TU, United Kingdom

MCCAFFERTY, JAMES ARTHUR, sociologist; b. Columbus, Ohio, Jan. 1, 1926; s. James A. and Marie Agatha (Gilchrist) McC.; m. Jane Roush, June 13, 1948 (dec. Oct. 1984); children: Lucinda Jane Martin, James Stanley Thomas, Bridget Anne Roush Green; m. Carolyn Ring Bradley, Nov. 7, 1987 (div. Apr. 1992); m. Irma Mae Prosser Nicholson, May 28, 1993 (dec. Nov. 1996). BS, Ohio State U., 1948, MA, 1954; postgrad., Am. U. Social rsch. analyst Ohio State Dept. Pub. Welfare, 1948-51; criminologist U.S. Bur. Prisons, Washington, 1951-63; ast. chief divsn. info. sys. Adminstrv. Office of U.S. Cts., Washington, 1963-77, chief statis. analysis and reports divsn., 1977-86; ret.; vis. lectr. Am. U., 1959, 62-64; adj. instr. Fordham U., 1978-89. Editor: Capital Punishment, 1972; contbr. articles on criminology and correctional stats. to profl. jours. Life mem. Md. State PTA; past pres. Potomac area coun. Camp Fire Girls of U.S., 1966-67; v.p. Prince George's County (Md.) Coun. PTAs, 1964-65; chmn. Prince George's County Youth Commn., 1970-72; past pres. Hypoglycemia Assn., past pres. Interfaith Cmty. Action Coun., Inc., 1991-93. Cpl. USAAF, 1944-46. Recipient Vol. award Prince George's Co., 1992. Mem. AAUP, Md. Soc. SAR (past pres., trustee), Am. Sociol. Assn., Am. Correctional Assn. (life), Assn. Correctional Rsch. and Info. Mgmt. (life, past pres., Ronald H. Beattie award 1997), Nat. Geneal. Soc., Nat. Geog. Soc., Am. Statis. Assn., Prince George's County Geneal. Soc. (life, past pres.), Ohio Geneal. Soc. (life, Nat. Capital Buckeye chpt., former editor newsletter), Judicature Soc., Md. State Beekeepers Assn. (life), DAV (life), Sons of Union Vets. Civil War (life, past camp comdr., former editor), Am. Legion (life), Army Airways Com. Sys. (life), Gallia County (Ohio) Hist. Geneal. Soc. (life), Nat. Congress Patriotic Orgns. (life), Rossmore Kiwanis. Presbyterian. E-mail: jirma@aol.com. Home: 613 Rosier Rd Fort Washington MD 20744-5554

MCCAFFREY, ANNE INEZ, author; b. Cambridge, Mass., Apr. 1, 1926; d. George H. and Anne (McElroy) McC.; m. Wright Johnson, Jan. 14, 1950 (div. Aug. 1970); children: Alec Anthony, Todd, Georgeanne. B.A. cum laude, Radcliffe Coll., 1947; student, U. City of Dublin, 1970-71. Copywriter, layout designer Liberty Music Shops, N.Y.C., 1948-50; copywriter, sec. Helena Rubinstein, N.Y.C., 1950-52. Author: Restoree, 1967, Dragonflight, 1968, Decision at Doona, 1969, Ship Who Sang, 1969, Mark of Merlin, 1971, Dragonquest: Being the Further Adventures of the Dragonriders of Pern, 1971, Ring of Fear, 1971, To Ride Pegasus, 1973, Cooking Out Of This World, 1973, A Time When, 1975, Dragonsong, 1976, Kilternan Legacy, 1975, Dragonsinger, 1977, Dinosaur Planet, 1977, Get Off the Unicorn, 1977, White Dragon, 1978, Dragondrums, 1979, Crystal Singer, 1981, The Worlds of Anne McCaffrey, 1981, The Coelura, 1983, Moreta: Dragonlady of Pern, 1983, Dinosaur Planet Survivors, 1984, Stitch in Snow, 1984, Killashandra, 1985, The Girl Who Heard Dragons, 1985, The Year of the Lucy, 1986, Nerilka's Story, 1986, The Lady, 1987, People of Pern, 1988, Dragonsdown, 1988, Renegades of Pern, 1989, (with Jody-Lynn Nye) The Dragonlover's Guide to Pern, 1989, The Rowan, 1990, Pegasus in Flight, 1990, (with Elizabeth Moon) Sassinak, 1990, (with Nye) The Death of Sleep, 1990, All the Weyrs of Pern, 1991, Generation Warriors, 1991, Damia, 1991, (with Margaret Ball) The Partnership, 1991, (with Nye) Crisis at Doona, 1991, Damia, 1992, (with Mercedes Lackey) The City Who Fought, 1993, (with Elizabeth Ann Scarborough) Powers That Be, 1993, Chronicles of Pern: First Fall, 1993, Lyon's Pride, 1994, (with Nye) The Ship Who Won, 1994, (with Scarborough) Power Lines, 1994, Dolphins of Pern, 1994, (with Scarborough) Power Play, 1995, Freedom's Landing, 1995, Black Horses for The King, 1996, Red Star Rising, 1996, Freedom's Choice, 1997, (with Margaret Ball) Acorna, 1997, Masterharper of Pern, 1998, Freedom's Challenge, 1998, (with Margaret Ball) Acorna's Quest, 1998, If Wishes Were Horses, 1998, Nimisha's Ship, 1999, The Tower and the Hive, 1999; editor: Alchemy and Academe, 1970; anthology: The Girl Who Heard Dragons, 1991; dir. musical Brecks Mill Cronies, 1962-65. Recipient Hugo award, 1967, Nebula award, 1968, E.E. Smith award, 1975, Ditmar award, 1979, Gandalf award, 1979, Eurocon/Streso award, 1979, Balrog award, 1980, Golden PEN award, 1981, Sci. Fiction Book Club award, 1986, 89, 91, 92, 93, 94, literary achievement award Margaret A. Edwards, 1999. Mem. PEN (Ireland), Sci. Fiction Writers Am. (sec.-treas. 1968-70), Authors' Guild. Office: Dragonhold Underhill, Timmore Ln Newcastle, Wicklow Ireland*

MCCALL, EDITH SANSOM, writer; b. Charles City, Iowa, Sept. 5, 1911; d. William John and Mary Catherine (May) Sansom; m. Merle Rederick McCall, June 7, 1935 (div. Jan. 1963); children: Constance Anita, Mary Edith. MA, U. Chgo., 1949. Cert. elem. educator, Ill. Tchr. Elmhurst (Ill.) Pub. Schs., 1930-35; tchr. Western Springs (Ill.) Pub. Schs., 1943-48; reading cons. LaGrange (Ill.) Pub. Schs., 1949-55; writer, 1953—. Author: Conquering the Rivers, 1982, Sometimes We Dance Alone, 1994, 52 other books for young readers; co-author: 30 textbooks; contbr. articles to profl. jours.; monthly column. Recipient Maritime Journalism award Inland Waterways Libr., St. Louis, 1992, Honor Book award Children's Reading Round Table, Chgo., 1989; named Disting. Alumnus U. Wis. Stevens Point, 1988; named to Mo. Writers' Hall of Fame, Springfield, 1996. Mem. Mo. Writers Guild (hon., life, pres. 1970, 2000, Best Book award 4 times 1960-89), Western Writers Am. (finalist non-fiction award 1985), Ozark Writers League (v.p.), Authors Guild, Inc. Home: PO Box 255 Hollister MO 65673-0255

MCCALL, LOUIS CHARLES JOHN, chief financial officer, financial advisor and executive; b. Irvington, N.J., Sept. 22, 1959; s. Louis C. and Joan M. (Zalewski) McC.; m. Vicki Lynn Braun; children: Heather Ashley, Louis, Christina Helen, Sean Thomas. BS, St. Joseph's U., 1981. CPA, Pa., N.J.; cert. fin. officer, mcpl. fin. officer. Pub. acct./auditor Merves & Co. CPAs, Phila., 1980-84; sr. audit mgr. Ernst & Young, LLP, Phila., 1984-94; CFO County of Camden, N.J., 1994-98; v.p. Advanta, 1998; sr. v.p., corp. contr. GMAC Mortgage, 1999—; pres. acctg. alumni bd. St. Joseph's U., 1993-94, acctg. alumni bd. 1993—, bd. govs., 1994—. Bd. dirs. Wenonah Planning/Zoneing Bd., 1995—; mem. Wenonah Hist. Soc., 1996—; pres. Lions Club, Wenonah, N.J., 1997-98. Recipient Cmty. Svc. award Borough of Wenonah, 1994, Outstanding Svc. award Wenonah Police, 1994, 97. Fellow N.J. Soc. CPAs (S.W. chpt. chmn. members in industry comm. 1991-94), Pa. Inst. CPA (Phila. chpt. bd. dirs., fin. svc. com. 1990-92); mem. N.J. County Fin. Officers Assn., South Jersey Assn. County Fin. Officers (founder).

MCCALLISTER, GARY LOREN, biology educator; b. Grand Junction, Colo., Feb. 26, 1945; s. Milfred Edward and Olive (Hammar) McC.; m. Gaydra Lea, Oct. 14, 1966; children: Sundy, Gaydra, Zane, Benjamin. BS in Zoology, Brigham Young U., 1970, MS in Zoology, 1972; D of Arts, U No. Colo., 1982. Chair biology dept. Mesa State Coll., Grand Junction, Colo., 1991-98; dir. Redlands Mosquito Control, Grand Junction, 1982-96; founder Robotics in Sci. Edn., 1999. Inventor Turbatrix T Test, 1984; contbr. articles to profl. jours. Recipient Boetcher fellowship Boetcher Found., U. No. Colo., 1977-78, Disting. Faculty Mesa States Coll.; 1988, Dixson scholar, 1996-98. Mem. Am. Mosquito Control, Am. Soc. Pan, Rocky Mountain Conf. of Parasitology (pres. 1982), Sigma Xi. Mem. LDS Ch. Avocations: guitar, pvt. music studio. Office: Mesa State Coll PO Box 2647 Grand Junction CO 81502-2647

MC CALLUM, CHARLES EDWARD, lawyer; b. Memphis, Mar. 13, 1939; s. Edward Payson and India Raimelle (Musick) McC.; m. Lois Ann Gowell Temple, Nov. 30, 1985; children: Florence Andrea, Printha Kyle, Chandler Ward, Sabra Nicole Temple. BS, MIT, 1960; JD, Vanderbilt U., 1964. Bar: Mich., Tenn. 1964. Assoc. Warner Norcross & Judd LLP, Grand Rapids, Mich., 1964-69, ptnr., 1969—, mng. ptnr., 1992-97; rep. assemblyman State Bar Mich., 1973-78; dir. Rsch. and Tech. Inst. West Mich., 1986-96, chmn., 1989-91; lectr. continuing legal edn. programs; chmn., bd. dirs. Butterworth Ventures, 1987-96; mem. West Mich. World Trade Week Com., 1988-99, chmn., 1990-91; mem. Mich. Dist. Export Coun., 1990-99, chmn., 1992-97. Chmn. Grand Rapids Area Transit Authority, 1976-79, mem., 1972-79; regional v.p. Nat. Mcpl. League, 1978-86, mem. coun., 1971-78; pres. Grand Rapids Art Mus., 1979-81, 96-98, trustee, 1976-83, 94-99; chmn. Butterworth Hosp., 1979-87, trustee, 1977-87; chmn. Butterworth Health Corp., 1982-89, dir., 1982-97, vice chmn., 1989-91, sec., 1991-97; vice chmn. Citizens Com. for Consolidation of Govt. Svcs., 1981-82; mem. nat. alumni bd. Vanderbilt U. Sch. Law, 1998—; chmn. Priority Health, 1995—, bd. dirs., 1995—. Woodrow Wilson fellow, 1960-61; Fulbright scholar U. Manchester, Eng., 1960-61. Fellow Coll. Law Practice Mgmt.; mem. ABA (com. on law firms bus. law sect. 1982-94, chmn. com. on law firms 1994-98, coun. mem. bus. law sect. 1998—, mem. fed. regulation of securities com., mem. internat. bus. law com.), Am. Bar Found., Am. Law Inst., Tenn. Bar Assn., Mich. Bar Assn. (mem. coun. bus. law sect. 1983-89, sect. chmn. 1988-89, ex-officio coun. bus. law sect. 1989—, chmn. takeover laws subcom. 1986-88, co-chmn. internat. bus. law com., internat. law sect. 1988-89), Grand Rapids Bar Assn., Internat. Bar Assn., Grand Rapids C. of C. (pres. 1975, bd. dirs. 1970-76), Univ. Club, Peninsular Club, Order of Coif, Sigma Xi. Home: 110 Bittersweet Ln NE Ada MI 49301-9552

MCCALLUM, EMMA MARGARET, sales executive; b. Cambridge, Eng., May 10, 1970; d. Ian Reid and Jennifer Mary Margaret Mathilde Robertson Fox McCallum. BA in History of Art, Design and Film with honors, U. Newcastle (Eng.), 1992. Roman Catholic. Avocations: dining, jazz, art. Home: 1 Pembridge Villas, 40 Viscount Ct, London W2 4XA, England Office: Pearson TV Internat, 1 Stephen St, London W1P 1PJ, England

MCCAMBRIDGE, JOHN JAMES, civil engineer; b. Bklyn., Oct. 27, 1933; s. John Joseph and Florence Josita (McDonnell) McC.; m. Dorothy Antoinette Cook, Mar. 17, 1962; children: Sharon J., John S., Patrick J., Kathleen C. BCE, Manhattan Coll., 1955; MS, Vanderbilt U., 1958; postgrad., UCLA, 1963-66. Civil engr. Raymond Concrete Pile Co., N.Y.C., 1955; commd. 2d lt. USAF, 1955, advanced through grades to col., 1972; exec. sec. Defense Com. On Rsch., Washington, 1971-73, DOD-NASA Supportive Rsch. Tech. Panel, Washington, 1972-74; asst. dir. Def. Rsch. and Engring. (for Life Scis.) Office Sec. Def., Washington, 1974-75; dir. Air Force Life Support Systems Program Office, Wright Patterson AFB, Ohio, 1975-79; ret. USAF, 1979; prin. Booz, Allen & Hamilton, Inc., Bethesda, Md., 1979-86; v.p. Espey, Huston & Assoc., Inc., Falls Church, Va., 1986-90; mng. prin. JMC Cons. Group, McLean, Va., 1990—; chmn. air panel on NBC Def., NATO, Evere, Belgium, 1970-71; def. dept. rep. to physics survey com., Nat. Acad. Scis., Washington, 1971. Contbr. articles to profl. jours. Decorated Legion of Merit with oak leaf cluster. Fellow Aerospace Med.

Assn. (exec. coun. 1972-73), Inst. Hazardous Materials Mgmt. (Disting. Diplomate, dir. 1984—, chmn. 1988-94); mem. Coun. Engring. and Sci. Splty. Bds. (dir., exec. com. 1995—, v.p. 2000), Acad. Cert. Hazardous Materials Mgrs. (pres. 1984-86), Survival and Flight Equipment Assn. (nat. sec. 1977-78), Air Force Ret. Officers' Cmty. (dir. 1997—), The Washington Assembly, River Bend Golf and Country Club, Fairfax Hunt Club, Black Tie Club, Tower Club, KC, Sigma Xi, Chi Epsilon. Republican. Roman Catholic. Office: JMC Cons Group 9200 Falls Run Rd Mc Lean VA 22102-1028

MCCAMY, CALVIN SAMUEL, optics scientist; b. St. Joseph, Mo., Sept. 22, 1924; s. Benjamin Samuel and Della Emma (Cervenka) McC.; m. Mabel Alice Bellerud, Nov. 4, 1945; children: Susan, Nicholas, Carter. BSChemE, U. Minn., 1945, M in Physics, 1950. Instr. math. U. Minn., Mpls., 1947-50; instr. physics Clemson (S.C.) U., 1950-52; chief image optics and photography Nat. Bur. Standards, Gaithersburg, Md., 1952-70; v.p. for rsch. Macbeth, Newburgh, N.Y., 1970-89; pvt. practice cons. in color sci. Wappingers Falls, N.Y., 1990—; leader in nat. and internat. standardization; adj. prof. chemistry Rensselaer Poly. Inst., Troy, N.Y., 1980-85; mem. adv. bd. Munsell Color Sci. Lab., Rochester (N.Y.) Inst. Tech., 1985—; pres. Kollmorgen Found., Hartford, 1979-89; photog. analyst Ho. of Reps. investigation of shooting of Pres. John F. Kennedy, Washington, 1978. Editor: Papers on Image Optics from National Bureau of Standards, 1973; contbr. over 100 articles to profl. jours., books and encys. Lt. (j.g.) USN, 1943-47. Fellow Optical Soc. Am. (chmn. color com. 1978), Soc. Photographic Scientists and Engrs. (v.p. sci. 1968-72, vis. lectr. 1986), Royal Photographic Soc. Gt. Britain, Soc. Motion Picture and TV Engrs., Washington Acad. Scis., N.Y. Acad. Scis., Inter-Soc. Color Coun. Unitarian. Achievements include improving Munsell color system; development of new principle of absolute radiometry, the compensated variable aperture; discovery of cause of redox blemishes threatening federal microfilm records; design of color test chart used internationally. Home: 44 All Angels Hill Rd Wappingers Falls NY 12590-1828

MCCAN, JAMES LAWTON, education educator; b. Plymouth, Ind., Aug. 10, 1952; s.Jean F. and Mildred P. (Hayn) McC.; m. Carolyn G. Splain, Jan. 16, 1971; children: Kendra, Brittany. B of Phys. Edn., Purdue U., 1974; MS in Edn., 1981, PhD, 1983. Tchr. reading and English Waynetown (Ind.) Mid. Sch., 1974-75, Yorkville (Ill.) H.S., 1979-80; reading specialist Purdue U., West Lafayette, Ind., 1983-89; program chair Basic Skills Advancement Ind. Voc-Tech. Coll., Lafayette, 1989-91; asst. prof., coord. student teaching Hillsdale (Mich.) Coll., 1991-95; dir. Student Achievement Zone, South Bend, Ind., 1995-96; assoc. prof. Nova Southeastern U., Ft. Lauderdale, Fla., 1996—. Contbr. articles and poetry to jours. Mem. Internat. Reading Assn., Fla. Reading Assn. Avocations: reading, music. Home: 1281 Blueberry Ct Altamonte Springs FL 32714-1256 Office: Nova Southeastern U Dept Edn Fort Lauderdale FL 33314

MCCANLESS, CHRISTEL LUDEWIG, library consultant; b. Peenemuende, Germany, Nov. 20, 1939; came to U.S. 1953.; d. Hermann Richard R. and Emmy Jaqlitz Ludewig; m. George F. McCanless, Jr., July, 11, 1963; 1 child, Katherine W. BA in English, U. Montevallo, 1961; MSLS, U. N.C., 1966. Libr. dir. U. Ala., Huntville, Ala., 1963-68; bookstore cons. U. Ala., 1968-75; libr. cons. Huntville Times, Huntville, 1985-90, Huntsville Mus. Art, Huntsville, 1999—; bd. dirs. Huntsville Libr. Assn., 1970-75, Friends Huntsville Pub. Libr., 1960s. Author: Faberge & His Works, 1994; co-author: Faberge Eggs: A Retrospective Encyclopedia, 2000; editor: Faberge Arts Foundation Newsletter, 1997—. Bd. dirs Monte Sano Sch. PTA, 1978-84, Burritt Mus. Park, Huntsville, 1980-94, Monte Sano Civic Assn., Huntsville, 1987-89; vol. instr. ARC, Huntsville, 1970's, 80's; vol. bookkeeper Monte Sano Pool Assn, Huntsville, 1980's. Recipient Libr. Volunteer of the Year, Women's Guild Huntsville Mus. Art, 1999. Mem. Ala. Libr. Assn., Ala. Mus. Assn., Friends of WLRH, Friends of Huntsville-Madison County Libr., Art Librs. Assn. North Am. Avocations: swimming, sailing, traveling, colored pencil drawing. Home and Office: 3218 Panorama Dr SE Huntsville AL 35801

MCCANN, CHRIS (CHRISTIAN DAVID MCCANN), software engineer, educator; b. Springfield, Mass., June 5, 1929; s. James Millard and Helen (Joblin) McC.; children: Nicole Fitzgerald, Adrienne Bashe, Gary McCann. Grad., GE Fin. Mgmt. Program, Schenectady, N.Y. With GE, Schenectady, 1947-66, indsl. educator in stats., probability, math., computers, 1966-80, work effectiveness instr., 1969-83, designer employee incentive programs, 1970-80, software designer, 1966-87; ret., 1987. Prodr., dir., stage mgr., performer, playwright, adminstr., treas. various cmty. theatre groups including Schenectady Light Opera Co., 1961-66; founder Merrimoppets Children's Theater, Schenectady, exec. dir. 1968-71; author: Master Pieces-The Art History of Jigsaw Puzzles, 1998; contbr. articles to antiques and collectibles mags.; designer computer database for golden age of jigsaw puzzles. Pres. Schenectady Civic Ballet Co., 1965-68; mem., officer Schenectady Young Adult Civic Coun., 1951-57; pres. N.Y. State Young Adult Civic Coun., 1952-54; mem. Schenectady GE/United Way liaison bd., 1974-77, chmn., 1976; stage mgr. U.S. Bicentennial celebration Schenectady County, 1976. Named to Schenectady honor roll of outstanding citizens, 1990. Avocation: research on jigsaw puzzle artists. Home: 658 Macelroy Rd Ballston Lake NY 12019-2202

MCCANN, JEAN FRIEDRICHS, artist, educator; b. N.Y.C., Dec. 6, 1937; d. Herbert Joseph and Catherine Brady (Ward) Friedrichs; m. William Joseph McCann, May 14, 1960; children: Kevin, Brian, Maureen McCann Breslin, William, James, Denis Gerard, Kathleen. Student, Caton-Rose Inst. Fine Arts, 1955-57; AAS, SUNY, Farmingdale, 1959; BS, SUNY-Empire State Coll., Binghamton, 1986; MA summa cum laude, Marywood Coll., 1987, MFA in Art summa cum laude, 1989; completed Kellogg Leadership Progam, Sch. Mgmt., SUNY, Binghamton, 1992; PhD, Nova Coll., 1995. Designer Patton Corp., N.Y.C., 1959-66; sub. art tchr. Owego-Apalachin Sch. Dist., 1968-88; tutor, evaluator Empire State Coll. SUNY, 1987—; dir. ArtSpace Gallery, Owego, N.Y., 1992-94; v.p. bd. dirs. Tioga County Coun. on Arts, 1990-91, pres., 1992-95; demonstrator for various schs., ednl. TV and county museums. One-woman shows include IBM, Owego, 1972, Tioga County Hist. Soc. Mus., Owego, 1975, Nat. Hist. Ct. House, 1982, Visual Arts Ctr., Scranton, Pa., 1989-90, ArtSpace Gallery, 1991, MacDonald Art Gallery of Coll. Misericordia, Dallas, Pa., 1992, Plaza Gallery, Binghamton, 1992, Krembs Gallery, Binghamton, 1993, 2000, Wilson Gallery, Johnson City, N.Y., 1994, 2001, Countryside Gallery, Owego, N.Y., 1996, Meml. Gallery, SUNY, Farmingdale, 1998; exhibited in numerous group shows, including IBM, Owego, 1970, Roberson Ctr., Binghamton, 1972, Arnot Art Mus., Elmira, 1974, 89, 92, Nat. Exhibits at Arena, Binghamton, 1974-76, Riise Gallery, St. Thomas, 1975-78, Pennino's Gallery, Burlington Vt., 1975-77, Wilson Gallery, Johnson City, N.Y., 1977, 99, 2000, Visual Arts Ctr., Scranton, Pa., 1987, Grand Concourse Gallery, Albany, N.Y., 1987, Tioga County Hist. Soc. Mus., 1990, ArtSpace Gallery, 1990, Contemporary Gallery, Scranton, 1992, 96, Meml. Gallery, SUNY, Farmingdale, 1997, Artists Guild Gallery, 1993, 99, 2000, Krembs Gallery, Binghamton, N.Y., 1999, 2001; art represented in numerous pvt. collections including those of Pres. George Bush, Congressman Matt McHugh, Senator Tom Libous, Gov. George Pataki, also pub. collections. Bd. dirs. Birthright of Owego, 1993—. Recipient N.Y. State Artisans award, 1982, Nat. Strathmore Silver award, 1989, 1st pl. in Graphic Arts award Jericho Arts Coun., 1994. Mem. Nat. Mus. Women in Arts (charter), Kappa Pi (pres. Zeta Omicron chpt. 1987-89, life), Artists Guild. Avocations: travel, read, visit museums. Home: 23 Paige St Owego NY 13827-1617

MCCANN, THOMAS RYLAND, JR., minister; b. Columbus, Miss., May 28, 1944; s. Thomas Ryland and Shirley Elizabeth (Jones) McC.; m. Beverly Jane Marshall, Nov. 26, 1966; children: Jane, Thomas Scott, Stephen. Student, U. Hawaii, 1962-64; BA in Polit. Sci., U. Richmond, 1966; MPA, U. N.C., Chapel Hill, 1971; MDiv, Southeastern Sem., 1985, DMin, 1990. Ordained to ministry So. Bapt. Conv., 1983. Pastor Wakefield Cen. Bapt. Ch., Zebulon, N.C., 1983-86; pastor 1st Bapt. Ch., Dunn, N.C., 1986-91, Martinsville, Va., 1991—; mem. gen. bd. Bapt. State Conv., Cary, N.C., 1990, mem. coun. on Christian life and pub. affairs, 1990, svcs.-needed com., 1990; sec. Dunn Ministerial Assn., 1989—; v.p. Mcpl. Advisors, Inc., Virginia Beach., Va., 1975-82; county adminstr. James City County, Va., 1973-75; budget dir. Alexandria, Va., 1970-73; dep. dir. Model Cities, Winston-Salem, N.C., 1967-70; mem. strategy planning com. Baptist Gen. Assn. Va., 1996-97, mem. com. on bds. and coms., 1998—, pres., 2000—; trustee Bapt. Theol. Sem., Richmond, Va., 1993-2000; chair exec. com. Va. Bapt. Mission Bd., 2000—. Co-chmn. Evening in the Park Com., Dunn, 1987-91; mem. City Planning Bd., Dunn, 1989-91; chmn. Dunn (N.C.) Drug Abuse Task Force, 1989—; mem., chmn. City Planning Commn., Martinsville, 1993—; bd. dirs., sec., exec. com. Piedmont Arts Assn., Martinsville, Va. Mem. Pi Sigma Alpha. Office: 1st Bapt Ch 23 Starling Ave Martinsville VA 24112-2921

MCCANNY, JOHN VINCENT, engineering educator, executive; b. Ballymoney, Northern Ireland, June 25, 1952; s. Patrick Joseph and Kathleen Brigid (Kerr) McC.; m. Maureen Bernadette, Mellon, July 1979; children: Damian Patrick, Kathryn Louise. BSc in Physics with honors, U. Manchester, Eng., 1973; PhD, New U. Ulster, Coleraine, No. Ireland, 1978; DSc, The Queen's Univ. of Belfast, Belfast, 1998. Chartered engr., physicist. Higher sci. officer RSRE, Malvern, Eng., 1979-80, sr. sci. officer, 1981-83, prin. sci. officer, 1983-84; lectr. Queen's U., Belfast, No. Ireland, 1984-87, reader Queen's U., Belfast, Ireland, 1987-88, prof. microelectronics engring., 1988—; dir. Audio Processing Tech., Ltd., Belfast, 1988-96, CTO Integrated Silicon Sys. Ltd., Belfast, 1990—, Inst. Advanced Microelectronics Ireland, 1989-92, Investments Belfast Ltd.; mem. U.K. Engring. and Phys. Scis. Rsch. Coun. Peer Rev. Coll. on Electronics and Photonics. Author 4 electronics rsch. books, some 200 sci. articles; patentee in field. Recipient No. Ireland Info. Tech. award, 1987, Best Demonstration award U.K. IT Forum, 1994, No. Ireland E-commerce Exporter of the Yr., 1999, Millenium Product award, 1999. Fellow IEEE (chmn. internat. conf. on systolic arrays 1989, tech. chair internat. workshop design and implementation signal processing sys. 1997, tech. dirs. com. on design and implementation of digital signal processing systems Signal Processing Soc. 1999—, 3rd Millennium medal 2000), Royal Acad. Engring. (Silver Medal 1996), Inst. Physics, Inst. Elec. Engrs., Royal Soc. Encouragement Arts, Mfg. and Commerce, No. Ireland Info. Age Initiative; mem. Clandeboye Golf Club. Avocations: golf, swimming, photography, sports, music. Fax: 001 908 771 8645. E-mail: j.mccanny@qub.ac.uk. Office: Queens U Belfast, Dept Electronics, Belfast BT9 5AH, Northern Ireland

MCCARGAR, ELEANOR BARKER, portrait painter; b. Presque Isle, Maine, Aug. 30, 1913; d. Roy and Lucy Ellen (Hayward) Barker; m. John Albert McCargar, Feb. 18, 1947; children: Margaret, Lucy, Mary. Cert. elem. sch. tchg., Aroostook State Normal Sch., Presque Isle, 1933; student, Acadia U., 1935-36; B of Sociology, Colby Coll., 1937; summer student, Harvard U., 1939; and, Cambridge Sch. Art, 1939; studied portrait painting with Kenneth Washburn, Thomas Leighton, Maria von Ridelstein, Jean Henry, 1957-67. Ltd. svc. credential in fine and applied arts and related techs. Calif. C.C. Tchr. sci. and geography Limestone (Maine) Jr. H.S., 1937-41; ins. claim adjuster Liberty Mut. Ins. Co., Boston, 1941-42, Portland, Maine, 1943; ARC hosp. worker 20th Gen. Hosp., Ledo, Assam, India, 1944-45; portrait painter Burlingame and Apple Valley, Calif., 1958—. Commns. include more than 650 portraits in 10 states and 4 fgn. countries. Recipient M. Grumbacher Inc. Merit award for outstanding contbn. to arts, 1977; named Univ. of Maine Disting. Alumnus in Arts, 1981. Avocations: canoeing, camping, travel, studying.

MCCARROLL, DANIEL, geography educator; b. Wishaw, Scotland, July 18, 1961; s. Gerald and Christina (Sinclair) McC.; m. Louise Anne Zelinka, Dec. 18, 1993; children: Bethan, Rhiannon. BA, U. Sheffield, Eng., 1983; PhD, U. Wales, 1986. Rsch. asst. U. Wales, Swansea, 1987-90; lectr. U. Wales, 1991—; tchg. fellow U. Southampton, Eng., 1990-91. Co-author: Geology of the Country Around Aberdaron, Including Bardsey Island, 1993; co-editor: The Isle of Man: Celebrating a Sense of Place, 1990; editor Jour. Earth Surface Processes and Landforms, 1996—; contbr. articles to profl. jours. Mem. Quaterary Rsch. Assn. (treas. 1996—), Brit. Geomorphological Rsch. Group (meetings officer 1995-98). Avocations: rock climbing, poetry. Office: Dept Geography U Wales, UWS Geography, Singleton Park SA2 8PP, Wales

MCCARRON, MERNE CHRISTINE, writer, public relations consultant; b. Milw., July 30, 1959; d. James Warren and Jean Miren (Jones) Schwerdt; divorced; children: Wesley, Madeleine. BA in Journalism and French, U. Wis., 1981. Comm. specialist Wis. chpt. Am. Heart Assn., Milw., 1982-83; with employee comm. dept. Pillsbury Co., Milw., 1985-86; coord. pub. rels. Ellerbe Becket Inc., Mpls., 1986-89; prin., owner, mgr. Savoir Faire Comm., Mpls., 1989—; mem. comm. adv. bd. Minnetonka (Minn.) Pub. Sch. Sys., 1996-99. Editor Minn. Splty. Physicians NetNews and Update newsletters, 1996-99; contbr. articles to profl. jours. Publicist Madison (Wis.) Art Ctr., 1983; mem. Encore adv. bd. YWCA, Mpls., 1989-91. Coll. scholar Homestead H.S., Mequon, Wis., 1977. Mem. Women in Comm., Profl. Women's Network, Internat. Assn. Bus. Communicators (internship coord. 1985-86). Avocations: international travel, art, photography, gardening, speaking French. Office: Savoir Faire Comm 5754 Holiday Ct Minnetonka MN 55345-5312

MCCARTHY, BARRY WAYNE, clinical psychologist; b. Chgo., Sept. 7, 1943; s. Edward Joseph and Dorothy (Small) McC.; m. Emily Jeannette McCabe, Nov. 19, 1966; children: Mark, Kara, Paul. BA, Loyola U., Chgo., 1965; PhD, So. Ill. U., 1969. Diplomate Am. Bd. Profl. Psychology; cert. sex therapist. Intern Wood VA Hosp., Milw., 1968-69; psychology cons. Mt. Vernon Ctr. for Cmty. Mental Health, Alexandria, Va., 1970-73; mem. faculty Am. U., Washington, 1969—, prof. psychology, 1978—; ptnr. Washington Psychol. Ctr., 1977—. Author: (with M. Ryan and F. Johnson) Sexual Awareness: A Practical Approach, 1975, What You Still Don't Know About Male Sexuality, 1977; (with Emily McCarthy) Sexual Satisfaction After Thirty, 1981, Sexual Awareness: Sharing Sexual Plreasure, 1984, Male Sexual Awareness: Increasing Sexual Pleasure, 1988, Female Sexual Awareness: Achieving Sexual Fulfillment, 1989, Couple Sexual Awareness: Building Sexual Happiness, 1990, Intimate Marriage: Developing a Life Partnership, 1992, Confronting the Victim Role: Healing from an Abusive Childhood, 1993, Sexual Awareness: Enhancing Sexual Pleasure, 1993. Mem. APA, Assn. for Advancement Behavior Thrapy, Am. Assn. Sex Educators, Counselors and Therapists, Am. Assn. Marital and Family Therapists. Home: 2827 Kennedy Rd Wilmington DE 19810-3446 Office: Washington Psychol Ctr 4201 Connecticut Ave NW Washington DC 20008-1158

MCCARTHY, BENEDICT, professional soccer player. Forward Ajax Amsterdam Football Club, 1998-99, Celta, 1999—. Office: R C Celta de Vigo, Avda de Balaidos S/N, ES-36210 Pontevedra Spain*

MCCARTHY, BILL DARCY, sociologist, criminologist; b. Guelph, Ont., Can., July 4, 1958. HBA, U. Guelph, 1979; BEd, U. Western Ontario, 1981; MA, U. Toronto, 1984, PhD, 1990. From asst. prof. to assoc. prof. sociology U. Victoria, 1989-95, assoc. prof. sociology, 1995—. Co-author: Mean Streets: Youth Crime and Homelessness, 1997 (C. Wright Mills award 1998, Michael J. Hindelang award, 1998). Office: U Calif Davis Dept Sociology 1 Shields Ave Davis CA 95616-5270

MCCARTHY, CHARLES R., bioethicist, consultant; b. St. Paul; s. Frederic D. and Florence Ruth (Milton) McC.; m. Estelle Rountree, July 23, 1971. BA, U. St. Thomas, St. Paul, 1947; MA, U. Toronto, 1956, PhD, 1961. Ordained priest, 1956. Priest Paulist Fathers; tchr. St. Paul's Coll., Cath. U. Am., George Washington U., Washington; program analyst NIH Divsn. Legis. Analysis, Bethesda, Md., 1971-74, chief legis. devel. br., 1975-78; dir. Office for Protection from Rsch. Risks NIH, Bethesda, Md., 1978-92; sr. rsch. fellow Kennedy Inst. Ethics Georgetown U., Washington; cons. to rsch. instns., 1992—; dir. Office Rsch. Compliance Va. Commonwealth U., 2000; fellow Hastings Ctr. Ethics, 1987—; bd. dirs. Pub. Responsiblity in Medicine and Rsch. Contbr. articles to profl. jours., chpts. to books; mem. editl. bd. Inst. Lab. Animal Rsch. Nat. Acad. Scis., 1995-99, issue editor, 1998. Group leader No. Ireland Peace Missions, Belfast, 1993, 96; mem. State of N.Y. Dept. Health Adv. Group on Human Subjects Rsch. Involving Protected Classes, N.Y.C., 1997-98. Recipient Exptl. Achievement award Asst. Sec. for Health, 1983, Pub. Health Superior Achievement award Surgeon Gen. of U.S., 1989, Spl. citation for 15 yrs. of leadership in protection of humans Commr. FDA, 1992, Outstanding Achievement award Sec. HHS, 1991, Harry C. Rowsell award Scientists Ctr. for Animal Welfare, 19999. Mem. Nat. Acad. Scis. Inst. Medicine (com. on legal and ethical issues relating to the inclusion of women in rsch. 1993-94), Scientists Ctr. for Animal Welfare (bd. trustees, v.p., 1993-99), Am. Fertility Soc. (mem. ethics com. 1989-94), Acad. Medicine, Kiwanis Internat. North Ctrl. Richmond (charter),. Roman Catholic. Avocations: fishing, golf, carpentry, travel. E-mail: chamcc@erols.com. Fax: 804-321-6478. Home: 3613 Hawthorne Ave Richmond VA 23222-1823

MC CARTHY, D. JUSTIN, emeritus college president; b. Brockton, Mass.; s. Denis Joseph and Jane Vincent (Dempsey) McC.; m. Rose Mary Hoye; children: Daniel Justin, Rosemary, John Emmet, Vincent Joseph. B.S., Bridgewater State Coll., 1938, Ed.M., 1939; Ed.D., Harvard U., 1955; LL.D. (hon.), Framingham State Coll., 1985. Tchr., prin. Hanover (Mass.) Pub. Schs.; tchr., asst. prin. Belmont (Mass.) Elem. Schs.; dean instrn. U. Maine, Farmington, 1947-48; extension lectr. U. Maine, Orono, 1947-48; supr. student teaching U. Mass. at Amherst, 1948-55; supr. edn., asst. dir. div. state colls. Mass. State Colls., 1955-56, dir. div. state colls., 1956-61; pres. Framingham (Mass.) State Coll., 1961-85; assoc. in edn. Harvard Grad. Sch. Edn., 1980-83; past sr. advisor Nat. Commn. on the Role and Future State Colls. and Univs. Contbr.: articles to profl. jours. including Harvard Educational Review. Chmn. evaluation Nat. Coun. Accreditation Tchr. Edn., Mass. Bd. Coll. Authority, New Eng. Assn. Colls.and Secondary Schs.; past pres. New Eng. Tchr. Prep. Assn.; former mem. 1202 Commn. Higher Edn. Mass. Mem. Assn. Supervision and Curriculum Devel. (past pres.), Phi Delta Kappa, Kappa Delta Pi (hon.). Address: 302 Washington St PO Box 1209 Duxbury MA 02331-1209

MC CARTHY, DANIEL CHRISTOPHER, JR., manufacturing company executive; b. St. Paul, May 10, 1924; s. Daniel Christopher and Isobel Beatrice (Wilmot) McC.; m. Gail Lloyd Allen, Mar. 9, 1951. B.Mech. Engring. with distinction, Cornell U., 1949. Mgr. profit planning Ford div. Ford Motor Co., 1949-56; dir. mfg. staff Chrysler Corp., 1956-58; controller Chrysler Internat., Geneva, Switzerland, 1958-59; exec. v.p. Pratt & Whitney Co., 1959-61, pres., 1961-64; v.p. bus. equipment group Litton Industries, Orange, N.J., 1964-65; pres. Monroe Internat., Inc. div., 1965-67; founder, v.p., dir. Keene Corp., 1967-74; founder, pres. Gale Corp., 1974-80; founder, chmn. Porta-Fab Corp., 1980-88, Norwood Mfg. Corp., 1980-88; pres., sole proprietor Gale Assocs., cons. and investments, Montclair, N.J., 1982—; founder, dir. Am. Mobile Systems, Inc., 1982-90; cons., dir. JJI Lighting Group Inc., 1980-97, M.H. Koomey subs. Maritime Group, AS, 1991-93; gen. ptnr. Fiduciary Capital Mgmt., L.P., 1989-98; founder, vice chmn. Glenco Holdings Inc., 1992-94. Mem. emeritus Cornell U. Council. Served with inf. AUS, 1942-46. Mem. ASME, Tau Beta Pi, Phi Kappa Phi, Pi Tau Sigma, Psi Upsilon. Home and Office: Gale Assocs 364 Fells Rd Essex Fells NJ 07021-1214

MCCARTHY, DANIEL WILLIAM, management consultant; b. Syracuse, N.Y., Apr. 15, 1952; s. William Cornelius and Ruth Francis (Geller) McC.; m. Mary Coleen Kisil, Jan. 17, 1987; children: Katherine M., Kevin D., Patrick W. BA in Polit. Sci., SUNY, Geneseo, 1974; MBA, NYU, 1982. Asst. buyer Abraham & Straus, Bklyn., 1976-78; buyer Lord & Taylor, N.Y.C., 1978-80; cons. Touche Ross, Newark, 1982-87; sr. mgr. Deloitte & Touche, N.Y.C., 1987-93; dir. Coach Leatherware, N.Y.C., 1993-94; prin. Greenvale Consulting Group, Poughkeepsie, N.Y., 1994-2000; pres. Retex Cons. Group, N.Y.C., 2000—. Author: Point of Sale - Current Trends and Beyond, 1986; contbr. articles to profl. jours. Mem. Town of Poughkeepsie Hist. Planning Commn., Town of Washington Hist. Soc. Mem. Nat. Retail Fedn., Inst. Mgmt. Cons. Roman Catholic. Avocations: wine collecting, ballet, fencing, architecture, investing.

MCCARTHY, DENISE MARIE, radiologist; b. N.Y.C.; d. John T. and Carol McCarthy; m. Carter Grant Abel. BA, Harvard and Radcliffe, 1985; MD, Columbia U., 1989. Diplomate Am. Bd. Radiology. Resident in radiology U. Pa., Phila., 1990-94; fellow in musculoskeletal radiology U. Ala., Birmingham, 1994-95; attending physician Med. U. S.C., Charleston, 1994—; asst. prof. Columbia Presbyn. Med. Ctr., N.Y.C., 1995—; attending physician Morristown (N.J.) Meml. Hosp., 1998—. Contbr. articles to profl. jours. Mem. Radiol. Soc. N.Am., Internat. Soc. Magnetic Resonance Imaging in Medicine, Am. Coll. Radiology, Am. Assn. Women Radiologists, N.Y. Roentgen Ray, Am. Roentgen Ray.

MCCARTHY, GEORGE A., Cayman Islands government executive; b. Cayman Islands, Jan. 22, 1950; m. Debra Thompkins McCarthy, Oct. 29, 1983; children: Schmarrah, Schwannah. Diploma in Govt. Acctg. and Audit, South Thames Coll., England, 1977; A in Applied Sci., Internat. Coll. Cayman Islands, 1978; BBA in Pub. Acctg., Pace U., N.Y., 1985. CPA. Clerical officer Cayman Islands Govt., 1974-77, higher exec. officer, 1977-79, internal auditor, 1979-82, dep. fin. sec., 1985-89; CPA Ernst & Young, Cayman Islands, 1989-91; fin. sec. Dept. Fin. and Devel. Govt. of Cayman Islands, George Town, Grand Cayman, 1992—; chmn. Govt. Pvt. Sector Cons. Cayman Islands, 1992—; chmn. Cayman Islands Monetary Authority, 1992—, Cayman Islands Pension Bd., 1992—; mem. Cayman Islands Legislative Assembly, Grand Cayman, 1992—. Trustee Cayman Islands Mus. Bd., Grand Cayman, 1992—. Named Officer of the Most Excellent Order of the British Empire, HRH Queen Elizabeth, U.K., 1994, Justice of Peace, Cayman Islands Govt., 1992. Mem. Cayman Islands Soc. Profl. Accts., Offshore Inst. Baptist. Avocations: reading, walking. Office: Govt Cayman Islands, Fin Sec Office Govt Adm Bld, Georgetown Grand Cayman, Cayman Islands*

MCCARTHY, JEAN JEROME, retired physical education educator; b. St. Paul, Sept. 11, 1929; s. Joseph Justin and Florence (Quirin) McC.; m. Norma Louise Shermer, July 30, 1955; children: Patrick J., Anne L., Kevin M. BS, U. Minn., 1956, PhD, 1986; MS, Wash. State U., 1958. Tchg. asst. Wash. State U., 1956-57; tchg. asst. U. Minn., 1957-59, adminstrv. asst., 1959-60; asst. prof. phys. edn. U. South Fla., 1960-62; asst. prof. phys. edn. Mankato State U., 1962-71, assoc. prof., 1971-86, prof., 1986-91, ret., 1991, baseball coach, 1962-77; cons. AAU. Contbr. articles to profl. jours. Mem. Minn. Gov.'s Phys. Fitness Adv. Com. With USAF, 1950-54. Recipient Outstanding Faculty award Mankato State U., 1979; named Region 2 Coach of Yr., NCAA, 1971, Outstanding Educators Am., 1970; named to Mankato State U. Athletic Hall of Fame, 1993; U. Minn. Grad. Sch. fellow, 1959-60; Lilly Found. scholar, 1974—; Rsch. Consortium fellow. Mem. AAPHER, Minn. Assn. Health, Phys. Edn., Recreation and Dance, Mensa, Phi Delta Kappa, Phi Epsilon Kappa (scholarship award 1972), Phi Kappa Phi. Roman Catholic.

MC CARTHY, JOHN EDWARD, bishop; b. Houston, June 21, 1930; s. George Gaskell and Grace Veronica (O'Brien) McC. Student, St. Mary's Sem., Houston, 1949-56; M.A., St. Thomas U., Houston, 1979. Ordained priest Roman Catholic Ch., 1956; served various Houston Cath. parishes; exec. dir. Nat. Bishops Com. for Spanish speaking, 1966-68; asst. dir. Social Action Office, U.S. Cath. Conf., 1967-69; exec. dir. Tex. Cath. Conf., Houston, 1973-79; ordained aux. bishop Diocese of Galveston-Houston, 1979-86; installed third bishop of Austin, 1986—; Bd. dirs. Nat. Center for Urban Ethnic Affairs, Mexican-Am. Cultural Center, Sisters of Charity of the Incarnate Word, Houston, from 1981, St. Thomas U., Houston, from 1980. Mem. Cath. Conf. for Urban Ministry. Democrat. Office: Chancery PO Box 13327 Austin TX 78711-3327

MCCARTHY, JOHN GILMAN, JR., international executive search consultant; b. Washington, Apr. 6, 1945; s. John Gilman and Lily (Lambert) McC.; m. Norah Angela Stowell, Oct. 8, 1968 (div. Feb. 1979); children: John Gilman III, Angela; m. Mary Aylwin Stratz Otto, July 24, 1979. BA, Williams Coll., 1968. Trainee Delafield & Delafield, Beirut, 1968-69; area pres. for Mid. East, U.S. Investment Svcs. Inc., Beirut, 1969-70; v.p. Mid-East Resources Engring & Mgmt. Internat. (REMI), Beirut, 1970-73; CEO, Tech. Bus. Svcs., Inc., Beirut, 1973-77; mng. dir. Russell Reynolds Assocs., London, 1977-85, Geneva, 1985-88; mng. dir. Korn/Ferry Internat. Search Group, Geneva, 1988-93; CEO John McCarthy Assocs. S.A.R.L., Geneva, 1993—; trustee Internat. Coll., Beirut, 1994—. Co-chmn. overseas George Bush for Pres. Nat. Fin. Com., London, Geneva, 1980, 88, 92; worldwide chmn. Reps. Abroad, Geneva, 1989-93; mem., sec. European adv. bd. Project HOPE, Geneva, 1991—; v.p. Royal Naval Mus., Portsmouth, 1997—. Mem. Swiss-Am. C. of C. (bd. dirs. Geneva chpt. 1990-96), Am. Internat. Club Geneva (pres. 1993, 94). Avocations: conservative political activist, swimming, hiking. Office: 6 ave de Frontenex, CH-1207 Geneva Switzerland

MCCARTHY, JOHN ROBERT, real estate firm officer; b. Carlisle, Pa., May 29, 1945; s. James Francis and Eleanor Marie (Harrington) McC.; m. Cathleen Ann Rice, Oct. 25, 1975; children: Kevin James, Michael John. BA in Bus. & Polit. Sci., St. Leo Coll., Fla., 1969. Mktg. rep. R.H. Donnelley Corp., N.Y.C., 1969-70; employee benefits rep. Marsh & McLennan Corp., N.Y.C., 1970-73; overseas sales rep. AMF, Inc., White Plains, N.Y., 1973-79; ptnr., sr. v.p. Rostenberg-Doern Co., White Plains, 1979-90; ptnr. pres. McCarthy-O'Callaghan Co Inc, White Plains, 1990—. Mem. Con Edison Sports Hall of Fame Com., White Plains, 1981—, St. Agnes Hosp. Children's Com., 1983-90; bd. dirs. Am. Diabetes Assn. Westchester, 1987-94, adv. bd. St. Vincents Hosp., Harrison, N.Y., 1998—, Lighthouse West County, 1999—; mem. Cardinals Com. of Laity, Westchester; pres. Archbishop Stepinac H.S. Crusader Mens Club, 1998—; fund raising chmn. Gt. Hunger Meml. Westchester County, 1999—; Grand Marhsall White Plains St. Patrick's Parade, 2000. Mem. Exch. Club (hon., past pres. Downtown chpt.), Friendly Sons St. Patrick (officer Westchester chpt. 1984-91, pres. 1990-91, bd. stewards 1990—), Orienta Beach Club (chmn. children's com. 1987-92, bd. dirs. 1992-98, pres. 1995-98), Winged Foot Golf Club. Roman Catholic. Avocation: sports, charitable fund raising. Home: 16 Ridgeway Cir White Plains NY 10605-4119 Office: 1 N Broadway White Plains NY 10601-2310

MCCARTHY, JONATHAN PAUL, economist; b. Britt, Iowa, Dec. 8, 1957; s. Henry Felix and Lucille McC.; m. Diana Marie Shaw, Aug. 23, 1997. BS summa cum laude, U. Wis., Parkside, 1980, MS, 1991; PhD, U. Wis., Madison, 1992. Teaching asst. U. Wis., Madison, 1986-87, rsch. asst., 1987-90; lectr. U. Wis., Whitewater, 1990-91; economist Fed. Res. Bank, N.Y.C., 1992—; vis. economist Bank Internat. Settlements, Basel, Switzerland, 1997-98. Contbr. articles to profl. jours. Mem. Am. Econ. Assn. Avocations: running, basketball, softball. Home: 395 S End Ave Apt 14E New York NY 10280-1029 Office: Fed Res Bank 33 Liberty St New York NY 10045-1003

MCCARTHY, MARY FRANCES, medical foundation administrator; b. Washington, Apr. 16, 1937; d. Joseph Francis and Frances (Oddi) McGowan; m. Charles M. Sappenfield, Dec. 14, 1963 (div. June 1990); children: Charles Ross, Sarah Kathleen; m. Daniel Fendrich McCarthy, Jr., Aug. 25, 1990 (dec. Apr. 1999). BA, Trinity Coll., Washington, 1958; cert. in bus. adminstrn., Harvard U.-Radcliffe Coll., 1959; MA, Ball State U., Muncie, Ind., 1984. Systems engr. IBM, Cambridge, Mass., 1959-61; editl. asst. Kiplinger Washington Editors, 1961-63; feature writer pub. info. dept. Ball State U., 1984-85, coll. editor Coll. Bus., 1985-86, coord. alumni and devel., 1986-88, dir. major gift clubs and donor rels., 1988-90; dir. devel. Sweet Briar (Va.) Coll., 1990-91; adminstr. St. Mary's Hosp. and Med. Ctr. Found., Grand Junction, Colo., 1991—. Editor: A History of Maxon Corporation, 1986, Managing Change, 1986, Indiana's Investment Banker, 1987; assoc. editor Mid-Am. Jour. Bus., 1985-86. Participant Leadership Lynchburg, 1990, Jr. League; mem. Sr. Companions Bd., Grand Junction, 1992—; mem. Mesa County Healthy Cmtys. Steering Com., 1992—; mem. Mesa County Health Assessment, 1994—; regional dir. IX, Assn. for Healthcare Philanthropy, 1996-98, found. bd. 1997—. Recipient Golden Broom award Muncie Clean City, 1989; svc. of distinction award Ball State U. Coll. Bus., 1990. Mem. Coun. for Advancement and Support of Edn., Assn. of Healthcare Philanthropy (regional 9 cabinet 1992—, bd. dirs. 1997—), Nat. Soc. Fundraising Execs. (cert., Colo. chpt. bd. dirs. 1994—), Rotary. Republican. Avocations: biking, walking, cross-country skiing, gardening. Office: St Marys Hosp/Med Ctr Found 2635 N 7th St Grand Junction CO 81501-8209

MCCARTHY, NEVILLE JOHN, retired pharmaceutical company executive; b. Melbourne, Australia, Feb. 17, 1929; s. Harold Louis and Jessica Mary (Edmonds) McC.; m. Margaret Patricia Vance, Sept. 27, 1928; children: Elizabeth, Gavan, Jennifer, Neil, Robert (dec.). MBBS, U. Melbourne, 1953, MA, 1980, M Adminstrn., Monash U., Melbourne, 1973, hon. LLD, 1999. Pvt. practice medicine Australia, 1953-68; sr. exec. Internat. Pharm. Industry, 1968-74; CEO, CSL, Melbourne, 1974-90; cons. in field of biotech. commercialization, 1990—; chmn. MABTECH, Ltd., Melbourne, 1996-97, Monash IVP Group of Cos., 1995—, Chiron Technologies Pty Ltd., Australia, 1993-98; mem. Nat. Health and Med. Rsch. Coun., Australia, 1974-86; exec. dir. Autogen Ltd., 1999—. Named Officer of the Order of Australia, 1984; disting. fellow Queensland Inst. Med. Rsch. Fellow Australian Acad. Tech. Scis. and Engring., Australian Inst. Co. Dirs. Avocations: music, reading, cattle raising, agroforestry.

MCCARTHY, SEAN MICHAEL, air force officer, pilot; b. Tacoma, Feb. 8, 1971; s. Lawrence Joseph and Mary Ann (Kramer) McC. BS with distinction, USAF Acad., Colorado Springs, 1993. Cadet USAF Acad., Colorado Springs, 1989-93; commd. capt. USAF, 1998; student pilot Undergrad. Pilot Tng., Del Rio, Tex., 1993-94; A-10 pilot USAF, Osan Air Base, Korea, 1995-96; air liaison officer 2d Infantry Divsn. USAF, Korea, 1997-98; squadron officer sch. USAF, 1997; strike eagle pilot USAF, Elmendorf AFB, Alaska, 1998—; summer intern Def. Mapping Agy., Alexandria, Va., 1992. Mem. Nat. Geographic Soc. (Dr. John Oliver LaGorce award 1993). Avocations: weight lifting, cycling, swimming, model building. Home: 9827 Little Diomede Cir Eagle River AK 99577 Office: Psc 3 Box 4321 APO AP 96266-0143

MCCARTHY, SHANNON ADRIAN, network engineer; b. Seymour, Ind., Aug. 26, 1969; s. William Joseph and Mary Lou McC. BS in Engring./Computer Sci., U. Louisville, 1993. Cert. Novell 5 adminstr., Novell groupwise 5-5 adminstr. Engring. technician Ben Franklin Retail Stores, Inc., Seymour, Ind., 1993-97; network engr., cons. Sirus Comics, Seymour, 1997-98, The Floor Store, Seymour, 1998; network adminstrn./tech. advisor Seymour Cmty. Schs. Corp., Seymour, 1997-98; engring. cons. Farm Credit Svcs., Louisville, 1998; network adminstrn./cons. Suburban Hosp., Louisville, 1998-99; Lan specialist No. Ariz. Regional Behavioral Health Authority, Flagstaff, Ariz., 1999—; network engr./cons. Brown, Todd & Heyburn PLCC, Louisville, 1995; dir. of info. svcs. U. Louisville, 1991-93. Mem. IEEE, Assn. Computing Machinery, Internat. Who's Who Info. Technology. Democrat. Lutheran. Avocations: snowboarding, travel, surfing, automobiles, weight-lifting. E-mail: cardinal@compuage.com. Office: No Ariz Regl Behav Hlth 125 E Elm Ave Flagstaff AZ 86001-3278

MCCARTHY, SISSEL W., journalist; b. Greenwich, Conn., Mar. 9, 1962; d. Jan O. and Grete (Brofos) Wivestad; m. Stephen Davis McCarthy, Nov. 9, 1985; children: Elliot, Connor, Julian, Justin. BA, Dartmouth Coll., 1984; MS, Columbia U., 1992, M in Internat. Arts, 1992. V.p. Bankers Trust, N.Y.C., 1984-88, Lehman Bros., N.Y.C., 1989-90; prodr. CNN, N.Y.C., 1992-93; corr. CNBC, London, 1994-95; anchor CNN Internat., London, 1996—.

MCCARTHY, THOMAS ANTHONY, philosophy educator; b. Springfield, Mass., Mar. 6, 1940; s. Alfred Lawrence and Minnie Josephine (Vivian) McC.; m. Patricia Perry, Aug. 3, 1963; children: Jennifer, Justin. BS in Math., Holy Cross Coll., 1961; MA in Philosophy, U. Notre Dame, 1963, PhD in Philosophy, 1968. Instr. U. Munich, Germany, 1968-72; from asst. to assoc. prof. Boston U., 1972-85; prof. philosophy Northwestern U., Evanston, Ill., 1985—, John Shaffer Disting. prof. in the Humanities, 1992—; dir. NEH summer seminar, Boston, 1982, 84. Author: The Critical Theory of Jurgen Habermas, 1978, Ideals and Illusions, 1991; co-author: Critical Theory, 1994; editor (series) Studies in Contempory German Social Thought, 1981—. Fellow Guggenheim Found., 1985, Alexander von Humboldt Found., Germany, 1975-76, Am. Coun. Learned Socs., 1989-90; grantee NEH, 1989-90. Mem. Am. Philos. Assn., N.Am. Kant Soc., Soc. for Phenomenology and Existential Philosophy. E-mail: t-mccarthy@nwu.edu. Office: Northwestern U Dept Philosophy 1818 Hinman Ave Evanston IL 60208-0810

MCCARTHY, WILLIAM HENRY, surgeon, educator; b. Nowra, NSW, Australia, Nov. 22, 1935; s. Harry Gerald and Margaret Mary (Mison) M.; m. Mavis Mary Boland; children: Sandra, Margot, Bronwyn, Marcus. MBBS, U. Sydney, Australia, 1958; FRACS, Coll. Surgeons, Australia, 1963; MEd, U. Ill., 1965. Sr. lctr. U. Sydney, 1968-76, assoc. prof., 1976-88, prof. surgery, 1988—; fellow in med. edn. U. Ill., Chicago, 1965-66; exec. dir. Melanoma Found., Sydney U., 1983—, Melanoma Skin Cancer Rsch. Inst., Sydney, 1993—; dir. Sydney Melanoma Unit Royal Prince Alfred Hosp., Sydney, 1985-98. Recipient The Order of Australia award, 1993. Fellow Royal Australian Coll. Surgeons; mem. Order of Australia, Clin. Oncological Soc. Australia, W.H.O. Melanoma Program, Australian Medical Assoc. Avocations: tennis, farming. Office: Royal Prince Alfred Hosp, Sydney Melanoma Unit, Sydney 2050, Australia

MCCARTNEY, (JAMES) PAUL, musician; b. Liverpool, Eng., June 18, 1942; s. James and Mary Patricia (Mohin) McC.; m. Linda Eastman, Mar. 12, 1969 (dec. 1998); 4 children. Hon., Univ. Sussex, Brighton, 1988. With John Lennon and George Harrison in groups Quarrymen, Moondogs, Silver Beatles, 1956-62, also with Ringo Starr in group The Beatles, 1962-70, solo performer and with group, Wings, 1970-80, The Paul McCartney World Tour, 1989, (TV) Here, There and Everywhere: a Concert for Linda, 1999; film appearances include: A Hard Day's Night, 1964, Help!, 1965, Let It Be, 1970, Give My Regards to Broad Street, 1984, Get Back, 1991; TV appearances include Doctor Who, 1965, Magical Mystery Tour, 1967, The Morecambe & Wise Show, 1968, Frost on Sunday, 1968, James Paul McCartney, 1973, Wings Over the World, 1979, Bread, 1986, (voice) The Simpsons, 1995, Saturday Night Live, 1998, V.I.P., 2000; videos include The Beatles: The First U.S. Visit, 1994, Paul McCartney: In the World Tonight, 1997, Twentieth Century Blues: The Songs of Noel Coward, 1998; producer animated film The Oriental Nightfish, 1978; composer numerous songs including (with John Lennon) Please Please Me, I Want To Hold Your Hand, All My Loving, Can't Buy Me Love, I Saw Her Standing There, Love Me Do, Yesterday, Michelle, She's a Woman, Here, There and Everywhere, Good Day Sunshine, Penny Lane, She's Leaving Home, Fool on the Hill, Back in the USSR, Martha My Dear, Blackbird, Helter Skelter, Hey Jude, Let It Be, The Long and Winding Road, Get Back, (solo) Maybe I'm Amazed, My Love, Live and Let Die, Band on the Run, Silly Love Songs, Another Day, No More Lonely Nights, With a Little Luck; rec. artist: (albums with The Beatles) Meet the Beatles, Introducing the Beatles, Hard Day's Night, Help!, Rubber Soul, Revolver, Sgt. Pepper's Lonely Hearts Club Band, Magical Mystery Tour, The Beatles, Yellow Submarine, Abbey Road, Hey Jude, Let It Be; solo albums include McCartney, 1970, Ram, 1971, Red Rose Speedway, 1973, Band on the Run, 1973, Venus and Mars, 1975, Wings Over America, 1975, Wings at the Speed of Sound, 1976, London Town, 1978, Wings Greatest, 1978, Back to the Egg, 1979, McCartney II, 1980, Tug of War, 1982, Press to Play, 1986, All The Best, 1987, Flowers in the Dirt, 1989, Jet, 1989, Tripping the Live Fantastic,1990, Unplugged/The Official Bootleg, 1991, Off the Ground, 1993, Paul is Live, 1993, Flaming Pie, 1997, Run Devil Run, 1999; composer The Liverpool Oratorio, 1991. Decorated Order of Brit. Empire, 1965, Knight Comdr., 1997; recipient Acad. award (with Beatles) for Best Original Song Score, Let It Be, 1970, 5 Grammy awards with Beatles, 2 solo, 1 with Wings, Ivor Novello award for outstanding services to Brit. music, 1989, (with Linda McCartney) Lifetime Achievement award People Ethical Treatment Animals, 1996; named to Rock and Roll Hall of Fame, 1988, Lifetime Achievement award, 1990. Fellow Royal Coll. Music. *

MCCARTY, DONALD K., electronic technician; b. Vermont, Ill., June 17, 1922; s. Harry H. and Olive Marie McCarty. Grad., Vt. H.S., 1940. Cert. electronic technician. Farmer Vermont, 1946-60; asst. engr. KWME Ednl. TV, U. N.Mex., Albuquerque, 1960-61; electronic technician FAA, Prescott, Ariz., 1961-72, ret., 1972. Author: Highlights of the Past, 1996. Tutor adult reading program Spoon River Coll., 1990s; mem. Friends of Macomb, Ill. Pub. Libr., 1994-99, Vermont Betterment, 1995-99; assoc. rep. Sppon River Scenic Dr., Lewistown, Ill., 1994-99. Cpl. U.S. Army, 1943-46. Mem. Philosophy Club. Avocations: radio, electronics, photography, writing. Home: 134 W Fifth St Vermont IL 61484

MCCARTY, TERRY SHANE, SR., real estate developer; b. Ft. Worth, Apr. 16, 1951; s. D.H. Jr. and Alma McC.; m. Suzanne Marie McCarty, Apr. 12, 1974; children: Terry S. Jr., Dustin Kyle. BBA in Acctg., U. Tex., 1975. V.p., owner Tex. Mail Svc., Inc., Ft. Worth, 1974-86, Overland Stagelines, Inc., Ft. Worth, 1983-86; pvt. practice real estate developer Ft. Worth, 1986—; pres. United Equity Investors, Inc., Ft. Worth, 1984-87. Bd. dirs. YMCA, Ft. Worth, 1984-86, Ft. Worth Jr. C. of C., 1982-86, Burleson (Tex.) Indep. Soccer Assn., 1985-87. Republican. Methodist. Avocations: golf, hunting, fishing. E-mail: tmccarty@flash.net. Home and Office: 2400 E Renfro St Burleson TX 76028-2202

MCCARTY, TIA RESHELL, educator; b. Kennett, Mo., Nov. 27, 1968; d. Isaac Clinton and Linda Carlean Bruton; m. Jeffrey McCarty, Aug. 18, 1990. BS, Grand Valley State U., 1992; M in Edn., Ind. U., South Bend, 2000. Tchr. Benton Harbor (Mich.) Schs., 1992—. Home: 106 Warren St La Porte IN 46350-2311 Office: King Jr HS 750 E Britain Ave Benton Harbor MI 49022-4118

MCCARTY, WILLIAM MICHAEL, JR., lawyer; b. Trenton, N.J., 1938. AB, Am. U., Dickinson Coll., 1964; JD, Dickinson Sch. Law, 1967. Bar: Vt. 1967, U.S. Dist. Ct. Vt. 1967, U.S. Ct. Appeals (2d cir.) 1973, U.S. Supreme Ct. 1978. Assoc. Fitts & Olson, Brattleboro, Vt., 1967-71; sole practice Brattleboro, 1971-76; ptnr. McCarty & Rifkin, Brattleboro, Wilmington, Vt., 1976-80; sr. ptnr., pres. McCarty Law Offices, P.C., Brattleboro, Wilmington, 1980—; presenter in various fields; dir. various corps. Mem. Brattleboro Zoning Bd. Adjustment, 1968-75; trustee Vt. Legal Aid, 1970-82, pres., 1979-80; pres. Brattleboro Winter Carnival, 1971-72; rep. Windham Regional Planning & Devel. Com., 1968-70, chmn. ch. coun., bench bar com., 1992-97, moderator Congl. Ch., 1990-94. With USMC, 1956-60. Mem. ABA, ATLA (advocate), Am. Bd. Trial Advocates, Vt. Bar Assn., Windham County Bar Assn. (pres. 1991-93, chair bench bar com. 1989-97), Am. Jud. Soc., Am. Law Student Assn. (nat. v.p., bd. govs.), Nat. Coun. Sch. Attys., Vt. Trial Laywers Assn. (outstanding litigation achievement award 1994), Am. Bd. Trial Advocates (advocate, Vt.), Inns of Ct., Vt. Criminal Def. Attys. Assn., Brattleboro C. of C. (bd. mgrs. 1971-72), U.S. Supreme Ct. Hist. Soc. (Vt. state chair 1999). Republican. Office: 76 High St Brattleboro VT 05301-6074

MCCASLIN, KATHLEEN DENISE, child abuse educator; b. Poughkeepsie, N.Y., Aug. 4, 1962; d. Nancy Ann (Starry) Gosselin; m. David Wayne McCaslin, Sept. 27, 1986 (wid. Oct. 1990); 1 child, LeAnn; m. Larry Thomas Ward, July 14, 1998. BA, Adelphi Coll., 1984. Pub. speaker Impact Seminars, Littlestown, Pa., 1987-96; exec. dir. McCaslin Internat., Florissant, Colo., 1994—; pub. speaker The Family Advocate, Guffey, Colo., 1997—; founder We the People, Colorado Springs, Colo., 1982; vol. counselor/facilitator Beginning Experience, Harrisburg, Pa., 1991-94. Author: (books) Trusting in God, 1993, Respecting Yourself, 1993, Loss and Recovery, 1992, (cd audio) One Child's Journey to Freedom, 1998. Troop leader Girl Scouts U.S., Guffey, Colo., 1998—. Recipient Outstanding Grad. award Adelphi Coll., Colorado Springs, 1984. Mem. ASCPA, World Wildlife Fedn., Arbor Day Found., S.W. Indian Found. Avocations: reading, hiking, needlework, gourmet cooking, gardening. Office: McCaslin Internat PO Box 696 Florissant CO 80816-0696

MCCAUL, JOSEPH PATRICK, chemical engineer; b. N.Y.C., May 11, 1952; s. Joseph and Marion (Sheehan) McC.; Kathleen Anne Crowley, Aug. 3, 1974 (div.); children: Kenneth, Christine; m. Nancy Marie Powell, May 28, 1977. BSChemE, Poly. Inst. Bklyn., 1973, M in Polymer Sci. and Engring., 1977; MBA, Case Western Res. U., 1987. Registered ofcl. baseball umpire Ill. H.S. Assn. Prodn. supr. Mobay Chem. Corp., Bayonne, N.J., 1973-77; process engr. Borg Warner Chems., Parkersburg, W.Va., 1977-78; process control engr. Borg Warner Chems., Ottawa, Ill., 1978-79, process control mgr. Linmar plant, 1979-82; mgr. tech. svc. Standard Oil Co., Cleve., 1982-87; mgr. internat. sales and tech. svc. Barex Group BP Chems., Cleve., 1987—, dir. sales and licensing, 1996-98; group v.p. sales and mktg. EVAL Co. Am., Lisle, Ill., 1998-2000, 2000—; bd. dirs. EVAL Co. Am. Contbr. articles to profl. jours., mags., ency.; patentee in field. Exec. bd. dirs. Mentor Lake Area Baseball, Mentor on the Lake, Ohio, 1988-89, pres. Mentor McMinn Area Baseball League, 1989-91; trustee Pinegate Homeowners Assn., Mentor, Ohio, 1988-89. Mem. Soc. Plastics Engrs. (award 1987), Pinegate Homeowners Assn. (past trustee), Am. Mensa. Republican. Roman Catholic. Avocations: fishing, boating, fitness, baseball, travel. Home: 1612 Pennsylvania Ct Naperville IL 60563-2600 Office: EVAL Corp Am 1001 Warrenville Rd Ste 201 Lisle IL 60532-1301

MCCAULEY, H(ENRY) BERTON, retired public health dentist; b. Duluth, Minn., Dec. 20, 1913; s. Henry Berton and Flora Agnes (Bourassa) McC.; m. Claire Ann Wolff, Dec. 20, 1937. DDS, U. Md., 1936. Lic. dentist, Md. Instr. oral roentgenology U. Md., Balt., 1936-40; Carnegie fellow in dentistry U. Rochester, N.Y., 1940-43, asst. prof. dentistry, cons. Manhattan Project, 1943-45; dir. dental care Balt. City Health Dept., 1949-75; health advisor Office of Mayor, Balt., 1975-77, gen. health adminstr., 1977-80; pres. North Balt. (Mental Health) Ctr., Balt., 1980; bd. visitors Balt. Coll. Dental Surgery, U. Md., 1997—. Contbr. more than 50 articles to profl. jours. Dir. Cooley's Anemia Found. Md., 1977-93. With USPHS, Nat. Inst. Dental Rsch., 1945-49. Fellow APHA, AAAS, Am. Coll. Dentists (J. Ben. Robinson award 1991), Internat. Coll. Dentists, Pierre Fauchard Acad.; mem. ADA (life, coun. on dental therapeutics 1943-48, chmn. sect. on pub. health 1968), Internat. Assn. Dental Rsch., Am. Soc. Dentistry for Children (Disting. Svc. award 1978), Am. Assn. Pub. Health Dentistry, Am. Acad. History of Dentistry (Hayden-Harris award 1988, pres. 1990-91), Md. Soc. Dentistry for Children (pres. 1954-55), Md. State Dental Assn. (historian 1959-87, Disting. Svc. award 1986), Md. Pub. health Assn. (pres. 1967-68), Balt. City Dental Soc. (pres. 1973), Nat. Mus. Dentistry (bd. visitors 1997—), Md. Hist. Soc., Walters Art Gallery, Balt. Mus. Art, Mil. Order World Wars (comdr. chpt. 1986-87, dept. 1994-95), Sigma Xi, Omicron Kappa Upsilon, Psi Omega. Roman Catholic. Avocations: history, travel, photography, gardening. Home: 3804 Hadley Sq E Baltimore MD 21218-1807

MCCAULEY, JANE REYNOLDS, journalist; b. Wilmington, Del., Oct. 22, 1947; d. John Thomas and Helen (Campbell) McC. BA, Guilford Coll., 1969. Editor, sr. writer Nat. Geographic Soc., Washington, 1970-90; freelance writer, editor, artist, 1990-96; exec. editor AM Quilter's Soc., 1996-97; freelance editor, writer, cons., profl. quilt restorer, 1997—; former owner Unique Native Crafts. Author of 15 children's books; co-author award-winning travel books. Mem. Children's Book Soc. of Am., Washington Ind. Writers. E-mail: ritstuff4u@aol.com.

MCCAWLEY, AUSTIN, psychiatrist, educator; b. Greenock, Scotland, Jan. 17, 1925; came to U.S., 1954; s. Austin and Anna Theresa (McBride) McC.; m. Gloria Klein, Feb. 15, 1958; children: Joseph, Tessa. MBCHB, U. Glasgow, 1948. Diplomate Am. Bd. Psychiatry and Neurology; DPM Royal Coll. London. Intern Glasgow Royal Infirmary, Scotland, 1948; resident Inst. Living, Harford, Conn., 1954-57, clin. dir., 1960-66; med. dir. Westchestor br. St. Vincent's Hosp., N.Y.C., 1966-72; dir. psychiatry St. Francis Hosp., Hartford, 1972-88; prof. psychiatry U. Conn. Med. Sch., Farmington, 1983-93; pvt. practice, West Hartford, Conn., 1988—; dir. psychiatry Kaiser Permanente of Conn., 1996-99. Co-author: The Physician, 1983; contbr. articles to profl. jours. Chmn. Bd. Mental Health, State of Conn., 1981-84, Search Com. for Commr. Mental Health, Conn., 1981; mem. Gov.'s Spl. Task Force on Mental health Policy, Conn., 1982. With RAF, 1948-50. Fellow Am. Psychiat. Assn., Am. Coll. Psychiatry (charter fellow, founder); mem. Conn. Psychiat. Soc. (pres. 1978-79), Hartford Golf Club. Democrat. Roman Catholic. Avocations: music, golf. Home and Office: 128 Westmont St Hartford CT 06117-2926

MCCHESNEY, SAMUEL PARKER, III, real estate executive; b. Oakland, Calif., July 30, 1945; s. Samuel Parker and Edna Margaret (McCorkle) McC.; m. Vicki Storrie, June 21, 1969; children: Nathan, Amanda, Jed. BA, Washington and Lee U., 1967; JD, Case Western Res. U., 1970. Lic. real estate broker, Mo., Kans. Urban intern and multifamily housing rep. HUD, Chgo., 1970-71; project loan mgr. 1st Home Investment Corp., Overland Park, Kans., 1971-72; v.p. devel. Northland Bldg. Corp., Gladstone, Mo., 1973-74; cons. Urban Equities, Kansas City, Mo., 1975; pres., co-owner McChesney Devel. Co., Inc., Edwardsville, Kans., 1976-78; pres., owner McChesney, Inc., Kansas City, 1978—; Managed Maintenance Inc., 1990-97. Pres. Lake Quivira (Kans.) Homeowners Assn. Inc., 1983-85; mem. planning and zoning com. City of Lake Quivira, 1983, mem. planning commn., 1992—; mem. real estate com. Quivira, Inc., 1986, nominating com., 1987-88, 90, restrictions & covenants update com., 1993-95; mem. patron's com. Tom Watson Golf Classic, Kansas City, 1984-85; mem. Lake Quivira Long Range Planning Com., 1987-88. Recipient cert. Nat. Assisted Housing Profl. Exec. Level. Mem. Johnson County Bd. Realtors, Affordable Housing Mgrs. Assn. (dir. region 7 1995—, v.p. region 7, mem. fin. com. 1995-96, chmn. 1995-96, mem. membership com. 1997—, mem. edn. com. 1997—), Lake Quivira Country Club (pres. 1983-85). Avocations: golfing, travelling, reading, gardening. Home: 510 Hillcrest Rd E Lake Quivira KS 66217-8781 Office: 9403 W 119th Ter Overland Park KS 66213-1699

MCCHRISTIAN, JOSEPH ALEXANDER, international business executive; b. Chgo., Oct. 12, 1914; s. Robert Lee and Lillian (Alexander) McC.; BS in Mil. Sci., U.S. Mil. Acad., 1939; grad. Command and Gen. Staff Coll., 1942, Armed Forces Staff Coll., 1951, Army War Coll., 1955, Army Lang. Sch., 1956; m. Dempsie Catherine Van Fleet, Sept. 26, 1940; children: Joseph Alexander, Anne, Lillian. Enlisted U.S. Army, 1933, commd. 2d lt., 1939, advanced through grades to maj. gen., 1961; various assignments 1933-44; successively armored inf. bn. comdr., asst. chief staff plans and ops., chief staff 10th Armored Div., ETO, 1944-45; asst. chief staff intelligence Hdqrs. 3d U.S. Army, Germany, 1945-47; dep. dir. intelligence U.S. Forces, Austria, 1947-48; comdg. officer 2d Bn., 3d Inf., "The Old Guard", Ft. McNair, D.C., 1948-49; spl. asst. to chief JUSMAG, Greece, 1949-50; S3 dept. tactics U.S. Mil. Acad., 1951-53, comdg. officer 1st Regt., U.S. Corp Cadets, 1953-54; U.S. Army attache, Greece, 1956-60; comdg. officer 1st Armored Regt. (tng.), also comdg. officer U.S. Army Tng. Ctr., Armor, Ft. Knox, Ky., 1960-61; chief Western div. Office Asst. Chief Staff-Intelligence, Dept. Army, 1962-63; asst. chief staff intelligence Hdqrs. U.S. Army Pacific, 1963-65; chief Army, Navy, Air Force and Marine Corps Intelligence, Hdqrs. U.S. Mil. Assistance Command, Vietnam, 1965-67; comdg. gen. 2d Armored Div., also III Corps, Ft. Hood, Tex., 1967-68; asst. chief of staff for intelligence Dept. Army, 1968-71; v.p. Overseas Basic Industries, Fla., 1972-74; v.p., gen. mgr. Société des Eaux, Athens, Greece, 1972-74; v.p. Ulen Mgmt. Co., Fla., 1972-75, Van Fleet Estates, Inc., Fla., 1970-77. Commr., Town of Jupiter Island (Fla.), 1975-83. Decorated D.S.M. with oak leaf cluster, Silver Star, Legion of Merit, Bronze Star with 3 oak leaf clusters, Air medal, Army Commendation, Am. Def., Am. Campaign, ETO Campaign with 3 bronze stars, WWII Victory, Nat. Def. with bronze oak leaf cluster, Vietnam Svc. with 4 oak leaf cluster, Vietnam Campaign, Combat Inf. badge; Croix de Guerre with gold star and bronze star (France); comdr. Royal Order King George 1st, also Disting. Svc. medal (Greece); Nat. Order 5th class and Disting. Svc. Order 1st class (Republic Vietnam); Mil. Merit medal, Chung Mu (Korea), Grand Cross of Mil. Merit with white ribbon (Spain), Medal of Metz (France). Mem. Mil. Order World Wars, Alumni Assn. U.S. Mil. Acad. Clubs: Army and Navy (Washington); Hobe Sound Yacht, Jupiter Island Club (Hobe Sound, Fla.); Ends of the Earth. Home: 365 S Beach Rd Hobe Sound FL 33455-2613

MCCLAIN, EDWARD FIFER, JR., retired physicist; b. Carrolton, Mo., Aug. 22, 1921; s. Edward Fifer and Corrine Carrie (Rahmoeller) McC.; m. Louise Cherry Shelby, Dec. 9, 1943; children: Deanna Louise, William Edward, Robert Jay. BSEE, George Washington U., 1950. With Naval Rsch. Lab., Washington, 1942-68, head radio astronomy br., 1956-68; ret., 1968; past chmn. commn. radio astronomy Internat. Scientific Radio Union; past adv. com. Nat. Radio Astronomy Obs.; cons. Nat. Acad. Sci., Interdept. Radio Adv. Com., Nat. Radio Astronomy Obs.; astronomy panel NSF. Contbr. articles to profl. jours.; patentee in field. Fellow AAAS, Washington Acad. Scis.; mem. IEEE (life), Internat. Astron. Union, Am. Astron. Soc., Scientific Rsch. Soc. Am., Sigma Tau. Achievements include conducting sea trials ST periscope radar in submarine; designed AN/APN67 self-contained doppler automatic navigator for aircraft; determined correct distance to radio source Cass A using galactic hydrogen absorption. Avocation: sound reproduction. Home: 4133 Maple Rd Morningside MD 20746-3514

MCCLAIN, GREGORY DAVID, minister; b. Anderson, S.C., June 6, 1957; s. Lemuel David and Mary Josephine (Hawkins) McC.; m. Anne Leigh Blackwell, May 21, 1983; children: Jonathan David, Sean Gregory. AS, Anderson Coll., 1977; BA, Erskine Coll., 1979; MDiv, Southeastern Bapt. Theol. Sem., Seminary, Wake Forrest, N.C., 1982; D of Ministry, Wesley Theol. Sem., Washington, 1996. Ordained Boulevard Bapt. Ch., 1983. Chaplain extern Bapt. Med. Ctr., Columbia, S.C., 1982; assoc. pastor First

Bapt. Ch., South Boston, Va., 1983-86; minister Corrottoman Bapt. Ch., Lancaster, Va., 1986-93, Colonial Beach (Va.) Bapt. Ch., 1993-98, Neill's Creek Bapt. Ch., Angier, N.C., 1998—; pres. Dan River Bapt. Pastors, Halifax, Va., 1984-85; preacher-jr. high weekend, Va. Bapt. Gen. Assn., 1986, faculty youth week, 1984-88; v.p. Lancaster Ministerial Assn., 1987-88; v.p. Little River Bapt. Pastor's Conf., Lillington, N.C., 2000—. Active CROP walk, South Boston, Va., 1984-85; coach youth soccer, South Boston, 1985, Westmoreland County, Va., 1995-97, Buics Creek, N.C., 1998; merit badge counselor Boy Scouts Am., Lancaster, 1990-93; mem. Lancaster Ednl. Task Force, 1988. Mem. Ruritan Club (chaplain 1990-93). Office: Neill's Creek Bapt Ch 4200 Neills Creek Rd Angier NC 27501-7063

MCCLAIN, JERRY RAY, lawyer; b. Perrin AFB, Tex., Nov. 12, 1960; s. Raymond Lee and Tiny Merel (Davis) McC. BA in Polit. Sci., U. Tex., Arlington, 1987; JD, U. Houston. Dock worker, truck driver Cen. Freight Lines, Inc., Irving, Tex., 1980-86; litigation legal asst. civil div. Tarrant County Dist. Atty., Ft. Worth, 1987; bankruptcy legal asst. Johnson and Johnson, P.C., Dallas, 1988; document analyst Heard, Goggan, Blair and Willaims, P.C., Dallas, 1988; faculty rsch. asst. U. Houston Law Ctr., 1990-91; atty. Law Office of Jerry R McClain, 1992—; assoc. McCreary & Assocs., 1999. Mem. ABA, State Bar Tex., U. Houston Law Ctr. Advocates, Denton County Bar Assn., Collin County Bar Assn. Republican.

MCCLAIN, THOMAS EMERSON, communications executive; b. East Liverpool, Ohio, July 26, 1950; s. Thomas E. and Helen Marie (Polinski) McC. BA, Case Western Reserve, Cleve., 1972; MA, Kans. State U., 1973. With intergovtl. rels. Ohio EPA, Columbus, 1974-77; legis. liaison Ohio Consumers Counsel, Columbus, 1977-80; dep. dir. Ohio Consumers Counsel, 1980-81; press sec. Ohio Atty. Gen., Columbus, 1982-83; asst. dir. Pub. Utilities Commn., Columbus, 1983; with instnl. rels. dept. Battelle Project Mgmt. Div., Chgo., 1983-84; mgr. instl. rels. Battelle Project Mgmt. Div., 1984-86; mgr/ comms. Battelle, Columbus, 1986-88, dir. corp. comm., 1989-95, v.p. corp. comms., 1995—; sec. devel. bd. Children's Hosp., Columbus, 1990-91. Vol. Ohio Youth Commn., Columbus, 1975-76; active ARC-Cen. Ohio chpt., 1986-87; mem. design rev. com. Ohio State U. Sci. and Tech. Park; active Colo. Energy Sci. Ctr. Bd.; amb. USAR Program; mem. Ohio State Bd. of Edn. Mem. Rotary (chmn. program com. 1991-93, bd. dirs. 1994-95, 2d v.p. 1996-97). Presbyterian. Avocations: basketball, golf. Home: 2689 Camden Rd Upper Arlington OH 43221-3221 Office: Battelle 505 King Ave Columbus OH 43201-2693

MCCLAIN, WILLIAM ANDREW, lawyer; b. Sanford, N.C., Jan. 11, 1913; s. Frank and Blanche (Leslie) McC.; m. Roberta White, Nov. 11, 1944. AB, Wittenberg U., 1934; JD, U. Mich., 1937; LLD (hon.), Wilberforce U., 1963, U. Cin., 1971; LHD, Wittenberg U., 1972. Bar: Ohio 1938, U.S. Dist. Ct. (so. dist.) Ohio 1940, U.S. Ct. Appeals (6th cir.) 1946, U.S. Supreme Ct. 1946. Mem. Berry, McClain & White, 1937-58; dep. solicitor, City of Cin., 1957-63, city solicitor, 1963-72; mem. Keating, Muething & Klekamp, Cin., 1972-73; gen. counsel Cin. br. SBA, 1973-75; judge Hamilton County Common Pleas Ct., 1975-76; judge Mcpl. Ct., 1976-80; of counsel Manley, Burke, Lipton & Cook, Cin., 1980—; adj. prof. U. Cin., 1963-72, Salmon P. Chase Law Sch., 1965-72. Mem. exec. com. ARC, Cin., 1978—; bd. dirs. NCCJ, 1975—. Served to 1st lt. JAG, U.S. Army, 1943-46. Decorated Army Commendation award; recipient Nat. Layman award, A.M.E. Ch., 1963; Alumni award Wittenberg U., 1966; Nat. Inst. Mcpl. Law Officers award, 1971, Ellis Island Medal of Honor, 1997. Fellow Am. Bar Found.; mem. ABA, FBA, Am. Judicature Soc., Cin. Bar Assn., Ohio Bar Assn., Nat. Bar Assn., Friendly Sons St. Patrick, Bankers Club, Masons (33d degree), Alpha Phi Alpha, Sigma Pi Phi. Republican. Methodist. Home: 2101 Grandin Rd Apt 904 Cincinnati OH 45208-3346

MCCLANAHAN, MICHAEL NELSON, systems analyst; b. Cin., Oct. 28, 1953; s. Roland Nelson and Jeanne Ann (Stevens) McC.; m. Tina Rosanne Swiecki, Mar. 8, 1986; 1 child, Sean Gabriel. Student, U. Cin., 1972-73, Goldenwest Coll., 1979-80, Riverside Community Coll., 1980-83, 90-92. Pres. Riverside (Calif.) Mktg., 1983-88; digital systems analyst Wyle Labs., Norco, Calif., 1988-93; systems analyst Ctr. for Environ. Rsch. and Tech. U. Calif., Riverside, 1993—. Author: (software) SDAS, 1989, HCSS DAS System, 1990, (book) HCSS Systems Operation, 1990, (manual) Software Quality Assurance, 1991. Recipient Svc. award Wyle Labs., 1991. Mem. IEEE, Assn. Computing Machinery, Instrument Soc. of Am., Soc. Automotive Engrs. Achievements include design of numerous software systems and integration of these with data acquisition hardware systems for the purposes of acquiring rsch. data from unique test systems in environ., aerospace, nuclear and def. industries; rsch. in ULEV hydrogen-powered vehicle devel. Office: U Calif Riverside CE-CERT 1200 Columbia Ave Riverside CA 92507-2129

MCCLARY, JAMES DALY, retired contractor; b. Boise, Idaho, July 19, 1917; s. Neil Hamaker and Myrtle (Daly) McC.; m. Mary Jane Munger, Feb. 2, 1939; children: Pamela, John. Student, Boise Jr. Coll., 1934-36, AA, 1957; AB, Stanford U., 1938; LLD, Gonzaga U., 1976. Laborer to supt. Morrison-Knudsen Co., Inc., Boise, 1932-42, project mgr., asst. dist. mgr., 1942- 47; gen. mgr. Mexican subs. Morrison-Knudsen Co., Inc., 1947-51, asst. to gen. mgr., 1951-53, asst. gen. mgr., 1953-60, dir., 1955-78, v.p., 1956-60, exec. v.p., 1960-72, chmn. bd., 1972-78; mem., vice chmn. Idaho Permanent Bldg. Fund Adv. Council, 1961-64, chmn., 1964-71. Treas. Idaho Rep. Cen. Com., 1964-70; presdl. elector, 1968; trustee Boise Jr. Coll., 1960-83, vice chmn., 1967-73, chmn., 1973-83; bd. dirs. Boise State U. Found., Inc., 1964-91, pres., 1970-81; bd. dirs. AGC Edn. and Rsch. Found., 1974-91, pres., 1974-90; elector Hall of Fame for Great Ams., 1976—; trustee St. Alphonsus Regional Med. Ctr., 1976-82, vice chmn., 1981-82. Recipient George Washington medal of honor Freedoms Found., Valley Forge, Pa., 1977, Disting. Alumnus award Boise State U., 1988, Silver medallion, 1996; decorated Chevalier and Legion of Honor, Order of DeMolay; named Disting. Alumnus of Yr. Boise State U. Alumni Assn., 1971, Ky. Col. Fellow ASCE, Am. Inst. Constructors; mem. Internat. Rd. Fedn. (bd. dirs. 1972-78, vice chmn. 1977-78), Soc. Am. Mil. Engrs., Assoc. Gen. Contractors Am. (bd. dirs. 1958—, mem. exec. com. 1961-78, pres. 1972), Cons. Constructors Coun. Am., Newcomen Soc., Conf. Bd. (sr. mem.), Idaho Assn. Commerce and Industry (bd. dirs., chmn. 1974-77, Harwood award 1994), Moles (hon., mem. award for Outstanding Achievement in Constrn. 1978), Hillcrest Country Club (bd. dirs. 1965-67, 69, pres. 1967), Arid Club (mem. exec. com. 1966), Ariz. Club (Scottsdale), Ariz. Country Club (Phoenix), Univ. Club (Mexico City), Stanford Club (Washington). Episcopalian. Home: 4903 Roberts Rd Boise ID 83705-2805

MCCLAUGHERTY, JOE L., lawyer, educator; b. June 1, 1951; s. Frank Lee and Elease (Terrell) McC. BBA with honors, U. Tex., 1973, JD with honors, 1976. Bar: Tex. 1976, N.Mex. 1976, U.S. Dist. Ct. N.Mex. 1976, U.S. Ct. Appeals (10th cir.) 1976, U.S. Supreme Ct. 1979, Colo. 1988. Assoc. Rodey, Dickason, Sloan, Akin & Robb, P.A., Albuquerque, 1976-81, ptnr., dir., 1981-87; resident ptnr. Rodey, Dickason, Sloan, Akin & Robb, P.A., Santa Fe, N.Mex., 1983-87, mng. ptnr., 1985-87; ptnr. Kemp, Smith, Duncan & Hammond, P.C., 1987-92, mng. ptnr., 1987-92; ptnr. McClaugherty & Silver, P.C., Santa Fe, 1992—; adj. prof. law U. N.Mex., Albuquerque, 1983—; faculty Nat. Inst. Trial Advocacy, so. regional, So. Meth. U. Law Sch., 1983—, Rocky Mt. regional, U. Denver Law Sch., 1986—, nat. session U. Colo. Law Sch., 1987; faculty Hastings Ctr. for Trial and Appellate Advocacy, 1985—; bd. dirs. MCM Corp., Raleigh, N.C., Brit.-Am. Ins. Co., Ltd., Nassau, The Bahamas, 1985-91. Mem. N.Mex. Bar Assn. (bd. dirs. trial practice sect. 1976-85, chairperson 1983-84, dir. young lawyers divsn. 1978-80), N.Mex. Assn. Def. Lawyers (pres. 1982-83, bd. dirs. 1982-85). Office: McClaugherty & Silver PC PO Box 8680 Santa Fe NM 87504-8680

MCCLEANE, GARY JOHN, physician; b. Belfast, Northern Ireland, Oct. 4, 1960; s. Ronald Norman and Lucy Sinton (Snoddy) McC.; children: Andrew, Robert, Emily. B Medicine B Surgery, Queens U., Belfast, 1984, B Obstetrics, 1984, MD, 1989. Intern Ulster Hosp., Dundonald, Northern Ireland, 1984-85; cons. anesthetist, cons. pain mgmt. Craigavon (Northern Ireland) Area Hosp., 1992—, hyperbaric med. officer, 1992—. Contbr. articles to profl. publs. Fellow Royal Coll. Surgeons Ireland (faculty anesthetics)mem. World Soc. Pain Clinicians, Interna. Soc. for Study of Pain, Ulster Med. Soc., Brit. Pain Soc. Home: 58 Kensington Manor, Dollingstown BT66 7MR, Northern Ireland

MCCLEARY, BENJAMIN WARD, investment banker; b. Washington, July 9, 1944; s. George William and Nancy (Grim) McC.; m. Dierdre Marsters, May 6, 1967 (div. 1977); children: Benjamin, Katherine; m. Jean Muchmore, Oct. 15, 1983. AB, Princeton U., 1966. With Chemical Bank, N.Y.C., 1969-81; trainee, asst. sec., asst. v.p., v.p., Chemical Bank; sr. v.p. Lehman Bros. Kuhn Loeb, N.Y.C., 1981-83; mng. dir. Shearson Lehman Bros., 1983-87, Shearson Lehman Hutton Internat., London, 1987-88, Shearson Lehman Hutton, Inc., N.Y.C., 1988-89; ptnr. McFarland Dewey & Co., LLC, N.Y.C., 1989—; dir. Detrex Corp., Detroit, Harvel Plastics, Easton. Lt. (j.g.) USN, 1966-69. Office: McFarland Dewey & Co LLC 230 Park Ave Rm 1450 New York NY 10169-1450

MCCLEERY, WINSTON THEODORE, computer consulting company executive; b. Mobile, Ala., Sept. 6, 1935; s. Robert Alton and Theadora K. (Kiebel) McC.; m. Sandra Thoss, Dec. 28, 1958; children: Winston T., Jacqueline McCleery McNeely. BS, Springhill Coll., 1957; postgrad., U. Ala., 1957-58. Logic design engr. Autonetics N.Am. Aviation, Anaheim, Calif., 1960-63; dirt. info. sys. Litton Industries, L.A., 1963-69; founder, owner Winston T. McCleery, Cons., 1969—; pres., CEO Mgmt. Resources, Inc., Mobile, 1979—. Patentee in field. With U.S. Army, 1958-60. Recipient Cert. for Heroism Boy Scouts Am., 1949. Mem. Data Processing Mgmt. Assn., Assn. Computer Machinery, Am. Mgmt. Assn., Ind. Computer Cons.'s Assn., Optimists (pres. 1972). Republican. Achievements include contributions to the design and development of the U.S. Army Field Artillery's first digital fire direction computer; member of design team of the centaur missile's guidance system that made the first soft landing on the moon; design and development of the first seamless, integrated, on-line and instant-time computer application system for main frame class computers; inventor of computer power and temperature enviroment control system, development of first automatic documentation system used to document computer programs written in the Cobol language. Home: 5213 Janekyn Dr Mobile AL 36693-4142

MCCLELLAN, JANET ELAINE, law educator; b. Salina, Kans., June 30, 1951; d. William Francis and Ethel Mary (Rinebold) McC. BA in Govt., Adminstrn., Park Coll., Parkville, Mo., 1976; MPA, U. Dayton (Ohio), 1978; postgrad., U. Kans., 1982-86. Police officer City of Leavenworth, Kans., 1970-71; narcotics agt. Kans. Bur. Investigation, Topeka, 1971-73; asst. to chief Police Dept., Ellensberg, Wash., 1973-76; dir. juvenile divsn. Police Dept., Centerville, Ohio, 1976-79; watch comdr. Police Dept., Douglas, Wyo., 1978-79; dir. criminal justice adminstrn. Park Coll., 1979—; directing advisor Tau Lambda Alpha Epsilon and Alpha Phi Omega, Park Coll., 1980-98; cons. Probation-Parole Dept., Kansas City, Mo., 1979-80, Police Dept., Leavenworth, 1981-82, Sheriff's Dept., Liberty, Mo., 1984-86; corrections adminstr. Kans. Dept. of Correction, 1988-96; police chief Pawnee Rock, Kans., 1996-98; prof. criminal justice, 1998—. Author mystery book series including K.C. Bomber, Murder in Cloud City, Penn Valley Phoenix, River Quay, Chimney Rock Blues, Windrow Garden; contbr. articles to profl. jours.; reviewer criminal justice textbooks, jours., reviewing editor book Introduction to Criminal Justice, 1984, Modern Police Management, Criminal Justice and Public Policy. Chmn. S.W. Montgomery County Youth Commn., Dayton, Ohio, 1977-79; bd. dirs. Synergy Youth Half-way House, Parkville, 1980-86. Mem. Internat. Assn. Chiefs of Police, Am. Soc. Criminology, Am. Criminal Justice Soc., Am. Correctional Assn., Mo. Polit. Sci. Assn., Am. Soc. Pub. Adminstrn., Mo. Acad. Sci., Pi Gamma Mu, Pi Sigma Alpha, Delta Tau Kappa. Democrat. Office: Southwestern Oreg CC 1988 Newmark Ave Coos Bay OR 97420-2911

MCCLELLAN, ROBERT EDWARD, civil engineer; b. Atlanta, Feb. 27, 1922; s. Robert Edward and Maria Elizabeth (Ameln) McC.; m. Mary Margaret Billetter, Oct. 21, 1944; children: Kathleen Mary, Mary Elizabeth, Patricia Maura, Eileen Mary, Robert Edward III, Mary Margaret, Thomas Francis. BCE, U. So. Calif., 1947, MSCE, 1956, PhD in Engring., 1970. Registered profl. civil and structural engr., Calif. Gen. supr. design Rocketdyne, Canoga Park, Calif., 1959-62; mem. tech. staff The Aerospace Corp., El Segundo, Calif., 1962-69, mgr. strategic studies, 1980-85; chief tech. staff The Ralph M. Parsons Co., Pasadena, Calif., 1969-80; v.p. research and devel. Apollo Systems Tech., Canyon Country, Calif., 1985-88, also bd. dirs. Served to lt. (j.g.) USN, 1943-46, PTO. Recipient Outstanding Civil Engring. Grad. award U. So. Calif., 1977. Mem. AIAA, Am. Def. Preparedness Assn., AAAS, N.Y. Acad. Scis., L.A. Athletic Club, Sigma Xi, Tau Beta Pi, Chi Epsilon. Republican. Roman Catholic.

MCCLELLAND, PATRICIA G., minister; b. Warsaw, Mo., July 12, 1944; d. Gail Raymond and Martha Carolyn (Lewis) Easton; m. Lester E. McClelland, Aug. 18, 1974; 1 child, Melody. BS, U. Mo., 1968; MA, Drury Coll., 1972. Cert. tchr., Mo., Kans., Ill.; lic. counselor; ordained to ministry Unity Ch., 1986. Instr. U. Mo., Kansas City, 1968, 71-74, Park Coll., Parkville, Mo., 1968-70; spl. cons. Kansas City Pub. Schs., 1970-71; author edn. materials, 1975-78; instr. U. Wis., 1978-79; min. Milw., 1979-81; instr. Sem. Unity Sch. Christianity, 1983-85; co-min. Unity Ch. Pitts., 1985-86; sr. min. Unity Ch., Anderson, Ind., 1986-87; sr. minister Unity Ch., Warren, Ohio, 1987-88, Massillon, Ohio, 1988-90; dir. housing Southwestern Coll., Winfield, Kans., 1990-91; min. specializing in ministry to women, cons., Lincoln, Nebr., 1991-93; co-min. Lindenwood Union Ch., Rockford, Ill., 1993—; founding min. Council Bluffs Unity Ch., Iowa; tchr. pub. schs., Rochelle, Ill., 1994—. Methodist. Mem. NAFE, Nat. Assn. Self-Employed, Internat. New Thought Alliance, Internat. Platform Assn. Methodist/Unity. E-mail: revpatmmcl@yahoo.com. Home and Office: 7399 Bermuda Dr Rockford IL 61108-4486

MCCLELLAND, RICHARD LEE, dentist; b. Pitts., May 18, 1927; s. William Noble and Pauline Elizabeth (Lee) McC.; m. Elizabeth Anne Michon, Dec. 6, 1958; children: Richard Scott, William Alfred, Robert Craig. BA, Princeton U., 1950; DDS, U. Pa., 1954. Pvt. practice Princeton, N.J., 1958-92; clin. instr. U. Pa. Dental Sch., Phila., 1958-62; mem. exec. com. Med. Ctr. Princeton, 1971-72, past chmn. dental dept.; elected Nat. Dental Surgeon Res. Officers Assn. of U.S., 1972-73. Lt. Dental Corps, USNR, 1954-57, capt., ret. Fellow Am. Coll. Dentists, Internat. Coll. Dentists, Acad. Gen. Dentistry, Acad. Dentistry Internat.; mem. ADA, Am. Prosthodontic Soc., Fedn. Dentaire Internat., Res. Officers Assn., Nassau Club, Princeton Club (N.Y.C.), Rotary (pres. Princeton 1978-79). Republican. Episcopalian. Avocations: sailing, photography. Home: 58 Governors Ln Princeton NJ 08540-3671

MCCLENAHAN, ROSHAN, speech and language therapist; b. Bombay, May 23, 1947; d. Latif Rajabally and Nergish (Mohammed) Patel; m. James Orr McClenahan, Feb. 5, 1980; children: Michael, Alasdair. MSc, Guy's Hosp., London, 1972, postgrad., 1994—. Speech & lang. therapist Ilea, England, 1969-72, Croydon Gen. Hosp., England, 1969-71; speech & lang. therapist Royal Free Hosp., England, 1972-74, sr. speech & lang. therapist, 1974—; vis. lectr. Ctrl. Sch. Speech & Drama, England, 1991-94. Rsch. grantee North Thames Rsch. Devel., 1994; Found. for Human Potential travel fellow, 1995. Mem. Royal Coll. Speech & Lang. Therapists. Avocations: reading, theatre, economics. Office: Royal Free Hosp, Pond St, London NW3 2QG, England

MCCLENDON, DENNIS EDWARD, retired air force officer; b. Nashville, July 8, 1922; s. Dennis Eugene and Loralee (Aswell) McC.; m. Vivian Eunette Youmans, May 13, 1944 (dec. 1989); children: Denise Diane Chastain, Lisa Linda Sims, Dennis Edward Jr. BS in Journalism, U. Houston, 1952. Commd. 2d lt. USAAF, 1943; advanced through grades to lt. col. USAF, 1967; pub. info. officer U.S. Strike Command, MacDill AFB, Fla., 1963-67; ret. USAF, 1967; dir. pub. info. St. Leo (Fla.) Coll., 1967-68; dir. info. svcs. U. South Fla., Tampa, 1968-73; pub. info. dir. Fla. Regional Med. Program, Tampa, 1973-75; pub. info. officer U.S. Readiness Command, Macdill AFB, Fla., 1975-80. Author: Lady Be Good, Mystery Bomber of WWII, 1962; co-author: Legend of Colin Kelly, First American Hero of WWII, 1995. Troop command pilot U.S. Army Air Corps, 1942-44. Recipient Journalism scholarship U. Houston, 1951; decorated Legion of Merit, Joint Svc. Commendation medal, Air medal, Air Force Commendation medal (2). Mem. Air Force Assn. (past chpt. pres., life, Outstanding award Wright Meml. chpt. 1958), Ret. Officers Assn. (life), Order of Daedalians (life), Fla. Pub. Rels. Assn. (past chpt. pres.), Res. Officers Assn. (past chpt. pres.), Phi Kappa Phi. Democrat. Avocations: writing, photography, travel. Home: 354 Inverness Dr SW Huntsville AL 35802-4571

MCCLENDON, FRED VERNON, real estate professional, business consultant, equine and realty appraiser, financial consultant; b. Vernon, Tex.; s. Guy C. and Lexie M. (Johnson) Mc C.; m. Dorothy J. Seibert, June 1943 (div. 1953); children: Cathy, Kent, Tracy; m. Ethel R. Cherry, Sept. 15, 1959; children: Tess, Rob, J.T. Assoc. in Commerce, Hannibal La Grange Coll., 1947; BBA, Baylor U., 1949; MBA, Harvard U., 1951, postgrad. in law, 1951; postgrad. in banking, Colo. U., 1951-52; postgrad., Denver U., 1951-52. Lic. ins. agt., Tenn.; cert. real estate broker, Tenn.; cert. internat. financier. Asst. cashier U.S. Nat. Bank, Denver, 1951; gen. mgr. Nat. Paper Band Co., Denver, 1952-53; personnel mgr. Houston Fire & Casualty Co., Ft. Worth, 1954-56; gen. sales mgr. City Lincoln/Mercury, Dallas, 1957-58; owner INS-Bank Personnel Agy., Dallas, 1959-61; mng. ptnr. Allen & Mc Clendon Ins., Dallas, 1959-63; owner, broker Mc Clendon Real Estate, Dallas, 1959-63; pres. Mc Clendon Realty Co., Hampton, Tenn., 1961—; gen. mgr. Eagle Nest Ranch, Roan Mountain, Tenn., 1963-88, Mile High Ranch, Roan Mountain, 1988—; pres. FMV Appraisal Co., Hampton, 1988—; cons. Gen. Adjustments Bur., 1981—, Debourdieux Corp., 1985—, Wachesaw Corp., 1985—, Hidden Lakes Devel. Corp., various ins. cos. and law firms in U.S. and Can., IRS, U.S. Marshals Svc., U.S. Customs, 1993—, Heartland Presbyn. Ctr.; exec. cons. El Dorado Ranch, 1991—; cons. IRS; lectr. to lodges and assns.; gen. ptnr. Flexnet Investments, Ltd., Dallas, 1988—; pres. Bus. Realty Internat. Cons., Roan Mountain, Tenn., 1990—; exec. v.p. OmniVue, Inc., S.C., 1992—; chmn. AmeriFund Ventures, Internat., Tenn., 1995—; pres. U.S. Med-Am. Bus. Svcs., 1995—. Contbr. articles to profl. jours. Recipient W.T. Grant fellow Harvard U., 1950-51. Mem. Am. Quarter Horse Assn. (life), Australian Appaloosa Assn., Appaloosa Horse Club U.S., Tenn. Walking Horse Breeders Assn., Am. Paint Horse Assn., Am. Soc. Equine Appraisers, Am. Horse Coun., Am. Soc. Appraisers (Accredited sr. appraiser, bd. examiners 1990—), Internat. Real Estate Inst., Nat. Assn. Real Estate Appraisers, Environ. Assessment Assoc. (cert. insp. 1991—), Appraisers Assn. Am. (cert. sr. appraiser), Internat. Soc. Financiers (cert. internat. financier). Republican. Mem. Seventh Day Adventists. Avocations: boating, travel, fishing, swimming. Home: Mile High Ranch 1580 State Highway 77 Hillsboro TX 76645-7285 Office: FMV Appraisal Co 1580 State Highway 77 Hillsboro TX 76645-7285

MCCLINTOCK, WILLIAM THOMAS, health care administrator, retired; b. Pittsfield, Mass., Oct. 23, 1934; s. Ernest William and Helen Elizabeth (Clum) M.; m. Wendolyn Hope Eckerman, June 22, 1963; children: Anne Elizabeth, Carol Jean, Thomas Daniel. BA, St. Lawrence U., Canton, N.Y., 1956; MBA, U. Chgo., 1959, MHA, 1962. Prodn. planner Corning (N.Y.) Glass, 1959-60; adminstrv. resident Alameda County Med. Instns., Oakland, Calif., 1961-62; adminstrv. asst. Univ. Hosps. of Cleve., 1962-65; asst. adminstr. Presbyn. Hosp., Whittier, Calif., 1965-68; regional asst. Kaiser Found. Hosps., Oakland, Calif., 1968-70; assoc. dir., exec. dir. Conn. Hosp. Planning Commn., New Haven, 1970-75; project dir., lectr. sch. health studies U. N.H., Durham, 1975-77; regional mgr. Tex. Med. Found., Austin, 1977-81; adminstr. Schick Shadel Hosp., Ft. Worth, 1981-87; mgmt. cons. George S. May Internat. Co., Park Ridge, Ill., 1987-88; mgr. Nat. Ctr. Rsch. Programs Am. Heart Assn., Dallas, 1988-89; adminstr. Ambulatory Svcs. Health Care of Tex., Ft. Worth, 1990-92; CEO Boundary Cmty. Hosp., Bonners Ferry, Idaho, 1992-2000, ret., 2000. 1st lt. U.S. Army, 1957. Fellow Am. Coll. Health Care Execs. (life); mem. Am. Hosp. Assn. (life), Am. Heart Assn. (bd. dirs. Idaho/Mont. affiliate 1993-95), Idaho Hosp. Assn. (bd. dirs. 1995-2000, sec.-treas. 1998, chmn. elect 1998, chmn. bd. dirs. 1999, immediate past chmn. 2000, Recognition of Retirement award 2000), Masons (Unity Lodge No. 9). Republican. Presbyterian. Avocations: book collections, gardening, photography, fly fishing. Home: County Rd 62C PO Box 1226 Bonners Ferry ID 83805-1226

MCCLINTON, JAMES ALEXANDER, state agency administrator, councilman; b. Milw., Nov. 18, 1961; s. James Henry O'Neal and Essie Marie (McClinton) Jones; m. Hazel Marie Walker, July 19, 1986 (div. 1998); children: Tawana Nicolette, Jameika Alexandra. AA, Washburn U., 1985, BA, 1987; MPA, U. Kans., 1997. Unit team supr. Kans. Neurol. Inst., Topeka, 1983-85; corrections officer Kans. Dept. Corrections, Topeka, 1985-87, corrections counselor, 1987-91, asst. tng. mgr., 1991-95; adminstr. Prison Health Svcs. Kans. Dept. Corrections, Lansing, 1995-96; personnel specialist City of Topeka, 1996-97; policy examiner Kans. Ins. Dept., Topeka, 1997-98; programs policy adminstr. Kans. Juvenile Justice Authority, Topeka, 1998—. Bd. dirs. Habitat for Humanity, Topeka, Kans. State Bd. Nursing, 1993-97, pres. 1995-96; ward capt., precinct com. mem. Shawnee County Dem. Party, Topeka, 1994—; commr. Topeka/Shawnee County Planning Commn., 1994-97, Jaycees, 1998—, Sertoma, 1999—; trustee Antioch Missionary Bapt. Ch. Fellow Washburn U. Alumni, 1998. Mem. Jaycees, Sertoma Club, Pi Alpha Alpha. Bapt. Avocations: fishing, boating, travelling, biking, baseball. Home: 1305 SE Washington St Topeka KS 66607-1304 Office: State of Kans Juvenile Justice Auth Jayhawk Walk 715 SW Jackson St Ste 300 Topeka KS 66603-3713

MCCLINTON, JAMES LEROY, city administrator; b. Longview, Wash., Oct. 14, 1949; s. James Delmer and Norma Jean (Ammons) McC.; m. Carmen Lassaphine Amador, Nov. 7, 1983; children: James Andrew, Ian Tyler, Kevin Riley. AA, SUNY, Albany, 1973; BA, Upper Iowa U., 1974; MA, Calif. State U., Carson, 1984; PhD, Calif. Coast U., 1985. Cert. mgr. Inst. Cert. Profl. Mgrs. With USCG, 1967-89, commd. officer, 1981-83, advanced through grades to comdr., 1987, ret., 1989; bur. mgr. adminstrv. svcs. Charleston (S.C.) County Sheriff's Office, 1989—; spkr. pro tem S.C. Criminal Justice Acad., Columbia, 1989—; mem. auditor selection com. Charleston County Govt., 1989—, computer users action com., 1989—; mem. various coms. County Govt. and Sheriff's Office, Charleston, 1989—. Editor (newsletter) The Badge, 1989—; newspaper columnist; contbr. articles to profl. jours. and mags. Mem. Charleston Police Pipes and Drums, 1994—; grad. Leadership S.C., 1993, Leadership Charleston, 1997. Recipient Achievement award Nat. Assn. Counties, Washington, 1993, 96, Golden Pen award The Post and Courier Newspaper, Charleston, 1996. Mem. ASPA, S.C. Law Enforcement Officers Assn., Rotary Internat. (bd. dirs. North Charleston). Republican. Avocations: bagpipes, writing.

MCCLINTON, SAMUEL IVOR, education educator; b. Belfast, Ireland, May 14, 1947; s. Thomas James and Elizabeth Horner McCleery; m. Irene Gibson, Aug. 6., 1969 (dec. Sept. 1994); children: Keira Sarah, Philip Ivor; m. Bea Gillespie, June 17, 1998. BSc, Queens U., Belfast, 1968, Diploma in Edn., 1969, MSc, 1984; BA with honors, Open U., 1978. Head math. dept. Dunmurry Secondary Sch., Belfast, 1969-75; from lectr. to sr. lectr. Ulster Poly., No. Ireland, 1976-84; lectr. U. Ulster, 1984-91, sr. lectr., 1991—; course dir. U. Ulster, 1988—. Recipient Disting. Tchg. award U. Ulster, 1991. Mem. Brit. Computer Soc. Avocations: walking, do-it-yourself, crossword puzzles, cooking. Office: Univ Ulster, Shore Rd Jordanstown, BT37 0QB Newtownabbey Northern Ireland

MCCLINTON, TRAVIS VICTOR, II, mathematics educator; b. Waco, Tex., July 13, 1951; s. Travis Victor and Jacqueline Joy (Lorenz) McC. BS in Indsl. Engring., U. Tex., Arlington, 1972; M of Physics and Math. Edn., U. North Tex., Denton, 1977. Cert. tchr., cert. master tchr., Tex. Tchr. St. Luke's Cath. Sch., Irving, Tex., 1972-75, Bishop Lynch H.S., Dallas, 1975-76, Irving Ind. Sch. Dist., 1977—, Dallas County Dist. Cmty. Colls., Dallas, 1982-97, Collin County Cmty. Colls., Plano, Tex., 1986-92, U. Tex., Arlington, 1989—; Master Tchr. Exam scorer Tex. Edn. Agy., Austin, 1990-92; spkr. in field. Author: (6 workbooks) Algebra I Card Games, 1997; co-author workbooks. Recipient awards Irving Schs. Found., 1995, 96, 98, Tex. Edn. Agy., 1985-90. Mem. Nat. Coun. Tchrs. Math., Greater Dallas Coun. Tchrs. Math., Tex. State Tchrs. Assn., Assn. Tex. Profl. Educators, Irving Edn. Assn., PTA . Avocations: crossword puzzles, piano, dancing, figure skating, gardening. Office: Travis Middle Sch 1600 Finley Rd Irving TX 75062-4349

MCCLOSKEY, THOMAS HENRY, mechanical engineer, consultant; b. Phila., Dec. 11, 1946; s. Thomas H. McCloskey; m. Rosemary Loscalzo, July 11, 1970. BSME, Drexel U., 1969. Rsch. engr. Westinghouse Elec. Corp., Phila., 1969-80; mgr. turbo-machinery Elec. Power Rsch. Inst., Palo Alto, Calif., 1980-92, cons. turbo-machinery, 1992—; mem. adv. bd. Internat. Pump Symposium, Houston, 1987—. Author: ASME Specification Guide-

lines for Large Steam Turbines, 1987; contbr. articles to profl. jours. Recipient George Westinghouse Gold medal Am. Soc. of Mechanical Engineers, 1995. Fellow ASME (dir. turbine design course 1988—, mem. rsch. bd. 1989—, Edison Elec. Prime Mover award 1984, 97, George Westinghouse Gold medal 1995). Achievements include 6 patents in turbomachinery design; development and field application of finite element/fracture mechanic techniques and erosion/corrosion resistant materials for life assessment/optimization of large turbine generators and pumps. Office: Elec Power Rsch Inst 3412 Hillview Ave Palo Alto CA 94304-1344*

MCCLOSKY, BARBARA HENNEBERGER, voice educator, therapist; b. Pasadena, Calif., Mar. 21, 1917; d. Herman and Vera (Jevne) Henneberger; m. David Blair McClosky, July 26, 1944 (dec.). Student piano, Mozarteum, Salzburg, Austria, 1936; AB, Vassar Coll., 1938. Tchr. piano Syracuse (N.Y.) U., 1945-46; tchr. voice Pvt. Practice, Syracuse, N.Y., 1945-52, Bradford (Mass.) Coll., 1966-74, U. Lowell (Mass.), 1967-85, Boston Conservatory of Music, 1974—; asst. dir. Plymouth Rock Ctr. Music and Drama, Duxbury, Mass., 1946-55; clin. voice therapist Mass. Eye and Ear Infirmary, Boston, 1951-66; chmn. bd. McClosky Inst. Voice. Co-author: Voice, In Song and Speech, 1975; singer: (Broadway musical) Mexican Hayride, 1943-45, Rhapsody, 1944; performer: Bradford Coll. Glee Club, Boston, U. Lowell, Middle Collegiate Ch., Marble Collegiate Ch., Syracuse U. Chorus and Orchestra, Marietta Coll. Chorus and Orchestra, The Cloisters N.Y. Mem. Music Tchrs. Nat. Assn., Music Tchrs. Nat. Conf., Mass. Music Tchrs. Assn.,Coll. Music Soc., Nat. Assn. Tchrs. Singing, Am. Assn. U. Profs., Duxbury (Mass.) Garden Club, Duxbury Rural and Hist. Soc., Sigma Alpha Iota (patroness).

MCCLUNE, (WILLIAM) ROSS, research physicist; b. Cape Girardeau, Mo., Dec. 26, 1940; s. William James and Luella Benjamin McCluney; m. Judith McCluney, June 15, 1969 (div. Jan. 1984); children: Alan Michael, Kevin Elliot. BA in Physics, Rhodes Coll., 1963; MS in Physics, U. Tenn., 1966; PhD in Physics, U. Miami, 1971. Devel. engr. Eastman Kodak Co., Rochester, N.Y., 1966-67; rsch. scientist NASA/Goddard Space Flight Ctr., Greenbelt, Md., 1971-76; prin. rsch. scientist Fla. Solar Energy Ctr., Cocoa, 1976—. Author: Daylighting-- Natural Light for passive Design, 1986, Introduction to Radiometry and Photometry, 1994; author, editor: The Environmental District of South Florida, 1971. V.p. Floridians for a Sustainable Population, Fla., 1998—. Mem. AAAS, Optical Soc. Am., Internat. Optical Engring. Soc. Avocations: tennis, swimming. Office: Fla Solar Energy Ctr 1679 Clearlake Rd Cocoa FL 32922-5703

MCCLURE, ANN CRAWFORD, judge, lawyer; b. Cin., Sept. 5, 1953; d. William Edward and Patricia Ann (Jewett) Crawford; m. David R. McClure, Nov. 12, 1983; children: Kinsey Tristen, Scott Crawford. BFA magna cum laude, Tex. Christian U., 1974; JD, U. Houston, 1979. Bd. cert. in family law and civil appellate law Tex. Bd. Legal Specialization. Assoc. Piro and Lilly, Houston, 1979-83; pvt. practice El Paso, Tex., 1983-92; ptnr. McClure and McClure, El Paso, 1992-94; justice 8th Ct. of Appeals, El Paso, 1995—; past mem. Tex. Bd. Law Examiners, Bd. Disciplinary Appeals; mem. Family Law Specialization Exam Com., 1989-93. Contbr. articles to profl. jours.; past editor The Family Law Forum; contbg. editor: Texas Family Law Service; mem. editl. bd. Tex. Family Law Practice Manual, 1982-93. Mem. State Bar Tex. (dir. family law sect. 1987-91, treas. 1993-94, vice chmn. 1995-96, chmn.-elect 1996-97, chmn. 1997-98), dir. appellate sect. 1991-95, treas. 1996-97, sec. 1997-98, vice-chmn. 1998-99, chmn.-elect 1999-2000, chmn. 2000—), Tex. Acad. Family Law Specialists (past dir.). Democrat. Presbyterian.

MCCLURE, DAVID H., utilities company analyst; b. Kennesaw, Ga., Apr. 29, 1948; s. Benjamin H. and Katherine E. (Reece) McC.; m. Judy King McClure; children: Christina Aldridge, John Robert Aldridge, Lori K. Aldridge, Charissa Diane Thomas. B in Indsl. Engring. Tech., So. Poly. U., 1976. Assoc. engr. Western Electric Co., Atlanta, 1972-75; jr. acct. Jack McPherson, CPA, Acworth, Ga., 1975-76; div. materials planner Southwire Co., Carrollton, Ga., 1976-78, indsl. engr., 1978-79; process engr. Alcan Cable, Tucker, Ga., 1979-82; rsch. specialist Ga. Power Co., Forest Park, 1982-86, staff rep., 1986-87, staff services engr., 1987-91, head of quality assurance sect., 1982-91, mgr. quality and support, 1991-94; bus. cons., 1994-96, bus. analyst, 1996—. Chmn. bd. dirs. Am. Diabetes Assn. Ga. Affiliate, Inc., Atlanta, 1985-87, nat. bd. dirs., 1988-91, mem. nat. com. on affiliate assocs., 1986-89, vice chmn., 1988-89, chmn. 1991-92, nat. So. region liaison, 1987-89; chmn. Nat. Com. on Fund Raising, 1989-91; nat. bd. mentor, 1989—, chmn. nat. bd. dirs., 1995-96, chmn. nat. strategic planning steering com., 1994-95, chmn. nat. nominating com., 1996-97, chmn. nat. alumni assn., 1996-97, ctr. for quality excellence adv. coun., 1987-92, chmn., 1989-90; chmn. Southeastern Quality Conf. Program, 1989, 90, 91, chmn. arrangements, 1992; mem. Ga. Dept. Human Resources Diabetes adv. com., 1989-92; chmn. bd. dirs. Am. Diabetes Rsch. Found., 1997-98, chmn. rsch. found. nominating com., 1998-99; nat. bd. dirs. Combined Health Appeal of Am., 1993-99, chmn. agy. rels., 1996-99. Staff sgt. USAF, 1968-72. Named Vol. of Yr., Am. Diabetes Assn. Ga. Affiliate, Inc., 1983-84, 84-85; recipient Ga. Power Co. R.W. Scherer award for leadership in cmty. svc., 1991, Am. Diabetes Assn. Charles H. Best award for disting. svc., 1996. Mem. Inst. Indsl. Engrs. (sec. 1976-77, v.p. seminars 1977-78), Am. Soc. Quality Control (cert. quality engr. 1983—, chmn. bd.-elect Greater Atlanta sect. exec. bd. 1989-92), Nat. Mgmt. Assn. (LDR chpt., profl. devel. com. 1989-91), Capital Area Kiwanis Club (bd. dirs. 1989—, pres. elect 1990-91, pres. 1991-92). Baptist. Home: 706 Singley Dr Lawrenceville GA 30044-5972

MCCLURE, HAL H., travel film producer; b. Indpls.; s. Harold Alonzo and Betty (Zemah Hays) McC.; m. Dorothea Vernell Millar, Jan. 15, 1949 (dec. 1994). AA, L.A. City Coll., 1941. Journalist various newspapers, Calif., 1949-56; newsman AP, L.A., 1956-58, N.Y.C., 1959-60; fgn. corr. AP, S.E. Asia and Middle East, 1961-76; bur. chief AP, Newark, 1976-77; prin., travel film producer Hal McClure Prodns., Laguna Woods, Calif., 1978—; adj. asst. prof. journalism Seton Hall U., S. Orange, N.J., 1976-77. Contbr. (book) Lightning Out of Israel, 1967; editor: Fire Over Suez, 1971; prodr. 10 travel films including Istanbul—Travels in Turkey, 1990, Land of Legend—England Scotland and Wales, 1993, Adventure Holland, 1994, Mystery Tales of Europe, 1996, Dracula-Travels in Transylvania, 1997, Story Book England, 1999; editor, co-owner Travelogue mag., 1978—; prodr. live electronic cinema for theater audience, 1994. Capt. USAFR, 1942-56. Recipient Rising Star award Program mag., 1978, Hall of Fame award, 1994; Ogden Reid Found. fellow, 1959. Mem. Internat. Motion Picture and Lectrs. Assn., Travel Adventure Cinema Soc. Home and Office: 686 Avenida Sevilla # C Laguna Beach CA 92653

MCCLURE, WILLIAM OWEN, biologist; b. Yakima, Wash., Sept. 29, 1937; s. Rexford Delmont and Ruth Josephine (Owen) McC.; m. Pamela Preston Harris, Mar. 9, 1968 (div. 1979); children: Heather Harris, Rexford Owen; m. Sara Joan Rorke, July 27, 1980. BSc, Calif. Inst. Tech., 1959; PhD, U. Wash., 1964. Postdoctoral fellow Rockefeller U., N.Y.C., 1964-65; rsch. assoc. Rockefeller U., 1965-68; asst. prof. U. Ill., Urbana, 1968-75; assoc. prof. U. So. Calif., L.A., 1975-79; prof. biology, prof. neurology U. So. Calif., 1979—; v.p. sci. affairs Nelson Rsch. & Devel. Co., Irvine, Calif., 1981-82; acting v.p. rsch. & devel. Nelson Rsch. & Devel. Co., 1985-86; dir. program. neurol. info. sci. U. So. Calif., 1982-92, dir. program in psychobiology, 1991—; dir. cellular biology U. So. Calif., 1979-81, dir. neurobiology, 1982-88, dir. prog. psychobiology, 1991—; cons. in field; dir. Marine & Freshwater Biomed. Ctr., U. So. Calif., 1982-83; co-dir. Baja Calif. Expedition of the R/V Alpha Helix, 1974, others; chmn. Winter Conf. on Brain Rsch., 1979, 80, others; lectr. in field; sci. adv. bd. Nelson R & D, 1972-91; mem. bd. commentators Brain and Behavioral Scis., 1978—. Co-editor: Wednesday Night at the Lab, 1972; patentee in field; mem. editorial bd. Neurochem. Rsch., 1975-81, Jour. Neurochemistry, 1977-84, Jour. Neurosci. Rsch., 1980-86; contbr. over 100 articles to profl. jours. Bd. dirs. San Pedro and Peninsula Hosp. Found., 1989-95, Faculty Ctr., U. So. Calif., 1991-95, San Pedro Health Svcs., 1992-97. Recipient John R. Hubbard award Univ. Assoc., 1993, Assocs. award for Outstanding Tchg., Univ. Assocs., 1994; Scripps Inst. fellow, 1958, NIH fellow, 1959-64, 64 -65, Alfred P. Sloan fellow, 1972-76, others; recipient rsch. grants, various sources, 1968—; Intersci. Rsch. Inst. fellow, 1989; West Coast Coll. Biol. Psychiatry fellow, 1983. Mem. AAAS, Am. Soc. Neurochemistry, Soc. for Neurosci., Am. Soc. Biol. Chemistry and Molecular Biology, Internat. Soc. Neurochemistry, Assn. Neurosci. Depts. and Programs, Univ. Park Investment Group, Bay Surgical Soc., N.Y. Acad. Scis, Phi Beta Kappa, Phi Kappa Phi. Republican. Presbyterian. Avocations: computing, travel, photography. Home: 30533 Rhone Dr Palos Verdes Peninsula CA 90275-5742 Office: U So Calif Dept Biol Scis Los Angeles CA 90089-0001

MCCLURE, WILLIAM PENDLETON, lawyer; b. Washington, May 25, 1925; s. John Elmer and Helen Newsome (Pendleton) McC.; children: Marilyn Alexander, Helen Pendleton, Elizabeth Ruffin, Melinda Geoghegan. BS, U. Pa., 1949; JD, George Washington U., 1951, LLM, 1954; postgrad., The Hague (Netherlands) Acad. Internat. Law, 1952. Bar: D.C. 1951. Sr. ptnr. McClure & Trotter, Washington, 1952-91, McClure, Trotter & Mentz, Washington, 1991-93, McClure, Trotter & Mentz, chartered, Washington, 1993-95; ptnr. White & Case, Washington, 1995—. Chmn. D.C. div. Crusade Against Cancer, Am. Cancer Soc., 1966, 67. Served from pvt. to 1st lt., inf. U.S. Army, 1943-46, PTO. Mem. Am. Bar Assn., Bar Assn. D.C., Am. Judicature Soc., Order of Coif, Phi Delta Phi, Phi Delta Theta. Clubs: Metropolitan (Washington), Columbia Country (Washington), Nat. Press (Washington). Home: 26201 Prescott Rd Clarksburg MD 20871-9163 Office: 601 13th St NW Ste 600 S Washington DC 20005-3807

MCCLURG, ROBERT JAMES, emergency nurse practitioner, educator; b. Warsaw, N.Y., Sept. 5, 1958; s. Robert and Elizabeth (Castiglia) McC.; m. Tina Marie Crawford, July 15, 1984; 1 child, Rose Marie. AAS, SUNY, Morrisville, 1978; ASN, SUNY, Albany, 1987; AAS, C.C. of the Air Force, Maxwell AFB, Ala., 1988; BSN, Brockport State coll., 1996; MS, U. Buffalo, 1999. RN, N.Y.; cert. paramedic. Enlisted USAF, 1980, advanced through grades to maj., 2000; med. technician 390 Tactical Fighter Squadron, Mountain Home AFB, Idaho, 1981-83; supr., shift leader David Grant USAF Med. Ctr., Travis AFB, Calif., 1983-84, USAF Hosp., Kirtland AFB, N.Mex., 1984-85; ind. duty med. technician USAF Survival Sch., Spokane, Wash., 1985-86, supr., field med. br., 1986-88; staff nurse St. Luke's Hosp., Spokane, 1987-88, Wyo. County Cmty. Hosp., Warsaw, N.Y., 1988-89; flight nurse, med. crew dir. USAFR, Niagara Falls, N.Y., 1989—; EMS coord. St. Jerome Hosp., Batavia, N.Y., 1989-96; emergency nurse practitioner Strong Meml. Hosp., Rochester, 1999—; clin. assoc. faculty U. Rochester, N.Y., 2000—; chmn. prehosp. adv. com. Western Regional EMS System, Buffalo, N.Y., 1993-95; mem. Wyo.-Erie Regional EMS Coun. Buffalo, 1993—; vice-chmn. Genesee County EMS Coun., Batavia, 1994-96; EMS coord. World Univ. Games, Buffalo, 1994; alternate rep. to N.Y. State EMS Coun.; mem. legis. com., regional activities com. N.Y. State EMS Coun. Vol. paramedic Perry Emergency Ambulance, N.Y., 1978-79, 88—; mem. Wyo. Co. Paramedic Task Force. Mem. Res. Officer Assn. (life), Air Force Assn. (life). Avocations: pvt. pilot, kayak instr., backpacking/camping, computers. Office: Strong Meml Hosp Emergency Dept 601 Elmwood Ave Rochester NY 14642-0002

MCCLUSKEY, NEIL GERARD, gerontologist, educator, literary agent; b. Seattle, Dec. 15, 1920; s. Patrick John and Mary Genevieve (Casey) McC.; m. Elaine Lituchy, June 5, 1977. AB, Gonzaga U., 1944, MA, 1945; Lic. in Sacred Theology, Gen. Theol. Union, Berkeley, 1952; PhD, Columbia U., 1957. Assoc. editor Am. (Nat. Cath. Weekly), N.Y.C., 1955-60; dean sch. edn. Gonzaga U., Spokane, 1960-62, dir. hons. program, 1963-65, v.p. acad., 1963-66; prof. U. Notre Dame, South Bend, Ind., 1966-71, dean, dir. Inst. Studies in Edn., 1968-71; prof., dean profl. studies Lehman Coll. CUNY, 1971-75; dir. Ctr. Gerontol. Studies CUNY Grad. Sch., 1975-81; exec. dir. BHRAGS Social Svcs. Ctr., Bklyn., 1981-84; sr. cons. Retirement Advisors, Inc., N.Y.C., 1985—; pres. Westchester Lit. Agy., 1991—. Author: Public Schools and Moral Education, 1958, Catholic Viewpoint on Education, 1959, Catholic Education Faces Its Future, 1969; author, editor: Aging and Society, 1980, Aging and Retirement, 1981. Bd. dirs. Cath. Big Bros. N.Y., 1985—. Home: 2533 Egret Lake Dr West Palm Beach FL 33413-2161

MCCOBB, ALLAN PAUL, not-for-profit organization executive; b. Russell, Kans.; s. Boyden and Doris Marie (Marsh) McC.; m. Ursula Fox, June 25, 1983 (div. Sept. 1991). BS in Phys. Edn., Kans. State U., 1967, BS in Bus. and Acctg., 1971; MS in Exercise Sci., Ft. Hays State U., 1986. Staff acct. Arthur Young & Co., Kansas City, 1972-74; gen. mgr., part owner McCobb Inc., Russell, Kans., 1974-80; grants mgr. N.W. Kans. Area Agy. on Aging, Hays, 1980-81; exec. dir. S.W. Kans. Area Agy. on Aging, Dodge City, Kans., 1981-85; grants mgr. N.W. Area Agy. on Aging, Hays, 1985-86; exec. dir. United Way of Enid and N.W. Okla., Enid, 1990—. Exec. dir. Wheatbelt Girl Scout Coun., 1987-90; presenter, group facilitator Meth. Divorce Support Group and Workshop, Enid, 1993—; youth coord. Enid Cmty. Children's Choir, 1994—; mem. initial bd. Enid Cmty. Free Health Clinic, Enid, 1996-99; small claims mediator N.W. Okla. Early Settlement, Fairview, 1998—. With U.S. Army, 1968-70, Vietnam. Recipient Bronze Star U.S. Army, 1970. Mem. Okla. Assn. United Ways (bd. dirs., treas. 1994-96), Garfield Coiunty Area C. of C., Fellowship of Christian Athletes. Methodist. Avocations: running, genealogy, youth work. Home: PO Box 771 Enid OK 73702-0771 Office: United Way Enid NW Okla 321 W Cherokee Ave Ste C Enid OK 73701-5603

MCCOID, NANCY KATHERINE, lawyer; b. Tacoma, July 30, 1953; d. Francis Patnck and Kathleen Grace McCoid; m. Tom Mash, Aug. 25, 1989; 1 child, Kelly Elizabeth. BS in Psychology summa cum laude, U. Wash., 1976; MA in Psychology summa cum laude, Western Wash. U., 1979; JD with high honors, U. Wash., 1983. Bar: Wash., U.S. Dist. Ct. (we. dist.) Wash., U.S. Ct. Appeals (9th cir.), U.S. Supreme Ct. Law clk. divsn. I Ct. Appeals, Seattle, 1983-85; assoc. Merrick, Hofstedt & Lindsey, Seattle, 1985-90, shareholder, 1991—; mentor to 1st-yr. law students U. Wash., Seattle, 1990—; arbitrator King County Superior Ct., Seattle, 1991—; mem. health-care panel counsel Tenet, 1996—; spkr. in field. Vol. atty. Bar Assn. Pro Bono Program, Seattle, 1991—, Fed. Pro Bono Program, Seattle, 1992; mem. Gov. Gary Locke's Transition Team. Mem. Am. Law Firm Assn. (health practices com., employment law com.), Wash. State Bar Assn. (com. on profl. liability 1995—, vol. spkr. 1998), Wash. Def. Trial Lawyers (com. on profl. liability 1995—), Def. Rsch. Inst. (com. on profl. liability 1990—), King County Bar Assn. (com. on professionalism 1995, gender bias com., com. on jud. evaluation 1998, pres.'s coun. mem.), Order of Coif. Avocations: jazz, theater, gardening, traveling. Office: Merrick Hofstedt & Lindsey 710 9th Ave Seattle WA 98104-2099

MCCOLL, HUGH LEON, JR., bank executive; b. Bennettsville, S.C., June 18, 1935; s. Hugh Leon and Frances Pratt (Carroll) McC.; m. Jane Bratton Spratt, Oct. 3, 1959; children: Hugh Leon III, John Spratt, Jane Bratton. B.S. in Bus. Adminstrn, U. N.C., 1957. Trainee NCNB Nat. Bank, Charlotte, 1959-61, officer, 1961-65, v.p., 1965-68, sr. v.p., 1968, div. exec., 1969, exec. v.p., 1970-73, vice chmn. bd., 1973-74, pres., 1974-83, also dir.; CEO NationsBank Corp., Charlotte, 1983—; CEO,pres. Barnet Banks, Miami, FL, 1998-; bd. dirs. Sonoco Products Inc., Hartsville, S.C. Trustee Heineman Found., Charlotte, 1976—, Queens Coll., Charlotte; bd. visitors Grad. Sch. Bus. U. N.C. at Chapel Hill; chmn. Charlotte Uptown Devel. Corp., 1978-81, 85. 1st lt. USMCR, 1957-59. Mem. Bankers Roundtable (mem. trialateral commn.), Am. Bankers Assn., N.C. Bankers Assn. (pres. 1974). Democrat. Presbyterian. Office: care Bank Am Corp 100 N Tryon St Charlotte NC 28255-0001

MCCOLLUM, ALVIN AUGUST, real estate company executive; b. L.A., Jan. 20, 1920; s. Nile Clarkson and Ida Martha (Kuhlman) McC.; m. Maxine Eleanor Seeberg, July 29, 1944; children: Robert Michael, James Alan, Patricia Kathleen. BA, UCLA, 1941; postgrad., U.S. Naval Acad., 1946, Southwestern U., 1949-50. Exec. v.p., dir. Strout Realty, N.Y.C., 1948-61, Del E. Webb Corp., Phoenix, 1961-67; pres., dir. Sahara Nev. Corp., Las Vegas, 1964-67, Devel. Svcs., Inc., Scottsdale, Ariz., 1967-69; pres., chmn. Recreation Leisure Land, Inc., Scottsdale, 1969-71; asst. pres., dir. A.J. Industries, Inc., L.A., 1971-74; pres., dir. Carefree (Ariz.) Ranch, Inc., 1974-76; pres., bd. dir. Cons. Internat., Scottsdale, 1976—; chmn. CEO Greenway Environ. Svs., Inc., Gilbert, Ariz., 1992—; pres., bd. dirs. Combined Assets, Inc., Westlake Village, Calif., First Realty Fin., Inc., L.A., Corp. Capital Resources, Inc., Westlake Village. Bd. dirs. Admiral Nimitz Found., Fredericksburg, Tex., 1970—, Boys Club Las Vegas, 1964-68, United Fund, Las Vegas, 1966; co-chmn. NCCJ, Las Vegas, 1966; elder Presbyn. Ch. USA, 1954—. Lt. USN, 1943-48, PTO. Mem. Masons, Shriners, Am. Legion, Mt. Shadows Country Club (bd. dirs. 1962-64). Republican. Avocations: golf, swimming, camping, sailing. Home: 215 N Power Rd Unit 180 Mesa AZ 85205-8442 Office: Greenway Environ Svcs Inc 644 E Southern Ave Ste 204 Mesa AZ 85204-4934

MCCOLLUM, CHARLES NEVIN, surgery educator; b. Stafford, Eng., Apr. 17, 1950; s. David Hugh and Jane (Boyd) McC.; m. Margaret Ludmilla Pak, Apr. 19, 1976; children: Samantha Jane, Nicola Claire. MB ChB, U. Birmingham, Eng., 1972, MD, 1981. Registrar in surgery St. James's U. Hosp., Leeds, Eng., 1974-78; lectr. in surgery U. Birmingham, 1978-83; sr. lectr., reader insurgery U. London, 1983-89; prof. surgery U. Manchester, Eng., 1989—; examiner univs. London, Glasgow and Manchester, 1989—; bd. dirs. Surgicare, U.K., 1989—. Mem. editorial bd. Jour. Vascular Surgery, Jour. Wound Care, Brit. Jour. Surgery; contbr. numerous articles to profl. jours. Recipient Moynihan prize Assn. Surgeons of Gt. Britain and Ireland, 1979; King Edward's Fund grantee, 1988. Fellow Royal Coll. Surgeons Eng. (Hunterian prof. 1985), Royal Coll. Surgeons Edinburgh; mem. Surg. Rsch. Soc. Great Britain and Ireland (treas., com. mem.). Avocations: skiing, tennis, country pursuits. Office: South Manchester U Hosp, Withington Hosp Nell Ln, West Didsbury, Manchester Lancs M20 2LR, England

MCCOLLUM, JAMES FOUNTAIN, lawyer; b. Reidsville, N.C., Mar. 24, 1946; s. James F. and Dell (Frazier) McC.; m. Susan Shasek, Apr. 26, 1969; children: Audra Lynne, Amy Elizabeth. BS, Fla. Atlantic U., 1968; JD, Fla. State U., 1972. Bar: U.S. Ct. Appeals (5th cir.) 1973, Fla. 1972, U.S. Ct. Appeals (11th cir.) 1982. Assoc. Kennedy & McCollum, 1972-73; prin. James F. McCollum, P.A., 1973-77, McCollum & Oberhausen, P.A., 1977-80, McCollum, Oberhausen & Tuck, L.L.P. (and predecessor firm), Sebring, Fla., 1977—; bd. dirs. Comml. Bancorp, Inc., Comml. Bank Highlands County; pres. Highlands Devel. Concepts, Inc., Sebring, 1982—; sec. Focus Broadcast Comm., Inc., Sebring, 1982-87; mng. ptnr. Highlands Investment Service. Treas. Highlands County chpt. ARC, 1973-76; vestryman St. Agnes Episcopal Ch., 1973—, chancellor, 1978—; mem. Fla. Sch. Bd. Atty.'s Assn., 1974—, bd. dirs., 1989-97, pres., 1995-96; mem. Com. 100 of Highlands County, 1975-83, bd. dirs., 1985-87, chmn., 1991-92; chmn. Highlands County High Speed Rail Task Force; chmn. bd., treas. Ctrl. Fla. Racing Assn., 1976-78; chmn. Leadership Sebring: life mem., past pres. Highlands Little Theatre, Inc.; bd. dirs. Palms of Sebring Nursing Home, 1988-90, Palms Estate Mobile Home Park, Sebring Airport Authority, 1988-90, treas., 1988, chmn. indsl. com., 1988, vice-chmn., 1989-90, chmn., 1990-91, Highlands County High Speed Rail Task Force, 1986-89; bd. dirs. Highlands County Family YMCA, 1985-93, pres. Sebring br., 1992-93, chmn. bldg. com., 1992-94; bd. dirs. Good Shepherd Hospice, Inc. Recipient ARC citation, 1974, Presdl. award of appreciation Fla. Jaycees, 1980-81, 82, 85, Outstanding Svc. award Highlands Coun. of 100, 1988, Most Valuable Player award Highlands Little Theatre, Inc., 1986, Zenon Significant Achievement award, 1991; named Jaycee of Year, Sebring Jaycees, 1981, Outstanding Local Chpt. Pres., U.S. Jaycees, 1977. Outstanding Service award Highlands Council of 100, 1988. Mem. ABA, ATLA, Comml. Law League Am., Am. Arbitration Assn. (comml. arbitration panel), Nat. Assn. Retail Credit Attys., Fla. Bar (jour. com.), Highlands County Bar Assn. (past chmn. legal aid com.), Fla. Sch. Bd. Attys. Assn. (dir. 1989—, v.p. 1993-94, pres. 1994-95), Greater Sebring C. of C. (dir. 1982-89, pres. 1986-87, chmn. transp. com. 1986—, Most Valuable Dir. award 1986, 87), Fla. Jaycees (life mem. internat. senate 1977—), Lions (bd. dirs. 1972-73, v.p. 1994-95, Disting. award 1984). Republican. Episcopalian. Office: 129 S Commerce Ave Sebring FL 33870-3602

MCCOLLUM, WILLIAM FRANKLIN, JR., sociology educator, private investigator; b. Wichita Falls, Tex., Apr. 2, 1942; s. William F. and Edna Marie McCollum; div.; children: Chris, Jeff. BBA, Midwestern State U., 1964; MA, U. Houston, 1996. Cert. rec. agt., Tex.; lic. pvt. investigator, Tex.; commd. security officer, Tex. V.p. Moody Nat. Bank, Galveston, Tex., 1965-80, Bank of the West, Galveston, Tex., 1980-81; pres. Bank of Sierra Blanca, Tex., 1981-82; ins. agt. McCollum Ins., Dickinson, Tex., 1982—; pvt. investigator Eagle Security Investigators, Dickinson, Tex., 1991—; instr. sociology Coll. of Mainland, Texas City, Tex., 1996—; instr. sociology, retention dir. ITT Tech. Inst., Houston, 1997—; sec.-treas. Galveston City Nat. Corp., 1970-78; dir. McCollum Inst. Criminology, Dickinson, 1999—. Newspaper columnist (religion page) Galveston Daily News, 1970-75. Dir., former pres. Noon Optimist Club, Galveston, 1967—; dir. Big Bros.-Big Sisters, Galveston, 1968-70; res./spl. dep. sheriff Galveston County Sheriff Dept., 1969-81. With N.G., 1965-67. Recipient Father of Yr. award Galveston County, 1972. Mem. AAUP, Am. Sociol. Assn., Tex. Assn. Lic. Investigators (jour. reporter 1992—), Tex. Jr. Coll. Tchrs. Assn. Republican. Baptist. Avocations: Sherlock Holmes Society, Galveston Gun Club. E-mail: Eta2g411@aol.com. Home: PO Box 1901 Dickinson TX 77539-1901 Office: ITT Tech Inst 2222 Bay Area Blvd Houston TX 77058-2070

MCCOLM, GEORGE LESTER, international agricultural consultant, journalist; b. Colby, Kans., Aug. 2, 1911; s. Theodore Harrison and Jane (Speirs) McC.; m. Emma Victoria Davis, Aug. 9, 1936 (dec. Sept. 1959); children: Carol Ann, Patricia Alice; m. Elizabeth Jane Gunder Funderburg, May 1, 1975. BS in Agr., Kans. State U., 1935; postgrad., U. Ariz., 1961-64. Cert. profl. agronomist Am. Soc. Agronomy. Various soil conservation and agrl. positions, 1935-41; dir. crop. prodn. War Relocation Authority, Topaz, Utah, 1942-43; chief agrl. officer planning invasion and occupation Japan Joint Chief's of Staff, 1944-45; officer in charge civilian govt. of Ponape Island USN, 1946; soil conservationist Bur. Indian Affairs, Shiprock and Window Rock, Ariz., 1947-52; soil conservationist Bur. Indian Affairs, Shiprock, 1949-52, dir. nursery, 1953-57; dir. B Square Ranch Expt. Sta., Farmington, N.Mex., 1958-61; educator U. Ariz., 1961-64; with U.S. Dept. State, India, 1964-66; tech. rep. internat. Mekong River devel. com. U.S. Dept. State, Vietnam, 1966-72; rancher Lewiston, Calif., 1973-87; owner Lewiston Nursery, 1987-95; part-time agrl. advisor Mex. Govt., 1976-81; with Office Strategic Svcs. in WWII conf., Washington, D.C., 1991. Contbr. articles to sci. jours. Bd. dirs. Trinity County Fair Assn. Lt. USNR, 1944-46, PTO; USN officer directing civilian govt. Ponape Island, 1946. Mem. NRA, CAST, Am. Soc. Agronomy and Soil Sci., Calif. Soc. Agronomy and Soil Sci., Am. Asst. Ret. Persons, Lewiston C. of C., Am. Legion, Alpha Gamma Rho, 4-H Club (Edison medal). Republican. Methodist. Achievements include direction of first U.S. Soil survey made with aerial photographs, 1936; development of method of taking water from a flowing stream without a diversion dam, 1939; perfection of method of constructing a stable roadbed or airfield through a swampy area, without limiting movement of ground water, 1939; wrote original draft of Japanese Land Reform Law, 1945. Avocations: fishing, fly tying, history research. Home: PO Box 330 Lewiston CA 96052-0330

MCCOMB, RONALD GRAEME, rolfer; b. Burns, Oreg., Jan. 6, 1938; s. Oliver Graham and Melba Viettta (Oard) McC.; m. Annie Bernice Duggan, Nov. 1968 (div.); 1 child, Siobhan Ariel Duggan. Student, Portland Art Mus. Sch., 1957-61; Cert., Rolf Inst., Boulder, Colo., 1971. Cert. rolfer. Artist, 1961-66; film maker Union Light Co., N.Y.C., 1966-70, Am. Film Inst., Hollywood, Calif., 1970; rolfer pvt. practice Portland, Seattle, 1971—. Contbr. articles to profl. jours. Mem. Rolf Inst.

MCCOMBS, MARK JAMES, lawyer; b. Blue Island, Ill., Sept. 28, 1959; s. James Marren and Yolanda Rose (Spinazzola) McC.; m. Kathryn Anne Crivolio, May 28, 1994; children: James John, Thomas Michael. BS, Am. U., 1981; JD, Northwestern U., 1984. Bar: Ill. 1984, U.S. Dist. Ct., no. dist., Ill., 1984. Assoc. Jerome H. Torshen, Ltd., Chgo., 1984-87, Arnstein & Lehr, Chgo., 1987-88; assoc., ptnr. Wildman, Harrold, Allen & Dixon, Chgo., 1998—; village atty. Village of Sauk, Ill., 1988—, Village of Phoenix, Ill., 1999—; adminstrv. hearing officer Village of Calumet Park, Ill., 1998—. Contbr. articles to profl. jours. Mem. South Suburban Mayors and Mgrs. Assn. (assoc. mem., chmn. attys. com.), Ill. State Bar Assn. Democrat. Roman Catholic. Office: Wildman Harrold Allen & Dixon William Harrold Allen & Dixon 225 W Wacker Dr Ste 3000 Chicago IL 60606-1224

MCCONAGHY, NATHANIEL (NEIL), psychiatrist, researcher; b. Brisbane, Australia, May 5, 1927; s. Nathaniel and Susan Angela (Mulroney) McC.; m. Helen Philomena Malony, May 2, 1962; children: Susan Jean, Finola Frances. MB, BS, U. Queensland, Brisbane, Australia, 1951; BSc, U. Melbourne, Australia, 1954, MD, 1965; DSc, U. South Wales, Sydney, 1990. Resident med. officer Brisbane Gen. Hosp., 1951-52; med. officer, sr. med. officer Mental Hygiene Dept., Ararat, 1952-55; rsch. scholar Alfred Hosp.,

Melbourne, 1961-64; lectr., sr. lectr. U. New South Wales, 1964-70, assoc. prof. sch. psychiatry, 1970-92, vis. prof. sch. psychiatry, 1992—; chmn. behavior therapy unit Prince of Wales Hosp., Sydney, 1970-90, chmn. biol. schizophrenia rsch., 1995—, chmn. sci. steering com. Neurosci. Inst. Schizophrenia and Allied Disorders, Sydney, 1994—. Author: Sexual Behavior, Problems and Management, 1993; editor: Liberation Movements and Psychiatry, 1974; contbr. chpts. to books, articles to profl. jours. Mem. Mental Health Rev. Tribunal of New South Wales, 1992—. Recipient Rsch. award Nat. Coun. of Problem Gambling, 1995. Fellow Royal Australian and New Zealand Coll. Psychiatrists, Internat. Acad. Sex Rsch.; mem. Polish Acad. Sexological Sci. (hon.). Home: 12 Gurner St Paddington, 2021 Sydney Australia Office: Prince of Wales Hosp, Avoca St Ranowick, 2031 Sydney Australia

MCCONCHIE, DAVID MURRAY, geochemist, educator, researcher, consultant; b. Wellington, New Zealand, Sept. 30, 1949; arrived in Australia, 1979; s. Stewart Donald and Margaret Loudon (Fastier) McC.; m. Fiona Gaye Davies, Dec. 22, 1986; children: Keetah, Jade. BSc, U. Canterbury, New Zealand, 1975, MSc, 1978; PhD, U. Western Australia, 1986. Tutor U. Western Australia, 1980-85, postdoctoral fellow, 1985-87; lectr. So. Cross U., East Lismore, 1987-90, sr. lectr., 1990-92, assoc. prof., 1992-99, prof., 1999—; dir. Risatec, Australia, 1999—, Virotec Internat., Australia, 2000—; presenter in field. Author: Practical Sedimentology, 1994, Analytical Sedimentology, 1994; inventor in field; contbr. more than 50 articles to profl. jours. Grantee Hamersley Iron Pty. Ltd., 1980, Western Australia Dept. Fisheries and Wildlife, 1984, Marine Sci. and Tech. Grants Com., Shark Bay, 1985, 86, Earthwatch U.S.A., 1988, Australian Rsch. Coun., 1989, 90, 91, 93, 94, 95, 96, 97, Great Barrier Reef Marine Park Authority, 1992, Queensland Alumina, 1995, Urban Water Rsch. Assn. Australia, 1996, Australian Inst. Nuclear Sci. and Engring., 1997, 99, 2000, Australian Tee Tree Oil Rsch. Inst., 1997, Risatec P/L, 2000; recipient Von Haast Geol. Hammer U. Canterbury, New Zealand, 1973, Vice chancellor's award, So. Cross U., 1995. Mem. Soc. Econ. Paleontologists and Mineralogists, Internat. Assn. Sedimentologists, Am. Geol. Inst., Soc. Econ. Geologists, Geol. Soc. New Zealand, Assn. Exploration Geochemists, Geol. Soc. Australia, Clay Minerals Soc., Australian X-Ray Analytical Assn., Minerals, Metals, and Materials Soc., N.Y. Acad. Scis. Avocations: climbing, hunting, playing bagpipes. Home: 14 Windsor Ct, Goonellabah NSW 2480, Australia Office: So Cross U, Military Rd, East Lismore NSW 2480, Australia

MCCONKEY, KEVIN MALCOLM, psychology educator; b. Gympie, Queensland, Australia, Mar. 7, 1952; s. Albert Edward and Hazel Irena (Aitken) McC.; m. Jacquelyn Cranney; children: Mahalia, Caillan. BA with honors, U. Queensland, Brisbane, Australia, 1976; PhD, U. Queensland, St. Lucia, Australia, 1980. Registered psychologist, NSW, Australia. Lectr. psychology Macquarie U., Australia, 1984-85, sr. lectr., 1986-89, asst. prof., 1990-92; prof. U. NSW, 1992—; head U. NSW Sch. Psychology, 1993-99, pres. acad. bd., 1999—; chair nat. com. for psychology Australian Acad. Sci., 1996-2000. Co-author: Readings in Australian Psychology, 1991, Hypnosis and Experience: The Exploration of Phenomena and Process, 1982 (Arthur Shapiro award Soc. for Clin. and Exptl. Hypnosis 1983), Hypnosis, Memory, and Behavior in Criminal Investigation, 1995; editor: Australian Psychology: Selected Applications and Initiatives, 1994, Truth in Memo's, 1998; book rev. editor Internat. Jour. Clin. and Exptl. Hypnosis, 1993-99. Fellow APA, Australian Psychol. Soc. (pres. 1993-94, Early Career award 1984), Am. Psychol. Soc., Acad. Social Scis. Australia. Avocation: films. Office: Univ NSW, Sch Psychology, NSW Sydney 2052, Australia

MCCONNELL, ARCHIBALD ALLISON, chemical pathologist consultant, educator; b. Ayr, Scotland, Nov. 15, 1943; s. Thomas Reid and Margaret Donald (Allison) McC.; m. Eva Karolina Josefine Semmelhofer, Aug. 8, 1983. BSc in Chemistry with 1st Class honors, U. Glasgow, Scotland, 1967, PhD, 1971, MBChB, 1980; LLB, U. Strathclyde, Glasgow, 1996. Chartered chemist and biologist. Jr. house officer in medicine Nat. Health Svc., Ayr, 1980-81; jr. house officer in surgery Nat. Health Svc., Alexandria, Scotland, 1981; registrar in pathology Nt. Health Svc.--Glasgow Royal Infirmary, 1981-84; sr. registrar Nat. Health Svc.-Southmead Hosp., Bristol, Eng., 1984-90; cons. chem. pathologist Nat. Health Svc.-Inverclyde Royal Hosp., Greenock, Scotland, 1990—; hon. sr. lectr. Glasgow U. Contbr. articles to sci. jours., including Jour. Chem. Soc., Nutrition and Food Sci., Brit. Med. Jour., Jour. Sci. Food and Agr., Lancet, Annals Clin. Biochemistry, Postgrad. Med. Jour., Today's Anaesthetist, Medicine, Sci. and Law, Alcohol, Drugs and Driving, West of Eng. Med. Jour., Jour. Clin. Pathology, Diabetic Medicine, Prospective, Scottish Medicine, Jour. Med. Ethics, Jour. Royal Coll. Surgeons Edinburgh, Hosp. Update, Occupl. Medicine. Fellow Royal Soc. Chemistry, Royal Coll. Pathologists, Inst. Biology; mem. Scottish Medico-Legal Soc. (sec.). Avocations: languages, history, law. Office: NHS-Inverclyde Royal Hosp, Dept Clin Biochemistry, Greenock PA16 0XN, Scotland

MCCONNELL, DAVID KELSO, lawyer; b. N.Y.C., July 12, 1932; s. David and Caroline Hanna (Kelso) McC.; m. Alice Schmitt, Dec. 26, 1953; children: Elissa Anne McConnell Henebry, Kathleen Anne, David Willet. BCE, CCNY, 1954; LLB, Yale U., 1962. Bar: Conn. 1962, U.S. Dist. Ct. Conn. 1963, U.S. Ct. Appeals (2d cir.) 1964, U.S. Ct. Appeals (3d cir.) 1966, U.S. Sup. Ct. 1970, U.S. Dist. Ct. (ea. dist.) Pa. 1971, Pa. 1975, N.Y. 1986. Asst. counsel N.Y.N.H. & H. R.R., New Haven, 1962-65; counsel N.Y.N.H. & H. R.R., 1966-68; asst. atty. gen. U.S. V.I., 1965-66; asst. gen. atty. Pa. Cen. Transp. Co., New Haven, 1969-70; asst. gen. counsel Pa. Cen. Transp. Co., Phila., 1970-71; sr. reorganization atty. Pa. Cen. Transp. Co., 1971, adminstrv. officer, spl. counsel to trustees, 1971-76, gen. atty., 1977-78; asst. to chmn., CEO The Penn Cen. Corp., N.Y.C., 1979-80; corp. sec. The Penn Cen. Corp., 1980-82; v.p., gen. counsel Gen. Cable Co., Greenwich, Conn., 1982-85; pvt. practice law Stamford, Conn., 1985-86, Pelham, N.Y., 1989-91, Greenwich, Conn., 1991-98; of counsel McCarthy, Fingar, Donovan, Drazen & Smith, White Plains, N.Y., 1986-89. Dep. supr., councilman Town of Pelham, N.Y., 1986-90; dep. mayor, trustee Village of Pelham, 1992-95, village atty., 1995-96, budget officer, 1996; clk. of session, elder, trustee, deacon Huguenot Meml. Ch., Pelham N.Y. With U.S. Navy, 1954-59, USNR, 1959-79. Mem. Conn. Bar Assn., Assn. of Bar of City of N.Y., Yale U. Law Sch. Assn. (exec. com. 1988-91), N.Y. State Bar Assn., The Corinthians (mem. afterguard, dir, The Corinthians Assn., Trustee, Pres. The Corinthians Endowment Fund), St. Andrews Soc. N.Y. (bd. mgrs. 1986-89, 96-99, chmn. bd. mgrs. 1988-89), Rotary Club (pres. 1993-94). Home: 68 1/2 Roseneath Ave Newport RI 02840-3849

MCCONNELL, GARY ALBERT, business executive, research consultant; b. Belfast, No. Ireland, Jan. 24, 1961; s. John Armstrong and Brenda (Robertsen) McC. Student, Maitland Sch., Cape Town, South Africa, 1979-81. Apprentice Hall Thermotank, Cape Town, South Africa, 1978-81; tech. asst. Hall Thermotank, Cape Town, 1981-83; CAD specialist HKS, Cape Town, 1983-85; product specialist McDonnell Douglas, Cambridge, Eng., 1985-88; systems advisor McDonnell Douglas, Hemel, Eng., 1988, Stockholm, 1988; mng. dir. GMC Graphics A/S, Bodo, Norway, 1988-91, 3DLIB, Bodo, 1991—; mgr. R&D Adv. Doc. Mgmt. A/S, Bodo, 2000—; dep. gov. A.B.I.R.A., 1995—; dep. dir. gen. Internat. Biog. Ctr., 1996—; mem. Condeco A/S, 2000—. Grantee NT-Programmet, Tromso, Norway, 1991, SND, Bodo, 1993; fellow Am. Biog. Assn., 1998—. Mem. AAAS, N.Y. Acad. Scis., Order Internat. Fellowship. Avocations: music, theater, travel, skiing. Office: 3DLIB, PO Box 872, 8001 Bodø Norway

MCCONNELL, JOHN EDWARD, electrical engineering company executive; b. Minot, N.D., July 28, 1931; s. Lloyd Waldorf and Sarah Gladys (Mathis) McC.; m. Carol Claire Myers, July 4, 1952 (dec. Feb. 1989); children: Kathleen Anne, James Mathis, Amy Lynn; m. Heidi Banziger, Sept. 29, 1990. Registered profl. engr., Pa. BSME, U. Pitts., 1952; MS, Drexel Inst. Tech., 1958. With mktg. and design depts. for turbomachinery Westinghouse Electric Corp., Lester, Pa., 1954-60, 63-67, Pitts., 1960-63; mgr. power generation equipment activities in U.S., ASEA Inc., White Plains, N.Y., 1967-79; regional mgr. power equipment activities Middle Atlantic and Southeastern U.S. regions, 1967-79, mgr. turbine generator dept., 1979-83, mgr. internat. ops. Power Systems div., 1983-84, mgr. transmission substas. dept., 1984-85; mgr. Eastern U.S. ops. ASEA Power Systems Inc., 1985-86, mgr. eastern ops. measurements div. GEC, 1986-91; mgr. eastern region Protection and Control div. GEC Alsthom T&D Inc., 1991-98; prin. JEMTECH Co., 1998—; adviser on energy matters to U.S. congressman 1968-74; speaker and author on energy and electric power topics. Served to 1st lt., C.E., U.S. Army, 1952-54. Mem. IEEE (sr.; energy com., past chmn. subcom. cogeneration, mem. power sys. relay com.), IEEE Power Engring. Soc. (sr.; past chmn. chpts. public affairs subcom.), ASME. Republican. Contbr. numerous articles on energy and electric power to industry publs.; developer analytical techniques for power systems performance characteristics and econs. of cogeneration systems. Home: 173 Remington Rd Ridgefield CT 06877-4324 Office: JEMTECH PO Box 229 Ridgefield CT 06877-0229

MCCONNELL, JOHN HOWARD, personnel management consultant, writer; b. Highland Park, Mich., June 18, 1933; s. Melvin William and Dorothy Marie (Miller) McC.; m. Dolores Ann Cooper, Oct. 29, 1955; children: Keith Ernest, Brian Howard, Eric William. BS, Wayne State U., 1957, MEd, 1963. Tchr. Detroit Bd. Edn., 1957-59, Highland Park Bd. Edn., 1959-60; personnel mgr. Wolverine Tube Co., Allen Park, Mich., 1960-69; personnel dir. Garan, Inc., N.Y.C., 1970-71; cons. Morristown, N.J., 1971-74; cons. human resource mgmt., pres. McConnell, Simmons & Co., Inc., Morristown, 1974—; bd. dirs. Circus Royale, Inc., Morristown. Author: How To Audit, 8 vols., 1974-85, Introduction to Human Resources, 1982, A Ring, A Horse and A Clown, 1994, Finders Keepers, 1999; prodr. London Follies, 1994, 96; contbr. articles to various publs. Pres. Morristown Civic Assn., 1980. Mem. Am. Psychol. Assn., Am. Mgmt. Assn., Acad. Magical Arts, Magic Castle Club (L.A.), Circus Hist. Soc. (bd. dirs.), Masons. Democrat. Methodist. Avocation: producing entertainment events. Home: 1 Skyline Dr Morristown NJ 07960-5146 Office: 73 E Hanover Ave Morristown NJ 07960-3161

MCCONNELL, JOHN HUNTER, marketing professional; b. Aliwal North, North Cape, South Africa, Jan. 12, 1948; s. John Hunter and Jean Maria (Bruce Brand) McC.; m. Helen Mary Theron, Dec. 18, 1971; three children. Diploma in advanced exec. program, U. South Africa, Pretoria, South Africa, 1985. Mgmt. trainee OK Bazaars, Johannesburg, Pretoria, South Africa, 1967-68; mgr. OK Bazaars, Johannesburg, Pretoria, 1969-70; sales rep. Royal Baking Powder, Johannesburg, 1970-74; retail ops. advisor SPAR, Pretoria, 1976-78; sales mgr., mktg. dir. Ruto Mills, Pretoria, 1978—; chmn. export com. Nat. Chamber Milling, South Africa, 1995, 98—; bd. dirs. Embany Bakery, Ermelo, South Africa. Sec. Inst. Mktg. Mgmt., Pretoria, 1974-77; mem. governing body Waterkloof Primary Sch., Pretoria, 1991-97. Mem. Alumni Univ. South Africa Sch. Bus. Leadership. Presbyterian. Avocations: videography, jogging, tennis. Office: Ruto Mills, 6 President Burgers St, Pretoria 0183, South Africa

MCCONNELL, MALACHY JAMES, programme executive; b. Edinburgh, Scotland, Oct. 11, 1972; s. Colm Patrick and Aileen (Russell) McC. BSc in Optoelectronics and Laser Engring, Heriot Watt U., Edinburgh, 1994. Divsn. mgr. Queensgate Instruments, Bracknell, Eng., 1994—. Mem. Inst. Physics. Avocations: mountain biking, swimming, studying, motorcycles.

MCCONNELL, PATRICIA LYNN, vocational consultant; b. Denver, Feb. 20, 1956; d. James Donald and Joyce Clemence (Wortman) McC.; m. Roger Tribble, 1989. BS, U. No. Colo., 1979. Mental health worker Arapahoe Mental Health Ctr., Littleton, Colo., 1977-79; work adjustment cons. recycling ctr. City of El Cerrito (Calif.), 1980-83; job developer, ind. contractor with Dept. of Rehab., Pleasant Hill, Calif., San Pablo, Vallejo, Calif., 1983-87; vocat. rehab. cons. Guitterez & Co., Oakland, Calif., 1987-89; owner, vocat. cons. JobPerfect, Berkeley, Calif., 1989—; owner, fundraiser Community Svcs. Mktg., Oakland; workshop leader Calif. Dept. of Rehab., Pleasant Hill, 1983-87, San Pablo, 1989. Author: (workbook) Job Search for the Disabled, 1985, JobPerfect Job Search manual Datebook and Organizer, 1999; dir., producer (video) JobPerfect, 1992, How To Improve Your Communication and Interview Skills, 1994, JobPerfect Job Search, 1995, Legacies, 1995, JobPerfect JobSearch Organizer, 1998; creator, producer (cable show) A Good Book to Live In, 1996, Homecare, 1996, HomeTours, 1996, CMO, 1996. Mem., fundraiser No. Calif. Recyclers Assn., Berkeley, 1982-87, Calif. Marine Mammal Ctr., Marine Headlands, Calif., 1987-90, Bay Area Cmty. Svcs., 1993-97. Recipient Dance award Englewood High Sch., Colo., 1974, Appreciation award Regional Occupational Program, San Pablo, 1989. Mem. Calif. Assn. for Rehab. Profls., Nat. Rehab. Assn. (bd. dirs. 1983-85). Avocations: filmmaking, video production, graphics, marine mammals, dance. Home: 5268B Locksley Ave Oakland CA 94618-1041 Office: JobPerfect at BFTI 1440 Broadway Ste 202 Oakland CA 94612-2022

MCCONNON, VIRGINIA FIX, dietitian; b. Aberdeen, S.D., July 20, 1932; d. Lavern Clyde and Janette Clare (Schmidt) Fix; m. Thomas James McConnon, Oct. 28, 1955; children: James Renaud, John Thomas, Paul Wilson. BS in Home Econ. (hon.), S.D. State U., Brookings, 1954. Registered dietitian Am. Dietetic Assn., 1955; cert. dietitian/nutritionist, N.Y., 1995. Dietetic intern U. Minn. Hosps., Mpls., 1955; therapeutic dietitian Northwestern Hosp., Mpls., 1955; dietitian Riley County Hosp., Manhattan, Kans., 1956; cons. dietitian Chautauqua County Office for the Aging, Mayville, N.Y., 1975-89; treas. Aging Svcs. Dietitians of N.Y. State, 1976-90; mem. Chautauqua County Nutrition Coun., 1990-98. Bd. dirs. Hall Meml. Housing Corp., Jamestown, N.Y., 1995—, Harbor House, Jamestown, N.Y., 1975-80, Chautauqua Region Multiple Sclerosis Soc., Jamestown, N.Y., 1983-86, Chautauqua Area Adult Day Care Ctrs., Jamestown, Dunkirk, N.Y., 1990—; ch. clk., 1990-93, diaconate, 1993-96, mem. ch. coun., 1997—, mem. ch. choir, 1946—. Named Chautauqua County Sr. Citizen of Yr., 1995. Mem. Am. Dietetic Assn., N.Y. State Dietetic Assn., Western N.Y. Dietetic Assn. Republican. Congregationalist. Avocations: church choir, bridge, reading, travel, grandchildren. Home: 4465 Baker Street Ext Lakewood NY 14750-9762

MCCORMACK, DONALD PAUL, newspaper consultant; b. Brockton, Mass., Jan. 15, 1926; s. Everett G. and Esther (Lufkin) McC.; m. Petronella Ruth Seger, Apr. 28, 1951; 1 son, Christopher Paul. B.A., U. Pitts., 1949. Corr. U.P.I., 1949-52; asst. city editor Pitts. Sun-Telegraph, 1952-56; pub. relations exec., 1956-64; copy reader N.Y. News, 1964-67, editorial writer, 1967-72, chief editorial writer, 1972-82; cons., 1982—. With USAAF, 1944-46, Pa. N.G., 1952-57. Home and Office: PO Box 3539 Westport CT 06880-8539

MCCORMACK, MARJORIE GUTH, psychology educator, career counselor, communications educator, public relations consultant; b. Jersey City; d. Joseph and Vera Guth; m. Kevin T. McCormack, 1961. BA, St. Peter's Coll., 1974; MA, Jersey City State Coll., 1990. Editor AT&T, N.Y.C., 1952-60, libr., 1960-67; libr. St. Peter's Coll., Jersey City, 1967-71; pub. rels. mgr. Blue Cross of N.J., Newark, 1971-81; instr. history, econs. St. Aloysius H.S., Jersey City, 1981-82; pub. rels. cons. Creative Pub. Rels. Assocs., Queensbury, N.Y., 1981—; prof. psychology Hudson County C.C., 1995-97; adj. instr. comm. St. Peter's Coll., 1982-88; copy editor Glens Falls, (N.Y.) Post-Star, 1986; dir. career placement Hudson County C.C., 1988-91. Bd. mgrs. Am. Cancer Soc., Jersey City, 1978-79; mem., sec. parish coun. St. Aloysius Ch., 1981-85; mem. Jersey City Tenants Orgn., 1981-98, Rent Leveling Bd. Jersey City, 1983-86, St. Peter's Coll. Cmty. Chorus, 1988-94; 2d v.p., pub. rels. chair Sodality of the Children of Mary of St. Teresa, 1993-95. Mem. AAUP, AAUW, NAFE (pub. rels. chmn. 1980-82), Mid Atlantic Career Counselors Assn., N.J. Assn. Counseling and Devel., N.J. Edn. Assn., Jersey City Bus. and Profl. Women's Assn. (legis. chmn. 1975-77, Nat. program award 1976, State Press award 1982), Hudson County Women's Network. Avocations: music, theatre, gourmet cooking.

MCCORMICK, DAVID ARTHUR, lawyer; b. McKeesport, Pa., Oct. 26, 1946; s. Arthur Paul and Eleanor Irene (Gibson) McC. BA, Westminster Coll., 1967; JD, Duquesne U., 1973; MBA, U. Pa., 1975. Bar: Pa. 1973, D.C. 1978, U.S. Ct. Appeals (3d cir.) 1977, U.S. Ct. Appeals (4th and D.C. cirs.) 1980, U.S. Supreme Ct. 1980. Asst. commerce counsel Penn Cen. R.R., Phila., 1973-76; assoc. labor counsel Consol. Rail Corp., Phila., 1976-78; atty. Dept. Army, Washington, 1978—. Author various geneal. and hist. works; contbr. articles to profl. jours. Mem. ATLA, Pa. Bar Assn., Phila. Bar Assn., D.C. Bar Assn., Assn. Transp. Practitioners, Soc. Cin. (Del. chpt.), SAR (Pitts. chpt.), Am. Legion, Res. Officers Assn., Masons, Phi Alpha Delta, Theta Chi. Presbyterian.

MCCORMICK, HOMER L., JR., lawyer; b. Frederick, Md., Nov. 11, 1928; s. Homer Lee McCormick and Rosebelle Irene Biser; m. Jacquelyn R.; children: Deidre Ann and Thomas Lee. Student, George Washington U., 1946-48; AB, San Jose State U., 1951; JD, U. Calif., San Francisco, 1961. Bar: Calif. 1961, U.S. Dist. Ct. Ctrl. Dist. Calif. 1972, U.S. Dist. No. Calif. 1961, U.S. Dist. Ct., So. Dist. Calif. 1976, U.S. Dist. Ct. of Appeals (9th cir. 1961), U.S. Tax Ct. 1977, U.S. Ct. Claims 1977, U.S. Supreme Ct. 1977. Atty. Holiway Jones State of Calif., 1961-63; atty. assoc. Rutan & Tucker, Santa Ana, Calif., 1963-66, atty. ptnr., 1966-70; atty., sr. ptnr. Rutan & Tucker, Costa Mesa, Calif., 1970-88, dept. head pub. law, 1974-88, mng. ptnr., 1984-88; founding ptnr., sr. ptnr. McCormick, Kidman & Behrens, Costa Mesa, 1988—; Arbitrator Am. Arbitration Assn., 1966-88; judge pro tem Orange County Superior Ct., 1975, 81, 84; spkr., lectr. Cal. Continuing Edn. of the Bar, 1976-88; profl. designation Internat. Right of Way Assn.; elected mem. Cal. Condemnation Lawyers, 1994—. Contbg. author: Real Property Remedies, 1982; contbr. articles to profl. jours. Mem. bd. govs. Bus. Com. Arts, Orange County Philharm. Soc. Lt. USMCR, 1951-56; pilot, Korea. Named Alumnus of Year Hastings Law Sch., 1992. Mem. ABA (com. chair 1991), Am. Bd. Trial Adv. (pres. O.C. chpt. 1973), Orange City Atty. Assn. (pres. 1972), Fed. Bar Assoc., Consumer Attys. Calif., Am. Judicature Soc., Orange County Bar Assn. (com. chair 1991-92), Orange County Bus. Trial Lawyers, Order Coif, Thurston Soc., Hastings Alumni Assn. (pres. 1973), Springs Country Club, Delta Theta Pi. Republican. Episcopalian. Avocations: boating, fishing, flying, golf, foreign travel.

MCCORMICK, KEN J., economics educator; b. Santa Maria, Calif., Sept. 25, 1954; s. Owen J. and Mary E. McCormick; m. Danita L. McCormick, 1984. BA, U. Calif., Riverside, 1976; PhD, Iowa State U. Asst. prof. U. No. Iowa, Cedar Falls, 1982-86, assoc. prof., 1986-91, prof., 1991—. Co-author: Essays on AD and AS, 1998; contbr. articles to profl. jours. including Eastern Econ. Jour., Rev. Social Economy, Jour. Theoretical Politics, Jour. Econs., History Polit, Economy. Grantee NEH, 1989, 93, 94; recipient rsch. award U. No. Iowa, 1989, tchg. excellnece award, 1993. Mem. Am. Econ. Assn., Hist. Econs. Soc., Eastern Econ. Assn., Internat. Torstein Veblen Assn. Office: U No Iowa Dept Econs Cedar Falls IA 50614-0001

MCCORMICK, QUEEN ESTHER WILLIAMS, clergyman; b. Apr. 5, 1941. BA in Theology, Internat. Sem., 1986; MA in Theology, Logos Bible Coll., 1993, PhD in Ministry, 1996. Adj. prof. Internat. Sem., Plymouth, Fla., 1987,91,98; founder, pastor New Birth House of Prayer for All People, Ft. Lauderdale, Fla., 1980—; radio/TV min., 1974-97; gospel singer, 1946—. Author: The Elect Lady in Ministry, 3d edit., 1998. Office: PO Box 5712 Fort Lauderdale FL 33310-5712

MCCORMICK, RICHARD, telecommunications company executive; b. Fort Dodge, Iowa, July 4, 1940; s. Elmo Eugene and Virgilla (Lawler) McC.; m. Mary Patricia Smola, June 29, 1963; children: John Richard, Matthew David, Megan Ann, Katherine Maura. B.S. in Elec. Engring., Iowa State U., 1961. With Bell Telephone Co., 1961-85; N.D. v.p., CEO Northwestern Bell Telephone Co., Fargo, 1974-77; asst. v.p. human resources AT&T, Basking Ridge, N.J., 1977-78; sr. v.p. Northwestern Bell, Omaha, 1978-82, pres., CEO, 1982-85; exec. v.p. U S West Inc., Englewood, Colo., 1985-86; pres., COO U S West Inc. (now Qwest), Englewood, Colo., 1986-90, pres., CEO, 1990-91, chmn., pres., CEO, 1992—; chmn. emeritus U S West Inc. (now Qwest), Englewood; bd. mem., pres.-elect Internat. C. of C.; bd. dirs. Norwest Corp., United Airlines Corp., Health Trio. Mem. Phi Gamma Delta. *

MCCORMICK, STEVEN THOMAS, insurance company executive; b. Phila., Dec. 18, 1955; s. Howard C. and Ruth Marion (Stahl) McC.; m. Helene Mary Trommler, Nov. 21, 1981; children: Matthew Thomas, Bria Helene. BBA, U. Ky., 1978; gen. ins cert., Ins. Inst. Am., 1980. Cert. adminstrv. mgr., purchasing mgr., ins. agt., Ky., 1980. Supr. trainee Ky. Farm Bur. Ins. Cos., Louisville, 1978-79, supr. micrographics dept., 1979-83, supr. adminstrv. svcs., 1983-85, mgr. adminstrv. svcs., 1985-89; asst. v.p. ops. and legis. agt., 1989—. Named to Hon. Order Ky. Cols., Outstanding Employee of Yr., Nat. Assn. of Mut. Ins. Cos., 1986; recipient Cert. of Excellence, Jefferson County Bd. Edn. Mem. Adminstrv. Mgmt. Soc. (internat. top recruiter 1985, chpt. pres. 1988, internat. dir. area 7 1990-91, internat. v.p. profl. devel. 1992-93), Acad. Adminstrv. Mgmt. (mem. bd. regents 1991-92, internat. v.p. 1992-93, internat. pres. 1993-94), U. Ky. Alumni Assn., Sigma Nu. Republican. Home: 706 Elsmere Cir Louisville KY 40223-2764 Office: Ky Farm Bur Ins Cos PO Box 20700 Louisville KY 40250-0700

MCCOWEN, ALEC, actor; b. Tunbridge Wells, May 26, 1925; s. Duncan and Mary (Walkden) McC. Ed. Skinners Sch., Tunbridge Wells, and Royal Acad. Dramatic Art. Appeared as Touchstone, Ford, Richard II, Mercutio, Malvolio, Oberon at Old Vic Theatre, 1959-60; appeared with R.S.C. as Fool in King Lear, 1964, Hadrian VII, 1968, The Philanthropist, 1970, The Misanthrope, 1972, as Dr. Dysart in Equus, 1972, as Henry Higgins in Pygmalion, 1974, as Ben in The Family Dance, 1976, Someone Who'll Watch Over Me, 1992, as Prospero in The Tempest, 1994, as Gaev in The Cherry Orchard, 1995; appeared with Prospect Co. as Antony in Antony and Cleopatra, 1977, in solo performance of St. Mark's Gospel, 1978, 81, as Frank in Tishoo, 1979, as Malvolio in Twelfth Night (TV), 1980, of Kipling, 1984, as Reilly in The Cocktail Party, 1986, as Nicolai in Fathers and Sons, 1987, as Vladimir in Waiting for Godot, 1987; appeared with Nat. Theatre and Abbey Dublin as Jack in Dancing at Cughnasa, 1990; appeared with Nat. Theatre as Crocker-Harris in The Browning Version, Arthur in Harlequinade, Capt. Corcoran in H.M.S. Pinafore, 1981, Adolf Hitler in The Portage to San Cristobal of AH, PTO, 1982; films: Frenzy, 1971, Travels with my Aunt, 1973, Stevie, 1978, Personal Services, Cry Freedom, 1987, The Age of Innocence, 1992; TV: Private Lives, 1976. Author: Young Gemini, 1979; Double Bill, 1980; Personal Mark, 1984. Named Best Actor, Evening Standard (now New Standard), 1968, 73, 82, Variety Club Stage Actor, 1970. Office: care Conway Van Gelder, 18-21 Jermyn St, London SW1 Y6HB, England

MCCOY, CHARLES CLIFFORD (CHIP MCCOY), engineering manager; b. Libertyville, Ill., Mar. 27, 1951; s. Charles Clifford and Helen Louise (Schloderbach) McC. AS, Triton Coll., 1971; BS in Physics, MIT, 1974, BSEE, 1975. Area svc. mgr. Chevrolet Motor Divsn., Chgo., 1976-79; engring. staff instr. GM Corp., Chgo., 1979-88; sr. program developer GM Corp., Warren, Mich., 1988-90; program developer Delco Elecs., Kokomo, Ind., 1990-94, svc. engr., 1994—; tech. writer GM Corp., 1983—, video scripting, 1988-90. Mem. Am. Soc. Physics Tchrs., Soc. Automotive Engrs. Avocations: computers, writing, HAM radio, robotics, reading. Home: 4206 Lance Ct Kokomo IN 46902-4109 Office: Delco Elecs 2700 S Goyer Rd Kokomo IN 46902-4167

MCCOY, JEANIE SHEARER, analytical chemist, consultant; b. Mancelona, Mich., May 27, 1921; d. Theophil R. and Goldie Margaret (Halladay) Schroeder; m. Theodore R. Shearer, June 14, 1958 (div. 1964); 1 child, Blair Barnett; m. George Altha McCoy, July 23, 1966. AA, North Pk. coll., 1941; BS, Northwestern U., 1944; MS, No. Ill. U., 1970. Jr. analytical chemist Buick Motor divsn. GM, Melrose Park, Ill., 1944-45; asst. rsch. chemist Hodson Oil Corp., Chgo., 1945-47; asst. analytical chemist Internat. Harvester Co., Melrose Park, 1947-49, analytical chemist, 1949-60, prin. chemist, 1960-74, supr. metal process control, 1974-82; cons. cutting fluid mgmt. divsn. JMT, Inc., Lombard, Ill., 1983—. Author: (monograph chpt.) Metalworking Fluids, 1993; editor: Lubrication Engring. Mag., 1979—. Fellow Soc. Tribologists and Lubrication Engrs. (Allan Mantafel award Chgo. sect. 1987, P.M. KU award, 1991, Internat. award 2000); mem. AAUW, Soc. Automotive Engrs., Am. Chem. Soc., Abrasive Engring. Soc. Avocations: shell and stamp collecting, fitness activities. Office: JMT Inc Cutting Fluid Mgmt Divsn 654 N West Rd Lombard IL 60148-1547

MCCOY, JOHN DENNY, artist; b. Columbus, Ohio, Dec. 13, 1945; s. Robert William and Dorothy Louise (Denny) McC.; children: Melinda Rene, Nathan Robert. Cert. of Grad., Columbus Coll. Art and Design, 1967; MFA, Washington U., St. Louis, 1969. Instr. Columbus Coll. Art and Design, 1969-73; program dir. Presidio of Monterey, Calif., 1975-78; gallery dir. Richard Danskin Gallery, Carmel, Calif., 1978-79, Bleich Gallery West, Carmel, 1979-80. One person shows include: Brunswick Gallery, Columbus, 1973, Seaside (Calif.) City Hall, 1978, Bleich Gallery, Carmel, 1980, Angles Gallery, Santa Monica, Calif., 1987, Hagger Gallery, Dallas, 1999, Flatbed Gallery, Austin, Tex., 2000; exhibited in group shows at Columbus Mus.

Art, 1965, Laclede Town Gallery, St. Louis, 1967, Merton Boyd Gallery, Columbus, 1970, Changing Scene Gallery, 1971, 72, Gallery Five, Columbus, 1972, Monterey Peninsula Mus. Art, 1976, 77, Angles Gallery, Santa Monica, 1989, Richard/Bennett Gallery, L.A., 1991, Arlington Mus. Art, 1998, Meridian Internat. Ctr., Washington, Vietnam, China, Singapore, Indonesia, 1999-2000, Haggerty Gallery, Dallas, 2000. Columbus Coll. Art and Design scholar, 1963; Ford Found. grantee, 1966; Washington U. fellow, 1968, 69. Home: 4606 Ave C Austin TX 78751-3026

MCCOY, VALERIE T., racial studies educator; b. Petersburg, Va., Sept. 23, 1949; d. Timothy and Dorothy T. Thweatt; widowed; children: Howard E., Devin R. AS, Va. Commonwealth U., 1975, BS, 1977, MPA, 1981; EdD, Va. Poly. Inst. and State U., 1998. Instr. John Tyler C.C., Chester, Va., 1989-91; tchg. asst. Va. Poly. Inst. and State U., Blacksburg, 1991-93; asst. prof. Va. State U., Richmond, 1996—; adj. instr. Va. Union U., Richmond, 1982-89; adj. instr. bus. edn. J.S. Reynolds C.C., Richmond, 1979-95; adj. prof. St. Paul's Coll., Lawrence, 1995-97; dean Va. Union U., Richmond, 1982. Bd. dirs. Powhatan-Goodland Cmty. Action Inc., 1994-95; assoc. dir. Urban League of Greater Richmond, 1986-89. Mem. Pub. Adminstrn. Club, Kappa Delta Pi (historian), Phi Delta Kappa (rsch. rep. 1999-2000), Pi Lambda Theta. Home: 3840 Pheasant Chase Dr Richmond VA 23231-7578

MCCOY, WILLIAM EARL, JR., economic development training consultant; b. Grand Rapids, Mich., Nov. 19, 1953; s. William Earl and Evelyn (Duke) McC.; m. Allene Denise Garrett, Aug. 20, 1977; children: Erin Nicole, Shannon Michele. BA, Alma Coll., 1975; MPA, Am. U., 1977; CID/CED, Am. Econ. Devel. Coun., 1989. Cert. indsl. and econ. developer; cert. violence interruption educator. Dep. city mgr. City of Benton Harbor, Mich., 1977-79; resident fellow Acad. Contemporary Problems, Columbus, Ohio, 1979-82; country dir. Peace Corps, Maseru, Lesotho, 1982-84; spl. asst. to Africa region dir. Peace Corps, Washington, 1984-85; pres. The McCoy Co., Columbus, 1985—; v.p. Econ. Devel. Council, Lima, Ohio, 1986-89; project dir. Columbus Found., 1989-91; planning, econ. devel., and tng. cons. in pvt. practice Columbus, 1985—; instr. Phoenix Coll. and South Mountain C.C., 1996—; cons. on rsch. Joint Ctr. Polit. Studies, Washington, 1976-77; cons. on small cities Nat. League Cities, Washington, 1978; cons. on urban affairs Ohio State U., Columbus, 1980-81; strategic planning, econ. devel. and tng. cons. City of Dayton, Ohio, 1985—, City of Lima, City of Kettering, Montgomery County, Ohio Commn. on Minority Health, Dayton Pub. Schs., Nat. Black Programming Consortium, Nat. Coun. Black Studies, Nat. Urban Policy Inst., Ctr. for Violence Interruption, Ohio Dept. Alcohol and Drug Addiction Svcs., Ohio Dept. Health, Nat. Women's Resource Ctr., NFL, others. Co-author: Managing Fiscal Retrenchment in Cities, 1980, Housing Problems of Black Mayor Cities, Planning Needs of Small Cities, Black Crime: A Police View. Dir. city drive United Way, Benton Harbor, 1978, Godman Guild, Columbus, 1980, ARC, Lima, 1987, Coun. for Arts Greater Lima, Lima Area Food Bank, 1988; chmn. bd. Lima-Allen County Full Employment Commn.; mem. fin. roundtable U.S. Econ. Devel. Adminstrn., Washington, 1980; mem. econ. devel. com. City of Lima, 1989; mem. Coun. on Urban Econ. Devel. Recipient Econ. Devel. Excellence award Ohio Devel. Assn., 1988, Jobs for Columbus Grads., 1991, PHA Cmtys. United, 1995. Mem. Am. Econ. Devel. Coun., Am. Soc. Pub. Affairs and Adminstrn., Nat. Bus. League, Internat. Traders, Internat. Downtown Assn., Am. Entrepreneurs Assn., Internat. City Mgmt. Assn., Nat. Main St. Network, Rotary, Pi Alpha Alpha. Home: 12 Westerville Sq Westerville OH 43081-2919 Office: The McCoy Co 5918 Sharon Woods Blvd Ste 200 Columbus OH 43229-2665

MCCRADY, BARBARA SACHS, psychologist, educator; b. Evanston, Ill., May 7, 1949; d. James Frederick and Margaret Maxine (Miller) Sachs; m. Dennis D. McCrady, June 13, 1969; 1 child, Eric Paul. BS, Purdue U., 1969; PhD, U. R.I., 1975. Lic. clin. psychologist. Clin. project evaluator Butler Hosp., Providence, 1974-75, chief psychol. assessment program, 1975-76, chief problem drinkers' project, 1976-83; assoc. prof. psychology Rutgers U., Piscataway, N.J., 1983-89, prof. psychology, 1989—; from instr. to assoc. prof. psychiatry Brown U., Providence, 1975-83; acting dir. Rutgers Ctr. Alcohol Studies, Piscataway, 1990-92; reviewer Nat. Inst. on Alcohol Abuse and Alcholism, Washington, 1979-82, extramural scientific adv. bd., 1989-93; cons. Inst. Medicine, Washington, 1988-89. Author: The Alcoholic Marriage, 1977; editor: Marriage and Marital Therapy, 1978, Directions in Alcohol Aubse Treatment Research, 1985, Research on Alcoholics Anonymous: Opportunities and Alternatives, 1993, Addictions: A Comprehensive Guidebook, 1999. Grantee Nat. Inst. on Alcohol Abuse and Alcoholism, 1979-83, 1988—. Fellow Am. Psychol. Assn. (pres.-elect divsn. addictions); mem. Assn. for Advancement Behavior Therapy, Rsch. Soc. on Alcoholism (bd. dirs., 1999-2003). Avocations: horseback riding, skiing, piano. Office: Rutgers U Ctr Alcohol Studies 607 Allison Rd Piscataway NJ 08854-8001

MCCRAE, SEAN CHRISTOPH, project manager; b. Wyomissing, Pa., Nov. 12, 1974; s. Richard Dean and Linda (Reed) McC. BBA, James Madison U., 1996; MBA, Tulane U., 1998. Cons. Strategic Reports Inc., Wyomissing, Pa., 1998—. Emergency room vol. Reading (Pa.) Hosp. Mem. James Madison U. (Phila. alumni chpt.), Beta Gamma Sigma. Avocations: soccer, percussion, BMW's. Home: 1904 Van Reed Rd Apt G19 Wyomissing PA 19610-1076

MCCRANOR, LAURIE S., residential designer; b. San Antonio, June 15, 1956; d. Ira Linwood and Hazel Elizabeth Shannon; m. William F. McCranor Jr., Oct. 22, 1983; children: William F. III, Shannon Lee. B cum laude in Environ. Design, Tex. A&M U., 1980. Cert. profl. bldg. designer, Tex. Owner, residential designer Shannon-McCranor Enterprise, Willis, Tex., 1981—. Tchr. CCE St. Joseph Cath. Ch., New Waverly, Tex., 1996—; coord., trainer altar svc., 1997—; mem. Am. Assn. U. Women, Montgomery County Br., Tex., 1996—, rec. sec., bd. dirs., 1998-99, chmn. com. pub. policy, 2000—. Mem. Am. Inst. Bldg. Design, Nat. Coun. Bldg. Designer Cert., Tex. Inst. Bldg. Design. Avocations: genealogy, clarinet, computer, water sports. E-mail: mccranor@earthlink.net. Home: 7662 County Line Rd Willis TX 77378-4798

MCCRARY, EUGENIA LESTER (MRS. DENNIS DAUGHTRY MCCRARY), civic worker, writer; b. Annapolis, Md., Mar. 23, 1929; d. John Campbell and Eugenia (Potts) Lester; m. John Campbell Howard, July 15, 1955 (dec. Sept. 1965); m. Dennis Daughtry McCrary, June 28, 1969; 1 child, Dennis Campbell. AB cum laude, Radcliffe Coll.-Harvard U., 1950; MA, Johns Hopkins U., 1952; postgrad., Harvard U., 1953, Pa. State U., 1953-54, Drew U., 1957-58, Inst. Study of USSR, Munich, 1964. Grad. asst. dept. Romance langs. Pa. State U., 1953-54; tchr. dept. math. The Brearley Sch., N.Y.C., 1954-57; dir. Sch. Langs., Inc., Summit, N.J., 1958-69; trustee Sch. Langs., Inc., Summit, 1960-69. Co-author: Nom de Plume: Eugenia Campbell Lester, (with Allegra Branson) Frontiers Aflame, 1987; film script adaptation (with John Gallagher) Frontier, 1998. Dist. dir. Ea. Pa. and N.J. auditions Met. Opera Nat. Coun., N.Y.C., 1960-66, dist. dir. publicity, 1966-67, nat. vice chmn. publicity, 1967-71, nat. chmn. public rels., 1972-75, hon. nat. chmn. pub. rels., 1976-99; bd. govs., chmn. Van Cortlandt House Mus., 1985-90. Mem. Nat. Soc. Colonial Dames Am. (bd. mgrs. N.Y. 1985-90), Met. Opera Nat. Coun., Soc. Mayflower Desc. (former bd. dirs. N.Y. soc., chmn. house com. 1986-89), Soc. Daus. Holland Dames (bd. dirs. 1982-87, 96—, 3d directress gen. 1987-92, directress gen. 1992-96), L'Eglise du St.-Esprit (vestry 1985-88, sr. warden 1988-90), Huguenot Soc. Am. (governing coun. 1984-90, 2000—, asst. treas. 1990-91, sec. 1991-95, 2d v.p. 1995-2000), Colonial Dames Am., Daus. of Cin., Colony Club (bd. govs. 1988-96), Causeries du Lundi. Republican. Episcopalian. Home: 24 Central Park S New York NY 10019-1629

MCCRAY, DOROTHY WESTABY, artist, printmaker, educator; b. Madison, S.D., Oct. 13, 1915; d. Robert Spencer and Annie Mary (Otter) Westaby; m. Francis F. McCray, Aug. 6, 1938 (dec. Jan. 1960); 1 child, Peter Michael. BA, State U. of Iowa, 1937, MA in Painting, 1939; MFA in Printmaking, Calif. Coll. Arts and Crafts, Oakland, 1955. Prof. art Western N.Mex. U., Silver City, 1948-81, prof. emeritus, 1981—; profl. painter/printmaker McCray Studios, Silver City. Solo exhbns. include Mezzanine Gallery, Oakland, Calif., Art Directions Gallery, N.Y.C., Lebanon Valley Coll., Pa., Coralles Art Assn., N.Mex., Richard Levy Gallery, Albuquerque, numerous others; group exhbns. include Art Inst. Chgo., 1940-41, Phila. Acad., 1941, Kansas City Art Inst., 1941, 42, Smithsonian Inst., Washington, 1941, 58, Am. Fine Arts Gallery, N.Y.C., 1943, Joslyn Meml. Art Mus., Omaha, 1947, Mus. Fine Arts, Santa Fe, 1950, 51, 52, 53, 54, 56, 57, 58, 59, 63, 66, Oakland (Calif.) Art Mus., 1955, Cin. Art Mus., 1956, 58, NAD, Newton, Kans., 1956, Dallas Mus. Fine Arts, 1956, 58, Roswell (N.Mex.) Art Mus., 1958, Bradley U., Peoria, Ill., 1960, Highlands U., Las Vegas, 1960, Bklyn. Mus., 1961, Pa. Acad. Art, Phila., 1965, Museo de Arte Historia, Juarez, Mexico, 1978, The Shellfish Collection, Silver City, N.Mex., 1990, 91, Deming (N.Mex.) Ctr. for Arts, 1991, Grant County Art Guild, Pinos Altos, N.Mex., 1991, 92, Carlsbad (N.Mex.) Mus. and Art Ctr., 1992, Richard Levy Gallery, Albuquerque, 1992, Jonathon Green Gallery, Naples, Fla., numerous others; represented in pvt. and mus. collections throughout the United States. Named Hon. Citizen of S.D., 1983; Western N.Mex. U. Art Building named Dorothy McCray Art Building, 1982; recipient N.Mex. Gov.'s Award for Excellence and Contbns. to the Arts, 1992, numerous art awards in exhbns. Office: PO Box 322 Silver City NM 88062-0322

MCCRAY, NIKKI KESANGAME, basketball player; b. Collierville, Tenn., Dec. 17, 1971. BA, U. Tenn., 1995. Basketball player USA Women's Nat. Team, 1996, Washington Mystics, 1998—. Office: Washington Mystics MCI Ctr 601 F St NW Washington DC 20004-1605

MCCREARY, DEBORAH DENNIS, oncology nurse; b. Washington, Ohio, Oct. 6, 1952; d. Eldon Hugh Dennis and Janice Sylvia (North) Saunders; m. James Leo McCreary, May 21, 1988. BSN, Ohio State Sch. Nursing, 1976. Nurse Ohio State U. Hosp., Columbus, 1976-77; asst. head nurse Riverside Meth. Hosp., Columbus, 1977-80; nurse Good Samaritan Hosp., San Jose, Calif., 1980-82; asst. head nurse Valley West Hosp., San Jose, 1982; outpatient oncology nurse Southbay Med. Oncology, San Jose, 1982-88; oncology nurse specialist, office mgr. Menlo Med. Clinic, Menlo Park, Calif., 1988-98; cons. Schering Corp., Dallas, 1991, Berlix, Menlo Park, 1992, spkr., 1994, Ortho Biotech, San Francisco, 1995. Mem. Oncology Nursing Soc. (Santa Clara chpt. sec. 1982-84, membership chair 1984-85, cert. oncology nurse). Republican. Avocations: classical music, piano, gourmet cooking, hiking, travel. Home: 23750 Ravensbury Ave Los Altos CA 94024-6341

MCCREE, PAUL WILLIAM, JR., systems design and engineering company executive; b. St. Louis, Oct. 27, 1926; s. Paul William and Hazel Elfrieda (Wilson) McC.; m. Carolyn Williams, Sept. 7, 1955; children—Brian, Paula, Ross. B.S. in Biochem. Scis., Harvard U., 1950. Mem. tech. staff System Devel. Corp., Santa Monica, Calif., 1956-62, Mitre Corp., Bedford, Mass., 1966-67; prin. engr., equipment div. Raytheon Co., Sudbury, Mass., 1963-66, 67-72; mem. tech. staff MIT Lincoln Labs., Lexington, 1972-76; mgr. Aerospace Systems div. Input Output, Waltham, Mass., 1976-79, tech. dir., 1979-80; mem. tech. staff Mitre Corp., Bedford, Mass., 1980-82; founder, pres. BPR Co., profl. cons. services (sci., engring. and bus. applications of computers), 1981—; sr. mem. tech. staff, mgr. subsystem design and devel. dept. GTE Strategic Systems Div., 1982-84; tech. dir. HH Aerospace and Design Co. Inc., Bedford, 1984-86; prin. engr., mem. tech. staff Raytheon Equipment div. Software Systems Lab., Sudbury, 1986-87; v.p. HH Aerospace and Design Co. Inc., Bedford, 1986-91. Mem. NAACP, Urban League. Served with U.S. Army, 1944. Recipient Black Achiever award Greater Boston YMCA, 1977. Mem. AAAS, IEEE, Math. Assn. Am., Am. Math. Soc., N.Y. Acad. Scis. Democrat. Club: Harvard (Concord); Harvard Faculty (Cambridge). Home: 173 Goodman's Hill Rd PO Box 77 Sudbury MA 01776-0077

MCCREERY, WILLIAM See RAMSEY, BILL

MCCREEVY, CHARLIE, Irish government official; b. Sept. 1949; married; 7 children. Grad., Univ. Coll. Dublin, Ireland. Ptnr. Tynan Dillon & Co., Dublin, Naas and Ballyhaunis; mem. Kildare County Coun., 1979-85; mem. Dáil, 1977—, min. for social welfare, 1992-93, min. for tourism and trade, 1993-94; min. for fin. Fianna Fáil, 1997—. Office: Govt Bldgs, Upper Merrion St, Dublin 2, Ireland

MCCREIGHT, SUSAN BUCKLEY, human resources executive; b. Oakland, Calif., Feb. 19, 1946; d. Milton Chester and Virginia Jean (Kincaid) Buckley. BS in Social Sci. summa cum laude, Fordham U., 1983. Mgr., adminstrn. and spl. projects ABC, Inc., N.Y.C., 1979-81, mgr. fair employment practices, 1981-84; dir. personnel Chilton Co., Radnor, Pa., 1984-85; dir. human resources Cahners Pub. Co., N.Y.C., 1987-89; v.p. human resources Warner Pub. Svcs., N.Y.C., 1990-95, AmeriChoice Health Svcs., N.Y.C., 1995-99; sr. dir. human resources Weill Med. Coll. of Cornell U., N.Y.C., 1999—. Mem. Soc. for Human Resources Mgmt., Slow Food, Phi Kappa Phi (life). Episcopalian. Avocations: cooking, reading, needlework, hiking, travel. Home: 600 W 111th St # 10F New York NY 10025-1813 Office: 445 E 69th St New York NY 10021-5664

MCCRERY, DAVID NEIL, III, lawyer; b. Ames, Iowa, Mar. 7, 1957; s. David Neil Jr. and Judith Ann (Purlee) McC.; m. Katherine Marie Meridith, June 9, 1979; children: Evelyn Judith, David Neil IV. BS in Agrl., U. Ill., 1979; JD, So. Ill. U., Carbondale, 1993. Bar: Ill. 1993, U.S. Dist. (ctrl. dist.) Ill. 1993. Dist. mgr. Ralston Purina Co., St. Louis, 1979-83; farmer, businessman McCrery Farms, Monmouth, Ill., 1984-90; grad. rsch. asst. So. Ill. U. Sch. Law, 1991-93; pvt. practice McCrery Law, Galesburg, Ill., 1993—; judge Knox County Teen Ct., 1997-99. Assoc. del. U.S.-Can. Gt. Lakes Conf., 1984; assoc. bd. dirs. Warren County Soil and Water Dist., Monmouth, 1986; bd. dirs., v.p. West Ctrl. Ill. Legal Assistance, 1996-98; bd. dirs. Head Start Ops. for Presch. Edn.-HOPE, 1996-98, Galesburg Youth Athletic Club, 1994-98; mem. Ill. Agr. Leadership Program, 1986-87. Recipient Outstanding State Dir. award Monmouth Jaycees, 1988. Mem. Knox County Bar Assn. Presbyterian. Avocations: hunting, fishing, collecting antiques, travel, mission work. Home: 105 N Carlysle Ave Abingdon IL 61410-1403 Office: 153 E Main St Galesburg IL 61401-4612

MCCRICKARD, ERIC EUGENE, customer service representative; b. Charlotte, N.C., May 20; s. Thomas Daniel and Claireen Aleta (Lawing) McC. Grad., Elon Coll., 1999. Customer svc. rep., asst. mgr. Flick's Video, Glen Raven, N.C., 1992-2000; with WXRA Radio, 1998; radio disc jockey Curtis Media Group, 1999-2000; customer svc. rep. Alamance Nat. Bank, Graham, N.C., 2000—. Mem. Epsilon Sigma Alpha, Alpha Kappa Psi, Alpha Phi Omega, Omicron Delta Kappa, Lambda Pi Eta, Epsilon Beta Epsilon. Baptist. Home: 2410 Delaney Dr Burlington NC 27215-5212

MCCRIMMON, BARBARA SMITH, writer, librarian; b. Anoka, Minn., May 3, 1918; d. Webster Roy and Jessie (Sargeant) Smith; m. James McNab McCrimmon, June 10, 1939; Children: Kevin Mor, John Marshall. B.A., U. Minn., 1939; M.S.L.S., U. Ill., 1961; Ph.D., Fla. State U., 1973. Asst. librarian Ill. State Nat. Hist. Survey, Champaign, Ill., 1961-62; research assoc. Bur. Community Planning, U. Ill., Champaign, 1962-63; librarian Ill. Water Survey, Champaign, 1964-65, Am. Meterol. Soc., Boston, 1965-67; edit. asst. Jour. Library History, Tallahassee, 1967-69, 73-74; adj. asst. prof. Sch. Library Sci., Fla. State U., Tallahassee, 1976-77. Author: Power, Politics and Print, 1981, Richard Garnett: The Scholar as Librarian, 1989; editor: American Library Philosophy, 1975; contbr. articles to profl. jours. Mem. ALA, Pvt. Libraries Assn., Beta Phi Mu, Manuscript Soc. Democrat. Home: 1330 W Indianhead Dr Tallahassee FL 32301-4763

MCCRINDLE, CHERYL MYRA, veterinarian; b. Johannesburg, Gauteng, S. Africa, Sept. 20, 1946; d. William Jean and Coral Gladys May (Robertson) Hay; m. Robert Ian McCrindle, Dec. 12, 1969; children: James, Alistair, Sarah-Jane. BVS, Faculty of Vet. Sci., Onderstepoort, 1969, BVS with honors, 1979; PhD, Faculty of Vet. Sci., 1996. Rsch. officer Onderstepoort Vet. Inst., South Africa, 1970-73, sr. lectr., 1973-76; pvt. practice Vet Clinic, Pretoria, 1976-80, Bklyn. Vet. Clinic, Pretoria, 1980-90; sr. lectr. Medunsa Vet. Faculty, Pretoria, 1990-96, assoc. prof., 1996-99, prof., 1999—; prof. U. Pretoria Vet. Faculty, 1999—; dir. SPCA Pretoria, S. Africa, hon. v.p.; judge Arabian Horses/Arab Horse Soc., 1976—; accredited animal behavior cons. Contbr. articles to profl. jours.; columnist Beeld Newspaper, 1982—. Recipient Chmn.'s award Medunsa Acad. Day, Medunsa, 1996. Mem. S.A. Vet. Assn. Animal Welfare, Gold Spurs Club (judge). Avocations: breeding, judging and riding horses, writing, reading. Office: Paravet Studies Pvt Bag X04, Vet Fac U Pretoria, Onderstepoort 0110, Republic of South Africa

MCCRUM, MICHAEL WILLIAM, educator; b. Gosport, Hampshire, Eng., May 23, 1924; s. Cecil Robert and Ivy Hilda Constance (Nicholson) McCrum; m. Christine Mary Kathleen fforde, Sept. 6, 1952; 4 children. Student, Corpus Christi Coll., Cambridge, 1946-48, MA, 1950; DEd (hon.), U. Victoria, 1989. Asst. master Rugby Sch., Warwickshire, Eng., 1948-50; tutor Corpus Christi Coll., 1950-62, master, 1980-94; head master Tonbridge Sch., Kent, 1962-70, Eton Coll., Berkshire, 1970-80; vice-chancellor Cambridge U., 1987-89; chmn. Cathedrals Fabric Commn. for Eng., 1991-99; gov. King's Sch., Canterbury, 1980-94, Sherborne Sch., 1980-94, United World Coll. Atlantic, 1981-94, Rugby Sch., 1982-94. Joint author Select Documents of the Principates of the Flavian Emperors A.D. 68-96, 1961, Thomas Arnold Head Master, 1989, The Man Jesus, 2000. Sub-lt. RNVR, 1943-45. Named comdr. Order de Isabel la Católica, 1988, CBE, 1996. Mem. Clubs: Athenaeum, United Oxford and Cambridge, East India and Pub. Schs., Hawks. Office: 32 Clarendon St, Cambridge CB1 1JX, England

MCCUAN, WILLIAM PATRICK, real estate company executive; b. Muskogee, Okla., Oct. 28, 1941; s. Lee L. and LaRee A. (Beverage) McC.; m. Jill Pamela Thomas, May 5, 1982; children: LaRee, Megan. Student, U. Tulsa, 1961-62; BA in Psychology, Baylor U., 1965; MRE, So. Sem., Louisville, 1967; MS, U. Louisville, 1969; postgrad., U. Md., 1971-73. Prof., asst. dean grad. sch. U. Md., Balt., 1969-73; lobbyist, cons. Washington, 1973-76; CEO KMS Group, Inc., Columbia, Md., 1976-84, MDG Cos. of Md., 1984—, MDG-Capital Ptnrs., Naples, Fla., 1992—, MDG Cos. W.Va., Berkeley Springs, 1991—; adj. prof. Cmty. Coll., Balt., 1969-72, U. Md. College Park, 1969-71; lectr. Univ. Coll.-Univ. Md., Balt., 1970-71, Howard C.C., Columbia, 1987-88; CEO Pet Holiday, Inc., Toledo, 1973-94; CEO Uniglobe Columbia Travel Ctr., 1986-94; non-lawyer mem. Atty. Grievance Commn., Md., 1990-96. Contbr. to numerous publs. Chmn., bd. dirs. Concert Soc. Md., 1988-98; chmn. United Way, Howard County, Md., 1984, Am. Presdl. Inaugural Com., Md., 1988, Howard County Cmty. Partnerships; fin. chmn. Rep. Ctrl. Com., Howard County, 1988-92; trustee Columbia Found.; mem. Pres.'s Commn. on Food, Nutrition and Health, Washington, 1970, Howard County Environ. Affairs Bd.; mem. bus. adv. coun. Howard C.C.; bd. dirs. Congl. Commn. on Mental Health of Children, Washington, 1973-75, Human Svcs. Inst. for Children and Families; pres., trustee McCuan Family Found., 1997—. Recipeint Alumni Fellows award U. Louisville, 1996. Mem. Nat. Assn. Home Builders (bd. dirs. 1979-87, fed. govt. affairs com.), Md. Builders Assn. (pres. 1981-82), Home Builders Assn. Md. (bd. dirs. 1977-82, Award of Honor 1979, Award of Excellence 1980, Presdl. award 1982), Howard County Home Builders Assn. (pres. 1978-80), Howard County C. of C. (pres. bd. dirs. 1984-86). Home: 4256 Snowberry Ln Naples FL 34119-8513 also: 11838 Farside Rd Ellicott City MD 21042-1526 Office: MDG Bldg 5550 Sterrett Pl Columbia MD 21044-2611

MCCUE, MICHAEL, manufacturing executive; b. Denver, Feb. 21, 1951; s. Ethan Roy and Mildred (Haag) McC. AB cum laude, Harvard U., 1973, MBA, 1975. Mgr. brands Brown & Williamson, Louisville, 1975-79; mgr. Northlich Stolley, Inc., Cin., 1979; nat. brand mgr. Brown-Forman Distillers, Louisville, 1980-83; pres. Columbus Holdings Corp., Columbus, N.C., 1983—; owner Photo Graphia Gallery of Fine Collectible Photography, Tryon; design arts panelist NEA. Pres. Louisville Hist. League, 1977; trustee Polk County Libr. System, Columbus, 1987—; bd. dirs. U. N.C.-Asheville Found. Mem. Water Tower Art Assn. (pres. Louisville 1982), Thermal Belt C. of C. (pres. 1986), Indsl. Designers Soc. of Am., Harvard Club (pres. 1997-99), Am. Hist. Prints Soc. (bd. dirs.). Democrat. Avocations: skiing, hiking, 19th Century prints. Home: 33 Forest Rd Asheville NC 28803-2943 Office: Kangaroo Golf Ltd 108 Mill Spring Rd Columbus NC 28722

MCCUEN, JOHN JOACHIM, building company and financial company executive; b. Washington, Mar. 30, 1926; s. Joseph Raymond and Josephine (Joachim) McC.; m. Gloria Joyce Seidel, June 16, 1949; children: John Joachim Jr., Les Seidel. BS, U.S. Mil. Acad., 1948; M of Internatl. Affairs, Columbia U., 1961; grad., U.S. Army War Coll., 1968. Commd. 2d. lt. U.S. Army, 1948, advanced through grades to col.; dir. internal def. and devel. U.S. Army War Coll., Carlisle Barracks, Pa., 1969-72; chief U.S. Def. Liaison Group, Jakarta, Indonesia, 1972-74; chief field survey office U.S. Army Tng. and Doctrine Command, Ft. Monroe, Va., 1974-76; ret. U.S. Army, 1976; mgr. tng. Chrysler Def., Center Line, Mich., 1977-82; mgr. modification ctr. Land Systems div. Gen. Dynamics, Sterling Heights, Mich., 1982-83; mgr. field ops. Land Systems div. Gen. Dynamics, Warren, Mich., 1983-94; pres. Mich. Econ. Devel. Corp., Birmingham, 1994—, The Magic Christmas Tree, Inc., Birmingham, 1994—; pres., CEO Laminar, Inc., Southfield, Mich., 1996—; owner Adventure and Exotic Travel Outfitters, Inc., Birmingham, 1995—; past pres. First Internat. Corp., Birmingham, 1995-97; ptnr. East West Connection, Birmingham, Mich.; past pres. Energy Resource Mgmt. Sys., Inc., Birmingham; armor advisor 3d Royal Thai Army, Utaradit, 1957-58; U.S. rep. users' com. NATO Missile Firing Installation Crete, Paris, 1964-66; advisor Vietnamese Nat. Def. Coll., Saigon, 1968-69; spkr. on terrorism and counter insurgency. Author: The Art of Counter Revolutionary War-The Strategy of Counter Insurgency, Faber 1966, Stackpole, 1967, Circulo Militar, 1967. Pres. Troy (Mich.) Cmty. Concert Assn., 1985—, bd. dirs., 1982—; past pres. Mich. Oriental Art Soc., Birmingham; pres. Grander View Found. Sr. Housing and Nursing, Milford, Mich., 1984-89; 1st reader First Ch. of Christ Scientist, Birmingham, 1989-92, chmn. bd. dirs. 2000—; past chmn. region VI N.E. unit Detroit United Way Campaign. Mem. Soc. Logistics Engrs., Nat. Mgmt. Assn., Assn. U.S. Army, Oriental Art Soc. Republican. Avocation: collecting and selling Oriental antiques, lecturing on terrorism and national security. Home: 32863 Balmoral St Beverly Hills MI 48025-3008 Office: Laminar Inc 802 S Worth St Birmingham MI 48009-6929 also: Mich Econ Devel Corp 802 S Worth St Birmingham MI 48009-6929

MCCULLEN, JOSEPH T., JR., venture capitalist; b. Phila., Mar. 15, 1935; s. Joseph Thomas and Sara Ellen (Berryman) McC.; m. Eleanor Joan Houder, July 5, 1958; children: Geoffrey, Jennifer, Justin. BA, Villanova U., 1957, PhD (hon.), 1976. Mgr. planning & acquisitions Merck & Co., Inc., Rahway, N.J., 1961-65; sr. v.p., ptnr. Spencer Stuart & Assocs., N.Y.C., 1965-71; spl. asst. to Pres. Richard M. Nixon, Washington, 1971-73; asst. sec. of The Navy, Washington, 1973-77; sr. v.p., sec. New Eng. Mut. Life, Boston, 1977-80; pres. McCullen Ptnrs. Inc., Boston, 1980—; mng. dir. OneLiberty Ventures, Boston, 1986-99, Whitney & Co., Boston, 1999—; bd. dirs. HealthShare Tech. Inc., Acton, Mass., TeleCorp, Inc., Arlington, Va., MetroPCS, Inc., Dallas, EXTRAPRISE Group, Boston, DIVEO Broadband Networks Inc., Washington, Argentina, Brazil, Colombia, Mex., Panama and Peru, Advanced TeleCom Group, Inc., San Francisco, Gabriel Comms. Inc., Chesterfield, Mo., Linx Comms., Newton, Mass., Carolina Broadband, Charlotte, N.C., Atlantis Wireless, Inc., Washington, PurePacket Comm., Alpharetta, Ga.; bd. advisors Ctr. for Photonics, Boston U., 1995—. Mem. selection com. White House Fellows Program, 1979-96; bd. dirs. World Affairs Coun., 1977-95, Boston Ballet, 1978-85, chmn., 1980-85; bd. trustees Goodwill Industries, 1979-95, Boston Biomed. Rsch. Inst., 1989-95; assoc. dir. Pres. Reagan Transition Team, 1980; advisor Pres. Bush Transition Team, 1988. Served with U.S. Navy, 1952-53; lt. U.S. Army, 1958-61. Recipient Disting. Pub. Svc. medals Exec. Office of Pres., 1973, U.S. Dept. Def., 1977. Home: 97 Essex Rd Chestnut Hill MA 02467-1316 Office: Whitney & Co One Liberty Sq 12th Fl Boston MA 02209

MCCULLEN, MICHAEL JOHN, advertising executive; b. Phila., Aug. 12, 1937; s. Joseph Thomas and Sara Ellen (Berryman) McC.; m. Kathleen Carol Flynn, Sept. 14, 1968; 1 child, Kelly Ann. BS in Mktg., Temple U., Phila., 1963. Creative liaison Phila. Inquirer, 1963-66; artist/writer The Phila. Bull., 1966-71; pres. Creative Creatures, Inc., Phila., 1971-79; advt. mgr. Eckerd Drug Co., Newark, Del., 1979-83; advt./sales promotion mgr. Eljo Products, Inc., Pennsauken, N.J., 1983-93; pres. McCullen & Assocs., Marlton, N.J., 1993—. Mem. Rep. Nat. Com., Washington, 1985-86. With USN, 1957-59. Mem. Am. Soc. Advt. and Promotion, Nat. Assn. Desktop Pubs., Mktg. Color Group, Phila. Advt. Club. Republican. Roman Catholic. Avocations: drawing, painting, reading, sports. Home: 268 Grisscom Ct Marlton NJ 08053-2011 Office: McCullen & Assocs 1 Eves Dr Ste 111 Marlton NJ 08053-3125

MCCULLOCH, ALISTAIR JOHN, research scientist, educator; b. Edinburgh, Scotland, Aug. 4, 1950; s. Robert Simpson and Mary Isobel (Mill) McC.; m. Gillian Elizabeth Reeves, Oct. 21, 1957; children: Robert Andrew, Lyndsay Mary, Jennifer Elizabeth. BA, U. Huddersfield, 1979;

PhD, Exeter U., 1986. Prof. Robert Gordon U., Scotland, 1987-97; head rsch. Edge Hill U. Coll., Lancashire, Eng., 1997—. Editor Greener Mgmt. Internat. Jour., 1995, Jour. Applied Mgmt. Studies, Sustainable Devel.; contbr. articles to profl. jours. Mem. Policy Studies Orgn. Avocations: reading, travel, walking. Office: Edge Hill Coll, Saint Helens Rd, Ormskirk L39 4QP, England

MCCULLOCH, DAPHNE LYNNE, optometrist; b. Sarnia, Ont., Can., Sept. 29, 1956; arrived in U.K., 1991; d. Earl Crawford and Margaret Josephine (Taylor) McC.; 1 child, Matthew Alan Tomlinson. OD, U. Waterloo, Can., 1979; PhD, Ind. U., 1988. Lic. optometrist, Ont., Can., Pa., Ind., U.K. Dir. visual electrophysiology unit dept. ophthalmology Hosp. Sick Children, Toronto, Ont., Can., 1987-90; rsch. assoc. Children's Hosp., L.A., 1990-91; lectr. dept. vision scis. Glasgow (Scotland) Caledonian U., 1992-96, sr. lectr., 1996—; hon. asst. prof. dept. ophthalmology U. Toronto, 1987-90; hon. rsch assoc. Royal Hosp. Sick Children, Yorkhill NHS Trust, Glasgow, 1994—. Contbr. articles to profl. jours. Rsch. devel. grantee Scottish Higher Edn. Funding Coun., 1994, 96, 99, rsch. grantee Chief Scientists Office Scottish Office of Home and Health Dept., 1992, 95, operating grantee Med. Rsch. Coun. Can., 1988, 90. Fellow Am. Acad. Optometry (com. mem. 1989—); mem. Internat. Soc. Clin. Electrophysics of Vision. Home: 23 Kirklee Rd, Glasgow G12, Scotland Office: Glasgow Caledonian U, Cowcaddens Rd, Glasgow G4 0BA, Scotland

MCCULLOUGH, EDWARD EUGENE, patent agent, inventor; b. Baldwin, N.D., June 4, 1923; s. Elmer Ellsworth and Emma Izelda (Nixon) McC. BA, U. Minn., 1957; postgrad., Utah State U., 1965. Machine designer Sperry Rand Corp., Mpls., 1952-58; patent adminstr. Thiokol Corp., Brigham City, Utah, 1958-86; patent cons. Thiokol Corp., Brigham City, 1986; pvt. practice, 1986—. Patentee 34 U.S. patents including instruments for making perspective drawings, apparatus for forming ignition surfaces in solid propellant motors, passive communications satellite or similar article, flexible bearings and process for their manufacture, rocket nozzel support and pivoting system, cavity-shaping machine, others. Pianist Aldersgate Meth. Ch., Brigham City, 1959—. Staff Sgt. U.S. Army, 1949-52. Decorated two battle stars. Avocations: philosophy, music composition, hiking in the mountains. Home: PO Box 46 Brigham City UT 84302-0046

MCCULLOUGH, FRANK WITCHER, III, lawyer; b. New Orleans, Dec. 13, 1945; s. Frank Witcher Jr. and Kathleen Elizabeth (Van Pelt) McC.; m. Barry Jean Bock, Mar. 7, 1981; children: William David Oat, Frank Witcher IV, Elizabeth Layton. BA, Stetson U., 1967; JD, W.Va. U., 1970. Bar: W.Va. 1970, Tex. 1970, U.S. Dist. Ct. (so. dist.) W.Va. 1970, U.S. Dist. Ct. (so. dist.) Tex. 1972, U.S. Ct. Appeals (5th cir.) 1972, U.S. Supreme Ct. 1980, U.S. Dist. Ct. (no. dist.) Calif. 1983, U.S. Dist. Ct. (we. dist.) Tex. 1987, U.S. Dist. Ct. (ea. dist.) Tex. 1993. Indsl. rels. specialist Continental Oil Co., Houston, 1970-72; asst. U.S. atty. U.S. Atty.'s Office, Houston, 1972-75; assoc. Baker & Botts, Houston, 1975-76, Austin, Tex., 1985-89; ptnr. Weiner Strother & Lamkin, Houston, 1983-85; regional counsel GATX Leasing Corp., Houston, 1976-78; ptnr. Walsh Squires Tompkins & McCullough, Houston, 1978-82; shareholder Sheinfeld, Maley & Kay, Austin, 1989—. Spl. commr. Harris County, Houston, 1982; mem. Bellaire (Tex.) Bd. Adjustment, 1982; bd. dirs. Big Bros. and Big Sisters of Austin, 1991-94. Mem. State Bar Tex. (grievance com. 1979-87, 95—), chmn. unauthorized practice law com. 1984-87), Austin Country Club, SAR. Republican. Episcopalian. Home: 6707 Bridge Hill Cv Austin TX 78746-1338 Office: Sheinfeld Maley & Kay 301 Congress Ave Austin TX 78701-2961

MCCULLOUGH, JOHN, consultant mechanical engineer; b. Glasgow, Scotland, Mar. 23, 1949; s. Henry Christie McCullough and Jessie Niven; m. Geraldine Mabel Gardner; children: Katherine, Alexander, Eleanor. MSc, Portsmouth (Eng.) U., 1976, PhD, 1979. Chartered engr., Fellow Instn. Mech. Engrs., European Engr. Dir. Cadogan Consultants, 1982—; expert witness, numerous cts., U.K., 1990—. Contbr. articles to numerous profl. jours. Mem. Acad. Experts U.K., Expert Witness Inst. U.K., Inst. Energy (chmn. 1984-85). Avocations: music, hill walking. Home: South Park, Kilmacolm PA13 4NN, Scotland Office: Corunna House, 39 Cadogan St, Glasgow G2 7AB, Scotland Office: 14 Clerkenwell Close, London EC1R 0PQ, England

MCCULLOUGH, KATHRYN T. BAKER, social worker; b. Trenton, Tenn., Jan. 5, 1925; d. John Andrew and Alma Lou (Wharey) Taylor; m. John R. Baker, Sept. 30, 1972 (dec. Oct. 1981); m. T.C. McCullough, May 14, 1988. BS, U. Tenn., 1945, MSW, 1954; postgrad., U. Chgo., 1950, Vanderbilt U., 1950-51. Lic. social worker, Tenn.; emeritus diplomate in clin. social work Am. Bd. Examiners. Home demonstration agt., agrl. extension svc. U. Tenn., Hardeman County, 1946-49; Dyer County, 1949-50; dir. med. social work dept. Le Bonheur Children's Hosp., Memphis, 1954-57; chief clin. social worker clinic mentally retarded children U. Tenn. Dept. Pediatrics, Memphis, 1957-59; clin. social worker Children's Med. Ctr., Tulsa, 1959-60; dir. med. social work dept. Coll. of Medicine U. Tenn., Memphis, 1960-69; dir. community svcs. regional med. program Coll. of Medicine, 1969-76; dir. regional clinic program Child Devel. Ctr. Coll. of Medicine, 1976-85; mem. faculty Coll. of Medicine, Coll. of Social Work U. Tenn., Memphis, 1960-85; social worker admissions rev. bd. Arlington Devel. Ctr., Memphis, 1976-98; cons. Tenn. Dept. Children's Svcs., 1999—. Author 14 books. Active Gibson County Fedn. Dem. Women, 1987—; commr. Dist. I, Gibson Utility Dist., 1990-98; former bd. dirs. Am. Heart Assn., Am. Cancer Soc., Am. Lung Assn., United Cerebral Palsy, Goodwill Industries, AGAPE Child and Family Svcs., Health and Welfare Planning Coun., Shelby County Head Start, Greater Memphis Day Care Assn.; advisor AGAPE Child and Family Svcs., 1998—. Fellow Am. Assn. Mental Retardation (life); mem. NASW (mem. steering com.), AAUP, Acad. Cert. Social Workers, Tenn. Conf. on Social Welfare, Sigma Kappa Alumni Found. (life). Mem. Ch. of Christ. Avocations: piano, organ, symphony. Home: 627 Riverside Yorkville Rd Trenton TN 38382-5917

MCCULLOUGH, RICHARD LAWRENCE, advertising agency executive; b. Chgo., Dec. 1, 1937; s. Francis John and Sadie Beatrice McCullough; m. Julia Louise Kreimer, May 6, 1961; children: Stephen, Jeffery, Julie. BS, Marquette U., 1959. Commd. U.S. Army, 1959, advance through grades to sgt., 1966; account exec. Edward H. Weiss Advt., Chgo., 1960-66; account supr. Doyle Dane Bernbach, N.Y.C., 1966-68; sr. v.p. J. Walter Thompson Co., Chgo., 1969-86; pres. E.H. Brown Advt., Chgo., 1986-97; exec. v.p. Space-Time Media Mgmt., Chgo., 1997-2000; ptnr. Callahan Group, Chgo., 2000—; developer Mktg. with Country Music nat. seminar, 1996. Author: Building Country Radio, 1986, A New Look at Country Music Audiences, 1988, (video) Country Music Marketing, 1989. Bd. dirs. Gateway Found., Chgo., 1976—, chmn., 1988-91; bd. dirs. Catholic Charities, Chgo. Mem. Country Music Assn. (Nashville bd. dirs. 1979—, pres. 1983-85, Pres.'s award 1987, elector Country Music Hall of Fame), NARAS (Nashville chpt.), North Shore Country Club (Glenview, Ill.), Dairymen's Country Club (Boulder Junction, Wis.), Quail Creek Country Club (Naples, Fla.). Roman Catholic. Home (summer): 2720 Lincoln St Evanston IL 60201-2043 also (winter): #304 6865 San Marino Dr Naples FL 34108-7541 Office: Space-Time Media Mgmt Inc 35 E Wacker Dr Chicago IL 60601-2103

MCCULLY, BRUCE CALVIN, videographer, director; b. Evanston, Ill., July 8, 1960. Student, Coll. Lake County, 1973. Cert. in TV prodn. 2nd shift computer ops. supr., 1st shift lead operator Americana Interstate, Mundelein, Ill.; computer problem solver, schedular AllState Ins., Northbrook, Ill.; sound engr. Cheyenne Winter (Country Rock Band), Vancouver, Can., 1979-85; videographer Cabac Prodns. Inc., Waukegan, Ill., 1986-97; dir. Reid Prodns., Evanston, 1988-92; videographer MainStream Prodns. Inc., Lindenhurst, Ill., 1988-2000; freelance videographer Chgo., 2000—. Avocations: travel, music, art, hiking. Office: PO Box 6173 Lindenhurst IL 60046-6173

MCCULLY, PATRICK WILLIAM, campaign director; b. Belfast, Northern Ireland, Mar. 17, 1965; came to U.S., 1993; s. William and Clare Barbara (Jenkinson) McC.; m. Angela Marie Gennino, Nov. 18, 1995 (div. Apr. 1999). BA with 1st class honors, Nottingham (Eng.) U., 1986. Asst. editor The Ecologist, Sturminster Newton, Eng., 1989-90, co-editor, 1990-92; editor Ngonet, Montevideo, Uruguay, 1992-93; campaigns dir. Internat. Rivers Network, Berkeley, Calif., 1993—; assoc. editor The Ecologist, 1993—; contbg. writer Multinat. Monitor, Washington, 1996—; editl. advisor Internat. Jour. on Water. Co-author: Imperiled Planet, 1990, The Road From Rio, 1992; author: Silenced Rivers, 1996, (jour.) World Rivers Rev., 1994—. Coord. Internat. Com. on Dams, Rivers and People, 1998—; mem. World Commn. on Dams Forum, 1998—. Avocations: cycling, hiking, Arsenal Football Club, Paraguayan history, foreign languages. E-mail: patrick@irn.org. Office: Internat Rivers Network 1847 Berkeley Way Berkeley CA 94703-1576

MCCUNE, PHILIP SPEAR, lawyer; b. Spokane, Wash., Sept. 14, 1965; s. Calmar A. McCune and Katrina Y. Spear; m. Joey Leigh Hankins, Jan. 15, 1993; children: Emma Sophia, Jackson Spear. BA magna cum laude, Dartmouth Coll., 1987; JD cum laude, U. Mich., 1991. Bar: Wash. 1991, U.S. Dist. Ct. (we. dist.) Wash. 1991, U.S. Ct. Appeals (9th cir.) 1992, U.S. Dist. Ct. (ea. dist.) Wash. 1993, U.S. Dist. Ct. Utah 1998. Law clk. hon. John C. Coughenour chief judge U.S. Dist. Ct. (we. dist.) Wash., Seattle, 1991-93; with Heller, Ehrman, White and Maculliffe, Seattle, 1993-97; ptnr., founder Summit Law Group, Seattle, 1997—. Author: The Forest Practices Act, Washington Environmental Law and Practice, 1997; sr. editor U. Mich. Jour. Law Reform, 1989-91; contbr. articles to profl. jours. Young leaders bd. mem. Seattle Art Mus., 1996-98; bd. mem. Cmty. Svc. for the Blind, Seattle, 1997—; jr. bd. Seattle Repatory Theater, 1999—. Mem. ABA (bd. dirs. young lawyers divsn. 1996), Washington State Bar Assn., King County Bar Assn., Wash. Athletic Club, U. Mich. Law Sch. Barristers. Avocations: hiking, running. Office: Summit Law Group 1505 Westlake Ave N Ste 300 Seattle WA 98109-6211

MCCURDY, LARRY WAYNE, automotive parts company executive; b. Commerce, Tex., July 1, 1935; s. Weldon Lee and Eula Bell (Quinn) McC.; m. Anna Jean Ogle, June 2, 1956; children: Michael, Kimberly, Laurie. BBA, Tex. A&M U., 1957. Jr. acct. Tenneco Inc., Houston, 1958-60; sr. acct. Tenneco Oil Co., Houston, 1960-64; acctg. supr. Tenneco Chems., Houston, 1964-69; from divsn. controller to v.p. fin. Tenneco Chems., Saddle Brook, N.J., 1970-78; sr. v.p. fin. Tenneco Automotive, Deerfield, Ill., 1978-80; pres. Walker Mfg. Co., Racine, Wis., 1980-81; exec. v.p. N.Am. ops. Tenneco Automotive, Deerfield, 1981-82; v.p. fin. Echlin Inc., Branford, Conn., 1983; pres., COO Echlin, Inc., Branford, Conn., 1983-85, pres., CEO, 1997—; pres., CEO Moog Automotive Inc., St. Louis, 1985-94; exec. v.p. ops. Cooper Industries, Houston, 1994-97; chmn. bd., pres., CEO Echlin, Inc., Branford, Conn., 1997-98; pres. Dana Automotive Aftermarket Group, 1998—; bd. dirs. Lear Seating Corp., Mohawk Industries, Inc., Breed Tech., Inc. Trustee Somerset County Coll., Somerville, N.J., 1974-78, Millikin U., Decatur, Ill., 1991-97; former mem. bd. dirs. Jr. Achievement, Chgo.; bd. dirs. Sam Houston coun. Boy Scouts Am., 1995-97; mem. adv. coun. Tex. A&M U. Engring. Sch., 1995-97. Mem. Fin. Execs. Inst., Nat. Assn. Accts., Motor Equipment Mfrs. Assn. (chmn. bd. dirs. 1989). Office: Dana Automotive Aftermarkets 741 Boston Post Rd Ste 150 Guilford CT 06437-2714

MCCURLEY, MARY JOHANNA, lawyer; b. Baton Rouge, La., Oct. 3, 1953; d. William Edward and Leora Elizabeth (Block) Trice; m. Carl Michael McCurley, June 6, 1983; 1 stepchild, Melissa Reneé Rockenbach. BA, Centenary Coll., 1975; JD, St. Mary's U., 1979. Bar: Tex. 1979; cert. family law 1984. Assoc. Martin, Withers & Box, Dallas, 1979-82, Raggio & Raggio, Inc., Dallas, 1982-83; ptnr. Bruner, McColl, McColloch & McCurley, Dallas, 1983-87; assoc., ptnr. Selligson & Douglass, Dallas, 1987-90; jr. ptnr. Koons, Fuller, McCurley & VanderEykel, Dallas, 1990-92; ptnr. McCurley, Kinser, McCurley & Nelson, Dallas, 1992—; Contbr. numerous articles to profl. jours. Adv. Women's Service League, Dallas, 1993—. Mem. Am. Acad. Matrimonial Lawyers (treas. Tex. chpt. 1995, sec. 1996, pres. 1997, nat. bd. dirs., bd. govs., pres. Tex. chpt. 1997-98), Dallas Bar Assn. (chairperson family law sect. 1985), Tex. State Bar Assn. (mem. family law coun.), Tex. Acad. Family Law Specialist, Dallas Bar Assn. Methodist. Avocations: golf, travel, jogging, horseback riding. E-mail: marjo@mkmn.com. Fax: 214-273-2470. Home: 4076 Hanover Ave Dallas TX 75225-7009 Office: McCurley Kinser McCurley & Nelson LLP 5950 Sherry Ln Ste 800 Dallas TX 75225-6533

MCCURRACH, JAMES CRAMPTON, professional squash player; b. Bklyn., June 8, 1934; s. James C. and Margaret (Means) McC.; m. Lynn Zabriskie (dec.); children: James C. III, Peter Zabriskie. V.p. Bankers Trust Co., N.Y.C., 1965-80; pres. Boxes Restaurant Inc., N.Y.C., 1980-82; exec. placement office Fanning, Inc., N.Y.C., 1982-84; recreation mgr. Printing Ho. Recreation, N.Y.C., 1984-90; assoc. recreational staff NYU, N.Y.C., 1989-90; squash profl. Cape Cod Recreation, Inc., 1991-94; pres. McCurrach Enterprises, Inc., San Francisco, 1991—; tchr., instr. San Francisco Bay Club, St. Dunstan's Sch., 1993-99; tchr., instr. Woodside Internat. Sch., 2000—. Mem. U.S. Squash Racquets Assn. (top five U.S. vets., 1979-83, #4 in U.S. 1986—), Met. Squash Racquets Assn. (ranked #1 Vet., Sr., N.Y.C., N.Y. State 1979—). Club: Univ. (N.Y.C.). Home: 500 9th Ave # 4 San Francisco CA 94118-3749 Office: McCurrach Enterprises 500 9th Ave San Francisco CA 94118-3779

MCCUTCHEN, CHARLES WILLIAM, chemical engineer; b. Wichita Falls, Tex., Nov. 20, 1928; s. William Urlin and Karis (Jameson) McC.; m. Joyce Forse, June 10, 1956; children: David William, Karis Ann. BSChE, MIT, 1949. Engring. trainee Dow Chem. Co., Midland, Mich., 1949; R&D engr. Dow Chem. Co., Freeport, Tex., 1949-68; sr. process engr. Dow Chem. Co., —, —, 1968-79, internal process cons., 1979-86; ret., 1986. Mem. AIChE. Achievements include 4 U.S. patents. Home: 109 Blossom St Lake Jackson TX 77566-4603

MCCUTCHEON, ALLAN LEE, sociology educator; b. Clarinda, Iowa, Mar. 15, 1950; s. Merle Marvin and Margaret Lucille (Larabee) McC.; m. Nancy Ann Cooper, June 13, 1970 (div. May 1975); 1 child, Jennifer; m. Elisabeth Jean Crockett, May 25, 1985. BS, Iowa State U., 1972; MA, U. Chgo., 1977, PhD, 1982. Asst. prof. sociology U. Del., Newark, 1982-88, assoc. prof. sociology, 1988-96, assoc. chair dept. sociology, 1989-95; Donald O. Clifton disting. prof. survey rsch. U. Nebr., Lincoln, 1996—, dir. Gallup Rsch. Ctr., 1996—; sr. scientist Gallup Orgn., 1996—; cons. Disaster Rsch. Ctr., Newark, 1986-88; vis. scientist Max Planck Inst., Freiburg, Germany, 1988-89; dozent U. Cologne (Germany), 1989; instr. European Consortium for Polit. Rsch. U. Essex (Eng.), 1990—; mem. sci. adv. coun. German Ctr. for Survey Rsch. and Methodology, 1998—. Author (book) Latent Class Analysis, 1987; editor (newsletter) States and Societies, 1988-95; contbr. articles to profl. jours. Resource cons. Leadership Del. United Way, Wilmington, 1991-92. U. Chgo. rsch. fellow, 1974-77; Deutscher Akademischer Austauschdienst scholar, 1990; Fulbright scholar, The Netherlands, 1995-96. Mem. World Assn. for Pub. Opinion Rsch., Coun. for European Studies, Am. Assn. for Pub. Opinion Rsch., Am. Statis. Assn., Am. Sociol. Assn., Sigma Xi. Avocations: German culture, literature. Office: U Nebr Gallup Rsch Ctr 200 N 11th St Lincoln NE 68508-1406

MCCUTCHEON, MARIE BURGESS ARLOUINE, town historian, retired; b. Ripley, N.Y., Dec. 19, 1920; d. Walter Casper and Florence Ellen (Walker) Burgess; m. Ralph W. McCutcheon Jr., July 11, 1942; children: Janet Marie, John Ralph, Walter Dennis. Student, Bus. Sch., Orlando, Fla., 1941. Sec. to prin. Ripley (N.Y.) Ctrl. Sch. Dist. # 1, 1941-71; local historian Town of Ripley, 1957—; presenter hist. events and programs, 1957—. Author, editor: Echoes from the Past, 1996, Golden Glow of History Past, 1995, 100 Year Hose Company History, 1980; contbr. articles to profl. publs. Mem. election bd. Town of Ripley, 1960s, mem. planning bd., 1960s. Recipient Person of Yr. award Ripley (N.Y.) Grange, 1980s, Open House Reception award Ripley Taxpayers Alliance, 1997, plaque Ripley Hose Co. # 1, 1981. Avocations: philately, antiques, music appreciation, history. Home: 123 W Main St Ripley NY 14775-9502

MCCUTCHEON, STEVEN CLIFTON, environmental engineer, hydrologist; b. Decatur, Ala., Oct. 29, 1952; s. Bernard Clifton and Rosa May (Askenburg) McC.; m. Sherry Lynn Sharp; children: Michael Ian, Alexander Tavis. BS, Auburn U., 1975; MS, Vanderbilt U., 1977, PhD, 1979. Hydrologist U.S. Geol. Survey, Bay St. Louis, Miss., 1977-86; environ. engr. U.S. EPA, Athens, Ga., 1986—; adj. asst. prof. Tulane U., New Orleans, 1984-85; panel mem. Nat. Rsch. Coun., Washington, 1989-92; adj. prof. Forestry U. Ga., Athens, 1994—; asst. prof. Clemson (S.C.) U., 1990-97; program evaluator Accreditation Bd. Engring. & Tech., 1992—. Author: Water Quality Modeling, vol. 1, 1989, (with others) Fate and Transport of Sediment-Associated Contaminants, 1989, Water Quality, Handbook of Hydrology, 1993; editor and author: (with others) Manual for Performing Estuarine Waste Load Allocations, 1990, Hydrodynamics and Transport for Water Quality Modeling, 1999; editor Jour. Environ. Engring., 1992-94; mem. editl. bd. Ecol. Engring., 1995—, Internat. Jour. Phytoremediation, 2000—; vice-chair editl. bd. Hazardous Toxic and Radioactive Waste Mgmt., 1996-97. Mem. Zoning Commn., St. Tammany Parish, La., 1984-85; vice=chmn. Planning Adv. Bd., St. Tammany Parish, 1985; asst. den leader Cub Scouts Am., Athens, pack 83, 1991-92, pack 96, 1998-99, den leader, 1999-2000. Recipient medal and plaque Korea Soc. Water Pollution Rsch. and Control, Seoul, 1986, Engr. of Yr. award in EPA, NSPE, 1992, EPA Sci. Achievement award in Waste Mgmt. Air and Waste Mgmt. Assn., 1995, EPA Sci. Achievement award in Chemistry Am. Chem. Soc., 1997, Richard R. Torrens award ASCE, 1994, Sci. and Tech. Achievement award EPA, 1999. Mem. ASCE (br. pres. 1983-84, Young Civil Engr. of Yr. award 1984, Torrens award 1994), Am. Geophys. Union, Internat. Soc. Environ. Ethics, Internat. Assn. Water Quality, Internat. Assn. Hydrologic Scis., Water Environ. Fedn., Sigma Xi (chpt. sec. 1982-84, membership com. 1984-85), Phi Kappa Phi, Phi Theta Kappa. Achievements include development of phytoremediation and ecological engineering to clean up federal facilities and response to Exxon Valdez oil spill. Home: 147 Spalding Ct Athens GA 30605-3716 Office: US EPA Nat Exposure Rsch Lab 960 College Station Rd Athens GA 30605-2720

MCDADE, JAMES RUSSELL, management consultant; b. Dallas, Jan. 15, 1925; s. Marion W. and Jeannette (Reneau) McD.; m. Elaine Bushey, Sep. 10, 1955. BSEE, So. Meth. U., Dallas, 1947; MBA, Northwestern U., Evanston, Ill., 1950. Asst. to pres. Davidson Corp., Chgo., 1951-52; asst. to pres. Mergenthaler Linotype Co., Bklyn., 1952-53, comml. works mgr., 1953-56; chief indsl. engr. Tex. Instruments, Inc., Dallas, 1956-57, product gen. mgr., 1958-60, v.p., 1961-64; chmn. bd. McDade Properties Co., Aspen (Colo.), Denver, Dallas, 1964—; bd. dirs. Pitkin County Bank, Aspen; chmn. bd. dirs. Harley-Davidson Tex., Westec Security of Aspen, Aspen Security, Inc. Founding mem. Aspen Art Mus., 1980; mem. Ballet Aspen, 1980—; pres. club Aspen Valley Hosp., 1984—. Served to 1st lt. USAF, 1943-46. Mem. Rep. Senatorial Inner Circle, Am. Mgmt. Assn., Presidents Assn. Avocations: skiing, horseback riding, camping, swimming. Home and Office: 1000 Red Mountain Rd PO Box 9090 Aspen CO 81612-9090

MCDAID, JIM, government official; b. Termon, Ireland, Oct. 3, 1949; married; 4 children. Student, U. Coll., Galway, Ireland. Sr. surg. ho. officer Letterkenny Gen. Hosp., 1974-79; founder, chmn. Donegal Hospice Movement, 1988—; min. Dept. Tourism & Trade, Dublin, 1997—. Office: Dept Tourism Sport & Rec, Kildare St, Dublin 2, Ireland*

MCDANIEL, CAROLYN MARIE (LYNN), secondary education educator; b. Nevada City, Calif., Jan. 25, 1951; d. Robert Carl and Mary Anne Peterson; m. William Charles McDaniel, July 16, 1972; children: James Robert, John William Michael Charles, Robert Carl. AA in Liberal Arts, Sierra Jr. Coll., Rocklin, Calif., 1971; BA, Calif. State U., Sacramento, 1973. Tchg. credential K-9, high sch. credential, Calif. Tchr. English, chair dept. English Nevada Union H.S., Grass Valley, Calif., 1985—, journalism adviser, 1986—; adviser Calif. Scholrship FEdn., Grass Valley, 1985—. Contbg. writer journalism curriculum guide. Registrar Gold County Soccer League, Grass Valley, 1983-93; pres. women's aux. Grass Valley Little League, 1985-92; charter mem., Nevada Union coord. Nevada County Peer Ct., Nevada City, 1995—, bd. dirs., 1995—. Named Educator of Yr., Ptnrs. in Edn., 1999. Mem. Nat. Coun. Tchrs. English, Calif. Tchrs. Assn., Journalism Education Assn. No. Calif. (sec. 1993—, v.p. 1996—, pres. 2000—, Newspaper Adviser of Yr. award 1997), Nevada Union H.S. Tchrs. Assn. Avocations: reading, writing, bridge, walking, travel. E-mail: lmcdaniel@jps.net. Home: 11671 Cathy Dr Grass Valley CA 95949-6559 Office: Nevada Union HS 11761 Ridge Rd Grass Valley CA 95945-5025

MCDANIEL, DONALD HAMILTON, lawyer; b. Washington, Apr. 26, 1948; s. Roy Hamilton and Mildred Dean (Borden) McD.; m. Eva Styron, Dec. 29, 1973; children: Sharon, Michelle. BS, La. State U., 1970; JD, U. Miss., 1973. Bar: Miss. 1973; bd. cert. tax atty., 1987—; bd. cert. estate planning & adminstrn. atty. Atty. IRS, Washington, 1974-77; tax law specialist Bourgeois Bennett Thokey, New Orleans, 1977-81; ptnr. McCloskey Dennery Page, New Orleans, 1981-85, Lemle & Kelleher, New Orleans, 1985—. Author: Estate Planning in Louisiana, 1991. Trustee St. Martins Episcopal Sch., New Orleans, 1993, East Jefferson Hosp. Found., New Orleans, 1995, United Meth. Found., New Orleans, 1995. Mem. ABA, La. State Bar Assn. (chmn. com. on trusts, estates and immovable property 1997—), Miss. State Bar Assn., New Orleans Estate Planning Coun. Avocations: golf, fishing. Office: Lemle & Kelleher LLP 601 Poydras St Ste 2100 New Orleans LA 70130-6021

MCDANIEL, JAMES EDWIN, lawyer; b. Dexter, Mo., Nov. 22, 1931; s. William H. and Gertie M. (Woods) McD.; m. Mary Jane Crawford, Jan. 22, 1955; children: John William, Barbara Anne. AB, Washington U., St. Louis, 1957, JD, 1959. Bar: Mo. 1959. Assoc. firm Walther, Barnard, Cloyd & Timm, 1959-60; assoc. firm McDonald, Barnard, Wright & Timm, 1960-63, ptnr., 1963-65; ptnr. firm Barnard, Timm & McDaniel St. Louis, 1965-73; ptnr. firm Barnard & Baer, St. Louis, 1973-82; ptnr. Lashly & Baer, St. Louis, 1982—, prosecuting atty., 1968—; city atty. City of Glendale, Mo., 1996—; bd. dirs. Eden. Theol. Sem.; lectr. Latvian U., Riga, Inst. Fgn. Rels., Banking in Am., 1992-93. Leader legal del. Chinese-Am. Comparative Law Study, People's Republic China, 1988, Russian-Am. Comparative Law Study, USSR, 1990; trustee, past chmn., past treas. 1st Congl. Ch. St. Louis. With USAF, 1951-55. Fellow Am. Bar Found. (life), St. Louis Bar Found. (life); mem. ABA (bd. govs. 1997-2000, ho. of dels. 1976-80, 84-92, 97-2000, state del. 1986-92, chmn. lawyers conf., jud. adminstrn. divsn. 1992-95, 8th cir. rep. standing com. on fed. jud. 1995-98, mem. standing com. on jud. qualification, tenure and compensation 1996-97), The Mo. Bar (pres. 1981-82, bd. govs. 1974-83), Mo. Assn. Def. Counsel, Bar Assn. Met. St. Louis (pres. 1972), Internat. Assn. Ins. Counsel, Assn. Def. Counsel St. Louis (past pres.), Phi Delta Phi. Home: 767 Elmwood Ave Saint Louis MO 63122-3216 Office: Lashly & Baer 714 Locust St Saint Louis MO 63101-1699

MCDANIEL, JARREL DAVE, lawyer; b. Clovis, N. Mex., Oct. 17, 1930; s. Raymond Lee and Blanch (Booth) McD.; m. Anne Louise McAllister; children: Jarrel Dave Jr., Julia Anne. A.A., Riverside Coll., 1951; B.A., U. Tex., 1956, LL.B., 1957. Bar: Tex. 1957. Assoc. Vinson & Elkins, Houston, 1957-69, ptnr., 1969-96; of counsel Sheinfeld, Maley & Kay, Houston, 1997—; author, lectr. in field. Served with USAF, 1950-54. Mem. ABA, Am. Coll. Bankruptcy, State Bar Tex., Am. Bankruptcy Inst., Tex. Bd. Legal Specialization in Bankruptcy (mem. adv. com. 1976-99, chair 1999—). Roman Catholic. Clubs: Houston Ctr. Home: 1217 Potomac Dr Houston TX 77057-1919 Office: Sheinfeld Maley & Kay PC 1001 Fannin St Ste 3700 Houston TX 77002-6709

MCDANIEL, JOHN STEPHEN, psychiatrist, educator; b. West Memphis, Ark., Jan. 27, 1959; s. Charles Woodrow and Geneva (Steakley) McD. BA with high honors, U. Ark., 1981, MD, 1986. Resident Emory U. Sch. Medicine, Atlanta, 1986-90; chief cons.-liaison psychiatry EMory U. Hosp., Atlanta, 1990-92; asst. prof. psychiatry EMory U. Sch. Medicine, 1990-96; med. dir. psychiat. svcs. Grady Infectious Disease Program, Atlanta, 1992—; project dir. Emory HIV Mental Health Tng. Project, Atlanta, 1992—, Emory Ctr. AIDS Mental Health Svcs., Atlanta, 1994—; asst. prof. family medicine Emory U. Sch. Medicine, 1994—, assoc. prof. psychiatry, 1996-2000, prof. psychiatry, 2000—; dir. Emory HIV Clin. Rsch. Tng. Program. Bd. dirs. Positive Impact, Atlanta, 1992-95, AIDS Rsch. Sonsortium, Atlanta, 1992-95; mem. AIDS coord. com. Fulton-DeKalb Hosp. Authority, Atlanta, 1992—. Rsch. fellow Emory U. Sch. Medicine, 1989-90, George Ginsberg fellow Assn. Dirs. Psychiat. Residency Tng., 1990; recipient So. Psychiat. Assn. Psychiatrist Tng. award, 1990, Ky. Mental Health Assn. Bingham Rsch. award, 1990. Fellow Acad. Psychosomatic Medicine, Am. Psychiat. Assn.; mem. AMA (Physician Recognition award 1996), Am. Psychosomatic Soc. Office: Emory Clinic-Psychiatry 1365 Clifton Rd NE Atlanta GA 30322-1013

MCDANIEL, SARA SHERWOOD (SALLY MCDANIEL), trainer, consultant; b. St. Louis, Apr. 24, 1943; d. Edward Leighton and Dolores Edic (Pitts) Sherwood; m. Allen Polk McDaniel, Dec. 29, 1967; children: James

Polk, Fontaine Maury. AA, Mt. Vernon Coll., 1963; BS, Vanderbilt U., 1965. Tchr. Kanawha Valley Schools, Charleston, W.Va., 1965-66, Fulton County Schools, Atlanta, 1966-68, Trinity Sch., 1969-71; tournament dir. Atlanta Classic, 1972-77; dir. alumni affairs Leadership Atlanta, 1988-89; pvt. practice cons., trainer Atlanta, 1988—; bd. dirs. AID Atlanta, The High Mus. Art, Leadership Coun. Kennedy Ctr. of Vanderbilt U., UNICEF-Atlanta, The Atlanta Women's Found., Leadership Atlanta. Bd. dirs. Girl Scouts U.S., Ga., High Mus. Art, Atlanta Opera, UNICEF Atlanta, Aid Atlanta, Fine Art Collectors; active Com. on Women and Minorities for 1996 Olympics; mem. exec. com. Leadership Atlanta, Jr. League; mem. Friends of Spelman; trustee Mt. Vernon Coll.; bd. chair Atlanta Women's Fund. Mem. Am. Soc. Trainers and Dirs., Atlanta Women's Network (bd. dirs., pres.), Vanderbilt U. Alumni Assn., Alumni Assn. Peabody Coll., The Atlanta Girls Sch. Presbyterian. Home and Office: 3777 Paces Ferry Rd NW Atlanta GA 30327-3003

MCDERMOTT, KEVIN R., lawyer; b. Youngstown, Ohio, Jan. 26, 1952; s. Robert J. and Marion D. (McKeown) McD.; m. Cindy J. Darling, Dec. 11, 1976; children: Ciara, Kelly. AB, Miami U., Oxford, Ohio, 1974; JD, Ohio State U., 1977. Bar: Ohio 1977, U.S. Dist. Ct. (so. dist.) Ohio 1978, U.S. Dist. Ct. (no. dist.) Ohio 1988, U.S. Dist. Ct. (we. dist.) Mich. 1993, U.S. Supreme Ct. 1990, U.S. Ct. Appeals (3rd cir.) 1996, U.S. Ct. Appeals (6th cir.) 1988. Assoc. ptnr. Murphey Young & Smith, Columbus, Ohio, 1977-88; ptnr. Squire Sanders & Dempsey, Columbus, Ohio, 1988-90, Schottenstein Zox & Dunn, Columbus, Ohio, 1990—; adv. bd. mem. Capital U. Legal Asst. Program, Columbus, Ohio, 1988—. Bd. pres. Easter Seal Soc. Ctrl. Ohio, Columbus, 1992-94, bd. mem. 1988-92; pres. Upper Arlington Civic Svc. Commn., Columbus, Ohio, 1988-93. Office: Schottenstein Zox & Dunn 41 S High St Ste 2600 Columbus OH 43215-6109

MCDERMOTT, THOMAS JOHN, JR., lawyer; b. Santa Monica, Calif., Mar. 23, 1931; s. Thomas J. Sr. and Etha Irene (Cook) McD.; m. Yolanda Amante Jatap; children: Jodi Friedman, Kimberly E., Kish S. BA, UCLA, 1953, JD, 1958. Bar: Calif. 1959. Ptnr. Gray, Binkley and Pfaelzer, L.A., 1964-67, Kadison, Pfaelzer, Woodward, Quinn and Rossi, L.A., 1967-87, Rogers & Wells, L.A., 1987-93, Bryan Cave, L.A., 1993-95, Manatt, Phelps & Phillips, LLP, L.A., 1995-99, Shanks and Herbert, San Diego. Served with U.S. Army, 1953-56, Korea. Fellow Am. Coll. Trial Lawyers; mem. ABA, Assn. Bus. Trial Lawyers (pres. 1980-81, mem. exec. com. 9th cir. jud. conf. 1993—, chair 1997), State Bar Calif. (chair litigation sect. 1993-94), UCLA Law Alumni Assn. (pres. 1961-62), Order of Coif. Office: Shanks & Herbert 4350 La Jolla Village Dr San Diego CA 92122

MCDEVITT, BRIAN PETER, history educator, educational consultant; b. Jersey City, Dec. 29, 1944; s. Bernard Aloysius and Veronica Sabina (Decker) McD.; m. Dorothy Helen Gilligan, Oct. 19, 1968; children: Peter David, Timothy Bernard. BS, Seton Hall U., 1966; MA, Columbia U., 1971; DLitt (hon.), Drew U., 2000. Tchr. history St. Patrick's High Sch., Elizabeth, N.J., 1966-68, Vail Deane High Sch., Elizabeth, N.J., 1968-70; fed. grant writer Alexian Bros. Hosp., Elizabeth, N.J., 1970-72, Union County Coll., Cranford, N.J., 1972-76; prin., owner Ednl. Svcs., Westfield, N.J., 1976—; adj. prof. history Union County Coll., Cranford, N.J., 1976—; adj. prof. classics Montclair (N.J.) State U., 1990—. Author: The Irish Librists, 1988, The Irish Librists and the Scrolls of Aristotle, 1993, A Historian's Thematic Study of Western Civilization, 1994, Evidence of an Ancient Greek Navigation System, 1995, The Irish Librists and The Vatican Library Mystery, 1996, A Definition of Western Civilization, 1997, Ancient Greeks: First Navigators, 2000, (video) The Minoans According to Sir Arthur Evans; contbr. articles to profl. jours. N.J. Dept. Higher Edn. grantee. Mem. Trireme Trust U.S.A. (internat. rowing team 1990), Friends of Trireme (London), Soc. Naval Architects and Marine Engrs., Assn. Ancient Historians, Soc. Ancient Greek Philosophy, Assn. Muslim Social Scientists, Classical Assn. of Atlantic States, Am. Soc. Naval Engrs., Westfield United Fund, Westfield P.A.L., Westfield Basketball Assn., Westfield Baseball Assn., Boy Scouts Am. Roman Catholic. Avocations: golfing, rowing, basketball, playing piano, stamp collecting. Home: 607 S Chestnut St Westfield NJ 07090-1369

MCDIARMID, ROBERT CAMPBELL, lawyer; b. N.Y.C., July 13, 1937; s. Norman Hugh and Dorothy (Shoemaker) McD.; m. Ruth Sussman, 1963 (div. 1996); children: Jennifer, Alexander Samuel; m. Frances Enseki Francis, 1996. BS in Mech. Engring., Swarthmore Coll., 1958; MS in Engring. Physics, Cornell U., 1960; LLB, Harvard U., 1963. Bar: D.C. 1964, Va. 1964, U.S. Supreme Ct. 1967, U.S. Ct. Appeals (4th, 6th and 9th cirs.) 1965, U.S. Ct. Appeals (3d, 5th and 10th cirs.) 1966, U.S. Ct. Appeals (7th, 8th and D.C. cirs.) 1967, U.S. Ct. Appeals (2d cir.) 1970, U.S. Ct. Appeals (1st cir.) 1979, U.S. Ct. Appeals (11th cir.) 1981. Assoc. Weaver & Glassie, Washington, 1963-64; trial atty. civil divsn. appellate sect. Dept. Justice, Washington, 1964-68; asst. to gen. counsel Fed. Power Commn., Washington, 1968-70; assoc. Law Office of George Spiegel, Washington, 1970-73; ptnr. Spiegel & McDiarmid, Washington, 1973—. Mem. alumni coun. Swarthmore Coll., 1986-89. Mem. ABA, Va. State Bar, Bar Assn. D.C., D.C. Bar, Energy Bar Assn. (exec. com. 1982-83, bd. dirs. 1997-2000). Democrat. Mem. Soc. of Friends. Home: 3625 Fulton St NW Washington DC 20007-1452 Office: Spiegel & McDiarmid 1350 New York Ave NW Ste 1100 Washington DC 20005-4798

MCDIVITT, KAREN LOUISE, psychologist, writer; b. Las Animas, Colo., Jan. 10, 1953; d. Frank Junior and Ida Ruth (Lopkoff) Woods; m. Michael Wayne McDivitt, June 20, 1977; children: David Eric, Elisabeth Kay. BA, U. Colo., 1974, MA, 1975; PhD, U. Denver, 2000. Spl. edn. tchr. Denver Pub. Schs., 1976-77; diagnostician Colo. Boys' Ranch, LaJunta, Colo., 1977-78; real estate developer LaJunta, 1980-87; bus. mgr. McDivitt Law Firm, Colorado Springs, Colo., 1989-94; freelance writer, 1994—. Sec. Nat. Charity League, Colorado Springs, 1996-97; den leader Boy Scouts Am., LaJunta, 1986-89; pres. PTA, Colorado Springs, 1993-94. Mem. AAUW, APA, Nat. Assn. for Edn. Young Children, U. Colo. Alumni Assn. (bd. dirs. 1986-89), Nat. Writers Club. Republican. Methodist. Avocations: piano, skiing, cooking, reading. Home: 545 Bear Paw Ln N Colorado Springs CO 80906

MC DONALD, ANDREW J., bishop; b. Savannah, Ga., Oct. 24, 1923; s. James Bernard and Theresa (McGrael) McD. AB, St. Mary's Sem., Balt., 1945, STL, 1948; JCB, Cath. U. Am., 1949; JCD, Lateran U., Rome, 1951. Ordained priest Roman Cath. Ch., 1948. Consecrated bishop Roman Cath. Ch., 1972; curate Port Wentworth, Ga., 1952-57; chancellor Diocese of Savannah, Ga., 1952-68, vicar gen., from 1968, vice officialis, 1952-57, officialis, 1956-72; pastor Blessed Sacrament Ch., Savannah, 1963-72; named papal chamberlain Roman Cath. Ch., 1956, named domestic prelate, 1959; bishop Diocese of Little Rock, 1972-2000, bishop emeritus, 2000—. Office: Diocese of Little Rock 2500 N Tyler St Little Rock AR 72207-3743

MCDONALD, ANGUS WHEELER, farmer; b. Washington, Apr. 21, 1927; s. John Yates and Dorothy Helen (Bosworth) McD.; m. Mary Joan Montgomery, May 8, 1952 (div. Sept. 1958); children: Mary Ann Hetzer, Paul Yates. BA, Columbia Union Coll., 1974. Farmer, owner Pleasant View Farm, Charles Town, W.Va., 1953—. Presdl. candidate Democratic Party, 1987-88, 92, 2000. With U.S. Army, 1946-47. Mem. AARP, Jefferson County Farm Bur., W.Va. State Hort. Soc., No. W.Va. Automobile Club, Am. Legion, The Moose. Avocations: photography, travel, attending historical events. Home and Office: Pleasant View Farm RR 3 Box 142 Charles Town WV 25414-9413

MCDONALD, BRIAN ROBERT, petroleum/electronics engineer; b. London, Nov. 2, 1945; s. William and Hilda Alice McD.; m. Christine Mary Allerton, Sept. 16, 1978; children: Ross, Howard, David. BS, Birmingham U., Eng., 1967; MS, Swansea U., Wales, 1973. Cert. profl. engr. Field engr. Schlumberger, Paris, 1967-72; design engr. Data Labs., London, 1974-75; sr. reservoir engr. UK Dept. Energy, London, 1976-78, 90-91; reservoir engring. advisor Mobil, Stavanger, Norway, 1979-86; petroleum engring. coord. Statoil, Stavanger, 1987-89; petroleum engring. mgr. UK Dept. Trade and Industry, London, 1992-98; mgr. LTR Tech. Ltd., 1998—; sec. IEA Collaboration on EOR, 1997-98; R&D Soc., London, 1993-98; presenter papers in field. Mem. Inst. Elec. Engrs., Soc. Petroleum Engrs. Avocations: travel, finance, computing, electronics, family life.

MCDONALD, BRONCE WILLIAM, community activist, advocate; b. Dayton, Ohio, Mar. 21, 1949; s. Lawrence and Pauline Elizabeth (Macknight) McD. Student, Wright State U., 1968-71, U. Dayton, 1971, Dayton Art Inst., 1967-68. Trainer, cons. Nat. Assn. Youth Orgns. United, Washington, 1971-73; program assoc. Dayton (Ohio) Model Cities, 1973-74; child care worker II Montgomery County Children's Svcs. Bd., Dayton, 1974-78; inventory control Mark Morris Tires, San Francisco, 1979-82; office mgr. Bio-Feedback Internat., San Francisco, 1978-84; speaker, bd. dirs. Dayton Area AIDS Task Force, 1987—, AIDS Found. Dayton, 1988-92; community activist People With AIDS, Dayton, 1987—; co-chair Dayton HIV Prevention Cmty. Planning Group Montgomery County Combined Health Dist.; com. mem. Direct Svcs. Dayton Area AIDS Task Force, 1987-92, speaker bur., 1987-92, edn. com., 1987-92, AIDS Found. Miami Valley, 1992—, speaker bur., 1992—, edn. com., 1992—, Pub. Policy and Conflict Mgmt., Ohio Statewide HIV Prevention Cmty. Planning Group, Ohio Dept. Health, The Prevention Summit: HIV Prevention Cmty. Planning Co-chairs meeting, Ctr. for Disease Control and Prevention, Nat. Alliance of State & Territorial AIDS Dirs., Nat. Minority AIDS Coun., Atlanta, 1995—; hotline vol. Dayton Lesbian & Gay Ctr., 1988—; mem. minority AIDS coalition Montgomery County Health Dept., Dayton, 1987—, minority health and social issues coalition, 1988—; bd. dirs. The African Am. Forum on AIDS, Dayton, 1990—, nat. AIDS awareness program So. Christian Leadership Conf., Dayton, 1993—; speaker numerous orgns. on AIDS; bd. dirs. Miami Valley AIDS Partnership, mem. membership, outreach, and needs assessment coms., 1995—. Founding mem., treas. Dayton Area People with AIDS Coalition, 1987-92, Men of All Colors Together, Dayton, 1988-90; co-chair Regional Cmty. Prevention Coord. Com., 1996—; bd. dirs. Ohio AIDS Coalition, 1997, mem. healing com. the leadership tng. program com., 1996—; co-chair AIDS Prevention Coun., Dayton; mem. bd. State of Ohio HIV Prevention Cmty. Planning Group, mem. cmty. info. com., 1996—; bd. dirs. Dayton Ryan White Consortium, mem. finance com., promotion evaluation com., 1994—, Dayton AIDS Prevention Group, membership com., mktg. com.; mem. exec. com. Consumer Adv. Coun. Recipient Pres.'s Citation, 1989, Ohio AIDS Svc. award Ohio Dept. Health, 1990, Cert. of Merit Ohio Dept. Health, Columbus, 1994, Plaque of Vol. Outstanding Merit Montgomery County Combined Health Dist., Dayton, 1995, Outstanding Vol. Svc. Plaque Ohio Dept. Health, 1995, Man of Yr. award Met. Cmty. Ch., Cmty. Unity Health and Wholeness Project, Dayton, 1995; named Miami Valley Hero, 1998. Mem. Nat. Assn. Black and White Men Together. Avocations: drawing, painting, writing, col. work. Home: 4301 Riverside Dr #A-1 Dayton OH 45405-1332

MCDONALD, CARL PETER, microbiologist; b. Billericay, Essex, Eng., May 17, 1958; s. Joseph Aidan and Irmgard (Lochner) McD.; children: Neal, Zoë. BSc in Applied Biology, Brunel U., 1980, MSc in Applied Immunology, 1988. Clin. scientist North London Blood Transfusion Svc., London, 1981—. Contbr. articles to profl. jours. Mem. Am. Soc. for Microbiology, Scottish Soc. for Contamination. Avocations: badminton, cooking, walking, football, travel. Office: North London Blood Ctr, Colindale Ave, London NW9 5BG, England

MCDONALD, CAROLYN ANN, dance educator, choreographer; b. Blytheville, Ark., Aug. 27, 1963; d. Travis Eugene and Barbara Jean (Myers) McD. BA in Dance, U. Calif., Irvine, 1987; MA in Edn., U. Iowa, 1998; choreographer, Coe Coll., 1998. Instr. dance Kirkwood C.C., Cedar Rapids, Iowa, 1987-90, choreographer, 1987—, artistic dir., 1990-96, 96—; owner, pres. McDonald Arts Ctr., Marion, Iowa, 1988—; instr. dance Coe Coll., Cedar Rapids, 1989—; choreographer show choir All Saints Mid. Sch., Marion, Iowa, 1998-2000; choreographer color guard dance ensemble Washington H.S., Cedar Rapids, 1996-97; cons. Jane Boyd Cmty. House, Cedar Rapids, 1993-94. Avocations: wine tasting, gourmet cooking, flying, gardening, song writing. Office: 105 Southview Dr Marion IA 52302-3055

MCDONALD, CRAYDON DEAN, psychologist; b. Denver, Dec. 22, 1946; s. Donald D. and Irene (Dunlavy) McD.; children: Ian, Brendan, Tavis, St. Morgynne. BFA, Parsons Sch. Design, N.Y.C., 1970; MDiv cum laude, St. Paul Sch. Theology, Kansas City, Mo., 1979; D of Ministry, Wesley Theol. Sem., Washington, 1982; PhD, Boston U., 1987. Diplomate Am. Bd. Profl. Psychology; lic. psychologist, Mass., Wis., Ill., Ariz.; approved supr. Am. Assn. Marriage & Family Therapy; ordained to ministry United Meth. Ch., 1982. Psychologist Worcester (Mass.) Pastoral Counseling Ctr., 1982-87; assoc. prof., asst. program dir. Loyola U., Chgo., 1987-88; clin. psychologist Lake Geneva, Wis., 1987-93; psychology faculty No. Ariz. U., 1993—; chief psychologist Drs. McDonald, Weston & Assocs., 1982—; examiner Am. Bd. Profl. Psychology. Author: Personality and Cognitive Theology, 1982, Type A Coronary Prone Behavior and Narcissism, 1987. Fellow The Acad. Family Psychology (bd. dirs.); mem. APA (program com. divsn. 43), Human Factors Soc., Am. Assn. Pastoral Counselors. Democrat. Office: 1100 N San Francisco St Ste C Flagstaff AZ 86001-3260

MCDONALD, IAN ARCHIE, sugar company executive, writer; b. St. Augustine, Trinidad and Tobago, Apr. 18, 1933; arrived in Guyana, 1955; s. John Archie and Thelma Camilla (Seheult) McD.; m. Myrna Camille Foster, 1960 (div. 1970); 1 child, Keith Ian; m. Mary Angela Callender, Sept. 14, 1984; children: Jamie Ian, Darren Christopher. BA in History with honours, Cambridge (Eng.) U., 1954, MA in History, 1957; DLitt, U. West Indies, 1997. Co. sec. Bookers Sugar Estates, Guyana, 1955-64, adminstrv. dir., 1964-76; dir. mktg. and adminstrn. Guyana Sugar Corp. Ltd., Georgetown, 1976-99; CEO Sugar Assn. of the Caribbean, 2000—; bd. dirs. Hand-in-Hand Ins. Co., Guyana, Guyana Nat. Coop. Bank Trust, Inst. Pvt. Enterprise Devel. Author: (novel) The Humming-Bird Tree, 1959 (award Royal Soc. Lit. 1959), (poetry) Mercy Ward, 1988, Essequibo, 1992 (Guyana prize for lit. 1992), Jaffo the Calypsonian, 1994; editor Kyk-Over-Al, lit. mag., 1984—; joint editor Heinemann Book of Caribbean Poetry, (anthology) They Came in Ships. Bd. dirs. Theatre Co., Guyana, 1981—; mem. mgmt. coun. Guyana Prize for Lit., 1987—, Nat. Art Collection, Guyana, 1992—; mem. adv. com. Nat. Archives, Guyana, 1993—; editl. cons. West Indian Commn., 1991-92. Recipient Arrow of Achievement, Nat. Awards Com., Guyana, 1959. Fellow Royal Soc. Lit.; mem. Georgetown Club, Georgetown Cricket Club. Roman Catholic. Avocations: playing tennis, cricket writing, reading, theatre. Office: Demerara Sugar Terminal, River View Ruimveldt, Georgetown Guyana

MCDONALD, JOHN FRANCIS PATRICK, electrical engineering educator; b. Narberth, Pa., Jan. 14, 1942; s. Frank Patrick and Lulu Ann (Hegedus) McD.; m. Karen Marie Knapp, May 26, 1979. BSEE, MIT, 1963; MS in Engring., Yale U., 1965, PhD, 1969. Instr. Yale U., New Haven, 1968-69, asst. prof., 1969-74; assoc. prof. Rensselaer Poly. Inst., Troy, N.Y., 1974-86, prof., 1986—; founder Rensselaer Ctr. for Integrated Electronics, 1980—. Contbr. more than 225 articles to profl. publs.; patentee in field. Recipient numerous grants, 1974—. Mem. ACM, IEEE (assoc. editor Transactions on VSLI Design 1995—), Optical Soc., Acoustical Soc., Vacuum Soc., Materials Rsch. Soc. Office: Rensselaer Poly Inst Ctr for Integrated Electronics Troy NY 12181

MCDONALD, JOHN GREGORY, financial investment educator; b. Stockton, Calif., 1937; m. Melody McDonald. BS, Stanford U., 1960, MBA, 1962, PhD, 1967. Mem. faculty Grad. Sch. Bus. Stanford U., Calif., 1968—; now The IBJ prof. fin. Grad. Sch. Bus. Stanford U.; vis. prof. U. Paris, 1972, Columbia Bus. Sch., 1975, Harvard Bus. Sch. 1986; vice chmn., bd. govs. NASD/NASDAQ Stock Market, 1989-90; mem. adv. bd. InterWest Venture Capital; dir. Investment Co. of Am., New Perspective Fund, Inc., Scholastic Corp., Varian, EuroPacific Growth Fund. Contbr. articles to profl. jours. Bd. overseers vis. com. Harvard U. Bus. Sch., Cambridge, Mass., 1994—. Fulbright scholar, Paris, 1967-68. Office: Stanford U Grad Sch Business Stanford CA 94305

MCDONALD, JOSEPH LEE, insurance broker; b. Bremerton, Wash., Aug. 15, 1931; s. Joseph Okane and Ida Elizabeth (Finholm) McD.; m. Glorietta Maness, Jan. 22, 1954 (dec. 1984); children: Holly Ann Chaffin, Andrew Lee McDonald; m. Beverly Mae Falkner, June 22, 1986. BS, U. Wash., 1954. Various mgmt. positions AT&T, 1956-62; broker, ptnr. McDonald & McGarry Co., Seattle, 1962-84; ptnr., exec. McDonald Ins. Group, Kirkland, Wash., 1984—; v.p., bd. dirs. Chimayo Inc., Seattle, 1990-94, Santa Fe Food Corp., Seattle, 1991-96. City councilman City of Bellevue, 1971-75; commr. Water Dist. #97, Bellevue, 1967-71, Lake Hills Sewer Dist., Bellevue, 1965-71; pres. Wash. State Assn. of Sewer Dists., Seattle, 1969. With U.S. Army, 1954-56. Mem. Coll. Club of Seattle, Overlake Golf and Country Club, Western Assn. of Ins. Brokers, Ind. Ins. Agts. Assn., Seattle Master Builders Assn., Nat. Wildlife Fedn., Nature Conservancy, Apt. Assn. of Seattle and King County, Roche Harbor Yacht Club, Chi Phi. Avocations: skiing, sailing, tennis. Home: 7235 91st Pl SE Mercer Island WA 98040-5803 Office: McDonald Ins Group 416 6th St S Kirkland WA 98033-6718

MCDONALD, LARI, secondary education educator, small business owner; b. Oak Forest, Ill., June 16, 1928; d. Haskell Laramie and Rose Veverka Laramie-Key; m. William J. McDonald, June 4, 1949 (div.); children: William James, Samuel Ellis, Arthur Thomas, Marianne McDonald Scott, Katherine McDonald Stuart. BS in Health and Phys. Edn., Ind. U., 1949; MA in Tchg., Phys. Edn. and Counseling, U. N.C., 1964-66, postgrad., 1966-74. Grad. asst., instr. health and phys. edn. U. N.C., Chapel Hill, 1964-74; rsch. dir. Family Adv. Coun. on Edn., Greensboro, N.C., 1992-98; sales rep. Nat. Fedn. Ind. Bus., 1998-99; tchr. Nat. Heritage Acad., Greensboro, Greensboro Acad.-Battleground. Rep. candidate N.C. Ho. of Reps., Greensboro, 1994, 96. Avocation: her grandchildren and great grandchild.

MCDONALD, MALCOLM WILLIS, real estate company executive; b. Mpls., Nov. 17, 1936; s. Malcolm Blanchard and Ruth Virginia (Stees) McD.; m. Judy Glynn Ballard, Aug. 22, 1959; children: Malcolm Scott, Margaret Alice, Philip Brian. BA magna cum laude with high honors and high orations, Yale Coll., 1958; MBA, Harvard U., 1960. V.p. First Nat. Bank of St. Paul, 1960-77; dir., sr. v.p., trustee Space Center, Inc., St. Paul, 1977—; adj. prof. grad. programs in mgmt. U. St. Thomas, St. Paul, 1975-94; dir. Firstar Bank of Minn., St. Paul, 1990-99, mem. adv. bd., 1999—; dir. Minntech, Inc., Plymouth, 1998—, Scherer Bros. Lumber Co., Mpls., 1988—; vice chair adv. coun. Minn. State Bd. of Investment, St. Paul, 1982—; adv. bd. Hill Monastic Manuscript Libr., St. John's U., Collegeville, Minn., 1980s-97. Mem. North Oaks Home Owners Assn., 1996; trustee, sec., chmn. audit com., investment com. Amherst H. Wilder Found., St. Paul, 1971—; trustee Bigelow & FR Bigelow Found., St. Paul, 1967-98; trustee Lee and Rose Warner Found., 1990—, Manitou Fund, 1990—, Adelaide and Harry G. McNeely Found., St. Paul, 1980-98; trustee, treas. mem., Grotto Found., St. Paul, 1980—; pres. Minn. Taxpayers Assn., 1994-96; former bd. dirs. Guthrie Theater, Minn. Orchestral Assn. Mem. Minn. Club of St. Paul, North Oaks Golf Club, White Bear Racquet & Swim Club, Yale Club of N.Y.C., St. Paul C. of C. (Bravo awards), Phi Beta Kappa, Phi Beta Kappa Assocs., Colony Found., U. Club of St. Paul, Phi Gamma Delta. Republican. Episcopalian. Avocations: physical fitness, gardening, travel, encouraging 3rd graders to read. E-mail: mmcdonald@spacecenterinc.com. Home: 21 E Oaks Rd North Oaks MN 55127-2527 Office: Space Center Inc 2501 Rosegate Saint Paul MN 55113-2717

MCDONALD, MARIANNE, classicist; b. Chgo., Jan. 2, 1937; d. Eugene Francis and Inez (Riddle) McD.; children: Eugene, Conrad, Bryan, Bridget, Kirstie (dec.), Hiroshi. BA magna cum laude, Bryn Mawr Coll., 1958; MA, U. Chgo., 1960; PhD, U. Calif., Irvine, 1975; doctorate (hon.), Am. Coll. Greece, 1988; diploma (hon.), Am. Archaeol. Assn.; DLitt (hon.), U. Athens, 1994, U. Dublin, 1994, Aristotle U., 1997, U. Thessalonika, 1997. Instr. Greek, Latin, English, mythology, cinema U. Calif., Irvine, 1975-79; founder, rsch. fellow Thesaurus Linguae Graecae Project, 1975-97; tchg. asst. U. Calif., Irvine, 1974; bd. dirs. Centrum. Author: Terms for Happiness in Euripides, 1978, Semilemmatized Concordances to Euripides' Alcestis, 1977, Cyclops, Andromache, Medea, 1978, Heraclidae, Hippolytus, 1979, Hecuba, 1984, Hercules Furens, 1984, Elecra, 1984, Ion, 1985, Trojan Women, 1988, Iphigenia in Taurus, 1988, Euripides in Cinema: The Heart Made Visible, 1983; translator: The Cost of Kindness and Other Fabulous Tales (Shinichi Hoshi), 1986, (chpt.) Views of Clytemnestra, Ancient and Modern, 1990, Classics and Cinema, 1990, Modern Critical Theory and Classical Literature, 1994, A challenge to Democracy, 1994, Ancient Sun/Modern Light: Greek Drama on the Modern Stage, 1990, Star Myths: Tales of the Constellations, 1996; contbr. numerous articles to profl. jours., chpts. to books. Bd. dirs. Am. Coll. of Greece, 1981-90, Scripps Hosp., 1981, Am. Sch. Classical Studies, 1986—; mem. bd. overseers U. Calif., San Diego, 1985—; nat. bd. advisors Am. Biog. Inst., 1982—; pres. Soc. for the Preservation of the Greek Heritage, 1990—; founder Hajime Mori Chair for Japanese Studies, U. Calif., San Diego, 1985, McDonald Ctr. for Alcohol and Substance Abuse, 1984, Thesaurus Linguarum Hiberniae, 1991—; vis. prof. U. Dublin, 1990—, U. C. Dublin, 1999, U. Ulster, Ireland, 1997; adj. prof. theatre U. Calif., San Diego, 1990, prof. theatre and classics, 1994—. Recipient Ellen Browning Scripps Humanitarian award, 1975, Disting. Svc. award U. Calif.-Irvine, 1982, Irvine medal, 1987, 3rd Prize Midwest Poetry Ctr. Contest, 1987; named one of the Cmty. Leaders Am., 1979-80, Philanthropist of Yr., 1985, Headliner San Diego Press Club, 1985, Philanthropist of Yr. Honorary Nat. Conf. Christians and Jews, 1986, Woman of Yr. AHEPA, 1988, San Diego Woman of Distinction, 1990, Woman of Yr. AXIOS, 1991; recipient Bravissimo gold medal San Diego Opera, 1990, Gold Medal Soc. Internationalization of Greek Lang., 1990, Athens medal, 1991, Piraeus medal, 1991, award Desmoi, 1992, award Hellenic Assn. of Univ. Women, 1992, Acad. of Achievement award AHEPA, 1992, Woman of Delphi award European Cultural Ctr. Delphi, 1992, Civis Universitatis award U. Calif., San Diego, 1993, Hypatia award Hellenic U. Women, 1993, Am.-Ireland Fund Heritage award, 1994, Contribution to Greek Letters award Aristotle U. Thessaloniki, 1994, Mirabella Mag. Readers Choice One of 1000 Women for the Nineties, 1994, Order of the Phoenix, Greece, 1994, citations from U.S. Congress and Calif. Senate, Alexander the Gt. award Hellenic Cultural Soc., 1995, made hon. citizen of Delphi and gold medal of the Amphiktuonon, Del. Bus. award for Fine Arts San Diego Bus. Jour., 1995, Vol. of Decade Women's Internat. Ctr., 1994, 96, Gold Star award San Diego Arts League, 1997, Golden Aeschylus award Inst. Nat. Drama Antkg. Siracusa, 1998, Women Who Mean Bus., Fine Arts award San Diego Bus. Jour., 1998, Fulbright award, 1999, Ellis Island award, 1999. Mem. MLA, AAUP, Am. Philol. Assn., Soc. for the Preservation of the Greek Heritage (pres.), Libr. of Am., Am. Classical League, Philol. Assn. Pacific Coast, Am. Comparative Lit. Assn., Modern and Classical Lang. Assn. So. Calif., Hellenic Soc., Calif. Fgn. Lagn. Tchrs. Assn., Internat. Platform Assn., Royal Irish Acad., Greece's Order of the Phoenix (commdr. 1994), KPBS Producers Club, Hellenic Univ. Club (bd. dir.). Avocations: karate, harp (medieval), skiing, diving. Home: PO Box 929 Rancho Santa Fe CA 92067-0929 Office: U Calif at San Diego Dept Theatre La Jolla CA 92093

MCDONALD, MARY ANN MELODY, investment management executive; b. Sandwich, Ill., Apr. 30, 1944; d. Theodore Harvey and Sarah Elizabeth (Irving) Larson; m. John G. McDonald, June 19, 1973. MusM, New England Conservatory, 1970; studied with Nadia Boulanger, Paris, 1971; MusD, Stanford U., 1975; MBA, Harvard U., 1986. Credit analyst Wells Fargo Bank, San Francisco, 1976-77, loan officer, 1977-79, asst. v.p., 1979-80; chmn. bd. dirs. Cornwall Corp., Stanford, Calif., 1980-84; dir. client svcs. RCM Capital Mgmt., San Francisco, 1986-92, ptnr., 1988-98, mng. dir., 1998—. Active Ill. Youth Commn., 1963-66. Recipient Rockefeller grantee Oberlin (Ohio) Coll. 1967; winner Miss Boston-Miss Am. Pageant, 1968. Mem. Senatorial Inner Cir. (life), Stanford Alumni Assn., Harvard Alumni Assn., Lincoln Club, Sigma Alpha Iota, Kappa Delta (Telford Cup). Republican. Lutheran. Office: DRCM Capital Mgmt 4 Embarcadero Ctr Ste 3100 San Francisco CA 94111-4106

MCDONALD, MICHAEL SCOTT, lawyer; b. Ft. Stockton, Tex., Feb. 6, 1962; s. Roland R. and Harriett L. McD.; m. Sara; children: Matthew, Michael. BA, U. Tex., El Paso, 1984; JD, U. Tex., Austin, 1987. Bar: Tex. 1987, U.S. Ct. Appeals (5th and 10th cirs.), U.S. Dist. Ct. (all dists.) Tex. With Littler Mendelson, Dallas; shareholder Littler, Mendelson, Dallas. Coauthor, editor: Chapter 9, The 1999 National Employer; The Texas Employer; contbg. editor, Covenents Not to Compete-A State by State Survey, 1995-99, Employee Duty of Loyalty, 1995-99, Trade Secrets - A State by State Survey, 1998-99; contbr. articles to profl. jours. Mem. ABA (litigation sect., labor and employment law sect.), Tex. Bar Assn. (labor and employment law sect.), Tex. Assn. Bus. (employee rels. chair Dallas chpt.), Dallas Bar Assn. (employment law sect., chmn. 2000, exec. com. 1994-2000). Office: Littler Mendelson 2001 Ross Ave Ste 2600 Dallas TX 75201-2931

MCDONALD, PEGGY ANN STIMMEL, retired automobile company official; b. Darbyville, Ohio, Aug. 25, 1931; d. Wilbur Smith and Bernice Edna

(Hott) Stimmel; m. George R. Stich, Mar. 7, 1953 (dec.); 1 child, Mark Stephen (dec.); m. Joseph F. McDonald Jr., Feb. 1, 1986 (dec.). Missionary diploma with honor, Moody Bible Inst., 1952; BA in Econs. cum laude (scholar), Ohio Wesleyan U., 1965; MBA with distinction, Xavier U., 1977. Lic. capt. USCG. Missionary in S.Am. Evang. Alliance Mission, 1956-61; cost acct. Western Electric Co., 1965-66; acctg. mgr. Ohio Wesleyan U., 1966-73; fin. specialist NCR Corp., 1973-74, systems analyst, 1974-75, supr. inventory planning, 1975, mgr. material planning and purchasing control, 1976-78; materials mgr. U.S. Elec. Motors Co., 1978; with Gen. Motors Corp., 1978-92; shift supt. materials Gen. Motors Corp., Lakewood, Ga., 1979-80; gen. ops. supr. material data base mgmt. Ctrl. Office Gen. Motors Corp., Warren, Mich., 1980; dir. material mgmt. GM Truck and Bus divsn. Gen. Motors Corp., Balt., 1980-91; dir. edn. and tng. GM Truck and Bus, Linden, N.J., 1991-92; ret., 1992; founder Creaciones Peggy Sport Jeans Mfg., Venezuela, 1993; vis. lectr. Inst. Internat. Trade, Jiao Tong U., Shanghai, China, 1985, Inst. Econs. and Fgn. Trade, Tianjin, China, 1986-87; part time instr. Towson (Md.) State U., 1986-87. Founder, pres. Capt.'s Challenge Corp., Global Christian Ministry of Econ. Devel., 1998; mem. 1st United Meth. Ch., Dunedin, Fla. Mem. AAUW, Am. Prodn. and Inventory Control Soc., Am. Soc. Women Accts., Balt. Exec. Women's Network, Balt. Coun. on Fgn. Rels. Methodist. Avocation: sailing. Home: 1524 Mahogany Ln Palm Harbor FL 34683-6526

MCDONALD, ROBERT DELOS, manufacturing company executive; b. Dubuque, Iowa, Jan. 30, 1931; s. Delos Lyon and Virginia (Kolck) McD.; m. Jane M. Locher, Jan. 16, 1960 (div. Jan. 1970); children: Jean, Patricia, Maria, Sharon, Rob; m. Marilyn I. Miller, July 4, 1978. BA in Econs., U. Iowa, 1953. With A.Y. McDonald Mfg. Co., Dubuque, 1956—, salesman, 1956-60, sales mgr., 1961-64, mgr. Dubuque wholesale br., 1965-72, v.p., 1971-72, v.p., corp. sec., 1972-83, sr. v.p., corp. sec., 1983-85, pres., 1985-95, chmn. bd., chief exec. officer, 1987—, also bd. dirs., 1964—; bd. dirs. Brock-McVey Co., Lexington, Ky.; sr. v.p., bd. dirs. A.Y. McDonald Industries, Inc., Dubuque, 1983—; chmn. bd., pres., CEO, bd. dirs. A.Y.M. Inc., Albia, Iowa, 1988—. Trustee, bd. dirs. A.Y. McDonald Mfg. Co. Charitable Found., 1978—, pres., 1982—; bd. dirs. Stonehill Care Ctr., Dubuque, 1984-92, chmn. bd., 1991-92; mem. Stonehill Renovation and Financing Task Force, 1994-97; bd. dirs. Boys and Girls Club of Greater Dubuque, 1989—, Dubuque Bank & Trust Co., 1994—, Save Iowa's Civil War Monument Restoration Fund, 1995—, Dubuque County Hist. Soc., 1996—, Grand Opera House Found., 1997—, Terrace Hill Found., 1997—; bd. govs. Iowa Coll. Found., 1997—; trustee United Way Svcs., Inc., Dubuque, 1989—; bd. dirs. Stonehill Benevolent Found., Dubuque, 1998—, vice chmn., 1989-92; mem. regional adv. coun. SBA, Cedar Rapids, 1984-89; mem. adv. bd. Jr. Achievement Tri-States, Inc., 1991—, Iowa State Fair Blue Ribbon Found., 1993—. Lt. USNR, 1953-56, Korea. Mem. Am. Mgmt. Assn., Am. Supply Assn., Am. Water Works Assn., Nat. Assn. Mfrs., Dubuque Area C. of C., Am. Legion, Dubuque Shooting Soc., Dubuque Golf and Country Club, Sigma Alpha Epsilon. Republican. Roman Catholic. Home: Fountain Hill 3399 Eagle Point Dr Dubuque IA 52001-8320 Office: AY McDonald Mfg Co PO Box 508 Dubuque IA 52004-0508

MCDONALD, ROBERT FRANCIS, broadcaster, writer; b. Vancouver, Can., Oct. 25, 1943; s. Francis William and Violet Rosa Alberta (Wilkins) McD.; m. Catherine Donna Napier McDonald. Assoc. Degree, Royal Conservatory of Toronto, Can., 1963; BA (hon.), UBC, 1964. Legis. corr. Toronto Star, 1965-66; freelance CBC, BBC, ABC, CBS, Athens, Greece, 1966-70, CBC, BBC, London, 1971-85, Fin. Times, London, 1983-87, Economist Intelligence Unit, London, 1986—, Viomichaniki Epitheorissis, Athens, 1991—. Author: Pillar and Tinder Box: The Greek Press and the Dictatorship, 1983, The Problem of Cyprus, 1988, Greece in the 1990's, 1991, Greek Privatisation, 1991. Mem. Royal Inst. Internat. Affairs, Commonwealth Journalists Assn. Home: 10 Chelwood Gardens, Richmond Surrey TW9 4JQ, England

MCDONALD, TANNY, actress; b. Princeton, Ind.; d. Douglas Hewitt and Irene Elizabeth (Codding) McD.; m. Robert D. Currie, Mar. 5, 1966 (div. Mar., 1986). BA cum laude, Vassar Coll., 1958. Actress Am. Savoyards, N.Y.C. and Tour, 1961—. Actress: (film) Hercules in New York, 1970, (plays) Broadway: Fiddler on the Roof, 1964, The Lincoln Mask, 1972, Clothes for A Summer Hotel, 1980, Macbeth (First Witch and Nurse), 1988, Man of La Mancha, 1992 and nat. tour, 1996-97, Medea (Woman of Corinth), 1994; Off-Broadway: Chelsea Theater Ctr. - the Beggar's Opera, 1972, Total Eclipse, 1974, Gorky, 1975, N.Y. Shakespeare Festival - Temptation, 1989, Titus Andronicus, 1989, Hamlet (Player Queen) also Great Performances, 1995; L.O.R.T. maj. roles (select): A Little Night Music, 1977, Three Penny Opera, 1979, Pal Joey, 1980, Tintypes, 1982, A Lesson From Aloes, 1982, Cloud Nine, 1984, Heartbreak House, 1986, The Bakkhai, 1995, Orpheus Descending, 1995, House of Bernarda Alba, 1997, Vassar to Vassar Cabaret, Road to Mecca, Long Day's Journey Into Night, 1998, WIT=NYC, Jekyll & Hyde, 1999; CBS Kate and Allie, NBC The Doctors, 1973, NCB spl. Duty Bound (Emmy award 1973). Reid Hall fellow, Paris, 1958, 59; recipient Frances Walker Prize for Excellence, Vassar Coll., 1958; named Best Actress Richmond (Va.) News Leader in 1978.

MCDONALD, THERESA MARIE, newswriter, broadcaster; b. Tuscaloosa, Ala., Nov. 25, 1964; d. John Luther Sr. and Lenora (Davis) McD.. Student, U. Ala. Dir. pub. affairs Sta. WDBB/FOX-TV, Tuscaloosa, 19987-90; owner McDonald Meteorol. Observation & Reporting, Tuscaloosa, 1993-97; nat. dir. Jellybean Ball & Auction, Tuscaloosa, 1999—, Outstanding Women Am. Pageant, Duncanville, Ala., 1998—; founder, dir. Let's Cure Diabetes, not just talk about it, Duncanville, Ala., 1999—. Mem. Am. Scholars Nat. Honor Soc. (Achievement award 2000), Golden Key Acad. and Leadership Soc., Phi Theta Kappa, Omicron Delta Kappa. E-mail: owiap@usa.net. Office: Outstanding Women Am Pageant 13127 Hummingbird Ln Duncanville AL 35456-1735

MCDONALD, THOMAS EDWIN, JR., electrical engineer; b. Wapanucka, Okla., June 19, 1939; s. Thomas Edwin and Rosamond Bell (Enoch) McD.; m. Myrna Kay Booth, Sept. 10, 1961; children: Stephen Thomas, Jennifer Kay, Sarah Lynn. BSEE, U. Okla., 1962, MSEE, 1963; PhDEE, U. Colo., 1969. Registered profl. engr., N.Mex. Asst. prof. elec. engring. U. Okla., Norman, 1969-70; planning engr. Okla. Gas and Electric Co., Oklahoma City, 1970-72; staff mem. Los Alamos (N.Mex.) Nat. Lab., 1972—, group leader, 1974-80, program mgr., 1980-92; program mgr. Centurion program Los Alamos (N.Mex.) Nat. Lab., Los Alamos, 1986-90; dep. program dir. inertial confinement fusion program Los Alamos (N.Mex.) Nat. Lab., 1990-92, program coord. mine detection and laser tech., 1992-93; project mgr. Nat. Ctr. for Advanced Mfg. Tech., 1993-96, project leader high-speed electronic imaging tech. devel., 1996—; adj. prof. elec. engring. U. Okla., 1970-72; cons. Los Alamos Tech. Assocs., 1980—, mgr. design sect., 1980-81. Rschr. in inertial confinement fusion, high-speed electronic imaging and neutron radiography; contbr. articles to profl. jours. Bd. dirs., mem. United Ch. Los Alamos, 1987— (chmn. fin. bd.), chmn. bd. elders, 1992. Served to capt. U.S. Army, 1963-67. Mem. IEEE (chmn. Los Alamos sect.), AAAS, Soc. for Info. Display, Soc. Photo-Optical Instrumentation Engrs., Los Alamos Gymnastics Club (treas., bd. dirs. 1980-88), Rotary (sec. Los Alamos, pres. 1999), Sigma Xi, Eta Kappa Nu. Republican. Avocation: computer science. Home: 4200 Ridgeway Dr Los Alamos NM 87544-3133 Office: Los Alamos Nat Lab PO Box 1663 Los Alamos NM 87544-0600

MCDONALD, TREVOR, newscaster, anchor; b. Trinidad, Aug. 16, 1939; married; 1 child. D (hon.), South Bank U., 1994; LHD (hon.), Plymouth U., 1995; LLD (hon.), U. West Indies, 1996; D (hon.), Open U., 1997; LHD (hon.), Nottingham U., 1997; D (hon.), Surrey U., 1997; LHD (hon.), Southampton Inst., 1997. Postions with newspapers and radio Trinidad; program mgr., reader news, interviewr local current affairs programs, 1962-69; reporter BBC World Svc., 1969-73; reporter ITN, 1973-78, sports corr., 1978-80, diplomatic corr., 1980-82, diplomatic corr. Channel 4 News, 1982-87, diplomatic editor Channel 4 News, 1987-89, presenter News at 5.40, Channel 4 News, weekend programs, 1989-90, co-presenter News at Ten, 1990-92, presenter News at Ten, 1992-99, presenter Evening News, 1999—, host Tonight with Trevor McDonald, 1999—; host chat show ITV2 Trevor McDonald Meets..., 1998—. Author: (autobiography) Fortunate Circumstances, 1993, other biographies, poems. Apptd. chancellor South Bank U., 1999; chmn. steering group to encourage use of better English in schs. and workplaces, 1998; chmn. inquiry set to encourage learning fgn. langs. Nuffield Found., 1998. Fellow (hon.) John Moores U., 1998; decorated officer Brit. Empire, knight; recipient Gold medal Royal TV Soc., 1998, Richard Dimbleby award for outstanding contbn. to TV Brit. Acad. Film and TV Arts, 1999; voted "best at job" newscaster Gallup poll commd. by Daily Telegraph, 1993; named Newscaster of Yr. TV and Radio Industries Club, 1993, 97, 99, Most Popular Newscaster Nat. TV Awards, 1996, most authoritative and trustworthy newsreader Radio Times survey, 1997. Mem. Surrey County Cricket Club. Avocations: tennis, golf, cricket. Office: ITN, 200 Grays Inn Rd, London WC1X 8X2, England

MCDONALD SMITH, PAUL, artist; b. Melbourne, Victoria, Australia, Nov. 26, 1956; s. John and Judith Anne (McDonald) S. Student, RMIT, 1976-78; studied in Europe; DFA hon., Washington U. Curator Alan Moore retrospective exhbn. Cato Gallery, Melbourne, 1994, Ludmilla Meilerts retrospective exhbn., Frater, Hammond and McCubbin Galleries, Melbourne, 1994, Melba Meml. Conservatorium of Music Centenary exhbn. 1995, The Bottlebrush Club, 1995 Cato Gallery, Len Annois, RWS retrospective exhbn./Cato Gallery, 1996; various judging, tutorial and lecturing appointments. One-man shows include: Mansourah Galleries Melbourne, 1980, Ash Tree Gallery, Melbourne, 1982, 83, Gallery 21, Melbourne, 1987, Cato Gllery, Melbourne, 1990, 93, Victorian Artist of the Yr. Exhbn. (finalist) 1990-94, 96-99, others; various group exhbns.; publs. include: Oils - The Medium of the Masters, 1989, Alan Moore/Biograph. Catalogue, 1994, Ludmilla Meilerts/Biograph. Catalogue, 1994, also nmerous editl. contbns. to newsletters and jours. Active numerous civic orgns., including Essendon Cmty. Group, 1981-98, Footscray Cmty. Arts Ctr., 1981-85, Williamstown Cmty. Outreach Ctr., 1981-95, Essendon Network for Employment and Tng., 1998—. Recipient over 100 awards for painting, including Norman Kaye Meml. medallion Victorian Artists Soc. and Kaye Family, 1998, 99, Ballarat 1998, Brighton 1998, Mt. Eliza Zonta 1998, Peninsula Arts Soc. 1998, Camberwell Club award 1998, Drysdale 1998, Sorrento 1998, award Mt. Waverley Art Com., 1999, Bright award Bright Art Gallery and Cultural Centre, 1999, Mildura Art award, Rural City of Mildura, 1999, numerous others; recipient Camberwell Travel scholarship Camberwell Rotary, 1986. Fellow Victorian Artists Soc. (pres. 1998—), Royal Soc. Arts (London); mem. Twenty Melbourne Painters Soc., Bottlebrush Club, Royal Art Soc. of New South Wales, Order of Internat. Fellowship, others. Avocations: classical and baroque music, biography, travel. E-mail: paulmcds@cosmos.net.au. Home: 3 Perry Ct, Kew, Victoria 3101, Australia

MCDONELL, NEIL EDWIN, lawyer; b. Johnson City, N.Y., May 30, 1952; s. Alexander Edwin McDonell and Loretta Arlene Terry; m. Margaret Lynn Moline, June 18, 1978; children: Adam, Aaron. AB in Philosophy and English Lit., U. Mich., 1974; PhD in Philosphy, Harvard U., 1979; JD, Columbia U., 1983. Bar: N.Y. 1984. Asst. prof. philosophy Middlebury (Vt.) Coll., 1979-80; assoc. Battle Fowler, N.Y.C., 1983-89; assoc. Marks & Murase, N.Y.C., 1989-92, ptnr., 1992-96; ptnr. Dorsey & Whitney LLP, N.Y.C., 1996—. Editor-in-chief Columbia Jour. Tranational Law, 1982-83, bd. dirs., 1989—; contbr. articles to profl. jours. Mem. ABA (internat., sci., tech., and antitrust sects.), N.Y. State Bar Assn., Internat. Trade Commn. Trial Lawyers Assn., Harvard Club, Phi Beta Kappa. Avocations: literature, history. Office: Dorsey & Whitney LLP 250 Park Ave New York NY 10177-0001

MCDONELL, ROBIN MURDOCH, film editor, producer; b. Dorking, Eng., Aug. 9, 1943; s. Fergus and Wendy Margaret (Hamblin) McD.; m. Anne-Marie Friend-Pereira, Aug. 15, 1970; children: Iain, Sophia, Teresa. Student, Ashbury Coll., Ottawa, Can., 1953-60, Marine Radio Coll., Kendal, 1961-62. Editor London, 1963-70, asst. dir., 1970-75; editor Yorkshire TV, Leeds, U.K., 1975-91; freelance editor London, 1991—; dir. Glengarry Films, London, 1964—. Contbr. articles to profl. jours. Avocations: walking, skiing, movies, reading. Home: 11 St James Rd, LS29 9PY Ilkley England

MCDONNELL, GAVIN VINCENT, physician; b. Belfast, No. Ireland, Feb. 12, 1967; s. Arthur and Martha Veronica (Mooney) McD. MB BCh, BAO, Queen's U., Belfast, 1990, MD, 1998. Jr. house officer in medicine and surgery Mater Hosp., Belfast, 1990-91; registrar in medicine Daisy Hill Hosp., Newry, No. Ireland, 1993-94; rsch. fellow Queen's U. Belfast, 1995-97; sr. house officer in medicine Royal Victoria Hosp., Belfast, 1991-93, registrar in neurology, 1994-95, specialist registrar in neurology, 1997—; mem. No. Ireland Jr. Drs. Com., 1998—; jr. dr. rep. Neuroscis. Specialist Adv. Com., 1998—. Contbr. articles to profl. jours. Patron, Fortwilliam Musical Soc. Royal Victoria Hosp. rsch. fellow, 1995-96; Action MS rsch. grantee, 1996-97. Fellow Royal Soc. Medicine; mem. Royal Coll. Physicians and Surgeons of Glasgow, Am. Acad. Neurology (corr. jr. mem.), Assn. Brit. Neurologists (assoc.), Internat. Med. Assn. of Lourdes. Roman Catholic. Avocations: golf, travel, theatre, cinema. Home: 48 Andersonstown Rd, Belfast BT11 9AN, Northern Ireland Office: Royal Victoria Hosp, Grosvenor Rd, Belfast BT12 6BA, Northern Ireland

MCDONNELL, LORENZO ROS, engineering educator, researcher; b. Murcia, Spain, Dec. 25, 1960; s. Diego and Geraldine Ros McDonnell. Mech. Engr., Murcia U., 1981, Elec. Engr., 1987; Indsl. Engr., Valencia (Spain) Poly. U., 1988, PhD, 1991. Pvt. cons. Cartagena, Spain, 1981-91; R & D dir. Blobis S.A., Valencia, 1990-91; lectr. Valencia Poly. U., 1991-98; master dir. Valencie Poly. U., 1993-98, head dept., 1997-98; prof. engring. Cartagena (Spain) Poly., 1999—, head dept., 1999—; subdir. Mediterranean U. Scis. and Tech., Valencia, 1996-97; chair UNESCO, Mexico Autonoma U., 1995. Author: Gestion de Sistemas Avanzados de Fabricacion, 1999; contbr. article sto profl. jours. Recipient grant Valencia Poly. U., 1989. Mem. Engrs. Assn., N.Y. Acad. Scis. Avocations: horseback riding, reading, swimming. Home: 12, 1-B, Paseo de Alfonso XIII, 30201 Cartagena Murcia, Spain Office: Paseo De Alfonso XIII, 22, 30201 Cartagena Murcia, Spain

MCDONOUGH, WILLIAM J., banker; b. Chgo., 1934; married. BS, Coll. of Holy Cross, 1956; MA, Georgetown U., 1962. With Dept. of State, 1961-67; with 1st Nat. Bank of Chgo., 1967-89, asst. v.p. internat. banking dept., 1967-70; v.p., gen. mgr. 1st Nat. Bank of Chgo., Paris, 1970-72; area head, Europe, Middle East and Africa 1st Nat. Bank of Chgo., 1972-73, sr. v.p., head internat. banking dept., 1973-75, exec. v.p., 1975-86, CFO, 1982-89, chmn. asset and liability mgmt. com., until 1989; vice chmn. 1st Chgo. Corp. and 1st Nat. Bank Chgo., 1986-89; exec. v.p., head markets group Fed. Res. Bank of N.Y., N.Y.C., 1992-93, pres., CEO, 1993—; vice chmn. fed. open market com. Fed. Res. Sys.; bd dirs. Bank for Internat. Settlements, chmn. basle com. on banking supervision. Bd. dirs. N.Y. Philharm. Orch.; mem. Trilateral Commn. Mem. N.Y. Acad. Scis. (bd. govs.), Fgn. Policy Assn., Coun. Fgn. Rels. (bd. dirs.), Econ. Club of N.Y., Ams. Soc. (chmn. bd. trustees), Fgn. Policy Assn. (bd. govs.). Office: Fed Res Bank of NY 33 Liberty St New York NY 10045-1003

MCDOUALL, RHODA MARY, immunologist, researcher; b. Kampala, Uganda, July 20, 1959; (parents U.K. citizens); d. Kenneth Willoughby and Edith Joan (Sears) McD.; m. Jeremy Stuart Stevenson, Aug. 14, 1982 (div. 1985); m. Andrew Neil David Eagles, Apr. 25, 1992; children: Ellen Joanna, Philip Mark. BA with honours in Biology, York (Eng.) U., 1980; MSc in Immunology, U. London, 1988, PhD, 1999. Rsch. asst. Muscle Rsch. Labs., Royal Postgrad. Med. Sch. Hammersmith Hosp., London, 1981-82, 85-88; rsch. asst. New Zealand Apple and Pear Mktg. Bd., Wellington, 1984-85; rsch. asst. immunology dept. Nat. Heart and Lung Inst., Harefield (Eng.) Hosp., 1988-96, rsch. asst. cell biology group Nat. Heart and Lung Inst., 1997-99. Contbr. articles to sci. jours., including Endothelium, Transplantation, Immunology, Microvascular Rsch., Clin. Exptl. Immunol., Jour. Neurol. Scis., Neuropath. Applied Neurobiology, Muscle and Nerve. Grantee Brit. Heart Found., 1991-96. Anglican. Avocations: walking, gardening, travel, crafts. Home: 14 St Johns Rd, Tylers Green, Penn Bucks HP10 8HW, England Office: Harefield Hosp (NHLI), Heart Sci Ctr, Harefield UB9 6JH, England

MCDOUGAL, STUART YEATMAN, comparative literature educator, author; b. L.A., Apr. 10, 1942; s. Murray and Marian (Yeatman) McD.; m. Menakka Weerasinghe, Apr. 29, 1967 (div. 1977); children—Dyanthe Rose, Gavin Rohan; m. Nora Gunneng, Aug. 4, 1979; children—Angus Gunneng, Tobias Yeatman. B.A., Haverford Coll., 1964; M.A., U. Pa., 1965, Ph.D., 1970. Lectr. U. Lausanne, Switzerland, 1965-66; asst. prof. Mich. State U., East Lansing, 1970-72; from asst. prof. to prof. English, comparative lit. and film /video U. Mich., Ann Arbor, 1972-85; dir. program in comparative lit. U. Mich., Ann Arbor, 1981-97, asst. to dean spl. projects, 1997-98; Dewitt Wallace prof. English, chair English Dept. Macalester Coll., St. Paul, Minn., 1998—; vis. prof. film Aegean Inst., Greece, 1994; vis. scholar Senapulli, Brazil, 1996. Author: Ezra Pound and the Troubadour Tradition, 1972 (Bredvold prize 1973), 2d edit. 1973; Made into Movies: From Literature to Film, 1985, 6th edit. 1995. Editor: Dante Among the Moderns, 1985; co-editor: Play It Again, Sam: Retakes on Remakes, 1998; contbr. articles to profl. jours. Am. Council of Learned Socs. fellow, 1974-75; U. Mich. Rackham Research grantee, 1975-76; Fulbright Assn. sr. lectr., Italy, 1978; recipient Faculty Recognition award, U. Mich., 1987. Fellow Dirs. Guild Am. (summr workshop, 1993); mem. MLA, Am. Comparative Lit. Assn. (sec.-treas. 1983-89, v.p. 1989-91, pres. 1991-93), Internat. Comparative Lit. Assn., Soc. Cinema Studies. Democrat. Office: Macalester Coll English Dept 1600 Grand Ave Saint Paul MN 55105-1801

MCDOUGALL, GERALD DUANE, lawyer; b. Hammond, Ind., Sept. 18, 1931; s. John and Carol Maxine (Lind) McD.; m. Ingrid Rosina Kempf, Jan. 26, 1960 (dec. 2000); children: Manfred, James. JD, Mercer U., 1971. Bar: U.S.V.I. 1972, Colo. 1973, Germany 1973, Tex. 1985. Atty. USVI Dept. Labor, St. Thomas, 1971-72; pvt. practice Denver, 1972-74, 76-84, Heilbronn, Neckar, Germany, 1974-76, Amarillo, Tex., 1985—. Precinct committeeman Rep. Ctrl. Com., Denver, 1978-84. Sgt. U.S. Army, 1951-54, ETO, 61-67, Vietnam. Mem. Nat. Assn. Criminal Defense Lawyers, Tex. Bar Assn., Tex. Criminal Defense Lawyers Assn., Amarillo Bar Assn., State Bar Coll. Home: 7910 Merchant Dr Amarillo TX 79121-1028 Office: PO Box 50898 Amarillo TX 79159-0898

MCDOUGALL, TREVOR JOHN, oceanographer; b. Adelaide, Australia, July 1, 1952; s. Jack Ronald and Violet Holly (McCloy) McD.; m. Brita Kathryn Hack, May 20, 1978; children: Karyn Elise, Amy Louise, Cameron John. Degree in Mech. Engring. with honors, U. Adelaide, 1973; PhD, U. Cambridge, 1978; Grad. Diploma in Econs., Australian Nat. U., 1982. Various positions to prin. rsch. scientist oceanography CSIRO, Hobart, 1987-91, tech. program mgr. Divsn. Oceanography, 1990-93, sr. prin. rsch. scientist Divsn. Oceanography, 1991-96, chief rsch. scientist Divsn. Marine Rsch., 1996—; vis. scientist Woods Hole Oceanographic Instn., 1994, Overseas Rsch. fellow 1985; rsch. fellow Rsch. Sch. of Earth Scis., ANU, 1980-83, others; mem. scientific coms. in oceanic rsch.; mem. Tasmanian Inventions Adv. Panael for the Assistance to Inventors Scheme, 1984-85; mem. scientific steering group World Ocean Circulation Experiment, 1986-92, scientific planning group Core Project 3, 1986-89, Australian scientific steering com., 1987—, chmn. 1993—, others. Assoc. editor: Deep-Sea Rsch., 1988-93; contbr. articles to profl. jours. Recipient Queen's fellowship in marine sci. Australian Nat. U., 1978-80, Frederick White prize Australian Acad. of Sci., 1988, Humboldt Rsch. award Alexander von Humboldt Found., 1997, M.R. Banks medal Royal Soc. of Tasmania, 1998. Fellow Australian Acad. of Sci. Office: CSIRO Marine Rsch, Castray Esplanade/Tasmania, Hobart 7000, Australia

MCDOWELL, ROBERT E., animal science educator; b. Charlotte, N.C., June 27, 1921; s. Robert and Grace W. (Bradford) McD.; m. Dorothy Gill, Dec. 8, 1945; children: Jean G. McDowell Burke, Ann G. Hickey, Robert G. BS, N.C. State U., 1942; MS, U. Md., 1949, PhD, 1955. Tchr. VA, Charlotte, 1946; rsch. investigator U.S. Dept. Agr., Beltsville, Md., 1946-67; prof. emeritus internat. animal sci. Cornell U., Ithaca, N.Y., 1967-86; vis. prof. internat. programs N.C. State U., 1986—; cons. FAO, Peace Corps, AID, Rockefeller Found., govts. of Venezuela, Dominican Republic, Taiwan, others. Author: Partnership for Humans and Animals, 1991, Dairying with Improved Breeds in Warm Climates, 1994, others; contbr. chpts. to books and articles to profl. jours. Bd. dirs. Internat. Found. for Sci., Sweden; chmn. bd. dirs. Internat. Livestock Ctr. for Africa, 1979-85, Ethiopia. Col. USMC, 1942-46. Decorated Bronze Star. Mem. AAAS, Am. Dairy Sci. Assn. (Internat. Dairy Prodn. award 1988), Am. Soc. Animal Sci. (award 1979), Ret. Officers Assn., Alpha Zeta. Home: 3336 Ocotea St Raleigh NC 27607-3140 Office: Nc State U Raleigh NC 27695-0001

MCDOWELL, SEAN ALISTAIR COURTNEY, chemistry educator, researcher; b. Kingston, Jamaica, Aug. 21, 1964; s. Owen and Constance (McCatty) McD.; m. Zanifa Mohammed, 1992; children: Kimberley, Sheri, Sasha. BSc, U. West Indies, Mona, Jamaica, 1985; PhD, U. Cambridge, Eng., 1992. Asst. editor Chem. Physics Letters, 1993; postdoctoral rsch. fellow U. Western Ont., London, Can., 1993-96; rsch. fellow U. West Indies, Barbados, 1996-97, lectr., 1997—. Internat. reviewer Jour. Chem. Edn.; contbr. articles to profl. jours. Cambridge Commonwealth Trust Tate and Lyle scholar, 1988; Royal Soc. Chemistry internat. authors grantee, 1998; recipient Lundgren rsch. award, Cambridge, 1991, Young Scientist award Caribbean Acad. Scis.-Third World Acad. Scis., 1999. Mem. Royal Soc. Chemistry, N.Y. Acad. Scis. Avocations: table tennis, Scrabble, reading, conjuring. E-mail: s.mcdowell@uwichill.edu.bb. Office: Dept Biol & Chem Scis, PO Box 64, Bridgetown Barbados

MCDYESS, ANTONIO, professional basketball player; b. Quitman, Miss.. Forward Denver Nuggets. Named to NBA All-Rookie First Team, 1995-96, All-NBA Third Team, 1998-99. Avocations: bowling, rythem and blues. Office: Denver Nuggets 1000 Chopper Cir Denver CO 80204-5809

MCELDOWNEY, ROLAND CONANT, gold mining company executive, photographer; b. Newton, Mass., Nov. 14, 1940; s. Richard Lancaster and Virginia Davis (Conant) McE.; m. Barbara Lynn Read, Mar. 26, 1966; children: Richard Read, Scott Roland, Kathryn Ramsay. AB in Geology, Franklin & Marshall Coll., 1963; MS in Geology, San Diego State U., 1971. Cert. geologist, Maine. Vol. geologist U.S. Peace Corps, Ghana, 1963-66; geologist U.S. Army C.E., San Francisco, 1966-68; sr. geologist Geodata Systems Inc., Orange, Calif., 1969-71; assoc. sr. geologist Dames & Moore, Denver, 1972-79; v.p. Apache Energy and Minerals Co., Lakewood, Colo., 1979-84; pres., owner Wolf Creek Exploration Co., Evergreen Colo., 1984—; sr. v.p. Internat. Gold Resources Corp., Houston, Tex., 1985-96; owner Image of Africa, Evergreen, Colo., 1999—; mng. dir. Internat. Gold Resources, Inc., Bibani, Ghana, 1990-96 (discovered Bibani Open Pit Gold Deposit). Artist, producer silver proof coin World Cup Skiing, Breckenridge, Colo., 1991-92; contbr. numerous articles to profl. geol. and engring. jours. Mem. Soc. Econ. Geologists, Soc. for Mining, Metallurgy and Exploration, Geol. Soc. Am., Kiwanis (past mem. bd. dirs. Blue Spruce). Republican. Avocations: artist, hunting, fishing, skiing, biking. E-mail: auexplore@aol.com. Home: 29434 Greenwood Ln Evergreen CO 80439-7446

MCELROY, HAL, television producer; b. Melbourne, Victoria, Australia, Apr. 6, 1946; s. James Carmichael and Clair Ethel (Smith) McE.; m. Diane Beverly Hann, July 16, 1976; children: Zoe, Rome, Jake. Student, Wesley Coll., Melbourne, 1962. Prodr. (feature film) The Cars That Ate Paris, 1973, Picnic at Hanging Rock, 1975, The Last Wave, 1976, Blue Fin, 1978, Razorback, 1983, The Sum of Us, 1993, (TV movie) Deadline, 1979, (TV series) Ratbags, 1981, Return to Eden, 1986, Blue Heelers, 1994-98, Water Rats, 1996-98, Murder Call, 1997-98, Above the Law, 1999, (comedy) Dogs Head Bay, 1999, (interactive serial) Going Home, 2000, (children's TV series) Amazing, 1994-98, (mini-series) The Last Frontier, 1986, A Dangerous Life, 1988, Which Way Home, 1990,. Avocations: swimming, family. Office: Mcelroy TV Hunters Hill, 37 Alexandra St, Sydney NSW 2110, Australia

MCELROY, MAURINE DAVENPORT, financier, educator; b. Eastland, Tex., Sept. 28, 1913; d. William Fred and Mary Ewell (Johnson) Davenport; m. Kennedy King McElroy, Aug. 9, 1937 (dec. Mar. 1996); children: Mary M., Kennedy King Jr. BA, Tex. Tech U., 1937; MA, Hardin-Simmons U., 1941; PhD, U. Tex., 1964. Tchr. Eastland West Ward Elem. Sch., 1933-39, Eastland H.S., 1939-41, Miller H.S., Corpus Christi, Tex., 1951-54, Ray H.S., Corpus Christi, 1954-57; instr. Del Mar Coll., Corpus Christi, 1957-59; prin. Birdville H.S., Ft. Worth, 1942-43; feature writer Ark. Dem.-Gazette, Little Rock, 1948-51; assoc. prof. emeritus dept. English U. Tex., Austin, 1964—; cons. in field. Contbr. articles to profl. publs. Patron art museums, theatrical orgns., hist. preservation; sponsor Shelter for Abused Women and Children; fin. mgr. trusts. Mem. AAUW, Am. Assn. Colls. Tchg. English, Coll. English Assn. (life), Renaissance Soc. Am. Avocations: travel, reading, theatre, horticulture. Home: 3215 Gilbert St Austin TX 78703-2221 Office: U Tex Austin Dept English Parlin Hall 108 Austin TX 78712

MCELVEEN, JOSEPH JAMES, JR., journalist, author, educator, mass media executive; b. Sanford, Fla., Feb. 23, 1939; s. Joseph James Sr. and Genevieve (Stoll) McE.; m. Mary Louise Young, Aug. 18, 1979; 1 child, Ryan Leighton. BA, Furman U., 1961; MA, U. S.C., 1968. Editor, pub. West Ashley News, Charleston, S.C., 1951-57; reporter, photographer Charleston Post, 1955-57; tchr. English and journalism St. Andrew's Parish High Sch., Charleston, 1961-65; dir. info., prof. journalism Columbia Coll., S.C., 1965-68; prof. journalism U. S.C., Columbia, 1968-79; staff pub. affairs FCC, Washington, 1979-81; dir. pub. affairs adminstrn. Nat. Cable TV Assn., Washington, 1981-87; dir. internal communications Corp. for Pub. Broadcasting, Washington, 1987-92, dir. program adminstrn., 1992-96, sr. program officer, 1996-99; media/comms. cons. Vienna, Va., 1999—; ombudsman, columnist Alexandria (Va.) Gazette, 1981-88. Author: Introduction to Creative Writing, 1963, Modern Communications, 1964; contbr. chpt. to Dictionary of Literary Biography (Mencken), 1986, Words, Words, Words: A Journalist's Memoir, 1997, Effective Writing and Editing, 2000, 1940s: Decade on the Threshold, 2000. Mem. Orgn. of News Ombudsmen, Soc. Profl. Journalists, Mencken Soc. Episcopalian. Avocations: photography, reading, desktop pub. Office: 1807 Hursley Ct Vienna VA 22182-2105

MCELVEIN, THOMAS IRVING, JR., lawyer; b. Buffalo, N.Y., Apr. 19, 1936; s. Thomas I. and Edith Marian (Bowen) McE.; m. Ernesta F. McElvein, June 26, 1965; children: Christopher, Andrew, Kathryn. BA, Antioch Coll., 1959; JD, Yale U., 1962. Bar: N.Y. 1962, U.S. Dist. Ct. (we. dist.) N.Y. 1969. Atty. Village Akron, N.Y., 1963-99; spl. project atty. Village Akron, 2000—. Mem. N.Y. State Bar Assn., Erie County Bar Assn. Home: 295 Nottingham Ter Buffalo NY 14216-3125 Office: 1500 Liberty Bldg Buffalo NY 14202-3612

MCELYEA, JACQUELYN SUZANNE, accountant, real estate consultant; b. Dallas, July 19, 1958; d. Owen Clyde and Mary Lou (Cockerill) Harvey; m. James E. McElyea, June 11, 1983. BBS, Tex. A&M U., 1980. CPA, Tex. Acctg. mgr. Oxford Tex. Devel., Dallas, 1980-81; staff to dir. PriceWaterhouseCoopers, Dallas, 1981—; pres. Nat. Assn. Corp. Real Estate, Dallas. Co-author: Real Estate Accounting Reporting, 1995. Bd. dirs. Am. Diabetes Assn., Dallas, 1996-97. Mem. AICPA, Nat. Assn. Real Estate Cos., Tex. Soc. CPAs. Presbyterian. Avocations: animals, cooking. Office: PriceWaterhouse Coopers 2001 Ross Ave Ste 1800 Dallas TX 75201-2933

MCENARY, JOHN WALTER, music educator; b. Minneapolis, Dec. 7, 1952; s. David Nye and Marilynn Sahlin M.; m. Allison Roberts, Mar. 25, 1988. BFA, U. Minn., Minneapolis, 1975; MFA, U. Minn., 1977. Cert. Calif. Cmty. Coll. Instr. Music. prof. Orange Coast Coll., Costa Mesa, Calif., 1978—; music dept. chair Orange Coast Coll., Costa Mesa, 1984—; program coord. Orange Coast Coll., 1986—; software developer Sound Source Unlimited, Agoura Hills, Calif., 1989-92, Midiman, Arcadia, Calif., 1989-98; content developer Coda Music Tech., Eden Prairie, Minn., 1992-94; midi cons. Roland Corp., L.A., 1990-96. Author: (books) Guide to Sequencers, 1992, Computers in Music, 1999, (software) Proteus Sound Manager, 1988, Interval, 1998. Mem. Bowers Mus., Santa Ana, Calif., 1999-2000; subscriber Old Globe Theatre, San Diego, 1991-98. Recipient Regents fellowship, U. Calif. San Diego, 1975. Mem. Music Assn. Calif. Cmty. Colls., (life) Orange Co. Guitar Cir. (pres. 1984-86). Avocations: reading, movies, theatre, tech., music. E-mail: jmcenary@mail.occ.cccd.edu. Office: Orange Coast Coll 2701 Fairview Rd Costa Mesa CA 92626-5563

MCENIERY, PAUL TIMOTHY, cardiologist; b. Collinsville, Australia, Sept. 23, 1952; s. Myles Joseph and Margaret Mary (Tunn) McE.; m. Pamela Ann McComb, Dec. 31, 1977; children: Jane, Peter, John, Elizabeth, David. MB, BChir, U. Queensland, Australia, 1975. Med. resident Princess Alexandria Hosp., Brisbane, Australia, 1975-77; med. registrar Prince Henry Prince of Wales Hosps., Sydney, 1978-79; cardiology registrar St. Vincent's Hosp., Sydney, 1980-81; cardiology rsch. fellow Royal North Shore Hosp., Sydney, 1982-84; cardiology fellow Cleve. Clin. Found., 1984-86, angioplasty fellow, 1986; sr. staff cardiologist Prince Charles Hosp., Brisbane, Australia, 1987—. Fellow Royal Australasian Coll. Physicians, Am. Coll. Cardiology, Soc. for Cardiac Angiography and Interventions (Founders award 1987); mem. Cardiac Soc. Australia and New Zealand. Roman Catholic. Avocations: share market, compost, wine. Office: Chermside Specialist Ctr, PO Box 505, Chermside South QLD 4032, Australia

MCENIRY, ROBERT FRANCIS, education educator; b. Milw., Feb. 22, 1918; s. Frank Michael and Mary (Brown) McE. BA, St. Louis U., 1941, Philosophiae Licentiatus cum laude, 1944, Theologiae Licentiatus cum laude, 1953, PhL, ThL cum laude, 1953; PhD, Ohio State U., 1972. Elem. sch. tchr. Howdershell Grade Sch., 1939-40; radio announcer Sta. inst., 1938-40; tchr. Howdershell Grade Sch., 1939-40; radio announcer Sta. WOW, St. Louis, 1941-43; instr. classics St. Louis U. High Sch., 1944-47, Creighton Prep. Sch., Omaha, 1947-48; asst. prof., chmn. classics Rockhurst Coll., Kansas City, Mo., 1953-58; retreat dir. White House Retreat, St. Louis, 1958-68; assoc. research prof. Creighton U., Omaha, 1972-89; ret., 1989; dir., facilitator Growth for Couples, 1975-89; lectr. Creighton Natural Family Planning Ctr.; facilitator groups Adult Children of Alcoholism and Dysfunctional Families, 1989-93; vis. lectr. San Francisco Sch. Theology, San Anselmo, Calif., 1985; more than 800 presentations (lectrs., papers, workshops and seminars) in 175 cities, 22 states and 12 fgn. countries on value decisions during high anxiety and stress in marriage, family, teaching and learning; exec. dir. Studies Adult Survivors of Abuse, 1993—; tchr., counselor in marriage and family issues. Editor and pub. Interaction Review, 1982-89; editor Scholar and Educator, 1974-76; mem. editorial bd. Counseling and Values, 1976-82; editor (book) Pastoral Counseling, 1977, Premarriage Counseling, 1978; contbr. over 180 articles to profl. jours.; literary agent, 1992-98. Mem. Bd. of Pastoral Ministry, Omaha, 1972-78. Research grantee Council for Theol. Reflection, 1975-77; recipient Research award Creighton U., 1977; 1st prize for "Pro and Con" in Queen's Work Play contest, 1945. Fellow Nat. Acad. Counselors and Family Therapists (editor book rev. 1979-91); mem. APA, Am. Assn. for Religious Values in Counseling (editor newsletter 1982-89, Outstanding Svc. award 1985, Meritorious Svc. award 1989, Edgar Dale award 1995), Phi Delta Kappa (exec. com. 1977-83, del. 1981-83). Avocations: barbershop quartets, photography, Civil War sites, yoga. Home: 3016 Paddock Rd Apt 12B Omaha NE 68124-2942 Office: Creighton U 2500 California St Omaha NE 68131-1676

MCENROE, JOHN PATRICK, JR., professional tennis player, commentator; b. Wiesbaden, Fed. Republic Germany, Feb. 16, 1959; s. John Patrick and Katy McEnroe; m. Tatum O'Neal, Aug. 1, 1986; children: Kevin Jack, Sean. Grad., Trinity Sch., N.Y.C., 1977; student, Stanford U. Winner numerous U.S. jr. singles and doubles titles; winner jr. titles French Mixed Doubles, 1977, French Jr. Singles, 1977, Italian Indoor Doubles, 1978; winner Nat. Coll. Athletic Assn. Intercollegiate U.S. Men's Singles title, 1978; professional tennis player, 1978-93; played on victorious U.S. Davis Cup Team, 1978, 79, 81, 82, 92; winner Stockholm Open, 1978, Benson and Hedges Tournament, 1978, Grand Prix Masters singles and doubles, Wembley, 1978, Grand Prix Masters Tournament, N.Y.C., 1979, New Orleans Grand Prix, 1979, WCT Milan Internat., Italy, 1979, Stella Artois Tournament, London, 1979, U.S. Open Men's Singles Championship, 1979, 80, 81, 84, World Championship Tennis Championship, 1979, 83, Australian Indoor Singles Championship, 1980-83, U.S. Indoor Singles Championship, 1980-83, Wimbledon Singles, 1981, 83, 84, Tournament of Champions, 1981, 83, AT & T Challenge, 1987, Japan Open, 1988, U.S. Hard Court Singles, 1989, Wimbledon Doubles, 1992; tennis sportscaster USA Network, 1993; mem. Men's Seniors' Tour Circuit, 1994; owner John McEnroe Gallery. Winner Quality Challenge, Worldwide Sr. Tennis Cir., 1999; Enducted, Tennis Hall of Fame, 1999. Office: RHB Ventures Inc Paul Weiss Rifkind Wharton & Garrison 1320 18th St NW Ste 100 Washington DC 20036-1822 also: The John McEnroe Gallery 41 Greene St New York NY 10013-5916*

MCEVOY, PAMELA T., clinical psychologist; b. Mar. 8, 1937; d. Renny T. and Pamela (Sweeny) McE.; m. Percy H. Johnston Jr. (dec.); children: Michael B. Anderson, Jeffery A. Thomas, Candy L. Watts, Kenneth L. Anderson. BA, U. La Verne, 1978, MS, 1980; PhD, U.S. Internat. U., 1982. Instr. psychology-sociology Allan Hancock Coll., Santa Maria, 1977-78; mental health asst. Santa Barbara City Alcoholism Dept., 1977-78; gen. mgr. Profl. Suites, San Diego, 1978-81; therapist Chula Vista (Calif.) Cmty. Counseling Ctr., San Diego, 1978-85; rsch. asst. U.S. Internat. U., 1979-82; rsch. coord. Mil. Family Rsch. Ctr., San Diego, 1981-82; assoc. dir. Acad. Assoc. Psychotherapists, 1982-86; pvt. practice San Diego, 1982—; pres. Borrego Springs Med. Clinic, 1993-95, Family Custody Santa Maria Superior Ct., 1994-95, Santa Barbara County Mental Health Assn., Santa Maria, Calif., 1995-96. Bd. dirs. Women's Internat. Ctr., 1984-86, San Diego County Mental Health Assn., 1978-79, Civic Fedn., 1993-95. State fellow, 1979, 80, 81, 82; Calif. State scholar, 1976-77. Mem. APA, Calif. State Psychol. Assn., Rotary Interant. Republican. Roman Catholic. Address: PO Box 28609 San Diego CA 92198-0609

MCEVOY-JAMIL, PATRICIA ANN, English language educator; b. Butler, Pa., June 26, 1955; d. Joseph Lawrence McEvoy and Janet Ann (McConnell) Beier; m. M. Jamal Jamil, Nov. 23, 1977; 1 child, Amirah M. MA in TESOL, Monterey Inst. Internat. Studies, 1984; MA in English, Coll. Notre Dame, 1995; EdD, U. San Francisco, 1996. Calif. C.C. credential for life. Instr. ESL City Coll. San Francisco, 1989-98, Canada Coll., Redwood City, Calif., 1989-98; lectr. ESL Stanford (Calif.) U., 1989-97, Coll. Notre Dame, Belmont, Calif., 1991-98; co-owner, v.p. bd. MPA Co. Investments, Inc., Houston, 1998—; presenter in field; vis. prof. EFL, Georgetown U., Washington, summer 1999; adj. ESL instr. U. Houston-Downtown, 2000. Recipient ELITE Patron of Honor award ELITE Stanford (Calif.) Hosp., 1989, 90. Mem. Nat. Coun. Tchrs. English, Tchrs. English to Speakers of Other Langs., Phi Delta Kappa. Avocations: tennis, swimming, bicycling.

MCEWAN, ROBERT NEAL, health facility administrator; b. Washington, Sept. 6, 1949; s. Thomas Cornealius and Esther (Johnson) McE.; m. Elizabeth Mary Ross, Aug. 24,, 1973; 1 child, Amy Elizabeth; stepchildren: Gary W. Tizard, Jacqueline A. Klein. BS, Va. Mil. Inst., 1971. Med. technician USPHS, Washington, 1971-72; biologist McGuire Va. Hosp., Richmond, 1972-75; rsch. assoc. Frederick (Md.) Cancer Rsch. Facility, 1975-84, The Upjohn Co., Kalamazoo, Mich., 1984-93; crit. care cons. The Upjohn Co., Balt., 1993-95; transplant specialist Roche Labs., Inc., 1995-96; adminstrv. dir. The Comprehensive Transplant Ctr., Johns Hopkins, 1996—; pres., chmn. bd. MEDBANK of Md., Inc., 2000 ; adj. faculty Med. Sch. Northwestern U., Chgo., 1984-87; mem. indsl. adv. bd. Cen. Va. Gov.'s Sch., 1992-95; founder, leader Inch by Inch Bayview Med. Ctr., 1995 ; bd. dirs. Comprehensive Transplant Ctr., 1999 . Exec. prodr., creator: (video for cable TV) You Can Climb Again, The Organ Transplant Challenge, 1995; patentee in field. Leader 4-H, Kalamazoo, Mich., 1988-90; founder, mem. Adventures in Spaces, pres. 1988-90; mem. Gull Lake Middle Sch. PTA, pres. 1987-89, Gull Lake Area Community Vols., pres. 1988. Recipient Outstanding Svc. award Middle Sch. Educators Assn., 1988, STAR award Kalamazoo Gazette, Vol. Action Ctr., 1989, Svc. Leadership award Gull Lake Area Community Vols., 1990. Mem. Am. Soc. Microbiology, Nat. 4-H Sci. Tech. Design Team. Avocations: golf, skiing, photography, horseback riding. Home: 3132 Laurel View Dr Abingdon MD 21009-2636 Office: Johns Hopkins Hosp Brady 416 600 N Wolfe St Baltimore MD 21287-0005

MCFADDEN, DANIEL LITTLE, economics educator; b. Raleigh, N.C., July 29, 1937; s. Robert S. and Alice (Little) McF.; m. Beverlee Tito Simboli, Dec. 15, 1962; children: Nina, Robert, Raymond. BS, U. Minn., 1957, PhD, 1962; LLD, U. Chgo., 1992. Mellon fellow U. Pitts., Pa., 1962-63; asst. prof. U. Calif., Berkeley, 1963-65, assoc. prof., 1965-67, prof., 1967-77; research prof. Yale U., New Haven, 1977-78; prof. MIT, Cambridge, Mass.; E. Morris Cox prof. of economics Coll. of Letters & Sci., U. Calif., Berkeley; dir. Econometrics Lab., U.Calif., Berkeley; mem. econs. adv. panel NSF, 1969-71, Universities Nat. Bur., 1974-77, rev. com. Calif. Energy Com. Forecasts, 1979, Sloan Found. Book Com., 1977-79, NAS Com. on Basic Research in Social Scis., 1982—, NAS Com. on Energy Demand Modeling, 1983-84; chmn. AEA Awards Com., 1981-84, NSF-NBER Conf. on the Econs. of Uncertainty, 1970—; bd. dirs. Nat. Bur. Econ. Research, 1976-77, 1980-83; dir. Econometrics Lab. U. Calif. Berkeley, 1991—; mem. NAS Commn. Behavioral and Social Scis. and Edn., 1989—. Editor: Jour. Statis. Physics, 1968-70, Econometric Soc. monographs, 1980-83; bd. editors: Am. Econ. Rev., 1971-74, Jour. Math. Econs., 1973-77, Transp. Research, 1978-80; assoc. editor: Jour. Econometrics, 1977-78. Mem. adv. com. Transp. Models Project, Met. Transp. Commn., 1975, City of Berkeley Coordinated Transit Project, 1975-76; exec. com. Transp. Research Bd., 1975-78. Recipient John Bates Clark medal, 1975, Outstanding Teacher award MIT Econ. Dept., 1981, Frisch medal, 1986, Nobel Prize in Economics, 2000. Mem. Am. Acad. Arts and Scis., Nat. Acad. Sci., Am. Econ. Assn. (exec. com. 1985-87, v.p. 1994), Econometric Soc. (exec. com. 1983-86, v.p. 1984, pres. 1985), Am. Statis. Assn., Math. Assn. Am., Transp. Rsch. Bd. Democrat. Avocations: biking, tennis, squash, sailing, skiing. Home: 1370 Trancas St # 152 Napa CA 94558-2912 Office: U Calif-Berkeley Dept Economics 549 Evans Hall # 3880 Berkeley CA 94720-1775

MCFADDEN, JAMES FREDERICK, JR., surgeon; b. St. Louis, Dec. 5, 1920; s. James Frederick and Olivia Genevieve (Imbs) McF.; m. Mary Cella Switzer, Sept. 15, 1956 (div. Sept. 1969); children: James Frederick, Kenneth Michael, John Switzer, Mary Cella, Joseph Robert; m. Deanne Nemec Puls, Apr. 29, 1989. AB, St. Louis U., 1941, MD, 1944. Intern Boston City Hosp., 1944-45; ward surgeon neurosurg. and orthopedics McGuire Gen. Hosp., Richmond, Va., 1945; ward surgeon in internal medicine Regional Hosp., Fort Knox, Ky., 1946; ward surgeon plastic surgery Valley Forge Gen. Hosp., Phoenixville, Pa., 1946-47; intern St. Louis City Hosp., 1947-48; resident in surgery VA Hosp., St. Louis, 1948-52; clin. instr. surgery St. Louis U., 1952-62; gen. practice medicine specializing in surgery St. Louis, 1952—; mem. staff St. Mary's Hosp., 1952-77, St. John's Mercy Hosp., 1952-74, St. Louis U. (Desloge) Hosp., 1952-62; Cardinal Glennon Children's Hosp., 1952-62; mem. staff Frisco RR Hosp., 1953-64, DePaul Hosp., 1954—, Christian Hosp., 1955-66, 83-91. Mem. St. Louis Ambassadors, 1979-81; officer St. Louis County Aux. Police, 1973-75. Served to capt. AUS, 1945-47. Recipient Eagle Scout award, Order of the Arrow Honor award Boy Scouts Am. Fellow ACS, Royal Soc. Medicine, Internat. Coll. Surgeons; mem. St. Louis Med. Soc., Am. Coll. Occupl. and Environ. Medicine, Am. Soc. Clin. Hypnosis, Internat. Soc. Hypnosis, Am. Assn. RR Surgeons, St. Louis U. Student Conclave, Alpha Sigma Nu, Phi Beta Pi. Roman Catholic. Avocations: hypnosis, photography. Home: PO Box 411933 Saint Louis MO 63141-1933 Office: 11500 Olive Blvd Saint Louis MO 63141-7143

MCFADDEN, P. MICHAEL, physician, surgeon; b. Hobbs, N.Mex., June 16, 1946; s. Paul Marion and Venita Lenora (Bowen) McF.; m. Jennifer Marie James, Apr. 8, 1990; children: Heather Anne, Jennifer Suzanne, Bryn Ellen, Callan Michael. BS, La. State U., 1968; MD, Tulane U., 1974. Diplomate Am. Bd. Surgery, Am. Bd. Thoracic Surgery. Surg. intern, resident Tulane U. Sch. Medicine, New Orleans, 1974-79, instr. surgery, 1974-79; resident in thoracic surgery Ochsner Clinic, New Orleans, 1979-81; cardiovascular and thoracic surgeon Stanford (Calif.) U. Hosp., 1981-91; chief cardiovascular surgery Palo Alto (Calif.) Med. Clinic, 1983-91; cardiovascular and thoracic surgeon Ochsner Clinic, 1991—, surg. dir. lung transplantaion, 1991—; clin. prof. surgery Tulane U. Sch. Medicine, 1991—. Contbr. articles to profl. jours. Bd. dirs. YMCA, Palo Alto area, 1988-91. Capt USNR, 1988-94. Fellow ACS, Am. Coll. Cardiology, Am. Coll. Chest Physicians; mem. AMA, Alton Ochsner Surg. Soc., Am. Assn. for Thoracic Surgery, Am. Heart Assn. (coun. on cardiovascular surgery), Assn. Mil. Surgeons U.S., Internat. Soc. for Cardiovascular Surgery, Internat. Soc. for Heart and Lung Transplantation, New Orleans Surg. Soc., Norman E. Shumway Surg. Soc., Orleans Parish Med. Soc., Pacific Coast Surg. Assn., So. Surg. Assn., So. Thoracic Surg. Assn., Southeastern Surg. Congress, So. Med. Assn., Surg. Assn. La., Thoracic Surgery Found., Tulane Surg. Soc., Tulane U. Med. Alumni Assn., Western Thoracic Surg. Assn., Alpha Omega Alpha, Alpha Epsilon Delta, Nu Sigma Nu, Kappa Alpha. Republican. Presbyterian. Home: 1707 Palmer Ave New Orleans LA 70118-6115 Office: Ochsner Clinic Dept Surgery Divsn Cardiothoracic Surg 1514 Jefferson Hwy New Orleans LA 70121-2483

MCFADDEN, ROBERT STETSON, hepatologist; b. Houston, Mar. 29, 1951; s. David Barnett and Phyllis Reed (Gowell) McF.; children: William Gordon, Elizabeth Stetson. BS in Biology, Baylor U., 1973; MD, U. Tex., Galveston, 1977. Diplomate Am. Bd. Internal Medicine; cert. gastroenterology Am. Bd. Internal Medicine. Intern in internal medicine La. State U. Med. Sch., New Orleans, 1977-78, resident in internal medicine, 1978-81; staff physician clinic Pub. Health Hosp., New Orleans, 1981; fellow gastroenterology U. Ala., Birmingham, 1981-83; fellow hepatology U. Miami, Fla., 1983-84; gastroenterologist Diagnostic Clinic Houston, 1984-87, Oklahoma City Clinic, 1987-92; hepatologist Okla. Transplantation Inst., Oklahoma City, 1993-2000; chief of hepatology Liver Disease Ctr., Good Samaritan Regional Med. Ctr., Phoenix, 2000—; cons. gastroenterology Diagnostic Clinic of Houston, 1984-87, Oklahoma City Clinic, 1987-92; cons. liver diseases and liver transplant medicine Okla. Transplant Inst., Oklahoma City, 1993-99. Contbr. articles to profl. jours. Mem. ACP, AMA, Am. Assn. for Study of Liver Diseases, Internat. Liver Transplantation Soc., Okla. State Med. Assn. Republican. Baptist. Avocations: Victorian antiques, gardening. Home: 14181 N 90th Pl Scottsdale AZ 85260-7506 Office: 1410 N 3d St Phoenix AZ 85004

MCFARLAND, JON WELDON, retired county commissioner; b. Wenatchee, Wash., Aug. 23, 1938; s. Charles Edward and Maud Elizabeth (Brennan) McF.; m. Kay Annette Erbes, Apr. 5, 1956; children: Colleen, Michael, Heather. BS in Edn., Eastern Wash. State U., 1961; MS in Personnel Adminstrn., George Washington U., 1966; Grad., Command and Gen. Staff Coll., Fort Leavenworth, Kans., 1970, U.S. Army War Coll., Carlisle Barracks, Pa., 1980. Commd. U.S. Army, 1961, advanced through grades to col., 1981, retired, 1988; ops. officer European Hdqtrs. U.S. Army, Heidelberg, Fed. Republic Germany, 1980-83; commdr. 16th mil. police brigade U.S. Army, Fort Bragg, N.C., 1983-85, provost marshal 18th Airborne Corps, 1983-85; asst. commandant, commdr. of troops U.S. Army Mil. Police Sch., Fort McClellan, Ala., 1985-88; county commr. Columbia County, Wash., 1989-96; ret., 1996; dir., owner Mr. Mc's Direct Mktg. Svcs., 1992—; owner, dir. Spectro-Optics of Ea. Wash., Dayton, 1994—; Wash. staff for courthouse security, 1995-96; Wash. gov. appointee bd. trustees Dist. 20 Cmty. Colls.; vice chmn. Southeastern Emergency Med. and Trauma Coun., Wash., 1990-94, chmn., 1995—; chmn. Columbia County Bd. Commrs., 1990, 96; bd. dirs. Emergency Mgmt. Svcs., Columbia County. Author: History of Civil Disturbance 1960-68, 1969. Bd. dirs. Columbia County Pub. Health Dist., Dayton, 1989-96, chmn., 1995-96; bd. dirs. Project Timothy Pub. Svcs., Columbia County Health Found., 1989—, Inland Counseling Network; vice chmn. Palouse Econ. Devel. Corp., 1990-92, chmn., 1993-95; bd. trustees Walla Walla C.C., 1998—. Decorated Legion of Merit, Bronze Star, numerous others. Mem. Assn. U.S. Army, Wash. State Assn. Counties, U.S. Army War Coll. Found., Kiwanis (bd. dirs. Dayton 1990—, treas. 1998—). Democrat. Roman Catholic. Avocations: woodworking, pottery, fishing, hunting, travel. Home: 150 S Touchet Rd Dayton WA 99328-8741 Office: Columbia County 205 S 4th St Dayton WA 99328-1411

MCFARLAND, LYNNE VERNICE, pharmaceutical executive; b. San Antonio, Tex., June 3, 1953; d. Earle Clifford and Avis Marie (Jones) Olson; m. Marcus Joseph McFarland, July 27, 1975. BS in Microbiology, Portland State U., 1975, MS, 1980; PhD in Epidemiology, U. Wash., 1988. Cert. Pub. Health. From rsch. asst. to lab. supr. U. Oreg. Health Sci. Ctr., Portland, 1977-82; intern Wash. State Pub. Health Labs, Seattle, 1983; from tchg. asst. dept. epidemiology to rsch. asst. U. Wash., Seattle, 1984-88, from rschr. to lectr. dept. med. chemistry, 1988, rsch. assoc. prof., 1991—; dir. scientific affairs Biocodex, Inc., Seattle, 1988—; reviewer McGraw-Hill Book Co., N.Y.C., 1982; editorial reviewer Ob-Gyn, L.A., 1989—, Jour. of Infect Diseases, 1991, 95—, Vet. Adminstrn., 1991; also review for gastroenterology 1990, clin. infectious diseases, 1995—. Reviewer Gastroenterology; contbr. articles to profl. jours. Lobbyist environ. issues Wash. State Biotech. Assn., Seattle, 1990; vol. Literacy Plus, Seattle, 1990. Recipient Poncin scholarshp, Seafirst Bank, Seattle, 1985-88. Mem. Am. Soc. Microbiology, Soc. for Epidemiol. Rsch., Soc. Microbiol. Ecology and Diseases (bd. dirs. 1997—), Wash. Assn. Epidemiology. Avocations: photography, musician (piano and flute), poet, outdoor sports, travel. Office: Biocodex Inc 1910 Fairview Ave E Ste 208 Seattle WA 98102-3620

MCFARLAND, ROBERT BRUCE, physician; b. Ames, Iowa, Sept. 18, 1929; s. Julian Ecwart and Winnie Florence (Goering) McF.; m. Zoë Euphrosyne Bucuvalas, June 1, 1958; children: Laura Ann, Bruce Damon. BA, Kenton Coll., 1950; MD, U. Iowa, 1954. Intern San Francisco Gen. Hosp., 1955; house officer Mass. Gen. Hosp., Boston, 1957-59; asst. resident U. Colo. Med. Ctr., Denver, 1959-61; physician pvt. practice, Boulder, Colo., 1961-76, 78-93; prof. U. Mo., Kansas City, 1976-78. Contbg. editor Jour. Psychohistory, 1996—; contbr. articles to profl. jours. Vestryman St. John's Episcopal Ch., Boulder, 1966-69; jail physician Boulder County, Kansas City, 1972-75, 76-78; co-founder Parenting Place, Boulder, 1984-95; cons., bd. health No. Cheyenne Tribe, Lame Deer, Mont., 1976-84; dir. Nat. Parenting Cmty., 1995—. Comdr. USNR-R, 1955-78. Avocations: skiing, hiking. Home: 2300 Kalmia Ave Boulder CO 80304-1931

MCFARLAND, ROBERT EDWIN, lawyer; b. St. Louis, July 25, 1946; s. Francis Taylor and Kathryne (Stephens) McF.; m. Jeannine M. Ghekiere, Feb. 26, 1982. BA, U. Mich., 1968, JD, 1971. Bar: Mich. 1971, U.S. Dist. Ct. (ea. dist.) Mich. 1971, U.S. Ct. Appeals (6th cir.) 1974, U.S. Supreme Ct. 1975, U.S. Ct. Appeals (D.C. cir.) 1978. Law clk. to chief judge Mich. Ct. Appeals, 1971-72; assoc. William B. Elmer, St. Clair Shores, Mich., 1972-74, James Elsman, Birmingham, Mich., 1974-75; ptnr. McFarland, Schmier, Stoneman & Singer, Troy, Mich., 1975-77; sr. ptnr. McFarland & Bullard, Bloomfield Hills, Mich., 1977-90, McFarland & Niemer, Farmington Hills, Mich., 1990-91; shareholder Foster, Swift, Collins & Smith, P.C., Farmington Hills, 1992—, mem. exec. com., 1995—. Chmn. bd. govs. Transp. Law Jour., U. Denver Coll. Law, 1981-83. Mem. bd. control Intercollegiate Athletics, U. Mich., 1966-68; mem. rulemaking study com. Mich. Pub. Svc. Commn., 1983-84, Motor Carrier Adv. Bd., 1984-88. Capt. USAR, 1971-80. Mem. ABA, Transp. Lawyers Assn. (officer 1998—, Disting. Svc. awad 1997), Assn. Transp. Law, Logistics and Policy, State Bar Mich. (vice-chmn. transp. law com. adminstrn. law sect. 1990—, sect. coun. adminstrv. law sect. 1994—), Am. Judicature Soc. Office: Foster Swift Collins & Smith PC 32300 Northwestern Hwy Ste 230 Farmington MI 48334-1571

MCFARLAND, THOMAS, English educator. AB, Harvard U., 1949; AM, Yale U., 1951, PhD, 1953; postgrad., Eberhard-Karls-Universität, Tübingen, Germany, 1953-54; MA status (hon.), Oxford U., Eng., 1986. Instr. in English Oberlin Coll., 1954-56, U. Va., 1956-58; asst. prof. Western Res. U., Cleve., 1958-62, assoc. prof., 1962-64, prof., 1964-67; prof. Grad. Ctr. CUNY, 1967-73, disting. prof. English lit., 1973-78; prof. Princeton U., N.J., 1978-81, Murray prof. English lit., 1981-89; Murray prof. English lit. emeritus Princeton U., N.J., 1989—; vis. prof. U. Colo., 1968, U. Va., 1972, Yale U., 1975; vis. fellow All Souls Coll., U. Oxford, Eng., 1986-87, Humanities Rsch. Ctr., Australian Nat. U., Canberra, 1992, Lechter Inst. for Lit. Rsch., Bar-Ilan U., Ramat Gan, Israel, 1989, U. Otago, Dunedin, New Zealand, 1992; The Ida Beam Lectures U. Iowa, 1985; mem. adv. bd. Bull. Rsch. in Humanities, 1978—, Studies in Romanticism, 1982—, Nineteenth-Century Lit., 1986—, Works of Thomas De Quincey, 1990, Romanticism, 1995—; hon. fellow Ctr. for European Romanticism, 1997—; mem. supervising com. English Inst., 1971-74, chmn. 1974; ; assoc. trustee The Dove Cottage Trust, The Lake Dist., Eng., 1982—; bd. advisors Milton and the Romantics, 1975—; seminar assoc. Columbia U., 1971—, 76—, 97—; cons., spkr. in field. author: Tragic Meanings in Shakespeare, 1966, Coleridge and the Pantheist Tradition, 1969, Shakespeare's Pastoral Comedy, 1972, Romanticism and the Forms of Ruin: Wordsworth, Coleridge and Modalities of Fragmentation, 1981, Originality and Imagination, 1985, Shapes of Culture, 1987, Romantic Cruxes: The English Essayists and the Spirit of the Age, 1987, William Wordsworth: Intensity and Achievement, 1992, Romanticism and the Heritage of Rousseau, 1995, Paradoxes of Freedom: The Romantic Mystique of Transcendence, 1996, The Masks of Keats: The Endeavor of a Poet, 1999; editor: The Opus Maximum of Samuel Taylor Coleridge; mem. editl. bd. Comparative Criticism, 1977—, European Romantic Rev., 1989—; contbr. articles to profl. jours. Fulbright scholar, 1953-54; fellow Guggenheim Found., 1964-65, 74-75, Am. Coun. Learned Socs., 1973-74, Ctr. for Advanced Study in Behavioral Scis., 1981-82, NEH, 1981-82, 86-87. Mem. MLA (exec. com. English 9 1970-73, chmn. 1974), Sydney Soc. for Literature and Aesthetics (hon. life). Fax: 609 279-9237. Home: 113 Westerly Rd Princeton NJ 08540-2623

MCFARLAND, WALTER GERARD, management consultant; b. Chicago Heights, Ill., June 28, 1952; s. Walter Louden and Rosemary (Voelker) McF. BA in Psychology, So. Ill. U., 1976, MPA, 1978; MA in Nat. Security, Georgetown U., 1991; EdD in Human Resource Devel., George Washington U., 1999. Program analyst USAF, San Antonio, 1978-82; program monitor CIA, Washington, 1982-85; spl. asst. to sec. of def. Dept.

of Def., Washington, 1985-88; mgmt. cons. Hay Mgmt. Consultants, Washington, 1988-97; prin. rsch. scientist Am. Insts. Rsch., Washington, 1997—; guest lectr. CIA, 1985-88, Georgetown U., 1995, Johns-Hopkins U., Washington, 1996. Elder Great Falls (Va.) Bible Ch., 1988-90; mem. Wakefield H.S. PTA, Arlington, Va., 1992-96. Mem. ASPA (nat. chpt. head 1985-86, chpt. dir. 1987), Acad. Mgmt. Republican. Baptist. Home: 2214 N Scott St Arlington VA 22209-1012

MCFARLAND, WILLELLYN SHAW, artist, educator; b. Compton, Calif., Nov. 14, 1934; d. William Bruce Shaw and Brenda Marguerite McKee; m. Jim McFarland, Apr. 9, 1960; children: Craig, Robin, Shawn. BFA, U. So. Calif., L.A., 1956; tchg. credentials, Calif. State U., Long Beach, 1978. Lifetime credentials in spl. secondary art, gen. jr. h.s., Calif. Tchr. elem. edn. Montebello Sch. Dist., 1972-92; adult sch. tchr. El Rancho Unified Sch. Dist., 1982-98; tchr. Downey (Calif.) Sch. Dist., 1983—; advisor Artists Mag., 1996. Featured in books Artists of California, 1993, The Artistic Touch 3, 1999, The Artists mag., 1999. Mem. Nat. Watercolor Soc. (pres. 1991-92, 96-97, exhbn. dir. 1991-92, 96-97, chmn. selection jury 1998 Ann. Exhbn. 1998, exhibited in juried art exhbns. 1995, corr. sec., advisor 1997-98), Women Painters West (exhibited in juried exhbns. 1986). Avocations: golf, painting on location.

MCGANN, LISA B. NAPOLI, language educator; b. West Hartford, Conn., Sept. 7; d. James Napoli; m. Edward Harrison McGann, Jr. BA, Vassar Coll., 1980; MA, Columbia U., 1983, postgrad., 1991-95; MA, Middlebury Coll., 1987. Cert. tchr. French, ESL and Italian, Conn. Cmty. English program coord. Tchrs. Coll. Columbia U., N.Y.C., 1982-83; mgr. English tchg. com. Jr. League N.Y., N.Y.C., 1983-84; asst. dir. ESL Fordham U., N.Y.C., 1988-89; ESL instr. Laguardia C.C., CUNY, Long Island City, N.Y., 1983—, Columbia U., 1983-96; ESL instr. Yale U., 1988, 89; ESL specialist, tchr. UN, N.Y.C., 1990. Big sister Highland Hts., New Haven, 1976-77; ESL tchr. Boys and Girls Club, Astoria, N.Y., 1992. Recipient awards and scholarships. Mem. Nat. TESOL Soc., Am. Assn. Tchrs. Italian, Italian-Am. Hist. Soc., Nat. Italian Am. Found. (coun.), The Statue of Liberty-Ellis Island Found., Inc.. Roman Catholic. Avocations: ballet, reading, travel, real estate, tennis.

MCGANN, MICHAEL GEYER, martial arts instructor, protection expert; b. Lafayette, La., Sept. 17, 1952; s. Robert Fred and Georgia Marie (Geyer) McG. M in Clin. Psychology, Internat. U., Athens, Greece, 1981, degree in oriental philosophy, 1985; D in Martial Arts, World Martial Arts Hall of Fame, Cleveland Heights, Ohio, 1995. Security supr. Don Cesar Beach Resort, St. Pete Beach, Fla., 1985-90; dir. security Sandpiper Beach Resort, St. Pete Beach, 1990-97; CEO, pres. Wa No Michi Ryu Karate/Kobudo, Clearwater, Fla., 1995—; dep. dir. Police Tactics Instrs. Am., St. Petersburg, Fla., 1995—; exec. adminstr. Sokeship coun. World Martial Arts Hall of Fame, Clearwater, 1995—; spl. dep. Pinellas County (Fla.) Sheriff's Dept., 1990-96; tech. advisor Isle of Man Karate Assn., Eng., 1977—. Editor Journey, 1995; contbr. poetry to lit. publs. (Grand award of honor 1990). Mem. WAR (Work Against Rape), St. Petersburg, 1985—. With U.S. Army, 1975-79. Recipient Pioneer/Founder award Fla. Hall of Fame Brotherhood of Martial Artists, 1998; named Nat. Master of Karate, Presdl. Coun. Sports and Phys. Fitness, Washington, 1988, Grandmaster of the Year Self Defense, 2000; inducted into Universal Martial Arts Hall of Fame. Fellow Soc. of Black Belt (tech. advisor 1977—); mem. Internat. Union Martial Artists (v.p. Am. 1990—, tech. advisor 1981—, Merit award 1996), World Kung Chung Do Self Defense Instn. (pres. 1977-79, Twain P. Marx Meml. award 1980). Democrat. Avocations: haiku poetry, sumie painting, chess, bonsai, iai jitsu. Home: 6100 150th Ave N Clearwater FL 33760-2138

MCGARRY, DOROTHY, librarian; b. Omaha, May 1, 1929; d. Moore and Ruth (Gorelick) Lasher. AB, UCLA, 1949, MLS, 1971. Catalog libr. UCLA, 1971-76, head cataloging divsn. phys. scis. and tech. librs., 1976-93, emerita, 1993—; mem. vocabulary task force for revision GeoRef Thesaurus 4th-9th edit. Am. Geol. Inst. Fellow Spl. Librs. Assn. 1994— (Hall of Fame 2000—); mem. AAAS, ALA (resources and tech. svcs . divsn., catalog form and function com. 1986-90), Assn. for Libr. Collections and Tech. Svcs. (chair com. on cataloging desc. and access 1985-86, orgn./by-law com., 1999—, cataloging and classification sect. policy and rsch. com. 1988-92, subject analysis com. 1993-96, mem.-at-large cataloging and classification sect. 1993-96, chair cataloging and classification sect. 1997-98), Am. Math. Soc. (libr. com. 1989-98), Am. Phys. Soc., Am. Soc. for Info. Sci. (L.A. chpt., chair by-laws com. 1986-89, 99-2000, sec. 1987-88, outstanding mem. yr. award 1990, 94, mem. other coms.), Assn. Coll. Rsch. Librs. (sci.-tech. sect., chair ad hoc com. designing conf. proc. style sheet 1984-87, mem. other coms.), Spl. Librs. Assn. (chair com. on cataloging 1983-89, 97-99, rep. CIP adv. group 1983-88, rep. Internat. Fedn. Libr. Assns. and Instns. sect. on classification and indexing 1988-95, rep. to sect. on cataloguing 1995—, chair physics astronomy-math. divsn. 1982-83, chair sci.-tech. divsn. 1991-92, rep. of the SLA geography and map divsn. Anglo-Amer. Cataloguin com. for Cartographic Materials, 1988—, internat. rels. com. 1989-97, bd. dirs. 1995-97, SLA del. to the Internat. Fedn. of Libr. Assns. and Instns., 1993-97, treas. So. Calif. chpt. 1991-93, rep. other coms., pres. So. Calif. Chpt. 1994-95, SLA John Cotton Dana award 1991, chair by-laws com. 2000), Calif. Acad. and Rsch. Librs., Calif. Libr. Assn., Geosci. Info. Soc., Internat. Fedn. Libr. Assns. and Instns. (chair sect. on classification and indexing 1989-93, sec. 1993-95, mem. sect. cataloging 1995—), Math. Assn. Am., N.Am. Serials Interest Group, Online Audiovisual Catalogers, South Calif. Tech. Processes Group. Office: UCLA Sci & Engring Libr 8251 Boelter Hl Los Angeles CA 90095-0001

MCGARRY, SHARON CHRISTINE, film company executive; b. Dublin, July 15, 1968; d. Liam and Frances (Walker) McG. Asst. adminstr. Temple Bar Gallery Studios, Dublin, 1988-91; acct. mgr. Mary Crotty, Dublin, 1991-94; publicity mgr. Columbia Tri Star, Dublin, 1994-98; product mgr. Sony Music, Dublin, 1998-99; gen. mgr. Twentieth Century Fox, Dublin, 1999—. Office: Twentieth Century Fox, 14 Kildare St, Dublin 2, Ireland

MCGARVEY, BRIAN, research scientist; b. Dublin; s. Seamus and Nora (Burke) McG. BSc, Univ. Coll. Dublin, 1989; MSc, Grenwich (U.K) U., 1991. Rsch. scientist Philips U.K., 1991-97; sr. engr. Gen. Semiconductor Ireland, Cork, 1998—. Contbr. articles to profl. jours.; patentee in field. Mem. Astronomy Ireland, Am. Inst. Physics. Avocations: astronomy, surfing. Office: Gen Semiconductor Ireland, Ovens, Cork Republic of Ireland

MCGARY, BETTY WINSTEAD, minister, counselor, individual, marriage, and family therapist; b. Louisville, June 21, 1936; d. Philip Miller and Mary Jo (Winstead) McG.; married, 1960 (div. 1979); children: Thomas Edward, Mary Alyson Griffith, Andrew Philip Pearce. BS, Samford U., 1958; MA, So. Bapt. Theol. Sem., 1961; EdD, U. Louisville, 1988. Ordained to ministry Bapt. Ch., 1986; cert. secondary tchr., Ky., Ga.; lic. profl. counselor, marriage and family therapist, Tex. Min. to youth Broadway Bapt. Ch., Louisville, 1958-60; learning disability and behavior disorders specialist Jefferson County Schs., Muscogee Schs., Cobb County Schs., Louisville, Columbus, Ga., Atlanta, 1964-88; min. to adults South Main Bapt. Ch., Houston, 1986-90; assoc. pastor Calder Bapt. Ch., Beaumont, Tex., 1991-96; psychotherapist pvt. practice, Beaumont, Tex., 1996—; marriage enrichment cons. Pastoral Inst., Columbus, 1973-76; co-founder and coord. Ctr. for Women in Ministry, Louisville, 1983-86, exec. bd. dirs., 1983-90; cons. Tex. Christian Life Commn., Ft. Worth, 1989-93; co-therapist pvt. practice, Houston, 1989—. Author: (with others) The New Has Come, 1988, A Costly Obedience: Sermons by Women of Steadfast Spirit, 1994; co-editor nat. newsletter Folio: A Newsletter for Southern Bapt. Women in Ministry, 1983-86. Vice-chairperson exec. bd. dirs. handicapped Boy Scouts Am., Houston, 1986-90; mem. leadership coun. Triangle Interfaith Project, Beaumont, 1995-97; mem. Leadership Houston, 2000—. Recipient citation for Disting. Svc. So. Bapt. Theol. Sem., 1984, Dean's citation Outstanding Achievement U. Louisville, 1988. Mem. The Alliance of Baptists (exec. bd. dirs. 1988-90, v.p. 1990-91), So. Bapt. Women in Ministry (pres. 1988-90, treas. 1995-96, archivist 1998—), Bapt. Gen. Conv. of Tex. (exec. bd. dirs. 1996—, adminstrv. com. 1998—), Leadership Beaumont. Avocations: gardening, interior design, travel. Home: 4112 Meyerwood Dr Houston TX 77025 Office: 5100 Westheimer Rd Ste 200 Houston TX 77056-5597

MCGAURAN, PETER, Australian government official. Min. sci. & tech. Govt. of Australia, 1996-97, min. arts & centenary of fedn., 1997—. Office: Min Arts & Centenary Fedn, Parliament House Ste MF 70, Canberra ACT 2600, Australia*

MCGEE, DOROTHY HORTON, writer, historian; b. West Point, N.Y., Nov. 30, 1913; d. Hugh Henry and Dorothy (Brown) M. Ed., Sch. of St. Mary, 1920-21, Green Vale Sch., 1921-28, Brearley Sch., 1928-29, Fermata Sch., 1929-31. Asst. Historian Inc. Village of Roslyn, N.Y., 1950-58; historian Inc. Village of Matinecock, 1966—. Author: Skipper Sandra, 1950, Sally Townsend, Patriot, 1952, The Boarding School Mystery, 1953, Famous Signers of the Declaration, 1955, Alexander Hamilton-New Yorker, 1957, Herbert Hoover: Engineer, Humanitarian, Statesman, 1959, rev. edit., 1965, The Pearl Pendant Mystery, 1960, Framers of the Constitution, 1968; author booklets, articles hist. and sailing subjects. Chmn. Oyster Bay Bicentennial Revolution Commn., 1971—, historian Town of Oyster Bay, 1982—, mem. Nassau County Am. Revolution Bicentennial Commn., hon. dir. The Friends of Raynham Hall, Inc., treas. Family Welfare Assn. Nassau County, Inc., 1956-58, dir. Family Svc. Assn. Nassau County, 1958-69. Recipient Cert. of award for outstanding contbn. children's lit. N.Y. State Assn. Elem. Sch. Prins., 1959, award Nat. Soc. Children of Am. Revolution, 1960, award N.Y. Assn. Supervision and Curriculum Devel., 1961, hist. award Town of Oyster Bay, 1963, Cert. Theodore Roosevelt Assn., 1976, Franklin D. Roosevelt award, Local Govt. Historian's Prof. Achievement award Office of State Historian and Assn. Pub. Historians N.Y. State, 1999. Fellow Soc. Am. Historians, mem. Soc. Preservation L.I. Antiquities (hon. dir.), Nat. Trust Hist. Preservation, N.Y. Geneal. and Biol. Soc. (dir., trustee), Oyster Bay Hist. Soc. (hon. pres. 1971-75, chmn. 1975-79, trustee), Theodore Roosevelt Assn. (trustee), Townsend Soc. Am. (trustee). Republican. Address: PO Box 142 Locust Valley NY 11560-0142

MCGEE, JAMES FRANCIS, lawyer; b. N.Y.C., Sept. 19, 1950; s. James F. and Elizabeth J. (Mooney) M.; m. Annamarie Saunders, Feb. 13, 1988; children: James, Brooke Nicole. BS, U. Penn., 1972; JD, Western State U., Fullerton, Calif., 1980. Bar: Calif. 1980. Founder McGee & Assocs., Newport Beach, Calif., 1980—. Chmn. Laguna Beach Bd. Adjustment, 1985-87, Laguna Beach Architecture Review Bd., 1985-87; pres. Junior All Am. Football, 1997—; pres. Pelican Hill Cmty. Assn., 1995—; pres. Newport Coast Cmty. Assn., 1997—, chmn. annexation com., 1998—; chief Indian Guides Chumash Tribe, 1996—; chief Newport Beach-Costa Mesa YMCA Indian Guides Dolphin Nation, 1997-99. Recipient 20-30 Internat. So. Calif. Man of Yr., 1985. Mem. ABA, ATLA, Calif. Bar Assn., Orange County Bar Assn., Calif. Trial Lawyers Assn., Orange County Trial Lawyers Assn. Avocations: sports, flying, public speaking. Office: 23 Corp Plaza Ste 230 Newport Beach CA 92660

MCGEHEE, THOMAS RIVES, paper company executive; b. Jacksonville, Fla., July 12, 1924; s. Clifford Graham and Ray (Sutton) McG.; m. Delia Houser, Nov. 3, 1950; children: Delia McGehee II, Thomas R. Jr. Student, Davidson Coll., 1942-43; BS in Chemistry, U. Ala., 1948. V.p. Jacksonville Paper Co., 1948-56, pres., 1956-64; pres. Mac Papers, Inc., Jacksonville, 1964-79, co-founder, chief exec. officer, chmn. bd., 1979—; co-chmn., chief exec. officer Mac Papers Converters, Inc., 1965—, pres., North Fla. TV-47, Inc., 1979-90; pres. Higley Pub. Co., 1968-90; bd. dirs. Barnett Bank of Jacksonville,, 1961-89; chmn. exec. com. Sta. WTLV-TV 12, 1972-78; numerous real estate interests. Chmn. and founder Greater Jacksonville Community Found., 1964-84, trustee, 1984-89; trustee Jacksonville U., 1959—, vice chmn., 1962-65, chmn., 1991-92; trustee Regent U., 1996—; mem. U. Fla. Pres.' Coun., U. Fla. Health & Sci. Ctr.; mem. post secondary edn. planning commn. State of Fla., 1987-90; bd. dirs. Dreams Come True, pres. and founder 1984-90, chmn. emeritus, 1990—; bd. dirs. Bapt. Hosp. Found., 1986-90; vice chmn. Every Home For Christ, 1987—; past mem., officer numerous other community orgs. Served with U.S. Army, 1943-46, ETO. Decorated 3 Battle Stars; recipient Fla. Gov.'s award as Outstanding Industrialist, 1962, Top Mgmt. award Sales and Mktg. Execs. of Jacksonville, 1981, Outstanding Vol. Leadership award, Patriot of Yr. award Duval County Rep. Party, 1991, Disting. Bus. Man award, Prime F. Osborne Disting. Citizen award U. North Fla., 1998, Disting. Citizen award Boy Scouts Am., 1999, others; named Philanthropist of Yr. Nat. Soc. Fundraising Execs., 1999. Mem. NAM (dir. 1964-66), Asso. Industries Fla. (dir. 1961-63), Nat. Paper Trade Assn., So. Paper Trade Assn., Nat. Assn. Broadcasters, Fla. State C. of C., Phi Gamma Delta (pres. 1948). Republican. Episcopalian. Clubs: River (dir. 1980-83), Fla. Yacht, Timuquana Country, Ponte Vedra, Blowing Rock Country (bd. dirs. 1991-94), Lodge Country Clubs. Home: Paul Plz Condos 6 505 Lancaster St Jacksonville FL 32204-4143 Office: MAC Papers Inc 3300 Phillips Hwy PO Box 5369 Jacksonville FL 32247-5369

MCGEHEE, THOMAS RIVES, JR., wholesale distribution company executive; b. Jacksonville, Fla., Aug. 25, 1959; s. Thomas Rives Sr. and Delia (Houser) McG.; m. Terri Ross, Nov. 30, 1985; children: Courtney Leigh, Ashley Ann, Mackenzie Rives. BS in Mgmt., U. Fla., 1981. Sales rep. Mac Papers, Inc., Jacksonville, Fla., 1981-82; gen. mgr. Mac Papers, Inc., Columbus, Ga., 1982-83; ops. mgr. Mac Papers, Inc., Montgomery, Ala., 1983-85; v.p. Mac Papers, Inc., Jacksonville, 1985—. Bd. dirs. ABC Bancorp, Moultrie, Ga., 1987-92, United Way of NE Fla., 1994-97, Jacksonville Chpt. of Navy League; exec. com. mem., sr. v.p. YMCA Bd. of Mgmt., 1992-95. Mem. Jacksonville C. of C. (mil. affairs/armed svcs. com., small bus. exec. coun. 1991-92, small bus. purchasing task force 1992-93), Jacksonville Fellowship of Christian Athletes (bd. dirs. 1997—), Leadership Jacksonville Class of 1994, Youth Leadership Jacksonville Coun., River Club, Fla. Yacht Club (bd. govs. 1993-95), Plantation Country Club, Ponte Vedra Inn and Club. Republican. Avocations: tennis, sailing, running, hunting, fishing. Office: Mac Papers Inc PO Box 5369 Jacksonville FL 32247-5369

MCGEOWN, MARY GRAHAM, physician; b. Lurgan, No. Ireland, July 19, 1923; d. James Edward and Sarah Graham (Quinn) McG.; m. Joseph Maxwell Freeland, Sept. 1, 1949; children: Peter, Mark, Paul. MB BCh, Queen's U., Belfast, No. Ireland, 1946, MD, 1950, PhD, 1953, DMS (hon.), 1990; DS (hon.), New U. Ulster, 1983. C.B.E., 1985. Cons. nephrologist Belfast Hosps., 1962-88; hon. reader Queen's U., Belfast, 1967-88; med. advisor No. Ireland Kidney Rsch. Fund, 1971-89; patron, 1989—; physician-in-charge Regional Dept. Nephrology, No. Ireland, 1968-88; chmn. U.K. Transplant Svc., 1983-90; profl. fellow Queen's U., Belfast, 1988—; Mem. Unrelated Live Transplant Regulatory Authority, 1990-96. Author: Clinical Management of Electrolyte Disorders, 1983; editor: Clinical Management of Renal Transplantation, 1992; contbr. over 300 articles to profl. jours. Decorated Commdr. Order British Empire. Fellow Royal Coll. Physicians London, Royal Coll. Physicians Edinburgh, Royal Coll. Physicians Ireland (Corrigan Gold medal 1990, J. Geery Ferguson Meml. Lecture gold medal 1997); mem. Renal Assn. (hon., pres. 1983-86), Brit. Transplantation Soc. (hon.), European Dialysis and Transplant Assn. (hon.), European Dialysis and Transplant Nurses Assn. (hon.), U.K. Unrelated Live Transplant Regulatory Authority. Presbyterian. Avocations: gardening, antique collecting. Home: 14 Osborne Gardens, Belfast BT9 6LE, Northern Ireland Office: Queens U, Hosp Whitla Med Bldg Rm 331, Belfast BT7 7AB, Northern Ireland

MCGERVEY, TERESA ANN, technical information specialist; b. Pitts., Sept. 27, 1964; d. Walter James and Janet Sarah (Donehue) McG. BS in Geology, Calif. U. Pa., 1986, MS in Earth Sci., 1988; MLS, Cath. U. Am., 1998. Phys. sci. technician U.S. Geol. Survey, Reston, Va., 1989-90; editor, indexer Am. Geol. Inst., Alexandria, Va., 1990-91; cartographer Def. Mapping Agy., Reston, 1991-93; tech. info. specialist Nat. Tech. Info. Svc., Springfield, Va., 1993-2000, Dept. of Def., Arlington, Va., 2000—; intern Dept. Mineral Scis., Smithsonian Instn., summers 1985, 1986. Mem. ALA, AAUW, Am. Soc. for Info. Sci., Spl. Librs. Assn., Geosci. Info. Soc.

MCGIBBON, IAN CALLUM, historian, editor, educator; b. Dannevirke, New Zealand, Dec. 7, 1947; s. Ian and Doreen Ethel (Hunt) McG.; m. Helen Mary Sherriff, July 8, 1972 (div. 1987); children: Kirstin Fiona, Morag Anna, Lorna Margaret; m. Sonia Liclican Ochoa, Mar. 28, 1998. BA, Victoria U., Wellington, New Zealand, 1968, BA with honors, 1969, MA, 1971, LittD, 1994. Def. historian Ministry of Def., Wellington, 1971-79; sr. historian Ministry of Culture and Heritage, Wellington, 1979—; assoc. lectr. in history Massey U., Palmerston North, New Zealand, 1990—. Author: Blue-water Rationale, The Naval Defence of New Zealand 1914-1942, 1981, The Path to Gallipoli, Defending New Zealand 1840-1915, 1991, New Zealand and the Korean War, Vol. I Politics and Diplomacy, 1992, Vol. II Combat Operations, 1996; contbr. articles to jours. in field; editor: Undiplomatic Dialogue, Letters Between Carl Berendsen and Alister McIntosh 1943-52, 1993, Unofficial Channels, Letters Between Alister McIntosh and Foss Shanahan, George Laking and Frank Corner, 1946-66, 1999, Oxford Companion to New Zealand Military History, 2000; mng. editor New Zealand Internat. Rev., Wellington, 1981—, New Zealand Hist Atlas, Wellington, 1990-97. Mem. standing com. New Zealand Inst. Internat. Affairs, Wellington, 1981—, hon. v.p., 1995—, mem. rsch. com., 1985—. Apptd. officer New Zealand Order of Merit, 1997. Mem. New Zealand Hist. Assn. Avocations: cricket, golf, jogging, reading, travel. Home: 26 Olivia Cres, Tawa Wellington New Zealand Office: Ministry Culture/Heritage, Box 5364, Wellington New Zealand

MCGINN, JAMES THOMAS, writer, producer; b. Evanston, Ill., Feb. 19, 1932; s. John Thomas and Mary (Kidney) McG.; m. Patricia Kay McMurtry, Apr. 4, 1959; children: Shannon, Michael, Sean. BS, Northwestern U., 1953, MA, 1958. Floor dir. Sta. WGN-TV, 1956-57; writer, dir. Ency. Britannica Films, Wilmette, Ill., 1957-58; pres. McGinn TV Prodns., Chgo., 1958-62; exec. producer Sta. WBBM-TV, Chgo., 1962-63; gen. program exec. Young and Rubicam, N.Y.C., 1963-69; dir. programming Bristol-Myers Squibb Co., Pacific Palisades, Calif., 1969-94; pres. Palisades Prodns., Inc., Pacific Palisades, Calif., 1994—; bd. dirs. Paulist Prodns., Pacific Palisades; faculty U. So. Calif. Sch. Cinema & TV. Producer: In Search Of...; writer: (TV film) Nadia, 1984, (TV spl.) Perry Como's Christmas in San Antonio, (TV series) Julia, Capital Cities Family Spls., Insight; playwright: Before You Go, The Singing Weatherman, Star Billing (with Alex Cohen), Viola: Seven Days in Selma, Grampa. Mem. Writers Guild Am., Dramatists Guild. Office: Palisades Prodns Inc 15219 W Sunset Blvd Ste 202 Pacific Palisades CA 90272-3607

MCGINN, RICHARD A., telecommunications company executive. Bachelor's degree, Grinnell Coll. With Ill. Bell, 1969; exec. positions internat. and computer sys. groups AT&T, 1978, CEO network sys.; CEO, pres. Lucent Techs., chmn., CEO; bd. dirs. Lucent Techs., Oracle Corp., Am. Express Co. Bus. Coun. Office: Lucent Technologies 600 Mountain Ave Murray Hill NJ 07974-2008

MCGINNIS, MICHAEL BOYD, chemistry educator; b. Balt., Mar. 3, 1970; s. Phyllis Lee (Miller) McG.; m. Maryann Lampert, Oct. 23, 1993. BS in Chem., Elizabethtown Coll., 1992; PhD in Organic Chemistry, U. Tenn., 1997. Postdoctoral rsch. assoc. U. Tenn., Knoxville, 1997, instr. chemistry, 1997; asst. prof. chemistry Georgia Coll. & State U., Milledgeville, 1997—. Contbr. to profl. jours. Instr. ARC, Milledgeville, 1997—; Faculty devel. workshop Ga. Coll. & State U., 1998; dir. State Sci. Bowl; active in various science fairs; bd. dirs. Ga. Jr. Acad. of Sci. Hoechst Celanese Sci. Outreach award Hoechst Celanese Corp., 1996. Mem. Am. Chem. Soc. (pub. outreach adv.), Younger Chemists Com., Sigma Xi. Democrat. Methodist. Avocations: whitewater canoeing, kayaking. Home: 1307 Clack Rd Madison GA 30650-4812 Office: Ga Coll and State U Dept Chemistry and Physics Milledgeville GA 31061

MCGINNIS, THOMAS MICHAEL, lawyer; b. Royal Oak, Mich., July 13, 1954; s. Donald Edward Sr. and Maryjane Carney (Jex) McG.; m. Tracy Chris, Mar. 4, 1993. BA, Regis U., 1976; JD, Thomas M. Cooley Sch. Law, 1980. Bar: Mich. 1981, U.S. Dist. Ct. (ea. dist.) Mich. 1981, U.S. Ct. Appeals 1984. Assoc. Wilson, Portnoy & Leader, 1980-83; pvt. practice Troy, Mich., 1983—; chairperson Lawyer Referral Svc., Pontiac, Mich., 1985-86. Mem. Soc. Irish/Am. Lawyers, Oakland County Bar (criminal law com. 1998-99, 99-2000). Avocations: water skiing, snow skiing, guitar. Office: 802 E Big Beaver Rd Troy MI 48083-1404

MCGLAMRY, MAX REGINALD, lawyer; b. Wilcox County, Ga., Sept. 12, 1928; s. Edgar Lee and Allie Bea (Faircloth) McG.; m. Jean Louise Hilyer, Dec. 28, 1950; children: Sharon Kay McGlamry Hendrix, Michael Lee. BS, Auburn U., 1948; LLB cum laude, Mercer U., 1952, JD cum laude, 1970. Bar: Ga. 1953, U.S. Dist. Ct. (mid. dist.) Ga. 1954, U.S. Ct. Appeals (5th cir.) 1964, U.S. Supreme Ct. 1972, U.S. Ct. Appeals (11th cir.) 1981, U.S. Ct. Appeals (4th cir.) 1985, U.S. Dist. Ct. (no. dist.) Calif. 1988, U.S. Dist. Ct. (no. dist.) Ga. 1989. Pvt. practice Columbus, Ga., 1953-64; from ptnr. to officer Swift, Pease, Davidson & Chapman (name changed to Page, Scrantom, Harris, McGlamry & Chapman, P.C.), Columbus, 1964-85; ptnr. Pope, Kellogg, McGlamry, Kilpatrick & Morrison, Columbus, 1985-90, Pope, McGlamry, Kilpatrick & Morrison, LLP, Columbus, 1990—. Mem. exec. com. Muscogee County Dem. Orgn., Columbus, 1956-60; bd. dirs. Columbus Jr. C. of C. Ens. USN, 1948-49. Am. Coll. Trust & Estate Counsel fellow, 1973, Lawyers Found. Ga. fellow, 1983. Mem. ABA, ATLA, State Bar Ga., Ga. Trial Lawyers Assn., Assn. U.S. Army, Ga. Golfers Sr. Assn., Metro Columbus Urban League, Inc., Columbus Lawyers Club (pres. 1964-65), Lions (Columbus chpt. pres. 1967-68), Chattahoochee River Club, Green Island Country Club, Phi Kappa Phi, Alpha Epsilon Delta, Phi Alpha Delta, Pi Kappa Alpha. Democrat. Methodist. Avocations: golf, fishing. Home: 6941 Wethersfield Rd Columbus GA 31904-3317 Office: Pope McGlamry Kilpatrick & Morrison LLP PO Box 2128 2d Fl 318 11th St Columbus GA 31902-2128

MCGLAUGHLIN, THOMAS HOWARD, publisher, retired naval officer, marine surveyor; b. Cin., Jan. 12, 1928; s. George Godden and Cordelia (Herrlinger) McG.; m. Moana Maharam-Stone, Jan. 4, 1984. BS in Elec. Engring., U.S. Naval Acad., 1950. Lic. master mariner. Commd. ensign U.S. Navy, 1950, advanced through grades to capt., 1970; White House aide to Pres. John F. Kennedy, Washington, 1960-63; exec. officer USS Prichett, Long Beach, Calif., 1963-65; comdg. officer USS Maddox, Long Beach, 1965-67; exec. officer USS Boston, Boston, 1967-70; chief naval ops. Comdr.-in-Chief, Pacific, Honolulu, 1970-74; chief of staff Mil. Sealift Command, N.Y.C., 1974-79; ret. U.S. Navy, 1979; pres. Falmouth Press, Honolulu, 1983—; marine surveyor R.W. Dickieson Internat., Inc., Honolulu, 1982—; master M.V. Rella Mae, Honolulu, 1981-90, Royal Taipan, Cebu, Philippines, 1990. Hon. police chief Boston Police Dept., 1969. Decorated Bronze Star, Navy commendation medal with combat "v", combat action ribbon, Vietnamese Disting. Svc. order; recipient medal for Outstanding Svc., Am. Legion, Pitts., 1942. Mem. Nat. Def. Transp. Assn., VFW (life), U.S. Naval Acad. Alumni Assn. (life), The Retired Officers Assn. Republican. Presbyterian. Avocations: flying, scuba diving, tennis, golf. Home: 118 Kiionioni Pl Honolulu HI 96816-4248 Office: RW Dickieson Internat Inc 46-208 Kahuhipa St Kaneohe HI 96744-3905

MCGLUE, ROBERT DAVID, foundation administrator; b. Sale, Cheshire, U.K., Feb. 22, 1947; s. Ernest Victor and Edith (Rangeley) McG.; m. Mary Hazel Cannon, Apr. 1, 1972; children: Hannah Mary, Adam Timothy. BA, Emmanuel Coll., Cambridge, 1968; MA, U. Sussex, Eng., 1969, PhD in Econs., 1971. Staff mem. Diplomatic Svc., London, 1971-73, Cabinet Office, London, 1973-75, Dept. Energy, London, 1975-80; adj. to dir. gen. for energy European Commn., Brussels, 1980-84, head energy systems analysis group, 1984-87, adviser on collaborative rsch. and internat. competitiveness, 1987-89, head divsn. financing instruments and policy, 1989-94; vice chmn. European Investment Fund, Luxembourg, 1994—. Co-author: Energy 2000; contbr. articles to profl. jours. Avocations: playing chamber music, tennis, skiing. Office: European Investment Fund, 43 Ave J F Kennedy, L-2968 Luxembourg Luxembourg

MCGLYNN, WILLIAM CHARLES, brokerage house executive; b. Hazelton, Pa., Apr. 4, 1944; s. William Charles and Mary McG.; m. Phyllis Marie Fotia, May 28, 1967; children: William Jason, Devon Laura, Robert Ryan, Kirsten Ann. BS in Bus. Mgmt., Farleigh Dickenson U., Madison, N.J., 1968, postgrad. studies in Fin. and Econs., 1968-69. V.p. William D. Witter, Inc., N.Y.C., 1970-75; v.p. Dillon Read & Co., Inc., N.Y.C., 1975-79, Tucker Anthony R. L. Day, N.Y.C., 1979-81; mng. dir. L.F. Rothschild, Inc., N.Y.C., 1982-88, Bear, Stearns & Co., Inc., N.Y.C., 1988—. Fund raiser Wall St. Charity Fund, N.Y.C., 1971-75; benefit com. Cath. Charities Home Bur., N.Y.C., 1980-90; trustee, exec. com. mem. Oak Knoll Sch. Holy Child, Summit, N.J., 1989—; fund raiser, mem. Fathers and Friends Delbarton Sch., 1993-98, Morristown Beard Sch. Assn., 1998-99; advisor, mem. Oak Knoll Fathers Bd., 1989—. Republican. Roman Catholic. Avocations: skiing, tennis, boating, reading. Home: 151 Deer Run

Watchung NJ 07060-6255 Office: Bear Sterns & Co Inc 245 Park Ave New York NY 10167-0002

MCGONIGLE, JOHN LEO, JR., civil engineer; b. Pitts., May 2, 1921; s. John L. and Marie (Cannon) McG.; m. Mary Frances McInerney, Oct. 10, 1953; children: Loretta, John III, Maureen, Charles, Thomas, Robert. BS in Civil Engring., Lehigh U., 1942. Registered profl. engr. N.Y., Pa., Conn. Field engr. Bethlehem Steel Corp., N.Y., Boston, 1947-50, resident engr., 1950-57; constrn. mgr. Bethlehem Steel Corp., San Francisco, 1957-67; mgr. estimates Bethlehem Steel Corp., Bethlehem, Pa., 1967-78; project mgr. C. F. Braun, Berkeley Heights, N.J., 1978-83; prin. resident engr. Berger-Lehman Assocs., Rye, N.Y., 1983-93; self-employed project mgmt. cons., 1993—; com. mem. Am. Inst. Steel Constrn., Pitts., 1970-73. Mem. Hanover Twp. (Pa.) Planning Commn. Fellow ACSE (life); mem. Lehigh U. Alumni Assn. (pres. San Francisco 1960). Republican. Roman Catholic. Achievements include resident engineer for high level bridges over Passaic River, N.J., Rappahonnock, Va., Missouri River, Annisquam River, Mass., Raritan River, N.J., and Newark Bay; also high rise buildings in Detroit, N.Y., S.I. Ferry Terminal, John Hancock, Boston.

MCGOVERN, DAVID CARR, lawyer; b. Taunton, Mass., Sept. 3, 1946; s. James Edward and Dorothea Elizabeth (Carr) McG.; m. Pamela Lee Compton, Mar. 22, 1975; 1 child, William David. AB, Coll. of Holy Cross, 1968; JD, U. Va., 1979. Bar: Calif. 1980, U.S. Dist. Ct. (ctrl. dist.) Calif. 1980, U.S. Dist. Ct. (so. dist.) Calif. 1981. Assoc. Rosenfeld, Meyer and Susman, Beverly Hills, Calif., 1979-81; ptnr. Engstrom, Lipscomb and Lack, L.A., 1981-90, Haight, Brown and Bonesteel LLP, Santa Monica, Calif., 1990—. Bd. dirs. United Cerebral Palsy/Spastic Children's Found., L.A., 1985-94; men's com. John Tracy Clinic Women's Aux., L.A., 1988-94; founding mem. Friends of John Tracy Clinic, L.A., 1996—. Mem. ABA, State Bar Calif., Aviation Ins. Assn. Avocations: running, reading, coaching youth sports, travel. Fax: (310) 829-5117. E-mail: mcgoverd@hbblaw.com. Home: 7812 W 80th St Playa del Rey CA 90293-7905 Office: Haight Brown and Bonesteel LLP 1620 26th St Ste 4000N Santa Monica CA 90404-4013

MCGOVERN, JAMES, author. BA in Journalism and Polit. Sci., U. Minn., postgrad. Radio talk show host "Let's Talk Turkey" WDGY, Mpls., 1950; news dir., TV news anchor, newscaster, reporter WDGY, KGTV, KSTP, KMSP-TV, WISN-CBS, SUN Newspapers; local news feed corres. NBC, CBS, ABC; instr. journalism Lakewood Jr. Coll., 1967-68; polit. advisor, speechwriter, nat. presdl. campaign advance man.; former speechwriter, news, pub. rels., mktg., video prodr. and orgnl. cons. various Minn. businesses and CEO's, including 3M, Honeywell, Control Data, others; trumpeter and leader Jim McGovern Swing Band. Writer, prodr., narrator PURSUIT series of tv documentarie; author 3 dramatic plays, 2 novels; contbr. articles to profl. jours. Mem. Twin Cities Musicians Union (local 30-73); hon. mem. Chinese (Nationalist) Air Force. With USAF. Decorated DFC with one oak leaf cluster, Air Medal with 2 oak leaf clusters; winner Nat. Headliners award for best pub.affairs documentary in U.S., 1963; recipient Award of Merit, Minn. Coll. Radio Network for outstanding leadership in radio news reporting through the "Behind the Parade" radio series on KSTP, 1960. Mem. ASCAP (assoc.), Am. Soc. Composers, Artists and Pubs., DFC Soc. (charter), 14th AAF Flying Tigers, Hump Pilots Assn., U. Minn. Alumni Assn., Irish Nat. Caucus (charter). Home: 777 Hamline Ave N Apt 709 Saint Paul MN 55104-1341

MCGOVERN, JOHN HUGH, urologist, educator; b. Bayonne, N.J., Dec. 18, 1924; s. Patrick and Mary (McGovern) McG.; m. Mary Alice Cavazos, Aug. 2, 1980; children by previous marriage: John Hugh, Robert, Ward, Raymond. BS, Columbia U., 1947; MD, SUNY, Bklyn., 1952. Diplomate Am. Bd. Urology. Rotating intern Bklyn. Hosp., 1952-53; asst. resident in surgery Bklyn. VA Hosp., 1953-54; with urology N.Y. Hosp., 1954-56; exchange surg. registrar West London Hosp., Eng., 1956-57; resident in urol. surgery N.Y. Hosp., 1957-58, rsch. asst. pediatric urology, 1958-59, asst. attending surgeon James Buchanan Brady Found., 1959-61, assoc. attending surgeon, 1961-66, attending surgeon, 1966—; asst. in surgery Med. Coll. Cornell U., 1957-59, asst. prof. clin. surgery, 1959-64, assoc. prof., 1964-72, prof., 1972—; attending staff in urology Lenox Hill Hosp., 1969—, in-charge urology, 1969-83; cons. urology Rockefeller Inst., St. Vincent's Hosp., Mercy Hosp., Phelps Meml. Hosp.; chmn. coun. on urology Nat. Kidney Found., 1982. Contbr. articles to profl. jours., chpts. to books. Lt. M.C., U.S. Army, 1942-45. Recipient Conatvoy mos medal Chile, 1975, Tree of Life award Nat. Kidney Found., 1990; named Huesped de Honor, Mimunicipalidad de Guayaquil (Ecuador), 1976; award in urology Kidney Found. N.Y., 1977, Sir Peter Freyer medal, Galway, Ireland, 1980. Fellow N.Y. Acad. Medicine (exec. com. urol. sect. 1968-72, chmn. 1972), ACS (credentials com. 1991—), Am. Acad. Pediatrics (urological); mem. AMA (diagnostic and therapeutic tech. assessment bd. 1991—, diagnostic and therepautic tech. assessment program panel 1991, DATTA panel 1991—), Am. Assn. G.U. Surgeons, N.Y. State Med. Soc. (chmn. urol. sect. 1975), Med. Soc. County N.Y., Am. Urol. Assn. (hon. mem. 1994—, pres.-elect 1988-89, pres. 1989-90, pres. N.Y. sect. 1979-80, N.Y. rep. exec. com. 1982-87, socioecons. com. 1987, chmn. fiscal affairs rev. com. 1987, chmn. awards com. 1990, time and place com. 1989-90), N.Y. State Urol. Soc. (exec. com. 1982—), Pan Pacific Surg. Assn., Am. Assn. Clin. Urologists (pres.-elect 1987-88, pres. 1988-89, bd. dirs. 1984—, mem. interpersonal rels. com. 1975—, govt. rels. com. 1989-90, program com. 1989-90, nominating com. 1989-90), Assn. Am. Physicians and Surgeons, Pan Am. Med. Assn. (diplomate 1981—), Urol. Investigators Forum, Soc. Pediatric Urology (pres.-elect 1979-80, pres. 1980-81), Am. Trauma Soc., Kidney Found. (med. adv. bd. N.Y. sect., trustee, 1979) Société Internationale d'Urologie (exec. com. U.S. sect.); hon. mem. Sociedad Peruana de Urologia, Sociedad Guatemale de Urologia, Sociedad Ecuadorians de Urologia, Royal Coll. Surgeons (London). Home and Office: 969 Park Ave Apt 5B New York NY 10028-0322

MCGOVERN, LIGAYA LINDIO, sociology and women's studies educator; b. Daraga, Albay, The Philippines, May 29, 1947; d. Teofilo and Monica Macasinag Lindio; m. James Ignatius McGovern, Apr. 26, 1980; 1 child, Paul Emmanuel. BA in Liberal Edn., St. Scholastica's Coll., Manila, 1969; MS in Sociology, Asian Social Inst., Manila, 1979; PhD in Sociology, Loyola U., Chgo., 1992. Mem. faculty St. Scholastica's Coll., 1969-75; vis. asst. prof. sociology Loyola U., 1991-92, Ferris State U., Big Rapids, Mich., 1993-94; assoc. prof. sociology Ind. U., Kokomo, 1994—, dir. women's studies, 1994-96, 98—; part-time faculty mem. in sociology Assumption Coll., Makati, The Philippines, 1978-79, Lewis U., Romeoville, Ill., 1990-91, Dominican U., River Forest, Ill., 1989-92; tchg. fellow Loyola U., 1990. Author: Filipino Peasant Women: Exploitation and Resistance, 1997; contbr. articles to profl. jours. Mem., co-founder GABRIELA Networ, Chgo. Rsch. grantee Fund for Advancement of Discipline/NSF, 1999, Ind. U., 1994, 95. Mem. Am. Sociol. Assn., Midwest Sociol. Soc. (mem. com. for acad. responsibility and freedom 1997—), Midwest Sociologists for Women and Soc., Soc. for Study of Social Problems. Avocations: reading, writing, swimming, concerts, dancing. Fax: (765) 455-9500. E-mail: LMcGover@iuk.edu. Office: Ind U 2300 S Washington PO Box 9003 Kokomo IN 46904-9003

MCGOVERN, THERESA M., law educator; b. Manhattan, N.Y., May 17, 1961; d. Lawrence Thomas and Ann Theresa (Walsh) McG. BA summa cum laude, SUNY, Albany, 1983; JD, Georgetown U., 1986. Atty. N.Y. Legal Aid Soc., 1986-87, Legal Aid Bur. Md., 1987-88, MFY Legal Svcs., Inc., 1988-89; founder, exec. dir. The HIV Law Project, Inc., 1989-99; faculty Columbia U. Sch. Pub. Health, 1999—; adj. prof. Rutgers U. Sch. Law, 1993-94, CUNY Law Sch., 1995—, Seton Hall Sch. Law, 1998; ind. judicial screening panel N.Y. State Supreme Ct., 1999; tech. adv. bd. perinatal transmision HIV U.S. Conf. Mayors, 1996—; adv. bd. Columbia U. HIV Ctr. for Clin. and Behavioral Studies, 1994—, Beth Israel Hosp., 1992-94; cons. Nat. Task Force on AIDS Drug Devel., 1994-96, Ctrs. for Disease Control-External Review Process; presenter in field. Contbr. articles to profl. jours. Open Soc. Inst. George Soros Found. fellow, 1999—; recipient Michael Hirsch award, 1992, History Maker award Bklyn. Hist. Soc., 1993, Libery award Lambda Legal Def. and Edn. Fund, 1993, Woman of Influence Cmty. Svc. Recognition award YWCA, 1994, Helen Hunt Neighborhood Leadership award N.Y. Women Found., 1995, Commr. FDA award, 1996, Pub. Interest award N.Y. State Bar Assn., 1996.

MCGOWAN, HAROLD, real estate developer, investor, scientist, author, philanthropist; b. Weehawken, N.J., June 23, 1909; s. Sylvester and Grace (Kalbfleish) McG.; m. Anne Cecelia McTiernan, Jan. 15, 1938; children—Linda Anne, Harold Charles, Janice Marie. Ed., Bklyn. Poly. U., Pratt Inst., N.Y. U.; student, N.Y. Tech.; ed., Hubbard U. (Eng.); D.Sc., Coll. Fla. Chmn. bd. Atomic Rsch. Inc.; pres. Harold McGowan Builders; owner, developer Central Islip Shopping Center, Central Islip Indsl. Center; developer, builder Brinsley Gardens, Rolling Green, Slater Park, Clover Green, Maple Acres, Wheeler Acres; owner-donor Little League Baseball Pks., 1950—. Sculptures include: Bless Them; Victory, Eternity, Love and Hate, Triumph; author: Green Flight, (originator) The Thoughtron Theory of Life and Matter, Race with Death across the Sahara, The Incorrigibles, The Frigid Trap, The Shah's Swiss Secret, Another World for Christmas, The Spirit of Christmas in Words and Sculpture, The Making of a Universalist, The Journeyman, $800,000 for Love, Beyond the Visible, Shock after Shock, Christmas Stories, Short Stories, Born Again, You Are Forever, Black Shroud Over Bagdad, The Gold Mine; mural Back to Creation; holder U.S. patent to form one-piece plywood corner units, U.S. patent apparatus for forming one-piece plywood corner units. Hwy. commr., Suffolk County; chmn. Recreation & Parks-Islip; past dir. Suffolk County Girl Scouts; land donor St. John of God R.C. Ch., The Episcopal Ch. of the Messiah, Ctrl. Islip Sch. Dist. Recipient Winston Churchill Medal of Wisdom, 1986, Wisdom Hall of Fame, Beverly Hills, Calif., 1970; Churchill fellow, 1989. Mem. AAAS, IEEE, Explorers Club, Mensa Internat. Avocations: sculpture, art, philanthropy. Address: 28 2nd Ave Central Islip NY 11722-3012

MCGOWAN, IAN DAVID, publishing educator, arts consultant; b. Glasgow, Scotland; s. John and Catherine (Ferguson) McG. BA, Oxford U., Eng., 1970; MA, Oxford U., 1974; PhD, Stirling U., 1981. Domus scholar Pembroke Coll., Oxford, 1968-70, Robert Browning sr. scholar, 1971-73; tutor English lit. Oxford, 1970-73; lectr., sr. lectr. English studies U. Stirling, 1973—, postgrad course dir. pub. studies, 1985—, dir. Ctr. Pub. Studies, 1988—; vis. prof. U. Malaya, Malaysia, 1988; dir. Internat. Assn. Pub. Edn., 1991-98; vis. lectr. Eng., 1988—, Malaysia, 1988, Australia, 1990, Japan, 1994, 99, China, 1997, 98, 99; exec. chmn. Stirling Univ. Press., 1986-90; adviser in field, expert assessor. Author: Charles Dickens: Little Dorrit, 1984; author, editor: The Restoration and Eighteenth Century, 1989, Principles and Practice in Book Publishing, 1999; editor: Journey to the Hebrides, 1996; contbr. articles to profl. jours. and reference works. Mem. exec. com. Book Trust Scotland, Glasgow, Edinburgh, 1986-93; apptd. mem., chmn. grants to pub. panel Scottish Arts Coun., Edinburgh, 1985-97, chmn. lit com., 1989-97; trustee Shepley Shepley Trust, Edinburgh, 1993-96, Arts Trust Scotland, 1996-97; mem. Scottish Arts Coun., 1993-97. Recipient E.C. Erasmus award European Cmty., Stirling, 1989-90; pub. scholar Paul Hamlyn Found., Eng., 1992-96. Mem. Assn. Learned and Profl. Soc. Pub. (elected), Boswell Soc. (pres. 1996-97), Internat. Writer's Conf. (chmn. 1990, 91, 93). Office: Ctr Pub Studies, U Stirling, Stirling FK9 4LA, Scotland

MCGOWAN, IAN DUNCAN, librarian; b. Liverpool, Eng., Sept. 19, 1945; s. Alexander and Dora (Sharp) McG.; m. Elizabeth Ann Weir, Oct. 30, 1971; children: Catherine, Margaret. BA, Exeter Coll., Oxford, 1967. FRSA, 1999. Asst. keeper Nat. Libr. of Scotland, Edinburgh, 1971-78, keeper, 1978-88, sec. of libr., 1978-90, libr., 1990—. Chmn. U.K. Nat. Preservation Adv. Com., 1995-96; chmn. Britain-Russia Ctr., Scotland, 1999—. Mem. Scottish Libr. Assn. (v.p. 1996-97, pres. 1998). Office: Nat Libr of Scotland, George IV Bridge, Edinburgh EH1 1EW, Scotland

MCGOWAN, JOAN YUHAS, development researcher; b. Trenton, N.J., Feb. 13, 1955; d. Bernard Joseph and Estelle (Gray) Yuhas; children: Matthew Sheehan, Allison Joo Ok. BA summa cum laude, Trenton State Coll., 1977. Cert. tchr., N.J. Tchr. Blessed Sacrament Sch., Trenton, 1977; intake officer Mercer County Juvenile Ct, Trenton, 1978-82; rsch. dir. Audits and Surveys, Princeton, N.J., 1982-85; project dir. The Gallup Orgn., Princeton, 1985-86, Hase/Schannen Rsch. Assocs., Princeton, 1986; devel. researcher Coll. NJ, 1986—; guest lectr., Thomas Jefferson U., Rutgers U., Helene Fuld Sch. Nursing; guest speaker local television programs. Author: Waiting: The Hopes and Frustrations of a Childless Couple, 1983; contbr. articles to various publs. Pres. Resolve, Inc., Phila, 1982; mem. Holt Internat. Children's Svcs., Trenton, 1984-85, Incarnation Altar Rosary Soc., Trenton, 1988—, Holy Name Soc., Trenton, 1989—; treas, area contact, Homeward Bound, Inc., 1996—. Recipient Think and Suggest award State of N.J., 1977, Meritorious award Trenton State Coll., 1989. Mem. Am. Fedn. Tchrs., Assn. Profl. Rschrs. for Advancement, New Eng. Devel. Rschrs. Assn., Operation Scarlet (assoc. mem. 1994—), Villa Park Civic Assn. Democrat. Roman Catholic. Avocations: reading, family activities, rescue dogs, piano, music. Home: 941 Lyndale Ave Trenton NJ 08629-2409 Office: The Coll NJ PO Box 7718 Ewing NJ 08628-0718

MCGOWAN, PETER ALAN, mechanical engineer, consultant; b. Adelaide, Australia, Feb. 25, 1955; s. Henry alan Whitworth and Adrienne Ethyl (Twyford) McG.; m. Loree Margaret Arthur, Dec. 23, 1979. B of Mech. Engring. with honors, U. Melbourne, 1976, PhD, 1988; grad. diploma in Material Engring., Monash U., Melbourne, 1990. Chartered mech. engr., materials engr. Design engr. Imperial Chemicals Industries Australia Engring., Melbourne, 1977-82; plant engr. Imperial Chems. Industries Australian OPs., Sydney, 1982; design engr. Imperial Chems. Industries Australia Engring., Melbourne, 1985-86; sr. engr. ICI Australia Engring. (now Orica Engring.), Melbourne, 1986-91, engring. cons., 1991-96, sr. cons., 1996—; part-time lectr. U. Melbourne, 1986-2000, Monash U., Melbourne, 1995-97, U. Tech., Melbourne, 1985-87; chmn. of standards Australia; com. on advanced pressure vessel design, 1997—. Contbr. articles and papers to profl. jours.; inventor in field. Fellow Inst. Engring. Australia; mem. Inst. Metals and Materials Australia. Seventh-Day Adventist. Avocations: musical arranging, ancient history, cycling, mathematics, trumpet. Office: Orica Engring, 1 Nicholson St, 3000 Melbourne Victoria, Australia

MCGOWAN, THOMAS RANDOLPH, retired religious organization executive; b. Balt., Apr. 19, 1926; s. Robert and Mary (Miller) McG.; m. Bernice A. Bernard, May 20, 1967 (dec. Nov. 1981); children: Howard, James, Terry; m. Roedean Olivia Oden, Feb. 9, 1985; children: Karen White, Kevin, Kurt. AA, Oakland Jr. Coll., 1964; postgrad., San Francisco State Coll., 1964-68; BS, U. Md., 1978. Lt. security police Oakland (Calif.) Army Base, 1955-60; chief motor pool San Francisco Procurement Agy., Oakland, 1960-64, contract specialist, 1964-68; contract specialist Harry Diamond Labs., Washington, 1968-79, br. chief procurement divsn., 1972-79; chief procurement directorate Yuma (Ariz.) Proving Ground, 1979-82; dir. ecumenism Roman Cath. Diocese of Oakland, 1983—; dir. African Am. Cath. Pastoral Ctr., Diocese of Oakland, 1991—. Convenor Interreligious Coun. of Oakland, 1988—; trustee Greater Oakland Interfaith Network, 1989-92; mem. East Oakland Renewal Task Force, 1990—; bd. dir. Columbia (Md.) Found., 1972-74, chmn., 1975-79; div. Bd. Cons., Graymoor, N.Y., 1990—; bd. dirs. Thea Bowman Manor, Oakland, 1989—, St. Mary's Ctr. With U.S. Army, 1944-46. Mem. Knights of Peter Claver, Rotary. Democrat. Avocations: tennis, woodworking. Home: 139 Pinto Dr Vallejo CA 94591-8451

MCGRAIL, JEANE KATHRYN, artist, educator, poet, curator; b. Mpls., May 1, 1947; d. Robert Vern and Mary Virginia (Kees) McGrail. BS, U. Wis.-River Falls, 1970; MFA, Cranbrook Acad. Art, 1972; postgrad., Sch. of Art Inst. of Chgo., 1985, Ill. Inst. Tech., 1993. Group exhbns. include Saginaw Art Mus., Mich., 1972, Met. Mus. Art, Miami, Fla., 1974, Lowe Mus. Art, Coral Gables, Fla., 1974, 76, Miller Galleries, Coconut Grove, Fla., 1978, 80, Cicchinelli Gallery, N.Y.C., 1980-82, Harper Coll., 1984, Contemporary Art Ctr. Arlington, Arlington Heights, Ill., 1984, 85, 86, 94, Evanston Art Ctr., 1985, South Shore Cultural Ctr., Chgo., 1990, N.A.M.E. Gallery, 1990, Artemisia Gallery, Chgo., 1991, 92, 93, 94, North Lakeside Art Ctr., Chgo., 1991, 94, 95, Ceres Gallery, N.Y.C., 1992, Harper Coll., Ill., 1993, Environ. Concerns, Chgo., 1993, North Pk. Coll., Chgo., 1993, Franklin Square Gallery, Chgo., 1994, 95, 96, Space 900 Gallery, Chgo., 1994, 95, 96, 97, 98, 99, Chuck Levitan Gallery, N.Y.C., 1995, Riverwest Art Ctr., Milw., 1995, Nat. Mus. Women in the Arts, Washington, 1996, Gallery 1040, 1997—, "Red", Chgo., 1998, Oakton Coll. Gallery, Ill., 1999—, Women's Works, Woodstock, Ill., 1999, "Paint It Sliver", ARC Gallery, Chgo., 1999, Past/Present, Chgo., 1999, "Blue", Northeastern Ill. U.,Chgo., 2000, Then and Now, Chgo., 1999, Norris Cultural Ctr., St. Charles, Ill., 1999, others; represented in permanent collections at Chgo. Mus. Sci. and Industry, U. Chgo., Mus. Photography, Chgo., Miami-Dade Pub. Libr., U. Wis.-River Falls, MacGregor Found., Printmakers Workshop, N.Y.C., Norman R. Eppnik Art Gallery Emporia State U., Kans., 2000, Mini Print Internat. Exhbn., Binghamton, N.Y., 2000, Yale U. Med. Libr., 2000, Columbia U. Med. Ctr., 2000, others; solo exhbns. include Gallery at the Commons, Chgo., 1982, Truman Coll. Gallery, Chgo., 1991, C.G. Jung Inst., Evanston, Ill., 1992, Carlson Tower Gallery, Chgo., 1994; pub. "Mosaic", 1992, The Best of Printmaking, 1997; contbr. publs. to profl. jours. Cranbrook Acad. Art scholar, 1971; CAAP grantee Dept. Cultural Affairs City Chgo, 1992; recipient Poster Competition award Vizcaya Mus., 1974; Print award Auction WPBT, 1979. Mem. Coll. Art Assn., Chgo. Women's Caucus for Art (bd. dirs. 1992-95, sec.), Chgo. Artists Coalition. Democrat. E-mail: jeanemcgrailstudios@mediaone.net. Studio: 1040 W Huron St LL5 Chicago IL 60622-6591

MCGRATH, EDWARD LEO, investment banker; b. N.Y.C., Apr. 5, 1947; s. Edward Philip McGrath and Mary M. (Kiley) Dennehy; m. Margaret M. Hart, Dec. 16, 1989; children: Philip B., Theresa F. BS, Fordham U., 1969; MBA, Columbia U., 1974. Chartered fin. analyst. With U.S. Peace Corps, Managua, Nicaragua, 1971-73; sr. fin. analyst Mellon Bank, N.A., Pitts., 1974-75; comptroller Mellon Bank, N.A., Tokyo, 1975-78; dep. gen. mgr. Mellon Bank, N.A., Hong Kong, 1978-80; mgr. internat. credit divsn. Mellon Bank, N.A., Pitts., 1980-82, chief internat. fin. officer, 1982-85; country mgr. Mellon Bank, N.A., Mexico City, 1985-89, comptroller trust dept., 1990-91; mgr. internat. mktg. and planning global asset mgmt. Mellon Bank, N.A., Pitts., 1991-93, dir. internat. planning, 1994-95, mgr. wholesale banking-Can., 1995-98; pres. Can. Mellon Asset Mgmt., 1996-98, group head, metals, 1999—; panelist ann. gen. meeting Investment Co. Inst., 1995. Author: Offshore Assembly Operations in Nicaragua, 1973. Dir., mem. fin. com. Braddock Gen. Hosp., Pitts., 1991-95; dir. Planning Forum, Pitts., 1993-95; dir., mem. exec. and fin. coms. Am. Brit. Cowdray Hosp., Mexico City, 1987-89. Mem. Assn. for Investment Mgmt. and Rsch., The Nat. Club Toronto, Princeton Club N.Y., Duquane Club Pitts., Am. Club Hong Kong, Fgn. Corrs. Club Hong Kong. Democrat. Roman Catholic. Avocations: sports cars, sailing, scuba diving, flying. Office: One Mellon Bank Ctr Rm 370 Pittsburgh PA 15258

MCGRATH, PAMELA DELLA, psychosocial researcher; b. Brisbane, Australia, Oct. 29, 1951; d. Andrew Lloyd and Iris Olive (Allen) Palmer; m. Philip William McGrath, May 13, 1972 (dec. Apr. 1988); children: Amy Beth, Emma Louise, Zoe Marisa, Bo Youn. B of Social Work, U. Queensland, Brisbane, Australia, 1972; MA, Queensland U. Tech., Brisbane, Australia, 1993; PhD, U. Queensland, 1996. Child care officer Dept. Children's Svcs., Brisbane, Australia, 1973-76, supr. child care officer, 1976; resource officer Dept. Family Svcs., Brisbane, Australia, 1989-90; tutor, lectr. Queensland U. Tech., Brisbane, Australia, 1992-94, U. Queensland, Brisbane, Australia, 1994-97; rsch. fellow Nat. Health and Med. Rsch., Brisbane, Australia, 1999—, Queensland U. Tech., Brisbane, 1997-99. Author: A Question of Choice, 1997, Confronting Icarus: A Psycho-Social Perspective on Haematological Malignancies, 1999; contbr. articles to profl. jours. Justice of peace, commr. declarations Dept. Justice, Brisbane, 1973—. Grantee Tertiary Edn. Inst., U. Queensland, 1995, Perpetual Trustees, Queensland, 1997, Gaming Machine & Cmty. Benefit Fund, Queensland, 1998, Queensland Cancer Fund, 1998, Royal Children's Hosp. Found., Queensland, 1999AMP, Queensland, 1999; Queensland Cancer Fund, 1998, rsch. fellow Ctr. Pub. Health Rsch., Brisbane, 1998-99; recipient Millenium Golden Internat. award Internat. Rsch. Promotion Coun., 1999; named Eminent Scientist of Yr. Asia-Pacific chpt. Internat. Rsch. Promotion Coun., 1999. Mem. Palliative Care Assn. Queensland (chair edn. and rsch. sub-com. 1997—), Cellink Leukemia found. Queensland (exec. mem. 1997—), Australian Bioethics Assn. Avocations: gardening, classical music, art. Office: Ctr Pub Health Rsch, QUT Kelvin Grove, Brisbane 4059, Australia

MCGRATH, THOMAS J., lawyer, writer, film producer; b. N.Y.C., Oct. 8, 1932; m. Mary Lee McGrath, Aug. 4, 1956 (dec.); children: Maura Lee, J. Connell; m. Diahn Williams, Sept. 28, 1974; 1 child, Courtney C. B.A., NYU, 1956, J.D., 1960. Bar: N.Y. 1960. Assoc. Milbank, Tweed, Hadley & McCloy, N.Y.C., 1960-69; ptnr. Simpson, Thacher & Bartlett, N.Y.C., 1970-95; retired, 1995; lectr., writer Practicing Law Inst., 1976—, Am. Law Inst. ABA, 1976-81; bd. dirs. Fast Food Devel. Corp. Author: Carryover Basis Under Tax Reform Act, 1977; contbg. author: Estate and Gift Tax After ERTA, 1982; producer: feature film Deadly Hero, 1977. Bd. dirs. N.Y. Philharm.; pres. Am. Austrian Found., Tanzania Wildlife Fund. With U.S. Army, 1953-54, Korea. Fellow Am. Coll. Trust and Estate Coun.; mem. ABA, N.Y. State Bar Assn., Assn. Bar City N.Y. Home: 988 5th Ave New York NY 10021-0143 Office: Simpson Thacher & Bartlett 425 Lexington Ave New York NY 10017-3954

MCGRAW, BRYAN KELLY, financial company executive; b. Ironton, Mo., Sept. 10, 1962; s. Robert Lee and Francine Clara McGraw; m. Elizabeth Adair Keck, Jan. 24, 1987; children: Kaitlyn Adair, Brendan Kelly. BS, S.E. Mo. State U., 1984; MPA, U. Okla., 1990; postgrad., St. Louis U., 1996—. Lic. residential contractor, N.C. Commd. 2d lt. USAF, 1984, advanced through grades to maj., 1998; svcs. officer, mgr. USAF, Pease AFB, N.H., 1985-87, Kadena AB, Okinawa, Japan, 1987-91; dep. chief svcs. K.I. Sawyer AFB, Mich., 1991-92; v.p. McGraw Builders, Inc., Goldsboro, N.C., 1992-95; exec. officer USAFR, Mitchell ARS, Wis., 1995-96; mgr. total quality Deutsche Fin. Svcs., St. Louis, 1998-99; dir. quality and process innovation Deutsche Fin. Svcs., 1999—. Mem. urban planning and real estate com. St. Louis U., 1997-98; coach U.S.A. Youth Hockey, St. Louis, 1998-99; mem. Heritage Found., Washington, 1996—. Recipient Young Alumni merit award S.E. Mo. State U., 1999. Mem. DAV, Assn. for Quality and Participation (bd. dirs. 1998—), Am. Soc. for Quality, Nat. Geog. Soc., Res. Officers Assn., U.S.A. Hockey. Republican. Roman Catholic. Avocations: hockey, racquetball, music, outdoors, military history. E-mail: bkmgraw@swbell.net. Home: 5346 Old Lemay Ferry Rd Imperial MO 63052-1919

MCGRAW, KENNETH WAYNE, financial executive; b. Cumberland, Md., May 15, 1935; s. Wesley Allen and Mary Catherine (Van Meter) M.; m. Diana Giles Renshaw, Aug. 1, 1959 (div.); children: Timothy York, Laura Kibler, Bryan Wayne. BA in Chemistry, Johns Hopkins U., 1957, M of Liberal Arts in Philosophy and Lit., 1965; MBA in Fin., Harvard U., 1960. Chemist W.R. Grace, Balt., 1957-59; staff asst. Balt. Gas & Electric Co., 1960-62; assoc. Alex Brown & Sons, Balt., 1963-70; v.p. Johns Hopkins Hosp., Balt., 1971-73; ptnr. Robert Garrett & Sons, Balt., 1973-75; pres. Corp. Fin. Cons., Balt., 1976-87; man. dir. Patricof & Co. Capital Corp., N.Y.C., 1988-98; pres. CFC Capital Corp., N.Y.C., 1998—; trustee Gen. Real Estate Shares, Detroit, 1980-85. Chmn. Balt. City Hosps. Commn., 1974-77; chmn. Balt. Choral Arts Soc., 1972-80. Sr. mem. Am. Soc. Appraisers; mem. Md. Club, Rolling Rock Club, Harvard Club of N.Y.C. Republican. Presbyterian. Avocation: farming. Home: Hayfields Farm McDowell VA 24458 Office: CFC Captl Corp 885 3rd Ave New York NY 10022-4834

MCGRAW, LAVINIA MORGAN, retired retail company executive; b. Detroit, Feb. 26, 1924; d. Will Curtis and Margaret Coulter (Oliphant) McG. AB, Radcliffe Coll., 1945. Mem. Phi Beta Kappa. Home: 2501 Calvert St NW Washington DC 20008-2620

MCGREGOR, ALAN GORDON, company executive; b. Adelaide, Australia, Aug. 29, 1936; s. William Wigham and Joan Mary (Smeaton) McG.; m. Skye Thyne Reid, June 8, 1963; children: Stirling William, Iona Mary, Thyne Wigham. Degree in econs. and law (hon.), Cambridge (Eng.) U., 1958; B Laws, U. Adelaide, 1962. Dir. South Australian Gas Co., 1978-88, Mutual Cmty. Ltd., 1969-91, chmn., 1984; with Elders IXL Ltd., 1979-90, Consort Pty. Ltd., 1983-94, F.H. Faulding & Co., Ltd., 1987—, chmn. 1989—, James Hardie Industries Ltd., 1989—, chmn. 1995—, Burns, Philp & Co. Ltd., 1993—, chmn. 1997—, Kinhill Ltd., 1987-97; chmn. BresaGen Ltd., 1987-98; with Minelab Electronics Pty. Ltd., 1995—; chmn. Australian Wool Testing Authority Ltd., 1992—; with Kidman Holdings Ltd., 1992—, numerous family and trust cos.; mem. fin. com. U. Adelaide, 1982—, Cos. and Securities Adv. Co., 1991-97; dir., chmn. bd. trustees, Ctr. Ind. Studies, 1991—; dir. Australian Stock Exch., 1992-95. Chmn. Inst. Med. and Vet. Sci., 1973-82; pres. Australian Polo Coun., 1972-78; capt. Adelaide Polo Club, chmn. com. mgmt., 1972-77, pres. 1986-95; mem. RAA Coun., 1973-

80, South Australia Coun. Inst. Dirs. in Australia, 1978-86; mem. South Australia Jubilee 150 Bd., 1981-87; mem. bd. govs. Adelaide Festival of Arts, 1972-86, dep. chmn., 1978-80, chmn., 1980-84, apptd. hon. life mem., 1986; dir. Australian Bicentennial Authority, chmn. South Australian Coun. 1980-89; chmn. Wilderness Sch. Found., 1985-89; dir. Art Exhbns. Australia Ltd., 1985-94; mem. Adelaide Festival Working Party, 1994; chmn. South Australian Rev. of Univ. Governance, 1995-96; dir. Winston Churchill Meml. Trust of Australia, 1988—. Office: GPO Box 2702, Adelaide SA 5001, Australia

MCGREGOR, BARBARA JOYCE, magazine publisher; b. Sydney, Australia, June 19, 1945; d. Frederick Prince and Eva (Wooding) Young; m. John Francis McGregor (div. Jan. 1983); children: Emily, John Scott. Cert. of mktg., U. NSW, Sydney. Br. mgr. Helene Curtis, Sydney, Australia, 1970-71, Yardley of London, Sydney, 1972-73; acct. dir. Grey Advt., Sydney, 1978-79; mktg. mgr. Blackmores Pl, Sydney, 1979-81; dir. Alpha Comms., Sydney, 1981-83; pub., founder WellBeing mag. Wellspring Publs., Sydney, 1983—; Editor: Never Give Up Hope, 1995. Fellow Australian Inst. Co. Dirs.; mem. Australian Inst. Mgmt., Australian Traditional Medicine Soc., Orthomolecular Med. Assn. Avocations: natural therapies, environmental protection. Office: WellBeing Holistic Ctr, 317 Pacific Hwy, North Sydney NSW 2060, Australia also: Private Bay 2102, North Sydney NSW 2059, Australia

MCGRORY, JOSEPH BENNETT, physicist; b. Phila., Feb. 23, 1934; s. John Reardon and Eleanor Custis (Bennett) McG.; m. Thelma Ruth Houk, July 20, 1957; children: Eleanor Ruth, William Dandridge. BS in Math., U. of the South, 1955; PhD in Physics, Vanderbilt U., 1963. Health physicist USPHS, Washington, 1957-60; nuclear theorist Oak Ridge Nat. Lab., 1963-76, sect. head for nuclear theory, 1976-90, asst. dir. physics div., 1990-91; program mgr. for nuclear theory U.S. Dept. Energy, Washington, 1991—. Contbr. articles to profl. jours. Pres. Oak Ridge Civil Music Assn., 1980; bd. dirs. numerous arts orgns. Fellow AAAS, Am. Phys. Soc.; mem. Phi Beta Kappa, Sigma Xi, Omicron Delta Kappa. Episcopalian. Home: 104 Westlook Cir Oak Ridge TN 37830-3820 Office: US Dept Energy ER 23 G420 GTN 19901 Germantown Rd Germantown MD 20874-1207

MCGRORY, MARY KATHLEEN, retired college president; b. N.Y.C., Mar. 22, 1933; d. Patrick Joseph and Mary Kate (Gilvary) McG. BA, Pace U., 1957; MA, U. Notre Dame, 1962; PhD, Columbia U., 1969; DHL, Albertus Magnus Coll., 1984; LLD, Briarwood Coll., 1990; DHL, Trinity Coll., 1991. Prof. English Western Conn. State U., Danbury, 1969-78; dean arts and scis. Ea. Conn. State U., Willimantic, 1978-80, v.p. for acad. affairs, 1981-85; pres. Hartford (Conn.) Coll. for Women, 1985-91; sr. fellow U. Va. Commonwealth Ctr., Charlottesville, 1991-92; exec. dir. Soc. Values in Higher Edn./Georgetown U., Washington, 1992-96; ret., 1996; pres. MKM Assocs., Holland, Ma., 1983—. Author: Yeats, Joyce & Beckett, 1975. Bd. dirs. Hartford Hosp., 1985-93; chmn. bd. govs. Greater Hartford Consortium Higher Edn., 1989-90. Fels Found. fellow, 1966-67, NEH summer fellow, 1975; Ludwig Vogelstein Found. travel grantee, 1973. Mem. New Eng. Jr. Community and Tech. Coll. Coun. (v.p. 1988-91), Am. Assn. Higher Edn., Med. Acad. of Am., Greater Hartford C. of C. (bd. dirs. 1989-91), Hartford Club (bd. dirs. 1988-91). Avocations: writing, swimming, piano. Address: RR 2 Box 1121 Holland MA 01521-9702

MCGUANE, FRANK L., JR., lawyer; b. White Plains, N.Y., July 10, 1939; s. Frank L. and Dorothy P. (McGrath) McG.; m. Carla L. Miller, June 26, 1993; children: Lauri Elizabeth, Molly Elizabeth. BA, U. Notre Dame, 1961; JD, U. Cin., 1968. Bar: Colo. 1968, U.S. Dist. Ct. Colo. 1968, U.S. Ct. Appeals (10th cir.) 1970, U.S. Supreme Ct. 1971. Shareholder McGuane and Malone, P.C., Denver, 1981-95; pres. Frank McGuane & Assocs., P.C., Denver, 1995—; ptnr. McGuane & Hogan, LLP, Denver, 1997—; lectr. in field. Author: Domestic Relations-Colorado Methods of Practice, 1983; co-author: Colorado Family Law and Practice, 1999; contbr. articles to profl. jours. Chmn. Denver area chpt. Nat. Eagle Scout Assn. Boy Scouts Am., 1980-82. With USMC, 1961-63. Fellow Am. Acad. Matrimonial Lawyers (jour. editor 1990-95, bd. govs. 1988-95, pres. Colo. chpt. 1988-89), Internat. Acad. Matrimonial Lawyers (founding fellow); mem. ABA, Colo. Bar Assn. (chmn. family law sect. 1977-78), Denver Bar Assn., Arapahoe County Bar Assn., Douglas-Elbert County Bar Assn., Pitkin County Bar Assn., Am. Coll. Family Trial Lawyers (diplomate), Cath. Lawyers Guild. Office: The Galleria 720 S Colorado Blvd Ste 910N Denver CO 80246-1935

MCGUINN, MICHAEL EDWARD, III, retired army officer; b. Spartanburg, S.C., Feb. 22, 1925; s. Michael Edward Jr. and Margaret Cordelia (Shackleford) McG.; m. Betty Gay Corn, 1948 (div. 1951); m. Phyllis Fryer, Oct. 7, 1952 (dec. July 1997); children: Michael Edward IV, Carol Anne McGuinn Branch. Student, Clemson U., 1941-43, 46, Coll. William and Mary, 1962-63. Served with U.S. Navy, PTO, 1943-46; commd. 2d lt. U.S. Army, 1949, advanced through grades to col., 1971; asst. mil. attache Am. Embassy, Copenhagen, 1958-61; posted to svc. British Army, Longmoor, Eng., 1964-66; served on U.S. Dept. Army Gen. Staff, Washington, 1966-68; comdr. 10th Transp. Bn. U.S. Army, Vietnam, 1968-69; chief transp. div. U.S. Readiness Command, MacDill AFB, Fla., 1969-72; ret. U.S. Army, 1972; state govt. svc. various locations, 1972-82; chief of staff Ga. State Def. Force, an Agy. of the State of Ga., Atlanta, 1987-95. Decorated Legion of Merit (2), Army Commendation medal (2), Naval Commendation medal. Mem. U.S. Army Transp. Mus. Avocations: military history, photography, home workshop. Home and Office: 6420 Tanacrest Ct NW Atlanta GA 30328-2837

MCGUINNESS, ROSAMOND ZEIGLER (CORKY), music educator; b. Bridgeport, Conn., Dec. 4, 1929; arrived in Eng., 1957; d. S. Howard and Adelaide (Zeigler) Cohan; m. Bernard Francis McGuinness (div. 1969); children: Catherine, Sara, Patrick, Lucy; m. George Charles Biddlecombe (div. 1981); 1 child, Elizabeth. BA in Music, Vassar Coll., 1951; MA, Smith Coll., 1952; postgrad., Harvard U., 1955, Cornell U., 1956-57; PhD in Music History, Oxford (Eng.) U., 1964. Lectr. music dept. Vassar Coll., 1955-57; tutor in music history Brasenose, Queen's, St. Peter's and St. Anne's/Oxford U., 1964-72; reader in music Birmingham (Eng.) U., 1969; lectr. music dept. Royal Holloway Coll., London U., 1969-82, sr. lectr., 1982—, prof., personal chair, 1990, emeritus prof., 1995—, project dir. computer register musical data, 1987—; vis. lectr. Royal Acad. Music, 1969-70,, Imperial Coll. Sci. and Tech., 1976-81, King's Coll., London U., 1979-82, Royal Coll. Music, 1999; mem. coun. Royal Hollow and Bedford New Coll., 1992; quality auditor Higher Edn. Quality Coun., Higher Edn. Funding Coun. for Eng.; alt. mem. Standing Conf. on Univ. Entrance Com. of Vice Chancellors and Prins., U.K., 1997, mem., 1998; chief external examiner Brunel U., West London Inst. Author: English Court Odes 1660-1820, 1971; contbr. articles to profl. jours., chpts. to books; project dir. register musical data London newspapers, 1660-1750. Chair Camden Lay Visitors Panel, Borough of Camden, London, 1990-95; dep. chair North-East London Lay Observers, 1996; mem. Cmty. and Camden Policy Consultative Coun., London, 1989-95. Harriet Boyd Hawes scholar, 1951-52; Louise Hart van Loon fellow, 1955-56, 60-61, Benjamin White Whitney fellow, 1955-56, Fredericka Schepp fellow, 1955-56, Leopold Schepp Found. fellow, 1956-57, Eliza Buffington fellow, 1957-58, Vassie James Hill fellow AAUP, 1958-59, Mary Richardson and Lydia Pratt Babbott fellow, 1960-61, Joanna Randall-MacIver rsch. fellow, 1967-69; named to Great Britain Women of Yr., 1996; recipient Hon. Mention John Lowell Osgood Meml. prize Oxford U., 1963; grantee Ctrl. Rsch. Fund U. London, 1977, Brit. Acad., 1977, Leverhulme Trust, 1978-79, Am. Coun. Learned Socs., 1978-79, Social Sci. Rsch. Coun., 1980-83. Fellow Royal Soc. Arts, mem. Brit. Soc. 18th Century Studies (pres. 1994-96), Am. Musicol. Soc., Royal Musical Assn., Am. Soc. 18th Century Studies, Sharp Studies, Royal Soc. Musicians. Avocations: walking, reading, the arts. Home: 23 Alma St, London NW5 3DJ, England

MCGUIRE, EDWARD DAVID, JR., lawyer; b. Waynesboro, Va., Apr. 11, 1948; s. Edward David and Mary Estelle (Angus) McG.; m. Georgia Ann Charuhas, Aug. 15, 1971; children: Matthew Edward, Kathryn Ann. BS in Commerce, U. Va., 1970; JD, Coll. William and Mary, 1973. Bar: Va. 1973, D.C. 1974, Md. 1990, Pa. 1995, U.S. Dist. Ct. (ea. dist.) Va. 1974, U.S. Dist. Ct. D.C. 1974, U.S. Dist. Ct. Md. 1990, Ct. Appeals (4th cir.) 1974, U.S. Ct. Appeals (D.C. cir.) 1974, U.S. Supreme Ct. 1993. Assoc. Wilkes and Artis, Washington, 1973-78; gen. corp counsel Mark Winkler Mgmt., Alexandria, Va., 1978-80; sr. contracts officer Amtrak, Washington, 1980-81; sr. real estate atty., asst. corp. sec. Peoples Drug Stores, Inc., Alexandria, 1981-88; of counsel Cowles, Rinaldi & Arnold, Ltd., Fairfax, Va., 1989-91; sr. assoc. Radigan, Rosenberg & Holmes, Arlington, Va., 1991; pvt. practice, Annandale, Va., 1992-97; sr. assoc. Stein, Sperling, Bennett, DeJong, Driscoll, Greenfeig Metro, Rockville, Md., 1997-99; of counsel Hodes, Ulman, Pessin & Katz, P.A., Annandale, 1999-2000; atty. pvt. practice, Alexandria, Va., 2000—; mng. dir., personal trust adminstr. Riggs Bank, N.A., Washington, 2000—. Co-author: Legacy: Plan, Protect and Preserve Your Estate, 1995, Generations: Planning Your Legacy, 1998. Bd. dirs. Dist. XVI Va. Student Aid Found., 1978-85, George Washington dist. Boy Scouts Am., 1986; active William and Mary Law Sch. Assn., bd. dirs., 1983-96, pres., 1987-88, treas., 1990-91. Capt. JAGC, USANG, 1973-79. Mem. ABA, Va. Bar Assn., Va. State Bar, D.C. Bar, Md. State Bar Assn., Fairfax Bar Assn., Am. Trial Lawyers Am., Arlington County Bar Assn., Va. Trial Lawyers Assn., No. Va. Estate Planning Coun., William and Mary Alumni Soc. (bd. dirs. D.C. chpt. treas. 1992-94), U. Va. Club of Washington (schs. com. chmn. 1995—, v.p. outreach 1997-99, pres.-elect 1998-99, bd. dirs. 1996-99), Rotary (treas. Springfield chpt. 1985-86, sec. 1986-87, pres.-elect 1987, chmn. World Affairs Conf. 1985-88, bd. dirs. 1984-88, 96-97, Dist. 7610 youth leadership awards chmn. 1994-97, Outstanding Rotarian award 1985). Greek Orthodox. Avocations: racquetball, coaching youth sports. Home and Office: 31 W Myrtle St Alexandria VA 22301-2422

MCGUIRE, JAMES GRANT, lawyer; b. Ashland, Ky., Nov. 9, 1955; s. Everett Earl and Martha Lou McGuire; m. P. Kheng Yap-McGuire, Dec. 29, 1984; children: Forrest, Loy. AB, Duke U., 1980; JD, Washington and Lee U., 1984. Bar: W.Va. 1984, Ky. 1985, D.C. 1984, Va. 1997. Adminstr. UN High Commn. for Refugees, Kuala Lumpur, Malaysia, 1980-81; mem. Campbell, Woods, Huntington, W.Va., 1984—; bd. dirs. 1st Nat. Bank, Grayson, Ky., Guaranty Bank, Huntington. Chmn. bd. dirs. Teubert Found. for Blind, Huntington, 1990—; mem. Huntington Area Devel. Coun., 1995—, Huntington Devel. Authority, 1999—. With U.S. Army, 1975-78. Luce scholar Henry Luce Found., N.Y.C., 1980. Mem. W.Va. C. of C. (bd. dirs. 1997—), City Club, Guyan Country Club, Gypsy Club, Huntington C. of C. (bd. dirs.), W.Va. Bar (bd. govs.), W.Va. State C. of C. (bd. dirs.), others. Avocations: golf, reading. E-mail: grant11955@aol.com. Home: 123 Ridgewood Rd Huntington WV 25701-4857 Office: Campbell Woods 517 9th St Ste 1000 Huntington WV 25701-2033

MCGUIRE, JOHN W., SR., advertising executive, marketing professional, author; b. Chgo., May 12, 1952; s. Eugene H. Sr. and Marjorie (Bolger) McG.; m. Mary Sue Roper, June 17, 1972 (div. 1977); 1 child, John William Jr.; m. Lynn L. Rembos, June 21, 1984 (div. April 1991); children: Kelly Lynn, Ryan Michael. AA, Chgo. City Colls., 1972; BA, Northeastern Ill., Chgo., 1974. Janitor Bd. of Edn., Chgo., 1970-74; sales rep. Motorola Comms., Inc., Schaumburg, Ill., 1974-76, Pattis Group, Chgo., 1976-77; midwest sales mgr. Harcourt Brace Jovanovich Pub. Co., N.Y.C., 1977-79; account sales mgr. Cosmopolitan Mag. Hearst Pub. Co., N.Y.C., 1979-81; midwest acct. mgr. Psychology Today Mag. Ziff-Davis Pub. Co., N.Y.C., 1981-82; midwest regional mgr. Pennwell Pub. Co., Tulsa, Okla., 1982-84; western regional sales mgr. Nursing Mgmt. Mag. SN Pub. Co., West Dundee, Ill., 1984-91; western regional sales mgr., midwest regional sales mgr. U.S. Pharmacist Mag. Jobson Pub. Co., N.Y.C., 1991-98; v.p. SK&A Info. Svcs., Irvine, Calif., 1998-99; assoc. pub. Health Mgmt. Technology Mag. Nelson Pub., Nokomis, Fla., 1999; pres., CEO Blossom Pub. Co., Wasco, Ill., 2000—. Author: (book) One Man's Life: A Poetic Review, 1995, singer (cassette tapes), designer (creative posters). With USN, 1970. Mem. VFW, Midwest Healthcare Mktg., Arlington Poetry Project. Republican. Roman Catholic. Avocations: writer, scuba, horsemanship, traveling, skydiving.

MCGUIRE, MICHAEL WILLIAM, communications executive; b. Pomona, Calif., Aug. 1, 1960; s. Frederick L. and Anna Belle (Crum) McG.; m. Victoria Jean Von Tobel; children: Gordon, Michael Jr. BA in Polit. Sci., U. San Diego, 1984. Spokesman, dir. Congl. affairs Voice of Am., Washington, 1986-88; owner, chief exec. officer McGuire Rsch. Svcs., Las Vegas, Denver and San Francisco, Washington, 1988—; cons. various U.S. and multinat. corps. Cons. various candidates for pub. office, 1988. Mem. Hiwan Golf Club. Home: 34123 Upper Bear Creek Rd Evergreen CO 80439-7816

MCGUIRE, ROGER ALAN, retired foreign service officer; b. Troy, Ohio, July 1, 1943; s. Charles M. and Mary L. (Coppock) McG.; m. Harriet H. Cooke, July 12, 1969; children: Sara, Casey. BA, Beloit Coll., 1965; MA, U. Wis., 1967. Country desk officer Dept. State, Washington, 1974-78; dep. chief of mission Am. Embassy, Maputo, Mozambique, 1978-80; congl. fellow Am. Polit. Sci. Assn., Washington, 1980-81; polit. officer Am. Embassy, Asuncion, Paraguay, 1981-83, Lusaka, Zambia, 1983-86; dep. dir. Office of West African Affairs Dept. of State, Washington, 1986-88; chief of mission Am. Embassy, Windhoek, Namibia, 1988-90; consul Am. Consulate, Porto Alegre, Brazil, 1990-92; U.S. amb. to Guinea-Bissau, 1992-95; counselor for polit. affairs Am. Embassy, Canberra, Australia, 1995-97; ret., 1997. Recipient Superior Honor award U.S. Agy. for Internat. Devel., 1969. Mem. Rotary Internat., Phi Beta Kappa. Home: 3007 Russell Rd Alexandria VA 22305-1719

MCGUIRE, SANDRA LYNN, nursing educator; b. Jan. 28, 1947; d. Donald Armstrong and Mary Lue (Harvey) Johnson; m. Joseph L. McGuire, Mar. 6, 1976; children: Matthew, Kelly, Kerry. BSN, U. Mich., 1969, MPH, 1973, EdD, 1988, MSN, 1997. Staff nurse Univ. Hosp., Ann Arbor, Mich., 1969; pub. health nurse Wayne County Health Dept., Eloise, Mich., 1969-72; instr. Madonna Coll., Livonia, Mich., 1973; pub. health coord. Plymouth Ctr. for Human devel., Northville, Mich., 1974-75; asst. prof. cmty. health nursing U. Mich., Ann Arbor, 1975-83; asst. prof. U. Tenn., Knoxville, 1983-88, assoc. prof., 1990—, gerontol. nurse practitioners program coord., 1998—; dir. Kids Are Tomorrow's Srs. Program, 1988—; resource person Gov.'s Com. Unification of Mental Health Svcs. in Mich.; spkr. profl. assns. and workshops. Author: (with S. Clemen-Stone and D. Eigsti) Comprehensive Community Health Nursing, 1981, 5th edit., 1998, 6th edit., 2000. Bd. dirs. Ctr. Understanding Aging, 1987-93, v.p., 1995—, bd. dirs. Mich. chpt. ARC, 1980-83, Knoxville chpt., 1984-85; founder Knoxville Intergenerational Network, 1989. USPHS fellow, 1972-73, Robert Woodruff fellow Emory U., 1996-97, Hewlett Innovative Tech. fellow U. Tenn., Knoxville, 1999-00, Profl. Devel. award U. Tenn. Knoxville, 1996-96, 99-2000. Mem. ANA, Tenn. Nurses Assn., Nat. Conf. Gerontol. Nurse Practitioners, Nat. Gerontol. Nursing Assn., Mich. Pub. Health Assn. (chmn. mental health sect. 1976, dir., co-chmn. residential svcs. com. 1976-79, chmn. health svcs. 1979-82), Nat. Assn. Retarded Citizens, Mich. Assn. Retarded Citizens, Nat. Coun. on Aging, Ctr. for Understanding Aging (v.p. 1994-95), Plymouth (chmn. residential svcs. com. 1975-77), Tenn. Assn. Retarded Citizens, So. Nursing Rsch. Soc., Sigma Theta Tau, Pi Lambda Theta, Phi Kappa Phi. Home: 11008 Crosswind Dr Knoxville TN 37922-4011 Office: 1200 Volunteer Blvd Knoxville TN 37916-3806

MCGUIRK, RONALD CHARLES, retired banker, economic advisor; b. Balt., Dec. 9, 1938; s. Charles F. and Grace E. (Delcher) McG.; m. Katherine Sauer, Oct. 1, 1960; children: Frank D., Ann E. Student, St. John's Coll., Annapolis, Md., 1956-59. Sr. data processing officer 1st Nat. Bank, Balt., 1966-72, v.p. data processing, 1972-76, v.p. mktg., 1976-80, sr. v.p. mktg., 1980-90, sr. v.p. corp. plan, chief of staff to CEO, 1990-94; sr. v.p., corp. sec. 1st Md. Bancorp, Balt., 1995-99; sr. econ. advisor Anne Arundel County, Md., 1999—. Bd. dirs., treas. North Arundel Hosp., Glen Burnie, Md., 1974—, Internet, Inc., 1990-95, Glen Burnie Town Ctr. Com., 1995—, Annapolis Symphony, 1991-92; trustee Mt. Washington Pediat. Hosp., 1997—; mem. adv. bd. Hist. Annapolis Found., 1982-85, dir., 1985-90; chmn. Annapolis Boundary Commn., 1983-84; mem. Anne Arundel County Coun., 1974-82, Anne Arundel County Libr. Bd., 1974-84; pres. Anne Arundel County Scholarship for Scholars/Bd. Edn., 1983-85, treas., 1985-88; mem. Anne Arundel County Charter Rev. Commn., 1986, Anne Arundel County Govt. Salary Commn., 1985, 89; chmn. Anne Arundel County Impact Fee Study Task Force, 1987; pres. Anne Arundel County YMCA, 1987-89, bd. dirs., 1982-87, 89-90; mem. Commn. for Ednl. Excellence, 1988-90; vice chmn. Ft. Meade Coordinating Coun., 1989-91; mem. Exec. Com. Md. Bus.-Industry PAC, 1991-99, Anne Arundel County Charter and Orgn. Transition Group, 1991; corp. ptnr. Sch. Bus. and Mgmt. Morgan State U., 1991-92; trustee Md. Hist. Soc., 1995-96; co-chair Anne Arundel County transition fin. com., 1998-99. Mem. Ctr. Club. Democrat. Roman Catholic. Office: Arundel Ctr Calvert St Annapolis MD 21401

MCHAFFIE, HAZEL ESTHER, medical ethics researcher; b. Ixworth Thorpe, England, Oct. 29, 1943; d. John and Myrtle (Nevard) Hayles; m. David John McHaffie, Aug. 24, 1968; 2 children. PhD, U. Edinburgh, Scotland, 1988. Nurse Western Gen. Hosp., Edinburgh, Scotland, 1967-68; midwife Simpson Meml. Maternity Pavilion, Edinburgh, 1968-71, 79-84; rschr. U. Edinburgh, 1984—; spkr. in field. Author: Holding On?, 1994, Life, Death & Decisions, 1996; co-author: The Midwifery Research Database, 1994; contbr. articles to profl. jours. Avocations: handicrafts, reading.

MCHALE, ANTHONY PATRICK, biological sciences educator, researcher; b. Castlebar, Ireland, Jan. 26, 1957; s. Laurence Christopher and Margaret Ellen (Duffy) McH.; ptnr. Ana Maria Rollan Haro; children: Fionnula, Tony, Ciarán, Daniel. BSc, Univ. Coll. Galway, Ireland, 1978, PhD, 1982. Postdoctoral fellow Baylor Coll. Medicine, Houston, 1982-84; lectr. Trinity Coll., Dublin, Ireland, 1985-91; lectr. biol. scis. U. Ulster, Coleraine, No. Ireland, 1991-98; reader applied biol. scis. U. Ulster, Coleraine, 1998—; founder Gendel Ltd., No. Ireland, 1998; mng. dir. Bioresources Ireland Ltd., Dublin, 1989-91; participant conf. in field. Contbr. more than 130 articles to sci. jours., including Jour. Irish Med. Sci., Internat. Jour. Biochemistry, Biochemistry Jour., Jour. Gen. Microbiology, Biotech. Bioengring., Applied Biochem. Biotech., Biochim. Biophys. Acta, Enzyme Microbiology Tech., Biochem. Soc. Trans., Cancer Biochemistry Biophysics, Biotech. Letters, Biotechnol. Techniques, European Jour. Surg. Oncology, Cancer Letters, Jour. Photochem. Photobiology, World Jour. Microbiol. Biotech., also chpts. to books. Mem. AAAS, Am. Chem. Soc., Soc. for Gen. Microbiology (com. mem. Irish area 1986-89), Biochem. Soc., Royal Irish Acad. (microbiology com. 1996—). Achievements include patents for solid component of distillery pot ale/spent wash as a metal/radionuclide biosorbent, use of carbohydrate-supplemented distillery pot ale/spent wash as a medium for ethanol production by a thermotolerant strain of yeast, nucleic acid delivery bioelectric systems for biorbmediation. Office: U Ulster Sch Appl Biol Scis, Cromore Rd, Co Derry Coleraine BT52 1SA, Northern Ireland

MCHALE, MICHAEL JOHN, lawyer; b. N.Y.C., Apr. 14, 1960; s. Michael Joseph and Mary Beatrice (Graddy) McH. BA, U. of the South, 1982; JD, Samford U., 1985. Bar: Ala. 1986, U.S. Dist. Ct. (no., mid. and so. dists.) Ala. 1986, U.S. Ct. Appeals (11th cir.) 1986, Fla. (cert. admiralty and maritime law) 1991, U.S. Dist. Ct. (mid. and so. dists.) Fla. 1991, U.S. Dist. Ct. (no. dist.) Fla. 1997, U.S. Supreme Ct. 1991; cert. admiralty and maritime lawyer Fla. Bar Bd. of Legal Specialization, mediator, arbitrator Fla. Supreme Ct. Assoc. Wagner, Nugent, Johnson, Roth, Romano, Eriksen & Kupfer, West Palm Beach, Fla., 1989-92; ptnr. Whalen & McHale, West Palm Beach, Fla., 1992-95, Daves, Whalen, McHale & Considine, West Palm Beach, Fla., 1995-98; sole practitioner Jensen Beach, Fla., 1998—; of counsel Deorchis, Corsa & Hillenbrand LLP, Miami, Fla., 1998—. Author: Strategic Use of Circumstantial Evidence, 2d edit., 1991, Evaluating and Settling Personal Injury Claims, 1992, supplement through present, Making Trial Objections, 1993, supplement through present, Expert Witnesses: Direct and Cross Examination, 1993, supplement through present; editor, author: Litigating TMJ Cases, 1993 and yearly supplements. Named one of Outstanding Young Men of Am., 1988. Mem. ABA (mem. admiralty com.), ATLA, Am. Acad. Fla. Trial Lawyers, Maritime Law Assn. U.S. (procter), Southeastern Admiralty Law Inst., Fla. Bar (admiralty law com. editl. bd., admiralty and maritime cert. com.), Palm. Beach Bar Assn., Martin County Bar Assn., Sigma Nu Phi. Avocation: vessel building. Fax: 305-571-9250. Home: 1905 NE River Ct Jensen Beach FL 34957-6423 Office: Deorchis Corsa & Hillenbrand LLP 2650 Biscayne Blvd Miami FL 33137-4531

MCHARG, JAMES FLEMING, retired psychiatrist; b. Hull, Yorkshire, Eng., Aug. 18, 1917; s. James and Jean (McGowan) McH. MB, ChB, U. Edinburgh, Scotland, 1940; MD, U. Edinburgh, 1959; Diploma in Psychol. Medicine, London U., 1948. Ho. surgeon Royal Infirmary, Edinburgh, 1941; asst. physician Royal Edinburgh Hosp., 1946-51; cons. psychiatrist, dep. physician supt. Glasgow (Scotland) Royal Hosp., 1951-59; hon. sr. lectr. U. St. Andrews, U. Dundee, 1959-82; cons. psychiatrist Brit. Nat. Health Svc., 1951-82; second opinion doctor Mental Welfare Commn. for Scotland. Author: In Search of Dr. John Makluire, Pioneer Edinburgh Physician, Forgotten for over 300 Years, 1997. Surgeon lt. Royal Naval Res., 1941-46. Recipient Vol. Res. Decoration Her Majesty the Queen. Fellow Royal Soc. Medicine, Royal Coll. Physicians Edinburgh (sr. fellow club), Royal Coll. Psychiatrists (fellow, examiner for membership); mem. Soc. Psychical Rsch. (mem. coun.). Episcopalian. Avocations: skiing, history of medicine, genealogy. Home: 33 Hazel Ave, Dundee DD2 1QD, Scotland

MCHENRY, MARTIN CHRISTOPHER, physician, educator; b. Feb. 9, 1932; s. Merl and Marcella (Bricca) McH.; m. Patricia Grace Hughes, Apr. 27, 1957; children: Michael, Christopher, Timothy, Mary Ann, Jeffrey, Paul, Kevin, William, Monica, Martin Christopher. Student, U. Santa Clara, 1950-53; MD, U. Cin., 1957; MS in Medicine, U. Minn., 1966. Diplomate Am. Bd. Internal Medicine. Intern Highland Alameda County (Calif.) Hosp., Oakland, 1957-58; resident, internal medicine fellow Mayo Clinic, Rochester, Minn., 1958-61, spl. appointee in infectious diseases, 1963-64; staff physician Henry Ford Hosp., Detroit, 1964-67; staff physician Cleve. Clinic, 1967-72, chmn. dept. infectious diseases, 1972-92, sr. physician infectious diseases, 1992-98; cons. infectious diseases, 1998—; asst. clin. prof. Case Western Res. U., 1970-77, assoc. clin. prof. medicine, 1977-91, clin. prof. medicine, 1991—; assoc. vis. physician Cleve. Met. Gen. Hosp., 1970—; cons. VA Hosp., Cleve., 1973-74. Contbr. more than 100 articles to profl. jours., also chpts. to books. Chmn. manpower com. Swine Influenza Program, Cleve., 1976. With USNR, 1961-63. Named Disting. Tchr. in Medicine, Cleve. Clinic, 1972, 90; recipient 1st ann. Bruce Hubbard Stewart award Cleve. Clinic Found. for Humanities in Medicine, 1985, Nightingale Physician Collaboration award Cleve. Clinic Found. Divsn. Nursing, 1995. Fellow ACP, Infectious Diseases Soc. Am. (Clinician award 2000), Am. Coll. Chest Physicians (chmn. com. cardiopulmonary infections 1975-77, 81-83), Royal Soc. Medicine of Gt. Britain; mem. Am. Soc. Clin. Pharmacology and Therapeutics (chmn. sect. infectious diseases and antimicrobial agts. 1970-77, 80-85, dir.), Am. Thoracic Soc., Am. Soc. Clin. Pathologists, Am. Fedn. Clin. Rsch., Am. Soc. Tropical Medicine and Hygiene, Am. Soc. Microbiology, N.Y. Acad. Scis., Assn. for Profls. in Infection Control and Epidemiology, So. Med. Assn. Home: 2779 Belgrave Rd Pepper Pike OH 44124-4601 Office: 9500 Euclid Ave Cleveland OH 44195-0001

MCHUGH, DAVID, psychology educator; b. Liverpool, Eng., Oct. 25, 1954; s. John Patrick and Mary (O'Malley) McH.; m. Christine Corcoran, Sept. 5, 1981; children: Roia Meriel, Anya Christine. BS in Social Psychology, Loughborough U., Eng., 1977; MA in Orgnl. Psychology, Lancaster U., Eng., 1980. Lectr. Edge Hill Coll., Ormskirk, Eng., 1982-86, Lancashire Poly., Preston, Eng., 1986-89; sr. lectr. U. Cen. Lancashire, Preston, 1989—; vis. lectr. Warwick U., Coventry, Eng., 1988—. Author: Work Organizations, 1990, 95. Mem. Brit. Acad. Mgmt. Roman Catholic. Avocations: collecting science fiction, guitar playing, English pool, tropical fish. Office: U Cen Lancashire Ctr Rsch on Employment, Dept Mgmt, PR1 2HE Preston England

MCHUGH, JAMES JOSEPH, lawyer; b. Phila., Sept. 15, 1961; s. James Joseph and Helene Anne (Kiernan) McH.; m. Colette Marie Taylor, May 20, 1989; children: Albert Taylor, James Joseph III, Cole Michael. BSME, Drexel U., 1985; JD magna cum laude, Villanova (Pa.) Law Sch., 1992. Bar: Pa. 1992, N.J. 1992, U.S. Dist. Ct. (ea. dist.) Pa., U.S. Dist. Ct. N.J. Ptnr. McHugh Plumbing & Heating, Phila., 1984-89; project mgr. Fluidics Mech Contractors, Phila., 1989-92; assoc. Pepper, Hamilton & Scheetz, Phila., 1992-94, Beasley, Casey & Erbstein, Phila., 1994—. Author, editor case notes. Mem. adv. com. Penn Pub. Svc. Program, Sch. Law, U. Pa. Named to Order of the Coif, Villanova Law Sch., 1992. Mem. ATLA, Pa. Bar Assn., Phila. Bar Assn. Home: 65 Brooks Rd Moorestown NJ 08057-3855 Office: Beasley Casey & Erbstein 1125 Walnut St Philadelphia PA 19107-4918

MCHUGH, JAMES T., bishop; b. Orange, N.J., Jan. 3, 1932. Educated at Seton Hall Univ., Immaculate Conception Sem. (Darlington, N.J.), Fordham Univ., Catholic Univ., Angelicum (Rome). Ordained priest, 1957; con-

secrated bishop, 1988. Asst. dir. Family Life Div., U.S. Cath. Conf., 1965-67, dir., 1967-75; dir. Office for Pro-Life Activities, Nat. Conf. Cath. Bishops, 1972-78; aux. bishop Newark, 1987-89; bishop Diocese of Camden, N.J., 1989-99, Rockville Centre, N.Y., 1999—. Home: 55 Columbia Rd Rockville Centre NY 11570-1319 Office: 50 N Park Ave Rockville Centre NY 11570-4129*

MCILWAIN, THOMAS DAVID, fishery administrator, marine biologist, educator; b. Pascagoula, Miss., Nov. 15, 1940; s. Julius Coleman and Kathleen (Folsom) McI.; m. Janet Ellen Chapman, Dec. 29, 1962; 1 child, Stacey Lee. BS in Biology and Psychology, U. So. Miss., 1964, MS in Biology, 1966, PhD in Zoology, 1978. Lab. aid U.S. Bur. Comml. Fisheries, Pascagoula, summer 1958; instr. biology U. So. Miss., Hattiesburg, 1964-66; tchr. sci. St. Martin (Miss.) High Sch., 1965-66; rsch. biologist Gulf Coast Rsch. Lab., Ocean Springs, Miss., 1966-67, sect. leader, 1967-78, asst. dir. fisheries, 1978-83, dir., 1989-94; legis. asst. U.S. Congressman Trent Lott, Washington, 1983-84; fishery adminstr. Nat. Marine Fisheries Svc., Pascagoula, Miss., 1994—; fishery cons. Gulf and South Atlantic Fishery Devel. Found., Tampa, Fla., 1984-86, Republic of Honduras, 1990; pres. bd. dirs. Miss.-Ala. Sea Grant Consortium, Ocean Springs, 1991-94. Contbr. numerous articles to profl. jours. Chmn. Harbor Commn., Ocean Springs, 1980—; bd. dirs. Jackson County United Way, Pascagoula, 1991-95, Walter Anderson Art Mus. Fellow Am. Inst. Fish Rsch. Scientists (regional bd. dirs. 1980); mem. Am. Fisheries Soc. (cert. fishery scientist), World Mariculture Soc., Miss. Acad. Scis. (bd. dirs. 1981), U.S. C. of C. (chmn. environ. com. 1990-95), So. Assn. Marine Labs. (pres. 1991-94). Presbyterian. Avocations: sailing, scuba diving, fishing. Office: Nat Marine Fisheries Svc Pascagoula Lab PO Box 1207 Pascagoula MS 39568-1207

MCINERNEY, JAMES EUGENE, JR., trade association executive; b. Springfield, Mass., Aug. 3, 1930; s. James Eugene and Rose Elizabeth (Adikes) McI.; m. Mary Catherine Hill, July 17, 1963; children: Anne Elizabeth, James Eugene, III. BS, U.S. Mil. Acad., 1952; MS in Engring., Princeton U., 1960; postgrad., Royal Air Force Staff Coll., 1964; MS in Internat. Affairs, George Washington U., 1970. Commd. 2d lt. USAF, 1952, advanced through grades to maj. gen., 1976; fighter pilot Korea, Japan and Ger.; comdr. tactical fighter squadron Thailand, 1967; tactical fighter wing Ger., 1971; sr. U.S. adviser Turkish Air Force, 1973; dir. mil. assistance and sales Hdqrs. USAF, 1975-78; comdt. Indsl. Coll. Armed Forces, 1978-79; dir. programs Hdqrs. USAF, 1979-80, asst. dep. chief of staff for programs and evaluation, 1980; dir. legis. liaison McDonnell Douglas Corp., Washington, 1980-83, dir. internat. affairs, 1983-86; from v.p. to exec. v.p. Am. League for Exports and Security Assistance, 1986-92, exec. v.p., 1989-92; v.p. Am. Def. Preparedness Assn., 1992-97, Nat. Def. Indsl. Assn., 1997—. Decorated Air Force Cross, D.S.M. (2), Silver Star (3), D.F.C. (7), Bronze Star, Air medal (18); Vietnamese Crosses of Gallantry with palm and star; Republic of Korea Cheongsu medal; comdr. Order of the Brit. Empire (CBE). Mem. Air Force Assn. (citation of honor 1968), Brit.-Am. Bus. Assn.-Washington (pres. 1982-94, chmn. 1994-96), Brit.-Am. Bus. Coun. (chmn. 1996-97), Am.-Air Mus. in Britain (exec. dir. 1984—), The Jefferson Islands Club, Capitol Hill Club, Congl. Country Club. Roman Catholic. Home: 1031 Delf Dr Mc Lean VA 22101-2009

MCINERNEY, JOHN PETER, agricultural economist, educator; b. Luton, Bedfordshire, Eng., Jan. 10, 1939; s. Peter and Eva Alice (Hooper) McI.; m. Audrey Margaret Perry, Aug. 12, 1961: children: Duncan Peter, Deborah Jane. BSc in Agr. with hons., U. London, 1960; MSc in Agrl. Econs., U. Oxford, Eng., 1961; PhD, Iowa State U., 1964. Nat. diploma in Agr. Lectr. Wye Coll., U. London, 1964-66; sr. lectr. U. Manchester, Eng., 1967-78; prof. U. Reading, Eng., 1979-84; prof., dir. agrl. econs. unit U. Exeter, Eng., 1984—; mem. Govt. Panel on Bovine TB and Badgers, 1985-87, Farm Animal Welfare Coun., Eng., 1996—; dir. Devon Environ. Bus. Initiative, Eng., 1994-98, Silsoe Rsch. Inst., Eng., 1996—; mem. U.K. Bd. Organic Food Stds., 1997—, Ind. Sci. Group on Cattle TB, 1998—. Author, editor: (books) The Food Industries: Economics and Policy, 1983, Livestock Disease: Economics and Policy, 1987, Agriculture at the Crossroads, 1998; contbr. numerous articles to profl. jours. Recipient Order of the British Empire, Her Majesty the Queen, Buckingham Palace, 1995, Massey Ferguson Nat. Agrl. award, 1998; named Fellow, Royal Soc. of Arts, London, 1995. Fellow Royal Agrl. Soc. Eng.; mem. Agrl. Econs. Soc. (pres. 1996-97), Rural Edn. and Devel. Assn., (pres. 1996-97), Internat. Agrl. Econs. Assn. (UK coun., 1987—), Soc. Vet. Epidemiology and Preventive Medicine. Avocations: furniture restoration, traditional farming, rural craft skills, winemaking, lying in a field. E-mail: J.P.McInerney@exeter.ac.uk. Office: U Exeter Agrl Econs Unit, Lafrowda Hse St Germans Rd, Exeter Devon EX4 6TL, England

MCINERNY, AUSTIN T., planner; b. L.A., Aug. 13, 1967; s. B. McInerny and L. LeMay. BA, U. Calif., Santa Cruz, 1990; MRP, Cornell U., 1997. With CONCUR Inc., Oakland, Calif. Mem. Am. Inst. Cert. Planners.

MCINNES, COLIN ROBERT, space scientist, researcher, educator; b. Glasgow, Scotland, Feb. 12, 1968; s. Ian Ronald and Marion (McDonald) McI.; m. Karen McLaughlin, Febr. 7, 1992; children: Calum, Gregor. BSc with honors, U. Glasgow, 1988, PhD, 1991. Lectr. U. Glasgow, 1991-96, reader, 1996-99, prof., 1999—; adv. House of Lords, 1994; cons. NASA, 1996. Contbr. numerous articles to profl. jours. Recipient Robert Cormack fellow Royal Soc. Edinburgh, 1988, Japanese Soc. for the Promotion of Science fellow, 1996; Rsch. grantee European Space Agy., 1995, Rsch. grantee Leverhuume Trust, 1994. Office: Dept Aerospace Engring, U Glasgow, G12 8QQ Glasgow Scotland

MCINTIRE, MARY, university administrator; b. Chgo., Nov. 23, 1943; d. Philip Thomas and Helen Marie McEnery; m. Larry Vern McIntire, July 5, 1969 (div. May 1995); m. James Robert Pomerantz, May 23, 1998; stepsons: Andrew, William. BA, U. Fla., 1965, MA, 1968; PhD, Rice U., 1975. Instr. U. Houston, 1970-71; instr. Rice U., Houston, 1977-78, program dir. Office Continuing Studies, 1977-81, dir., 1981-86, dean Sch. Continuing Studies, 1986—; cons. Tex. Internat. Edn. Consrtium, Austin, 1998—; pres. adv. bd. Tex. Humanities Resource Ctr., Austin, 1992-93. Commr. Harris County Hist. Commn., Houston, 1978-81, 85-87; mem. exec. com. San Jacinto Girl Scouts, 1998—, bd. dirs., 2000—; mem. allocations com. Gulf Coast United Way, 1991-98; mem. adv. bd. Casa de Esperanza, 2000—; pres. Emerald Cir., 2000—. Recipient Meritorious Svc. award Rice U. Alumni Assn., 1998; named YWCA Woman of Yr. in Edn., Houston, 1994, Woman of Distinction, Greater Houston Women's Found., 1997, Woman on the Move, Tex. Exec. Women, 1999. Mem. Univ. Continuing Edn. Assn. (commr. 1998—), Rsch. Univ. Deans of Continuing Edn., Tex. Assn. Cmty. Svc. and Continuing Edn. (pres. 1986). Avocations: aerobics, swimming, hiking. Home: 5000 Montrose Blvd Unit 18F Houston TX 77006-6564 Office: Rice U Sch Continuing Studies MS 550 PO Box 1892 Houston TX 77251-1892

MCINTOSH, AMY BENNETT, telecommunications company executive; b. Cin., Apr. 14, 1958; d. Robert Charles McIntosh and Nancy Allensworth Drysdale; m. Jeffrey Ross Toobin, May 31, 1986; children: Ellen Frances Toobin, Adam Jerome Toobin. AB, Harvard U., 1980, MBA, 1984. Various positions Am. Express, N.Y.C., 1984-91, v.p. mktg., 1991-93, sr. v.p. mktg., 1993-95; v.p. consumer mktg. Bell Atlantic (previously Nynex), N.Y.C., 1995-98, pres., CEO, Network Data, Inc., 1998—; rsch. analyst Bain & Co., Boston, 1980-82. Chmn. bd., Teach for Am.-N.Y., N.Y.C., 1997—. Mem. Internet Industry Assn. Am. (bd. mem. 1998—). Office: Bell Atlantic 1095 Ave of Americas New York NY 10036

MCINTOSH, CECILIA ANN, biochemist, educator; b. Dayton, Ohio, Apr. 30, 1956; d. Russell Edward McIntosh and Geraldine Rita (Cochran) Slemp; m. Kevin Smith Schweiker, May 28, 1978 (div. Mar. 1989); children: Katrina Lynn McIntosh Schweiker, Rebecca Sue McIntosh Schweiker. BA in Biology cum laude, U. South Fla., 1977, MA in Botany, 1981, PhD in Biology, 1990. Rsch. assoc. U. South Fla., Tampa, 1981-86; sci. mentor Ctr. for Excellence, U. So. Fla., Tampa, 1984-90; tchg. and rsch. asst. dept. biology U. South Fla., Tampa, 1986-90; postdoctoral fellow dept. biochemistry U. Idaho, Moscow, 1990-93; asst. prof. dept. biol. scis. East Tenn. State U., Johnson City, 1993-98, assoc. prof., 1998—, grad. student coord., 1997—; adj. assoc. prof. dept. biochemistry Quillen Coll. Medicine East Tenn. State U., Johnson City, 1995—; sci. mentor U. So. Fla. Ctr. for Excellence, Tampa, 1984-90; rsch. forum judge Coll. Medicine Rsch. Forum, East Tenn. State U., Johnson City, 1994—. Contbr. articles to sci. jours. including Plant Sci., Plant Physiology, Archives Biochemistry and Biophysics. Sci. fair judge East Tenn. Regional Sci. Fair, Johnson City, 1994—. Strengthening program grantee USDA, 1994-95, 97-98, Seed grantee, 1995-97, plant genetic mechanisms grantee, 1998—; rsch. devel. grantee East Tenn. State U. Rsch. Devel. Coun., 1994-96, 97-98; grantee USDA NRI, 1998—; co-grantee Howard Hughes Med. Inst., 2000-2004. Mem. Am. Assn. Women in Sci., Am. Soc. Plant Physiologists, Phytochem. Soc. N.Am. (treas. 1998—), Sigma Xi (sci. fair workshop coord. Appalachian chpt. 1995, Dissertation award 1991). Achievements include characterization of new enzyme in plant flavonoid biosynthesis; biochemical characterization of plant mitochondrial membrane tricarboxylate and phosphate transporters and TCA cycle enzymes. Avocations: outdoor activities, sports, mysteries. Office: East Tenn State U Dept Biol Scis Box 70 703 Johnson City TN 37614-0703

MCINTOSH, DENNIS KEITH, veterinary practitioner, consultant; b. Newark, June 12, 1941; s. Sheldon Weeks and Enid Nicholson (Casey) McI.; children: Kevin, Jamie. BS in Animal Sci., Tex. A&M U., 1963, BS in Vet. Sci., 1967, DVM, 1968. Asst. county agrl. agt. Cleburne, Tex., 1963-65; owner, operator Park North Animal Hosp., San Antonio, 1970-75, El Dorado Animal Hosp., San Antonio, 1973—; co-chmn. vet. tech. adv. coun. Palo Alto Coll. tchr. Animal Health Tech., San Antonio Coll., 1985-95; pres., mgr. Bexar County Emergency Animal Clinic, Inc., 1978-81; cons. vet. practice mgmt., mktg., client rels.; spkr. for vet. meetings, assns.; co-host Ask the Vet, Adopt a Pet, Sta. KENS-TV, 1980-93; vet. mem. Tex. Bd. Health, 1984-89, chmn. disease control com., pers. com.; mem. environ. health, hosps. com. Team capt. Alamo Roundup Club and Pres.' Club of San Antonio C. of C., 1970-75; mem. Guadalupe County Youth Fair Bd., 1978-80. Contbg. author: Mosby's Review Questions and Answers for Veterinary Boards, 1998, Chicken Soup for the Pet Lover's Soul, 1998; contbr. articles to profl. jours. With Vet. Corps, USAF, 1968-70. Recipient Alumnus award Guadalupe County 4-H Club, 1979, Outstanding Svc. award San Antonio Coll., 1986-87, Outstanding Bus. Ptnrs. award N.E. Ind. Sch. Dist., 1995-96. Mem. AMVA, Tex. Vet. Med. Assn. (pres., chmn. bd. dirs.), Tex. Acad. Vet. Practice (pres.), Am. Assn. Human-Animal Bond Vets., Vet. Hosp. Mgrs. Assn., San Antonio C. of C. (life), Tex. County Agrl. Agts. Assn. (4th v.p. 1964), Delta Soc. (pres. San Antonio chpt. 1989-90). Office: 13039 Nacogdoches Rd San Antonio TX 78217-1960

MCINTOSH, EDWIN DAVID GEORGE, pediatrician, educator, pharmaceutical physician; b. Sydney, NSW, Australia, Feb. 7, 1955; s. Edwin Kevin and Beris Olwyn (Mayer) McI. MB BS, U. Sydney, 1979, MPH, 1986; diploma in ob-gyn., London U., 1984, diploma in child health, 1984, PhD, 1997. Registrar The Children's Hosp., Sydney, 1988-90, fellow in preventive medicine, 1991-93; assoc. lectr. U. Sydney, 1995-96; Churchill fellow St. Mary's Hosp., London, 1994-95, rsch. scientist, hon. sr. registrar, 1996-2000; sr. med. adviser vaccines Wyeth; vis. lectr. 1st faculty medicine Charles U., Prague, 1997—; hon. clin. lectr. Imperial Coll. Sch. Medicine at St. Mary's, 1998—. Author: (with others) A Practical Approach to Paediatric Infections, 1996; contbr. articles to profl. jours. Artistic dir. The Glebe Music Festival, Sydney. Fellow St. Andrew's Coll. U. Sydney, 1988—; recipient Australian Coll Paediatrics award, 1993. Fellow Royal Soc. Tropical Medicine and Hygiene, Royal Australian Coll. Physicians, Australian Faculty Pub. Health Medicine; mem. Royal Coll. Paediatrics and Child Health. Home: 36B King Henrys Rd, London NW3 3RP, England Office: Wyeth, Huntercombe Ln South, Taplow Maidenhead Berks SL6 0PH, England

MCINTOSH, MOLLY JEAN, interior designer; b. Spokane, Wash., Feb. 4, 1951; d. Keith L. and Dolores J. (Hensel) Yates; m. Forrest E. McIntosh, Dec. 18, 1971; children: Jennifer, Brandon. Student, N.W. Christian Coll., 1971. Archtl. signage salesperson Clarke & Assoc., Santa Ana, Calif., 1983-84; interior designer Precept Design, Worthington, Ohio, 1984-85, Gracious Living, Redmond, Wash., 1985—. Recipient Silver award Master Builder Assn., 1994. Mem. Am. Soc. Interior Designers (allied mem., showhouse com. 1998), N.W. Soc. Interior Designers (profl. mem., 2d pl. for residential design 1994). Mem. Disciples of Christ. Avocation: traveling. Fax: (425) 836-0311.

MCINTOSH, RICHARD TURNER, construction consultant, wood worker; b. Salem, Mass., Mar. 20, 1926; s. Perley Turner and Frmcuca Edson (Manning) McI.; m. Oct. 10, 1952; children: Susan, Sandra, Stephen, Sally. BA in History, Salem (Mass.) State, 1999. Bldg. inspector; constrn. inspector; home inspector. Treas. Mass. Bldg. Commn. and Inspectors Assn., 1986-96, Manning Assn., North Billerica, Mass., 1994—, Kilwining Orgn. of Boston, Swampscott, Mass., 1996—; Mem. planning bd. Town of Swampscott, 1994—. Cpl. U.S. Army, 1944-46. Mem. Scotts Charitable Soc. Avocations: woodworking, reading biographies, swimming, education. Home and Office: 250 Essex St Swampscott MA 01907-1149

MCINTOSH, WILLIAM ALAN, financier; b. Billericay, Essex, Eng., Nov. 2, 1967; s. Ian George and Felicity Noel (Campbell) McI. MA with honours, Aberdeen (Scotland) U., 1989. Acct. Deloitte Touche, Aberdeen, 1990-93; corp. fin. exec. Hill Samuel Bank, London, 1993-95; financier London, 1995—; bd. dirs. Wellington Pub Co. Plc, Punch Group Plc, Topps Tiler PLc, X-centric. Mem. Inst. Chartered Accts. Scotland, Cobden Club (founder). Avocations: business and finance. Office: 54 Baker St, London W1M 1DJ, England

MCINTURFF, FLOYD M., retired state agency administrator; b. Greenback, Tenn., May 1, 1923; s. Samuel Floyd and Hazel Agnes (Vaden) M.; m. Merle Celeste Sosna, May 27, 1950; children: Judith Margaret, Laura Ellen, Melissa Ann. BS, U. Tenn., Knoxville, 1950. Asst. to the chief engr., missiles Rockwell Internat., Columbus, 1957-73; chief, targeted jobs tax credit program Ohio Bur. Employment Svcs., Columbus, 1974-88; ret., 1988. Commd. officer U.S. Army Signal Corps., 1942-46, 51-52. Mem. Opera Columbus, Columbus Astron. Soc., Soc. Separationists, Sons of Revolution, First Families of Tenn. Avocations: music, astronomy, photography, elderhostel. Home: 4985 Beatrice Dr Columbus OH 43227-2114

MCINTYRE, ANITA GRACE JORDAN, lawyer; b. Louisville, Ky., Jan. 29, 1947; d. Blakely Gordan and Shirley Evans (Grubbs) Jordan; m. Kenneth James McIntyre, Oct. 11, 1969; children: Abigail, Jordan Kenneth. BA, Smith Coll., 1969; JD, U. Detroit, 1975. Bar: Mich. 1975, U.S. Dist. Ct. (ea. dist.) Mich. 1975, U.S. Dist. Ct. (we. dist.) Mich. 1979, U.S. Ct. Appeals (6th cir.) 1979. Ptnr. Rollins White & Rollins, Detroit, 1975-79; vis. assoc. prof. Detroit Coll. Law, 1979-81; assoc. Tyler & Canham, Detroit, 1981-82; prin. Anita G. McIntyre, P.C., Grosse Pointe, Mich., 1982-87, 91—; of counsel Nederlander Dodge & Rollins, Detroit, 1987-90; assoc. Damm & Smith, P.C., Detroit, 1990-91; hearing panel chmn. Atty. Discipline Bd., 1985—. Editor, author (case notes) U. Detroit Jour. Urban Law, 1975; contrbr. articles to profl. jours. Sec. Berry Subdivsn. Assn., Detroit, 1975-77; pres. Smith Coll. Club Detroit, 1982-86; mem. parents bd. U. Liggett Sch., Grosse Pointe, Mich., 1991-95; chmn. polit. action com. Jr. League Detroit, 1998-99. Mem. State Bar Mich., Wayne County (Mich.) Probate Bar Assn., Wayne County Juvenile Trial Lawyers Assn., Edgmont Park Assn. (sec.), Jr. League Detroit (chair pub. affairs com. 1998—, vice chair Mich. state pub. affairs com. 1999). Episcopalian. Avocations: skiing, swimming, needle point. Office: 15324 Mack Ave Ste 201 Grosse Pointe Park MI 48224-3397

MCINTYRE, BERNICE KAY, lawyer, management consultant; b. Worcester, Mass., Aug. 9, 1950; d. William James and Theodora Grace (McCullough) M.; m. Michael Henry Pete, June 25, 1994. BA, Oberlin Coll., 1972; JD, Boston U., 1977. Bar: Mass. 1977. Asst. gen. counsel Dept. Pub. Welfare, Boston, 1977-78; asst. gen. counsel Coastal Zone Mgmt., Boston, 1978-79, gen. counsel, 1979-81; gen. counsel Exec. Office Environ. Affairs, Boston, 1981-83, asst. sec., 1982-83; commr. Dept. Pub. Utilities, Boston, 1983—; appointed by gov. chmn. Pub. Utilities Commn., Boston, 1987-90; active Clinton Gore Energy Transition Team, 1992-93; mgr., sr. cons. Arthur D. Little, Inc., 1991-95; prin., pres. B.K. McIntyre & Assocs., Inc., 1995—; assoc. prof. mgmt. dept. Southeastern U., Washington. Contbr. chpts. to books. Office: BK McIntyre & Assocs Inc 1250 24th St NW Ste 350 Washington DC 20037-1124

MCINTYRE, DOUGLAS CARMICHAEL, II, congressman; b. Lumberton, N.C., Aug. 6, 1956; s. Douglas Carmichael and Thelma Riley (Hedgpeth) McI.; m. Lola Denise Strickland, June 26, 1982; children: Joshua Carmichael, Stephen Christopher. BA, U. N.C., 1978, JD, 1981. Bar: N.C. 1981, U.S. Dist. Ct. (ea. dist.) N.C. 1984, U.S. Dist. Ct. (mid. dist.) N.C. 1985., U.S. Ct. Appeals (4th cir.) 1987, U.S. Supreme Ct., 1987. Assoc. Law Office Bruce Huggins, Lumberton, 1981-82, McLean, Stacy, Henry & McLean, Lumberton, 1982-86; ptnr. Price & McIntyre P.A., Lumberton, 1987-89; prin. McIntyre Law Firm, P.A., Lumberton, 1989-96; congressman U.S. Ho. of Reps., 1997—; mem. law-focused edn. adv. com. N.C. Dept. Pub. Instrn., 1986-87; mem. U.S. Ho. Com. on Agr., 1997—, Nat. Security Com., 1997—; co-chmn. Coalition Task Force on Edn., 1997-98, Congrl. Task Force on Promotion of Fatherhood, Rural Health Care Coalition, 1999—, Democratic Task Force on Children, 1999—; mem. President's Summit on Am.'s Future, 1997. Del. Dem. Nat. Conv., N.Y.C., 1980, N.C. Dems., Raleigh, 1974—; pres. Robeson County Young Dems., Lumberton, 1982; sec.-treas. 7th Congl. Dist. Young Dems., N.C., 1983, chmn., 1984; 2d vice chmn. 7th Congl. Dist. Dems. So. N.C., 1986-89, 1st vice chmn., 1989; mem. state adv. bd. North Carolinians Against Drug and Alcohol Abuse, Raleigh, 1984-85; chmn. Morehead Scholarship Selection Com., Robeson County, 1985-94; deacon, elder, clk. of session Presbyn. Ch.; active Boy Scouts Am., Lumberton, 1983; mem. N.C. Commn. on Children and Youth, 1987-89, N.C. Commn. on the Family, 1989-91; mem. Young Life Lumberton com., 1987-89; chmn. Robeson County U.S. Constn. Bicentennial com., 1986-87; mem. lawyers' adv. com. to N.C. Commn. on Bicentennial of U.S. Constn., 1986-89; bd. dirs. Robeson County Group Home, Lumberton, 1984-87, Lumberton Econ. Advancement for Downtown, Inc., 1987-90, pres., 1988-89, 89-90; chmn. legis. affairs com. C. of C., 1991, 92, 93, bd. dirs., 1992-94; mem. N.C. Mus. of History Assocs., 1987-89; mem. regional selection com. Gov.'s Award for Excellence in Teaching Social Studies, 1991. Morehead Found. scholar, 1974-78; named one of Outstanding Young Men in Am., 1981, 84, 85, 88; Outstanding Young Dem. Robeson County Young Dems., 1984-85; one of State's Outstanding Young Dems. Young Dems. N.C., 1984, 85; recipient Algernon Sydney Sullivan award U. N.C., 1978, Outstanding Young North Carolinian award N.C. Jaycees, 1988, Outstanding Young North Carolinians, Heart Robeson Jaycees, 1988, Nat. Bicentennial Leadership award for Individual Achievement Coun. for Advancement of Citizenship and Ctr. for Civic Edn., Washington, 1987, Gov.'s Outstanding Vol. Svc. award, 1989, Thomas Jefferson award Food Distbrs. Internat., 1998, Guardian of Small Bus. award, Nat. Fedn. Independent Bus., 1997-99, Nat. Rural Health Legislative award, 1999, Outstanding Health Svc. award Cmty. Ptnrs. Health Net, Spirit of Enterprise award, U.S. C. of C., 1997-98. Mem. ABA (exec. com. citizenship edn. com. 1985-87, nat. cmty. law week com. 1982-83), Internat. Platform Assn., N.C. Bar Assn. (chmn. youth edn. and constn. bicentennial com. 1986-87, youth edn. com., exec. coun. young lawyers divsn. 1986-87), Robeson County Bar Assn. (founder, chmn. citizenship edn. com. 1982-94, law day com.), 16th Jud. Dist. Bar Assn., N.C. Acad. Trial Lawyers, N.C. Coll. Advocacy, Christian Legal Soc. (state adv. bd. 1986-90, state pres. 1987), Lumberton C. of C. (bd. dirs. 1992-94), Order of Old Well, Lumberton Rotary Club (bd. dirs. 1995-96), Phi Beta Kappa, Phi Eta Sigma. Avocations: tennis, snow skiing, softball, dancing, Bible study. Home: 1701 N Chestnut St Lumberton NC 28358-3839 Office: 1405 Longworth Washington DC 20515-0001

MCINTYRE, JAMES ERIC, chemist, educator; b. Auchterarder, Scotland, May 7, 1928; s. John Charles and Henrietta Mary (Mitchell) McI.; m. Pauline Brocklehurst, Sept. 14, 1957; 1 child, Neil. BS, U. St. Andrews, 1948; DSc (hon.), Heriot-Watt U., 1994. Rsch. scientist ICI, 1952-77; prof. U. Leeds, Eng., 1977-93; ret., 1993; dir. Gelectrix, Leeds, 1996—. Author: The Chemistry of Fibers, 1971; editor: The Production of Man-Made Fibres, 1976, Textile Terms and Definitions, 10th edit., 1995; inventor in field. Fellow Royal Soc. Chemistry, Inst. Materials, Royal Soc. Arts, Textile Inst. (v.p. 1991-94, Carothers medal 1996); mem. Soc. Dyers and Colourists. Avocations: golf, local history. Home: 3 Rossett Gardens, Harrogate HG2 9PP, England

MCINTYRE, JOHN ANDREW, environmental and economic planner, geography educator; b. Chgo., Mar. 4, 1958; s. Donald Merrill McIntyre and Rosemary Martha (Windgassen) Peters; m. Nancy Lynn Curtis, Sept. 17, 1983. Ba in Geog. Studies, So. Ill. U., 1988, MS in Geography, 1993; diploma in econ. devel., U. Okla., 1993. Cert econ. developer. Sales mgr. Bally Mfg. Inc., Chgo., 1981-87; dir. econ. devel. Riverbend Growth Assn., Godfrey, Ill., 1987-91; dir. Argonne Regional Consortium, Palos Hills, Ill., 1991-93; cmty. devel. dir. Homer Twp., Lockport, Ill., 1993—; adj. faculty dept. natural scis. Joliet (Ill.) Jr. Coll., 1994—; mem. mktg. com. I&M Canal Nat. Heritage Corridor, Lockport, 1993—; bd. dirs. Applied Geography Conf., Denton, Tex., 1993—. Contbr. articles to profl. jours. Trustee Village Orland Hills, Ill., 1992-94; instr. Jr. Achievement, Orland Park, 1993; facilitator Riverbend in 90's, Alton, Ill., 1989-91. Sgt. USAF, 1977-81. Recipient Superior Lit. award Mid-Am. Econ. Devel. Coun., Deerfield, Ill., 1993. Mem. Assn. Am. Geographers (meteorology splty. group), Am. Econ. Devel. Coun. (Howard Roepke award 1994), Am. Planning Assn. (environ. splty. group), Am. Inst. Cert. Planners. Libertarian. Achievements include research on geographic information systems as applied to economic development, on economic impacts of federal research laboratories at local and regional levels; research on environmental and geological aspects of the Illinois and Michigan canal national heritage corridor. Home: 9212 Quail Ct Orland Hills IL 60477-5916 Office: Homer Twp 14350 W 151st St Lockport IL 60441-6776

MCINTYRE, LOUISE S., income tax consultant; b. Cin., Jan. 29, 1924; d. George Washington and Bertha (McDaniels) Sullivan; m. Harry McIntyre Jr., Jan. 18, 1947; children: Carol L., Patricia A., Harriet L., Harry J., Brenda R. AA, Mira Costa Coll., Oceanside, Calif., 1972; grad. in auditing, Nat. Tax Practice Inst., 1989. Enrolled agt. Hydraulic testor Paterson Field, Fairfield, Ohio, 1942-45; control clk. Hickam Field, Honolulu, 1945-47; clk.-typist Patterson Field, Fairfield, 1947-49, Camp LeJeune, Jacksonville, N.C., 1951-56; sec., bookkeeper Mission Bowl, Oceanside, 1973-79; income tax cons. Oceanside, 1974—. Mem. Oceanside Human Rels. Commn., 1970; bd. dirs. Armed Forces YMCA, Oceanside, 1969-71, Oceanside Christian Women's Club, 1988-91, North County Concert Assn. Aux., 1993-96; active PTA, Girl Scout U.S. Mem. Inland Soc. Tax Cons. (bd. dirs. 1988—), Am. Soc. Women Accts. (v.p. 1989-90), Enrolled Agts. Palomar, Nat. Assn. Enrolled Agts., Nat. Soc. Pub. Accts., Calif. Assn. Ind. Accts., Palmquist PTA (hon. life). Avocations: bowling, dancing, crafts, interior decorating, cake decorating. Home: 328 Camelot Dr Oceanside CA 92054-4515

MCIVOR, LEE, public relations consultant; b. Port Moresby, Papua New Guinea, Jan. 6, 1958; arrived in Australia, 1972; d. Colin and Beverley (Nielsen) McI. B of Bus. Comm., 1982; BA, Sydney U., 1995. Tutor, sr. lectr. Queensland U. Technology, Brisbane, Australia, 1987-89; news editor ABC Radio, Australia, 1989-91; exec. prodr. Shot in the Dark Prodns., Sydney, 1991-92; journalist Campus Rev., Sydney, 1992; media officer U. Western Australia, Sydney, 1994-95; dir. Maximum Exposure, Sydney, 1996—; dir. Venus Awards, 1997-98, arts publicist 1996-98; news editor 101FM, Brisbane, 1987-89. Avocations: scuba diving, fast cars, photography. Office: Maximum Exposure, PO Box 78, Bundeena SYD 2230, Australia

MCKAY, DONALD ARTHUR, mechanical engineer; b. June 10, 1931; s. Benjamin Arthur and Florence (Heeney) McK.; m. Janette Capellaro, Dec. 30, 1978; children by previous marriage: Susan Deeb, Barbara Albury, Laura Lower, Douglas. AB, Harvard U., 1952. Registered profl. engr., Mass. Sales engr. C.P. Blouin, Cambridge, Mass., 1955-60; contract mgr. to v.p. Limbach Co., Boston, 1960-68; exec. v.p. Tougher Heating & Plumbing Co., Albany, N.Y., 1968-74; chmn., CEO Tougher Industries, Albany, 1986—, pres., 1974—; v.p. Spunduct Inc. Pres. Fifty Group (Albany), 1991-92; mem. corp. gifts com. Albany Med. Ctr., 1978-84; chmn. 25th reunion fund raising com. of upstate N.Y., Harvard Class '52; mem. curriculum adv. bd. Hudson Valley C.C.; trustee Coll. St. Rose, sec.; bd. dirs. Samaritan Hosp. N.E. Health, treas.; bd. dirs. Albany Meml. Hosp., chmn., 1988-91. With USN, 1951-54. Recipient Albany Meml. Hosp. Found. award, 1998. Mem. ASHRAE, NSPE, Am. Soc. Sanitary Engrs., Am. Soc. Plumbing Engrs., Mech. Contractors Assn. Am. (pres. capital dist. 1981-82, pres.-elect 1988, pres. 1989-90), Mech. Contractors Assn., N.Y. State (v.p. 1981-82, pres.

1981-82), Subcontractors Assn. N.Y. (bd. dirs.), N.Y. State Subcontractors Assn. (bd. dirs.), Aircraft Owners and Pilots Assn., Exptl. Aircraft Assn., Albany-Colonie Regional C. of C. (bd. dirs., mem. exec. com., James Michael's Envoy salute 1993, chmn. 1998), Clan McKay Soc. N.Am., Heating Ventilating Contractors Assn. of U.K. (hon. past pres. 1995), Harvard Club (pres. N.E. N.Y. chpt. 1987-88) , Masons (Dorchester, Mass.), Wolferts Roost Country Club, Am. Su bcontractors Assn. (N.Y. chpt.). Congregationalist. Home: 312 Presidential Way Guilderland NY 12084-9536 Office: Tougher Industries PO Box 4067 175 Broadway Albany NY 12204-2734

MC KAY, EMILY GANTZ, civil rights professional; b. Columbus, Ohio, Mar. 13, 1945; d. Harry S. and Edwina (Bookwalter) Gantz; m. Jack Alexander McKay, July 3, 1965. BA, Stanford U., 1966, MA, 1967. From pub. info. specialist to rsch. assoc. Cmty. Action Pitts., 1967-70; freelance cons., 1969-70; pub. rels. & materials specialist Met. Cleve. JOBS Coun., 1971-72; rsch. & mgmt. cons. BLK Group, Inc., Washington, 1970-73; dir. tech. products Am. Tech. Assistance Corp., McLean, Va., 1973-74; rsch. and mgmt. cons. CONSAD Rsch. Corp., Pitts., 1974-76, v.p., 1976-78; spl. asst. to pres. for planning and eval. Nat. Coun. La Raza, Washington, 1978-82, v.p. rsch., advocacy & legislation, 1981-88, exec. v.p., 1983-88, cons. to pres., 1988-90, v.p. instl. devel., 1991-93, sr. v.p. instl. devel., 1993-94; pres. Mosaica Ctr. for Nonprofit Devel. and Pluralism, 1994—; cons. resource devel. New Israel Fund, 1989-91; cons. City of Cleve., Nat. Assn. Cmty. Devel., Nat. Coun. La Raza, 1975-78, Ford Found., 1989, Nat. AIDS Network, 1988-89, Am. Cultural Ctr., Israel, 1990, 2000, Nat. Hispana Leadership Inst., 1993; vol.orgnl. cons. SHATIL, Jerusalem and cmty. based groups in Israel, 1987—; guest faculty Union Inst. Grad. Sch.; adj. faculty Sch. Internat. Rels. Am. U., Washington, 1995—. Author devel. tng. materials and HIV/AIDS tech. assistance materials. Co-chmn. Citizens Adv. Com. to D.C. Bar, 1986-87; mem. Mayor's Commn. Coop. Econ. Devel., 1981-83; non-lawyer mem. bd. govs. D.C. Bar, 1982-85; exec. com., bd. dirs. Indochina Resource Action Ctr., 1982-92; bd. dirs. exec. com. Southeast Asia Resource Action Ctr., 1993-97; co-chmn. Citizens Commn. Adminstrn. Justice, 1982-84; exec. com. Coalition on Human Needs, 1981-88; mem. Washington area steering com. New Israel Fund, 1989-91; co-chmn. adv. com. to Washington dist. office dir. Immigration and Naturalization Svc., 1984-88; chair Refugee Women in Devel., 1987-90, vice-chair, 1990-94; nat. adv. bd. Project Blueprint United Way of Am., 1992-94, diversity com., 1994-96; vice-chair, treas. Fund for the Future of Our Children, 1994—; sec. bd. dirs. New Bosnia Fund, 1995-99, U.S. vice-chair, 1997—; bd. advisors Internat. Ctr. for Residential Edn., 1994-96; bd. dirs. Mary's Ctr. Maternal and Child Care, 1995—, treas., 1996—; treas., bd. dirs. AVODAH: The Jewish Svc. Corps., 1996-99; bd. dirs. Nat. Hispana Leadership Inst., 1997—, treas., 1998—; mem. working group Memorandum of Understanding between HHS and Israeli Ministry of Labour and Social Welfare, 1990-94, chair subcom Youth at Risk, 1992-94; adv. merit sel. panel Superior Ct. D.C., 1987-90; mem. US-Israel Women to Women planning task force, 2000. Recipient I. Pat Rios award Guadalupe Ctr., 1988; Ford Found. nat. honors fellow, 1966-67. Mem. NAACP, Nat. Coun. La Raza, Phi Beta Kappa. Democrat. E-mail: emily@mosaica.org. Home: 3200 19th St NW Washington DC 20010-1006 Office: 1522 K St NW Ste 1130 Washington DC 20005-1225

MCKAY, JOHN JUDSON, JR., lawyer; b. Anderson, S.C., Aug. 13, 1939; s. John Judson and Polly (Plowden) McK.; m. Jill Hall Ryon, Aug. 3, 1961 (div. Dec. 1980); children: Julia Plowden, Katherine Henry, William Ryon, Elizabeth Hall; m. Jane Leahey, Feb. 18, 1982; children: Andrew Leahey, Jennifer McFaddin. AB in History, U. S.C., 1960, JD cum laude, 1966. Bar: S.C. 1966, U.S. Dist. Ct. S.C. 1966, U.S. Ct. Appeals (4th cir.) 1974, U.S. Supreme Ct. 1981, U.S. Dist. Ct. (so. dist.) Ga. 1988, U.S. Ct. Appeals (11th cir.), 1990. Assoc. Haynsworth, Perry, Bryant, Marion & Johnstone, Greenville, S.C., 1966-70; ptnr. Rainey, McKay, Britton, Gibbes & Clarkson, P.A., and predecessor, Greenville, 1970-78; sole practice, Hilton Head Island, S.C., 1978-80; ptnr. McKay & Gertz, P.A., Hilton Head Island, 1980-81, McKay & Mullen, P.A., Hilton Head Island, 1981-88, McKay & Taylor, Hilton Head, 1988-91; pvt. practice, 1991—. Served to lt. (j.g.) USNR, 1961-64; lt. comdr. Res. (ret.). Mem. ABA, S.C. Bar Assn. (pres. young lawyers sect. 1970, exec. com. 1971-72, assoc. mem. grievance and disciplinary com. 1983-87), S.C. Bar, Beaufort County Bar Assn., Hilton Head Bar Assn., Assn. Trial Lawyers Am., S.C. Trial Lawyers Assn., S.C. Bar Found. (pres. 1977), Blue Key, Wig and Robe, Phi Delta Phi. Episcopalian. Clubs: Poinsett (Greenville). Editor-in-chief U. S.C. Law Rev., 1966; contbr. articles to legal jours. Home: 17 Foxbriar Ln Hilton Head Island SC 29926 Office: 203 Watersedge Hilton Head Island SC 29928-3541

MCKAY, MICHAEL WENDELL, lawyer; b. Beaufort, S.C., Dec. 14, 1949; s. John W. and Alice (Thornhill) M.; m. Leah H. McKay; children: Wendell, Slater, Watson, Harris. BA, La. State U., Baton Rouge, 1971, JD, 1974. Assoc./ptnr. Brewer & McKay, Baton Rouge, 1974-80; ptnr. Roy, Kiesel, Patteshon & McKay, Baton Rouge, 1980-84; pvt. practice Baton Rouge, 1984-88; dir. Hoffman Sutterfield, Baton Rouge, 1988-97; of counsel Shows, Cali & Burns, Baton Rouge, 1997-99; ptnr. McKay Williamson & Lutgring, Baton Rouge, 1999—. Bd. dirs. Baton Rouge Area Found., 1994-97; treas., bd. dirs. Capital Area Legal Svcs. Corp., Baton Rouge, 1978-83. Mem. ABA, La. State Bar Assn. (treas. 1999—, Pres.'s award for outstanding svc. 1997, Pro Bono Publico award 1994), Baton Rouge Bar Assn. (pres., sec., treas. 1989-93), La. Bar Found. (bd. dirs. 1998—), La. Assn. Def. Counsel (bd. dirs. 1999—), Am. Inns of Ct. Democrat. Episcopalian. Avocation: tennis. Home: 1558 Ingleside Dr Baton Rouge LA 70808-1200 Office: McKay Williamson & Lutgring 637 Saint Ferdinand St Baton Rouge LA 70802-6152

MCKAY, RENEE, artist; b. Montreal, Que., Can.; came to U.S., 1946, naturalized, 1954; d. Frederick Garvin and Mildred Gladys (Higgins) Smith; m. Kenneth Gardiner McKay, July 25, 1942; children: Margaret Craig, Kenneth Gardner. BA, McGill U., 1941. Tchr. art Peck Sch., Morristown, N.J., 1955-56. One woman shows include Pen and Brush Club, N.Y.C., 1957, Cosmopolitan Club, N.Y.C., 1958; group shows include Weyhe Gallery, N.Y.C., 1978, Newark Mus., 1955, 59, Montclair (N.J.) Mus., 1955-58, Nat. Assn. Women Artists, Nat. Acad. Galleries, 1954-78, N.Y. World's Fair, 1964-65, Audubon Artists, N.Y.C., 1955-62, 74-79, N.Y. Soc. Women Artists, 1979-80, Provincetown (Mass.) Art Assn. and Mus., 1975-79; traveling shows in France, Belgium, Italy, Scotland, Can., Japan; represented in permanent collections: Slater Meml. Mus., Norwich, Conn., Norfolk (Va.) Mus., Butler Inst. Am. Art, Youngstown, Ohio, Lydia Drake Libr., Pembroke, Mass., many pvt. collections. Recipient Jane Peterson prize in oils Nat. Assn. Women Artists, 1954, Famous Artists Sch. prize in watercolor, 1959, Grumbacher Artists Watercolor award 1970, Solo award Pen and Brush, 1957, Sadie-Max Tesser award in watercolor Audubon Artists, 1975, Peterson prize in oils, 1980, Michael Engel prize Nat. Soc. Painters in Casein and Acrylic, 1983. Mem. Nat. Assn. Women Artists (2d v.p. 1969-70, adv. bd. 1974-76), Audubon Artists (pres. 1979, dir. oils 1986-88), Artist Equity (dir. 1977-79, v.p. 1979-81), N.Y. Soc. Women Artists, Pen and Brush, Nat. Soc. Painters in Casein and Acrylic M.J. Kaplan prize 1984, Nat. Arts Club, Provincetown Art Assn. and Mus., Key West Art Assn., Cosmopolitan Club.

MCKEAN, JOHN MAULE, architecture educator, historian, critic; b. Glasgow, Scotland; s. John Laurie and Nancy Burns (Lendrum) McK.; children: Jerome, Sophie, Jack. BArch, U. Strathclyde, Scotland, 1968; MA in Archtl. History & Theory, U. Essex, Eng., 1971. Architect Inner London Edn. Auth., 1969-70; asst. editor The Architect's Jour., London, 1971-75; lectr. North East London Polytechnic, 1976-80; tutor The Archtl. Assn., London, 1976-80; sr. lectr. U. North London, 1980-90; prin. lectr. U. Brighton, Sussex, Eng., 1990-96, prof., reader in architecture, 1996—; external examiner Nottingham Trent U., 1984-87, U. East London, 2000—, South Bank U., London, 2000—; course dir. Architecture U. North London, 1987-90, Interior Architecture, Brighton, 1990-96; originator, dir. MA Interior Design, Brighton, 1995—; specialist assessor archtl. history The Higher Edn. Funding Coun. Eng., 1996—. Author: Learning from Segal, 1989, The Royal Festival Hall, 1992, Leicester Engineering Building, 1994, Crystal Palace, 1994 (Am. Inst. Architect's Internat. Book award), C.R. Mackintosh: A Pocket Guide, 1998, C.R. Mackintosh: Architect, Artist, Icon, 2000; co-author: Architecture of the Western World, 1980, Alexander "Greek" Thomson, 1994 (AIA Internat. Book award). Jr. sch. gov., Brighton, 1992-96, secondary sch. gov., 1997-99. Fellow Royal Soc. Arts; mem. Internat. Union Architects (elected mem. critics circle), Royal Inst. Brit. Architects (assoc.), Royal Incorporation Architects in Scotland (assoc.), Sri Lankan Inst. Architects (assoc.), Chartered Soc. Designers. Green Party. Avocations: music, painting, photography. Office: U Brighton Sch Architecture, Mithras House Lewes Rd, Brighton BN2 4AT, England

MCKEAN, RODERICK HUGH ROSS, solicitor; b. Edinburgh, Scotland, Mar. 13, 1956; s. Hugh Ross and Louise Muriel (Haldane) McK. LLB with honors, Edinburgh U., 1978. Trainee solicitor W&J Burness, Edinburgh, U.K., 1978-80; solicitor Maclay, Murray & Spens, Glasgow, 1980-84, Lovell, White & King, London, 1984-88; ptnr. Lovell White Durrant, London, 1988-96; mng. ptr./Asia Lovells, Hong Kong, 1996—. Mem. Law Soc. of Scotland, Law Soc. Eng. and Wales, Law Soc. Hong Kong. Avocations: skiing, sailing, golf, tennis. Office: Lovells, 2 Queens Rd Ctrl, 23F Cheung Kong Ctr Hong Kong Hong Kong China

MCKEAND, PATRICK JOSEPH, newspaper publisher, educator; b. Anderson, Ind., June 10, 1941; s. William Dale and Iva Pearl (Shaw) McK. BA, Ind. U., 1963; MA, Ball State U., 1983. Staff writer The St. Petersburg (Fla.) Times, 1963; mng. editor The Anderson (Ind.) Herald, 1968-79; adminstr. analyst Ind. Medicaid Program, Indpls., 1980-81; assoc. prof. Defense Info. Sch., Ft. Ben Harrison, Ind., 1981-89; owner p.m. ink!, Indpls., 1989—; pub. bd. dirs. Student Pub. at Ind. U., Purdue U. at Indpls., 1992—; bd. dirs. Miss Indpls. Scholarship Pageant, Indpls, 1994—. Capt. U.S. Army, 1964-68. Decorated Bronze Star, Army Commendation medal with 1 Oak leaf cluster, recipient disting. Newspaper award from CMA, 1998. Mem. Soc. Profl. Journalists (bd. dirs.), Soc. Newspaper Design, Assn. Educators in Journalism and Mass Comm., Associated Press Mng. Editors Assn., Ind. Collegiate Press Assn. (bd. dirs., exec. dir.), Coll. Media Advisors (Disting. Newspaper Adviser award 1998). Home: 4450 E 56th St Indianapolis IN 46220-5710 Office: Sch of Journalism 902 W New York St Indianapolis IN 46202-5197

MCKEE, GEORGE MOFFITT, JR., civil engineer, consultant; b. Valparaiso, Nebr., Mar. 27, 1924; s. George Moffitt and Iva (Santrock) McK.; m. Mary Lee Taylor, Aug. 11, 1945; children: Michael Craig, Thomas Lee, Mary Kathleen, Marsha Coleen, Charlotte Anne. Student, Kans. State Coll. Agr. and Applied Sci., 1942-43, Bowling Green State U., 1943; BSECE, U. Mich., 1947. Registered profl. civil engr., Kans., Okla., registered land surveyor, Kans. Draftsman Jackson Constrn. Co., Colby, Kans., 1945-46; asst. engr. Thomas County, Colby, 1946; engr. Sherman County, Goodland, Kans., 1947-51; salesman Oehlert Tractor & Equipment Co., Colby, 1951-52; owner, operator George M. McKee, Jr.; cons. engrs. Colby, 1952-72; sr. v.p. engring. Contract Surety Cons., Wichita, Kans., 1974-2000; engring. cons. Wichita, 2000—. Adv. rep. Kans State U., Manhattan, 1957-62; mem. adv. com. N.W. Kans. Area Vocat. Tech. Sch., Goodland, 1967-71; chmn. ofcl. bd. Meth. Ch., 1966-67. With USMCR, 1942-45. Mem. Kans. Soc. Profl. Engrs. (pres. N.W. profl. engrs. chpt. 1962-63, treas. cons. engrs. sect. 1961-63), Kans. County Engr.'s Assn. (dist. v.p. 1950-51), N.W. Kans. Hwy. Ofcls. Assn. (sec. 1948-49), Nat. Soc. Profl. Engrs., Kans. State U. Alumni Assn. (life, pres. Thomas County 1956-57), Am. Legion (Goodland 1st vice comdr. 1948-49), The Alumni Assn. U. Mich. (life), Colby C. of C. (v.p. 1963-64), Goodland Jr. C. of C. (pres. 1951-52), Masons (32 degree, Shriner), Order of the Ea. Star. Home: 8930 Suncrest St # 502 Wichita KS 67212-4069

MCKEE, MARGARET JEAN, federal agency executive; b. New Haven, June 20, 1929; d. Waldo McCutcheon and Elizabeth (Thayer) McKee; A.B., Vassar Coll., 1951. Staff asst. United Rep. Fin. Com., N.Y.C., 1952; staff asst. N.Y. Rep. State Com., N.Y.C., 1953-55; staff asst. Crusade for Freedom (name later changed to Radio Free Europe Fund), N.Y.C., 1955-57; researcher Stricker & Henning Research Assocs., Inc., N.Y.C., 1957-59; exec. sec. New Yorkers for Nixon (name later changed to N.Y. State Ind. Citizens for Nixon Lodge), N.Y.C., 1959-60; asst. to Raymond Moley, polit. columnist, N.Y.C., 1961; asst. campaign com. Louis J. Lefkowitz for Mayor, N.Y.C., 1961; research programmer, treas. Consensus, Inc., N.Y.C., 1962-67; spl. asst. to U.S. Senator Jacob K. Javits, N.Y., 1967-73, adminstrv. asst., 1973-75; dep. adminstr. Am. Revolution Bicentennial Adminstrn., 1976, acting adminstr., 1976-77; chief of staff Perry B. Duryea (minority leader) N.Y. State Assembly, 1978; public affairs cons., 1979-80; dir. govt. relations Gen. Mills Restaurant Group, Inc., 1980-83; exec. dir. Fed. Mediation and Conciliation Service, 1983-86; mem. Fed. Labor Rels. Authority, 1986-89, chmn., 1989-94; mem. Nat. Partnership Coun., 1993-94; bd. dirs. Interam. Life Ins. Co., 1979-86, VNNC, Inc., 1992-97 (treas.); chmn. adv. bd. Workplace Solutions, 1996—. Mem. N.Y. State Bingo Control Commn., 1965-72, U.S. Adv. Commn. on Public Diplomacy, 1979-82; pres. Bklyn. Heights Slope Young Rep. Club, 1955-56; co-chmn. Bklyn. Citizens for Eisenhower-Nixon, 1956; chmn. 2d Jud. Dist. Assn. N.Y. State Young Rep. Clubs, Inc., 1957-58, vice-chmn., mem. bd. govs., 1958-60, v.p., 1960-62; pres., 1962-64; mem. exec. com. Fedn. Women's Rep. Clubs N.Y. State, Inc., 1960-64, mem. council, 1964-70; mem. exec. com. N.Y. Rep. State Com. 1962-64; co-chmn. spl. assts. Rockefeller for Pres. Nat. Campaign com., N.Y.C., 1964; co-dir. N.Y. Rep. State Campaign Com., 1964; asst. campaign mgr. Kenneth B. Keating for Judge Ct. Appeals, N.Y., 1965; dir. scheduling Gov. Rockefeller campaign, 1966, Sen. Charles E. Goodell campaign, 1970; dir. scheduling and speakers' bur. N.Y. Com. to Re-elect the Pres., 1972; dir. planning and strategy, Conn. Reagan-Bush campaign, Hartford, 1980; mem. annual fund adv. com. Vassar Coll., 1992-96, 50th Reunion chmn. 2001. Mem. bd. govs. Women's Nat. Rep. Club, N.Y.C., 1963-66. Mem. Jr. League of Bklyn. (past (dir.), Exec. Women in Govt. (chmn. 1986), Nat. Women's Edn. Fund (mem. bd.), Am. Newspaper Women's Club, Nat. Soc. Colonial Dames Am. Episcopalian. Club: Vassar (past dir., Bklyn.). Home: 532 S Brooksvale Rd Cheshire CT 06410-3515 also: 3001 Veazey Ter NW Apt 1225 Washington DC 20008-5407

MCKEIGHEN, RONALD EUGENE, physicist; b. Marion, Ill., Oct. 17, 1942; s. George A. and Aileen (Reach) McK.; m. Loretta M. Ward, Sept. 3, 1966; children: Kevin, Christy. BS in Engring. Physics, U. Ill., 1964, MS in Nuclear Engring., 1965, PhD in Physics, 1971. Postdoctoral in cancer rsch. and nuclear medicine Oak Ridge Nat. Lab., 1972-73; sr. prin. rsch. scientist Searle/Siemens Ultrasound, Des Plaines, 1973-79; sr. R&D engr. KB-Aerotech, Lewistown, Pa., 1979-83; staff scientist Advanced Diagnostic Rsch., Tempe, Ariz., 1983-85; prin. staff engr. Motorola Space Elect, Scottsdale, Ariz., 1985-86; mgr. advanced devel. Advanced Tech. Labs., Bothel, Wash., 1986-93; dir. advanced devel. Acoustic Imaging inc., Phoenix, 1993—. Contbr. articles to profl. jours. and chpts. to books. Spl. fellow in nuclear engring. AEC. Mem. IEEE. Mem. Pentecostal Ch. Achievements include patent for concept of digital beamformer for ultrasonic phased array, developed ultrasonic transducer arrays and sensors. Home: 1432 E Desert Flower Ln Phoenix AZ 85048-5932 Office: Acoustic Imaging 10027 S 51st St Ste 101 Phoenix AZ 85044-5207

MCKELLEN, IAN, actor; b. Burnley, England, May 25, 1939; s. Denis Murray and Margery (Sutcliffe) McK. Student, St. Catharine's Coll., Cambridge. Prof. Oxford U., 1990-91. First stage appearance as Roper in A Man for All Seasons, Belgrade Theatre, Coventry, Eng., 1961; numerous other parts include title roles in Henry V, Luther, Ipswich, 1962-63, Aufidius in Coriolanus, Arthur Seaton in Saturday Night and Sunday Morning, title role in Sir Thomas More, Nottingham Playhouse, 1963-64; London debut as Godfrey in A Scent of Flowers, 1964, Claudio in Much Ado About Nothing, Andrew Cobham in Their Very Own and Golden City, 1966; title part in O'Flaherty, V.C. and Bonapart in The Man of Destiny, 1966, (Broadway debut) Leonidik in the Promise, London, 1966-67, Richard II, Edward II, Hamlet, Prospect Theatre Co., 1968-71; Captain Plume in The Recruiting Officer; founder-mem. Actors' Co., Edinburgh Festival, 1972 and touring as Giovanni in Tis Pity She's a Whore, Page-Boy in Ruling the Roost, title role Wood Demon; debut with R.S.C. as Dr. Faustus, Edinburgh Festival, 1974; title role in The Marquis of Keith, Philip the Bastard in King John, 1974-75, Young Vic Colin in Ashes, 1975; Royal Shakespeare Co.: Burglar in Too True to be Good, Romeo, MacBeth, Leontes in the Winter's Tale, Face in the Alchemist, Bernick in Pillars of the Community, Langevin in Days of the Commune, 1976-78, Ivanov in Every Good Boy Deserves Favour, Toby Belch in Twelth Night, Andrei in The Three Sisters, Max in Bent, 1979, Amadeus, N.Y.C., 1980, Iago in Othello, The Other Place, Stratford, 1989; European tour of one-man show Acting Shakespeare, 1983, also L.A., N.Y.C., 1984, one-man show A Knight Out at the Lyceum (devised especially for Gay Games IV U.K. and South Africa tour), 1994; assoc. dir. Nat. Theatre, London, 1984-86, plays include: Venice Preserved, Wild Honey, Coriolanus, Duchess of Malfi, The Cherry Orchard, King Lear, Richard III, Napoli Milionaria, Uncle Vanya, An Enemy of The People, Peter Pan, others; dir. first prodn. The Prime of Miss Jean Brodie, Liverpool Playhouse, 1969, A Private Matter, 1973, The Clandestine Marriage, 1975; films include: Alfrred the Great, 1969, The Promise, 1969, A Touch of Love, 1969, The Keep, 1982, Plenty, Zina, 1985, Scandal, 1988, The Ballad of Little Jo, 1992, I'll Do Anything, 1992, Last Action Hero, 1993, Six Degrees of Separation, 1993, The Shadow, 1994, Jack and Sarah, 1994, Restoration, 1994, Richard III, 1995, Cold Comfort Farm, 1995, Bent, 1996, Swept From the Sea, 1996, Apt Pupil, 1997, Gods and Monsters, 1997; TV appearances include: David Copperfield, 1965, Ross, 1969, Richard II, Edward II and Hamlet, 1970, Hedda Gabler, 1974, Macbeth, Every Good Boy Deserves Favour, Dying Day, 1979, Acting Shakespeare, 1981, The Scarlet Pimpernel, 1982, And the Band Played On, 1993 (Emmy nomination, Supporting Actor, 1996). Recipient Clarence Derwent award, 1964, Variety and Plays and Players awards, 1966; Actor of Year, Plays and Players, 1976, Soc. of West End Theatres for Best Actor in Revival award, 1977, for Best Comedy Performance, 1978, for Best Actor in a New Play, 1979, Tony Award for Best Actor, Drama Desk award, Outer Critics Circle award, N.Y. Drama League award, 1981, Performer of the Yr. award Royal TV Soc., 1983; decorated comdr. Order Brit. Empire, knight Bachelor. Mem. Brit. Actors' Equity (coun. 1970-71).

MCKELLOP, HARRY ALDEN, biomechanical engineering educator; b. L.A., Nov. 7, 1945; s. Thomas and Opal Nina (Brown) McK.; m. Tovya Wager, Nov. 5, 1989; 1 child, Rachelle Tashi. BS in Mech. Engring., UCLA, 1970, MS in Mech. Engring., 1972; PhD in Mech. Engring., U. So. Calif., 1988. Adj. asst. prof. surgery U. Calif., 1979-80; instr. rsch. orthopaedics U. So. Calif., L.A., 1980-89; dir. J. Vernon Luck Orthopaedic Rsch. Ctr., L.A., 1993—; asst. prof. orthopaedics JVL Orthopaedic Rsch. Ctr., L.A., 1989-95, asst. prof. biomed. engring., 1993-95, assoc. prof. orthopaedics and biomed., 1995-98, dir. rsch., 1994-98; v.p. rsch. Orthopaedic Hosp., L.A., 1996—. Contbr. over 75 articles to profl. jours. Recipient John Charnley award, 1994, 2000; NIH grantee, 1994-97; awardee Kappa Delta, 1998. Fellow Am. Inst. Med. and Biol. Engring.; mem. Orthopaedic Rsch. Soc., Am. Acad. Orthopaedic Surgeons, Hip Soc. Achievements include development of wear resistant Polythylene for Joint Replacements; developed total system for fixing complex femur fractures. Office: Orthopaedic Hospital 2400 S Flower St Los Angeles CA 90007-2629

MCKELVEY, GERALD, public relations executive; b. Waynesboro, Pa., June 27, 1943; s. Gerald Campbell and Mary Lou (Dunn) McK.; m. Lynn Brenner. BA, Wash. Coll., 1965. Reporter The Record Herald, Waynesboro, Pa., 1965-67; reporter, editor Phila. Inquirer, 1967-76; night city editor Newsday, Melville, 1976-81; dep. met. editor N.Y. Newsday, 1981-88; spl. asst. Manhattan Dist. Atty.'s Office, N.Y.C., 1988-96; sr. v.p. Rubenstein Assocs., Inc., N.Y.C., 1996—. Trustee Ch. of St. Mary Virgin, N.Y.C., 1996—. Mem. SAR, The Inner Cir. Office: Rubenstein Assocs Inc 1345 Avenue Of The Americas New York NY 10105-0302

MCKELVY, MICHAEL JOHN, materials chemist, research scientist; b. Berkeley, Calif., Apr. 19, 1954; s. Andy Milton and Dagmar Marie (Johnson) McK.; m. Margaret Knight Riddall, Aug. 2, 1975; children: Robin, Adam, Evan. BS in Chemistry, U. Calif., Berkeley, 1975; MS in Chemistry, Ariz. State U., 1981, PhD in Chemistry, 1985. Engr. crystal growing lab., ctr. solid state sci. Ariz. State U., Tempe, 1976-82, materials sci. engr. II, 1982-84, rsch. specialist, 1984-90, mgr. materials facility, 1986-94, assoc. rsch. scientist, 1990-99, affiliate assoc. prof. sci. & engring. of materials PhD program, 1993-99, dir. materials facility, 1994—, dir. Goldwater materials sci. labs., 1995—, acting dir. ctr. solid state sci., 1997, sr. rsch. scientist, 1999—, affiliate prof. sci. and engring. materials PhD program, 1999—; invited asst. prof. Institut des Matériaux de Nantes, U. Nantes, France, 1993; proposal reviewer Petroleum Rsch. Fund, Washington, 1992-94, U.S. Dept. Energy, 2000—. Contbr. articles to profl. jours.; manuscript reviewer Chemistry of Materials, 1994—, Jour. Physics and Chemistry of Solids, 1995, Jour. Solid State Chemistry, 1996—, Molecular Crystals and Liquid Crystals, 1997-98, Jour. Am. Chem. Soc., 1998—. Coach Chandler (Ariz.) Youth Baseball, 1988-95, Chandler Am. Little League, 1996-97; chair Cub Scout pack com., Boy Scouts Am., Mesa, Ariz., 1992, mem. Boy Scout com., Chandler, 1993-95. Rsch. grantee NSF, 1986—, Petroleum Rsch. Fund, 1992-95, Dept. Energy, 1995—. Mem. Am. Chem. Soc., Materials Rsch. Soc. Democrat. Presbyterian. Achievements include patents for Method for Detection of Chemical Components, Chemical Switch and Method for Detection of Chemical Compounds, and Chemical Switch for Detection of Chemical Components; co-development of atomic-level imaging of Lamellar Intercalation Reaction processes using dynamic high-resolution transmission electron microscopy and scanning tunneling microscopy/spectroscopy; research in new materials synthesis, materials reaction mechanisms, carbon dioxide mineral sequestration, intercalation chemistry, thermal chemistry and analysis, materials sci. edn. Office: Ariz State U Ctr for Solid State Science Tempe AZ 85287-1704

MCKENNA, FREDERICK GREGORY, lawyer, consultant; b. Chgo., Oct. 4, 1952; s. Frederick Hilary and Jean Elizabeth (Henneberry) McK.; m. Cornelia Ann Burns, Nov. 17, 1984; children: Kieran Padraig, Conor Burns. BA with honors, Coll. Holy Cross, 1974; JD, Georgetown U., 1978; postgrad., U. Nev., Las Vegas, U. Denver. Bar: D.C. 1978, Md. 1981, Nev. 1986, U.S. Supreme Ct. 1987, Colo. 1993. Assoc. Joseph, McDermott et al, Washington, 1979-82, Hudson & Creyke, Washington, 1982-85; sr. counsel Reynolds Elec. & Engring. Co., Inc., Las Vegas, 1985-90; dep. gen. counsel EG&G Rocky Flats, Golden, Colo., 1990-92, v.p., gen. counsel, 1992-96; ptnr. Hall & Evans, Denver, 1996—. Mem. Community Svc. Commn., Md., 1984-85. Mem. ABA, D.C. Bar Assn. (D.C. procurement com.), Mensa. Republican. Roman Catholic. Avocation: history. Home: 5594 Wood Sorrel Way Littleton CO 80123-6758 Office: Hall & Evans 1200 17th St Ste 1700 Denver CO 80202-5817

MCKENNA, JOHN FRANCIS, media executive; b. Bakersfield, Calif., Feb. 18, 1961; s. Frank Joseph and Linda Rae (Antongiovanni) McK.; m. Diana McKenna, May 31, 1997. Portuguese Lang., Curso Sao Joao Bosco, São Paulo, Brazil, 1979-80. Youth dir. Blue Army of Our Lady of Fatima, São Paulo, Brazil, 1981-87; mng. dir. Cath. Radio and TV Network, Brussels, 1988-97; mgr. Fedn. Field Sports Assns. of the European Cmty., 1998-99; network adminstr. Edgemail Techs., Bakersfield, Calif., 2000; cons. Sts. Cyril and Methodius Ctr., Paris, 1990-98, Internationaler Hilfsfonds e.V., Frankfurt, Germany, 1990-97, Conservative Caucus Found., Washington, 1991; western Europe corr. Lithuanian Weekly, Vilnius, Lithuania, 1992-93. Producer documentary film A Hill Apart, 1995; contbr. articles to profl. jours. Recipient Diploma for Outstanding Orgn., Kaunas Tech. U., 1995. Mem. INITIO (dir. 1994-96), Cath. Radio and TV Network (pres. 1993-99), Internat. Lithuanian Ctr. (mng. dir. 1990-99), Serbon Sound Systems. Roman Catholic. Avocations: judo, reading, learning langs., concerts, theater.

MCKENNA, KEVIN PATRICK, newspaper editor; b. Santa Monica, Calif., May 1, 1955; s. John Stephen and Patricia (Williams) M.; m. Laura Gail Scanlon, Dec. 16, 1995; 1 child, Felicity Beatrice. BA, U. So. Calif., 1976; MS, Columbia U., 1977. Reporter AP, Raleigh, N.C., 1977-78; copy editor Internat. Herald Tribune, Paris, 1978-84; editorial staff The New York Times, N.Y.C., 1984-95; editorial dir. N.Y. Times Electronic Media Co., 1995-97; asst. to dep. mng. editor N.Y. Times, 1998, technology editor, 1999—. Knight Journalism fellow Stanford U., 1997-98. Mem. Am. Soc. Newspaper Editors. Home: 175 W 73rd St Apt 4A New York NY 10023-2931 Office: NY Times 229 W 43rd St New York NY 10036-3959

MCKENNA, MARGARET ANNE, college president; b. R.I., June 3, 1945; d. Joseph John and Mary (Burns) McK.; children: Michael Aaron McKenna Miller, David Christopher McKenna Miller. BA in Sociology, Emmanuel Coll., 1967; postgrad., Boston Coll. Law Sch., 1968; JD, So. Meth. U., 1971; LLD (hon.), U. Upsala, N.J., 1978, Fitchburg (Mass.) State Coll., 1979, Regis Coll., 1982; D Community Affairs, U. R.I., 1979. Bar: Tex. 1971, D.C. 1973. Atty. Dept. Justice, Washington, 1971-73; exec. dir. Internat. Assn. Ofcl. Human Rights Agys., Washington, 1973-74; mgmt. cons. Dept. Treasury, Washington, 1975-76; dep. council to Pres. White House, Wash-

ington, 1976-79; dep. undersec. Dept. Edn., Washington, 1979-81; dir. Mary Ingraham Bunting Inst., Radcliffe Coll., Cambridge, Mass., 1981-85; v.p. program planning Radcliffe Coll., Cambridge, 1982-85; pres. Lesley Coll., Cambridge, 1985—; bd. dirs. Dominion Resources, Inc., Cisco Learning Inst., The Jason Found. for Edn. Bd. dirs. Coun. Ind. Colls., Washington, Am. Coun. Edn.; chmn. higher edn. task force Clinton Transition, 1992-93; chmn. edn. task force Mayor Thomas Menino Transition Com., 1994; bd. overseers Peabody Essex Mus. Recipient Outstanding Contribution award Civil Rights Leadership Conf., 1978; named Woman of Yr. Women's Equity Action League, 1979, Outstanding Woman of Yr. Big Sister Assn., 1986, Pinnacle award for Lifetime Achievement, Lelia J. Robinson award Women's Bar Assn. Mass., 1996, Valeria Addams Knapp award, The Coll. CLub, 1995; named Margaret A. McKenna Day, Gov. DePrete, R.I. Mem. Boys Scouts Am., Big Sisters Ass. Boston, Y.W.C.A. Cambridge, Women's Equity Action League, Nat. Women's Polit. Conf., Nat. Assn. Official Human Rights Agencies. Democrat. Office: Lesley Coll Office of the President 29 Everett St Cambridge MA 02138-2702

MCKENZIE, DAVID CHARLES ROBB, carpenter, music teacher; b. Woodville, New Zealand, Aug. 25, 1936; s. Kenneth Luxford and Clare Mertyle (Olsen) Robb; adopted Duncan Alexander Pringle and Ivy Amelia (Olsen) McK.; m. Gwen Tyler, Mar. 14, 1970 (div. May 1981); children: Christopher, David; m. Marlene June Glennie, Jan. 30, 1982. Student, Wesley Coll., Paerata, 1950-54, Auckland (New Zealand) U., 1955-56. Cert. tchr. woodwork, higher tech. tchr., trained tchr. Carpenter, draftsman C.H. Giles & Son, Auckland, 1956-58; pipe organist Kingsland Meth. Ch., Auckland, 1957-58; men's sect. pianist Lyric Harmonists Choir, Auckland, 1957-59; carpenter W.G. Archer, Auckland, 1958-60; carpenter, joiner W. Dickson, Masterton, New Zealand, 1960-62; carpenter Rigg-Zchoke, Masterton, 1962-63; student tchr. Tchrs. Coll., Auckland, 1964-65; tchr. woodwork Wellington Edn. Bd., Carterton-Featherston, New Zealand, 1965-92; carpenter, tchr. music Carterton, 1992—. Pianist Open Brethren, Masterton, 1960-63; pipe organist Anglican Ch., Carterton, 1962-63; pianist, band master Salvation Army, Carterton, 1973—; founding mem., conductor, pianist Dutch Reformed Choir, 1995—. Leader bible class Meth. Ch., Auckland, 1964; v.p. Cobblestones Early Settlers Mus., 1995—. Mem. Gideons. Avocations: restoring antique furniture, playing piano, accordion and electric piano. Home: 54 Costley St, Carterton New Zealand

MCKENZIE, DONALD CYRIL, management consultant; b. Melbourne, Victoria, Australia, Sept. 13, 1946; s. Kenneth Donald and Irene Hazel (Fitzgerald) McK.; m. Bonnie Connor Seamonds, Dec. 14, 1988; children: Shelly Anne, Justin Phillip, Carissa Lee. Degree in Indsl. Engring., Footscray Inst. Tech., Melbourne, 1972; BA, Monash U., Melbourne, 1978, diploma in gen. studies (psychology), 1978. Registered psychologist, NSW. Trainer indsl. engring. Olympic Cables, Sunshine, Victoria, Australia, 1966-69; indsl. engr. Massey Ferguson, Sunshine, 1969-72, Cottees Gen. Foods, Ringwood, Victoria, 1972-74; indsl. engr. REPCO, Melbourne, 1974-76, indsl. psychologist, 1976-78; cons. Arthur Young & Co., Melbourne, 1978-80; ptnr. Arthur Young & Co., Sydney, NSW, Australia, 1980-86, N.Y.C., 1986-89; group CEO Gadens Lawyers, Sydney, 1991—; trustee Com. for Econ. Devel. Australia. Pres. Northbridge Br. Liberal Party Australia, Sydney, 1994-96. Fellow Australian Inst. Co. Dirs.; mem. Univ. and Schs. Club, Victorian Racing Club (assoc.). Avocations: scuba diving, traveling, wine collecting. E-mail: dmckenzie@nsw.gadens.com.au. Fax: 02 9931 4756. Office: Gadens Lawyers, 77 Castlereagh St, Sydney NSW 2000, Australia

MCKENZIE, HARRY JAMES, cardiothoracic surgeon, surgical researcher; b. Meyersdale, Pa., Aug. 7, 1960; s. Henry Sadrus and Betty Elaine (Reiber) McK.; m. Judith Palmieri, July 6, 1985; children: Henry James, Anne Christine. BS, Duquesne U., 1984; postgraduate, U. Pitts., 1986-87; MD, Hahnemann U., 1992. Surg. intern Temple U., Conemaugh Med. Ctr., Johnstown, Pa., 1992-93, surg. resident, 1993-97; cardiothoracic resident Med. Coll. Ga., Augusta, 1997-99; mem. problem task force Conemaugh Med. Ctr., 1992-93. Contbr. articles to profl. jours.; presenter in field. Hosp. vol. Ctrl. Med. Pavilion, Pitts., 1981-84, Presbyn. Hosp., Pitts., 1986-87; med. exam. officer, Phila. Special Olympics, 1989-90; grad. banquet spkr. Salisbury (Pa.) H.S., 1993.. Recipient 3d place rsch. competition award, ACS Region III com. on trauma, Norfolk, Va., 1993; recipient 1st place rsch. competition award ACS-Pa. com. on trauma, Hershey, 1993. Mem. ACS, AMA, Am. Soc. Gen. Surgeons, Soc. Am. Gastrointestinal Endoscopic Surgeons, Soc. Thoracic Surgeons. Avocations: skiing, golfing, jogging, fishing, hiking. Home: 4130 N Tara Cir Wichita KS 67226-3367

MCKENZIE, KATHLEEN JULIANNA, artist; b. Jan. 20, 1957. Artist Torrington, Conn., 1987—; paintings featured in 7th, 9th and 11th Encyclopedia of Living Artist. Address: 1655 Mountain Rd Torrington CT 06790-2750

MCKENZIE, KEVIN PATRICK, artistic director; b. Burlington, Vt., Apr. 29, 1954; s. Raymond James and Ruth (Davison) McK. Grad. high sch., Washington. Mem. corps de ballet Nat. Ballet of Washington, 1972-74; prin. Joffrey Ballet, N.Y.C., 1974-78, Am. Ballet Theatre, N.Y.C., 1979-91; artistic assoc. Washington Ballet, 1991-92; artistic dir. Am. Ballet Theatre, N.Y.C., 1992—; pres. bd. dirs. Am. Ballet Theatre Dancers Fund, Inc., 1982-89; assoc. dir. New Amsterdam Ballet, N.Y.C., 1984—. Appeared in film Unicorn, Gorgon and Monticore, Sta. WETA-TV, Washington, 1971; guest dancer Houston Ballet, 1978, Spoleto Festival, 1980, 84, Theatre des Champs Elysees, Paris, 1981, Sadler's Wells Theatre, London, 1981, Asami Maki Ballet Co., Tokyo, 1983, Aspen Festival, 1982; producer, dir. The Party of the Year, 1982; choreographer Groupo Zambaria Ballet, 1984, Liszt Etudes, 1991, Lucy and the Count, 1992, The Nutcracker, 1993; created roles in Adrienne Dellos' The Blind Man's Daughter, Seoul, Korea, 1986, Amnon V'Tamar, S.P.E.B.S.Q.S.A.; appeared with Martine Van Hamel in Swan Lake, Nat. Ballet of Cuba, Havanna, 1986, Merrill Ashley in Tchaikowsky Pas de Deux, Bolshoi Theater, Moscow, 1986; repertoire as dancer includes La Bayadere, Carmen, Cinderella, Coppelia, Dim Lustre, Don Quixote, Giselle, The Garden of Villandry, Jardin aux lilas, The Leaves Are Fading, Pillar of Fire, Raymonda, Requiem, Rodeo, Romeo and Juliet, The Sleeping Beauty, Swan Lake, La Sylphide; other dances include Paquita, Sylvia Pas de Deux, Theme and Variations. Recipient Silver medal Varna (Bulgaria) Internat. Ballet Competitions, 1972, Artistic Achievement medal Dept. State, U.S. Govt., 1972, Artistic Achievement medal Mayor of Burlington, Vt., 1974, Performing Arts award, Am. Ireland Fund, 1994; Kevin McKenzie Day proclaimed by City of Burlington, 1985. Office: Am Ballet Theatre 890 Broadway New York NY 10003-1211

MCKENZIE, PAUL DOUGLAS, lawyer; b. Vancouver, B.C., Can., Aug. 26, 1963; s. Allan Douglas and June Bowen (Perry) McK. BA with honors, U. Toronto, Ont., Can., 1985, LLB, 1989. Barrister, solicitor, B.C. Assoc. Ladner Downs, Vancouver, 1990-93; assoc. Baker & McKenzie, Beijing, 1993-96; assoc. Baker & McKenzie, Hong Kong, 1997, ptnr., 1997-00; ptnr. Perkins Coie LLP, Hong Kong, 2000—. Contbr. articles to profl. jours. Mem. Can. Bar Assn. E-mail: mckep@perkinscoie.com. Office: Perkins Coie LLP, 4 Des Voeux Rd Ctrl, Hong Kong Hong Kong

MCKENZIE, RICHARD LLOYD, atmospheric physicist, researcher; b. Reefton, Westland, New Zealand, Sept. 24, 1950; s. Donald Stewart and Joan Margaret (Gregory) McK.; m. Louise Anne Lynch, May 8, 1972; children: Andrew, David (dec. 1993), Hamish. MSc in Physics, U. South Pacific, Suvu, Fiji, 1979; PhD in Atmospheric Physics, Oxford (Eng.) U., 1986; BSc in Physics with honors, U. Canterbury, Christchurch, New Zealand, 1972. Cert. tchr. Tchr. Kaiapol (New Zealand) H.S., 1974-76; lectr. U. South Pacific, Suvu, 1977-79; scientist Dept. Sci. and Indsl. Rsch., Lauder, New Zealand, 1980-83, Nat. Inst. for Water and Atmospheric Rsch., Omakau, New Zealand, 1987—; mgr. UV radiation program Nat. Inst. for Water and Atmospheric Rsch., Lauder, New Zealand, 1989—; mgr. Nat. Inst. for Water and Atmospheric Rsch., Lauder, 1992-93; leader World Meteorological Orgn./United Nations Environ. Programme (WMO/UNEP) Sci. Assessment of Ozone, 1991—; mem. UNEP Ef fects Panel, Geneva, Switzerland, Nairobi, Kenya, 1994—; presenter in field. Contbr. chpts. to books and articles to profl. jours. Treas. Ctrl. Otago Compassionate Friends, Alexandra, 1996—. Nat. Rsch. Adv. Coun. fellow Oxford U., 1984-86. Mem. Am. Geophys. Union, Royal Soc. New Zealand, New Zealand Meteorol. Soc., Alexandra Basketball Club (sec. 1997—), Rotary Club. Avocations: golf, basketball, tennis, tramping, reading.

MCKENZIE, STANLEY DON, academic administrator, English educator; b. Yakima, Wash., July 10, 1942; s. Don Guy and Jean Elizabeth McKenzie; m. Michal A. Koehler, Sept. 21, 1968 (div. Sept. 1974); 1 child, Thomas Charles. BS, MIT, 1964; MA, U. Rochester, 1967, PhD, 1971. Prof. lit. Rochester (N.Y.) Inst. Tech., 1967—, asst. to v.p. student affairs/judicial affairs, 1972-87, 92-94, acting dean, Coll. Liberal Arts, 1987-88, provost, v.p. acad. affairs, 1994--; vice-chair bd. dirs. RIT Rsch. Corp., Rochester, 1994--; bd. dirs. CIMS Print, Rochester, Am. Coll. Mgmt. & Tech., Dubrovnik, Croatia. Author: Shakespeare Studies, 1987; (with others) The Practice of Theory, 1992, Other Voices, Other Views, 1999. Mem. ACLU, AAUP, MLA. Democrat. Avocations: hiking, reading. E-mail: SDMPRO@RIT.edu. Office: Rochester Inst Tech 6 Lomb Memorial Dr Rochester NY 14623-5604

MCKEOWN, H. MARY, lawyer, educator; b. West Palm Beach, Fla., Sept. 17, 1952; d. Honore Stephen McKeown and Margaret Berg McKeown Growney; m. Jon Henry Barber, Sept. 18, 1981; children: Sean Patrick, Mary Kathleen. AA, St. Petersburg Jr. Coll., Fla., 1970; BA in Polit. Sci. and Sociology, U. South Fla., 1972; JD cum laude, Samford U., 1976. Bar: Fla. 1976, U.S. Dist. Ct. (mid. dist.) Fla. 1977, U.S. Ct. Appeals (5th and 11th cirs.) 1981, U.S. Supreme Ct. 1992. Asst. state atty. 6th Jud. Ct., Clearwater, Fla., 1976-90; ptnr. Growney, McKeown & Barber, St. Petersburg, 1976—; adj. prof. Stetson Coll. of Law, St. Petersburg, 1990—. Chairperson Child Welfare Std. and Tng. Coun., 1995-98; mem. Health and Human Svcs. Bd., nominee qualifications review com. Dist. 5, 1992—; mem. Study Commn. Child Welfare, 1990-91; Suncoast Girl Scout leader, 1991—. Recipient Victim Advocacy award Pinellas County Victims Rights Coalition, 1984, Law and Order award Elks, Pinellas County, 1991. Mem. ABA, ATLA, Acad. Fla. Trial Lawyers, Fla. Bar Assn., St. Petersburg Bar Assn., Phi Alpha Delta. Office: 7455 38th Ave N Saint Petersburg FL 33710-1228

MCKEOWN, LORRAINE LAREDO, travel company executive, writer; b. N.Y.C., Mar. 20, 1928; d. Frank A. and May (Collins) Laredo; m. William Taylor McKeown, July 9, 1964; children: Beth Ellison, Kate Taylor, Suzanne Harris. Talent agt. Carl Eastman, N.Y.C., 1960-65; cooking/travel columnist Camping Jour./Boating Jour., N.Y.C., 1968-70; travel agt. Beecher Travel, N.Y.C., 1968-70; founding ptnr. Computer Travel Info., N.Y.C., 1984; v.p., pres. Computer Travel Info., 1985-90, CEO, 1990—. Contbr. articles to various publs. Bd. dirs. Chapin-Brearley Exch., N.Y.C., 1980. Mem. Freelance Assocs., Beacon Conservation Coun.

MCKERRACHER, DANIEL WALLACE, psychologist, consultant, researcher; b. Renfrew, Scotland, Jan. 2, 1935; arrived in New Zealand, 1973; s. Angus Mathie and Catherine Munn (Foulds) McK.; m. Anne Finlay Hamilton Thornbury, Aug. 4, 1959 (dec. Aug. 1996); children: Graham Angus James, Sheila Agnes Catherine, Angus Finlay Hamilton, Kenneth Daniel. MA with honors, Glasgow U., Scotland, 1957, MEd, 1961; PhD, Sheffield U., Eng., 1968. Secondary sch. tchr., libr. Knightswood Comprehensive, Glasgow, 1958-62; rsch. clin. psychologist Rampton Hosp., Notts, Eng., 1962-65, sr. clin. psychologist, 1965-68; asst. prof. ednl. psychology U. Calgary, Alberta, Can., 1968-71, assoc. prof., 1971-73; prof. edn. U. Otago, Dunedin, New Zealand, 1973-97, dir. ednl. psychology tng. programme, 1978-97, prof. emeritus, 1997—; applied psychologist Otago Medico-Psychol. Assocs., Dunedin, 1997—; assoc. lectr. Nottingham U., Notts, 1967-68; dir. Assessment Vocat. Rehab. Rsch. Inst., Calgary, 1968-70; dir. psychology Woods Homes Children, Calgary, 1970-73, Holy Cross Hosp., Calgary, 1970-73; sr. clin. psychologist Family Health Counseling Ctr., Mosgiel, New Zealand, 1978-97. Editor: Jour. Spl. Edn., 1967-68; contbr. articles to profl. jours. and chpts. to books. Bd. mem. Taieri H.S., Mosgiel, 1978-82; mem. Otago Hosp. Bd., 1982-86. Glasgow U. history scholar, 1954. Fellow Royal Soc. New Zealand; mem. Brit. Psychol. Soc. (hon.), Brit. Royal Coll. Psychiatry (hon.), New Zealand Psychol. Soc. (coun. mem., hon.). Social Democrat. Presbyterian. Avocations: sheep farming, gardening, travel, reading, writing poetry. Home: Levencorrach Farm, 26 Dickson St Macandrew Bay, Dunedin M2, New Zealand Office: Otago Medico Psychol Assocs, PO Box 24, Dunedin New Zealand

MCKERROW, AMANDA, ballet dancer; b. Albuquerque; d. Alan and Constance McKerrow; m. John Gardner. Student, Met. Acad. Ballet, Bethesda, Md., Washington Sch. Ballet. With Washington Ballet Co., 1980-82; with Am. Ballet Theatre, N.Y.C., 1982—, soloist, from 1983, prin. dancer, 1987—. Toured Europe with Washington Ballet; danced in Margot Fonteyn Gala at Metropolitan Opera House; featured in Pavlova Tribute film, also many guest appearances; leading roles in Ballet Imperial, La Bayadere, Manon, Birthday Offering, Dim Lustre, Donizetti Variations, Giselle, Graduation Ball, The Leaves Are Fading, Nine Sinatra Songs, The Nutcracker, Pillar of Fire, Requiem, Romeo and Juliet, The Sleeping Beauty, Les Sylphides, Push Comes to Shove, Symphony Concertante, Symphonic Variations, Theme and Variations, Stravinsky Violin Concerto, Swan Lake, Triad, Duets, Etudes, Coppelia, Voluntaries and Rodeo; created leading role in Bruch Violin Concerto No. 1, Some Assembly Required and Agnus De Mille's The Other. Recipient N.Y. Woman award for dance, 1991; co-winner gold prize for women Moscow Internat. Ballet Competition, 1981. Office: Am Ballet Theatre 890 Broadway New York NY 10003*

MCKEY, WINSTON JACKSON (JACK MCKEY), artist, boat designer, builder; b. Biloxi, Miss., Feb. 15, 1942; s. Winston Carlile and Dorothy Mae (Jackson) McK.; m. Betty Jean McKey, Dec. 3, 1973. Student, Gordon Mil. Coll., Barnesville, Ga., 1958-61, Valdosta State Coll., 1962. Owner, operator Wilderness Guide Svc., Valdosta, Ga., 1964-69; outdoor writer, photographer Valdosta, Ga., 1964-73; asst. dr., dir. dept. recreation and tourism Coastal Plain Area Planning and Devel. Commn., Valdosta, Ga., 1968-73; boat designer, builder for recreation and comml. use Fla. and Alaska, 1973-82, 90-94; artisan, rsch. ancient tech. Blackfeet Reservation, Mont. Tlingit Villages, S.E. Alaska, Nez Perce Reservation, Idaho, 1982—; cons. most phases of Native Am. lifeways, Ga., Fla., Mont., Alaska, Idaho, 1961—; lectr., presenter ancient tech. mus., hist.-ednl. groups, Ga., Fla., Mont. Alaska, Idaho, 1964—; writer Native Am. culture, 1964—; instr., mentor Native Am. tech., 1986-99; cons. PBS Lewis and Clark--The Journey of the Corps of Discovery, Orofino, Lewiston, Idaho, 1997; dug-out canoe expert Idaho PBS documentary Lewis and Clark in Idaho, Boise, 1997-98; acknowledged expert in Indian weapons and early Indian tech.; bd. dirs. ZI.KI.A., Inc. Mem. Lewis and Clark Bicentennial Com., 1997—. Mem. Soc. Primitive Tech., Glacier County Hist. Soc. (life), J.W. Schultz Soc. (life). Avocations: hunting, fishing, canoeing, birdwatching, reading, Western horseman. Home: PO Box 24 Weippe ID 83553-0024

MCKIBBEN, BILL, writer; b. Palo Alto, Calif., Dec. 8, 1960; s. Gordon Charles and Margaret Hayes McK.; m. Sue Halpern, Mar. 6, 1988; 1 child, Sophie Crane. BA, Harvard Coll., 1982; PhD (hon.), Lebanon Vly. Coll., 1992, Given Mtn. Coll., 1995. Author: The End of Nature, 1989, The Age of Missing Information, 1992, Hope, Human and Wild, 1995. Trustee Paul Smith's Coll., N.Y.C., 1997—, TV-Free Am., Washington, 1995-99, Future Generations, Franklin, W.Va., 1999—, Florence & John Schumann Found., N.Y.C., 1999—. Fellow Guggenheim Found., 1994, Lyndhurst Found., 1990. Methodist. Home: 46 Garnet Lake Rd Johnsburg NY 12843-2501

MCKINLEY, JOHN MCKEEN, retired physics educator; b. Wichita, Kans., Feb. 1, 1930; s. Lloyd and Ruth Muriel (McKeen) McK.; m. Martha Ann Dicker, Feb. 7, 1953; children: Susan, Kathi, Kevin Michael. BS, U. Kans., 1951; PhD, U. Ill., 1962. Asst. prof. Kans. State U., Manhattan, 1960-66; assoc. prof. Oakland U., Rochester, Mich., 1966-71, prof., 1971-92, ret., 1992; rsch. assoc. Goddard Space Flight Ctr. NASA, Greenbelt, Md., 1980-81, 82-83. Author: Solutions Manual to Accompany Tipler's Modern Physics, 1978; assoc. editor Am. Jour. Physics, 1978-81. 1st lt. U.S. Army, 1951-55, Korea. Avocations: family history and genealogy.

MCKINLEY-HAAS, MARY, artist; b. St. Louis; d. Lee Carrington and Florence (Dowden) McK.; m. Saul Haas; children: Christopher, Matthew. BA, Smith Coll.; student, Art Students League, 1973-74, Nat. Acad. Design, 1965-66, Studio and Forum Stage Design. Head costume design dept. ABC-TV, NYC, 1968-73. Solo exhbns. include Tarlowe Gallery, Westhampton Beach, N.Y., 1974, Fontbonne Gallery, St. Louis, 1977, Gallery Yssa, N.Y.C., 1979, Vered Gallery, East Hampton, N.Y., 1981, Netherlands Bank & Ludlow-Hyland Gallery, N.Y.C., 1981, U. Tex., Austin, 1988, RVS Fine Art, Southampton, N.Y., 1990, TSS Gallery, N.Y.C., 1992, U. Tex., Austin, 1992, TAI Gallery, N.Y.C., 1999; group exhbns. include Guild Hall, East Hampton, N.Y., 1974, 75, 76, 78, 81, 85, 96, Parrish Art Mus., Southampton, 1975, 76, 78, 81, Water Mill Mus., 1983, 92, Vared Gallery, East Hampton, N.Y., 1985, Queens Coll. Art Ctr., Flushing, N.Y., 1991, Stony Brook U. Art Gallery, N.Y., 1994, Women in Art and Culture, Beijing, 1995, Elite Gallery, Moscow, 1995, Nat. Mus. Women in Arts, Washington, 1996, Soho 20 Gallery, N.Y.C., 1998—, others; represented in permanent collections at Nat. Mus. of Women in the Arts, Washington, Tari Women's Cultural Ctr., Papua, New Guinea, Fontbonne Coll., St. Louis, No. Trust Naples (Fla.); also numerous pvt. collections; costume designer for Broadway and network TV shows, Harkness Ballet, Holiday on Ice, others. Mem. United Scenic Artists, Women in the Arts, N.Y. Artists Equity. Address: 280 Lafayette St Loft5B New York NY 10012-3303

MCKINNELL, ROBERT GILMORE, zoology, genetics and cell biology educator; b. Springfield, Mo., Aug. 9, 1926; s. William Parks and Mary Catherine (Gilmore) McK.; m. Beverly Walton Kerr, Jan. 24, 1964; children: Nancy Elizabeth, Robert Gilmore, Susan Kerr. AB, U. Mo., 1948; BS, Drury Coll., 1949, DSc (hon.), 1993; PhD, U. Minn., 1959. Research assoc. Inst. Cancer Research, Phila., 1958-61; asst. prof. biology Tulane U., New Orleans, 1961-65; assoc. prof. Tulane U., 1965-69, prof., 1969-70; prof. zoology U. Minn., Mpls., 1970—; prof. genetics and cell biology U. Minn., St. Paul, 1976—; vis. scientist Dow Chem. Co., Freeport, Tex., 1976; guest dept. zoology U. Calif., Berkeley, 1979; Royal Soc. guest rsch. fellow Nuffield dept. pathology John Radcliffe Hosp., Oxford U., 1981-82; NATO vis. scientist Akademisch Ziekenhuis, Ghent, Belgium, 1984; faculty rsch. assoc. Naval Med. Rsch. Inst., Bethesda, Md., 1988; secretariat Third Internat. Conf. Differentiation, 1978; mem. amphibian com. Inst. Lab. Animal Resources, NRC, 1970-73, mem. adv. coun., 1974; mem. panel genetic and cellular resources program NIH, 1981-82, spl. study sect., Bethesda, 1990. Author: Cloning: Amphibian Nuclear Transplantation, 1978, Cloning, A Biologist Reports, 1979; sr. editor: Differentiation and Neoplasia, 1980, Cloning: Leben aus der Retorte, 1981, Cloning of Frogs, Mice, and other Animals, 1985, (with others) The Biological Basis of Cancer, 1998; mem. editorial bd. Differentiation, 1973—; assoc. editor: Gamete Research, 1980-86; contbr. articles to profl. jours. Served to lt. USNR, 1944-47, 51-53. Recipient Outstanding Teaching award Newcomb Coll., Tulane U., 1970; Disting. Alumni award Drury Coll., 1979, Morse Alumni Teaching award U. Minn., 1992; Research fellow Nat. Cancer Inst., 1957-58, Prince Hitachi award Japanese Found. Cancer Rsch., 1998; Sr. Sci. fellow NATO, 1974. Fellow AAAS, Linnean Soc. (London); mem. Am. Assn. Cancer Rsch. (emeritus), Am. Assn. Cancer Edn. (sr.), Am. Inst. Biol. Scis., Indian Soc. Devel. Biology (lifetime emeritus mem.), Internat. Soc. Differentiation (exec. com., sec.-treas. 1975-92, pres. elect 1992-94, pres. 1994-96), Gown-in-Town Club, Sigma Xi. Home: 2124 Hoyt Ave W Saint Paul MN 55108-1315 Office: U Minn Dept Genetics Cell Bio Saint Paul MN 55108-1095

MCKINNEY, BRIDGET MCARDLE, lawyer; b. Highland Park, Ill., June 14, 1952; arrived in Egypt, 1995; d. Robert Patrick McArdle and Patrician Ann (Rice) Cameron; m. Robert Carlton McKinney, Oct. 23, 1982. BA magna cum laude, U. Mass., 1977; JD, Ind. U., 1982. Bar: Ind. 1982, U.S. Dist. Ct. Ind. 1982. Lawyer Mallor & Mills, Bloomington, Ind., 1982-84; vis. prof. U. Khartoum, Sudan, 1984-86; project officer USAID, Muscat, Oman, 1987-89; sr. atty. Fox & Gibbons, Muscat, 1989-95; resident mgr., sr. atty. Fox & Gibbons, Cairo, 1995-98; resident ptnr., sr. atty. Denton Fox & Gibbons, Cairo, 1998—. Contbr. articles to profl. jours. V.p. Am. Bus. Coun., Muscat, Oman, 1990-95; commr. Human Rights Com., Bloomington, 1980-82. Named one of World's Leading Energy and Resources Lawyers, Euromoney, 1995, 97, 99, Lawyer's Lawyer in Mid. East, Global Law and Bus. Rev., 1996. Mem. ABA, Am. C. of C. in Egypt (gov., v.p. 1997—), Ind. Bar Assn., Internat. Bar Assn., Arab Regional Forum (coun. 1989—). Democrat. Roman Catholic. Avocation: equestrian sports. Home: 5 Dr Mahmoud Azmi St, Zamalek Cairo, Egypt Office: Denton Fox & Gibbons, 19 Yehia Ibrahim St, Zamalek Cairo, Egypt

MCKINNEY, CHARLES MICHAEL, artist, educator; b. Clinton, Okla., Dec. 1, 1951; s. Charles Bert and Catherine Georgene McKinney; m. Denise Ann Wardell Kirkes, Apr. 15, 1972 (div. Sept. 1983); children: Gary Michael, Charles Justin; m. Rose Caterina Vartuli, Aug. 15, 1992; children: Sean Patrick, Catherine Maedb, Paul Devon Ross. BA in Journalism, U. Okla., Norman, 1987; MFA in Creative Writing, McNeese State U., 1990. Freelance journalist The Daily Oklahoman, Oklahoma City Times, Oklahoma City, 1972-75; editor Wyo. Outdoor Reporter, Buffalo, 1979-82; profl. photographer Paseo Photo Works, Oklahoma City, 1982-86; grad. tchg. asst. McNeese State U., Lake Charles, La., 1987-90, U. Southwestern La., Lafayette, 1990-91; instr. IV Southwestern Okla. State U., Sayre, Okla., 1991—; copy editor Westview: A Jour. of Western Okla., Southwestern Okla. State, Weatherford; cons. Arts in Prisons program Instn. Programs Inc., Oklahoma City. Mem. citizen's adv. commn. Okla. State Reformatory, Granite, 1994—; pres.-elect faculty senate Southwestern Okla. State U., 1998—. With U.S. Army, 1976-79. Recipient Addy award for photography Oklahoma City Advt. Club, 1985. Mem. Phi Theta Kappa Internat. (faculty advisor Beta Iota Gamma chpt. 2000—). Democrat. Avocations: flyfishing, wildflower taxonomy and collecting, collecting antiques, gardening. Home: PO Box 145 Leedey OK 73654-0145 Office: Southwestern Okla State U 409 E Mississippi Ave Sayre OK 73662-1236

MCKINNEY, DENNIS KEITH, lawyer; b. Ottawa, Ill., May 12, 1952; s. Robert Keith and Delroy Louise (Clayton) McK.; m. Patricia Jean Boyle, Oct. 4, 1986; 1 child, Geoffrey Edward. BS, Ball State U., 1973; JD, Ill. Inst. Tech., 1976. Bar: Ind. 1977, U.S. Dist. Ct. (so. dist.) Ind. 1977, U.S. Supreme Ct. 1993. Appellate dep. Ind. Atty. Gen, Indpls., 1977-78, trial dep., 1978-79, sr. trial dep., 1979-81, chief real estate litigation sect., 1981-94; clk. to Hon. James S. Kirsch Ind. Ct. Appeals, Indpls., 1994-95; staff atty. Ind. Supreme Ct. Disciplinary Commn., Indpls., 1995—. Author: Eminent Domain, Practice and Procedure in Indiana, 1991, A Guide to Indiana Easement Law, 1995, A Railroad Ran Through It, 1996; contbg. author: Indiana Real Estate Transactions, 1996; contbr. articles to profl. jours. Active Indpls.-Scarborough Peace Games, 1983-84. Avocations: reading, volleyball, wargaming. Office: Ind Supreme Ct Disciplinary 115 W Washington St Indianapolis IN 46204-3420

MCKINNEY, GEORGE HARRIS, JR., training systems analyst; b. Birmingham, Ala., Nov. 23, 1943; s. George Harris and Elizabeth Dickey (Fikes) McK.; m. Lynda Jeanne Ponder, June 26, 1965 (div. Aug. 18, 1992; children: Michael Thomas, Carol Elizabeth; m. Tambri Sue Hillis, Aug. 19, 1992. BS in Polit. Sci., U.S. Air Force Acad., 1965; MS in Psychology, Troy State U., 1977. Commd. 2d lt. U.S. Air Force, 1965, advanced through grades to lt. col., 1981; fighter pilot U.S. Air Force, worldwide, 1965-85; ret. U.S. Air Force, 1985; tng. sys. cons. in pvt. practice, Milton, Fla., 1985—. Author tech. reports. Decorated D.F.C. (5), Air medal (26), Purple Heart, Meritorious Svc. medal (3). Mem. Order of Daedalians, USAFA Assn. Grads., Air Force, Assn., Am. Def. Preparedness Assn. Avocations: whitetail deer hunting, fishing. Home: 3101 Chippewa Dr Milton FL 32571-9603

MC KINNEY, MICHAEL WHITNEY, trade association executive; b. San Angelo, Tex., Aug. 23, 1946; s. Wallace Luster and Mitzi Randolph (Broome) McK.; m. Martha LaNan Hooker, Feb. 24, 1973; children: Wallace Blake, Lauren Brooke. BA in Govt., U. Tex., Austin, 1973. Adminstrv. asst. to lt. gov. State of Tex., Austin, 1968-69, adminstrv. asst. to gov., 1969-73; asst. to dir. Tex. Water Quality Bd., Austin, 1973-76; chief of staff Tex. Alcoholic Beverage Commn., 1976-83; v.p. for industry affairs Wholesale Beer Distbrs., Tex., 1984-88, exec. v.p., chief exec. officer, 1989—. Bd. dirs. Tex. Alpha Edn. Found., Inc., Austin, 1969—; bd. govs. Keep Tex. Beautiful, 1997-98; mem. Travis County Zoo Task Force, 1986; mem. Senate Com. on Fees and Grants, 1982-83; bd. dirs. Friends of Gov.'s Mansion, 1993-97. Recipient Bert Ford award Tex. Alcholic Beverage Commn., 1996, Pres. award for legis. excellence Nat. Beer Wholesalers Assn., 1998. Mem. Sam Houston Soc., Knights of the Symphony, Austin Assembly, Masons (32 deg., K.T.), Austin Country Club, Austin Club (bd. dirs. 1989—, exec. com. 1994—, Mem. of Yr. 1994), Phi Kappa Psi. Home: 1708 Intervail Dr Austin TX 78746-7630 Office: 823 Congress Ave Ste 1313 Austin TX 78701-2434

MCKINNON, JAMES BUCKNER, real estate sales executive, writer, researcher; b. Tacoma, Dec. 5, 1916; s. James Mitchell and Rochelle Lenore (Buckner) McK.; m. Mary C. Corbitt, Dec. 1961 (div. June 1963); 1 child, James H.C.; m. Marylyn Adelle Coote, Mar. 12, 1967 (div. May 1977); 1 child, Michelyn; m. Martha Sackmann, June 12, 1977. BA in Internat. Studies, U. Wash., 1983, H.M. Jackson Sch. Police detective Los Angeles Police Dept., 1946-50; bn. security officer 1st med. bn. 1st Marine div. Fleet Marine Force, 1950-53; owner, operator, mgr., dir. promotional sales The Saucy Dog Drive-In, Venice, Calif., 1953-63; salesman new car sales and leasing Burien Mercury, Seattle, 1963-66; real estate salesman and appraiser various firms Seattle, 1966—; instr., lectr. U.S. Naval Support Activity, Sandpoint, Wash., 1964-74; mem., lectr. NRC 11-8, Naval Postgrad. Sch., Monterey, Calif., 1975-76; Burien Mercury announcer KOMO TV. Author: (poetry) On the Threshold of a Dream, Vol. III, 1992, Best Poems of the 90's, 1992; contbr. to anthologies: Where Words Haven't Spoken, 1993, Fire From Within, 1994; contbr. articles to various newspapers and mil. jours. Mem. br. adv. com. Wash. State YMCA, Seattle, 1994—, treas., 1986-94, 95, mem. so. dist. fin. bd., 1989-93, 94, 95-96. With USN, 1939-53, PTO, Korea. Recipient Wilmer Culver Meml. award Culver Alumni Fictioneers, Seattle, 1979, Silver Poet award World of Poetry Press, 1986, Golden Poet award, 1987-92, Best Poet of the 90's Nat. Libr. of Poetry, 1992, First Place with Editor's Preference award Creative Arts and Scis. Enterprises, 1996; Occidental Coll. scholar, 1935; named to Honorable Order Ky. Cols., 1976; named One of Best New Poets, Am. Poetry Assn. Anthology, 1988; inducted into the Internat. Poetry Hall of Fame, 1996. Mem. Internat. Soc. Authors and Artists (1st place award for 1997 poem), Internat. Platform Assn., U.S. Naval Inst. (life), Internat. Soc. Poets (life), N.W. Writers Conf., Ret. Officers Assn. (life), Mensa, Acad. Am. Poets, KP, Masons. Republican. Home: 2312 41st Ave SW Seattle WA 98116-2060

MCKINSTRY, RONALD EUGENE, lawyer; b. Bakersfield, Calif., Aug. 11, 1926; s. Melville Jack and Lillian Agatha (Saner) McK.; m. Shirley Danner, June 19, 1948; children: Michael R., Jill I. McKinstry Epperson, Jeffrey A., Carol A. McKinstry Sundquist. BS, U. Wash., 1950, JD, 1951. Bar: Wash. 1951, U.S. Ct. Claims 1970, U.S. Ct. Appeals (D.C. cir.) 1981, U.S. Supreme Ct. 1982. Assoc. Evans, McLaren, Lane, Powell & Beeks, Seattle, 1951-55, Bogle, Bogle & Gates, Seattle, 1955-61; ptnr. Bogle & Gates, Seattle, 1962-91, chmn. litigation dept., 1970-91; sr. trial ptnr. Ellis Li & McKinstry, Seattle, 1992—; apptd. spl. master by U.S. Dist. Ct. (we. dist.) Wash., 1976-81, apptd. settlement mediator, 1980—. Editor-in-chief Washington Civil Procedure Before Trial Deskbook, 1981, Supplement to Deskbook, 1986; contbr. articles to profl. jours. Attends Christ Meml. Ch., Poulsbo, Wash. With USN, 1944-46, PTO. Recipient Svc. award Western Ctr. for Law and Religious Freedom, 1990. Fellow Am. Coll. Trial Lawyers (regent 1978-82); mem. ABA, Internat. Assn. Def. Counsel (mem. exec. com. 1974-78, voted Best Lawyers in Am., 1983—), CPR Panels of Disting. Legal Neutrals, AAA Club Wash. (mem. exec. com. 1983-98). Mem. Christ Meml. Ch. Avocations: golf, traveling. Office: Ellis Li & McKinstry Two Union Square 601 Union St Ste 4900 Seattle WA 98101-3906

MCKINZIE, CARL WAYNE, lawyer; b. Lubbock, Tex., Dec. 3, 1939; s. J. Clyde and Flora (Cates) McK.; m. Rowena Ann Williams; children: Wayne, Clinton, Morgan (dec.). BBA, Tex. Tech U., 1962, MBA, 1963; JD, So. Meth. U., 1966. From assoc. to ptnr. Nossaman, Guthner & Knox, L.A., 1966-80; prin. Riordan & McKinzie, L.A., 1980—. Contbr. articles to law jours. Trustee Jaquish Found.; bd. visitors Sch. Law So. Meth. U., Dallas, 1979-82, 90—, bd. dirs., 1970-73, 84-89, chmn. exec. com., 1996-98; bd. visitors Ariz State U. Coll. Law, 1990-98; bd. dirs. Riordan Found., Rx for Reading; bd. dirs., pub. counsel Calif. Cmty. Found., 1994-98; bd. advisors Coll Law, U. Wyo., 1987-91. Recipient disting. alumni award So. Meth. U., Dallas, 1994. Mem. ABA (chmn. current devel. subcom., com. tax problems 1978-80), Nat. Assn. Real Estate Investment Trusts (bd. govs. 1986-89), Calif. Bar Assn., Los Angeles County Bar Assn., Jonathan Club, City Club on Bunker Hill, L.A. Country Club. Republican. Home: 527 21st Pl Santa Monica CA 90402-3047 Office: Riordan & McKinzie 29th Fl 300 S Grand Ave Ste 29 Los Angeles CA 90071-3110

MCKISSOCK, DAVID LEE, retired manufacturing company executive; b. Boston, Mar. 27, 1933; s. Allan and Elizabeth (Lee) McK.; m. Diana Parish, Sept. 1, 1956; children: David Lee Jr., Christopher Lee. BA, Middlebury Coll., 1955. Salesman Am. Flange and Mfg. Co., N.Y.C., 1957-62; asst. to v.p. sales Am. Flange and Mfg. Co., Linden, N.J., 1962-64, salesman rip cap closures, 1964-73, v.p. rip cap closures, 1973-89, also bd. dirs. With USNR, 1955-57. Mem. Rumson Country Club, Seabright Lawn Tennis and Cricket Club. Republican. Unitarian. Avocations: tennis, golf, platform tennis. Home: 20 Hance Rd Fair Haven NJ 07704-3210

MCKITTRICK, NEIL VINCENT, lawyer; b. Framingham, Mass., June 21, 1961; s. Harold Vincent and Dorothy Frances (Alexander) McK.; m. Karen Beth Hoffman, May 30, 1987; children: Kerry Alexandra, Brian Hoffman, Robert Hoffman. AB magna cum laude, Brown U., 1983; JD, U. Va., 1987. Bar: Mass. 1988, U.S. Dist. Ct. Mass. 1989, U.S. Ct. Appeals (1st cir.) 1989, U.S. Supreme Ct. 1999. Law clk. to Hon. Frank M. Johnson Jr. U.S. Ct. Appeals (11th cir.), Montgomery, Ala., 1987-88; assoc. Hill & Barlow, Boston, 1988-95, mem., 1995—; pub. defender Suffolk County (Mass.) Bar Advocate, 1990-91; asst. dir. White House sec. rev. U.S. Dept. Treasury, 1994-95; case conf./mediator Boston Mcpl. Ct. Alternative Dispute Resolution Program, 1997—; mem. steering com. Lawyers' Com. Civil Rights Under Law, 1998—. Editor U. Va. Law Rev., 1985-87. Dillard fellow U. Va., 1985-86; recipient Arc Mass. Disting. Citizens award, 1996. Mem. ABA, Mass. Bar Assn., Fed. Bar Assn. (exec. com. 1997—), Boston Bar Assn. (lawyers' com. civil rights, steering com., 1998—), Order of the Coif, Phi Beta Kappa, Theta Delta Chi. Office: Hill & Barlow One International Pl Boston MA 02110

MCKUSICK, MARSHALL KIRK, computer scientist; b. Wilmington, Del., Jan. 19, 1954; s. Blaine Chase and Marjorie Jane (Kirk) McK.; domestic ptnr. Eric P. Allman. BSEE with distinction, Cornell U., 1976; MS in Bus. Adminstrn., U. Calif., Berkeley, 1979, MS in Computer Sci., 1980, PhD in Computer Sci., 1984. System designer Hughes Aircraft Co., 1977-79; software cons., 1982—; rsch. computer scientist U. Calif., Berkeley, 1984-93. Author: The Design and Implementation of the 4.4BSD Operating System, 1996 (trans. into German, 1997, Japanese, 1997, French, 1997); contbr. articles to profl. publs. Mem. IEEE, Usenix Assn. (Lifetime Achievement award 1992, pres. 1990-92, bd. dirs. 1986-92), Assn. Computing Machinery. Democrat. Avocations: swimming, scuba diving, wine collecting. Office: 1614 Oxford St Berkeley CA 94709-1608

MCLACHLAN, JOHN JAMES, investment company executive; b. Wirral, Eng., Aug. 28, 1942; s. William and Helen (Duffy) McL.; m. Heather Joan Smith, Sept. 24, 1966; children: Deborah Gail, Alexander George William. Chartered acct., FCA, investment analyst, AIIMR. Articled clerk Poulson & Co., Liverpool, Eng., 1960-66; mgmt. acct. Norwest Holst, Liverpool, 1966-67; investment analyst Barclays Bank, Martins Bank Trust Co., Ltd., Liverpool, 1967-74; investment mgr., dir. British Rail Pension Fund, London, 1974-84; corp. investment mgr. Reed Internat. plc, London, 1984-88; investment dir. United Friendly Group plc, London, 1988-99, Refuge Assurance PLC, 1996-99, United Assurance Group, 1996-99; non-exec. dir. Schroder Ventures Internat. Investment Trust plc, London, 1995—, Invesco Income Growth Trust plc, 1996. Fellow Inst. Chartered Accts. (chartered).

MCLACHLIN, BEVERLEY, Canadian supreme court chief justice; b. Pincher Creek, Alta., Can., Sept. 7, 1943; m. Roderick McLachlin (dec. 1988); 1 child, Angus; m. Frank E. McArdle, 1992. B.A., U. Alta., MA in Philosophy, LLB, LLD (hon.), 1991; LLD (hon.), U. B.C., 1990, U. Toronto, 1995, York U., 1999, Law Soc. Upper Can., 2000, U. Ottawa, 2000, U. Calgary, 2000, Brock U., 2000, Simon Fraser U., 2000. Bar: Alta. 1969, B.C. 1971. Assoc. Wood, Moir, Hyde and Ross, Edmonton, Alta., Can., 1969-71, Thomas, Herdy, Mitchell & Co., Fort St. John, B.C., Can., 1971-72, Bull, Housser and Tupper, Vancouver, B.C., 1972-75; lectr., assoc. prof., prof. with tenure U. B.C., 1974-81; appointed to County Ct., Vancouver, 1981; justice Supreme Ct. of B.C., 1981-85, B.C. Ct. of Appeal, 1985-88; chief justice Supreme Ct. of B.C., 1988; justice Supreme Ct. Can., Ottawa, Ont., 1989-2000, chief justice, 2000—. Co-author: B.C. Supreme Court Practice, B.C. Court Forms, Canadian Law of Arch. and Engring.; contbr. numerous articles to profl. jours. Office: Supreme Ct Bldg, 301 Wellington St, Ottawa, ON Canada K1A 0J1

MCLAFFERTY, FRED WARREN, chemist, educator; b. Evanston, Ill., May 11, 1923; s. Joel E. and Margaret E. (Keifer) McL.; m. Elizabeth E. Curley, Feb. 5, 1948; children: Sara L., Joel E., Martha A., Samuel A., Ann E. BS, U. Nebr., 1943, DSc (hon.), 1983, MS, 1947; PhD, Cornell U., 1950; DSc (hon.), U. Liege, Belgium, 1987, Purdue U., 1995. Fellow U. Iowa, 1949-50; rsch. chemist, divsn. leader Dow Chem. Co., 1950-56; dir. Eastern Rsch. Lab., 1956-64; prof. chemistry Purdue U., 1964-68; prof. chemistry Cornell U., 1968-92, Peter J.W. Debye prof. chemistry emeritus, 1992—; chem. sci. and tech. bd., numerical data adv. bd., bd. Army sci. tech., bd. radioactive waste mgmt. NRC; chem. co-chmn. World Bank's Chinese Univ. Devel. Project. Author: Mass Spectrometry of Organic Ions, 1963, Mass Spectral Correlations, 2d edit., 1981, Interpretation of Mass Spectra, 4th edit., 1993, Tandem Mass Spectrometry, 1983, Advances in Analytical Chemistry and Instrumentation; (with C.N. Reilley), Vols. 4-7, 1967-70, Index and Bibliography of Mass Spectrometry, (with J. Pinzelik), 1967, Atlas of Mass Spectral Data; (with E. Stenhagen and S. Abrahamsson), 1969, Registry of Mass Spectral Data, 1974; (with D.B. Stauffer) Wiley/NBS Registry of Mass Spectral Data, 1989, Important Peak Index of Mass Spectral Data, 1991; editor: Accounts of Chemical Research, 1986-94; co-editor: (with E. Stenhagen and S. Abrahamsson) Archives of Mass Spectral Data, 1969-72. With AUS, 1942-45, ETO. Decorated Purple Heart, Combat Inf. badge, Bronze Star with 4 oak leaf clusters; recipient Pitts. Spectroscopy award Spectroscopy Soc. Pitts., 1975, Gold medal U. Naples, 1989, Robert Boyle Gold medal Royal Soc. Chemistry, 1992, Bijvoet medal U. Utrecht, 1997, W.L. Evans award Ohio State U., 1987, Jaroslav Heyrovsky Gold medal Czech Acad. Scis., 1999, Giulio Natta Gold medal Italian Chem. Soc., 2000; John Simon Guggenheim fellow, 1972, Overseas fellow Churchill Coll., Cambridge (Eng.) U., 1979,. Fellow NAS, AAAS, N.Y. Acad. Scis., Am. Acad. Arts and Scis.; mem. Soc. Analytical Chemists (Pitts. Analytical Chemist award 1987, Pioneer Analytical Instrumentation award 1994), Am. Chem. Soc. (chmn. analytical chem. divsn. 1969, chmn. Midland sect. 1956, Northeastern sect. 1964, award chem. instrumentation 1971, award analytical chemistry 1981, Nichols medal N.Y. sect. 1984, Oesper award Cin. sect. 1986, award mass spectrometry 1989), Internat. Spectrometry Orgn. (Sir J. J. Thomson medal 1985), Assn. Analytical Chemists (Anachem award 1985), Am. Soc. Mass Spectrometry (founder, sec. 1957-58), Am. Inst. Chemists (Chem. Pioneer award 1996), Sigma Xi, Phi Lambda Upsilon, Alpha Chi Sigma. Home: 103 Needham Pl Ithaca NY 14850-2120

MCLAIN, JOHN LOWELL, resource specialist, consultant; b. Havre, Mont., Jan. 23, 1942; s. Woodrow B. and Ann Teresa (Bolta) McL.; m. Carolyn Louise Peterson, June 27, 1964; children: Nicole Rachelle, Tanya Lynn. BS in Range Mgmt., Mont. State U., 1969. Cert. range mgmt. cons.; cert. soil erosion & sediment control specialist. Soil conservationist USDA Soil Conservation Svc., Miles City, Mont., 1969-71; range conservationist USDA Soil Conservation Svc., Glendive, Mont., 1971-74; area range conservationist USDA Soil Conservation Svc., Minden, Nev., 1974-76, dist. conservationist, 1976-78; co-founder, prin. resource specialist Resource Concepts Inc., Carson City, Nev., 1978—; bd. dirs. Range Mag., Carson City; keynote spkr. Desert Tech. IV Internat. Conf., 1997; mem. governing bd. Policy Analysis Ctr. for Western Pub. Lands. Mem. citizens adv. bd. U. Nev.-Reno, 1981—; Nev. del. Coun. for Agrl. Rsch. Ext. and Tchg., Washington, 1983-97, 99—. Recipient Outstanding Achievement award Carson Valley Conservation Dist., 1978; named Man of 1980s Nevada Appeal City newspaper, 1980. Fellow Soc. for Range Mgmt. (pres. Nev. sect. 1980, Rangeman of Yr. Nev. sect. 1987); mem. Soil and Water Conservation Soc. (pres. Nev. sect. 1982), Soc. Range Mgmt (dir. 1993-96), Soc. Range Mgmt. (pres. 2000), Resource Restoration Internat. (mem. adv. com. 1992), Range Edn. Inst. (dir. 1995—). Roman Catholic. Avocations: fishing, guitar/singing, horseback riding, skiing, hunting. Home: 2424 Manhattan Dr Carson City NV 89703-5416 Office: Resource Concepts Inc 340 N Minnesota St Carson City NV 89703-4152

MCLAIN, THELMA LOUISE, retired college librarian, artist; b. Sparks, Okla., Nov. 18, 1918; d. Grant Leroy and Emma Evelyn (Ellington) Spoonemore; m. Bruce McLain, Nov. 27, 1943 (div. June 1948). BA, Tex. Woman's U., Denton, 1940; MLS, U. Tex., 1959. Cert. tchr., Tex. Sch. libr. supr. Works Progress Adminstrn., Waco, Tex., 1940-41; tchr. 5th grade Donna (Tex.) Pub. Schs., 1941-42; h.s. libr. Rosenburg (Tex.) Pub. Schs., 1942-43; bookmobile libr. Houston Pub. Libr., 1943-44; county libr. Morgan County Libr., Versailles, Mo., 1946-49; h.s. libr. Harlingen (Tex.) Pub. Schs., 1950-52; asst. order libr. U. Tex. Libr., Austin, 1953-56; head rsch. and reference Pan Am. U. Libr., Edinburg, Tex., 1957-74; asst. prof. Pan Am. U., Edinburg, 1970-74; co-owner Custom Ladies Dress Designs, McAllen, Tex., 1972-75; selling arts and crafts, 1975—. Exhibited paintings oil and acrylics spons. by McAllen Art Mus., Hidalgo County Art Legue, McAllen, McAllen Jr. League, Rio Grande Valley Art League, Harlingen, Willacy County Art League, Raymondville, Tex., others; author: Long Trail Awinding--My Family's History, 1993. Vol. Thrift Shop, La Grange, Tex., 1992-95. Recipient awards for art. Mem. Order of the Daus. of the King (sec. chpt. 1992—). Episcopalian. Avocation: needlecrafts, especially cloth dolls of original design.

MCLAIN, WILLIAM ALLEN, lawyer; b. Chgo., Oct. 19, 1942; s. William Rex and Wilma L. (Raschka) McL.; divorced; children: William A., David M., Heather A.; m. Kristine R. Zierk. BS, So. Ill. U., 1966; JD, Loyola U., Chgo., 1971. Bar: Ill. 1971, U.S. Dist. Ct. (no. dist.) Ill. 1971, U.S. Ct. Appeals (7th cir.) 1971, Colo. 1975, U.S. Dist. Ct. Colo. 1975, U.S. Ct. Appeals (10th cir.) 1975. Law clk. U.S. Dist. Ct. (no. dist.) Ill., Chgo., 1971-72; assoc. Sidley & Austin, Chgo., 1972-75; ptnr. Welborn, Dufford, Brown & Tooley, Denver, 1975-86; pres. William A. McLain PC, 1986—; ptnr. McLain & Singer, Denver, 1990—. Mem. Dist. 10 Legis. Vacancy Commn., Denver, 1984-86. Served with U.S. Army, 1966-68. Recipient Leadership and Scholastic Achievement award Loyola U. Alumni Assn., 1971. Mem. Colo. Bar Assn. (lobbyist 1983-85), Denver Bar Assn., Colo. Assn. Commerce and Industry (legis. policy coun. 1983-88), Colo. Mining Assn. (state and local affairs com. 1978-88), Inst. Property Taxation, Mt. Vernon Country Club, Roundup Riders of the Rockies Club, Masons, Shriners, Scottish Rite, York Rite. Republican. Home and Office: 3962 S Olive St Denver CO 80237-2038

MCLAIN, WILLIAM TOME, principal; b. Washington, July 10, 1935; s. Ronald Alpha and Dorothy Smithson (Tome) McL.; m. Meurial Claire Webb, Nov. 20, 1977; 1 child, Laura Louisa McLain. BA, U. Del., 1957, MEd, 1966. Secondary Prin. Cert., Del. Math. tchr. Newark Sch. Dist., 1957-69, high sch. adminstrv. asst., 1969-78; high sch. assoc. prin. New Castle County Sch. Dist., Newark, 1978-81; high sch. asst. prin. Christina Sch. Dist., Newark, 1981-84, middle sch. asst. prin., 1984-87, prin. adult edn. program, 1987—. Treas., past chmn. Del. Coalition for Literacy; past pres. Del. Assn. for Adult and Cmty. Edn. Recipient Tchrs. medal Freedom's Found., 1968, Silver Beaver award Boy Scouts Am., 1967, Walace Johnson Community Svc. award New Castle County C. of C., 1979, Adult, dFamily Lit. Outstanding Svc. award State of Del., 1992. Mem. Interagency Coun. on Adult Lit. United Methodist. Avocations: travel, history. Home: 95 Dallas Ave Newark DE 19711-5123 Office: Christina School District 925 Bear Corbitt Rd Bear DE 19701-1323

MCLANE, WILLIAM DELANO, mechanical engineer; b. Ralls, Tex., Aug. 22, 1936; s. Clyde and Lillian Helen (Earp) McL.; m. Mary Ann Clark, Feb. 17, 1962; children: William Devin, Keri, Kristi, Mandy. BSME, Tex. Tech. U., 1961. Profl. engr. Tex. Engr. Texaco Inc., Tulsa, 1961-63; plant engring. mgr. Owens-Corning Fiberglas Corp., Toledo, 1963-72; pres., CEO Tucker-McLane Tire Corp., Waxahachie, Tex., 1972-89; commr. County of Ellis, Waxahachie, 1989-93; engr. Morrison Knudsen Corp., Dallas, 1993-94, MK-Ferguson, Albuquerque, 1994-95, Parsons Brinckerhoff, Dallas, 1995-96; quality control mgr. Sedalco, Inc., Ft. Worth, Tex., 1996-97; engring. mgr. Fortra Fiber-Cement, LLC., Waxahachie, Tex., 1997—; mem. adv. bd. Guaranty Fed. Bank, Waxahachie, 1993—, Citizens Nat. Bank, Waxahachie, 1991-92, City of Waxahachie, 1990-91, Tex. State Tech. Coll., Inc., Waco, 1998—, Navarro Coll., Corsicana, 1998—, Portland Cement Assn., Skokie, Ill., 1998—. Sec. bd. Waxahachie Sch. Dist., 1979-88; vice chmn. Ctrl. Tex. Econ. Devel. Dist., Waco, 1989-93; mem. adv. com. Tex. State Tech. Coll., Waco, 1998—. Mem. ASME, ASCE, NSPE, Tex. Soc. Profl. Engrs., So. Bldg. Code Congress Internat., Internat. Soc. Tribologists and Lubrication Engrs., Internat. Conf. Bldg. Officials, Waxahachie C. of C. (pres. 1977). Republican. Presbyterian. Avocations: civic and political volunteer work, varmint hunting, photography, cooking. Home: 1612 Alexander Dr Waxahachie TX 75165-1902 Office: Fortra Fiber-Cement LLC 2425 N Highway 77 Waxahachie TX 75165-6222

MCLAREN, ARCHIE CAMPBELL, JR., marketing executive; b. Atlanta, Sept. 25, 1942; s. Archie Campbell and Virginia Lynn (Sides) McL.; m. Georgia Mae Blunt, 1969 (div. 1971); 1 child, Leslie Michelle; m. Yvette Rubio, June 17, 1995. BA, Vanderbilt U., 1964; JD, Memphis State U., 1968. Clk. FBI, Memphis, 1965-66; tchr., tennis coach Memphis U. Sch., 1966-68; tchr. Hunt High Sch., Columbus, Miss., 1968-69; tennis coach Miss. State U., Starkville, Miss., 1968-69; concierge The Roosevelt Hotel, New Orleans, 1969-70; sales rep. West Pub. Co., St. Paul, 1970-84, adminstr. internat. mktg. The Orient, 1985-90; freelance wine cons., 1985—; cons. Calif. Ctrl. Coast Wine Growers Assn., Santa MAria, 1987-91; lectr. advanced wine appreciation Calif. Poly. U. Extended Edn., San Luis Obispo, 1986-90; dir. KCBX Ctrl. Coast Wine Classic, San Luis Obispo, 1985—, KHPR Wine Classic, Honolulu, 1987-91, Winesong, Ft. Bragg, Calif., 1987-96, WETA Washington Wine Classic, 1989-90, KCRW Summerday, 1991, Santa Barbara Wine Auction, 1997-98, auction dir., 1992-94, 97, 98—; auction cons. Am. Inst. of Wine And Food, 1994—; chmn. Edna Valley Arroyo Grande Valley Vinters' Assn., 1999—. Host talk show Pub. Radio Sta. KCBX, San Luis Obispo, 1984—; columnist (newspaper) San Luis Obispo Telegram-Tribune, 1992-95, New Times San Luis Obispo, 1995-96; contbg. writer: Adventures in Dining, 1994-95, Santa Barbara Mag., 1998—. Bd. dirs. Avila Beach County Water Dist., 1992-95, pres., 1992-94; bd. dirs. San Luis Obispo (Calif.) Mozart Festival, 1988-92, pres., 1991-92; dir. Internat. Festival Champagne and Sparkling Wine, 1992-98; mem. Avila Valley Adv. Coun., 1993-95; bd. dirs. Guild South County Ctr. for Performing Arts, 1993-94, San Luis Obispo County Arts Coun., 2000—, San Luis Obispo County Visitors and Confs. Bur. (annual award for tourism promotion, 2000); mem. City of San Luis Obispo Tourism Coun., 2000—; founder Avila Drum Day, 1999; chmn. Avila Beach Cmty. Arts Com., 2000—. Mem. Calif. Cen. Coast Wine Soc. (pres. 1985), Am. Soc. Wine Educators, German Wine Soc. Honolulu, Vintners Club San Francisco, Avila Bay Wine Soc., Cen. Coast Chaine des Rotisseurs (chpt. pres. 1987, 88, 89), Marin County Food and Wine Soc., Edna Valley Arroyo Grande Valley Vintners Assn. (chmn. 1999), Internat. Food, Wine and Travel Writers' Assn., Austrian Wine Brotherhood, Avila Bay Club. Avocations: racquetball, tennis, squash racquets, collecting wine, basketball. Office: PO Box 790 Avila Beach CA 93424-0790

MCLAREN, IAN KENNETH, cardiovascular researcher; b. Hale, Cheshire, Eng., Jan. 18, 1945; s. George and Anne Lowe (Cowan) McL. PhD in Cardiovascular Sci. (hon.), Mercian Order of St. George, 1997, DDiv, 1997, PhD in Cell Migration Therapy (hon.), 1998, PhD in Diabetic Therapy-Options (hon.), 1999. Prodn. engr. Carlson-Ford Ltd., Manchester, Eng., 1969-70; avionics commissioning engr. Royal Saudi Air Force, Dhahran, 1970; electronic technician Cadbury-Schweppes, Birmingham, Eng., 1971-74; electronic R&D technician Cobra Electronic Svcs., Birmingham, 1974-91, cardiovascular cons., 1995—; cons. in cardiovascular disease Mercian Order of St. George, 1994-97; minister Universal Life Ch., Birmingham, 1997—. Author: Venture-Misadventure, 1994, An Investigation of Cardiovascular Disease, 1997. Dep. custodian Mercian Order of St. George, Birmingham, 1994-97. With RAF, 1965-69. Fellow Royal Meteorol. Soc., Royal Geog. Soc.; mem. Royal Inst. Navigation. Eclectic Unitarian. Avocations: sport parachuting, paragliding, naturism, adventure travel, flying light aircraft. Office: Smethwick, 12 Grange Rd, Smethwick B66 4NH, England

MCLAREN, JOHN DAVID, literature educator, editor; b. Melbourne, Australia, Nov. 7, 1932; s. David Lawrence and Katherine Euphemia (McDonald) McL.; m. Shirley Marion Stewart (dec. 1999); children: James, Cameron. BA with honors, Melbourne U., 1954, BEd, 1959, PhD, 1983; MA, Monash U., Australia, 1972. Tchr. and lectr. Dept. Edn., Victoria, Australia, 1956-71; head of humanities DDIAE, Toowoomba, Australia, 1972-76, Footscray Inst. Tech., Australia, 1976-89; prof. lit. Victoria U., Melbourne, 1991-97, hon. prof. Faculty Arts, 1997—; editor Australia Book Rev., Melbourne, 1978-86; assoc. editor Overland, Melbourne, 1966-92, editor, 1993-97; cons. editor, 1997—. Author: Australian Literature: an Historical Introduction, 1989, The New Pacific Literatures, 1993, Writing in Hope and Fear, 1996. Fulbright sr. scholar Australian-Am. Edn. Found., 1990. Office: Victoria U Fac of Arts, PO Box 14428/MCMC, 8001 Melbourne Australia

MCLAREN, KAREN LYNN, advertising executive; b. Flint, Mich., Feb. 14, 1955; m. Michael L. McLaren, June 18, 1974. AA, Mott Community Coll., Flint, 1976; BA, Mich. State U., 1978. Writer Sta. WGMZ-FM, Flint, 1979-84; writer, producer Tracy-Stephens Advt., Flint, 1984-87; pres. McLaren Advt., Troy, Mich., 1987—. Contbr. articles to profl. jours. Mem. centennial com. Wolverine region ARC, 1981, pub. rels. com., 1981-84; vol. coord., pub. rels. tour guide Whaley Hist. Ho., Flint, 1980-91; home designer, tour guide Romeo (Mich.) Hist. Home Tour, 1992; mem. Nat. Trust for Hist. Preservation, 1991-95; com. chair Crim Festival of Races, Flint, 1992, 93, 94, 95; active Sta. WFUM-Pub. TV, Flint, 1980-91; panelist career fair Modona U., Livonia, Mich., 1994, 95, 96, 97; ad book chair Juvenile Diabetes Found./Detroit Evening of Brilliance, 1997; mem. Oakland Regional Bd. Barbara Ann Karmanos Cancer Instn., 1999. Recipient 3 awards, 2 Nat. Health Care Mktg. Competition awards, Women's Adv. Club Detroit Pres.'s award, 1994. Mem. NAFE, Women's Advt. Club Detroit (scholar chmn. 1988-88, bd. dirs. 1989, 92-93, chmn. scholarship fundraiser 1991, co-chmn. career fair 1989, 90, 92, career fair panelist 1993, v.p. 1990, pres. 1991, amb. 1992, chmn. woman of yr. award 1994-96, by-laws chmn. 1994), Women's Econ. Club Detroit (progam com. 1996, workplace of tomorrow com. 1996, vice chair 1997, chair 1999). Office: 3001 W Big Beaver Rd Ste 306 Troy MI 48084-3104*

MCLARTY, THOMAS F., III (MACK MCLARTY), business executive; b. Hope, Ark., June 14, 1946; s. Thomas Franklin and Helen (Hesterly) McL.; m. Donna Kay Cochran, June 14, 1969; children: Mark Cochran, Franklin Hesterly. BA, U. Arkansas, Fayetteville, 1968. Founder, pres. McLarty Leasing System Inc., Little Rock, 1969-79; pres. McLarty Cos., 1979-83; with Arkla Inc., Shreveport, from 1983, pres., CEO Arkla Gas divsn., 1983; pres., COO Arkla Gas divsn. Arkla, Inc., Shreveport, 1984, chmn. bd., pres., CEO, from 1985; chief of staff The White House, Washington, 1993-94, sr. adviser to President Clinton, 1994—, counselor to pres., spl. envoy for Ams.; vice chmn. Kissinger McLarty Assocs., Washington, D.C., 1998—; chmn. Arkla Energy Mktg. Co., Shreveport, La., Arkla Chem. Corp., Shreveport, AER-Ark. Gas Transit Co., Shreveport; chmn., chief exec. officer, Miss. River Transmission Corp., St. Louis, MRT Energy Mktg. Co., St. Louis, Ark. La. Fin. Corp., Shreveport. Mem. Ark. Ho. of Reps., 1970-72; chmn. Ark. Dem. Com.; mem. Dem. Nat. Com., 1974-76; treas. David Pryor Gubernatorial Campaign, 1974, Gov. Bill Clinton campaign, 1978; bd. dirs. Hendrix Coll., Conway, Ark.; bd. visitors U. Ark., Little Rock; former chmn. United Negro Coll. Fund Campaign, fund-raising campaign Ark. Symphony. Mem. Greater Little Rock C. of C. (pres. 1983). Office: Kissinger McLarty Assocs 1775 Pennsylvania Ave NW Washington DC 20006-4605 also: The McLarty Cos 425 W Capitol Ave Ste 3810 Little Rock AR 72201-3460

MCLAUCHLAN, SYLVIA JUNE, charity organization executive; b. Hornchurch, Essex, Eng., June 8, 1935; d. Sydney George and Muriel May (Treweek) Smith; m. Derek John A. McLauchlan, Aug. 6, 1960. MB, ChB, U. Bristol, Eng., 1959; MSc, U. Manchester, Eng., 1979. Gen. practitioner Bristol, 1960-66; med. officer Portsmouth (Eng.) City Coun., 1970-76; pub. health physician Univ.-Regional Health Authority, Manchester, 1976-85, S.W. Thames Regional Health Authority, London, 1985-91; dir. pub. health Ealing (Eng.) Health Authority, 1991-93; dir. gen. The Stroke Assn., London, 1993-97; cons. in pub. health medicine. Fellow Faculty Pub. Health Medicine.

MCLAUCHLIN, TAMMY DENISE, protective services official; b. Greenville, S.C., July 14, 1964; d. William Kenneth and Martha Jo Pritchard; m. Henry Otho McLauchlin, Oct. 20, 1996. Cert. police officer, S.C. Merchandiser K-Mart Automotives/Sporting Goods, Greenville, 1981-84;

comms. specialist Greenville County Sheriff's Office, Greenville, 1984-86; police sgt. Greenville Police Dept., 1986—. Named Vince Perone Office of the Yr., Greenville Police Dept., 1994. Avocations: running, weight lifting, reading. Home: 103 Riverside Chase Cir Greer SC 29650-2535

MCLEAN, EPHRAIM RANKIN, information systems educator; b. Jan. 7, 1936; married; 3 children. BME, Cornell U., 1958; SM in Mgmt., MIT, 1967, PhD in Mgmt., 1970. Mfg. mgmt., then sys. analyst positions Procter & Gamble Co., 1958-65; instr. tracked vehicle sect. automotive br. U.S. Army Ordnance Sch., Aberdeen Proving Ground, Md., 1959; sys. analyst Cambridge (Mass.) Thermionic Corp., 1966-67; rsch. asst. Sloan Sch. Mgmt. MIT, Cambridge, 1966-69, instr. info. sys., 1969; asst. prof. Grad. Sch. Mgmt. UCLA, 1969-75, assoc. prof., 1975-87; prof., George E. Smith eminent scholar's chair Ga. State U., Atlanta, 1987—; dir. computing svcs. Grad. Sch. Mgmt., UCLA, 1970-74, chmn. computers and info. systems, 1972-73, 77-80, 83-84, 86-87, founder/dir. computers and info. systems rsch. program, 1978-87; mem. adv. bd. Info. Inst., Internat. Acad. Santa Barbara, Calif., 1983-87; mem. adv. com. Info. Systems Faculty Devel. Inst., Am. Assembly Collegiate Sch. Bus. and U. Minn., Mpls., 1982, 84; cons. numerous bus. and ednl. orgns., 1967—; vis. prof. U. South Australia, Adelaide, 1993. Author: (with J.V. Soden) Strategic Planning for MIS, 1977; (with E. Turban and J. Wetherbe) Information Technology for Management, 1996, 2d edit., 1999; co-editor: Management Applications in APL, 1981, Decision Support Systems: A Decade in Perspective, 1986, The Management of Information Systems, 1989, 2nd edit., 1994, prof. conf. procs.; assoc. editor Data Base, 1990-94, co-editor, 1994—; mem. editl. bd./adv. bd., referee many profl. publs. and pub. cos.; contbr. numerous articles and revs. to profl. jours., mags., other publs. 2nd lt. ordnance corps USAR, 1958-59; 1st lt. ordnance corps N.J. Army N.G., 1959-65; capt. ordnance corps Mass. Army N.G., 1965-68. NDEA doctoral fellow MIT, 1967-69; recipient 1st prize nat. engring. design contest Lincoln Arc Welding Found., 1958; rsch. grantee IBM Corp., 1985, McCormick & Co., Hunt Valley, Md., 1989, InformationWEEK mag., Manhasset, N.Y., 1989, Sellinger Sch. Bus. and Mgmt. Loyola Coll. Md., Balt., 1992. Fellow Assn. for Info. System (founding mem., v.p. affiliated orgns. 1995-97, exec. dir. 1998—); mem. Internat. Acad. Info. Mgmt. (bd. dirs. 1992—), EDUCOM (affiliate) Decision Scis. Inst., Internat. Fedn. Info. Processing (founding mem. working group on decision support sys. 1981—), Internat. Conf. on Info. Sys. (founding mem. adv. bd. 1980—, chmn. exec. com. 1986-87, 96-98, exec. dir. 1998—, co-chmn. exec. com. 1998), Soc. for Info. Mgmt. (Atlanta chpt., mem. nat. pres.'s coun. 1985-98, mem. nat. exec. com. 1976-79, 85-87, v.p. chpt. devel. and alliances 2000—, 3d pl. juried paper award competition 1987), Inst. Mgmt. Scis., ACM, Mensa, Sigma Xi. Home: 2257 Old Brooke Pt Dunwoody GA 30338-3173 Office: Ga State U Computer Info Sys Dept Box 4015 Atlanta GA 30302-4015

MCLEAN, JANELLE ANNETTE, elementary education educator; b. Freeport, Ill., Aug. 15, 1955; d. Leonard Burdette and Janet Elaine (Baxter) Bastian; m. Richard McLean, Jan. 18, 1997. BA, U. No. Iowa, Cedar Falls, 1976, MA in Edn., 1987. Cert. tchr., Iowa, Calif. Librarian, English tchr. Walnut Ridge Bapt. Acad., Waterloo, Iowa, 1977-78, tchr. 3d grade, 1978-88; tutor Grace Community Sch., Sun Valley, Calif., 1989—, tchr. 2d and 3d grades, 1989—; leader various seminars; instr. etiquette Logos Bible Inst. Author: Honeycomb Tapestry, 1988; contbr. articles to profl. jours. Named to Outstanding Young Women of Am., 1991; Waterloo Women of Today reading grantee, 1987. Republican. Avocations: reading, travel, hosting parties, writing, walking. Office: Grace Community Sch 13246 Roscoe Blvd Sun Valley CA 91352-3739

MCLEAN, JOHN BONWELL, SR., government official; b. Feb. 18, 1950; s. Joseph Berkley Sr. and Vella Victorine (Watler) McL.; m. Stephanie Ameleta, Feb. 6, 1971; children: John Bonwell Jr., Shannon Dianne, Ronald Reagan. Bank officer Royal Bank Can., 1967-73, N.W. Bank, 1973-74; with dept. acctg. Kirkconnell Bros. Ltd., 1974-81; legis. rep. Govt. Cayman Islands, 1976—, mem. exec. coun., 1980-84; min. agriculture Govt. Cayman Islands, Grand Cayman, 1992—; owner, gen. mgr. M.Lmac Leasing Co. Ltd., 1979—. Apptd. Justice of Peace Govt. Cayman Islands, 1980. Decorated Order Brit. Empire by Queen Elizabeth II. Mem. Rotary Club (charter). Avocations: hunting, fishing. Office: Cayman Islands Ministry Agr Comm & Works, Govt Adminstrn Bldg, Georgetown Grand Cayman, Cayman Islands*

MCLEAN, MICHAEL JOHNSON, quality assurance professional; b. Winston Salem, N.C., Jan. 30, 1951; s. Ernest Shaw and Irene (Coram) McL.; m. Laura Alice Perry, July 3, 1976; children: Jenny Johnson, Matthew Russell. BSChemE, N.C. State U., 1973. Prodn. engr. Mallinckrodt, Inc., Raleigh, N.C., 1974-75; health and safety engr. Mallinckrodt, Inc., Raleigh, 1975-77, sr. process engr., 1977-78, prodn. supr., 1978-80; fermentation and separation mgr. Ajinomoto USA, Raleigh, 1980-86, quality assurance mgr., 1986-89, quality assurance assoc. dir., 1989-98, quality assurance dir., 1998—; mem. adv. bd. pharm. tech. Wake C.C., Raleigh, 1989-99; trustee Wake C.C. Found., Raleigh, 1998-99; adv. bd. Chem. Engring. dept. N.C. State U., 1999. Vol. coord. Hot Hoops Tournament, Raleigh, 1988-98. Mem. AIChE, Internat. Soc. Pharm. Engrs., Am. Soc. Quality, Capital City Club. Presbyterian. Avocations: golf, fishing, skiing, boating. Office: Ajimomoto USA 4020 Ajinomoto Dr Raleigh NC 27610-2917

MCLEAN, ROBERT, III, real estate company executive; b. Balt., May 23, 1928; s. Robert Jr. and Mary Somerville (Iglehart) McL.; m. Elizabeth Madison Lewis, May 21, 1960; children: Elizabeth, Alexander, Mary, John. BA, Yale U., 1950; MA, U. Pa., 1965. Mktg. exec. Owens-Ill., Toledo, Ohio, 1957-65; mktg. cons. Old Phila. Devel. Corp., Phila., 1966-70; vice chmn., mem. bd. Cushman & Wakefield, N.Y.C., 1970—; mem. real estate investment com. Yale U., New Haven, Conn., 1982-90; mem. bd. Cushman & Wakefield/Healey & Baker joint venture, N.Y.C., 1990-94. Author: Countdown to Renaissance II, The New Way Corporate America Builds, 1984. Chmn. Nat. Bldg. Mus., Washington, 1992-95; mem. bd. Washington Nat. Cathedral, 1981-87. S/Sgt. USMC, 1953-56. Mem. Rolling Rock Club, Allegheny Country Club, Metropolitan Club, Center Club, Gibson Island Club. Republican. Episcopalian. Avocations: tennis, golf, skiing. Fax: (703) 84702798. E-mail: robert mclean@cushwake.com. Home: 631 Stillwater Rd Gibson Island MD 21056 Office: Cushman & Wakefield 1650 Tysons Blvd Ste 450 Mc Lean VA 22102-4841

MCLEAN, ROBERT JAMES CAMERON, microbiologist, educator; b. Toronto, Sept. 18, 1956; came to U.S., 1993; s. James Campbell and Blanche Alice Violet (Harrison) McL.; m. Martha Elaine Law, May 21, 1988; children: Malcolm Albert Campbell, Alistair Ian Law. BSc, U. Guelph, Ont., Can., 1978; PhD, U. Calgary, Alta., Can., 1986. Asst. prof. Queens U., Kingston, Ont., 1988-93; from asst. prof. to assoc. prof. S.W. Tex. State U., San Marcos, 1993—; cons. Kingston Techs., Trenton, N.J., 1991, Q-Life Systems, Inc., Kingston, 1992-93, ICET, Inc., Norwood, Mass., 1995, Sulzer Carbomedics Inc., Austin, Tex., 1999. Author: Immobilized Biosystems, 1994; mem. editl. bd. Applied and Environ. Microbiology, 1999—, Bioresource Tech., 1997—, Geomicrobiology Jour., 1999—; contbr. articles to profl. jours. Recipient Pres. award Microscopical Soc. Can., 1986. Mem. Am. Soc. for Microbiology, Can. Soc. Microbiologists (chmn. morphology and structure sect. 1994-96). Presbyterian. Achievements include first experimental bacterial biofilm formation during space flight; co-discovery of quorum sensing signal molecules in naturally occurring biofilms; research on slow growth starvation survival and quorum sensing genes in biofilm growth. E-mail: RM12@swt.edu. Office: SW Tex State Univ Dept Biology San Marcos TX 78666

MCLEAN, ROGER FAIRBAIRN, geographer, educator; b. Wellington, New Zealand, Oct. 9, 1938; m. Margaret Ruth Barrett, Aug. 26, 1961; children: Susan, Caroline, Alison. BA, U. New Zealand, 1960, MA, 1961; PhD, McGill U., 1965. Lectr. U. Canterbury, New Zealand, 1964-71; rsch. fellow Australian Nat. U., Canberra, 1972-77; sr. lectr. U. Auckland, New Zealand, 1978-85; prof., head depts. geography & oceanography Australian Def. Force Acad., Canberra, 1986—. Mem. Inst. Australian Geography (pres.), Australian Geosci. Coun., Australian Acad. Sci. Office: Univ Coll NSW Dept Geog, Northcott Dr, Canberra ACT 2601, Australia

MCLEAN, SUSAN RALSTON, lawyer; b. Fayetteville, Tenn., Feb. 28, 1948; d. Joseph Frederick and Clara (Robertson) Ralston; m. Arthur Edward McLean, Apr. 16, 1983. AB, Randolph-Macon Woman's Coll., 1970; MAT in English, Vanderbilt U., 1971; JD, U. Tenn., 1979; LLM in Taxation, So. Meth. U., 1984. Bar: Tenn. 1979, Tex. 1981, Ark. 1984. Assoc. Rose Law Firm, Little Rock, 1984-85, Brice & Mankoff, Dallas, 1986-87; counsel tax divsn. Dept. Justice, Dallas, 1987-96. Contbr. articles to profl. jours. Advocate for treatment of reactive attachment disorder. Mem. ABA (tax, litigation, bus. law sects.), Tex. Bar Assn. (tax and litigation sects.), Randolph-Macon Woman's Coll. Alumnae (pres. 1992-94). Presbyterian. Avocations: swimming, golf, art, music, hiking. Home: 4025 McFarlin Blvd Dallas TX 75205-1723

MCLEES, JOHN ALAN, lawyer; b. Mpls., Jan. 19, 1948; s. Alan L. and Marian G. (Melby) McL.; m. Bozena Nowicka, June 25, 1993; children: Alexandra, Thomas. BA, U. Chgo., 1970, MBA, 1973, JD, 1974; MS in Econs., London Sch. Econs., 1971. Bar: D.C., 1974, Ill., 1975. Assoc. Keck Mahin & Cate, Chgo., 1975-79; atty. advisor office of sec. U.S. Dept. Energy, Washington, 1979-81; mng. atty. Sidley & Austin, Muscat, Oman, 1981-83; assoc. Sidley & Austin, Chgo., 1983-88, Morgan Lewis & Bockius, Washington, 1988-91; dir. Latin Am. tax svc. Coopers & Lybrand, Chgo., 1991-97; ptnr. Baker & McKenzie, Chgo., 1997—; organizer, chmn. confs. on Mex. and Latin Am. tax laws, 1992—. Editor (loose leaf treatise) CCH Latin Am. Tax Guide, 2000; contbr. articles to profl. jours. Adv. bd. Com. for Pub. Autonomous Schs., Washington, 1989—; chmn. of bd. dirs. Mid Am. Chpt., U.S. Mex. C. of C., 1993-97. Named Leading Tax Advisor, Euromoney Guide to Leading U.S. Tax Lawyers, 1997, Euromoney Guide to the World's Leading Tax Advisors, 1999, Leading Advisor on Latin Am. Tax, Internat. Tax. Review, 1996-2000. Mem. ACLU, ABA, Internat. Fiscal Assn. Episcopalian. E-mail: John.A.McLees@Bakernet.com. Home: 1434 S Plymouth Ct Chicago IL 60605-2729 Office: Baker & McKenzie 130 E Randolph Dr Ste 3700 Chicago IL 60601-6342

MCLELLAN, A. ANNE, Canadian government official; b. Hants County, N.S., Can., Aug. 31, 1950; d. Howard Gilmore and Joan Mary (Pullan) McL. BA, Dalhousie U., LLB, 1974; LLM, King's Coll., U. London, 1975. Bar: N.S., 1976. Asst. prof. law U. N.B., Can., 1976-80; assoc. prof. law U. Alta., Edmonton, Can., 1980-89, assoc. dean faculty of law, 1985-87, prof. law, 1989-93, acting dean, 1991-92; M.P. for Edmonton West Ho. of Commons, Can., 1993—; min. Natural Resources Can., Ottawa, Ont., Can., 1997—, Justice and Atty. Gen., Can.; commentator on Can. Charter of Rights and Freedoms and on human rights issues. Contbr. articles to profl. publs. Past bd. dirs. Can. Civil Liberties Assn., Alta. Legal Aid; past v.p. U. Alta. Faculty Assn. Office: Canada Justice Bldg, 284 Wellington St, Ottawa, ON Canada K1A 0H8

MCLELLAN, JOHN PAUL, lawyer; b. London, Feb. 13, 1964; s. John Michael and Shiela Rosena McLellan. LLB in Bus. Law with 2d class honors, Guildhall U. Solicitor, Eng. and Wales 1988, Hong Kong 1989, Australian Capital Territory, 1989. From trainee solicitor to assoc. solicitor Sheridans, U.K., 1986-89; assoc. solicitor Haldanes, Hong Kong, 1989-92, equity ptnr., 1992—; legal advisor Hong Kong Performing Actors Guild, Hong Kong Dirs. Guild, Music Pubs. Assn. of Hong Kong, MIDEM Asia and MIP Asia Confs., France. Mem. Internat. Assn. Entertainment Lawyers (mem. Asia coun.). Office: Haldanes, 11 Duddell St, Hong Kong China

MCLELLAND, LORI ANN, music educator; b. Williamston, N.C., Mar. 12, 1968; d. Delton Jack and Liza Daniels McLelland. MusB, East Carolina U., 1990; postgrad., Appalachian State U., 1991-93, 2000. Cert. kindergarten-12th grade music tchr., N.C. Freelance vocalist, pianist, 1985—, pvt. voice and piano tchr./coach, 1985—; children's choir dir. Immanuel Bapt. Ch., Greenville, N.C., 1987-89; grad. asst. elem. music, piano, choral tchr. Broyhill Music Ctr., Appalachian State U., Boone, N.C., 1991-93; choral dir. Pinecrest H.S., So. Pines, N.C., 1993-96; pianist Kellum Bapt. Ch., Jacksonville, N.C., 1996-97; choral dir., gen. music tchr., musical theatre dir. Hunters Creek Middle Sch., Jacksonville, 1996—; tchr., counselor East Carolina U. Summer Choral Camp, Greenville, 1988, 89, 90, 91, 95-99; staff mem. Silver Burdett Ginn Elem. Music Workshop, Boone, N.C., 1992-95, 97; guest singer Glenn Miller Orch., Pinehurst, N.C., 1995—. Vol. musician various chs., N.C., 1980—; vol., mem. steering com. Habitat for Humanity, Greenville, 1989-90. Mem. NEA, N.C. Assn. Educators, Am. Choral Dirs. Assn. (collegiate pres., v.p., sec. 1987-90), N.C. Music Educators Assn., Music Educators Nat. Conf. (collegiate pres., sec., v.p. 1988-90), East Carolina Univ. Sch. Music Alumni Profl. Soc. (v.p., sec., mem.-at-large 1995—), Sigma Alpha Iota (pres., rec. sec., corr. sec. 1988-90, Sword of Honor 1990). Methodist. Avocations: music, travel, reading, movies, Broadway. E-mail: panthers@onslowonline.net. Home: 203 N Carole Dr # 72 Jacksonville NC 28546-4845 Office: Hunters Creek Middle Sch 4040 Hunters Trl Jacksonville NC 28546-4852

MCLELLAND, MALCOLM HERBERT, retired judge; b. Sydney, Australia, July 5, 1937; s. Charles and Helena Muriel (Willcock) McL.; m. Margaret Roslyn Newell, Jan. 8, 1965; children: Margot Catherine, Nicola Gail, Kim Caroline. BA, U. Sydney, 1958, LLB with honors, 1961. Bar: 1963. Solicitor Sly and Russell, Sydney, 1961-63; barrister Sydney, 1963-79, queens counsel, 1974-79; judge Supreme Ct. N.S.W., Sydney, 1979-97; chief judge Equity Supreme Ct. N.S.W., 1993-97; rule com. N.S.W. Supreme Ct., 1981-97; mem. Joint Law Cts. Libr. Mgmt. Com., 1991-93; councillor N.S.W. Bar Coun., Sydney, 1967-72. Contbr. articles to profl. jours. Mem. N.S.W. Bar Assn. (hon. sec. 1970-72). Avocations: music, metaphysics, science, history, tennis.

MCLEMORE, HARRY KIMBRELL, retired real estate developer; b. Nashville, June 23, 1929; s. Richard Aubrey and Nannie (Pitts) McL.; m. Monita Prine, Mar. 9, 1952; children: Risa Lyn, Richard Alby. BS, U. So. Miss., 1950. Cert. indsl. developer. Rsch. economist N. Miss. Indsl. Devel. Assn., W. Point, 1953-57; exec. v.p. Indsl. Devel. Com., Shreveport, La., 1957-64; mgr. econ. devel. dept. Little Rock C. of C., 1964-74; mgr. Ctr. S., Jackson, Miss., 1974-80; exec. dir. Pensacola (Fla.) Escambia Devel. Commn., 1980-90; mgr. econ. devel. Jackson County Port Authority, Pascagoula, Miss., 1990-93; ret., 1993; spl. assignment IESC, Armenia, 1999. Fellow Am. Econ. Devel. Coun. (hon. life); mem. SAR (pres. Gulf Coast chpt.), SCV (v.p. 1699 hist. com.), So. Econ. Devel. Coun. (hon. life) (pres.), Miss. Econ. Devel. Coun. (hon. life). Methodist. Avocations: travel, flying, amateur radio. Home: 110 Winchester Dr Ocean Springs MS 39564-5419

MCLENDON, SUSAN MICHELLE, lawyer, nurse; b. N.Y.C., Mar. 5, 1964; d. James U. McLendon, Sr. BSN, Binghamton U., 1986; JD, Hofstra U., 1990. Bar: N.Y., N.J., D.C.; RN, N.Y., 1986. Asst. regional counsel Social Security Adminstrn., Office Gen. Counsel, N.Y.C., 1990-98; RN All Care Nursing Corp., N.Y.C., 1998—; pvt. law practice All Care Nursing Corp., 2000—; RN L.I. Jewish Hosp., Roosevelt, N.Y., 2000—; mentor Practicing Attys. for Law Students, N.Y.C., 1992—. Fundraiser Race for the Cure, March Dimes.

MCLEOD, GUY COLIN, aerospace company executive; arrived in Singapore, 1968; s. Ian and Janet (Angus) McL. Degree in chem. engring., Edinburgh (Scotland) U., 1990. Dir. area sales Airbus Industry, Beijing, 1995-98, v.p., 1998—. Capt. 6th Gurkha Rifles, Her Majesty's Armed Forces, 1990-95. Avocations: scuba diving, reading, trekking, sky diving. Office: Airbus Industry China Ltd, Internat PO Box 9072, Beijing 100 600, China

MCLEOD, STEPHEN GLENN, education educator, language educator; b. Pensacola, Fla., Mar. 30, 1949. AA, Pensacola Jr. Coll., 1969; BA, U. West Fla., 1971; MA, Vanderbilt U., 1973; EdD, Nova Southeastern U., 1992. Commd. 2d lt. U.S. Army, 1978, advanced through grades to capt., 1981, resigned, 1984; sr. assoc. prof. mil. edn. program St. Leo Coll., Hurlburt Field, Fla., 1984-92; adj. instr. Pensacola Jr. Coll., 1984-86, 91—; West Fla. cluster adminstr. programs for higher edn. Nova Southeastern U., Pensacola/Ft. Lauderdale, Fla., 1994—. Contbr. articles to profl. publs. Capt. U.S. Army, 1975-84. Recipient Rsch. award Phi Delta Kappa, 1989. Mem. Two-Year Coll. English Assn. Southeast, Nat. Coun. Tchrs. English. Avocations: golf, writing, travel. Home: 1313 Wisteria Ave Pensacola FL 32507-2250

MCLEOD, WALTON JAMES, lawyer, state legislator; b. Walterboro, S.C., June 30, 1937; s. Walton James Jr. and Rhoda Lane (Brown) M.; m. Julie Edwina Hamiter, Feb. 15, 1969; 1 child, Walton James IV. BA, Yale U., 1959; LLB, U. S.C., 1964. Bar: S.C. 1964, U.S. Supreme Ct. 1974. Law clk. to Chief Judge Clement Haynsworth U.S. Ct. Appeals (4th cir.), Richmond, Va., 1964-65; assoc. Pope and Schumpert, Newberry, S.C., 1965-67; asst. U.S. Atty. Columbia, S.C., 1967-68; gen. counsel S.C. Dept. Health & Environ. Ctrl., Columbia, 1968-94, spl. counsel, 1994-96; dep. S.C. atty. gen. Columbia, 1987-88; magistrate Newberry County, Little Mountain, S.C., 1973-81; mcpl. judge Town of Little Mountain, 1981-83, mayor, 1983-89, 93-96; mem. S.C. Ho. of Reps., Columbia, 1996—. Author: Legal Perspectives of Environmental Health, 1973; co-author: Environmental Quality Law, 1975, Hospital Franchising Law and Regulation, 1979. Pres. Newberry (S.C.) Jaycees, 1967; bd. dirs. S.C. Housing Fin. & Devel. Authority, Columbia, 1977-96; chair Ctrl. Midlands Coun. Govts., Columbia, 1981-82; trustee S.C. State Mus., Columbia, 1981-85. Lt. (j.g.) USN, 1959-61, Capt. USNR, 1961-92. Recipient Outstanding Jaycee award Newberry Jaycees, 1967, Howell Excellence award Naval Res. Law Program, Washington, 1991; named Outstanding Freshman Rep. of Yr. Carolina Hist. Found. Soc., Inc., 1997. Fellow S.C. Bar Found.; mem. S.C. Magistrates Assn. (pres. 1976-77, Disting. Jud. Svc. award 1975, 77), Judge Advs. Assn. (nat. pres. 1991-92), S.C. Res. Officers Assn. (state pres. 1981-82, Res. Officer of Yr. 1998), S.C. Soc. (pres. 1990-93). Democrat. Luth. Avocations: jogging, reading. Fax: 803-345-0770. Home: 308 Pomaria St Little Mountain SC 29075-9003 Office: SC House of Reps PO Box 11867 Columbia SC 29211-1867

MCLEOD, WILLIAM LASATER, JR., lawyer, former judge and state legislator; b. Marks, Miss., Feb. 27, 1931; s. William Lasater and Sara Louise (Macaulay) McL.; m. Marilyn Qualls, June 16, 1962; children: Sara Nelson Judson, Martha Ellen Livanec, Ruth Elizabeth. AB, Princeton U., 1953; JD, La. State U., 1958. Bar: La. 1958, U.S. Supreme Ct. 1980. Pvt. practice, Lake Charles, La., 1958-90, 97—; ptnr. McLeod & Little, 1976-90; dist. judge Calcasieu Prish, 1991-96; mem. La. Ho. of Reps., 1968-76; mem. La. Senate, 1976-90. Chmn. adv. bd. Lake Charles Salvation Army, 1965-66; pres. Calcasieu Area coun. Boy scouts Am., 1978; elder Presbyn. Ch. With U.S. Army, 1953-55. Recipient Disting. Svc. award Lake Charles Jaycees, 1963, Civic Svc. award S.W. La. C. of C., 1986. Mem. La. Bar Assn., S.W. La Bar Assn. (pres. 1980), Masons. Democrat. Office: 120 W Pujo St Lake Charles LA 70601-4257

MCLOUGHLIN, JAMES PATRICK, bishop; b. Galway, Ireland, Apr. 4, 1929; s. Patrick and Winifred (McDermott) McL. BA, St. Patrick's Coll., Maynooth, Ireland, 1950; Higher Diploma in Edn., Univ. Coll., Galway, 1955. Ordained priest Roman Cath. Ch., 1954; ordained bishop, 1993. Prof. St. Mary's Coll., Galway, 1954-65; diocesan sec. Galway (Ireland) Diocese, 1965-83; parish priest Galway (Ireland) Cathedral, 1983-93, bishop, 1993—. Home: Mount St Marys, Taylors Hill, Galway Ireland Office: Diocesan Office The Cathedral, Galway Ireland

MCMAHON, EILEEN MARIE, art agent; b. Jersey City, July 15, 1953; d. William John and Marie Rita (Stringer) M. BA in Art, Jersey City State Coll., 1974; postgrad., Rutgers U., 1974-76, New Sch. for Social Research, 1976-77, Sch. of Visual Arts, 1976. Asst. curator Jersey City Mus., 1975-77; curator Ian Woodner Family Collection, N.Y.C., 1977-78; assoc. rep. Artist's Assocs., Inc., N.Y.C., 1978-81; sr. rep. Gerald and Cullen Rapp, Inc., N.Y.C., 1981-86; mktg. dir. Corey Chaloner Millen, N.Y.C., 1986-88; assoc. rep. John Locke Studios Inc., N.Y.C., 1988-97; pres. Eileen McMahon & Co., Bayonne, N.J., 1997—. Co-author, designer: mus. catalog, August Will: Scenes of Old Jersey City, 1976, Jersey Jour. Woman of Achievement, 1977. Named Jersey Jour. Woman of Achievement, 1977. Office: Eileen McMahon & Co PO Box 1062 Bayonne NJ 07002-1062

MCMAHON, PAUL FRANCIS, finance company executive; b. Malone, N.Y., Apr. 28, 1945; s. Philip Francis and Shirley (Roy) M.; m. Sheila Ann Lester, Nov. 30, 1963; children: Michael, Marsha. BS, Syracuse U., 1968. CPA, N.Y., Oreg.; cert. mgmt. acct., mgmt. cons. With Ernst & Young, Syracuse, N.Y., 1968-73, mgr., 1975-79; ptnr. in charge of mgmt. cons. in Europe Ernst & Young, Brussels, 1979-84; vice-chmn. Ernst & Young, Cleve., 1984-87; exec. ptnr. Ernst & Young Internat., N.Y., 1987-93; chmn. Ernst & Young Ea. Europe, 1990-93; regional dir. Asia/Pacific Ernst & Young Internat., Singapore, 1994-96; contr. Coop. Mktg. Agy., Syracuse, 1973-75; COO Amrop Internat., Brussels, 1997—; steering com. Oreg. Emerging Bus. Initiative. Treas. Bus. Coun. for Internat. Understanding. Mem. AICPA, Oreg. Inst. CPA's, Oreg. Emerging Bus. Initiative, N.Y. Soc. CPA's, Inst. Mgmt. Acctg., Assn. Mgmt. Cons. Firms (bd. dirs.), Coun. Cons. Orgns. (past chmn.), Art Harvest (bd. dirs.). Democrat. Roman Catholic. Avocations: photography, sculpture, travel, gardening, biographies. Home: 35680 NE Wilsonville Rd Newberg OR 97132-7181

MCMAHON, ROBERT LEE, JR. (BOB MCMAHON), semi-retired investor, retired aerospace and information systems executive; b. Weatherford, Tex., Feb. 19, 1944; s. Robert Lee Sr. and Gusta Rosann (Collins) McM. AA, Weatherford Coll., 1964; BA, U. Tex., Arlington, 1970; postgrad. in mgmt., Tex. Christian U., 1970-73. Announcer Sta. KZEE, Weatherford, Tex., 1963-65; asst. gen. mgr. Sta. KZEE, Weatherford, 1972-75; programmer Gen. Dynamics, Ft. Worth, 1967-68, sr. programmer, 1968-72, sr. engr., 1975-78, project engr., 1978-79, group supr., 1979-80, sect. chief, 1980-83, dept. mgr., 1983-93; staff specialist Lockheed Ft. Worth Co., 1994-95, retired, 1995; mem. adv. bd. Mfg. Tech. Directorate, USAF, Dayton, Ohio, 1981-91, Automation and Robotics Rsch. Inst., Ft. Worth, 1986-91. Editor: Manufacturing Engineer's Handbook, 1988; mem. editorial bd. Mfg. Engring. mag., 1989-91. Dir. adult edn. program Parker County, Tex., 1972-75; chmn. Weatherford City Charter Revision Commn., 1974-75; mem. Weatherford Planning and Zoning Bd., 1984-88; chmn. 4th precinct Parker County Dem. Com., 1982-92, 27th precinct, 1992-98; foreman Grand Jury, 1993. Mem. Soc. Mfg. Engrs. (cert., sr.), Robotic Industries Assn. (sr., bd. dirs. 1984-88), Computer and Automated Sys. Assn. (sr.), Robotics Inst. (sr.), Am. Inst. Indsl. Engrs., Nat. Mgmt. Assn., Masons (33d degree, past master), Phi Theta Kappa (v.p. Weatherford chpt.), Ego Omega, Beta Alpha Psi. Mem. Ch. of Christ. Avocations: photography, pocket billiards, reading, model railroading. Home: 1418 E Bankhead Dr Weatherford TX 76086-4607

MCMAHON, WILLIAM EDWARD, philosophy educator; b. Chgo., Sept. 25, 1937; s. Daniel Patrick McMahon and Mary Lois Hurley; m. Mary Louise Owens, Dec. 29, 1962; children: Elizabeth Maura, Coleman William. AB, U. Notre Dame, 1959, PhD, 1970; AM, Brown U., 1961. Instr. St. Vincent Coll., Latrobe, Pa., 1961-64; asst. prof. John Carroll U., Cleve., 1967-69; asst. prof. U. Akron, 1969-77, assoc. prof. to prof., 1977-99, dept. chair, 1985-96, prof. emeritus, 1999—. Fellow Pullman Found., 1955-59, Brown U., 1960-61; grantee for Inst. in Medieval Philosophy, NEH, 1980. Mem. Internat. Naval Rsch. Orgn., Soc. for Am. Baseball Rsch., N.Am. Assn. for History of Lang. Scis., Am. Philos. Assn., Soc. for Medieval and Renaissance Philosophy, Ohio Philos. Assn. (v.p. 1985-91), Henry Sweet Soc. Democrat. Roman Catholic. Avocations: baseball and naval history, stamp collecting. E-mail: mcmahon@uakron.edu. Home: 606 Nome Ave Akron OH 44320-1681 Office: U Akron Philosophy Dept 302 Olin Hl Akron OH 44325-0001

MCMANIS, JAMES, lawyer; b. Haverhill, Mass., May 28, 1943; s. Charles and Yvonne (Zinn) McM.; m. Sara Wigh, Mar. 30, 1968. BA, Stanford U., Palo Alto, Calif., 1964; JD, U. Calif., Berkeley, 1967. Bar: Calif. 1967, U.S. Dist. Ct. (no. dist.) Calif. 1967, U.S. Ct. Appeals (9th cir.) 1967, U.S. Supreme Ct. 1971. Dep. dist. atty. Santa Clara County Dist. Atty., 1968-71; mem. McManis, Faulkner & Morgan, San Jose, Calif., 1971—; spl. master tech. equities litigation, 1987—; spl. examiner State Bar Calif., 1995-98; prof. law Lincoln U. Law Sch., San Jose, 1972-82; lectr. Calif. Continuing Edn. of Bar, 1989-90; instr. U. Calif. Law Sch., 1992-96, Stanford U. Sch. Law, 1994-99. Pres. Santa Clara County Bar Assn. Law Found., 1996, dir., 1987—. Fellow Am. Coll. Trial Lawyers; mem. ABA, State Bar Calif., Calif. Trial Lawyers Assn., Santa Clara County Bar Assn., Boalt Hall Alumni Assn. Avocations: history, books, travel, running. Fax: 408-279-3244. E-mail: jmcmanis@mfmlaw.com. Office: McManis Faulkner & Morgan Inc 160 W Santa Clara St Fl 10 San Jose CA 95113-1701

MCMANUS, CLARENCE ELBURN, judge; b. New Orleans, June 3, 1934; s. Otis Clarence and Odell (Hawsey) McM.; m. Barbara Isabella Edmundson, Apr. 3, 1976; children: Elizabeth Ann, Bryan Stephen. BBA,

Tulane U., 1958, JD, 1961. Bar: La. 1961, U.S. Ct. Appeals (5th cir.) 1961, U.S. Dist. Ct. (ea. dist.) La. 1961, U.S. Supreme Ct. 1987. Sole practice Metairie, La., 1961-69; asst. dist. atty. Jefferson Parish, La., 1969-82; state dist. judge 24th Jud. Dist. Ct., Gretna, La., 1982-99; judge La. Ct. Appeals (5th cir.), 1999—. Republican. Home: 824 Bonnabel Blvd Metairie LA 70005-2059 Office: Gretna Courthouse Annex Gretna LA 70053

MCMANUS, FRANCIS, law educator; b. Edinburgh, Scotland, Jan. 5, 1952; s. Frank McManus and Alma Santini; m. Caroline Charters, Aug. 29, 1989. MLitt, U. Edinburgh, 1984, LLB, 1991. Cert. educator. Environ. health officer West Lothian Dist. Coun., Edinburgh, 1974-75, lectr. in environ. health, 1975-91, sr. lectr. in law, 1991—. Author: Environmental Health Law in Scotland, 1989, Environmental Health Law, 1994; co-author: Noise and Noise Law, 1994, Delict, 1998. Fellow Royal Inst. of Pub. Health and Hygiene; mem. Royal Environ. Health Inst. of Scotland. Mem. Labour Party. Roman Catholic. Avocations: soccer, jogging. E-mail: f.mcmanus@napier.ac.uk. Office: Napier U, Sighthill Ct Rm 139, Edinburgh EH11 4BN, Scotland

MCMEEN, ALBERT RALPH, III, writer, technical trainer, multimedia programmer, financial services executive; b. Lewistown, Pa., Oct. 4, 1942; s. Albert Ralph and Margaret McDowell (Parker) McM.; m. A. Mary Kelley, June 6, 1965 (div.); children: Albert Ralph, Christopher Benjamin. BA in Econs., Williams Coll., 1964; MBA in Fin., Columbia U., 1966. Asst. v.p. Chem. Bank, N.Y.C., 1966-75; v.p. Irving Leasing Co., N.Y.C., 1975-80, USI Capital and Leasing, N.Y.C., 1980-83; pres. Tng. Assocs., Inc., 1983—; mgr., owner guest house 222 West 88th Assocs., 1990—; assoc. adj. prof. NYU, 1979-93; asst. prof. L.I. U., 1986-93; tng. cons. Citibank, 1986-87 Barclay's Bank, 1986-89; lectr. Am. Mgmt. Assn., 1986-93, Am. Bankers Assn., 1992-94, Kocbank, Istanbul, 1993, Fund Democracy and Devel., Moscow, 1995; computer based tng. cons. Depository Trust Co., 1998. Author: Treasurers and Controllers New Equipment Leasing Guide, 1984, Equipment Leasing Guide for Lessees, 1990, Debt Repayment Capacity, 1992, Financial Statement Analysis, 1993, Guide to Consumer Lending Computer-Based Training, 1995, Commercial Credit for Lenders, 1998. Mem. legis. com. Citizens' Union, 1968-75; bd. dirs. Columbia U. Alumni Assn., 1970-75; sec. Gay Fathers Inc. Scholar Columbia Internat. Fellows, 1964; recipient Columbia Bus. Sch. svc. award, 1966. Democrat. Home: 333 W 88th St New York NY 10024-2219

MCMEEN, ELMER ELLSWORTH, III, lawyer, guitarist; b. Lewistown, Pa., June 3, 1947; s. Elmer Ellsworth II and Frances Josephine McM.; m. Sheila Ann Taenzler, July 31, 1971; children: Jonathan Ellsworth, Daniel Biddle, James Cunningham and Mary Josephine (twins). BA cum laude, Harvard U., 1969; JD cum laude, U. Pa., 1972. Bar: 1973, U.S. Ct. Appeals (2nd cir.) 1973, U.S. Dist. Ct. (so. and ea. dists.) N.Y. 1975. Assoc. Cravath, Swaine & Moore, N.Y.C., 1972-75; assoc. LeBoeuf, Lamb, Greene & MacRae, LLP, N.Y.C., 1975-78, ptnr., 1979-99, of counsel, 2000—; lectr. Editor U. Pa. Law Rev., 1970-72. Author numerous guitar books; editor: U. Pa. Law Rev., 1970-72; contbr. articles to profl. jours.; solo guitar recordings Of Soul and Spirit, Irish Guitar Encores by Shanachie Records, Solo Guitar Serenade, Playing Favorites, El McMeen Live, Acoustic Guitar Treasures by Piney Ridge Music, solo instructional audio and video lessons and performance videos for Stefan Grossman's Guitar Workshop and Rounder Records. Chmn. N.Y.C. regional com. U. Pa. Law Sch., 1984-86; class sec. Northfield Mt. Hermon Sch. Class of 1965, Mass., 1984-91. Fellow Am. Coll. Investment Counsel; mem. ABA, N.Y State Bar assn. (mem. bus. law com.), Rockaway River Country Club, Harvard Club. Office: 30 Oak Ln Mountain Lakes NJ 07046-1343

MCMENAMIN, HELEN MARIE FORAN, home health care, pediatric, and maternal nurse; b. Buffalo, May 21, 1943; d. John Michael and Helen Marie (McCarty) Foran; m. John Patrick McMenamin, Aug. 21, 1965; children: Maureen Regina, Kathleen Noelle, Terence Michael, Amy Colleen, Shannon Rosemary, Barry Patrick. BSN, Niagara U., 1965; cert. instr. natural family planning, St. Margaret's Hosp., Boston, 1983. RN N.Y., N.H., Maine, D.C., Va., Md., Pa.; cert. childbirth educator; cert. Motherwell instr./trainer. Instr. perinatal, neonatal nursing Mercy Hosp. Sch. Nursing, Portland, Maine, 1981-83; staff/charge nurse neonatal intensive care unit Georgetown U. Hosp., Washington, D.C., 1984-93, 99; staff nurse neonatal ICU, renal unit, home care case mgr. Children's Hosp. Nat. Med. Ctr., Washington, 1986-93; educator infant APNEA/CPR, Fairfax Hosp. Infant APNEA Program, Fairfax, Va., 1988-89; pediatric and maternal-child case mgr. Vis. Nurse Assn. No. Va., Arlington, 1992; staff nurse pediatric emergency room Mercy Hosp., Balt., 1992-93; case mgr. maternal-child pediatrics, high-risk neonatal home care Bay Area Health Care, Balt., 1993-95; mgr. maternal-child/neonatal and pediatric program 1st Am. Home Care, Hanover, Pa., 1994-95; coord. high risk maternal-child and pediatric program Future Health Corp., Timonium, Md., 1995-97; mgr. sch.-based clinic U. Md. Sch. Nursing, Balt., 1998; maternity staff nurse Hanover (Pa.) Hosp., 1998; pvt. duty home care, in-hosp. staff Mt. Washington Pediat. Hosp., Balt., 1995-99; case mgr. for high-risk neonates Sierra Mil. Health Svcs., Balt., 1999; NICU, nursery and maternity staff nurse Adventist Preferred Nursing Svcs., Silver Spring, Md., 1999-2000; RN II, maternity nurse St. Agnes Health Care, Balt., 2000—; organizer, co-dir. health clinics Cathedral Elem. Sch., Portland, Maine, 1981-83; breastfeeding instr. tng. St. Margaret's Hosp., Boston, 1982. Block capt. Am. Cancer Assn., Springfield, Va., 1986-90; mem. Healthy Mothers/Health Babies and Teen Pregnancy Coalition York County; leader 4-H Club, Limerick, Maine, 1977-84; active pro-life and outreach coms. Annunciation of BVM Ch., McSherrystown, Pa., 1997—, Eucharistic min., 2000—. Fellow Am. Bd. Disability Analysts (cert.); mem. Nat. Assn. Pro-Life Nurses (bd. dirs. of Pa.), Nat. Assn. Pediatric Nurses, Assn. Womens Health, Obstetrics, Neonatal Nurses. Roman Catholic. Avocations: art, gardening, knitting, piano, baking. Home: 1075 Hobart Rd Brodbecks PA 17329-9757

MCMENAMIN, MARK ALLAN, paleontologist, geologist, educator; b. Portland, Oreg., Feb. 4, 1958; s. Milton James and Ann Marie (O'Farrell) McM.; m. Dianna Lyn Schulte, Aug. 8, 1981; children: Sarah, Amy. BS in Geology, Stanford U., 1979; PhD in Geology, U. Calif., Santa Barbara, 1984. Prof. Mount Holyoke Coll., South Hadley, Mass., 1984—; guest curator and new exhibit cons., Peabody Mus. of Natural History, Yale U., New Haven, Conn., 1996-98. Author: (books) The Emergence of Animals, 1990, Hypersea, 1994, The Garden of Ediacara, 1998; founder Meanma Press, 1996. Water commr. Fire Dist. No. 2, South Hadley, Mass., 1994-97. Recipient Presidential Young Investigator award, NSF, Washington, 1988. Mem. Paleontol. Soc. Achievements include development of Hypersea Theory (with Dianna McMenamin), 1993; discovery of oldest animals and Ediacaran fossils, Sonora, Mex., 1995; elucidation of the morphology of enigmatic Ediacaran fossils using the concept of metacellularity, 1997. Avocations: internat. travel, cycling, gardening, archeology, hiking. Home: 63 Silver St South Hadley MA 01075-1617 Office: Mount Holyoke Coll Dept Earth and Environment South Hadley MA 01075

MCMICHAEL, JEANE CASEY, real estate company executive, educator; b. Clarksville, Ind., May 7, 1938; d. Emmett Ward and Carrie Evelyn (Leonard) Casey; m. Norman Kenneth Wenzler, Sept. 12, 1956 (div. 1968); m. Wilburn Arnold McMichael, June 20, 1978. Student Ind. U. Extension Ctr., Bellermine Coll., 1972-73; student, Ind. U. S.E., 1973—, Kentuckiana Metroversity, 1981—; grad. Realtors Inst., Ind. U., 1982. Grad. Leadership Tng., Clark County, Ind.; lic. real estate broker, Ind., Ky.; master Grad. Realtors Inst., Cert. Residential Splst., Cert. Real Estate Broker. Owner, pres., mgr. McMichael Real Estate, Inc., Jeffersonville, 1979-88, 91-98; mgr., owner Buzz Bauer, 1979-88, 88-91; mng. broker Parks & Weisberg Realtors, Jeffersonville, Ind., 1989-96; instr. pre-license real estate Ivy Tech. State Coll., 1995-96, ISTR Real Estate Tng. Concepts, Inc. Pres. congregation St. Mark's United Ch. of Christ, 1996, mem. long range plan and property acquisition, 1996-98; pres. Mr. and Mrs. Class, chmn., fin. trustee, bus. adv., chmn. devel. com., 1993, 94, chmn. com. long range planning, 1997; chmn. bd. trustees Brooklawn Youth Svcs., 1988-95, chmn., 1994-96; bd. dirs. Noah's Ark, Inc., 1998-99, sec./treas., 1999—; chmn. social com. Rep. party Clark County (Ind.); v.p. Floyd County Habitat for Humanity, 1991, 94-95. Recipient cert. of appreciation Nat. Ctr. Citizen Involvement, 1983; award Contact Kentuckiana Teleministries, 1978. Mem. Nat. Assn. Realtors (nat. dir. 1989—), Ind. Assn. Realtors (state dir. 1987—, quick start spkr. 1989-91), Nat. Women's Coun. Realtors (state pres., chmn. coms., state rec. sec. 1984, state prs. 1985-86, Nat. Achievement award 1982, 83, 84, 85, 86, 87, 88, 89, 90, nat. gov. Ind. 1987, v.p. region III 1988, Ind. Honor Realtor award 1982—), Women's Coun. of Realtors (spkr. 1990-94, Mem. of Yr. 1988), Ky. Real Estate Exch., So. Ind. Bd. Realtors (program chmn. 1986-87, bd. dirs., pres. 1988—, Realtor of Yr. 1985, instr. success series 1989-92, Snyder Svc. award 1987, Omega Tau Rho award 1988, excellence in Edn. award 1989), Ind. Assn. Realtors (state dir. 1985—, bd. govs. instr./trainer, spkr. 1989-94, chair bd. govs. 1991), Toastmasters (pres. Steamboat chpt.), Psi Iota Xi. Office: McMichael Real Estate Inc 1402 Blackiston Mill Rd Jeffersonville IN 47129-2279 Address: 23 Arctic Spgs Jeffersonville IN 47130-4701

MCMILLAN, HELEN BERNEICE, sales executive; b. Huntington, Ark., Jan. 27, 1932; d. James Louis and Edna Lorene (Repass) Harrison; m. James Edward McMillan, May 10, 1950; children: Dianna Kaye Carter, Connie Sue Sadler. BBA, Dallas Bapt. U., 1993. Sewing machine operator Bobbinoak Corp., Fort Smith, Ark., 1949-50; greeting card decorator Hallmark Corp., Leavenworth, Kans., 1950-54; office clk. Sears Roebuck & Co., Lawton, Okla., 1955-57; grocery checker Safeway Grocery, Moberly, Mo., 1957-58; asst. retail mgr. Army & Air Force Exch., Leesville, la., 1962-74; buyer ladieswear Army & Air Force Exch., Dallas, 1974-90; merchandise mgr. Army & Air Force Exch., Munich, 1990-93; sales assoc. Hallmark Cards, Grand Prairie, Tex., 1994—. Recipient Achievement award Nat. Assn. Purchasing Mgmt., Dallas, 1988. Mem. NAFE, Fashion Group Internat. Republican. Avocations: doll collecting, ceramics, aerobics, gardening, fashion. Home: 609 Redwood Dr Grand Prairie TX 75052-6734

MCMILLAN, THOMAS MURRAY, psychology educator; b. Prestwick, Scotland, Mar. 3, 1954; s. Thomas Murray and Edith Jellet (Paton) McM.; m. Sarah Louise Wilson, Jan. 10, 1983; 1 child, Catriona. BS with honors, U. Aberdeen, Scotland, 1976; M of Applied Sci., U. Glasgow, Scotland, 1983; PhD, U. London, 1982. Lectr. in clin. psychology Inst. Psychiatry, London, 1983-89; head clin. neuropsychology St. Georges Healthcare, London, 1989-99; prof. clin. psychology U. Surrey, Guildford, England, 1996-99; prof. clin. neuropsychology U. Glasgow, Scotland, 1999—. Assoc. editor: Neuropsychology Rehabilitation, 1993, Coma and Vegetative State, 1993. Fellow Brit. Psychol. Soc.; mem. European Brain Injury Soc., Internat. Neuropsychology Soc. Avocation: cross-country running. Office: U Glasgow, 1055 Great Western Rd, Glasgow G12 0XH, Scotland

MCMILLEN, ROBERT PAUL, agricultural engineer; b. Mansfield, Tex., Nov. 20, 1952; s. Charles William and Janie Lee (Dixon) McM. BS in Agrl. Engring., Tex. Tech. U., 1978. Reg. profl. engr., Tex. Agrl. engr. U.S. Dept. Agr.-Soil Conservation Svc., Lubbock, Vernon, Tex., 1978-82; design engr. Parkhill, Smith & Cooper, Inc., Lubbock, 1982-88, project mgr., 1988-96, corp. assoc., 1996—. Mem. adv. bd., tech. subcom. Reese Air Force Base Restoration, Lubbock, 1995-2000. Mem. NSPE, ASCE, Am. Soc. Agrl. Engrs., Nat. Ground Water Assn., Tex. Soc. Profl. Engrs. (chpt. dir. 1995-99), Water Environ. Assn. Tex. (chpt. sec. 1995-99, chpt. pres. 1999-2000). Avocations: piloting. Home: 5502 56th St Apt 214 Lubbock TX 79414-2039 Office: Parkhill Smith & Cooper Inc 4222 85th St Lubbock TX 79423-1930

MCMILLER, ANITA WILLIAMS, logistics management consultant; b. Chgo., Dec. 23, 1946; d. Chester Leon and Marion Claudette (Martin) Williams; m. Robert Melvin McMiller, July 29, 1967 (div. 1980). BS in Edn., No. Ill. U., 1968; MBA, Fla. Inst. Tech., 1979; M of Mil. Arts and Sci., U.S. Army Command & Gen. Staff Coll., 1990; postgrad., U.S. Army War Coll., Carlisle, Pa., 1993-94. Social worker Cook County, Chgo., 1968-69; recruiter analyst, dir. pers. State of Ill., Chgo., 1969-75; commd. 1st lt. U.S. Army, 1975, advanced through grades to col., 1996; dep. comdr., ops. officer Bremerhaven (Germany) Terminal, Ft. Eustis, Va. and Okinawa; comdr. 1320th Port Batt, 1991-93; comdr. 1320th Port Battalion U.K. Terminal, Felixstowe, Great Britain, 1991-93; dep. legis. asst. to Chmn. Joint Chiefs of Staff The Pentagon, Washington, 1994-98; pres., CEO Trove Internat.; v.p. ATC Leasing, Kenosha, Wis., 1999—; instr. Ctrl. Tex. Coll., Hanau, Germany, 1981-83, Phillips Bus. Coll., Alexandria, Va., 1983-84, City Colls. Chgo., 1987-89. Editor: Rocks, Inc. Pictoral Album, 1996, Alpha Kappa Alpha 75th Commemorative Album, 1997; contbr. articles to profl. jours. Child adv., foster mother Army Cmty. Svc., Hanau, 1980-83; tutor Parent-Tchr. Club Hanau Schs., 1981-83; vol. Vis. Nurses Assn. No. Va., 1983-85; coord., English tutor Adopt-a-Sch. Project, Washington, 1983-85; treas. Bremerhaven Girl Scouts Coun., 1987-89, mem. ARC, Big Sisters, Internat. Platform Assn. Mem. Nat. Def. Transp. Assn., World Affairs Coun., Assn. U.S. Army, Am. Mgmt. Assn., Fedn. Bus. Profl. Women, Rocks, Inc., Am. Legion, British Legion, Am. Hist. Assn., Internat. Platform Assn., Army Women's Profl. Assn., Jr. League Washington, Nat. Coun. of Negro Women, Nat. Assn. Women Bus. Owners, Army-Navy Club (Washington), Alpha Kappa Alpha. Avocations: skiing, golf, running, hist. rsch. Home: 3623 17th St Kenosha WI 53144-3341 Office: ATC Leasing Co 4316 39th Ave Kenosha WI 53144-1962

MCMULLAN, DENNIS, physicist, consultant; b. Reading, Berkshire, Eng., May 3, 1923; s. George and Muriel Watkins (Wells) McM.; m. Marie Ottilie Sander, Apr. 3, 1959. BA, Cambridge U., 1944, MA, 1948, PhD, 1953. Fellow Inst. of Physics; chartered physicist; mem. Inst. Elec. Engrs.; chartered engr. Head simulation dept. Can. Armaments R&D Establishment, Valcartier, PQ, 1953-56; scientific advisor The Rank Orgn., London, 1956-59; electronic designer British Nat. Hydrogen Bubble Chamber Imperial Coll., London, 1959-63; head operating team CERN, Geneva, 1963-65; sr. lectr. Imperial Coll., London, 1965-68; head of instrumentation divsn. Royal Greenwich Observatory, Herstmonceux, Eng., 1969-80; sr. asst. in rsch. Cavendish Lab. Cambridge U., 1980-83, cons., 1983—. Developer 1st modern form of scanning electron microscope, 1948-53, low-light level detectors for astronomy, 1965-80, instrumentation for electron spectroscopy in electron microscopes; contbr. articles to profl. jours. Fellow Royal Astron. Soc., Royal Microscopical Soc. (hon.); mem. Microscopy Soc. Am. (hon., Disting. Scientist 1994), Royal Instn. (life), Royal TV Soc. Avocations: music, reading, skiing. Home: 59 Courtfield Gardens, London SW5 0NF, England Office: Cavendish Lab Cambridge U, Madingley Rd, Cambridge CB3 0HE, England

MCMULLAN, THOMAS ANDREW, magazine editor; b. Cuckfield, Sussex, Eng., Apr. 4, 1971; s. William Francis and Deirdre (Tierney) McM. 1st class honors, Oxford (Eng.) U., 1989-93. Diamond sorter DeBeers, London, 1993-94; copywriter Gold Star Publs., Ltd., Whyteleafe, Eng., 1994-96, editor, 1996—. Editor (adult mags.) Journal of Love, Raider, Exclusive, Derriere. Office: Gold Star Publs Ltd, Gadoline Ho Godstone Rd, Surrey Whyteleafe CR3 0EA, England

MCMULLAN, WILLIAM PATRICK, III, investment banker; b. Newton, Miss., Dec. 29, 1952; s. William Patrick Jr. and Rosemary (Lyons) McM.; m. Rachel Smiley McPherson, Oct. 16, 1982. BA, Vanderbilt U., 1974; MBA, U. Pa., 1976. V.p. Lehman Bros. Kuhn Loeb, N.Y.C., 1976-82; assoc. dir. Prudential-Bache Securities, N.Y.C., 1982-85; mng. dir. Donaldson, Lufkin & Jenrette Securities Corp., N.Y.C., 1985—. Bd. dirs. Lar Lubovitch Dance Co. Mem. Met. Club, Mashomack Fish and Game Club, Confrerie des Chevaliers du Tastevin. Home: 607 6th St Brooklyn NY 11215-3701 Office: Donaldson Lufkin & Jenrette Securities Corp 277 Park Ave Fl 7 New York NY 10172-3400

MCMULLIN, RUTH RONEY, publishing executive, trustee, management fellow; b. N.Y.C., Feb. 9, 1942; d. Richard Thomas and Virginia (Goodwin) Roney; m. Thomas Ryan McMullin, Apr. 27, 1968; 1 child, David Patrick. BA, Conn. Coll., 1963; M Pub. and Pvt. Mgmt., Yale U., 1979. Market rschr. Aviation Week Mag., McGraw-Hill Co., N.Y.C., 1962-64; assoc. editor, bus. mgr. Doubleday & Co., N.Y.C., 1964-66; mgr. Natural History Press, 1967-70; v.p., treas. Weston (Conn.) Woods, Inc., 1970-71; staff assoc. GE, Fairfield, Conn., 1979-82; mng. fin. analyst, credit analyst corp. GECC Transp., Stamford, Conn., 1982-85; credit analyst corp. fin. dept. GECC, Stamford, Conn., 1984-85; sr. v.p. GECC Capital Markets Group, Inc., N.Y.C., 1985-87; exec. v.p., COO John Wiley & Sons, N.Y.C., 1987-89, pres., CEO, 1989-90; pres., CEO Harvard Bus. Sch. Pub. Corp., Boston, 1991-94; mem. chmn.'s com., acting CEO UNR Industries Inc., Chgo., 1991-92, also bd. dirs.; mgmt. fellow, vis. prof. Sch. Mgmt. Yale U., New Haven, 1994-95; chairperson trustees Eagle-Picher Personal Injury Settlement Trust, 1996—; chairperson Claims Procesing Facility, Inc., 1998—; bd. dirs. Bausch & Lomb, Rochester, N.Y.; vis. prof. Sch. Mgmt., Yale U., New Haven, 1994-95; chair bd. trustees Eagle Picher Personal Injury Settlement Trust, 1996—. Mem. dean's adv. bd. Sch. Mgmt. Yale U., 1985-96; bd. dirs. Yale U. Alumni fund, 1986-92, Yale U. Press, 1988-99, Math. Scis. Edn. Bd., 1990-93, Mighty Eighth Air Force Heritage Mus., treas., 2000—; bd. dirs. Savannah Tree Found. Mem. N.Y. Yacht Club, Stamford Yacht Club. Avocations: sailing, skiing, golf, tennis. Home: 8 Breckenridge Ln Savannah GA 31411-1701 Office: Eagle Picher Trust P O box 206 652 Main St Cincinnati OH 45202-2542

MCMURPHY, MICHAEL ALLEN, energy company executive, lawyer; b. Dothan, Ala., Oct. 1, 1947; s. Allen L. and Mary Emily (Jacobs) McM.; m. Maureen Daly, Aug. 8, 1970; children: Matthew, Kevin, Patrick. BS, USAF Acad., 1969; MA, St. Mary's U., San Antonio, 1972; JD, U. Tex., 1975. Bar: Tex. 1975, U.S. Supreme Ct. 1977, U.S. Ct. Mil. Appeals, D.C. 1978, U.S. Ct. Appeals (fed. cir.) 1982. Commd. 2d lt. USAF, 1969, advanced through grades to capt.; instr. Air U., Ala., 1975-79; resigned USAF, 1979; atty., advisor Oak Ridge (Tenn.) ops. U.S. Dept. Energy, 1979-83; gen. counsel COGEMA, Inc., Washington, 1983-87, v.p., 1987-88; pres., chief exec. officer COGEMA, Inc., Bethesda, Md., 1988—; pres., CEO Va. Fuels, Inc., Lynchburg, 1987-92; bd. dirs. Nuclear Energy Inst., Washington, SGN S.A., St. Quentin, France, U.G./USA, Atlanta, Transnuclear, Inc., Hawthorne, N.Y., Cogema Resources, Inc, Casper, Wyo., Cogema Engring. Co., Richland, Wash., Numatec Hanford Co., Wash., Framatome Cogema Fuel Co., Lynchburg, Va.; bd. govs. Duke Cogema Stone & Webster, LLC, Charlotte, N.C., 1998—; pres. Uranium Producers Am., 1991-92. Mem. editorial bd. Air Force Law Rev., 1977-79. Decorated chevalier Nat. Order of Merit (France). Avocation: skiing. Office: COGEMA Inc 7401 Wisconsin Ave Bethesda MD 20814-3400

MCMURRAY, DAVID GORDON, compliance and financial regulation expert; b. Glasgow, Scotland, Aug. 20, 1959; 2 children. Grad. high sch., Glasgow. Banker Royal Bank of Scotland, Glasgow and Edinburgh, 1977-85, Barclays Bank Plc, Glasgow, 1985-87; settlements mgr. Murray Johnstone Ltd., Glasgow, 1987-88, project mgr., 1988-90, systems analyst, 1990-91, group compliance officer, head internal audit, 1991-97; dir. regulatory svcs. and performance verification KPMG, London, 1997-2000; gen. mgr. Walter Scott & Ptnrs., Ltd., Edinburgh, Scotland, 2000—; bd. dirs., mng. dir. NRS Regulatory Svcs. Ltd., Glasgow, NRS Sys. Ltd., Glasgow; assoc. London Coll. Music; spkr. in field. Contbr. articles to profl. jours. Mem. expert advisor's bd., Securities Inst., London; tutor, verifier investment subjects, Chartered Inst. Bankers, Scotland. Fellow Royal Soc. for Encouragement of Arts, Manufactures and Commerce; mem. Chartered Inst. Bankers in Scotland, Securities Inst. (bd. dirs. 1995-97, pres. Scottish nat. br. 1996-97), Inst. Dirs. (London). Avocations: golf, shooting and country pursuits, music. Home: 25 Netherauldhouse Rd, Glasgow G43, Scotland

MCMURRY, WILLIAM MORTIMER, retired sales executive; b. Miami, Dec. 30, 1926; s. Charles Taylor and Elizabeth Lucille (Lemmon) McM.; m. Vivian Smolorski, Dec. 2, 1950 (div. Nov. 1979); children: Charles Michael, Nancy Jane, William Patrick. BS in Chemistry, U. Fla., 1950. Lic. pvt. pilot. Pharm. sales rep. Charles Pfizer & Co., N.Y.C., 1950-57; pharm. sales rep. Hoffman-LaRoche Labs., Nutley, N.J., 1958-65; med. electronics sales IVAC, Jacksonville, Fla., 1966-67; stock broker Hayden-Stone, Inc., Jacksonville, 1967-70; store mgr. Rhodes Furniture Co., Jacksonville, 1971-78; pres. McMurry & Company (import/export), Jacksonville, 1980-89. Libr., mem. ch. coun. West Normandy Bapt. Ch., Jacksonville, 1996—. With U.S. Navy, 1945-47. Mem. Mensa (co-founder chpt. 1952), Phi Gamma Delta. Baptist. Avocations: astronomy, particle physics, Actinides/Lanthanides rsch., gardening, computering. Home: 1624 Brier Way E Jacksonville FL 32221-1433

MCMURRY, WILLIAM SCOTT, retired allied health educator; b. Poteau, Okla., Apr. 10, 1921; s. Ulysses Scott and Syntha Alice (McDonald) McM.; m. Kathryn Elizabeth Robison, Feb. 2, 1946. BS, N.E. U., Okla., 1942; DDS, U. Mo., 1950, MS, 1966; PhD, Columbia Pacific U., 1983. Commd. 2d lt. USAF, 1941, advanced through grades to lt. col., 1963, ret., 1969; assoc. chief of staff edn. VA, Dayton, Ohio, 1973-79; asst. dean vets. affairs Wright State Med. Sch., 1975-79, assoc. prof. surgery and continued edn.; prof. St. Petersburg (Fla.) Jr. Coll., 1967-73; adj. prof. Ohio State U., 1973-79; assoc. prof. allied health So. Ill. U., 1979-98, prof. emeritus, 1998—. Contbr. articles to profl. jours. Fellow Internat. Assn. Oral and Maxillofacial Surgeons; mem. Coun. Occupl. Edn., Midwestern Oral Surgeons, Ill. Assn. Oral and Maxillofacial Surgeons, Okla. State Dental Assn., Ill. Police Assn., Ret. Officers Assn., Assn. Mil. Surgeons, Assn. Ret. Fed. Employees, Air Force Assn., Masons, Lions, Am. Legion. Republican.

MC MURTRY, JAMES GILMER, III, neurosurgeon; b. Houston, June 11, 1932; s. James Gilmer and Alberta Elizabeth (Matteson) McM.; student Rice U., Houston, 1950-53; M.D. cum laude, Baylor U., Houston, 1957. Intern, Hosp. U. Pa., Phila., 1957-58; resident gen. surgery Baylor U. Affiliated Hosps., Houston, 1958-59; asst. neurol. surgery Coll. Physicians and Surgeons, Columbia U., N.Y.C., 1959-60; asst. resident neurol. surgery and neurology Neurol. Inst. N.Y., Columbia Presbyn. Med. Center, N.Y.C., 1960-62, chief resident neurol. surgery, 1962-63; Nat. Inst. Neurol. Disease and Blindness spl. fellow neurol. surgery Coll. Physicians and Surgeons, Columbia U., N.Y.C., 1963-64, instr. neurol. surgery, 1963-65, assoc., 1965-68, asst. prof. clin. neurol. surgery, 1968-73, assoc. prof., 1973-89, prof., 1989—; asst. attending neurol. surgeon Neurol. Inst. N.Y., N.Y.C., 1964-73, assoc. attending neurol. surgeon, 1973-89, attending neurol. surgeon, 1989—; chief neurol. surgery clinic Vanderbilt Clinic, Columbia Presbyn. Med. Center, N.Y.C., 1964-68; attending-in-charge neurosurgery Lenox Hill Hosp., N.Y.C., 1970-91; assoc. cons. neurol. surgery Englewood (N.J.) Hosp., 1964—; asst. cons. neurol. surgery Harlem Hosp., N.Y.C., 1964—; cons. neurol. surgery Bronx (N.Y.) VA Hosp., 1964-65; mem. NIH Parkinson Research Group, Columbia U., 1965—; mem. med. adv. bd. N.Y. State Athletic Commn. Jesse H. Jones scholar Baylor U. Coll. Medicine, 1953-57, Allen fellow dept. neurol. surgery Columbia U., 1964-65. Diplomate Am. Bd. Neurol. Surgery. Fellow ACS, Linnean Soc. (London); trustee Glimmerglass Opera, Morris-Jumel, Opera Manhattan. Mem. AAUP, AAAS, AMA, Am. Assn. Neurol. Surgeons, European Congress Pediatric Neurosurgery, Am. Soc. Stereotaxic Surgeons, Pan Am. Med. Assn., N.Y. State Soc. Surgeons, N.Y. State Neurosurgery Soc., N.Y. Acad. Sci., N.Y. Neurosurg. Soc., Med. Soc. State N.Y., N.Y. County Med. Soc., Osler Soc., Baylor U. Coll. Medicine Alumni Assn., Med. Strollers, The Med. Soc. of London, The Harveian Soc., Alpha Omega Alpha. Presbyn. Clubs: The Union (N.Y.C.), The Garrick (London), The Atheneum (London), The Met. Opera (N.Y.C., dir. 1998), The Norfolk Yacht and Country. Author: Medical Examination Review Book-Neurological Surgery, 1970, rev. edit., 1975; Neurological Surgery Case Histories, 1975; contbr. articles to profl. jours. Home: 1 Cobb Ln Tarrytown NY 10591-3003 Office: 710 W 168th St New York NY 10032-2603

MCMURTRY, LARRY JEFF, author; b. Wichita Falls, Tex., June 3, 1936; s. William Jefferson and Hazel Ruth (McIver) McM.; m. Josephine Ballard, July 15, 1959 (div. 1966); 1 child, James. BA, N. Tex. State Coll., 1958; MA, Rice U., 1960. Instr. Tex. Christian U., Ft. Worth, 1961-62; lectr. in English and creative writing Rice U., Houston, 1963-69; co-owner Booked Up Book Store, Washington, from 1970; vis. prof. George Mason Coll., 1970, Am. Univ., 1970-71. Author: (novels) Horseman, Pass By, 1961 (Jesse H. Jones award Texas Inst. of Letters 1962), Leaving Cheyenne, 1963, The Last Picture Show, 1966, Moving On, 1970, All My Friends Are Going to be Strangers, 1972, Terms of Endearment, 1975, Somebody's Darling, 1978, Cadillac Jack, 1982, The Desert Rose, 1983, Lonesome Dove, 1985 (Pulitzer prize for fiction 1986), Texasville, 1987, Anything for Billy, 1988, Some Can Whistle, 1989, Buffalo Girls, 1990, The Evening Star, 1992, Streets of Laredo, 1993, (with Diana Ossana) Pretty Boy Floyd, 1994, The Late Child, 1995, Dead Man's Walk, 1995 (with Diana Ossana) Zeke and Ned, 1997, Commanche Moon, 1997; (essays) In a Narrow Grave: Essays on Texas, 1968, It's Always We Rambled: An Essay on Rodeo, 1974, Film Flam: Essays on Hollywood, 1987; screenwriter: (with Peter Bogdanovich) The Last Picture Show, 1971 (Academy award nomination best adapted screenplay 1971), Texasville, 1990, Montana, 1990, Falling From Grace, 1992, (with Cybill Shepard) Memphis, 1992; also articles, essays, book revs. in N.Y. Times, Saturday Rev., Washington Post, Am. Film, others. Wallace Stegner fellow, 1960, Guggenheim fellow, 1964; recipient Barbara

McCombs/Lon Tinkle award Texas Inst. of Letters, 1986. Mem. Tex. Inst. Letters (Jesse H. Jones award 1962). Office: Simon & Schuster 1230 Avenue of the Americas New York NY 10020-1586 also: care Saria Co Inc 2509 N Campbell Ave # 95 Tucson AZ 85719-3304

MCNAB, ALAN ANGUS, ophthalmologist; b. Kilmore, Victoria, Australia, June 17, 1956; s. Douglas Robert and Betty Isabel (Hannam) McN.; m. Briar Goessi; children: Hugh, Michael, George. MB BS, U. Melbourne, Australia, 1979. Intern, resident Royal Melbourne Hosp., 1980-82, ophthalmologist, 1989—; vis. lectr. anatomy Stanford (Calif.) U., 1983; opthalmology registrar Royal Victorian Eye & Ear Hosp., Melbourne, 1984-86; head orbit, plastic and lacrimal clinic Royal Victorian Eye and Ear Hosp., Melbourne, 1990—; fellow orbital, lacrimal & ocular plastic surgeon Moorfields Eye Hosp., London, 1987-89; ophthalmologist Royal Children's Hosp., Melbourne, 1990—. Author: Manual of Orbital and Lacrimal Surgery, 1994, 2d edit., 1999; editor: Australian and New Zealand Jour. Ophthalmology, 1992-95; contbr. articles to profl. jours. Fellow Royal Australian Coll. Ophthalmologists, Royal Australian Coll. Surgeons, Royal Coll. Ophthalmologists (Eng.), Am. Soc. Ophthalmic Plastic and Reconstructive Surgery; mem. Orbital Soc., European Soc. Ophthalmic Plastic and Reconstructive Surgery. Office: 200 Drummond St, Carlton 3053, Australia

MCNABB, TALMADGE FORD, religious organization administrator, retired military chaplain; b. Johnson City, Tenn., Mar. 22, 1924; s. Robert Pierce and Dora Isabelle (Bailey) McN.; m. Nesbia Orlene Boswell, Dec. 3, 1950 (dec.); children: Darlene Roberta, Marla Dawn; m. Pirkko Marjotta Pelttari, Nov. 11, 1962; children: Valerie Anne, Lisa Rhea, Marcus Duane. Student, East Tenn. State U., 1941-43, 46; BA, Southwestern U. Assemblies of God, Waxahachie, Tex., 1947, BTh, 1949; BS, Birmingham Southern Coll., 1952; MA, U. Ala., 1957; HHD (hon.), S.E. Univ., Greenville, S.C., 1978. Ordained to ministry Assemblies of God, 1950. Evangelist Assemblies of God, 1948-49; pastor 1st Assembly of God, Warrior, Ala., 1949-53, Tuscaloosa, Ala., 1955-56; commd. 1st lt. U.S. Army, 1955, advanced through grades to lt. col., 1966; chaplain U.S. Army, Ft. Rucker, Ala., 1953-54, Korea, 1954-55, Ft. Benning, Ga., 1957-59, France, 1959-61, Ft. Knox, Ky., 1961-66, Ft. Dix, N.J., 1967-69; chaplain William Beaumont Hosp. U.S. Army, El Paso, Tex., 1971-72; ret. U.S. Army, 1972; writer, evangelist, speaker, 1973—; founder, pres. Worldwide Christian Ministries, Browns Mills, N.J., 1981—; ministered in Ecuador, India, Russia, China, France, Belgium, The Netherlands. Contbr. articles on religious and ethnic topics to newspapers and mags. Mem. DAV (life), Mil. Ret. Officers Assn. (life), Mil. Chaplains Assn. (life, del.). Republican. Home and Office: Worldwide Christian Ministries 1 Springfield Rd Browns Mills NJ 08015-6709

MCNAMARA, ROBERT STRANGE, former banking executive, cabinet member; b. San Francisco, June 9, 1916; s. Robert James and Clara Nell (Strange) McN.; m. Margaret Craig, Aug. 13, 1940 (dec.); children: Margaret Elizabeth, Kathleen, Robert Craig. AB, U. Calif., 1937; MBA, Harvard U., 1939; LLD (hon.), U. Calif., U. Mich., Columbia U., Harvard U., George Washington U., Princeton U., Amherst Coll., Williams Coll., U. Ala., Ohio State U., NYU, U. Notre Dame, U. Pa., U. St. Andrews, U. Philippines, Aberdeen U., Oxford U., U. S.C. Asst. prof. bus. adminstrn. Harvard U., 1940-43; exec. Ford Motor Co., 1946-61, pres. co., 1960-61, co. dir., 1957-61; sec. U.S. Dept. Def., 1961-68; pres. World Bank, 1968-81; mem. , trustee pub. and pvt. instns. including Overseas Devel. Coun., Urban Inst., Enterprise Found., Brookings Inst.; spl. cons. War Dept., 1942. Author: The Essence of Security, 1968, One Hundred Countries-Two Billion People, 1973, The McNamara Years at the World Bank, 1981, Blundering Into Disaster, 1986, Out of the Cold, 1989, In Retrospect, 1995, Argument Without End, 1999. Served as lt. col. USAAF, 1943-46. Decorated Legion of Merit, D.S.M.; recipient Presdl. Medal of Freedom with distinction, Christian A. Herter Meml. award, Albert Pick Jr. award U. Chgo., 1979, Franklin D. Roosevelt Freedom from Want medal, 1983, Onassis Athinai prize, 1988. Mem. Phi Beta Kappa. Office: 1350 I St NW Washington DC 20005-3305

MCNAMARA-RINGEWALD, MARY ANN THÉRÈSE, artist, educator; b. Hempstead, N.Y., Apr. 11, 1935; d. William George Schlichtig and Alice Agnes Rakeman; m. Raymond Anthony McNamara, Apr. 22, 1957 (div. Sept. 1975); children: Thomas William, Raymond Gerard, William Daniel, James Francis Jude; m. John Drew Ringewald, Feb. 17, 1984. BS, Fordham U., 1957; M in Studio Arts, Adelphi U., 1972; postgrad., Parsons Sch. Design, 1973-75; student, Art Students League, N.Y.C., 1973-74; postgrad., Goddard Coll., 1986-87; student, Progoff Intensive Jour. Program, N.Y.C., 1999—. Cert. elem. edn. and art N.Y. State Dept. Edn. Elem. sch. art tchr. Dept. Edn., Freeport, N.Y., 1957-58; jr. and high sch. art tchr. Massapequa (N.Y.) Sch. Dist., 1970-90; owner, pres. South Shore Creative Arts Ctr., Massapequa, 1975; pvt. art tchr. various locations, 1970-90; illustrator Doubleday, Inc., N.Y.C.; profl. artist, judge, lectr., Md., Fla., 1975—; mem. art advisory bd. Chesapeake Coll, Wye Mills, Md., 1995—. One-person shows include Fordham U., 1954, Andonia Gallery, Massepequa, N.Y., 1974, Isis Gallery, Islip, N.Y., 1974, For the Birds, Salisbury, Conn., 1978, Harguen Gallery, Pt. Jefferson, N.Y., 1979, Adelphi U., Garden City, N.Y., 1992, Acad. of Arts, Easton, Md., 1993, Wohlfarth Gallery, Washington, 1994-95, Gallery 44, Millbrook, N.Y., 1997-98; works exhibited at Kennedy Gallery, Key West, Fla.; represented in pvt. collections GM, The Benedictines, Prudential Life, St. Michael's Maritime Mus., Yupo Corp., Japan; illustrator: From a Lighthouse Window, Chesapeake Bay Maritime Mus., 1992 (Best of Balt. Book award 1993, Book award Tabasco N.Y.C. 1994). Pres. AAUW, L.I., 1969-71; bd. mem. L.I. (N.Y.) Art Tchrs. Assn., 1973-76; docent U.S. Fish and Wildlife Svc., Washington, 1994-95; mem. Am. Farmland Trust. Recipient Nat. Middle Sch. Art Tchrs. award Middle Sch. Art Tchrs. Assn., 1988; named to Outstanding Young Women of Am., 1969. Mem. Internat. Welcome Fla. Assn. Series (lectr. 1994—), Nat. League Am. Pen Women (founder, pres. Naples, Fla. br. 1995—), Nat. Gallery Art (copyist 1993—), Order of the Benedictines (oblate 1990—), Working Artists Forum (Easton, Md.), Am. Farmland Trust. Roman Catholic. Avocations: horticulture, traveling, illuminations, music. Address: Marafour 5493 Anderby Dr Royal Oak MD 21662 Office: Marafour Studio 27098 Del Lu Bonita Springs FL 34135-4409

MCNAMEE, LAWRENCE ROSS, manufacturing executive. Supr. Gen. Dynamics, Pomona, Calif., 1958-61; mem. staff Arthur D. Little, Inc., L.A., 1961-65; dir. Booz Allen & Hamilton, L.A., 1965-70; gen. mgr. Hydril Co., L.A., 1970-76; pres. Diogenes Group, L.A., 1976-91; chmn., CEO Radiant Tech. Corp., Fullerton, Calif., 1991—. With U.S. Army, 1952-54. Mem. Semiconductor Equipment and Materials Internat., Turn Around Mgmt. Assn., Ops. Rsch. Soc. Am., Calif. Yacht Club. Avocations: sailing, fishing, photography, art collecting. Fax: 714-991-0600. Office: Radiant Tech Corp 1335 S Acacia Ave Fullerton CA 92831-5315

MCNAUGHT, JUDITH, author; b. San Luis Obispo, Calif., May 10, 1944; d. Clifford Harris and Rosetta (Prince) Spath; m. J. Michael McNaught, June 1, 1974 (dec. 1983); children: Whitney, Clayton. BS, Northwestern U., 1966. Pres. Pro-Temps, Inc., St. Louis, 1983-84, Eagle Syndication, Inc., Dallas, 1987—. Author Tender Triumph, 1983 (Critics Choice award 1983); Double Standards, 1984; Whitney, My Love (Best Hist. Novelist 1985), Once and Always, 1987 (Best Hist. Novel 1987), Something Wonderful 1988 (N.Y. Times Best seller, Critics Choice award Best Hist. Novel 1988), A Kingdom of Dreams, 1989 (N.Y. Times Bestseller, Award for Best Hist. Novel 1989), Almost Heaven, 1990 (N.Y. Times #1 Bestseller, Persie award, Romantic Times award), Paradise, 1991 (N.Y. Times Bestseller award for best hardcover contemporary romance, Romantic Times award), Perfect , 1993 (N.Y. Times Bestseller), Until You, 1994, Holiday of Love, 1996, (N.Y. Times Bestseller), Remember When, 1996 (N.Y. Times Bestseller). Mem. Novelists, Inc. Roman Catholic. Avocations: racquetball, skiing.*

MCNAUGHTAN, DAVID PRINGLE, investment banker; b. Glasgow, Scotland, Mar. 6, 1950; came to Bahamas, 1988; s. James and Helen (Duff) McN.; m. Anne Patricia McNaughtan, June 26, 1980; children: James, Eleanor. BA with honors, U. Strathclyde, Glasgow, 1972. Grad. trainee Nat. and Grindlays Bank, Beirut and New Delhi, 1972-74; jr. corp. exec. Slater Walker Securities, London, 1974-76; dir. Deltec Securities (U.K.) Ltd., London, 1976-88; chmn. Deltec Bank and Trust, Nassau, Bahamas, 1988—, Deltec Panam. Trust Co., Nassau, 1988—. Treas. The Lyford Cay Sch., Nassau, 1989-91. Mem. Lyford Cay Club (Bahamas), R.A.C. London. Avocations: horseback riding, swimming, scuba diving. Office: The Deltec Banking Corp Ltd, Deltec Bank & Trust, Deltec House, PO Box N3229, Nassau Bahamas

MCNAUGHTON, KENNETH JOHN, publisher; b. Melbourne, Australia, July 22, 1940; arrived in U.S., 1970; s. Charles Dudley and Lilian May (Besant) McN.; m. Victoria Ann Yocum, Oct. 28, 1972 (div. Oct. 1982); children: Aurelius John, Candace Ann. B chem. engr., Univ. Melbourne, 1961; M in engr. sci., Monash Univ., Clayton, Australia, 1964. Dir. communications network Found. Faith, N.Y., 1966-77; asst. editor Chemical Engring., N.Y., 1976-81, assoc. editor, 1981-86; editor-in-chief Industrial Chemist, N.Y., 1986-89; dir. new publs. divsn. sci. and tech. Warren Gorham & Lamont, N.Y., 1989-90; mng. editor Physics Today, N.Y., 1991-94; assoc. pub. The Industrial Physicist, College Park, Md., 1995—; pres. McNaughton Communications, N.Y., 1978—. Contbr. over 100 articles to profl. jours. Mem. Friends of Benjamin Banneker Historical Park, Oella, Md., 1996—; founder Campaign to Save the Trees, Roosevelt Island, N.Y., 1991; pres. PTA H.S. for the Humanities, N.Y., 1990-91; mem. Romnet Newsgroup, 1997-99. Recipient Broadcast awards Coun. of Chs., 1976, 78, 79, Golden Mike awards Am. Legion, 1978, 79. Mem. Port Philip Pioneers Group, Univ. Melbourne Alumni Assn. (founding pres. 1988-90, northeastern br. pres. 1992-94), Australia Soc. Phila. Avocations: music, dance, film, swimming, walking, traveling. Home: 3778 College Ave Ellicott City MD 21043-4662 Office: Am Inst Physics One Physics Ellipse College Park MD 20740-3843

MCNAUGHTON, PETER ANTHONY, pharmacology educator, neuroscience researcher; b. Auckland, New Zealand, Aug. 17, 1949; came to Great Britain, 1971; s. Anthony Henry and Dulcie Helen (Maiden) McN.; m. Linda Margarita Ariza, Feb. 22, 1985; children: Monica, Daniel, Anna. BS with honors, U. Auckland, 1971; PhD, U. Oxford, Eng., 1974; MA, U. Cambridge, Eng., 1976. Rsch. fellow Clare Coll., Cambridge, 1974-78; demonstrator U. Cambridge, 1978-83, lectr., 1983-91; fellow Christ's Coll., Cambridge, 1983-91; Halliburton prof. physiology King's Coll., London, 1991-99, dean basic med. scis., 1993-96; Sheild prof. pharmacology U. Cambridge, Eng., 1999—. Contbr. articles to profl. jours. Mem. Physiol. Soc., Pharmacol. Soc. Office: U Cambridge Dept Pharmacology, Tennis Court Rd, Cambridge CB2 1QJ, England

MCNAUGHTON, WILLIAM FRANK, translator, educator; b. Westboro, Mo., May 21, 1933; s. Frank McNaughton and Ruth Ellen (Flanders) Francis; m. Margaret Orminski, Apr. 4, 1956 (div. 1971); children: John Ferenc, Dorothy Ellen; m. Li Ying, Apr. 8, 1990. Student, U. Mo., 1951-53; studied poetry and translation with, Ezra Pound, 1953-56; student, Georgetown U., 1953-54; BA, Bklyn. Coll., 1961; PhD, Yale U., 1965. Asst. prof. Oberlin (Ohio) Coll., 1965-70; lectr. Exptl. Coll., Oberlin, 1970-71; vis. lectr. Bowling Green (Ohio) State U., 1972-74, Denison U., Granville, Ohio, 1972-78; prof. Program for Afloat Coll. Edn. (PACE) USN, Norfolk, Va., 1978-84; vis. prof. King Saud U., Abha, Saudi Arabia, 1984-85; sr. lectr. English, translation City Poly. Hong Kong, 1986-89, prin. lectr. translation, 1989-94; univ. sr. lectr. City U., Hong Kong, 1994-95, assoc. prof., 1995-98; retired, 1998; guest lectr., U. degli Studii, Venice, Italy, 1975; coord. Tri-Coll. Chinese program, Gt. Lakes Colls. Assn., Ann Arbor, 1965-68; cons., Asian Lit. program, Asia Soc., N.Y.C., 1967-80, Nat. Translation Ctr., Austin, Tex., 1965-68, Ballantine Books, N.Y.C., 1985, Princeton U. Press, 1965; presenter papers at lit. confs. Author: Reading and Writing Chinese, 1979, rev. edit., 1999, Pound's Usura and the Islamic Concept of Riba, 1996; co-translator: Poem Without a Hero and Selected Poems of Anna Akhmatova, 1989, As Though Dreaming: The Tz'u...of Li Ch'ing-chao, 1977, A Gold Orchid: The Love Poems of Tzu Yeh, 1972; editor, translator: Light from the East, 1978, The Confucian Vision, 1974, The Book of Songs, 1971, The Taoist Vision, 1971, Guerilla War, 1971; contbr. articles to profl. publs., translations to various lit. mags.; editor-in-chief: City Univ. Bull., 1995-98; mem. editl. bd. City Univ. Press, 1996-98. Woodrow Wilson Found. fellow, 1961-62; modern fgn. lang. fellow, NDEA, 1962-65; grantee, Nat. Translation Ctr., Austin, 1967, Gt. Lakes Colls. Assn., Ann Arbor, 1965, 67-68, Asia Soc., N.Y.C., 1971-72, 74; Fulbright fellow, 1968-69. Avocations: sailing, music, Venetian culture and history. Home and Office: Flat 20C Block 26, Baguio Villa 555 Victoria, Pokfulam Hong Kong

MCNAUGHTON, WILLIAM JOHN, bishop; b. Lawrence, Mass., Dec. 7, 1926; s. William John Sr. and Ruth Irene (Howe) McN. BA, U. of State of N.Y., Ossining, 1948, B of Sacred Theology, 1953; M in Religious Edn., Maryknoll Sem., Ossining, 1953. Ordained Maryknoll priest, 1953; cert. in Korean Lang. Studies, Yale U., 1954. Pastor Pouk Moun Ro Cath. Ch., Chong Ju Diocese, Korea, 1955-57, Nae Duk Dong Cath. Ch., Chong Ju Diocese, Korea, 1957-60; consultor Chong Ju Diocese, 1958-59, vicar gen., 1959-60; consecrated bishop Inchon (Korea) Diocese, 1961—. Home: Bishop's House, 3 Tap Tong Chung Ku, Inchon 400-090, Republic of Korea

MCNEELY, CAROL J., dentist; b. Chgo., July 17, 1954; d. Lewis W. and Jessie O. (Woodfin) McN.; divorced; 1 child, Matthew. Student, U. Chgo., 1972-74; DDS, U. Ill., Chgo., 1979; cert. in cosmetic dentistry, Case Western Res. U.; M of Mgmt., Northwestern U., 1995. Cert. cosmetic dentistry, 1993. Pvt. practice, Chgo., 1979—; pres. HealthS.M.A.R.T. Strategies, 1995—; ptnr. Provident Dental Assocs., Chgo., 1983-85; owner Soulful Expressions, Chgo., 1987—; dental cons. Dental Network Am., Oakbrook Terrace, Ill., 1988-92. Mem. assoc. bd. dirs. Chgo. Child Care Soc., 1982-85; mem. scholarship fund com. Chgo. Urban League, 1989. Recipient Ptnrs. in Community award Nat. Bar Assn., 1985. Mem. ADA (task force on women and minorities 1992-93), Acad. Cosmetic Dentistry, Am. Assn. Dental Cons., Nat. Dental Assn., Chgo. Assn. Black Women Dentists (pres. 1992-94), U. Chgo. Alumni Assn. (minority mentor program). Office: 7931 S King Dr Chicago IL 60619-3701

MCNEELY, PATRICIA GANTT, journalism educator; b. Winnsboro, S.C., Dec. 2, 1939; d. William Adolphus and Alice (Woodson) Gantt; m. Alfred Raymond McNeely, Apr. 8, 1960; children: Allison Patricia, Alan David. BA, Furman U., 1960; MA, U. S.C., 1975. Reporter Greenville (S.C.) News, 1958-60; reporter Columbia (S.C.) Record, 1960-66, 66-72, news editor, 1979-80; reporter The State, Columbia, 1965-66; prof. journalism U. S.C., Columbia, 1972—, Eleanor M. and R. Frank Mundy prof. of journalism, 2000—, dir. print and electronic sequence, 2000—; state mgr. Voter News Svc., N.Y., 1972—; workshop dir. Reader's Digest, Pleasantville, N.Y., 1985—. Mem. Assn. for Edn. in Journalism and Mass Comm. (sec. mag. divsn. 1995-96, head newspaper divsn. 1988-89, standing prof. freedom and responsibility com. 1995—). Office: Univ SC Coll Journalism Mass Comm Blossom At Assembly Sts Columbia SC 29208-0001

MCNEIL, EDWARD WARREN, real estate executive; b. Alhambra, Calif., Jan. 5, 1942; s. Murray Charles and Helen Katherine (Curtis) McN.; m. Jutta Bocking, Apr. 1, 1941; children: Anja Britt, Bradley Stuart. Student, U. Calif., Berkeley, 1960-63. Structures engr. Peter Kiewit Sons Co., various cities, Calif., 1961-63; project engr. Huntington Harbour, Sunset Beach, Calif., 1963-64; project supt. Coordinated Realty, Inc., Anaheim, Calif., 1964-65; field ops. mgr. Lear Siegler, Saigon, Vietnam, 1965-67; project engr. Constructora Emkay, Rio Blanco, Chile, 1968-69; ptnr. The Pyramid Cos., Syracuse, N.Y., 1969-75; ptnr. The Pioneer Group, Syracuse, 1975-95, ret., 1995. Past chmn., bd. dirs. Crouse Irving Meml. Hosp. Found., Syracuse, 1986—; trustee, past vice-chmn. Everson Mus. of Art, Syracuse, 1981-94; bd. dirs. Syracuse Stage, 1981-93, past chmn., vice-chmn.; chmn. Adirondack chpt. Nature Conservancy, 1994—, Adirondack Land Trust, 1994—; trustee Manlius Pebble Hill Sch., 1984-86, 1994-99, emeritus, 1999—. Recipient award for svc. to the arts, Cultural Resource Coun., Syracuse, 1987. Mem. Seaplane Pilots Assn., Slocum Soc., Century Club, Royal Cornwall Yacht Club (Eng.), Lake Amphibian Flyers Club, Warbirds of Am. Avocations: ocean sailing, canoeing, fly fishing, seaplane flying, aerobatics.

MCNEIL, HELEN JO CONNOLLY, nursing educator, public health administrator; b. Olympia, Wash., June 15, 1925; d. James Ambrose and Corinne Marie (Bordeaux) Connolly; m. Robert Phillip McNeil, Aug. 16, 1947; children: Sheryl Ann Andrews, Robert John, Maureen Connolly, Kevin Charles. BSN, Seattle Coll., 1947; MSN, U. Wash., 1961, postgrad., 1974-80. RN, Wash., S.C., Tex., Va.; cert. pub. health nurse. Clinic nurse Schutt Clinic, Bremerton, Wash., 1947-49; staff nurse Providence Hosp., Seattle, 1950-60, Overlake Hosp., Bellevue, Wash., 1961-62; pub. health nurse Seattle King County Health Dept. and Vis. Nurse Svc., 1962-64, pub. health nurse supr., 1964-65, assoc. dir. pub. health nursing and vis. nurse svc., 1965-70, health planning and evaluation specialist, 1970-73, adminstr. S.E. dist., 1973-78, adminstr. Ctrl. dist., 1979-81, adminstr. N. dist., 1981-84, dir. nursing rsch., 1984-85; lectr. Sch. Nursing U. Wash., Seattle, 1985-87; mem. faculty S. Puget Sound C.C., Olympia, 1987-88; vis. faculty Sch. Nursing Clemson (S.C.) U., 1988; instr. coll. nursing allied health U. Tex., El Paso, 1988-90; dir. pub. health nursing Commonwealth Va., Richmond, 1990-93; lectr. Sch. Nursing Seattle U., 1995; cons. Seattle, Seaview, Wash., 1995—; adj. assoc. prof. Sch. Pub. Health, U. N.C., Chapel Hill, 1980-92; adj. asst. prof. U. Wash. Sch. Nursing, 1965-85; rev. com. nursing census USPHS, 1970-72; health care cons., Kuwait, 1976; lectr. Congress on Nutrition, Rio de Janeiro, Brazil, 1978. Author: Reaching Out, 1998; contbr. articles to profl. jours., chpts. to books. Mem. task force Seattle Health Policy, 1981, Seattle 2000 Commn., 1973; lectr. Internat. Congress Social Psychiatry, Athens, 1974; with Project Hope Internat. Approaches in Health Care of Elderly, Milwood, Va., 1983, 84; co-project dir. occupl. health con. edn. for cmty. nurses divsn. nursing U. Wash., 1983-86; mem. ARC Disater Team, Seattle, 1995-97, Parent and Home Health Bd., Richmond, Va., 1990-93. With U.S. cadet nursing corps USPHS, 1943-47. Stress Rsch. grantee Heath Resources Adminstrn., 1974; W. K. Kellog Found. grantee U. Tex., El Paso, 1990, grantee U. Wash., 1983-86; recipient Nursing Adminstrn. recognition award Jour. Nursing Adminstrn., 1993. Fellow APHA (nursing sect. pres. 1992-93, Ruth B. Freeman Dising. Career award 1998); mem. Am. Assn. Colls. of Nursing (mem. panel in nursing ed. 1985-87), Assn. Cmty. Health Nurse Educators (founder, pres. 1985), Wash. State Pub. Health Assn. (pres. 1976-77, Adminstrn. Svc. award 1975), Seattle Mgmt. Assn. (pres. 1976, Disting. Adminstrv. Svc. award City of Seattle 1976), Seattle U. Alumni (mem. nursing adv. bd. 1993-96, Cmty. Svc. Alumni award 1992), Assn. State and Terr. Dirs. Nursing (emeritus), Am. Coll. Nursing (panel 1985-87), VNA (mem. instructive visitors parent and home health bd. 1990-93), Sigma Theta Tau (internat. rsch. conf. Seoul, South Korea 1984), Alpha Tau Delta. Avocations: renovating low income housing, skiing, gardening, traveling, writing. Home and Office: PO Box 173 Seaview WA 98644-0173

MCNEIL, PAUL JOSEPH, JR., employment security interviewer; b. Winthrop, Mass., Oct. 11, 1941; s. Paul Joseph Sr. and Helen Margaret (Carr) McN. Cert. in ins., U. R.I., 1965; cert. in travel agts., Travel Sch. of Am., 1968; cert., Labor Sch. of Boston, 1976, Labor Studies Inst., 1989. Field investigator R.I. Food Stamp Unit, Providence, 1965-68; cmty. rels. Coordinator Ecology Action for Rhode Island, 1970-71; sec. and rsch. asst. R.I. Worker Assn., 1973-74; enumerator R.I. Polk & Co., Providence, 1970-83; sr. employment security interviewer R.I. Dept. Employment Tng., Providence, 1984-96; sr. employment & tng. interviewer R.I. Dept. Labor & Tng., Providence, 1996—; rec. sec. Local 189 New Eng. chpt., Boston, 1973-76, treas., 1989—; mem. bd. dirs. of R.I. Workers Assn., 1973-74, 75-76, census enumerator U.S. Census Bur., Providence, 1990; mail handler U.S. Post Office, Providence, 1980; claims interviewer R.I. Dept. Employment Security, Providence, 1979-84; rec. sec. R.I. Employment Security Alliance, Providence, 1980-90; v.p. Community Econs. Edn. Ctr., Providence, 1988-91. Exec. com. R.I. State Employees Assn., 1966-68, Community Labor Organizing Com., Providence, 1983-89, Sane Freeze, Washington, 1989-90; shop steward Local 401 SEIU, Providence, 1990-92, 1st v.p., 1992-96; rec. sec. R.I. Sane Freeze, Providence, 1988-94; mem. Nat. Com. Peace Action, 1993—; v.p. Peace Action R.I., 1994-95, pres., 1995—; coord. R.I. Nation Readers Group, 1995—; state committeeman Amvets Dept. R.I., 1965-69, 96—, adj. posts, 1965-68, trustee post 6, 1995-96; v.p. Labor Party R.I., 1994-97, treas., 1997—, pres., 1999, chmn., 1999; exec. bd. R.I. Coalition for Consumer Justice, 1997—; bd. dirs. Injured Workers R.I., 1996—, Warwick Cmty. Action, 1967-69, R.I. Legal Svcs., 1967-69; founder East Greenwich Dem. Youth Club, 1959; co-chmn. Human Rights Action Coun., Warwick, 1968-70; del. R.I. Dem. State Conv., 1976, 78; mem. R.I. Dem. State Com., 1980-86, bd. dirs., 1985-87; mem. Dem. Study Group R.I., 1986-88; organizer United Farm Workers, 1968-71; mem. Fox Point Neighborhood Housing Corp. Dirs., 1980-87, pres., 1981-83, sec., 1983-87. With U.S. Army, 1960-63, ETO. Mem. Internat. Assn. Pers. in Employment Security (R.I. chpt. bd. dirs. 1989-93, sec. 1991-93), Greater R.I. Indsl. Rels. Rsch. Assn., R.I. ACLU (bd. dirs. 1974-80, bd. sec. 1975-77, exec. com. 1979-80), Union of Peace Profls. (exec. bd. 1988-90), Nat. Writers Union, R.I. Cen. Am. Network, Cath. Peace Fellowship, Pax ChristiAncient Order, Order of Hibernians (rec. sec. Providence chpt. 1990-91, 97-98, v.p., 1998—, pres. 1991-92, state sec. 1993-96, pres. 1996—), K. of C., Sierra Club, Newport Mus. Irish History, Am. Irish Hist. Soc., R.I. Hist. Soc., R.I. Labor History Soc., Gaspee Days Com., Americans for Dem. Action, Debs Found., Edward Bellamy Meml. Assn., R.I. Irish Famine Meml. Com., Am. Legion, Indsl. Rels. Rsch. Assn., Assn. Can.-Am., Am. French Geneal. Soc., Irish Nat. Caucus, Am. Irish Polit. Edn. Com., Friendly Sons of St. Patrick (East Greenwich, R.I.). Democrat. Avocation: writing. Home: PO Box 945 Providence RI 02901-0945

MCNEILL, JOHN, botanist; b. Edinburgh, Scotland, U.K., Sept. 15, 1933; s. Thomas and Helen Lawrie (Eagle) McN.; m. Bridget Mariel Winterton, July 29, 1961 (div. 1990); children: Andrew Thomas, Douglas Paul; m. Marilyn Lois James, Apr. 6, 1990. BSc with honors, U. Edinburgh, 1955, PhD, 1960. Asst. lectr. dept. agrl. botany U. Reading, Eng., 1957-60, lectr. agrl. botany, 1960-61; lectr. dept. botany U. Liverpool, Eng., 1961-69; rsch. scientist Plant Rsch. Inst. Agr., Ottawa, Ont., Can., 1969-77; sr. rsch. scientist Biosystematics Rsch. Inst. Agr., Ottawa, 1977-81; prof. dept. biology U. Ottawa, 1981-87; regius keeper Royal Bot. Garden, Edinburgh, 1987-89, hon. assoc., 1998—; assoc. dir. Royal Ont. Mus., Toronto, 1989-90, acting dir., 1990-91, dir., 1991-97, dir. emeritus, 1997—, hon. assoc., 1998—; prof. dept. botany U. Toronto, 1991—; curator herbarium U. Liverpool, 1964-69, dep. sr. tutor faculty sci., 1967-69; vis. assoc. prof. dept botany U. Wash., Seattle, 1969; acting assoc. prof. dept. population and environ. biology U. Calif., Irvine, 1969; chief taxonomy and econ. botany sect. Plant Rsch. Inst. Agr., Ottawa, 1969-73; sessional lectr. dept. biology U. Ottawa, 1977, chmn. dept. biology, 1981-87, mem. faculty sci. tchg. pers. com., 1987, mem. univ. rsch. com., 1986-87, mem. univ. adv. com. on computing, 1984-87, mem. sch. grad. studies, adj. prof., 1987-91; vis. prof. dept. botany U. Toronto, 1978; adj. prof. dept. biology Carleton U., 1973-79; hon. prof. dept. botany U. Edinburgh, 1989, hon. fellow faculty sci., 1988-89; dir. George R. Gardiner Mus. Ceramic Art, Toronto, 1991-96; pres. Royal Ont. Mus. Found., 1992-97; presenter in field. Author: (with others) Grasses of Ontario, 1980, The Genus Atriplex (Chenopodiaceae) in Canada, 1983, Preliminary Inventory of Canadian Weeds, 1988, also book chpts.; editor: (with others) Phenetic and Phylogenetic Classification, 1964, International Code of Botanical Nomenclature, 1983, 88, 94, French edit., 1988, 95, German edit., 1989, 95, Japanese edit., 1992, 97, Slovakian edit., 1996, Italian edit., 1998, Flora of North America, Vols. 1 and 2, 1993, Vol. 3, 1997, vol. 22, 2000, International Code of Nomenclature for Cultivated Plants, 1995, Draft BioCode, 1996, 97, Russian edit., 1997, Italian edit., 1999; mem. editl. com. Flora of N.Am., 1985—, mem. mgmt. com., 1997—, chair mgmt. com., 1998—, nomenclature advisor, 1987—; contbr. articles to profl. jours.; mem. internat. bd. editors Edinburgh Jour. Botany, 1996—; nomenclature editor Taxon, 1999—. V.p. XVI Internat. Bot. Congress, St. Louis, 1999, rapporteur-gen. for bot. nomenclature, 1999—. NSERC Operating grantee, 1982-92. Fellow Linnean Soc. London; mem. Am. Soc. Plant Taxonomists, Biol. Coun. Can. (v.p. 1984-85, v.p., pres.-elect 1985-86, pres. 1986-87), Can. Coun. Univ. Biology Chmn. (v.p. 1982-84, pres. 1984-85, past pres. 1985-86), Bot. Soc. Brit. Isles, Bot. Soc. Edinburgh (v.p. 1987-89), Can. Bot. Assn. (chmn. systematics and phytogeography sect. 1981-83, dir. 1995—), Natural Scis. and Engring. Rsch. Coun. Can. (population biology grant selection com. 1981-84), Classification Soc., Hennig Soc., Hunt Inst. Bot. Documentation, Internat. Union Biol. Scis. (voting mem. exec. 1985-88, alt. mem. exec. 1991-94), Internat. Assn. Bot. and Mycological Socs. (sec. 1986-93, chmn. 1993-99), Internat. Union Biol. Scis., Internat. Union Microbiol. Socs. (internat. com. for bionomenclature 1994—), Internat. Assn. Plant Taxonomy (mem. coun. 1981-87, 93—, adminstr. fin. 1987-93), Internat. Congress Systematic and Evolutionary Biology (internat. com. 1980-90), Internat. Orgn. Plant Biosystematists (mem. coun. 1989-92), Internat. Orgn. for Plant Info. (vice-chmn. 1993-96, chmn. 1996—), Internat. Orgn. for Systematics and Evolutionary Biology (treas. 1996—), Annales Botanici Fennici (adv. bd. 1987-92), Acta Botanica Fennica (adv. bd. 1987-92), Internat. Assn. Bot. Gardens, Internat. Weed Sci. Soc., Orgn. for Phyto-Taxonomic Investigation of Mediterranean Area (bd. dirs. 1989—), Royal Caledonian Hort. Soc., Royal Hort. Soc., Soc. Systematic Biology, Systematics Assn. (mem. coun. 1959-62, 64-66, gen. sec. 1966-69), Ottawa Field Naturalists Club, Scottish Rock

Garden Club. Office: Royal Bot Garden, 20A Inverleith Row, Edinburgh EH3 5LR, Scotland

MCNELLEY, JUDY ANNE, small business owner; b. Commerce, Ga., Oct. 19, 1956; d. Marvin Ellis and Florence Evelyn Duncan; m. Harold Michael McNelley, Aug. 14, 1977; children: Jeremy Michael, James Todd, Joshua Duncan. Student, Young Harris Coll., 1976-77. Co-owner M & J Vending, Tunnel Hill, Ga., 1988—. Columnist Banks County News, 1992. Chmn. Whitfield County Rep. Party, 1995—, precinct capt., 1991-93, 1st vice chmn. 1993-95, conv. del., 1988—; cons. Dalton State Coll. Reps., 1998—; exec. com. 9th Congl. Dist. Ga. Rep. Party, 1995—, conv. del., 1989—; 2d v.p. Rep. Women N.W. Ga., 1993-97; mem. sex. edn. adv. com. Whitfield County Schs., Dalton, Ga., 1991-98, mem. sys. level media adv. bd., 1995-96; Sunday sch. tchr. Tunnel Hill United Meth. Ch., 1986-97; charter mem. Coun. Women Advisors to Congress, Washington, 1995. Named Hon. Life Mem. Ga. PTA, 1991, Rep. Woman of Yr., Rep. Women N.W. Ga., 1995, Cmty. Hero Torchbearer, Atlanta Com. Olympic Games, 1996; recipient Ronald Reagan award 9th Congl. Dist. Ga. Rep. Party, 1997, Vol. of Yr. award Tunnel Hill Elem. Sch., 1991. Republican. Christian. Avocations: volunteer work, collecting autographed memorabilia, reading, concerts. Home: 306 Scenic Dr Tunnel Hill GA 30755-9712

MC NELLY, FREDERICK WRIGHT, JR., psychologist; b. Bangor, Maine, Apr. 14, 1947; s. Frederick Wright and E. Frances (Cutter) McN.; 1 adopted son, Roger; foster children: Joseph, Ronald, Michael, Jeffrey. BA magna cum laude, U. Minn., 1969; MA, U. Mich., 1971, PhD, 1973. Registered clin. psychologist, Ill.; cert. profl. qualification, state and provincial bds. of psychology; cert. early intervention program provider, Ill. Rsch. coord. NSF project U. Minn., Morris, 1968-69, lab. instr., 1969, trainee USPHS, 1969-70, 72; teaching fellow psychology U. Mich., Ann Arbor, 1970-72; ednl. examiner Ann Arbor Pub. Schs., 1971; dir. psychol. svcs. Children Devel. Ctr., Rockford, Ill., 1972-82, program dir., 1982-86; cons. psychologist, 1986—; lectr. Rock Valley Coll., Rockford, 1974-75; part-time pvt. practice psychology, Rockford and Belvidere, Ill., 1980-86, Beloit, Wis., 1985-86, full time, 1986—; mental health cons. Rockford Head Start, 1982—, United Cerebral Palsy, Blackhawk Region, 1986—, Access Svcs., Mendota, Ill., 1992—; mem. health svcs. adv. com. human resources dept., City of Rockford, 1985—; presenter state and regional workshops and confs. Contbr. articles to profl. jours. Active Boy Scouts Am., 1978-83; chmn. spl. edn. regional advisory com. Bi-County Office of Edn., Rockford, 1976-78; mem. Nat. and Ill. Com. on Child Abuse, 1975-85; co-chmn. Winnebago County Child Protection Assn., 1980; elder Willow Creek United Presbyn. Ch., Rockford, 1980-83; mem. stronghold renovation session com. Presbytery of Blackhawk, Oregon, Ill., 1985. Named U.S. Jaycees Outstanding Young Man of 1977. Mem. Ill. Psychol. Assn., No. Ill. Psychol. Assn. (chmn. 1976-77), Wis. Psychol. Assn., No. Ill. Pvt. Practice Mental Health Assn. (v.p. 1993-94, pres. 1994-96), Coun. for Exceptional Children, Nat. Register Health Svc. Providers in Psychology, State Provincial Bds. in Psych., Nat. Assn. of Disability Examiners, Nat. Assn. Mentally Ill, No. Ill. Alliance for Mentally Ill. Home: 11591 Beverly Ln Belvidere IL 61008-8708 Office: Childrens Devel Ctr 650 N Main St Rockford IL 61103-6994 Office: 972 N Main St Rockford IL 61103-9652

MCNULTY, MARK, professional golfer; b. Harare, Zimbabwe, Oct. 25, 1953; m. Allison McNulty; atherine. Profl. golfer U.S.A., European & South African PGA Tours, 1977—; mem. Pres. Cup Team, 1994. Worldwide winner 42 times with 14 victories on PGA European Tour. Avocations: piano, fine arts, koifish. Office: IMG Pier House, Strand on the Green, Chiswick W4 3NN, England

MCNULTY, ROBERT HOLMES, non-profit executive; b. Oakland, Calif., June 20, 1940; s. Frederick James and Ruth (Holmes) McN.; m. Penelope Cuff, Dec. 27, 1964; children: Maria, Abigail. BS in Bus. Administrn., U. Calif., Berkeley, 1962, JD, 1965. Bar: Calif. 1965. Property acquisition planner Safeway Stores, Internat., Oakland, 1962; archeol. asst. Colonial Williamsburg, Va., 1968; rsch. asst. Nat. Mus. of History and Tech. The Smithsonian Instn., Washington, 1968-69, asst. to the dir., 1969-70; environ. advisor GSA, Washington, 1970-71; asst. dir. architecture and environ. arts program NEA, Washington, 1971-78; acting dir. grad. program in hist. preservation Sch. Architecture Columbia U., N.Y.C., 1978-79; pres. Ptnrs. for Livable Communities, Washington, 1979—; cons. Task Force on Land Use and Urban Growth, 1972, Task Force on Neighborhood Economic Development, 1976, German Marshall Fund, Washington, 1978; bd. visitors U. Ind. Sch. Pub. Adminstrn., 1991—; mem. NY St. Council of the Arts, Architecture & Enviromental Arts Prgm (panelist 1973-74, advisor 1974-75), Taskforce under President Reagan on Private Sector Initiatives, 1981, Urban Land Inst. Cultural Fac. (co-chair adv. comm.) 1984, The Micronesian Inst. (adv. council) 1985—, Oversight Comm. of L'Axe Majeur de Cergy-Pontoise, Paris, 1988, Internat. Prgm. Adv. Comm. to the Natl. Endowment for the Arts, 1990-92, Internat. Ecotourism Soc., 1992-99, City Innovation Natl. Adv. (bd. mem.) 1993—, President's Natl. Preparatory Comm. for the Human Settlements Conference, Istanbul, 1996, Inst. for the Regl. Community (bd. trustees) 1997-98, Am. Assembly on Improving the Economic Hlth. of Am. Distressed Communities, 1997; lect. in field. Author: Neighborhood Conservation: A Handbook of Methods and Techniques, 1976, Economics of Amenity, 1985, Entrepreneurial American City, 1985, Return of the Livable City, 1986; editor: (book) Better Cities Book, 1989, (report) State of the American Community, 1994; contrib. articles to profl. journals. Pres. Brookmont and Vicinity Civ. League, 1976-77, bd. mem., 1975-76, 77-78, 91-92; served to capt. U.S. Army, 1966-68. Smithsonian Inst. grantee, 1972, 73, Graham Found. grantee 1978; Loeb fellow Harvard U., 1973-74, Pierson Coll. guest fellow, Yale U., 1985, adj. sr. fellow Hudson Inst., 1989—; recipient AIA Gold Medal to the Architecture, Planning & Design Prgm. of NEA, 1979. Mem. Calif. Bar Assn., Nat. Press Club., Royal Soc. for the Arts in the U.S. (fell. 1992—), Inst. of Current World Affairs, Lambda Alpha Internat. Office: Ptnrs for Livable Community 1429 21st St NW Washington DC 20036-5902

MCNULTY, WILLIAM JOSEPH, solicitor; b. Strabane, Ireland, Oct. 29, 1956; s. Michael and Jeannette (Maxwell) McN.; m. Assumpta Catney, July 30, 1990; 1 child, James Michael. BA, Trinity Coll., Dublin, 1979, MA, 1994. Prin. solicitor Bogue & McNulty, Ireland, 1983—. Mem. Coun. of the Law Soc. No. Ireland, Balmoral Golf Club. Avocations: golf, music, association football, Gaelic football.

MCPARTLAND, PATRICIA ANN, health educator and administrator; b. Passaic, N.J.; d. Daniel and Josephine McP. BA, U. Mo., 1971; MCRP, Ohio State U., 1975, MS in Preventive Medicine, 1975; EdD in Higher and Adult Edn., Columbia U., 1988. cert. health edn. specialist. Sr. health planner Merrimack Valley HSA, Lawrence, Mass., 1977-79; planning cons./adminstr. Children's Hosp., Boston, 1979-80; exec. dir. Southeastern Mass. Area Health Edn. Ctr., Marion, Mass., 1980—; v.p., cons. New Bedford (Mass.) Cmty. Health Ctr., 1993-94; chmn. edn. and tng. com. Health and Human Svc. Coalition, 1988-89; mem. project expert panel Office of Minority Health, 1997—; mem. New Eng. Regional Minority Health Conf. Com., 1997—; vis. lectr. Bridgewater State Coll.; lectr. in field; project expert panel Office Minority Health's Culturally and Linguistically Appropriate Svcs. Mem. editl. bd. Jour. Healthcare Edn. and Tng., 1989-93; author: Promoting Health in the Workplace, 1991; reviewer Qualitative Health Rsch. Jour.; contbr. articles to profl. jours. Vol. speaker March of Dimes Found., Wareham, Mass., 1992-93; coll.-wide vocat. Cape Cod C.C., Hyannis, Mass., 1989—; planning adv. 2nd Internat. Symposium, Pasco, Wash., 1992; v.p. New Bedford chpt. Am. Cancer Soc., 1985-90. Recipient award Excellence in Continuing Edn. Nat. AHEC Ctr. Dirs. Assn., 1994, 95, 96, 97, Sec.'s awards for Outstanding Progam in Community Health, Nat. Cancer Inst., Washington, 1990. Mem. Am. Pub. Health Assn., Inst. for Disease Prevention (steering com. 1982—), Southeastern Mass Health Planning (bd. dirs., sec., 1982-87), Nat. Planning Conf. (mem. com. 1984-85, 86-87). Avocations: writing, acting, dance, theatre, travel, hiking. Home: PO Box 1116 Marion MA 02738-0020 Office: Southeastern Mass AHEC PO Box 69 2 Spring St Marion MA 02738-1519

MCPHAIL, JOANN WINSTEAD, writer, publisher, art dealer; b. Trenton, Fla., Feb. 17, 1941; d. William Emerson and Donna Mae (Crawford) Winstead; m. James Michael McPhail, June 15, 1963; children: Angela C. McPhail Morris, Dana Denise McPhail Gaizutis, Whitney Gold McPhail Casso. Student, Fla. So. Coll., 1959-60, St. John's River Jr. Coll., Palatka, Fla., 1960-61, Houston (Tex.) C.C. With Jim Walter Corp., Houston, 1961-62; receptionist, land lease sec. Oil and Gas Property Mgmt. Inc., Houston, 1962-63; sec. to mng. atty. State Farm Ins. Co., Houston, 1963-64; saleswoman, decorator Oneil-Anderson, Houston, 1973; sec. Law Offices of Ed Christensen, Houston, 1980-82; advt. mgr. Egalitarian Houston (Tex.) C.C. Systems, 1981; fashion display artist, 1985-86; entrepreneur, writer, art agt. Golden Galleries and Antiques, Houston, 1990-95; owner, property mgr. APT Investments, 1994-98; lyricist, publisher Anna Gold Classics, 1995—, writer song lyrics, 1996—. Freelance writer, photographer: Elegance of Needlepoint, 1970, S.W. Art Mag., A Touch of Greatness, 1973, Sweet 70's Anthology, The Budding of Tomorrow, 1974 (award); columnist, photographer: Egalitarian: Names Can be Symbols, Design Your Wall Covering, Student Profile, 1981, National Library of Poetry, Fireworks (award), 1995; contbr. poetry various publs.; playwright, 1993—; screenwriter, 1996—; writer, pub. The Missing Crown, religious drama World Wide Christian Radio, Sta. KCBI-FM, KYND-AM, and other radio stas., 1996—, baby publ. Hello...World...Hello, 1997; author: (poetry) The Budding of Tomorrow, 1997; music pub., 1999—. Vol. PTO bd. Sharptown Middle Sch. Mem. ASCAP, Manuscriptors Guild. Methodist. Home: 361 N Post Oak Ln Apt 333 Houston TX 77024-5950

MCPHERSON, KENNETH JOHN, art director; b. Aberdeen, Scotland, Dec. 24, 1954; s. John and Phyllis (Campbell) McP. Dipl. art, Dartington Coll., 1976, postgrad., 1977; postgrad., Goldsmiths Coll., 1978. Owner Screenheat, Aberdeen, 1980-99, Virtu, 1999—; radio presenter NorthSound, Aberdeen, 1991-92. Exhibit of photographs, Kans.; musical composition, Edge. Avocations: chess, football, soccer, jazz and folk music. Avocations: chess, football, soccer, jazz and folk music.

MCPHERSON, NORMAN ANGUS, shipbuilding company executive; b. Bellshill, Scotland, July 3, 1948; s. McIntyre Wilson and Jean Burnett Strathearn (Henderson) McP.; m. Jessie Hunter Gordon, July 3, 1974; 1 child, Morven Fiona. BS, U. Strathclyde, Glasgow, Scotland, 1970, PhD, 1976, MBA, 1987. Chartered engr. Metallurgist British Steel, U.K., 1973-78, sect. mgr., 1978-85, tech. mgr., 1985-86; tech. mgr. Thor Ceramics, U.K., 1986-90; quality mgr. Kvaerner Govan, Glasgow, 1990—; bd. dirs. SMC, Glasgow; vis. prof. Glasgow Caledonian U., 1997—. Author: Tundish To Mould Transfer, 1992, Non-metallic Inclusions in Continuously Cast Steels, 1995, Transverse Cracking in Continuous Cast Products, 1997, also over 50 papers. Recipient Sidney Gilchrist Thomas medal Metals Soc., London, 1982, Steelmaking Conf. award Iron and Steel Soc. and AIME, U.S., 1985, Frank B. McKune award, 1987. Fellow Welding Inst., Inst. Engrs. and Shipbuilders in Scotland, Inst. Materials; mem. Scottish Assn. for Metals (pres. 1998-2000). Mem. Ch. of Scotland. Avocations: travel, gardening, photography, sports. Home: 2 Strathclyde View, Bothwell Glasgow G71 8NJ, Scotland Office: BAE Sys, 1048 Govan Rd, Glasgow G51 4XP, Scotland

MCPHERSON, SAMUEL DACE, III, computer scientist, instructor, consultant; b. Durham, N.C., May 22, 1957; s. Samuel Dace Jr. and Margaret Courtauld (Finney) McP.; m. Grace Carroll Gilliam, Oct. 11, 1986; children: Stuart Dace, Katherine Finney, Rebecca Banks. BA in Edn., U. N.C., 1979; MEd, U. S.C., 1981. Data entry operator Olsten svcs. No. Telecom, Durham, 1985; computer operator GTE Data Svcs., Durham, 1985-86, sr. computer operator, 1986-87, svc. technician, 1987-88; systems tng. analyst GTE Data Svcs., Tampa, Fla., 1988-90, sr. systems tng. analyst, 1990-92; sr. sales tng. specialist Ascom Timeplex, 1992-93; tech. tng. specialist Fujitsu Network Switching, Raleigh, N.C., 1994-95; founder, pres. Technology Tng. Solutions, Inc., 1995—; presenter pub. and ednl. workshops Wake Tech.; instr./lectr. Am. Rsch. Group. Vol. U.S. Olympic Festival, Durham, 1987, GTE Suncoast Classic, Tampa, 1989-91; instr. Jr. Achievement Tampa, 1989; active Village Presbyn. Ch., Tampa, 1990. Recipient Personal Best Group award GTE, 1992, Quest for Quality award, 1992, Outstanding Achievement award Ascom Timeplex, 1993; Cameron scholar U. N.C., 1978-79. Mem. ASTD (spl. projects com. Suncoast chpt. 1989-90, appreciation award 1989), Data Processing Mgmt. Assn. (dir. mem. edn. 1989-91, presenter local workshop 1991). Republican. Avocations: racquetball, golf, tennis, music, working with others. Home: 12416 Mayhurst Pl Raleigh NC 27614-8803 Office: Tech Tng Solutions Inc 5201 Lovell Ct Raleigh NC 27613-5618

MCQUAID, JOHN GAFFNEY, lawyer; b. N.Y.C., Jan. 4, 1918; s. Paul Augustine and Louise (Gaffney) McQ.; m. Betty Frances Seay, May 27, 1989; children from previous marriage: John G. Jr., Catherine M., Elizabeth L. BA, Yale Coll., 1940, LLB, 1947. Bar: N.Y. 1948, U.S. Supreme Ct. 1954. Assoc. Townley Updike Carter & Rodgers, N.Y.C., 1947-52; with Nat. Prodn. Auth., Washington, 1952-54; pvt. practice White Plains, N.Y., 1954-60; ptnr. Fingar & McQuaid, White Plains, 1960-65; ptnr. McCarthy, Fingar, Donovan, Drazen & Smith, White Plains, 1965-94, counsel, 1995—; dir., asst. sec. Dewey Electronics Corp., Oakland, N.J., 1955—. Co-author, editor: New York Wills and Trusts, 2d edit., 1961, 3d edit., 1990; nat., N.Y. co-editor: Will Manual Svc. Bd. advisors Westchester County Found.; bd. advisors Westchester Nonprofit Loan Fund. 2d lt. U.S. Army, 1942-46. Fellow Am. Coll. Trust and Estate Counsel, Am. Bar Found., N.Y. Bar Found.; mem. N.Y. State Bar Assn. (chmn. trusts and estates law sect. 1981), White Plains Bar Assn. (pres. 1961), Westchester County Bar Assn., Ardsley Country Club, Yale Club (N.Y.C.). Home: Hudson House PO Box 11 Ardsley on Hudson NY 10503-0011 Office: McCarthy Fingar Donovan Drazen & Smith 11 Martine Ave White Plains NY 10606-1934

MCQUAID, RONALD WILLIAM, economic development educator, consultant, researcher; b. Ont., Can., 1955. BA with honors, Lancaster (U.K.) U., 1977; MS in Econs. with distinction, London Sch. Econs., 1979; PhD, Harvard U., 1984. Head dept. econs. Coun., Stirling, Scotland, 1985-87, Strathkelvin, Scotland, 1987-90; sr. lectr. Napier U., Edinburgh, U.K., 1990—. Treas. Scout Group, Stirling. Mem. Regional Sci. Assn. Internat. (Brit. and Irish br. treas. 1997—). Office: Napier U Merchiston Campus, 10 Colinton Rd, Edinburgh EH10 5DT, United Kingdom

MCQUILLAN, WILLIAM ROBERT, association administrator, minister, lecturer; b. Belfast, No. Ireland, Feb. 13, 1942; arrived in Australia, 1974; s. Isaac and Elizabeth (Gray) McQ.; m. Maureen McGeown, July 7, 1961; children: Wendy, Robert Stuart. Dux grad., Crusade Bible Coll., Adelaide, Australia, 1977; Cert. in Theology, Launceston Coll. Theology, Tasmania, Australia, 1978; diploma in Theology, Vision Coll., Sydney, Australia, 1982; B in Bible Theology, Jubilee Internat. Bible Coll., Brisbane, Australia, 1989, M in Ministry, 1989, LittD, 1989; DD (hon.), MA, Pacific Coast Christian Coll., L.A., 1998; LHD, Regent Theol. Coll., L.A., 1998. Mktg. mgr. Charlicks, Adelaide, 1976-80; sr. minister Christian Life Ctr., Adelaide, 1978-85; editor Australian Evangel Assemblies of God in Australia, Adelaide, 1985-89; editor Australian Evangel Assemblies of God in Australia, Melbourne, 1991-98, nat. publs. dir., 1991-98; founder, dir. Life Focus Ministries, Inc., 1998—; sr. minister Life Focus Centre, 1999—; state sec. Assemblies of God, South Australia, 1988-89; rep. Heads of Chs., 1988-89. Editor Minister's Bulletin, 1985-89, 91-98, Missions Update, 1989-98. Bd. mem. Children's Bible Ministries. Adv. bd. mem., Internatl. Pentecostal Press Assn., 1985-89, 91-98, Renewal Jour., Dayspring Ministries Internat., Challenge Ministries Internat.; magazine publications consultant. Avocations: reading, golf, travel, old movies. E-mail: Lifocus@bigpond.com.

MCQUOWN, JUDITH HERSHKOWITZ, author, financial advisor; b. N.Y.C., Apr. 8, 1941; d. Frederick Ephraim and Pearl (Rosenberg) H.; m. Michael L. McQuown, Jan. 13, 1969 (div. 1980); m. Harrison Roth, Dec. 8, 1985 (dec. 1997). AB, Hunter Coll., 1963; postgrad., N.Y. Inst. Fin., N.Y.C., 1965-67. Chief underwriting div. mcpl. securities City of N.Y., 1972-73; CEO Judith H. McQuown & Co., Inc., N.Y.C., 1973—. Author: Inc. Yourself: How to Profit by Setting Up Your Own Corporation, 9th edit., 1999, Tax Shelters That Work for Everyone, 1979, The Fashion Survival Manual, 1981, Playing the Takeover Market, 1982, How to Profit After You Inc. Yourself, 1985, Keep One Suitcase Empty: The Bargain Shopper's Guide to the Finest Factory Outlets in the British Isles, 1987, Keep One Suitcase Empty: The Bargain Shopper's Guide to the Finest Factory Outlets in Europe, 1988, Use Your Own Corporation to Get Rich, 1991; contbg. editor Boardroom Reports, Physician's Fin. News, Physician's Guide to Money Mgmt.; seminars The Learning Annex, The Discovery Ctr., Boston Ctr. for Adult Edn., First Class, Learning Connection, Knowledge Network. Mem. Am. Soc. Journalists and Authors. Home and Office: 315 E 72d St New York NY 10021-4625

MCREYNOLDS, ALLEN, JR., investment company executive; b. Carthage, Mo., Dec. 25, 1909; s. Allen and Maude (Clark) McR.; m. Virginia Madeliene Hensley, Jan. 17, 1946; children: Sharron Anne, Amy Elizabeth, Mary Armilda, Allen IV. Student, N.Mex. Mil. Inst., 1926-29, U. Mo., 1929-31. Pres. Joplin (Mo.) Stockyards, Inc., 1945-83; v.p., dir. First Nat. Bank, Monett, Mo., 1943-80; v.p., cashier First Nat. Bank, Golden City, Mo., 1950-56; dir. First Nat. Bancorp, Joplin, 1982-87; asst. adminstr. Mo. State Coun. Civil Defence, 1941-44. Pres. Jasper County Assn. for Soc. Services, 1976-78, Mo. State Southern Coll. Found., Joplin, 1984-85. Mem. Sigma Nu. Democrat. Episcopalian. Avocation: farming. Home: 1202 Mississippi Ave Joplin MO 64801-5344 Office: Lower Level Firstar Bldg Rm 021 Joplin MO 64801

MCREYNOLDS, MARY ARMILDA, lawyer; b. Carthage, Mo., Sept. 2, 1946; d. Allen and Virginia Madeliene (Hensley) McR. BA, Mt. Holyoke Coll., 1968; JD, Georgetown U., 1971; LLM, Harvard U., 1973. Bar: D.C. 1971, U.S. Ct. Appeals (D.C. cir.) 1971, U.S. Ct. Appeals (2d cir.) 1975, U.S. Ct. Appeals (4th cir.) 1979, U.S. Ct. Appeals (1st, 5th, 6th, 9th 10th cirs.) 1980, U.S. Supreme Ct. 1980, U.S. Ct. Appeals (11th cir.) 1981, U.S. Ct. Appeals (3rd, 7th, 8th cirs.) 1983, U.S. Ct. Appeals (fed. cir.) 1988. Law clk. U.S. Ct. Appeals for D.C. cir., 1971-72; assoc. Wilmer, Cutler & Pickering, Washington, 1973-77; sr. trial atty. civil divsn. fed. program br. U.S. Dept. Justice, 1977-79, mem. appellate staff, 1979-81; ptnr. McReynolds & Mutterperl, Washington, 1981-83, Wilner & Scheiner, Washington, 1983-89, Haley, Bader & Potts, 1989-92; prin. Law Offices of Mary A. McReynolds, P.C., 1992—; bd. dirs., gen. counsel Washington Bach Consort, 1977-81, 1985-92, pres. 1981-82, 89-90; pres. Calla, 1993—. Contbr. articles to profl. jours. Bd. dirs., gen. counsel Washington Bach Consort, 1977-81, 85-92, pres. 1981-82, 89-90; pres. Calla, 1993—. Mem. ABA, Fed. Comms. Bar Assn., Kenwood Club, City Tavern Club. Episcopalian. Home: 2101 Connecticut Ave NW Apt 26 Washington DC 20008-1754 Office: 888 16th St NW Ste 400 Washington DC 20006-4103

MCTEER, ROBERT D., JR., banker. Pres., CEO, Fed. Res. Bank Dallas, Tex. Office: Fed Res Bank Dallas 2200 N Pearl St Dallas TX 75201-2284

MCVAY, BARBARA CHAVES, secondary education mathematics educator; b. Dallas, July 6, 1950; d. Joe M. and Dorothy May (Nock) Chaves; m. David Clyde McVay, Dec. 23, 1968; 1 child, Kathryn McVay Hearn. BS in Math., U. Tex., Arlington, 1971, MS in Math., 1999. Cert. secondary tchr. math., English, Tex. Tchr. math. C.W. Nimitz High Sch. Irving (Tex.) Ind. Sch. Dist., 1972—; bldg. rep. Dallas Tchrs. Credit Union, 1982—; part time lab. instr. North Lake/Dallas County Community Coll., Irving, 1988—. Tchr. Sunday sch. North Dallas Bapt. Ch., 1971-80; ch. tng. leader 1st Bapt. Ch., Irving, 1981-85. Mem. NEA, Tex. State Tchrs. Assn., Irving Edn. Assn. (rep. 1980—), Nat. Coun. Tchrs. Math., Tex. Coun. Tchrs. Math., Greater Dallas Coun. Tchrs. Math., Math. Assn. Am., Delta Kappa Gamma. Republican. Avocations: crafts, sewing, needlework. Office: CW Nimitz High Sch 100 W Oakdale Rd Irving TX 75060-6833

MCVEIGH, JOSEPH, lawyer, geologist; b. N.Y.C., May 24, 1954; s. Joseph and Magdalene McVeigh; m. Denise; 1 child, Brendan. BS, Rutgers U., 1976; JD, Gonzaga U., 1984. Bar: N.Y., N.J., Colo., Idaho. Attorney Ebasco Svcs., N.Y.C., 1985-87, U.S. Envriron. Protection Agy., N.Y.C., 1987—; hydrogeologist Cleve. Cliffs Iron Co., Casper, Wyo., 1976-80, Wahler Assocs., Denver, 1980-81. Office: US Environ Protection Agy 290 Broadway New York NY 10007-1823

MCVEY, TRAVIS LYNN, manufacturing technician; b. Scottsburg, Ind., Apr. 4, 1970; s. John Richard and Karen Sue McV.; m. Lori Carol McVey, Aug. 24, 1996. Student, Vol. State U., Nashville, 1993-94. Operating technician Bridgestone/Firestone, Morrison, Tenn., 1994—. Sgt. USMC, 1989-93. With USMCR, 1993-96. Tchr. North Warren Ch. of Christ, McMinnville, Tenn., 1997—. Mem. Am. Legion Nashville Post. Recipient Humanitarian Svc. medal Dept. Navy, 1996. Republican. Mem. Ch. of Christ. Avocations: reading, walking, writing, SCUBA diving. Home: 425 Parkhurst Rd Mc Minnville TN 37110-7608 Office: Bridgestone/Firestone Old Wells Rd Morrison TN 37110

MCVIE, JOHN GORDON, research administrator, oncologist; b. Glasgow, Scotland, Jan. 13, 1945; s. John and Lindsaye Woodburn (Mair) McV.; children: Malcolm John, Tammas Angus, Douglas Gordon; m. Claudia Joan Burke, Aug. 31, 1998. BS in Pathology with honors, Edinburgh (Scotland) U., 1967, MBChB, 1969, MD, 1978; DSc (hon.), Abertay U., Dundee, Scotland, 1996, Nottingham U., 1997, Portsmouth U., 1999; F Med. Sci., 1998, FRCS Edn., 2000. Lectr. therapeutics Edinburgh (Scotland) U., 1971-76; sr. lectr. clin. oncology Glasgow (Scotland) U., 1976-80; head clin. rsch. unit The Netherlands Cancer Inst., Amsterdam, 1980-84, clin. rsch. dir., 1984-89; sci. dir. Cancer Rsch. Campaign, London, 1984-96, dir. gen., 1996—; chmn. Pharmacokinetics and Metabolism Group, 1984-87, fellowship program Internat. Union Against Cancer, Geneva, 1990— ; mem. Med. Rsch. Coun. Cancer Therapy Ctr., Eng ., 1984-92. Co-author: Cancer Assessment and Monitoring, 1979, Autologous Bone Marrow Transplantation and Solid Tumours, 1984, Microspheres and Drug Therapy, 1984, Clinical and Experimental Pathology and Biology of Lung Cancer, 1985; European editor: Jour. Nat. Cancer Inst., Bethesda, Md., 1994—. Mem. European Orgn. Rsch. and Treatment of Cancer (lung cancer coop. group 1981-88, protocol rev. com. 1984-91, pres. 1994-97, exec. com., bd. dirs. 1997-00). Avocations: opera, theatre, cooking, Italian wine, Scottish poetry. Office: Cancer Rsch Campaign, 10 Cambridge Terr, NW1 4JL London England

MCWHIRTER, NORRIS DEWAR, publisher, author, broadcaster; b. London, Aug. 12, 1925; s. William Allan and Margaret Moffat (Williamson) McW.; m. Carole Eckert, Dec. 28, 1957 (dec. 1987); children: Jane Margaret, Alasdair William; m. Tessa Mary Pocock, Mar. 26, 1991. Student Marlborough Coll., 1939-43; BA in Econs., Trinity Coll., Oxford, 1947, MA in Contract Law, 1950. Founder and dir. McWhirter Twins Ltd., London, 1951—; athletics corr. The Star, 1951-64, The Observer, 1951-67; editor and pub. Athletics World, 1952-57; dir. Guinness Superlatives Ltd. (now Guinness Publs. Ltd.), London, 1954-96; mng. dir., 1954-76; commentator Olympic Games BBC radio, 1952-56, TV, 1960-72; presenter BBC TV Record Breakers, London, 1972-92; founding editor Guinness Book of Records, London, 1954-86; founder, chmn. Redwood Press, Trowbridge, Wiltshire, England, 1966-72; dir. Gieves Group plc, 1972-95; chmn. William McWhirter & Sons, Glasgow, 1955-87, Ross Films Ltd., 1998—. Publications include: Get To Your Marks, 1951; Guinness Book of World Records (founder, editor and compiler in 37 langs. 1955-86); Dunlop Books of Facts, 1964, 1966; Guinness Book of Answers, 1976-93; Ross, Story of a Shared Life, 1976, Treason at Maastricht, 1994, Time and Space, 1998. Parliamentary candidate Conservative Party, Orpington, Kent, 1962-66; mem. Sports Coun. for England, 1970-74; co-founder, chmn. The Freedom Assn., London, 1975—. Served sub.-lt. R.N.V.R., 1943-46. Named Comdr. Order Brit. Empire, 1980; recipient Free Enterprise Spl. award Aims of Industry, London, 1983. Anglican. Clubs: Vincent's (Oxford); Carlton (London). Office: Guinness Pub, 222 The Strand, London WC2R 1BB, England*

MCWHORTER, JERRY EVAN, accountant; b. Kaufman, Tex., Nov. 8, 1947; s. Evan McWhorter and Frances Louise Tidwell; m. Edith Faye Struck, Mar. 1, 1969 (div. Jan. 1989); children: Brandon Keith, Kevin Bradley, Vincent Kyle; m. Mary June Madison, Aug. 5, 1989. BBA in Acctg., U. Tex., Arlington, 1972. CPA. Acct. City of Dallas, 1973-79, gen. ledger supr., 1981-85, acting mgr. water acctg. and fin., 1985-86, fixed asset mgr., 1986, asst. city controller, 1986-98, spl. project acct., 1999; cons. MWS Cons., Inc., Chgo., 1979-80, EBASCO Bus. Consulting, N.Y.C., 1980-81. Chief warrant officer U.S. Army, 1970-2000. Mem. Govt. Fin. Officers Assn., Govt. Fin. Officers Assn. Tex., Tex. Soc. CPA. Baptist. Home: 506 Bermuda Ct Arlington TX 76011-2222

MCWHORTER, SHARON LOUISE, business executive, inventor, consultant; b. Feb. 22, 1951; d. Leroy Byron Harris Jr. and Josiebell (Richards) Harris Aaron; m. Abner McWhorter II, Mar. 15, 1969 (div. Aug. 1974); 1 child, Abner III. BA, Wayne State U., 1988; cert., SBA, Detroit, 1978; cert.

in sound engring., Detroit Rec. Inst., Warren, Mich., 1982. Directory asst. Mich. Bell Telephone Co., Detroit, 1969; quality control clk. Chevrolet Gear & Axle, Detroit, 1971-74; circulation clk. Wayne County C.C., Detroit, 1977-85, mem. libr. standing com. and open house com., 1983-84; pres. Galactic Concepts & Designs, Detroit, 1977-88, cons., 1983—; gen. ptnr., mgr. S.M.J. Corridor Devel., Detroit, 1982—, hist. rschr., 1982; del. Small Bus. Conf., 1981; ad hoc mem. Minority Tech. Coun., 1981-82; elected alt. Mich. del. White House Conf. on Small Bus., Washington, 1985-86; lectr., cons. Author, editor: Creative Dilemma newsletter, 1985—; co-patentee cup holding apparatus. Vol. counselor Barat House/March of Dimes, Detroit, 1977; active Concerned Citizens Cass Corridor, Detroit, 1982-87, Cass Corridor Citizen's Patrol, Detroit, 1983-84, Empowerment Zone Devel. Corp., Detroit, 1996—, bd. dirs., corp. chair, 1997—; pres. Wayne County chpt. MADD, Mich., 1987-88; apptd. citizen rev. com, 1988—; mem. adv. bd. Neighborhood Family Initiative, Southeastern Cmty. Found.; pres. Am. Res. Tng. Sys., Inc., 1990—. Recipient Hist. Landmark award Dept. Interior, 1983, cert. appreciation Tri-County Substance Abuse Awareness Com., 1984. Mem. Inventors Coun. Mich. (bd. dirs. 1985-88), Black Women in Bus. (sec. 1984-85), Greater Detroit C. of C., South Cass Bus. Assn. (v.p. 1987-88, pres. 1988-89), Detroit Econ. Club. Democrat. Methodist. Avocations: inventing, photography, video production. Office: SMJ Corridor Devel Co 453 Myrtle St Ste 102 Detroit MI 48201-2311

MCWILLIAMS, CHARLES HENRY (SIR CHARLES HENRY MCWILLIAM), educational administrator, researcher; b. Coral Gables, Fla., Sept. 11, 1952; s. Charles McWilliams and Suzanne Jones; m. Susan Robinson, oct. 13; children: Carla, Angela. D Acupuncture, Inst. Modern Scis., Mexico City, 1980; D Homeopathic Medicine, Internat. Inst. Homeopatia, Mexico City, 1981; diploma in herbal medicine, Nat. Inst. Chinese Medicine, Hong Kong, 1982; MD, Open Internat. U., Sri Lanka, 1992; DLitt honoris causa, Open Internat. U., 1997, Hon. Prof. Medicine, 1997; MB, BS, U. Med. Scis., Colombo, Sri Lanka, 1998. Dir. Am. Sch. Oriental and Homeopathic Medicine, Miami Beach, Fla., 1979-86, Jade Acad., Charlestown, St. Kitts and Nevis, 1992—, Pan Am. Sch. Bioenergetics, Charlestown, 1994—; pres. Universal Tech. Ltd., Charlestown, 1989—. Author: Treatise of Acupuncture and Homeopathy, 19 vols., 1981—, (paperback) Photobiotics, 1995, Your Cure for Cancer, Only Skin Deep, 1997. Named Knight of Malta, 2000. Mem. Knights of Malta. Home and Office: Pan Am Sch Bioenergetics, PO Box 553, Charlestown Saint Kitts and Nevis

MCWILLIAMS, CHRIS PATER ELISSA, elementary school educator; b. Cin., Oct. 23, 1937; d. Ray C. and Mary Loretta (Collins) Pater; m. Nabeel David Elissa, Aug. 15, 1964 (dec. Aug. 1975); children: Sue Renee Caplan, Ramsey Nabeel; m. Jim Bill McWilliams, Apr. 14, 1977 (dec. Sept. 1993). BA, Our Lady of Cin. Coll., 1959; MEd, Xavier U., 1965. Cert. tchr. elem., social studies, environ. edn., Tex. Elem. tchr. Cin. Parochial Schs., 1960-64, Champaign County Schs., Urbana, Ohio, 1968; tchr. social studies St. Mary's Elem. Sch., Urbana, 1968-73; tchr. Granbury (Tex.) Ind. Sch. Dist., 1981—; instr. Tarleton State U., Stephenville, Tex., 1989-90. Contbr. (text) Texas: Yesterday, Today and Tomorrow, 1988; music editor (newspaper) Jerusalem Star, 1966. Me. Hood Gen. Hosp. Aux., 1978—; chmn. Hood County Blood Drive, Granbury, 1978-82. Recipient scholarship Our Lady of Cin. Coll., 1955, Betty Crocker Homemaker award, Gen. Mills, 1955. Mem. Tex. Alliance for Geog. Edn., Phi Delta Kappa, Delta Kappa Gamma (pres. Lambda Pi chpt. 1988-90, 96-98). Roman Catholic. Avocations: piano, reading, needlework, cooking, walking. Home: 204 Northwood Ct Granbury TX 76049-5732

MCWILLIAMS, NANCY RILEY, psychotherapist, educator; b. Abington, Pa., Oct. 26, 1945; d. Howard Gordon and Millicent (Wood) Riley; m. Wilson Carey McWilliams, Sept. 16, 1966; children: Susan Jane, Helen Elizabeth. AB, Oberlin Coll., 1967; MS, Rutgers U., 1973, PhD, 1976. Dir. Camp Edith Newell, 1968, 69; lectr., instr., co-adj. prof. Bklyn. Coll., 1970, Fordham U., 1970, Livingston Coll., 1972-79, Rutgers Coll., 1973-74, Douglas Coll., 1975; mental health clinician Rutgers Mental Health Center, Coll. Medicine and Dentistry N.J., Piscataway, 1973-74; pvt. practice psychotherapy, Flemington, N.J., 1978—; vis. prof. Grad. Sch. Applied and Profl. Psychology, Rutgers U., New Brunswick, N.J., 1981—, supr., 1978—. Author: Psychoanalytic Diagnosis, 1994, Psychoanalytic Case Formation, 1999. V.p. Flemington-Raritan Bd. Edn., 1987-91; bd. dirs. Flemington Free Pub. Libr., 1994—, Anderson House Halfway House. Mem. APA, Nat. Psychol. Assn. Psychoanalysis, Inst. Psychoanalysis and Psychotherapy of N.J. (bd. dirs. 1989—), Assn. Advancement Psychology, Rotary Internat. Democrat. Home and Office: 9 Mine St Flemington NJ 08822-1515

MDA, ZANEMVULA KIZITO, film producer, writer, educator; b. Herschel, Ea. Cape, South Africa, Oct. 6, 1948; s. Ashby Peter and Rose Nompumelelo (Mtshula) M.; m. Margaret Mpho Seema, Dec. 22, 1978 (div. May, 1991); children: Neo, Thandi, Dini; m. Adele Madikoma Mavuso, Feb. 22, 1992; children: Zukile, Zukiswa. MA, MFA, U. Ohio, Athens, Ohio, 1984; PhD, U. Cape Town, South Africa, 1989. Program dir. Radio Lesotho, Maseru, Southern Africa, 1984-85; prof. U. Lesotho, Roma, Lesotho, Southern Africa, 1985-92; vis. rsch. fellow Yale U., New Haven, Conn., 1992-93; prof. U. Vermont, Burlington, 1993-94, U. Witwatersrand, Johannesburg, South Africa, 1994-95; dramaturg Market Theatre, Johannesburg, 1995—; mem. bd. govs. Fuba Acad., Johannesburg, South Africa, 1994—; editor Vivlia Publishers, Johannesburg, 1994—; dir., producer, Thapama Prodns., Johannesburg, 1995—; bd. dirs. Dalro (Pty) Ltd., Johannesburg, 1996. Playwright: The Road, 1983 (Christina Crawford award 1984), The Nun's Romantic Story, 1992 (Olive Schreiner award 1996); author (novels) She Plays with the Darkness, 1995 (Sanlam award 1995), Ways of Dying, 1995 (CNA honorable mention 1996, M-Net Book prize 1997). Mem. Task Force on Migrant Labour, Maseru, Lesotho, 1988, U.S. Postal Svc. Customer Adv. Coun., Burlington, Vt., 1993-94. Named Amstel Playwright of Yr., Johannesburg, 1979, Hon. Mem. Internat. Understanding Honor Soc., Ohio U. chpt., 1984; recipient Fulbright-Hayes fellowship, U.S. Govt., 1983. Mem. Screenwriters Inst. (bd. dirs. 1985-92), Internat. Fedn. for Theatre Rsch., Royal Soc. of Lit. Avocations: music, painting, composing. Home: 15 Besembos Ave, Gauteng Weltevreden Park 1715, South Africa Office: Thapama Prodns CC Ste 109, Postnet X9, Gauteng Melville 2109, South Africa

MDLADLANA, SHEPERD, South African government official. Minister of labor Govt. of South Africa, Pretoria, 1998—. Office: Ministry Labor Laboria Bldg, Schoeman St Pvt Bag X499, Pretoria 0001, South Africa*

MEACHIN, DAVID JAMES PERCY, investment banker; b. Teignmouth, Devon, Eng., Jan. 1, 1941; came to U.S., 1969; s. James Alfred and Ena Annie Meachin; m. Barbara Marshall Maxwell, Sept. 25, 1971; children: Jonathan J.M., Philip D.M. BS in Phys. Sci., U. Natal, Republic of South Africa, 1960; BSChemE, U. Cape Town, Republic of South Africa, 1963; MS in Petroleum Engring., French Petroleum Inst., Paris, 1965; diploma in Indsl. Mgmt., Cambridge (Eng.) U., 1966; MBA with distinction, Harvard U., 1971. Project engr. Humphreys and Glasgow Ltd., London, 1966-69; 2nd v.p. investment banking Smith Barney and Co. Inc., N.Y.C. and Tokyo, 1971-75; v.p., gen. mgr. internat. corp. fin. Salomon Bros., N.Y.C. and London, 1975-81; mng. dir. investment banking divsn. Merrill Lynch Capital Markets, N.Y.C., 1981-91; chmn., CEO, Cross Border Enterprises L.L.C., 1991—; dir. Millennium Chemicals Inc.; bd. dirs. Millenium Chems. Inc. Dir. Spartek Emerging Opportunities of India Fund; dir., past chmn. Brit. Am. Ednl. Found.; elder Brick Presbyn. Ch., N.Y.C., 1988—; bd. dirs., vice-chmn. U. Cape Town Fund, N.Y.C., 1985—. Mem. Misquamicut Club (bd. govs.), Watch Hill Yacht Club, Hurlingham Club (U.K.), United Oxford and Cambridge Club (U.K.), Harvard Club, Union Club, Sky Club, Kelvin Grove Club (South Africa). Avocations: sailing, golf, tennis, squash. Home: 40 E 94th St New York NY 10128-0709 Office: Cross Border Enterprises LLC 441 Lexington Ave New York NY 10017-3910

MEAD, CARL DUANE, gallery owner, educator; b. Hastings, Mich., June 1, 1939; s. Kenneth N. and Ruth B. (Martz) M. BS, Albion Coll., 1961. Cert. secondary sch. tchr. Dir., owner The Rendezvous Gallery, Aberdeen, Scotland, 1975-99; dir. scholarship program The Rendezvous Gallery, Aberdeen, 1995-99; head master, organizer Am. Sch. Great Yarmouth, Eng., 1968-72; founder, organizer Am. Sch. Aberdeen, 1972-75; headmaster Taymouth Castle Summer Internat. Sch., Kenmore, Eng., 1973-75; educator The Ormes Sch. Mayer, Ariz., 1967-71, Internat. Sch. The Hague (The Netherlands), 1971-72. Author over 100 exhibn. catalogues. Mem. Aberdeen Art Gallery. Address: 100 Forest Ave, Aberdeen AB15 4TL, Scotland

MEAD, DANA GEORGE, diversified industrial manufacturing company executive; b. Cresco, Iowa, Feb. 22, 1936; s. George Francis and Evelyn Grace (Derr) M.; m. Nancy L. Cooper, Apr. 12, 1958; children: Dana George Jr., Mark Cooper. B.S. (Disting. Cadet), U.S. Mil. Acad., 1957; Ph.D., M.I.T., 1967. Commd. 2d lt. U.S. Army, 1957, advanced through grades to col., 1974; service in W. Ger. and Vietnam; White House fellow, 1970-71; staff asst. to Pres. Nixon, 1970-72; assoc. dir., then dep. dir. Domestic Council, White House, 1972-74; permanent prof. social sci. dept., dep. head U.S. Mil. Acad., 1974-78; ret., 1978; v.p. human resources Internat. Paper Co., N.Y.C., 1978-81, v.p., group exec., 1981-87; sr. v.p. Internat. Paper Co., Purchase, 1987-89, exec. v.p., dir, 1989-92; pres., COO Tenneco, Inc., Houston, 1992-93, chmn., CEO, 1994-99, also bd. dirs.; chmn. Pactiv and Tenn. Auto, 1999—; bd. dirs. Logistics Mgmt. Inst., Washington, Pfizer, Inc. Zürich Allied, Zürich Ins., Switzerland. Author articles on nat. security, domestic policy, bus. and mfg. planning, econ. growth and leadership. Mem. Pres.'s Commn. on White House Fellowships, West Point Soc., N.Y., 1980—, pres., 1981-83; mem. White House Fellows Assn. and Found., 1981-98; bd. dirs. White House Fellows Found., 1978-83, pres., 1978; mem. MIT Corp. and Vis. Com. Polit. Scis. Nuc. Engring.; mem. bus. coun., chmn. bus. roundtable, 1998-99; trustee George C. Marshall Found.; chmn. Transatlantic Bus. Dialogue, 1996-97; U.S. chair French-Am. Bus. Com.; chmn. The Mfg. Inst.; nat. bd. girs. Boys and Girls Clubs. Decorated Legion of Merit with oak leaf cluster, Bronze Star with oak leaf cluster, Meritorious Service medal, Air medal with 3 oak leaf clusters, Army Commendation medal, Presdl. Service badge, Combat Inf. badge; Vietnam Cross Gallantry with palm, silver and bronze stars; recipient John J. McCloy award, Mfg. Ledership award, Woodrow Wilson award, Boy Scouts Am. Leadership award, others. Mem. Am. Soc. Corp. Execs., Nat. Assn. Mfg. (chmn. 1995-96), Coun. Fgn. Rels., Assn. Grads. West Point (trustee, life), Univ. Club, Met. Club (N.Y.), Blind Brook Club (Rye), Greenwich Country Club, John's Island Club, Redstick Club (Vero Beach). Republican. Home: 290 Coconut Palm Rd John's Island Vero Beach FL 32963 Office: Ste 100 Eight Sound Shore Dr Greenwich CT 06830

MEAD, FRANK WALDRETH, taxonomic entomologist; b. Columbus, Ohio, June 11, 1922; s. Arlington Alfred and Edith May (Harrison) M.; widowed; children: David Harrison, Gregory Scott. BS, Ohio State U., 1947, MS, 1949; PhD, N.C. State U., 1968. Rsch. asst. dept. physiology Ohio State U., Woods Hole, Mass., summer 1941; rsch. asst. dept. entomology Ohio State U., Columbus, 1948-50; Japanese beetle scout bur. entomology and plant quar. USDA, Columbus, summer 1948, biol. aid bur. entomology and plant quar., 1950-53; entomologist div. plant industry Fla. Dept. Agr., Gainesville, 1953-58, 60, biologist IV, 1983-95, emeritus, 1995—; rsch. asst. N.C. State U., Raleigh, 1958-60; state survey entomologist Fed.-State Coop. Survey, Gainesville, 1969-80; courtesy assoc. prof. dept. entomology U. Fla., Gainesville, 1973-95, emeritus, 1995—, Fla. A&M U., Tallahassee, 1977-95, emeritus, 1995—. Co-editor Tri-ology Technical Report; contbr. articles to profl. jours. Bd. dirs., treas. Alachua Audubon Soc., Gainesville, 1968-75, 77-82; bd. dirs. Alachua County Hist. Soc. (hon. lifetime mem. 1998), Gainesville, 1980-82; former mem. steering com. Civitan Regional Blood Bank, Gainesville, 1977-79; vol. photographer P.K. Yonge Devel. Rsch. Sch. U. Fla., Gainesville, 1978—; vol. Project Graduation, U. Fla., 1994—. Ohio Acad. Sci. fellow, 1966. Mem. VFW, Internat. Order of Merit, Cambridge, Entomol. Soc. Am. (bd. dirs. S.E. br. 1978-79), Ga. Entomol. Soc., Fla. Entomol. Soc. (hon., sec. 1968-82, Cert. of Appreciation 1975, 82, 91, Cert. of Merit 1986), Fla. Mosquito Control Assn., Entomol. Soc. Washington, Soc. Systematic Biologists, SAR (Benjamin Franklin chpt. Columbus, Ohio), The Am. Legion (life), Sierra Club, Fla. Track Club, Military Book Club. Avocations: photography, history, birding. Home: 2035 NE 6th Ter Gainesville FL 32609-3758 Office: Fla Dept Agr and Cons Svcs Divsn Plant Industry PO Box 147100 Gainesville FL 32614-7100

MEAD, JAMES MATTHEW, insurance company executive; b. Erie, Pa., June 10, 1945; s. James Leonard and Olga (Richter) M.; m. Rhoda Ginsburg, Sept. 2, 1967 (div. 1971); m. Elaine Margaret Lytle, Mar. 8, 1975. BS, Pa. State U., 1967, MA, 1970. Instr. bus. Pa. State U., Middletown, 1968-71; asst. to ins. commr. Commonwealth of Pa., Harrisburg, 1971-74; asst. to pres. Capital Blue Cross, Harrisburg, 1974-78, sr. v.p., 1978-84, pres., CEO, 1984—; bd. dirs. Blue Cross & Blue Shield Assn., Chgo., BCS Fin., Chgo., Mellon Bank Com. Reg., Fed. Res. Bank Phila., chmn. 1994-95. Contbr. articles on health care to profl. publs. Mem. bd. advisors Pa. State U., 1985-93; chmn. savs. bond campaign for Ctrl. Pa., U.S. Treasury Dept., Harrisburg, 1986-87; bd. dirs. United Way Capital Region, 1994-98, pres. 1994. Paul Harris fellow Rotary Internat., 1988. Mem. Capital Region C. of C. (bd. dirs., treas. 1987-90), Country Club of Harrisburg, Blue Ridge Country Club. Home: 201 Hearth Rd Camp Hill PA 17011-8455

MEAD, WALTER RUSSELL, editor, foreign policy organization fellow; b. June 12, 1959; s. Loren Benjamin and Polly Ayers Mead. BA in English, Yale U., 1976. Chief writer Cuomo Commn. on Competetiveness and Trade, N.Y.C., 1987-88; contbg. editor L.A. Times, N.Y.C., 1991—; contbg. editor Worth Mag., N.Y.C., 1993-96, sr. contbg. editor, 1996—; pres.'s fellow World Policy Inst., New Sch. U., N.Y.C., 1994-97; sr. fellow U.S. fgn. policy Coun. on Fgn. Rels., N.Y.C., 1997—. Author: Mortal Splendor, 1987; chief staff writer: U.S.-Cuban Relations in the 21st Century: Report of an Independent Task Force Council on Foreign Relations, 1999; contbr. articles to profl. jours. Bd. dirs. New Am. Found., Washington, Arca Found., Washington. Finalist L.A. Times Book award, 1986, finalist for essays and commentary Nat. Mag. awards, 1998; fellow Breadloaf Writers' Conf., 1987; recipient NYU Olive Br. award, 1993. Fellow Fgn. Policy Assn. (hon.); mem. Author's Guild, Coun. Fgn. Rels. Office: Coun on Fgn Rels 58 E 68th St New York NY 10021-5953

MEADER, JOHN DANIEL, judge; b. Ballston Spa, N.Y., Oct. 22, 1931; s. Jerome Clement and Doris Luella (Conner) M.; m. Joyce Margaret Cowin, Mar. 2, 1963; children: John Daniel Jr., Julia Rae, Keith Alan. BA, Yale U., 1954; JD, Cornell U., 1962. Bar: N.Y. 1963, U.S. Dist. Ct. (no. dist.) N.Y. 1963, U.S. Ct. Appeals (2d cir.) 1966, U.S. Supreme Ct. 1967, U.S. Ct. Mil. Appeals 1973, Ohio 1978, U.S. Dist. Ct. (no. dist.) Ohio 1979, Fla. 1983, U.S. Ct. Appeals (4th cir.) 1992, U.S. Ct. Appeals (fed. cir.) 1993. Sales engr. Albany (N.Y.) Internat. Corp., 1954-59; asst. track coach Cornell U., 1959-62; asst. sec., asst. to pres. Albany Internat. Corp., 1962-65; asst. atty. gen. State of N.Y., Albany, 1965-68; ops. counsel, attesting sec. GE, Schenectady, 1968-77; gen. counsel, asst. sec. Glidden div. SCM Corp., Cleve., 1977-81; chmn. bd., pres. Applied Power Tech. Co., Fernandina Beach, Fla., 1981-84; pres. Applied Energy, Inc., Ballston Spa, 1984-88; judge N.Y. State Workers Compensation Bd., Albany, 1988—; dir. Saratoga Mut. Fire Ins. Co. Author: Labor Law Manual, 1972, Contract Law Manual, 1974, Patent Law Manual, 1978. Candidate U.S. Ho. of Reps., 29th Dist. N.Y., 1964, N.Y. Supreme Ct., 1975, 87, 93. Col. JAGC, USAR, 1968—, dep. staff judge adv. 3d U.S. Army & Cen. Command, 1984. Nat. AAU High Sch. 1000 Yard Indoor Track Champion, 1949, Nat. AAU Prep. Sch. 440 and 880 Yard Indoor Track Champion, 1950, Nat. AAU Outstanding Performer award, Melrose Games Assn., 1950, Heptagonal Track 880-Yard Champion 1954. Mem. ABA, N.Y. State Bar Assn., Fla. Bar, Amelia Island Plantation Club, Cyprus Temple Club, Yale Club Jacksonville (pres.), Masons. Republican. Presbyterian. Home: 271 Round Lake Rd Ballston Lake NY 12019-1714 Office: NY State Workers Compensation Bd 100 Broadway Albany NY 12241-0001

MEADOR, CHARLES LAWRENCE, management and systems consultant, educator; b. Dallas, Oct. 7, 1946; s. Charles Leon and Dorothy Margaret (Brown), m. Diane E. Collins, May 18, 1985. BSME with honors, U. Tex., 1970; MSME, MS in Mgmt., MIT, 1972. Engring. staff Union Carbide Corp., Houston, 1967-68; instr. Alfred P. Sloan Sch. Mgmt. MIT, Cambridge, 1972-75, asst. dir. Ctr. Info. Systems Rsch., 1976-78, lectr. Sch. Engring., co-dir. Macro-Engring. Rsch. Group, 1978-99; founder, pres. Decision Support Tech., Inc., 1974-92; co-founder, vice-chmn., dir. Software Productivity Rsch., Inc., 1985-87; pres., dir. The Softbridge Group, 1989-92; founder, CEO, Mgmt. Support Tech. Corp., 1992-99; sr. v.p., chief info. officer CIGNA Property and Casualty, 1995-98; vice-chmn., dir. Condor Tech. Solutions, Inc., 1998—; co-founder, chmn., dir. Clinician Support Tech., Inc., 1999—. Editor: How Big and Still Beautiful? Macro-Engineering Revisited, 1980, Macro-Engineering: The Rich Potential, 1981, Macro-Engineering and the Future: A Management Perspective, 1982, Macro-Engineering: Global Infrastructure Solutions, 1992, Macro-Engineering: MIT Brunel Lectures on Global Infrastructure, 1997; mem. editorial bd. Computer Comm., 1979-91; contbr. articles to profl. jours. NSF trainee, 1970; MIT Wilfred Lewis fellow, 1971, Draper Lab. fellow, 1974. Mem. Computer Soc. IEEE (vice-chmn. Ea. Hemisphere and Latin Am. area com. 1977-83), Am. Soc. for Macro-Engring. (bd. dirs. 1992-96), Cosmos Club, St. Botolph's Club, Sigma Xi, Tau Beta Pi, Pi Tau Sigma. Home: 3 Windy Hill Ln Wayland MA 01778-2612 Office: Clinician Support Tech Inc 3 Speen St Framingham MA 01701-4679

MEADOR, DANIEL JOHN, law educator; b. Selma, Ala., Dec. 7, 1926; s. Daniel John and Mabel (Kirkpatrick) M.; m. Janet Caroline Heilmann, Nov. 19, 1955; children: Janet Barrie, Anna Kirkpatrick, Daniel John. BS, Auburn U., 1949; JD, U. Ala., 1951; LLM, Harvard U., 1954; LLD (hon.), U. S.C., 1998. Bar: Ala. 1951, Va. 1961. Law clk. to Justice Hugo L. Black U.S. Supreme Ct., 1954-55; assoc. firm Lange, Simpson, Robinson & Somerville, Birmingham, Ala., 1955-57; faculty U. Va. Law Sch., Charlottesville, 1957-66, prof. law, 1961-66; prof., dean U. Ala. Law Sch., 1966-70; James Monroe prof. law U. Va., Charlottesville, 1970-94, prof. emeritus, 1994—; asst. atty. gen. U.S., 1977-79, dir. grad. program for judges, 1979-95; Fulbright lectr., U.K., 1965-66; vis. prof. U.S. Mil. Acad., 1984; chmn. Southeastern Conf. Assn. Am. Law Schs., 1964-65; chmn. Cts. Task Force Nat. Adv. Commn. on Criminal Justice, 1971-72; dir. appellate justice project Nat. Ctr. for State Cts., 1972-74; mem. Adv. Coun. on Appellate Justice, 1971-75, Coun. on Role of Cts., 1978-84; bd. dirs. State Justice Inst., 1986-92; exec. dir. commn. on structural alternatives Fed. Ct. Appeals, 1998-99. Author: Preludes to Gideon, 1967, Criminal Appeals-English Practices and American Reforms, 1973, Mr. Justice Black and His Books, 1974, Appellate Courts: Staff and Process in the Crisis of Volume, 1974, (with Carrington and Rosenberg) Justice on Appeal, 1976, Impressions of Law in East Germany, 1986, American Courts, 1991, (with J. Bernstein) Appellate Courts in the United States, 1994, His Father's House, 1994, Unforgotten, 1999, (with Rosenberg and Carrington) Appellate Courts: Structures, Functions, Processes, and Personnel, 1994; editor: Hardy Cross Dillard: Writings and Speeches, 1995; editor Va. Bar News, 1962-65; contbr. articles to profl. jours. 1st lt. U.S. Army, 1951-53; col. JAGC, USAR ret. Decorated Bronze Star.; IREX fellow German Dem. Republic, 1983. Mem. ABA (chmn. standing com. on fed. jud. improvements 1987-90), Ala. Bar Assn., Va. Bar Assn. (exec. com. 1983-86), Am. Law Inst., Am. Judicature Soc. (bd. dirs. 1975-77, 80-83), Soc. Pub. Tchrs. Law, Am. Soc. Legal History (bd. dirs. 1968-71), Order of Coif, Raven Soc., Phi Delta Phi, Omicron Delta Kappa, Kappa Alpha. Presbyn. Office: U Va Sch Law 580 Massie Rd Charlottesville VA 22903-1738

MEADOWS, PATRICIA BLACHLY, art curator, civic worker; b. Amarillo, Tex., Nov. 12, 1938; d. William Douglas and Irene Bond Blachly; m. Curtis Washington Meadows, Jr., June 10, 1961; children: Michael Lee, John Morgan. BA in English and History, U. Tex., 1960. Program dir. Ex-Students Assn., Austin, Tex., 1960-61; co-founder, dir. Dallas Visual Art Ctr., 1981-86, curator, 1987-98, bd. dirs., 1981-99, pres. bd. dirs., 1982-85, founder The Collectors, 1988; founder, prin. cons. Art Connections, Dallas, 1996—; sr. v.p. Hall Fin. Group Ltd., 1999—; exhbn. dir. Tex. bd. Nat. Mus. Women in Arts, Washington, 1986-91; mem. acquisition com. Dallas Mus. Art, 1988-92; chmn. adv. bd. Oaks Bank and Trust, 1993-96; juror numerous exhibits, Dallas and Tex.; spkr. on arts subjects; cons. city, state and nat. project concerning arts; chmn. bd. dirs. State-Thomas TIF Zone #1, 1994-99, bd. dirs. 1989-99; art cons. Art Connections, 1996—. Author: (art catalogues) Critic's Choice, 1983-97, Texas Women, 1989-90, Texas: reflections, rituals, 1991; organizer many exhbns. including Presenting Nine, D-Art Visual Art Ctr., 1984, Mosaics, 1991-97, Senses Beyond Sight, 1992-93. Bd. dirs. Mid-Am. Arts Alliance, Kansas City, Mo., 1989-93, Tex. Bd. Commerce, Austin, 1991-93, Women's Issues Network, Dallas, 1994-96; bd. dirs. Dallas Summit, 1989-95, pres., 1993-94, mem. 1988—; mem. Charter 100, 1993—, Dallas Assembly , 1993—, Leadership Tex., 1987; co-founder, mem. steering com. Emergency Artists Support League, Dallas, 1992-99; mem. originating task force Dallas Coalition for Arts, 1984; also others. Recipient Dedication to Arts award Tex. Fine Arts Assn., 1984, Assn. Artists and Craftsmen, 1984, Southwestern Watercolor Soc., 1985, Flora award Dallas Civic Garden Ctr., 1987, James K. Wilson award TACA, 1988, Maura award Women's Ctr. Dallas, 1991, Disting. Woman award Northwood U., 1993, Excellence in the Arts award Dallas Hist. Soc., 1993, Legend award Dallas Visual Art Ctr., 1996. Mem. Tex. Assn. Mus., Arts Dist. Mgmt. Assn. (bd. dirs., exec. com. 1984-92, Artists and Craftsmen Assn. (pres. bd. dirs. 1982-83), Dallas Art Dealer's Assn. (pres. 1997-99). Presbyterian. Office: Hall Financial Group 6801 Gaylord Pkwy Ste 100 Frisco TX 75034-8545

MEADS, DONALD EDWARD, management services company executive; b. Salem, Mass., Sept. 23, 1920; s. Laurence G. and Gertrude F. Meads; m. Jane Lightner, June 15, 1943; children: Edward G., Robert C., Laurence G., Judith C. Antrim, Suzanne M. O'Neil, Clifford L., Nancy Chapin. AB in Pre-Law, Dartmouth Coll., 1942; MBA in Fin., Harvard U., 1947. V.p., vice chmn. investment com. N.Y. Life Ins Co., N.Y.C., 1947-61; v.p. fin., chmn. investment com. Investors Diversified Svcs. Inc., Mpls., 1961-65; pres., CEO Internat. Basic Economy Corp., N.Y.C., 1965-67, chmn., CEO, 1967-71; exec. v.p., dir., CFO, chmn. investment com. INA Corp., Phila., 1971-74; chmn. bd., CEO CertainTeed Corp., Valley Forge, Pa., 1974-78, dir., 1973-78; chmn. Mateer-Burt Co., Inc., Plymouth Meeting, Pa., 1984-87, Phila. First Group Inc., 1982-90, Carver Assocs., Inc., West Conshohocken, Pa., 1978—. Hon. life trustee Valley Forge Mil. Acad. and Coll., Wayne, Pa.; trustee emeritus Thomas Jefferson U., Phila.; trustee Connelly Found., Phila.; bd. dirs. Independence Hall Assn., Phila.; hon. dir. Marine Corps Scholarship Found., Princeton, N.J.; mem. Phila. Com. on Fgn. Rels.; mem. adv. bd. World Affairs Coun. Phila. Served to capt. USMC, 1942-45. Decorated DFC, Air medals (6). Mem. Harvard Club N.Y.C., Sunday Breakfast Club, Union League (Phila.).

MEAGHER, DAVID JAMES, psychiatrist, researcher; b. Birmingham, Eng., Nov. 1, 1964; arrived in Ireland, 1976; s. James Marie and Maureen Teresa (Singleton) M.; m. Catherine Noreen O'Boyle; children: James, Emer, Helen. MB, BCh, BAO, Univ. Coll., Dublin, 1988; MSc in Neurosci., U. London, 1996. Diplomate in psychol. medicine. Gen. med. dr. Mater Hosp., Dublin, 1988-90; psychiatry trainee Eastern Health Bd., Dublin, 1990-94; lectr. Univ. Coll., Dublin, 1994-95; sr. registrar St. Ita's Hosp., Dublin, 1995-96, St. Vincent's Hosp., Dublin, 1996-97, St. Davnet's Hosp., Monaghan, 1997—; lectr. tng. body Irish divsn. Royal Coll. Psychiatry, 1994—; lectr. Dublin City U., 1997; cons. psychiatrist St. Ita's Hosp., Dublin, 1998-99, Dept. Clin. Rsch., Crichton Royal Hosp., Dumfries, Scotland, 1999—. Contbr. articles to profl. jours. Mem. Royal Coll. Surgeons, Royal Coll. Psychiatrists, Assn. Psychiatrists Tng. in Ireland (chmn. 1995-97), British Neuropsychiatry Assn., British Assn. Psychopharmacology. Roman Catholic. Avocations: music (guitar), athletics (marathon running), triathlon. Office: Univ Coll Dublin Dept Psych, Dept Clin Rsch, Crichton Royal Hosp, Dumfries DG1 4TG, Scotland

MEAGHER, ROBERT FRANCIS, international economic law consultant; b. Bklyn., May 13, 1927; s. Frances Xavier and Marie Janet (Tallent) M.; m. Donna Marie Dowsett, May 21, 1973 (div. Mar. 1974). B Social Sci., CCNY, 1949; JD, Yale U., 1952. Bar: N.Y. Assoc. Winthrop Stimson Putnam & Roberts, N.Y.C., 1954-58; lawyer UN Relief & Works Agy., Beirut, Lebanon, 1958-60; vis. and adj. prof., assoc. dir. internat. legal rsch. Columbia U. Law Sch., N.Y.C., 1961-73; internat. econ. law cons. Somerville, Mass., 1964—; prof. internat. law Fletcher Sch. Law and Diplomacy Tufts U., Medford, Mass., 1967-92, prof. emeritus, 1992—; legal advisor India Interest Group, 1993—; vis. sr. fellow Overseas Devel. Coun., Washington, 1975-76; vis. prof. Law Harvard Law Sch., Cambridge, Mass., 1984, 89, Melbourne (Australia) U., Monash U., Australia, 1981, Indian Law Inst., New Delhi, 1987-88; lectr. on fgn. policy, fgn. aid, fgn. investment; mem. study groups Coun. Fgn. Rels.; coord. Peace Corps tng. program for lawyers going to Somalia, 1967; coord. workshops in field; lectr. on various

fgn. policy issues Asia, Africa, Mid. East and U.S., 1952—. Editor, contbr. chpt.: Law and Social Change, 1988; co-author: International Financial Aid: A Comparative Study of Policies, Institutions and Methods, 1966; author: An International Redistribution of Wealth and Power: A Study of the Charter of Economic Rights and Duties of States, 1979, Proposed Options for the Future Activities of the U.S. Office of International Activities of the Environmental Protection Agency, 1979; contbr. articles, revs. to profl. publs. Chmn. fgn. policy com. N.Y. Young Dems., N.Y.C., 1956-58; exec. dir. Citizens for Johnson & Humphrey, N.Y.C., 1964; fgn. policy cons. Michael Dukakis, Boston, 1988. With U.S. Army, 1945-46, ETO. Fulbright scholar Bombay (India) Sch. Econs., 1952-53, Indian Law Inst., 1987-88, Ford Found., 1961; Rockefeller grantee, 1975. Mem. ABA (African law subcom., Mid. Eastern law subcom.), African Studies Assn., Am. Fgn. Law Assn., Am. Soc. Internat. Law (bd. rev. and devel. 1980-85, panel on pvt. investment in less developed countries), Asia Soc. (India coun., program com. 1967-69), Assn. Asian Studies, Assn. Bar City of N.Y. (fgn. law com. 1956-58, 65-68, internat. commn. jurist com. 1965-67, lawyers' role in search for peace com. 1976-78, 80-82), Inter-Am. Affairs (program com. 1977-79), Coun. African-Am. Inst., Coun. Fgn. Rels., Internat. Law Assn. (com. fgn. investment), Soc. Internat. Devel., Trade Policy Rsch. Ctr., UN Assn. (bd. dirs. greater Boston/Mass. 1978—), World Peace Through Law Ctr (com. fgn. investments 1967-74). Avocation: wine tasting. E-mail: rfm2@erols.com. Home and Office: 108 Curtis St Somerville MA 02144-1242

MEAL, LARIE, chemistry educator, researcher, consultant; b. Cin., June 15, 1939; d. George Lawrence Meal and Dorothy Louise (Heileman) Fitzpatrick. BS in Chemistry, U. Cin., 1961, PhD in Chemistry, 1966. Rsch. chemist U.S. Indsl. Chems., Cin., 1966-67; instr. chemistry U. Cin., 1968-69, asst. prof., 1969-75, assoc. prof., 1975-90, prof., 1990—, rschr., 1980—; cons. in field. Contbr. articles to profl. jours. Mem. AAAS, N.Y. Acad. Scis., Am. Chem. Soc., NOW, Planned Parenthood, Iota Sigma Pi. Democrat. Avocations: gardening, yard work. Home: 2231 Slane Ave Norwood OH 45212-3615 Office: U Cin 2220 Victory Pky Cincinnati OH 45206-2822

MEALIE, CARL A., physician, educator; b. Astoria, N.Y., Jan. 26, 1948; s. Patrick and Natalie (Previti) M.; m. Maureen Frances Maybury, Apr. 24, 1993; children: David, Ian, Daniel. BA, NYU, 1969; MD, N.Y. Med. Coll., 1974. CCRN. Chmn. Dept. Emergency Medicine St. Mary's Hosp., Roswell, N.Mex., 1975-83; emergency dept. attending physician Guadalupe Med. Ctr., Carlsbad, N.Mex., 1979-83; emergency dept. attending physician L.I. Jewish Med. Ctr., New Hyde Park, N.Y., 1993—, chmn. disaster preparation com., 1991—, asst. chief emergency dept., 1989-95, chief clin. ops., 1995; asst. prof. emergency medicine Albert Einstein Coll. Medicine, N.Y.C., 1995; mem. ambulance adv. bd. Chavez County Med. Soc., Roswell, 1980-83, ambulance bd., 1981-87. Mem. City Roswell EMS Bd., 1981-93. Grantee Min. Health Guatemala Pediat. Inst., 1993. Fellow Am. Coll. Emergency Physicians (key contact 1987—), N.Y. Acad. Medicine; me,. AMA, Am. Acad. Emergency Medicine, N.Y. State Med. Soc., Soc. Acad. Emergency Medicine. Roman Catholic. Avocations: skiing, sailing, hunting, golf. Home: 33 Heights Rd Northport NY 11768-2629 Office: LI Jewish Med Ctr Lakeville New Hyde Park NY 11040

MEALY, J. BURKE (), psychological services administrator. MA in Guidance and Psychology, Assumption Coll., 1966, CAS in Counseling Psychology, 1967; PhD in Clin. Psychology, Duquesne U., 1972. Lic. psychologist, Md; diplomate Profl. Acad. Custody Evaluators,Am. Acad. Forensic Examiners. Clin. psychologist Woodville State Hosp., Carnegie, Pa., 1969-70; dir./psychologist Western State Sch. and Hosp., Canonsburg, Pa., 1970-72; asst. prof. human devel. Calif. State U., Hayward, 1972-73; pvt. practice Md., 1973—; clin. community psychologist Montgomery County Health Dept., Rockville, 1974-78; forensic psychologist Montgomery County Ct., 1978-84; cons. dist., cir. cts. Montgomery County, 1984-88. Mem. APA, Am. Orthopsychiat. Assn., Md. Psychol. Assn. Office: 15817 Crabbs Branch Way Rockville MD 20855-2635

MEANLEY, SARAH, prosthetist, orthotist, consultant; b. Stourbridge, Eng., Dec. 3, 1956; d. George R. Graeme and Joan (Simpson) M. B Engring., Sheffield (Eng.) U., 1978; MSc, Surrey U., Guildford, Eng., 1979; PhD, North Staffordshire Poly., Stoke-on-Trent, Eng., 1984; postgrad. certs. prosthetics & orthotics, Northwestern U., Chgo., 1992; BSc, Strathclyde (Scotland) U., 1999. Rsch. asst. North Staffordshire Poly., Stoke-on-Trent, Eng., 1979-83; rsch. bioengr. The Leprosy Mission Internat., India and U.K., 1984-85; overseas worker orthotics Seconded to Internat. Nepal Fellowship by Tear Fund, 1986-90, overseas worker, appliance design technologist, 1993-97; con. prosthetics Tear Fund, Bangladesh, 1991, 95, 96, cons. cmty. based rehab., Uganda, 1997; prosthetist/orthotist RRC, Birmingham, Eng., 1999—. Mem. Internat. Soc. Prosthetics and Orthotics, Brit. Assn. Prosthetists and Orthotists. Baptist. Avocations: committed Christian, squash, crafts, gardening, do-it-yourself. Office: Oak Tree Ln Centre, Selly Oak, Birmingham England

MEANS, ERIK, editor; b. Mankato, Minn., Nov. 8, 1963; s. Gordon Paul and Ingunn (Norderval) M.; m. Mette Otto, July 7, 1990; children: Matias, Maia. BA in Internat. Politics, U. Western Ont., 1985. Journalist Noroil Pub. Ho., Stavanger, Norway, 1986-88; news editor Noroil mag., Stavanger, 1988-90; editor European Offshore Petroleum newsletter, Stavanger, 1988-90; journalist Tradewinds, Aarhus, Denmark, 1990-96; editor Upstream (internat. oil and gas newspaper), Oslo, 1996-99, editor-in-chief, 1999—. Avocations: basketball, skiing, golfing, squash, travel. Home: Hiltonveien 1C, Slependen 1341, Norway Office: Upstream, PO Box 1182 Sentrum, Oslo 0107, Norway

MEANS, GEORGE ROBERT, organization executive; b. Bloomington, Ill., July 5, 1907; s. Arthur John and Alice (Johnson) M.; m. Martha Cowart, Aug. 5, 1950. B.Ed., Ill. State U., 1930; A.M., Clark U., 1932; HHD (hon.), Rikkyo U., Tokyo; H.H.D. (hon.), Ill. State U.; HHD (hon.), Ill. Wesleyan U., Ky. Wesleyan Coll. Cartographer, map editor, 1932-35; with Rotary Internat., 1935—; beginning as conv. mgr., successively head Middle Asia office Rotary Internat., Bombay, India; asst. gen. sec. Rotary Internat., 1948-52, gen. sec., 1953-72; sec. Rotary Found., 1953-72; dir. Washington Nat. Corp., 1972-80, 4 Way Test Assn., Hertzberg-New Method, Inc., Ind State Retirement Home Guaranty Fund, 1982-95. Author: Rotary's Return to Japan, also numerous articles. Mem.-at-large nat. council Boy Scouts Am. Served as comdr. USNR, 1942-46. Decorated Legion of Honor France; Chilean Order of Merit; Japanese Order of Rising Sun; Italian Order of Merit; recipient Disting. Service award Geog. Soc. Chgo., 1972; Paul Harris fellow The Rotary Found. Fellow Am. Geog. Soc.; mem. Rotary Club (Evanston, Bloomington, Ill., Kyoto, Osaka and Tokyo, Japan, Seoul, Korea, Cape Town, South Africa, Ituzaingo, Saavedra, Argentina, Greenwood, Ind.), Gamma Theta Upsilon. Home: 295 Village Ln Apt 246 Greenwood IN 46143-2475

MEANS, JOHN BARKLEY, foreign language educator, association executive; b. Cin., Jan. 2, 1939; s. Walker Wilson and Rosetta M. Miller (Barkley) M. BA, U. Ill., 1960, MA, 1963, PhD, 1968. U.S. govt. intelligence rsch. analyst on Brazil CIA, Washington, 1962-64; assoc. prof. Spanish and Portugese Temple U., Phila., 1972-82, prof. Portuguese and critical langs., 1982—, co-chmn. dept. Spanish and Portuguese, 1971-75, dir. Center for Critical Langs., 1975—, dir. Inst. for Langs. and Internat. Studies, 1987—, chmn. dept. Germanic and Slavic Langs. and lit., 1992-94, chair univ. core programs, 1995-97; cons. on Brazilian-Portuguese and second lang. acquisition and self-instrnl. programs for less commonly taught langs., 1968—; cons. to founds., pubs., univs. acad. assns. and govt. agys., sch. dists. Editor: Essays on Brazilian Literature, 1971; author: (with others) Language in Education: Theory and Practice, 1988—; contbr. numerous articles to profl. jours. Trustee Bristol (Pa.) Riverside Theatre, 1990—; mng. trustee Means Charitable Trust, 1993—. 1st lt. U.S. Army, 1960-62. NDEA fellow, 1962, 64; grantee U.S. Dept. Edn., 1979-83, Japan Found., 1980, 82, 89-91, ARCO Chem. Found., 1991, 93. Mem. MLA, S.E., S.R., Nat. Coun. on Langs. and Internat. Studies (bd. dirs.), Joint Nat. Com. for Langs. (bd. dirs.), Nat. Assn. Self-Instrnl. Lang. Programs (exec. dir. 1977-98, editor jour. 1978-94, exec. dir. emeritus 1999—), Am. Coun. on Teaching Fgn. Lang., Nat. Coun. Orgns. Less Commonly Taught Langs. (exec. sec.-treas. 1991-2001), Nat. Assn. State Univs. and Land Grant Colls., Pi Kappa Phi, Phi Lambda Beta, Sigma Delta Pi. Home: PO Box 829 Washington Crossing PA 18977-0829 Office: Temple U Ctr for Critical Langs Anderson Hall 1114 W Berks St Philadelphia PA 19122-6007

MEANS, ROSALINE, business executive, business educator; b. Xiamen, Fukien, China; came to U.S., 1952; d. Cheng Peng and Lu Chong (Siy) Limtiuco; m. Cyril Chestnut Means, Jr., Nov. 8, 1958 (dec. Oct., 1992); children: Elizabeth Rose Thayer Means, Annette Thayer Means, Cyril III. AA in Pre-law, U. Santo Tomas, Manila, The Philippines, 1949; BS in Comm. Edn., U. East, Manila, 1951; MA in Edn., U. Iowa, 1953; postgrad., CUNY, 1956-58. Tchr. Chinese Rep. Sch., Manila, 1947-52; corp. dir. and officer various cos. and corps., 1950-70; edn. specialist U. Hosp. Sch., Iowa City, 1952-53; lectr. SUNY Urban Ctr., Bklyn., 1967-73; adj. lectr. cmty. coll. CUNY, 1969-72, various positions, 1973-84; adj. prof. L.I. U., Bklyn., 1978; lectr. Ednl. Opportunity Ctr., Bklyn., 1973-95. Author: First Steps in Conversation, 1954; stage performances include Two for the Seesaw, The Defender, Stage Door. Mem. Legis Adv. Com. N.Y. State Senate, 11th. Dist., 1990; treas. PSC/CUNY. Recipient Cmty. Leaders and Noteworthy Ams. award, 1975-76, Achievement of Recognition award Bus. and Profl. Women of Cape Ann, 1996. Mem. Liedenkranz of City of N.Y., Music Librarian. Avocations: classical music, fishing, boating; candidate Mrs. N.Y. Am. Beauty Pageant, 1990. Home: 44 Fairview Ave Great Neck NY 11023-1224

MEANS, TINA, police officer, consultant; b. L.A., June 9, 1961; d. Melvin Julian and Theresa Alberta Means; m. Marvin Alton Hatchett, July 7, 1995; children: Ciyani, Taliya. AA in Liberal Arts, Santa Monica Coll., 1982; BSBA, Calif. State U.-Dominguez Hill, Carson, 1984; MPA, City U., Bellevue, Wash., 1996; postgrad., Fielding Inst., Santa Barbara, 1998—. Basic, intermediate and advance certs., Calif. Commn. on Peace Officers and Tng.; cert. cons. Police officer trainee, police officer City of Pasadena, Calif., 1990-91; police officer sch. police dept. Pasadena Unified Sch. Dist., 1991—; cons. Pasadena Prep. Sch., 1999—, Internat. Outreach Ministry, Inc., Pasadena, 1999—. Bd. dirs. Pasadena Family Ctr. Mem. ASPA, ASTD, Justice Rsch. and Stats. Assn. Avocations: reading, cooking, singing, planning training seminars. Fax: 626-969-1867. E-mail: tmeans@lalc.k12.ca.us. Home: 350 W Annandale Ln Azusa CA 91702-1432 Office: Pasadena Unified Sch Dist Sch Police Dept 351 S Hudson Ave Pasadena CA 91101-3599

MEANS COLEMAN, ROBIN RENEE, communications educator; b. Pitts., Feb. 26, 1969; d. Marcel Theodore Sr. and Patricia (Lloyd) M.; m. Randy Tyrone Coleman, July 28, 1996. BA in Comm., Chatham Coll., 1991; MA in Comm., U. Mo., Columbia, 1993; PhD in Mass Comm., Bowling Green State U., 1996; postgrad., U. Pitts., 1996-98. Adminstrv. asst. Bethesda Adult Literacy Program, Pitts., 1990; tchg. fellow U. Mo., 1991-93; tchg.-adminstrv. fellow Bowling Green State U., 1993-96; rsch. assoc. U. Pitts., 1996-98; asst. prof. media ecology NYU, 1998—; project cons. Ctr. Family Excellence, Pitts., 1996—. Author: African American Viewers and the Black Situation Comedy: Situating Racial Humor, 1998; contbr. profl. articles to The Bulletin, 1996. Ballot counter Boone County, Columbia, 1992; vol. voter registration Urban League, Pitts., 1988. Postdoctoral fellow U. Pitts., 1996. Mem. Internat. Comm. Assn., Speech Comm. Assn. Democrat. Baptist. Avocations: cinema, African-Am. literature, travel, 5K walk races, concerts. Home: 15 Washington Pl Apt 4J New York NY 10003-6645 Office: NYU Dept Culture and Comm 239 Greene St # 735 New York NY 10003-6674

MEASHAM, DONALD CHARLES, small press company administrator; b. Birmingham Warwickshire, Eng., Jan. 19; s. Charles Henry and Elsie Winifred (Knowles) M.; m. Joan Doreen Barry, Dec. 15, 1954; children: Caitlin Joy, Jonathan Michael. BA with honors, Birmingham U., 1953; MPhil, Nottingham (Eng.) U., 1971. Cert. tchr., U.K. English tchr. Kilburn High Sch., London, 1956-58, Netteswell High Sch., Essex, Eng., 1958-60; dept. head Hockley High Sch., Essex, 1960-63; sr. English lectr. Matlock Coll., Derbyshire, Eng., 1963-68, dept. head, chair, 1968-83; chair, head of sch. Derbyshire Coll., 1983-89; co-editor, pub. Staple New Writing, Matlock, Eng., 1982—; co. sec., bd. dirs. Staple New Writing, Cromford, Eng., 1997—. Editor: Fourteen: Autobiography of a Yeargroup, 1965; author: English Now and Then, 1965, John Ruskin: The Last Chapter, 1989; editor, co-editor various lit. articles, poetry and fiction monographs. Home and Office: 81 Cavendish Rd Tor Cottage, Matlock DE4 3HD, England

MEATES, STEPHEN RUTHVEN, insurance company executive; b. Melbourne, Australia, July 13, 1958; s. Claude William and Aileen (Young) M. Clk. TG Life Soc., Melbourne, Australia, 1977-80; facultative & treaty broker Golding Collins MGA Reins., London, 1981-82; facultative & treaty br. mgr. MGA Reins Brokers, Sydney, Australia, 1982-84; mgr. facultative underwriter Gerling Global, Sydney, Australia, 1984-95; asst. gen. mgr. Gerling Australia, Sydney, 1995-99; regional mgr. Facultative Property for ZurichRe, Sydney, 1999—; treas., sec. Reins. Discussion Group, Sydney; treas., pres. Mgmt. Devel. Group, Sydney; assoc. Australian Inst. Mgmt., Sydney, 1993-96. Fellow Australian Ins. Inst. Avocations: swimming, tennis, squash, running, horseback riding. Office: Zurich Reins, Australia Sq, 264 George St, Sydney NSW 2000, Australia

MECH, ROLAND, research engineer; b. Hamm, NRW, Germany, Mar. 4, 1969; s. Friedhelm and Heidrun Elisabeth (Beckers) M.; m. Michaela Ina Schäfer, Apr. 26, 1996. M in Computer Sci., U. Dortmund, Germany, 1995; postgrad., U. Hannover, Germany, 1995—. Rsch. engr. U. Hannover, Germany, 1995—; active mem. European Project Acts, Momusys, 1998—, European Project Cost-211, 1997—; active ISO/MPEG, 1996—; lectr. U. Hannover, 1996—. Contbr. articles to profl. publs.; patentee in field. Lance corporal, Supply Detachment, 1988-89. Mem. German Stardardization Orgn. Roman Catholic. Avocations: travelling, inline skating, cycling, jogging, dancing. Home: Lettow-Vorbeck-Allee 67, D-30455 Hannover Germany Office: U Hannover TNT, Appelstr 9A, D-30167 Hannover Germany

MECHALLEN, ELLIS, writer; b. June 23, 1977. Writer N.Y.C., 1996—. Home: 104 Kingsberry Dr Apt B Rochester NY 14626-2256

MECHL, ZDENEK, oncologist; b. Brno, Czech Republic, Oct. 20, 1928; s. Victor and Milada (Mechlova) M.; m. Eva Stouracova; children: Marek, Zdenek. MD, Faculty of Medicine, Brno, 1953, Internal Medicine I, 1957, PhD, 1964; Internal Medicine II, Charles U., Prague, Czech Republic, 1970. Jr. asst. Dist. Hosp., Ostrava, Czech Republic, 1953-57, Oncol Inst., Brno, 1957-64; sr. asst. Cancer Inst., Brno, 1964-75, head med. oncology, 1975-92; head med. oncology dept. Kuwait Cancer Control Ctr., Shuwaikh, 1992-98. Author: (book) Prirucka prakticke chemotherapie, 1986, (textbook) Chemotherapy of Advanced Cancer, 1993; editor Clin. Oncology. Mem. N.Y. Acad. Scis., European Soc. Med. Oncology, European Assn. for Cancer Rsch. Avocations: skiing, treking. Home: Chorvatska 13, 61200 Brno Czech Republic

MECKE, WILLIAM MOYN, public affairs consultant; b. Detroit, May 7, 1957; s. Theodore Hart McCalla Jr. and Mary Eleanor (Flaherty) M. BA, Georgetown U., 1979; MA, Am. U., 1982; postgrad., Oxford U., 1982, U. N.C., 1982-85. Asst. dir. Found. Study Presdl. and Congrl. Terms, Washington, 1979-82; acct. exec. Hill and Knowlton, Inc., Chgo., 1985-86; tchr. The Bolles Sch., Jacksonville, Fla., 1986-88, St. Andrew's Sch., Savannah, 1988-91, Joseph Walker Sch., Marietta, Ga., 1991-92; polit. cons. various Democratic candidates, 1992-95; tech. writer Total Sys. Svcs. Inc., Columbus, Ga., 1995; dir. mktg. Habitat for Humanity Internat., Americus, Ga., 1995-2000, media svcs. mgr., 2000—. Co-author, editor: Presidential and Congressional Term Limitation: The Issue That Stays Alive, 1981. Asst. dir. Found. Study Presd. and Congl. Terms, Washington, 1979-82. Mem. Pub. Rels. Soc. Am. Office: Habitat for Humanity Internat 121 Habitat St Americus GA 31709-3498

MECOCCI, ALESSANDRO, engineering educator, researcher; b. Grosseto, Italy, Apr. 25, 1958. B in Elec. Engring. cum laude, Florence U., 1983. Head SW devel. Data Processing Sys., Florence, Italy, 1984-86, Officine Galileo SpA, Florence, 1986-90; rschr. U. Florence, 1990-91; assoc. prof. U. Pavia, Italy, 1991-95, U. Siena, Italy, 1995—; mem. Telematic Environment Min. Rsch., Rome, 1995-96; Italian del. European Union; dir. Etruria Innovazione S.p.A. for tech. transfer to SME, Tuscany Region; mem. Nat. Commn. Min. Rsch. for Cultural Heritage. Author: Informatica, 3 vols., 1989; patentee in field. Co-founder Ctr. Studi Uoma-Macchina, Florence, 1993. Recipient Renato Mariani award Italian Assn. Electronic Engrs., 1984. Avocations: computer applied art and cultural heritage, electronic toys. Office: U Siena, via Roma 56, 53100 Siena Italy

MÉCS, IMRE GYULA, biotechnologist, researcher; b. Mako, Csanad, Hungary, Feb. 19, 1931; s. Jozsef and Erzsébet (Bugyán) M.; m. Etelka Anna Széll; children: Zsusa, László, Erzsébet. Diploma, Jate U., Szeged, Hungary, 1954, PhD, 1958. Tchr. Gymnasium, Kisvárda, Hungary, 1954-56; asst. prof. Med. U., Szeged, 1957-68, reader, 1969-89; chmn. Jate U. Inst. Biotech., 1989-96; sr. scientist Bay Found., Inst. Biotech., Szeged, 1996—; vis. scientist Nat. Inst. Med. Rsch., London, 1965-66, Sloan-Kettering Cancer Ctr., N.Y.C., 1981-84. Contbr. articles to profl. jours. Senator Local Parlament Szeged, 1990-94. Excellent scholar Med. U. Szeged, 1977, Pro Educatione Jate U., Szeged, 1996. Mem. Internat. Soc. Interferon Rsch. Mem. Hungarian Democratic Forum. Roman Catholic. Avocations: classical music, archeology, gardening. Home: 10 Szivárvány, 6725 Szeged Csongrad, Hungary Office: Bay Inst Biotech, 2 Derkovits, 6726 Szeged Csongrad, Hungary

MEDALIE, SUSAN DIANE, lawyer, management consultant; b. Boston, Oct. 7, 1941; d. Samuel and Matilda (Bortman) Abrams; m. Richard James Medalie, June 5, 1960; children: Samuel David, Daniel Alexander. BA, Sarah Lawrence Coll., 1960; MA, George Washington U., 1962, Cert. Pubs. Spec., 1977; JD, Am. U., 1986. Bar: Pa., 1987, D.C., 1987. Pres. Medalie Cons., Washington, 1980—; dep. dir. U.S. Holocaust Meml. Coun., Washington, 1980-82; assoc. pub. Campaigns & Elections, Washington, 1983-84; legis. analyst Subcom./House Energy and Commerce, Washington, 1985; ea. regional dir. Josephson Found. for Adv. Ethics, L.A., 1986-88; asst. dean for external affairs George Washington U. Nat. Law Ctr., Washington, 1988-90; exec. dir. Internat. Soc. Global Health Policy, Washington and Paris, 1990-93; pvt. practice, Washington, 1993—; exec. dir. Women's Campaign Fund, Washington, 2000—; corp. liaison First Hosp. Corp., Norfolk, Va., 1986-88; assoc. producer and cons. Prof. Arthur Miller's "Headlines on Trial" (NBC), N.Y.C., 1987-91. Editor/pub.: Getting There mag., 1977-80; sr. editor: Am. Univ. Law Rev., Washington, 1984-86. Nat. dep. fin. dir. Edward M. Kennedy for Pres. Com., Washington, 1979-80; del. D.C. Ward 3 Dem. Ctrl. Com.; mem. exec. bd., D.C. Bar rep. D.C. Coalition Against Drugs and Violence, 1997—; bd. dirs., mem. exec. com. Women's Campaign Fund, 1999—. Mem. ABA, D.C. Bar. Office: Womens Campaign Fund 1734 15th St NW Washington DC 20009-3814

MEDCALF, PETER GORDON, publishing consultant; b. Harrow, Eng., May 16, 1922; s. John Gordon and Cecilia Malid (Boole) M.; m. Dora Helen Norris; children: Sally, Nigel (dec.), Paul, Tim. Cert. diploma acctg. & fin., Chartered Inst. Cert. Accts., London, 1975. Trainee Hunt Barnard & Co. Ltd., Aylesbury, 1938-39, prodn. mgr., 1946—; chmn. Hunt Barnard Group of Cos., Aylesbury, Bedford, London, The Peter House Press, Brill, Bucks, 1981-99. Flying officer Royal Air Force, 1939-46. Fellow Inst. Printing; mem. Brit. Printing Industries Fedn. (pres. 1979-80), Little Ship Club, North Devon Yacht Club. Liberal Democrat. Avocations: amateur radio, computers, jazz. Home: The Old Sunday School Brill, Aylesbury HP18 952, England Office: 10 Windmill St, Brill-Aylesbury HP18 952, England

MEDDENS, MARC JOHANNES, medical association administrator, virologist; b. Haelen, The Netherlands, Mar. 25, 1950; s. Johannes Jacobes Meddens and Maria Elisabeth Scheymans; m. Diet Nijhoff, May 15, 1981; children: Marjolein, Claartje, Annemarie, Laura. Diploma in Biochemistry, Utrecht (The Netherlands) U., 1979; PhD in Medicine, Leiden (The Netherlands) U., 1983. Cert. in immunology and virology. Virologist Clin. Microbiology SSDD, Delft, The Netherlands, 1983-89; product mgr. Eurodiagnostics, Apeldoorn, The Netherlands, 1989-92; pres. Meddens Diagnostics, Vorden, The Netherlands, 1992—. Author: Role of granulocytes and monocytes in experimented bacterial endoconalitis, 1983, Techniques in Diagnostic Pathology, 1989. Mem. Vorden basic sch. bd., 1983-98. Officer, Dutch Air Arty., 1970-71, Ede. Mem. Diagnostic Assn. Netherlands, European Group for Clin. Virology, Lions. Roman Catholic. Avocations: bridge, sailing, volleyball, astronomy. Home: Rondweg 1, NL7251RT Vorden The Netherlands Office: Meddens Diagnostics, Het Jebbink 15, NL7251BJ Vorden The Netherlands

MEDEARIS, MILLER, lawyer; b. Liberty, Mo., Jan. 19, 1921; s. Thomas Whittier and Mara (Miller) M.; children: Christy Crochet, Kellee Reed. LLB, Cumberland U., 1948; JD, Stamford U., 1969. Bar: Okla. 1948, Calif. 1957. Claims adjustor Transit Casualty Co., L.A., 1950-56, atty., trial counsel, 1956-58; ptnr. Hagenbaugh, Murphy & Medearis, L.A., 1958-69, Medearis and Grimm, L.A., 1969—. Sec., Bd. Med. Quality Assurance, Sacramento, 1979-84, v.p., 1984-86; bd. dirs. Pico Rivera Cmty. Hosp., 1975-85; mem. Dem. Bus. Council, L.A., 1980; commr. L.A. Bd. Transp., 1986-92. With USN, 1945-46. Mem. ABA, State Bar Calif., Calif. Trial Lawyers Assn., Okla. Bar Assn., Lawyers Club L.A. Democrat. Baptist. Avocations: boating, water skiing, downhill skiing. Home: 2175 Ridge Dr Los Angeles CA 90049-1153 Office: Medearis and Grimm 1331 W Sunset Blvd Los Angeles CA 90026-4499

MEDEIROS, M. JOYCE, community health educator; b. Boston, Feb. 17, 1954; d. Raymond A. and D. Jean (Russell) Harrington; m. Joseph A. Medeiros, July 26, 1977; children: Jessica A., Jo Ellen. Grad., Youville Hosp. Sch. Practical Nursing, 1973; BS in Cmty. Health Edn., U. Maine, Farmington, 1992. Staff nurse Goddard Meml. Hosp., Stoughton, Mass., 1973-87; dist. dir. Somerset Family YMCA, 1988-90; ITV aide Skowhegan (Maine) H.S., 1990-91; intern Somerset Residential Care Ctr., 1991-92, WARNACO, 1992; dir. edn. Sebasticook Valley Hosp., 1992-96; spl. needs edn. tech. transition III MSAD # 59 Madison (Maine) H.S., 1996-99; children's case mgr. Youth & Family Svcs., 1999—; camp nurse, dir. 4-H Camp Farley, 1982-87, Camp at Eastward Starks, Maine, 1990. Mem. gov. coun. U. Maine, Farmington. Mem. AAHPERD, ASHA, MPHA, Eta Sigma Gamma, Phi Sigma Pi. Avocations: camping, bowling, photography, ceramics, collecting music boxes. Home: 241 Dill Rd Starks ME 04911

MEDEIROS, WALTER EUGENIO, science educator; b. Augusto Severo, Brazil, Oct. 5, 1959; s. Máximo Walter Medeiros and Alexandrina Elim Soares; m. Geneci Cavalcanti Moura, May 27, 1981; children: Máximo, Rafaela. BSc in Engring., Fed. U. Rio Grande Norte, Natal, Brazil, 1981; MSc in Geophysics, Fed. U. Bahia, Salvador, Brazil, 1987; PhD in Geophysics Distinction and Laud, Fed. U. Para, Belém, Brazil, 1993. Prof. Fed. U. Rio Grande Norte, Natal, 1982—; rschr. CNPq, Brazil, 1997—; MSc and PhD thesis advisor Fed. U. Rio G. Norte, 1996—. Contbr. articles to sci. jours. Mem. Soc. Exploration Geophysicists (assoc.), Brazilian Geophys. Soc. Office: U Fed Rio Grande Norte, Caixa Postal 1641, 59072970 Natal Brazil

MEDEN, ANTON, chemistry educator; b. Ljubljana, Slovenia, Sept. 4, 1963; s. Anton Meden and Marija (Popek) M.; m. Terezija Glavač, July 29, 1989; children: Ana, Janez, Ema. Diploma chemistry, U. Ljubljana, 1987, M in Chemistry, 1990, Dr. Chem. Sci., 1994. Asst. prof. U. Ljubljana, 1996—; cons. Nat. Inst. of Chemistry, Ljubljana, 1993—. Pvt. Infantry, 1982-83. Mem. Internat. Ctr. for Diffraction Data, European Crystallographic Assn., Slovenian Chem. Soc. Roman Catholic. Avocations: mountain climbing, cycling, snorkling. Office: U Ljubljana, Askerceva 5, 1000 Ljubljana Slovenia

MEDER, CORNEL, national archives director; b. Esch/Alzette, Luxembourg, Sept. 23, 1938; s. Nicolas and Susan (Hecker) M.; m. Nicole Wagner, Apr. 10, 1965; children: Charles, Françoise. Grad., State U., Luxembourg, D of Philosophy & Philology. Prof. Lycée de Garçons Esch/Alzette, Esch/Alzette, 1966-69; headmaster Lycée Mathias Adam Petange, Petange, Luxembourg, 1969-87; dir. Nat. Archives, Luxembourg, 1987—. Author 15 books in letters, philology and history. Sen. Senate of Luxembourg, 1978-99. Decorated grand officer Order de la Couronne de Chêne (Luxembourg). Mem. Institut Grand-Ducal (pres. linguistics and ethnological sect. 1976-91). Mem. Social Dem. Party. Avocation: lecture. Home: Prinzenberg L-Niederkorn, L-4650 Luxembourg Luxembourg Office: Nat Archives, PO Box 6, L-2010 Luxembourg Luxembourg

MEDGYESI, IVÁN PÁL, chemical engineer; b. Budapest, Hungary, Feb. 21, 1929; s. Pál and Antónia (Vida) M.; m. Katalin Varga, Feb. 16, 1951; children: András, Tibor. Chem. Engr., U. Engring., Budapest, 1952; PhD, U. Chem. Industry, Veszprém, 1977. Dir. lab. Underground Builder Co., Budapest, 1952-54, office mgr., 1954-89; mng. dir. Buildcorr, Budapest, 1970-89; exec. mgr. SOFORT Ltd., Budapest, 1990—; cons. Engring. Ltd. Budapest. Author: Mechanism of concrete Corrosion, 1977, Corrosional Protection of buildstructures, 1983; contbr. over 220 articles to profl. jours. Expert Nat. Tech. Devel. Com., Budapest, 1970-90; mem. com. RILEM, 32-RCA (Resistance of Concrete to Chem. Attack), Paris, 1980-92. Mem. Hungarian Chemists Assn. (mgr. dept. 1969-94). Office: SOFORT LTD, Sóvári 34, 1031 Budapest Hungary

MEDGYESSY, PETER, Hungarian government official; b. Budapest, Hungary, 1942. Ed., Karl Marx U. Polit. Economy. With Ministry Fin., 1987-88, minister, 1988-89; dep. prime minister Hungary, Budapest, 1990-94; chief exec. MAGYAR Paribas Sarl., Budapest, 1994-96; chmn., CEO Hungarian Bank for Investment and Devel., Budapest, 1996-98; pres. Inter-Europa Bank, Budapest, 1998—; mem. Internat. Inst. Pub. Finance, 1973—; bd. mem. fin. sect. Hungarian Econ. Soc. Office: Ministry of Finance, Jozsef Nador ter 2-4, 1051 Budapest Hungary Office: Inter-Europa Bank, Szabadsag ter 15, H-1054 Budapest Hungary*

MEDHUS, ASLE WILHELM, physician, researcher; b. Växjö, Sweden, Sept. 23, 1969; arrived in Norway, 1971; s. Magne K. and Ilse (Bachrodt) M. MD, U. Oslo, Norway, 1995. Rschr. U. Oslo, 1995—.

MEDICI, ROCHELLE, psychologist, brain researcher; b. Morris, Minn., Dec. 31, 1933; d. Albert and Johanna (Ulvestad) Johnson; m. Michael A. Medici, July 4, 1970 (div. 1995); 1 child, Bianca Cristina. BA magna cum laude, U. Minn., 1954, PhD, 1962. Lic. psychologist, Calif. USPHS postdoctoral fellow U. Minn., Mpls., 1965-67; asst. biologist Calif. Inst. Tech., Pasadena, 1967-68; assoc. prof. anatomy Brain Rsch. Inst., UCLA, 1968-79; pvt. practice neuropsychology, San Marino, Calif., 1980—; cons. AEC, Washington, 1976, WHO, Washington, 1976, Neuroscis. Rsch. Program, Boston, 1977. Rschr. numerous publs.; contbr. articles to profl. jours (Nature, Brain Research, et al). Mem. APA, AAAS, Explorers Club, Phi Beta Kappa. Democrat. Avocations: music, art, travel, politics, literature. Home: 2220 El Molino Pl San Marino CA 91108-2317

MEDICUS, GERHARD, psychiatrist; b. Salzburg, Austria, June 12, 1950; s. Karl and Inge (Friedel) M.; m. Elisabeth Happacher, Feb. 15, 1980; children: Philipp, Gertraud, Thomas. MD, U. Innsbruck, Austria, 1981. Clin. tng. U. Hosp. Innsbruck, Austria, 1985-88; psychiat. tng. Psychiat. Hosp. Tyrol, Hall, Austria, 1989-93; neurol. tng. U. Innsbruck, 1993-94; psychiatrist Psychiat. Hosp. Tyrol, 1994—; vis. physician U. Innsbruck, 1983; free-lance rsch. unit human ethology Max-Planck-Inst., Andechs, Germany, 1988—; lectr. in behavioral biology U. Innsbruck, 1990—; rschr. Zool. Inst. U. Vienna, 1983-85. Co-author: (1 chpt.) Pedophilia, Biosocial Domensions; contbr. articles to profl. jours. Mem. Internat. Soc. Human Ethology, Human Behavior and Evolution Soc. Achievements include contributions to the interdisciplinarity of neural sciences, to biological bases of psychotherapy and other applied anthropological sciences, to the special behavioral positions of human beings among species. Home: Stollenstrasse 23 A, A-6065 Thaur Austria Office: Psychiat Hosp Tyrol, Thurnfeldgasse 14, A-6060 Hall Austria

MEDICUS, HILDEGARD JULIE, retired dentist, orthodontist, educator; b. Frankfurt, Germany, July 25, 1928; came to U.S., 1961, naturalized, 1995; d. Gustav and Elizabeth Berta (Neunhoeffer) Schmelz; m. Heinrich Adolf Medicus, June 15, 1961. DMD, U. Marburg, W. Germany, 1953; orthodontics diploma, U. Düsseldorf, W. Germany, 1957. lic. dentist, N.Y. Postdoctoral fellow dental sch. U. Zürich, Zürich, Switzerland, 1957; postdoctoral fellow U. Liège, Belgium, 1958; postdoctoral fellow Forsyth Dental Ctr., Boston, 1959, orthodontics rsch. affiliate, 1963-74; sch. dentist Pub. Sch. System, Zürich, 1975-76; dental hygiene instructor Hudson Valley Community Coll., Troy, N.Y., 1976-77; pvt. practice Troy, N.Y., 1977-89. Active Hudson Mohawk Swiss Soc. Mem. AAUW, ADA, European Orthodontic Soc., German Orthodontic Soc. Presbyterian. Achievements include study of functional orthodontic appliances and growth and development. Home: 1 The Knoll Troy NY 12180-7284

MEDIN, A. LOUIS, computer company executive; b. Balt., Oct. 2, 1925; s. Nathan and Bessie (Zell) M.; m. Julia A. Levin, Dec. 24, 1950; children: Douglas, David, Thomas, Linda. BSChemE, Johns Hopkins U., 1948; PhDChemE, Ohio State U., 1951. Registered profl. engr., Md. Chmn. engr. AEC, Wilmington, Del., 1951-53; rsch. engr. Ford Motor Co., Dearborn, Mich., 1953-55; chief chem. nuclear reactor tech. ALCO Products, Schenectady, 1955-58; head nuclear rsch. engr. U.S. Steel, Monroeville, Pa., 1958-63; project mgr. missile design AVCO Corp., Wilmington, Mass., 1963-65; mgr. sci. applications IBM, Manassas, Va., 1965-72; mgr. advanced applications IBM, Manassas, 1975-87; exec. dir. Inst. for Simulation and Tng., Orlando, Fla., 1987-2000; sr. assoc. Mgmt. and Ednl. Tech. Assocs., 2000—; chmn. symposia on def. research and devel.; asst. dir. environment and life scis. Dept. Def., 1972-74; lectr. in field. Contbr. articles to profl. and tech. jours. Mem. Monroeville Parks and Recreation Commn., 1960; chmn. Monroeville Mental Health Assn., 1961; mem. Monroeville Zoning and Planning Commn., 1961; dep. precinct chmn. Montgomery County Rep. Com., 1982. With USN, 1944-46, PTO. Recipient award Am. Chem. Soc., 1957. Fellow Am. Inst. Chemists; mem. Nat. Security Indsl. Assn., Am. Inst. Chem. Engrs., Am. Def. Preparedness Assn. (chmn. sci. and engring. tech. divsn. 1981-90, ednl. advisor Def. Jour., Am. Def. award 1984, Gold medal 1990, Lifetime Achievement award Intersvc. Industry Tng. Simulation and Edn. Com. 1999), Am. Metall. Soc., John's Hopkins U. Alumni Assn., Ohio State U. Alumni Assn. Home: 11401 Ridge Mist Ter Potomac MD 20854-7002

MEDIN, JULIA ADELE, mathematics educator, researcher; b. Dayton, Ohio, Jan. 16, 1929; d. Caroline (Feinberg) Levitt; m. A. Louis Medin, Dec. 24, 1950; children: Douglas, David, Thomas, Linda. BS in Maths. Edn., Ohio State U., 1951; MA in Higher Edn., George Washington U., 1977; PhD in Counseling and Edn., Am. U., 1985. Cert. tchr., Fla., Md. Rsch. engr. Sun Oil Co., Marcus Hook, Pa., 1951-53; tchr. maths. Montgomery County Pub. Schs., Rockville, Md., 1973-88; asst. prof. maths. U. Ctrl. Fla., Orlando, 1988-90, sr. ednl. technologist Inst. for Simulation and Tng., 1990-99; sr. assoc. Mgmt. Ednl. Tech. Assocs., 1999—; mem. adv. steering com. U.S. Dept. Edn. Title II, Washington, 1985-89; sr. math. educator, rschr. Inst. for Simulation and Tng., Orlando, 1988-90; judge, co-chair GII Nar. Awards; co-acad. advisor I/ITSEC Conf.; spkr. in field. Author: Loc. of Cont. and Test Anxiety of Mar. Math. Studies, 1985; contbg. author: Math for 14 & 17 Yr. Olds, 1987; editor: Simulation and Computer-Based Technology for Education; contbr. articles to profl. jours. Dem. committeewoman Town of Monroeville, Pa., 1962; religious sch. dir. Beth Tikva Religious Sch., Rockville, 1971; cons. Monroeville Mental Health, 1960. Mem. Nat. Coun. Tchrs. Math., Math. Assn. Am. (task force on minorities in math.), Women in Math. in Edn., Nat. Coalition for Tech. in Edn. and Tng., Phi Delta Kappa, Kappa Delta Pi. Home: 11401 Ridge Mist Ter Potomac MD 20854-7002

MEDIN, LOWELL ANSGARD, management executive; b. Shafer Twp., Minn., Aug. 28, 1932; s. Ansgaard Phillip Magnus and Adelaide Marie Christine (Grandstrand) M.; m. Frances Irene Knutson, Sept. 13, 1958; children: Kimberly June, James Lowell. AS in Liberal Arts, U. Minn., 1957, BBA, 1959. Dairy farmer Medin Farm, Franconia Twp., 1951-53; silo builder Lindstrom Silo, 1956-58; employment mgr. John Wood Co., St. Paul, 1959; salesperson Diversey Co., LaCrosse, Wis., 1959-60; rebuyer, inventory mgr. Montgomery Ward, St. Paul, 1960-67; rebuyer, rebuyer mgr. Montgomery Ward, Chgo., 1967-85; with sales dept. J.T. Gen. Store, Palatine, Ill., 1986; rebuying mgr. Sportsmen's Guide, Golden Valley, Minn., 1987; inventory mgr. Donald Bruce and Co., Chgo., 1988-91; supr. Pinkerton Security Ops., 1992-96; pics coord. Hickory Farms, Itasca, Ill., 1995-99. Author: (with others) Shafer Swamp to Village, 1978, The Pioneers of Chisago County 1838-1870, 1992, The Knutson/Stavenau Family Roots, 1994. Candidate for polit. office, Mpls., 1967; del. Minn. State Dem.-Farm Labor Conv., 1956, 58; chmn. cancer drive Village of Palatine, 1968, mem. dist. 6 adv. coun., 1989-97; mem. Homeowners Coun., Palatine, 1976-77; mem. coun. Christ Luth. Ch., Palatine, 1981-86; officer Chicago County DFL Party, 1956-60; del. Chicago County DFL Conv., 1956, 58; pres. Palonis Park Homeowners Assn., Palatine, 1976-82. Cpl. U.S. Army, 1953-55, ETO. Mem. No. Ill. Civil War Roundtable (chartered officer 1983-86, trustee, sec., 2d v.p.), VFW (life, post 981, Arlington Hts.), Am. Legion (life, post 690, Palatine), Alpha Phi Omega. Republican. Lutheran. Avocations: genealogy, gardening, Am. history, Civil War period. Home: 121 S Linden Ave Palatine IL 60067-6342

MEDINA, FERNANDO HECTOR, physician, oncologist, researcher; b. Buenos Aires, Argentina, May 21, 1957; s. Fernando Aquiles and Helena (Bradford) M.; m. Sandra Elizabeth Sanchez, Aug. 28, 1961; children: Nicolas Fernando Medina Sanchez, Mathias Javier Medina Sanchez. BSc, Domingo F. Sarmiento, Buenos Aires, 1974; MD, Buenos Aires Nat. U., 1980. Diplomate in inernal medicine and oncology. Chmn. in oncology O.S.M.O. y S.P., Buenos Aires, 1989-91; mem. oncol. staff Spanish Hosp., Buenos Aires, 1981—; assoc. rschr. Med. Coll. Buenos Aires, 1983-86, P.I. CONICET, Buenos Aires, 1989-90; med. adv. Lederle Labs., Buenos Aires, 1991-95; med. advisor, CRA John Wyeth Lab., 1995-97, Astra Zenoca Pl, 1997—. Mem. AAAS, Argentinian Med. Assn., Argentinian Soc. med. Genetics, Am. Soc. Clin. Oncology. Home: Av La Plata 3966 PB Dpto D, 1676 Santos Lugares Argentina Office: Circulo Medico Artentina, Paraguayo Urquiza 141, 1215 Buenos Aires Argentina

MEDINA, SORIQUEZ FLORANTE, construction engineer, administrator; b. Calapan, The Philippines, June 6, 1942; s. Francisco Mendoza and Flora Albanez (Medina) S.; m. Silvana Sansone La Valle (div. 1979); children: Francesco, Ruben, Cristiano, Leizl, Larra, Tessa. BS in Civil Engring., Mapua Inst. Tech., Manila, The Philippines, 1966; tng. in bridge engring., Carl Duisberg Soc., West Germany, 1970; M in Mgmt., Philippine Christian U., Manila, 1985; numerous tngs. and seminars relative to project mgmt. and civil engring. profession, The Philippines and abroad, 1969-94. Cert. civil engr., Philippine Profl. Regulation Commn., 1967. Laborer to foreman to civil engring. aide in the constrn. of various locally-funded roads and bridges in Metro Manila Dept. Pub. Works and Hwys., The Philippines, 1962-68, assoc. civil engr. to supr. civil engr. II mng. constrn. of various locally-funded bridge projects in the country, 1968-80, head civil engr. ADB-funded nationwide road contrn., 1980-82, asst. project dir. to profect dir. ADB, DANIDA, KfW, GTZ, USAID-funded nationwide road, port and water supply projects under Palawan Integrated, 1982-93, asst. regional dir., region IV-B, 1988-89, foreign-funded integrated area devel. project offices, 1989-92; project dir.and program dir. ADF, KICA, KfW, USAID, Dutch, OECF, CIM, IBRD, SDR-funded anti-lahar and flood control, road, bridge, and social infrastructure project under Mt. Pinatubo emergency and rehab. offices, The Philippines, 1991-2000; profect dir. World Bank-funded nat. road improvement and mgmt. project The Philippines, 2000—. Commendations for integrity, dedication and efficiency in Govt. Svc. and in completing infrastructure project in record time from former Philippine Pres. Fidel Ramos, 1993; from former Dept. Sec. of Public Works and Hwys. Manuel Siquio, 1971; Gregorio Vigilar, 1997, Jose de Jesus, 1998; Recipient plaques of appreciation City Peñafrancia Contractors Assn., 1989, City of Angeles, 1994, numerous other citations and recognitions. Mem. Road Engring. Assn. Asia and Australia, Philippine Inst. Civil Engrs., Carl Duisberg Soc.-Philippines, Manila Royale Lions Club (pres. 1984-85), Internat. Lions club (chmn. zone II region XIII 1983-84), Tau Alpha. Roman Catholic. Avocations: reading, chess, swimming, movies, photography. Fax: 9245825. Home: Project 8, 76 Congressional Ave, Quezon City The Philippines Office: Dept Pub Works and Hwys, Bonifacio St Port Area, Manila The Philippines

MEDINA FILHO, HERCULANO PENNA, agronomist; b. Campinas, Brazil, June 4, 1950; s. Herculano Penna and Dixier (Marozzi) Medina; children from previous marriage: Daniel, Rodrigo, Mariana; m. Rita Bordignon, Mar. 1, 1985; children: Marina, Ricardo. BS in Agronomy, U. Sao Paulo, 1973; PhD in Genetics, U. Calif., Davis, 1980. Rschr. Inst. Brasileiro do Café, Campinas, 1973-75, Inst. Agronomico, Campinas, 1975-78, 78—; rsch. asst. Tomato Genetics Stock Ctr., Davis, Calif., 1977-80; grad. prof. U. Campinas, 1983—; cons. DNA Plant Technology Co., Cinnaminson, N.J., 1983-87, Internat. Rsch. Inst. USAID, Stamford, Conn., 1993, 95-96. Recipient Tech. Achievement award Specialty Coffee Assn. of Am., 2000. Mem. Brazilian Soc. Genetics, Nat. Geographic Soc. Roman Catholic. Avocations: soccer, tennis, plants. Home: Rua Paiquere 766 Casa 50, Valinhos Sao Paulo 13271600, Brazil

MEDLAND, MAURICE BLUE, writer, educator; b. Centerville, Iowa, Sept. 29, 1936; s. William C. and Avis N. (Blue) M.; m. Karen A. McFarland, Aug. 7, 1965; children: Melissa A., Steven W. BS, Truman State U., 1961; MBA, Pepperdine U., 1977. Mgmt. sys. analyst Rockwell Internat. Corp., Downey, Calif., 1961-70; dir. Fluor Corp., Irvine, Calif., 1970-85; v.p. PacifiCare Health Sys., Cypress, Calif., 1985-87; novelist Calif., 1987—; instr. U. Calif., Irvine, 1998—; adv. Calif. State U. Fullerton Writer's Program, 1998—. Author: Point of Honor, 1997. With USN, 1954-57. Recipient Apollo Achievement award NASA, 1969. Mem. The Authors Guild. Fax: 714 779-9831. E-mail: mauricemedland@msn.com. Home: 19842 Villager Cir Yorba Linda CA 92886-4454

MEDLAND, WILLIAM JAMES, college president; b. Logansport, Ind., Jan. 1, 1944; s. Thomas Gallagher and Mary Elizabeth (Hassett) M.; m. Donna Lee Bahnaman, Mar. 12, 1977; children: Bridget Marie, Mark David, Jeanne Nicole. BA, U. Notre Dame, 1966; student, St. Louis U., 1972-74; MA in History, Ball State U., 1967, MA in Edn., 1979, PhD in History, 1980; postgrad., Inst. for Mgmt. Lifelong Edn., Harvard U., 1985, Ctr. Internat. Cooperation and Security Studies, U. Wis., 1988, Ctr. Internat. Studies, MIT, 1989, Freie Universitat, Berlin, 1991. Instr. history and philosophy Donnelly coll., Kansas City, Kans., 1967-70; curricular advisor Ball State U., Muncie, Ind., 1970-71, teaching fellow, 1977-80; asst. dean St. Louis (Mo.) U., 1971-75; employee supr. Wilson, Inc., Logansport, 1975-76; ops. mgr. Watson-Jenkins, Inc., Indpls., 1976-77; dean of coll., asst. prof. history Springfield (Ill.) Coll., 1980-81; acad. dean, assoc. prof. history and edn. Marymount Coll., Salina, Kans., 1981-86; exec. v.p., provost, prof. history St. Mary's U., Winona, Minn., 1986-91; pres., prof. history Viterbo U., LaCrosse, Wis., 1991—; also bd. dirs., CEO Viterbo U., LaCrosse, 1991—; edn. cons. Am. Inst. Banking, Springfield, 1980-81; advisor Adv. Com. to Sch. Bd., Salina, 1984, Salina Diocesan Bd. Edn., 1981-83; evaluator North Ctrl. Assn., Chgo., 1987-2000. Author: Cuban Missile Crisis of 1962-Needless or Necessary?, 1988, reprint, 1990, A Guide to Writing College Research Papers, 1989, The Catholic School: A Bibliographical Resource Guide, 1990; editor: Ind. Acad. Social Scis. jour., 1979, Perspectives: A Liberal Arts Exchange (faculty jour.), 1988. Coll. solicitor United Way, St. Louis, 1973; coord. Coll./Cmty. Artist Series, Salina, 1981-84; bd. dirs. Immaculate Heart of Mary Sem., Winona, 1987-91, La Crosse Med. Health Sci. Consortium, 1993—; bd. dirs. Wis. Found. for Ind. Colls., 94-98, Assn. Franciscan Colls. and U., 1999—; chair La Crosse Diocesan Edn. mmn., 1994—. Fellow Ctr. Internat. Studies, MIT/Harvard U., 1989. Mem. KC, Am. Assn. Higher Edn., Am. Assn. Coll. Pres., Am. Assn. Ind. Coll. Pres., Wis. Assn. Ind. Colls. and Univs. (bd. dirs.), Wis. Assn. of Ind. Colls. and Univs. (bd. dirs. 1991—), Rotary, Phi Alpha Theta (rsch. award Ball State U. 1979), Phi Delta Kappa. Roman Catholic. Avocations: reading, research. Home: 119 Calla Ct Onalaska WI 54650-8317 Office: Viterbo Univ Office of Pres 815 9th St S La Crosse WI 54601-4777

MEDLEY, ALEX ROY, executive minister; b. Columbus, Ga., Aug. 4, 1948; s. Howard and Clois Mildred (Chumney) M.; m. Patricia Stauffer, May 10, 1975; children: James Ethan, Christopher Jordan. BA magna cum laude, U. Chattanooga, 1970; cert., Grad. Sch. Ecumenical Studies, Celigny, Switzerland, 1973; MDiv, Princeton Sem., 1974. Ordained to ministry Bapt. Ch., 1975. Assoc. pastor First Bapt. Ch. Trenton, N.J., 1974-77; adminstrv. intern Nat. Ministries Am. Bapt. Chs. U.S.A., Valley Forge, Pa., 1977, nat. dir. Christian ctr., 1978-85; min. of world mission support, area min. Am. Bapt. Chs. N.J., East Orange, 1986-92, exec. min., 1992—; intern World Coun. Chs., Geneva, Switzerland, 1973; rep. N.Am. Bapt. Fellowship, Washington, 1975-77; mem. domestic hunger/poverty working group Nat. Coun. Chs. of Christ, 1978-85, mem. gen. assembly; conf. speaker Am. Bapt. Chs., 1979; Am. Bapt. Ch. U.S.A. del. to Nat. Coun. Chs. of Christ. Editor (newsletter) Social Edn. for Action Newsletter, 1978-79. Bd. dirs. Ch. World Svc./CROP, N.J., 1975-77, Occupational Tng. Ctr., Burlington, N.J., 1992—; sec. Key Inmate Edn. Project, Trenton, 1986; participant Nat. Religious Leadership Program, 1997-99. Mem. Am. Bapt. Regional Exec. Mins. Coun. Avocations: reading, fishing, hiking. Home: 22 Story Ct Freehold NJ 07728-5322 Office: Am Bapt Chs NJ 3752 Nottingham Way Ste 101 Trenton NJ 08690-3802*

MEDNEY, TANIA LEVY, advertising agency executive; b. Rio de Janeiro, June 19, 1955; d. Samuel and Paulette (Schinazi) L.; children: Matthew Levy, Samantha Jennifer. BA cum laude, SUNY, Albany, 1977. Sec. Benton & Bowles, Inc., N.Y.C., 1977-78, network coord., 1978-79, sr. media planner, 1979-81; sr. media planner Young & Rubicam, Inc., N.Y.C., 1981-82, media supr., 1982-87; media dir. Young & Rubicam Bravo, N.Y.C., 1987-88; sr. media supr. Young & Rubicam, N.Y.C., 1987-89, tng. specialist, 1983-89, mktg. and media cons., tng. specialist, 1989—; media supr. Foote, Cone & Belding, N.Y.C., 1998-99; assoc. media dir. Bates USA, N.Y.C., 1999—; song specialist, dance and guitar instr. Author: Supervisory Skills Manual, 1984. Democrat. Avocations: dancing, playing guitar. Office: Bates USA 498 7th Ave New York NY 10018-6702

MEDNIKAROV, BORISLAV DIMITROV, chemist; b. Varna, Bulgaria, Dec. 8, 1940; s. Dimitar Marinov and Maria Petrova Mednikarov; m. Olga Ivanova Kalpaktchieva, Mar. 12, 1952; children: Slavov Ivailo Svetoslavov, Viktor Borislavov. Student, Higher Inst. Chem. Tech., Sofia, 1962-67; PhD, Bulgarian Acad. Sci., 1984. Engr. Ctrl. Lab. Photoprocesses, Bulgarian Acad. Scis., Sofia, 1967-70, rsch. assoc., 1970-90, sr. rsch. assoc., 1990—, chief of group, 1976-94, dep. dir. R&D, 1994—. Contbr. numerous articles to profl. jours.; patentee in field. Supporter Union of Dem. Forces in Bulgaria. Recipient Gold medals Plovdiv Internat. Tech. Fair, 1985, 87, Bronze medal World fair of Invention, Rsch. and Indsl. Innovation, Eureka, Brussels, 1991. Orthodox Ch. Avocations: literature, music. E-mail: bormed@CLF.BAS.BG. Home: Mladost 4 Bl 451/5, 1715 Sofia Bulgaria Office: Ctrl Lab Photoprocesses, Acad g Bontchev str bl 109, 1113 Sofia Bulgaria

MEDRONHO, RICARDO DE ANDRADE, chemical engineering educator; b. Rio de Janeiro, Sept. 24, 1951; s. Jayr da Rocha and Neuza Jose de Andrade Medronho; m. Leda Reis Castilho, Dec. 21, 1996; children: Viviane, Vinicius, Vitor. BSc, Fed. U. of Rio de Janeiro, 1974, MSc, 1979; PhD, U. Bradford, Eng., 1984. Head chem. engring. dept. Fed. U. Rio de Janeiro, 1987-89, dir. sch. of chemistry, 1990-94, supt. of undergrad. studies, 1994-98; invited rschr. GBF, Germany, 1998-2000; cons. CNPQ/Ministry of Sci. and Tech., Brasilia, 1989—, Capes/Ministry of Edn., Brasilia, 1991—, Faperj/Govt. of Rio de Janeiro, 1997—. Mem. Brazilian Assn. of Chem. Engring., Brazilian Soc. for the Sci. Devel. Home: Rua Pedro de Carvalho 691/1402, 20725231 Rio de Janeiro Brazil Office: U Fed Rio de Janeiro Escola de Quimica, Centro de Tecnologia, 21949900 Rio de Janeiro Brazil

MEDSGER, BETTY, journalist, educator; b. Johnstown, Pa., Mar. 14, 1942; d. Richard J. and Alice J. (Wilson) M.; m. Ben H. Bagdikian, Feb. 24, 1973 (div. 1982); m. John T. Racanelli, Apr. 14, 1984. BA, Grove City Coll., 1964; doctoral equivalency, San Francisco State U., 1982. Reporter Tribune-Democrat, Johnstown, 1964-66; med. writer Temple U., Phila., 1967; reporter The Evening Bulletin, Phila., 1967-69, Washington (D.C.) Post, 1970-73; freelance reporter, photojournalist various nat. mags. and newspapers, 1973-81; prof. San Francisco (Calif.) State U., 1982-94, journalism dept. chair, 1985-94; vis. prof. Stanford U., 1981-82; judge Freedom Forum Scholarship Com., 1989-93; mem. adv. bd. Hearst Found., Progressive Mag., Calif. Lawyer Mag. Photographer: (photodocumentary books) Women at Work, 1974; author: Framed: The New Right, Attack on Chief Justice Rose Bird and the Courts, 1983, Winds of Change: Challenges Confronting Journalism Education, 1996. Mem. Accrediting Coun. on Edn. in Journalism and Mass Comm., Assn. for Edn. in Journalism and Mass Communication, Soc. Profl. Journalists, Investigative Reporters and Editors. Avocation: biking. Home and Office: 252 Seventh Ave #5Q New York NY 10001

MEDVEDKIN, GENNADIY ALEKSANDROVICH, physicist, researcher; b. St. Petersburg, Russia, Oct. 30, 1954; s. Aleksandr Trofimovich Zabolotny and Polina (Aleksandrovna) M.; m. Anna Ivanovna Grishaeva, Dec. 1981 (div. May 1989); 1 child; m. Elizaveta Nikolaevna Antonova, Sept. 1990; 2 children. MSc, Elec. Engring. U., St. Petersburg, 1977; PhD, Ioffe Phys. Tech. Inst., St. Petersburg, 1981, DSc, 1993. Lab. asst. Elec. Engring. U., St. Petersburg, 1972-77, probationer-rschr., 1977-79, jr. rschr., 1979-86, rschr., 1986-99, sr. scientist, 1999—; dir. gen. Joint-St. Co. Standard, St. Petersburg, 1997-98; vice-dir. PROFIT, Ltd., St. Petersburg, 1999—; vis. prof. Tokyo U. Agr. Tech., 1999—. Author: Semiconductor Crystals for Photosensors of Linearly Polarized Radiation, 1992; patentee in field. Grantee Internat. Sci. Found., N.Y., 1993, Internat. Rich Found., Paris, 1994-95; Uppsala (Sweden) U. scholar, 1996; Japanese Soc. Promotion Sci. fellow, 1999-2000. Avocations: sports, philately. E-mail: gen@medv.ioffe.rssi.ru. Home: Apt 18, Tikhoretskiy Prospect 5-2, 194064 Sankt Petersburg Russia Office: IOFFE Phys Tech Inst, Polytechnicheskaya St 26, 194021 Sankt Petersburg Russia

MEDVINSKY, ALEXANDER BEREL'EVICH, biophysicist; b. Kiev, USSR, Aug. 21, 1945; s. Berel Avram-Movshevich and Vita Shaevna (Velixon) M.; m. Faina Semenovna Berezovsky, Aug. 8, 1968 (div. Oct. 1980); 1 child, Kirill; m. Natalia Igorevna Grishchenko, Apr. 8, 1986; children: Lidia, Victoria. MS in Nuclear Physics, Kiev U., 1974; PhD in Biophysics, Inst. Biophysics, Pushchino, Russia, 1985; DSc in Biophysics, Inst. Theoret. and Exptl. Biophysics, Pushchino, Russia, 1993. Sr. lab. asst. Inst. Biophysics, 1975-76, engr., 1976-84, jr. rsch. scientist, 1984-90, rsch. scientist, 1990-94; sr. rsch. scientist Inst. Theoret. and Exptl. Biophysics, 1991-94, leading rsch. scientist, 1994, head lab., 1994—; mem. sci. coun. Inst. Theoret. and Exptl. Biophysics, 1995-96, 96—. Recipient grant Russian Acad. Scis., 1994, 97. Mem. Soc. Chaos Theory in Psychology and Life Scis. Avocation: history. Home: PO Box 45, 142290 Pushchino Russia Office: Inst Theoret and Exptl Biophysics, 142290 Pushchino Russia

MEDZIHRADSZKY, KALMAN, organic chemistry educator, researcher; b. Rakoscsaba, Hungary, Apr. 20, 1928; m. Hedvig Schweiger, Sept. 9, 1950; children: Denes, Sophie. MSc, Eotvos U., Budapest, Hungary, 1950; DSc, Hungarian Acad. Sci., 1970. Diplomate in chemistry. Asst. prof. organic chemistry Eotvos U., Budapest, 1950-65, assoc. prof., 1966-70, prof., 1971-98; prof. emeritus, 1999—; prorector Eotvos U., Budapest, 1981-83, dean Faculty of Sci., 1983-89, dir Inst. of Chemistry, 1989-93; head rsch. group of peptide chemistry Hungarian Acad. Sci., 1990-98. Contbr. more than 140 articles to internat. jours. Recipient State Prize of Hungary, 1970, Heyrovsky medal Czechoslovak Acad. Sci., 1982, Gold medal of the Univ., Eotvos U., 1989, Middle Cross of the Order of the Hungarian Rep., 1998. Mem. Hungarian Acad. Sci. Home: Goz-U 19, H-1214 Budapest Hungary Office: Rsch Group Peptide Chemistry, Pazmany P Setany 2, H-1117 Budapest Hungary

MEE, AENEAS DAVID, urologist; b. Dunedin, New Zealand, Dec. 5, 1940; s. Stanley Edward and Ellen Veronica (Henaghan) M.; m. Rita Mary O'Dea, Oct. 16, 1965; children: Antonia Frances, Christopher David. MB ChB, Otago U., 1964. Vis. urologist Waikato Hosp., Hamilton, New Zealand, 1974-80; sr. lectr. Royal Postgrad. Med. Sch. U. of London, 1980-82; hon. cons. urologist Hammersmith Hosp., London, 1980-82; cons. urologist Charing Cross Hosp., London, 1982-93, Northwick Park Hosp., Harrow, Eng., 1982—. Contbr. articles to profl. jours. Fellow Royal Coll. Surgeons; mem. British Assn. Urol. Surgeons, British Med. Assn. Office: Northwick Pk & St Marks NHS Trust, Watford Rd, Harrow HA1 3UJ, England

MEEHAN, RICHARD THOMAS, JR., lawyer; b. Bridgeport, Conn., Jan. 11, 1949; s. Richard Thomas and Elvira (Avola) M.; m. Kathy Lynn Mucci, Aug. 23, 1969; children: Michael, Brian, Daniel, Timothy, Richard. BA, U. Notre Dame, 1970; JD with honors, U. Conn., 1974. Bar: Conn. 1974, U.S. Dist. Ct. Conn. 1975, U.S. Ct. Appeals (2d cir.) 1975, U.S. Supreme Ct. 1980; cert. criminal trial specialist Nat. Bd. Trial Advocacy. Clk. Conn. Supreme Ct., Hartford, 1974-75; ptnr. Meehan and Meehan, Bridgeport, 1975—; adj. assoc. prof. paralegal program Sacred Heart U., Fairfield, Conn., 1976-79; lectr. Fairfield U., 1988—, Coun. Trial Lawyer's Assn. The People's Law Sch., 1990—, Fairfield County Detective Sch., 1988—; adj. prof. Quinnipiac Coll. Law Sch., 1997—. Bd. editors U. Conn. Law Rev., 1972-73, rsch. and spl. projects editor, 1973-74. Alderman City of

Bridgeport, 1975-79; commr. Airport Commn., Bridgeport, 1977-79; pres. Common Coun., Bridgeport, 1977-79; mem. exec. bd. North End Little League, Bridgeport, 1983; mgr. Shelton Am. Little League, 1985-92; v.p. Flag Football League, Shelton, 1991—; varsity basketball coach Shelton Cath. Regional Jr. H.S., 1991-95; pres., adv. bd. Cath. Family Svcs. Fairfield County, 1997—. Recipient Am. Jurisprudence award for torts Lawyers Coop, 1972, Am. Jurisprudence award advance criminal procedure Lawyers Coop, 1972, Am. Jurisprudence award contracts Lawyers Coop, 1972. Mem. ATLA, Conn. Bar Assn. (exec. com. criminal law 1981-83), Conn. Trial Lawyers Assn., Bridgeport Bar Assn. (exec. com. 1982-85, chmn. criminal law sect. 1981-82, 84-85, pres.-elect 1985-86, pres. 1986-87), Nat. Coun. Bar Pres., Conn. Coun. Bar Pres's. Democrat. Roman Catholic. E-mail: thefirm@meehanlaw.com. Home: 28 Elderberry Ln Shelton CT 06484-3757 Office: Meehan and Meehan 76 Lyon Ter Bridgeport CT 06604-4022

MEEKER, DAVID ANTHONY, public relations executive; b. Akron, Ohio, June 1, 1939; s. Charles Anthony and Lucia Pauline (Schweikert) M.; m. Anita Marie De Jacimo, June 24, 1961; children: Christine Marie, Elizabeth Ann, Eileen Louise, David Edgerton. BS in Indsl. Journalism, Kent State U., 1961, postgrad., 1963-64; MS in Comms. Mgmt., Syracuse U., 1998. Editor Recordak Record, Eastman Kodak Co., N.Y.C., 1961-62; journalist Akron Beacon Jour., 1962-66, St. Louis Post-Dispatch, 1966-69; exec. sec. to mayor City of St. Louis, 1969-71; asst. dir. Ohio Dept. Natural Resources, Columbus, 1971-73; exec. dir. Ohio Dem. Party, Columbus, 1973-74; pres. Urbanistics, Inc., 1974-76; ptnr. Meeker-Mayer Pub. Rels., 1976-84; pres. David A. Meeker & Assocs., Inc., Akron, 1984-89; sr. counselor Edward Howard & Co., Akron, 1989—; also bd. dirs. Bd. dirs. Akron Regional Devel., Ohio Alliance for the Environment, St. Edward Home; Dem. candidate for mayor City of Akron, 1987; mem. regional environ. priorities project pub. com. Kent State U. Sch. Journalism, 1996-97; mem. adv. bd. Kent State U. Sch. Journalism and Mass Comm.; chmn. Summit County Charter Commn., 1995. Recipient Con Lee Kelliher award Kent State U., 1966, Disting. Alumnus award Sch. Journalism, 1983. Fellow Pub. Rels. Soc. Am. (nat. honors and awards com. 1981-83, chmn. 1983, nat. membership com. 1980-81, chmn. 1984, past del.-at-large nat. assembly, chmn. Counselors Acad. spring conf. 1987, pres. Akron chpt. 1982, immediate past chmn. and dir. environ. sects., chmn. Coll. of Fellows); mem. SAR, Internat. Pub. Rels. Assn., Soc. Profl. Journalists (past pres. Buckeye chpt., John S. Knight award 1999). Roman Catholic. Avocations: tennis, fishing, antiques. Home: 269 S Rose Blvd Akron OH 44313-7843 Office: One Cascade Pla 19th Fl Akron OH 44308

MEEKER, GUY BENTLEY, banker; b. Calcutta, India, Nov. 4, 1945; (parents Am. citizens); s. Lincoln Voght and Fortune Helen (Bentley) M.; m. Lavenia Yale Nelson, Apr. 27, 1967 (div. 1979); children: G. Bentley Jr., Melissa Anne ; m. Marcia Lee Zink, Nov. 4, 1984 (div. 1993). BSBA, Georgetown U., 1967; MBA, George Washington U., 1970. Cons. OAS, Washington, 1971-73; v.p. The Deltec Banking Corp., Nassau, Bahamas & N.Y.C., 1973-78, Comml. Credit Internat. Banking Corp., Balt., 1978-82; sr. v.p., gen. mgr. Union Planters Internat. Bank, N.Y.C., 1982-84; exec. v.p., gen. mgr. Worthen Bank Internat., N.Y.C., 1984-86; exec. v.p. and chief exec. officer N.Am. Bank Cen. Asia, N.Y.C., 1984-95; supervisory dir. BCA Bank Europe N.V., Amsterdam, The Netherlands, 1993-95; pres. G.B. Meeker & Co., N.Y.C., 1996—. Author articles and monographs in field. Mem. Bankers Assn. Fgn. Trade (internat. adv. coun. 1992-95, vice chmn. IAC 1994-95), Inst. Internat. Bankers (legis. and regulatory com. 1992-94, bd. trustees 1994-95), Asia Soc. (corp. coun. 1987-95), River Club, Dutch Treat Club. Roman Catholic.

MEEM, JAMES LAWRENCE, JR., nuclear scientist; b. N.Y., Dec. 24, 1915; s. James Lawrence and Phyllis (Deaderick) M.; m. Buena Vista Speake, Sept. 5, 1940; children: James, John. B.S., Va. Mil. Inst., 1939; M.S., Ind. U., 1947, Ph.D., 1949. Aero. research sci. NACA, 1940-46; dir. bulk shielding reactor Oak Ridge Nat. Lab., 1950-53, in charge nuclear operation aircraft reactor expt., 1954-55; chief reactor sci. Alco Products, Inc., 1955-57; in charge startup and initial testing Army Package Power Reactor, 1957; prof. nuclear engring. U. Va., Charlottesville, 1957-81; dept. chmn., dir. reactor facility U. Va., 1957-77, prof. emeritus, 1981—; cons. U.S. Army Fgn. Sci. and Tech. Ctr., 1981-90; vis. cons. nuclear fuel cycle programs Sandia Labs., Albuquerque, 1977-78; vis. staff mem. Los Alamos Sci. Lab., 1967-68; mem. U.S.-Japan Seminar Optimization of Nuclear Engring. Edn., Tokai-mura, 1973. Author: Two Group Reactor Theory, 1964. Fellow Am. Nuclear Soc. (sec. reactor ops. div. 1966-68, vice chmn. 1968-70, chmn. 1970-71, Exceptional Service award 1980); mem. Am. Phys. Soc., Am. Soc. Engring. Edn., SAR. Home: University Village # 1201 500 Crestwood Dr Charlottesville VA 22903-4890

MEENGS, WILLIAM LLOYD, cardiologist; b. Zeeland, Mich., Dec. 23, 1942; s. Lloyd Stanley and Gertrude (Wyngarden) M.; m. Helen Delores Van Dyke, June 10, 1964; children: Michelle Rene, William Lloyd, Lisa Ann. AB, Hope Coll., 1964; MD, U. Mich., 1968. Intern in internal medicine U. Hosp., Ann Arbor, Mich., 1968-69, resident in internal medicine, 1971-73, fellow in cardiology, 1973-75; practice medicine specializing in cardiology Petoskey, Mich., 1975—; cardiologist Burns Clinic Med. Center, Petoskey, 1975-99, chmn. dept. cardiology and cardiac surgery, 1978-89; med. dir. No. Mich. Heart Center, 1989-95; pres. Petoskey Cardiology, P.C., 1999—; chief sect. cardiology No. Mich. Hosps., 2000—; cardiologist Little Traverse Hosp., Petoskey, 1975—, dir. coronary care unit, 1986-89; dir. cardiac catheterization lab. No. Mich. Hosps., Petoskey, 1985-87, 92—, adult spl. care units, 1986-89; vice chmn. bd. dirs. Burns Clinic Med. Ctr., 1989-92. Contbr. med. articles to profl. jours. Trustee Mich. Heart Assn., 1979-83. Served as surgeon USPHS, 1969-71. Fellow Am. Coll. Cardiology, Soc. Cardiovasc. Angiography and Interventions; mem. Am. Heart Assn. (fellow Coun. on Clin. Cardiology), Am. Soc. Echocardiography, Alpha Omega Alpha. Home: 1224 Autumn Ln Petoskey MI 49770-9019 Office: Petoskey Cardiology 560 W Mitchell St Ste 400 Petoskey MI 49770-2274

MEER, FAROOQ AMJAD, lawyer; b. Lahore, Pakistan, May 27, 1959; s. Muhammad Ashrad M. and Naseem Akhtar; m. Samina Naz Qureshi, Apr. 7, 1986; children: Aiziz, Ahmad, Aleema. LLB, U. Law Coll., Lahore, Pakistan, 1983; LLM, Kings Coll., London, 1985. Advocate Subordinate Cts., Lahore, Pakistan, 1984-86, High Ct., Lahore, Pakistan, 1986-97, Supreme Ct., Islamabad, Pakistan, 1997-99; vis. lectr. U. Law Coll., Lahore, 1988-94; vis. prof. Punjab Law Coll., Lahore, 1995-97, Pakistan Coll. Law, Lahore, 1997-99. Gen. sec. Pakistan Tehreek-E-Insaf, Punjab, 1997-98, pres., Lahore, 1998-99. Mem. Lahore High Ct. Bar Assn. (hon. sec. 1994-95), Internat. Bar Assn., Lions Club (pres. 1996-97). Avocation: reading. Office: Meer Law Assocs, 1 Farid Kot Rd, Lahore 54000, Pakistan

MEERKAMP VAN EMBDEN, IAN CIRKSENA, chemical engineer, consultant; b. Malang, Java, Indonesia, Dec. 30, 1929; s. Johannes and Irene (Jennings) Meerkamp van E.; m. Ingeborg Bruener, Mar. 13, 1957; children: Arne and Vera (twins), Andrea. Degree in chem. engring., Fed. Inst. Tech., Zurich, 1953; DSc, U. Treiburg, Germany, 1957. Rsch. chemist Unilever, Vlaardingen, The Netherlands, 1953-59; gen. mgr. Schucharodt, Munich, Germany, 1960-72; dir. Metallgesellschaft AG, Frankfurt, Germany, 1972-80; dep. mgr. divsn. Soc. German Chem. Industry, Frankfurt, 1980-94; pres. Alpenforum, Murau, Austria, 1995—; v.p. Altrosenbergian-er, 1976—; pvt. cons. Frankfurt, 1995—; chmn. Econ. Coun., Frankfurt, 1976-84; bd. dirs. Wirtschaftsrat Hessen, Frankfurt. Contbr. articles to profl. jours. Recipient hon. plaque Econ. Coun., 1987, Ludwig-Ehrhard medal, 1990, hon. Merit Cross Germany, Bundesrerdienstkrenz am Bande, 1991. Mem. GdCh, DECHEMA, AGU, Austria Club (Frankfurt). Avocations: amateur film, classical piano, mountain hiking, political science, paleo-anthropology. Office: Lutzmannsdorf 14 St Georgen ob Murau Germany

MEERPOHL, HANS GERD, obstetrics and gynecology educator; b. Beckum, Westfalen, Germany, July 6, 1946; s. Franz and Agathe (Boller) M.; m. Ursula Blecke, Jan. 9, 1950; children: Jörg, Hella, Thomas. MD, U. Freiburg, Germany, 1972, PhD, 1986. Postdoctoral fellow Inst. Immunology, Freiburg, 1974-76; pres. dept. ob-gyn. U. Freiburg, 1976-81, asst. prof., 1986-93; head dept. ob-gyn. St. Vincentius Hosp., Karlsruhe, Germany, 1993—. Author, editor: Recurrent Disease in Gynecological Oncology, 1990, Ovarian Carcinoma, 1992, Clinic and Practice of Gynecologic Oncology, 1999. Lt. German armed forces, 1966-67. Mem. Am. Soc. Clin. Oncology, Internat. Gynecol. Cancer Soc., German Soc. Ob-Gyn. (sec. 1993), German Gynecol. Oncology Group (sec. 1987-93). Avocations: skiing, biking. Fax: 0721/8108 3644. E-mail: prof.meerpohl@gmx.de. Office: St Vincentius-Krankenhauser, Südendstrasse 32, 76137 Karlsruhe Germany

MEESE, CLAUS O., chemist; b. Bergreichenstein, Czech Republic, July 17, 1945; arrived in Germany, 1945; s. Othmar and Hilde (Thomas) M.; m. Ulla Paschen, Dec. 27, 1978; children: Jan, Isabelle. BSc in Chemistry, U. Hamburg, Germany, 1970, PhD in Chemistry, 1978. Lectr. U. Hamburg, 1973-76; rsch. assoc. Health Adminstrn., City of Hamburg, 1976-78, Fischer-Bosch Inst. Clin. Pharmacology, Stuttgart, Germany, 1979-93; head dept. chemistry Schwarz Pharma, Monheim, Germany, 1993—. Contbr. over 90 articles to profl. jours.; patentee in field. Grantee German Rsch. Coun., Robert Bosch Found. Mem. German Chem. Soc. Office: Schwarz Pharma AG, Alfred-Nobel-Str 10, D-40789 Monheim Germany

MEESSEN, KARL M., commercial law educator; b. Freiburg, Germany, July 30, 1939; s. Hubert and Margarete (Hein) M.; m. Heidi Boie, Aug. 22, 1964; children: Franziska, Maximilian. JD, U. Bonn, Germany, 1965. Prof. U. Cologne, Germany, 1975-76; prof. U. Augsburg, Germany, 1976-96, pres., 1979-83; prof. European and internat. comml. law U. Jena, Germany, 1996—; adviser Am. Law Inst., Phila., 1982-86; vis. prof. U. Chgo., 1985, Grad. Inst., Geneva, Switzerland, 1986-92, U. Paris, 1992. Author: Völkerrechtliche Grundsätze des Internationalen Kartellrechts; editor Wirtschaft und Wettbewerb, 1997—. Chmn. Friends and Sponsors of Deutsches Nat. Theater, Weimar, 1998. Decorated Fed. Order of Merit. Avocations: hiking, skiing. Home: Am Horn 55, D-99425 Weimar Germany Office: Jean-Monnet-Chair, Carl-Zeiss-Str 3, D-07740 Jena Germany

MEESSEN, MICHEL JOSEPH, surgeon; b. Thimister, Belgium, Apr. 12, 1939; s. Gaston and Nelly (Domken) M.; m. Anne Marie Doneux, Sept. 10, 1964; children: Dominique, Benoît, Bruno, Vincent, Olivier. MD, U. Liege, Belgium, 1964. Diplomate Am. Bd. Surgery. Physician-in-chief Ctr. Social Medicine, 1965-68; asst. resident Sinai Hosp., Balt., 1968-71; attending surgeon CHRVS, Aubelias, Belgium, 1977-83; chief resident in surgery Sinai Hosp., Balt., 1971-72; surgeon Univ. Hosp., Liege, 1972-77; surgeon-in-chief CHRVS, Auvelais, Belgium, 1983-97; head med. info. dept. Ch Basse Sambre Bib Med. Ctr., Sambreville, Belgium, 1998—. Roman Catholic. Avocations: reading, travel. Home: 6 Rue Bois St Martin, 5060 Tamines Belgium Office: Ch Basse Sambre Bib Med Ctr, 75 Rue Chère Voie, 5060 Sambreville Belgium

MEESTERS, YBE, psychologist, psychotherapist, researcher; b. Oosterwolde, Friesland, The Netherlands, Mar. 5, 1951; s. Sjoerd and Kornelia (Westerhof) M.; m. Johanna Sybrigje Borger, May 12, 1986; children: Sjoerd Ferdinand Sjieuwe, Alie Nynke Roelie. RN, Acad. Hosp., Groningen, The Netherlands, 1979; MSc, State U., Groningen, The Netherlands, 1988, PhD, 1994. Electronic engr. Tektronix Ltd., Heerenveen, The Netherlands, 1973-75; nurse Acad. Hosp., Groningen, 1975-89, psychologist, rschr., behavioral therapist, 1989—. Contbr. articles to profl. jours. Mem. Soc. Light Treatment and Biol. Rhythms, Nederlands Inst. van Psychologen, Vereniging voor Gedragstherapie. Home: Washuisterweg 7, 9791 TE Ten Boer The Netherlands Office: Acad Hosp Groningen, PO Box 30 001, 9700RB Groningen The Netherlands

MEFFRE, PATRICK RENE, chemistry educator; b. Marseille, France, Oct. 10, 1964. Degree in engring., ENSCP, Paris, 1987; D. U. Paris VI, 1991; postgrad., U. Montreal, Can., 1992. Lectr. ENSCP, Paris, 1993—. Contbr. chpts. to books in field; mem. editl. bd. Amino Acids Jour., 1999. Recipient prize Assn. Francaise Rsch. Therapeutique, 1991. Mem. French Chemical Soc., Soc. Chemical Industry. Home: 14 Rue Des Hautes Formes, 75013 Paris France Office: ENSCP, 11 Rue P et M Curie, 75005 Paris France

MEGAHY, DIANE ALAIRE, physician; b. Des Moines, Iowa, Oct. 12, 1943; d. Edwin Dare and Georgiana Lee (Butcher) Raygor; m. Mohamed H. Saleh Megahy, Sept. 20, 1969; children: Hassan, Hamed, Hala, Heba. MD, U. Alexandria, Egypt, 1981. Diplomate Am. Bd. Family Practice. Intern Univ. Hosps., Alexandria, Egypt, 1982-83; resident Siu Family Practice, Belleville, Ill., 1987-90; physician St. Joseph's Hosp., Highland, Ill., 1988—; mem. 3rd jud. cir. ct. steering com. on domestic violence, domestic violence med. subcom. Mem. AMA, AAUW, Am. Coll. Forensic Examiners, So. Ill. Med. Assn., Ill. State Med. Soc. (com. for CME accreditation, chmn. internat. med. grad. com.), Assn. Emergency Room Physicians. Avocations: student education in local schools. Home: 812 S Virginia Ave Belleville IL 62220-3689 Office: 109 W Legion Ave Columbia IL 62236-2341

MEGAN, MIHAIL, mathematician, researcher; b. Zegaia, Mehedinti, Romania, Jan. 2, 1947; s. Gheorghe and Eugenia (Popescu) M.; m. Nicoleta Angheloni, Nov. 8, 1970; children: Mihaela, Diana. BA, U. Timisora, Romania, 1969. Asst. prof. U. Timisoara, 1969-90, assoc. prof., 1990-92, prof., 1992—, vice dean, 1981-90, dean, 1996—; doctoral adviser U. Timisoara, 1993—; mem. Nat. Coun. Sci. Rsch. Romania, 1998—. Author: Introduction to Mathematical Analysis by Exercises and Problems, 1976, Differential Calculus by Exercises and Problems, 1981, Real Mathematical Analysis, 1981, Integral Calculus by Exercises and Problems, 1984, Tests of Mathematics and Physics, 1993, Foundations of Mathematical Analysis by Exercises and Problems, 1994, Mathematical Analysis, vols. 1,2,3, 1995-97, monographs; editor Seminar Math. Analysis and Applications Control Theory, 1990. Capt. Romanian Army Res., 1992—. Mem. Romanian Math. Soc. (pres. Timisoara br. 1992-96, Centenary Jubilee medal, 1995), Timisoara Coun. Scholars Acad. Avocations: football, reading, trips. Home: 1B Cozia, 1900 Timisoara Romania Office: U Timisoara, 4 Parvan, 1900 Timisoara Romania

MEGARBANE, BRUNO, physician; b. Alepoo, Syria, Nov. 9, 1966; s. Noel and Claude (Samman) M. MD, U. Paris V, 1997. Fellow Hosp. Lariboisiere, Paris, 1997-98, asst., 1998-99; physician Hosp. Lariboisiere, 1997—. Home: 46 Rue Henri Huchard, 75018 Paris France Office: Hosp Lariboisiere, 2 Rue Ambroise Pare, 75010 Paris France

MEGARRY, SIR ROBERT, retired judge, writer, lecturer; b. Croydon, Surrey, England, June 1, 1910; s. Robert Lindsay and Irene Marion Edgar (Clark) M.; m. Iris Davies, Nov. 14, 1936; children: Katherine Lindsay, Susanna Briony, Esther Jacquetta. BA, U. Cambridge, Eng., 1932, LLB, 1933, LLD, 1959; LLD (hon.), U. Hull, Eng., 1963, U. of Nottingham, Eng., 1979, The Law Soc. of Upper Can., 1982, U. of London, 1988, U. Essex, Eng., 1991. Cert. solicitor, 1935, barrister, 1944, Queen's Counsel, 1956. Lectr. Coll. of Law, London, 1935-39, prin., 1940-44, asst. sec., 1944-46, ministry of supply; barrister Chancery Bar, London, 1946-67; vis. prof. NYU, 1960-61, Osgoode Hall Law Sch., Toronto, Ont., Can., 1964; asst. reader in equity Inns. of Ct., 1946-51, reader, 1951-70; high ct. judge Chancery Div., 1967-76, vice-chancellor, 1976-85; ret.; mem. jud. com. Privy Coun., 1978—; Regents' fellow UCLA, 1983; chmn. Inc. Coun. of Law Reporting, 1972-87, comparative law sect. Br. Inst. of Internat. and Comparative Law, 1977-82; The Visitor, Essex U., 1983-90, Clare Hall, Cambridge, 1984-89. Asst. editor, book rev. editor The Law Quarterly Review, 1944-67; author: The Rent Acts 1939, 11th edit., 1988-89, A Manual of the Law of Real Property, 1946, 7th edit., 1993, Miscellany-at-Law, 1955, A Second Miscellany-at-Law, 1973; joint author The Law of Real Property, 1957, 6th edit., 2000; contbr. articles to profl. jours. Chmn. Notting Hill Housing Trust, London, 1967-68, Friends of Lancing Chapel, Sussex, 1969-93. Created knight, 1967; Privy Counsellor, 1978; named to Bench Lincoln's Inn, 1962, treas. 1981; named hon. fellow Trinity Hall Cambridge U., 1973—. Fellow The Brit. Acad.; mem. The Soc. of Pub. Tchrs. of Law (pres. 1965-66), Selden Soc. (pres. 1976-79), Can. Bar Assn. (hon.), Am. Law Inst. (hon.), The Lancing Club (pres. 1974-98). Home: 5 Stone Bldgs, Lincoln's Inn, London WC2A 3XT, England Office: Inst Advanced Legal Studies, 17 Russell Sq, London WC1B 5DR, England

MEGONE, CHRISTOPHER BRUCE, philosophy educator; b. Cape Town, South Africa, May 10, 1958; s. Cyril Bruce and Hilary (Crowther) M.; m. Deborah Janet Barker, Sept. 17, 1988; children: Julia Catherine, Helen Felicity Siphokhazi. BA in Lit. Humaniores with honors, Oxford (Eng.) U., 1980, BPhil, 1982, DPhil, 1991. Lectr. in philosophy U. York, Eng., 1983-91; lectr. in philosophy U. Leeds, Eng., 1991-96, sr. lectr. in philosophy, 1997—, fin. officer Ctr. Bus. and Profl. Ethics, 1991—. Author: Encyclopaedia of Applied Ethics, 1997; contbr. articles to profl. jours. Mem. Deanery Synods, York, 1993—. Conservative. Mem. Anglican Ch. Avocations: cricket, squash, film, reading, walking. Office: U Leeds, Sch Philosophy, Leeds LS2 9JT, England

MEGUID, AHMED ESMAT ABDEL, government official; b. Alexandria, Egypt, Mar. 22, 1923; m. Eglal Abou-Hamda, 1950; 3 sons. Licence en Droit, Alexandria U., 1944; diploma of Higher Studies in Pub. Law, Paris U., 1947, diploma of Higher Studies in Econs., 1948, diploma of Comparative Law Inst., 1949, diploma of Polit. Sci. Inst., 1949, Ph.D. in Internat. Law, 1951; postgrad., Acad. Internat. Law, The Hague, summer 1949, Inst. Advanced Legal Studies, London U., 1951-52; Doctorate (hon.), L'U. Catholique de Louvain, Belgium. Atty. legal dept. Egyptian Govt., 1944-45; attaché and 3d sec. Embassy of Egypt, London; polit. adviser Anglo Egyptian Agreement, 1954-56; head U.K. desk Ministry Fgn. Affairs, Cairo, 1954-57, dept. dir. legal dept., 1961-63; counsellor Permanent Mission of Egypt to European Office of UN, Geneva, 1957-61; minister plenipotentiary at Egyptian Embassy Paris, 1963-67; chef de cabinet of Under-sec. of State for Fgn. Affairs Cairo, 1968; sec.-gen. high interministerial com. of cultural relations and tech. assitance of Arab Republic of Egypt, 1969; head of cultural and tech. assistance dept. Ministry of Fgn. Affairs, Cairo, 1968-69; head State Info. Service, ofcl. spokesman of Egyptian Govt. with rank of dep. minister, 1969, ambassador of Egypt to France, 1970, minister of State for Cabinet Affairs, 1970-72, ambassador permanent rep. of Arab Republic of Egypt to UN, 1972-83, minister fgn. affairs, 1984-91, dep. prime minister, 1985-91; sec. gen. League of Arab States, 1991—; external examiner internat. law Faculty of Law, Cairo U. and Alexandria U., 1962-63; charge de cours on diplomacy Faculty of Econs. and Polit. Sci., Cairo, U., 1962; mem. internat. rivers com., ILA; head numerous ministerial coms.; lectr. in field; mem., rep., head various delegations to confs., councils; mem. Inst. Internat. Studies Stanford U. Author: Period of Defeat and Victory, 1999; contbr. articles to profl. jours. Pres. Egyptian com. for Tut-Ankh-Amon Exhbn. Le Petit-Palais, Paris, 1966; presided over dedication of Sackler Wing housing Egyptian Temple of Dendur at Met. Mus. Art, N.Y.C., 1978; mem. bd. trustees Am. U., Cairo; chmn. Cairo Internat. Ctr. for Arbitration. Decorated Grand Croix Govt. of France, 1st Class Arab Republic of Egypt, Govt. of Yugoslavia, Ordre de Merite Govt. of France, Grand Cordon of Order of Merit, Govt. Greece, Cavaliere de Gran Croce de L'Ordina Al Merito Della Republica Italianna, Grande Croix de L'Ordre du Dannebrog, Govt. Denmark, La Gran Cruz de la Orden de Boyaca, Govt. Colombia, Con Decoracion de la Orden del Aguila Azteca, Govt. Mexico, Grande Croix ler Classe de L'Ordre du magen, Order of Crown of Brunei, Sudan, Libya, Lebanon, Yemen, Morocco; fellow Aspen Inst. Humanistic Studies. Mem. Egyptian UN Assn., French-Egyptian Friendship Soc., Egyptian Bar Assn., Internat. Law Assn., Egyptian Soc. Internat. Law (past bd. dirs.). Home: 78 El Nile St Apt 23, Giza Cairo, Egypt Office: League of Arab States, Cairo Egypt

MEGWARA, JOHN, physicist; b. Owerri, Imo, Nigeria, Oct. 17, 1974; s. Samuelson and Joystella M. BTech in Physics, Fed. U. Tech., Akure, Nigeria, 1997; MTech in Geophysics, Fed. U. Tech., Minna, Nigeria, 1999; postgrad., Fed. U. Minna, 2000—. Instr. physics Fed. U. Tech., Akure, 1996; mgr. Data Computers, Abuja, 1997-98; dir. Mega Pearl Nigeria Ltd., 1998—; cons. Prime Comms., Nigeria, 1995, Zenol Computers, Nigeria, 1998; workshop/seminar Nigeria Internet Group, Abuja, 1998. Contbr. articles to profl. jours. Participant Nat. Tree Planting, Nigeria, 1985-99, Road Safety Awareness, Nigeria, 1990-99, Nat. Anti-Drug Abuse Campaign, Nigeria, 1990-99, Environ. Protection Awareness, Nigeria, 1986-99. Mem. Nat. Assn. Physicists, Protect Environ. Club (pres. 1998-99), Physics, Computer and Telecoms Club. Democrat. Avocations: football, singing/listening to music, drama, lawn tennis, athletics. Office: c/o K Megwara FIRS/PMB 33, Garki/Abuja Nigeria

MEGYER, ORS, communication company executive; b. Budapest, July 22, 1947; s. Szabolis Megyer and Gudit Varga; m. Edit Borosi, July 22, 1981; children: Csenge, Zsombor. Grad. in econs., Coll. Trade and Industry, Budapest, 1971; degree in econs., U. Econs., Budapest, 1979, Master's, 1986. Acct. Matur, Budapest, 1971-75, dir. commerce, 1975—, dir. prodn., 1987-89, dep. gen. dir., 1989-90; mng. dir. DDB Budapest, 1991-98, group chmn., 1999—; pres. Hungarian Advt. Self-Regulating Bd., 1998—. Mem. Hungarian Advt. Assn. (bd. dirs. 1994—), Internat. Assn. Advt. (bd. dirs. 1995—), Assn. Advt. Agys. (v.p. 1997—). Avocations: canoeing, running, cabinet work, house building. Home: Nedu Eg, 1028 Budapest Hungary Office: DDB Budapest, Obudai Sziget, 1033 Budapest Hungary

MEHAN, JULIE ELLEN, information systems specialist, consultant; b. New Orleans. BS in History and Lang., SUNY, Albany, 1987; MA in Internat. Rels. and Law cum laude, Boston U., 1994; cert. in AMSC, Army Mgmt. Staff Coll., 1996. Intelligence spl. project officer U.S. Army, Berlin, 1985-90; chief security and ops. 1st personnel commd. U.S. Army, Schuetzingen, Germany, 1990-94; IO/IA divsn. chief, Hdqs. U.S. Army, Heidelberg, Germany, 1994-97; dep. divsn. chief land info. warfare U.S. Army, Ft. Belvoir, Va., 1997-99; program mgr. EWA land info. group Heindon, Va., 1999—; advisor Pres.'s Partnership for Critical Info. Security, Washington; co-chair proof concept team Internat. Security Trust and Privacy Alliance, Washington. Author: (handbook) Information Operations Vulnerabiltiy Assessment and Red Team Concept, 1998. Counselor victims of domestic violence ACTS, Dumfries, VA. Mem. Info. Systems Security Assn., Internat. Systems Security Engring. Assn. (program chair), Boston U. Alumni Assn. Avocations: language study, sports, hiking with dog. E-mail: JMehan@ewa.com.

MEHENDALE, HARIHARA MAHADEVA, toxicologist, educator; b. Phiyla, India, Jan. 12, 1942; s. Shinginakodlu Mahadeva Bhat and Narmada M. (Tahmankar) M.; m. Rekha N. Joshi, May 10, 1968; children: Roopa, Neelesh. BS, Karnataka U., Dharwar, India, 1963; MS in Entomology, N.C. State U., 1966, PhD in Physiology, 1969. Diplomate Am. Bd. Toxicology (bd. dirs. 1986-90, sec. 1987-90). Asst. prof. dept. pharm. & toxicology U. Miss. Med. Ctr., Jackson, 1975-78, assoc. prof., 1978-80, prof., 1980, dir. toxicology tng. program, 1982-92; prof., Kitty DeGree chair toxicology Coll. Pharmacy U. La., Monroe, 1992—; dir. La. Inst. Toxicology, Monroe, 1995—; fellow Acad. Toxicological Scis., 1989—, vis. prof. dept. forensic medicine Karolinska Inst., Stockholm, 1983-84; adj. prof. Geriatric Edn. Ctr., 1986-91; mem. toxicology study sect. NIH, 1983-87, ad hoc study sects., 1983—, sci. adv. panel Fed. Fungicide Rodenticide and Insecticide Act, EPA, FIFRA, 1992-97; trustee Toxicology Edn. Found., 1997-99, sec.-treas., 1998-99; mem. com. on toxicology Nat. Acad. Scis., 2000—. Contbr. over 255 articles to profl. jours.; mem. editl. bd. Fundamental and Applied Toxicology, 1983-86, Jour. Toxicology and Environ. Health, 1986-93, Jour. Biochem. Toxicology, 1988-93, Toxicology and Applied Pharmacology, 1989—, Indian Jour. Environ. and Toxicology, 1990-94, Indian Jour. Toxicology, 1997—; overseas editor Indian Jour. Pharmacology, 1984-94, Toxicology, 1996—, Jour. Am. Coll. Toxicology, 1996; editor-in-chief Internat. Jour. Toxicology, 1997—. Grantee NIH, EPA, Air Force Office of Scientific Rsch., Burroughs Wellcome Fund, Dept. Energy, Agy. for Toxic Substances and Disease Registry, Miss. Lung Assn., Miss. Heart Assn.; Postdoctoral fellow toxicology U. Ky., Lexington, 1969-71, vis. fellow Nat. Inst. Environ. Health Sci., 1971-72, staff fellow, 1972-75, Acad. Toxicol. Scis. fellow, 1994—. Fellow AAAS; mem. Am. Soc. Pharmacology and Exptl. Therapeutics (chmn. divsn. toxicology 1993-96), Am. Assn. Study of Liver Diseases, Soc. Toxicology (awards com. 1996-97, Burroughs Wellcome Toxicology scholar 1988-92, Zeneca Internat. Travel award 1993, Bd. Publs. Best Paper award 1999), Am. Chem. Soc., Am. Coll. Toxicology (coun. mem. 1996—, mem. editl. bd. 1995-96, bd. chair publs. com. 1997—), Internat. Soc. Study Xenobiotics Am. (mem. publ. com. 1991-96, chmn. 1994-96), Am. Thoracic Soc., Internat. Union Pharmacologists, South Ctrl. Soc. Toxicology (v.p. 1986-87, pres. 1987-88), Assn. Scis. Indian Origin in Am. (founding pres. 1981, Disting. Svc. award 1990, Outstanding Scientist award 1992), Acad. Environ. Biology India (pres. 1990-93), Soc. Toxicology (India), Indian Pharm Soc., Soc. Neuroscis. (India), Indian Sci. Congress Assn., Entomol. Soc. India, Miss. Acad. Sci. (Outstanding Contbns. to Sci. award 1986), Hindu Temple Soc. Miss. (life, sec. bd. trustees 1991-92, chmn. bd. trustees 1992-95), Heritage of India (founding pres. 1998-99), Sigma Xi (chpt. v.p. 1981-82, 99-2000, pres. 1982-83, pres.-elect U. La. at Monroe chpt. 1999, pres. 2000—). Home: 207 Winterpark Dr West Monroe LA 71292-1107 Office: U La at Monroe Coll Pharmacy Monroe LA 71209-0001

MEHER, PRAMOD KUMAR, computer scientist, educator; b. Jarashingha, India, Mar. 10, 1955; s. Shesadev and Sindhu (Kumari) M.; m. Meera, May 11, 1986; children: Sudhir, Subrat. BSc, Rajendra Coll., 1976; MSc, Gangadhar Meher Coll., 1978; MPhil, Sambalpur U., 1981, PhD, 1996. Lectr. Panchayat Coll., Bargarh, India, 1981, Gangadhar Meher Coll., Sambalpur, India, 1981-89, Govt. Coll., Rourkela, India, 1989-92; tchg. fellow Regional Engring. Coll., Rourkela, India, 1992-93; reader in elec. sci. Berhampur U., India, 1993-97; prof. computer sci. Utkal U., India, 1997—; vis. prof. Sambalpur U., 1997—. Hindu. Home: Jarasingha, 767 067 Bolangir Orissa, India Office: Utkal U Dept Computer Application, Vani Vihar, 751 004 Bhubaneswar Orissa, India

MEHL, ROLAND, journalist, pharmacist; b. Paris, Nov. 18, 1923; s. Simon and Berta Mehl; m. Florence Kupper, July 9, 1970; children: Patrice, Arnaud. Pharm, U. Paris, 1950. Pharmacist, 1949-87; adminstr. Trade Union Pharmacists, Paris, 1950-85; founder Galien Award, 1970—, sec. gen., 1970-97; expert cons. Group Havas Medimedia, Levallois-Perret, France, 1983—; sec. gen. Prix Épidaure in Medicine and Ecology. Editor-in-chief Pharmacie Française, 1945-46, Moniteur des Pharmacies, 1957-68, Revue Technique Pharmaceutique, 1958-66, Pharmacie Mondiale, 1967-74, Tonus, 1975-82. Adminstr. Social Office, Paris. Decorated chevalier Ordre Arts et Lettres, chevalier Ordre Nat. du Merite, comdr. Civil Svc. (France); recipient Gold medal City of Paris, 1988. Mem. Soc. Expert Chemists, French Nat. Acad. Bd. Pharmacy, N.Y. Acad. Scis., Nat. French Press Fedn., Press Club France, Lions (bd. dirs. Paris club 1982-91). Avocations: travel, music. Office: Group Havas Medimedia, 140 Rue Jules Guesde, 92300 Levallois-Perret France

MEHLENBACHER, DOHN HARLOW, civil engineer; b. Huntington Park, Calif., Nov. 18, 1931; s. Virgil Claude and Helga (Sigfridson) M.; m. Nancy Moss; children: Dohn Scott, Kimberly Ruth, Mark James, Matthew Lincoln. BSCE, U. Ill., 1953; MS in City and Regional Planning, Ill. Inst. Tech., 1961; MBA, U. Chgo., 1972. Registered profl. engr., Ill.; lic. structural engr., Ill. Structural engr., draftsman Swift & Co., Chgo., 1953-54, 56-57, DeLeuw-Cather Co., Chgo., 1957-59; project engr. Quaker Oats Co., Chgo., 1959-61, mgr. constrn., 1964-70, mgr. real property, 1970-71; mgr. engring. and maintenance Quaker Oats Co., L.A., 1961-64; chief facilities engr. Bell & Howell Co., Chgo., 1972-73; v.p. design Globe Engring. Co., Chgo., 1973-76; project mgr. I.C. Harbour Constrn. Co., Oak Brook, Ill., 1976-78; dir. estimating George A. Fuller Co., Oak Brook, 1978; pres. Food-Tech. Co., Willowbrook, Ill., 1979-80; dir. phys. resources Ill. Inst. Tech., Chgo., 1980—; cons. Exec. Svc. Corp., Chgo., 1994—; arbitrator Am. Arbitration Assn. With USAF, 1954-56. Fellow ASCE. Home and Office: 436 Leitch Ave La Grange IL 60525-6126

MEHMOOD, KHALID, career officer, diplomat; b. Mian Channu, Punjab, Pakistan, Dec. 25, 1952; s. Aley and Fatima (Khatoon) A.; m. Maliha Jamil Khalid, Nov. 26, 1977; 3 children. BSc (hon.), Air War Coll., Karachi, Pakistan, 1988; MSc (hon.) in War Studies, Nat. Def. Coll., Islamabad, Pakistan, 1993; MBA, Islamabad Coll. Mgmt. and Commerce, Islamabad, 1997. Cert. fighter instr. Commdg. officer operation conversion unit PAF, Mianwali, Pakistan, 1986-88; commdg. officer flying instr. sch. PAF, Risalpur, Pakistan, 1989-90, commdg. officer Cadets Wing, 1990-92; commdg. officer Air Superiority Wing PAF Base, Quetta, Pakistan, 1993-94; dir. recruitment PAF, Peshawar, Pakistan, 1994-95; group capt. Pakistan Air Force, 1990—; def. attache Pakistan Embassy, Abu Dhabi, 1998—. Avocations: computer, music, golf. Home: Culshan Rd Link Paf Rd, 29-B Sargodha Pakistan Office: Embassy Pakistan, PO Box 846, Abu Dhabi Pakistan

MEHNERT, HELLMUT, physician; b. Leipzig, Sachsen, Germany, Feb. 22, 1928; s. Manfred and Annalies (Richter) M.; m. Ulrike Erika Wallem, Dec. 10, 1966; children: Stephanie, Katrin, Andrea, Friederiyke. Student, U. Munich, 1949-54; Tátigkeit Medizinischeny Poliklinik, 1957; State Exam, Promotion magna cum laude, Ludwig-Maximilians-U. Munich, 1954; Fachart Innere Krankheiten, 1961. Assoc. prof. internal medicine, 1964, prof., 1968; chefarzt der III Medizinischen Abteilung des Krankehauses München-Schwabig, 1966, 93; with Inst. Diabetesforschung, 1968; with Vertreter der Bundesrepublik Deutschland Diabetes-Experten-Komitee Welgesundheitsorgn., 1965-90; Mitglied Fortbildungsausschusses Bundesárztekammer, 1975-91; Leiter Konservatives Zentrums im Krankenhaus München-Schwabing, 1971-74;. Contbr. numerous articles to profl. jours. Recipient Ernst-von-Bergmann medal Deutschen Ärztenschaft, Bundesverdienstkreuz 1. Klasse, Bayerische Verdienstorden, München leuchtet gold medal, Jülich prize Düsseldorfer Diabetesforschungsinsts. Mem. Deutschey Diabetes-Union (pres., ehrenprásident 1999), Deutschey Gesellschaft Innere Medizin (pres. 1980-81, Ehrenmitglied 1993), Deutschel Diabetes-Gesellschaft (pres. 1973, ehrenmitglied 1994, Gerhard-Katsch medal), Internat. Diabetes-Vereinigung (v.p. 1975-82), Europáaischey Diabetes Gesellscahft (pres. congress 1975), Kassenárztlichey Vereinigung Bayerns (Bezirksvertreter 1992—), Rotary. Home: Drosselweg 16, 82152 Krailling Germany Office: Inst Diabetesforschung, Kölner Pl 1, 80804 Munich Bayern, Germany

MEHRA, JAGDISH, economics educator; b. Amritsar, Punjab, India, Nov. 12, 1934; came to U.S., 1962; s. Manmohan and Savitri (Devi) M.; m. Sneh L. Mehra, May 19, 1949; children: Reena, Benu. BA, Birla Inst. Tech., Pilani, Rajasthan, 1955, MA, 1957; PhD, SUNY, Buffalo, 1970. Asst. prof. econs. Banasthali U., Rajasthan, 1959-60; rschr. Nat. Coun. Applied Econ. Rsch., New Delhi, 1960-61; asst. prof. Econs. Birla Inst. Tech., Pilani, 1961-62; grad. asst., econs. instr. SUNY, Buffalo, 1962-65; asst. prof. econs. Youngstown (Ohio) U., 1965-71, assoc. prof. econs., 1971-81, prof. econs., 1981—. Contbr. articles to profl. jours. Avocations: reading, tennis. Home: 4892 Westchester Dr Apt 2 Youngstown OH 44515-6515 Office: Youngstown State U Dept Econs Youngstown OH 44515

MEHRAJ, MUHAMMAD ILYAS, company executive; b. Lahore, Punjab, Pakistan, June 21, 1955; s. Main Mehraj Din and Bano Begum; m. Shehzadi Ilyas; children: Zainab, Haseeb, Zakia, Siddra, Muhammad Abduccrh, Muhammad Yousaf. BSc, Punjab U.; BSc in Engring., Middlesex (Eng.) Tech. Inst., 1980. Dir. Ittefaz Group, Lahore, 1981-92; chief exec. Hasseb Waqas Group, Lahore, 1992—. Home: 183 H Block Modeltown, Lahore Pakistan Office: Haseeb Wawas Group, 103-B-1 MM Alam Rd, Lahore Punjab, Pakistan

MEHRAN, FIROUZEH, psychologist, researcher; b. Teheran, Iran, Apr. 11, 1946; d. Manoutchehr Mehran and Monir (Asfia) Djazani; married, Jan. 21, 1971 (div. 1992); children: Sam Ghobad, Sétareh Ghobad. BA, U. Social Svc., Paris, 1968; M in Adminstrn. Social Svcs., U. Social Svc. Mgmt., Teheran, 1974; PhD in Psychology, Fla. Inst. Tech., 1978; Diploma in Clin. and Pathol. Psychology, U. René Descartes, Paris, 1994. Cert. clin. psychologist, Ministry Nat. Edn., France. Creator, staff Behavioral Cognitive Psychotherapy unit Paul-Brousse Hosp., Villejuif, France, 1976—; founder 1st Ctr. Psycho-Family Psychotherapy, Teheran, 1977-79; cons. in psychotherapy Sainte-Anne Hosp., Paris, 1993—; clinician psychologist, pvt. practice Paris, 1995—; mem. scientific commn. behavioral-cognitive diploma, U. René Descartes, 1995—, mem. thesis jury, 1995-97; lectr. Iranian univs., 1969-78; lectr. U. René Descartes, 1993—; rschr. Vallé Found. and CNRS, France, 1986-88; organizer seminar on cognitive-behavioral psychotherapy, Univ. and Hosp. Ctr. Sainte-Anne, 1995-96. Contbr. articles to profl. jours. and conf. procs. Recipient Royal medal of Culture, Ministry Royal Affairs, Iran, 1976, cert. pres. of U. Chemiran, Iran, 1977. Mem. French Assn. Cognitive-Behavioral Psychotherapy, Iranian Drs. in Paris, Internat. Soc. Study of Personality Disorders. Avocations: oil painting, cooking, flower arrangement, swimming. Home: No 10 Rue Valentin Haüy, F-75015 Paris France Office: 50 Blvd de la Tour-Marbourg, F-75007 Paris France

MEHROTRA, NAVEEN, pediatrician; b. May 18, 1968. MD, SUNY, Stony Brook, 1992. Intern U. Chgo. Hosps., 1992-93, resident, 1993-95; attending physician, pediatrician S.I. (N.Y.) Univ. Hosp., 1996-98; attending physician Raritan Bay Med. Ctr., Perth Amboy, N.J., 1998—. Home: 3 Hageman Rd Somerset NJ 08873-7348

MEHROTRA, RADHEY SHYAM, metallurgist, researcher; b. Allahabad, India, Sept. 11, 1947; s. Shiva Narain and Bimla Debi (Tandon) M.; m. Rashmi Mehrotra, Feb. 7, 1973; children: Amit, Puneet. BSc, Allahabad U., 1965; B in Engring., Roorkee U., 1969; PhD in Metall. Engring., Indian Inst. Tech., Bombay, 1990. Grad. trainee Bhabha Atomic Rsch. Ctr., Bombay, 1969-70, sci. officer SC, 1970-75, sci. officer SD, 1975-81, sci. officer SE, 1981-87, sci. officer SF, 1987-94, sci. officer SG, 1994—, group leader, 1984-2000, sect. head, 2000—; PhD examiner Indian Inst. Tech., Bombay, 1995. Contbr. articles to profl. jours. including Materials Rsch. Bull., Trans. Powder Metallurgy Assn. India, Nuclear Tech., among others. Mem. Powder Metallurgy Assn. India (life), Indian Nuclear Soc. (life), Navi Mumbai Sports Assn. (life), Bhabha Atomic Rsch. Ctr. Officers Assn. (life). Avocations: photography, reading, meditation. Home: 10-A Nandadevi, Anushaktinagar, Mumbai Maharashtra 400094, India Office: Bhahba Atomic Rsch Ctr, Radiometallurgy Divsn, Mumbai Maharashtra 400085, India

MEHROTRA, RAM CHARAN, chemistry educator; b. Kanpur, India, Feb. 16, 1922; s. Ram Bharose and Chameli Devi (Tandon) M.; m. Suman Khanna, Dec. 11, 1944; children: Patil Rashmi, Mehrotra Piyush, Khanna Shalini. MSc, U. Allahabad, India, 1943, DPhil, 1948; PhD, U. London, 1952, DSc, 1965; DSc (hon.), Meerut (India) U., 1976, Kanpur (India) U., 1996, Jhansi (India) U., 2000. Lectr., reader Allahabad U., LKO U., India, 1944-58; prof., head chem., dean sci. Gorakhpur U., India, 1958-62; prof., head chem., dean sci. Rajasthan U., India, 1962-82, prof. emeritus, coord. spl. assistance program, 1982—; vice-chancellor Delhi (India) U., 1974-79, Allahabad U., 1991-94; governing body Commonwealth Sci. & Indsl. Rsch., 1963-66, 76-80; grants com., rev. com. Indian Parliament, India, 1974-78; higher edn. com., univ. act ammendment com. U. Rajasthan U., 1994-96; lectr. 1st Internat. Conf. Advanced Ceramics, Kyoto, 1990, Symposium for Aerogels, 1991, XXXIX Internat. Conf. on Coordination Chemistry, Lausanne, Switzerland, 1992, Better Ceramics through Chemistry Symposium, Paris and Chgo., 1993, ICCC, Kyoto, 1994, numerous others; presenter in field. Author: Text Book of Organometallic Chemisty, 1991, 2d edit., 1999; mem. editl. bd. internat. jours.; contbr. articles to profl. jours. Exec. com. Assn. of Commonwealth, 1976-79; chmn. pay com. UGC, Govt. India, Delhi, 1983-86; gen. pres. India Sci. Congress Assn., Hyderabad, 1979; pres. India Chem. Soc., Calcutta, 1978-79. Lt. India mil., 1950-54. Recipient Bhatanagar Laureate award CSIR, 1965, P.C. Ray award Indian Chem. Soc., 1988, Ind. Sci. Congress, 1998, Popularisation Sci. award Central H. Orgn., 1988, Life-time medals Platinum Jubilee Indian Chem. Soc., 2000, lifetime medal Chem. Rsch. Soc., 2000. Fellow Nat. Acad. Sci., India Nat. Sci. Acad., India Acad. Sci., Fedn. Asian Chem. Soc., Royal Inst. Chemistry (Eng.), Royal Soc. Chemistry (Eng.); mem. NCERT (chmn. book writing project 1985—), UNESCO (Indian del.). Avocation: photography. Home: 4/682 Jawahar Nagar, 302004 Jaipur India Office: Univ Rajasthan, 302004 Jaipur India

MEHROTRA, SEEMA, anesthesiologist; b. Bombay, Mar. 7, 1964; d. Chander Kishore and Sarla M.; m. Suresh Kumar Dargan, Apr. 14, 1993; 1 child, Shreya. BS in Biology, M.L.B. Coll., Bhopal, India, 1982; MBBS, Gandhi Med. Coll., Bhopal, India, 1988; MD, Gandhi Med. Coll., 1991. Intern Gandhi Med. Coll., Bhopal, 1987-88, resident house officer, 1988-89, demonstrator (anesthesia), 1989-91; sr. resident (anesthesia) Maulana Azad Med. Coll., Delhi, India, 1991-94; specialist (anesthesia) Govt. Gen. Hosp., Rafha, Saudi Arabia, 1995—; cons. (anesthesia) Lifeline Hosp., Bhopal, 1994, Wadhwa Medicare Ctr., Delhi, 1995. Contbr. articles to profl. jours. Recipient Certs. of Excellence Gandhi Med. Coll., G.B. Pant Hosp., Delhi, 1991. Mem. Indian Soc. Anesthetists, Indian Med. Assn., Delhi Med. Assn. Avocations: music, travel, cooking. Home: 265 A Pocket J&k, Dilshad Garden, 110095 Delhi India Office: Govt Gen Hosp Rafha, Rafha Saudi Arabia

MEHROTRA, SURESH CHANDRA, physics educator, researcher; b. Lucknow, India, Jan. 15, 1951; s. Krishna Narain and Shail Kumari (Tandon) M.; m. Uma Suresh Tandon, Sept. 1, 1953; children: Samit, Sudeep. BSc, Allahabad U., India, 1968, MSc, 1970; PhD, U. Tex., 1975. Vis. fellow Tata Inst. Fundamental Rsch., Bombay, 1977-79; prof. dept. electronics and computer sci. Dr. Babasaheb Ambedkar Marathwade U., Aurangabad, India, 1979-95, 1998—. Contbr. articles to profl. publs. Fellow Nat. Acad. Scis. E-mail: mehrotrascm@hotmail.com. Home: R1/1 University Campus, Aurangabad Maharastr 431004, India Office: Univ Campus, Physics Dept, Aurangabad Maharastr 431004, India

MEHRTENS, HERBERT, history educator; b. Bremen, Germany, May 5, 1946; s. Kurt and Ursula (Erlenhof) M. Diploma Math., U. Hamburg, 1974, Dr.rer.nat., 1977. Asst. prof. Tech. U., Berlin, 1979-85; prof. Tech. U., Braunschweig, Germany, 1992—. Author: (book) Moderne-Sprache-Mathematik, 1990; editor: Social History of Mathematics, 1981, Naturwissenschaft, Technik und NS-Ideologie, 1980. Fellow Inst. Advanced Study, Berlin, 1986, Dibner Inst. for History of Sci., 1996-97. Avocation: photography. Office: Technische Univ, Pockelsstr 14, D-38023 Braunschweig Germany

MEHTA, ANILKUMAR DHONDILAL, publishing executive; b. Nipani, India, Mar. 3, 1941; s. Dhondilal Valchand and Akkatai Dhondilal (Saudamini) M.; m. Anjali Anil Shah, Feb. 26, 1963; children: Sharmila, Sunil. B of Commerce, Pune (India) U., 1963. Chmn. Marathi Prakashak, Pune, India, 1975-80; v.p. Fedn. Indian Publs., Pune, 1990-95; publ. Mehta Publishing House, Pune, 1995—; trustee Marathi Prakashak, Sanghatha-Pune. Mem. exec. com., Fedn. Indian Publishers, 1995—. Avocations: badminton, reading, traveling.

MEHTA, CHAITANYA HARILAL, oil company executive, geophysicist; b. Bombay, June 6, 1945; s. Harilal Jeshanker and Jasumati Harilal (Shastri) M.; m. Mamta C. Mundra, May 31, 1974; children: Manjari, Shuchi. BSc, U. Bombay, 1964, MSc, 1966; PhD in Physics, U. Calif., San Diego, 1972. Rsch. physicist U. Calif., San Diego, 1972; Coun. Sci. and Indsls. Rsch. officer U. Bombay, 1972-76; mathematician Inst. Petroleum Exploration Oil and Natural Gas Co., Dehradun, India, 1976-93; head regional computer ctr., mgr. Oil and Natural Gas Co., Bombay, 1993-96; gen. mgr. Geopic Oil and Natural Gas. Co., Dehradun, 1996—; tchr. dept. physics U. Bombay, 1973-76; rschr. Inst. Petroleum Exploration, Oil and Natural Gas Co., Dehradun, 1976-93. Contbr. articles to profl. jours. Recipient Merit award for outstanding contbn. KDM Inst. Petroleum Exploration, Dehradun, 1989, Nat. Mineral award in geophysics Ministry Mines, Govt. India, New Delhi, 1993. Mem. Soc. Petroleum Geophysicists, Computer Soc. Indian, Nat. Geographic Soc. Avocations: yoga, music, literature, homeopathy. Home: 20/1 Prakash Nagar, Idgah, Dehradun 248001, India Office: Geodata Processing ONGC, Kaulagarh Rd, Dehradun 248195, India

MEHTA, CHAMPAT RAJ, agricultural engineer, researcher; b. Sirohi, Rajasthan, India, June 23, 1965; s. Bhim Raj and Rukmani Devi (Sanghvi) M.; m. Anita Gandhi, Dec. 2, 1988; children: Shruti, Shrecha. B in Agrl. Engring. with honors, Coll. Tech. and Agrl. Engring., Udaipur, India, 1987, M in Agrl. Engring. with honors, 1993; PhD in Farm Machinery and Power Engring., Indian Inst. Tech., Kharagpur. Rsch. assoc. Krishi Vigyan Kendra, Jalore, India, 1987-88; sr. tech. asst. Coll. Tech. and Agrl. Engring., Udaipur, 1988; scientist Ctrl. Inst. Agrl. Engring., Bhopal, India, 1989—. Author: Soil and Water Management, 1997; contbr. articles to profl. jours. Merit scholar Mrs. Kusum Rathore Meml. Trust, Udaipur, 1983-86, Gate-87 scholar Ministry of Human Resource Devel., New Delhi, 1988-89. Mem. Indian Soc. Agrl. Engrs. (life). Jain. Avocations: cricket, table tennis, philately, numismatics, movies. Office: Ctrl Inst Agrl Engring, Nabi Bagh, Bhopal 462 038, India

MEHTA, EILEEN ROSE, lawyer; b. Colver, Pa., Apr. 1, 1953; d. Richard Glenn and Helen (Wahna) Ball; m. Abdul Rashid Mehta, Aug. 31, 1973. Student, Miami U., 1971-73; BA with distinction, Fla. Internat. U., 1974; JD cum laude, U. Miami, 1977. Bar: Fla. 1977, U.S. Dist. Ct. (so. dist.) Fla. 1977, U.S. Ct. Appeals (11th cir.) 1981. Law clk. to presiding judge U.S. Dist. Ct. (so. dist.) Fla., Miami, 1977-79; asst. atty. County of Dade, Miami, 1979-89; shareholder Fine Jacobson Schwartz Nash Block & England, Miami, Fla., 1989-94; ptnr. Eckert Seamans Cherin & Mellott, Miami, 1994-98, Bilzin Sumberg Dunn Price & Axelrod, Miami, 1998—; lectr. in field; v.p., bd. dirs. Mehtatron Enterprises, Inc., Miami, Shalimar Homes Inc., Anderson, S.C. Miami U. scholar, 1971-73. Mem. Fla. Bar Assn., Dade County Bar Assn. Office: Bilzin Sumberg Dunn Price & Axelrod 2500 First Union Fin Ctr Miami FL 33131

MEHTA, HIMATLAL KARSANJI, business executive; b. Chhattar, Gujarat, India, May 2, 1935; s. Karsanji Mavji and Kastur Karsanji (Sheth) M.; m. Urmila Himatlal Vora, Feb. 9, 1961; children: Nisha, Chetan. BSc, U. Bombay, 1957, BSc Tech., 1959, Diploma in Indsl. Engring., 1969, Diploma in Ops. Mgmt., 1971. Plant mgr. Indian Dyestuff Industries Ltd., Kalyan, India, 1959-77; porject mgr. Sahyadri Dyestuff & Chems., Dewas, India, 1977-79, Indian Dyestuff Industries Ltd., Bangkok, 1979-82, 1979-82; CEO Mafatlal Plywood Industries Ltd., Bombay, 1982-85; sr. v.p. Indian Dyestuff Industries Ltd., Bombay, 1985-88; exec. dir. Nat. Peroxide Ltd., Bombay, 1988-98; vis. mgmt. faculty U. Bombay, 1972-84. Mem. Indian Instn. Indsl. Engring., Bombay Productivity Coun., Garware Club (life). Home: A/17 Saurabh Apts, Parshwanath Nagar, Mulund, Bombay 400 080, India

MEHTA, NARINDER KUMAR, marketing executive; b. Lahore, Punjab, India, Feb. 18, 1938; came to U.S., 1959; s. Puran Chand and Raj Rani Mehta; m. Narayanaswamy Sampath; children: Kiren, Ravi. B of Commerce, U. Delhi, India, 1958; MA, U. Minn., 1961. Program dir. All India Mgmt. Assn., New Delhi, India, 1963-67; with Am. Express Co., Chgo., 1968-82; nat. sales dir. Am. Express Co., N.Y.C., 1975-80, v.p. sales, 1980-82; sr. v.p. Shearson Lehman/Am. Express, Boston, 1982-85; sr. v.p. mktg. & sales Capital Credit Corp., Fairfield, N.J., 1985-94; sr. v.p. internat. mktg. Outsourcing Solutions, Inc., 1994-97; pres. Mehta Cons. Group, Dover, Mass., 1997—; sr. v.p. Temporary Investment Funds, 1982-85, Trust for Short Term Fed. Securities, 1982-85, Mcpl. Fund for Calif. Investors, 1983-85; conducted seminars for profl. assns., colls. and univs. Contbr. articles to profl. jours. Nat. v.p. Muscular Dystrophy Assn., N.Y.C., 1984-86; student body pres. U. Delhi, India, 1958-59. Recipient 1st prize inter-coll. debate, 1958. Mem. Am. Mgmt. Assn., Tau Kappa Epsilon. Avocations: running, swimming, traveling, reading. Office: Mehta Cons Group PO Box 547 4 Bryant Ln Dover MA 02030-2401

MEHTA, NAWZER HOSHANG, science foundation director; b. Nairobi, Kenya, Nov. 12, 1958; came to U.S., 1987; s. Hoshang D. and Najoo H. M.; m. Clare Elizabeth, July 4, 1987; children: Tajel Yasmin, Christopher William. BSc, U. Surrey, Guildford, England, 1981; PhD, U. London, 1987. Post doctoral rsch. asst. St. George's Hosp. Med. Sch., London, 1987-88; dir. clin. rsch. Corazonix Corp., Oklahoma City, 1988-91; v.p. product devel. Corazonix Corp., 1991-93; new projects mgr. Microsystems Engring., Lake Oswego, Oreg., 1993-96; dir. clin. rsch. Biotronik Inc., Lake Oswego, 1996—. Contbr. articles to profl. jours. Avocations: tennis, squash, reading, skiing. E-mail: nawzerm.@att.net. Office: Biotronik Inc 6024 Jean Rd Lake Oswego OR 97035-5308

MEHTA, NIRBHAY KUMAR, computer software developer; b. Durg, India, July 2, 1950; s. N.S. and K. (Dave) M.; m. Vrinda Dhagat, Dec. 19, 1977; 1 child, Vivek. BE, Engring. Coll., Jabalpur, India, 1971; PGDIE, NITIE, Bombay, 1974; PhD, Lehigh U., 1980. Faculty mem. NITIE, Bombay, 1982-83; mgr. NTPC, New Delhi, 1983-86; sr. con. Tata Consultancy, New Delhi, 1987-90; resident mgr. Tata Consultancy, Sydney, 1991-92, Bangalore, India, 1993-95; info. tech. cons. qV Systems, Bhopal, India, 1995-98; v.p. IIS Infotech Ltd., Madras, 1998—; panel mem. Union Pub. Svc. Commn. Govt. of India, 1988—; resource profl. CSI, India, 1996; panel mem. Indian Inst. Sci., Bangalore, 1994. Contbr. articles to profl. jours.; reviewer European Jour. OR, 1983-90. Treas. Indian Assn. Lehigh Valley, Bethlehem, Pa., 1979. Nat. scholar Govt. India, 1977. Mem. Assn. Computing Machinery, Computer Soc. India (sr.). Avocations: sightseeing, fabrication and repair, quiz programs. E-mail: mehta@iis.stpn.soft.net. Home: M-7/3 Ankur Complex, Shivajinagar Bhopal 462 016, India Office: IIS Infotech Ltd, 12 Khader Nawaz Khan Rd, Chennai 600 006, India

MEHTA, PESHOTAN RUSTOM, magnetotherapist and holisticologist; b. Bombay, Mar. 4, 1956; s. Rustom Nowroji and Aimai (Mahaluxmivala) M.; m. Amanda Gordon-Smith, Apr. 8, 1991. BS in Math., Physics, Biology with honors, U. Bombay, 1976; DS in Fundamental Biophysics, Inst. Theoretical Physics, 1995; PhD in Internat. Rels., Ala. A&M U., 1997. Pvt. practice in magnetomedicine, holistic, Tibetan, Ayurved, Unani and Chinese medicine; prof. U. Peace, Brussels, 1996; amb. plenipotentiary, permanent rep. UN, N.Y., Geneva, Vienna; ofcl. spl. advisor House of Lords, Eng., 1999—; invited lectr. numerous symposiums, seminars, workshops; pres., chmn. Albert Einstein Internat. Acad. Found., 1999; prof. U. Global and Religious Studies, U.S., 1998, Internat. U. 1992, 93, Tilak U., 1991, Ashtang Ayurved U., 1988-89; prof. emeritus Inst. Hist. and Mediaeval Studies, Cataluna, Spain, 1992; disting. prof.-at-large Open Internat. U., Colombo, Sri Lanka, 1994—; disting. prof. psychobioenergetic scis.; hon. prof. Internat. U., 1990—, Flinders U., 1993-94, U. St. Petersberg, 1995, U. Moscow, 1995, U. Rio de Janeiro, 1995, Chinese Acad. Scis., 1995, Ayurved Edn. Acad., 1992-93; spl. adv., hon. consul 1st Children's Embassy of World, Moldova, 1998; adv. com., hon. dir. med. rsch. Indo Japanese Med. Trust, Osaka, Japan, 1979; cons., internat. expert, v.p.-at-large United Town Agencies for North South Cooperation, Switzerland, 1999; cons., rsch. scholar The Vedi Rsch. Inst., Poona, India, 1977-78; rschr. St. Xaviers Coll., Caius Labs., Bombay, 1974-75, Tata Inst. Fundamental Rsch.-Basic Dental Rsch. Unit, Bombay, 1973-79, Tata Meml. Cancer Rsch. Ctr. and Hosp., Bombay, 1973-79; sr. rsch. fellow depts. applied maths. and electronic and elec. engring., U. Adelaide, 1992-93, lectr. Royal Adelaide Hosp., 1995, vis. clinican, vis. physician, 1991, adv., cons., 1995, vis. rsch. scholar, 1992-93; vis. scholar Hera's Inst., India, 1974-75, Tibetan Med. and Astrology Inst., 1986-87; vis. cons., physician North Melbourne Football Club, Collingwood Football Club, Adelaide Football Club, Sydney Football Club, Brisbane Football Club, Geelong Football Club, Carlton Football Club, Hawthorn Football Club, Port Adelaide Football Club, 1992-93, Kirke Paraplegic Home, Poona, 1990; vis. physician and magnetotherapist Children's Orthopedic Hosp., Bombay, 1977-78; chief internat. exec. councillor, chief internat. med. councillor St. Lukas Akademie, Germany, 1999; spl. consular of presidency and laureate Universal Movement of Artists for Peace, 1999; counsel-actif Confedn. European Judiciary and Magistrature of Europe, 1999; counsel, adv., mem. coun. for pres. United Towns Agy. for North South Dialogue, Geneva, 1999; sci. collaborator Ctr. Sci. Doc. Pres. Romania, 1989; dep. mem. assembly U.S.A. Parliamentary Group of Internat. States Parliament, Italy, 1997, min. del. Okla., 1998; ofcl. rep. to UN, Women's Health and Econ. Assn. Nigeria, 1999, N.Y., Geneva, Vienna, 1999; internat. corr. World Press Orgn., Brussels, 1999; judge-at-large Internat. Supreme Ct. for Protection of Life, 1999; spl. envoy of pres., v.p.-at-large, v.p. for U.S. and Can., internat. expert intercultural dialog, internat. expert interreligious dialog Coun. for Human Rights and Religious Freedom, Belgium, Switzerland, 1999; del. 52d UNDPI/NGO Conf., UN Hdqs., N.Y.C., 1999; mem. numerous adv. bds., couns. and coms.; cons., sci. advisor and expert in field. Editl. advisor the New Physician, 1992; author: The Nature of Cancer, What is Cancer?, How to Deal With the Cancer Problem, The Role of the Oncologost in Cancer Morbidity and Mortality, The Psychological Impact of the Word Cancer, The Biological Effects of the Magnetic Field, Magnetism and Its Effects on the Human Organism, The Gathas of Zarathustra, Space Travel as Revealed in the Zarathustrian Religion and the Pahlavi Texts, The Zend Avesta, vols. 1-4, The Significance of Fire Worship, Tibetan Mysticism - A Critical Anthology, A Collection of Poems, vols. I and II, Shirdi, Some Personal Experiences, Flying Saucers (UFO's) Declassified; author 220 papers, articles, monographs, reviews, and study aids. Recipient Pax Mundi award, 1994, Silver Medallion, Brit. Inst. Homoeopathy, 1994, Fellowship Award for Profl. Excellence, Acad. Diplomatique de la Paix, UN, 1994, Lifetime Achievement award, European Acad. Arts, 1997, Regional Recognition award, 1997, Humanitarian award Royal Order of Medicines, 1998, Recognition diploma Commn. de Educacion a Distancia, 1998, diplomas of Honor, Acad. Ecologica, Liga Culturala Pentru Unitatea Romanilor de Pretutindeni, 1998, cert. Honor, UNICEF, UNDPI, UNCED, 1996, 98, 2000 Millennium medal of Honor, 1997, Internat. diploma Honor, 1996, diploma Recognition, 1996, cert. Recognition, World Peace Acad., 1998, Cert. Merit, Five Element award medal, The Southern Star, Medicina Alternativa, 1998; numerous other awards, honors, and decorations. Fellow World Found. Integrated Medicine, Internat. Magnetotherapy Assn., Internat. Inst. Fine Mechanics and Optics, Internat. Inst. Natural Medicine (hon., cert. appreciation 1998), Internat. Soc. of ECIWO Biology, Internat. Soc. for Bioelectricity, Internat. Biog. Assn., Commonwealth Inst. Acupuncture and Natural Therapies, Royal Order of Natural Medicines, Royal Astron. Soc., Royal Soc. Medicine, Indian Found. Devel. of Integrated Medicine, Australian Charter for Natural Medicine Practitioners, Chinese Acad. Sci., Brit. Inst. Homoeopathy, Brit. Homoeopathic Assn.,

Homoeopathic Found., Found. of Oriental Medicine, Acupuncture Found. Sri Lanka and Register, Medicina Alternativa, Soc. Natural Therapists and Rschrs., Theosophical Soc., Coptic Orthodox Cultural Ctr., Monterey Inst. Study of Alternative Healing Arts, Kirlian Aura Rsch. Ctr. at St. Petersburg; mem. AAAS, Universal Assn. Peace through Cooperation (permanent rep., sci. adv. 1996), World Fedn. Holistic Medicine, World Health Fedn., World Assn. Integrative Medicine, World Inst. Achievement (hon. life), World Assn. Bioenergetics, World Directions in Sci. and Medicine, World Parapsychology New Ethics of Consciousness, Internat. Assn. Educators for World Peace (diploma of honor 1998, state chancellor for Okla. 1999, internat. liason 1999, adv. sci. and medicine/sci adv. 1996), Internat. Soc. for Bioelectricity, Internat. Soc. for Preventive Oncology, Internat. Soc. for Study of Subtle Energies and Energy Medicine, Internat. Rsch. Inst. Natural Medicine, Internat. Magnetotherapy Assn., Internat. Inst. Acupuncture and Complementary Medicines, Internat. Found. Alternative Medicine, Liga Medicorum Homoeopathic Internat., Internat. Inst. Traditional Medicine, Internat. Sci. Acad. (prof. magnetomedicine, comparative religion, physics, and biophysics 1997, 99), Internat. Assn. Biologically Closed Electric Circuits in Biology and Medicine (spl. adv. pres. 1999, charter mem. bd. dirs. 1999), Internat. Acupuncture Sci. Inst., Internat. Coun. Cmty. Chs., Internat. Homoeopathic Med. Orgn., Inst. Internat. Affairs (Serge Jurasunas Accolade and Gold medal 1996, diplomas honor 1996, cert. honor 1998, corr., academic, mem. coun. hon., permanent rep 1997, adv. science and medicine, sci. adv. 1996), Academic Sci. Acad. Internat. U., Acupuncture Assn. Australia, New Zealand and Asia, Asian Homeopathic Med. Assns. in Medicine, Asian Homoeopathic Med. Orgn., Asian Homoeopathic Med. League, Australian Coll. Phys. Scientists and Engrs. in Medicine, Australian Inst. Holistic Medicine, Australian Fedn. Homoeopaths, Australian Charter for Natural Med. Practitioners (internat. adv. magnetomedicine 1995), Scandinavian Acupuncture Found., U.K. Homoeopathic Med. Assn., Brit. Homoeopathic Assn., Brit. Holistic Med. Practitioners, All India Magnetotherapy Assn. (sci. adv. 1985-86), Indian Homoeopathic Orgn., Indian Assn. Surg. Oncology., Indian Bd. Alternative Medicine, Cardiol. Soc. India, Indian Cancer Soc., Bombay Assn. Sci. Edn., Ratheshtra Mandal, Rahnumae Mazdayasnan Sabha, The K.R. Cama Oriental Inst. (rsch. scholar), Brazilian Acad. Oriental Scis., Acad. Scis. Tech. Cybernetics of Ukraine (disting. prof. med. cybernetics, 1999, adv 1999), Assn. Artistic Promotion of Moldova (hon.), Spanish Assn. Profls. in Occupl. Health and Environment (hon. mem., registered in Spanish Min. Labor), Am. Phys. Soc., Am. Biog. Rsch. Assn. (dep. gov., mem. bd. govs.), FDIC U. Am., N.Y. Acad. Scis., Whole Health Inst., East and West U. Holistic Health Scis., Sokhao-In Found. Oriental Medicine, Royal Soc. Health, Acad. Peace, Soc. Homoeopaths, Inst. Complementary Medicine, Meteoritic Soc., Acupuncture Assn., Inst. Agrl. and Rural Devel., Theosophical Soc., Culture and Art of Healing Assn., Acad. Med. Tech. Scis. (disting. prof. frontier medicine 1999, adv. 1999). Achievements include the development of a new independent system of medicine: magnetomedicine which successfully treated over 300,000 individuals globally; expertise in implementing and applying magnetic fields for maintenance and restoration of homeostasis or in agriculture, interpreting bioeffects of electromagnetic field exposure, and the causes and explanations for these effects, prevention/remedy of electormagnetic pollution, holistic interpretation of phenomena and application of all therapies to the whole individual; expertise in intercultural negotiations, interreligious negotiations, international liasoning; invention of Magnet Arrangement, Biopulse/Pico Pulse; successfully treated over 300,000 individuals worldwide using magnetomedicine. Avocations: cosmology, meteoritics, paranormal phenomena, conducting, comparative religion.

MEHTA, RAJENDRAPRASAD MANILAL, librarian; b. Baroda, Gujarat, India, Nov. 11, 1940; s. Manilal Tulsidas and Chanchalben (Manilal) M.; m. Kamal Mohanlal Shah, May 15, 1960; children: Kirti, Meeta, Kunjalata, Prabodh. BA, M.S. U. Baroda, India, 1960, LLB, 1965, BLS first class, 1965. Supt. ref., circulation, acquisition, catalogue/periodicals Smt. Hansa Mehta U. Libr., M.S. U. Baroda, 1960-71, lectr. libr. sci. faculty arts, 1968-70; head catalogue dept. Vikram Sarabhai Libr., Indian Inst. Mgmt., Ahmedabad, 1971-76, head acquisition dept., 1976-92, dep. libr., 1993—; examiner Gujarat State Exam Bd., Govt. Gujarat, Ahmedabad, 1979-83; test adminstrn. Indian Inst. Mgmt., Ahmedabad, 1974, coord. and assistance in adminstrn., enquiring officer, mem. interview coms., pers. policy, staff evaluation coms., libr. com., 1978-92; lectr. various orgns. Contbr. articles to profl. jours. Avocations: reading, writing, advising, consultancy, computer applications. Home: 41/492 Adarshnagar, Ahmedabad 380 013, India Office: Indian Inst Mgmt, Vastrapur, Ahmedabad 380 015, India

MEHTA, RAKESH KUMAR, physician, consultant; b. Gidderbaha, Punjab, India, Aug. 18, 1952; came to U.S., 1985; s. Parkash Chander and Sheela (Thukral) M.; m. Anita Gupta; children: Sonika Deepali Mehta, Shivam Parkash Mehta. MB BS with gold and silver medal, Med. Coll., Amritsar, Punjab, 1975; MD, Postgrad. Inst. Med. Edn., Chandigarh, 1978. Diplomate Am. Bd. Internal Medicine. Intern Victoria Jubilee, Amritsar, 1975; resident in medicine Hosp. Postgrad. Inst., Chandigarh, India, 1976-78; sr. resident in medicine Hosp. Postgrad. Inst., Chandgarh, India, 1978-79, All India Inst. of Med. Scis., New Delhi, 1979-81, U. Alta., Edmonton, Can., 1981-83; clin. fellow in oncology Cross Cancer Inst., Edmonton, 1984-85, N.Y. Med. Coll., N.Y.C., 1985-86; cons. med. oncologist Vets. Affairs, Castle Point, N.Y., 1986-97; clin. asst. prof. medicine N.Y. Med. Coll., Valhalla, 1990—; chief oncology program Vets. Affairs Hudson Valley, 1986—. Contbr. articles to professional jours. Fellow ACP, Royal Coll. Physicians and Surgeons of Can., Am. Coll. Internat. Physicians; mem. Am. Soc. of Clin. Oncologists, Can. Assn. Med. Oncologists, Med. Staff Soc. (pres. 1994—). Avocations: travel, jogging, photography. Office: Vets Affairs VA Med Ctr Castle Point NY 12511

MEHTA, RAMAN, pharmaceutical executive; b. Amritsar, India, Sept. 14, 1947; s. Puran Chand and Leela M.; m. Nidhi Chaudhary, Aug. 3, 1974; children: Bharat, Diyya, Neha. BSChemE, Punjab U., Chandigarh, 1970; MS in Indsl. Engring., Columbia U., N.Y., 1972. V.p. Alchem Internat., Ltd., Delhi, 1986-97, sr. v.p., 1997—; sr. v.p. Lepro Herbals, Panipat, 1991—. Avocations: golf, photography. Home: 3 Empire Estate, Mehrauli-Gurgon Rd, 110030 New Delhi India

MEHTA, RAVI RAVINDER SINGH, international trade finance consultant, banking trainer and researcher, trade specialist; b. Rawalpindi, Punjab, Pakistan, May 20, 1945; s. Harbans Singh and Swinder Kaur (Duggal) M.; m. Davinder Kaur Kohli, Nov. 7, 1977; 1 child, Gurpreet. BSc, Delhi U., 1967, MSc, 1970; MLitt, Punjabi U., Patiala, India, 1976; PhD, Panjab U., Chandigarh, India, 1991. Cert. trade specialist. Rsch. scholar Panjabi U., Patiala, 1971-74; officer operational banking Punjaband Sind Bank, Bombay, 1977-80; officer trainer Punjaband Sind Bank, Chandigarh, 1980-96, mgr. internat. banking tng., 1996-2000; retail mktg. rsch. assoc. Wal-Mart Stores, Inc., 1999—; fac. mem. Internat. Trade and Banking Inst. (Canada), online teaching internat. trade fin., 2000—, correspondent, Documentary Credits Insight Mag., Internat. C. of C., France. Author: Sociology of Banking, 1976, Autobiography of a Cheque, 1982, Fundamentals of Banking, 1984, Signature Verification, 1990, Journey Through British Banking, 1991, Banking on Lombard Street, 1993, Bank Training in the U.K., 1994, Pictorial Biography of a Bank Training Centre in Switzerland, 1994, Early Banking in England, 1994, Expertly Handling of Export Letters of Credit: A Handbook For The Exporter and His Banker and Freight Forwarder, 2000; mem. editorial bd. LC Monitor Mag. (Ontario, Canada); contbr. articles to profl. and trade jours. Recipient several awards. Mem. Indian Inst. Bankers (life), Internat. Trade Assn., Inst. Export, bd. dirs., Internat. Trade and Banking Inst. Sikh. Avocations: travel, gardening, philately. Address: 1025 S Beach St Apt 141 Daytona Beach FL 32114-6278 Office: Wal-Mart Supercenter Punjab and Sind Bank 1590 Dunlawton Ave Port Orange FL 32127-4752

MEHTA, YAGNESH MANUBHAI, chemistry educator, researcher; b. Nadiad, Gujarat, India, June 1, 1939; s. Manubhai Devprasad and Bhanuben Manubhai M.; m. Meena Yagnesh Kaushik, June 8, 1963; 1 child. BSc, J. & J. Coll. Sci., Nadiad, India, 1960, MSc in Organic Chemistry, 1962, PhD in Organic Polymer Chemistry, 1995; LLB, Bhagat & Sonawala Law Coll., Nadiad, India, 1963. Tutor J. & J. Coll. Sci., Nadiad, India, 1962-77, lectr., 1977—, head dept. chemistry, 1991—, prin., 1994—; mem. bd. of studies Gujarat U., Ahmedabad, Nadiad, India, 1996, staff selection com., 1996, ct.; dir. Dr. Y.R. Patel Inst. Med. Tech., Nadiad, 1994. Author, editor: Organic Chemistry, 1994, Analytical Chemistry, 1994; contbr. articles to profl. jours.; rschr. in field. Trustee religious temples, pub. libr.; mem. pub. rels. com., Charutar Vidya Mandal, Vidyanagar, India; mem. ct., senate Gujarat U. Recipient cert. Jour. Oriental Chemistry, certs. Indian Coun. Chemists Conf., 1996-97. Fellow N.Y. Acad. Scis., Indian Coun. Chemists (life); mem. Planetary Soc., Chemistry and Environ. Rsch. India. Home: Fulaji Pole Dabhan Bhagol, Nadiad Gujarat 387001, India Office: J & J Coll Sci, College Rd, Nadiad Gujarat 387001, India

MEHTA, YATIN, anesthesiology consultant; b. Changa, Gujarat, India, Mar. 16, 1955; s. Chandrakant Mehta; m. Usha Ray, Nov. 25; children: Nihar Ranjan, Manan. MBBS, Univ. Coll. Med. Scis., New Delhi, 1976; MD in Anesthesia, All India Inst. Med. Scis., New Delhi, 1980. Med. diplomate; fellow Royal Coll. Anesthetists. Registrar in anesthetics All India Inst. Med. Scis., New Delhi, 1981-82; sr. house officer in anesthetics Scarbrough (Eng.) Hosp., 1982-83; registrar Nottingham (Eng.) Tchg. Hosps., 1983-85; sr. registrar Odense (Denmark) U. Hosp., 1985-87; locum cons. cardiac anesthesiologist Mafraq Hosp., United Arab Emirates, 1995; sr. cons. Escorts Heart Inst. and Rsch. Ctr., New Delhi, 1988—; locum cons. Eksjo Hosp., Sweden, 1985-88, Uppsala U. Hosp., Sweden; guest lectr. European Assn. Cardiothoracic Anesthesiologist, others. Chief editor Annals of Cardiac Anesthesia, 1998; mem. editl. bd. Indian Heart Jour., 1997—; contbr. articles to profl. jours. Fellow Royal Coll. Anesthetists (U.K.); mem. Nat. Acad. Med. Scis., Indian Soc. Anesthetists. Home: Villa 59, Block III, Erosgarden, Faridabad, Haryana 121 009, India Office: Escorts Heart Inst/Rsch Ctr, Okhala Rd, New Delhi 110 025, India

MEHTA, ZUBIN, conductor, musician; b. Bombay, India, Apr. 29, 1936; came to U.S., 1961; s. Mehli Nowrowji and Tehmina (Daruvala) M.; m. Nancy Diane Kovack; children: Zarina, Merwan. Student, St. Xavier's Coll., Bombay, 1951-53, State Acad. Music, Vienna, Austria, 1954-60; LL.D., Sir George Williams U., Montreal, 1965; D.Mus. (hon.), Occidental Coll.; hon. doctorate, Colgate U., Brooklyn Coll., Westminster Choir Coll., Juilliard Sch., Weizmann Inst. Sci. (Israel). Music dir. Montreal Symphony Orch., 1961-67, L.A. Philharm. Orch., 1962-78; mus. dir. Israel Philharmonic, from 1969, appointed dir. for life, 1981; music dir. N.Y. Philharm., 1978-91, Munich Opera, 1998—; guest condr. Met. Opera, Salzburg (Austria) Festival, Vienna Philharmonic, Berlin Philharmonic, La Scala, Milan, Italy, music dir., Maggio Musicale Florence, Italy, rec. artist for, Decca, CBS, RCA, New World Records, (recipient 1st prize Liverpool (Eng.) Condrs. Competition 1958); gen. music dir. Barian State Opera, Munich, 1998—. Decorated Padma Bhushan India, 1967, commendatore of Italy. *

MEIDANI, REXHEP, president of Albania; b. Tirana, Aug. 17, 1944; married; 2 children. Grad., U. Tirana, 1966, D in Scis., 1984; postgrad., U. Cannes, U. Paris, 1973-76. Lectr. in physics U. Tirana, U. Pristina, Albania, 1966-96; gen. sec. Socialist Party of Albania, 1996; dep. socialist party mem. People's Assembly, Albania, 1997; pres. Republic of Albania, 1997—; vis. scientist, lectr., prof. univs. and internat. rsch. ctrs.; participant commns., sci. couns., orgns. dealing with univ. edn. and sci. rsch. Pub. monographs, books and articles in Albanian and internat. sci. jours. Office: Office of Pres, Bulevardi Deshmoret e Kombit, Tirana Albania

MEIDANIS, JOAO, computer scientist; b. Sao Paulo, Brazil, Aug. 27, 1960; s. Panayote Charalambos and Vassilikoula Meidanis; m. Lucrecia Mendonca, Oct. 8, 1983 (div. Oct. 1996); m. Maria Aparecida Alves Diniz, Dec. 1998. BSc in Math., U. Sao Paulo, 1980, MSc in Math., 1984; MSc in Computer Sci., U. Wis., 1989, PhD in Computer Sci., 1992. Lectr. U. Sao Paulo, 1980-84; asst. prof. U. Campinas, Brazil, 1996—. Author: Introduction to Computational Molecular Biology, 1997. Mem. Brazilian Computing Soc. Avocation: swimming. Office: Unicamp, Av Albert Einstein 1251, 13083970 Campinas SP, Brazil

MEIER, ANTON EMIL, physicist, researcher; b. Lucerne, Switzerland, July 3, 1951; s. Anton and Alma (Gasser) M.; m. Verena Pezzotta, Sept. 10, 1987; children: Fabia, Rico. Matura, Kantonsschule Lucerne, Switzerland, 1970; Dipl. phys. ETH, Swiss Fed. Inst. Tech., Zurich, 1978; Dr.Phil.Nat., U. Bern, Switzerland, 1988. Rsch. scientist U. Bern, 1979-90; sr. rsch. scientist Paul Scherrer Inst., Villigen, Switzerland, 1990—. Contbr. articles to profl. jours. Office: Paul Scherrer Inst, Solar Tech, CH 5232 Villigen PSI, Switzerland

MEIER, HANS, chemist; b. Fuerth, Germany, Aug. 18, 1927; s. Eugen and Rosa (Denk) M.; m. Ingrun Schnittger, Aug. 15, 1964; 1 child, Kerstin. BSc, U. Erlangen, 1967. Dir. Staatliches Forschunginstitut fur Geochemie, Bamberg, Germany, 1960-92; ausserplanmässiger prof. Universitaet Erlangen-Nuernberg, 1972—. Author: Organic Semiconductors, 1974; contbr. articles to profl. jours. Home: Himmelreichstrasse 10, D-96120 Bischberg Germany

MEIER, HERBERT, writer; b. Solothurn, Switzerland, Aug. 29, 1928; s. Albert and Anna (Mueller) M.; m. Yvonne Haas, Sept. 23, 1954; children: Jonas, Livia, Titus. PhD, U. Fribourg, Switzerland, 1954. Chief dramaturg Schauspielhaus, Zurich, Switzerland, 1977-82; writer-in-residence U. So. Calif., L.A., 1986. Author: (novels) Ende September, 1959, Verwandtschaften, 1962, Stiefelchen, 1970, Winterball, 1996, (poems) Siebengestirn, 1956, Sequenzen, 1969, (poems and stories) Aufbrüche Reisen von dorther, 1998; (plays) Theater I-III, 1993. Recipient Bremer Literaturpreis, 1955, Solothurner Kunstpreis, 1975, Schillerpreis, 1997. Mem. PEN Club. Office: Appenzeller Strasse 73, CH-8049 Zurich Switzerland

MEIER, PAUL DANIEL, psychiatrist, writer; b. Saginaw, Mich., May 5, 1945; s. Alexander and Elizabeth M.; m. Janice Evonne Verkler, Aug. 27, 1966; children: Daniel, Cheryl, Brian, Mark, Brent, Elizabeth. MS in Cardiovascular Physiology, Mich. State U., 1968; MD, U. Ark., 1974; MA in Bibl. Studies, Dallas Theol. Sem., 1985. Resident in psychiatry Duke U. Med. Sch., Durham, N.C., 1974-75; co-founder Minirth-Meier Clins., nationwide, 1976-94; med. dir. New Life Clins., U.S. and Can., 1994—. Author over 50 books and novels including Happiness is a Choice, Love is a Choice, Windows of the Soul, The Third Millennium, The Secret Code. Mem. Christian Med. and Dental Soc., Focus on the Family Physician Resource Coun. Republican. Avocations: golf, hiking. Office: 2100 N Collins Blvd Richardson TX 75080-2661

MEIER, THOMAS, electrical engineer, researcher; b. Wetzikon, Zürich, Switzerland, Oct. 7, 1968; s. Jakob Meier and Gisela Otto. BEE, Swiss Fed. Inst. Tech., Zürich, 1993; PhD distinction in Elec. Engring., U. Western Australia, Perth, 1999. Software engr. Holliger & Meister Engring., Zürich, 1993-95; rsch. fellow U. Western Australia, Perth, 1999—; publicity chair, sec. Internat. Conf. on Visual Comm. and Image Processing, Perth. Author: Advanced Video Coding, 1999; contbr. articles to profl. jours. Mem. IEEE. E-mail: thomas.meier@ieee.org. Fax: 61-8-9380 1065. Office: Univ Western Australia, Stirling Hwy, Nedlands WA 6907, Australia

MEIER-RUGE, WILLIAM ALFRED, pathologist; b. Rudolstadt, Thür, Germany, July 28, 1930; s. Artur Robert and Herta (Kruger) M.-R.; m. Jutta Ruge, May 28, 1955; children: Peer, Cora, Tilman, Anja. MD, U. Berlin, 1954. Clin. asst., intern Gen. Hosp., Potsdam-Babelsberg, Germany, 1954-56; rsch. asst. Pathology Inst., U. Berlin, 1956-61; rsch. assoc. Pathology Inst., U. Basel, Switzerland, 1963—, assoc. prof., 1965; head Lab. Exptl. Pathology and Histochemistry dept. biology Sandoz Ltd., Basel, 1967-69; head dept. basic med. rsch. Sandoz Ltd., 1969-79, head gerontol. brain rsch. divsn. preclin. rsch., 1979-83; head Lab. Gerontol. Brain Rsch dept. neuropathology U. Basel, 1984—. Author: Medikamentose Retinopathie, 1967, CNS-Aging and Its Neuropharmacology, 1979, Teaching and Training in Geriatric Medicine, Vol. 1, 1987, Vol. 2, 1990, Vol. 3, 1992. Recipient Rudolf Virchow prize, 1960. Mem. German Soc. Pathology, Swiss Soc. Pathology, Royal Soc. Medicine (London), German Histochem. Soc., Swiss Gerontol Soc., N.Y. Acad. Scis. Home: 12 Oberwilerstrasse, CH-4103 Bottmingen/BL Switzerland Office: U Med Sch Basel Dept Pathol, Schoenbeinstrasse 40, CH-4003 Basel Switzerland

MEIGAS, KALJU, biomedical engineer, educator; b. Tallinn, Estonia, Feb. 20, 1951; s. Bernhard and Salme (Kalju) M.; m. Riita Lepik, Aug. 11, 1973; children: Marko, Risto. Diploma in engring., Tallinn Poly. Inst., 1974; MSc, Tallinn Tech. U., 1993, PhD in Elec. Engring., 1997. Chartered engr. Engr. Tallinn Poly. Inst., 1973-78; head designer Tallinn Indsl. Enterprises, 1978-86; rschr. Tallinn Tech. U., 1986-90; dir. Sm. Bus. Enterprises, Kvantel, Estonia, 1990-92; sr. rschr., assoc. prof. Tallinn Tech. U., 1992-96, prof. biomed. engring., head of chair, 1998—. Co-author: Lazernaja Dalhometrija, 1995; contbr. articles to profl. jours. Mem. IEEE, IFMBE (secs. com.), Estonian Soc. Biomed. Engrs. (sec. gen.), Estonian Assn. Engrs. (bd. dirs.). Office: Tallinn Tech U Biomed Engring Ctr, Ehitajate tee 5, 19086 Tallinn Estonia

MEIGEL, DAVID WALTER, retired career officer, retired musician; b. Chgo., Feb. 27, 1957; s. Thomas Arent and Annie Elizabeth (Thomas) M. Diploma, USAF NCO Leadership Sch., Chanute AFB, Ill., 1981, USAF/CAP SQD Officer Sch., 1987, USAF NCO Acad., Norton AFB, Calif., 1991. Enlisted USAF, 1976; major CAP, Travis AFB, Calif., 1998; ret., 1996; percussionist 724th USAF Band, McChord AFB, Wash., 1976-78, 752d USAF Band, Elmendorf AFB, Alaska, 1978-80, 505th USAF Band, Chanute AFB, Ill., 1980-84, 504th USAF Band, Travis AFB, 1984-90; prin. percussionist, chief of adminstrn. Am.'s Band in Blue, USAF, Travis AFB, 1990-92. Prin. percussionist San Diego (Calif.) Civic Orch., 1973-76, Poway (Calif.) High Sch. Band, 1974-75; percussionist Anchorage (Alaska) Civic Opera, 1979-80, Anchorage (Alaska) Scottish Soc., 1979-80, Fairfield Civic Theatre, Fairfield, Calif., 1984—; communications officer USAF Civil Air Patrol, Travis AFB, 1986—. Recipient Gov.'s medal Youkon Internat. Invitational Scottish Games, Whitehorse City Coun., B.C., 1980; decorated USAF Achievement medal 1989, 93, USAF Commendation medal 1996, Comdrs. Commendation medal 1993, 98; named one of Outstanding Young Men Am., 1988, 92, CAP Meritorious Svc. medal, 1989. Mem. CAP, USAF Aux. Avocations: amateur radio, golf, bowling, computer ops. Home: 8341 Crestshire Cir Orangevale CA 95662-3861 Office: Intel Corp Intel Corp 1900 Prairie City Rd Folsom CA 95630-9599

MEIGNAN, FRANCIS GEORGES, rheumatologist; b. Sete, France, Sept. 19, 1945; s. André Joseph and Rose Gabrielle (Sarrou) M.; m. Anne Marie Vieilledent, July 31, 1945; children: Benoit, Vincent, Olivia, Astrid. MD, U. Lyon, France, 1971; med. helper, Paris, 1975, med. specialist, 1980. Gen. practitioner, infirmary, Nimes, France, 1972-75; helper Ctr. Hosp. Univ. Cocody, Abidjan, Côte d'Ivoire, 1976-78, Hôpital d'instruction des Armées Desgenettes, Lyon, 1975-76, 78-80; specialist in rheumatology HIA Desgenettes, Lyon, 1984—, asst. mgr., 1984-88, dept. mgr., 1989—; expert in aeronautic medicine, CEMPN, Marseille, 1980-84; founder Pain Study Ctr., Lyon, 1990. Med. chief svcs. Svc. de Santé des Armées, 1985—. Decorated knight Legion of Honor (France). Mem. Med. Soc. of Paris Hosp. Office: HIA Desgenettes, 108 Blvd Pinel, 69998 Lyon Rhone, France

MEIJER, WIM, bank executive. Chmn., bd. dirs. Rabobank Group, Utrecht, The Netherlands. Office: Rabobank Group, P Box 17100, 3500 HG Utrecht The Netherlands*

MEIJLER, FRITS LOUIS, cardiologist, educator; b. Den Ham, The Netherlands, Apr. 29, 1925; m. Annemarie P. Schendstok, Apr. 4, 1953; children: Annejet P., Gerda, Theo Dirk. HBS-B, Almelo, Eindhoven, 1947; MD, U. Amsterdam, 1957, PhD, 1960. Tng. in internal medicine and cardiology U. Amsterdam, The Netherlands, 1957-62; mem. staff Wilhelmina Gasthuis, Amsterdam, 1962-67; prof. cardiology State U. Utrecht, The Netherlands, 1968-85; prof. cardiology Interuniv. Cardiology Inst., 1973-85, chmn. sci. council, 1983-93; retired, 1993. Co-author: Kun Jij een Aardappel Maken?, 1968, Electrocardiografie voor Intensive Bewakingseenheden, 1971, Nederlands Leerboek der Cardiologie, 1978, 2d edit. 1983, Elektrocardiografe voor de Hartbewaking, 1980, Th.W. Engelmann, Some Papers and his Bibliography, 1984, Professor Dirk Durrer, 35 Years of Cardiology in Amsterdam, 1986, Kun Jij een Aardappel Maken? Herinneringen van een Onderduiker en Andere Verhalen, 1987, Waarom ven een Walvis?, 1989, Van Aardappel naar Walvis, 1993; contbr. articles to profl. publs., Dutch newspapers; editor: Brains for Hearts, 1997. Served with Royal Dutch Army, 1947-49. Decorated Wounded in Action Svc. decoration, House Order of Orange, Order of Dutch. Lion. Fellow Am. Coll. Cardiology, Am. Heart Assn., European Soc. Cardiology; mem. Dutch Cardiac Soc. (hon.), Royal Netherlands Acad. Arts Scis., Royal Acad. Medicine Belgium. E-mail: denham@euronet.nl. Home: 20 G Stadhouderskade, 1054 ES Amsterdam The Netherlands Office: Interuniv Cardiology Inst Netherlands, PO Box 19258, 3501 DG Utrecht The Netherlands

MEIKAN, SEKI, gynecologist, educator; b. Walien, Taiwan, July 5, 1947; s. Seki and Seki (Chang) Choi.; m. Seki Wu, Nov. 15, 1969; children: Masamichi, Masanori. M in Agriculare, Kyushu U., Japan, 1974; MD, Kumamoto U., Japan, 1980; PhD, Kyusyu U., 1989. Resident in Ob/Gyn. Kyushu U., Japan, 1979-82, med. staff. supr., 1982-87; instr. Kyushu U., 1987-90; asst. prof. U. Environ. Health, 1991-99; vis. prof. Taipei Med. Coll., Taiwan, 1992-99; cons. Uei Hosp., 1990—, Inst. Life Sci., Japan, 1995—, Psychosomatic Soc. Japan, 1996—. Contbr. articles to profl. jours. Mem. Japan Soc. ObGyn, Japan Soc. Fertility and Sterility. Office: U Occup/Environ Health, Isegaoka 1-1, 807-0804 Kitakyushy Japan

MEINANDER, MARTIN, city official; b. Grankulla, Finland, Feb. 17, 1940; s. Nils and Gunnel (Estlander) M.; m. Kerstin D. Bondfolk, Sept. 19, 1970p; children: Anna M., Christel D., Martina J., Petra S. BSc, U. Helsinki, 1963, MSc, 1964, Lic.Sc., 1970, PhD, 1972. Curator Zool. Mus., Helsinki, 1963-72, sr. curator, 1972-79; prof. zoology U. Helsinki, 1980-89; dir. Finnish Mus. Natural History, Helsinki, 1989-96; dep. mayor City of Helsinki, 1996—; docentship in zoology U. Helsinki, 1972-79, 89—. Mem. City Coun., Helsinki, 1985-96, mem. city bd., 1989-96. Recipient Golden Medal of Honor, League of Finnish Res. Officers, 1967, The Acad. Res. Officers, 1965. Fellow Societas Scientiarum Fenniae; mem. Societas Entomologica Helsingforsiensis (hon., pres. 1983-97), Scandinavian Soc. Entomology (chmn. 1985—), Internat. Assn. for Neuropterology (chmn. 1994-97). Swedish Peoples Party of Finland. Lutheran. Home: Håkansvägen 4A, FI 00420 Helsingfors Finland Office: City of Helsinki, City Hall, N Esplanaden 11-13, FIN00099 Helsinki Finland

MEINCKE, JENS PETER, university rector. Pro-rector U. Cologne, Germany. Office: U Cologne, Albertus-Magnus Platz, D-50931 Cologne Germany*

MEINDERS, AREND EDO, internal medicine educator; b. Apeldoorn, Gelderland, The Netherlands, Dec. 1, 1939; s. Arend and Carla (Sasse) M.; m. Johanna Groeneveld, Mar. 26, 1966; children: Arend Jan, Jeroen, Bastiaan. MD, Med. Sch., Amsterdam, The Netherlands, 1966, PhD, 1969. Rsch. fellow London Hosp., 1963-64; resident in internal medicine U. Amsterdam, 1966-71, asst. prof., 1972-73, assoc. prof., 1973-74; cons. in internal medicine Arnhem, The Netherlands, 1974-87; prof. medicine U. Leiden, The Netherlands, 1987—; chmn. dept. medicine U. Leiden, 1988—, chmn. dept. endocrinology and metabolism, 1992—; vis. prof. Ind. Med. Sch., Indpls., 1971-72; gen. health coun mem., The Netherlands; chmn. diagnostic strategies in medicine Dutch Ins. Cie. Editor in chief: Therapy in Internal Medicine, 1994; mem. editl. bd. several jours.; contbr. articles to profl. jours. Recipient award NWO, The Hague, The Netherlands, 1990, award Dutch Fund for Prevention in Diseases, The Hague, 1996. Mem. European Assn. for the Study of Diabetes, European Soc. for Intensive Care Medicine, Dutch Soc. for the Tng. in Internal Medicine (chmn. 1995—), Dutch Soc. for Internal Medicine (bd. mem.), Netherlands Orgn. Scientific Rsch. Avocations: painting, literature, sports. Office: Leiden Univ Med Ctr, PO Box 9600, 2300 RC Leiden The Netherlands

MEINER, SUE ELLEN THOMPSON, gerontologist, nurse practitioner, nursing educator and researcher; b. Ironton, Mo., Oct. 24, 1943; d. Louis Raymond and Verna Mae Thompson; m. Robert Edward Meiner, Mar. 5, 1971; children: Diane Romeril, Suzanne Elaine. AAS, Meramec C.C., 1970; BSN, St. Louis U., 1978, MSN, 1983; EdD, So. Ill. U., Edwardsville, 1991. RN, Mo.; cert. gerontol. nurse practitioner; cert. clin. specialist in gerontol. nursing. Staff RN St. Joseph's Hosp., St. Charles, Mo., 1976-78; nursing supr. Bethesda Gen. Hosp., St. Louis, 1975-76, 71-74; adult med. dir. Family Care Ctr.-Carondelet, St. Louis, 1978-79; program dir., lectr. Webster Coll./Bethesda Hosp., Webster Groves, Mo., 1979-82; diabetes clin. specialist Washington U. Sch. Medicine, St. Louis, 1982; chmn. dept. nursing, asst. prof. St. Louis C.C., 1983-88, Barnes Hosp. Sch. Nursing, 1988-89; instr. U.

Mo., St. Louis, 1989; assoc. prof. St. Charles County C.C., St. Peters, Mo., 1990-92, Deaconess Coll. of Nursing, 1991-93; patient care mgr. Deaconess Hosp., St. Louis, 1993-94; assoc. prof. Jewish Hosp. Coll. of Nursing and Allied Health, 1994-99; gerontol. nurse, rschr. Wash. U. Sch. Med., St. Louis, 1996-2000; asst. prof. nursing U. Nev., Coll. of Health Scis., Las Vegas, 2000—; nat. dir. edn. Nat. Assn. Practical Nurse Edn. and Svc., Inc., St. Louis, 1984-86; mem. task force St. Louis Met. Hosp. Assn., 1987-88; mem. adv. com. Bd. Edn. Sch. Nursing, St. Louis, 1986-90; grant coord. Kellogg Found. Gerontology and Nursing, 1991-92; project dir. NIH Grant Washington U., St. Louis, 1996—; mem. editorial bd. geriatric Nursing Journ., 1999—; legal nurse cons. Author and editor profl. books; contbr. articles to profl. jours. Chmn. bd. dirs. Creve Coeur Fire Protection Dist. Mo., 1984-89; vice chmn. Bd. Cen. St. Louis County Emergency Dispatch Svc., 1985-87; asst. leader Girl Scouts U.S., St. Louis, 1975; treas. Older Women's League, St. Louis, 1992-93. Recipient Woman of Worth award Gateway chpt. Older Women's League, 1993. Mem. ANA, Am. Acad. Nurse Practitioners, Am. Coll. Nurse Practitioners, Am. Nurses Found., Nat. League for Nursing, Am. Soc. of Aging, Am. Acad. Nurse Practitioner, Am. Coll. Nurse Practitioner, Mid-Am. Congress on Aging, Creve Coeur C. of C., Order Ea. Star (chaplain 1970), Jobs Daus. (guardian 1979-80), Sigma Theta Tau (fin. chmn. 1984, archivist 1985-87), Sigma Phi Omega (pres. 1990-91), Kappa Delta Pi. Avocations: travel, reading. Home and Office: 3722 Violet Rose Ct Las Vegas NV 89147-7400

MEINRATH, GÜNTHER, nuclear waste disposal consultant; b. Heilbronn, Germany, Aug. 21, 1961; m. Andrea Elisabeth Schweinberger, July 31, 1995. Diploma in chemistry, Karlsruhe U., 1987; Dr.rer.nat., München Tech. U., 1991; habilitation, Tech. U. Bergahademie Freiberg, 2000. Rschr. Tech. U. Munich, 1987-91; rsch. fellow Atomic Energy Rsch. Inst., Tokai, Japan, 1991-92; prin. cons. RER Cons., Passau, Germany, 1993—; rsch. fellow Rsch. Ctr. Karlsruhe, 1994-95; lectr. U. Bergakademie, Freiberg, Germany, 1996-98, rsch. fellow, 1997; invited fgn. rschr. Japan Atomic Energy Rsch. Inst., 1997; guest lectr. Mickiewicz U., Poznan, Poland, 1999. Contbr. articles to profl. jours. Fellowship German Soc. for Promotion of Sci., 1997, Japan Atomic Energy Rsch. Inst., 1991-92. Mem. Gesellschaft Deutscher Chemiker. Avocations: music, painting. Office: TU Bergakademie Freiberg, Gustav-Zeuner Strasse 12, D-09596 Freiburg Germany

MEIRA, DILMAR MALHEIROS, telecommunications executive, system engineer, consultant, researcher, educator; b. Guanambi, Brazil, Jan. 25, 1951; s. Benjamin de Souza and Valdelourdes M.; m. Zilda Maria Alves, Jan. 18, 1975; children: Guilherme, Anália, Alexandre. BSEE, Fed. U. Minas Gerais, 1973, MS in Computer Sci., 1989, PhD In Computer Sci., 1997. From trainee to rschr. Telemig, Belo Horizonte, Brazil, 1973-93; vis. scholar U. B.C., Vancouver, Can., 1994-95; sr. mgr. Telemig, 1995-99, sr. telecoms. cons., 1999—. Mem. IEEE. Achievements include contributions to the fields of network operations and management. Avocations: woodworking, music, cinema, jogging. Home: Rua Julio Ferraz 397, Belo Horizonte 31270160, Brazil Office: Telemig SA, Av Afonso Pena 4001, Belo Horizonte 30130008, Brazil

MEIRELLES, RICARDO MARTINS DA ROCHA, endocrinologist; b. Sao Paolo, Brazil, Dec. 17, 1946; s. Walter and Lobelia (Martins de Rocha) M.; m. Lucia Maria de Castro Noronha, Apr. 28, 1973; 1 child, Tatiana Noronha de Meirelles. Degree in medicine, Fed. U. Rio de Janeiro, 1971. Coord. dept. nutrition and dietetics Brazilian Beneficient Rehab. Assn., Rio de Janeiro, 1972-73; staff endocrinologist Nat. Inst. Med. Care of Social Welfare, Rio de Janeiro, 1976-89; staff endocrinologist State Inst. Diabetes and Endocrinology, Rio de Janeiro, 1976-90, dir., 1990—; assoc. prof. endocrinology Cath. U., Rio de Janeiro, 1981—; dir. 18th Brazilian Congress of Endocrinology, Rio de Janeiro, 1986-88; cons. endocrinology Financier of Studies and Projects, Brazil, 1993—. Editor: Clinical Endocrinology, 1988; co-editor Brazilian Archives of Endocrinology and Metabolism, 1991—. Cultural attache Carlos Chagas Acad. Ctr., Rio de Janeiro, 1967-68; mem. ethical commn. Regional Coun. Medicine, Rio de Janeiro, 1985-87; del. 2d Mcpl. Health Conf., Rio de Janeiro, 1993. Recipient Citation, Gov. of State of Rio de Janeiro, 1982. Mem. Brazilian Soc. Endocrinology and Metabolism (regional pres. 1984-86, nat. v.p. 1988-90), Brazilian Soc. for Study of Obesity (v.p. 1990-92), Endocrine Soc. (educator). Avocations: theater, music, reading, movies, computers.

MEIS, NANCY RUTH, marketing and development executive; b. Iowa City, Aug. 6, 1952; d. Donald J. and Theresa (Dee) M.; m. Paul L. Wenske, Oct. 14, 1978; children: Alexis Meis Wenske, Christopher Meis Wenske. BA, Clarke Coll., 1974; MBA, U. Okla., 1981. Cultural program supr. City of Dubuque, Iowa, 1974-76; cmty. svcs. dir. State Arts Coun. of Okla. City, 1976-78, program dir., 1978-79; mgr. Cimarron Circuit Opera Co., Norman, Okla., 1979-82, bd. dirs., 1982-86; accout exec. Bell System, Kansas City, Mo., 1982; mgr. spl. svcs. Children Internat., Kansas City, 1983-86, dir. mktg. and fund raising, 1986-87, dir. devel., 1987-88, v.p. devel., 1988-90; dir. mktg. and consulting svcs. Unimedia divsn. Universal Press Syndicate, Kansas City, 1990-95; dir. mktg. Universal New Media divsn. Andrews McMeel Universal, 1996-2000; v.p. content and licensing Nerds, Inc., N.Y.C., 2000—; cons., speaker in field. Co-founder Girls to Women.

MEISALO, VEIJO P. JUHANI, education educator; b. Helsinki, Finland, Oct. 12, 1938; s. Paul Hjalmar and Aino Linnea (Manni) M.; m. Leena Inkeri Suomaa, 1961; children: Timo, Martti, Marja. BS, U. Helsinki, 1960, MS, 1961, LicPhil, 1964, PhD, 1967. Postdoctoral fellow NRC, Ottawa, Ont., Can., 1967-69; assoc. prof. U. Oulu, Finland, 1976-77; sr. lectr. U. Helsinki, 1969-76, assoc. prof., 1977-98, prof., 1998—, head dept. tchr. edn., 1987-92, dean Faculty Edn., 1992-98, dir. Ctr. for R & D in Pedagogy Math. Scis., 1999—; vis. prof. U. Tartu, Estonia, 2000. Decorated Officer Order of Lion of Finland, Badge of Merit, State of Finland. Mem. Internat. Sailing Schs. Assn. (past pres.). Avocation: sailing. Home: Runeberginkatu 28B20, FIN00100 Helsinki Finland Office: U Helsinki Dept Tchr Edn, Box 38 Ratakatu 6A, FIN00014 Helsinki University, Finland

MEISEL, JOHN, political scientist; b. Vienna, Austria, Oct. 23, 1923; s. Fryda and Ann M. BA, U. Toronto, 1948, MA, 1950; PhD in Polit. Sci., London Sch. Econs., 1959; LLD, Brock U., 1983, U. Guelph, 1985, Carleton U., 1990, U. Toronto, 1993, Queen's U., 1996, U. Regina, 1999, U. Calgary, 2000; DU (hon.), U. Ottawa, 1983; D of Social Scis. (hon.), Laval U., 1988; LittD (hon.), U. Waterloo, 1998. Head dept. polit. studies Queen's U., Kingston, Ont., Can., 1963-67, Hardy prof. polit. sci., 1963-80, Sir Edward Peacock prof. polit. sci., 1983-93; prof. emeritus Queen's U., Kingston, Can.; former chmn. Can. Radio-TV and Telecomms. Commn.; moderator symposia on finding common grounds for polit. issues confronting Yugoslavia, UN, Vienna, 1995. Author: The Canadian General Election of 1957, 1962, Papers on the 1962 Election, 1964, Ethnic Relations in Canadian Voluntary Associations, 1972, Working Papers on Canadian Politics, 1975; editor: Internat. Polit. Sci. Rev., 1979-95, (with Jean Laponce) Debating the Constitution/Débat sur la constitution, 1994. Decorated companion Order of Can.; recipient Killam award Can Coun., 1968-73; sr. rsch. fellow Ctr. for the Study of Democracy Queens U. Fellow Royal Soc. Can. (pres. 1992-95); mem. Rideau Club (Ottawa), Univ. Club (Toronto). E-mail: meiselj@politics.queensu.ca. Home: Colimaison, Tichborne, ON Canada K0H 2V0 Office: Queen's U, Kingston, ON Canada K7L 3N6

MEISNER, G. MICHAEL, researcher, anesthetist; b. Bayreuth, Germany, Feb. 27, 1963; s. Robert P. and Agnes Meisner. MD, U. Erlangen-Nuremberg, Germany, 1988; postgrad., Harvard Med. Sch., 1988. Cert. Nat. Bd. Anesthesiologists, Ednl. Commn. of Fgn. Med. Grads. Resident in internal medicine dept. internal medicine U. Erlangen-Nuremberg, 1988-90, anesthetist, fellow dept. anesthesiology, 1990-98; rschr., anesthetist dept. anesthesiology U. Jena, Germany, 1998—. Author: (books) Procalcitonin—A New Innovative Infection Parameter. Biochemical and Clinical Aspects, 1996, Procalcitonin, 1999; reviewer: Intensive Care Medicine, 1999. Mem. German Soc. for Anesthesiology and Intensive Medicine. Avocations: writing, music, painting, trekking. Fax: 493641933256. E-mail: meisner@med.uni-jena.de. Office: U Jena Dept Anesthesiology, Bachstr 18, 07743 Jena Germany

MEISNER, JOACHIM CARDINAL, archibishop; b. Breslau, Germany, Dec. 25, 1933; s. Walter and Hedwig Meisner. Ed. U. Erfurt, Pastoral Sem. at Neuzelle. Ordained priest Roman Cath. Ch., 1962. Chaplain St. Agidien, Heiligenstadt, 1963-66, St. Crucis, Erfurt, 1966; rector Diozesencaritas of Erfurt, 1966-76, suffragan bishop, 1975-80; bishop of Berlin, 1980-89; pres. Berliner Bischofskonferenz, 1982-89; elevated to cardinal, 1983; archibishop of Cologne, 1989—. Author: Das Auditorium Coelicum am Dom zu Erfurt, 1960; Nachreformatorische katholische Frommigkeitsformen in Erfurt, 1971; Sein, wie Gott uns gemeint hat-Betrachtungen zu Maria, 1988; contbr. articles to mags. Address: Generalvikariat, Marzellenstrasse 32, S0668 Cologne Germany*

MEISSNER, JOACHIM, electrical engineer, educator; b. Berlin, Nov. 18, 1950; s. Herbert and Editha (Otterstein) M.; m. Sabine Herm, July 30, 1982; 1 child, Jana. Diploma in engring. with honors, Tech. U. Berlin, 1979, DEng, 1985. Rschr. Tech. U. Berlin, 1979-84; mem. R & D staff Deutsche Aerospace, Berlin, 1985-93; prof. Fachhochschule Deutsche Telekom, Berlin, 1993-95, Fachhochschule für Technik und Wirtschaft, Berlin, 1996—. Mem. IEEE (sr.). Avocation: electromagnetics. Home: Benekendorffstrasse 11, 13469 Berlin Germany Office: Fachhochschule Tech-Wirt, Allee der Kosmonauten 20-22, 10315 Berlin Germany

MEISSNER, JOERN, physicist, consultant; b. Hamburg, Germany, Mar. 21, 1968; s. Hartwig and Elfi Meissner; m. Francesca Primas, June 22, 1998. MS, U. Notre Dame, 1992, PhD, 1996; diploma in physics, Tech. Univ. Munich, 1993. Rsch. asst. U. Notre Dame, South Bend, Ind., 1991-96; electron beam cons. Ion Beam Applications, Louvain-La-Neuve, Belgium, 1996-99, dir. engring., 1999—; mem. organizing com. internat. conf., 1996. Contbr. articles to profl. jours. Counselor Youth for Understanding, Munich, 1986-91. Grantee Nat. Acad. Sci., 1994-96; scholar Rotary Internat., 1991-92. Mem. Am. Phys. Soc. Avocations: pvt. pilot, skiing, hiking. Office: Chemin Du Cyclotron 3, Ion Beam Applications, B-1348 Louvain-la-Neuve Belgium

MEISSNER, RUDOLF OTTO, geophysicist, educator; b. Dortmund, Germany, June 15, 1925; s. Alfred Richard and Gertrud Maria (Auffermann) M.; m. Sofia Theresa Hitzegrad, Oct. 15, 1954; children: Monika, Gunter. Diploma, U. Frankfurt, 1953, doctor, 1955, habilitation, 1966. Party leader Prakla, Europe, Africa, 1955-59; supr. Shell Oil Co., Tripolis, Libya, 1959-61; asst. prof. Univ. Frankfurt, Hesse, Germany, 1961-69; lectr. Univ. Frankfurt, Hesse, 1966-69, Univ. Mainz, Rhineland, Germany, 1966-69; vis. prof. Hawaiian Inst. Geophysics, 1969-70; prof., dir. Inst. Geophysics, Kiel Univ., Schleswig-Holstein, 1971-96; dean math.-sci. faculty U. Kiel, 1981-83; chmn. working group Internat. Lithosphere Project, 1987-90; chmn. FKPE, Germany, 1991-93. Author: Der Mond, 1969, Seismische Messungen, 1976, The Continental Crust, 1986; co-author: The Dekorp Atlas, 1990; chief editor: Continental Lithosphere, 1992; contbr. articles to profl. jours; mem. editorial bd. 4 sci. jours. Mem. steering com., bd. dirs. Dekorp, 1985-97; pres. Alfred Wegener Found., 1994-97. Recipient Stitching award Schlumberger Co., 1990, Schmidt medal Russian Acad., 1993, Kapitsa award Russian Acad. Natural Scis., 1998. Mem. European Geophys. Soc. (pres. 1985-87), Europe Acad., Assn. Royal Astron. Soc., Internat. Geologic Correlation Program, Geophys. Gesellschaft (hon.). Avocations: music, piano. Home: Struckbrook 2, D-24161 Altenholz Germany Office: Inst Geophys, Otto Hahn Platz 1, D-24098 Kiel Germany

MEISTAS, MARY THERESE, endocrinologist, diabetes researcher; b. Grand Rapids, Mich., July 22, 1949; d. Frank Peter and Anne Therese (Karsokas) M. MD, U. Mich., 1975. Diplomate Am. Bd. Internal Medicine, Am. Bd. Endocrinology. Intern, then resident in internal medicine Cleve. Clinic Hosp., 1975-78, endocrinology fellow, 1978-79; fellow in pediatric endocrinology Johns Hopkins Hosp., Balt., 1979-81; diabetes researcher Joslin Diabetes Ctr., Boston, 1981-86; assoc. in medicine Brigham and Women's Hosp., Boston, 1981-86; asst. in medicine, diabetes researcher Mass. Gen. Hosp., Boston, 1986-92; staff endocrinologist Emerson Hosp., Concord, Mass., 1989—. Mem. ACP, Am. Diabetes Assn., Am. Fedn. Clin. Research, Endocrine Soc. Office: Emerson Hosp 747 Main St Ste 111 Concord MA 01742-3325

MEISTER, HARTMUT, research engineer; b. Siegen, Germany, Oct. 28, 1963; s. Artur and Helga (Kohl) M. Diploma, U. Siegen, 1987, U. Wuppertal, Germany, 1991; PhD, U. Cologne, 1999. Lectr. HDT-Essen, Germany, 1991-92, educator, 1992—; rschr. ENT-Clinic, Cologne, Germany, 1992—. Inventor complete middle ear prosthesis, 1997; contbr. articles to profl. jours. Mem. German Soc. Acoustics, German Audiolog. Soc. Office: ENT Clinic U Cologne, JOS Stelzmann Str 9, 50931 Cologne Germany

MEITZLER, LELAND KEITH, executive editor; b. Enumclaw, Wash., Apr. 13, 1950; s. Theodore Canfield and Virginia Francis Cornett-Feller; m. Patty Sue Daffern, Sept. 1, 1968; children: Leland Neal, Dale Ralph. AA with honors, Green River C.C., Auburn, Wash., 1983. Mgr. Meitzler's Greenhouse & Nursery, Puyallup, Wash., 1970-72; sales mgr. Meitzler's Wholesale Greenhouses, Orting, Wash., 1972-75; terminal mgr. Green Thumb Products Corp., Apopka, Fla., 1975-76; owner, mgr. Northwest Tropicals, South Prairie, Wash., 1976-82; pres. Meico Assocs., South Prairie, Wash., 1982-84; co-founder, pres. Heritage Quest Mag., Orting, 1985-92; mng. editor Heritage Quest Mag., Bountiful, Utah, 1992-95, exec. editor, 1996—, touring editor, 1993-00; v.p., print publs. and acquisitions Heritage Quest, a mem. of the SierraHome family, North Salt Lake, Utah, 2000—. Mem. Assn. Profl. Genealogists, Tacoma-Pierce County Geneal. Soc. (corr. sec. 1982-83, pres. 1983-85), South Prairie Hist. Soc. (pres. 1982-85). Republican. Avocations: country music, genealogy, collecting political and national recovery act memorabilia. Office: Heritage Quest 669 West 900 North North Salt Lake UT 84054 Address: PO Box 540193 North Salt Lake UT 84054-0193

MEIXNER, MICHAEL, communications design engineer; b. Regensburg, Bavaria, Germany, Oct. 27, 1972; s. Walter and Ernestina (Sauerer) M. Engring. diploma, Friedrich-Alexander U., Erlangen, Germany, 1997. Asst. engr. Inst. for Integrated Cirs., Erlangen, 1993-96, Inst. Nat. Scientific Rsch., Montreal, Can., 1997; design engr. Ericsson Eurolab, Nuremberg, Germany, 1998—; chmn. design focus group Ericsson Mobile Comms., Lund, Sweden, 1999—. Patentee controllable filter. Avocations: volleyball, badminton, skiing, guitar. Office: Ericsson Eurolab Deutschland, Gebertstr 5, 90411 Nuremberg Germany

MEJDOUB, NOUREDDINE, diplomat; married; 3 children. PhD, U. Paris. Charge de mission Min. Fgn. Affairs, 1960-62; spokesman Min. Fgn. Affairs, Washington, 1962-63; press officer Tunisian Embassy, London, 1963-65; counselor Embassy of Tunisia, Washington, 1966-70; dep. dir. polit. affairs Min. Fgn. Affairs, 1970; min. plenipotentiary, dep. chief of mission Embassy of Tunisia, Paris, 1971-73; amb. Tunisian Embassy, Vienna, Austria, 1973-77; dir. polit. affairs for Europe and America Min. Fgn. Affairs, 1977-80; amb. Govt. of Tunisia, Prague, 1980-86, Rome, 1986-89; diplomatic counselor, chmn. nat. com. Tunisia's rels. ECC, 1990; sec. of state Min. Fgn. Affairs, 1991-92; amb. Govt. of Tunisia, Tokyo, 1992-97, Washington, 1997—; grand officer Republic Order, 1997—. Office: Embassy of Tunisia 1515 Massachusetts Ave NW Washington DC 20005-1801*

MEJIA, CARMEN, biologist; b. Mex., Dec. 21, 1964; d. Arturo and Carmen (Vazquez) M.; m. Luis Cabral Rosetti, June 13, 1992. MS, Faculty Sci., Mexico City, Mex., 1994; PhD, Faculty Sci., Valencia, Spain, 1999. Lab. asst. Mex. Inst. Social Security, Mexico City, 1990-91; prof. inorganic chemistry, biology Tech. Inst. Higher Studies Monterrey, Mexico City, 1991, prof. inorganic chemistry, 1993; prof. biology Arturo Rosenblueth Found., Mexico City, 1993; with faculty medicine U. Valencia, Spain, 1999. Contbr. articles to profl. jours. Avocations: reading, music, movies, theatre, opera. Office: U Valencia Dept Pathol, Av Blasco Ibanez 17, 46010 Valencia Spain

MEJIA, CECILIA, Colombian government official, publisher; b. Bogota, Colombia, Mar. 27, 1945; d. Jorge and Julia (Hernandez) Mejia-Salazar. BFA, U. Andes, Bogota, 1969; MBA, Columbia U., 1977. Researcher Fedesarrollo, 1977-81; dir. bus. mgmt. programs U. Andes, 1981-84; exec. Resurgir, Bogota, 1985-86; dir. Nat. Bldg. Fund Ministry Pub. Works, Bogota, 1987-89; dir. Nat. Landmarks & Partimony Cokultura, Colcultura, 1989-90, Vol. Ret. Execs. Found., Bogota, 1991—; cons., 1993—; amb. Columbia U. Bus. Grads. Abroad, Bogota, 1987—. Bd. dirs. Nat. Landmarks Commn., Bogota, 1987-89, Nat. Calamities Prevention Fund, Bogota, 1987-89. Mem. Jockey Club, Bogota Country Club. Mem. Liberal Party. Avocations: horseback riding, photography, painting, travel. Home: Carrera 9 75-50, Bogota Colombia Office: Nat Landmarks & Patrimony, Carrera 9 74-08, SF 401 Bogota Colombia

MEJIA, LUIS FERNANDO, ophthalmologist; b. Medellin, Colombia, Sept. 4, 1963; s. Camilo A. and Clara (Echavarria) M. MD, CES, Medellin, Colombia, 1986; Fellow, Clinica Barraquer, Bogotá, Colombia, 1992. Chief resident Clinica Barraquer, Bogotá, Colombia, 1991-93; pvt. practice ophthalmologist SOMA, Medellin, Colombia, 1993—; asst. prof. CES, Medellin, Colombia, 1993—. Contbr. articles to profl. clin. jours. Named Best Intern in promotion Acad. Antioqueña de Medicina, 1987. Mem. Am. Acad. Ophthalmology, Castroviejo Cornea Soc., SAOO. Office: Clinica SOMA Cons 310, Calle 51 #45-93, Medellin Colombia

MEJIA, LUIS GONZALO, engineer, consultant; b. Andes, Colombia, May 19, 1950; s. Augusto Mejia and Ligia Canas; m. Gloria Isabel Valencia, Nov. 22, 1974; children: Carlos Federico, Maria Isabel. CE, U. Nacional, Medillin, Colombia, 1973; MS, T.H. Karlsruhe, Germany, 1977. Structural engr. Ingenieria y Construcciones, Medellin, 1971-75; cons. engr., dir. Luis Gonzalo Mejia C. y Cia, Medellin, 1978—; prof. Universidad Nacional, 1973-82. Contbr. articles to profl. jours. Mem. Am. Concrete Inst., Verein Deutscher Ingenieure, Asociacion Colombiana de Ingenieria Sismica, Goethe Inst., Sociedad Ecologica Colombiana, Amigos de Alemania. Roman Catholic. Office: Calle 49B-77B12, AA 54173 Medellin Colombia

MEJÍA, MARIO ERNESTO, electronic engineer, entrepreneur; b. Bogota, Colombia, May 29, 1963; s. Mario and Aida Mercedes (Torres) M. Grad. in Electronic Engring., Javeriana U., Bogota, 1988. Prof. Javeriana U., 1986-88; field engr. Equipos y Controles, Bogota, 1990-98; sr. engr. SCS Foxboro, Colombia, 1998—; thesis dir. Javeriana U., 1993-95; engr. COM3 Ltd., Bogota, 1992—. Mem. IEEE. Avocations: astronomy, science, psychology. Home: Calle 122 # 8A-17, Bogota Colombia Office: SCS Foxboro Colombia, Cll 69A # 4-77, Bogota Colombia

MEJIAS, CRISTINA, sociologist; b. Buenos Aires, Apr. 4, 1946; d. Edgardo and Teresa Lauro Mejias. Lic. in Sociology, Univ. Catolica Argentina. Pres. CM Sociologia De Empresa, Buenos Aires, 1973—. Author: Entre Usted y Yo, 1988, Claves Para Empleo, 1989, El Sillon Vacio, 1990. Mem. Internat. Assn. Outplacement Cons. (bd. dirs.), European Mgmt. Assn. (bd. dirs.), Am. Mgmt. Assn. (bd. dirs.). Roman Catholic. Avocations: painting, golf. Home: Virrey Del Pino 2086, C1426EGJ Buenos Aires Argentina Office: CM Sociologia, Tucuman 1321 # 8, C1050AAA Buenos Aires Argentina

MEJSNAR, JIŘÍ ANTONÍN, physiologist, educator; b. Prague, Czech Republic, Feb. 13, 1941; s. Jiří and Milada (Pavlová) M.; m. Blanka Alexandra Buchtová, July 1, 1967; children: Jiří, Jakub. RNDr in Biology, Charles U., Prague, 1970, MSc in Math., 1976, PhD, 1991; DSc, Czech Acad. Scis., Prague, 1993. Asst. prof. Charles U., 1963-65, sr. asst. prof., 1965-91, assoc. prof. physiology, 1991-97, prof. physiology, 1997—; co-investigator 4 projects, 1963-80; prin. investigator 3 projects, 1976-90; faculty contractor 33 applied projects, 1965-90; vis. prof. C. Bernard U., Lyon, France, 1995. Capt. lt., Tank Army, 1963-64, West Mil. Circle of Warsaw Pact. Grantee USSR Acad. Med. Sci., Novosibirsk, 1978, 81, Zyma Found., U. Geneva, Switzerland, 1984, Muscular Dystrophy Found., U. Wash., Seattle, 1988, Swiss Nat. Found., U. Geneva, 1991. Mem. Czech Med. Assn. (exec. com.). Roman Catholic. Avocations: chamber and philharmonic music, wine, sports. E-mail: mejsnar@natur.cuni.cz. Home: Chlumínská 5, CZ-18100 Prague 8, Czech Republic Office: Charles U Fac Sci, Dept Physiology, CZ-12800 Prague 2, Czech Republic

MEKALANOS, JOHN J., microbiology educator. PhD, UCLA, 1978. Prof., chmn. dept. microbiology and molecular genetics Harvard Med. Sch., Boston; invited spkr. Centenary Symposium of the Pasteur Inst., 1987; mem. vaccines and related biol. products adv. com. FDA, 1988. Recipient Eli Lilly & Co. Microbiology and Immunology Rsch. award Am. Soc. Microbiology, 1991, Milton Fund award, 1981, Am. Cancer Soc. Faculty Rsch. award 1986, NIH Merit award, 1989, AAAS Newcomb Cleve. prize, 1994, City of Medicine prize Durham, N.C., 1997, Ledlie prize Harvard U., 1997. Office: Harvard Med Sch 200 Longwood Ave Boston MA 02115-5701*

MEKEEL, ROBERT K., lawyer; b. Ossining, N.Y., Mar. 21, 1950; s. Ira III and Carmen E. (Munson) M.; m. Martha J. Keller, Sept. 29, 1979; 1 child, Meryl Fox. BA, Wesleyan U., Middletown, Conn., 1972; JD, U. Puget Sound, 1978. Bar: N.H. 1978, N.Y. 1979, U.S. Dist. Ct. (so. dist.) N.Y. 1980, U.S. Ct. Appeals (2d cir.) 1981, U.S. Dist. Ct. N.H. 1983, U.S. Ct. Appeals (1st cir.) 1983. Asst. dist. atty. Westchester County N.Y. Dist. Atty., White Plains, N.Y., 1979-82; assoc. Craig Wenners & McDowell, Manchester, N.H., 1983-84; clk. ct. Coos County Superior Ct., Lancaster, N.H., 1985; ptnr. McKible & Mekeel, P.A., Concord, N.H., 1986-89, Cullity Kelley & McDowell, Manchester, 1989-93, McDowell & Mekeel P.A., Manchester, 1994-96; prin. Robert K. Mekeel, P.A., Concord, 1996—; mem. mentor program Franklin Pierce Law Sch., Concord, 1992; lectr. Nat. Bus. Inst., Eau Claire, Wis., 1993-95; mem. Million Dollar Advocates forum; mediator N.H. Superior Cts.; pvt. mediator, arbitrator disputes involving personal injury claims. Fellow N.H. Bar Found.; mem. ATLA (N.H. rep.), N.H. Trial Lawyers Assn. (amicus com. 1994-96), N.H. Bar Assn. (com. on cooperation with cts., lectr. evidence seminar 1994). Democrat. Avocations: running, biking, swimming, drawing, wood working. Home: 73 Main St Hopkinton NH 03229-2628 Office: Century Bldg 185 N Main St Concord NH 03301-5039

MĚKOTA, KAREL, anthropologist; b. Brno, Czech Republic, Mar. 24, 1932; s. Metoděj and Anna (Hudlaská) M.; m. Jarmila Radvanová, Nov. 12, 1955; children: Hana, Jarmila. MA, Masaryk U., Brno, 1953; PhD, Charles U., Prague, 1964, Habilitation, 1969. Asst. prof. Tech. U., Ostrava, Czech Republic, 1953-66; asst. prof. Palacky U., Olomouc, Czech Republic, 1966-70, assoc. prof., 1970-91, prof. faculty of phys. culture, 1991—. Co-author: Physical Efficiency of Czechoslovak Students, 1965, Motor Tests in Physical Education, 1983, Unifittest (6-60) Tests and Norms of Motor Performance and Physical Fitness in Youth and in Adult Age, 1995, Motor Performance of Candidates to University Study of Physical Education in Olomouc, Katowice, Bratislava, Ljubljana, and Innsbruck: A Comparative Study, 1999; editor-in-chief Acta Universitatis Palackianae Olomucensis, Gymnica, 25 vols., 1970-95. Mem. acad. coun. Czechoslovak Union of Phys. Edn. and Sports, 1965-69. Mem. Internat. Assn. Sport Kinetics (v.p. 1991—), Soc. for Kinanthropology. Avocation: skiing. Home: Slavoninska 22, 779 00 Olomouc Czech Republic Office: Palacky U Faculty Phy Culture, Třída Míru 115, 771 11 Olomouc Czech Republic

MELANDRI, PIERRE CHRISTIAN, history educator; b. Nice, France, June 15, 1946; s. Henri and Mireille (Noat) M.; m. Anne Catherine Thyss, Sept. 9, 1967; children: Fabrice, Priscille. Master, Sorbonne U., 1968, doctorat D'Etat, 1977; PhD, U. Nice, 1972. Asst. prof. U. Paul Valéry, Montpellier, France, 1970-77; assoc. prof. U. Paul Valéry, Montpellier, 1977-79, Ecole Normale Supérieure, Paris, 1979-81; prof. Am. civilization U. Lille III, France, 1981-88; prof. contemporary history U. Paris, Nanterre, France, 1988-95; prof. Am. Civilization Sorbonne, 1995—; mem. Commn. Publn. Des Documents Diplomatiques Français, 1984—. Author: Les Etats-Unis Face à l'Unification de l'Europe, 1980, Histoire des Etats-Unis depuis 1865, 1975, L'Alliance Atlantique, 1979, La Politique Extérieure des Etats-Unis de 1945 à Nos Jours, 1982, Reagan, 1988, Une incertaine alliance: Les Etats-Unis et l'Europe. 1973-1983, 1988; mem. editorial bd. Vingtiéme Siécle, Relations Internationales; contbr. articles to profl. jours. Augustus Clifford Tower fellow Harvard U., 1969-70, ACLS scholar, 1974; Fulbright scholar French-Am. Co., 1978, 99 , guest scholar Wilson Ctr., 1983, 87. Mem. Assn. Française d'Etudes Américaines (v.p. 1984-87), Société d'Etudes Nord-Américaines (pres. 1995-98), Soc. d'Histoire des Relations Internat. Contemporaines. Roman Catholic. Home: 68 Cours de Vincennes, 75012 Paris France Office: Paris III, IMA, 5 Rue de l Ecole Medicine, 75006 Paris France

MELBARDIS, WOLFGANG ALEXANDER, lawyer; b. Bayreuth, Ger., June 21, 1946. BA, Hartwick Coll., 1968; JD, St. John's U., 1971; MBA,

L.I. U., 1977. Bar: N.Y. 1972, U.S. Dist. Ct. (ea., no. and so. dists.) N.Y. 1979, U.S. Ct. Mil. Appeals 1972, U.S. Supreme Ct. 1977. Asst. prof. law U.S. Mil. Acad., 1974-77; asst. atty. gen. Appeals and Opinions Bur. State of N.Y., Albany 1977-79; ptnr. Gramer & Melbardis, Coram, N.Y., 1979-96; served as arbitrator of personal injury cases for Am. Arbitration Assn., 1991-94;justice Village of Poquott N.Y. ethics com., 1999—, mem. Mather Meml. Hosp., Port Jefferson, N.Y., 1999—. Office: 2780 Middle Country Rd Lake Grove NY 11755-2124 also: 194 Main St East Setauket NY 11733-2945

MELBARZDE, ELFRIDA, publishing executive, interpreter, translator; b. Kordimovo, Russia; arrived in Latvia, 1946; d. Janis and Elina (Berzina) Krauze; m. Janis Melbarzdis, Mar. 21, 1967; children: Elizabete, Evelina. Diploma, Latvian State U., Riga, 1964. Corr. Radio Riga, 1962-68; fiction editor Liesma Pub. House, Latvia, 1968-82; head dept. dictionaries Avots Pub. House, Latvia, 1982-92; mgr. fgn. rights Artava Pub. House, Latvia, 1993—; interpreter ABA, Ctrl. and Ea. European Law Initiative, Latvia, 1996. Translator (English to Latvian) Alice in Wonderland, others. Avocations: reading, travel. Home: Miera St 91-20, LV-1013 Riga Latvia Office: Artava Ltd, Bezdeligu 12, LV-1007 Riga Latvia

MELBERG, ATLE, neurologist; b. Halden, Norway, July 13, 1953; s. Håkon and Anne-Kari (Lislegard) M.; m. Xin Fu, Aug. 6, 1992; 1 child, Amanda. BS in Biochemistry, U. Wis., 1976; MD, Royal Coll. Surgeons, Dublin, Ireland, 1984; Specialist in Neurology, Uppsala (Sweden) U., 1993, PhD, 1996. Intern various hosps. and dists., Lillehammer, Skjåk, Norway, 1984-86; med. staff Förde (Norway) Hosp., 1986-87, Mil. Camp, Lahaugmoen, Norway, 1987-88, Ulleväl Hosp., Oslo, 1988, Univ. Hosp., Umeå, Sweden, 1988-90; med. staff U. Uppsala Hosp., 1990—, assoc. prof. neurology, 2000—. Fellow Royal Soc. Medicine, Swedish Neurol. Assn., Swedish Med. Assn., Norwegian Med. Assn. Avocation: swimming. Office: Uppsala Univ Hospital, Dept Neurosci & Neurology, S-751 85 Uppsala Sweden

MELCHER, JERRY WILLIAM COOPER, clinical psychologist, army officer; b. Bloomington, Ill., Oct. 17, 1948; m. Margaret Frances Orban; children: Heather, Shawna, Jay. BS, Lincoln U., Mo., 1975; MS, Tex. A&I U., 1976; PhD, Tex. A&M U., 1980. Psychometrist Lamar U., Beaumont, Tex., 1978-79, psychologist, 1979-81; commd. 1st lt. U.S. Army, 1981, advanced through grades to lt. col., 1987; clin. intern William Beaumont Army Med. Ctr., 1981-82; psychologist 1st Cav. Divsn., Fort Hood, Tex., 1982-84; chief psychology svc. Darnall Army Community Hosp., Fort Hood, 1984-85, Blanchfield Army Community Hosp., Fort Campbell, Ky., 1986-87; clin. psychologist, owner Area Counseling Assocs., Millington, Tenn., 1987—; clin. psychologist U.S. Army Res., Memphis, 1988-93; comdr. 1451st Combat Stress Detachment, Jackson, Miss., 1997—; clin. dir. Genesis Treatment Ctr., Memphis, 1990-94; clin. dir., co-owner Mid-South Alcohol and Drug Edn. Ctr., Memphis, 1998—; tng. coord. CETA, Beaumont, 1980-81; rsch. psychologist Operation Desert Storm, Fort Gordon, Ga., 1991. Bd. dirs. Family Aid Network, Killeen, Tex., 1984-85; vol. Rape Crisis Ctr., Beaumont, 1979. Decorated Bronze Star with valor device, Meritorious Svc. medal; Cross of Gallantry with palm (Vietnam). Mem. APA. Avocations: physical wellness, travel, boating, computer games. Office: Area Counseling Assocs 8222 Us Highway 51 N Millington TN 38053-1708

MELCHINGER, ALBRECHT EUGEN, science educator; b. Aalen, Germany, Mar. 4, 1949; s. Hans and Ursula (Mack) M.; m. Iris Herrschner, 1983. Diploma in math., U. Stuttgart, Germany, 1977; D of Agrl. Scis., U. Hohenheim, Stuttgart, 1984. Cert. in plant breeding. Univ. prof. U. Hohenheim, Stuttgart, 1991—.

MELCHIOR, IB JORGEN, author, television and motion picture writer, director; b. Copenhagen, Sept. 17, 1917; came to U.S., 1938; s. Lauritz Lebrecht Hommel and Inger Thora (Nathansen) M.; m. Harriet Hathaway Kale, Mar. 15, 1942 (div. 1960); 1 child, Leif; m. Cleo Baldon-Chute, Jan. 18, 1964; stepchild, Dirk Arin. Postgrad., U. Copenhagen, 1937. Actor, stage mgr., co-dir. The English Players, Paris, 1937-39; stage mgr. Radio City Music Hall, Ctr. Theater, N.Y.C., 1941-42; actor, writer N.Y.C., 1946-49; assoc. dir. CBS-TV, N.Y.C., 1949-50, dir., 1951-56; assoc. prodr. G-L Enterprises, N.Y.C., 1952-53; screenwriter, dir., novelist, 1957—. Author: (novels) Order of Battle, 1973, Sleeper Agent, 1975, The Haigerloch Project, 1977, The Watchdogs of Abaddon, 1979, The Marcus Device, 1980, The Tombstone Cipher, 1983, Eva, 1984, V-3, 1985, Code Name: Grand Guignol, 1987, (biography) Quest, 1990, Order of Battle: Hitler's Werewolves, 1991, (autobiography) Case by Case, 1993; author: (with Cleo Baldon) Steps & Stairways, 1989, Reflections on the Pool, 1997; screenwriter Live Fast, Die Young, 1957, The Angry Red Planet, 1959, Reptilicus, 1962, Journey to the 7th Planet, 1962, Ambush Bay, 1965, Robinson Crusoe on Mars, 1964, The Time Travelers, 1964, others; dir. Angry Red Planet, The Time Travelers; translator, narrator (tapes) Hans Christian Andersen Fairy Tales, 1986; creator Space Family Robinson (spl. advisor Lost in Space, 1997-98). Mem. adv. bd. Mayor's Narcotics Info. Clinic, L.A., 1972-73; adv. coun. Danish Immigrant Mus., Elk Horn, Iowa, 1985—. With U.S. Army Mil. Intelligence, 1943-46. Decorated Bronze Star, Knight Commander Cross, Militant Order of St. Brigitte of Sweden, 1965; recipient King Christian X Erindringsmedalje, 1948, Medal of Merit Old Guard, 1965, Golden Scroll award Best Writing Acad. Sci. Fiction, 1976, Hamlet award Best Legitimate Play Shakespeare Soc. Am., 1982. Mem. Writers Guild Am. West, Dirs. Guild Am., Acad. Sci. Fiction (hon.), Manuscript Soc., Authors Guild Inc., Royal Danish Guard Assn., Danish Lucheon Club (L.A.), Adventures Club (L.A.). Home and Office: 8228 Marmont Ln Hollywood CA 90069-1624

MELCHIOR, PAUL JACQUES, astronomer, educator; b. Mont-sur-Marchienne, Belgium, Sept. 30, 1925; m. Anne Marie Bary, Sept. 30, 1950; 3 children. DSc, Free U. of Brussels, 1950; DrIng honoris causa, U. Darmstadt, 1988. Astronomer Royal Obs. of Belgium, 1949—, dir., 1981-90, hon. dir., 1990—; mem. faculty Cath. U. Louvain, Belgium, 1964—, prof. geodesy, gravimetry and geodynamics, 1972-90, prof. emeritus, 1990—; hon. prof. Inst. of Geodesy and Geophysics, Academia Sinica, Wuhan, China, 1979—; sec.-gen. Internat. Union Geodesy and Geophysics, 1973-91, hon. sec.-gen., 1991—. Author: The Tides of the Planet Earth, 1983, The Physics of the Earth's Core, 1986. Decorated chevalier Order of Merit (Italy); officer, comdr., grand. officer Order Leopold II, chevalier Order of Leopold, grand. officer Order of the Crown (Belgium); grand officer Order of Merit, officer Order of the Crown (Luxembourg); Baron by royal favour King Baudouin of Belgium, 1993; recipient awards Royal Acad. of Belgium, 1948, U. Libre Brussels,; Marin Drinov medal Acad. Scis. of Bulgaria, 1987, K Okkrid medal U. Sofia, 1987, also Lagrange prize, 1950, Stroobant prize, 1967, others. Fellow Am. Geophys. Union; mem Royal Belgian Soc. Astronomy, Meteorology and Earth's Physics (pres.), Royal Astron. Soc. London, Deutsche Geodaetische Commn. (corr.); fgn. mem. Acad. Scis. of Finland, Spain, Romania, Netherlands. Office: Obs Royal de Belgique, Ave Circulaire 3, B-1180 Brussels Belgium

MELCHIOR, STEFAN, soil scientist, environmental engineer, consultant; b. Geisenheim, Germany, Nov. 19, 1958; s. Guenther and Frede (Herkel) M.; m. Susanne Senkel, Sept. 16, 1988; children: Jakob, Moritz. Diploma on geography, U. Hamburg, Germany, 1985, Dr.rer.nat., 1993, Dr.rer.nat.habil., 1999. Rsch. asst. dept. soil sci. U. Hamburg, 1985-89, rsch. assoc. dept. soil sci., 1989-95; sr. cons. IGB Hamburg, 1996—; tchr. courses in soil sci. U. Hamburg, 1990—; cons., mem. com. German Inst. Constrn. Tech. Contbr. over 65 articles to sci. publs. Recipient Kurt-Hartwig-Siemers prize Hamburger Wissenschaftl-Stiftung, 1993. Mem. German Soil Sci. Soc., Assn. Environ. Engrs., German Geotech. Soc. Avocations: sports, wildlife, travel. Home: Klosterallee 51, 20146 Hamburg Germany Office: IGB, Heinrich-Hertz-Strasse 116, 22083 Hamburg Germany

MELCONIAN, JERRY OHANES, engineering executive; b. Cairo, Egypt, Jan. 22, 1934; came to U.S., 1967; s. Melik Melconian and Zarouca Papazian; m. Veronique Kocifay, June 12, 1998; 1 child, Terran Kirk. BSc, U. London, 1957. Section leader Otis Elevator Co., London, Eng., 1957-61, Rolls Royce Ltd., Derby, Eng., 1961-66; program coord. Textron Lycoming, Stratford, Conn., 1967-74; mgr., TF34 Design to Cost Gen. Electric Co., Lynn, Mass., 1974-77; mgr. mktg. No. Rsch. and Engring. Co., Woburn, Mass., 1977-82; pres. SOL-3 Resources Inc., Reading, Mass., 1982—. Editor: Design and Development of Gas Turbine Combustors, 1980; patentee in field. Mem. Am. Inst. Aeronautics and Astronautics. Office: SOL-3 Resources Inc 76 Beaver Rd Reading MA 01867-1310

MELCONIAN, RUBEN DARIO, chemicals executive; b. Buenos Aires, Argentina, Oct. 12, 1951; s. Garabet Helconian and Maria Rosa Markarian; m. Rina Teresa Islas; children: Rina, Lucia. Diploma in chem. engring., U. Buenos Aires, 1976. With tech. svc. divsn. Grace Argentina S.A., Quilmes, 1976-79, sals supr., 1979-80, devel. mgr., 1980-87, devel. and sales mgr., 1987-92, ops. mgr., 1992-94, product line mgr., 1994—. Avocation: golf. E-mail: ruben.d.melconian@grace.com. Office: Grace Argentina SA, Primera Junta 550, 1878 Quilmes Argentina

MELDRUM, BRIAN STUART, neuroscientist, educator; b. Ipswich, Suffolk, Eng., Aug. 20, 1935; s. Frederick Stephen and Mary (Singleton) M.; m. Mary Ann Fryer, Jan. 4, 1958 (div. 1975); children: Julian, Judith, Andrew; m. Astrid Grønneberg Chapman, Aug. 14, 1981; 1 child, Hannah. BA, Cambridge (Eng.) U., 1956, MBBChir, 1959; PhD, London U., 1964; DSc (hon.), U. R. Desartes, Paris, 1994. House officer Guy's Hosp., London, 1959-60; rsch. asst. dept. physiology U. Coll., London, 1961-63; mem. sci. staff neuropsychiatry unit MRC, Carshalton, Eng., 1963-73; sr. lectr. exptl. neurology London U., 1981-84, reader exptl. neurology, 1984-88, prof. exptl. neurology, 1988—. Co-editor: Recent Advances in Epilepsy, vols. 1-6, 1983-95, Antiepileptic Drugs, 3rd edit., 1989, 4th edit., 1995; mng. editor jour. Epilepsy Rsch., 1990—; contbr. rsch. articles to profl. jours. Trustee Fund for Epilepsy, London, 1995. Recipient Michael prize Stiftung Michael, 1980-81, Epilepsy Rsch. award Am. Epilepsy Soc., 1999; named First Alfred Meyer Lectr., Brit. Neuropathol. Soc., 1995. Mem. Am. Neurol. Assn. (assoc.), Internat. League Against Epilepsy (amb. epilepsy 1987), Brit. Pharmacol. Soc.

MELEG, CSILLA, sociologist, educator; b. Baja, Hungary, Dec. 25, 1947; d. Meleg József and Katay Ilona; m. Vastagh Zoltan, July 3, 1980; children: Gerda, Noemi. DA, Szeged (Hungary) U., 1972-76; PhD, Budapest U., 1976-80; first asst., Janus Pannonius U., Pecs, Hungary, 1980-87; prof. sociology, Janus Pannonius U., 1987—. cons. Fact Found., Pecs, 1990—; bd. dirs. Hungarian Rsch. Found. Author: School and Society, 1996; editor: Anthology of Political Sociology, 1996. Mem. Hungarian Sociol. Assn. (bd. dirs. 1988—), Hungarian Rsch. Found. (bd. dirs. 1997—), Stress and Anxiety Rsch. Assn., Internat. Assn. Intercultural Edn., European Union Sch. and Univ. Health Medicine. Calvinist. Office: Janus Panonius U, 48-as tér 1, 7601 Pécs Hungary

MELEGH, BÉLA, pediatrician, geneticist, researcher; b. Kömlö, Hungary, June 27, 1954; s. Bèla and Terezia (Ágoston) M.; m. Maria Pap, June 24, 1958; children: Bèla, Márton. MD, Univ. Med. Sch., Pécs, Hungary, 1978; PhD, Hungarian Acad. Scis., Budapest, 1991, DSc, 1999. Postdoctoral fellow dept. biochemistry Univ. Med. Sch., Pécs, 1978-81, resident in pediatrics, 1981-85, lectr., 1985-97, asst. prof. pediat., clin. chemistry, molecular biology, 1992—, assoc. prof., 1997-99, prof., assoc. chair med. genetics and pediats., 1999—; chief ctrl. lab., dept. pediatrics and med. genetics Univ. Pécs, 1992-99. Contbr. articles to profl. jours., chpts. to books; editl. bd. Paediatrics Hungary, 1993—. Grantee: Hungarian Nat. Sci. Found., Ministry of Welfare, Ministry of Edn. Mem. Internat. Assn. for Pediatric Lab. Medicine, European Soc. for Pediatric Rsch., Am. Assn. for Clin. Chemistry, Hungarian Biochem. Soc., Hungarian Pediatric Soc., World Muscle Soc. Office: Pécs Dept Med Genet, József A 7, 7623 Pécs Hungary

MELENDEZ, EDWIN MANUEL, orthopaedic hand surgeon; b. Rio Piedras, P.R., Jan. 2, 1958; s. Manuel and Olga (Martinez) M.; m. Mari Lopez, Feb. 23, 1985; children: Andre G., Gian-Franco, Stephan A. BS in Chemistry magna cum laude, U. P.R., 1978, MD, 1982, grad. in Orthop. Surgery, 1987. Diplomate Am. Bd. Orthopaedic Surgery, sub.-bd. Surgery of the Hand, also Nat. Bd. Med. Examiners. Gen. surgery intern U. P.R. Sch. Medicine, resident in orthopaedic and fracture surgery; fellowship in hand surgery Hosp. for Joint Diseases, Orthop. Inst., N.Y.C., 1988; pvt. practice hand and orthop. surgeon Tampa, Fla., 1991—; chmn. emergency/trauma liaison St. Joseph's Hosp., Tampa, 1996—. Contbr. articles to profl. jours. Maj. USAF, 1988-91. Fellow Am. Acad. Orthop. Surgeons; mem. Am. Assn. for Hand Surgery, Fla. Med. Assn., Fla. Hand Soc., Hillsborough County Med. Assn. Roman Catholic. Avocations: tennis, piano. Office: 4602 N Armenia Ave Ste D-3 Tampa FL 33603-2624

MELENDEZ, JOAQUIN, retired orthopedic assistant; b. San Gabriel, Calif., Aug. 16, 1929; s. Guadalupe and Gudelia (Maldonado) M.; m. Lola Hester Harris, Sept. 3, 1954. BS, Instituto del Estado, Chihuahua, Mex., 1949; AA, Foothill Coll., Los Altos Hill, Calif., 1973. Enlisted U.S. Army, 1950, advanced through grades to sgt. 1st class, ret., 1971; orthopedic asst. St. Vrain Valley Orthopedics (name now Longmont Orthopedics and Sports Medicine Clinic), Longmont, Colo., 1973-93; ret., 1973; translator Mcpl. Ct., Police Dept. and City of Longmont; tchr. pub. spkg. and Spanish for med. office use. Author: (poems) Saturday Night, 1990, Reflections, 1991, Freedom, 1992, Season of Life, 1998; translator: Video Parliamentary Procedure. With U.S. Army, 1950-71. Decorated Bronze Star with V, Meritorious Svc. medal with V; recipient marathon awards. Mem. Colo. Acad. Physician Assts., Nat. Assn. Parlimentarians, Colo. Assn. Parliamentarians (2d v.p. 1998-99), Toastmasters (named Outstanding Divsn. Gov. 1988-89, Divsn. Gov. of Yr. 1995-96, Silver Level of Recognition 1995, recipient speech awards), Internat. Soc. Poets. Republican. Roman Catholic. Avocations: pub. speaking, writing, photography, running, hist. rsch. Home: 3331 Mountain View Ave Longmont CO 80503-2155

MELES, ZENAWI, Ethiopian government official; b. Adua, May 9, 1955. Pres. Ethiopia, Addis Ababa, 1991-95, also chmn. Coun. of Reps.; founder, chmn. EPRDF, 1991—; prime min. Govt. of Ethiopia, Addis Ababa, 1995—; founder Marxist Leninist League of Tigre, Tigre People's Liberation Front; founder, chmn. Ethiopian People's Revolutionary Democratic Front, 1991. Office: Office of the Prime Min, PO Box 1031, Addis Ababa Ethiopia*

MELESHKO, EVGUENI ALEKSEEVICH, electronician; b. Moscow, Feb. 1, 1932; s. Aleksey Vasilievich and Aleksandra Viktorovna (Nikiforova) M.; m. Valentina Konstantinovna Jeltova, Apr. 22, 1933; 1 child, Natali. Degree in elec. engring., Tech. U. Comm. & Info., Moscow, 1955; D of Tech. Sci., Russian Rsch. Ctr., Moscow, 1970. Engr. Russian Rsch. Ctr., Kurchatov Inst., Moscow, 1955-72, sr. scientific rschr., 1972-77, head lab., 1977—; deputy dir. Scientific-Tech. Comlex Electronics, 1993—. Co-author: Two-Frequency Precession of Mounium in Magnetic Field, 1975; author: Measurement Generators in Nuclear Electronics, 1981, Nanosecond Electronics in Experimental Physics, 1987. Home: St Maksimova 6-49, 123098 Moscow Russia Office: Russian Rsch Ctr, Kurchatoc Sq 1, 123182 Moscow Russia

MELEZINEK, ADOLF, engineering educator; b. Vienna, Austria, Oct. 3, 1932; s. Rudolf and Franziska Melezinek; m. Vera Vysansky, July 21, 1952; children: Adolf, Vera. MEE, Tech. U. Prague, 1957; PhD, U. Prague, 1969; DSc (hon.), U. Liberec, 1996; VDSc (hon.), Tech. U., Baumann, Moscow, 2000. Rsch. asst. Tech. Rsch. Inst., Prague, 1952, chief engr., 1957-61, assoc. prof., 1961-69; prof. HTBLVA, Vienna, 1969-71, full prof.; prof. U. Klagenfurt, Austria, 1971—; head Inst. Ednl. Tech. and Engring. Edn.; guest prof. U. Karlsruhe, 1971, Tech. U. Vienna, 1972—, Tech. U. Graz, 1977—, Tech. U. Zurich, 1974—, Tech. U. Budapest (Hungary), 1985—, Tech U., Prague, 1990—, Tech U., Liberec, 1993—. Contbr. numerous articles to profl. publs., books; contbr. to films, videotapes, slide series in field. Recipient Golden Felber medal Czech Tech. U., Prague, 1991, Great Golden medal Govt. Carinthia, 1992; named hon. sen. Tech. U., Budapest, 1994. Mem. Internat. Soc. Engring. Edn. (pres. 1972—, Golden Ring award 1992), Soc. Motion Picture and TV Engrs., Czechoslovakian Cybernetics Soc., Soc. for Programmed Instrn. (bd. dirs. 1976-79). Avocations: flying, music. E-mail: adolf.melezinek@unin-k.blu.ac.at. Home: Akazienhofstr 79, A 9020 Klagenfurt Austria Office: U Klagenfurt, Universitatsstr, A 9020 Klagenfurt Austria

MELGAR, HAROLDO RODAS, associations executive. Sec. gen. Ctrl. Am. Common Market, Guatemala City, Guatemala. Office: Mercado Comun Centro Am, 4A Avda 10-25 Zona 14, Guatemala City 01901, Guatemala*

MELHEM, GEORGES ABDALLAH, chemical engineer; b. Kafarhazir, Lebanon, Nov. 7, 1961; came to the U.S., 1980; s. Abdallah N. and Georgette M. (Karam) M.; m. Lucie L. Leveille, Sept. 12, 1992. BSChE, Northeastern U., 1984, MSChE, 1986, PhD, 1988. Lectr. in chem. engring. Northeastern U., Boston, 1986-88; cons. Arthur D. Little Inc., Cambridge, Mass., 1988-89, sr. cons., 1989-91, mgr. N.Am. safety and risk, 1991—, assoc. dir., 1988-92; dir. Arthur D. Little Inc., Cambridge, 1992—, v.p., 1997-2000; pres., COO Pyxsys Corp. (an Arthur D. Little Co.), 2000—. Contbr. articles to profl. jours. Mem. AIChE (chair safety of chem. processes and hazardous materials subcom.), Design Inst. for Emergency Relief Sys. Users Group, Am. Chem. Soc., Sigma Xi, Omega Chi Epsilon, Alpha Pi Mu., Tau Beta Pi. Office: Arthur D Little Inc 20 Acorn Park Cambridge MA 02140-2328

MELIAN, VICTOR MANUEL, engineering educator, researcher; b. Las Palmas G.C., Spain, Oct. 12, 1966; s. Jorge Melian and Josefa Santana; m. Pino Peña Lopez, Aug. 2, 1997; 1 child, Victor Melian Lopez. Cert. telecomm. engr., ETSIT, Las Palmas, 1992, DEng in Telecomm., 1997. Staff ETSIT-ULPGC, Las Palmas G.C., 1996-99, prof., 1999—. Author: Problems of Optical Communications, Vol. I, 1999. Mem. COIT. Roman Catholic. Avocations: football, rugby, boat races, basketball, golf. Office: ETSI Telecomm, 35017 Las Palmas GC LP, Spain

MELICAN, JAMES PATRICK, JR., lawyer; b. Worcester, Mass., Sept. 8, 1940; s. James Patrick and Abigail Helen (Donahue) M.; children: Marlane, James P., David, Molly, Megan. BA, Fordham U., 1962; JD, Harvard U., 1965; MBA, Mich. State U., 1971. Bar: Mich 1966, Calif. 1983. Supervising atty. product liability sect. Gen. Motors Corp., Detroit, 1971-73; atty.-in-charge trade regulation Gen. Motors Corp., 1973-77, atty.-in-charge mktg. and purchasing, 1977-80, asst. gen. counsel, 1980-81; gen. counsel Toyota Motor Sales, U.S.A., Inc., Torrance, Calif., 1981-82, v.p., gen. counsel, 1982-84; v.p., gen. counsel Internat. Paper Co., N.Y.C., 1984-87, sr. v.p., gen. counsel, 1987-91; exec. v.p. legal and external affairs Internat. Paper Co., Purchase, N.Y., 1991—; bd. dirs. Scitex Corp., Ltd.; bd. trustees Fordham Prep. Sch. Mem. ABA, NAM (bd. dirs., exec. com.), Am. Law Inst., Assn. Bar City of N.Y., Assn. Gen. Counsel, Industry Sector Adv. Com. on Paper and Paper Products for Trade Policy Matters. Roman Catholic. Home: 39 Willowmere Cir Riverside CT 06878-2503 Office: Internat Paper Co 2 Manhattanville Rd Purchase NY 10577-2113

MELICHERCIK, JURAJ, cardiologist; b. Bratislava, Czechoslovakia, Apr. 15, 1952; arrived in Germany, 1992; s. Andrej and Viera (Zathurecka) M.; m. Kornelia Kovarovicova, Nov. 24, 1973; children: Andrea, Katarina. MD, Comenius U., 1976; PhD, Postgrad. Inst. Bratislava, 1992. Intern, resident Derer's Hosp., Bratislava, 1976-79; resident, staff internist, cardiologist, dep. head dept. Inst. Cardiovasc. Disease, Bratislava, 1979-92; rsch. fellow U. Heidelberg, Germany, 1992-95; head dept. clin. electrophysiology, sr. staff cardiologist Heart Ctr., Lahr, Germany, 1995—. Fellow European Soc. Cardiology, Internat. Coll. Angiology (Young Cardiologist award, 1986, Young Investigation award, 1994), Slovakian Soc. Cardiology; mem. AAAS, N.Y. Acad. Sci.

MELIKHOV, SERGEY VSEVOLODOVITCH, radio engineering educator; b. Tomsk, Russia, Apr. 12, 1950; s. Vsevolod Sergeevitch and Maria Grigorjevna (Maisack) M.; m. Tatyana Nickolaevna Voronko, Apr. 6, 1974; 1 child, Olga Sergeevna. Degree in Engring., Tomsk State U. Control Sys. and Radioelectronics, 1972, PhD, 1979, DSc, 1998. Asst. Tomsk State U. Control Sys. and Radioelectronics, 1972-75, asst. prof., 1978-82, 97-99, head of the chair, 1982-94, chair prof., 1999—. Co-author: (M.K. Nazarenko) Sensitivity of Radio Receivers, 1995; contbr. articles to profl. jours. Mem. A.S. Popov Sci. Soc. Achievements include patentee in field. Avocations: popular music, skiing, building summer house. Office: Tomsk State Univ Control, 40 Lenin St, 634050 Tomsk Russia

MELING, TORSTEIN R., neurosurgeon, researcher; b. Stavanger, Norway, Mar. 21, 1968; s. Torjer R. and Wenche (Helgoe) M.; m. Eva Oedegaard, Sept. 21, 1991; children: Trym, Tord. MD, U. Oslo, 1995, PhD, 1997. Rschr. Norwegian Cancer Soc., Oslo, 1991-92, Rsch. Forum Ullevaal Hosp., Oslo, 1995; intern Sarpsborg (Norway) Hosp., 1996; intern dept. internal medicine VAMC, Washington, 1994; resident dept. neurosurgery Nat. Hosp., Oslo, 1998—. Lt. Norwegian Navy, 1996-97, Oslo. Grantee The Norwegian Cancer Soc., Oslo, 1991, 92, The Nobel Found., Stockholm, 1993. Mem. Norwegian Med. Assn., N.Y. Acad. Scis. Avocations: tennis, sailing. Home: Eddaveien 37, 0772 Oslo Norway Office: Dept Neurosurgery, Nat Hosp, 0027 Oslo Norway

MELIOS, CRISTO BLADIMIROS, chemistry educator; b. Araçatuba, Sao Paulo, Brazil, Nov. 22, 1942; s. Bladimiros Papantoniou and Kiriácula (Condos) M.; m. Vilma Carli, Jan. 28, 1978. Lic. in Chemistry, Inst. Chemistry, Araraquara, Brazil, 1965, B Chemistry, 1966, PhD in Chemistry, 1974, Privat-Dozent, 1987. Tchg. asst. Inst. Chemistry, Araraquara, 1966-71, asst. prof., 1971-74, assoc. prof., 1974-87, prof. chemistry, 1987—; rsch. fellow NRC, Brasilia, Brazil, 1979—; vis. prof. chemistry U. Liege, Belgium, 1990; mem. Commn. on Equilibrium Data, IUPAC, Oxford, Eng., 1992-95; dir., prin. Inst. Chemistry, Univ. Estadual Paulista, 1992-96; mem. Commn. on Solubility Data, IUPAC, N.C., 2000—; chemistry grants com., 1990-92. Contbr. articles to profl. jours. Recipient sr. award Univ. Estadual Paulista, Araraquara, Brazil, 1993, 96. Mem. Brazilian Com. Tech. Recommendations, Brazilian Chem. Soc. (cons. 1990-92, merit award 1997). Avocations: classical and popular music, stamp collecting, soccer games. Home: Avenida Portugal 156 Apt 34, 14801075 Araraquara Brazil Office: Inst Quimica UNESP s/no, Rua Prof Francisco Degni, 14800900 Araraquara Brazil

MELITZ, JACQUES, economist, educator; b. Paris, Dec. 23, 1935; s. Morris and Czyporah (Shapiro) M.; m. Susan Layton, May 15, 1987. BA, UCLA, 1956, MA, 1957; PhD, Princeton U., 1963. Sr. economist rsch. dept. INSEE, Paris, 1974—; prof. Inst. des Etudes Politiques, Paris, 1981—. Home: 1 Rue Erlanger, Paris 75016, France Office: CREST-INSEE, 15 Blvd Gabriel Peri, 92245 Malakoff France

MELKEBEEK, JAN AUGUSTE ARTHUR, engineering educator; b. Gent, Belgium, Feb. 20, 1952; s. Albert Melkebeek and Josephine Marescau. Degree in electro-mech. engring., Ghent U., 1975, D Applied Scis., 1980, D Habilitus, 1986. Asst. prof. U. Ghent, 1975-82, lectr., 1982-85; sr. lectr. U. Gent, 1985-87; prof. engring. U. Ghent, 1987—, head dept. elec. power engring., 1991—; mem. sci. com. Nat. Fund Sci. Rsch., Belgium, 1996. Contbr. articles to profl. jours. Recipient Ednl. award U. Wis., 1982. Fellow Inst. Elec. Engrs.; mem. IEEE (sr., mem. elec. mach. com. 1983), Koninklyke Vlaamse Ingenieursvereniging (student award 1975). Avocations: swimming, flying. Home: Duilhoekstraat 25, B-9230 Wetteren Belgium Office: Ghent U, Sint-Pietersnieuwstraat 41, B-9000 Ghent Belgium

MELKERT, AD P W, Dutch government official; b. Gouda, The Netherlands, Feb. 12, 1956; married; 2 children. BA in Polit. Sci., U. Amsterdam, The Netherlands, MA in Internat. Rels., 1981. Gen. sec. European Youth Forum, European Cmtys., Brussels, 1981-84; coord., dir. internal affairs Orgn. for Internat. Devel. Cooperation, 1984-86; chmn. Netherlands Platform Internat. Youth Work Coun. European Nat. Youth Coms. Nat. Working Group Youth Yr., 1985; bd. mem. Radical Party Com., 1979-81; Labor Party mem. Lower House, 1986-94; fin. spokesperson Parliamentary Labor Party, bd. mem.; mem. Permanent House Coms. for Fgn. Affairs & European Affairs; dep. chmn. Fin.Com.; Min. Social Affairs and Employment Dutch Govt., 1994-98; fl. leader labor party Lower House Dutch Parliament, The Hague, The Netherlands, 1998—. Office: PO Box 20018, 2500 EA The Hague The Netherlands*

MELKONIAN, ARMEN, consul general of Armenia; b. Yerevan, Armenia, June 19, 1958; came to U.S., 1998; s. Ashot and Joanna (Sogomonian) M.; m. Yevgenia; children: Ashot, Ani. Magister, Yerevan State U., 1980; PhD, Inst. Oriental Studies, Yerevan, 1990. Aide to the Pres. of Armenia Rep. of Armenia, Yerevan, 1992-94; 1st sec. Ministry Fgn. Affairs, Yerevan, 1994; councellor Embassy of Armenia, Cairo, 1994-97; chief of dept. Ministry of

Fgn. Affairs, Yerevan, 1997-98; consul gen. Consulate Gen. of Armenia, L.A., 1998—. E-mail: armconla@aol.com. Office: Consulate Gen of Armenia 50 N La Cienega Blvd Beverly Hills CA 90211-2227

MELLA, ARTHUR JOHN, insurance company executive; b. New York, N.Y., Sept. 25, 1937; s. Anthony Arthur and Angela Helen (Morrongiello) M.; m. Louise Vetere, May 5, 1962; children: Douglas James, Gregory Arthur. BS, Fordham U., 1959. CPCU. Supr. Liberty Mut. Ins. Co., N.Y.C., 1960-70; v.p. The Home Ins. Co., N.Y.C., 1970-80, Skandia Am. Reinsurance Co., N.Y.C., 1980-85; sr. v.p. Reliance Reinsurance Corp., Phila., 1985-2000; ret., 2000; cons. in field. With USNG, 1960-63. Mem. Fedn. Ins. and Corp. Counsel, Excess Surplus Lines Claims (pres. 1988-89, v.p. 1987-88, bd. dirs. 1986-87), Broker and Reins. Underwriting, Soc. CPCU. Republican. Roman Catholic. Avocations: gardening, book collecting, golf.

MELLANDRI, GIOVANNA, government official; b. N.Y.C., Jan. 28, 1962. Min. Constitutional Reform, Rome, 1998—. Office: Office of Prime Min, Piazza Colonna 370, 00100 Rome Italy*

MELLBRING, GÖRAN OLOF LENNART, surgeon; b. Götene, Sweden, Aug. 12, 1945; s. Gunnar Alfred and Anna Cecilia (Magnusson) M.; m. Eva Elisabeth Reuterskiöld, Nov. 28, 1970; children: Olof Carl Gunnar, Johan Peter Gustaf. MB, Uppsala U., Sweden, 1967, MD, 1972; PhD, Umeå U., Sweden, 1984. Resident in surgery Kärnsjukhuset, Skövde, Sweden, 1973-79; fellow in surgery Univ. Hosp., Umeå, 1979-81, dir. surg. edn., 1981-91, head sect. gastroent. surgery, 1987-91; head dept. surgery Kärnsjukhuset, 1992; chmn. dept. surgery Kärnsjh, Skövde, 1993-99; assoc. prof. surgery Umeå Univ., 1986—; sci. advisor Nat. Bd. Health and Welfare, 1997-99, regional med. supr., 1999—. Contbr. numerous articles to profl. jours. Fellow Swedish Soc. Medicine, Swedish Surg. Soc.; mem. Swedish Med. Assn. Avocations: fly fishing, classical music, fine art. Home: S Bergv 54, S-54131 Skövde Sweden Office: Socialstyrelsen Box 2163, S-55002 Jönköping Sweden

MELLENDORF, PATRICIA JEAN, retired personnel professional; b. Terre Haute, Ind., Mar. 12, 1948; d. LeRoy Benjamin and Sue Jean (Nickerson) Patterson; m. Loren D. Mellendorf; 1 child, Peggy Marie. BA, U. Iowa, 1971, MA in English, 1973, EdS, 1973. Cert. sr. profl. human resources. Related edn. chair Ivy Tech Coll., Richmond, Ind., 1974-84; sec. Am. Water Sys., Richmond, 1984-86, cmty./employee rels. mgr., 1986-88, asst. dir. pers. devel., 1988-96, dir. pers. svcs., 1996-98; ret., 1998; lectr. EEOC, N.Y.C., Phil. Health Maintenance, 1991-95. Editor mag. Am. Water, 1994-96. Mem. econ. edn. adv. coun. Ind. U. East, Richmond, 1988. Mem. Soc. Human Resource Mgmt., ASTD (dir. utilities industry group 1992-95), Am. Water Works Assn., Phi Beta Kappa. Presbyterian.

MELLING, JACK, biotechnologist; b. Aspull, Lancashire, Eng., Feb. 8, 1940; s. John and Mary (Marsden) M.; m. Susan Melling, May 27, 1967. BSc, Manchester U., Eng., 1963, MSc, 1965; PhD, Bath U., Eng., 1968. Rsch. asst. Bath U., Eng., 1965-68; lectr. Heriot-Watt U., Scotland, 1968-69; sr. sci. officer Ministry of Def., Eng., 1969-73, prin. sci. officer, 1973-79; dir. vaccine rsch. and product lab. Pub. Health Lab. Svc., Eng., 1979-87; head biologics div. and dep. dir. Ctr. for Applied Microbiology & Rsch., Porton Down, Salisbury, England, 1987-92; dir. Ctr. for Applied Microbiology & Rsch., Porton Down, Salisbury, Eng., 1992-96, Salk Inst., Swiftwater, Pa., 1996—; vis. prof. Rutgers U. 1979-84, Aston U., 1981-96, Westminster U., 1995—, Zurich U., 1999—; mem. MRC Vaccine Com., 1979-96; sec. Brit. Coord. Com. for Biotech., London, 1981-85; mem. Com. Safety of Medicines, Biologic, London, 1982-99, Ministry of Agr. Toxicants in Foods com., London, 1982-94; counsellor, tutor Open U., Salisbury, 1971-74; sr. scientific adv. Internat. AIDS Initiative, N.Y.C., 1999—. Editor: Microbial Adhesion, 1980; editor Chem. Tech. and Biotech. Jour., 1985—; contbr. more than 100 articles to profl. jours. Mem. Swiss Diasaster Relief Orgn. Fellow Royal Pharm. Soc. G.B., Inst. of Biology. Fellow Royal Soc. Medicine, Royal Coll. Pathologists; mem. Soc. Chem. Industry (coun. mem. 1975-83, 98—, sec. 1975-81, chmn. biotech. group 1981-83, chmn. publs. com. 1999—). Avocations: skiing, walking. Office: Salk Inst Biol Studies PO Box 250 Rt 611 N Swiftwater PA 18370

MELLING, JOHN KENNEDY, accountant; b. Westcliff-on-sea, Essex, Eng., Jan. 11, 1927; s. John Robert and Ivy Edith May (Woolmer) M. Chartered acct.; chartered tax cons. Audit clk. Younghusband, Taft & Co., Derby, Eng., 1942-43; articled clk., chartered acct. Jones, Shinner & Co., London and Southend, Eng., 1943-53; sr. asst. Howard, Howes & Co., London, 1953-59; pvt. practice London & Westcliff, Eng., 1959—; dramatic critic The Stage, Eng., 1957-90, Fur Weekly News, Eng., 1968-73; lectr., radio and TV broadcaster in field; columnist Crime Time, Eng., 1996—. Author: Southend Playhouses Since 1793, 1969, Discovering Lost Theatres, 1969, Discovering London's Guilds and Liveries, 1973, 5th edit., 1995, Discovering Theatre Ephemera, 1974, She Shall Have Murder, 1987, Alchemy of Murder, 1993, Gwendoline Butler-Inventor of the Women's Police Procedural, 1993, Murder Done to Death, 1996, (plays) George-From Caroline, Murder at St. Dunstan's, The Toast Is series, also filmscripts, audio books; co-author: Scaling the High C's, 1996; editor: The Farrier & His Craft, 1981, Crime Writers' Practical Handbook, 1989 (CWA Spl. award); editor The Liveryman Mag., 1970-75, Black Dagger Series, 1986-91; contbr. articles to profl. jours. Gov. Corp. of the Sons of the Clergy, Eng., 1981—; hon. life internat. v.p. Am. Fedn. Police, 1985—; com. mem. Crime Writers' Assn., Eng., 1985-88; spl. agt., hon. chief police Nat. Drugs Task Force, 1989—. Decorated knight Order St. Basil the Great (Russia); knight comdr. Order Knights of Justice, knight grand cross Order St. Michael the Archangel, 1980-81; master Worshipful Co. of Poulters; liveryman Farriers and Bakers Cos.; freeman Constructors Co.; recipient Award Police medal of Honor 1984. Fellow Faculty of Bldg., Royal Soc. Arts; mem. Brit. Acad. Film and TV Arts, City Livery Club (editor and coun. mem. 1970-75), Cookery and Food Assn., Marylebone Rifle & Pistol Club, Westcliff Film and Video Club (founder, pres. 1962, first hon. life mem. 1999), Edinburgh Press Club. Conservative. Anglican. Avocations: reading, shooting, collecting crime fiction. Home: 44A Tranquil Vale, Blackheath, London SE3 0BD, England Home: 85 Chalkwell Ave, Westcliff-on-sea Essex SS0 8NL, England

MELLIS, MICHAEL J., lawyer; b. White Plains, N.Y., Aug. 31, 1965; m. Martha Lee Joseph, May, 30, 1998. BA in History, Williams Coll., 1987; JD, Harvard U., 1991. Bar: N.Y. 1992, N.J. 1992, U.S. Dist. Ct., ea. dist., so. dist., N.Y., 1992, 2d circuit, 1993. Jud. clerk Hon. John R. Bartels U.S. Dist. Ct., Bklyn., 1991-93; assoc. Patterson, Belknap, Webb & Tyle, LLP, N.Y.C., 1993-98; new media counsel Major League Baseball Enterprises, N.Y.C., 1998—. Office: Major League Baseball Enterprises 245 Park Ave New York NY 10167-0002

MELLIS, WERNER, education educator; b. Oberhausen, Germany, Jan. 19, 1951; m. Vincenza Pignataro, Dec. 29, 1984; 1 child, Enrico. State Exam in Math., U. Cologne, Germany, 1978, Doctor rer.nat., 1980. Asst. U. Cologne, 1980-84, prof., 1993—; systems engr. Nixdorf Computer, Paderborn, Germany, 1984-85, mgr., 1986-89; mgr. Daimler Benz AG, Stuttgart, 1989-92; dir. BIFOA, Cologne, 1994-96; owner SIGMA QM Consulting, Konigswinter and Cologne, Germany, 1996. Author: TQM, 1996, Quality Function Deployment, 1997. Mem. IEEE. Office: U Cologne, Albertus Magnus Platz, D-50923 Cologne Germany

MELLISH, GORDON HARTLEY, economist, educator; b. Toronto, May 3, 1940; came to U.S., 1958; s. Gordon Day and Catherine (Hartley) M.; m. Nancy Bernice Newell (div. Nov. 1972); m. Diane Evelyn Bostow, Jan. 1, 1978 (div. 1999); children: Jennie Bostow, Luke Bostow. BA, Rockford (Ill.) Coll., 1962; PhD, U. Va., 1965. Econs. educator U. South Fla., Tampa, 1965-89; pvt. practice Tampa, Fla., 1966—; vis. prof. U. Va., 1969, Hillsborough Jr. Coll., 1968; vis. lectr. U. Tampa, 1965, 74. Contbr. articles to profl. jours. Mem. Tampa Yacht and Country Club, Tampa Club, Leadership Tampa Alumni. Democrat. Avocations: sailing, skiing. Home: 2510 W Shell Point Pl Tampa FL 33611-5033

MELLO, JOAO CANELLAS, energy company official, energy consultant; b. Rio de Janeiro, May 11, 1936; m. Duplar Pires and Edina Canellas (Moura) M.; m. Ruth Benevides Oliveira, Aug. 7, 1959; children: Joao Carlos, Ana Ruth Mello Oliva. BS, Nat. Sch. Engring., Barzil, 1958. Registered elec. engr., Brazil. Engr. Rio Light, Brazil, 1959-61; head dept. engring. CHESF-HID, Sao Francisco, Brazil, 1961-74; v.p. Monasa Consultoria, Brazil, 1974-85; energy mgr. Alcoa Aluminio, Brazil, 1985-97; supt. dir. Machadinho Energetica, Sao Paulo, Brazil, 1997—; prof. Nat. Sch. Engring., 1959-65, Fed. U. Fluminense, 1961-71, Cath. U., Brazil, 1964-65; v.p. Internat. Conf. Large Elec. Networks (CIGRE), Brazil, 1991-95; seminar presenter in field in Brazil and fgn. countries. Author: Electricity Distribution, 1962 (merit award); contbr. over 75 articles on energy to Brazilian and internat. jours. Roman Catholic. Avocation: horseback riding. Office: Machadinho Energetica 13 Fl, 2100 Alexandre Dumas St, 04717004 Sao Paulo Brazil

MELLO, MARIA LUIZA SILVEIRA, cell biologist, educator; b. Bauru, Sao Paulo, July 14, 1943; d. José Silveira and Rosa (Petrocine) M.; m. Benedicto de Campos Vidal, Jan. 13, 1994. BS, U. Sao Paulo State, Rio Claro, Brazil, 1965; PhD, U. Sao Paulo, Ribeirão Preto, Brazil, 1969. Asst. prof. U. Sao Paulo, 1969; assoc. prof. State U. Campinas, Brazil, 1969-81, prof., 1981—, mem. bd. inst. devel. and evaluation, 1994-98, dir. Inst. of Biology, 1998—; vis. scientist Mich. Cancer Found., Detroit, 1985, Autonomous U., Madrid, 1985, Tech. U. Munich, 1992. Author: Practice in Cell Biology, 1980, Cell Biology, 1987; contbr. over 150 articles to sci. jours. Recipient CNPq-30 Yrs. award Brazilian R&D Coun., 1981, Zeferino Vaz award for outstanding acad. performance, 1996, 98. Mem. AAAS, Brazilian Soc. Genetics (Rafael Beiguelman award 1977), Am. Assn. Cancer Rsch. Avocation: piano. Office: UNICAMP Inst Biology, Dept Cell Biology, 13083970 Campinas Sao Paulo, Brazil

MELLO-FRANCO, AFFONSO ARINOS DE, diplomat; b. Belo Horizonte, Brazil, Nov. 11, 1930; s. Affonso Arinos and Anna Guilhermina (Pereira) Mello-F.; m. Beatriz Fontenelle, Aug. 15, 1955; children: Virgilio (dec.), Cesario, Afranio, Caio, Silvia, Afonso. PhD, Nat. Law Sch., Rio de Janeiro, 1955; postgrad., Brazilian Inst. Economy, 1975. State legislator State Assembly, Rio de Janeiro, 1960-62; congressman Ho. of Reps., Brasilia, Brazil, 1964-66; sec. Brazilian Embassy, Rome, 1956-59; sec. Embassy, Vienna, 1959-60, Brussels, 1963, The Hague, 1964; consul Brazilian Consulate, Geneva, 1966-69; counsel, min. Brazilian Embassy, Washington, 1969-74; consul-gen. Brazilian Consulate Gen., Oporto, Portugal, 1977-79; amb. Brazilian Embassy, La Paz, Bolivia, 1980-82, Caracas, Venezuela, 1983-85, Vatican, 1986-90, The Hague, The Netherlands, 1990-94. Author: Primo Canto, 1976, Tres Faces da Liberdade, 1988, Atras do Espelho, 1994, Tempestade no Altiplano, 1998, Ribeiro Couto e Afonso Arinos, 1999, Afonso Arinos no Congresso, 1999. Decorated Grand Cross of the Order of Rio-Branco, Grand Cross of the Order of Pius IX, Grand Cross of the Order of Orange-Nassau, Grand Cross of Order of Condor de los Andes, 1st class of Order of Francisco de Miranda, Grand Cross of Order of Malta. Mem. Brazilian Hist. and Geog. Inst., Brazilian Bar Assn., Brazilian Pen Club, Brazilian Acad. Lit. Roman Catholic. Home: Praia de Botafogo 130 #801, 22250040 Rio de Janeiro Brazil

MELLON, GWEN GRANT, foundation executive; b. Englewood, N.J., July 22, 1911; d. William Wright Grant and Katherine Hall; m. John Rawson (div.); children: Michael, Jenifer, Ian; m. William Larimer Mellon Jr., 1946. BA, Smith Coll., 1934, LHD (hon.), 1959; HHD (hon.), Bethany Coll., 1976; D in Pub. Svc. (hon.), Chatham Coll., 1999. V.p. The Grant Found., 1954-89, pres., 1989—. Author: My Road to Deschapelles, 1997; author, editor: Letters From St. Marc, 1995. Recipient Elizabeth Blackwell award Hobart and William Smith Colls., Geneva, N.y., 1958, Citation for Creative Svc., The Shipley Sch., Bryn Mawr, Pa., 1963, Margaret Bailey Speer award The Shipley Sch., Bryn Mawr, 1981, award in recognition of creative leaderhip and dedicated svc. The Family of Man, World Conv. Chs. of Christ, 1985, Reverence for Life award Boston Konbit Clinic, 1992, Reverence for Life Commendation, Albert Schweitzer Inst. for the Humanities, Quinnipiac Coll., Hamden, Conn., 1994, Schweitzer Inst. award for excellence Chapman U., Orange, Calif., 1996, L'Ordre Nat. Honneur et Mérite au Grade de Chevalier, Republic Haiti, 1996, Smith Coll. medal Smith Coll., Northampton, Mass., 1997, Reconnaissance du Mérite award La Fondation Haitienne, Boston, 1997, Lifetime Achievement award Assn. Haitian Physicians Abroad, Chgo., 1997, Honneur et Mérite award Vallée de l'Artibonite, Haiti, 1999, Brooke Astor award for women in sci. Rockefeller U., N.Y.C., 2000. Office: Hosp Albert Schweitzer c/o Agape Flights Inc 7990 15th St E Sarasota FL 34243-2718

MELLO NETO, GUSTAVO ADOLFO RAMOS, psychology educator; b. Neves Paulista, Sao Paulo, Brazil, Apr. 9, 1957; s. Gustavo Adolfo Ramos and Dinah Naxara (Souza) Mello Filho; m. Arlanza Rodrigues Rodrigues Rebello, July 11, 1979 (div. Apr. 1986); m. Viviana Velasco Martinez, Sept. 21, 1986; 1 child, Gustavo Adolfo. D, U. Sao Paulo, 1993; postgrad., U. Paris VII, 1996. Cert. psychologist. Prof. U. Estadual de Maaringá, Brazil, 1983——. Author: Oardil da crianée, 1994, Le social dans la construction freudienne de la psychanalyse, 1997. Mem. APA. Avocation: writing short tales. Home: Rua Paranguá, 565, Rua Prof Ney Marques n 21, 87020300 Maringá Brazil Office: U Estadual de Maaringá, 88702090 0aringá Brazil

MELLOR, MARJORIE LOTH, art and museum education consultant; b. Newark, July 6, 1934; d. Rudolph David and Katharine (Egleston) Loth; m. Clifford Warren Mellor, July 2, 1955; children: Jill Mellor Carey, Wayne Clifford Mellor. BA, Douglass Coll., 1957; MS in Art Edn., Syracuse U., 1975. Cert. tchr., Syracuse (N.Y.) Sch. Dist. Part-time art tchr. Syracuse City Sch. Dist., 1968-85, full-time art tchr., 1985-90; curator student svcs. Everson Mus., Syracuse, 1979-85, Stickley Project coord., 1990-96; docent tng. cons. Everson Mus., 1979—, Stickley cons. Syracuse City Sch. dist. and Everson Mus., 1990—; mem. edn. com. of bd. Everson Mus., 1995—; liaison Syracuse City Sch. Dist. to Everson Mus., 1983-96. Author: (text and workbook) Louis Comfort Tiffany, 1993. Chair Friends of Art Syracuse U., 1974; mem. bd. Met. Sch. Arts, Syracuse, 1973-79, Found. to Advance Arts and Athletics, Syracuse, 1981-83; bd. chair Unitarian Universalist Ch., Syracuse, 1996-97. Grantee N.Y. State Coun. Arts, Syracuse, 1993-94, 94-95, 95-96. Mem. Syracuse Stage, Syracuse Symphony, Jr. League Syracuse, Syracuse Corinthian Club, Kappa Pi Upsilon. Avocations: painting, tennis, old movies, walking. Home: 122 Fairfield St Fayetteville NY 13066-2211

MELLORS, ROBERT CHARLES, physician, scientist, educator; b. Dayton, Ohio, 1916; s. Bert S. and Clementine (Steinmetz) M.; m. Jane K. Winternitz, Mar. 25, 1944; children: Alice J., Robert C., William K., John W. Ph.D., Western Res. U., 1940; M.D., Johns Hopkins, 1944. Diplomate Am. Bd. Pathology. Intern Nat. Naval Med. Ctr., Bethesda, Md., 1944-45; rsch. fellow medicine Meml. Center Cancer and Allied Diseases, N.Y.C., 1946-50; rsch. fellow pathology Meml. Ctr. Cancer and Allied Diseases, 1950-53, asst. attending pathologist, 1953-57, assoc. attending pathologist, 1957-58; sr. fellow Am. Cancer Soc., 1947-50; sr. clin. rsch. fellow Damon Runyon Meml. Fund, 1950-53; asst. attending pathologist Meml. Hosp., N.Y.C., 1953-57, assoc. attending pathologist, 1957-58; asst. attending pathologist Ewing Hosp., N.Y.C., 1953-57, assoc. attending pathologist, 1957-58; instr. biochemistry Western Res. U., 1940-42; rsch. assoc. Poliomyelitis Rsch. Ctr. and Dept. Epidemiology Johns Hopkins U. Sch. Hygiene, 1942-44; asst. prof. biology Meml. Ctr. Cancer and Allied Diseases, N.Y.C., 1952-53; asst. prof. pathology Sloan Kettering div. Cornell U., 1953-57, assoc. prof., 1957-58; prof. pathology Cornell U. Med. Coll., 1961-90, prof. emeritus, 1990—; adj. prof. pathology N.Y. Med. Coll., 1997—; assoc. attending pathologist N.Y. Hosp., 1961-72, attending pathologist, 1972-86; pathologist-in-chief, dir. labs., 1958-84, emeritus, 1984-85, hon. staff, 1986—; assoc. dir. rsch. Hosp. for Spl. Surgery, N.Y.C., 1958-69, dir. rsch., 1969-84, emeritus, 1984-85, scientist emeritus, 1986—; mem. rsch. adv. com. NIH, 1962-66; adv. com. Nat. Inst. Environ. Health Sci., 1966-69; com. nomenclature and classification of disease Coll. Am. Pathologists, 1960-64. Author: Analytical Cytology, 1955, 2d edit., 1959, Analytical Pathology, 1957. Served as lt. (j.g.), M.C. USNR, 1944-46. Recipient Kappa Delta award Am. Acad. of Orthopedic Surgeons, 1962. Fellow Royal Coll. Pathologists, Molecular Medicine Soc., Am. Soc. Clin. Pathology; mem. Internat. Soc. for Optical Engring., Am. Assn. Pathologists, Am. Assn. Immunologists, Am. Soc. Biochemistry and Molecular Biology, Am. Coll. Rheumatology, Am. Orthopedic Assn. (hon.). Home: 3 Hardscrabble Cir Armonk NY 10504-2222

MELLOTTÉE, HENRY, chemical engineer, researcher; b. Mantes-la-Jolie, France, July 7, 1941; s. Robert and Madeleine (Talabot) M.; m. Sabine Revel, June 21, 1980; children: Benoit, Claire. PhD in Phys. Sci., U. Paris, 1968. Cert. chem. engr. Rsch. dir. CNRS, 1978—; dir. Lab. Combustion and Reactive Sys. CNRS, Orleans, 1982-94; sci. advisor Ecodev program CNRS, Meudon, France, 1995—. Mem. French Soc. Chemistry, Combustion Inst. (gen. sec. French sect. 1984-94). Home: 11 Boulevard Davout, 75020 Paris France Office: CNRS-Ecodev, 1 Rue du Cerf, 92195 Meudon France

MELLOUL, ABRAHAM J., hydrogeologist; b. Fez, Morocco, Oct. 15, 1943; arrived in Israel, 1964; s. Jacob and Esther (Assouline) M.; m. Nov. 28, 1992; 3 children. BSc in Geology, diploma in hydrogeology, Hebrew U., Jerusalem, 1970; 3d cycle cert. in operational hydrology, Ecole Polytech. Fed., Lausanne, Switzerland, 1973; PhD in Hydrogeology, Neuchatel U., Switzerland, 1979. Cert. in hydrogeology, ground water quality, ecology. Sr. hydrogeologist Hydrol. Svc., Jerusalem, 1970—, rschr., 1993—; lectr. in hydrochemistry, ecology and Israel groundwater mgmt., 1970—; mem., advisor, referee Water Commn., Israel, 1970—; manuscript reviewer, 1995—. Author: Principal Components Analysis for Construction of Conceptual Model of Deep Aquifer with Scarce Data, 1979; contbr. articles to profl. jours. Mem. Israel Soc. Geology, Israel Soc. Hydrology, Israel Soc. Ecology. Avocation: painting. Office: Hydrol Svc, Yaffo 234 Str, 91063 Jerusalem Israel

MELNICK, IGOR VASILYEVICH, researcher; b. Gorlovka, Donetzk, Ukraine, May 3, 1962; s. Vasiliy Nikolayevich and Nadezhda Terentyevna Melnick; m. Natasha Vladimirovna Melnick, Oct. 8, 1992 (div. July 1994). Physician, Med. Inst., Kiev, Ukraine, 1985; PhD, Bogomoletz Inst. Physiology, Kiev, 1992. Cert. in medicine. Rsch. asst. Bogomoletz Inst. Physiology, Kiev, 1988-92; postdoctoral fellow Max Planck Inst. Psychiatry, Martinsried, Germany, 1993-94, Pasteur Inst., Paris, 1994-96; sci. rschr. Bogomoletz Inst. Physiology, Kiev, 1996—. Contbr. articles to profl. jours. Mem. Ukrainian Neurosci. Soc. Orthodox. Avocations: sports, literature, music. Fax: 293-6458. Office: Bogomoletz Inst Physiol, Bogomoletz str 4, Kiev 252024, Ukraine

MELNIK, BORIS EFIM, science educator; b. Briceni Village, Moldova, Feb. 11, 1928; s. Efim Dumitru and Vera (Braguta) M.; m. Ana Vitiu, Aug. 29, 1953; children: Liudmila, Victoria. MS, Chisinau State U., Moldova, 1951, PhD in Physiology and Biochemistry of Man, 1955; D Honoris Causa, Internat. Free U., Moldova, 1994, State Med. U., Moldova, 1994, Acad. Econ. Studies of Moldova, 1996, State Pedagogical Inst., 2000. Prof. biology and chemistry Chisinau State U., dean, 1955-64, v.p., 1964-74, pres., 1974-92; chair physiology dept. Moldova State U.; chmn. Superior Attestation Bd. of Republic of Moldova, 1992—; mem. coun. sci. problems and durable human devel. under Pres. Republic of Moldova, 1996. Contbr. numerous sci. works, including 7 manuals, 9 monographs, 8 books and booklets, including Physiology of Man and Animals, Medical and Biological Forms of Stress, MSH and Adaptation, The Formation of Human Qualities, The Man in the Objective of Science, 1996, Chemistry, Stress and Tumor, 1997, The Man-The Genesis of The Human Existance, 1998, Science News Man and Nature. Mem. parliament Republic of Moldova, dep. of parliament, 1980-85; dep. Chisinau Municipality, 1975-85. Recipient 3 govtl. awards, 3 medals, Laureate of State Sci., Technics and Prodn. award Republic of Moldova, 1996, award of the Republic, Moldova, 1996. Mem. Internat. Assn. European Dimensions, 1992 (mem. sci. com. 1992), Acad. Scis. of Republic of Moldova (mem. presidium 1980-90, 96—), Internat. Acad. Scis. of Nature and Soc., Internat. Acad. Ecology and Life Protection Scis., Ctrl. European Acad. Sci. and Art. Avocations: journalism, prose, radio. Home: Ap 5 Serghei Lazo 26, 2004 Chisinau Moldova

MELNIK, RODERICK V. NICHOLAS, mathematician; b. Shepetivka, Ukraine, June 1, 1963; arrived in Australia, 1994, naturalized, 1997; s. Nick and Maya M.; m. Katerina N. Zotsenko, Oct. 5, 1985; children: Vitaly, Roman. MSc, Nat. U. Kiev, 1985, PhD, 1989. Chartered mathematician. Lectr. Nat. Tech. U., Kiev, Ukraine, 1989-94, assoc. prof., 1992—; lectr. U. South Australia, 1994-97, U. So. Queensland, Australia, 1997-99; sr. mathematician Commonwealth Sci. and Indsl. Rsch. Org., Sydney, Australia, 1999—; mem. com. Queensland divsn. Australian and New Zealand Indsl. Applied Math., 1998. Author book; contbr. over 60 articles to profl. jours. Grantee Australian Rsch. Coun., 1998. Fellow Inst. Math. and Its Applications; mem. Am. Math. Soc., London Math. Soc., European Math. Soc., Australian Math. Soc. E-mail: roderick.melnik@cmis.csiro.au. Office: CSIRO Math & Info Scis, Bldg E6B Macquarie U Campus, NSW 2113 Sydney Australia

MELNIKOV, BORIS EVGENIEVICH, engineer, researcher, educator; b. Pskov, Russia, Jan. 1, 1948; s. Evgenij Alexandrovich and Lidija Afanasjevna (Kravchenko) M.; m. Irina Sergeevna Zelig, Jan. 21, 1983; 1 child, Anna Borisovna. Diploma, Leningrad Polytech. Inst., 1972; PhD, Tech. U., St. Petersburg, 1977, D in Tech. Scis., 1993. Engr. Scientist Shipbuilding Inst., St. Petersburg, 1972-78; asst. prof. Leningrad Polytech. Inst., St. Petersburg, 1979-86; asst. prof. St Petersburg State Tech. U., 1986—, prof., 1996—; mem. acad. coun. Inst. Mech. Engring. Rsch. Russian Acad. Scis., Moscow, 1997—; sci. sec. Acad. Coun. Tech. U. for Sci. Programs and Grants, 1996—, head dept. strength of material, 1998—; bd. dirs. Ltd. Triada, St. Petersburg. Contbr. articles to profl. jours. Grantee Russian Found. Fundamental Rschs., 1995-97, Moscow Airline Inst., 1997-98. Avocations: literature, skiing, boxing. Home: Bryantseva 2/1-295, 195269 Saint Petersburg Russia Office: St Petersburg State Tech U, Polytechnical 29, 195251 Saint Petersburg Russia

MEL'NIKOV, YURIY PAVLOVICH, physicist, educator; b. Rostov, Yaroslavl, Russia, Mar. 26, 1947; s. Pavel Fiedorovich and Anna Gerasimovna (Strokina) M.; m. Elena Vladimirovna Schietkina, Apr. 10, 1970; children: Marina, Dmitriy. Cert. in physics, Perm (Russia) U., 1971; D of Physics and Math., Poly. Inst., St. Petersburg, Russia, 1989. Tchr. Tech. Sch., Rostov, Russia, 1971-72; engr. Engine Works, Rybinsk, Russia, 1973-74; tchr. Rybinsk State Acad. Aviation Tech., 1974-76, 79-92, rschr., 1983-86, 90-92, docent of physics, 1992—. Author (textbook) Atomic and Nuclear Physics, 1995; co-author: (textbook) Mathematical Questions of the Organization of Physical Experiments, 1990; contbr. numerous articles to profl. jours. Grantee Russian Found. for Basic Rsch., Moscow, 2000. Avocations: audio and video electronics, swimming, cycling, travel. Home: 182 21 Lenin Ave, 152907 Rybinsk Russia Office: Rybinsk State Acad, Aviation Tech 53 Pushkin St, 152934 Rybinsk Russia

MELNYCHUK, DMYTRO OLEKSIYOVICH, biochemist, educator; b. Ghashkiv, Cherkasy, Ukraine, Nov. 5, 1943; s. Oleksiy Prokhorovich and Hanna Pavlivna Melnychuk; m. Tetyana Fedorivna Lisitsa, 1969; children: Sergiy, Maxim. Vet. MD, Ukrainian Agrl. Acad., Kyiv, 1964, Candidate of Biol. Scis., 1968; D in Biol. Scis., O.V. Palladin Rsch. Inst., Kyiv, 1978. Asst. lectr. biochemistry dept. Ukrainian Agrl. Acad., Kyiv, 1968-69; rschr. O.V. Palladin Rsch. Inst. Biochemistry, Kyiv, 1969-82, head metabolism regulation dept., 1986-97; head biochemistry dept. Nat. Agrl. U. Ukraine, Kyiv, 1979-84, pres., 1984—; prof. Ukrainian Agrl. Acad., Kyiv, 1984—; v.p. Urkainian Acad. Agrl. Scis., Kyiv, 1995-96; mem. bur. molecular biology divsn. Nat. Acad. Scis., Kyiv, 1996—; hon. prof. Iowa State U., Ames, 1996; hon. state senator La. State Senate, 1999; hon. advisor of Pres. Internat. Parliamentarian Assn. for Agr. and Fisheries, 2000. Author: Carbon Dioxide Role in Geterotrophic Organisms' Metabolism, 1978; mem. editl. bd. Archive of Animal Nutrition, 1986—, Ukrainian Biochem. Mag., 1990—; contbr. articles to profl. jours. Mem. Com. on State Prizes of Ukraine, Kyiv, 1990—, State Accreditation Commn., Kyiv, 1995—, Commn. of the Ministry of Edn. of Ukraine on Awarding Sci. Degrees, Kyiv, 1995—. Recipient medal for labor valour Supreme Soviet of USSR, Moscow, 1973, State prize of Ukraine in the field of sci. and tech. Cabinet of Mins. of Ukraine, 1985, Order of Merit of 2nd and 3rd Grade, Honorary Distinction reward Pres. of Ukraine, 1997; named Merited Worker in Sci. and Tech. of Ukraine, Supreme Soviet of Ukraine, Kyiv, 1990. Mem. NAS, Ukrainian Acad. Agrl. Scis., Ukrainian Biochemistry Soc., Global Consortium Agrl. Univs. (v.p. internat. consortium), N.Y. Acad. Scis., Acad. Scis. Ukraine, Global Consortium Higher Edn. Rsch. for Agr. Avocations: fishing, hunting. E-mail: rector@nauu.kiev.ua. Office: Nat Agrl Univ Ukraine, 15 Heroyiv St, 03041 Kyiv Ukraine

MELO, STELLA MARIS LUDOVICO, physicist; b. Goiania, Goias, Brazil, Feb. 2, 1961; d. Ivo P. and Suzete L. Melo; m. Marden Herbert Silva Souza; children: Gustavo S., Camille S. Undergrad. degree in Physics, U. Fed. de Goiás, Brazil, 1986; MSc in Phys. Chemistry, U. Fed. de Santa Catarina, Brazil, 1989; PhD in Space Sci., Inst. Pesquias Espaciais, Brazil, 1994. Vis. rschr. INPE, Sjcampos, Brazil, 1994-96; postdoctoral fellow York U., North York, Ont., Can., 1996-97, U. Western Ont., London, Ont., 1997—. Contbr. articles to profl. jours. Recipient Sci. Project grantee Fundação Amparo Pesquisa, Brazil, Inpe, 1995-96. Mem. Am. Geophys. Union, Brazilian Soc. Physics. Avocations: literature, plastic arts. Office: U Western Ont, Dept Physics and Astronomy, London, ON Canada N6A 5B7

MELONE, JOSEPH JAMES, retired insurance company executive; b. Pittston, Pa., July 27, 1931; s. Dominick William and Beatrice Marie (Pignone) M.; m. Marie Jane DeGeorge, Jan. 23, 1960; children—Lisa, Carol. BS, U. Pa., 1953, MBA, 1954, PhD in Econs, 1961. C.P.C.U., 1964, ChFC, 1984. Assoc. prof. ins. U. Pa., 1959-66, mem. pension rsch. coun., 1961-66; rsch. dir. Am. Coll. Life Underwriters, 1966-68; v.p. Prudential Ins. Co., Boston, 1969-76; sr. v.p. Prudential Ins. Co., Newark, 1976-81, exec. v.p., 1981-84, pres., 1984-90; pres., COO, bd. dirs. The Equitable Life Assurance Soc. U.S., 1990-94; pres., COO The Equitable Life Assurance Soc. of U.S., 1990-94, also bd. dirs.; pres., COO The Equitable Cos., Inc., 1992-96, now bd. dirs.; pres., CEO The Equitable Cos., Inc., N.Y.C., 1996-98; chmn. The Equitable Life Assurance Soc. U.S., N.Y.C., 1994-98; chmn., CEO Equitable Variable Life Ins. Co.; bd. dirs. Foster Wheeler Corp.; chmn. emeritus The Equitable Cos. Author: Collectively Bargained Multi-Employer Pension Plans, 1961; co-author: Risk and Insurance, 1963, Pension Planning, 1966. Trustee Newark Mus.; chmn. ins. divsn. Cardinal's Commn. Laity N.Y. Archdiocese; ptnr. N.Y.C. Partnership; bd. overseers Wharton Sch. U. Pa.; bd. dirs. Greater N.Y. couns. Boy Scouts Am. Mem. Am. Risk and Ins. Assn., Am. Soc. CLUs, Am. Coll. (trustee), Internat. Ins. Soc., Internat. Acad. Mgmt., Morris County Country Club, Baltusrol Golf Club, Alpha Tau Omega. Home: Gen Delivery New Vernon NJ 07976-9999 Office: Equitable Cos Inc 1290 Ave of Americas New York NY 10104

MELOTTI, UMBERTO, sociologist, educator; b. Milan, Italy, Apr. 6, 1940; s. Paolo Melotti and Luisa Brambilla; m. Elena Elvira Sala; children: Marxiano, Libero. Polit. scientist, U. Pavia, 1963; D of Sociology, U. Milan, 1968. Lectr. Acad. di Brera, Milan, 1969-78; assoc. prof. U. Pavia, Italy, 1978-87; prof. U. Rome I, 1987—. Author: Marx and the Third World, 1979, Ego e i Suoi Cugini, 1986, L'Uomo tra Natura e Storia, 1979, Ethnicity, Nationality and Citizenship, 2000, The Multicultural Dazzle, 2000; editor Third World Jour., 1968—; dir. Centro Studi Terzo Mondo, 1964—. Pres. Assn. Religious Freedom, Milan, 1990—. Mem. Italian Assn. Sociology, Swiss Acad. Devel., Inst. Maghreb-Europe. Avocation: mountain climbing. E-mail: melotti.uml@uniroma1.it. Home: via GB Morgagni 39, I 20129 Milan Italy Office: Facolta di Sociologià, via Salaria 113, I 00198 Rome Italy

MELOUN, MILAN, chemistry educator; b. Stoky, Czech Republic, Feb. 3, 1943; s. Frantisek and Miloslava (Prochazkova) M.; m. Helena Leichmanova, Sept. 25, 1946; children: Martin, Ivan. MS, Purkyne U., 1965; PhD, U. Pardubice, 1973; DS, U. Chem. Tech., 1989. Asst. U. Pardubice (Czech Republic), 1965-68, lectr., 1968-89; prof. U. Baghdad (Iraq), 1989-91; assoc. prof. U. Pardubice, 1989-95; prof. Royal Inst. Tech., Stockholm, 1988-90, U. Pardubice, 1995—; cons. in field. Co-author: (with J. Havel and E. Hogfeldt) Computation of Solution Equilibria, 1988, (with J. Militky and M. Forina) Chemometrics for Analytical Chemistry, vol. 1, 1991, vol. 2, 1994. Mem. Czech Chemometrical Soc. (chmn. 1995—). Roman Catholic. Avocations: photography, opera. Home: Kpt Bartose 410, 53009 Pardubice Czech Republic Office: U Pardubice, Nam Cs Legii 565, 53210 Pardubice Czech Republic

MELROSE, BARRY JAMES, sportscaster, former professional hockey team coach; b. Kelvington, Sask., Can., July 15, 1956. Player various minor league teams, 1973-77, 82-83, 83-86, 86-87; player Cin. Stingers, 1976-79, Winnipeg Jets, 1979-81, Toronto Maple Leafs, 1981-82, 82-83, Detroit Red Wings, 1983-84, 85-86; former gen. mgr., head coach Adirondack Red Wings; now head coach L.A. Kings, 1992-94; sportscaster ESPN, 1995—. Office: care ESPN Inc 935 Middle St Bristol CT 06010-1001

MELROSE, GRAHAM JOHN HAMILTON, researcher; b. East Fremantle, Australia, Feb. 11, 1934; s. Claude William Staniforth and Ethel Isobel (Hamilton) M.; m. Olga Mary Wilson, July 16, 1960; children: Michele Keryn, Fiona Elizabeth. BS with honors, U. Western Australia, 1955, PhD in Chemistry, 1960; MBA, Macquarie U., 1978. Rsch. chemist I.C.I. Ltd., Sydney, Australia, 1960-62; sr. lectr. chemistry U. NSW, Sydney, Australia, 1963-72; exec. dir., v.p. rsch. Johns & Johnson Ltd., Sydney, Australia, 1973-78; exec. chmn. Melrose & Assoc. Ltd., Sydney, Australia, 1979-87, Biopolymers Ltd., Perth, Australia, 1988-89, Chemeq Ltd., Perth, Australia, 1990—; vis. rsch. scientist Oxford (Eng.) U., 1971; dir. Western Capital Ltd., Perth, 1985-86; chair, mem. Confederation of Industry, Sydney, 1973-78; cons. Unisearch Ltd., Sydney, 1963-72. Contbr. articles to profl. jours. Chmn. Australian Indsl. Rsch. Group, Sydney, 1977; mem. adv. com. State Min. for Tech., Perth, 1985-86; v.p. Australian Soc. Cosmetic Chemists, Sydney, 1977; councillor C. of C., Perth, 1984-86. Commonwealth Undergrad. scholar U. Western Australia, 1951; Hon. Sr. Rsch. fellow Curtin U., Australia, 1983—. Fellow Royal Australian Chem. Inst., Australian Inst. Mgmt., Australian Inst. Co. Dirs.; mem. N.Y. Acad. Sci. Presbyterian. Avocation: jogging. Home: 20 Nardina Crescent, Dalkeith 6009, Australia Office: Chemeq Ltd, 8/3 Brodie Hall Drive, Techology Park 6102, Australia

MELSEN, BIRTE, orthodontics educator; b. Fredericia, Denmark, June 9, 1939; d. Otto Emil and Kjerstine (Caspersen) P.; m. Flemming Melsen, Apr. 5, 1963; children: Michael, Christian. DDS, Royal Dental Coll., Aarhus, Denmark, 1964, specialist, 1971, Doctor Odont, 1974. Asst. tchr. Inst. of Cariology, Royal Dental Coll., Aarhus, 1964-65; rsch. assoc. Inst. Orthodontics, Royal Dental Coll., Aarhus, 1965-67, asst. prof., 1967-72, acting head, 1971—, assoc. prof., 1972-75, prof., head, 1975—; orthodontist SCh. Dental Clinics, Silkeborg, 1965-67, cons., orthodontist, 1967-88; pvt. practice orthodontics, 1980—; vis. prof. U. Padova, Italy, 1981-84; contract prof. U. Naples, Italy, 1990—. Contbr. more than 150 articles to profl. jours. Decorated knight of Dannebrog; recipient Zendium prize, 1991, The Jarabak Mem. Orthodontic Tchrs. and Rsch. award, 1995, the "Dandy" price, 1996, Am. Assn. of Orthodontists Found. PARC, 1997, The SIDO World Price, Rome, 1999. Mem. Scandinavian Orthodontic Soc. (pres. 1976), Danish Orthodontic Soc. (pres. 1988-90, head 1995—), European Orthodontic Soc. (v.p. 1990), Austrian Dental Soc. (hon.), Deutsche Kieferorthopädische Gesellschaft (hon. mem.), Egyptian Orthodontic Soc. (hon. mem.). Office: Royal Dental Coll, Vennelyst Blvd, 8000 Århus Denmark

MELTEBEKE, RENETTE, career counselor; b. Portland, Oreg., Apr. 20, 1948; d. Rene and Gretchen (Hartwig) M. BS in Sociology, Portland State U., 1970; MA in Counseling Psychology, Lewis and Clark Coll., 1985. Lic. profl. counselor, Oreg.; nat. cert. counselor. Secondary tchr. Portland Pub. Schs., 1970-80; project coord. Multi-Wash CETA, Hillsboro, Oreg., 1980-81; coop. edn. specialist Portland C.C., 1981-91; pvt. practice career counseling, owner Career Guidance Specialists, Lake Oswego, Oreg., 1988—; mem. adj. faculty Marylhurst (Oreg.) Coll., 1989-93, Portland State U., 1994—; assoc. Drake Beam Morin Inc., Portland, 1993-96; career cons. Managed Health Network, 1994—, Career Devel. Svcs., 1990—, Life Dimensions, Inc., 1994; presenter Internat. Conf., St. Petersburg, Russia, 1995. Rotating columnist Lake Oswego Rev., 1995-99; creator video presentation on work in Am. in 5 langs., 1981. Pres. Citizens for Quality Living, Sherwood, Oreg., 1989; mem. Leadership Roundtable on Sustainability for Sherwood, 1994-95; bd. dirs. Bus. for Social Responsibility for Oreg. and Southwestern Wash., 1999. Recipient Esther Matthews award for outstanding contbn. to field of career devel., 1998. Mem. Assn. for Psychol. Type, Nat. Career Devel. Assn., Oreg. Career Devel. Assn. (pres. 1990), Assn. for Humanistic Psychology (presenter nat. conf. Tacoma 1996), Willamette Writers. Avocations: walking, swimming, bicycling, cross-country skiing, photography. Home: 890 SE Merryman St Sherwood OR 97140-9746 Office: Career Guidance Specialists 15800 Boones Ferry Rd Ste C104 Lake Oswego OR 97035-3492

MELTZER, BERNARD DAVID, law educator; b. Phila., Nov. 21, 1914; s. Julius and Rose (Welkov) M.; m. Jean Sulzberger, Jan. 17, 1947; children: Joan, Daniel, Susan. A.B., U. Chgo., 1935, J.D., 1937; LL.M., Harvard U., 1938. Bar: Ill. 1938. Atty., spl. asst. to chmn. SEC, 1938-40; assoc. firm Mayer, Meyer, Austrian & Platt, Chgo., 1940; spl. asst. to asst. sec. state, also acting chief fgn. funds control div. div. State 1941-43; asst. trial counsel U.S. stafff Internat. Nuremberg War Trials, 1945-46; from professorial lectr. to disting. svc. prof. law emeritus U. Chgo. Law Sch., 1946—; counsel Vedder, Price, Kaufman & Kamnholz, Chgo., 1954-55, Sidley and Austin, Chgo., 1987-89; hearing commr. NPA, 1952-53; labor arbitrator; spl. master U.S. Ct. Appeals for D.C., 1963-64; bd. publs. U. Chgo., 1965-67, chmn., 1967-68; mem. Gov. Ill. Adv. Commn. Labor-Mgmt. Policy for Pub. Employees in Ill., 1966-67, Ill. Civil Service Commn., 1968-69; cons. U.S. Dept. Labor, 1969-70. Author: Supplementary Materials on International Organizations, 1948, (with W.G. Katz) Cases and Materials on Business Corporations, 1949, Labor Law Cases, Materials and Problems, 1970, supplement, 1972, 75, 2d edit., 1977, supplements, 1980, 82 (with S. Henderson), 3d edit. (with S. Henderson), 1985, supplement, 1988; also articles. Bd. dirs. Hyde Park Community Conf., 1954-56, S.E. Chgo. Commn., 1956-57. Served to lt. (j.g.) USNR, 1943-46. Mem. ABA (co-chmn. com. devel. law under NLRA 1959-60, mem. spl. com. transp. strikes), Ill. Bar Assn., Chgo. Bar Assn. (bd. mgrs. 1972-73), Am. Law Inst., Coll. Labor and Employment Lawyers, Am. Acad. Arts and Scis., Order of Coif, Phi Beta Kappa. Home: 1219 E 50th St Chicago IL 60615-2908 Office: U Chgo Law Sch 1111 E 60th St Chicago IL 60637-2776

MELUCCI, ALBERTO, sociologist, educator, clinical psychologist; b. Rimini, Italy, Nov. 27, 1943; s. Nicola and Matilde (Aluigi) M.; m. Anna Maria Fabbrini, Oct. 19, 1969; children: Alessandra, Marta. MA in Philosophy, Cath. U., Milan, 1967; postgrad., State U., Milan, 1970; PhD in Sociology, U. Paris-Sorbonne, Paris, 1977; PhD in Clin. Psychology, U. Paris VII, 1981. Asst. prof. Cath. U., Milan, 1969-73; assoc. prof. U. Sassari, Italy, 1973-76, State U., Milan, 1976-87; prof. sociology State U., 1987-90, U. Trento, Italy, 1988-91; prof. sociology State U., Milan, 1991—, prof. grad. Sch. Clin. Psychology, 1990—; vis. prof. New Sch. for Social Rsch., N.Y.C., 1985, 86, 95, MIT, Cambridge, 1994; assoc. supr. vis. prof. Ecole des Hautes Etudes en Scis. Sociales, Paris, 1988. Author: Lotte sociali e mutamento, 1974, Classe dominante e industrializzazione, 1974, Movimenti di rivolta, 1976, Sistema politico, partiti e movimenti sociali, 1977, L'invenzione del presente, 1982, 91, Nazioni senza stato, 1983, 92, Altri codici, 1984, Corpi estranei, 1984, Libertà che cambia, 1987, Nomads of the Present, 1989, Il gioco dell'io, 1991, I luoghi dell'ascolto, 1991, L'età dell'oro, 1992, Protogiovani, 1993, Creatività, Miti, discorsi, processi, 1994, Passaggio d'epoca, 1994, The Playing Self, 1996, Challenging Codes, 1996, Verso una sociologia riflessiva, Ricerca qualitiva e cultura, 1998, Fine della modernità?, 1998, Accion colectiva, vida cotidiana y democracia, 1999, Culture in gioco, 2000, Parole chiave, Per un nuovo, lessico delle scienze sociali, 2000, Divemtare persone, 2000; contbr. articles to profl. jours., collective vols. With Italian Air Force, 1968-69. Mem. Italian Sociol. Assn., Italian Psychol. Soc., Internat. Sociol. Assn., European Assn. for Gestalt Therapy, Internat. Gestalt Therapy Assn., Internat. Assn. for Human Rels. Avocations: trekking, climbing, clowning. Home: Corso di Porta Romana 91, 20122 Milano Italy 2ffice: State U Dept Soc & Polit Studies, Via Conservatorio 7, I-20122 Milan Italy

MELUZÍN, JAROSLAV, cardiologist; b. Brno, Czech Republic, Feb. 24, 1955; s. Jaroslav and Marta (Součková) M.; m. Hana Kalová, Aug. 1, 1962; children: Martin, Petr. MD, Masaryk's U., Brno, 1980, PhD, 1991. Asst. prof. Masaryk's U., 1986-96, assoc. prof., 1996—, chief echocardiographic lab. 1st internal dept., 1998—. Contbr. articles to profl. jours. Mem. European Soc. Cardiology (mem. working group on echocardiography 1997—). Office: St Anna Hosp Internal Dept, Pekařská 53, 656 91 Brno Czech Republic

MELVILLE, JENNIE See BUTLER, GWENDOLINE WILLIAMS

MELVIN, ALEC, engineer, consultant; b. Hull, Yorkshire, Eng., Sept. 2, 1933; s. John Alexander and Ellen (Ingram) M.; m. Marjorie Elizabeth Midgley, Apr. 21, 1962; children: Andrew, Robert, Iain, Jennifer. BSc with honours, Birmingham (Eng.) U., 1954; PhD, Hull U., 1959. Chartered engr.; chartered physicist. Rsch. scientist I.C.I. Ltd., Manchester, Eng., 1958-60, Battelle Meml. Inst., Geneva, 1960, Unilever Rsch., Port Sunlight, Eng., 1960-62; sci. adviser, physics mgr. Brit. Gas. plc, London, 1962-93; owner Seicomb, Maidenhead, Eng., 1994—; chmn. thermodynamics com. Groupe Européene de Récherches Gazieres, 1972-89. Author: Natural Gas: Basic Science and Technology, 1987; contbr. articles to profl. jours.; patentee in field. Sch. gov., local schs., Maidenhead, 1979-91. Mem. Inst. of Physics (mem. combustion physics group com. 1979-80). Avocations: classical music, piano playing. Office: Seicomb, 16 The Pagoda, Maidenhead SL6 8EU, England

MEMEZAWA, HAJIME, physician, educator; b. Koiwa, Tokyo, Nov. 4, 1953; s. Toshio and Akiko (Takahashi) M.; m. Masako Hirose, Mar. 1, 1954; children: Akane, Haruka. MD, Nippon Med. Sch., Tokyo, 1986; PhD, Lund (Sweden) U., 1994. Resident Nippon Med. Sch., 1981-83, sr. resident, 1983-86, 92-94, asst. prof., 1994-97, chief mgr. 2d dept. internal medicine, 1993-97; rsch. fellow Lund U., 1988-92; co-chmn. Ctr of Neurological Disease, Stroke Care Unit Chiba-Hokusoh Hosp., Nippon Med. Sch., Chiba, Japan, 1998-99; officer Memezawa Med. Clinic, Tokyo, 1999—. Author: Focal Cerebral Ischemia in the Rat, 1993; contbr. articles to profl. jours. Office: Memezawa Med Clinic, 4-5-8 Kitakoiwa, Edogawa Tokyo 133-0051, Japan

MEMEZAWA, MASAKO, dentist, educator; b. Tokyo, Mar. 3, 1954; d. Shin-ya and Miyoko (Sasa) Hirose; m. Hajime Memezawa, Oct. 25, 1981; children: Akane, Haruka. PhD, Nihon U., Matsudo, Japan, 1998. Dir. Miyabi Dental Clinic, Tokyo, 1980—; asst. prof. dept. periodontology Nihon U. Sch. Dentistry, Matsudo, 1998—; sr. instr. Japanese dance Bando Miyabi. Author: Masako's Sky, 2000; contbr. articles to profl. jours. Office: Miyabi Dental Clinic, 4-12-3 Kitakoiwa, Edogawa Tokyo 133-0051, Japan

MEMON, AAMIR AZIZ, dermatologist, consultant, educator; b. Khahi Qasim, Sind, Pakistan, Jan. 24, 1961; arrived in the U.K., 1988; s. Abdul Aziz and Zahida (Rana) M.; m. Jennifer Price, Mar. 9, 1994; 1 child, Zara Amber. MB, BChir, U. Sind, Pakistan, 1985; diploma in dermatol. scis., U. Wales, Cardiff, 1988; MD, U. Liverpool, Eng., 1996. House officer Liaquat Med. Coll. Hosp., Hyderabad, Pakistan, 1985-86; sr. house officer Liaquat Med. Coll. Hosp., Hyderabad, 1986-87; hon. registrar Royal Liverpool U. Hosp., 1990-94, rsch. registrar, 1994-95; cons. dermatologist Southport (U.K.) and Formby Nat. Health Svc. Trust, 1995—; cons. dermatologist Ormskirk (U.K.) and Dist. Gen. Hosp., 1995—. Contbr. articles to profl. jours. Mem. Brit. Assn. Dermatologists, Brit. Soc. Investigative Dermatology (Best Poster award 1995). Islamic. Avocations: computers, squash, cooking, animal welfare, travel. Home: 5 Camberley Close, Southport PR8 2PP, England Office: Southport Dist Gen Hosp, Town Lane Kew, Southport PR8 6PN, England

MEMORY, JASPER DURHAM, academic administrator, physics educator; b. Raleigh, N.C., Dec. 10, 1936; s. Jasper Livingston and Margaret Moore (Durham) M.; m. Carolyn Hofler, June 4, 1961; children—Margaret Carolyn, Jasper William. B.S. summa cum laude, Wake Forest U., 1956; Ph.D., U. N.C., 1960. Successively asst. prof., assoc. prof. physics U. S.C., Columbia, 1960-64; assoc. prof. N.C. State U., Raleigh, 1964-67, assoc. dean, physics and math. scis., 1973-82, prof., 1967-98, vice-provost, grad. dean, 1982-86, dir. corp. and govtl. affairs, 1998-99; v.p. for research U. N.C. System, Chapel Hill, 1986-98; bd. govs. Research Triangle Inst., Research Triangle Park, N.C., 1983-84, Triangle Area rsch. dir., 1981-98; cons. NASA Langley, Hampton, Va., 1970-74, Ohio Bd. Regents, 1993-95, Ark. Bd. Regents, 1987, Mass. Bd. Regents, 1998; N.C. State U. rep. Oak Ridge Associated Univs., 1982-85, Grad. Record Exam. Bd., 1985-90, chair, 1989, Policy Coun., Test of English as a Fgn. Lang., 1987-88, chair, 1988. Author: Quantum Theory of Magnetic Resonance Parameters, 1968; (with others) NMR of Aromatic Compounds, 1982, High Resolution NMR in the Solid State: Fundamentals of CP/MAS, 1994. Recipient Outstanding Tchr. award N.C. State U., 1967, Disting. Alumni Service award Wake Forest U., 1981. Fellow Am. Phys. Soc.; mem. Am. Assn. Physics Tchrs., Phi Beta Kappa, Sigma Xi. Democrat. Presbyterian. E-mail: jmemory@nc.rr.com. Home: 124 Talon Dr Cary NC 27511-8604

MEMOS, CONSTANTINE DEMETRIUS, marine engineer, educator; b. Patras, Greece, Nov. 26, 1946; s. Demetrius and Georgia (Vassilopoulos) M.; m. Maria Antonopoulou, Sept. 22, 1973; children: Demitris, Arion. MSc, Nat. Tech. U., Athens, Greece, 1969; diploma, Patras (Greece) U., 1972; PhD, Imperial Coll., London, 1977, diploma, 1978. Engr. J.D. & D.M. Watson, Athens, 1977-79; from lectr. to asst. prof. Nat. Tech. U. Athens, Zografos, 1979-94, assoc. prof., 1994—; pvt. practice Athens, 1979-88; engr. Doxiadis Assoc., Athens, 1972-73; cons. in field. Author: Port Engineering, 1999; contbr. articles to profl. jours. With Greek Air Force, 1970-72. Grantee Greek Govt., Athens, 1969, Greek Scholarships Found., Athens, 1972, scholar, London, 1973-76. Fellow ASCE; mem. Internat. Assn. Hydraulic Engrng. and Rsch., Internat. Navigation Assn. (working group). Avocations: swimming, mountain climbing, travel. Home: 32A St George St, 15123 Amaroussion Greece Office: Nat Tech Univ Athens, 15780 Zografos Greece

MENA, F. XAVIER, economics educator, consultant; b. Vielha, Spain, Jan. 10, 1958; s. Aquilino Mena and Angela Lopez-Serradell. License in Econs. with hons., U. Barcelona, Spain, 1980, PhD in Econs., 1992; Lic. in Law, U. Madrid, 1999. Economist Bank Sabadell, Spain, 1980; rschr. D.G. Politica Cientifica, Barcelona, Spain, 1981-83; economist Govt. Catalonia, Barcelona, 1983-85; dir. Consultur, Barcelona, 1985-86; prof. Esade, Barcelona, 1986-89, asst. dean, 1990-92, dept. head, 1992—; vis. prof. Jiaotong U., Shanghai, 1995, 98; dir. AECI Tourism, San Jose, Costa Rica, 1997. Author: Market Structure and Tourism Industry, 1992; contbr. articles to profl. jours. Home: P Maritimo 10, 08860 Castelldefels Spain Office: Esade, Av Pedralbes 60, 08034 Barcelona Spain

MENAKER, RONALD HERBERT, retired bank executive; b. N.Y.C., Dec. 17, 1944; s. Harold L. Menaker and Gladys (Bleiberg) Ross; m. Kathleen Sager Thomas, Sept. 11, 1966; children: Meredith E., Kyri D. Student, Queen's Coll., 1965-66. Mng. dir. J.P. Morgan & Co., Inc., N.Y.C., 1966-2000. Trustee Sinai/NYU Med. Ctr. and Health Sys., N.Y.C., 1991—; trustee St. Huberts Giralda Animal Welfare and Edn. Ctr., Madison, N.J., The Dog Mus., St. Louis, 1989—; bd. dirs. Am. Kennel Club, N.Y.C.; trustee, past chmn. NYU Downtown Hosp., 1991—; dir. ATALanta Sosnoff Capital Corp., N.Y.C., 1999. Mem. Westminster Kennel Club (gov., show chmn. 1990—), Am. Kennel Club (past bd. dirs.). Avocations: sporting art, judging dogs.

MENAMPARAMPIL, THOMAS S.D.B., archbishop; b. Palai, India, Oct. 22, 1936; s. Cheriathu and Annamma Menamparampil. M in English Lit., Calcutta U., 1969, M in History, 1970. Prin. Don Bosco Tech. Sch., Shillong, India, 1975-81; bishop Diocese of Dibrugarh, Assam, India, 1981-92; archbishop of diocese of Guwahati Assam, 1992—; spl. sec. Asian Synod, Vatican, 1998. Author several books. Originator, builder of 30 schs. in Assam. Recipient Maschio award for Peace and Reconciliation, 1998. Fax: 361 520588. E-mail: bishop@gw1.vsnl.net.in. Home and Office: Archbishop's House, Box 100, Guwahati Assam 781 001, India

MENANTEAU, BERNARD PAUL, medical educator; b. Angers, France, Apr. 24, 1939; s. Charles and Simone (Deveaux) M.; m. Marie-Therese Puig, Dec. 30, 1976. Diploma in Radiology, U. Paris, 1967; MD, U. Reims, France, 1969. Resident Univ. Hosp., Reims, 1965-69, asst., 1969-74; asst. prof. U. Sherbrooke, Can., 1974-78; prof. diagnostic radiology, chmn. dept. radiology U. Reims, 1978—; expert Supreme Ct. of Appeal, Paris, 1991—; v.p. U. Reims, 1971-74; pres. med. commn. Univ. Hosp., Reims, 1998. Coauthor: Chest Radiology, 1989; contbr.: Vocabulary of Signs and Symptoms of the Musculo-Skeletal System, 1992. Recipient Decoration, Ministry of Edn., Reims, 1994. Mem. Radiol. Soc. N.Am., Am. Roentgen Ray Soc., French Soc. Radiology (pres. ea. sect. 1992-95). Avocations: history and political science, forensic medicine, travel, music. Home: 9 Rue Piper, 51100 Reims France Office: Robert Debre Hospital, Rue General Koenig, 51092 Reims France

MENCER, HELENA JASNA, chemical engineer, researcher, scientist; b. Zagreb, Croatia, Apr. 3, 1943; d. Juraj Stjepan and Nada Stefanija (Konfic) Postruzin; m. Petar Mencer, Dec. 26, 1964 (dec.); children: Martina, Helena. MSc, U. Zagreb, 1973, PhD, 1976; postgrad., CNRS, Strasbourg, France, 1978-79, Katholieke U., Leuven, Belgium, 1991-92. Rschr. U. Zagreb, 1966-71, asst. prof., 1971-78, assoc. prof., 1978-86, prof., 1986—, vice dean, 1993-95, vice rector, 1994—; mem. adv. bd. Nat. Sci. Coun., Govt. Croatia, 1994—. Contbr. articles to profl. jours. Mem. Croatian Soc. Chem. Engrng. (pres. divsn. macromolecules 1988-92). Achievements include development of a widely used method of polymer fractionation; research solubility, miscibility, phase separation, polidispersity of polymers, university management and development. Home: Rockefellerova 20, 10000 Zagreb Croatia

MENCK, JOHANNES HERWIG, physician, researcher; b. Kiel, Germany, Dec. 27, 1961; s. Herwig Klaus-Friedrich and Petra Astrid M. MD, U. Hamburg, Germany, 1988. Scientist U. Hamburg, 1988-95; gen. practitioner Bargteheide, Germany, 1988—; cons. in field. Med. Commdr. German Army, 1993—; candidate for profl. chair of gen. medicine, U. Leipzig, 1998-99. Grantee Biomechanic Ctr., U. Hamburg, 1992, 93. Mem. German Soc. Osteology, Anatomical Soc., Soc. for Sci. Devel., Namibia. Roman Cath. Avocations: chicken-pheasant hybridization, athletics, Christian rels. Office: Alte Landstrasse 72, D-22941 Bargteheide Germany

MENCWEL, ANDRZEJ, literature and culture educator; b. Tarnobrzeg, Poland, Sept. 11, 1940; s. Antoni and Stanislawa (Walkowiak) M.; m. Anna Maria Gettlich, July 5, 1970; children: Stanislaw, Jan. Magister, Warsaw U., 1963, Doctor, 1976, Prof., 1992. Asst. Warsaw U., 1963-68; journalist Poland, 1969-73; asst. prof. Warsaw U., 1974-92, prof., 1992—, head dept. Polish culture, 1991-98, dir. Inst. Polish Culture, 1998—; expert Ministry of Edn., 1998; v.p. bd. Found. of Polish dept. Jerusalem U., 1998. Author: Stanislaw Brzozowski, 1976, Etos Lewicy, 1990, Przedwiosnie czy potop, 1997; editor-in-chief Meritum, Warsaw, 1980-81; contbr. to jours., TV and radio. Recipient fellowship and grants. Mem. Internat. Assn. Criticism and Letters, Janusz Korczak Internat. Soc., Com. of Lit. Sci. of Polish Acad. Scis. Roman Catholic. Home: Wyspowa 18/8, 03-687 Warsaw Poland

MENDE, HOWARD SHIGEHARU, mechanical engineer; b. Hilo, Hawaii, Nov. 19, 1947; s. Tsutomu and Harue (Kubomitsu) M. BSME, U. Hawaii, 1969; MSME, U. So. Calif., 1975. Registered profl. engr., Calif. Mem. tech. staff I Rockwell Internat., Anaheim, Calif., 1970-71; mem. tech. staff I Rockwell Internat., L.A., 1971-73, mem. tech. staff II, 1973-77, mem. tech. staff IV, 1984-86; devel. engr. AiRsch. Mfg. Co., Torrance, Calif., 1977-83; mech. engr. Def. Contracts Mgmt. Dist. West, Santa Ana, Calif., 1987-94, electronics engr., 1994—; lectr. Pacific States U., L.A., 1974-75. Mem. ASME. Democrat. Buddhist. Home: 1946 W 180th Pl Torrance CA 90504-4417 Office: Def Contracts Mgmt 2525 W 190th St Torrance CA 90504-6002

MENDE, MICHAEL, historian, educator; b. Schleswig, Germany, June 23, 1945; s. Gerhard and Ingeborg (Turné) M.; m. Marlies Buers Van Treeck, Nov. 17, 1943. State exam., art sch., Berlin, 1970; PhD, Technical U., 1978. Asst. Technical U., Berlin, 1974-78; lectr. Art Sch., Braunschweig, Germany, 1978-80; univ. prof. Art Sch., Brannschweig, 1980—; cons. U. Bremen, Germany, 1970-73; researcher Fed. Inst. Vocat. Tng., Berlin, 1972-73. Author: Denkmale der Industrie, 1990, K.K. Nationalfabrikproductenkabinett, 1995; author, editor: Sturm's Muehlenbaukunst, 1991; contbr. article to jour. Bd. dir. Gesellschaft fuer Arbeit Tech. U. Wirtshaft im Unterricht, Oldenburg, 1977-87; mem. adv. bd. Verein Dentscher Ingenieure, Dusseldorf, Germany, 1987—, mcpl. mus., Delmenhorst, Germany, 1998—; mem. Hist. Commn. Lower Saxony and Bremen, Hanover, Germany, 1993—. Mem. Gesellschaft fuer Technikgeschichte, The Internat. Com. Conservation Indsl. Heritage (nat. rep. 1997—), Soc. History Technology. Office: Brannschweig Sch Art, Johannes Selenka Platz 1, 38118 Braunschweig Germany

MENDEL, TADEUSZ ANDRZEJ, neurologist; b. Warsaw, Poland, Sept. 3, 1960; s. Tadeusz and Janina (Gussnar) M. Physician diploma, Med. Acad., Warsaw, 1985; PhD, Inst. Psychiatry and Neurology, Warsaw, 1991, degree in neurology, 1989; degree in neurology, Inst. Psychiatry and Neurology,

Warsaw, 1992. Mem. staff various hosps., Warsaw, 1985-86; asst. dept. cerebrovascular diseases Inst. Psychiatry and Neurology, 1986-90, sr. clin. asst., 1990-92, asst. prof. 2d dept. neurology, 1992—; observer physician dept. clin. neurol. scis. Western U. Hosp., London, Ont., Can., 1991; clin. fellow dept. pediat. and pediat. neurology Children's Hosp., Albany Med. Ctr., 1991-92; vis. physician McGill U., Montreal, Can., 1992; vis. scientist dept. neurology Utrecht (The Netherlands) U., 1996. Contbr. over numerous articles and abstracts to profl. jours. Recipient 1st degree award Sci. Coun. Inst. Psychiatry and Neurology, 1999. Mem. Polish Soc. Neurology (treas. Warsaw br. 1993-96), Internat. Atherosclersis Soc., Polish Neurosci. Soc. Roman Catholic. Avocations: biking, walking, gardening, classical music. Home: Apt 57, Al Niepodleglosci 121/123, 02-585 Warsaw Poland Office: Inst Psychiatry/Neurology, Al Sobieskiego 1/9, 02-957 Warsaw Poland

MENDELEEV, VLADIMIR YAKOVLEVICH, optician, researcher; b. Kamenets-Podol'sk, Former USSR, Aug. 26, 1946; s. Yakov Iosifovich and Etya Borisovna (Borisonik) M.; m.Lubov Aleksandrovna Ivanenko; children: Ludmila, Dmitrii. Degree in engring., Mil. Acad., Kharkov, Ukraine, 1974, PhD in Radioelectronics, 1988. Officer Ministry of Def., Former USSR, 1967-91; sr. rschr. Russian Acad. Scis., Inst. High Temperatures, Moscow, 1991—. Contbr. articles to profl. jours. Lt. col. Army of USSR, 1986-91. Mem. Optical Soc. Am. Avocation: skiing. Home: Govorova 15 #338, 121596 Moscow Russia Office: Russian Acad Scis Inst High Temps, Izhorskaya 13/19, 127412 Moscow Russia

MENDELEVICH, TAMARA MARIA, secretary, accountant; b. Genoa, Italy, July 25, 1954; d. Giacomo and Luisa (Ferretti) M.; m. Giuseppe Martino Inchingolo, Dec. 11, 1980. Cert. acct., ITC Avanzini, Genoa, 1975. CPA. Cons./sci. sec. Nat. Rsch. Coun., Genoa, 1981-82; cons./dir.'s sec. INFM, Genoa, 1988-89; cons./sci. sec. U. Genoa, 1980-88, 91—, cons. European Union projects, 1997-99, sec. polis dept., 1999—. Avocations: science fiction, fairy tales and folk stories. Fax: 1-651-6465. E-mail: inkta@yahoo.com. Home: Via San Bernardo 17, 16123 Genoa Italy Office: PO Box 575, I-16100 Genoa Italy

MENDELSOHN, STUART, lawyer, elected official; b. Jersey City, N.J., Aug. 8, 1952; s. Norman and Florence M.; m. Laura Dick, May 30, 1987; children: Michelle, Sarah. BS in Ocean Engring., Fla. Inst. Tech., 1974, MS in Environ. Engring., 1975; JD, George Mason U., 1984. Project mgr. Naval Facilities Engring. Command, Washington, 1975-80; divsn. mgr. Analysis & Tech., Inc., Arlington, Va., 1980-87; mng. prin. Mendelsohn & Ishee, P.C., Fairfax, Va., 1987-99; supr. Fairfax County Bd. Suprs., Mclean, Va., 1996—; of counsel Piper Marbury Rudnick & Wolfe, Reston, Va., 1999—. Bd. suprs. Fairfax County, 1996—; No. Va. Planning Dist. commn., 1996—; coord. coun. Transportation, 1997—; task force Fairfax county Tree Preservation, 1997—; active Boy Scouts Am., Patowomack Dist., 1996, 97; vice chair, sch. bd. mem. Fairfax County, 1993-95; sunday sch. tchr. Andrew Chapel United Meth. Ch., 1994—, adminstrv. bd. 1997—, staff-parish resl. com. 1995-97; cmty. roundtable on edn. WJLA-TV, 1992-93. Recipient Gold Medal award Spl. Olympics, Va., 1985, Spirit of Spl. Olympics award, 1987,. Mem. Fairfax County C. of C. (bd. dirs. 1991—, exec. com. 1992-95, dir. 1994-95, com. co-chair 1991-93, edn. com. 1987—, legis. affairs com. 1988—, edn. subcom. 1991—, congressional affairs com. 1988—), Herndon C. of C., McLean C. of C., Westbriar Elem. Sch. PTA, Fairfax Bar Assn., Kiwanis (lt. gov. 1983-84, charter pres. Fair Oaks club 1988, pres. McLean Club 1980-81). Republican. Methodist. Avocation: tennis. E-mail: stuart.mendelsohn@p.perruduick.com. Office: Piper Marbury Rudnick & Wolfe, LLP 1850 Centennial Park Dr # S610 Reston VA 20191-1524

MENDENHALL, HARLAN VINCENT, research veterinary surgeon; b. Gulfport, Miss., Oct. 21, 1944; s. Harlan Harry Mendenhall and Catherine Rose (Cunningham) Cowell; m. Toni (Meglitsch) Winch, July 29, 1979 (div. May 1988); m. Diann Marie Frederick, Aug. 15, 1992; children: Tai Justin, Tiffany. DVM, Colo. State U., 1968, PhD, 1981. Staff surgeon Rangitaiki Plains Dairy Co., Edgecume, New Zealand, 1968-71; grad. student exptl. surgery Colo. State U., Fort Collins, 1971-75; surg. rsch. specialist 3M, St. Paul, Minn., 1975-91; owner/operator Veterinary Surg. Specialists, Stillwater, Minn., 1977-93; sr. rsch. surgeon Primedica Corp., Worcester, Mass., 1993—; cons. biomed. surg. rsch., Stillwater, 1992-93; lectr. surg. anatomy Colo. State U., 1973; animal care cons. St. Paul Ramsey Hosp., 1980-85; working group mem. Health Industry Mfrs. Assn./Orthopedic Surg. Mfrs. Assn. FDA panel, 1987. Author: Anterior Cruciate, 1987; author, editor: Handbook Biomaterials, 1986, 2d edit., 1998; contbr. articles to Jour. Am. Vet. Med. Assn., Clin. Orthopedic Related Rsch. Mem. Soc. for Biomaterials (PhD students award 1982), Acad. Surg. Rsch. (mem. bd. 1996-97). Achievements in orthopedics include development of the concept of isometricity in ACL replacement surgery; achievements in ophthalmics include development of the importance of posteriorly convex lenses and haptics; achievements in microsurgery include development of the microvascular anastomotic system for small vessel anastomosis; leading research in chronic laboratory animal access. Home: 26 Grover Rd Ashland MA 01721-2510 Office: Primedica Corp 57 Union St Worcester MA 01608-1182

MENDES, NELSON FIGUEIREDO, physician, educator, researcher; b. São Paulo, Aug. 3, 1942; s. Ernesto Vieira and Julia (Figueiredo) M.; m. Cibele Barros, Dec. 12, 1998. MD, U. São Paulo, 1966, PhD, 1969; law degree, Fac. Metropolitans Unidas, São Paulo, 1998. Intern Hosp. de Clínicas de Faculdade de Medicina U. São Paulo, 1966, tchg. instr. faculty medicine, 1967-68, asst. prof. faculty medicine, 1969-70; postdoctoral rsch. fellow Duke U., Durham, 1967-68; assoc. prof. Escola Paulista de Medicina, São Paulo, 1970-78, prof., chmn. immunology, 1978-96; prof. immunology faculty medicine U. Marília, São Paulo, 1997—; lLatin Amer. Assn. Immunology (pres. 1987-1990). Contbr. numerous sci. papers to profl. jours. Recipient Lafi prize Fundacão Lafi, 1971, Academia de Medicina São Paulo prize, 1976, Veco-Aids prize 1989. Mem. Brazilian Soc. Allergy and Immunopathology (v.p. 1998—, pres.-elect 2000—). Home: Rua Caicara 385, 17502620 Marilia SP, Brazil Office: Av Rio Branco 936 CJ 71, 17502000 Marilia Brazil

MENDES, SAM (SAMUEL ALEXANDER MENDES), film director; b. Redding, Eng., Aug. 1, 1965; s. James Peter and Valerie Helene (Barnett) M. Student, U. Cambridge, Eng. Dir. original stage prodn. Little Voice, 1998; dir. film American Beauty, 1999 (Outstanding Directorial Achievement in Feature Film Dirs. Guild Am. 1999, Golden Globe for best dir. 1999, Best Dir. award Dallas-Ft. Worth Film Critics Assn. 1999, Best Dir. award Online Film Critics Soc. 1999, Best Dir. award Broadcast Film Critics Assn. 1999, Best Dir. award L.A. Film Critics Assn. 1999, Oscar for best dir. 2000, Dir. of the Yr. London Film Critics Cir. 2000). Office: Dirs Guild Great Britain, Acorn House 314-320 Grays Inn Rd, London WC1X 8DP, England

MENDEZ, CELESTINO GALO, mathematics educator; b. Havana, Cuba, Oct. 16, 1944; came to the U.S., 1962; naturalized, 1970.; s. Celestino Andres and Georgina (Fernandez) M.; m. Mary Ann Koplau, Aug. 21, 1971; children: Mark Michael, Matthew Maximilian. BA, Benedictine Coll., 1965; MA, U. Colo., 1968, PhD, 1974, MBA, 1979. Asst. prof. maths. scis. Met. State Coll., Denver, 1971-77, assoc. prof., 1977-82, prof., 1982—, chmn. dept. math. scis., 1980-82, adminstrv. intern office v.p. for acad. affairs, 1989-90. Assoc. editor Denver Met. Jour. Math. and Computer Sci., 1993—; contbr. articles to profl. jours. including Am. Math. Monthly, Procs. Am. Math. Soc., Jour. Personalized Instrn., Denver Met. Jour. Math. and Computer Sci. and newspapers. Mem. advt. rev. bd. Met. Denver, 1973-79; parish outreach rep. S.E. deanery, Denver Cath. Cmty. Svcs., 1976-78; mem. social ministries com. St. Thomas More Cath. Ch., Denver, 1976-78, vice-chmn., 1977-78, mem. parish coun., 1977-78; del. Adams County Rep. Conv., 1972, 74, 94, Colo. 4th Congl. Dist. Conv., 1974, Colo. Rep. Conv., 1982, 88, 90, 92, 96, 98, 2000, Douglas County Rep. Conv., 1980, 82, 84, 88, 90, 92, 94, 96, 98, 2000; alt. del. Colo. Rep. Conv., 1974, 76, 84, 2000, 5th Congl. dist. conv., 1976, mem. rules com., 1978, 80, precinct committeeman Douglas County Rep. Com., 1976-78, 89-92, mem. ctrl. com., 1976-78, 89-92; dist. 29 Rep. party candidate Colo. State Senate, 1990; mem. Colo. Rep. Leadership Program, 1989-90, bd. dirs., 1990—; Douglas county chmn. Rep. Nat. Hispanic Assembly, 1989—; bd. dirs. Rocky Mountain Better Bus. Bur., 1975-79, Rowley Downs Homeowners Assn., 1976-78, Colo. Rep. Leadership Program, 1990-98; trustee Hispanic U. Am., 1975-78; councilman Town of Parker, Colo., 1981-84, chmn. budget and fin. com., 1981-84; chmn. joint budget com. Town of Parker-Parker Water and Sanitation Dist. Bds., 1982-84; commr. Douglas County Planning Commn., 1993-97; dir. Mile High Young Scholars Program, 1995-98. Recipient Excellence in Tchg. award U. Colo. Grad. Sch., 1965-67; grantee Benedictine Coll., 1964-65, Math. Assn. Am. SUMMA grantee Carnegie Found. N.Y., 1994, NSF, 1995-98; nominated candidate for first v.p Math. Assn. Am. Mem. Math. Assn. Am. (referee rsch. notes sect. Am. Math. Monthly 1981-82, gov. Rocky Mountain sect. 1993-96, investment com. 1995—, devel. com. 1995—, task force on reps. 1994-96, sci. policy com. 2000—), Am. Math. Soc., Nat. Coun. Tchrs. Math., Colo. Coun. Tchrs. Math. (bd. dirs. 1994-96), Colo. Internat. Edn. Assn., Assoc. Faculties of State Insts. Higher Edn. in Colo. (v.p. 1971-73). Republican. Roman Catholic. Home: 39 Hummingbird Dr Castle Rock CO 80104-9047 Office: PO Box 173362 Denver CO 80217-3362

MENDEZ, JOSÉ SANCHEZ, military officer; b. Corca, Caceres, Spain, Apr. 27, 1936; s. Jose Sanchez and Maria Mendez; m. Maria Teresa Gomez Rubio; children: Javier, Teresa, Eva. Master Degree, U. Complutense, Madrid, 1957; 1st lt., Air Force Acad., Spain, 1959; staff officer, Air War Coll., Spain, 1977; intelligence analyst, Intelligence D.I.A. Sch., 1981. Flight comdr. 12th Tactical Wing, Torreson AFB, Spain, 1960-76; staff officer Spanish Air Force Hdqrs., 1977-87; dep. comdr. Air War Coll., Spain, 1987-89; dep. dir. Nat. Def. Policy, Spain, 1989-93; dep. comdr. Ctrl. Air Command, Spain, 1993-96; dir. Hist. and Cultural Svc., Spanish Air Force, 1997—; cons. Internat. Avion Revue, 1983-86, Spanish Def. Rev., 1990-93; dir. Revista Aeronautica and Astronautica, Spain, 1996; lectr. U. Complutense, Madrid, 1994-99, U. Salamanca, Spain, 1995-96, U. Menendez y Pelayo, Valencia, Spain, 1995, Diplomatic Sch., Madrid, 1995, NATO Def. Coll., Rome, 1995. Author: European Organizations, 1977 (Aero. medal 1978), Strategic Intelligence, 1983 (Army Cross 1983), Security and Defence Policy, 1993; contbr. articles to mags. and newspapers. Maj. gen. Spanish Air Force, 1993-99. Mem. IISS. Roman Catholic. Avocations: research, writing. Office: Servicio Historico/Cultural, Princesa 88 Bis, 28008 Madrid Spain

MENDEZ, RUBEN POLICARPIO, diplomat, educator; b. Manila, Philippines, June 28, 1933; came to U.S., 1948; s. Mauro and Paz Policarpio M.; m. Matilda Currier McEwen, Apr. 8, 1961; children: Katherine McEwen, Tomas Currier. BA cum laude, Harvard U., 1953; MA, Columbia U., 1959; PhD, NYU, 1984. Economist Merrill Lynch, Pierce, Fenner & Smith, N.Y.C., 1959-63; econ. adviser to chmn. Nat. Econ. Coun., Manila, 1964-66; project officer UN Spl. Fund, N.Y.C., 1963-65; various positions UN Devel. Program, N.Y.C., Africa, Asia, 1966-93; chief econ. advisor UN Environ. Program, Nairobi, Kenya, 1977-81; prin. officer, historian UN Devel. Program, N.Y.C., 1993—; adj. prof., fellow, vis. lectr. NYU, 1991—, Columbia U., 1992, Yale U., 1994—; cons. Oxford U. Press, N.Y., 1999—. Author: International Public Finance: A New Perspective on Global Relations, 1992; contbr. articles to profl. jours., chpts. to books. Yale rep. Acad. Coun. on UN Sys. Grantee Carnegie Corp., N.Y.C., 1995-98, Internat. Devel. Rsch. Ctr., Ottawa, Can., 1994-97. Mem. Am. Econ. Assn., N.Y. Acad. Scis., Soc. Internat. Devel., Harvard Club (N.Y.C.), Harvard Faculty Club, Riverdale Yacht Club, United Kenya Club (Nairobi). Avocations: history, philosophy, classical music, sailing, personal computers. E-mail: rpmendez@post.harvard.edu. Home: 313 W 263d St Riverdale NY 10471 Office: UN Devel Programme 304 E 45th St New York NY 10017-3425

MENDGEN, KURT WALTER, plant pathologist, educator, researcher; b. Hummelshain, Germany, Dec. 17, 1944; s. Karl Otto and Madlen (Meyer) M. PhD, U. Göttingen, Germany, 1971. Asst. U. Göttingen, 1971-79; prof. U. Konstanz, Germany, 1979—. Recipient Heisenberg prize Deutsche Forschungsgemeinschaft, 1978, Julius Kühn prize Deutsche Phytomedizinische Gesellschaft, 1982. Home: Fischerstr 32, 78464 Konstanz Germany Office: U Konstanz, Universitätsstr 10, 78434 Konstanz Germany

MENDIETA, MARCELO VENTECOL, journalist, public relations and press advisor; b. Argentina, Jan. 16, 1937; s. José Ventecol and Maria Mendieta. Columnist La Nación, Buenos Aires, 1958-84; correspondent La Mañana and El Diario, Montevideo, Uruguay, 1972-76; editor-dir. weekly newsletter Temas, 1980-98; asst. dir. weekly mag. Las Noticias, Buenos Aires, 1980; press advisor to pres. Coca-Cola, 1987-92; editor-dir. weekly publ. Internet Temas, 1995-96, editor-dir. weekly newsletter in e-mail, 1996-97; asst. editor La Prensa, Buenos Aires, Argentina, 1998; obituaries editor La Prensa, Buenos Aires, 1998—; press advisor National Congress, 2000—; internat. promoter Inst. Cardiology and Cardiovascular Surgery Fundacion Rene Favaloro; press advisor IV Conference of Ministers, Bosses of Planning, Latin Am., Caribbean, V Summit Meeting of Ministers UNCTAD; press advisor in field. Recipient Nat. prize in journalism, 1968. Mem. Circulo de la Prensa. E-mail: mendieta@impsat1.com.ar. Office: Paraguay 2421-CP, 1121 Buenos Aires Argentina

MENDOLA, LOUIS ANDRÉ MANTEGNA, genealogist; b. Rochester, N.Y., Apr. 1, 1961; arrived in Italy, 1991; s. Giuseppe Mendola and Giuseppina La Paglia. BA, SUNY, Albany, 1986. Dir. Italian Geneal. and Heraldic Inst., Palermo, Italy, 1990-96; pres. Mendola Design, 1996—; guest lectr. NYU, 1990. Contbr. articles to profl. jours. Vol. Am. Cancer Soc., N.Y., 1985-88. Named Knight, Constantian Order of St. George, Royal House of the Two Sicilies, Naples, 1988, Knight, Order of Civil Merit of Savoy, Royal House of Savoy, Italy, 1990, Knight, Order of Sts. Maurice and Lazarus, Royal House of Savoy, Italy, 1991, Knight Comdr., Order of Menelik II, Ethiopia, 1998, Knight, Order of Merit of Sovereign Mil. Order Malta, 2000. Avocations: martial arts, mountain climbing, weightlifting, painting. Home: Via Massimo DAzeglio 9-B, 90143 Palermo Italy

MENDOUGA, JEROME, diplomat; b. Aug. 15, 1938; married; 6 children. BA in Internat. Affairs, George Washington U.; postgrad., American U. With Ministry External Rels., Washington; 1st sec., acting chief mission, attaché Cameroon Embassy, Ottawa, Ont., Can.; acting dir. to tech. and econ. affairs sect. Fgn. Ministry, Yaounde, Cameroon, 1966-67, divsn. chief internat. orgns., 1967-70; econ. counselor Moscow, Bonn, Addis-Ababa, 1970-79; head Cameroon's econ. mission to E.C. Brussels, 1971-84; amb. to Senegal, 1984-89, amb. to Zaire, Burundi and Rwanda, 1989-94; amb. to U.S. Washington, 1994; pres. bd. dirs. Internat. Eye Found., Washington, 1999-2000; analyst Ministry Fgn. Affairs, 1979-81. Office: Embassy of Republic of Cameroon 2349 Massachusetts Ave NW Washington DC 20008-2853

MENDOZA, GEORGE, poet, author; b. N.Y.C., June 2, 1934; s. George and Elizabeth Mendoza; m. Ruth Sekora, 1967; children: Ashley, Ryan. BA, State Maritime Coll., 1953; postgrad., Columbia U., 1954-56. Author over 100 books for children and adults published worldwide; many included in Boston U.'s George Mendoza Collection, established 1984; children's books on display at the Centre Nat. d'Art et de Culture Georges Pompidou. Works include: And Amedeo Asked, How Does One Become a Man?, (illustrated by Ati Forberg), 1959, The Puma and the Pearl, 1962, The Hawk Is Humming: A Novel, 1964, A Piece of String, Astor-Honor, 1965, Gwot! Horribly Funny Hairticklers (illustrated by Steven Kellog), 1967, The Crack in the Wall and Other Terribly Weird Tales (illustrated by Mercer Mayer), 1968, Flowers and Grasses and Weeds (illustrated by Joseph Low), 1968, The Practical Man (illustrated by Imero Gobbato), 1968, Hunting Sketches (illustrated by Ronald Stein), 1968, A Beastly Alphabet (illustrated by J. Low), 1969, The Digger Wasp (illustrated by Jean Zallinger), 1969, Herman's Hat (illustrated by Frank Bozzo), 1969, The Starfish Trilogy (illustrated by Ati Forberg), 1969, (compiler) The World From My Window: Poems and Drawings (children's writings), 1969, Are You My Friend? (illustrated by F. Bozzo), 1970, The Marcel Marceau Alphabet Book, 1970, The Thumbtown Toad (illustrated by Monika Beisner), 1970, The Inspector, 1970, The Good Luck Spider & other bad luck stories, 1970, The Fearsome Brat (illustrated by F. Bozzo), 1971, Fish in the Sky (illustrated by Milton Glaser), 1971, Moonfish and owl scratchings, 1971, Moonstring, 1971, The Hunter, the Tick and the Gumberoo, 1971, The Marcel Marceau Counting Book, 1971, The Scarecrow Clock (illustrated by Eric Carle), 1971, Big Frog, Little Pond, 1971, The Scribbler, 1971, The Christmas Tree Alphabet Book, 1971, Shadowplay, 1974, Lord, Suffer me to Catch a Fish, 1974, Fishing the Morning Lonely, 1974, (with Carol Burnett) What I Want to Be When I Grow Up, 1975, (with Zero Mostel) The Sesame Street Book of Opposites, 1975, Norman Rockwell's Americana ABC (illustrated by N. Rockwell), 1975, Doug Henning's Magic Book, 1975, Lost Pony, 1976, Norman Rockwell's Boys and Girls at Play, 1976, Secret Places of a Trout Fisherman, 1977, Norman Rockwell's Diary for a Young Girl (illustrated by N. Rockwell), 1978, Magic Tricks, 1978, Mon livre de magic (French edit. of My Book of Magic), Norman Rockwell's Scrapbook for a Young Boy (illustrated by N. Rockwell), 1979, (with Andres Segovia) Segovia, My Book of the Guitar, 1979, Need a House? Call Ms. Mouse! (illustrated by Doris Susan Smith), 1981, Alphabet Sheep (illustrated by K. Reidy), 1982, The Sheepish Book of Opposites, 1982, Silly Sheep and other sheepish rhymes, 1982, Norman Rockwell's Four Seasons, 1982, Norman Rockwell's Happy Holidays, 1983, Henri Mouse (illustrated by Joelle Boucher), 1985, Henri La Souris, 1987, Norman Rockwell's Patriotic Times, 1986, (with Ivan Lendl) Hitting Hot, 1986, (with Sam Snead) Slammin' Sam, 1986, Norman Rockwell's Love and Remembrance, 1986, Top Tennis, 1987, L'Album des Noeuds, 1988, Norman Rockwell's Old Fashioned American Cookbook, 1988, Hairticklers (illustrated by Gahan Wilson), 1989, The Hunter I Might Have Been, reprint 1989, Were You a Wild Duck, Where Would You Go? (illustrated by Jane Osborn-Smith), 1990, Traffic Jam (illustrated by David Stoltz), 1990; also author screenplays for Petals from a Poem Flower, You Show Me Yours and I'll Show You Mine and scripts for Sesame Street; numerous others; over 15 books of poetry including The Hunter I Might Have Been (Lewis Carroll Shelf award 1968), The Mist Men, Goodbye, River, Goodbye; also dozens of articles in The N.Y. Times, Herald Tribune, Stern, Vogue, Harper's Bazaar, Ms., Esquire, Town & Country, Sports Afield, Men's Journal, Philadelphia Inquirer; special travel corr. Toronto Globe & Mail, 1991-94. Cited by Pres. Reagan for Norman Rockwell's Patriotic Times. Avocation: trout and salmon fishing. Worldwide fishing expeditions recorded for TV spls.

MENDOZA, GEORGE JOHN, college administrator, public speaker; b. Governors Island, N.Y., Apr. 1, 1955; s. George John Mendoza and Lucinda Marion Huber; m. Maria Rosario Escobedo, May 14, 1982; children: Michael George, Maria Guadalupe. B in Individualized Studies, N.Mex. State U., 1978. Coord. handicapped svcs. N.Mex. State U., Las Cruces, 1985—; Mem. Govs. Com. Concerns Handicapped, Santa Fe, 1986—; keynote speaker UCLA Upward Bound, 1987, Dallas County Community Coll., 1986, S.W. Assn. Students Assistance Programs, San Antonio, 1989. Author (screenplay) Blinding Speed, 1988, (lyrics) (with Pamela Polland) Chimayo; subject (PBS documentary) The George Mendoza Story, 1989, (biography) Running Toward the Light, 1994, also numerous mag. articles;. Athlete Olympics for Disabled, The Netherlands, 1980, Internat. Games for Disabled, N.Y., 1984. Named One of Outstanding Young Men Am., 1980; recipient Outstanding Blind Athlete Award State N.Mex., 1980, Nat. Trio Achievers Award U.S. Dept. Edn., 1986, N.Mex. Hispanic Heritage Award Las Cruces Fed. Agys., 1983; nat. record holder 1500 meter run, 1979, 800 meter run, 1980; proclaimed George Mendoza Day Gov. Gary Carruthers, 1989. Mem. Assn. Handicapped Student Svc., U.S. Assn. Blind Athletes. Republican. Lutheran. Avocations: running, hiking, playing guitar. Office: NMex State U Student Devel Office PO Box 3001 Las Cruces NM 88003-3001

MENDOZA, GERMAN DAVID, nutritionist, educator; b. Mexico City, Dec. 29, 1958; s. Javier Mendoza and Martinez Georgina; m. Elizabeth Barrera, Sept. 27, 1985; children: Elizabeth, German. Student, Autonomous Met. U., Mexico, 1976-81; MSc, Postgrad. Coll., Montecillo, Mexico, 1985; PhD, U. Nebr., 1991. Tech. staff SEP, Mexico City, 1981-82; tchr. Autonomous Met. U., Mexico City, 1983-85; prof. Postgrad. Coll., Montecillo, 1985—, coord. animal sci. dept., 1994-98. Author: Alimentacion de Bovinos, 1997, Lananaderia Familiar, 1998. Named rschr. CONACYT, Mexico, 1991-99. Mem. Am. Soc. Animal Sci., Mexican Soc. Animal Prodn. Avocations: classical music, wildlife. Office: Colegio de Postgraduados, Carr Mexico Texcoco km 36.5, 56230 Montecillo Mexico

MENDOZA, JUAN FRANCISCO, telecommunications company executive; b. Huaraz, Ancash, Peru, Aug. 9, 1967; s. Juan Flavio Mendoza and Ada Loretta Ramirez. Degree electronic engr., Univ. Nacional de Ingenieria-UNI, 1995. Cert. engr. Postmaster APROTEC, Lima, Peru, 1993-96; networking specialist Programa Nacional de Informatica Comms., UNDP, Lima, 1996-97; cons. Lima, 1997-98; LAN/WAN specialist Nextel del Peru, Lima, 1998-99, tech. support supr., 1999—. Recipient Premio Voluntario Sobresaliente Oscar C. Fernandez, IEEE Latin Am., 2000. Mem. IEEE (RAB Achievement award 1997), Colegio de Ingenieros del Peru-CIP. Roman Catholic. Avocations: Pelota court, photography, cycling. Office: Nextel del Peru, Calle Los Nardos 1018 7th Fl, San Isidro Lima Peru

MENDOZA, RYAN, artist; b. N.Y.C., Oct. 29, 1971; s. George and Ruth (Sekora) M. Student, Yale U., 1989, Washington U., St. Louis, Mo., 1990-91, Ind. U., 1991-92, Parsons Sch. Art and Design, Paris, 1992-94. One-person shows include Galleria Studio Legale, Caserta, 1997, Galleria In Arco, Torino, 1997, Studio Cannaviello, Milan, 1998, Galerie Bernd Klüser, Munich, 1999, Museum Modern and Contemporary Art, Trento, 2000; subject of art books: Cadaver Dog (Cristiana Perrella), 1997, Oh, Big Fishy (Sergio Bertaccini), 1997, Ryan Mendoza (Tullio Pironti and Alberto Fiz), 1998, Ryan Mendoza: A Cake for the Dead (Hubertus Gassner), 1999, Ryan Mendoza (Skira), 2000. Office: Galerie Bernd Klueser, Georgenstr 15, 80799 Munich Germany

MENDOZA, SAMUEL JOSE, chemical engineer, educator; b. Santo Domingo, Dominican Republic, May 16, 1965; s. Hugo Rafael and Rosaleda (Valdes) M.; m. Maria Dolores Valiente, Nov. 23, 1991; children: Joan Samuel Mendoza Valiente, Carla Victoria Mendoza Valiente. BChemE, U. Nat. Pedro Henriquez Urena, Santo Domingo, 1989; postdoctoral degree in prodn. mgmt., Inst. Tech. Santo Domingo, 1991. Registered profl. chem. engr. Process engr. Refineria Dominicana Petroleo, Santo Domingo, 1988-92; prodn. mgr. Multiquimica Dominicana, Santo Domingo, 1992-94; tech. rep. NALCO Chem. Co., Santo Domingo, 1994—; prof. reactor design U. Nat. Pedro Henriquez Urena, Santo Domingo, 1991-98; prof. indsl. water treatment Inst. Tech. Santo Domingo, 1992-93. Mem. AIChE, Am. Water World Assn., Colegio Dominicano de Ingenieros. Home: Ave Enriquillo 114 Apt 304, Santo Domingo Dominican Republic

MENDOZA, TONY CHAVEZ, insurance company official; b. Roswell, N.Mex., June 1, 1950; s. Dennis and Mary Inez M.; m. Juanita Ann Sosa, June 10, 1972; children: Theresa Renee, Benjamin Anthony, Selina Marie. BBA in Acctg., Ea. N.Mex. U., 1973. Acct. Arthur Andersen & Co., Dallas, 1973-74, North Vista Med. Ctr., Hobbs, N.Mex., 1974-75, Armstrong & Armstrong, Roswell, 1975-78; salesman Duran Floor Coverings, Roswell, 1978-84; agt. Allstate Ins. Co., Roswell, 1984—. Fellow Life Underwriters Tng. Coun.; mem. Nat. Assn. Life Underwriters, Roswell C. of C. (life Red Coats), KC. Roman Catholic. Avocations: golf, tennis. Home: 1905 W Juniper St Roswell NM 88203-1623 Office: Allstate Ins Co 200 W 1st St Ste 100 Roswell NM 88203-4672

MENDOZA GOMEZ, CELIA XOCHIQUETZAL, astrophysicist, mathematician, researcher; b. Cambridge, U.K., July 18; d. Eugenio E. Mendoza and Celia Gomez de Mendoza; m. Eric Hoekstra; 1 child, Maria Teresa Idskjen. Mathematician, U. Mex., Mexico City, physicist; PhD, U. Leiden, The Netherlands. prof. U. Mex.; promovenda U. Leiden, The Netherlands; postdoc. Space Rsch. Orgn. of Netherlands; free lance astrophysicist The Netherlands and Mex. Co-editor: The Chemistry of Life's Origins; contbr. numerous articles to profl. jours. Grantee U. Mex., Inst. Math., Min. Edn. and Scis., The Netherlands, U. Mex. Inst. Astronomy, U. Leiden, The Netherlands. Mem. Internat. Soc. for Study of Origin of Life.

MENDRELA, ERNEST ANDRZEJ, electrical engineering educator, consultant; b. Katowice, Silesia, Poland, Aug. 26, 1943; s. Ernest and Anna (Spalek) M.; m. Elzbieta Maria Baranski, Nov. 29, 1969; children: Malgorzata, Ewa, Adam. MSc, Silesian U. Tech., Gliwice, Poland, 1968; PhD, Wroclaw (Poland) U. Tech., 1975; DSc, Lodz (Poland) U. Tech., 1984. Diplomate in elec. engring. Deisgner Elec. Machine Repair Plant, Lubliniec, Poland, 1967-68; lectr. Wroclaw U. Tech., 1968-77; sr. lectr. Kielce (Poland) U. Tech., 1977-85; asst. prof. Czestochowa (Poland) U. Tech., 1985-89; sr. lectr. U. Sydney, Australia, 1989-92; prof. Opole (Poland) U. Tech., 1993—; vis. prof. Lodz U. Tech., 1993-96, Kielce U. Tech., 1998; cons. Energoserwis, S.A., Lubliniec, 1994-98. Author: Induction Motors with Two Degrees of Mechanical Freedom, 1985; contbr. articles to profl. jours.; patentee magnetic separator and rotary-linear and X-Y electric motors. Head of

Solidarity at Kielce U. Tech., 1980-81. Recipient Edn. award Polish Ministry Edn., 1970, Rsch. award Polish Acad. Sci., 1984. Mem. IEEE (sr.), PTETIS, Polish Soc. Applied Electromagnetics. Roman Catholic. Avocations: skiing, hiking, music, philosophy. E-mail: emen@polo.po.opole.pl. Home: Okolna 83E, 42-200 Czestochowa Poland Office: Opole U Tech, Luboszycka 7, 45-951 Opole Poland

MENEES, JOHN ROBERT, mechanical engineer; b. Chgo., Mar. 15, 1928; s. Thomas Orville and Elda Ruth (Johnston) M.; s. Patricia June Kyle, July 28, 1950; children: Gillian Sue, John Robert. BS in Mech. Engring., U. Ill., 1952. Corp. mgr. heavy industry sales Sinclair Refining Co., N.Y.C., 1953-67; sales Rogers (Conn.) Corp., 1967-92; prin. J.R. Menees Assocs., Olympia Fields, Ill., 1992—. Mem. Soc. Plastics Engrs. Republican. Presbyn. Avocations: golf, travel, family genealogy, alumni activities. Home and Office: 3617 Ionia Ave Olympia Fields IL 60461-1316

MENEFEE, FREDERICK LEWIS, advertising executive; b. Arkansas City, Kans., Oct. 22, 1932; s. Arthur LeRoy and Vera Mae (Rather) M.; m. Margot Leuze, Sept. 16, 1955; children: Gregory S., Christina Menefee-Anderson. AA, Arkansas City Jr. Coll., 1952; BA, U. Wichita, 1958. Sports editor, bus. mgr. Ark. Light and Tiger Tales, 1949-52; sports reporter Arkansas City Daily Traveler, 1950-52; advt. mgr. Derby Star, Haysville Herald and Sedgwick County News, 1956-57; v.p., account exec. Associated Advt. Agy., 1958-64; with McCormick-Armstrong Adv. Agy. (now Menefee and Ptnrs., Inc.), Wichita, 1964—, agy. mgr., 1964—, account. supr., 1965—, gen. mgr., 1972—, pres., CEO, 1979—, chmn. bd., 1989-96. Vol. Wichita River Festival, 1974-98; pub. rels. chmn. Wichita Centennial Nat. Art Show and Exhibit, 1969-70. With AUS, 1953-55. Named Advt. Man of Yr., Advt. Club of Wichita, 1964, Advt. Man of Yr., 9th Dist. Am. Advt. Fedn. Colo., Nebr., Iowa, Mo., Kans., 1965, Adm. Windwagon Smith III Wichita Festivals Inc., 1976. Mem. Am. Advt. Fedn. (nat. bd. dirs. 1969-70, dist. gov. 1968-69, chmn. nat. coun. govs. 1969-70), Wichita Wagonmasters (founding mem., capt. 1974-75, dir., charter, founder), Wichita Advt. Club (bd. dirs. 1958-68), v.p. awards 1961-62, v.p. membership 1962, v.p. programs 1963, pres. 1964-65), PAWS Inc. (founder, 1st pres. 1978-86), Alpha Delta Sigma (pres. 1957-58, Outstanding Svc. award 1958). Home: 2235 Red Bud Ln Wichita KS 67204-5346 Office: Menefee & Ptnrs Inc 1065 N Topeka St Wichita KS 67214-2913

MENEFEE, SAMUEL PYEATT, lawyer, anthropologist; b. Denver, June 8, 1950; s. George Hardiman and Martha Elizabeth (Pyeatt) M. BA in Anthropology and Scholar of Ho. summa cum laude, Yale U., 1972; diploma in Social Anthropology, Oxford (Eng.) U., 1973, BLitt, 1975; JD, Harvard U., 1981; LLM in Oceans, U. Va., 1982, SJD, 1993; MPhil in Internat. Rels., U. Cambridge, Eng., 1995. Bar: Ga. 1981, U.S. Ct. Appeals (11th cir.) 1982, Va. 1983, La. 1983, U.S. Ct. Mil. Appeals 1983, U.S. Ct. Internat. Trade 1983, U.S. Ct. Claims 1983, U.S. Ct. Appeals (10th cir.) 1983, U.S. Ct. Appeals (fed., 1st, 3d, 4th, 5th, 6th, 7th, 8th and 9th cirs.) 1984, D.C. 1985, Nebr. 1985, Fla. 1985, U.S. Supreme Ct. 1985, U.S. Ct. Appeals (D.C. cir.) 1986, Maine 1986, Pa. 1986. Assoc. Phelps, Dunbar, Marks, Claverie & Sims, New Orleans, 1983-85; of counsel Barham & Churchill PC, New Orleans, 1985-88; sr. assoc. Ctr. for Nat. Security Law U. Va. Sch. Law, 1985—, fellow Ctr. for Oceans Law and Policy, 1982-83, sr. fellow, 1985-89, Maury fellow, 1989—, adv. bd., 1997—; vis. lectr. U. Cape Town, 1987; vis. asst. prof. U. Mo.-Kansas City, 1990; law clk. Hon. Pasco M. Bowman, U.S. Ct. Appeals (8th cir.), 1994-95; vis. prof. Regent U., 1996-97, scholar-at-large, 1997—, prof., 1998—; adv. The Am. Maritime Forum/The Mariners' Mus., 1997-98; lectr. various nat. and internat. orgns.; mem. ICC Consultative Task Force on Comml. Crime, 1996—. Author: Wives for Sale: An Ethnographic Study of British Popular Divorce, 1981, Contemporary Piracy and International Law, 1995, Trends in Maritime Violence, 1996; co-editor: Materials on Ocean Law, 1982; contbr. numerous articles to profl. jours. recipient Katharine Briggs prize Folklore Soc., 1992; Bates traveling fellow Yale U., 1971, Rhodes scholar, 1972; Cosmos fellow Sch. Scottish Studies U. Edinburgh, 1991-92, IMB fellow, ICC Internat. Maritime Bur., 1991—, Piracy Reporting Ctr. fellow, Kuala Lampur, 1993—, Huntington fellow The Mariners Mus., 1997. Fellow Royal Anthrop. Inst., Am. Anthrop. Assn., Royal Asiatic Soc., Royal Soc. Antiquaries of Ireland, Soc. Antiquaries (Scotland), Royal Geog. Soc., Soc. Antiquaries; mem. ABA (vice-chmn. marine resources com. 1987-90, chmn. law of the sea com. subcom. naval warfare, maritime terrorism and piracy 1989—, mem. law of the sea com. steering com. 1996—, mem. working group on terrorism), Southeastern Admiralty Law Inst. (com. mem.), Maritime Law Assn. (proctor, com. mem., chmn. subcom. law of the sea 1988-91, vice chmn. com. internat. law of the sea 1991— , chair working group piracy 1992—, UNESCO study group, 1998—), Marine Tech. Soc. (co-chmn. marine security com. 1991—), Selden Soc., Am. Soc. Internat. Law, Internat. Law Assn. (com. mem., rapporteur Am. br. com. EEZ 1988-90, rapporteur Am. br. com. Maritime Neutrality 1992, observer UN conv. on Law of the Sea meeting of States Parties 1996, chmn. Am. br. com. on Law of the Sea 1996—), rapporteur joint internat. working group on uniformity of the law of piracy 1998—, (Com. Maritime Internat.), Am. Soc. Indsl. Security (com. mem.), U.S. Naval Inst., USN League, Folklore Soc., Royal Celtic Soc., Internat. Studies Assn., Royal Scottish Geog. Soc., Royal African Soc., Egypt Exploration Soc., Arctic Inst. N.Am., Internat. Studies Assn., Am. Hist. Soc., Internat. Assn. Rsch. on Peasant Diaries (nat. editor 1996—), Nat. Eagle Scout Assn., Raven Soc., Jefferson Soc., Fence Club, Mory's Assn., Elizabethan Club, Yale Polit. Union, Leander Club, Cambridge Union, United Oxford and Cambridge Univ. Club, Yale Club (N.Y.C.), Paul Morphy Chess Club, Pendennis Club, Round Table Club (New Orleans), Phi Beta Kappa, Omicron Delta Kappa. Republican. Episcopalian. Avocations: anthropology, archaeology, social history, crew, hill walking. Office: U Va Ctr Nat Sec Law 580 Massie Rd Charlottesville VA 22903-1738

MENEGAZZI, PASCAL CHRISTOPHE, automotive engineer; b. Libourne, Gironde, France, Apr. 9, 1964; s. Rino Geno and Louise (Cerrato) M.; m. Aude Liorzou, June 24, 1989; children: Camille, Céleste. D of Mech. Engring., U. Bordeaux, France, 1989. Rsch. engr. Institut Francais du Pétrole, Rueil-Malmaison, 1991-98; project mgr. Institut Francais du Pitrole, Rueil-Malmaison, 1998—. Contbr. articles to profl. jours. Recipient VTMS Conf. Best Paper award Soc. Automotive Engrs./Instn. Mech. Engrs., 1997. Home: 37 ave de la Concorde, 78500 Sártrouville France Office: Inst Francais du Pétrole, 1 & 4 ave de Bois-Préau, Rueil-Malmaison France 92500

MENENDEZ, ANGEL NICOLAS, hydraulics engineer; b. Buenos Aires, Argentina, Sept. 23, 1952; s. Angel and Rafaela (De Simone) M.; m. Maria Ines Schlieper, Mar. 15, 1979 (div. Dec. 1994); children: Sofia, Laura; m. Graciela Myriam Sordetti, Nov. 21, 1996. BSc, U. Buenos Aires, 1975; PhD, U. Iowa, 1983. Tchg. asst. U. Buenos Aires, 1973-80; jur. rschr. Nat. Inst. Water & Environment, Ezeiza, Argentina, 1977-80; from rsch. asst. to postdoctoral assoc. Iowa Inst. Hydraulic Rsch., Iowa City, 1980-84; head dept. Nat. Inst. Water & Environment, 1984—; assoc. prof. U. Buenos Aires, 1985—; cons. in field. Mem. Internat. Assn. Hydraulic Rsch., Argentinian Assn. Computational Mechs. Avocations: dancing tango, playing tennis. Office: INA Autop Ezeiza Cañuelas, Tramo J Newbery km 1620 1802 Aeropuerto, Ezeiza CC21, Argentina

MENENDEZ DEL VALLE, EMILIO, ambassador; b. Madrid, June 20, 1945; m. Marisa Gonzalez Mostoles, Apr. 25, 1981; children: Irene, Alejandra. MA in Law, Madrid U., 1961; postgrad., Columbia U., 1973-75. Ambassador to Italy Rome; mem. European Parliament, Brussels, Belgium, 1999—. Socialist. Office: European Parliament, Rue Wiertz, ASP 11G346 Brussels B-1047, Belgium*

MENESES, ERNESTO, religious educator; b. Cordoba, Veracruz, Mexico, July 30, 1915; s. Jose Meneses and Concepcion Morales. MA, Ysleta Coll., 1939; lic. in theology, St. Louis U., 1947; MEd, Fordham U., 1949, PhD, 1995; D Scientiarum (hon.), U. Iberoamericana, Mexico City, 1981. Dir. Ctr. Psychol. Evaluation U. Iberoamericana, Mexico City, 1955-65, dir., 1955-65, vice-rector, 1965-68, rector, 1968-77, prof., 1969, prof. emeritus, 1978—; assoc. prof. Ysleta Coll., El Paso, Tex., 1949-51. Author: Revista Latinoamericana de Estudios Educativos, 1971, Revista de Educacion Superior, 1977, Umbral XXI, 1993, Umbral XXI, 1996, Educar Comprendiendo al Nino, 1995, Ensenanzas de la historia de la educacion en Mexico, 1999, Tendencias Educativas Oficiales en Mexico (5 vols.), 1983-97. Recipient OEA award in edn., 1988, Tlamatini award in edn., 1996, ANUIES award in higher edn. Mem. Am. Psychol. Assn., Colegio Nacional de Psicologos. Roman Catholic. Avocations: music, archaeology, literature. Home: Margaritas 143, 05330 Cuajimalpa DF, Mexico Office: Univ Iberoamericana, Prolongacion Pas reform 880, 01210 Mexico City DF, Mexico

MENEZES, IGNATIUS, bishop; b. Mangalore, India, Jan. 3, 1936; s. Jacob and Concepta (D'Mello) M. MA in History, Agra (India) U., 1971, MA in Lit., 1973. Tchr. psychology St. Paul's Sem., Lucknow, India, 1964; vice prin. St. Francis Coll., Lucknow, 1965-66, prin., 1977-78; parish priest, prin. St. Joseph's Cathedral and Cathedral Sch., Lucknow, 1966-76; bishop Diocese of Ajmer-Jaipur, Ajmer, India, 1979—; mem. Cath. Coun. India. Author: I Have Come to Do Thy Will, 1995; contbr. articles to profl. jours. Avocations: reading, studying, badminton, basketball. Home: Bishops House, Ajmer 305001, India Office: Diocesan Soc Ajmer-Jaipur, Kaiserganj, Ajmer 305001, India

MENEZES, SISTER MARY NOEL, religious organization administrator, history educator; b. Georgetown, Guyana, July 14, 1930. BA in History, Coll. Misericordia, 1964; MA, Georgetown U., 1965; PhD in History, U. London, 1973; LHD, Coll. Misericordia, 1983. Prin. Sacred Heart Girls' Sch., Georgetown, Guyana, 1957-63; lectr. Coll. Misericordia, Dallas, Pa., 1966-67; lectr. U. Guyana, Georgetown, 1967-77, sr. lectr., 1977-80, chmn. dept. history, 1977-89, chief supr. grad. programme history, 1973-90, prof. history, 1980—; pres. Assn. Caribbean Historians, 1978-80; dir. Can. Orgn. for Devel. Edn., Guyana, 1989-93, Demerara Pub. Ltd., Guyana, 1988-90, St. Joseph Mercy Hosp., Guyana, 1988—, Food for the Poor, Guyana, 1990-96. Author: British Policy Towards the Amerindians in British Guiana, 1803-1873, 1977, The Portuguese of Guyana: A Study in Culture and Conflict, 1994, 11 others; contbr. numerous articles to profl. jours. Mem. Cheshire Home Com., Guyana, 1973-2000, Ptnrs. of the Americas, Guyana, 1992-93, Adoption Bd. Ministry of Labor, Guyana, 1992, Adv. Com./Ministry Amerindian Affairs, Guyana, 1992—. Recipient Ford Found. fellowship, 1970-73, Govt. of India Vis. fellowship, 1982, Golden Arrow Achievement award Govt. of Guyana, 1982, Senator Hicks fellowship Dalhousie U., 1986, Outstanding Guyanese Women award U. Guyana, 1989, Internat. Woman of Yr. award, 1994-95. Fellow Inst. Latin Am. Studies, Henry Chapman Vis. fellowship; mem. Assn. Caribbean Historians, Guyana Heritage Soc. (mem. exec. com. 1985—). Avocations: reading, researching, writing, listening to clasical music. Home: Saint John Bosco Convent, Plaisance ECD Guyana

MENG, GUANG JUN, librarian, educator; b. Beijing, Feb. 2, 1934; s. Shao Meng and Lian Sun; m. Yu Wang, Nov. 25, 1962; two children. Grad., Inst. Fgn. Langs., China, 1954, Info. Sci. Dept. U. Su-Tech, China, 1960. From asst. libr. to prof., instr. PhD students Documentation and Info. Ctr. Chinese Acad. Scis., Beijing, 1958—. Author: An Introduction to Library and Information Science, 1982, 2d edit., 1991, Selected Works of Meng Guangjun, 1988, An Introduction to Information Resources Management, 1998, Advance in Library and Information Science Research in Foreign Countries, 1999; editor-in-chief Libr. and Info. Svc.; contbr. articles to profl. jours.

MENG, XIANMIN, dermatologist, researcher; b. Benxi, Liaoning, China, Jan. 31, 1967; s. Zhaojun Meng and Sufan Wang; m. Yuhong Xiao; 1 child, Qingyu. MD, Dalian (China) Med. U., 1989, M Medicine, 1994; PhD in Med. Sci., Hirosaki (Japan) U., 1999. Physician dept. dermatology Dailan Med. U., 1989-91; rsch. fellow dept. dermatology Hirosaki U. Sch. Medicine, 1994-95; postdoctoral fellow dept. dermatology Thomas Jefferson U., Phila., 1999—. Contbr. numerous articles to profl. jours. Mem. AAAS, Japanese Dermatol. Assn., Japanese Soc. for Investigative Dermatology (diploma of dermatol. sci. 1998). Avocations: sports, auto camps, music, movies. E-mail: mengderm@yahoo.com. Home: 520 Collings Ave Apt B706 Oaklyn NJ 08107-1642 Office: Thomas Jefferson U Dept Dermatology 233 S 10th St Rm 450 Philadelphia PA 19107-5541

MENGEL, CHRISTOPHER EMILE, lawyer, educator; b. Holyoke, Mass., Sept. 11, 1952; s. Emile Oscar and Rose Ann (O'Donnell) M.; m. Ellen Christine Creager, Dec. 6, 1991; children: Meredith Anne, Celia Claire; stepchildren: Cara Elizabeth Creager, Kristen Michele Creager. Student, U. Notre Dame, 1970-71; BA, Holy Cross Coll., 1974; JD, Detroit Coll. Law, 1979. Bar: Mich. 1979, U.S. Dist. Ct. (ea. dist.) Mich. 1989, U.S. Ct. Appeals (6th cir.) 1990. Tchr. Holyoke Pub. Schs., 1974-76; assoc. Fried & Sniokaitis P.C., Detroit, 1980-82; prof. Detroit Coll. Law, 1982-85; pvt. practice Detroit, 1982-91; mng. ptnr. Berkley, Mengel & Vining, PC, 1992—. Mem. coun. St. Ambrose Parish, Grosse Pointe Park, Mich., 1985-88, pres. 1986-87. Matthew J. Ryan scholar, 1970; recipient Disting. Brief award Thomas M. Cooley Law Rev., 1996. Mem. ABA, Mich. Bar Assn., Detroit Bar Assn. Democrat. Roman Catholic. Avocations: baseball, sailing, photography. Home: 1281 N Oxford Rd Grosse Pointe MI 48236-1857 Office: Berkley Mengel & Vining PC 3100 Penobscot Bldg Detroit MI 48226

MENGUTURK, MUHSIN, government agency administrator; b. Mugla, Turkey, Sept. 12, 1948; s. Cahit and Leman (Ertuglu) M.; m. Aysu Terzibasoglu; children: Levent, Murat. BS, Robert Coll., Istanbul, 1970; MS, Duke U., 1971, PhD, 1974. Sr. engr. Westinghouse, Pitts., 1974-76; faculty mem. Bogazici U., Istanbul, Turkey, 1976-84; prof., vice chmn. Istanbul Tech. U., 1984-88; prof. bus. adminstrn. Bilkent U., Ankara, Turkey, 1991-97, Middle East Tech. U., Ankara, 1992-97; sr. v.p. Turk Eximbank, Ankara, 1988-92; gen. mgr., bd. dirs. Bayindir Life Ins., Ankara, 1992-96; mgmt., investment cons. Ankara, 1996-97; chmn., ceo Capital Markets Bd. Turkey, Ankara, 1997—. Author: International Finance, 1995; contbr. over 45 articles to international publications. Office: Capital Markets Bd, Doc Dr Bahriye Ucok CD # 13, Besevler Ankara 06500, Turkey

MENICUCCI, RAFAEL GUILLERMO, beverage company executive; b. Dominican Republic, Apr. 8, 1943; came to U.S., 1955; s. Rafael Guillermo and Dolores (Vila) M.; m. Olga Padilla, Dec. 2, 1966; children: Angelo, Joanne Menicucci de Perez. BSME, U. P.R., 1965. Engr. Refrescos Nacionales CxA, Santo Domingo, Dominican Republic, 1965-68; dir. engring. Cerveceria Nacional Dominicana CxA, Santo Domingo, Dominican Republic, 1968-78, genl. mgr., 1978-82, exec. v.p., 1982-93, pres., 1993—. Mem. Asociacion de Industrias de la Republica Dominicana (v.p.), Camara Americana de Comercio (exec. com), Asociacion Latinoamericana Fabricantes Cerveza (exec. com.), Asociacion Dominicana Fabricantes Cerveza (pres.). Roman Catholic. Avocations: boating, water sports. Home: Paseo de los Framboyanes 15, Los Pinos, Santo Domingo Dominican Republic Office: Cerveceria Nac Dominicana, Profl Avenida Ind Km 6 1/2, Santo Domingo Dominican Republic

MENIGOZ, RON EARL, manufacturing executive; b. L.A., Sept. 22, 1964; s. Leslie Leland and Marilyn Louise (Tustin) M.; m. Melissa Lynn Haka Smith, Aug. 16, 1984 (div. May 1989). BSEE, U. Calif., Davis, 1988, Calif. Poly., San Luis Obispo, 1993. Registered profl. engr., Calif. Mgr. Kettlehut Svcs., Mission Viejo, Calif., 1984-89; pres. Santa Lucia Engring., Atascadero, Calif., 1989-94; mgr. 3Com, Santa Clara, Calif., 1994-96, Bay Networks, Santa Clara, 1996-98; dir. Gadzoox Networks, San Jose, Calif., 1998—. Author: Manufacturing for Fun and Profit, 1998; editor: Managing for Results, 1998. Vol. tchr. Fremont High Sch., Milpitas, Calif., 1995; vol. big brother Big Bros. and Sisters, Beaverton, Oreg., 1984. Mem. IEEE, Am. Water Ski Assn., U.S. Parachute Assn. Republican. Methodist. Avocations: water skiing, sky diving, teaching. Home: 1660 Riverlake Rd Discovery Bay CA 94514-9496 Office: Gadzoox Networks 5850 Hellyer Ave San Jose CA 95138-1004

MENIPAZ, EHUD, business administration educator, engineer; b. Jerusalem, Israel, May 2, 1946; s. David Zlotnik and Tova (Charpak) M.; m. Esther Rosenbaum, May 1969; children: amit Reuven, Liat, Ronen Shmuel. BSc in Engring., Technion-Israel Inst. Tech., 1968, MSc in Engring., 1972; MBA, U. Cin., 1974, PhD, 1975. Registered profl. engr., Israel, chmn. Sr. ptnr. Ernst & Young, Can., 1984—; prof. engring. and mgmt., chmn. Ben Gurion U., Raanana, Israel, 1994—; pres. RTI, Can., 1975—; dir. Kao-Didak, Can., 1982-85; chmn. IE com. NRC, Can., 1981-84. Dir. Young Entrepreneurs Ltd., 1998. Lt. Israel armed forces, 1968-72. HTZ fellow Friends of Technion, 1972-75. Avocations: piano, skiing, tennis, travel.

MENKERIOS, HAILE, diplomat; b. Asmara, Eritrea, Oct. 1, 1946; s. Drar Menkerios and Neguse Giorgis; m. Hebret Berhe, Nov. 14, 1979 (div. 1996); children: Selam, Solomon; m. Ghennet Tesfamariam, Jan. 27, 1998. BA, Brandeis U., 1970; MA, Harvard U., 1971, postgrad., 1971-73. Dir. Eritrean Rsch. Ctr., Eritrea, 1986-87; dir. rsch. and policy Govt. Fgn. Rels. Dept., Eritrea, 1987-90; gov. South & East Zone (Province), Eritrea, 1990-91; spl. rep. Ethiopia and Somalia Govt. Eritrea, Addis Ababa, Ethiopia, 1991-93, amb. Ethiopia and Orgn. African Unity, 1993-96; spl. envoy to Great Lakes Govt. Eritrea, various African countries, 1996-97; amb. Eritrea, permanent rep. UN, N.Y.C., 1997—; mem. Horn of Africa high level com. on Somalia, 1992-95; mediator Oromo Liberation Front, Ethiopian Peoples Dem. Revolutionary Front, 1993-95; M.P. Eritrean Nat. Coun., 1993—; polit. advisor, pres. Dem. Republic of Congo, Kinshasa, 1997. Author various govt. documents, 1970-95. Mem. ctrl. coun. Eritrean Peoples Liberation Front, 1977—. Platoon comdr., Eritrean Liberation Army, 1973-74. Christian. Avocations: reading, travel. E-mail: hmenkerios@aol.com. Home: 241 Ardsley Rd Scarsdale NY 10583-2626 Office: Eritrean Mission to UN 800 2nd Ave Fl Dave18 New York NY 10017-4709

MENNEN, ULRICH, hand surgery and orthopaedics educator, surgeon; b. Barberton, Mpumalanga, South Africa, July 1, 1947; s. Erich and Frieda (Steinberg) M.; m. Johanna Margaretha Louw, Jan. 15, 1971; children: Albert Menno, Mathilda Christina, Abraham Faure. MBChB, Pretoria (S. Africa) U., 1970, MMedOrth, 1979, PhD in Orthopaedics, 1983. Lic. orthop. surgery. Intern Krugersdorp (South Africa) Hosp., 1971; med. officer Lahr Krankenhaus, Schwarzwald, Germany, 1972; sr. houseman Brook Gen. Hosp., London, 1973-74; registrar Kalafong Hosp., Pretoria, 1975-77; registrar Pretoria Acad. Hosp., 1978-79, sr. surgeon, 1980, assoc. prof., prin. surgeon, 1981; prof., head Dept. Hand and Microsurgery Med. U. Southern Africa and Ga-Rankuwa Hosp., Pretoria, 1985—; acting head orthopaedic surgery Med. U. So. Africa and Ga-Rankuwa Hosp., Pretoria, 1990-91; pvt. practice in hand surgery, Pretoria, 1992—; vis. prof. hand surgery L.A., 1994, Hong Kong, 1996, Australia, 1998, Vietnam, 1999, South Korea, 1999, Iran, 1999, Botswana, 2000; lectr. and presenter in field. Author: Chirurgiese Sinopsis, 1978, The History of the South African Society for Surgery of the Hand, 1969-1994, 1994; (with others) Surgical Synopsis, 1983; editor: The Hand Book, 1988, 3d edit., 2000; (with others) Principles of Surgical Patient Care, 1990, 2d edit., 2000; contbr. numerous chpts. to books and articles to profl. jours.; patentee internal fixation bone fractures (Mennen clamp-on plate sys.), Researcher/promoter End-to-Side Nerve Suture. Chamber of Mines Rsch. grantee, 1987; finalist Med. Rsch. Coun. award, 1991; recipient South African Bur. Standards Design Inst. Chmn. award for Excellence, 1998, also several lit. and rsch. awards. Fellow Royal Coll. Surgeons Edinburgh and Glasgow, Coll. Medicine South Africa (orthop. surgery); mem. South African Med. Assn. (mem No. Gauteng br. coun.), South African Soc. Surgery of the Hand (chmn. No. Gauteng br., mem. nat. exec. pres.), Internat. Fedn. Socs. for Surgery of the Hand (mem. exec. coun.; nat. del., chmn. com. on treatment ctrs. for hand surgery). Home: 374 Lawley St, Waterkloof 0181 Pretoria South Africa Office: Med U So Africa & Ga-Rankuwa Hosp, U Pretoria Dept Orthop Surgery, Pretoria 0204, South Africa also: Jacaranda Hosp Pretoria Hand Inst, Ste 8, Pretoria South Africa

MENNICKEN, LOTHAR, animal and poultry scientist, researcher; b. Aachen, Germany, July 17, 1962; m. Choon Nin Tee, 1992; children: Christabel, Cecil, Charles. Diplom-agraringenieur, U. Bonn, Germany, 1989; D in Agrl. Sci., Humboldt U., Berlin, 1995. Rsch. fellow vet. svc. dept. Ministry of Agr., Johor Bahru, Malaysia, 1990-92; rsch. fellow Humboldt U., Berlin, 1992-95; sci. asst. Bonn U., 1995—. Author: Haltungstechnische und züchterische Möglichkeiten zur Reduzierung der Hitzebelastung von Broiler-Elterntieren am tropischen Standort, 1995 (Best Dissertation award World's Poultry Sci. Assn. German Br. 1996); co-author: Herkunftsnachweis von Eiern aus verschiedenen Haltungssystemen für Legehennen, 1998. Chmn. Young Adul's Movement, Johor Bahru, 1990-92. Pvt. German Air Force, 1981-82. German Acad. Exch. Svc. postgrad. grant/scholar, 1990-92. Mem. German Agrl. Scientists Assn., German Agrl. Soc. (poultry sci. coun.), World's Poultry Sci. Assn. (rep. working group 4). Office: U Bonn Inst Animal Sci, Endenicher Allee 15, D-53115 Bonn Germany

MENNIN, DOUGLAS STEVEN, psychologist; b. N.Y.C., May 21, 1972; s. Gerald Stanley and Miriam Juliet (Kobrin) M. BA, Oberlin Coll., 1994; MA, Temple U., 1999, postgrad., 1995. Clin. rsch. analyst Mass. Gen. Hosp., Boston, 1994-96; clin. rsch. assoc. Adult Anxiety Clinic Temple U., Phila., 1996-2000; clin. psychology fellow N.Y. Presbyn. Hosp.-Cornell Med. Coll., 2000—. Ad hoc reviewer Cognitive Therapy and Rsch., 1996-99; contbr. articles to profl. jours. Recipient psychology fellow N.Y. Presbyn./Cornell Med. Ctr., 2000—, Congl. medal of merit U.S. Congress, Scarsdale, N.Y., 1990. Mem. APA (student), Assn. Advancement of Behavior Therapy (student), Anxiety Disorders Assn. Am. (student), Sigma Xi. Home: #6115 221 S 12th St # 6115 Philadelphia PA 19107-5556 also: 301 E 63rd St Apt 3K New York NY 10021-7735 Office: Temple Univ Dept Psychology Weiss 419 1701 N Broad St Philadelphia PA 19122-6002

MENNIN, GERALD STANLEY, ophthalmologist; b. N.Y.C., Mar. 20, 1932; s. Daniel and Sadie (Krieger) M.; children: Danielle, Douglas. BA, NYU, 1954; MD, SUNY, N.Y.C. Intern Beth Israel Hosp., N.Y.C., 1958-59; resident Bronx Mcpl. Hosp. Ctr./Einstein Coll. Medicine, 1050-62; pvt. practice Yonkers; chief ophthalmology Yonkers Gen. Hosp., 1986—; attending ophthalmologist Montefiore Hosp., Bronx, 1962—, Bronx Mcpl. Hosp., 1962—, St. John's Hosp., Yonkers, 1981—, Yonkers Gen. Hosp., 1962—, Manhattan Eye and Ear Hosp., N.Y.C., 1990—. Fellow ACS, Am. Acad. Ophthalmologists, Nat. Arts Club. Avocation: art. Office: 45 Ludlow St Yonkers NY 10705-1947 also: 710 Park Ave New York NY 10021-4944

MENON, HARILAL BHASKARA, oceanographer, researcher, educator; b. Thiruvalla, Kerala, India, July 31, 1962; s. Parameswaran Bhaskara and Chellamma (Leelavathiamma) M.; m. Lalitha Radhakrishna Menon, Apr. 22, 1990; children: Athul Harilal, Aathira Harilal. Grad., Devaswom Bd. Coll., Kerala, India, 1982; MS, Cochin U. Sci. and Tech., Kerala, India, 1984, PhD, 1990. Jr. rsch. fellow Cochin U., 1985-86; jr. rsch. fellow Nat. Inst. Oceanography, Panjim, 1986-87, sr. rsch. fellow, 1987-88; lectr. Goa U., Panjim, 1988-93, sr. lectr., 1993-97, reader, 1997—; vis. scientist Inst. Oceanography, Hamburg, Germany, 1994-96; cons. Indian Space Rsch. Orgn., Bangalore, 1999—, Cochin U., 2000—. Contbr. articles to profl. jours. Warden Boy's Hostel, Goa U., Panjim, 1997-99. With Nat. Cadet Corps, 1975-82. Recipient German Acad. Exch. award DAAD, 1994. Mem. Indian Assn. for Phys. Scis. Ocean, Am. Geophys. Union. Hindu. Avocations: music, reading, films, cricket. Office: Goa U Dept Marine Sci, Taleigao Plateau, Panjim Goa 403206, India

MENON, KARUNAKARA CHITLANCHERY, electronic engineer; b. Chitlanchery-Palakkad, Kerala, India, Nov. 28, 1932; s. Raman Menon Thottekkat and Yesoda Chitlanchery Pathiyil (Yesoda) M.; m. Annu Karunakar Anandavalli Parijathamma, Sept. 13, 1960; children: Dipen K., Brinda A., Venugopal K. Grad., Instn. Elec. & Radio Engrs., U.K., 1955; grad. def. svcs., Staff Coll., Wellington, India, 1969. Chartered engr., Eng. Commd. pilot officer Indian Air Force, 1957, advanced to wing comdr., 1973, aero. engr., 1957-74; mgr. devel. and engring. Bharat Electronics, Bangalore, India, 1974-76; dep./additional gen. mgr. Bharat Electronics, Bangalore, 1976-84, gen. mgr. R&D, 1985-86, exec. dir., 1986-90; cons. Bangalore, 1990-95; COO Spectrum Infotech, Bangalore, 1995—; head project team Air Hdqrs. Indian Air Force, New Delhi, 1966-68; leader devel. team Air Def. Radar, 1971-80. Named Disting. fellow Soc. Electronic Engrs., Bangalore, India, 1990. Mem. IEEE, Instn. Elec. Engrs. (U.K.), Instn. Electronic and Telecom. Engrs. India (chmn. Bangalore Ctr. 1988-90). Hindu. Avocations: photography, chess. Home: 233 Jalvayu Vihar, Kalyananagar, Bangalore 560043, India Office: Spectrum Infotech Ltd, 5 Victoria Rd, Bangalore 560047, India

MENON, MAMBILLIKALATHIL GOVIND KUMAR, physicist; b. Aug. 28, 1928; s. Kizhekepat Sankara and Mambillikalathil Narayaniamma Menon; m. Indumati Patel, 1955; 2 children. Grad., Jaswant Coll., Jodhpur, India, Royal Inst. Sci., Bombay, India, U. Bristol, Eng.; MSc, PhD, DSc (hon.), U. Jodhpur, U. Delhi, Sardar Patel U., U. Roorkee, Banaras Hindu U., Jadavpur U., Sri. Venkateswara U., Allahabad U., Andhra U., Utkal U.

Aligarh Muslim U., North Bengal U., Guru Nanak Dev U., Indian Inst. Tech., Madras and Kharagpur, U. Bristol; D in Engring. (hon.), Stevens Inst. Tech. Dir. Tata Inst. Fundamental Rsch., Bombay, 1966-75; chmn. Electronics Commn., sec. Govt. India Dept. Electronics, 1971-78; sci. adviser to Min. of Def., sec. for def. rsch., dir. gen. Def. R&D Orgn., 1974-78; dir.-gen. Coun. Sci. and Indsl. Rsch., 1978-81; sec. Dept. Sci. and Tech., 1978-82, Dept. of Environment, 1980-81; chmn. Commn. for Additional Sources Energy, 1981-82; chmn. sci. adv. com. Indian Cabinet, 1982-85; mem. Govt. Planning Commn., 1982-89; sci. adviser to Prime Min., 1986-89; min. state sci. & tech. Govt. India, 1989-90; pres. Internat. Coun. Sci. Unions, 1988-93; M.P. Indian Parliament, 1990-96; pres. Indian Statis. Inst., Calcutta, 1990—, disting. prof. dept. space, 1999—; chmn., bd. govs. Indian Inst. Tech., Bombay, 1997—. Recipient Sr. award Royal Commn. for Exhbn. of 1851, 1953-55, Shanti Swarup Bhatnagar award for phys. scis. Coun. Sci. and Indsl. Rsch., 1960, Abdus Salam medal 3d World Acad. Scis., 1997, Repub. Day (nat.) awards Govt. India, Padma Shri, 1961, Padma Bhushan, 1968, Padma Vibhushan, 1985, numerous other awards. Fellow NAS (pres. 1987-88, M. N. Saha Disting. fellow 1994-99), Indian Acad. Scis. (pres. 1974-76), Indian Nat. Sci. Acad. (pres. 1981-82), Royal Soc., Inst. Physics U.K. (hon. fellow); mem. IEEE (hon.), AAAS (fgn. hon.), Pontifical Acad. Scis., Asia Electrons Union (pres. 1973-75), Russian Acad. Scis. (hon.). Address: C-63 Tarang Apts 19, I P Ext Mother Dairy Rd, Delhi 110092, India

MENON, SANJAY THEKKECHERUVATH, management educator; b. Thrissur, Kerala, India, Mar. 26, 1963; came to U.S., 1995; s. Madhavan Ayyappath and Remadevi Thekkecheruvath; m. Ammini S. Kumar, Dec. 4, 1992; 1 child, Mihika P. B in Engring., South Gujarat U., Surat, India, 1984; MBA, Indian Inst. Mgmt., Calcutta, India, 1987; PhD, McGill U., Montreal, Canada, 1995. Jr. exec. Dunlop India Ltd., Calcutta, 1987-1990; instr. mgmt. McGill U., 1991-95; asst. prof. Clarkson U., Potsdam, N.Y., 1995—. Contbr. articles to profl. jours. Mem. Acad. Mgmt., Internat. Soc. Study of Work and Orgnl. Values (life, sci. com. 1998—). E-mail: menons@clarkson.edu. Office: Clarkson U PO Box 5790 Potsdam NY 13699-0001

MENSAH, SAMUEL KWAME, clergyman, educator; b. Mampong, Ghana, Oct. 8, 1948; s. Yaw Sarfo and Yaa Amoah; m. Mary Aboraa, Aug. 3, 1981; children: Josephine Mensah, Samuel Sarfo-Mensah, Mark Atta-Mensah, Raheal Ataa-Mensah, Kofi Tawia-Mensah, Mary Mensah. BA with honors, U. Cape Coast, Ghana, 1976, MA in Geography, 1984; DipTh, Trinity Coll., Legon, Ghana, 1994. Ordained minister Presbyn. Ch., 1994; cert. tchr. Acad. adviser, tutor Bechem Bus. Coll., Ghana, 1972-73; house master, counselling coord., tutor Adisadel Coll., Ghana, 1976-79; sr. tutor, counsellor Apisadel Coll., Cape Coast, 1980; sr. tutor, house master Ghana Nat. Coll., Cape Coast, 1981-82; asst. lectr., acad. counsellor dept. geography U. Cape Coast, Cape Coast, 1982-84; head dept. edn. St. Andrew's Coll., Mampong-Ashanti, Ghana, 1984-90, dir. edn., 1991-92; regional mgr. Presbyn. Ednl. Unit, Ashanti, Kumasi, 1994—; prin. Presbyn. Tng. Coll., Akropong-Akuapem, 1997-99; dist. dir. edn. Akuapem North Dist., 1999-2000; mem. mgmt. bd. Amaniapong Secondary Sch., 1992-95; Presbyn. Ch. of Ghana rep. Agogo Tng. Coll. Bd., 1994, Prempeh Coll. Bd., Kumasi, 1994; mem. Presbyn. U. planning com., 1998, implementation com., 1998-2000; mem. bd. trustees Akrofi-Christaller Meml. Ctr. for Mission Rsch. and Theology, 1997-2000. Author: Inter-Urban Passenger Movement, 1984. Sec. adv. bd. Nurses' Christian Fellowship, Accra, 1976-86. Recipient Prin.'s Svc. award Trinity Coll. Bd., 1993, 94. Mem. Ghana Nat. Assn. Tchrs., Scripture Union (area chmn. 1986-92, Svc. award 1990), Ghana Fellowship of Evang. Students (local coord. 1984-94). Avocations: reading, gardening, indoor games, tree planting. Home: House No B 113, Benim-Mampong Ghana Office: Dist Edn Office, PO Box 102, Akropong-Akuapem Ghana

MENSCHER, BARNET GARY, steel company executive; b. Laurelton, N.Y., Sept. 5, 1940; s. Samuel and Louise (Zaimont) M.; m. Diane Elaine Gachman, June 12, 1966; children: Melissa Denise, Corey Lane, Scott Jay. Student, Centenary Coll., 1958-59; B.B.A., U. Tex., 1963. Vice pres. mktg. Ella Gant Mfg., Shreveport, La., 1964-66; warehouse mgr., dir. material control Gachman Steel Co., Fort Worth, 1966-68; gen. mgr. Gachman Steel Co., Houston, 1968-70; v.p. sales Gachman Metal Co., Houston, 1971-76; pres. Menko Steel Service, Inc., Houston, 1979—; CEO NEXTLEVEL, Houston, 1998—; investment cons. D & L Enterprises, 1966—. Mem. solicitation com. United Fund, 1969-76; mem. Nat. Alliance of Businessmen Jobs Program, 1969—. Served with AUS, 1963-65. Mem. Tex. Assn. Steel Importers, Purchasing Agts. Assn. Houston, Credit Assn. Houston, Am. Mgmt. Assn., Assn. Steel Distbrs., Nat. Assn. Elevator Contractors, Phi Sigma Delta, Alpha Phi Omega. Home: 314 Tealwood Dr Houston TX 77024-6113 Office: PO Box 40296 Houston TX 77240-0296

MENSES, GERARD, foundation executive; b. Sydney, NSW, Australia, Mar. 31, 1957; s. G. H. and S. Menses; m. Philippa Mary Croll, May 8, 1982; children: Lachlan, Oliver. BA with honors, Macquarie U., Sydney, 1979, MA, 1988. Lic. psychologist Psychol. Bd., SA and Psychologists Bd. Queensland. Asst. to chaplain, rsch. asst. Macquarie U., Sydney, 1980; sch. counselor Trinity Grammar Sch., Sydney, 1981-83; coord. CareForce Youth Care Team, Sydney, 1983-87; pvt. practice Dulwich Centre, Adelaide, Australia, 1987; exec. dir. South Australian Coun. Social Svc., Adelaide, 1988-90; CEO Anglicare-SA, Adelaide, 1990-99, Endeavour Found., Brisbane, Queensland, Australia, 1999—; dep. chair Anglicare Australia, 1990-98; dir. Cmty. Info. Strategies Australia, Adelaide, 1987-88. Editor: (jour.) Case Studies, 1984-86. Commr. South Africa Devel. Assessment Commn., Adelaide, 1994-96; chair key advisors group City and Soc. Adelaide 21, 1996; bd. dirs. SA Bus. Leadership Found., Adelaide, 1998; trustee SA Bus. Vision 2010, Adelaide, 1987—. Fellow Australian Inst. Mgmt.; mem. Australian Inst. Co. Dirs., Australian Psychol. Soc. Avocations: photography, wine. Fax: 61738741047. E-mail: g.menses@endeavour.com.au. Office: Endeavour Found, 38 Jordan TC Bowen Hills, Queensland 4006, Australia

MENTEER, DAVID HILTON, producer, production manager; b. L.A., Apr. 7, 1939; s. Charles Hilton Greene and Virginia Rose (Kershner) Menteer; m. JoAnne Letty Bagwell, Dec. 30, 1960 (div. June 1986); children: Jon-David, Kevin James; m. Kathryn Jan Severson, May 30, 1987. BS, U. Miami, 1964. Tv cameraman WTVJ, Miami, Fla., 1962-65; tv engr. ABC Network, L.A., 1965-66, stage mgr., assoc. dir., 1966-68; freelance stage mgr., assoc. dir. L.A., 1968-73; asst. dir., second unit dir., prodn. mgr. Universal Studios, L.A., 1973-79; freelance producer, prodn. mgr. L.A., 1979—. With USN, 1957-61, PTO. Mem. Dirs. Guild Am. Avocations: profl. diver, comml. pilot. Home: 4515 Park Serena Calabasas CA 91302-1775

MENTEN, JOHAN JOZEF, radiotherapist; b. Zutendaal, Belgium, July 8, 1955; m. Veronique Boelen, Aug. 20, 1982. MD, Cath. U., Leuven, Belgium, 1980, diploma in radiotherapy, 1984. Staff mem. radiotherapy Univ. Hosp. Gasthuisberg, Leuven, 1984—, dir. palliative support team, 1996—; dir. palliative care unit UZ Leuven, 1999—; pres. sci. com. Internat. Comprehensive Cancer Care Congress, Cyprus, 1997. Author: Palliative and Terminal Care, 1996; co-author: Eso Manual Practical Pain Management, 1996; reviewer Radiation-Oncology, 1995—. Mem. Belgium Soc. Palliative Care (bd. dirs. 1994-96), Flemmish Fed. Palliative Care (bd. dirs. 1996—), European Assn. Palliative Care (mem. rsch. network 1996—), European Soc. for Therapeutic Radiology and Oncology. Office: Univ Hosp Gasthuisberg, Herestraat 49, B3000 Leuven Belgium

MENTHE, ERICH, automotive company executive; b. Eschwege, Hessen, Germany, Jan. 7, 1964; s. Rudolf and Dagmar Menthe. Diploma, Tech. U. Braunschweig, Germany, 1992, Dr.-Ing., 1999. Scientist Tech. U. Braunschweig, 1992—, ANSTO, Sydney, Australia, 1997-98; rschr. DaimlerChrysler, Ulm, Germany, 1999—. Author: Plasmanitrieren von Austenitischen Stählen, 1999. Deutscher Akademischer Austauschdienst scholar, 1997-98. Mem. Verein Deutscher Ingenieure, Deutsche Gesellschaft für Oberflächentechnik. Office: DaimlerChrysler AG FT4ST, Wilhelm-Runge Str 11, 89081 Ulm Germany

MENTON, ARTHUR FRANCIS, information services specialist; b. Bronx, N.Y., Aug. 6, 1932; s. Alexander and Mildred (Sahr) M.; m. Nancy G. Guralnick, Aug. 3, 1986; children from previous marriage: Marc, Deborah. MBE, CCNY, 1954, MME, 1959; postgrad., NYU, 1964-67; D Mgmt., Derek Inst., 1970. Engr. RCA, Moorestown, N.J., 1954-55; sr. engr. Fairchild Engine and Aircraft Corp., Deer Park, N.Y., 1955-59; chief mech. engr. Servo Corp. Am., Hicksville, N.Y., 1960-63; mgr. adv. devel. Veeco, Plainview, N.Y., 1963-64; prin. engr. corp. planning Grumman Corp., Bethpage, N.Y., 1965-90; pres. Menton Assoc., Inc., Cold Spring Harbor, N.Y., 1990—; v.p. The Huntington (N.Y.) Group, Inc.,1 968-72. Author: Probability and Statistics for Management Engineers, 1969, The Book of Destiny: Toledot Charlap, 1996, Ancilla To Toledot Charlap, 1999; editor newsletter B'Rayshit, 1989—, The Huntington Jewish Bull., 1965-72 (Solomon Schecter award 1969). Avocations: tennis, sailing, theater, music. Office: Menton Assocs Inc PO Box 108 Cold Spring Harbor NY 11724-0108

MENTSCHL, JOSEF, retired educator; b. Vienna, Austria, Feb. 23, 1926; s. Josef and Berta (Schefzik) M.; m. Margarete Pichler, July 26, 1958; children: Christoph, Elisabeth, Georg. Grad, Handelsakademie, Vienna, 1944; PhD, U. Vienna, 1948, Magister, 1949. Cert. secondary sch. tchr., Austria. Vocat. sch. tchr. Vienna, 1951-81, H.S. tchr., 1953-87; lectr. U. Econs., Vienna, 1974—. Author: (text) Deutsch-Rechtschreiben und Ausdruck, 12th edit., 1956, (with G. Otruba) Österreichische Industrielle und Bankiers, 1965, (with E. Fijala) Zeiten, Völker und Kulturen, 1973; author, editor jour. GdW-Informationen, 1965—. Chmn. Südtiroler Jugendhilfe, Vienna, 1959-69; founder, chmn. Gemeinschaft der Wohnungseigentümer, Vienna, 1964—. With Germany armed forces, 1944-45. Recipient Goldenes Ehrenzeichen fur Verdienste um die Republik, Ministry of Economy, Vienna, 1989, Ehrenkreuz fur Wissenschaft und Kunst 1st Klasse, Ministry of Sci., Vienna, 1995, Goldenes Doktordiplom der U. Wien, 1998. Roman Catholic. Avocation: cross country skiing.

MENTZ, BARBARA ANTONELLO, lawyer; b. Kansas City, Mo., July 4, 1944; d. John Francis and Eleanor Barbara (Vagnino) Antonello; m. Lawrence Mentz, Nov. 10, 1973; children: Kathleen Elizabeth, Lawrence Goodwin. BA in Econs., U. Kans., 1965; JD magna cum laude, U. Notre Dame, 1973. Bar: N.Y. 1974, U.S. Dist. Ct. (so. and ea. dists.) N.Y. 1974, U.S. Ct. Appeals (2d cir.) 1974, U.S. Supreme Ct. 1977, U.S. Ct. Appeals (9th cir.) 1981, U.S. Ct. Appeals (3d cir.) 1983, N.J. 1985, U.S. Dist. Ct. N.J. 1986. Various positions with ins. cos. Chgo., 1965-68, Kansas City, Mo., 1968-70; assoc. Sullivan & Cromwell, N.Y.C., 1973-77, Forsyth, Decker, Murray and Hubbard, N.Y.C., 1977-79; ptnr. Hall, McNicol, Hamilton & Clark, N.Y.C., 1979-86; sr. litig. counsel CBS, 1986-88; assoc. gen. counsel, prin. Deloitte & Touche USA LLP, N.Y.C., 1988—. Contbr. articles to profl. jours., chpt. to supplements, publs. Mem. ABA (antitrust sect. 1979-90), Nat. Futures Assn. (panel of arbitrators 1985—), Assn. Bar City of N.Y. (prof. discipline com. 1983-86, antitrust and trade regulation com. 1988-91). Home: 140 W 86th St Apt 2B New York NY 10024-4067 Office: Deloitte & Touche USA LLP 1633 Broadway New York NY 10019-6708

MENTZ, LAWRENCE, lawyer; b. N.Y.C., Nov. 5, 1946; s. Joseph Walter and Audrey Cecilia (Armstrong) M.; m. Barbara Antonello, Nov. 10, 1973; children: Kathleen Elizabeth, Lawrence Goodwin. BS in Physics, Rensselaer Poly. Inst., 1968; JD, U. Notre Dame, 1973. Bar: N.Y. 1973; Washington 1974. Assoc. Condon & Forsyth, N.Y.C., 1973-80, ptnr., 1981-89; ptnr. Biedermann, Hoenig, Massamillo & Ruff, N.Y.C., 1990—; counsellor at law; speaker Worldwide Airlines Customer Rels. Assn. Conf., Singapore, 1983, 2d Cir. Speakers Bur., Com. on BiCentennial of U.S. Constn., 1987; arbitrator U.S. Dist. Ct. (ea. dist.) Bklyn., 1986—. With USNR, 1969-70. Mem. ABA, Fed. Bar Coun., N.Y. State Bar Assn. (exec. com. sect. on comml. and fed. litigation, fed. judiciary com., 1993, com. Supreme Cts.), Assn. of Bar of City of N.Y. (com. on aeronautics law, task force on N.Y. Constl. Conv., com. on state legis.), Wings Club. Roman Catholic. Avocations: swimming, running, philately. Office: Biedermann Hoenig Massamillo & Ruff 90 Park Ave New York NY 10016-1301

MENTZEL, THOMAS DIETRICH WILHELM, histopathologist; b. Saalfeld, Germany, May 25, 1962; s. Hans Martin and Rosemarie (Bartnick) M.; m. Kirstin Beleites, Sept. 30, 1995. Diploma in medicine, U. Jena, Germany, 1989, MD, 1990. Cert. pathologist. Resident in surgical pathology U. Jena, Germany, 1989-95, sr. lectr. dept. pathology, 1996-99; sr. lectr. dept. dermatopathology U. Friedrichshafen, Germany, 1999—; postdoctoral fellow, London, 1992-94, Boston, 1996; mem. edn. com. German divsn. Internat. Acad. Pathology, 1997—. Contbr. articles to profl. jours. Roman Catholic. Avocations: choral and chamber choir singing. E-mail: tmentzel@w-4.de. Office: Dept Dermatopathology, D-88048 Friedrichshafen Germany

MENTZELOPOULOS, SPYROS DENNIS, anesthesiologist, researcher; b. Athens, Greece, Nov. 21, 1964; s. Dennis Spyros and Eleni Gerassimos (Minettos) M. MD, Med. Sch. of Athens, 1992. Med. diplomate. Mil. dr. Greek Infantry, Athens, 1992-93, resident in psychiatry, 1993-94; cmty. dr. Greek Ministry of Health Ag., Nikolaos, Greece, 1994-95; resident in pulmonology Greek Ministry of Health, Iraklion, Greece, 1995-96; resident in anesthesiology Greek Ministry of Health, Athens, 1996-99; rsch. assoc. Eqion General Hosp., Egion, Greece, 1998-99. Author: Combined Techniques of Airway Mangagement, 1998, New Technique of Difficult Airway Management, 1999, New Technique of Airway Management in Tracheal Resection, 1999. Recipient Second Best Free Paper award European Soc. Regional Anaesthesia, Athens, 1998. Mem. N.Y. Acad. Scis. Avocations: chess, billiards. Home: 2A Kypseli St, 11362 Athens Greece

MENU, JEAN-CHRISTOPHE, publisher; b. Amiens, Somme, France, Aug. 23, 1964; s. Edouard and Bernadette (Mangin) M.; m. Jeanne Valerie, 1988; children: Séraphine, Ophēlie, Raphaëlle, Thēophile. BA, Lycee La Bruyere, Versailles, 1982; MA, Paris I, Sorbonne, 1988, DEA in Arts Plastiques, 1989. Foundator Edn. L'Assn., Paris, 1990—. Author: Meder, 1988, Livret de Phamille, 1995 (Nominated Best Album of Yr., Angoulême 1996), Gnognottes, 1999, others.

MENZEL, JIŘI, film director; b. Prague, Czechoslovakia, Feb. 23, 1938; s. Josef and Bozena Menzel. Specialized in film directing, Film Acad. of Performing Arts, 1957-61. Film dir. and actor, 1962—; head of dept. of film directing Film Acad. of Performing Arts, Prague, 1990-92; prodr. Studio 89, 1991-98; artistic dir. Theater on Vinohrady, Prague, 2000—. Dir.: (films) Pearls of the Deep, 1965, Crime at a Girl's School, 1965, Closely Watched Trains, 1966 (Best Fgn. Lang. Film Acad. award), Capricious Summer, 1968, Crime in a Night Club, 1968, Larks on a String, 1969, Who Looks for Gold?, 1974, Seclusion Near a Forest, 1976, Those Wonderful Men with a Crank, 1978, Short Cut, 1980, The Snowdrop Festival, My Sweet Little Village, 1986, The End of Old Times, 1989, The Beggar's Opera, 1991, The Life and Extraordinary Adventures of Private Ivan Chonkin, 1994.

MENZEL, WILLIAM CLARENCE, JR., nuclear engineer; b. Chgo., July 17, 1942; s. William Clarence and Iris Johnston M.; m. Margaret Ann Lagle, Apr. 3, 1964 (div. June 1977); children: Kimberly Menzel Bramlett, William Edward, Timothy Ian; m. Constance Ellen Carter, Mar. 27, 1992. BS in Math., U. Montevallo, 1965. Sr. field engr. reliability & quality assurance Bendix Launch Support Divsn., Kennedy Space Ctr., Fla., 1967-77; engr. quality assurance Rockwell Internat., Kennedy Space Ctr., Fla., 1977; mgr. supplier evaluation program Tenn. Valley Authority, Knoxville, TN, 1977-80; Tenn. Valley Authority, Chattanooga, TN, 1981-94; supr. vendor audits Brown & Root, Houston, TX, 1980-81; cons. nuclear engr., 1994—. vol. fireman Bellwood (Fla.) Vol. Fire Dept., 1972-73, vol. fire chief, 1973-74; coach Shirley Temple Softball, Titusville, Fla., 1975. With U.S. Army Rserve, 1961-67. Baptist. Avocations: reading, water sports. Home and Office: 2613 Hills Chapel Rd Dandridge TN 37725-6809

MENZIES, JAMES IAN, retired science educator; b. London, May 2, 1928; s. John and Margaret (Maxton) M.; m. Ann Ronald, Aug. 15, 1962. BSc, U. London, 1955, MSc, 1960. Edn. officer Govt. of Sierra Leone, 1956-62; lectr. U. Ife, Nigeria, 1963-67; prof. Nat. U. Lesotho, 1978-82; curator Nat. Mus. Papua New Guinea, 1982-87; sr. lectr. sci. U. Papua New Guinea, University P.O., 1968-77, assoc. prof., 1988-99, environ. cons., 1988-99; ret., 1999. Author: Handbook of New Guinea Frogs, 1976, Handbook of New Guinea Marsupials and Monotremes, 1991, Flora of Motupure Island (jointly with H. Fortune), 1996; editor Sci. in New Guinea, 1987—; contbr. articles to sci. jours. Avocations: ceramics, painting, woodwork. Home: 5 Oatlands Dr, Paignton TQ4 5JL, England Office: U Papua New Guinea, Box 320, University PO Papua New Guinea

MENZIES, MARGARET ANNE, aerospace engineer; b. Cin., May 8, 1963; d. James Harley and Patricia (Socrates) M. BS in Naval Arch., U.S. Naval Acad., 1985; MS in Mech. Engring., Naval Postgrad. Sch., 1991; PhD in Aerospace Engring., Old Dominion U., 1996. Grad. rsch. asst. Old Dominion U., Norfolk, Va., 1993-96; aerospace engr. Avionics Specialties, Inc., Charlottesville, Va., 1996—. Mem. Chesapeake Bay Found., Norfolk. Lt. USN, 1981-92. Recipient N.Am. Rsch. Soc. award Sigma Xi, 1996; named Outstanding Young Women of Am.; Va. Space Grant Consortium fellow, 1993-95; Coll. of Engring. fellow, 1994-96. Mem. AIAA. Avocations: sailing, skiing, biking. Achievements include patents on improvements to multifunction aircraft probes; aircraft probe with integral air temperature sensor. Home: 183 Spring Oaks Ln Ruckersville VA 22968-3643 Office: Avionics Specialties Inc PO Box 6400 Charlottesville VA 22906-6400

MENZINGER, GUIDO, endocrinology educator; b. Perugia, Italy, Feb. 12, 1934; s. Carlo and Sylvia (Jucker) M.; m. Anna Carusi, 1967; children: Guilio, Sara, Constanza. MD, Rome, 1958. Asst. prof. med. clin. U. Rome, 1960-80; prof. U. Naples, Italy, 1980-83; prof. tor vergata metabolism U. Rome, 1983, prof. endocrinology, 1990—. Fellow Royal Coll. Physicians; mem. Romanian Soc. Nutrition-Diabetes (hon.). Avocations: history of gardens, classical music, walking. Home: Via Bormida 1, 00198 Rome Italy Office: U Rome Vergata, Div Metabolica Via Moscati, 00168 Rome Italy

MER, FRANCIS PAUL, steel executive; b. Pau, Basses-Pyrénées, France, May 25, 1939; s. René and Yvonne (Casalta) M.; m. Catherine Bonfils, July 6, 1964; children: Grégoria, Suzanne, Renée. Student, École Polytech.; diploma, Sch. Mines; degree in econs. Engr. mining corps. Mining engr. directorate mines Min. Industry Govt. France, 1966; tech. cons. guarantees, Coun. Agreements Govt. France, Abidjan, 1967-68; dep. office sec. gen. interministerial com. on questions European econ. coop. Govt. France, 1969-70; head planning Saint-Gobain Industries, 1971, dir. planning, 1973, dir. gen.; dir. planning Compagnie Saint-Gobain-Pont-à-Mousson, 1973, asst. dir. gen., 1978-82; pres., chmn. Pont-à-Mousson s.A., 1982-86; dir. divsn. canalisations and mechanics Group Saint-Gobain, 1982-86; chmn., CEO USINOR, 1986—. Decorated chevalier Legion of Honor, officer Nat. Order Merit (France). Mem. Fedn. Française de l'Acier (pres.), Assn. Nationale de la Recherche Technique (pres. 1991—), Ctr. d'Etudes et d'Informations Internationales (pres. 1995—). Home: 9 rue Bobierre-de-Vallière, 92340 Bourg-la-Reine France Office: Grp Usinor Pacific TSA, 11-13 Cours Valmy La Defense 7, 92070 Puteaux La Defense Cedex, France*

MERA, IBRAHIM KHALIL, oil company exeucutive; b. Suez, Egypt, Dec. 28, 1942; s. Khalil Ibrahim and Bahia Mohamed (Mogaze) M.; m. Hoda Abdelsamee Elsebae, Oct. 1, 1972; children: Ahmed, Dalia, Samaa. BSME, Cairo U., 1964, diploma in Prodn. Mgmt. and Orgn., 1992, diploma in Mgmt., 1994. Mgr. Shokir (Eqypt) sector Petroleum Pipelines Co., 1983-84; mgr. projects sector Petroleum Pipelines Co., Suez, 1984-87, mgr. op. sector, gen. mgr. Suez region, 1987-96; gen. mgr. planning and computer dept. Petroleum Pipelines Co., Cairo, 1996-99, gen. mgr. Cairo region, 1999—. Mgr. Egyptian Wrestling Fedn., Suez, 1991; sub. mgr. Horus Social Soc., Egypt, 1994; mem. El Watany Party, Suez, 1982. Gen. maj. Egyptian Army, 1964-79. Mem. Egyptian El Seid Club, Egyptian Army Club, Suez Club. Home: 11 El Tahrer St Dokky, Cairo Egypt Office: PP Co, PO Box 1104, Cairo Egypt

MERAB, JULIE ATIENO, administrator; b. Nairobi, Kenya, Nov. 4, 1950; d. David Macmillan and Mary Gladys (Kasuku) Odera; 1 child, Avril Adoncia. Grad., Temple Secretarial Coll., Nairobi, 1969, Regent Inst., London, 1972, U. Droit d'Economie Et Scis., Aix en Provence, France, 1983. Personal asst. to sec. gen. East African Legis. Assembly East African Cmty., Arusha, Tanzania, 1970; pers. asst., dir. E.A. Meteorol. Dept. East African Cmty., Nairobi, 1971-75; adminstrv. asst. UNESCO, Nairobi, 1976—. Recipient cert. UNESCO Secretariat, Paris, 1976. Mem. Internat. Assn. for Children Internat. Summer Villages (life), Kenya Mus. Soc. Anglican. Avocations: reading, swimming, music, cookery, dancing. Home: PO Box 14185, Nairobi Kenya Office: UNESCO, PO Box 30592, Nairobi Kenya

MERAFHE, MOMPATI S., Botswana government official; b. Serowe, June 6, 1936; married; 5 children. Student, Khama Meml. Sch., 1954-59, Internat. Sch. Careers, 1962-64, U.K., 1969, 72; B of Law, U. South Africa. Police officer, dep. commr., 1960-77, dept. commr. police, 1973-77, army commdr., 1977-90; min. presdl. affairs Govt. Botswana, Gaborone, 1990-94, min. fgn. affairs, 1994—. Chmn. Botswana Nat. Sports Coun., 1980-89, Botswana Nat. Olympic Com., 1980-89; exec. com. mem. Assn. Nat. Olympic Coms. of Africa representing southern Africa, 1984-89, pres. 1987-89; pres. Botswana Amateur Athletics Assn., 1978-80; patron BDF Tennis Club, BDF XI Football Club, Botswana Family Welfare Assn., Botswana amateur Athletics Assn., Miscellaneous Sporting Club, Serowe, Gaborone Choral Choir. Office: Min Fgn Affairs, Pvt Bag 00368, Gaborone Botswana*

MÉRAL, JEAN, educator; b. St. Maurin, France, Oct. 19, 1934; s. Joseph Henri and Yvonne Jeanne (Martory) M.; m. Régine Vincente Beau, Aug. 28, 1968; 1 child, Jean-Laurent. BA, MA, Univ. Toulouse, France, 1958; PhD, Mich. State, 1965; D, Paris III Sorbonne, Paris, 1980; Agregation, 1967. Instr. Mich. State Univ., Lansing, 1962-64; asst. prof. U. Western Ontario, London, Can., 1964-66, McGill Univ., Montreal, Can., 1966-68; asst., prof. Toulouse Univ., Toulouse, France, 1968-83, prof., 1983-97, prof. emeritus, 1997—; chmn. English dept. Toulouse, 1985-88, UFR English Studies, 1994-95; vis. prof. Agnes Scott Coll., Decatur, 1977, Ohio U., Athens, Ohio, 1992. Author: Paris dans la Littérature Americaine, 1983, Paris In American Literature, 1989. With Nato Interpreter, 1961-62. Recipient Chevalier des Palmes Académiques French Min. of Edn., 1986, Officier des Palmes Académiques French Ministry of Edn., 1993. Avocation: sailing. Home: 3 Ave St Exupéry, 31820 Pibrac France Office: Univ de Toulouse Le Mirail, 31058 Toulouse-Cedex France

MERCADO, MARY GONZALES, cardiologist; b. Houston, July 9, 1959; d. Frank Reyes and Joyce (Byrd) Gonzales; m. Antonio Gonzalez Mercado, May 25, 1985. BS magna cum laude, U. Tex., San Antonio, 1987; MD with honors, Baylor Coll. of Medicine, 1992. Diplomate Am. Bd. Internal Medicine, Am. Bd. Cardiovascular Diseases. Intern U. Tex. Affiliated Hosps., San Antonio, 1992-93, resident, 1993-95, chief resident, 1995-96, fellow in cardiology, 1996-99; presenter confs. and symposiums. Contbr. articles to med. publs. Mem. AMA, Am. Soc. Echocardiography, Am. Coll. Cardiology, Am. Soc. Nuc. Cardiology, Tex. Med. Assn., Bexar County Med. Soc. Office: Ctrl Cardiovasc Inst 927 Mccullough San Antonio TX 78215-1630

MERCADO-BOSCH, MARIA CARMEN, pediatrician; b. Rio Piedras, P.R., Nov. 6, 1939; d. Clodomiro Mercado and Antonia Bosch. MD, U. Barcelona, 1963, Pediatrician, 1966, Sport's Medicine Physician, 1970; Nutritionist, Health/Social Security Dept., Barcelona, 1979. Gen. practitioner Spanish Health Inst., Barcelona, 1966-68, pediatrician, 1968-78; sport's medicine physician Sport's Gen. Dept., Barcelona, 1970—, sophrologist, 1975—; pediatrician Spanish TV, Barcelona, 1975—, Catalonian Health Inst., Barcelona, 1978—; lectr. U. Barcelona, 1988-96, Catalonian Sch. of Sports, Barcelona, 1981-83, Nat. Inst. pf Phys. Edn., Barcelona, 1981-84, U. Sch. of Sport's Medicine, Barcelona, 1988-96. Author: Emergency Paediatrics, 1967, We Can Live Better, 1987; co-author: Handbook of Children Sport's Aptitude, 1987; inventor: The Game of Health, 1991. Mem. Catalonian Pediatric Soc., Catalonian Sport's Medicine Soc. (charter mem.), Internat. Soc. for Advancement of Kinanthropometry. Roman Catholic. Avocations: playing piano, travel, book's collector, sport's practice. Office: Barcelona Sports Med Ctr, Passatge Permanyer 3, 08009 Barcelona Spain

MERCAU SAAVEDRA, ANDRES JUAN, lawyer; b. Buenos Aires, Argentina, Mar. 30, 1965; s. Eduardo and Maria Justa (Gonzalez Victorica) Mercau S.; m. Silvana Santa Maria, Dec. 30, 1990; children: Tomas, Maria, Catalina. JD, U. Buenos Aires, 1988. Ptnr. Cueto Rua Landaburu & Lynch, Buenos Aires, 1988—; fgn. legal cons. Fox, Horan & Camerini, N.Y.C., 1996-97; officer Civil and Comml. Ct., San Isidro, Argentina, 1985-88; clk. Labor Ct., San Isidro, 1982-85. Mem. Buenos Aires Bar Assn., San Isidro Bar Assn. Roman Catholic. Avocations: soccer, squash, skiing, paddle tennis, water sports. Office: Cueto Rua Landaburu & Lynch, Cerrito 866 10th Fl C1010AAR, Buenos Aires Argentina

MERCE, ANA LUCIA, chemical engineer, educator; b. Rio de Janeiro, Jan. 9, 1960; d. Norton Bueno and Lygia Ramalho Merce; m. Mario Cesar Maia, July 12, 1986; 1 child, Rodrigo R. Merce Maia. Degree in Chem. Engring., U. Estado Rio de Janeiro, 1983; MS in Organic Chemistry, U. Fed. Rio de Janeiro, 1988; DSc in Analytical Chemistry, Pontificia U. Catolica, Rio de Janeiro, 1994. Cert. chem. engring. Chem. engr. Companhia de Pesquisa de Recursos Minerais-CPRM-DNPM, Rio de Janeiro, 1984-90; prof. U. Fed. do Parana, Curitiba, Brazil, 1992—; cons. Companhia de Pesquisa de Recursos Minerais-CETEM-DNPM, Rio de Janeiro, 1984-86, Petrosix-Petrobras, Sao Mateus do Sul, 1998—. Contbr. articles to profl. jours. Avocations: swimming, bicycling, reading, working out at gym. E-mail: anamerce@quimica.ufpr.br. Fax: 55 41 263-3399. Home: Rua Almirante Tamandare, 1352-606, 80040110 Curitiba Brazil Office: U Fed do Parana, Dept Quimica Centro Politec, Curitiba 81531990, Brasil

MERCER, BETTY DEBORAH, electrologist, poet, writer, proofreader; b. N.Y.C., Sept. 10, 1926; d. Cecil Boyce and Martha (Romanoff) Fishbein; m. Frank Berthold Mercer, Dec. 22, 1957 (dec. Aug. 1979); children: Kenneth Arnold, Stephen Harry. BS, NYU, 1948; cert. in psychology, child guidance, vocat. guidance, Cornell U., 1951; cert. in libr. sci., Queens Coll., 1954, 55; cert., Hoffman Inst. Electrolysis, N.Y.C., 1955; cert. piano and honors theory II, Royal Conservatory of Music, Toronto, 1965. Cert. clin. electrologist. Pvt. tutor English N.Y.C., 1948, proofreader, copyholder various firms, 1951-54; freelance book reviewer Viking Press, N.Y.C., 1954; clin. electrologist, 1955—; pvt. tchr. piano Muskegon, Mich., 1967—; sales rep. Beauty Counselor and Studio Girl, Sudbury, Ont., Can., 1963-64, Blair Products, Muskegon, 1967-68, 78-80; chair Muskegon Writers, 1979-80; freelance proofreader, 1988, 89; invited Third Coast Writers Conf. Western Mich. U. Author: (poetry) Toward A Brighter Tomorrow!: A First Collection of Twenty-Seven Published Poems, 1980; contbr. poetry to anthologies Moments of Reflection, A Celebration of Poets, Love is an Awesome Thing, Treasured Poems of America, Serenity at Daybreak, The Blush of Morning, The Bright Horizon, Best Friends, Home Is Where the Heart Is, A Time to Be Free, Time Pieces, Mirrors of the Mind; contbr. to mags. including New Writers Mag., Time Pieces II, Poets at Work, Bardic Echoes, Poetry Plus. Leader Girl Guides, Sudbury,1958, local chpt. Girl Scouts U.S.A., Muskegon, 1967; libr., cart Sudbury Meml. Hosp., 1963-65; libr. Temple B'nai Israel, Muskegon,1969-78; vol. Hospice Respite Svc., Muskegon, 1989; chairperson Jewish Nat. Fund, Muskegon Hadassah, 1971-72. Recipient Silver Poet award, 5 Golden Poet awards, 10 Merit awards World of Poetry, Sacramento, 1984—, Editors Choice award Nat. Library Poetry, Owings Mills, Md., 1988, 89, Poet of Yr. award Nat. Poetry Pubs. Assn., L.I., N.Y., 1974, 76, Bronze cert. Creative Enterprises, Carson City, Nev., 1986, 87, 5th pl. prize Poetry Unltd., 1991, cert. Poetic Achievement Amherst Soc. Fellow World Lit. Assn.; mem. AAUW (publicity com. 1987-88, membership com. 1985-86), Internat. Soc. Poets (disting. mem.), Clover Internat. Poetry Assn. (life, DANAE title cert. 1974-75), Am. Electrology Assn., Internat. Guild Profl. Electrologists, Region II Electrolysis Assn., Internat. Platform Assn., NYU Alumni Assn., Muskegon Writers, Poetry Soc. of Mich., Hadassah Women's Zionist Orgn. (life), NYU Club, Mich. Electrolysis Assn. Jewish. Avocations: piano, crafts, needlework, art, reading. Home: 1422 New St Muskegon MI 49442-5372

MERCER, JAMES LEE, management consultant; b. Sayre, Okla., Nov. 7, 1936; s. Fred Elmo and Ora Lee (Davidson) M.; m. Karolyn Lois Prince, Nov. 16, 1962; children: Tara Lee, James Lee. BS, U. Nev., 1964, MBA, 1966; postgrad. exec. devel. program, Cornell U., 1979. Cert. in mcpl. adminstrn. U. N.C., 1971; cert. mgmt. cons. Methods and results supr. Pacific Tel. & Tel., Sacramento, 1965-66; prodn. control supr. Gen. Dynamics, Pomona, Calif., 1966-67; nuclear submarine project mgr. Litton Industries, Pascagoula, Miss., 1967-70; asst. city mgr. City of Raleigh, N.C., 1970-73; nat. program dir. Pub. Tech., Inc., Washington, 1973-76; gen. mgr. Battelle So. Ops., Atlanta, 1976-79; v.p. Korn/Ferry Internat., Atlanta, 1979-81; pres. James Mercer & Assocs. Inc.; mgmt. cons. Atlanta, 1981-86; chief Indsl. Ext. Divsn., Ga. Inst. of Tech., Atlanta, 1981-83; dir. govtl. cons. svc. Coopers & Lybrand, 1983-84; regional v.p. Wolfe & Assocs., Inc., 1984-86; pres., CEO, chmn. Mercer, Slavin & Nevins, Inc., 1986-90, The Mercer Group, Inc., 1990—; ad hoc prof. N.C. State U., 1972-73; bd. dirs. Taratec Corp., Columbus. Author: Public Management Systems, 1978, Public Technology, 1981, Managing Urban Government Services, 1981, Strategic Planning for Public Managers, 1990, Public Management in Lean Years, 1992; contbr. numerous articles to profl. jours. Chmn. Raleigh Mayor's Civic Ctr. Authority Study Commn., 1971; founding bd. dirs. Mordecai Sq. Hist. Soc., Nat. Civic League; founding mem. U. S.C. Master of Pub. Adminstrn. adv. bd., 1987-97; founding mem. Calif. Poly. State U., adv. coun. Coll. of Bus. Adminstrn., San Luis Obispo, 1980-95; lectr., pub. spkr.; founding mem., bd. trustees U. Nev. Found., Reno, 1985-91. With USN, 1955-59. Mem. Internat. City Mgmt. Assn., Am. Soc. Pub. Adminstrn., Am. Inst. Indsl. Engrs. (past pres.'s award 1970, pres. chpt. 1969-70), Tech. Transfer Soc. (dir. 1978-87, treas. 1985-86), Ga. Indsl. Devel. Assn., U. Nev. Alumni Assn. (exec. com. 1969-79), Atlanta C. of C., Rotary, Masons, Shriners, Contract Svcs. Assocs. of Am. (bd. dirs. 1994—). Home: 28 Sierra del Sol Santa Fe NM 87505-2136 Office: 551 W Cordova Rd Ste 726 Santa Fe NM 87501-4100

MERCHANT, CAROLYN, environmental history educator; b. Rochester, N.Y., July 12, 1936; d. George Eugene and Elizabeth Merchant; m. Hugh Iltis, Aug. 5, 1961 (div.); children: David Iltis, John Iltis; m. Charles Grier Sellers, Sept. 5, 1993. AB, Vassar Coll., 1958; MA, U. Wis., 1962, PhD, 1967; D (hon.), Umeå (Sweden) U., 1995. From asst. to assoc. prof. U. San Francisco, 1969-78; from asst. prof. to prof. U. Calif., Berkeley, 1979—; chancellor's prof. environ. history, philosophy and ethics, former chair dept. conservation and resource studies U. Calif., Berkeley; vis. prof. Ecole Normale Superieure, Paris, 1986; vis. fellow Sch. Social Scis., Murdoch U., Perth, Australia, 1991; lectr., cons. in field. Author: The Death of Nature: Women, Ecology and the Scientific Revolution, 1980, 2d edit., 1990 (also Japanese, German, Italian, Swedish and Chinese edits.), Ecological Revolutions: Nature, Gender and Science in New England, 1989, Radical Ecology: The Search for a Livable World, 1992 (also Japanese edit.), Earthcare: Women and the Environment, 1996; editor, contbg. author: Major Problems in American Environmental History: Documents and Essays, 1993, Key Concepts in Critical Theory: Ecology, 1994, Green Versus Gold: Sources in California's Environmental History, 1998; contbr. numerous articles to profl. jours. Fellow Am. Coun. Learned Socs., 1978, Ctr. for Advanced Study in the Behavioral Scis., 1978, John Simon Guggenheim fellow, 1995; Fulbright sr. scholar, 1984; grantee NEH, 1977, 1981-83, NSF, 1976-78, Nathan Cummings Found., 1992, Calif. Coun. for the Humanities, 1997-98. Office: Dept Environ Sci Policy and Mgmt U Calif 207 Giannini Hall Berkeley CA 94720-3310

MERCHANT, ISMAIL NOORMOHAMED, film producer and director; b. Bombay, Dec. 25, 1936; arrived in U.S., 1958; s. Noormohamed and Hazrabi (Memon) Rehman. BA, St. Xavier's Coll., Bombay, 1958; MBA, NYU, 1960. V.p. Merchant Ivory Prodns. Inc., N.Y.C., 1962—. Prodr.: (films) The Householder, 1963, Shakespeare Wallah, 1965, The Guru, 1969, Bombay Talkie, 1970, Adventures of a Brown Man in Search of Civilization, 1971, Savages, 1972, Helen, Queen of the Nautch Girls, 1973, Autobiography of a Princess, 1975, The Wild Party, 1975, Sweet Sounds, 1976, Roseland, 1977, Hullabaloo Over Georgie and Bonnie's Pictures, 1978, The Europeans, 1979, The Five-Forty-Eight, 1979, Jane Austen in Manhattan, 1980, Quartet 1981, Heat and Dust, 1983, The Bostonians, 1984, A Room With A View, 1986, The Deceivers, 1988, Slaves of New York, 1988, Mr. and Mrs. Bridge, 1990, Howards End, 1992, The Remains of the Day, 1993, Jefferson in Paris, 1995, Surviving Picasso, 1996, A Soldier's Daughter Never Cries, 1998, The Golden Bowl, 2000; dir.: Creation of Woman, 1960, Mahatma and the Mad Boy, 1973, Feast of July, 1995, The Courtesans of Bombay, 1982, In Custody, 1993, The Proprietor, 1996, Cotton Mary, 1999; author: Ismail Merchant's Indian Cuisine, 1986, The Making of the Deceivers, 1988, Ismail Merchant's Vegetarian Cuisine, 1991, Ismail Merchant's Florence, 1993, Ismail Merchant's Passionate Meals: The New Indian Cuisine for Fearless Cooks and Adventurous Eaters, 1994, Once Upon A Time...The Proprietor, 1996, Ismail Merchant's Paris: Filming and Feasting in France, 1999. Decorated comdr. des Arts and Lettres (France). Home: 400 E 52nd St New York NY 10022-6404 Office: 250 W 57th St Ste 1825 New York NY 10107-1899

MERCHANT, ROLAND SAMUEL, SR., hospital administrator, educator; b. N.Y.C., Apr. 18, 1929; s. Samuel and Eleta (McLymont) M.; m. Audrey Bartley, June 6, 1970; children: Orelia Eleta, Roland Samuel, Huey Bartley. BA, NYU, 1957, MA, 1960; MS, Columbia U., 1963, MSHA, 1974. Asst. statistician N.Y.C. Dept. Health, 1957-60, statistician, 1960-63; statistician N.Y. Tb and Health Assn., N.Y.C., 1963-65; biostatistician, adminstrv. coord. Inst. Surg. Studies, Montefiore Hosp., Bronx, N.Y., 1965-72; resident in adminstrn. Roosevelt Hosp., N.Y.C., 1973-74; dir. health and hosp. mgmt. Dept. Health, City of N.Y., 1974-76; from asst. adminstr. to adminstr. West Adams Cmty. Hosp., L.A., 1976; spl. asst. to assoc. v.p. for med. affairs Stanford U. Hosp., Calif., 1977-82, dir. office mgmt. and strategic planning, 1982-85, dir. mgmt. planning, 1986-90; v.p. strategic planning Cedars-Sinai Med. Ctr., L.A., 1990-94; cons. Roland Merchant & Assocs., L.A., 1994—; clin. assoc. prof. dept. family, community and preventive medicine Stanford U., 1986-88, dept. health rsch. and policy Stanford U. Med. Sch., 1988-90. With U.S. Army. 1951-53. USPHS fellow. Fellow Am. Coll. Healthcare Execs., APHA; mem. Am. Hosp. Assn., Nat. Assn. Health Svcs. Execs., N.Y. Acad. Scis. Home: 27335 Park Vista Rd Agoura Hills CA 91301-3639

MERCHANT, RUTH NELMS, retired accountant; b. West Palm Beach, Fla., Feb. 17, 1930; d. Fredrick William and Anna Spader (DuBois) N.; m. James Brady Budesheim, June 19, 1949 (div. Oct. 1970); children: Deborah Anne, Mary Louise; m. Lloyd Keith Merchant, Sept. 10, 1978. Student, Fla. State U., 1947-49, Palm Beach Jr. Coll., 1972-73; BBA, Fla. Atlantic U., 1979. CPA, Fla. Sec.-treas. Union Congl. Ch., West Palm Beach, Fla., 1967-70; internal bookkeeper Coopers & Lybrand, Palm Beach, Fla., 1970-73; CPA Cherry, Bekaert & Holland, West Palm Beach, 1973-87; pvt. practice West Palm Beach, 1987—. Vol. tchrs. aide/asst. Berkshire Elem. Sch.; vol. VA Med. Ctr.-West Palm Beach; trustee, treas., registrar, fin. sec., ch. clk., deaconess, mem. various coms. Union Congl. Ch., West Palm Beach; day camp supr., day camp leader, first aider, leader jr. and brownie troops Girls Scouts Am.; local unit pres., various coms. PTA; participant Christmas in April, Habitat for Humanity. Mem. Am. Legion Aux. (treas., pres., membership chmn. unit 12). Avocations: volunteering, traveling, sewing. Home: 2534 Boundbrook Dr S Apt 116 West Palm Beach FL 33406-8683

MERCHES, IOAN, physicist, educator; b. Campulung, Moldova, Romania, Apr. 16, 1937; s. Octavian and Iulia (Stefureac) M.; m. Dorina Anghelutza, July 13, 1963; 1 child, Oana Roberts. Licentiate, U. Iasi, Romania, 1959; PhD in Physics, U. Cluj, Romania, 1970. Tchr. high sch. Botosani, Romania, 1959-61; asst. Dept. Physics, Ai Cuza U., Iasi, 1961-67, lectr., 1967-74, asst. prof., 1974-92, prof. physics, chair dept. theoretical physics, 1992—. Author: Applied Analytical Mechanics, 1995, 8 textbooks; contbr. articles to profl. jours. Grantee Fulbright Found., 1968-69, 1992-93, Brit. Coun., 1972. Mem. N.Y. Acad. Scis., Romanian Soc. Gravitation, Phi Beta Delta. Orthodox. Avocations: jogging, driving, reading. Home: Ciurchi nr 105 Bl F5, Scara E Etaj 2 Apt 1, 6600 Iasi Romania Office: Alex Ioan Cuza Univ, Bulev Copou nr 11, 6600 Iasi Romania

MERCIECA, JOSEPH, archbishop; b. Victoria, Gozo, Malta, Nov. 12, 1928; s. Saverio and Giovanna (Vassallo) M. Ordained priest Roman Cath. Ch., 1952. Rector Gozo Sem., 1958-69; judge Roman Rota, Rome, 1969-74; aux. bishop of Malta, 1974-76, archbishop of Malta, 1976—; mem. Apostolic Segnatura, Rome, 1991—. Home: Archbishop's Palace, Mdina Malta Office: Archbishop's Curia, PO Box 29, Valletta Malta

MERCIER, CLAUDE PAUL, vascular surgeon, educator; b. Lyon, France, Nov. 7, 1932; s. Jean and Suzanne (de Bouillanne) M.; m. Christine Thevenot, Mar. 30, 1964; children: Frederic, Vincent. MD, Faculté de Medicine, 1956. Intern hosps. Marseilles, France, 1956-63; chief clinic Faculty of Medicine, Marseilles, 1963, prof. vascular surgery, 1970—; pres. U. Aix-Marseille, 1989-94. Author: Deep Venous Thrombosis, 1973, Thoracic Outlet Syndrome, 1979. Pres. Med. Com. Hosps., Marseille, 1988. Named Officer Ordre Nat. du Merite, 1991. Mem. Acad. de Chirurgie, Internat. Soc. Vascular Surgery, Internat. Soc. Surgery, Rotary (gov. 2000—). Roman Catholic. Avocation: golf. Home: 12 rue de Comdt Rolland, 13008 Marseille France

MERCURIO, ANTONINO MARCO, anthropologist, philosophy educator; b. Nov. 8, 1930; s. Paolo and Maria (Urso) M.; m. Paola Sensini, Dec. 28, 1974. Doctor in Classical Literature, State U. Messina, 1958; Lic. in Philosophy, Jesuit Faculty of Messina, 1953; Doctor in Theology, Cath. U. Paris, 1964. Prof. theology Gregorian Pontifical U., Rome, 1969-70; founder, dir. Inst. Analytical Psychotherapy, Rome, 1970—, Inst. Existential Anthropology; founder, pres. Associazione Psicoterapeuti Italiana, Rome, 1974-78; founder, rector Sophia U., Rome, 1978—; founder Sophia U., Geneva, 1980, Sophia U., Brussels, 1981, Sophia U., Paris, 1984, European Ctr. Research in Life as a Masterpiece of Art, 1986; sci. supr. several insts. psychotherapy, Italy, 1974—; founder, dir. Internat. Weeks of Sophia-Analysis, Geneva, 1981—, Paris, 1984—, Intelligent Weekends of Sophia-Art, Rome, 1987—, Internat. Meetings of Existential Anthropology, Assisi, 1987, Paris, 1989, Taranto, 1991, Lecce, 1993, Brussels, 1995, Internat. Weeks of Sophia-Art, Belgium, 1992, Lab. of Existential Anthropology, Rome, 1994, Lab. of Cosmo-Art, Rome, 1996. Author: Amore e Persona, 1976, Teoria della Persona, 1978, Amore Liberta e Colpa, 1980, La vita come opera d'arte, 1988, Antropologia Esistenziale e Metapsicologia Personalistica, 1992, Teoria Dell'Inconscio Esistenziale, 1995, Ricerca Corale Sulle Leggi Della Vita, 1995, La Vita Come Opera D'Arte e La Vita Come Dono Spiegate in 41 Films, 1995, Gli Ulissidi, 1997, La sophia-analisi e l'Edipo, 2000; founder, dir. sci. mag. Persona, 1978; inventor sophia-analysis, 1970; inventor sophia-art, 1987; inventor Olimpiadi Della Forza Amorosa, 1993; inventor cosmo-art, 1996; contbr. articles in field to profl. publs. Mem. European Assn. Humanistic Psychology (co-founder 1979). Home: 12 Via Pantanelle, 00043 Ciampino Rome Italy Office: 73 Via Potenza, 00043 Ciampino Rome Italy

MEREDITH, ARCHIBALD L., banker. Gov. Bank of Guyana. Office: Bank of Guyana, 1 Church St & Ave of Republic POB 1003, Georgetown Guyana*

MEREDITH, MERI HILL, reference librarian, educator; b. Riverside, Calif., May 30, 1943; d. William Beans and Marie Louise (Zantzinger) Hill; m. William Rinehardt Meredith, Mar. 17, 1970 (div.); children William Rinehardt III, Sarah Daingerfield Meredith. AB in French, George Washington U., Washington, 1967; MLS, Ind. U., 1980. Cataloger Ind. U., Bloomington, 1980-81; bus. libr. Cummins Engine Co., Columbus, Ind., 1981-88; pres. Info. and Comm. Rsch., Inc., Columbus, 1989-92; reference libr. Ohio State U. Bus. Libr., 1992—; bd. dirs. Sch. of Libr. and Info. Sci., Ind. U., Bloomington; pres., co-founder Ind. On-Line Users Group, Indpls. Mem. AAUP, Spl. Librs. Assn., Acad. Libr. Assn. of Ohio. Republican. Roman Catholic. Home: 1800 Lafayette Pl Apt A1 Columbus OH 43212-1609 Office: Ohio State U Bus Libr Raymond E Mason Hall 250 W Woodruff Ave Columbus OH 43210-1133

MERENDA, PETER FRANCIS, psychologist, emeritus educator; b. Everett, Mass., July 18, 1922; s. Frank and Sarah (Lino) M.; m. Rose Cafasso, Aug. 31, 1946; children: Anne, Rosemary, Pamela. BS, Tufts U., 1947, MA, 1948; CAS, Harvard U., 1951; PhD, U. Wis., 1957. Asst. prof. psychology U. R.I., Kingston, 1960-63, assoc. prof., 1963-65, assoc. dean Grad. Sch., 1965-68, univ. coord. rsch., prof., 1965-84, prof. emeritus, ret., 1985—; sr. psychologist W.V. Clarke Assocs., Providence, 1957-88, Pitts., 1988-97.

MERENDA, ROBERTO, surgeon; b. Caracas, Venezuela, Oct. 31, 1957; s. Paolo and Rosetta (Pezze) M. MD, Padua Sch. Medicine, Italy, 1982, diploma in Gen. Surgery, 1987, diploma in Pediatric Surgery, 1992. Assoc. prof. III Surg. Padua (Italy) Sch. Medicine, 1991—; cons. Liver Transplant Unit, 1st Gen. Surgery Inst., Padua Sch. Medicine, Italy. Author: Cancer of the Lung, 1989; contbr. articles to profl. jours. Mem. European Soc. for Organ Transplantation, European Liver Transplant Assn., Italian Soc. Chirurgia, Italian Soc. Organ Transplantation. Avocations: sailing, skiing. E-mail: surgeon@uxl.unipd.it. Fax: 00-39-49-8212254. Office: III Surg Clinic, 2 Giustiniani, 35100 Padua Italy

MERFELD, GERALD LYDON, artist; b. Des Moines, Feb. 19, 1936; m. Carol L. Fiser; 1 child, Elizabeth Ann. Studied with William Mosby, Chgo. Studio asst. Dean Cornwell; combat artist USN. Group exhbns. include Mass. Mus. of Fine Arts, Springfield, Smithsonian Inst., Audubon Artists, N.Y.C., Nat. Acad. of Western Art, others; represented in permanent collections Marietta Coll., USN Archives, John J. McDonough Collection of Am. Art, John Deere & Co. Bd. dirs. Frontier Pathway Scenic Byway, Colo., 1995-98. Recipient Gold Medal of Honor, Am. Artist Profl. League, 1989, Am. Artists Mag. award Knickerbocker Artists, 1989, 2 Gold medals Washington Sq. Exhibit, N.Y.S., Painting award Okal. Mus. of Art, 1975, Mainstreams Juror's award of Merit, Marietta Coll., 1976, Mainstreams award of Distinction, 1977, First prize Hope Show, 1980, First prize Butler Inst. of Am. Art. Office: Brookwood Gallery 2302 Muddy Rd Westcliffe CO 81252

MERGLER, H. KENT, investment counselor; b. Cin., July 1, 1940; s. Wilton Henry and Mildred Amelia (Pulliam) M.; m. Judith Anne Metgzer, Aug. 17, 1963; children: Stephen Kent, Timothy Alan, Kristin Lee. BBA with honors, U. Cin., 1963, MBA, 1964. CFA, C.I.C. Portfolio mgr. Scudder, Stevens & Clark, Cin., 1964-68; exec. v.p. Scudder, Stevens & Clark, Chgo., 1970-73; v.p. Gibralter Rsch. and Mgmt., Ft. Lauderdale, Fla., 1968-70; ptnr. Stein Roe & Farnham, Ft. Lauderdale, 1973-84; ptnr., pres., dir., prin. Stein Roe & Farnham, Inc., Chgo., 1984-91, also mem. exec. com.; pres. Stein Roe Investment Trust, Chgo.; mng. ptnr., chief investment officer Loomis, Sayles & Co., L.P., Palm Beach Gardens, Fla., 1992-2000; pres., dir., CEO Northstar Capital Mgmt., Inc., 2000—; arbitrator Nat. Assn. Security Dealers, Inc., 1976-82. Chmn. adminstrv. bd. Christ United Meth. Ch., Ft. Lauderdale, 1981-83; mem. fin. com. Kenilworth Union Ch., 1989-92, Broward Cmty. Found., 1999—, mem. investment com., 1992—, chmn., 1994-99, bd. dirs., 1994-99; mem. Martin County Econ. Coun., 1992-2000; bd. dirs. Pine Crest Prep. Sch., 1982-84, mem. bd. advisors, 1984-87; mem. corp. adv. bd. U. Cin. Coll. Bus. Adminstrn., 1991-94; bd. dirs. Hibiscus House Children's Found., 1993-99, chmn. investment com., 1994-99; bd. dirs. Coral Ridge Little League, 1976-84, pres., 1980-81. Mem. Fin. Analysts Soc. So. Fla. (bd. dirs. 1974-78, pres. 1975), Bond Club Ft. Lauderdale (bd. dirs. 1978-82), Willoughby Golf Club, Cullasaja Club (Highlands, N.C.), City Club Palm Beach, Beta Gamma Sigma. Republican. Home: 3980 SE Old Saint Lucie Blvd Stuart FL 34996-5119 Office: 4400 PGA Blvd Ste 600 Palm Beach Gardens FL 33410-6559

MERGNER, HANS KONRAD, zoology educator; b. Lemgo, Germany, May 8, 1917; s. Konrad Johannes and Luise Johanna (Tasche) M; m. Maria Theresia Zieger, July 16, 1933; children: Hans Joachim, Wolfgang Christian, Andreas. D in Natural Scis., U. Tübingen, Fed. Republic Germany, 1956. Researcher Max Planck Inst. Hirnforschung, Giessen, Fed. Republic Germany, 1956-58; from asst. to assoc. prof. Zool. Inst. U. Giessen, 1958-70; prof. Inst. Spezielle Zoologie, Bochum Ruhr U., Fed. Republic Germany, 1970-84, emeritus prof., 1984—; initiator Agaba Coral Reef Project, 1972—; sci. dir. UNESCO Course for Ecology of Red Sea and Adjacent Waters, Gardagha, Egypt, 1977; dean faculty biology Ruhr U., Bochum, 1974-75, 78. Author: Schlechter: Orchideen, 1970—, Reverberi: Experimental Embryology of Marine and Fresh-Water Invertebrates, 1971; author, editor: Mergner: Orchideenkunde, 1992; contbr. numerous articles on embryology of hydroids, brain anatomy, exptl. physiology of sponges and ecology of coral reefs to profl. jours. Maj. German mil., 1936-45, prisoner of war 1944-49, Russia. Mem. Internat. Soc. Reef Studies, Deutsche Zoologische Gesellschaft. Lutheran. Avocations: traveling, literature, painting, classical music. Home: Hansstrasse 1, 44797 Bochum Germany Office: Inst Spez Zoology Ruhr U, Universitatsstrasse 150, 44780 Bochum Germany

MERHAUT, JOSEF, electroacoustics educator; b. Prague, Czech Republic, Nov. 5, 1917; s. Vaclav and Marcela (Jansenova) M.; m. Bezouskova Merhaut, June 26, 1942 (div. 1951); 1 child, Jan; m. Kristkova Merhaut, Dec. 29, 1951. Degree engring., T.U., Prague, 1946, Doctor, 1959. Techniquer Telegrafia Co., Pardubice, Czech Republic, 1940-45; audioengr. Tesla Co., Prague, 1945-58; prof. T.U., Prague, 1958-90, ret., 1990; chmn. Internat. Electrotechnic Commn., Geneva, Switzerland, 1976-84, v.p., 1978-84. Author: Theory of Electroacoustics, 1981; contbr. articles to Jour. of Audioengring., 1982-90. Fellow Acoustical Soc. of Am.; mem. Audio Engring. Soc. of Am. Home: Dvouletky 341, 10000 Prague Czech Republic

MERI, LENNART, president of Estonia; b. Tallinn, Estonia, Mar. 29, 1929; s. Georg-Peeter and Alice-Brigitta (Engmann) M.; m. Helle Pihlak; children: Mart, Kristjan, Tuule. Grad. in History cum laude, Tartu U., 1953; DLitt (hon.), Helsinki U. Min. fgn. affairs Republic of Estonia, Tallinn, 1990-92, also mem. Coun. of Estonia, 1990-92; amb. to Finland, 1992; pres. Republic of Estonia, 1992—; hon. mem. bd. dirs. Acad. of Scis. and Arts in Europe; hon. mem. Writers Union Finland, 1982, head of Manuscript Sec Theatre Vanemuine, 1953-55. Scriptwriter and dir.: Tallinnfilm; editor: Estonian Radio; author: numerous travel stories and literary essays; author: (books) Silverwhite, Hobevalge, 1976, 1984, Approaching Coasts, 1977, others. Active Estonian Popular Front, Estonian Heritage Soc., 1980—. Decorated Order of the Renaissance (Jordan), Order of the Elephant (Denmark), Order of the White Rose (Finland), Royal Order of The Seraphim (Sweden), Order of The Aztec Eagle (Mex.), Grand Cross and Collar of the Order of Three Stars (Latvia), Order of Merit (Italy), Grand Cross Order of Merit (Hungary), Golden Order of Liberty (Slovenia), Order of Vytautas the Gt. (Lithuania), Order of White Eagle (Poland), Order of the Falcon (Iceland), grand cross Order of St. Olaf (Norway), Grand Cross Order of Redeemer (Greece); recipient Coudenhove-Kalergi European award, Coudenhove-Kalergi Found., 1996, East-West Freedom award Inst. for East-West Studies, N.Y., 1996, Crans-Montana Universal Forum Found. award, 1997, Silver medal Jagellonian U., Cracow, Poland, 1998. Mem. Estonian Writers' Union., Writer Union of Finland (hon.), Estonian Cinematographers Union, Internat. Coun. Meml. Found. for Victims of Communism, Inter-Parliamentary Coun. Against Antisemitism, others. Authority on the history of the Finno-Ugric peoples.

MERIC, RENE PIERRE, JR., shipbuilding marine construction executive; b. Ama, La., Sept. 21, 1925; s. Rene Pierre and Frances Elizabeth (Sellers) M.; m. Ruth Elizabeth Rasch Meric, Nov. 24, 1945 (widowed Dec. 3, 1991); children: Nancy, Ruth, Robin, R. Pierre III, Philip; m. Millicent Clesi Meric, May 22, 1993. BEE, Tulane U., New Orleans, 1947; student, LSUNO Grad. Sch., New Orleans, 1967. Profl. engr., La. Tech. asst. to price negotiator to ship supv. Todd Johnson Drydocks, Inc., New Orleans, La., 1947-51; floor broker Loop-Weaver & Co., 1951-55; project engr. Avondale Industries, Inc., New Orleans, La., 1955, chief engr., 1968, asst. v.p., 1969, v.p. contract adminstrn, 1972, group v.p. contract adminstrn., 1978, group v.p. indsl. divsn., 1985, group v.p. indsl. group, 1987, corp. v.p. indsl. group, 1990, corp. v.p. indsl./comml. group, 1992-98; retired, 1998—; cons. Avondale Industries, Inc., New Prleans, 1998-99. Avondale rep. Jr. Achievement, New Orleans, 1950. Mem. Soc. Naval Architects and Marine Engrs., Am. Bur. Shipping (Engring. Com. 1978-82), The Propeller Club, Navy League of the U.S., Sigma Alpha Epsilon. Republican. Roman Catholic. Avocations: real estate, home improvement, secondary residence, genealogy. Home: 5863 Marcia Ave New Orleans LA 70124-1121

MĚŘIČKA, JIŘÍ, electrical engineer, consultant; b. Plzeň, Bohemia, Czech Republic, Jan. 22, 1929; s. Josef and Marie (Henžlíková) M.; m. Marie Veselá, Aug. 8, 1956; children: Pavel, Petr. Degree in Elec. Engring., Czech Tech. U., Prague, 1952, Candidate of Sci., 1962. Asst. prof. Faculty Elec. Engring., Prague, 1952-64, assoc. prof., 1964-74, 91-94; dir. Rsch. Inst. for Engring. Edn., Prague, 1974-91; cons. Czech Tech. U., Prague, 1994—; vis. prof. U. Okla., Norman, 1966-67; liaison officer Ednl. Sci. & Cultural Orgn. UN—European Ctr. Higher Edn., Bucurest, Romania, 1976-90; mem. sci. coun. Czech Tech. U., Prague, 1991-94; mem. accreditation for requalification Com. of Ministry of Edn., Prague, 1991—. Co-author: Theory of the Generalized Electric Machine, 1974, Electric Machines, 1964, 94; co-editor: Visions and Strategies for Europe Vols. 1 and 2, 1994. Mem. Internat. Soc. for Engring. Edn. (pres. regional group 1992—, sec. nat. monitoring com. 1994—, Engring. Edn. award 1990, honorary mem. 1997), Elec. Engring. Soc. (hon.). Home: Na Spojce 7, 101 00 Prague 10, Czech Republic Office: Elec Engring Faculty, Technická 2, 16627 Prague 6, Czech Republic

MERIDITH, DENISE PATRICIA, government official; b. N.Y.C., Apr. 14, 1952; d. Glenarva C. and Dorothy (Sawyer) M. BS, Cornell U., 1973; MPA, U. So. Calif., 1993. Various positions Bur. Land Mgmt., various locations,

1973-79; chief divsn. resources Bur. Land Mgmt., Alexandria, Va., 1980-83; dep. state dir. Bur. Land Mgmt., Alexandria, 1983-86, Sante Fe, 1986-89; assoc. state dir. Bur. Land Mgmt., Sante Fe, Calif., 1989-91, state dir. Ea. states, 1991-93; dep. dir. BLM, Washington, 1993-95; state dir. Ariz., 1995—. Pres. Greater Phoenix Black C. of C., 1998-99; bd. dirs. Phoenix Black, Girl Scouts; mem. bd. trustees Cornell U. Recipient Ray Gildea Conservation award Soil Conservation Svc., 1972,, Meritorious Svc. award Dept. Interior, 1987, SBA Minority Bus. Vision 2000 award, 1999, Disting. Woman award, 2000; named Individual Minority Advocate of Yr., 1999. Mem. NAFE, Wildlife Soc. (cert.), Soc. Am. Foresters, Soc. Range Mgmt., Federally Employed Women. Avocations: photography, writing, art, movies, public speaking. Home: PO Box 7305 Phoenix AZ 85011-7305 Office: Bur Land Mgmt 222 N Central Ave Phoenix AZ 85004-2203

MERIKOSKI, JORMA KAARLO, mathematics educator; b. Helsinki, May 12, 1942; s. Antti Johannes Siimes and Ilona Marjatta Merikoski; m. Ulla Inkeri Kuhanen, Aug. 14, 1971; children: Marppa, Raisa, Tanja. MSc, U. Helsinki, 1964; PhLic, U. Jyväskylä, Finland, 1970; PhD, U. Tampere, Finland, 1976. Mathematician Finnish Cable Co., Helsinki, 1963-66; teaching asst. U. Helsinki, 1963-64; teaching asst. Tampere U. Tech., 1967, spl. tchr., 1974-75; lectr. math. U. Tampere, 1966—, docent, 1983—, head dept. math. sci., 1993-94, 96-98, assoc. prof., 1995—; vis. asst. prof. McGill U., Montreal, Que., Can., 1980; vis. rsch. fellow U. Coimbra, Portugal, 1985, Technion-Israel Inst. Tech., Haifa, 1988, Czechoslovak Acad. Scis., Prague, 1989, 93, 95. Co-author 34 math. textbooks for lower and upper secondary schs.; contbr. articles to math. jours. 2d lt. inf. Finnish Army, 1965. Mem. Internat. Linear Algebra Soc., Finnish Math. Soc., Am. Math. Soc., Soc. for Indsl. and Applied Math., European Math. Soc. Avocations: jogging, literature. Home: Ylisenkatu 3 B 16, FIN-33710 Tampere Finland Office: Dept Math Stats and Philos, U Tampere, FIN-33014 Tampere Finland

MERIMEE, JEAN-BERNARD, diplomat; b. Toulouse, France, 1936; married; 3 children. Grad., Inst. d'Etudes Politique, Paris, Ecole Nationale d'Adminstrn., Paris. Joined Fgn. Svc., 1965; from 2nd to 1st sec. French Embassy, London, 1966-72; head cooperation mission Côte d'Ivoire, 1975-78; head protocol French Govt., 1978-81; amb. to Australia, 1981-85, amb. to India, 1985-87, amb. to Morocco, 1987-91; permanent rep. of France UN, N.Y.C., 1991-95; amb. to Italy, 1995—; under-sec. gen., spl. advisor on European matters UN, N.Y.C., 1999—. Decorated officer Legion of Honor (France), officer Nat. Order of Merit (France). Office: UN Office Spokesman Sec-Gen UN S-378 New York NY 10017*

MERIN, SAUL CVI, ophthalmologist; b. Bedzin, Poland, Aug. 25, 1933; arrived in Israel, 1949; s. Isaac and Gitl (Grun) M.; m. Rachel Siton, May 28, 1958; children: Isaac, David Ofer, Guy. MD, Hebrew U., Jerusalem, 1960. Resident in ophthalmology Hadassah U. Hosp., Jerusalem, 1963-68, specialist in ophthalmology, 1968; fellow U. Toronto, 1970-71; sr. lectr. Hebrew U., Jerusalem, 1972-75, assoc. prof., 1975-79, prof. ophthalmology, 1979—; ophthalmic surgeon Queen Elizabeth Hosp., Blantyre, Malawi, 1965-67; head unit ophthalmology Hadassah Mt. Scopus, Jerusalem, 1979-98; vis. prof. U. Ill., Chgo., 1983-84. Author: Inherited Eye Diseases, 1991; contbr. over 100 articles to profl. jours. Chmn. Israel Bd. Ophthalmology, 1989-96. Lt. col. M.C., Israel Def. Forces. Recipient Oscar Hirsch prize Faculty of Medicine Jerusalem, 1960, Jacob Landau prize Sci. Coun. Israel, 1965; numerous rsch. grants, 1973-92. Mem. Israel Ophthalmol. Soc. (pres. 1976-82), Israel Soc. for Eye and Vision Rsch. (pres. 1985-90), Am. Acad. Ophthalmology. Jewish. Office: Hadassah U Hosp, PO Box 12079, 91120 Jerusalem Israel

MERINI, RAFIKA, foreign language and literature educator; b. Fès, Morocco; came to U.S., 1972; d. Mohamed and Fatima (Chraibi) M. BA in English cum laude, U. Utah, 1978, MA in Romance Langs. and Lits., 1981; postgrad., U. Wash., 1980-82; cert. in translation, SUNY, Binghamton, 1988, PhD in Comparative Lit., 1992. Tchg. asst. U. Utah, Salt Lake City, 1978-80, U. Wash., Seattle, 1980-82; adminstrv. asst., tchr. French, interpreter The Lang. Sch., Seattle, 1982-83; lectr. Pacific Luth. U., Tacoma, Wash., spring 1983; instr. Ft. Steilacoom C.C. (now Pierce C.C.), 1983-85; tchg. asst. dept. romance langs. SUNY, Binghamton, 1985-87, tchg. asst. women's studies dept., summer 1988, tchg. asst. comparative lit. dept., 1986-88; vis. instr. Union Coll., Schenectady, N.Y., 1988-89; vis. instr. dept. fgn. langs. and lits. Skidmore Coll., Saratoga Springs, N.Y., 1989-90; asst. prof. dept. fgn. langs. State Univ. Coll. (SUCB), Buffalo, 1990-96, assoc. prof. dept. fgn. langs., 1996—; coord. BSC women's studies interdiscipinary unit SUCB, Buffalo, 1993-99, adviser French Club, 1990-93. Author: Two Major Francophone Women Writers, Assia Djébar and Leila Sebbar: A Thematic Study of Their Works, 1999; contbr. articles to profl. pubs.; presenter at seminars, workshops, confs. Grantee Nat. Defense Student award U. Utah, 1974; also numerous other grants and awards. Mem. Modern Lang. Assn., Am. Assn. Tchrs. French, Women in French, Conseil Internat. d'Etudes Francophones, Pi Delta Phi, Soc. Hon. Française, Kappa Theta (hon.). Home: PO Box 1063 Buffalo NY 14213-7063 Office: State Univ Coll-Buffalo Dept Fgn Langs 1300 Elmwood Ave Buffalo NY 14222-1004

MERINO, FERNANDO, economist, researcher, educator; b. Alicante, Spain, Nov. 7, 1966; s. Cipriano and Esperanza (De Lucas) M. B in Econs., U. de Alicante, 1989; MSc in Econs., Ctr. Monetary and Fin. Study, Madrid, 1991. Econs. rschr. Fundacion Empresa Publica, Madrid, 1992—; assoc. prof. U. de Alcala, 1995—. Co-author: Las Empresas Industriales Espanolas, 1992, rev. edit., 1995::::; contbr. articles to profl. jours. including Strategic Mgmt. Jour., Barcelona Mgmt. Rev., The Econ. Jour. Office: Fundacion Empresa Publica, Ave Burgos 8B, E-28036 Madrid Spain

MERINO, PEDRO, chemist, researcher; b. Zaragoza, Aragon, Spain, Nov. 11, 1962; s. Pedro and Rosa (Filella) M.; m. Rosa Pilar Matute, July 7, 1995; children: Pedro, Javier. B, El Pilar Zaragoza, 1997; chemistry degree, U. Zaragoza, 1986, MSc, 1986, PhD, 1989. Fellow U. Zaragoza, Spain, 1986-89, U. Ferrara, Italy, 1989-91; asst. prof. U. Zaragoza, 1991-92, lectr., 1992—. Author: Organic Chemistry, 1997; contbr. chpt. in book and articles to profl. jours. Mem. Am. Chem. Soc., Internat. Soc. Heterocyclic Chemistry, Spanish Royal Soc. Chemistry. Avocations: cycling, tennis, swimming. Office: Univ Zaragoza Sci Dept Organic Chem Dept Sci Fac, Plza S Francisco S/N, E-50009 Zaragoza Aragon, Spain

MERISALO, OUTI KAIJA, romance philologist; b. Helsinki, Finland; s. Paavo Martti A. and Kaija Anita (Kolari) M. MA, U. Helsinki, Finland, 1981, lic. in Philosophy, 1982, PhD in Philosophy, 1988. Asst. in Latin Lang. and Roman Lit. U. Helsinki, Finland, 1981-82; rsch. asst. Acad. Finland, 1985-91; asst. in Romance Philology U. Helsinki, Finland, 1988-93; jr. rsch. fellow ad interim Acad. Finland, 1993-94; prof. Romance Philology U. Jyväskylä, Finland, 1994—. Author: La Langue et les Scribes, 1988, L Poggio Bracciolini, De Varietate Fortunae, 1993, Le collezioni medicee nel 1495, 1999; editor: Mare Balticum-Mare Nostrum, 1994, Actes du XIIIe Congrès des romantistes Scandinaves, 1998. Vice chair Jyväskylä Summer Festival, 1998—; mem. Com. Internat. Paléographie Latine, 2000—. Alexander von Humboldt Foundation scholar 1994, 97. Avocations: music, reading, travel. E-mail: merisalo@tukki.jyu.fi. Fax: 358-14-2601-401. Office: ILRC U Jyväskylä, PO Box 35, FIN40351 Jyväskylä Finland

MERKER, RICHARD J., economist, educator, consultant; b. Gelsenkirchen, Germany, July 27, 1964; s. Ludwig and Felizitas (Herx) M.; m. Bettina Verhoeven. Diploma, Ruhr U., 1991, DSc in Bus. Adminstrn., 1997. Rschr. in bus. adminstrn. & working econs. Inst. Applied Innovation Rsch., Bochum, Germany, 1991-93; rschr., lectr. Ruhr U., Bochum, 1993-95; rschr., lectr. Rsch. Ctr. Human Resources Devel., Bochum, 1995-97, CEO, 1997—; lectr. bus. adminstrn. & working econs. Ruhr U., 1997—. Author: The Organization of Small Business Enterprises, 1997. Mem. Assn. Working Scientists Bochum (v.p. 1995—), Friends of the Maple, Can. Club (pres.). Home: Bertastr 29, D-45883 Gelsenkirchen Germany Office: Ruhr U Bochum, Univeritaetstr 150 NB1/168, D-44780 Bochum Germany

MERKIN, DONALD H., internist; b. Bronx, N.Y., Nov. 12, 1945; s. Eugene and Hortense Ruth (Erdrich) M.; children: Daniel Hansen, Andrew David. BA, Parsons Coll., 1968; MS, Colo. State U., 1972; PhD, Cornell U., 1974; MD, U. Autonoma de Ciudad, Juarez, Mexico, 1978. Asst. prof. U. So. Colo., Pueblo, 1973-74, Bethel Sch. of Nursing, Colorado Springs, 1973-74, U. Colo., Colorado Springs, 1973-74, So. Ill. U. Sch. Medicine, Springfield, Ill., 1975-76; internist Westside Med. Assocs., Bradenton, Fla., 1982-84, pvt. practice, Sarasota, Fla., 1984-88, Superior (Wis.) Clinic, Ltd., 1989-91; internist Gulf Coast Ortho. Ctr.- Inst. for Spl. Surgery, Hudson, Fla., 1991-94, dir. orthopedic medicine, 1992-94; pvt. practice Internal Medicine Assocs. of Pasco County, Hudson, Fla., 1995-96; internist St. Luke's Cataract & Laser Inst., Tarpon Springs, Fla., 1998—; med. dir. Physicians Injury and Wellness Ctr., Inc., New Port Richey, Fla., 1999, Suncoast Spinal Med. and Rehab. Ctrs., Clearwater, Fla., 1999—, Suncoast Clin. Rsch., Inc., New Port Richey, Fla., 1999—; mem. elder affairs advisor com. to Fla. state rep. Heather Fiorentino, 1999—. Author: Pregnancy as a Disease, 1976. Officer candidate USMC, 1969. Nat. Inst. Child Health and Human Devel. fellow Cornell U., 1970-73; Fulbright fellow Nat. Assn. Colls. for Tchr. Edn., India, 1974. Mem. AMA, Fla. Med. Soc., Pasco County Med. Soc., Am. Soc. Internal Medicine, Fla. Soc. Internal Medicine. Lutheran. Avocations: tennis, snorkeling, travel, photography. Office: Suncoast Spinal Med & Rehab Ctrs Inc 24945 US Highway 19 N Clearwater FL 33763-3927

MERKL, HEINRICH, literary critic; b. Legau, Fed. Republic Germany, July 15, 1951; s. Josef Franz and Liselotte (Sepp) M.; m. Kathryn Lesley Hawken, Apr. 21, 1984; children: Piran Timothy, Padryk Elwyn. PhD, U. Heidelberg, 1981. Wissenschaftlicher angestellter U. Heidelberg, 1978-80; wissenschaftliche hilfskraft U. Regensburg, 1980-82, akademischer rat auf zeit, 1983-88; pvt. scholar, 1989—. Author: Sor Juana Inés de la Cruz Ein Bericht zur Forschung, 1951-81, 1986; contbr. articles to profl. jours. Mem. Internat. Comparative Lit. Assn., Asociación Internacional de Hispanistas. Home: 10 im Grund, L-6917 Roodt-sur-Syre Luxembourg

MERKULOV, IGOR ALEXANDROVICH, physicist, researcher; b. Leningrad, USSR, July 16, 1947; s. Alexandr Iosifovich and Ekaterina Vladimizovna (Sheinina) M.; m. Galina Yakovlevna Levich, Sept. 26, 1969; 1 child. M degree, U. Leningrad, 1971; PhD in Physics, Ioffe Physics-Tech. Inst., Leningrad, 1975, PhD, 1983; diploma, Phys. Tech. Inst., St. Petersburg, 1991, Russian Acad. Scis., Moscow, 1993. Rschr. Phys. Tech. Inst., Leningrad, 1975-79, sr. rschr., 1979-85, prin. rschr., 1985-91; exec. sec. Phys. Tech. Inst., St. Petersburg, 1991-96; prof. Tech. U., St. Petersburg, 1993—; cons. Coll. Phys. Tech. Sch., St. Petersburg, 1987-97. Author: Optical Orientation, 1984; contbr. more than 100 articles to profl. jours. including Jour. Solid State Physics. Mem. United Phys. Soc. of the Russian Fedn., St. Petersburg Scientists Assn. Avocations: writing poetry, skiing, music. Home: Fl 60, Ave Moris Torez 36/2, 194021 Saint Petersburg Russia Office: Phys Tech Inst, Polytechnicheskaya St 26, 194021 Saint Petersburg Russia

MERKURYEV, YURI, computer modeling and simulation and industrial logistics managment educator; b. Riga, Latvia, Apr. 30, 1954; s. Anatoly and Anastasia (Shalina) M.; m. Galina Korneyeva, June 16, 1953; 1 child, Lena. Elec. engr., Riga Polytech. Inst., 1976, D of Engring., 1992, D.Habil. in Engring., 1997. Rsch. asst. Riga Polytech. Inst., 1976-78, 81-82, asst. prof., 1982-85, lectr., 1985-91; assoc. prof. Riga Tech. U., 1991-97, prof., 1997—; pres. Mt Simulation Ltd., Riga, 1992—; dir. Latvian Ctr. of the McLeod Inst. of Simulation Scis., Riga, 1995—; head dept. of modeling and simulation of Riga Tech. U., 1993—. Author: (with others) Bounding Approaches to System Identification, 1996; co-author: Managing and Controlling Growing Harbour Terminals, 1997; contbr. articles to profl. jours. Rsch. grant Latvian Coun. of Sci., 1994-96, 97—; recipient Best Paper award 1992 European Simulation Symposium, 1992, award Latvian Nat. Org. on Automatics, 1997. Mem. Latvian Simulation Soc. (pres. 1992—), Latvian Nat. Orgn. of Automatics (bd. dirs. 1994-99), Baltic Ops. Rsch. Soc. (pres. elect 1998—), Soc. for Computer Simulation (internat. mem. steering com. European coun. 1995—). Avocations: painting, traveling, fishing. E-mail: merkuz@itl.ztu.lv. Home: Jasmuizhas St 2-131, Riga LV-1021, Latvia Office: Riga Tech Univ, Kalku Street 1, Riga LV-1658, Latvia

MERL, STEPHAN, historian, history educator; b. Hamburg, Germany, Sept. 7, 1947; s. Stephan and Else (Meyer) M.; m. Bettina Dabelstein, Sept. 8, 1983; children: Christoph, Tobias. Abitur, Waldörfergymnasium, Hamburg, Germany, 1967; First State Examination, U. Hamburg (Germany), 1975, DrPhil, 1979; Habilitation, Freie U. Berlin, 1990; D (hon.), State Pedagog. U., Yaroslavl, 1998. Lectr. U. Hamburg/U. Bielefeld (Germany), 1981-82; asst. prof. Freie U. Berlin, 1982-88; asst. prof. U. Giessen, 1988-91, assoc. prof., 1991; prof. U. Bielefeld (Germany), 1991—, dean Faculty History and Philosophy, 1996-98. Author: Agricultural Market and the "New Economic History", 1981, The Beginning of Collectivisation in the Soviet Union, 1985, Peasants under Stalin, 1990, Social Advancement in the Soviet System?, 1990. Rsch. grantee FAZIT-Stiftung, 1980, Deutsch Forschungsgemeinschaft, 1987. Mem. Am. Assn. Advancement Slavic Studies, Verband Deutscher Historiker, Deutsche Gesellschaft Osteuropakunde. Home: 39 Ohlendorffs Tannen, D-22359 Hamburg Germany Office: U Bielefeld Fakultat Geschi, Postfach 10 01 31, D-33501 Bielefeld Germany

MERLE, MICHEL PAUL, plastic surgeon, orthopedic surgeon, educator; b. Belley, Ain, France, July 12, 1943; s. Roger F. and Anne-Marie (Fey) M.; m. Sylvie Michon, July 8, 1968. MD, U. Nancy, France, 1970. Resident Univ. Hosp., Nancy, 1969-70, asst. head staff, 1975-79; prof. orthopedics and plastic surgery CHU Nancy, 1979-2000; head dept. plastic and reconstructive surgery CHU, Nancy, 1988-2000; dir. European Inst. Biomaterials and Microsurgery, Nancy, 1987-94, 99-2000, European Inst. of Hand Surgery, 2000—. Author: (with Ch. Destrez) Hand, Art and Science, 1992, (with G. Dautel) Hand Injury, 1992, Wrist Injury, 1995. Capt. French Health Care Svc., 1969-70. Decorated knight Nat. Order of Merit, knight Legion of Honor (France). Mem. French Acad. Surgery, Royal Belgian Acad. Medicine (hon.), French Acad. Medicine (corr.), French Soc. for Surgery of Hand, Belgian Soc. for Surgery of Hand, Indian Soc. for Surgery of Hand, Brit. Soc. for Surgery of Hand, Am. Soc. for Surgery of Hand, Argentine Soc. for Surgery of Hand, European Confedn. Emergency Treatment of Hand (founding). Roman Catholic. Avocations: classical music, tennis, painting, sculpture. Home: 5 Allée des Roches, 54000 Nancy France Office: Inst European Rein, 13 rue Blaise Pascal, 54320 Maxeville-Nancy France

MERLET, THOMAS JEAN, physics engineer, researcher; b. Bois Colombes, Frande, July 31, 1968; s. Joseph Henri and Nicole Renée (Brault) M.; m. Emmanuelle Noelle Guerin, Sept. 3, 1994; 1 child, Nicolas. Degree in engring., ESPCI, Paris, 1993; PhD, U. Paris, 1997. Rschr. Thomson-CSF Lab. Ctrl. Rsch., Orsay, France, 1993-97; engr. Thomson-CSF Airsys, Limours, France, 1997—. Office: Thomson CSF Airsys, Hameau Roussigny, 91410 Limours France

MERLONI, VITTORIO, electronics executive; b. Fabriano, Ancona, Italy, Apr. 30, 1933; m. Franca Carloni; 4 children. Degree in Econs., U. Perugia, Italy, 1959. With Ariston, 1960; pres. Merloni Elettrodomestici S.p.A., 1970; founder merloni Progetti S.p.A., 1973; pres. Industrialists Assn. Ancona (Italy), 1976, Industrialists' Fedn. Marche Region, 1979, Confindustria, 1980-84, Centromarca, 1984; pres., chmn. bd., CEO Merloni Elettrodomestici S.p.A., Fabriano, Ancona, Italy; chmn. Merloni Elettrodomestici S.p.A., Fabriano; bd. dirs. IBM Italia, Mondadori, Alitalia, Philco, Ferruzzi Finanziaria; joint pres. LUISS; bd. mgrs. harvard Bus. Sch., Olivetti Inst. Bus. Studies, Aristide Merloni Found., Censis; chmn. Finanziaria Italiana de Partecipazione. Decorated Knight of the Order of Labour Merit of the Italian Republic, 1984. Avocations: racing cars, boats. Office: Merloni Elettrodomestici SPA, Viale Aristide Merloni 45, 60044 Ancona Fabriano, Italy*

MERMOD, NICOLAS P., biochemist, educator; b. Geneva, Sept. 26, 1958; s. Ronald and Sylvie (Binet) M.; m. Annie Monique Jeanine Bourrel; children: Thomas, Eric, Aude. BSc in Biochemistry, U. Geneva, 1981, BSc in Chemistry, 1982, MSc in Biochemistry, 1982, PhD, 1986. Asst. Med. Faculty U. Geneva, 1982-86; postdoctoral fellow U. Calif., Berkeley, 1986-89; Start group leader U. Lausanne, Switzerland, 1989-95, privat-docent, 1990-93, asst. prof., 1993-95; prof. U. Lausanne, 1995—; on-line expert for analysis of protein structure by the PROSITE computer package, 1991—. Contbr. articles to profl. jours. Recipient Georges F. Janbert prize U. Geneva, 2000; Deutsche Forschungsgemeinschaft fellow U. Goettingen, 1982, Swiss Nat. Sci. Found. fellow U. Calif., 1986, Swiss Nat. Sci. Found. fellow U. Lausanne, 1989. Mem. Swiss Soc. for Microbiology, Swiss Soc. Biochemistry. Office: U Lausanne Inst Animal Biol, Ctr Biotech UNILEPFL, CH-1015 Lausanne Switzerland

MERMOZ, JORGE FRANCISCO, secondary education educator, researcher; b. Buenos Aires, Nov. 14, 1954; s. Jorge Alberto Mermoz and Eva Yolanda Paci; m. Anita Maqueda, Apr. 19, 1986; children: Javier Ignacio, Maria Belén, Juan Pablo. Lic. in ecology, U. Buenos Aires, 1984. Field rsch. Mus. Natural History, Buenos Aires, 1974-94; tchr. sci. secondary bilingual schs., Buenos Aires, 1987—; dep. headmaster Belgrano Day Sch., Buenos Aires, 1995—; advisor to fisheries sec. Govt of Argentina, 1976-91; instr. fisheries biology Instituto Tecnologico de Buenos Aires, 1985-91; organizer, author, lectr. tchr. conf. Space Scis. in Edn., 1999. Mem. AAAS, Am. Astron. Soc., Am. Geophys. Union, Planetary Soc. Avocations: reading, naval modeling, rock and shell collecting, seashore ecology. Home: Diaz Velez 1020, 1636 La Lucila BA, Argentina Office: Belgrano Day Sch, Juramento 3035, 1428 Buenos Aires Argentina

MERNA, GERALD FRANCIS, advertising executive, retired marine officer, retired postal executive; b. N.Y.C., Apr. 1, 1930; s. George F. Merna and Geraldine (Byers) Kraus; m. Dorothy May Sedlack, Feb. 10, 1951; children: Linda Carol Figura, Gerald Thomas. BS, George Washington U., 1973, MS, 1977; postgrad., U. So. Calif., 1975, U. Va., 1983. Enlisted USMC, 1947, advanced through grades to master gunnery sgt., 1966, commd. 2d lt., 1966, promoted to 1st lt. in Vietnam, 1967; with USMC, Korea, 1952-53, Vietnam, 1966-67; ret. USMC, 1968; various positions U.S. Postal Svc., Washington, 1968-82, exec. asst. to Postmaster Gen., 1978-82; sectional ctr. mgr. U.S. Postal Svc., No. Va., 1982-87; ret., 1987; advt. dir. Signal mag.-Jour. Armed Forces Communications and Electronics Assn., Fairfax, Va., 1987-93; assoc. pub. Nat. Def. Mag., Arlington, Va., 1993-98; v.p. Nat. Def. Indsl., Arlington, 1993-98; ret., 1998; publs. cons. Nat. Def. Indsl. Assn., 1998—. V.p. ops. Va. Hills Civic Assn., Alexandria, 1971-72; mem. covenants com. Cascades Comm. Assn., 1998-00, chair 2000—. Mem. The Ret. Officers Assn. (life), Marine Corps League, Marine Corps Res. Officers Assn. (life), 1st Marine Divsn. Assn. (life), 3rd Marine Divsn. Assn. (life), Nat. Def. Indsl. Assn. (life), Am. Legion, USMC Mustang Assn., VFW, Armed Forces Communications and Electronics Assn., Nat. League Postmasters U.S. (v.p. 1989-92). Home and Office: The Cascades 46386 Bluestem Ct Potomac Falls VA 20165-6461

MEROLLI, ANTONIO, orthopedic surgeon, consultant; b. Frosinone, Lazio, Italy, Feb. 22, 1962; s. Arduino Franco and Luciana (Tomassetti) M. Degree in medicine, Cath. U., Rome, 1986, cert. in orthopedic surgery, 1991. Resident in orthopedic surgery Cath. U., Rome, 1986-91, mem. staff orthopedic dept., 1995—; pvt. practice Rome, 1991—; cons. European Union, Brite-Euram Project on Biomaterials, Rome, 1990-93. Editor: Three Dimensional Analysis of Spinal Deformities, 1995. Mem. Forza Italia, Rome, 1994. Lt. Army Med. Corps Res., 1988—. Recipient scholarship Italian Scoliosis Soc., 1988, European Fedn. Orthopedic Socs., 1990; grantee European Soc. Biomechanics, 1994. Mem. Internat. Rsch. Soc. Spinal Deformity (exec. bd. dirs. 1994-98), European Soc. Biomaterials (auditor 1997—), Nat. Geog. Soc., Planetary Soc., Italian Soc. Biomaterials (exec. bd. dirs. 1997—, treas. 1998—). Roman Catholic. Avocations: scuba diving, skiing, piano playing.

MERONI, RUDOLF, lawyer; b. Zurich, Switzerland, Apr. 26, 1953; s. Francesco and Hedwig (Fischer) M. Lic.iur., U. Zurich, 1978, JSD, 1982; M in Comparative Jurisprudence, NYU, N.Y.C., 1981. Ptnr. Meroni & Schmid, Attys. at Law, Zollikon/Zurich, 1995—; chmn. Merohaus Verwaltungs-AG, Zurich, 1977—, Domaine du Château du Val de Mercy S.A., Chablis, France, 1992—. Co-author: Lawyers' Guide to Transnational Corporate Acquisitions, 1990, International Franchising Option, 1991, International Franchising Law, 1993; co-editor: Bankers' Liability, 1993. Mem. Internat. Bar Assn. (chmn. sub-com. 1986-93), Internat. C. of C. Avocations: wine growing, horse breeding, history. Office: Meroni & Schmid, Dufourstrasse 13, CH-8702 Zollikon Zurich Switzerland

MERRIAM, JOHN GOODWIN, political scientist, educator; b. Lausanne, Switzerland, Mar. 27, 1933; parents U.S. citizens; s. Gordon Phelps and Eunice Wilbur (Brandt) M.; m. Kathleen Howard, June 20, 1961 (div. 1989); children: Heather S., Christopher H., Jennifer S. Truax; m. Nancy J. Fox, Nov. 27, 1993. BA, Hamilton Coll., 1955; postgrad., Harvard U., 1961; MA, Boston U., 1962; PhD, Ind. U., 1970. Instr. Ricker Coll., Houlton, Maine, 1960-61, 64; teaching fellow Am. U. in Cairo, Egypt, 1964-66, asst. prof., 1966-67; instr., asst. prof., assoc. prof. polit. sci. Bowling Green (Ohio) State U., 1967-93, assoc. prof. emeritus, 1993—; part-time prof. Lourdes Coll., 1993—; bd. dirs. Alliance Francaise de Toledo, 1986-93, Ohio Middle East Policy Coun., 1987—. With U.S. Army, 1955-58. Grantee Ind. U., Bloomington, 1961-62; Ford Found fellow, 1962-64. Mem. Middle East Inst., Middle East Policy Coun., Pi Sigma Alpha, Delta Tau Kappa. Democrat. Episcopalian. Avocation: walking. Home: 3033 Hopewell Pl Toledo OH 43606-3105 Office: Bowling Green State U Dept Polit Sci Bowling Green OH 43403-0001

MERRIAM, JOHN L., consulting water management engineer; b. Corona, Calif., Nov. 27, 1911; s. George H. and Bessie (Baird) M.; m. Sarah Elizabeth Gridley, Oct. 2, 1938; children: Andrew G., Elisabeth Merriam Farley. AA, San Bernardino Valley Coll., 1932; BSCE, Calif. Inst. Tech., 1938. Registered civil, agrl. engr., Calif. Engr. Soil Conservation Svc., USDA, Calif., 1939-56; sr. irrigation engr. Ralph M. Parsons Co., Saudia Arabia, 1956-58; prof. Calif. Poly. State U., San Luis Obispo, 1958-78; pvt. practice cons., irrigation engr. Sri Lanka, India, Can., U.S., Mex., Egypt, Pakistan, Tunisia, 1978—; cons. FAO, Saudi Arabia, 1969; Peace Corps trainer, Thailand, 1971; vis. prof. Katholieke U., Leuven, Belgium, 1982. Author: (with others) Design and Operation of Farm Irrigation Systems, 1981, (with Jack Keller) Farm Irrigation System Evaluation: A Guide for Management; contbr. articles to profl. jours.; patentee in field. Mem. adv. com. County Flood Control Commn., San Luis Obispo, 1973-78, Calif. State Office Water Conservation, Sacramento, 1980-86. Named Outstanding Prof. Calif. Poly. State U., 1964, Conservationist of Yr SCSA Calif. chpt., 1978. Fellow ASCE (various offices, Royce J. Tipton award 1979, Outstanding Svc. award 1994); mem. Am. Soc. Agrl. Engrs. (sr., Engr. of Yr. 1981/Calif.), Calif. Irrigation Inst. (pres. 1967-68, Engr. of Yr. 1980); mem. Internat. Com. on Irrigation and Drainage, U.S. Com. on Irrigation and Drainage. Achievements include establishing an endowment for irrigation and water mgmt. and the fund for furthering flexible irrigation at Calif. Poly State U., the Merriam Irrigation Edn. Found. and the Am. Soc. Agrl. Engring. award for the advancement of surface irrigation. Home and Office: 235 Chaplin Ln San Luis Obispo CA 93405-1932

MERRIER, HELEN, actress, writer; b. Chgo., Mar. 10, 1932; d. Miner Thompson and Helen (Hembree) Coburn; m. Tim Meier, Dec. 23, 1954; 1 child, William Frank. BA, Mills Coll., 1954; BS, Northwestern U., 1955. Radio roles include Ma Perkins, One Man's Family, Standard School House of the Air, 1934-52; stage roles include Finian's Rainbow, 1952, The Happy Time, 1952, The Night of January 16th, 1952, No Exit, 1953, Tiger at the Gates, 1953, Caeser and Cleopatra, 1953, The Cocktail Party, 1953, Streetcar Named Desire, 1953, Misalliance, 1956, Cry the Beloved Country, 1956, Cat in a Tin Roof, 1963, Take Me Along, 1966, Caucasian Chalk Circle, 1967, The Devils, 1968, Electra, 1969, Jean Harlow and Billy the Kid, 1969, Three-Penny Opera, 1969, A Shot in the Dark, 1970, Private Lives, 1970, The Importance of Being Earnest, 1971, Forty Carats, 1972, Paris is Out!, 1972, A Christmas Carol, 1973, The Sea Gull, 1975, Something more than Ordinary, 1976, Three Dollar Bill, 1976, Maid to Marry, 1977, Scrooge, the musical, 1984, Prisoner of Second Avenue, 1985, Tom Sawyer, 1986, Comedy of Errors, 1987, Juno and the Paycock, 1987, Woman of the Year, 1989, Time and the Conways, 1991, Cinderella, 1991, Sweney Todd, 1991, The Birds, 1993, Dreams of Defiance (rev.), 1994, Lady Lucinda's Scrapbook (solo play), 1996-98, As You Like It hike, 1998-99, A Midsummer Night's Dream hike, 1999, Vieux Carre, 1999, Woman Talk (cabaret), 1999, Healthy-Minded Little Old Lady Songs (solo cabaret), 2000, William Inge Festival, 2000, Robin Hood Hike, 2000. Recipient The Spirit of Theater award, 2000. Mem. Victory Svcs. Club (London), Arts Club Chgo. Home: 915 Linden Ave Wilmette IL 60091-2712

MERRIFIELD, DUDLEY BRUCE, business educator, former government official; b. Chgo., June 13, 1921; s. Fred and Anna (Marshall) M.; m. Paula

Sorensen, June 8, 1949; children: Bruce, Robert, Marshall. AB in Chemistry, Princeton U., 1942; MS in Chemistry, U. Chgo., 1948, PhD in Chemistry, 1950. Disting. vis. prof. Georgetown U. Bus. Sch., Washington. Sr. rsch. chemist Monsanto, St. Louis, 1950-56; mgr. polymer rsch. Tex.-U.S. Chem. Co., Parsippany, N.J., 1956-63; dir. R & D Petrolite Corp., St. Louis, 1963-68; v.p. tech. and ventures Occidental Petroleum Co., Houston, 1968-77; v.p. tech. and venture mgmt. Continental Group, Stamford, Conn., 1977-82; asst. sec. for productivity, tech. and innovation Dept. Commerce, Washington, 1982-89; undersec. econ. affairs, 1986-87; Walter Bladstrom prof., emeritus Wharton Bus. Sch., U Pa., Phila., 1989-94; pres., CEO Pinnacle Rsch. Inst. Devel. Co., 1991—; adv. bd. Binat R & D Found., U.S., Israel, France, India, 1979—. Contbr. articles to profl. jours.; patentee in field. Exec. coun. Episcopal Ch., 1973-79; chmn. Princeton Alumni Coun., 1968-72. With USMC, 1943-46. Fellow AAAS, Inst. for Chemists; mem. Am. Chem. Soc., Indsl. Rsch. Inst. (dir., pres.-elect 1977-82 M. Holland award), Am. Mgmt. Assn. Hall of Fame (trustee, chmn. rsch. coun.), Dirs. Rsch., Sigma Xi. Republican. Episcopalian. Office: Pridco Mgmt Corp Ste 604 1316 New Hampshire NW Washington DC 20036

MERRIFIELD, ROBERT BRUCE, biochemist, educator; b. Ft. Worth, Tex., July 15, 1921; s. George E. and Lorene (Lucas) M.; m. Elizabeth Furlong, June 20, 1949; children: Nancy, James, Betsy, Cathy, Laurie, Sally. B.A., UCLA, 1943, Ph.D., 1949; Ph.D. (hon.), U. Colo., 1969, Uppsala U., 1970, Yale U., 1971, Newark Coll. Engring., 1972, Med. Coll. Ohio, 1977, Boston Coll., 1984, Fairleigh Dickinson U., 1985, N.J. U. Medicine & Dentistry, 1985, U. Barcelona, 1986, Adelphi U., 1987, U. Montpellier, 1988, Delaware Valley Coll., 1991, Scripps Rsch. Inst., 1998, Rockefeller U., 1998. Chemist Park Research Found., 1943-44; research asst. Med. Sch., UCLA, 1948-49; asst. Rockefeller Inst. for Med. Research, 1949-53, assoc., 1953-57; asst. prof. Rockefeller U., 1957-58, assoc. prof., 1958-66, prof., 1966-92, John D. Rockefeller prof., 1984-92, emeritus prof., 1992—; Developed solid phase peptide synthesis; completed (with B. Gutte) 1st total synthesis of an enzyme, 1969. Assoc. editor: Internat. Jour. Peptide and Protein Research; contbr. articles to sci. jours. Recipient Lasker award biomed. rsch., 1969, Gairdner award, 1970, Intra-Sci. award, 1970, Nichols medal, 1973, Alan E. Pierce award Am. Peptide Symposium, 1979, Nobel prize in chemistry, 1984, Rudinger award European Peptide Soc., 1990, Chem. Pioneer award Am. Inst. Chemists, 1993, Assn. Biomolecular Resource Facilities award, 1998; named one of Top 75 Contbrs. to Chem. Enterprise during past 75 yrs., Chem. & Engring. News, 1998. Mem. Am. Chem. Soc. (award creative work synthetic organic chemistry 1972, Hirschmann award in peptide chemistry 1990, Glenn T. Seaborg award 1993), NAS USA, Am. Soc. Biol. Chemists, Sigma Xi, Phi Lambda Upsilon, Alpha Chi Sigma. Office: Rockefeller Univ Dept Chemistry 1230 York Ave New York NY 10021-6307

MERRILL, GEORGE VANDERNETH, lawyer, investment executive; b. N.Y.C., July 2, 1947; s. James Edward and Claire (Leness) M.; m. Janice Anne Humes, May 11, 1985; children: Claire Georgina, Anne Stewart. Student, Phillips Exeter Acad., 1960-64; AB magna cum laude, Harvard U., 1968, JD, 1972; MBA, Columbia U., 1973. Bar: N.Y. 1973, U.S. Dist. Ct. (so. and ea. dists.) N.Y. 1974, U.S. Ct. Appeals (2d cir.) 1974. Assoc. Cleary, Gottlieb, Steen & Hamilton, N.Y.C., 1974-77, Hawkins, Delafield & Wood, N.Y.C., 1977-79; v.p. Irving Trust Co., N.Y.C., 1980-82; v.p., gen. counsel Listowel, Inc., N.Y.C., 1982-84; bd. dirs., exec. v.p., gen. counsel Listowel, Inc., 1984-93; v.p. instl. portfolio mgmt. Shawmut Investment Advisors, 1993-95; also co-mgr. Shawmut Growth & Income Equity Mut. Fund; v.p. instl. portfolio mgmt. Fleet Investment Advisors, 1995-96, also co-mgr. Galaxy Growth U Income Equity Mut. Fund.; v.p. trust and intsl. portfolio mgmt. No. Trust Corp., Chgo., 1996-2000; v.p., sr. personal investment officer Bank of N.Y., N.Y.C., 2000—; bd. dirs. Pres. Arell Found., N.Y.C., 1985-93, also bd. dirs., pres. Northfield Charitable Corp., N.Y.C., 1986-93; v.p., sec. Brougham Prodn. Co., N.Y.C., 1986-89, bd. dirs., sr. v.p., sec., 1990-93; v.p., sec. Marinetics Inc., N.Y.C., 1988-90, sr. v.p., sec., 1991-93, also bd. dirs., 1989-93; v.p. Sci. Design and Engring. Co., Inc., N.Y.C., 1987-88, bd. dirs., exec. v.p., 1989-93. John Harvard scholar; recipient Detur award Harvard U., 1968. Mem. ABA, Am. Mgmt. Assn., Assn. Bar City N.Y., Nat. Cum Laude Soc., The Brook, Union Club (N.Y.C.), Down Town Assn., Racquet and Tennis Club, Somerset Club (Boston), Signet Soc. (Cambridge), Pilgrims of U.S. Home: 2 Pierce Rd Riverside CT 06878 Office: The Bank of NY 5th Fl 1290 Ave of the Americas New York NY 10000

MERRILL, MARY LEE, professional society administrator; b. Wilmington, Del., Dec. 6, 1925; d. Claude William and Sue Athelia (Savage) Sutton; m. Alan Douglas Merrill, Sept. 1, 1962; 1 child, Stephen Andrew. Grad. high sch., Wilmington, 1944. Exec. sec. E.I. du Pont de Nemours, Wilmington, 1950-65; founder, gov. Pilgrim Edward Doty, Wilmington, 1982-87, The Fuller Soc., Friendship, Maine, 1992—. Pres. United Meth. Women, Waldoboro, Maine, 1992-99, gov., 1992-00, gov. ex-officio, 2000—; vol. Farnsworth Mus., Rockland, Maine, 1995; docent Olson House, Cushing, Maine, 1995; gov. Fuller Soc., 1992-99; chmn. publicity Maine Fedn. Women's Clubs, 2000—, pub. rels. chmn., 2000—. Mem. Nat. Mayflower Soc. (historic sites com. 1995—), Del. Mayflower Soc. (councillor 1986-88), Daus., Founders, Patriots (treas. 1992—), Daus. of 1812 (registrar 1991-92), Maine Mayflower Soc. (chmn. pub. rels. 1992-95), Waldoboro Woman's Club (chmn. pub. rels. 1993—), Fuller soc. (gov. 1992-99, founder). Republican. Avocations: genealogy, travel, reading, civic work. Home: 514 Martin Point Rd Friendship ME 04547-4343

MERRINGTON, OLIVER J., information scientist; b. London, Dec. 13, 1951; s. William and Maxine (Venables) M. BSc, U. London, 1973, MSc, 1974. Head libr. scis. Schering Agrochems. Ltd., Saffron Walden, England, 1977-94; mgr. ICSU World Data Ctr. Glaciology, Cambridge, England, 1995-98; mgr. NERC Arctic Environ. Metadata Ctr., Cambridge, 1997-99; website mgr. Scott Polar Rsch. Inst., 1998—. Mem. Inst. Biology, Inst. Info. Scis. Office: U Cambridge Scott Polar Rsch, Lensfield Rd, Cambridge CB2 1ER, England

MERRITT, JOE FRANK, industrial supply executive; b. Paris, Tex., Dec. 9, 1947; s. Henry Grady and Margaret Leon (Murrell) M.; m. Barbara Jean Sands (div. May 1973); 1 child, Daniel Joe; m. Bonnie Louise McLure, Feb. 1, 1975; 1 stepchild, David Wright Dwyer. BA in Govt., U. Tex., Arlington, 1970; attending, All-Inclusive Sch., 1999. Cert. contractor Dept. Def. USA and Can. With purchasing A.F. Holman Boiler Works Inc., Dallas, 1970-77; supply salesman Stanco Indsl. Supply, Dallas, 1977-79, Tool Specialty Indsl. Supply, Dallas, 1979-80, Briggs-Weaver Indsl. Supply, Dallas, 1980-81; owner, pres. Joe F. Merritt & Co., Inc., Carrollton, Tex., 1981; v.p., gen. mgr. Abrasives & Buffs Co., Dallas, 1981-83; owner, pres. Buff, Polish & Grind Indsl. Supply Co., Inc., Argyle, Tex., 1984—; cons. The Broadway Collection, OLathe Kans., 1990, Offenhauser Co., Houston, 1993, 94, 98, Innovation Industries, Russellville, Ark., 1994; instr. buff, polish and grind methods quality control dept. Rsch. Facility, Peterbilt Motors Co., 1994; trainer Peterbilt Madison-Tenn. plant, 1997, DBC Indsl., Garland, Tex., 1999, Am. Ironhorse Motorcycle Co., Ft. Worth, Tex., 2000, Chgo. Iron and Bridge, Tex., 2000. Creator State of the Art Rsch. and Tchg. Facility, 1984, 100% Virgin Lambswool Buffing Belt, 1987, spl. extra wide spindle buffers to be manufactured by Baldor Electric, Ft. Smith, Ark., 1995, 97, 98; contbr. article to profl. jour. Recipient Cert. of Appreciation, City of Carrollton, Tex., 1981. Republican. Methodist. Avocations: travel, animals, Landrover-4 wheel drive vehicle. Fax: (940) 455-7385. Office: Buff Polish & Grind Indsl Supply 1907 E FM407 Argyle TX 76226-9447

MERRITT, JOHN HOWARD, secondary school educator; b. Salisbury, Md., May 19, 1948; s. Robert Wilson and Iris Amy (Horsey) M.; m. Carole A. Tramontana; children: Robert W. II, John H. Jr.; 1 stepchild, Stephen A. Capelli Jr. BS, Salisbury State Coll., 1971; MEd, Salisbury State U., 1990. Cert. secondary tchr., Md. Propr. constrn. bus. Salisbury, 1977-86; high sch. math. tchr. Wicomico Count Schs., Salisbury, 1986—; instr. math. NROTC Prep Sch., San Diego, 1988-91. Capt. USNR, 1970—. Mem. Nat. Coun. Tchrs. of Math., ASCD, Kappa Delta Pi. Republican. Methodist. Avocations: swimming, gardening, residential real estate investments, commodity futures trading.

MERRY, BRUCE CARMICHAEL, education educator, writer; b. Birmingham, Eng., July 3, 1944; arrived in Australia, 1987; s. John Michael and Diana Constance (Milman) M.; m. Jean Marquard, Aug. 8, 1980 (widowed Dec. 28, 1984); m. Gina Roseanne Curro Merry, June 28, 1997; children: ludovica, Natalie. BA, Oxford U., Eng., 1966; MA, Stanford U., 1968; PhD, Nat. U. Ireland, 1976. Instr. Stanford U., 1966-68; lectr. U. Kent, Eng., 1968-72, U. Coll. Dublin, Ireland, 1972-79; prof. U. Witwatersrand, South Africa, 1980-87; assoc. prof. James Cook U., Australia, 1987-97, Kuwait U., 1997—. Author: Anatomy of the Spy Thriller, 1977, Women in Modern Italian Literature, 1990, Dacia Maraini and the Written Dream of Women in Italian Literature, 1997; co-author: English in Action, 1994. Avocations: road running, painting, chess. Home and Office: Kuwait U, PO Box 23558, 13096 Safat Kuwait

MERRY, PAUL ROBERT, statistics educator; b. Kansas City, Mo., May 15, 1921; s. Paul Horace Merry and Hallie Etta Haxton; m. Berneice Roberta Lyddon, June 25, 1943; children: Marcia Paulette, Mark Lyddon. AB, Baker U., Baldwin City, Kans., 1942; MBA, U. Denver, 1947; PhD, Northwestern U., 1949. From asst. prof. to assoc. prof. U. Denver, 1949-60, prof., 1960-80, prof. stats. and rsch. emeritus, 1980—, assoc. dir. Bur. Bus. and Social Rsch., 1949-58, chmn. dept. stats. and rsch., 1961-80, asst. dean Coll. Bus. Adminstrn., 1960-64, dir. USAF divsn. ops. analysis standby unit, 1964-71. Lt. USN, 1941-45, PTO. Grad. fellow U. Denver, 1946-67, fellow Inst. for Basic Math. for Application to Bus., Ford Found., Harvard U., 1959-60; univ. scholar Northwestern U., 1947-49. Mem. Beta Gamma Sigma. Methodist. Avocations: travel, hiking, bird watching. E-mail: latierra@compuserve.com. Home: 5182 County Road 523 Bayfield CO 81122-9606

MERSEL, MARJORIE KATHRYN PEDERSEN, lawyer; b. Manila, Utah, June 17, 1923; d. Leo Henry and Kathryn Anna (Reed) Pedersen; AB, U. Calif., 1948; LLB, U. San Francisco, 1948; m. Jules Mersel, Apr. 12, 1950; 1 son, Jonathan. Admitted to D.C. bar, 1952, Calif. bar, 1955; Marjorie Kathryn Pedersen Mersel, atty., Beverly Hills, Calif., 1961-71; staff counsel Dept. Real Estate State of Calif., Los Angeles, 1971—. Active L.A.-Guangzhou Sister City. Mem. Beverly Hills Bar Assn., L.A. County Bar Assn., Trial Lawyers Assn., So. Calif. Women Lawyers Assn. (treas. 1962-63), L.A.-Guangzhou Sister City Assn., Beverly Hills C. of C., World Affairs Coun., Current Affairs Forum, L.A. Athletic Club, Sierra Club. Home: 13007 Hartsook St Sherman Oaks CA 91423-1616 Office: Dept Real Estate 107 S Broadway Ste 8107 Los Angeles CA 90012-4402

MERSMAN, RICHARD KENDRICK, III, lawyer; b. Des Moines, Sept. 14, 1949; s. Richard K. Jr. and Mary Jane Mersman; children: Richard K. IV, Thomas R. BA, Tulane U., 1971, JD, 1975. Bar: Mo. 1976. Atty. Boyce & Mersman, St. Louis, 1976-81; gen. counsel Mason Group, Inc., St. Louis, 1981-90; CFO The Forsythe Group, St. Louis, 1990-92; atty. The Stolar Partnership, St. Louis, 1992—. Roman Catholic. Avocations: golf, soccer coaching. Office: The Stolar Partnership 911 Washington Ave Ste 700 Saint Louis MO 63101-1290

MERSON, MICHAEL HOWARD, public health physician, epidemiologist; b. N.Y.C., June 7, 1945; s. Leo and Paula Enid (Katz) M.; 1 child: Jonathan. BA, Amherst Coll., 1966; MD, SUNY, Bklyn., 1970. Commd. officer USPHS, 1972, advanced through grades to capt.; chief enteric disease br. Ctrs. for Disease Control, Atlanta, 1974-75; chief epidemiologist Cholera Rsch. Lab., Dacca, Bangladesh, 1977-78; dir. diarrheal diseases control program WHO, Geneva, 1978-90, dir. global program on AIDS, 1990-95; prof., dean pub. health Sch. Medicine Yale U., New Haven, 1995—; trustee, bd. dirs. Internat. Ctr. for Diarrheal Diseases, Dacca, 1985-90. Recipient Arthur Fleming award U.S. Jaycees, 1975. Mem. Royal Soc. Tropical Medicine and Hygiene, Internat. Epidemiol. Assn., Am. Soc. for Epidemiology, Soc. Scholars. Office: Yale U Sch Med Dept Epidemiology & Pub Health PO Box 208034 New Haven CT 06520-8034

MERT, ALI, physician, educator; b. Mersin, Turkey, Nov. 22, 1955; s. Mahmut and Pembe Mert. MD, Istanbul U., 1982. Physician Istanbul U., Edirne, 1982-92, internist, 1992-97; assoc. prof. Istanbul U., 1997—. 2st lt. Turkish Land Forces, 1984-85. E-mail: rosaras@yahoo.com. Office: Cerrhpasa Med Faculty, Istanbul 34303, Turkey

MERTEN, JENS, physicist; b. Freiburg, Breisgau, Germany, June 6, 1965. Diploma degree, Tech. U. Munich, 1993; PhD cum laude, U. Barcelona, 1996. Prof. Sarria U. Sch., Barcelona, 1996-97; sr. rschr. U. Barcelona, 1996—; head R&D dept. Trama TecnoAmbiental, Barcelona, 1997—. Contbr. chpt. to book and articles to profl. jours. Office: TTA Rsch and Devel Dept, Ripolles 46, E-08026 Barcelona Spain

MERTEN, KLAUS RAINER, humanities educator; b. Potsdam, Germany, July 31, 1940; s. Rolf and Margarethe (Ocholt) M.; m. Frogard Barbara Nölting, Apr. 19, 1971; children: Jan, Christoph. Diploma in sociology, U. Bielefeld, Germany, 1971, Dr. rer. soc., 1975. Asst. prof. Faculty of Sociology, U. Bielefeld, 1975-79; prof. Faculty of Sociology, U. Giessen, 1979-84; prof. Faculty of Philosophy, U. Muenster, 1984—. Author: Fortran IV, 1975, Communication, 1977, Content Analysis, 1983, The Picture of Foreigners in the German Press, 1986, Empirical Communication Research, 1991, The Reality of Mass Media, 1995, (with S. J. Schmidt) Introduction to Communication, 1999, Violence by Violence in the Media?, 1999, Handbook Public Relations, 1999, Handbook of Organized Communication II, 2000; editor: Handbook of Organized Communication; contbr. articles to profl. jours. Recipient Top award Thyssen Found., 1990. Mem. Internat. Comm. Assn. (Top award), German Assn. for Publ. and Comm., German Sociol. Soc. Home: Raesfeldstr 38, D 48149 Münster Germany Office: U Münster Inst Comm Sci, Bispinghof 9-14, D 48143 Münster Germany

MERTEN, THOMAS, clinical neuropsychologist, researcher; b. Stralsund, Germany, Dec. 11, 1959; s. Helmut and Ingrid (Mielke) M. Diploma in psychology, Humboldt U., Berlin, 1986; Dr phil, Free U., Berlin, 1991. Cert. clin. psychologist, clin. neuropsychologist. Rsch. scientist Humboldt U., 1985-87, sci. asst., 1993-94, external mem. faculty, 1994—; psychotherapist various orgns., Germany, 1988-89; rsch. scientist Free U., 1990-91; rsch. coord. project Longitudinal Assessment Intervention U. Lisbon, Portugal, 1990-92; clin. neuropsychologist Hosp. in Friedrichshain, Berlin, 1992—. Contbr. articles on schizophrenia, neuropsychology, creativity, and computers to sci. jours., including Nervenarzt, Diagnostica, Creativity Rsch. Jour.; author manuals, software. Avocation: languages. Office: Hosp im Friedrichshain, Landsberger Allee 49, D-10249 Berlin Germany

MERTON, ROBERT C., economist, educator; b. N.Y.C., July 31, 1944; s. Robert K. and Suzanne (Carhart) M. BS in Engring. Math., Columbia U., 1966; MS in Applied Math., Calif. Inst. Tech., 1967; PhD in Econs., MIT, 1970; MA (hon.), Harvard U., 1989; LLD (hon.), U. Chgo., 1991; Prof. honoris causa degree, HEC Sch. Mgmt., Paris, 1995; D Econ. Sci. (hon.), U. Lausanne, Switzerland, 1996; Dr honoris causa, U. Paris Dauphine, 1997; D of Mgmt. Sci. (hon.), Nat. Sun Yat-sen U., Kaoshiung, Taiwan, 1998. Instr. econs. MIT, Cambridge, 1969-70; asst. prof. fin. Alfred P. Sloan Sch. Mgmt., 1970-73, assoc. prof., 1973-74, prof., 1974-80, J.C. Penney prof. mgmt., 1980-88; vis. prof. fin. Harvard U., Boston, 1987-88, George Fisher Baker prof. bus. adminstrn., 1988-98, John and Natty McArthur University prof., 1998—; rsch. assoc. Nat. Bur. Econ. Rsch., 1979—; mem. internat. bd. sci. advisors Tinbergen Inst.; co-founder Long-Term Capital Mgmt., L.P., Greenwich, Conn., 1993-99. Author: Continuous-Time Finance, 1990, rev. edit., 1992; co-author: Casebook in Financial Engineering: Applied Studies of Financial Innovation, 1995, The Global Financial System: A Functional Perspective, 1995, Finance, 2000; editor: The Collected Scientific Papers of Paul A. Samuelson, vol. III, 1972; mem. editl. bd. Internat. Econ. Rev., 1972-77, Jour. Fin., 1973-77, Jour. Money, Credit and Banking, 1974-79, Jour. Fin. Econs., 1974-83, Jour. Banking and Fin., 1977-79, 92—, Fin. India, 1988—, Geneva Papers on Risk and Ins., 1989-96, Jour. Fixed Income, 1991—, Fin. Rev., 1992-97, Jour. Fin. Edn., 1995—, European Fin. Rev., 1997—; mem. adv. bd. The New Palgrave Dictionary of Money and Finance, Math. Fin., Rev. Derivatives Rsch., Nihon Finance Gakkai, The Brookings-Wharton Papers on Financial Policy, Internat. Jour. Theoretical & Applied Finance; contbr. articles to profl. jours. Recipient Leo Melamed prize U. Chgo. Sch. Bus., 1983, Roger Murray prize Inst. for Quantitative Rsch. in Fin., 1985, 86, Disting. Scholar award Ea. Fin. Assn., 1989, Internat. INA-Nat. Acad. Lincei prize Nat. Acad. Lincei, Rome, 1993, FORCE award for fin. innovation Fuqua Sch. Bus., Duke U., 1993, Fin. Engr. of Yr. award Internat. Assn. Fin. Engrs., 1993, Alfred Nobel Meml. Prize in Econ. Scis., 1997, Heroes Among Us award Boston Celtics, 1997, Michael Pupin medal Columbia U., 1998, Disting. Alumni award Calif. Inst. of Tech., 1999, MFD Lifetime Achievement award Boston U., 1999; inducted Derivatives Hall of Fame, 1998. Fellow Internat. Assn. Fin. Engrs. (sr.), Econometric Soc., Am. Acad. Arts and Scis., Inst. Quantitative Rsch.; mem. NAS, Am. Fin. Assn. (dir. 1982-84, pres. 1986), Bachelier Fin. Soc., Soc. for Fin. Studies (v.p. 1993), Hon. Order Ky. Cols., Tau Beta Pi, Sigma Xi. Office: Harvard U Grad Sch Bus Adminstrn Morgan 397 Soldiers Field Rd Boston MA 02163

MERTON, ROBERT K., sociologist, educator; b. Phila., July 4, 1910; s. Harry David and Ida (Rosoff) Schkolnick; m. Suzanne Carhart, 1934 (sep. 1968, dec. 1992); children: Stephanie, Robert C., Vanessa; companion Harriet Zuckerman, 1968-92, m. June, 1993. AB, Temple U., 1931, LLD (hon.), 1956; MA, Harvard U., 1932, PhD, 1936, LLD (hon.), 1980; LHD (hon.), Emory U., 1965, Loyola U., Chgo., 1970, Kalamazoo Coll., 1970, Cleve. State U., 1977, U. Pa., 1979, Brandeis U., 1983, SUNY-Albany, 1986, New Sch. Social Rsch., 1995, Long Island U., 1996; Dr. honoris causa, U. Leyden, 1965, Jagiellonian U., Cracow, Poland, 1989; LLD (hon.), Western Res. U., 1966, U. Chgo., 1968, Tulane U., 1971, U. Md., 1982; LittD (hon.), Colgate U., 1967, SUNY, 1984, Columbia U., 1985, SUNY, Albany, 1986, Oxford U., 1986; Dr. Social Sci. (hon.), Yale U., 1968; DSC in Econ. (hon.), U. Wales, 1968; PhD (hon.), Hebrew U. of Jerusalem, 1980, U. Oslo, Norway, 1991; D of Polit. Sci. (hon.), U. Bologna, 1996; D honoris causa, U. Madrid, 1999, U. Athens, 1999. Tutor, instr. sociology Harvard U., 1936-39; prof., chmn. dept. Tulane U., 1939-41; from asst. prof. to prof. Columbia U., 1941-63, Giddings prof., 1963-74, univ. prof., 1974-79, spl. svc. prof., 1979-84, Univ. prof. emeritus, 1979—; assoc. dir. Bur. Applied Social Rsch., 1942-71; adj. faculty Rockefeller U., 1979—; George Sarton prof. hist. sci. U. Ghent, Belgium, 1986-88; adv. editor sociology Harcourt Brace 1947-98; ednl. adv. bd. Guggenheim Found., 1963-79, chmn., 1971-79. Author: Science Technology and Society in 17th Century England, 3rd edit., 2000, Mass Persuasion, 2d edit., 1971, Social Theory and Social Structure, rev. edit., 1968, On the Shoulders of Giants, 1965, vicennial edit., 1985, post-Italianate edit., 1993, On Theoretical Sociology, 1967, The Sociology of Science, 1973, Sociological Ambivalence, 1976, Sociology of Science: An Episodic Memoir, 1979, Social Research and the Practicing Professions, 1982, Opportunity Structure, 1995, On Social Structure and Science, 1996; co-author: the Focused Interview, rev. edit., 1956, 3d edit., 1990, Freedom to Read, 1957, I Viaggi e le Avventura della "Serendipity", 2000; co-editor, co-author: Continuities in Social Research, 1950, Social Policy and Social Research in Housing, 1951, Reader in Bureaucracy, 1952, The Student-Physician, 1957, Sociology Today, 1959, Contemporary Social Problems, 4th edit., 1976, The Sociology of Science in Europe, 1977, Toward a Metric of Science, 1978, Qualitative and Quantitative Social Research: Papers in Honor of Paul F. Lazarsfeld, 1979, Sociological Traditions from Generation to Generation, 1980, Continuities in Structural Inquiry, 1981; co-editor Social Sci. Quotations, 2000. Trustee Ctr. Advanced Study Behavioral Scis., 1952-75, Temple U., 1964-68, Inst. Sci. Info., 1968—; mem. bd. guarantors Italian Acad. for Advanced Studies in Am., 1992—. Recipient MacArthur Prize fellow, 1983-88, Nat. Medal of Sci., 1994, Common Wealth award for Disting. Svc. to Sociology, 1979, award Meml. Sloan-Kettering Cancer Ctr., 1981, Derek Price award Scientometrics, 1995, Sutherland award Am. Soc. Criminology, 1996, Dinerman prize World Assn. Pub. Opinion Rsch., 2000; Disting. scholar in humanities Am. Coun. Learned Socs., 1962, Russell Sage Found. scholar, 1979-99, emeritus, 1999—, Haskins lectr., 1994; NIH lectr. in recognition of outstanding sci. achievement, 1964; Guggenheim fellow, 1962. Fellow Am. Acad. Arts and Scis. (Talcott Parsons prize 1979), Brit. Acad. (fgn.); mem. NAS, Am. Philos. Soc., Sociol. Rsch. Assn. (pres. 1968), Nat. Acad. Edn., Nat. Inst. Medicine, Am. Sociol. Assn. (pres. 1957, Disting. Scholarship award 1980, Cooley-Mead Award in social psychology 1997), Ea. Sociol. Soc. (pres. 1969), History of Sci. Soc., World Acad. Arts and Scis., Soc. Social Studies of Sci. (pres. 1975, Bernal prize), Royal Swedish Acad. Scis. (fgn.), Academia Europaea (fgn.), Polish Acad. Scis. (fgn.), N.Y. Acad. Scis. (hon. life mem.). Home: 71 Hither Ln East Hampton NY 11937-2634

MERVILLE, LAWRENCE JOSEPH, finance educator; b. Nashville, Apr. 7, 1943; s. Lawrence Augustus Merville and Emma June (Collier) Park; m. Sheryl Wolff, Aug. 9, 1968; 1 child, Lauren Anne. BA, Vanderbilt U., 1965; MBA, U. Tex., 1968, PhD, 1971. Fin. analyst Tex. Instruments, Dallas, 1968-70; asst. prof. fin. Ind. U., Bloomington, 1971-73; prof. fin. U. Tex., Dallas, 1973—; pres. Merville & Assocs., Dallas; cons. Tex. Pub. Utility Com., Austin, 1983-85. Author: Economics and Finance, 1990; contbr. articles to profl. jours. Dir. Pub. Utility Programs, Dallas, 1978-82, Pub. Utility Ctr., Dallas, 1981-87. NSF fellow U. Tex., Austin, 1965. Mem. Am. Fin. Assn., Fin. Mgmt. Assn. (program com.), Western Fin. Assn. (program com.), Soc. for China Studies, Dallas Economist Club (membership com.), Phi Beta Kappa. Republican. Avocations: travel, jogging, fishing, theatre. Office: Univ Tex Dallas 2601 N Floyd Rd Richardson TX 75080-1407

MERWIN, JOHN DAVID, retired lawyer, former governor; b. Frederiksted, St. Croix, V.I., Sept. 26, 1921; s. Miles and Marguerite Louise (Flemming) M.; m. Marjorie Davis Spaulding, Feb. 18, 1993. Student, U. Lausanne, Switzerland, 1938-39, U. P.R., 1939-40; BSc, Yale U., 1943; LLB, George Washington U., 1948. Bar: Conn., V.I. 1949. Practice law St. Croix, V.I., 1949-50, 1953-57, 67-85; gen. counsel, v.p. Rob't L. Merwin & Co., Inc., 1953-57; senator-at-large V.I. Legislature, 1955-57; govt. sec. for V.I., 1957-58, gov. V.I., 1958-61; rep. Chase Manhattan Bank, Nassau, Bahamas, 1961-65; exec. v.p. Equity Pub. Corp. Orford, N.H., 1965-67. Chmn. V.I. Port Authority, 1972-75; Rep. candidate for Pres. N.H. Primary Election, 1992; pres. The Nason Found., Cleve., 1981—. Served from 2d lt. to capt. F.A. AUS, 1942-46, 50-53. Decorated Bronze Star; Croix de Guerre with silver star. Mem. Conn., N.H., V.I. bar assns., Phi Delta Phi. Episcopalian. Clubs: Tennis of St. Croix (V.I.), Yale (N.Y.C.), Cosmos (Washington). Home and Office: PO Box 2213 New London NH 03257-2213

MERZ, MONIKA, economics educator; b. Montabaur, Germany, Nov. 2, 1963; came to U.S., 1989; d. Alfons and Margret Merz; m. Thomas Paul Gehrig, July 27, 1996; 1 child, Teresa Louise. MA in Econs., U. Bonn, Germany, 1988; PhD, Northwestern U., 1994. Rsch. assoc. Kiel (Germany) Inst., 1989; asst. prof. econs. Rice U., Houston, 1994—. Contbr. articles to profl. jours. Jean Monnet rsch. fellow European Univ. Inst., 1998. Mem. Am. Econ. Assn., European Econ. Assn., Soc. for Econ. Dynamics. Avocations: foreign languages, classical music, playing guitar. E-mail: mmerz@rice.edu. Office: Rice U 6500 S Main St Houston TX 77005-1892

MERZER, MOSHE, physicist; b. London, Apr. 5, 1946; s. Lew and Roza (Steinhaus) M.; m. Yiska Lange, Apr. 5, 1973; children: Shmuel, Malka, Arieh, Hadassah, Yitzhak, Shulamit, Asher, Yael. BA, U. Cambridge, 1967, MA, 1971, PhD, 1971. Lectr. U. Tel-Aviv, Israel, 1971-76; sr. lectr. Technion, Haifa, Israel, 1976-81; sr. rsch. scientist Rafael, Haifa, 1981—; session co-chmn. European Seismological Commn. Assembly, Tel Aviv, 1998, IEEE-EMC Regional Symposium, Tel-Aviv, 1992; assoc. prof. Technion R&D Found., Haifa, 1987-89; cons. Inst. for Halacha & Tech., Haifa, 1979-81. Contbr. articles to profl. jours.; patentee in field. Scholarship Churchill Coll., 1964-67. Fellow Royal Astron. Soc. Jewish. Office: Rafael, POB 2250 (87), 31021 Haifa Israel

MESA, MARÍA ELENA, librarian; b. Ciego de Avila, Cuba, Sept. 9, 1953; d. Rafael and Enélida Fleitas; m. Manuel Romero Fiallo, Dec. 13, 1971 (divorced); m. Carlos Moya, Oct. 15, 1987; children: Dayamis Romero, Manuel Romero Mesa. Grad., Havana (Cuba) U., 1991. Technician in sci. info. Acad. Sci., Havana, 1971-75; info. specialist Nat. Inst. Sci., Havana, 1975-95, Nat. Ctr. Animal Plant Health, Havana, 1995—. Contbr. articles to profl. jours. Mem. Ministerio de Educación Superior. Avocation: growing ornamental plants. Office: Nat Ctr Animal Plant Health, St Autopista Nat y, Carretera de Tapaste, Havana 32700, Cuba

MESA ORAMA, JESÚS DE LA CARIDAD, research scientist; b. Havana, Marianao, Cuba, Oct. 28, 1952; s. Alfredo Mesa Alfonso and Lázara de la Caridad Orama Alvarez; m. Virginia Beatriz Paz San Pedro, Feb. 23, 1990. BS in Physics, Havana (Cuba) U., 1979; digital systems specialist, J.A.E. Superior Poly. Inst., Havana, 1982, microelectronics specialist, 1985; M in Econs., Havana (Cuba) U., 1997; Diploma in Mktg., Havana U., 2000. Rsch. scientist Cuban Digital Rsch. Inst., Havana, 1983-87, sr. scientist,

1987-90; sr. scientist Cuban Rsch. Inst. for Sugar Cane By-Products, Havana, 1990-98, mem. sci. coun., 1992—, sec. sci. coun., 1993-98, automation project mgmt., 1995-98; mem. sci. com. rsch. sci. evaluation Telecomms. Ctrl. Lab., Havana, 1990—, sci. sec. diversification Internat. Congress, 1996. Recipient 2 gold medals Inst. Cen. de Investigacion Digital, 1993. Avocations: sports, music, philatelic and numismatic. Home: José A Saco # 275 Apt 10, 10500 Ciudad Habana Vibora, Cuba Office: ICIDCA, PO Box 5134, 10500 Ciudad Habana Cuba

MESAROVIC, SINISA DJORDJE, materials engineer, mechanical engineer; b. Belgrade, Yugoslavia, Apr. 19, 1962; s. Djordje Borislav and Zlatija Vitomir (Stefanovic) M.; m. Svetlana Miroslav Vukovic, Apr. 13, 1995; 1 child, Vasilije. Diploma in engring., U. Belgrade, 1987; MS, Case Western Res. U., Cleve., 1990; PhD, Harvard U., 1996. Rsch. engr. Resource Internat., Inc., Columbus, Ohio, 1990-91; rsch. assoc. Cambridge U., Eng., 1996-99; sr. scientist U. Virginia Materials Sci. Engrg., 1999—. Contbr. articles to profl. jours. Recipient Craig J. Miller Meml. award Case Western Res. U., 1990. Mem. Materials Rsch. Soc. (invited spkr. fall meeting 1998). E-mail: sm9vw@virginia.edu. Office: Dept Materials and Engrg U Virginia Charlottesville VA 22904-0001

MESCHEDE, DIETER H.K., geneticist, researcher; b. Arnsberg, Germany, Mar. 21, 1963; s. Alfred and Doris (Ludwig) M.; m. Kerstin Kebsch, July 9, 1993; children: Anna-Maria, Christian. MD, U. Munster, 1989. Rschr. Inst. Reprodv. Medicine, Munster, 1991-93; rschr./clinician Inst. Human Genetics, Munster, 1993—. Contbr. articles to profl. jours., chpts. to books. Lt. German Air Force, 1990-91. Deutsche Forschungsgemeinschaft Sci. Tng. grantee, 1991. Mem. German Soc. Human Genetics, European Soc. Human Reprodn. and Embryology, German Soc. Study of Fertility. Roman Catholic. Avocations: classical music, literature, cycling. Office: Inst Human Genetics, Vesaliusweg 12-14, 48149 Münster Germany

MESCHER, ROBERT J., technology executive; b. Jan. 14, 1963. AS in Bus. Mgmt., El Camino Coll., Lawndale, Calif., 1993; BS in Acctg., Calif. State U., Dominguez Hills, 1996, MBA, 1998. Sr. acct. Hilton at Walt Disney World, Lake Buena Vista, Fla., 1983-87; asst. controller L.A. Airport Hilton, 1987-89; contr. Pasadena (Calif.) Hilton, 1989-90; v.p. fin. and adminstrn. Imperial Tech., El Segundo, Calif., 1990—. Treas. region 92 Am. Youth Soccer Orgn., El Segundo, 1996-2000. Office: Imperial Tech 2305 Utah Ave El Segundo CA 90245-4803

MESCHIA, JAMES FREDERICK, neurologist, researcher; b. Denver, June 16, 1965; s. Giacomo Meschia and Irene Rose Battaglia; m. Diana Lee, May 24, 1992; children: Catherine, Camille. BA, Columbia U., 1987; MD, Johns Hopkins U., 1992. Diplomate Am. Bd. Psychiatry and Neurology. Intern U. Colo., Denver, 1992-93; resident Washington U., St. Louis, 1993-96; fellow Ind. U., Indpls., 1996-97; sr. assoc. cons. Mayo Clinic, Jacksonville, Fla., 1997; asst. prof. Mayo Clinic, Rochester, Minn., 1998—. Mem. Am. Acad. Neurology, Am. Heart Assn. Stroke Coun. Home: 8123 Woodgrove Rd Jacksonville FL 32256-7314 Office: Mayo Clinic 4500 San Pablo Rd S Jacksonville FL 32224-3899

MESCHKOW, JORDAN M., lawyer; b. Bklyn., Mar. 25, 1957; s. Gerald Meschkow and Florence Y. (Katz) Silverman; m. Susan G. Scher, Aug. 10, 1980; children: Sasha Hayley, Alisha Sadie. BS in Biology, SUNY, Stony Brook, 1979; JD, Chgo. Kent Coll. Law, 1982. Bar: Ariz. 1982, Fla. 1983; registered U.S. Patent and Trademark Office 1983. Assoc. James F. Duffy, Patent Atty., Phoenix, Ariz., 1982; ptnr. Duffy & Meschkow, Phoenix, 1983-84; sole practice Phoenix, 1984-92; sr. ptnr. Meschkow & Gresham, P.L.C., Phoenix, 1992—; frequent talk radio guest and spkr. at seminars on patent, trademark and copyright law. Contbr. article series to profl. jours.; patentee in field. Exec. bd. City of Phoenix Fire Pub. Awareness League, 1996—. Mem. Am. Intellectual Property Law Assn., State Bar Ariz. (intellectual property sect. 1982—), State Bar Fla. Avocations: gardening, motorcycling, bicycling, skating, swimming. E-mail: M&GPatent@mcimail.com. Office: 5727 N 7th St Ste 409 Phoenix AZ 85014-5818

MESEKE, CORNELIA BEATE, psychologist, researcher; b. Bremen, Germany, Feb. 14, 1952; came to U.S., 1961, returned to Germany, 1974, arrived in Poland, 1990; d. Siegfried Meseke and Helga Blazkova. BA in Psychology, U. So. Calif., L.A., 1974; BA in Geology, U. Tübingen, Germany, 1980; MA in Psychology, U. Osnabrück, Germany, 1984. Rsch. asst. U. Tübingen, Germany, 1977-80; rsch. asst. U. Osnabrück, 1982-84, asst. prof., 1984-86; asst. prof. Cath. U., Lublin, Poland, 1990-91; cons. Med. Acad., Lublin, 1991-93; dir. Inst. Health, Edn. and Human Welfare, Lublin, 1993—; human engring. cons. works coun., 1984-90 ; coll. instr., Marburg, Germany, 1986-89. Author: Aspects of Environmental Dissonance, 1998, Bibliographies of Polish Nursing Theses, (in Polish) 2000, A Bibliography of Masters Theses in Lublin, (in English) 2000; contbr. articles to profl. jours. Grantee Daimler-Benz scholarship, Germany, 1988, Tempus scholarship, Poland, 1992. Mem. Bahai Faith. Achievements include research in community health and environmental studies. Home: ul Peowiaków 8/13, 20-007 Lublin Poland Office: Inst Health Edn & Human Wel, ul Peowiaków 8/2a, 20-007 Lublin Poland

MESERVE, JOHN SHACKFORD, II, retirement housing executive; b. Newark, Oct. 5, 1940; s. Julien Hill and Jane (Brydges) M.; m. Mary Ellen Meserve, Mar. 11, 1964; children: Michele Avella, John, Elizabeth. BS in Nautical Sci., Merchant Marine Acad., 1963; MS in Computer Sci., U.S. Naval Postgrad. Sch., 1975. Cert. retirement housing profl. Commd. USN, 1964, advanced through grades to capt.; commanding officer Naval Air Sta., Mayport, Fla., 1987-90; ret.; exec. dir. Beachers C. of C., Jacksonville, Fla., 1990-93, Fleet Landing, Atlantic Beach, Fla., 1993—. Mayor/commr. City of Atlantic Beach, 1995—; chmn. bd. Dean's Coun., Coll. of Health, Jacksonville, 1995—; chmn. Mayport (Fla.) Waterfront Partnership, 1996—. Decorated DFC. Mem. Beaches C. of C. (chmn. bd. 1993—), Meninak Club. Republican. Roman Catholic. Avocations: computers, woodworking, jogging. Home: 2126 Beach Ave Atlantic Bch FL 32233-5933 Office: Fleet Landing Retirement Cmty One Fleet Landing Blvd Atlantic Beach FL 32233

MESFIN, SEYOUM, Ethiopian government official; b. Tigrai, Jan. 25, 1949. Diploma in industrial chem., Bahir Dar Gojjam, Ethiopia, 1971; diploma in physical sci., U. Addis Ababa, Ethiopia, 1974. Mem. politobur. of C.C., head dept. fgn. affairs Tigrai People's Liberation Front, 1975-88; mem. exec. coun., head dept. fgn. affairs Ethiopian People's Revolutionary Democratic Front, 1988-91; min. fgn. affairs Govt. of Ethiopia, 1991—; mem. Tigrai People's Liberation Front; chmn. fgn. affairs com. Ethiopian People's Revolutionary Democratic Front. Office: Ministry Fgn Affairs, PO Box 393, Addis Ababa Ethiopia*

MESHBESHER, RONALD I., lawyer; b. Mpls., May 18, 1933; s. Nathan J. and Esther J. (Balman) M.; m. Sandra F. Siegel, June 17, 1956 (div. 1978); children: Betsy F., Wendy S., Stacy J.; m. Kimberly L. Garnaas, May 23, 1988; 1 child, Jolie M. BS in Law, U. Minn., 1955, JD, 1957. Bar: Minn. 1957, U.S. Supreme Ct. 1966. Prosecuting atty. Hennepin County, Mpls., 1958-61; pres. Meshbesher and Spence Ltd., Mpls., 1961—; lectr. numerous legal and profl. orgns.; mem. adv. com. on rules of criminal procedure Minn. Supreme Ct., 1971-91; cons. on recodification of criminal procedure code Czech Republic Ministry of Justice, 1994. Author: Trial Handbook for Minnesota Lawyers, 1992; mem. bd. editors Criminal Law Advocacy Reporter; mem. adv. bd. Bur. Nat. Affairs Criminal Practice Manual; contbr. numerous articles to profl. jours. Mem. ATLA (bd. govs. 1968-71), ABA, Minn. Bar Assn., Internat. Acad. Trial Lawyers, Am. Coll. Trial Lawyers, Am. Bd. Trial Advs., Am. Bd. Criminal Lawyers (v.p. 1983), Am. Acad. Forensic Scis., Nat. Assn. Criminal Def. Lawyers (pres. 1984-85), Minn. Trial Lawyers Assn. (pres. 1973-74), Minn. Assn. Criminal Def. Lawyers (pres. 1991-92), Trial Lawyers for Pub. Justice, Calif. Attys. for Criminal Justice. Avocations: biking, photography, travel, flying. Home: 2010 Sugarwood Dr Orono MN 55356-9339 Office: Meshbesher & Spence 1616 Park Ave Minneapolis MN 55404-1695

MESHCHEROV, BORIS RAKHIMOVICH, physicist; b. Moscow, July 20, 1956; s. Rakhim Ainudinovich and Irina Vladimirovna (Davydova) M.; m. Irina Mikhailovna Mikheeva, July 1, 1978; 1 child, Kirill Borisovich. MSc, Moscow State U., 1980; PhD, Kurchatov Inst., Moscow, 1991. Engr. Kurchatov Inst., 1980-83, minor sci. fellow, then sci. fellow, 1983-94, sr. sci. fellow, 1994-97, leading sci. fellow, 1997—; lectr. Moscow Inst. Physics and Tech., 1993—. Contbr. articles to sci. jours. (Kurchatov prize 1992). Grantee, Am. Phys. Soc., 1993, Internat. Sci. Found., Washington, 1994, Russian Found. for Basic Rsch., Moscow, 1995. Avocations: reading, music, theatre, travel, sports. Home: 7-2-19 Klyaz'minskaya Str, 127644 Moscow Russia Office: Kurchatov Inst, Kurchatov Sq, 123182 Moscow Russia

MESHKE, GEORGE LEWIS, drama and humanities educator; b. Yakima, Wash., Oct. 7, 1930; s. George Joseph and Marye Elizabeth (Lopas) M. BA, U. Wash., 1953, MA, 1959, PhD in Drama, 1972. Cert. tchr., Wash. Tchr. English and drama Zillah High Sch., Wash., 1955-58; tchr. English and drama high sch., Bellevue, Wash., 1958-60, Federal Way, Wash., 1960-70; dir., actor Old Brewery Theatre, Helena, Mont., 1962-66; prof. drama Yakima Valley C.C., Yakima, 1970—; casting dir., dir. summer seminar Laughing Horse Summer Theatre, Ellensburg, Wash., 1989-96; adj. prof. grad. studies Ctrl. Wash. U., Tchr. Exch., London, 1995, People-to People Exch., China, 2000; lectr. Inquiring Mind series Wash. State Humanities, 1989-91; regional dir. Am. Coll. Theatre Festival, Washington, 1980-86; arts dialogue J.F. Kennedy Ctr., Washington, 1987—; casting dir., actor Hollywood Ind. Prodns.; mem. adv. coun. Kennedy Ctr. Author, producer Towers of Tomorrow, 1985, The Halls of Yesterday-Yakima Hist. drama; appeared in Yakima, Washington, 1998. Regional bd. dirs. Common Cause, Yakima, 1971-73; active Nat. Hist. Soc., Nat. Wilderness Soc., Roosevelt Meml. Found., Wash. State Commn. Humanities, Drama League. With U.S. Army, 1953-55, Austria. Recipient Gold medallion Kennedy Ctr., 1985, Wash. State Humanities medal, 1983, NISAD medallion, 1989, Wash. State Drama award, 1999. Mem. ACLU, Wash. Edn. Assn., N.W. Drama Assn., Am. Edn. Theatre Assn., Am. Fedn. Tchrs., Kennedy Libr., Libr. Congress (assoc.), Truman Libr. (honor mem.), Phi Delta Kappa. Democrat. Avocations: travel, mountain climbing, skiing, reading. Home: 5 N 42nd Ave Yakima WA 98908-3214 Office: Yakima Valley CC 16th And Nob Hill Blvd Yakima WA 98907

MESHKOV, YURY YAKOVLEVICH, metallurgist; b. Zaporozhye, Ukraine, May 3, 1932; s. Yakov Borisovich Zagorsky and Anna Andreyevna Meshkova. Diploma in metallurgy, Kiev, 1955; postgrad., Inst. Metal Physics, NAS, Kiev, Ukraine, 1957-60, candidate of sci., 1961; DSc, Ural Poly. Inst., Sverdlovsk, 1973. From jr. rschr. to sr. rschr. Inst. Metal Physics, NAS, 1961-75, head dept. physics of strenght fracture of metals, 1975-2000, prof. phys. metallurgy, 1981—; expert Higher Cert. Commn. Ukraine, 1993-99. Author: Physical Fundamentals of Brittleness of Steel Structures, 1980, Structure of Metals and Brittleness of Steel Products, 1985. Recipient State award Ukraine Soviet Socialist Republic, 1974, State award USSR, 1986. Home: 2-4/7 Pushkinskay St, Kiev 252034, Ukraine

MESKAUSKAS, ARTURAS, molecular geneticist, researcher; b. Ukmerge, Lithuania, Aug. 31, 1953; s. Alfonsas and Albina (Aleksandraviciute) M. B in Sci., State U. Vilnius, Lithuania, 1977; PhD, Inst. Biochemistry, Vilnius, 1991. Sr. scientist Inst. Botany, Vilnius, Lithuania, 1988—; vis. scientist U. Medicine and Dentistry N.J. Contbr. articles to profl. jours. Mem. European Molecular Biology Orgn. Workshop. Home: Sausio 13-sios 21-67, LT 2050 Vilnius Lithuania Office: Inst of Botany, Zaliuju Ezeru 49, LT 2021 Vilnius Lithuania also: U Medicine and Dentistry NJ Dept Molecular Gen Microbio 675 Hoes Ln Piscataway NJ 08854

MESKHI, APOLLO, obstetrician, gynecologist, researcher, educator, manager; b. Tbilisi, Georgia, USSR, May 31, 1959; s. Tengiz and Mzia (Iashvili) M.; m. Tinatin Kldiashvili, Nov. 17, 1970; children: Elaine, Tengiz Max. MD with honors, Tbilisi State Med. Inst., 1982; postgrad., Inst. Perinatal Medicine, Ob-Gyn., Tbilisi; PhD, Moscow Inst. Medicine and Stomatology, 1988. active projects of cooperation between the former Soviet Union and western countries. Author two books in obstetrics and gynecology; contbr. articles to profl. jours. Fellow Royal Soc. Medicine; mem. Royal Coll. Ob-Gyn. (London), Georgian Med. Assn. (organizing group 1988-91), Young Rsch. Scientist Club (organizing com. 1977-80), Brit. Soc. Coloposcopy and Cervical Pathology. Avocations: music, sports, travel. Home: 8 The Fold, Urmston Manchester M41 5SP, England Office: Fl 34 Block 17, Kv 2 Digomi Mass, Republic Georgia Tbilisi 380059, Republic of Georgia

MESKILL, VICTOR P., college president, educator; b. Albertson, N.Y., May 9, 1935; s. James Joseph and Ida May (Pfalzer) M.; m. Gail King Heidinger, 1986; children by previous marriage—Susan Ann, Janet Louise, Gary James, Glenn Thomas, Kenneth John, Matthew Adam. BA, Hofstra U., 1961, MA (grad. scholar), 1962; PhD, St. John's U., 1967; postgrad. insts., Ohio State U., 1968; postgrad., Harvard U., 1972, NYU, 1973; DSc (hon.), Samara State Aerospace U., Russia, 1993; LHD (hon.), St. John's U., 1995; DCL (hon.), Moscow Internat. U., Russia, 1996; DCL (hon.), D Ecology/Biosphere (hon.), Coll. Puschino State U., Moscow, 1996; D of Pedagogy (PdD) (hon.), Dowling Coll., 1997; D of Econs. (hon.), U. Istanbul, Turkey, 1997; D of Sci., Yanshan U., Peoples' Republic of China, 1998. Lab. asst., instr. biology Hofstra U., 1960-62; N.Y. State teaching fellow St. John's U., 1962-63; instr. biology Nassau (N.Y.) C.C., 1963-64; tchr. sci. Central H.S. Dist. 2, Floral Park, N.Y., 1963-64; lectr. biology C.W. Post Coll., Greenvale, N.Y., 1963-64, instr. biology, 1964-67, asst. prof., 1967-68, assoc. prof., 1968-74, assoc. dir. Inst. for Student Problems, supr. student tchrs., 1967-68, asst. dean Coll., dean summer sch., coordinator Admissions Office, coordinator adult and continuing edn. programs, 1968-69; dean adminstrn. C.W. Post Ctr. of L.I. U., 1969-70, v.p. adminstrn., 1970-77, prof. biology, 1975-77; pres. Dowling Coll., Oakdale, L.I., 1977-2000, pres. emeritus, 2000—; cons. in edn. and biology; chem. technician, detective Tech. Rsch. Bur., Nassau County Police Dept., 1958-63, mem. sci. adv. com., 1970; mem. adv. coun. Aerospace Edn. Coun. Inc., 1968; trustee, mem. state legis. com. Commn. Ind. Colls. and Univs.; mem. evaluation teams Mid. States Assn., 1971—; mem. higher edn. adv. com. N.Y. State Senate; mem. Nassau-Suffolk Comprehensive Health Planning Coun.; chmn. Internat. and Mediterranean Studies Group Conf. Author book; contbr. articles to profl. jours. Founding mem., vice-chmn. bd. trustees Nassau Higher Edn. Consortium; bd. dirs. Suffolk County coun. Boy Scouts Am.; mem. N.Y. State Energy Rsch. and Devel. Authority, Town of Islip Devel. Commn.; chmn. bd. trustees L.I. Regional Adv. Coun. Higher Edn.; chmn. L.I. Mid Suffolk Bus. Action; bd. dirs. Southside Hosp., N.Y.; v.p. L.I. Forum for Tech.; former commr. Suffolk County Vanderbilt Mus.; mem. Bus. Coun. N.Y.; hon. mem. U. Pau and Pays de l'Adour, Pau, France, 1994; hon. prof. Minjiang U., Fuzhou, Peoples Republic of China, 1994; active mem. Universal Life Keeping Problems Acad., Dept. Justice Russian Fedn., Moscow. Decorated commendatore dell'Ordine al Merito (Italy); NSF rsch. grantee, 1967-69; Named Tchr. of Year, Aesculapius Med. Arts Soc., C.W. Post Coll. of L.I. U., 1967; Disting. Faculty Mem. of Year, C.W. Post Ctr. L.I. U., 1977, Educator of Yr. WLIW Channel 21, 1996; recipient George M. Estabrook award Hofstra U., 1978, Higher Edn. Leadership award Corning Glass Works, 1987, Disting. Leadership award L.I., 1989, Diploma Merito, Garibaldi Inst., Rome, Diploma of Honor, Rsch. Ctr. for Islamic History, Art and Culture, Istanbul, Turkey, Advancement for Commerce and Industry Disting. Svc. award in field of edn., 1997. Mem. AAAS, Coun. Advancement and Support of Edn., Am. Assn. Collegiate Registrars and Admissions Officers, Am. Assn. Higher Edn., Am. Inst. Biol. Scis., Am. Soc. Zoologists, Am. Assn. U. Adminstrs., Commn. on Ind. Colls. and Univs. (trustee), Nat. Assn. Biology Tchrs., Nat. Sci. Tchrs. Assn., Soc. Protozoologists, N.Y. Acad. Scis., Camilo Josè Cela Found. (hon.), Met. Assn. Coll. and Univ. Biologists (founder, mem. steering com.), Bus. Coun. N.Y., Oakdale C. of C. (founding mem., dir.), Russian Soc. Plant Physiologists (corr.), Universal Life Keeping Problems Acad. Moscow, Tsiolkovski Space Acad. Moscow (fgn.), Univ. Club (N.Y.C.), Wings Club (N.Y.C.), Nat. Arts Club (N.Y.C.), L.I. Coun. Fgn. Rels., L.I. Assn. Commerce and Industry (v.p. edn., dir.), Alpha Chi, Kappa Delta Pi, Phi Delta Kappa, Sigma Xi, Beta Beta Beta, Alpha Eta Rho, Delta Mu Delta, Kappa Delta Rho.

MESKO, IVAN, economist, mathematician, educator; b. Zg Leskovec, Slovenia, Apr. 1, 1933; s. Jozef and Filomena (Rudolf) M.; m. Tatjana Gortnar, July 13, 1963; children: Tjasa, Majda, Metoda. B in Math., U. Ljubljana (Slovenia), 1961, M in Econ., 1971; D in Econ., U., Ljubljana, Slovenia, 1974. Tchr. Coll., Ptuj, Slovenia, 1961-65; rschr. Aluminum Factory, Kidricevo, Slovenia, 1965-68; lectr. U. Maribor, Slovenia, 1968-74; prof. U. Maribor, 1974—. Author: Business Optimization, 1990, (computer program) Linear Optimization, 1982, Fractional Piecewise Linear Optimization, 1994. Mem. N.Y. Acad. Sci. Office: U Maribor EPF, Razlagova 14, SI 2000 Maribor Slovenia

MESLIER, FRANCOIS HENRI, electrical utility executive; b. Viroflay, France, July 23, 1949; s. Pierre and Paulette (Coutant) M.; m. Catherine Ghislaine Goudey, Sept. 7, 1973; three children. Grad., Ecoly. Poly. Paris, 1969; DSc, U. Paris, 1976. From engr. to mng. dir overseas depts. EDF, La Défense, France, 1972—. Mem. IEEE, Conf. Internat. des Grands Reseaux Electriques (chmn. study com. 37), Rotary. Home: 91 rue du Cherche-Midi, 75006 Paris France

MESNIAEFF, GREGORY, economist; b. N.Y.C., Jan. 13, 1958; s. Peter G. and Maria A. (Voropajeff) M.; m. Elizabeth Burke, June 18, 1989. BBA, CUNY, N.Y.C., 1986; MA in Econs., Trinity Coll., Hartford, 1989. Market rschr. Blair TV, N.Y.C., 1989-90; industry analyst telecomms. Northern Bus. Info./McGraw Hill, N.Y.C., 1990-94; assoc. v.p. equity rsch. Wheat First Butcher & Singer, Richmond, Va., 1994-96; sr. v.p. equity rsch. Robinson-Humphrey Co., LLC, Atlanta, 1996—. Fellow Trinity Coll. Bd. Fellows, Hartford, 1994-96. Recipient All-Star Analyst Telecom. Equipment Wall St. Jour., 1998. Fellow The Frick Collection; mem. Nat. Assn. Bus. Econs., Comms. Tech. Analysts Assn., Trinity Club Atlanta, N.Y. Athletic Club, Russian Nobility Assn. Am., Nat. Trust for Hist. Preservation, English-Speaking Union. Republican. Russian Orthodox. Avocations: skiing, sailing, cycling, historic preservation. Home: PO Box 53074 Atlanta GA 30355-1074 Office: Robinson-Humphrey Co LLC 3333 Peachtree Rd NE Atlanta GA 30326-1070

MESSENGER, NIGEL JAMES, molecular biologist, researcher; b. London, Feb. 1, 1958; s. James Teasdale and Joyce Dorothy (Smyth) M.; m. Georgina Gabrielle Ruth Kelly, Sept. 16, 1995. BSc in Biochemistry, Kent (Eng.) U., 1979. Rsch. technician U. Coll. London, 1980-86, sr. rschr., 1986—; rsch. asst. Wellcome/CRC Inst., Cambridge, Eng., 2000—. Contbr. articles to profl. jours. Mem. TVR Car Club, British Film Inst., Jaguar Drivers Club. Avocations: writing, ornithology, cinema.

MESSER, ANDREA ELYSE, anthropologist, archaeologist, science writer; b. Freeport, N.Y., Apr. 4, 1952; d. Julius and Gloria Rhoda (Epstein) M. BA in Sci. and Culture, Purdue U., 1973; MA in Journalism and Sci. Comm., Boston U., 1976; MS in Anthropology, Pa. State U., 1995, postgrad., 1995—. Reporter Attleboro (Mass.) Sun Chronicle, 1975; tech. editor, writer Bell Labs., Whippany, N.J., 1976-79; editor Freund Pub. Co., Tel Aviv, 1980; pub. info. officer ASME, N.Y.C., 1981-88; sci. and rsch. comm. officer Pa. State U., State College, 1988—; ad hoc mem. WISE Network, State College, 1994—. Contbr. articles to profl. jours. Mem. AAAS, Nat. Assn. Sci. Writers, Soc. of Am. Archaeology, Am. Geophys. Union, Am. Anthropological Assn. Office: Sci and Rsch Comm 201 Rider House University Park PA 16802

MESSER, JANICE GRABOWSKI, academic administrator; b. Wilmington, Del., July 24, 1939; d. Stanley Joseph and Helen (Pajewski) Grabowski; m. Robert Gerard Messer, Aug. 24, 1963; children: Edward C., Helen Messer Ventouris, Elizabeth S. Tanner, Allison S. Shea, Robert Gerard Jr., Jonathan P., Victoria C., Lloyd. BA, Chestnut Hill Coll., Phila., 1961; postgrad., Inst. for Advanced Study, 1962, Adelphi U., 1961-62, Antioch-New Eng. Coll., 1989-91; MS in Mgmt., 1991. Owner Ambiance, party planning, Wilmington, 1973-87; co-owner, mgr. Colonial Printing Co., Bennington, Vt., 1979-99; dir. audience devel. Oldcastle Theatre Co., Bennington, 1983-87; campaign coord. Bennington Coll., 1987-88, acting dir. alumni rels., 1988-89, assoc. dir. alumni rels. and ann. giving, 1989-90; dir. devel. Northern Berkshire Coun. of Arts, North Adams, Mass., 1991-93; adminstr., cons. projects for Holden-Leonard Mill, 1990; cons. ARC, 1990-96; chief alumni and devel. officer Mass. Coll. Liberal Arts, 1994-98, dir. alumni devel. and programs, 1998—. Trustee Bennington Mus., 1981-2000; founder, vol. dir. Arts Alive!, Bennington, 1985-89; mem. nominating com. Vt. coun. on Arts, Montpelier, 1986-87; bd. dirs., v.p. Oldcastle Theatre Co., 1988-91; bd. dirs. United Way; founder, bd. dirs. Bennington Area Arts Coun., 1988-91; bd. dirs. Green Mtn. chpt. ARC, 1990-96; Parish coun. St. Francis de Sales Ch., Bennington, 1991-96. Recipient best actress award Del. Theatre, Newark, 1971; grantee Vt. Coun. on Arts, 1984-86. Mem. Coun. for Advancement and Support Edn. (grantee 1988), Nat. Soc. Fundraising Execs., AAUW, Bennington C. of C. (bd. dirs. 1981-85). Roman Catholic. Avocations: theatre, arts, reading, gourmet cooking, tennis. E-mail: jmesser@mcla.mass.edu. Home: 125 Grandview St Bennington VT 05201-2433

MESSER, THOMAS MARIA, museum director; b. Bratislava, Czechoslovakia, Feb. 9, 1920; came to U.S., 1939, naturalized, 1944; s. Richard and Agatha (Albrecht) M.; m. Remedios García Villa, Jan. 10, 1948. Exch. student, Inst. Internat. Edn., 1939; student, Thiel Coll., Greenville, Pa., 1939-41; BA, Boston U., 1942; degree, U. Sorbonne, Paris, 1947; MA, Harvard U., 1951; DFA (hon.), U. Mass., 1962, U. of Arts, Phila., 1988. Dir. Roswell (N.Mex.) Mus., 1949-52; asst. dir. Am. Fedn. Arts, N.Y.C., 1952-53, dir. exhbns., 1953-55, dir. fedn., 1955-56, trustee, 1972-75; hon. prof. Johane Wolfgang Goethe U., Frankfurt, Germany, 1997, prof., 1998—; dir. Inst. Contemporary Art, Boston, 1957-61, Solomon R. Guggenheim Mus., N.Y.C., 1961-88, Peggy Guggenheim Collection, Venice, Italy, 1980-88, Solomon R. Guggenheim Found., N.Y.C., trustee, 1980-90, dir. emeritus, 1990—; chief curator Schirn Kunsthalle, Frankfurt, 1994-99; adj. prof. Harvard U., 1960, Barnard Coll., 1966, 71; prof. Hochschule für Angewandte Kunst, Vienna, Austria, 1984; pres. Assn. Art Mus. Dirs., 1974-75, hon. mem., 1988—; pres. Ind. Com. Med. Art Mus., 1976-80, hon. mem., 2000—; trustee Inst. Internat. Edn., 1990-98, hon. mem., 1998—; founding mem. Am. Arts Alliance, Washington, 1978-81; pres. The MacDowell Colony Inc., 1977-78; mem. adv. bd. Palazzo Grassi, Venice, 1986-97; trustee Fontana Found., Milan, 1996—, The Isamu Noguchi Found., N.Y.C. & Tokyo, 1988—; sr. cultural advisor Am.'s Soc., 1988-96; sr. advisor visual arts Caixa Found., 1991-96, guest curator 1998—; mem. coun. Nat. Gallery, Czech Republic, 1994-99. Author: Edvard Munch, 1973, Vasily Kandinsky, 1997; contbr. to mus. catalogues, art jours. Decorated chevalier Legion d'Honneur, France, 1980, Officier Legion d'Honneur, France, 1989; recipient Goethe medal Fed. Republic Germany; spl. fellow for study in Brussels Belgian-Am. Ednl. Found., 1953; sr. fellow Ctr. Advanced Studies, Wesleyan U., 1966. Mem. Internat. com. for Mus. and Collections Modern Art, Met. Opera (N.Y.C.), Century Assn. (N.Y.C.). Home: 35 Sutton Pl New York NY 10022-2464 Office: 205 E 77th St New York NY 10021-2061

MESSERE, KENNETH CHARLES, international civil servant; b. Richmond, Surrey, Eng., Apr. 16, 1928; arrived in France, 1964; s. Charles and Marie (Newman) M.; m. Elizabeth Humphrey, May 3, 1954 (div. Nov. 1981); children: Martin, Philip, Tom, Kevin; m. Brunehilde Lequesne, June 16, 1984. MA, Oxford U., 1951. Asst. prin. HM Customs and Excise, London, 1951-55, prin., 1955-64; prin. adminstr. Orgn. Econ. Coop. Devel., Paris, 1964-71, head fiscal affairs divsn., 1971-91; retired, 1991; cons. World Bank, IMF, Orgn. Econ. Coop. Devel., 1991—. Author: Tax Policy in OECD Countries, 1993, Tax Systems in Industrialized Countries, 1998; contbr. over 50 articles to profl. publs. Recipient: Order British Empire. Avocations: internat. corr. chess master, bridge, reading, classical music, theatre. Home: 118 rue Lauriston, 75116 Paris France

MESSERSCHMIDT, ALBRECHT MATTHIAS, x-ray crystallographer, educator; b. Wippra, Germany, Jan. 31, 1945; s. Wilhelm and Margot Hedwig (Lange) M.; m. Beate Dorothea Selm, Nov. 10, 1967; 1 child, Nadja. M in Crystallography, Humboldt-U., Berlin, 1968, Dr.rer.nat., 1972; Dr.rer.nat.habil., U. Konstanz, Germany, 1996. Postdoctoral fellow Humboldt U., Berlin, 1972-75; rsch. assoc. Acad. Scis. German Dem. Republic, Berlin, 1975-81; postdoctoral fellow Max Planck Inst. for Biochemistry, Martinsried, Germany, 1983-90; sr. scientist Max Planck Inst. for Biochemistry, Martinsried, 1990—; lectr. faculty of biology U. Konstanz, 1996—. Editor: Multi-Copper Oxidases, 1997, Handbook of Metalloproteins. Polit. prisoner Prison Brandenburg, 1981-83. Office: Max Planck Inst Biochem, Am Klopferspitz 18A, D-82152 Martinsried Bavaria, Germany

MESSERSCHMIDT, GERALD LEIGH, pharmaceutical industry executive, physician; b. Vancouver, B.C., Can., Feb. 2, 1950; s. George Gus and Joan May (Chapman) M.; children: Jacqueline Diane, Victoria Leigh, Jonathan Leigh. BS, Portland State U., 1972; MD, U. Oreg., Portland, 1976. Diplomate Am. Bd. Internal Medicine, Am. Bd. Med. Oncology, Am. Bd. Hematology. Resident in internal medicine Letterman Army Med. Ctr., San Francisco, 1976-79; fellow in oncology and hematology NIH, Bethesda, Md., 1979-82; head exptl. hematology Nat. Cancer Inst., NIH, Bethesda, Md., 1981-82; dir. bone marrow transplants for Dept. of Def. Wilford Hall Med. Ctr., San Antonio, 1982-88; dir. bone marrow transplants U. Mich. Med. Ctr., Ann Arbor, 1988-90; dir. med. affairs Ciba-Geigy Pharm., Summit, N.J., 1990-92, exec. dir. med. affairs, 1992-93; v.p. med. and regulatory affairs DNX Corp., Princeton, N.J., 1993-94; corp. v.p. C.R. Bard Inc., Murray Hill, N.J., 1994-95, sr. v.p., 1995-96; CEO, pres. Kimeragen, Inc., Newtown, Pa., 1996-2000; exec. chmn. Wild-Type Enterprises Worldwide, 2000—. Maj. USAF, 1982-88. Fellow ACP; mem. Am. Soc. Med. Oncology, Am. Soc. Hematology. Office: Wild-Type Worldwide LLC 270 Curwen Rd Bryn Mawr PA 19010-1617

MESSERSCHMIDT, ULRICH FRANZ GEORG, physicist; b. Berlin, June 26, 1938; s. Wilhelm Arnold Otto and Margot Gerda Hedwig (Lange) M.; m. Heike Hanson, Aug. 7, 1941; children: Bettina, Bernhard. Diploma in physics, Martin Luther U., Halle, Germany, 1962, D of Natural Scis., 1968, D habilitation, 1987. Cert. prof. Acad. Scis., Berlin, 1989. Sci. asst. Martin Luther U., 1962-68; head of rsch. group Acad. Sci., Halle, 1968-89, head of dept., 1989-91; head of rsch. group Max Planck Inst. Microstructure Physics, Halle, 1992—. Editor: (book) Electron Microscopy in Plasticity and Fracture Research of Materials, 1990, (jour. vol.) Plastic Deformation of Structural Materials at High Temperatures, 1997; mem. editl. bd.: European Phys. Jour.; contbr. numerous articles to sci. jours. and books. Mem. German Phys. Soc., German Soc. Electron Microscopy (bd. dirs. 1996-97), German Soc. Material Scis. Avocation: playing flute. Office: Max Planck Inst Micro Phys, Weinberg 2, D-06120 Halle Germany

MESSERSCHMIDT, WILLIAM HARCLERODE, army noncommissioned officer, percussionist; b. Lebanon, Pa., Apr. 30, 1947; s. Harry Edgar and Sylva (Harclerode) M.; m. Janice Andersen, Dec. 28, 1971; children: William F., Ann K., Dorothy R., Edward D. MusB with distinction, Eastman Sch. Music, 1969; postgrad., Cath. U. Am., 1983, Va. Theol. Sem., 1992-96. Enlisted man U.S. Army, 1969, advanced through grades to sgt. maj., 1994; percussionist U.S. Army Field Band, Ft. George G. Meade, Md., 1969-74; percussionist U.S. Army Band (Pershing's Own), Ft. Myer, Va., 1974-85, asst. sect. leader, 1985-89, leader percussion sect., 1989-94, leader percussion group, 1994—; pvt. tchr. percussion, Springfield and Woodbridge, Va., 1973—; adj. instr. percussion No. Va. C.C., Woodbridge, 1983—; percussionist Prince William Symphony Orch., Lake Ridge, Va., 1989-93; timpanist, percussionist Nt. Christian Choir Orch., Gaithersburg, Md., 1990—. Choir dir. Grace Ref. Presbyn. Ch., Woodbridge, 1985-93. Mem. Percussive Arts Soc., Am. Fedn. Musicians, Internat. Assn. Rudimental Percussionists, Smithsonian Assocs., Kappa Delta Pi. Avocations: reading literature, philosophy and art history, tennis, collecting baseball cards. Home: 60 Hergelrode Dr Myerstown PA 17067-2513

MESSIAS, JOSÉ AUGUSTO DA SILVA, medical educator, physician; b. Rio de Janeiro, May 31, 1949; s. Tarcisio Torres and Marina Tati (Da Silva) M.; m. Katia Maria Montaury De Souza, Mar. 24, 1979; children: Gustavo, Gabriel José, Pedro. Diplomate med. scis., State U. Med. Sch., Rio de Janeiro, 1973. Auxiliary prof. State U. Med. Sch., 1973-84, asst. prof., 1984-89, adj. prof., 1989-94, univ. counsellor, 1993—, full prof. medicine dept. internal medicine, 1994—, dir Adolescent Health Care Program, 1995—; med. dir. Casa de Saude Grajau, Rio de Janeiro, 1981—. Home: Josue de Castro 140, 22793-260 Rio de Janeiro Brazil

MESSIER, JEAN-MARIE, construction executive. CEO, chmn. Vivendi, Paris. Office: 42 Ave de Friedland, 75380 Paris France*

MESSIN, MARLENE ANN, plastics company executive; b. St. Paul, Oct. 6, 1935; d. Edgar Leander and Luella Johanna (Rahn) Johnson; m. Eugene Carlson (div. 1972); children: Rick, Debora, Ronald, Lori; m.. Willard Smith (dec. 1975); m. Frank Messin, Sept. 24, 1982; 5 stepchildren. Bookkeeper Jeans Implement Co., Forest Lake, Minn., 1952-53, part-time bookkeeper, 1953-57; bookkeeper Great Plains Supply, St. Paul, 1960-62; bookkeeper Plastic Products Co., Inc., Lindstrom, Minn., 1962-75, pres., 1975—; co-owner, treas. Gustaf's Fine Gifts, Lindstrom, 1985—. Bookkeeper Trinity Luth. Ch., Lindstrom, 1976-81. Mem. Soc. Plastic Engrs., Swedish Inst., Soc. Plastic Industry, Minn. State Hist. Soc., Chgo. County Hist. Soc. Home: 28968 Olinda Trl Lindstrom MN 55045-9429 Office: 30355 Akerson St Lindstrom MN 55045-9456

MESSINA, BONNIE LYNN, lawyer; b. Lima, Ohio, Mar. 17, 1961; m. Dominick Messina. BA, We. Md. Coll., 1983; JD magna cum laude, U. Balt., 1991. Bar: Md. 1991. Claim adjuster The Hartford, Hunt Valley, Md., 1983-86; claim supr. The Hartford, Hunt Valley, 1986-88; assoc. Venable, Baetjer & Howard, Balt., 1991-94; sr. counsel U.S. Fidelity & Guaranty Co., Balt., 1994-98; sr. counsel St. Paul Fire & Marine Ins. Co., Balt., 1999—, group claims counsel, 1999—. Assoc. editor U. Balt. Law Rev., 1990-91. Mem. jud. selection com. Women's Law Ctr., Balt., 1993—; mentor U. Balt. Sch. of law, Balt., 1993-97. Recipient Am. Jurisprudence award Balt., 1989, 90 (2). Mem. ABA (vice chair fidelity and surety sect.), Md. State Bar Assn., Balt. County Bar Assn., Md. Assn. Def. Trial Counsel, Def. Rsch. Inst., Inc., Psi Chi. Office: St Paul Fire & Marine Ins Co Ins Co 6225 Smith Ave Baltimore MD 21209-3652

MESSINA, PAUL FRANCIS, education consultant; b. Newport, R.I., Aug. 31, 1962; s. Nunzio Francis and Ilse Ingeborg (Maibaum) M. BS, SUNY, Albany, 1988; MS, Tex. A&M, Texarkana, 1992. Cert. tchr., Tex., La. Instr. math and physics St. Mary's High Sch., Natcitoches, La., 1989-91, Liberty-Eylau High Sch., Texarkana, Tex., 1991-93; chm. dept. sci. Liberty-Eylau High Sch., Texarkana, 1992-93; preventive medicine officer U.S. Army, 1993-98; edn. cons. Hewlett-Packard Co., Irving, Tex., 1998—; adj. instr. physics Northwestern State U., Natchitoches, 1989-91; adj. instr. math. Texarkana Coll., 1991-93; mem. Merrill Pub. Physics Adv. Coun., 1990-93; adj. instr. physics Ga. Mil. Coll., 1993-95. With U.S. Army, 1988-89, USAR. Tandy Tech. scholar Tandy Corp., 1992; grantee Eisenhower minigrant, Liberty-Eylau Ind. Sch. Dist., Texarkana, 1992. Mem. NEA, Tex. State Tchrs. Assn. (bldg. rep.), Am. Assn. Physics Tchrs., Tex. Acad. Sci., Sci. Tchrs. Assn. Tex., Cen. La. Astronomy Soc., U.S. Profl. Tennis Registry, Nat. Tennis Acad. Roman Catholic. Avocations: tennis, computing, music. Home: 5124 Timber Park Dr Flower Mound TX 75028-2217 Office: Hewlett-Packard Co 3301 W Royal Ln Irving TX 75063-6042

MESSING, STEN INGMAR, agricultural studies educator; b. Brazzaville, Congo, Aug. 4, 1953; s. Carl Emil and Inga Elisabet (Löfgren) M. MSc in Agronomy, Swedish U. Agrl. Scis., Uppsala, 1981, lic. hydrotech., 1989, PhD in Hydrotech., 1993. Assoc. rschr., tchr. Swedish U. Agrl. Scis., Uppsala, 1981-93, sr. rschr., 1993—, assoc. prof. environ. physics, 1998—. Contbr. articles to profl. jours. Avocations: African, Latin and Oriental percussion, Tai Chi. Office: Swedish U Agrl Scis, PO Box 7014, S-750 07 Uppsala Sweden

MESSINIS, LAMBROS, clinical health psychologist; b. Patras, Greece, May 15, 1968; s. Thomas and Paraskevi (Christopoyloy) M.; m. Maria Issaias, Sept. 9, 1994; 1 child, Thomas. BA, Rand Afrikaans U., South Africa, 1993, BA with honors, 1994, MA, 1995, PhD, 1997. Lectr. Tei Patras Sch. Speech Therapy, Greece, 1997—, U. Wales, Athens, 1997-99; clin. health psychologist U. Hosp. Larisa, Greece, 1999—; cons. in field. Editor, translator: Abnormal Psychology, 1999; contbr. articles to profl. jours. With Greek Mil., 1997. Ctr. Sci, Devel. scholar, South Africa, 1996; rsch. fellow R.A. U., Johannesburg, South Africa, 1995-97. Mem. APA, Greek Psychol. Assn. Greek Orthodox. Avocations: reading poetry, water activities. Office: Tei of Patras Sch Health, Dept Speech Therapy, 26334 Patras Greece

MESSMER, KONRAD FRIEDRICH WILHELM, surgical researcher; b. Breisach, Germany, Mar. 16, 1937; s. Wilhelm Konrad and Ilse Messmer (Buchberger) M.; m. Maria José García Castellanos; children: Geraldine, Catalina. MD, U. Munich, 1964, PhD, 1969; PhD (hon.), U. Zaragoza, Spain, 1993, U. Granada, Spain, 1994, U. Santiago, Spain, 1998, U. Cordoba, Argentina, 1999. Prof., chmn. U. Heidelberg, Germany, 1981-90, dean clin. medicine, 1983-85, 87-89; prof., chmn. U. Munich, Germany, 1990—, dir. Inst. for Surg. Rsch., 1990-92; adj. prof. surgery U. Calif., San Diego, 1978-92. Editor-in-chief European surg. Rsch., Progress in Applied Microcirculation. Recipient Premio Gimbernat award Catalanian Soc. Surgery, 1995, Lingen Found. award, 1996. Mem. Acad. Nat. Medicine Mex. (hon.), European Acad. Scis. and Arts. Avocations: sailing, music, languages. Office: U Munich Inst Surg Rsch Clin Grosshadern, Marchioninistrasse 15, 81366 Munich Germany

MESSMER, MARIETTA E., English educator; b. Augsburg, Bavaria, Germany, June 22, 1966; d. Siegfried and Lieselotte C. (Eckhardt) M. MA, Eichstätt (Germany) U., 1991, state exam for secondary edn., 1992; PhD, York U., Toronto, Can., 1997. Cert. secondary edn., Bavaria, Germany. Asst. prof. Göttingen (Germany) U., 1997—. Author: Reconstructing Dickinson's Epistolary Subject Positions, 1997 (Mary McEwan Meml. award 1998). German Acad. Exch. Svc. scholar, Cardiff, Wales, 1987-88, Entrance scholar York U., Toronto, 1992-93, Pres.' Dissertation scholar York U., Toronto, 1996-97. Mem. MLA, German Assn. Am. Studies, Soc. Early Americanists, Emily Dickinson Soc. Avocations: hiking, languages. Home: Zimmermannstr 13 #39, D-37075 Göttingen Germany Office: Göttingen Univ SFB 529, Humboldtallee 17, D-37073 Göttingen Germany

MESSNER, PAUL, microbiologist, educator; b. Amstetten, Austria, May 22, 1949; s. Paul Jakob and Elfriede (Enengl) M.; m. Reinhild M. Daxbacher, Nov. 8, 1980; children: Reinhild A., Michael P. Dipl.Ing., U. Bodenkultur, Vienna, Austria, 1978, Dr., 1980. Asst. prof. U. Bodenkultur, Vienna, 1980-86, assoc. prof. ultrastructure rsch., 1987—, univ. prof., 1996—; Schroedinger rsch. fellow Austrian Sci. Found., Edmonton, Alta., Can., 1988-89; guest prof. U. Guelph, Ont., Can., 1989, 97. Editl. adv. bd. Jour. Bacteriology, 1990-96; co-editor: Crystalline Bacterial Cell Surface Layers, 1988, Immobilised Macromolecules: Application Potentials, 1993, Crystalline Bacterial Cell Surface Proteins, 1996; contbr. over 135 articles to profl. jours., chpts. to books. Recipient Sandoz (Austria) Rsch. Inst. award, 1988, Hygiene prize Austrian Soc. for Hygiene, Microbiology and Preventive Medicine, 1993, Philip Morris Rsch. award, 1998. Mem. Royal Microscopical Soc., Am. Soc. for Microbiology. Achievements include patent on application of crystalline bacterial cell surface layers as a vaccine carrier system. Home: Ameisgasse 63/3/10, A-1140 Vienna Austria Office: U Bodenkultur Wien/Zentrum Ultrastrukturforschung, Gregor Mendel Str 33, A-1180 Vienna Austria

MESSNER, SABINE, technology executive; b. Wels, Austria, May 17, 1954; d. Jakob and Erika (Hauser) M. Diploma in engring., U. Tech., Vienna, 1978. Cert. engr. tech. math. Rsch. asst. Internat. Inst. for Applied Sys. Analysis, Laxenburg, Austria, 1979-83, rsch. scholar, 1983-86, 90-98, sr. rsch. scholar, 1998-99; exec. mgr. Temaplan, Austria, 1987—; exec. mgr. Integrated Resource Mgmt., Vienna, 1998—, also bd. dirs.; cons. Temaplan, Austria and Germany, 1981-98, bd. dirs. Co-author: (book) Global Energy Perspectives, 1998, (book chpt.) Sustainable Development of the Atmosphere, 1986. Mem. Internat. Assn. Energy Economists, Österreichische Gesellschaft für Ops. Rsch., Soroptimist Internat. Office: IRM GmbH, Wienerbergstr 31-39, A-1120 Vienna Austria

MESTAS, JEAN-PAUL, engineer, consultant; b. Paris, Nov. 15, 1925; s. Michel Mestas and Paule Mounet; m. Christiane Schoubrenner, Dec. 23, 1977. BA, LLB, U. Paris, 1947; postgrad., Inst. Polit. Studies, 1947. Cert. in engring. Asst. Compagnie Constrns. Civiles et Industrielles, Paris, 1948-53; dir. Viasphalte, Algeria, Algiers, 1953-62; chief sec. Constrn. Moderne, Chamarande, France, 1962-64; chief dir. Setfina, Paris, 1964-85; corr. Alto Madeira, Brazil, 1999. Author 60 books of poetry and essays including Soleils Noirs, 1965, Part de Vivre, 1968, Château de Paille, 1971, Treize Ballades Le Retour D'Ulysse, 1974, Mémoire D'Exil, 1978, Au Fond Des Choses, 1981, Entre Deux Temps, 1983, Ismène, 1984, Chambourg à Deux Voix, 1985, Avec L'Eau de Ce Fleuve, 1986, Pluies de Juillet, 1988, Chant Pour Chris, 1989, La Lumière Arriva des Mains, 1990, Aliénor, 1992, Soirée Bleu-Noir, 1994, Le Livre de la Retenue, 1995, Le LIvre des Crépuscules, 1998, Apologie de Pierre Corneille, 1999. Recipient Premio della Cultura Alianello, 1991, Main prize of Internat. Poetry, 1996, 97, Grand Priz Internat. de Poésie, Seoul, Korea, 1997; named Cultural Personality of the World, 1996. Home: 43 Quai Magellan, 44000 Nantes France

MESTECHKIN, MIKHAIL MARKOVICH, math physicist; b. Kiev, Russia, June 2, 1932; s. Mark Mikhailovich and Bella Grigorjevna (Greben') M.; m. Liya Semenovna Gutyrya, Apr. 23, 1955; 1 child, Tanya. MS, Odessa State U., 1955; PhD in Math./Physics, Leningrad State U., 1961, ScD in Math./Physics, 1970. Tchr. high and mid. sch. Railway Sta., Yasinovataja, Ukraine, 1955-57; asst. prof. Mordovian State U., Saransk, 1960-65; head theoretical chemistry dept., prof. Inst. Phys. Organic and Coal Chemistry, Donetsk, Ukraine, 1965-96; ret. Author: Density Matrix Method in theory of Molecules, 1977, Spin-Extended Hartree-Fock Method, 1983 (Bronze medal of Soviet Ind. Exhbn. 1990), Hartree-Fock Instability Theory and Molecular Stability, 1986; contbg. author: Density Matrices and density Functionals, 1987, Fullerene Science and Technology, 1997; contbr. 200 articles to profl. jours. Home: 2875 Cowley Way Apt 201 San Diego CA 92110-1009

MESTEL, LEON, retired astronomy educator; b. Melbourne, Victoria, Australia, Aug. 5, 1927; arrived in U.K., 1931; s. Solomon and Rachel (Brodetsky) M.; m. Sylvia Louise Cole, Nov. 15, 1951; children: Anne Leonora, Andrew Jonathan, Rosemary Judith, Benjamin David. BA, Cambridge (Eng.) U., 1948, PhD, 1952; MSc, Manchester (Eng.) U., 1967. I.C.I. rsch. fellow dept. math. U. Leeds, Eng., 1951-54; Commonwealth fund fellow Princeton U. Obs., 1954-55; asst. lectr., lectr. Cambridge U., 1955-58, 58-66; fellow St. John's Coll., Cambridge, 1957-66; prof. applied math. Manchester U., 1967-73; prof. astronomy U. Sussex, Brighton, Eng., 1973-92; prof. emeritus U. Sussex, Brighton, 1992—; vis. mem. Inst. for Advanced Study, Princeton, 1961-62; vis. fellow Weizmann Inst., Rehovoth, Israel, 1966-67; pres. commn. 35 Internat. Astron. Union, 1973-76. Co-author: Magnetohydrodynamics, 1974; author: Stellar Magnetism, 1999; contbr. articles to profl. jours. Fellow Royal Astron. Soc. (coun. mem. 1968-71, 90-92, Eddington medal 1993). Fellow Royal Soc. Jewish. Avocations: reading, music. Home: 13 Prince Edward's Rd, Lewes BN7 1BJ, England Office: Astronomy Ctr Univ Sussex, Falmer, Brighton BN1 9QJ, England

MESTEL, MARK DAVID, lawyer; b. May 15, 1951; s. Oscar L. and Katherine (Waldner) M.; m. Linda Antonik, Jan. 6, 1984; children: Brenton V., Spenser Andrew. BA, Northwestern U., 1973; JD, U. Mich., 1976. Bar: Mich. 1976, D.C. 1977, Wash. 1978, U.S. Dist. Ct. (we. dist.) Wash. 1979, U.S. Ct. Appeals (9th cir.) 1984, U.S. Dist. Ct. (ea. dist.) Wash. 1986, U.S. Supreme Ct. 1991; cert. criminal trial specialist Nat. Bd. Trial Advocacy, 1982, 86, 91. Atty. EPA, Washington, 1976-77; pvt. practice Washington, 1977-78, Everett, Wash., 1981-84; staff atty. Snohomish County Pub. Defender, Everett, 1978-80, dir., atty., 1980-81; ptnr. Mestel & Muenster, Everett, 1984-94; pvt. practice, 1994—. Mem. ATLA, Nat. Assn. Criminal Def. Lawyers, Wash. Trial Lawyers Assn., Wash. Assn. Criminal Def. Lawyers. E-mail: markmestel@bigfoot.com. Office: Mark D Mestel Inc PS 3221 Oakes Ave Everett WA 98201-4407

MESTER, TÜNDE, microbiologist, researcher; b. Pécs, Baranya, Hungary, Dec. 16, 1961; d. Zoltán and Ilona Csepregi; children: Zoltán, Anna. MSc, Kossuth U., Debrecen, Hungary, 1985, Inst. Hydraulic/Environ. Engr., Delft, The Netherlands, 1992; PhD, Wageningen Agrl. U., The Netherlands, 1997. Lectr. Agrl. U., Debrecen, 1985-93. Office: Penn State U Ctr Biomed Structure & Function Dept Biochem Molecular Biology University Park PA 16802

MESTRALLET, GÉRARD, professional society administrator; b. Paris, Apr. 1, 1949; arrived in Belgium, 1991; s. Georges Julien Marie and Paule Andrée Augustine (Besnard) M.; m. Joëlle Emilienne Renée Arcens, Sept. 7, 1974; children: Stephanie, Caroline, Bastien. Student, Ecole Polytech., Paris, 1968, Ecole Aviation Civile, Paris, 1971, Inst. for Study of Politics, Toulouse, France, 1973, Ecole Nat. d'Adminstrn., Paris, 1978. Counsellor Minister Transp., Econs., Fins., & Budget, Paris, 1973-84; chargé de mission Suez, Paris, 1984-86, dél. adjoint indsl. affairs, 1986-91, dir. gen. adjoint, 1991—; CEO Soc. Gen. de Belgique, Brussels, 1991; chmn., CEO Compagnie de Suez, Paris, 1995-97; CEO, pres. exec. bd. Suez Lyonnaise des Eaux, Paris, 1997—. Office: Suez Lyonnaise des Eaux, 1 rue d'Astorg, 75008 Paris France

MESTRE, DANIEL, economics consultant; b. Barcelona, Catalonia, Spain, June 14, 1937; s. Lluis and Joaquima (Solana) M.; married, June 6, 1969; children: Oriol, Laia. Degree, Escuela de Altos Estudios Mercantiles, Barcelona, 1955; Programa Alta Direccion de Empresas, Instituto Estudios Superiores da la Empresa, Barcelona, 1972. V.p. Banco Condal, Barcelona, 1969-75, Banco de Madrid, Barcelona, 1975-77; pvt. practice mgmt. cons. Barcelona, 1977-81, Andorra la Vella, Andorra, 1981—. Author: Tax Planning Andorra, 1989. Sec. presidence Govt. of Andorra, 1985. Mem. Spanish Fin. Law Assn., Econ. Bus. Assn., Catalonia Auditors Assn., Moore Rowlands Internat. Office: Consultors Profls Assocs SL, Bonaventura Armengol 15, Andorra la Vella Andorra

MEŠTROVIĆ, JULIJE, pediatrician; b. Split, Croatia, July 10, 1959; s. Slavko and Marija (Škare) M.; m. Marija Martinić, Dec. 12, 1994. MD, Zagreb (Croatia) U., 1984, MS, 1989, cert. in pediatrics, 1994; cert. pediatric intensivist, U. Cattolica, Rome, 1996. Gen. physician Emergency, Split, 1984-89; resident Clin. Hosp., Split, 1989-94, pediatrician intensive care unit, 1994-96, dir. pediat. intensive care unit, 1996—; cons. pediatrician Clin. Hosp., Split, 1994—; presenter in field. Contbr. articles to profl. jours. Mem. European Soc. Parenteral and Enteral Nutrition, Croatian Soc. Allergology, Croatian Soc. Naval, Undersea and Hyperbaric Medicine, Croatian Cultural Literary Soc. (collaborator 1992—). Roman Catholic. Avocations: drawing, swimming. Home: Kneza Višeslava 1, 21000 Split Croatia Office: Clin Hosp Split, Spinčićeva 1, 21000 Split Croatia

MESZAROS, MILAN, astrophysicist; b. Devavanya, Hungary, Oct. 3, 1954; s. Istvan and Istvanne (Vozary Klara) M.; children: Balazs, Veronika. Cert. physicist, Roland Eotvos U., 1980, cert. philosopher, 1984. Rsch. scientist dept. logic Roland Eotvos U., Budapest, 1980-86; rsch. scientist inst. physics Tech. U. Budapest, 1986-94; rsch. head, sci. advisor Rsch. Inst. and Innovation Co. for Telecom., Budapest, 1994-97; chief counsellor Data Processing Office, Hungarian Ministry Interior, Budapest, 1997-99; chief counsellor Hungarian Ministry of EPA, Budapest, 1999—; chmn. curatorium 137 Found. for Theoretical Phys. Rsch., Budapest, 1995—; head dept. physics Real Green Soc., Hungary, 1992—. Editor: The Enigmatic Photon, Vol. 5: Photon and Poincare Group, 1999; contbr. articles to profl. jours. and books. Buddhist priest, 1989. Named Man of the Yr. Am. Biol. Inst., 1997, Key award, 1997, World Lifetime achievement award, 1997, Man of the Yr., 1998, 2000 Millennium Medal of Honor, 1998, Internat. Man of the Yr. award Internat. Biol. Ctr., 1997-98, Gold Star award, 1997, 20th Century award for achievement, 1998. Mem. London Diplomatic Acad. (founder mem. of diplomatic coun., 2000), Nat. Geographic Soc., N.Y. Acad. Scis., IEEE Nuclear and Plasma Scis. Soc., Planetary Soc., Internat. Union Radio Sci. Avocation: family activities. Home: 11 Rutafa St, H-1165 Budapest Hungary Office: Alpha Group Labs Inc, 11 Rutafa St Bldg H, H-1165 Budapest Hungary

MÉSZÁROS, SÁNDOR, agricultural economist; b. Miskolc, Borsod, Hungary, Mar. 25, 1937; s. Gusztáv and Gusztávné (Péter) M.; m. Sándorné Varró, Aug. 13, 1963 (div. 1977); children: Adrienne, Krisztina. Agronomist, Agrl. U., Gödöllő, 1960, agrl. economist, 1965; DSc, Hungarian Acad. Sci., 1987. Agronomist State Farm, Miskolc, 1960-61; agrl. economist County Coun., Miskolc, 1962-67; head of dept. Ministry of Agrl., Budapest, 1968-77; sci. adviser Rsch. Inst. Agrl. Economist, Budapest, 1978—. Author (in Hungarian): Efficiency and Optimal Rates of Fertilizers, 1972; Projection of World's Fertilizer Production and Consumption, 1985, Competitiveness of Agriculture and Food Industry, 1986; author, editor: O Operation Research Methods in Agriculture, 1981 (Acad. award 1982). Recipient Honor Ministry of Agrl., 1988. Mem. European Assn. of Agrl. Economists, Acad. Sci. Hungary (agrl. econ. com.). Achievements include first calculation of times series of nominal protection coefficient, effective protection coefficient, domestic resource costs, producer subsudy equivalent, consumer subsidy equivalent measures for Hungarian agriculture. Home: Beregszász 56/D, H-1112 Budapest Hungary Office: Rsch Inst Agrl Econ, PO Box 5, H-1355 Budapest Hungary

MESZÉNA, GEORGE, mathematics educator; b. Kiskomarom, Hungary, Mar. 13, 1931; s. Eugen and Rosette (Horvath-Gaal) M.; m. Maria Meszaros, July 21, 1960; children: Zsolt, Thomas. MA in Math. and Physics, Kossuth Lajos U., 1953; MSEE, Tech. U., Budapest, 1966. Tchr. Fazekas Secondary Sch., Debrecen, Hungary, 1953-57; rschr. Nuclear Rsch. Inst., Debrecen, Hungary, 1957-61; asst. prof. U. Econs., Budapest, 1961-75, assoc. prof., 1975-92, prof., 1992—; cons. Ministry of Post, Budapest, 1960-72, Ctrl. Planning Bd., Budapest, 1972-82, Ctrl. Office of Water Supply, Budapest, 1965-77, Ministry of Industry, Budapest, 1970-80. Author: Probability Theory and Mathematical Statistics, 1981, Stochastic Methods and Models, 1982, Statistical Methods of Multivariate Data Analysis, 1986; co-author: Economic Risk and its Measurement, 1975; editor: Quantitative Methods for Investment Analysis, 1985; patentee in field. Recipient Honours of Work Coun. of Ministries, 1985, Acad. prize Acad. of Scis., 1986. Mem. Soc. for Econ. and Modelling (pres. 1994—). Avocations: tourism, gardening, tarot. Home: Bartok Bela-U 57, H-1114 Budapest Hungary Office: Univ of Econs, POB 489 Fovam-Ter 8, H-1828 Budapest Hungary

METALLO, THOMAS JOSEPH, language and political science educator; b. Balt., Sept. 27, 1951; s. Dominick Francis and Betty Jean Metallo; m. Joyce Katherine Metallo, Sept. 18, 1983. AB, Ind. Wesleyan U., 1986; MA in Pub. Policy, Regent U., 1990; PhD in Internat. Studies, U. Miami, 1998. Cons. Microleague Sports Assn., Newark, Del., 1987-88; rsch. asst. Regent U., Virginia Beach, 1989-90; tchr. Virginia Beach Pub. Schs., 1990-91; rsch. analyst N./S. Ctr. U. Miami, Coral Gables, Fla., 1991-95; asst. prof. Oral Roberts U., Tulsa, Okla., 1996-2000, Ind. Wesleyan U., Marion, Ind., 2000—; rsch. analyst U.S. News and World Report, 1994; adj. prof. Fla. Internat. U., Miami, 1996; faculty advisor Oral Roberts U., Tulsa, 1996—. Tchr., asst. dir. Youth With A Mission, 1980-86. Bowman Divisional scholar Ind. Wesleyan U., 1987-88, Acad. Merit scholar Regent U., 1988-90, N.S. Ctr. scholar U. Miami, 1991-95. Mem. Am. Polit. Sci. Assn., Latin Am. Studies Assn., Internat. Alliance Christian Polit. Parties and Movements. Presbyterian. Avocations: bird-watching, international travel, calligraphy, running. Home: 4509 S Selby St Marion IN 46953-5328 Office: Indiana Wesleyan U 4201 S Washington St Marion IN 46953-4974

METCALF, DEAN ANDREW, plant pathologist, researcher; b. Bendigo, Victoria, Australia, Aug. 3, 1969; s. Robert W. and Gail E. (Crawford) M.; m. Sharon Kemp, 1998; 1 child, Angus. B in Applied Scis., U. Adelaide (Australia), 1989; Grad. Diploma in Agrl. Scis. with honors, U. Tasmania (Australia), 1992, PhD, 1997. Tech. officer Australian Hop Marketers, Australia, 1990-91; sr. plant pathologist Tasmanian Inst. Agrl. Rsch., Australia, 1996—; diagnostic svc. plant pathologist Tasmanian Inst. Agrl. Rsch., 1998—; project leader onion white rot and onion neck rot rsch., Tasmania, 1996—; expert in plant disease caused by fungi. Developer biol. control agents; contbr. articles to profl. jours., including Plant Pathology. Australian postgrad. rsch. award fellow, 1993, fellow Australian Rsch. Coun., 1997. Mem. Australian Plant Pathology Soc., Australian Onion Industry Assn. E-mail: Dean.Metcalf@dpiwe.tas.gov.au. Office: Newtown Rsch Labs, GPO Box 192 B, Hobart 7001, Australia

METCALF, ROGER DALE, SR., dentist; b. Ft. Worth, July 24, 1950; s. Frank Dean and Fannie Pauline (Yarbrough) M.; m. Linda Susan Cervenka, June 15, 1974; children: Roger Dale, Kelli Anne, Ryan David. BS, Baylor U., 1973, DDS, 1977; postgrad., U. No. Tex. Health Sci. Ctr., 1987. Pvt. practice dentistry Arlington, Tex., 1977—; owner Medicalc, Arlington, Tex., 1980—; pres. Metcalf & Metcalf Family Clinic, 1996—. Pres., chmn. Am. Cancer Soc., 1983, 84. Named one of Outstanding Young Men Am., 1984. Mem. ADA, Nat. Med. Assn., Tex. Dental Assn., Fort Worth Dist. Dental Soc., Acad. Gen. Dentistry, Am. Acad. Gold Foil Ops., Tex. Lyceum Assn. (bd. dirs. 1986), Mensa, Alpha Epsilon Delta. Republican. Baptist. Avocations: photography, music, antique fishing tackle. E-mail: metcalfdd-

s@aol.com. Home: 5126 Bridgewater Dr Arlington TX 76017-2782 Office: 3808 Jason Dr 1115 W Arkansas Ln # A Arlington TX 76013-6325

METCHIK, MORTIMER J., retired lawyer; b. N.Y.C.; s. Joshua and Jenny Metchik; m. Evelyn Metchik, Aug. 6, 1950; children: Eric Wendell, Judith R. BA, Queens Coll., 1946; LLB, Columbia U., 1948; JD, 1958. Bar: N.Y. 1949. Assoc. Sherman, Citron & Karasik, N.Y.C., 1964-90. Pres. Dem. Club, Oceanside, N.Y., 1963-64. Sgt. USAF, 1943-45, ETO. Mem. Jewish War Vets. Home: 650 Shore Rd Apt 3T Long Beach NY 11561-4673

METKA, WOLFGANG ERNST, plastic surgeon; b. Austria, Jan. 12, 1945; s. Ernst and Agnes (Briem) Metka; m. Inge Friede; 1 child, Susi. DM, U. Innsbruck, Austria, 1969. Tng. in surgery U. Innsbruck, 1976; tng. in plastic surgery Vienna, 1979; head aesthetic plastic surgery Döling, Vienna, 1990-99; tng. in aesthetic surgery U. Paris, NYU, Loma Linda (Calif.) U., 1996; pvt. practice, Vienna and Linz, 1982—; prof. aesthetic surgery U. Trencin, Slovakia, 1999—. Contbr. numerour articles to med. jours. Mem. Austrian Soc. Plastic, Reconstructive and Aesthetic Surgery. Avocation: painting. Office: Opernring 23, A-1010 Vienna Austria also: Badgasse 7, A-4020 Linz Austria

METODIEV, KRASSIMIR TIHOMIROV, medical educator, researcher; b. Veliko Tarnovo, Bulgaria, Dec. 18, 1950; s. Tihomir Metodiev and Zdravka (Stoilova) Kamburova; m. Silvia Ivanova, Apr. 7, 1974 (div. Sept. 1988); 1 child, Kalin; m. Pavla Lazarova Georgieva, July 10, 1990; children: Kalin, Alexander. MD, MEd. Faculty, Varna, Bulgaria, 1974; PhD, Inst. Transplantation, Moscow, 1983; DS in Medicine, Inst. Nephrology, 1989. Asst. prof. Med. Faculty, Varna, Bulgaria, 1975-89; assoc. prof. Med. U., Varna, Bulgaria, 1990-94, prof., 1995—; guest prof. Sheba U. Hosp., Tel Aviv, Israel, 1992, Munich U., Germany, 1995, 97, 99, Chiang Mai U., Thailand, 1993, Norwegian Cancer Ctr., Oslo, 1998, 99; hon. prof. Hebrew U., Hadassah Med. Ctr., Jerusalem, 2000. Author: Dictionary of Immunology, 1984, 2nd edit., 1992, Early Diagnosis and Treatment of Kidney Disease, 1990, Immunodermatology, 1993, (poem) Around The World, 2000; editor Scripta Scientifica Medica jour., 1979-88; chief editor Annual Jour. IMAB, 1994—. Mem. Bulgarian Soc. Young Scientists (pres. 1980-90), European Assn. Young Med. Scientists (v.p. 1988-91), Union Bulgarian Physicians (bd. dirs. 1990—, Golden medal 1989), Internat. Soc. Chemotherapy (assoc. bd. dirs. 1996—), Internat. Med. Assn. Bulgaria (pres. 1993—), European Com. on Antibiotics (London 1997—). Avocations: geography, travel. Home: St No 12 No 22 Zvezditza, 9103 Varna Bulgaria Office: Med U, 55 m Drinov Str, 9002 Varna Bulgaria

METSCH, WERNER WALTER, mechanical engineer, consultant; b. Berlin, Mar. 15, 1928; came to U.S., 1951; s. Walter and Ida (Baier) M.; m. Barbara Katharina Buhlemann, Nov. 11, 1954. BSME magna cum laude, Fairleigh Dickinson U., 1964. Registered profl. engr., N.Y., N.J., Calif., Ga., Fla. Design engr. Syska & Hennessy, Inc., N.Y.C., 1957-65; mgr. European ops. Hydrotherm, Inc., N.J., also Germany, 1965-67; design engr. Parsons Brinckerhoff et al, N.Y.C., 1967-77; dir. mech./elec. engring. Wigton Abbott, Plainfield, N.J., 1977-79; mgr. projects Parsons Brinckerhoff et al, 1979-83, v.p., tech. dir. mech./elec., 1983-89; value engring. program mgr. Bechtel/Parsons Brinckerhoff, Boston, 1987-89; consulting engr. Tampa, Fla., 1989-98; conceptual ventilation design Underground Hwy., Seoul, Korea, 1991-92; value engring. program mgr., Kaoshiung MRT, Taiwan, 1992; mech./elec. engring. mgr. Underground Hwy., Singapore, 1992-93. Contbg. author: (handbook) Subway Environmental Design, 1975, ASHRAE Handbook/Applications, 1987; contbr. articles to profl. jours. Cpl. U.S. Army, 1953-55. Mem. ASHRAE (life). Achievements include managment of over 20 significant engineering projects; directed the mechanical engineering design for over 100 projects; developed concepts and in charge of design of ventilation, climate control, and fire/life safety systems for major U.S. and international transportation projects and "hardened" underground facilities. Home and Office: Werner W Metsch PE 18537 N Villa Bella Dr Surprise AZ 85374-5496

METSSALU, REIN, microbiologist; b. Jõgeva, Estonia, Nov. 13, 1957; s. Edgar and Virve (Petersell) M.; m. Pirkko Liisa Ahola, May 19, 1984. MS, Tartu (Estonia) U., 1980. Diplomate biology/microbiology. Microbiologist Esmar Biotech. Lab., Tallinn, Estonia, 1980-87; microbiologist, product mgr. Labsystems Corp., Helsinki, Finland, 1988-96; gen. mgr. Transgalactic ltd., Vantaa, Finland, 1996—; cons. automation in microbiology, hardware, software and methods Labsystems Corp., Hensinki, 1988-96. Inventor Wastewater Treatment Disk, 1979, Wastewater Treatment Spiral, 1980. Mem. Mikrobiologikilta Ry. Avocation: making home movies.

METTLER, NORMA EVANGELINA, research scientist; b. Larroque, Entre Rios, Argentina, Jan. 26, 1932; d. Ernesto Rodolfo and Catalina Geronima (De Merlier) M. MD, U. Buenos Aires, 1958, PhD in Medicine, 1960; MPH, Yale U., 1968, DPH, 1970. Med. diplomate, Argentina. Med. practitioner Children's Hosp., Buenos Aires, 1953-58; asst. to chief practical work U. Buenos Aires, 1954-66; ind. rschr. Conicet, Buenos Aires, 1962-66; postdoctoral fellow Govt. Med. Sci./U.S.A./Yale, New Haven, 1966-69; mem. faculty Yale U., New Haven, 1969-71; rschr. CIC Buenos Aires Province, 1978-96; cons. virology Pan Am. Health Orgn./WHO, Chile, Brazil, Venezuela, 1971-77; prof. virology Universidad Nacional Centro Pro Vincia Buenos Aires, Tandil, Argentina, 1977-84; prof. immunology Facultad Ciencias Veterinarias-U. Buenos Aires, 1984-87; bd. dirs. dept. microbiology Facultad Medicina/U. Buenos Aires, 1989-96; cons. infectious disease dr. Florencio Escardo Pediatric Svc., Children's Hosp., Ricardo Gutierrez, 1963-66. Author: Argentine Hemorragic Fever, 1969, Los Virus en Medicine Humana y Veterinaria, 12 parts, 1978-83, Virus Trasmitidos al Hombre por Alimentos, 1990, El Universo, 1992; author over 70 publs. in profl. jours. Recipient fellowship Conicet/Argentina, Rockefeller Inst., 1960-62, grante Rockefeller Found., 1962. Fellow Royal Soc. Health; mem. AAAS, Argentine Assn. Microbiology (life), Argentine Med. Assn., Assn. Former Internat. Civil Servants (life), Am. Soc. Microbiology, N.Y. Acad. Scis. Roman Catholic. Avocations: card games, writing poetry, readings. Home: M Larumbe (Ex-San Juan) 571, 1640 Buenos Aires Martinez, Argentina also: Cordoba 2077 2o A, 1120 Buenos Aires Argentina

METTLER-VON MEIBOM, BARBARA ELISABETH, political science educator; b. Düsseldorf, Germany, 1947; d. Hanspeter and Irmgard (Stoltenhoff) von Meibom; children: Nathalie, Pascale. MA, U. Konstanz, Germany, 1971, PhD, 1974; Habilitation, Privat Dozent, U. Hamburg, Germany, 1985. Lectr. U. Tübingen, Germany, 1974-75; rschr., Paris, 1975-77; chief divsn. Socialdata, Munich, 1978-82; chief rschr. telecom. in polit. sci. U. Hamburg, 1982-85; chief OPTEK, Hamburg, 1985-88; prof. polit. sci. U. Gesamthochschule Essen, Germany, 1989—; chief Communio, cons. for comm. and cooperation, Essen, 1997—. Author 11 books, including Kommunikation in der Mediengesellschaft, 1996; co-editor Jahrbuch Ökologie, 1992—. Pres. Stadtforum Essen, 1990-93; bd. dirs. Gemeinschaftswerk der Evgl. Publizistik, Frankfurt, Germany, 1994-96. Mem. German Assn. Pub. Comm. and Comm. Studies (v.p. 1995-96), German Assn. Polit. Sci. (adv. bd. 1975), Internat. Gesellschaft für Tiefenpsychologie. Avocations: performing, painting, poetry. Office: U GH-Essen, Universitätsstrasse 12, D-45117 Essen Germany

METZ, CRAIG HUSEMAN, legislative administrator; b. Columbia, S.C., Aug. 26, 1955; s. Leonard Huseman and Annette (Worthington) M.; m. Karen Angela McCleary, Aug. 11, 1984; 1 child, Preston Worthington. BA, U. Tenn., 1977; JD, U. Memphis, 1986; cert., U.S. Ho. of Reps. Rep. Leadership Parlimentary Law Sch., 1987. Bar: S.C., D.C., U.S. Ct. Claims, U.S. Supreme Ct., U.S. Ct. Appeals (4th cir.). Canvass coord., liaison Campaign to Re-elect Congressman Floyd Spence, 1978; del., chmn. Shelby County Del. to 1983 Tenn. Young Rep. Fedn. Conv.; vice chmn. Shelby County Young Reps., 1983-84, chmn., 1984-85; Shelby County adminstr., asst. to Tenn. state exec. dir. Reagan-Bush Campaign, 1984; field rep. Campaign to Re-elect Congressman Floyd Spence, 1986; spl. asst. to Congressman Floyd Spence, 1986-88; counsel com. on labor and human resources U.S. Senate, 1988-90; commr.'s counsel U.S. Occupational Safety and Health Rev. Commn., Washington, 1990-91; spl. asst. to asst. sec. for legis. and congl. affairs; dep. asst. sec. for congl. liaison U.S. Dept. Edn., Washington, 1991-93; asst. dir. Divsn. Congl. Affairs AMA, Washington, 1993; chief of staff Congressman Floyd Spence, Washington, 1993—. Judge nat. writing competition U.S. Constn. Bicentennial, S.C. 1987-88; mem. Ch. of the Ascension and Saint Agnes, Washington. Recipient award of merit Rep. Party of Shelby County, 1985, Outstanding Leadership award Shelby County Young Reps., 1985. Mem. Rep. Nat. Lawyers Assn. (state chmn. S.C. chpt. 1987-90), Freedoms Found. Valley Forge, Va. Hist. Soc., Assn. for Preservation Va. Antiquities, Va. Geneal. Soc., U. South Caroliniana Soc., Palmetto Trust for Historic Preservation, Lowcountry Heritage Soc., Orangeburg County Hist. Soc., Nat. Trust for Hist. Preservation (assoc. Capital region), SAR, St. David's Soc., St. Andrew's Soc. Washington, Mil. Soc. War of 1812, Vet. Corps Arty. State of N.Y., Gen. Soc. War of 1812, Mil. Order Loyal Legion of U.S., Order of St. John (Hospitaller), SCV, Mil. Order Stars and Bars, Sons and Daus. Colonial and Antebellum Bench and Bar 1565-1861, Sons of the Revolution, Nat. Cathedral Assn., U. Tenn. Nat. Alumni Assn., Sigma Alpha Epsilon, Phi Alpha Delta (v.p. McKellar chpt., Outstanding Svc. award 1983). Republican. Episcopalian. Home: 8505 Westown Way Vienna VA 22182-2513 Office: 2405 Rayburn Bldg Washington DC 20515-4002

METZ, LAURENT DOMINIQUE, health products company executive; b. Nancy, France, June 21, 1963; s. Roland and Micheline (Ecuter) M. MD, U. Nancy, 1990, MSc, 1992; MBA, HEC, Paris, 1994. Product mgr. Johnson & Johnson-Ethicon, France, 1996-98, dir. health econs., 1998—. Served with French Air Force, 1991-92. Office: Ethicon-Johnson & Johnson, 1 Rue Camille Desmoulins TSA 81002, 92787 Issy-Les-Moulineaux France

METZ, RONALD IRWIN, retired priest, addictions counselor; b. Walthill, Nebr., Aug. 11, 1921; s. Harry Elmer and Emma Rilla (Howe) M.; m. Helen Chapin, July 14, 1951; children: Mary Selden Metz Evans, Helen Winchester Metz Ketchum, Grace Chapin Metz Hunton. BA in Chinese and Far Ea. Studies, U. Calif., Berkeley, 1945; MA in Mid. Ea. Studies, Am. U., Beirut, 1954; M Div., Yale U., 1969, STD, 1975. Ordained priest Episcopal Ch., 1969. Intelligence officer various govtl. intelligence agys., Far East and Washington, 1944-52; exec. Arabian/Am. Oil Co., Dhahran and Riyadh, Saudi Arabia, 1954-66; deacon Grace Cathedral, San Francisco; priest St. George's Cathedral, Jerusalem, 1969; exec. asst. to archbishop Jerusalem and Mid. East Archbishopric, 1969-75; rector Ch. of the Holy Spirit, Erie, Pa., 1976-81; chaplain Brent Sch., Baguio, Philippines, 1981-82; counselor of chemically dependent Washington, 1982—; addictionologist, vol. New Beginnings Treatment Ctr., P.I.W. Hosp., Washington, 1989-90, Found. Next Step Outpatient Treatment Ctr., Washington, 1991-92; adj. clergy St. Margaret's Ch., Washington; mem. D.C. Diocesan Commn. on Alcohol and Drug Abuse, Washington, 1982-89. Bd. dirs. Mid. East Inst., Washington, 1959-60, Pub. Broadcasting System, n.w. Pa., 1976-81; mem. adv. bd. Children's Aid Internat., 1988-89. Served to col. U.S. Army, 1942-45, CBI, OSS. Decorated Bronze Star. Mem. Iran Diocesan Assn. U.S.A, Phi Beta Kappa, Sigma Chi (chaplain D.C. alumni assn. 1982-99). Democrat. Avocations: home movies, double crostics. Home: 3001 Veazey Ter NW Apt 334 Washington DC 20008-5455

METZ, STEVEN KENT, federal agency administrator, writer; b. Charleston, W.Va., June 30, 1956; s. David N. and Carolyn Ann (Powell) M.; m. Jayne Godwin Nelson, Aug. 14, 1977; children: Rachel Elizabeth, Stephanie Eleanor. BA, U. S.C., 1977, MA, 1981; PhD, Johns Hopkins U., 1985. Vis. prof. polit. sci. Va. Tech, Blacksburg, Va., 1984-87; prof. internat. rels. U.S. Army Command and Gen. Staff Coll., Ft. Leavenworth, Kans., 1987-91; prof. low intensity conflict and Third World studies Air War Coll., Maxwell AFB, Ala., 1991-93; rsch. prof. nat. security affairs Strategic Studies Inst. U.S. Army War Coll., Carlisle Barracks, Pa., 1993—, Henry L. Stimson prof. mil. studies, 1993-95; lectr., cons. in field. Contbr. articles to profl. jours., chpts. to books. Republican. Home: 134 Fieldstone Dr Carlisle PA 17013-9036 Office: Strategic Studies Inst US Army War Coll Carlisle Barracks PA 17013

METZ, WILLIAM CLINTON, program manager; b. Leominster, Mass., Oct. 13, 1944; s. William Dewitt and Clarice Styles (McKenney) M.; m. Carol Ann Giles; children: William Christopher, Jennifer Giles. B of History, Bates Coll.; M in Geography, U. R.I.; PhD in Geography, U. Pitts., 1974; MBA, Dowling Coll., 1985; M of Info. Scis., Aurora U., 1987. Sr. scientist Westinghouse, Pitts., 1974-78; prin. investigator Brookhaven Nat. Lab., Upton, N.Y., 1978-84; program mgr. Argonne (Ill.) Nat. Lab., 1984—, deputy to divsn. dir., 1990-93. Contbr. articles to profl. jours. Avocations: American history, antique cars, hiking. Office: Argonne Nat Lab 9700 Cass Ave Bldg 900 Argonne IL 60439-4803

METZDORFF, CARL HEINRICH, executive search executive; b. Viby, Jylland, Denmark, Oct. 28, 1938; arrived in Belgium, 1989; s. Carl and Carla (Petersen) M. Sales mgr. Upjohn, Denmark, 1976-79; mktg. dir. Astra, Denmark, 1979-81; mng. dir. Searle, Denmark, 1981-88; dir. European govt. affairs Mosanto-Searle, Brussels, 1988-91; dir. Metzdorff Assoc., Brussels, 1991—; sr. ptnr. Aces Internat., Brussels, 1994—. Capt. Royal Danish Air Force, 1958-67. Office: Aces Health Care, Ave Louise 109, B-1050 Brussels Belgium

METZELAAR, WILLEM-FREDERIK GEERT, environmental consultant; b. Rotterdam, The Netherlands, Mar. 12, 1966; s. Frederik and An (Venema) M.; m. Jessica Blok, May 1, 1998. Atheneum, Inst. Vrybergen, The Netherlands, 1987; degree in sociology, U. Rotterdam, 1996. Cons. Socrates Consultancy, The Netherlands, 1995-96; strategic environ. cons. ENW, The Netherlands, 1996-99; integration mgr. NUON, The Netherlands, 1999-2000; strategic environ. cons. NUON, 2000—. Mem. Roundtable, Noordwjkse Golf Club, Erasmus Liga. Home: Voorstraat 58A, 2201 HX Noordwijk The Netherlands

METZGEN, FREDERICK WILLIAM, communications company executive; b. Belize City, Central America, June 3, 1945; s. Monrad Sigfried and Elsa McKensie (Weir) M.; m. Gloria Jean Dowsett, June 5, 1970 (div. May 1995); children: Paul James, Richard Alistair, Timothy Charles, Nicholas David. BS in Computer Sci., Fich Inst. Technology, London, 1963. Investment banker WE Hutton & Co., London, 1963-65; from computer programmer to sales & mktg. dir. Europe IBM, London, 1965-88; pres., CEO EDIMATRIX, London, 1988-90; dir. gen. France Telecom Transpac UK, London, 1990-95; internat. bus. devel. dir. BT Europe, Paris, 1995-2000; CEO Omniticket Network, Inc., Paris, 2000—. Author: Killing the Paper Dragon, 1990, Same Back, 1999. Mem. Inst. Dirs. Avocations: writing, jogging, golf, sailing. Office: Omniticket Network Inc, 86 Rue Régnault, 75013 Paris France

METZGER, CATHERINE Z., global marketing administrator; b. Canton, Ohio, Mar. 22, 1961. BSBA, Miami U., 1983. Systems edn. coord. Smyth Bus. Systems, North Canton, Ohio, 1983-85; tech. instr. Diebold, Inc., North Canton, Ohio, 1985-89, product mgr., 1989-93, sr. product mgr., 1993-95, global mktg. mgr., 1995—. Mem., alumnus Leadership Stark County, Canton, 1998. Mem. Smart Board Forum, Electronic Funds Transfer Assn. Avocations: mentoring high school youths, white water rafting, community volunteering. E-mail: metzgec@diebold.com. Office: Diebold Inc Dept 9-B-10 5995 Mayfair Rd Dept 9-b10 North Canton OH 44720-1597

METZGER, DIRK, physicist; b. Idar-Oberstein, Germany, Jan. 20, 1966; s. Klaus Wolfgang and Hildegard (Wagner) M. Diploma in physics, U. Heidelberg, Germany, 1993, PhD in Physics, 1997. Scientist, rschr. U. Heidelberg, 1992-97; responsible for devel. sys. Systeme Anwendungen Produkte AG, Walldorf, Germany, 1997-99, quality mgr. internat. lang. support, 1999—. Contbg. author for hydrodynamics Lexikon der Physik, 1996—. Exec. Götzplatz Music Festival, Idar-Oberstein, 1984-90. 1st lt. arty. German Army, 1985-87. Office: SAP AG, Neurottstrasse 16, 69190 Walldorf Germany

METZGER, HENRY, federal research institution administrator; b. Mainz, Germany, Mar. 23, 1932; came to U.S., 1938; naturalized, 1945; s. Paul Alfred and Anne (Daniel) M.; m. Deborah Stashower, June 16, 1957; children: Eran D., Renée V., Carl E. MD, Columbia U., 1957. Chief chem. immunology sect. Nat. Inst. Arthritis & Musculoskeletal & Skin Disease/NIH, Bethesda, Md., 1973—; br. chief USPHS, Bethesda, 1983-94, sci. dir., 1987-98, med. officer grade VI, 1975-98; with Sr. Biomed. Rsch. Svc., 1999—; Carl Prausnitz Meml. lectr., 1982; Ecker Meml. lectr. Case Western Res. U., Cleve., 1984; Harvey Soc. lectr., 1984; Eli Nadel Meml. lectr. St. Louis U., 1987; Rodney Porter Meml. lectr., 1993; Burroughs-Wellcome lectr., 1994; R.E. Dyer lectr.; mem. health rsch. coun. BMFT, German Govt., 1994-97. Editor: Fc Receptors & the Action of Antibodies, 1990; assoc. editor Ann. Rev. Immunology, 1982-96; contbr. numerous articles to profl. jours.; mem. editorial bd. numerous sci. jours. Recipient Meritorious Svc. award USPHS, 1978, Disting. Svc. award, 1985, 97, Joseph Mather Smith prize Columbia U., 1984. Fellow AAAS, Am. Acad. Allergy and Immunology; mem. NAS, Am. Assn. Immunologists (pres. 1991-92), Am. Soc. Biol. Chem. Molecular Biology, Am. Soc. Cell Biology, Am. Rheumatism Assn., Internat. Union Immunol. Soc. (pres. 1992-95), Found. for Advanced Edn. in the Scis. (pres. 1990-92), Alpha Omega Alpha. Home: 3410 Taylor St Bethesda MD 20815-4024 Office: NIH 9000 Rockville Pike Rm 9n228 Bethesda MD 20892-0003

METZGER, H(OWELL) PETER, writer; b. N.Y.C., Feb. 22, 1931; s. Julius Radley and Gertrude (Fuller) M.; m. Frances Windham, June 30, 1956 (div. July 1987); children: John, James, Lisa, Suzanne; m. Valerie A. Farnham, Jan. 12, 1990 (div. Sept. 1995). BA, Brandeis U., 1953; PhD, Columbia U., 1965. Host radio talk show KTLN, Denver, 1966-68; mgr. advanced programs Ball Bros. Rsch. Corp., Boulder, 1968-70; rsch. assoc. dept. chemistry U. Colo., Boulder, 1966-68; sr. rsch. scientist N.Y. State Psychiat. Inst., N.Y.C., 1965-66; syndicated columnist N.Y. Times Syndicate, 1972-74, Science Critic, Newspaper Enterprise Assn., 1974-76; sci. editor Rocky Mt. News, Denver, 1973-77; mgr. public affairs planning Public Svc. Co. Colo., Denver, 1977-96; cons. Environ. Instrumentation, 1970-72; dir. Colspan Environ. Sys., Inc., Boulder, Colo., 1969-72. Author: The Atomic Establishment, 1972; contbr. articles in field to profl. jours., nat. mags. Pres. Colo. Com. for Environ. Info., Boulder, 1968-72; mem. Colo. Gov.'s State Health Planning Coun., 1969-72, Colo. Gov.'s Adv. Com. on Underground Nuc. Explosions, 1971-74; mem. spl. project on energy policy mgmt. Heritage Found., 1980; mem. 1981 U.S. Presdl. Rank Rev. Bd., U.S. Office Pers. Mgmt., 1981; bd. dirs. Wildlife-2000, 1970-72, Colo. Def. Coun., 1972-75. USPHS fellow, 1959-65; prin. investigator, 1968; archivee Hoover Instn. Stanford U., 1982. Mem. ACLU (state bd. dirs. 1968-71), Am. Alpine Club, Sigma Xi, Phi Lambda Upsilon. Address: 2595 Stanford Ave Boulder CO 80305-5332

METZGER, PHILIP WILLIAM, artist, author; b. Bklyn., Oct. 9, 1931; s. Jacob and Marie Barbara (Friedle) M.; m. Barbara Ann Hance, May 1, 1954; children: Jeffrey, Cindy, Lori, Scott. BS, Union Coll., 1953. Programming mgr. IBM, Gaithersburg, Md., 1955-71; ret., 1971; art instr., Rockville, Md., 1972-81; mgmt. instr. IBM, 1968-71. Author: Managing a Programming Project, 1973, 3d edit., 1996, Managing Programming People, 1987, Perspective Without Pain, 1992, Enliven Your Paintings with Light, 1993, North Light Guide to Materials and Techniques, 1996; exhibited at numerous art shows (numerous awards). With USAF, 1953-55. Avocations: racquetball, gardening. Home: PO Box 10746 Rockville MD 20849-0746

METZLAFF, MICHAEL HEINZ, plant molecular biologist, researcher; b. Genthin, Germany, Nov. 26, 1954; arrived in Eng., 1993; arrived in Belgium, 1999; s. Egon Otto and Ursula Eva (Tech) M.; m. Liane Adeline Heine, May 21, 1977 (div. Apr. 1994); children: Oliver, Benjamin, Fabian; m. Karin Gutberlet, Dec. 16, 1995; 1 child, Julia. Diploma in biology, Martin Luther U., Halle, Germany, 1980, D Natural Sci. in Genetics, 1983, Habilitation, 1987. Rsch. asst. Martin Luther U., 1980-86, lectr., 1987-91, dir. for biology rsch., 1990-92; higher sci. officer John Innes Ctr., Norwich, Eng., 1993-99; group leader functional genomics Aventis Crop Sci. N.V., Gent, Belgium, 1999—. Author: Wörterbücher der Biologie Biotechnology, 1991, Ergebnisse und Trends der Gentechnologie, 1991, Methoden der Gentechnologie, 1990, Gene Silencing in Higher Plants and Related Phenomena in Other Eukaryotes, 1995, Epigenetics, 1998. Recipient Carl Correns medal Biol. Soc. Germany, 1987. Home: Irislaan 26, 3080 Tervuren NR9 3QJ, Belgium Office: Aventis Crop Sci NV, Jozef Plateaustraat 22, B-9000 Gent Belgium

METZLER, PAUL RAYMOND, electrical engineer, consultant; b. St. Louis, Sept. 19, 1949; s. Raymond Herman and Rita Fanny (Morton) M.; m. Barbara Mary Dolan, May 18, 1974 (div. Dec. 1985); children: Tammi Marie, Julie Lynn, Brian Keith; m. Roxy Susan Clark, Dec. 20, 1987. BSEE, U. Mo., Rolla, 1973. Registered profl. engr., Tenn., Nev., Mo. Elec. engr. Titanium Pigment div. NL Industries, St. Louis, 1974-76, Reynolds Elec. & Engring. Co., Inc., Las Vegas, Nev., 1983-88; sr. elec. engr. Carborundum Environ. Systems div. Kennecott Corp., Knoxville, Tenn., 1976-81; instrument and control project engr. Chem. Separations Corp., Knoxville, 1981-82; cons. engr. PM Engring. Assocs., Knoxville, 1982-84; quality control engr. C.R. Fedrick, Inc., Kaneohe, Hawaii, 1988-89; cons. PM Engring. Assocs., Pearl City, Hawaii, 1989-92, Lawton, Okla., 1992-94; v.p. Pacific Rim Cons. & Inspection Corp., Aiea, Hawaii, 1991-92; elec. inspector Sverdrup-CRSS Jacob Facilities, Inc., St. Louis, 1996-2000; cons. engr. Criterium-McMahon Engrs., St. Louis, 2000—. Mem. vestry Grace Episcopal Ch., Kirkwood, Mo. Fellow: Internat. Biog. Assn. (life); mem. NSPE, Illuminating Engring. Soc. N.Am. (assoc.), Silver State Computer Users Group (v.p. 1984-86, libr. 1986-88), Instrument Soc. Am., Nat. Fire Protection Assn., Brotherhood of St. Andrew Inc. (life), Order of Engr. (charter), Nat. Model R.R. Assn. (editor Rail Post Office 1997—), Big Bend R.R. Club, Kirkwood R.R. Assn. (pres. 1997—). Home: 5404 Medalion Way Saint Louis MO 63128-3531 Office: 13503 Coliseum Dr Chesterfield MO 63017-3004

METZLER, RUTH HORTON, genealogical educator; b. Eden, N.Y., Aug. 4, 1927; d. John Morris and Bernice Louise Horton; m. Henry George Metzler, Sept. 4, 1948; children: Kathleen, Ronald, Janice, Margaret. Student, Wheaton Coll., 1945-48; AB cum laude, Wilmington Coll., 1956; MLS, SUNY, Geneseo, 1962. Cert. tchr., libr. media specialist, N.Y. Cataloging typist Peoria (Ill.) Pub. Libr., 1949-52; cataloging asst. Wilmington (Ohio) Coll. Libr., 1953-56; sch. libr. K-12 Nunda (N.Y.) Cen. Sch., 1956-65; head Libr. Media Ctr. Irondequoit H.S., Rochester, 1965-84; pres. Rochester (N.Y.) Geneal. Soc., 1989-93; instr., lectr. Rochester Mus. and Sci. Ctr., 1990—. Author several family histories. Organizing instr. Genealogy Workshops, Rochester Mus. and Sci. Ctr; contbg. lectr. Nat. Geneal. Conf. in Rochester, 1990, others. Mem. N.Y. Libr. Assn., N.Y. State Tchr.'s Retirement System, New Eng. Hist. and Geneal. Soc., Kodak Geneal. Soc., N.Y. State Coun. of Geneal., Genealogy Round Table of Monroe County (del. 1996—), Rochester Geneal. Soc. Republican. Baptist. Avocations: family history photography, geneal. rsch., writing.

METZLER-ARNOLD, RUTH, federal official; b. Balgach, Switzerland, May 23, 1964. B in Acctg., Freibourg U. Swiss chartered acct. Acct. United Bank Switzerland, Bern, Switzerland, 1989-90, PricewaterhouseCoopers AG, St. Gallen, Switzerland, 1990-99; dist. judge Appenzell, Switzerland, 1992-95; cantonal judge Appenzell I. Rh, 1995-96, councilor, dir. fin., 1996-99, also bd. dirs.; chmn. Fed. Dept. Justice and Police, Bern, 1999—. Roman Catholic. Office: Bundeshaus West, CH-3003 Bern Switzerland

METZNER, BARBARA STONE, university counselor; b. St. Louis, June 9, 1940; d. Wendell Phillips and Lois Custer (Rake) Metzner. AB, Ind. U., 1962, MS, 1964, EdD, 1983; BA, Purdue U., 1979. Asst. dean students U. Ill., Urbana, 1964-68; undergrad. advisor UCLA, 1968-69; asst. dean students Ohio State U., 1969-72; student affairs officer San Diego State U., 1972-76; sr. counselor Ind. U. - Purdue U., Indpls., 1976—; supr. Ednl. Testing Svc., Indpls., 1980-90; cons. editorial bd. Nat. Acad. Advising Assn., Manhattan, Kans., 1987-93; adj. prof. Ind. U., 1987—; mgr. Info. Svcs., Ind. U.-Purdue U., 1989-91. Contbr. articles to profl. jours., chpts. to books. Mem. Marion County Precinct Election Bd., 1980-92; mem. exec. com. Ind. Allied Health Assn., 1983-84; VIP escort Pan Am. Games, 1987. Spencer Found. grantee, 1985. Mem. AAAS, APA, Am. Edn. Rsch. Assn., Assn. Instl. Rsch., Kappa Alpha Theta (vol. charity benefits 1980-90), Phi Beta Kappa. Avocations: tennis, Chinese cooking, fine arts. Office: IUPUI 815 W Michigan St Indianapolis IN 46202-5199

MEULING, WIM J.A., biochemist, toxicologist; b. The Hague, The Netherlands, Aug. 23, 1946; s. Wim J.A. and Truus (Nicolaas) Löhl; m. Alma ter Riet, Sept. 28, 1970; children: Myrthe, Martyn Willem Frederik. HBO in Analytical Chemistry, 1973, HBO in Biochemistry, 1976, Toxicology I, 1992, HLO in Biochemistry, 1993. Rschr. TNO, Zeist, The Netherlands, 1969—; mgr. TNO, Zeist, 1995—. Co-chair Soil Pollution

Comm., Maassluis, 1991—. Mem. Percutaneous Penetration Congress (sci. com., adv. bd.), Dutch Soc. Toxicology, Netherlands Soc. Cosmetic Chemists, Drug Info. Assn. Avocations: music, tennis, theatre. Home: Churchilldreef 16, 3146BB Maassluis Zuid-H, The Netherlands Office: TNO, Nutrition & Food Rsch Inst, 3700 AJ Zeist The Netherlands

MEURIS, MARC ALFONS, physicist; b. Lier, Belgium, Sept. 19, 1961; s. Georges and Yvonne (Guldentops) M.; m. Annick Maria Van den Berghe, Aug. 1, 1985; three children. M in Physics, Catholic U. Leuven, 1983, PHD, 1990. From rschr. to sr. scientist IMEC, Leuven, Belgium, 1985—. Mem. Electro Chem. Soc.

MEURMAN, JUKKA HEIKKI, medical educator; b. Helsinki, Finland, Sept. 14, 1947; m. Elisabet Kristina Hellberg, June 4, 1971; children: Anna, Kristian. DDS, U. Helsinki, 1972, MD, 1980, D Odont., 1977, PhD, 1993. Lic. dentist, physician. Prof. U. Kuopio, 1992-96, U. Helsinki, 1996—. Recipient La Medaille d'Argent Ville de Paris, France, 1991, Pehr Gadds prize Odontologiska Samfundet, 1992, Pohjola prize Pohjola Mut. Ins. Co., 1992. Home: Westendintie 67C, FIN02160 Espoo Finland Office: U Helsinki, PO Box 41, Helsinki FIN-00014, Finland

MEWBORN, WILLIE MAE, publisher, writer; b. Dover, NC, May 26, 1959; d. Joshua and Bertha Mattie Ruth M. BA in English, Atlantic Christian Coll., 1982. Author: Through the Storms & Through the Rain, 2000, Resting in God's Love, 2000; pub.: What Do You Do Once God Delivers You?. Avocations: reading, writing, volunteering. Home: 1528 London Cir Durham NC 27701-2738

MEY, JACOB LOUIS, linguistics educator; b. Amsterdam, The Netherlands, Oct. 30, 1926; arrived in Denmark, 1952; s. Jacob Louis and Wynanda (Meyer) M.; m. Kari Lothe, July 15, 1957 (div. 1964); m. Inger Hansen, Sept. 18, 1965; children: Kari Anne, Sara Katrine, Jacob Louis IV, Inger Elise, Alexandra Rebecca, Kristianna Henrikke. Lic. in philosophy, U. Nymegen, The Netherlands, 1951; PhD, U. Copenhagen, Denmark, 1960; PhD (hon.), U. Zaragoza, Spain, 1993. Lectr. linguistics Oslo U., 1960-66; assoc. prof. U. Tex., Austin, 1966-72; prof. Odense (Denmark) U., 1972-96, J.W. Goethe U., Frankfurt, Germany, 1996-97, U. Campinas, Brazil, 1997, U. Haifa and Haifa Technion, Israel, 1998, Söderstörn Univ. Coll., Stockholm, 1999; vis. assoc. prof. Georgetown U., Washington, 1967; rsch. fellow Rand Corp., Santa Monica, Calif., 1963; rsch. scientist Charles U., Prague, Czechoslovakia, 1965; vis. fellow Yale U., New Haven, 1979, Northwestern U., Evanston, Ill., 1989, 94-95, Warwick (Eng.) U., 1991; vis. scientist City U., Hong Kong, 1993-94. Author: La Catégorie du Nombre en Finnois Moderne, 1961, Whose Language: A Study in Linguistic Pragmatics, 1985, Pragmatics: An Introduction, 1993, When Voices Clash: A Study in Literary Pragmatics, 1999; editor: Pragmalinguistics: Theory and Practice, 1979; co-editor: Encyclopedia of Language and Linguistics, 1995; editor-in-chief Jour. Pragmatics, Amsterdam, 1977—, Concise Ency. of Pragmatics, 1998. Mem. adv. bd. Discourse and Soc., 1990—, Psyke & Logos, 1988—, Revue de Sémantique et Pragmatique, 1997—, Text, 1998—, Miscellanea (Zaragoza), 1997—. Japan Found. scholar Tsukuba U., Ibaraki, Japan, 1983; fellow Sloane Found., 1979, Sasakawa Found., 1985, Andersen Cons., 1993. Mem. Linguistic Cir. Copenhagen, Linguistic Soc. Am., Internat. Pragmatics Assn. (mem. cons. bd. 1987—), Cognitive Technology Soc. (v.p. 1998—). Roman Catholic. Avocations: outdoor activities, water sports, bicycling, music, Japanese calligraphy. Address: 1100 W 29th St Austin TX 78703-1915 Office: U of So Denmark Inst Lang/, Comm Campusvej 55, DK-5230 Odense Denmark

MEYBECK, ALAIN LOUIS, research director; b. Rouen, France, Aug. 4, 1938; s. Jean and Laurence (Fraisse) M.; m. Anne Scheveleff de Suzor, Dec. 21, 1962; children: Alexandre, Aude, Agnès. Ingenieur chimiste, Ecole Nat. Superieure de Chimie, Mulhouse, France, 1960; DSc, U. Louis Pasteur, Strasbourg, France, 1966. Rsch. fellow CNRS, Mulhouse, 1961-67, 68-72, USDA, Albany, Calif., 1967-68; dir. rsch. Orlane, Nanterre, France, 1972-75; tech. dir. Jeanne Gatineau, Bezons, France, 1975-78; dir. labs. Christian Dior Perfumes, St. Jean De Braye, France, 1978-83; del. dir. LVMH Recherche, Nanterre, 1983-98; dir. ext. rsch. natl. prod. L'Oreal, Clichy, France, 1999—. Contbr. chpts. to books and articles to profl. jours.; patentee in field. Recipient award Internat. Fedn. Soc. Cosmetic Chemists, Sydney, 1978. Mem. AAAS, Am. Chem. Soc., Assn. Nationale des Docteurs es Scis., Soc. Française de Chimie, N.Y. Acad. Scis., Soc. Française de Cosmetologie, Soc. Cosmetic Chemists, Soc. Cosmetic Chemists of Japan. Home: Apt 242, 20 Ter Rue De Bezons, 92 400 Courbevoie France

MEYBERG-SOLOMAYER, GABRIELE CHRISTINE, physician, researcher; b. Ludwigsburg, Germany, Aug. 21, 1964; d. Bernhard Ulrich and Lotte (Essig) Meyberg; m. Erich Franz Solomayer, May 25, 1996. Student, U. Ancona, Italy, 1984-85, Free U. Berlin, 1985-86; MD, U. Heidelberg, 1992. Physician/rschr., dept. ob-gyn. U. Heidelberg, 1992—; chmn. Fedn. Internat. Ob-Gyn. World Congress, 1997. Contbr. chpts. to books, articles to profl. jours. Mem. German Soc. for Ultrasound in Medicine, German Soc. for Gynecology and Obstetrics, German Soc. for Doppler Ultrasound, German Soc. for Echocardiography in Ob-Gyn. Avocations: reading, dancing, painting, sports, playing piano. Home: Leipzigerstrasse 1, 69181 Leimen Germany Office: U Heidelberg Dept Ob Gyn, Voss strasse 9, 69115 Heidelberg Germany

MEYER, ALVIN FELIX, environmental consultant; b. Shreveport, La., Sept. 3, 1920; s. Alvin Felix and Bertha (Weil) M.; married June 1941 (widowed Oct. 1987); children: A.F. Meyer III, Carolyn Rhode; m. Grace W. Weil, Sept. 15, 1995. BS in Civil and Sanitary Engring., Va. Mil. Inst., 1941; DSc in Optometry (hon.), Ill. Coll. Optometry, 1969. Commd. 2d lt. USAF, 1941, advanced through grades to col., 1957, sanitary engr., 1941-48, chief indsl. hygiene Air Material Command, 1948-54, chief sanitary/indsl. hygiene engring. Strategic Air Command, 1954-61, chief USAF Biomed. Scis. Corp., Dept. of Def., 1962-69, ret., 1970; dir. environ. health svc. USPHS, 1969-70; dep. asst. adminstr. noise control U.S. Environ. Protection Agy., 1970-75; pres. A.F. Meyer & Assocs. Inc., McLean, Va., 1975—. Fellow ASCE, APHA, Soc. Am. Mil. Engrs., Aerospace Med. Assn. (assoc.); mem. Am. Acad. Envron. Engrs. (diplomate). Office: AF Meyer and Assocs Inc 400 Kilkenny Way Cantonment FL 32533-6815

MEYER, ANDREA PEROUTKA, small business owner; b. Prague, Czechoslovakia, Nov. 29, 1963; came to U.S. 1970; d. George and Alena Peroutka; m. Dana Charles Meyer, Oct. 16, 1983. BA in Liberal Arts, U. Tex., 1985, M in Libr. of Info. Sci., 1986. Libr. IBM, Austin, Tex., 1985-86; rsch. specialist Career Track Seminars, Boulder, Colo., 1986-88; founder, pres. Working Knowledge, Boulder, 1988—; project mgr. Interesting Orgns. Database for MIT, 1995—; cons. The Tom Peters Group, Palo Alto, Calif., 1989-95. Author: (workbooks) Stress Management Strategies, 1987, How to Give Presentations, 1988; co-author: (audio tape) How to Set Up a Corporate Library, 1989; co-editor Briefing Book for Inventing the Organizations of the 21st Century, 1995-96; assoc. editor Inside Decisions, 1995-96; contbr. chpts. to 3 books. Recipient Ray C. Janeway scholarship, Tex. Libr. Assn., 1985, Philip Morris scholarship, 1981-85. Mem. Planning Forum (v.p. comm., bd. dirs. Denver chpt.), Product Devel. and Mgmt. Assn. (newsletter editor), Toastmasters, Mensa (chmn. scholarship com.), Pres.'s Assn., European Consortium of Info. Cons.; Phi Beta Kappa. Avocations: reading, hiking, writing, travel. Home and Office: 515 Forest Ave Boulder CO 80304-2550

MEYER, AXEL, science educator; b. Mölln, Germany, Aug. 4, 1960; came to U.S., 1982, permanent resident, 1993; s. Diethard and Ingrid (Ollmann) M. BA, U. Marburg, Germany, 1982; student, U. Kiel, Germany, 1982, U. Miami, 1982; postgrad., Harvard U., 1986-87; MS in Zoology, U. Calif., Berkeley, 1984, PhD in Zoology, 1988. Alfred P. Sloan postdoctoral fellow in molecular evolution U. Calif., Berkeley, 1988-90; asst. prof. dept. ecology and evolution SUNY, Stony Brook, 1990-93, assoc. prof., 1993-97; prof. dept. biology U. Konstanz, Germany, 1997—; Miller vis. rsch. prof. depts. integrative biology and molecular and cell biology U. Calif., Berkeley, 1996-97; vis. prof. Hopkins Marine Sta., Stanford U., 1997—. Assoc. editor Molecular Biology and Evolution, 1997—, Jour. Molecular Evolution, 1998—; mem. editl. bd. Zoology-Analysis of Complex Sys., 1998—, Jour. Exptl. Zoology-Molecular Devel. Evolution, 1998—, Comparative Biochemistry and Physiology, 1995—; contbr. numerous articles to sci. jours., including Nature, Proceedings of NAS, others. Recipient G.C. Jordan award Am. Cichlid Assn., 1986, Young Investigator prize Am. Soc. Naturalists, 1990; grantee NATO, 1991-94, NSF, 1991—, others; Fulbright fellow, 1982-84, U. Calif. fellow, 1986-87; Simon Guggenheim Meml. fellow 1996-97. Fellow Linnean Soc.; mem. AAAS, Am. Soc. Ichthyologists and Herpetologists, Soc. Molecular Biology and Evolution, Soc. Systematic Biologists, Genetics Soc. Am., Soc. Integrative and Comparative Biologists, Soc. Study of Evolution, Gesellschaft Biol. Sytematik, Deutsche Zool. Gesellschaft, European Soc. Evolutionary Biology, Fisheries Soc. British Isles. Avocation: opera, pets. Fax: +49-07531-88-3018. E-mail: axel.meyer@uni-konstanz.de. Office: Dept Biology, U Konstanz, 78457 Konstanz Germany

MEYER, BILL, newspaper publisher, editor; b. Pratt, Kans., Aug. 6, 1925; s. Otto William and Ruth Clarinda (Jones) M.; m. Joan Aileen Wight, Sept. ll, 1949; l child, Eric Kent. BS in Journalism, U. Kans., 1948. News editor Marion County Record, Hoch Pub. Co., Inc., Marion, Kans., 1948-67, editor, pub., 1967—; owner Cottonwood Valley Agy., Marion, 1990-98, Hoch Pub. Co., Inc., Marion, 1998—; editor 99th Inf. Divsn. Assn., Marion, 1971—, pres., 1998-99; lectr. media law Wichita (Kans.) State U., 1985; polit. interviewer St. KPTS-TV, Wichita, 1983-98; bd. dirs. Ctrl. Nat. Bank, Junction City, Kans.; mil. cons., travel agt. Battlefield Tours, Slidell, La., 1990—. Past pres. Marion Sch. dist. Bd. Edn., Marion County Hosp. Dist.; bd. dirs. Marion Manor Nursing Home, Kans. Hist. Soc., 1985-94; trustee, past pres. William Allen White Found., Lawrence, Kans. With U.S. Army, 1943-45, ETO. Recipient commendation Kans. Ho. of Reps., 1982, 99th Inf. Div. Assn., 1986, 89, named Kans. Master Editor, recipient Clyde Reed Kans. Master Editor award Kans. Newspaper Found., 1997, Mentor award Kans. Newspaper Found., 2000; named Hon. Col. Kans. Calvary, 1987, Hon. Ky. Col., 1990. Mem. Nat. Newspaper Assn., Kans. Press Assn. (pres. 1982-83, Boyd Community Svc. award 1979, Outstanding Mentor award 1999), Marion C. of C. (past bd. dirs.), Marion Country Club, Masons, Shriners, Kiwanis (pres. Marion 1957), 99th Infantry Divsn. Assn. (pres. 1998), Soc. Profl. Journalists. Republican. Methodist. Avocation: military history. Home: PO Box 99 Marion KS 66861-0099 Office: Hoch Pub Co Inc 117 S 3rd St Marion KS 66861-1621

MEYER, CAROL FRANCES, pediatrician, allergist; b. Berea, Ky., June 2, 1936; d. Harvey Kessler and Jessie Irene (Hamm) Meyer; m. Daniel Baker Cox, June 5, 1955 (div. Apr. 1962). AA, U. Fla., 1955; BA, Duke U., 1957; MD, Med. Coll. Ga., 1967. Diplomate Am. Bd. Pediatrics, Am. Bd. Allergy and Immunology. Intern in pediat. Med. Coll. Ga., Augusta, 1967-68; resident in pediat. Gorgas Hosp., Canal Zone, 1968-69; fellow in pediat. respiratory disease Med. Coll. Ga., 1969-71, instr. pediat., 1971-72; med. officer pediat. Canal Zone Govt., 1972-79; med. officer pediat. Dept. of Army, Panama, 1979-82, med. officer allergy, 1982-89, physician in charge allergy clinic, 1984-89; asst. prof. pediat. and medicine Med. Coll. Ga., Augusta, 1990-2000; med. dir. Telemedicine Ctr. Med. Coll. Ga., 2000—; mem. Bd. of Canal Zone Merit Sys. Examiners, 1976-79. Contbr. articles to profl. jours. Mem. First Bapt. Ch. Orch., 1992—; founding mem., violoncello Curundu Chamber Ensemble, 1979-89. Recipient U.S. Army Exceptional Performance awards, 1985, 86, 89, Merck award Med. Coll. Ga., 1967; U. Fla. J. Hillis Miller scholar, 1954. Mem. Am. Coll. Rheumatology, Allergy and Immunology Soc. Ga., Hispanic-Am. Allergy and Immunology Assn., Ga. Pediat. Soc., Am. Coll. Allergy, Asthma and Immunology, Am. Acad. Allergy, Asthma and Immunology, Am. Acad. Pediat., Panama Canal Soc. Fla., Ga. Ornithol. Soc., Ga. Thoracic Soc., Am. Lung Assn. (Ga. East Ctrl. br. exec. bd. 1990-98), Am. Assn. Ret. Persons, Nature Conservancy, Royal Soc. for Preservation Birds, Nat. Assn. Ret. Fed. Employees, Nat. Audubon Soc., Augusta Audubon Soc., Willow Run Homeowner's Assn. (pres. 1994-99), Alpha Omega Alpha.

MEYER, SIR CHRISTOPHER J.R., diplomat; b. Beaconsfield, Eng., Feb. 22, 1944; m. Catherine Meyer; 5 sons. Student, Lancing Coll., Cambridge, Eng., Peterhouse, Cambridge, Eng., Paul Nitze Sch., Bologna, Italy. Joined Diplomatic Svc., London, 1966-68; with Diplomatic Svc., Moscow, 1968-70, Madrid, 1970-73; head Soviet sect. East European and Soviet dept. Diplomatic Svc., London, 1973-76, speech-writer to fgn. sec. policy planning staff, 1976-78; mem. UK rep. to European cmtys. Diplomatic Svc., Brussels, 1978-82; polit. counselor Diplomatic Svc., Moscow, 1982-84; fgn. office spokesman, press sec. to fgn. sec. Diplomatic Svc., London, 1984-88; min. Diplomatic Svc., Washington, 1989-92; min., dep. head mission Diplomatic Svc., 1992-94; govt. spokesman, press sec. to prime min. Diplomatic Svc., London, 1994-97; Brit. amb. to Fed. Rep. Germany Diplomatic Svc., 1997; amb. to the U.S. Govt. U.K., Washington; vis. fellow Harvard U. Ctr. for Internat. Affairs, 1988-89. Named Knight Comdr. of the Order of St. Michael and St. George, 1997-98. Avocations: squash, tennis, watching football, listening to jazz music. Fax: 202-588-7870. Office: Embassy of the UK of Gt Britain and No Ireland 3100 Massachusetts Ave NW Washington DC 20008-3689

MEYER, DANIAL RONALD, association executive; b. Cape, South Africa, May 2, 1955; s. Victor Leonard and Katerina Aletta (Steyn) M.; m. Theadora Gysberta Froon, Sept. 1, 1979; children: Danial, Elizabeth, Jonathan, Malcolm, Heidi. Diploma in mktg. mgmt., Cape Technicon, Cape Town, South Africa, 1977; EDP, U. Zimbabwe, Harare, 1988. Mgmt. trainee Protea Med., Cape Town, 1974-77; sales mgr. Glaxo Surg., Cape Town, 1977-78; gen. mgr. Eschmann, Harare, 1978-82; mng. dir., CEO Surgimed, Harare, 1982—; chmn. Trinidad Industries, Harare, 1996—, Meymed Holdings Ltd., Harare, 1989—; dir. Danny Meyer Family Trust, 1994—, Zimbabwe Investment Ctr., Harare, 1996—; mem. faculty of com. adv. U. Zimbabwe; bd. dirs. Suburban Med. Ctr., 1996—. Mem. Harare City Coun., 1991—. Recipient Industrialist of Yr. Confedn. Zimbabwe Industries, 1993, Mktg. Man. of Yr. Inst. Mktg. Mgmt., 1988. Fellow Inst. Dirs., Inst. Personal Mgmt.; mem. African, Pacific and Caribbean Assoc. C. of C. (pres.), Zimbabwe Nat. C. of C. (pres. 1995-98), Rotary CLub Harare (pres. 1994-95), Royal Harare Golf Club, Harare Club. Roman Catholic. Avocations: regional politics, golf, reading, community service, outdoor activities. Home: PO Box 5908, Harare Zimbabwe

MEYER, DANIEL KRAMER, real estate executive; b. Denver, July 15, 1957; s. Milton Edward and Mary (Kramer) M. Student, Met. State Coll., Denver, 1977-78, U. Colo., 1978-80. Ptnr., developer RM & M II (Ltd. Partnership), Englewood, Colo., 1981-87; pres. Centennial Mortgage and Investment, Ltd., Englewood, Colo., 1984-87; prin. Capriole Properties, Greenwood Village, Colo., 1983—. Alumni mem. bd. trustees Kent Denver Country Day Sch., 1981-83; sec. dist. 37 ctrl. and vacancy com. Colo. Ho. of Reps., 1991-92. Recipient Pamela Davis Beardsley devel. award Kent Denver Sch., 1995. Mem. Greenwood Athletic Club. Republican. Avocations: climbing, rollerblading, political economy, 20th century English lit., metaphysics.

MEYER, EDMOND GERALD, energy and natural resources educator, resources scientist, entrepreneur, former chemistry educator, university administrator; b. Albuquerque, Nov. 2, 1919; s. Leopold and Beatrice (Ilfeld) M.; m. Betty F. Knobloch, July 4, 1941; children: Lee Gordon, Terry Gene, David Gary. BS in Chemistry, Carnegie Mellon U., 1940, MS, 1942; PhD, U. N.Mex., 1950. Chemist Harbison Walker Refractories Co., 1940-41; instr. Carnegie Mellon U., 1941-42; asst. phys. chemist Bur. Mines, 1942-44; chemist research div. N.Mex. Inst. Mining and Tech., 1946-48; head dept. sci. U. Albuquerque, 1950-52; head dept. chemistry N.Mex. Highlands U., 1952-59; dir. Inst. Sci. Rsch., 1957-63; dean Grad. Sch., 1961-63; dean Coll. Arts and Sci., U. Wyo., 1963-75, v.p., 1974-80, prof. energy and natural resources, 1981-89, prof. and dean emeritus, 1989—; exec. cons. Diamond Shamrock Corp., 1980; bd. dirs. Carbon Fuels Corp., First Nat. Bank, Laramie; sci. adviser Gov. of Wyo., 1964-90; pres. Coal Tech. Corp., 1981—; mng. gen. ptnr. Coal Tech. Internat., LLC, 1999—; cons. Los Alamos Nat. Lab., NFS, HHS, GAO, Wyo. Bancorp; contractor investigator Rsch. Corp., Dept. Interior, AEC, NIH, NSF, Dept. Energy, Dept. Edn.; Fulbright exch. prof. U. Concepcion, Chile, 1959. Co-author: Chemistry-Survey of Principles, 1963, Legal Rights of Chemists and Engineers, 1977, Industrial Research & Development Management, 1982; contbr. articles to profl. jours.; patentee in field. Chair, Laramie Regional Airport Bd., 1989-93, treas., 1994-97, chair; active Laramie City Coun., 1997—, vice mayor, 1998—. Lt. comdr. USNR, 1944-46, ret. Recipient Disting. Svc. award Jaycees; rsch. fellow U. N.Mex., 1948-50. Fellow AAAS, Am. Inst. Chemists (hon. fellow; pres. 1992-93, chmn. 1994-95); mem. Assoc. Western Univs. (chmn. 1972-74), Am. Chem. Soc. (councilor 1962-90, chmn. Wyo. sect. 1997), Biophys. Soc., Coun. Coll. Arts and Scis. (pres. 1971, sec.-treas. 1972-75), dir. Washington office 1973), Laramie C. of C. (pres. 1984), Sigma Xi. Home: 1058 Colina Dr Laramie WY 82072-5015 Office: U Wyo Coll Arts Scis Laramie WY 82071-3825

MEYER, GEORGE REX, retired freelance educational consultant, author; b. Croyden, N.S.W., Australia, Mar. 15, 1928; s. Robert Gribbon and Emma Rae (Wilkins) M. BSc, Sydney U., 1951, BA, 1954, MEd, 1955, MA, 1984; PhD, London, 1959; MSc in Society, U. N.S.W., Australia, 1986. From teaching fellow zoology to sr. lectr. zoology, biology Sydney U., 1952-66; dir. Centre Advancement Teaching, Macquarie U., Sydney, 1967-78; fellow continuing edn. Macquarie U., 1978-88; freelance ednl. cons. Beecroft, Australia, 1988-95; writer, 1995—. Co-author: Field Work in Animal Biology, 1954, Science and the Environment of Man, 1966, Quiz Yourself About African Mammals, 1974; editor: Practical Work in Animal Biology, 1966, The Jacaranda Dictionary of Scientific Terms, 1971, Overcoming Constraints on Teaching Biology, 1984, Bioethics in Education, 1991, Teaching Biology for Social Relevance, 1996, Scientific Orientation Test (S.OR.T.), 1996, Meyer Family History, 1998—; contbr. numerous articles to profl. jours. Mem. syllabus and exam. com. in sci.for secondary schs., N.S.W., 1952-78; pioneer devel. field biology studies for schs.; mem. state com. to supervise inservice tng. tchrs., N.S.W., 1973-83; UNESCO cons. in curriculum devel., 1968-95. Grantee Nuffield Found., Carnegie Corp., Australian Govt. Fellow Australian Coll. Edn.; named Mem. Order of Australia, 1981. Mem. Australian and New Zealand Assn. Advancement Sci. (vice chmn. 1967-75), Sydney Sci. Film Soc. (v.p. 1967-80), Assn. Environ. Edn. (founding pres. 1972-75), Australian Returned Servicemen's League (assoc. Epping br. 1967—), Internat. Union Biol. Scis. (lifetime emeritus 1989—, mem. edn. commn. 1978-89). Avocations: music appreciation, family history. Home: PO Box 154, Beecroft 2119, Australia

MEYER, HANS BERNHARD, liturgy educator, priest; b. Mannheim, Baden, Fed. Republic Germany, Dec. 23, 1924; s. Karl and Klara (Reich) M. Student, U. Freiburg, Fed. Republic Germany, 1945-46; lic. phil., Jesuitenhochschule, Munich, 1951; D. in Theology, U. Innsbruck (Austria), 1959. Ordained priest in Roman Cath., 1956; joined Soc. of Jesus, 1946. Prof. moral-theology U. Innsbruck, 1966-69, dir. Inst. Moral Theology, 1966-69, co-dir. Inst. Pastoral Theology, 1970-78, prof. liturgy, 1969-95; bd. dirs. Inst. for Liturgiewissenschaft, Innsbruck; dean Faculty of Cath. Theology, Innsbruck, 1967-68, 79-81; rector Collegium Canisianum, Innsbruck, 1986-93. Dir. Zeitschrift für Katholische Theologie, 1963-98, (series) Studien und Arbeiten der Theologischen Fakultät, 1967—; editor: (series) Pastoralliturgische Studien, 1974—, (handbook, 15 vols.) Gottesdienst der Kirche, 1983—; author 18 books; contbr. numerous articles to profl. jours. Mem. Societas Liturgica. Avocations: art, architecture, liberal arts. Home: Sillgasse 6, A 6020 Innsbruck Austria

MEYER, IRWIN STEPHAN, lawyer, accountant; b. Monticello, N.Y., Nov. 14, 1941; s. Ralph and Janice (Cohen) M.; children: Kimberly B., Joshua A. BS, Rider Coll., 1963; JD, Cornell U., 1966. Bar: N.Y. 1966; CPA, N.J. Tax mgr. Lybrand Ross Bros. & Montgomery, N.Y.C., 1966-71; mem. Ehrenkranz, Ehrenkranz & Schultz, N.Y.C., 1971-74; prin. Irwin S. Meyer, 1974-77, 82-96; mem. Levine, Honig, Eisenberg & Meyer, 1977-78, Eisenberg, Honig & Meyer, 1978-81, Eisenberg, Honig, Meyer & Fogler, 1981-82, Janow & Meyer, LLC., 1997—. With U.S. Army, 1966-71. Mem. ABA, N.Y. Bar Assn., Am. Assn. Atty.-CPA, N.Y. Assn. Atty.-CPA, N.J. Soc. CPA. Office: 1 Blue Hill Plz Ste 1006 Pearl River NY 10965-3100

MEYER, J. THEODORE, lawyer; b. Chgo., Apr. 13, 1936; s. Joseph Theodore and Mary Elizabeth (McHugh) M.; m. Marilu Bartholomew, Aug. 16, 1961; children: Jean, Joseph. BS, John Carroll U., 1958; postgrad., U. Chgo.; JD, DePaul U., 1962. Bar: Ill. 1962. Ptnr. Bartholomew & Meyer, Chgo., 1963-83; mem. Ill. Gen. Assembly, Ho. of Reps. 28th Legis. Dist., 1966-72, 74-82; chmn. House environ. study com., 1968; chmn. energy environ. com. and natural resources com.; mem. appropriations and exec. com.; chmn. Joint House/Senate com. to review state air and water plans, 1968; mem. Fed. State Task Force on Energy; chmn., founder Midwest Legis. Coun. on Environ., 1971; mem. Joint Legis. Com. on Hazardous Waste in Lake Calumet Area, 1987; chmn. Gov.'s adv. com. to streamline the Ill. environ. protection act, 1999—, Ill. Regulatory Revision Commn., 1999—; mem. Ill. Pollution Control Bd., Chgo., 1983-98, Ill. EPA, 1998-99; lectr. in field. Recipient Appreciation award Ill. Wildlife Fedn., 1972, Environ. Quality award Region V, EPA, 1974, Pro Bono Publico award Self-Help Action Ctr., 1975, Merit award Dept. Ill. VFW, 1977, Environ. Legislator of Yr. award Ill. Environ. Coun., 1978-79; named Disting. Lawyer Legislator of Yr., Hon. Tex. Citizen, hon. lt. aide-de-camp Ala. State Militia. Fellow Chgo. Bar Found.; mem. ABA, Ill. Bar Assn., Chgo. Bar Assn., Nat. Rep. Legis. Assn., Nat. Trust Hist. Preservation, Nat. Wildlife Fedn., Ill. Hist. Soc. Republican. Roman Catholic. Office: State of Ill Ctr 100 W Randolph St Ste 4-900 Chicago IL 60601-3218

MEYER, JEAN-PIERRE, psychiatrist; b. Paris, Apr. 3, 1949; s. Henry Jules and Jacqueline Suzanne (Roux).; m. Marie Elisabeth Buisan, June 25, 1977; children: Arnaud Jean, Gauthier Henri. MD, Broussais U., Paris, 1975; Cert. of Maritime Medicine, 1976; Cert. of Med. Expertise, Cochin U., Paris, 1978; specialist in psychiatry, Necker U., Paris, 1978. Intern Fontainebleau (France) Hosp., 1974, Enfants Malades Hosp., 1975, Melun (France) Hosp., 1976, Mohamed V Hosp., Rabat, Morocco, 1976, Lagny (France) Hosp., 1977; intern psychiatrist infirmary of police Paris, 1977, sole practice medicine, specializing in psychiatry, 1979—; cons. Paris Hosp., 1986—; expert cons. Securite Sociale, Paris and Creil, 1984—; expert cons. Ct. of Appeals, Paris, 1988; archbishopric, Paris, 1979—. Author: Relaxation Therapeutique, 1986; co-author: Le Projet en Psychotherapie, 1983, Abrege de Neuro-Psychiatrie, Conduites Pratiques de Psychiatrie, 1994. Contbr. articles to profl. jours. V.p. Mutual Ins.'s, Paris, 1972—. Mem. Intergroupe de Formation en Relaxation, Med. Assn. Paris., Soc. Français de Relaxation (treas.). Roman Catholic. Avocations: golf, skiing, surfing. Fax: 33-1-40-71-99-25. Office: 9 Rue Du Général Delestraint, 75016 Paris France

MEYER, JON KEITH, psychiatrist, psychoanalyst, educator; b. Springfield, Ill., May 6, 1938; s. Samuel Barclay and Finela Hermoine (Roehl) M.; m. Eleanor Fumie Yamashita, June 6, 1964; children: David Christopher, Laura Tamiko. AB summa cum laude, Dartmouth Coll., 1960; MD, Johns Hopkins U., 1964; grad., Washington Psychoanalytic Inst, 1980. Intern internal medicine Johns Hopkins Hosp., Balt., 1964-65, resident in psychiatry, 1965-67, 69; resident in psychiatry St. Elizabeth's Hosp., Washington, 1968; spl. asst. to dir. NIMH, Bethesda, Md., 1969-71; asst. prof. psychiatry Johns Hopkins Med. Sch., Balt., 1971-76, assoc. prof., 1976-83; prof. psychiatry Med. Coll. Wis., Milw., 1983—, prof. psychoanalysis, 1996—, prof. family medicine, 1990—; tng. and supervising analyst Chgo. Inst. for Psychoanalysis, 1987—; vice chmn. Dept. of Psychiatry, 1993—; chief psychiatry Froedtert Meml. Luth. Hosp., Milw., 1994-97; med. dir. Wis., Psychoanalytic Found., Milw., 1987-91, sec. bd. dirs., 1988-91. Author books; editl. bd. Jour. Am. Psychoanalytic Assn., 1991-94; nat. editor: The American Psychoanalyst, 1997—; contbr. chpts. to books, numerous articles to profl. jours. Comdr. USPHS, 1967-71. Daniel Webster Nat. scholar Dartmouth Coll., 1956-60, sr. fellow, 1959-60, Dennison rsch. fellow Johns Hopkins Med. Sch., 1964; Erik Erikson scholar-in-residence Austen Riggs Ctr., Stockbridge, Mass., 1991-92, Edith Sabshin Tchg. award, 1999. Fellow Am. Psychiat. Assn., Am. Coll. Psychoanalysts, Am. Coll. Psychiatrists; mem. Internat. Psychoanalytic Assn. (com. on constn. and by-laws 1997—, com. on procedural codes 1997—, ho. dels. 1998—, chair ho. of dels. 1999-2000, task force on structure and mission 1998—, task force on governance 2000—), Am. Psychoanalytic Assn. (exec. councilor 1993-97, chmn. com. on exec. coun. structure and function 1995-98, sec. 1997—, exec. com. 1997—, adminstrv. bd. Jour. Am. Psychoanalytic Assn. 1997—, chmn. com. on cmty. clinics 1997—, com. on insts. 1998—), Wis. Psychoanalytic Soc. (pres. 1989-91). Avocations: photography, hiking, kayaking. Office: Med Coll Wis 2025 E Newport Ave Fl 4 Milwaukee WI 53211-2906

MEYER, LUTZ-MICHAEL, physician; b. Stuttgart, Germany, May 8, 1961; s. Wolfgang M. and Gisela (Fleischmann) M.; m. Hildegard Josephine Holl, May 7, 1993; children: Julia, Moritz. Degree in medicine, Albert-Ludwigs U., Freiburg, Germany, 1990; doctorate, Rupert-Karls U., Heidelberg, Germany, 1993; diploma in tropical medicine & hygiene, Royal

Coll. Physicians, Eng., 1993. Diplomate Am. Bd. Pediatrics, Am. Bd. Neonatologists, German Bd. Pediatrics, German Bd. Neonatologists, German Bd. Critical Care. Jr. ho. officer Inst. Tropical Hygiene Heidelberg U., 1990-92; scholar London Sch. Hygiene & Tropical Medicine, 1993; resident Med. Ctr. Hosp. Vt., Burlington, 1993-96; sr. officer Stadtklinik Baden-Baden, Germany, 1996-97; fellow in pediatraic critical care Queen Olga Hosp., Stuttgart, Germany, 2000—; fellow in neonatology Queen Olga Hosp., Stuttgart, 1997-99; emergency flight surgeon German Air Ambulance, Stuttgart, 1997—. Scholar Deutscher Akademischer Austauschdienst, 1993; Rsch. grantee Beit Trust , 1993; Intensive Care Traveller scholar Deutsche Interdisziplinaere Vereinigung fuer Intensivmedizine, 1999. Fellow Am. Acad. Pediatrics; mem. Deutsche Tropenmedizinische Gesellschaft. Avocations: antique furniture, travel. E-mail: thebabydoc@web.dc. Home: Teckweg 6, D-73269 Hochdorf Germany Office: Queen Olga Hosp ICU, Bismarckstr 87, D-70176 Stuttgart Germany

MEYER, MARION M., editorial consultant; b. Sheboygan, Wis., July 14, 1923; d. Herman O. and Viola A. (Hoch) M. BA, Lakeland Coll., 1950; MA, NYU, 1957. Payroll clk. Am. Chair Co., Sheboygan, 1941-46; tchr. English and religion, dir. athletics Am. Sch. for Girls, Baghdad, Iraq, 1950-56; edn. and publ. staff United Ch. Bd. for Homeland Ministries, United Ch. Press/Pilgrim Press, 1958-64, sr. editor, 1965-88, ret., 1988; cons. in field. Editor Penney Retirement Cmty. Newsletter, 1990-98; contbr. articles to various publs.; writer hymns Look to God, Be Radiant, 1989, Be Still, 1990, Come, God, Creator, 1992, Something New! (extended work), 1993, Our Home is PRC, 1996. Incorporating mem. Contact Phila., Inc., 1972, bd. dirs., 1972-75, v.p., chmn. com. to organize cmty. adv. bd., chmn. auditing com., editor newsletter, 1972-74, pres., 1974-75, assoc. mem., 1977—; mem. ofcl. bd. Old First Reformed Ch., Phila., 1984-89, Penney Meml. Ch., Penney Farms, Fla., 1997-2000, chmn. bd., 1998-2000; del. to coun. Nat. Interfaith Coalition on Aging as rep. of United Ch. of Christ, 1996-98; deacon United Ch. Christ, 1984—, Mid.-East Com. of Pa. SE Conf. United Ch. Christ, 1986-88. Honored as role model United Ch. of Christ, 1982, 85. Mem. AAUW, NOW, Nat. Mus. Women in the Arts (charter mem.), Nat. Trust for Hist. Preservation. Home: PO Box 656 Penney Farms FL 32079-0656

MEYER, MICHEL BERNARD, philosophy educator; b. Brussels, Nov. 11, 1950; s. Serge and Simone (Samdam) M.; m. Corinne Hoogaert, Sept. 11, 1993; children: Alexandre, Patrick. BA in Philosophy, U. Brussels, 1972, BA in Econs., 1973, PhD in Philosophy, 1977; MA Arts and Scis., Johns Hopkins U., 1975. Prof. State U. of Mons, 1980—; vis. fellow Yale U., 1982, European Inst. at Florence, 1990; vis. prof. U. Montreal, 1986, U. Calif., Berkeley, 1987, 88, U. Lausanne, 1992; pres. European Ctr. in the Study of Argument, 1988. Author: Découverte et justification en science, 1979, Logique, langage et artumentation, 1982, Meaning and Reading: A Philosophical Essay on Language and Literature, 1992, De la problématologie: language, science et philosophie, 1986, Science et métaphysique chez Kant, 1995, Le philosophe et les passions, 1991, Pour une critique de l'ontologie, 1991, Questions de rhétorique: Language, raison et séduction, 1993, Rhetoric, Language and Reason, 1994, De l'insolence: essai sur la morale et le politique, 1995, Qu'est-ce que la philosophie?, 1997; editor: (series) Philosophy and Language, 1983-90, L'Interrogation philosophique; editor Revue Internationale de Philosophie, Library of Rhetoric. Recipient Chevalier de l'Ordre de Leopold. Office: U Brussels CP 188, 50 Avenue F Roosevelt, 1050 Brussels Belgium

MEYER, NORVA, history educator; b. N.Y.C., Sept. 17, 1941; d. Max Wilson and Dorothy Louise (Cox) Lintecum; m. E.R. Meyer, Jan. 17, 1964 (div. Dec. 1980); children: Carrie Elizabeth, N. Patrick. BS, Ind. U., 1964; MA, Ariz. State U., 1972. History tchr. Ind. U. Lab Sch., Bloomington, 1964-66, Jeffersonville (Ind.) H.S., 1966-68; Western civilization instr. Glendale (Ariz.) C.C., 1970-72, Va. Commonwealth U., Richmond, 1973-74, J. Sargent Reynolds C.C., Richmond, 1973-74; history chair The Steward Sch., Richmond, 1982—; sponsor, organizer Model UN Soc., Richmond, 1983—; organizer, guide Europe study trips, The Steward Sch., 1988, 90, 92. Editor: Vietnam Blues, 1990, (poetry) Sarge's Little Book of Haiku, 1994. Troop com. mem. Boy Scouts Am., Richmond, 1988-95, troop mother, 1989-94, merit badge counselor, 1988-98. Mem. Nat. Coun. for History Edn., Nat. Coun. for the Social Studies, Va. Assn. Ind. Schs., Va. Assn. History Tchrs., UN Assn. U.S.A., Phi Alpha Theta. Avocations: travel, reading, music, theater. Home: 1696 Liberty Bell Ct Richmond VA 23233-4330 Office: 11600 Gayton Rd Richmond VA 23233-3423

MEYER, PAUL A., lawyer; b. Milton, Fla., Feb. 3, 1957; s. Robert T. and Edna (Cadmus) M.; m. Tracey Leigh Whitaker, Aug. 2, 1986. BA cum laude, U. Pitts., 1979; JD, Case Western Res. U., 1983. Bar: Pa. 1983, U.S. Dist. Ct. (we. dist.) Pa. 1983, Ohio 1984, Md. 1986, D.C. 1986, U.S. Dist. Ct. Md. 1986, Va. 1992, U.S. dist. Ct. (ea. dist.) Va. 1992. Assoc. Houston, Cohen, Narbaugh & Lippard, Pitts., 1983-85; mem. staff Decklebaum, Wolpert & Ogens, Washington, 1985-86; assoc. Hirschman & Wasser, Landover, Md., 1986-87, Ridgway & Griffin Chartered, Rockville, Md., 1987-89, Graham & James, Washington, 1989-92; dep. gen. counsel Direct Response Consulting Svcs., McLain, Va., 1993-94; of counsel Watson Wyatt Worldwide, Bethesda, 1994—; with U.S.-Yugoslav Econ. Coun., 1990-91. Assoc. editor Case & Res. Law Rev., 1982-83. Can. U.S. Law Inst. scholar Case Western Res. U., 1982. Mem. Am. Corp. Counsel Assoc. Home: 2401 Bermondsey Dr Bowie MD 20721-4222 Office: Watson Wyatt Worldwide 6707 Democracy Blvd Bethesda MD 20817-1129

MEYER, PETER, sociology educator; b. Forbach, Germany, June 19, 1941; s. Brunhilde Chrusciel; m. Maria Perger. MA, U. Heidelberg, Germany, 1968, PhD, 1971; Habilitation, U. Augsburg, Germany, 1982. Rsch. asst. U. Augsburg, 1972-80, prof. sociology, 1988—; prof. sociology U. Nuremberg, Germany, 1980-81, U. Mainz, Germany, 1985; lectr. sociology U. Wuerzburg, Germany, 1986-87. Author: Sociology of War and the Military (in German), 1977, Evolution and Violence (in German), 1981, Sociobiology and Sociology (in German), 1982; co-author: The Sociobiology of Ethnocentrism, Ethnocentrism in Human Social Behavior, 1986, Evolutionary Theory in Social Science Basic Structures in Human Action, 1987, The Nature of Culture; On Human Universals, 1989, Sociology and Conflict, Human Nature and the Function of War in Social Evolution, 1990, Evolutionary Theory and Human Social Institutions, 1997; co-editor: Sociobiology and Politics, Research in Biopolitics, Vol. 6, 1998, The Sociobiology of Human Cooperation: The Interplay of Ultimate and Proximate Causes, 1999; contbr. Politics and the Life Sciences, Vol. 13, 23-25, 1994. Mem. Assn. for Politics and Life Scis., European Sociol. Soc. (chmn.). Home: Eichenstr 14, D86356 Neusaess Bavaria, Germany Office: U Augsburg, Universitaetsstr 16, D86159 Augsburg Bavaria, Germany

MEYER, PHILIP GILBERT, lawyer; b. Louisville, June 26, 1945; s. Henry Gilbert and Adele (Gutermuth) M.; m. Jackie Darlene Watson, Jan. 30, 1971 (div. Apr. 1976); m. Sylvia Saunders, Oct. 9, 1976. BBA, U. Mich., 1967; JD, U. Tex., 1970. Bar: Tex. 1970, Mich. 1971, U.S. Tax Ct. 1972, U.S. Dist. Ct. (ea. dist.) Mich. 1971, U.S. Ct. Appeals (6th cir.), 1972, U.S. Dist. Ct. (no. dist.) Ohio 1976, U.S. Dist. Ct. (we. dist.) Mich. 1993, U.S. Dist. Ct. (no. dist.) Ill. 1998. Law clk. Wayne County Cir. Ct., Detroit, 1970-72; atty. Leonard C. Jaques, Detroit, 1972; assoc. Christy & Robbins, Dearborn, Mich., 1972-73; ptnr. Foster, Meadows & Ballard, Detroit, 1973-79; of counsel Christy, Rogers & Gantz, Dearborn, 1979-81, Rogers & Gantz, Dearborn, 1981-86; prin. Philip G. Meyer and Assocs., Dearborn, 1986—; adj. prof. U. Detroit Sch. Law, 1979. Mem. ABA (com. vice chmn. rules and procedure 1982-88), Maritime Law Assn. U.S., Mich. Bar Assn. (vice chmn. admiralty sect. 1978), Tex. Bar Assn., Detroit Bar Assn. (vice chmn. admiralty com. 1991-93, chmn. admiralty sect. 1993-95), Propeller-Port of Detroit Club (pres. 1984-85). Republican. Home: 5905 Independence Ln West Bloomfield MI 48322-1854 Office: Ste 113 30300 Northwestern Hwy Farmington Hills MI 48334-3212

MEYER, RACHEL ABIJAH, foundation director, artist, theorist, poet; b. Job's Corners, Pa., Aug. 18, 1963; d. Jacob Owen and Velma Ruth (Foreman) M.; children: Andrew Carson, Peter Franklin. Student, Lebanon Valley Coll. Restaurant owner Purcy's Place, Ono, Pa.; restaurant mgr. King's Table Buffet, Citrus Heights, Calif.; product finalizer TransWorld Enterprises, Blaine, Wash.; dir., support svcs. adminstr. Tacticar Found., Sacramento, 1991—; tchr. Tacticar Inst., 1995; chair Coniréms, Sacramento, 1996—. Author: Year of the Unicorn, 1994. Avocations: researching, writing, painting. Studio: 2013 Kathryn Way Sacramento CA 95821-5517

MEYER, ROBERT ERNEST, veterinary educator; b. Buffalo, N.Y., Mar. 16, 1951; s. Ernest J. Jr. and Ruth L. M.; m. Sharon Adair, Jan. 1, 1977; 1 child, Anna Adair. BA in Biology, SUNY, Buffalo, 1973; DVM, Cornell U., 1980. Diplomate Am. Coll. Vet. Anesthesiologists; lic. veterinarian, N.Y. Asst. prof. Coll. Vet. Medicine N.C. State U., Raleigh, 1983-89; assoc. prof. N.C. State U., 1989-92, 1993—; vis. scientist radiation oncology Duke U. Med. Ctr., Durham, 1992-93; assoc. prof.; Mem. Bd. of Scientific Reviewers Am. Jour. Vet. Rsch., Schaumburg, Ill., 1999-2001, Vet. Surgery/Anesthesia, 1996-98. Patentee in field. Mem. AVMA, Am. Coll. Vet. Anesthesiologist, N.Am. Hyperthemia Soc., Cornell U. Coll. Vet. Medicine Alumni Assn. (life). Avocations: flatwater canoeing, reading. E-mail: robert meyer@ncsu.edu. Office: Coll Vet Medicine Box 8401 NC State U 4700 Hillsborough St Raleigh NC 27606-1428

MEYER, ROBERT LEWIS, investment company executive; b. Orange, N.J., Nov. 4, 1949; s. Mortimer Washington Jr. and Jean Hasna (Lewis) M.; m. Deborah Elaine Abraham, Sept. 6, 1984 (dec.); children: Michael Mordecai, Benjamin Abraham; m. Viviane Therese Lachaud, Feb. 12, 1987 (div.); 1 child, Rachelle Deborah. BA, Columbia U., 1971, JD, 1974. Bar: Ga. 1974, Fla. 1975, N.Y. 1977. Law clk to presiding justice Atlanta, 1974-76; assoc. Coudert Bros., N.Y.C., 1976-78, Hong Kong, 1978-81; exec. dir. 1st Pacific Group, Hong Kong, 1981-98; mng. dir. Spl. Assets Ltd., Hong Kong, 1985—. Mem. ABA, Hong Kong Mgmt. Assn., Am. Club, Aberdeen Marina Club. Home: 8A Bowen Rd 8th Fl, Hong Kong Hong Kong Office: 6th Fl Terr, 8 Duddell St, Central Hong Kong

MEYER, ROBERTA, mediator, communication consultant; b. San Francisco, July 27, 1936; d. Theodore Robert and Virginia (Organ) M.; m. G. William Sheldon; children: Megan McDougall Radeski, Deborah Ann Guerra. Student, U. Utah, 1974. Cert. mediator. Founder, pres., exec. dir. Roberta Meyer Communication Cons., Inc., San Francisco, 1977—; presenter numerous workshops in field of alcoholism and communication; nat. speaker Nat. Found. for Alcohlism Communicaton; keynote speaker Calif. Women's Commn. on Alcoholism, 1981; mem. adv. bd. Soviet Am. Alliance on Alcoholism and Other Addictions; founder Youter Dance Experience, 1999. Author: Facts About Booze and Other Drugs, 1980, The Parent Connection: How To Communicate With Your Child About Alcohol and Other Drugs, 1984, Listen to the Heart, 1989, (film) Understanding Addiction, 1988, Better Relationships Through Effective Communication, 1991; numerous radio and TV appearances; creator, dir. Meyer Method dance program for ballroom dancers, One Meyer Method dance tng. video, 1998. Mem. adv. bd. Marin Svcs. for Women, 1980; vol. Calif. Pacific Med. Ctr., San Francisco Ballet Aux.; mem. N.Y.C. and San Francisco Ballet Cos., 1950-56; mem. faculty San Francisco Ballet Sch., 1956-65; founder, dir. Ballet Arts of San Francisco, 1965-78, San Francisco Ballroom Dance Theatre and the accelerated dance program, 1994—. Recipient award Optimists Club, 1978; named 56th Point of Light, Pres. Bush, 1990. Mem. Nat. Ctr. for Collaborative Planning and Community Svc. (cert.), Nat. Coun. on Alcoholism (co-chmn. pub. info. com. 1985—, v.p. Bay area 1988—, bd. dirs. Teen Kick Off 1987—, Alcoholism and Drug Rsch. Communications Ctr. 1990—; pres. 1988—, creator, cons. youth aware program 1974—), San Francisco Womens Rehab. Assn. (pres. 1975-76, dir., founder Youth Dance Project 1999), Nat. Coun. on Alcoholism and Drug Dependence Calif. (pres. 1988-91), Childrens Theatre Assn., San Francisco C. of C.

MEYER, ROSALIND MAE, community volunteer; b. Fremont, Nebr., Jan. 7, 1927; d. Elwood A. P. and Emma Prince Murray; m. Richard P. Meyer, June 11, 1950; children: Susan Eldredge, Kimberly Landaal, William Meyer. BA in Psychology, U. Denver, 1949. Tchr. Denver Pub. Schs., 1949-51; journalist, columnist Trenton (Mich.) Times, 1971-79. Photographer Grosse Ile Golf and Country Club, Mich., 2000. Pres. Downriver Coun. Arts, Wayne County, Mich., 2000—; mem. steering com. Grosse Ile Libr. campaign, 1999—. Named Outstanding Woman in Arts, Hist., and Culture, Wayne County, 1999, Citizen of Yr. Grosse Ile Rotary, 1979, Woman of Yr. Grosse Ile Jaycettes, 1972, Women of Achievement Yr. Downriver Profile, 2000. Mem. Detroit Symphony Coffee Concert (founding mem.), Downriver Town Hall (founding mem.), Grosse Ile Founders Soc. (founding mem.), Grosse Ile Nature and Land Conservancy (founding mem.), Grosse Ile Questers, Book Club and Musicale. Republican. Presbyterian. Avocations: family, travel, photography, music, gardening. Home: 20769 Thorofare Rd Grosse Ile MI 48138-1248

MEYER, STEFAINE MICHELLE, environmental scientist; b. Fort Lauderdale, Fla., Oct. 20, 1974; d. Paul Franklin and Linda (Helms) M. BS, U. Fla., 1997, postgrad., 1997—. Technician Dept. Agr. State of Fla., Gainesville, 1997-98; sci. tchr. Dunnellon (Fla.) Mid. Sch., 1998-99; technician Dept. Transp. State of Fla., Gainesville, 1999; technician Dept. Environ. Protection State of Fla., Tallahasee, 1999; technician St. John's River Water Mgmt. Dist., Palatka, Fla., 1999—. Mem. Wildlife Soc. (treas. 1996-97). Avocations: reading, crocheting, hiking, camping, fishing. E-mail: S-Felis@yahoo.com.

MEYER, VERONIKA RUTH, chemist; b. Berne, Switzerland, Apr. 25, 1951; d. Theodor Paul and Maria Ruth (Schär) Gerber; m. Otto Meyer, Dec. 23, 1974. BSc, Engring. Sch. Burgdorf, Switzerland, 1974; lic. natural scis., U. Berne, 1989, D of Nat. Scis., 1989, privat-docent, 1996. Asst. Engring. Sch. Burgdorf, 1974-75; asst. U. Berne, 1976-89, sr. asst., 1990-98; postdoctoral fellow Weizmann Inst., Rehovot, Israel, 1989-90, U. Del., Newark, 1990; lectr. U. Basel, Switzerland, 1993, U. Innsbruck, 1999; sr. scientist EMPA, St. Gallen, 1998—. Author: Praxis der HPLC, 1979, 8th edit., 1999, Practical High-Performance Liquid Chromatography, 3d edit., 1999, Fallstricke und Fehlerquellen der HPLC, 1996, 2d edit., 1999; Pitfalls and Errors of HPLC, 1997; mem. editl. bd. Acad. Press, London, 1992-95; contbg. editor Analytical Chemistry, Am. Chem. Soc., 1997—; contbr. articles to profl. jours. Mem. Swiss Alpine Club (climbing leader). Avocations: mountain climbing, classical music. Home: PO Box 1453, Felsenstrasse 89, CH-9001 Saint Gallen Switzerland Office: EMPA St Gallen, Dept Chem, CH-9014 Saint Gallen Switzerland

MEYER-HENTSCHEL, GUNDOLF, management consultant, futurist; b. Andernach, Germany, May 16, 1953; s. Gerhard and Elisabeth (Heil) M-H.; m. Hanne Freidinger, July 16, 1983; children: Linda, Michael, Andrea. MBA, U. Saarland, 1976, PhD in Econs., 1983. Asst. prof. U. Saarland, Germany, 1977-84; CEO Meyer-Hentschel Mgmt. Consulting, Saarbruecken, Germany, 1985—. Author: Better Advertising, 1996; co-author: Influencing Consumer Behavior, 1982, Marketing to the 60+ Consumer, 1992; editor: Handbook 60 plus Marketing, 2000. Mem. Am. Mktg. Assn. (exec. mem. 1983—), World Future Soc. Roman Catholic. Avocation: swimming. E-mail: info@meyer-hentschel.com. Office: Meyer Hentschel Mgmt Cons, Kirchweg 44, D-66133 Saarbrücken Germany

MEYER-HERMANN, MICHAEL, physicist, researcher; b. Germany, July 29, 1967; s. Andreas and Madeleine (Martini) M-H.; m. Ulrike Ruttmann, Sept. 2, 1996. Student, U. Pierre et Marie Curie, Paris, 1989-90; MSc in Physics, Johann Wolfgang Goethe U., Frankfurt, Germany, 1994; PhD, Goethe U., Frankfurt, Germany, 1997. Asst. sci. worker Inst. Theoretical Physics Goethe U., Frankfurt, 1991-93, scientist, 1994-97; asst. prof. Tech. U., Dresden, Germany, 1998—; programmer, Germany, 1992-99. Contbr. articles to profl. jours. Mem. Amnesty Internat., Germany, 1999—. Fellow German Nat. Merit Found., 1990-94. Roman Catholic. Avocations: photography, philosophy, singing. Office: Tech U Dresden, Zellescher Weg 17, D-01062 Dresden Germany

MEYER-HILBERG, JOCHEN, systems engineer; b. Berlin, Fed. Republic Germany, Feb. 19, 1960; s. Rudolf and Roswitha (Schreier) Meyer; m. Steffi Hilberg, Dec. 7, 1990; children: Lukas, Leila, Annika, Jakob. Diploma, Tech. U., Darmstadt, Germany, 1984, PhD, 1989. Rsch. asst. Tech. U., Darmstadt, 1984-89; sys. engr. EADS Deutschland GmbH, Ulm, Germany, 1990—. Contbr. articles to profl. jours.; patentee efficient storing of huge amounts of text. Mem. German IEEE, Greenpeace Germany, German Bicycle Club. Avocations: travelling by bicycle, playing electric guitar, PC. Office: EADS Deutschland GmbH, Woertstrasse 85, 89077 Ulm Germany

MEYERINK, VICTORIA PAIGE, film producer, actress; b. Santa Barbara, Calif., Dec. 27, 1960; d. William Joseph Meyerink and Jeanne Baird; m. Lawrence David Foldes, Apr. 24, 1983. Student, U. So. Calif., 1978-80. Actress, 1962—; v.p. Star Cinema Prodn. Group, Inc., 1981-85; pres. Star Entertainment Group, Inc., L.A., 1985—; mem. faculty Internat. Film & TV Workshops, 1991—; lectr. colls. & film festivals. Prodr. (motion pictures) The Great Skycopter Rescue, 1982, Young Warriors, 1984, Night Force, 1987, Prima Donnas, 1996; actress (TV series) The Danny Kaye Show, Green Acres, My Three Sons, Family Affair, The FBI, Adam 12, (motion pictures) Speedway, Night of The Grizzly, Seconds, Brainstorm, The Littlest Hobo, (TV spl.) It Isn't Easy Being a Teenage Millionairess, numerous commls. Recipient Mayoral Proclamation for Outstanding Achievement, City of L.A., Cert. of Recognition for 25 Yrs. Outstanding Contbns. to the Entertainment Industry, City of L.A., Outstanding Achievement award Acad. Family Films & TV. Mem. Acad. Motion Picture Arts & Scis. (exec. com. Student Acad. Awards 1996—), L.A. Film Tchrs. Assn. Avocations: languages, travel, music, scuba diving, gourmet cooking.

MEYER-ORTMANNS, HILDEGARD, physics educator; b. Duisburg, Germany; d. Hubert and Gertrud Meyer; m. Karl-Peter Ortmanns; children: Lara Celine, Anne Sophie. PhD in physics, 1983. Postdoctoral rschr. Max-Planck-Inst., Munich, 1984-86; fellow CERN, Switzerland, 1986-87; postdoctoral rschr. U. Zurich, Switzerland, 1987-90, U. Heidelberg, Germany, 1990-94; prof. physics U. Wuppertal, Germany, 1996—.

MEYERS, DOROTHY, education consultant, writer; b. Chgo., Jan. 9, 1927; d. Gilbert and Harriet (Levitt) King; m. William J. Meyers, Oct. 9, 1947; children: Lynn, Jeanne. BA, U. Chgo., 1945, MA, 1961; postgrad., Columbia U., Northwestern U. New Sch. Social Rsch. Instr. sr. adults Chgo. Bd. and/City Colls., Chgo., 1961-78; coord. pub. affairs forum and health maintenance program City Colls. Chgo.-Jewish Community Ctrs., Chgo., 1975-78; lectr. adult program City Colls. Chgo., 1984; tchr. Dade County Adult Edn. Program, Miami, Fla., 1983-85; discussion leader Brandeis U. Adult Edn., 1985-86; cons., lectr. in field. Contbr. articles to profl. jours. Chmn. legis. PTA; discussion leader Great Decisions, 1984-86, chmn. civic assembly Citizens Sch. Com.; v.p. community rels. Womens Fedn. and Jewish United Fund; discussion leader LWV, Gt. Decisions, Fgn. Policy Assn.; program chmn. Jewish Community Ctrs., 1966-67, mem. sr. adult. com.; bd. dirs. coun. Jewish Elderly, Open U.; mem. art and edn. com. Chgo. Mayor's Com. for Sr. Citizens and Handicapped; mem. com. on media Met. Coun on Aging; active Bon Secour's Villa Maria Hosp.; founder Mt. Sinai Hosp., Miami Beach; sponsor Miami Heart Inst.; bd. mem. Royal Notable Alzheimer Care Unit-Douglas Home Miami; com. mem. March of Dimes; amb. Project Newborn U. Miami Prenatal Unit; bd. dirs. Alzheimer Day Care Ctr. Douglas Garden Home, 1995—, Villa Maria Found. Archdiocese, Miami, 1998—, Angels Villa Maria, 1998—. Recipient Prima Donna awrd Men's Opera Guild, Fla., 1995, 99, Miami Children's Hosp. honor, 1996. Mem. ASA, Gerontol. Assn., Nat. Coun. Aging, Nat. Coun. Jewish Women, Women's Auxiliary Jewish Community Ctr., Chgo. Met. Sr. Forum (media com.), Coun. Women Chgo. Real Estate Bd., Women in Comms., Chgo. Real Estate Bd., Nat. Assn. Real Estate Bds., Cultural Ctr., Miami, Mus. Art Ft. Lauderdale, Miami Internat. Press Club, Gastrointestinal Rsch. Found., Brandeis U., Art Inst., Chgo., Mus. Contemporary Art (life), Mus. Art Boca Raton, Brandeis Women's Auxiliary, Circumnavigator Club (Chgo. and Fla. chpts.). Office: 77 W Washington St Chicago IL 60602-2801

MEYERS, HANNES, JR., judge; b. Muskegon, Mich., Dec. 11, 1932; s. Hannes Sr. and Anna Meyers; m. Marjorie Meyers, Mar. 22, 1958; children: Hannes IV, Steven Arthur, Mark Cameron. AB, Calvin Coll., 1955; JD, U. Mich., 1958. V.p., shareholder Roper, Meyers, Bauer & Forman, P.C., Holland and Zeeland, Mich., 1959-92; judge Ottawa County Dist. Ct., Holland, 1992—. Chmn. Mich. State Officers Compensation Commn., Lansing, 1975, Mich. State Hwy. Commn., Lansing, 1975-78; chmn., commr. Mich. State Transp. Commn., Lansing, 1978-92. Named to Transp. Hall of Honor, Mich. Dept. Transp., 1994. Mem. Mich. State Bar Assn., Mich. Dist. Judges Assn., Ottawa County Bar Assn. (pres.), Zeeland Rotary Club (pres., sec., Paul Harris fellow 1993). Republican. Christian Reformed. Avocations: travel, flying, auto racing, golf. Office: Holland Dist Ct 57 W 8th St Holland MI 49423-3147

MEYERS, JAN E., lawyer; b. Hasselt, Belgium, Sept. 24, 1951; s. Jan Meyers and Alice Huyghen; m. Dominique Van Canneyt, May 16, 1987; children: Sebastian, Nicholas, Julia. Lic. in law, Cath. U., Louvain, 1974; LLM, Harvard U., 1975; JSD, Stanford U., 1982. Bar: Brussels. Assoc. Cleary, Gottlieb, Steen & Hamilton, Brussels, 1976-77, 79-85, ptnr., 1985—; mem. Banking and Fin. Commn., Belgium, 1998—. 2d lt. Belgian Army Res., 1978. Office: Cleary Gottlieb Steen et al, Rue de la Loi 23, 1040 Brussels Belgium

MEYERS, JOHN THOMAS, JR., academic administrator; b. L.A., Oct. 17, 1963; s. John Thomas and Maria Ceil (Borger) M.; m. Kristen Andersen Wisnewski. BA, Am. U. of Paris, France, 1986; cert. language, UCLA, 1986; MA, Columbia U., 1995; MLS, Rutgers U., 1997. Bibliographic asst. Columbia U. Librs., N.Y.C., 1988-89, preservation supr., 1989-90; periodicals asst. Pace U. Libr., N.Y.C., 1989-90; human resources asst. Howard Hughes Med. Inst., N.Y.C., 1990-91; dir. external rels. Coun. on Internat. Ednl. Exch., 1992-97; dir. devel. Bank St. Coll. of Edn., 1998-99; dir. rsch. and donor rels. Dartmouth Coll., Hanover, N.H., 1999—; mem. U.S. delegation to Asia, Pacific Econ. Coop. Human Resource Devel. Working Group, 1997. Pres. Student Govt. Assn. Am. U. Paris, 1984-86, trustee, 2000—; trustee Reach the World, inc., 1998—; mem. adv. bd. Nat. Com. on Disability and Exch., 1996-98. Scholar Am. U. Paris, 1983-86; fellow, Am. Coun. of Learned Studies, 1986, fgn. lang. and area studies fellow Columbia U., 1992. Mem. Am. Ednl. Rsch. Assn., Univ. Continuing Edn. Assn. (internat. rels. com. 1996-97), Global Alliance for Transnat. Edn. (corp. adv. bd.). Democrat. Roman Catholic. Avocations: long distance running, stamp collecting, wine tasting, book collecting. Office: Dartmouth Coll 63 S Main St Hanover NH 03755

MEYERS, MARC ANDRE, research center administrator; b. Belo Horizonte, Brazil, Aug. 10, 1946; came to U.S., 1970; s. Henri and Marianne Meyers; m. Suzanne Claire Meyers, Sept. 1972 (div. 1979); children: Marc Henri, Maria Cristina. BS, Fed. U. Minas Gerais, Brazil, 1969, MS, 1972, PhD, 1974. Tchng. asst. dept. metallurgy Fed. U. Minas Gerais, Brazil, 1969; grad. rsch. asst. Denver Rsch. Inst., 1969-70; Brazilian Govt. fellow U. Denver, 1972-74; prin. investigator Ctr. for Materials Rsch. Mil. Inst. Engring., Rio de Janeiro, 1974-76; asst. prof. dept. metallurgy engring. S.D. Sch. Mines and Tech., 1977-79; assoc. prof. dept metallurgy engring. N.Mex. Inst. Mining and Tech., Socorro, 1979-88; assoc. dir. Ctr. for Explosives Tech. Rsch., Sorroco, N. Mex., 1983-88; advisor to dir. material sci. divsn. U.S. Army Rsch. Office, Durham, N.C., 1985-86; prof. materials sci. UCSD, 1989—; assoc. dir., dir. Inst. Mechanics and Materials, 1993—; vis. scientist Nat. Chem. Lab. for Industry, Tsukuba, Japan, 1985. Author: Dynamic Behavior of Materials, 1994; (with K.K. Chawla) Principios de Metalurgia Mecanica, 1982, Mechanical Metallurgy: Principles and Applications, 1984, Mechanical Behavior of Materials, 1999; editor: (with L.E. Murr) Shock Waves and High Strain-Rate Phenomena in Metals: Concepts and Applications, 1981; (with O.T. Inal) Frontiers in Materials Technologies, 1985; (with L.E. Murr and K.P. Straudhammer) Metallurgical Applications of Shock-Wave and High-Strain-Rate Phenomena, 1986; contbr. over 220 articles to profl. jours. Served with engring. corps, Brazilian Army, 1964-66. Recipient 1st prize Alliance Francaise, Belo Horizonte, Brazil, 1963, BE award N.Mex. Inst. Tech., 1986, Humboldt Sr. Scientist award, 1997. Fellow Am. Soc. Metals Internat.; mem. AIME (bd. reviewers Metall. Transactions 1981—), Brazilian Soc. Metals, Sigma Xi, Alpha Sigma Mu. Roman Catholic. Avocations: triathlon, kayaking. Office: UCSD Dept MAE Mail Code 0411 La Jolla CA 92093

MEYERS, PETER, retired history educator; b. Klinkum, Germany, June 13, 1933; s. Heinrich and Katharina (Theissen) M.; m. Alice Schmelzer, Mar. 18, 1959; 1 foster child, Tuan Ngoc Huynh. Grad., U. Bonn, Germany, 1959; EdD, Coll. Edn., Germany, 1982. Tchr. secondary sch., Cologne, Germany, 1959-68; lectr. Coll. Edn., 1968-80; prof. history didactics and media edn. U. Bonn, 1980-2000. Author: From the Industrial Revolution until to the First World War, 1979, Frederic II of Prussia in the View of History in the Soviet Zone and GDR, 1983, Film in History Teaching, 1998;

editor: The National Sozialism in School and Adult Education, 1979, Stages of a University Life, 1999; contbr. numerous articles to profl. jours., including Geschichte in Wissenschaft und Unterricht, Geschichtsdidaktik, Storia contemporanea, Politische Meinung, Geschichte, Politik und ihre Didaktik. Mem.Internat. Soc. History Didactics, Assn. Historians Germany, Assn. History Didactics Germany. Roman Catholic. Fax: 02226/2938. E-mail: 022262632@t-online.de. Home: Burgacker 13, 53359 Rheinbach Germany Office: Rhein Friedrich-Wilhelms U, An der Schlosskirche-1, 53113 Bonn Germany

MEYERS, ROBERT ALLEN, chemist, publisher; b. L.A., May 15, 1936; s. Jack B. Meyers and Pearl (Cassell) Thorpe; m. Roberta Lee Hart, June 24, 1961 (div. 1976); children: Tamara, Robert Jr.; m. Ilene Braun, Feb. 27, 1977; children: Jenifer, Jacalyn. BA, San Diego State U., 1959; PhD, UCLA, 1963. Postdoctoral fellow, mem. faculty Calif. Inst. Tech., Pasadena, 1963-64; rsch. scientist Bell & Howell Rsch. Ctr., Sierra Madre, Calif., 1965; project mgr. TRW Def. & Space, Redondo Beach, Calif., 1966-81; bus. area mgr. TRW Energy Group, Redondo Beach, 1981-86; mgr. process devel. TRW Def. & Space, Redondo Beach, 1986-88, mgr. new projects devel., 1988-95; pres. Ramtech Ltd., Tarzana, Calif., 1995—; del. U.S.-USSR Working Group, Washington and Moscow, 1973-80; chmn. adv. bd. Guide to Nuclear Power Tech., N.Y.C., 1982-84; mem. adv. coun. chemistry dept. UCLA, 1991—. Author: Coal Desulfurization, 1977; editor: Coal Handbook, 1981, Coal Structure, 1982; editor: Handbook of Petroleum Refining Processes, 1986, 2d edit., 1996, Handbook of Synfuels Technology, 1984, Handbook of Energy Technology and Economics, 1983, Handbook of Chemicals Production Processes, 1986, others; editor-in-chief Ency. of Phys. Sci. and Tech., 1987, 92, Ency. of Modern Physics, 1990, Ency. of Lasers and Optics, 1991, Encyclopedia of Telecommunications, 1989, Molecular Biology and Biotech., 1995, Encyclopedia of Molecular Biology and Molecular Medicine, 1995, Encyclopedia of Environmental Analysis and Remediation, 1998, Encyclopedia of Analytical Chemistry, 2000. Mem. Am. Chem. Soc., Am. Inst. Chem. Engrs. Avocations: swimming, bicycling, running. Office: Ramtech Ltd 3715 Gleneagles Dr Tarzana CA 91356-5622

MEYERS, TEDSON JAY, lawyer; b. Bayonne, N.J., May 6, 1928; s. Irving and Norma Miriam (Anson) M.; m. Patricia Elizabeth Sullivan, Apr. 10, 1965 (div. Apr. 1978); children: Mary, John, Katherine; m. Lynn Scholz, Aug. 6, 1978 (div. Oct. 1992). Student, Ohio State U., 1945-47; BA, NYU, 1949, MA, 1950; JD, Harvard U., 1953. Bar: D.C. 1953, N.Y. 1957, U.S. Supreme Ct. 1971. Asst. counsel Office Gen. Counsel, Dept. Navy, Washington, 1955-56; assoc. Liebman, Eulau & Robinson, N.Y.C., 1956-58; staff counsel for govt. regulations ABC, N.Y.C., 1958-61; adminstrv. asst. to chmn. FCC, Washington, 1961-62; asst. to dir., dir. overseas edn1. TV projects Peace Corps, Washington, 1962-68; pvt. practice Washington, 1968-70; ptnr. Sullivan Beauregard Meyers & Clarkson, Washington, 1970-74, Peabody Lambert & Meyers, Washington, 1974-84, Reid & Priest, Washington, 1984-96, Coudert Brothers, Washington, 1996—; adj. prof. comm. San Diego State U., 1993—; founding pres. Harvard Legis. Rsch. Bur., 1952-53; mem. White House Task Force on Ednl. TV Overseas, 1966-68, adv. panel on internat. telecomm. law U.S. State Dept., 1987—; bd. govs. Internat. Coun. for Computer Comm., 1986—, pres., 2000—; bd. dirs. AfriSpace, Inc., Cyber Century Forum. Contbr. conf. papers and articles to profl. publs. Mem. City Coun. Washington, 1972-75; bd. govs. Met. Washington Coun. Govts., 1973-75; chmn. Bicycle Fedn. of Am., 1977—; bd. dirs. U.S. Coun. for World Comm. Yr. 83, 1982-84; dir. The Arthur C. Clarke Found. of the U.S. Inc., 1987—. Lt. USMC, 1953-55, Korea. Rsch. fellow Carnegie Found., 1949. Mem. ABA (co-founder and chmn. internat. telecomm. com., sect. sci. and tech. 1982-85, coun. mem. sect. sci. and tech. 1983-87), Fed. Comm. Bar Assn., Internat. Inst. Comm., Royal TV Soc., Pacific Telecom. Coun., Soc. Satellite Profls., Cosmos Club (pres. 1988-90), Cosmos Club Found. (trustee, chmn. 1985-88, 90—), Army and Navy Club, Potomac Boat Club, Alpha Epsilon Pi. Avocations: computers, sculling, bicycling, motorcycling, military music. E-mail: tmeyers@tedson.com. Office: Coudert Brothers 1627 I St NW Ste 1200 Washington DC 20006-4093

MEYERSON, CHRISTOPHER CORTLANDT, law scholar; b. Princeton, N.J., July 7, 1962; s. Dean and Beatrice Meyerson; m. Megumi Kawaguchi; 1 child, Kenneth. BA in Govt. magna cum laude, Harvard U., 1985, cert. in L.Am. studies, 1985, MA in History, 1985; MPhil in Polit. Sci., Columbia U., 1993; LLM, Kyoto (Japan) U., 1994. Intern Bur. Inter-Am. Affairs, Office Policy Planning/Coord. U.S. State Dept., Washington, summer 1982; rsch. asst. Harvard U., 1982-83; intern, rschr. macro econ. rsch. dept. Banco Itau, São Paulo, 1983-84; human rights intern Coalition for Homeless, N.Y.C., summer 1988; legal intern gen. counsel Mus. Modern Art, N.Y.C., summer 1989; law clk. Office of Chief Counsel for Internat. Commerce U.S. Commerce Dept., Washington, summer 1991; editl. asst. Kyoto Comparative Law Ctr., summer 1994, 95; vis. scholar Associated Kyoto Program, 1996; summer assoc. Venable, Baetjer, Howard & Civiletti, Washington, 1998; law clk. Office of Chief Counsel for Import Adminstrn., U.S. Commerce Dept., Washington, 1999-2000. Contbr. articles to bus. jours., Columbia Internat. Affairs Online. Mem. Am. Soc. Internat. Law, Soc. Legislation Comparee, Am. Polit. Sci. Assn. (presenter papers ann. meetings), Internat. Studies Assn. (Internat. Polit. Economy Jr. Scholar award 2000, presenter papers ann. meetings), Assn. for Asian Studies (presenter papers ann. meetings), Assn. Japanese Bus. Studies (Young Scholar 1996), Internat. House of Japan. Episcopalian. Home: 7306 Summit Ave Chevy Chase MD 20815-4030

MEYLER, MARK ZINOVYEVICH, dentist; b. Odessa, Ukraine, June 6, 1948; came to U.S., 1989; s. Zinoviy and Liya (Keselman) M.; m. Anna Zilberman, Feb. 19, 1955; 1 child, Zinovy. D Stomatology, Odessa Med. Inst., 1971; Stomatologist, Surgeon 1st Degree, Ukraian Inst. Doctors, Kharkov, 1984; DDS, NYU, N.Y.C., 1991. Stomatologist, surgeon Stomatology Clinic #7, Odessa, 1971-88; dentist Beach Haven Dental Office, Bklyn., 1992-94, M/M Dental, Bklyn., 1994—. Inventor New Americans collected sci. reports, 1991. Mem. ADA. Office: M/M Dental 50 Shore Blvd Brooklyn NY 11235-4057

MEYLER, WILLIAM ANTHONY, financial executive; b. Newark, Oct. 29, 1944; s. Raymond Francis and Margaret (Loveless) M.; BS, St. Joseph's Coll., 1966; MBA, Fairleigh Dickinson U., 1974; m. Dana Irene Brennan, May 3, 1975; children: Daniel, Diana. CPA, N.J. Sr. acct. Ernst & Young, Trenton, N.J., 1970; dir. acctg. Baker Industries, Inc., Parsippany, N.J., 1971-72; mgr. corp. acctg. Witco Chem. Corp., N.Y.C., 1973-75, asst. to controller, 1976-79, asst. controller world-wide ops., 1977-82, asst. controller mgmt. info. systems, 1982-84; ptnr. Letters, Meyler & Co., CPAs, 1984-91; cons., exec. v.p. Investment Techs., Inc., Edison, N.J., 1985-91, also bd. dirs.; pvt. practice, Middletown, N.J., 1991—; exec. v.p., CFO Gateways to Space, Inc., 1994-96, also bd. dirs.; adj. prof. Monmouth Coll., 1983-85. Fellow N.J. Soc. CPA's; mem. AICPA, Am. Acctg. Assn., Middletown C. of C., Rotary. Home: 30 Southview Ter S Middletown NJ 07748-2415 Office: One Arin Park 1715 Highway 35 Middletown NJ 07748-1867

MEYNET, ROLAND, religious studies educator; b. Thonon-les Bains, France, July 7, 1939; s. Joseph and Henriette (Bochaton) M. M in Arabic, U. Aix-en-Provence, France, 1969, DS, 1986. Joined Jesuits, 1959, ordained priest Roman Cath. Ch., 1972. Prof. U. St. Joseph, Beyrut, Lebanon, 1972-86; rschr. Pontifical Biblical Inst., Jerusalem, 1987-91, Faculty of Theology of Jesuits, Paris, 1991; rschr. Pontifical Gregorian U., Rome, 1992—, dir. dept. Bibl. theology, 1997-2000. Author: L'Évangile selon saint Luc., 1988, L'Analyse rhétorique, 1989, Rhetorical Analysis, 1998; (with others) Analyse rhétorique et herméneutique, 1993, Le livre du prophète Amos, 1994, Rhétorique Sémitique, 1998, Jésus passe, 1999. Mem. Internat. Soc. History Rhetoric, Assn. Cath. Francaise de la Bible, Studiorum Novi Testamenti Soc. Home and Office: Pontificia U Gregoriana, Piazza della Pilotta 4, 00187 Rome Italy

MEYYANATHAN, SUBRAMANIA NAINAR, pharmaceutical analyst, educator; b. Tiruppattur, Tamilnadu, India, May 27, 1967; s. Subramania Nainar and Jeyalakshmi Meyyanathan; m. Dhaksnamurthy Rajeswari, Sept. 11, 1995; children: M. Jayalakshmi preetha, M.Vijaya harini. B in Pharmacy, C.L. Baid Metha Coll. Pharmacy, Chennai, Tamilnadu, 1989; PharmM, J.S.S. Coll. Pharmacy, Ooty, Tamilnadu, 1993. Cert. pharmacist. Drug mfg. trainee, chemist Cheena, 1989-90; asst. prof. J.S.S. Coll. Pharmacy, Ooty, 1990-2000. Mem. N.Y. Acad. Scis., Indian Pharm. Assn. (life), Assn. Pharm. Tchrs. India (life), Assn. Pharm. Analysts India. Avocations: internet viewing, enjoying scenarios. Fax: 91-423-442937. Home e-mail: myys@usa.net; office e-mail: jssphamooty@md3.vsnl.net.in. Home: 137f 69a Emerald Apts Devisdale, Ooty Tamilnadu 643001, India Office: JSS Coll Pharmacy, Rocklands, Ooty Tamilnadu 643001, India

MEZHIKOVSKII, SEMYON MARKOVICH, chemist, educator; b. Odessa, Ukraine, Nov. 18, 1936; s. Mark Iosifovich Mezhikovskii and Feiga Shlyomovna Vitis; m. Olga Alekseevna Kozdoba, Nov. 10, 1964 (dvi. Mar. 1988); 1 child, Andrey Kozdoba-Mezhikovskii; m. Marina Ivanovna Tokar, Nov. 4, 1989; 1 child, Dmitry Tokar-Mezhikovskii. Chemist, U. Odessa, 1958; Candidate of Sci., Inst. Chem. Physics, Moscow, 1967, DSc, 1984, prof., 1996. Lic. chemist. Engr. Rezinotekhnika plant, Yaroslavl, Russia, 1958-60; chemist Sanitary and Epidemiol. Inspection, Odessa, 1961-64; prof. Inst. Chem. Physics, Moscow, 1964—; tchr. Chem. Coll., Yaroslavl, 1959-60, Poly. Inst., Moscow, 1968-71; expert C. of C., Odessa, 1962-63; cons. Engring. Ctr., Kazan, Russia, 1992-94; lectr. various confs. on chemistry of oligomers. Author monographs on phys. chemistry of oligomers; holder numerous patents in field; contbr. numerous sci. papers to profl. jours. Named Hon. Inventor of USSR, 1985; recipient Bronze medal Exhbn. of Nat. Economy Achievements, 1974, Silver medal, 1980, award for popularization of sci. Academician N.N. Semyonov, 1979. Mem. G.V. Vinogradov Rheol. Soc., N.Y. Acad. Scis., Moscow Soc. Dog Fanciers. Avocations: collecting books by and about A.S. Pushkin, collecting small bells. Office: N N Semyonov Inst Chem Phys, Russian Acad S Kosygin St 4, 117334 Moscow Russia

MEZHZHERIN, VITALIY, zoologist, researcher; b. Dnepropetrovsk, USSR, Feb. 1, 1933; s. Aleksey and Ekaterina (Ryabova) M.; m. Lidiya Zimbalevskaya (dec. 1996). Student, Kiev State U., USSR, 1950-55. Cert. in biology. Asst. Sumy Pedagog. Inst., 1955-56; sr. scientist Zool. Mus. Kiev State U., 1956-62, asst., 1962-65, assoc. prof., 1965—. Contbr. numerous articles to sci. publs. including Russian Jour. Ecology, Acta Theriol. Mem. Ukrainian Soc. Theriologists. Avocations: gardening, mushrooms. Office: Schevchenko U, Vladimirskaya str 60, 01017 Kiev Ukraine

MEZIANE, MOULAY AHMED, physician; b. Taza, Morocco, Aug. 28, 1952; came to U.S., 1979; s. Abdelmadjid and Khedoudja (Senouci) M.; m. Anissa Venessa Schweiger, Dec. 13, 1990; children: Brahim, Tarik, Malik, Amina, Nabil. BS, Lycee El-Mokrani, Algiers, Algeria, 1972; MD, U. Algiers, 1979. Intern Algiers U. Hosp., 1978-79; resident in diagnostic radiology Johns Hopkins HOsp., Balt., 1980-84; mem. staff Johns Hopkins Hosp., Balt., 1984-87; mem. staff, co-head thoracic imaging Cleve. Clin. Found., 1987-90, mem. staff, head thoracic imaging, 1990—. Author: High Resolution CT of the Lung, 1986 (gold medal); contbr. articles to profl. jours. Avocations: competitive running, painting, photography. Office: Cleve Clin Found 5500 Euclid Ave Cleveland OH 44195-0001

MEZNIK, IVAN, mathematician, educator; b. Brno, Czech Republic, July 17, 1942; s. Frantisek and Kvetuse M.; m. Zora Meznikova; children: Ondrej, Borek. BSc, Palacky U., Olomouc, Czech Republic, 1964; MSc, Masaryk U., Brno, Czech Republic, 1970; PhD, Czechoslovak Acad. Scis., Prague, 1975. Lectr. Tech. U. Brno, 1964-75, assoc. prof., 1975-93, prof. math., 1993—, head dept. math., 1973-91, vice dean, 1984-89, 96—; prof. Charles U., Prague, 1993-96; vis. assoc. prof. U. Sulaimaniyah, Iraq, 1977-80; lectr. in field. Author: Mathematics for Mechanical Engineering, 1992, also 23 textbooks; contbr. some 45 articles to profl. jours. Recipient medal of honour Czech Tech. U., Prague, 1987, Sulaimaniyah U., 1980; rsch. scholar, Belgium, 1971, Finland, 1987, Israel, 1993. Mem. Gesellschaft fur Angewandte Mathematik und Mechanik, European Assn. for Theoretical Computer Sci., European Soc. for Engring. Edn., Czech Math. Sci. Soc., Am. Math. Soc. Avocations: philately, sports, tourism, music. Office: Tech U Brno Bus Mgmt Fac, Technicka 2, 61669 Brno Czech Republic

MEZOGHI, MILAD OMAR, engineer, researcher; b. Tripoli, Libya, Sept. 18, 1958; s. Omar Mohamed and Amna Mohamed Mezoghi; m. Zineb Ahmed Garbaj, Nov. 6, 1986; children: Iman, Manal, Mohamed, Nadeen. BSc in Aero. Engring., Tripoli U., 1982; BSc in Acctg., Open U., Tripoli, 1996. Cert. engring. and maintenance aircraft engr. Acct. Wahda Bank, Tripoli, 1980-82; flight engr. Libyan Arab Airlines, Tripoli, 1982-88, maintenance engr., 1988-93, rsch., 1993—; cons. Ministry of House and Urban Devel., Tripoli, 1984-90, Ministry of Planning, Tripoli, 1990-92. Author: Aerodynamics of Helicopter, 1981, The Accounting in Joint Stock Companies, 1995. Active HANA Benefit Soc., Tripoli, 1990—, WAFA Benefit Soc., Tripoli, 1995—, Libyan Air Transport Guild-Bldg. Soc., 1999. Recipient air frame cert. Libyan Civil Aviation, Tripoli, 1989, jet engine cert., 1990, Engine Type Licece: JT8D, 1999. Mem. Soc. Automotive Engrs., Arab Physicians Orgn., Aviators Guild. Muslim. Avocations: poetry, traveling, literature. Office: Libyan Arab Airlines, Haiti St PO Box 13145, Tripoli Libya

MEZVINSKY, EDWARD M., lawyer; b. Ames, Iowa, Jan. 17, 1937; m. Marjorie Margolies; 11 children. BA, U. Iowa, 1960; MA in Polit. Sci., U. Calif., Berkeley, 1963, JD, 1965. State rep. Iowa State Legislature, 1969-70; U.S. congressman 1st Dist., Iowa, 1973-77; U.S. rep. UN Commn. on Human Rights, 1977-79; chmn. Pa. Dem. State Com., 1981-86. Author: A Term to Remember; contbr. articles to law jours. Mem. Pa. Bar Assn., Bar of the Supreme Ct. of U.S., Omicron Delta Kappa. Office: 815 N Woodbine Ave Narberth PA 19072-1430

MEZZINA, MAURU, research scientist; b. Rome, Italy, Aug. 19, 1949; arrived in France, 1977; s. Antonio and Carmela (Cracas) M.; m. MArtine Thibaut, Aug. 5, 1980; children: Diana, Nigry. PhD, U. Rome, 1974, U. Paris, 1986. Assoc. rschr. U. Rome, 1972-82, CNRS, Paris, 1982—; asst. rschr. Stanford (Calif.) U., 1988-91; rschr. SNRS, Willejuif, France, 1991-98, Evry, France, 1999—. Contbr. articles to profl. jours. Avocations: movies, music, cooking. Home: 42 Ave Pasteur, 91550 Paray-Vielle Poste France Office: Genethin, 1 rue de L'internationale, 91002 Evry France

MHETAR, VIJAY, chemical engineer; b. Ichalkranji, India, Mar. 31, 1971; s. Ramchandra and Rajani Hogade M.; m. Savita Musale. B Engring., U. Poona, 1992; M Tech, Indian Inst. Tech., Bombay, 1994; PhD, Tex. A&M U., 1997. Rsch. assoc. Indian Inst. of Tech., Bombay, 1992-94; lectr. Tex. A&M U., College Station, 1994-96, rsch. assoc., 1994-97; analytical technology leader Gen. Electric Plastics, Selkirk, N.Y., 1997-98; product devel. Gen. Electric Plastics Europe, The Netherlands, 1998-99; technology assessment specialist GE Co., Pittsfield, 1999—; rsch. scientist in field. Recipient award FIE Found., 1998. Mem. Soc. Rheology, Am. Inst. Chem. Engring., Am. Phys. Soc., Soc. Plastics Engrs. (pres. Tex. A&M chpt. 1996-97, Future Technology award 1996). Office: GE Co 1 Plastics Ave Pittsfield MA 01201-3662

MHIMID, ABDALLAH, engineering educator; b. Souassi, Mahdia, Tunisia, Aug. 17, 1957; s. Ali and Mabruuka (Mabrouk) M.; m. Louiza Arami, Aug. 8, 1988; children: Kiajdi, Imen. BS, H. Shoaf, Mahdia, 1977; MA in Sci., F. Monastir (Tunisia), 1982; D.E.A., F. Tunis (Tunisia), 1984, postgrad. doctorate, 1991. Temporary A lectr. Monastir, 1982-86, A. lectr., 1989-91, jr. lectr., 1991-98; h.s. tchr. Sousse, Tunisia, 1986-89; lectr. Sur, Oman, 1998—. Author: Theoretical Study of Heat and Mass Transfer During Drying, 1996; contbr. articles to profl. jours. Moslem. Avocation: football. Home: Ecole Nat d'Ingenieurs, Route de Kairouan, 5019 Monastir Tunisia Office: Ecole Nat d'Ing, Route de Kairoan, 5019 Monastir Tunisia

MIA, LOKMAN, educator; b. Rajargaon, Chandpur, Bangladesh; arrived in Australia, 1980; s. Haider Ali and Lutfa Nisa; m. Nargis Mia; 1 child, Tusar. B in Commerce with honors, Dhaka (Bangladesh) U., 1968, M in Commerce, 1969; MBA, Ind. U., 1972; PhD in Acctg. Commerce, U. Queensland, Brisbane, Australia, 1985. Lectr. U. Tasmania, Hobart, Australia, 1985; sr. lectr. U. Tasmania, Hobart, 1987-90, U. Otago, New Zealand, 1985-87, La Trobe U., Melbourne, Australia, 1990-93; assoc. prof. Griffith U., Brisbane, Australia, 1993-94; prof. Griffith U., Brisbane, 1994—, head of sch., 1993-96. Contbr. articles to profl. jours. Merit scholar Govt. Pakistan, East Pakistan, 1965-70; scholar Ford Found., Dhaka, 1970. Mem. AAA, ASCPA, AAANZ. Avocations: running, music, fishing, theatre. Office: Sch Acctg and Fin, Griffith Univ Gold Coast, Gold Coast Qld, Australia

MIAH, MUHAMMAD ABDUL AZIZ, physicist; b. Pabna, Bangladesh, Jan. 5, 1949; s. Muhammad Arman Ali and Golapjan Ali; m. Shamsunnahar, June 3, 1976; children: Nisho, Sonia. BS, Rajshahi U., Bangladesh, 1969, MS, 1972, PhD, 1992. Lectr. Rajshahi U., Bangladesh, 1974-78, asst. prof., 1978-89, assoc. prof., 1989-94, prof., 1994—, chmn. dept. applied physics and electronics, 1998—; provost Rajshahi U., 1994-95, adminstr. computer ctr., 1997. Co-author: Applied Optics, 1992; contbr. articles to profl. jours. Organizer Children's Culture Forum, Bangladesh, 1992—. Mem. Bangladesh Elec. Soc. (joint sec. 1994-98), Bangladesh Phys. Soc., Bangladesh Assn. Advancement Sci. Avocations: gardening, fishing. Office: Dept Applied Physics & Elecs, Rajshahi U, Rajshahi 6205, Bangladesh

MIAN, AJMAL, chief justice. Chief justice Pakistan Supreme Ct, Islamabad. Office: Supreme Ct, Constitution Ave, Islamabad Pakistan*

MIAN, FAROOQ UMAR, precision engineer, consultant; b. Faisalabad, Punjab, Pakistan, July 24, 1941; s. Mian Muhammad and Qadeer Nurullah (Amtul) Nurullah; m. Seemeen Mir Ishaq, Nov. 6, 1965; children: Syma, Shehma, Salaar, Sonia. BS, Karachi (Pakistan) U., 1974, BS with honors, 1976; MSc of War Studies, Islamabad (Pakistan) U., 1978; Doctor, Royal Coll. Def. Studies, London, 1983. Chartered Inst. Transp., London; cert. pilot. Chmn. AL-SHIFA, Pakistan, 1993—; mng. dir. Pakistan Internat. Airlines Corp., Karachi; pres. Hockey Fedn., Pakistan, 1993—; v.p. Pakistan Olympics Assn., Lahore, Pakistan, 1995—; dir. gen. Pakistan Aero. Complex, Kamra, Pakistan, 1986-89; mng. dir. Shaheen Air Internat., Rawalpindi, Pakistan, 1990-93. Contbr. articles to profl. jours. Patron-in-chief Al-Shaoor Welfare Assn., Faisalabad, 1987—, Awakening, Lahore, 1995—; mem. Environ. Protection Coun., Islamabad, 1995—. Air vice marshal Pakistan Air Force, 1958-93. Recipient Sword of Honor, Pakistan Air Force, Risalpur, 1960, Top Gun award Fighter Leader Sch., Karachi, 1971, Sitara-e-Jurat award Govt. Pakistan, 1971, Hilal-e-Imtiaz Mil. award Govt. Pakistan, 1988. Fellow Royal Aero. Soc. London; mem. Pacific Asian Tourism Assn. (chmn. 1994-96, Best Chpt. award 1995), Pakistan Hockey Fedn. (pres. 1993-96, Shield of Honour 1996, Roll of Honour 1996), Chartered Inst. Transp. (pres. 1994-96, chmn. 1994—, Shield of Honour 1996). Muslim. Avocations: environmental protection, developmental awakening, lecturing on youth development, sports development, flying. Home: House 710 Z Sector, St 7 Phase III LCCHS, Lahore Pakistan also: House No 1 Air Force Housing Societ, Tufail Rd, Lahore Cantt Lahore Pakistan Office: H-297 St40 Sector F-10/4, Islamabad Pakistan also: House 75/12, Sarfraz Rafiqui Rd, Lahore Cantt Pakistan

MIAN, WASEEM SHAFIQ, accountant; b. Karachi, Sind, Pakistan, Jan. 8, 1963; s. Shafiq Saad Mian and Tahera Hayat Begum; m. Arefa Waseem Baig, Feb. 28, 1997; 1 child, Zafir Waseem. B Commerce, Karachi (Pakistan) U., 1985. Trainee Kammer Furgam Ali & Co. Chartered Accts., Karachi, 1986-90; project acct. Dynamic Tech. Svcs. (Pvt.) Ltd., Karachi, 1990-93; audit sr. Anjim Asin Shahid & Co. Chartered Accts., Karachi, 1993-94; sr. acct. Toyola Ctrl. Motor, Karachi, 1994-95; asst. mgr. credit Network Leasing Corp. Ltd., Karachi, 1995-99; sr. accts. and adminstrn. officer Small Medium Enterprises Devel. Authority, Karachi, 1999—; cons. North Star Gen. Ins., Karachi, 1998-99, Genesis Mgmt. Cons., Karachi, 1997, Fiair Cons., Karachi, 1998-99. Mem. Assn. Acct. Tech. Pakistan, Inst. Corp. Secs. Pakistan, Inst. Taxation Mgmt. Pakistan (cert. acctg. tech.). Home: S-2/816 Saud Abad, 75080 Karachi Sind, Pakistan

MIANO, ELIPHELET, consulting civil engineer; b. Meru, Kenya, Nov. 18, 1932; s. Henry Kahare and Joanna Wanjuugu; m. Zipporah Murugi M'Thura, Feb. 28, 1959; children: Jane, Peter, Joyce, David, Catherine. Student, Makerere U., Kampala, Uganda, 1950-52; BS in Civil Engring., U. Alberta, 1965. Registered profl. engr., Kenya, Uganda. Articled engring. apprentice Mowlem Constrn. Co., Uganda, 1953-56; engring. asst. Mowlem Constrn. Co., Uganda, Kenya, 1956-61; civil engr. Mowlem Constrn. Co., Kenya, 1965-67; chief civil engr. East African Engring Cons., Nairobi, Kenya, 1967-69; bd. dirs. East African Engring. Cons., Nairobi, 1969—, chmn. bd., 1978—. Decorated Elder of the Order of Burning Spear, Republic of Kenya, 1985. Fellow Instn. Engrs. Kenya; mem. Assn. Consulting Engrs. Kenya, Nairobi Club, United Kenya Club. Avocations: photography, reading. Home: PO Box 21045, Nairobi Kenya Office: E African Engring Cons, PO Box 30707, Nairobi Kenya

MIANO, JAMES GIKONYO, information systems specialist; b. Nairobi, Kenya, Mar. 2, 1969; s. Christopher Miano Mathaiya and Agnes Nyawira (Kangaru) Miano. BSc, Kenyatta U., Nairobi, 1991; MSc in Info. Sys., Nairobi U., 2000. Cert. computer sys. analyst. Programmer, instr. NCR, Nairobi, 1991-92; mgmt. trainee Barclays Bank, Nairobi, 1993-94, team supr., 1995-96; asst. info. tech. mgr. Transnational Bank, Nairobi, 1996—. Roman Catholic. Avocations: soccer, athletics, chess, traveling, music. Home: PO Box 32564, Nairobi Kenya

MIAOULIS, IOANNIS NIKOLAOS, mechanical engineer, educator; b. Athens, Greece, July 24, 1961; came to U.S., 1980; s. Nikolaos Ioannis and Titika Photini (Kokkinopoulou) M.; m. Beth Karen, Sept. 23, 1984; children: Marina, Katrina. BSME, Tufts U., 1983, MA in Econs., 1986, PhD, 1987; SMME, MIT, 1984. Asst. prof. mech. engring. Tufts U., Medford, Mass., 1987-93, assoc. prof., 1993-97, prof., 1997—, assoc. dean engring., 1993-94, dean Sch. Engring., 1994—; cons. in field. Contbr. over 95 articles to sci. jours. Elected mem. Mass. Tech./Engring. Edn. Adv. Bd., 1999—, chair 2000—; elected mem. Mass. Math. & Sci. Edn. Bd., 1995-99, Tufts Alumni Coun., Medford, 1994—; elected coun. mem. Pompostiticut Sch., Stow, Mass., 1993-98. Recipient Presdl. Young Investigator award NSF, 1991, Inventor's Assn. award, New. Eng., 1990, William P. Desmond award Citizen's Edn. Resource Ctr., Mass., 1996, Cmty. & Leadership award Toastmasters Internat., Mass., 1995, Jaycees Outstanding Young Leader award, 1999. Mem. ASME, AAAS, Am. Soc. Engring. Edn., Materials Rsch. Soc. Achievements include 2 U.S. patents; research in area of heat transfer in materials processing, microscale heat transfer, comparative biomechanics. Office: Tufts U Coll Engring Anderson Hall Medford MA 02155

MICALE, FRANK JUDE, lawyer; b. Pitts., Jan. 10, 1949; s. Frank Jacob and Catherine Anna (Wagner) M. BA, Duquesne U., 1971, JD, 1977. Bar: Pa. 1977, U.S. Dist. Ct. (we. dist.) Pa. 1977, U.S. Ct. Appeals (3rd cir.) 1978, U.S. Supreme Ct. 1986. Law clk. to judge U.S. Ct. Appeals (3rd cir.), 1977-78, U.S. Dist. Ct. (we. dist.) Pa., 1978-79; assoc. Egler & Reinstadtler, Pitts., 1979-80; dep. atty. gen., sr. dep. atty. gen. in charge torts litigation sect. western region Office of Atty. Gen. Commonwealth of Pa., 1980-92; pvt. practice, 1992—. Mem. ABA, Am. Arbitration Assn., Pa. Bar Assn., Allegheny County Bar Assn., Acad. Trial Lawyers Allegheny County. Home: 555 S Negley Ave Apt 9 Pittsburgh PA 15232-1634 Office: 200 One Williamsburg Pl Warrendale PA 15086

MICALLER, ALBERTO BASCO, engineering manager; b. Camarines Norte, The Philippines, Oct. 16, 1956; arrived in Saudi Arabia, 1987; s. Jesus Buasan Micaller and Asuncion Vegas Basco; m. Josie Dizon Dela Cruz, July 27, 1980; children: Jobert, Christian, John Michael. BSEE, Far Ea. U., Manila, 1979. Engr. II Constrn. & Devel. Corp. of the Philippines, Makati, 1979-81; sr. engr. Westinghouse Internat. Projects Co., Makati, 1981-86; asst. engr. Al-Yusr Townsend & Bottum Co. Ltd., Jubail, Saudi Arabia, 1987-89; project mgr. Arabian Consulting Engring. Ctr., Al-Khobar, Saudi Arabia, 1989—. Mem. Internat. Soc. for Measurement and Control (sr. mem.), N.Y. Acad. Scis. Roman Catholic. Avocations: reading, jogging. Fax: 9663-882-5452. E-mail: albert.micaller@swme.com, Jcmicaller@prime.net.sa. Home: Lot 2-B Mangosteen St, Trinidad Village Angeles City 2009, The Philippines Office: Arabian Cons Engring Ctr, PO Box 3790, Al-Khobar 31952, Saudi Arabia

MICCA, GIORGIO, researcher; b. Torino, Italy, May 28, 1951. Laurea in Computer Sci. with honors, U. Torino, 1976. Sr. rschr. CSECT, Torino, 1997%; project leader Euroscom, Heidelberg, Germany, 1996-97. Contbr. articles to profl. jours. Mem. IEEE. Home: cso Vittorio 229, 10139 Torino Italy Office: CSELT, Via G Reiss Romoli 274, 10148 Torino Italy

MICELI, MOTHER IGNATIUS, retired nun, missionary; b. N.Y.C., Mar. 14, 1918; d. Joseph and Cecelia (Torre) M. BS, Regis Coll.; MEd, Loyola

U., New Orleans; M Religious Edn., Seattle U.; postgrad., U. Denver, 1968-69. Various housemother/missionary assignments Orphanage, West Park, N.Y., 1942-44; tchr. St. Donato's Sch., Phila., 1944-48, local sch., Scranton, Pa., 1948-52, Cabrini H.S., N.Y.C., 1952-54; prin. sch./orphanage, Denver, 1954-65; coordinator religious programs All Souls Ch., Englewood, Colo., 1968-71, dir. home instr. for adults, 1971-72, dir. adult edn., 1972—; dir. religious edn. Assumption, Welby, Colo., 1973-77, Holy Cross, Thornton, Colo., 1971-73; instr. religion various missions, 1968—. Author: (poems) Leaves Of Thought, 1978, Random Thoughts and Meditations, 1975, Colorado and St. Francis Xavier Cabrini, M.S.C., 1980, (poetry and photography book) Life's Seasons, 1989, Short History of Cabrini Shrine, 1992, Cabrini Colorado Missions, 1996, Welcome to My World, 1996; (VCRs) Welcome to Colorado, 1971, The Life of St. Frances Xavier Cabrini, 1986, The History and Meditations on the Rosary, 1990. Mem. Internat. Bibl. Assn., Religious Edn. Assn. U.S., Religious Edn. Assn. Can., Nat. League Am. Pen Women, Kappa Delta Pi. Avocations: photography, camping, hiking, fishing, jeeping. Home: Mountain Vista Village 4700 Tabor St Apt 2C Wheat Ridge CO 80033 Office: All Souls Ch Religious Edn Office 435 Pennwood Cir Englewood CO 80110-6921

MICHAEL, CECIL FRANCIS, JR., pediatrician; b. Albuquerque, June 3, 1950; s. Cecil F. and Gene (Clairmont) M.; m. Karen Sara Dworkin, June 28, 1975; children: Kristen, Jonathan. BA in Chemistry, U. N.M., 1972, MD, 1976. Resident in pediats. Phoenix Affiliated Pediat. Program, 1976-79; pvt. practice Cactus Children's Clinic, Glendale, Ariz., 1979—; chmn. pediat. dept. Thunderbird Samaritan Hosp., Glendale, 1981-83; mem. grievance com. Maricopa County Med. Soc., Phoenix, 1987. Contbr. article to profl. jour. Recipient Top Doctor Nurse's List award, Phoenix Mag. Poll, 1997, Top Doctor Doctor's Poll, 1998. Fellow Am. Acad. Pediats.; mem. AMA, Ariz. Med. Assn., Maricopa County Med. Soc. Democrat. Roman Catholic. Avocations: golf, exercise, gardening, mountain biking. Office: Cactus Childrens Clinic 5310 W Thunderbird Rd Ste 300 Glendale AZ 85306-4710

MICHAEL, DIANN DEE, psychologist, educator; b. Charleston, W.Va., July 19, 1947; d. Esber John Michael and Asma Deebie Radwan; 1 child, Gianna Christiane. BA, W.Va. State Coll., 1969; PhD, U. Akron, 1978; DEA, U. Paris The Sorbonne, 1984. Lic. psychologist, Fla. Psychologist, dir. Ea. Mahoning County Mental Health Ctr., Youngstown, Ohio, 1971-77; psychologist Youngstown Psychol. Assocs., 1977-81, Fla. Mental Health Inst., Tampa, 1981-83; mem. faculty European divsn. U. Md., Heidelberg, Brussels, Turkey, 1984-91; psychologist in pvt. practice Paris, 1984-91; psychologist, clin. dir. Fla. Biodyne, Ft. Lauderdale, 1991-94; mem. faculty Nova Southeastern U., Ft. Lauderdale, 1994—; psychologist Child and Family Psychologists, Ft. Lauderdale, 1996—; co-chmn. adv. bd. Tropical Elem. Sch., Plantation, 1997-98; mem. success team Seminole Mid. Sch., Plantation, 2000—. Mem. Broward Psychol. Assn. (newsletter editor 2000—), Kfeirian Reunion Found. (Reunion scholar 1964-65; newsletter editor, pres. bd. dirs.). Avocations: painting, writing, photography, travel. Office: Child and Family Psychologists 7250 NW 5th St Plantation FL 33317

MICHAEL, GARY G., retail supermarket and drug chain executive; b. 1940; married. BS in Bus., U. Idaho, 1962. Staff acct. Ernst & Ernst, CPA's, 1964-66; with Albertson's, Inc., Boise, Idaho, 1966—, acct., 1966-68, asst. controller, 1968-71, controller, 1971-72, v.p., controller, 1972-74, sr. v.p. fin., treas., 1974-76, exec. v.p., 1976-84, vice chmn., CFO, corp. devel. officer, 1984-91, chmn., CEO, 1991—; also dir. Albertson's Inc. Served to 1st lt. U.S. Army, 1962-64. Office: Albertsons Inc PO Box 20 250 E Parkcenter Blvd Boise ID 83726

MICHAEL, JERROLD MARK, public health specialist, former university dean, educator; b. Richmond, Va., Aug. 3, 1927; s. Joseph Leon and Esther Leah M.; m. Lynn Y. Simon, Mar. 17, 1951; children: Scott J., Nelson L. BCE, George Washington U., 1949; MSE, Johns Hopkins U., 1950; MPH, U. Calif., Berkeley, 1957; DrPH (hon.), Mahidol U., 1983; ScD (hon.), Tulane U., 1984. Commd. ensign USPHS, 1950, advanced through grades to rear adm., asst. surgeon gen., 1966; ret., 1970; dean Sch. Pub. Health, U. Hawaii, Honolulu, 1971-92, prof. pub. health, 1971-95; emeritus prof. pub. health U. Hawaii, Honolulu, 1995—; adj. prof. internat. health George Washington U., 1997—; bd. dirs. Nat. Health Coun., 1967-78, Nat. Ctr. for Health Edn., 1977-90; mem. nat. adv. coun. on health professions edn., 1978-81; chmn. bd. dirs. Kuakini Med. Ctr., Honolulu; sec., treas. Asia-Pacific Acad. Consortium Pub. Health; vis. prof. U. Adelaide, 1993, George Washington, 1994; hon. prof. Beijing Med. U., 1994; adj. prof. health svcs., mgmt. and policy Goerge Washington U., 1997—. Contbr. articles to profl. jours.; assoc. editor Jour. Environ. Health, 1958-80, Asia-Pacific Jour. of Pub. Health, 1986-95. Pres. Commissioned Officers Found., 2000—. Served with USNR, 1945-47. Decorated Meritorious Svc. medal, comdr. Royal Order of Elephant (Thailand); recipient Walter Mangold award, 1961, J.S. Billings award for mil. medicine, 1964, Gold medal Hebrew U., Jerusalem, 1982, San Karcil Gold medal, Malaysia, 1989, Disting. Svc. award Pacific Island Health Officers Assn., 1992, USPHS awards, Commd. Officers Assn. Brutsche award, 1999, others. Fellow Am. Public Health Assn.; mem. Am. Acad. Health Adminstrn., Am. Soc. Cert. Sanitarians, Nat. Environ. Health Assn., Am. Acad. Environ. Engrs. Democrat. Jewish. Club: Masons. Home: 16736 Gooseneck Ter Olney MD 20832-2456

MICHAEL, MARY AMELIA FURTADO, freelance writer, retired educator; m. Eugene G. Michael; children: David, Douglas, Gregory. BA, Albertus Magnus Coll.; MS, U. Bridgeport, 1975; CAS, Fairfield U., 1982. Cert. secondary sch. sci. tchr., ednl. adminstr. Housemaster, sci. tchr. Fairfield (Conn.) Pub. Schs., adminstrv. housemaster, sci. tchr., sci. dept. coord., 1992, retired, 1992; freelance fin. rsch. and investment writer and cons., 1994—. Author: The Art and Science of Cooking, 1996; contbr. articles to profl. jours. Mem. Discovery Mus., Conn. Arts & Sci. Mus. Mem. AAUW (bd. dirs. 1998-2000), LWV, Conn. Assn. Suprs. and Curriculum, Fairfield Sch. Adminstrs. Assn., Retired Educators of Fairfield, Fairfield Hist. Soc., Alpha ONE Antitrypsin Assn. Avocations: collecting antiques, gourmet cooking, collecting old cookbooks and recipes, photography, writing. Home: 942 Valley Rd Fairfield CT 06432-1671

MICHAEL, MILAD ISHAK, biologist, educator; b. Luxor, Egypt, Jan. 15, 1930; s. Ishak and Fahima (Makar) El-Deeb; m. Hilda Maurice Hanna, Sept. 20, 1964; children: Maged, Maha. BSc, Cairo U., 1949; MSc, Alexandria U., 1953, PhD, 1956. From demonstrator zoology to ast. prof. zoology Alexandria U., 1949-72, prof. devel. biology, head zoology dept., vice dean, 1972-90. Co-author: Normal Table of Xenopus Laevis, 1956, Discipline: Regeneration and Wound Healing in Vertebrates; contbr. articles to profl. jours. Mem. Egyptian Zool. Soc., Sporting Club Alexandria. Avocations: walking, photography, reading, cycling. Office: Alexandria U Dept Zoology, 21511 Moharram Bey, Alexandria Egypt

MICHAELIDES, DOROS NIKITA, internist, medical educator; b. Nicosia, Cyprus, Jan. 7, 1936; came to U.S., 1969; s. Nikita P. and Elpinike (Taliadorou) M.; m. Eutychia J. Loizides, Feb. 27, 1965; children: Nike-Elsie, Joanna-Doris. MD magna cum laude (Royal Greek Govt. scholar), U. Athens, 1962; D.T.M. and H. (Greek State Scholarship Found. scholar), U. Liverpool (Eng.), 1967; MSc in Clin. Biochemistry (Greek State Scholarship Found. scholar), U. Newcastle-upon-Tyne (Eng.), 1969. Clk., intern U. Uppsala (Sweden), 1962; resident Nicosia Gen. Hosp., 1963-66; fellow U. Liverpool Hosps., 1967; fellow internal and clin. medicine Royal Infirmary, U. Edinburgh, 1967-68; research fellow Royal Victoria Infirmary, U. Newcastle-upon-Tyne, 1968-69; resident internal medicine Bapt. Meml. Hosp., Memphis, 1969-72; fellow in chest diseases Western Okla. Chest Disease Hosp., 1970-71; chief clin. immunology and respiratory care center, Erie, Pa.; chief respiratory care center VA Med. Ctr., Erie, 1972-84, acting chief dept. medicine, 1980-81; asst. clin. prof. medicine Hahnemann Univ. Sch. Medicine, Phila., 1977—; asst. clin. prof. medicine Gannon U., Erie, 1977—; mem. staff internal medicine Hamot Med. Ctr., immunology & chest diseases Metro Health Ctr., Erie; preceptor medicine St. Vincent's Health Ctr.; affiliate staff Cleveland Clinic Found; vol. physician Greek Nat. Guard, Cyprus, 1964. Recipient citation for outstanding services to vets. DAV, 1975, citation Adminstr. U.S. Vets. Affairs, 1978. Diplomate Am. Bd. Family Practice, Am. Bd. Allergy and Immunology; qualified Am. Bd. Internal Medicine; cert. in infectious diseases and immunochemistry, Eng. Fellow ACP (life), Am. Assn. Cert. Allergists, Am. Coll. Allergy and Immunology (com. autoimmune diseases), Am. Assn. Clin. Immunology and Allergy (pulmonary com.). Am. Coll. Chest Physicians (life; critical care com.), Royal Soc. Medicine, Am. Coll. Angiology, N.Y. Acad. Scis., Am. Coll. Clin. Pharmacology, Am. Assn. Cert. Allergists. Greek Orthodox. Author: The Occurrence of Proteolytic Inhibitors in Heart and Skeletal Muscle, 1969; Blood Gases, Acid-Base and Electrolytes Disturbances, 1980; Immediate Hypersensitivity: The Immunochemistry and Therapeutics of Reversible Airway Obstruction, 1980; The Equivalent Potency of Corticosteroid Preparations used in Reversible Airway Obstruction, 1981; contbr. articles to med. jours. Home: 4107 State St Erie PA 16508-3129 Office: Allergy Immunology & Chest Diseases 1611 Peach St Ste 220 Erie PA 16501-2121

MICHAELIDES, EFSTATHIOS EMMANUEL, mechanical engineer; b. Thessaloniki, Greece, Feb. 13, 1955; s. Emmanuel Efstathios and Eleni M.; m. Maria-Laura Garcia, July 31, 1982; children: Emmanuel Alexandros, Dimitris Nicolas, Eleni Guadalupe. BA, Oxford U., 1977, MA honoris causa, 1983; MS, Brown U., 1979, PhD, 1980. Asst. prof. U. Del., Newark, 1980-85, assoc. prof., 1985-89, acting chmn., 1985-86; head of mech. engring. Tulane U., New Orleans, 1990-92, prof., 1990—, assoc. dean, 1992—, sr. Fulbright fellow, 1997, Leo S. Weil prof. mech. engring., 1998—; cons. DuPont, Chevron, Exxon, TASA; chair Internat. Conf. on Multiphase Flow-2001. Editor nine books, presenter more than 100 conf. papers; contbr. more than 80 articles to profl. jours.; patentee in field. Mem. ASME, ASEE, APS. Avocation: stained glass windows/master craftsman. Office: Sch Engring Tulane Univ New Orleans LA 70118

MICHAELIDES, MICHAEL ALEXANDROU, retail executive; b. Nicosia, Cyprus, Sept. 30, 1932; m. Thelma Christodoulides, June 12, 1965; children: Alexander, Phryne. Cypher officer Ministry Fgn. Affairs, Cyprus, 1961; co-owner MAM, 1965—, Cyprus Bibliographic Info. Bank, 1997—. Founder Cyprus Youth Coun., Assn. Protection Cypriot Environment, Assn. Books Children-Youth. Mem. Soc. Cypriot Studies, Cyprus Greek Intellectual Group, Cyprus Philatelic Soc., Cyprus Numismatic Soc., Cyprus Bibliog. Soc., Cyprus Soc. Hist. Studies. Home: 18 Procopiou St, 1085 Nicosia Cyprus Office: 46 Phaneromeni St, 1011 Nicosia Cyprus

MICHAELIS, BERND, computer science educator; b. Magdeburg, Germany, Sept. 18, 1947; s. Hermann and Walli (Kauffeld) M. Diploma in Engring., Advanced Coll. Tech., Magdeburg, 1971, D Engring., 1974; D Engring. Habilitation, Tech. U., Magdeburg, 1980. Lectr. Advanced Coll. Tech., Magdeburg, 1973-80; scientist Joint Inst. Nuclear Rsch., Dubna, Russia, 1980-83; dozent Tech. U., Magdeburg, 1984-93; prof. tech. computer sci. U. Magdeburg, 1994—, chair tech. computer sci., 1994; head Inst. for Measurement Techs. and Electronics, Magdeburg, 1995. Mem. IEEE, European Neural Network Soc., Verband deutsche Ingenieure. Home: Am Weidenring 12, D-39175 Biederitz Germany Office: Otto-von-Guericke U, Postfach 41 20, D-39016 Magdeburg Germany

MICHAELIS, KAREN LAUREE, law educator; b. Milw., Mar. 30, 1950; d. Donald Lee and Ethel Catherine (Stevens) M.; m. Larry Severtson, Aug. 2, 1980 (div. Aug. 1982); 1 child, Quinn Alexanda Michaelis. BA, U. Wis., 1972, BS, 1974; MA, Calif. State U., L.A., 1979; MS, U. Wis., 1985, PhD, 1988, JD, 1989. Bar: Wis., U.S. Dist. Ct. (we. dist.) Wis. Asst. prof. law Hofstra U., Hempstead, N.Y., 1990-93; assoc. prof. law Ill. State U., Normal, 1993-95; asst. prof. law Wash. State U., Pullman, 1995—. Author: Reporting Child Abuse: A Guide to Mandatory Requirements for School Personnel, 1993, Theories of Liability for Teacher Sexual Misconduct, 1996, Postmodern Perspectives and Shifting Legal Paradigms: Searching For A Critical Theory of Juvenile Justice, 1998; Student As Enemy: A Legal Construct of the Other, 1999; editor Ill. Sch. Law Quarterly, 1993-95; mem. editl. bd. Nat. Assn. Profs. of Ednl. Adminstrn., 1994-95, Planning and Changing, 1993-95, Jour. Sch. Leadership, 1991—, People & Education: The Human Side of Edn., 1991-96. Mem. ABA, State Bar of Wis., Nat. Coun. Profs. Ednl. Adminstrn. (program com. 1994-95, morphet fund com. 1993—), Nat. Orgn. Legal Problems in Edn. (publs. com. 1993—, program com. 1995, exec. bd.), Edn. Law Assn. (bd. dirs. 1998, co-chair publs. com.). Office: Wash State U Dept Ed Leadership & Co Psy Pullman WA 99164-0001

MICHAELOWA, AXEL, economist, researcher; b. Heidelberg, Germany, Apr. 8, 1968; s. Ulrich and Helma (Wernery) Schmidt-Rohr; m. Katharina Michaelowa, Aug. 14, 1993; 1 child, Sascha. Diploma, Mannheim (Germany) U., 1993; PhD, Hamburg (Germany) U., 1996. Rschr. Hamburg Inst. Econ. Rsch., 1994-97, Internat. Ctr. for Rsch. on Environ. and Devel., Paris, 1998-99; head rsch. program internat. climate policy Hamburg Inst. for Internat Econ., 1999—; cons. Ministry Econ. Affairs, Bonn, Germany, 1994-95, 98, UNCTAD, 1998, World Bank, 1999, U.N. Climate Change Secretariat, 1999, German Agy. Tech. Coop., 2000. Contbr. articles to profl. jours. Del. F.D.P. State Party Conv., Hamburg, 1995-98; v.p. German Fedn. Liberal Students, Bonn, 1992-93; mem. senate Mannheim U., 1991-93. With German mil., 1987-88. Grantee German Nat. Scholarship Found., 1989-93. Mem. Vereinigung für Ökologische Ökonomie, Internat. Soc. Ecol. Econs., Am. Econ. Assn., Assn. German Speaking Economists. Avocations: skiing, mountain photography, numismatics. Home: 177 Bd de la Republique, 92210 Saint-Cloud France

MICHAELS, ALAN J., safety, occupational health and training executive; b. Stowe, Pa., Nov. 29, 1946; s. Joseph and Helen (Arena) Pavelish; m. Glenda Jo Becton Lewis; children: Catherine Michaels, Victoria Anne Desireé Michaels. AA with high honors, Mesa Community Coll., 1967; BA with high honors, Ariz. State U., 1970; MS with highest honors, Colo. State U., 1979. Cert. safety profl. Tchr. Phoenix Area Pub. Schs., 1970-78; supr. safety and tng. Amax Inc., Greenwich, Conn., 1980-84; supr. employee rels. and safety Colowyo Coal Co., Meeker, Colo., 1984-86; corp. dir. safety and tng. Tenneco/Echo Bay Minerals, Reno, 1986-88; mgr. safety and human resources various locations Occidental Chem. Corp., 1979-80, 86-94; dir. safety, fire protection, indsl. hygiene, security, pub. rels. Rayon divsn. Courtaulds/Acordis Cellulosics Fibers Inc., Axis, Ala., 1994-98; safety mgr. Goodyear-Dunlop Tire Corp., Huntsville, Ala., 1998-99; dir. of safety-health Lafarge Constrn. Materials, Denver, 1999—; mem. exec. bd. Copper Devel. Assn., N.Y., 1980-82, Am. Traffic Safety Svc. Assn., 1980, 1999—; mem. exec. safety com. Fla. Phosphate Coun., Orlando, 1989-90; mem. exec com safety and health Tex. Chem. Coun., 1990-91. Contbr. articles to profl. jours. Mem. steering com. Drug Free Mobile Coalition, 1993-94; mem. Mobile Area Tng. and Edn. Symposium, 1992-95, S.E. Consortium for Minorities in Engring., 1991-98, Edn. 2000, 1996-98; mem. adv. coun. Dist. Magnet Sch., 1994; pres. Alhambra Sch. Dist. of Classroom Tchrs., 1973-74; mem. LeMoyne Cmty. Adv. Panel, 1994-98; mem. transp. safety com. LeMoyne Indsl. Park, 1997-98. Recipient Medallion of Merit, Ariz. State U., 1967; NIOSH fellow, 1978-79. Mem. AARP, Am. Soc. Safety Engrs. (prof., Pres. Cir. 1990, Mobile chpt. sec. 1995-96, treas. 1997-98, v.p. 1998), Bus. Coun. Ala., Indsl. Pers. Assn. Mobile, Chickasaw C. of C. (pres. 1994), Ala. Textile Mfg. Assn. (health and safety sect. 1994-98), Nat. Stone Assn., Colo. Contractors Assn., Colo. Ready Mix Concrete Assn., Colo. Rock Prodrs., Joseph Holmes Safety Assn. (founding mem. corp. chpts. 1984, 86, 99), Colo. State U. Alumni Ambassadors, Mensa. Avocations: comic classical movies, music, restoring old automobiles, pet animals, sports trivia. Home: 12340 Ivanhoe St Brighton CO 80602-8034 Office: Lafarge Corp 1590 W 12th Ave Denver CO 80204-3410

MICHAELS, MARION CECELIA, writer, editor, news syndicate executive; b. Black River Falls, Wis.; d. Leonard N. and Estelle O. (Payne) Doud; m. Charles Webb (div.); children: Charles, David, Robert; m. Mark J. Michaels (div.); 1 child, Merry A. Student, MIT, 1962-64, U. Wis., 1971-76; BS in Bus. Edn., U. Wis., 1978, MS in Spl. Edn., 1981. Mgr., instr. bus. program Blackwell Job Corps Ctr., 1987-89; mgr. Michaels Secretarial Svc., Black River Falls, Wis., 1979-83; columnist, editor Michaels News, Black River Falls, 1983—, pres., 1989—; hon. appt. rsch. bd. advisors Am. Biog. Inst., 1996—. Author: The Little Cowboy: Pursuing Dana's Dream, 1998; columnist: Single Parenting, 1983-94, Parenting Plus, 1990—; editor, contbr. (column) Surviving Single, 1990-95, To Read or Not, Report From Planet Earth, 1989—, Travel Tidbits, 1991-95, Surviving Sane, 1995-98. Chmn. Brockway Community Orgn., 1969-71; chair, counselor Brockway Youth Group, 1970-72; chmn. labor com. Dem. Platform Com., Wis., 1975-76; candidate State Assembly, 1978, 82; co-founder Franklin Delano Roosevelt Meml., 1997. Named to Internat. Poetry Hall of Fame, 1997. Mem. AAUW, Pub. Citizen, Internat. Platform Assn., Internat. Soc. Poets (Poet of Yr. nominee 1997, 99, 2000, Poet of Merit award 1999), Union Concerned Scientists, Physicians for Social Responsibility, Am. United, Nat. Parks, Pi Omega Pi, Phi Delta Kappa. Avocations: singing, dancing, walking, swimming, travel. Office: Michaels News RR 5 Box 367 Black River Falls WI 54615-9160

MICHAELS-PAQUE, JOAN MARIE, artist, educator; b. Menominee, Mich., July 24, 1936; d. Frank E. and Gertrude (Pfotenhauer) Michaels; m. Henry Paul Paque, July 13, 1957; children: Juliann Marie, Elaine Marie. Student, Layton Sch. of Art, 1955-58, Marquette U., 1955-58. Art tchr. Kawashima Sch., Kyoto, Japan, 1983, Bellas Artes, San Miguel de Allende, Mex., 1985, Am. U., Washington, 1992, Peters Valley Craft Ctr., Layton, N.J., 1993-94, Cardinal Stritch U., Milw., 1990-95, Milw. Inst. Art & Design, 1993—, The Clearing Sch. of Arts, Nature and Humanities, Ellison Bay, Wis., 1995-98; art tchr., lectr. Peninsula Art Sch., Fish Creek, Wis., 1997-98; bd. dirs. Artists Working in Edn., Inc., 2000; mem. adv. bd. Women's Caucus for Art, Madison, Wis. Designer Craftsmen, Milw.; mem. artists' adv. bd. Milw. Art Mus., 1993; artist advisor, co-chair Milw. AIDS Project, 1991-92; vis. artist Australia, 1989, 1998, Arrowmont Sch. Arts & Crafts, Gatlinburg, Tenn., 1999, Wisc. Designer Crafts Coun. 75th Invitational Exhbn., Luth. Coll., Milwaukee, Wisc., 1998. One-person shows include St. Norbert Coll., De Pere, Wis., 1991; one-person shows (sculptural portraits) include Wis. Layton Gallery of Cardinal Stritch U., Milw., 1998, Wis. Luth. Coll., Milw., 2000; exhibited in group shows U. Wollongong, NSW, Australia, 1989, Artworks, Milw. Art Mus., 1992, H2O Gallery, Milw., 1999; author, pub.: (books) Visual Instructional Knotting, 2d edit., 1971, Design Principals/Fiber Techniques, 2d edit., 1973, A Creative/Conceptual Analysis of Textiles, 2d edit., 1979; writer, reviewer Fiberarts Mag., 1970-2000. Jurist Cancer Care Ctr., Milw., 1991; artist cons. African Am. Childrens Theatre, Milw., 1997, 98, 99, 2000; artist, jurist Wis. State Fair, Milw., 1994-97, 2000; donated time and art works Women's Exptl. Theatre, Milw., 1994-2000. Named Most Interesting Person, Milw. Mag., 1986; grantee Internat. Forum of Arts, 1998, Eli Lilly grantee, 1993, grantee Roundy's Corp. Arts Grant, 2000. Mem. Internat. Sculpture Ctr., Australian Forum for Textile Arts (vis. artist, writer, reviewer Textile Fiber Forum 1989, 98, 99, 2000), Arrowmont Sch. Arts and Crafts (vis. supporter, tchr. 1970-99), Shuttle Spindle and Dypot Handweavers Guild of Am., Inc. (writer, reviewer Shuttle mag. 1984-93), Milw. Art Mus. (exhibitor, bd. dirs.). Avocations: traveling, learning, swimming, meeting new people, dog. E-mail: joanmichaels@paque.com. Home and Studio: JMP Atelier 4455 N Frederick Ave Milwaukee WI 53211-1653

MICHAILIDIS, SOUSANA, English educator, history educator; b. Batumi, Republic of Georgia, Feb. 9, 1948; arrived in Greece, 1991, naturalized, 1992; d. Antonious and Valeria (Tkachenko) M.; m. Constantine Antoniadis, Feb. 7, 1991 (dec. Oct. 1996). BA, State U., Tbilisi, Georgia, 1971; PhD, Acad. Scis., Moscow, 1989. Tchr. English H.S., Rustavi, Georgia, 1968-73; sr. rschr. Acad. Scis., Tbilisi, 1973-91; assoc. prof. Modern Info. Systems-English Acad., Athens, Greece, 1992—; asst. prof. world history and sociology U. Indianapolis, Athens, 1994—, asst. prof. comparative lit. and literary criticism, 1995—, assoc. prof., 1997—; rsch. and thesis supr. Acad. Scis., Tbilisi, 1986-91, Unity Indianapolis, Athens, 1994—; assoc. prof. dept. English U. Indpls., summer 1997. Author: American Short Story, 1982, Modern Nigerian Criticism, 1992, Contemporary Georgian Literature, 1993, Women in Medieval Georgian Epic, 1999; contbr. articles to profl. jours. Mem. Sci. Coun. African Studies, Scholars Soc. on Comparative Lit. Acad. Scis., Georgian Inst. in Athens, Hellenic-Georgian Assn., Hellenic-Am. Union, Amer. Comparative Lit. Assn., Yale Univ., Georgian-Greek Assn. Avocations: classical music, swimming, reading. Home: 44 Plapouta St, 16561 Ano Glyfada Greece Office: Univ Indianapolis, 29 Voulis St, 10557 Athens Greece

MICHALCZONEK, MACIEJ ZBIGNIEW, publisher; b. Gdynia, Poland, Feb. 24, 1950; s. Mikolaj and Marianna (Zglinicka) M.; m. Irena Czerwinska, Nov. 15, 1975; children: Maja, Iwona. Journalist Gdańsk, Warsaw, Budapest, Munich, 1966—; publisher MZM Publications Co., Sopot, Poland, 1989—; participant many nat. and internat. fairs, bus. and sci. confs., speaker in field. Editor: Socialist World Shipping Directory, 1984, MZM World Business Directory (ex-Socialist World Bus. Directory), 1986—, Industrial and Service Contacts in Poland, 1990, Standard World's Business Information Sources Directory, 2000—. Office: MZM Publications Co, PO Box 465, PL81705 Sopot 5, Poland

MICHALEK, HILMA ADELHEID LEONORE, histopathology educator, researcher, consultant; b. Vienna, Dec. 21; d. August and Maria Michalek; 1 child, Fatima. MD, U. Vienna, 1965. Pathologist-in-chief Mama Yemo Hosp., Kinshasa, Zaïre, 1972-74; pathologist, assoc. prof. U. Hawaii Postgrad. Edn. Program, Okinawa, Japan, 1974-77; sr. pathologist U. Vienna, 1977-82, U. Graz, Austria, 1982-84; prof., cons. postgrad. edn. program U. Hawaii, Okinawa, Japan, 1985; prof., co-chmn. King Abdul Aziz U. Univ., Jeddah, Saudi Arabia, 1986-91, Sultan Qaboos U., 1992, Al-Thawra U. Hosp., Yemen, 1993-98; rschr. comparative studies of lymphomas between West, Middle and Far East; internat. cons.; deputy dir. gen. Europe IBC. Named Woman of Yr. award ABI, 1995, IBC Cambridge, 1994, 95. Mem. N.Y. Acad. Sci., Order Internat. Fellowship. Avocations: poetry, deep sea diving, geological studies, history, archaeology. Home: Schardorf # 13, Trofaiach Austria A-8793 Office: Top 102, 164-168, Brigittenauer Laende, Vienna Austria A-1200

MICHALIK, JOHN JAMES, legal educational association executive; b. Bemidji, Minn., Aug. 1, 1945; s. John and Margaret Helen (Pafko) M.; m. Diane Marie Olson, Dec. 21, 1968; children: Matthew John, Nicole, Shane. BA, U. Minn., 1967, JD, 1970. Legal editor Lawyers Coop. Pub. Co., Rochester, N.Y., 1970-75; dir. continuing legal edn. Wash. State Bar Assn., Seattle, 1975-81, exec. dir., 1981-91; asst. dean devel. and cmty. rels. Sch. of Law U. Wash., 1991-95; exec. dir., CEO Assn. Legal Adminstrs., Vernon Hills, Ill., 1995—. Fellow Coll. Law Practice Mgmt.; mem. Am. Soc. Assn. Execs., Am. Mgmt. Assn., Nat. Trust Hist. Preservation, Coll. Club Seattle. Lutheran. Office: Assn Legal Adminstrs #325 175 E Hawthorn Pkwy Ste 325 Vernon Hills IL 60061-1460

MICHALOPOULOS, CHRISTOS DEMETRIUS, cardiologist; b. Lyrkeia, Argolis, Greece, Aug. 30, 1931; s. Demetrius Christos and Angelike Sotirios (Colovos) M.; m. Vasiliki Petros Mitrakos, Feb. 21, 1965; children: Angela, Katherine. MD, U. Athens, Greece, 1969. Med. diplomate. Commd. 2d lt. Greek Army, 1956, advanced through grades to brig. gen., 1985; dir. 204-212 Med. Bn., Alexandroupolis, Greece, 1966-68; chief editor Hellenic Armed Forces Med. Rev., Athens, 1968-72; head dept. cardiology Athens Gen. Mil. Hosp., 1972-74; dir. med. dept. various mil. units, Athens, Corinth, Edessa, Greece, 1974-77; head dept. cardiology Athens Gen. Mil. Hosp., 1978-81; dir. 411th Gen. Mil. Hosp., Tripolis, Greece, 1981-82; head dept. cardiology NIMTS Hosp., Athens, 1983-87; ret., 1987, pvt. practice, 1983-2000. Chief author and editor: Dictionary of Cardiological Terms, 1996; 1st author: Dictionary of Cardiological Terms of the Hellenic Society of Cardiology, 1996; translator: The Heart (Hurst), 1978; translator, editor: Cardiology Clinics, 1990-97, Heart Disease (Braunwald), 5th edit., 1996; exec. editor Hellenic Jour. Cardiology, 1989-95; mem. editl. bd. European Heart Jour., 1991-95. Mem. Hellenic Cardio. Soc., Hellenic Armed Forces M.C. Sci. Assn. (bd. dirs. 198-92), Hellenic Com. Against Thromboembolic Diseases (gen. sec. 1976-2000), N.Y. Acad. Scis., Am. Coll. Angiology. Avocations: chess, gardening, desktop pub. Office: 9 Neoph Metaxa Str, 104-39 Athens Greece

MICHALOPOULOU, NIOVI, psychologist, educator; b. Athens, Greece, Dec. 17, 1969; d. Themistocles and Nora (Santama) M. BA in Psychology, Deree Coll., Athens, 1991; MA in Clin. Psychology, Widener U., 1995, D of Psychology, 1997. Intern in psychology Child Psychiatry, Phila., 1995-96, New Directions, Phila., 1996-97; cons. Rsch. Internat., Athens, 1997-98; pvt. practice Athens, 1997—; mem. faculty SUNY, Athens, 1998—; mem. adj. faculty U. Indpls., Athens, 1999—. Mem. APA (internat. affiliate). Office: 3 Kapsali St, 10674 Athens Greece

MICHALOWICZ, ROMAN PIOTR, child neurologist; b. Warsaw, Poland, May 20, 1926; s. Alexander and Stanistawa Michalowicz. MD, U. Lublin, 1949, U. Szczecin, 1952. Jr. asst. U. Neurol. Clinic, Szczecin, Poland, 1949-55; asst. U. Neurol. Clinic, Warsaw, 1955-60; sr. asst. U. Pediatric Clinic, Warsaw, 1960-64; adj. and asst. prof. Rsch. Inst. for Child a. Mather, Warsaw, 1965-77; prof. head clinic Child's Health Ctr., Warsaw, 1977—. Author/co-author 24 books; contbr. more than 550 articles to profl. jours. Mem. N.Y. Acad. Sci., Polish Acad. of Scis. (commn. devel. neurology 1986-90), Polish Pediatric Assn., Polish Neurol. Assn. Avocations: art, music, travelling. Home: ul Chocimska 31 m 19, 00-791 Warsaw Poland Office: Child's Health Ctr Inst, Al-Dzieci Polskich 20, 04-736 Warsaw Poland

MICHALSKI, JACEK ANDRZEJ, chemist; b. Warsaw, Mazowsze, Poland, Feb. 9, 1957; s. Jan and Zofia (Synowiecka) M.; m. Bozena Osińska, Sept. 11, 1997; 1 child, Stanislaw. MSc, Warsaw Tech. U., 1982, PhD, 1991. Shift engr. Sugar Refinery, Marlbork, Poland, 1981; chemist Inst. Phys. Chemistry, Warsaw, 1982-89, rsch. assoc., 1989-91, asst. prof. chemistry, 1993—; trainee GE, Lebanon, U.S.A., 1991-93. Contbr. articles to profl. jours.; patentee in field. Mem. PZK, Dx Century Club. Roman Catholic. Avocations: ham radio, electronics, informatics, painting, art. Fax: 048 22 632 52 76. Office: Inst Physical Chemistry, Kasprzaka 44/52, 01-224 Warsaw Poland

MICHALTSOS, GEORGE THEODORE, civil engineering educator, researcher; b. Athens, Greece, June 28, 1944; s. Theodore George and Penelopes Theodore (Athanasopulu) M.; m. Helen George Kriezi, Oct. 14, 1971; 1 child, Ekaterini. MA in Civil Engirng., Nat. Tech. U. Athens, 1967, PhD in Civil Engring., 1976. Rschr. asst. Nat. Tech. U. Athens, 1970-80, lectr., 1981-87, asst. prof., 1988-95, assoc. prof., 1996—; cons. engr. Helliniki Techniki S.A., Athens, 1970-78, Hellenic Power Corp., Athens, 1985-90. Author: Thin Walled Beams--Methods of Calculation, 1994, Thin Walled Beams--Applications on Civil Engineering, 1999. Ensign, Greek Navy, 1967-70. Mem. ASCE, SSRC, N.Y. Acad. Scis. Greek Orthodox. Office: Nat Tech U Athens, 42 Patission Str, 10682 Athens Greece

MICHEL, ALIX JAMES, Seychelles government official; b. Seychelles, Aug. 16, 1944. Student, tchr. tng. coll., Victoria, Seychelles, 1960-61. Tchr. primary and secondary schs. Anse Boileau, 1960-61; with Cable & Wireless Ltd., 1961-71, Hotel des Seychelles, 1971-74; min. adminstrn. and info., 1977-79; editor ofcl. party newspaper The People, 1971—; min. edn. and info. Govt. Seychelles, 1979-89, min. finance and comm., min. def., now min. fin., comm., def. and environment; v.p., 1996—; mem. exec. com. Seychelles People's United Party, 1974; dep. sec.-gen. Seychelles People's Progressive Front, 1984-94, sec.-gen., 1994—. Recipient Outstanding Civilian Svc. medal U.S. Army, 1995. Office: State House, PO Box 655, Victoria Mahe, Seychelles

MICHEL, DANIEL JOHN, broadcast educator, writer, photographer, artist; b. New Orleans, June 18, 1949; s. Nolan Joseph and Evelyn Marie (Breaux) M. Diploma, Sta. WKG-TV, 1986; BA in Mktg. Mgmt., Kensington U., 1989; cert. diploma photography, Media West, 1990; cert., Art Instrn. Schs. Inc., 1991, Brit.-Am. Sch. of Writing, 1991. Instr. English East Baton Rouge Sch. Bd., 1982-84; instr. broadcast prodn. Sta. WKG-TV, Baton Rouge, 1986—; freelance writer Baton Rouge, 1987—; technician, photographer Evangeline Downs Race Track; announcer Nat. Sports Festival, Baton Rouge, 1985. Writer song lyrics including I've Sat So Long, Now I Became Lonely, stage plays, works in Libr. of Congress, 1982—. Camera dir. La. Pub. Broadcasting Fund Raising, Baton Rouge, 1986—; instr. TV broadcasting Boy Scouts Am., Baton Rouge, 1986—. Mem. Lafayette Art Assn. (2d v.p. 1994). Roman Catholic.

MICHEL, ELIZABETH CHENEY, communications strategist, educator, consultant; b. Pitts., Feb. 11, 1951; d. George Philip and Charlotte Elizabeth (Cowser) Cheney; m. Raymond Joseph Michel, Oct. 21, 1973 (div. June 1997); children: Keith Raymond, Grant Petersen. BA, Rollins Coll., 1973; M in Comm., U. Ctrl. Fla., 1988, PhD, 1992. Vis. prof. Univ. Ctrl. Fla., Orlando, Fla., 1989-92; assoc. prof., chair comm. program Mars Hill (N.C.) Coll., 1993-99; comms. cons., v.p. Comms. Strategies-Healthcare.com, Corp., 1998-2000; cons. Kairos Comm. Strategies, Kennesaw, Ga., 1998—; bd. dirs. Mars Hill Inst., 1997—, cons. 1996—; bd. dirs. Commn. on Industries of the Mind, Atlanta; vice-chair 21st Century Comm., 1996—; project coord. for joint comms. with Chinese Acad. Social Scis., China; del. to Consortium for Global Edn., China, 1998; vis. prof. comms. Kennesaw State U.; mem. internat. del. to China Internat. Conf. on Sustained Devel., 2000; v.p. Systems and Strategies. Author: 4 Simple Steps to Communications that Connect! and Kairos Community Strategies Interactive CD-ROM, 2000; chief editor: An Orchestra of Voices: Making the Argument for Press and Speech Freedom in the People's Republic of China, 2000; contbr. articles to mag. Mem. edn. com. Industries of the Mind, 1999—; bd. advisors Atlantic Univ. Chinese Medicine, 2000—; bd. dirs. Atlanta Women's Network, 2000—. Internat. Rsch. grant Appalachian Coll. Assn., 1994, 96, 97, Mellon Found., 1994, 95, 96, 97; Vis. Rsch. fellow Chinese Acad. Social Scis., 1996, 97. Mem. Nat. Comm. Assn., Am. Educators Journalism and Mass Comm., Nat. Spkrs. Assn., Ga. Spkrs. Assn., Brit. Am. Bus. Group, Women's Network, Metro Atlanta C. of C., Women's Commerce Club, Atlanta Women's Network-Strategic Planning, Ga. Exec. Women's Network, Phi Kappa Phi, Kappa Delta Phi. Presbyterian. Avocations: acting, music, postmodernism. Office: Healthcare.com Corp 1850 Parkway Pl SE Ste 1100 Marietta GA 30067-8265

MICHEL, HARTMUT, biochemist; b. Ludwigsburg, Germany, July 18, 1948; m. Ilona S. Leger, 1979; 2 children. Doctorate, U. Wurzburg, 1977. With Max Planck Inst. Biochemistry, Martinsried, Federal Republic of Germany, 1979-87. Co-recipient Nobel prize for chemistry, 1988. Office: Max Planck Inst Biophysics, Heinrich-Hoffmann Str 7, 60528 Frankfurt Germany

MICHEL, HENRY LUDWIG, civil engineer; b. Frankfurt, Germany, June 18, 1924; s. Maximilian Frederick and Loschka (Hepner) M.; m. Mary Elizabeth Strolis, June 5, 1954; children: Eve Musette, Ann Elizabeth. BSCE, Columbia U., 1949. Registered profl. engr., Pa., N.Y. Pres., CEO, Parsons Brinckerhoff, Inc., 1975-90, chmn., 1990-94, chmn. emeritus, 1994—; dir. Parsons Brinckeroff Internat., Inc., 1975—; chmn. Pegasus Consulting, Inc.; guest lectr. NYU, Columbia U., Colo. State U., Cornell U., U. Ark.; industry prof. N.Y. Poly. U.; sr. lectr. MIT; vice chmn. Bldg. Futures Coun., 1980—; instrumental in devel. and mgmt. of maj. transp. and pub. works project in U.S. and abroad; mem. Nat. Acad. Engrs., 1995—; adv. bd. Rentmakers.com. Contbr. numerous articles on mgmt. and transp. engring. to engring. jours. Fellow ASCE, Soc. Am. Mil. Engrs., Am. Cons. Engr. Coun., Instn. Civil Engrs.; mem. Internat. Rd. Found. (hon. life, chmn. 1989-92, bd. dirs. 1977—), World Exec. Bd., Constrn. Industry Pres. Forum (bd. dirs. 1989-94, chmn. 1990-91), Civil Engring. Rsch. Found. (bd. dirs. 1990—, chmn. 1992-96), Columbia U. Engring. Sch. Alumni Assn. (Egelston medal 1992, Alumni medal 1991, Pupin medal 2000), Am. European Cmty. Assn. (bd. dirs. 1983—, chmn. 1999—). Home: 35 Sutton Pl New York NY 10022-2464 Office: Parsons Brinckerhoff Inc One Penn Plaza New York NY 10119

MICHEL, KEITH, solicitor, author; b. London, May 19, 1948; s. George Richard and Winifred (Eve) M.; m. Rosemary Suzannah Simons, Dec. 16, 1972; 1 child, Edward Richard. MA, Cambridge (Eng.) U., 1970. Trainee solicitor Clifford Chance, London, 1971-73; asst. solicitor Clyde & Co., London, 1973-75; ptnr. Holman Fenwick & Willan, London, 1975—. Author: (novels) Contraband, 1988, Countdown, 1991, Caracara, 1995, Karakan, 2000; contbr. articles to profl. jours. Mem. City of London Solicitors Co., Hawks Club. Avocations: history, wildlife conservation, calligraphy. Home: Thatchdale, Thatchdale, Pennymead Dr, East Horsley Surrey KT24 5AH, England Office: Holman Fenwick & Willan, Marlow House Lloyds Ave, London EC3n 3AL, England

MICHEL, OLAF GERT, surgeon, educator; b. Bad Langensalza, Germany, Oct. 24, 1956; s. Gert R. Michel. MD, Free U. Berlin, 1983; Habilitation, U. Cologne, Germany, 1992. Cert. specialist ENT-surgery, specialist on voice disorders and plastic surgery. Ltd. Oberarzt ENT dept., prof. U. Cologne, 1992—. Author: Sudden Deafness, 1994, Menière's Disease, 1998; co-editor: The Facial Nerve, 1992. Grantee Heinrich-Hertz-Stiftung NRW, 1991, 92, 93, 98, Deutsche Forschungsgemeinschaft, 1991, 96, 99, 00, Jean-Uhrmacher-Stiftung, 1995, 96, 97, 98, 99, 00. Mem. Sir Charles Bells Soc., German Skull Base Soc., German Soc. Oto-Rhino-Laryngology. Office: U Cologne, Dept Oto-Rhinolaryngology, D-50924 Cologne Germany

MICHEL, PATRICK, astrophysicist, researcher; b. Saint-Tropez, France, Feb. 25, 1970; s. Jean-Paul and Marie-Claire (Giordana) M. Diploma in Engring., Superior Sch. Aero. Technics., Paris, 1993; MS, Nice (France) U., 1994, PhD in Physics, 1997. Rschr. in Astrophysics Observatory of Torino, Pino Torinese, Italy, 1997-99; astrophysicist C te d'Azur Observatory Scientific Rsch. Nat. Ctr., Nice, 1999—. Affiliate mem. Am. Astronomical Soc., Dept. Planetary Scis.; mem. N.Y. Acad. Scis., French Soc. of Specialists in Astronomy. Avocations: golf, piano, skiing, hiking. Home: Grand Hotel Residence, 45 Blvd of the Croisette, 06400 Cannes France Office: CNRS/UMR 6523 Cassini, BP 4229, 06304 Nice France

MICHEL, ROLF, physics educator; b. Tambach-Dietharz, Thuringen, Germany, Jan. 21, 1945; s. Heinz and Luise (Weber) M.; m. Elke Besenthal, Sept. 24, 1971; children: Stephanie, Florian. Diploma in physics, U. Cologne, 1971, Dr.rer.nat., 1975. Scientific asst. Inst. of Nuclear Chemistry, U. Cologne, 1971-84; scientific cons. PATI GmbH, Cologne, 1984; univ. prof. U. Hannover, head Ctrl. Inst. for Radiation Protection, 1984-93, head Ctr. of Radiation Protection and Radioecology, 1994, univ. prof., 1984. Contbr. over 350 articles to profl. publs. Mem. Fachverband Strahlenschutz, Gesellschaft deutscher Chemiker, European Phys. Soc., Deutsche Physikalische Gesellschaft, Meteoritical Soc., Internat. Radiation Physics Soc. Home: Wilh-Henze-Weg 14, D-31303 Burgdorf Germany Office: U Hannover, Am Kleinen Felde 30, D-30167 Hannover Germany

MICHELACCI, GIACOMO ADRIANO, mathematician, researcher; b. Asmara, Eritrea, former Italian colony, Mar. 30, 1939; s. Mauro Michelacci and Rosa Caffo. Degree in math., U. Trieste, Italy, 1967. Rschr. Dept. Naval Engring., Trieste, 1968-85, Dept. Maths., Trieste, 1985—. Contbr. sci. papers to profl. jours. Home: Via F Severo 71, 34127 Trieste Italy Office: Univ Trieste, Dept Math Sci Via Valerio 1, 34100 Trieste Italy

MICHEL-BRIAND, YVON, microbiologist; b. Besancon, France, May 20, 1934; s. Roger and Liliane (Py) M-B. MD, U. Montpellier, France, 1960, PhD, 1967. Chief of lab. Faculty of Medicine, Montpellier, 1959-62, asst., 1964-68; chief of works Faculty of Medicine, Brest, France, 1968-70; prof. bacteriology-virology Faculty of Medicine, Besancon, France, 1970-95; prof. emeritus Faculty of Medicine, Besancon, 1995—. Author: Molecular Mechanisms of Antibiotic Action, 1986 (Nat. Acad. Medicine award 1987). Mem. AAAS, Am. Soc. Microbiology, Brit. Soc. Antimicrobial Therapy, French Soc. Microbiology, French Nat. Acad. Medicine (corr. mem.). Avocation: lit. Office: Faculty of Medicine, Hosp J Minjoz, 25030 Besançon France

MICHELENA, GEORGINA LOURDES, chemical engineer, researcher; b. Havana, Cuba, July 19, 1964; d. Benigno Silvio Michelena and Georgina Gabina Alvarez; m. Leonardo Emilio Pacios, May 6, 1986; children: Anabel Pacios Michelena, Sandra Pacios Michelena. B in Chem. Engring., Polytech. U. Havana, Cuba, 1987; DSc, 1997. Cert. chem. engr. Rschr. Cuban Inst. Rsch. on Sugar Cane By-Products, Havana, 1987—. Author: Handbook of Sugarcane Byproducts, 1993; contbr. articles to profl. jours. Mem. N.Y. Acad. Scis. Avocations: movies, books, classical music, paintings. Office: Cuban Inst Rsch/Sugar Cane Prods, Via Blanca 804 PO Box 4026, Havana Cuba

MICHELET, JORGEN GEORG, financial executive; b. Oslo, Mar. 17, 1956; s. Christian Fredrik and Ragna Grieg (Grung) M.; m. Elisabeth Moystad, Oct. 8, 1983; children: Erica, Kristin. Lic. Oec., Hochschule St. Gallen, Switzerland, 1981; Authorized Pub. Acct., Norwegian Coll. Bus., 1983. Authorized pub. acct. Arthur Andersen & Co., Oslo, 1981-86; contr. Veidekke ASA, Oslo, 1986-90, sr. v.p. fin., 1990—. Home: Charlotte Audersensver 1B, 0374 Oslo Norway Office: Veidekke ASA, PO Box 505 Skoyen, 0214 Oslo Norway

MICHELI, ENRICO, federal official; b. Terni, Italy, May 16, 1938. Min. Pub. Works, Rome, 1998—, undersec. for the cabinet. Office: Palazzo Chigi, Piazza Colonna 370, 00100 Rome Italy*

MICHELS, RICHARD STEPHEN, microbiologist; b. Bridgeport, Conn., Dec. 27, 1951; s. Edward Joseph and Mary (Morawski) M.; m. Kathleen Bagoly (div. June 1979); 1 child, Wade Emery; m. Linda Marie Wolak, Oct. 1984; children: Steven Douglas, Lauren Elizabeth. AA, Housatonic C.C., Bridgeport, 1973; BS in Biology, So. Conn. State U., New Haven, 1975. Microbiologist Chesebrough Ponds Inc., Clinton, Conn., 1975-80; rsch. microbiologist Chesebrough Ponds Inc., Oriskany Falls, N.Y., 1980-86; mgr. lab. control ctr. Sherwood Med., Oriskany Falls, 1986-91; microbial quality assurance mgr. Sherwood, Davis, & Geck, Oriskany Falls, 1991-97, Kendall Co., Oriskany Falls; staff microbiologist Ortec Internat., N.Y.C., 1999—. Mem. ASTM, AAAS, Am. Soc. Microbiology, N.Y. Acad. Scis., Assn. for Advancement of Med. Instrumentation, Trout Unltd. (bd. dirs. 1985-91, pres. 1985, 87). Office: 3960 Broadway New York NY 10032-1543

MICHELSEN, CHRISTOPHER BRUCE HERMANN, surgeon; b. Boston, Aug. 18, 1940; s. Jost Joseph and Ingeborg Elizabeth (Dilthey) M.; m. Amy Lee; children: Heidi Elizabeth, Matthew Christopher, Joshua Jost. BA, Bowdoin Coll., 1961; MD, Columbia U., 1969. Diplomate Am. Bd. Orthop. Surgery, Am. Bd. Forensic Medicine. Intern Columbia Presbyn. Med. Ctr., N.Y.C., 1969-70, resident, 1970-71; orthop. resident N.Y. Orthop. Hosp., N.Y.C., 1971-73, jr. Anne C. Kane fellow, 1973-74, sr. Anne C. Kane fellow and hip fellow, 1974-75, traveling fellow, 1975-76; intenrat. A-O fellow, postgrad. fellow in biomechanics Case Western Res. U., N.Y.C., instr. biomed. engring.; prof. clin. orthop. surgery, orthop. surgeon Columbia Coll. Physicians and Surgeons, 1976—; chief orthop. svc. Allen Pavillion, Columbia Presbyn. Med. Ctr., 1993—, chief orthop. spine surgery svc., 1998—; chief orthop. svc. Individual Mobilization Designees Fitzsimmons Army Med. Coll., 1995—. Col. USAR, 1961—. Fellow ACS, Am. Assn. for Surgery of Trauma, Am. Orthop. Assn., N.Am. Spine Soc., Am. Acad. Orthop. Surgeons, Internat. Coll. Surgeons, N.Y. Acad. Medicine; mem. AMA, Am. Coll. Physicians Execs., Orthop. Rsch. Soc., Am. Soc. Bone and Mineral Rsch., Royal Soc. Medicine (affiliate). Home: 102 Shearwater Ct E Jersey City NJ 07305-5423 Office: 5141 Broadway New York NY 10034-1159

MICHELSTETTER, STANLEY HUBERT, lawyer; b. Milw., July 8, 1946; s. Donald Lee and Gloria (Menke) M.; m. Joyce Bladow, Apr. 29, 1972; children: Chad S., Chris E. BA in Math., U. Wis., 1968, JD, 1972. Bar: Wis. 1972, U.S. Dist. Ct. (we. dist.) Wis. 1972. Staff atty. Wis. Employment Rels. Commn., Milw., 1972-80; pvt. practice, Milw., 1980—; adminstrv. law judge, equal rights div. adminstrat. Wis. Dept Industry, Labor & Human Rels., Milw., 1992-93. Chmn. North Shore Rep. Club, Milw., 1984-86. Served to 2d lt. Wis. N.G., 1968-74. Mem. Wis. Bar Assn. (chmn. 1993), Milw. Bar Assn., Nat. Acad. Arbitrators, Indsl. Rels. Rsch. Assn. (bd. dirs. 1987—), Rotary. Republican. Jewish. Home: 1500 W Green Brook Rd Milwaukee WI 53217-1515 Office: 1568 N Farwell Ave Milwaukee WI 53202-2366 also: 601 S Lasalle St Ste M786 Chicago IL 60605-1700

MICHENFELDER, ALBERT A., lawyer; b. St. Louis, July 21, 1926; s. Albert A. and Ruth Josephine (Donahue) M.; m. Lois Barbara Sullivan, Sept. 03, 1949 (div. May 2, 1967); children: Michael J., Ann C. Michenfelder Yancey, Elizabeth D. Michenfelder Brown; m. Ramona Jo Dysart, July 12, 1968 (dec. Jan. 2, 1998); 1 child, Julie D. Michenfelder Wolfe. B of Naval Sci., Marquette U., 1946; LLB, St. Louis U., 1950. Bar: Mo. 1950, U.S. Dist. Ct. (ea. dist.) Mo. 1950, U.S. Supreme Ct. 1975. Assoc. Flynn & Challis, St. Louis, 1950-54; pvt. practice St. Louis, 1954-55; prin., chmn. Ziercher & Hocker, P.C., St. Louis, 1955—; mem. 21st Cir. Jud. Commn., St. Louis, 1981-87. Contbr. articles to profl. jours. City atty. City of Webster Groves, Mo., 1966-79; mem. John Marshall Club, St. Louis. Lt. (j.g.) USNR, 1944-47. Mem. Mo. Bar Assn., Bar. Assn. Met. St. Louis, St. Louis County Bar Assn. (pres. 1966), Westborough Country Club. Republican. Avocations: golf, tennis. Office: Ziercher and Hocker PC 231 S Bemiston Ave Saint Louis MO 63105-1914

MICHLER, MARKWART WALDEMAR, orthopedist, surgeon; b. Breslau, Silesia, Apr. 30, 1923; s. Waldemar Karl-Arthur and Leonie Frieda (Olleck) M.; student U. Breslau, 1942-44, U. Berlin, 1946-49; Dipl. in surgery, 1957, Dipl. in orthopedics, 1958, M.D., 1958; m. Inge Stemmler, Dec. 20, 1957; children: Waldemar, Karl-Friedrich; Intern, Städt. Krankenhaus Berlin Neukölln, 1950-51; resident Städt. Auguste-Viktoria-Krankenhaus Berlin-Schöneberg, 1951-56; orthopedic clinician Evangelisches Waldkrankenhaus, Berlin-Spandau, 1956-61, chief physiotherapy Orthopedic Clinic, 1958-61; sci. asst., lectr. med. history Inst. Friedrich Wilhelms U. Bonn, Fed. Republic Germany, 1961-64; lectr. Med. History Inst., U. Hamburg, Fed. Republic Germany, 1964-65, habilitation history medicine, 1965; prof. history of medicine Justus Liebig U., Giessen, Fed. Republic Germany, 1965-73, ret., 1973; pvt. practice as orthopedist and spa physician, Bad Brückenau, Fed. Republic Germany, 1974-90; dir. Inst. History of Medicine Justus Liebig U. Giessen and leader Ludwig Schunk Meml. Library, 1965-73. Served with Tank Corps, German Army, World War II. Mem. Deutsche Gesellschaft für Geschichte d Medizin d Naturwissenschaften und der Technik; Gesellschaft f Wissenschaftsgeschichte, Schweizerische Ges Geschichte d Med und d Naturwissenschaften, History of Sci. Soc., AAAS, Société Internat. d'Histoire de la Médecine, N.Y. Acad. Scis., Internat. Acad. History Medicine, Deutsche Gesellschaft für Orthopädie und Traumatologie, Société Internat. de Chirurgie Orthopédique et de Traumatologie. Author: numerous books; contbr. articles to profl. jours. Home: 36 Ernst Putz Str, D-97769 Bad Brückenau Germany

MICHLER, ROBERT E., heart surgeon; b. July 8, 1956; m. Sally Radcliffe Sandercock, May 28, 1983; children: Alexandra Keats, Sarah Radcliffe, Elizabeth Tamsin. BA magna cum laude, Harvard U., 1978; MD, Dartmouth U., 1981. Diplomate Am. Bd. Surgery, Am. Bd. Thoracic Surgery, Am. Bd. Surgery-Critical Care. Intern Columbia-Presbyn. Med. Ctr., N.Y.C., 1981-82, resident gen. surgery, 1982-86, chief resident gen. surgery, 1986-87, resident cardiothoracic surgery, 1987-88, chief resident cardiothoracic surgery, 1988-89; chief resident pediat. cardiothoracic surgery Boston Children's Hosp., Harvard Med. Sch., 1989-90, attending surgeon, 1990-97, dir. cardiac transplant svc., 1993-97; assoc. prof. surgery Columbia U., 1990-97, dir. cardiac transplantation rsch. lab., 1991-97; Karl P. Klassen prof. surgery, chief thoracic surgery Ohio State U., Columbus, 1997—; dir. cardiothoracic transplantation and rsch. Ohio State U. Med. Ctr., Columbus, 1997—, co-dir. heart and lung inst., 1997—; dir. Heart Hosp., 2000—; rsch. fellow cardiopulmonary transplantation Columbia U., Coll. Physicians and Surgeons, N.Y.C., 1984-85; presenter and lectr. in field; founder, chmn. Heart Care Internat., 1994—. Contbr. chpts. to books and articles to profl. jours. Exec. coun. mem. Second Congl. Ch., Greenwich, Conn., 1994—. Recipient Claire Lucille Pace Humanitarian award, 1996; named Person of Week, ABC World News Tonight, 1995; Leopold Schepp scholar Dartmouth Med. Sch., Hanover, N.H., 1981. Fellow ACS, Am. Coll. Cardiology, Am. Coll. Chest Physicians; mem. AMA, Am. Bd. Surgery, Am. Bd. Thoracic Surgery, Soc. Thoracic Surgeons, Internat. Soc. for Heart and Lung Transplantation, Soc. Pediat. Cardiac Surgery, Soc. Critical Care Medicine, Am. Soc. for Artificial Internal Organs, N.Y. Soc. for Thoracic Surgery, N.Y. Transplantation Soc., Riverside Yacht Club (Greenwich, Conn.). Avocations: sailing, sculling, squash, tennis. Office: Ohio State U Med Ctr Doan Hall N825 410 W 10th Ave Columbus OH 43210-1228

MICKA, JENNIFER LEIGH, university program director; b. Monroe, Mich., Nov. 25, 1973; d. Harry James Micka and Christine Marie McCollum. BEd, U. Toledo, 1996, postgrad., 1998—. Cert. spl. edn. K-12, Ohio. Spl. edn. tchr. Toledo (Ohio) Pub. Schs., 1997-98; coord. admissions recruitment U. Toledo, 1999—. Recruitment advisor Kappa Delta chpt. Chi Omega Sorority, Bowling Green State U. Mem. Nat. Assn. Student Pers. Adminstrs., Am. Coll. Pers. Assn., Higher Edn. Student Assn. (treas. 1998-99), Ohio Assn. Coll. Admission Counselors, Chi Omega, Omicron Delta Kappa, Order of Omega. E-mail: jmicka@utnet.utoledo.edu. Home: 4648 Talmadge Rd Apt 2B Toledo OH 43623-3043 Office: Univ Toledo Toledo OH 43606

MICKELSON, PHIL (PHILIP ALFRED MICKELSON), professional golfer; b. San Diego, June 16, 1970; m. Amy; 1 child, Amanda. Student, Ariz. State U., 1992. Profl. golfer PGA, 1992—. Recipient Fred Haskins award, 1990, 91, 92, Jack nicklaus award, 1990, 91, 92; won NCAA Championships, 1989, 90, 92, No. Telecom Open, 1991, 95, Buick Invitational Calif., The Internat., 1993, Mercedes Championships, 1994, Nortel Open, 1996, Phoenix Open, 1996, Byron Nelson Classic, 1996; 1st team All-Am. with Sun Devils; one of 4 collegians ever to win NCAA crown as freshman; 1st left-hander to win U.S. Amateur, 1990; 1st player in PGA history to win same tournament as amateur and profl. (No. Telecom Open); NEC World Series of Golf, 1996; Bay Hill Invitational, 1997; Sprint International, 1997; Mercedes Championships, 1998; AT&T Pebble Beach National Pro-Am, 1998, Buick Invitational, 2000, Bell South Classic, 2000, MasterCard Colonial, 2000. Office: care PGA Box 109601 100 Avenue Of Champions Palm Bch Gdns FL 33418-3653

MICKENAUTSCH, STEFFEN, dentist, consultant; b. Leipzig, Germany, May 27, 1968; s. Helmut and Renate (Müller) M.; m. Riante Wolhuter, Aug. 5, 1998; 1 child, Maxine. B, U. Leipzig, 1994. Dentist, supr. Dept. Cmty. Dentistry, Johannesburg, South Africa, 1995—; dentist, coord. German-African Assn., Johannesburg, 1996-98; oral health cons. Neemcor Logistics Ltd., Gibraltar, 1998—; coord. DAFRIG, Accra, Ghana, 1996-97. Vol. Kenyan Voluntary Devel. Assn., Nairobi, 1991-92, Ghana Red Cross Soc., Accra, 1992, German African Assn., Leipzig, 1993-96. Mem. Oral Health Alliance, S. African Fgn. Qualified Drs. Assn. Avocations: social anthropology, travel, arts and culture, geography, history. Office: Neemcor Logistics Ltd, 26 Main St, Gibraltar Gibraltar

MICKLIN, PHILIP PATRICK, science educator, consultant; b. Gig Harbor, Wash., May 8, 1938; s. Thomas Michael and Doris Mae Micklin; m. Mollie, Mar. 25, 1961 (div. 1975); 1 child: Sean Patrick; m. Constance Russell, Mar. 12, 1977; 1 child, Claire Elizabeth. BA, U. Wash., 1960, MA, 1965, PhD, 1971. Instr. Western Mich. U., Kalamazoo, 1966-67, 70-71, asst. prof. to assoc. prof., 1971-83, prof., 1983-99, emeritus, 1999; task mgr. U.S. Agency Internat. Devel., Tashkenet, Uzbekistan, 1996-97. Author: Water Management in Central Asia, 2000; editl. adv. bd. Soviet Geography and Successor Jours., 1976-99; co-editor Aral Sea Problems, 1996; contbr. articles to profl. jours. Mem. S.W. Mich. Land Trust, 1998-99, Environ. Concerns, chmn., 1974-80. With U.S. Army, 1961-62. Mem. AAAS, Assn. Am. Geographers, Auduhon Soc. Democrat. Avocations: running, nature and environmental study. E-mail: Micklin@wmich.edu. Home: 1618 Grove St Kalamazoo MI 49006-4467 Office: Western Mich U Dept Geography Kalamazoo MI 49008

MICLAT, AUGUSTO NELMIDA, JR., business executive; b. Baguio, The Philippines, Jan. 21, 1957; s. Augusto Corum and Agrinelda (Nelmida) M.; m. Thelma Reyes, Oct. 10, 1989; children: Mithilaya, Mikoel Augusto, Maya Sarani. BA in Humanities, Ateneo de Davao, The Philippines, 1978, postgrad., 1984; postgrad., U. of the Philippines, 1985. Instr. Ateneo de Davao U., 1978-85; coord. Mindanao-Sulu Pastoral Conf., Davao, 1980-85; program officer Asian Coun. for Peoples Culture, Manila, The Philippines, 1985-86; exec. editor Media Mindanao News Svc., Manila, 1985-88; co-dir. Initiatives for Internat. Dialogue, Manila, 1988-93, exec. dir., 1993—; chairperson Kulturang Atini Fedn., Inc., Davao, 1979-865, Trainors Collective, Inc., Manila, 1994-99; cons. Devel. Edn. Media Svcs., Davao, 1981-84; bd. mem. Alfredo Navarro Salanga Fedn., Manila, 1988—. Author: Breaking the Silence, 1995; editor, contbr.: Beyond the Cold War, 1992; editor, conceptualizer: Globalization: A Primer, 1997, East Timor for Beginners, 1997; editor: Burma for Beginners, 1998. Sec.-gen. Mindanao Nationalist and Dem. Opposition, The Philippines, 1984; coord. Asia-Pacific Coalition for East Timor, 1994-2000, Regional Peoples Working Group on Bimp-Eaga, 1997-2000; steering com., co-founder Alternative Asean Network on Burma, Bangkok, 1996. Mem. Nat. Press Club. Roman Catholic. Avocations: traveling, reading, music, sports, movies. Office: Initiatives Internat Dial, 27G Galaxy St G515 Hts, Matina Davao 8000, The Philippines

MICROYANNAKIS, EMMANUEL JOHN, history educator; b. Herakleion, Crete, Greece, July 19, 1935; s. John and Euterpe (Caraconst) M.; m. Theoni Christopoulou, Oct. 8, 1963; children: John, Christina, George. Grad., U. Athens, Greece, 1960, PhD, 1968; postgrad., U. Göttingen,

Germany, 1963-66. Lectr. history U. Athens, 1966-82, asst. prof., 1982-85, assoc. prof., 1985-88, prof., 1993—, chmn. dept. history and archaeology, 1989-94, 97—; head all Nat. Schs. Tourist Guides, Athens, Crete, Corfu, Rhodes, Mytilene of Lesbos, 1988—; guest prof. Greek civilization U. Taipei, Taiwan, 1995-96. Author: Hellenistic Crete, 1967, Inter-state Relations in Antiquity, 1969, Pathology of Constitutions, 1990. Fellow Hellenic Philol. Assn., Hellenic Humanistic Soc.; mem. Byzantine Music Assn. (chmn. 1974-77). Avocations: mountain climbing, ecclesiastical music. Home: 3d Septemvriou 77, 104 34 Athens Greece Office: U Athens, University Campus, 157 84 Athens Greece

MIDDELHOEK, ANDRÉ J., international organization administrator, auditor; b. The Netherlands, 1931; m. Geertruida Johanna Van den Broek; 2 children. Degree, U. Amsterdam, 1957. Various posts Netherlands Cen. Planning Bur., The Hague, 1958-66; lectr. Internat. Inst. for Social Studies, 1960-69; dep. dir. Netherlands Cen. Planning Bur., 1966-69; dir. gen. budget Ministry of Finance, 1969-77; mem. ct. of auditors The European Cmty., 1977-95, pres. ct. of auditors, 1993-95; mem. bd. dirs. Koninklijke Ned. Hoogovens N.V., Hoogovens Ijmuiden B.V., 1970-77; mem. Nat. Phys. Planning Com., 1966-77; mem., v.p. econ. policy com. European Cmty., 1969-77, mem., vice chmn. staff establishment com., 1969-77, chmn. com. for devel. of policy analysis, 1970-77, mem. extraordinary sci. coun. for govt. policy, 1972-77. Contbr. articles to profl. jours. Recipient comdr. Order of the Netherlandse Leeuw, knight Orde Van de Nederlandse Leeuw; Grand Croix Ordre Grand-Ducal de la Couronne de Chêne (Luxemburg).

MIDDELHOFF, THOMAS, publishing executive; b. Düsseldorf, Germany, Nov. 5, 1953; married; 5 children. MBA, U. Munster, 1979. Rsch. asst. Inst. Mktg. Munster U., 1980-83; mng. asst. Mohndruck Graphische Betriebe BhmH, Gütersloh, Germany, 1986; mng. dir. Elsnerdruck BmbH, Berlin, 1987, Mohndruck, 1989, Calendar Pub. Co., 1989; bd. industry divsn. Bertelsmann AG, Munster, 1990—, mem. exec. bd., head corp. devel., coord., 1994—; mem. bd. America Online Inc, 1995—; chmn., CEO Bertelsmann AG, 1997—; bd. dirs. Am. Online, Inc. Office: Bertelsmann AG, Carl-Bertelsmann-Str 270, D-33311 Gulersloh Germany Address: Bertelsmann 1540 Broadway Fl 24 New York NY 10036-4039

MIDDELL, MATTHIAS, comparative history educator, researcher; b. Leipzig, Germany, Apr. 17, 1961; s. Eike and Gudrun Middell; m. Katharina Middell. PhD in History, U. Leipzig, 1989. Asst. prof. comparative history U. Leipzig, 1989-94, gen. sec. Rsch. Ctr., 1995—; vice-dir. French Studies Ctr., U. Leipzig, 1994—. Author 3 books; editor: Deutsch-Französische Kulturbibliothek, 14 vols., 1993—, Beitraege fur Universalgeschichte und Vergleichende Gesellschaftsforschung, 19 vols., 1992—; editor-in-chief (jour.) Comparativ, 1991—. Mem. Karl-Lamprecht-Gesellschaft, Société des Etudes Robespierristes. Office: U Leipzig Ctr Advanced Stud, Augustusplatz 10/11, D-04109 Leipzig Germany

MIDDENDORF, ALICE CARTER, volunteer; b. Balt., Dec. 7, 1940; d. John William and Alice Temple (Carter) M. BA, Wellesley Coll., 1963, Oxford U., Eng., 1972. Libr. Boston Athenaeum Libr., 1963-66; editor Houghton Mifflin Co., Boston, 1966-69; bd. dirs. Balt. Zool. Soc., 1976; cons. Nat. Zoo, Washington, 1976-77, G. Ward & Assocs., Ridgefield, Conn., 1976-79; from bd. dirs. to bd. govs. Nat. Aquarium in Balt., 1976-88, sec. bd. govs., 1987-88, chmn. animal policy com., 1982-88; bd. dirs. Total Health Care (merger Constant Care and West Balt. Cmty. Health Ctrs.), Balt., 1981—; sec. bd. dirs. Total Health Care (merger Constant Care Med. Ctr. and West Balt. Constant Health Ctr.), Balt., 1990-93, 97-98; treas., 1998; adv. bd. Nat. Aquarium in Balt., 1989-94, 99—, bd. govs., 1994-99, sec. bd. govs., 1995-99; bd. dirs. Constant Care Med. Ctr., Balt., Park Heights Street Acad., Balt., sec., 1988-90; pres. Fulmar Corp., Cayman Islands, Brit. West Indies, 1991-99; pres., chmn. bd. dirs. Lystra Hill Farms, Inc., Goleta, Calif., 1996-97. Recipient Pres.'s Citation, Pres. City Coun. Balt., 1974, 76, Award of Appreciation, Mayor of Balt., 1981. Avocations: scuba, underwater photography, marine biology, malacology, travel, reading. Home and Office: 1301 Hillside Rd Stevenson MD 21153-2019

MIDDENDORF, HENRY STUMP, JR., lawyer; b. Balt., Feb. 23, 1923; s. Henry Stump and Sarah Kennedy (Boone) M. Student, McDonogh (Md.) Sch., 1934-35, Groton (Mass.) Sch., 1935-41; AB, Harvard U., 1945, JD cum laude, 1952; LLM, NYU, 1957. Bar: N.Y. 1953. Assoc. Milbank, Tweed, Hope & Hadley, N.Y.C., 1952-56, Gilbert & Segall, N.Y.C., 1956-59; pvt. practice N.Y.C., 1959—; sec., dir. The Van Waveren Corp., N.Y.C., 1959-61, M. Van Waveren & Sons, Inc., Holland, 1961-71. Editor: Law Today, 1963-69. Bd. dirs. Youth Found., 1970—, sec., 1980—; mem. N.Y. County Rep. Com., 1955-61, exec. com. 9th assembly dist., 1956-61; gen. counsel Goldwater for Pres. com., 1964; former mem., chmn. N.Y. County com. Conservative Party; former mem. State com. N.Y. Conservative Party, former mem. exec. com. 1st Lt. inf. AUS, 1945-46. Mem. ATLA, ABA, Assn. Bar City N.Y., N.Y. Bar Assn., Bronx Bar Assn., Independent Bar Assn. (pres. 1962-64, chmn. bd. govs. 1964-69), Am. Bar Found., N.Y. County Lawyers Assn., N.Y. Geneal. and Biog. Soc. (mem. heraldry com., pres. 1989-98), SR (N.Y., pres. 1996-99), Soc. Colonial Wars, Pilgrims of U.S., Union Club. Episcopalian. Address: 175 W 12th St # 15 New York NY 10011-8275

MIDDENDORF, J. WILLIAM, II, investment banker; b. Balt., Sept. 22, 1924; m. Isabelle Paine, Mar. 7, 1953; children: Frances, Amy, John W. IV, Ralph Henry. B in Naval Sci., Holy Cross Coll., 1945; AB, Harvard U., 1947; MBA, NYU, 1954; LLD (hon.), Troy State U.; LittD (hon.), Sch. of Ozarks, Am. Christian Coll.; D. Social Scis. (hon.), Netherlands-Am. Inst. Commd. ensign USN, 1945, advanced through grades to lt. (j.g.), ret., 1946; with credit dept. Chase Manhattan Bank, 1947-52; ptnr. Wood Struthers and Co., 1958-61; sr. ptnr. Middendorf, Colgate and Co., 1962-69; ambassador to The Netherlands, 1969-73; sec. USN, 1974-77; pres., CEO Fin. Gen. Bankshares, Inc., 1977-81; ambassador to Orgn. Am. States, 1981-85, European Communities, 1985-87; chmn. Middendorf & Assocs., Inc., 1989—; chmn. presdl. task force Project Econ. and Social Justice, 1986-90; mem. U.S. Del. to supervise elections in Suriname, 1988; treas. Internat. Rep. Inst. Composer 8 symphonies, 100 marches, (opera) King Richard, nat. independence march for Belize, other compositions for Latin Am. countries; guest condr. Boston Pops, St. Louis Symphony, Ind. U., others; contbr. articles to profl. jours. Mem. U.S. Olympic com., 1979-89, U.S. Olympic Selection com. for field hockey; judge field hockey Olympics, Rome, 1960; former mem. vis. com. dept. Am. paintings Met. Mus. Art, N.Y.C., vis. com. dept. Am. Art, Mus. Fine Arts, Boston; hon. v.p. Naval Hist. Found.; treas. Goldwater for Pres. com., 1962-64, Presdl. Transition com. 1968, Rep. Nat. Com., 1964-69; alt. del. for Gov. Reagan, 1980; del. State of Conn., 1964, 68, State of Va., 1996; co-chmn. Virginians for Reagan, 1980, fin. com. Va. GOP, 1980-81; coordinator internat. econ. and naval adv. com. Reagan for Pres. campaign, 1980; chmn. Congl. Boosters com., 1978-81; chmn. CIA Transition Team, 1980-81; chmn. fin. com. Pres. Reagan's 1981 Inaugural com.; trustee NavaL War Coll. Found., Heritage Found., Washington; past trustee Hoover Instn. for War Revolution and Peace, Corcoran Gallery, N.Y. Hist. Soc., Balt. Mus. Art, Greenwich Hist. Soc., Boston Symphony, Middlesex Sch., Concord, Mass., Nat. Symphony Orch., Mass. Gen. Hosp., Boys Club N.Y.; bd. electors Ins. Hall of Fame; bd. dirs. Georgetown U., John Philip Sousa Meml. Found.; chmn. bd. dirs. council statesmen Ludwig von Mises Inst.; bd. dirs. Newport Art Mus. and Mariners' Mus., Norfolk, Va.; chmn. Netherlands-Am. Amity Trust; chmn. Com. for Monetary Research and Edn. Inc.; chmn. Def. Forum Found.; former mem. com. Dept. State Fine Arts Com.; chmn. Navy League Awards com., 1977—; founding chmn. U.S. Navy Meml. Found.; past chmn. Netherlands-Am. Inst., Wolf Trap Farm Park, John Carter Brown Library Assocs., Providence, Asian Composers Expo., European Council of Boy Scouts. Recipient Superior Honor award Dept. State, 1974, Disting. Pub. Service award Dept. Def., 1975, 76, Navy Disting. Pub. Service award, 1976, Naval Disting. Service medal Republic Brazil, 1976, Ludwig von Mises Free Market award, 1985, Inter-Am. Music Council award, 1985, Edwin Franko Goldman award Am. Bandmasters Assn., 1987, Assn. Harvard Clubs Am. award, Disting. Service medal Purdue Univ. Bands, Netherlands Soc. Phila. Gold medal, Good Citizenship medal Nat. Soc. SAR, Medal of Honor, Midwest Nat. Band Assn., Invest in Am. Am. Eagle award, 1988, Eugene J. Keogh Disting. Pub. Svc. award NYU, 1989, Nat. Commendation award Pres.' Coun. Phys. Fitness and Sports, 1989, Leadership award Am. Friends of Turkey, 1989, Adm. Arleigh Burke Leadership award, 1998, Arleigh Burke award 1998; decorated Grand Master Order of Orange Nassau, Netherlands, Order of Arab Republic of Egypt, 1979, Grand Master of Order of Naval Merit, Republic Brazil, 1974; named Alumnus of Yr. NYU, 1978; Nat. Masters Sculling champion, 1979, Gold medal The Holland Soc. Mem. Am. Antiquarian Soc., Harvard Alumni Assn. (permanent class com. 1947), Soc. Cin. (hon.), ASCAP, Walpole Soc., Co. Mil. Historians, Mil. Order Loyal Legion, SAR, Soc. of SAR, Field Hockey Assn. Am. (past pres., player/mgr. nat. team 1963), U.S. Naval Inst., Navy League. Clubs: Angler's, Downtown Assn., Union (N.Y.C.); Army-Navy, Capitol Hill, Met., Potomac Boat (Washington); Sakonnet Golf (Little Compton, R.I.); Somerset (Boston). Office: Middendorf & Assocs Inc PO Box 159 Great Falls VA 22066-0159

MIDDLEBROOKS, EDDIE JOE, environmental engineer; b. Crawford County, Ga., Oct. 16, 1932; s. Robert Harold and Jewell LaVerne (Dixon) M.; m. Charlotte Linda Hardy, Dec. 6, 1958; 1 child, Linda Tracey. BCE, U. Fla., 1956, MS, 1960; PhD, Miss. State U., 1966. Registered profl. engr., Ariz., Miss., Utah; registered land surveyor, Fla. Asst. san. engr. USPHS, Cin., 1956-58; field engr. T.T. Jones Constrn. Co., Atlanta, 1958-59; grad. teaching asst. U. Fla., 1959-60; research asst. U. Ariz., 1960-61; asst. prof., then assoc. prof. Miss. State U., 1962-67; research engr., asst. dir. San. Engrng. Research Lab., U. Calif.-Berkeley, 1968-70; prof. Utah State U., Logan, 1970-82, dean Coll. Engrng., 1974-82; Newman chair natural resources engrng. Clemson U., 1982-83; provost, v.p. acad. affairs Tenn. Tech. U., 1983-88; provost, v.p. acad. affairs U. Tulsa, 1988-90, prof. chem. engrng., 1988-92, Trustees prof. chem. engrng., 1990-92, acting pres., 1990; prof. civil engrng. U. Nevada, Reno, 1992-97; mem. nat. drinking water adv. council EPA, 1981-83; cons. EPA, UN Indsl. Devel. Orgn., Calif. Water Resources Control Bd., also numerous indsl. and engrng. firms. Author: Modeling the Eutrophication Process, 1974, Statistical Calculations-How To Solve Statistical Problems, 1976, Biostimulation and Nutrient Assessment, 1976, Water Supply Engineering Design, 1977, Lagoon Information Source Book, 1978, Industrial Pollution Control, Vol. 1: Agro-Industries, 1979, Wastewater Collection and Treatment: Principles and Practices, 1979, Water Reuse, 1982, Wastewater Stabilization Lagoon Design, Performance and Upgrading, 1982, Reverse Osmosis Treatment of Drinking Water, 1986, Pollution Control in the Petrochemicals Industry, 1987, Natural Systems for Waste Management and Treatment, 1988, 2d edit., 1995; mem. editl. adv. bd. Lewis Pubs. Inc., Environment Internat., Environ. Abstracts; contbr. tech. articles to profl. jours. Fellow ASCE; mem. AAAS, Water Environment Fedn. (dir. 1979-81, 91-92), Eddy medal 1969), Assn. Environ. Engrng. Profs. (pres. 1974), Utah Water Pollution Control Assn. (pres. 1976), Internat. Assn. on Water Quality, Am. Soc. Engrng. Edn., Am. Acad. Environ. Engrs. (diplomate, trustee 1992-95, v.p. 1995, pres. 1997-98), Sigma Xi, Omicron Delta Kappa, Phi Kappa Phi (Disting. mem.), Tau Beta Pi, Sigma Tau. Home and Office: 360 Blackhawk Ln Lafayette CO 80026-9392

MIDDLEDITCH, DARREN PAUL, economist; b. London, May 20, 1971; s. Frank Eric and Sylvia Wendy (Young) M. BSc in Econ. and Statistics, U. Keele, 1992; MPhil in Econ., St. Edmund Hall, Oxford, Eng., 1993; MSc in Econ., U. Coll., London, 1995. Rsch. asst. James Capel Strategy, London, 1993-94; economist Carnegie Emerging Markets Ltd, London, 1995-97; economist, editor Middle East and North Africa The Economist Intelligence Unit, London, 1997-2000; freelance econ. cons. EconomistOnline.com, 2000—; nominee mem. Royal Inst. Internat. Affairs. Avocations: current affairs, theatre, cinema, fine foods & restaurants, consumer rights. Home: 141 Colson Rd Loughton, Essex 1G10 3QY, England

MIDDLEMISS, DEREK NEIL, pharmacologist, research scientist; b. Sunderland, England, Mar. 1, 1948; s. Hugh and Dorothy (Herring) M.; m. Marilyn Scott, Aug. 8, 1970 (div. Sept. 1999); children: Aimee Louise, Lucie Kate, Jennie Elisabeth. BA in Chemistry, York U., England, 1969; PhD in Chemistry, U. Newcastle, England, 1973; DS, York U., 1993. Biochem. pharm. ICI Pharms., Macclsfield, England, 1975-82; sr. pharm. Merrell-Dow, Strasbourg, France, 1982-85; sr. group leader G.D. Searle, St. Louis, 1985-87; assoc. dir. MSD, England, 1987-93; group dir. rsch. Smith Kline Beecham, England, 1993—; prof. U. Nottingham, England, 1995—. Contbr. articles to profl. jours. Mem. Brit. Pharm. Soc., Serotonin Club. Avocations: cooking, reading, music, drinking, walking. Office: Smithkline Beechamh, New Frontiers Sci Park, Harlow England

MIDDLETON, ANTHONY WAYNE, JR., urologist, educator; b. May 6, 1939; s. Anthony Wayne and Dolores Caravena (Lowry) M.; m. Carol Samuelson, Oct. 23, 1970; children: Anthony Wayne, Suzanne, Kathryn, Jane, Michelle. BS, U. Utah, 1963; MD, Cornell U., 1966. Intern U. Utah Hosps., Salt Lake City, 1966-67; resident in urology Mass. Gen. Hosp., Boston, 1970-74; practice urology Middleton Urol. Assocs., Salt Lake City, 1974—; mem. staff LDS Hosp., chmn. divsn. urology, 1995—; chmn. divsn. urology Salt Lake Regional Med. Ctr., 1977-79, 84-86; assoc. clin. prof. surgery U. Utah Med. Coll., 1977—; vice-chmn. bd. govs. Utah Med. Self-Ins. Assn., 1980-81, 96—, chmn., 1985-87; chmn. med. adv. bd. Uroquest Co., 1996-99; med. dir. Uromed, prostate microwave co., 1999—. Editor: (monthly publ.) AACU-FAX, 1992—; assoc. editor Millenial Star Brit. LDS mag., 1960-61; contbr. articles to profl. jours. Bd. dirs. Utah chpt. Am. Cancer Soc., 1978-86; bishop, later stake presidency Ch. Jesus Christ Latter-day Saints; vice chmn. Utah Med. Polit. Action Com., 1978-81, chmn., 1981-83; chmn. Utah Physicians for Reagan, 1983-84; del. Utah State Rep. Conv., 2000; mem. U. Utah Coll. Medicine Dean's Search Com., 1983-84; bd. dirs. Utah Symphony, 1985—, Primary Children's Found., 1989-96; mem. Utah Crime Reparations Bd., 2000—. Capt. USAF, 1968-70. Mem. ACS, AMA (alt. del. to Ho. of Dels. 1987-88, 89-92, 94, 96-98, del. 1998—), Utah Med. Assn. (pres. 1987-88, disting. svc. award 1993), Am. Urologic Assn. (socioecons. com. 1987-90, chmn. western sect. socioecons. com. 1989-90; western sect. health policy com. chmn. 1990—, pres. elect western sect. 1999-2000), Salt Lake County Med. Assn. (sec. 1965-67, pres. liaison com. 1980-81, pres.-elect 1981-83, pres. 1984), Utah Urol. Assn. (pres. 1976-77), Salt Lake Surg. Soc. (treas. 1977-78), Am. Assn. Clin. Urologists (bd. dirs. 1989-90, nat. pres.-elect 1990-91, pres. 1991-92, nat. bd. chmn. urologic polit. action com. UROPAC 1992-98, Disting. Svc. award 2000), Phi Beta Kappa, Alpha Omega Alpha, Beta Theta Pi (chpt. pres. Gamma Beta 1962). Republican. Home: 2798 Chancellor Pl Salt Lake City UT 84108-2835 Office: 1060 East 1st South Salt Lake City UT 84102-1520

MIDDLETON, DAVID, physicist, applied mathematician, educator; b. N.Y.C., Apr. 19, 1920; s. Charles Davies Scudder and Lucile (Davidson) M.; m. Nadea Butler, May 26, 1945 (div. 1971); children: Susan Terry, Leslie Butler, David Scudder Blakeslee, George Davidson Powell; m. Joan Bartlett Reed, 1971; children: Christopher Hope, Andrew Bartlett, Henry H. Reed. Grad., Deerfield Acad., 1938; AB summa cum laude, Harvard U., 1942, AM, 1945, PhD in Physics, 1947. Tchg. fellow electronics Harvard U., Cambridge, Mass., 1942, spl. rsch. assoc. radio rsch. lab., 1942-45, NSF predoctoral fellow physics, 1945-47, rsch. fellow electronics, 1947-49, asst. prof. applied physics, 1949-54; cons. physicist Cambridge, 1954—, Concord, Mass., 1957-71, N.Y.C., 1971—; adj. prof. elec. engring. Columbia U., 1960-61; adj. prof. applied physics and comm. theory Rensselaer Poly. Inst., Hartford Grad. Ctr., 1961-70; adj. prof. communication theory U. R.I., 1966—; adj. prof. math. scis. Rice U., 1979-89; U.S. del. internat. conf. Internat. Radio Union, Lima, Peru, 1975; lectr. NATO Advanced Study Inst., Grenoble, France, 1964, Copenhagen, 1980, Luneburg, Germany, 1984; mem. Naval Rsch. Adv. Com., 1970-77; mem., cons. Inst. Def. Analyses; mem. sci. adv. bd. Supercomputing Rsch. Ctr., 1987-91; cons. physicist since 1946, orgns. including Johns Hopkins U., SRI Internat., Rand Corp., USAF, Cambridge Rsch. Ctr., Comm. Satellite Corp., Lincoln Lab., NASA, Raytheon, Sylvania, Sperry-Rand, Office Naval Rsch., Applied Rsch. Labs., U. Tex., GE, Honeywell Transp. Sys. Ctr. of Dept. Transp., Dept. Commerce Office of Telecom., NOAA, Office Telecom. Policy of Exec. Office Pres., Nat. Telecom. and Info. Adminstrn., Sci. Applications Inc. (SAIC), Naval Undersea Warfare Ctr., Lawrence Livermore Nat. Labs., Planning Rsch. Corp., Applied Physics Labs. U. Wash., 1992—, Kildare Corp., 1995—, Karmanos Cancer Inst., 1997—, others. Author: Introduction to Statistical Communication Theory, 1960, 3d edit., 1996, Russian edit. Soviet Radio Moscow, 2 vols., 1961, 62, Topics in Communication Theory, 1965, 87, Russian edit., 1966; sci. editor English edit. Statistical Methods in Sonar (V.V. Ol'shevskii), 1978; mem. editl. bd. Info. and Control, Advanced Serials in Electronics and Cybernetics, 1972-82; contbr. articles to tech. jours. Recipient award (with W.H. Huggins) Nat. Electronics Conf., 1956; Wisdom award of honor, 1970; First prize 3d Internat. Symposium on Electromagnetic Compatibility Rotterdam, Holland, 1979; awards U.S. Dept. Commerce, 1978. Fellow AAAS, IEEE (life, awards 1977, 79), Am. Phys. Soc., Explorers Club, Acoustical Soc. Am., N.Y. Acad. Scis., Electromagnetics Acad. MIT; mem. Am. Math. Soc., Nat. Acad. Engring., Author's Guild Am., Harvard Club (N.Y.C.), Cosmos Club (Washington), Dutch Treat (N.Y.C.), Phi Beta Kappa, Sigma Xi. Achievements include research in radar, telecommunications, underwater acoustics, oceanography, seismology, systems analysis, electromagnetic compatibility, communication theory; pioneering research in statistical communication theory. Office: MIND 48 Garden St Cambridge MA 02138-1561 also: 127 E 91st St New York NY 10128-1601

MIDDLETON, ELLEN LONG, family nurse practitioner, educator; b. Danville, Pa., June 14, 1954; d. Samuel Murray and Dorothy Morgan (Wasley) Long; m. Jeffrey Long Middleton, Sept. 5, 1981; children: Matthew Long, Andrew Long, Douglas Long, Samuel Long. BS, U. Vt., 1976; MN, U. Wash., 1982; postgrad., Boston Coll., 1995—. Cert. family nurse practitioner. Nurse practitioner emergency dept. Hosp. of U. Pa., Phila., 1985-88, nursing dir. admission evaluation ctr., 1988-90; nursing dir. Family Practice Clinic Family Health Svcs., Worcester, Mass., 1990-94; family nurse practitioner U. Mass. Meml. Health Care, 1990—; instr. Boston Coll., 1994-98; co-project dir. MassHealth Workforce Devel. Plan U. Mass. Med. Sch., 1998—; nursing fellow Children's Hosp. of Boston, 1999-2000; lectr. U. Pa., 1985-89. Recipient Nat. Rsch. Svc. award Nat. Inst. Nursing Rsch., 1997-2000. Mem. Sigma Theta Tau.

MIDDLETON, GEORGE, JR., clinical child psychologist; b. Houston, Feb. 26, 1923; s. George and Bettie (McCrary) M.; m. Margaret MacLean, Nov. 17, 1953. BA in Psychology, Birmingham-Southern Coll., 1948; MA in Psychology, U. Ala., Tuscaloosa, 1951; PhD in Clin. Psychology, Pa. State U., 1958. Lic. psychologist, La.; diplomate Am. Coll. Forensic Examiners, Am. Bd. Psychol. Specialities. Asst. clin. psychology Med. Coll. Ala., Birmingham, 1950-52; dir. dept. psychology Bryce Hosp., Tuscaloosa, 1952-54; instr. counseling Coll. Bus. Adminstrn. Pa. State U., 1956-58; asst. prof. spl. edn. McNeese State U., 1962-65, assoc. prof. spl. edn., 1962-65; dir. La. Gov.'s Program for Gifted Children, 1963—; prof. spl. edn. McNeese State U., 1965-73, prof. psychology, 1973-74; pvt. practice clin. psychology and neuropsychology, 1974—; cons. psychologist Calcasieu Parish Sch. Bd., 1975—; vis. scholar U. Victoria, BC, Can., 1970-71. Mem. Am. Psychol. Assn., Nat. Acad. Neuropsychology, Internat. Neuropsychol. Soc., La. Psychol. Assn. (pres. 1973-74), La. Sch. Psychol. Assn., S.W. La. Psychol. Assn. (pres. 1965, 73, 84), La. State Bd. Examiners Psychologists (chmn. 1977-78), Coun. for Exceptional Children, Am. Coll. Forensic Examiners, 1996. Assn. for the Gifted. Episcopalian. Home and Office: 2001 Southwood Dr Ste A Lake Charles LA 70605-4139

MIDDLETON, JAMES BOLAND, lawyer; b. Columbus, Ga., Aug. 19, 1934; s. Riley Kimbrough and Annie Ruth (Boland) M.; 1 child, Cynthia. BA in Psychology, Ga. State U., 1964; JD, Woodrow Wilson Coll. Law, 1972. Bar: Ga. 1972, U.S. Patent Office. Draftsman, paralegal and office mgr. to patent atty. Atlanta, 1955-68; draftsman, paralegal and office mgr. Jones & Thomas, Atlanta, 1968-72, assoc., 1972-76; pvt. practice intellectual property Decatur, Ga., 1976-98; ret., 1998. Mem. editl. bd. Atlanta Lawyer, 1973-82, assoc. editor, 1978-81, editor-in-chief, 1981-82. Dir. arts coun. Unitarian-Universalist Congregation Atlanta, 1989-91; bd.d irs. Unitarian-Universalist Endowment Fund, 1993-96, vice chair, 1994-95, sec., 1995-96; bd. dirs., sec. Decatur Arts Alliance, 1990-94. With U.S. Army, 1957-59. Mem. ABA, Am. Intellectual Property Law Assn., Am. Arbitration Assn. (comml. panel 1983-94), DeKalb Bar Assn., State Bar Ga. (editl. bd. jour. 1985-92, patent trademark and copyright sect. 1972-2000, chmn. 1982-83, pub. rels. com. 1982-88), Fed. Cir. Bar Assn. Office: PO Box 1968 Decatur GA 30031-1968

MIDDLETON, JOHN ALBERT, retired communications executive; b. Bradford, Yorkshire, Eng., Mar. 20, 1915; came to U.S., 1922; s. Albert Henry and Priscilla (Lambert) Ml; m. Marjorie Frances Crossett, May 29, 1942; children: John Gary, Pamela Mary, Gregory Chester, Susan Jeanne. Grad. H.S., Manchester Ctrl. H.S., Manchester, 1934. Repair supr. New Eng. Telephone, Claremont, N.H., 1946-77; ret., 1977. City councilor, Claremont, 1986-94, asst. mayor, 1987-88, 90, 93-94, mayor, 1991; state rep., Concord, N.H., 1989-92; Justice of the Peace, N.H., 1990—; vice-chair fin. Sullivan County Delegation, N.H., 1989-92; mem. Sullivan County Econ. Devel. Coun., 1986-95; mem. Claremont Indsl. Devel. Authority, 1994, chmn. traffic com., 1987-90; chmn. health com., Claremont, 1993-94; mem. strategic planning com. Claremont Sch. Dist., 1994-95; sr. warden Union Ch., Claremont; grand marshall Independence Day Parade, July 4, 1997. With U.S. Army, 1942-46, PTO. Mem. VFW (life), Am. Legion (life), Am. Vets. (life), Shrine Legion of Honor (life), Hist. Soc. (writer historical document Civil War Tablets at City Hall 1987), Telephone Pioneers Am. (pres. 1985-86, 95), Anniversary Lodge (charter), William Pitt Tavern Lodge (charter), Sullivan Hugh-De Payens (treas. 1979-89), Hiram Lodge (Master Hiram # 9, 1963,83, 84, 85, 86, sec. 1987-89), Masons (Maj. Gen. John Sulivan medal, Disting. Svc. award 1986, Cheshire/Webb chpt. # 4 High Priest 1987-88, Columbian/St. Johns chpt. # 2 master 1983-90). Republican. Episcopalian. Avocation: woodworking. Home: 4 S Park St Claremont NH 03743-2842

MIDDLETON, SIR PETER (EDWARD), bank executive; b. Apr. 2, 1934; m. Valerie Ann Lindup, 1964; 2 children (1 dec.); m. Constance Owen, 1990. BA, Sheffield U., England, DLitt (hon.), 1984; student, Bristol U., England. Sr. info. officer HM Treasury, 1962, prin., 1964; asst. dir. Ctr. for Adminstrv. Studies, 1967-69; private sec. Chancellor of the Exchequer, 1969-72; press sec. Treasury, 1972-75; head Monetary Policy Divsn., 1975, undersecretary, 1976, dep. sec., 1980-83, permanent sec., 1983-91; dep. chmn., bd. dirs. GCB (formerly KCB), 1989-98; chmn. BZW Barclays Bank, 1991-98; dir. Bass Plc., 1992—; chmn. Barclays Bank, 1998—, United Utilities, 1993—; dir. Barclays Globe Investors, 1997—; adv. bd. Nat. Econ Rsch. Assocs., 1991; exec. com. Ctr. Econ. Policy Rsch.; vis. fellow Nuffield Coll., Oxford, Eng., 1981-89. Chmn. Inst. Contemporary Brit. History, 1992—; mem. coun. Manchester (Eng.) Bus. Sch., 1985-92, chancellor Sheffield U., 1984-91; gov. London Bus. Sch., 1984-90, Ditchley Found., 1985—, NIESR, 1991—; dir. English Chamber Orch. and Music Soc., 1984-91. Mem. Civil Svc. Sailing Assn. (commodore 1984-92), fin. reporting coun. Office: Barclays Bank Plc, 54 Lombard St, London EC3P 3AH, England

MIDGLEY, JOHN MORTON, pharmaceutical educator, researcher, consultant; b. York, Eng., July 14, 1937; s. John Wilfred and Evelyn May (Grayson) M.; m. Jean Mary Tillyer, July 17, 1965; children: Duncan Simon, Mark Richard. BSc in Pharmacy with 1st class honors, U. Manchester, Eng., 1959, MSc in Pharmacy, 1962; PhD in Pharmacy, U. London, 1965. Asst. lectr. Sch. Pharmacy U. London, 1962-65, lectr., 1965-73, sr. lectr., 1973-83; prof. U. Strathclyde, Glasgow, Scotland, 1984—, chmn., head dept. pharmacy, 1985-90, prof. emeritus, 1999; rsch. assoc. MIT, Cambridge, 1965-66; cons., 1967—; vis. prof. U. Fla., 1978-83, 85-89, U. Punjab, India, 1981, U. Lodz, Poland, 1985, U. Alexandria, Egypt, 1987-88; hon. prof. China Pharm. U., Nanjing, 1987—; sci. engring. rsch. coun. Engring. & Phys. Scis. Rsch. Coun., 1980—; mem. Com. on Rev. Medicine, 1984-92; mem. Com. on Safety of Medicines, 1990—; mem. Br. Pharmacopoeia Commn., 1984—, chair com. C., 1984—, com. L., 1991—, vice chair com. B., 1985—; U.K. del. to European Pharmacopoeia Commn., 1998—; mem. European Panel Experts on Human Medicines, 1995; mem. European Pharmacopoeia Commn. group experts IOB. Contbr. numerous articles to profl. jours. Decorated Officer of the Most Excellent Order Brit. Empire, 1998. Fellow Royal Pharm. Soc. Gt. Britain, Royal Soc. Chemistry. Avocations: gardening, music, fly fishing, fisheries management, golf. Home: 116 Old Greenock Rd, Bishopton PA7 5BB, Scotland Office: U Strathclyde Dept Pharm, SIBS 27 Taylor St, Glasgow G4 0NR, Scotland

MIDKIFF, KIMBERLY ANN, paralegal; b. Kingsport, Tenn., Nov. 27, 1958; d. Harold Douglas and Mary Lou (Carden) M. Student, U. Tenn., 1976-80, 94—. Cert. legal asst. Nat. Assn. Legal Assts. Legal sec. Gilreath & Rowland, Knoxville, Tenn., 1981-83, Tenn. State Atty. Gen.'s Office, Knoxville, 1983-84, Bond, Carpenter & O'Connor, Knoxville, 1984; paralegal Gilreath & Assocs., Knoxville, 1984-89, Lewis, King, Krieg, Waldrop & Catron, P.C., Knoxville, 1989—. Active Westminster Presbyn. Ch., Knoxville. Mem. Nat. Assn. Legal Assts., Tenn. Paralegal Assn., Knoxville Paralegal Assn., Delta Gamma Alumnae Assn., Golden Key Nat. Honor

Soc., Phi Kappa Phi, Phi Alpha Theta. Democrat. Presbyterian. Avocations: vocal and piano music, horseback riding, reading, theater, hiking. Office: Lewis King Krieg Waldrop & Catron PC One Centre Square 5th Fl 620 Market St Knoxville TN 37902-2231

MIDLER, BETTE, singer, entertainer, actress; b. Honolulu, Dec. 1, 1945; m. Martin von Haselberg, 1984; 1 child, Sophie. Student, U. Hawaii. Debut as actress film Hawaii, 1965; mem. cast Fiddler on the Roof, N.Y.C., 1966-69, Salvation, N.Y.C., 1970, Tommy, Seattle Opera Co., 1971; nightclub concert performer on tour, U.S., from 1972; appearance Palace Theatre, N.Y.C., 1973, Radio City Music Hall, 1993; TV appearances include The Tonight Show, Bette Midler: Old Red Hair is Back, 1978, Gypsy, 1993 (Golden Globe award best actress in a mini-series or movie made for television 1994, Emmy nomination, Lead Actress - Special, 1994), Seinfeld, 1996, Diva Las Vegas, 1997, Murphy Brown, 1998; appeared Clams on The Half-Shell Revue, N.Y.C., 1975; recs. include The Divine Miss M, 1972, Bette Midler, 1973, Broken Blossom, 1977, Live at Last, 1977, The Rose, 1979, Thighs and Whispers, 1979, Songs for the New Depression, 1979, Divine Madness, 1980, No Frills, 1984, Mud Will Be Flung Tonight, 1985, Beaches (soundtrack), 1989, Some People's Lives, 1990; motion picture appearances include Hawaii, 1966, The Rose, 1979 (Academy award nomination best actress 1979), Divine Madness, 1980, Jinxed, 1982, Down and Out in Beverly Hills, 1986, Ruthless People, 1986, Outrageous Fortune, 1987, Oliver and Company (voice), 1988, Big Business, 1988, Beaches, 1988, Stella, 1990, Scenes From a Mall, 1991, For the Boys, 1991 (Academy award nomination best actress 1991), Hocus Pocus, 1993, Get Shorty, 1995, The First Wives Club, 1996, That Old Feeling, 1997, Get Bruce, 1999, Isn't She Great, 1999; appeared in cable TV (HBO) prodn. Bette Midler's Mondo Beyondo, 1988; author: A View From A Broad, 1980, The Saga of Baby Divine, 1983. Recipient After Dark Ruby award, 1973; Grammy awards, 1973, 1990; spl. Tony award, 1973; Emmy award for NBC Spl., Ol' Red Hair is Back, 1978; 2 Golden Globe awards for The Rose, 1979, Golden Globe award for The Boys, 1991; Emmy award The Tonight Show appearance, 1992. Fax: 818-866-5871. Office: c/o All Girl Prodns 100 Universal City Plz Universal City CA 91608 also: c/o Warner Bros Records 3300 Warner Blvd Burbank CA 91505

MIDYA, PALLAB, electrical engineer. BTech with honors, Indian Inst. Tech., Kharagpur; MS in Elec. Engring., Syracuse U., 1990; PhD in Elec. Engring., U. Ill., 1995. Grad. rsch. asst. Syracuse (N.Y.) U., 1988-90; grad. rsch./tchg. asst. dept. elec. and computer engring. U. Ill., Urbana-Champaign, 1990-95; intern IBM/T.J. Watson Rsch. Labs., Yorktown Heights, N.Y., 1992; sr. engr., staff engr., sr. staff engr. IC Design Lab./Motorola Corp. Rsch. Labs., 1995—. Contbr. articles to profl. jours.; patentee in field. Mem. IEEE (sr.), AES, Sigma Xi, Eta Kappa Nu. E-mail: midya@ieee.org. Address: 929 Casey Ct Apt 6 Schaumburg IL 60173-5243

MIEGEL, WOLFGANG HERBERT PAUL, civil engineer, educator; b. Berlin, Germany, Jan. 4, 1952; s. Herbert and Hildegard (Sasse) M.; m. Ellinor Trzeciok, Dec. 11, 1981; children: Marlen, Maximilian. Abitur, Waldoberschule, Berlin, 1972; engr., Tech. Univ., Berlin, 1979. Mgmt. Harzwasserwerke, Hildesheim, Germany, 1979-80, Firms of Pipeline Bldgs., Hamburg, Germany, 1980-86, Stadtentwaesserung, Hamburg, Germany, 1986-90; mng. dir. Building Auth., Norderstedt, Germany, 1990-92; prof. U. Applied Scis., Hamburg, 1993—; mgr. Engr. Office IWM, Hamburg, 1993—. Co-author: Rehabilitation of Waste Water Pipes with Relining, 1994, The Glassy Subsoil, 1997; inventor in field; co-author: German Inst. of Standard Specifications DIN 18319, 1992, LB085, 1997. Recipient First place award Youth Rsch., 1972. Mem. Hamburg Engring. Assn., German Soc. for Trenches Tech. (adv. com.), engring. Soc. Avocation: sailing. Office: Engring Office IWM, Grotenbleken 8, D 22391 Hamburg Germany

MIEHLING, KLAUS, composer, harpsichord player, musicologist; b. Stuttgart, Germany, Aug. 24, 1963. Diploma in music, Schola Cantorum Basiliensis, Basel, Switzerland, 1988; DMus, Albert Ludwigs U., Freiburg, Germany, 1993. Author: Das Tempo in der Musik von Barock und Vorklassik, 1993; composer numerous compositions including Requiem, 1987, Psalmi Poenitentiales, 1996, also Lieder, sonatas and suites, concertos for instruments including recorder, violin, viola da gamba, harpsichord. Mem. Tonkunstler Verband Baden Wurttemberg, Gesellschaft fur Musikforschung. Home: Friedrichring 23, D-79098 Freiburg Baden, Germany

MIELE, RUDOLPH, manufacturing executive; b. Gütersloh, Germany, Nov. 4, 1929. Ptnr., Miele & Cie. GmbH & Co., Gütersloh. mem. adminstrn. bd. Sparkasse Gütersloh. Co-pres., owner Miele & Cie Gmbtt & Co., Gütersloh, Germany. Mem. Industrialists Assn. (chmn. Gütersloh dist.). Home: Thesingallee 8, D-4830 Gütersloh Germany Office: Miele & Cie GmbH & Co, Carl Miele Str 29, D-33332 Gütersloh Germany*

MIELI-VERGANI, GIORGINA, physician; b. Como, Italy, Aug. 19, 1946; arrived in Eng., 1977; d. Walter M. and Liderica Salina; m. Diego Vergani, Aug. 24, 1972. MD, U. Milan, 1971, Specialist in Immunology, 1977; Specialist in Paediats., Joint Com. on Higher Med. Edn., London, 1985; PhD, London U., 1985. Prof. Paediat. Hepatology, London U., 1994. House officer dept. medicine and surgery U. Hosp. Policlinico, Milan, 1971-73; sr. house officer dept. pediats. Milan U., 1971-73, registrar dept. pediats., 1973-75, registrar dept. pediat. dermatology, 1973-75, lectr. dept. pediats., 1975-76; rsch. fellow dept. child health and liver unit King's Coll. Hosp., London, 1977-79, locum clin. rsch. asst. liver unit, 1979-80, clin. rsch. asst. liver unit, 1980-81, Michael McGough Found. lectr. pediat. hepatology dept. child health, hon. sr. registrar, 1981-85, sr. lectr. pediat. hepatology dept. child health, hon. cons. pediatrician, 1985-94, prof. pediat. hepatology dept. child health, hon. cons. pediatrician, 1994—, svc. head pediat. liver/ITU svcs., 1992—, dir. Supra Regional Pediat. Liver Svc., 1995—. Contbr. 30 chpts. to med. books, 203 papers, revs., editls. to med. jours. Fellow Royal Coll. Physicians, Royal Coll. Paediatric and Child Health. Roman Catholic. Avocations: music, cycling, visual art, gardening, travel. Office: U London Kings Coll Hosp, Dept Child Health Denmark, Hill London SE5 9RS, England

MIENO, TETSU, physicist, educator; b. Ooita, Kyushu, Japan, June 24, 1956; s. Hiroshi and Miyoko (Mori) M.; m. Mie Goto; children: Satoshi, Midori. BS, Shizuoka (Japan) U., 1979; M in Engring., Tohoku U., Sendai, Japan, 1981, D in Engring., 1984. Rsch. assoc. dept. electronic engring. Tohoku U., Sendai, 1984-87; rsch. assoc. dept. physics Shizuoka U., 1987-92, assoc. prof. dept. physics, 1992-99, prof. dept. physics, 1999—. Author: Double Layers and Other Nonlinear Potential Structures in Plasma; contbr. articles to profl. jours. Mem. Red Cross Sect. Japan, Shizuoka, 1992—. Grantee Ministry Edn.-Japan, 1995-96, 98—, Nat. Inst. Space Sci., Japan, 1995-99. Mem. Phys. Soc. Japan, Japan Soc. Applied Physics (organizer Plasma Electronics br. 1994-95, 97-98), Japan Soc. Plasma Sci., Japan Electronics Soc. (mem. com. of next age plasma tech. 1996-98), Chem. Soc. Japan (com. mem. Fullerene Rsch. Assn.). Avocations: bicycling, hiking, reading, computers. Office: Shizuoka U Dept Physics, 836 Ooya, Shizuoka 422-8529, Japan

MIENO, YASUSHI, Japanese central banker; b. Tokyo, Mar. 17, 1924; s. Masaru and Fumiko Mieno; m. Kazuko Mori, 1951; 2 children. Student, U. Tokyo. With Bank of Japan, Tokyo, 1947—, dir. dept. policy planning, 1973-75, dir. dept. mkt. ops., 1975-78, exec. dir., 1978-84, sr. dep. gov., 1984-89, gov., chair policy bd., 1989-94. Avocations: reading, walking, art. Office: care Bank of Japan 2-1-1, Hongoku-cho Nihonbashi, Chuo-ku Tokyo 100-8630, Japan

MIERMONT, JACQUES GEORGES JEAN, psychiatrist, researcher; b. Sancoins, Cher, France, Nov. 9, 1946; s. Marc and Cecile (Rausis) M.; m. Dominique Grente, Oct. 30, 1971; children: Gregory, Aurelie. MD, Med. Faculty, Clermont-Ferrand, France, 1974; psychiatrist, Paris VI U., 1976; univ. doctor law-economy-scis., U. Aix-Marseille, 1993, rsch. dir. habilitation, 1993. Intern Psychiat. Hosp., Paris, 1974-77; med. asst. Psychiat. Hosp., Villejuif, France, 1982-87; psychiatrist Psychiatre des Hosp., Villejuif, 1987—; assoc. rsch. dir. Groupe Rsch. L'Adaptation, Systemique et la Complexite Econ., Aix en Provence, France, 1993—; pvt. practice psychotherapist, psychoanalyst and family therapist, Paris, 1977—; trainer family therapy Ctr. d'Étude et de Rsch. sur la Famille, Paris, 1979—; coord. Family Therapy Establishments Fedn., Villejuif, 1995—. Author: The Dictionary of Family Therapy, 1987, English edit., 1995, Ecology of Relationships, 1993, The Autonomous Man, 1995, Psychosis and Family Therapy, 1997, Contemporary Psychotherapies: History, Evolution, Prospect, 2000, The Tricks of Mind, or the Mysteries of Complexity, 2000. Mem. Soc. Française de Therapie Familiale (founder, pres. 1993—), European Family Therapy Assn. (founder), L'Evolution Psychiatrique (titular mem.). Avocations: piano, do-it-yourself activities. Home: 65-67 Ave Gambetta, 75020 Paris France Office: Fedn Svcs Family Therapy, 80 Rue de Verdun, 94800 Villejuif France

MIERNOWSKI, JAN, foreign language educator; b. Warsaw, Poland, Apr. 24, 1959; s. Stanislaw and Ewa (Fedorów) M.; m. Ewa Filipczyńska, June 16, 1979; children: Marysia, Tomek, Michal. M, U. Warsaw, 1980; Doctorat, U. Paris X-Nanterre, 1988. Lectr. U. Warsaw, 1980-83, asst. prof., 1983-89, assoc. prof., 1996—; asst. prof. U. Wis., Madison, 1989-94, assoc. prof. French and Italian, 1994-99, prof., 1999—. Author: Dialectique et Connaissance dans La Sepmaine Du Bartas, 1992, Signes Dissimilaires. La quête des noms divins dans la poésie française, 1997, Le Dieu Néant. Théologies négatives à l'aube des temps modernes, 1998; co-editor: Anteros, 1994. Mem. Solidarność, Poland, 1980-89. NEH fellow, 1994-95; KBN grantee, Komitet Badań Naukowych, 1997-98. Mem. Société Française des Seiziémistes, Renaissance Soc. Am. Roman Catholic. Home: Lowicka 51 M 7, 02-535 Warsaw Poland Office: U Wis Madison Dept French and Italian 1220 Linden Dr Dept And Madison WI 53706-1525

MIERTUS, STANISLAV, chemist, researcher; b. Banky, Slovakia, Apr. 26, 1948; arrived in Italy, 1992; s. Koloman and Augusta (Javorska) M.; m. Janka Risová, Aug. 7, 1971; children: Stanislava, Jan. MSc in Chemistry, Slovak Tech. U., Bratislava, Slovakia, 1971; PhD in Chemistry, Slovak Acad. Scis., Bratislava, Slovakia, 1975; DSc in Chemistry, Tech. U., Bratislava, Slovakia, 1988; Doctorate (hon.), U. Pisa, Italy, 1997. Rschr. Polymer Inst., Slovak Acad. Sci., Bratislava, 1971-81; from asst. to assoc. prof. Tech. U., Bratislava, 1981-88; full prof. Slovak Tech. U., Bratislava, 1989-92; sr. rschr. UN Indsl. Devel. Orgn.-Internat. Ctr. for Sci. & High Tech., Trieste, Italy, 1992-93; area coord., deputy dir. UN Indsl. Devel. Orgn.-Internat. Ctr. for Sci. & High Tech., Trieste, 1996—; project dir. Polybios/Polytech, Trieste, 1993-96; dep. dir. UN Indsl. Devel. Orgn. Internat. Ctr. Sci. and High Tech., Trieste, 1999—; vis. rschr. U. Pisa, 1977-78, Inst. Chem. Biophysics, Paris, 1977-78; vis. prof. Mount Sinai Sch. Medicine, CUNY, 1988; contr. prof. U. Trieste Faculty Pharmacy, 1993—; nat. coord. AIDS project Ministry of Health, Rome and Trieste, 1994—. Author: Molecular Spectroscopy, 1990; co-author: Polarized Continum Medium Theory of Solvent Effect, 1981; co-editor: Combinatorial Chemistry and Techniques, 1998; contbr. articles to profl. jours.; inventor composite biosensors; patentee in field. Recipient Gold medal Arab Soc. for Material Sci., Alexandria, Egypt, 1997; named Best Jr. Rschr. in Czechoslovakia, Czecho-Slovak Acad. Scis., Prague, 1977. Mem. AAAS. Roman Catholic. Avocations: tennis, skiing, windsurfing. Office: UN Indsl Orgn Ctr Sci Tech, UNIDO-ICS Padriciano 99, 34012 Trieste Italy

MIETZ, HOLGER, ophthalmologist; b. Guetersloh, Germany, June 30, 1962; s. Alfred and Brunhild (Scheid) M.; 1 child, Carl Rettig. MD, U. Bonn, Germany, 1987. Resident U. Dusseldorf, Germany, 1988-89, U. Koeln, Germany, 1990, 92-95; asst. prof. U. Cologne, Germany, 1996—; asst. in ocular pathology U. Cologne, 1990-95, dir. ophthalmic pathology, 1996—. Fellow Johns Hopkins, Balt., 1991, Baylor Coll., Houston, 1995-96. Mem. German Ophthalmological Soc. (glaucoma rsch. award 1996), Assn. Rsch. Vision and Ophthalmology.

MIFFLIN, FRED JOHN, Canadian government official; b. Bonavista, Nfld., Can., 1938; m. Gwenneth Davies; children: Cathy, Mark, Sarah. Grad., Can. Navy's Venture Tng. Program, U.S. Naval War Coll., Nat. Def. Coll., Kingston, Ont. Enlisted Can. Navy, 1954, advanced through ranks to rear admiral, 1985, head nat. def. secretariat; mem. parliament Canadian Govt., 1988-96, parliamentary sec. to min. nat. def. & vet. affairs, 1993, min. fisheries & oceans, 1996-97; min. vet. affairs and sec. of state Atlantic Can. Opportunities Agy., 1997-99. Avocations: country music, cooking. Office: Confederation Bldg, Rm 207, Ho of Commons, Ottawa, ON Canada K1A OA6*

MIFSUD, FRANCIS MONTANARO, ambassador; b. Valletta, Malta, Dec. 19, 1925; s. Henry and Mary (Montanaro) M.; m. Erminia Malavasi, July 24, 1971. LLD, U. Malta, 1952; MA (hon.), Oxford U., Eng., 1956. Dist. officer, dist. commr. H.M. Overseas Civil Svc., Tanzania, 1952-61, customary law adv., 1962-63; legal and staff adminstrn. FAO, Rome, 1964-83, chief legis. br., 1984-87; cons., profl. work pvt. practice, 1988-91; ambassador to FAO, IFAD and WFP Rome, 1991—; chmn. Gen. Fisheries Commn. for the Mediterranean, 1997—; mem. FAO Com. on Constnl. and Legal Matters, 1998—, alt. chmn. FAO Appeals Com., 1999—. Author: Customary Land Law in Africa, 1967, reprinted 1985; contbr. articles to profl. jours. Avocations: reading, music, travel, languages. Home: Piazza Grazioli 5, 00186 Rome Italy Office: Permanent Rep of Malta to FAO, Lungotevere Marzio 12, 00186 Rome Italy

MIGAL, YURI FEDOROVICH, physicist, educator; b. Krasnodar, Russia, Sept. 20, 1947; s. Fedor Grigorievich and Maria Andreevna (Kudryavets) M.; m. Nadezhda Vladimirovna Sentyurina, July 4, 1970; 1 child, Mikhail. D of Phys.-Math. Sci., Rostov State U., Rostov-on-Don, Russia, 1970. Rschr. Rostov State U., 1970-81, Rostov Inst. Rwy. Transport, 1981-85; assoc. prof. Don State Tech. U., Rostov-on-Don, 1985-99, prof., 1999—. Contbr. articles to profl. jours. Grantee Russian Basic Rsch. Found., 1996-01. E-mail: ymigal@mail.ru. Home: Apt 45, Kommunisticheskу Prosp 43/4, 344091 Rostov-on-Don Russia Office: Don State Tech U, 1 Gagarin Sq, 344010 Rostov-on-Don Russia

MIGITAKA, MASATOSHI, engineering educator; b. Kasugai, Kizuki, Japan, June 29, 1931; s. Masanori and Kagi (Katoh) M.; m. Toshiko Yamazaki, Nov. 25, 1964; children: Toshiya, Sonoko. BS, Nagoya (Japan) U., 1955, PhD, 1967. Rsch. ctrl. lab. Hitachi Ltd., Kokubunji, Japan, 1958-65, sr. rschr. ctrl. lab., 1965-76; head lab. 1 coop. lab. VLS TRA, Kawasaki, Japan, 1976-80; sr. rschr. ctrl. lab. Hitachi Ltd., Kokubuji, 1980-83; prof. Toyota Tech. Inst., Nagoya, Japan, 1983-89, prof. dir. semiconductor ctr., 1989-99; dept. head of contol and info. Engring. Toyota Tech Inst., Nagoya, 1995-98. Author: (book) Solid-State Microwave Devices, 1973, Semiconductor Lithgraphy Technology, 1984, Introduction to New LSI Engineering, 1992; author, editor: LSI Process Engineering, 1982. Recipient IEEJ Tech. Devel. award, 1996, Odaira Meml. award Oma Orgn., Tokyo, 1996, Toyota Scholarship award Toyota Tech. Inst., 1997, Schlumberger Awd., Schlumberger Co., Inc., 1998. Fellow IEEE. Office: 2-12-1 Hisakata Tempaku, Nagoya 468, Japan

MIGNANI, ROBERTO, physics educator, researcher; b. Messina, Italy, Jan. 28, 1946; s. Pietro and Maria Antonietta (Parise) M.; m. Rosa Amato, June 17, 1976; children: Ruggero, Diana. PhD in Physics, U. Palermo (Italy), 1970. Fellow, Inst. for Theoretical Physics, Catania U. (Italy), 1971-73, dept. physics, Università La Sapienza, Rome, 1974, assoc. prof. physics, 1977-80, prof. electrodynamics, 1981-92; assoc. prof. dept. physics L'Aquila U. (Italy), 1975-76; prof. theoretical physics Inst. for Basic Research, Palm Harbor, Fla., 1981-91; prof. theoretical physics dept. physics E. Amaldi III Univ. di "Roma Tre", 1993—; research assoc. Sicilian Ctr. for Nuclear Physics and Structure of Matter, Catania, 1971-74, Italian Nat. Inst. for Nuclear Physics (INFN), Rome, 1971—, Italian Nat. Orgn. for Nuclear Energy (ENEA), Rome, 1984, Interuniv. Ctr. Cognitive Elaboration in Natural & Artificial Systems, Rome, 1995—. Contbr. articles on physics to profl. jours.; editor Hadronic Jour., 1981-91; (book) Selected Papers of Italian Physicists: Piero Caldirola vols. I-IV, 1986, Test di Fisica, vol. I-II, 1997. Fellow Italian Phys. Soc. Office: Dept Fisica E Amaldi U Roma Tre, via della Vasca Navale 84, 00146 Rome Italy

MIGONE, GIAN GIACOMO, history educator, Italian senator; b. Stockholm, May 25, 1940; s. Bartolomeo Migone and Jacquette Hamilton; m. Donata Origo (div. 1982); children: Bartolomeo, Sebastiano, Thi-Sao; m. Anna Viacava. MA in Polit. Sci., Cath. U. Milan, 1965; MA in Modern HIstory, Harvard U., 1966. Asst. prof. N.Am. history U. Turin, Italy, 1969-77, assoc. prof. N.Am. history, 1977-87, prof. N.Am. history, 1987—; chmn. Centro Universitario Sportivo, Rome, 1961; Lauro de Bosis Lectr. Italian Civilization, Harvard U., Cambridge, Mass., 1990. Author: Problemi di storia nei rapporti tra Italia e Stati Uniti (Problems of History in the Relations Between Italy and the U.S.), 1970, I Banchieri americanie Mussolini, Aspetti internazionale della Quota Novanta (The American Bankers and Mussolinis International Aspects of Quota Novanta), 1979, Gli Stati Uniti e il Fascismo (The United States and Fascism), 1980; editor L'Indice dei Libri del Mese, 1984-90; co-editor Liber, 1987-90; contbr. articles to profl. jours. and daily newspapers. City councillor, Turin, 1990-92; sen., Rome, 1992—, dep. chmn. fgn. rels. com., 1992-94, undersec. of state for fgn. affairs, 1999, chmn. fgn. rels. com., 1994—; also chmn. civilian affairs com., North Atlantic assembly, 1997-99, chmn. adv. bd. UN Staff Coll. Project, Turin. Recipient Knight Grand Cross award; Harkness fellow, Commonwealth Fund, N.Y., 1964-66, Fulbright fellow, 1968, 69, 75. Democratici di Sinistra. Roman Catholic. Avocations: cross-country skiing, athletics. Home: Via della Rocca 47, I-10123 Turin Italy Office: Senato della Repubblica, Rome Italy

MIGUEL, LUIS, musician; b. Genre, Mex.. Recordings include Soy Como Quiero Ser, 1989, Romance, 1991, El Idolo De Mex., 1992, Am. & En Vivo [EP], 1992, Los Idolos De Mex.--16 Super Exitos, 1993, Aries, 1993, Segundo Romance, 1994, Romantico Desde Siempre, 1994, El Concierto video, 1995, El Concierto, 1995, Nada Es Igual, 1996, Romances, 1997, Fiebre De Amor, 1998, Collezione Privata, 20 Anos, 14 Grandes Exitos, Amarte Es Un Placer (Album of the Yr. award Latin Grammy Awards, Best Pop Album award Latin Grammy Awards. Recipient three Grammy awards, numerous platinum records; named Best Male Pop Vocal Performance, Latin Grammy Awards. Office: care WEA Latina Inc 10950 Ventura Blvd Studio City CA 91604-3340*

MIGUEL, PAULO CAUCHICK, educator; b. Ribeirao Preto, Brazil, Oct. 15, 1962; s. Augusto Henrique and Maria (Cauchick) M.; m. Erica Fernandes Garbo, July 20, 1964; children: Caio, Lucas. MS, UNICAMP, Caminas, Brazil, 1992; PhD, U. Birmingham, England, 1996. Mfg. engr. VARGA, Limeira, Brazil, 1985-87, Oriente, Artur Nogueira, Brazil, 1987-88, BENDIX, Campinas, Brazil, 1988-90, UNICAMP, Campinas, Brazil, 1992; assoc. prof. UMMEP, Santa Barbara, Brazil, 1990—; tech. dir. QFO Inst., Brazil, 1999—. Mem. ASQ. Avocations: tennis, jogging. Office: UNIMEP Campus Santa Barbara, Rodovia SP 306 KM 1, 13450000 Santa Barbara D'Oeste Brazil

MIGUEL NECOECHEA, GRACIA, film producer, writer; b. Mexico City, Mex., Oct. 26, 1949; s. Miguel Mecoechea and Ageles Gracia; m. Ivania Chavez; 1 child, Miguel Jr. Student, London Film Sch., 1972. Free-lance scriptwriter Mex., 1973-76, free-lance film editor, 1973-76; dir. programming Nat. Inst., Mex., 1976-79; gen. dir. Audiovisual Media, Nicaragua, 1979-89; head prodn. Mex. Film Inst., 1990-94; pres. Ivanai Films, Mex., 1995-99; tutor Media Bus. Sch., Spain, 1997-99; cons. in field. Producer (films) Married Life, 1993, Deep Crimson, 1996, A Sweet Scent of Death, 1998; exec. producer (film) Perdita Durango, 1997. Mem. Mex. Film Prodrs. Assn. (v.p.). Office: IVania Films, Plaza San Jacinto 23-D, 01000 Mexico City Mexico

MIHAI, DUMITRU GRIGORE, veterinary medicine educator; b. Stoina, Gorj, Romania, Mar. 19, 1936; s. Grigore Ion and Ioana Ion (Alecu) M.; m. Mariana Stefan Istrate, Aug. 5, 1962; children: Alexandru, Nicoleta. DVM, Faculty Vet. Medicine, Bucharest, Romania, 1961, PhD, 1970. DVM Vet. Dispensary, Turburea, Romania, 1961-64; asst. prof. U. Agrl. Sci., Bucharest, 1964-70; rschr. Kans. State U., Manhatan, 1970-71; assoc. prof. U. Agrl. Sci., Bucharest, 1971-90, prof., 1991-99; sr. lectr. Inst. Namibia, 1973-79. Author: Nutritional and Metabolic Diseases, 1966, 84, Dismineralogis on Animals, 1979 (Romanian Acad. award 1981), Differential Diagnosis, 1984, Internal Veterinary Medicine, 1994. Fulbright scholar Kans. State U., 1970-71. Mem. N.Y. Acad. Scis., Agrl. Scis. Bucharest, AGMVR. Avocations: literature, sports. Home: Sandu Aldea 4 Bloc 2, ap 6, 71338 Bucharest Romania Office: USAMV, Bd Mărăsti 59, 71331 Bucharest Sector 1, Romania

MIHAILOV, RADU MIHAIL, agricultural company executive; b. Constanta, Romania, July 24, 1965; s. Mihai and Liana Felicia (Amzulescu) M.; m. Ileana Claudia Constantin, Sept. 5, 1987; 1 child, Ciprian. Diploma in engring., Fac. Mechanics, Craiova, Romania, 1986; MBA, Open U., Oxford, Eng., 1999. Engr. CJRBB, Sibioara, 1986-89; investment exec. Arguc Oil Plant, Constanta, 1990-92; gen. mgr. Romcereal Import/Export Agy., Constanta, 1993-95; CEO Savellys Argo, Constanta, 1995—. Dunarea Trade Internat., Bucharest, 1997-98; CEO, v.p. Lois Cont, Bucharest, 1994-98. Grantee USAID, 1996, 98, N.Y. Acad. Scis., 1998. Mem. Am. Mktg. Assn., Am. Mgmt. Assn., Chamber Agr., Rotary. Avocations: travel, informatics, training. Office: Savellys Agro, General Manu NR 02, 8700 Constanta Romania

MIHAL, SANDRA POWELL, distance learning specialist; b. Balt., Dec. 15, 1941; d. Sanford William and Mary Louise (Barry) Powell; m. James George Anderson, June 15, 1963; children: Robin Marie, James Brian, Melissa Lee, Derek Clair; m. Charles Turner Barber, Apr. 18, 1978; stepchildren: Gretchen Jayco, Katrina Hope; m. Ladislaw Paul Mihal, May 25, 1991; stepchildren: Alexander Paul, Suzie May, Natasha Elizabeth, Rudy Darius. BA, Mt. St. Agnes Coll., 1963; MA, N.Mex. State U., 1970, Purdue U., 1975; EdD, Vanderbilt U., 1990. Cert. tchr., Md. Tchr. Ridgely-Dulaney Jr. H.S., Towson, Md., 1964; grad. asst. N.Mex. State U., Las Cruces, 1967-69; acad. advisor, instr. polit. sci. Purdue U., West Lafayette, Ind., 1974-78; prof., acad. sys. analyst U. So. Ind., Evansville, 1978-82; assoc. prof., chair dept. computer info. sys. Henderson (Ky.) C.C., 1982-88; prof. computer tech., divsn. chair Anne Arundel C.C., Arnold, Md., 1988-91; computer sys. analyst Immigration & Naturalization Svc., Dept. of Justice, Washington, 1991-92, Glynco, Ga., 1995—; bd. dirs. Ind. Polit. Sci. Assn., Muncie, 1984-88, Internat. Studies Assn.-Midwest, Chgo., 86-88; pres. Ky. Acad. Computer Users' Group, Lexington, 1985-86; mem. telecom. adv. bd. C.C. Sys., Annapolis, Md., 1990-91; computer syst. network analyst CLARC Svcs., Pt. Charlotte, Fla., 92-95; adj. prof. history and polit. sci. Edison C.C., Punta Gorda, Fla., 1993-95. Author: Learning By Doing BASIC, 1983, Computers Learning By Doing, 1984; contbr. to several profl jours. 1980-90; author, spkr. series Faculty/Staff Edison CC 94, Ednl. Tech. Nova U., 1995. Block coord. several neighborhood assns.; mem. Henderson County Sch. Computer Adv. Bd. 1982-88; chmn. Newburgh (Ind.) Youth Orgn., 78-86; judge Sci. Fair, Annapolis, 1988-90; mem. nomination bd. Ky. Higher Edn. Assn., 1989-91; mem. Charlotte Chorale, Port Charlotte, 1992-94, Peace River Power Squadron, Port Charlotte, 1994-96. Coast Guard Aux., 1995-97. Md. State Tchr. Bd. Edn. scholar, 1960-63; fellow Sloan Found., 1973-75, U. Ky., 1984. Mem, Soc. Applied Learning Tech., Assn. Computing Machinery (v.p. 85—), Am. Legion, Pi Gamma Mu. Democrat. Roman Catholic. Avocations: sailing, singing, swimming, cooking. Home: 112 Oak Ridge Rd Brunswick GA 31523-9741 Office: Dept Treasury Media Support Divsn FLETC Bldg 18 Rm 216 Glynco GA 31524

MIHALACHE, DUMITRU, physicist, researcher; b. Vilcele, Romania, June 24, 1948; s. Marin and Maria (Ionescu) M.; m. Adriana Nicolae, Apr. 22, 1972; children: Monica-Manuela. Diploma in physics, Bucharest (Romania) U., 1971, diploma in math., 1977; PhD in Physics, Inst. Atomic Physics, Bucharest, 1986. Physicist Inst. Atomic Physics, Bucharest, 1971-88, rschr., 1988-90, sr. rschr. III., 1990-91, sr. rschr. II., 1991-93, sr. rschr. I., 1993—; vis. prof. Rome U., 1986, 90, Jena (Germany) U., 1992, 95, 96, 98, 99, 2000, Poly. U. Catalonia, Barcelona, 1993, 95, 96. Author: Nonlinear Planar Optical Waveguides, 1990; contbr. chpts. to books; mem. adv. editl. bd. Optics Comm., 1997—. Recipient Constantin Miculescu prize Romanian Acad., Bucharest, 1985; rsch. grantee NATO, Barcelona, 1997-98. Mem. Optical Soc. Am., European Phys. Soc. (ordinary). Office: Inst Atomic Physics Theoret, Physics Dept PO Box MG-6, 76900 R Bucharest Romania

MIHALACHE, VALERIA, software engineer; b. Calimanesti, Vilcea, Romania, Apr. 12, 1969; d. Ion and Veronica (Busui) Danila; m. Cicerone N. Mihalache, Dec. 24, 1988. MSc, U. Bucharest, Romania, 1992; PhD, Turku Ctr. for Computer Sci., Finland, 1998. Software developer Rsch. Inst. for Computer Sci., Bucharest, 1992-93; asst. U. Bucharest, 1993-95; software devel. engr. C Level Design, Inc., Campbell, Calif., 1999—. Contbr. articles to profl. jours. Achievements in research on formal languages and automata, natural language processing, DNA computing. Avocations: piano, nature.

Office: C Level Design Inc 3425 S Bascom Ave Ste 230 Campbell CA 95008-7300

MIHAN, RICHARD, retired dermatologist; b. Dec. 20, 1925; s. Arnold and Virginia Catherine (O'Reilly) M. MD, St. Louis U., 1949. Diplomate Am. Bd. Dermatology. Intern L.A. County Gen. Hosp., 1949-51, resident in dermatology, 1954-57; pvt. practice in dermatology L.A., 1957-95; prof. emeritus U. So. Calif., 1989—. Lt. Comdr. USNR, 1951-53. Fellow ACP; mem. AMA, Soc. Investigative Dermatology, Pacific Dermatol. Assn. (exec. bd. 1971-74), Am. Acad. Dermatol., Calif. Med. Assn. (chmn. dermatol. sect. 1973-74), L.A. Dermatol. Soc. (pres. 1975-76), L.A. Acad. Medicine (pres. 1988-89), Order of St. John of Jerusalem, of Rhodes, and of Malta, Order of St. Lazarus (comdr.), Calif. Club. Roman Cath. Home: 3278 Wilshire Blvd Apt 503 Los Angeles CA 90010-1431

MIHAYLOV, DIMITER MIHAYLOV, surgeon; b. Sofia, Bulgaria, May 10, 1956; s. Mihail and Maria Dimitrova (Minova) M.; m. Marlena Racheva Stoilova, Jan. 29, 1989; 1 child, Maria. MD, Med. Acad., Sofia, Bulgaria, 1982, Specialist in Surgery, 1990; MD, U. Groningen, The Netherlands, 2000, PhD, 2000. Surgeon Transport Hosp., G. Oriahovitca, Bulgaria, 1982-86; heart surgeon Med. Acad., Sofia, 1986-93; rschr. U. Groningen, The Netherlands, 1995—; coord. heart transplantation, Med. Acad., Sofia, 1986-93. Contbr. articles to profl. jours. Avocations: computers, cars, music, photography, videos. Home: Marshallplein 260, 2286LTM Rijswijk ZH The Netherlands Office: Divsn for Artificial Organs, Bloemsingel 10, 9712 KZ Groningen The Netherlands

MIHAYLOV, NIKOLAY, lawyer; b. Sofia, Bulgaria, Nov. 3, 1941; s. Vladimir Mihaylov and Borka (Pancheva) Vukadinov; children: Vladimir Nikolaev, Liubomir Nikolaev. LLB, Sofia U., 1970, LLM, 1972. Legal adviser Technocomplect, Sofia, 1971-74; prof. Sofia U., 1974-87, 91-92; rsch. fellow Bulgarian Acad. Scis., Sofia, 1987-2000; vis. scholar NYU Sch. Law, 1979-80; Bulgarian del. Third UN Conf. of Law of the Sea, 1979-80; expert Bulgarian Del. at UNESCO gen. conf., Sofia, 1985. Author: Public International Law Problems in Prevention of Pollution of the Sea by Oil, 1983, Higher Education in the U.S.A., 1985, Legal Status of Persons Belonging to National, Ethnic, Linguistic and Religious Groups/Minorities, 1986, Minorities. International Treaties and Normative Acts, 1995, Glossary of Bulgarian Diplomatic Dictionary, 1978, Public International Law, vols. 1 and 2, 1974; co-author: Legal Status of Bulgarians Abroad, 1990; contbr. articles to profl. jours. CEO Permanently Neutral Bulgaria Found., 1994—, Turnovo Constn. Found., 1994—, Basic Inst. for Rsch. & Def. of Human Rights, 1996; expert minorities problems Coun. Europe, 1995-96. Mem. Union Dem. Lawyers (sec. 1992-93, v.p. 1993—), Union Bulgarian Scientists, Soc. for Ecol. and Indsl. Def. of kv. Vrazhdebna, Rule of Law Inst. Mem. Liberal Congress Party. E-mail: nikolay-mihaylov@usa.net. Home: 6 10th St kv Vrazhdebna, 1839 Sofia Bulgaria

MIHAYLOVA, EMILIA MITKOVA, physicist, educator; b. Trud, Plovdiv, Bulgaria, July 28, 1959; d. Mitko Panajotov Mihaylov and Carevka Vasileva Kashlakeva. B Math., Plovdiv U., 1981, MS in Physics, 1982. Secondary sch. physics tchr. Plovdiv, 1982-84; asst. prof. physics Agrl. U., Plovdiv, 1984—. Contbr. articles to profl. jours.; patentee in field. Fellow N.Y. Acad. Scis. E-mail: Emiliam@au-plovdiv.bg. Office: Agrl U, Mendeleev St 12, 4000 Plovdiv Bulgaria

MIHAYLOVA, LARISA GRIGORYEVNA, humanities educator, researcher; b. Moscow, Sept. 1, 1954; d. Grigory Antonovitch Mihaylov and Anastasia Ivanovna Tarasova; m. Vladimir Vasilyevitch Guerassimenko, July 21, 1979; children: Yasen, Eeva, Dar. MA, Lomonosov Moscow State U., 1977, PhD, 1982. Cert. fgn. lit. Lectr. journalism dept. Moscow State U., 1980-86, jr. rschr. journalism dept., 1986-90, rschr. journalism dept., 1990—. Editor: (biobibliog. guide) Science Fiction Writers Look at the World, 1986, Abstracts of Russian Society for American Culture Studies Conferences, 1986-2000, Sverkhnovaya amerikanskaya fantastika mag., 1994-96, Sverkhnovaya F&SF, 1997—. Bd. mem. Moscow State U. Scientists Club, 1978-92; mem. Non Govt. Orgn. Zensky Forum, Moscow, 1992—; hon. senator Senate, La., 1995. Travel grantee Orgn. Com. 1st European Feminist Rsch. Conf., Aalborg, Denmark, 1991, Orgn. Com. 2nd European Feminist Rsch. Conf., Graz, Austria, 1994; grantee Summer Inst. in Am. Studies, USIA, 1995. Mem. Sci. Fiction Rsch. Assn., Russian Soc. Am. Culture Studies (acting sec. 1994—). Avocation: folk dancing. Office: Supernova Mag Lab Magnetism Phys Dept, Moscow State U, 119899 Moscow Russia

MIHELICH, EDWARD DAVID, chemist; b. Coeur D'Alene, Idaho, June 24, 1950; s. Joseph Anthony and Alma Josephine (Folden) M.; m. Loren Marie O'Connor, May 20, 1972; children: Christopher Colin, Patrick Joseph. BS, Ill. Inst. Tech., Chgo., 1972; PhD, Colo. State U., 1975. Postdoctoral rsch. assoc. Harvard U., Cambridge, Mass., 1975-77; chemist Procter & Gamble Co., Cin., 1977-83; rsch. scientist Eli Lilly and Co., Indpls., 1983-90, sr. rsch. scientist, 1991—. Contbr. articles to profl. jours. bd. dirs. Sycamore Sch., 1993-96. Mem. Am. Chem. Soc. Office: Lilly Rsch Labs DC 0548 Lilly Corp Ctr Indianapolis IN 46285-0001

MIHUL, ALEXANDRU LEONIDA MIHAI, physicist, educator, researcher; b. Iasi, Romania, June 1, 1928; s. Constantin and Irina (Suruceanu) M.; m. Eleonora Mihu, Aug. 6, 1949. Grad. in Engring., Poly. Inst., Iasi, 1950; grad. in Physics, U. Iasi, 1953, PhD, 1957. Engr. R.R. Co., Iasi, 1951-52; main rschr. Joint Inst. for Nuclear Rsch., Dubna Su, Romania, 1957-62; dept. head Inst. for Atomic Physics, Bucharest, Romania, 1962-70, Joint Inst. for Nuclear Rsch., 1970-75; prof. dept. physics Bucharest U., 1970—; dep. dir. Joint Inst. for Nuclear Rsch., Dubna Su, 1970-73. Author 5 books; contbr. over 250 articles to profl. jours. Fellow Am. Phys. Soc.; mem. N.Y. Acad. Sci. Home: C-P 1-447, Bucharest Romania Office: U Bucharest Faculty Phy, Platforma Magurele, Bucharest MG 11, Romania

MIJATOVIC, MIROSLAV, financial company executive; b. Zagreb, Croatia, May 5, 1967; arrived in Australia, 1969; s. Bozo and Milka (Kalinic) M.; m. Monika Jandrek, Apr. 9, 1994. B in Econs., Macquarie U., 1989, JD, 1990; assoc. dipl., U. Tech., Sydney, Australia, 1991. Mktg. asst. IBM, Sydney, 1988-90; solicitor Sly & Weigall, Sydney, 1990-93, Graham & James, Deacons, Tokyo, 1993; sr. assoc. Deacons, Graham & James, Sydney, 1994; sr. project officer Nippon Steel Trading Co. Ltd., Tokyo, 1994—; mng. dir. Indus Pipeline Ltd., Pakistan, 1997—, NS Energy Project Fin. Ltd., Ireland, 1998—; cons. Mitsui & Co., Ltd., Tokyo, 1992-93. Contbr. articles to profl. jours. Fellow Australian Govt., 1993. Mem. Internat. Bar Assn., Law Soc. Australia, Law Coun. Australia. Office: Nippon Steel Trading Co Ltd, 1-Chome Kameido ND Tower 5-7, Tokyo 136, Japan

MIJATOVIC, PREDRAG, soccer player; b. Podgovica, Serbia, Jan. 19, 1976. Forward Real Madrid Football Club, Yugoslavia Nat. Team, Beograd, AC Fiorentina, Firenze, Italy. Office: Yugoslav Football Assn, 35 Terazije, CP 263 Beograd 11000, Yugoslavia*

MIKA, OTAKAR JIŘÍ, chemist, consultant; b. Opava, N. Moravia, Czechoslovakia, Jan. 26, 1953; s. Otakar and Vlastimila (Ziffer) M.; m. Naděžda Marie Jiříček, Aug. 7, 1976; children: Andrew, Susan, Terri. Degree in chem. engring. sci., Mil. Acad., Brno, 1977, PhD, 1990. Head chem. svc. Army Regiment, Stribro, Czech Republic, 1977-80; dep. head chem. svc. Army Divsn., Plzen, Czech Republic, 1980-86; sr. tchr. Mil. Acad., Brno, Czech Republic, 1989-97; chemist Tech.-People-Environment, Brno, Czech Republic, 1997—; environ. cons. Czechoslovak Environ. Soc., Prague, 1991-92, Czech Environ. Soc., 1993—; cons. nuclear, biol., chem. and arms control Czech Peace Soc., Prague, 1997—. Author: Terrorism and NBC Weapons, 1995 (special cert. 1995), (brochures) Chem. Instrs., 1985 (gold medal 1985), Chem. Observers, 1983 (silver medal 1983); contbr. articles to Choice of Essays jour. (acknowledgement for best writer 1998). Lt. col. Czech Chem. Corps., 1977-97. Scholar Cambridge U., 1996, Oxford U., 1998. Mem. Czech Chem. Soc., Czech Soc. for Environment, Czech Peace Soc. Avocations: music, playing guitar, writing articles and essays. Home: Vlcnovska St No 2, 62900 Brno Moravia, Czech Republic

MIKALOW, ALFRED ALEXANDER, II, deep sea diver, marine surveyor, marine diving consultant; b. N.Y.C., Jan. 19, 1921; m. Janice Brenner, Aug. 1, 1960; children: Alfred Alexander, Jon Alfred. Student, Rutgers U., 1940; MS, U. Calif., Berkeley, 1948; MA, Rochdale U. (Can.), 1950. Owner Coastal Diving Co., Oakland, Calif., 1950—, Divers Supply, Oakland, 1952—; dir. Coastal Sch. Deep Sea Diving, Oakland, 1950—; capt. and master rsch. vessel Coastal Researcher I; mem. Marine Inspection Bur., Oakland. marine diving contractor, cons. Mem. adv. bd. Medic Alert Found., Turlock, Calif., 1960—. Author: Fell's Guide to Sunken Treasure Ships of the World, 1972; (with H. Rieseberg) The Knight from Maine, 1974. Lt. comdr. USN, 1941-47, PTO, 1949-50, Korea. Decorated Purple Heart, Silver Star. Mem. Divers Assn. Am. (pres. 1970-74), Treasury Recovery, Inc. (pres. 1972-75), Internat. Assn. Profl. Divers, Assn. Diving Contractors, Calif. Assn. Pvt. Edn. (no. v.p. 1971-72), Authors Guild, Internat. Game Fish Assn., U.S. Navy League, U.S. Res. Officers Assn., Tailhook Assn., U.S. Submarine Vets. WWII, Explorer Club (San Francisco), Calif. Assn. Marine Surveyors (pres. 1988—), Soc. Naval Archs. and Marine Engrs. (assoc.), Masons, Leions, Am. Legion, VFW. Office: 52 Mira Loma Rd Orinda CA 94563-2332

MIKAMI, MASAO, meteorologist, researcher; b. Kawaguchi-Shi, Japan, Nov. 25, 1954; s. June and Michiko (Komori) M.; m. Akemi Nakagawa, Mar. 28, 1987; children: Gaku, Fumi. BS, Meteorol. Coll., Kashiwa, Japan, 1978; PhD, Tokoku U., Sendai, Japan, 1996. Engr. Miyakojima Local Meteorol. Obs., Okinawa, Japan, 1978-82, Osaka (Japan) Dist. Meteorol. Obs., 1982-85; rschr. Meteorol. Rsch. Inst., Tsukuba, Japan, 1985-92, sr. rschr., 1992—. Editl. bd. Jour. Met. Soc.; author monographs. Mem. Japan Soc. Hydrology and Water Resources (dir. 1996—). Avocations: camping, skiing. E-mail: mmikami@mri-jma.go.jp. Office: Meteorol Rsch Inst, Meteorol Rsch Inst, Nagamine 1-1, 305-0052 Tsukuba Japan

MIKATA, YOZO, mechanical engineer, software engineer; b. Nichinan, Miyazaki, Japan, Jan. 29, 1956; came to U.S., 1981; s. Chotaro and Fumiko (Kato) M. BS in Civil Engring., U. Tokyo, 1979, MS in Civil Engring., 1981; PhD in Mech. Engring., U. Del., Newark, 1984. Postdoctoral fellow Northwestern U., Evanston, Ill., 1984-87; postgrad. rsch. engr. U. Calif. San Diego, LaJolla, Calif., 1987-89; rsch. assoc. U. Ill., Urbana-Champaign, 1989-90; asst. prof. Old Dominion U., Norfolk, Va., 1990-96; sr. rsch. scientist ICAM, NASA Langley Rsch. Ctr., Hampton, Va., 1996-99; software engr. Bell Atlantic Network Svcs., Silver Spring, Md., 1999—. Contbr. articles to profl. jours. Rsch. grantee Engring. Found., Washington, 1992, NASA Langley Rsch. Ctr., Hampton, 1993, 94. Mem. ASME, Soc. Indsl. and Applied Math., Am. Acad. Mechanics. Achievements include research on micromechanics of coated fiber composite materials providing analytical solutions, and thereby contributed to the understanding of local mechanical behavior of coatings; research on wave propagation, fracture mechanics, dynamic phase transformation; avocations: tennis, swimming, jazz, astronomy, number theory. Home: 3564 Powder Mill Rd Apt 303 Beltsville MD 20705-3520 Office: Bell Atlantic Network Svcs Inc 13100 Columbia Pike Fl 4 Silver Spring MD 20904-5296

MIKEL, THOMAS KELLY, JR., laboratory administrator; b. East Chicago, Ind., Aug. 27, 1946; s. Thomas Kelly and Anne Katherine (Vrazo) M.; BA, San Jose State U., 1973; MA, U. Calif.-Santa Barbara, 1975. Asst. dir. Santa Barbara Underseas Found., 1975-76; marine biologist PJB Labs., Ventura, Calif., 1976-81; lab. dir. CRL Environ., Ventura, 1981-88; lab. dir. ABC Labs, Ventura, 1988—; instr. oceanography Ventura Coll., 1980-81. Chair joint task group, section author 20th edit. Std. Methods Examination Water & Wastewater APHA, 1996. With U.S. Army, 1968-70. Mem. Assn. Environ. Profls., Soc. Population Ecologists, ASTME (rsch. contbr. 10th ann. symposium 1986), Soc. Environ. Toxicology and Chemistry (bd. dirs.). Biol. coord. Anacapa Underwater Natural trail U.S. Nat. Park Svc., 1976; designer ecol. restoration program of upper Newport Bay, Orange County, Calif., 1978; rsch. contbr. 3d Internat. Artificial Reef Conf., Newport Beach, Calif., 1983, Ann. Conf. Am. Petroleum Inst., Houston. Democrat.

MIKELS, RICHARD ELIOT, lawyer; b. Cambridge, Mass., July 14, 1947; s. Albert Louis and Charlotte Betty (Shapiro) M.; m. Deborah Gwen Katz, Aug. 29, 1970; children: Allison Brooke, Robert Jarrett. BS in Bus. Adminstrn., Boston U., 1969, JD cum laude, 1972. Bar: Mass. 1972, U.S. Dist. Ct. Mass. 1974, U.S. Ct. Appeals (1st cir.) 1978. Legal examiner ICC, Washington, 1972-74; ptnr. Riemer & Braunstein, Boston, 1974-80; ptnr., chmn. comml. law sect. Peabody & Brown, Boston, 1980-88; mem., chmn. comml. law sect. Mintz, Levin, Cohn, Ferris, Glovsky and Popeo, P.C., Boston, 1988—. Contbr. articles to profl. jours. Tng. adv. com. Jewish Vocat. Svc., Boston, 1991, 95, 96, bd. dirs., 1995-99, vice chair microenterprise adv. com. 1997; vice-chair lawyers com. Combined Jewish Philanthropies, 1994, 95. Fellow Am. Coll. Bankruptcy; mem. ABA, Am. Bankruptcy Inst. (bd. dirs. 2000—), Assn. Comml. Ins. Attys., Comml. Law League Am., Mass. Bar Assn., Boston Bar Assn., Boston U. Law Alumni Assn. (mem. exec. com., v.p. exec. com. 1999-2000, pres. exec. com. 2000—). Office: Mintz Levin Cohn Ferris Glovsky & Popeo PC 1 Financial Ctr Fl 39 Boston MA 02111-2657

MIKHAIL, WILLIAM MESIHA, economist, educator; b. Fayoum, Egypt, May 31, 1935; s. Mesiha M. and Foutnah Mikhail; m. Nariman Marei, Dec. 23, 1983; children: Fadi, Monia. Ph.D. in Stats., London Sch. Econs., 1969. Assoc. prof. Cairo U., 1970-76; prof. econometrics Am. U., Cairo, 1976—; bd. dirs. Comml. Internat. Bank, Egypt; cons. econ. modeling, devel. planning and econometrics UN Devel. Program, Internat. Labour Orgn. and numerous internat. orgns. Mem. Econometric Soc., Am. Statis. Assn., Egyptian Statis. Assn. Author articles in field. Home: PO Box 623, Cairo 11511, Egypt Office: 113 Kasr El-Aini St, Cairo 11511, Egypt

MIKHAILIDIS, DIMITRI PHILIP, pathologist, educator, consultant; b. Cairo, Apr. 13, 1948; came to U.K., 1966; s. Philip and Chryssanthi (Philippou) M.; m. Alice Maria Efstratiadis, Jan. 21, 1979; 1 child, Philip George. BS, U. London, 1971, MB, BS, 1976, MS, 1981, MD, 1989, cert., 1990. House physician Royal Free Hosp., London, 1976-77; house surgeon Whipps Cross Hosp., London, 1977; sr. house physician Royal Free Hosp., 1977-78, Royal Marsden Hosp., London, 1978; sr. house officer Royal Free Hosp., 1978-79, registrar, 1979-80, Wellcome Trust fellow, hon. lectr., 1980-83, lectr., hon. sr. registrar, 1983-90, sr. lectr., hon. cons., 1990-97, reader, hon. cons., 1997—; vis. prof. Kingston U., London, 1994—, U. Ioannina (Greece) Med. Sch., 1995—; European fellow Med. Angiology, 1999. Revs. editor Prostaglandins, Leukotrienes and Essential Fatty Acids, 1988—; prin. editor Platelets, 1989—; editor-in-chief Hellenic Med. Jour., 1996—, Current Med. Rsch. and Opinion, 1999—; regional editor Current Drug Targets; mem. editl. bd. Jour. Roy Soc. Health; contbr. over 200 articles to profl. jours. Assessor for Queen's award for higher and further edn., London, 1994—. Recipient grant Nordisk, London, 1983, 96. Fellow Royal Soc. Health (mem. editl. bd. Jour. Royal Soc. Health), Royal Soc. Medicine (v.p. sect. pathology 1995-97, editl. bd. 1997—), Royal Coll. Pathologists, Am. Coll. Angiology; mem. Brit. Med. Assn. (award for vascular rsch. 1995). Greek Orthodox. Avocations: travel, music, motion pictures. Office: Royal Free Hosp, Pond St Dept Chem Pathology, NW3 2QG London England

MIKHAILOV, ALEKSEI ALEKSEEVICH, physicist, researcher; b. Chukar, Russia, Aug. 16, 1945; s. Aleksei Nikolaevich and Marie Petrovna (Nikolaeva) M.; m. Ludmila Pavlovna Pavlova, Oct. 2, 1971 (dec. Apr. 1985); children: Leonid, Natasha, Masha. BS, Tomsk (Russia) State U., 1971; MS Phys. Inst., Russian Acad. Scis., Moscow, 1980, PhD Engring., 1984. Jr. rschr. Inst. Cosmophys. Rsch. and Aeronomy, Yakutsk, Russia, 1971-90, sr. rschr., 1990—; chmn. Commn. Study of Anomalios Phenomenon. Co-authro: Ultra-High Energy Cosmic Radiation, 1991; contbr. papers to profl. jours. Grantee Soros Found., N.Y.C., 1994, 95. Mem. Znanie Soc. Avocations: chess, running, hunting, draughts. E-mail: mikhailov@sci.yakutia.ru. Fax: 4112-445551. Office: Inst Cosmophys Rsch Aeron, Lenin Ave 31, 677891 Yakutsk Yakutia, Russia

MIKHAILOV, ALEXANDER SERGEEVICH, physicist; b. Maksatikha, Tver, Russia, June 1, 1950; s. Sergei A. and Larisa A. (Grebenshchikova) M.; m. Elena O. Karaulova, May 17, 1986; 1 child, Anastasia-Elisabeth. Diploma in Physics, Moscow State U., 1973, Cand. of Scis., 1976, ScD in Physics, 1984. Rsch. assoc. physics Moscow State U., 1976-84, sr. rsch. assoc., 1984-91; vis. prof. Inst. Physics, U. Stuttgart, Germany, 1990-91; vis. scientist Fritz-Haber-Inst. der Max-Planck-Gesellschaft, Berlin, 1992-95; rsch. group leader Fritz-Haber-Inst. der Max-Planck Gesellschaft, Berlin, 1995—. Author: Self-Organization in Non-Equilibrium Physico-Chemical Systems, 1983, Foundations of Synergetics I. Distributed Active Systems, 1990, 2d edit., 1994, Foundations of Synergetics II, Chaos and Noise, 1991, 2d edit., 1996; editor: Interdisciplinary Approaches to Nonlinear Complex Systems, 1993. Recipient Alexander von Humboldt-Stiftung Rsch. award, 1993. Orthodox Christian. Office: Fritz-Haber Inst der MPG, Faradayweg 4-6, D-14195 Berlin Germany

MIKHAILOV, ALEXANDER TROFIMOVICH, biologist, researcher; b. Moscow, Aug. 31, 1945; s. Trofim Vasilevich M. and Taissia Ivanovna Khodorevskaya; m. Irina Avelinovna Rey-Carro, Sept. 13, 1966; 1 child, Marina Alexandrovna. MD, 2nd Moscow Med. Inst., 68; PhD, Inst. Human Morphology, Moscow, 1973; DSc in Biology, Inst. Devel. Biology, Moscow, 1985. Diploma in medicine, embryology. Intern, rsch. student Inst. Human Morphology USSR Acad. Med. Scis., Moscow, 1968-70, pre, postdoct. Inst. Human Morphology, 1970-75, rsch. officer Koltzov Inst. Devel. Biology, 1975-80, sr. rsch. officer, group leader Koltzov Inst. Devel. Biology, 1980-87, chief Lab. Organogenesis Koltzov Inst. Devel. Biology, 1987-98; prof. embryology, histology and cytology Russian Acd. Scis., 1992; rsch. dir. Inst. Health Scis. U. La Coruña (Spain), 1995—; vis. prof. dept. cell and molecular biology U. La Coruña (Spain), 1992-93; grant-aided rschr. Ministry of Edn. and Sci., Spain, 1993-94; participant med. projects, Finland and Germany; dep. chmn. Sci. Coun. on Developmental Biology USSR/Russian Acad. Scis., 1986-98; mem. Coun. Biol. Scis. Superior Certifying Commn. Coun. Mins. USSR, 1987-93, Sci. Coun. Embryology, Histology and Cytology Moscow U., 1986-95; mem. organizing com. Soviet-Finnish Symposia on Developmental Biology, Inductive Processes and Cell Interactions, Tallinn, Estonia, 1981, membrane and cell interactions during devel., Tbilisi, Georgia, 1984, cell differentiation and gene expression, Tashkent, Uzbekistan, 1988, signal molecules and cell differentiation, Suzdal, Russia, 1991, Soviet/Russian Symposia on Developmental Biology, Moscow, 1982, 87, 90, Pushchino-on-Oka, 1988, Spanish Symposium, La Coruña, Spain, 1995; lectr., rschr., presenter in field. Author: (in Russian) Embryonic Inducers, 1988, Immunochemical Methods in Developmental Biology, 1991, (in Spanish) Immunochemical Analysis: Bases and Protocols, 1994; editor: Immunological Aspects of Developmental Biology, 1984, Hemopoetic Stem Cells, 1988; Developmental Biology in Russia, 1997 (in English); editor-in-chief: Soviet/Russian Jour. Developmental Biology (Ontogenez), 1988-95; mem. editl. bd. Russian Jour. Developmental Biology (Ontogenez), 1995—; mem. adv. bd. Internat. Jour. Developmental Biology, 1994—; patent for diagnostic method for early stages of ascarid infection, 1980; contbr. over 100 articles to profl. jours. Grantee Deutsche Forschungsgemeinschaft, 1993-95, Internat. Sci. Found., 1993-95. Mem. Internat. Soc. Developmental Biologists (bd. dirs. 1989-98), Internat. Cytoskeleton Club, Domus Human House (mem. internat. com. 1993—), Am. Biograph. Inst. (mem. rsch. bd. advs. 1994—), Spanish Soc. Developmental Biology (founder 1995—), AAAS, Internat. Biograph. Ctr. (dep. dir. gen. 1997), N.Y. Acad. Scis., Russian Acad. Natural Scis. (assoc.). Avocations: jazz, car travel, playing with dogs.

MIKHAILOV, GENNADY MIKHAILOVICH, physicist, educator; b. Astrakhan, Russia, May 20, 1955; s. Mikhail Iakovlevich and Valentina Grigorievna (Kobzeva) M.; m. Olga Evgenievna Oleynikova, July 19, 1975; 1 child, Mikhail. Master, Inst. Physics Tech., Russia, 1978; PhD, Inst. Chem. Physics, Moscow, 1985; sr. scientist (hon.), Inst. Microelectronics Tech., Chernogolovka, Russia, 1992. Engr. Inst. Chem. Physics, Chernogolovka, Russia, 1978-80, sr. engr., 1980-83, jr. rschr., 1983-85, sr. rschr., 1985-87; sr. rschr. Inst. Microelectronics Tech., Chernogolovka, Russia, 1987-96, acting head lab., 1996-98; head lab. Inst. Microelectronics Tech., Chernogolovka, 1999—; lectr. Technol. U., Moscow, 1993—. Co-author: Chemical Bonding and Molecular Structure, 1984; contbr. articles to profl. jours. Recipient Kapitza fellowship Royal Soc. London. Home: Institutsky prospect 11-65, 142432 Chernogolovka Russia Office: Inst Microelectronics Tech, Institutsky prospect, 142432 Chernogolovka Russia

MIKHAILOV, MIKHAIL DMITRIEVITCH, chemist, researcher; b. Sudoma, Russia, Dec. 1, 1949; s. Dmitry Sysorvitch and Maria Alexervna (Alexeeva) M.; m. Margarita Belkova, Dec. 3, 1970; children: Dmitry, Alexander. MS, State U., Leningrad, USSR, 1971, PhD, 1977, DSc, 1993. Rschr. State U., Leningrad, 1971-89; lead rschr. Optical Inst., St. Petersburg, Russia, 1989-97, Corning Sci. Ctr., St. Petersburg, 1997—; prof. Tech. U., Kirov, Russia, 1993-97, Mariner U., St. Petersburg, 1994-96. Author: Chemistry in Exercises, 1988, Chemistry of Glasses and Melts, 1998. Home: Korablestroiteley 39-522, 199397 Saint Petersburg Russia Office: Corning Sci Ctr, West PO Box 109, 53101 Lappeenrata Finland

MIKHAILOV, OLEG VASILEVICH, chemist, educator; b. Kharkov, Ukraine, Apr. 7, 1950; s. Vasiliy Yakovlevich and Mariyam Nikolaevna (Abakirova) M.; m. Tatiana Iosifovna Fishkina, Dec. 22, 1979; 1 child, Ekaterina Olegovna. Grad. in Chemistry, Kazan (USSR) State U., 1972, PhD in Chemistry, 1977, D in Chem. Sci., 1993. Jr. rsch. worker Kazan Cinema-Photo Inst., 1976-79, sr. rsch. worker, 1979-87; sr. rsch. worker Kazan Inst. Chem. Tech., 1988-92; assoc. prof. Kazan State Technol. U., 1992-94; prof., leading rsch. worker Kazan State Tech. U., 1994—. Author: (with V.K. Polovnyak) Coord. Compounds in Silver Halide Photography, 1992, Complex Formation Processes in #d-Metal hexacyanoferrate (II) gelatin-immobilized matrices, 1995, MHF-GIM Complexing: Novel Synthetic and Applied Horizons, 1997, Coordination Compounds as Components of Silverless Photographic Systems, 1999; contbr. over 400 articles to profl. publs.; holder 120 patents in field. Grantee Russian Found. Fundamental Rsch., 1996, Ctr. Fundamental Sci. of Ministry of Edn. of Russian Fedn., 1997, Internat. Soros Sci. Found., 1998; recipient Medal USSR Inventor, 1985. Mem. N.Y. Acad. Sci. Avocations: reading, traveling, football. Office: Kazan State Tech U, K Marx St 68, 420015 Kazan Russia

MIKHAILOV, SERGEY ANATOLIEVICH, physicist, researcher; b. Volgograd, Russia, Dec. 24, 1958; s. Anatoly Ivanovich and Lidia Pavlovna (Parsheva) M.; m. Nadejda Alexandrovna Savostianova, Sept. 5, 1981; 1 child, Vladislav. Engr.-physicist, Moscow Physical Tech. Inst., 1982; PhD in Physics, Russian Acad. Scis., Moscow, 1987. Jr. scientific rschr. Inst. Radioengring. and Electronics, Russian Acad. Scis., Moscow, 1986-88, scientific rschr., 1988-92, sr. rschr., 1992-95; guest rschr. LMU Munich, 1993; Alexander von Humboldt fellow U. Regensburg (Germany), 1995-97; guest rschr. Max-Planck-Inst. PKS, Dresden, Germany, 1997-99, U. Regensburg, 1999—. Contbr.: Landau Level Spectroscopy, 1991, Recent Research Developments in Applied Physics, 1999; contbr. papers to scientific jours.; sci. referee Jour. Abstracts, Physics; sci. editor Jour. Abstracts, Physics, All-Union Inst. Sci. and Tech. Info., Russian Acad. Scis., 1991-93; referee Phys. Rev. B. Recipient rsch. grants Internat. Sci. Found., 1994, Internat. Sci. Found. and Russian Found. Fundamental Rsch., 1995. Mem. APS. Avocations: photography, family. Office: Max-Planck Institut für Physik Komplexer Systeme, U Regensburg Inst Theoretische Physik, 93040 Regensburg Germany

MIKHALENKOV, VICTOR SERAFIMOVICH, physicist; b. Perevalsk, Ukraine, Dec. 15, 1930; s. Serafim Petrovich and Xeniya Ivanovna (Subbotina) M.; m. Tamara Georgievna Shleimer, Mar. 12, 1955; 1 child, Konmstantin. BS, Inst. Metal Physics, Kiev, Ukraine, 1958, DS, 1982. Jr. rschr. Inst. Metal Physics, Kiev, Ukraine, 1958-61, sr. rschr., 1961-82, leading rschr., 1983-89, head lab., 1990-94, chief rschr., 1995—. Author: Electronic Structure and the Properites of Metals and Alloys, 1988. Avocations: rowing, travel. Home: O Gonchar str 15/3 apt 8, 252025 Kiev Ukraine Office: Inst Metal Physics, Vernadskii str 36, 252680 Kiev Ukraine

MIKHALEVICH, VALERIA-ALLA JOSIPHOVNA, zoologist, poet; b. St. Petersburg, Russia, Dec. 18, 1936; d. Joseph Kafailovich Perlin and Nina Ksenofontovna Popova Perlina; m. Igor Felixovich Mikhalevich, Feb. 17, 1959 (div. Feb. 1976); m. David Josiphovich Raskin, Jan. 21, 1998. Magistr, Leningrad State U., Russia, 1961; magistr with distinction, Pedagogical U., Leningrad, 1959; PhD, Min. of Higher and Mid. Edn., Moscow, 1975; D, Soviet of Mins., Moscow, 1993. Cert. biology, geography, chemistry. Lab. asst. Zool. Inst. RAS, Leningrad, 1960-76, jr. res. officer, 1976-86, rsch. officer, 1986-90, sr. rsch. officer, 1990-92, chief rsch. officer, 1992—. Author: Classification and Phylogeny of Foraminifera, 1999; author (poetry) Echo, 1990; co-author: Russian-Am. Anthology, 1996 (Hon. Mention Peter Meinke and Open Poetry Soc. 1996). Recipient Vet of Work, Govt. of USSR, 1987, 50 Yrs. of Victory in Great Patriotic War medal Govt. of Russia, 1995, Ofcl.

Document of Presidium RAS, 1999. Mem. All Russian Protozoological Soc., All Russian Paleontol. Soc., Union of Writers of St. Petersburg (sec. sect. poetry). Avocations: visiting painting exhibitions, going to forests. Home: Morskaja naberezhnaja, 17 fl 291, 199226 Saint Petersburg Russia Office: Zool Inst Russian Acad Scis, Univ naberezhn 1, 199034 Saint Petersburg Russia

MIKHALSKI, EVGUENI VITAL'EVICH, geologist; b. St. Petersburg, Russia, Jan. 12, 1956; s. Vitaliy and Galina (Vetkova) M.; m. Alla Zubova, Oct. 19, 1984; 1 child. B in Mining Engring., Leningrad Mining Inst., Russia, 1978; PhD, All Russian Geol. Inst., St. Petersburg, 1995. From engr. to prin. rsch. scientist VNIIOkeangeologia, St. Petersburg, Russia, 1997—. Mem. Nat. Geographic Soc. Office: VNIIOkeangeologia, Angliysky Ave 1, 190121 Saint Petersburg Russia

MIKI, KENJU, physiologist, educator; b. Nagao, Kagawa, Japan, Aug. 6, 1953; s. Shigeyoshi Akitomo and Fusako Miki; m. Mino Okamoto, Apr. 25, 1981; children: Maori, Ayumi. BS, Tokushima (Japan) U., 1976, MS, 1978; PhD, Kyoto Prefectural U. Medicine, Japan, 1983. Assoc. prof. physiology U. Occpl. and Environ. Health, Kitakyushu, Japan, 1983-93; prof. physiology Nara (Japan) Women's U., 1993—; rsch. asst. prof. physiology SUNY, Buffalo, 1984-85. Author: Text of Physiology, 1988; contbr. articles to profl. jours. Mem. AAAS, Physiol. Soc. Japan, Richard Bright Soc. Avocations: triathlon, scuba diving. Office: Nara Womens U Dept Environ Health, Kitauoya Nishimachi, Nara 630-8506, Japan

MIKI, YOSHITSUGU, oncologist; b. Neyagawa, Japan, Jan. 1, 1954; s. Atsushi Setsuko (Nagata) M.; m. Machiko Tsuchiya, Nov. 26, 1989. MD, Osaka U., 1984. Pres. Miki Clinic, Neyagawa, 1985—. Mem. Japanese Soc. Immunology, Japanese Cancer Assn. Avocation: fine arts. Fax: 81-72-838-6568. Office: Miki Clinic, 2-2-1 Kuzuhara, 572-0075 Neyagawa Osaka, Japan

MIKIN, ILYA, media planner; b. Feb. 19, 1974. From media buyer to media planner Ogilvy & Mather, Moscow, 1994-99; media planner MindShare, Moscow, 1999—. Office: MindShare, B Afansyevsky per 8/3, 121019 Moscow Russia

MIKKELSEN, ERICH OLAF, pharmacologist; b. Varde, Jylland, Denmark, Oct. 19, 1933; s. Kaj and Elna Kristine (Madsen) M.; m. Gertrud Ester Fleissig Hammelsvang, Mar. 31, 1958 (div. Jan. 7, 1972); 1 child, Frank; m. Inge Jensen Gade, June 21, 1973; 1 child, Anders. MD, U. Aarhus, Denmark, 1966, DMSc, 1980. Surgeon dept. surgery and internal medicine Esbjerg Hosp., Denmark, 1966-68; physician dept. internal medicine Viborg Hosp., Denmark, 1968-69, sr. physician, 1969-70; cardiologist dept. cardiology Aarhus Kommunehospital, U. Aarhus, Denmark, 1972-73; psychiatrist dept. psychiatry Statshospital, Viborg, 1971-72; asst. prof. clin. pharmacology U. Aarhus, Denmark, 1973-80, assoc. prof. pharmacology, 1979—, specialist in clin. pharmacology, 1999—; examiner in pharmacology U. Copenhagen, 1988—, in med. rsch., 1992—; rschr. Cardiovascular Rsch. Ctr., Denmark, 1991—. Referee to med. jours. Blood Pressure, 1992, Ethnopharmacology, 1991—, Pharmacology and Toxicology, 1980—, Pharmacy and Pharmacology, 1993—, Jour. Vascular Rsch., 1997, Comparative Biochemistry and Physiology, 1998; contbr. chpts. to med. book. Lt. Danish armed forces, 1967-68. Grantee Danish Med. Rsch. coun., 1978-88, Lundbeck Fonden, 1989. Mem. AAAS, Danish Med. Assn., Danish Soc. Pharmacology and Toxicology, Danish Soc. Clin. Pharmacology, N.Y. Acad. Scis. Avocations: painting, entomology. Home: Fritz Sybergsvej 16, 8270 Højbjerg Jylland, Denmark Office: U Aarhus, Dept Pharmacology, C Jylland Ålborg 8000, Denmark

MIKKELSON, DEAN HAROLD, geological engineer, writer; b. Devils Lake, N.D., July 25, 1922; s. John Harold and Theodora (Eklund) M.; m. Delphene Doss, May 30, 1946; 1 child, Lynn Dee Hoffman. Student, N.D. State Coll., 1940-41; midshipman, U.S. Naval Acad., 1942-45; BS in Geological Engring., U. N.D., 1956. Registered profl. engr., Okla. 2d officer U.S. Lines, Quaker Lines-States Lines, Portland, Oreg., 1945-48; ptnr. J.I. Case Farm Machinery & Packard Automobile Franchises, Devils Lake, N.D., 1948-52; oil and gas lease broker Devils Lake, N.D., 1952-54; geologist Sohio Petroleum Co., Oklahoma City, 1956-58; geol. engr. Petrobras, Belem do Para, Brazil, 1958-60; pvt. practice Oklahoma City, 1961-78; pres., owner Dogwatch Petroleum, Inc., Oklahoma City, 1978-98; owner Spindrift Press, 1998—; agrl. pilot, N.D., Mont., Tex., N.Mex., summers, 1952-56. Author: (as Dee Geo) Danny; contbr. articles to profl. jours. Candidate Okla. Rep. State Legislature, Oklahoma City, 1958; del. various county and state conv., N.D. and Okla., 1948-68. With N.D. N.G., 1938-40, U.S. Army Air Corps., 1942. Mem. Oklahoma City Geol. Soc., Masons, Shriners, Jesters, Am. Legion, Sportsmans Country Club. Republican. Avocations: hunting, fishing, golf, oil painting, singing. Office: Spindrift Press 4430 NW 50th St Ste H Oklahoma City OK 73112-2295

MIKKOLA, KARI JUHANI, scientist; b. Salla, Finland, May 13, 1959; arrived in Sweden, 1962; s. Eero Mikaeli Soppela and Helvi Orvokki (Mikkola) Leinonen. Diploma in nursing, Vårsta, Märnösand, Sweden, 1979; diploma in theology, H.S., Karlskoga, Sweden, 1983; degree in history, U. Linköping, Sweden, 1996. Process operator Munksjö AB, Aspabruk, Sweden, 1980—; dep. gov. Am. Biograph. Inst., Raleigh, N.C., 1997—, ambassador, 1998—; dep. dir. gen. Internat. Biograph. Ctr., Cambridge, Eng., 1996—. Contbr. articles to profl. jours. Congl. asst. Swedish State Ch., Lerbo-Valla-Sköldinge, 1979, theology tchr., 1979—; founder Rehabs. in Alcoholics, Karlskoga, Sweden. Recipient Presdl. Seal of Honor, U.S., 1997. Mem. AAAS, Nat. Geog. Soc., N.Y. Acad. Scis., London Diplomatic Acad. (diplomatic counselor). Avocations: social anthropology, quantum physics, cosmology, theology, history. Office: Studys in Tehology & Sci, Parkvägen 3, SE-69673 Aspabruk Sweden

MIKKOLA, KAURI EINO FREDRIK, museum curator, entomologist; b. Helsinki, Finland, May 9, 1938; s. Eino Fredrik and Katri Eliisa (Sainio) M.; m. Tarja Liisa Lahtinen, 1966 (div. 1980); children: Melina, Matti; m. Maarit Irmeli Louekari, Dec. 23, 1983 (div. 2000); 1 child, Reija. BSc, U. Helsinki, 1963, MPh, 1965, PhD, 1973. Rschr. U. Helsinki, 1966-83, asst. tchr. dept. zoology, 1980-92, sr. curator Finnish Mus. Natural History, 1981-82, 93—; rschr. Biosystematics Inst., Ottawa, Can., 1985-86, 92-93; specialist on invertebrates Finnish Broadcasting Co., 1974—. Author: (in Finnish) Finnish Lepidoptera: Noctuidae 1-2, Geometridae 1-2, 1977-89; contbr. 150 articles to profl. jours. V.p. Lepidopterists Soc., New Haven, 1994-96; mem. coun. Societas Europaea Lepidopterologica, Basel, Switzerland, 1986-92, v.p., 1990-92. Rsch. grantee Acad. Finland, 1966-83. Fellow Royal Entomol. soc.; mem. Russian Entomol. Soc. (hon.), Polish Entomol. Soc. (hon.), Finnish Lepidopterol. Soc. (hon., chmn. 1980-84, prof. honoris causa). Avocations: Baroque and classical music, fishing, cottage activities, bird watching. Office: U Helsinki Zool Mus, PO Box 17, FIN00014U Helsinki Finland

MIKKONEN, KAUKO KALERVO, geographer, educator; b. Nivala, Finland, Dec. 31, 1941; s. Kaarlo Ilmari and Valma Alina M.; m. Leena Marjatta Rantala, Oct. 31, 1964; children: Jouni Kalervo, Janne Ilmari. Lic. phil. in Geography, U. Turku, Finland, 1971; DSc in Econs., Vaasa (Finland) Sch. Bus., 1975. Head rsch. inst. Vaasa Sch. Bus. Studies, 1974-76; acting prof. U. Vaasa, 1976-88, lectr., 1988-90, head rsch. inst., 1991-93, assoc. prof., 1993-96, prof., 1996—, vice rector, 1995—. Editor Proceedings of the U. Vaasa, 1975-92, chmn. editl. bd., 1995—. Mem. leading group Network U. Tourism, Finland, 1996—; mem. coun. S.E. Asia Network U., Finland, 1996—. Mem. Geog. Soc. Finland, Rotary. Avocations: singing, tourism. Office: U Vaasa, Wolffintie 34 PO Box 700, 65200 Vaasa Finland

MIKLA, VICTOR, science laboratory administrator, educator; b. Mukachevo, Ukraine, July 31, 1953; s. Ivan and Elena (Krishtofori) M.; m. Ottilia Kajnc, Nov. 15, 1975; 1 child, Victor. PhD, Odessa (Ukraine) State U., 1984; DSc, Nat. Acad. Scis., Kiev, Ukraine, 1998. Cert. physicist. Engr. lab. multicomponent semicondr. Uzhgorod State U., Ukraine, 1976-79, sci. worker lab. multicomponent semicondr., 1979-85, sr. sci. worker lab. multicomponent semicondr., 1985-92, head of lab. Inst. Solid State Physics and Chemistry, prof., 1992—; sr. rschr. Uzhgorod State U., 1985. E-mail: mikla@iss.univ.uzhgozod.ua. Fax: 38 03122 32339. Office: Uzhgorod State U, Voloshina St 54, 88000 Uzhgorod Ukraine

MIKLAS, HEINZ FRANZ ALFRED, Slavonic philology educator, scientist; b. Graz, Styria, Austria, Oct. 28, 1948; s. Hassan Cumbouroglu and Emma Karoline Miklas; m. Ivonn Stegmann, Dec. 14, 1979; 1 child, Angela. Dr.phil., U. Graz, Austria, 1975; Dr.habil., U. Freiburg, Germany, 1988; Dr. h.c., U. Sofia, Bulgaria, 1997. Scientific cooperator U. Würzburg, Germany, 1975-76; scientific asst. U. Freiburg, Germany, 1976-81, acad. adviser, 1981-93, sr. acad. advisor, 1993-94; prof. U. Vienna, Austria, 1994—, head Inst. for Slavonic studies, 1996-99; Author, editor: Berlinski Sbornik, 1988, The Four Gospels of Makarije of the Year, 1512, 1999; contbr. articles to profl. publs. Mem. Austrian Acad. of Scis. (Balkan com.), Assn. of Austrian Slavicists, Societas Linguistica Europaea. Avocations: singing, sports. Office: U Wien Inst Slawistik, Spitalgasse 2-4, A-1090 Vienna Austria

MIKLAVCIC, STANLEY JOSEPH, mathematician, educator; b. Sydney, Australia, May 18, 1959; s. Joseph and Maria (Vadnjal) M.; m. Marianne Granfelt, Feb. 17, 1991; children: Marcus, David, Jacob. Surveying Cert., Sydney Tech. Coll., Australia, 1979; BS with honors, U. New South Wales, Sydney, 1985; PhD, Australian Nat. U., Canberra, 1989. Postdoct. fellow Lund (Sweden) U., 1989-90, rsch. assoc., 1991-94; rsch. fellow Ian Wark Rsch. Inst. U. South Australia, Adelaide, 1995; sr. rsch. fellow Ian Wark Rsch. Inst. U. South Australia, 1997; vis. rsch. fellow Linköping (Sweden) U., 1996, assoc. prof., 1997—. Contbr. articles to profl. jours. Queen Elizabeth II rsch. fellow Australian Rsch. Coun., 1997. Mem. European Coll. Interface Soc., Royal Australian Chem. Inst., Australian Inst. Physics. Office: U Linköping, Dept Sci and Engring, S-60174 Norrköping Sweden

MIKLOSHAZY, ATTILA, bishop. Ordained priest Roman Cath. Ch., 1961, consecrated bishop, 1989. Titular bishop Castel Minore; bishop Apostolate to Hungarians, Scarborough, Ont., Can., 1989—. Mem. Jesuit Soc. Office: St Augustine's Sem, 2661 Kingston Rd, Scarborough, ON Canada M1M 1M3

MIKOLAJCZAK, BOLESLAW, computer science educator, researcher, consultant; b. Poznan, Poland, June 30, 1946; came to U.S., 1986; s. Walenty and Maria (Piechocka) M; m. Urszula Hajdrowska, Aug. 14, 1971; children: Maciej, Wojciech Rafal. MS in Control Engring. summa cum lauda, Tech. U., Poznan, 1970, PhD, 1974, Dr.Habilitis in Computer Sci., 1979; MS in Math., Adam Mickiewicz U., Poznan, 1972. Lectr. Inst. Control Engring., Poznan, 1970-74, asst. prof., 1974-79, assoc. prof., 1980-85; assoc. prof. Computer Sci. Ctr., Poznan, 1985-86; vis. lectr. dept. computer sci. Southea. Mass. U. (now U. Mass.), Dartmouth, 1986-87, assoc. prof., 1987-91; assoc. prof. dept. computer and info. sci. U. Mass. (formerly Southeastern Mass. U.), Dartmouth, 1991—; prof. computer sci. U. Mass., Dartmouth, 1993—, chmn. computer and info. sci. dept., 1995—; sci. cons. Elana, Torun, Poland, 1980-85, Tekoma, Warsaw, Poland, 1982-84, Lenin's Steelwork, Cracow, Poland, 1984-85, Mercomp, Warsaw, 1985-86; vis. scholar Cornell U., Ithaca, N.Y., 1976-77. Author: Transformations of Automata and Computational Complexity of Some Problems in Automata Theory, 1988, Algebraic and Structural Automata Theory, 1989, Algebraic and Structural Automata Theory Eng. edit., 1991; others; contbr. articles to profl. jours.; patentee in field. Active Polish Tchrs. Assn., 1964-80, Trade Union Solidarnosc, 1980—. Recipient award Ministry of Sci. and Tech., 1980, Gen. Tech. Orgn., 1980, Polish Acad. Scis., 1981, 84, Ministry of Higher Edn., 1982. Mem. Am. Math. Soc., Computer Soc. of IEEE, Polish Math. Soc., Assn. for Computing Machinery, Polish Computer Soc., Mass. Tchrs. Assn., Math. Revs. (reviewer 1976—). Roman Catholic. Achievements include patents for digital systems; research in algebraic and structural automata theory, in computational complexity of some problems in automata theory, in analysis and design of parallel algorithms, analysis and design of distributed software systems using Patri nets. Office: U Mass Old Wesport Rd Dartmouth MA 02747

MIKOŁAJCZYK, ZOFIA STANISLAWA, management educator; b. Lublin, Poland, Jan. 26, 1931; d. Stanisław and Maria (Mozgawa) Maj; m. Mieczisław Wiesław Mikołajczyk, Feb. 27, 1954; children: Maria, Adam. M. Higher Sch. Economy, Łódź, Poland, 1959; PhD, U. Łódź, 1965, D in Mgmt. Sci., 1972. Chief dept. Dyes Industry Factory, Zgierz, Poland, 1954-60; asst. U. Łódź, 1960-64; from lectr. to asst. prof. U. Łódź, 1965-83; prof., chair inst. U. Łódź, 1983—. Author: Method of Work Orgnization in Condition of Modern Industry, 1973, Organizational Techniques, 1977, How to Manage the Enterprise in Market Economy, 1993, European and International Management, 1995. Mem. nat. com. for sci. degrees Prime Minister of Polish Govt., Warsaw, 1990-00. Scholar The Brit. Con., London, 1969-70; rsch. fellow Oxford (Eng.) U., 1986, U. Pitts., 1994. Mem. Polish Acad. Scis. (com. mgmt. scis. 1977), Sci. Assn. Łódź, Sci. Soc. for Orgn. and Mgmt. (sci. coun. 1992). Avocations: classical music, theater, touring, books. Home: 26 Grunwaldzka str, 91-335 Lodz Poland Office: U Łódź, 39Rewolucji 1905, 90-214 Lodz Poland

MIKOŚ, MATJAŽ, civil engineer, educator; b. Ljubljana, Slovenia, Dec. 6, 1959; s. Boris and Biserka (Dovšak) M.; m. Zagorka Simić, July 12, 1985 (div. 1994); 1 child, Val; m. Urska Petje, Jan. 20, 1999; 1 child, Jon. Diploma in Civil Engring., U. Ljubljana, 1983, MS in Civil Engring., 1988; DSc, Swiss Fed. Inst. Tech., Zurich, Switzerland, 1993. Registered profl. civil engr. EURO-ING. Rschr. Inst. for Water Mgmt., Ljubljana, 1983-93; asst. prof. U. Ljubljana, 1994-99, assoc. prof., 1999—, vice-dean for rsch., 1999—; sr. cons. Inst. for Water Mgmt., Ljubljana, 1994—; dep. head of chair U. Ljubljana, 1994—, vice dean for rsch., 1999—; mem. Commn. on Snow Avalanches Ministry of Environ. and Phys. Planning, Republic of Slovenia. Editor Acta hydrotechnica, 1996—; contbr. articles to profl. and sci. jours. Mountain guide Slovene Alpine Assn., Ljubljana, 1977-81, inst. edn., 1981-88. Swiss Fed. fellow, 1988-89; recipient Silver Deserving medal Slovene Alpine Assn., 1988. Mem. Am. Soc. Civil Engrs., Am. Geophysical Union, Internat. Assn. Hydraulic Rsch., Internat. Assn. Hydrological Scis., Internat. Assn. Sedimentologists, Soil and Water Conservation Soc., Verein der Diplomingenieure der Wildbach-und Lawinen Verbauung Österreichs, Deutscher Verband Für Wasserwirtschaft Und Kulturbau, N.Y. Acad. Scis., Internat. Assn. Erosion Control, Slovenian Interpraevent Com. (pres.), Slovenian Assn. of Geodesy and Geophysics, Slovenian Assn. of Tech. and Natural Scis. Avocations: stamp collecting, mountaineering, skiing. Office: U Ljubljana FGG, Jamova 2, SI 1000 Ljubljana Slovenia

MIKULASEK, PETR, chemical engineering educator; b. Zlin, Czechoslovakia, Aug. 14, 1958; s. Stanislav and Miroslava (Hnojilova) M.; m. Lenka Kourilova, Sept. 11, 1982; children: Jan, Jiri. MS, U. Chem. Technology, Pardubice, Czechoslovakia, 1982, PhD, 1991. Lectr. U. Chem. Technology, 1983-86; sr. lectr. U. Pardubice, 1986-97, assoc. prof., 1997-2000, prof., 2000—; cons. NATO ASI, Curia, Portugal, 1993. Inventor in field; contbr. articles to profl. jours. Chmn. Univ. Sports Assn., Pardubice, 1995. Grantee Grant Agy. of the Czech Rep., Prague, 1993, 97, 2000. Mem. The Czech Soc. Chem. Engring. (bd. dirs. 1983—), N.Y. Acad. Scis., European Membrane Soc. Avocations: sports, handyman. Home: Studanecka 1276, 530 03 Pardubice Czech Republic Office: Univ of Pardubice, Nam Cs legii 565, 532 10 Pardubice Czech Republic

MIKULIK, KAREL, microbiologist; b. Prague, Czech Republic, Oct. 25, 1935; s. Joseph and Marie (Kupková) M.; m. Ludmila Hronová, Nov. 20, 1963; children: Lenka, Martin. MSc, Charles U., Prague, 1961; PhD, Czechoslovak Acad. Scis., Prague, 1966, DSc, 1986. Fellow Nat. Rsch. Coun. Can., Ottawa, 1966-67; sci. officer Czechoslovakia Acad. Sci./Inst. Microbiology, Prague, 1967-74; head dept. molecular biology Inst. Microbiology, Prague, 1974-84; sr. sci. officer Czechoslovakia Acad. Sci., Prague, 1984—; cons. UNESCO, 1983—. Contbr. articles to profl. jours.; patentee in field. Czechoslovak Acad. Sci. award 1972, 86. Mem. N.Y. Acad. Sci., Czechoslovakia Biochem. Soc. Roman Catholic. Avocation: classical music. Office: Inst Microbiology, Videňská 1083, 14220 Prague 4 Czech Republic

MIKUMO, TAKESHI, geophysist; b. Kyoto, Japan, Mar. 23, 1929; m. Yoko Okamoto, May 30, 1958; children: Mikumo Mariko, Mikumo Akira. BSc, Kyoto U., 1953, MSc, 1955, DSc, 1960. Rsch. assoc. Kyoto U., 1958-60, assoc. prof. geophysics, 1960-73, prof. seismology, 1973-92, prof. emeritus, 1992—; Japan Internat. Coop. Agy. expert Cenapred, Mex., 1992-94, Universidad Nacional Autonoma de, Mexico City, 1994-98; prof. geophysics Universidad Nacional Autonoma de Mex., Mexico City, 1998—; pres. nat. com. for seismology Sci. Coun. Japan, 1985-91; mem. Coord. Com. for Earthquake Prediction, Japan, 1989-92; rsch. fellow Calif. Inst. Tech., 1962-63, U. Calif., Berkeley, 1963-64. Co-author: Numerical Modelling of Realistic Fault Rupture Processes in Strong Motion Synthetics, 1987. Mem. Seismol. Soc. Japan (hon., pres. 1974-75), Am. Geophys. Union, Seismol. Soc. Am. Home: Jose Marie Olloqui #119-702, Col del Valle, 03100 Mexico City Mexico Office: UNAM Inst Geoficia, Cuidad Universitaria, 04510 Mexico City Mexico

MILAM, WILLIAM BRYANT, diplomat, economist; b. Bisbee, Ariz., July 24, 1936; s. Burl Vivian and Alice Vera (Pierce) M.; m. Faith Adele Handley; step-children: Erika, Fred. AB, Stanford U., 1959; MA, U. Mich., 1970; postgrad., Am. U., 1973. Polit. officer Dept. State, Washington, 1967-69; fin. economist Dept. State and Am. Embassy, Washington and London, 1970-75; energy economist Dept. State, Washington, 1975-77, dep. office dir., 1977-80, office dir., 1980-83; dep. chief of mission Am. Embassy, Yaounde, Cameroon, 1983-85; dep. asst. sec. Dept. State, Washington, 1985-90; U.S. amb. to Bangladesh, 1990-93; spl. negotiator oceans environ. sci. Dept. State, Washington, 1993-95; chief of mission Am. Embassy, Monrovia, Liberia, 1995-98; U.S. amb. to Pakistan, Am. Embassy, Islamabad, 1998—. Calif. State scholar, 1956-59; recipient James Clement Dunn award Dept. of State, 1981, Superior Honor award, 1983, Pres.'s Meritorious Svc. award U.S. Govt., 1990, Pres. Outstanding Svc. award, 1991. Avocations: reading, golf. Home and Office: Am Embassy Islamabad Unit 62200 Box 1 APO AE 09812-2200

MILAZZO, PAOLO MARIA, physicist, researcher; b. Bologna, Italy, July 10, 1966; s. Salvatore and Maria Teresa (Frigieri) M. MS, U. Bologna, 1989, PhD, 1992. Postdoc. fellow Nat. Inst. Nuclear Physics, Bologna, 1993; rschr. Nat. Inst. Nuclear Physics, 1996—; postdoc. fellow U. Bologna, 1994-95. Office: Via A Valerio 2, I 34100 Trieste Italy

MILBERG, JOACHIM, automotive executive. CEO Bayerische Motoren Werke, Munich; chmn. mgmt. bd. BMW. Office: BMW, Petuelring 130, 80788 Munich Germany*

MILBURN, HARRY GEORGE WILLIAM, science educator; b. Wallasey, Cheshire, England, Nov. 25, 1934; s. Harry George Thomas and Audrey (Parkinson) M.; m. Jean Muriel Howells, Mar. 17, 1962; children: Jonathan Henry, Jessica Anne. Degree, Liverpool Coll. Tech., England, 1959; PhD, Leeds U., England, 1966; D (hon.), Polytech. U., Budapest, Hungary, 1988. Lab. tech. Shell Refining Co., Ellesmere Port, England, 1954-59; staff demonstrator Leeds U., 1963-66; fellow Sydney U., Australia, 1966-67; sr. sci. officer Agrl. Rsch. Coun., London, 1967-68; lectr. Plymouth Poly., England, 1968-70; sr. lectr. Sheffield Poly., England, 1970-73; head dept. Napier U., Edinburgh, England, 1973-97, dean sci. faculty, 1987-90, rsch. advisor, rsch. prof., 1997-99; retired, 1999; ptnr. Milburn Assocs., Edinburgh, 1982—; vis. lectr. Imatra Poly., Finland, 1991-99; coord. Tempus projects European Union, 1992-94, 94-97; hon. lectr. Internat. Sch. Advanced Sci. in Polymer Studies, Ferrara, Italy, 1992-93; lectr., judge Scottish Photographic Fedn., 1992-99; mem. acad. bd. Napier U., quality and Stds. com.; chmn. rsch. degrees com., sci. faculy bd.; chief external examiner Newcastle Poly., Dundee Coll. Tech.; examination bd. Rennes U., France; external examiner U. West of England. Author: X-ray Crystallography, 1972, Photographic Techniques in X-ray Crystallography Photographic Techniques, 1978, Molecular Modelling Monograph, 1993; patentee in new light emitting materials; contbr. articles to profl. jours. Sci. advisor Lothian Region, Edinburgh, 1978-86, mem. emergency planning; hon. rep. Rubber and Plastics Rsch. Assn., Napier Poly.; mem. Scottish Coll. Textiles Acad. Coun., Coll. Structure Review com., Soc. Europeane pour la Formation des Ingenieers Curriculum Devel. Working Group, Royal Soc. Chemistry Edn Divsn. Coun., Internat. Union Pure and Applied Chemistry Working Party, rsch. com. Coun. Nat. Acad. Awards insts. and programs com.; bd. dirs. Royal Soc. Chemistry Qualifications and Edn., Coun. Nat. Acad. Awards Chemistry. Capt. Royal Corps of Signals, 1959-63, res. 1970-74; mem. project mgmt. com. TEMPUS JEP Shipping, Hungary, Italy, 1991, coord., 1992-94, european coord., 1994-97; coord. Hungarian Rsch. Collaboration-British Coun., 1995-98. Recipient Hon. silver star Interprom, 1996. Fellow Royal Soc. Chemistry (edn. divsn. coun. 1987-90, qualifications and edn. bd. 1987-90), British Inst. Mgmt., Royal Soc. Arts and Tech. Avocations: golf, bridge, photography, guitar. Home: 9 Orchard Ct, Longniddry EH32OPE, Scotland

MILCH, WOLFGANG E., physician, researcher, analyst; b. Hagen, Germany, Sept. 10, 1950; s. Werner E. and Ursula (Kayser) M.; m. Anne Schliephake, Dec. 24, 1981; children: Jonas, Lena. MD, U. Giessen, 1976. Physician Bundeswehr Krankenhaus, Giessen, 1978-80, Psychiatrisches Kramkenhaus, Giessen, 1980-83; physician Neurologische Klinik U. Giessen, 1983-86, sr. physician Psychosomatische Klinik, 1992—; physician psychiatrists Kranherhaus, Giessen, 1986-88, registrar psychiatrists, 1988-92. Coeditor books; contbr. articles to profl. jours. Avocation: tennis, art. Office: Friedrichstr 33, 35372 Giessen Germany

MILDNER, VESNA, speech educator; b. Zagreb, Croatia, July 6, 1953; d. Janko and Ana (Pavelic) Popovic; m. Boris Mildner, July 5, 1980. BA, Zagreb U., 1977, PhD, 1996; MA, U. Pa., 1986. Pub. rels. univ. computing ctr. U. Zagreb, 1980-89, lectr. faculty philosophy, 1989-97, sr. lectr., 1997-98, asst. prof., head phonetics dept., 1998—; rsch. assoc. univ. computing ctr. U. Zagreb, 1986-89, rsch. assoc. ministry sci. & tech., 1989—. Editor Govor, 1997—; editor-in-chief: Strani jezici, 2000; contbr. articles to profl. jours. Fulbright scholar U. Pa., 1984-86. Mem. Internat. Phonetic Assn., Internat. Clin. Phonetics & Linguistics Assn., Croatian Applied Liguistics Soc. (v.p. 1998—). Avocations: reading, travel, sports. Home: Kopernikova 34, 10020 Zagreb Croatia Office: U Zagreb, I. Lucica 3, 10000 Zagreb Croatia

MILES, ALEXANDER CHARLES, correspondent, journalist, author; b. Hempstead, N.Y., July 5, 1958; s. Samuel A. and Helen (Scherer) M. Attended, Bard Coll., Annandale, N.Y., 1977-78, McGill U., Montreal, Can., 1979-80. Staff reporter Nor'Wester Mag., Cayman Islands, 1980-81; corr. United Press Internat., Cayenne, French Guiana, 1988, Reuters, Cayenne, French Guiana, 1989—. Author: Devil's Island, 1988; contbr. articles to profl. jours. Mem. Associated Photographers Internat. E-mail: miles107@wanadou.fr. Home and Office: Impasse du 8 mai 1945, 97300 Cayenne French Guiana

MILES, ANDREW, senior health scientist; b. Cardiff, Wales, Aug. 10, 1963; s. Kenneth and Averil (Bardugoni) M. BSc, U. Wales, 1985; MSc, U. Wales Coll. Medicine; PhD, U. Wales; MPhil, U. Wales Coll. Medicine. Postgrad. rsch. fellow U. Wales Coll. Medicine, Cardiff, 1985-87; postgrad. rsch. scientist U. Wales, Cardiff, 1987-90; health data analyst Mid Glamorgan Health Auth., Wales, 1990-91; head dept. med. audit Llandough Hosp., Cardiff, 1991-93; head dept. med. audit, prof. health svcs. rsch. Whipps Cross Hosp., U. Westminster, London, 1993-96; dep. dir. Ctr. Advancement of Clin. Practice, prof. U. Surrey and East London, 1996—; cons. in field. Editor: Effective Clinical Practice, 1996, NICE, CHI and the NHS Reform, 2000, Clinical Goverance and the NHS Reforms, 2000; editor Jour. Evaluation in Clin. Practice, 1995—. Fellow Royal Soc. Medicine London, Med. Soc. London, Royal Soc. Health London; mem. Nat. Conf. Univ. Profs. Socialist. Avocations: classical piano music, counter-reformation art, neoclassical architecture, food, wine. Office: Ctr Health Svs Rsch, U East London 33 Shore Rd, London E97TA, England

MILES, ARNOLD IAN, physician; b. Leeds, Eng., June 18, 1931; arrived in U.S., 1967; S. Myer and Fanny (Solomon) M. BChD, LDS, Leeds Dental Sch., Eng., 1955; MRCS, LRCP, Royal Free Hosp. London U., 1965. Diplomate Am. Bd. Internal Medicine, Am. Bd. Pulmonary Diseases. Med. dir. emergency svcs. Health Ins. Plan Greater N.Y., N.Y.C., 1971-74; assoc. prof. Fairleigh Dickinson U., 1974-80; med. dir. R & D Johnson & Johnson, N.J., 1977-80; med. dir. ICU Shaare Zedek Hosp., Jerusalem, 1980-83; chief pulmonary svc., med. dir. ICU ACOS VA Hosp. Med. Ctr., Lyons, N.J., 1984-87; pvt. practice, London, 1987—; med. cons. Seton Hall U. Sch. Grad. Med. Edn., 1994-97, asst. dean, 1997—. Co-founder, editor: DMD, 1979-84. Capt. RADC, 1955-57, U.K. Fellow ACP. Avocation: archaeological research. Home: 95 Eyre Ct Finchley Rd, London NW89TX, United Kingdom

MILES, EDWARD HARRY, optometrist; b. Bklyn., Feb. 16, 1936; s. Bernard Ralph and Esther (Ungarten) M.; m. Ina Beth Goldberg, June 4, 1970; children: Bradley Samuel, Jamie Lauren, Michael Jared. Student, Bklyn. Coll., 1957-59, L.I. U., 1959, NYU, 1959, Roosevelt U., 1962; BS in Optics, Ill. Coll. Optometry, 1962, D in Optometry, 1962; postgrad., N.Y. Tech. Coll., 1981. Mem. staff orthopedic ward Baimbridge (Md.) Hosp., 1955, dir. med. sick call rm., 1955-57; pvt. practice N.Y.C., 1964—; contract physician Health Ins. Plan Greater N.Y., 1975—; sec.-treas. Comprehensive Profl. Systems, N.Y., 1980—, United Dental Systems, N.Y., 1989-92, Comprehensive Purchasing Group, N.Y., 1990—; trustee Local 408 Optical Workers Union, N.Y., 1986—. Author: Chauffeurs Badges and Auto-Related Badges of the World, vol. I, 1991, vol. II, 1992, vol. III, 1993, Keychain Tag News-Many License Plate Collectors newsletter, 1984—. Mem. Nassau Civic Club, N.Y., 1986—, Bnai Brith Teamsters Lodge, N.Y., 1986—; bd. dirs. N.Y. Consumer Assembly, 1992—, Greater N.Y. Safety Coun., 1992—. With USN, 1954-57. Mem. Execs. Assn. Greater N.Y., State Revenue Soc. (bd. dirs. 1980-92), Am. Revenue Assn., N.Y. State Optometric Assn., Mini License Plate Collectors Assn. (editor newsletter). Avocations: collecting license plates, chauffeurs badges, license plate key chain tags, registration inspection windshield stickers. Home and Office: 888 8th Ave New York NY 10019-5704

MILES, FRANCIS JAMES, management consultant; b. Twickenham, England, Mar. 18, 1939; s. Francis Gerald and Mollie Catherine (Briggs) Elborough; m. Patricia Violet Dyer, Sept. 16, 1961 (dec. Nov. 1997); children: Anthony David, Stephen James. Trainee mgr. F.W. Woolworth, South East, Eng., 1956-62, retail mgmt., 1962-77; co. training mgr. Woolworth Holdings, 1977-84; training mgr. Motorola Ltd., Basingstoke, 1984-88; mgr. Motorola Univ., Geneva, London, 1988-91; owner James Miles Cons., Epsom, 1992—; contract instr., 1992—; assoc. Motorola Univ., 1992—, GE Capital Svcs., 1995—, Dell Computers, 1998—. Author, designer Training Programs for Mgmt. and Process inprovement. Mem. Inst. of Pers. and Devel., Assn. of Mgmt. Edn. and Devel. Ch. of Eng. Avocations: horse riding, travel, gardening, wind surfing. Office: James Miles Cons, 36 Lower Hill Rd, KT198LT Epsom England

MILES, JOHN BILL, accountant, tax advisor; b. Knox County, Ky., Sept. 18, 1931; s. John Ishmael and Allie Arizona (Engle) M.; m. Mary Patricia Wilson, May 25, 1963; children: Melanie, Jennifer, Dennis. BSC, Salmon P. Chase Coll., Highland Heights, 1962; BS in Acctg., U. Cin., 1972. CPA; accredited tax advisor; enrolled agt. Cost acct. Avco Corp., Cin., 1956-58; chief auditor Pepsi-Cola Bottling Co., Cin., 1958-64; property acct. Monsanto Co., Addyston, Ohio, 1964-66; sec.-treas. Shur-Good Biscuit Co., Inc., Cin., 1966-79; acct. Fabritec Internat. Corp., Cold Spring, Ky., 1980-98; ind. practice acctg., 1999—. Lt. Col. Ohio Mil. Res. Mem. Am. Inst. CPAs, Ohio Soc. CPAs, Nat. Soc. Accts., Ohio Assn. Ind. Accts., Am. Legion, Assn. U.S. Army, Ohio Mil. Res. Assn., Accts. for Pub. Interest, NRA, Fur Takers Am., Cheviot Rep. Club. Home: 3816 Roswell Ave Cheviot OH 45211-3329

MILES, PHILIP ALLINGTON, stockbroker; b. London, Jan. 2, 1967; s. Philip and Edith M. BA with hons., U. London, 1990. Stockbroker NatWest Stockbrokers Ltd., London, 1991—. Coord. London Festival of Greek Drama, 1988-89. Mem. Univ. London Polo Club (founder 1988, pres. 1989-90, capt. 1989-91), The Securities Inst., East India Club, Dorchester Club, Freeman City of London St. Redemption, Freeman Worshipful Co. Basket Makers, Freedom City of London. Avocations: riding, polo, shooting, food, music. Home: Flat 1B 224 Old Brompton Rd, London SW5 ODA, England Office: NatWest Stockbrokers Ltd, 55 Mansell St, London E1 8AN, England

MILES, RAY, telecommunications executive, educator; b. Sarajevo, Bosnia-Herzegovina, Mar. 24, 1952; arrived in U.S., 1996; BSc in Elec. Engring./Computer Sci., U. Sarajevo, 1974; MSc in Elec. Engring./Computer Sci., U. Zagreb, Croatia, 1981; PhD in Elec. Engring./Computer Sci., U. Sarajevo, 1987; MBA, So. Meth. U., 1999. Prof. computer sci. U. Sarajevo, 1974-92; divsn. dir. R & D and engring., corp. IT advisor Energoinvest Sarajevo, 1977-92; sr. rsch. fellow, advisor for strategic devel., internat. bus. devel. mgr. British Telecom, London, 1992-96; strategy mgr., mgr. internet tech. br. Tex. Instruments, Dallas, 1996—, mgr. internet DSP; mem. bd. U. Sarajevo, 1989-91, Nextpromet, Sarajevo, 1989-92, Dallas Coun. on World Affairs, 1998—, MCC, Austin, Tex., 1999—; dir. CERD, Sarajevo, 1989-92; prin. IT cons. Dept. Def., Belgrade, former Yugoslavia, 1987-92. Author: Programming in Pascal, 1986, Programming in Macro-II, 1987, Global Currency, 1995; editor: Experience with Management, 1990; adv. editor Engring. Applications of Artificial Intelligence-Elsevier, 1988-95. Various leading vol. roles Red Cross, former Yugoslavia, 1973-92. Lt. Navy, 1979-80. Mem. IEEE (sr.), Assn. for Computing Machinery, European-Atlantic Group, East-European Trade Coun., British Assn. for Ctrl. and East Europe. Avocations: classical music, art, skiing, photography, hiking. Office: Tex Instruments MS 8373 PO Box 655303 Dallas TX 75265-5303

MILES, RICHARD R., writer, curator; b. Tokyo, Apr. 1, 1938; s. Robert Henri and Eleanor Alfrida Perreau-Saussine; m. Xuong-Hong Quach, Feb. 1, 1994. BA, Georgetown U., 1958, UCLA, 1960; MFA, UCLA, 1980. Cert. tchr., Calif.; cert. adminstrv., Calif. Actor L.A., 1945-60; novelist, 1965-72; pres. Burbank (Calif.) Tchrs. Assn., 1977-79; dir. Meilinki Enterprises Ltd., L.A., 1982—. Author: (novels) That Cold Day In The Park, 1965, Angel Loves Nobody, 1969, The Moon Bathers, 1972, (non-fiction) Prints of Paul Jacoulet, 1980, Watercolors of Paul Jacoulet, 1988, Elizabeth Keith-The Printed Works, 1992; contbr. articles to profl. jours. Recipient Samuel Goldwyn award, UCLA, 1979, 80. Mem. Writers Guild Am., New England Appraisers Assn. Avocations: reading.

MILES, THOMAS CASWELL, aerospace engineer; b. Atlanta, Mar. 21, 1952; s. Franklin Caswell and Eugenia Frances (Newsom) M.; m. Linda Susan Duggleby, Aug. 10, 1980. BMET, So. Poly. State U., 1977; postgrad., Troy State U., 1978-80. Assoc. engr. aircraft design Lockheed Martin Aero. Co., Marietta, Ga., 1980-82, engr., aircraft design, 1982-85, sr. engr., aircraft design, 1985-89, group engr., 1989-90, specialist engr., 1990-98; sr. specialist eng., 1998—; mem. SAE-A-6 Mil. Aircraft & Helicopter Panel, 1987-91, SAE-A-10 Aircraft Oxygen Equipment Com., 1996—. Mem. AIAA, (assoc. fellow), ASME, ASTM, Nat. Mgmt. Assn. (bd. dirs. 1996-2000), Soc. Automotive Engrs. (SAE co. rep., SAE Atlanta sect. vice chmn. aircraft), Oxygen Standardization Coord. Group, Assn. Fraternity Advisors (affiliate), Wick's Lake Homeowners Assn. (pres. 1995, v.p. 1996, 97), Tau Kappa Epsilon (Providence advisor 1999—, dist. pres. 1987-88, dist. v.p. 1984-99, chpt. advisor 1980-87, key leader 1985, 90, So. Order of Honor 1989). Avocations: sailing, screen printing. Home: 1926 Wicks Ridge Ln Marietta GA 30062-6777

MILES-CLARK, JEARL, olympic athlete, track and field; b. Gainesville, Fla., Sept. 4, 1966; m. J.J. Clark, Nov. 30, 1997. BA in Business, Ala. A&M, 1988. Winner N.C.A.A. Divsn. II Nats. 400m, 1985; mem. U.S.A. Olympic Team, 1992, 1996. Achievements include world Champion 400m, 1993. Office: c/o USA Track & Field 1 Rca Dome Ste 140 Indianapolis IN 46225-1023

MILEV, NIKOLAY KOLEV, petroleum engineer; b. Stara Zagora, Bulgaria, Aug. 28, 1949; s. Kolio and Maria M.; m. Velitchka Milina, July 30, 1983; children: Nikolay, Mila. Tech. Power Networks, Power Tech. Sch., Bulgaria, 1968; MS in Petroleum Engring., Oil & Gas Acad., Moscow, 1973, PhD in Petroleum Engring., 1981; Cert. in Econs., Coll. of Petroleum Studies, Oxford, U.K., 1997. Jrs. rschr. Bulgargas, Sofia, 1975-76; sr. rschr. Oil & Gas R&D Ctr., Bojurishte, Bulgaria, 1977-84, 87, 90; sr. tech. expert Gasstrojmontaj, Damascus, Syria, 1985-86, Bulgargeomin, Jbissa, Syria, 1988-90; pres. Petroconsult, Sofia, 1991—; sr. tech. expert European Commn. Multi-Country Energy Programe, Bucharest, Romania, 1994-98; tech. cons. Quad Engring., London, 1991-94; tech. expert BCEOM, Paris, 1997-98; head R&D divsn., Bulgargaz EAD, Sofia, 1998—. Author: Maintenance of Oil and Gas Pipelines, 1983, Technical Diagnostic of Oil and Gase Pipelines, 1984; inventor: Inhibitor of H2S Corrosion, 1983. Mem. Soc. Petroleum Engrs./USA, Inst. of Gas Engrs./UK. Avocations: skiing, yachting, mountain tourism. Office: Petroconsult, PO Box 2, 1712 Sofia Bulgaria

MILEY, STEFANY ANN, lawyer; b. Austin, Tex., Dec. 19, 1970; d. Andrew Martin and Judith Clara TeWell. BA in Journalism, Tex. A&M U., 1993; JD, Calif. Western Sch. Law, 1995. Bar: Nev. Law clk. Judge Nancy Oesterle, Las Vegas, Nev., 1995, Barker, Gillock, Koning, Brown, Las Vegas, Nev., 1995-96; assoc. atty. Pynh, Eglet and Silvestri, Las Vegas, Nev., 1996-97, Edwards, Hale, Sturman and Parkid, Las Vegas, Nev., 1997-98, Jolley, Urga, Wirth and Woodbury, Las Vegas, Nev., 1998—; clk. County Bar Assn., Las Vegas, 1996—. Fundraising chmn. Las Vegas Jr. League, 1996—, Univ. Med. Ctr., Las Vegas, 1996—, U. Nev. Women's Ctr., Las Vegas, 1996—. Mem. ABA, Clark County Bar Assn. Office: Jolley Urga Wirth and Woodbury 3800 Howard 16th Fl Las Vegas NV 89109

MILGRIM, DARROW A., insurance broker, recreation consultant; b. Chgo., Apr. 30, 1945; s. David and Miriam (Glickman) M.; m. Laurie Stevens, Apr. 15, 1984; children: Derick, Jared, Kayla. BA, Calif. State U., San Bernardino, 1968; postgrad., U. So. Calif., 1972. Accredited ins. adv.; cert. ins. counselor; cert. sch. adminstr. Tchr. Rialto (Calif.) Unified Sch. Dist., 1969-70, Las Virgenes Unified Sch. Dist., Westlake Village, Calif., 1970-78; instr. Calif. State U., Northridge, Calif., 1980-84; pres. Darrow Milgrim Ins. Svcs., Inc.; ins. broker, dir. Speare Ins. Brokers, Blade Ins. Svcs., Brentwood, Calif., 1984—; dir. Calamigos Star C Ranch Summer Camp, Malibu, Calif., Calamigos Environ. Edn. Ctr., Malibu. Editor: Legislation and Regulations for Organized Camps, 1987. Pres. Calif. Camping Adv. Coun., Long Beach, 1985-87; bd. dirs. Calif. Collaboration for Youth, Sacramento, 1985—, Camp Ronald McDonald for Good Times, 1989-95; commr. dept. parks and recreation City of Agoura Hills, Calif., 1987-93; cons. So. Calif. Children's Cancer Svcs., L.A., 1986-95, ACA Legis Task Force and Nat. Pub. Policy Com. Mem. Am. Camping Assn. (bd. dirs. So. Calif. sect., chmn. nat. pub. policy com. Martinsville, Ind., 1980-98, nat. bd. dirs. 1990-95, legis. liaison, regional honor 1986), Ins. Brokers and Agts. of L.A. Coun., Agts. and Brokers State Legis. Coun. E-mail: dmilgrim@speare.com. Office: Speare Co Ins Brokers PO Box 250024 Los Angeles CA 90025-0660

MILI, SAMIR, agricultural economist; b. Jemmel, Monastir, Tunisia, Oct. 5, 1964; arrived in Spain, 1987; s. Mohamed and Selma (Chergui) M. Agronomist, Agrl. Engring. Sch., Sousse, Tunisia, 1987; MS, Advanced Mediterranean Agr., Zaragoza, Spain, 1990; PhD in Agrl. Econs., Polytech. U., Madrid, Spain, 1995. Rsch. asst. Advanced Mediterranean Agronomic Studies, Zaragoza, 1988-89, Polytech. U., Madrid, 1990-92, Spanish Coun. Sci. Rsch., Madrid, 1993-95; rschr. Inst. Econs. & Geography, Madrid, 1995—. Recipient nat. prize for agrl. publs. Spanish Ministry Agr., Madrid, 1995. Office: Instituto Economia y Geog, c/Pinar 25, 28006 Madrid Spain

MILIC, BOŽIDAR LJUBIŠA, chemistry educator, researcher; b. Kraljevo, Yugoslavia, Apr. 29, 1935; s. Ljubiša Janko and Caja Milorad (Neškovic) M.; m. Mirjana Ljubomir Alimpic, Apr. 7, 1960 (div. Mar. 7, 1967); 1 child, Marijana; m. Nevena Ilija Runjevac, Apr. 20, 1969; 1 child, Natasha. BD, U. Belgrade, Yugoslavia, 1961, MD, 1975, PhD, 1978. Asst. rschr. faculty vet. U. Belgrade, 1959-61; rschr. Yugoslav Inst. Food Industry, Novi Sad, Yugoslavia, 1962-70; tchg. asst. dept. organic chemistry faculty tech. U. Novi Sad, Yugoslavia, 1970-78, tchr. dept. organic chemistry faculty tech., 1978-83, assoc. prof. dept. organic chemistry faculty tech., 1983-88, prof. dept. organic chemistry faculty tech., 1988—; vice dean Faculty of Tech., 1982-86, dean, 1986-90; vice rector U. Novi Sad, 1991-94. Author: Experimental Organic Chemistry, 1982, 2d edit., 1985, 3d edit., 1996, Organic Chemistry, 1987, 3d edit., 1992, Nonenzymatic Browning Reaction of Foods, 1988, Terpenes, 1997, Alkaloids, 1998, Chemistry of Hallucinogens, 1999, Plant Phenolycs, 2000. Mem. Internat. Electron Spin Resonance Soc., Internat. Food and Tech. Soc., Serbian Chem. Soc. Avocation: history of Renaissancial music. Home: Dusana Vasiljeva No 7, YU-21000 Novi Sad Yugoslavia Office: U Novi Sad Faculty Tech, Bulevar Cara Lazara 1, YU-21000 Novi Sad Yugoslavia

MILICHOVSKY, MILOSLAV JOSEF, chemistry educator; b. Babice, Czechoslovakia, Feb. 13, 1945; s. Josef Jan and Marie Frantiska (Hajkova) M.; m. Svatava Milada Dostalova, June 21, 1968; children: Karel, Pavel. Engr., Inst. Chem. Technology, Pardubice, Czechoslovakia, 1968, Inst. Chem. Technology, Praha, Czechoslovakia, 1975; CS, Inst. Chem. Technology, Pardubice, 1977, DS, 1989. Rsch. and devel. profl. Jihoceske Papirny, Vetrni, Czechoslovakia, 1968-75; asst. prof. Inst. Chem. Technology, Pardubice, 1976-85, head of dept., 1986-93, head of dept. wood, pulp and paper, 1994—; cons. Ministry of Forest, Water and Environment, Praha, 1988-90; adv. group The Sustainable Paper Cycle, London, 1994-96. Contbr. articles to profl. jours. Mem. Chem. Soc. Praha, Tech. Assn. of Pulp and Paper Industry, Pulp and Paper Assn. Avocations: music, gardening. Office: U Pardubice Dept Wood Pulp & Paper, Cs Legii 565, CZ 53210 Pardubice Czech Republic

MILINAIRE, GILLES JEAN, French diplomat; b. Paris, France, Apr. 6, 1944; s. Henri and Nicole (Schneider) M.; m. Louise Egolf, July 1992 (div. 1996); children: Galaad, Thea Gabriella Nicole. Diploma, Acad. Art Drama Ctr., London, 1967, Sony Inst. at Am. Film Inst., Hollywood, Calif., 1986. Actor, 1967-89, ind. prodr., 1986-95; hon. consul from France to N.Mex., Tesuque, 1991—. Appeared in Repertory Theater, Eng., roles in The Boxer, La Ronde, The Knack, Catherine the Great, Macbeth, others; in France mem. co. Theatre du Soleil, 1989, 93; appeared in films Slogan, Desire, Irresistible, Adventure of Gerard, Red, Last Program, Mimi Bluette, Salvador; appeared on TV in The Avengers, Delius, Reconciliation, The Hitchhiker, Hart to Hart, Bret Maverick, others; ind. film and video prodr. Jerry Lewis, Les Grands Chefs, Oliver Stone, Pow Wow, Regine, others. E-mail: gmilinaire@aol.com. Office: Consulate of France PO Box 247 Tesuque NM 87574-0247

MILIOU, ELENA D., advertising consultant; b. Athens, Greece, Feb. 3, 1956; d. Dimitrios G. and Marieta S. (Tsirigoti) M.; m. Dimitrios S. Semsis, (div. 1997); children: Alexandros Milios Serbetis, Dimitrios Milios Semsis. Diploma in Advt., Mktg., Coll. Distributive Trades, London, 1974; diploma in Pub. Rels., CAM, London, 1975; diploma in Advt., R.S.A., London, 1975; diploma in Mktg., C.C.E.I., London, 1975. Client svcs. in ADEL S&S, ABC, BATES, ALECTOR, 1976; acc. dir. J.W.T., Athens, Greece, 1984-86; client svcs. dir. DDB Needham, Athens, 1986-87; group acc. dir. BBDO, Athens, 1989-90; mng. dir. D'Arcy, Athens, 1990—. Mem. Am. Hellenic C. of C. and Industry, WWF, Greek Soc. Mgmt. Avocation: gardening. Office: D'Arcy, Pentelis Ave 73, 15234 Halandri Greece

MILITKY, JIŘÍ, engineering educator; b. Kalna Voda, Trutnov, Czech republic, June 16, 1949; s. Lubomír and Erna (Kolbe) M.; m. Dagmar Medvědová, July 7, 1998; children: Michal, Jaroslava, Kateřina. Dipl. Engring., Tech. U. Liberec, Czech Republic, 1973, PhD, 1982. Rschr. State Rsch. Inst., Liberec, 1973-75; head dept. Rsch. Inst., Dvur, 1975-89; tchr. Tech. U. Liberec, 1990—, assoc. prof., 1990-93, prof., 1993—, vice rector, 1992-94, faculty dean, 1995-2000, vice rector, 2000—; academician Kiev Inst., 1996; hon. prof. Ivanovo Acad., 1995. Author: Modified Pet Fibers, 1993; co-author: Experimental Data Treatment, 1995. Head com. FEANI, Paris, 1995; bd. dirs. Textile Acad., Switzerland, 1995. Mem. AUTEX (Belgium). Avocations: running, weight lifting. Home: Seifertova 2374, 54402 Dvur Králové Czech Republic Office: Technical Univ, Hálkova 6, 461 17 Liberec Czech Republic

MILK, JARED MARC, real estate company executive, writer; b. Gt. Neck, N.Y., Dec. 24, 1969; s. Richard H. Milk and Hattie (Fuld) Milk Solymosy. AA in Bus., SUNY, 1990; BA in Theater & Comms., SUNY, Old Westbury, 1992; AA in Bus., Nassau C.C. Real estate sales N.Y., real estate broker N.Y. Broker Surf Realty, 1995-96; owner Milk and Assocs., 1996—, Hamajama Wood Boxes and Bags, 1996—, Castlecove Vending Machines, 1988—. Author: Flying Feathers, 1993; co-author: (book-on-cassette) Cinderella Cockroach, 1990, A Christmas Tale, 1994, A Chanukah Tale, 1995, The Mystery of the Old Fishing Shack, 1999, Legally Raped, 1999, Confessions on the Psycho Lane, 1999. Mem. N.Y. State Real Estate Assn., Nassau Rep. Club. Democrat. Jewish. Avocations: tennis, collecting, ice-skating, golf, travel, antiques.

MILKEY, JAMES R., environmental lawyer; b. Hartford, Conn., Dec. 17, 1956; s. Robert K. and Ruth M. Milkey; m. Cathie Jo Martin, July 7, 1990; children: Julian M., Jonathan R. AB magna cum laude, Harvard U., 1978; M City Planning, MIT, 1983; JD magna cum laude, Harvard U., 1983. Bar: Mass. 1983, U.S. Ct. Appeals (1st cir.) 1984, U.S. Dist. Ct. Mass. 1984, U.S. Supreme Ct. 1990. Law clk. Mass. Appeals Ct., Boston, 1983-84; asst. atty. gen. Office of the Atty. Gen., Boston, 1984-94, 95—, dep. chief environ. protection divsn., 1990-94, dir. land use and environ. protection, 1995-96, chief environ. protection divsn., 1996—; vis. assoc. prof. Pace Law Sch., White Plains, N.Y., 1994-95; seminar instr. Harvard U., Cambridge, 1990, 92; mem. Bronnfields Adv. Group, Boston, 1999—. Author: (book chpt.) Massachusetts Environmental Law, 1991, 93, 96, 99. Mem. Mass. Bar Assn., Boston Bar Assn. (mem. environ. steering com. 1996—), Environ. League of Mass. (Unsung Hero award 1998), Mass. Audubon Soc., Mass Pub. Interest Rsch. Group, Environ. League of Mass. E-mail: jim.milkey@ago.state.ma.us. Home: 34 Woodcliff Rd Newton MA 02461-1825 Office: Office of Atty Gen 200 Portland St Boston MA 02114-1722

MILKOV, BORYS OLEGOVYCH, physician, educator; b. Kholm, Lublin, Poland, Apr. 2, 1932; s. Oleg Orestovych and Nina Stepanovna (Hrushko) M.; m. Violla Herasymivna Hutsa, July 13, 1956 (div. Oct. 1977); children: Milkov Serhiy, Milkova Iryna; m. Lidia Ivanovna Tronko, Oct. 14, 1977. ENT specialist, U. Ukraine, Dnipropetrovsk, 1956; postgrad., Inst. Pectoral Surgery, Moscow, 1960-62; Candidate Med. Sci., Inst. Dnipropetrovsk, 1967, D Med. Sci., 1976. Chief pectoral unit Hosp. Dnipropetrovsk, 1962-69; asst. prof. Inst. Dnipropetrovsk, 1972-78, prof., 1978-79; prof. Inst. Chernivtsi, Ukraine, 1979-80, chief faculty surgery, 1980-97, prof., 1997—. Author: Injury of Organs of the Thorax, 1982, Urgent Thorax Surgery, 1989, Acute Suppurative Peritonitis, 1997, Acute Surgery Diseases of the Abdominal Cavity, 1999. Recipient Honored Sci. and Engring. Worker of Ukraine, Presidium of Kiev Supreme Coun., 1990. Mem. Surgeon Soc. Kiev, Surgeon Sci. Soc. Kiev, Regional Surgeon Soc. Chernivtsi (chmn.). Avocations: Christian philosophy, outdoors. Home: Kyivska 32a, 58004 Chernivtsi Ukraine Office: Bukovinian State Med Acad, Theatrical 2, 58004 Chernivtsi Ukraine

MILKS, WILLIAM WOODS, lawyer; b. Bradford, Pa., Aug. 16, 1943; s. William Woods and Irene Marie (Chisholm) M.; m. Marie Nakanishi, June 10, 1969; children: Alicia Leilani, William Woods III. BA, Boston Coll., 1965; JD, Georgetown U., 1971. Pvt. practice law Honolulu, 1973—; consumer advocate Hawaii State Govt., Honolulu, 1979-88. Office: Hui Enekinia Hawaii 1001 Bishop St # 2810 Honolulu HI 96813-3429

MILKY, IMRAN FARUK, import/export company executive; b. Dhaka, Bangladesh, Nov. 19, 1966; s. Abdul Halim and Farrukh Ara Milky. B of Commerce. Cargo officer Thai Airways Internat., Dhaka, Bangladesh, 1985-86; mng. dir. World Cargo Svc. Ltd., Dhaka, 1987—. Mem. Assn. Cargo Agts. of Bangladesh (founding mem.), Lions Club (pres. Dhaka chpt. 1995-96). Avocations: travel, singing, reading, acting, playing cricket. Home: House No 69/2 Rd No 7A, Dhanmondi R/A, Dhaka 1209, Bangladesh

MILLA GRAVALOS, EMILIO, industrial engineer; b. Zaragoza, Spain, Apr. 1, 1944; s. Pablo Milla Mallo and Emilia Grávalos Gil. Diploma in Indsl. Engring., Higher Tech. Sch. Indsl. Engrs., Madrid, 1972; Dr. in Indsl. Engring., Higher Tech. Sch. Indsl. Engrs. U. Politecnica, Madrid, 1977; diploma in Physics Sci., Complutense U., Madrid, 1984, diploma in History, 1989. Diplomate engring. divsn. Junta de Energia Nuclear, Madrid, 1973-78, inspector of nuclear power plants, 1978-82, project dir. air treatment Nuclear Systems divsn., 1982-86; safety engr. Nuclear Tech. Inst. Ctr. Energetic, Environ. Tech. Rsch. (CIEMAT), Madrid, 1986-91; project leader nuclear & radioactive facilities decommissioning Nuclear Tech. Inst. Ctr. Energetic, Environ. Tech. Rsch., Madrid, 1991—; mem. coordinating com. on fast breeder nuclear reactors, Europe, 1991-94; lectr. in atmospheric pollution Trade and Indsl. Chamber, Madrid, 1992—. Contbr. articles and revs. to profl. jours. Mem. AAAS, Internat. Assn. for Aerosol Rsch., Amnesty Internat., UNICEF, N.Y. Acad. Scis. Avocations: lecturing, history, travel, mountains, music. Home: Maria Benitez 25, Pozuelo de Alarcon, 28224 Madrid Spain

MILLAR, RICHARD WILLIAM, JR., lawyer; b. L.A., May 11, 1938. LLB, U. San Francisco, 1966. Bar: Calif. 1967, U.S. Dist. Ct. (cen. dist.) Calif. 1967, U.S. Dist. Ct. (no. dist.) Calif. 1969, U.S. Dist. Ct. (so. dist.) Calif. 1973, U.S. Supreme Ct. Assoc. Iverson & Hogoboom, Los Angeles, 1967-72; ptnr. Eilers, Stewart, Pangman & Millar, Newport Beach, Calif., 1973-75, Millar & Heckman, Newport Beach, 1975-77, Millar, Hodges & Bemis, Newport Beach, 1979—. Fellow Am. Bar Found.; mem. ABA (litigation sect., trial practice com., ho. of dels. 1990—), Calif. Bar Assn. (lectr. CLE), Orange County Bar Assn. (sec. 1999, treas. 2000, chmn. bus. litig. sect. 1981, chmn. judiciary com. 1988-90, dir. charitable fund 2000), Balboa Bay Club, Bohemian Club (San Francisco), Pacific Club, Palm Valley Country Club (Palm Desert, Calif.). Home: 2546 Crestview Dr Newport Beach CA 92663-5625 Office: Millar Hodges & Bemis One Newport Pl Ste # 900 Newport Beach CA 92660

MILLARD, NEAL STEVEN, lawyer; b. Dallas, June 6, 1947; s. Bernard and Adele (Marks) M.; m. Janet Keast, Mar. 12, 1994; 1 child, Kendall Layne. BA cum laude, UCLA, 1969; JD, U. Chgo., 1972. Bar: Calif. 1972, U.S. Dist. Ct. (cen. dist.) Calif. 1973, U.S. Tax Ct. 1973, U.S. Ct. Appeals (9th cir.) 1987, N.Y. 1990. Assoc. Willis, Butler & Schiefly, Los Angeles, 1972-75; ptnr. Morrison & Foerster, Los Angeles, 1975-84, Jones, Day, Reavis & Pogue, Los Angeles, 1984-93, White & Case, L.A., 1993—; instr. Calif. State Coll., San Bernardino, 1975-76; lectr. Practising Law Inst., N.Y.C., 1983-90, Calif. Edn. of Bar, 1987-90; adj. prof. USC Law Ctr., 1994—. Citizens adv. com. L.A. Olympics, 1982-84; trustee Altadena (Calif.) Libr. Dist., 1985-86; bd. dirs. Woodcraft Rangers, L.A., 1982-90, pres., 1986-88; bd. dirs. L.A. County Bar Found., 1990-2000, pres., 1997-98; mem. Energy Commn. of County and Cities of L.A., 1995-99; bd. dirs. Inner City Law Ctr., 1996-99; mem. jud. procedures commn. L.A. County, 1999—, chair, 2000—. Mem. ABA, Calif. Bar Assn., N.Y. State Bar Assn., L.A. County Bar Assn. (trustee 1985-87), Pub. Counsel (bd. dirs. 1984-87, 90-93), U. Chgo. Law Alumni Assn. (pres. 1998—), Calif. Club, Phi Beta Kappa, Pi Gamma Mu, Phi Delta Phi. Office: White & Case 633 W 5th St Ste 1900 Los Angeles CA 90071-2087

MILLARES RODRIGUEZ, MANUEL, Cuban government official; b. Havana, Cuba, Jan. 9, 1934. Grad., U. Havana. CPA, Cuba. With ctrl. planning office Govt. of Cuba, Havana, 1963-69, vice min. mines, oil and metal industries, 1969, v.p. ctrl. planning office, 1974, min. fgn. trade, 1980-85, v.p. state fin. com., 1985-95, min. of finance & prices, 1995—. Communist. Office: Min of Finance & Prices, Caya Obispo No 211, Esq Havana Cuba*

MILLER, ALAN, physicist, educator; b. Dunfermline, Scotland, June 5, 1949; s. Henry Mushet and Christina Caird (Walkinshaw) M.; m. Susan Linklater Abbott, Dec. 16, 1976; children: Lisa Anne, Ruth Elaine, Janet Rachel. BSc, U. Edinburgh, Scotland, 1971; PhD, U. Bath, Eng., 1975. Chartered physicist, U.K. Rsch. fellow Heriot-Watt U., Edinburgh, 1974-79; vis. asst. prof. North Tex. State U., Denton, 1979-81; sr. prin. sci. officer Royal Signals and Radar Estab., Malvern, Eng., 1981-89; prof. U. Ctrl. Fla., Orlando, 1989—, prof. semiconductor physics, 1993—, head sch. physics and astronomy, 1997—; prof. U. St. Andrews, Scotland, 1993—. Editor, co-author: Nonlinear Optics and Signal Processing, 1992; editor: Nonlinear Optical Materials and Devices, 1995, Laser, Sources and Applications, 1996, Semiconductor Quantum Optoelectronics, 1999; guest editor Ultrafast Phenomena in Jour. Modern Optics, 1989; editor Optical and Quantum Electronics, 1987—; series editor Series on Modern Optics, 1993—. Fellow IEEE (outstanding chpt. chmn. of Orlando sect. 1991), Royal Soc. of Edinburgh, Inst. Physics (U.K.); mem. Optical Soc. Am, Com. Scottish Profs. Physics (chmn.), Scottish Chpt. Lasers and Electro-Optics Soc. (chmn.). Avocation: classical music. Office: Univ of St Andrews, Sch of Physics & Astronomy, St Andrews KY16 9SS, Scotland

MILLER, ALAN M., editor, educator, writer; b. N.Y.C., July 24, 1934; s. Philip and Sylvia (Lubash) M.; children: Neil, Peter, Stephanie, Douglas; m. Sharon A. Tanenbaum, Aug. 29, 1996; step-children: Holly Harouche, Becky Theodoratos. AB, Syracuse U., 1955, LLB, 1958, JD, 1968. Asst. counsel 3 joint legis. coms. N.Y. State Legislature, 1968-70; counsel to minority Nassau County Bd. Suprs., 1974-75; prin. atty. editor West Group, Westbury, N.Y., Eagan, Minn., 1985—; adj. faculty screenwriting Mpls.

Coll., 1999—, Hofstra U., 1990-97, Discovery Ctr., 1990-94, N.Y. Inst. Tech., Old Westbury, 1987-89; presenter 2nd ann. Internat. Conf. on Law and Psychiatry, Jerusalem, 1986. columnist South Shore Record, Woodmere, N.Y., Another Viewpoint, 1985-99 (awards N.Y. Press Assn. 1988, 89, 94, Best column award 1992), Single-Minded, 1991-92, N.Y. Bowler, 1991-93 (Bowling Mag. awards 1990-93, Best column award 1992), Nostalgia Mag., 1990-91, Never Too Late, Writer's Digest (award winning screenplay 1992), Paradox (Screenplay awards 1994-95, Maui Writing conf. Quarter Final, Nicholls Screenwriting fellow), The Sharks, Loss of Reason; writer-editor USCAdvantage, 1995-99 (Immy awards 1996, 97); editor: Beyond the Bar, West Group, 2000; contbr. numerous articles to publs., including N.Y. Times, Newsday, Newsday Mag., Mpls. Star-Tribune, Nat. Press Assn. Assembly dist. leader N.Y. State Dem. Com., 1965-76; commr. Village of Woodsburgh, N.Y., 1980, City of Eagan, Minn., 2000—; mem. citizens adv. com. for Minn. Twins, 2000—. Recipient awards for coverage of Persian Gulf War from Israel, 1991, nat. coun. Jewish Women, 1991, Five Towns Sr. Couns. Mem. Am. Film Inst., Screenwriters Workshop. Jewish. Fax: 651-905-1980. E-mail: alan.miller@earthlink.net. Home: 4316 Aries Ct Eagan MN 55123-1825 Office: 610 Opperman Dr Eagan MN 55123-1340

MILLER, ALEX GORDON, nuclear engineer; b. Newcastle, Eng., Apr. 29, 1950. BA, Cambridge U., 1972, PhD, 1975. Profl. tech. officer AEA, Risley, Windscale, Eng., 1975-79; rsch. officer CEGB, Berkeley, Eng., 1979-88; insp., prin. insp. NII, Bootle, Eng., 1988-92; adminstr. OECD-NEA, Paris, 1992-99. Office: HSE, St Peter's House, Balliol Rd, Bootle L20 3LZ, England

MILLER, ARTHUR, playwright, author; b. N.Y.C., Oct. 17, 1915; s. Isadore and Augusta (Barnett) M.; m. Mary Grace Slattery, Aug. 5, 1940 (div. 1956); children: Jane Ellen, Robert; m. Marilyn Monroe, June 1956 (div. 1961); m. Ingeborg Morath, Feb. 1962; children: Rebecca Augusta, Daniel. AB, U. Mich., 1938, LHD, 1956; LittD (hon.), Oxford U., 1995, Harvard U., 1997, Brandeis U., 1998. Assoc. prof. drama U. Mich., 1973-74. Author: (plays) Honors at Dawn, 1936 (Avery Hopwood award for playwriting U. Mich. 1936), No Villain: They Too Arise, 1937 (Avery Hopwood award for playwriting U. Mich. 1937), Man Who Had All the Luck, 1944 (Nat. prize Theatre Guild 1944), That They May Win, 1944, All My Sons, 1947 (N.Y. Drama Critics Circle award 1947, Tony award best play 1947, Donaldson award 1947), Death of a Salesman, 1949 (N.Y. Drama Critics Circle award 1949, Tony award best play 1949, Donaldson award 1949, Pulitzer prize in drama 1949), The Crucible, 1953 (Tony award best play 1953, Donaldson award 1953, Obie award 1958), A View from the Bridge, 1955 (Antoinette Perry award Best Revival), A Memory of Two Mondays, 1955, After the Fall, 1964, Incident at Vichy, 1964, The Price, 1968, Fame, 1970, The Reason Why, 1970, The Creation of the World and Other Business, 1972, Up From Paradise, 1974, The Archbishop's Ceiling, 1976, The American Clock, 1980, Some Kind of Love Story, 1983, Elegy for a Lady, 1983, Playing for Time, 1986, Danger: Memory!, 1986, The Last Yankee, 1990 (BBC Best Play award 1992), The Ride Down Mt. Morgan, 1991, Broken Glass, 1994 (Olivier award Best Play London 1995), Mr. Peter's Connections, 1998; (play adaptation) Enemy of the People (Ibsen), 1950; (screenplays) The Story of G.I. Joe, 1945, The Misfits, 1961, The Hook, 1975, Everybody Wins, 1990, The Crucible, 1995; (teleplays) Death of a Salesman, 1966, The Price, 1971, Fame, 1978, Playing for Time, 1980 (George Foster Peabody award 1981, Outstanding Writing Emmy award 1981), All My Sons, 1987, An Enemy of the People, 1990, The American Clock, 1994; author: Situation Normal, 1944, Focus, 1945, Jane's Blanket, 1963, I Don't Need You Anymore, 1967, In Russia, 1969, In the Country, 1977, The Theatre Essays of Arthur Miller, 1978, Chinese Encounters, 1979, Salesman in Beijing, 1987, Timebends: A Life, 1987, The Misfits and Other Stories, 1987, (novella) Homely Girl, 1994; exec. prodr. Death of a Salesman, 1985 (Outstanding Drama/Comedy Spl. Emmy award 1985). Recipient Bur. New Plays prize Theatre Guild, 1938, Nat. Assn. Ind. Schs. award, 1954, Gold Medal for drama Nat. Inst. Arts and Letters, 1959, Anglo-Am. award, 1966, Creative Arts award Brandeis U., 1970, Lit. Lion award N.Y. Pub. Libr., 1983, John F. Kennedy Lifetime Achievement award, 1984, Algur Meadows award So. Meth. U., 1991, Antoinette Perry Lifetime Achievement award, 1999, Prix Molière, 1999, Dorothy and Lillian Gish award, 1999.

MILLER, ARTHUR HAROLD, lawyer; b. Plainfield, N.J., Sept. 21, 1935; s. Leon Daniel and Bertha Zelda (Madoff) M.; m. Lynn Fieldman, Aug. 24, 1958; children: Jennifer, Jonathan. BA, Princeton U., 1957; JD, Columbia U., 1960. Bar: N.Y. 1961, U.S. Supreme Ct. 1965, N.J. 1969. Assoc. Wachtel & Michaelson, N.Y.C., 1961-65, Netter, Lewy, Dowd, N.Y.C., 1965-67, Dannenberg Hazen & Lake, N.Y.C., 1967-69; ptnr. Clarick, Clarick & Miller, New Brunswick, N.J., 1971-78, Miller & Miller, New Brunswick, N.J., 1979—; chmn. Middlesex County Legal Svcs. Corp., New Brunswick, 1975-83. Mem. Sch. Bd. Highland Park, N.J., 1981-84. Mem. N.J. Bar Assn. (chmn. availibility legal svcs. com. 1983-85, lawyer referral com. 1986-88), MIddlesex County Bar Assn. (pres. 1993-94, lawyer achievement award 1996), Middlesex County Bar Found. (pres. 1997-98), Middlesex County C. of C. (trustee and legal counsel 1990-93). Democrat. Jewish. Home: 145 N 9th Ave Highland Park NJ 08904-3627 Office: Miller & Miller 96 Paterson St New Brunswick NJ 08901-2109

MILLER, ARTHUR MADDEN, lawyer, investment banker; b. Greenville, S.C., Apr. 10, 1953; s. Charles Frederick and Kathryn Irene (Madden) M.; m. Roberta Beck Connolly, Apr. 17, 1993; children: Isabella McIntyre Madden, Roberta Beck Connolly. AB in History, Princeton U., 1973; MA in History, U. N.C., 1976; JD with distinction, Duke U., 1978; LLM in Taxation, NYU, 1982. Bar: N.Y. 1979, U.S. Dist. Ct. (so. dist.) N.Y. 1979. Assoc. Mudge Rose Guthrie Alexander & Ferdon, N.Y.C., 1978-85; v.p. pub. fin. Goldman, Sachs & Co., N.Y.C., 1985—. mem. adv. bd. Mary Baldwin Coll., Staunton, Va., 1982-86; trustee Princeton U. Rowing Assn., N.J., 1980—, pres., 1986-95; trustee Rebecca Kelly Dance Co., N.Y.C., 1984-86; mem. Power Ten, N.Y., steward, 1992-95. Mem. ABA (tax sect. com. on tax exempt financing 1985—), Nat. Assn. Bond Lawyers (lectr. 1985—), Pub. Securities Assn. (cons. 1985—), Practising Law Inst. (lectr. 1980, editor/author course materials 1980—), Bond Attys. Workshop (editor/author course material 1983—, lectr. 1983—), Princeton Club. Office: Goldman Sachs & Co 85 Broad St New York NY 10004-2456

MILLER, AUDREY THORNTON, vice principal elementary school; b. Glassboro, N.J., June 22, 1937; d. Aubrey and Rebecca Thornton; m. Kenneth C. Miller, Sr., Nov. 20, 1967; children: Yvette A. West, Kenneth C. Jr. BS, Cheyney U., 1963; MEd, Rutgers U., 1974; EdD, Nova Southeastern U., 1998. Cert. prin., supr. N.J. Tchr. Camden (N.J.) Bd. Edn., 1963-74, asst. to prin., 1974-97, vice prin., 1997—; advisor Theta Chi City Wide chpt. Rowan U., 1980-85, Sharp Sch. Safety Patrol, Camden, 1991-95, Network III Drug Program, Camden, 1993-96; mem. adv. bd. Carter's Psychol. Svc., Camden County, 1995—. Author: (Practicum Report) Using the Writing Process to Enchance Elementary Students Writing Proficiency and Teachers' Instructional Strategies, 1998. V.p. Garden City Alumnae of Delta Sigma Theta Sorority, Inc., Sicklerville, N.J., 1989-91; chairperson Career Women's Ministry, St. Matthews Bapt. Ch. Williamstown, N.J., 1993-96; mem. proclamation bd. Chosen Freeholders Camden County, 2000—. Recipient Set a Good Example award Gov. Christie Whitman, Trenton, 1994, Disting. Achievement award, Camden Bd. Edn., 1994, 96, Educator's award N.J. Confedn. Colord Women, 2000. Mem. NAACP, AFL-CIO, Black Women's Edn. Alliance (Educator's award 1992), Camden City Fedn. Sch. Adminstrs. (Local #39), N.J. State Fedn. Colored Women's Club (Outstanding Svc. in Edn. award 2000), Cheyney U. Alumni (life mem.), Nova S. Ea. U. Alumni, Delta Sigma Theta Sorority, Inc. (life mem.), Kappa Delta Pi. Democrat. Avocations: interior decorating, travel, tennis. E-mail: milerau@.aol.com. Home: 4 Pierson Pl Sicklerville NJ 08081-2006 Office: HC Sharp Sch 928 N 32d St Camden NJ 08105

MILLER, BARNEY EARL, biochemist; b. Chattanooga, Tenn., Apr. 3, 1952; s. Gilbert R. and Marcella (Wear) M.; m. Merry A. Noel, June 11, 1983; Children: Corwin Andrew, Melanie Kay. BA in chemistry, U. Tenn., Chattanooga, 1975; PhD in biochemistry, U. Tenn., Memphis, 1983; post doctoral in biochemistry, Duke U., 1985. Rsch. assoc. Duke U. Hughes Med. Inst., Durham, N.C., 1985-88; project leader Abbott Labs, North Chgo., 1988-90, sr. sci., 1990-92; lab chief Molecular Geriat., Lake Bluff, Ill., 1992-94; sec. Neurosci. Cons. Inc., Libertyville, Ill., 1992—; v.p. rsch. Nymox Labs, Johnson City, Tenn., 1994-95, Med. Toolworks, Inc., Evanston, Ill., 1995—; assoc. prof. psychiatry East Tenn. State U., Johnson City, 1994—; cons. Med. Toolworks, 1994—, Neurosci. Cons., Libertville, 1992—. Contbr. articles to profl. jours. Mem. AAAS, N.Y. Acad. Scis., Am. Chem. Soc., Soc. for Neurosci. Republican. Presbyterian. Avocations: rafting, hiking, animation, computer programing. Home: 504 W Maple St Johnson City TN 37604-6604 Office: East Tenn State U W Memorial Ctr Rm 213 University Pkwy Johnson City TN 37604-7328

MILLER, BEVERLY, marketing consultant; b. Osaka, Japan, Sept. 22, 1952; d. Aldee and Helen Miller. BA magna cum laude, U. Md., 1976; JD, Georgetown U., 1982. Corp. devel. officer Folger Shakespeare Libr., Washington, 1982-83; nat. mktg. cons. Blue Cross Blue Sheild Assns., Washington, 1983-86; change mgmt. cons. Sewell Mktg. and Promotions, Göteborg, Sweden, 1986-87; CEO Tng. Connexion/Market Mgmt. Spectrum, Göteborg, 1987—; chmn., CEO Absormatic, The Connexion Internat., Stockholm, 1997—; adj. prof. Internat. Bus. Coll., Göteborg campus Johnson & Wales U., 1994—; fundraising cons. Swedish Jr. C. of C., Göteborg, 1987-90; orgnl. cons. Götaverken Energy/Kvaerner Pulping Techs., Karlstad, Sweden, 1991-93; internal mktg. cons. Neste/Borealis, Copenhagen, 1993-97. Host, scriptwriter corp. promotional film: SKF: The Constant Quest, 1997 (2d pl. Silver Screen award Internat. Film and Video Festival 1998); author: (manuals) A Guide to Strategic Interpersonal Communications, 1987, Coaching, Communicating and Marketing for Excellence, 1997. Fundraiser Washington City Coun. campaign, 1982, campaign mgr., 1990; vol. Big Sisters Nat. Capitol Area, Washington, 1985-86. Recipient Cert. of Achievement and Appreciation, FINA/Swedish Swimming Fedn., 1996, Cert. of Achievement and Outstanding Contbn., Corp. Pub. Affairs-SKF, 1997. Mem. Swedish-Am. C. of C.m Am. Mktg. Assn., Am. Mgmt. Assn., European Assn. Internat. Edn. Office: Market Mgmt Spectrum, Kristinehöjdsgatan 8, S-412 82 Göteborg Sweden

MILLER, BILLIE ANTOINETTE, Barbadian government official; b. Jan. 8, 1944. Student, U. Durham, Eng. Lawyer, 1969-76; M.P. from Bridgetown Ho. of Commons, 1976-86, 91—; min. health Govt. of Barbados, 1976-81, min. of edn. and culture, 1981-86; leader opposition bus. Senate, 1986-89; dep. prime min., min. fgn. affairs, fgn. trade and internat. bus. Govt. of Barbados, Saint Michael, 1994-95, dep. prime min., min. fgn. affairs, tourism and internat. transport, 1995—; bd. dirs. Life of Barbados Ins. Co.; mem. Gray's Inn of Ct., London, Commonwealth Parly. Mem. U.N. Fund for Population Activities; adv. panel Activities Concerning Woment; bd. dirs. Internat. Inst. Women's Polit. Leadership; pres. we. hemisphere region Internat. Planned Parenthood Fedn. Mem. Barbados Bar Assn., Inter-Am. Parly, Commonwealth Parly, Group on Population and Devel., Barbados Nat. Trust, Barbados Mus. and Hist. Soc., Barbados Flower Arranging Soc., Barbados Family Planning Assn. Office: Ministry of Fgn Affairs, Culloden Rd F Walcott Bldg, Saint Michael Barbados*

MILLER, BRIAN JOHN, surgeon, educator; b. London, Sept. 25, 1946; arrived in Australia, 1988; s. Roy and Mary Miller; m. Rosemary Good, Apr. 11, 1970. MB, BS, U. London, 1969. House officer King's Coll. Hosp., London, 1970-71; registrar Jamaican Govt., Montego Bay, 1971-73, U. Saskatchewan, Saskatoon, Can., 1974-79; staff surgeon U. Saskatchewan, 1979-81, 1984-88; provincial surgeon Govt. Kenya, Mombasa, 1981-83; sr. lectr. U. Queensland, Brisbane, 1988—. Contbr. articles to profl. jours. Fellow Royal Australian Coll. Surgeons (cert. merit 1991), Royal Coll. Surgeons Can.; mem. Gen. Med. Coun., Assn. Surgeons East Africa. Avocations: sailboarding, scuba, photography, band-playing, golf. Home: 50 Moreton St, Brisbane 4170, Australia Office: Princess Alexandra Hosp, Dept Surgery, Brisbane 4102, Australia

MILLER, BURTON LEIBSLE, construction executive; b. L.A., July 17, 1944; s. Kenneth Wilbur and Dorothy (Leibsle) M.; m. April Suydam, Dec. 22, 1969 (div. 1983); children: Brandon, Gregory; m. Linda L. Reynolds, Aug. 11, 1990. BSCE, San Jose State U., 1968; MS in Engring., U. So. Calif., 1977. Civil engr. USN, San Bruno, Calif., 1968-74; cost engr. Bechtel Corp., L.A., 1974-79; supr. Bechtel Corp., Saudi Arabia, 1979-81; project mgr. Bechtel Corp., San Francisco, 1981-84, Bay Area Contractors, San Francisco, 1984-94; dist. sales mgr. ISC, San Francisco, 1994-98; constrn. supt. Cannon Constructors, San Francisco, 1998—; cons. KMD/Kimco Mgmt. Co., San Francisco, 1989-90. Mem. World Affairs Coun., San Francisco, 1991, C. of C., San Francisco, 1986. Recipient Commendation, V.P. Dan Quayle, 1992, Cert. of Appreciation, Pres. George Bush, 1989, Cert. of Appreciation, Congressman Bob Mitchel, 1991. Mem. Olympic Club, Project Mgmt. Inst. Republican. Avocations: snow skiing, scuba diving, woodworking. Home: 634 28th Ave San Francisco CA 94121-2817 Office: Cannon Constructors 301 Howard St San Francisco CA 94105-2252

MILLER, CHARLES E. (CHUCK MILLER), judge; b. Washington, Sept. 26, 1944; s. Charles Edward Miller and Mary (Cox) M.; divorced; 1 child, Samantha Mcgill Cox. BA, So. Meth. U., 1971, JD, 1972. Bar: Tex. 1972. Assoc. Roseborough & Curlee, Dallas, 1972-77; judge County Criminal Ct. #7, Dallas, 1977-82, Ct. Criminal Appeals, Austin, Tex., 1983-94; state judge at large State of Tex., 1995—; adj. prof. criminal law So. Meth. U. Law Sch., Dallas, 1980-82. Author and lectr. in field. Mem. nat. adv. coun. Nat. victim Ctr., N.Y.C. and Washington; mem. nat. steeringcom. Victims Constitutional Amendment Network; mem. adv. bd. victims Organized to Ensure Rights and Safety; mem. victim assistancecom. Tex. Young Lawyers Assn.; parliamentarian state exec. bd. People Against Violent Crime. With U.S. Army, 1966-70. Named Disting. Mil. Grad., Officer Candidate Sch., Ft. Sill, Okla., 1968, Best Dallas Misdemeanor Ct. Judge, Dallas Bar Assn., 1982, Best Dallas Criminal Ct. Judge, Dallas County Criminal Bar Assn., 1982; decorated Army Commendational medal, 1970; recipient Sunny von Bulow Nat. Victim Advocacy Ctr. Appreciation cert., 1987, U.S. Dept. Justice Victims of Crime Appreciation cert., 1992, Victims Organized to Ensure Rights and Safety Advocate for Justice award, 1993, People Against Violent Crime Appreciation cert., 1993. Mem. SAR, State Bar Tex. (chmn. criminal law sect. 1981-82, course dir. advanced criminal law course 1990, chmn. crime victim com. 1992-94, crime victim & witness, 1994, cert. specialist in criminal law), Coll. State Bar Tex., Tex. Bar Found. Republican. Home and Office: 1701 Foggy Glen Cv Austin TX 78733-1541

MILLER, CHARLES WALLACE, historian, environmental geologist, educator; b. Phoenix, July 7, 1946; s. Charles W. and Emabel O. Miller; m. Connie Raschke, June 3, 1972; 1 child, Geoffrey Wallace. BA, U. Md., 1969; MA, U. Tex., 1970; BS, SUNY, Albany, 1978; PhD, Union Inst., 1990. Tchr. pub. schs. San Antonio, 1971-76; instr. San Antonio Coll., 1972-78, St. Mary's Univ., San Antonio, 1976-78, Cochise Coll., Sierra Vista, Az., 1989-90; environ. geologist U.S. Geol. Survey, Metairie, La., 1978-80; field geologist U.S. Bur. Land Mgmt., Moab, Utah, 1980-84; historian U.S. Bur. Reclamation, Salt Lake City, 1990-94; environ. scientist USAF, Tucson, 1994—; instr. Pima C.C., Tucson, 1998—; mineral cons., Tucson, 1984-89; instr. Pima C.C., 1998—. Author: Stake Your Claim! The Tale of America's Enduring Mining Law, 1991, The Spirit of the Pioneers Still Rules, 1997, The Automobile Gold Rushes, 1998. Vol. Christ Comty. Ch., Tucson, also various youth orgns. including Boy Scouts; group coord. Combined Fed. Campaign. Mem. Nat. Eagle Scout Assn., Mining History Assn., Mensa, Hist. Soc., Golden Key, Phi Alpha Theta, Pi Sigma Alpha. Avocations: backpacking, scuba diving, photgraphy. Home: 136 S Shadow Creek Pl Tucson AZ 85748-3278 Office: USAF 355 CES CEVA Davis Monthan A F B AZ 85707

MILLER, CYNTHIA ANN, mathematics educator; b. Thomasville, Ga., Oct. 17, 1951; d. James Peyton and Mildred Virginia (Simpson) M.; m. George H. Gibson Jr.; children: Casey Ann Miller Gibson, Patrick Peyton Miller Gibson. BS cum laude, U. Tenn., Chattanooga, 1972; MEd cum laude, West Ga. Coll., 1978; EdS, Ga. State U., 1980, PhD, 1983; postgrad., Ga. Inst. Tech., 1980-81. Math tchr. Cobb City Bd. Edn., Marietta, Ga., 1978-80; prof. math. edn. Ga. State U., Atlanta, 1981-82, prof. math., 1982-83, asst. prof., 1987-93; prof. math. and computer sci. DeKalb Coll., Atlanta, 1980-84; prof. math. Spelman Coll., Atlanta, 1984-87, Mercer U., Atlanta, 1985-87; adj. math. prof. Christian Bros. U., 1993-95, U. Memphis, 1998-99, Ark. State U., 2000—; rschr. NASA Jet Propulsion Lab., Pasadena, Calif., 1985, 86, cons., 1985—; rschr. Navy Personnel R&D Ctr., San Diego, 1987—. Nat. Meris scholar, 1969. Mem. Nat. Coun. Tchrs. Math., Math. Assn. Am., Ga. Coun. Tchrs. Math., Assn. for Women in Math., Internat. Orgn. Women in Math., Mensa, Pi Mu Epsilon, Kappa Delta Pi. Avocations: water skiing, hiking, reading, travel, photography. Office: Ark State U State Univ Math Dept Jonesboro AR 72401

MILLER, DENNIS DAVID, publications administrator, consultant; b. Milw., June 26, 1941; s. Clyde Harry and Ruth Mae (Krekel) M. Student, U. Va., 1962-63; BS, U. Wis., Milw., 1967. Asst. prodn. mgr. KVPD Inc. Advt., Milw., 1967-69; asst. sales promotion mgr. Oster Corp., Milw., 1969-74; collateral account exec. Lawler-Ballard Advt., Norfolk, Va., 1974-75; account exec. Comml. Art Svc., Norfolk, 1975-77; dir. printing and publs. Old Dominion U., Norfolk, 1977-83, dir. publs., 1983-87; dir. publs. Nat. Ctr. for State Courts, Williamsburg, Va., 1987-93; cons. City of Norfolk, Va. Printing Dept., 1980; instr. continuing edn. Old Dominion U., Norfolk, 1983-85; judge NCAA Football Program Competition, 1985. Creative dir.: (devel. publ.) A Briefcase, 1977 (Bronze medal 1977), (recruitment publ.) ODU Viewbook, 1982 (Gold medal 1983). Non-profit coord. Williamsburg United Way, 1989. With USN, 1960-64. Mem. Va. Assn. Printing, Publs. and Pub. Rels. (pres. 1978-80), Coun. for the Advancement and Support Edn. (lectr. 1982, Gold award, Award of Merit 1980), Assn. Coll. and Univ. Printers, Nat. Sch. Pub. Rels. Assn. (Nat. Bronze award 1982).

MILLER, DONALD ANDREW, II, psychologist; b. Indpls.; s. Donald A. Sr. and Julia Elizabeth (Stewart) M.; m. Eiko Martin, Sept., 1981 (div. June, 84); 1 child, Shabaka Jamal. AB, Ind. U., 1974, MS, 1978; PhD, LaSalle U., 1997; doctoral tng., U. Cin., 1983-84. Cert. sch. psychologist, mental health counselor, profl. counselor, clin. hypnotherapist. Social worker Children's Bur. of Indpls., 1979-81; dir. V.C. Hilligoss Child Abuse Prevention Ctr., Anderson, Md., 1983; pediatric psychology intern U. Md., Balt., 1984-85; clin. child psychologist Franklin Sq. Hosp. dept. psychiatry, Balt., 1985-86; sch. psychologist Howard County Pub. Schs., Columbia, Md., Montgomery County Pub. Schs., Rockville, Md.; pvt. practice counselor Columbia, 1997—; asst. adj. prof. pastoral counseling dept. Loyola Coll., 1997—; coord. Near Eastside Multiservice Ctr., Indpls., 1978-79; disability claims adjuster Ind. Rehab. Svcs., Indpls., 1977-78; counselor Atterbury (Ind.) Job Corps Ctr., 1975-76; layout operator Otis Elevator Co., Bloomington, Ind., 1976-77. Musician/composer : (compact disk) With You In Mind, 1998; poet: Poetic Voices of Am.- Village News, 1992-96. Dir. cultural identity project, Mark Twain Sch., 1991-97; dir. Cultural Identity Project, curator Gallery African Am. History and Culture; musical dir. African Am. Art Ensemble, 1990-98; fellow in child & youth svcs. Internat. Coun. of Sex Edn. and Parenthood of Am. U., 1982—. Recipient minority fellowship U. Md., 1984-86, grad. minorities scholars and fellows award U. Cin., 1983-84; named one of Outstanding Young Men Am., 1981. Fellow Am. Bd. Child Mental Health Svc. Providers; mem. Am. Assn. Christian Counselors, Am. Counseling Assn., Am. Mental Health Counselors Assn., Assn. Non-White Concerns, Am. Personnel & Guidance Assn. Baptist. Avocations: musical performance, composition, recording & instrn., running, weightlifting. Home: 10534 William Tell Ln Columbia MD 21044-2425 Office: Montgomery County Pub Schs Mark Twain Sch 14501 Avery Rd Rockville MD 20853-3601

MILLER, DONALD KENNETH, engineering consultant; b. St. Louis, Oct. 18, 1925; s. Henry Edward and Ernestine Elizabeth (Schmeer) M.; m. Arline Louise Heckman, Feb. 27, 1953; children: Garry Edwin, Kristine Louise Miller Morris. BSChemE, Mo. U., 1950. Registered profl. engr., Pa. Application engr. York (Pa.) Corp., St. Louis, Houston, York, 1951-62; mgr. quality control York divsn. Borg Warner Corp., 1962-65, chief engr., 1965-85; refrigeration specialist York Internat. Corp., 1985-88; pres. MDK Engring. Corp., York, 1988—. Author: (with others) Plant Engineering Handbook, 1959, ASHRAE Handbook, 1981-94, Applied Thermal Design, 1989; contbr. articles to ASHRAE Jour. and IIR/IIF Internat. Congress Procs.; inventor desuperheater control in a refrigeration apparatus. With USNR, 1944-46. Mem. AIChE, NSPE, ASHRAE (life mem., cen. Pa. chpt., sec. 1972-73, treas. 1973-74, v.p. 1974-75, pres. 1975-76, Disting. Svc. award 1992), U.S. Nat. Com. Internat. Inst. Refrigeration. Republican. Presbyterian. Avocations: sketching, computers. Office: MDK Engring Corp 2036 Wyntre Brooke Dr York PA 17403-4545

MILLER, DOROTHY ELOISE, education educator; b. Ft. Pierce, Fla., Apr. 13, 1944; d. Robert Foy and Aline (Mahon) Wilkes. BS in Edn., Bloomsburg U., 1966, MEd, 1969; MLA, Johns Hopkins U., 1978; EdD, Columbia U., 1991. Tchr. Cen. Dauphin East H.S., Harrisburg, Pa., 1966-68, Aberdeen (Md.) H.S., 1968-69; asst. dean of coll., prof. Harford C.C., Bel Air, Md., 1969—; owner Ideas by Design, 1995—; mem. accreditation team Mid. States Commn., 1995— ; statewide writing skills assessment com., statewide English stds. com. Md. Higher Edn. Commn. 1997—, English composition com., 1997—. Editor: Renewing the American Community Colleges, 1984; contbr. articles to profl. jours. Pres. Harlan Sq. Condominium Assn., Bel Air, 1982, 90-96, Md. internat. divsn. St. Petersburg Sister State Com., 1993—; edn. liaison AAUW, Harford County, Md., 1982-92; cen. com. mem. Rep. Party, Harford County, 1974-78; crusade co-chair Am. Cancer Soc., Harford County, 1976-78; mem. faculty adv. com. Md. Higher Edn. Commn., 1993-96; people's adv. coun. Harford County Coun., 1994—. Recipient Nat. Tchg. Excellence award Nat. Inst. for Staff and Orgn. Devel., U. Tex.-Austin, 1992. Mem. Nat. Mus. Women in the Arts (charter). Republican. Methodist. Avocations: skiing, swimming, golf, reading, image consulting. Office: Harford Community Coll 401 Thomas Run Rd Bel Air MD 21015-1627

MILLER, DOUGLAS ANDREW, lawyer, educator; b. Chgo., May 10, 1959; s. Walter William and Jean (Johnson) M.; m. Birgitte Jorgensen, Aug. 4, 1984. BS, Boston Coll., 1981; JD, Ill. Inst. Tech. Chgo., 1986. Bar: Fed. Trial, Ill., U.S. Dist. Ct. (no. dist.) Ill. Assoc. Bresnahan, Garvey, O'Halloran & Colman, Chgo., 1986-90; ptnr. Williams & Montgomery, Ltd., Chgo., 1990—; adj. prof. law Loyola U., Chgo., 1997—. Contbr. articles to profl. jours. Mem. ABA, Ill. State Bar Assn. (civil practice sect., torts sect.), Chgo. Bar Assn. (vice-chmn. bench and bar com., trial techniques sect., ins. law sect.), Ill. Assn. of Def. Trial Counsel. Avocation: distance running. Office: Williams & Montgomery Ltd 20 N Wacker Dr Ste 2100 Chicago IL 60606

MILLER, DWIGHT MERRICK, archivist, historian; b. Keosauqua, Iowa, July 25, 1932; s. Leo Albert and Beryl Irene (Merrick) M.; m. Frances Florine Olney, Nov. 19, 1961 (dec. Sept. 1977); 1 child, Dianne; m. Judith Spencer, 1979 (div. 1988); m. Pauline K. Leaverton, 1999. BA, U. Iowa, Iowa City, 1959; MA, Truman State U., Kirksville, 1961; attended, The American U., Washington, 1963-64. Asst. archivist Manuscript Divsn., Library of Congress, Washington, 1961-64; sr. archivist Herbert Hoover Presdl. Libr., West Branch, 1964-99. Compiler, asst. editor: (book) The Public Papers of the Presidents: Herbert Hoover; 1929-1933 (6 vols.), 1974-77; co-editor: (book) Herbert Hoover and Harry S. Truman: A Documentary History, 1992, Historical Materials in the Herbert Hoover Presidential Library, 1996, Herbert Hoover and Franklin D. Roosevelt: A Documentary History, 1998. Co-chmn. Iowa Sesquicentennial Commn. Cedar Cty., Tipton, 1995-97. Mem. Nat. Trust for Hist. Preservation, Univ. Athletic Club, Friends of the Univ. of Iowa Libraries (adv. bd. 1976-81), Manuscript Soc., Ft. Ticonderoga Assn. (adv. bd. 1991—), The Manuscript Soc. Presbyn. Avocations: book collecting, historical Iowa pottery. Home: 10 Rita Lyn Ct Iowa City IA 52245-3504

MILLER, DWIGHT RICHARD, personal care industry executive, cosmetologist, consultant; b. Johnstown, Pa., Jan. 24, 1943. Grad., Comer & Doran Sch., San Diego; DSci. (hon.), London Inst. for Applied Rsch., 1973. Cert. aromatherapist; lic. cosmetologist., instr.; Brit. Mastercraftsman. Styles dir. Marinello-Comer, Hollywood, Calif., 1965-67; expert Pivot Point Internat., Chgo., 1967-68; styles dir. Lapins, L.A., 1969; dir. Redken, L.A., 1970, Vidal Sassoon, London, 1971-74; world amb. Pivot Point, New Zealand and Australia, 1974-75; internat. artistic dir. Pivot Point, Chgo., 1975-78; internat. dir., co-founder Hair Artists Inst. & Registry, 1978-81; internat. artistic dir. Zotos Internat., Darien, Conn., 1981-87, Matrix Essentials, Inc., Solon, Ohio, 1987-92; bd. dirs., founder, v.p. creative Anasazi Exclusive Salon Products, Inc., Dubuque, Iowa, 1992-96; pres. Anasazi Salon Sys., Santa Fe, N.Mex., 1996-98; cons., 1998—; judge hairdressing competitions including Norwegian Masters, Australian Nat. Championships; pres. Intercrimpers, London, 1974-75; cons. Amos, Clairol, John Frieda, John Sahag, J.C. Penney, NCA, Matrix, Zotos/ISO, 1998—. Author: Sculptic Cutting Pivot Point 75, Prismatics, 1983, Milady's Standard System of Salon Skills,

1998; prod., dir. 15 documentaries, numerous tech. and industry videos; contbr. articles, photographs to popular mags.; developer several profl. product lines including Vidal Sassoon-London, Design Freedom, Bain de Terre, Ultra Bond, Vavoom!, Systeme Biolage. Cons. American Crew; with USMC, 1960-64. Named Artistic Dir. Yr. Am. Salon mag., Intercoiffure Educator of the Century; presented with Order of White Elephant, 1976; recipient London Gold Cup for Best Presentation London Beauty Festival, 1982, Dr. Everett G. McDonough award for Excellence in Permanent Waving, World Master award Art and Fashion Group, 1992, N.Am. Hairstylist of the Yr. award, 2000. Mem. Cercle des Arts et Techniques de la Coiffure, Intercoiffure, Haute Coiffure Franchaise, Soc. Cosmetic Chemists, Hair Artists Great Britain, Internat. Assn. Trichogists, Nat. Cosmetologists Assn. (HairAmerica, cert. instr.), Am. Soc. Phytotherapy and Aromatherapy, HairChicago (hon.), Art and Fashion Group (pres. 1993), 'Dressers MC (pres. 1990—), London's Alternative Hair Club (patron), The Salon Assn., Am. Beauty Assn., Beauty and Barber Suppy Inst. Home and Office: 707 Don Gaspar Ave Santa Fe NM 87501-4429

MILLER, DWIGHT WHITTEMORE, lawyer; b. Worcester, Mass., July 8, 1940; s. Fred Hamilton and Jeanette (Lewis) M.; m. Mary Francisco, June 22, 1963; children—Rebecca, David. A.B., Colgate U., 1962; J.D., Boston Coll., 1965. Bar: Vt. 1965, MO. 1969, Law clk. U.S. Dist. Ct. Vt., 1965-66; sole practice, Brattleboro, Vt., 1966-68; with Monsanto Co., St. Louis, 1968-72; gen. counsel Stromberg Carlson Communications, Inc., St. Louis, 1972-75, Pott Industries, Inc., St. Louis, 1975-85; gen. solicitor Mo. Pacific R.R., St. Louis, 1985-86, Union Pacific R.R., 1991—; ptnr. Thompson & Mitchell, St. Louis, 1987-91; Mem. ABA, Order of Coif. Unitarian. Office: 210 N 13th St Saint Louis MO 63103-2329

MILLER, GARY H., lawyer; b. New Orleans, Mar. 11, 1957; s. Leo Jr. and Suzanne Robinowitz (Meltzer) M.; m. Ellen Baldwin Hoffman, Oct. 18, 1986; children: Matthew Hilliard, Katherine Elise. BA magna cum laude, New Eng. Coll., 1979; JD cum laude, Tulane U., 1982. Assoc. Jones Walker, New Orleans, 1982-89, ptnr., 1990—; mem. moot ct. bd. Tulane U. Sch. Law, 1980-82; lectr. in field. Bd. dirs. Golden Retriever Club Greater New Orleans, Inc., 1980, Burtheville Cmty. Assn., Inc., 1997—. Mem. La. Bar Assn. (treas. consumer protection, lender liability and bankruptcy sect. 1990-91, chmn. consumer protection, lender liability and bank sect. 1991-92), Phi Tau Beta. Democrat. Jewish. Avocations: Retriever and obedience training, fishing, hunting, guitar. Office: Jones Walker 201 Saint Charles Ave Ste 5200 New Orleans LA 70170-5100

MILLER, GENEVIEVE, retired medical historian; b. Butler, Pa., Oct. 15, 1914; d. Charles Russell and Genevieve (Wolford) M. AB, Goucher Coll., 1935; MA, Johns Hopkins U., 1939; PhD, Cornell U., 1955. Asst. in history medicine Johns Hopkins Inst. History of Medicine, Balt., 1943-44, instr., 1945-48, rsch. assoc., 1979-94; asst. prof. history of sci. Case Western Res. U. Sch. Medicine, Cleve., 1953-67, assoc. prof., 1967-79, assoc. prof. emeritus, 1979—; rsch. assoc. med. history Clevel. Med. Libr. Assn., 1953-62; curator Howard Dittrick Mus. Hist. Medicine, 1962-67, dir., 1967-79; corr. mem. fgn. socs. history of medicine. Author: William Beaumont's Formative Years: Two Early Notebooks 1811-1821, 1946; The Adoption of Inoculation for Smallpox in England and France, 1957 (William H. Welch medal Am. Assn. History Medicine 1962), Bibliography of the History of Medicine of the U.S. and Canada, 1939-1960, 1964, Bibliography of the Writings of Henry E. Sigerist, 1966, Letters of Edward Jenner and Other Documents Concerning the Early History of Vaccination, 1983; assoc. editor Bull. of History of Medicine, 1944-48, acting. editor, 1948, mem. adv. editl. bd., 1960-92; mem. bd. editors Jour. History of Medicine & Allied Scis., 1948-65; editor Newsletter Am. Assn. History of Medicine, 1986-96; contbr. articles to profl. jours. Alumna trustee Goucher Coll., Balt., 1966-69; trustee Judson Retirement Cmty., Clevel., 1993-99,. Am. Coun. Learned Socs. fellow, 1948-50, Dean Van Meter fellow, Goucher Coll., 1953-54. Fellow Cleve. Med. Libr. Assn. (hon.); mem. Am. Assn. History Medicine (pres. 1978-80, mem. coun. 1960-63, Lifetime Achievement award 1999), Am. Hist. Assn., Internat. Soc. History of Medicine, Soc. Archtl. Historians, Phi Beta Kappa. Democrat. Home and Office: Judson Manor 1890 E 107th St Apt 816 Cleveland OH 44106-2245

MILLER, GEORGE, film director; b. Brisbane, Australia, Mar. 3, 1945. MD, U. NSW, Australia, 1970. Former physician St. Vincent's Hosp., Sydney, Australia. Films include: dir., writer: Violence in the Cinema, Part I, 1971, Mad Max, 1979, The Road Warrior-Mad Max II, 1982, Mad Max: Beyond the Thunderdome, 1985, Lorenzo's Oil, 1992 (Acad. award nominee for best original screenplay 1992), White Fellas Dreaming, 1996, (host, narrator) 40,000 Years of Dreaming, 1996, (exec.) Heaven Before I Die, 1997, Babe: Pig in the City, 1998; dir.: Devil in Evening Dress, 1973, Twilight Zone: The Movie, 1983, The Witches of Eastwick, 1987; editor Frieze, an Underground Film, 1973; assoc. prodr.: Chain Reaction, 1980; prodr.: The Year My Voice Broke, 1988, Dead Calm, 1989, Flirting, 1990, Video Fool For Love, 1996; prodr., writer: Babe, 1995 (Acad. award nominee for best film and for best screenplay 1996). Office: Kennedy Miller Prodns, 30 Orwell St Kings Cross, Sydney 2011, Australia Office: Gang Tyre & Brown Inc c/o Jeff Mandell 132 S Rodeo Dr Beverly Hills CA 90212*

MILLER, G(ERSON) H(ARRY), research institute director, mathematician, computer scientist, chemist; b. Phila., Mar. 2, 1924; m. Mary Alexa Heath, Jan. 28, 1961; children: Byron, Alexandra. BA, Pomona Coll., 1949; MEd in Counseling and Pers., Temple U., 1951; PhD. in Ednl. Psychology, U. So. Calif., 1957; MS in Math., U. Ill., 1982, postgrad., 1963-65. Jr. high sch. and jr. coll. instr. math. L.A. Sch. Dist., 1953-57; assoc. prof. Western Ill. U., Macomb, 1957-60; prof. Towson State U., Balt., Md., 1960-61; prof. math. and edn. Parsons Coll., Fairfield, Iowa, 1961-65; prof. Tenn. Technol. U., Cookeville, 1966-89; prof. math. and computer sci. Edinboro (Pa.) U., 1968-71, 81-89, asst. dir. Institutional Rsch., 1972-80; dir. Studies On Smoking, Inc. and SOS Stop Smoking Clinic, Edinboro, 1972—; spkr. state, nat. and internat. profl. meetings; condr. seminars on smoking and health London, Fed. Republic Germany, Alaska, New Brunswick, N.J., Chgo., Costa Rica, Nice, Washington; dir. Nat. Study Math. Requirements for Scientists and Engrs., 1966-73; condr. Nat. Seminars for Biologists, Chemists & Engrs., 1970-75. Contbr. numerous articles to profl. jours. Pres. Edinboro YMCA, 1972-83; bd. dirs. Common Cause, Harrisburg, Pa., 1975-80; Sgt. USAAF, 1943-46, PTO. Grantee U.S. Office Edn., 1968, 70, No Other World, 1973, NAS, 1980, ITT Life Ins. Corp., 1983, Erie Cmty. Found., 1987. Fellow Am. Inst. Chemists (cert. profl. chemist), AAAS; mem. APHA, Am. Assn. World Health, Am. Chem. Soc., Am. Soc. Engring. Edn., Internat. Assn. Pure and Applied Chemists, Internat. Soc. for Preventive Oncology, Math. Assn. Am., Am. Diabetes Assn., Nat. Coun. Tchrs. Math., Sch. Sci. and Math. Assn., N.Y. Acad. Scis. (hon.), Acad. Sr. Profls. (hon.). Home and Office: Studies on Smoking Inc 125 High St Edinboro PA 16412-2552 also: 25 Crescent Pl S Saint Petersburg FL 33711-5118

MILLER, HARRY FREEMAN, university administrator; b. Vallejo, Calif., Aug. 27, 1946; s. Theodore Harry and Grace (Eubank) M.; 1 child, Charissa Rainie. BA, Howard U., 1969; JD, U. Calif., Davis, 1972; cert., Harvard U., 1989, U. Chgo., 1998. Assoc. gen. sec. Stanford U., Palo Alto, Calif., 1973-79; asst. dean, lectr. law Syracuse (N.Y.) U., 1979-81; dir. devel. Georgetown U. Law Ctr., Washington, 1981-83; v.p. instnl. advt. Morgan State U., Balt., 1983-91; assoc. v.p., dir. planned giving U. South Fla., Tampa, 1991-95; assoc. v.p. devel. Tex. So. U., Houston, 1996—. Host Lou Rauls Telethon for United Negro Coll. Fund, Syracuse, 1981, mem. adv. com., Tampa, 1993-95; mem. Nat. Sports Festival Com., Syracuse, 1981. Mem. Nat. Soc. Fund Raising Execs., Assn. Fund Raising Officers (bd. dirs. 1984-90), Am. Inst. Parliamentarians, Tampa Urban League (bd. dirs. 1993-95), Phi Alpha Delta. Office: Tex So U Office of Devel 3100 Cleburne St Houston TX 77004-4501

MILLER, HERBERT H., lawyer; b. Balt., May 24, 1921; s. Louis Miller and Rebecca Platt; m. Irene R. Rosen, Aug. 27, 1944; children: Rose, Marjorie, Fran. JD cum laude, U. Balt., 1942; ABA in Acctg., Balt. Coll. of Commerce, 1947. Bar: Md. 1943, U.S. Dist. Ct. Md. 1944, U.S. Supreme Ct. 1986; notary pub., Md. Law clk. Rubenstein and Rubenstein, Balt., 1938-39, Joel J. Hochman, Balt., 1939-40, Feikin & Talkin, Balt., 1940-42; atty. Sherbow, Harris & Medwedeff, Balt., 1942-43, Harris & Medwedeff, Balt., 1943-45; pvt. practice Balt. and Towson, Md., 1946—; mem. inquiry panel Atty. Grievance Com. Md., Balt. County, 1985—; panel chmn. Health Claims Arbitration, Balt., 1994—. Bd. trustees Balt. Coll. Commerce, 1948-52, Beth El Congregation, Balt. County, 1990-94; youth advisor B'nai B'rith, Balt., 1943-88, mem. B'nai B'rith Youth Orgn., pres., 1940-42. Mem. Md. State Bar Assn., Balt. City Bar Assn., Balt. County Bar Assn., Mensa Internat. (arbitrator Md.). Avocations: reading, handyman work, walking. Office: 200 E Joppa Rd Ste 205 Towson MD 21286-3107

MILLER, HERMAN LUNDEN, retired physicist; b. Detroit, Apr. 23, 1924; s. Josiah Leonidas and Sadie Irene (Lunden) M.; m. Dorothy Grace Sack, Sept. 15, 1951. BS in Engring. Physics, U. Mich., 1948, MS in Physics, 1951. Registered profl. engr., Mich. Physicist Ethyl Corp., Ferndale, Mich., 1948-49, Dow Chem. Co., Denver, 1950-55; mem. project rsch. staff Princeton (N.J.) U., 1955-65; physicist Bendix Aerospace, Ann Arbor, Mich., 1965-72; nuclear engr. Commonwealth Assocs., Jackson, Mich., 1973-80. Author: Lewiston in the Lumbering Era, 1992, Lumbering in Early Twentieth Century Michigan, The Kneeland-Bigelow Company Experience, 1995.; contbr. articles to profl. jours. With USAF, 1943-46, PTO, lt. col. Res. Mem. IEEE, Am. Phys. Soc., Am. Nuclear Soc.

MILLER, JACQUES FRANCIS, medical researcher; b. Nice, France, Apr. 2, 1931; s. Maurice Eugene and Fernande Eugenie (Debarbnot) M.; m. Margaret Denise Houen, Mar. 17, 1956. BSc in Medicine, U. Sydney, Australia, 1953, MB, BS, 1955; MD (hon.), U. Sydney, 1986; PhD, London U., 1960, DSc, 1966; BA, Melbourne U., Australia, 1985. Medical Diplomate. Intern Royal Prince Alfred Hosp., Sydney, 1956-57; asst. prof. Chester Beatty Rsch. Inst. and London U., 1961-64; assoc. prof. (reader) Beatty Rsch. Inst. and U. London, 1965-66; head exptl. pathology unit Walter and Eliza Hall Int. Med. Research, Melbourne, Australia, 1966—; cons. task force on immunology of malaria, WHO, Geneva, Switzerland, 1976-79, expert advisor on immunology, 1984—; cons. Internat. Agy. Rsch. on Cancer, Lyon, France, 1976-80. Contbr. over 400 articles to sci. jours. Recipient Langer-Bertha Teplitz Meml. prize for cancer rsch., 1965, Gairdner Found. Internat. award, 1966, Ency. Britannica award, 1966, Paul Ehrlich-Ludwik Darmstaedter prize, 1974, Rabbi Shai Shacknai Meml. prize Hebrew U., 1978, Internat. St. Vincent prize for med. sci. UNESCO, WHO and Republic of Italy, 1983, 1st Sandoz prize for immunology, 1990, 1st Medawar prize Transplantation Soc., 1990, J. Alwyn Taylor Internat. prize for medicine John. P. Roberts Rsch. Inst., 1995; named Officer of Order of Australia. Fellow Royal Soc. (London) (Croonian prize 1992), Australian Acad. Sci. (council mem. 1976-79, v.p. 1979), Royal Soc. Arts; mem. U.S. NAS (fgn. assoc.), Internat. Agy. Research Cancer (sci. council 1976-80, pres. 1980), Internat. Union Immunol. Socs. (counsellor 1977-83), Australian Soc. Immunology, Am. Assn. Immunologists (hon.), Transplantation Soc. Avocations: art, photography, music, literature. Office: Walter & Eliza Hall Inst Med Rsch, PO Royal Melbourne Hosp, Melbourne Victoria 3050, Australia

MILLER, JAMES CLIFFORD, III, economist; b. Atlanta, June 25, 1942; s. James Clifford and Annie (Moseley) M.; m. Demaris Humphries, Dec. 22, 1961; children: Katrina Demaris, John Felix, Sabrina Louise. BBA, U. Ga., 1964; PhD in Econs., U. Va., 1969; LLD (hon.), U. of Pacific, 1987; PhD (hon.), Kennesaw Coll., 1988. Asst. prof. Ga. State U., Atlanta, 1968-69; economist U.S. Dept. Transp., Washington, 1969-72; assoc. prof. econs. Tex. A&M U., College Station, 1972-74; economist U.S. Coun. Econ. Advs., Washington, 1974-75; asst. dir. U.S. Council Wage and Price Stability, Washington, 1975-77; resident scholar Am. Enterprise Inst., 1977-81; adminstr. Office Info. and Regulatory Affairs, Office Mgmt. and Budget and exec. dir. Presdl. Task Force on Regulatory Relief, Washington, 1981; chmn. FTC, Washington, 1981-85; dir. Office Mgmt. and Budget, Washington, 1985-88; disting. fellow, chmn., counsellor Citizens for a Sound Economy, 1988—; disting. fellow Ctr. for Study of Pub. Choice George Mason U., 1988—; pres., chmn. bd. Econ. Impact Analysts, Inc., 1978—. Author: Why the Draft?: The Case for a Volunteer Army, 1968, Economic Regulation of Domestic Air Transport: Theory and Policy, 1974, Perspectives on Federal Transportation Policy, 1975, Benefit-Cost Analyses of Social Regulation: Case Studies from the Council on Wage and Price Stability, 1979, Reforming Regulation, 1980, The Economist as Reformer, 1989, Fix the U.S. Budget: Urgings of an "Abominable No-Man," 1994, Monopoly Politics, 1999. Candidate for Rep. nomination for U.S. Senate for Va., 1994, 96. Thomas Jefferson fellow, 1965-66, DuPont fellow, 1966-67, Ford Found. fellow, 1967-68. Mem. Am. Econ. Assn., Pub. Choice Soc., So. Econ. Assn. (exec. com. 1980-81, v.p. 1990-91), Adminstrv. Conf. U.S. (vice chmn. 1987-88). Republican. Presbyterian. Office: Citizens for Sound Economy 1250 H St NW Ste 700 Washington DC 20005-5938

MILLER, JANEL HOWELL, psychologist; b. Boone, N.C., May 18, 1947; d. John Estle and Grace Louise (Hemberger) Howell; m. C. Rick Miller, Nov. 24, 1968; children: Kimberly, Brian, Audrey, Rachel. BA, DePauw U., 1969; postgrad., Rice U., 1969; MA, U. Houston, 1972; PhD, Tex. A&M U., 1979. Lic. clin. psychologist, sch. psychologist, Tex. Assoc. sch. psychologist Houston Ind. Sch. Dist., 1971-74; rsch. psychologist VA Hosp., Houston, 1972; assoc. sch. psychologist Clear Creek (Tex.) Ind. Sch. Dist., 1974-76; instr. psychology, counseling psychology intern Tex. A&M U., 1976-77; clin. psychology intern VA Hosp., Houston, 1977-78; coord. psychol. svcs. Clear Creek Ind. Sch. Dist., 1978-81, assoc. dir. psychol. svcs., 1981-82; pvt. practice Houston, 1982—; faculty U. Houston-Clear Lake, 1984—; adolescent suicide cons., 1984—. DePauw U. Alumni scholar, 1965-69; NIMH fellow U. Houston, 1970-71. Mem. APA, Am. Assn. Marriage and Family Therapists, Soc. for Personality Assessment, Am. Coll. Forensic Examiners, Internat. Rorschach Soc., Tex. Psychol. Assn., Tex. Assn. Marriage and Family Therapists, Houston Psychol. Assn. (media rep. 1984-85), Houston Assn. Marriage and Family Therapists. E-mail: shrink-skate@prodigy.net. Home: 806 Walbrook Dr Houston TX 77062-4030 Office: Ste 270 16815 Royal Crest Dr Houston TX 77058-2552

MILLER, JEAN PATRICIA SALMON, art educator; b. Little Falls, Minn., Sept. 28, 1920; d. Albert Michael and Wilma (Kaestner) Salmon; m. George Fricke Miller, Sept. 8, 1951 (dec. Apr. 1991); children: Victoria Jean, George Laurids. BS, St. Cloud State Tchrs. Coll., 1942; MS, U. Wis., Whitewater, 1976. Lic. cert. secondary English, art, Wis. Tchr. elem. and secondary art Pub. Schs. Sauk Center, Minn., 1943; tchr. secondary art Bd. Edn., Idaho, 1945; tchr. elem. and secondary art Elkhorn (Wis.) Area Schs., 1950-78; tchr. art adult edn. Kenosha Tech. Coll., Elkhorn, Wis., 1969; cooperating tchr., supr. art majors in edn. U. Wis., Whitewater, 1970-77; coord. Art Train Project, Walworth County. Represented in permanent collections Irwin L. Young Auditorium, U. Wis., Whitewater. Sec. Walworth County Needs of Children and Youth, Williams Bay, Wis., 1956-57; co-chair, sponsor Senate Bill 161-art requirement for h.s. grad., 1988-89. Recipient Grand award painting Walworth County Fair, 1970, 3rd award painting Geneva Lake Art Assn., Lake Geneva, Wis., Acrylic Painting First award Badlants Art Assn., 1994. Mem. Nat. Art Edn. Assn., Wis. Women in Arts, Wis. Art Edn. Assn., Wis. Regional Artists Assn. (co-chmn. Wis. regional art program 1992, 93, corr. sec. 1992—), Walworth County Art Assn. (bd. dirs. 1979-94, pres. 1986-87), Badlands Art Assn., Kiwanis, Elks, Alpha Delta Kappa (pres. Theta chpt. Wis. 1968-70), Delta Kappa Gamma (Iota chpt.). Home and Office: 215 5th St N Richardton ND 58652-7107

MILLER, JEANNE-MARIE ANDERSON (MRS. NATHAN J. MILLER), English language educator, academic administrator; b. Washington, Feb. 18, 1937; d. William and Agnes Catherine (Johns) Anderson m. Nathan John Miller, Oct. 2, 1960. BA, Howard U., 1959, MA, 1963, PhD, 1976. Instr. dept. English Howard U., Washington, 1963-76, asst. prof., 1976-79, assoc. prof., 1979-92, prof., 1992-97, prof. emeritus, 1997—, asst. dir. Inst. Arts and Humanities, 1973-75, asst. acad. planning, office v.p. for acad. affairs, 1976-90; cons. Am. Studies Assn., 1972-75, Silver Burdett Pub. Co., Nat. Endowment for Humanities, 1978—; adv. bd. D.C. Libr. for Arts, 1973—, John Oliver Killens Writers Guild, 1975—, Afro-Am. Theatre, Balt., 1975—. Editor, Black Theatre Bull., 1977-86; Realism to Ritual: Form and Style in Black Theatre, 1983; assoc. editor Theatre Jour., 1980-81; contbr. articles to profl. jours. Mem. Washington Performing Arts Soc., 1971—, Friends of Sta. WETA-TV, 1971—, Mus. African Art, 1971—, Arena Stage Assos., 1972—, Washington Opera Guild, 1982—, Wolf Trap Assocs., 1982—, Drama League N.Y., 1995—. Ford Found. fellow, 1970-72, So. Fellowships Fund fellow, 1973-74; Howard U. rsch. grant, 1975-76, 94-97, ACLS grant, 1978-79, NEH grant, 1981-84. Mem. AAUP, ACLU, MLA, Nat. Coun. Tchrs. English, Coll. English Assn., Am. Studies Assn., D.C. LWV, Common Cause, Am. Acad. Polit. and Social Sci., Coll. Lang. Assn., Am. Assn. Higher Edn., Nat. Assn. for Women in Edn., Friends of Kennedy Ctr. for Performing Arts, Ibsen Soc. Am., Langston Hughes Soc., Zora Neale Hurston Soc., Nat. Trust Historic Preservation, D.C. Preservation League, Hist. Soc. Washington, Winterthur Guild, Nat. Bldg. Mus., Nat. Mus. Women in Arts, Studio Mus. Harlem, Am. Theatre and Drama Soc., Acad. Am. Poets, Sierra Club, Pi Lambda Theta. Democrat. Episcopalian. Home: 504 24th St NE Washington DC 20002-4818

MILLER, JEROME M., civic worker; b. New Brunswick, N.J., Mar. 16, 1917; s. Edward I. and Beatrice (Kalisch) M.; m. Dorothy Tishler, Apr. 29, 1921; children: David G., Eliot K. Student, Pa. State U., 1935-37, Rutgers U., 1935-39. With E.I. DuPolnt De Nemours & Co., N.J. Dept. Transp., N.Y. Shipbuilding; agt. Equitable Life Assurance Soc.; owner Sally's Steak House, Highland park, N.J., 1952-73; adv. bd. Pan-Am Bank, 1980-84, Broward Fed. Savs. and Loan, Lauderdale, Fla., 1984-89. Chmn. Planning and Zoning Bd., City of Lauderhill, Fla., 1987—; bd. dirs. Garden Lakes of Inverrary Condominium Assn., 1978-81, pres., 1980; bd. dirs. Ornada of South Fla.; pres. Inverrary Assn., 1980—; mem. Fla. State Dem. Exec. Com.; founder Highland Park (N.J.) Lions Club, pres., 1960, past zone chmn., dep. dist. gov.; active Down's Syndrome Program, N.J., 1968-71; mem. exec. bd. Inverrary Tournament, LPGA, Ed Kranpoll Am. Diabetes Assn. Golf Tournament; chmn. Urban Forestry Com., Lauderhill. Sgt. U.S. Army, 1942-46. Recipient Community Service award, Inverrary Assn., 1988, others. Mem. B'nai B'rith, Jewish War Vets. Democrat. Jewish. Office: 5625 Hammock Ln Lauderhill FL 33319-5112

MILLER, JERRY HUBER, retired university chancellor; b. Salem, Ohio, June 15, 1931; s. Duber Daniel and Ida Claire (Holdereith) M.; m. Margaret A. Setter, 1958; children: Gregory, Joy, Carol, Beth, David. BA, Harvard U., 1953; MDiv., Hamma Sch. Theology, 1957; DD (hon.), Trinity Luth. Sem., 1981. Ordained to ministry Luth. Ch., 1957. Research assoc., intern Cornell U., Ithaca, N.Y., 1955-56; instr. Wittenberg U., Springfield, Ohio, 1956-57; parish pastor Ch. of Good Shepherd, Cin., 1957-62; asst. to pres. Ohio Synod Luth. Ch. Am., 1962-66; sr. campus pastor, dir. campus ministry U. Wis., Madison, 1966-69; regional dir. Nat. Luth. Campus Ministry, Madison, 1969-76; exec. dir. Nat. Luth. Campus Ministry, Chgo., 1977-81; pres. Calif. Luth. U., Thousand Oaks, 1981-92, chancellor, 1992-94, pres. emeritus, 1994—; ret. Ventura County Maritime Mus., Channel Islands Harbor, Calif., 1993-95; chmn. Los Robles Bank, Thousand Oaks, 1987-2000; mem. exec. com. Coun. Ind. Colls., Washington, Assn. Ind. Calif. Colls. and Univs., 1981-92, Coun. Luth. Colls., Luth. Ednl. Conf. N.Am., 1977-94; vice chair bd. behavioral sci. State Calif.; bd. dirs. Santa Barbara Bank and Trust. Editor: The Higher Disciplines, 1956; contbr. articles to profl. jours. Bd. dirs. Wittenberg U., Augustana Coll., Rock Island, Ill., United Way, Thousand oaks, Ventura County chpt. ARC, Thousand Oaks, YMCA; chmn. bd. dirs. Los Robles Hosp.; vice chair Stagecoach Inn Mus. Found., 1998—. Named Man of Yr., Salem, 1975, Man of Yr. Conejo Valley, 1999; Siebert Found. fellow, 1975. Mem. Am. Assn. Higher Edn., Council Advancement and Support Edn., Harvard Alumni Assn., Western Coll. Assn. (bd. dirs.), Conejo Valley C. of C. (bd. dirs.), Conejo Symphony Orch. (bd. dirs.), Conejo Valley Hist. Soc. (bd. dirs. 1995—). Club: Harvard (Ill., Ohio, Wis., Calif.), YMCA (regional bd. dirs., vice chair 1996-99), Rotary. Avocations: skiing, golfing, hiking, travelling.

MILLER, JOHN PENDLETON (JACK MILLER), publishing company executive; b. Middletown, Ohio, Sept. 11, 1931; s. John William and Helena Bernice (Pendleton) M.; m. Barbara Elaine Stutsman, Jan. 19, 1952; children: Stacy Lynn, John Dewey, Tamara Leigh, Mark Douglas, Matthew Scott, Delano Mitchell. BS in Civil Engring., Wash. State U., Pullman, 1958. Sales engr. Armco Steel Corp., Middletown, Ohio, 1958-64; v.p., dir. mktg. Mes-Tex, Houston, 1964-67, Kirby Bldg. Sys., Houston, 1967-69; pres. Group Comm., Inc., Houston, 1969-81; chmn. bd. dirs. Group Comm., Inc., 1981—; lectr. in field; condr. seminars in field. Author: Selling Building Systems, 1970, Profitable Management Techniques for Contractors, 1973, A Professional Approach to Marketing for the Construction Industry, 1977, Design/Build, Build/Lease, and Financing Building Projects, 1977, Human Stress ... How to Turn It Into Success, 1978, Advanced Negotiating Skills and Strategies, 1979, The Jack Miller Reports, 1985, Rules You Should Know About Investing, 1988, 16 Opportunities in Build/Lease, 1988, Rules You Should Know About Motivation, 1988, Rules You Should Know to be a Better Manager, 1988, Rules You Should Know About Investing in Real Estate, 1988, Rules You Should Know About Time Management and Speed Reading/Speed Learning, 1988, The Important Steps that Take You to Health, Wealth and Happiness, 1992, Rules You Should Know Before You Build Your Important Project, 1993, Total Quality Management for the Construction Industry, 1993, Guide Manual for a Win/Win Negotiator, 1999. Elder Pines Presbyn. Ch., Houston, 1996—. With USAF, 1950-54. Mem. ASCE, Associated Builders and Contractors, Associated Gen. Contractors, Am. Soc. for Quality, The Jack Miller Network, Tau Beta Pi, Phi Kappa Phi. Republican. Presbyterian. Office: Group Comm 10417 Rockley Rd Houston TX 77099-3565

MILLER, JOHN T., JR., lawyer, educator; b. Waterbury, Conn., Aug. 10, 1922; s. John T. and Anna (Purdy) M.; children: Kent, Lauren, Clare, Miriam, Michael, Sheila, Lisa, Colin, Margaret. AB with high honors, Clark U., 1944; JD, Georgetown U., 1948; Docteur en Droit, U. Geneva, 1951; postgrad., U. Paris, 1951. Bar: Conn. 1949 (inactive), D.C. 1950, U.S. Ct. Appeals (2d, 3d, 5th, 10th, 11th and D.C. cirs.), U.S. Supreme Ct. 1952. With Econ. Cooperation Adminstn. Am. Embassy, London, 1950-51; assoc. Covington & Burling, 1952-53, Gallagher, Connor & Boland, 1953-62; pvt. practice Washington, 1962—; adj. prof. law Georgetown U. Law Ctr., Washington, 1959—; mem. Panel on Future of Internat. Ct. Justice. Co-author: Regulation of Trade, 1953, Modern American Antitrust Law, 1948, Major American Antitrust Laws, 1965; author: Foreign Trade in Gas and Electricity in North America: A Legal and Historical Study, 1970, Energy Problems and the Federal Government: Cases and Material, 8th edit., 1996, Deregulating the Interstate Natural Gas and Electric Power Industries, 1998; contbr. articles, book revs. to legal publs. Trustee Clark U., 1970-76; bd. trustees De Sales Sch. of Theology, 1993-97; bd. advisors Georgetown Visitation Prep. Sch., 1978-94, bd. trustees, 1994-96, emeritus trustee, 1996—; former fin. chmn. troop 46 Nat. Capital Area coun. Boy Scouts Am.; pres. Thomas More Soc. Am., 1996-97. 1st lt. U.S. Army, 1943-46, 48-49. Decorated Bronze Star; recipient 10 yr. teaching award Nat. Jud. Coll., 1983. Mem. ABA (coun., chmn. adminstrv. law sect. 1972-73, ho. dels. 1991-93), AAUP, D.C. Bar Assn., Fed. Energy Bar Assn. (pres. 1990-91), Congl. Country Club (bd. govs. 2000—), Army and Navy Club (bd. govs. 2000—), DACOR, Prettyman-Leventhal Am. Inn of Ct. (master 1988-99, pres. 1995-96), Sovereign Mil. Order of Malta (knight). Republican. Roman Catholic. Home: 4721 Rodman St NW Washington DC 20016-3234 Office: 1001 Connecticut Ave NW Washington DC 20036-5504

MILLER, J(OHN) WESLEY, III, lawyer, writer; b. Springfield, Mass., Oct. 3, 1941; s. John Wesley Jr. and Blanche Ethel (Wilson) M. AB, Colby Coll., 1963; AM, Harvard U., 1964, JD, 1981. Bar: Mass. 1984, U.S. Dist. Ct. Mass. 1984, U.S. Supreme Ct. 1993. Instr. English Heidelberg Coll., Tiffin, Ohio, 1964-69, U. Wis., 1969-77; real estate broker, 1977-84; founder Miller-Wilson Family Papers, U. Vt., Madison (Wis.) People's Poster and Propaganda Collection, St. Hist. Soc. Wis. Author: History of Buckingham Junior High School, 1956, The Millers of Roxham, 1958, Giroux Genealogy, 1958, Symphonic Heritage, 1959, Community Guide to Madison Murals, 1977, Aunt Jennie's Poems, 1986; founding editor: Hein's Poetry and the Law Series, 1985—; editor: The Curiosities and Law of Wills, 1989, The Lawyers Alcove, 1990, Famous Divorces, 1991, Legal Laughs, 1993, Coke in Verse, 1999; founding editor: Law Libr. Microform Consortium Arts Law Letters Collection, 1991—; exhibitor A Salue to Street Art, State Hist. Soc. wis., 1974; represented in permanent collections U. Vt., Colby Coll. Archives, State Hist. Soc. Wis., Boston Pub. Libr., Pierpont Morgan Libr.; contbr. The Poems of Ambrose Philips, 1969, Dictionary of Canadian Biography, 1980, Collection Building Reader, 1992, Oxford English Dictionary, 1995—; contbr. numerous articles on Am. street lit., bibliography, ethics, history, edn., law, religion, librarianship, mgmt. of archives, gay studies. Fellow Wisdom Hall of Fame; recipient Cmty. Activism award Bay State Objectivist, 1993, 94, 95. Mem. MLA, Am. Philol. Assn., Milton Soc., New Eng. Historic Geneal. Soc., Vt. Hist. Soc., Wis. Acad. Scis., Arts & Letters, Social Law Library, Pilgrim Soc., Ancient and Hon. Arty. Co., Mayflower Soc., Soc. Colonial Wars, Sons and Daus. of the Victims of Colonial Witch Trials,

Mensa, Springfield Renaissance Group. Office: 5 Birchland Ave Springfield MA 01119-2708

MILLER, JONATHAN WOLFE, theater and film director, physician; b. London, July 21, 1934; s. Emanuel Miller; m. Helen Rachel Collet, 1956; 3 children. Ed., St. John's Coll., Cambridge U.; MB Ch, Univ. Coll. Hosp. Med. Sch., London, 1959; DLitt (hon.), U. Leicester, 1981, Cambridge U., 1996; Dr. (hon.), Open U., 1983. Dir. Nottingham Playhouse, 1963-69; assoc. dir. nat. Theatre, 1973-75; mem. Arts Coun., 1975-76; artistic dir. Old Vic, 1988-90; lectr. Nat. Gallery, 1995, Met. Mus., N.Y.C., 1995; curator major exhbn. Nat. Gallery, London, 1998; vis. prof. drama Westfield Coll., U. London, 1977-78; lectr. wide variety of subjects. Co-author, actor in Beyond the Fringe, 1961-64; dir. Under Plain Cover Royal Ct. Theatre, 1962, The Old Glory, N.Y.C., 1964, Prometheus Bound, Yale Drama Sch., 1967, Oxford and Cambridge Shakespeare Co. prod. of Twelfth Night, on tour in U.s., 1969; dir. for Nat. Theatre, London: The Merchant of Venice, 1970, Danton's Death, 1971, The School for Scandal, 1972, The Marriage of Figaro, 1974; other prodns. include: The Tempest, London, 1970, Prometheus Bound, London, 1971, The Taming of the Shrew, Chichester, Eng., 1972, The Seagull, Chichester, 1973, The Malcontent, Nottingham, Eng., 1973, The Family in Love, 1974, The Importance of Being Earnest, 1975, All's Well That Ends Well, Measure For Measure, Greenwich Season, 1975, Three Sisters, 1977; dir. operas Arden Must Die, 1973, Sadler's Well Theatre, 1974, The Cunning Little Vixen, Glyndebourne, 1975, 77, Marriage of Figaro, Vienna State Opera, 1991, Robert Devereux, Monte Carlo, 1992, Die Gezeichnete, Zurich, 1992, Maria Stuarda, Monte Carlo, 1993, the Secret Marriage, Opera North, 1993; dir. for English Nat. Opera: The Marriage of Figaro, 1978, The Turn of the Screw, 1979, 91, Arabella, 1980, Othello, 1981, Rigoletto, 1982, 85 (alwo at Met. Opera, N.Y.C.), Fidelio, 1982, 83, Don Giovanni, 1985, The Magic Flute, 1986, Tosca, 1986, The Mikado, 1986, 88, The Barber of Seville, 1987, Cosi fan Tutte, 1995, Carmen, 1995; dir. for Kent Opera: Cosi Fan Tutte, 1975, Rigoletto, 1975, Orfeo, 1976, Eugene Onegin, 1977, La Traviata, 1979, 96, Falstaff, 1980, 81, Fiedlio, 1982, 83, 88; dir. for La Scala Milan: La Fanciulla del West, 1991, Manon Lescaut, 1992; dir. for Maggio Musicale, Florence: Don Giovanni, 1990, Cosísi fan Tutte, 1991, 94, Marriage of Figaro, 1992, La Bohéme, 1994, La Bohéme, which transfered to La Bastille, 1995, dir., Strass Ariadne auf Naxos, 1997; dir. Met. Opera, N.Y.: Katya Kabanova, 1991, Pelléas et Mélisande, 1995; dir in co-prodn. with L.A. Music Ctr. and Houston Grand Opera House Der Rosenkavalier, 1994; dir. Broadway play Long Day's Journey Into Night, 1986, The Taming of the Shrew at Royal Shakespeare Co., Stratford, 1987, Andromache, One Way Pendulum, Bussy D'Ambois, all at Vic, 1988, The Tempest, 1988, Turn of the Screw, 1989, Kimg Lear, 1989, The Liar, 1989; films include: Take a Girl Like You, 1969; TV films include: Whistle and I'll Come to You, 1967, Alice in Wonderland, 1967, The Body in Question Series, 1978, Henry the Sixth, part I, 1983, States of Mind Series, 1983; exec. prodr. Shakespeare TV series, 1979-81; author (TV) McLuhan, 1971, The Body in Question, 1978, States of Mind, The Facts of Life, Subsequent Performances, 1986, Who Cares, Born Talking, Museums of Madness, Anthropology, Opera Works; editor: Freud: The Man, His World, His Influence, 1972, The Don Giovanni Book, 1990; actor (TV) Jonathan Miller on Reflection, 1998, (TV mini-series) The Talk Show Story, 2000. Decorated Order of Brit. Empire; named Dir. of Yr., Soc. West End Theatre Awards, 1976; recipient Silver medal Royal TV Soc., 1981; fellow Univ. Coll. London; hon. fellow St. John's Coll., Cambridge U.; rsch. fellow in history of medicine Univ. Coll., London U., 1970-73. Fellow Royal Coll. Physicians (London and Edinburgh); mem. AAAS (fgn. mem.). Office: care IMG Artists, 616 Chiswick High St, London 5RX UK, England*

MILLER, JOSEPH ALFRED, printing executive; b. Richmond, Va., Feb. 23, 1907; S. Ernest Hutchinson and Caroline (lipscombe) M.; m. Berenice K. Moss. Student, U. N.C., Chapel Hill, 1953-54. Pres. Miller Printing Co., Asheville, N.C., 1930-71; hon. dir. First Union Nat. Bank, Asheville; bd. trustee, U. N.C., Asheville, 1958-63, Montreat-Anderson Coll., Montreat, N.C., 1961-65. Chmn. Asheville Redevel. Commn., 1961-70; chmn. bd. deacons Presbyn. Ch., 1954. Recipient Spl. award City of Asheville, 1970, Chancellor's Medallion U. N.C., 1990. Mem. Printing Industry of the Carolinas (pres. 1955, hon.), Blue Ridge Pkwy. Assn. (pres. 1963-64), Asheville C. of C. (dir. 1957-62, spl. award 1950), Am. Bus. Club (pres. Asheville chpt. 1938), Rotary, Country Club Asheville (pres. 1949-50). Democrat. Home: Givens Estates 100 Wesley Dr Apt 710 Asheville NC 28803-2092

MILLER, JOSEPH ARTHUR, retired manufacturing engineer, educator, consultant; b. Brattleboro, Vt., Aug. 28, 1933; s. Joseph Maynard and Marjorie Antoinette (Hammerberg) M.; m. Ardene Hedwig Barker, Aug. 19, 1956; children: Stephanie L., Jocelyn A., Shana L., Gregory J. BS in Agrl., Andrews U., Berrien Springs, Mich., 1955; MS in Agrl. Mechs., Mich. State U., 1959; EdD in Vocat. Edn., UCLA, 1973. Constrn. engr. Thornton Bldg. & Supply, Inc., Williamston, Mich., 1959-63, C & B Silo Co., Charlotte, Mich., 1963-64; instr. and dir. retraining Lansing (Mich.) C.C., 1964-68; asst. prof./prog. coord./coop coord. San Jose State U., 1968-79; mfg. specialist Lockheed Martin Missiles and Space (and predecessor cos.), Sunnyvale, Calif., 1979-81, rsch. specialist, 1981-88, NASA project mgr., 1982-83, staff engr., 1988-96, rsch. staff engr., 1996-98, coord. flexible mfg. system simulation project, 1994-96, team mem. federally funded AIMS Agile Mfg. project, 1995-97, team mem. corp funded machining outsource initative project, 1995-97, coord. productivity improvement program, 1996-98; engring. and constrn. cons., Berry Creek, Calif., 1998—; agrl. engring. cons. USDA Poultry Expt. Sta., 1960-62; computer numerical control cons. Dynamechtronics, Inc., Sunnyvale, 1987-90; machining cons. Lockheed, Space Sys. Div., 1986-96; instr. computer numerical control DeAnza Coll., Cupertino, Calif., 1985-88, Labor Employment Tng. Corp., San Jose, Calif., 1988-93; instr. computer-aided mfg. and non traditional machining San Jose (Calif.) State U., 1994-97; team leader Pursuit of Excellence machine tool project Lockheed Martin Missiles and Space, Sunnyvale, Calif., 1990-95, coord. safety award program, 1997-98, mem. quality awareness program screening com., 1998. Author: Student Manual for CNC Lathe, 1990; contbr. articles to profl. jours. Career counselor Pacific Union Coll., Angwin, Calif., 1985-92. UCLA fellow, 1969-73. Mem. Soc. Mfg. Engrs. (sr. mem. 1980-92, chmn. edn. com. local chpt. 1984-85, career guidance counselor 1986-88), Nat. Assn. Indsl. Tech. (pres. industry divsn. 1987-88, bd. cert. 1991-92, mem., chmn. accreditation visitation teams 1984—), Calif. Assn. Indsl. Tech. (pres. 1974-75, 84-85), Am. Soc. Indsl. Tech. (pres. 1980-81). Seventh-day Adventist. Avocations: violin, camping, designing and building homes, traveling. Home: PO Box 190 Berry Creek CA 95916-0190

MILLER, JOSEPH BAYARD, lawyer; b. Highland, La., Feb. 25, 1920; s. Harrison Coleman and Jeannette (Donaldson) M.; m. Gloria Berthelot, Dec. 31, 1950; children: Joseph Bayard Jr., Melinda May. BA in Arts and Scis., Tulane U., 1939, LLB, 1941. Bar: La. 1941, U.S. Dist. ct. (ea. dist.) La. 1941, U.S. Ct. Appeals (5th cir.) 1941, U.S. Supreme Ct. 1969. Assoc. Milling, Godchaux, Saal & Milling, New Orleans, 1941-47; ptnr. Milling, Benson, Woodward, Hillyer, Pierson & Miller, New Orleans, 1948—; bd. dirs. Continental Land & Fur Co., Inc., New Orleans. Maj. USAF, 1942-46, PTO. Mem. New Orleans Country Club, City Energy Club. Episcopalian. Avocations: hunting, fishing, horses. Home: 7399 Agate St New Orleans LA 70124-3512 Office: Milling Benson Woodward Hillyer Pierson & Miller 909 Poydras St Ste 2300 New Orleans LA 70112-1010

MILLER, JOSEPH IRWIN, automotive manufacturing company executive; b. Columbus, Ind., May 26, 1909; s. Hugh Thomas and Nettie Irwin (Sweeney) M.; m. Xenia Ruth Simons, Feb. 5, 1943; children: Margaret Irwin, Catherine Gibbs, Elizabeth Ann Garr, Hugh Thomas, II, William Irwin. Grad., Taft Sch., 1927; AB, Yale U., 1931, MA (hon.), 1959, LHD (hon.), 1979; MA, Oxford (Eng.) U., 1933; LLD, Bethany Coll., 1956, Tex. Christian U., Ind. U., 1958, Oberlin Coll., Princeton, 1962; LL.D., Hamilton Coll., 1964, Columbia, 1968, Mich. State U., 1968, Dartmouth, 1971, U. Notre Dame, 1972, Ball State U., 1972, Lynchburg Coll., 1985; L.H.D. (hon.), Case Inst. Tech., 1966, U. Dubuque, 1977; Hum.D., Manchester U., 1973, Moravian Coll., 1976. Assoc. Cummins Engine Co., Inc., Columbus, Ind., 1934—; v.p., gen. mgr. Cummins Engine Co., Inc., 1934-42, exec. v.p., 1944-47, pres., 1947-51, chmn. bd., 1951-77, chmn. exec. com., 1977-95; dir., 1995-97; hon. chmn. Cummins Engine, 1997—; pres. Irwin-Union Bank & Trust Co., 1947-54, bd. dir., 1937—, chmn., 1954-75; chmn. exec. com. Irwin Union Corp., 1976-90, hon. chmn., 1997—; bd. dirs. Irwin Fin. Corp., 1990—; mem. Commn. Money and Credit, 1958-61, Pres.'s Com. Postal Reorgn., 1968, Pres.'s Com. Urban Housing, 1968; chmn. Pres.'s Com. on Trade Rels. with Soviet Union and Eastern European Nations, 1965, Nat. Adv. Commn. on Health Manpower, 1966; vice chmn. UN Commn. on Multinat. Corps., 1974; adv. council U.S. Dept. Commerce, 1976; mem. Study Commn. on U.S. Policy Toward So. Africa, 1979-81. Pres. nat. Coun. Chs. of Christ U.S.A., 1960-63; trustee Nat. Humanities Ctr., 1978-90, Carnegie Instn., Washington, 1988-91; mem. cen. and exec. coms. World Coun. Chs., 1961-68; trustee Ford Found., 1961-79, Yale Corp., 1959-77, Urban Inst., 1966-76, Mayo Found., 1977-82; fellow Branford Coll. Recipient Rosenberger award U. Chgo., 1977, 1st MacDowell Colony award, 1981; hon. fellow Balliol Coll., Oxford (Eng.) U.; Benjamin Franklin fellow Royal Soc. Arts. Fellow Am. Acad. Arts and Scis., Royal Inst. Brit. Architects (hon.); mem. AIA (hon.), Am. Philos. Soc., Ind. Acad., Bus. Coun., Conf. Bd. (sr.), Phi Beta Kappa, Beta Gamma Sigma. Mem. Christian Ch. Office: 301 Washington St Columbus IN 47201-6743

MILLER, L. MARTIN, accountant, financial planning specialist; b. N.Y.C., Sept. 17, 1939; s. Harvey and Julia (Lewis) M.; m. Judith Sklar, Jan. 21, 1962; children: Philip, Marjorie. BS, Wharton Sch., U. Pa., 1960. CPA; CFP; accredited fin. planning specialist. Jr. acct. Deloitte, Haskins & Sells, N.Y.C., 1960-62; sr. acct. Deloitte, Haskins & Sells, Phila., 1962-64; mng. ptnr. Cogen, Sklar LLP, Phila., 1964—; treas. Coronet Container Co., Inc., Phila., Val Mar Realty Corp., N.Y.C.; dir. Penn Internat. Trading Co., Phila.; mng. dir. CPA Tax Forum, 1966-69; underwriting mem. Lloyds of London, 1978-95, chmn. Mid-Atlantic region, 1991-92; mem. faculty Wharton Sch. U. Pa., 1992-99; lectr., discussion leader on fin. and taxation; columnist Montgomery and Bucks County Dental News. Author: Accountants Guide to S.E.C. Filings, 1968, Salaries, Penn. Non-Profit Report, 1997, Worker Compensation, Practical Tax Strategies, 2000; contbr. articles to profl. jours. Mem. Phila. Rep. Com., 1963-67, treas. Daerr-Bannon for state rep. com., 1997; chmn. Lower Merion Twp. scholarship fund, 1975-78; bd. dirs. Main Line Br. ARC, 1997-2000; bd. dirs. Penn Valley Civic Assn., 1973-79, Gladwyne Civic Assn., 1992-95; mem. Lower Merion Planning Commn., 1978-82, Gov.'s Tax Study Commn.; pres. Mensa Edn. and Rsch. Found., 1984-86; mem. SEC Forum on Small Bus. Capital Formation, 1983, Pa. Impact, 1995; apptd. to Pa. State Bd. Accountancy, 1985-94, chmn., 1990-91; elected sch. bd. dir. Lower Merion Twp., 1993-97, also chmn. fin. com. Served with U.S. Army, 1961-62. Recipient Outstanding Achievement award Germantown Civic Assn., 1965. Mem. Pa. Inst. CPAs (edn. com. 1975-78, bd. dirs. 1979-81, by-laws chmn. 1980-83, mem. non-profit orgns. com. 1995—), Nat. Assn. State Bds. Accountancy (edn. com. 1987, nominating com. 1989, experience com. 1990, continuing edn. com. 1995—), Cert. Fin. Planner (bd. ethics 1995-97), AICPAs (nat. tax commn. 1979-82, exec. com. self regulation divsn. for CPA firms 1984-87, acctg. and rev. svcs. com. 1985-88, long range planning com., ethics divsn. 1985-88, specialization bd. 1989-90, ethics exec. com. 1990-93, mem. curriculum and acctg. edn. 1993-96, chmn. fin. assistance task force 1995, bd. dirs. Estate Planning Coun. 1998—, nomination com. 1999), Little 10 Acctg. Assn. (edn. chmn. 1980-84), Main Line C. of C. (govt. affairs com. 1991—), Mensa (internat. fin. officer 1970-74), Masons (past master), Plays and Players Club (treas. 1978-79), Beta Alpha Psi. Home: 204 Dove Ln Haverford PA 19041-1902 Office: Cogen Sklar LLP 150 Monument Rd Bala Cynwyd PA 19004-1702

MILLER, LIA VERENA REYES, management services executive; b. Pasay City, Manila, Philippines, Sept. 1, 1966; d. Rudy San Pedro and Cecilia San Pedro (Suarez) Reyes; m. Thomas Michael Miller, Oct. 3, 1998; stepchildren: Michael Bradley, Brenton Joseph. BS, Marymount Coll., 1988. Creative dir. Pacific Design, Indpls., 1989-91; v.p. ops. Park Kwik Corp. of Am., Indpls., 1988-92; self-employed parking cons. N.Y.C., 1992-95; dir. Internat. Parking Profls., Singapore, 1997—; pres. ParkAsia, Inc., Philippines, 1995—, Parking Co. Asia, Philippines, 1999—; cons. Fort Bonifacio Devel. Corp., Manila, Philippines, 1995-99, Kerry Properties, Hong Kong, 1997-98, Metro Pacific Land Corp., Manila, Philippines, 1997, Totsuka Station, Japan, 1997. Chmn. Bus. Encouraging Students for Tomorrow, Ind., 1989-90 (recipient Leadership award 1990); vol. Kiwanis Club Indpls., 1986; counselor, leader Eli Lilly Project Leadership, Ind., 1984; mem. Women's Round Table, Ind., 1989-92, Commn. for Downtown Indpls., 1989-91. Mem. Nat. Parking Assn., Internat. Parking Inst. Avocations: scuba diving, drawing and painting, tennis, traveling.

MILLER, LINDA KAREN, educator; b. Kansas City, Jan. 22, 1948; d. Bennie Chris and Thelma Jane (Richey) M. B of Secondary Edn., U. Kans., 1970; M of Secondary Edn., U. Va., 1978, EdD, 1991. Tchr. social studies Pierson Jr. High Sch., Kansas City, 1970-72; substitute tchr. Fairfax (Va.) Pub. Schs., 1972-73; reading aide Lake Braddock Secondary Sch., Burke, Va., 1973-74; tchr. social studies Mark Twain Intermediate Sch., Alexandria, Va., 1974-75, Herndon (Va.) Intermediate Sch., 1975-78, Fairfax High Sch., 1978-86, 87—; cons. in field. Recipient George Washington medal Valley Forge Freedom Found., 1998, Excellence in Tchg. award U. Kans. Sch. of Edn., 1999; named Pre-Collegiate Tchr. of Yr., Orgn. Am. Historians, 1996, Secondary Tchr. of Yr., Nat. Coun. for Social Studies, 1996, Secondary Tchr. of Yr., U. Va., 1997, Outstanding Secondary Tchr., Va. Hist. Soc., 1998, Celebrating Tchg. Excellence award Am. Coun. Tchrs. Russian, 1998, Va. Geography Tchr. of Yr., 1999, Global Teachnet Tchr. of Yr., Nat. Rease Corps. Assn., 1999; Korean Soc. fellow, 2000. Mem. Nat. Coun. Social Studies (curriculum com. 1991-94), Am. Legal History Soc., Orgn. Am. Historians, Va. Coun. Social Studies, Washington Area Women Historians, U. Va. Alumni Assn. Republican. Episcopalian. Avocation: doll collecting. Office: Fairfax High Sch 3500 Old Lee Hwy Fairfax VA 22030-1888

MILLER, LISA ANN, oceanographer; b. Mpls., Apr. 9, 1965; d. Russel Leonard and Kathleen Claire (Krieg) M.; m. Conrad Stewart Cooper. BS, Humboldt State Univ., 1988; PhD, Univ. Calif., 1994. Billing clerk Stoner & Welsh, AAL, Pacific Grove, Calif., 1981-83; shipping clerk Social Security Adminstr., Carmel, Calif., 1983-84; waiter Deli-Icious, Pacific Grove, Calif., 1985; rsch. fellow Univ. Calif., Santa Cruz, 1987, teaching asst., 1988-93, grad. student researcher, 1988-94; rsch. scientist Univ. Bergen, Bergen, Norway, 1994-97; sr. scientist Inst. of Marine Rsch., Bergen, Norway, 1997-99; rsch. scientist Inst. Ocean Scis., Dept. Fisheries and Oceans, Can., 1999—; Eng. editor, internet rsch. specialist Amnesty Internat., Bergen, 1995-97. Contbr. articles to profl. jours. Chair mailing com. Info. Tabling Com. Women's Internat. League for Peace and Freedom, 1991-94; legis. alert phone tree Citizens for Social Responsibility, 1985-88, tour guide chem. demonstrations Annual Conf. on Women in Sci. Humboldt State Univ., Arcata, Calif., 1984-86. Decorated Antarctic Svc. medal U.S. Navy, 1992; grad. rsch. fellow Nat. Sci. Found., 1989-92, regent's fellowship Univ. Calif., 1988-89, Analytical Chem. award Am. Chemical Soc., 1987. Mem. Am. Geophysical Union, The Oceanography Soc. Avocations: piano, sailing. Fax: 1 250 363 6476. E-mail: millerli@pac.dfo-mpo.gc.ca. Office: Inst Ocean Scis, 9860 W Saanick Rd Box 6000, Sidney, BC Canada U8L 4B2

MILLER, LOUIS H., lawyer; b. Lampeter, U.K., Apr. 22, 1945; m. Diane Matuszewski, Dec. 31, 1973; children: Margaret, Anthony. BA in History, Rutgers Coll., 1967; JD, Temple U., 1970. Bar: N.J. 1970, U.S. Dist. Ct. N.J. 1970, U.S. Supreme Ct. 1996. Law clk. to Judge Thomas Beetel Hunterdon County Ct., Flemington, N.J., 1970-71; law clk. to Judge Baruch Seidman Superior Ct. N.J. Chancery, Trenton, N.J., 1971-72; assoc. Jefferson, Jefferson & Vaida, Flemington, 1972-75; ptnr. Vaida & Miller, Flemington, 1975-78; pvt. practice Flemington, 1978-81, 88—; judge Superior Ct. N.J., Flemington, 1981-88; of counsel Levinson Axelrod Wheaton & Grayzel, Flemington, 1990-97; spl. dep. atty. gen. N.J. Hunterdon County Prosecutor Office, Flemington, 1972-73; condemnation commr. Appt. Superior Ct. N.J., Flemington, 1988—, assembly spkrs. commr.; commr. N.J. State Commn. Investigation, Trenton, 1993-97; arbitrator U.S. Fed. Dist. Ct. N.J., 1989—. Twp. committeeman Alexandria Twp. Com., R.D. Milford, N.J., 1978-81. Mem. Am. Judges Assn., Am. Judicature Soc., N.J. State Bar Assn. (mem. dist. ethics com. 1980-81, mem. mcpl. ct. practice com. 1996—), Hunterdon County Bar Assn., Warren County Bar Assn., Consular Law Soc., Welsh Am. Geneal. Soc., Welsh North Am. C. of C. (bd. dirs.). Republican. Avocations: paleontology, traveling, hiking. Office: PO Box 850 40 Main St Flemington NJ 08822-1411

MILLER, LUTHER GORDON, III, tourism executive; b. Barbados, W.I., Dec. 5, 1946; s. Frederick Edward and Mildred Miriam (Lashley) M.; m. Suzanne Arore Meloche, June 30, 1973; children: Luther Jason, Mandy Miriam. B Commerce, Sir George Williams U., Montreal, Que., Can., 1973, MBA in Fin., 1975. Mgr. ops. Barbados Devel. Bank, Bridgetown, W.I., 1977-79; dep. sec. gen. Caribbean Tourism Research and Devel. Ctr., Bridgetown, 1979—; dir. L.G. Miller & Sons, Bridgetown, Millbrand Products Ltd., Bridgetown. Author tourism publs. Dir. hospitality div. Barbados Communiity Coll., Bridgetown, 1983—. Fellow Econ. Devel. Inst. of World Bank, Barbados Turf Club (Bridgetown). Methodist. Avocations: thoroughbred horse breeding and racing, swimming. Home: 20 Risk Rd, Fitts Village, Saint James Barbados West Indies

MILLER, MARGERY SILBERMAN, psychologist, speech/language pathologist/educator; b. May 7, 1951; d. Bernard and Charlotte (Schatzberg) Silberman; m. Donald F. Moores; children: Kip Lee, Tige Justice. BA, Elmira Coll., 1971; MA, NYU, 1972; EdS, MS, SUNY-Albany, 1975; MA, Towson State U., 1987; PhD, Georgetown U., 1991. Lic. speech pathologist, N.Y., Md.; lic. psychologist, Md.; cert. tchr. nursery-6th grades, spl. edn., N.Y.; nationally cert. sch. psychologist. Speech and lang. pathologist Mental Retardation Inst. Flower and Fifth Ave. Hosp., N.Y.C., 1971-72; cmty. speech/lang. pathologist, dir. speech and hearing svc. N.Y. State Dept. Mental Hygiene, Troy, 1972-74; instr. comm. disorders dept. Coll. St. Rose, Albany, N.Y., 1975-77; clin. supr. U. Md., College Park, 1978; speech/lang. pathologist Md. Sch. for Deaf, Frederick, 1978-84; auditory devel. specialist Montgomery County Pub. Schs., Rockville, Md., 1984-87; coord. Family Life program Nat. Acad. Gallaudit U., Washington, 1987-88, interim dir., 1988-89; dir. Counseling & Devel. Ctr. N.W. Campus, Washington, 1989-93; prof. psychology Gallaudet U., Washington, 1993—; lic. practicing psychologist Ctr. for Families in Transition, Washington, 1998—; instr. sign lang. program Frederick C.C.; dance instr. for deaf adolescents; diagnostic cons. on speech pathology. Author: It's O.K. To Be Angry, 1976; contbr. chpt. to Cognition, Education, and Deafness: Directions for Research and Instruction, 1985; mem. editl. rev. com. Gov.'s Devel. Disabilities Coun. Md., 1984; presenter at confs.; contbr. articles to profl. jours. Vol., choreographer Miss Deaf Am. Pageant, 1984. Office of Edn. Children's Bur. fellow, 1971. Mem. Am. Speech, Lang. and Hearing Assn. (cert. clin. competence in speech/lang. apthology), Md. Speech, Lang. and Hearing Assn., D.C. Speech, Lang. and Hearing Assn., Nat. Assn. of Deaf, Nat. Assn. Sch. Psychologists, Am. Psychol. Assn. Jewish. Home: 368 Broadview Ln Annapolis MD 21401-7240 Office: Gallaudet U 800 Florida Ave NE Washington DC 20002-3660

MILLER, MARY JEANNETTE, office management specialist; b. Washington, Sept. 24, 1912; d. John William and David Evengeline (Hill) Sims; m. Cecil Miller, June 17, 1934 (dec.); children: Sylvenia Delores Doby, Ferdi A., Cecil Jr. (dec.). Student, Howard U., 1929-30, U. Ill., 1940-42, Dept. Agr. Grad. Sch., 1957-59, U. Md., 1975; cert. in Vocat. Photography, Prince George's C.C., 1986. Chief mail processing unit Bur. Reclamation, Washington, 1940-57; records supr. AID, Manila, Korea, Mali, Guyana, Dominican Republic, Indonesia, Laos, 1957-71; office engr. Bechtel Assocs., Washington, 1976-79; real estate assoc; tchr. English as 2d lang. Ministry of Edn., Seoul, Korea, 1960-61, Ministry of Fin., Laos, 1968-70; cons. to Ministry of Fin. Royal Lao Govt., 1971-74; cons. AID missions to Yemen, Sudan, Somalia, 1982; records mgmt. cons. AID, Monrovia, Liberia, 1980-81, Sri Lanka, 1984; docent Mus. African Art Smithsonian Inst., Washington, 1986-89; circulation asst. Prince George County Meml. Libr. System, Hyattsville, Md., 1987-91, ret.; mem. Friends of Internat. Edn. Com., 1985-92; sec./treas., bd. dirs. Miller Transitional, Inc. Author handbooks on office mgmt.; publs. to travel book. Mem. NAFE, Am. Assn. Ret. Persons (bd. mem. Fla. chpt. 1357), Mayor's Internat. Adv. Coun. Mem. AARP (bd. dirs.), Soc. Am. Archivists, Am. Mgmt. Assn., Montgomery County Bd. Realtors, Am. Fgn. Svc. Assn., Nat. Trust Hist. Preservation, Assn. Am. Fgn. Svc. Women's Writer Group, Consumer Mail Panel, Zeta Phi Beta. Roman Catholic. Home: 5597 Seminary Rd Apt 510S Falls Church VA 22041-3520

MILLER, MARY LOIS, retired nurse midwife; b. Altoona, Pa., Feb. 21, 1933; d. Isaac Emory and Lucinda Jane (Brumbaugh) Miller. Diploma, West Suburban Hosp. Sch., 1953; BSN, Wheaton (Ill.) Coll., 1955; MRE, Grace Theol. Sem., 1957; nurse midwife, Frontier Nursing Svc., 1959. Cert. nurse midwife. Nurse obstetrics Delnor Hosp., St. Charles, Ill., 1953-55; head nurse McDonald Hosp., Warsaw, Ind., 1955-57; med. missionary Fgn. Missionary Soc. Grace Brethren Ch., Winona Lake, Ind., 1959-79; cert. nurse midwife Lewistown (Pa.) Hosp., 1979-97; ret., 1997. Recipient Ordre du Merit du Chevalier, Ctrl. African Rep., 1972. Mem. APHA, Am. Coll. Nurse Midwives (sec.), Nat. Perinatal Assn., Pa. Perinatal Assn., Nat. Assn. Childbearing Ctrs. Home: 1007 N 2nd St Juniata Altoona PA 16601-5613

MILLER, MICHAEL JAMES, radiation oncologist; b. Hammond, Ind., Apr. 30, 1961; s. James Richard and Margaret Joan Miller; m. Gretchen Therese Miller; children: Megan Joan, Eric James, Maria Kathryn. BA in Chemistry, Hanover Coll., 1983; MD, Ind. U., Indpls., 1987. Diplomate Am. Bd. Radiation Oncology. Intern Blodgett meml. Med. Ctr., Grand Rapids, Mich., 1987-88; resident Ind. U. Med. Ctr., Indpls., 1988-91; physician Assocs. in Radiation Oncology, P.C., Kalamazoo, Mich., 1991-92, Lafayette (Ind.) Radiation Oncology, LLC, 1992-99, Oncology-Hematology Assocs., Evansville, Ind., 1999—; treas. med. staff St. Elizabeth Hosp., Lafayette, 1997, v.p. med. staff, 1998. Mem. St. Marys Cathedral, Lafayette, 1992-99, Good Sheperd Ch., Evansville, 1999—. Mem. Am. Coll. Radiology, Am. Soc. Therapeutic Radiation Oncology, Am. Coll. Radiation Oncology. Republican. Roman Catholic. Avocations: bicycling, skiing, reading, playing with my children. Home: 11630 Blue Grass Rd Evansville IN 47725-7017 Office: St Marys Radiation Oncology 3801 Bellemeade Ave Evansville IN 47714-0100

MILLER, NEAL ADRIAN, periodontist; b. Stockton, Calif., Nov. 1, 1946; s. Robert Wilson Miller and Marquerite Jeanne Adrian; m. Catherine Lamey; children: Claire, Marc, Marie, Anne. DCD, U. (France) Nancy, 1971; CES in Periodontology Dentistry, U. Paris, 1973; DSO, U. France (Nancy), 1980; DEO, U. (France) Strasbourg, 1987. Instr. dept. periodontology U. Nancy, 1976-83; asst. prof. Idem, 1983-87, assoc. prof., 1987—, chmn., 1990—. Mem. Soc. Française Paradontogie, Soc. Lorraine Parodontie (pres. 1981-84), Assn. Parodontistes Libéraux Nancy, Lafayette Days (founder). Home: 12 rue du Haut Bourgeois, 5400 Nancy France Office: Dept Perio faculte Chirurgie-Dentaire, rue du Docteur Heydenreich, 54000 Nancy France

MILLER, NICHOLAS, business development executive, scientist; b. Braintree, Essex, Eng., Aug. 16, 1964; s. Colin Leonard and Ena Rose (Bereman) M. BSc with 1st class honours, U. Bristol, Eng., 1985; PhD, U. Wales, Cardiff, 1991; diploma French lang. studies 1st degree, Edexcel, Geneva and London, 1997. Postdoctoral fellow Imperial Cancer Rsch. Fund, London, 1991-94; rsch. scientist Glaxo-Wellcome, Geneva, 1994-96; mem. staff Arthur Andersen, Cambridge, Eng., 1996-97; mgr. bus. devel. Cambridge Antibody Tech., 1997-2000; bd. dirs., co. sec. Eladon Ltd., U.K., 1990—; referee for sci. articles Brit. Jour. Cancer, 1991-94; spkr., presenter various confs. in field, U.S., U.K., 1991-96. Contbr. articles to sci. jours., including Jour. Steroid Biochemistry and Molecular Biology, Human Gene Therapy, Glycoconjugate Jour., Virology, FASEB Jour., Melanoma Rsch., Gen. Therapy, Parasitology Tody, Jour. Insect Physiology. Vol.Cyreneans, Bristol, 1983. Scholar Wellcome Trust, 1985-89. Avocations: French, skiing, snooker, literature, Chinese boxing (black belt).

MILLER, PETER DANIEL, artist, printmaker; b. Phila., Aug. 14, 1945; arrived in Japan, 1982; s. Marvin J. and Theresa Miller; m. Yuko Itami, June 17, 1979; 1 child, Neil Satoru. BA, Columbia Coll., 1967; PhD, U. Calif., Berkeley, 1974. Founder, dir. Kamakura Print Collection, 1991—. Represented in mus. collections Sackler Gallery at Smithsonian Instn., Nat. Gallery of Am. Art, N.Y. Pub. Lib Cleve. Mus. Art, Portland Art Mus., Bibliothèque Nationale de France, Musée Jenisch (Switzerland), Kamakura Mus. Modern Art, Japan; pub. more than 130 ltd.-edition gravure prints. Coll. Women's Assn. of Japan Print Show selection, 1994-00. Avocations: bicycling, cross-country skiing. Home and Office: Kamakura Print Collection, 4-23-12 Jomyoji, 248-0003 Kamakura Japan

MILLER, PETER JAMES, zoologist, educator; b. Liverpool, Eng., Feb. 1, 1936; s. Peter and Matilda (Kontzle) M.; m. Beryl Margaret Swift, Sept. 11, 1964; children: Lucy Zenobia, Edward James. BS with honors, Liverpool U., 1958, PhD, 1964; DSc, Bristol (Eng.) U., 1993. Asst. in zoology Glasgow (Scotland) U., 1961-64, lectr. in zoology, 1964-66; lectr. in zoology

Bristol U., 1966-80, reader, 1980-98, prof., 1998—. Author: Collins Pocket Guide to the Fish of Britain and Europe, 1997; co-author: Collect Fish on Stamps, 1999; editor: Fish Phenology, 1979, Miniature Vertebrates, 1996; editor, translator: Field Guide to the Mediterranean Seashore, 1976. Mem. Fisheries Soc. Brit. Isles, Am. Soc. Ichthyologists and Herpetologists, Japanese Ichthyological Soc., Bristol and Avon Archeol. Soc. (chmn. 1991-93). Avocations: reading, collecting, constructing. Office: U Bristol, Sch Biol Scis, BS8 1UG Bristol England

MILLER, PHILIP HAROLD, linguistics educator; b. Brussels, Nov. 5, 1959; s. Lee Hart and Liliane Germaine (Massau) M. M in Romance Philology, U. Brussels, 1983; PhD in Linguistics, U. Utrecht, 1991. Asst. U. Brussels, 1985-91; postdoctoral rschr. Ohio State U., Columbus, 1991-92; maitre de conferences U. Lille 3, France, 1992-95, prof., 1995—; dir. Unité Mixte de Recherche 8528, CNRS, Lille. Author: Clitics and Constituents in Phrase Structure Grammar, 1992, Strong Generative Capacity: The Semantics of Linguistic Formalism, 1999; mem. editl. bd. Grammars: A Jour. of Mathematical Rsch. on Formal and Natural Langs., Lexique; contbr. articles to profl. jours. Rsch. grantee Région Nord-Pas de Calais, 1995-97, NSF and Ctr. Nat. Rsch. Scientific, 1995-97. Mem. Linguistic Soc. Am. Home: Rue des Prêtres 15, B-1000 Brussels Belgium Office: U Lille 3, BP 149, 59653 Villeneuve Cedex, France

MILLER, RANDAL J., lawyer, educator; b. Joliet, Ill., Apr. 16, 1952; s. William D. Jr. and Joyce N. Miller; m. Mary Kaluzny, Oct. 4, 1980; children: Randal J. Jr., Hayley K., Hannah S. AA, Joliet Jr. Coll., 1973; BS, Lewis U., Lockport, Ill., 1975; JD, John Marshall Law Sch., Chgo., 1978. Bar: Ill. 1978, U.S. Dist. Ct. (no. dist.) Ill. 1982, U.S. Ct. Appeals (7th cir.) 1982. Real estate and trust atty. Heritage Bank, Crest Hill, Ill., 1978-79; asst. state's atty. County of Will, Joliet, 1979-86, asst. pub. defender, 1986-89; ptnr. Dunn, Martin & Miller, Ltd., Joliet, 1991—; adj. prof. Joliet Jr. Coll., 1980-84, U. St. Francis, Joliet, 1988—. cons. atty. Reflex Sympathetic Dystrophy Assn., Chgo., 1996—. Mem. exec. com. Will County Rep. Orgn., Joliet, 1985-90. Mem. Ill. State Bar Assn. (assemblyman 1991-97, standing com. supreme ct. rules 1997—), Will County Bar Assn. (bd. dirs. 1992-95, pres. 1999-2000), Masons. Avocations: music, collectibles, fine art. Home: 2604 Glasgow St Joliet IL 60435-1335 Office: Dunn Martin & Miller Ltd 15 W Jefferson St Ste 300 Joliet IL 60432-4301

MILLER, RANDY M., marketing professional; b. Aug. 2, 1966. BS in Mktg. Mgmt., U. R.I. Founder, chmn. Ready & Motivated Minds LLC, N.Y.C., 1996—. Office: Ready & Motivated Minds LLC 50 W 23d St New York NY 10010-5205

MILLER, RENÉE JACQUES, accountant, administrator; b. Rochester, N.Y., Jan. 12, 1963; d. Montraville Allan and Shirley May (Peterson) Jacques; m. David Keith Miller, Dec. 26, 1981; children: Kendall Peterson, Jed Baron. AA in Bus., Pensacola (Fla.) Jr. Coll., 1983; BA in Acctg. cum laude, U. West Fla., 1985, postgrad., 1990—. Accounting clk. U. West Fla., 1983-84; staff acct. Mo. Money Assn., 1984-85; acct., office mgr. Kerrigan, Estess & Rankin, Pensacola, Fla., 1985-89; acct. Wengor of Panama City (Fla.), Inc., 1989-93, Sunshine Cellular, 1990-94; legal adminstr. Kerrigan, Estess, Rankin & McLeod, Pensacola, Fla., 1989-98; co-owner, adminstr. Miller Arcadia Self Storage/Arcadia Culverts, 1999—; co-owner, adminstr. Miller & Miller Contractors, Pensacola, Fla., 1988—; tour planner Sunshine Express Tours Inc., Pensacola, 1995—. Mem. office systems tech. adv. com. Pensacola Jr. Coll., 1990-99, legal secretarial tech. adv. com., 1990-91; dep. campaign treas. Fla. State Rep., Pensacola, 1986; care group leader Olive Bapt. Ch., Pensacola, 1987—. Kahn scholar U. West Fla., 1984. Mem. Inst. Mgmt. Accts., Internat. Platform Assn., Concerned Women for Am. Democrat. Baptist. Avocations: traveling, visiting with friends, sports. Office: Miller & Miller Contractors 9525 Baron Miller Rd Pensacola FL 32514-5696

MILLER, RICHARD BRUCE, electronics company executive; b. Bryn Mawr, Pa., Jan. 2, 1947; s. Robert and Kathryn (Marks) M; m. Nedra Lynn Herbert, Aug. 28, 1971; children: Sean Patrick and Ryan Cameron. BA in Polit. Sci., Shippensburg State U., 1969, MA in Polit. Sci., 1975. Asst. city mgr. City of Chambersburg, Pa., 1970-72; city mgr. City of New Cumberland, Pa., 1972-76, Montgomery Twp., N.J., 1976-78; from internal control mgr. to contr. Xerox Corp., Harrisburg, Pa., 1978-83; field adminstrn. ops. mgr. Xerox Corp., Stamford, Conn., 1983-85; ctr. mgr. City of N.Y.C., N.Y.C., 1985-88; transition mgr. bus. ops. Stamford, Conn., 1988-89; mgr., ops. support Ea. region, 1989-90; mgr. quality/customer satisfaction Xerox Corp., Stamford, 1990-91; mgr. customer svc. ops. Xerox Corp., Stamford, Conn., 1991-92; mgr. sys. products adminstrn. Xerox Corp., Rochester, N.Y., 1992-93, mgr. customized solutions adminstrn., 1993-94, market to collection, 1994-95; from infrastructure delivery mgr. to applications mgr. Office Document Products, 1995-97, applications mgr., 1997; applications framework mgr. Year 2000 Program Office Xerox Corp. Info. Mgmt., Rochester, 1997-2000; mgr. productivity office Xerox Corp., 2000—; mem. All Star Club Xerox Corp., 1982-83, 85-86, 87-88, 89-90, grad. Astronaut VII, 1987, chief info. officer Leadership award, 1995. Bd. dirs. So. Conn. Child Guidance Ctr., 1988-90, Child Care Ctrs., Stamford, 1990-92; cubmaster Boy Scouts Am., Fairport, N.Y., 1994-95; youth sports coach Southeast YMCA, Pittsford, N.Y., 1993-96, Fairport Youth Lacrosse, 1994—; registrar Perinton Youth Hockey, 1998-2000. Republican. Roman Catholic. Avocations: tennis, boating, amateur radio, reading. Home: 60 Vineyard Hl Fairport NY 14450-4629 Office: Xerox Corp 200 Canal View Blvd Ste 300 Rochester NY 14623-2896

MILLER, RICHARD WALTER, consulting engineer; b. Greenfield, Mass., Feb. 16, 1935; s. Wilfred E. and Ruth B. (Booker) M.; m. Barbara J. Mushovic, May 2, 1960; children: Pamela J., Brenda M., Jennifer E. BS, Northeastern U., 1958, MS, 1960. Registered profl. engr., Mass. Design engr. Walworth Co., Braintree, Mass., 1960-62; sr. flow cons. The Foxboro Co., Foxboro, Mass., 1962-88; cons., pres. R.W. Miller & Assocs., Foxboro, 1988-98, Venice, Fla., 1998—. Author: Flow Measurement Engineer Handbook, 1983, 87, 96; contbr. tech. papers to profl. jours. Bristol fellow The Foxboro Co., 1987. Fellow ASME (chmn. 1980—, Dedicated Svc. award 1985, v.p. 1986-89). Achievements include patents in field on an inline powered viscometer, a vortex flowmeter, an annular target flowmeter, and a mass flowmeter apparatus. Avocations: sailing, golf, oil painting. Home and Office: 512 Pennyroyal Pl Venice FL 34293-7233

MILLER, ROBERT CARL, retired library director; b. May 9, 1936; m. Jeanne M. Larson. BS in History and Philosophy, Marquette U., 1958; MS in Am. History, U. Wis., 1962; MA in Libr. Sci., U. Chgo., 1966. Head telephone reference Library of Congress, Wash., 1959-60; reference librarian Marquette U., Milw., 1960-62, acquisition librarian, 1962-66; head tech. services/librarian Parsons Coll., Fairfield, Iowa, 1966-68; head acquisitions dept. U. of Chgo. Library, Ill., 1968-71; assoc. dir (reader services) U. of Chgo. Library, 1971-73; assoc dir (gen. service) U. of Chgo., 1973-75; dir. of libraries U. Mo., St. Louis, 1975-78; dir of libraries U. of Notre Dame, Ind., 1978-97, ret., 1997; vis. prof. IBIN-U. Warsaw, Poland, 1992, 93, 97, 2000. Contbr. to prof. jour. Fellow Woodrow Wilson Found. (sr.), Coun. on Libr. Resources; mem. ALA, Polish Inst. of Arts and Letters of Am. Roman Catholic. E-mail: miller.1@nd.edu. Home: 4540 W Binner Dr Chandler AZ 85226-2949

MILLER, ROGER ALLEN, physicist; b. Chillicothe, Ohio, June 27, 1934; s. Joseph Perrin and Mary Josephine (Sowers) M.; m. Barbara Pauline Rice, Aug. 31, 1957; children: Erich Rice, Gretchen Rice, Carl Rice. BS, Ohio U., 1956; PhD, Case Inst., 1963. Rsch. assoc. Case Inst., Cleve., 1963-64; rsch. physicist Corning (N.Y.) Inc., 1964-71, sr. rsch. physicist, 1971-79, devel. assoc., 1979-87, sr. rsch. assoc., 1987—; spl. lectr. physics Elmira Coll., N.Y., 1966-69; mem. edit. bd. Fiber and Integrated Optics, Pasadena, Calif., 1976-86, mem. adv. bd. 1986-88. Contbr. articles to profl. jours. AART award Assn. for the Advancement Radiation Tech., 1990. Mem. Am. Phys. Soc., Optical Soc. Am., Am. Assn. Physics Tchrs., Sigma Xi, Phi Beta Kappa, Phi Kappa Phi. Achievements include contributions to the development of lead free Steuben crystal; development of optical waveguide coatings and coating applicators; design and development of the first, all dielectric, low-loss optical waveguide cable; patentee in field. Office: Corning Inc Sullivan Pk Sp Fr 03 # 1 Corning NY 14831-0001

MILLER, RONALD WRIGHT, pharmaceutical scientist; b. Pottstown, Pa., Dec. 8, 1947; s. Wright Reninger and Marcelle (Scholler) M.; m. Carol Catherine Grove, Mar. 27, 1971. BS in Chemistry, Lebanon Valley Coll., 1970; MBA, Temple U., 1977, PhD in Pharmaceutics, 1988. Asst. to prodn. mgr. Glenbrook Labs. Divsn., Sterling Drug, Trenton, 1971-74; asst. prodn. mgr. Elkins-Sinn Co., Cherry Hill, N.J., 1974-75; sr. compounding supr. Richardson-Merrell Co., Hatboro, Pa., 1975-80; sr. rsch. scientist Whitehall Labs. Divsn., Am. Home Products, Hammonton, N.J., 1980-88; assoc. dir. Worldwide Pharm. Tech. Bristol-Myers Squibb Co., New Brunswick, N.J., 1988—. Lt. col. USAR, 1970-95, ret. Mem. Am. Chem. Soc. (cert.), Am. Assn. Pharm. Scientists. Achievements include patents for coated aspirin tablets decomposition inhibited by incorporation of citric, alginic and glutamic acid mixtures thereof, for enteric coated aspirin tablets rendered shock-insensitive by providing a protective coat of hydroxypropyl methylcellulose of at least 1.5% by weight of the tablet core; pharmaceutical research on compaction with vacuum deparation system and its technological advantages and NIR spectroscopy in-process mapping of roller compaction. Home: 126 Fox Hollow Dr Langhorne PA 19053-2492 Office: Bristol-Myers Squibb PO Box 191 New Brunswick NJ 08903-0191

MILLER, SANDRA A. CARAMELA, gerontologist, educator; b. Painesville, Ohio, June 1, 1957; d. Paul M. and Jane E. (Zaffuto) Caramela; m. Charles S. Miller, May 3, 1985; 1 child, Shannon; stepchildren: Carrie J., Charles A. BA in Psychology, U. Akron, 1980, MA in Psychology, 1991, cert. in gerontology, 1991, PhD in Psychology, 1997. Instr. U. Akron, Ohio, 1989-92, fellow, adj. Inst. Life-Span Devel., 1997—, adj. faculty, 2000—; coord. dir. pediatric rsch. St. Luke's Hosp., Cleve., 1992-94; statistician, epidemiologist All Kids Count Consortium, Cleve., 1993-94; dir. forensic tng. Cuyahoga County Coroner's Office, Cleve., 1995—, rschr., project dir., 1997—. Mem. consortium Child Protection Coalition, Cuyahoga County, Ohio, 1993-96, All Kids Count, Cleve., 1993-94; mem. adv. bd. Cmty. Medicine Forum Violence, 1993-94; dir., pres. bd. dirs. Safe and Secure Home, Inc., Macedonia, Ohio, 1996-00. Mem. APA, Gerontol. Soc. Am., Assn. Death Edn. and Counseling, Inst. Trauma and Loss in Children, Soc. Psychol. Study Social Issues, Assn. Health Svcs. Rsch., Sigma Phi Omega. Home: 8375 N Boyden Rd Sagamore Hls OH 44067-1711 Office: Cuyahoga County Coroners Office 11001 Cedar Ave Cleveland OH 44106-3043

MILLER, SANFORD ARTHUR, academic administrator, biochemistry educator; b. Bklyn., NY, May 12, 1931; s. Howard and Lillian (Kenter) Epstein; m. Judith W. Cohen, Aug. 17, 1958; children: Wallis Jo, Debra Lauren. BS in Chemistry and Biology, CCNY, 1952; MS in Psychology and Biochemistry, Rutgers U., 1956, PhD, 1957. Jr. chemist electronics br. Army Chem. Ctr., Edgewood, Md., summer 1951; chemist applied rsch. br. Army Chem. Ctr., Edgewood, 1952; asst. to chief toxicology Army Med. Ctr., Washington, 1953-54; tchg. asst. in physiology and biochemistry Rutgers U., 1955-57; rsch. assoc. dept. food tech. MIT, 1957-59, asst. prof. nutritional biochemistry, 1959-65, assoc. prof., 1965-70, prof., dir. tng. program in oral sci., 1970-83; dir. Ctr. Food Safety and Applied Nutrition FDA, Washington, 1978-87; prof. biochem. and medicine, dean grad. sch. biomed. scis. U. Tex. Health Sci. Ctr., San Antonio, 1987—; adj. fellow Ctr. for Food and Nutrition Policy Georgetown Univ., Wash., 1999—; vis. lectr. in nutrition Tufts U. Sch. Dental Medicine, 1963-85, Boston U. Sch. Medicine, 1963-87, Harvard U. Sch. Medicine, 1963-87; sr. lectr. MIT, 1983-84; cons. to food and drug cos., U.S. and abroad; chmn. ad hoc com. Nat. Inst. Neurol. Disease and Stroke, 1972-77; mem. meetings com. Fedn. Am. Socs. Exptl. Biology, 1972, chmn. conf., 1973, expert com. on generally recognized as safe substances, 1972-78; mem. com. on maternal and child health Nat. Inst. Child Health and Human Devel., 1973-77, com. on contraceptive steroids, 1973-81, com. on growth and devel., 1972-76; mem. adv. com. on nutrition Nat. Inst. Dental Rsch., 1973-78; bd. sci. advs. FDA, 1972-78; mem. Food Update Bd. Govs. Food and Drug Law Inst., 1978-82; trustee toxicology forum; mem. Nat. Adv. Environ. Health Scis. Coun., 1988-92, U.S. Nestle Adv. Bd., 1990, Food Forum, Inst. Med., Nat. Acad. of Scis., 1993—; co-chmn. USDA-FDA working group on food safety legis., 1980-87; coord. nutrition initiatives for Pub. Health Svc., 1982-87; co-chmn. Cancer Risk Assessment Task Force, 1984-87; U.S. co-coord. Codex Alimentarius, 1984-87. Contbr. numerous articles, revs., chpts. to profl. publs.; mem. editl. bd. Drug-Nutrient Interactions, 1981—. Cpl. U.S. Army, 1953-54. Recipient Outstanding Tchr. of Yr. award MIT, 1975, Pub. Health Svc. Superior Svc. award, 1982, Award of Merit, FDA, 1987, Esther Peters Conumer Svc. award Food Mktg. Inst., 1988; recipient numerous grants and fellowships including Nat. Acad. Scis., 1959, NIH, 1960-78, AEC, 1965, Disting. Svc. award HHS, 1983. Fellow Mark L. Morris Animal Care Panel (hon.); mem. Am. Chem. Soc. (Sterling B. Hendricks award 1989), W.O. Atwater Meml. Lectureship, Agrl. Rsch. Svc., Glenn W. Kilpatrick Meml. Address, Assn. of Food and Drug Offcls. (nat. councilor 1966-69, nat. chmn. com. on nutrition edn. 1969-72, Babcock-Hart award 1991), Animal Care Panel, Am. Inst. Nutrition (chmn. fellows com. 1977-78, chmn. biochem. nutrition com. 1967-69, nat. program com. 1967-72, chair pub. affairs com. 1989-91, Conrad Elvehjem award 1981), Soc. Teratology, Perinatal Rsch. Soc., Am. Inst. Dental Rsch., Soc. Pediatric Rsch., Gordon Rsch. Confs. (chmn. 1973, vice chmn. 1972), Western Hemisphere Nutrition Congress (program com. 1977, chair WHO-FAO joint food safety com. 1990, world food conf. planning commn. 1990-92), Commn. on Health and Environ. (panel on food and agriculture 1990), Corp. Culinary Inst. Am. (life), Cosmos Club (Washington), New Century Club (Boston), Sigma Xi. Jewish. Office: U Tex Health Sci Ctr 7703 Floyd Curl Dr San Antonio TX 78229-3901

MILLER, SHANNON, Olympic athlete; b. Rolla, Mo., Mar. 10, 1977. Silver medalist, All-Around Competition Barcelona Olympic Games, 1992, Silver medalist, Balance Beam, 1992, Bronze medalist, Uneven Bars, 1992; Gold medalist all-around competition Birmingham Great World Championships, Britain, 1993, Brisbane Austrlia World Championships, St. Petersburg, Russia, 1994. Bronze medalist in floor exercise, Olympics, 1992; World Champion Gold medalist in all around, 1993, 94, in uneven bars and fl. exercise, 1993, in balance beam, 1994; Gold medal Team competition Atlanta Olympics, 1996, gold medal balance beam, 1996; recipient Up & Coming award Women's Sports Found., 1991, Steve Reeves Fitness award Downtown Athletic Club, 1992, Comeback award Nuprin, 1992, Dial award, 1994; named Athlete of Yr. USA Gymnastics Congress, 1994. Christian Scientist. Address: c/o USA Gymnastics Pan Am Plz 201 S Capitol Ave Ste 300 Indianapolis IN 46225-1058

MILLER, SHELBY ALEXANDER, chemical engineer, educator; b. Louisville, July 9, 1914; s. George Walter and Stella Katherine (Cralle) M.; m. Jean Adele Danielson, Dec. 26, 1939 (div. May 1948); 1 son, Shelby Carlton; m. Doreen Adare Kennedy, May 29, 1952 (dec. Feb. 1971). BS, U. Louisville, 1935; PhD, U. Minn., 1943. Registered profl. engr., Del., Kans., N.Y. Asst. chemist Corhart Refractories Co., Louisville, 1935-36; teaching, rsch. asst. chem. engring. U. Minn., Mpls., 1935-39; devel. engr., rsch. chem. engr. E.I. duPont de Nemours & Co., Inc., Wilmington, Del., 1940-46; assoc. prof. chem. engring. U. Kan., Lawrence, 1946-50; prof. U. Kan., 1950-55; Fulbright prof. chem. engring. King's Coll. Durham U., Newcastle-upon-Tyne, Eng., 1952-53; prof., chem. engring. U. Rochester, 1955-69, chmn., 1955-68; assoc. lab. dir. Argonne (Ill.) Nat. Lab., 1969-74; dir. Ctr. Ednl. Affairs, 1969-79, sr. chem. engr., 1969-84, ret., cons., 1984—; vis. prof. chem. engring. U. Calif., Berkeley, 1967-68; vis. prof. U. of Philippines, Quezon City, 1986; cons. in field. Editor: Chem. Engring. Edn. Quar, 1965-67; sect. editor: Perry's Chem. Engrs.' Handbook, 5th edit., 1973, 6th edit., 1984, 7th edit. 1997; contbr. to McGraw-Hill Ency. Sci. and Tech., 5th edit., 1982, 6th edit., 1987, 7th edit., 1992; contbr. articles to profl. jours. Sec. Kans. Bd. Engring. Examiners, 1954-55; mem. adv. com. on tng. Internat. Atomic Energy Agy., 1975-79; treas. Lawrence (Kans.) League for Practice Democracy, 1950-52; sec. Argonne Credit Union, 1994-97. Fellow AAAS, Am. Inst. Chemists, Am. Inst. Chem. Engrs. (past chmn. Kansas City sect.); mem. Am. Chem. Soc. (past chmn. Rochester sect.), Soc. Chem. Industry, Am. Soc. Engring. Edn. (past chmn. grad. studies div.), Am. Nuclear Soc., Filtration Soc., Triangle, Sigma Xi, Sigma Tau, Phi Lambda Upsilon, Tau Beta Pi, Alpha Chi Sigma. Presbyterian. Home: 825 63rd St Downers Grove IL 60516-1962 Office: Argonne Nat Lab Chem Tech Divsn Argonne IL 60439-4837

MILLER, STEFAN, mechanical engineer; b. Podkonce, Radom, Poland, May 28, 1929; s. Stanisław and Maria Miller; m. Sylwia Kanert, Aug. 15, 1958; children: Adam, Renata. Student, Tech. U., Wrocław, Poland, 1950-56, PhD, 1961, prof., 1975. Registered engr. Docent dept. mech. Tech. U., Wrocław, 1968-74, prof. dept. mech., 1974-84, full prof. dept. mech., 1984—. Author 6 books; patentee in field; contbr. numerous papers to profl. jours. Decorated Order Złoty Krzyż Zasługi, 1977, Order Krzyż Orderu Odrodzenia Polski, 1977; recipient reward Didaks-Film, 1985, Min. of Edn., 1970, 73, 74, 82, 87, 90; medal Edukacji Narodowej, 1981. Mem. Internat. Fedn. for Theory of Machines and Mechanisms, Polish Acad. Scis. (mem. com. on machine constrn. 1988—), Polish Com. on Mechanism and Machine Theory. Roman Catholic. Avocation: travel. Home: ul Kolbuszowska 26, 53-404 Wroclaw Poland Office: Tech U, ul Łukasiewicza 7/9, 50-371 Wroclaw Poland

MILLER, STEPHEN GAYLORD, archaeology educator; b. Goshen, Ind., June 22, 1942; s. Gaylord Wesley and Dorothy (Detweiler) W.; m. Stella Grobel, Nov. 3, 1971 (div. Aug. 1984); m. Effie Davlantes, Oct. 17, 1999. AB in Ancient Greek, Wabash Coll., 1964; AM in Classical Archaeology, Princeton U., 1967, PhD in Classical Archaeology, 1970; PhD (hon.), U. Athens, Greece, 1996. Rsch. asst. Inst. Advanced Study, Princeton, N.J., 1972-73; dir. Am. Sch. Classical Studies, Athens, 1982-87, Nemea (Greece) Excavations, 1973—; from asst. prof. to prof. U. Calif., Berkeley, 1973—; bd. dirs. Min. of Culture, Athens; vis. scholar Phi Beta Kappa, 1992-93. Author: The Prytaneion, 1978, Arete: Greek Sport, 1991; author, editor: Nemea I: The Sacred Square, 1992. Cultural advisor Gov. of Korinthia, Greece, 1994—. Named Hon. Citizen, Ancient Nemea, 1981, Comdr. of Order of Honor, Hellenic Republic, Greece, 1996. Mem. Deutsches Archäologisches Institut (corr. mem.), Academia Scientiarum et Artium Europaeae, Archaeol. Soc. Athens (hon.). Avocations: college athletics, concerts/opera. Office: Univ Calif Dept Classics Mc # 2520 Berkeley CA 94720-0001

MILLER, STEPHEN RALPH, lawyer; b. Chgo., Nov. 28, 1950; s. Ralph and Karin Ann (Olson) M.; children: David Williams, Lindsay Christine. m. Sheila L. Krysiak, Feb. 2, 1998. BA cum laude, Yale U., 1972; JD, Cornell U., 1975. Bar: Ill. Assoc. McDermott, Will & Emery, Chgo., 1975-80, income ptnr., 1981-85, equity ptnr., 1986—, mgmt. com. mem., 1992-95; mem. spl. task force on post-employment benefits Fin. Acctg. Standards Bd., Norwalk, Conn., 1987-91. Contbr. articles to profl. jours. Mem. Chgo. Coun. on Fgn. Rels., 1978—, mem. devel. com., 1997—, chair mem. devel. subcom., 1999—; trustee police pension bd., Wilmette, Ill., 1992-98; trustee Seabury We. Theol. Sem., Evanston, Ill., 1994—, chancellor, 1996-97, chair trusteeship com., 2000—. Mem. ABA, Ill. Bar Assn., Yale Club Chgo., Hundred Club Cook County, Lawyers' Club of Chgo. Avocations: sailing, water skiing, cross-country skiing. Office: McDermott Will & Emery 227 W Monroe St Ste 3100 Chicago IL 60606-5096

MILLER, STEPHEN WARREN, dean; b. Rockville Centre, N.Y., July 23, 1954; s. Warren Harding Miller and Carol Simon; m. Laurie Robin Hogan (div. July 1988); 1 child, James Warren. AA, Indian River C.C., 1974; BS, Fla. State U., 1977, MS, 1982. Cert. career devel. facilitator master instr. Nat. Occupl. Info. Coord. Com.; cert. instr. Zenger/Miller Tng. Corp. Sports reporter WECA/ABC, Tallahassee, Fla., 1976-77, WXLT/ABC, Sarasota, Fla., 1980-82; 7th and 8th grade sci. tchr. St. Anastasia Sch., Ft. Pierce, Fla., 1978-80; dir. student life Macon (Ga.) C.C., 1981-86; assoc. dean continuing edn. Fla. Atlantic U., Ft. Lauderdale, 1986—; bd. dirs. Am. Coll. Testing, Iowa City, Iowa, 1995—; bd. advisors PACE Ctr. for Girls, Ft. Lauderdale, 1996—. Contbr. to book: High Technology and the 3 Rs, 1985; contbr. articles to profl. jours. Mem. Broward Rep. Leadership, Ft. Lauderdale, 1997—; bd. dirs. SAILS Found., Macon and Ft. Lauderdale, 1995—; chpt. advisor Phi Delta Kappa, Boca Raton, 1988-89; mem. career adv. bd. Broward County Sch. Bd., Ft. Lauderdale, 1991—; chmn. Broward County Americorp., 1995-96; mem. bus. devel. com. Broward Econ. Devel. Bd., 1988—, pres. A Child is Missing. Named Disting. Pres., Kiwanis Internat., 1985, Kiwanian of Yr., 1984, Outstanding Young Man of Am. U.S. Jaycees, 1983. Mem. Ft. Lauderdale C. of C. (bd. govs. 1995-97, Proclamation award). Republican. Episcopalian. Avocations: jet skiing, golf, guitar, reading. Fax: (954) 351-4176. Office: Fla Atlantic U 1515 W Commercial Blvd Fort Lauderdale FL 33309-3095

MILLER, STEPHEN WILEY, lawyer; b. Washington, Feb. 27, 1958; s. Robert Wiley and Betty Ruth (Brown) M.; m. Andrea Brill, Feb. 12, 1982; children: Ashley, Craig, Kevin. BA, Denison U., 1980; JD, U. Va., 1984. Bar: Va. 1984, U.S. Dist. Ct. (ea. dist.) Va. 1987, U.S. Ct. Appeals (4th cir.) 1984. Assoc. Hunton & Williams, Richmond, Va., 1984-87; asst. U.S. atty. U.S. Atty.'s Office, U.S. Dept. Justice, Richmond, 1987—. Contbr. articles to profl. jours. Mem. ABA, Va. State Bar, Va. Bar Assn., Phi Alpha Delta (chpt. pres. 1982-83, state coordinator 1986—, outstanding svc. award 1983). Office: US Attys Office 600 E Main St Richmond VA 23219-2441

MILLER, SUSAN JANET, business educator, researcher; b. Hillingdon, Middlesex, Eng., 1955; d. Ronald Frank and Joyce Pamela (West) M. BA with honors, Bradford & Ilkley Coll., 1985; MBA, Bradford U., 1986, PhD, 1990. Various positions in adminstrn. in pub. and pvt. orgns. BBC and Taylor Woodrow, 1974-85; rschr. Bradford (Eng.) U., 1990-91; sr. lectr. Durham (Eng.) U., 1991—. Co-author, contbr.: Handbook of Organization Studies, 1996, Encyclopedic Dictionary of Organization Behavior, 1995; contbr. articles to profl. jours. including Am. Behavioral Scientist and Exec. Devel. Jour. (MCB Press Lit. award 1993). Grantee U.S. Army, Rsch. Isnt., 1995. Avocations: walking, badminton. Office: Durham U Bus Sch, Mill Hall Ln, Durham DH1 3LB, England

MILLER, SUZANNE MARIE, state librarian, educator; b. Feb. 25, 1954; d. John Gordon and Dorothy Margaret (Sabatka) M.; 1 child, Altinay Marie. B.A. in English, U. S.D., 1975; M.A. in Library Sci., U. Denver, 1976, postgrad. in law, 1984. Librarian II U.S.D. Sch. of Law, Vermillion, 1977-78; law libr. U. LaVerne, Calif., 1978-85, instr. in law, 1980-85; asst. libr. tech. svcs. McGeorge Sch. Law, Calif., 1985-99, prof. advanced legal rsch., 1994-99; state librarian S.D. State Library, Pierre, S.D., 1999—. Co-author (with Elizabeth J. Pokorny) U.S. Government Documents: A Practical Guide for Library Assistants in Academic and Public Libraries, 1988; contbr. chpt. to book, articles to profl. jours. Recipient A. Jurisprudence award Bancroft Whitney Pub. Co., 1983. Mem. ALA, S.D. Libr. Assn., Am. Assn. Law Librs., So. Calif. Assn. Law Librs. (arrangements com. 1981-82), No. Calif. Assn. Law Librs. (mem. program com., inst. 1988), Western Pacific Assn. Law Librs. (sec. 1990-94, pres. elect 1994-95, pres. 1995-96, local arrangements chair 1997). Roman Catholic. Home: 505 N Grand Ave Pierre SD 57501-2014 Office: SD State Library 800 Governors Dr Pierre SD 57501-2235

MILLER, THOMAS EUGENE, lawyer, writer; b. Bryan, Tex., Jan. 4, 1929; s. Eugene Adam and Ella Lucille (Schroeder) M. BA, BS, Tex. A&M U., 1950; MA, U. Tex., 1956, JD, 1966; postgrad., U. Houston, 1956-58, U. Calif., 1983. Bar: Tex. 1966. Rsch. technician M.D. Anderson Hosp., Houston, 1956-58; claims examiner trainee Social Security Adminstrn., New Orleans, 1964; trademark examiner U.S. Patent and Trademark Office, Washington, 1966; editor Bancroft-Whitney Co., San Francisco, 1966-92. Author: (under pseudonym Millard Thomas) Home From 7-North, 1984. Contbg. mem. Dem. Nat. Com., 1981-2000; mem. Celebrate Bryan Com. Mem. ABA, World Lit. Assn., World Inst. Achievement, United Writers Assn. India, Nat. Trust for Hist. Preservation, Tex. Bar Assn., African Wildlife Found., World Wildlife Fund, Internat. Platform Assn., Nat. Writers Assn., Scribes, Press Club, Commonwealth Club, Rotary Club (Paul Harris fellow), Menninger Found., Tex. A&M U. Faculty Club, Phi Kappa Phi, Psi Chi, Phi Eta Sigma. Methodist. Home: 101 N Haswell Dr Bryan TX 77803-4848

MILLER, TOBY A., engineering executive, system engineer; b. Baton Rouge, July 27, 1969; s. Allen Bruce Miller and Dolores Ann Roy. BS in Gen. Studies Applied Sci., U. La., 1994, BS in Elec. and Computer Engring., 1995. Registered engr. in tng., La. VCR technician Garico Electronics, Galvez, La., 1987-89; delivery man Domino's Pizza, Lafayette, La., 1989-91; sporting goods salesman Athletic Ctr. of Lafayette, 1991-93; lab. technician Ambar Labs., Lafayette, 1993-95; rsch. asst. microelectronics rsch. lab. U. La., Lafayette, 1993-96; project engr. Point Eight Power, New Orleans, 1996-98; tech. dir. Basler Electric, Wasselonne, Strasbourg, France, 1998—. Mem. Phi Kappa Psi (treas. La. Beta chpt. 1998, pres. 1989-91), Soc. Physics

Students. Avocations: cinema, travel, home electronics projects, science and technology. Home: 5 Rue Thiergarten, Strasbourg 67000, France

MILLER, URI, information specialist; b. Moscow, June 4, 1947; s. Yliya and Nadezda Ratner; m. Roza Bayvel, Jan. 3, 1948; children: Dani. MA, U. Moscow, 1970; PhD, Inst. of Culture, Peterburg, 1978. Rschr. USSR Acad. of Scis., Moscow, 1969-82, U. Sci. and Tech. Info. Nat. Ctr., Tel-Aviv, 1988-89; sr. indexer Wingate Inst., Israel, 1989—; thesaurus constructor Mofet Inst., Tel Aviv, Israel, 1993—; Cons. The Encyclopedia of Russian Jewry, Israel, Russia, 1995—. Author: The Methodological Problems of Subject Indexing, Sport in the History of Jews and Jews in the History of Sport; translator: I. Bashevis Singer, A. Einstein; contbr. articles to profl. jours. Avocations: cinema, theatre, belle letter reading. Home: 11 Kaplan Str, 49451 Petah Tiqwa Israel Office: Wingate Inst Phys Edn/Sport, Wingate POB 42902, Netanya Israel

MILLER, WALTER JAMES, English and humanities educator, writer; b. McKee City, N.J., Jan. 16, 1918; s. Walter Theodore and Celestia Anna (Simmons) M.; m. Bonnie Elizabeth Nelson, July 9, 1969 (div.); children: Naomi, Jason, Robin, Jared, Elizabeth. BA, CUNY, 1941; MA, Columbia U., 1952. Instr. English Poly. Inst. Brooklyn, N.Y., 1946-53, asst. prof., 1953-55; asst. prof. English and modern langs. Colo. State U., Ft. Collins, 1955-56; assoc. prof. English NYU, N.Y.C., 1958-66, prof. English, 1966-84, prof. emeritus, 1984—; Dir. Summer Writers Conf. Hofstra U., Hempstead, N.Y., 1972-79, NYU, N.Y.C., 1983-85. Author: 1001 Ideas for English Papers, 1994, Making an Angel: Poems, 1977, Engineers as Writers, 1953; author, translator: Annotated Jules Verne, 1995; editor, translator: Verne's 20,000 Leagues Under the Sea, 1993; contbg. editor Simon and Schuster, 1969-97. Recipient Spl. award Engrs. Coun. Profl. Devel., 1966, Charles Angoff award The Lit. Rev., 1983, Gt. Tchr. award NYU Alumni Assn., 1980, Fisher Second Harvest award CUNY Alumni Assn., 1997; Ruttenberg Found. fellow, 1999—. Democrat. Avocations: hiking, fishing, traveling. Office: NYU 50 W 4th St New York NY 10012-1156

MILLER, WALTER RICHARD, JR., banker; b. N.Y.C., Nov. 20, 1934; s. Walter Richard and Ann M. (Phelan) M.; m. Joan M. Groark; children: Kathryn A., Margaret E., Jennifer M., Walter Richard III. AB, Dartmouth Coll., 1955; MBA, Columbia U., 1957; PhD, NYU, 1965. Dir. mktg., v.p. Mellon Nat. Corp., Pitts., 1965-78; sr. v.p. First Atlanta Corp., 1979-81; exec. v.p. Norwest Corp., Mpls., 1981-86; pres., chief exec. officer First Constn. Fin. Corp., New Haven, 1987-91, also bd. dirs.; pres., CEO First Constn. Bank, New Haven, 1987-90; pres. Fin. Mktg. and Planning Co., Whitneyville, Conn., 1990—; exec.-in-residence Quinnipiac Coll., 1990-91, prof. fin. and mktg., 1991-95; pres. CIRRUS Sys., Inc.; exec. dir. Wright Investors' Svc., Milford, Conn., 1995—. Contbr. articles, chpts. to profl. pubs. Bd. dirs. St. Paul Chamber Orch., Minn. Pub. Radio, Sci. Mus. Minn., Quinnipiac Coll., Hamden, Conn., Quinnipiac Coun. Boy Scouts Am., The Mus. of AM. Theatre; chmn. bd. Orchestra New England. With USAF, 1958. Teaching fellow NYU, N.Y.C., 1960; Ford Found. fellow NYU, 1962. Mem. Interbank Card Assn. (internat. chmn., bd. dirs.), Am. Mktg. Assn. (contbg. editor), Bank Mktg. Assn. (bd. dirs., chmn. mktg. planning council, chmn. mktg. mgmt. council), Somerset Club, New Haven County Club, Quinnipiack Club, Lawn Club. Home 2 Marshall Rd Hamden CT 06517-3505 Office: Fin Mktg-Planning Co 3 Marshall Rd Whitneyville CT 06517-3505

MILLER, WILLIAM FRANKLIN, instrumentation engineer; b. Houston, Oct. 27, 1942; s. Robert William and Edith Grace (Bell) Miller; m. Joyce Kay Sams, Aug. 27, 1966; children: Robert, Christina, Paul. BS in Mech. Engring., U. Houston, 1970. Registered profl. engr., Tex. Instrumentation cons., v.p., controller Strong Engr., Inc., Houston, 1976-78; self-employed instrumentation cons. Houston, 1978-84, 87; field constrn. instrumentation engr. Lummus Constrn. Co., Bloomfield, N.J., Saudi Arabia, 1984-87; sr. instrument engr. Chemstress Cons. Co., Houston, 1987-88; sr. instrument splst., refinery engr. Saudi Aramco, Ras Tanura, Saudi Arabia, 1988—. Co-author: Applied Instrumentation in the Process Industries, 1974. Webelos leader pack 80 Sam Houston area coun. Boy Scouts Am., Houston, 1977, asst. scout master Sam Houston area coun. troop 80, Houston, 1978-82. Recipient Wood Badge Tng. award Sam Houston area coun. Boy Scouts Am., 1981. Mem. ASME, Instrument Soc. Am. (sr.), Nat. Soc. Profl. Engrs., Soc. Petroleum Engrs., Nat. Eagle Scout Assn. (Eagle Scout 1958), Century Club U. Houston Alumni Orgn. Republican. Roman Catholic. Avocations: camping, hiking, fishing, scuba diving. Home: care Saudi Aramco, Box 1960, 31311 Ras Tanura Eastern, Saudi Arabia Office: RT Refinery Engring Dept, care Saudi Aramco W-2620, 31311 Ras Tanura Eastern, Saudi Arabia

MILLER, WILLIAM GREEN, ambassador; b. N.Y.C., Aug. 15, 1931; m. Suzanne Lisle; 2 children. BA, Williams Coll., Oxford U., U.K.; MA, Oxford U., U.K.; postgrad., Harvard U. Tutor Winthrop House Harvard U., 1956-59; with Fgn. Svc., 1959; vice consul, polit. officer Isfahan, Iran, 1959-62; polit. officer Tehran, Iran, 1962-64; line officer, exec. secretariat Dept. of State, 1965-66; mem. Sr. Interdepartmental Group, 1966-67; spl. asst. fgn. affairs and def. Senator John Sherman Cooper, 1967-73; staff dir. Senate Select Com. Emergency Powers, 1973-75, Senate Select Com. to Study Govtl. Ops. with Respect to Intelligence Communities, 1975-76, Senate Select Com. Intelligence, 1976-81; assoc. dean, adj. prof. internat. politics Fletcher Sch. Law and Diplomacy, 1981-83, rsch. assoc., 1983-85; faculty assoc. Harvard Ctr. Middle Eastern Studies, 1983-86; pres. Am. Com. U.S.-Soviet Rels., 1986-92; U.S. amb. to Ukraine, 1993-98; cons. D.H. Sawyer and Assocs., Ltd., N.Y.C., 1985; bd. dirs. Internat. Found., pres. 1986-92; pres. Com. Am.- Russian Rels., cons. Catherine T. MacArthur Found., 1992-93. Contbr. articles to profl. jours. Rsch. fellow Harvard Ctr. Sci. and Internat. Affairs, 1984-86, John F. Kennedy Sch. of Govt. fellow Harvard U., 1986. Fellow Rsch. Inst. of Politics; mem. Nat. Acad. Pub. Diplomacy, Nat. Acad. Pub. Adminstrn., Internat. Inst. Strategic Studies, Coun. Fgn. Rels., Children of the 21st Century, Middle East Inst., Soc. Iranian Studies, Search For Common Ground. Office: Woodrow Wilson Internat Ctr Scholars 1 Woodrow Wilson Plaza 1300 Pennsylvania Ave NW Washington DC 20004-3002

MILLER, WOODBURN DAVIDSON, educational administrator, retired, consultant; b. Rock River, Jamaica, Feb. 24, 1929; s. John Nathaniel and Lavinia (Parker) M.; m. Inez Viola Thompson Miller, Dec. 29, 1956. BA (hon.), UCWI, London, 1962; diploma in Edn., UWI, Jamaica, 1967, higher diploma in Edn., 1971; diploma in Ednl. Adminstrn., U. Leeds, Eng., 1974. Tchr. Crofts Hill Elem. Sch., Clarendon, 1952-53; tchr., sr. tchr. Wolmer's Boys' Sch., Kingston, 1953-74; vice prin. Kingston Tech. H.S., 1974-75; prin. DeCateret Coll., Mandeville, 1975-79, Kingston Coll., Kingston, 1980-86; sec. gen. Jamaica Tchrs. Assn., Kingston, 1986-94; pres. Jamaica Tchrs. Assn., 1979; chmn. Jamaica Publ. House, Joint Trade Union Rsch. Devel. Ctr., 1996; treas. Workforce Devel. Consortium, Kingston, 1997—; mem. Nat. Coun. on Edn., 1994—. Lay reader Anglican Ch., Jamaica, 1952—; pres. Christian Aux. Movement of Jamaica, Traralgar Park Citizens Assn., 1988—, Harbour View Citizens Assn., 1960-73. Lt. Col. Jamaica Combined Cadet Force, 1981—. Recipient Order of Distinction, Govt. Jamaica, 1984, 92; named Justice of Peace Govt. of Jamaica, 1990—. Jamaican Tchrs. Assn. (trustee 1993—), Jamaica Combined Cadet Force 2nd in command, 1991—). Anglican. Avocations: gardening, swimming, dominoes, scrabble. Home: 1 Breary Ave, Kingston 10, Jamaica

MILLER, ZOYA DICKINS (MRS. HILLIARD EVE MILLER, JR.), civic worker; b. Washington, July 15, 1923; d. Randolph and Zoya Pavlovna (Klementinovska) Dickins; m. Hilliard Eve Miller, Jr., Dec. 6, 1943; children: Jeffrey Arnot, Hilliard Eve III. Grad., Stuart Sch. Costume Design, Washington, 1942; student, Sophie Newcomb Coll., 1944, New Eng. Conservatory Music, 1946, Colo. Coll., 1965; grad., Internat. Sch. Reading, 1969. Lic. pvt. pilot. Instr. Stuart Summer Sch. Costume Design, Washington, 1942; fashion coord. Julius Garfinckel, Washington, 1942-43; fashion coord., cons. Mademoiselle mag., 1942-44; star TV show Cowbelle Kitchen, 1957-58, Flair for Living, 1958-59; model mags. and comml. films, also nat. comml. recs., 1956-80; dir. rsch. devel. Webb-Waring Inst. for Biomed. Rsch., Denver, 1973—. Contbr. articles, lectrs. on health care sys. and fund raising. Mem. exec. com., bd. dirs. El Paso County chpt. Am. Lung Assn. Colo., 1965-84, bd. dirs., 1965-87, chmn. radio and TV coun., 1963-70, mem. med. affairs com., 1965-70, pres., 1965-66, procurer found. funds, 1965-70; developer nat. radio ednl. prodns. for internat. use Am. Lung Assn., 1963-70, coord. statewide pulmonary screening programs Colo., other states, 1965-72; chmn. benefit fund raising El Paso County Cancer Soc., 1963; co-founder, coord. Colorado Springs Debutante Ball, 1967—; coord. Nat. Gov.'s Comprehensive Health Planning Coun., 1967-74, chmn., 1971-72; chmn. Colo. Chronic Care Com., 1969-73, chmn. fund raising, 1970-72, chmn. spl. com. conl. studies on nat. health bills, 1971-73; mem. Colo.-Wyo. Regional Med. Program Adv. Coun., 1969-73; mem. Colo. Med. Found. Consumers Adv. Coun., 1972-78; mem. decorative arts com. Colorado Springs Fine Arts Ctr., 1972-75; founder, state coord. Nov. Noel Pediat. Benefit Am. Lung Assn., 1973-87; founder, chmn. bd. dirs. Newborn Hope, Inc., 1987—; mem. adv. bd. Wagon Wheel Girl Scouts, 1991-94, Cmty. in Schs., 1995—; mem. cmty. adv. coun. Beth-El Nursing Sch., 1998—. Zoya Dickins Miller Vol. of Yr. award established Am. Lung Assn. of Colo., 1979; recipient James J. Waring award Colo. Conf. on Respiratory Disease Workers, 1963, Nat. Pub. Rels. award Am. Lung Assn., 1979, Gold Double Bar Cross award, 1980, 83, Jefferson award Am. Inst. Pub. Svc., 1991, Thousand Points of Light award The White House, 1992, Recognition award So. Colo. Women's C. of C., 1994, Silver Spur Cmty. award Pikes Peak Range Riders, 1994, Silver Bell award Assistance League Colorado Springs, 1996, Svc. to Mankind award Centennial Sertoma Club, 1997, Help Can't Wait award Pikes Peak chpt. ARC, 1997, Cmty. Weaver award The Independent News, 1997, Apgar award Colo. March of Dimes, 1998; named Humanitarian of Yr., Am. Lung Assn. of Colo., 1987, One of 50 Most Influential Women in Colorado Springs by Gazette Telegraph Newspaper, 1990, One of 5 Leading Ladies Colo. Homes & Lifestyles Mag., 1991. Mem. Colo. Assn. Fund Raisers, Denver Round Table for Planned Giving, Nat. Soc. Fund Raising Execs., Nat. Cowbell Assn. (El Paso county pres. 1954, TV chmn., chmn. nat. Father of Yr. contest Colo. 1956-57), Broadmoor Garden Club. Home: 74 W Cheyenne Mountain Blvd Colorado Springs CO 80906-4336

MILLER-PODRAZA, HALINA, biochemist, researcher; b. Warsaw, Poland, May 2, 1948; d. Juliusz and Halina (Liscocka) M.; m. Stanislaw Podraza. MSc, U. Warsaw, Poland, 1972, PhD in Biochemistry, 1980. Asst. Inst. Hematology, Warsaw, 1972-80, rschr., 1982-86, asst. prof., 1985; lectr. Med. Acad., Warsaw, 1986-90; rschr. Góteborg (Sweden) U., 1990—; vis. fellow NIH, Bethesda, Md. , 1980-82. Contbr. over 40 articles and over 20 abstracts to profl. jours.; speaker, panel mem., internat. confs. Group award Polish Acad. Scis., 1977, 2d degree didactic group award Med. U. Warsaw, 1989. Home: Lantmilsgatan 20, 421 37 Vastra Frolunda Sweden Office: Göteborg Univ D Biochem, Box 440, SE 40530 Göteborg Sweden

MILLETT, JOHN ANTILL, lawyer, accountant, poet; b. Sydney, Australia, Feb. 3, 1921; s. John Millett and Doris Ruth Antill; m. Enid Simshauser (div. 1961); m. Marion Beatrice Moss, 1961; children: Scott, Shelley, Michelle. LLB, Sydney U., 1952. Law practice Sydney and the Gold Coast, Queensland, Australia. Author 14 books of poetry; editor, mng. editor Poetry Australia, 1970—. With RAF, 1941-46. Decorated Order of Australia; recipient Book of Yr. awards Australian Poetry Soc., 1974; 1st prize for short story Royal Soc. Lit., 1999, prize, 1998; Salmon Run Book of Yr., 1995, Short Listed New Premier's award, 1982, 94; winner Scottish Internat. Open Poetry Composition award, 1993, Max Harris Literary award, 1999. Office: South Head Press, Market Pl, Berrima NSW 2577, Australia

MILLETT, TERRY BRIAN, financial services executive; b. Frankston, Victoria, Australia, Dec. 2, 1959; s. Brian Gerald and Kath Louise (McLennon) M.; m. Marie Louise Morgan, Oct. 1, 1988. BS, LaTrobe U., Melbourne, 1981, M in Agrl. Sci., 1983; grad. diploma computing, Chisholm Inst., Melbourne, 1985; MBA, Melbourne U., 1993. Product mgr. superamuation Nat. Mutual, strategy mgr., distbn. support mgr.; head sales and mktg. Fin. Svcs. Group; chief mgr. Fin. Svcs. Group Bank New Zealand; program advisor global pvt. banking Nat. Australia Bank, Melbourne. Mem. Australian Inst. Mgmt., Australian Inst. Co. Dirs., Melbourne Bus. Sch. Alumni. Avocations: current affairs, travel, business management. Office: Nat Australia Bank, Level 21 500 Bourk St, Melbourne VIC 3001, Australia

MILLIGAN, GLENN EDWARD, poet; b. Detroit, Aug. 21, 1949; s. George Edwin and Doris Ann M. BBA in Econ., Western Mich. U., Kalamazoo, 1984. Disabled american vet., 1974—. Author: Lust, Love, Life, 1986, Nocturnes, 1988, Beyond Bamboo, 1998, Passage, 1999, Lament, 2000. Mem. Disabled Am. Vets., Battle Creek, Mich., 1979—. Home: 600 E Emmett St Apt 12 Battle Creek MI 49017-5733

MILLIGAN, ROBERT LEE, JR., computer company executive; b. Evanston, Ill., Apr. 4, 1934; s. Robert L. and Alice (Connell) M. BS, Northwestern U., 1958; m. Susan A. Woodrow, Mar. 23, 1957; children: William, Bonnie, Thomas, Robert III. Account rep. IBM, Chgo., 1957-66; sr. cons. L.B. Knight & Assocs., Chgo., 1966-68; v.p. mktg. Trans Union Systems Corp., Chgo., 1968-73; sr. v.p. sales mktg., sec. Systems Mgmt. Inc., Rosemont, Ill., 1973-87, dir., 1980-87; pres., CEO, owner Target Data, Inc., Northbrook, Ill., 1987; pres. CEO Wireless Spectrum Tech., Inc., Northbrook, Ill., 1993—; mng. dir. L. William Teweles & Co., 1996-98; treas. Systems Mgmt. Inc. Svc. Corp., 1981-84; dir. Nanofast, Inc., Chgo., 1982—. Div. mgr. North Suburban YMCA Bldg. Fund, 1967; area chmn. Northfield Twp. Rep. Party, 1965-71. Bd. dirs. United Fund, Glenview, Ill., 1967-69, Robert R. McCormick Chgo. Boys Club, 1974—; pres. Glenview Amateur Hockey Assn., 1974-79, bd. mgrs., 1982-86; gen. mgr. Glenbrook South High Sch. Hockey Club, 1973-78. With AUS, 1953-55. Mem. Data Processing Mgmt. Assn., Assn. for Info. and Image Mgmt., Chgo. High Tech. Assn., Info. Industry Coun. of Met. Chgo., Consumer Credit Assn. (bd. dir., sec. 1969-70), Cellular Telecomm. Industry Assn., Personal Comm. Industry Assn., Telecomms. Industry Assn., Winforum, Phi Kappa Psi. Presbyterian. Clubs: Northwestern (bd. dir. 1973-75) (Chgo.); Glen View (Ill.). Home: 19 Ct Of Island Point Northbrook IL 60062-3210 Office: Wireless Spectrum Tech Inc PO Box 1417 Northbrook IL 60065-1417

MILLIKAN, CLARK HAROLD, physician; b. Freeport, Ill., Mar. 2, 1915; s. William Clarance and Louise (Chamberlain) M.; m. Gayle Margaret Gross, May 2, 1942 (div. Apr. 1966); children: Terri, Clark William, Jeffry Brent; m. Janet T. Holmes, July 21, 1966 (div. Dec. 1987); m. Nancy Futrell, Dec. 28, 1987. Student, Parsons (Kans.) Jr. Coll., 1935; MD, U. Kans., 1939. Diplomate Am. Bd. Psychiatry and Neurology. Intern St. Luke's Hosp., Clev., 1939-40, asst. resident medicine, 1940-41; from resident neurology to asst. prof. neurology State U. Iowa, Iowa City, 1941-49; staff Mayo Clinic, Rochester, Minn., 1949—, cons. neurology, 1958—; dir. Mayo Center for Clin. Rsch. in Cerebrovascular Disease; prof. neurology Mayo Sch. Medicine; physician-in-chief pro tem Cleve. Clinic, 1970; prof. neurology U. Utah Sch. Medicine, Salt Lake City, 1976-87, U. Miami (Fla.) Sch. Medicine, 1987-88; scholar in residence, dept. neurology Henry Ford Hosp., Detroit, 1988-92; prof. neurology Sch. of Medicine Creighton U., Omaha, 1992-94; clin. prof. neurology Med. Coll. Ohio, Toledo, 1994-97; dir. acad. affairs Intermountain Stroke Rsch. Found., Salt Lake City, 1997—; Asst. chmn., editor trans. 2d Princeton Conf. Cerebrovascular Disease, 1957, chmn. confs., 1961, 64; chmn. com. classification and nomenclature cerebrovascular disease USPHS, 1955-69; mem. council Nat. Inst. Neurologic Diseases and Blindness, NIH, USPHS, 1961-65, div. regional med. program, 1965-68; A.O.A. lectr. Baylor U., Waco, Tex., 1952; James Mawer Pearson Meml. lectr., Vancouver, B.C., Can., 1958; Conner Meml. lectr. Am. Heart Assn., 1961; Peter T. Bohan lectr. U. Kans., 1965, 73. Editor: Jour. Stroke, 1970-76, assoc. editor, 1976—. Recipient Outstanding Alumnus award U. Kans., 1973. Fellow ACP, Am. Acad. Neurology (founding chmn. sect. on stroke and vascular neurology 1994), Royal Soc. Medicine; mem. AMA, AAUP, AAAS, Assn. Rsch. Nervous and Mental Disease (pres. 1961), Am. Neurol. Assn. (1st v.p. 1969-70, pres. 1973-74), Minn. Med. Assn., Four County Med. Soc. South Minn., Cen. Neuropsychiat. Assn., N.Y. Acad. Sci., Am. Heart Assn. (chmn. coun. cerebrovascular disease 1967-68, Gold Heart award 1976, Spl. Merit award 1981), Nat. Stroke Assn. (pres. 1986, editor Jour. Stroke and Cerebrovascular Disease 1990—), Sigma Xi.

MILLIKEN, JOHN GORDON, research economist; b. Denver, May 12, 1927; s. William Boyd and Margaret Irene (Marsh) M.; m. Marie Violet Machell, June 13, 1953; children: Karen Marie, Douglas Gordon, David Tait, Anne Alain. BS, Yale U., 1949, BEng, 1950; MS, U. Colo., 1966, PhD, 1969. Registered profl. engr., Colo. Engr. U.S. Bur. Reclamation, Denver, 1950-55; asst. to plant mgr. Stanley Aviation Corp., Denver, 1955-56; prin. mgmt. engr., dept. mgr. Martin-Marietta Aerospace Divsn., Denver, 1956-64; mgmt. engr. Safeway Stores, Inc., Denver, 1964-66; sr. rsch. economist, prof., assoc. div. head U. Denver Rsch. Inst., 1966-86; pres. Univ. Senate, 1980-81; prin. Milliken Chapman Rsch. Group, Inc., Littleton, Colo., 1986-88, Milliken Rsch. Group, Inc., Littleton, 1988—; vis. fellow sci. policy rsch. unit U. Sussex, Eng., 1975-76; bd. dirs. Sci. Mgmt. Corp.; cons. mgmt. engr. Author: Aerospace Management Techniques, 1971, Federal Incentives for Innovation, 1974, Recycling Municipal Wastewater, 1977, Water and Energy in Colorado's Future, 1981, Metropolitan Water Management, 1981, Technological Innovation and Economic Vitality, 1983, Water Management in the Denver, Colorado Urban Area, 1988, Benefits and Costs of Oxygenated Fuels in Colorado, 1990, Water Transfer Alternatives Study, 1994, Colorado Springs Water Resources Plan Alternative Assessment Study, 1995, Colorado Springs Utilities Wastewater Infrastructure Alternatives Study, 1998; contbr. articles to profl. jours. Bd. dirs. S.E. Englewood Water Dist., 1963—, South Englewood San. Dist., 1965—; bd. dirs. South Suburban Pk. and Recreation Dist., 1971-96, chmn., 1990-92; chmn. Dem. Com. of Arapahoe County, 1969-71, 5th Congl. Dist. Colo., 1972-73, 74-75; mem. exec. com. Colo. Faculty Adv. Coun., 1981-85; mem. Garrison Diversion Unit Commn., 1984; trustee Colo. Local Govt. Liquid Asset Trust, 1986—, chmn., 1991-93; bd. dirs. Colo. Spl. Dist. Assn. Property and Liability Pool, 1989—, pres. 1997-98. With M.C., U.S. Army, 1945-46. Recipient Adlai E. Stevenson Meml. award, 1981, cert. of Appreciation for svc. to Nation, U.S. Sec. Interior, 1984, hon. title "Amicus Universitatis," U. Denver, 1994, Disting. Svc. award Spl. Dist. Assn. Colo., 1995; Milliken Park named in his honor for svcs. to Littleton cmty., 1996. Mem. Acad. Mgmt., Nat. Assn. Bus. Economists, Yale Sci. and Engring. Assn., Am. Water Works Assn., Sigma Xi, Tau Beta Pi, Beta Gamma Sigma, Sigma Iota Epsilon. Congregationalist. Home and Office: 6502 S Ogden St Littleton CO 80121-2561

MILLING, MARCUS EUGENE, SR., geologist; b. Galveston, Tex., Oct. 8, 1938; s. Robert Richardson and Leonora Mildred (Currey) M.; m. Sandra Ann Dunlay, Sept. 21, 1959; 1 child, Marcus Eugene Jr. BS in Geology, Lamar U., 1961; MS in Geology, U. Iowa, 1964, PhD in Geology, 1968. Cert. petroleum geologist. Rsch. geologist Exxon Prodn. Rsch. Co., Houston, 1968-76; prodn. geologist Exxon Co. U.S.A., Kingsville, Tex., 1976-78; dist. exptl. geologist Exxon Co. U.S.A., New Orleans, 1978-80; mgr. geol. rsch. Arco Oil and Gas Co., Plano, Tex., 1980-86; chief geologist Arco Oil and Gas Co., Dallas, 1986-87; assoc. dir. Bur. Econ. Geology U. Tex., Austin, 1987-92; exec. dir. Am. Geol. Inst., Alexandria, Va., 1992—; vice-chmn. Offshore Tech. Conf., Dallas, 1984-87; dir. Geosci. Inst. for Oil and Gas Recovery Rsch., Austin, 1988-91. NSF fellow, 1966. Fellow Geol. Soc. Am. (councilor 1986-89); mem. Am. Assn. Petroleum Geologists, Soc. Petroleum Engrs., Am. Inst. Profl. Geologists (Ben H. Parker Meml. medal 1997), Blue Key, Sigma Xi. E-mail: mmilling@dgiweb.org. Home: 11457 Hollow Timber Ct Reston VA 20194-1980 Office: Am Geol Inst 4220 King St Alexandria VA 22302-1507

MILLIS, NANCY FANNIE, university administrator; b. Melbourne, Victoria, Australia, Apr. 10, 1922; d. Frank Ormonde and Annie Beryl (Ellis) M. M of Agrl. Sci., U. Melbourne, 1948; PhD, U. Bristol, Eng., 1951; DSc, U. Melbourne, 1993. From lectr. to reader to prof. U. Melbourne, 1953-87, prof. emeritus, 1987—; chancellor LaTrobe U., Bundoora, Victoria, 1992—; pres. Australian Soc. Micro., 1978-80; mem. UNESCO Nat., 1975-86; chair Recombinant DNA Monitoring Com., 1981-88, Genetic Manipulation Adv. Com., 1989—. Co-author: (textbook) Biochemical Engineering, 1965, 2d edit., 1973. Mem., chair Fairfield Hosp. Bd., Melbourne, 1982-93; mem. PANCH Bd., Melbourne, 1990-95, Australian Inst. Marine Sci., Townsville, 1988-94; dir. Melbourne Water Corp., 1992-94; mem., pres. Univ. House, 1984-85. Named Order of Brit. Empire, Australia, 1977, Companion, Order of Australia, 1990; travel grantee Fulbright Found., 1954. Fellow Australian Acad. Technol. Scis. and Engring.; mem. Beefsteak. Avocations: gardening, traveling. Home: 8 Grandview Rd, 3186 Brighton Victoria, Australia Office: LaTrobe U, Chancellor's Office, 3083 Bundoora Victoria, Australia

MILLNS, ANTHONY THOMAS COWLING, financial and maritime consultant; b. Brentwood, Essex, Eng., Oct. 7, 1935; s. Cecil Thomas and Lissie Muriel (Simons) M.; m. Elizabeth Ann Way, Aug. 20, 1959 (div. Oct. 1963); children: Tina, Richard; m. Pamela Ann Donne, Apr. 9, 1966; children: Philip, Geoffrey. Grad. in nav., U. Southampton, 1952. Cert. master on fgn. going S.S. Navigating officer Alfred Holt & Co., Liverpool, Eng., 1953-56, Union Castle Mail S.S. Co. Ltd., London, 1956-65; area mgr. Esso Petroleum Co. Ltd., London, 1965-90; sr. adviser Hill Samuel, London, 1965-93; fin. cons. DGR Hunt Ind. Fin. Svcs., Bishop's Waltham, Eng., 1993-99; prin. A.T.C. Millns Ind. Fin. Consultancy, 1999—; presenter Nat. Conf. on Preventing Collisions at Sea, 1996. Contbr. articles to profl. jours., including Jour. Nav. Pres. Henleaze Neighbourhood Soc., Bristol, Eng., 1986-88. Named freeman City of London, 1968. Mem. Life Ins. Assn. (diplomate), Royal Inst. Nav. Avocations: sailing, swimming, walking. Home: 3 Rockside Dr, Henleaze, Bristol BS9 4NW, England Office: ATC Millns Ind Fin Consultancy, 3 Rockside Dr Henleaze, Bristol BS9 4NW, England

MILLON, CHARLES MARIE ANDRÉ PHILIPPE, French government official; b. Belley, Ain, France, Nov. 12, 1945; s. Gabriel Millon and Suzanne Gunet; m. Chantal Delsol, June 6, 1970; children: Thomas, Béatrice, Charlest-Etienne, Marie-Contance, François-Xavier, Philippe. Degree in Law, Econ., U. Lyon; lic. Econ. Teaching asst., 1969, juridical & fiscal counsel, 1970—; mayor Belley, 1977—; counsel-gen. Ain, 1985-88; v.p. Nat. Assembly, 1986-88; pres. Fed. Dept. Republican Party, UDF, asst., sec.-gen., 1983-84; mem. PR Polit. Bur., 1984—; dep. UDF-PR, Ain, 1978—; sec.-gen. Assn. Dept. des Maires; treas. Assn. des Maires de France, v.p., 1981; pres. Regional Coun. Rhône-Alpes, 1988-98, Parlementary Group, UDF, 1989—, la Droite, 1998; Min. State Def., Paris, 1995-97, La Paix Civile, 1998. Author: L'Extravagante Histoire des Nationalisations, 1984, La Tentation du Conservatisme, 1995. Office: Office of the Mayor, 11 bis rue de Barons, 01300 Belley France

MILLOY, FRANK JOSEPH, JR., surgeon; b. Phoenix, June 26, 1924; s. Frank Joseph and Ola (McCabe) M. BS, Notre Dame U., 1946; MS, Northwestern U., 1949, MD, 1947. Diplomate Am. Bd. Surgery and Thoracic Surgery. Intern Cook County Hosp., Chgo., 1947-49, resident, 1953-57; practice medicine, specializing in surgery Lake Forest, Ill., 1958—; assoc. attending staff Presbyn.-St. Lukes Hosp.; attending staff Cook County Hosp.; mem. staff U. Ill. Rsch. Hosp.; clin. assoc. prof. surgery, U. Ill. Med. Sch.; assoc. prof. surgery Rush Med. Sch. Contbr. more than 35 articles to profl. jours., chpts. to books. Cons. West Side Vet. Hosp. Served as apprentice seaman USNR, 1943-45; lt. M.C., USNR, 1950-52; PTO. Mem. A.C.S., Chgo. Surg. Soc., Internat. Soc. Surgery, Am. Coll. Chest Physicians, Soc. Thoracic Surgeons, Phi Beta Pi. Clubs: Metropolitan, University (Chgo.). Past president Illinois Thoracic Surgical Society; past secretary Warren Cole Surgical Society (Surgical Alumni University of Illinois); secretary Karl Meyer Surgical Society (Cook County Hospital Surgical Alumni Association). Home: 574 Jackson Ave Glencoe IL 60022-2036

MILLS, ALICE CATHERINE, literature educator, writer; b. Liverpool, Eng., BA (hon.), U. Adelaide, Australia; MLitt, Cambridge (Eng.) U. Sr. lectr. U. Ballarat, Australia; tutor U. New Eng., Australia. Editor: Random House Treasury of Children's Literature, 1997, Favourite Bedtime Stories, 1998. Office: BSSH, U Ballarat, Ballarat 3353, Australia

MILLS, BARBARA, barrister; b. Chorley Wood, Hertsfordshire, Eng., Aug. 10, 1940; d. John and Kitty Warnock; m. John Angus Donald Mills, July 28, 1962; children: Sarah, Caroline, Elizabeth, Peter. MA, Lady Margaret Hall, U. Oxford, Eng., 1962; LLD, Hull U., 1993; LLD (hon.), Nottingham Trent U., 1993, London Guildhall U., 1994. Called to Bar, Middle Temple, 1963, bencher, 1990. Jr. treasury counsel Cen.Criminal Ct., 1981-86; mem. Criminal Injuries Compensation Bd., 1988-90; mem. Parole Bd., 1990; dir. pub. prosecutions Crown Prosecution Svc., London, 1992-98; with The Adjudicator (ind. ombudsman), 1999—. Hon. fellow Lady Margaret Hall, 1993; decorated Dame Comdr. of Brit. Empire, 1996; recipient Dame Commdr. Brit. Empire New Year Honors, 1996. Fellow Soc. Advanced Legal Studies (hon.); mem.

Inst. Mgmt. (companion of honor), Inst. for Study and Treatment of Delinquency (hon. v.p. 1996). Avocation: family.

MILLS, BELEN COLLANTES, early childhood education educator; s. Ricardo and Epifania (Tomines) C.; children: Belinda Mills Keiser, Roger A. BSE, Leyte Normal Coll., Tacloban, Leyte, Philippines, 1954; MS in Edn., Ind. U., 1955, EdD, 1967. Prof. early childhood edn. Fla. State U., Tallahassee; early childhood cons. to ednl. agys. and orgns. Author books on early childhood edn., phonics-based children's books and acad. readiness computer programs; contbr. articles to profl.jours. Smith-Mundt Fulbright scholar. Mem. Nat. Assn. for the Edn. of Young Children, Nat. Assn. of Early Childhood Tchr. Edn., World Coun. for Curriculum and Instruction, Assn. of Childhood Edn. Internat. Home: PO Box 20023 Tallahassee FL 32316-0023

MILLS, CAROL MARGARET, business consultant, public relations consultant; b. Salt Lake City, Utah, Aug. 31, 1943; d. Samuel Lawrence and Beth (Neilson) M. BS magna cum laude, U. Utah, 1965. With W.S. Hatch Co., Woods Cross, Utah, 1965-87, corp. sec., 1970-87, traffic mgr., 1969-87; dir. publicity W.S. Hatch Co., Woods Cross, 1974-87, cons. various orgns., 1988—; dir. Hatch vc. Corp., 1972-87, Nat. Tank Truck Carriers, Inc., Washington, 1977-88; bd. dirs. Intermountain Tariff Bur. Inc., 1978-88, chmn., 1981-82, 1986-87; bd. dirs. Mountainwest Venture Group. Fund raiser March of Dimes, Am. Cancer Soc., Am. Heart Assn.; active senatorial campaign, 1976; gubernatorial campaign, 1984, 88, congl. campaign, 1990, 92, 94, vice chair voting dist., 1988-90, congl. campaign, 1994, chmn. 1990-92, chmn. party caucus legis. dist.; witness transp. com. Utah State Legislature, 1984, 85; apptd. by gov. to bd. trustees Utah Tech. Fin. Corp., 1986—, corp. sec., mem. exec. com., 1988—; mem. expdn. to Antaractica, 1996, Titanic '96 expdn.; mem. Pioneer Theatre Guild, 1985—. Recipient Svc. awards W.S. Hatch Co., 1971, 80; VIP chpt. Easter Seal Telethon, 1989, 90, Outstanding Vol. Svc. award Easter Seal Soc. Utah, 1989, 90. Mem. Nat. Tank Truck Carriers Transp. Club Salt Lake City, Am. Trucking Assn. (mem. pub. rels. coun.), Utah Motor Transport Assn. (bd. dirs. 1982-88), Internat. Platform Assn., Traveler's Century Club, Titanic Internat., Beta Gamma Sigma, Phi Kappa Phi, Phi Chi Theta. Home: HC 11 Box 329 Kamiah ID 83536-9410 Office: PO Box 1495 Kamiah ID 83536-1495

MILLS, DON HARPER, pathology and psychiatry educator, lawyer; b. Peking, China, July 29, 1927; came to U.S., 1928; s. Clarence Alonzo and Edith Clarissa (Parrett) M.; m. Lillian Frances Snyder, June 11, 1949; children: Frances Jo, Jon Snyder. BS, U. Cin., 1950, MD, 1953; JD, U. So. Calif., 1958. Diplomate Am. Bd. Law in Medicine. Intern L.A. County Gen. Hosp., 1953-54, admitting physician, 1954-57, attending staff pathologist, 1959—; pathology fellow U. So. Calif., L.A., 1954-55, instr. pathology, 1958-62, asst. clin. prof., 1962-65, assoc. clin. prof., 1965-69, clin. prof., 1969—, clin. prof. psychiatry and behavioral sci., 1986—; asst. in pathology Hosp. Good Samaritan, L.A., 1956-65, cons. staff, 1962-72, affiliating staff, 1972-91; dep. med. examiner Office of L.A. County Med. Examiner, 1957-61; instr. legal medicine Loma Linda (Calif.) U. Sch. Medicine, 1960-66, assoc. clin. prof. humanities, 1966-95; cons. HEW, 1972-73, 75-76, Dept. of Def., 1975-80; bd. dirs. Am. Bd. Law in Medicine, Inc., Chgo., 1980-86; med. dir. Profl. Risk Mgmt. Group, 1989—. Column editor Newsletter of the Long Beach Med. Assn., 1960-75, Jour. Am. Osteopathic Assn., 1965-77, Ortho Panel, 1970-78; exec. editor Trauma, 1964-88, mem. editl. bd., 1988—; mem. editl. bd. Legal Aspects of Med. Practice, 1972-90, Med. Alert Comms., 1973-75, Am. Jour. Forensic Medicine and Pathology, 1979-87, Hosp. Risk Control, 1981-96; contbr. numerous articles to profl. jours. Bd. dirs. Inst. for Med. Risk Studies, 1988—; mem. adv. bd. Pacific Ctr. for Health Policy and Ethics, 1997—, chmn., 1999—. Recipient Ritz Heerman award Calif. Hosp. Assn., 1986, Disting. fellow Am. Acad. Forensic Scis., 1993, Genesis award Pacific Ctr. for Health Policy and Ethics, 1993, Founder's award Am. Coll. Med. Quality, 1994. Fellow Am. Coll. Legal Medicine (pres. 1974-76, bd. govs. 1970-78, v.p. 1972-74, chmn. malpractice com. 1973-74, jour. editl. bd. 1984—, gold medal 1999), Am. Acad. Forensic Sci. (gen. program chmn. 1966-67, chmn. jurisprudence sect. 1966-67, 73-74, exec. com. 1971-74, 84-88, v.p. 1984-85, pres. 1986-87, ethics com. 1976-86, 91—, chmn. ethics com. 1994—, long-term planning com. 1990—, jour. editl. bd. 1965-79); mem. AMA (jour. editl. bd. 1973-77), AAAS, ABA, Am. Coll. Med. Quality (hon. life), Calif. Med. Assn., L.A. County Med. Assn., L.A. County Bar Assn., Am. Soc. Hosp. Attys., Calif. Soc. Hosp. Attys. E-mail: donharpermills@pol.net. Home: 700 E Ocean Blvd Unit 2606 Long Beach CA 90802-5039 Office: 911 N Studebaker Rd Ste 250 Long Beach CA 90815-4959

MILLS, ELIZABETH SHOWN, genealogist, editor, writer; b. Cleve., Miss., Dec. 29, 1944; d. Floyd Finley Shown and Elizabeth Thulmar (Jeffcoat) Carver; children: Clayton Bernard, Donna Rachal, Daniel Garland. BA, U. Ala., 1980. Cert. genealogist, geneal. lectr. Profl. geneal. writer, educator, 1972—; editor Nat. Geneal. Soc. Quar., Arlington, Va., 1987—; faculty Samford U. Inst. of Genealogy and Hist. Rsch., Birmingham, Ala., 1980—; trustee Assn. for Promotion of Scholarship in Genealogy, N.Y., 1984-90; contract dir., cons. U. Ala., 1985-92; faculty Nat. Inst. of Geneal. Rsch., 1985-97. Author, editor, translator Cane River Creole Series, 6 vols.; author: Evidence: Citation and Analysis for the Family Historian, 1997; editor: Professional Genealogy: A Manual for Researchers, Writers, Editors, Lecturers, and Librarians, 2000; contbr. articles to profl. jours. Trustee Nat. Bd. Certification Genealogists, 1984—, v.p., 1989-94, pres., 1994-96; trustee Assn. Profl. Genealogists, 1984-90, 92-94, regional v.p., 1988-89. Named Outstanding Young Women of Am. Jaycees, Gadsden, 1976, Outstanding Alumna award U. Ala. New Coll., Tuscaloosa, 1990. Fellow Am. Soc. of Geneal. (sec. 1992-95, v.p. 1995-98, pres. 1998—), Nat. Geneal. Soc. (councilor 1987-92), Utah Geneal. Assn., Grady McWhiney Rsch. Found. (sr.); mem. Assn. of Profl. Geneal. (Smallwood Svc. award, 1989). Republican. Roman Catholic. Office: Nat Geneal Soc Quarterly 1732 Ridgedale Dr Tuscaloosa AL 35406-1942

MILLS, GEORGE MARSHALL, insurance consultant; b. Newton, N.J., May 20, 1923; s. J. Marshall and Emma (Scott) M.; m. Dorothy Lovilla Allen, Apr. 21, 1945; children: Dianne (Mrs. Thomas McKay III), Dorothy L.A. (Mrs. Edward Sphatt). BA, Rutgers U., 1943; MA, Columbia U., 1951. CLU, CPCU; chartered fin. cons.; cert. govt. fund mgr. Pres. George M. Mills Inc., North Brunswick, N.J., 1946-75; pres. CORECO, Inc., Newark, 1960-78; risk mgr. N.J. Hwy. Authority, Woodbridge, 1976-95; pres. Assoc. Risk Mgmt., North Brunswick, N.J., 1995—; cons. Govs.'s Com. on Bus. Efficiency in Pub. Schs., 1979-80; cons. Risk Mgmt. Ins., Real Estate. Bd. dirs. Alpha Chi Rho Edni. Found., vice-chmn. 1991-95; workshop Easter Seal Soc.; mem. Gov.'s Task Force on Sound Mcpl. Govt., 1981-82; pres. Nat. Interfrat. Conf., 1979-80. With USNR, 1943-46. Mem. Am. Coll. Life Underwriters, Am. Coll. Property Liability Underwriters, Internat. Bridge Tunnel and Turnpike Assn. (chmn. risk mgmt. com. 1980-95, mem. bus. ins. risk mgmt. bd. 1988-95, Matthew J. Lenz Jr. medal 1989, Paul K. Addams award 1992), New Brunswick Hist. Soc., English Speaking Union, Rutgers Club, Alpha Chi Rho (nat. councillor 1964-70, nat. pres. 1970-73, nat. treas. 1975-78), Kappa Kappa Psi, Tau Kappa Alpha, Phi Delta Phi. Mem. Reformed Ch. Am. Home: 1054 Hoover Dr New Brunswick NJ 08902-3244

MILLS, GREGORY JOHN BARRINGTON, think-tank executive; b. Cape Town, South Africa, May 9, 1962; s. Denis Arthur Barrington and Nanette Mary How (Elliott) M.; m. Janet Margaret Wilson, Dec. 30, 1994. BA, Cape Town U., 1983; BA with honors in African Studies, U. Cape Town, 1985; MA, Lancaster U., Eng., 1986; PhD in Internat. Rels., Lancaster U., 1990. Part-time lectr. Lancaster U., 1988-89; lectr. U. of the Western Cape, 1990-94; dir. studies South African Inst. Internat. Affairs, Johannesburg, 1994-96, nat. dir., 1996—; rsch. assoc. Inst. for Def. Policy, 1992—; rsch. assoc. Ctr. for Def. and Internat. Security Studies, Lancaster, 1991—. Co-author, editor: From Pariah to Participant: South Africa's Evolving Foreign Relations, 1994, South Africa in the Global Economy, 1995, Maritime Policy for Developing Nations, 1995, South African Yearbook of International Affairs, 1996; contbr. articles to profl. jours. Chmn. South African Inst. Internat. Affairs, Cape Region, 1992-94; capt. The Alfred Rowing Club, 1991-93. Recipient Philip Andrew Meml. scholarship Lancaster U., 1989, Human Scis. Rsch. Coun. doctoral merit bursary, 1987-89; selected as participant European Union Visitor's programme, 1996; vis. fellow Australian Nat. U., 1997-98; ACU Symons fellow U. Kent, U.K., 1999-2000. Mem. South African Polit. Studies Assn., African Studies Assn. of South Africa (coun. mem. 1993-95), The Africa Inst. Avocations: rowing, running, tennis, squash, reading. Office: South African Inst Internat Affairs, Jan Smuts House, Wits U, Johannesburg South Africa

MILLS, HELEN RACHEL, biotechnologist; b. Hucknall, Nottingham, England, May 22, 1962; d. Brian and Janice (Staniforth) Measures; m. Laurence Robert Mills, Sept. 30, 1989; children: Joshua, Adam. BSc in Biochem., Imperial Coll., 1983; PhD, Southampton U., 1988. Higher sci. officer NERC Inst. Virology, Oxford, England, 1988-91; rsch. scientist Brit. Biotech, Oxford, 1991-93, sr. rsch. scientist, 1993-97, rsch. liaison mgr., 1997-99, rsch. liason mgr., 1997-99; med. rsch. assoc., mgr. Parexel, 2000—. Mem. Royal Coll. Sci. Anglican. Avocations: swimming, gardening, campanology. Office: Br Biotech, Parexel, River Court 50 Oxford Rd, Denham Uxbridge UB9 4DL, England

MILLS, HELENE AUDREY, education educator; b. Oct. 6, 1933; d. Paul Albert and Mabel Meister; m. Ray Mills, Apr. 17, 1954; children: Keith, Katherine (dec.), Kevin. BS in Family Life Edn., Wayne State U., 1954, MEd in Human Resources, 1965, EdD in Gen. Adminstrn., 1980. Supr., instr. Wayne State Coll. Edn., 1958-67; tchr. life studies, health edn. Seaholm H.S., Birmingham, Mich., 1967-72, 74-77, asst. to prin., 1974-77, asst. prin., 1978-79, prin., 1990-97; prin. Derby Mid. Sch., Birmingham, 1980-90; asst. prof. Oakland U., Rochester Hills, Mich., 1997—; adj. prof. Wayne State U., Detroit, 1989-91, Oakland U., Rochester, 1985-89, asst. prof., 1997—. Consulting editor Clearing Ho., 1985-97; contbr. articles to profl. jours. Mem. steering com. Meadowbrook Leadership Acad., 1984-87; mem. Detroit Strategic Planning Task Force, 1986-88; mem. exec. bd. Oakland County Youth Assistance, 1987-90; program chairperson women's group Northbrooke Ch., 1997-99, mem. adult minstries purpose com., 1998-99. Recipient PTSA Coun. Pres. award, 1982, Celebration of Women award Greater Detroit Coun. NA'AMAT USA, 1986, Exemplary Secondary Sch. award State Mich., 1991. Mem. NASCD, Nat. Staff Devel. Assn., Nat. Secondary Prins. Assn., Mich. Assn. Supervision and Curriculum Devel., Mich. Coun. Family Rels., Mich. Secondary Prins. Assn., Oakland County Secondary Prins. Assn. (pres. 1983-85, Prin. of the Yr. 1991), Phi Delta Kappa (chmn. mem. Oakland br. 1998—). E-mail: mill@oakland.edu. Office: Oakland U 311 Odowd Hall Rochester Hls MI 48309-4423

MILLS, JOHN EVANS ATTA, Ghanaian government official. V.p. Govt. of Ghana, 1997—. Office: Office of Pres, The Castle, PO Box 1627 Osu Accra, Ghana*

MILLS, LOIS JEAN, company executive, former legislative aide, former education educator; b. Chgo., Oct. 20, 1939; d. Martin J. and Annabelle M. (Hrabik) Rademacher; m. Frederick V. Mills, Dec. 1, 1974; children: Todd, Susan, Randal, Merre, Mollie, Michael, Mark (dec.). BS in Edn., Ill. State U., Normal, 1962, MS in Edn., 1969. Lectr. elem. curriculum Ill. State U., 1973-90; in-svc. advisor for elem., gifted, critical thinking and study skills, coop. learning Title I State Bd. Edn., Springfield, Ill., 1969-90; elem. tchr., supr. Metcalf Lab. Sch. Ill. State U., 1962-72; legis. aide to Asst. Majority Leader Senator John Maitland, Jr., Ill. Gen. Assembly, 1990-95; pres., ptnr. Mills Design Assocs., 1996—; mem. state rep. Dan Rutherford's house task force for statute repeal, 1995—, adv. roundtable, 1995—, legis. task force for cmty. residential svcs. deaf adults, 1995—; campaign coord. Asst. Majority Leader Senator John Maitland, Jr., 1995—; county campaign coord. for Ill. Comptroller Loleta Didrickson, 1994-98. Contbr. articles to profl. jours. Pres. Leadership Ill., 1994—, pres.-elect, 1993-94; past pres. governing bd. Lake Bloomington Assn., v.p., 1993-94, pres., 1994-95; mem. mgmt. com. McLean County 21st Century commn., 1991-92, vice chair cmty. rels., 1991-92; commr. McLean County Regional Planning commn., vice chair 1994-95; charter bd. govs. Ill. Lincoln Excellence in Pub. Svc. Series, 1994—, other civic activities; mem. Ill. steering com. Beijing-UN Women's Conf. One Yr. Later, 1996; mem. gov.'s commn. on status of women, Econ. Opportunities Working Group, 1998—. Recipient Exemplary Tchr. awards Ill. State U. Student Elem. Edn. Bd., Women of Distinction award YWCA of McLean County, Ill. State Univ. Alumni Assn. Svc. Awd. Mem. NAFE, Ill. State U. Alumni Assn. (bd. dirs. 1982—, internat. pres. 1992-94, 1994—), McLean County Rep. Women's Club (v.p. 1986, pres. 1987, past pres. 1988), Ill. Rep. Committeewoman's Roundtable, Ill. Fedn. Rep. Women, Nat. Fedn. Rep. Women, Internat. Platform Assn. Home: K-162 Lake Bloomington RR 2 Box 60A Hudson IL 61748-9414

MILLS, PAUL CHRISTIAN, research scientist, veterinarian; b. Bolton, Lancashire, Eng., Mar. 2, 1965; s. Brian and Julie (Nelson) M.; m. Sally Ann Brindley, Sept. 17, 1993; 1 child, Siena. B.Vet.Sci. (hons.), U. Queensland, Brisbane, 1987, PhD, 1993; M.Vet.Sci., U. Sydney, 1999. Vet. surgeon Rockhampton Vet. Hosp., 1987-90; staff veterinarian Animal Emergency Ctr., Brisbane, 1993; sr. scientist Animal Health Trust, Newmarket, Eng., 1993-97; rsch. officer dept. medicine U. Queensland, Brisbane, 1997—; cons. Boehringer Ingelheim, Sydney, 1999—; vet. rep. Atlanta Olympic Games, 1996; lectr. in field. Contbr. articles to profl. jours. NHMRC Rsch. grantee, 1999; Half-Blue award U. Queensland, 1984. Mem. Australian Vet. Assn., Australian Coll. Vet. Scientists. Roman Catholic. Avocations: triathlons, scuba diving, travel. Office: Univ Queensland, Princess Alexandra Hosp, Woolloongabba QLD 4102, Australia

MILLS, RUSSELL ANDREW, newspaper publisher; b. St. Thomas, Ont., Can., July 14, 1944; s. Gerald Armond and Phyllis Marie (Hulse) M.; m. Judith Elizabeth Zimmerman, Mar. 25, 1967; children: Lara, Colin, Patrick. BA, U. Western Ont., London, 1967, MA, 1968. Reporter London (Ont.) Free Press, 1964-67; city editor The Oshawa (Ont.) Times, 1970; asst. city editor, night editor, asst. mng. editor The Ottawa (Ont.) Citizen, 1971-85, exec. editor, 1975-76, editor, 1977-84, gen.mgr., 1984-86, pub., 1986-89, pres., publ., 1992—; pres. Southam Newspaper Group, Toronto, Ont., 1989-92. Office: Ottawa Citizen, 1101 Baxter Rd, Ottawa, ON Canada K2C 3M4

MILLS, SUSAN C., sculptor; b. Chgo., Dec. 13, 1962; d. Ronald Richard Miesowicz/Mills and Marie Eleana Post; domestic ptnr. Carol Lynn Dichtenberg, Feb. 14, 1994. BFA, U. Ill., 1986; MFA, So. Ill. U., 1989. Tech. instr. SUNY, Buffalo, 1994-97; museum preparator Ariz. Hist. Soc., Tempe, 1998—.

MILLS, TEHERAN L. (TERRY MILLS), sociology educator; b. N.Y.C., Feb. 5, 1949; s. Lehman R. and Shirley Marie MIlls; m. Antonia Allen, Feb. 10, 1968; children: Brion K., Dion L. BA in Polit. Sci., L.I. U., 1974; MA in Sociology, U. So. Calif., 1995, PhD in Sociology and Gerontology, 1996. Asst. prof. U. Fla., Gainesville, 1996—; editl. bd. Jour. Family Issues, Gainesville. Faculty advisor Alpha Kappa Delta Sociology Honor Soc., Gainesville. Avocations: hiking, golf, travel. Fax: (352) 392-6568. E-mail: tlmills@soc.ufl.edu. Office: U Fla PO Box 117330 Gainesville FL 32611-7330

MILMAN, NILS, respiratory physician; b. Copenhagen, Nov. 17, 1939; s. Hans Helmuth and Gudrun Kirstine (Maansson) M.; m. Inge Lauridsen; children: Katrine, Nikolai, Ditte, Elisabeth, Marianne. MD, U. Copenhagen, 1968. Diplomate Danish Bd. Internal Medicine, Danish Bd. Respiratory Diseases, Danish Bd. Allergology. Registrar dept. infectious diseases Rigshospitalet, U. Copenhagen, 1975-77; registrar dept. neurology Frederiksberg Hosp., 1977-79; registrar dept. medicine Bispebjerg Hosp., U. Copenhagen, 1979-82, registrar dept. respiratory medicine, 1982-86; staff physician dept. respiratory medicine Gentofte Hosp., U. Copenhagen, 1986-94; chief physician dept. respiratory medicine Naestved (Denmark) Hosp., 1994—; study visitor dept. hepatology Kings Coll. Hosp., London, 1980, Lungenklinik Heckeshorn, Berlin, 1987, Chest Diagnostic Ctr., Johns Hopkins U., Balt., 1995. Contbr. articles to profl. jours., chpts. to books. Mem. Danish Respiratory Soc. (tchr. postgrad. courses 1987-2000), Danish Med. Assn., European Respiratory Soc., World Assn Against Sarcoidosis and Other Granulomatous Disorders, World Assn. Bronchology. Fax: 45 55 73 12 83. Office: Naestved Hosp, Dept Respiratory Medicine, DK 4700 Naestved Denmark

MILMAN, VITALI D., mathematics educator; b. Odessa, Ukraine, Aug. 23, 1939; arrived in Israel, 1973; s. David P. and Nemo E. M.; m. Ludmila; children: Larissa, Emanuel, Anat. BS, Kharkov U., USSR, 1959, MSc, 1961, PhD, 1965; DSc, Phys. Inst. Low Temperatures, Kharkov, USSR, 1970. Lectr. Kharkov U., 1961-65; sr. rschr. Inst. Chem. Physics, USSR Acad. Scis., Moscow, 1965-73; prof. Tel Aviv U., 1973—, Argentinian chair in math.; vis. prof. U. Paris VI, 1984-85, Inst. Advanced Studies, Princeton, N.J., 1988, Ohio State U., Columbus, 1990-95, Institut Hautes Etudes Scientifiques; bd. dirs. Inst. Indsl. Math., Beer-Sheva, Israel; internat. bd. govs. Coll. Judea and Samaria, Ariel, Israel, 1994—. Editor Geometric and Functional Analysis, Birkhauser, Basel, Switzerland, 1990—; contbr. articles to profl. jours. Mem. Israel Math Union, Am. Math. Soc.

MILNE, DAVID, IV, lawyer; b. Phila., July 19, 1932; s. David Milne and Constance Green; m. Elizabeth Straubmmuller Congdon, Dec. 8, 1996; children: James, Brooks, Zebullon; m. Karen Walgreen; children: David, Caleb. BS, Wharton Sch.; LLB, U. Va.; LLM, Georgetown U.; SRS, U. London. U. S. Supreme Ct. CEO Holmes Oil Co., Huntingdon Valley, Pa., Petroleum Mgmt. Assn., Hopewell, NJ; ptnr. Pepper Hamilton & Scheetz, Phila.; atty. U.S. Treas. Dept., Wash.; chmn. com. mgmt. svcs., Inc., Ft. Lauderdale, Fla.; mem. adv. bd. Callery- Judge Grooe Lt., Loxahatchee, Fla. Office: David Milne & Assocs 118 Church St Philadelphia PA 19106-2201

MILNE, HENRY JAMES OGSTON, education educator; b. Moshi, Tanganyika, Jan. 31, 1942; arrived in Australia, 1969; s. Henry Ogston and Patience Sarah (Pidgeon) M.; m. Heather Lexie Wilkinson, Apr. 7, 1969; children: Henry Robert Ogston, Richard James Ogston. B of Ednl. Studies, U. Queensland, 1975, M of Ednl. Studies, 1983; Grad. Diploma in Spl. Edn., Mt. Gravatt Coll. Advanced Ed., 1976; Grad. Diploma in Distance Edn., S. Australian Coll. Adv. Edn., 1987; MA in Edn./Gifted and Talented, U. Conn., 1996. Mem. Faculty of Edn., Sch. of Cognition, Language, Spl. Edn. Mt. Gravatt campus Griffith U., Nathan, Australia, 1990—; rsch. assoc. U. Conn., Storrs, 1997-98. Contbr. articles to profl. jours. Mem. European Coun. for High Ability, World Coun. for Gifted and Talented Chldren, Internat. Assn. for Spl. Edn., Australian Assn. for Edn. of Gifted and Talented, Australian Assn. for Spl. Edn. (nat. v.p. 1989), Queensland Assn. for Gifted and Talented Children, Nat. Assn. for Gifted Children (U.S.). Office: Griffith U, Faculty of Edn, Nathan Queensland 4151, Australia

MILNE-KUHN, MICHELLE DAWN, artist; b. Bloomington, Minn., June 23, 1967; d. William and Karen Jean Milne; m. Daniel James Kuhn, June 29, 1995. Psychologist, U. Wis., 1991; postgrad. in Fine Arts, Art Inst. of Chgo. Artist Ariz., 1994-99; vol. U.S. Peace Corps, Zambia, Africa, 1995-96; artistic dir. The Many Faces of HIV/AIDS, Phoenix. Creator: The Many Faces of HIV/AIDS presentation, 1998 (Vibrant Arts grantee). Mem. Internat. Sculpture Ctr.

MILNER, ALEXANDER, physicist, researcher; b. Kharkov, Ukraine, Jan. 4, 1947; arrived in Israel, 1994; s. Abram and Rachel (Feldman) M.; m. Alla Bogdanovich, Dec. 18, 1968; children: Valery, Natalya. MSc, State U., Kharkov, 1970; PhD in Physics, Inst. Low Temperature Physics, Kharkov, 1977. Engr. Inst. for Low Temperature Physics and Enginrg., Kharkov, 1970-73, rschr., 1973-83, sr. rschr., 1983-94; sr. rschr. Tel Aviv U., 1994—. Contbr. articles to profl. jours. Office: Sch Physics & Astronomy, Tel Aviv U Ramat Aviv, Tel Aviv 69978, Israel

MILNER, ARTHUR DAVID, psychology educator; b. Leeds, Yorkshire, Eng., July 16, 1943; s. Arthur and Sarah Ellen (Gaunt) M.; m. Christine Armitage, July 24, 1965; children: Benedict Jon, Edward. BA, U. Oxford, Eng., 1965, MA, 1970; dipl. psych., U. London, 1966. Rsch. asst. U. London, 1966-70; lectr. U. St. Andrews, Scotland, 1970-82, sr. lectr., 1982-85, reader, 1985-90, prof. neuropsychology, 1990-2000; prof. cognitive neurosci. U. Durham, 2000—; head dept. psychology U. St. Andrews, 1983-88, 94-97, dean faculty of sci., 1992-94; hon. rsch. psychologist Tayside Health Bd., Dundee, Scotland, 1990—; F.C. Donders lectr. Max Planck-Inst., 1999. Author: The Visual Brain in Action, 1995; editor: The Neuropsychology of Consciousness, 1992, Comparative Neuropsychology, 1998. Trustee Dundee (Scotland) Sci. Ctr., 1998-2000. Leverhulme trust rsch. fellow Leverhulme Trust, 1998-99. Fellow Royal Soc. of Edinburgh; mem. Experimental Psychology Soc. (com. 1989-92), Internat. Neuropsychol. Symposium (com. 1992-97), European Brain and Behavior Soc. (com. 1996-99). Mem. Labour Party U.K. Avocations: walking, jazz, writing. Home: 5 Northside, Durham DHG 1LJ, England Office: U Durham Dept Psychology, South Road, Durham DH1 3HP, England

MILNER, CHARLES FREMONT, JR., manufacturing company executive; b. Durham, N.C., July 21, 1942; s. Charles Fremont and Eloyse (Sargent) M.; m. Molly Franc Wakefield, Aug. 28, 1965; children: Bernadette Ann Milner Gardner, Eloyse Lee. BA, Guilford Coll., 1963; MBA, Harvard U., 1965. Asst. to comptroller Harvard U., 1965-66; instr. Northeastern U., Boston, 1965-66; with Burlington Hosiery Co. divsn. Burlington (N.C.) Industries, 1966-71, asst. v.p., 1970-71; exec. v.p. Parklane Hosiery Co., Inc., New Hyde Park, N.Y., 1971-74; pres. Rudin & Roth, Inc. divsn. NCC Industries, N.Y.C., 1974-75; v.p. apparel group M. Lowenstein and Sons, N.Y.C., 1975-76; pres., CEO BBC, Inc. and Camp Industry divsns. Genesco, Inc., 1976-80; gen. mgr. Johnston and Murphy Shoe Co. divsn., 1979—; gen. mgr. footwear mktg. and mfg. Genesco, Inc., 1980-81, v.p., 1981-82; pres., CEO Hope Hosiery Mills and C.M. Industries, Inc., Adamstown, Pa., 1983—. Trustee Friends Acad., Locust Valley, N.Y., 1974-79, Guilford Coll., 1982-97, vice chmn., 1989, chmn., 1990-97; mem. class chief fund agt. Harvard Bus. Sch., 1986-91, alumni bd., 1992—, v.p., 1995-97, pres., 1997-99, past pres., 1999—. Mem. Nat. Assn. hosiery Mfrs. (dir. 1978-82, 87—, exec. com. 1989-93, 99—, 2d vice chmn. 1991-92, vice chmn. 1992, chmn. 1993), Lancaster Country Club, Hamilton Club, Moselem Springs Golf Club. Home: 158 Hamilton Rd Lancaster PA 17603-4734 Office: PO Box 487 Adamstown PA 19501-0487

MILNER, FABIO AUGUSTO, mathematics educator; b. Buenos Aires, Aug. 27, 1954; s. Isaac Arnoldo and Teresa Adela (Dubcovsky) M.; children from previous marriage: Sasha, Eric, Daniel; m. Diana Ivette Soto García, Aug. 5, 1998; children: Mónica Teresa, Mikhail Alexander. Lic. in math. sci., U. Buenos Aires, 1976; MS, U. Chgo., 1979, PhD, 1983. Lectr. Elmhurst (Ill.) Coll., 1981-82; instr. DePaul U., Chgo., 1982-83; lectr. Chgo. State U., 1983-84; asst. prof. Purdue U., West Lafayette, Ind., 1983-89, assoc. prof., 1989-94, prof., faculty convenor for human ecology, 1994—; assoc. prof. U. Rome II, 1987-92. Lily Found. grantee 1994; recipient award NSF, 1999—, U.S.-France Bi-nat. award NSF, 1995-99. Mem. Assn. L.Am. Biomatematica (alternate exec. bd. dirs. 1998—), Soc. Math. Biology (Best Paper of Internat. Congress 1995), Soc. Hispanic Profl. Engrs. (faculty advisor 2000—). Avocations: photography, movies, flying. Fax: (765) 494-0548. E-mail: milner@math.purdue.edu. Office: Purdue U Dept Math West Lafayette IN 47907-1395

MILNES COATES, ANTHONY ROBERT, medical microbiology educator; b. Cambridge, Eng., Dec. 8, 1948; s. Robert Edward James Clive and Patricia Ethel Milnes Coates; m. Harriet Ann Burton, Sept. 28, 1978; children: Sara, Sophie, Tom. BSc in Anatomy, U. London, 1971, MB BS, 1973, MD, 1984. Med. Rsch. Coun. tng. rsch. fellow dept. bacteriology Royal Postgrad. Med. Sch., London, 1979-82, sr. registrar in bacteriology, 1982-84; sr. lectr., hon. cons. dept. med. microbiology London Hosp., 1984-90; prof. med. microbiology St. George's Hosp. Med. Sch., 1990—; dir. Pub. Health Lab. Svc., London, 1990-98. Councillor Royal Borough of Kensington and Chelsea, London, 1980—. Fellow Royal Coll. Pathologists, Royal Coll. Physicians; mem. Royal Coll. Surgeons. Home: Hereford Cottage, 135 Gloucester Rd, London SW7 4TH, England Office: St Georges Hosp Med Sch, Cranmer Terr, London SW17 ORE, England

MILO, HJALMAR TAEKE, arbiter, forensic data processing auditor; b. Leeuwarden, Friesland, The Netherlands, Oct. 19, 1945; s. William Lodewijk and Jacoba (De Jager) M.; m. Catharina Elisabeth Luijkx; children: Michael, Bauke, Hjalmar, Martijn. Grad., Polytechnics Electro HTS-E, The Hague, 1965. Cert. informatics expert. Jr. economist Bakkenist Spits & Co., Amsterdam, 1967-68; tech. staff Bakkenist/Auerbach, Amsterdam, 1968-69; project leader Ford Motor Co., Cologne/London, 1969-72; data processing cons. Automation Centre Volmac, Rotterdam, 1972-77; profit centre mgr. Dataskil Nederland, Amsterdam, 1977-81; mgr. Samsom Data Systemen, Alphen aan den Rijn, 1981-83; ind. cons. Milo/Van Vessem Inf. Advs., Alphen aan den Rijn, 1983—; chmn. CJB, Alphen aan den Rijn, 1987-89; expert witness, arbiter in various informatics ct. procedures; com. mem. local

enterprises assn., Holland, 1987—. Co-author: Onderneming and Automatisering, 1993. With Netherlands Army, 1965-67. Mem. ACM, Dutch Assn. for Info. Sci., Orgn. of Sworn Data Processing Cons. (chmn. 1987). Liberals. Avocations: sailing, windsurfing. Home: Loevestein 1, 2403 JC Alphen aan den Rijn The Netherlands

MILONE, ANTHONY M., bishop; b. Omaha, Sept. 24, 1932. Grad., North American Coll. (Rome). Ordained priest Roman Catholic Ch., 1957. Ordained titular bishop of Plestia and aux. bishop Diocese of Omaha, 1982; bishop Diocese of Great Falls-Billings, Great Falls, Mont., 1987—. Office: Diocese Gt Falls Billings PO Box 1399 121 23rd St S Great Falls MT 59403

MILONE, JAMES MICHAEL, occupational health-safety forensic engineering technology executive, environmental engineer; b. Welfare Island, N.Y., Sept. 1, 1942; s. Michael James and Winifred Patricia (Rhenos) M.; m. Lois Esther Polinsky, Sept. 30, 1967; 1 child, Michelle Elena Milone. ABA, St. John's U., 1963; MPH Engring., MS in Environ. Scis., La Salle U., 1993, PhD in Indsl. Hygiene and Environ. Policy and Resource Mgmt., 1994; PhD in Environ. Safety and Health, Western State U., 1997. Registered profl. indsl. hygienist, constrn./re-engring. occupl. health and safety engr., forensic engr. Integrated Pest Mgmt. expert, cons.; cert. environ. auditor/insp. environ./food sanitarian environ./hazardous materials and waste mgmt. mgr. sonc., econs./biol. entomologist; lic. air sample technologist, remediation supr., project monitor, mgmt. planner; cert. comml. applicator, profl. mgr. blds. and grounds; lic. accident prevention and loss control cons., N.Y.; diplomate Am. Bd. Forensic Engring. and Tech., Am. Coll. Forensic Examiners. Sales, mktg. and bus. devel. cons., sales mgr. Profl. Porter Svc., Lynbrook, N.Y., 1963-69; dir. environ. svcs. Cross and Brown Co., N.Y.C., 1969-71; v.p., gen. mgr. Cert. Bldg. Maintenance Corp., N.Y.C., 1971-76; gen. mgr. Orkin Ext. Co., Inc., L.I., N.Y., 1976-80; sr. v.p., gen. mgr., environ.-occupl. health-safety engr., sr. project mgr., dir. constrn. sys., safety and loss prevention, risk mgmt. Envirotronics Ltd., Wilmington, Del., 1980—, human resources mentor, trainer, safety & occpl. health adminstr. instr., trainer; adj. faculty/prof. Nat. and Internat. Diplomate for LaSalle U., Kent Coll., Southland Law Sch., Nova U., LaSalle U. Internat. Practical Tng. Program U.S. Dept. Edn., Coun. on Post Secondary Christian Edn.; cons. Fed. Govt., Gen. Svcs. Adminstr., Dept. VA, Ben Gilman House of Reps., Sen. Joseph Holland/N.Y., others; corp. risk mgr., profl. cons., sys. safety mgr.; safety and health adminstr. OSHA, cert. trainer, instr. Author/lectr.: Integrated Pest Management Systems In A Government Hospital Metroplex, 1994. Appt. environ. occupl. health and safety officer World Safety Orgn. for UN, deputy dir. gen. Internat. Biographical Ctr., Cambridge, Eng., eminent fellow Am. Biographical Inst. Served with U.S. Army, 1961-69. Mem. AAAS, Am. Indsl. Hygiene Assn., Am. Soc. Safety Engrs., Environ. Mgmt. Assn., Entomol. Soc. Air and Waste Mgmt., Am. Assn. for Standards and Testing of Materials, Products, Svcs. and Systems, Nat. Safety Coun., Am. Coll. Forensic Examiners, N.Y. Acad. Scis., Inst. of Forensic Sci., numerous other environ., occupl. health, safety assns. and orgns. Roman Catholic. Achievements include invention of non-toxic biodegradeable odor counteractant and the development of an inter-disciplinary building maintenance green building system. Fax: 718-380-6354. Home: 16151 Jewel Ave Apt 3C Flushing NY 11365-4331

MILORI, DEBORA MARCONDES BASTOS PEREIRA, physicist; b. Sao Paulo, Brazil, Jan. 9, 1966; d. Sebastiao Bastos and Enoi Paiva Marcondes Bastos (Pereira) P.; m. Marcius Milori, Jan. 16, 1988; children: Giulia Marcondes Bastos Pereira Milori, Felipe Marcondes Bastos Pereira Milori. Physicist, USP, Sao Carlos, Brazil, 1983-86, M in Physics, 1987-89, Doctor in Physics, 1990-94; postgrad., Embrapa, Sao Carlos, Brazil, 1998-99. Rschr. Sao Paulo U., 1996-97; fellowship Embrapa-CNPDIA, Sao Carlos, 1998-99; cons. CNPq, Brazil, 1994-95. Contbr. articles to profl. jours. Recipient Bernhard Gross prize, USP, Sao Carlos, 1984. Mem. Physics Brazilian Soc., Brazilian Metrology Soc., Brazilian Soc. Nikeis Rschrs. Office: Embrapa-CNPDIA, Rua XV de novembro 1452, Sao Paulo 13560970, Brazil

MILORO, PROTOPRESBTER FRANK, church official, religious studies educator; b. Wilmington, Del., Jan. 26, 1947; m. Constance Ann Evanisko, Apr. 20, 1969; children: Alexandra, Stephanie, Christopher. Grad. summa cum laude, Saviour Sem., 1969; grad. with high honors, St. Vincent Coll., 1972; attended, U. Pitts. Ordained to Diaconate and Priesthood, 1969. Assigned St. John's Ch., Ligonier, Pa., 1969-72, St. Stephen's Ch., Latrobe, Pa., 1969-72, St. John's Ch., Rahway, N.J., 1972-76; dir. Camp Nazareth, diocesan dir. youth, 1976-86; dean Christ the Saviour Sem.; elevated to dignity of Very Rev., 1985, sec. to bishop, instr. homiletics and parish administrn.; diocesan chancellor Am. Carpatho-Russian Orthodox Diocese, 1990—; dean Christ the Savior Cathedral, 1997—; chaplain Ea. Orthodox residents Polk Ctr., Commonwealth Pa., established chapel. Assoc. editor The Ch. Messenger. Office: 312 Garfield St Johnstown PA 15906-2122

MILOSAVLJEVIC, IVAN DJORDJE, gas industry executive; b. Belgrade, Yugoslavia, Apr. 29, 1963; arrived in France, 1995; s. Djordje and Angelina (Kuburovic) M.; m. Dragana Comic, Sept. 17, 1988; children: Iva, Filip. BSc, Belgrade U., 1987, postgrad., 1987-89; MSc, Brown U., Providence, 1991, PhD, 1994. Rsch. engr. Vincha (Yugoslavia) U., 1987-89; rsch. asst. Brown U., Providence, 1989-94, tchg. asst., 1990-93; cons. AFR Inc., East Hartford, Conn., 1994; rsch. engr. Air Liquide, Countryside, Ill., 1995-99; bus. devel. mgr. Air Liquide, Les Loges En Josas, France, 1999—. Patents pending in field.; contbr. articles to profl. jours. With Yugoslav Army, 1980-81. Brown U fellow, Providence, 1989. Mem. Am. Chem. Soc. (fuel chemistry divsn.), Combustion Inst. Home: 2 Rue de L'Etang, 78960 Voisins Bretonneux France Office: Air Liquide, 11 Rue de la Croix Blanche, 78350 Jouy-en-Josas France

MILOSAVLJEVIC, ZLATOLJUB DRAGAN, electrical engineer, educator; b. Knjazevac, Yugoslavia, Aug. 19, 1968; s. Dragan Miroslav and Danka Dusan (Marinkovic) M.; m. Vesna Milutin Jeremic, May 1, 1995; 1 child, Misa. Dipl.-Ing. in Elec. Engring., Fac. Elec. Engring., Nis, Yugoslavia, 1993, MS, 1997. Rsch. asst. Fac. of Electronic Engring., Nis, 1993-95, tchg. and rsch. asst., 1995—. Author: The Theory of Electrical Circuits, 1998; contbr. articles to profl. jours. Mem. IEEE, Yugoslav Microwave Theory and Techniques Assn. Avocations: basketball, football, tennis, travel. Fax: 881-18-46-180. E-mail: ZLATKO@ELFAK.NI.AC.YU. Home: Sretena Mladenovica 112/1, 18000 Nis Yugoslavia Office: Faculty Electronic Engring, Beogradska 14, 18000 Nis Yugoslavia

MILOSZ, CZESLAW, poet, writer, educator; b. Lithuania, June 30, 1911; came to U.S., 1960, naturalized, 1970; s. Aleksander and Weronika (Kunat) M. M Juris, U. Wilno, Lithuania, 1934; LittD (hon.), U. Mich., 1977; honoris causa, Cath. U. Lublin, 1981, Brandeis U., 1985, Harvard U., 1989, Jagiellonian U., Poland, 1989, U. Rome, 1992. Programmer Polish Nat. Radio, 1935-39; diplomatic service Polish Fgn. Affairs Ministry, Warsaw, 1945-50; vis. lectr. U. Calif., Berkeley, 1960-61; prof. Slavic langs. and lits. U. Calif., 1961-78, prof. emeritus, 1978—. Author: The Captive Mind, 1953, Native Realm, 1968, Post-War Polish Poetry, 1965, The History of Polish Literature, 1969, Selected Poems, 1972, Bells in Winter, 1978, The Issa Valley, 1981, Separate Notebooks, 1984, The Land of Ulro, 1984, The Unattainable Earth, 1985, Collected Poems, 1988, Provinces, 1991, Beginning With My Streets, 1992, A Year of the Hunter, 1994, Facing the River, 1995, A Book of Luminous Things, 1996, Striving Towards Being, 1996, Roadside Dog, 1998. Recipient Prix Littéraire Européen Les Guildes du Livre, Geneva, 1953, Neustadt Internat. prize for lit. U. Okla., 1978, citation U. Calif., Berkeley, 1978, Nobel prize for lit., 1980, Nat. Medal of Arts, 1990; Nat. Culture Fund fellow, 1934-35; Guggenheim fellow, 1976. Mem. AAAS, Am. Acad. Arts and Scis., Am. Acad Arts and Letters, Polish Inst. Letters and Scis. in Am., PEN Club in Exile. Office: U Calif Dept Slavic Langs Lits Berkeley CA 94720-0001

MILOSZEWSKA, JOANNA JOZEFA, biologist, researcher; b. Warsaw, Poland, Aug. 27, 1958; d. Tadeusz and Stanislawa M.; m. Wojciech Piotr Baranowski, Sept. 10, 1989. MS in Biology, Warsaw U., 1982, PhD in Biochemistry, 1991; postgrad., U. London, 1986. Asst. Warsaw Med. Sch., 1982-85; asst. Inst. Oncology, Warsaw, 1985-91, adj., 1991-92; vis. scientist Roswell Park Cancer Inst., Buffalo, 1992-93; vis. fellow NIH, Bethesda, Md., 1993-95; adj. Cancer Ctr., Warsaw, 1995—; tchr. seminars, lectures Warsaw Med. Sch., 1982-85, 86-89; sec. commn. tumor biology Polish Acad. Scis., 1988-92. Contbr. articles to profl. jours. Recipient 1st degree award for work on the tumor promotion Polish Acad. Scis., 1991; Fogarty fellow Fogarty Internat. Ctr., Bethesda, 1993; rsch. grantee Fulbright Commn., 1992. Mem. Polish Soc. Cell Biology. Avocations: theater, literature, journeys, jogging. Office: Cancer Ctr, M Sklodowska-Curie Inst Onc, Warsaw Poland

MILSTAM, KARL ÖSTEN, Swedish government official; b. Arboga, Sweden, Dec. 3, 1928; s. Karl Alfred Josef and Helga Alexandra (Oskarsson) M. BA, Stockholm U., Sweden, 1954, M of Polit. Sci., 1962. Adminstrv. ofcl. Statens Biltrafiknämnd, Stockholm, 1949-56; sr. adminstrv. officer Konjunkturinstitutet, Stockholm, 1957-62, Ministry of Fin., Stockholm, 1963, Ministry of Transport & Communication, Stockholm, 1964-71; prin. adminstrv. officer Nat. Rd. Adminstrn., Stockholm, 1972-78; prin. adminstrv. officer State Power Bd., Stockholm, 1979-90, cons., 1991—. Author: Väljarinflytande, 1975, Väljare, skärp kraven på riksdagspartierna!, 1977. Avocations: reading, sailing. Home: Enspännargatan 58, 165 57 Hässelby Sweden

MILSTEIN, CÉSAR, molecular biologist; b. Oct. 8, 1927; s. Lázaro and Máxima Milstein; m. Celia Prilleltensky, 1953. Ed., Colegio Nacional De Bahia Blanca, U. Nacional de Buenos Aires, Fitzwilliam Coll., Cambridge; D (hon.), Vigo U., Spain, 1999, Cambridge (Eng.) U., 1999, Helsinki U., 2000. Brit. Council fellow, 1958-60; staff Instituto Nacional de Microbiologia, Buenos Aires, 1957-63; head Div. de Biologia Molecular, 1961-63; mem. staff Lab. Molecular Biology, Med. Rsch. Coun., Cambridge, Eng., 1963-95, dep. dir., 1988-95. Contbr. articles to profl. jours. Decorated Companion of Honour to the Queen; recipient Rozenberg prize, 1979, Mattia award, 1979, Gross Howit prize, 1980, Koch prize, 1980, Wolf prize in medicine, 1980, medal Wellcome Found., 1980, Gimenez Diaz medal, 1981, Sloan prize GM Cancer Rsch. Found., 1981, Gardner award Gardner Found., 1981, Nobel prize for medicine, 1984. Fellow Royal Coll. Physicians (hon.), Royal Soc. (Royal medal 1982, Copley medal 1989), Royal Coll. Pathologists (hon.); mem. NAS (fgn. assoc.). Avocation: cooking. Office: Med Rsch Coun Lab Mol Biol, Hills Rd, Cambridge CB2 2QH, England

MILTENBURG, DARLENE MARGARET, surgeon; b. Hamilton, Ont., Can., Jan. 21, 1963; d. Cornelis and Margaret (Zonneveld) M. BS, McMaster U., 1984, MD, 1989. FRCSC, FACS. Asst. prof. surgery Baylor Coll. of Medicine, Houston, 1997—. Contbr. articles to profl. jours. Mem. Assn. for Acad. Surgery, Am. Assn. Breast Surgeons. Fax: 713-798-8070. Office: Baylor Coll of Medicine 6550 Fannin St Ste 1625 Houston TX 77030-2767

MILTON, CORINNE HOLM, art history educator; b. Nogales, Ariz., Oct. 16, 1928; d. Walter and Louise (Oates) Holm; m. Lee B. Milton, July 17, 1950 (dec. Oct. 1986); children: Bruce, Marina, Alan, Stuart. BA in Polit. Sci., U. Ariz., 1951, MLS, 1982; tchg. cert., U. N.Mex., 1973. Cert. secondary sch. tchr., Ariz., C.C. tchr., Ariz., Calif. Real estate sales agt. Walter Holm & Co., 1951-67; French and history tchr. Dept. State Overseas Schs., Washington, 1968-76; Sci. Tran Sci. Translating Co., Santa Barbara, Calif., 1976-78; libr. City of Nogales, 1982-83, City of Tucson, 1990-93; lectr. U. Ariz. Extension, Tucson, 1984—; Spanish instr. Pima Coll., Tucson, 1990-93; mem. Ariz.-Sonora Gov.'s Commn., Phoenix, 1993—; evaluator Ariz. Coun. for Humanities. Author, abstracter ABC Clio Press, 1976-78. Mem. Ariz. Opera Guild, 1989-96; bd. dirs. Hilltop Gallery, Nogales, 1989—; hostess, translator Tuscon Internat. Vis. Coun., 1994-96; lectr. on art history to cmty. schs. and retirement homes, Tucson, 1989—. Mem. UN Coun., Tucson Mus. Art (docent 1989—), Sunbelt World Trade Assn., Pimeria Alta Hist. Soc., Sierra Club. Democrat. Episcopalian. Avocations: hiking, raising greyhounds. Home: 6981 E Jagged Canyon Pl Tucson AZ 85750-6196

MILTON, DELISHA, professional basketball player; b. Riceboro, Ga., Sept. 11, 1974. Degree in sports mgmt., U. Fla., 1997. Forward L.A. Sparks, Womens Nat. Basketball League, 1997—. Office: Los Angeles Sparks Great Western Forum 3900 W Manchester Blvd Inglewood CA 90305-2200

MILTON, HAROLD W., JR., lawyer; b. Detroit, Oct. 5, 1935; s. Harold W. and Una Mae Milton; m. Barbara Ann Milton, Oct. 4, 1958 (div. Nov. 1977); m. Lynn B. Rose, June 18, 1994; children: Lisa, Kristin, Staci. BS in Aero. Engring., Purdue U., 1957; JD, Georgetown U., 1964. Atty. Barnard, McGlynn, Reising, Birmingham, Mich., 1964-69, McGlynn, Reising, Milton and Ethington, Troy, Mich., 1969-73, McGlynn & Milton, Troy, 1973-83, Reising, Ethington, Perry and Milton, Troy, 1983-95, Howard & Howard, Bloomfield Hills, Mich., 1995—. Author: Handbook for Preparation of Patent Application, 1999; patentee in field. Fundraiser Abraham for Senate, Mich., 1999—, Knollenberg for Congress, Mich., 1999—. Recipient Commendation medal USAF, 1961. Mem. Ocean Reef Club. Republican. Avocations: private pilot, photography, skiing, bicycling. Office: Howard & Howard 1400 N Woodward Ave Ste 101 Bloomfield Hills MI 48304-2855

MILTON, JOHN CHARLES DOUGLAS, nuclear physicist; b. Regina, Sask., Can., June 1, 1924; s. William and Frances Craigie (McDowall) M.; m. Gwendolyn Margaret Shaw, Oct. 10, 1953; children: Bruce F., Leslie J.F., Neil W.D., Theresa M. A.M. in Music, U. Man., 1943, B.Sc. with honors, 1947; M.A., Princeton U., 1949, Ph.D. in Physics, 1951. Asst. rsch. officer Atomic Energy Can., Ltd., Chalk River, Ont., 1951-57; assoc. rsch. officer Atomic Energy Can., Ltd., 1957-62, sr. rsch. officer, 1962-70, prin. rsch. officer, 1970-91, head nuclear physics br., 1967-83, dir. physics div., 1983-85, v.p. physics and health scis., 1986-90, researcher emeritus, 1990-97; vis. scientist Lawrence Berkeley Lab., 1960-62, Centre de Recherches, Strasbourg & Bruyeres-le-Chatel, 1975-76; chmn. nuclear physics grants Natural Sci. and Engring. Research Council, 1977-82; adv. bd. TRIUMF 1984-92; bd. dirs. Can. Fusion Fuels Tech., 1986-90, Tokamak de Varennes, 1986-90. Pres. Deep River Hort. Assn., 1997-98. Fellow Royal Soc. Can., Am. Phys. Soc.; mem. Can. Assn. Physicists (pres. 1992). Home: 3 Alexander Pl, Deep River, ON Canada K0J 1P0

MILTON, JOSEPH PAYNE, lawyer; b. Richmond, Va., Oct. 24, 1943; s. Hubert E. and Grace C. Milton; children: Michael Payne, Amy Barrett, David King; m. Cela Cabler Milton, Apr. 8, 1989. BS in Bus. Adminstrn., U. Fla., 1967, JD, 1969. Bar: Fla. 1969, U.S. Ct. Appeals (5th cir.) 1971, U.S. Supreme Ct. 1972, U.S. Ct. Appeals (11th cir.) 1981. Assoc. Toole, Taylor, Moseley & Gabel, Jacksonville, 1969-70; ptnr. Toole, Taylor, Moseley, Gabel & Milton, Jacksonville, 1971-78, Howell, Liles, Braddock & Milton, Jacksonville, 1978-89, Milton & Leach, Jacksonville, 1990-95, Milton, Leach & D'Andrea, Jacksonville, 1996—. Mem. Mayor's Blue Ribbon Task Force; mem. Law Ctr. Coun., U. Fla. Coll. Law, 1972-78, mem. alumni coun., 1995—; campaign chmn. N.E. Fla. chpt. March of Dimes, 1973-74, v.p., 1974-75; pres. Willing Hands, 1974-75; chmn. attys.' divsn. United Way, 1977; pres. Civic Round Table of Jacksonville, 1980-81; mem. exec. com. Jacksonville Area Legal Aid, Inc., 1982-83; chmn. pvt. bar involvement com. Legal Aid Bd. Dirs., 1982-83. Recipient Outstanding Svc. award for individual contbns. in support of legal svcs. for the poor, 1981. Fellow Am. Bar Found., Internat. Soc. Barristers, Southeastern Admiralty Law (com., dir. Port, Jacksonville 1996-99); mem. ATLA, ABA, Fla. Chpt. Am. Bd. Trial Advs. (treas. 1999, mem. exec. com. 1997—), Am. Bd. Trial Advs. (charter, pres. Jacksonville chpt. 1997, FLABOTA bd. mem. 1997—, treas. 1999, pres.-elect 2000, nat. bd. mem. 1999—, chpt. selected as Best in the Nation 1997, Selected as Fla. Trial Lawyer of Yr. 2000), Jacksonville Bar Assn. (pres. 1980-81, pres. young lawyers sect. 1974-75, Lawyer of Yr. award 1999), Fla. Bar (bd. cert. civil trial lawyer, bd. cert. admiralty and maritime law, grievance com. 1975-77, chmn. 1976, 4th jud. cir. nominating commn. 1980-82, mem. exec. coun. for trial sect. 1982-89, voluntary bar liaison com. 1982-83, chmn.-elect 1986-87, chmn. 1987, 88, bd. govs. 1988-90, charter mem. admiralty and maritime law bd. cert. 1996—, chmn. 1997, chmn. 4th jud. cir. professionalism com. 1998—, chmn. recipient of Outstanding Professionalism Program 1999), Fla. Coun. Bar Assn. Pres. (exec. com. 1982-88, v.p. 1984, pres. 1985-86), Jacksonville Assn. Def. Counsel (pres. 1981-82, lectr. CLE programs, guest lectr. U. Fla. Nat. Assn. R.R. Trial Counsel), Nat. Assn. R.R. Trial Counsel (exec. com. 1979—, v.p. southeastern region 1984-86, pres.-elect 1989-90, pres. 1990-91), Maritime Law Assn. U.S. (mem. com. professionalism 1996—), Acad. Fla. Trial Lawyers, Am. Judicature Soc., San Jose Country Club, Univ. Club, Gulf Life Tower Club, Country Club Sapphire Valley (N.C.). Republican. Home: 4655 Corrientes Cir N Jacksonville FL 32217-4329 Office: Milton Leach & D'Andrea 1660 Prudential Dr Ste 200 Jacksonville FL 32207-8181

MILTON, SHULMAN, writer, journalist, critic; b. Toronto, Can.; s. Samuel and Ethel (Raisberg) S.; m. Drusilla Beyfus; children: Alexandra, Nicola, Jason. BA, U. Toronto, 1934; barrister-solicitor, Osgood Hall, Toronto, 1937. Columnist London Evening Std., 1950-97, theater critic, 1951-96; book, TV and film critic Evening Std., Sunday Express (London), Vogue. Author 3 children's books; contbr. numerous articles to jours. and mags. Recipient IPC Critic of Yr. award. Mem. Garrick Club, Hurlingham Club, Chelsea Arts Club. Fax: 0171-823-1766.

MILUTINOVIC, MILAN A., President Republic of Serbia; b. Belgrade, Yugoslavia, Dec. 19, 1942; s. Aleksandar Milan Milutinovic and Ljubica Vladimir Jokic; m. Olga Branko Sapasojevic, Dec. 6, 1970; 1 son, Veljko. LLM, U. Belgrade, 1965. Mem. presidency Yugoslav Socialist Youth Union, Belgrade, 1969-71; M.P. Belgrade, 1969-74; sec. Communal Com. of League of Communists, 1972-74; sec. for ideology City Com. of League of Communists of Belgrade, 1974-77; Republican sec. for edn. and sci. Govt. of Serbia, 1977-82, dir. Nat. Library of Serbia, 1983-87; ambassador, head sector for press info. and culture Fed. Secretariat for Fgn. Affairs, 1987-89; mem. fgn. affairs com. Fed. Assembly, 1969-74; ambassador to Greece Fed. Republic of Yugoslavia, 1989-95, minister for fgn. affairs, 1995-97; pres. Republic of Serbia, 1997—; mem. or chief 55 Yugoslav meetings and dels. to UN, OECD, UNESCO. Author: UniversityúúEppur si muove, 1985; also articles. Decorated Order of Merit with Silver Star, 1974, medal for work with gold coronet, 1980. Avocation: philately. Home: Koste Glavinica 9, 11000 Belgrade Yugoslavia Office: Presidency of Republic, Serbia Andricev Venac 1, 11000 Belgrade Yugoslavia

MILVIDSKII, MIKHAIL GRIGOR'EVICH, chemical engineer, educator; b. Moscow, Aug. 2, 1932; s. Gregory Semionovich Milvidskii and Paulina Ionovna Sheveliova; m. Alla Georgievna Braginskaya, Feb. 10, 1984; 1 child. Engr., Tech. U. Steel and Alloys, Moscow, 1956; cand. sci., Tech. U. Steel and Alloys, 1962, DS, 1969. Scientist, dept. chief, vice-dir. State Inst. Rare Metals, Moscow, 1956-92; vic.-dir. State Inst. Chem. Problems for Microelectronics, Moscow, 1992—; prof. Lomonosov Acad. Fine Chem. Tech., Moscow, 1978—. Author: Physical Chemical Foundation of Semiconductor Compound Preparation, 1974, Structural Defects in Semiconductor single Crystals and Epitaxial Layers, 1984, 85, Semiconductor Materials in the Modern Electronics, 1986; editor: Actual Problems of Semiconductor Materials Technology, 1998; patentee in field; editl. staff Jour. Crystallography, 1983—, Jour. Physics and Tech. of Semiconductors, 1987—, Jour. Material Sci., 1996—, Jour. Materials of Electronics Engring., 1997—; contbr. articles to profl. jours. Grantee NASA, 1997-98; recipient State Lenin prize for semiconductor technology, 1964, State prize for tech. and physics, 1975, 84, State Medals, 1965, 85. Mem. Russian Phys. Soc., Russian Acad. Sci. (grantee 1998). Avocations: running, skiing. Home: Krupskaya str 8 k 1 64, 117311 Moscow Russia Office: Inst Chem Problems Microele, Bolshoy Tolmachevsky 5, 109017 Moscow Russia

MILYAEVA, ELVINA LEONIDOVNA, biologist; b. Vladivostok, Russia, Sept. 22, 1936; d. Leonid Matveevich and Olga Danilovna Milyaeva; 1 child, Veronika. MSc, Moscow State U., 1959; PhD, Main Bot. Garden, Moscow, 1964. Asst. Main Bot. Garden, Moscow, 1959-61; sr. asst. K.A. Timiryazev Inst. Plant Physiology, Moscow, 1964-67, jr. sci. rschr., 1967-77, sr. sci. rschr., 1977—, substitute lab. leader, 1999—. Co-author: Biology of Plant Development, 1975, Hormonal Regulation of Plant Ontogenesis, 1984, Plant Growth and Resistance, 1988, Saffron Crocus, 1999. Grantee Soros Found., Russia, 1994. Mem. Russian Soc. Plant Physiologists (Chailakhyan's award 1996). Avocations: sports, traveling. E-mail: e milyaeva@worldmailer.com and ifr@ippras.ru. Fax: 7 095 9761685. Home: Bolshoi Afanasievskii, pereulok 5/12-47, 121019 Moscow Russia Office: KA Timiryazev Inst Plant Physiology, Botanicheskaya Str 35, 127276 Moscow Russia

MIMA, KUNIOKI, physicist, educator; b. Anan, Tokushima, Japan, Aug. 17, 1945; s. Shigeru and Toyo Mima; m. Kazuko Saito, Oct. 20, 1970; children: Chifumi, Joji, Tomoya, Yohei. B in Physics, Kyoto U., Japan, 1968; M in Physics, Kyoto U., 1970, PhD of Physics, 1973. Rsch. assoc. Hiroshima (Japan) Univ., 1973-75; from rsch. assoc. to assoc. prof. Inst. Laser Engring., Osaka (Japan) Univ., 1975-83, prof., 1983—, dir., 1995-99; cons. AT&T Bell Labs., Murray Hill, N.J., 1975-76; rsch. assoc. Plasma Physics Lab., UCLA, 1976-77; physics sub-com. mem. Japanese Acad. Sci., Tokyo, 1989—; chmn. rsch. com. Osaka Sci. and Tech. Found., 1986-90. Editor: Proceedings of 14th Free Electron Laser Internat. Conf., 1992, Research Textbook, 1991. Fellow Am. Phys. Soc. (Excellence in Plasma Physics Rsch. award 1993, Osaka Sci. prize 1995); mem. Japanese Phys. Soc., Laser Soc. Japan (chmn. evaluation com. of laser fusion energy). Home: 1-15-30 Okutenjin, Takatsuki 569, Japan Office: Osaka U Inst Laser Engring, 2-6 Yamada-oka, Suita 565-0871, Japan*

MIMICA, MARKO, gynecologist, researcher; b. Split, Croatia, Oct. 29, 1960; s. Ivan and Ruth (Fischbach) M.; m. Radojka Ulić, May 14, 1994; children: Dorotea, Bianka. MD, U. Zagreb, Croatia, 1985; MSc, U. Rijeka, Croatia, 1996; specialist in ob-gyn., U. Zagreb, 1996. Rsch. fellow Clin. Hosp., Split, 1988-92, ob-gyn. staff, 1992-96, gynecologist, 1996—. Contbr. articles to profl. med. jours. Mem. Croatian Med. Assn. Avocations: photography, sports. Home: Šime Ljubica 14, 21000 Split Croatia Office: Clinical Hospital Split, Spinčiceva 1, 21000 Split Croatia

MIMICA, NINOSLAV, psychiatrist; b. Zagreb, Croatia, June 20, 1959; s. Milorad-Miro and Nikica-Nine (Majstorovic) M.; m. Nevenka-Nena Vajdić, May 8, 1982; children: Nina, Mislav. MD, U. Zagreb, Croatia, 1987; postgrad., Inter U. Ctr., Dubrovnik, Croatia, 1987; MSc, U. Zagreb, 1994. Physician Clin. Hosp. (now Sestre Milosrdnice), Zagreb, Croatia, 1988-89, Clin. Psychiat. Hosp. Vrapce, Zagreb, Croatia, 1989-94; cons. psychiatrist U. Dept. Psychiatry, Psychiat. Hosp. Vrapče, Zagreb, Croatia, 1994—; guest investigator Psychiat. Inst. Columbia U., N.Y.C., 1991; cons. psychiatrist Gen. Hosp. Knin, Croatia, 1996; cons. rschr. Croatian Inst. Brain Rsch., Zagreb, 1994—, Dept. Psychiat. Rsch., Zagreb, 1994—; lectr. in field. Roche edn. grantee, Budapest, Hungary, 1993; recipient Young Scientist award Biennial European Workshop Schizophrenia, Switzerland, 1994, 96. Mem. Croatian Psychiat. Soc., Croatian Assn. Biol. Psychiatry and Psychopharmacology, Croatian Assn. Med. Anthropology. Avocations: movies, gardening, walking, fishing. Home: Bolnicka cesta 29, HR 10090 Zagreb Croatia Office: U Dept Psy/Psy Hosp Vrapce, Bolnicka cesta 32, HR 10090 Zagreb Croatia

MIMIKOS, MICHAIL GEORGE, marketing, advertising agency executive; b. Nea Artaki, Evia, Greece, Mar. 26, 1965; s. George Mihail and Loula George (Kokopipi) M.; m. Vana Dimitriou Georgala, May 6, 1989; children: George Mihail, Synthia Mihail. BSc, L.I. U., N.Y., 1986; MBA in Mktg., St. John's U., N.Y., 1987. Prodn. supr. Mimikos Bros. SA, Chalkis, Evia, Greece, 1988, mktg. mgr., 1990-99, bd. dirs., 1994-99; pres. Com Advt., 1996—; cons. Asterias Fisheries, 1992; bd. dirs. Goody's Restaurant. Contbr. articles to profl. jours. With Greek Air Force, 1988-89. Fgn. Student scholar L.I. U., 1982-86. Mem. Mgmt. Ctrl. Europe, Greek C. of C. (bd. dirs. 1994—), Advertisers Assn. Greece, Greek Poultry Assn., European Poultry Assn. (rep. 1992—), Athletic Club of Nea Artaki (v.p.).

MIMMS, THOMAS BOWMAN, JR., lawyer; b. Atlanta, Oct. 11, 1944; s. Thomas Bowman and Alice Buehl Mimms; m. Alison Hayward, July 22, 1967; children: Karen Mimms Swift, Christina Mimms Couret. BA, U. N.C., 1965; JD, Columbia U., 1969. Bar: Fla. 1969, Ga. 1999, U.S. Dist. Ct. (mid. dist.) Fla. 1972, U.S. Supreme Ct. 1973, U.S. Ct. Appeals (11th cir.) 1981, Ga. 1999. Assoc. atty. Fleming O'Bryan, Fort Lauderdale, Fla., 1969-72; shareholder Macfarlane Ferguson & McMullen, Tampa, Fla., 1972-99. Fellow Am. Bar Found.; mem. Fla. Bar Assn. (exec. coun. bus. law sect. 1987-99, bus. law legislation com. 1995-99, chair bus. law bankrupty/UCC com. 1988-89), Tampa Bay Bankruptcy Bar Assn. (pres. 1992-93), Columbia U. Alumni Club (dir. 1991-99). Democrat. Episcopalian. Office: Mimms Enterprises 85A Mill St Ste 100 Roswell GA 30075-4910

MIMURA, GORO, medical educator, researcher; b. Fukuoka, Japan, May 7, 1926; s. Takajiro and Haruko (Murakami) M.; m. Setsuko Haraguchi;

children: Kazuo, Mayumi, Mariko. MD, Kumamoto Medical Coll., Kumamoto, Japan, 1953; PhD, Kumamoto U., Kumamoto, Japan, 1960. Assoc. prof. Kumamoto U., Kumamoto, Japan, 1961-81; rsch. fellow Munich U., Munich, Germany, 1963-64; dir. Ryukyu U. Hosp., Okinawa, Japan, 1980-81; prof. U. Ryukyus, Okinawa, 1976-92; adv. prof. Harbin Medical U., Harbin, China, 1984—, China Medical U., Shenyang, China, 1991—; hon. dir. Jinnouchi Hosp., Kumamoto, 1992-93; pres. Shokei Jr. Coll., Kumamoto, 1993—; prof. emeritus U. Ryukus, 1992; mem. Sci. Coun. Japan, 1988-91. Dir. Japan Diabetes Soc., 1971-96, chmn. Kyushu br. 1971-96; pres. Japanese Soc. Constitutional Medicine, 1980—. Recipient Prize of Sakaguchi, Japan Diabetes Soc., 1992, Prize of Health Care and Culture Japan Ministry of Health & Welfare, 1992, Disting. Leadership award Am. Biographical Insts., 1996, 20th Century award for Achievement Internat. Biographic Ctr., Cambridge, Eng., 1996. Mem. Japan Assn. Health Care and Edn. (v.p. 1992—, Kyokai prize 2000), Chinese Med. Assn. (hon.), Japan Diabetes Soc. (hon.). Home: 1-13 Higashihonmachi, Kumamoto 862 0902, Japan Office: Shokei Jr Coll, 2-6-78 Kuhonji, Kumamoto 862-8678, Japan

MIN, GEH, surgeon; b. Singapore, Jan. 30, 1950; s. Geh Ik Cheong and Lee Seok Tin; m. Tong Ming Chuan, Nov. 26, 1976; 1 child, Tong Wen Fei. MB BS, U. Singapore, 1974. Cons. eye surgeon Mount Elizabeth Med. Ctr., Singapore, 1985—; vis. cons. Singapore Nat. Eye Ctr., 1991—, Nat. U. Hosp., Singapore, 1998—. Dir. Singapore Art Mus., 1995, Singapore Dance Theatre, 1987, Sculpture Sq. Ptd. Ltd., 1998, Save the Children Singapore, 1989. Fellow Royal Coll. Surgeons (Edinburgh); mem. Glaucoma Soc. (pres. Singapore chpt. 1999—). E-mail: tmcgm.singnet.com.sq. Office: Mount Elizabeth Med Ctr, 3 Mount Elizabeth/#17-11, Singapore 228510, Singapore

MIN, MART, electronics educator; b. Tallinn, Estonia, May 9, 1943; s. Walter and Ida (Menkoff) M.; m. Rhine Yksine, Sept. 17, 1971; 1 child, Randel. Diploma in engr., Tallinn Tech. Univ., 1969; PhD, Kiew Polytech., Kiew, Ukraine, 1984. Researcher Tallinn Tech. Univ., Tallinn, 1984-88, assoc. prof., 1988-92, prof., 1992—; dir. Inst. of Elec., Tallinn, 1995-99; vis. prof. Univ. der Bunderswehr, Munich, 1993; guest scientist Tech. Univ. Munich, 1992; cons. Rohde & Schwarz Co., Munich, 1993, Pacesetter AB, Stockholm, 1997, Karolinska Inst., Stockholm, 1997—, St. Jude Med. Inc., 2000—. Contbr. articles to profl. jours.; patentee in field. Recipient Award of Yr. Eng. Sci. of Repubic of Estonia, 1993, Award in Engring. Gov. of Estonia, 1986. Mem. IEEE, Nordic Bio-Impedance Club (internat. com.). Avocations: biomedical rsch., engring., sports, bodybuilding. Home: Sopruse str 188A-4, 13424 Tallinn Estonia Office: Tallinn Tech Univ, Ehitajate Tee 5, 19086 Tallinn Estonia

MIN, ZHENG, dermatology educator; b. Hangzhou, Zhejiang, China, Apr. 19, 1956; parents Jinzhang Zheng and Qiyu Chen; m. Sui-qing Cai, Feb. 16, 1993; 1 child, Yuxing Zheng. B of Medicine, Zhejiang Med. U., Hangzhou, 1982, M of Medicine, 1988; D of Medicine, Kiel (Germany) U., 1995. Cert. in medicine. Resident 2d Tchg. Hosp. of Zhejiang Med. U., Hangzhou, 1982-90, vis. dr., lectr., 1990-96, assoc. prof., 1996-99, prof. dermatology dept., 1999—; dir. dermatology dept. Med Sch., Zhejiang U., Hangzhou, 1999. Contbr. articles to sci. jours. Mem. Zhejiang Provincial Dermatology Assn. (vice-chmn. 1999—). Fax: 0086 571 7215882. E-mail: minz@mail.hz.zj.cn. Office: 2d Affil Hosp Zhejiang U, Jie-fang Rd 68, 310009 Hangzhou Zhejiang, China

MINA, MIKHAIL VALENTINOVICH, zoologist; b. Ordzhonikidze, N. Ossetia, USSR, July 1, 1939; s. Valentin Nikolaevich and Elena Sergeevna (Karzinkina) M; m. Galina Alexandrovna Klevezal, Dec. 4, 1962. Candidate of Scis. in Biology, Moscow State U., 1967; D of Scis. in Biology, All Union Rsch. Inst. of Marine Fishery and Oceanography, Moscow, USSR, 1987. Jr. scientist All-Union Rsch. Inst. of Marine Fishery and Oceanography, Moscow, 1961-64; from jr. to sr. scientist dept. ichthyology Moscow State U., 1964-77; from sr. to leading scientist Inst. Devel. Biology Russian Acad. of Scis., Moscow, 1977—. Author: (with G.A. Klevezal) Growth of Animals, 1976, Microevolution of Fishes, (Russian) 1986, (English) 1991 (I.I. Schmalhausen prize 1998); contbr. over 100 articles to profl. jours. Avocations: bird hunting, gundogs. Home: Obrucheva Str 12-83, 117421 Moscow Russia Office: Inst Devel Biology, Vavilova Str 26, 117334 Moscow Russia

MINAEV, BORIS FILIPPOVICH, chemist; b. Ekaterinbourg, Russia, Sept. 21, 1943; d. Filipp Prokopjevich and Tatjana Nikolaevna (Manohina) M.; m. Valentina Alexandrovna Banina, Nov. 29, 1971; 1 child, Alexandr. BA, Tomsk (Russia) State U., 1967, PhD, 1974; DSc, Chem. Physics Inst., Moscow, 1984. Rschr. Sibirian Phys. Inst., Tomsk, 1970-73; assoc. prof. theoretical physics U. Karaganda, Kazakhstan Republic, 1974-76, prof., head chair phys. chemistry, 1976-83, head chair quantum chemistry, 1984-89; prof. Tech. and Engr. Inst., Cherkassy, Ukraine, 1989—; vis. rschr. J.Heyrovsky Inst., Praha, 1979-80; vis. rschr., educator inst. physics and measurement tech. U. Linköping, Sweden, 1993-98; vis. rschr. Royal Inst. Tech., Stockholm, 1999—. Author: Optical and Magnetic Properties of the Triplet State, 1983; co-author: Quantum electrochemistry of Alkaloids, 1986, Electronic Structure of Molecules: New Aspects, 1987; contbr. articles to profl. jours. Dep. regional soviet Karaganda, 1985-88. Grantee Swedish Royal Acad. Sci., Stockholm, 1993, European Sci. Found., Brussels, 1994; named Water Polo champion Kazakhstan Rep., 1961-62. Mem. AAAS, N.Y. Acad. Scis. Mem. Russian Orthodox Ch. Home: Smeljanskaja 2 k 392, 257002 Cherkassy Ukraine Office: Tech and Engring Inst, bvd Shevchenko 460, 257006 Cherkassy Ukraine

MINAGAWA, MASATOMO, chemist, educator, researcher; b. Niigata, Japan, Apr. 10, 1946; s. Eisuke and Mie Minagawa; m. Sumie Shibuya, Mar. 30, 1978; children: Ariko, Erika. BE, Yamagata U., Yonezawa, Japan, 1969, ME, 1971; PhD, Tokyo Inst. Tech., 1991. Rsch. asst. Yamagata U., 1971-82, 85-91, lectr., 1992-95, assoc. prof., 1997—; domestic rschr. Tohoku U., Sendai, Japan, 1983-84; vis. prof. Poly. U., N.Y.C., 1996; mgr. Interdisciplinary Rsch. Coun. Japan, Tokyo, 1996—. Contbr. articles to profl. jours. Grantee Mitsubishi Rayon Co., Ltd., Hiroshima, 1994, Asahi Chem. Industry Co., Ltd., Osaka, Japan, 1995, Tohoku Rubber Co. Ltd., Sendai, 1996. Mem. Am. Chem. Soc., Soc. Polymer Sci. Japan, N.Y. Acad. Scis. Home: Rinsenji 2-1-1, Yonezawa 992, Japan Office: Yamagata U Faculty Engring, Dept Materials Sci & Engrin, Yonezawa 992, Japan

MINAGAWA, SITIRO, applied mathematics educator; b. Kashiwazaki, Japan, Jan. 2, 1928; s. Koji and Kiyono (Aida) M.; m. Miyako, Apr. 24, 1960; 1 child, Rima. B of Engring., U. Tokyo, 1952, D of Engring., 1965. Lectr. U. Tokyo, 1964; assoc. prof. Tohoku U., Sendai, Japan, 1964-74; prof. U. Electro-Comm., Tokyo, 1974-93, prof. emeritus, 1993—; prof. Niigata (Japan) U. Internat. and Info. Studies, 1994-99; rsch. assoc. Northwestern U., 1970-72. Adv. editor Internat. Jour. Engring. Scis.; contbr. articles to sci. jours. Mem. Materials Sci. Soc. Japan (pres. 1995-97), Phys. Soc. Japan, Japan. Soc. Mech. Engrs. Fax: 03-5999-7786. E-mail: minagawa@hi-ho.ne.jp.

MINAGAWA, TEIICHI, molecular biologist; b. Kamo, Niigata, Japan, Oct. 28, 1924; s. Ryozo Taguchi and Tatsu Minagawa; m. Sachiko Isahaya, Apr. 13, 1952; 1 child. BS, Kyoto (Japan) U., 1947, MS, 1949, DSc, 1957. Assoc. prof. Kobe (Japan) U., 1953-64; postdoctoral Syracuse (N.Y.) U., 1957-58; rsch. assoc. Carnegie Inst. Wash., Cold Spring Harbor, 1958-60; assoc. prof. Kyoto U., 1965-70, prof., 1970-88, emeritus prof. molecular biology, 1988—. Author: T-Phages, 1991, Genetics and Evolution, 1995, Dictionary of Molecular Cell Biology, 1997, Virology, 1997. Mem. Am. Soc. Microbiology. Avocations: gardening, listening to classics. Fax: 075-351-3567. Home: Bukkojidori Teramachi, Higashi, Shimokyoku, Kyoto 600-8032, Japan

MINAKAMI, KOREBUMI, medical school educator; b. Kumamoto, Japan, Apr. 17, 1944; s. Masatoshi and Kinu (Ishibashi) M.; m. Michiko Tanoue, Mar. 25, 1970; children: Kanae, Yoshie. BF, Kagoshima (Japan) U., 1967, DF, 1968, PhD, 1994; MSc, Kumamoto (Japan) U., 1970. Asst. prof. Kagoshima (Japan) U., 1970-86, assoc. prof., 1986-93, prof., 1993—; JICA expert U. Ghana, Accra, 1980-81; vis. prof. Aston U., Birmingham, Eng., 1995. Contbr. articles to profl. jours. Grantee Ministry of Edn., 1995. Mem. Zoological Soc. Japan, 1970, Japanese Pharmacological Soc., Brit. Assn. Psychopharmacology. Avocations: reading, music, painting, mountain climbing, sightseeing. Office: Kagoshima U Sch Health Sci, 8-35-1 Sakuragaoka, Kagoshima 890-8506, Japan

MINALE, CARMINE, cardiovascular surgeon; b. Naples, Italy, Sept. 21, 1943; s. Gaetano and Lucia (Orso) M.; m. Nadia Bolla, Jul. 8, 1972; 1 child, Mario. Med. degree, U. Naples (Italy), 1968. Resident Univ. Hosp., Zurich, 1969-73, Children Hosp., Naples, 1973-78; assoc. Univ. Hosp., Aachen, Germany, 1978-89; chief Univ. Hosp., Wuppertal, Germany, 1989-97, Univ. Hosp. S. Martino, Geneo, Italy, 1997-2000; chief cardiovasc. surgery Hosp. S. Carlo, Potenza, Italy, 2000—; prof. Medical Faculty Aachen, 1987-90, Medical Faculty, Düsseldorf, Germany, 1990—. Contbr. over 120 articles to profl. jours. Avocation: sailing, flying, skiing. Office: Hosp S Carlo, Dept Cardiovasc Surgery, 85100 Potenza Italy

MINAMI, MASARU, pharmacologist; b. Oyabe, Toyama, Japan, Dec. 15, 1938; s. Kosaku and Tatsue (Ito) M.; m. Yumiko Matsuoka, June 9, 1962; children: Atsushi, Hideko. BA in Medicine, Hokkaido U., Sapporo, Japan, 1964, PhD in Medicine, 1969. Med. diplomate, Japan. Asst. prof. mech. tech. Hokkaido U., Sapporo, 1969-81, asst. prof. medicine, 1981-82, assoc. prof., 1982-86; prof. pharmacy, health scis. Hokkaido U., Ishikari-Tobetsu, Japan, 1986—. Editor: Progress in Hypertension, Vol. 2, 1992; author: Serotonin and the Scientific Basis of Anti-emetic Therapy, 1995. Recipient acad. award Hokkaido Newspaper Co. Ltd., 1995. Mem. Pharm. Soc. (br. dir. 1995-96). Home: Kita-40 Higashi 5-2-7, Sapporo 007-0840, Japan Office: Health Scis U Hokkaido, Kanazawa 1757, Ishikari-Tobetsu 061-0293, Japan

MINAMI, NOBUYA, electric power industry executive. CEO Tokyo Electric Power. Office: Tokyo Electric Power, 1-1-3 Uchisaiwaicho, Tokyo 100-0011, Japan*

MINAMI, TOSHIHIRO, electronics company executive, accountant; b. Kyoto, Japan, Feb. 14, 1960; m. Chizuru Shimizu, Apr. 21, 1984; children: Eri, Hiromasa. LLB, U. Tokyo, 1983; MBA, Georgetown U., 1991. CPA; cert. fin. planner. Sales rep. Hitachi, Ltd., Tokyo, 1983-89, mktg./sales mgr., 1991-96; gen. mgr. Philips Japan Ltd., Tokyo, 1997—. Mem. alumni admissions com. Georgetown U., 1995—. Mem. Fin. Planners Assn. Japan. Avocations: golf, American film. Home: 3-13-14 Oyamadai, Setagaya-ku, 158-0086 Tokyo Japan Office: Philips Japan Ltd, 13-37 Kohnan 2-chome, Tokyo 108-8507, Japan

MINAR, PAUL G., design consultant; b. Phoenix, July 12, 1932; s. Aaron Crowther and Ione Anna (Schmid) Mortensen. Student, Ariz. State U., 1950-54, John F. Kennedy U., 1978-80, Antioch West U., 1980. Sound effects technician, TV stage mgr. Sta. KHJ-AM-TV, L.A., 1955-63; displayer W.&J. Sloane Furniture Co., Beverly Hills, Calif., 1963-66, Bullock's Dept. Store, L.A., 1966-68, Macy's Dept. Store, San Francisco, 1968-70; interior designer Lloyd's Furniture Co., San Diego, 1970-71, Bonynge's Furniture Co., Oakland, Calif., 1971-72, Breuner's Furniture Co., Oakland, 1972-74; design cons. The Other Artist, San Francisco, 1974—; archival rschr. and conservation Petaluma Hist. Mus., 1994—; profl. numerologist; lectr. in onomatology. Author: Numerology For People Who Don't Understand It, 1997; writer, producer (documentary) The Modern Nursing Home, 1959. Vol. talent agt. San Francisco Symphony Black and White Ball, 1983; bd. dirs. Akasha Personal Projects; mem. Fine Arts Mus. of San Francisco. Mem. Inst. Noetic Scis., Petaluma Mus. Assn. Democrat. Roman Catholic. Avocations: wilderness exploration, tennis, classical music, parapsychology, world history. Office: The Other Artist 3200 Buchanan St San Francisco CA 94123-3517

MINASI, ANTHONY, software company executive; b. N.Y.C., July 9, 1948; s. Dominic A. and Mary (De Rosa) M.; m. Patricia Ann Gallagher, Oct. 3, 1976; children: Christopher, Marie Elizabeth. BA, Hunter Coll., 1971; MBA with distinction, Pace U., 1982, postgrad., 1988. Bus. analyst Am. Internat. Group, N.Y.C., 1971-75; systems mgr., officer Fiduciary Trust Co., N.Y.C., 1975-79; systems mgr. Flexivan Leasing, N.Y.C., 1979-84; group mgr., v.p. Drexel Burnham, N.Y.C., 1984-89; mng. dir. tech. Vista Concepts, Inc., N.Y.C., 1989-93; sr. prin., mgr. N.Am. investment industry sales/svc. Am. Mgmt. Systems, Inc., N.Y.C., 1994-95; practice mgr. Investment Industry Group, N.Y.C., 1996-97, v.p., engagement mgr. corp. banking and securities practice, 1997-98; v.p. engagement mgr. utilities industry practice Am. Mgmt. Sys., Inc., Roseland, N.J., 1999—. Avocations: photography, tennis. Office: Am Mgmt Sys 75 Livingston Ave Roseland NJ 07068-3701

MINASYAN, GEORGIY R., acoustical engineer, computer programmer; b. Tbilisi, Ga., USSR, Oct. 31, 1962; s. Robert G. Minasyan and Valentina D. Podlesnova; 1 child. MsD, Moscow Inst. Radio Engring. Electronics and Automation, 1986; PhD Acoustics Inst., Russian Acad. Scis., Moscow, 1994. Engr., rschr. Acoustics Inst., 1986-91, scientist, 1991-94, sr. scientist, 1994-97; sr. scientist Telefactor Corp., West Conshokochen, Pa., 1997—. Contbr. chpt. to book: Full Field Inversion Methods, 1995, also articles to sci. jours. Small Bus. Rsch. grantee NIH, 1998. Mem. IEEE, Computer Soc. of IEEE, EMBS, Acoustical Soc. Am., Signal Processing Soc., Internat. Neural Network Soc. Avocations: chess, automobiles, music. E-mail: gminasyan@yahoo.com. Home: 2042 Spring Mill Rd Lafayette Hill PA 19444-2110 Office: Telefactor Corp 1094 New Dehaven St West Cnshohocken PA 19428-2713

MINATO, ATSUSHI, physicist, educator; b. Hitachi-ota, Ibaraki, Japan, Oct. 23, 1961; s. Ken and Masako Minato; m. Keiko Minato, Mar. 26, 1993; children: Tadashi, You, Hiroshi. BSc, Kyoto (Japan) U., 1984; ME, U. Tokyo, 1988, DE, 1994. Engr. Hitachi Koki Co., Ltd., Katsuta, Japan, 1984-85; rschr. Nat. Inst. for Environ. Studies, Tsukuba, Japan, 1988-95; asst. prof. Ibaraki U., Hitachi, Japan, 1995-98, assoc. prof., 1998—. Contbr. articles to Applied Optics, Optics Letters, Optical Rev., others. Mem. Optical Soc. Am., Japan Soc. Applied Physics, Laser Soc. Japan. Avocation: fishing. Office: Ibaraki U, 4-12-1 Nakanarusawa, Hitachi, Ibaraki 316-8511, Japan

MINCATO, VITTORIO, gas, oil industry executive. CEO, chmn. ENI S.P.A., Rome, mng. dir., CEO. Office: ENI SPA, Piazzale E Mattei, 00144 Rome Italy*

MINCHEY, SAMUEL BONE, research scientist; b. Nashville, July 7, 1955; s. Ruth Minchey. BA, U. Tenn., 1973, MS, 1975, PhD, 1978. Postdoctoral fellow NIH, Bethesda, Md., 1978-81; scientist Liposome Co., Princeton, N.J., 1981-83, sr. scientist in animal studies, 1983-85, dir. membrane rsch., 1985-91, exec. dir. rsch., 1991—. Contbr. over 40 articles to profl. jours. Mem. Biophys. Soc., N.Y. Acad. Scis. Mem. Reform Party. Achievements include 14 U.S. and 16 international patents in field. Office: Liposome Co 1 Research Way Princeton NJ 08540-6690

MINCHIN, NICK, administrator; b. Sydney, Australia, Apr. 15, 1943; m. Kerry Minich; children Jack, Oliver and Anna. B of Econ., Australian Nat. U., LLB. Dir. South Australian Liberal Party, 1985-93; mem. Australian Senate, 1993—, parliamentary sec. to leader of opposition, 1994-96; parliamentary sec. Office of Prime Min., Australia, 1993-97, min. asst. prime min., 1997-98; min. Dept. Industry, Sci. & Tourism, Australia, 1998—. Office: Dept Industry Sci & Tourism, Parliament Ho Ste MF21, Canberra ACT 2600, Australia*

MINDERMANN, THOMAS FRIEDRICH GERHARD, neurosurgeon, researcher; b. Schopfheim, Germany, Mar. 10, 1955; arrived in Switzerland, 1975; s. Fritz and Gisela (Boldt) M. MD, U. Basel, Switzerland, 1983. Med. diplomate; bd. cert. neurosurgeon, Switzerland, 1995. Resident in neurosurgery Univ. Hosps., Basel, 1990-92, 94, attending neurosurgeon, 1995-99; sr. pituitary rsch. fellow U. Calif., San Francisco, 1992-93; privatdozent U. Basel, Switzerland, 1999—; dir. Gamma Knife Ctr., Zurich, Switzerland, 2000—. Author: (book) Indications for Single-Dose Antibiotic Prophylaxis in Surgery and Gynecology, 1985, Single-Dose Antibiotikaprophylaxe, 1991, (book chpts.) Neurosurgery 96, Manual of Neurosurgery, 1996, Cancer Medicine, 4th edit., 1997; contbr. articles to profl. jours. Pvt. West German Army, 1974-75. M. & W. Lichtenstein-Stiftung grantee U. Basel, 1992, Ciba-Geigy-Jubiläumsstiftung grantee, 1992, 93, Freiwillige Akademische Gesellschaft grantee, 1992, 93. Mem. Swiss Neurosurg. Soc., Swiss Med. Assn., Congress of Neurol. Surgeons (U.S.), Am. Assn. Neurol. Surgeons, Pituitary Soc. (U.S.), Leksell Gamma Knife Soc. Avocation: contemporary Australian Aboriginal art, antique Portuguese tiles, contemporary American art. Office: Klinik Im Park, Seestrasse 220, 8027 Zürich Switzerland

MINDIN, VLADIMIR YUDOVICH, information systems specialist, chemist, educator; b. Tbilisi, Georgia, USSR, June 6, 1939; came to U.S., 1992; naturalized U.S. citizen, 1997; s. Yuda Isaakovich and Sofia Markovna (Ioffe) M.; m. Irina Alexandrovna Pleshivaia, July 1, 1964; children: Liya, Yakov. MS, Georgian Tech. U., Tbilisi, 1961, PhD, 1969. Sr. rsch. scientist Georgian Tech. U., 1970-80, assoc. prof. phys. chemistry, 1980-92; head computational chemistry lab. Georgian Acad. Sci., Tbilisi, 1980-92; investigator Beltran Inc., Bklyn., 1993-94, prin. investigator, 1994-95; statistician AFP, Inc., Manhasset, N.Y., 1995-98, info. systems dir., 1998—; cons. DNS Sci., Inc., Bklyn., 1992-97; chief scientific officer, BioNova, Inc., Forest Hills, N.Y., 1997—. Author: (with A.G. Morachevskii and A.S. Avaliany) Liquid Cathodes, 1978, (A.V. Sarukhanishvily and J.S. Galuashvily) Inorganic Substances Thermodynamic Parameters Calculation on Computers by Landia Method, 1987, (S.M. Mazmishvily and D.V. Eristavy) Album of Compositions of Condensed and Gaseous Phase of Silica-Carbon System, 1988 (Georgian Chem. soc. award 1989), (A.V. Sarukhanishvily) Chemical Thermodynamics, 1990, (D.V. Eristavy) Investigation on Thermodynamics of Interaction in Boron and Silicon Containing Systems By Means of Digital Chemistry Methods, 1994; contbr. numerous articles to profl. jours. Grantee Dept. Def., 1994-95. Mem. Am. Statis. Assn., Minerals, Metals, Materials Soc., Assn. Engrs. and Scientists for New Ams. (assoc. exec. dir. 1993-94). Achievements include co-development of the first complete phase diagram of the silica-carbon system; patents (with others): Method of Manganese Salt Solutions Obtaining, Method of Manufacturing of Porous Electrodes, Method of Manganese Obtaining, Device for Electrochemical Measurement During Electrolysis of Melted Media, Working of Sulphur Ores, Nonferrous Metals Sulphate Ores Roasting Process, Unhydrous Manganese Chloride Producing Process, A Way of Working Sulphide Ores Containing Nonferrous Metals, Furnace Charge for Silicomanganese Obtaining, The Batch for the Medium Carbonic Ferromanganese Smelting. Home: 70 Dahill Rd Apt 5A Brooklyn NY 11218-2232 Office: AFP Inc 111 E Shore Rd Manhasset NY 11030-2902

MINDLIN, PAULA ROSALIE, retired reading educator; b. N.Y.C., Nov. 27, 1944; d. Simon S. and Sylvia (Naroff) Bernstein; m. Alfred Carl Mindlin, Aug. 14, 1965; 1 child, Spencer Douglas. BA in Edn., Bklyn. Coll., 1965; MS in Edn., Queens Coll., 1970, Specialist Sch. Adminstrn, 1973. Tchr. Dist. 16 Pub. Sch., Bklyn., 1965-68; reading tchr. Dist. 29 Pub. Sch. and Dist. 16, Bklyn., 1968-85; instr. insvc. courses Comty. Sch. Dist. 29, Queens Village, N.Y., 1984-93; reading coord. Reading/Comms. Arts Program Comty. Sch. Dist. 29, Queens, N.Y., 1985-90; dir. reading Cmty. Sch. Dist. 29, Queens Village, N.Y., 1990-94; ednl. cons.; adj. lectr. York Coll., 1989; dir. chpt. 1 program (Nat. Recognition 1994) U.S. Sec. Edn., 1993; curriculum cons., 1997-98. Recipient svc. award N.Y. State Reading Assn. Coun., 1996. Mem. Internat. Reading Assn., Queensboro Reading Coun. (pres. 1994-96, Educator of Yr. award 1994). Avocations: reading, gardening, boating.

MINE, KATSUTOSHI, engineering educator; b. Fukuoka-ken, Japan, Apr. 28, 1928; s. Tsuneo and Chiyoko (Yoshimura) M.; m. Kazuko Yamauchi, Feb. 5, 1956; 1 child, Satoshi. Diploma, Meiji Tech. Coll., Kitakyushu, Japan, 1949; D of Engring., Kyoto (Japan) U., 1978. Engr. Mitsubishi Chem. Co. Ltd., Kitakyushu, 1949-50, Dantani Plywood Co. Ltd., Kitakyushu, 1955-56; assoc. prof. Ube (Japan) Tech. Coll., 1962-72, prof., 1972-80; prof. Kyushu Inst. Tech., Kitakyushu, 1980-92; prof. Kyushu Kyoritsu U., Kitakyushu, 1992-99, gen. mgr. libr., 1996-98, dean engring., 1997-99, JICA splst., 1999—. Author: T.EMC, IEEE, 1994; inventor in field. Recipient Acad. award Fukuhara Gakuen U. Consortium, Kitakyushu, 1993, disting. svc. medal Internat. Cooperation JICA, 1999. Mem. IEEE (reviewer indsl. electronics 1992), IEEE Japan, Soc. Instrumentation and Control Engrs. (bd. dirs. 1990-92), Japan Soc. Med. and Biol. Engrs. (gen. chmn. 6th conf. 1991-92, bd. dirs. 1993-99, congress 1992), Kitakyushu Med. and Engring. Coop. Assn. (pres. 1989-93), Kitakyushu Techno-coop. Assn. (bd. dirs. 1992-99), N.Y. Acad. Sci. Avocations: classical music, skiing, hiking. Home: 296-2 Mushiozu, Onga-cho Fukuoka 811-43, Japan Office: Kyushu Kyoritsu Univ, 1-8 Jiyugaoka Yahatanishiku, Kitakyushu 807, Japan

MINEEV, KONSTANTIN PETER, traumatologist, orthopedist; b. Ichalkovo, Mordovia, Russia, July 12, 1950; s. Peter Andrew and Lukerya (Mironova) M.; m. Alexandra Merkulova, Dec. 22, 1988; children: Konstantin, Vladimir, Peter. Diploma med. officer, Mil.-Med. Acad. Kirov, Leningrad, USSR, 1972-78; BS in Med. Scis., U. Saransk, Russia, 1985; postgrad., Russian Acad. Natural Scis., Moscow, 1997, Internat. Acad. Authors Sci., Moscow, 1998. Candidate-asst. Mordovia State U., Saransk, 1981-87; sci. collaborator Sci. Ctr., Sverdlovsk, Russia, 1987-92; hon. prof. Eurouniversity, Moscow, 1999. Author: Guidance on Orthopedics, 1998; inventor abilities of vascular anastomoses to function during the fertilization period; author 16 monographs, numerous articles in field. Capt. Russian armed forces. Recipient Silver medal of Peter the Great, Presidium of Internat. Acad., 1997, Golden medal of Peter the Great, 1998, Gold and Silver medals of P.K. Kapitsa, Presidium of Russian Acad., 1998, Silver medal of I.P. Pavlov, Presidium of Russian Acad., 1999, Merited Doctor award of Russian Federation, 1999. Mem. Soc. Traumatists and Orthopedists, N.Y. Acad. Scis. Home: 2-41 Sozidatelei St, 432059 Ulyanovsk Russia Office: 23 Orenburgskaya St, 432010 Ulyanovsk Russia

MINEHART, JEAN BESSE, tax accountant; b. Cleve., Nov. 8, 1937; d. Ralph and Augusta Besse; m. Ralph Conrad Minehart, Aug. 28, 1959; children: Patricia Minehart Miron, Deborah, Elizabeth, Stephen. BA, Mass. Wellesley Coll., 1959; MEd, U. Va., 1971. Rsch. assoc. Age Ctr. of New Eng., Boston, 1959-61; substitute tchr. Charlottesville (Va.) Sch. System, 1976-81; tax acct. H&R Block, Charlottesville, 1982-94, Huey & Bjorn, Charlottesville, 1994—. Past pres. Ephphatha Village Housing for the Deaf, Charlottesville, 1984-87; bd. dirs. Tues. Evening Concert Series, Charlottesville, 1990-94; sec., bd. dirs. Family Svc., Inc., Charlottesville, 1987-91; bd. dirs. Westminster Organ Concert Series, 1998—; elder Westminster Presbyn. Ch., 1979-81, 94-96. Mem. LWV (v.p., treas. 1991-95) Blue Ridge Wellesley Club (pres. Charlottesvillechpt. 1989-91, dorm rep. 1996-99). Avocations: reading, music. Home: 1714 Yorktown Dr Charlottesville VA 22901-3034 Office: Huey & Bjorn 408 E Market St Ste 207 Charlottesville VA 22902-5261

MINER, JACQUELINE, political consultant; b. Mt. Vernon, N.Y., Dec. 10, 1936; d. Ralph E. and Agnes (McGee) Mariani; B.A., Coll. St. Rose, 1971, M.A., 1974; m. Roger J. Miner, Aug. 11, 1975; children: Laurence, Ronald Carmichael, Ralph Carmichael, Mark. Ind. polit. cons., Hudson, N.Y.; instr. history and polit. sci. SUNY, Hudson, 1974-79. Rep. county committeewoman, 1958-76; vice chmn. N.Y. State Ronald Reagan campaign, 1980; candidate for Rep. nomination for U.S. Senate, 1982; co-chair N.Y. state steering com. George Bush for Pres. campaign, 1986-88; vice chmn. N.Y. State Rep. Com., 1991-93; del. Rep. Convention, 1992; chmn. Coll. Consortium for Internat. Studies; mem. White House Outreach Working Group on Central Am.; co-chmn. N.Y. State Reagan Roundup Campaign, 1984-86; mem. nat. steering com. Fund for Am.'s Future, 2d cir. Hist. Com. Mem. U.S. Supreme Ct. Hist. Soc., P.E.O. Address: 1 Merlins Way Hudson NY 12534-4157

MINER, MARY ELIZABETH HUBERT, retired secondary school educator; b. Provident City, Tex., Mar. 25, 1921; d. Fred Edward and Charlotte Alice (Haynes) Hubert; m. Daniel Bowen Miner, Jan. 29, 1945 (dec. Aug. 1979); children: Charlotte Martelia Miner Williams, Daniel Bowen Jr., Mary Elizabeth Miner Martinez, Joseph Frederick, William McKinley (dec.). BA, Rice U., 1942; postgrad., U. Houston, East Tenn. State U., 1959, U. Tenn., 1961. Cert. tchr. math., English, French, history, Tex., 8th grade, math., English, French, Am. history grades 9-12. Math. tchr. Crosby (Tex.) H.S., 1942-43; office mgr. Uvalde Rock Asphalt, Houston, 1943-44; tchr. math., English, health Rogersville (Tenn.) H.S., 1947-49, 55-58; tchr. math., English, French Ch. Hill (Tenn.) H.S., 1949-51, 53-55; tchr. 8th grade Rogersville (Tenn.) City Schs., 1951-53; tchr. math. Cherokee Comprehensive H.S.,

Rogersville, 1978-84; chmn. math. and sci. planning com., Hawkins County, Tenn., 1977-79; pvt. tutor, Rogersville. Tchr. ladies Bible class Rogersville United Meth. Ch., 1952—, mem. choir, 1979—, sec., 1967-96, sec. adminstr. bd. dirs.; blood donor ARC, Rogersville, 1974-75; leader Girl Scouts Am., 1956-58, 65-72, Cub Scout den mother Boy Scouts Am., 1951-53, 66-68, 68-70. Lt. Women's Corps USNR, 1944-47. Recipient Apple award Sta. WKGB, 1956. Mem. NEA (life), Tenn. Edn. Assn. (life), Rogersville Bus. and Profl. Women (pres. 1953-55, treas. 1948-53), Am. Legion Aux. (pres.), Delta Kappa Gamma (Alpha Iota chpt. pres.), Hawkins Ret. Tchrs. Assn. (pres. 1984-85). Republican. Avocations: bridge playing, playing piano, teaching, sewing, visiting children.

MINER, ROGER JEFFREY, federal judge; b. Apr. 14, 1934; s. Abram and Anne M.; m. Jacqueline Mariani; 4 children. BS, SUNY; LLB cum laude, N.Y. Law Sch., 1956; postgrad., Bklyn. Law Sch., Judge Advocate Gen.'s Sch., U. Va.; LLD (hon.), N.Y. Law Sch., 1989, Syracuse U., 1990, Albany Law Sch./Union U., 1996; attended, Emory U. Bar: N.Y. 1956, U.S. Ct. Mil. Appeals 1956, Republic of Korea 1958, U.S. Dist. Ct. (so. and ea. dists.) N.Y. 1959. Ptnr. Miner & Miner, Hudson, N.Y., 1959-75; corp. counsel City of Hudson, 1961-64; asst. dist. atty. Columbia County, 1964, dist. atty., 1968-75; justice N.Y. State Supreme Ct., 1976-81; judge U.S. Dist. Ct. (no. dist.) N.Y., 1981-85; judge U.S. Ct. Appeals (2d cir.), Albany, N.Y., 1985—, now sr. judge; adj. assoc. prof. criminal law State U. System, N.Y., 1974-79; adj. prof. law N.Y. Law Sch., 1986-96, Albany Law Sch. Union U., 1997—; lectr. state and local bar assns.; lectr. SUNY-Albany, 1985; N.Y. Law Sch. Bd. Trustees, 1991-96; mem. jud. coun. 2d Cir., 1992-96; chmn. 2d Cir. Com. on Hist. and Commemorative Events, 1989-94; Cameras in the Courtroom Com., 1993-96, No. Dist. Hist. Com., 1981-85; State, Fed. Jud. Coun. of N.Y., 1986-91, chmn., 1990-91; Jud. Conf. of U.S. com. on fed.-state jurisdiction, 1987-92; trustee Practicing Law Inst. Mng. editor N.Y. Law Sch. Law Rev.; contbr. articles to law jours. 1st lt. JAGC, U.S. Army, 1956-59, capt. USAR ret. Recipient Dean's medal for Disting. Profl. Svc., N.Y. Law Sch., Disting. Alumnus award, Charles W. Froessel award for Valuable Contbn. to Law. Albany Jewish Fedn. award, Abraham Lincoln award, Community Svc. award Kiwanis, others; named Columbia County Man. of Yr., 1984, Ellis Island medal of Honor. Mem. ABA, N.Y. State Bar Assn., Assn. of Bar of City of N.Y., Columbia County Bar Assn., Am. Law Inst., Am. Judicature Soc., Fed. Judges Assn., Fed. Bar Coun., Am. Soc. Writers on Legal Subjects, Assn. Trial Lawyers Am., Columbia County Magistrates Assn., Supreme Ct. Hist. Soc., Columbia County Hist. Soc., N.Y. Law Sch. Alumni Assn. (hon. mem., bd. dirs.), B'nai Brith, Elks (past exalted ruler). Jewish. Office: US Ct Appeals 445 Broadway Ste 414 Albany NY 12207-2926

MINETTI, MAURIZIO, chemist, researcher; b. Rome, Sept. 25, 1945; s. Marcello and Margherita (Folinea) M.; m. Maria Robbiati, Mar. 30, 1968; children: Martina, Giulia Claudia. Chemistry, Univ. Rome, 1969. Researcher Istituto Superiore di Sanita, Rome, 1974-84, head of rsch., 1984—; head of membrane sect. Istituto Superiore De Sanita, Rome, 1982—. Contbr. articles to profl. jours. Recipient AIDS Nat. project grant Istituto Superiore Di Sanita, 1991-94, Oncology project grant CNR, 1984-87, NATO grant for Collaborative Rsch., 1984-86. Fellow Oxygen Soc. Office: Istituto Superiore di Sanita, V Regina Elena 299, 00161 Rome Italy

MINETTI, RODOLPHE HENRI, chemistry educator; b. Brussels, Belgium, June 15, 1943; s. Peter Heinrich and Liliane (Van Mol) M.; m. Janine Piteus, Dec. 10, 1966; children: Nathalie, Vincent, Marc, Christophe. PhD in Chemistry, U. Louvain, Belgium, 1969. Chartered chemist. Prof. U. Kinshasa, Congo, 1969-72, U. Bujumbura, Burundi, 1978-87, U. Lille, France, 1987—; dir. Lab. Applied Phys. Chemistry, Bruay, France, 1999—. Fellow Royal Soc. Chemistry.; mem. Am. Chem. Soc., Combustion Inst. Roman Catholic. Home: 283 Residence Flandre, 59170 Croix France Offce: U LIlle, C11, 59655 Villeneuve D'Ascq France

MING, RUISEN, educator; b. Hubei, China, Apr. 8, 1959; s. Ting Yue Ming and Lian Ying Yue; m. Yi Qing Wang, Feb. 6, 1996; children: Xiao, Tian. BS, Huibei U., Wuhan, China, 1982; M in Engring., Northwestern Poly. U., Xian, China, 1986; PhD, Heriot-Watt U., Edinburgh, Scotland, 1993. Asst. lectr. Wuhan TV U., 1982-83; vis. fellow Inst. Sound and Vibration, Southampton (U.K.) U., 1988-90; rsch. asst. acoustic rsch. unit Liverpool (U.K.) U., 1990-91; lectr., assoc. prof. Zhejiang U., Hangzhou, China, 1994-96; postdoctoral fellow U. Western Australia, Perth, 1996—. Author: Sound Intensity Techniques, 1996. Recipient Third award State Edn. China, 1994. Mem. Chinese Soc. Vibration Engring. (com. mem. 1996—), Chinese Soc. Bldg. Engring. (com. mem. 1994-98), Acoustical Soc. Am. Achievements include research in structural acoustics, noise control and architectural acoustics. Avocations: reading, music. E-mail: rming@mail.mech.uwa.edu.au. Fax: 61-8-93801024. Home: 56 Broadway, Nedlands WA 6009, Australia Office: Univ Western Australia, Nedlands WA 6907, Australia

MINGER, TERRELL JOHN, public administration and natural resource institute executive; b. Canton, Ohio, Oct. 7, 1942; s. John Wilson and Margaret Rose M.; m. Judith R. Arnold, Aug. 7, 1965; 1 child, Gabriella Sophia. BA, Baker U., 1966; MPA, Kans. U., 1969; Urban Exec. Program, MIT, 1975; Loeb fellow, Harvard U., 1976-77; Exec. Devel. Program, Stanford U., 1979; MBA, U. Colo., 1983. Asst. dir. admissions Baker U., 1966-67; asst. city mgr. City of Boulder, Colo., 1968-69; city mgr. City of Vail, Colo., 1969-79; pres., chief exec. officer Whistler Village Land Co., Vancouver, B.C., Can., 1979-81; v.p., gen. mgr. Cumberland S.W. Inc., Denver, 1981-83; exec. asst. dep. chief of staff to Gov. Colo., 1983-87; pres., chief exec. officer Sundance (Utah) Inst. for Resource Mgmt., 1986—, Sundance Enterprises Ltd., 1988-91; adj. prof. grad. sch. pub. affairs U. Colo., 1983—, Sch. Bus. U. Denver, 1992—; bd. dirs. Colo. Open Lands, Inc., 1986—; participant UN Conf. on Environment and Devel., Rio de Janeiro, 1992; chmn. environ. adv. bd. Wal-Mart, Inc., 1990—; co-chmn. task force sustainable consumption World Bus. Coun. Sustainable Devel.; co-chmn. N.Am. Telecom./Environ. Taskforce; chmn. Environ. Excellence Task Force Telecomm. Industry; environ. advisor Salt Lake City Olympic Com.; bd. dirs. Piton Found., 1996. Editor: Greenhouse/Glasnost-The Global Warming Crisis, 1990, Val Symposium Papers, 1970-79; author, editor: Growth Alternatives for Rocky Mountain West, 1976, Future of Human Settlements in the West, 1977. Spl. del. UN Habitat Conf. Human Settlements, spl. rep. to UN Environ. Program, 1992, coord. UN Global Youth Forum, 1993, 94, co-chmn. conf. on environ. and mktg., N.Y.C., 1993; founder Vail Symposium, advisor UN Environ. Program Telecom. Charter, Nairobi, Kenya, 1999; co-founder, bd. dirs. Colo. Park Found., 1985—; chair World Alpine Championship Conf., Vail, Colo., 1999; founding mem. Greenhouse/Glasnost U.S./USSR Teleconf. with Soviet Acad. Scis., 1989—; mem. pres. task force Commn. on Sustainable Devel., 1994—; co-chmn. Golf and Environ. Conf., Pebble Beach, Calif., 1995; founder, pres. Western Rendezvous, 1995—. Nat. finalist White House Fellowship, 1978; named one of B.C.'s Top Bus. Leaders for the '80s, 1980. Mem. Urban Land Inst., Colo. Acad. Pub. Adminstrn. (charter, founding mem. 1988), Colo. City Mgmt. Innovation award 1974-76), Western Gov.'s Assn. (staff coun., chmn. adv. com. 1985-86), Flatirons Athletic Club. Home: 785 6th St Boulder CO 80302-7416 Office: Ctr for Resource Mgmt 1410 Grant St Ste 307C Denver CO 80203-1846

MINGES, JOHN FRANKLIN, III, non-profit management consultant; b. Greenville, N.C., Mar. 27, 1963; s. John Franklin II and Thorburn (Whitehurst) M.; m. Sarah Jo Poindexter, Aug. 2, 1986. BSW, East Carolina U., 1986. Adminstr. pers. and pub. rels. Pepsi-Cola Bottling co., Greenville, 1986-89, v.p., 1990-98; non-profit mgmt. cons. Minges & Assocs., 1998—; exec. dir. The Greater Greenville Found., 1999—; adv. com. mem. Z. Smith Reynolds Found., 1999—. Bd. dirs. Pitt-Greenville Crime Stoppers, First Citizens Bank & Trust (Greenville br.), Greenville Industries Bd., Greenville Cmty. Shelter, Boys and Girls Clubs of Pitt County, 1989-96, 98; mem. Gov.'s Crime Commn., Raleigh, 1995—. Recipient Outstanding Cmty. Svc. award Greenville City Coun., 1988, Outstanding Svc. to N.C. award Gov. N.C., 1995, Medallion for Unusually Devoted Svc. to Youth Boys and Girls Clubs Am., 1993; named Civitan Citizen of Yr. Greenville Civitan, 1990, Greenville C. of C., 1996. Mem. Greenville-Pitt County C. of C. (bd. dirs.), Rotary Internat. (Paul Harris fellow 1991). Avocations: metal detecting, coin collecting.

MINGUS, CHARLES, III, playwright, artist; b. L.A.; s. Charles and Jeanne (Gross) M. Playwright-in-residence Ensemble Studio Theatre Johnson (Vt.) State Coll., 1975; guest lectr. Towson (Md.) State U., 1993; artist selection panelist, City of Dallas, 1994; adj. tchr. Empire State Coll., SUNY, N.Y.C., 1996—. Playwright: Cheap Trick, 1970, Out of the Death Cart, 1971, The Atlantic Crossing, 1972, The Chair, 1985; prodr. (films) A Tribute to Dr. Martin Luther King, 1969, Wilmington Ten, 1980; curator (multi-media art) Reflections, A Legacy Unearthed, Discovery of the Duane St. Burial Site, 1993, African Burial Ground; exhibited in group shows at Allan Stone Gallary, N.Y.C., 1980—. Office: Mingus Designs 1691 2nd Ave Apt 4N New York NY 10128-3293

MINGUS, LOIS KAGAN, actor, dancer, singer, choreographer, playwright; b. Boston; d. Bert S. and Edith B. (Greene) Kagan. Co. mem., actor, dancer, singer The Living Theatre, N.Y.C., 1988—; acting co. mem. Dadanewyork, N.Y.C., 1993—; acting co. mem., singer The Wycherly Sisters, N.Y.C., 1993—; acting co. mem. The Theatre of Dreams, N.Y.C., 1996—; co-prodr. The Living Theatre at the Jewish Mus., N.Y.C., 1996; choreographer, Dadanewyork and The Living Theatre, 1993—. Actor (plays) The Tablets, 1990, We Should...(A Lie), 1991, Humanity, 1991, Utopia, 1996, Mysteries and Smaller Pieces, 1996, (cabarets) Dadanewyork, 1997, The Theatre of Dreams, 1996-97. Actor/activities The Living Theatre, N.Y.C. and Europe, 1988—; co-founder of the theatre workshop Mighty Action Racket and Action Racket Lab.

MINGXIA, FU, Olympic athlete. Winner platform competition Goodwill Games, 1990; Gold medal winner in platform competition Olympic Games, Barcelona, 1992; winner gold medal springboard Olympic Games, Atlanta, 1996, winner gold medal platform, 1996. Holder world record youngest world champion platform diver, 1991, youngest gold medalist, 1992.

MING ZHONG, XIA, agricultural educator, researcher; b. Renshou, Sichuan, China, Apr. 1, 1956; s. Xia Ai Xiang and Deng Man (Rong) Z.; m. Xiong Fang Qiu, May 1, 1984; 1 child, Xia Li Wei. Diploma, Xichang Agrl. Coll., Liangshan, China, 1981; tchr.'s vocat. studies, Jiangsu Agrl. Coll., Yangzhou, Jiangsu, China, 1982. Dir. crop lab. Xichang Agrl. Coll., 1983-86, dir. dept. agr., 1986-90, lectr., 1987, head of exptl. farm, 1990-91, assoc. prof., 1991, asst. pres., 1991-92, dep. pres., 1993—; sci. cons. Liangshan State, China, 1992-97, agrl. cons., 1993-95, prof., 1995. Author: (books) Southwest China Crop Breed Science, 1992, Southwest China Crop Culture Science, 1992, Proceedings of Plateau Plant, 1992, Proceedings of Crop Physiology, 1993; chief editor: Principle of Crop Planting for High Yield, 1992 (award 1993), Physiology of Faba Bean, 1992, Crop Culture in Panxi Region, 1993, Economic Plant Culture, 1994, Agriculture Research in Panxi Region, 1994, Plant Culture Manual, 1996, Crop Culture and Tillage Science, 1996; editor: Research of Crop Breed; contbr. articles to profl jours. including: Jour. of Xichang Agrl. Coll., S.W. China Jour. of Agrl. Sci., Jour. of Agrl. Sci. Cambridge, Jour. of Agronomy and Crop Sci. (Berlin and Hamburg), Jour. of Yunnan Agrl. U., Resource Devel. and Conservation, Acta Phytoecologica et Geobo Sci., Soil and Fertilizer, Soybean Sci. (China), Sichuan Agrl. Sci, Sichuan Crop Sci., Plant Physiology Comm., World Agr. (China), Tropical Agriculture (Trinidad), Crop Culture and Tillage Sci., Sichuan Sugar Cane Sci., Australia Jour. Agrl. Sci. (13 awards for jour. articles). Rep. Sichuan Congress of Sci., Chengdu City, 1991, Xichang People's Congress, Xichang City, 1993. Recipient Model Educator Honor Sichuan Province Govt., Chengdu, 1985, 2d award of sci. Lingshan State Govt., Xichang, 1988, 90, Sichuan Province Govt., Chengdu, 1990, Model Young Rschr. award Sichuan Province Govt., Chengdu, 1991, 3d award of sci., 1993, Model Agronomist award, Liangshan State Govt., Xichang, 1991, Model scientist honor, 1992, Model Advanced Educator honor, State Coun. of China, Peking, 1992, 2d award of sci. Sichuan Edn. Com., Chengdu, 1992, Model Young Sci. award Sichuan Province Govt., Chengdu, 1995, 3rd award of Sci., China Edn. Com., Peking, 1996, 1st award of tchg. achievement Sichuan Province Govt., 1996, 2d award of tchg. achievment State Coun. China, Peking, 1996. Mem. Sichuan Assn. Crop Sci., (permanent dir. 1990-95, award 1992, dep. pres. 1995—), Sichuan Assn. Tillage (dir. 1991-96), China Assn. Agrl. Colls. and Industry, (permanent dir., 1994-98). Achievements include: Comprehensive study of the physiology, ecology and culture of the faba bean; finding the photosynthetic compensation of different leaves and the relationship between sugar-nitrogen ratio and organs abscission in faba bean; establishing the physiology of the faba bean; breeding new cultivars of rice and faba bean. Avocations: travel, flower cultivation, photography, literature, stamp collecting. Home: Xichang Agrl Coll, Xichang Sichuan 615013, China Office: Office of Xichang Agrl Coll, Ma Ping Ba, Xichang 615013, China

MINKER, WOLFGANG MANFRED, computer science researcher, educator; b. Ulm/Donau, Germany, Feb. 12, 1967; s. Manfred and Gabriele Maria (Höhn) M. BS, U. Karlsruhe, Germany, 1991, MS, 1993, PhD, 1997; diploma d'etudes approfondies (hon.), U. Paris, 1993, PhD, 1998. Cert. electronic sys. engr., computer sci. Rschr. Nat. Ctr. Sci. Rsch.-Lab. Info. Mech. and Engring. Scis., Orsay, France, 1993—; asst. prof. U. Paris, Orsay, 1999—, attachétemporaire d'enseignement et de recherche, 1997-98; asst. prof. Ecole Superieure d'Info. Electronique et Automatique, Paris, 1998—; permanent jour. reviewer European Speech Comm. Assn., 1996—, European Assn. for Computational Linguistics, 1996—, European Network in Lang. and Speech, 1996—. Author: (books) Speech Understanding for Spoken Language Systems, 1998, Compréhension automatique de la parole spontanée, 1999, Stochastically-Based Semantic Analysis, 1999, (book chpt.) Computational Models of Speech Pattern Processing, 1998. Active mem. Sinfonic Orch. Baden-Württemberg, Germany, 1983-91, Sinfonic Orch. Ulm, 1992—. Recipient ERASMUS award, 1991-93; French fellow Min. Nat. Edn., 1993-96. Mem. ESCA (Student Paper award 1997). Avocations: clarinet, biking, trekking. Office: CNRS-LIMSI, BP 133, 91403 Orsay France

MINKIEWICZ, MARIAN RAJMUND, banker; b. Zaracze, Braslaw, Poland, Apr. 26, 1927; s. Kazimierz and Eugenia (Szostak) M.; m. Irena Lewandowska, Oct. 26, 1982. M in Econs., Main Sch. Planning & Stats., Warsaw, Poland, 1953. Chief sec. internat. agreements Narodowy Bank Polski, Warsaw, 1953-60; dir. fin. dept. Ministry for Fgn. Trade, Warsaw, 1961-78; exec. pres. Bank Handlowy, Warsaw, 1978-82; adviser to Fin. Min. Warsaw, 1982-86, adviser to Min. for Fgn. Econ. Rels., 1986-93; adviser, exec. bd. dirs. Bank Rozwoju Eksportu S.A., Warsaw, 1993—. Roman Catholic. Avocations: geography, travel, foreign languages. Office: Bank Rozwoju Eksportu SA, Senatorska 18, 00-950 Warsaw Poland

MINKLER, BLATE JONES, information technology consultant; b. Ogden, Utah, Aug. 25, 1959; s. Rodney Jones and Lorna Vern Olsen; m. Pamela Ruth Stratton, Feb. 19, 1982; children: Meridy, Mandy, Aaron Blate, Andrew Garrett, Jarom Killian. BS in Math., Weber State U., 1978; MBA, U. Utah, 1985. With Systematics, Inc., 1980-93; data ctr. account mgr. Systematics, Inc., Portland, Oreg., 1989-91; corp. tng. dept. mgr. Systematics, Inc., Little Rock, 1991-93; dir. ops. Europe, Mid. East and Africa region Alltel Info. Svcs., Ltd., London, 1993-96; sr. info. tech. cons. Alltel Info. Svcs., Inc., Little Rock, 1996-2000; project mgr. yr. 2000 Bank of Norway, Oslo, 1997-2000; sr. project cons. ALLTEL Fin. Svcs. Divsn. Project Mgmt. Office, Little Rock, 2000—. Republican. Mem. LDS Ch. Achievements include development of project management methodology, a specialized approach for managing larger projects. Avocations: travel, bass guitar, hiking, reading, tennis. Office: 2240 W Sunset Pointe Dr Cedar City UT 84720-1814

MINKOFF, ALICE SYDNEY, interior designer, showroom owner; b. Washington, Jan. 29, 1948; d. Lawrence and Ellen (Altman) Glassman; children: Adam Pollin, Shane Pollin, Jacob, Sam. Student, U. Md. Owner Fredrick, Miley & Assocs., Inc., 1983—, Showroom at Washington Design Ctr.; interior designer for homebuilders, 1975-82; interior designer high end residential homes and hotel interiors, 1980—. Vol. Food and Friends, Washington, 1991—; chair Heartstrings, Washington, 1990; active AIDS awareness, Leadership Coun. of the Retreat, East Hampton, N.Y. Mem. NOW, ACLU, Nat. Trust Hist. Preservation, Nature Conservancy, Amagansett Village Improvement Soc., Human Rights Campaign. Avocations: gourmet cooking, antique collecting, dolls, quilts. Home: PO Box 7064 Amagansett NY 11930-7064 also: Watergate West Penthouse 1 2700 Virginia Ave NW Washington DC 20037-1908 Office: Matches at Miley 300 D St SW Ste 401 Washington DC 20024-4705

MINKOV, DORIAN ASENOV, science educator; b. Gabrovo, Bulgaria, June 11, 1957; arrived in Japan, 1996; s. Asen Trivonov Minkov and Velichka Dimova Dimitrova; m. Mariana Dancheva Vasileva; 1 child, Asen. MSc in Physics, Sofia (Bulgaria) U., 1980; PhD in Physics, Bulgarian Acad. Scis., Sofia, 1988. Cert. in physics. Rsch. assoc. Inst. Microelectronics & Optoelectronics, Botevgrad, Bulgaria, 1980-88, sr. rsch. assoc., 1988-91; postdoctoral fellow Rand Afrikaans U., Johannesburg, South Africa, 1991-92; postdoctoral fellow U. Natal, Durban, South Africa, 1992-94, sr. lectr., 1994-96; assoc. prof. Tohoku U., Sendai, Japan, 1996—. Contbr. articles to profl. jours. Mem. Optical Soc. Am. Avocations: tennis, working out at gym, jogging, swimming, table tennis. Office: Tohoku U, Fracture Rsch Inst, Aoba-ku Sendai 980-8579, Japan

MINKOWSKI, ALEXANDRE, neonatology educator, retired; b. Paris, Dec. 5, 1915; s. Eugeniusz and Franciszka (Brockmann) M.; m. Marcelle Thiedot, 1942 (div. 1943); 1 child, Marianne; m. Mary-Ann Wade, Apr. 2, 1950; children: Anoine, Nicolas, Marc, Laurent. MD, U. René Descartes, Paris, 1944. Rockefeller fellow Harvard U., Cambridge, Mass., 1946-47; chief of staff Faculté Cochin, Paris, 1962; prof. pediatrics U. René Descartes, 1966-80, prof. emeritus, 1980, ret., 1980; dir. Ctr. for Rsch. in Biology of the Foetus and the Newborn INSERM, 1962-80. Author: Le Mandarin aux Pieds nus: Entretiens avec Jean Lacouture, 1975, Pour un Nouveau-né Sans Risque, 1983, Ce que je Crois Grasset, 1997. Mem. UNICEF, 1977—; counsellor Conseil Regional D'Ile de France, 1992—; sci. counselor Partage Avec les Enfants du Monde, Paris, 1992—. With French Army, 1939-45. Recipient Prix Monthion Acad. Scis., 1965, Prix de la Maternité European Perinatal Soc., 1987, Nils Rosen von Rosenstein Medal, U. Uppsala, 1999. Fellow Royal Coll. Physicians, Royal Coll Pediatrics and Child Health (London); mem. Am. Pediat. Soc. (hon.), Neonatal Soc. U.K. Avocations: music, sports, skiing, mountain climbing, tennis. Office: Partage Avec Enfants Monde, 27 BD Saint-Michel, 75007 Paris France

MINNA, ANTHONY JOSEPH, lawyer; b. Toronto, Ont., Can., Aug. 13, 1964; arrived in Switzerland, 1999; s. Antonio and Anne (Capicciotti) M. Student, Johannes-Gutenberg U., Mainz, Germany, 1985-86; BA with honours, U. Toronto, 1987, LLB, 1991; LLM with distinction, U. Brussels, 1992. Bar: N.Y. 1992, Ont. 1994. Articling student Siskind, Cromarty, Ivey & Dowler, London, Ont., 1992-93; lawyer Copeland, McKenna, Toronto, 1995, Walch & Schurti, Vaduz, Liechtenstein, 1996-99; compliance ofcr., company sec. Clariden Trust Mgmt., Zurich, Switzerland, 1999—. Avocations: cycling, swimming, tennis.

MINNER, THOMAS O., marketing executive; b. Chgo., Jan. 3, 1956; s. Robert Schermerhorn and Arleen Minner; m. Mary Anderson; children: Allison, Brent, Courtney, Drew, Summer. BS in Bus. Adminstrn., U. Ill., 1978; MBA, Northwestern U., 1980. Mktg. mgmt. trainee PPG Industries, Inc., Pitts., 1978-79; market devel. mgr. Gould Inc., Mpls., 1980-89; v.p., gen. mgr. Automotive Battery Div. GNB, Inc., Atlanta, 1990-96; pres., CEO GNB Technologies, Inc., Atlanta, 1997—. Bd. dirs. Students in Free Enterprise. Mem. Battery Coun. Internat. (bd. dirs.). Home: 3485 Newport Bay Dr Alpharetta GA 30005-7820 Office: GNB Tech 13000 Deerfield Pkwy Bldg 200 Alpharetta GA 30004-5026

MINNERLY, ROBERT WARD, retired headmaster; b. Yonkers, N.Y., Mar. 21, 1935; s. Richard Warren and Margaret Marion (DeBrocky) M.; m. Sandra Overmire, June 12, 1957; children: Scott Ward, John Robert, Sydney Sue. AB, Brown U., 1957; MAT, U. Tex., Arlington, 1980. Tchr., coach Rumsey Hall Sch., Washington, Conn., 1962-64; tchr., coach Berkshire Sch., Sheffield, Mass., 1964-70, asst. head, 1969-70, headmaster, 1970-76; dir. Salisbury (Conn.) Summer Sch. Reading and English, 1970; prin. upper sch. Ft. Worth Country Day Sch., 1976-86; headmaster Charles Wright Acad., Tacoma, Wash., 1986-96; ednl. cons. The Edn. Group, 1996-2000; cons. Tarrant County Coalition on Substance Abuse, 1982-84; mem. mayor's task force Tacoma Edn. Summit, 1991-92. Contbr. articles to profl. jours. Bd. dirs. Tacoma/Pierce County Good Will Games Art Coun., 1989; mem. exec. com. Am. Leadership Forum, 1991-95; bd. dirs. Broadway Ctr. for Performing Arts, Tacoma, 1988-94, 96-98, mem. exec. com., 1990-93; elected Wash. State Bd. Edn., 1996—. Named Adminstr. of Yr. Wash. Journalism Edn. Assn., 1991. Mem. Pacific N.W. Assn. Ind. Schs. (chmn. long-range planning com. 1989-92, exec. com. 1990-92, 91, v.p. 1994). Republican. Presbyterian. Home and Office: 4214 39th Avenue Ct NW Gig Harbor WA 98335-8029

MINO DE KASPAR, HERMINIA, microbiologist, researcher; b. Asuncion, Paraguay, Apr. 26, 1947; arrived in Germany, 1977; d. Julio Mino and Sabina Sotelo; m. Peter Kaspar, June 16, 1977; children: Karin, Christina, Sonja. D in Biochemistry, U. Nat. Asuncion, 1973; diplome d'etudes aprofondues, U. Tech. de Lille, France, 1975; PhD in Biochemistry, Free U. Berlin, 1980. Rsch. investigator Inst. Nat. Tech. and Normalization, Asuncion, 1976-77, Schering AG, Berlin, 1977-80, Boehringer Mannheim GMBH, Tutzing, Germany, 1981-85; cons. Inst. Investigations in Scis. and Health, Asuncion, 1986-89; head microbiol. rsch. lab. Eye Clin. of Univ. Hosp., Munich, 1989—; cons. eye dept. Kenyatta Hosp., Nairobi, Kenya, 1993—, Inst. Investigations in Scis. and Health, Asuncion, 1992—, eye dept. Hosp. Gen. of Mex., Mexico City, 1996—, Stanford (Calif.) U. Sch. Medicine, 1999—. Mem. ARVO, Germany Mycology Assn. Office: Stanford U Sch Medicine Boswell Bldg Rm A-157 Stanford CA 94305-5308

MINOGUE, KENNETH ROBERT, political science educator, writer; b. Palmerston North, New Zealand, Sept. 11, 1930; arrived in England, 1951; s. Dennis Francis Minogue and Eunice Pearl Porter; m. Valerie Pearson Hallett, June 14, 1954; children: Nicholas Robert, Eunice Karen Addis. BA, Sydney (Australia) U., 1949; BSc in Econs., London Sch. Econs., 1955. Asst. lectr. pub. adminstrn. U. Exeter, Eng., 1955-56; asst. lectr. polit. sci. London Sch. Econs., 1955-60, from lectr. to sr. lectr. to reader, 1960-85, prof., 1985-95, prof. emeritus, 1995—; cons. in field. Author: The Liberal Mind, 1963, Nationalism, 1967, The Concept of a University, 1974, Alien Powers: The Pure Theory of Ideology, 1985, Politics: A Very Short Introduction, 1995, The Silencing of Society: The True Cost of the Lust for News, 1997, Waitangi Morality Reality, 1998; editor: Essays in Conservative Realism, 1996; co-editor: (with A.R. de Crespigny) Contemporary Political Philosophies, 1976. Chmn. Bruges Group, 1991-93. Mem. Garrick Club. Avocations: tennis, walking, opera. Home: 43 Perrymead St. London SW6 3SN, England Office: London Sch Econs, Houghton St, London WC2A 2AE, England

MINOLA, GIUSEPPE GIANLUIGI, chemist; b. Como, Italy, Apr. 14, 1954; s. Luciano Minola and Milena Bresciani; m. Marina Bergna, Sept. 15, 1984; children: Stefano, Silvia. Degree in chemistry, U. Milan, 1979; degree in chem. prof., Tech. Init., Como, 1973. With Roche, Mi, Italy, 1981-84, product mgr., 1984-87, project leader, 1987-89, head, 1989-92, divsnl. mgr., 1992-98, gen. mgr., 1999—; v.p. Ambisuredice, Mi, 1998. With Italian Nat. Army, 1979-80. Home: Via Trento 14, 22044 Invericio Italy Office: Roche Diagnostics, V G G B Stueeli 110, 20052 Monza Italy Address: Roche Diagnostics spa, Viale GB Stucchi 110, 20052 Monza Italy

MINOR, MARIAN THOMAS, elementary and secondary school educational consultant; b. Richmond, Va., Apr. 16, 1933; d. James Madison and Florence Elwood (Edwards) M. BS, U. Va., 1955; MEd, William and Mary Coll., 1968; postgrad., Va. Commonwealth U., 1987-88. Cert. guidance, health and phys. edn. Educator Richmond (Va.) Pub. Schs., 1955-90, ednl. cons., 1990—; educator Sch. Nursing Med. Coll. Va., Richmond, 1958-68; camp dir. Manakin, Va., 1956-68; nat. basketball ofcl. Richmond (Va.) Bd. Ofcls., 1952-77; mem. faculty adv. com. Albert Hill Middle Sch., Richmond, 1965-90, dept. chmn., 1960-90, Tchr. of Yr., 1980; textbook adoption Richmond (Va.) Pub. Sch., 1975, 85, curriculum planner, 1978-79, 82-83, 84-85; PTA coord. Albert Hill Middle Sch., Richmond, 1985-89, chmn. self-study and accreditation team, 1987-88. Mem. Sherwood Park Civic Assn., Richmond, 1960-98; v.p. alumni weekend Mary Washington Alumni Assn., Fredericksburg, Va., 1965, 66, v.p. annual giving, 1967; chmn. basketball ofcl. examiners Richmond Bd. Women Ofcls., 1966-76; bd. dirs., homeowner adv., constrn. crewman, family svcs. com. Habitat for Humanity, 1994—, Blitz Builds 2000 adv. chmn.; mem. Albert Hill PTA (Outstanding Svc. award 1988); mem. exec. com. Northminster Bapt. Ch., 1991-94, 99—, deacon, clk., 97-97, premises chair, 1991-94, mem. by-laws revision com., 1986, 98, 99, srs. task force chmn., regional Befriender Ministry adv. coun.

Recipient J.C. Penney Golden Rule award, 1996, Outstanding Vol. award Habitat for Humanity, 1998. Mem. AAUW, AAHPERD, Va. Health Phys. Edn. Assn., Va. Ret. Tchrs. Assn., Train Collectors Assn., King and Queen Hist. Soc., Mortar Bd., Alpha Phi Sigma, Kappa Delta Pi. Republican. Avocations: gardening, genealogy, local history, historical preservation, antiques. Home and Office: 1507 Brookland Pky Richmond VA 23227-4707

MINOR, THOMAS, medical researcher; b. Limburg/Lahn, Hessen, Germany, June 4, 1961; s. Ernst and Ursula (Steup) M. MD, U. Cologne, Germany, 1989, PhD, 1995. Physician Svc. de Cardiologie Clermont, France, 1986-87; med. officer NATO, Brunssum, The Netherlands, 1987-88; rsch. assoc. Inst. for Exptl. Medicine, U. Cologne, 1988-90, rschr., 1991—, physician II dept. surgery, 1990-91, sr. rschr. exptl. surgery, 1992-97; prof. surg. rsch., head divsn. Surg. Clinic, U. Bonn, 1997—. Contbr. articles to profl. jours. Capt. German Mil., 1987-88. Recipient Forum award Soc. NRW Surgery, 1992, 94, German Soc. Surgery, 1998, Folkert O. Belzer award Internat. Soc. for Organ Sharing, 1999. Mem. German Soc. Surgery, European Soc. for Surg. Rsch., Internat. Pathophysiol. Soc., Transplantation Soc., European Soc. for Organ Transplantation. Office: U Bonn Divsn Surg Rsch, Sigmund Freud Str 75, 53127 Bonn Germany

MINOR-EVANS, LESLIE, psychology educator, writer; b. Seattle, Jan. 29, 1955; d. Jack Kaylor and Barbara Anne Minor; m. Robert Evans, May 20, 1995; children: Demitrius, Zamir, Jawan. BA, U. Wash., 1982; MA, U. Calif., Irvine, 1990, PhD, 1995. Assoc. prof. Ctrl. Oreg. C.C., Bend, Oreg., 1992—; adj. prof. U. Oreg., Eugene, Linfield Coll., McMinnville, Oreg., Oreg. State U., Corvallis, U. Calif., Irvine, Concordia U., Irvine, San Bernardino State U., 1982—; rsch. cons. Sustainable Resources Devel. Group, Hood River, Oreg.; program evaluator J Bar J Youth Svcs., Bend, Oreg.; field site supr. Vt. Coll. Norwich U., Montpelier, Vt.; rsch. supr. Lindenwood U., St. Charles, Mo. Co-author: Human Relations: Strategies for Success, 1995, Working with People, 1997. Mem. adv. bd. Big Bros./Big Sisters, Bend, Oreg.; bd. dirs. Seattle-King County Head Start, Seattle, Neighborhood House Social Svcs., Seattle. Mem. APA, Western Psychol. Assn., Pacific Sociol. Assn., Soc. for Psychol. Study Social Issues, Coun. for Tchg. Undergrad. Psychology, Oreg. Psychol. Assn. Avocation: outdoor recreational activities.

MINOVES-TRIQUELL, JULI, diplomat, economist, political scientist, writer; b. Andorra la Vella, Andorra, Aug. 15, 1969; s. Juli Minoves-Pallerola and Pilar Triquell-Seró. Lic. in Econ. and Social Scis., Fribourg (Switzerland) U., 1991; MA in Polit. Sci., Yale U., 1993, MPhil in Internat. Rels., 1994. Adviser staff orgn. Elec. Forces of Andorra, Encamp, 1988; econ. adviser Ministry of Fin., Andorra la Vella, 1989, BBV Bank, Brussels, 1990; 1st Andorran diplomat, 1993; min. plenipotentiary, dep. permanent rep., chargé d'affaires UN, N.Y., 1994-95, amb. extraordinary/plenipotentiary permanent rep. Andorra, 1995—; amb. extraordinary/plenipotentiary permanent rep. Andorra U.S., 1996—, Can., 1996—; part-time writer Andorra 7 Mag., 1986-88; prof. Catalan, Migrosklubschule, Bern, Switzerland, 1989-91; tchg. asst. constnl. law Yale U., New Haven, 1993; part-time adviser UN, N.Y., 1993, part-time counselor, 1993-94, chmn. Western European and other states group, N.Y., 1994, v.p. UN Pledging Conf. for World Food Programme, 1994, alt. head del. of Andorra, World Summit for Social Devel., Copenhagen, 1995, pres. VINCI Group, N.Y., 1995, v.p. UN Pledging Conf. for Devel. Activities, N.Y., 1995, chmn. Western European and other states group, N.Y., 1996, v.p. Gen. Assembly UN, N.Y., 1996—. Author: (novel) Segles de Memèria, 1989, (short stories) Les pedres del diable, 1992. Recipient Nat. Lit. award Fiter i Rossell, 1988, El futur de les Valls for works in econ. and social scis., 1989, Lit. award Sant Carles Borromeau, 1991; Credit Andorra fellow, 1991. Mem. Ofcl. Bd. Economists Andorra, Am. Polit. Sci. Assn., Mory's (New Haven), Yale Club (N.Y.C.). Office: Permanent Mission of Principality of Andorra UN 2 United Nations Plz Fl 25 New York NY 10017-4403*

MINOW, JOSEPHINE BASKIN, civic volunteer; b. Chgo., Nov. 3, 1926; d. Salem N. and Bessie (Sampson) Baskin; m. Newton N. Minow, May 29, 1949; children: Nell, Martha, Mary. BS, Northwestern U., 1948. Asst. to advt. dir. Mandel Brothers Dept. Store, Chgo., 1948-49; tchr. Francis W. Parker Sch., Chgo., 1949-50; vol. in civil and charitable activities, 1950—; bd. dirs. Juvenile Protective Assn., Chgo., 1958—; pres. Juvenile Protective Assn., 1973-75; bd. dirs. Parnham Trust, Beaminster, Dorset, Eng. Author: Marty the Broken Hearted Artichoke, 1997. Founder, coord. Children's div. Hospitality and Info. Svc., Washington, 1961-63; mem. Caucus Com., Glencoe, Ill., 1965-69; co-chmn. spl. study on juvenile justice Chgo. Community Trust, 1978-80; chmn. Know Your Chgo., 1980-83; bd. dirs. Chgo. Coun. Fgn. Rels.; trustee Chgo. Hist. Soc., Ravinia Festival Assn.; mem. women's bd. Field Mus., U. Chgo.; founding mem., v.p. women's bd. Northwestern U., 1978; bd. govs. Chgo. Symphony, 1966-73, 76—; mem. Citizens Com. Juvenile Ct. of Cook County, 1985-96; exec. com. Northwestern U. Libr. Coun., 1974-96; co-chair grandparents' adv. com. Chgo. Children's Mus., 1999; bd. dirs. Jane Addams Juvenile Ct. Found. Recipient spl. award Chgo. Sch. and Workshop for Retarded, 1975, Children's Guardian award Juvenile Protective Assn., 1993. Mem. Hebrew Immigrant Aid Soc. (bd. dirs. 1977-98, award 1988), Friday Club, Northmoor Country Club. Democrat. Jewish. Office: Chgo Hist Soc Clark St at North Ave Chicago IL 60614

MINSKER, KARL SAMOJLOVICH, chemistry educator; b. Kiev, Ukraine, June 14, 1929; came to Russia, 1930; s. Samuel Sergeevich and Dina Mikhaelevna (Chudinskaja) M.; m. Faina Ivanovna Deltzova, Nov. 12, 1969; children: Sergey, Vladimir. Diploma in Engring. Tech. Chemistry, Inst. Fine Chem. Tech., Moscow, 1952; DSc in Organic Chemistry, State U., Niznii Novgorod, Russia, 1958; PhD in Polymer Sci., Karpov's Phys.-Chem. Inst., Moscow, 1968; Academician, Bashkoztostan Rep. Acad. Sci., Russia, 1991. Superior shift chem. factory Dzerzhinsk, Gorkii, Russia, 1952-53; sci. collaborator, chief lab. Kazgin's Rsch. Inst. Chem. & Tech. of Polymers, Dzerzhinsk, 1953-68; head chair macromolecular and colloide chemistry, prof. Bashkir State U., Ufa, 1968—, head problem lab., 1979—; sci. head lab. ionic polymerization Inst. Chem. Bashkir Br. Acad. Sci., USSR, Ufa, 1968-83; head divsn. chem. and biochem. problems Rsch. Inst. Problems Transport Energy Resources, Ufa, 1993-96; vice-chmn. Ecological-Sci.-Technic Assn. Acad. Sci. Bachkortostan Republic, Ufa, 1993—; mem. Main Commn. Permanent Exhbn. Nat. Econ. USSR. Author: Destruction and Stabilization of Poly(Vinyl)chloride, in Russian, 1972, 79, in Chinese, 1985, Degradation and Stabilization of Polymers on the Base of Vinyl Chloride, in Russian, 1982, in English, 1988, The Second Time Treatment of Polymer, 1985, Isobutilene and Their Polymers, 1986, Complex Processing of Second Time Products of Working up of Cotton-Plant in Production of Polymers Materials, in Russian, 1988, Fast Polymerization Processes, in English, 1996, The New Unification-Energy and Resource Saving up High Productive Technologies Elevating Ecological Cleanness on the Basis Tube Turbulent Reactors, in Russian, 1996, Quantum-Chemicals Aspects of the Cationic Polymerization, in Russian, 1996, in English, 1997, Ceulluloses: The Cellulose Esters and Plastics on her Base (for Examples of the Acetate Celluloses), in Russian, 1996, The Chemistry of Chlorin-Containing Polymers: Degradation, Stabilization, Syntheses, New Horizons, in English, 2000; mem. editl. bd. Bashkir Chem. Jour., Russian Polymer News, Chem. & Biochem. Kinetics; contbr. numerous articles to profl. jours.; patentee in field. Named Hon. Sci. Worker, Bashkortostan Republic, 1977, Russia Fedn., 1987, Man. of Yr., U.S., 1994-95, Internat. Man of Yr., Eng., 1995-96; recipient diploma of honor, 1991, gold medal of laureate, 1993, 2 silver medals, 1982, 89, bronze medal, 1968, 74, silver medal 20th Century award for achievement in field of tng. and sci., 1900-2000, U.S., Kargins Premium of Russian Acad. Sci., 1999, signature sign of honor of Mendeleev's Russian Chem. Soc., 1996, Main Commn. Permanent Exhbn. Nat. Econ. USSR and Russia, Exhbn. Achievement Silver medal. Mem. Acad. Sci. Bashkortostan Republic (academician-sec. chem. divsn., 1999—), N.Y. Acad. Sci., Soc. Plastics Engrs., Russian Mendeleev's Union Chem. (vice-chair Bashkortostan Repub. 1992—). Avocations: science, stamps, sports, coins, ballet. Home: 1 Frunze Str App 19, 450076 Ufa 76, Russia Office: Chem Div Acad Sci Bashkort, 15 Kizov Str, 450077 Ufa 77, Russia

MINSKY, BRUCE WILLIAM, lawyer; b. Queens, N.Y., Sept. 28, 1963; m. Jill R. Heinter, May 1992; children: Aryeh Hanan, Elisheva Yael, Calev Betzalel, Rephel Akive. BA in Polit. Sci., Boston U., 1985; JD, Southwestern U., 1988; LLM in Am. Banking, Boston U., 1989. Bar: Calif. 1988, Conn. 1989, N.Y. 1990, U.S. Dist. Ct. (ea. and so. dist.), U.S. Ct. Appeals. Assoc. Quirk & Bakalor, N.Y.C., 1989-91; house counsel, v.p. Banco Popular N.Am., N.Y.C., 1991—, Banco Poplur N. Am., 1999. Atty. Monday Night Law Pro Bono Svcs., N.Y.C. Mem. Assn. of Bar of City of N.Y. (mem. young lawyers com. 1993-95). Avocations: music, sports, literature. Office: 7 W 51st St New York NY 10019-6910

MINTER, ALAN HUNTRESS, lawyer; b. San Antonio, Feb. 21, 1939; s. Merton Melrose Minter and Katherine Logan Huntress; m. Patricia West, May 31, 1964; children: Katherine Ruth, Patricia West. Student, Brown U., 1957-59; BA, U. Tex., 1962, JD, 1965. Bar: Tex., U.S. Supreme Ct. 1971, U.S. Tax Ct. 1969, U.S. Ct. Claims 1969, U.S. Ct. Mil. Appeals 1971, U.S. Ct. Customs and Patent Appeals 1971, U.S. Ct. Appeals (5th cir.) 1986, U.S. Dist. Ct. (no. and we. dists.) Tex. 1967, U.S. Dist. Ct. (ea. dist.) Tex. 1968, U.S. Dist. Ct. (so. dist.) Tex. 1970. Asst. atty. Atty. Gen.'s Office, State of Tex., Austin, 1965-71; pvt. practice Austin, 1971—. Mem. adv. com. History Aviation Collection U. Tex., Austin; bd. dirs. Young Man's Bus. League, Austin, 1972, St. Andrew's Episcopal Sch. Austin, 1973-76, Tex. Hist. Found., 1983-85, Les Patrons Paramount Theatre Performing Arts, 1978-82; mem. ad hoc hist. zoning com. City of Austin, 1973; mem. citizen adv. com. Tex. Constl. Revision Com., 1973; bd. dirs. Austin Heritage Soc., 1974-81, chmn. properties com., 1975-76, co-chmn. properties com., 1976-77, 2d v.p., 1978-79; mem. steering com. Tex. Heritage Coun. Tex. Hist. Found., 1977-80, 81-83, v.p. edn., 1978-80; mem. adv. coun. Winedale Hist. Ctr. U. Tex., 1978-87, treas., 1984-85; vice-chmn. City Austin Tex. Libr. Commn., 1980-81, chmn., 1981-84; trustee Elisabet Ney Mus. Assn., 1980-81. Fellow Tex. Bar Found.; mem. ABA (vice chmn. 1981-85, hist. preservation and easement com. real property, probate and trust law sect.), ATLA, SCV, Comml. Law League Am., State Bar Tex., Sheriff's Assn. Tex. (assoc.), Tex. Old Fts. and Missions Restoration Assn., Old Trail Drivers Assn. Tex., State Assn. Tex. Pioneers, Sons Republic Tex., Travis County Bar Assn. (bd. dirs. chmn. estate planning and probate law sect. 1994—, bd. dirs. estate planning and probate law sect. 1995-96), Order Alamo, Order Sons Hermann State Tex., German Club, Phi Alpha Delta. Avocations: hunting, fishing, travel, reading, writing. Home: 1602 W Lynn St Austin TX 78703-3446

MINTON, KENNETH JOSEPH, company director; b. Jan. 17, 1937; s. Henry and Lilian (Moore) M.; m. Mary Wilson, 1961; 1 child. BSc in Mining Engring., 1st class honors, Leeds (Eng.) U. Mgmt. position Unilever, Eng. and France, 1960-68; mgmt. position Laporte Plc, 1968-79, chief exec., mng. dir., 1979-95; dir. John Mowlem & Co. Plc, Middlesex, Eng., 1994-98, chmn. bd. dirs., 1995-98; bd. dirs., chmn. SGB Group Plc, London, 1996—; dir. Solvay, S.A., 1996—; bd. dirs. Jeyes Group Plc, chmn. bd. dirs., 1993-96; chmn. bd. dirs. Arjo Wiggins Appleton p.l.c., 1997—. Trustee Industry and Parliament Trust, 1997—. Mem. Soc. Chem. Industry (pres. 1996-98, Centenary medal 1994), European Coun. Fedns. of Chem. Industry (bd. dirs. 1991-95). Avocations: gardens, fine art, walking, charity. Office: Arjo Wiggins Appleton plc, Times Place 45 Pall Mall, Isleworth London SW1Y 5JG, England

MINTSIS, MOISEY YAKOB, metal products company executive; b. Samarkand, Uzbekistan, Apr. 25, 1928; s. Yakob Moisey and Klara Efim (Slavina) M.; m. Adelaida Taras Denisenko, Feb. 1, 1953; 1 child, Alla. Electrical engr. degree, Tasehkent, 1951; candidate of sci., Leningrad, 1973. From master to tech. dir. Aluminium Plant, Novokuznetsk, 1952-95; prof. Tech. U., Novokuznetsk, 1995—. Author: Ecologue of Production of Aluminium, 1997, Metallurgy of Secondary Aluminium, 1998, Metallurgy of Aluminum, 1999. Mem. Acad. Ecology. Avocation: pencil collector. Home: POB N622, Novokuznetsk 654034, Russia Office: Tech U, Kirov St 42, Novokuznetsk 654007, Russia

MINTZ, JEFFRY ALAN, lawyer; b. N.Y.C., Sept. 15, 1943; s. Aaron Herbert and Lillian Betty (Greenspan) M.; m. Susan Politzer, Aug. 22, 1979; children: Jennifer, Melanie, Jonathan. AB, Tufts U., 1964; LLB, Rutgers U., 1967; postgrad., U. Pa. Law Sch., 1968-70. Bar: D.C. 1968, N.Y. 1970, U.S. Supreme Ct. 1972, N.J. 1973, Pa. 1983; registered mediator, N.J. Law clk. to judge U.S. Ct. Appeals, New Orleans, 1967-68; asst. defender Defender Assn. Phila., 1968-70; asst. counsel NAACP Legal Def. and Ednl. Fund, N.Y.C., 1970-74; dir. Office Inmate Advocacy, N.J. Dept. Pub. Adv., Trenton, 1974-81; pvt. practice Haddonfield and Medford, N.J, 1982; ptnr. Stein & Shapiro, Medford, 1982-83, Cherry Hill, N.J., 1983-84; ptnr. Mesirov, Gelman, Jaffe, Cramer & Jamieson, Cherry Hill, Phila., 1984-90, Schlesinger, Mintz & Pilles, Mt. Holly, N.J., 1990-92; pvt. practice Mt. Holly, 1992—. Trustee Congregation M'Kor Shalom, Cherry Hill, 1990-97; mem. Burling County and Mt. Laurel Dem. Coun. Com., 1993-95; chair Moorestown Dem. Com., 1995—. Mem. ABA, ATLA, N.J. Bar Assn. (del., gen. coun. 1986-88, 89-91), D.C. Bar Assn., Camden County Bar Assn., Burlington County Bar Assn. (trustee 1989-92), Assn. Trial Lawyers N.J. (bd. govs. 1990-95), Barrister, Burlington Am. Inn. of Ct. (founding mem., vice chair, 1999-2000, dist. fee arbitration com. 1997-01, chair 2000-01). Jewish. Home: 224 Quakerbridge Ct Moorestown NJ 08057-2823 Office: 129 High St Mount Holly NJ 08060-1401

MINTZ, KENNETH ANDREW, librarian; b. Plattsburgh, N.Y., Mar. 15, 1951; s. Max Manuel and Mildred Patricia (O'Rourke) M.; m. Melinda Lou Harris, Jan. 12, 1974 (div. Oct. 31, 1975). BA, U. Redlands, 1973; MLS, So. Conn. State U., 1978. Cert. profl. libr., N.J. Temporary cataloger Medford (Mass.) Pub. Libr., 1980; libr. Bayonne (N.J.) Pub. Libr., 1980-88; cataloger Hoboken (N.J.) Pub. Libr., 1991-99, head tech. svcs. dept., 1999—, newsletter editor, 1999—; book reviewer Libr. Jour., N.Y.C., 1988-93; head drama group Community Ch. of N.Y., N.Y.C., 1993—. Author: The Holy Ghost, 1980, (play) Black Fire in the Chalice, 2000; newsletter editor Unitarian Soc. Rutherford, N.J., 1984-85; asst. newsletter editor First Unitarian Soc. New Haven, 1979-80; contbr. book revs. to Am. Book Rev., Wilson Libr. Bulletin, Libr. and Culture. Mem. ch. coun. Cmty. Ch. of N.Y., 1988-90; mem. Friends of the N.Y. Pub. Libr., 1997—, Mark Twain House, Hartford, Conn., 1999—. Recipient Quill Poetry award Quill Books, 1991, Essay prize Hudson County Writing Festival, Bayonne, 1994, Bayonne Writers Legion of Honor award, 1989, 98, Editor's Choice award Nat. Libr. Poetry, 1989, 96, Garden state writing Challenge Poetry award, 1998, awards N.J. Superbowl of Writing, Halloween Story, 1995, Playwriting, 1995, Essay, 1996, 97, Short Story, 1997, Bayonne Writers Spl. Legion award, 1996, Christmas Story prize Hudson County Writing Festival, Bayonne, 1997, Bayonne Writers Group Founder's Comp. award, 1997, Garden State Writing Challenge Essay award, 1997, N.J. Olympics of Writing essay award, 1998; N.J. Olympics of Writing playwriting award, 1998, Legion of Honor award Bayonne Poetry Writers', 1997, Legion of Honor award Bayonne Essay Writers, 1998, award Bayonne Writers Group Short Story Reading Competition, 1998, award Bayonne Writers Group Short Story Reading competition, 1999, others; named Poet of Yr., 1994, Writer of Yr., 1995, N.J. Essay Writer of Yr., 1997; named to Bayonne Writers' Wall of Fame, 1996, Honor Soc. Bayonne Writer's Group, 1997. Mem. ALA, N.J. Libr. Assn., Poetry Soc. of Am., Bayonne Writers Group (v.p. 1986), Acad. of Am. Poets, Modern Poetry Assn., Hoboken Creative Alliance, N.Y. Acad. Scis., Poets House, Poet's Guild, House Seven Gables Settlement Assn., Irish Am. Cultural Inst., Irish Am. Partnership. Democrat. Unitarian-Universalist. Avocations: history, piano, chess, bowling, fishing. Office: Hoboken Pub Libr 500 Park Ave Hoboken NJ 07030-3906

MINTZ, RONALD STEVEN, lawyer, photojournalist; b. Bklyn., Aug. 16, 1947; s. Herbert and Phoebe (Gilman) M.; children: Raymond, Gloria. JD, Western State U., Fullerton, Calif., 1978. Bar: Calif. 1978, U.S. Dist. Ct. (no., so., ea. and cen. dists.) Calif. 1978, U.S. Ct. Appeals (9th cir.) 1979, U.S. Supreme Ct. 1982. Pvt. practice law Berkeley, Calif., 1978-80, Canyon Country, Calif., 1980-83, Chino, Calif., 1983-84, Ontario, Calif., 1984-88, Pomona, Calif., 1988-91, San Fernando, Calif., 1991-92; pvt. practice Joshua Tree, Calif., 1993-94, Hollywood, Calif., 1994—; founder legal aid orgn. to protect civil rights Tactical Law Command. Producer film on air pollution: State of Emergency, 1971, videotape documentary: America-A True Glimpse, 1979; publisher opposition newspaper: Ten Penny Press. Recipient Am. Jurisprudence awards Bancroft Whitney Law Book Pub. Co., 1977, 78. Mem. Lawyers in Mensa (charter), State Bar Calif. (criminal law sect. 1983-84, police misconduct lawyer referral service), Mensa. Avocations: photography, film, video, guns, cars. Fax: 323-733-3768. Office: PO Box 3151 Hollywood CA 90078-3151

MINTZ, SAMUEL ISAIAH, English language educator, writer; b. N.Y.C., Nov. 20, 1923; Nathan and Anna (Sheinkman) M.; m. Eleanor Streichler, Mar. 2, 1947; children: Joel Alan, Jonathan. BA, Bklyn. Coll., 1948; MA, Columbia U., 1949, PhD, 1958. Prof. City Coll. N.Y., N.Y.C., 1948-86, prof. doctoral faculty, 1965-86, prof. emeritus, 1986—; prof. emeritus CUNY Grad. Ctr., N.Y.C., 1986—; English faculty Cambridge U., Eng., 1964-65; vis. prof. Columbia U., N.Y.C., 1969-70, Barnard Coll., N.Y.C., 1987-89; vis. fellow Wolfson Coll. Oxford U., 1973. Author: The Hunting of Leviathan, 1962, 2d edit., 1996; editor: From Smollett to Henry James, 1980; founder, editor History Ideas Newsletter, N.Y.C., 1954-60; contbr. articles to profl. jours. With Army Air Force, 1943-46. Fulbright fellow Cambridge U., 1956-57, rsch. scholar, 1964-65, Guggenheim fellow, 1964. Office: City U NY Grad Sch 365 5th Ave New York NY 10016-4309

MINTZER, EDWARD CARL, JR., lawyer; b. Phila., Sept. 17, 1949; s. Edward Carl and Jean Marie (McGinnis) M.; m. Colleen Anne Marie Hanratty, June 6, 1975; children: Catherine Marie, Elizabeth Seton, Edward Carl III, Conor Andrew. BA, St. Charles Coll., 1971; MA, Villanova U., 1974; JD, Temple U., 1979. Bar: Pa. 1979, U.S. Dist. Ct. (ea. dist.) Pa. 1979, U.S. Ct. Appeals (3d cir.) 1980, U.S. Claims Ct. 1990, U.S. Supreme Ct. 1982; cert. civil trial advocate. Exec. dir., program dir. Programs for Exceptional People, Inc., Phila., 1973-78; assoc. McWilliams and Sweeney, Phila., 1979-82; ptnr. McWilliams and Mintzer, Phila., 1982—. chmn. bd. CATCH, Inc., Phila., 1981—, C.M.S., Inc., 1715 Properties, Inc. Mem. Pa. Bar Assn., Phila. Bar Assn. (med. and legal sub-com.), Pa. Trial Lawyers Assn., Phila. Trial Lawyers Assn. Democrat. Roman Catholic. Avocations: reading, tennis, karate. Office: McWilliams & Mintzer PC 8 Penn Ctr 20th Fl 1628 John F Kennedy Blvd Philadelphia PA 19103-2125

MINUTH, WILL WOLFGANG, anatomist, educator; b. Heidenheim, Germany, Aug. 13, 1949; s. Wilhelm Eugen and Erika (Conradi) M.; m. Katharina Lorenz, Mar. 2, 1990; 1 child, Kaija. Dipl. biology, U. Cologne, 1974, Dr. rer. nat., 1978. Rschr. dept. biochemistry and molecular biology Free U., Berlin, 1974-78; lectr. dept. anatomy U. Heidelberg, 1978-86; prof. U. Heidelberg, Germany, 1986-89, U. Regensburg, Germany, 1989—. Patentee in field. Recipient Philip Morris Rsch. award, 1992, Forschungspreis H. Doerenkamp-Zbinden Found., 1996. Avocation: horseback riding. Office: U Regensburg Dept Anatomy, University St 31, D-93053 Regensburg Bavaria, Germany

MIODOŃSKI, ADAM JAN, biology researcher, otorhinolaryngologist; b. Cracow, Poland, July 20, 1935; s. Jan Józef and Maria (Michalewska) M.; m. Krystyna Zofia Miodońska, Mar. 12, 1966; 1 child, Katarzyna. PhD in Zoology, Jagiellonian U., Cracow, 1965; MD, Copernicus Med. Acad., Cracow, 1974. Asst. in zoology Jagiellonian U., Cracow, 1961-70, asst. lectr. neuroanatomy, 1971-83, assoc. prof. neuroanatomy, 1984-90, assoc. prof. otorhinolaryngology, leader SEM lab. Collegium Medicum, 1992-98, prof., 1999—; asst. lectr. otorhinolaryngology Copernicus Med. Acad., 1964-89, assoc. prof. otorhinolaryngology, leader SEM lab., 1990-92; postdoctoral fellow IBRO/UNESCO Ctrl. Netherlands Inst. Brain Rsch., Amsterdam, 1970-71; dir. histol. lab. Ctrl. Netherlands Inst. Brain Rsch., 1975-76; dir. dept. neuroanatomy Jagiellonian U. Inst. Zoology, 1980-90; vis. rschr. Max-Planck-Inst. Sys. Physiology, Dortmund, Germany, 1983-84; vis. rschr. U. Salzburg (Austria) Inst. Zoology, 1980. Contbr. articles to science jours.; inventor in field; mem. editl. adv. bd. Scanning Microscopy Internat., 1990. Recipient Cavalier Cross "Polonia Restituta", Polish Coun. of State, 1988. Mem. Am. Assn. Anatomists, Microscope Soc. Am., Collegium Oto-Rhino-Laryngologicum Amicitae Sacrum, Polish Oto-Rhino-Laryngological Soc. Avocations: history of Cracow, Judaica, photography.

MIODUSHEVSKY, PAVEL VLADIMIROVICH, utilities executive; b. Kiev, Ukraine, Sept. 22, 1935; arrived in Italy, 1996; s. Vladimir Alexandrovich Miodushevsky and Sheina Davidovna London; m. Margarita Alexandrovna Rudina, May 20, 1965 (div. Aug. 1979); m. Galina Michailovna Syssoeva, Jan. 22, 1981; 1 child, Miodushevsky Alexandr. Diploma in engring., Aviation U., Kazan, Russia, 1959; PhD, Ctrl. Aerohydrodynamic Inst., Moscow, 1970. Rschr. Raduga Design Bur., Dubna, Russia, 1959-60; chief designer rep. at Far East Raduga Bur., Azseniev, Russia, 1961-63; leading engr. TsAGI, Zhukovski, Russia, 1964-67; head lab. TsAGI, Zhukovski, 1968-77, head dept., 1977-85, head divsn., 1985-95; dir. rsch. Powerco, Brindisi, Italy, 1996—; dep. dir. TsAGi, Zhukowski, 1991-96. Achievements include 45 patents. Mem. AAAS, Internat. Acad. Engring. (corr.), N.Y. Acad. Scis. Avocations: tennis, skiing, diving, swimming. Home: via Montebello, 72100 Brindisi Puglia, Italy Office: Powerco SpA, SS7 per Mesagne km 7t300, 72100 Brindisi Puglia, Italy

MIOSSEC, PIERRE JEAN, immunologist, rheumatologist; b. Quimper, France, Sept. 27, 1955; s. Herve and Yvonne (Diraison) M.; m. Marie Coatalem, June 26, 1982; children: Vincent, Philippe. MD, U. Brest, France, 1983; PhD in Immunology, U. Marseille, France, 1987. Rsch. fellow U. Tex., Dallas, 1983-85; asst. in rheumatology U. Montpellier, France, 1985-89; assoc. in clin. immunology U. Lyon, France, 1989-96, prof. clin. immunology, 1996—; rschr. Nat. Inst. Med. Rsch., Lyon, 1989—. Contbr. articles to profl. jours. Mem. Am. Coll. Rheumatology, N.Y. Acad. Scis., French Soc. Rheumatology, French Soc. Immunology (Alessandro Robecchi prize 1995). Home: 16 rue de Reims, 69500 Bron France Office: Dept Immunology and Rheumatology, Hosp Edouard Herriot, 69437 Lyon France

MIR, MOHAMMAD MUZAFFAR, biochemist, researcher; b. Handwara, Kashmir, India, Jan. 3, 1961; s. Mohammad Ramzan and Farzana (Bhat) M.; m. Ashia Muzaffar, Nov. 17, 1974; children: Sameer, Zameer, Saba. BS, U. Kashmir (India), 1981, MS, 1984; MPhil, AMU-Aligarh, India, 1986, PhD, 1989. Jr. rsch. fellow AMU Aligarh, India, 1984-86, sr. rsch. fellow, 1987-89; asst. prof. Sheri-kashmir U. of Agrl. Scis. and Tech., Srinagar, India, 1989-93; asst. prof., cons. Sheri-kashmir Inst. Med. Scis., Srinagar, India, 1993—. Contbr. articles to profl. jours. in field. Organizer Rural Ednl. Soc., Handwara, India, 1989-93; mem. sec. Role of Hygiene in Pub. Life, Srinagar, India, 1993-94. Recipient Young Scientist award Dept. Sci. and Tech., Srinagar, India, 1994. Mem. Assn. of Clin. Biochemists of India (India, life), Soc. of Biol. Chemists (India, life), Internat. Fedn. Clin. Chemistry. E-mail: mirmuza77ar@hotmail.com. Avocations: mass awareness programs, gardening. Office: SK Inst Med Scis, Clin Biochemistry PO Box 27, Soura Srinagar, India

MIRA, CHRISTIAN, engineering educator, researcher; b. Meknes, Morocco, Mar. 6, 1934; s. Fernand and Renee (Pidot) M.; m. Nicole Drillon, Oct. 18, 1958; children: Odile, Christine, Jacques. Degree in Engring., Toulouse, 1957; D es-Scis. Physiques, Faculte des Scis., U. Toulouse, 1961. Maitre asst. INSA, Toulouse, 1962-65, prof. titulaire, 1965-90, prof. classe exceptionnelle, 1990—; head rsch. group LAAS, Toulouse, 1964-74, INSA, Toulouse, 1976-96; mem. editl. bd. Internat. Jour. Bifurcation and Chaos, 1991—; sci. expert NATO, 1990—. Author: Chaotic Dynamics, 1987; co-author: Optimization in Control Theory and Practice, 1968, Dynamique Chaotique, 1980, Chaotic Dynamics in Two-Dimensional Noninvertible Maps, 1996. Sous-lt. Artillery, France and Algeria, 1961-62. Recipient Campaign Medal Algeria French Army, 1962, Bronze medal Societe d'Encouragement au Progres, 1971. Avocations: theology, philosophy, bibliophily, judo. Office: Inst Nat des Scis Appliquees, Complexe Sci Rangueil, 31077 Toulouse France

MIRABELLI, CESARE, judge, member of parliament; b. Gimigliano, Italy, Dec. 29, 1942. Mem. parliament Rome, Italy, 1991—. Office: Corte Costituzionale, Piazza del Quirinale 41, 00187 Rome Italy*

MIRABELLO, MARK LINDEN, history educator; b. Toledo, May 6, 1955; s. Paul Joseph and Regina Joan (Baranski) M. BA, U. Toledo, 1977; MA, U. Va., 1979; PhD, U. Glasgow (Scotland), 1988. Instr. honors program U. Toledo, 1984-87; sr. instr. European history Shawnee State U., Portsmouth, Ohio, 1987-88, asst. prof. European history, 1988-93, chair honors program, 1990—, assoc. prof. European History, 1993—; vis. assoc. prof. European history Nizhni Novgorod State U., Russia, 1994; dir. Ian B. Cowan Award for Outstanding Work in Hist. Studies, Shawnee State U., Portsmouth, 1990—; cons. The Open Air, Shawnee State U. newspaper, Portsmouth, 1992—, The Univ. Chronicle Shawnee State Univ. Newspaper, Portsmouth, 1992—; co-founder, advisor Ar Tyr Ar Fraternity Shawnee State U., Port-

smouth, 1992—. Author: The Odin Brotherhood: A True Narrative of a Dialogue with a Mysterious Secret Society, 1992, The Crimes of Jehovah: A Brief Selection from the Bible, 1996. Co-founder, adviser Delta Tau Omega fraternity, Shawnee State U., Portsmouth, 1992—. Honored by Asatru Sogulega Bokasafn, 1996; named Hon. Ky. Col. by Gov's. Office, 1998. Mem. Am. Hist. Assn., Ohio Acad. History, Fortean Soc. (London), Internat. Fortean Orgn., Planetary Soc.. Avocation: Fortean research. Home: 940 2nd St Portsmouth OH 45662-4303 Office: Dept History Shawnee State U Portsmouth OH 45662

MIRACLE, GORDON ELDON, advertising educator; b. Olympia, Wash., May 28, 1930; s. Gordon Tipler and Corine Adriana (Orlebeke) M.; m. Christa Stoeter, June 29, 1957; children: Gary, Gregory, Glenn. BBA, U. Wis., 1952, MBA, 1958, PhD, 1962. Case officer, civilian intelligence analyst U.S. Army, Fed. Republic Germany, 1955-57; instr. commerce U. Wis. Grad. Sch. Bus., Madison, 1958-60; instr., then asst. prof. mktg. U. Mich., Ann Arbor, 1960-66; assoc. prof. advt. Mich. State U., East Lansing, 1966-70, chmn. PhD program in mass media, 1973-74, chmn. dept., 1974-80, prof. advt., 1970-99, prof. emeritus, 1999—; vis. prof. mktg. mgmt. N. European Mgmt. Inst., Oslo, 1972-73; cons., lectr. in field. Author: Management of International Advertising, 1966; co-author: International Marketing Management, 1970, Advertising and Government Regulation, 1979, Instructor's Manual for International Marketing Management, 1971, European Regulation of Advertising: Supranational Regulation of Advertising in the European Economic Community, 1986, Voluntary Regulation of Advertising: A Comparative Analysis of the United Kingdom and the United States, 1987, (in Korean) Cultures in Advertising: Advertising in Cultures, 1990; contbr. articles to scholarly and profl. jours.; editor: Marketing Decision Making: Strategy and Payoff, 1965, Sharing for Understanding, Proc. Ann. Conf. Am. Acad. Advt., 1977. Served with AUS, 1952-55. Recipient first Biennial Excellence in Advt. award, U. Ill., 1995; Ford Found. fellow, 1961-62, 64, Am. Assn. Advt. Agys. fellow Marsteller, Inc., 1967, Advt. Ednl. Found. fellow McCann-Erickson Hakuhodo, 1985, Fulbright rsch. fellow Waseda U., Tokyo, 1985; recipient numerous grants; recipient Viktor-Mataja medal Austrian Advt. Rsch. Assn., Vienna, 1999. Fellow Am. Acad. Advt. (treas., exec. com. 1978-79); mem. Acad. Internat. Bus. (sec., exec. com. 1973-75), Am. Mktg. Assn., Internat. Advt. Assn. (ednl. accreditation com. 1993-95, internat. advt. edn. group 1996—), Adcraft Club Detroit. Home: 10025 Oak Island Dr Laingsburg MI 48848-8718 Office: Mich State U Dept Advt East Lansing MI 48824

MIRACLE, ROBERT WARREN, retired banker; b. Casper, Wyo.; m. Maggie Zanoni; children—Mark, John. BS in Law, U. Wyo., 1951; grad. with honors, Pacific Coast Banking Sch., 1960. With Wyo. Nat. Bank (now Norwest Bank Casper N.A.), 1954-91; exec. v.p. Wyo. Nat. Bank of Casper, 1967; pres., chief exec. officer Wyo. Nat. Bank of Casper (now Norwest Bank Casper N.A.)ú, 1968-87; chmn. Wyo. Nat. Bank of Casper (formerly Norwest Bank Casper N.A.), 1983-91, also bd. dirs.; pres., chief exec. officer, dir. Wyo. Nat. Bancorp. (formerly Affiliated Bank Corp Wyo.), Casper, 1970-91; mgr. Kemmerer LaBarge Royalties LLC, 1999—; instr. bank mgmt. U. Colo., 1971-75. Bd. dirs. United Fund of Natrona County, Wyo., 1963-85, campaign co-chmn., 1973-78; trustee The Myra Fox Skelton Found., 1963—, Goodstein Found., 1992—; bd. dirs., pres. Investment in Casper, 1967-70; Wyo. treas. Radio Free Europe, 1967-72; trustee Casper Coll. Foun., 1967-91, pres., 1973-75, 85-91; trustee U. Wyo. Found., 1972-87; chmn. Casper Downtown Improvement Assn., 1974-75; bd. dirs. Cen. Wyo. Fair Bd., 1974-79, pres., 1977-78; dir. Mountain States Employers Coun., 1979-91; bd. dirs. Wyo. Natural Gas Pipeline Authority, 1991-97; trustee Meml. Hosp. Natrona County, 1993-96, pres. 1995-96; bd. dirs. Wyo. Med. Ctr., 1996-99. Capt. USMC, 1951-53. Recipient James C. Scarboro Meml. award Colo. Sch. Banking., 1977; Disting. Service in Bus. award U. Wyo. Coll. Commerce and Industry, 1980. Mem. Wyo. Bankers Assn. (chmn. legis. com. 1969-80, pres. 1974-75), Am. Bankers Assn. (mem. governing coun. 1974-75, 81-83), Am. Mgmt. Assn., Rocky Mountain Oil and Gas Assn., Newcomer Soc. in N.Am., Casper C. of C. (pres. 1965-66, Disting. Svc. award 1981), VFW, Casper Petroleum Club, Casper Country Club (pres. 1993-94), Casper Rotary Club (hon. Rotarian award 1996-97), Masons, Lions.

MIRALLES, VICENTE JOSE, biochemist, researcher, educator; b. Valencia, Spain, Nov. 28, 1956; s. Vicente and Carmen (Fernandez) M.; m. Inma Vivo, Sept. 25, 1992; 1 child, Lydia. BS in Chemistry, U. Valencia, 1978, MD in Organic Chemistry, 1979, PhD in Biochemistry, 1983. Postdoctoral fellow Consejo Superior Investigaciones Cientificas, Valencia, 1986-87, Robert Wood Johnson Med. Sch., N.J., 1987-90; postdoctoral fellow U. Valencia, 1991-92, asst. prof., 1992-95, prof., 1995—; rsch. scientist CSIC, Valencia, 1993-94, U. Valencia, 1995—. Contbr. articles to profl. jours. Sgt. Spanish Arty., 1979-80. Fellow Ayuntamiento de Valencia, 1984, NATO, 1987. Avocations: music, literature, football. Office: U Valencia Fac de Farmacia, Vicent Andres Estelles S/N, 46100 Burjassot Valencia, Spain

MIRAMS, WILLIAM C., construction executive; b. Alhambra, Calif., Apr. 24, 1934; s. William Roy Mirams and Mary Louise Clarke; m. Judith Ann Hamilton, Feb. 20, 1956 (div. 1961); children: Deborah, Sheryl, Bruce, Lisa; m. Lisa Ann Richmond, Dec. 5, 1979. BS in Engring., Stanford U., 1956. Pres., owner various cos., Calif. & Idaho, 1961—. Capt., USMC, 1956-60. Avocations: skiing, sailing. E-mail: mirams@sunvalley.net.

MIRANDA, BRINSTON ADRIAN, communications executive, management consultant; b. Bombay, Sept. 8, 1945; s. Lawrence and Nora (Rebello) M.; m. Filomena Bernice Sequeira, Oct. 18, 1969; children: Michelle, Michael. BA, U. Bombay, 1965, MA, 1967, MBA, 1968. Sr. account dir. Chaitra Leo Burnett, Bombay, 1975-78; sr. group mgr. Ogilvy & Mather, Bombay, 1978-80; sr. v.p. RK Swamy/Batten Barton Durstine & Osborne, Bombay, 1980-85; gen. account dir. Hindustan Thompson Assocs., Bombay, 1985-87; CEO Frank Simoes Advt., Bombay, 1987-89, Brinston Miranda Assocs., Bombay, 1989—. Editor, pub. Promotion-Jour. Advt. Agys. Assn. India; contbr. over 500 articles to profl. jours. Mem. Bombay Mgmt. Assn. (life, editor, pub. jour.), Advt. Club Bombay (life, editor, pub. jour.), Indo-Am. Soc. (life), Am. Coun. Libr. (life). Avocations: communication, music, literature, theatre. Fax: 4460624. E-mail: brinmir@yahoo.com. Home: 10 Sea View, 35 Shivaji Pk, Bombay 400028, India Office: Sea View, 35 Keluskar Rd N, Shivaji Park Bombay 400028, India

MIRANDA, CARLOS SA, food products company executive; b. Fall River, Mass., Nov. 16, 1929; s. Carlos Sa and Annette (Pratt) M.; m. Natalie Cardoso, Jan. 5, 1949; children: Carla, Lucy, John. BS in Mech. Engring., Marquette U., 1956. With internat. div. Kellogg Co., Battle Creek, Mich., 1964-65; gen. mgr. Kellogg Co., Brazil, 1965-80, Kellogg's Spain, 1983-84; v.p. Kellogg Internat., Battle Creek, 1980-89; country dir. internat. exec. svc. corps. Costa Rica, 1990-91; mediator Fla. County Cts., 1994—. Recipient Pero Vaz Caminha award, Brazil, 1976; conferred title Comdr. of Legion of Honor of Marshal Rondon, Brazil, 1971. Mem. ASME. Republican. Roman Catholic. Home: Apt 614 988 Boulevard Of The Arts Sarasota FL 34236-4840

MIRANDA, ENRIQUE NESTOR, physicist, philospher of science; b. Mendoza, Argentina, Nov. 15, 1959; s. Nestor and Esther (Martinez) M. M in Physics, Instituto Balseiro, Bariloche, Argentina, 1984, PhD, 1989. Rsch. asst. Centro Atomico Bariloche, 1984-90; instr. Inst. Balseiro, 1984-90; vis. rschr. KFA, Jülich, Germany, 1990-91, Institut fuer Physik, Mainz, Germany, 1991-92; assoc. prof. Univ. Nacional San Luis, Argentina, 1992—; ind. rschr. CRICYT, Mendoza, 1994—. Contbr. articles to Europhysics Letters, Jour. of Physics, Physica, Jour. Statis. Mechanics, others. Roman Catholic. Home: Olascoaga 2215, Mendoza 5500, Argentina Office: CRICYT, Mendoza 5500, Argentina

MIRANDA, MICHELE RENEE, optometrist; b. Springfield, Mass., Jan. 6, 1960. BS, Springfield Coll., 1982; OD, New Eng. Coll. Optometry, 1986; postgrad., Johns Hopkins U. Diplomate Internat. Assn. Bd. Examiners in Optometry. Resident VA Med. Ctr., Roxbury/Brockton, Mass., 1988; optometrist Med. Eye Care Assoc., Norwood, Mass., 1987-95, Bassett Healthcare, Cooperston, N.Y., 1995-96, Baystate Eye Care, PC, Springfield, Mass., 1996-99, John Papale, MD PC, Springfield, 1999—; liaison New Eng. Coun. Optometrists, Boston, 1989-91, bd. corporators, 1991-93; spkr. in field. Recipient Alumni Assn. award New Eng. Coll. Optometry, 1986, Barnes Hind Student Recognition award New Eng. Coll. Optometry, 1986. Mem. Am. Optometric Assn., N.Y. State Optometric Assn., Mass. Soc. Optometrists (pres. 1990-91), Beta Sigma Kappa.

MIRANTE, ARTHUR J., II, real estate company executive; b. Hackensack, N.J., Aug. 25, 1943; s. Arthur J. and Mildred (Spaluzzi) M.; m. Elizabeth McMillan, Oct. 2, 1993; children: Arthur, Claudia, Matthew. BS, Coll. of the Holy Cross, 1965; JD, St. John's U., 1968. Bar: 1968. Sole practice N.Y.C., 1966-71; asst. to gen. counsel Cushman & Wakefield, N.Y.C., 1971-77, gen. counsel, 1977-81, nat. dir. asset mgmt., 1981-82, exec. v.p., dir. N.Y. area, 1982-84, pres., chief exec. officer, 1984—. Home: 211 E 70th St New York NY 10021-5205 Office: Cushman & Wakefield Inc 51 W 52nd St Rm 700 New York NY 10019-6119

MIREA, MIHAIL DOLORIS, physics researcher, educator; b. Vintila-Voda, Buzau, Romania, Feb. 9, 1961; s. Constantin and Sidonia (Burtel) M.; m. Doina Demetrescu, Aug. 20, 1990; 1 child, Mirela-Cristina. Degree in engring. and physics, U. Bucarest, Romania, 1985; D, Inst. Atomic Physics, Bucarest, 1994. Engr. Inst. for Nuc. Reactors, Pitesti, Romania, 1985-87; asst. rschr. Inst. Atomic Physics, Bucarest, 1987-90, rschr., 1990-94, prin. rschr., 1994—. Avocation: theatre. Office: Inst Atomic Physics, Atomistilor, 76900R Bucarest Romania

MIRI, AMIR MANSOUR, engineering educator, dean; b. Ahwaz, Khousestan, Iran, July 2, 1935; arrived in Germany, 1979; s. Seid Mohsen and Jamileh (Fathi) M.; m. Irandokht Safi; 1 child, Raz. Diploma in engring., U. Hannover, Germany, 1960; PhD in Engring., U. Karlsruhe, Germany, 1965. Assoc. prof. U. Teheran, Iran, 1966-72; full prof. faculty engring. U. Teheran, 1972-79, dean of students faculty engring., 1967-68, chmn. dept. elec. engring., 1968-72, dir. Inst. Elec. Engring., 1971-79, dean faculty engring., 1972-79; sr. rschr. Inst. Elec. Energy Systems & High-Voltage Tech. U. Karlsruhe, 1979-84, hon. prof., 1984—; mem. Iranian Electrotechnical Stds. Com., 1972-79, pres., 1978-79; rector Poly. U. Teheran, 1978-79; bd. mem. PhD Found. Superconductivity, U. Karlsruhe, 2000—, PhD Found. Numerical Electromagnetic field calculation, 1998—; mem. indsl. chair on atmospheric icing of power network equipment U. Que., Chicoutimi, 1996—. Contbr. articles to profl. jours. Recipient Iranian Homajun medal, 1975, Bundesverdienstkreuz der Bundesrepublik Deutschland, Fed. Republic Germany, 1976. Mem. CIGRE (task force 23-03 1991—), OPTIM (co-chmn. and hon. chmn. 2000 conf.), Short Cir. Curents Conf. (sci. com. 1992—). Avocations: classical music, opera and operettas. Office: U Karlsruhe Inst Electro, Kaiserstrasse 12, D-76128 Karlsruhe Germany

MIRICK, ROBERT ALLEN, military officer; b. Kingston, N.Y., June 26, 1957; s. Harry Lawrence and Jean Alice (Erickson) M.; m. Pamela Ann Warburton, July 24, 1982; children: Kristen E., Kathryn A., Meredith W., Abigail S. BS in Oceanography, U.S. Naval Acad., 1979; MS in Engring. Acoustics, Naval Postgrad. Sch., 1989. Commd. ensign USN, 1979, cmmdr., 1994; navigator, propulsion asst. USS McCandless, 1979-82; diving and deck officer USS Pigeon, 1983-85; exec. officer, navigator USS Bolster, 1985-87; commdg. officer USS Hoist, 1990-92; cmty. mgr., assignment and placement officer USN Spl. Ops., 1993-95; exec. officer U.S. Naval Activities, Guam, 1995-97; base ops. support officer US Naval Forces, Marianas, Guam, 1997-98; commdg. officer Mobile Diving and Salvage Unit 1, Pearl Harbor, Hawaii, 1998-99; chief staff officer, comdr. Explosive Ordnance Disposal Group One, San Diego, 1999—; vol. staff diver Monterey (Calif.) Bay Aquarium, 1987-89; field asst. Scripps Inst., San Diego, 1985. Contbr. article to Jour. of Acoustical Soc. Am. Pres. Parents Assn. of L.A., San Pedro, Calif., 1986. Decorated Meritorious Svc. medal USN, 1992, 95, 98, 99; recipient Nat. Partnership for Reinventing Govt. Silver Hammer award for diving and salvage work, U.S. Vice-Pres., 1999. Mem. Acoustical Soc. Am., Am. Soc. Naval Engrs., U.S. Naval Inst., Soc. Colonial Wars. Republican. Achievements include research in sediment acoustics; development of apparatus to determine the complex mass of a viscous fluid contained in a rigid porous solid from acoustic pressure measurements; contributor to certification of USN MK2 Mod1 Deep Diving System to 850 feet; sr. salvage officer and command center watch commander for survivor rescue, and search and recovery phase of KAL flight 801 disaster, Guam, 1997; sr. fleet salvage officer for recovery of Alaska Air Flight 261 Disaster Offshore, L.A. area, 2000. E-mail: mirickr@ndu.edu. Office: Commdr Explosive Ordnance Disposal Group One 2424 Rendova Rd San Diego CA 92155-5400

MIRILAS, PETROS, pediatric surgeon; b. Athens, Greece, May 6, 1964; s. Spiridon and Sofia (Samioti) M. MD, U. Patras, Greece, 1988; MChir, U. Paris, 1996; PhD, U. Patras, 1997. Intern Pediatric Hosp., Patras, Greece, 1991-93; rsch. trainee Inst. Pasteur, Paris, 1995-98; attache U. Hosp. St. Vincent de Paul, Paris, 1995-96, U. Hosp. Bicetre, Paris, 1996-97; vis. asst. prof. U. Crete, Helaklion, Greece, 1998-2000, lectr., 2000—; asst. U. Paris, 1995-96; rsch. assoc. Assn. Claude Bernard Ecole Chirgirgie, Paris, 1997-98. Contbr. articles to profl. jours. Mem. Gen. Med. Coun., England, 1991, Ordre des Medecins, Paris, 1996. With Greek Air Force, 1989-90. Doctiral fellow French Govt., Paris, 1992-95, Postdoctoral fellow Lemos Found., Athens, London, 1997-98, Grand Prix fellow Inst. Elec., Paris, 1997. Mem. Med. Soc. Greece, N.Y. Acad. Scis. Avocations: literature, dogs, sea moto. Office: U Crete Med Sch, PO Box 1393 Herakleion, 71110 Crete Greece

MIRISOLA, LISA HEINEMANN, air quality engineer; b. Glendale, Calif., Mar. 25, 1963; d. J. Herbert and Betty Jane (Howson) Heinemann; m. Daniel Carl Mirisola, June 27, 1987; 1 child, Ian Cataldo. BSME, UCLA, 1986. Cert. engr.-in-tng., Calif. Air quality engr. South Coast Air Quality Mgmt. Dist., Diamond Bar, Calif., 1988—. Chancellor's scholar UCLA, 1981. Mem. ASME, NSPE, Soc. Women Engrs. Office: South Coast Air Quality Mgmt Dist 21865 Copley Dr Diamond Bar CA 91765-4178

MIRK, JUDY ANN, retired elementary educator; b. Victorville, Calif., June 10, 1944; d. Richard Nesbit and Corrine (Berghoefer). BA in Social Sci., San Jose (Calif.) State U., 1966, cert. in teaching, 1967; MA in Edn., Calif. State U., Chico, 1980. Cert. elem. edn. tchr., Calif. MFT trainee John F. Kennedy U., Orinda, Calif.; tchr. Cupertino (Calif.) Union Sch. Dist., 1967-95; lead tchr. lang. arts Dilworth Sch., San Jose, 1988-90, mem. supt.'s adv. team, 1986-90, mem. student study team, 1987-95; ret.; mem. student study team, 1987-95; mem. Dilworth Sch. Site Coun., 1981-95. Mem. The Commonwealth Club of Calif, Phi Mu. Republican. Avocations: photography, natural history, watercolors. Home: 2075 Redwood Dr Santa Cruz CA 95060-1238

MIRKOWSKI, JAN ANDRÉ, occupational safety and health manager; b. Birmingham, Eng., Apr. 14, 1959; s. Roman and Anne Isabel (Hall) M.; m. Margaret Eleanor Gooding, Aug. 30, 1987. BSc, Aston U., Birmingham, 1981; MBA, Open Univ., Eng., 1996, Open Univ., Eng., 1996. Registered Safety Practitioner, Instn. Occupl. Safety and Health, Leicestershire, Eng., 1994, cert. environ. mgmt. specialist Nat. Examining Bd. Occupational Safety and Health. Health and safety mgr. Vickers Plc., Leeds, Eng., 1981-84; co-health and safety advisor Spicers Ltd., Cambridge, Eng., 1984-89; group health and safety mgr. Reed Internat., Maidstone, Eng., 1989-92; group health safety and environ. mgr. Unipart, Oxford, Eng., 1992—; dangerous goods safety advisor Scottish Qualifications Authority, 1999. Author: Materials Movement and Storage, 1994. Mem. Instn. Occupl. Safety and Health, Instn. Environ. Mgmt. and Assessment. Office: Unipart Group Cos., Unipart House Cowley, Oxford OX4 2PG, England

MIROLI, ALFREDO AMERICO, immunologist; b. San Miguel De Tucuman, Argentina, July 20, 1951; s. Miguel Angel and America (Arca) M.; m. Celia Fatima Griet, Jan. 4, 1974; children: Lautaro, Celia, Alejandra, Veronica. Diploma faculty medicine, Nat. U., Argentina, 1974. Med. Diplomate Immunologist. Tutor faculty medicine Nat. U., Tucuman, Argentina, 1971-74; instr. immunology Nat. U., Tucuman, 1975-81, prof. immunology, 1982—; hon. prof. U. Flores, Buenos Aires, 1998—; scientific dir. Inst. Retroviruses, Tucuman, 1987—; dir. Nat. Aids Programme, Nat. Ministry Health, Argentina, 1992-93, Under Sec. Prevention and Assistance, Nat. Sec. Drugs, 1996-98; pres. Am. States Orgn. Coun. Against Drug Abuse, 1997. Author/Editor: (books) HIV-AIDS: Handbook for Everybody, 1993, Drugs: Handbook for Everybody, 1996. Recipient Disting. Citizen award, San Miguel De Tucuman, 1991, Gen. San Martin award, Gov. State of Tucuman, 1991. Mem. Argentinian Assn. Allergy and Immunology (mem. of honor), Assn. Allergy and Immunology Tucuman (pres.). Avocations: cycling, model cars. E-mail: miroli@jetnet.com.ar. Home: Pasaje Benito Lynch 4636, 4000 San Miguel de Tucuman Argentina

MIRONE, LUISA, rheumatologist, researcher; b. Palermo, Sicilia, Italy, June 15, 1959; d. Domenico and Germana (Palma) M.; m. Lorenzo Capaldi, Sept. 10, 1988. MD, Cath. U., Rome, 1983, specialist in gastroenterology, 1988, specialist in rheumatology, 1994. Rschr. Cath. U., Rome, 1986—, cons. rheumatologist rheumatology dept., 1994—; prof. occupl. therapist Specialization Sch. Rheumatology, Cath. U., Rome, 1997, prof. rheumatology, 1998. Active Lions Club, Rome, 1997. Mem. Italian Rheumatology Soc. (Best Exptl. Work award 29 Italian Congress Rheumatology 1992), Italian Internal Medicine Soc. Avocations: skiing, diving, riding horses, traveling. Office: Complesso Integrato Columbus, Via G Moscati 31, 00168 Rome Italy

MIRONESCU, MIRCEA TOMA, structural designer; b. Odobesti, Vrancea, Romania, Mar. 28, 1934; s. Toma Panaite and Anastasia Constantin (Mazilu) M.; m. Silvia Gheorghe Ionescu, Dec. 20, 1965. Grad., Civil Engring. Coll., 1958. Engr. Bldg. Co., Constanta, Romania, 1958-62, Bucharest, Romania, 1962-67; designer Design Carpati Office, Bucharest, 1967-95, mgr., 1995—; cons. Rsch. Inst., Bucharest, 1993—; adv. bd. Hist. Monuments, Bucharest, 1993-97. Contbr. articles to profl. jours. Maj. Artillery, 1958-94. Avocations: vegetable growing, tennis, music. Home: Vitejiei No2 Bloc 1 Sector2, Etaj 1 Ap 38, Bucharest Romania Office: Miro Group SRL Et 4 Ap 131, 90-96 Mihai Bravu-Bloc D17, 732651 Bucharest Romania

MIRONOVA, ANTONINA PETROVNA, cell biologist, cytoecologist, researcher; b. Chimkent, Kazakhstan, Soviet Union, Nov. 28, 1948; s. Peter Ivanovich and Lubov Vasilievna (Ushakova) M.; 1 child, Eugenia Sergeevna. MS cum laude, U. Leningrad, 1971; postgrad., Inst. Cytology, 1973. Sr. technologist Radiol. Inst. Leningrad, 1971-73; jr. rschr. Inst. Cytology, Russian Acad. Sci., St. Petersburg, 1976—. Contbr. articles to profl. jours. Fellow Scientists Union. Avocations: reading, playing with dog, spending time with daughter, composing poems for friends. Office: Inst Cytology, 4 Tikhoretsky Ave, 194064 Saint Petersburg Russia

MIRONOVSKY, LEONID ALEXEEVITCH, engineering educator; b. Orel, Russia, Feb. 8, 1939; s. Alexey Ivanovitch Mironovsky and Galina Leonidovna Tzvetkova; m. Nina Georgievna Burtzeva, Jan. 29, 1962; children: Anna, Alexey, Maria. MS, St. Petersburg Tech. U., 1962; PhD, St. Petersburg Acad. Airspace Syss., 1969, D in Sci. and Tech., 1980. Cert. elec. engring. Asst. prof. St. Petersburg Airspace Acad., Russia, 1965-73, pvt. prof., 1973-82, prof., 1982—; chief rsch. lab. St. Petersburg Airspace Acad., 1982—. Author: Fault Detection in Dynamic Systems, 1998; co-author: Fault Detection and Identification in Robotics Systems, 1985; editor: Automation and Remote Control, 1989—; contbr. articles to profl. jours. Lt. Mil. Airforce, 1965-68. Grantee Russian Sci. Acad. Mem. Russian Acad. Navigation and Motion Control, Russian Acad. Metrology. Avocations: kayaking, skiing, fine arts. Home: Serebristy Blvd 15-537, 197 227 Saint Petersburg Russia Office: St Petersburg Airspace Acad, Bolshaya Morskaya 67, 190 000 Saint Petersburg Russia

MIROTIN, ADOLF, mathematics researcher; b. Gomel, USSR, May 5, 1952; s. Ruvim and Gita (Televevich) M.; m. Rimma Feigina, Jan. 2, 1982; 1 child, Eugene. M, Gomel State U., 1974; D, Voronezh State U., 1987. Math. diplomate. Asst. prof. math. Gomel State U., 1974-87, assoc. prof., 1987—. Co-author: Laboratory Practical Work in Mathematical Analysis, 1991; contbr. articles to profl. jours. Mem. Am. Math. Soc. Home: Flat 65, Starochernigovskaya Str 6, 246028 Gomel Belarus Office: Gomel State U, Sovietskaya 104, 246699 Gomel Belarus

MIRREN, HELEN, actress; b. London, 1946. First appeared with Nat. Youth Theatre; appeared as Cleopatra in Antony and Cleopatra, Old Vic, 1965; joined Royal Shakespeare Co., 1967; appeared as Castiza in The Revenger's Tragedy and Diana in All's Well That Ends Well; other roles include: Cressida in Troilus and Cressida, Royal Shakespeare Co., Stratford, Eng., 1968; Hero in Much Ado About Nothing, Stratford, 1968; Win-the-Fight Littlewit in Bartholomew Fair, Aldwych, 1969; Lady Anne in Richard III, Stratford, Ophelia in Hamlet, Julia in The Two Gentlemen of Verona, Stratford, 1970 (last part also at Aldwych); Tatyana in Enemies, Royal Shakespeare Co., Aldwych, 1971; title role in Miss Julie, Elynae in The Balcony, The Place, 1971; with Peter Brook's Centre Internationale de Recherches Theatrales, Africa and U.S., 1972-73; Lady Macbeth, Royal Shakespeare Co., Stratford, 1974, and Aldwych, 1975; Maggie in Teeth 'n' Smiles, Royal Ct., 1975; Nina in The Seagull and Ella in The Bed Before Yesterday, Lyric for Lyric Theatre Co., 1975, Antony and Cleopatra, The Roaring Girl, Henry VI-Parts 1, 2, 3, 1977-78, Measure for Measure, 1979, The Duchess of Malfi, 1980-81, Faith Healer, 1981, Royal Shakespeare Co., Barbican, 1983, Extremities, 1984, Madame Bovary, 1987, Two Way Mirror, 1988, Sex Please We're Italian, 1991, A Month in the Country, 1994 (Tony nominee - Lead Actress in a Play, 1995); films include: Age of Consent, 1969, Savage Messiah, O Lucky Man!, 1973, Caligula, 1977, The Long Good Friday, Excalibur, 1981, Cal, 1984 (Best Actress award Cannes Film Festival 1984), 2010, 1984, White Knights, 1984, Heavenly Pursuits, 1985, The Mosquito Coast, 1986, Pascali's Island, 1987, When The Whales Came, 1988, Bethune, Making of a Hero, 1988, The Cook, The Thief, His Wife, and Her Lover, 1989, The Comfort of Strangers, 1990, Where Angels Fear to Tread, 1991, The Gift, 1991, The Hawk, 1991, The Prince of Jutland, 1991, The Madness of King George, 1994 (Acad. award nominee for Best Supporting Actress), Critical Care, 1996; Painted Lady (tv miniseries), 1997; Sidoglin Smithee, 1998; The Passion of Ayn Road (tv), 1998; Killing Mrs. Tingle, 1998; Prince of Egypt (voice), 1998; TV appearances include: Behind the Scene, Cousin Bette, Coffin for the Bride, Jackanory, The Changeling, Bellamira, The Philanthropist, Mussolini And Claretta Petacci, The Collection, The Country Wife, Blue Remembered Hills, The Serpent Son, Quiz Kids, Midsummer Night's Dream, After the Party, Cymbeline, Coming Through, Cause Celebre, Miss Julie, The Apple Cart, The Little Minister, As You Like It, Mrs. Reinhardt, Soft Targets, 1982, Heavenly Pursuits, 1985, Red King White Knight, 1988, Prime Suspect, 1991 (Best Actress award BAFTA 1991), Prime Suspect 2, 1992, (Best Actress award BAFTA 1992), Prime Suspect 3, 1993 (Best Actress award BAFTA 1994), Prime Suspect 4, 1994 (Emmy award Best Actress 1996), Prime Suspect 5, 1996, Chase in Losing Chase, 1995 (Golden Globe award), Some Mothers Son, 1995. Mem. PTO. Address: 2003 La Brea Ter Los Angeles CA 90046-2313*

MIRRLEES, SIR JAMES ALEXANDER, economics educator; b. Minnigaff, Scotland, July 5, 1936; s. George Barlas MacNab and Nan Lindsay (Purdie) M.; m. Gillian Marjorie Hughes, July 29, 1961 (dec. 1993); children: Catriona, Fiona. MA, Edinburgh (Scotland) U., 1957; BA, Cambridge (Eng.) U., 1959, PhD, 1963; D Litt (hon.), Warwick U., Eng., 1982, Portsmouth U., 1997, Brunel U., 1997, Edinburgh U., 1997, Oxford U., 1998. Lectr. in econs. U. Cambridge, 1963-68; Edgeworth prof. econs. U. Oxford, Eng., 1968-95; prof. polit. economy U. Cambridge, Eng., 1995—. Author: Project Appraisal and Planning for Developing Countries (with Little), 1974; contbr. articles to profl. publs. Recipient Nobel Meml. prize in econs., 1996. Fellow Brit. Acad., Fellow Roy. Soc. of Edinburgh, Econometric Soc. (pres. 1983-84); mem. Royal Econ. Soc. (pres. 1989-92), Foreign Assoc. of Natl. Acad. Scis., Am. Econ. Assn. (hon.), Am. Acad. Arts and Scis., Assn. Univ. Tchrs. Econs. (chmn. 1983-87). Office: U Cambridge Faculty Econs, Sidgwick Ave, Cambridge CB3 9DD, England

MIRSHAHI, MASSOUD, biomedical researcher; b. Dizbad, Nishabour, Iran, May 19, 1954; arrived in France, 1979; s. Farvardin and Nosrat (Badakhshani) M.; m. Shahsoltan Mirshahi, Nov. 29, 1986; children: Sam Qiumars, Anahita. Diploma, Higher Nat. Sch. Shahreza, Mashhad, Iran; MD, Limburg U., Maastricht, The Netherlands, 1984; PhD in Immunology, U. Paris VII, Paris, 1986, diploma in cancerology, 1982. Rschr. Nat. Ctr. for Sci. Rsch., Paris, 1986. Contbr. articles to profl. jours. Pres., organizer Congress in Indo-Iranian Civilization Congress Tajikestan Acad. Sci., 1996, Amersfourt, The Netherlands, 1997, Hamburg (Germany) U., 1998, Dushanbe (Tajikistan), 1999. Rsch. grantee Retinite Pigmantosa Assn., 1991-93, Assn. Cancer Rsch., 1994-95. Mem. N.Y. Acad. Sci., Assn. for Rsch. in Vision and Ophthalmology, Internat. Soc. for Fibrinolysis and

Thrombolysis, Assn. Rudaki (pres. 1993). Achievements include contributions to detection of fibrin-fibrinogen degradation products by plasmin, differentiation antigens in the hematopoietic tissue and acute lymphoblastic Leukemia, retinal S-antigen, autoimmune uveoretinaitis, arrestin in retinal and pineal gland, arrestin like proteins in non photosensitive cells (brain, lung, kidney, platelets, heart) and plants kingdom mineralocorticoid receptor in heart, lung, kidney, brain, human Leukemic cell, ocular tissue, plant cells and alga, protease in corneal wound healing plasminogen receptor. Home: 24 rue Jean Lurcat, 94800 Villejuif Paris France Office: INSERM U E9912 Faculty Med, 15 rue d'Ecole de Medicine, 75006 Paris France

MIRYALA, MURALIDHAR, physicist; b. Karvena, A.P., India, Nov. 26, 1963; s. Narayana Gupta and Chandrakala Miryala; m. Radha rani Miryala, Aug. 30, 1996; 1 child, Santosh Kumar. BSc, Osmania U., Badepally, India, 1984; MSc, Osmania U., Hyderabad, India, 1987; PhD, Osmania U., 1992. Postdoctoral rsch. fellow Osmania U., Hyderabad, 1993-94, young scientist, 1995; vis. rsch. scientist Superconductivity rsch. Lab./ISTEC, Tokyo, 1996-97; chief rsch. scientist Superconductivity rsch. Lab./ISTEC, Morioka, 1997—; project investigator Osmania U., 1995, lectr., 1993-95; lectr. in field. Contbr. numerous articles to profl. jours. and books; patentee in field. Pres. Osmania U., Mahbubnagar, 1987. With Indian Mil., 1992-93. ICTP guest scientist, trieste, Italy, 1991, U. Bursary fellow Osmania U., 1995-96; named Young Scientist Dept. Sci. and tech., Govt. of India, 1995, Dirs. award SRL-ISTEC, 1998, Award of Excellence PASREG, 1999. Mem. Soc. for Advancement of Solid State Scis. India (founder). Avocations: charitable works, collecting stamps, reading. Office: Superconductivity Rsch Lab, 3-35-2 Iioka-Shinden, Morioka 020-0852, Japan

MIRZA, MOHAMMAD SAMIUDDIN, power and desalination engineer; b. Karolli State, Rajputana, India, Mar. 12, 1946; migrated to Pakistan, 1947; arrived in United Arab Emirates, 1974; s. Mohammad Alimuddin and Ahsan Jehan (Begum) Khan; m. Hummera Mumtaz, Mar. 15, 1975; children: Nigar Sami, Nida Sami, Hina Sami. BSc in Physics, Chemistry and Math., Govt. Coll. Karachi U., Pakistan, 1964; BE in Mech. Engring., Nadir Shah Edulji din Shah, Karachi, Pakistan, 1968. Asst. mgr. Pakistan Machine Tools, Karachi, 1968-70; exec. engr. Karachi Electric Supply Corp., Karachi, 1970-74; maintenance supt. Water and Electricity Dept., Abu Dhabi, United Arab Emirates, 1974-80, gen. supt. power and desalination plants, 1980-82, mgr. projects, 1982-87, chief engr. projects, 1987—; mgmt. shareholding Providence Modaraba Ltd., Karachi, 1988—. Contr. article to Ency. of Life Support Systems. Pres. Overseas Pakistani Investors Forum, Abu Dhabi, 1991—; mem. Thinkers Forum, Abu Dhabi, 1990—; pres. Math. Soc. Govt. Coll., Karachi, 1963-64. Mem. Instn. Engrs. Pakistan (life), Engring. Coun. Pakistan (life), Internat. Desalination Assn. U.S.A. Avocations: reading technical journals and religious books, badminton, table tennis, home appliance maintenance, watch repair, social work. Home: PO Box 43158, Abu Dhabi United Arab Emirates also: A-19/8 Federal B Area, Karachi 79950, Pakistan

MIRZAEI, SIROOS, health facility administrator; b. Mashhad, Iran, Apr. 22, 1963; arrived in Austria, 1980; s. Mohamed and Sakineh M.; m. Estelle Apffel, Aug. 27, 1967; children: Sarah, David. MD, U. Vienna, Austria, 1987. Asst. med. dir. Inst. Nuclear Medicine, Wilhelminenspital, Vienna, 1999; vice chmn. Rehab. Ctr. for Victims of Torture and War, Vienna, 1999; med. coord. Amnesty Internat. Med. Group, Vienna, 1990-94. Contbr. articles to profl. jours. Recipient Programer award Elscint User Group, 1996, Mallinckrodt award Austrian Nuc. Medicine Soc., 1999. Avocations: chess, soccer. Office: Wilhelminenspital Inst, Nuc Med Montleartstr 37, A-1171 Vienna Austria

MISAKI, MASAO, atmospheric science researcher; b. Tokyo, Feb. 23, 1921; s. Kaneji and Fumi (Torii) M.; m. Sumiko Hosokawa, Jan. 5, 1953; children: Akiko, Keiko. Student, Meteorol. Tng. Coll., Tokyo, 1941, postgrad., 1947; DSc, Kyoto (Japan) U., 1962. Mem. Kakioka Magnetic Obs., Ibaraki Prefecture, Japan, 1941-58; rschr. Meteorol. Rsch. Inst., Tokyo, 1958-60, sect. chief, 1960-76, head divsn., 1976-81; prof. Tokyo Kasei U., Tokyo, 1989-91; lectr. Tokyo Sci. U., 1981-89, Nihon U, 1991—. Author: Aerosols Change the Global Climate, 1992. Recipient prize Meteorol. Soc. Japan, Tokyo, 1970. Roman Catholic. Avocation: painting. Home: 7-73 Higurashi, Matsudo Chiba 270-2253, Japan

MISAN, GARY MICHAEL, pharmacist, lecturer; b. Adelaide, Australia, Jan. 21, 1958; s. Henry Aaron and Miriam Gabbai (Petrook) M.; m. Debra Ann Harvey, oct. 13, 1979; children: Benjamin, Daniel. B of Pharmacy, South Australian Inst. Tech., Adelaide, Australia, 1979; PhD, U. Adelaide, 1997. Trainee pharmacist Flinders Med. Ctr., Adelaide, Australia, 1979; pharmacist Gippsland Base Hosp., Sale, Australia, 1980-81; pharmacist Royal Adelaide (Australia) Hosp., 1982-86, sr. pharmacist, 1987-93, dir. pharmacy, 1994-95; exec. editor Australian Medicines Handbook, Adelaide, 1996—; dir. clin. svcs. and info. tech. SA Ctr. for Rural and Remote Health, U. Adelaide, 1999—. Exec. editor Australian Medicines Handbook, 1996-99; contbr. articles to profl. jours. Mem. Soc. Hosp. Pharmacists of Australia, Australasian Soc. Clin. & Exptl. Pharmacologists & Toxicologists, Health Informatics Soc. Australia (sec.). Avocations: family, caravaning, swimming. E-mail: gary.misan@adelaide.edu.au. Home: 35 Calomba Crescent, Happy Valley 5159, Australia Office: South Australian Ctr, Univ Adelaide, Adelaide SA 5000, Australia

MISAR, ZDENEK, geology educator; b. Krucemburk, Czech Republic, Mar. 6, 1926; s. Antonin and Frantiska (Fialova) M.; m. Dana Martinu, Oct. 15, 1951; 1 child, Irena. MS, Charles U., 1950, PhD, 1954; DSc, Acad. Sci., Czech Republic, 1970. Asst. Charles U., Praha, Czech Republic, 1953-57, sr. lectr., 1957-61, dr. habilitatis, 1961-71, prof. geology, 1971-93, prof. emeritus, 1993—; rsch. fellow U. New South Wales, Kensington, Australia, 1961-62; geologist Gronlands Geol. Undersokelse, Copenhagen, 1964-65; prof. regional geology U. Wis., Madison, 1982; head dept. geology Charles U., 1970-91. Author: Geology of Czechoslovakia, 1983, Ransko-gabbro-peridotite massif, 1974, Regional Geology of the World, 1984 (Univ. medal 1985); co-author: Mineral Deposits of the World, 1994, Geology of the Czech Republic and Geology of Mongolia, 1996, Pre-PErmian Geology of Central and Eastern Europe, 1995. Mem. Geol. Soc. Czechoslovakia (pres. 1982-90), U.S. Geol. Soc., Geol. Soc. Finland. Avocation: fishing. Home: kpt Stranskeho 983/23, 19800 Praha 9, Czech Republic Office: Charles U Faculty Sci, Albertov 6, 12843 Praha 2, Czech Republic

MISAWA, GIICHI, special education educator; b. Ina, Naganoken, Japan, Nov. 1, 1929; m. Haruko Misawa; children: Ikuko, Yoko. Diploma, Tokyo U. Lit. and Sci., 1953. Psychologist Tokyo Met. Govt., 1953-58, Ministry of Health, Tokyo, 1958-66; assoc. prof. Mie U., Mie-Ken, Japan, 1966-73, prof., 1973-77; prof. Tokyo U. Edn., 1977-78, U. Tsukuba, 1978-93; prin. U. Tsukuba Elem. Sch., 1989-93; prof. emeritus U. Tsukuba, 1993—; prof., dean Tsukuba Internat. U., 1994-99; pres. Kinjo U., Matto, Japan, 2000—. Author: Psychology and Education of the Handicapped, 1984; editor Education for Motor Handicapped Children, 1993. Chmn. Coun. on Employment Promotion for the Handicapped, 1995-99; mem. Ctrl. Coun. for Promotion of Measures for Disabled Persons, 1994—. Mem. Japanese Psychol. Assn., Japanese Assn. Spl. Edn. Avocation: swimming. Home: 530-255 2 Chome Karasuyama, Tsuchiura-shi 300-0836, Japan Office: Kinjo U, 1200 Kasama-cho, Matto Ishikawa-Ken 924-8511, Japan

MISAWA, MIWA, pharmacology educator; b. Toyama, Japan, Feb. 3, 1946; d. Bunji and Fumiko (Takata) Yamatake; m. Sachiko Misawa, Nov. 16, 1974; children: Tamako, Moko. BS, U. Tokyo, 1968, MS, 1970, PhD, 1973. Lic. pharmacist, Japan. Postdoctoral fellow Kans. Univ. Med. Ctr., 1979-81; prof. applied pharmacology Hoshi U., Tokyo, 1986-92, prof. pharmacology, 1992—; mem. Japan Pharmacists Edn. Ctr., 1994-95; vis. rschr. Nat. Inst. Environ. Studies, 1990—; vis. prof. Beijing Med. U., China, 1993; mem. nat. evaluation team for Burma Drug Devel. Ctr., 1985; mem. nat. exam for pharmacist com., Japan, 1998—. Author: Japanese Scientific Terms - Pharmacy and Pharmaceutical Sciences, 1993—. Recipient Iwaki award Iwaki Found., Tokyo, 1986; named Disting. Educator, Japan Pvt. Sch. Promotion Found., 1994, 97. Fellow Japanese Pharmacol. Soc. (bd. dirs. 1998—), Japanese Soc. Allergology, Japanese Soc. History of Pharmacy. Office: Hoshi Univ Dept Pharmacology, 2-4-41 Ebara Shinagawa, Tokyo 142, Japan

MISAWA, SETSUO, physicist; b. Ina, Japan, Dec. 7, 1931; s. Chuji and Yoshino (Kurata) M.; m. Mieko Koyama; children: Michio, Tatsuki, Akiko. DSc, U. Tokyo, 1962. From rsch. assoc. to assoc. prof. Nihon U., Tokyo, 1961-76, prof., 1976—; lectr. Chiba U., 1980—. Co-author: Landolt-Börnstein, 1986, 3d edit., 1997. Sr. fellow U. Sheffield, Eng., 1963-64, Rsch. fellow MIT, Cambridge, 1964-65; Rsch. grantee Ministry Edn., Sci. and Culture, Japan, 1977-78. Avocations: tennis, chorus. Home: 3-2-7 Kikuna Kohoku-ku, 222-0011 Yokohama Japan Office: Nihon Univ, Dept Physics, 101-8308 Tokyo Japan

MISCHO, JEAN, international justice; b. 1938. Degrees in law and polit. sci., U. Montpellier, U. Paris, Cambridge U. Mem. Legal Svc. of Commn.; prin. adminstr. Mems. of Legal Svc. of Commn.; sec. of embassy in contentious affairs and treaties Dept. of Ministry of Fgn. Affairs, Grand Duchy of Luxembourg; dep. permanent rep. of Luxembourg European Cmtys.; dir. polit. affairs Ministry of Fgn. Affairs, sec. gen.; advocate gen. Court of Justice of European Cmtys., 1986-91, 97—. Office: Ct Justice European Cmtys, Palais de Cour de justice, Kirchberg L-2925, Luxembourg

MISCOVICH, PETER JOHN, consulting company executive; b. Seattle; s. John A. and Mary Miscovich. BS in Civil Engring., U. Ariz., 1984. Project dir. Interior Space Design, 1985-90; dir. nat. accounts Interior Space Internat., L.A., 1990-92, mng. dir., 1992-94; pres. Interior Space Internat., Chgo., 1994-96; dir. Arthur Andersen, N.Y.C., 1996-2000, ptnr., 2000—. Contbg. author: Guide to Human Capital, 1998, Future of the Work Place, 1999. Mem. Internat. Rsch. Devel. Coun. E-mail: peter.j.miscovich@us.arthurandersen.com. Office: Arthur Andersen 1345 Ave Americas New York NY 10105

MISE, JESSE SHERDEN, structural engineer, consultant; b. Jonesville, Va., July 13, 1933; s. Clabe Moss and Gladys Elizabeth (Orr) M.; m. Betty Joy Curtiss, July 8, 1984; children: Nancy Miller, Linda Andrews, Doug Hinshaw. BS in Math., Tenn. Tech, 1957. Registered profl. engr., Tenn., Mo. Road designer Va. Dept. Hwys., Petersburg, Va., 1958-64; structural designer various archtl., engring. firms, 1964-67; structural engr. Combustion Engring., Windsor, Conn., 1967-72, Tenn. Eastman, Kingsport, 1973-76, Tenn. Valley Authority, Knoxville, 1976-87, ABB Environ., Knoxville, 1988-91; cons. Jesse S. Mise, P.E., Knoxville, 1992—; chief engr. James Thomas Engring., Knoxville, 1992—. Author: Engineers Guide to Unusual Opportunities, 1972. Mem. Patriots of East Tenn., Knoxville, 1996—. Mem. ASCE, Nat. Coun. of Examiners for Engring. and Surveying, 1993—. Home and Office: 5704 Melstone Dr Knoxville TN 37912-4629

MISELSON, ALEX J. (JACOB) (JACOB MISELSON), portfolio manager, securities analyst, investment theorist; b. N.Y.C., Feb. 23, 1926; s. Aaron and Bertha (Guskin) M. BS in Social Sci. with honors in History, CCNY, 1947; MA in History, Columbia U., 1950; MA in Econs., Queens Coll., 1975. Instr. dept. history CCNY, 1949-55; tchr. Kearny (N.J.) High Sch., 1955-57, Uniondale High Sch., L.I., N.Y., 1957-76; reg. rep. Herzfeld and Stern, N.Y.C., 1977-81, Haas Securities Corp., N.Y.C., 1981-83, Fahnestock and Co., N.Y.C., 1983-85, Dominick and Dominick, N.Y.C., 1985; dir. rsch. A.T. Brod and Co., Inc., N.Y.C., 1986-94, Investors Assocs., N.Y.C., 1994-96, Paragon Capital Corp. (now Drake and Co.), N.Y.C., 1996-2000; dir. investment strategy Drake and Co., 2000—; instr. econs. Nassau Community Coll., 1969-75; head coach basketball Kearny High Sch., 1955-57; asst. coach basketball C.W. Post Coll., Greenvale, L.I., 1958-59; spl. guest TV talk shows; commentator in fin. field, 1988—. Contbr. articles to profl. publs., regularly interviewed by talk shows on special occasions, regularly interviewed by The Wall Street Transcript as part of its series on successful money managers, recognized as leading proponent of sophisticated long-term quality investing, with a unique highly unconventional selection technique and strategy. Active L.I. Coun. for Econ. Edn., Hofstra U., Hempstead, N.Y., 1968-75. With U.S. Army, 1944-45. Mem. Phi Delta Kappa, Phi Alpha Theta, Phi Beta Kappa. Avocations: reading, writing, theatre.

MISERY, LAURENT, dermatologist, biologist; b. St. Etienne, Loire, France, July 23, 1963; s. Laurent and Yvette (Bougault) M. MD, U. Lyon I, France, 1992, PhD in Biology, 1995. Physician Hosps. of Lyon, 1992-97, Hosps. of St. Etienne, 1998—. pres. rsch. commn. Parti Republicain, Paris, 1991-97, fed. sec., Loire, 1995-98; nat. sec. Movement of Young Republicans, Paris, 1989-92. Recipient L'Oreal prize, 1996. Mem. InterSyndicat Nat. des Chefs de Clinique-Assts. (v.p. 1995-96). Avocations: skiing, history, music. E-mail: laurent.misery@univ-st-etienne.fr. Home: 38 rue Saint Maximin, 69003 Lyon France Office: Dept Dermatology, North Hosp, 42055 Saint-Étienne France

MISHCHENKO, ALAN, computer scientist and engineer; b. Kiev, Ukraine, Sept. 1, 1970; came to U.S., 1998; s. Andrey Tikhonovich and Nadiya Mikhaylivna M. MS in Applied Math./Info. Tech., Moscow Inst. Physics & Tech., 1993; PhD in Computer Sci., Glushkov Inst. Cybernetics, Kiev, 1997. Jr. rsch. worker Glushkov Inst. Cybernetics, Kiev, 1993-98; instr. PhysTech Ctr., Kiev Dept. of Moscow Inst. Physics & Tech., 1997-98; vis. asst. prof. Portland (Oreg.) State U.; chmn. ann. Oreg. Symposium on Logic, Design, and Learning, 2000. Contbr. articles to profl. jours. Intel faculty fellow, 1999. Mem. IEEE, IEEE Computer Soc. Avocations: hiking, travel, reading, programming.

MISHNAEVSKY, LEON L., JR., mechanical and civil engineer, researcher; b. Kiev, Ukraine, May 14, 1964; s. Leonid L. and Simona L. (Gekhtmann) M.; m. Slava Kulenko, 1995; 1 child, Lennart. Diploma in engring., Civil Engring. U., Kiev, 1987; D. of Engring., Inst. of Mining North, Yakutsk, Russia, 1990. Engr. Inst. Superhard Materials, USSR Acad. Scis., Kiev, 1981-87; rschr., 1987-94; rsch. scientist Tech. U. Vienna, Austria, 1994-95, Max-Planck Inst. fuer Metallforschung, Stuttgart, 1997; rsch. fellow State Material Testing Inst. U. Stuttgart, Germany, 1996-97, rsch. scientist, 1997—; mem. internat. organizing com. 2d Internat. Conf. Mesofracture-96, Tomsk, Russia, 1996; mem. internat. organizing com. Internat. Conf. Mesomechanics-98, Tel Aviv, 1998. Author: Theory of Fragmentation of Permafrost and Brittle Rocks in Drilling, 1991, Damage and Fracture of Heterogeneous Materials, 1998; contbr. over 70 articles to profl. publs. Activist Animal Protection Campaign, Germany and Ukraine, 1996. Recipient Best Rsch. Work award Inst. for Superhard Materials, 1990, 92, Internat. Sci. Found. Travel award 1993; Alexander von Humboldt Rsch. fellow, Bonn, Germany, 1995-97, Engring. Found. Conf. fellow, N.Y.C., 1996, Japan Sci. and Tech. Agy. fellow Nagoya, Japan, 2000, Japan Soc. Promotion Sci. fellow Tokyo, 2000, Japan Sci. and Tech. Agy. fellow Synergy Ceramics Lab., Nagoya, 2000; travel grantee European Phys. Soc., Geneva, 1996; vis. grantee dept. math. Goeteborg U. and Chalmers U. Tech., Sweden, 1996; travel grantee NATO Advanced Rsch. Workshop, 1997, CECAM Workshop, Lyon, France, 1998. Mem. Internat. Soc. Structural Optimization, Gesellschaft fur Angewandte Math. and Mechanik, Internat. Soc. Rock Mechanics (organizing conf. com., 1996, 1998). Fax: 049-711-685-26-35. E-mail: impgmish@mpa.uni-stuttgart.de. Home: Nauheimerstr 8, Frankfurt am Main D-60486, Germany Office: MPA U Stuttgart, Pfaffenwaldring 32, Stuttgart D 70569, Germany

MISHRA, ASHOK KUMAR, economist, educator; b. Jaunpur, India, Aug. 5, 1967; came to U.S., 1990; s. Shambhu N. and Chandrawati P. Mishra; m. Venita S. Mishra, Dec. 29, 1990; children: Sachin, Megna. BSc in Agrl., G.B. Pant U. Agr. and Tech., Pantnagar, India, 1988; MSc in Agrl. Econs., U. Aberdeen, Scotland, 1989; PhD in Econs., N.C. State U., 1996. Econs. instr. N.C. State U., Raleigh, 1993-95, grad. rsch. asst. agrl. econs., 1991-95; economist II Dept. Environment, Health and Natural Resources, State Govt., Raleigh, 1995-97; economist Econ. Rsch. Svc. USDA, Washington, 1997—. Contbr. articles to profl. jours. including Am. Jour. Agrl. Econs. Treas. Econ. Grad. Student Assn., N.C. State U., Raleigh, 1993. Recipient merit scholarship G.B. Pant U. Agr. and Tech., 1985-88, univ. sports scholarship, 1987-88, scholarship Overseas Devel. Adminstrn. (Eng.), 1988-89; Sir Vincent Meridith fellow McGill U. (Can.), 1989-90. Mem. Am. Agrl. Econs. Assn., So. Agrl. Econs. Assn., Am. Econs. Assn. Avocations: gardening, sports, cooking. E-mail: amishra@ers.usda.gov. Office: ERS/USDA 1800 M St NW Washington DC 20036-5802

MISHRA, CHANDRA S., finance educator, consultant; b. India, Jan. 5, 1962; came to U.S., 1986; s. K.C. and S. Mishra; m. Karabi Mishra, June 23, 1985; children: Mitushi, Sachit. BS, Saurastra U., India, 1982; MS, Nat. Inst. Tng. Indsl. Engr., India, 1984; PhD, U. Tex., Dallas, 1991. Asst. prof. fin. Loyola U., Chgo., 1990-96; assoc. prof. fin. Oreg. State U., Corvallis, 1996—; cons., Corvallis, 1996—. Home: 1798 SW Otana Dr Corvallis OR 97333-1369 Office: Coll Bus Oreg State U 200 Bexell Hall Corvallis OR 97331-8527

MISHRA, KAUSHALA PRASAD, biologist; b. Allahabad, India, July 2, 1941; s. Ram Narain and Shokali (Devi) M.; m. Usha Kaushala, Apr. 19, 1951; children: Rajesh, Abha, Anil. BSc, U. Allahbad, 1966, MSc, 1968; PhD, Gujarat U., 1979. From officer trainee to scientific officer, head biology Bhabha Atomic Rsch. Ctr., Mumbai, India, 1968—. Home: Nari Seva Sadan Rd, 400 084 Mumbai India Office: Bhabha Atomic Rsch Ctr, Trombay, 400 085 Mumbai India

MISHRA, LALIT KUMAR, physics educator; b. Gaya, Bihar, India, Oct. 25, 1956; s. Gansh Dutt and Malti (Devi) M.; m. Chanchala, Mar. 10, 1978; 2 children. BSc, Magadh U., Gaya, 1972, MSc, 1975; PhD, Inst. Physics, Bhubaneswar, India, 1991. Lectr. S.V.P. Coll., Bhabhua, India, 1977-83; postgrad. Inst. of Physics, Bhubanaswar (Jrissa), 1983-84; reader S.V.P. Coll. Bhabhua, 1990-91; reader dept. physics Magadh U., Bodh Gaya Bihar, India, 1991-95, prof. dept. physics, 1995—. Contbr. articles to profl. jours. Avocations: chess playing, music listening, movies watching. Home: New Area, Bisar Taleb, Gaya 823001, India Office: Magadh Univ, Dept Physics, Bodh Gaya Bihar 824234, India

MISHRA, SANAK, steel company executive, researcher; b. Berhampur, Orissa, India, Dec. 18, 1945; s. Harihar and Indumati (Rath) M.; m. Veena Paralkar, Sept. 27, 1973; children: Apurva, Ashish. BSc with honours in Physics, Ravenshaw Coll., Cuttack, India, 1965; BEng in Metallurgy, Indian Inst. Sci., Bangalore, 1968; MS, U. Ill., 1970, PhD, 1973. Dep. mgr., then sr. mgr. Steel Authority India Ltd., 1973-86, prin. rsch. mgr., 1986-89, asst. gen. mgr., 1989-91, dep. gen. mgr., 1991-93, gen. mgr., 1993-96, exec. dir., 1996—; Alexander von Humboldt fellow Aachen (Germany) Tech. U., 1981-82, vis. scholar U. Pitts., 1991, Carnegie-Mellon U., 1992; co-chmn. Indian Deep Drawing Rsch. Group, 1996—. Chief editor Steel India, 1978—; contbr. over 100 articles to internat. jours., chpts. to books. Pro-vice chmn. governing body Delhi Pub. Sch. Soc. Secondary Sch., Ranchi, 1993—. Recipient Nat. Metallurgist award Govt. of India, 1988, 89, Metallurgy and Materials Sci. medal, 1992, SAIL Gold medal, 1993. Fellow Indian Inst. Metals (nat. coun. 1996—, editor Trans. 1991—, G.D. Birla Meml. award 1995, Kamani gold medal 1984), Indian Nat. Acad. Engring., Indian Instn. Engrs. (Visvesvaraya gold medal); mem. NAS, Computer Soc. India (chmn. Ranchi chpt. 1995-97), Materials Rsch. Soc. India (medal), Bur. Indian Standards (chmn. steel products sectional com.). Avocations: classical and pop music. Home: House #A-342 Asian Games V, New Delhi 110049, India Office: Steel Authority India Ltd, Ispat Bhawan Lodi Rd, New Delhi 110003, India

MISHRA, SURENDRA PRASAD, medical physicist; b. Gorkhpur, India, Nov. 5, 1953; s. Sheo Pujan and Chitragupta Mishra; m. Rambha Pandey, June 13, 1973; children: Akhilesh, Pratika. BS, U. Gorakhpur, India, 1975, MS, 1977; diploma in radiological physics, U. Bombay, 1979; PhD, U. Allahabad, India, 1997. Cert. course in med. physics Abdus Salam Ctr. for Theoretical Physics, Italy; med. physicist Bhabha Atomic Rsch. Ctr., Bombay. Physicist, radiol. safety officer Cancer Hosp. and Rsch. Inst., Goa, India, 1979-81, Gwaliar, India, 1981-83; sr. physicist, radiol. safety officer Regional Cancer Ctr., Kamala Nehru Meml. Hosp., Allahabad, 1983—, head dept. med. physics, 1992—; expert panel Dept. Sci. and Tech., India, 1996—; acad. counselor Indira Gandhi Nat. Open U., India, 1995—; mem. governing coun. Regional Cancer Ctr., Allahabad, 1993—. Author book chpts.: Diagnostic Imaging and Quality Control, 1995, Medical Physics and Human Health, 1996; mem. editl. bd. Jour. Med. Physics, 1995—; contbr. articles to profl. jours. Social worker Soc. for Rural Health, Allahabad, 1995; sec. UP-Delcha, Allahabad, 1995-97. Rsch. fellow Abdus Salam Ctr. for Theoretical Physics, 1992. Mem. Assn. Med. Physicist India (exec. com. 1995-97, organizing sec. 1997), Indian Assn. for Radiation Protection (organizing sec. 1991, Best Paper award 1991), Lions Club (sec. 1992-93). Mem. Indian Nat. Congress. Avocations: sports, social work, environment, promotion of science, female welfare. Home: Sri Mahavir Jute Mills, 272209 Sahjanwa India Office: KN Meml Hosp Regional Cancer Ctr, Hashimpur Rd, 211002 Allahabad India

MISHRA, VIJAY CHANDRA, English literature educator, researcher; b. Suva, Fiji, May 4, 1945; arrived in Australia, 1970; s. Hari Karan and Lila Wati (Singh) M.; m. Nalini Singh, June 29, 1973; children: Rohan, Paras. BA, Victoria U., Wellington, New Zealand, 1966; diploma in tchg., Christchurch Tchrs. Coll., 1967; BA with honors, Macquarie U., Australia, 1971; MA with honors, Sydney (Australia) U., 1976; PhD, Australian Nat. U., Canberra, 1981, Oxford U., 1990. Tchr. Labasa Coll., Fiji, 1968-69; sr. edn. officer Ministry of Edn., Fiji, 1972-73; tutor English, Women's Coll.-Sydney U., 1974-75; lectr. English, Murdoch U., Perth, Australia, 1976-91, assoc. prof., 1992-97; prof. English, U. Alberta, Can., 1998-99; prof. English and comparative literature Murdoch U., 1999—; vis. prof. U. Calif. Santa Cruz, 1996. Author: The Gothic Sublime, 1994, Devotional Poetics and the Indian Sublime, 1998; co-author: Dark Side of the Dream, 1991; editor: Rama's Banishment, 1979; contbr. over 50 articles to profl. publs. and books. Fellow U. Wales, Cardiff, 1989, U. Calif. Santa Cruz, 1993-94, U. Delhi, India, 1997. Hindu. Avocations: walking, classical music, golf, Indian harmonium. Home: 92 Hensman St, South Perth WA 6151, Australia Office: Murdoch U, Sch Humanities, Perth WA T6G 2E5, Australia

MISHURIS, GENNADY, applied mathematician, educator; b. Khmelnicki, USSR, Jan. 30, 1959; arrived in Poland, 1995; s. Samoil Boris and Eva (Zinger) M.; m. Victoria Zhyrnova, Nov. 15, 1961; 1 child, Victor. Master, Leningrad (Russia) State U., 1982, PhD, 1985; DSc, Cracow U. Tech., 1999. Prof. math. Vologda (Russia) U. of Tech., 1986-91; sci. rschr. Warsaw (Poland) U., 1991-92; prof. math. Rzeszów (Poland) U. of Tech., 1993—; Alexander von Humboldt fellow, chair applied mechanics Erlangen-Nuremberg U., Germany, 1999-2000. Contbr. articles to profl. jours. Mem. Am. Math. Soc., Polish Math. Soc., Euromech. Office: Rzeszów U of Tech Dept Math, W Pola 2, 35 959 Rzeszów Poland

MISIEK, DALE JOSEPH, oral and maxillofacial surgeon; b. Hartford, Conn., Dec. 10, 1952; s. Joseph John and Jadwiga Magdelena (Wojtowicz) M.; m. Patricia Ann Munson, June 28, 1975; children: Matthew Bryan, Stacy Lynne, Michael Stephen. BA magna cum laude, U. Conn., Storrs, 1974; DMD, U. Conn., Farmington, 1978; cert. advanced tng. oral and maxillofacial surgery, La. State U., 1982. Diplomate Am. Bd. Oral and Maxillofacial Surgery. Resident oral surgery Charity Hosp. of La., New Orleans, 1978-82, mem. clin. surgery com., 1984-86, mem. surgery com., 1986—, mem. credentials com., 1988—; asst. prof. dept. oral and maxillofacial surgery Sch. Dentistry, La. State U., New Orleans, 1984-87, assoc. prof., 1987-94; prof. dept. oral and maxillofacial surgery Sch. Dentistry La. State U., New Orleans, 1994-98; also mem. various coms. Sch. Dentistry, La. State U., New Orleans; practice dentistry specializing in oral surgery New Orleans, 1982-84; pvt. practice Charlotte, 1998—; mem. staff Ear, Eye, Nose and Throat Hosp., New Orleans, 1982-98, chmn. dental dept., also mem. exec. com., credentials com. and instrument com., 1983-84; mem. staff East Jefferson Gen. Hosp., Metairie, 1982-98, chmn. dental dept., 1990-94, med. records com., 1983-85, credentials com., 1994-98; mem. staff Univ. Hosp., New Orleans, 1982—; courtesy staff Children's Hosp., New Orleans, 1982—, Mercy Hosp., New Orleans, 1982-98, So. Bapt. Hosp., New Orleans, 1983-98, Our Lady of the Lake Regional Med. Ctr., Baton Rouge, 1985-98, Kenner (La.) Regional Med. Ctr., 1986-98, Dr.'s Hosp., Metairie, 1986—; cons. VA Med. Ctr., New Orleans, 1984—, Carolinas Med. Ctr., Charlotte, 1998—, Presbyn. Med. Ctr., Charlotte, 1998—, U. Hosp., Charlotte, 1998—, Northeast Med. Ctr., Concord, 1999—; lectr. in field. Contbr. articles and abstracts to profl. jours. Recipient C.V. Mosby Book award. Fellow Am. Assn. Oral and Maxillofacial Surgeons (mem. spl. com. for devel. stds. and criteria for care 1986—, spl. com. on oral and maxillofacial surgery self-assessment program 1990), Am. Coll. Oral and Maxillofacial Surgeons; mem. ADA (cons. commn. on dental accreditation 1986—), Am. Bd. Oral and Maxillofacial Surgery (adv. com. 1990-95, regional advisor Dist. III 1996-99), Am. Acad. Cosmetic Surgery, La. Soc. Oral and Maxillofacial Surgeons (anesthesia com. 1983-85, advanced cardiac life support com. 1986-88, sec./

treas. 1991-95, v.p. 1996—), Internat. Assn. Oral and Maxillofacial Surgery, Acad. Osseointegration, Charlotte Dental Soc., 2d Dist. Dental Soc., N.C. Dental Soc., N.C. Soc. Oral and Maxillofacial Surgeons, Orleans Parish Med. Soc., Am. Heart Assn. (instr.), Phi Beta Kappa, Phi Kappa Phi, Omicron Kappa Upsilon. Republican. Roman Catholic. Avocations: baseball, weightlifting, fishing. Office: 8738 University City Blvd Charlotte NC 28213-3558

MISKIMEN, ROBERT IVAN, retired pastor; b. Alliance, Nebr., Oct. 25, 1925; s. Elmo L. and Lena Magdalena (Panwitz) M.; m. Lois Magdalena Hoffmeyer, Aug. 19, 1951; children: Victoria, Carolyn, Elizabeth, Grace, Robert Jr., Christine, Eunice, Carl, Karen. Student, Concordia Theol. Sem., 1952. Pastor Faith Luth. Ch., Council Bluffs, Iowa, 1952-58, Trinity Luth., Cherokee, Iowa, 1958-64; assoc. pastor St. John Luth., Racine, Wis., 1964-73; head pastor St. Stephen Luth., Horicon, Wis., 1973-86; part-time pastor Immanual Luth., Burns, Wyo., 1988-94; interim pastor St. John, Brule and Zion Luth., Big Springs, Nebr., 1998-99; ret.; chmn. Commn. on Adjudication, So. Wis. Dist. Luth. Ch.-Mo. Synod Dist. Office, Horicon, Milw., 1978-86. Mem. Am. Assn. Ret. Persons (chmn. 1996-2000), SAR (chaplain Wis. state 1975-86, chaplain Wyo. state 1988-2000). Avocations: photography, writing. Home: 2228 E Pershing Blvd Cheyenne WY 82001-4111

MISKIN, RAYMOND JOHN, retired mechanical engineer; b. Ipswich, Suffolk, England, July 4, 1928; s. Sidney George and Hilda (Holdsworth) M.; m. Betty Tavener, July 14, 1951 (div. Nov. 1981); 1 child, Karen; m. Brenda Elizabeth Mills, June 3, 1991. Cert. in mech. engring., Southall Tech. Coll., Middlesex, Eng., 1951. Chartered mech. engr., Eng. Apprentice Fairey Aviation Co. Ltd., Hayes, Middlesex, 1945-49, devel. engr., 1949-54, sect. leader devel. engr., 1956-59, dep. chief inspector, 1959-63; dep. chief technician Self Priming Punp Co. Ltd., Slough, Bucks, Eng., 1954-56; quality mgr. Graviner (Colinbrook, Eng.) Ltd., 1963-69; sec., CEO Inst. Quality Assurance, London, 1969-73; dep. sec. Inst. Prodn. Engrs., London, 1973-76, sec., CEO, 1976-87; cons. Royal Acad. Engring., London, 1987-89; CEO Cadlas Ltd., Chesterfield, Derbyshire, Eng., 1989-93; cons. quality assurance Sheffield, Eng., 1993—. Vice chmn. Nat. Coun. for Quality and Reliability, London, 1973-75, chmn., 1975-77. Recipient Internat. Indsl. Tech. Mgmt. award San Fernado Valley Engrs.' Coun., 1978, Internat. Contbns. award L.A. Coun. Engrs. and Scientists, First Shuttle Flight Achievement award, 1982, Internat. Interprofl. Achievement award NSPE, 1983, Outstanding Tech. Transfer award Calif. Coun. Indsl. and Bus. Assns., 1984, Internat. Tech. Comms. award Calif. Engring. Found., 1985, Gold medal Hungarian Soc. Mech. Engrs., 1985, Disting. Econs. Devel. Programs award Soc. Mech. Engrs., 1992. Fellow Instn. Mech. Engrs., Inst. Elec. Engrs., Inst. Quality Assurance, Indian Instn. Prodn. Engrs. (hon.), Soc. Mfg. Engrs.; mem. Royal Aero. Soc. Mem. Ch. of England. Avocations: golf, photography, model making. Home: 36 Hayes Dr, Mosborough Sheffield S20 4TR, England

MISNER, CAROL DEAN, mathematics educator; b. Kansas City, Mo., Jan. 18, 1943; d. Howard Edward and Thelma Irene (Creps) M.; m. Ronald William Umphrey, Aug. 6, 1966 (div. Jan. 1983); children: Clinton Howard Umphrey, Lorna Soonhee Umphrey. BA in Math, Sterling Coll., 1966; MA in Edn., Emory U., 1970. Tchr. math. Wyandotte County Unified Sch., Kansas City, Kans., 1965-66, Fulton County Unified Schs., Atlanta, 1966-71; lectr. Okla. State U., Stillwater, 1982-85; curriculum coord. Morongo Valley Unified Schs., Yucca Valley, Calif., 1985-87; tchr. math. Morgan Hill Unified Schs., San Jose, Calif., 1987-89; prof. math. Hartnell Coll., Salinas, Calif., 1989-95; chair math. dept., prof. Mohave C.C., Bullhead City, Ariz., 1995-99; coord. instrnl. tech. Porterville (Calif.) Coll., 1999—; multimedia cons. Porterville, 1999—; presenter at numerous confs. incl. League of Innovation, Ariz. Math. Assn., Calif. Math. Consortium of Cmty. Colls. Author, instrnl. technologist: Multimedia-Using Power in the Classroom, 2000; contbr. numerous articles to profl. jours. Recipient Tchg. Excellence award Calif. Coun. C.C.s, 1994; named Tchr. of Yr., Alpha Chi Psi, 1997, Advisor of Yr., Phi Theta Kappa, 1998. Avocations: drawing, hiking, reading. Fax: (559) 789-9300. E-mail: cmisner@pc.cc.ca.us. Office: Porterville Coll 100 E College Ave Porterville CA 93257-6058

MISRA, AJIT KUMAR, dairy microbiology educator, researcher; b. Ballia, India, July 20, 1957; s. Bankey Behari and Radha Rani (Dubey) M. m. Poonam Tewari, Dec. 6, 1982; 1 child, Stuti. BSc, Kanpur (India) U., 1976; MSc in Dairy Sci., Nat. Dairy Rsch. Inst., Karnal, India, 1978; PhD, Bidhan Chandra Agr. U., Nadia, India, 1990. Cert. in evaluation, examination and methodology Assn. Indian Univs. Dairy bacteriologist Pradeshik Coop. Dairy Fedn., Moradabad, India, 1979-81; lectr. Bidhan Chandra Agrl. U., Nadia, India, 1981-88, reader, 1989-94, head dept. dairy bacteriology, 1983-94; reader dairy microbiology West Bengel U. Animal and Fishery Scis., Calcutta, India, 1995—, head dept. dairy bacteriology, 1995—, exec. coun. mem., 1996—; mem. adv. group NRC, Washington, 1991; counsellor Indira Gandhi Nat. Open U., New Delhi, 1989—. Contbr. articles to sci. jours., including Milchwissenschaft, Australian Jour. Daily Tech., Cultured Dairy Products Jour., Lait. Mem. governing body Kalyani (India) Springdale Welfare and Edn. Soc., 1995—. Mem. Indian Dairy Assn. (life, editor 1994-96), Assn. Food Scientists and Technologists, Agrl. Rsch. Comm. Ctr. (regional editor 1989—), West Bengal Coll. and Univ. Tchrs. Assn. Avocations: social work, chess, badminton, science journalism. Home: B10/271, Nadia Kalyani 741235, India Office: WB U Animal and Fishery Sci, Mohanpur Campus, Nadia 741235, India

MISRA, BAIDYANATH, physicist, researcher; b. Pithapotal, Orissa, India, Aug. 25, 1937; s. Durga Prasad and Sindhu Kumari (Dash) M.; m. Beenapani Nanda, Feb. 11, 1968; children: Purabi, Surabhi, Shubhada. BS with honors, Utkal U., India, 1956; MS, U. Delhi, 1958; DSc, U. Geneva, 1965. Rschr. U. Geneva, 1962-67, pvt. docent, 1967-69; asst. prof. U. Rochester, N.Y., 1969-70; prof. Sambalpur U., India, 1970-71; assoc. prof. U. Colo., Boulder, 1971-75; rsch. prof. Internat. Solvay Inst., Brussels, 1976—; mem. syndicate Sambalpur U., 1970-71; dean Sch. Phys. Scis., Jawaharlal Nehru U., New Delhi, 1986-88. Contbr. articles to profl. jours. Recipient Da Vinci award Royal Belgian Acad. Sci. and Internat. Rotary Club, 1986. Fellow Nat. Acad. Sci. India. Avocations: philosophy, chess, listening to classical music. Home: 6 Narang Colony Janakpuri, New Delhi 58, India

MISRA, BASANT KUMAR, neurosurgeon, consultant; b. Bhubaneshwar, India, Jan. 18, 1953; s. Baidyanath and Basanti Misra; m. Sasmita Kar, Feb. 1, 1981; children: Sarthak, Siddharth. B in Medicine, B in Surgery, Veer Surendra Sai Med. Coll., Sambalpur, India, 1975; MS in Surgery, Delhi U., 1980; M of Surgery in Neurosurgery, All India Inst of Med. Scis., Delhi, 1983; diploma in Neurosurgery, Nat. Bd. Examinations, Delhi, 1984. Nat. Bd. Examiners. Lectr. neurosurgery Sree Chitra Tirunal Inst. of Med. Sci. and Tech., Trivandrum, India, 1984-85; asst. prof. neurosurgery Sree Chitra Tirunal Inst. and Med. Sci. and Tech., Trivandrum, India, 1986; Commonwealth med. scholar U. Edinburgh, Scotland, 1985-87; assoc. prof. neurosurgery Sree Chitra Tirunal Inst. of Med. Sci. and Tech., 1987-90; additional prof. neurosurgery Sree Chitra Tirunal Inst. and Med. Sci. and Tech., 1991—; cons., neurosurgeon Hinduja Nat. Hosp. and Med. Rsch. Ctr., Bombay, 1995—, cons., HOD neurosurgery, HOD Gamma knife surgery; vis. faculty neurosurgery All India Inst. of Med. Scis. and Tech., Delhi, 1992, Tex. Tech. U., Lubbock, 1993; vis. prof. neurosurgery Himeji (Japan) Heart and Brain Ctr., 1993, George Washington U., Washington, 1994. Contbr. over 70 articles to profl. jours. Recipient 3 Gold medals Sambalpur U., 1975, Gold medal Pfizer Ltd., 1978, scholarship Commonwealth Scholarship Comm., London, 1984, grant. dept. of sci. and tech. Govt. India, 1994. Mem. Neurology Soc. India (life), Congress Neurol. Surgeons (USA), Skull Base Soc. India (founding mem.), N.Y. Acad. Scis. Avocations: lecturing tours, acting, basketball. Home: 701 Carlton Ct Plot # 139, Junction Peri Rd & Pali Rd, Bandra Bombay 400 050, India Office: PD Hinduja Nat Hosp, VS Marg Mahim, 400 016 Bombay India

MISRA, DEBENDRA KUMAR, retired pulp and paper industry executive, consultant; b. Cuttack, Orissa, India, Dec. 9, 1924; arrived in Cyprus, 1987; s. Satyabadi and Sabitri (Mohapatra) M.; m. Olga Momirski, May 4, 1957; children: Guru Prasad, Gali. BSc in Indsl Chemistry and Chem. Engring, Banaras (India) Hindu U., 1947; PhD in Chem. Engring., U. Beverly Hills, L.A., 1979. Process and tech. engr. various pulp and paper mills, India, 1948-53; R & D officer Forest Rsch. Inst., DehraDun, India, 1949-51; pulp and paper technologist various, Yugoslavia, Austria, Germany, Belgium, 1953-57; mill supt., tech. exec. Parsons & Whittemore Inc., N.Y.C., 1966-77, sr. v.p. internat. ops., 1978-82, cons., tech. advisor, 1983-86; cons. Roya. Inst. Tech., 1978-79; chief spkr. of del. Ministry of Light Industry, Beijing, 1978-79; tech. advisor UNIDO, Vienna, 1990-91; cons. pulp and paper cos., Delhi, India, Dubai, United Arab Emirates, 1992-94. Inventor in field. Scholar Govt. Orissa, DehraDun, 1948; fellow Govts. India and Yugoslavia, 1953-56. Mem. AIChE. Avocations: reading magazines, technical literature, science, fiction. Home: 28th Otober St 25, Apt 41 Delta Ct, 2012 Strovolos Nicosia Cyprus Home: 15426 Smithaven Pl Centreville VA 20120-1162

MISRA, RABINDRA, thermal power station administrator; b. Sambalpur, India, Jan. 30, 1956; s. Srinath and Snehamayee (Pujari) M.; m. Baridhi Mund, Feb. 18, 1984; children: Soma, Smrutiman. BEE, Bangalore (India) U., 1979; Postgrad. Diploma in Indsl. Mgmt., Sambalpur U., 1984. Engring. asst. Indian Aluminium Co. Ltd., Sambalpur, 1980-85, asst. supt., 1985-88, supr. elec., 1988-91, mgr. engreing., 1991-95, plant mgr., 1995-97, works mgr., 1997—. Mem. IEEE, Rotary Club. Home: SSB 1 Indal Colony, Hirakud, 768 016 Sambalpur, Orissa India

MISRA, RABINDRA KUMAR, root scientist, soil scientist; b. Bhubaneswar, Orissa, India, Oct. 21, 1954. BSc in Agr., Orissa U. Agr. and Tech., 1975; MSc in Agrl. Physics, Indian Agrl. Rsch. Inst., New Delhi, 1977; PhD, U. Adelaide, Australia, 1987. Rsch. fellow U. Melbourne, Australia, 1986-88, Griffith U., Australia, 1988-92; root scientist U. Tasmania, Australia, 1992-98; lectr. in soil sci. U. Sunshine Coast, Queensland, Australia, 1999—. Contbr. articles to profl. jours. Recipient State Merit scholarship Dept. Edn., Orissa, India, 1966-70, Nat. Merit scholarship Dept. Edn., India, 1971-75; fellow Indian Coun. Agrl. Rsch., 1975-77; Commonwealth scholarship and fellowship, Australia, 1982-86. Mem. Australian Soc. Soil Sci. Avocations: cricket, table tennis, tennis. Office: Faculty Sci, U Sunshine Coast, Maroochydore DC Queensland 4558, Australia

MISSANA, LILIANA RAQUEL, oral pathologist; b. Cordoba, Argentina, Sept. 8, 1957; d. Victorio and Maria Ester (Lattanzi) M.; m. Cesar Guido Filippone, Sept. 7, 1989; 1 child, Bruno (dec.). DDS, Cordoba Dental Sch., 1979; PhD Dentistry, Okayama (Japan) Dental Sch., 1994. Asst. Cordoba U., 1978-80; asst. prof. Tucuman (Argentina) U., 1981-90, head prof., 1995—; Mombusho scholar Okayama U., 1988-94; Fulbright scholar Kansas U. Med. Ctr., 1998; rsch. career adj. CONICET, Argentina, 1997—; rsch. project dir. CIUNT, Tucuman, 1997—. Mem. IADR. Roman Catholic. Avocations: tai-chi-chuan, Oriental arts and philosophy. Home: Pasaje Leopoldo Lugones 80, 4.000 Tucuman Argentina Office: Tucuman U Dental Sch, Av Benjamin Araoz 800, 4.000 Tucuman Argentina

MISSANA, MARCO ORSO, astronomer; b. Ceriale, Savona, Italy, Mar. 13, 1941; s. Natale and Eleonora (Merlo-Ceriale) M.; m. Lea Slerca, 1969; children: Natalia, Michela. D of Physics, U. Torino, 1964. Tech. laureato Obs. Torino, Italy, 1966; astronomer Obs. Milan, Italy, 1966—; dir. I.P.M.S., Carloforte, Italy, 1968-69. Contbr. articles to profl. jours. Fellow NATO, 1973-74. Mem. Soc. Astronomers Italy, Soc. Italian Physicists. Home: via Cremagnani 13/11, 20059 Vimercate Milan, Italy Office: Obs Astronomico di Brera, via Brera 28, 20121 Milan Lombard, Italy

MISTIAEN, WILHELM PETER, surgeon, researcher; b. Antwerp, Belgium, Jan. 15, 1959; s. David and Hannah Luise (Verkerk) M.; m. Hilde Maria Van Roie, Aug. 31, 1985; children: Rebecca, Dominic. MD, U. Antwerp (Belgium), 1984, PhD, 1999. Resident U. Hosp. Antwerp (Belgium), 1984-85; researcher U. Antwerp, 1985-87; surg. trainee Middelheim Hosp., Antwerp, 1987-94, 1994-97; surgeon St. Augustinus Hosp., Antwerp, 1994-98; rschr., dept. morphology U. Antwerp, 1998—; guest prof. anatomy for physiotherapists, Antwerp, 1999. Contbr. articles to profl. jours. Mem. Royal Coll. Surgeons Belgium. Avocations: reading about astrophysics and nuclear physics, playing clarinet. Home: Koning Albertstr 9, 2610 Antwerp Belgium Office: U Antwerp Dept Morph, Groenenborgerlaan 121, 2020 Antwerp Belgium

MISTRY, PERCY SHIAVAK, investment banker; b. Bombay, July 22, 1947; arrived in United Kingdom, 1987; s. Shiavak P. and Banoo S. (Engineer) M.; m. Pauline Earnshaw, Oct. 15, 1969. B of Tech. with honors, Loughborough (U.K.) U., 1969; MBA, U. Toronto, 1970, MPhil, 1971. Sr. advisor to exec. v.p. Internat. Fin. Corp., Washington, 1977-78; mng. dir. SGV-SUN Hung Kai Corp. Fin., Hong Kong, 1978-81; dir., sr. fin. advisor The World Bank, Washington, 1981-87; sr. fellow Oxford (Eng.) U., 1987-92; chmn. Oxford Internat. Assoc., 1988—, Oxford Internat. Fin., 1992-97; CEO Synergy Power Corp., 1998-2000; chmn. Ukraine Fin. Corp., 1995-98, D.C. Gardner & Co., London, 1992-93; bd. dirs. Indsl. Credit & Investment Corp. India, Bombay, 1993-97,Forum on Debt & Devel., The Hague, Holland, 1988-98; bd. dirs.Synergy Power Corp., Hong-Kong, 1987; columnist The Banker, 1987-91; adv. DBSA, UN-ECA, 1999—. Author: Adjustment, Investment and Development Finance in Southern Africa, 2000, Regional Integration & Economic Development, 1996, Resolving Africa's Multilateral Debt Problem, 1996, Multilateral Development Banker, 1995, Multilateral Debt: An Emerging Crisis, 1994, The Financial Condition of the African Development Bank, 1993, Economic Integration in Southern Africa, 1993, Inflation in Ethiopia, 1992, African Debt Revisited: Procrastination or Progress?, 1991, African Debt: The Case for Relief, 1988, Multilateral Development Banks, 1995; co-author: Adjusting Privatization, 1992 (Acad. Book of Yr. 1993), The Conversion of Official Bilateral Debt, 1992, Financing the Multilateral System, 1991, Zambia: Exchange Rate Policy, 1989, Development Finance in Southern Africa; contbr. articles to profl. jours. Dir. US-Caresbac, Atlanta, 1988-92; trustee The P.C. Mistry Found., Bombay, 1987—. Mem. The Reform Club, The Willingdon Club, Newbury Race Club, Cricket Club of India, The Royal Western India Turf Club. Avocations: breeding thoroughbreds, swimming, squash, tennis, reading.

MISU, KUNIHIRO, planner, architect, engineer; b. Yokohama, Kanagawa, Japan, Mar. 26, 1941; s. Kenzo and Kin (Asai) M.; m. Masako Watanabe, June 25, 1966 (dec. Aug. 1995); children: Yoshiko Hirabayashi, Kenichi, Namiko. BSc in Architecture, Tokyo Inst. Tech., 1963; MSc in Architecture, Ill. Inst. Tech., 1966; DHL (hon.), Barat Coll., Lake Forest, 1997. Registered architect, Singapore; registered 1st class architect, Japan. Architect Nikken Sekkei Ltd., Bunkyo-ku, Tokyo, Japan, 1968-89, dir., 1989-97, mng. dir., 1997-99, sr. mng. dir., 1999-2000, pres., 2000—; ptnr. Nikken Sekkei Partnership, Singapore, 1988—; lectr. Tokyo Inst. Tech., 1985-86. Co-author: Super High Rise Office Building, 1987, Office Renaissance, 1986; designer C. Itoh Bldg., 1980 (Bldg. Contractors Soc. prize 1982), NEC Super Tower, 1990 (Bldg. Contractors Soc. prize 1991). Recipient Nikkei BP award Nikkei Bus. Publ. Inc. Japan, 1991, award Architects Regional Coun. Asia, 1996. Mem. Singapore Inst. Architects, Japan Inst. Architects (coun. mem. 1987—). Office: Nikken Sekkei Ltd, 2-1-3 Koraku, Bunkyo-ku 112 8565, Japan

MISU, MASAFUMI, electrical engineering executive; b. Kamitonda, Wakayama, Japan, Nov. 30, 1913; s. Bin and Taka Misu; m. Kimiko Tsuiki, June 13, 1941; children: Masaharau, Keiko, Reiko. Degree in Elec. Engring., Tokyo U., 1936. Gen. mgr. South Am., Buenos Aires, 1963-65; bd. dirs. Hitachi Ltd., Tokyo, 1967-69; exec. mng. dir. Hitachi Ltd., Tokyo, 1969-75, exec. v.p., 1975-81, sr. advisor, 1981-93; sr. advisor emeritus Hitachi Ltd., 1993-98; coun. mem. Ministry Internat. Trade and Industry, 1980-84; vice-chmn. Japan Machinery Ctr., 1975-94, sr. advisor. Named to The 3rd Order of Merit, 1985. Office: care Hitachi Ltd Nihon Bldg, 6-2 Ontemachi 2, Chiyoda-KU Tokyo 100, Japan

MISU, TOSHIHIKO, engineer, researcher; b. Gotemba, Shizuoka, Japan, Oct. 6, 1971; s. Einosuke and Chiyuki (Yamamoto) M.; m. Hitomi Kawabata, Aug. 9, 1998. B in Engring., U. Tokyo, 1994, M in Engring., 1996, DEng, 1999. Rsch. fellow Japan Soc. for Promotion of Sci., Tokyo, 1996-99; rschr. NHK Sci. and Tech. Rsch. Labs., Japan Broadcasting Corp., Tokyo, 1999—. Contbr. articles to profl. publs. Grantee-in-aid for JSPS fellows Ministry of Edn., Sci. and Culture, Govt. of Japan, 1996-99. Mem. Inst. Electronics, Info. and Comm. Engrs. Avocations: web page making, travel, photography. Office: NHK Sci and Tech Rsch Labs, 1-10-11, Kinuta, Setagaya Tokyo 157-8510, Japan

MISZTAL, GENOWEFA, science educator; b. Męciszów, Poland, Jan. 5, 1950; d. Stanisław and Rozalia (Podsiadła) Pionka; m. Stanisław Misztal, Nov. 29, 1975; 1 child, Katarzyna. Grad. pharmacy, Med. Acad.-Faculty Pharmacy, Lublin, Poland, 1973, D of Pharm. Scis., 1981. Specialist in medicinal chemistry. Prof. Med. Acad., Lublin, 1992, 2000. Contbr. papers and articles to profl. jours.; patentee in field. Mem. Solidarity Trade Union. Mem. Polish Acad. Scis. (mem. drug analysis com.), Polish Pharm. Soc., N.Y. Acad. Sci. Roman Catholic. Office: Chodźki 6, 20-093 Lublin Poland

MISZTAL, TOMASZ, zoologist, researcher; b. Warsaw, Poland, Sept. 5, 1965; s. Zdzisław and Zofia (Zduniak) M.; m. Anna Wasilewska; 1 child, Mateusz Aleksander. M in Animal Sci., Warsaw Agrl. U., 1989; PhD in Agrl. Scis., Polish Acad. Scis., 1995. Rsch. asst. The Kielanowski Inst. Animal Physiology and Nutrition, 1989-95, lectr., 1996—. Contbr. articles to profl. jours. Recipient prize of the sec. Polish Acad. Scis., 1998. Mem. Biology of Reproduction Soc. Avocations: traveling, allotment garden. Office: Kielanowski Inst Animal Phy, and Nutrit Polish Acad Scis, 05-110 Jabłonna Warsaw, Poland

MITA, KATSUSHIGE, former electronic and electrical equipment company executive; b. Tokyo, Apr. 6, 1924; s. Yoshitaro and Fuji M.; m. Toriko Miyata, May 27, 1957 (dec. Nov. 1989); children: Yoko, Makiko. B in Engring., U. Tokyo, 1949; DSc, Tufts U., 1991. With Hitachi, Ltd., Tokyo, 1949—, gen. mgr. Kanagawa Works, 1971-76, group exec. computer group, 1976-77, exec. mng. dir., 1977-79, sr. exec. mng. dir., 1979-80, exec. v.p., 1980-81, pres., 1981—, chmn. emeritus bd. dirs. Recipient blue ribbon medal Japan, 1985, DSPN Dato award Malaysia, 1993, Will Rogers award, 1994; named Officier Legion d'honneur, 1993. Mem. Keidanren (vice chair 1992-96). Buddhist. Office: Hitachi Ltd, 4-6 Kanda-Surugadai, Chiyoda Tokyo 101-10, Japan*

MITARAI, FUJIO, electronics company executive; b. Sept. 23, 1935. Grad., Chuo U., 1961. Exec. dir. Canon Inc., 1961—; pres., CEO Canon Inc., Tokyo. Office: Canon Inc, 30-2 Shimomaruko 3-chome, Ohta-ku Tokyo 146-8501, Japan*

MITARAI, OSAMU, physics educator; b. Fukue, Nagasaki, Japan, Nov. 14, 1950; s. Iwao and Kito Mitarai; m. Akiko Tani. BSME, Kyushu U., Fukuoka, Japan, 1974, MSME, 1976, D of Nuclear Engring., 1979. Postdoctoral fellow dept. physics U. Saskatchewan, Saskatoon, Can., 1981-83, rsch. assoc. dept. physics, 1983-84; lectr. Kumamoto (Japan) Inst. Tech., 1985-87, assoc. prof., 1987-93; prof. Kyushu Tokai U., 1994—. Author: Invention of "Alternating Current (AC) Tokamak Reactor: Nuclear Fusion, Fusion Technology, 1984, Invention of "Ignition Access Condition for a Tokamak Reactor" Fusion Technology, 1990. Mem. AAAS, IEEE, Am. PHys. Soc., Japan Phys. Soc., Japan Soc. Plasma, Sci. and Nuclear Fusion Rsch., Atomic Energy Soc. Japan. Achievements include pioneer work on D-3He tokamak reactor; first experimental demonstration of AC operation in the STOR-1M tokamak; design, building and experiments of first Canadian tokamak STOR-1M; first 1.5 cycle AC operation in STOR-M tokamak; ignition analysis on tokamak fusion reactor including ITER; burn contol algorithm with diagnostics in ITER, plasma current start-up by a vertical field in a spherical tokamak reactor. Office: Kyushu Tokai U Sch Eng Gen Dept EE, 9-1-1 Toroku, Kumamoto 862, Japan

MITCHAM, JULIUS JEROME, accountant; b. Pine Bluff, Ark., Jan. 2, 1941; s. James Vernon and Bertha Lee (Robertson) M.; m. Janet Claire Berry, Mar. 31, 1970 (div. Sept. 1981); m. Marsha Lee Henderson, Oct. 22, 1983; 1 child, Timothy John. BBA, U. Cen. Ark., 1971. CPA, Ark.; cert. healthcare fin. mgr. Br. mgr. Comml. Nat. Bank, Little Rock, 1961-66; auditor, acctg. supr. Ark. Blue Cross and Blue Shield, Little Rock, 1971-77; contr. Riverview Hosp., Little Rock, 1977-81; pvt. practice acctg. Little Rock, 1981-82; contr. Henryetta (Okla.) Med. Ctr., 1982-83; fin. report supr. Am. Med. Internat., Inc., Houston, 1983; dir. corp. acctg. Ft. Myers (Fla.) Cmty. Hosp., 1984-86; contr. Med. Ctr. of Southeast Okla., Durant, 1986-87; CFO Gulf Coast Cmty. Hosp./Qualicare of Miss., Inc., 1987-88; asst. adminstr. fin. S.W. Gen. Hosp., San Antonio, 1988-89; pvt. practice San Antonio, 1989-90; CFO Bapt. Meml. Hosps. of Mississippi County, Blytheville, Ark., 1991-94, Med. Arts Hosp., Texarkana, Tex., 1994-96, Healthsouth Rehab. Hosp., Texarkana, Tex., 1997-98; pres. Mitcham & Assocs., 1998—. Served with USN, 1959-61. Mem. AICPA, Ark. Soc. CPAs, Healthcare Fin. Mgmt. Assn. (cert. fellow), Lions (sec. 1985-86, 2d v.p. 1995-96), Masons. Republican. Baptist.

MITCHELHILL, JAMES MOFFAT, civil engineer; b. St. Joseph, Mo., Aug. 11, 1912; s. William and Jeannette (Ambrose) M.; BS, Northwestern U., 1934, MSCE, 1935; m. Maurine Hutchason, Jan. 9, 1937 (div. 1962); children: Janis Maurine Mitchelhill Leas, Jeri Ann Mitchelhill Riney; m. Alicia Beuchat, 1982; registered profl. engr., Mont., P.R., Tex.; Engring. dept. C., M., St. P. & P.R.R. Co., Chgo. and Miles City, Mont., 1935-45; asst. mgr. Ponce & Guayama R.R. Co., Aguirre, P.R., 1945-51, v.p., gen. mgr., 1969-70; mgr. Cen. Cortada, Santa Isabel, P.R., 1951-54; r.r. supt. Braden Copper Co., Rancagua, Chile, 1954-63; staff engr. Coverdale & Colpitts, N.Y.C., 1963-64; asst. to exec. v.p. Central Aguirre Sugar Co., 1964-67; v.p., gen. mgr. Coddea, Inc., Dominican Republic, 1967-68; asst. to gen. mgr. Land Adminstrn. of P.R., La Nueva Central Aguirre, 1970-71, for Centrals Aguirre Lafayette and Mercedita, 1971-72; asst. to gen. mgr. Corporacion Azucarera de P.R., 1973-76, asst. to exec. dir., 1977-79, asst. exec. dir. for environ., 1979-82; engring. cons., 1982-92; Kendall County engr., 1985-97; county engring. cons., 1997. Fellow ASCE; mem. Am. Ry. Engring. Assn., Colegio de Ingenieros y Agrimensores de P.R., Explorers Club, Circumnavigators Club, Travellers Century Club, Sigma Xi, Tau Beta Pi. Home: PO Box 506 Boerne TX 78006-0506

MITCHELL, ADA MAE BOYD, legal assistant; b. Nov. 23, 1927; d. Allen T. Boyd and Marjorie (Bigger) Mills Boyd; 1 child, Joseph W. Student, NYU, 1972-73. Supr. Faberge, Inc., Mahwah, N.J.; mgr. Demostration Svcs. and Promotional Monies; mgr. accts. receivables, credit mgr. Faberge, Inc., Mahwah, N.J., 1946-89; legal asst. Wright Patterson Med. Ctr., Dayton, Ohio, 1990—. Pres. Urban League Guild, Bergen County, N.J., 1982-83, bd. dirs., 1982-83; treas. Bethany Presbyn. Ch., Englewood, N.J., 1975, fin. sect., 1966-67, chair bldg. and renovation com., 1978-81, choir mem., elder, 1979—, clk. of session, 1980-85; founder N.J. Coalition of 100 Black Women, 1982; 1st Black woman moderator Presbytery of Palisades-Presbyn. Ch., 1986; mem. self devel. of people com. Presbyn. Ch. Miami Presbytery, Dayton; dir. Isis Akbar Ct. # 33, 1995—; vol. WPAFB, Ohio-Legal Office/Med. Group, 1990—, Heroines of Jericho P.H.A. Burning Bush Ct., 1997, Truth Guild #2 Heroines of Templar Crusades, 1997; active Jarvis Soc. Nat. Presbyn. Ch., Dayton Urban League Guild, 1991. Mem. NAFE, NAACP, Order Eastern Star (Queen of Sheba chpt. 4, Worthy Matron 1972-73).

MITCHELL, ALISON, textile artist; b. Oxford, England, Sept. 16, 1947; d. Alan and Christine (Fox) M.; 1 child, Danny. Diploma A.D., Loughborough Coll., England, 1969. Tchr. Harlow Coll. Art, Harlow, England, 1974-80; tchr. Ravensbourne Coll. Art, London, 1974-80; self-employed artist, weaver England, 1974—, lectr. various guilds and art schs., 1980—; dyer-ikat weaver wall hangings for refectory U. Leeds, 1978, W.H. Smiths, Swindon, Eng., 1985, The Lady Chapel, Christ Ch. Cathedral, Oxford, 1989, The Jeffreys Bldg., St. John's Coll. Innovation Ctr., Cambridge, 1993, Enron Europe Ltd., London, 2000; numerous exhbns. and pvt. customers. Contbr. articles to profl. jours. Ea. Arts grantee for completion of studio, East Anglia, Eng., 1980; studied ikat weaving and dyeing in Japan, Indonesia aided by grants from Ea. Arts and Royal Soc. Arts travel bursary. Socialist. Avocations: observation, travel.

MITCHELL, ALLAN EDWIN, lawyer; b. Okemah, Okla., May 13, 1944; m. Neva G. Ream; children: Brian E., Amy E. BA in Mass. Comm., Northwestern Okla. State U., Alva, 1991; JD, U. Okla., 1994. Bar: Okla. 1994, U.S. dist. ct. (we. and no. dists.) 1994. Asst. state mgr. Oklahomans for Right to Work, Oklahoma City, 1967-68; exec. dir. London Sq. Village, Oklahoma City, 1968-73; dist. mgr. Farmland Ins. Svc., Oklahoma City, 1974-80, Nat. Farmers Union, Oklahoma City, 1980-85; dist. agt. Prudential Ins., Cherokee, Okla., 1985-89; atty. Hughes & Grant, Oklahoma City, 1994-96, Collins & Mitchell, Cherokee, Okla., 1996 ; asst. dist. atty Alfalfa County, Okla., 1996—. Mem. Cherokee Bd. Edn., 1985-90; mem. fin. com.

Rep. Party of Okla., 1995, state com., 1997 ; scoutmaster, 1981-86, bd. mem. Great Salt Plains Coun. Boy Scouts Am.; adult advisor Girl Scouts Am.; pres. United Way Cherokee, 1984; mem. Okla. Sch. Bd. Mems. Legis. Network, 1985-90, state com. Okla. Rep. Party, 1997; vol. Okla. Spl. Olympics, 1996, 97. Mem. Ch. of the Nazarene. Avocations: public speaking, politics, civic activities. Office: Collins & Mitchell 214 S Grand Ave Cherokee OK 73728-2030

MITCHELL, ANDREW JOHN, advertising agency executive; b. Abyad, Egypt, Mar. 24, 1952; s. Colin and Joyce Mary (Stone) M.; m. Barbara Carolyn McKay; chidlren: Clare Jessica, Chloe Rose. Student, Prior's Ct., Chieveley, Eng., 1962-65, Kingswood Sch., Bath, Eng., 1965-71; BA in Hotel Mgmt., U. Strathclyde, Glasgow, Scotland, 1974, BA in Mktg., 1975. Mktg. exec. Western Geophys. Co. of Am., London, 1975-76; advt. exec. Grey Advt., Ltd., London, 1976-78; advt. account dir. Young & Rubicam Advt., London, 1978-83; group vice chmn. Publicis, London, 1983-90; founder, mng. ptnr. Mitchell Patterson Grime Mitchell Ltd., London, 1990—. Carnegie scholar, 1974. Home: 74 Stamford Brook Rd, London W6, England

MITCHELL, AUSTIN VERNON, member of parliament; b. Sept. 19, 1934. BA, Manchester U., 1956; MA, Nuffield Coll., Oxford, 1957. Lectr. history Otago U., Dunedin, New Zealand, 1959-63; sr. lectr. politics U. Canterbury, Christchurch, New Zealand, 1963-67; fellow Nuffield Coll., Oxford, 1967-69; journalist Yorkshire TV Leeds, 1969-71, Sta. BBC TV, 1972; presenter Yorkshire TV, 1973-77; mem. of parliament Great Grimsby, 1977—; co-presenter Target, Sky TV, 1989-98; lectr. history Otago U., Dunedin, New Zealand, 1959-63. Author: Whigs in Opposition 1815-30, 1969, People and Politics in New Zealand, 1969, Westminster Man, 1982, The Case for Labour, 1983, Britain: Beyond the Blue Horizon, 1989, Competitive Socialism, 1989, Teach Thissen Tyke, 1979, Last Time Labours Lessons from the Sixties, 1997, Parliament in Pictures, 1999, Farewell My Lords, 1999. Opposition spokesman for Trade and Industry, 1987-89. Mem. Labour Party. Mem. Ch. of Eng. Avocations: photography, contemplating exercise. Home: 15 New Cartergate Rd, Grimsby DN31 1RB, England Office: House of Commons, London SW1A OAA, England

MITCHELL, BETTY JO, writer, publisher; b. May 2, 1931; d. Edith Darrah McWilliams. BA, S.W. Mo. State U.; MSLS, U. So. Calif. Asst. acquistions librarian Calif. State U., Northridge, 1967-69, librarian for pers. and fin., 1969-71, acting assoc. libr. dir., 1971-72, assoc. dir. univ. librs., 1972-81; mgr. info. sys. Sity Santa Monica Rent Control, 1984-93; owner Viewpoint Press, Tehachapi, Calif.; cons. Western Interstate Commn. for Higher Edn. USOE Inst. for Tng. in Staff Devel. Problem Solving; participant workshops in field; spkr. at profl. confs. in field; bd. dirs. Tehachapi Cmty. Orch. Author: ALMS: A Budget Based Library Management System, 1982, The Secret of Hilhouse: An Adult Book for Teens, 1993; co-author: Cost Analysis of Library Functions: A Total System Approach, 1978, How to See the U.S. on $12 a Day; contbr. writings to profl. publs.; editor Staff Development column in Spl. Librs., 1975-76. Bd. dirs. San Fernando Valley coun. Girl Scouts U.S., 1974-77, employed pers. com., 1979-81; bd. dirs. Bear Valley Springs Condo. Owners Assn., 1978, Empyrean Found., 1978-81, Tehachapi Cmty. Orch. Found., 1998—. Mem. AAUP, AAUW, ALA (mem., chmn. various coms.), Assn. Women in Computing (bd. dirs. 1987-89), Nat. Libr. Assn., Author's Guild, Calif. Libr. Assn., Assn. Calif. State U. profs. (sec., mem. exec. com. 1971-72), Phi Beta Chi, Alpha Mu Gamma. Office: PMB 400 785 Tucker Rd Ste G Tehachapi CA 93561-2523

MITCHELL, CHARLES BASIL, accountant, company director; b. Warrington, Eng., Sept. 2, 1939; s. Charles Mitchell and Ruth (Tilsdon) Woolley; m. Wendy Ogden, Apr. 28, 1962; children: Charles, Ian, John. Grad. pvt. sch., Cumbria, Eng. Chartered acct. Ptnr. Mitchell Charlesworth, Chartered Accts./Corp. Fin. Advisers, Liverpool, Eng., 1960—; bd. dirs. Westcombe Trust Co. Ltd., Warrington Cricket Ground Co. Ltd., Hi-Tech Svcs. (Warrington) Ltd.; vice chmn. bd. dirs. Warrington Indsl. Tng. Trust Ltd., 1984—; chmn. Warrington Bus. Park Ltd., 1988—; v.p. St. Rocco's Hospice, 1984—; sec. Master Tanners Assn., Liverpool, 1975—. Fellow Inst. Chartered Accts. in Eng. and Wales; mem. Inst. Taxation (assoc.), Liverpool Soc. Chartered Accts. (bd. dirs. 1986-89, past pres.), Athenaeum Club, Warrington Club. Mem. Conservative Party. Anglican. Avocations: golf, skiing, swimming. Home: Amberley, Greenway, Appleton, Cheshire, Warrington WA4 3AD, England Office: Mitchell Charlesworth, Victoria House, 488 Knutsford Rd, Warrington WA4 1DX, England

MITCHELL, CHARLES EDWARD, lawyer; b. Seymour, Ind., July 7, 1925; s. Edward Charles Mitchell and Lula Belle (Thompson) Browning; m. Julia Viola Sarjeant, Sept. 15, 1951; children: Charles Leonard, Albert Bascom. Student, Morehouse Coll., Atlanta, 1943-44, 46-47, NYU, 1949; JD, Temple U., Phila., 1954. Bar: D.C. 1970, U.S. Ct. Appeals (3d cir.) 1971, Pa. 1972, U.S. Supreme Ct. 1973, U.S. Ct. Appeals (6th cir.) 1984; cert. labor arbitrator, Am. Arbitration Assn., Fed. Mediation and Conciliation Svc. Tchr. City of Phila., 1954-55; mgmt. trainee Office of Dir. of Fin., Budget Bur., Phila., 1955-56; legal asst. Office of Phila. Dist. Atty., 1956-60; claims rep., claims authorizer U.S. HEW, Social Security Adminstrn., Phila., 1960-64; atty., examiner NLRB, Phila., 1964-72; mgmt. labor counsel E.I. duPont de Nemours & Co., Phila., 1972-92; pvt. practice Phila., 1993-99; mem. mgmt./labor panel Am. Arbitration Assn.; mem. roster of arbitrators Fed. Mediation and Conciliation Svc. 1st class seaman USN, 1944-46. Mem. ABA (mem. mgmt. sect. labor and employment law, practice and procs. com. 1973-92), Fed. Bar Assn. (pres. Del. chpt. 1974-76, nat. chpt. del. 1973-78), Indsl. Rels. Rsch. Assn. (v.p. 1970-72), Phila. Bar Assn. Democrat. Episcopalian. Avocations: golf, tennis, chess, bridge, travel.

MITCHELL, SIR DEREK, company director; b. Wimbledon, Eng., Mar. 5, 1922; s. Sidney George and Gladys Nellie (Newman) M.; m. Miriam Dorothy Jackson, Apr. 1, 1944 (d. Aug. 1993); children: Sarah, Julia, Anthony. MA with honors, Christ Church Oxford U., Eng., 1947. Asst. prin. His Majesty's Treasury, London, 1947-51; prin. pvt. sec. to chancellor of exchequer London, 1962-64, prin. pvt. sec. to prime minister, 1964-66; dep. sec. Dept. Econ. Affairs and Ministry of Agr., London, 1966-69; minister econ. Brit. Embassy, Washington; exec. dir. IMF and World Bank, 1969-72; 2nd permanent sec. Her Majesty's Treasury, London, 1973-78; sr. advisor Shearson Lehman-Hutton, London, 1979-87; bd. dirs. Bowater Inc., Greenville, S.C., 1984-93; ind. dir. The Observer, 1981-93. Bd. dirs. Royal Nat. Theatre, London, 1977-95; governing trustee Nuffield Trust, London, 1978-98. Served to maj. Royal Army Corps., 1942-45. Mem. Garrick Club. Avocations: opera, theatre, travel. Home: 9 Holmbush Rd, London SW15 3LE, England

MITCHELL, EDWARD WILLIAM, mental health researcher; b. London, Nov. 20, 1972; s. David Smith and Karin (Hall) M. BA with honors, U. Oxford, Eng., 1995, MA, 1999; MPhil, U. Cambridge, 1997, postgrad. Rsch. asst. dept. zoology Oxford U., 1993, rsch. asst. dept. psychiatry, 1994-96; doctoral rschr. U. Cambridge, 1997—, tutor, 1999; vis. Fulbright rsch. fellow Harvard U. Med. Sch., 1999—; rsch. assoc. program in psychiatry and law Harvard Med. Sch., Boston, 1999—. Mem. editl. team Brit. Psychol. Soc. publ. Forensic Update, 1998—; contbr. articles to profl. jours. Computer cons. Henley Royal Regatta, 1998, 99. Nightingale scholar Cambridge U., 1997, Fulbright scholar, 1999, Wingate scholar, 1999. Mem. Am. Soc. Criminology, Cambrdige U. Pitt Club, Friends of Magdalene Boat Club (founder). Avocations: rowing, scuba diving, bass, skiing, falconry. Home and Office: Cambridge U, Trinity Hall, Cambridge CB2 1TJ, England

MITCHELL, GEORGE CHARLES, diplomat, international consultant, mediator, educator, writer; b. Aug. 6, 1920; s. Charles Peter and Athena N. (Kapotas) M.; m. Nina Catherine Chaconas, Oct. 22, 1955; children: Martina, Marlena. BS, U. Nebr., Kearney, 1941; postgrad., U. Nebr., Lincoln, 1941-42; cert., Oxford U., 1947; MA, Georgetown U., 1947; cert., Acad. Internat. Law, The Hague, The Netherlands, 1948; PhD summa cum laude, Sorbonne U., Paris, 1949; postgrad., Inst. d'Etudes Politiques, Paris, 1947-49, George Washington U. Law Sch., 1959-61, Fgn. Svc. Inst., 1962, 69, U. Pitts., 1974, U.S. Army War Coll., 1980, U.S. Naval War Coll., 1981. News corr. Washington and Western Europe, 1946-49; polit. analyst U.S. Dept. State, Washington, 1951-54, specialist, 1954-56; dep. prin. officer, econ. com. officer, consul Am. Consulate Gen., Belfast, No. Ireland, 1955-58; fgn. rels. officer U.S. Dept. State, Washington, 1958-62; prin. officer, polit. officer, consul Am. Consulate, Arequipa, Peru, 1962-67; dean Consular Corps, 1965-66; polit.-mil. officer, lst sec. Am. Embassy, Santo Domingo, Dominican Republic, 1967-68; prin. officer, polit.-econ. officer, consul Am. Consulate, San Luis Potosi, Mex., 1968-71; chief Speakers Bur. U.S. Dept. State, Washington, 1971-72, plans officer, 1971-72; exec. dir. World Affairs Coun. Pitts., 1973-91; internat. con., mediator Pitts., 1989—; exec. dir. internat. mgmt. tng. Lang. Ctr., Pitts., 1990-91; adj. prof. grad. internat. bus. mgmt. Point Park Coll., 1991—; internat. mgr. U.S. Arbitration and Mediation, Pa., 1992-93; bd. dirs. Stas. KGFW and KQKY, Kearney, Stas. KKAR and KQKQ, Omaha, KXNP-KODY, North Platte, 1954-96; leader del. to China, World Affairs Coun., 1978, to Taiwan and Philippines, Nat. Coun. World Affairs, 1988. Author: Matthew B. Ridgway: Soldier, Statesman, Scholar, Citizen, 1999; editor World Affairs Coun. newsletter, Nat. Coun. World Affairs Orgns. newsletter; co-editor Asian/Pacific Dynamics--Economic, Political, Security, 1984; radio interviewer on internat. affairs; judge Battle of Wits (TV program); contbr. articles to U.S. govt. publs., profl. jours., newspapers. Founder, pres. Atheneum Soc., Washington, 1952; founder Am. Soc. Arequipa, 1963, Prescott Sch., Arequipa, 1964; mem. Western Pa. Dist. Export Coun., Pitts., 1979-92. Lt. (j.g.) USNR, 1942-45, ETO. Recipient Meritorious Honor award U.S. Dept. State, 1966; AHEPA scholar, 1939, U. Nebr. scholar, 1941. Mem. Am. Fgn. Svc. Assn., Com. on Present Danger (founding), Nat. Coun. World Affairs Orgns. (v.p. 1985-87, pres. 1987-89, bd. dirs., exec. com. 1974-91), Fgn. Affairs Res. Corps, Internat. Exec. Svc. Corps, Nat. Inst. Dispute Resolution, Soc. Profls. in Dispute Resolution, Midwest Conf. on World Affairs (adv. coun. 1988-90, Disting. Svc. award U. Nebr., Kearney, 1972, 88), Am. Arbitration Assn., Mortar Bd., Rotary. Avocations: reading, writing, public speaking, antiques, travel. Home and Office: 3416 Brookdale Dr Upper Saint Clair Pittsburgh PA 15241-1558

MITCHELL, GEORGE TRICE, physician; b. Marshall, Ill., Jan. 20, 1914; s. Roscoe Addison and Alma (Trice) M.; m. Mildred Aletha Miller, June 21, 1941; children: Linda Sue, Mary Kathryn. BS, Purdue U., 1935; MD, George Washington U., 1940. Intern Meth. Hosp., Indpls., 1940-41; gen. practice medicine, Marshall, 1946—; mem. courtesy staff Union and Regional Hosps., Terre Haute, Ind.; clin. assoc. Sch. Basic Medicine, U. Ill.; mem. recruitment and retention com. U. Ill. Coll. Medicine, Rockford; chmn. bd. dirs. 1st Nat. Bank, Marshall. Author: Dr. George-An Account of the Life of a Country Doctor, 1993. Mem. adv. coun. premedicine Eastern Ill. U., 1965-69; alt. del. Rep. Conv., 1968, del., 1972; trustee Lakeland Jr. Coll., 1978-92. Lt. col. USAAF, 1941-45. Named Health Practitioner of Yr. Ill. Rural Health Assn., 1993; recipient Disting. Svc. award, Lake Land Coll., 1992, Purdue Alumni Assn. Citizenship award, 1996. Fellow Am. Acad. Family Physicians (Family Physician of Yr. 1993); mem. AMA, Ill. Med. Soc. (2d v.p. 1980-81), Clark County Med. Soc. (pres.), Aesculapian Soc. of Wabash Valley (pres. 1965), Nat. Rural Health Assn. (Practitioner of Yr. 19951999 Disting. Svc. award), Ill. Rural Health Assn. (bd. dirs.), Clark County Hist. Soc. (pres. 1968-70), Masons (32 degree), Shriners. Methodist. Home: 15923 N Oak Crest Rd Marshall IL 62441-4332 Office: 410 N 2d St Marshall IL 62441-1010

MITCHELL, GRAHAM RICHARD, government engineering executive; b. Oxford, Eng., Sept. 14, 1938; came to U.S., 1968; s. David and Doris (Clarke) M.; m. Patricia Mary Garside, Jan. 11, 1963; children: Claire Helen, Iain Andrew. BSc, U. Westminster, London, 1962, PhD, 1968. Mgr. rsch., bus. devel. and engring. GE, Phila., 1968-76; cons. GE Corp. R&D Ctr., Schenectady, N.Y., 1976-80; dir. planning & forecasting GTE Labs., Waltham, Mass., 1980-93; asst. sec. of commerce for tech. policy U.S. Dept. Commerce, Washington, 1994-97; Bladstrom vis. prof. The Wharton Sch./U. Penn., Philadelphia, 1998—; bd. dirs. Indsl. Rsch. Inst. Contbr. articles to books and profl. jours.; patentee in field. Recipient Ayerton Premium Inst. of Elec. Engring., London, Maurice Holland award IRI, 1993. Mem. IEEE, Am. Mgmt. Assn. (mem. mgmt. coun. 1990—), Internat. Assn. for Mgmt. of Tech. (bd. dirs.). Home: 538 W Moreland Ave Philadelphia PA 19118-4221 Office: Univ Pa 317 Vance Hall 3733 Spruce St Philadelphia PA 19104-6301

MITCHELL, HAROLD CHARLES, media specialist; b. Trafalgar, Victoria, Australia, May 13, 1942; s. Harold Earnest Mitchell and Lorna Joyce Banks; m. Beverley Joan Donnelly, Dec. 21, 1963; children: Stuart, Amanda. Grad. h.s., Australi. Media mgr. USP, Melbourne, Australia, 1966-69; regional media dir. Masius Wynne-Williams, Melbourne, 1969-76; chmn. Mitchell & Ptnrs., Melbourne, 1976—. Pres. Asthma Found. Victoria, Melbourne, 1995-97, Melbourne Internat. Festival of Arts, Melbourne, 1995-97, chmn. 1997—; dir. Opera Australia, Sydney, 1997, Nat. Gallery Australia Coun., 1998. Fellow Australian Inst. Mgmt.; mem. Victoria Racing Club, Mooney Valley Racing Club, Athanaeum Club. Avocations: reading, opera, music, camping, collecting. Office: Mitchell and Ptnrs, 105 York St, 3205 South Melbourne Victoria, Australia

MITCHELL, IAN MOORHOUSE, consultant cardiac surgeon; b. Guildford, Surrey, Eng., Feb. 25, 1957; s. R. G. Bruce and Sheila M. (Dean) M.; m. Johanna Elizabeth Allflatt, Aug. 7, 1982; children: James, Annelies, David. BSc with honours, Leeds (Eng.) U., 1979, MB ChB, 1979, MD with distinction, 1994. Rsch. fellow Royal Hosp. for Sick Children, Glasgow, Scotland, 1989-91; sr. registrar Yorkshire Regional Health Authority, Leeds, 1991-95; cons. cardiac surgeon Nottingham (Eng.) City Hosp., 1995—. Rsch. grantee Tenovus-Scotland, 1990, Assn. for Children with Heart Diseases, 1990. Fellow Royal Coll. Surgeons Glasgow; mem. Soc. Cardiothoracic Surgeons. Avocations: golf, traveling. Office: Nottingham City Hosp, Dept Cardiothoracic Surgery, Hucknall Rd, Nottingham NG5 1PB, England

MITCHELL, SIR JAMES FITZALLEN, prime minister Saint Vincent and The Grenadines, agronomist, hotelier; b. Bequia, Grenadines, Mar. 15, 1931; s. Reginald Fitzgerald M. and Lois Gooding Baynes; divorced; children: Sabrina, Gretel, Louise, Gabija. Grad., Imperial Coll. of Tropical Agr., Trinidad, 1954, U. B.C., 1954-56. Cocoa agronomist St. Lucia, 1957; agrl. rsch. officer St. Vincent, 1958-61; sci. lectr. various schs., Eng., 1962-64; tech. editor on pest control Ministry of Overseas Devel., London, 1964-65; elected mem. St. Vincent Labour Party, 1966-67, elected as ind., 1972-74, premier, 1972-74; founder New Dem. Party, 1975, pres., 1975-2000; min. fin. and planning Govt. St. Vincent and the Grenadines, 1984—; prime min., 1984—; chmn. Hotel Frangipani, Plumeria Investments; lectr. Cornell U., Ind. U., Princeton U. Author: Caribbean Crusade, 1989, Concepts, Guiding Change in the Islands, 1996. Pres., founder New Dem. Party, privy councillor, 1985; chmn. Caribbean Dem. Union, Caribbean Cmty. Heads of Govt., 2000; vice chmn. Internat. Dem. Union. Decorated Order of Liberator (Venezuela), 1972, Knight Commdr. of Order of St. Michael and St. George, 1995, Chevalier d'Honneur, 1995, Order of Propitious Clouds, 1995, Order of the Great Cross of Infante Dom Henrique (Portugal), 1998; recipient Alumni award of distinction U. B.C., Can., 1988. Mem. Bequia Sailing Club. Anglican. Avocations: sailing, gardening. Office: Office of Prime Min, Kingstown Saint Vincent and the Grenadines

MITCHELL, JANET ALDRICH, fund raising executive, reference materials publisher; b. Providence, Jan. 12, 1928; d. Norman Ackley and Janet (Gordon) Aldrich; m. Raymond Warren Mitchell, Jan. 9, 1954 (div. 1967); children: Lydi Aldrich, Polly Mitchell Ranson. AB, Smith Coll., 1949; MEd, Rutgers U., 1975. Engaged in devel. various non-profit orgns., 1954-72; dir. devel. Wilson Fellowship Found., Princeton, N.J., 1972-74; dir. spl. projects N.J. Dept. Higher Edn., Trenton, 1974-96; pub., editor-in-chief Mitchell Guide, 1967-87, 93—, pres., chmn., 1987—; cons. numerous non-profit orgns., 1976-86; lectr. Adult Sch., Princeton, 1983-84. Editor: Directory of Woodrow Wilson Fellows, 1968, A Community of Scholars, 1980. Exec. officer Princeton Cmty. Dem., 1984-86; mem. Princeton Twp. Com., 1987-89; mem. NAACP Legal Def. Fund, 1980-86; trustee N.J. Hist. Soc., 1984-86. Mem. Smith Coll. Club (pres. 1968-70), Princeton Dog Club (bd. dirs. 19962-68). Episcopalian. Avocation: breeding and showing standard poodles. E-Mail: grantsnj@aol.com. Home and Office: 430 Federal City Rd Pennington NJ 08534-4209

MITCHELL, JOHN CAMPBELL, financial broker; b. Glasgow, Scotland, June 4, 1947; arrived in Zimbabwe, 1965; s. John Steel and Doris (Cope) M.; m. Bonita Arlene Bennett; children: Murray Steel, Shiona Joy. Student, Lenzie Acad., Scotland, 1952-63. Police cadet Dunbartonshire Constabulatory, Scotland, 1963-65; police officer Brit. South Africa Police, Rhodesia, 1965-81; pers. officer Morenear, Zimbabwe, 1981-82; pers. and tng. mgr. Turnall, Zimbabwe, 1982-84, mktg. dir., 1984-86; sales mgr. Genkem, Zimbabwe, 1986-87; mng. dir. Freight Internat., Zimbabwe, 1987-90, Chloride, Zimbabwe, 1990-92, James North, Zimbabwe, 1992-93; chmn. Diamond Plant Hire, Zimbabwe, 1992—; regional mgr. Mondial Internat. Fin. Svcs., Zimbabwe, 1993-97; area mgr. Britex Internat., Zimbabwe, 1997—. Mem. Inst. Pers. Mgmt., Inst. Orgn. and Methods, Harare Club, Royal Harare Golf Club. Presbyterian. Avocation: golf. Home: 285 Water End Close, Glen Lorne PO Chisipite, Harare Zimbabwe

MITCHELL, JOHN DANIEL, taxonomist, ecologist; b. N.Y.C., Nov. 30, 1957; s. John Dietrich and Miriam (Pitcairn) M.; m. Beth Ann Trowbridge, Aug. 4, 1979; children, George Trowbridge, Charles Arthur. BS in Biology, Muhlenberg Coll., 1979. Wildlife mgr. Pennypack Watershed Assn., Huntingdon Valley, Pa., 1979-80; hon. research assoc. N.Y. Bot. Garden, Bronx, N.Y., 1983-95, hon. curator, 1995—; bd. dirs. Beneficia Found., Jenkintown, Pa.; mem. botan. scis. com. N.Y. Botan. Garden. Sr. author: The Cashew and Its Relatives, 1987; co-author: Topic-Plant Ecology, 1986; illustrator: Search for Style, 1982, MacBeth Unjinxed, 1985; contbr. articles to profl. jours.; co-author: Guide to the Vascular Plants of Central French Guiana, 1997. Fellow Linnean Soc. London; mem. Internat. Assn. Plant Taxonomists, Ecol. Soc. Am., AAAS, BAT Conservation Internat. (vice-chmn. 1987—), Pennypack Watershed Assn. (bd. dirs. 1981-90), Inst. for Advanced Studies in the Theatre Arts (adv. bd. 1987-95), Phila Bot. Club, New Eng. Bot. Club, Explorers' Club, Orgn. for Flora Neotropica. Democrat. Avocations: birdwatching, hiking, photography, travel, sketching.

MITCHELL, JOHN DIETRICH, theatre arts institute executive; b. Rockford, Ill., Nov. 3, 1917; s. John Dennis Royce and Dora Marie (Schroeder) M.; m. Miriam Pitcairn, Aug. 25, 1956; children: John Daniel, Lorenzo Theodore, Barbarina Mitchell Heyerdahl. BSS, Northwestern U., 1939, MA, 1941; EdD, Columbia U., 1956; HHD (hon.), Northwood U., 1986. Dir., producer Am. Broadcasting Co., N.Y.C., 1942-46; assoc. editor Samuel French, Publ., N.Y.C., 1946-48; assoc. prof. Manhattan Coll., N.Y.C., 1948-58; pres. Inst. for Advanced Studies in the Theatre Arts, N.Y.C., 1958-97; founder, pres. Eaton St. Press, Key West, Fla., 1994; bd. dirs. Beneficia Found., Jenkintown, Pa. Author: Staging Chekhov, 1990, Actors Talk, 1991, Gift of Apollo, 1992, Staging Japanese Theatre: Noh and Kabuki, 1995, Men Stand on Shoulders, 1996; author: (aka Jack Royce) The Train Stopped at Domodossola, 1993, Murder at the Kabuki, 1994, Dressed to Murder, 1997, Way to the Towers of Silence, 1997, Bewitched by the Stage, 1997, Troubled Paradise, 1998, The Wallpaper Murder, 1998, Death in the Suit of Lights, 1999. Trustee emeritus Northwood U., Midland, Mich., 1972-91; patron Met. Opera, N.Y.C.; golden donor Am. Ballet Theatre. Named hon. conch Key West (Fla.) Commrs., 1994. Mem. Met. Mus., Key West Arts and Hist. Soc., Spencer Family Assn. Mayflower Soc., Key West Literary Seminar (emeritus), Nippon Club N.Y.C., N.Y. Athletic Club. Mem. Community Ch. Avocations: Tai Chi Chuan, swimming, collecting musical recordings, books. Fax: 305-296-5827. E-mail: jdm@keysdigital.com. Home and Office: 703 Eaton St Key West FL 33040-6843

MITCHELL, JOHN DOUGLAS, clinical neurologist, educator; b. Amersham, Buckinghamshire, England, June 30, 1951; s. Thomas and Constance M.; m. Christine Elizabeth Aitken, June 25, 1983; children: Susan Helen Mary, Catriona Jane. MB, ChB, U. Aberdeen, Scotland, 1975; MRCP, Royal Coll. Physicians, 1978; FRCP, Royal Coll. of Physicians and Surgeons, 1989; MD, U. Aberdeen, Scotland, 1991; FRCP, Royal Coll. Physicians, Edinburgh, 1992, Royal Coll. Physicians, London, 1993. Registrar in neurology Addenbrooks Hosp. Cambridge, 1979-80; sr. registrar in neurology No. Gen. Hosp., Edinburgh, 1980-84; sr. lectr. in med. neurology U. Edinburgh, Scotland, 1984; cons. neurologist Royal Preston Hosp., 1986; hon. prof. clin. neurology U. Cen. Lancashire, 1993; mem. motor neurone disease subcom. World Fedn. of Neurology, 1990—; vice-chmn. Lancashire Ctr. for Med. Studies, 1992-98; med. adv. com. Migraine Trust, 1993-96; chmn. rsch. adv. panel Motor Neuron Disease Assn., 1994-97. Contbr. chpt. to books. Avocations: playing piano and violin. Office: Royal Preston Hosp, Sharoe Green Ln, PR2 9HT Fulwood Preston Lancashire England

MITCHELL, JOHN NOYES, JR., retired electrical engineer; b. Pownal, Maine, Dec. 16, 1930; s. John Noyes and Frances (Small) M.; m. Marilyn Jean Michaelis, Sept. 1, 1956 (dec.); children: Brian John, Cynthia Lynn Mitchell Tumbleson, Stephanie Lee Mitchell Judson; m. Jacqueline A. Starr, Sept. 10, 1999. BSEE, Milw. Sch. Engring., 1957. Registered profl. engr., Ohio. Elec. rsch. engr. Nat. Cash Register Co., Dayton, Ohio, 1957-65; sr. engr. Xerox Corp., Rochester, N.Y., 1965-70, area mgr., 1970-73; area mgr. Xerox Corp., Dallas, 1973-76; area mgr. Xerox Corp., El Segundo, Calif., 1976-79, tech. program mgr., 1979-85, competitive benchmarking mgr., 1985-92, quality mgr., 1992-97. With USN, 1949-53. Mem. IEEE, Mason. Republican. Episcopalian. Home: 5545 Downham Meadow Sarasota FL 34235-0971

MITCHELL, JOSEPH PATRICK, architect; b. Bellingham, Wash., Sept. 29, 1939; s. Joseph Henry and Jessie Delila (Smith) M.; m. Marilyn Ruth Jorgenson, June 23, 1962; children: Amy Evangeline, Kirk Patrick, Scott Henry. Student, Western Wash. State Coll., 1957-59; BA, U. Wash., 1963, BArch, 1965. Cert. Nat. Coun. of Architectural Registration Bd. Assoc. designer, draftsman, project architect Beckwith Spangler Davis, Bellevue, Wash., 1965-70; prin. J. Patrick Mitchell, AIA & Assocs./Architects/Planners/Cons., Kirkland, Wash., 1970—. Chmn. long range planning com. Lake Retreat Camp, 1965-93; charter mem., bldg. chmn. Northshore Bapt. Ch., 1969, 80-96, elder, 1984-90; mem. bd extension and ctrl. com. Columbia Bapt. Conf., 1977-83; del. to Bapt. World Alliance 16th Congress, Seoul, Korea, 1990, 17th Congress, Buenos Aires, 1995, 18th Congress, Melbourne, Australia, 2000; trustee Bakke Libr./Cultural Ctr., 1994-96; vice-moderator Columbia Bapt. Conf., 1995-96, moderator, 1996-97, overseer ch. ministries bd., pres., 1997-99; charter mem. Cascade Cmty. Ch., 1997—, mem. bldg. com., 1999—; mem. Deming Hist. Cemetery Assn., 1997—, IFRRA Arch. Edn. Tour, Finland and St. Petersburg, 1998, Japan, 2000. Recipient Internat. Archtl. Design award St. John Vianney Parish, 1989. Mem. AIA, Constrn. Specification Inst., Interfaith Forum Religion, Art, and Architecture, Nat. Fedn. Bus., Christian Camping Internat., Wash. Farm Forestry Assn., Woodinville C. of C., Kirkland C. of C. Office: 12620 120th Ave NE Ste 208 Kirkland WA 98034-7511

MITCHELL, KEITH CLAUDIUS, Grenada government official. Student, Presentation Coll., Grenada, U. West Indies; M of Math., Howard U., 1975; PhD in Math. and Stats., American U., Washington, 1979. MS, PhD. Gen. sec. New Nat. Party, Grenada, 1984-89, leader, 1989—; min. comm., works, pub. utilities, transp., civ. aviation Govt. of Grenada, 1984-87, min. comm., works, pub. utilities, coops., cmty. devel., 1988-89, prime min., 1995—. Candidate for Grenada Nat. Party in 1972 elections; capt. Grenada Nat. Cricket Team, 1971-74. Office: Office Prime Minister, Bot Gardens, Tanteen Saint Georges Grenada*

MITCHELL, KEITH RONALD, accountant, politician; b. Chingford, Essex, U.K., July 9, 1946; s. Edward John and Nellie Louise (Brigden) M. Chartered acct. Dir. LSA Ltd., London, 1968-75, ATC Ltd., London, 1975-87; mng. dir. ATC (Publs.) Ltd., Oxford, U.K., 1987-90; ptnr. K R Mitchell & Co., Oxford, U.K., 1968—. Elected mem. Oxfordshire County Coun. of Oxfordshire, 1989—, Cherwell Dist. Coun. Oxfordshire, 1990—; non-exec. dir. Oxfordshire Health Authority, 1985—. Fellow Inst. Chartered Accts.; mem. Carlton Club, Frewen Club, United and Cecil Club. Mem. Conservative Party. Avocations: music, hunting, freemasonry, good food and wine, reading. Home: Nell Bridge, Adderbury OX17 3NU, United Kingdom

MITCHELL, LEE MARK, communications executive, investment fund manager, lawyer; b. Albany, N.Y., Apr. 16, 1943; s. Maurice B. and Mildred (Roth) M.; m. Barbara Lee Anderson, Aug. 27, 1966; children: Mark, Matthew. AB, Wesleyan U., 1965; JD, U. Chgo., 1968. Bar: Ill. 1968, D.C. 1969, U.S. Supreme Ct. 1972. Assoc. Leibman, Williams, Bennett, Baird & Minow, Chgo. and Washington, 1968-72; assoc. Sidley & Austin, Washington, 1972-74, ptnr., 1974-84, 92-94; exec. v.p. and gen. counsel Field Enterprises, Inc., Chgo., 1981-83, pres., CEO, 1983-84; pres., CEO Field Corp., 1984-92; prin. Golder, Thoma, Cressey, Rauner, Inc., Chgo., 1994-98; ptnr. Thoma Cressey Equity Ptnrs., Inc., Chgo., 1998—; bd. dirs. Paging

Network, Inc., Chgo. Stock Exch., Inc.; chmn. Cognitive Arts Corp. Author: Openly Arrived At, 1974, With the Nation Watching, 1979; co-author: Presidential Television, 1973. Mem. LWV PResdl. Debates Adv. Com., Washington, 1979-80, 82; U.S. del. Brit. Legis. Conf. on Govt. and Media, Ditchley Park, Eng., 1974; bd. visitors U. Chgo. Law Sch., 1984-86, Medill Sch. Journalism, Northwestern U., 1984-91; bd. govs. Chgo. Met. Planning Coun., pres., 1988-91; mem. midwest regional adv. bd. Inst. Internat. Edn., 1987—; trustee Ravinia Festival Assn., 1989-97, Northwestern U. Mem. ABA, Fed. Comm. Bar Assn., Econ. Mid-Am. Club, Chgo. Club, Comml. Club Chgo. Home: 135 Maple Hill Rd Glencoe IL 60022-1252 Office: Thoma Cressey Equity Ptnrs Sears Tower Ste 9200 233 S Wacker Dr Chicago IL 60606-6306

MITCHELL, LUCILLE ANNE, retired elementary school educator; b. Dayton Corners, Ill., Oct. 19, 1928; d. Roy Rollin and Edna May (Whitehouse) Sheppard; m. Donald L. Mitchell; children: David, Diane, Barbara Rock, Patricia Reaves. BSin Edn., Augustana Coll., 1966; MS in Edn., Western Ill. U., 1972, Edn. Specialist, 1974. Tchr. Carbon Cliff (Ill.) Elem. Sch., 1962-65, Moline (Ill.) Bd. Edn., 1967-92; mem. textbook selection com. Moline Bd. Edn., 1967-84; tchr. of gifted Moline Bd. Edn., 1985-87. Named Ill. Master Tchr., State of Ill., 1984. Mem. Ill. Edn. Assn. (various coms.), Moline Edn. Assn. (various coms.), Delta Kappa Gamma (program chmn. 1978-79, recording sec. 1980-81). Avocations: organ, piano, oil and water color painting. Home: 3214 55th Street Ct Moline IL 61265-5740

MITCHELL, MALCOLM, journalist; b. London, Feb. 7, 1933; s. Frank and Nellie Florence (Watts) M.; m. Elizabeth Anne Judith Mitchell, Nov. 23, 1974; children: James, Harriet, Justin. Reporter/editor Mid Kent (U.K.) News, 1954-56; reporter Kentish Express, Kent, 1956-60; reporter/chief reporter/dep. editor Kentish Gazette, Kent, 1960-75; editor Extra Newspapers, Kent, 1975-82, East Kent Mercury, 1982-88. Cpl. RAF, 1951-54. Mem. Sr. Common Rm. of U. Kent at Canterbury (hon. mem.). Anglican Ch. Avocations: jazz, botany, archaeology, crosswords, travel. Home: Old Cottage The Street, Bishopsbourne Kent CT4 5HT, England

MITCHELL, MALCOLM STUART, physician, researcher; b. N.Y.C., May 6, 1937; s. Max E. and Sylvia Mitchell; m. June Kan, Aug. 14, 1976; 1 child, Ian Douglas; children by previous marriage—Jeffrey Scott, Roderick Keith, Derek James. A.B. magna cum laude, Harvard Coll., 1957; M.D., Yale U., 1962. Diplomate Am. Bd. Internal Medicine. Instr. to assoc. prof. of medicine and pharmacology Yale U. Sch. Medicine, New Haven, 1968-78; chief of med. oncology, dir. clin. investigations U. So. Calif. Sch. Medicine and Cancer Ctr., Los Angeles, 1978-84; prof. medicine and microbiology U. So. Calif. Sch. Medicine and Cancer Ctr., 1978-94; prof. medicine, dir. Ctr. for Biol. Therapy-Melanoma Rsch., U. Calif. at San Diego Sch. Medicine and Cancer Ctr., La Jolla, 1994-98; prog. leader biol. therapy, Herrick Chair cancer immunology Karmanos Cancer Inst., Detroit, 1998—, interim dir. clin. rsch.; cons various panels Nat. Cancer Inst., Bethesda, Md., 1975—; mem. adv. com. Am. Cancer Soc., N.Y.C., 1975-79, U.S. Pharmacopeia, Washington DC, 1975-80; chmn. sci. adv. com. Nat. Cancer Cytology Ctr., N.Y.C., 1981-86; mem. Expert Panel on Unprofl. Med. Conduct, Calif., 1981—, prof. med., immunology and microbiol. Author: Hybridomas in Cancer Diagnosis and Treatment, 1982, The Modulation of Immunity, 1985, Immunity to Cancer, 1985, Human Tumor Antigens and Specific Tumor Therapy, 1989, Immunity to Cancer II, 1989, Biological Approaches to Cancer Treatment: Biomodulation, 1992; editor-in-chief Yale Jour. Biology and Medicine, 1976-78; contbr. articles to profl. jours. Pres., founder Philanthropic: Am. Melanoma Found. Recipient Research Career Devel. award Nat. Cancer Inst., 1974-79; Leukemia Soc. Am. scholar, 1968-73; Fulbright scholar, Oxford, 1959-60. Mem. Am. Assn. Immunologists, Am. Soc. Clin. Investigation, Am. Soc. Clin. Oncology, Soc. Biol. Therapy (bd. dirs. 1986-89), Am. Radium Soc. (2d v.p. 1979-80), Am. Assn. Cancer Rsch., Phi Beta Kappa, Sigma Xi. Democrat. Avocations: classical and jazz piano; tennis; skiing. Office: Karmanos Cancer Inst 110 E Warren Ave Detroit MI 48201-1312

MITCHELL, MARY ANN CARRICO, poet; b. Louisville, Aug. 1, 1937; d. Bernard and Catherine (Steinlocker) Carrico; m. William Ray Mitchell, Aug. 25, 1962; children: Michael, Anne Marie, Katherine. RN, St. Joseph Sch. Nursing, Louisville, 1958; BSN, U. Colo., 1962. Head nurse Our Lady of Peace Hosp., Louisville, 1960; mgr. collections Point Loma Credit Union, San Diego, 1974-77; charge nurse Mercy Hosp., San Diego, 1977-78; managerial sec. Gulf Oil, Denver, 1977-81; exec. sec. Phillips Petrol, Denver, 1981-82; adminstrv. asst. Reliance Petroleum, Denver, 1982-84; Mem. Nat. League Am. Pen Women (founder, pres. Bluegrass of KY branch), 2000. Author: (poems) Meeshak, 1997, My First Vertical, 1997, White Tail-a-Flyin', 1997, Friends, 1997. Mem. DAR, AAUW. Roman Catholic. Avocations: painting, sewing, quilting, gardening, poetry. Home: 494 Lea View Ave Campbellsburg KY 40011-7545

MITCHELL, MOZELLA GORDON, English language educator, minister; b. Starkville, Miss., Aug. 14, 1936; d. John Thomas and Odena Mae (Graham) Gordon; m. Edrick R. Woodson, Mar. 20, 1951 (div. 1974); children: Cynthia LaVern, Marcia Delores Woodson Miller. AB, LeMoyne Coll., 1959; MA in English, U. Mich., 1963; MA in Religious Studies, Colgate-Rochester Divinity Sch., 1973; PhD, Emory U., 1980. Instr. in English and Speech Alcorn A&M Coll., Lorman, Miss., 1960-61; instr. English, chmn. dept. Owen Jr. Coll., Memphis, 1961-65; asst. prof. English and religion Norfolk State Coll., U. Norfolk, Va., 1965-81; assoc. prof. U. South Fla., Tampa, 1981-93, prof., 1993—; pastor Mount Sinai AME Zion Ch., Tampa, 1982-89; presiding elder Tampa dist. AME Zion Ch., 1988—; pastor, founder Love of Christ AME Zion Tabernacle, Branden, Fla., 1993—; vis. assoc. prof. Hood Theol. Sem., Salisbury, N.C., 1979-80, St. Louis U., 1992-93; vis. asst. lectr. U. Rochester, N.Y., 1972-73; co-dir. Ghent VISTA Project, Norfolk, 1969-71; cons. Black Women and Ministry Interdenominational Theol. Ctr; lectr. Fla. Humanities Coun., 1994-95; Meml. lectr. Mordecai Johnson Inst., Colgate Rochester Div. Sch., 1997. Author: Spiritual Dynamics of Howard Thurman's Theology, 1985, Howard Thurman and the Quest for Freedom, Proc. 2d Ann. Howard Thurman Convocation (Peter Lang), 1992, African American Religious History in Tampa Bay, 1992;, New Africa in America: The Blending of African and American Religious and Social Traditions Among Black People in Meridian, Mississippi and Surrounding Counties (Peter Lang), 1994, also articles, essays in field; editor: Martin Luther King Meml. Series in Religion, Culture and Social Devel.; editorial bd. Cornucipia Reprint Series. Mem. connectional coun. A.M.E. Zion Ch., Charlotte, 1984—, staff writer Sunday sch. lit., 1981—, mem. jud. coun.; mem. Tampa-Hillsborough County Human Rels. Coun., 1987—; pres. Fla. Coun. Chs., Orlando, 1988-90, pres.-elect, 1998—, pres., exec. bd., 2000; del. 7th assembly World Coun. Chs., Canberra, Australia, 1991, 17th World Meth. Coun., Rio de Janiero, 1996; founder Women at the Well, Inc. Recipient ecumenical leadership citation Fla. Coun. Chs., 1990, Inaugural lectr. award Geddes Hanson Black Cultural Ctr. Princeton Theol. Sem., 1993; fellow Nat. Doctoral Fund, 1978-80; grantee NEH, 1981, Fla. Endowment for Humanities, 1990—, U. South Fla. Rsch. Coun., 1990—. Mem. Coll. Theology Soc., Am. Acad. Religion, Soc. for the Study of Black Religion (pres. 1992-96), Joint Ctr. for Polit. Studies, Black Women in Ch. and Soc., Alpha Kappa Alpha. Phi Kappa Phi. Democrat. Methodist. Avocations: piano, poetry, tennis, bicycling, Scrabble. Office: U South Fla 301 CPR Religious Studies Dept Tampa FL 33620

MITCHELL, PAMELA, writer; b. Huddersfield, England, Dec. 3, 1924; d. Brian Lynn and Mary Gwendolin (Middlemost) Broadbent; m. Sidney Gordon Mitchell, Sept. 8, 1954 (dec. July 1988); 3 children; m. Laurence Geoffrey Castagnola, Jan. 18, 1996. Author: The Tip of the Spear, 1993, Chariots of the Sea, 1998. With English Mil., 1942-45. Avocations: crafts, writing, grandchildren.

MITCHELL, PAUL ENGLAND, solicitor; b. St. Albans, U.K., Nov. 2, 1951; s. Ronald England and Katia Patricia (Hannay) M.; m. Catherine Anne Ros-Jones, Aug. 18, 1984; children: Charlotte Daniele, Mark England. B of Laws, Bristol (U.K.) U., 1973. Cert. Solicitor. Articled clerk Joynson-Hicks, London, 1974-76, solicitor, 1976-78; ptnr. Joynson-Hicks, Taylor Joynson Garrett, London, 1978—; mem. adv. bd. The Roald Dahl Found., London, 1992—. Co-author: Joynson-Hicks Copyright Law, 1988. Freeman City of London. Mem. The Copinger Soc., Fishmongers' Co., The Copyright Soc. U.S.A. Anglican. Avocations: family, sailing, food and wine. Office: Taylor Joynson Garrett, 50 Victoria Embankment, London EC4Y 0DX, England

MITCHELL, PAUL JAMES, journalist, writer; b. San Bernardino, Calif., Dec. 25, 1962; s. James Richard and Marie Magdalen Mitchell. BA in Econs., U. Md., Budingen, Germany, 1987; MS in Film Prodn. and Writing, FAMUL, Prague, Czech Republic, 1993. Freelance journalist McMullen/Argus Pub., Placentia, Calif., 1994-98, Sports Car Internat. mag., Novato, Calif., 1998-99; writer ELogicty.com., Plesanton, Calif., 1999—; contbg. broadcast journalist AutoTalk, Riverside, Calif., 1995-99,. Contbf. articles to mags. Avocations: collecting classic sports care,flying sailplanes. E-mail: paul.mitchell@elogicity.com. Home: 105 Shoreline Cir Apt 419 San Ramon CA 94583-5500 Office: eLogicity.com 4457 Willow Rd Ste 100 Pleasanton CA 94588-8554

MITCHELL, PAULA RAE, nursing educator, college dean; b. Independence, Mo., Jan. 10, 1951; d. Millard Henry and E. Lorene (Denton) Gates; m. Ralph William Mitchell, May 24, 1975. BS in Nursing, Graceland Coll., 1973; MS in Nursing, U. Tex., 1976; EdD in ednl. Adminstrn., N.Mex. State U., 1996. RN, Tex., Mo.; cert. childbirth educator. Instr. nursing El Paso (Tex.) C.C., 1979-85, dir. nursing, 1985—, acting divsn. chmn. health occupations, 1985-86, divsn. dean, 1998-99, dean health occupations, 1999—, curriculum facilitator, 1984-86; ob-gyn. nurse practitioner Planned Parenthood, El Paso, 1981-86, mem. med. com., 1986-98; cons. in field. Author: (with Grippando) Nursing Perspectives and Issues, 1989, 93; contbr. articles to profl. jours. Founder, bd. dirs. Health-CREST, El Paso, 1981-85; mem. pub. edn. com. Am. Cancer Soc., El paso, 1983-84, mem. profl. activities com., 1992-93; mem. El Paso City-County Bd. Health, 1989-91; mem. Govt. Applications Rev. Com., Rio Grande Coun. Govts., 1989-91; mem. collaborative coun. El Paso Magnet H.S. for Helath Care Professions, 1992-94, co-chair health and human svcs. task force, Unite El Paso Health, 1996-98, mem. steering com. 1999—; co-chair health taskforce El Paso Cmty. Legis. Agenda, 1997-99; mem. adv. com. Ctr. for Border Health Rsch., Paso del Norte Health Found., 1998—; mem. Leadership El Paso, 1999. Capt. U.S. Army, 1972-78. Decorated Army Commendation medal, Meritorious Svc. medal. Named to Women's Hall of Fame, El Paso Commn., 1999. Mem. Nat. League Nursing (resolutions com. Assocs. Degree coun. 1987-89, accreditation site visitor, AD coun. 1990—, mem. Tex. edn. com. 1991-92, Tex. 3d v.p. 1992-93, Tex. 1st v.p. 1997-99, nominating com. 1999—), Am. Soc. Psychoprophylaxis Obstetrics, Nurses Assn. Am. Coll. Ob-Gyn. (cert. in ambulatory women's healthcare, chpt. coord. 1979-83, nat. program rev. com. 1984-86, corr. 1987-89), Advanced Nurse Practitioner Group El Paso (coord. 1980-83, legis. com. 1984), Am. Phys. Therapist Assn. (commn. on accreditation, site visitor for phys. therapist asst. programs 1991—), Orgn. Assoc. Degree Nursing (Tex. membership chmn. 1985-89, chmn. goals com. 1989—, mem. nat. bylaws com. 1990-95), Am. Vocat. Assn., Am. Assn. Women Cmty. and Jr. Colls., Tex. Orgn. Nurse Execs., Nat. Coun. Occupational Edn. (articulation task force 1986-89, program standards task force 1991-93), Nat. Coun. Instrnl. Adminstrs., Tex. Soc. Allied Health Profls., Tex. Nurses Assn., Nat. Soc. Allied Health Profls. (edn. com. 1993-96), El Paso C. of C., Sigma Theta Tau, Phi Kappa Phi. Mem. Christian Ch. (Disciples of Christ). E-mail: paulam@epcc.edu. Home: 4616 Cupid Dr El Paso TX 79924-1726 Office: El Paso C C PO Box 20500 El Paso TX 79998-0500

MITCHELL, PETER LAWRENCE, psychology educator; b. Southport, U.K., Apr. 15, 1959; s. Gordon Herbert and Kathleen (Wright) M.; m. Rita Mary Proctor, Aug. 11, 1979; 1 child, Andrew Keith. BA in Psychology with honors, Liverpool (U.K.) U., 1984, PhD in Psychology, 1987. Rsch. fellow U. Birmingham, U.K., 1987-90; lectr. U. Swansea, Wales, 1990-94; lectr. U. Birmingham, 1994-97, sr. lectr., 1997-98; prof. in psychology U. Nottingham, Eng., 1998—. Author: Psychology of Childhood, 1992, Acquiring a Conception of Mind, 1996, Introduction to Theory of Mind, 1997; co-editor: Children's Early Understanding of Mind, 1994, Children's Reasoning and the Mind, 2000; assoc. editor Brit. Jour. Devel. Psychology, 1996—. Recipient Rsch. grants ESRC, Eng., 1992, 95, 96. Mem. Brit. Psychol. Soc., Soc. Rsch. in Child Devel., Exptl. Psychol. Soc. Avocations: aviation and aerodynamics, playing badminton. Office: Univ Nottingham, Sch Psychology Univ Pk, Nottingham NG7 2RD, United Kingdom

MITCHELL, RIE ROGERS, psychologist, counselor, educator; b. Tucson, Feb. 1, 1940; d. Martin Smith and Lavaun (Peterson) Rogers; m. Rex C. Mitchell, Mar. 16, 1961; 1 child, Scott Rogers. Student, Mills Coll., 1958-59; BS, U. Utah, 1962, MS, 1963; postgrad., San Diego State U., 1965-66; MA, UCLA, 1969, PhD, 1969. Diplomate Am. Bd. Psychology; registered play therapist, supr.; cert. sandplay therapist. Tchr. Coronado (Calif.) Unified Sch. Dist., 1964-65; sch. psychologist Glendale (Calif.) Unified Sch. Dist., 1968-70; psychologist Glendale Guidance Clinic, 1970-77; asst. prof. ednl. psychology Calif. State U., Northridge, 1970-74, assoc. prof., 1974-78, prof., 1978—; chmn. dept. ednl. psychology, 1976-80, 2000—, acting exec. asst. to pres. Calif. State U., Dominguez Hills, 1978-79; cons. to various Calif. sch. dists.; pvt. practice psychology, Calabasas, Calif. Author: Sandplay: Past Present & Future, 1994; contbr. numerous articles to profl. jours. Recipient Outstanding Educator award Maharishi Soc., 1978, Woman of Yr. award U. Utah, 1962, Profl. Leadership award Western Assn. Counselor Edn., 1990, Disting. Tchg. award Calif. U. Northridge, 1994. Mem. APA, Calif. Assn. Counselor Edn., Supervision and Adminstrn. (dir. 1976-77), Western Assn. Counselor Edn. and Supervision (officer 1978-82, pres. 1980-81), Assn. Counselor Edn. and Supervision (dir. 1980-81, program chmn. 1981-82, treas. 1983-86, Presdl. award 1986, Leadership award 1987), UCLA Doctoral Alumni Assn. (pres. 1974-76), Am. Ednl. Rsch. Assn., Calif. Women in Higher Edn. (pres. chpt. 1977-78), Calif. Concerns (treas. 1984-86), Sandplay Therpists of Am. (fin. officer 1996—, bd. mem. 1993—, media chair, 1995, bylaws chair, 1994-96, exceptions com. chair, 1995-96), Pi Lambda Theta (pres. chpt. 1970-71, chairwoman nat. resolutions 1971-73). Home: 4503 Alta Tupelo Dr Calabasas CA 91302-2516 Office: Calif State U Counselor Edn Dept Northridge CA 91330-0001

MITCHELL, ROBERT LEE, III, auditor; b. Smyrna, Tenn., July 31, 1957; s. Robert Lee Jr. and Mary Helen (Lee) M. BA, U. Nebr., 1978. Div. sales mgr. J.L. Brandeis, Omaha, 1978-80; asst. mgr. Postal Thrift, Omaha, 1980-82; br. mgr. Security Pacific Fin. Svcs., Council Bluffs, Iowa, 1982-84; internal auditor Security Pacific Fin. Svcs., San Diego, 1984-91; branch mgr. Security Pacific Fin. Svcs., Omaha, 1991-94, sr. employee dev. spec., 1994-95, v.p. Bank America, 1995-97; dist. mgr. Avco Fin. Svcs., 1998-99; mgr. Comml. Fed. Bank, 1999—. Decorated Nat. Def. medal. Mem. U.S. Naval Inst., U.S. Naval Reserve. Democrat. Avocations: traveling, hiking, golf, photography, genealogy. Office: 8644 NW Waukomis Dr Kansas City MO 64154-2423

MITCHELL, RONNIE MONROE, lawyer, educator; b. Clinton, N.C., Nov. 10, 1952; s. Ondus Corneilius and Margaret Ronie (Johnson) M.; m. Martha Cheryl Coble, May 25, 1975; children: Grant Stephen, Mitchell, Meredith Elizabeth Mitchell. BA, Wake Forest U., 1975, JD, 1978. Bar: N.C. 1978, U.S. Dist. Ct. (ea. dist.) N.C. 1978, U.S. Ct. Appeals (4th cir.) 1983, U.S. Supreme Ct. 1984. Assoc. atty. Brown, Fox & Deaver, Fayetteville, N.C., 1978-81; ptnr. Harris, Sweeny & Mitchell, Fayetteville, 1981-91, Harris, Mitchell & Hancox, 1991-96, Harris & Mitchell, 1997-98, Harris, Mitchell, Burns & Brewer, 1998—; adj. prof. law Norman Adrian Wiggins Sch. of Law, Campbell U; bd. dirs. Mace, Inc. Contbr. chpts. to books. Chmn. Cumberland County Bd. Adjustment, 1985-92, Cumberland County Rescue Squad, 1986-93; bd. dirs. Cumberland County Rescue Squad, Fayetteville, 1983-91. Recipient U.S. Law Week award Bur. Nat. Affairs, 1978. Mem. ABA, ATLA, Twelfth Judicial Dist. Bar Assn. (pres. 1988-89), N.C. Bar Assn. (councillor Young Lawyers divsn. 1982-85), N.C. Legis. Rsch. Commn. (family law com. 1994), Cumberland County Bar Assn. (mem. family law com., N.C. State Bar Bd. legal specialization), N.C. Acad. Trial Lawyers, Fayetteville Ind. Light Infantry Club, Dem. Men's Club (pres. 1993-94), Moose, Masons. Home: RR 1901 Water Oaks Dr Fayetteville NC 28301-9125 Office: Harris Mitchell Burns & Brewer 308 Person St Fayetteville NC 28301-5736

MITCHELL, ROY DEVOY, industrial engineer; b. Hot Springs, Ark., Sept. 11, 1922; s. Watson W. and Marie (Stewart) M.; m. Jane Caroline Gibson, Feb. 14, 1958; children: Michael, Marilyn, Martha, Stewart, Nancy. BS, Okla. State U., 1948, MS, 1950; B of Indsl. Mgmt., Auburn U., 1960. Registered profl. engr., Ala., Miss. Instr. Odessa (Tex.) Coll., 1953-56; prof. engrng. graphics Auburn (Ala.) U., 1956-63; field engr. HHFA, Cmty. Facilities Adminstrn., Atlanta and Jackson, Miss., 1963-71; area engr. Met. Devel. Office, HUD, 1971-72, chief architecture and engrng., 1972-75, chief program planning and support br., 1975, dir. archtl. br., Jackson, 1975-77, chief archtl. br. and engrng. br., 1977-84, cmty. planning and devel. rep., 1984-88; prin. Mitchell Mgmt. and Engrng., 1988—; cons. Army Balistic Missile Agy., Huntsville, Ala., 1957-58, Auburn Rsch. Found., NASA, 1963; mem. state tech. action panel Coop. Area Manpower Planning System; elected pub. ofcl., chmn. Bd. of Election Commrs., Rankin County, Miss. Mem. Cen. Miss. Fed. Personnel Adv. Council; mem. House and Home mag. adv. panel, 1977; trustee, bd. dirs. Meth. Ch., 1959-60; docent Miss. Mus. Art, 1993—; bd. dirs. Am. Heart Assn., Rankin County, 1994. Served with USNR, 1943-46. Recipient Outstanding Achievement award HUD, Commendation by Sec. HUD. Mem. NSPE, Am. Soc. for Engrng. Edn., Miss. Soc. Profl. Engrs., Nat. Assn. Govt. Engrs. (charter mem.), Jackson Fed. Execs. Assn., Ctrl. Miss. Safety Coun., Am. Water Works Assn., Iota Lambda Sigma. Club: River Hills (Jackson). Deceased. Home and Office: HUD 706 Forest Point Dr Brandon MS 39047-6220

MITCHELL, SHAWNE MAUREEN, author; b. Tacoma, Wash., Jan. 9; d. F. King and Nona Margaret Burnside (Hayes) M.; m. J.D. Cook, Spt. 4, 1982; children: Travis, Austin. BA, U. Wash., 1972; postgrad., U. Santa Monica, 1997—. CEO Adventures of the Spirit, Santa Barbara, Calif., 1994—; author, spkr. Soul Style, 1995—; columnist Feng Shui-Soul Style, Calif., 1996—; cons. real estate, Wash., Calif., 1980—; dir. Small Luxury Hotels, L.A., 1986-87; internat. spkr., author on subject of higher consciousness; internat. spkr. on Feng Shui. Author: Soul Style, 1997, Soul Style, Creating Sanctuaries and Altars, 2000; editor: Home Sanctuaries mag.; contbr. articles to profl. jours. Bd. dirs. Montecito (Calif.) Ednl. Found., 1997-99, Los Positas Park Found., Santa Barbara, 1995, Nuclear Age Peace Found. Fellow Master Minds of Montecito (vice-chair); mem. DAR, Montecito Instn. Group (sec.), Womens Exec. Network, Seattle Tennis Club. Avocations: boating, hiking, sailing, traveling. Office: Adventures of the Spirit Inc PO Box 5765 Santa Barbara CA 93150-5765

MITCHELL, SUZANNE JUNE, editor; b. Sydney, N.S.W., Australia, June 25, 1950; d. Albert Leslie and Betty Estelle (Crofts) Chandler; m. Richard Walter Mitchell, Jan. 21, 1972; children: Kara Danielle, Benjamin Luke, Joel Richard. BA, U. New Eng., Armidale, N.S.W., 1990, Grad. Diploma in Edn., 1993; MA in Pub. History, Sydney U., 1998. Tchr. history various schs., Sydney, 1990-92; editor Christian Parent Controlled Schs., Sydney, 1993—. Co-editor: Reclaiming the Future - An Australian Perspective on Christian Schooling, 1996, The Crumbling Walls of Certainty - Towards a Christian Critique on Postmodernity and education, 1997; editor Nurture Jour., 1993—; mng. editor The Christian Tchrs. jour. Bd. dirs. John Wycliffe Christian Sch., Sydney, 1988-90. Mem. Oral History Assn. Australia, Profl. Historians Assn. Office: Christian Parent Cont Schs, PO Box 7000, Blacktown NSW 2148, Australia

MITCHELL, VINCENT-WAYNE, management educator; b. Carlisle, Cumbria, Eng., Apr. 18, 1964. BSc with honors, Manchester (Eng.) U., 1985; MSc, U. Manchester Inst. of Sci. and Tech., 1986, PhD, 1991. Prof. U. Manchester Inst. of Sci. and Tech., 1989—. Contbr. articles to profl. jours. Mem. Chartered Inst. Mktg. (diploma), Brit. Acad. Mgmt., Acad. Mktg. Sci. Anglican. Avocations: exercise, theatre, poetry. Office: Manchester Sch Mgmt, UMIST PO Box 88, Manchester M60 1QD, England

MITCHELL, WAYNE LEE, health care administrator; b. Mar. 25, 1937; s. Albert C. and Elizabeth Isabelle (Nagel) M.; m. Marie Galletti. BA, U. Redlands, Calif., 1959; MSW, Ariz. State U., 1970, EdD, 1979. Social worker various county, state, and fed. agys., 1962-70; social worker Bur. Indian Affairs, Phoenix, Ariz., 1970-77, USPHS, 1977-79; asst. prof. Ariz. State U., 1979-84; with USPHS, Phoenix, 1984—; lectr. in field. Contbr. articles to pubis. Bd. dirs. Phoenix Indian Cmty. Sch., 1973-75, ATLATL, 1994-98, Partnership for Cmty. Devel. Ariz. State U.-West, 1996—, Cen. Ariz. Health Sys. Agy., 1982-85; mem. Phoenix Area Health Adv. Bd., 1975, Cmty. Behavioral Mental Health Bd., 1976-80, Fgn. Rels. Com., Phoenix; trustee Heard Mus. Anthropology, Phoenix, 1996; apptd. Bd. Behavioral Health Examiners, 2000—. With USCG, 1960-62. Recipient Cmty. Svc. award Ariz. Temple of Islam, 1980, Ariz. State U., 1996, Dir. Excellence award Phoenix Area IHS Dir., 1992, 93. Mem. NASW, Fgn. Rels. Coun., Am. Hosp. Assn., U.S.-China Assn., Kappa Delta Pi, Phi Delta Kappa, Chi Sigma Chi, Nucleus Club. Democrat. Congregationalist. Home: PO Box 9592 Phoenix AZ 85068-9592 Office: DHHS IHS Two Renaissance Sq 40 N Central Ave Phoenix AZ 85004-4424

MITCHELL, WILLIAM EDWARD ALEXANDER, industrial chemist, consultant; b. Edinburgh, Scotland, Aug. 23, 1929; s. Edward Irving and Barbara Lockie (Anderson) M.; m. Margaret Longstaff, Nov. 17, 1956; children: Kathryn Anne, Graham Irving. BS in Chemistry with honors, Edinburgh U., 1950, PhD in Carbohydrate Chemistry, 1953. Cert. organic chemist. Devel. mgr. Atomic Energy Authority, Sellafield, Eng., 1953-55; R&D dept. ICI, Billingham, Eng., 1955-59; prodn. devel. Olefine Works ICI, Wilton, Eng., 1959-64; project mgr. tech. dept. ICI, Billingham, 1964-72, group mgr. hydrocarbons/oil/bulk chems., 1973-84; rsch. & tech. mgr. petrochemicals ICI, Wilton, 1984-90; cons., 1991—; cons. numerous U.S. and European cos., 1990—. Patentee in petrochemical field; contbr. articles to profl. jours. Mem. Royal Soc. Chemistry (C.Chem/MRSC awards 1951), Wilton Castle Club, Norton Hall Club, Synthonia Badminton Club, Synthonia Golf Club. Presbyterian. Avocations: golf, badminton, fell walking, gardening. Home: 26 Junction Rd, Norton, Stockton-on-Tees TS201PL, England

MITCHELL, WILLIAM GRAHAM CHAMPION, lawyer, business executive; b. Raleigh, Dec. 24, 1946; s. Burley Bayard and Dorothy Ford (Champion) M.; children: William Graham, Margaret Scripture. AB, U. N.C., 1969, JD with highest hons., 1975. Bar: N.C. 1975, U.S. Dist. Ct. (ea., mid. and we. dists.) N.C. 1976, U.S. Ct. Appeals (4th cir.) 1978. Ptnr. Womble, Carlyle, Sandridge & Rice, Winston-Salem, 1975-87; sr. v.p. for external affairs RJR Nabisco, Atlanta, 1987-89; exec. v.p. R.J. Reynolds Tobacco Co., Winston-Salem, 1988-89; ptnr. Howrey & Simon, Washington, 1990-94; spl. counselor to chmn. bd. True North Comm., Inc., Chgo., 1996; chmn. bd., CEO Global Exch. Carrier Co., Leesburg, Va., 1997-2000; pres., CEO Global Comms. Techs. Inc., Reston, Va., 1999-2000; chmn. bd., CEO Convergence Equipment Co., Manassas, Va., 1999-2000; chmn. bd. Webnet-Mktg. Inc., 2000—; bd. dirs. Fed. Agrl. Mortgage Corp., Washington; chmn. bd. Webnet-Mktg. Inc., 2000—, QFactor, Inc., 2000—. Mem. Pres.'s Adv. Com. on Trade Policy and Negotiations, Indsl. Policy Adv. Com., Washington, 1991—; exec. com. Nat. Assn. Mfrs., Washington, 1988-89, Nat. Fgn. Trade Coun., 1988-89; chmn. Tobacco Inst., Washington, 1988-89; bd. dirs. Washington Performing Arts Soc., 1988-92; bd. advisors Dem. Leadership Coun., 1988—; founding trustee Progressive Policy Inst., 1988—; vice chmn. fin. Bush Campaign. Mem. ABA (vice chmn. antitrust sect., pvt. litigation com. 1987-89, chmn. subcom. of FTC com. 1986), Georgetown Club, City Club of Washington, Forsyth Country Club, Order of the Coif.

MITCHEM, MARY TERESA, publishing executive; b. Atlanta, Aug. 31, 1944; d. John Reese and Sara Letitia (Marable) Mitchem. BA in History, David Lipscomb Coll., 1966. Sch. and library sales mgr. Chilton Book Co., Phila., 1972-79; dir. market devel. Baker & Taylor Co. div. W.R. Grace, N.Y.C., 1979-81; dir. mktg. R.R. Bowker Co. div. Xerox Corp., N.Y.C, 1981-83, dir. mktg. research, 1983-85; mktg. mgr. W.B. Saunders Co. div. CBS, Inc., Phila., 1985-87; mktg. dir. Congl. Quarterly Inc., Washington, 1987-89; dir. mktg. rsch. and devel. Bur. Nat. Affairs, Inc., Washington, 1990-96; account exec. Hughes Rsch. Corp., Rockville, Md., 1996; vice pres., ptnr. The Psychological Advantage, Inc., Atlanta, GA, 1997—. Mem. Book Industry Study Group, Inc. (chairperson stats. com. 1984-86), Mktg. Research Assn., Soc. Competitive Intelligence Profls.

MITCHISON, JOHN MURDOCH, retired zoology educator; b. Oxford, Eng., June 11, 1922; s. Lord and Naomi M. Haldane; m. Rosalind Mary Wrong, 1947; chilldren: Sally, Neil, Harriet, Amanda. Student, Winchester Coll.; ScD, Trinity Coll., Cambridge, Eng. With Army Operational Rsch., 1941-46; sen., rsch. scholar Trinity Coll. Cambridge (Eng.) U., 1946-50,

fellow, 1950-54; lectr. zoology Edinburgh (Scotland) U., 1953-59, reader, 1959-62, prof., 1963-88, dean. faculty of sci., 1984-85, prof. emeritus, univ. fellow, 1988—; Mem. of Ct., 1971-74, 85-88, J.W. Jenkinson Meml. lectr. Oxford U., 1971-72; Working Group on Biol. Manpower, Dept. of Edn. Sci. 1968-71. Author: The Biology of the Cell Cycle, 1971; contbr. articles to profl. jours. Mem. Royal Commn. Environ. Pollution, 1974-79; adv. com. Safety Nuclear Installations, Health and Safety Exec., 1981-84. Maj. Army Operational Rsch., 1942-46, ETO. Fellow Royal Soc., Inst. Biology; mem. Sci. Rsch. Coun. (biology com. 1972-75, sci. bd. 1976-79), Internat. Soc. Cell Biology (exec. com. 1964-72), Academia Europaea, Scottish Marine Biology Assn. (coun. 1961-67), Brit. Soc. Cell Biology (pres. 1974-77). Home: Great Yew, Ormiston, East Lothian EH35 5NJ, England

MITCHISON, SALLY, psychiatrist; b. Oxford, U.K., Dec. 22, 1948; d. J. Murdoch and Rosalind M. (Wrong) M.; m. John D. Charlton; children: Siobhán C. Neale, Mark E., Davey N. BA with honors, U. York, 1971; MBBS, U. London, 1978; M in Med. Sci. in Clin. Psychiatry, U. Leeds, 1990; diploma in group analysis, Inst. of Group Analysis, London, 1995. Sr. registrar in psychiatry Yorkshire Region, 1990-95, sr. registrar in psychotheraphy, 1996; cons. psychiatrist with spl responsibility for psychotherapy Priority Healthcare Wearside, Sunderland, 1996—. Mem. Assn. for Learning Langs. in the Family, Group Analytic Soc. (London). Office: Upper Poplars, Cherry Knowle Hosp Ryhope, Sunderland SR 2 ONB, United Kingdom

MITCHUM, BETH, bookstore manager, freelance editor, author; b. Logansport, Ind., Sept. 11, 1959; d. Normagene N. (Overmyer) M. BA, Southeastern Coll., Lakeland, Fla., 1981; MLA, U. N.C., Asheville, 1993. Childcare worker Fla. Bapt. Children's Home, Lakeland, 1981-85; asst. mgr. Walden Books, Seattle, Wash., 1993—; journalist Comm. Connections, Asheville, N.C., 1992-93. Author: (books) The Diary of Allie Katz, 1993, Artemesian Artist, 1997, Driftwood, 1997, Higher Love, 1997. Valedictorian Southeastern Coll., Lakeland, 1981. Mem. AAUW, NOW. Avocations: songwriting, singing, bicycling, playing guitar, drawing. Office: Waldenbooks 270 Southcenter Blvd Seattle WA 98188-2895

MITCHUM, CASSANDRA, poet, writer; b. Greensboro, N.C., June 11, 1950; m. Preston Mitchum Sr., Dec. 17, 1973; children: Preston Jr., Cynthia, Vanessa. Bus. cert., Monroe Bus. Inst., 1970. Receptionist, typist Royal Nat. Bank, N.Y.C., 1970-72, Metcalf & Eddie Engrs., N.Y.C., 1972-74; sec. Bendix Internat., N.Y.C., 1975-80; receptionist Chrysler Corp., N.Y.C., 1980-81; sec. Nat. Assn. Securities, Washington, 1981-83; word processor, sec. Lewis, Kominers & James, Counselors-at-Law, 1983-84, 86. Author numerous poems. Recipient Merit certificate World of Poetry, Sacramento, 1990, Editor's Choice award Nat. Libr. Poetry, 1996-97; named Golden Poet, World of Poetry, Sacramento, 1991; named to Internat. Poetry Hall of Fame, 1997; named one of Best Poets of 1997, 98, Outstanding Poet of 1998. Mem. Internat. Soc. Poets. Democrat. Penecostal. Home: 3225 Powder Mill Rd Adelphi MD 20783-1030

MITELMAN, BONNIE COSSMAN, editor, writer, lecturer; b. Flint, Mich., Feb. 15, 1941; d. Maurice B. and Frieda H. (Ragir) Cossman; student U. Mich., 1958-61; BA, Northwestern U., 1969; MA, Manhattanville Coll., 1977; m. Stanley D. Lelewer, Mar. 12, 1961 (div. 1969); children: Joanne, Stephen (dec.); m. Alan N. Mitelman, July 23, 1972; 1 son, Geoffrey. Copywriter trainee Dancer-Fitzgerald-Sample, Inc., Chgo., 1956-60; advt. copywriter Spiegel, Inc., Chgo., 1961-63; freelance advt. and public relations writer, Chgo., N.Y., 1963-72; co-founder Mitelman & Assocs., Briarcliff Manor, N.Y., 1972-92, pub. rels. assoc., 1992-94, asst. dir. pub. rels., 1994-97; dir. internal comms. Anti-Defamation League, N.Y.C., 1997—; adj. lectr. dept. history Mercy Coll., Dobbs Ferry, N.Y., 1979-85; contbr. articles to N.Y. Times, Am. Experiences, Vol. II, Am. History Illustrated, Working Mother, Reform Judaism, 1977—. Mem. Am. Hist. Assn., Women in Comm., Authors Guild. Author: Mothers Who Work: Strategies for Coping; mem. editl. bd. Reform Judaism, 1977—.

MITMAN, STEWART PHIPARD, retired purchasing officer; b. Huntington, N.Y., Feb. 2, 1925; s. Samuel Thomas and Marie Louise (Phipard) M.; m. Anne Carruthers Cochrane, Aug. 15, 1953; children: Suzanne Marie, Nanette Louise, Lucille Anne. BSBA, Lehigh U., 1949. Cert. pub. purchasing officer. Engring. sales rep. Gen. Cable Corp., N.Y.C., 1949-59; dir. purchasing County of Suffolk, Riverhead, N.Y., 1960-72; adminstrv. officer grants Town of Huntington, N.Y., 1972-79; dir. purchasing SUNY, Stony Brook, 1979-88; ret., 1988; part-time instr. Nat. Inst. Govtl. Purchasing, Reston, Va., 1988—; Fla. Supreme Ct. cert. mediator Fifth Jud. Cir. Ct., 1994—. Contbg. author: Public Purchasing and Materials Management, 1983. Flight officer USAAF, 1943-45, ATO. Mem. Nat. Inst. Govtl. Purchasing (bd. dirs. 1968-72, 82-88, life mem., Disting. Svc. award 1990). Avocations: swimming, golf, bowling.

MITRA, ASOKE NATH, retired physicist, educator; b. Rajshahi, India, Apr. 15, 1929; s. Jatindra Nath and Rama Rani (Bose) M.; m. Anjali Ghosh, Nov. 27, 1956; children: Bani, Gargi. BA with honors in Math., Ramjas Coll., Delhi, 1947, MA in Math., 1949; PhD in Physics, Delhi U., 1952, Cornel U., 1955. Lectr. physics U. Delhi, 1949-52; ctrl. states scholar Govt. India, Cornell U., Ithaca, N.Y., 1952-55; reader in physics Aligarh Muslim U., India, 1955-60, Delhi U., 1960-62; vis. prof. physics Ind. U., Bloomington, 1962-63; prof. physics Delhi U., 1963-69, sr. prof., 1969-89; ret., freelance writer-rschr., 1996—; profl. cons. Rutherford Lab., 1968; vis. scientist UCLA, 1967, CERN, 1968, 83, 85, U. Tex.-Austin, 1971, Bonn, 1974, U. Paris, 1977, Deutsche Elektronen Synchrotron, 1979, Internat. Ctr. for Theoretical Physics, Trieste, 1962, 65, 67, 68, 69, 70, 71, 74, 77, 83, Tubingen, 1985, Ind U., Bloomington, 1986; nat. lectr. Univ. Grants Commn., India, 1973; vis. prof. U. Ill., Chgo., 1986-87, Nat. Inst. Adv. Studies, Bangalore, 1995; vis. lectr. Nuffield Found., Australia, 1973; mem. internat. adv. coms. for successive internat. conf. series on few body problems in nuc. and particle physics and other internat. confs.; convenor, organizer 7th Internat. Conf. on Few Body Problems, Delhi U., 1975-76; sr. exch. visitor U.S. univs., Indo-U.S. Joint Program, 1976; sr. exch. visitor Brit. univs., Indian Nat. Sci. Acad. Royal Soc. Exch. Programme, 1979. Editor: Few Body Dynamics, 1976, Niels Bohr-A Profile, 1985, Quantum Field Theory, 2000; bd. editors: Few Body Systems, 1985-2000; contbr. over 200 articles to revs. to profl. jours. Mem. physics panel Univ. Grants Commn., India, New Delhi, 1974-76, 80-82; mem. coun. Raman Rsch. Inst., Bangalore, India, 1978-88; mem. Nat. Bd. for Higher Maths., Bombay, 1982-88; mem. phys. adv. com. dept. sci. and tech. Govt. India, 1982-87; mem. physics coms. Coun. for Sci. and Indsl. Rsch., New Delhi, 1974-78, 81—; mem. nat. accelerator com. Dept. Atomic Energy, India, 1979-83. Recipient S.S. Bhatnagar award Coun. for Sci. and Indsl. Rsch. India, New Delhi, 1969, Megh Nad Saha award Univ. Grants Commn., New Delhi, 1975, S.K. Mitra Birth Centenary medal Indian Sci. Congl. Assn., 1999; nat. fellow Univ. Grants Commn., 1975-78; assoc. Internat. Ctr. for Theoretical Physics, Trieste, 1967-70, sr. assoc., 1972-77, hon. assoc., 1978-83. Fellow Third World Acad. Scis., Indian Nat. Sci. Acad. (sec. 1975-79, editor publ. 1983-86, Albert Einstein rsch. prof. 1989-94, S.N. Bose medal 1986), Indian Acad. Sci. (coun. 1975-78), Am. Phys. Soc. Avocations: stamp and coin collecting, philosophy of science. Home: 244 Tagore Park, Delhi 110009, India

MITRA, SUNIRMAL, accountant, consultant; b. Calcutta, India, Mar. 1, 1953; s. Santosh and Manjari (Ghosh) M.; m. Diali De, Sept. 19, 1985; 1 child, Shimontini. BS, Calcutta U., 1973; chartered accountancy degree, Inst. Chartered Accts. India, Calcutta, 1979; postgrad. diploma in systems devel., Nat. Inst. Info. Tech., Calcutta, 1989. CPA, Inst. CPAs Kenya, Nairobi, Kenya, 1991; MIIA, IIA, Fla., 1987. Mgr. Deloitte Haskins & Sells, Calcutta, 1980-87; ptnr. Deloitte & Touche, Calcutta, 1987-90; ptnr.-designate Kassim-Lakha Abdulla & Co., Nairobi, 1990-93; fin. dir. Lyons Maid (EA) Ltd., Nairobi, 1993-98; ptnr. Kassim-Lakha Abdulla & Co., Nairobi, 1998—. Mem. Computer Soc. India (assoc.), Inst. Internal Auditors (mem. Inst. Internat. Auditors 1987), Calcutta Club. Avocations: yoga, philosophy, music, travel, current affairs.

MITRANY, DEVORA, marketing consultant, writer; b. Oak Park, Ill., Mar. 20, 1947; d. John Joseph and Frances Elizabeth (Kirke) Lang. BA cum laude, Beloit Coll., 1969; postgrad., Boston U., 1971-72. Elem. and presch. tchr. Boston, Oak Park, Ill., 1969-72; regional adminstr. TRW Fin. Sys., Wellesley, Mass., 1972-76; mgr. mktg. comms. Computer Sharing Svcs., Denver, 1976-82; dir. corp. comms. Corp. Mgmt. Sys., Denver, 1982-85; sr. copywriter On-Line Software Internat., Ft. Lee, N.J., 1985-86; mgr. corp. comms. Health Mgmt. Sys., N.Y.C., 1986-89; dir. pub. rels. Am. Sephardi Fedn., 1989-92; pres. The Mitrell Group, 1992-94; U.S. mktg. dir. The Best of Israel, 1994-95; publs. specialist PCS Health Sys., Inc., 1995—; press release chmn. Nassau Region Hadassah, 1992-94; bd. dirs. Chabad Women, 1995-98, Companion Animal Assn. Ariz., 1999-2000. Bd. dirs. Talia Hadassah, 1986-94, co-pres., 1990-92; v.p. edn. Long Beach Hadassah, 1992-94; dir. pub. rels. Bus. Roundtable on Nat. Security, Colo., 1983-84. Recipient Nat. Leadership award Long Beach Hadassah, 1991-92, Nat. Leadership award Talia Hadassah, 1993-94; named Woman of Yr., Talia Hadassah, 1993. Mem. Denver Advt. Fedn. (bd. dirs. 1981-83, Alfie award 1984), Colo. Conf. Communicators (Denver Advt. Fedn. liasion 1981-84), Am. Sephardi Fedn. (edn. com. 1987-89). Jewish.

MITRELIAS, THANOS, solid state physicist, surface chemist; b. Athens, Greece, Mar. 28, 1969; s. Dimitrios and Eleni (Kakogeorgou) M. Degree in physics, U. Ioannina, Greece, 1991; MSc in Engring. with distinction, U. Liverpool, Eng., 1992; PhD in Phys. Chemistry, U. Cambridge, 1997. Post-grad. rschr. U. Cambridge, Eng., 1992—; presenter at confs. Contbr. articles to profl. jours. Fellow European Union, Cambridge, 1992. Achievements include design of experimental system that was used to show a remarkable 8-fold increase of the rate of catalytic reactions by means of acoustic wave excitation. E-mail: tmitrelias@aol.com. Home: 4 York St, Cambridge CB1 2PY, England

MITRI, KARIM TAWFIC, petroleum reservoir engineer, geoscientist; b. Beirut, Lebanon, Sept. 8, 1951; s. Tawfic S. and Wajiha M. (Khoury) M.; m. Nohad Kahouaji, Jan. 8, 1977; children: Ragheed, Zahi. BS in Chemistry, Am. U., Beirut, 1971; MS in Chem. Engring., N.C. State U., Raleigh, 1975. Tchr./rsch. asst. Am. U., Beirut, 1971-72; asst. petroleum engr. ADPC, Abu Dhabi, United Arab Emirates, 1975-76, petroleum engr., 1976-78, reservoir engr., 1979-81, lead reservoir engr. (SIM/studies), 1982-91, lead reservoir engr., 1992-94, sr. reservoir engr. spl. studies, 1995—; assignment in reservoir studies ADNOC, Abu Dhabi, 1982-92; presenter Abu Dhabi Internat. Petroleum Conf., 1998. Contbr. rsch. articles to profl. jours. in Macromolecular Sci., Reservoir Formation Evaluation and Engring. Asst. leader First Abu Dhabi Scout Group, 1991-92. UN Relief and Works Agy. scholar, 1967-71; Am. Friends of the Middle East fellow, 1972-75. Mem. AIChE, SPE of AIME, Petroleum Soc. of CIM (Can.), N.Y. Acad. Scis., Soc. of Core Analysts. Christian Orthodox. Achievements include research in physical chemistry, chemical engineering/polymer research. Avocations: strategy games, photography, poetry, swimming, tennis. E-mail: ktm@starmail.com. Home: Fanar, Osta Bldg 2d Fl, Beirut Lebanon Office: PO Box 6172 Stn D, Calgary, AB Canada T2P 2C8 also: Abu Dhabi Co Onshore Oil Ops Petroleum Devel Divsn, PO Box 270, Abu Dhabi United Arab Emirates

MITROFANOVA, IRINA VJACHESLAVOVNA, biotechnologist; b. Yalta, Ukraine, Jan. 19, 1965; d. Vjacheslav Ivanovich and Olga Vladimirovna (Dmitrieva) M. MS, Godollo Agrl. U., Hungary, 1989; PhD in Biotech., State Nikita Bot. Garden, Yalta, Ukraine, 1994. Lab. asst. State Nikita Bot. Garden, Yalta, Ukraine, 1990, rschr., 1994-96, sr. rschr., 1996—; cons. in field. Contbr. articles to profl. jours. Mem. Internat. Assn. Plant Tissue Culture, N.Y. Acad. Scis. Avocations: painting, tennis, cultivating ornamental plants, reading. Office: State Nikita Bot Garden, Nikita, 98648 Yalta Ukraine

MITROVIC, DRAGISA, mathematics educator; b. Valjevo, Yugoslavia, Mar. 16, 1922; s. Radomir and Anka (Ignjatovic) M.; m. Melita Klakocar, Oct. 17, 1946; 1 child, Zoran. BS, U. Zagreb, Croatia, 1949, DS, 1958. Tchr. Zagreb Secondary Sch., 1951-55; teaching asst. U. Zagreb, 1955-60, asst. prof., 1960-63, assoc. prof., 1963-67, prof., 1967-87, rsch. counsellor, 1987-91. Author: Distributions and Analytic Functions, 1989, Fundamentals of Applied Functional Analysis, 1998; contbr. rsch. papers on Dirichlet series, analytic function theory, theory of distributions to profl. jours. Fellow Alexander von Humboldt, Mainz, Germany, 1966-67. Mem. Am. Math. Soc., Croatian Math. Soc. Avocation: reading. Home: Šestinska Cesta 7B, Zagreb 10000, Croatia

MITSAKIS, KARIOFILIS, humanities educator; b. Thessaloniki, Greece, May 12, 1932; d. Christos and Krystalli (Kernopoulou) M.; m. Anthoula Chalkias, Aug. 14, 1966; children: Christos, Aristides. BA, U. Thessaloniki, 1956, PhD, 1963; DPhil, U. Oxford, Eng., 1965, MA, 1968. Assoc. prof., chmn. comparative lit. U. Md., 1966-68; prof. U. Oxford, 1968-72, U. Thessaloniki, 1972-75, U. Athens, Greece, 1977—; dir. Inst. Balkan Studies, Thessaloniki, 1972-80. Author: The Language of Romanos The Melodist, 1967, Byzantine Hymnography, 1971, March Through the Time, 1981, The Living Water, 1983, The Boston Essays, 1993, The Oxford Essays, 1995. Grantee Schillizzi Found., 1962-65, grantee Alex von Humboldt Stiftung, 1965-66; recipient award Internat. Herder prize, 2000. Mem. Modern Greek Lit. Soc. (pres. 1990—), Soc. Translators Lit. (pres. awards com. 1986—), Hellenic Indian Soc. (v.p. 1993—), Soc. Promotion Greek Lang. (pres. 1993—). Mem. Christian Orthodox Ch. Avocations: painting, music, creative writing. Home: 25 Troados Str, 15342 Aghia Paraskevi Athens, Greece Office: U Athens, Campus, 15784 Zografou Athens, Greece

MITSÁNYI, ATTILA, physiologist; b. Budapest, Oct. 26, 1933; s. Ferenc and Ferencné (Utyumova) M.; m. Margit Dóda, July 18, 1959; children: Attila, Zoltán, Gábor. MD, Budapest U. Med. Sch., 1958; PhD, Hungarian Acad. of Scis., 1971; Dr.med.habil., Semmelweis U. Med. Sch., 1994. Asst. prof. Dept. Physiology, Budapest U. Med. Sch., 1958-67; sr. rsch. fellow dept. exptl. physiology Nat. Inst. Occupl. Health, Budapest, 1967-76, head of dept. dept. applied physiology, 1976-86; sr. rsch. scientist dept. physiology Semmelweis U. Med. Sch., Budapest, 1986—; scientific adviser Ministry of Health, Budapest, 1972-79; lectr. Postgrad. Med. Sch., Budapest, 1976-86, Tech. U. of Budapest, 1979-85, U. Vet. Sch., Budapest, 1992—. Co-author: Occupational Health, Industrial Health, 1981, Medical Physiology, 1997, 99; editor Procs. of the Internat. Union of Physiological Scis., Vol. 14, 1980; mng. editor Ctrl. European Jour. Occupl. and Environ. Medicine, 1999—. Trustee, sec. Hungarian Physiol. Fund, Budapest, 1991—. Recipient Presdl. Rsch. award Hungarian Acad. of Sci., 1966, 73; recipient Scientific Prize Postgrad. Med. Sch., 1978, Award for Excellent Work Ministry of Health, 1984. Mem. Hungarian Physiol. Soc. (treas. 1990-98), Hungarian Soc. for Exptl. and Clin. Pharmacology, N.Y. Acad. Scis., Hungarian Neurosci. Soc., European Neurosci. Assn., Internat. Brain Rsch. Orgn. Achievements include (with others) the first description of the sympathetic C-reflex. Office: Semmelweis U Med Sch, Dept Physiol PO Box 259, H-1444 Budapest Hungary

MITSCH, HEINZ, mathematician; b. Vienna, Austria, Aug. 10, 1944; s. Oskar and Adele (Fitscha) M.; children: Andreas, Christoph. PhD, U. Vienna, 1967; postgrad., U. Paris, 1970. Asst. math. dept. U. Vienna, 1967-75, lectr., 1975-80, prof., 1980—, dept. head, 1988-90; guest prof. math. dept. U. Merida, Venezuela, 1972-73; vis. prof. math. dept. U. Hamilton, Can., 1985, U. Lecce, Italy, 1986-89, U. Siena, Italy, 1986-89, U. Braga, Portugal, 1997—, U. Vila Real, Portugal, 1997—. Author: Linear Algebra, 1978, Algebra, 1982; contbr. over 30 articles to profl. jours. Mem. Austrian Math. Soc., Unione Matematica Italiana, European Math. Soc. Avocations: piano, literature, sports. Office: U Vienna Inst fur Math, Strudlhofgasse 4, 1090 Vienna Austria

MITSEK, ALEXANDR IVANOVICH, physicist; b. Donetsk, Ukraine, Aug. 29, 1938; s. Ivan and Vitalia (Fishman) M.; m. Tatiana Shubina, 1958 (div. 1968); children: Sergei, Maria; m. Valentina Pushkar, Nov. 20, 1971; 1 child, Valentin. PhM, Ural State U., Sverdlovsk, Russia, 1960, PhD, 1964; DS, Inst. Metal Physics, Sverdlovsk, 1978. Rschr. Inst. Metal Physics, Sverdlovsk, Russia, 1964-72; rschr. Inst. Metal Physics, Kyiv, Ukraine, 1972-80, chief rschr., 1980—; lectr. Ural State U., 1964-70; vis. prof. physics Tech. U., Kyiv, 1978-82. Author: The Real Crystals with Magnetic Order, 1978, The Phase Transitions in Crystals with Magnetic Structure, 1989; contbr. articles to profl. jours. Avocations: cycling, gardening. Home: Sagaidachny St 14 ap 2, 04070 Kyiv Ukraine Office: Inst Metal Physics, Vernadzky St 36, 03680 Kyiv Ukraine

MITSELMAKHER, GUENAKH, physics educator, researcher; b. Vilnius, Lithuania, Dec. 5, 1945; came to U.S., 1991; s. Viktoras and Anna (Bannikova) M.; m. Antonina Lavrova, Aug. 22, 1970; children: Irina, Victor. M Physics, Moscow State U., 1968; PhD in Physics, Joint Inst. Nuclear Rsch., Dubna, Russia, 1974; DS, USSR State Com. Higher Edn., Moscow, 1987. Rsch. asst. Joint Inst. for Nuclear Rsch., Dubna, 1968-70, rsch. scientist, 1970-74, sr. rsch. scientist, 1974-83, dept. head, 1983-91, dep. dir. lab., 1987-89; staff scientist Superconducting Supercollider Lab., Dallas, 1991-94, Fermi Nat. Accelerator Lab., Batavia, Ill., 1994-98; prof. physics U. Fla., Gainesville, 1995—; mem. adv. com. Program Fundamental Nuclear Physics, Ministry of Sci. of Russian Fedn., Moscow, 1993—; mem. steering com. compact muon solenoid CMS, experiment European Ctr. for Nuclear Rsch., CERN, Geneva, 1997—; cons. to dir. Joint Inst. Nuclear Rsch., Dubna, Russia, 2000—. Contbr. over 150 articles to profl. publs. Mem. AAAS, Am. Phys. Soc. Achievements include contributions to physics of pions and muons, study of electroweak interactions, particle detectors development. Home: 4929 SW 95th Ter Gainesville FL 32608-4189 Office: U Fla Dept Physics Gainesville FL 32611

MITSIS, FOTIS JOHN, dentist, educator; b. Phiniki, Filiaton, Greece, Sept. 1, 1926; s. John Gregory and Efterpi (Lagou) M; 1 child, Evi. DDS, U. Athens, 1951, MD, 1964, ScD, 1962; cert. in endodontics and periodontics, U. Pa., 1965. Asst. dept. dental pathology and therapeutics Dental Sch./U. Athens, 1956-62, assoc., 1962-66, assoc. prof., 1966-69, prof., 1969-94, dean, 1975-77, 83-88, prof. emeritus, 1995—; rector U. Athens, 1978-81; pres. Gen. Hosp. Evangelismos, 1987-89, 97—; vis. prof. Tufts U., 1977-78; mem. Nat. Coun. Health; mem. Adv. Com. on Dental Tng. in EEC, 1981-90; mem. Nat. Drug Orgn., Nat. Com. for AIDS, Piezze Fauchard Acad. Author: Atlas of Dental Histology, 1963, 2d edit. 89, Dental Pathology and Therapeutics, 1972, Introduction in Dentistry and History of Dentistry, 1975, Endodontics, 1987, Periodontology, 1980, 2d edit., 1990; contbr. sci. papers to profl. confs. and internat. and Greek jours.; rschr. in field. With Greek Army, 1952-55. NIH fellow USPHS, 1965. Mem. Am. Acad. Periodontology, Am. Assn. Endodontists, Fedn. Dentaire Internat., Internat. Assn. Dental Rsch., Greek Assn. Odontostomatol. Rsch. (pres. 1970-72), Hellenic Soc. of Perio (pres. 1997-99), European Fedn. Perio. Office: Athinisin Ethnikon Kai Kapodistriakon, Panepistimion O dos Panepistimiou 30, 143 Athens Greece

MITSUI, TAKETOMO, mathematician, educator; b. Tokyo, Mar. 30, 1944; parents Tametomo and Miwako (Nakayama) M.; m. Shoko Takizawa, Oct. 10, 1970; children: Naomi, Masashi. BA, U. Tokyo, 1967, MS, 1969; DSc, Kyoto U., 1981. Rsch. assoc. Kyoto U., Japan, 1969-83; from asst. prof. to assoc. prof. Fukui U., Japan, 1983-86; from assoc. prof. to prof. Nagoya U., Japan, 1986—; dean grad. sch. human informatics Nagoya U., 1998—. Editor: Numerical Analysis of Ordinary Differential Equations and its Application, 1995; contbr. articles to profl. jours. Mem. Japan Soc. Indsl. & Applied Maths., Soc. Indsl. & Applied Maths. Avocation: photography. Office: Nagoya U Grad Sch Human Informat, Furo-cho Chikusa-ku, Nagoya Japan 4648601

MITSUKE, KOICHIRO, chemistry educator; b. Tokuyama, Yamaguchi, Japan, Feb. 2, 1959; s. Tatsuo and Atsuko (Oyane) M. BS, U. Tokyo, Japan, 1981, MS, 1983, DSc, 1986. Rsch. assoc. U. Tokyo, Japan, 1986-91; assoc. prof. Inst. for Molecular Sci., Okazaki, Japan, 1991—. Mem. Japan Chem. Soc., Japan Phys. Soc., Am. Phys. Soc. Home: Tatsumi-Minami 2-5-1-1-42, Okazaki 444-0874, Japan Office: Inst for Molecular Sci, Myodaiji, Okazaki 444-8585, Japan

MITSUOKA, MASAHIRO, surgeon, researcher; b. Saga, Japan, Sept. 1, 1964; s. Masatsugu and Teruko (Kudo) M.; m. Masae Haranosono, Nov. 8, 1992; children: Nagiko, Masamu. MD, Kurume (Japan) U., 1989. Fellow Kurume U., 1989-91, rschr., 1993-95, staff, 1998-99; resident Kyusyu Cancer Ctr., Fukuoka, 1991-92; staff Yame (Japan) Pub. Hosp., 1992-93; rsch. fellow U. Calif., San Diego, 1995-97. Contbr. articles to profl. jours. Recipient Encouragement of Young Scientists award Ministry Edn., Japan, 1999. Mem. Am. Coll. Chest Physicians, Japan Surg. Soc., Japanese Assn. for Thoracic Surgery. Avocations: judo, skiing, scuba diving. Office: Kurume U Dept Surgery, 67 Asahi-machi, Kurume Fukuoka 830-0011, Japan

MITTAL, DUTT KUMAR, commerce educator, researcher; b. Lahore, Pakistan, Feb. 16, 1945; s. Brikh Bhan and Janak Dulari Mittal; m. Aruna Gupta, Apr. 19, 1969; children: Megha, Luv. M in Commerce, Delhi (India) U., 1968; LLB, Mahanand Misssion Hari Coll., Meerut, India, 1968, MA in Econs., 1971; PhD, Delhi U., 1981. Reader Shri Ram Coll., Delhi U., 1966-81; assoc. prof. commerce Xavier Labour Rels. Inst., Jamshedpur, India, 1981-82; prin. lectr. Inst. Mgmt. and Tech., Enugu, Nigeria, 1982-84; reader Shri Ram Coll. Commerce, Delhi U., 1984—. Author: Employment in Public Enterprises, 1989, Price Control, 1991, Fertiliser Industry, 1994; co-author: Indian Financial System, 1997. Mem. Indian Acctg. Assn. (sec. 1989-91). Home: 5/3 Bl 41 Singh Sabha Rd, Shakti Nagar, Delhi 110007, India Office: U Delhi Shri Ram Coll Comm, Dept Commerce, Delhi 110007, India

MITTAL, RAMA DEVI, biochemistry educator; b. Lucknow, India, May 22, 1954; d. Pyarelal and Ramshree Devi Gupta; m. Balraj Mittal, Mar. 22, 1952; children: Tulika, Nimisha. Degree, Loreto Coll., Lucknow, 1969; BS, Lucknow U., 1971, MS, 1973; PhD, Banaras Hindu U., Varanasi, India, 1979. Post doctorate Indsl. Toxicology Rsch. Ctr., Lucknow, 1979-80; rsch. specialist Coun. Sci. and Indsl. Rsch. Ctr. for Biotechnology, Delhi, India, 1980-81; Coun. Sci. and Indsl. Rsch. pool scientist Sanjay Gandhi Post Grad. Inst. Med. Scis., Lucknow, 1988-91, asst. prof., 1991-97; assoc. prof. Sanjau Gandhi Post Grad. Inst. Med. Scis., Lucknow, 1998—; rsch. assoc. Temple U., Phila., 1981-84; rsch. PDF Temple U. Med. Sch., 1986-88; cons. Temple U., 1984-86. Contbr. articles to profl. jours. Mem., activist Women Scientists of Indian Origin, Phila., 1987. Recipient Pub. Svc. award NIH, 1987. Mem. Soc. Biol. Chemists, Assn. Clin. Biochemists, N.Y. Acad. Scis., Am. Assn. Clin. Chemistry, Sigma Xi. Avocations: field hockey, softball (nat. player), writing. Home: V B/22, Sanjay Gandhi Postgrad Inst, 226014 Lucknow India Office: Sanjay Gandhi Inst Med Scis, Rae Bareli Rd, 226014 Lucknow India

MITTAL, RAMESH CHAND, mathematics educator, researcher; b. Sabalgarh, India, Sept. 5, 1952; s. Laxmi Narayan and Savitri Devi Mittal; m. Rama Modi, Dec. 6, 1980; children: Ratnesh, Pragya. BSc, Govt. Sci. Coll., Gwalior, India, 1973; MSc, I.I.T., Delhi, 1975, PhD, 1979. Rsch. assoc. I.I.T., Delhi, 1979-80; lectr. Roorkee (India) U., 1980-93, asst. prof., 1993-97, assoc. prof., 1997—. Contbr. articles to profl. jours. Avocations: reading, swimming. Home: Univ Roorkee, 31/3 Niti Nagar, Roorkee India Office: Univ Roorkee Dept math, 247 667 Roorkee India

MITTAL, SUNEETA, obstetrics and gynecology educator; b. Pilani, Rajasthan, India, July 17, 1950; d. Shriram and Kantadevi Mittal; m. Nirmal Kumar, Apr. 17, 1979; children: Pakhee, Paras. Grad., Maharani Coll., Jaipur, India, 1967; B Medicine B Surgery, Lady Hardinge Med. Coll., New Delhi, 1972, MD in Ob-Gyn., 1977. Pool officer Coun. Scientific & Indsl. Rsch., New Delhi, 1980-82; sr. rsch. officer Indian Coun. Med. Rsch., New Delhi, 1982-83; asst. prof. All India Inst. Med. Scis., New Delhi, 1983-87, assoc. prof., 1987-91, additional prof., 1991-96, prof. ob-gyn., 1996—, project sec., 1987-92. Author: Cancer Detection in Women, 1987; editor: Assessment in Medical Education, 1995; contbr. over 100 articles to profl. jours., chpts. to textbooks. Mem. Nat. Acad. Med. Sci., Assn. Ob-Gyns. Delhi (life), Fedn. Obstet. and Gynecol. Socs. India (life), Indian Soc. Perinatology and Reproductive Biology (life), Nat. Assn. Voluntary Sterilization and Family Welfare (treas. 1991). Avocations: music, embroidery, photography, gardening. Home: DII/4 Ansari Nagar, AIIMS Campus (W), New Delhi 110029, India Office: All India Inst Med Scis, Dept Ob-Gyn Ansari Nagar, New Delhi 11029, India

MITTE, ROY F., finance company executive. BS, S.W. Tex. State U., 1953, MEd, 1956. Founder Fin. Industries Corp., Austin, 1972; chmn., CEO Fin. Industries Corp., Austin, Tex., 1985. Establisher Roy F. and Joann Cole Mitte Found. Scholarship program S.W. Tex. State U., 1997. Recipient Disting. Alumnus award S.W. Tex. State U., 1982. Office: Fin Industries Corp Austin Ctr 701 Brazos St Austin TX 78701-3258

MITTEL, JOHN J., economist, corporate executive; b. L.I., N.Y.; s. John and Mary (Leidolf) M.; 1 child, James C. BBA, CUNY. Rschr. econs. dept. McGraw Hill & Co., N.Y.C.; mgr., asst. to pres., Indsl. Commodity Corp., J. Carvel Lange Inc., and J. Carvel Lange Internat., Inc., N.Y.C., 1956-64, corp. sec., 1958-86, v.p., 1964-80, exec. v.p., 1980-86; pres. I.C. Investors Corp., N.Y.C., 1972—, I.C. Pension Adv., Inc., N.Y.C., 1977—; bd. dir. several corps.; plan adminstr., trustee Combined Indsl. Commodity Corp. and J. Carvel Lange Inc. Pension Plan, 1962-86, J. Carvel Lange Internat. Inc. Profit Sharing Trust, 1969-86, Combined Indsl. Commodity Corp. and J. Carvel Lange Inc. Employees Profit Sharing Plan, 1977-86. Co-author: How Good a Sales Profit Are You, 1961, The Role of the Economic Consulting Firm. Mem. grad. adv. bd Bernard M. Baruch Coll., CUNY, 1971-72. Mem. Conf. Bd., Am. Statis. Assn., Newcomen Soc. N.Am., Union League (N.Y.C.). Office: 10633 Saint Andrews Rd Boynton Beach FL 33436-4714

MITTELMAN, MOSHE, internist, hematologist, educator; b. Petah-Tikva, Israel, Oct. 2, 1952; s. Israel and Lea M.; m. Edit Benov, Sept. 27, 1978; children: Shaked, Ben, Gefen. MD, Israel, 1978. Med. diplomate. Dir. dept. medicine Hasharon Hosp., Petah-Tikva, Israel, 1994—; clin. assoc. prof. Tel-Aviv U., 1998—. Office: Hasharon Hosp, PO Box 121, 49372 Petah Tikva Israel

MITTELSTAEDT, ARTHUR HOWARD, JR., educational educator; b. N.Y.C., Sept. 25, 1936; m. Sue Carol Olsen, 1962; children: Kurt Arthur, Karen Maria. BS, Syracuse U., 1958; MPA, NYU, 1963, EdD, 1977. Self-employed landscape designer N.Y. State, 1954-58; asst. landscape architect N.Y.C. Housing Authority, 1959; landscape architect Nassau County Dept. Public Works, 1959-62, Office Joseph Gangemi, N.Y.C., 1959; landscape architect, planning cons. Urban Planning Assocs., Port Washington, N.Y., 1960—, Planning Assocs., Mineola, N.Y., 1961—; chmn. bd. P.A. Edn. and Recreations Cons., Inc., leisure systems planner, Hempstead, Bohemia and Ronkonkoma, N.Y., 1966—; adj. asst. prof. NYU, 1965-70, Hunter Coll., 1971, So. Conn. State Coll., 1975-77; prof. Merrimack Valley C.C., 1973; assoc. prof. C.W. Post Ctr., L.I. U., 1978-85; participant confs. in field. Contbr. numerous articles, reports to profl. publs. Exec. bd. Nassau County coun. Boy Scouts Am., 1978-84; usher, vestryman St. Stephen's Epis. Ch., Port Washington, 1975-80; corp. bd. dirs. Nassau-Suffolk YMCA, 1975-78; trustee Dikaia Found., 1977-80; trustee Sci. Mus. of L.I. Health and Safety Comm. Nat. Boy Scouts of Am.; mem. Cmty. Safety Divsn., vice-chmn. Nat. Safety Coun. Capt. USAR, 1958-65. Disting. fellow N.Y. State Recreation and Park Soc. (chmn. various coms. 1973—, pres. 1983-84); mem. Am. Soc. Landscape Architects, Am. Inst. Cert. Planners, Coun. Park and Recreation Cons. (pres.), Nat. Park and Recreation Assn., Comml. Recreation and Tourism Soc. (pres. 1992-98), AAHPER (trustee nat. found. 1974-76), Nassau Recreation, Park and Conservation Soc. (chmn. civic affairs com. 1970-84; profl., presdl. and hon. mention awards 1963-83), recipient numerous nat. awards. Office: Planning Assocs 39 Shadyside Ave Port Washington NY 11050-2416

MITTENDORF, ROBERT, physician, epidemiologist; b. Ironton, Ohio, Aug. 6, 1943; s. Robert William and Martha Jane (Whitley) M.; m. Marguerite Jean Herschel, Nov. 10, 1979; children: Jeffrey David, Robert William II, Inga. BS, Ohio State U., 1966; MD, U. Ky., 1974; MPH, Harvard U., 1987, D Pub. Health, 1991. Diplomate Am. Bd. Ob-Gyn. Attending physician St. Margaret's Hosp., Boston, 1977-87; chief of surgery Winthrop (Mass.) Hosp., 1986-88; project dir., collaborative breast cancer study Harvard U., Boston, 1989-91; dir. Office Clin. Rsch. Tufts Sch. Medicine, Boston, 1991-92; dir. health studies, dept. ob-gyn. U. Chgo., 1992-99; assoc. prof. Loyola U. Med. Ctr., Maywood; dir. divsn. gen. ob-gyn Loyola U. Med. Ctr., Maywood, Ill., 2000—; mem. sci. adv. com. anti-epileptic drugs in pregnancy registry Mass. Gen. Hosp., Boston, 1997—; cons. Nat. Ctrs. for Disease Control and Prevention, Atlanta, 1994; bd. dirs. U. Chgo. Health Plan, Chgo., Quadrangle Club, U. Chgo.; manuscript reviewer for The Lancet, 1998—. Author: Control of Transmissible Diseases in Health Care, 1995; contbr. articles to profl. jours. Med. dir. Cambridge Econ. Opportunity Com., 1977-78. Capt. USAF, 1966-70. Mem. AMA, Soc. Maternal Fetal Medicine, Soc. Epidemiol. Rsch. Democrat. Achievements include devel. of a linear regression model that permits the more precise determination of the estimated date of confinement in pregnant women (Mittendorf-Williams Rule); discovery that strenuous phys. activity is associated with a reduced risk of breast cancer, using a multivariable logistic regression model. Prin. investigator of the MAGnet Trial (magnesium and neurologic endpoints randomized control trial) to determine if using antenatal magnesium sulfate is associated with the prevention of severe cerebral palsy. Through statis. meta-analysis, discovered that certain prophylactic antibiotics are highly efficacious in preventing the serious infections associated with total abdominal hysterectomy. Home: 5634 S Woodlawn Ave Chicago IL 60637-1623 Office: Dept Ob-Gyn Loyola U Med Ctr 2160 S 1st Ave Maywood IL 60153-3304

MITTENECKER, ERICH FELIX PAUL, psychology educator; b. Wiener Neustadt, Austria, June 26, 1922; s. Felix and Anna (Vukovich) M.; m. Ilse Stigleitner, May 15, 1940; children: Georg, Sonja. PhD, U. Vienna, Austria, 1948. Univ. asst. U. Vienna, 1948-53, univ. dozent, 1953-62, univ. prof., 1962-65; full prof. U. Tuebingen, Fed. Republic of Germany, 1965-68; full prof. U. Graz, Austria, 1968-90, prof. emeritus, 1990—. Author: (books) Design and Evaluation of Experiments, 1952, 83, Methods and Results of Psychological Accident Research, 1962, Video in der Psychologie, 1987; co-author: (book) Informationstheorie F. Psychologen, 1973; contbr. articles to profl. jours. Mem. German Soc. Psychology, Profl. Assn. Austrian Psychologists (hon.). Avocation: Alpine skiing. Home: Tullbachweg 5, A-8044 Graz Austria Office: U Graz Dept Psychology, Univ Platz 2, A-8010 Graz Austria

MITTER, PARTHA, educator; b. Calcutta, West Bengal, India, 1938; arrived in Eng., 1962; s. Rabindra Nath and Pushpa Lata (Dé) M.; m. Swasti Sanyal, Aug. 7, 1960; children: Rana Shantashil Rajyeswar, Pamina Radha. BA with honors, Presidency Coll., Calcutta, 1954-58, London U., 1962-65; PhD, London U., 1965-70; MA, Cambridge U., Eng., 1968. Jr. research fellow Churchill Coll. Cambridge U., 1968-69, research fellow Clare Hall, 1970-74; lectr. in history Sussex U., Brighton, Eng., 1974-95, reader in art history, 1995-2000, prof. art history, 2000—; Radhakrishnan Meml. lectr. All Souls Coll., Oxford, 1992—. Author: Much Maligned Monsters, 1977, Art and Nationalism in Colonial India: 1850-1922, 1995; compiler and author exhbn. History of Indian Photography, London, 1982; contbr. articles to profl. jours. Reader of the Brit. Acad., 1985-87; Mellon fellow Inst. for Advanced Study, Princeton, 1981-82. Fellow Royal Soc. of Arts. Mem. Labour Party. Avocations: painting, photography. Home: 25 Norfolk Rd, Brighton Sussex BN1 3AA, England

MITTER, WOLFGANG ANDREAS, education educator, researcher; b. Trautenau, Czech Republic, Sept. 14, 1927; s. Karl Michael and Margarete Helene (Rebhann) M.; m. Sylvia Saenger, Apr. 18, 1957; children: Doris, Sonja. Diploma in secondary edn., U. Mainz, Germany, 1953; PhD, Free U., Berlin, 1954. Tchr. h.s., Kassel, Germany, 1954-64; prof. Coll. of Edn., Lueneburg, Germany, 1964-72; prof., head dept. German Inst. Internat. Ednl. Rsch., Frankfurt, Germany, 1972-98, prof., dir., 1978-81, 87-95, prof. emeritus, 1995—; prof. U. Hamburg, Germany, 1965-72, U. Frankfurt, 1973—. Author: Secondary School Graduation: University Entrance Qualification in Socialist Countries, 1978, Education for All, 1984, Schule Zwischen Reform Und Krise, 1987, Pädagogische Reisen in Polen, 1989-95, 1997; editor: Wege Zur Hochschulbildung in Europa, 1996. Named to L'Ordre Leopold II, Belgian Govt., Brussels, 1986; recipient Goethe-Plakette award Govt. of Hessen, Germany, Wiesbaden, 1992, Land Medal of 650 Years Charles U., Prague, 1998; hon. fellow Charles U., Prague, Czech Republic, 1992. Mem. World Coun. Comparative Edn. Socs. (pres. 1991-96), Russian Acad. Edn., Academia Europaea, World Assn Ednl. Rsch. (pres. 1997-2000). Avocations: piano, concerts, hiking, reading, swimming. E-mail: Mitter@dipf.de. Office: German Inst Internat Ednl Rsch, Schloss-Strasse 29, D-60486 Frankfurt Germany

MITTERAND, HENRI C., education educator, writer; b. Vault-De-Lugny, Yonne, France, Aug. 7, 1928; s. Joseph and Helene (Dangauthier) M.; m. Helene T. D'Afflitto, Dec. 24, 1955; children: Marie-Helene, Jacques-Olivier. Lic., U. Paris, 1969, Maitrise, 1950, Agregation, 1951, PhD, 1969. Asst. to assoc. prof. U. Besancon, France, 1957-65; assoc. prof. U. Reims, France, 1965-68; prof. U. Paris 8, 1968-78, U. Paris 3, 1978-90, Columbia U., N.Y.C., 1990—; vis. prof. U. Toronto, Can., 1970-93, U. Pa., 1999; editl. cons., Paris, 1971—; mem. numerous advisory bds. in field. Editor: (books) Zola, 5 Vols., 1959-67 (award 1968), Zola, 15 Vols., 1970; author: (books) Le Discours du roman, 1980, L'Illusion réaliste, 1994, Zola et le Naturalisme, 1986, Le Regard et le Signe, 1987, Le Roman á l'oeuvre, 1998, (biography) Zola, 1999. Officier des Palmes Acads., France, 1987, Chevalier de la Legion d'Honneur, France, 1989. Mem. Soc. des Amis de Zola (pres. 1990—), Inst. Pierre Larousse (pres. 1990), Acad. du Morvan, Soc. of Fellows/Columbia U. Avocations: sailing, music, films, books. Office: Columbia U Broadway/116th St W New York NY 10027

MITTERAUER, BERNHARD JOSEF, psychiatrist, educator, neuroscientist; b. Salzburg, Austria, Oct. 31, 1943; s. Josef and Maria Christine (Brötzner) M.; m. Gertraud Antonia Laemboeck, Sept. 9, 1970; children: Stilla, Tobias. MD, U. Innsbruck, Austria, 1969. Lic. psychoanalyst, psychotherapist. Gen. physician Salzburg Gen. Hosp., 1969-71; asst. neurologist Salzburg Psychiat. Clinic, 1971-76, asst. psychiatrist, 1976-78, dep. dir., 1978-83; asst. prof. U. Graz, Austria, 1983-89; prof. and dir. psychiatry U. Salzburg, 1989—; pvt. practice neuropsychiatry Salzburg, 1979—; supr. for psychotherapy Gen. Psychiat. Hosp., Salzburg, 1979—; ct. expert Austrian Legal Sys., 1984—. Contbr. articles to profl. jours. Achievements include patentee in field; research in biocybernetics. Avocation: horseback riding. Office: Inst Forensic Neuropsychiat, Ignaz-Harrer Str 79, 5020 Salzburg Austria

MITTERMAYER, HELMUT WOLFGANG, physician, clinical microbiologist; b. Linz, Austria, July 13, 1947; s. Helmut O.W. and Marianne MIttermayer; m. Liselotte Ambos, July 13, 1972; children: Ursula, Fritz, Werner. MD, U. Vienna, Austria, 1972. Tng. in microbiology and hygiene Hygiene Inst., U. Vienna, 1972-75; splty. tng. in lab. medicine Elisabethinen Hosp., Linz, 1976-80, hosp. hygienist, chmn. infection control com., 1976—, in charge clin. microbiology, 1977—, cons. for chemotherapy, 1977—, head dept. med. microbiology and hygiene, 1984—; asst. prof. hygiene, microbiology and preventive medicine U. Vienna, 1987-91, prof. hygiene, micrbiology and preventive medicine, 1991—; lectr. in postgrad. med. edn.; presenter papers to sci. meetings. Contbr. articles on infection control, clin. microbiology, anaerobic bacteria to med. jours. Mem. Austrian Soc. Hygiene, Microbiology and Preventive Medicine (chmn. working group for clin. microbiology), Am. Soc. for Microbiology, Austrian Soc. Clin. Chemistry, Assn. Italian Clin. Microbiologists, Hosp. Infection Soc. (London), Paul Ehrlich Soc. Chemotherapy, German Soc. for Hygiene and Microbiology, European Soc. for Clin. Microbiology, European Study Group on Antibiotic Resistance (com. mem.). Office: Elisabethinen Hosp, 1 Fadingerstrasse, A-4010 Linz Austria

MITTWOCH, URSULA, genetics educator; b. Berlin, Mar. 21, 1924; arrived in Eng., 1939; d. Eugene and Anna Hermine (Lipmann) M.; m. Bernard Victor Springer, Dec. 21, 1954; 1 child, Caroline. BSc, Chelsea Poly., London, 1947; PhD, Univ. Coll. London, 1950, DSc, 1978. Rsch. staff Med. Rsch. Coun., London, 1958-62; lectr. genetics Univ. Coll. London, 1963-80, reader, 1980-85, prof., 1985-89, prof. emeritus, 1989—; vis. prof. Queen Mary and Westfield Coll., London, 1989—. Author: Sex Chromosomes, 1967, Genetics of Sex Differentiation, 1973. Fellow Inst. Biology, Royal Soc. Medicine, Zool. Soc.; mem. Brit. Genetical Soc. Home: 73 Leverton St, London NW5 2NX, England Office: Galton Lab U Coll London, Wolfson House 4 Stephenson Way, London NW1 2HE, England

MITTY, TODD JAY, financial services company executive; b. N.Y.C., Sept. 1, 1965; s. Neil Henry and Talma Helen (Bourkoff) M. BS, Rensselaer Poly. Inst., 1986, MS, 1987, MA, 1990; PhD, Princeton U., 1993. Sr. rsch. engr. AESOP, Inc., Princeton, N.J., 1993-94; mgr. Deloitte & Touche Consulting Group, N.Y.C., 1994-97; v.p. strategic devel. NetDox, Inc., Deerfield, Ill., 1997-98; mng. dir. Invengen LLC, Murray Hill, N.J., 1998-99; v.p., gen. mgr. US Interactive, Inc., Murray Hill, 1999-2000; prin. Morgan Stanley Dean Witter, N.Y.C., 2000—. Recipient Luigi Crocco tchg. award Princeton U., 1990, AIAA Paul E. Hemke award, Rensselaer Polytech. Inst., 1986. Mem. Assn. Princeton Grad. Alumni (pres. 1999—), N.Y. Acad. Scis. (fin. affairs com. 1994—), Princeton Club N.Y., Tau Beta Pi, Sigma Gamma Tau. Home E-mail: tjmitty@princeton.edu. Office E-mail: todd.jay.mitty@msdw.com. Fax: 212-761-3027. Home: Two Charlton St Apt 5H New York NY 10014 Office: Morgan Stanley Dean Witter 1585 Broadway New York NY 10036-8200

MITZ, NINA, government communications advisor; b. Wels, Austria, Oct. 4, 1947; d. Serge Mitz and Regina Maria Mincberg; m. Daniel Alexandre Marchac, June 26, 1985; children: Alexandre Charles Vadim, Nathalie Anne Erika. Degree, Law U.-Assas, Paris, European Inst. Adminstrn. Affairs INSEAD, Fontainebleau, France, 1992, Inst. Hauts Elindes Securité Inteuieure, Paris, 1994. Account mgr. Leo Burnett/EDI Agy., Paris, 1965-68; mgr. advt. and sales promotion Nat. Cash Register, Paris, 1968-70; dir. corp. comm. Japan Airlines/JAL Group, Paris, 1970-92; pres. NMC Internat., Paris, 1992-94; v.p. fin. and corp. comm. SOREMA/GROUPAMA, Paris, 1994-97; advisor for internat. comm. to French Minister of Economy, Fins. and Industry, Paris, 1997—. Avocations: primitive and modern art, skiing, archaeology. Home: 130 rue de la Pompe, 75116 Paris France Office: Cabinet of French Min of Econ, 139 rue de Bercy, 75112 Paris France

MIURA, HAJIME, physiology educator; b. Takada, Japan, June 4, 1966; s. Atsushi and Reiko Miura. PhD, Chukyo U., Japan, 1996. Asst. prof. U. Tokushima, Japan, 1995—; vis. prof. U. Pa., 1998. Fax: 81-88-656-7288. Office: U Tokushima, 1-1 Minamijosanjima, Tokushima 770-8502, Japan

MIURA, KIYOHIRO, English language educator, writer; b. Muroran, Hokkaido, Japan, Sept. 10, 1930; s. Yoshiharu and Kiyoko (Kobayashi) M.; m. Emiko Takigawa, Dec. 6, 1964; children: Genta, Toné. Student, Tokyo U., 1950-52; BA, San Jose State U., 1957; postgrad., U. Iowa, 1957-58. Clk. Miyazaki Travel Agy., N.Y.C., 1958-60, Pan Am. Airways, Paris, 1960-62; mgr. Taiheiyo TV, Tokyo, 1962-63; instr. Meiji U., Tokyo, 1963-67, asst. prof., 1967-83, prof., 1983—; Ida Bean Disting. scholar U. Iowa, Iowa City, 1991; lectr. Lit. Soc. Muroran, Japan, 1994-2000, Asahi Culture Ctr., Tamashi, Tokyo, 1994-96. Author: He's Leaving Home, 1988 (Akutagawa award 1988), The Indian on Top of a Skyscraper, 1991, Going Into the British Mist, 1983, A Literary Apprenticeship, 1988. Mem. Japan Am. Lit. Assn., Japan Writers' Assn., Soc. Psychical Rsch. U.K., Japan Psychic Sci. Assn. (bd. dirs. 1991-99), Japan PEN Club. Zen Buddhism. Home: 405 1-4-5 Tonoyama-cho, Hitachinaka-City, Ibaraki-ken 311-1212, Japan Office: Meiji Univ, 1-1-1 Higashi-Mita, Tama-ku, Kawasaki-shi 214, Japan

MIURA, TAKEO, electronic engineer; b. Kyoto, Japan, Oct. 1, 1926; s. Eitaro and Nao M.; m. Akiko Haruyama, Nov. 24, 1953; children: Chiaki, Koji. B in Engring., Kyoto U., 1949, D in Engring., 1959. From gen. mgr. sys. devel. lab. to sr. adv. Hitachi Ltd., Tokyo, 1973—. Author, editor: Contemporary System Engineering. V.p. Internat. Fedn. for Info. Processing. Mem. Info. Processing Soc. Japan (hon.), Internat. Fedn. Info. Processing (hon.). Home: 2-32-9 Kamiasao, Aso-ku Kawasaki, Kanagawa-Ken 215, Japan Office: Hitachi Ltd 4-6, Kanda-Surugadai Chiyoda-ku, Tokyo 101, Japan

MIURA, TOKUHIRO, English and American literature educator; b. Sukumo, Japan, May 30, 1928; s. Harukichi and Sueno (Enoki) M.; m. Masako Matsumoto, Nov. 5, 1959; children: Tokutaka Miura, Yuri Joguchi. Student, Kochi (Japan) Tchrs. Coll., 1945-48, Waseda U., Tokyo, 1949-51, 52-53; BA, U. Calif., Berkeley, 1956; MA, Truman State U., 1959. Reporter and mem. editl. staff. Japan Times, Tokyo, 1960-63; instr. English Hosei U., Tokyo, 1961-65; prof. English and Am. Lit., Hosei U., 1965-99, chmn. dept. English and grad. divsn. English, 1986-88, chmn. grad. divsn. English, 1993-94, 96-97, prof. emeritus, 1999—. Author: Robinson Jeffers' Quest in The Double Axe, 1967, Poetics of Robinson Jeffers, 1977, Literary Phenomena: A Conceptual Framework of Literature, 1979; Selected Poems of Robinson Jeffers (in Japanese translation), 1986. Mem. MLA, English Lit. Soc. Japan, Am. Lit. Soc. Japan. Buddhist. Home: 23-28 4-chome, Naruse-dai Machida-shi, Tokyo 194-0043, Japan Office: Hosei U, 17-1 2-chome Chiyoda-ku, Tokyo 102-0071, Japan

MIWA, HIROHIDE, electronics company executive; b. Himeji, Hyogo-Ken, Japan, Jan. 12, 1924; s. Yuzoh and Kiyo (Abe) M.; m. Miyoko Koike, Apr. 24, 1949; children: Hiroaki, Keiko Ishida, Kenichiro. B of Physical Engring., Tokyo Imperial U., 1946; PhD, Tokyo U., 1959. Cert. radiation protection supr. Vice mgr. Kobekogyo Atomic Energy Divsn., Kobe, Japan, 1956-66; vice pres. Kobekogyo Lab., Kobe, Japan, 1966-69; gen. mgr. Fujitsu Ltd., Tokyo, 1969-78; dir. Fujitsu Labs., Tokyo, 1978-86; exec. dir. Crown Corp., Tokyo, 1986-88; pres. Cosmos R&D Co., Ltd., Tokyo, 1989-95, Miwa Sci. Lab., Kawasaki, 1995—; chmn. DGPS com., Japan GPS Coun., Tokyo, 1993—; vice chmn. Electronic Application Club, Tokyo, 1970—; dir. Matsushita Graphic Sci. Sys., Inc., Tokyo, 1973-81; exec. dir. Inst. Hosp. Sys. Devel., Tokyo, 1977-80. Author: Applied Radiation Gauging, 1961 (Ohkohchi Meml. prize 1968); inventor 100 products in field; patentee in field. Recipient Invention prize Japan Inst. Invention and Innovation, Tokyo, 1952, 69, Chmn. prize C. of C., Hyogo, Japan, 1954, Best Paper of Yr. award Japan Soc. Med. Electronics, 1986. Mem. IEEE (sr. mem., U.S.), Japan Radioisotope Assn. Buddhist. Avocations: haiku, calligraphy, swimming, world fruits collective cultivation, archaeology. Office: Miwa Sci Labs, 6-7-10 Miyazaki Miyamae-ku, Kawasaki 216-0033, Japan

MIWA, KUNIHISA, cardiologist, researcher; b. Toyama, Japan, Jan. 21, 1950; s. Hirohisa Hatakeyama and Sadako M.; m. Takako Mitsuji Miwa; children: Eriko, Sakiko, Kunihide. MD, Kyoto (Japan) U., 1975, PhD, 1983. Resident Kyoto (Japan) U. Hosp., 1975-76; doctor internal medicine Shizuoka (Japan) City Hosp., 1976-79; postgrad. student Kyoto (Japan) U., 1979-83; asst. prof. Dept. Internal Medicine, Fukui, Japan, 1983-85; vis. asst. prof. U. Cinn., 1985-87; asst. prof. Toyama (Japan) Med. and Pharm. U., 1987-99; lectr. dept. cardiovasc. medicine Kyoto (Japan) U. Grad. Sch., 1999—; doctor in chief dept. internal medicine Kansai Elec. Power Hosp., Japan, 1999—. Contbr. articles to profl. jours. Recipient The Japan Rsch. Found. for Clin. Pharm, 1990, The 5th, 8th and 12th Coronary Heart Disease and Heart Failure Rsch. Conf. award, 1990, 93, 97. Mem. Toyama Internat. Nonsmoking Club. Avocations: tennis. Home: Shintomicho 1-4-3, Toyama 930-0002, Japan Office: Toyama Med & Pharm Univ, 2630 Sugitani, Toyama 930-0194, Japan

MIX, EILHARD, biomedical laboratory chief; b. Rostock, Germany, Apr. 8, 1949; s. Hermann and Ilse-Maria (Plagemann) M.; m. Monika Christine Schroeder, July 24, 1972; children: Corinna, Johanna. MD, U. Rostock, Germany, 1977; PhD, Karolinska Inst., Stockholm, 1994. Specialist for immunology, electrotechnics. Scientific asst. Univ. Inst. for Med. Biochemistry, Rostock, Germany, 1977-81; scientific asst. dept. neurology Univ. Rostock, 1981-91, mem. staff, 1982-88, chief of lab., 1991—; guest researcher Karolinska Inst., Stockholm, 1988-93; cons. German Neurol. Soc., Divsn. for Diagnostics of Cerebrospinal Fluid and Clin. Neurochemistry, Germany, 1993-95. Co-author: Procedure for Manufacturing of a Tumor Antigen, 1983 (patent 1983), Durchflusszytometrie in der Klinischen Zelldiagnostik Schattauer, 1994; co-editor: Klinische Neuroimmunologie Aktuelle Aspekte De Gruyter, 1999, others. Del. Trade Union Rostock, 1985-89. Capt. Med. Svc., 1975-77, Germany. Mem. German Soc. Immunology, German Soc. Neurology, German Soc. for Diagnostics of Cerebrospinal Fluid and Clin. Neurochemistry, German Soc. Cytometry, AAAS, N.Y. Acad. Sci. Avocations: hist. studies, canoeing, fishing, collecting stamps, gardening. Home: Waechterstrasse 25, Rostock D-18057, Germany Office: Dept Neurology, PO Box 100888 GehlsheimerStr 20, Rostock D-18055, Germany

MIXER, RONALD WAYNE, minister; b. Mpls., Jan. 22, 1954; s. Joseph William and Faith Amour (Minor) M.; m. Glenda Renae Fjordbak, June 22, 1974; children: Rachelle Renae, Danielle Kaye. BA, North Cen. Bible Coll., 1977; M in Ministry, Internat. Bible Sem., 1983. Ordained to ministry. Dir. ch. ministry Rock River Christian Ctr., Rock Falls, Ill., 1977-79; dir. christian edn. Cen. Assembly of God, Tulsa, 1979-80; sr. pastor Manchester (Iowa) Assembly of God, 1980-83, Richmond (Mo.) Assembly of God, 1983-84, Odessa (Mo.) First Assembly of God, 1984-87; field rep. Am. Bible Soc., N.Y.C., 1988-97, program mgr. 1999 Yr. of the Bible,, 1997-99; asst. dir. vol. ministries Am. Bible Soc., Olathe, Kans., 1999—; assoc. dir. Bible reading programs Am. Bible Soc., Olathe, 1999-2000; dir. church relations Cross Pointe Net., Olathe, 2000—. Commr. Olathe (Kans.) Human Rels. Commn., 1990—, chair, 1996-97. Named one of Outstanding Young Men in Am., U.S. Jaycees, 1986. Mem. Internat. Platform Assn., Assemblies of God Ministers (Kansas City, Kans. chpt.), Toastmasters Internat. Republican. Avocation: racquetball. Office: Am Bible Soc 15720 W 150th Ter Olathe KS 66062-4732

MIXSON, WILLIAM TUNNO, retired gynecologist; b. Gainesville, Fla., May 22, 1924; s. William Tunno and Mabel Gray (Currell) M.; m. Katherine Louise Hoffman, June, 1948 (div. 1977); children: William T. III, Richard Allyn, Robert David; m. Beverly Jean Armstrong, 1977. BS, U. Miami, Coral Gables, Fla., 1946; MD, Temple U., 1948, MSc in Ob-gyn., 1953. Diplomate Am. Bd. Ob-gyn. Intern Phila. Gen. Hosp., 1948-50; residency Temple U. Hosp., Phila., 1950-53; pvt. practice ob-gyn. Coral Gables, 1953-72, pvt. practice gynecology, 1972-89; pvt. practice gynecology South Miami, Fla., 1989-96; retired, 1996; clin. assoc. prof. ob-gyn. Sch. Medicine, U. Miami, 1954-95; chief staff Dr.'s Hosp., Coral Gables, 1968-69; exec. com. Nat. Practitioner Data Bank, Rockville, Md., 1990—. Contbr. articles to profl. jours. Exec. bd., Planned Parenthood Greater Miami, 1989—. Fellow Am. Coll. Obstetricians and Gynecologists (bd. govs. 1977-87, pres. 1985-86, Miles lectr. 1985, Dist. Svc. award 1985), ACS (bd. govs. 1979-84); mem. South Atlantic Assn. Obstetricians and Gynecologists (pres. 1984-85), Fla. Obstet. and Gynecol. Soc. (pres. 1985). Republican. Avocations: golf, travel, fishing, skin diving, swimming. Home: 8820 SW 67th Ct Miami FL 33156-1700

MIYACHI, IWAO, electrical engineering educator; b. Kochi, Japan, Sept. 27, 1916; s. Sakaki and Asami (Taniwaki) M.; m. Kazuko Nagano, Apr. 4, 1943; children: Yukiko Tanaka, Reiko Yamashita. B in Engring., U. Tokyo, 1940, D in Engring., 1953. From lectr. to prof. Nagoya U., Aichi, 1940-80, prof. emeritus, 1980—; prof. Aichi Inst. Tech., Toyota, 1980—. Author: Power Transmission and Distribution, 1958, Electrical Power Engineering, 1965, Electrical Power Generation, 1988. Decorated 2d Order of Nat. Merit, 1990. Mem. Inst. Elec. Engrs. of Japan (hon., pres. 1977, Power Engring. award 1968, Best Treatise award 1973, Disting. Svcs. award 1980, Advanced Tech. award 1990), Elec. Coop. Rsch. Inst. Japan (adviser 1989—), Soc. des Electriciens et des Electroniciens, Conf. Internat. des Grands Reseaux Electriques (disting.). Avocations: driving, worldwide sightseeing. Home: 3-6-5 Nishizaki-cho, Chikusa, Nagoya 464-0825, Japan Office: Aichi Inst Tech, 1247 Yachigusa Yakusa-cho, Toyota 470-0392, Japan

MIYACHI, JUN-ICHI, mathematics educator; b. Fukuoka, Japan, Dec. 1, 1958; s. Hitoshi and Fumiko (Satoh) M.; m. Nobuko Takeuchi, Dec. 22, 1991. PhD, U. Tsukuba, Japan, 1995. Lectr. Tokyo Gakugei U., 1990-95, assoc. prof., 1995—. Contbr. articles to profl. jours. Mem. Math. Soc. Japan. Home: Suginami-ku Takaido Nishi, 2-14-36, Tokyo 168-0071, Japan Office: Tokyo Gakugei U, Koganei-shi 4-1-1, Tokyo 184-8501, Japan

MIYAGAWA, MASAO, radiologist, researcher; b. Matsuyama, Shikoku, Japan, Aug. 24, 1957; s. Hiroshi and Fumiko (Idai) M.; m. Naoko Mino, Apr. 19, 1989; 1 child, Shu. MD, Ehime U., Japan, 1983, PhD, 1991. Resident in radiology Ehime U. Hosp., 1983-84; chief radiologist Uwajima City Hosp., Ehime, 1985-87, Ehime Nat. Hosp., 1991—. Contbr. articles to profl. jours. Mem. Japanese Soc. Nuclear Medicine (Nuclear Medicine award 1996, bd. trustees 1997-99), Japanese Soc. Nuclear Cardiol. (bd. trustees 1998-99), Japanese Soc. Radiology, Soc. Nuclear Medicine (U.S.A.). Office: Ehime Nat Hosp, Dept Radiology, Shigenobu Ehime 791 0281, Japan

MIYAGAWA, YUKIO, dentistry educator; b. Oomiya, Japan, Mar. 26, 1950; s. Mitsuyuki and Noriko (Sekita) M.; m. Keiko Nakatomi, Nov. 21, 1981; children: Rei, Rina. DDS, Nippon Dental Univ., Tokyo, 1974, PhD, 1978. Asst. Nippon Dental Univ., Niigata, Japan, 1978-79; vis. scholar Univ. Mich., 1979-81; asst. prof. Nippon Dental Univ., Niigata, 1981-85, assoc. prof., 1985-99, prof., 1999—; mng. dir. Alumni Soc. Nippon Dental Univ., 1991-95; com. mem. dental materials standards Japan Dental Assn., 1994-2000; assoc. dir. acad. affairs Nippon Dental Univ., 1997—. Author: Current Dental Materials Science, 1996, Dental Statistics and Dental Epidemiology, 1985; contbr. articles to profl. jours. Fellow Acad. Dental

Materials; mem. Internat. Assn. Dental Rsch., Sigma Xi, Japanese Soc. Dental Materials & Devices (dir. 1999—). Home: 1-2-16 Shindori-nishi, 950-2036 Niigata Japan Office: Nippon Dental Univ, 1-8 Hamaura-cho, 951-8580 Niigata Japan

MIYAGUCHI, SHINGO, physician; b. Kyoto, Japan, July 29, 1959; s. Yoshiyuki and Yoshiko (Kusui) Matsumoto; m. Naoko Miyaguchi, Sept. 28, 1986; children: Kazuya, Yuri. D. Yamagata (Japan) U., 1985; MD, Keio U., Tokyo, 1993. Resident Keio U., Tokyo, 1985-87; physician Nat. East Saitama Hosp., 1987-89; asst. Keio U., Tokyo, 1989-91; physician Nat. Kurihama Hosp., 1991-92; vice dir. Otawara Red Cross Hosp., 1992-95; dir. Otsuka Met. Hosp., 1995—. Contbr. articles to profl. jours. Recipient rsch. award Japanese Soc. Hepatology, excellent award Japanese Liver Cancer Study Group, 1999. Home: Hikarigaoka 3-3-6-601, Nerimaku 179-0029, Japan Office: Tokyo Met Otsuka Hosp, Minami-Otsuka 2-8-1, Toshimaku Japan

MIYAHARA, KENJI, investment company executive. Pres., CEO, Sumitomo Corp., Osaka, Japan. Fax: 81-03-3217-6997. Office: Sumitomo Corp, 4-5-33 Kitahama Chuo-ku, Osaka 540-8666, Japan*

MIYAISHI, SATORU, forensic pathologist; b. Nagoya, Japan, Apr. 3, 1960. BA, Okayama (Japan) U., 1986, MD, 1986, PhD, 1991. Resident Okayama (Japan) U. Hosp., 1986-87, rsch. assoc. dept. legal medicine, 1991-92, asst. prof. dept. legal medicine, 1992-96, assoc. prof., 1996—; guest prof. U. Hamburg, Germany, 1997. Author: Encyclopedia of Analytical Science, 1995; contbr. articles to profl. jours. Fax: 81-86-235-7201. Office: Okayama U Med Sch, 2-5-1 Shikata-cho, Okayama 700-8558, Japan

MIYAJIMA, HIDEAKI, education educator; b. Ota-ku, Tokyo, Japan, May 8, 1955; s. Hiro and Hisami (Ukai) M.; m. Mizuho Nagasawa, Sept. 3, 1989; children: Daichi, Taiga. BA in Econ., Rikkyo U., Tokyo, 1978, MA in Econ., 1980; postgrad., Tokyo U., 1980-85. Rsch. assoc. Tokyo U. Inst. Social Scis., 1985-87; from lectr. to assoc. prof. Waseda U. Sch. Commerce, Tokyo, 1987-94, prof., 1995—; vis. scholar Harvard U. Reischauer Inst. Japanese Studies, 1992-94; cons. The World Bank, Washington, 1994-95, Hawaii U., 1995-96, Hebrew U., 1997-98, Ministry of Trade and Industry, 1997-98, Minstry of France 1999—. Avocation: tennis, F1 racing. Home: 4-3-18-206 Tsurumaki, Setagaya-ku 154-0016, Japan Office: Waseda Univ, 1-6-1 Nishi-Waseda, 169 Tokyo Japan

MIYAKAWA, TORU, computer science educator; b. Kamakura, Kanagawa, Japan, Sept. 11, 1931; s. Funao and Yoshiko (Abe) M.; m. Michiko Shigeno, Oct. 16, 1961; children: Haruko, Akira. BS, Tokyo U., 1953, MS, 1955, DSc, 1967. Lectr. The Nat. Def. Acad., Yokosuka, 1958-62; assoc. prof. The Nat. Def. Acad., Yokosuka, Japan, 1962-70, prof., 1970-97, dean grad. sch., 1988-92, acad. dean, 1992-96, prof. emeritus, coun. Found. for Promotion Rsch. and Edn., 1997—; rsch. assoc. U. Rochester, N.Y., 1967-69; prof. computer sci. Chiba Inst. Tech., Narashimo, Japan, 1997—. Author: Excercises in Solid State Physics for Electronics, 1975, Excercises in Electromagnetic Theory for Electronics, 1980, Electronics for Information Science, vol. 1 & 2. Mem. Phys. Soc. Japan, Japanese Inst. Electronics Communication and Infor., Am. Phys. Soc., Japanese Soc. Applied Physics, Kanagawa Acad. Sci. and Tech. (adv. bd. 1998—). Home: 734 Kawashimacho Hodogayaku, Yokohama 240-0045, Japan Office: Chiba Inst Tech, 2-17-1 Tsudanuma, Narashimo 275-0016, Japan

MIYAKE, AKIO, biologist, educator; b. Kyoto, Japan, June 29, 1931; s. Yoshikazu and Yukie (Yamazaki) M.; m. Sadako Harada, Mar. 15, 1965 (dec. June 1986); children: Akiko, Toshio; m. Terue Harumoto, Dec. 30, 1988; 1 child, Yuka. BS, Kyoto U., 1953, D of Science, 1959. Asst. Osaka (Japan) City U., 1953-63; visiting scholar Ind. U., Bloomington, 1959-61; lectr. Kyoto (Japan) U., 1963-70; group leader Max-Planck Inst. for Molecular Genetics, West Berlin, 1970-74; visiting scholar U. Pisa, Italy, 1975-77, U. Münster, West Germany, 1978-83; prof. U. Camerino, Italy, 1983—. Contbr. articles on sexual reprodn. in microorganisms to profl. jours. and books. Recipient Zool. Soc. of Japan Prize, 1981. Mem. Zool. Soc. Japan, Genetics Soc. of Japan, AAAS, Soc. Protozoologists, Planetary Soc. Avocations: origin and evolution of life, Italian opera music. Home: Corso Italia 150, I-62022 Castelraimondo Italy Office: U Camerino Dept Cell Biol, Via F Camerini 2, I-62032 Camerino Italy

MIYAKE, YASUJI, computer science educator; b. Nagoya, Aichi Pref, Japan, Nov. 28, 1936; m. Sugako Yamada, Apr. 29, 1971; 1 child, Shigemitsu. B in Engring., Nagoya (Japan) U., 1960, M in Engring., 1962, D in Engring., 1968. Rsch. assoc. Nagoya (Japan) U., 1965-68, asst. prof., 1968-69, assoc. prof., 1969-78; prof. engring. Mie (Japan) U., 1978-2000; dir. Computation Ctr. Mie U., 1982-87, counselor, 1997-99; prof. and chairperson, computer sci. dept. engring. Chubu Univ., Japan, 2000—. Inventor, patent applicant, 1990; contbr. articles to profl. jours., 1985—. Recipient 1st prize Inst. for character recognition technique contests, Inst. Posts and Telecomms., Ministry of Posts and Telecomms. Japan, 1992, 93, 94, commendation from dir. Tokai Elec. Comm. Control. Mem. Inst. Electronics, Info. Comm. Engrs. Japan, Info. Processing Soc. Japan, Japanese Soc. Med. Electronics Biol. Engring. Buddhist. Avocations: photography, collecting cameras, driving. Office: Chubu U, 1200 Matsumoto-cho, Kasugai Aichi 489-8501, Japan

MIYAKE, YOSHIO, health facility administrator; b. Kurashiki, Okayama, Japan, Sept. 9, 1945; s. Toshio and Michiko (Miyaji) M.; m. Yoko Kobayashi, Feb. 1, 1976; 1 child, Maiko. MD, Kyoto (Japan) U., 1971; diploma, Nat. Inst. Pub. Health, Tokyo, 1977. Intern, resident Amagasaki (Japan) Gen. Hosp., 1971-73; med. officer Ministry of Health and Welfare, Tokyo, 1974-77; med. adviser Kyoto (Japan) Prefectural Office, 1977-80; physician Horikawa Gen. Hosp., Kyoto, 1980-87; chief geriatric medicine Ohta Gen. Hosp., Koriyama, Japan, 1987-94; dir. Yasaka Nat. Health Ins. Hosp., Kyoto, 1994-99; vice dir. Kyoto Minami Hosp., Kyoto, Japan, 1999—. Author: Understanding the Mind of the Elderly, 1987, Nursing for the Ill Elderly, 1994, 13 + 1 Short Stories in Aging, 1995, Introduction of Geriatrics, 1996. Mem. Alzheimer's Disease Internat. (com. mem.), Internat. Psychogeriatrics Assn. Avocations: playing piano, skiing, mountain driving. Home: 1-6-7 Goryo-Minegado-cho, Nishikyo, Kyoto 610-1103, Japan

MIYAKO, YOSHIHITO, physics educator; b. Nagaike, Tokushima, Japan, June 9, 1936; s. Shigeyuki and Shigeko Miyako; m. Naoko Tsukinoki, May 2, 1965; children: Kōsuke, Junko, Shinko. BA, Osaka (Japan) U., 1959, MA, 1963, PhD, 1972. Lectr. Hokkaido U., Sapporo, Japan, 1975-80; from assoc. prof. to prof. Hokkaido U., Sapporo, 1980-91; prof. Osaka U., 1991-2000, prof. emeritus, 2000—, dir. low temperature ctr., 1993-95, 97-99; guest prof. Grenoble (France) U., 1988. Mem. The Phys. Soc. (bd. dirs. 1992-94). Fax: 81 722-73-3897. Home: Kōnocho 3-3-26, Sakai Osaka 593-8308, Japan Office: Osaka U Grad Sch Sci, Machikaneyama-cho, Toyonaka Osaka 560-0043, Japan

MIYAMAE, KAZUHIRO, linguist, language educator; b. Takefu, Fukui, Japan, Feb. 3, 1955; s. Kunita and Sueko (Mizuno) M.; m. Masae Inoue, Jan. 15, 1976. BA in Econs., Hosei U., Tokyo, 1981; MA in Linguistics, U. Kans., 1991. Asst. dir. English Conversation Ctr., Shibuya, Japan, 1983-87; dir. of instrn. Total of Fgn. Langs. (TOFL) Seminar, Yokohama, Japan, 1991—; lectr. in English Musashi U., Tokyo, 1992—. Author: (books) Eitango Magic, 1988, TOEFL Taisaku Meikai Reading, 1995, Zenchisi no Bunpo, 1997, TOEFL TEST Vocabulary Tetteikoza, 1999; co-author: (book) TOEFL Taisaku Jissen Mondaishu, 1995. Mem. English Linguistic Soc. Japan, Linguistic Soc. Japan. Home: 3-2-12-402 Ochiai, Tokyo Tama 206-0033, Japan

MIYAMOTO, HIROSHI, retired chemist, educator; b. Hitachi-ohta, Ibaraki, Japan, Oct. 31, 1929; m. Shikako Sakamoto, Apr. 7, 1962; children: Ryo, Kei. PhD, Tohoku U., Sendai, Japan, 1962. Asst. Ibaraki U., Mito, Japan, 1952-62; assoc. prof. Niigata (Japan) U., 1962-75, prof., 1975-95, prof. emeritus, 1995—; vis. prof. Emory U., Atlanta, 1981-82; vice-chmn. 8th Internat. Symposium on Solubility Phenomena, Internat. Union of Pure and Applied Chemistry, Niigata, 1998, assoc. mem. solubility data commn., Oxford, Eng., 1991-95, mem. solid solubility subcom., Oxford, 1975—. Author, editor: (with M. Salomon and H. L. Clever) Alkaline Earth Metal Halates, 1983, (with M. Salomon) Alkal: Metal Hatales, Ammonium Iodate and Iodic Acid, 1987, (with E. M. Woolly and M. Salomon) Copper and Silver Halates, 1990; contbr. articles to books and jours. Mem. AAAS, Am. Chem. Soc., Chem. Soc. Japan, Rare Earth Soc. Japan.

MIYAMOTO, RICHARD TAKASHI, otolaryngologist; b. Zeeland, Mich., Feb. 2, 1944; s. Dave Norio and Haruko (Okano) M.; m. Cynthia VanderBurgh, June 17, 1967; children: Richard Christopher, Geoffrey Takashi. BS cum laude, Wheaton Coll., 1966; MD, U. Mich., 1970; MS in Otology, U.So. Calif., 1978. Diplomate Am. Bd. Otolaryngology. Intern Butterworth Hosp., Grand Rapids, Mich., 1970-71, resident in surgery, 1971-72; resident in otolaryngology Ind. U. Sch. Medicine, 1972-75; fellow in otology and neurotology St. Vincent Hosp. and Otologic Med. Group, L.A., 1977-78; asst. prof. Ind. U. Sch. Medicine, Indpls., 1978-83, assoc. prof., 1983-88; prof. 1988—; chmn. 1987—, chief Otology and Neurotology dept. Otolaryngology, Head and Neck Surgery, Ind. U., 1982—, chmn. dept. Otolaryngology, 1987—, Arilla DeVault prof., 1991; chief Otolaryngology, Head and Neck Surgery Wishard Meml. Hosp., 1979—. Mem. editorial bd. Laryngoscope, Am. Jour. of Otology, Otolaryngology-Head and Neck Surgery, European archives of Oto-Rhino-Laryngology, Anales de Otorrinolaringologia Mexicana; contbr. articles to profl. jours. Mem. adv. coun. Nat. Inst. Deafness and other communication disorders, 1989-94; mem. med. adv. bd. Alexander Graham Bell Assn. for the Deaf, The Ear Found. Served to maj. USAF, 1975-77. Named Arilla DeVault Disting. investigator Ind. U., 1983. Fellow Am. Acad. Otolaryngology (gov. 1982—), ACS, Am. Otological, Rhinological, and Laryngological Soc. (Thesis Disting. for Excellence award), Am. Neurotology Soc. (pres. elect 1999-2000, pres. 2000-01), Am. Auditory Soc. (mem. exec. com. 1985—); mem. Am. Acad. Pediats., N.Y. Acad. Scis., Otosclerosis Study Group (coun. 1993—), Am. Otol. Soc. (coun. 1992—), Marines Meml. Assn., Assn. Rsch. Otol. (pres. elect 2000), Wheaton Coll. Scholastic Honor Soc., Cosmos Club of Washington, Columbia Club of Ind., Royal Soc. Medicine London, Collegium Oto-Laryngologicum Amecitiae Sacrum; Alpha Omega Alpha. Office: Ind U Sch Med 702 Barnhill Dr Indianapolis IN 46202-5128

MIYAMOTO, TADAOMI-ALFONSO MATSUMOTO, neurobiologist; b. Iguala, Oct. 6, 1936; s. On and Hisashi (Matsumoto) M.; m. Kazue Kato, Oct. 3, 1975; three children. MD, Nat. U. Mex., 1960. Diplomate Am. Bd. Surgery, Am. Bd. Thoracic Surgery. Intern Grasslands Hosp., Valhalla, N.Y., 1961-62; resident in gen. surgery Montefiore Hosp., Bronx, N.Y., 1962-65; resident in thoracic surgery Montefiore Hosp., Bronx, 1967-69; fellow in cardiac surgery Tokyo Women's Med. Coll., 1965-67, resident in thoracic surgery, 1967-69; fellow in anesthesiology Iwate Med. U., Japan, 1969-71; assoc. investigator Nat. Inst. Cardiology, Mexico City, 1971-72; asst. head cardiovasc. surgery City of Hope Nat. Med. Ctr., Duarte, Calif., 1972-74; sr. staff surgeon Cedars-Sinai Med. Ctr., L.A., 1974-82; prof. thoracic and cardiovasc. surgery Saga U. Med Sch., Japan, 1982-84; head dept. cardiovasc. surgery Kokura Meml. Hosp., Kitakyushu City, Japan, 1984-91, head rsch., 1991—. Fellow ACS; mem. Am. Soc. Thoracic Surgeons, Am. Assn. Thoracic Surgery. Achievements include active in neuroprotection research. Avocations: carving, making research tools. Office: Kokura Meml Hosp Dept Rsch, 1-1 Kifunecho Kokurakitaku, 802-8555 Kitakyushu Fukuoka, Japan

MIYAMOTO, YASUMI, law educator; b. Tokyo, Apr. 14, 1930; s. Kazuyasu and Matsu (Adachi) M.; m. Michiko Suzuki, Feb. 24, 1965; children: Yasuko, Yoshiko. BA in Polit. Sci., Gakushuin U., Tokyo, 1953; MA in Law, Keio U., Tokyo, 1959, SJD, 1996. Grad. fellow Inst. Labor and Indsl. Rels., U. Ill., Champaign, 1965-67; asst. prof. labor law Keio U., Tokyo, 1968-69, assoc. prof. labor law, 1969-76, prof. labor law, 1976-96, assoc. dir. Inst. Labor Mgmt. Studies, 1989-96; prof. emeritus Keio U., 1996—; prof. law Heisei Internat. U., Saitama-ken, Japan, 1996—; mem. Tokyo (Japan) Met. Labor Rels. Commn., 1987-99; acting chmn. Kanagawa Prefectural Vocatinal Ability Devel. Deliberative Coun., Yokohama, Japan, 1990—. Author: Contemporary Problems of Labor Relations Law, 1993; co-author: Equal Employment Opportunity Between Men and Women, 1988, Commentaries on Japanese Trade Union Law and Labor Relations Adjustment Law, 1989. Home: 3-8-6 Tsuchihashi Miyamae-ku, Kawasaki 216-0005, Japan Office: Heisei Internat U, 2000 Ohtateno Mizufuka, Kazo-shi Saitama 347-8504, Japan

MIYAMOTO, YOSHIYUKI, pharmacologist, toxicologist, researcher; b. Arida-gun, Wakayama, Japan, Feb. 25, 1958; s. Hachiroh and Setsuko (Misaki) M.; m. Kaori Miyamoto, Oct. 10, 1985; 2 children. BS, Gifu (Japan) U. Sch. Pharmacy, 1980; PhD, Wakayama (Japan) U. Sch. Med., 1985. Instr. Wakayama U. Sch. Medicine, 1981-93; postdoctoral rschr. U. Minn., Mpls., 1990-92; asst. dir. Dainippon Pharm. Co., Ltd., Osaka, Japan, 1993-98; pres. Vision CL Ltd., Wakayama, 1998—. Contbr. articles to profl. jours. Recipient travel award Coll. on Problems of Drug Dependence, Colo., 1992. Mem. AAAS, N.Y. Acad. Scis., Japanese Pharmacol. Soc. (mem. com. 1980—), Japanese Soc. Neuropsychopharmacology. Avocations: fishing, tennis, motorcycle. E-mail: RXE06332@nifty.ne.jp. Home: 527-4 Kimiidera, Wakayama-shi 641-0012, Japan Office: Vision CL Ltd, 527-7 Kimiidera, Wakayama-shi 641-0012, Japan

MIYANDA, GODFREY, Zambian government official. V.p. Govt. of Zambia, 1996—, minister of edn. Office: Ministry of Edn, PO Box 50093, Lusaka Zambia*

MIYARA, FEDERICO SALOMÓN, electronics engineering educator, composer; b. Rosario, Argentina, Sept. 4, 1958; s. José and Julia Elvira (Verdeja) M.; m. María Victoria Gómez, Feb. 15, 1990; children: Francisco Nicolás, Andrés Pedro. Electronics Engr., U. Nac. de Rosario, 1984. Prof. electronics engring., acoustics and noise control U. Nac. de Rosario, 1986—; mem. directive coun. Faculty Engring., U. Nac. de Rosario, 1990-98, founder, dir., Web master Acoustics and Electroacoustics Lab., rschr. on urban noise Faculty Arch. Author: (novel) El Experimento, 1999, Las Leyes de Méndez, 1996, Control De Ruido, 1996, Acústica y Sistemas de Sonido, 1999; composer: (chamber music) Borborigmos, for flute and piano, 1991, Kinesis II, for flute and piano, 1987, (piano music) Six Piano Sonatas, 1977-95. Gov. of Province of Santa Fe rsch. grantee, 1994, 97; recipient First prize 1997 Composition Contest Radio Clásica Rosario; Nat. Govt. grantee, 2000, Agencia Española de Cooperación Internacional grantee, 1999. Mem. Assn. Docents of U. Nac. Rosario, Acoustical Soc. Am. (assoc.), Assn. Santafesina de Compositores (sec. 1992-94). Avocations: playing piano and synthesizer, writing, painting, computer programming. Home: Centeno 1217, 2000 Rosario Argentina Office: U Nac de Rosario Dept Elec Engring, Riobamba 245 Bis, 2000 Rosario Argentina

MIYASAKA, KENJI, mechanical engineering educator, researcher; b. Osaka, Japan, July 14, 1948; s. Sadaharu and Michie (Morii) M.; m. Naoko Yamagata, Nov. 27, 1986; children: Shuji, Yu. B Engring., U. Osaka Prefecture, 1971, M Engring., 1973; PhD, U. Tokyo, 1982. Rsch. assoc. Osaka U., 1973-79; postdoctoral fellow Northwestern U., Evanston, Ill., 1979-82; asst. prof. So. Ill. U., Carbondale, 1982-85; assoc. prof. mech. engring. Fukui (Japan) U., 1985-89, prof., 1989—; rsch. scholar dept. mech. engring., U. Calif., Berkeley, 1994—. Avocations: flying, radio control airplanes, classic vacuum tube amplifier. Home: 4-19-16 Ninomiya, Fukui 910-0015, Japan Office: Fukui U, Fukui U, 3-9-1 Bunkyo, Fukui 910-8507, Japan

MIYASAKA, MASAO, automotive parts company executive; b. Maruko, Japan, Feb. 20, 1950; s. Norimasa and Fukuko M.; m. Kimiko Miyasaka, Oct. 24, 1981. BA, Waseda U., Tokyo, 1973; postgrad., Harvard U. Mgr. Hakuhodo Inc., Tokyo, 1973-80; from exec. mgr. to sr. v.p. Asama Automotive Parts Co., Ltd., Tokyo, 1980-94, pres., CEO, 1994—. Co-author: Revolutionary Management of Entrepreneurs, 1995; co-translator: Essentials of Accounting, 1999. Mem. Japan Auto Parts Union Soc. (bd. dirs. 1994—), Tokyo Auto Parts Assn. (dir. 1994—), Tokyo Jingu Rotary Club. Office: Asama Automotive Parts Co, 2-4-11 Nishi-shimbashi, Minato-ku, Tokyo 105-0003, Japan

MIYASAKA, TSUTOMU, chemical engineer; b. Kamakura, Kanagawa, Japan, Sept. 10, 1953; s. Teruo and Teiko (Soda) M.; m. Yayoi Kiyota, Apr. 18, 1985; children: Kotaro, Tohru. BS in Engring., Waseda U., Tokyo, 1976; MS in Engring., U. Tokyo, 1978, PhD in Engring., 1981. Rschr. Ashigara Rsch. Labs. of Fuji Photo Film Co., Kanagawa, 1981-91, mgr., 1991—; abstractor Chem. Abstract Svc., 1985-91; lectr. Tokai U., Kanagawa, 1995, 2000. Author: Organic Thin Films and Surfaces, 1995, Molecular Biology and Biotechnology, 1995; editor Jour. Electrochem. Soc. Japan, 1993-95; contbr. articles to profl. jours. including Science; patentee in field. Mem. Chem. Soc. Japan, Electrochem. Soc. Japan. Achievements include research in molecular electronics and design of artificial retina. Avocations: violin playing, appraisal in old Italian violins. Office: Ashigara Rsch Lab Fuji Pho, Nakanuma Minamiashigara, Kanagawa 250-0193, Japan

MIYASHITA, SEIJI, physics educator; b. Himeji City, Hyogo, Japan, Feb. 9, 1954; s. Koukitsu and Kyoko (Honsho) M.; m. Ami Suzuki, Mar. 15, 1981; children: Hiroyuki, Sana. MS, U. Tokyo, 1978, DSc, 1981. Asst. U. Tokyo, 1981-89; assoc. prof. Kyoto (Japan) U., 1989-95; prof. Osaka (Japan) U., 1995-99, U. Tokyo, 1999—. Author: Netsu Toukeirikigaku, 1993, Netsurigigakuno kiso, 1995, Kaiseki Rikigaku, 2000; editor (jours.) Progress of Theoretical Physics, 1991—, Mag. of Phys. Soc. Japan, 1984-86; contbr. articles to profl. jours. Mem. Phys. Soc. Japan. Office: U Tokyo Grad Sch Engring, 7-3-1 Hongo Bunkyo-ku, Tokyo 113-8656, Japan

MIYASHITA, YOSHIYUKI, lawyer; b. Aizuwakamatsu City, Fukushima, Japan, Dec. 1, 1958; s. Takasi and Kazuko (Yamaguchi) M.; m. Takako Suzuki, Nov. 15, 1986; 2 children. LLB, Tohoku U., Miyagi, Japan, 1982; grad., Legal Rsch. and Tng. Inst., Tokyo, 1984; LLM, Cornell U., 1990. Bar: N.Y., 1991, Japan, 1984. Assoc. Yagi Fukushima & Yamanouchi, Tokyo, 1984-85, Showa Law Office, Tokyo, 1985-91, O'Melveny & Myers, N.Y.C., 1990-91; ptnr. Showa Law Office, Tokyo, 1992—; mem. Copyright Coun./Agy. for Cultural Affairs, Japan, 1995—. Mem. ABA, Federation of Bar Assns. Japan (vice-chmn. computer rsch. com. 1994-97), Dai-ni Tokyo Bar Assn. Office: Showa Law Office T Hachiman, 5F 2-4 Kojimachi Chiyoda-ku, Tokyo 102-0083, Japan

MIYATA, HIDEO, science educator, researcher; b. Osaka, Japan, Mar. 16, 1943; p. Koichi and Yoneko (Shimamoto) M.; m. Michiko Kawakatsu; children: Mariko, Nanako, Yuichi. BA, Kyoto (Japan) U., 1965, MA, 1967, DSc, 1973. Lectr. Kanazawa Inst. Tech., Ishikawa, Japan, 1970-71; asst. prof. Kanazawa Inst. Tech., Ishikawa, 1971-73, prof., 1973—. Author: Introduction to Virtual Machine, 1983; contbr. articles to profl. jours. Buddhist. Avocations: skiing, railroads, go game, walking. Home: Yokogawa 1-185-2, Kanazawa 921-8163, Japan Office: Kanazawa Inst Tech, Ogigaoka 7-1, Nonoichi 921-8501, Japan

MIYAUCHI, FUMIHISA, obstetrician and gynecologist, researcher; b. Nomura, Ehime, Japan, Nov. 30, 1948; s. Ryosaku and Misao (Horike) M.; m. Hiromi Matsuura, Apr. 29, 1973; children: Kennichi, Yuji. MD, Yamaguchi U., Ube, Japan, 1973, PhD, 1979. From asst. prof. to assoc. prof. Yamaguchi U., Ube, 1984-89; dir. Ehime Rosai Hosp., Niihama, Japan, 1989—; vis. scientist Mich. U., Ann Arbor, 1984-86. Mem. Japan Soc. Ob-Gyn., Japan Endocrine Soc., Japan Soc. Fertility and Sterility. Office: Ehime Rosai Hosp, 13-27 Minami Komatsubara, 792 Niihama Ehime, Japan

MIYAUCHI, JUN, pathologist, researcher; b. Kuki, Japan, Aug. 30, 1951; s. Yoshiya and Yoshiko (Kurihara) M.; m. Hiromi Nakasato, May 30, 1981; children: Rie, Mari. MD, Keio U., Tokyo, 1977, DMS, 1984. Asst. dept. pathology Keio U., 1977-85, 1987-88; rsch. fellow divsn. of biorsch. Ont. Cancer Inst., Toronto, Can., 1985-87; dir. dept. lab. medicine Nat. Children's Hosp., Tokyo, 1988—. Contbr. articles to profl. jours. Recipient Sanshikai award Keio U., 1991. Mem. Am. Soc. Hematology, Japanese Soc. Pathology (councillor), Japanese Soc. Hematology (councillor), Japanese Soc. Clin. Hematology (councillor), Japanese Soc. Pediat. Oncology (councillor). Avocations: bird watching, mountain walking, photography. Home: 1-11-15 Motomachi, Urawa Saitama-ken 336-0003, Japan Office: Nat Childrens Hosp, 3-35-31 Taishido, Setagaya-ku Tokyo 154-8509, Japan

MIYAWAKI, SHIGEKI, geneticist; b. Osaka, Japan, Sept. 2, 1950; s. Mitsuo and Norie (Hanafusa) M.; m. Mariko Bessho, May 6, 1979; children: Hiroyuki, Keisuke, Eri. BS, Nagoya U., 1973, MS, 1975, PhD, 1987. From scientist to mgr. Nippon Shinyaku Co., Ltd., Kyoto, 1975—. Home: 73-31 Terada-Ohgawara, Joyo City Kyoto 610-0121, Japan Office: Nippon Shinyaku Co Ltd, 3-14-1 Sakura, Tsukuba-shi, Ibaraki 305-0003, Japan

MIYAZAKI, KOICHI, economics educator; b. Yokohama, Japan, Dec. 7, 1949; s. Yoshikazu and Teruko (Inukai) M.; m. Mizuyo Muto, Jan. 16, 1993. BA, Yokohama Nat. U., 1972; MA, U. Tokyo, 1974. Prof. dept. econs. Hosei U., Tokyo, 1986—. Contbr. articles to profl. jours. Mem. Am. Econ. Assn., Tokyo Ctr. for Econ. Rsch., Japanese Econ. Assn. Avocation: tennis. Home: 565-10-202 Kitano-Machi, Hachioji-Shi Tokyo 192-0906, Japan Office: Hosei U Dept Econs, 4342 Aihara-Machi, Machida-Shi Tokyo 194-0298, Japan

MIYAZAKI, NOBUYOSHI, computer scientist, educator; b. Okazaki, Aichi, Japan, Nov. 13, 1948; s. Toshio and Etsu (Hasebe) M.; m. Yuriko Muramatsu, June 18, 1977; children: Maho, Maki. BSc, Kyoto U., 1973, DEng, 1990; MSc in Computer Sci., U. Ill., 1979. Sr. rschr. Inst. for New Generation Computer Tech., Tokyo, 1982-85; engr. Oki Electric Industry, Tokyo, 1973-82, rsch. mgr., 1985-94; prof. Chiba Inst. Tech., Narashino, Japan, 1994—; mem. tech. working group Inst. for New Generation Computer Tech., 1985-91. Co-author: (in Japanese) Introduction to Distributed Knowledge Processing, 1989, New Databases, 1994; also articles. Mem. IEEE Computer Soc., Info. Processing Soc. Japan (editorial com. 1988-97), Assn. for Computing Machinery, Japan Soc. Artificial Intelligence (editorial com. 1990-92), Inst. Electronics, Info. and Comm. Engrs. (exec. com. 1992-94), Sigma Xi, Phi Kappa Phi. Avocation: fruit gardening. Home: 7-18-4 Takinoi, Funabashi, Chiba 274, Japan Office: Chiba Inst Tech Dept Computer Sci, 2-17-1 Tsudanuma, Narashino 275-0016, Japan

MIYAZAKI, SHIGEKI, university official; b. Nigata-Shibata, Japan, Oct. 21, 1925; s. Shigesaburo Miyazaki and Akiko Kojima; m. Setsuko Yamamoto, May 27, 1951; children: Shigemoto, Takaki. JD, Meiji U., Tokyo. Prof. Sch. of Law Meiji U., Tokyo, 1959-65, dean for students, 1965-75, dean Sch. of Law, 1975-87; pres. Assn. of World Law, Tokyo, 1987-91, Assn. of Internat. Human Rights Law, Tokyo, 1991-93; chancellor Meiji U., Tokyo, 1992-96, chief dir. Ctr. for Human Rights Affairs, 1997—, now prof. emeritus. Author: (book) International Law (10th edit.), 1995, editor book in field, 1995. Chmn. Conseil for DOA-Problema, Tokyo, 1993—. Avocation: stamp collecting. Home: 26-19 Daita 5-Chome, Setagaya-ku Tokyo 155-0033, Japan Office: Ctr for Human Rights Affair, MT Bild 5-5 Shimbashi 2 chome, Chiyoda-ku Minato-ku Tokyo 105-0004, Japan

MIYAZAKI, SHUICHI, materials scientist, educator; b. Sumoto City, Japan, Feb. 28, 1950; s. Takizo and Imako (Amano) M.; m. Mie Shibamura, Mar. 29, 1981; 1 child, Maki. BSc, Himeji (Japan) Inst. Tech., 1972; MS, Osaka (Japan) U., 1974, PhD, 1979. Asst. prof. materials sci. U. Tsukuba, Japan, 1979-90, assoc. prof. materials sci., 1990-98, prof. materials sci., 1998—; vis. scientist U. Ill., Urbana, 1985-86; Gredden vis. sr. fellow, U. Western Australia, Nedlands, 1989; hon. fellow U. Minn., Mpls., 1990; vis. prof. U. Franche-Comte, Besancon, France, 1997; vis. rsch. advisor Nat. Inst. Metals, Tsukuba, 1990-99. Author: Shape Memory Alloys, 1987, 96, Mechanical Properties of Shape Memory Alloys, (in Japanese) 1993; author, editor: Shape Memory Alloys—From Microstructure to Macroscopic Properties, 1998. Recipient Muramatsu Acad. Deed award Acad. Shape Memory Materials for Med. Use, Japan, 1991, Acad. Deed award Japan Inst. Metals, 1995, Best Poster prize, Internat. Conf. on Microstructures and Functions of Materials, 1996, Internat. Metallographic Contest prize Internat. Metallographic Soc. and ASM Internat., 1998, Metallographic Contest award Japan Inst. Metals, 1998, Metall. and Materials Sci. award Metall. Rsch. Aid Assn., 1998. Avocations: reading, travel. Office: U Tsukuba, Inst Materials Sci, Tsukuba 305-8573, Japan

MIYAZAWA, KIICHI, Japanese government official; b. Tokyo, Oct. 8, 1919; married; 2 children. Grad., Tokyo Imperial U., 1941. With Japanese Fin. Ministry, Tokyo, 1942-52, govt. rep. to San Francisco Peace Conf., 1951; mem. Ho. of Councillors, 1053-65; parliamentary vice min. edn., 1959-60; min. of state, dir. gen. Econ. Planning Agy., 1962-64, 66-68, 77-78; mem. Ho. of Reps., 1967—; min. internal trade and industry, 1970-71, min. fgn. affairs, 1974-76, min. state, chief cabinet sec., 1980-82, min. fin., 1986-88,

93—, dep. prime min., 1987-88, prime min., 1991-93. Author: Tokyo-Washington Secret Talk, 1956, Challenge for Beautiful Japan, 1984. Chmn. exec. coun. Liberal Dem. Party, 1984-86. Office: Ministry of Fin, 3-1-1 Kasumigaseki Chiyoda-ku, Tokyo 100-8940, Japan*

MIYAZAWA, SHINTARO, manufacturing company executive, researcher; b. Nagoya, Japan, June 19, 1942; m. Kyoko Miyazawa, Aug. 18, 1945. BS, Waseda U., Tokyo, 1966, MS, 1968; PhD, Tohoku U., Sendai, Japan, 1978. Staff engr. NTT Elec. Comm., Musashino, Japan, 1974-85; head device materials sect. NTT LSI Labs., Atsugi, Japan, 1985-87, exec. rsch. engr., 1988-89; rsch. fellow NTT Sys. Electronics Labs., Atsugi, Japan, 1989-98; dep. dir., sr. chief rschr. USHIO, Inc., Shizuoka, Japan, 1998-2000, Shinkosha Co., Ltd., Yokohama, Japan, 2000—; vis. rschr. France Telecom-Bagneux, Paris, 1976-77, ICMCB/CNRS, Bordeaux, 2000; invited prof. Tohoku U., Sendai, 1985-86, Waseda U., Tokyo, 1990-92, Yamanashi U., Kohfu, Japan, 1992-93, Tokushima (Japan) U., 1997. Co-editor: (book) Semi-Insulating III-V Materials, 1987; co-editor, author: (handbook) Handbook of Materials for Advanced Devices, 1993; author: (book) Optical Crystals, 1995; editor, author: (handbook) Crystal Growth Handbook, 1995. Recipient Devel. of New Tech. award Japan Soc. Metallurty, 1985. Mem. Japan Soc. Applied Physics, Materials Rsch. Soc., Japanese Assn. Crystal Growth (Best Paper award 1997), Optical Soc. of Am. Avocations: modeling of trains, collection of lithography. Office: Shinkosha Co Ltd, 2-4-1 Kosugaya Sakae-ku, Yokohama 247-0007, Japan

MIYAZU, JUN-ICHIRO, telecommunications industry executive. CEO Nippon Telegraph. Fax: 81-3-5359-1603. Office: Nippon Telegraph and Tel Co, 3-1 Otemachi 2-chome, Chiyoda-ku Tokyo 100-8116, Japan*

MIYOSHI, MASAO, English literature educator, writer; b. Tokyo, May 14, 1928; came to U.S., 1952; s. Katsunai Miyoshi and Hisae Takahama; m. Elizabeth Ann Lester, July 27, 1953 (div. 1977); m. Martha L. Archibald, Apr. 8, 1977; children: Kathy Michele, Owen Malcolm, Melina Cybele. BA, U. Tokyo, 1951; MA, NYU, 1955, PhD, 1963. Instr., lectr. Gakushin U., Tokyo, 1951-52, 54-55; from asst. prof. to assoc. prof. to prof. English U. Calif., Berkeley, 1963-87; Edwin O. Reischauer prof. Japanese studies Harvard U., Cambridge, Mass., 1984-85; Hajime Mori prof. lit. U. Calif., San Diego, 1986—; vis. prof. U. Chgo., 1978-81; dir. regional seminar and Japanese studies U. Calif., Berkeley, 1980-86; dir. program for Japanese studies U. Calif., San Diego, 1989-95; dir. council on East Asian Studies U. Calif at San Diego, 1997—. Author: The Divided Self, 1969, Accomplices of Silence, 1975, As We Saw Them, 1979, Off Center, 1991; editor: Postmodernism and Japan, 1989, Japan in the World, 1993, The Cultures of Globalization, 1998, (book series) Asia-Pacific: Culture, Politics, and Society. Guggenheim fellow, 1971-72, 75-76. Mem. MLA, Assn. for Asian Studies, Internat. Comparative Lit. Assn. Office: U Calif 9500 Gilman Dr La Jolla CA 92093-5004

MIYOSHI, SAKUICHIRO, retired anatomy educator; b. Uwajima, Ehime, Japan, May 31, 1932; s. Hichizo and Chizu (Utsunomiya) M. DDS, Osaka (Japan) U., 1958, PhD, 1968. Assoc. prof. oral anatomy Hiroshima (Japan) U., 1968-70, Osaka U., 1970-78; prof. oral anatomy Fukuoka Dental Coll., 1978-98, prof. emeritus, 1998—; tchr. Japanese lang., Edn. Info. Inst., 1999—.

MIYOSHI, SHUNKICHI, steel industry engineering executive; b. Mar. 16, 1929. Grad. 1st Faculty of Engring., Tokyo U., 1951. With Nippon Kokan K.K., 1951; various mgmt. positions NKK Corp., 1951-82, dir., 1982-85, mng. dir., 1985-88, sr. mng. dir., 1988-90, exec. v.p., 1990-92, pres., 1992-97, also chmn. bd. dirs., 1997—; mem. adv. panel for Prime Min. Elec. Power Devel. Coord. Coun., 1996—; mem. adv. panel coal mining coun. Min. of Internat. Trade and Industry, 1992-97; mem. adv. panel Trade Coun., 1997—; mem. Ctrl. Environ. Coun., 1997-99, mem. Weights and Measures Administrn. Coun., 1998—. Mem. Iron and Steel Inst. of Japan (pres. 1992-94), Japan Fedn. Econ. Orgns. (exec. bd. dirs. 1992-97), Japan Iron and Steel Fedn. (vice chmn. 1993-94, 96-97, bd. dirs. 1992-97), Japan Assn. Corp. Execs. (trustee 1995—), Japan Fedn. Employer's Assn. (vice chmn. 1997—), Japan Inst. Construction Engring. (chmn. 1997—). Japan Vocat. Ability Devel. Assn. (chmn. 1998—). Office: NKK Corp, 1-1-2 Marunouchi, Chiyoda 100-8202, Japan

MIYOSHI, TORU, retired chief justice; b. Oct. 31, 1927. Student, U. Tokyo. Asst. judge Tokyo Dist. Ct., Tokyo Family Ct., 1955; judge Hakodate Dist. Ct., Hakodate Family Ct., 1965; judge, presiding judge divsn. Tokyo Dist. Ct., 1975, pres. rsch. & tng. ct. clks., 1982; pres. Oita Dist. Ct., Oita Family Ct., 1985, Nagano Dist. Ct., Nagano Family Ct., 1986; chief judicial rsch. ofcl. Japanese Supreme Ct., 1987; pres. Sapporo High Ct., 1990, Tokyo High Ct., 1991; justice Supreme Ct., 1992, chief justice, 1995-97; ret., 1997.

MIZEN, PAUL DAVID, economist researcher; b. Coventry, Eng., Feb. 12, 1968; s. David John and Jean Valerie (Davenport) M. BSc in Econs., U. Wales, Abersystwyth, Wales, 1989; PhD, Loughborough (Eng.) U., 1992. Lectr. U. Nottingham, Eng., 1992-99, reader, 1999—; cons. Bank Eng., 1997—; mem. Ctr. Econ. Policy Rsch.; vis. fellow U. Warwick, Eng.; 1994; vis. scholar Johns Hopkins U., Balt., 1995, Internat. Monetary Fund, 1995, 96, Ohio State U., 1995; vis. scholar Res. Bank Australia, 1998, Res. Bank New Zealand, 1998, U. S. Australia, 1998, Czech Nat. Bank, 1999, IMF, 1999. Author: (book) Buffer Stock Models and the Demand for Money, 1994; (with M. K. Lewis) Monetary Economics, 2000; contbr. articles to profl. jours. Mem. Royal Econ. Soc., Am. Econ. Assn., European Econ. Assn. Avocations: classical guitar, reading and collecting second hand books, hill walking, cycling. Home: 15 Ambleside Close, Loughborough LE11 3SH, England Office: U of Nottingham, University Pk, Nottingham NG7 2RD, England

MIZER, RICHARD ANTHONY, technology company executive; b. San Francisco, Jan. 7, 1952; s. Conrad Xavier and Sally Jo (Hagan) M. BA in Bioengring. and Econs., U. Calif., San Diego, 1977. Founding ptnr. Microdoctors, Palo Alto, Calif., 1974-94; mgr., ptnr. K-Family Corp. dba Harlow's Night Club, Fremont, Calif., 1977-79, Restaurants Unique Inc. dba Bourbon St., Mountain View, Calif., 1980-83; engring. mgr. Pacific Bell, San Ramon, Calif., 1983-89; tech. staff advanced tech. Pacific Bell, 1989-92, developer advanced video svcs., 1992-96; asst. v.p. Nuko Info. Sys., Inc., San Jose, Calif., 1996-98; pres., CEO Digital Ventures Diversified Inc., San Jose, Calif., 1998—. Exec. prodr.: Cinema of the Future sm, 1992; assoc. prodr. Soccer Fest: World Cup Soccer Final in HDTV to Europe and U.S. theaters from Pasadena Rose Bowl, 1994; exec. in chg. prodn. 50th Anniversary of Signing of UN Charter, 1995. Mem. security staff Republican Task Force, San Francisco, 1984, tech. staff U.S. Olympic Com., Los Angeles, 1984. Mem. IEEE, Nat. Assn. Broadcasters, Soc. Motion Picture and TV Engrs. (western region gov. 1999—). Roman Catholic. Avocations: martial arts, auto racing, skiing, triathlon. Office: Digital Ventures Diversified Inc 990 Richard Ave Ste 112 Santa Clara CA 95050-2828

MIZRACH, AMOS, scientist; b. Haifa, Israel, May 5, 1944; m. Orna Mizrach; children: Ronit, Yifat, Chen. BSc, Technion, Haifa, 1970, MSc, 1977, DSc, 1993. Scientist Inst. Agrl. Engring., Agrl. Rsch. Orgn., Bet Dagan, Israel, 1970—; dept. head Agrl. Rsch. Orgn., Bet Dagan. Contbr. articles to sci. publs.; patentee in field. Mem. Am. Assn. Agrl. Engrs., Israeli Assn. Agrl. Engrs. Fax: 972 3 9603704. E-mail: amos@agri.gov.il. Home: 18 Pninat HaYam, Rishon Lezion 75404, Israel Office: Inst Agrl Engring, PO Box 6, Bet Dagan 50250, Israel

MIZRAHI, ABRAHAM MORDECHAY, retired cosmetics and health care company executive, physician; b. Jerusalem, Apr. 16, 1929; came to U.S., 1952, naturalized, 1960; s. Solomon R. and Rachel (Haliwa) M.; m. Suzanne Eve Glasser, Mar. 15, 1956; children: Debra, Judith, Karen. B.S., Manchester Coll., 1955; M.D., Albert Einstein Coll. Medicine, 1960. Diplomate: Am. Bd. Pediatrics, Nat. Bd. Med. Examiners. Intern U. N.C., 1960-61; pediatric resident Columbia-Presbyn. Med. Center, N.Y.C., 1961-63; NIH fellow in neonatology Columbia-Presbyn. Med. Center, 1963-65; assoc. dir. Newborn Service Mt. Sinai Hosp., N.Y.C.; also dir. Newborn Service Elmhurst Med. Center, 1965-67; staff physician Geigy Pharm. Corp., N.Y.C., 1967-69; head cardio-pulmonary sect. Geigy Pharm. Corp., 1969-71; sr. v.p. corp. med. affairs USV Pharm. Corp., Tuckahoe, N.Y., 1971-76; v.p. health and safety Revlon, Inc., N.Y.C., 1976-89, sr. v.p. human resources, 1989-94; ret., 1994; assoc. in pediatrics Columbia U., 1963-67; cons. in neonatology Misericordia-Fordham Med. Ctr., 1967-89; clin. affiliate N.Y. Hosp.; clin. asst. prof. Cornell U. Med. Coll., 1982—. Contbr. articles to profl. jours. Trustee Westchester (N.Y.) Jewish Center. Mem. AMA, N.Y. State and County Med. Soc., Am., N.Y. acads. medicine, Am. Soc. Clin. Pharmacology and Therapeutics, Am. Pub. Health Assn., Am. Occupational Med. Assn. Home: 7 Jason Ln Mamaroneck NY 10543-2108

MIZRAHI, ISAAC, fashion designer; b. Bklyn., Oct. 14, 1961; s. Zeke and Sarah M. Attended, Parsons Sch. Design, 1982. Design asst. Perry Ellis, 1982-84, Jeffrey Banks, 1984-85, Calvin Klein, 1985-87; founder Isaac Mizrahi, 1987—, added menswear line, added eyewear, 1990—. Designed costumes Twyla Tharp's ballet Brief Fling, Am. Ballet Theatre. Recipient Perry Ellis new fashion talent award Coun. Fashion Designers Am., 1989; named Best Womenswear Designer 1989 Coun. Fashion Designers Am., 1990. Office: 876 Centennial Ave Piscataway NJ 08854-3917*

MIZUKAMI, YOSHIHIRO, theoretical chemist; b. Tokyo, Oct. 8, 1961; s. Tomio and Toyoko (Hirose) M.; m. Yasumi Maekawa, Mar. 21, 1991; 1 child, Mayuri. Degree in Sci., Kyoto (Japan) U., 1986, PhD, 1991. Postdoctoral fellow Inst. for Fundamental Chemistry, Kyoto, 1991-92; lectr. Shiga U., Hiratsu, Japan, 1992-95, assoc. prof. environ. sci., 1995—. Mem. Am. Chem. Soc. Avocation: Japanese chess problems. Home: Kokubu 1-7-30-634, Otsu 520-0844, Japan Office: Shiga U Fac Lib Arts/Edn, Hiratsu 2-5-1, Otsu 520-0862, Japan

MIZUNO, ATSUSHI, economist; b. Handa, Aichi, Japan, Aug. 18, 1959; came to U.S., 1984; s. Yosei and Kimiko (Nagasaka) M. BA in Econs., Waseda U., Tokyo, 1984; postgrad., Brown U., 1984-85; MPhil in Econs., CUNY, 1988, PhD in Econs., 1989. Predoctoral visiting scholar Nat. Bur. Econs. Rsch., N.Y.C., 1986-89, postdoctoral visiting scholar, 1989; sr. economist The Nomura Securities Co., Ltd., Tokyo, 1989-94, chief strategist, 1995-97; chief fixed income strategist Deutsche Morgan Grenfell Capital Markets Ltd., Tokyo Br., 1997—; chief fixed income strategist Deutsche Securities Ltd. Tokyo Br., 1998—, mng. dir., chief fixed income strategist, 1999—; adj. instr. Baruch Coll., N.Y.C., 1987, Rutgers U., Newark, 1987, Manhattan Coll., Riverdale, N.Y., 1988. Named Best Fixed Income Strategist, Nikkei Newsletter on Bond and Money, 1996, 97, 98, 99; CUNY fellow, 1985-87; first team of Japanese fixed-income strategy/1997, 98, 99 All-Asia Rsch. Team. Avocations: tennis, golf. Home: 6-19-23-307 Akasaka, Minato-ku Tokyo 107-0052, Japan 107-0052

MIZUSAWA, JUN-ICHI, engineering educator; b. Tokyo, June 10, 1943; p. Keitaro and Seki Mizusawa; m. Yumi Morita, Mar. 23, 1972; children: Yuka, Toru, Satoru. Bachelor Degree, U. Tokyo, 1967, D in Engring., 1989. Cert. telecom. chief engr. With Nippon Tel. and Telegraph Corp., Tokyo, 1967-90; assoc. prof. faculty engring. U. Tokyo, 1990-93; rsch. fellow NTT Multimedia Network Labs., Musashino-shi, Japan, 1993-98; fellow engr. NTT Advanced Tech. Corp., 1999; prof. Aoyama gakuin U., Tokyo, 2000—. Author: Intelligent Network and Network Operations, 1991 (Ookawa Found. Publ. prize 1994), Communication Network, 1998, Japanese Telecommunication Network, 1994,. Mem. IEEE (sr.), Inst. Electronics, Info. and Comm. Engrs. Fax: 81-47-390-9774. E-mail: mizu@ieee.org. Home: 3-20-15 Maihama, Urayasu-shi Chiba 279-0031, Japan Office: Aoyama gakuin Univ, 6-16-1 Chitosedai, Setagaya-ku Tokyo 157-8572, Japan

MIZUTANI, HITOSHI, planetary science educator; b. Tokyo, Feb. 27, 1942; s. Hisao and Shukuko (Shiraishi) M.; m. Teruko Tanaka, May 30, 1967; children: Shin, Gen. BSc, U. Tokyo, 1964, MSc, 1966, DSc, 1971. Asst. U. Tokyo, 1966-78; assoc. prof. Nagoya (Japan) U., 1978-81, prof., 1981-87; prof. Inst. Space and Astronautical Sci., Sagamihara-shi, Japan, 1987—; rsch. fellow Calif. Inst. Tech., Pasadena, 1971-73; vis. scientist U. Colo., Boulder, 1976-77. Mem. Japanese Soc. for Planetary Sci. (v.p. 1991—), Seismol. Soc. Japan, Am. Geophys. Union. Office: Inst Space-Astronaut Sci, 3-1-1 Yoshino-dai, Kanagawa Sagamihara-shi 229-8510, Japan

MIZUTANI, TOMOHIKO, neurology educator; b. Tokyo, Mar. 4, 1945; s. Nobuo and Kimiko (Ito) M.; m. Machiko Miyoshi, Sept. 28, 1974; children: Yukiko, Saneyuki, Junko. MD, Tokyo Med. and Dental U., 1969; PhD, Tokyo Women's Coll. Medicine, 1983. Bd. cert. Am. Bd. Psychiatry and Neurology, Am. Bd. Pathology, Japanese Bd. Neurology. Resident in medicine Toranomon Hosp., Tokyo, 1970-72; intern in medicine D.C. Gen. Hosp., Washington, 1972-73; resident in neurology Upstate Med. Ctr., Syracuse, N.Y., 1973-76; fellow in neuropathology Hosp. of U. of Pa., Phila., 1976-79; staff in neurology Toranomon Hosp., Tokyo, 1979-83; assoc. prof. neurology Nihon U. Sch. Medicine, Tokyo, 1983-99; prof. neurology Nihon U. Sch. Medicine, 1999—. Mem. Am. Acad. Neurology, Am. Assn. Neuropathologists, Japanese Soc. Neurology. Avocations: judo, igo. Office: Nihon U Sch Medicine, 30-1 Ohyaguchi-Kamimachi, 173-8610 Itabashi-ku Tokyo, Japan

MIZUTANI, YUKIO, engineering educator, mechanical engineer; b. Osaka-shi, Osaka, Japan, Jan. 23, 1935; s. Shin'ichi and Otei (Haba) M.; m. Mariko Hirai, Oct. 10, 1964; children: Hideki, Satoko, Yuichi. B Engring., Osaka (Japan) U., 1957, M Engring., 1961, D Engring., 1964. Engr. Kurashiki Rayon Co., Okayama, Japan, 1957-58; rsch. assoc. Osaka (Japan) U., 1964, assoc. prof., 1964-74, prof., 1974-96; prof. mech. engring. Kinki U., Osaka, Japan, 1996—. Author: Combustion Engineering, 2nd edit., 1989, Combustion Engineering Handbook, 1995; mem. editl. bd. Progress in Energy and Combustion Sci., 1976-86. Mem. Japan Soc. Mech. Engrs. (dir. thermal engring. divsn. 1992-93. Kansai br. 1994-95, editor Internat. Jour. 1988-91, v.p. 1997-98, award 1966, 75, 94, 97), Gas Turbine Soc. Japan. Avocations: swimming, classical music, gardening, jogging. Home: 1-45-8 Tsutsumi-cho, Yao 581-0832, Japan Office: Kinki U Fac Sci and Engring, 3-4-1 Kowakae, Higashi Osaka 577-8502, Japan

MIZZI, JOANN M., nurse; b. Detroit, Feb. 17, 1965; d. George and Ruth Ann (Silas) M.;. BSBA, Wayne State U., 1988, BSN, 1991, MBA, 1999. Pediat nurse St. John Hosp. & Med. Ctr., Detroit, 1991-97, emergency nurse, 1997—. Golden Key Nat. Hon. Soc. (lifetime mem.). Office: 22101 Moross Rd Detroit MI 48236-2148

MJOLSNESS, RAYMOND CHARLES, retired physicist, researcher; b. Chgo., Apr. 22, 1933; s. Raymond and Emma Pearl (McCormick) Veseth; m. Patricia M. McGeary, Oct. 6, 1957; children: Eric, Ingrid, Kirsten. BA, Reed Coll., 1953, Oxford (Eng.) U., 1955; PhD, Princeton U., 1963. Rsch. assoc. Los Alamos (N.Mex.) Nat. Lab., 1958-61; asst. prof. math. Reed Coll., Portland, Oreg., 1961-62; staff scientist GE Space Sci. Ctr., King of Prussia, Pa., 1962-63; staff mem. Los Alamos Nat. Lab., 1963-67; assoc. prof. astronomy Pa. State U., State College, 1967-69; staff mem. Los Alamos Nat. Lab., 1969-92; adj. prof. physics Los Alamos Nat. Lab., 1983-84. Contbr. articles to profl. jours. including Phys. Rev., Physics of Fluids, Turbulent Shear Flow II. Mem. Am. Phys. Soc. Achievements include research in plasma stability theory and collision theory, electron-atom and electron-molecule collisions, cosmology, hydrodynamics (turbulence, stability theory, code development, low gravity flows), and foundations of quantum mechanics. Avocations: jogging, weightlifting, music, chess, investing. Home: 207 Dos Brazos St Los Alamos NM 87544-2426

MKAPA, BENJAMIN WILLIAM, president of Tanzania; b. Ndanda, Nov. 12, 1938; s. William Matwani and Stephania Nambanga; m. Anna Joseph Maro, 1966; 2 children. Ed., Makerere U. Coll. adminstrv. officer Mekerere U., 1962, fgn. svc. officer, 1963; mng. editor Tanzania Nationalist and Uhuru, 1966; mng. editor The Daily News and Sun News, 1972, press sec. to pres., 1974; founding dir. Tanzania News Agy., 1976; minister fgn. affairs Tanzania, 1977-80, 84—, minister info. and culture, 1980-82; high commr. to Canada, amb. to U.S., 1982-84; mem. Parliament, 1985—; CCM chmn., 1996—; mem. nat. exec. com. Chama Cha Mapinduzi, 1987—; now pres. of Tanzania. Office: Presidents Office, PO Box 9120, Dar es Salaam Tanzania*

MKHITARYAN, NVER MNATSAKANOVICH, construction company executive; b. Yerevan, Armenia, June 16, 1960; s. Mnatsakan Vardanovich and Jenia Mamikovna (Mkrtchyan) M.; m. Ruzanna Razmikovna Kagramanyan, Sept. 29, 1979; children: Astkhik, Arthur. Diploma of Engr., Yerevan Poly. Inst., Yerevan, 1982; PhD, Kiev Civil Engring. Inst., 1989; DSc, Yerevan Archtl.-C.E. Inst., 1996. Cert. prof. bldg. materials and structures Aerospace Acad. Ukraine. Master Armvodstroy Trust, Yerevan, 1982-87; chief engr. Ehegnutsk Plant of Reinforced Concrete Structures, Armenia, 1988-92; sr. lectr. Yerevan Archtl.-Civil Engring. Inst., Yerevan, 1992-93; chmn. corp. Poznyakizhylstroy, Kiev, Ukraine, 1996—; cons., mem. sci. coun. for granting PhDs, Kiev Nat. U. Constrn., 1999—; rschr. Sci. Inst. for Binders and Materials, Kiev Nat. U. Constrn. and Architecture, 1996—. Author: The Solar Energy Treatment of Thin-Walled Reinforced Concrete Slabs and Their Manufacturing Under Package Technology, 1994, The Bases of Solar Energy Treatment of Alkaline Concretes, 1996, (with P.V. Krivenko) The Physical and Chemical Bases of Solar Technology of Alkaline Concretes, 1997. Recipient Cert. of Honor, Cabinet of Ministers of Ukraine, 1999, 2d silver class order for Labour Achievements, 1999, numerous other awards; named The Honorable Builder of Ukraine, Pres. of Ukraine, 1999; mem. Order of St. Prince Vladimir, Ukrainian Orthodox Ch., 1999. Fellow Acad. Constrn. of Ukraine, Internat. Acad. Egnring.; mem. ASCE, Acad. Engring. Scis. Ukraine. Home: Dragomanova 17 Apt 300, 03068 Kiev Ukraine

MLADENOV, GEORGY MICHAILOV, physics educator; b. Sofia, Bulgaria, May 10, 1941; s. Michail Stefanov and Elena Ivanova (Semerdjieva) M.; m. Vera Petrovna Ivanova, Nov. 6, 1966; children: Elena, Anastassia. BEE, St. Petersburg State U., Russia, 1967, PhD in Elec. Engring., 1972; DSc in Physics, Inst. Electronics Acad. Scis., Sofia, Bulgaria, 1986. Engr. Inst. Electronics, Bulgarian Acad. Scis., Sofia, 1967-69, rsch. fellow electron and ion divsn., 1972-81, sr. rsch. fellow, head of lab., 1981-97; founder, gen. dir. Tech. Ctr. Electron and Plasma Techs. and Techniques, Sofia, 1987—; prof., head of lab. phys. problems of electron beam techs. Inst. Electronics Bulgarian Acad. Scis., Sofia, 1987—. Author: Electron and Ion Methods for Analysis and Treatment of Materials, 1981, Microprocessor Control of Beam Technologies, 1988 (Best Sci. Monograph award Kiev Polytech. U., 1989); contbr. articles to profl. jours.; 22 inventions of processes and equipment for treating materials with charged particles. Pres. Assn. Tech. Ctrs. and Bus. Incubators in Sofia, Bulgaria, 1992—. Recipient Tech. awards Bulgarian Com. for Tech. Success, 1977, 84; named Prof. G. Nadjakov, Sofia U. and Bulgarian Acad. Scis., 1988. Mem. Internat. Engring. Acad., N.Y. Acad. Scis., Bulgarian Union of Electronics, Electrotechnics and Comms. (v.p. 1992-98), Fedn. Sci. and Tech. Assns. of Bulgaria (governing bd. 1991-98). Office: Inst Electronics BAS, Tzarigr Shosse 72, 1784 Sofia Bulgaria

MLADINIC-VULIC, DENIS, pediatrician, researcher; b. Split, Croatia, Sept. 5, 1960; d. Zeljko and Paskvalina (Ivancic) Mladinic; m. Nenad Vulic, Aug. 16, 1986; 1 child, Marko. MD, Med. Faculty, Zagreb, Croatia, 1985, Specialist, 1996. Diplomate in Pediatrics. Physician Health Inst., Split, Croatia, 1986-92; resident in pediatrics Clin. Hosp. Firule, Split, 1992-96; pediatrician Pediatric Group Practice Mertojak, Split, 1996-99; pediatric ofcr. Denis Mladinic-Vulic, 2000—. Contbr. articles to profl. jours. Mem. Internat. Pediatric Chat, Acad. for Devel. Rehab. Zagreb, Pediatric Sect. of Croatia. Roman Catholic. Avocation: fitness. Home: Sukoisanska 37, 21000 Split Croatia Office: Denis Mladinic-Vulic, Doverska bb, 21000 Split Croatia

MLAMA, PENINA MUHANDO, theater educator; b. Kilosa, Morogoro, Tanzania, Mar. 3, 1948; d. Phinehas Daudi Muhando and Noa Abby Chiduo; m. Raphael Dominic Mlama; children: Mota Cecilia, Huila Calvin. BA in Edn., U. Dar es Salaam, Tanzania, 1971, MA in Theatre, 1973, PhD, 1983. Mem. faculty dept. theatre U. Dar es Salaam, prof., 1984-98, head dept., 1982-88, assoc. dean faculty arts, 1989-90, dean, 1990-91, dep. vice chancellor, 1991—; exec. dir. Orgn. for African Women Educationalists, Kenya, 1998—; bd. dirs. AGIPTanzania Ltd.; advisor to African panel Social Sci. Rsch. Coun., U.S., 1997—; v.p. Econ. and Social Rsch. Found., Tanzania, 1994—. Author: (plays) Hatia, 1969, Lina Ubani, 1984 (Shaabon Robert award 1998), Culture and Development, The Popular Theatre Approach in Africa, 1991; lead actress in film Mama Tumaini, 1986 (SADC Film Festival best actress award). Chmn. Kilosa Edn. Found., 1996—; coordinator Edn. for Dem. for Girls Caucus, Tanzania, 1996—. Grantee Rockefeller Found., 1986. Mem. Assn. African Women R & D, Internat. Children's Theatre Assn. (exec. bd. 1994-97), Theatre for Devel. Assn. Tanznia (bd. dirs. 1980—), Tanzania Writers Assn., Tanzania Theatre Ctr. Avocations: playriting, music, reading, theatre production. Office: U Dar es Salaam, Box 35091, Dar es Salaam Tanzania

MLCZOCH, JOHANNES KARL, cardiologist; b. Hochegg, Austria, Mar. 23, 1945; s. Felix and Dorli (Pernter) M.; m. Traudi Aigner, Oct. 23, 1971; children: Barbara, Elisabeth, Marie-Theres, Stephan. MD, U. Vienna, Austria, 1969. Asst. med. faculty U. Vienna, 1971-76; rsch. fellow CVP rsch. lab. UCMC, Denver, 1975-76; oberarzt dept. cardiology U. Vienna, 1976-81, assoc. prof. medicine, 1981-87, prof. medicine, 1987—; head dept. medicine KH Lainz, Vienna, 1991—. Editor: Pulmonary Circulation, 1985; mem. editorial bd. European Heart Jour., 1991—; contbr. articles to profl. jours. Fellow Am. Coll. Chest Physicians, European Soc. Cardiology (chmn. working group on pulmonary circulation 1980-86); mem. Austrian Soc. Cardiology (bd. dirs. 1989-99, pres. 1990),. Office: KH Lainz 4 Med Abteilung, Wolkersbergen Str 1, 1130 Vienna Austria

MLDRUM, BRIAN STUART, research neuroscientist; b. Ipswich, Suffolk, Eng., Aug. 20, 1935; s. Frederick Stephen and Ada Mary (Singleton) M.; m. Mary Anne Fryer, Jan. 4, 1958 (div.); children: Julian, Judith, Andrew; m. Astrid Gronneberg Chapman, Aug. 14, 1981; 1 child, Hannah. BA, Cambridge (Eng.) U., 1956, MB, BCh, 1959; PhD, London U., 1964; DSc, Paris V, 1994. Rsch. asst. dept. physiology Univ. Coll., London, 1961-63; mem. sci. staff neuropsychiatry unit Med. Rsch. Ctr., Carshalton, Eng., 1963-73; sr. lectr. dept. neurology Inst. Psychiatry, London, 1973-84; reader exptl. neurology London U., 1984-87, prof., 1988—; William G. Lennox lectr. Am. Epilepsy Soc., 1980, D. Mattson lectr., 1994, A. Meyer lectr., 1995. Editor: Recent Advances in Epilepsy, Vols. 1-6, 1983-95; contbr. articles to med. jours. Recipient basic rsch. award Am. Epilepsy Soc., 1999. Office: Inst Psychiatry Dept Neur, De Crespigny Park, London SE5 8AF, England

MLEKO, STANISLAW WACLAW, food scientist; b. Cracow, Poland, Apr. 20, 1964; s. Wladyslaw and Stefania (Gawel) M.; m. Anna Truchlinska, July 27, 1991; children: Jan, Piotr. MSc, Agrl. U., 1992, PhD, 1995. Asst. Agrl. U., Cracow, 1991-92; asst. Agrl. U., Lublin, Poland, 1992-95, lectr., 1995—; vis. scientist U. B.C., Vancouver, Can., 1997; rsch. scientist N.C. State U., Raleigh, 1997-2000. Contbr. articles to profl. jours. Mem. Polish Soc. of Food Technologists (sec. Lublin's br. 1992—), Soc. of Rheology Am. Inst. of Physics, Inst. Food Technologists (profl.). Achievements include patent for methods of forming whey protein products; research in the field of understanding of process of whey protein functionality in food systems. Avocations: art, classical music, writing dramas. Home: Krolowej Jadwigi 2/8, 20-282 Lublin Poland Office: Agrl U Dept Food Tech, Akademicka 13, 20-950 Lublin Poland

MLINARIC-GALINOVIC, GORDANA, microbiologist; b. Fužine, Croatia, Feb. 15, 1950; d. Ivan and Ana (Subotić) Mlinarić; m. Mili Galinović, Feb. 23, 1974; children: Ivana, Andro. MD, U. Zagreb, Croatia, 1973, MSc, 1978, DSc, 1985. Gen. practitioner Clin. Hosp. Ctr., Zagreb, 1974-75; from asst. lectr. to asst. prof. U. Zagreb Med. Sch., 1975-97, assoc. prof., 1997—; prin. investigator on respiratory syncytial virus infections Ministry of Sci., Zagreb, 1986—; chief WHO Virus Collaborating Ctr., Zagreb, 1988—. Contbr. articles to profl. jours. British Coun. fellow RVI, New Castle Upon Tyne, 1985; P.L. Ogra grant U. Tex., Galveston, 1991-92. Mem. European Soc. Clin. Virology, Croatian Med. Soc., Croatian Soc. Med. Microbiology. Roman Catholic. E-mail: gordana.mlinaric-galinovic@med-fakzg.tel.hr. Home: Bartolici 33, 10 000 Zagreb Croatia Office: U Zagreb Med Sch, Rockefellerova 4, 10 000 Zagreb Croatia

MLOSTON, GRZEGORZ, chemist; b. Pabianice, Poland, Oct. 6, 1950; s. Franciszek and Wtadyslawa (Werfel) M.; m. Jadwiga Filarska, July 17, 1977; children: Anna, Ewa, Katarzyna. PhD, U. Lodz, Poland, 1982. Rsch. scientist U. Lodz, Poland, 1974-91, assoc. prof., 1991-98, prof., 1999—.

Contbr. articles to profl. jours. Recipient Scientific award Min. Edn. Poland, 1999; Humboldt fellow, Munich, 1983-85, 87-88, Disting. Vis. fellow U. So. Calif., 1996-97, Swiss Govt. fellow, 1995. Mem. Polish Chem. Soc., Lodz Scientific Soc. Avocations: gardening, fine arts. Home: Hippiczna 6, PL 90049 Lodz Poland Office: U Lodz, Narutowicza 68, PL 90136 Lodz Poland

MŁYNARSKA, MARIA STANISŁAWA, physiologist, researcher; b. Cracow, Poland, Apr. 27, 1925; d. Ludwik Marian and Janina Zofia (Chmielewska) Chrobak; m. Marian Franciszek Młynarski, June 8, 1951; children: Jan-Kajetan, Barbara Kapturkiewicz. Physician's Diploma, Med. Acad. Cracow, 1952, MD, 1963; Specialist in Gen. Medicine, Med. Acad. Lublin, 1973. Physician Mcpl. Cardiol. Clinic, Cracow, 1952-56; rsch. asst. Inst. Physiology, Cracow, 1954-62, Inst. Pathology, Cracow, 1962-65; physician S. Zeromski Hosp. and Cardiol. Clinic, Cracow, 1965-69, Univ. Med. Ctr., Cracow, 1968-76, Specialist Indsl. Health Ctr., Cracow, 1976-86; asst. prof. dept. physiology Inst. Pharmacology, Polish Acad. Scis., Cracow, 1986—. Author: Electromagnetic-mechanic Computing, 1998; contbr. articles to profl. jours. Mem. Acad. Sports Assn., Cracow, 1945-51, Assn. Med. Student, Cracow, 1946-52, Trade Union of Health Svc. Workers, Cracow, 1952-81, Solidarity/Solidarność, 1981-86. Recipient Badge of Excellence in Health Svcs., Minister of Health and Social Welfare, 1981. Mem. Polish Physiol. Soc., Polish Cardiol. Soc., Polish Soc. Hypertension, Polish Gastroen. Soc., Cracowian Med. Soc. Roman Catholic. Avocations: gardening, piano playing, Chopin's music. Office: Inst Pharmacology, ul Smętna 12, 31-343 Cracow Poland

MNTUNGWA, MOSES MILTON, insurance executive; b. Eshowe, Zulunatal, South Africa, Jan. 1, 1945; s. Mtobozi Cleopas and Ntombi Flora (Zungu) M.; m. Nozimvo Eunice Nongingi, Dec. 27, 1980; 3 children. Diploma in Bldg. Carpentry, Olifantsfontein Trade Ctr., Pretoria, South Africa, 1977. Clk. Bantu Adminstrn., Durban, South Africa, 1966-79; salesman Ellerine Holdings, Durban, South Africa, 1977-80; rep. Met. Life Ins., Durban, South Africa, 1981-83; sr. br. mgr. AA Life Ins., Durban, 1985-97; life ins. cons. African Life Ins., Durban, 1999, Mktg. Strategic Mgmt. Investment (Pty) Ltd., Durban, 1999—; bd. dirs. Insabelele Property Investments, Durban, South Africa, 1997—. Recipient Best Performance award Dale Carnegie, Durban, South Africa, 1981. Jehova's Witness. Avocations; reading, TV, sports. Home: AA 80 Umlazi PO Box UM/A21, Durban 4031, South Africa Office: Insabelele Property Invest, 199 Smith St, Durban 4001, South Africa

MO, LOAR KA-KEUNG, geriatrician, consultant, educator; b. Hong Kong, Sept. 11, 1962; s. Kam Wah Mo and Sau Fong Wong; m. Yee Man Chan; children: Cheuk Yan, Cheuk Hei. MBChB, Chinese U. Hong Kong, 1986, MBA, 1996. Reg. med. practitioner. Intern Med. & Health Dept., Hong Kong, 1986-87; med. officer Hosp. Svcs. Dept., Hong Kong, 1987-92; sr. med. officer Hosp. Svcs. Dept./Hosp. Authority, Hong Kong, 1992-96; cons. Hosp. Authority, Hong Kong, 1996—; hon. clin. tutor, hon. lectr. Faculty of Medicine, The Chinese U., Hong Kong, 1988-89, 95-96, hon. assoc. prof., 1996-97, adj. assoc. prof., 1997—; part-time lectr. Hong Kong Bapt. U., 1998—; part-time instr. The Open U. of Hong Kong, 1997—; hon. adv. elderly svcs. Internat. Buddhist Progress Soc. (Hong Kong) Ltd., 1997—; profl. adv. Cmty. Rehab. Network Hong Kong Soc. Rehab., 1996-99; honorable advisor Hong Kong Neuromuscular Disease Assn., 1999—; honorable advisor Hong Kong Stroke Assn., 1997-99; hon. med. advisor Yan Chai Nursing Home, 1998—; hon. clin. supr. Hong Kong Coll. Family Physicians, 1997—. Reviewer Hong Kong Jour. Gerontology, 1993. Mem. coun. Ch. of Mt. Carmel, 1995-97. Fellow Hong Kong Coll. Physicians, Hong Kong Acad. Medicine; mem. Royal Coll. Physicians, Hong Kong Alzheimers Disease and Brain Failure Assn. (coun. 1996-97), Hong Kong Assn. Gerontology (coun. 1991-92), Hong Kong Geriatrics Soc. (coun. 2000-01). Avocations: badminton, bowling, swimming, stamp collecting. Office: Yan Chai Hosp, 7-11 Yan Chai St, Tsuen Wan Hong Kong China

MO, NING, medical educator; b. Wuzhou, Guangxi, China, May 13, 1944; d. Zhi-Liang Mo and Bi-Ju Liao; m. Xiao-Qiang Huan, Feb. 1, 1971; 1 child, Huan Hiu. MD with hons., Guangxi Med. Coll., 1968; PhD, Walles U., Cardiff, U.K., 1993. Vis. scholar Loyola U., Chgo., 1983-87; assoc. prof. Guangxi Med. U., Nanning, 1990-93, prof., 1993—; dir. Guangxi Scinence, 1995—, Guangxi Medicine, 1996—. Contbr. articles to profl. jours. Grantee NSF, 1988, 95, British Heart Found., 1991; fellow Walles U., 1991-93. Mem. Chinese Pharmacological Soc. (dir. chpt. 1990—). Avocations: music, sports. Home: 6 Bin Hu Rd, Nanning Guangxi 530021, China

MOATAMEDI, MOJTABA, safety engineer, researcher; b. Zanjan, Iran, May 18, 1969; s. Parviz Moatamedi and Fatemah Adl. BSc, K.N. Toosi U. Tech., Tehran, Iran, 1992; MSc in Engring., Sheffield (Eng.) U., 1994, PhD in Engring., 1997. Cert. Instn. Chem. Engrs. U.K. in process safety engring. Rschr. Nissan, Tehran, 1990-91; rschr., project mgr. Aerodynamics Rsch. Ctr., Tehran, 1992-93; rschr. Sheffield U., 1996—, postdoctoral rsch. assoc., 1997—; pvt. cons. safety engring., 1994—; contbr. 1st European Congress on Chem. Engring., 1997. Contbr. articles to Process Plant Safety Symposium, ISME Internat. Conf. 1996, Metallurgy and Materials Conf. 1994, and Industry and Safety Jour. Named Grad. of Yr. K.N. Toosi U. Tech., 1992; recipient rsch. grant Ministry Culture and Higher Edn., Tehran, 1993. Mem. ASME (co-chair various confs. 1997, PVP Student Competition award 1997), Instn. Chem. Engrs. U.K. (Rsch. Event award 1997), Am. Soc. Safety Engrs. Achievements include development of safe design criteria for cylindrical structures under impulsive loading. Home: 41 Summer St, Sheffield S3 7NS, England Office: Univ Sheffield, Mappin St, Sheffield S1 3JD, England

MOATEZ, MOATASSEM ABDELWAHED, civil engineering executive; b. Guiza, Egypt, Mar. 19, 1953; s. Abdelwahed Ashmawy Moatassem and Mossa El Komy Horria; m. Maha Ahmed Fahmy, Nov. 14, 1978; children: Moatassem Jr., Ahmed Jr. Bachelor in Civil Engring., Cairo U., 1976. Prodn. mgr. Moatassem for Marble and Granite, Cairo, 1976, 85, dep. mgr., 1985-87, mgr., 1987—. Mem. Rotary. Office: Moatassem Marble & Granite, 183 El Tahrir St, Cairo Egypt

MOBASHERI, ALI, cell biologist, educator; b. Tehran, Iran, July 13, 1968; arrived in U.K., 1983; s. Dariush and Mahnaz (Farzaneh) M.; m. Denise Elaine Baigent, Mar. 21, 1991; children: Soraya, Roxana. BSc, U. London, 1990; MSc, U. Toronto, Can., 1993; PhD, U. Oxford, Eng., 1997. Lectr. U. Westminster, London, 1997-98, sr. lectr., 1998-2000; lectr. Faculty Vet. Sci., U. Liverpool, Eng., 2000—; mem. common room Wolfson Coll., Oxford, Eng., 1993—; cons., scientist Intersep Ltd., Wokingham, U.K., 1998—, Vivasci./Sartorius, Gloucestershire, U.K., 1999—. Contbr. articles to profl. jours. Open fellow U. Toronto, Can., 1990; grad. scholar Arthritis Rsch. Campaign, Oxford U., 1993. Mem. Royal Coll. Sci. (assoc.), Physiol. Soc. U.K., Royal Soc. Medicine U.K., Biochem. Soc. Office: U Liverpool, Faculty Veterinary Sci, Liverpool L69 3BX, England

MOBBS, SIR GERALD NIGEL, property investment executive; b. Birmingham, Eng., Sept. 22, 1937; s. Gerald Aubrey and Elizabeth (Lanchester) M.; m. Pamela Jame Marguerite Berry, Sept. 14, 1961; children: Christopher William, (twins) Virginia Elizabeth and Penelope Helen. Student, Oxford (Eng.) U., 1956-59; DSc (hon.), City Univ., London, 1988; D. Univ (hon.), U. Buckingham, Eng., 1993; LLD (hon.), Reading U. Exec. Slough (Eng.) Estates plc, 1960-63, dir., 1963-71, mng. dir., 1971-76, chmn., CEO, 1976-99; chmn. Bovis Homes, 1999—; chmn. Charterhouse Group, London, 1977-83; bd. dirs. Howard of Walden Estates, London, Barclays Bank, London, Kingfisher plc, London, chmn., 1995-96. Pres. Brit. Property Fedn., London, 1979-81; chmn. Property Services Agy., Adv. Bd., London, 1980-86, U. Buckingham, 1987-98; mem. Commonwealth War Graves Commn., London, 1988-97; mem. constrn. task force DETR, 1997—; Lord Lt. of Buckinghamshire, 1997-98; chmn. Wembley Task Force, 1999—. Mem. RICS (hon.), Comm. on Corporate Governance. Office: Slough Estates plc, 234 Bath Rd, Slough SL1 4EE, England

MOBBS, KENNETH WILLIAM, musician; b. Higham Ferrers, Northants, Eng., Aug. 4, 1925; s. George William and Grace Elsie (Pack) M.; m. Barbara Joyce McNeill, Sept. 2, 1950 (div. Apr. 1979); children: Sheelagh, Barbara, Patricia; m. Mary Jeanette Randall, May 18, 1979. MusB, Cambridge U., 1949, MA in Natural Scis. and Music, 1950; Licentiate in Pianoforte, Royal Acad. Music, Eng., 1941. Asst. lectr. music U. Bristol, Eng., 1950-53, lectr., 1953-64, sr. lectr., 1964-83; mus. dir. Bristol Opera Sch., 1954-64, Bristol Intimate Opera, 1981-84; freelance performer, lectr., 1983—; dir. Mobbs Keyboard Collection and Keyboard Photog. Archive, Bristol, 1976—. Contbr. articles on keyboard instruments to profl. publs.; composer, arranger Engaged!, 1963. Organ scholar Clare Coll., Cambridge, 1943, hon. scholar, 1948; fellow Royal Coll. Organists, 1949. Mem. Galpin Soc. for Study Mus. Instruments (mem. com. 1986-89), Inc. Soc. Musicians (mem. coun. 1997-2000), Assn. Univ. Tchrs., Musicians' Union, Fellowship Makers and Restorers Hist. Mus. Instruments, Am. Mus. Instrument Soc, Internat. Coun. of Museums. Avocations: photography, "O" gauge model trains. Home: 16 All Saints Rd, Bristol BS8 2JJ, England

MOBLEY, CLEON MARION, JR. (CHIP MOBLEY), physics educator, real estate executive; b. Reidsville, Ga., July 14, 1942; s. Cleon M. and Lucile (Anderson) M.; m. Martha Hewlett, 1962 (div. 1970); children: Lisa Anne, Arthur Marion; m. Delia Braswell, 1997. AS, So. Poly. U., 1961; BS, Oglethorpe U., 1963; MS, U. Mo., 1966; PhD, The Union Inst. Ohio, 1987. Lic. airplane pilot. Faculty rsch. assoc. Ga. Inst. Tech., Atlanta, 1963-65; faculty fellow NASA, 1967-68; from asst. to assoc. prof. physics Ga. So. U., Statesboro, 1968-95, dir. planetarium, assoc. prof. emeritus, 1995—; pres. Mobley Sci. Co., Statesboro, 1993—; pres. Assoc. Income Properties, Inc., Statesboro, 1982—, Savannah Properties Mgmt., Inc., 1983-87; sci. cons. AEC fellow, 1965; sec. Ga. Acad. Sci., 1990-94. Contbr. articles to profl. jours. NASA-ASEE fellow, 1970. Mem. Statesboro Home Builders Assn., Am. Inst. Physics, Ga. Acad. Sci., Sigma Phi Epsilon. Methodist. Office: PO Box 2053 Statesboro GA 30459-2053

MOBLEY, EMILY RUTH, library dean, educator; b. Valdosta, Ga., Oct. 1, 1942; d. Emmett and Ruth (Johnson) M. AB in Edn., U. Mich., 1964, AM in Libr. Sci., 1967, postgrad., 1973-76. Tchr. Ecorse (Mich.) Pub. Schs., 1964-65; adminstrv. trainee Chrysler Corp., Highland Park, Mich., 1965-66, engring. libr., 1966-69; libr. II Wayne State U., Detroit, 1969-72, libr. III, 1972-75; staff asst. GM Rsch. Labs. Libr., Warren, Mich., 1976-78, supr. reader svcs., 1978-81; libr. dir. GMI Engring. & Mgmt. Inst., Flint, Mich., 1982-86; assoc. dir. for pub. svcs. & collection devel., assoc. prof. libr. sci. Purdue U. Librs., West Lafayette, Ind., 1986-89, acting dir. librs., assoc. prof. libr. sci., 1989, dean librs., prof. libr. sci., 1989—; Esther Ellis Norton Disting. Prof. Libr. Sci. Purdue U., West Lafayette, Ind., 1997—; adj. lectr. U. Mich. Sch. Libr. Sci., Ann Arbor, 1974-75, 83-86; grants reader Libr. of Mich., 1980-81; project dir. Mideastern Mich. Region Libr. Cooperation, 1984-86; cons. Libr. Coop. of Macomb, 1985-86, Clark-Atlanta U., 1990-91; search com. for new dir. of libr. Smithsonian Instn., 1988; mem. GM Pub. Affairs Subcom. on Introducing Minorities to Engring.; presenter in field. Author: Special Libraries at Work, 1984, numerous other publs.; mem. editl. bd. Reference Svcs. Rev., 1989—, Infomanage, 1993-97. Mem. corp. vis. com. for librs. MIT, 1990—, Carnegie-Mellon U., 1998—; mem. Ind. Statewide Libr. Automation Task Force, 1989-90; mem. state tech. strategy subcom. on info. tech. and telecomms. Ind. Corp. for Sci. & Tech., 1989; mem. nat. adv. com. Libr. of Congress, 1988; trustee Libr. of Mich., 1983-86, v.p., 1986, long range plan com., 1979-82, task force on document access and delivery, 1977-79; info. project mem. Rep. Nat. Conv., 1980; bd. dirs. Small Farms Assn., Southfield, Mich., Lafayette Symphony Orch., YWCA. Recipient Bausch & Lomb award for sci. achievement, 1960, Cert. for Outstanding Performance in Acad. Achievement State of Mich. Ho. of Reps., 1976, Spl. Tribute for Outstanding Contbns. Libr. of Mich. Bd. Trustees, 1986, Disting. Alumnus award U. Mich. Sch. Info. & Libr. Studies, 1989; U. Mich. Regents Alumni scholar, 1960-64; CIC doctoral fellow in libr. sci., 1973-76. Mem. ALA (com. on accreditation, subcom. to rev. 1972, standards for accreditation 1988-89, OLOS minority internship com. 1988-89, nominating com. 1992-93, mem. coun. resolutions com. 1993-97), Assn. Coll. & Rsch. Librs. (task force on libr. sch. curriculum 1988-89, com. on profl. edn. 1990-92), Libr. Adminstrn. & Mgmt. Assn., Assn. Rsch. Librs. (bd. dirs. 1990-93), Spl. Librs. Assn. (pres. 1987-88, fellow 1991, com. mem.), Alpha Kappa Alpha, Phi Kappa Phi, Iron Key. Office: Purdue U Librs Stewart Ctr Purdue University IN 47907

MOBLEY, TONY ALLEN, university dean, recreation educator; b. Harrodsburg, Ky., May 19, 1938; s. Cecil and Beatrice (Bailey) M.; m. Betty Weaver, June 10, 1961; 1 child, Derek Lloyd. BS, Georgetown Coll., 1960; MS, Ind. U., 1962, D Recreation, 1965; MRE, So. Sem., Louisville, 1963. Chmn. dept. recreation and pks. Western Ill. U., Macomb, 1965-72, Pa. State U., University Park, 1972-76; prof., chmn. recreation and pks., dean Sch. Health, Phys. Edn. and Recreation Ind. U., Bloomington, 1976—; chair health adv. coun. White River Park Commn., State of Ind., 1979—; v.p Ind. Sports Corp., Indpls., 1983-89; bd. dirs. Nat. Inst. for Fitness and Sport, Indpls., 1984-93; J.B. Nash scholar, lectr. Am. Assn. Leisure and Recreation, Reston, Va., 1985. Contbr. over 50 articles to profl. jours. Bd. dirs. Monroe County YMCA, Bloomington, 1984-88, United Way, Bloomington, 1994—; mem. Gov.'s Coun. for Phys. Fitness and Sport, 1991—. Am. Coun. Edn. adminstrv. internship fellow, N.C. State U., 1970-71. Fellow Am. Acad. Pk. and Recreation Adminstrn. (pres. 1985-86); mem. Nat. Recreation and Pk. Assn. (pres. 1978-79, Nat. Disting. Profl. award 1981), Assn. Rsch., Adminstrn., Profl. Couns. and Socs. (pres. 1986-87, award 1987), Am. Alliance Health, Phys. Edn., Recreation and Dance (Coll. and Univ. Adminstrs. Coun. Honor award 1986, R. Tait McKenzie award 1996), Soc. Pk. and Recreation Edn. (pres. 1974-75, award 1978), Ind. Pk. and Recreation Assn. (Outstanding Profl. award 1985). Avocations: golf, travel. Office: Ind U Sch Health Phys Edn & Rec Recreation Rm 111 Bloomington IN 47405

MOBLEY, WILLIAM HODGES, management educator, researcher, author, executive; b. Akron, Ohio, Nov. 15, 1941. BA, Denison U., 1963; PhD, U. Md., 1971. Mgr. employee rels. rsch. PPG Industries, Pitts., 1971-73; prof. U. S.C., Columbia, 1973-80; head dept. of mgmt. Tex. A&M U., College Station, 1980-83, dean. Coll. of Bus. Adminstrn., 1983-86, exec. dep. chancellor, 1986-88, pres., 1988-93; chancellor Tex. A&M U. Sys., College Station, 1993-94; prof. mgmt. Tex. A&M U., College Station, 1980-96; pres. PDI Global Rsch. Consortium, Ltd., Hong Kong, Dallas, London, 1996—; vis. fellow Cornell U., 1994, vis. prof. Hong Kong U. Sci. and Tech., 1995-97. Author: Employee Turnover, 1982, Advances in Global Leadership, 1999. Bd. dirs. Internat. Food and Agrl. Devel. and Econ. Coop., U.S. AID, 1992-94; mem. tri-lateral task force on N.Am. Higher Edn. Coop., USIA, 1993-95; trustee SIOP Found., 1998—, AMMA Found., Denison U.; mem. Pres. Bush's Commn. on Minority Bus. Devel., 1990-92, U.S. Com. of the Pacific Econ. Coop. Coun., 1995—; bd. dirs. Medici Med. Ctr., 1992—, Concept Tech. Ltd., 1999—. Sr. Fulbright scholar Found. for Scholarly Exchange, Republic China, 1978-79; recipient DAAD, Rep. Germany, 1984; Fellow NDEA U.S. Dept. of Edn., 1968-71. Fellow APA, Am. Psychol. Soc. Home: 4317 Fannin Dr Irving TX 75038-6234 Office: PDI Global Rsch Ltd 600 Las Colinas Blvd E Ste 1700 Irving TX 75039-5624

MOCANU, DIANA, Olympic athlete; b. Braila, Romania, July 19, 1984. Recipient Gold medal 100-meter backstroke, 200-meter backstroke Sydney Olympics, 2000; 3d pl. women's 100-meter butterfly, 6th pl. women's 200-meter backstroke European Championships, Istanbul, Turkey, 1999, 2d pl. women's 100-meter backstroke, 2d pl. women's 200-meter backstroke European Championships, Helsinki, Finland, 2000. Avocations: music, dance, gymnastics, swimming. Office: Romania Swimming Fedn, Str Maior Coravu Nr 34-36 2, Bucharest 73403, Romania*

MOCEANU, DOMINIQUE, gymnast, Olympic athlete; b. Hollywood, Calif., Sept. 30. Mem. Nat. Team, 1992-93, 93-94, 1994-95, 95-96, 1999; Competitions include U.S. Classic, 1991, 92, 93, U.S. Gymnastics Championships, 1992, Am. Classic, 1993, U.S. Olympic Festival, 1993, Coca-Cola Nat. Championships, 1993, 94, 95, 96, Am. Classic/World Championships, 1994, Am. Classic/Pan Am. Games, 1995, World Team Trials, 1995, U.S. Olympic Trials, 1996, John Hancock U.S. Gymnastics Championships, 1997, 98; mem. Olympic team, Sydney, Australia, 2000. Recipient Silver and Bronze medals World Championships, 1995, Gold medal team competition Olympic Games, Atlanta, 1996; placed 1st in balance beam U.S. Classic, Salt Lake City, 1991, 2d in balance beam jr. divsn. U.S. Gymnastics Championships, Columbus, 1992, 2d in all around, 1st team, vault, uneven bars and floor exercise Jr. Pan Am. Games, 1992, 1st in team and balance beam, 3rd in uneven bars Internat. Tournament of Jr. Women's Gymnastics, Charleroi, Belgium, 1993, 1st in all around, vault and team floor exercise, 3rd in uneven bars and balance beam jr. divsn. Coca-Cola Nat. Championships, Nashville, 1994, 1st in team all around, 1st in vault, 3rd in balance beam and floor exercise Am. Classic-Pan Am. Games Trials, Oakland, Calif., 1995, 1st in all around, 2d in floor exercise, 3rd in vault Coca-Cola Nat. Championships, New Orleans, 1995, 1st in all around World Team Trials, Austin, 1995, 1st in uneven bars, 3rd in balance beam Reese's Internat. Gymnastics Cup, Portland, 1995, 1st in all around, team and floor exercise, 3rd in vault and balance beam, 2nd in uneven bars Visa Challenge, Fairfax, Va., 1995, 3rd all around for team, 2d for team balance beam World Championships, Sabae, Japan, 1995; named USOC SportsWoman of Month, Apr. and Sept. 1995; named individual all-around finalist World Championships Team, 1997, gold medalist Goodwill Games, 1998. Avocations: swimming, reading, listening to music. Home: 5959 Fm 1960 Rd W Apt 1437 Houston TX 77069-4197

MOCHEL, MYRON GEORGE, mechanical engineer, educator; b. Fremont, Ohio, Oct. 9, 1905; s. Gustave A. and Rose M. (Minich) M.; m. Eunice Katherine Steinicke, Aug. 30, 1930 (dec. Dec. 1982); children: Kenneth R., David G., Virginia June. BSME, Case Western Res. U., 1929; MSME, Yale U., 1930. Registered profl. engr. N.Y., Mass., Pa. Devel. engr. nitrogen div. Allied Chem. Corp., Hopewell, Va., 1930-31; devel. engr. R&D dept. Mobil Corp., Paulsboro, N.J., 1931-37; design and devel. engr. gearing div. Westinghouse Electric Corp., Pitts., 1937-43; rsch. assoc. underwater sound lab. Harvard U., Cambridge, Mass., 1943-45; supr. of tng. steam turbine div. Worthington Corp., Wellsville, N.Y., 1945-49; prof. mech. engr. Clarkson U., Potsdam, N.Y., 1949-71; prof. emeritus Clarkson U., Potsdam, 1971—; lect. U. Pitts., 1938-43, N.Y. State U. Adult Edn., Wellsville, 1946-49, Oswego, 1965, N.Y. State High Sch. Enrichment Program, Potsdam, 1962-71; cons. Designers for Industry, Cleve., 1953, rsch. engr. Morris Machine Works, Baldwinsville, N.Y., 1954, design engr. Racquette River Paper Co., Potsdam, 1955. Author: Fundamentals of Engineering Graphics, 1960, Pre-Engineering and Applied Science Fundamentals, 1962, Fortran Programming, Programs and Schematic Storage Maps, 1971; co-author: (with Eunice S. Mochel) Funds For Fun, 1983, (with Donald H. Purcell) Beyond Expectations, 1985; contbr. articles to profl. jours. and on internet. Officer, vol. St. Lawrence Valley Hospice, 1983; pres. Mayfield Tenants Assn., 1989-91. Mem. ASME, Am. Soc. Engring. Edn. (advt. mgr. Jour. Engring. Graphics 1963-66, sec. 1966-67, high schs. liaison on engring. graphics 1962-65, awards com. chmn. 1965-66), Am. Assn. Ret. Persons (founder St. Lawrence County chpt., income tax counselor 1988-89, medicare/medicaid assistance program counselor 1988—, pres. 1989-90). Republican. Mem. Unitarian Universalist Ch. Home and Office: 931 Mayfield Dr Potsdam NY 13676-4222

MOCHIZUKI, KAZUHIRO, engineering researcher; b. Tokyo, May 3, 1963; s. Sakae and Kazue (Sekiguchi) M.; m. Kiyoko Asakura, Sept. 26, 1992; 1 child, Miho. B of Electronic Engring., U. Tokyo, 1986, M in Electronic Engring., 1988, D in Electronic Engring., 1995. Rschr. Ctrl. Rsch. Lab., Hitachi Ltd., Tokyo, 1988-99, sr. rschr., 2000—; vis. rsch. scholar electrical and computer engring. U. Calif., San Diego, 1999-2000; sr. rschr. Ctrl. Rsch. lab., Hitachi Ltd., Tokyo, 2000—. Contbr. articles to profl. jours. Mem. IEEE (sr.). Office: Ctrl Rsch Lab Hitachi Ltd, 1-280 Higashi-Koigakubo, Tokyo 185-8601, Japan

MOCHIZUKI, TAKESHI, artist, art critic; b. Japan, 1937; arrived in Spain, 1965, became Spanish citizen, 1989; BA in Lit., Gakushuin U. Tokyo, 1962; postgrad. in art and sci., NYU, 1963-64, postgrad. in govt. and internat. rels., 1964. Personal sec. to Prince Irakly Bagration (Royal Crown Prince in exile/Ga.), 1966-77; rschr., biographer, writer; treas. Madrid Assn. of Art Critics, 1996—. Author: Ramon de Zubiaurre, Artist and Man, 1981; contbr. articles to profl. jours.; works exhibited in shows, Spain, 1972—. Mem. Spanish Assn. of Art Critics, Internat. Assn. Art Critics.

MOCHIZUKI, YOHICHI, medical educator; b. Sapporo, Hokkaido, Japan, May 17, 1936; s. Toshimasa and Miyo (Maruko) M.; m. Sachiko Oomori; children: Tamaki, Takafumi, Chihiro, Ryusei. M, Sapporo Med. U., 1963, PhD, 1968. Med. diplomate. Asst. prof. Sapporo Med. U., 1968-71, instr., 1971-76, assoc. prof., 1976-88, prof., 1988—; bd. dirs. Inst. Med. Rsch. Sapporo Med. U., 1992-94, 97—. Contbr. articles to profl. jours. Mem. Japanese Soc. Pathology (councilor). Buddhist. Home: Midorimach 1-1-20-402, Minami-ku, Sapporo 005-0013, Japan Office: Sapporo Med U Dept Pathology, Cancer Rsch Inst/S-1 W-17, Sapporo 060-8556, Japan

MOCK, DAVID CLINTON, JR., internist; b. Redlands, Calif., May 6, 1922; s. David Clinton and Eithel (Benson) M.; m. Marcella Enriqueta Fellin, Nov. 13, 1952. A.B., U. So. Calif., 1944; M.D., M.H.D., Hahnemann Med. Coll., 1948. Intern Hahnemann Hosp., Phila., 1948-49; resident San Mateo (Calif.) County Hosp., 1949-51, 54, VA Hosp., Oklahoma City, 1954-55; research fellow in exptl. therapeutics U. Okla., Oklahoma City, 1956-57, L.N. Upjohn fellow, 1958, dir. exptl. therapeutics unit, 1959-62; dir., preceptorship program, 1968-76; assoc. prof. medicine U. Okla., Oklahoma City, 1963-72, prof., 1972-84, emeritus prof. medicine, 1984—, assoc. dean med. student affairs, 1970-76, assoc. dean postdoctoral edn., 1976-82, dir. continuing med. edn., 1980-83, dir. Transitional Yr. program, 1980-84, dir. History of Medicine program, 1982-84; assoc. mem. Faculty of Homeopathy Royal London Homeopathic Hosp., Eng.; pres., dir. Coachella Valley Fruit Co., Inc., Indio, Calif. Capt. USPHS, 1951-53; now ret. Fellow ACP; mem. Am. Fedn. Medical Rsch., N.Y. Acad. Scis. Unitarian. Home: 570 Alameda Blvd Coronado CA 92118-1617

MOCK, ROBERT CLAUDE, architect; b. Baden, Germany, May 3, 1928; came to U.S., 1938, naturalized, 1943; s. Ernest and Charlotte (Geismar) M.; m. Belle Carol Bach, Dec. 23, 1952 (div.); children: John Bach, Nicole Louise; m. Marjorie Reubenfeld, Dec. 20, 1964. BArch, Pratt Inst., 1950; MArch, Harvard U., 1953. Registered arch., N.Y., Conn., N.J., Nat. Coun. Archtl. Registration Bds. Arch. George C. Marshall Space Ctr., Huntsville, Ala., 1950-51; archtl. critic Columbia Sch. Architecture, N.Y.C., 1953-54; dir. facility design Am. Airlines, N.Y.C., 1955-60; founder Robert C. Mock & Assocs., N.Y.C., 1960—; Mem. Mayor's Panel of Archs., N.Y.C. Prin. works include: Shine Motor Inn, Queens, N.Y., 1961 (recipient 1st prize motel category Queens C. of C. 1961), temporary terminal bldg. Eastern Air Lines , La Guardia Airport, N.Y.C., 1961, cargo bldgs United Airlines and Trans World Airlines, Kennedy Airport, N.Y.C., Bridgeport (Conn.) Airport, 1961, Eastern Air Lines Med. Ctr., Kennedy Airport, 1962, ticket office Trans World Airlines Fifth Ave., N.Y.C., 1962, terminal bldgs. Eastern Air Lines and Trans World Airlines , La Guardia Airport, N.Y.C., 1963, 7 bldgs. Mfrs. Hanover Trust Co. , 1964-66, kitchen and commissary bldg. Lufthansa German Airlines, 1964, Ambassador Club, La Guardia Airport, 1964, Happyland Sch., N.Y.C., 1965, cargo bldgs. Alitalia and Lufthansa German Airlines, Kennedy Airport, 1965, FAA-Nat. Prototype Air Traffic Control Tower, 1966; Lufthansa German Airlines; Irish Internat. Airlines, El Al Israel Airlines, Varig Brazilian Airlines; passenger terminals Kennedy Airport, 1970; Swiss Air Cargo Terminal, Lufthansa German Airlines, cargo terminals El Al Israel airline cargo terminal, Kennedy Airport, 1972, passenger terminal Aerolineas Argentina, 1974, N.Am. hdqrs. Aerolineas Argentinas, N.Y.C., 1974, corp. hdqrs. Am. Airlines, 1977, N.Am. hdqrs. Varig Brazilian Airlines, N.Y.C., 1977, Norel-Ronel Indsl. Pk., Hollywood, Fla., 1979, N.Am. hdqrs. Irish Internat. Airlines , N.Y.C., 1979, corp. hdqrs. Bankers Trust Co., N.Y.C., 1980, cargo terminal Air India, cargo terminal Flying Tiger, Kennedy Airport, 1982, 2 flight kitchen bldgs. Ogden Food Corp., Kennedy Airport, 1984, 88 and LaGuardia Airport, 1987, Greenwich Assn. Retarded Citizens Sch., 1983, passenger terminal extension Varig Brazilian Airlines , 1985, 3 restaurants La Guardia Airport, 1987, residences Palm Beach, Fla., 1989-92, Bethesda, Md., 1993, 97, 98, 99, (named best custom residence in U.S., Profl. Builder Mag. 2000), Fenwick Island, Del., 1994, Potomac Falls, Md., 1995. Recipient Vol. of Yr. award United Way, 1984. Mem. Am. Arbitration Assn., Harvard Club, Admirals Cove Club. Office: 185 Byram Shore Rd Greenwich CT 06830-6909

MOCKARY, PETER ERNEST, clinical laboratory scientist, researcher, medical writer; b. Zghorta, Lebanon, Jan. 6, 1931; came to U.S., 1953; s. Ernest Peter and Evelyn (Kaddo) M.; m. Yvette Fadlallah, Aug. 27, 1955; children: Ernest, Evelyn, Paula, Vincent, Marguerite. BA in Philosophy, Coll. des Freres, Tripoli, Lebanon, 1948; MB, Am. U. Beirut, 1950, postgrad., 1950-52. Cert. clin. lab. scientist, Calif.; cert. clin. lab. scientist Nat. Certification Agy. Chief hematology unit VA Wadsworth Med. Ctr., West Los Angeles, Calif., 1956-81; CEO Phoenicia Trading Co., 1981-88; dir. Coagulation Lab. Orthopaedic Hosp., L.A., 1988-97; lab. supr. Westside Hosp., L.A., 1964-79; lectr. hematology UCLA, West Los Angeles, 1970-78.

Pres. World Lebanese Cultural Union, L.A., 1978-79. With U.S. Army, 1954-56. Recipient outstanding performance award lab. svc. VA Wadsworth Med. Ctr., 1972-76. Republican. Roman Catholic. Avocations: billiards, reading, classical music. Home: 3103 Gilmerton Ave Los Angeles CA 90064-4319

MOCKER, HANS WALTER, physicist; b. Teplice, Czech Republic, Feb. 22, 1929; came to U.S., 1960; s. Emil and Marie (Schubert) M.; m. Carol Virginia Vines, Feb. 13, 1981; children: Peter, Nancy. MS in Physics, Inst. Tech., Darmstadt, Germany, 1954; PhD in Physics, U. Innsbruck, Austria, 1959. Sr. rsch. scientist rsch. dept. Honeywell, Mpls., 1960-65, prin. rsch. scientist sys. and rsch., 1965-69, sect. chief sys. and rsch., 1969-78, prin. rsch. fellow sys. and rsch., 1978-93; Ctr. fellow Tech. Ctr.-Alliant Tech. Sys., Mpls., 1991-93; cons. Electro-Optics Laser Sys., Dothan, Ala., 1994—; physicist Farbenfabriken Bayer, Krefeld, Germany, 1959-60; mem. advanced group on electronic devices Undersec. of Def., Washington, 1977-78; presenter in field. Co-author: Design of Infrared and Laser Systems, 1981; contbr. articles to profl. jours. including Laser Focus, Applied Optics, Applied Physics Letters, IEEE Jour. Quant. Electr. Coach Minn. Soccer Assn., Mpls., 1981-83. Recipient H.W. Sweatt award, 1968, ir-100 award Indsl. Rsch. Mag., 1969, 77, Excellence in Oral Presentation, Soc. Automotive Engrs., 1993; named one of 7 Wonders of Engring., Minn. Soc. Profl. Engrs., 1970. Achievements include patents for apparatus for supervising proportion of magnetically active component in a fluid, for ring laser biased to permit two equal intensity transition frequencies to be generated in opposite directions, for optical system for laser doppler homodyne detection, for relaxation laser synchronizer for pulsed laser operation, for rapidly tunable laser, for method and means for removing claddings from optical fibers, for rapid wavelength switching of IR lasers with Bragg Cells, for laser doppler velocimeter using stable semiconductor or solid-state lasers, for scanning laser helmet mounted sight, for laser cavity helmet mounted sight, for solid-block homodyne interferometer, for look-ahead windshear detector by filtered Raleigh-scattered light. Avocations: skiing, travel, woodworking. Home: 204 Westbrook Rd Dothan AL 36303-2952

MOCKLER, ADELE, educator; b. N.Y.C., June 12, 1927; d. Max and Rose (Zipkin) R.; m. Nils E. Mockler, Feb. 26, 1954; children: P. Anna, Michael W. ABD, SUNY, Albany, 1979; BA, Hunter Coll., 1949, MA, 1957. Tchr. Putnam Valley Cmty., Putnam Valley, N.Y., 1963-67, Duanesburg Central, Delanson, N.Y., 1967-79; sales Northwestern Mutual Life, Latham, N.Y., 1980—. Pres. League of Women Voters Putnam Valley, 1966, Hunter Coll. Alumni Assn., Albany, 1990-95; chmn. Cong. Gates of Hearon, 1999—. Mem. CLU. Democart. Jewish. Avocations: book group, torah study.

MOCTEZUMA, EDGAR, chemical engineering educator; b. Cardenas, Mexico, Mar. 30, 1955; s. Manuel Moctezuma and Virginia Velazquez; m. Elisa Leyva; children: Elizabeth, Elena, Edgar. BSChemE, UASLP, San Luis Potosi, Mexico, 1978; MSChemE, Ohio State U., 1987, PhD in Chem. Engring., 1991. Quality control engr. UNIROYAL, Queretaro, Mexico, 1978-79; rsch. engr. HYLSA, Monterrey, Mexico, 1979-82; process engr. ASARCO, Chihuahua, Mexico, 1983-84; tchg. asst. Ohio State U., Columbus, 1984-91; faculty UASLP, San Luis Potosi, 1991—. Contbr. articles to profl. jours. Scholar Conacyt-Mexico, San Luis Potosi, 1991-92; fellow Fulbright-UCLA, 1998-99. Mem. AIChE, ACS, AMIDIQ-Mexico (nat. treas. 1996-98). Office: Univ San Luis Potosi, Sucorsal 3 Apt Postal 77, 78250 San Luis Potosi Mexico

MOCUMBI, PASCOAL MANUEL, prime minister of Mozambique; b. Maputo, Mozambique, Apr. 10, 1941; m. Adelina Mocumbi; 4 children. Grad. in medicine, U. Lausanne, Switzerland. Founding mem., head info. and propaganda dept. FRELIMO, 1963; elected to Mozambique People's Assembly, mem. cen. com., 1983; provincial health dir., prin. physician Sofala Province, 1976-80; min. health Govt. of Mozambique, Maputo, 1980-87, min. for fgn. affairs, 1987-94, prime min., 1995—. Office: Praça da Marinha, CP 272, Maputo Mozambique*

MOCZKO, JERZY ANDRZEJ, biophysicist, researcher, educator; b. Poznań, Poland, Feb. 18, 1951; s. Stefan Mirosław and Wanda Maria (Michejda) M.; m. Alina Elzbieta Wietrzykowska, Aug. 9, 1975. MS with honors, Jagiellonian U., Cracow, Poland, 1973; PhD, U. Med. Scis., Poznań, 1982, habilitation, 1990, assoc. prof., 1992; full prof., U. Med. Scis., 1998. Jr. asst. Inst. Physics, Polish Acad. Scis., Poznań, 1973-74, asst., 1974-75, asst. lectr. physics, 1975-77; lectr. biophysics U. Med. Scis., Poznań, 1977-82, tutor in biophysics, 1982-90, assoc. prof. biophysics, 1990-98, prof. biophysics, 1998—; head lab. computer sci., U. Med. Sci., Poznań, 1977—, plenipotentiary of rector, 1981—; cons. sci. coun. bd. Inst. Tech. and Med. Instruments, Zabrze, Poland, 1995—; cons. sci. coun. bd. Supercomputer and Network Ctr., Poznań, 1993—. Recipient 2d prize European Soc. Perinatal Medicine, 1986. Mem. Internat. Soc. Perinatal Obstetrics, Soc. Math. Sci. Application in Clin. Rsch., State Com. for Scientific Rsch., Polish Soc. Medical Physics. Roman Catholic. Achievements include applications of digital signal processing in frequency and joined time-frequency domain of fetal and neonatal heart rate signals, statistical and artificial inteligence methods of classification of power spectra. Fax: (48) (61) 8411-116. E-mail: jmoczko@usoms.poznan.pl. Home: Os Rusa 125/11, 61-245 Poznań Poland Office: Univ Med Scis, JM Dabrowskiego 79, 60-529 Poznań Poland

MODANESE, GIOVANNI, theoretical physicist, consultant; b. Bolzano, Italy, Aug. 16, 1964; s. Angelo and Ottorina (Pregnolato) M.; m. Nadia Oberhofer, Sept. 25, 1993; 1 child, Isabella. M Physics, U. Trento, Italy, 1988; PhD in Physics, U. Pisa, Italy, 1992. Rschr. MIT, Boston, 1993, Max-Planck Inst., Munich, 1994, 95, European Ctr. Theoretical Studies Nuclear Physics, Villazzano, Italy, 1997, 98; rsch. assoc. Calif. Inst. Physics and Astrophysics, Palo Alto, 1999-2000; vis. scientist MIT, Boston, 1996; spkr. in field. Contbr. articles to profl. jours. With Italian mil., 1989-90. Mem. A. Von Humboldt Found., I.N.F.N. Home: Via Villa 8, 39011 Lana Italy Office: ECT, 38050 Villazzano Italy

MODANO, MICHAEL, professional hockey player; b. Livonia, Mich., June 7, 1970. Right wing/ctr. Minn. North Stars, 1988-93, Dallas Stars, 1993—; player World Hockey League East All-Star Game, 1988-89, NHL All-Rookie Game, 1989-90, NHL All-Star Game, 1993; mem. Stanley Cup Championship Team, 1999. Office: Dallas Stars HockeyClub Inc Dr Pepper Star Ctr 211 Cowboys Pkwy Irving TX 75063-5931

MODE, VINCENT ALAN, research executive, computer scientist; b. Gilroy, Calif., May 25, 1940; s. Vincent Allan and Jewel (Clary) M.; m. Sue A. Oleson, Feb. 14, 1964 (div. Feb. 1975); 1 child, Nicolle A.; m. Jackie Sue Hill, Dec. 23, 1976. BA magna cum laude, Whitman Coll., 1962; PhD in Inorganic Chemistry, U. Ill., 1965; MBA, Golden Gate U., 1980. Chemist Lawrence Livermore Nat. Lab., Livermore, Calif., 1965-69, group leader, 1969-72, sect. leader, 1972-80, facility mgr., 1984-85, dep. assoc. dir., 1985-96; divsn. leader, prin. Alan Mode Assocs., Vancouver, Can., 1993—; exec. dir. B.C. Rsch., Vancouver, Can., 1980-84; B.C. Sci Council, Vancouver, 1982-84; mem. B.C. Research Council, Vancouver, 1984—. Also lectr. sci. presentations. Contbr. articles to profl. jours. Named one of Outstanding Young Men Am., 1969; Alfred P. Sloan Nat. Scholar Whitman Coll., 1958-62, Ford Teaching fellow Whitman Coll., 1960-62. Mem. Soc. Computer Simulation (chmn. northwest region, 1982-84, vice-chmn. W. region, 1985-86), Interactive Fin. Planning System Users Assn., Sigma Xi (pres. chpt. 1998-99). Avocations: birding, gardening. Home: 2610 Gapwall Ct Pleasanton CA 94566-4520 Office: Lawrence Livermore Nat Lab PO Box 808 Livermore CA 94551-0808

MODÉER, THOMAS, pediatric dentistry educator; b. Stockholm, Dec. 23, 1945; s. Owe and Bibbi (Winell) m. Ingrid Olofsson, Aug. 14, 1971; children: Henrik, Andreas. DDS, Karolinska Inst., Stockholm, 1970, PhD in Dentistry, 1976. Asst. prof. Karolinska Inst., Stockholm, 1977-83, prof., 1983—, dean dental sch., 1993-96. Editor: (textbook) Pedodontics: A Clinical Approach, 1991; mem. editl. bd. Internat. Jour. Pediatric Dentistry., 1991. Mem. Internat. Assn. Pediatric Dentists London, Nordic Pediatric Soc. (v.p. 1982-96), Internat. Assn. Dental Rsch., Found. Acta Odontologica Scandinavia (chmn. 1996-98, assoc. editor 1999—). Avocations: sailing, golf. Home: Karlavägen 20, 114 31 Stockholm Sweden Office: Karolinska Inst, Dept Ped Dentistry Box 4064, SE-14104 Huddinge Sweden

MODELL, STEPHEN MARK, medical researcher, educator; b. Detroit, June 22, 1958; s. Richard Martin and Sola Jane (Hamburger) M.; m. Wanpen Prasoptham, Jan. 14, 1988; 1 child, Marrisa Lynne. AB in Philosophy, Stanford U., 1980; MD, Med. Coll. Ohio, 1984; MS in Clin. Rsch. Design/Statis.Analysis, U. Mich., 1991. Asst. coord. The Resource for Pub. Health Policy U. Mich. Sch. Pub. Health, Ann Arbor, 1987-89; rsch. asst., dept. psychiatry U. Mich., Ann Arbor, 1989-90, rsch. assoc. Genome Ethics Com., 1992-94; rsch. assoc. Coun. Genetics and Soc. U. Mich. Dept. Health Mgmt. and Policy, Ann Arbor, 1995-98, rsch. dir. genetics policy, 1999—; mem. Pres.'s Coun., Med. Coll. Ohio, 1992—. Genome studies sect. editor Ultimate Reality and Meaning, 1995—; editor Studies in Biophilosophy, 1997. Recipient honorable mention Nellie Westerman prize competition in clin. rsch. ethics, Am. Fedn. Clin. Rsch., 1995. Mem. AMA, Am. Fedn. Med. Rsch., N.Y. Acad. Scis., Maimonides Soc., Internat. Soc. Study of Human Ideas on Ultimate Reality and Meaning (bd. dirs. 1994—, treas. 1999—). Avocations: book discussion groups, water sports, jogging, hiking, travel. Home: 3086 Deer Creek Ct Ann Arbor MI 48105-9664 Office: U Mich Sch Pub Health SPH-II HMP M3048 109 S Observatory St Ann Arbor MI 48109-2029

MODENA, STEFANO PAOLO EMILIO, financial executive; b. Ancona, Italy, Oct. 3, 1962; arrived in Spain, 1997; s. Mario and Caterina (Cimberle) M.; m. Ana Nadal de Bolos, July 16, 1988; children: Lea, Marc. MBA, U. Bocconi, Milan, 1986. Cert. auditor and economist. Sr. auditor Coopers & Lybrand, Milan, 1986-90; stock exch. reporter Montedison, Milan, 1990-92; contr. Alitalia, Rome, 1992-97; fin. dir. Albright & Wilson Iberica SA, Barcelona, 1997—. Author: Barcelona Olimpica, 1992. Mem. Bocconi U. Alumni Assn. (area leader). Avocations: golf, skiing. Home: Consell de Cent 377, 08009 Barcelona Spain Office: Albright & Wilson Iberica P I, Zona Franca Sector F c/43 n 10, 08040 Barcelona Spain

MODI, JAGDISH JAMNADAS, computer company executive; b. Kakamega, Kenya, Nov. 10, 1956; arrived in Eng., 1968; s. Jamnadas Gordhandas and Champaben (Khimji) M. BSc with honors, Aston U., Birmingham, Eng., 1978; postgrad. diploma, Cambridge (Eng.) U., 1979; PhD, London U., 1982. Research asst. Oxford (Eng.) U., 1983-84; sr. research assoc. Cambridge U., 1984—; mng. dir. Parallel Computing Corp., London and Cambridge, 1986—; dir. IDEA global, 1990—. Author: Parallel Algorithms and Matrix Computation, 1988; contbr. articles to profl. jours. Fellow Inst. Math. and Applications, Cambridge Philos. Soc. Home: 7 Rushey Close, Leicester LE4 7PT, England Office: DAMTP, Silver St, Cambridge CB3 9EW, England

MODI, TARUN KUMAR, distilling and manufacturing executive; b. Patiala, Punjab, India, May 6, 1968; s. Sudershan Kumar and Rani Sarup (Aggarwal) M.; m. Shivani Gupta, Feb. 3, 1995; 1 child, Aayush. Pre. engring., Punjab U., Patiala, India, 1987; BA, Punjab U., 1990, MA in Polit. Sci., 1992. Mgmt. trainee M/S Patiala (India) Distillers & Mfrs. Ltd., Punjab; dir. M/S Patiala (India) Distillers & Mfrs. Ltd., 1992-93, exec. dir., 1993-95, joint mng. dir., 1995—. Avocations: adventurous activities, arms and amunation. Home: Modi Bhawan, Passi Rd, Patiala Punjab, India Office: Patiala Distillers & Mfrs, Bahera Rd off Fire Brigade, Patiala Punjab 147001, India

MODI, VINOD, microbiologist; b. Baroda, India, May 10, 1929; s. Venilal N. and Vidya (Pratap) M.; m. Bharati Gandhi, Feb. 17, 1957; children: Mayuranki, Chaula. MSc, U. Baroda, 1951; PhD, Liverpool U., 1955. Scientific officer Hanna Rsch. Inst., Ayr, U.K., 1956; reader in biochemistry U. Baroda, 1957-60; rsch. assoc. U. Ill., Urbana, 1961-62; prof., head dept. microbiology Maharaja Sayajirao, Baroda, 1964-89, chief coord. biotech., 1986-89; vis. prof. U. Nagoya. Contbr. numerous articles to profl. jours. Pres. Soc. for Clean Envrion., 1984—, Heritage Trust 1994—, Swar Vilas, 1981—, Internat. Friendship League, 1980. Fellow Indian Nat. Scis. Acad.; mem. Assn. of Microbiologists of India (life), Soc. of Biol. Chemists of India. Avocations: listening to music, sports, group discussion, science education. Home: AALAP, 12-A Pratapgunj, Baroda 390 002, India

MODIGLIANI, FRANCO, economics and finance educator; b. Rome, June 18, 1918; came to U.S., 1939, naturalized, 1946; s. Enrico and Olga (Flaschel) M.; m. Serena Calabi, May 22, 1939; children: Andre, Sergio. D. Jurisprudence, U. Rome, 1939; D. Social Sci., New Sch. Social Rsch., 1944; LLD (hon.), U. Chgo., 1967; D. honoris causa, U. Louvain, Belgium, 1974, Istituto Universitario di Bergamo, 1979, Hartford U.; LHD (hon.), Bard Coll., 1985, Brandeis U., 1986, New Sch. Social Research, 1989; LLD, Mich. State U., 1989; D (hon.), U. Ill., 1990, U. Valencia, Spain, 1992; D in Managerial Engring. (hon.), U. Naples, 1998. Instr. econs. and statistics N.J. Coll. Women, New Brunswick, 1942; instr., then assoc. econs. and statistics Bard Coll., Columbia, 1942-44; lectr., asst. prof. math. econs. and econometrics New Sch. Social Rsch., 1943-44, 46-48; rsch. asso., chief statistician Inst. World Affairs, N.Y.C., 1945-48; rsch. cons. Cowles Commn. Rsch. in Econs. U. Chgo., 1949-54; asso. prof., then prof. econs. U. Ill., 1949-52; prof. econs. and indsl. adminstrn. Carnegie Inst. Tech., 1952-60; vis. prof. econs. Harvard U., 1957-58; prof. econs. Northwestern U., 1960-62; vis. prof. econs. MIT, 1960-61, prof. econs. and finance, 1962—, Inst. prof., 1970-88, Inst. prof. emeritus, 1988—; fellow polit. economy U. Chgo., 1948; Fulbright lectr. U. Rome, also, Palermo, Italy, 1955. Author: The Debate Over Stabilization Policy, 1986, Il Caso Italia, 1986, The Collected Papers of Franco Modigliani, 3 vols., 1980, 4th and 5th vols., 1989; co-author: National Incomes and International Trade, 1953, Planning Production, Inventories and Work Forces, 1960, The Role of Anticipations and Plans in Economic Behavior and Their Use in Economic Analysis and Forecasting, 1961, New Mortgage Designs for Stable Housing in an Inflationary Environment, 1975, (with Frank J. Fabozzi) Capital Markets: Institutions and Instruments, 1991, (with Frank J. Fabozzi) Mortgage and Mortgage-Backed Security Markets, 1992, (with Frank J. Fabozzi, Michael G. Ferri) Foundations of Financial Markets and Institutions, 1994, Le Avventure di un Economista: La Miarita, Le Miee Idee, La Nostra Epoca, 1999. Recipient Nobel prize in econ. sci., 1985; Cavaliere Di Gran Croce Repubblica Italiana, 1985, Premio Coltura for Econs., Repubblica Italiana, 1988, Premio APE award, 1988, Graham and Dodd award, 1975, 80, James R. Killian Jr. Faculty Achievement award, 1985, Lord Found. prize, 1989, Italy Premio Columbus, 1989, Italy Premio Guido Dorso, 1989, Italy Premio Stivale D'oro, 1991, Italy Premio Campione D'Italia, 1992, Premio Scanno, 1997; named hon. citizen of Town of Modigliana, Italy, 1993, Hon. Citizen of Town of Chiavari, Italy, 1996, Jan Timbergen Meml. Lect., Rotterdam, 1994; named honorary citizen of the Town of Chiavari, Italy, 1996. Fellow NAS, Am. Econ. Assn. (v.p. 1971, pres. 1976), Econometric Soc. (coun. 1960, v.p. 1961, pres. 1962), Am. Acad. Arts and Scis., Internat. Econ. Assn. (v.p. 1977-83, hon. pres. 1983—); mem. Am. Fin. Assn. (pres. 1981), Accademia Nazionale dei Lincei (Rome), Shadow Fin. Regulatory Com., Boston Security Analysts Soc. (hon.).

MODIS, THEODORE, technological forecaster; b. Florina, Greece, Aug. 11, 1943; s. Georges and Theodosia (Panayotidou) M.; m. Carole G. Moore, Feb. 11, 1972 (div. 1986); children: Yorgo, Thea. BS, Columbia Engring. Sch., N.Y.C., 1966, MS, 1968; PhD, Columbia U., 1973. Rsch. assoc. Columbia U., N.Y.C., 1968-73; rsch. fellow CERN, Geneva, Switzerland, 1973-76; asst. prof. U. Geneva, 1977-84; mgmt. sci. cons. Digital Equipment Co., Geneva, 1984-95; pres. Growth Dynamics, Geneva, 1995—. Author: Predictions, 1992, Conquering Uncertainty, 1998, An S-Shaped Trail to Wall Street, 1999. Mem. N.Y. Acad. Scis. (mem. adv. bd. technol. forecasting and social change), World Futures Studies Fedn. Avocations: music, philosophy. E-mail: tmodies@compuserve.com. Office: Growth Dynamics, 2 rue Beau Site, 1203 Geneva Switzerland

MODLIN, CHARLES TREVOR, physician, medical hypnoanalyst; b. Johannesburg, South Africa, Mar. 9, 1945; s. Jack and Ann (Meyerson) M.; m. Joan Susan Wason, Mar. 28, 1969 (div. Mar. 1980); children: Stevan Bradford, Melissa Cara; m. Beverley Joy Ferreira, Nov. 7, 1982; 1 child, Roderick Adam. MB, B of Surgery, U. Witwatersrand, South Africa, 1969. Author: Prisoners of Our Perceptions, 1999; contbr. articles to profl. jours. Vice chmn. South African Coun. for Alcohol and Drug Addiction Johannesburg Soc., 1981-87. 2d lt. South African Armored Corps, 1963. Recipient Cert. of Appreciation, Lions, South Africa, 1988, Continuing Med. Edn. Jour., South Africa, 1990. Mem. South African Soc. Clin. Hypnosis (diplomate, chmn. tng. 1995-99, vice chairperson 2000—), Am. Acad. Med. Hypnoanalysts, Endangered Wildlife Trust, Glendower Golf Club. Avocations: wildlife, golf, astronomy, biological sciences.

MODROW, HANS, German Democratic Republic government official; b. Jasenitz, Germany, Jan. 27, 1928. D Econs., Humboldt U., Berlin, German Dem. Republic, 1966. Apprentice locksmith, 1942-45; mem. Socialist Unity Party Germany, 1949—, 1st sect. East Berlin dist. com. Free German Yough Orgn., 1953-61; mem. East Berlin city coun. Socialist Unity Party Germany, Berlin, 1953-71, dep. to People's Chamber, from 1958, 1st sec. city dist. com. in Berlin-Köpenick, 1961-67; full mem. Cen. Com. Socialist Unity Party Germany, from 1967, head dept. agitation Cen. Com., 1967-71, 1st sec. Dresden dist. com., from 1973; chmn. in honour of party Cen. Com. Socialist Unity Party Germany, 1990—; chmn. Coun. Mins., Berlin, 1989-90; mem. parliament, 1990—; mem. European parliament, Brussels, Belgium. Chmn. People's Chamber Friendship Group, German Dem. Republic-Japan, from 1972; dep. chmn. German Dem. Republic-Japan Friendship Soc., from 1976. With German Army, World War II, prisoner of war. Decorated bronze, silver gold medals Fatherland's Merit Order, Karl Marx Order. Address: 1 rue de Malbeck 7/69, B-1000 Bruxelles Belgium*

MODWEL, PRADEEP BEHARI, agro-meteorologist; b. Etawah, India, Aug. 20, 1952; s. Jyoteswari Prasad and Krishna Kumari (Pradhan) M.; m. Sharad Jauhari, Nov. 27, 1982; children: Siddharth, Geetika. BSc, K.K. Coll., Etawah, 1971; MSc, D.B.S. Coll., Kanpur, India, 1974. Sr. computor scientist Indian Agrl. Statis. Rsch. Inst., New Delhi, 1975, scientist, 1975-81; scientist Indian Grassland and Fodder Rsch. Inst., Jhansi, 1981-91, scientist sr. scale, 1991—. Mem. Range Mgmt. Soc. India (life). Avocations: table tennis, cricket, social service, movies, playing cards. Home: 100/F Shiv Sagar, Balaji puram, Shirpuri Rd, Jhasi 284 003, India Office: Indian Grassland and Fodder, Rsch Inst/Gwalior Rd, 284 003 Jhansi India

MODY, ZIA JAYDEV, lawyer; b. Mumbai, India, July 19, 1956; d. Soli Jehangir and Zena Soli (Fozdar) Sorabjee; m. Jaydev Mukund Mody; children: Anjali J., Aarti J., Aditi J. BA in Law, Cambridge (Eng.) U., 1978; LLM, Harvard U., 1979. Bar: N.Y. 1980. Assoc. Baker & McKenzi, N.Y.C., 1979-83; pvt. practice Mumbai, 1984—. Mem. Local Spiritual Assembly of the Baha'is of Bombay, Mumbai, 1989—; dir. Advt. Stds. Coun. India, Mumbai, 1999—; trustee New Era H.S., Panchgani, 1997—, J.N. Petit Trust, Mumbai, 1998—, J.B. Petit H.S., Mumbai, 1998—. Mem. Willingdon Club. Bahai. Avocation: reading. Home: Westhill 27 Nepean Sea Rd, Mumbai 400 036, India Office: Chambers of Zia Mody, 16 Alli Chambers NM Rd, Fort Mumbai 400 001, India

MOE, HENRY STANLEY RAWLE, supreme court justice; b. St. James, Barbados, W.I., Apr. 18, 1935; s. Cecil Stanley and Odessa Marion (Marshall) M.; m. Constance Elizabeth DeLisser, May 25, 1963; children: Cecile, Michael, Vanessa. BA with honors, Durham U., Eng., 1958, Diploma in Edn., 1959; postgrad. in Social Adminstrn., Oxford U., Eng., 1962-63; Barrister, Lincoln's Inn, Eng., 1970; LLM, Leicester (Eng.) U., 1994. Lectr. Cornwall Coll., Jamaica, 1959-62; asst. master Grimsbury Secondary, Oxon, U.K., 1963-64; head dept. Tolworth Secondary, Surbiton, Surrey, Eng., 1964-69; asst. master Inner London Edn. Authority, Eng., 1969-70; edn. officer Ministry of Edn., Barbados, W.I., 1970-71; head law dept. Barbados Community Coll., W.I., 1971-78; legal cons. Internat. Bus. & Edn. Cons., U.K., 1978-79; prin. law lectr. Inner London Edn. Authority, U.K., 1979-85; pres., judge Indsl. Ct., Antigua, Barbuda, W.I., 1985—. Social sec. J.C.R. Henderson Hall, King's Coll., Newcastle-Upon-Tyne, 1958, 63, Capt. Brit. Coun. Overseas Student Cricket XI, N/CE, Tyne, 1956-59; pres. London W.I. Cricket Club, 1966-70; chmn. edn. com. Luton W.I. Assn., Bedfordshire, 1983-85. Fellow Inst. Commerce; mem. Brit. Inst. Mgmt., Chartered Inst. Secs. and Adminstrs., Assn. Law Tchrs., Internat. Bar Assn. Anglican. Avocations: gardening, walking, cricket, museums. Home: Paradise View Dr, Saint John's Antigua and Barbuda Office: Judge's Residence, PO Box 1722, Saint John's Antigua and Barbuda

MOE, JOHANNES, engineering educator; b. Modalen, Norway, Apr. 24, 1926; s. Knut and Maria (Mo) M.; m. Astrid Sigrun Christiansen, June 6, 1952; children: Kirsti, Bjarte, Heidi. MSc in Civil Engring., Tech. U. Norway, 1952, D in Engring., 1957, 61; D (hon.), Heriot-Watt U., Edinburgh, 1989. Asst. prof. Tech. U. Norway, Trondheim, 1952-53, rector, 1972-76, prof. ship structures, 1962-76; engr. Lindboe, Kristiansand, 1953-55; mgr. Norwegian Inst. Wood Tech., Oslo, 1959-62; vis. prof. U. Mich., Ann Arbor, 1967-68; pres. Found. for Engring. Rsch.(Sintef), Trondheim, 1976-89; sci. advisor Statoil, Stavanger, 1990-93; sci. adv. SINTEF, 1997, chmn. Norwegian Fisheries Rsch. Coun., 1972-79, chmn. Royal Commn. on Offshore Cost Escallations, 1979-80; chmn. co. assembly Norsk Hydro, Oslo, 1986-89. Author: Analysis of Ship Structures, Vol. 1-2, 1964-67, Pa tidens skanser, 1999; editor: Fra Kardemomme by til Cyberspace, 1995, Optimization and Automated Design, 1971. Bd. mem. Coun. Mem. Parliament and Scientists, 1977-91; mem. Royal Commn. on Bravo Blowout, 1977; chmn. Com. on Energy Rsch., Ministry of Energy, 1980-82; chmn. jury design competition Norway Main Airport, 1989; mem. Royal Com. on Norwegian Rsch. Coun. Sys., 1990-91, mem. Coun. Royal Norwegian Order of St. Olav, 1978-96, 2d lt. Norwegian Mil. Decorated Comdr. Royal Norwegian Order of St. Olav, 1976; recipient gold medal Norwegian Engring. Soc., 1990. Mem. Norwegian Acad. Engring. (hon., pres. 1993-98), Royal Norwegian Acad. Scis. and Letters (Gunnerus medal 1988), Nat. Acad. Engring. (fgn. assoc.), Russian Acad. Engring (hon. fgn. mem.). Avocations: slalom skiing, swimming. Home: Solhogdveien 18, 7021 Trondheim Norway Office: SINTEF, 7465, Trondheim Norway

MOE, RONALD CHESNEY, public administration researcher; b. San Diego, May 28, 1937; s. Chesney R. and L. Bernice (Weston) M.; m. Carolyn Carr, May 18, 1962 (div. Feb. 1974); children: Steven, Cynthia; m. Grace Tyler, Apr. 30, 1976. BA, Claremont Coll., 1959; MA, Columbia U., 1962, PhD in Pub. Law and Govt., 1968. Asst. prof. San Diego State U., 1967-70; sr. policy advisor Office of Econ. Opportunity, Exec. Office of the Pres., Washington, 1970-71, Cost of Living Coun., Exec. Office of the Pres., Washington, 1971-73; specialist govt. orgns. and mgmt. Congl. Rsch. Svc. Libr. of Congress, Washington, 1973—; cons. OECD, Paris, 1996—. Contbr. chpts. in books, articles to profl. jours. Mem. exec. bd. Congregational Chs. of Am., Milw., 1985-89. Capt. U.S. Army Res., 1961-63. Ctr. Study of Am. Govt. fellow Johns Hopkins U., Washington, 1993—; recipient ASPA Louis Brownlow award, 1988, 91, 95-96. Fellow Nat. Acad. Pub. Adminstrn.; mem. Acad. Polit. Sci., Cosmos Club (Washington), Phi Beta Kappa. Republican. Home: 4700 Connecticut Ave NW Apt 407 Washington DC 20008-5609 Office: Congl Rsch Svc Libr Of Congress Washington DC 20540-0001

MOE, STANLEY ALLEN, architect, consultant; b. Fargo, N.D., May 28, 1914; s. Ole Arnold and Freda Emily (Pape) M.; m. Doris Lucille Anderson, July 25, 1937; children: Willa Moe Crouse, Myra Moe Galther. BArch, U. Minn., 1936; D of Engring. (hon.), U. N.D., 1993. lic. architect several states; cert. Nat. Coun. Archtl. Registration Bds. Project architect several firms in Midwest, 1936-42; project architect U.S. Army Corps Engrs., Africa, 1942-43; ptnr. H.S. Starin, Architects & Engrs., Duluth, Minn., 1943-47; sr. ptnr. Moe & Larsen, Architects & Engrs., L.A., 1947-54; ptnr., gen. mgr., exec. v.p. Daniel, Mann, Johnson & Mendenall, L.A., 1954-71, corp. v.p., 1972-79; prin. Stanley A. Moe, AIA, L.A., 1979—; dir. design of major mil. projects in Eritrea, Sudan, Egypt, Yemen for Allied Forces, 1942-43; chmn. control com. DMJM & Assocs., dir. design prototype, tng. & operational facilities Titan I Intercontinental Ballistic Missiles Program USAF, 1958-63; project dir. Space Shuttle facilities Kennedy Space Ctr., 1973; project dir. for design of aircraft maintenance complex Iranian Aircraft Industries, 1978; project mgr. for design of major med. facility program Min. of Def. and Aviation, Saudi Arabia, 1975-76; project mgr. design of Boufarik Internat. Airport, Algeria, 1983. Pres. San. Fernando Valley Young Reps., 1952, Van Nuys (Calif.) Jaycees, 1950. Recipient Disting. Svc. award for cmty. svc. Van Nuys Jaycees, 1949, Sioux award U. N.D. Alumni Assn., 1985, Trustees Soc. award U. Minn., 1992; inducted into N.D. Entrepreneur Hall of Fame, 2000. Mem. AIA (Calif. coun.), Rotary, Delta Tau Delta. Republican. Presbyterian. Avocations: world travel, hunting, fishing, historic restoration, woodworking. Home and Office: 447 S Plymouth Blvd Los Angeles CA 90020-4706

MOECKEL, REGINA, research scientist; b. Bonn, Germany, Apr. 15, 1964; d. Wilhelm Friedrich and Irmentraut M. Diploma in Chemistry, U. of Cologne, Germany, 1987, U. of Cologne, 1991; PhD in Natural Sci., U. of Cologne, 1993. Tchr. U. Cologne, 1990-93, sci. asst., 1990-93; sci. co-worker U. Klinikum Mannheim, Heidelberg, Germany, 1994—; trainer MTA-Schule, Klinikum Mannheim, Mannheim, 1996-98. Contrb. articles to profl. jours; patentee in field. Mem. Gesellschaft Deutscher Chemiker, Deutsche Röntgengesellschaft. Mem. Evangelical Ch. Avocations: badminton, reading, photography. Office: U Heidelberg, Theodor-Kutzer-Ufer 1-3, 68167 Mannheim Germany

MOEEN, NADEEM, mechanical engineer; b. Rawalpindi, Punjab, Pakistan, Oct. 8, 1953; s. Ghulam and Tahira (Jabeen) Mohyuddean; m. Zeerak Farzana, Mar. 19, 1981 (dec. Dec. 1993); children: Omar, Osman, Farooq, Ibaad, Nafae; m. Waqar Fatimah, June 1, 1994; children: Fadzeela, Itteqa. B Engring. in Mech. Engring., Ned U. Engring. and Tech., Karachi, Pakistan, 1978. Site engr. M. Binladin Orgn., Abu Dhabi, United Arab Emirates, 1978-80; workshop mgr. M. Binladin Orgn., Dubai, United Arab Emirates, 1980; mgmt. trainee Albhar, Sharjah, United Arab Emirates, 1980-83; engring. instr. Allied Engring., Karachi, 1983-84; area plant mgr. Binladin Orgn., Medina, Saudi Arabia, 1984-87; dir. Karam Internat. (Pvt.) Ltd., Karachi, 1987-98, pres., 1998—. Designer arts and crafts (1st prize 1977). Mem. Pakistan Engring. Coun., Trade Leader Club. Avocations: fretwork, reading, designing. Office: Karam Internat 9-10 2d Fl, Haider Plz Rashid Minhas Rd, Karachi 75300, Pakistan

MOEHRING, FRED ADOLF, fastener distribution company executive; b. Bklyn., Nov. 4, 1935; s. Fred Henry Christian and Elsa Martha (Klein) M.; m. Marilyn Agnes Rieber, June 7, 1958; 1 child, Donna. Grad. high sch., Jamaica, N.Y. Salesman Miller-Charles and Co., Mineola, N.Y., 1956-63, Century Fasteners Corp., Elmhurst, N.Y., 1963-65; gen. mgr. Stewart Air Industries, Syosset, N.Y., 1965-70; salesman Supreme Lake Mfg. Co., Plantsville, Conn., 1971, Allmetal Screw Products Inc., Garden City, N.Y., 1971-72; cab driver Scull's Angels, Flushing, N.Y., 1972-74; gen. mgr. Empire Fasteners, L.I.C., N.Y., 1974-83, Mar-Lin Sales, Bklyn., 1983-97, Fred A. Moehring, Inc., Bklyn., 1998—. Mem. ASME, ASTM, NRA, ASM Internat., Soc. Automotive Engrs., Met. Fastener Distbrs. Assn. (pres. 1991-92), Steuben Soc. Am., United German-Am. Com. of U.S.A., Inc., German-Am. Steuben Parade Com. Republican. Lutheran. Avocation: golf. E-mail: fred35@qualityservice.com. Office: Fred A Moehring Inc 208 N 8th St Brooklyn NY 11211-2008

MOELBY, LARS, nephrologist, internist; b. Aalborg, Jutland, Denmark, July 14, 1956; s. Poul Joergen and Karen (Moelby) Jensen; m. Lone Joergensen, Aug. 22, 1987; children: Anne Cathrine, Jens Christian. Graduation, U. Aarhus, Denmark, 1985. Specialist in internal medicine, specialist in nephrology. Physician Dept. Internal Medicine, Dronninglund, Denmark, 1985-87; physician dept. hematology Aalborg Hosp., 1987-90, physician dept. nuclear medicine, 1991, physician dept. nephrology, 1992-97, chief physician dept. nephrolgoy, 1999—; physician dept. nephrology Odense U. Hosp., 1997-98. Contbr. sci. articles to profl. jours. Mem. Danish Soc. Internal Medicine, Danish Soc. Nephrology. Avocations: rock and blues music, painting, outings in the woods. Office: Aalborg Hosp, Dept Nephrology, 9100 Ålborg Denmark

MOELIONO, ANTON MOEDARDO, retired linguistics educator; b. Bandung, West Java, Indonesia, Feb. 21, 1929; s. Prawirohardjo and Maria Amat (Igno) M.; m. Cecile Soeparni Josowidagdo; children: Miriam Dian Pramesti, Isbia Nilam Paramita. Doctorandus, U. Indonesia, Jakarta, 1958, LHD, 1981; MA, Cornell U., 1965; LittD (hon.), U. Melbourne, Australia, 1995. Chair Indonesian dept. U. Indonesia, Jakarta, 1960-63, sr. lectr. faculty letters, 1973-82, prof., 1982-94, chair grad. program linguistics, 1987-96, chair Germanistic studies, 1991-94; dean Faculty Edn. Atma Jaya U., Jakarta, 1964-70; dir. Atma Jaya Rsch. Inst., Jakarta, 1974-86, 91-94, Nat. Ctr. for Lang. Devel. and Cultivation, Jakarta, 1984-89; governing bd. mem. Seameo Regional Lang. Ctr., Singapore, 1983-89. Editor: General Manual of the Perfected Indonesian Spelling, 1975, General Manual of Indonesian Terminology, 1975, Large Dictionary of Indonesian Language, 1988; author, editor: Standard Grammar of Indonesian Language, 1988. Founding mem. Atma Jaya U., Jakarta, 1960. Named knight Order of St. Gregory, Pope John Paul II, 1994, knight officer Order of Orange-Nassau, Queen Beatrix, 1996. Mem. Royal Dutch Inst. Linguistics and Anthropology, Linguistics Soc. Am., Linguistics Soc. Indonesia (vice chair 1975-78). Roman Catholic. Avocations: charity services, classical plays and music. Home: Jalan Kertanegara 51, Jakarta 12110, Indonesia Office: Atma Jaya Found, Jln Sudirman 51, Jakarta 12930, Indonesia

MOELJOPAWIRO, SUGIONO, plant breeder, researcher; b. Yogyakarta, Indonesia, Nov. 25, 1947; s. Moegihardjo and Soemirah (Wirosoekarto) M.; m. Asseta Suhatma, June 15, 1976; children: Aditya Anggoro-Adhie, Shanti Resmi-Anggari. BSc, Gadjah Mada U., Yogyakarta, Indonesia, 1970, Insinyur, 1973; MSc, U. of The Philippines, Los Baños, 1979; PhD, U. Ark., 1986. Jr. breeder Sukamandi (Indonesia) Rsch. Inst. for Food Crops, 1973-77, rice breeder, 1977-89; rschr. Ctrl. Rsch. Inst. for Food Crops, Bogor, Indonesia, 1989-95; rschr., head molecular biol. and gen. engring. divsn. Rsch. Inst. for Food Crops Biotech., Bogor, 1995-99, rsch. dir., 1999—; lowland rice program coord. CRIFC, 1986-89, biotech. program coord., 1990-95; leader team for drafting biosafety guidelines for planned release of GMOs, 1997—. Rockefeller Found. grantee, 1990, 93, 97, 99. Mem. Am. Soc. Agronomy, Internat. Soc. Plant Molecular Biology, Indonesian Soc. Agrl. Biotechnology (pres. 1997—). Avocations: easy music, cooking. Home: Jalan Cimanggu 7A Bogor, 16114 West Java Indonesia Office: RIFCB, Jalan Tentara Pelajar 3A Bogor, 16111 West Java Indonesia

MOELLER, ANDREAS, soccer player; b. Sept. 2, 1967. Midfielder Borussia Dortmund (Germany) Football Club, 1994—. European champion, 1996; recipient World Cup, 1998. Address: Westfalen Stadion, Postfach 10 05 09, 44005 Dortmund Germany*

MOELLER, FLOYD DOUGLAS, lawyer; b. Safford, Ariz., Aug. 16, 1949; s. Floyd Albert and Helen Lou (Posey) M.; m. Tyra Brown, Dec. 18, 1970; children: Kristin, Sam, John, Susan. BS in Police Sci., Brigham Young U., 1972, JD, 1977; MS in Mgmt., Lesley Coll., 1985, MA in Counseling Psychology, 1987; LLM in Tax, Washington Sch. Law, 1992. Bar: N.Mex. 1978, U.S. Dist. Ct. N.Mex. 1978, U.S. Dist. Ct. Ariz. 1978, U.S. Ct. Appeals (10th cir.) 1979 , U.S. Tax Ct. 1981, U.S. Supreme Ct. 1981, Navajo Nation, Hopi Tribe, Jicarilla Apache Tribe, White Mountain Apache Tribe, So. Ute Tribe, Ute Mountain Tribe, So. Paiute Coun., Ft. Belknap Indian Ct., Gila River Indian Ct., Mescalaro Apache Ct., S.W. Inter Tribal Ct. Appeals. Assoc. Wade Beavers & Assocs., Farmington, N.Mex., 1978-79; ptnr. Nunn & Moeller, Farmington, 1979; sole practice Farmington, 1979-80, 87—; ptnr. Moeller & Burnham, Farmington, 1980-87. Mem. exec. com. Better Bus. Bur. of 4 Corners, 1978, bd. dirs., 1978—; bd. dirs. Farmington Pub. Library Bd., 1979-86, San Juan Med. Found., San Juan Pub. Library Found., Halvorson House; chmn. local troop coms. Boy Scouts Am., Farmington, 1985—. Capt. USMC, 1972-75. Named diplomat Nat. Bd. Trial Advocacy, 1986. Mem. ABA, J. Reuben Clark Law Soc., Nat. Panel Consumer Arbitrators, Am. Arbitration Assn., N.Mex. Trial Lawyers Assn., N.Mex. State Bar Assn. (CLE, fee arbitration coms. 1985, pres. trial practice sect. 1988), Navajo Nat. Bar Assn., San Juan County Bar Assn., 4 Corners Inn of Ct. Republican. Mormon. Avocations: reading, poetry, gardening, knot tying. Office: PO Box 15249 Farmington NM 87401-5249

MOELLER, ROBERT CHARLES (BUD MOELLER), management consultant; b. Washington, Sept. 5, 1954; s. Charles Edward and Ann Joan (Federico) M.; m. Carol Elizabeth Buchanan, June 19, 1976; children: Melaine Elizabeth, Robert Kehne. BChemE, Ga. Inst. Tech., 1976; MBA, Harvard U., 1978. Cons. ERT, Concord, Mass., 1977-78; assoc. Booz, Allen & Hamilton, Bethesda, Md., 1978-81, sr. assoc., 1981-83; prin. Booz, Allen & Hamilton, San Francisco, 1983-88, v.p., 1988-92; mng. officer Asia/Pacific Energy Practice, Singapore, 1992-97; ptnr. Andersen Consulting, San Francisco, 1998—; chmn. bd. dirs. Nat. Capital YFC, Olney, Md., 1981-83. Contbr. articles to energy and bus. pubs. Chmn. bd. dirs. East Bay Youth for Christ, Concord, Calif., 1983-91; mem. Rep. Presdl. Task Force, Washington, 1984-91; advisor Montgomery County (Md.) Health Dept., 1981; mem. World Affairs Coun., San Francisco Mayor's Fiscal Adv. Com.; adv. YFC Internat., 1992-97; bd. dirs. Emerging Young Leaders. Mem. Am. Inst. Chem. Engrs., Mensa, Ferrari Owners Club, Sports Car Club of Am., Harvard Bus. Sch. Club (Singapore and San Francisco). Republican. Avocation: profl. auto racing. Address: 4555 Kingswood Dr Danville CA 94506-6034 Office: Andersen Consulting Spear St Tower 1 Market Plz Fl 37 San Francisco CA 94105-1196

MOELLER, SUSAN ELAINE, artist; b. Akron, Ohio, Jan. 27, 1949; d. Guy Raymond and June Elaine (Inherst) Walker; m. Robert Allen Moeller, Aug. 13, 1988. BFA, BA in Edn., Akron U., 1972. Art tchr., dept. head Manchester Sch. Sys., Akron, 1972-79; ad exec. The Repository, Canton, Ohio, 1979-81; art dir. Vic & Walt's, Akron, 1981-85; illustrator Collector's Marketplace Mag., Atwater, Ohio, 1983-85; freelance artist, graphic designer Akron, 1985-94; fine artist, co-owner Creative Images Studio, Cuyahoga Falls, Ohio, 1994-98, Nogal, N.Mex., 1998—; owner Paz de Nogal Gallery and Studio, Nogal, 1998—; co-owner Creative Images Assocs., Cuyahoga Falls, 1986-98; Nogal, N. Mex., 1998—; graphic cons. Advanced Analytical and Computational Solutions, Inc., Cleve., 1996-97, Akron Chess Club, 1989-97; art juror Cuyahoga Falls H.S., 1997; owner, organizer Paz de Nogal Fine Art Shows, 1998—. Artist, designer: (bd. game) Barnes Publishing, 1984; contbr. poetry and drawing to Cat Fancy Mag., 1994; illustrator: (mag.) Collector's Marketplace, 1983-85, (newspaper) Canton Repository, 1979-81; exhibited N.E. Ohio Fine Art Guild shows, 1996-97. Donor of fine art to various charities, Akron, 1996-98. Recipient Hon. Mention award Kent (Ohio) Art-in-the-Park Com., 1996. Mem. ASPCA, Humane Soc. U.S., Humane Soc. Summit County, Pet Ptnrs. Rescue City (Pet Angel 1997), Lincoln County Humane Soc., Creative Connection, Ohio Arts and Crafts Guild, Cuyahoga Valley Soc. Fine Arts, Lincoln County Soc. Artists. Avocations: antiques, lapidary arts, gardening, writing. Studio: Paz de Nogal PO Box 190 Nogal NM 88341-0190

MOELLERING, HELEN S., retired social worker; b. St. Elizabeth, Mo., Dec. 6, 1939; d. James Patrick and Mildred Irene (Rane) Howard; m. Robert Kenneth Moellering, Sept. 17, 1960 (dec. Jan. 1995); children: Michael, Carla. BS in Psychology with honors, Lindenwood Coll., 1976; MSW, St. Louis U., 1978; cert., Family Therapy Inst., St. Louis, 1992. Lic. clin. social worker, Mo. Social worker Divsn. Family Svcs., St. Charles and St. Louis, 1978-89; family preservation therapist Children's Svcs., St. Charles, 1990-97; primary mental health project worker Rochester (N.Y.) Sch. 7, 1998—; field instr. Washington U., St. Louis, 1989-97. Contbr. articles to profl. jours. Past leader Girl Scouts Am., Bowling Green, Ky., St. Charles Mo.; leader 4-H; vol. Sch. # 25, Rochester. Mem. Am. Assn. Marriage and Family Therapists, MAHBS (sec. 1992-94). Presbyterian. Avocations: studying classical piano, studying writing. Home: 33 Menlo Pl Rochester NY 14620-2717 Office: Sch # 7 Bryan & Dewey Rochester NY

MOELY, BARBARA E., psychology researcher, educator; b. Prairie du Sac, Wis., July 17, 1940; d. John Arthur and Loretta Ruth (Giese) M.; children: John Jacob Moely Wiener, David Andrew Moely Wiener. Student, Carroll Coll., 1958-60; BA, U. Wis., 1962, MA, 1964; PhD, U. Minn., 1968. Asst. prof. U. Hawaii, Honolulu, 1967-71; rsch. psychologist UCLA, 1971-72; asst. prof. Tulane U., New Orleans, 1972-75, assoc. prof. psychology, 1975-85, prof., 1985—, dept. chmn., 1992-96. Contbr. articles to profl. jours. Grantee U.S. Office Edn., Handicapped Pers. Preparation, 1977-80, Tulane U., 1973, 75, 77, 78, 83-84, Inst. for Mental Hygiene, City of New Orleans, 1983-84, 2000, Nat. Inst. Edn., 1983-84, La. Edn. Quality Support Fund, 1988, 89, 91, 92, 96, HUD, 1997—, Annenberg, 1997, DHHS, 1997—, U.S. Dept. Edn., 1999—. Mem. AAUP (v.p. La. conf. 1992-93, sec. 1993-97, v.p. 1998-2000, pres. Tulane 1992-94), APA, Soc. Rsch. in Child Devel., Am. Ednl. Rsch. Assn., Southwestern Soc. for Rsch. in Human Devel. (pres. 1986-88), Phi Beta Kappa (pres. Alpha chpt. La. 1981-82, sec. 1995-99). E-mail: moely@mailhost.tcs.tulane.edu. Office: Tulane Univ Dept Psychology New Orleans LA 70118

MOEN, BENTE ELISABETH, physician; b. Kongsvinger, Norway, June 6, 1956; d. Sverre and Agnes (Skotterud) Nytorpet; divorced; 1 child, Erik Moen. Cand. Med., U. Bergen, 1981, MD, 1991. Psychiatrist Solli, Bergen, 1983-84, gen. practice, 1984, neurologist, 1985-90; asst. prof. U. Bergen, 1990—, prof., 1996; with Divsn. Occupl. Medicine, Bergen, 1996; specialist in occupl. medicine, 1991—. Author: (books) Morbidity Among Seamen on Tankers, 1991, Handbook for BHT, 1993.; contbr. 100 articles to profl. jours. Mem. Internat. Com. Occupational Health. Avocations: painting, walks in the mountains. Office: Divsn Occupational Med, Ulriksdal 8C, N-5009 Bergen Norway

MOEN, JON PETER GUNNAR, research scientist; b. Härnösand, Sweden, Aug. 9, 1960; s. John O. and Britta H.M. M.; m. Elisabeth Darstedt, June 20, 1992; 1 child, Nora. BS, Umeå U., 1986, PhD, 1993. Asst. prof. Umeå U., 1995—; adj. faculty Idaho State U., Pocatello, 1996—. Contbr. articles to profl. jours. Mem. Ecol. Soc. Am., Brit. Ecol. Soc., Nordic Soc. of Okios. Office: Dept Ecology & Environ Sci, Umeå University, Umeå 901 87, Sweden

MOEN, OLE O., American studies scholar; b. Hell, Norway, Aug. 3, 1940; s. Odd Margido and Olga (Romuld) M.; m. Solveig Helene Solberg Moen, Oct. 10, 1970; 1 child, Stine Marit. MA, U. Oslo, 1971, U. Minn., 1974; PhD, 1978. Tchr. Nordby Jr. High, Jessheim, Norway, 1971-73; lectr. Lillehammer Sr. H.S., 1974-79; asst. prof. U. Oslo, Norway, 1979-90; assoc. prof., 1990—; owner, dir. AmFact, Lillehammer Norway, 1986—; exec. sec. Vaernes Flying Club, Norway, 1966-69; expert commentator Am. affairs Nat. Radio and TV; vis. fellow Inst. for Rsch. in Humanities, U. Wis., 1998; vis. prof. George Washington U., 1988. Contbg. editor Norway: Journal of American History; author: Inside the USA, 1994; co-author: Hands-On, 1996; co-editor: Frontiers and Visions: A Casebook of American Civilization Studies, 1996; contbr. articles to profl. jours. Dir. edn. Student Polit. Orgn., 1966-69. Fulbright grant, 1973-74, 76-77; fellow Norman Johnson Dewitt, 1977-78, Torske Klubben, 1973-74, 77-78, U. Minn.; grantee NEH, 1996. Mem. Orgn. Am. Historians, European Assn. for Am. Studies, Nordic Assn. for Am. Studies, Am. Studies Assn. Norway (v.p. 1998—), Phi Kappa Phi. Avocations: skiing instructor, flying instructor. E-mail: Ole.Moen@iba.uio.no. Fax: 4722856804. Home: Sidsel Sidserks VEI 9, N2615 Lillehammer Norway Office: Dept British & Am Studies, U Oslo PO Box 1003 Blindern, N0315 Oslo Norway

MOËNE, YVES PAUL, neurologist; b. Lyon, France, Jan. 16, 1941; s. Georges and Marie Therese (Bouvier) M.; m. Marie Claude Olivier, Feb. 12, 1969; children: Coralie, Cyril, Alexa. BS, Lycee Ampere Lyon, 1958, MD, 1969. Intern Hosp., Lyon, France, 1964-70; chief Clinic de Neurologie, Lyon, 1970-72, Svc. de Neurologie, Annecy, France, 1973—. Contbr. articles to profl. jours. Mem. Lions Club (pres. 1995). Office: Service de Neurologie, 1 Av De Tresum, 74000 Annecy France

MOENKE-WEDLER, THURID CORA, scientist, researcher; b. Jena, Thuringia, Germany, May 30, 1968; d. Horst Heinz Werner Moenke and Lieselotte Emilie Marie-Luise Born Blankenburg; m. Wolfgang Gerhard Wedler, Dec. 5, 1991; children: Christopher Martin, Stepha nie Maya, Franziska Denise. Diploma in chemistry, U. Halle, Germany, 1991; MS, U. Massach, 1994; PhD, U. Mass., 1999. Cert. rschr. in natural scis. Rschr. Sensobi Sensor GmbH, Halle, Germany, 1999—. Contbr. articles to sci. jours. Home: Rennbahnring 40, D-06124 Halle Germany

MOENS, GUIDO FRANS, epidemiologist, scientific director, educator; b. Aalst, Belgium, Mar. 30, 1949; s. Gustaaf and Godelieve De Smedt M.; m. Hildegarde Van Kerckhoven, Sept. 18, 1974; children: Thomas, Erik. MD, U. Louvain, Belgium, 1974, MPH, 1980, D Med. Scis., 1990. Various certs. in epidemiology and med. stats. Gen. practitioner Ain Defla (Algeria) Health Sector, 1975-77; rsch. asst. U. Louvain, 1977-84, assoc. prof., 1990—; lectr. Rega Sch., Louvain, 1983-88; occupl. physician, epidemiologist Occupl. Health Svc. for Employers, Louvain, 1988—, sci. dir., 1996—; lectr. in field.; scientific adv. coun. Flemish Ministry of Health, 1992—, ethical adv. com., 1994—. Contbr. over 120 articles to profl. jours.; mem. editl. bd. Archives Pub. Health; referee various internat. med. jours. including Internat. Jour. Epidemiology. Recipient Jean Van Beneden prize, U. Liège, Belgium, 1996. Mem. Internat. Commn. on Occupl. Health, Flemish Sci. Assn. for Occupl. Health (bd. dirs. 1997—). Avocations: jogging, playing guitar, biking. Fax: 32 16 400 236. E-mail: guido.moens@idewe.be. Office: IDEWE, Interleuvenlaan 58, B-3001 Leuven Belgium

MOERBEEK, STANLEY LEONARD, lawyer; b. Toronto, Ont., Can., Nov. 12, 1951; came to U.S., 1953; s. John Jacob and Mary Emily Moerbeek; m. Carol Annette Mordaunt, Apr. 17, 1982; children: Sarah, Noah. BA magna cum laude, Calif. State U., Fullerton, 1974; student, U. San Diego-Sorbonne, Paris, 1977; JD, Loyola U., 1979. Bar: Calif. 1980; cert. in internat. bus. transactions, bankruptcy and bus. rehab., and civil trial practice. From law clk. to assoc. McAlpin Doonan & Seese, Covina, Calif., 1977-81; assoc. Robert L. Baker, Pasadena, Calif., 1981-82, Miller Bush & Minnott, Fullerton, 1982-83; prin. Law Office of Stanley L. Moerbeek, Fullerton, 1984—; judge pro tem Orange County Superior Ct., Calif., 1984—; notary pub., lt. gov. 9th cir. law student divsn. ABA, 1979. Mem. Heritage Found., Washington, 1989—. Calif. Gov.'s Office scholar, 1970; recipient Plaque of Appreciation, Fullerton Kiwanis, 1983. Mem. Calif. Assn. Realtors (referral panel atty. 1985—), Orange County Bar Assn. (Coll. of Trial Advocacy 1985), Calif. C. of C., Phi Kappa Phi. Roman Catholic. Avocations: history, politics, sports. Office: 1370 N Brea Blvd Ste 210 Fullerton CA 92835-4128

MOERDLER, CHARLES GERARD, lawyer; b. Paris, Nov. 15, 1934; came to the U.S., 1946, naturalized, 1952; s. Herman and Erna Anna (Brandwein) M.; m. Pearl G. Hecht, Dec. 26, 1955; children: Jeffrey Alan, Mark Laurence, Sharon Michele. BA, L.I.U., 1953; JD, Fordham U., 1956. Bar: N.Y. 1956, U.S. Supreme Ct. 1962. Assoc. Cravath, Swaine & Moore, N.Y.C., 1956-65; spl. counsel coms. City of N.Y. and judiciary N.Y. State Assembly, 1960-61; commr. bldgs. City of N.Y., 1966-67; sr. ptnr., chmn. litigation dept. Stroock & Stroock & Lavan, N.Y.C., 1967—; bd. dirs., gen. counsel, dir. N.Y. Post Co., Inc., 1987-92; cons. housing, urban devel. and real estate to Mayor of N.Y.C., 1967-73; mem. com. on character and fitness of applicants for admission to Bar, Appellate divsn. 1st Dept., N.Y., 1977—, vice chmn. 1998—; mem. disciplinary com. (policy com.) appellate divsn. 1st Dept., N.Y., 1998—, commr. N.Y. State Ins. Fund, 1978-97, vice chmn., 1986-94, chmn., 1995-97; mem. Mayor's Com. on Judiciary, 1994—; mem. N.Y.C. Housing Devel. Corp., 1997—; bd. dirs. N.Y.C. Residential Mortgage Ins. Corp., 1997—; chmn. bd. dirs. Bank Austria Creditanstalt Am.; mem. N.Y.C. Bd. Collective Bargaining, 2000—. Mem. editorial bd. N.Y. Law Jour., 1985—; assoc. editor Fordham Law Rev., 1956. Asst. dir. Rockefeller nat. presdl. campaign com., 1964; adv. bd. Sch. Internat. Affairs Columbia U., 1977-80; bd. govs. L.I.U., 1966, trustee, 1985-91; chmn. Cmty. Planning Bds. 8 and 14, Bronx County, 1977-78; nat. bd. govs. Am. Jewish Congress, 1966; bd. overseers Jewish Theol. Sem. Am., 1993-95; trustee St. Barnabas Hosp., Bronx, N.Y., 1985—. Recipient Walker Metcalf award L.I. U., 1966. Mem. Am. Bar Assn., N.Y. State Bar Assn., N.Y. County Lawyers Assn., Internat. Bar Assn., Assn. of Bar of City of N.Y., Free Sons of Israel, World Trade Ctr. Club, Metro. Club. Home: 7 Rivercrest Rd Bronx NY 10471-1236 Office: Stroock Stroock & Lavan 7 Hanover Sq New York NY 10004-2616

MOERS, JOYCE ANN, bookkeeper, day camp administrator; b. Evansville, Ind., Sept. 4, 1956; d. Lawrence Burns and Virginia Frances London; m. John Michael Moers, June 7, 1980; children: Michael J., Rachel N. Legal sec., Lockyear Bus. Bookkeeper Reitz Drug Store, Evansville, Ind., 1970-75; plant mgr. sec. Carhartt Mfg., Evansville, 1975-76; bookkeeper, day camp adminstr. Burdette Park, Evansville, 1976—, day camp adminstr., 1989—. Recipient County Achievement award Ind. Assn. Counties, Vanderburgh County, 1992; grantee Mead Johnson, Evansville, 1992—. Mem. Nat. Assn. Concessionaires, Ind. Assn. Sch. Age Child Care (bd. mem. 1996-98), Evansville 4-C, Go-Fishin. Roman Catholic. Avocations: camping, family activities, walking. E-mail: broke4evr@dellnet.com. Office: Burdette Park 5301 Nurrenbern Rd Evansville IN 47712-8534

MOERSCHEL, BLANCHE LENORE, pianist, composer, educator; b. Oak Park, Ill., Dec. 2, 1915; d. Henry Arnold and Estelle Redd Hollnagel; m. Eugene Moerschel, Apr. 17, 1943; children: Richard, Paul, Eugene, Joel, Daniel. MusB in Composition, Cosmopolitan Sch. Music, Chgo., 1940, MusB in Piano, 1941; postgrad., U. Wis., Stevens Point, 1979-83. Instr. piano, theory, and organ, collegiate dept. Cosmopolitan Sch. Music, 1941-43; pianist Oak Park Playground, Village of Oak Park, 1955-58; dir. music Timothy Christian Grade Sch., Cicero, Ill., 1958-72; pvt. tchr. piano, theory, and organ Waupaca, Wis., 1974-98; accompanist U. Wis., 1981-95. Composer sonatas for cello, suite for violin and piano, songs; writer poetry, pub. in Nat. Libr. Poetry. Charter mem. Rural Hist. Soc.; organist Christian Ch., Oak Park, 1936-38, Euclid Ave. Meth. Ch., Oak Park, 1932-35, Willard Meth. Ch., Oak Park, 1939-43, Berean Bible Students Ch., Cicero, Ill., 1954-72. Mem. Nat. Music Tchrs. Assn., Wis. Music Tchrs. Assn., Wis. Alliance for Composers (charter, performing). Avocations: writing poetry, prose, journals, Bible study. Home and Office: N1637 County K Waupaca WI 54981

MOESSNER, JOERG MANFRED, law educator, tax court judge; b. Cologne, Germany, Oct. 1, 1941; s. Erich and Margret (Kriegelmann) M.; m. Helgard Wolff, Feb. 23, 1967; children: Stephan, Jutta. Abitur, U. Hoelderlin, Cologne, 1961; JD, U. Cologne, 1967; 1st law exam., Cologne, 1965; 2d law exam., Duesseldorf, Germany, 1969. Asst. U. Cologne, 1969-73; prof. internat. law Univ. Armed Forces, Hamburg, Germany, 1973-83; prof. tax law U. Osnabrück, Germany, 1983-2000; judge Tax Ct., Hannover, Germany, 1986-2000; dir. Osnabrück Inst. Tax Law, 1987—; vis. prof. U. Stockholm, 1992, U. Tilburg, The Netherlands, 1996—, Sorbonne, Paris, 1997—, U. Vienna, 1997—; vis. scholar NYU, 1999—; chmn. European Assn. Tax Law Profs., 1999. Author 8 books on constnl., internat., and tax law; contbr. over 100 articles to various internat. legal jours. Mem. Internat. Fiscal Assn. (permanent sci. com.), Am. Soc. for Internat. Law, Internat. Law Assn., Deutschen Staatsrechtslehrer, Deutsche Gesellschaft für Völkerrecht. Avocation: music. Home: Uhlandstr 53, D-49134 Wallenhorst Germany Office: Inst fur Finanz, U Steuerrecht Martinistr 10, D-49069 Osnabrück Germany

MOEZI, AMIR-NASER, neuropsychiatrist; b. Tehran, Iran, June 28, 1932; s. Karam and Aziz Moezi; m. Fariba Alizadeh, Feb. 15, 1981; children: Amir-Mansour, Amir-Masoud. Gen. practitioner, Med. Coll., 1952, neurology, 1958, neuropsychiatry, 1960; neurophysiology, Med. Coll./Inst. of Neurology, 1970. Diplomate Neuropsychiatry, Neurophysiologist. Asst. prof. Tehran U., 1958-61, assoc. prof., 1961-64; cons., treas. Iran-Neuropsychiatry Soc., Tehran, 1963-79; advisor, rschr. Iran Bur. for Retarded and Gifted Children, Tehran, 1959-79; rschr. Iran Neuropsychiatry Soc., Tehran, 1979-97; counsellor Iran Mental Health Orgn., Tehran, 1969-81, John F. Kennedy Ctr. for Retarded Children, Tehran, 1965-75; programming advisor Com. of Mental Health Broadcasting, Tehran, 1965-70. Author: Psychoanalysis of Famous Persian Poets and European Writers, 1967; contbr. articles to profl. jours.; co-editor Mental Health Jour., 1965-79. Columnist, polit. interpretor Tehran Local Newspapers, 1960-80. Mem. Mental Health, R.S.H., Psychiatry Soc. Avocations: chess, mountain climbing, penmanship, swimming. Home: Hormozan St Saadi Tower, Shahrak Gharb, Tehran Iran Office: 37-32 Hashemi Far St, Amirakram Valiasr Ave, Tehran Iran

MOFFAT, SIR BRIAN, steel company executive; b. Jan. 6, 1939; s. Festus and Agnes Moffat; m. Jacqueline Mary Cunliffe, 1964; 2 children. With Peat Marwick Mitchell & Co., 1961-68; with Brit. Steel plc (formerly Brit. Steel Corp.), London, 1968—, mng. dir., fin., 1986-91, chief exec., chmn., 1992-99; chmn. Corus Group plc (formerly Brit. Steel plc), London, 1999; non-exec. dir. Enterprise Oil plc, 1996, HSBC Holdings plc, 1998; mem. Ct. of Bank of Engl., 2000. Avocations: farming, fishing, shooting. Office: Corus Group plc, 15 Gt Marlborough St, London W1V 2BS, England*

MOFFAT, DAVID ANDREW, otologist, otoneurosurgeon, consultant; b. Cardiff, Glamorgan, South Wales, June 27, 1947; s. James Graham and Myra Constance (Paul) M.; m. Jane Elizabeth Warwick; children: Claire, Simon, Mark. BSc, U. London, 1968, MB, BChir, 1971; MA, U. Cambridge, 1985. Cons. surgeon Westminster Hosp., London, 1981-82, Addenbrooke's Hosp., Cambridge, Eng., 1982—; lectr. U. Cambridge, 1982—; Brit. rep. Internat. Fedn. Otorhinolaryngol. Soc., 1996—; chmn. Intercollegiate Faculty Bd. in Otolaryngology, 1998—. Author: Recent Advances in Otolaryngology, vol. 7, 1995; contbr. articles to profl. jours. Fellow Royal Coll.

Surgeons, Royal Soc. Medicine Eng. (treas. otology sect. 1993—); mem. European Acad. Otology and Otoneurosurgery (founder). Avocations: golf, music, theatre, motor sports, skiing. Home: Millington Lodge, 3 Millington Rd Newnham, Cambridge CB3 9HW, England Office: Addenbrookes Hosp Clinic 10, Hills Rd, Cambridge CB2 2QQ, England

MOFFAT, MARYBETH, automotive company executive; b. Pitts., July 25, 1951; d. Herbert Franklin and Florence Grafe (Knerem) M.; m. Brian Francis Soulier, Nov. 30, 1974 (div.). BA, Carroll Coll., 1973. Indsl. engring. technician Wis. Centrifugal Co., Waukesha, Wisc., 1976-77; indsl. engr. Utility Products, Inc., Milw., 1977-79; mgr. indsl. engring. Bear Automotive (divsn. SPX Corp.), Bangor, Pa., 1980-90; program mgr. Toyota Johnson Controls, Inc. Automotive Systems Group, 1990—. Group home house parent Headwaters Regional Achievement Ctr., Lake Tomahawk, Wis., 1974. Mem. Am. Inst. Indsl. Engrs., MTM Assn. for Standards Rsch., Indsl. Mgmt. Soc., Alpha Gamma Delta (standards chmn. 1971-72). Republican. Methodist. Avocations: skiing, horseback riding, swimming, reading. Office: Johnson Controls Inc Automotive Systems Group One Quality Dr Georgetown KY 40324-2011

MOFFATT, HENRY KEITH, applied mathematician, educator; b. Edinburgh, Scotland, Apr. 12, 1935; s. Frederick Henry and Emmeline Marchant (Fleming) M.; m. Katharine Stiven, Dec. 17, 1960; children: Fergus (dec. 1987), Peter, Hester, Penelope. BSc, Edinburgh U., 1957; BA, Cambridge U., 1959, PhD, 1962, ScD, 1987; DSc (hon.), Ecole Nat. Polytech. Grenoble, 1986, SUNY, 1990. Lectr. Cambridge (Eng.) U., 1965-77, prof., 1980—; prof. Bristol (Eng.) U., 1977-80, Ecole Polytechnique, Paris, 1992-99; dir. Isaac Newton Inst., Cambridge, 1996—. Author: Magnetic Field Generation in Electrically Conducting Fluids, 1978; co-editor: Topological Aspects of the Dynamics of Fluids and Plasmas, 1991; editor Jour. Fluid Mechanics, 1966-83; contbr. articles to profl. jours. Officier des Palmes Academiques, France, 1998. Fellow Royal Soc., Royal Soc. Edinburgh; mem. Royal Netherlands Acad. (fgn. mem.), Acad. des Scis. (Paris). Office: Isaac Newton Inst Math Sci, 20 Clarkson Rd, Cambridge CB3 0EH, England

MOFFATT, JOYCE ANNE, performing arts executive; b. Grand Rapids, Mich., Jan. 3, 1936; d. John Barnard and Ruth Lillian (Pellow) M. BA in Lit., U. Mich., 1957, MA in Theatre, 1960; HHD (hon.), Profl. Sch. Psychology, San Francisco, 1991. Stage mgr., lighting designer Off-Broadway plays, costume, lighting and set designer, stage mgr. stock cos., 1954-62; nat. subscription mgr. Theatre Guild/Am. Theatre Soc., N.Y.C., 1965-67; subscription mgr. Theatre, Inc.-Phoenix Theatre, N.Y.C., 1963-67; cons. N.Y.C. Ballet and N.Y.C. Opera, 1967-70; asst. house mgr. N.Y. State Theater, 1970-72; dir. ticket sales City Ctr. of Music and Drama, Inc., N.Y.C., 1970-72; prodn. mgr. San Antonio's Symphony/Opera, 1973-75; gen. mgr. San Antonio Symphony/Opera, 1975-76, 55th St. Dance Theater Found., Inc., N.Y.C., 1976-77, Ballet Theatre Found., Inc./Am. Ballet Theatre, N.Y.C., 1977-81; v.p. prodn. Radio City Music Hall Prodns., Inc., N.Y.C., 1981-83; artist-in-residence CCNY, 1981—; propr. mgmt. cons. firm for performing arts N.Y.C., 1983—; exec. dir. San Francisco Ballet Assn., 1987-93; mng. dir. Houston Ballet Assoc., 1993-95; gen. mgr. Chgo. Music and Dance Theater, Inc., 1995—; cons. Ford Found., N.Y. State Coun. on Arts, Kennedy Ctr. for Performing Arts.; mem. dance panels N.Y. State Coun. on Arts, 1979-81; mem. panels for Support to Prominent Orgns. and Dance, Calif. Arts Coun., 1988-92. Appointee San Francisco Cultural Affairs Task Force, 1991; chmn. bd. dirs. Tex. Inst. for Arts in Edn., 1994—; trustee Internat. Alliance of Theatrical Stage Employees Local 16 Pension and Welfare Fund, 1991-94; bd. dirs. Rudolf Nureyev Dance Found., Chgo., 1998—. Mem. Assn. Theatrical Press Agts. and Mgrs., Actors Equity Assn., United Scenic Artists Local 829, San Francisco Visitors and Conv. Bur. (bd. dirs.), Argyle Club (San Antonio). Office: Chicago Music & Dance Theater Mezz Level 203 N La Salle St Chicago IL 60601-1210

MOFFATT, MICHAEL ALAN, lawyer; b. Indpls., Feb. 22, 1964; s. James L. Kelso and Peggy A. Tackett; m. Nancy Norman, Sept. 23, 1989; children: Patricia Margaret, Michael Alan, Nicole Elizabeth, Michelle Ann. BA in Polit. Sci., Depauw U., 1986; JD, Ind. U., 1989. Bar: Ind. 1989, U.S. Dist. Ct. (so. and no. dists.) Ind. 1989, U.S. Ct. Appeals (7th cir.) 1991, U.S. Supreme Ct., 1999. Law clk., assoc. White & Raub, Indpls., 1987-94; assoc. Wooden McLaughlin & Sterner, Indpls., 1994-95, Barnes & Thornburg, Indpls., 1995—; lectr. litigation, paralegal program, Ind. U./Purdue U., Ind. CLE Forum & labor/employmemt seminars. Contbr. articles to legal jours. Cons. pediatric ethics com. Meth. Hosp., Indpls., 1990-92; co-chmn. Keep Am. Beautiful, Greencastle, Ind., 1986, bd. dirs., sec., 1990-94; mem. devel. control com. Geist Harbors Property Owners' Assn., Indpls., 1993-94, cons., 1994, pres., 1997—; winners cir. mentor U.S. Auto Club. Mem. ABA (labor and employment sect.), Fed Bar Assn., Ind. Bar Assn., Indpls. Bar Assn. (exec. coun. labor law sect., vice chmn.), Exch. Club (pres.-elect 1997-98, pres. 1998-99). Avocations: golf, basketball, war gaming, softball. Office: Barnes & Thornburgg 11 S Meridian St Indianapolis IN 46204-3535

MOFFETT, DONALD R., artist, retired sales and marketing executive; b. Tacoma, Wash., July 29, 1924; s. Donald Romaine and Gundrieda (Cottrell) M.; m. Mary Warren, Dec. 29, 1953; children: Donald W., James S. Sales rep. IBM, N.Y.C. and Poughkeepsie, N.Y., 1944-49; v.p. Great Bull Mkts., Kingston, N.Y., 1949-50; sales rep., dist. mgr. Varco, various cities, 1950-60; saleesman, v.p. sales Wallace Computer Supplies, Chgo., N.Y.C., 1960-75; v.p. mktg., graphics divsn. Am. Std., Balt., 1975-77; mgr., v.p. nat. accts. Varco, Chgo., 1977-87; cons. Chgo., Nantucket, Mass., 1987-88; self-employed cons., Siasconset, Mass., 1987-88. Bd. dirs. Ecumenical Inst., Inst. Cultural Affairs, 1967-92; bd. dirs. Hospice of Nantucket. With Brit. 8th Army, 1942-44. Avocations: art, history, tennis, jogging, walking. Winter home: PO Box 425 Siasconset MA 02564-0425

MOFFETT, FRANK CARDWELL, architect, civil engineer, real estate developer; b. Houston, Dec. 9, 1931; s. Ferrell Orlando and Jewell Bernice (Williams) M.; m. Annie Doris Thorn, Aug. 1, 1952 (div.); children: David Cardwell (dec.), Douglas Howard; m. Darlene Adele Alm Sayan, June 7, 1985 (div.); m. Vicki Lynn Schultz Harris, May 1, 1999. BArch, U. Tex., 1958. Registered arch.; profl. engr.; cert. Nat. Council Archtl. Registration Bds., U.S. Dept. Def., Fallout Shelter Analysis, environ. engring. Arch. Seattle, Harmon, Pray & Dietrich, Arnold G. Gangnes, Ralf E. Decker, Roland Terry & Assocs., 1958-64; ptnr. Heideman & Moffett, AIA, Seattle, 1964-71; chief arch. Wash. State Dept. Hwys., Olympia, 1971-77, Wash. State Dept. Transp., Olympia, 1977-87; owner The Moffett Co., Olympia, WA, 1987-90, pres., 1991—; adv. Wash. State Bldg. Code Counc., 1975-95, instr. civil engrng. tech., Olympia Tech. Commty. Coll., 1975-77; adv. mem. archtl. barriers subcom. Internat. Conf. Building Ofcls.; founder, treas. T.A.A., Inc., P.S., 1988; presenter in field. Archtl. works include hdqrs. Gen. Telephone Directory Co., Everett, Wash., 1964; Edmonds Unitarian Ch., 1966; tenant devel. Seattle Hdqrs. Office, Seattle First Nat. Bank, 1968-70; Wash. State Dept. Transp. Area Hdqrs. Offices, Mt. Vernon, Selah, Raymond, Colfax and Port Orchard 1973-87; Materials Lab., Spokane, Wash., 1974; Olympic Meml. Gardens, Tumwater, Wash., 1988, City Anacortes emergency power stas., 1989, L. Albert Residence, 1990, F. Gasperetti Residence, 1991; archtl. barriers cons. State of Alaska, 1978, State of Wash., 1972-94. Co-author: An Illustrated Handbook for Barrier-Free Design, 2nd edit., 1985, 3rd edit., 1987, 4th Edit., 1989, Accessibility Design for All, 1992, 2nd edit., 1995, 3d edit., 1998; Housing and Building Accessibility: The Law in Washington, 1992. Chmn. Planning Commn. of Mountlake Terr., Wash., 1963, 64, mem., 1961-67; mem. State of Wash. Govs. Task Force on Wilderness, 1972-75, Heritage Park Task Force, Olympia, Wash., 1986—; trustee Cascade Symphony Orch., 1971; incorporating pres. United Singles, Olympia, 1978-79; capt. CAP, fin. ofcr. Olympia Squadron; mem. nat. panel profl. advisors to Nat. Multiple Sclerosis Soc., 1993—; bd. dirs. Wash. Coalition Citizens with Disabilities; expert witness Ams. with Disabilities Act of 1990. With USN, 1951-54. Fellow ASCE; mem. AIA (dir. S.W. Wash. chpt. 1980-82, pres.-elect 1985, pres. 1986, dir. Wash. council 1986, archs. in govt. nat. com. 1978-87, chmn. N.W. and Pacific region conf. 1991), Am. Public Works Assn., Inst. Bldgs. and Grounds , Constrn. Specifications Inst., Am. Arbitrations Assn. (invited panelist), Washington Soc. (pres. 1978-80, 85-87, 95-99), Gen. Soc. Mayflower Descs. (gov. Wash. Soc. 1982-83, dep. gov. gen. Gen. Soc., 1998—), Nat. Huguenot Soc., SAR (state treas. 1984-85), SCV Sons and Daus. of Pilgrims (gov. Wash. Soc. 1984), Baronial Order of Magna Charta, Aircraft Owners' and Pilots' Assn., Rotary (pres. Edmonds, 1969-70), Olympia, Coll. Club of Seattle. Republican. Baptist. Home and Office: PO Box 2422 Olympia WA 98507-2422

MOFFETT, J. DENNY, lawyer; b. Atlanta, Sept. 20, 1947; s. James Denny Moffett Jr. and Dorothy (Mckenzie) McCall; m. Mary F. Ray, June 6, 1987; children: David, Jenny. BA, U. Okla., 1969; JD with honors, George Washington U., 1972, LLM in Taxation, 1974. Bar: Okla. 1972, U.S. Tax Ct. 1973. Legis. asst. U.S. Senate, Washington, 1973-74; ptnr. Conner & Winters, Tulsa, 1974-90, McKenzie, Moffett, Elias & Books, Tulsa, Oklahoma City, 1990-97, Moffett & Assocs., P.C., Tulsa, 1997—; adj. faculty U. Tulsa Law Sch., 1978; arbitrator Nat. Assn. Securities Dealers. Commr. Ark.-Okla. River Compact Commn., 1990-94; pres. Nicholas Club Tulsa, 1984; endowment com. Trinity Episcopal Ch., 1990—. 2d lt. U.S. Army, 1972-74; bd. dirs. Am. Cancer Soc., Tulsa, 1991-94. Mem. Am. Arbitration Assn., Tulsa Tax Club (pres. 1981, 94). Republican. Home: 2132 E 32nd Pl Tulsa OK 74105-2222 Office: Moffett & Assocs PC 1000 Philtower Bldg Tulsa OK 74103

MOFFETT, SEAN PATRICK, property developer; b. Johannesburg, Transvaal, South Africa, Feb. 13, 1971; s. Patrick John and Judith Mary (Simpson) M.; m. Keryn Anne Booysen, Nov. 2, 1996; 1 child, Aidan. Mgr. Aero Trucking, Johannesburg, 1990-93; dir., owner Davis & Moffett Projects, Johannesburg, 1994—, also bd. dirs. Avocations: model ships, cycling. Home: Ste 122 Postnet X9, 2109 Johannesburg Melville, Republic of South Africa Office: Davis & Moffett Projects, 11 7th Ave Melville, 2109 Johannesburg Gauteng, Republic of South Africa

MOFFLY, JOHN WESLEY, IV, magazine publishing executive; b. Phila., Aug. 5, 1926; s. John W. III Moffly and Audrey (Kane) Chancellor; m. Donna Jeanette Clegg, July 11, 1959; children: Jonathan Wesley, Audrey Kane Lkotz. BA, Princeton U., 1949; student, Woodrow Wilson Sch. Mem. staff Woodrow Wilson Sch. Time Inc., Cleve., 1954-62; N.Y. advt. mgr. House & Home Mag. Time Inc., N.Y.C., 1962-66, N.Y. advt. exec. LIFE Mag., 1967-73, v.p. selling areas mktg. divsn., 1973-87; pres., owner Moffly Publs., Inc., 1987—; pub. Greenwich and Westport mags. Hon. trustee Greenwich Hist. Soc.; bd. dirs. Boys and Girls Club Greenwich, Community Answers, Greenwich, United Way, Greenwich Emergency Med. Svc., Greenwich Adult Day Care, Greenwich Green & Clean; mem. Amb.'s Round Table-Foru, World Affairs. With USAAF, 1944-45. Mem. Greenwich C. of C. (chmn. 2000, Small Businessman of Yr. 1991), Riverside Yacht Club, Cruising Club Am., Indian Harbor Yacht Club. Republican. Episcopalian. Avocations: sailing, tennis, clay bird shooting, skiing, international studies. Home: 100 Meadow Rd Riverside CT 06878-2520 Office: GREENWICH mag 39 Lewis St Ste 8 Greenwich CT 06830-5558

MOFIZ, UDDIN AHMED, plasma scientist, fusion and space physicist; b. Hatiya, Bangladesh, Dec. 9, 1954; s. Abdur Rashid and Khatun (Firoza) M.; m. Amber Shameem Malik, Feb. 7, 1978; children: Ehtesham, Sanwal, Moutushi. HSC, Dhaka Coll., Bangladesh, 1972; MS, People's Friendship U., Moscow, 1979, PhE, 1983. Asst. prof. engring. & technology Bangladesh U., 1984-85; sr. scientific officer Bangladesh Atomic Energy Commn., 1985-91, principal scientific officer, 1991-95; prof. Bangladesh Open U., Dhaka, 1995—; dean Sch. Sci. & Technology, Bangladesh Open U., 1995—. Mem. Bangladesh Assn. for Advancement of Sci., Bangladesh Astronomical Assn. (past pres. 1992), Bangladesh Physical Soc. (sec. 1994-95), Bangladesh Acad. Avocations: music, gardening, fishing, reading, theatre. Home: Bangladesh Open U, Prof Quarters Flat A1-5, Gazipur 1704, Bangladesh Office: Sch Sci and Technology, Bangladesh Open U, Gazipur 1704, Bangladesh

MOGAE, FESTUS GONTEBANYE, Botswana government official; b. Serowe, Botswana, Aug. 21, 1939; s. Dithabano and Dithunya M.; m. Marbara Gemma Modise, 1968; 3 children. MA, Univs. Oxford and Sussex, U.K. Planning officer Ministry of Devel. Planning, Botswana, 1968-69; planning officer Ministry of Fin. and Devel. Planning, Botswana, 1970-71, sr. planning officer, 1971-72, dir. econ. affairs, 1972-74, permanent sec., 1975-76; min. Ministry of Fin. and Devel. Planning, 1989—; alt. exec. dir. IMF, 1976-78, exec. dir., 1978-80; gov. Bank of Botswana, 1981-82; permanent sec. to pres. Office of Pres. Govt. of Botswana, 1982-89, min. fin. and devel. planning, 1989-92, former v.p., now pres., 1992—; chmn. SADC Coun. of Minis., 1992—; mem. Global Coalition for Africa, Washington, 1992—; mem. internat. adv. bd. Transparency Internat., Berlin, 1993—. Rep. Commonwealth Fund for Tech. Cooperation, 1971—. Avocations: reading, tennis, music. Office: Ministry Fin and Devel Plan Office Pres, Pvt Bag 001, Gaborone Botswana*

MÔGE, PHILIPPE PIERRE, telecommunications company executive; b. Angeoulê,e, Cjaremte, France, May 18, 1942; s. Abel roger and Juliette (Mathelié-Guinlet) M.; m. Yovnne Charlotte Hélène Baillet, Feb. 22, 1965; 1 child, Caroline. Degree in Math. and Physics, Orsay (France) U., 1962, Lic. Maitrises, 1967, PhD in Electronics, 1969. Telecom. engr. ITT (France), 1972-78; engring. expert Thomson-CSF/LTT, France, 1978-85; mgr. for Am. Alcatel, France, 1985-86, advisor, 1987; mgr. for Africa SAT, France, 1987-89; internat. mktg. mgr. Thomson-CSF, Gennevilliers, France, 1992—; cons. in field, Paris, 1989-91; prof. math. Internat. H.S., France, 1967-69. Co-author: (handbook of ITU) Spectrum Monitoring, 1995, (for CAPTEF) Principles of Spectrum Management Implantaation, 1999. Capt. French Army, 1969-70. Decorated Ordre National du Merite Chevalier, France, 1998. Roman Catholic. Office: Thomson-CSF/RSC, 66 Rue du Fosse Blanc, 92231 Gennevilliers France

MOGENSEN, CHARLES RAY, JR., food service administrator; b. Elizabeth, N.J., May 7, 1946; s. Charles Ray Sr. and Hellen Oakley (Holland) M.; m. Linda Diane Friezer, Apr. 25, 1970; children: Charles Ray III, Jason C., Eric S., Lindsey H. Student, Middlesex County Vocat. Coll., 1972. Cert. food executive, 1979, 1987. Chef St. Elizabeth Hosp., Elizabeth, N.J., 1969-70; dir. food svcs. Cornell Hall Conv. Ctr., Union, N.J., 1970-96; dir. food svc. Corrections Corp. Am., Elizabeth (N.J.) Detention Ctr., 1996—; pres. C.R.M. Food Enterprises, Ltd., Kenilworth, N.J., 1971-89. Author: (recipes) Escargots Without Shells, 1979 (citation merit 1979). Mem. Rep. Nat. Com., Washington, 1988; mem. adv. bd. Episcopalian Program for Homeless, Elizabeth, 1990, Union County (N.J.) Coalition for Homeless, 1991. Cpl. USMC, 1964-68, Vietnam. Named N.Y. Dist. winner Gen. Foods Corp., 1981; recipient Cert. of Appreciation Roselle Park (N.J.) First Aid Squad, 1986, award of merit USNR, 1990. Mem. VFW, Vets. of Vietnam War, Am. Legion (cert. of appreciation 1999), Masons, Internat. Food Svc. Exec. Assn. (pres. 1977, 79, 85, 86, bd. dirs., treas. 1989-91, Royal Order of Skillet 1987, Humanitarianism award 1987), Am. Correctional Food Svc. Assn. Avocations: antiques, coins, Oriental art. Home: The Harbor Club The Harbour Club 708 Sunshine Ct Parlin NJ 08859 Office: Corrections Corp Am Elizabeth Detention Ctr 625 Evans St Elizabeth NJ 07201-2008

MOGGRIDGE, HARRY TRAHERNE, landscape architect; b. London, Feb. 2, 1936; s. Harry Weston and Helen Mary Ferrier (Taylor) M.; m. Catherine Grevile Herbert, Dec. 1, 1962; children: Harriet, Geoffrey, Lawrence. AA diploma, Archtl. Assn., London, 1959. Asst. Jellicoe, Ballantyne & Coleridge, London, 1960-63; site architect Sir William Halcrow & Ptnrs., Tema, Ghana, 1963-65; landscape architect Greater London Coun., 1965-67; pvt. practice London, 1967-69; ptnr. Colvin and Moggridge, Lechlade, Eng., 1969-97; cons., 1997—; prof. landscape arch. U. Sheffield, 1983-85; landscape cons. for Inner London Royal Parks and Castle Cement, Ltd. Prin. works include landscape design of Brenig Reservoir, Wales, Gale Common Waste Ash Hill, Yorkshire, Eng., JCB Factory and Offices, Staffs, Eng., White Horse Hill Archaeol. Monuments; (hist. parks) Blenheim, Eng., Castle Hill, Eng., Castletown Cox Eire. Commr. Royal Fine Art Commn., London, 1988-99; architects panel Nat. Trust, U.K., 1991—; founding bd. dirs. Landscape Found., U.K., 1993-99, chmn. 1995-99. Recipient Order of Brit. Empire, Her Majesty the Queen, 1986, Victoria medal of Honor Royal Hort. Soc., 2000. Mem. Landscape Inst. (hon. sec. 1971-75, v.p. 1975-79, pres. 1979-81, chmn. internat. com. 1987-92), Internat. Fedn. Landscape Architects (U.K. del. 1981-92). Office: Colvin and Moggridge, Filkins, Lechlade Gloucestershire GL7 3JQ, England

MOGHIMI, SEYED MOEIN, biochemist, educator, researcher, consultant; b. Iran, Dec. 24, 1962; arrived in U.K., 1978; s. Seyed Morteza and Forough (Foroughi); m. Anne Mette Jakobsen, Aug. 19, 2000. BSc, U. Manchester, Eng., 1985; PhD, U. London, 1989. Rsch. scientist U. Nottingham, Eng., 1989-92, univ. rsch. fellow, 1992-96; sr. lectr. biopharm. and molecular targeting Brighton U., 1998—; cons. contractor drug delivery and gene transfer systems pharm. biotech. diagnostic imaging industry in Europe, Japan, U.S., 1995—; vis. lectr. Liverpool John Moores U., 1996-2000. Guest editor: Advanced Drug Delivery Reviews, 1995, 99; contbr. more than 50 articles to biomed. jours.; patentee in field. Recipient rsch. grants. Mem. Biochem. Soc. U.K., Acad. Pharmacy Group, Royal Pharm. Soc. Great Brit., Med. Rsch. Soc. Achievements include pioneer research in drug delivery systems and molecular and cellular targeting. Avocations: music, soccer, tennis, water sports. Home: 28 Clumber Ct, Clumber Crescent South, Nottingham NG7 1EE, England Office: U Brighton, Sch Pharmacy and Biomolecular Sc, Brighton BN2 4GJ, England

MOGOS, CONSTANTIN, engineer, consultant; b. Negrea, Galatzi, Romania, May 22, 1943; s. Stroea and Maria Ene Mogos; m. Stela Jipa, June 13, 1969 (div. Sept. 1984); 1 child, Claudia-Diana (dec. 1970); m. Eugenia Stroe, Jan. 29, 1989; 1 child, Octavian. Student, The Bldg. Inst., Bucharest, Romania, 1961-67. Cert. engring. Stagiar engr. The Bldg. Trust, Galati, 1968-69; project engr. Inst. for Projekting of Rolling Metalurgic, Bucharest, 1969-75; prof. engring. The Sch. Inspectorat of Galati County, 1975-85; technology engr. The Bldg. Co. for Metalurgical Combinant, Galati, 1985-94; QC engr. bldg. installation Apaterm, Galati, 1994-97. Lt. Orgn. for Rebuilding of Bucharest, 1986. Mem. Nat. Geog. Soc. Penticostal. Avocations: traveling, plants, history, biology. Home: Strada Siderurgistilor 19, 6200 Galati Romania

MOGYORÒSY, GÀBOR, pediatric cardiologist; b. Miskolc, Hungary, May 1, 1960; s. Ferenc and Mària (Szabo) M.; m. Gabriella Kertèsz (div. 1993). MD, Med. Sch. Debrecen, Hungary, 1984. Resident Med. Sch. Debrecen, 1984-88, staff pediatrician, 1988-91, staff pediat. cardiologist, 1991—. Co-author: Methods of Developing Guidelines, 1997. Home: 6 Kürtgyarmat, 4032 Debrecen Hungary Office: Med Sch Debrecen Dep Pediat, 98 Nagyerdei Krt, 4012 Debrecen Hungary

MOHAIDEEN, A. HASSAN, surgeon, healthcare executive; b. Ramanathapuram, India, Aug. 14, 1940; s. Abdul and Mariam (Pitchai) Kader; m. Zarina M. Meera, May 30, 1965 (dec. July 1986); children: Ahamed, Mariam, Najeeba, Azeema; m. Laurie J. Kucich, June 23, 1989; children: Yasmin Sara, Leila Jahan. MD, U. Madras, India, 1965; MBA, Wagner Coll., 1996. Diplomate Am. Bd. Surgery, Am. Bd. Quality Assurance and Utilization; cert. physician exec. Am. Coll. Physician Execs. Intern Govt. Stanley Hosp., Madras, 1965-66, Good Samaritan Hosp., West Islip, N.Y., 1967-68; resident in gen. and vascular surgery L.I. Coll. Hosp., Bklyn., 1968-73, asst. attending surgeon, 1973-76, assoc. attending surgeon, 1976-78, attending surgeon, 1978—, chief divsn. vascular surgery, 1980-93, dir. vascular lab., 1981-93; v.p. Bklyn.-Caledonian Hosp. Ctr. (affiliate of NYU), 1994-95; sr. v.p., managed care and exec. vice-chmn. dept. surgery The Bklyn.-Caledonian Hosp. Ctr. (affiliate of NYU), 1995-96; asst. surgeon G.H.Q. Hosp., Ramnad, India, 1966-67; assoc. attending surgeon Meth. Hosp., Bklyn., 1982-90, attending surgeon, 1991-97; asst. attending surgeon Bklyn. Caledonian Med. Ctr., 1973-85, mem. courtesy staff, 1985-94, 97—, attending surgeon, 1994-96; attending surgeon Victory Meml. Hosp., Bklyn., 1982—; vis. physician Kings County Hosp. Ctr., Bklyn., 1973-94; clin. instr. in surgery Downstate Med. Ctr., SUNY, Bklyn., 1973-78, clin. asst. prof. surgery, 1978—; mem. exec. com. of med. staff L.I. Coll. Hosp., Bklyn., 1979-93, treas. med. staff, 1982-85, pres., 1985-87, med. chmn. Guild Ball com., 1981, mem. quality assurance com. dept. surgery, 1988-94, chmn. credentials com., 1990-93, quality assurance and risk mgmt. com., 1990-93; bd. dirs. Aetna Health Plans of N.Y., AIDS adv. com., 1987-93, stds. com., 1986-94, quality assurance com.; bd. dirs. Aetna-U.S. Healthcare, 1997; mem. credentials com. Prucare, 1988-92; sr. v.p. managed care Bklyn. Hosp., 1995-96; mem. quality mgmt. com. Oxford Health Plans, 1995—; mem. quality improvement com. Chubb Health, N.Y., 1994-96, Cigna (HealthSource), 1997; ; mem. credentials com. United Healthcare, 1997—; exec. dir. Mayan Health, PPO, Atlantic Med. Assocs. IPA. Contbr. articles to med. jours. Fellow ACS (com. on Long Island dist. applicants, 1988-99, bd. dirs. Bklyn.-L.I. chpt.), Royal Coll. Physicians and Surgeons Can. (cert.), Internat. Coll. Surgeons; mem. AMA (Physician's Recognition award), AAAS, Am. Coll. Physician Execs., Med. Soc. of State of N.Y., N.Y. State Soc. of Surgeons, N.Y. Acad. of Scis., Med. Soc. of County of Kings (mediation com., 1979-85), Bklyn. Surg. Soc., Soc. for Non-Invasive Vascular Technicians, Kings Physicians I.P.A. (pres./med. dir., 1985-95), Bklyn. Physicians I.P.A. (v.p., 1985-96, pres.). Avocations: photography, computers, walking. Office: 348 13th St Ste 202 Brooklyn NY 11215-5004 also: 142 Joralemon St Ste 11B Brooklyn NY 11201-4709

MOHAMAD, MAHATHIR, government executive; b. Alor Setar, Kedah, Malaysia, Dec. 20, 1925; married; 5 children. MBBS, King Edward VII Coll., 1952; postgrad., Harvard U., 1967. Med. officer Malaysian Govt. Svc.; physician pvt. practice, Malaysia, 1957-72; Malaysian rep. UN, 1963; elected MP, Kota Setar, Malaysia, 1964-69; mem. IMNO Supreme Coun., Malaysia, 1965-69, senator, 1973-76; elected MO, Kubang Pasu, Malaysia, 1974, 78, 82 86; min. edn. Malaysia, 1974-81; v.p. IMNO, Malaysia, 1975-78; deputy prime min., min. trade & Industry Malaysia, 1978-81; pres. UMNO, Malaysia, 1981—; min. home affairs Malaysia, 1981-99; prime min., 1981—; chmn. Higher Edn. Coun., Nat. U. Coun. Office: Office Prime Min, Halan Dato Onn, Kuala Lumpur 50502, Malaysia*

MOHAMED, AHMED NUR, geology educator; b. Marka, Somalia, Dec. 12, 1958; s. Nur Mohamed Abdi and Madina Hassan Shidey; m. Furqan Moallim Mursal, July 22, 1991; children: Aisha-lul, Madina, Batula-Rahma, Nur. Laurea in Geology, Somali Nat. U., Mogadishu, Somalia, 1986; Cert. in Computer-Aided Expln. Geophys., Free U. Berlin, 1989; MSc in Applied Geophysics, U. Nigeria, Nsukka, 1991; PhD in Applied Geophysics, Rivers State U. of Tech., Pt. Harcourt, Nigeria, 1995. Asst. prof. geology dept. Somali Nat. U., Mogadishu, 1986—; sr. lectr. geology dept. Fed. U. Tech., Yola, Nigeria, 1995—; chmn. dept. geology rsch. bd., 1995-96, acting head dept. geology, 1996-97, 99—, mem. senate Fed. U. Tech., Yola, 1996-97, 99—. Muslim. Avocations: reading, swimming, football, news, travel. Office: Fed U Tech, Dept Geology, Yola Adamawa, Nigeria also: Somali Nat U, Dept Geology, Mogadishu Somalia

MOHAMED, ISMAIL HASSAN, bank executive; b. Cairo, July 2, 1936; s. Hassan Mohamed and Fatma Ashour; m. Fatma Mostafa Sayed, Mar. 9, 1966; children: Yasser, Ahmed, Mostafa. BSc in Commerce, Ein Shams U., Cairo, 1959; diploma in statis. studies, Cairo U., 1965. Adviser IMF, Aden, Yemen, 1975-78; gen. mgr. banks control dept. Ctrl. Bank Egypt, Cairo, 1980, gov., 1993—; vice chmn. Capital Market Authority, Cairo, 1980-83; commr. Islamic Internat. Devel. Bank, Cairo, 1986; chmn. MISR Am. Internat. Bank, Cairo, 1988-93, Bank Alexandria, Egypt, 1991-93. Home: 83 Abdel Aziz Fahmy St, Heliopolis Egypt Office: Ctrl Bank Egypt, 31 Kasr el-Nil St, Cairo Egypt*

MOHAMED, KUMANKATTIL AHAMED, physics educator; b. Kottayi, Kerala, India, Apr. 10, 1946; s. Kumankattil Kattubavan Ahamed; m. Rameez Nazereen, Sept. 29, 1983. BSc, Kerala U., 1967; MSc, Calicut U., India, 1970; PhD, Manchester (Eng.) U., 1977. Lectr. physics Aligarh (India) Muslim U., 1977-84, reader physics, 1984-98, prof. physics, 1998—; vis. scientist Inst. for Atomic and Molecular Physics, Amsterdam, 1980-81; vis. fellow Bologna (Italy) U., 1991-92. Contbr. rsch. papers and monographs to profl. publs. Mem. Indian Soc. for Atomic and Molecular Physics (life), Internat. Ctr. for Theoretical Physics (assoc.), Univ. Grants Commn. (nat. assoc.). Muslim. Avocations: listening to music, reading, watching TV, going out with wife. Office: Aligarh Muslim U, Dept Physics, 202002 Aligarh India

MOHAMED, MOHD-ZAIN BIN, management educator, consultant, researcher; b. Kota Bharu, Malaysia, Aug. 12, 1952; s. Mohamed Hussain and Siti-Pura Karim; m. Susan Ardis Keeney, Feb. 3, 1979; children: Johan, Sarah, Sabrina. BS, U. Calif., Davis, 1977; MS, W.Va. U., 1978, MBA, 1979; PhD, Manchester (Eng.) Bus. Sch., 1993. Rsch. asst. MARDI, Serdang, Malaysia, 1973-74; mgmt. info. sys. cons. Andersen Consulting, Kuala Lumpur, Malaysia, 1979-80; lectr. U. Putra Malaysia, Serdang, 1980-94, assoc. prof. mgmt., 1994-98, prof. mgmt., dep. dean, dir. MS and PhD

programs, 1999—; cons. Agro-industry Devel. Authority of Pahang, Kuantan, Malaysia, 1995-97, Telekom Malaysia, Kuala Lumpur, 1994-95. Editor-in-chief Malaysian Jour. Small and Medium Enterprises. Lance cpl., Malaysian Volunteer Corps, 1971-73. Assn. Commonwealth Univs. (Eng.) scholar, 1989-93. Mem. Malaysian Nat. Computer Confedn. Avocations: travel, woodworking, reading, scuba diving, super biking. Home: 2 Jalan Hilir Enam, Taman Ampang Hilir, Kuala Lumpur 55100, Malaysia Office: U Putra Malaysia, Grad Sch Mgmt, Serdang Selangor 43400, Malaysia

MOHAMED, YASIEN ALLI, language educator; b. Johannesburg, South Africa, July 21, 1954; s. Alli Mohamed and Gadija Isaacs; m. Zaida Latief; children: Khalid, Nabil, Ilham. Diploma in edn., U. Durban, Westville, South Africa, 1979; postgrad diploma, U. King Saud, 1981; diploma in tchg. of Arabic, U. Riyadh, Saudi Arabia, 1981; MA, U. Cape Town, South Africa, 1985; Doctorandus, Free U. Amsterdam, The Netherlands, 1992; Doctorate, Johan Wolfgang Goethe U., Frankfurt, Germany, 2000. Tchr. Arabic Durban Girls' H.S., 1981-83; lectr. in Islam U. Cape Town, 1986-88; lectr. in Arabic U. Western Cape, South Africa, 1984—. Co-author: First Steps in Arabic Grammar, 1989; author: Fitrah: The Islamic Concept of Human Nature, 1995; translator: The Noisy Neighbour: Three Moral Plays, 1995; editor: The Teaching of Arabic in South Africa, 1997. Ednl. Opportunities Coun. fellow, 1991-92; Ctr. for Sci. Devel. scholar, 1998-99. Islam. Avocations: swimming, chess, travel. Home: 32 Osterley Rd, 7764 Crawford Cape Town Republic of South Africa Office: U Western Cape, Dept Fgn Langs, 7535 Bellville Republic of South Africa

MOHAMMAD, ALI NASSER, politician; b. Dathina Modia, Yemen, Dec. 31, 1940; arrived in Syria, 1990; s. Nasser Mohammad Sulieman and Sheika Mohammad Nasser; m. Meriam Ubad Nasser; children: Jamal, Arwa, Tariq, Lamia, Amal; m. Reem Faud Abdulghani; 1 child, Maysan. Diploma in Edn. Pedagogy, Tchr.'s Imaging Ctr., Aden, 1960. Tchr. Min. of Edn., So. Yemen, 1960-62, head tchr., 1962-64, min. of def., 1969-77; prime min. PDRY, So. Yemen, 1971-85; head of state Parliament/PDRY, 1980-86, pres., 1980-86; head Arab Ctr. for Strategic Studies, Damascus, Syria, 1995—. Author: (book) Revolutionary Changes in Yemen, 1984. Gen. sec. Socialist Yemni Party, 1980-86; pres. Yemeni Presidency Coun. Bd., 1980-86. Moslem. Avocations: swimming, walking, table tennis. Office: Arab Ctr Strategic Studies, PO Box 36843/Mezzeh Jabal, Damascus Syria also: 1 Sad Aaly, Midan Aljala Dukki, Cairo Egypt

MOHAMMAD, ISLAM AMIRUL DALIM, career officer, economist, educator, researcher; b. Rangpur, Bangladesh, Apr. 30, 1951; arrived in Brazil, 1986; s. Mortuza Syed Golam and Mortuza Syeda Rakiba. B in Econs. with honors, Dhaka U., Bangladesh, 1971; MA, Mil. Acad., USSR, 1976. Capt. Air Force, Dhaka, 1972-83; first sec., diplomat Min. External Affairs, Dhaka, 1983-86; first sec., head chancery Embassy of Bangladesh, Brasilia, Brazil, 1986-89; prof. Edn. Found., Brazil, 1993—; rschr., cons. in field; resident dir. South Asian Regional Coop. Summit, Dhaka, 1985; dir. Diplomatic Cir. Brasilia, 1986-88, sec. gen., 1988-90; spkr. in field; tourism cons., tour guide, 1991—. Freedom fighter Bangladesh Liberation Army, 1971. Decorated Campaign Star medal, War medal, Victory medal, Constn. medal, Nirapatta medal. Mem. Bangladesh Flying Acad. (life), Bangladesh Officers Club. Avocations: reading, traveling, sports, meditation. Address: SQ 15 Q 14 C 65, CID Ocidental, 72880000 Brasilia Brazil

MOHAMMAD, SYED YOUNUS, educator; b. Karachi, Sindh, Pakistan, Dec. 31, 1948; s. Syed Mohammad Yousuf and Sugra Shiekh Bibi; m. Zubeda Younus Begum, Feb. 7, 1975; children: Tariq, Aysha, Amna, Haleemah, Hirrah, Abdulkarim. HSC, Jinnah Coll., Karachi, 1969; BSc, U. Karachi, 1971; MBA, Delariman U., U.K., 1985; DSc, Eurotech U., Calif., 1989. Cert. mgmt., engring. and med. industries. Mktg. exec. Unilever, Bahrain, 1974-84; v.p., gen. mgr. IBS, Bahrain, 1986-87, chmn., 1989-90; comml. mgr. Almutlaq S.A., Saudi Arabia, 1990-94; cons., advisor Lt. Gen. Yahya A.M., Saudi Arabia, 1994-97; pres. A.I.M., Manila, The Philippines, 1997—. Author: Job in Overseas, 1994, Winner or Loser, 1996. Chmn. Overseas Svcs. Forum, Oslamabad, 1985—; dir. gen. Fgn. Tng. Svcs., Lahore, Pakistan, 1997. Avocations: writing, advising on educational social affairs, expert on Middle East business development. E-mail: dr younus@yahoo.com. Home: A-72 Irfan Corner, Near Taleemi Bagh, Karachi Pakistan Office: AIM GPO Saddar, PO Box 8888, Karachi Pakistan

MOHAMMAD, TUFAIL, pediatrician, child rights activist; b. Marghuz, Pakistan, May 15, 1952; s. Fazal Mohammad and Padam (Sultan) Khan; m. Nighat Durrani, Oct. 17, 1981; children: Shehriyar Khan, Mariya Khan, Haris Khan. MB, BS, Kyhber Med. Coll., Peshawar, Pakistan, 1975; diploma in Child Health, Peshawar U., 1980; diploma in clin. pathology, Khyber Med. Coll., 1984. Intern in medicine, surgery Lady Reading Hosp., Peshawar, 1976; demonstrator in anatomy Khyber Med. Coll., 1977-80, registrar in pediat., 1980-83, postgrad. trainer in pathology, 1980-83; from dep. prin. to prin. Regional Tng. Inst., Peshawar, 1983—; advisor Swabi Women Welfare Soc., Pakistan, 1992—, All Pakistan Women Assn. Family Planners Project, 1998—; dir. ILO/IPEC Automobile Workshop Project, 1994—; hon. advisor AIDS Awareness Project, Physicians Forum, Peshawar, 1991—. Author: Manual on Safety and Health in Autoworkshops, 1994, Your Amazing Baby, 1998, (booklet) Child Abuse, 1992; editor Pakistan Paediatric Jour., 1990—; contbr. over 100 articles to profl. jours. Chmn. Child Rights Com., Pakistan, 1991-98; dir. Children in the Prision Project, Peshawar, 1992-98, Children in Autoworkshops Project, Peshawar, 1992-98; advisor Cmty. Based Family Planning, Swabi, 1998. Recipient Gold medal U. Peshawar, 1980, Gold medal Lions Club, Peshawar, 1984. Mem. Coll. Physicians and Surgeons, NGO's Coalition on Child Rights (chmn. 1996-98), Faculty Family Medicine (sec. gen. 1992-98, Doctor of Yr. award in reproductive health 1998). Avocations: travel, social work. Home: House 16 K-3, Phase 3 Hyabahad, 25100 Peshawar NWFP Pakistan

MOHAMMAD, YOUSUF HASAN J., economist, educator; b. Kuwait, June 25, 1955; s. Hasan Jawad Mohammad and Fatemah Darweesh Zainal; m. Gloria Patricia Escudero, Nov. 19, 1980; children: Hamza, Mehdi, Ghadeer. BSEE, Iowa State U., 1977; MSEE, U. Calif., Santa Barbara, 1979, MA in Econs., 1979, PhD in Econs., 1983. Elec. engr. Ministry of Comms., Kuwait, 1977-83; tchg. asst. U. Calif., Santa Barbara, 1981-83; asst. prof. Kuwait U., 1983-92, assoc. prof., 1992-98, prof., 1998—, chmn. econs. dept., 1993-96; assoc. dean grad. studies and rsch., dir. MBA program Kuwait U. Coll. Adminstrv. Scis., 1998—; cons. Nat. Assembly, Kuwait City, 1995-96, Ministry of Oil, 1992-93. Co-author: (book) World Oil Prices: Demand, Supply and Substitutes, 1990; author: (book) Energy and Petroleum Industries: Fundamentals and Economics, 1988; contbr. articles to profl. jours. Recipient Scientific Achievement award Kuwait Found. for Advancement of Scis., Kuwait, 1992. Fellow Econ. Rsch. Forum; mem. Kuwait Econ. Soc. Avocations: table tennis, soccer, walking, travel. E-mail: yhmohammad@cas.kuniv.edu.kw. Fax: (965) 251-7294. Office: Kuwait U Coll Adminstrv Scis, PO Box 5486 Safat, 13055 Kuwait Kuwait

MOHAMMADIAN, PARVANEH, pharmacology educator; b. Tehran, Iran, Aug. 24, 1965; came to U.S., 1992; d. Morteza Mohammadian and Hajieh Barzegari; m. M. Hassan Rezaie-Boroon, Sept. 3, 1993; 1 child, Parnaz Rezaie-Boroon. BS, MS in Pharmacy, Erlangen (Germany) U., 1992, PhD in Human Biology, 1996. Cert. pharmacist. Pharmacist-intern Ring-Pharmacy, Erlangen, 1991-92, pharmacist, 1993-96; scientific rsch. asst. Aalborg (Denmark) U., 1992-97; ind. pharm. cons. ENV Consulting Co., Roseville, 1997-98; chair, dir. undergrad. program Cleveland Chiropractic College, L.A., 1998—. Contbr. articles to profl. jours. Rsch. grantee Pohl-Boskamp Pharm. Co., Germany, 1996. Mem. AAUP, Nat. Assn. Advisors for Health Professions, Assn. Clin. Rsch. Profls., Am. Pain Soc., Grantsmanship, Persian Club (L.A.), Soc. Neurosci. Avocations: reading, stock trading, walking. E-mail: Mohamp@Cleveland.edu. Office: Cleveland Chiropractic Coll 590 N Vermont Ave Los Angeles CA 90004-2196

MOHAMMAD MOKHTAR, HAITHAM KAMAL, food services executive; b. Alexandria, Egypt, Oct. 21, 1972; s. Abdel-Aty Kamal Mokhtar and Ahmad Hoda Abdel-Ra'ouf. BSc in Mech. Power Engring., Alexandria (Egypt) U., 1995; postgrad., 1996. Sales mgr. Sun Blinds Co., Alexandria, 1993-95; mechanic Santa Fe Internat. Drilling, Alexandria, 1995-97; maintenance mgr. The Egyptian Co. Foodstuff Industries, Alexandria, 1997—, also bd. dirs.; with The Egyptian Co. For Foodstuff Industries, 1997-98; maint. mgr. Agiba Petroleum Co., 1998; maint. eng. Belayem Petroleum Co., 1998—, proj. eng., 1998—. Mem. ASME, Egyptian Engrs. Syndicate, Egyptian Soc. Mech. Engrs. Muslim. E-mail: enghaitham@hotmail.com. Avocations: bicycling, rowing, traveling, fishing. Home: 19 Zaifal St, Alexandria 21121, Egypt Office: El Mkhayam El Dayem St, PO Box 7074, 11768 Nasr City Egypt

MOHAMMED, BABAGANA, engineering lecturer, consulting engineer; b. Maiduguri, Borno, Nigeria, May 10, 1964; s. Modu Mohammed and Hauwa Modu (Abba-Gana) Tela. BSc in Agrl. Engring., U. Maiduguri, 1988, M of Indsl. and Labour Rels., 1996; MSc in Agrl. Engring., U. Ibadan, Nigeria, 1991, postgrad., 1995—. Chartered and registered engr., Nigeria. Asst. store officer Ministry of Edn., Maiduguri, 1982-83; rsch. assoc. Nat. Root Crops Rsch. Inst., Umuahia, Nigeria, 1988-89; lectr. Borno Coll. Agr., Maiduguri, 1989; grad. asst. U. Maiduguri, 1989-91, asst. lectr., 1991, lectr., 1991—; chmn., mng. dir. Ultikonsults Ltd., Maiduguri, 1993—. Contbg. author: Monitoring the Nigerian Environment, 1996; author conf. procs. Mem. ward electoral coll. Nat. Electoral Commn. of Nigeria, 1996, mem. local govt. electoral coll., 1996. John Holt scholar, 1986, Fed. Govt. scholar, 1989, U. Maiduguri fellow, 1989. Mem. Nigerian Soc. Agrl. Engrs., Nigerian Soc. Engrs. (sec. gen. Maiduguri br. 1997—, nat. exec. com. and coun. 1999—), N.Y. Acad. Scis. Islamic. Avocations: table tennis, football, movies. Home: No 311, Aji Kolo St, (off Nimeri Rd) PO Box 756, Maiduguri Nigeria Office: U Maiduguri, Dept Agrl Engring, PMB 1069 Maiduguri Nigeria

MOHAMMED, FAROUK AHMED, geology educator; b. Ummdom, Khartoum, Sudan, Jan. 1, 1943; s. Ibrahim Ahmed and Aisha (Ahmed) M.; m. Fatima El Amin Kisha; children: Ahmed, Sarya, Salma, Sahar, Hagir. BSc with honors, Khartoum U., 1965, MSc, 1968; PhD, Khartoum/Leeds U., 1972. Teaching asst. Khartoum U., 1965-72; postdoctoral fellow Leeds (Eng.) U., 1973; lectr., assoc. prof. Khartoum U., 1974-89; prof. Sebha U., Libya, 1990-92; head dept. Internat. U. Africa, Sudan, 1993—; cons. BCI-Geonetic, 1989; overseas assoc. Globex Inc., 1983—. Author: Field Mapping for Geology Students, 1983; co-author: Field Guide to the Geology of Sabaloka Inlier, 1993. Fellow Geol. Soc. London; mem. AGID, Am. Geophys. Union. Avocations: field trips, walking, reading. Home: PO Box 416, Khartoum Sudan Office: U Khartoum Geology Dept, PO Box 321, Khartoum Sudan

MOHAMMED, HUSSEIN RAAFAT, public relations executive; b. Cairo, Egypt, July 18, 1935; s. Mohammed Mohammed Ahmed and Nour Ali Gabr; m. Soad Hussein Shiboksi, Oct. 10, 1959 (dec. 1966); 1 child, Maysa; m. Siham Said Raslan; children: Yasser, Nader. Deg., Bus. & Adminstrn. Cairo, 1955, U. Mich., Detroit, 1993, N.Y. Acad Scis., 1997. Clk. Suez Oil Refinery, 1955-58; head gen. sect. E.G.P.C., Cairo, 1958-61; mgr. pub. rels. Pipeline Petroleum Co., Cairo, 1961-68, Suez/Gulf Pipeline Project, Cairo, 1968-74, Sumed Co., Alexandria, Egypt, 1974-89; gen. mgr. pub. affairs Sumed Co., Alexandria, 1989-95, chmn., cons., bd. sec., 1995—; adminstrn. advisor Sadat Group Cos., 1998-2000. With Egyptian Army, 1956-57. Mem. Am. Mgmt. Assn., Pub. Rels. Soc. Am., N.Y. Acad. Scis., Shooting Club Cairo, Sporting Club Alexandria. Home: 50B Dokki St, Giza Egypt

MOHAMMED TAIB, PEHIN DATO HAJI ABDUL RAHMAN BIN, minister of industry, primary resources of Brunei; b. Kuala Belait, Dec. 5, 1942; married; 3 children. BA, U. Malaysia, 1966; student, U. Oxford, Eng., 1979-80. Lang. officer Brunei Govt. Svc., 1966-67, adminstrv. officer, 1966-71; dep. establishment officer Establishment Office, 1971-73, dir., 1975-79; sr. adminstrv. officer Sultan, 1973-75; head Diplomatic Svc. Dept., 1981; acting state sec. Govt. Brunei, 1981-83, min. devel., 1984-86, min. edn., 1986-88, min. industry, primary resources, 1989—. Office: Min Industry, Jalan Menteri Besar, Bandar Seri Begawan 1220, Brunei*

MOHAN, ANNETTE IMELDA, producer, educator; b. Bombay, India, Sept. 17, 1950; came to U.S., 1983; d. Joseph Alexander and Amy Vaz Gonsalves. BA, U. Bombay, 1971; MA, Andrews U., 1980, Norfolk State U., 1990. Prodr. Bombay TV, 1972-83; v.p. L.I.F.E., Inc., Virginia Beach, Va., 1983-98, Lathika Internat., Huntsville, Ala., 1998—; asst. prof. Oakwood Coll., Huntsville, 1998—. Prodr. (shows) Young World, 1975-79, Magic Lamp, 1979-82; exec. prodr. (documentary) Hanged on a Twisted Cross, 1996 (Chris award Columbus (Ohio) Film Festival 1996), (film) Nazaraana-The Gift, 1997 (Bronze award Columbus Film Festival 1997). Avocations: travel, stamps, coins, cooking. E-mail: LIFEINCVA@aol.com. Office: Lathika Internat PO Box 5042 Huntsville AL 35814-5042

MOHAN, CHANDER, mathematics educator; b. Jehlum, Punjab, Pakistan, Oct. 8, 1939; arrived in India, 1947; s. Krishan Gopal and Vidya Wanti; m. Tripta Kumari, Sept. 27, 1968; children: Kumar Rajive, Kavita. BA in Math. with honors, Panjab U., India, 1957, MA in Math., 1960; PhD, Roorkee (India) U., 1967. Lectr. math. M.M. Postgrad. Coll., Modinagar, India, 1961-64; lectr. math. Roorkee U., 1964-69, reader math., 1969-84, prof. math., 1984—, head math. dept., 1994-99; visitor Manchester (Eng.) U., 1973, Baghdad (Iraq) U., 1976-79. Contbr. articles to profl. jours. Mem. Internat. Astron. Union, Indian Soc. for Indsl. and Applied Math. (mem. exec. com.), Operational Rsch. Soc. India. Avocations: reading, traveling, listening to music. Home: Univ Roorkee, 105 Vigyan Kunj, Roorkee 247667, India Office: Dept Math, Univ Roorkee, Roorkee 247667, India

MOHAN, HARSCH, pathologist; b. Ambala, India, July 18, 1953; s. Ram and Maya (Ahuja) Khetarpal; m. Praveen Sharma, July 4, 1979; children: Tanya, Sugandha. MBBS, Med. Coll., Rohtak, India, 1976, MD, 1980. Demonstrator pathology Med. Coll., Rohtak, 1977-83; cons. pathologist Escorts Med. Ctr., Faridabad, India, 1983-84; from lectr. to reader pathology Med. Coll., Rohtak, 1984-93; prof., head pathology Govt. Med. Coll., Chandigarh, 1994—. Author: Textbook of Pathology, Essential Pathology for Dental Students. Avocations: badminton, cooking. Home: 1112 Sector 32-B GMC Campus, Chandigarh 160047, India Office: Govt Med Coll, Dept Pathology, 160047 Chandigarh India

MOHAN, JAG, chemist, educator, researcher; b. Karnal, Haryana, India, Apr. 3, 1945; s. Sumer Chand and Prem Lata; m. Neelam Gupta Aggarwal, Dec. 30, 1978; children: Sonal, Manika. BSc with honors, Kurukshetra (India) U., 1966, MSc in Organic Chemistry, 1969, PhD in Chemistry, 1974. Lectr. M.D. U., Rohtak, India, 1975-85, reader, 1985-94, prof., 1994—; postdoctoral rsch. assoc. U. Ill., Chgo., 1989-90; dean faculty pharm. scis. M.D. U., Rohtak, 1995-96; collaborator Uniroyal Chem. Rsch. Labs., Can., Cyanamid India Ltd., DuPont Agrl. Products, Sline-Haskett Rsch. Ctr. Contbr. over 100 articles to profl. jours.; author: Advanced Practical Organic Chemistry, vols. I and II, Organic Spectroscopy. Programme officer NSS-Unit univ. tchg. dept. M.D. U. Rohtak, 1977-83. Recipient Golden Record of Achievement award. Fellow Instn. Chemists, Indian Chem. Soc.; mem. Indian Sci. Congress Assn., Nat. Acad. Scis. India, Am. Chem. Soc., Royal Soc. Chemistry Eng. (assoc.). Home: Type IV Duplex/30, M D Univ, Rohtak 124001, India Office: M D Univ, Dept Chemistry, Rohtak 124 001, India

MOHAN, MANJU, environmental engineer; b. Agra, India, June 30, 1959; d. Manek and Santosh (Devi) Maheshwari; m. Sharad Mohan, Jan. 29, 1989. BSc, Rajasthan U., 1978, MSc, 1980; PhD, Indian Inst. Technology, Delhi, 1986. From sr. rsch. asst. to assoc. prof. Indian Inst. Technology, Delhi, 1984—. Mem. Indian Meteorol. Soc., Indian Sci. Congress Assn. Avocations: badminton, music, reading. Office: Indian Inst Technology, Hauz Khas, 110016 New Delhi India

MOHAN, SUBBURAMAN, biochemist, educator; b. Salem, India, June 15, 1951; came to U.S., 1979; s. Subburama and Pavayee Gounder; m. Shanthi Mohan, Nov. 4, 1985; children: Shilpa, Ashwin. BSc, Bangalore (India) U., 1972, MSc, 1974, PhD, 1978. CSIR rsch. fellow Bangalore U., 1974-78, CSIR postdoctoral fellow, 1978-79; Am. Heart Assn. rsch. fellow U. So. Calif., L.A., 1979-80; lectr., rsch. assoc. Calif. Poly. U., Pomona, 1980-82; asst. rsch. prof. Loma Linda (Calif.) U., 1982-87, assoc. rsch. prof., 1987-91, rsch. prof., 1991—, asst. dir. molecular genetics divsn., 2000—; lectr. in field; presenter symposia. Mem. editl. bd. Endocrinology, 1993—; contbr. numerous articles to sci. publs. Mem. Am. Soc. Biochemistry and Molecular Biology, Am. Soc. Cell Biology, Am. Soc. Clin. Rsch., Am. Soc. Bone and Mineral Rsch., Sigma Xi (Rsch. Merit award Loma Linda chpt. 1990). Avocations: tennis, hiking, reading. Office: Pettis Vets Hosp 151 11201 Benton St Loma Linda CA 92357-1000

MOHAN, TUNGESH NATH, television and film producer, film educator; b. Lucknow, India, Oct. 30, 1949; came to U.S., 1979; s. Bhola Shambu and Saraswati P. (Devi) Nath; m. Annette Gonsalves; 1 child, Lathika. BS, Kampur (India) U., 1969; diploma in Cinema, Film and TV Inst. India, Poona, 1972; MA, Andrews U., 1980. Producer Bombay TV, 1972-75, 77-79; asst. prof. Film and TV Inst. India, Poona, 1975-77; TV producer 700 Club, Virginia Beach, Va., 1980-82; producer spl. projects Christian Broadcasting Network, Virginia Beach, 1982-86, Christian Broadcasting Network Cable Prodns., Inc., Virginia Beach, 1986-87; dir. Internat. CBN Producers Group, 1987-89, Internat. NorthStar Entertainment Group, L.A., 1989-92; mgr. Adventist Comm. Network, Silver Springs, Md., 1992-93; pres. Tri-Angel Media Corp., Thousand Oaks, Calif., 1992-94; adj. prof. Film and TV Inst. India, Poona, 1975-79, Spicer Coll., Poona, 1975-79, Hampton (Va.) U., 1980-92; pres. Producers Unit-One, Virginia Beach, 1982—, L.I.F.E. Inc., 1993—; cons. Global Comm. Assocs., Virginia Beach, 1987-88, Global TV Syndication, 1996-97, dir. Telecomms. Ctr., Huntsville, 1998—. Prodr., dir. (films) Even So, 1972, Dishantar (cert. Proficiency 1975), Raktajeevee (Golden Lion award 1977), (documentary) Afghanistan: Under the Iron Claw, 1982; prodr., dir., writer (film) U-Turn (Garima award 1973); exec. prodr. Stand at Ease, 1989-90; co-exec. prodr. Rin Tin Tin K-9 Cop, 1988-89; prodr. Touching the Supernatural, 1992, Midnight Cry, 1994, Master Control, 1994, The Way We Were, 1995, Bought at a Price, 1996, Hanged on a Twisted Cross, 1996 (Chris award for best film, Bronze Medal for screenplay Columbus Internat. Film Festival 1996), Inn Keeper, 1996, The Invitation, 1997, The Gift, 1997 (Bronze Plaque for 2nd pl. Columbus Internat. Film Fest 1997). Mem. NATAS, Writers Guild Am., Dirs. Guild Am., Lions. Mem. Seventh-Day Adventists. Avocations: collecting stamps, music, camping, traveling, tennis. E-mail: lifeincva@aol.com. Home: 118 Hunters Hill Trl Toney AL 35773-6947 Office: PO Box 5042 Huntsville AL 35814-5042

MOHANAN, PARAYANTHALA VALAPPIL, toxicologist, researcher; b. Kannur, Kerala, India, May 20, 1962; s. P.V. Kunhambu Nair and P.P. Parvathi Amma; m. Mohan Bindu, July 30, 1968; 1 child, Anushka Mohan. BSc, Govt. Brennen Coll., Kannur, 1984; MSc, Sree Narayana Coll., Kannur, 1986; diploma in computers, Gokul Computer Ctr., Bangalore, India, 1988; PhD, Kerala U., Trivandrum, India, 1997. Tchr. biology Ednl. Soc., Kannur, 1986-88; rsch. fellow Rallis Rsch. Sta., Bangalore, 1988-89; sci. asst. Sree Chitra Tirunal Inst., Trivandrum, 1989-94, scientist, 1994—. Contbr. articles to jours. in field. Bd. dirs. Ednl. Soc., Kannur, 1986-92. Internat. travel fellow Com. Sci. and Tech. in Developing Countries and Internat. Bioscis. Networks, 1995, fellow Govt. Japan, 2000. Mem. Soc. Toxicology (life), Environ. Mutagen Soc. (life), Japanese Soc. Promotion Sci. Avocations: football, cricket, cinema, poems, touring. Home: B-2 Faculty Quarters, Trivandrum 695012, India Office: Sree Chitra Tirunal Inst, Poojapura, Trivandrum 695012, India

MOHANAN, TARA WARRIER, linguistics educator, researcher; b. Kerala, India; d. Unnikrishna and Ammini Warrier; m. Karuvannur Puthanveettil Mohanan, 1976; 1 child, Malavika. PhD, Stanford U., 1990. Author: (juvenile) The Hunter and the Mermaid, 1979, Argument Structure in Hindi, 1994, (with Lionel Wee) Grammatical Semantics: Evidence for Structure in Meaning, 1999. Office: Nat U Singapore, Dept English Lang and Lit, Kent Ridge 117570, Singapore

MOHANTY, AARON, neurosurgeon, educator; b. Cuttack, Orissa, India, June 30, 1962; s. Upendra Narayan and Girishbala (Pattnaik) M.; m. Mary Reeni Mathew George, Feb. 28, 1992; 1 child, Alina. Intermediate degree in sci., Ravenshaw Coll., Cuttack, India, 1979; MB BS, SCB Med. Coll., Cuttack, 1986; MCh in Neurosurgery, Nat. Inst. Mental Health, Bangalore, India, 1991. Sr. resident in neurosurgery Nat. Inst. Mental Health and Neuro Scis., Bangalore, 1991-93, asst. prof. neurosurgery, 1993-97, fellow in pediat. neurosurgery, 1997-99; assoc. prof. neurosurgery Nat. Inst. Mental Health & Neurosci., Bangalore, 1997—. Contbr. articles to profl. jours. Mem. Congress Neurol. Surgeons, Asian Soc. Stereotactic and Functional Neurosurgery, Indian Soc. Stereotactic and Functional Neurosurgery. Avocations: cricket, Indian music. Office: NIMHANS Dept Neurosurgery, Hosur Rd, Bangalore Karnataka 560 029, India

MOHANTY, BIBHUTI BHUSAN, communications educator, consultant; b. Kesol, Orissa, India, Oct. 1, 1931; s. Raj Kishor and Indurekha (Pattanayak) M.; m. Krishna Choudhury, July 14, 1958; children: Kalpana, Kasturi, Aseem (dec.), Amlan. BSc in Physics with honors, Utkal U., Bhubaneswar, India, 1950; MSc in Radiophysics & Electronics, Calcutta U., India, 1953; diploma in audio-visual aids, U. London, 1964; diploma in distance edn., Indira Gandhi Nat. Open U., New Delhi, 1988. Registered profl. engr. Audio-visual edn. officer cmty. project, Junagarh, India, 1954-55, chief social edn. organizer, 1955-56; dist. social edn. organizer Kalahandi, Dhenkanal, India, 1956-60; instr. ext. and social edn. Orientation and Study Ctr., Mysore, Bhubaneswar, India, 1960-67; vice prin. Tribal Orientation & Study Ctr., Bhubaneswar, India, 1967; ext. officer farmers tng. Govt. India, New Delhi, 1967; audio-visual aids specialist Indian Coun. Agrl. Rsch., New Delhi, 1967-68; info. specialist Agrl. Fin. Corp., Bombay, 1968-70; expert in cmty. devel. UNESCO, Jayapura, Irian Jaya, Indonesia, 1970-73; mgr. Indian Express, Chandigarh, India, 1977-78; dir. State Resource Ctr. for Adult Edn., Angul, India, 1978-84; prof., head dept. audio-visual comm. Indian Inst. Mass Comm., New Delhi, 1984-93; resident dir. Indian Inst. Mass Comm., Dhenkanal, Orissa, India, 1993-96; internat. cons. in edn., comm. Angul, India, 1996—; cons. ednl. radio, TV, UNICEF, Kabul, Afghanistan, 1981; resource person mass media for adult edn. UNESCO, Hanoi, Vietnam, 1982; cons. Jamaican village devel. project Rotary Found., Blue Mt., Jamaica, 1984; cons. in distance edn. UN Devel. Program, Jakarta, Indonesia, 1995. Author: A Handbook of Audio-Visual Aids, 1962, The World Changes Every Moment, 1962, Adult Education: Some Reflections, 1989; editor Indian Jour. of Adult Edn., CHETANA Jour. Vol. VITA, Va., 1978; hon. advisor Devel. News of India, Bhubaneswar, 1980; exec. pres. Bajiraut Chhatravas Angul, India, 1994—; v.p. Indian Adult Edn. Assn., New Delhi, 1994—. Recipient Nehru literacy award Indian Adult Edn. Assn., New Delhi, 1992, Sardar Patel Literacy award Internat. Assn. Educators for World Peace, Indian Chpt., Ahmedabad, 2000; fellow Ford Found., 1963-64; Fulbright scholar U.S. govt., 1966. Mem. Worldview Internat. Found. (v.p., mem. ctrl. coun.), Asian Media Info. and Comm. Ctr., Commonwealth Assn. for Edn. in Journalism and Comm., Indian Inst. Pub. Adminstrn. (life), Indian Adult Edn. Assn. (life, v.p.). Achievements include languages known Oriya (mother tongue), English, Bengali, Hindi, Bahasa Indonesia, Bahasa Malay. Avocations: photography, writing, public speaking, choral singing. Home and Office: Bajiraut Chhatravas, PO Box 35, Angul Orissa 759 122, India

MOHANTY, KAILASH CHANDRA, physician; b. Gandibed, India, Apr. 4, 1948; s. Arjun Charan and Kamala (Raul) M.; Suravi Naik, July 11, 1974; children: Anurag, Lucyann. MBBS, SCB Med. Coll., 1972; MD, Delhi U., 1977. Med. registrar Nat. Health Svc., U.K., 1978, sr. registrar, 1979, cons. physician, 1982—; mem. indsl. tribunal Dept. of Employment, London, 1991; mem. ct. U. Bradford; chmn. KCM Textiles. Author: Sexual Behavior and Sexual Dysfunction in Men, 1997; editl. bd. Jour. of Sexual Health, 1990—; contbr. articles to profl. jours.; inventor inosine pranobex in warts. Justice of the Peace British Judiciary Bradford City Cts., 1987. Recipient Merit award C Nat. Health Svc., 1995. Mem. British Med. Assn. (pres. Yorkshire Regional Coun. 1995-97, Bradford divsn. sec. 1990). Avocations: jogging, aerobic exercises. Home: 137 Bradford Rd, Shipley BD18 3TB, England Office: Saint Lukes Hosp, Little Horton Ln, Bradford BD5 0NA, England

MOHANTY, RAMANARAYAN BANSHIDHAR, chemical company executive; b. Dasarathpur, Orissa, India, Feb. 26, 1952; s. Banshidhar and Premlata (Nayak) M.; m. Dopati Ramanarayan Basumallick, Feb. 5, 1977; children: Mayukh, Mayuri. BS in Physics, Utkal U., India, 1971; BS in Electronics, Inst. Engrs., India, 1980. Cert. engring. Asst. project engr. Fertilizer Corp. of India, Talcher, 1973-82; plant engr. Zuari Agro Chem., Goa, India, 1982-88; v.p. Vinyl Chems. (I) Ltd., Maharashtra, India, 1988—; mem. exec. coun. Dr. B.A. Technol. U.; nat. chmn. tech. devel. com., in-

strument sub-com.; chmn. Intelligent Automation User's Group, India. Contbr. articles to profl. jours. Convenor Konkan Industries Fedn.; mem. exec. body Maharashtra Econ. Devel. Coun. Mem. Mahad Mfrs. Assn. (pres. 1993—), Maharashtra C. of C. and Industry (mem. governing coun. 1995—, chmn. industry com.), Rotary Club (pres. Mahad 1995-96), Instrument Soc. for Measurement and Control (pres. 1996-97), Tech. Devel. Com. E-mail: rnmohanty@pidilite.com. Home: Bungalow F-2 RX1 MIDC, Mahad Dist Raigad, Maharashtra 402 309, India Office: Vinyl Chems I Plot A/21, MIDC Mahad Dist Raigad, Maharashtra 402 309, India

MOHANTY, SURESWAR, neurosugeon, educator; b. Cuttack, India, Oct. 15, 1942; s. Bisheshwar Mohanty and Haripriya Devi; m. Brinda Rathore, Dec. 26, 1969; 1 child, Aprajita. MBBS, SCB Med. Coll., Cuttack, 1966; MS in Gen. Surgery, AIIMS, New Delhi, 1969, MChir in Neurosurgery, 1974. Lectr. in neurosurgery Inst. of Med. Scis., Banaras Hindu U., Varanasi, India, 1975-78, reader in neurosurgery, 1978-81, prof. and head dept. neurosurgery, 1981—, head dept. surgery, 1995-98, dean faculty of medicine, 1998—; fellow Nat. Hosp. for Nervous Disease, Inst. of Neurology, London, 1981-82, U. Nagoya and U. Okayama, Japan, 1985, Inst. Neuropathology, U. Dusseldorf, Germany, 1987, Henry Ford Hosp., Detroit, 1990, NIH, Bethesda, 1990, Cleve. Clinic Found., 1990, dept. neurosurgery U. Graz, Austria, 1991; examiner in neurosurgery Nat. Bd. Univs. of Delhi, Bombay, Lucknow, Jaipur, others. Contbr. articles to profl. jours.; editor Quar. Jour. Surg. Scis., 1995-98. Fellow Nat. Acad. Med. Scis., Internat. Coll. Surgeons, Assn. Indian Surgeons, Found. of Integrated Medicine; mem. Indian Med. Assn., Internat. Brain Rsch. Orgn., Neurolog. Soc. India, Congress of Neurological Surgs., Indian Soc. for Advancement of Med. Edn., Indian Acad. Neuroscis., Indian Soc. for Study of Pain (founder), UP Neuroscis. Soc. (pres. 1998), Neurotrauma Soc. India (sec.). Hindu. Avocations: reading, history of medicine, stamp collecting, travel. E-mail: mohanty@banaras.ernet.in. Home: B 31/7 Malviya Kung, Varanasi 221005, India Office: Banaras Hindu U, Inst Med Scis, Varanasi 221005, India

MOHATO SEEISO See LETSIE, III

MOHD-AMBIA, ABU FATAH SANUSI BIN, telecommunication engineer; b. Penang, Malaysia, Jan. 21, 1952; s. Mohd-Ambia Bin Tajuddin and Saleha Bt. Redzuan; m. Latifah Nadzrah Bte Abdullah, Jan. 6, 1982; children: Mohd-Fahmi, Mohd-Faisal, Anisa Nadhirah, Alianna Nadiah. BS Elec./Electronic Engring. with honors, Portsmouth U., U.K., 1978; advance diploma in computer sci., U. Keb, Malaysia, 1983; diploma in comm., U. Tek. Mal, Malaysia, 1974; diploma in mgmt., M.I.M., Malaysia, 1982. Cert. in engring. Asst. contr. Telecom Dept., Malaysia, 1978-83; bus. devel. mgr. Kump. Akz, Malaysia, 1983-84; gen. mgr. Rimman Internat., Malaysia, 1984-85, Kilatcom, Malaysia, 1986-89; chief exec. Radionet, Malaysia, 1989-93; mng. dir. PTT Unitrunk, Malaysia, 1993—; bd. dirs. Unitello, Malaysia, Alfin Ocean, Malaysia, Alfin Oriental, Malaysia. Exco mem. Kuala Lumpur Tourist Assn., Malaysia, 1986-90. Mem. Inst. Engrs. Malaysia, Malaysian Inst. Mgmt., Kelub Golf Negara Subang, Kuala Lumpur Golf & Country Club. Avocations: reading, traveling, golf, rugby, football. Home: 13 Jalan 22/38, 46300 Petaling-Jaya Selangor, Malaysia Office: PTT Unitrunk Sdn Bhd, 30-3 Jalan Bangsar Utama, 59000 Kuala Lumpur Malaysia

MOHIDEEN, UMAR, physicist, educator; b. Trichy, India, Dec. 29, 1960; p. Nainar Mohamed and Haseena Nainar; m. Namita Pandiri, July 31, 1993; children: Kabir, Naveen. B of Tech., Banaras Hindu U., Varanasi, 1983; MS, Pa. State U., 1987; PhD, Columbia U., 1993. Prof. physics U. Calif., Riverside, 1994—. Office: Dept Physics U Calif 3401 Watkins Dr Riverside CA 92521-0001

MOHIUDDIN MOHAMMAD, GALIB ASADULLAH, engineer; b. Pabna, Bangladesh, July 1, 1972; s. Akbar Ali M.S. and Monowara Khatun. Diploma of Japanese langs., Tokyo U., 1993; BSEE, Nagoya (Japan) U., 1997, MSEE, 1999. Engr. Ericsson, Yokosuka-shi, 1999—. Contbr. rsch. articles to profl. jours. Monbusho scholar Ministry of Edn., 1992-96, 97-98. Mem. IEEE, Inst. Electronics, Info. and Comm. Engrs. Avocations: cricket, movies, reading books. Home: Awata 2-32-5, Mason Nobi B 102, 239-0895 Yokosuka Kanagawa, Japan

MOHL, ALLAN S., social worker; b. Passaic, N.J., Feb. 10, 1933; s. Milton and Ruth (Meisler) M.; m. Judith Klein, Dec. 21, 1958; children: Barbara, Eric, Adam. BA, NYU, 1954, MA, 1956, MSS, 1960; PhD, Columbia Pacific U., 1991. Diplomate Clin. Social Work. Dir. residential social svcs., adminstr. Queens (N.Y.) Soc. for Prevention of Cruelty of Children, N.Y., 1977-80; psychotherapist in pvt. practice Ardsley, N.Y., 1966—; cons., dir. family svcs. Tip Neighborhood House, Bronx, N.Y., 1980-84; sch. social worker Com. on Spl. Edn., Dist. 28, N.Y.C., 1984—; condr. workshop on incestuous families and child sexual abuse; unit dir. Children's Village, Dobbs Ferry, N.Y., 1971-77; cons. Parents Anonymous, South Bronx, N.Y., 1983-84; com. mem. Crisis Intervention Dist. 28, 1995—; mem. Queens regional staff devel. com., 1995-98; mem. Queens regional social work awards com., 1996-98. Contbr. articles to profl. jours. Former chmn. Gen. Social Svcs. Adv. Coun. # 6, 1982-83; active participant Bronx Task Force on Child Abuse and Neglect; group leader Project Enable, South Bronx, N.Y., 1965-67; sponsor Parents' Anonymous group, Bronx, 1982-84. With U.S. Army, 1956-58. NIMH grantee; recipient Editor's Choice award Internat. Libr. Poetry, 1999, 2000. Mem. NASW (awards com. Queens, N.Y. chpt.), Am. Assn. Marriage and Family Therapy, Am. Orthopsychiat. Assn., N.Y. State Soc. Clin. Social Wk. Psychotherapists, Internat. Assn. Counselors and Therapists, Am. Group Psychotherapy Assn. (assoc. clin. mem.), Internat. Soc. Poets (disting. mem.). Home: 8 Shorthill Rd Ardsley NY 10502-2020

MÖHL, DIETER ERNST PAUL, physicist, researcher; b. Munster, Westfalia, Germany, Dec. 14, 1936; s. Ernst Josef and Annemarie (Rheinlander) M.; m. Lieselotte Hummelsiep; children: Karin, Andrea. Diploma, Tech. U., Brunswig, 1960, Free U. Berlin, 1964; D in Natural Scis., Free U. Berlin, 1966; cert. specialization in human ecology, U. Geneva, Switzerland, 1976. Asst. lectr. Free U. Berlin, 1964-66; rsch. physicist CERN, Geneva, 1966—; rschr. Lawrence Lab., Berkeley, Calif., 1971; mem. sci. coun. Deutsches Elektronen Synchrotron, Hamburg, 1997-99; mem. adv. coun. Cooler Synchrotron in Rsch. Ctr., Julich, 1994-99; mem. European Study Group on Fusion, Darmstadt, 1992-98. Co-author: Advances of Accelerator Physics, 1993; mem. editl. bd. Particle Accelerators, 1989—. Mem. Orlov (Human Rights) Com., CERN, 1976-85. Recipient Sr. Physicist award CERN, Geneva, 1982. Mem. German Phys. Soc., AAAS, European Phys. Soc. Office: CERN, CH 1211 Geneva Switzerland

MÖHLER, HANNS, pharmacologist executive, biochemist educator; b. Ehingen, Germany, Mar. 8, 1940; m. Moira Claire Woods, 1972; children: Christine, Fiona. BSc, U. Bonn, Germany, U. Tübingen, Germany; MSc, U. Tübingen, Germany, 1966; PhD, U. Freiburg, Germany, 1968. Cert. biochemist, pharmacologist. Rsch. scientist U. Mich., East Lansing, Med. Rsch. Coun., London; asst. prof. biochemistry, pharmacology U. Freiburg, Germany; dir. rsch. unit Hoffmann-La Roche, Basle, Switzerland, 1976-88; prof. biochemistry, pharmacology Federal Inst. Tech. Eidgenossische Tech. Hochschule, Zürich, Switzerland, 1988—, U. Zürich, Switzerland, 1988—; dir. Inst. Pharmacology, Zürich, Switzerland, 1988—. Author (with K. Jungermann) Biochemie, 1980; editor: (with M. Da Prada) The Challenge of Neuropharmacology, 1994; co-author more than 200 articles to sci. jours. including Science, Nature, Proceedings, National Academy Sciences. Mem. European Acad. Sci., Swiss Acad. Med. Scis. Home: Haltenstr 146, Feldmeilen 8706, Switzerland Office: Inst Pharm & Toxic U Zurich, Winterthurerstrasse 190, Zurich 8057, Switzerland

MÖHLMANN, DIEDRICH THEODOR FRIEDRICH, physicist, researcher; b. Greifswald, Germany, Apr. 10, 1942; s. Hubert and Gerda (Brümmer) M.; m. Monika Fänder, Dec. 1966; children: Sabine, Susanne, Tobias. Diploma in physics, Tech. U., Dresden, Germany, 1967; D of Natural Scis., U. Leipzig, Germany, 1972; DSc, Acad. Scis., Germany, 1977, prof., 1981. Sci. co-worker Acad. Scis., Potsdam/Berlin, 1967-81; head of br. Acad. Scis., Berlin, 1981-91; head of group German Aerospace Ctr., Cologne, Germany, 1991—. Author: Kometen-Himmelskörper aus den Anfängen des Sonnensystems, 1997; co-author: Origin and Evolution of Planetary and Satellite Systems, 1989, Kometen, 1989; contbr. articles to profl. jours. Mem. IAU, COSPAR, EGS. E-mail: dirk.moehlmann@dlr.de. Home: Luckenwalder Str 4, D-14552 Wildenbruch Germany Office: German Aerospace Ctr, D-51170 Cologne Germany

MOHNEY, NELL WEBB, religion educator, speaker, author; b. Shelby, N.C., Oct. 31, 1921; d. John Wonnie and Maude (Ferree) Webb; m. Ralph Wilson Mohney, Dec. 31, 1948; children: Richard Bentley, Ralph Wilson Jr. BA, Greensboro Coll., 1943; LHD (hon.), Tenn. Wesleyan Coll., 1982. Dir. youth work Western N.C. Conf., Salisbury, 1945-48; dir. Christian edn. 1st United Meth. Ch., Lenoir, N.C., 1943-45, Washington Pike United Meth. Ch., Knoxville, Tenn., 1952-56; dir. adult ministries 1st Centenary United Meth. Ch., Chattanooga, 1967-73, dir. membership devel., 1973-81; dir. membership devel. 1st Broad St. United Meth. Ch., Kingsport, Tenn., 1981-87; speaker, seminar leader for bus., profl., religious orgns. S.E. U.S., 1960—; spkr. Internat. Women's Conf., Crystal Cathedral, 1991; adj. staff Bd. Discipleship Sect. on Evangelism, Nashville, 1987-96. Author: Inside Story, 1979, Single Out Singles for Ministry, 1989, Don't Put a Period Where God Put a Comma, 1993, How to be Up on Down Days, 1995, Keep on Kicking as Long as You Are Ticking, 1999, Get A Faith Lift, 2000; co-author: Parable Churches, 1989, Churches of Vision, 1990, 365 Meditations for Grandmothers, 1996, 365 Meditations for Women, 1997; contbr. weekly article Chattanooga Free Press, 1977—, Kingsport Times, 1981—. Recipient Freedom Founds. award for writing, Valley Forge, Pa., 1973, for speaking, 1974, Key to City of Chattanooga, 1979; named Disting. Alumnae Greensboro Coll., 1988, Woman of Distinction in Chattanooga, 1992, Woman of Distinction Hall of Fame, 1993, Tenn. Woman of Yr., 1999. Republican. Home: 1004 Northbridge Ln Chattanooga TN 37405-4214

MOHR, FRIEDEMANN ALBERT, engineering educator; b. Hardheim, Germany, Dec. 24, 1947; s. Friedrich and Erika Anna (Horn) M.; m. Birgitta Franziska Hollerbach, May 17, 1974; children: Andreas, Roland. Diploma in engring., U. Karlsruhe, Germany, 1975, doctor in engring., 1984. Mem. tech. staff RC/ITT-SEL, Stuttgart, Germany, 1977-84; sect. head RC/ALCATEL-SEL, Stuttgart, 1984-87; dept. head Kissling, Wildberg, Germany, 1987-88; R&D dir. Polytec, Waldbronn, Germany, 1988-92; prof. optoelec. and laser measurement FH, Göttingen, Germany, 1992-96; prof. measurement sci., optoelectronics U. Applied Scis. Pforzheim, Germany, 1996—; dean elec. engring. dept. U. Pforzheim, Germany, 1997. Mem. IEEE, Verband Deutscher Elektrotechniker. Achievements include research in fiber-based rotation sensors and optical transmission systems, esp. polarization effects in high-bit rate transmission (PMD) and environmental perturbatious, polarization mode dispersion in high-bit rate systems, optical coherent transmission concepts and laser interferometric measurement systems for displacement and vibration. E-mail: mohr@fh-pforzheim.de. Office: U Appl Scis Elc Engring Dpt, Tiefenbronner Str 66, D-75175 Pforzheim Germany

MOHR, GEOFFREY ARNOLD, academic administrator, mathematics consultant; b. Cape Town, South Africa, Feb. 8, 1946; arrived in Australia, 1947; s. Courtney Balthazar Oppenheim and Christina Mary (Fear) M.; m. Patricia Lynne Cook, Jan. 10, 1970 (div. 1987); children: Richard Sinclair, Peter Edwin. B in Engring., Melbourne (Australia) U., 1968, M in Engring. Sci., 1970; PhD, Cambridge (Eng.) U., 1976; M in Bus. Sci., Internat. Arts & Scis. Coll., Melbourne, 1996, D in Bus. Sci., 1998. Dir. Engring., planning & archl. cons. Inst. Engring., Melbourne, 1969—; cons. engr. Meinhardt Internat., Melbourne, 1971-80; lectr. Monash U., Melbourne, 1977-79; sr. lectr. Auckland (New Zealand) U., 1980-85; cons. Multicon P/L, Melbourne, 1969-74; dir. Neotec P/L, Melbourne, 1970-86; mem. IE Australia com., Melbourne, 1979-80; cons. Monash U., 1983—. Author: A Microcomputer Introduction to the Finite Element Method, 1986, 87, A Treatise on the Finite Element Method, 1989, Finite Elements for Solids, Fluids, and Optimization, 1992, Numerical Methods for Management Science, 1996. Cons. Aborigines Advancement League, 1988-89. Anglican. Office: IASC, 7 Marine Ave St Kilda, Melbourne VIC 3182, Australia

MOHR, JANET ANN, psychiatrist; b. Defiance, Ohio, Feb. 13, 1958; d. Leo Arnold and Keiko Takahashi Mohr; m. Timothy Lyn Hunsucker, Aug. 4, 1984; 1 child, James Hunter Hunsucker. BS, U. Toledo, 1979; MD, Ohio State U., 1982. Diplomat Am. Bd. Psychiatry and Neurology. Intern Baylor and Affiliates, Houston, 1982-83, resident, 1983-86, fellow in child and adolescent psychiatry, 1986-88; pres., psychiatrist Assocs. of Psychiatry P.A., Sugar Land, Tex., 1988-96, Golden Isles Psychiatric Assocs., P.C., Brunswick, Ga., 1996—. Fellow Nat. Psychiatric Endowment Fund, 1986. Mem. AMA, Am. Psychiatric Assn., Am. Acad. Child and Adolescent Psychiatry, N.Y. Acad. Scis., Glynn County Med. Soc., Phi Kappa Phi. Office: Golden Isles Psychiatric Assoc PC 1421 Lee St Brunswick GA 31520-7132

MOHR, LAWRENCE CHARLES, physician; b. S.I., N.Y., July 8, 1947; s. Lawrence Charles Sr. and Mary Estelle (Dawsey) M.; m. Linda Johnson, June 14, 1970; 1 child, Andrea Marie. AB with highest honors, U. N.C., 1975, MD, 1979. Diplomate Am. Bd. Internal Medicine. Commd. 2d lt. U.S. Army, 1967, advanced through grades to col., 1989; med. intern Walter Reed Army Med. Ctr., Washington, 1979-80, resident in medicine, 1980-82, chief resident, 1982-83, attending physician, 1984-86, pulmonary fellow, 1986-87; command surgeon 9th Inf. Div., Ft. Lewis, Wash., 1983-84; med. cons. Madigan Army Med. Ctr., Tacoma, 1983-84; physician The White House, Washington, 1987-93; asst. prof. medicine Uniformed Svcs. U. of the Health Scis., Bethesda, Md., 1984-91; assoc. prof. medicine Uniformed Svcs. U. Health Scis., Bethesda, Md., 1991-94; assoc. clin. prof. medicine George Washington U., Washington, 1990-94; prof. medicine Med. U. S.C., Charleston, 1994—, dir. environ. hazards assessment program, 1995—; attending physician Med. U. Hosp., Charleston, 1994—, Charleston Meml. Hosp., 1994—; mem. Working Group on Disability in U.S. Presidents, 1995—. Editor: International Case Studies in Risk Assessment and Management, 1997, Biomarkers, Medical and Workplace Applications, 1998; contbr. articles to profl. jours. and books. Bd. dirs. Internat. Lung Found., Washington; mem. adv. bd. Nat. Mus. Health and Medicine, Washington; mem. sci. adv. bd. Consortium in Environ. Risk Evaluation; prin. investigator Consortium in Molecular Epidemiology and Biomarker Rsch. Decorated Silver Star, Bronze Star with 2 V devices and 3 oak leaf clusters, Purple Heart, Meritorious Svc. medal with oak leaf cluster, Air medal, Army Commendation medal with oak leaf cluster, D.S.M.; recipient Erskine award Walter Reed Army Med. Ctr., 1982; named Outstanding Med. Resident, 1982. Fellow ACP, Am. Coll. Chest Physicians; mem. AMA, Army and Navy Club, Order Mil. Med. Merit, Harbour Club, Phi Beta Kappa. Episcopalian. Avocations: mountain climbing, skiing. Home: 673 Lake Francis Dr Charleston SC 29412-4345 Office: Med U S C Environ Hazards Assess Program 171 Ashley Ave Charleston SC 29425-0001

MOHR, THOMAS, research scientist; b. Vienna, Austria, Sept. 30, 1964; s. Gerhad Julian Georg and Maria Mohr; m. Ingrid Massier, Dec. 12, 1989; 1 child, Elisabeth Daniel. Diploma in engring., U. for Agr. and Forestry, Vienna, 1995. Staff scientist Inst. for Tumorbiology-Cancer Rsch., Vienna, 1992—; cons. Mucos Pharma EmulsionsgesmbH, Vienna. Contbr. articles to profl. jours. V.p. K.OE.H.V. Franco Bavaria, Vienna, 1985, pres., 1986. Mem. AAAS, Austrian Orgn. Vascular Biology Rsch., N.Y. Acad. Scis. Roman Catholic. Fax: 43(2236)56793. E-mail: thomas.mohr@magnet.at. Home: Enzianweg 10a, A-2353 Guntramsdorf Austria Office: Inst Tumorbiology, Borschkegasse 8a, A-1090 Vienna Austria

MOHR, WERNER, electronics and communication technology engineer; b. Hann Munden, Germany, June 2, 1955; s. Helmut and Rosemarie (Heinemann) M. Diploma in elec. engr., Univ. Hannover, Hannover, Germany, 1981, PhD, 1987. Engr. Brigitta and Elwerath Betriebsfuhrungsgesellschaft GmbH, Hannover, 1981-82; rsch. group mem. Inst. of High Frequency Tech., U. Hannover, 1982-86, sr. engr., 1987-90; rsch. engr. Siemens AG, Munich, 1991-95, tech. expert cons. and group leader, 1995-97, dir. strategic pre-devel., 1997-98; v.p. pre-engring., chief tech. office Siemens ICM MC, Munich, 1998—; organizer of presentations VDE ITG, Hannover, 1989-90, participant RACE II ATDMA Project European Commn., Munich, 1992-95, project mgr. ACTS FRAMES Project European Commn., 1996-99, ETSI SMG5 European Standardization Body, Sophia Antipolis, France, 1995-96; head European rsch. projects Siemens ICM MC, 1999—. Contbr. articles to profl. jours.; patentee in field. With German Armed Forces, 1974-75. Mem. VDE ITG (award 1990), IEEE (sr.). Lutheran. Avocations: hiking, travelling, reading. Home: Josef-Beiser Strasse 12, D 81737 Munich Germany Office: Siemens AG Bus Unit ICM MC, Hofmannstrasse 51, D 81359 Munich Germany

MOHRI, HITOSHI, surgeon, educator; b. Taihoku City, Japan, July 28, 1930; s. Tetsuo and Sonoko (Oda) M.; m. Yoko Murayama, Mar. 28, 1963; children: Alidè Chihiro, Alvin Chikafusa, Melissa June. MD, Tohoku U., 1955, PhD, 1962. Asst. dept. surgery Tohoku U., Sendai, Japan, 1959-63; chief cardiothoracic surgery Katta Gen. Hosp., Shiroishi, Japan, 1963-64; vis. scientist dept. surgery U. Wash., Seattle, 1964-68, asst. prof., 1968-71, assoc. prof., 1971-76; assoc. prof. cardiothoracic surgery Tohoku U., Sendai, 1976-79, prof., chmn. dept. cardiothoracic surg., 1987-94, prof. emeritus, 1994—; prof., chmn. 1st dept. surgery Yamaguchi U., Ube, Japan, 1979-87; established investigator Am. Heart Assn., 1970-75; exec. cons. Tohoku-bunka, Gakuen, 1994-97; pres. Tohoku Coll. Sci. Tech., 1997-2000, Tohoku Bunka Gakuen U., 1999—. Author: Hypothermia for Cardiovascular Surgery, 1981; adv. editl. bd. Jour. Cardiovasc. Surgery, 1983-99; contbr. articles to profl. jours. Wash. Heart Assn. fellow, 1967-70; grantee NIH, 1968-75, Japanese Dept. Edn., 1962, 77-79, 81. Mem. Am. Assn. Thoracic Surgery, Internat. Cardiovasc. Soc., Japanese Soc. Artificial Organs, Japan Surg. Soc., Japanese Assn. Thoracic Surgery, Sigma Xi. Fax: 81 22 233 7941. E-mail: hmohri@office.tbgu.ac.jp. Home: 5-20-3 Moniwadai, Taihaku-ku, Sendai 982-0252, Japan Office: 6-45-16 Kunimi, Aoba-ku Sendai 981-8551, Japan

MOHRI, MEHRYAR, computer scientist. Diplome d'ingenieur, Ecol. Poly., Palaiseau, France, 1987; M in Applied Math. and Computer Sci., Ecole Normale Superieur Rue, Paris, 1989; M in Computer Sci., Paris 7, 1989, PhD in Computer Sci., 1993. Rsch. engr. IBM France, Paris, 1988-91; rsch. asst. Ecole Poly., Palaiseau, 1991-92; asst. prof. computer sci. U. Paris 7, 1992-93; assoc. prof. computer sci. U. Marne-la-Vallee and U. Paris 7, 1993-95; mem. tech. staff AT&T Bell Labs., Murray Hill, N.J., 1995-97; sr. mem. tech. staff AT&T Labs. Rsch., Florham Park, N.J., 1997-98; prin. mem. tech. staff AT&T Labs. Rsch., Florham Park, 1998—; adj. prof. Columbia U., N.Y.C., 1998-2000. Scholar Ministry Fgn. Affairs, Paris, 1985-87, rsch. scholar Ecole Polytechnique, Paris, 1991-92. Mem. European Assn. Theoretical Computer Sci., Assn. Computational Linguistics. E-mail: mohri@research.att.com. Fax: 973-360-8092. Office: AT&T Labs Rsch 180 Park Ave Rm E147 Florham Park NJ 07932-1004

MOHRI, MITSUNOBU, pharmacologist, researcher; b. Ishikawa, Japan, Feb. 19, 1962; s. Matatoshi and Yaeko (Motoya) M.; m. Yuka Nishimoto, Feb. 25, 1996; 1 child, Rima. BS, Kanazawa (Japan) U., 1984, MS, 1986; D Pharm., U. Shizuoka, Japan, 1998. Cert. pharmacology. Rschr. Lab. Pharm., Asahi Chem. Industry, Fuji, Japan, 1986-88; rschr. clin pharmacology Dana-Faber Cancer Inst., Boston, 1988-90; rschr. Lab. Pharmacological Rsch., Fuji, 1990-92; sr. rschr. 1st Lab. Pharmacology, Oh-hito, Japan, 1992-98; asst. rsch. mgr. Lab. Pharmacology, Oh-hito, 1998—. Contbr. articles to profl. jours. Mem. Japanese Soc. Haematology, Japanese Soc. Thrombosis and Hemostasis. Office: Asahi Chem Industry Co Ltd, Lab Pharm, 632-1 Mifuku, Oh-hito, Tagata 4102321, Japan

MOHSEN, ZOHAIR HUSEIN, entomologist, research scientist; b. Baghdad, Iraq, Jan. 8, 1948; s. Husein Mohsen and Armouta Mousa Al-Kazzaz; m. Sawsan Mostafa El-Gamal, July 28, 1970; children Mohammad, Abeer, Ali. BSc, Al-Azhar U., Cairo, 1970; MSc, Baghdad U., 1973; PhD, U. Calif., Riverside, 1981. Dir. gen. Sci. Rsch. Coun., Baghdad, 1982-86, head sci. photographic unit, 1987-90; rsch. scientist Biol. Rsch. Ctr., Baghdad, 1981-87, sr. rsch. scientist, 1987-90; sr. entomologist Agrl. & Consultation Svc. Bur., Iraq, 1990-91; tech. cons. Arab Pest Control Ctr., Amman, Jordan, 1991-99; adj. lectr. dept. natural scis. U. Mich., Dearborn. Contbr. numerous articles to profl. jours. Mem. Entomological Soc. Am., Soc. Invertebrate Pathology, Soc. Vector Ecology. Avocations: photography, music, reading, travel. E-mail: zmohsen@mediaone.net. Home: 1391 S Hidden Creek Dr Saline MI 48176-9021

MOI, DANIEL T. ARAP, president of Kenya; b. Sacho, Baringo Dist., Kenya, 1924. Ed., African Mission Sch., A.I.M. Sch., Govt. African Sch. Tchr., 1945-57; head tchr. Govt. African Sch., Kabarnet, Kenya, 1946-48, 55-57; now pres. Govt. of Kenya, Nairobi; tchr. Tambach Tchr. Tng. Sch., Kabarnet, 1948-54; African rep. mem. Legis. Council, 1957-63; chmn. Kenya African Dem. Union, 1960-61; mem. Ho. of Reps., 1961—; Parliamentary sec. Ministry of Edn., 1961; minister of edn., 1961-62, minister of local govt., 1962-64, minister of home affairs, 1964-67; pres. Kenya African Nat. Union for Rift Valley Province, 1966-78; min. home affairs, v.p. of Kenya, 1967-78; pres. of Kenya, comdr.-in-chief of Armed Forces, 1978—. Mem. Rift Valley Edn. Bd., Kalenjin Lang. Com.; chmn. Rift Valley Provincial Ct. Office: Office of Pres, PO Box 30510, Harambee House, Harambee A, Nairobi Kenya*

MOIA, PATRICIA INES, mathematician, educator, researcher; b. Capital Federal, Buenos Aires, Dec. 5, 1944. Licentiate in math. scis., U. Buenos Aires, 1968. Prof. U. Buenos Aires, 1970—; prof. Nat. Technol. U., Argentina, 1971—, dir. of prof.'s chair, 1985—; gons. Air Force, Argentina, 1978-94; rschr. in field. Co-author: Syndrom of secondary disadaptability to flight. Mem. N.Y. Acad. Scis.

MOIDA, RAMANA MURTY VENKATA, research scientist; b. Adra, India, Mar. 26, 1964; s. Viswanadham Kasi and Savitriamma (Routhu) M.; m. Vijaya Goparaju, Sept. 5, 1996; 1 child, Rubhavan. BS, Andhra U., Visakhapatnam, India, 1984, MS, 1986; diploma in remote sensing, Dept. of Space, Dehradun, India, 1987. Jr. scientist Orissa Remote Sensing Application Ctr., Bhubaneswar, India, 1988-90; project scientist AP State Remote Sensing Applications Ctr., Hyderabad, India, 1990-98; scientist Commn. Rural Devel., Hyderabad, 1998-99, AP Cyclone Hazard Mitigation Project WL/Delft Hydraulics, Hyderabad, 1999—. Author: Geomorphological Studies for Disaster Mitigation, 1993; co-author: Suggested Alternate Feasible Outfall of Coastal Drain, 1994, Flood Hazard Zoning in Pennar River Delta, 1995. Mem. Indian Soc. Remote Sensing, Deccan Geog. Soc. Avocations: social work, chess, crossword and jumble puzzles, reading, television. Home: Plot No 26/7, Kartik Enclave Sikh Rd, Secunderabad AP 500 009, India Office: APCHMP Meredian Plz, 6-3-853/1 Ameerpet, Hyderabad AP 500 016, India

MOIOLA, JORGE LUIS, electrical engineer and researcher; b. Rosario, Santa Fe, Argentina, Aug. 3, 1961; s. Bernardo Lorenzo and Lidia Celestina (Alonso) M.; m. Mariela Antonieta Cerella, Mar. 4, 1989; children: Melissa, Franco. B. Elec. Engr., U. Nacional Del Sur, Bahia Blanca, Buenos Aires, 1986, PhD in Control Sys., 1992; MSc in Elec. Engring., U. Houston, 1991. Rschr. CONICET (Nat. Coun. Sci. and Technol. Investigations), Bahia Blanca, 1987-90; teaching asst. U. Nacional Del Sur, Bahia Blanca, 1987-90, rschr., 1991—, sec. grad. studies (vice-dean) dept. elec. engring., 1992-94, prof., 1994—; teaching/rsch. asst. U. Houston, 1990-91. Assoc. editor L.Am. Applied Rsch., 1991-99, editor in chief, 1999—; contbr. articles to profl. jours. Fulbright scholar, 1998. Fellow Rotary (scholar 1990-91), CONICET; mem. IEEE (sr.), N.Y. Acad. Sci. Roman Catholic. Achievements include study of oscillatory behavior in nonlinear systems applying techniques derived from control theory. Avocations: painting, reading. Home: Güemes 136, 8000 Bahia Blanca Argentin, Argentina Office: Univ Nacional Del Sur, Dept Elec Engring, Avda Alem 1253, 8000 Bahia Blanca Argentina

MOIR, JAMES MARCUS, finance company executive; b. Muchwenlock, U.K., Jan. 10, 1965; s. Ian James and Priscilla Mary (Minton-Beddoes) M.; m. Lucy Mary Milner, Nov. 12, 1993; 1 child, James Edward Victor, 1998. BA in Arch. with honors, Manchester (U.K.) U., 1987; MBA, Manchester Bus. Sch., 1990. Mfg. mgr. Pilkington Glass Ltd., St. Helens, U.K., 1987-88; exec. asst. to chmn. Conder Group Plc., London, 1990-91; dir. Livingstone Guarantee Plc., London, 1992-98; mng. dir. Livingstone Guarantee Plc., 1998—. Charity trustee P.L.A.C.E., Buxton, Derbs., U.K., 1993—. Capt. (T.A.) Royal Armoured Corps, 1984-94. Chmn. Manchester Bus. Sch. Alumni Assn. (steering group 1994-99), Assn. MBAs., Travellers Club. Office: Livingstone Guarantee Plc, 15 Adam St, London WC2, England

MOISE, THEODORE SIDNEY, IV, engineering educator; b. Rochester, N.Y., Aug. 17, 1965; s. Theodore Sidney III and Phyllis (Hayward) M.; m. Elizabeth Muik, Feb. 27, 1993; 1 child, Emily Meagan. BS, Trinity Coll., 1987; MS, Yale U., 1988, PhD, 1992. Sr. mem. tech. staff Tex. Instruments, Dallas, 1992—; adj. prof. So. Meth. U., Dallas, 1994-98. Adv. bd. Trinity Coll., Hartford, Conn., 1998—. Mem. IEEE, Phi Beta Kappa.

MOISES, HANS WERNER, psychiatrist, molecular geneticist; b. Celle, Germany, July 3, 1948; s. Hans Ludwig and Sophia Aloisia (Schorler) M.; m. Joan Wang, June 8, 1999; children: Miriam, Maurice. Student, U. Louvain, Belgium, 1973; MD, U. Heidelberg, 1980. Diplomate in medicine; lic. psychiatrist. Rsch. asst. in psychiatry Ctrl. Inst. Mental Health, Mannheim, Germany, 1978-86; fellow in genetics/molecular genetics Stanford U. Sch. Medicine, 1987-89; attending dept. psychiatry Univ. Hosp., Kiel, Germany, 1989—; lectr. U. Kiel, 1994—, dir. Molecular Genetics Lab. dept. psychiatry, 1989—; Contbr. articles to profl. jours. Rsch. Career Devel. awardee, 1980. Mem. German Soc. Biol. Psychiatry, Soc. Biol. Psychiatry.

MOISEYENKO, VASILIJ NIKOLAYEVICH, physicist; b. Krasnograd, Kharkov, Ukraine, Dec. 12, 1951; s. Nikolaj Antonovich and Serafima Vasiljevna (Pelihova) M.; m. Lyudmila Efimovna Solovjova, Aug. 4, 1973 (div. Apr. 1986); 1 child. Diploma in Engring., Moscow State Inst. Engr./Phys., 1975; postgrad. P.N. Lebedev Phys. Inst., Russian Acad. Scis., Moscow, 1975-78; candidate of sci., Moscow State Inst. Engring. and Physics, 1978, DSc, 1993. Sci. worker Kemijski Inst., Ljubljana, Slovenija, 1982-83; jr. sci. worker, then sr. sci. worker Dniepropetrovsk State U., 1978-86, reader, 1986-88, chairperson optoelectronics dept., 1988—, prof., 1995—. Inventor in field; contbr. articles and revs. to sci. publs. Mem. SPIE, Spectroscopists Assn. Russia. Avocations: artistic photography, swimming, hiking. E-mail: mois@ff.dsu.dp.ua. Office: Dniepropetrovsk State Univ, Naukovy 13, 49625 Dniepropetrovsk 10, Ukraine

MOISEYEV, ALEKSEY, software engineer; b. Moscow, Jan. 22, 1963; came to U.S., 1999; s. Anatoly Fridland and Ludmila Moiseyeva; m. Tatyana Goganskaja, Aug. 2, 1997. PhD, Moscow Railway Transp. Inst., 1992, MA, 1995. Asst. prof. Moscow Rlwy. Transp. Inst., 1991-96; sr. engr. Joint Stock HGS Ctr., Moscow, 1996-99; sr. software engr. Parametric Tech. Corp., Waltham, Mass., 1999—. Author: Macintosh in Computer Prepress, 1996; co-author: Computer Fonts: Creation and Using, 1997. Avocation: books. Home: 166 Ridgewood Dr Norwood MA 02062-5630 Office: Parametric Tech Corp 128 Technology Dr Waltham MA 02453-8938

MOITINHO DE ALMEIDA, J. C., judge. Judge Ct. Justice European Communities, Luxembourg, 1986-. Office: Ct Justice European Communities, Cour de Justice-Batiment C, 2925 Luxembourg Luxembourg

MOITRA, DEEPENDRA, software company executive, researcher; b. Calcutta, India, Jan. 21, 1970; s. Rathindra Kumar and Deepali (Chakraborty) M.; m. Nandita Sen, Nov. 20, 1995. B Tech. with honors, Calicut (India) U., 1992. Self-employed cons. Bilaspur, India, 1992-93; scientist Indian Space Rsch. Orgn., Ahmedabad, India, 1993-96; sr. exec. Siemens, Bangalore, India, 1996-97; dep. gen. mgr. quality Lucent Technologies, Bangalore, 1997—; core group mem. Bangalore Software Process Improvement Network; dep. regional councilor India region, Software Divsn. Am. Soc. Quality, 1998—; mem. industry adv. bd. IEEE Software. Reviewer IEEE Software, 1995—, IEEE Computer, 1997—; mem. editl. rev. bd. Software Quality Profl. Jour.; editl. bd. Knowledge and Process Mgmt. Jour.; guest editor IEEE Computer, 1999. Mem. IEEE Computer Soc., IEEE TSCE, Assn. Computing Machinery, IEEE Standards Assn., Am. Soc. Quality (sr.). Hindu. Avocations: books, Western classical music, sports. Office: Lucent Techs India Ltd, Golf View Campus Wind Tunnel Rd, Bangalore 560 017, India

MOIX QUERALTÓ, JENNY, psychologist, educator; b. Sabadell, Spain, Oct. 30, 1963; d. Joan Moix and Joana Queralto; m. Emiliano Ayala, Sept. 2, 1989; children: Ingrid, Eric. MA, U. Autonoma Barcelona, Bellaterra, Spain, 1986, PhD, 1990. Asst. prof. U. Autonoma Barcelona, 1986-91, prof. psychology, 1991—. Author (chpt. in book) Memory and Awareness in Anaesthesia III, 1996. Mem. Spanish Soc. Study of Anxiety and Stress, Med. Sci. Acad., Catalonia Psychologist Acad. Avocation: traveling. Office: U Autonoma Barcelona, PO Box 29, 08193 Bellaterra Spain

MOIZE, JERRY DEE, lawyer, government official; b. Greensboro, N.C., Dec. 19, 1934; s. Dwight Moody and Thelma (Ozment) M.; m. Margaret Ann Wooten, Aug. 13, 1976; 1 child, Jerry Dee Jr. AB cum laude, Elon (N.C.) Coll., 1957; JD, Tulane U., New Orleans, 1960; diploma, Army Command & Gen. Staff Sch., USAR, 1981. Bar: Colo. 1961, U.S. Dist. Ct. Colo. 1961, U.S. Ct. Mil. Appeals 1962, U.S. Supreme Ct. 1965, N.C. 1965. Legal clk. Air Def. Commd., Colorado Springs, Colo., 1960-61, assistance officer, 1962-63; chief legal assistance divsn. 2nd Army, Ft. Meade, Md., 1964-65; staff JAG, Indiantown Gap Mil. Reservation, 1965; law clk. to hon. Eugen Gordon U.S. Dist. Ct. (mid. dist.) N.C., Winston-Salem, 1965-66; dir. Legal Aid Soc. Forsyth County, Winston-Salem, 1966-69; exec. dir. Forsyth Bail Project, Winston-Salem, 1968-69, Lawyer Referral Svc. of Bar of 21st Jud. Dist., Winston-Salem, 1968-69; staff atty. office of gen. counsel FAA, Washington, 1969-70, acting chief admin. & legal resources, 1970-71; staff atty. office of gen. counsel Dept. Housing & Urban Devel., Washington, 1971; counsel Jackson (Miss.) area office Dept. Housing & Urban Devel., 1971-83, chief counsel Jackson (Miss.) field office, 1983-94; chief counsel Office Gen. Counsel Miss., Jackson, 1994—; HUD del. Miss. Fed. Exec. Assn., 1997—; lectr. U. W.Va. Conf. on Poverty Law, 1968; program svcs. adviser, 2000—. Editor N.C. Legal Aid Reporter, 1968-69, N.C. Legal Aid Directory, 1968, Avlex Legal Index (2nd supplement), 1971, developed Miss. low income housing financing mechanism 1975-76; contbr articles to profl. jours., articles to splty. mags. Dem. candidate N.C. Ho. of Reps., Guilford County, 1964; mem. mil. com. Forsyth County N.C. Red Cross, 1967-68; pack leader Andrew Jackson coun. Boy Scouts Am., 1986-92; active Project Adv. Group U.S. Office Econ. Opportunity Legal Svcs. Program, 1968-69, Adv. Com. on Housing & Urban Devel., Miss., Law Rsch. Inst., 1980-81, Pilot Mountain Preservation & Park Com., Winston-Salem, 1968-70; mem. Race Com. Whitworth Hunt Races, 1973-76; Am. Master of Foxhounds Assn., 1976-79; adv. Order DeMolay, 1997—; sec. Miss Scottish Games, 1999—; patron Miss. Church #366, 1999-2000. Capt. AUS, 1960-65; ret. lt. col. USAR, 1966-87. Decorated Meritorious Svc. medal, Army Commendation medal with oak leaf cluster, Army Res. Forces Achievement medal with three oak leaf clusters, Nat. Def. Svc. medal, Armed Forces Res. medal; named Hon. Knight Mason, 1999. Mem. NRA, Fed. Bar Assn., N.C. State Bar, Miss. Hist. Assn., Miss. Track Club, Iron Bridge Hunt (v.p. 1964-65), Whitworth Hunt (founder, master of foxhounds 1975-76), The Austin Hunt (joint master of foxhounds 1976-79), Caledonian Soc. Miss., Sons of Confederate Vets., Mason (sec. 1999—, 32 degree), KT, Order Eastern Star, Shriner, Rosicrucian, Capital Club (Jackson, Mo.), Pi Gamma Mu. Republican. Episcopal. Avocations: riding to hounds, running, book collecting. Home: Ivanhoe 935 Bellevue Pl Jackson MS 39202 Office: Miss State Dept Housing & Urban Devel Fed Bldg 100 W Capitol 9th Flr Jackson MS 39269

MOJICA, JOSE ALVIN PARDIÑAS, rehabilitation medicine specialist; b. Davao City, Philippines, Oct. 12, 1957; s. David Quiñones and Dolores Oropesa (Pardiñas) M.; m. Maria Georgina Diaz, Mar. 14, 1992; children: Felicia Marie Jemima, Isabelle Kezia, Jose Emmanuel. BS, U. Philippines, 1978, MD, 1982. Diplomate Philippine Bd. Rehab. Medicine (bd. govs. 1999-2000). Resident physician Dept. Rehab. Medicine, Philippine Gen. Hosp., Manila, 1984-86; postgrad. scholar Tohoku Univ. Sch. of Medicine, Miyagi, Japan, 1987-89; assoc. prof. Coll. of Medicine, U. of the Philippines, Manila, 1989—; attending physiatrist Philippine Gen. Hosp., Manila, 1989—; fellow in cardiovascular rehab. Cumberland Coll. of Health Scis., U. Sydney, New South Wales, NSW, Australia, 1991; coord. for rsch. Dept. of Rehab. Medicine, Philippines Gen. Hosp., Manila, 1989-92, coord. for tng., 1992-99, vice chmn., 1994-99; dean Brent Coll. Phys. Therapy, Zamboanga City, Philippines, 1994-99; dean Nat. Tchr. Tng. Ctr. for the Health Professions, U. Philippines, Manila, 1999—; cons. Jose P. Rizal Med. Rsch. Found., Cavite, Philippines, 1989—, St. Clare's Hosp., Makati, Philippines, 1992—; mem. active staff Manila Drs. Hosp., 1994—, De La Salle-U. Med. Ctr., Cavite, 1994-99. Contbr. articles to profl. jours. Trainer community based rehab. svcs. Dept. of Health, Manila, 1992-93; vol. extension svcs. U. Philippines Manila, 1994. Fellowship in cardiovascular and rehab. Lidcombe Hosp. and Cumberland Coll. of Health Scis., U. Sydney, 1991; postgrad. scholar in rehab. Japan Ministry of Edn., Tohoku Imperial Univ., 1987-89. Fellow Philippine Acad. Rehab. Medicine (chmn. sci. com. 1993-94, rsch. com. 2000-01); mem. Am. Coll. Sports Medicine, Philippine Assn. of Japan Ministry of Edn. Scholars, Assn. Med. Doctors for Asia, Mu Sigma Phi. Roman Catholic. Avocations: swimming, reading, watching movies, gardening. Office: Dept Rehab Medicine, Philippine Gen Hosp Dept, Rehab Medicine, Taft Ave, Manila The Philippines

MOK, HENRY TAI KEE, social work educator; b. Hong Kong, Jan. 3, 1953; s. K.I. and P.Y. (Wong) M.; m. Ann O.Y. Wong, 1982. B of Social Sci. with honors, Hong Kong U., 1975, MSW, 1977; MSc, London Sch. Econs., 1984, PhD, 1987. Registered social worker. Social worker Ecumenical Agy., Hong Kong, 1977-78; asst. lectr. Hong Kong Bapt. Coll., Kowloon, 1978-83, lectr., 1983-88, sr. lectr., 1988-93; dir. Key of Ctr., Hong Kong, 1978-81; assoc. prof., assoc. head Hong Kong Poly. U., 1993-97; prof., head Hong Kong Bapt. U., 1998—; subject panelist Hong Kong Examination Authority, 1988—; examiner Hong Kong City Univ., 1990—. Author: Youth Policy and Practice, 1992, Poverty and Social Security in Hong Konng, 1993, Citizen Participation: Foundation of Social Policy, 1995, Poverty Eradication-Policy Formation, 1999, Medical System and Health Policy in Hong Kong, 1999; co-author: Youth Work in Hong Kong, 1982, Social Work and Labour, 1983, Social Security in Hong Kong, 1986, Policy Debates of Social Security in Hong Kong, 1991, Proverty Alleviation and Employment, 1996, New Youth Work in Hong Kong, 1995, Social Development in China, 1995, Social Welfare in China, 1998; co-editor: Civic Education in Hong Kong, 1988; editor Acad. Jour. Hong Kong Bapt. Coll., 1986—. Active Red Cross, Hong Kong, 1990, Hong Kong Social Security Soc., 1983, Hong Kong Children and Youth Svcs., 1988, Hong Kong Workers Health Ctr., 1990. Recipient Jardines scholarship Hong Kong U., 1973-75, Y.P. Pao award, 1974-75, BR Coun. scholarship, Hong Kong, 1983-84, social work tng. fund, Hong Kong Govt., 1984-86. Mem. Hong Kong Social Workers Assn., others. Office: Hong Kong Bapt Univ, Attn Head Prof Social Work, Kowloon Tong Hong Kong

MOKEROV, VLADIMIR GRIGORIEVICH, physicist, educator; b. Kirov, Russia, May 2, 1940; s. Grigorii Ivanovich and Mariya Sergeevna (Beresneva) M.; m. Julia Alekseevna Popova, Mar. 9, 1963; 1 child, Vladimir Vladimirovich. Grad. in physics, State U., Leningrad, Russia, 1963; MSc, Inst. Microdevices, Moscow, 1970; D Phys.-Math. Scis., Inst. Electronics, Moscow, 1983. Prof. State High Qualification Com., Russia, 1989. Engr., rschr. Inst. Microdevices, 1963-65; scientist Inst. Molecular Electronics, Moscow, 1965-71, head lab., 1965-80, head divsn., 1980-88; head divsn., dep. dir. Inst. Radio Engring. and Electronics, Russian Acad. Scis., Moscow, 1988—; prof., head dept. electronics and automatics Tech. U. Radio Engring., Moscow, 1989—; expert UN, Delhi, India, 1994-95. Mem. editl. bd. Jour. Microelectronics, 1990—, Jour. Radio Engring. and Electronics, 1997—; contbr. over 150 articles to sci. jours., including Solid State Physics, Semicondr. Physics, Exptl. and Theoretical Physics, Tech. Physics, Microelectronics, Quantum Electronics, Jour. Applied Physics, Optics and Spectroscopy, Radio Engring. and Electronics; numerous inventions in field. Decorated Friendship of Nations medal (Russia). Mem. IEEE, Russian Acad. Scis. (corr.), Russian Acad. Electrotech. Scis. Avocations: classical music, painting, sports. Office: Inst Radio Eng-Electronics, 11 Mokhovaya St, 103907 Moscow GSP-3, Russia

MOKHTAR, MOHAMAD, financial executive; b. Negri Sembilan, Malaysia, May 30, 1939; s. Mohamad Shafie and Maimunah (Rahman) M.; m. Anizah Abdullah, Apr. 30, 1976; children: Faizal, Fadzil, Mazlan. BSc in Econs., U. London, 1960; MBA, U. Bath, 1968. Cert. corp. sec., U.K., profl. internat. financier, U.S., profl. internat. cons., U.S. Area rep. Std. Oil Co., N.Y.C. and Kuala Lumpur, Malaysia, 1960-63; mktg. and sales promotion exec. Colgate Palmolive, Petalina Jaya, Malaysia, 1963-68; comml. officer Brit. High Commn., Kuala Lumpur, Malaysia, 1968-72; sr. mgr., corp. sec. Maltraco Industries, Kuala Lumpur, Malaysia, 1972-74; sr. superscale officer, dir. Statutory Authorities Govt. of Malaysia, Kuala Lumpur, 1975-83; prin. assoc., dir. R-A-Crider & Assocs., St. Louis, 1983—; bd. dirs. spl. investigation unit Law Enforcement Intelligence, Asia-Pacific, 1983—. Office: R-A-Crider & Assocs PO Box 3459 Saint Louis MO 63143

MOKKAMAKKUL, SAKDA, supreme court president Thailand. LLB, Thammasat U., Bangkok, Thailand. Judge Maha Sarakham Provincial Ct., Nakhon Ratchasima Provincial Ct.; chief justice Udon Thani Kwaeng Ct.; judge Civil Ct.; sr. judge Criminal Ct.; dep. permanent sec. State for Justice; justice Supreme Ct., sr. justice; chief justice Ctrl. Labour Ct, Civil Ct.; v.p. Supreme Ct., pres.; chmn. Judicial Svc. Commn. Office: Thanon Rathchadamnoen Nai, 10200 Bangkok Thailand*

MOKKEN, ALEXANDER HUGO, metallurgy consultant; b. Pretoria, Gauteng, South Africa, July 10, 1915; s. Jan and Jaantje (Kotterer) M.; m. Edwina Mary White, Sept. 8, 1956. BS in Engring. cum laude, U. Witwatersrand, Johannesburg, South Africa, 1937; Diploma, Sch. Accountancy, Johannesburg, South Africa, 1941. Profl. engr. Grad. engr. Union Corp., South Africa, 1937-48, works mgr., 1949-59, asst. cons. metallurgist, 1959-65, cons. metallurgist, 1965-78; ret., 1978, cons. metallurgist, 1978—. Contbr. 21 articles to profl. jours. Nuffield postgrad. travelling scholar Nuffield Found., 1947. Fellow South African Inst. Mining and Metallurgy (Gold Medal 1976, vet. contbr., Brigadier Stokes Meml. award platinum medal 2000), South African Corrosian Inst. Avocations: playing piano, composing. Home: 35 Lakefield Ave, 1501 Benoni Gauteng, South Africa

MOKRY, JAROSLAV, histologist; b. Nové Město na Mor, Moravia, Czech Republic, Oct. 14, 1964; s. Jaroslav and Františka (Koudelová) M.; m. Michaela Pánková, Dec. 18, 1993; 1 child, Marek. MD, Charles U., Hradec Králové, Czech Republic, 1990, PhD, 1995. Head dept. histology embryology Med. Faculty Charles U., Hradec Králové, 1998—; assoc. prof., 1999. Mem. editorial bd. Lékařské Zprávy LFUK, 1995—. With Czech Mil., 1990-91. Recipient Young Histochemist award Internat. Fedn. of Socs. of Histochemistry and Cytochemistry, 1996, Eastern European award European Tissue Culture Soc., 1997. Mem. Czech Anatomical Soc., Czech Soc. of Histochemistry and Cytochemistry, Czech Neurosci. Soc., Czechoslovak Biologic Soc., Czech Med. Chamber. Office: Dept Histology Embryology, Charles U Šimkova 870, 500 01 Hradec Králové Czech Republic

MOKWENA, CISCO FRANS LESUIRA, promotions company executive; b. Soweto, Gauteng, Republic of South Africa, Nov. 24, 1955; s. Tseko Zacharia and Topi Femiria (Nhcapo) M.; m. Tumi Maria Mokwena; children: Thapelo, Palesa, Tshepang. Grad., Naledi U., Republic of South Africa, 1992. CEO Lesuira Promotions, Johannesburg, Republic of South Africa, 1994—. Campaign worker ANC, Soweto, 1980—. Baptist. Avocations: soccer, home movies, singing, reading, writing. Home: PO Box 6052, 2000 Soweto Gauteng Republic of South Africa Office: Lesuira Promotions, Sikotsi St, 1868 Soweto Gauteng Republic of South Africa

MOLA, FRANCO ANTONIO, engineering educator; b. Olgiate Olona, Italy, Jan. 24, 1946; s. Guido Enrico and Angela Carolina (Aliverti) M.; m. Anna Maria Bruno, Sept. 3, 1975; 1 child, Elena. D Engring., Politecnico, Milan, Italy, 1971. Rsch. asst. Politecnico, Milan, 1973-81, assoc. prof., 1981-86, prof., 1989—; prof. Sch. for Reinforced Concrete Structures, Milan, 1975, Arch. U., Venice, Italy, 1986-89; head Inpro Cons. Engring., Milan, 1978. Co-author: Comité Eurointernational du Beton Bull. 142, 1984, Limit States Design for R.C. Structures, 1984, Advanced Problems in Bridge Engineering, 1991, American Concrete Institute Special Publication 160, 1996. Lt. Italian Engring. Corps., 1971-72. Recipient prize Ready Mixed Concrete Assn. Singapore, 1990. Mem. Internat. Assn. for Bridge and Structural Engring. (award 1985), Am. Concrete Inst., Concrete Soc. Roman Catholic. Avocations: symphonic music, literature, historical monuments, theory of structural mechanics and mathematics. Fax: 0039-02-3271133. Home: Via Amendola 19, 21057 Olgiate Olona Italy Office: Inpro Cons Engring, Viale Certosa 34, 20155 Milan Italy

MOLDAVSKAY, ANNA ARKADJEVNA, anatomy educator; b. Astrakhan, Russia, Apr. 17, 1937; d. Arkadiy Tiosifovich and Michailovna Schvartsman (Faina) Zelikson; m. Nikolay Tefimovich Moldavskiy, Nov. 4, 1967. Grad., Med. Inst., Astrakhan, Russia, 1961. Med. diplomate. Physician regional hosp., Russia, 1961-63; aspirant of anatomy chair Med. Inst. Astrakhan, 1963-66, asst. of anatomy chair, 1966; prof. anatomy chair Med. Acad., Astrakhan, 1994, 99—. Author numerous reports and articles in field. Mem. N.Y. Acad. Scis., Nature Acad. Russia, Soc. Anatomists, Histologists and Embryologists (grantee). Home: St Zvezdnaja 41/1 n 116, 414022 Astrakhan Russia Office: Med Acad, St Bakinskaja 121, 414000 Astrakhan Russia

MOLDEN, A(NNA) JANE, retired counselor; b. Weeping Water, Nebr.. BS, Schauffler Coll.; MA, Princeton (N.J.) Theol. Sem. Cert. adminstr., Iowa. Dir. outreach Chgo. City Union; dir. campus ministry Iowa State U., Ames; dir. Christian edn. 1st Congl. Ch., Ames; dir. community outreach Congl. Chs., Kansas City, Mo.; ctrl. regional dir. Am. Friends Svc., Des Moines; dir. acad. support counseling Grand View Coll., Des Moines; dir. Consortium of Higher Edn., Des Moines; mem. Health Planing Coun. Ctrl. Iowa; mem. Gov.'s Vocat. Rehab. Adv. Coun., 1993—; mem. Protection and Adv. Pair Adv. Coun., 1993—; bd. dirs. Iowa Protection and Adv. Bd. Dir. Grand View Coll. Dems., 1971-93; active devel. com. for handicapped HUD, Des Moines; bd. dirs. Plymouth Pl.; mem. Dr. Martin Luther King Com., Des Moines, Internat. Black Children's Conf., Iowa Vocat. Rehab. Coun., Iowa Protection and Adv. Coun.; chair Des Moines Human Rights Commn.; mem. study com. LWV; past pres. Citizens Disability Coun.; mem. community adv. bd. McKinley Sch.; mem. George Washington Carver com. Simpson Coll.; bd. dirs. Bernie Lorenz House, Community Focus, Greater Des Moines YWCA, Christian Ednl. Plymouth Congl. Ch. Named Outstanding Educator Jack and Jill, Inc., Des Moines, Supporting Friend, Learning Disability Coun. Ctrl. Iowa. Mem. AACD, Torch Club Internat. (pres.), Delta Kappa Gamma. Democrat. Mem. United Ch. of Christ. Home: The Ramsey 1611 27th St # 212 Des Moines IA 50310-5400

MOLDENHAUER, NANCY A., social worker, consultant, educator. BSEd, Valparaiso U., 1976; MSW, U. Mich., 1984, cert. specialist in aging, 1984. Instr. Meiji Gakuin and Tokyo Med. and Dental U., 1977-81; corp. communication trainer Saito Internat., Inc., Tokyo, 1981-82; conf. coord. Ctr. for Japanese Studies U. Mich., Ann Arbor, 1982-84; gerontol. social worker Turner Geriatric Clinic U. Mich. Hosps., Ann Arbor, 1983-84; med. social worker Mo. Bapt. Med. Ctr., St Louis, 1985-88; geriatric social work specialist Program on Aging Jewish Hosp. Wash. U. Med. Ctr., St. Louis, 1988-92; dir. case mgmt. and corp. svcs. Aging Consult, St. Louis, 1993-95; adj. prof. Wash. U., St. Louis, 1991-95; trainee in aging NIH, 1983-84; dir. Nat. Adult Day Svc. Assn., Nat. Coun. Aging, Washington, 1995-96; registration mgr. Landmark Edn. Corp., Alexandria, Va., 1997-98. Co-author: Positive Attitudes, Positive Aging: A Guide for Positive Actions in Later Life, NASDA Curriculum for Directors and Administrators, Adult Day Services - The Next Frontier, Handbook of Home Health Care Administration. Del. White House Conf. Aging, 1995. Named OWL Woman of Worth, 1993. Mem. Nat. Assn. Social Workers, Acad. Cert. Social Workers, Gerontol. Soc. Am., Am. Soc. Aging, Nat. Coun. on Aging, Alzheimer's Assn., Older Women's League (local bd. dirs., pres. 1991-95, nat. bd. dirs., v.p. 1993-96), Challenge Metro (bd. dirs., pres. 1986-90). Avocations: gourmet cooking, restaurants, wine, fishing, gardening. Office: Ageless Solutions 6103 Larkspur Dr Alexandria VA 22310-1511

MÖLDER, LEEVI, chemical engineer; b. Tudulinna, Estonia, July 4, 1933; s. Johannes and Julie (Nahkur) M.; m. Maila Vägi, Dec. 27, 1961; children: Toomas, Taimi, Tauno. MS in Chem. Engring., Tallinn Tech. U., 1957, PhD, 1963. Rschr. Tallinn (Estonia) Tech. U., 1957-62, assoc. prof., 1962-73, prof., 1973-85, 92—; dept. head inst. chemistry Estonian Acad. Scis., Tallinn, 1983-97; vice chmn. Coun. Oil Shale Estonian Acad. Scis., Tallinn, 1989-99; chmn. Commn. Liquid Fuels Quality Specification Ministry Econs., Tallinn, 1994-97; cons. RAS Kiviter Chem. Co., Kohtla-Jarve, Estonia, 1995-98, Environ. Health Project, Arlington, Va., 1996. Author: Technology of Heavy Chemicals, 1970, English-Estonian-Russian dictionary of Chemistry, 1998; co-author: Chemical Nomencature, 2000; contbr. articles to profl. jours. Bd. dirs. Virumaa Found., Rakvere, Estonia, 1989-92; active Estonian Soc. Nature Conservation, Tallinn, 1975—. Recipient Paul Kogerman medal Estonian Acad. Scis., 1987. Mem. ASTM, Estonian Chem. Soc., Union Estonian Scientists, Coun. Energetics Estonian Acad. Scis. Lutheran. Achievements include invention of method for cobalt recovery, methods for separation and extraction of resorcinol derivatives. Office: Tallinn Tech U, 5 Ehitajate tee, Tallinn 19086, Estonia

MOLDOFF, WILLIAM MORRIS, retired lawyer; b. Phila., Jan. 1, 1921; s. David and Pauline (Arcusin) Moldoff; m. Irene Morstad, June 1946 (div. 1950); m. Doris Elaine Johnson (dec.); children: Phillip Douglas, Laura Ellen, Janet Susan Sayers, Allan William. BA, U. Iowa, 1943; JD cum laude, U. Miami, 1950; LLM, U. Mich., 1955. Law editor Lawyers Coop. Pub. Co., Rochester, N.Y., 1952-54, 57-60; instr. Ohio Northern U. Coll. of Law, 1955-57; proofreader N.Y. Codes, Rules and Regulations State of N.Y., 1960, adminstrv. asst. to exec. dep. Sec. of State, 1961-63; pvt. practice Nassau, N.Y., 1963-66; veterans claims examiner, rating bd. Vets. Adminstrn. Regional, N.Y.C., 1966-85; ret., 1985. Lt. (j.g.) USNR, 1943-46. Republican. Jewish. Home: PO Box 151 Nassau NY 12123-0151

MOLENBERGHS, GEERT, biostatistics educator, consultant; b. Antwerp, Belgium, Feb. 5, 1965; s. Louis and Maria A. (Van Nieuwenmove) M.; m. Conny C. Aerts, Sept. 29, 1990; children: An, Jasper. BS with greatest distinction, U. Antwerp, 1988, PhD with greatest distinction, 1993. Rsch. asst. Sci. Found., Antwerp, 1988-93; vis. fellow Harvard U., Boston, 1993; asst. prof. Limburgs U. Ctr., Diepenbeek, Belgium, 1994-97, assoc. prof., 1997—; spkr. in field. Editor: Linear Mixed Models in Practice, 1997; assoc. editor Biometrics, 1995—, Applied Stats., 1997—; editor: Biometric Bull., 1998—; contbr. articles to profl. jours. Recipient Sci. grant NATO, 1995. Mem. Belgian Statis. Soc. (treas.). Office: Limburgs Univ Ctr, Univ Campus, 3590 Diepenbeek Belgium

MOLENDIJK, LEENDERT WILLEMMINUS, obstetrician, gynecologist; b. Deventer, Overijssel, The Netherlands, Oct. 23, 1957; arrived in Belgium, 1982; s. Willemminus Johannes Molendijk and Digna Elisabeth Van Santen; m. Mireille Lucy Louise Fifi, Mar. 3, 1979; children: Sebastien, Rebecca, Laura. MD, Erasmus U., Rotterdam, The Netherlands, 1982. Cert. med. specialist in ob-gyn. Med. officer Nikolas Hosp., Eupen, Belgium, 1983-85; registrar Siegburg Hosp., Cologne, Germany, 1985-89; cons., head dept. ob-gyn. Knappschafts Hosp., Wurselen, Germany, 1989—, head cytology lab., 1989-96; dir. dept. gynecol. pharmacology Chemist Commn., Bochum, Germany, 1993—; cons. Regional Cancer Ctr., Aachen, Germany, 1993—; clin. rsch. scientist Cancer Inst., Aachen, 1993—. Author: Effect of Plasma Expanders in Toxemia in Pregnancy, 1996; translator Rodzynek edits. med. books, 1992-95; corr. editor Netherlands Jour. Medicine, 1993—; contbg. author Belgian Med. Jour., 1993—. 1st lt. NATO Armed Forces, The Netherlands, 1982-83. Mem. German Doppler Soc. (founder, New Techniques award 1992), German-Namibien Friendship Assn., Theol. Philosophy Assn., European Orgn. for Rsch. and Treatment of Cancer. Christian-Democrat. Mem. Dutch Reformed Ch. Achievements include development of clinical Hemorheology in pregnancy, new methods surgical therapy of ovarian cancer. Home: 10 Rue Mathysart, B-4053 Embourg Liège, Belgium Office: Knappschafts Hosp, CMB, rue Selys 2, B 4000 Liège Belgium

MOLER, DONALD LEWIS, educational psychology educator; b. Wilsey, Kans., Jan. 12, 1918; s. Ralph Lee and Bessie Myrtle (Berry) M.; B.S., Kans. State Tchrs. Coll., Emporia, 1939; M.S., U. Kans., Lawrence, 1949, Ph.D., 1951; m. Alta Margaret Ansdell, Nov. 6, 1942; 1 son, Donald Lewis Jr. Tchr., Centralia (Kans.) High Sch., 1939-42, Carthage (Mo.) High Sch., 1946-48; asst. dir. Reading Clinic, U. Kans., 1948-51; dir. reading program Ea. Ill. U., 1951-70, prof. dept. ednl. psychology and guidance, 1963—, chmn. dept., 1963-84, dean Sch. Edn., 1980; vis. scholar U. Fla., 1965. Served with Signal Corps, U.S. Army, 1942-46. Recipient C.A. Michelman award, 1974; Disting Svc. award Ill. Assn. Counselor Educators, 1985. Mem. Ill. Guidance and Pers. Assn. (pres. 1968-69), Ill. Counselor Educators and Suprs., Ill. Coll. Pers. Assn., Am. Pers. and Guidance Assn. (senator 1970-71), Assn. Counselor Edn. and Supervision, Assn. Humanistic Edn. and Devel., Phi Delta Kappa, Xi Phi, Pi Omega Pi, Pi Kappa Delta, Sigma Tau Gamma. Methodist. Assoc. editor Ill. Guidance and Pers. Assn. Quar., 1970-84, mng. editor, 1984—. Home: 407 W Hayes Ave Charleston IL 61920-3303 Office: Ea Ill U Dept Ednl Psychology and Guidance Charleston IL 61920

MOLEV, ALEXANDER SERGEEVICH, theoretical physicist, researcher; b. Blagoveshchensk, Russia, Nov. 28, 1959; s. Sergei Ivanovich and Nina Petrovna (Komkova) M.; m. Victoria Igorevna Kovalyova, Sept. 5, 1985; 1 child, Elena Alexandrovna. Grad., Kharkov (Russia) State U., 1983; PhD,

Kiev (Russia) State U., 1986. Asst. lectr. Kharkov State U., 1983-86, jr. rschr., 1986-88, lectr., 1986-89, rschr., 1988-89, sr. rschr., 1989—. Contbr. articles to profl. jours. Recipient Gold medal Ukrainian Ministry of Edn., 1977, Lenin grant Ukrainian Ministry of Edn., 1981-83, grant Internat. Sci. Found., Ukraine, 1993. Mem. Coun. Young Scientists at Kharkov State U. (mem. bur. 1985-87), Coun. Young Scientists at Phys. Tech. Dept. of Kharkov U. (chmn. 1986). Avocation: collecting of Azerbaijanian and Georgian teas. Home: Apt 12, Saltovskoye shosse 240 B, 310171 Kharkov Ukraine Office: Kharkov State Univ, Svoboda Sq 4, 310077 Kharkov Ukraine

MOLIN, ERIC JOHANNES ELISABETH, social research educator, researcher; b. Margraten, Limburg, The Netherlands, May 11, 1964; s. Jef and Jeannette (Blom) M.; m. Anneke Petronella Kwak, Mar. 29, 1999; 1 child, Pieke Loys. MA in Sociology, Cath. U. Nijmegen, The Netherlands, 1989; PhD, Eindhoven U. Tech., The Netherlands, 1999. Researcher Netherlands Statistics, Heerlen, 1989-91, Maastricht (The Netherlands) U., 1991-92, Eindhoven U. Tech., 1992-97; asst. prof. Delft (The Netherlands) U. Tech., 1997—. Contbr. articles to scientific jours. Avocations: drumming, sports climbing, cycling.

MOLINA, MARIO JOSE, physical chemist, educator; b. Mexico City, Mexico, Mar. 19, 1943; came to U.S., 1968; s. Roberto Molina-Pasquel and Leonor Henriquez; m. Luisa Y. Tan, July 12, 1973; 1 child, Felipe. Bachillerato, Acad. Hispano Mexicana, Mexico City, 1959; Ingeniero Químico, U. Nacional Autónoma de México, 1965; postgrad., U. Freiburg, Fed. Republic Germany, 1966-67; Ph.D., U. Calif., Berkeley, 1972. Asst. prof. U. Nacional Autónoma de México, 1967-68; research assoc. U. Calif.-Berkeley, 1972-73; research assoc. U. Calif.-Irvine, 1973-75, asst. prof. phys. chemistry, 1975-79, assoc. prof., 1979-82; sr. rsch. scientist Jet Propulsion Lab., 1983-89; prof. dept. earth, atom and planet sci., dept. chemistry MIT, Cambridge, 1989-96, Martin prof. atmospheric chemistry, 1997—, Inst. prof., 1997—. Recipient Tyler Ecology award, 1983, Esselen award for chemistry in pub. interest, 1987, Max-Planck-Forschungs-Preis, Alexander von Humboldt-Stiftung, 1994, Nobel Prize in Chemistry, 1995, Sasakawa prize UNEP, 1999. Mem. NAS, Am. Chem. Soc., Am. Phys. Soc., Am. Geophys. Union, Pres.'s Com. on Advisors on Sci. and Tech., Inst. of Medicine. Achievements include discovering the theory that fluorocarbons deplete ozone layer of stratosphere. Home: 8 Clematis Rd Lexington MA 02421-7117 Office: MIT Dept of EAPS 77 Mass Ave # 54-1814 Cambridge MA 02139-4307

MOLINA, MISAEL, biologist, educator; b. Merida, The Andes, Venezuela, Jan. 1, 1968; s. Ponciano and Felina Molina; m. Ana Grismel Ruiz Pena, June 23, 1995; children: Yovanny Andres, Ricardo Samuel. Degree in biology, U. de Los Anges, Merida, Venezuela, 1996; MSc, U. Los Llanos Occidentales Ezequiel Zamora, 1999. Field biologist Nat. Inst. Parks/Andean Bank, Merida, 1996-97; wildlife mgr. Forestry, Geog., Environ. and Agrl. Svc. Offering Unit, Merida, 1997-98; appraiser diamond-gold mining impace on wildlife Guaniamo Mining Co., Caicara del Orinoco, 1997-98; prof. wildlife mgmt. Dept. Forestry and Environ. Scis. U. de Los Andes, Merida, 1996—, coord. investigation unit, 1998—; assessor on animal endangered species Nat. Inst. Parks, Merida, 1998—. Juvenile sec. Dem. Action, Merida, 1991-93; pres. Chamita's Sportive and Cultural Club, Merida, 1993-95; exec. coord. Edn. Orgn. for Gestion of Environment and the Sustainable Use of Natural Resources (BIOTROPICOS), Merida, 1999—. Recipient scholarship U. Los Anges, 1987-91; internat. grantee Superior Studies Found. (Colombia), 1993; nat. grantee Found. for the Def. of Nature (FUDENA), 1992, The Gran Mariscal de Ayacucho Found., 1997-99. Fellow Assn. Profs. U. Los Andes; mem. Venezuelan Assn. for Study Mammals, Educative Assn. for Conservation Nature. Democrat. Roman Catholic. Avocations: football, camping, fishing, photographing nature. E-mail: mmolina@forest.ula.ve. Office: U Los Andes/For & Environ, Via Chorros de Milla, 5101 Ciclo Basico Merida, Venezuela

MOLINARI, SANDRO, bank executive. Ceo Cariplo, Milan, chmn.; dep. chmn. Banca Intesa. Office: Bank Intesa, Piazza Paolo Ferrari 10, Milan 20121, Italy*

MOLINARI, TODD MICHAEL, priest; b. Portland, Oreg., Oct. 29, 1968; s. Joseph Charles Molinari and Joan Marie Campbell. BA in Philosophy, Franciscan U., Steubenville, Ohio, 1990; Sacrae Theologiae Baccelaureate, Gregorian U., Rome, 1993, Sacrae Theoligiae Licentiate, 1996. Lic. moral theology. Parochial vicar St. John Bapt. Ch., Milw., 1995, St. Anne Ch., Grants Pass, Oreg., 1996-99; pastor St. Francis Ch., Roy, Oreg., 1999—. Mem. Fellowship Cath. Scholars, Cath. League, KC (chaplain 1996—). Avocations: reading, golf, hiking, guitarist. Home and Office: Saint Francis Parish 39135 NW Harrington Rd Banks OR 97106-8210

MOLINARO, ALBERT FRANCIS, actor; b. Kenosha, Wis.; s. Ralph Frank and Teresa (Marrone) M.; m. Betty Sydney; 1 child, Michael Martin. Grad. high sch., Kenosha. Appeared in (tv series) as Murray in The Odd Couple, 1969, as Al Delvecchio in Happy Days, 1975 and Joanie Loves Chachi, 1985, as Joe in Family Man, 1990. Home: PO Box 9218 Glendale CA 91226-0218

MOLINIE, PHILIPPE GERMAIN ANDRE, chemist, researcher; b. Paris, Jan. 24, 1946; s. Philippe Albert and Suzanne Cecile (Helbert) M.; m. Chantal Odette Jonquet, July 21, 1971; children: Roland and Viviane (twins). Engr. in Chemistry, Nat. Inst. Applied Scis., Lyon, France, 1970; PhD in Solid State Chemistry, U. Nantes, France, 1977. Attaché de recherche Solid Chemistry Lab. CNRS, Nantes, 1975-79, head of rsch. Mixed Unit of rsch., 1980-91, dir. rsch. Material Inst., 1991—, mgr. rsch. group, 1989-95, chief magnetic measurement dept., 1980—; assoc. rschr. Cornell U., Ithaca, N.Y., 1978. Contbr. articles to profl. jours.; patentee in field. Mem. Neutronic French Soc., Mecanosynthesis French Soc., ACS. Avocation: sailing. Office: Inst Materials de Nantes, 2 rue de la Houssiniere, 44322 Nantes France

MOLINO, GIANPAOLO, health facility executive; b. Campertogno, Piemonte, Italy, Aug. 2, 1936; s. Giacomo Molino and Lidia Fornara; m. Maria Cantoni; children: Andrea, Francesca. Degree in Medicine, Torino (Italy) U., 1961, Degree in Gastroenterology, 1965, Degree in Occupl. Medicine, 1970, Degree in Internal Medicine, 1975. Asst., registrar, rschr. Torino U., 1970-80, assoc. prof., cons., rschr., 1980-94; med. divsn. leader Torino Hosp., 1994-97, dept. leader, 1997—. Contbr. articles to profl. jours. Capt. Italian Mil. Health Svc., 1961-62. Recipient Internat. Huspi award for clin. application of artificial intelligence, 1985; rsch. fellow Torino U., 1956-61. Mem. European Soc. for Med. Decision Making (pres. 1994-96), Am. Med. Info. Assn., Am. Gastroent. Assn., Italian Assn. for Study of Liver, European Assn. for Study of Liver, Internat. Assn. for Study of Liver, European Assn. for Artificial Intelligence in Medicine, Italian Soc. Internal Medicine, Italian Assn. for Info. in Medicine, Assn. Italiana Studi Fegato. Avocations: photography, carving and sculpture, folk studies. Home: via Ventimiglia 108, 10126 Torino Italy Office: Azienda Ospedaliera San Giovanni Battista, Corso Bramante 88, 10126 Torino Italy

MOLINO, MARIO, caterer, writer; b. Naples, Italy, Apr. 26, 1942; came to Eng., 1962; s. Giovanni and Chiara (Segreto) M.; m. Ilse Huber, May 26, 1967; children: Maurizio, Marco. Student, Oriental U., Naples, 1961. Gen. mgr. Pizza Express, London, 1965-72; dir. Mario e Peppe Ltd., London, 1972-85, Mario Molino Import Export Ltd., London, 1976—; dir., advisor Pizza Express Ltd., London, 1972—. Roman Catholic. Avocations: swimming, tennis, country life. Home: 43 St Johns Wood Rd, London NW8 8QJ, England Office: Mario e Peppe Ltd, 15 Gloucester Rd, London 5W7 4PP, England

MOLL, CLARENCE RUSSEL, retired university president, consultant; b. Chalfont, Pa., Oct. 31, 1913; s. George A. and Anna A. (Schmidt) M.; m. Ruth E. Henderson, Nov. 19, 1941; children: Robert Henderson, Jonathan George. BS, Temple U., 1934, EdM, 1937; LHD, Pa. Mil. Coll., 1949; PhD, NYU, 1956; LLD, Temple U., 1963; ScD, Chungang U., Seoul, Korea, 1969; LLD, Swarthmore Coll., 1970, Gannon U., 1981; LittD, Delaware Valley Coll., 1976; Ped D, Widener U., 1981. Instr. physics and chemistry Conshohocken (Pa.) H.S., 1935-37; instr. sci. Freehold (N.J.) H.S., 1937-38; instr. physics, chemistry Meml. H.S., Haddonfield, N.J., 1938-42; instr. electronics and radar USN, Phila., 1942-43; assoc. prof. physics and elec. engring. Pa. Mil. Coll., Chester, Pa., 1943-45; registrar, coord. engring. program Pa. Mil. Coll., 1945-47, dean admissions, student pers., prof. edn., 1947-56, v.p., dean pers. svcs., 1956-59, pres. coll., 1959-72; pres. Widener U. (formerly PMC Colls.), 1972-81, chancellor, 1981-88, pres. emeritus, 1988—; pres. RC Assocs., Inc., 1981—; instr. electronics Temple U., 1944-46; headmaster Pa. Mil. Prep. Sch., 1945-47; bd. dirs., trustee Fedders Corp., Ironworkers Bank., trustee Found. of Project Mgrs. Author: History of PA Military College, 1955; contbr. numerous mag. articles. Chmn. Pa. Commn. Ind. Colls., 1969, Found. for Ind. Colls. Pa., 1970; chmn. Com. for Financing Higher Edn. in Pa., 1975; trustee Pa. Inst. Tech., 1985—; commr. Am. Assn. Homes for Aging Cont. Care Accrediting Commn., 1985-95. Recipient Horatio Alger award, 1962, Disting. Alumnus award Temple U., 1964, Cert. of Honor Temple U., 1997, B'nai B'rith Citizen Service award, 1966, Distinguished Citizen award, 1971, Themis award Del. County Bar, 1976, Good Citizenship award Phila. Bar, 1976, Exec. of Yr. award Soc. Advancement Mgmt., 1978, Gallery of Success award, Temple U., 1999. Mem. Assn. Mil. Colls. and Schs. (pres. 1969), Pa. Assn. Colls. and Univs. (chmn. 1970, Sheepskin award 1982), Am. Soc. Engring. Edn., Springhaven Club (Wallingford, Pa.), Tau Beta Pi, Phi Delta Kappa, Alpha Sigma Lambda, Phi Kappa Phi. Lutheran. Home: 1960 Dog Kennel Rd Media PA 19063-1008 Office: Widener U Pres Emeritus Office Chester PA 19013

MOLL, FRIEDRICH HEINRICH, urologist; b. Stolberg, NRW, Germany, Oct. 10, 1959; s. Heinrich B. and Margaretha A. (Theisen) M. MD, Rheinisch Westfaelische Technische Hochschule, Aachen, Germany, 1986. Cert. urologist, German Bd. of Urology. Urologist Univ. Urology Clinic, Aachen, 1984-89; urologist surg. dept. St. Josef Hosp., Linnich, Rhenania, 1989-91; urologist Cologne (Germany) Med. Ctr., 1991—; vis. lectr. Cologne Med. Ctr. Nursing Coll., 1991—, cons. urologist Klinikum Merheim Cologne Med. Ctr., 1997—; head Matthias-Pullem-Haus Nursing Sch., 1999—. Author: (chpts in books) Minimal Invasive Chirurgie, 1994, Jahrbuch der Urologie, 1995, 96, Rheinische Lebensbilder, 1995, 96, Historia Urologia Europaeae V, 1998, Streiflichter aus der Geschichte der Urologie, 1999, Urologie im Wandel, 1999, 2000. Advising med. dir. Matthias-Pullem-Haus Sr. Citizen Homes, Cologne, 1991—. Fellow European Bd. of Urology; mem. Am. Urol. Assn. (corr.), Berufs-verband Dt Urologen, Deutsche Gesellschaft für Urologie. Office: Cologne Med Ctr Urol Dept, Neufelder Str 32, 51067 Cologne NRW, Germany

MOLL, MARTIN ANDREAS, office supplies wholesale trade company executive; b. Graz, Styria, Austria, Feb. 16, 1961; s. Gerhard and Brigitte (Walzer) M.; m. Gabriele Hildegard Platzer, Oct. 3, 1961 (div. May 1996); children: Martina, Elisabeth, Theresa. PhD, U. Graz, Austria, 1987. Dep. chmn. Papier-Moll KG, Graz, 1986—. Contbr. articles to profl. jours. Chmn. Aktionsgemeinschaft, Graz, 1984-85; mem. U. Parliament, Graz, 1983-86. Sgt. Austrian Inf., 1980—. Recipient grant for rsch. Ministry Sci., Vienna, 1996-99. Mem. German Hist. Assn. Roman Catholic. Home: Wilhelm-Kienzlgasse 33, A-8010 Graz Styria, Austria Office: Papier-Moll KG, Fischergasse 23B, A-8010 Graz Styria, Austria

MOLLAH, ABDUS SATTAR, physicist, researcher; b. Munshigonj, Dhaka, Bangladesh, Nov. 1, 1954; s. Manir Uddin and Azimun Nessa (Begum) M.; m. Begum Aleya, Feb. 21, 1986; children: Sabiha Sattar, Sabbir Ahmad, Samiha Sattar. BSc, U. Dhaka, 1974, MSc, 1976; MPhil in Physics, Bangladesh U. Engring. Tech., 1987, PhD in Physics, 1997. Sci. officer Bangladesh Atomic Energy Commn., Dhaka, 1981-84, sr. sci. officer, 1985-92, prin. sci. officer, 1993—, head sec. std. dosimetry lab., 1993-99, head radiation control and waste mgmt. divsn., 1997-99, head radiation control sect., 2000—. Contbr. articles to profl. jours. Mem. Internat. Orgn. of Med. Physics, Bangladesh Atomic Energy Scientist Assn., Bangladesh Assn. of Scientists and Sci. Professions, Bangladesh Med. Physics Assn. (sec.). U. Dhaka Merit scholar, 1977, 1978. Mem. Bangladesh Assn. Sci., Bangladesh Phys. Soc., Am. Assn. Physicsts in Medicine, Internat. Union of Ecology, N.Y. Acad. of Scis. Achievements include development of shielding materials; TL dosimeters. E-mail: asmollah@dhaka.agni.com. Office: Bangladesh Atomic En Commn, Ramna PO Box 158, 1000 Dhaka Bangladesh

MOLLAMUSTAFAOGLU, OSMAN LEVENT, industrial engineer; b. Trabzon, Turkey, Mar. 1, 1961; parents Mehmet and Melek M.; m. Ferihan Fevrin Ipek, Sept. 1, 1988; children: Berk, Bora. BS, Bogazici U., 1982, PhD, 1990, BS, 1984. Software engr. Komili Inc., Istanbul, 1984; software dir. Logo Software Inc., Istanbul, 1984-89; asst. prof. Bogazici U., Istanbul, 1990-93; rsch. assoc. Harvard U., Cambridge, Mass., 1991-92; assoc. prof. Bogazici U., 1993-96; sr. scientist NATO C2 Agy., The Hague, The Netherlands, 1996—. Author: Object-Oriented Programming, 1995; contbr. articles to profl. jours. Mem. Soc. Computer Simulation, 1990—.

MØLLENDAL, HARALD, chemistry educator; b. Ålesund, Norway, Mar. 1, 1941; s. Harald and Aasta (Nilsen) M.; m. Wenche Anita Langseth, Nov. 26, 1966; children: Lise, Siri, Endre. BS, U. Oslo, 1964, MS, 1967, PhD, 1974. Rschr. U. Oslo, 1967-76, assoc. prof., 1976-91, prof., 1991—; postdoctoral fellow U. Tex., Austin, 1970-71. Contbr. sci. papers to profl. publs. Rsch. grantee Rsch. Coun. Norway and Norwegian Acad. Sci. and Letters. Mem. Chem. Soc. Norway. Lutheran. Home: Konglestien 8, N-3440 Røyken Norway Office: U Oslo Dept Chemistry, PO Box 1033 Blindern, N-0315 Oslo Norway

MOLLENKOTT, VIRGINIA RAMEY, English literature and language educator, author, guest lecturer; b. Phila., Jan. 28, 1932; d. Robert Franklin and May (Lotz) Ramey; m. Frederick H. Mollenkott, June 17, 1954 (div. July 1973); 1 child, Paul F. BA, Bob Jones U., 1953; MA, Temple U., 1955; PhD, NYU, 1964; D in Ministries (hon.), Samaritan Coll., 1989. Chair English dept. Shelton Coll., Ringwood, N.J., 1955-63, Nyack (N.Y.) Coll., 1963-67; prof. of English William Paterson Coll. of N.J., Wayne, 1967-97, English dept. chair, 1972-76, prof. emeritus, 1997—; asst. editor Seventeenth Century News, N.Y.C., 1965-75; stylistic cons. New International Version of the Bible, Am. Bible Soc., 1970-78; mem. translation com. An Inclusive Language Lectionary, Nat. Coun. Chs., 1980-88; bd. dirs. Pacem in Terris, Warwick, N.Y., 1980—, Kirkridge Conf. Ctr., Bangor, Pa., 1980-91, Upper Room AIDS Ministry, Harlem, N.Y.C., 1989-94; mem. adv. bd. Program on gender and soc. Rochester (N.Y.) Divinity Sch., 1993—; manuscript evaluator Jour. of Feminist Studies in Religion, Cambridge, Mass., 1994—; contbg. editor The Witness, 1994—; frequent guest lectr. at various colls., seminaries, civic and religious groups. Author: (books) Adamant and Stone Chips, 1967, In Search of Balance, 1969, Women, Men and the Bible, 1977 1st rev. edit. 1988, Korean translation, 1981, Speech, Silence, Action, 1980, (with others) Is the Homosexual My Neighbor? A Positive Christian Response, 1978, rev. edit. 1994 (Integrity award 1979), The Divine Feminine: Biblical Imagery of God as Female, 1983, in German 1985, French, 1990, Italian, 1993, (with others) Views from the Intersection, 1984, Godding: Human Responsibility and the Bible, 1987, Sensuous Spirituality: Out from Fundamentalism, 1992 (N.J. Lesbian and Gay Achievement award 1992); editor: Women of Faith in Dialogue, 1987, Adam Among the Television Trees, 1971. Recipient Lifetime Achievment award Sr. Action in a Gay Environ., 1999. Mem. MLA (exec. com. religion and lit. 1976-80), Women's Inst. for Freedom of the Press (assoc.), Milton Soc. Am. (exec. com. 1974-76). Democrat. Episcopalian. Avocations: travel, gardening, grandmothering. Home and Office: 11 Yearling Trl Hewitt NJ 07421-2510

MÖLLER, ÅKE JOHAN RICHARD, oral microbiologist, endodontist, educator; b. Göteborg, Sweden, Sept. 25, 1916; s. Axel Richard and Anna Justina (Fredlund) M.; m. Margit Ingegerd Olsson, July 15, 1939; children: Barbro, Lars, Jan. DDS, Dental Sch. Stockholm, 1941; D in Odontics, Dental Sch. Malmö, 1966; specialist degree in endodontology, 1968. Asst. tchr. Dental Sch. Stockholm, 1941-43; pvt. dental practice, 1943-65; asst. tchr. Med. Faculty Göteborg, Sweden, 1954-66, assoc. prof. med. microbiology, 1966, acting prof., 1968-68, prof. oral microbiology, Odontologic faculty, 1970-83; prefekt Inst. Med. Microbiology, Göteborg, 1974-81; cons. in field for assns. and labs., 1958-90. Contbr. articles to profl. jours. Mem. Swedish Physician Soc., Göteborg Dental Soc. (Elander prize 1958), Odontol. Inst. (chmn. hygiene com. 1970-83), Swedish Dental Soc. (Grand prize 1968), others. Avocations: nature, sailing. Home: Bävervägen 16, S-43370 Sävedalen Sweden Office: Inst Oral Microbiology, Box 450, S-40530 Göteborg Sweden

MØLLER, BIRGER LINDBERG, biochemist, educator; b. Frederiksberg, Copenhagen, Denmark, Nov. 17, 1946; s. Henry Christensen and Ragnhild Lindberg (Hansen) M.; m. Birte Kloppenborg Skrumsager, Mar. 19, 1975; children: Inge Skrumsager Møller, Lene Skrumsager Møller. MSc, U. Copenhagen, 1972, PhD, 1975, DSc, 1984. Postdoctoral fellow U. Calif., Davis, 1975-77; sr. rsch. scientist dept. physiology Carlsberg Lab., Copenhagen, 1977-83, Niels Bohr fellow dept. physiology, 1983-84; rsch. prof. dept. plant physiology Royal Vet. and Agrl. U., Copenhagen, 1984-89, prof. plant biochemistry, dept. plant biology, 1990—; head Ctr. for Molecular Plant Physiology Danish Nat. Rsch. Found., 1998—. Recipient Hans Gram medal Royal Danish Acad. Scis. and Letters, 1985, Pedersholm Legat, 1988, Carlsberg Mindelegat for Brygger J.C. Jacobsen, 1994, numerous grants. Achievements include research in plant natural products, photosynthesis, starch. Home: Kongstedvej 5, DK-2700 Brønshøj Denmark Office: Royal Vet and Agrl U, 40 Thorvaldsensvej, DK-1871 Copenhagen Denmark

MÖLLER, ERNA BIRGITTA IRMGARD, immunologist; b. Stockholm, Mar. 14, 1940; d. Gunnar and Irmgard (Nilsson) Lindell; m. Goran Moller, June 10, 1960; children: Gunnar, Elisabeth. MD, PhD, Karolinska Inst., Stockholm, 1966; degree (hon.), Turku U., 1996, Helsinki U., 2000. Scientist MRC, Stockholm, 1969-75; sr. lectr. Karolinska Inst., Stockholm, 1975-83, prof. transplantation immunology, 1983-86, prof. clin. immunology, 1986—. Contbr. articles to profl. jours. Mem. Swedish Acad. Engring. Home: Morabergsv 14, S-13333 Saltsjobaden Sweden Office: Huddinge Hosp/Karolinska U, Divsn Clin Immunology, S-14186 Huddinge Sweden

MÖLLER, GÖRAN, immunology educator; b. Vittangi, Sweden, Aug. 30, 1936; s. Sven and Edla (Falck) M.; m. Erna Lindell, June 10, 1960; children: Gunnar, Elisabeth. MD and PhD, Karolinska Inst., Stockholm, 1963. Lic. physician, Sweden. Scientist Swedish Cancer Soc., Stockholm, 1963-69; prof. Karolinska Inst., Stockholm, 1969-85, Stockholm U., 1985—; mem. Nobel Com., Stockholm, 1976-78, Nobel Assembly, Stockholm, 1977-85, vice chmn., 1985. Editor Jour. Immunol. Revs., 1969-96, Scandinavian Jour., 1990—; contbr. articles to profl. jours. Recipient A. Jahres prize Oslo U., 1976. Mem. Royal Acad. Medicine Belgium (fgn. mem.), Am. Assn. Immunology (hon. mem.), Scandinavian Soc. Immunology (hon. mem., pres. 1978-82). Home: Morabergsvagen 14, 133 33 Saltsjobaden Sweden Office: Stockholm U, 106 91 Stockholm Sweden

MÖLLER, HENRIK EINAR, business executive, acoustics consultant; b. Fredriksberg, Denmark, Dec. 27, 1961; arrived in Finland, 1987; s. Henning and Anna Elsebeth (Sörensen) M.; m. Sirpa Tuulikki Hämäläinen, 1987; children: Julia, Jonas. BA in Engring., Aalborg (Denmark) U., 1986; MSc in Tech., Helsinki U. Tech., 1991. acoustics tchr. dept. light and sound design Theatre Acad. Finland, 1989—. Tchr. asst. Aalborg Univ. Ctr., 1986-87; acoustics cons. Finnish Acoustics Ctr., 1987-88, 91-94; tchr. sci. Sipoo Swedish H.S., 1988-91; acoustics cons., mng. dir. Akukon Cons. Engrs., Finland, 1994—. Mem. Finnish Acoustic Soc., Danish Acoustic Soc., Audio Engring. Soc. (vice chair Finnih sect.), Acoustic Soc. Am. Office: Akukon Cons Engrs Ltd, Kornetintie 4 A, FIN00380 Helsinki Finland

MOLLER, MARIANNE, retired primary school educator; b. Copenhagen, Apr. 12, 1929; arrived in Australia, 1968; d. Axel and Kamma Edith (Norholt) M. Child care cert., London, 1951, qualified tchr., 1961. Child care worker Wycliffe Bible Translators, Ukarumpa, Papua New Guinea, 1972-76; primary tchr. Trinity Christian Sch., Adelaide, Australia, 1977-78, Cowman Coll., Canberra, Australia, 1980-81; nanny pvt. homes, Adelaide, 1982-83, 85-89; staff nursery nurse Kindy, Adelaide, 1983-84; ret., 1989. Singer Woodville Choral Group, Salford Choral Soc., others. Avocation: singing.

MOLLER, SVEND ERIK, pharmacology company executive; b. Copenhagen, Nov. 20, 1941; s. Svend and Elisabeth (Larsen) M.; m. Bente Hedegaard Christensen, Sept. 21, 1968; children: Thomas, Jacob. MSc in Pharmacy, Royal Danish Sch. of Pharmacy, Copenhagen, 1967, PhD in Pharmacology, 1971; DSc in Medicine, U. Copenhagen, 1986. Traveling substitute Danish Pharm. Assn., Copenhagen, 1967-68; head dept. clin. pharmacology St. Hans Psychiat. Univ. Hosp., Roskilde, Denmark, 1971-94; clin. rsch. mgr. H. Lundbeck A/S, Copenhagen, 1994-95, clin. rsch. dir., 1995-97, internat. med. mktg. dir., 1997—. 1st lt. Royal Danish Navy, 1960-62. Mem. Internat. Coll. Neuro-Psychopharmacology, European Coll. of Neuropsychopharmacology, Serotonin Club, Rotary Internat. Avocation: playing trombone in traditional jazz band. Office: H Lundbeck A/S, Ottiliavej 9, DK-2500 Valby Copenhagen, Denmark

MOLLER, THORSTEN JENS, physicist, researcher; b. Kassel, Germany, Apr. 2, 1967. Diploma in physics, U. Göttingen, Germany, 1993, PhD, 1996. Rschr. Max-Planck-Inst. for Fluidmechanics, Göttingen, 1993-94, German Aerospace CTr., Göttingen, 1994—. Contbr. articles to profl. jours.; inventor in field.

MOLLISH, JACK JAMES, retired insurance executive; b. Dudley, Pa., June 10, 1918; s. Martin and Helen M.; m. Helen Kocik, Aug. 23, 1947; 1 child: Mary Anne Mollish Seckman. Pres. CEO Nat. Ins. Mgmt. Corp., Clarksburg, W.Va., 1957-2000, Home Crafts Corp., Clarksburg, W.Va., 1981-95; sec., pres. Clarksburg Life Underwriters, 1968, 69. Mem. Serra Club (pres. 1977—), Lions. Republican. Roman Catholic. Avocations: golf, baseball, reading, hunting. Home: PO Box 2146 Clarksburg WV 26302-2146

MOLLISON, DENIS, mathematics educator, conservationist; b. Carshalton, Surrey, Eng., June 28, 1945; s. Patrick Loudon and Margaret Doreen (Peirce) M.; m. Jenny Hutton, June 1, 1978; children: Clare, Hazel, Daisy, Charles. MA in Math., Cambridge (Eng.) U., 1966, PhD in Math., 1971, Sc.D. in Math., 1994. Rsch. fellow Cambridge U., Kings Coll., 1969-73; lectr. Heriot-Watt U., Edinburgh, Scotland, 1973-79, reader, 1979-86, prof. applied probability, 1986—; vis. profl. fellow Newton Inst., Cambridge, 1993; vis. fellow commoner Trinity Coll., Cambridge, 1993;. Editor: Epidemic Models: Their Structure and Relation to Data, 1995; contbr. numerous papers to profl. jours. on epidemic and population dynamics and wave energy statistics. Co-founder John Muir Trust, U.K., 1983, trustee, 1986—; chair Mountain Bothies Assn., U.K., 1978-94 (hon. life mem. 1995); coun. mem. Nat. Trust for Scotland, 1979-84, 99—. Recipient Smiths prize Cambridge U., 1968. Fellow Royal Statis. Soc.; mem. Bernoulli Soc., various conservation orgns. Scottish Liberal Democrat. Rationalist. Avocations: mountaineering, photography, racket games, music. Home: Laigh House Inveresk Vill, Musselburgh EH21 7TD, Scotland Office: Heriot-Watt U, Dept Actuarial Math/Stats, Edinburgh EH14 4AS, Scotland

MOLNÁR, GÁBOR, psychiatrist, neurologist, researcher; b. Debrecen, Hungary, July 17, 1951; s. Lajos and Sarolta (Diénes) M.; m. Elena Aseva, Jan. 3, 1974; children: Dénes, Lajos, Léna. MD, Sechenow Med. Sch., Moscow, 1975. Med. diplomate, spl. cert. in psychiatry and neurology. Sr. asst. prof. Debrecen Med. Sch., 1975-90; sr. registrar City Hosp., Debrecen, 1990-94; cons. in psychiatry and neurology Debrecen, 1994-98; psychiatrist, neurologist Budapest Social Ctr., 1998—. Active Amnesty Internat., 1991-93. Fellow Internat. Coll. Neuro-Psychopharmacology; mem. N.Y. Acad. Scis., Internat. Soc. of Psychoneuroendocrinology. Achievements include research in incidence of pathological postmenopausal estrogen deficiency in mental disorders of the involution, emotional cognitive interactions focusing on the diagnostic possibilities of detecting interhemispherical communications, further development of M. Bleuler's endocrine psycho-syndrome concept; work on some problems of psychonosologics, psychiatric nosology, stress-psychiatry. Avocations: paleolithic art, human development, swimming, videoclips. Home: Solymarvolgyi ut 78, H-1037 Budapest Hungary Office: Budapest Soc Ctr, Dozsa Gyorgy ut 152, H-1134 Budapest Hungary

MOLNAR, GABOR, mechanical engineer; b. Belisce, Croatia, June 9, 1942; s. Josip and Paulina (Timaric) M.; m. Dusanka Jerosimic, Feb. 16, 1980; 1 child, Zoltan. Diploma in engring., U. Zagreb, 1973. Designer Tehnomehanika factory, Marija Bistrica, Croatia, 1980-84, Koncar Generators, Zagreb, Croatia, 1984-90. Home: Ul Kralja Zvonimira 24, 10410 Velika Gorica Croatia

MOLNAR, ILDIKO, internist, allergist, immunologist; b. Debrecen, Hungary, May 28, 1953; s. Lajos and Lajosne (Dienes Sarolta) M. MD, U. Debrecen, 1977; PhD, Hungarian Acad. Scis., Budapest, 1992; specialization in allergology, Budapest, 1993, specialization in clin. immunology, 1993. Internist Kenezy County Tchg. Hosp., Debrecen, Hungary, 1977—; chief physician Kenezy County Tchg. Hosp., Debrecen, 1994—; sec. endocrinology com. Hungarian Acad. Scis. Mem. Found. Hungarian Immunology Soc. (fin. com.), Hungarian Internal Soc., Hungarian Endocrinology and Metabolism, European Thyroid Assn., N.Y. Acad. Scis. E-mail: molil@mail.matav.hu. Office: Kenezy County Tchg Hosp, Bartok B ut 2-26, H-4043 Debrecen Hungary

MOLNÁR, IMRE, agricultural engineer, agricultural consultant; b. Timár, Hungary, Mar. 21, 1941; s. Ferenc and Ferencné (Mária Vattamány) M.; m. Imréné Ildikó Dobai, Aug. 8, 1963; 1 child, Krisztina. MSc, U. Agr., Debrecen, Hungary, 1963; Specialist MSc, U. Agr., Gödöllö, Hungary, 1966, PhD, 1969; Candidate, Hungarian Acad. Scis., Budapest, Hungary. Agrl. engr. Ctr. Plant and Soil Health of Hajdu-Bihar County, Debrecen, Hungary, 1964-90; dir. HID Co., Budapest, 1992, Uj Élet Agrl. Coop. Farm, Hencida, Hungary, 1992—; agrl. cons. Judiciary Debrecen, 1993—; cons. Hungarian Quality Control Co., Budapest, 1994. Contbr. articles to profl. jours. Avocations: reading, playing tennis, swimming, listening to music, travel. Home: 3 Ispotály utca, 4025 Debrecen Hungary Office: U Szeged Coll Agr, 15 Andrássy u, 6800 Hodmezovásdrhely Hungary

MOLNAR, LASZLS GIZA, microbiologist, researcher; b. Tiskevar, Hungary, Nov. 19, 1939; s. Jszsef Molnar and Jszsefni Berzsenyi Jolan; m. Laszlsni Michliva, Jan. 31, 1968; children: Jszsef, Monika, Laszls. Grad., U. Budapest, Hungary, 1967, PhD, 1986. Rschr. Inst. Hungarian Acad. Sci., Budapest, 1967-70; rschr. Vet. Sci. and Med. U., Budapest, 1970-80, first asst., 1980-86, reader, 1986—; vis. prof. Fedn. U. Para, Belim, Para, Brazil, 1994—. Contbr. articles to profl. jours. Sgt. Armed Forces, 1959-62. Recipient Medal of Honor, Brasilian Assn. Saude, Belem, 1996, Mencao Honrosa, Assn. Vet. Medicine, Belem, 1997. Mem. Assn. Hungarian Microbiologists, Assn. Hungarian Vet. Medicine, Conselho Vet. Medicine. Roman Catholic. Avocations: literature, history. E-mail: eva@cbio.ufpa.br. Fax: 55 091 211 1773. Home: Av Visconde Sousa Franco, 1144, 66053000 Belim Par, Brazil Office: U Fed do Para, Campus Univ do Guama, 66075900 Belam Para, Brazil

MOLNAR, LAWRENCE, lawyer; b. Czygand, Hungary, Apr. 14, 1927; came to U.S., 1954; s. Alexander and Marie (Vavra) M.; m. Virginia Hampton Broome, July 16, 1999. Juris Utriusque Candidatus, Charles U., Prague, Czechoslovakia, 1951; JD, NYU, 1962; LLM, LLD (hon.), Charles U., 1991. Bar: N.Y. 1962, U.S. Dist. Ct. (so. and ea. dists.) N.Y. 1970, Czech Republic, 1991. With U.S. Intelligence, Berlin, 1951-54, Lansen, Naeve Corp., N.Y., 1955-56; asst. mgr. export traffic Intra-Mar Shipping Corp., N.Y., 1957-58; mgr. export traffic Melchior, Armstrong, Ridgefield, N.J., 1958-59; assoc. Hamburger, Weinschenk, N.Y.C., 1963-69; ptnr. Hamburger, Weinschenk, Molnar & Fisher, N.Y.C., 1969—. Mem. ABA, Assn. of Bar of City of N.Y., Consular Law Soc. (v.p. 1980—), Fgn. Law Assn., Queens Bar Assn. Office: Hamburger Weinschenk Molnar & Fisher 36 W 44th St New York NY 10036-8102

MOLNAR, MARK, psychophysiologist; b. Pecs, Hungary, Aug. 19, 1949; s. Laszlo and Maria (Pump) M.; m. Judit Miklossy, 1974 (div. 1980); children: Barbara, Mark; m. Magdolna Kovari, Nov. 27, 1987; 1 child, Tamas. MD, Univ. Med. Sch. Debrecen, Hungary, 1973; PhD, Budapest Acad. Scis., 1988. Neurologist Univ. Med. Sch., Pecs, Hungary, 1973-76; rsch. fellow Inst. Psychology Acad. Sci., Budapest, 1976-95, head. psychophysiology dept., 1995—; neurologist St. Stephen's Hosp., Budapest, 1977-79; head EEG dept. St. Rokus Hosp., Budapest, 1988—. Mem. European Fedn. Psychophysiol. Scis., Soc. Neurosci., Soc. Psychophysiol. Rsch. Office: Inst Psychology, Terez krt 13, H-1394 Budapest Hungary

MOLNAR, ROWAN RUSTEM, anesthesiologist; b. London, Nov. 7, 1961; arrived in Australia, 1963; s. Robert Rustem and Lorraine Margaret (Briggs) M.; m. Julianne Margaret Kiel, Oct. 13, 1990; children: Ella, Hamish, Lucy. MBBS, Melbourne U., 1984. Intern St. Vincent's Hosp., Melbourne, 1985, jr. resident med. officer, 1986, anaesthetic registrar, 1988, 90, staff anaesthetist, 1992, sr. staff anaesthetist, 1993—; anaesthetic registrar Geelong Hosp., 1987, Royal Women's Hosp., 1989, Royal Children's Hosp., 1989; sr. clin. fellow in anaesthesia Mass. Gen. Hosp., 1991; instr. in anaesthesia Harvard U. Med. Sch., Boston, 1991; lectr. Melbourne U. Sch. of Medicine, 1993—. Author: Clinical Anaesthesia Procedures of the Massachusetts General Hospital, 4th edit., 1993, 5th edit., 1997; contbr. articles to profl. jours. Fellow Australian and New Zealand Coll. Anesthesiologists (treas. 1994—, lectr. part II course 1992—), Australian Med. Assn. (councillor 1997—), Australian Soc. Anesthetists, Victoria Racing Club. Avocations: horse racing, fly fishing. Office: Dept Anesth St Vincents Hos, Victoria Parade, Fitzroy VIC 3065, Australia

MOLNAR, THOMAS FERENC, thoracic surgeon, consultant, educator; b. Pecs, Hungary, Oct. 4, 1953; s. Ferenc and Brigitta (Royko) M.; m. Eve Hadhazi, Mar. 17, 1983; children: Thomas, Gitta. MD, Med. U. Pecs, Hungary, 1979; PhD, Acad. Scis. of Hungary, 1995. Diplomate European Bd. Thoracic Cardiovasc. Surgeons. Asst. surgeon dept. surgery Town Hosp., Marcali, Hungary, 1979-81; resident, registrar, dept. surgery County Hosp. of Pecs, 1981-91; trainee, sr. house officer dept. thoracic surgery Frenchay Hosp., Bristol, Eng., 1991; sr. house officer, registrar dept. thoracic surgery Hairmyres Hosp., Glasgow, Scotland, 1994; sr. registrar dept. surgery County Hosp. of Pecs, 1994-95; asst. prof., head dept. thoracic surgery, cons. Med. U. Pecs, First Clinic of Surgery, 1995—; head thoracic surgery unit County Hosp. of Pecs, 1994-95; sr. lectr., asst. prof. surgery Med. U. Pecs, 1994—; lectr. mil. history U. Pecs, 1988-89. Author: How to stop smoking, 1991; author articles and lectures. Capt. res. Hungarian Army, 1979-80. Mem. European Soc. Thoracic Surgeons (regent), European Assn. for Cardiothoracic Surgery (postgrad. edn. com.). Roman Catholic. Avocations: war games, military history. Home: Lanc U 14, H-7624 Pécs Hungary Office: Med U Pecs First Clinic of Surgery, PO Box 99, H-7624 Pécs Hungary

MOLNAR, VERA (VERONIQUE MOLNAR), visual artist, educator; b. Budapest, Hungary, Jan. 5, 1924; arrive in France, 1947; d. Eugen and Elisabeth (Pollatschek) Gacs; m. Francois Ferenc Molnar (dec. 1993). Grad., H.S. Visual Arts, Hungary, 1947. Founding mem. Groupe de Recherche D'Art Visuel, Paris, 1960, Art & Informatique, Paris, 1967; with ARTA, Centre G. Pompidou, Paris, 1979-82; founding mem. Centre de Recherche des Arts Visuels U. Paris I-Sorbonne, 1980, prof. art dept., 1985-90. Author: 1 % of Disorder, 1980, Out of Square, 1994, Tango, 1996, Solo d'untrait noir, 1999; contbr. articles to profl. jours.; one-woman shows include Musée d' Art Moderne d'Ottendorf, Studio A, Germany, 1990, Galerie St.-Johann, Saarbrücken, Germany, 1990, Musée Vasarely, Budapest, Hungary, 1990, Stiftung für konkrete Kunst, Reutlingen, Germany, 1990, Gesellschaft für Kunst und Gestaltung, Bonn, Germany, 1991, 94, Galerie St. Charles de Rose, Paris, 1991, Galerie St. Johann, Saarbrücken, 1992, Cloître du CRDP Poitou-Charentes, Poiters, France, 1993, Kunst im Herrenhof, Neustadt, Germany, 1993, Galerie März, Mannheim et Ladenburg, Germany, 1994, Musée Wilhelm-Hack, Ludwigshafen, Germany, Galerie Quadri, Brussels, 1994, Found. pour l'art concret, Zurich, Switzerland, 1994, Galerie März, Mannheim, Germany, 1994, 95, Galerie Oniris, Rennes, France, 1995, Muséee d'Art et d'Historie, Cholet, France, 1995, 96Galerie Its-art-Ist, Brussels, 1996, Galerie März, Mannheim et Ladenburg, Germany, 1996, Galerie le Faisant, Strasbourg, France, 1996, Ecole des Beaux-Arts (vitrines), Valenciennes, France, 1996, others. Home: 54 R Halle, 75014 Paris France

MOLNÁR, ZOLTÁN, neuroscientist, anatomy educator; b. Nagykörös, Hungary, Aug. 20, 1964; arrived in Eng., 1988; s. Elek and Julianna (Szabó) M.; m. Nadia Pollini, 1994; children: Matyas, Thomas. MD, Albert Szent-Györgyi Med., Szeged, Hungary, 1988; DPhil, Oxford (Eng.) U., 1994, MA, 1995. Neurosurgical resident Albert Szent-Györgyi Med. Sch., Szeged, 1988; Soros-Has scholar Oxford U., Hertford Coll., 1988-89; Wellcome trust rsch. asst. U. Lab. of Physiology, Oxford, Eng., 1989-92; jr. rsch. fellow Merton Coll. Oxford and U. Lab. Physiology, Oxford U., 1992-96; postdoctoral fellow Inst. Cellular Biology and Morphology, U. Lausanne (Switzerland) Faculty Medicine, 1998-99; univ. lectr. dept. human anatomy and genetics U. Oxford, 2000—, tutor anatomy St. John's Coll., 2000—; chmn. sci. forum undergrad. students, dept. physiology, Albert Szent-Györgyi Med. Sch., Szeged, 1986-88; vis. postdoctoral fellow Prefectural Med. Sch., Kyoto, Japan, 1992-93; jr. dean Merton College, Oxford, 1994—. Author: Development of Thalamocortical Connections, 1998; editor: Humsirc Elective Programme Book, 1988. Co-sec. Oxford Hungarian Soc., 1989. Recipient Cortical Explorer prize Cajal Club of Am. Anat. Soc., 1999, Biennial Rolleston Meml. prize Oxford and Cambridge Univs., 1995; Med. Rsch. Coun. fellow, 1994-98, CIBA Found. fellow U. Queensland, 1995, U. Calif., David, 1997. Avocations: tennis. Home: St John's Coll, St Giles St, Oxford OX1 3JP, England Office: U Oxford Dept Human Anatomy, and Genetics, S Parks Rd, Oxford OX1 3QX, England

MOLODTSOV, DMITRI, mathematician; b. Moscow, June 2, 1949; s. Anatoliy and Julia (Sedova) Molodtsov; m. Helena Molodtsova; children: Daria, Anatoliy. Honors Degree, Moscow U., 1971, Candidate of Sci., 1974, DSc, 1990. Cert. mathematician. Rschr. Computer Ctr. Russian Acad. Sci., Moscow, 1974—. Author: Stability of Optimality Principles, 1987; author of the theory of soft sets. Home: Maliy Predtechenskiy 6-12, 123242 Moscow Russia Office: Vavilova St 40, 117967 Moscow Russia

MOLODTSOV, SERGUEI L'VOVICH, educator; b. Leningrad, Russia, Dec. 2, 1961; s. Lev Anatol'evich and Lina Nikolaevna (Ivanova) M.; m. Olga Vital'evna Korzova, Oct. 27, 1984; children: Maria, Alexandra. M of Physics, Leningrad State U., Russia, 1984, PhD, 1987; Dr.rer.nat., Freie U., Berlin, 1991; Dr.habil., St. Petersburg State U., Russia, 1993. Rsch. assoc. Leningrad State U., Russia, 1987-89; sr. rsch. assoc. St. Petersburg State U., Russia, 1990—; assoc. prof. Tech. U. Dresden, Germany, 2000—; guest prof. Tech. U. Dresden, Germany, 1994-96, 97-99, Inst. de Ciencia de Materiales, Madrid, 1997. Contbr. articles to profl. jours. Mem. Russian-German Adv. Com. Application of Synchrotron Radiation, Berlin, Moscow, 1995—. Alexander von Humboldt Found. fellow, 1991. Mem. Alexander Von Humboldt Club. Avocations: tennis, skiing, hiking. Office: Inst f Oberflächen, u Mikzostruktuzphysik, D-01069 Dresden Germany

MOLOKANOVA, NATALIA ALEKSANDROVNA, nuclear research scientist; b. Dubna, Russia, Dec. 22, 1974; d. Aleksandr Grigorievich and Tatiana Aleksandrovna (Agudina) M. MSc, Engring. Physics Inst., Moscow, 1997; postgrad., Univ. Ctr., Dubna, 1997—. Sci. rschr. Joint Inst. for Nuclear Rsch., Dubna, 1995—. Contbr. article to Czechoslovak Jour. Physics. Mem. Assn. Young Scientists and Specialists of Joint Inst. for Nuclear Rsch. (sci. sec.). Avocations: music, swimming, windsurfing, gardening. Fax: 7 09621 66666. E-mail: molokan@sunse.jinr.ru. Home: Pontecorvo 17 Apt 1202, 141980 Dubna, Moscow Region Russia Office: Joint Inst for Nuclear Rsch, Joliot-Curie 6, 141980 Dubna, Moscow Region Russia

MOLOTKOV, LEV ANATOLIYEVICH, physicist, researcher; b. Leningrad, Russia, Nov. 11, 1932; s. Anatolii Yevgenyevich and Charlotta Rudolfovna (Steinmann) M.; m. Irina Aleksandrovna Kholodilina, Mar. 21, 1959 (dec. Apr. 1994); 1 child, Sergei. Degree in physics, U. Leningrad, USSR, 1955, PhD, 1962, DSc, 1975. Jr. rschr. Leningrad Math. Inst. (now St. Petersburg Math. Inst.), 1955-68, sr. rschr., 1968-86, leading rschr., 1986—; prof. Tech. Inst., St. Petersburg, 1997—. Author: Matrix Method in the Theory of Wave Propagation in Elastic and Fluid Media, 1984; co-author: Waves in Layered Homogeneous Isotropic Elastic Media, vol. I, 1982, vol. II, 1985, Effective Seismic Models of Fractured and Porous Media, 1998; contbr. over 170 articles to profl. jours. Recipient State Prize of USSR, 1982; grantee Soros, 11994, 95, Russian Fund Fundamental Investigations, 1993. Mem. European Assn. Geoscientists and Engrs., European-Asian Geophys. Soc. Avocations: travel, skiing, bicycling, philately. Home: Chernyshevskii Sq 8 Ap 5, 196070 Saint Petersburg Russia Office: POMI, Fontanka 27, 191011 Saint Petersburg Russia

MOLSON, ERIC H., beverage company executive; b. Montreal, Sept. 16, 1937; s. Thomas Henry Pentland and Celia Frances (Cantlie) M.; m. Jane Mitchell, Apr. 16, 1966; 3 children. AB, Princeton U., 1959. With Molson Inc., Montreal, chmn. bd., 1988—. Office: Molson Inc, 1555 Notre Dame St E, Montreal, PQ Canada H2L 2R5

MOLTERER, WILHELM, administrator; b. Steyr, Austria, May 14, 1955; married. Grad. in social econs., Johannes Kepler U., Linz, 1980. Econ. policy advisor Austrian Farmers' Fedn., 1981-85; with Stae Govt. Upper Austria, 1985-87; pvt. sec. then chief staff Office min. of Agrl., 1987-89; CEO Austrian Farmers' Fedn., 1989-93; min. agrl., forestry, and water mgmt. Austria, 1994-2000, min. agrl., forestry, environment, and water mgmt., 2000—. E-mail: wilhelm.molterer@bmlf.gv.at. Office: Fed Min Agrl & Forestry, Stubenring 1, A-1012 Vienna Austria

MOLTZAU, TROND, NATO official; b. Oslo, Dec. 12, 1944; m. Lisbeth Moltzau; 2 children. Grad., Flight Sch., Norway, 1965, Air Force Acad., 1971; postgrad., Norwegian Air Force Staff Coll, 1983-84. Commd. 2d lt. Royal Norwegian Air Force, 1965, advanced through grades to lt. gen., 1999, early career assignments include pilot 334th squadron, 1965-69, pilot, then flight comdr., 1971-76, inspection officer Air Force Acad., 1976-78, flight comdr. 336 squadron, 1978-79, dep. comdg. officer 332 squadron, then squadron comdr., 1979-83, staff officer Hdqrs. Def. Command, Air Staff, 1984; with Tactical Sch. Royal Norwegian Air Force, Rygge Main Air Sta.; comdr. Norwegian Air Force Acad. Royal Norwegian Air Force, 1989-91, comdr. Norwegian Air Force Staff Coll., 1992-93; chief of staff, Hdqrs. Def. Command Royal Norwegian Air Force, North Norway, 1993-94; dep. chief of staff Ops. and Plans, Hdqrs. Def. Command Royal Norwegian Air Force, 1994-96, dep. chief of staff, Plans and Policy Divsn., 1996-99; Norwegian mil. rep. to NATO's Mil. Com. Royal Norwegian Air Force, Brussels, 1999—; also Norwegian mil. del. to Western European Union, 1999—. Decorated Def. Svc. medal with 2 stars, Nat. Svc. medal with 3 stars, Comdr. with star, Icelandic order of Falcon. Office: NATO Hdqrs, Blvd Leopold III, 1110 Brussels Belgium*

MOLYNEAUX, JAMES HENRY, retired government official; b. Aug. 27, 1920; s. William Molyneaux. Grad., Aldergrove Sch. Vice-chmn. mng. com. Eastern Spl. Care Hosp., Ireland, 1966-73; hon. sec. S. Antrim Unionist Assn., Ireland, 1964-70; v.p. Ulster Unionist Council, 1974; mem. No. Ireland Assembly, 1982-86; leader Ulster Unionist Party House of Commons, 1974-95; M.P. from Antrim South, 1970-83, M.P. from Lagan Valley, 1983-97. Served with Royal Air Force, 1941-46. Decorated Grand Master of Orange Order, Hon. PGM of Can., Sovereign Grand Master. Avocations: gardening, music. Office: Aldergrove, Crumlin Co, Antrim Northern Ireland also: House of Lords, London SW1A 0PW, England*

MOLZ, FRED JOHN, III, hydrologist, educator; b. Mays Landing, N.J., Aug. 13, 1943; s. Fred John Jr. and Viola Violet (MacDonald) M.; m. Mary Lee Clark, Dec. 17, 1966; children: Fred John IV, Stephen Joseph. BS in Physics, Drexel U., 1966, MCE, 1968; PhD in Hydrology, Stanford U., 1970. Hydraulic engr. U.S. Geol. Survey, Menlo Park, Calif., 1970; asst. prof. Auburn (Ala.) U., 1970-74, alumni asst. prof., 1974-76, alumni assoc. prof., 1976-80, asst. dean research, 1979-84, dir. Eng. exptl. sta., 1981-84, prof., 1980-84, Feagin prof., 1984-89, Huff eminent scholar, 1990-95; Dept. Energy disting. scientist Clemson U., 1995—; cons. Battelle N.W., Richland, Wash., 1982-83, 84-85, Argonne (Ill.) Nat. Labs., 1983-85, Electric Power Rsch. Inst., Menlo Park, Calif., 1984-85, U.S. NRC, 1991-97. Author: (with others) Numerical Methods in Hydrology, 1971, Modeling Wastewater Renovation, 1981; contbr. articles to profl. jours. Recipient Disting. Faculty award Auburn U. Alumni Assn., 1987; grantee EPA, 1986, 90, 97, DOE, 1980, 83, 98, U.S. Dept. Edn., 1991, NSF, 1992, 94, 97. Fellow Am. Geophys. Union (Horton award 1992); mem. Am. Soc. Agronomy, Nat. Ground Water Assn., Am. Inst. Hydrology. Avocations: reading, travel, investing. Home: 213 Amethyst Way Seneca SC 29672-6851 Office: Clemson U Dept Environ Engring & Sci 342 Computer Ct Anderson SC 29625-6510

MOLZ, PHILIP JACK, management consultant; b. N.Y.C., Jan. 28, 1929; s. Philip and Mary H. Molz; m. Margaret J. Ralph, July 29, 1978; 1 child, Philene M. BS in Math., CCNY, 1953; PhD in Internat. Bus. Adminstrn., Ky.-Western. Cert. quality auditor; cert. ISO/Q5 9000 lead assessor; cert. MBTI instr.; cert. SYMLOG instr.; cert. team facilitator. Accountant, auditor GE, Schenectady, N.Y., 1953-61; treas. GE, Rio, Brazil, 1961-65; CFO GE, Wolfenbûttel, Germany, 1965-68; corp. fin. analyst ITT, N.Y.C., 1968-70; CFO, v.p. fin. adminstrn. Xerox Latin Am., Stamford, Conn., 1970-74; CFO Abbott Labs. Internat., N. Chicago, Ill., 1974-78; sr. CFO Macmillan Pub., N.Y.C., 1978-80; pres., owner TSI Co., Bridgeport, Conn., 1980-85; pres. IJ Cos., Knoxville, Tenn., 1985-89; pres., owner PMP Internat. Group, Knoxville, 1989-94, Kansas City, Kans., 1994—; ind. NIKKEN distbr. Co-author: Controller's Handbook, 1974, Treasurer's Handbook, 1976, Quality Manual Reference, 1988. With CIC U.S. Army, 1951-53, Korea. Republican. Roman Catholic. Avocations: skiing, racquetball, rancher, tree farmer, oil painting. Home and Office: 11930 Stearns St Overland Park KS 66213-1962

MOMAH, DAVID N., physiotherapist; b. Aug. 1, 1960. BS, U. Ibadan, Nigeria, 1986; MS, Columbia State U., 1994, PhD, 1996. Pres., CEO Universal Therapeutics, Bronx, N.Y., 1993—, Christ for the Widows and Orphans, N.Y.C., 1997—, Peace Towers Corp., N.Y.C., 1997—. Home: 100 Sprain Valley Rd Scarsdale NY 10583-3156

MOMAH, ETHEL CHUKWUEKWE, women's health nurse; b. Iyi-Enu, Ogidi, Nigeria, May 28, 1934; d. Zaccheus C. and Victoria U. (Orizu) Obi; m. Christian C. Momah, Nov. 21, 1959; children: Chukwudi, Adaora, Azuka. SRN, Harrow Hosp., Middlesex, U.K., 1956; SCM, Mothers Hosp., London, 1957; MTD, Midwife Tchrs. Coll., Surrey, U.K., 1964; BS, Upsala Coll., 1988. Cert. inpatient obstetric nurse Nat. Cert. Corp. Nurse-midwife Guy's Hosp., London, 1959; nursing sister, head nurse labor/delivery Univ. Coll. Hosp., Ibadan, Nigeria, 1960-62; midwife tutor Lagos (Nigeria) Island Maternity Hosp., 1963-66; nurse-midwife Brit. Hosp., Paris, 1966, Hosp. Cantonal, Geneva, Switzerland, 1967-78; patient care coord. St. Peter's Med. Ctr., New Brunswick, N.J., 1985-90, antenatal testing nurse, 1990—. Named Nurse of Yr. Women's Ambulatory Care Svc. St. Peters Univ. Hosp., 1997. Mem. Assn. of Women's Health, Obstetric and Neonatal Nurses. Office: St Peters Med Ctr New Brunswick NJ 08901

MOMANI, OMAR HAMID, military officer, pilot instructor; b. Amman, Jordan, May 2, 1958; s. Hamid Mufleh and Ameera Rasheed (Nihlawi) M.; m. Randa Faisal Zaghloul, July 3, 1983; children: Rania, Tariq, Nada, Nirmeen, Neveen. Aviation diploma, King Hussain Air Coll., Mafraq, Jordan, 1977; safety mgmt., U. So. Calif., L.A., 1981; BSc in Mil. Sci., Motah U., Jordan, 1991. Cert. fighter pilot, fighter weapons and electronic warfare instr., flight safety mgmt. Commd. officer Royal Jordanian Air Force, 1974, advanced through grades to col.; fighter pilot Royal Jordanian Air Force, Safawi, 1977-81, unit flight safety officer, 1981-84; fighter weapons instr. Royal Jordanian Air Force, Azraq, 1985-90; squadron comdr. Royal Jordanian Air Force, Safawi, 1991-94; dir. air safety br. Royal Jordanian Air Force, Amman, 1994-97; fighter instr. pilot United Arab Emirates Air Force, Dubai, 1997—; mem. bd. inquiry Royal Jordanian Air Line, Amman, 1994-97; bd. dirs. Golden Falcon Establishment, Ammam. Author: Human Factors in Air Accidents, 1996; editor Falcon Safety Jour., 1995-97. Fellow Middle East Bird Control Orgn., Jordan, 1996-97. Decorated Faithfull Svc. medal Royal Jordan Air Force, 1995. Fellow Nature and Wildlife Preservation; mem. Nat. Geog. Soc. Avocations: reading, traveling, nature observation, flying. Home: Alkhan St, Sharjah 28855, United Arab Emirates

MOMBA, MAGGY NDOMBO-BENETEKE, microbiology educator, researcher; b. Kinshasa, Zaire, Sept. 10, 1958; arrived in South Africa, 1991; d. Michel Eyeye Ndombo and Antoinette Amba Beneteke; 1 child, Tresor Bomba. BA, Inst. Superieur Pedagogique, Bombe, Kinshasa, 1982; BSc, U. Kisongani, Congo, 1983, MSc in Biology, 1985; MSc in Microbiology, U. Pretoria, South Africa, 1995, PhD in Microbiology, 1998. Chief lab. Dépot Ctrl. Médico-Pharmaceutique, Kinshasa, 1987-89; rsch. asst. Inst. Zairoise Pour la Conservation de la Nature, Kinshasa, 1989-92; rsch. asst. U. Pretoria, 1993-95, rschr., 1995-97; rschr. Coun. for Sci. and Indsl. Rsch., Pretoria, 1995-97; lectr., rschr. U. Ft. Hare, South Africa, 1997—; internat. referee Water Rsch., 1997—, Water South Africa, 1998—; mem. internat. adv. bd. South Africa Ctr. for Essential Cmty., 1999—. Contbr. articles to profl. jours. Mem. Water Rsch., Water South Africa. Avocations: healing ministry, evangelism, Bible study. Office: U Ft Hare P/Bag 1314, Dept Biochem & Microbiology, 5700 Alice Eastern Cape South Africa

MOMČILOVIĆ, BERISLAV, clinical research scientist, consultant; b. Zagreb, Croatia, Feb. 27, 1942; s. George and Nada (Gložić) M.; m. Marijana Dubravka Brinzej, June 25, 1966; 1 child, Rastko. MD, Med. Sch., Zagreb, 1966; MSc, Inst. Med. Rsch./Occup. Health, Zagreb, 1969; PhD, Med. Sch., Zagreb, 1973. Cert. specialist in internal medicine and occupational health. Rsch. asst. Inst. for Med. Rsch. and Occupational Health, Zagreb, 1969-77, assoc. prof., 1977-80, prof., 1980—, head dept. occupational health/toxicology, 1985-88; rsch. leader Inst. for Med. Rsch. and Occupational Health, 5, 1988—; temporary advisor WHO-Europe, Copenhagen, 1985—; mem. trace element metabolism in man and animals Parent Com. Aberdeen, Scotland, 1990—; vis. rsch. scientist USDA Human Nutrition Rsch. Ctr., Grand Forks, N.D., 1992-95; vis. rsch. scientist dept. physics, 1996. Editor: Trace Elements in Man and Animals 7, 1991; mem. editorial bd. Archives of Occupational Health and Toxicology, 1988-92. Wellcome Trust grantee, 1985. Mem. Yugoslav Radiation Protection Soc. (v.p. 1978-80, pres. 1980-82), Am. Inst. Nutrition, Am. Coll. Clin. Nutrition, Sigma Xi. Republican. Avocations: metaphysics, popular science, political history. Office: Inst Med Rsch and Occup Health, Ksaverska c2, Zagreb Croatia

MOMEN, MOOJAN, physician, researcher; b. Tabriz, Iran, Jan. 25, 1950; arrived in U.K., 1955; s. Sedratullah and Gloria (Iman) M.; m. Wendi Cunningham Worth Wirtshafter; children: Sedrhat Attar, Carmel Cunningham. BA, U. Cambridge, Eng., 1971, BChir, 1974, MB, MA (hon.), 1975. Affiliate prof. faculty grad. studies, dept. religion Landegg Acad., Switzerland, 1997—; bd. dirs. Primary Care Group, Ivel Valley, Eng., 1999—. Author: The Babi and Baha'i Religions, 1844-1944, 1981, Introduction to Shi'i Islam, 1985, The Phenomenon of Religion, 1999; editor: Studies in Babi and Baha'i History, vol. 1, 1982, vol. 2, 1984, vol. 5, 1988. Fellow Royal Asiatic Soc.; mem. Brit. Soc. Middle Ea. Studies, Brit. Assn. for Study of Religion. Baha'i. Avocation: travel. Office: c/o George Ronald Pub, 46 High St Kidlington, Oxford OX5 2DN, England

MOMIN, ALHAJ BABUL AHMED, investigation bureau director; b. Dhaka, Bangladesh, Jan. 1, 1956; arrived in The Netherlands, 1978; s. Sultan Ahmed Shorkar and Begum Ahmed (Rohisunnesa) Sultan; m. Begum Sheila Anwara, Apr. 12, 1990; children: Sultana Beatrix Ahmed, Antiqul Alexander Ahmed. BS, Dhaka U., 1975; postgrad. in agrl. engring., Nat. Aq. Coll., The Netherlands, 1983; D of Advance Thought, Internat. Acad. for Planetary, Planning and Mgmt., 1985. Gen. sec. Social Welfare Assn., Bangladesh, 1975-77; telexist The Royal Dutch Army, The Netherlands, 1987-89; with comms. UN Peace Keeping Force, Israel and Egypt, 1989-90; security planning officer to advisor Randstad Bewaking BV, The Netherlands, 1990-92; civil servant The Royal Dutch Marine, The Netherlands, 1993-94; investigator Amsterdam Onderzoek Bur., The Netherlands, 1996—; vice chmn. Found. Anjuman, The Netherlands, 1994; adminstrv. exec. Content Profl. BV, The Netherlands, 1995; 3rd World Agrl. advisor Stichting Vrijheid Matschapij, The Netherlands, 1985; journalist News Net-Work, 1997; chief advisor NGO-Prova. Author, editor: (documentary) Cry for One World, 1980, Press Card Journalist, bonafied mem., Int. Press Corps., AGORO Int., USA, 1999—. Human rights rschr. Amnesty Internat., The Netherlands, 1979; minority rights advisor Progressive Minority, The Netherlands, 1993; active Bangladesh Embassy Cmty. Ctr., Dhaka, 1989; mem. Provincial Govt., North Holland for Dutch Water Bd. Authority, 1997—; foundeing chmn. Dutch Human Rights Party. 2d lt. Bangladesh Rakkhi Bahini Mil., 1975-76; freedom fighter Liberation War of Bangladesh, India-Pakistan War, 1971; referee FIF/KNVB: Royal Dutch Football. Mem. VISA (sec. push in push back berodi com. Bangladesh Freedom Fighter Assn. (Liberation War of Bangledash 1971, human rights negotiator 1980), Stichting Freedom Soc. (mem. restoration of democracy in Bangladesh), Royal Air Force Assn. (life), Internat. Assn. for Identification, Oxford Club. Avocations: speaker human rights and peace, traveling, football referee, first aid and swimming. Fax: 880-2-9882466. Office: Am-

sterdam Onderzoek Bur, PO Box 12592, 1100 AN Amsterdam The Netherlands

MOMIRLAN, MAGDALENA, chemistry researcher; b. Bucharest, Romania, Feb. 15, 1944. Student, U. Bucharest, 1962-67; PhD, Poly. Inst. Bucharest, 1984. Chemist Inst. Rare and Non-Ferrous Metals, Bucharest, 1967-71, scientific researcher, 1971-85; scientific researcher PhD Inst. Phys. Chemistry "I.G. Murgulescu" Romanian Acad., Bucharest, 1985-90, sr. scientific researcher, 1990—; assoc. prof. Faculty Chem. Engring. Ecol. U., Bucharest, 1990-91, Faculty Chemistry Poly. U. Bucharest, 1996; vis. researcher dept. chemistry Imperial Coll. Sci., Tech. and Medicine, London, 1991, dept. chemistry Brookhaven Nat. Lab., 1995, U. Miami, 1995, dept. physics and astronomy U. Coll. London, 1998; internat. steering com. 3d Internat. Renewable Energy Congress, Reading, Eng., 1994, 5th World Renewable Energy Congress, Florence, Italy, 1998. Co-author: Defects in crystaline phase. Applications in physical chemistry, 1998; rev. jour. Energy, 1999; contbr. numerous articles to profl. jours.; patentee in field. Mem. internat. steering com. Internat. Energy Found., Can., 1996. Mem. Soc. Promotion Inexhaustible, Renewable and New Energies Poly. Inst. Bucharest, Inst. Energy (Eng.), Internat. Assn. Hydrogen Energy, Royal Soc. Chemistry (chartered),. Address: Str Brasov 24 Bloc 717, Sc A Apt 15 Sect 6, Bucharest 77372, Romania also: Romanian Acad Inst Physical Chemistry, Spl Independentei 202, Bucharest 77208, Romania

MOMOSE-SATO, YOKO, physiology educator; b. Tokyo, May 2, 1964; d. Hirofumi and Keiko (Matano) Momose; m. Katsushige Sato, Dec. 4, 1990; 1 child, Muneaki. MD, Tokyo Med. and Dental U., 1989, PhD, 1993. Asst. prof. Sch. Medicine Tokyo Med. and Dental U., 1993-98, assoc. prof., 1998-99, assoc. prof. Grad. Sch., 1999—. Contbr. articles to profl. jours. Recipient Inoue Rsch. award for young scientists Inoue Found. for Sci., Tokyo, 1994, Ochanomizu Med. award Ochanomizu Med. Alumni Assn., Tokyo, 1995. Mem. Soc. Neurosci., Physiol. Soc. Japan, Japan Neurosci. Soc. Avocations: music, theater, travel, tea ceremony. Home: 1-47-7-101 Shibamata, Tokyo 125-0052, Japan Office: Tokyo Med and Dental U, 1-5-45 Yushima Bunkyo-ku, Tokyo 113-8519, Japan

MOMOTAZ, ALIYA, plant breeder; b. Bogra, Bangladesh, Mar. 18, 1964; d. Mobarak Ali and Sahara Banu; m. A. B. M. Golam Rabbany, July 20, 1989; 1 child, Asif Sadik. MSc in Agr., Bangladesh Agrl. U., Mymensingh, 1986; MS in Biotechnology, Ehime U., Matsuyama, Japan, 1997, PhD, 2000. Sci. officer Bangladesh Agrl. Rsch. Inst., Joydebpur, 1990—, coord. spl. maize project plant breeding divsn., 1990-91. Contbr. articles to profl. jours. Natinal Sci. and Tech. fellow Bangladesh Agrl. U., 1988-90; Monbusho scholar Japanese Govt., 1994-00. Mem. Soc. Breeding Sci., Soc. Genetics and Plant Breeding (life). Avocations: travelling, reading, music. Home: Dr. Ishaque Ln, 5800 Bogra Bangladesh Office: Bangladesh Agrl Rsch Inst, Joydebpur, 1701 Gazipur Bangladesh

MONAGHAN, JESSINE ADRIENNE, lawyer; b. Floral Park, N.Y., May 5, 1953; d. Francis Adrian and Jessine Marion (Cordes) M. BA, Wellesley Coll., 1975; JD, Washington & Lee U., 1979. Bar: Va. 1979, D.C. 1980. Jud. clk. FTC, Washington, 1979-81; counsel Hunton & Williams, Richmond, Va., 1981-92, Environ. Health and Safety Progams GE Plastics, The Netherlands, 1992-95; with GE Corp. Environ. Programs Europe, 1995-98; dir. and European compliance officer Sotheby's, London, 1998—. Chmn. subcom. magnet sch. task force Richmond Pub. Schs., 1989; lawyer Church Hill Pro Bono Office, Richmond, 1990-92. Mem. Omicron Delta Kappa. Avocation: violin. Office: Sotheby's, 34-35 New Bond St, London W1A 2AA, England

MONAHAN, THOMAS PAUL, accountant; b. Pitts., Feb. 27, 1951; s. Thomas Andrew and Patricia (Tompkins) M.; m. Ellen McKeithan Easterby, Aug. 2, 1975; children: Kelley Kathleen, Thomas Patrick, Kyle Easterby, Tessa Elizabeth. BS in Acctg., U. S.C., 1973. CPA, S.C. Staff acct. Rogers, Brigman, Peterson & Co., Columbia, S.C., 1972-75, ptnr., 1975-82; treas., prin. GMK Assocs., Columbia, 1982—; bd. dirs., treas. Devel. Properties Inc.; trustee Town Theater Trust; lectr., cons. Mem. Com. of 100. Mem. bus. coun. S.C. Dems., 1986—. Mem. AICPA, S.C. Assn. CPAs, Columbia Stage Soc. (trustee, bd. dirs.), Spring Valley Country Club, Faculty House Club, Capital City Club, Sertoma, Zeta Beta Tau (trustee emeritus). Home: 1117 Adger Rd Columbia SC 29205-1942 Office: GMK Assoc 1333 Main St Ste 400 Columbia SC 29201-3201

MONAKHOV, VLADIMIR GENRIKHOVICH, biologist, researcher; b. Sukhobezvodnoe, Gorky, USSR, Mar. 30, 1954; s. Genrikh Ivanovich and Evpraxia Ignatievna M.; m. Galina Nikolaievna Urakova, Apr. 15, 1978; children: Dennis, Ilya. Biologist, Agr. Inst., Kirov, USSR, 1976; D in Biol. Scis., Inst. Plant and Animal Ecology, Sverdiovsk, 1984. Researcher Inst. Hunting and Fur Farming, Sverdlovsk, 1978-85, group researcher, 1985-94; group researcher Inst. Plant and Animal Ecology, Ekaterinburg, 1994—. Author: (monograph) Sable of the Urals, Probye and the Eniseyskaya Siberia: Results of 1995. Sgt. in radiotech., 1976-77. Avocations: filately, football. Office: Inst Plant and Animal Ecology, 202 8 Marta, Ekaterinburg 620144, Russia

MONASTERIO, ANGEL ALBERTO, gas company executive; b. Buenos Aires, Dec. 8, 1942; s. Angel Antonio Monasterio and Aida Auria; m. Mabel Norma Canatelli, Feb. 5, 1971; children: Andrea Laura, Cecilia Soledad. Diploma in Mech. Engring., U. Tech. Nat., Buenos Aires, 1969. Tech. rep. Dem. S.A., Buenos Aires, 1976-79, Consercio Pazio - Dem. Spinazzold, Buenos Aires, 1979-80; tech. mgr. Coest - Constructora de Oleoductos y Servicios Tecnicos, Buenos Aires, 1980; works dir. and tech. rep. Somerfin SaticF, Buenos Aires, 1981-86; works and svcs. mgr. IDESA Ingeniera S.A., Buenos Aires, 1986-94; constrn. mgr. Arcan Ingenieria Construcciones S.A., Buenos Aires, 1994—; cons. STE-Servicios Technicos de Engring., Porto Alegre, Brazil; tech. rep. Anker, Buenos Aires, 1989—. Office: Arcan Ingenieria Construcci, Riuadauia 875 8th Flr, 1002 Buenos Aires Argentina

MONATERI, PIER GIUSEPPE, law educator; b. Turin, Italy, Jan. 15, 1958; s. Pier Carlo and Emma (Actis-Perinetti) M.; m. Maria Letizia Tosco, July 8, 1985; children: Francesca, Valentina. Grad. cum laude, Turin Law Sch., 1981; diploma, Internat. Law Sch., Strasbourg, France, 1982. Asst. prof. U. Bocconi, Milan, 1981-85; prof. law sch. Trento, Italy, 1985-90; prof. Internat. Law Sch., 1990—; prof. law U Turin, 1990—; Jean Monnet prof. law sch., Trento, 1994, vice chancellor, 1987-90. Author: La Sineddo Che, 1984, Il Quantum Nel Danno a Persona, 1989, Pensare Il Diritto Civile, 1994, Il Modello di Civil Law, 1996, La Responsabilita Civile, 1998, La Responsabilitá Contrattuale, 1998, gen. edit. le Digesto, CD-Rom edit., 2000. Mem. Internat. Acad. Comparative Law, Soc. de Legislation Comparee. Home: Corso Einaudi 2, 10128 Turin Italy Office: U Turin Faculty Law, Via S Ottavio 20, 10138 Turin Italy

MONATH, NORMAN, publishing company executive; b. Toronto, Ont., Can.; came to U.S., naturalized, 1944; m. Pauline K. Farber, Aug. 30, 1952 (dec. Feb. 1972); children—Richard, Robert, Bruce. Dir. subsidiary rights Simon & Schuster, Inc., 1957-59; now cons.; founding pres. Cornerstone Library, Inc., N.Y.C., 1960—. Composer (with Walt Kelly) Songs of the Pogo; author: Know What You Want And Get It!; How To Play Popular Piano, 1984, How To Play Popular Guitar, 1994, (with William Cole) Folk Songs of England, Ireland, Scotland and Wales; editor (with Bobby Short) unpublished songs of Cole Porter; writer songs with Hal David, Sammy Cahn; recs. by Dionne Warwick, Supremes, Mitch Miller, Burns and Allen, Burl Ives. Served with Signal Corps AUS, 1942-45. Mem. ASCAP. Inventor Bali word game, 1954. Home: 3545 S Ocean Blvd Apt 101 Palm Beach FL 33480-5716

MONCLARO, ANTONIO CARLOS MENNA BARRETO, communications security company executive; b. Port Alegre, Brazil, Feb. 12, 1942; s. José Maria and Marieta (Menna Barreto) M.; m. Maria Cristina Vieira, Dec. 18, 1981; children: Thomaz, Antonielle. Comms. officer, Mil. Acad., Brazil, 1962; comm. engr., IME, Rio de Janeiro, 1979. Cert. in engring. Rschr. IMBEL, Rio de Janeiro, 1969-78, tech. dir., 1978-84; tech. dir. CEPESC, Brazilia, 1984-90, ACRON, Brazilia, 1990—. Lt. col. Brazilian Army, 1957-85. Decorated Ordem do Mérito Militar Grade Knight, Brazilian Army, 1997. Avocations: classical, jazz and Brazilian music, philosophy of science. Home: Sqn 304 Bloco A Apt 204, 70736010 Brazilia Brazil

MONDADORI, CESARE, neurobiologist, researcher; b. Zug, Switzerland, Jan. 2, 1946; s. Max and Dolores (Quadri) M.; m. Brigitte Joller, June 29, 1972; children: Patrick, Claudia. MSc, U. Zurich, 1971; PhD, Fed. Inst. Tech. (ETH), Zurich, 1977. Postdoctoral fellow U. Zurich, 1977-78; rschr. Ciba-Geigy, Switzerland, 1979-80; vis. prof. U. Toronto, 1981-82; head psychopharmacology Ciba-Geigy Basel, Switzerland, 1983-94; head pharmacology Marion Merell Dow, Strasbourg, France, 1994-96; head neuroscis. Hoechst-Marion-Roussel, Bridgewater, N.J., 1997-99; v.p., head neuroscis. Aventis, Bridgewater, N.J., 1999—; vis. prof. McMaster U., Hamilton, Ont., Can., 1989—. Contbr. articles to profl. jours.; behavioral and neural biology rschr. Mem. AAAS, ACNP, European Neurosci. Assn., European Brain Behavior Soc. Home: 44 Hartley Ln Basking Ridge NJ 07920-3707 Office: Aventis PO Box 6800 Bridgewater NJ 08807-0800

MONDAINI, MARCO, banker; b. Esch Alzette, Luxembourg, Apr. 2, 1966; s. Vincenzo and Maria Louisa (Curzietti) M.; m. Sabina Di Franco, July 20, 1989; children: Vanessa, Steve. BAC, Lycee Technique, Esch Alzette; Ecole Commerce, Grand Jean, Luxembourg. Cons. Ital/UIL, Esch Alzette, 1985-86; asst. Banque Internat. Luxembourg, Luxembourg, 1986-90, conseiller, 1990-98; gen. mgr. Banque Internat. Luxembourg, Dublin, Ireland, 1998—. Treas. Italian Olympic Com., Luxembourg. Avocations: golf, car collection, tennis.

MONDALE, WALTER FREDERICK, former Vice President of United States, diplomat, lawyer; b. Ceylon, Minn., Jan. 5, 1928; s. Theodore Sigvaard and Claribel Hope (Cowan) M.; m. Joan Adams, Dec. 27, 1955;children: Theodore, Eleanor, William. BA cum laude, U. Minn., 1951, LLB, 1956. Bar: Minn. 1956. Law clk. Minn. Supreme Ct.; pvt. practice law, 1956-60; atty. gen. State of Minn., 1960-64; U.S. senator from Minn., 1964-77, v.p. of U.S., 1977-81; mem. Nat. Security Council, 1977-81; mem. firm Winston & Strawn, 1981-87; ptnr. Dorsey & Whitney, Mpls., 1987-93; U.S. amb. to Japan Tokyo, 1993-96. Author: The Accountability of Power—Toward a Responsible Presidency, 1975; mem. Minn. Law Rev. Dem. nominee for Pres. U.S., 1984. With U.S. Army, 1951-53. Presbyterian.

MONDELLO, DIMA, conductor, educator, musician; b. Bedford, Eng., Sept. 27, 1960; s. Angelo and Filomena Melchionna; 1 child, Davide Angelo. Student, Kneller Hall Music Sch., London, 1983-84. tchr. improvisation.; session musician Jazz, Classical. Tchr. music schs., Germany, 1990—; condr. Angelo/German Orch., Celle, Germany, 1999. With Brit. Army, 1982-90. Roman Catholic. Avocation: composing. E-Mail: d.mondello@t-online.de. Office: Musikschule Mondello, Blumlage 50, 29221 Celle Germany

MONDLIN, MARVIN, retail executive, antiquarian book dealer; b. Bklyn., July 1, 1927; s. Samuel and Thelma (Schultz) M.; m. Phyllis Grossman, Oct. 23, 1962 (div. 1968); 1 child, Gerri; m. Irene Szmulewicz, Sept. 4, 1970. Student, Cornell U., 1945; student of Aesthetic Realism, with Eli Siegel, 1945-68; student, CCNY, 1948, Bklyn. Coll., 1969-71. Ptnr. Amory Books, N.Y.C., 1953-59; clk. Strand Book Store, N.Y.C., 1951, estate book buyer, 1959-71, 74-76, sr. exec. v.p., 1976—; bus. mgr. Definition Press., N.Y.C., 1957; cataloger U. Cath. de Louvain, Belgium, 1972. Author: Appraisals: A Guide for Bookmen, 1997; proofreader, copy editor Dover Publs., N.Y.C., 1958; editor Yearbook of Internat. Assocs., 1974. Mem. Antiquarian Booksellers Assn. Am., Appraisers Assn. Am., Bibliog. Soc. Am., Bibliog. Soc. London, Am. Photog. Hist. Soc., European Soc. History of Photography, The Ephemera Soc. Am., The Typophiles. Avocations: photography, non-silver processes lab. work, natural history, horticulture, music. Home: 889 Broadway Apt 3C New York NY 10003-1219 Office: Strand Book Store 828 Broadway New York NY 10003-4805

MONDUL, DONALD DAVID, patent lawyer; b. Miami, Fla., Aug. 24, 1945; s. David Donald and Marian Wright (Heck) M.; children: Alison Marian, Ashley Megan; m. Anna Marie Towle, Oct. 12, 1996. BS in Physics, U.S. Naval Acad., 1967; MBA, Roosevelt U., 1976; JD, John Marshall Law Sch., 1979. Bar: Ill. 1979, Fla. 1980, Tex. 1998; U.S. Patent Office 1980; U.S. Ct. Appeals (fed. cir.) 1982; U.S. Supreme Ct. 1990. Commd. ensign USN, 1967, advanced through grades to comdr., 1977; mktg. rep. Control Data Corp., Chgo., 1977-79; patent atty. Square D Co., Palatine, Ill., 1979-81; group patent counsel Ill. Tool Works Inc., Chgo., 1981-87; assoc. Cook, Wetzel & Egan, Chgo., 1987-89; ptnr. Foley & Lardner, Chgo. and Milw., 1989-95; sr. patent atty. IBM, East Fishkill, N.Y., 1995-96; gen. patent counsel Ericsson, Inc., Richardson, Tex., 1996-99; pvt. practice Dallas, 1999—. Patentee in methods and apparatus for multiplying plurality of numbers, N numbers, determining the product of two numbers, air baffle appartus, electrical encoding device. Commander, USNR, 1967-87. Office: 6631 Lovington Dr Dallas TX 75252-2519

MONEER, MOHAMED MOHAMED, surgery educator; b. Cairo, Egypt, May 1, 1952; m. Manal El-Hefnawy; children: Mahy, Maie, Marihan. MBBCh, Cairo Med. Sch., Egypt, 1976, MS in Surgery, 1983, MD (PhD) in Surgery, 1993. Intern Cairo U. Hosps., Egypt, 1976-77; gen. practitioner Mil. Hosps., Egypt, 1977-80; resident in surgery Ahmed Maher Teaching Hosp., Cairo, 1981-82; resident NCI, Cairo U., 1982-85, Clin. Attachment, Royal Infirm, Lowmore Hosp., Edinburgh, U.K., 1986-87; rsch. registrar NCI, Cairo U., 1988-92; lectr. surgery Mataria Teaching Hosp., Cairo, 1994-98, asst. prof. surgery, head of breast unit, 1999—. Contbr. articles to profl. jours. Mem. Egyptian Soc. Surgeons, Egyptian Soc. Cancer, Modern Egyptian Soc. Surgeons. Achievements include introducing a new technique for preperitoneal inguinal hernial repair and extension of McBurny's Incision: postulation of a mechanism by which Locally Advanced Breast Cancer (LABC) regress under the effect of Neoadjuvant Chemotherapy and suggested a new strategy for breast conservation in Locally Advanced Breast Cancer to achieve adequate locoregional control of the disease. Avocations: chess, judo. Office: 35 El-Galaa St, Cairo Egypt

MONEGRO, FRANCISCO, psychology educator, alternative medicine consultant; b. La Vega, Dominican Republic, Apr. 20, 1949; s. Francisco Monegro-Fdez and Ana A. (Pena) Monegro. Grad. cum laude, Pontifical U., Santiago, Dominican Republic, 1973; grad. psychology, Autonomous U. Santo Domingo, 1978, MD, 1986; MA in Ednl. Psychology, Tech. Inst. Santo Domingo, 1981; PhD in Nutrition, LaSalle U., Mandeville, La., 1993. Cert. natural health profl., hypnotherapist, profl. biofeedback profl.; diplomate in behavioral medicine, diplomate in pain mgmt.; lic. in psychology Autonomous U. Santo Domingo, 1978. Tchr. Peace H.S., Santo Domingo, Dominican Republic, 1975-76; dir. dept. psychology Holy Trinity Ednl. Ctr., Santo Domingo, 1978-80; prof. Sch. Medicine Tech. Inst. Santo Domingo, 1986-87; dir. dept. psychology Interam. U., Santo Domingo, 1988-89; prof. psychology and medicine Autonomous U. Santo Domingo, 1978-89, psychologist, counseling dept., 1979-84; staff mem. spl. edn. Bd. Edn. Dist. X, Bronx, N.Y., 1991-93; founder, chmn. N.Y. Inst. for Holistic Life, N.Y.C., 1991—; prof. psychology CUNY at HCC, Bronx, 1990—; founder, pioneer in behavioral medicine Behavioral Medicine Clinic, Santo Domingo, 1987-94. Author: Biofeedback-Bio-retroalimentacion, 1988, Holistic Behavioral Medicine, 1993, Biomagnetic Medicine: Secrets and Power of Magnetic Energy, 1996, Psychology and Life Mind, Body and Society, 1997, (interactive CD-ROM) Psychology and Life, 2000; editor, pub.: BOEST, 1978, Dominican Bull. Behavioral Medicine, 1987, Holistic Life/Vida Holistica, 1991, others. Mem. Dominican Psychol. Assn. (treas. 1978-79), Soc. Behavioral Medicine, Assn. for Advancement of Behavior Therapy, Am. Acad. Pain Mgmt., Assn. for Applied Psychophysiology and Biofeedback. Democrat. Roman Catholic. Avocations: computers, golf, basketball, swimming, travel. Home: PO Box 302 Bronx NY 10458-0302 Office: NY Inst for Holistic Life 976 Mclean Ave Ste 370 Yonkers NY 10704-4105

MONES, REYNALDO AMIGAN, information technology professional, consultant; b. Manila, Philippines, Nov. 28, 1954; s. Filemon Mones and Rosalina (Amigan) M.; m. Emily Resurreccion, Jan. 5, 1985; children: Marie Bernard, Regine Marie. BS in Commerce, De La Salle U., Philippines, 1986, postgrad, 1998—. Project mgr. System Resources, Inc., Makati, Philippines, 1981-85; chief oper. officer System Tech. Inst., Quezon City, Philippines, 1985-91; adminstr. Glaucoma Rsch. Found., Manila, 1991-92; EDP mgr. The Westin Philippine Plaza, Manila, 1992-95; cons., 1995; chmn. and pres. Electronic Info. Sys. Assoc., Inc., Makati City, 1994—; shareholder Sys. Tech. Inst., Makati, 1983—; v.p., treas. Dux Holdings, Inc.; chmn. Paco Cath. Sch. Alumni Assn. Inc.; instr. info. tech. De La Salle U., 1997—, registrar, Saint benilde, 1998—. Designer 7-in-1 toy for children; web page designer. Lector, commentator Parish of San Fernando de Dilao, Manila, 1970—; adviser The Knights of the Altar, Manila, 1969—; dir. PCS Class 1971, Inc. U. Philippines govt. scholar, 1971-73. Mem. IEEE Computer Soc., Philippine Computer Soc., N.Y. Acad. Sci., Planetary Soc. Roman Catholic. Avocations: photography, graphic design, tennis. E-mail: ram@i-next.net. Home and Office: 2356 Febo St and Flerida St, Pandacan 1011 Manila, The Philippines

MONGE-ARGILES, J. ANTONIO, neurologist; b. Almoradi, Spain, Feb. 18, 1960; s. Antonio Monge and Francisca Argiles; m. Maria Garcia; children: Victoria, Sonia. Grad., Almoradi U., St. Luc, Spain, 1977; MD, Alicante U., 1983. Neurologist Alicante Hosp., 1991, Lovain U., Brussels, 1986-91, Alicante Hosp., 1991, Elche (Spain) Hosp., 1992-94, Rosell Hosp., Cartagena, Spain, 1995—. Author: Test del Frio en ACV, 1986, Heart Rate Variability in MS, 1998. Bayern grant for neurol. specialization, 1987, Fondo Investigaciones Sanitarias grant, 1994. Fellow Spanish Neurol. Soc.; mem. Valencia Neurol. Soc., Murcia Neurol. Soc. Home: Maisonnave 25 1o, 03003 Alicante Spain

MONGELLI, MAX, medical educator; b. Bari, Apulia, Italy, Oct. 5, 1956; arrived in Singapore, 1997; s. Domenico Mongelli; m. Wei Zhen Lu. BSc in Medicine, Sydney (Australia) U., 1980, MB BChir, 1981; MD, Nottingham (Eng.) U., 1997. Rsch. fellow U. Nottingham, 1992-95; assoc. prof. Chinese U. Hong Kong, 1995-97, Nat. U. Singapore, 1997—; sr. cons. Nat. Univ. Hosp., 1997—. Contbr. rsch. articles to profl. jours. Rsch. grantee Oriental Press Found., Hong Kong, 1995, Singapore Cancer Soc., 1998. Fellow Royal Australian and New Zealand Coll. Ob-Gyn.; mem. Royal Coll. Obstetricians and Gynecologists U.K., Perinatal Soc. Singapore (treas. 1999). Office: Nat Univ Hosp Dept Ob-Gyn, Lower Kent Ridge Rd, 119074 Singapore Singapore

MONGE-NAJERA, JULIAN ANTONIO, ecologist; b. San Jose, Costa Rica, June 6, 1960; s. Victor M. and Angela M. (Gonzalez) Monge-N.; m. Patricia A. Valverde (div. 1995); m. Zaidett M. Barrientos, Aug. 17, 1996; children: Andres, Estefanie. BS in Biology, U. Costa Rica, 1985, MSc, 1989. Prof. U. Costa Rica, San Jose, 1989—; dir. rsch. Open U., San Jose, 1994-95; adviser Nat. Geog. Soc., 1992, BBC, London, 1989—, CR Oil Co., San Jose, 1989-90; rsch. fellow Smithsonian, Panama, 1986. Author: Insects of Panama, 1992, Biodiversity Arthropods, 1997; contbr. articles to scientific jours. Mem. Intersci. Assn. (biotech. editor 1996—), Med. Law Assn., Legal Medicine Assn., Ondontol. Assn. Avocations: photography, camping. Office: U Costa Rica, Biologia Tropica, 2060 San José Costa Rica

MONGIN, PHILIPPE, philosopher, economist, educator; b. Marseille, France, July 18, 1950; s. Maurice and Micheline (Genevet) M.; m. Françoise Forges. Diploma, Inst. Polit. Studies, 1971; D in Social Scis., E.H.E.S.S., Paris, 1978; Doctorat d'Etat, U. Aix-Marseille, 1984. Jr. civil servant Ecole Normale Superieure, Paris, 1969-74; jr. rschr. C.N.R.S., Paris, 1978-88, sr. rschr., 1988—; invited prof. U. Cath. Louvain, Belgium, 1988-96, Ecole Superieure Scis. Econs. Comml., 1996—. Co-editor Econs. and Philosophy, 1994—; assoc. editor other jours.; contbr. articles to profl. jours. Recipient Order of Merit, 1995. Office: Thema, Ctr Nat Rsch Sci U. Cergy, F-95011 Cergy France

MONHART, VÁCLAV, nephrologist, consultant; b. Prague, Czech Republic, Apr. 5, 1942; s. Stanislav and Františka (Strnadová) M.; m. Jana Šulcová, June 30, 1964 (dec. 1991); children: Pavel, Zdeněk; m. Magdalena Budilová, June 20, 1995. MD, Charles U., Hradec Králové, Czech Republic, 1965; PhD, Charles U., Prague, 1981. Resident Ctrl. Mil. Hosp., Prague, 1965-67, sr. resident, 1968-72, med. asst., 1973-81, attending physician, 1982-87, assoc. prof., 1988-93, prof. internal medicine, 1994—; head dept. internal medicine Ctrl. Mil. Hosp., Prague, 1985—. Author: Hemoperfusion, 1985 (Czech Lit. Fund award 1987), Hypertension and Kidney, 1999; patentee in field. Col. Czech Mil., 1982—. Mem. Internat. Soc. Nephrology, Czech Soc. Nephrology (v.p. 1996—, awards 1984, 95), European Dialysis and Transplant Assn., N.Y. Acad. Scis., Czech Kidney Found. (pres. 1999—). Home: 206/51 U druhe baterie, 162 00 Prague Czech Republic Office: 1200 U vojenske nemocnice, 169 02 Prague Czech Republic

MONHEMIUS, ANDREW JOHN, hydrometallurgy educator; b. Belfast, Ulster, No. Ireland, Oct. 3, 1942; s. Frank André and Edna Rowlands (Goodhall) M.; m. Johanna Werson, Aug. 6, 1966; children: Simon, Lucy. BSc in Minerals Engring., U. Birmingham (Eng.), 1964; MASc in Metall. Engring., U. B.C. (Can.), 1966; PhD in Metallurgy, U. London, 1972. Chartered engr. Asst. lectr. Imperial Coll., London, 1966-69, lectr., 1969-86; vis. prof. Fed. U. Rio de Janeiro, 1973-76; reader Imperial Coll., London, 1986-96, prof. of mineral and environ. engring., 1996—; dean Royal Sch. Mines, 2000—; bd. dirs. Consort Rsch. Ltd., London. Editor: Iron Control in Hydrometallurgy, 1986; co-inventor, patentee hydrolytic stripping. Fellow Instn. Mining and Metallurgy. Office: Imperial Coll Dept Mineral, TH Huxley Sch Environ/Engrs, Imperial Coll/Royal Sch Mns, London SW7 2BP, England

MÓNICA, ANTÓNIO DE CARVALHO GODINHO, lawyer; b. Lisbon, Portugal, Aug. 2, 1951; s. José António and Maria Margarida (Carvalho) M.; m. Isabel Sacadura, Ju ne 16, 1984; children: Martim, Duarte, Isabel. Lic. by Faculty of Law, Lisbon U., Lisbon, 1976. Mem. legal dept. Supa SA, Lisbon, 1973-77; pvt. practice in civil, comml. banking, environ. and oil law, 1976—; Internat. Bankers Course of Midland Bank, London, 1979—; mem. internat. and legal dept. Banco Totta Acore, Lisbon, 1979-84. Advisor to Portuguese State Sec. of Treasury, 1981; chief of staff External Trade Sec. of State, Lisbon, 1988-89; del. to 3d and 4th Portuguese Congress of Lawyers. Decorated Italian Grande Officiale Order of Merit, 1989. Mem. Portugese Bar Assn. Lisbon County, Ginasio Clube Portugues, Automovel Clube Portugal, Clube Naval Cascais, Portugese C. of C. and Industry (Sec. gen. 1979, Portugal del. to Internat. C. of C. 1991-95). Avocations: water skiing, motorycles, reading, antiques. Fax: 3511 213882554. Office: Av Alvares Cabral no 84 2, 1250 Lisbon Portugal

MONIPPALLY, MATHUKUTTY MATTHEW, business communication educator; b. Pala, Kerala, India, Mar. 1, 1949; s. Matthew Joseph and Thressiamma Matthew (Ettathotte) M.; m. Philomina Mathukutty James, Jan. 10, 1952; children: Preeti, Manu. Lic. in Philosophy, Pontifical Atheneum, Pune, India, 1971; MA, Poona U., Pune, India, 1974; MLitt, Ctrl. Inst. English/Fgn. Lang., Hyderabad, 1977; PhD, Manchester (Eng.) U., 1983. Lectr. T.C. Coll., Baramati, India, 1974-75; lectr. Ctrl. Inst. English and Fgn. Langs., 1977-80, assoc. prof., 1990-99, prof., 1999—; vis. prof. Indian Inst. Mgmt., 2000—; lectr. Higher Inst. Tech., Brak, Libya, 1983-85, asst. prof., 1985-88; cons. Drucker Coll. Mgmt., numerous other cos., Hyderabad, 1995—. Author: English for Adults, 1980, Writing, 1990, The Craft of Business Letter Writing, 1997; lead author: Business and Technical Writing in English, 1999; contbr. articles to profl. jours. and newspapers. Univ. Grants Commn. fellow, 1976-77; Brit. Govt. grantee, 1980-81. Mem. Soc. for Accident Free Environment (founder 1995), Hyderabad Mgmt. Assn., Nat. Human Resources Devel. Network, Hyderabad Mktg. Assn. Syro Malabar Catholic. Avocations: reading, walking. Home: IIM Vis Faculty Guest Ho, FPM 15 IIM Campus, Ahmedabad 380015, India Office: Comms Area, Indian Inst Mgmt, Ahmedabad Gujarat 380015, India

MONIRUZZAMAN, MOHAMMED, chemical engineer; b. Rajshahi, Bangladesh, Feb. 15, 1960; came to U.S., 1994; s. Mohammed Abdul Majid and Khukon Bibi. BS, U. Dhaka, Bangladesh, 1982, MS, 1983; D of Engring., Kanazawa U., Japan, 1993. Microbiologist Pfizer Labs. (Bangladesh) Ltd., Dhaka, 1987-88, Rhone-Poulenc (Bangladesh) Ltd., Dhaka, 1988-89; rsch. assoc. dept. chem. engring. Tex. A&M U., College Station, 1994-96; rsch. assoc. dept. microbiology U. Fla., Gainesville, 1996-98; cons. BC Internat., Jennings, La., 1998—; vis. scientist fermentation biochemistry rsch. unit USDA, Peoria, Ill., 1995-96. Author: (book chpts.) Fuels and Chemicals from Biomass, 1997, Recent Research Developments in Biotechnology and Bioengineering, 1998; patentee in field; reviewer: Applied Biochemistry

and Biotechnology, 1995—; contbr. numerous articles and papers to profl. jours. Monbusho scholar Japanese Ministry of Edn., 1989. Mem. Am. Soc. for Microbiology. Achievements include development of cellobiose fermenting bacterial strain by genetic engineering; design and publication of new model for bacterial saccharide metabolism; optimization of steam explosion and ammonia fiber explosion processes for lignocellulose pretreatment; development of unique process for lignocellulose hydrozates fermentation to ethanol by genetically engineered bacteria. Avocations: tennis, reading, travel. Office: BC Internat PO Box 389 11107 Campbell Wells Rd Jennings LA 70546

MONIZ, ERNEST JEFFREY, government official, former physics educator; b. Fall River, Mass., Dec. 22, 1944; s. Ernest Perry and Georgina (Pavao) M.; m. Naomi Hoki, June 9, 1973; 1 child, Katya. BS, Boston Coll., 1966; PhD, Stanford U., 1971. Prof. physics MIT, Cambridge, 1973-97; dir. Bates Linear Accelerator Ctr. MIT, Middleton, 1983-91, head physics dept., 1991-95, 97; under sec. U.S. Dept. Energy, Washington, 1997—; cons. Los Alamos Nat. Lab., 1975-95; assoc. dir. for sci. Office of Sci. and Tech. Policy, Exec. Office of the Pres., 1996-97. Contbr. articles to profl. jours. Office: Office of UnderSecretary US Dept Energy 1000 Independence Ave SW Washington DC 20585-0001

MONK, ANTHONY JOHN, engineer; b. Coulsdon, Eng., Nov. 14, 1923; s. Frank Leonard and Barbara (Ashby) M.; m. Elizabeth Ann Samson, Apr. 14, 1951; children: Michael Frank, Anstace Elizabeth (dec.), Peter John Oliver, Andrew Anthony, Jonathan Patrick Bruce. BSc in Engring., London U., 1950; MSc, Cranfield U., 1972. Chartered engr. Engr. officer Royal Navy, 1941-78, rear admiral, 1974-78; dir. gen. Brick Devel. Assn., 1979-83; appeals organiser Royal Marsden Hosp., London, 1984-87; cons. Engring. Industry Tng. Bd., Watford, 1987-89. Recipient CBE Her Majesty the Queen, 1973. Fellow Royal Aeronautical Soc., Instn. of Mech. Engrs., Inst. of Marine Engrs., Royal Soc. of Arts; mem. Royal Instn., Worshipful Co. Engrs. (liveryman). Avocations: swimming, service pilot. Home: 1 Cissbury, Windsor Rd, Ascot SL5 7LF, England

MONK, DIANA CHARLA, artist, stable owner; b. Visalia, Calif., Feb. 25, 1927; d. Charles Edward and Viola Genevieve (Shea) Williams; m. James Alfred Monk, Aug. 11, 1951; children: Kiloran, Sydney, Geoffrey, Anne, Eric. Student, U. Pacific, 1946-47, Sacramento Coll., 1947-48, Calif. Coll. Fine Arts, San Francisco, 1948-51, Calif. Coll. Arts & Crafts, Oakland, 1972. Art tchr. Mt. Diablo Sch. Dist., Concord, Calif., 1958-63; pvt. art tchr. Lafayette, Calif., 1963-70; gallery dir. Jason Aver Gallery, San Francisco, 1970-72; owner, mgr. Monk & Lee Assocs., Lafayette, 1973-80; stable owner, mgr. Longacre Tng. Stables, Santa Rosa, Calif., 1989—. One-person shows include John F. Kennedy U., Orinda, Calif., Civic Arts Gallery, Walnut Creek, Calif., Vallery Art Gallery, Walnut Creek, Sea Ranch Gallery, Gualala, Calif., Jason Aver Gallery, San Francisco; exhibited in group shows at Oakland (Calif.) Art Mus., Crocker Nat. Art Gallery, Sacramento, Le Salon des Nations, Paris. Chair bd. dirs. Walnut Creek (Calif.) Civic Arts, 1972-74, advisor to dir., 1968-72; exhibit chmn. Valley Art Gallery, Walnut Creek, 1977-78; juror Women's Art Show, Walnut Creek, 1970, Oakland Calif. Art. Home and Office: Longacre Tng Stables 1702 Willowside Rd Santa Rosa CA 95401-3922

MONK, PAUL MALCOLM SPENSER, physical chemistry educator, researcher; b. London, Aug. 30, 1965; s. Michael John and Mary Frances (Glossop) M.; m. Joanne Bakehouse, July 29, 1995. BSc, U. Exeter, Eng., 1986, PhD, 1990. Postdoctoral fellow U. Aberdeen, Scotland, 1989-91; sr. lectr. Manchester (Eng.) Met. U., 1991—. Author: Electrochromism: Fundamentals and Applications, 1995, The Viologens, 1998, Fundamentals of Electroanalytical Chemistry, 2000; contbr. over 40 articles to profl. jours. Methodist. Avocations: theology, art, fiction, French. Home: 52 Shore Mount, Littleborough OL15 8EW, England Office: Manchester Met U, Chester St, Manchester M1 5GD, England

MÖNKÄRE, SINIKKA, Finnish government official; b. Sippola, Finland, Mar. 6, 1947; 2 children. MD. Asst. phys. Salo Regl. Hosp., 1973-74; health ctr. phys. City of Torku, 1974-75; sr. phys. Hyatra Regl. Hosp., 1975-77, Tiuru Hosp., 1977-85; specialist, 1985-95; Min. of social affairs and health Govt. of Finland, Helsinki, 1995, Min. of Housing, now minister of social affairs and health, min. trade and industry. Mem. Imatra City Coun., 1981-95; mem. City Exec. Bd., 1981-83; mem. Parliament 1987-91, 95—. Office: Min Social Affairs & Health, PO Box 267, FIN00171 Helsinki Finland Address: PO Box 230, FIN00171 Helsinki Finland*

MÖNKEMÜLLER, KLAUS ERIK, physician, researcher; b. Guatemala City, Guatemala, Apr. 10, 1965; came to U.S., 1992; s. Klaus Dieter and Julia Odily (Porras) M.; 1 child, Kirsten Odily. BS, U. Francisco Marroquin, Guatemala, 1987, MD, 1991. Diplomate Am. Bd. Internal Medicine; diplomate gastroenterology; cert. Ednl. Commn. for Fgn. Med. Grads. Intern in internal medicine U. Tenn., Memphis, 1992-93, resident in internal medicine, 1993-95, chief med. resident, 1995-96; assoc. fellow in gastroenterology U. Ala., Birmingham, 1996-99, asst. prof. medicine, 1999—; chief gastrointestinal endoscopy Vets. Hosp., 1999—; attending physician Bapt. Meml. Hosp.-Monroe Clinic, Memphis, 1995-96, Vets. Hosp., Memphis, 1995-96, Vets. Hosp., Birmingham, 1997—; vis. lectr. U. Francisco Marroquin, 1996; vis. prof., L.Am. Congress Surgery, Guatemala City, 1997; instr. dept. emergency medicine U. Ala., 1997-99. Inventoro in field of gastrointestinal endoscopy; contbr. articles to profl. jours. and books. Mem., dir. med. activities Rotaract, Guatemala, 1986; pres. Med. Sch. Class, Guatemala, 1987-91; mem. exec. com. U. Tenn., 1992-95, ethics com., 1995-96. Recipient Young Investigator award DuPont and Am. Coll. Chest Physicians, 1995, Honor diploma Ministry of Health, Guatemala, 1996, Outstanding Vis. Scholar award U. Ala., 1989, ACG/ASTRA Pharms. award, 1998, othrs. Mem. Am. Coll. Gastroenterology, Assn. for Study of Liver Diseases, Am. Soc. Gastrointestinal Endoscopy, Am. Coll. Physicians, Guatemalan Coll. Physicians and Surgeons (Best Clin. Investigation award 1989), Internat. Assn. Pancreatology, Club Aleman Guatemala. Roman Catholic. Avocations: photography, reading, bicycling, travelling. Home: 2042 Wild Flower Dr Birmingham AL 35244-1723 Office: Univ Ala Dvsn Gastroenterology 633 Zrb Uab Sta Birmingham AL 35294-0001

MONKMAN, GARETH JOHN, engineer, educator; b. Beverley, Yorkshire, Eng., Apr. 8, 1956; came to Germany, 1992; s. Arthur and Dorothy (Whitelock) M. BA, Open U., Milton Keynes, Eng., 1984; BS, Hull (Eng.) U., 1986, MS, 1987, PhD, 1990. Sr. tech. NASA, Winkfield, Eng., 1975-77; radio officer Brit. Merc. Marine, Eng., 1977-79; elec. officer Brit. Merc. Marine, 1979-83; rsch. asst. Hull U., 1986-89, comml. devel. officer, 1989-92; vis. prof. U. Applied Sci., Regensburg, Germany, 1992-95, prof., 1996—; pres. Internat. Phoretics, Hull and Regensburg, 1992—; non-exec. dir. Protoform, Ltd., Leeds, UK, 1995—; chmn. Coil Winding Internat. Conf., Berlin, 1996-98; press officer AXON, Bremen, 1996-99; bd. editors Mechatronics Sensor Rev., 1998—. Contbr. articles to profl. jours.; numerous patents in field. Mem. Registered Engrs. for Disaster Relief, 1990-93. Rsch. grant EEC, 1992. Mem. German Union Electrotech. Avocations: hiking, cycling, antiques. Home and Office: FH Regensburg, Prüfeninger Strasse 58, 93049 Regensburg Bavaria, Germany

MONKS, PAUL SAVILLE, anaesthetist, consultant; b. London, May 1, 1938; s. Kenneth Walter and Marcelle Anne (Laver) M.; m. Sandra Wentworth, Sept. 8, 1962; children: Julia, Michele. BA, Oxford (Eng.) U., 1960, MA, B Med., B of Surgery, 1964. Anaesthetic sr. house officer Sutton Gen. Hosp., London, 1966-67; registrar anaesthetist St. Helier Hosp. Carshalton, London, 1967-68, St. Thomas' Hosp., London, 1968-69; sr. registrar anaesthetist Hammersmith Hosp., London, 1969-72; cons. anaesthetist The London Hosp. (now Royal London), 1973—, St. Bartholomew's Hosp., London, 1995—; tchr. U. London, 1973—. Contbr. articles to profl. jours. Fellow Royal Coll. Anaesthetists; mem. Assn. Anaesthetists Gt. Britain and Ireland, French Soc. Anaesthetists. Avocation: genealogy.

MONLEONE, RICHARD DONATO, engineering company executive; b. Geneva, Switzerland, Jan. 26, 1962; s. Giulio V. and Heidi R. Monleone; m. Carmela Bianchi. Engring. diploma, Swiss Fed. Poly. Inst., Zurich, Switzerland, 1986; postgrad., U. N.C., 1988. R&D engr. Agie Ltd., Losone, Switzerland, 1986-88, Elox Corp., Davidson, N.C., 1988; R&D project engr. Agie Ltd., Losone, 1989-95; mng. dir. Meet Ltd., Coldrerio, Switzerland, 1995—. Patentee in field; contbr. articles to profl. jours. Mem. IEEE, Swiss Engr. and Archs. Soc. Avocations: skiing, swimming, sailing.

MONNA, NAOKI, sociology educator; b. Haibara, Sizuoka, Japan, June 7, 1942; s. Yoshio and Katsumi (Kawamura) M.; m. Reiko Iida, Sept. 15, 1973. BA, Doshisha U., Kyoto, Japan, 1965, MA, 1968. Lectr. Doshisha U., Kyoto, 1971-73; assoc. prof. Momoyama-Gakuin Jr. Coll., Niihama, Japan, 1975-78; assoc. prof. Rikkyo U., Tokyo, 1978-84, prof., 1984—, dir. MA course, 1990-91, dir. sociology course, 1992-96, dean Coll. Sociology, 1997—; cons. on mass comm. sect. Japan Press Ctr., Tokyo, 1992-95; cons. on media studies Japan br. Brit. Coun., Tokyo, 1993—. Author: History of People's Press, 1983, Journalism in Britain and Japan, 1993, The Press Control in Okinawa Island under American Administration, 1996, Contemporary Sociology, vol. 22, 1996. Mem. adult edn. com. Tokorozawa City Office, Saitama-Ken, 1996. Fellow Internat. Assn. for Mass Comm. Rsch.; mem. Japan Soc. for Studies in Journalism (dir. 1995-97), Japan Press Club. Social Democrat. Buddhist. Avocations: playing Go, listening to classical music, chess. Home: Kita-yurakucho, 3-18 Tokorozawa-shi 359, Japan Office: Rikkyo U, Nishi-Ikebukuro 3 chome, 171 Tokyo Japan

MÖNNIG, HANS-ULRICH, civil engineer, researcher, educator; b. Markneukirchen, Saxonia, Germany, Apr. 19, 1943; s. Willy and Mariechen (Dick) M.; m. Karla Langguth, Aug. 29, 1964; children: Falk, Ulrike. Diploma, U. Weimar, Germany, 1968, Diploma, Dr. Ing., 1968, 73, Dr. sci., 1982, prof., dr. habil., 1986, 91. Engring. diploma. Asst. HAB Weimar, Germany, 1968-73; cons. Planning Staff, Vietnam, 1973-75; sr. asst. HAB Weimar, Germany, 1975-76, scientist, 1980-82, asst. prof., 1982-86, prof., 1986-96, rector, 1989-92; dept. mgr. Spezialbaukombinat, Germany, 1976-80; chmn. Bauhaus Weimar Stiftung e. V. Weimar, 1990—; lectr. U. Kaiserslautern, 1993-96; internat. cons. structural civil engring., 1993—. Coauthor: Bemessung von Strassenkonstruktionen, 1978, 2d edit., 1981; coauthor, editor: Planning and Building in the Tropics, 1990-92; editor Wissenschafliche Zeitschrift, 1989-92; contbr. articles to profl. jours. Avocations: writing, photography, travel, painting. Home: Lenbachweg 2, 99425 Weimar Germany Office: Bauhaus Weimar Stiftung, Belvederer Allee 25, 99425 Weimar Germany

MONNINGER, ROBERT HAROLD GEORGE, ophthalmologist, educator; b. Chgo., Nov. 5, 1918; s. Louis Robert and Katherine (Lechner) M.; m. Anna Evelyn Turnen, Sept. 1, 1944; children—Carl John William, Peter Louis Philip. A.A., North Park Coll., 1939; B.S., Northwestern U., 1941, M.A., 1945; M.D., Loyola U., Chgo., 1953, Sc.D. (hon.), 1968. Diplomate Am. Bd. Cosmetic Plastic Surgery. Intern St. Francis Hosp., Evanston, Ill., 1953-54; resident Presbyterian-St. Luke's, U. Ill. Research and Eye, Va. hosps., 1954-57; mem. leadership council Ravenswood Hosp. Med. Ctr.; instr. chemistry Lake Forest Coll., Ill., 1946-47; instr. biochemistry, physiology Loyola U. Dental Sch., 1948-49; clin. assoc. prof. ophthalmology Stritch Sch. Medicine, Loyola U., Maywood, Ill., 1957-72; practice medicine specializing in ophthalmology Lake Forest, 1957—; clin. prof. ophthalmology Finch U. Health Scis./Chgo. Med. Sch.; guest lectr. numerous univs. med. ctrs. U.S., Can., Europe, Central and S.Am., Orient; resident lectr. Klinikum der Goethe-Universitat, Fed. Republic Germany, 1981; mem. panel Nat. Disease and Therapeutic Index; cons. Draize eye toxicity test revision HEW, cons. research pharm. cos. Nat. Assoc. Smithsonian Instn.; bd. dirs. Eye Rehab. and Research Found.; postgrad. faculty Internat. Glaucoma Congress; lectr. Hopital Dieu, Paris; lectr. postgrad. courses for developing nations physicians WHO; life mem. Postgrad. Sch. Medicine U. Vienna; cons. Nat. Acad. Sci.; adv. bd. Madera Del Rio Found. Cons. author Textbook of Endocrinology. Editorial bd. Clin. Medicine, 1958—, EENT Digest, 1958—, Internat. Surgery, 1972—, profl. jours. Served with USMCR, 1941-44. Recipient citation Gov. Bahamas, 1960, Ophthalmic Found. award, 1963, Sci. Exhibit award Ill. State Med. Soc., 1966, Franco-Am. Meritorious citation, 1967, Paris Post No. 1 Am. Legion award, 1967, citation Pres. Mexico, 1968, Sightsaving award Bausch & Lomb, 1968, exhibit award Western Hemisphere Congress Internat. Surgeons, 1968, Research citation Japanese Soc. Ophthalmology, 1969; Barraquer Gold Medallion; Physician's Recognition award AMA, Bicentennial citation Library of Congress Registration Book; Pres.'s medal of merit; meritorious citation Gov. Ill., citation and medal Lord Mayor of Rome, also Pres. of Italy, 1981, Civic Ctr. of Evanston, Ill., 1981, commendation and citation Ill. Gen. Assembly, 1982, cert. of accomplishment Loyola U. Alumni Assn., Chgo., 1983; Catherine White Scholarship fellow, 1945-46. Fellow Internat. Coll. Surgeons (postgrad. faculty continuing edn.), Am. Coll. Angiology, Oxford Ophthal. Congress and Soc. (lectr. 1960-61), Royal Soc. Health, Internat. Acad. Cosmetic Surgery (editorial bd.), Sociedad Mexicana Ortopedia (hon.), C. Puestow Surg. Soc.; mem. AAAs, Internat. Soc. Geog. Ophthalmology (program course coordinator, lectr. ocular electrophysiology VI Internat. Congress, Rio de Janiero), Pan Am. Assn. Ophthalmology, Assn. for Research Ophthalmology, Am. Assn. Ophthalmology, Am. Soc. Contemporary Ophthalmology, Internat. Glaucoma Soc., Ill. Soc. for Med. Research, Ill. Assn. Ophthalmology, Internat. Soc. clin. electrophysiology of Vision (hon., lectr. 1978), Brazilian Soc. Ophthalmology (hon. corr.), German Ophthal. Soc., Internat. Fedn. Clin. Chemists (lectr.), Primum Forum Ophthalmologicum (lectr.), European Ophthal. Soc. (lectr.), Internat. Congress Anatomists (lectr.), Assn. des Diabetologues Francise (lectr.), German Soc. for Internal Medicine (lectr.), Met. Opera Guild, Fedn. Am. Scientists, N.Y. Acad. Scis., Ill. Acad. Scis., AAUP, Nat. Soc. Lit. and Arts, Nat. Hist. Soc., Rush Med. Sch.-Presbyn. St. Luke's Alumni Assn., Sociedad Poblana Oftalmologia (hon, silver placue, commemorative prestige lectr. 1982) (Mex.), Internat. Platform Assn., Cousteau Soc., Sigma Xi, Sigma Alpha Epsilon, Phi Beta Pi, Theta Kappa Psi.

MONOD, JÉRÔME, diversified financial services company executive; b. Paris, Sept. 7, 1930; m. Françoise Gallot, Dec. 21, 1963; children: Fabrice, Guillaume, Donatien. Degree in law and letters, U. Paris, 1952; diploma, Inst. d'Etudes Politiques, Paris, 1953; student, Ecole Nat. d'Admnstrn.; degree, Wesleyan U., 1950. Auditor Court of Audit, 1957-58; reporter at inquiry commn. Secretariat for Algerian Affairs, 1958-59; sr. staff mem. Prime Min. Michel Debré Govt. of France, 1963, appeal advisor to Prime Min. Michel Debré audit office, 1959-62; dir. Regional Planning and Devel. Agy., France, 1967-75; chief staff to Prime Min. Jacques Chirac Govt. of France, 1975-76; sec. gen. Rassemblement pour la République Party, 1976-78; vice chmn. Lyonnaise des Eaux, 1979-80, chmn., CEO, 1980-97; prof. Auguste Comte Inst., 1980-83; chmn. supervisory bd. Suez Lyonnaise des Eaux, 1997—; chmn. Sino French Holding, China, 1996, Lyonnaise des Eaux de Casablanca, Marocco, 1997—, Hisusa, Spain, Lyonnaise Am. Holding, U.S.; hon. supervisory chmn. Suez Lyonnaise Eaux, 2000; bd. dirs. Total (Compagnie Française des Pétroles), Métropole TV, SMEG, Monaco, France, EEC, New Caledonia, EDT, Tahiti, Aguas de Barcelone, Spain, Dumez-GTM, Groupe GTM, Sino. French Holding, Lyonnaise Am. Holding; pres. European Round Table, 1989-96, mem. consultive coun. Banque de France, 1990—; mem. bus. adv. coun. IFC, U.S.; mem. consultative com RWE, Germany. Co-author: Transformation d'un Pays-Pour une géographie de la Liberté, 1975, Propositions pour la France, 1977, L'Aménagement du Territoire, 8th edit., 1996. Mem. European Round Table Industrialists (mem. steering com., chmn. 1992-95). Avocations: swimming, climbing. *

MONOHAN, EDWARD SHEEHAN, IV, lawyer; b. Frankfort, Ky., Feb. 12, 1940; s. Edward Sheehan III and Mary (Lally) M.; m. Marilyn Louise Diebold, Aug. 31, 1963; children: Meredith, Edward, Patrick, Megan. B-SChemE, Purdue U., 1962; JD, Georgetown U., 1965. Bar: D.C. 1966, Ky. 1966, Ohio 1990, U.S. Supreme Ct. 1975. Assoc. Vest & Ware, Covington, Ky., 1967-74; ptnr. Ware & Monohan, Florence, Ky., 1974-80, Monohan, Hertz & Blankenship, Florence, 1993-2000, Monohan & Blankenship, Florence, 2000—; pres. Boone County Bar Assn., Florence, 1980-81. City councilman City of Crestview Hills, Ky., 1972-78. Mem. Ky. Bar Assn., Ky. Trial Lawyers Assn., No. Ky. Bar Assn., Louisville Bar Assn., Am. Inns of Ct. (master), Rotary (pres. 1981). Republican. Roman Catholic. Avocations: sailing, jogging, reading, French. Fax: 859-283-5155. E-mail: ed@kyattys.com. Home: 21 Winding Way Covington KY 41017-2227 Office: Monohan & Blankenship 7711 Ewing Blvd Ste 100 Florence KY 41042-1814

MONOSSON, IRA HOWARD, physician; b. N.Y.C., Mar. 23, 1937; adopted s. Henry M.; s. I. Easer Rosenfield and Yetta Malvin; m. Aviva May Sokol, Sept. 20, 1970; children: Elana, Danielle, Ari. BA, Stanford U., 1959, MD, 1962. Diplomate Am. Bd. Preventive Medicine; cert. in occupational medicine. Intern Montefioro Hosp., Bronx, N.Y., 1962-63; resident L.A. County Gen. Hosp., 1963-64, Cedars of Lebanon Hosp., L.A., 1964-65; fellow Scripps Clinic and Rsch. Found., La Jolla, Calif., 1965-66; resident U. Calif., Irvine, 1976-77; pvt. practice San Diego, 1966-68, Southington, Conn., 1968-69; pvt. practice Ctrl. Med. Group, L.A., 1969-71; prin., owner Mid-City Med. Group, L.A., 1971-73; ptnr., physician Foley Med. Group, L.A., 1973-74; pub. health physician City of L.A., 1975; pub. health med. officer, chief Calif. State Divsn. Occupational Safety & Health, L.A., 1976-82; pvt. practice various, Calif., 1982—; asst. clin. prof. medicine UCLA Sch. Medicine; asst. clin. prof. preventive medicine U. So. Calif. Sch. Medicine; com. mem. UCLA Inst. Biosafety Com., 1982—; adv. bd. Hazardous Substances Task Force, City of L.A., Calif. State Divsn. Indsl. Accidents, 1984-86, Occupl. Medicine Calif. Med. Assn., 1985-88; cons. in field; spkr. in field. Mem. Environ. Occupl. Health com. Am. Lung. Assn. Calif., 1986-89; steering com. of L.A. 2000 project, 1980-81; adv. com. Del Amo/Montrose Superfund Site, 1995—, Permanent Disability Study, Calif. State Commn. Health and Safety and Workers Compensation; mem. L.A. Unified Sch. Dist. Bd. Edn. Ind. Commn. regarding The Belmont Learning Ctr., 1999, mem. Ind. Commn. for Belmont Learning Ctr., 1999—. Author: (with others) A Practical Approach to Occupational and Environmental Medicine, 1994; contbr. articles to profl. jours. Fellow Am. Coll. Preventive Medicine, Am. Coll. Occupl. Environ. Medicine, Royal Soc. Medicine, Am. Acad. Occupl. Medicine; mem. AMA (Calif. chpt., L.A. chpt.), Calif. Soc. Indsl. Medicine and Surgery (pres. 1995, bd. dirs.), Calif. Indsl. Med. Coun. (mem. state regulatory bd. 1990—, chmn. 1990-93). Fax: 310-570-0110. Office: Ste 268W 2001 Santa Monica Blvd Santa Monica CA 90404-2102

MONPLAISIR, MALCOLM HAROLD, maintenance and management specialist; b. Demerara, Guyana, Apr. 15, 1956; s. Harold and Gwendolyn Leila (Jacobs) M. BS in Mech. Engring. with honors, U. West Indies, 1979, MS in Prodn. Engring. & Mgmt., 1990. Chartered engr. Brit. Engring. Coun. Engr.-in-tng. Guymine, Linden, Guyana, 1979-80, project engr., 1980-84, sr. project engr., 1984-86, maintenance supt., 1986-87; maintenance cons. G.E.T.S., Linden, Guyana, 1987-91, pvt. practice, Guyana & Caribbean, 1991—; maintenance cons. MMA-ADA, Onverwagt, Guyana, 1987; job. evaluation cons. Caribbean Cmty. Secretariat, Georgetown, 1995; orgnl. devel. cons. Guyana Nat. Co-op Bank, Georgetown, 1991-92; human resource cons. GT&T, Georgetown, 1993, compensation cons. IDB, Washington, 1994, 95, 97, 98; human resource cons. CARDI, St. Augustine, Trinidad, 1994-96, Guyana Sugar Corp. Ltd., Georgetown, 1997; compensation cons. Iwokrama Internat. Ctr. for Rain Forest Conservation, Guyana, 1997, compensation cons., Commonwealth Sec., London. Contbr. articles to Jour. Operational Rsch. Soc. Mem. ASME, Inst. Mech. Engrs. Avocations: reading, travel, cricket, soccer. Home and Office: Guyhoc Park NE La Penitence, 180 Apaiqua Ln, Georgetown Guyana

MONRO, JAMES LAWRENCE, cardiac surgeon; b. Singapore, Nov. 17, 1939; s. John Kirkpatrick and Landon Carter (Reed) M.; m. Caroline Jane Dunlop, Sept. 29, 1973; children: Charles, Rosanne, Andrew. MB BS, London Hosp. Med. Coll., 1964. Sr. house officer St. James' Hosp., London, 1966-67; registrar surg. unit London Hosp., 1967-69, sr. registrar cardiothoracic surgery, 1972-73; resident surg. officer Brompton Hosp., London, 1969; sr. registrar Green Ln Hosp., Auckland, New Zealand, 1970-72; cons. cardiac surgeon Gen. Hosp., Southampton, Eng., 1973—. Author: A Colour Atlas of Cardiac Surgery: Acquired Heart Disease, 1982, A Colour Atlas of Cardiac Surgery: Congenital Heart Disease, 1984; contbr. numerous articles to profl. pubs. Fellow Royal Coll. Surgeons; mem. European Assn. Cardiothoracic Surgery, Soc. Cardiothoracic Surgeons of Gt. Britain and Ireland (pres.), Brit. Cardiac Soc. Avocations: skiing, tennis, golf, horseback riding. Office: Gen Hosp, Dept Cardiac Surgery, Southampton SO16 6YD, England

MONROE, HASKELL MOORMAN, JR., university educator; b. Dallas, Mar. 18, 1931; s. Haskell M. and Myrtle Marie (Jackson) M.; m. Margaret Joan Phillips, June 15, 1957; children: Stephen, Melanie, Mark, John. BA, Austin (Tex.) Coll., 1952, MA, 1954; PhD, Rice U., Houston, 1961. From instr. to prof. Tex. A&M U., 1959-80; asst. dean Tex. A&M U. (Grad. Sch.), 1965-68, asst. v.p. acad. affairs, 1972-74, dean faculties, 1974-80, assoc. v.p. acad. affairs, 1977-80; pres. U. Tex., El Paso, 1980-87; chancellor U. Mo., Columbia, 1987-91, prof. history, 1987-97, chancellor emeritus, prof. history, 1997—; dean faculties emeritus, dir. heritage preservation program Tex. A&M U., College Station, 1998; instr. Schreiner Inst., Kerrville, Tex., summer 1959; vis. lectr. Emory U., summers 1967, 72; faculty lectr. Tex. A&M U., 1972; alumni lectr. Austin Coll., 1980; bd. dirs. Southwestern Bell Corp., Boone County Nat. Bank, SBC Comms., Inc.; history adv. com. Sec. Air Force, 1987-87; orientation com. Dept. Def.-Joint Chiefs, 1986; adv. bd. Army Command and Gen. Staff Sch., 1986-88. Contbr. articles, revs.; editor: Papers of Jefferson Davis, 1964-69; adv. editor: Texana, 1964-71; bd. editorial advisers: Booker T. Washington Papers, 1965-85 . Bd. dirs. Brazos Valley Rehab. ctr., 1975-77, Salvation Army, El Paso, 1984-87, Columbia, Mo., 1988-97, Crime Stoppers of El Paso, United Way Columbia, 1988-94; trustee Bryan Hosp., 1976-79, chmn., 1979; bd. ch. visitors Austin Coll., 1977-78; deacon First Presbyn. Ch., Bryan, 1961-63, elder, 1965-67, 69-71, 73-74, clk. of session, 1973-74, chmn. pulpit nominating com., 1971-72; mem. presbytery's coun. Presbytery of Brazos, 1969-71, mem. resources for the 80s steering com., 1978-80; elder 1st Presbyn. Ch., El Paso, 1984-87, 1st Presbyn. Ch., Columbia, 1994-96; mem. exec. bd. Great Rivers coun. Boy Scouts Am., 1990-97; mem. Pres. Coun. NCAA, 1986-87; chmn. Jefferson Davis award com. Confederate Mus., 1996-97; bd. dirs. Salvation Army, 1989-97. Recipient Citation of Appreciation, LULAC, 1982, Honor award Salvation Army, 1997, also numerous achievement awards; grantee Social Sci. Rsch. Coun., Tex. A&M U., Huntington Libr., Intrafraternity and Sorority Outstanding Tchr. award, 1997; named Ky. Col., 1967; named to Legends of Aggieland, 1998. Mem. Am. Hist. Assn., Orgn. Am. Historians, So. Hist. Assn. Hist. Found. Presbyn. and Reformed Chs. (pres. 1970-72), Coll. Football Assn. (chmn. bd. 1989-90, bd. dirs.), Truman Scholarship Panel, Soc. Conf. Deans Faculties and Acad. V.P.s (pres. 1978), Rotary (El Paso, hon. Columbia, Mo., Bryan, Tex.). Home: 1005 Sonoma Cir College Station TX 77845-7907 Office: Tex A&M U 610 Ellis Libr College Station TX 77845-5000

MONROE, MELROSE, retired banker; b. Flowery Branch, Ga., Apr. 13, 1919; d. Willis Jeptha and Leila Adell Cash; m. Lynn Austin, June 14, 1942. AB in Edn., Ga. State U., 1968. Negotiator Trust Co. Bank, Atlanta, 1962-89, ret., 1989. Mem. Nat. Women's C. of C. (pres. 1987-88), Atlanta Women's C. of C. (dir. 1965-66, pres. Fidelis SS class 1962-63), Nat. Am. Legion Aux. (so. divsn. chmn. aux. Americanism 1995-96, so. divsn. chmn. aux. emergency fund 1996-97, cmty. svc. com.), Am. Legion Aux. (pres. 5th dist. 1986-87, Ga. state chaplain 1989-90, state historian 1991-92, state 2d v.p. 1992-93, 1st v.p. 1993-94, pres. 1994-95, Americanism chmn. so. divsn. 1995-95, chmn. emergency fund 1996-97, mem. cmty. svc. com. 1997-98, nat. historian 1999-00, v. chmn. nat. poppy com. 2000-01), Order Ea. Star (worthy matron 1951-52). Democrat. Home and Office: 6243 Spout Springs Rd Flowery Branch GA 30542-5032

MONROE, MURRAY SHIPLEY, lawyer; b. Cin., Sept. 25, 1925; s. James and Martha (Shipley) M.; m. Sally Longstreth, May 11, 1963; children: Tracy, Murray, Courtney, David. BE, Yale U., 1946, BS, 1947; LLB, U. Pa., 1950. Bar: Ohio 1950, U.S. Dist. Ct. (so. dist.) Ohio 1954, U.S. Dist. Ct. (mid. dist.) Tenn. 1981, US. Dist. Ct. (mid. dist.) N.C. 1974, U.S. Dist. Ct. (mid. dist.) Pa. 1986, U.S. Dist. (ea. dist.) Pa. 1960, U.S. Dist. Ct. (we. dist.) Mo. 1974, U.S. Dist. Ct. Mass. 1978, U.S. Dist. Ct. (ea. dist.) La. 1979, U.S. Dist. Ct. (no. dist.) Ill. 1980, U.S. Ct. Appeals (4th cir.) 1984, U.S. Ct. Appeals (6th cir.) 1969, U.S. Supreme Ct. 1977, U.S. Ct. Appeals (3d cir.) 1990. Assoc. Taft, Stettinus & Hollister, Cin., 1950-58, ptnr., 1958-96; of counsel, 1997—; mem. lawyers com. Nat. Ctr. for State Cts., 1985-96; faculty Ohio Legal Ctr. Inst., 1970-93. Contbr. articles to profl. jours. Trustee, treas. The Coll. Prep. Sch., 1972-76, Episcopal Sch. Cin., 2000—; trustee The Seven Hills Schs., 1982-88, chmn. bd., 1982-85. 2d lt. USNR, 1943-46. Recipient award Seven Hills Schs., 1985. Fellow Ohio Bar Found.; mem. ABA (speaker symposiums), Ohio Bar Assn. (coun. dels. 1977-82, bd. govs. antitrust sect. 1960-95, dir. emeritus 1995—, chmn. bd. govs. 1973-75, Merit award 1976, speaker symposiums), Bankers Club (Cin.), Cin. Country Club, Met. Club, Tau Beta Pi. Republican. Episcopalian. Avocations: sailing, tennis.

MONROE, SUSAN MACGREGOR, chemist; b. Greenville, N.C., May 17, 1948; d. Calvin W. MacGregor and Lullah Cox Pringle; m. James Louie Monroe, Feb. 21, 1969; children: Matthew James, Michael Christopher. BS in Math., Chemistry and Physics, Mesa State U., 1987; PhD in Bioinorganic Chemistry, U. Denver, 1996. Quality control chemist Ricon Resins, Inc., Grand Junction, Colo., 1985-92; environ. chemist Quanterra, Inc., Arvada, Colo., 1992; rsch. chemist Matheson Gas Products, Longmont, Colo., 1996-98; quality control supr. Sulzer Biologics Inc., Wheat Ridge, Colo., 1998—. Contbr. articles to profl. jours. including Biochemistry, Biochim. Biophys. Acta, and Jour. Inst. Environ. Scis. and Tech. Named Richardson Leadership Found. scholar East Carolina U., 1968-69; recipient Chemistry award Dickinson State Coll., 1985. Mem. AAAS, Am. Chem. Soc. (alt. councilor 1998-99, councilor 1999—). Office: Sulzer Biologics 4056 Youngfield St Wheat Ridge CO 80033-3862

MONSEN, TOR JOHAN, bacteriologist, researcher; b. Mo i Rana, Norway, Nov. 3, 1955; arrived in Sweden, 1978; s. Torbjørn and Ingrid (Bernhartsen) M.; children: Line, Petter. Degree, Umea (Sweden) U., 1980, med. degree, 1990, splty. degree in clin. bacteriology, 1997. Physician dept. clin. bacteriology U. Umea, 1992—. Contbr. articles to profl. jours. Office: Dept Clin Bacteriology, U Umea, S-90185 Umea Sweden

MONSERRAT, JOSÉ HIGINIO, business executive, engineer; b. Cordoba, Argentina, Jan. 12, 1919; s. José and Angela Elvira (Farre) M.; m. Victoria Digna Carciofini, Dec. 6, 1945; children: Silvia María, Cecilia Beatriz María, Adriana Victoria María, María Alejandra, Pablo José Javier. B Humanities, Nat. Coll. Monserrat, Cordoba, 1937; grad. mech.-elec. engr., Nat. U. Cordoba, 1943, grad. mech.-aero. engr., 1950. Proyect. engr. Fábrica Military de Aviones, Argentina, 1942-56; dir., tech. sec. Fábrica Automotores, Argentina, 1955-56; dir. Banco Ind. República Argentina, 1958-62; pres. Empresa Provincial Energia Cordoba, Cordoba, 1962-63; v.p. MOLOBO S.A., Argentina, 1981—; pres. ORMAS S.A.I.C.I.C., Buenos Aires, 1978—. Mem. ASME, Soc. Automotive Engrs., Cordoba Engrs. Ctr., Agua y Energia Electrica Argentina. Roman Catholic. Office: ORMAS SAICIC, Carlos Pellegrini 1023 11, 1009 Buenos Aires Argentina

MONSON, CAROL LYNN, osteopath, psychotherapist; b. Blue Island, Ill., Nov. 3, 1946; d. Marcus Edward and Margaret Bertha (Andres) M.; m. Frank E. Warden, Feb. 28, 1981. B.S., No. Ill. U., 1968, M.S., 1969; D.O., Mich State Coll. Osteo. Medicine, 1979. Lic. physician, Mich., diplomate Am. Bd. Osteo., Am. Bd. Family Physicians, Am. Bd. Osteo. Gen. Practice, diplomate MSUCOM. Expeditor-psychotherapist H. Douglas Singer Zone Ctr., Rockford, Ill., 1969-71; psychotherapist Tri-County Mental Health, St. Johns, Mich., 1971-76; pvt. practice psychotherapy, East Lansing, Mich., 1976-80; intern Lansing Gen. Hosp., Mich., 1979-80, residency dir. family practice, 1988—; pvt. practice osteo. medicine, Lansing, 1980—; mem. staff Ingham Med. Hosp., Lansing Gen. Hosp. (now Ingham Regional Med. Ctr.), chmn. gen practice, 1987-89; field instr. Sch. Social Work, U. Mich., 1973-76; clin. instr. Central Mich. Dept. Psychology, 1974-75; clin. prof. Mich. State U., 1980-88, asst. prof., 1988—, tng. supr. family medicine residency, 1988-97, faculty devel. fellow, 1994-95, residency dir. family medicine, 1994-97; mem. adv. bd. Substance Abuse Clearinghouse, Lansing, 1983-85, Kelly Health Care, Lansing, 1983-85, Americor Health Svcs., Lansing, 1984-88, Lansing Home Care, 1988-94. Fellow Am. Coll. Family Practice (osteo.); mem. Am. Osteo. Assn. (del. 1994—, health policy fellow 1997-98), Am. Coll. Family Practice, Osteo., Am. Acad. Family Practice, Internat. Transactional Analysis Assn., Mich. Osteo. Assn. (formerly Mich. Assn. Osteo. Physicians and Surgeons, program com. 1992—, governance coun., 1996-1997, bd. trustees 1997—), Ingham County Osteo. Assn. (pres. 1993-95, 96-97), Nat. Assn. Career Women (conv. com. 1984—), Lansing Assn. Career Women, Soc. Tchrs. of Family Medicine, Mich. Assn. Osteo. Family Physicians (pres.-elect 1994, pres. 1995-96), Am. Coll. Family Physicians (residency insp. 1991—), Mich. Coun. Grad. Med. Edn. (appointee 1998—), Zonta (chmn. service com. Mid Mich. Capital Area chpt.). Avocations: gardening; orchid growing; antique collecting. Office: 2445 Jolly Rd Ste 400 Okemos MI 48864-4572

MONSON, DIANNE LYNN, literacy educator; b. Minot, N.D., Nov. 24, 1934; d. Albert Rachie and Iona Cordelia (Kirk) M. BS, U. Minn., 1956, MA, 1962, PhD, 1966. Tchr. Rochester (Minn.) Pub. Schs., 1956-59, U.S. Dept. Def., Schweinfurt, West Germany, 1959-61, St. Louis Park (Minn.) Schs., 1961-62; instr. U. Minn., Mpls., 1962-66; prof. U. Wash., Seattle, 1966-82; prof. literacy edn. U. Minn., Mpls., 1982-97, prof. emeritus, 1997—; chmn. curriculum and instrn. U. Minn., 1986-89. Author: Reading, 2000; co-author: New Horizons in the Language Arts, 1972, Children and Books, 6th edit., 1981, Experiencing Children's Literature, 1984, (monograph) Research in Children's Literature, 1976, Language Arts: Teaching and Learning Effective Use of Language, 1988, Reading Together: Helping Children Get A Good Start With Reading, 1991, Scott Foresman Reading, 2000; assoc. editor: Dictionary of Literacy, 1995. Recipient Outstanding Educator award U. Minn. Alumni Assn., 1983, Alumni Faculty award U. Minn. Alumni Assn., 1991. Fellow Nat. Conf. Rsch. in English (pres. 1990-91); mem. ALA, Nat. Coun. Tchrs. English (exec. com. 1979-81), Internat. Reading Assn. (dir. 1980-83, Arbuthnot award 1993, Reading Hall of Fame 1997), U.S. Bd. Books for Young People (pres. 1988-90). Lutheran. Home: 740 River Dr Apt 6F Saint Paul MN 55116-1045

MONSON, JOHN PATRICK, endocrinologist, educator; b. London, July 11, 1950; s. Joseph Patrick and Margaret (Connor) M.; m. Eva-Helena Maria Lind, Oct. 12, 1974; children; Kevin T.P., Andrew F. B Medicine B Surgery, U. London, 1973, MD, 1983. House physician Guy's and Greenwich Hosps., U.K., 1973-74; sr. house physician Croydon Hosp., U.K., 1974-75; registrar in medicine St. George's Hosp., London, 1975-78; lectr. in medicine London Hosp. Med. Coll., 1978-82, sr. lectr. in endocrinology, 1982-94; reader in metabolism and endocrinology St. Bartholomew's Hosp., Royal London Sch. Medicine, 1994-99, prof. clin. endocrinology, 1999—; mem. exec. sci. com. Kims Surveillance Program of Treatment in Adult Hypopituitarism, Stockholm, 1994—. Author, editor: Challenges in Growth Hormone Therapy, 1999; contbr. articles to profl. jours. Fellow Royal Coll. Physicians; mem. Soc. Endocrinology, Endocrine Soc., Med. Rsch. Soc., European Neuroendocrine Assn., European Soc. Clin. Investigation. Office: St Bartholomew's Hosp, Dept Endocrinology, London EC1A 7BE, England

MONSON, JOHN RUDOLPH, lawyer; b. Chgo., Feb. 4, 1941; s. Rudolph Agaton and Ellen Louise (Loeffler) M.; m. Susan Lee Brown, May 22, 1965; children: Elizabeth Louisa, Christina Lee, Donald Rudolph. BA with honors, Northwestern U., 1963; JD with distinction, U. Mich., 1966. Bar: Ill. 1966, N.H. 1970, Mass. 1985. Atty. assoc. Chapman & Cutler, Chgo., 1966-68, Levenfeld, Kanter, Baskes & Lippitz, Chgo., 1968-70, Nighswander, Martin & Mitchell, Laconia, N.H., 1970-71; mem., ptnr. Wiggin & Nourie, P.A., Manchester, N.H., 1972—; pres. Wiggin & Nourie, P.A., Manchester, 1991-94; sec., gen. counsel Rock of Ages Corp., 1996-2000. Mem. N.H. Fish and Game Commn., Concord, 1980-94, chmn., 1983-93; sr. bd. dirs. Brown-Monson Found., 1991—; incorporator Cath. Med. Ctr., 1988-95, Optima Health, 1994-99; commr. N.H. Land and Cmty. Heritage Commn., 1998-2000. Fellow Am. Coll. Trust and Estate Counsel, Safari Club Internat. (v.p. 1999—, dir.-at-large 1997-99). Republican. Avocations: skiing, hunting, running. Home: 24 Wellesley Dr Bedford NH 03110-4531 Office: Wiggin & Nourie PA 20 Market St Manchester NH 03101-1931

MONTAGNIER, LUC ANTOINE, virologist; b. Chabris, Indre, France, Aug. 18, 1932; 3 children. Cert. of Studies on Natural Scis., U. Poitiers, France, 1953, BS, 1955; MD, U. Paris, 1960. Asst. Faculté des Scis, Paris, 1955-60; attaché de recherche Nat. Ctr. Sci. Rsch., Paris, 1960-63, chargé de recherche, 1963-67, maitre de recherche, 1967-72, dir. research, 1974—; head lab. Nat. Ctr. Sci. Rsch., Orsay, France, 1965-72; head viral oncology unit Institut Pasteur, Paris, 1972—, head virology dept., 1982-85, prof., 1974—, head dept. AIDS and Retroviruses, 1990-96; disting. prof., dir. Ctr. for Molecular and Cellular Biology Queens Coll. of the CUNY, 1997—; dir. virology course Institut Pasteur, 1980-85, head dept. AIDS and Retrovirus, 1991-97; mem. responsible research team CNRS; discovered HIV-1 virus, 1983 and HIV-2 virus, 1985; pres. adminstrv. coun. European Fed. for AIDS Rsch., 1988. Author: Vaincre le Sida, 1987, Des virus et des hommes, 1994, AIDS, Oxidative Stress and Cancer, 1997, Virus, in English, 2000. Pres. World Found. for AIDS Rsch. and Prevention, Paris, 1993—. Decorated Comdr. Legion of Honor, comdr. Ordre Nat. du Mérite; recipient Lasker prize, 1986, Gairdner prize, 1987, Japan prize, 1988, Warrent Alpert Found. prize, 1998, also others. Mem. Acad. Nat. de Médecine, French Acad. Scis. Co-discoverer (with Robert Gallo) of AIDS virus. Office: Inst Pasteur, 25-28 rue du Dr Roux, 75015 Paris France

MONTAGUE, JOEL GEDNEY, public health officer; b. N.Y.C., July 6, 1932; s. William Pepperrell and Jean Lois (Gedney) M.; m. Shahnaz Emami-Nikou, Dec. 16, 1963; children: Jahan, Maryam. BA, Oberlin Coll., 1956; MA, Johns Hopkins U., 1960; MS in Pub. Health, U. N.C., 1970; postgrad., U. Tehran, 1961. Field rep., mission chief CARE, Iran, Egypt, Tunisia, 1961-68; regional dir. CARE, N.Y.C., 1968-69, The Population Coun., N.Y.C., 1971-76; dep. dir. Project for Strengthening Health Delivery Systems in Ctrl. and West Africa, Boston, also Ivory Coast, 1976-79; regional dir. Mgmt. Scis. for Health, Boston, 1979-80; head health and hosps. Secretariat of His Highness The Aga Khan, Aiglemont, France, 1980-85; v.p. John Snow Pub. Health, Boston, 1985-89; dir. Am. Friends of AICF, Washington, 1990-92; country rep. John Snow, Cambodia, Cambodia, 1994-97; pvt. pub. health cons., Wellesley, Mass., 1997—. Contbr. articles to profl. jours. Bd. dirs. Nat. Coun. for Internat. Health, 1993-96, Am. Coun. for Nationalities Svcs., 1992-95, U.S. Com. for Refugees, 1991-94; chmn. bd. Ptnrs. for Devel., 1996—. With signal corps U.S. Army, 1956-58. Decorated Medal of Honor, Iranian Red Cross, officer Order of the Republic (Tunisia) Fund; Fulbright grantee, 1961; Ford Found. fellow, 1970-71; Aspen Fund grantee, 1993; hon. fellow Inst. Advanced Study Humanities, U. Edinburgh, Scotland, 1997. Fellow Royal Soc. Tropical Medicine and Hygiene. Home: 24 Maugus Ave Wellesley MA 02481-7617

MONTALVO, GABRIEL, archbishop; b. Santafé de Bogota, Columbia, Jan. 27, 1930. D in Canon Law, Lateran U., Rome. Ordained priest Archdiocese of Santafé, Bogota, 1953. With Holy See, Bolivia, Argentina and El Salvador, 1957-64; sec. of state sect. Ea. Eurpean Countries Holy See, 1964-74; apostolic nuncio Nicaragua and Honduras, 1974; apolstolic pronuncio Algeria and Tunisia, 1980-82; apostolic del. Lybia, 1980-82; from mem. to head Papal Mediation Office, 1982-86; apostolic pro-nuncio Yugoslavia, 1986-96; 1st apostolic nuncio Belarus, 1993; pres. Pontifical Ecclesiastical Acad., 1993; apostolic nuncio U.S., 1998; permanent observer Holy See to Org. of Am. States, 1998—. Recipient Episcopal Ordination by Pope John Paul VI, 1974. Home and Office: 3339 Massachusetts Ave NW Washington DC 20008-3610*

MONTANARI, CARLOS ALBERTO, chemistry educator; b. Canitar, Sao Paulo, Brazil, Feb. 17, 1958; s. Flavio and Iraci Peres da Silva Montanari; m. Maria Luiza Montanari, July 29, 1985. BSc, Faculty Oswaldo Cruz, São Paulo, 1984; MSc, U. São Paulo, 1987, PhD, 1991. Lectr. Faculdades Oswaldo Cruz, São Paulo, 1983-87, U. Fed. de Ouro Preto, Brazil, 1987-94, U. Fed. de Minas Gerais, Belo Horizonte, Brazil, 1994—; vis. prof. U. Kent, Canterbury, U.K., 1995; rschr. in field. Contbr. articles to profl. jours. Mem. Soc. Brasileira de Qummica (adv. bd. 1994—). Avocation: cycling. E-mail: montana@dedalus.lcc.ufmg.br. Fax: 31-499-5700. Office: Fed Univ Minas Gerais, Av Pres Antonio Carlos 627, 31270901 Belo Horizonte MG, Brazil

MONTANARI, FRANCO, classicist, educator; b. Sannazzaro de' Burgondi, PV, Italy, May 24, 1950; s. Renzo and Maria (Rastaldi) M.; m. Daniela Manetti, Sept. 21, 1978. Diploma liceale, Liceo Classico U. Foscolo, Pavia, Italy, 1969; laurea in lettere, U. Pisa, Italy, 1973; diploma, Scuola Normale Superiore, Pisa, 1973, perfezionamento, 1974. Contrattista quadriennale U. Pisa, Italy, 1975-77, prof. incaricato, 1977-82, prof. associato, 1982-86; prof. ordinario U. Genova, Italy, 1987—; pres. XL Entretiens Fondation Hardt, Geneva, 1993; treas. Bur. of the Fedn. Internat. des Assn. des Etudes Classiques (FIEC), 1994—; mem. Conseil de Fondation and Conseil Scientifique of the Fondation Hardt (Geneva); dir. Centro Italiano dell'Année Philologique. Author: Studi di filologia omerica antica I, 1979, I frammenti dei grammatici Agathokles, Hellanikos, Ptolemaios, Epithetes, 1988, Introduzione a Omero, 1990, 92, Studi di filologia omerica antica II, 1995, GI. Vocabolario della lingua greca, 1995, Storia della Letteratura Greca, 1998; editor: Da Omero agli Alessandrini, 1988, La philologie grecque à l'époque hellénistique et romaine, 1994, Omero. Gli aedi, i poemi, gli interpreti, Firenze, 1998; mem. editl. bd. Corpus Papiri Filosofici, Florence. Mem. Soc. Internat. de Bibliographie Classique. Home: via Studiati 6, I-56127 Pisa Italy Office: Facoltà di Lettere, U Genova Via Balbi 4, 16126 Genova Italy

MONTANDON, DENYS, plastic surgeon; b. Geneva, Oct. 22, 1938; m. Cleopatra Pastirmatzi, Jan. 9, 1964. Student in medicine, U. Geneva, 1957-63; MD, 1967, specialization plastic surgery, 1975, privatdozent, 1977; assoc. prof., U. Geneva, 1994. Diplomate Am. Bd. Plastic Surgery. Head Dept. Plastic and Reconstructive Surgery U. Hosp. Geneva, 1982—, assoc. prof., 1982—; Tchg. asst. NYU, 1968, instr. clin. surgery, 1969. Office: Univ Hosp Plastic Surgery, 112 Route Florissant, 1206 Geneva Switzerland

MONTANEZ, MARY ANN CHAVEZ, counselor, consultant, writer; b. Pasadena, Calif., July 16, 1936; d. Vincent Chavez-Trujillo-Mendibles and Trinidad (Huerta-Molina) Chavez; m. R.E. Montanez, Nov. 17, 1956 (div. June 1976); children: Robert, Eric, (twins) Michael and Manuel. AA, Pasadena City Coll., 1980; BA, Pacific Oaks Coll., 1985, MA in Human Devel., 1988; cert. counseling, Calif. State U., L.A., 1994. Life cert. C.C. counseling and instrn. Placement officer Pasadena (Calif.) C.C. Dist., 1981-90, coll. instr., 1986-90; vocat. rehab. counselor Calif. Dept. Rehab., L.A., 1990—; exec. dir. Latins Writers & Film Makers, 1998—; mem. outreach bd. Pasadena Mental Health Assn., 1976-79; field rep. El Centro De Accion Social, Inc., 1976-77; dir. program Pasadena Unified Sch. Dist., 1977-78; coord. outreach, crisis counselor Pasadena Mental Health, 1978-81; cons., field reader Women's Ednl. Equity Act, Washington, 1981; out-placement coord. PCC, 1984; staff recruitment program Pasadena C.C., 1987-88; acad. counselor Multi Cultural Ctr.-Cerritos Coll. Dist., 1990-91. Commr. Commn. on Disabilities, 1990—; adv. bd. mem. Fiesta Educativa, 1991-99; bd. mem. West Side Ctr. on Ind. Living, L.A., 1993-99; mem. credit com. Pasadena Employees Credit Union, 1996; active Huntington Libr.; mem. Christian Calvery Chapel. Recipient Golden Angel award, 1995. Mem. Soc. Hispanic Hist. Ancestral Rsch. Democrat. Roman Catholic. Avocations: writing, history, art. Home: 2533 Glenrose Ave Altadena CA 91001-5049

MONTANUS, HANS, mathematics educator; b. Loon op Zand, The Netherlands, July 7, 1958; s. Jan Montanus and Elizabeth VanTol; m. Daniele Van den Burg, Oct. 1, 1992; children: Jenny, Romy. M in Physics, U. Amsterdam, The Netherlands, 1987. Rschr. Delft Hydraulics, Vollenhoven, The Netherlands, 1987-90; physics tchr. High Sch., Naarden, The Netherlands, 1991-94; math. tchr. High Sch., Almere, The Netherlands, 1994—. Contbr. articles on the foundations of physics to profl. jours. Avocations: synesthesia, painting. Home: Bunuellaan 16, 1325PL Almere The Netherlands

MONTANUS, MARY ROSAMOND, accountant; b. Meriden, Conn., July 22, 1957; d. Robert James Jr. and Rosamond Gertrude (Ernst) Hearn. BS, U. N.C., 1986. CPA, Md., Calif. Bus. mgr. Allegro Music Svc., Silver Spring, Md., 1986-93; acct. Foxx & Co., CPAs, Bethesda, Md., 1993-95, Maraney, Leslie & Gibbons, LLP, CPAs, Irvine, Calif., 1997-98, Maxwell & Co. CPAs, Irvine, Calif., 1998—. Vol. Friends of the Nat. Zoo, Washington, 1991, The Nature Conservancy, Chevy Chase, Md., 1994-95, Whitbread Chesapeake, 1996. Mem. AICPA, Calif. Soc. CPAs, Md. Assn. CPAs, Women's Sailing Assn. (co-founder Chesapeake Bay 1996). Avocations: sailing, snow skiing. Home: 32821 Pointe Stirling Apt G Dana Point CA 92629-1171

MONTASSE, MOSTAFA KAMEL, construction company executive; b. Tanta, Gharbia, Egypt, Sept. 6, 1944; s. Fahim and Mohamed and Hanem Ali (Abu Shady) M.; m. Samia Mohamed Gaber, Nov. 29, 1973; 1 child, Sherif. BSc in Civil Engring., Ain Shams U., Cairo, 1971. Execution mgr. Montasser Constrn. Co., Cairo, 1971-77, gen. mgr., 1977-84; v.p. Montasser Group, Cairo, 1984-97, chmn., 1997—. Mem. Am. C. of C., German C. of C., Businessmen Assn. Avocations: reading, walking, photography, travel. Home: 34 Gamat El Dwl Arab Flr, Cairo Egypt Office: Montasser Group, 122 Tahrir St-Dokki, Giza 12311, Egypt

MONTASSER, AMR M.K., physician, anaesthesiologist consultant, researcher; b. Cairo, Giza, Egypt, May 26, 1954; s. Mahmoud Kamel Montasser and Awatef Mohamed Bishara; m. Azza Ahmed Hassan, Jan. 29, 1982; children: Farah, Alia. MB, BCh, Cairo U., Cairo, 1977, MSc in Anaesthesia, 1981; DA, Royal Coll. Surgeons, London, 1983, FRCA, 1983. Resident of Anaesthesiology Cairo U. Hosps., 1979-81; registrar Royal Hallamshire Hosp., Sheffield, England, 1982, Middlesex Hosp. & Med. Sch., London, 1982-83; asst. lectr. Rsch. Inst. Ophth., Giza, 1983-87, lectr., 1987-92, asst. prof., 1992-98, prof., 1998—; Founder, dir., chief anesthesiologist, Specialized Surg. Unit, As Sallam Internatl. Hosp. for Spiral, Neuro, Orthopedic Surgs., 1998—. Recipient The Ideal Doctor medal The Egyptian Med. Syndicate, 1980, The Nuffield prize The Faculty of Anesthetists of the Royal Coll. Surgeons, 1982. Mem. Am. Soc. Anesthesiologists, Internat. Anesthesia Rsch. Soc. Moslem. Avocations: tennis, computers, motorcars, fishing. Home: 22 Abdel-Hameed Lotfy St, Dokki 12311 Cairo Egypt Office: Rsch Inst of Opthalmology, 2 Al-Ahram St, Giza Cairo Egypt

MONTASSER, MAGDY SHABAN, molecular virologist, educator; b. Damanhour, Behera, Egypt, Feb. 5, 1949; arrived in Kuwait, 1993; s. Shaban Ali and Zakiya Attia (Ghorab) M.; m. Omayma Ibrahem Abo-Ouf, Jan. 31, 1978; children: Monty, Shireef, Rania. BSc with honors, Alexandria (Egypt) U., 1971; MSc, Minia (Egypt) U., 1979; PhD, Rutgers U., 1988. Cert. agrl. engring. Instr., plant pathologist Minia (Egypt) U., 1974-83; rsch., tchg. asst. Rutgers U., New Brunswick, N.J., 1983-87; rsch. assoc. U. Md., College Park, 1987-91; molecular virologist Biotech. Ctr., Md., 1991-93; assoc. prof. U. Kuwait, Khaldiya, 1993—; cons. NASA/Goddard Space Flight Ctr., Md., 1990, Nat. Germplasm Resources, USDA, Beltsville, Md., 1990-91, Cancer Diagnostics, Inc., Fairfax, Va., 1991-93. Author: Experimental Protocols in Virology and Immunology, 1999; contbr. articles to profl. jours. Recipient award cert. sci. Ministry Edn., Egypt, 1965; rsch. grantee U. Kuwait, 1998. Mem. Am. Phytopathol. Soc., Radiation Safety Ctr., N.J. Acad. Sci. Avocations: swimming, hiking, stamp collecting. Email: m montasser@hotmail.com. Home: 319 Overbrook Rd Hagerstown MD 21742-3483 Office: U Kuwait Dept Biol Sci, PO Box 5969, Safat 13060, Kuwait

MONTEFIORE, ALAN CLAUDE, retired philosophy educator; b. London, Dec. 29, 1926; s. Leonard Nathaniel and Muriel Jeannetta (Tuck) M.; m. Hélène Denise Pivant, Mar. 25, 1952 (div. Sept. 1984); children: Anne, Claire, Paul; m. Catherine Audard, Nov. 24, 1984. Student, Clifton Coll., Bristol, Eng., 1941-45; BA, Balliol Coll., Oxford, Eng., 1950, MA, 1957. Asst. lectr. U. Keele/U. Coll., North Staffordshire, Eng., 1951-54, lectr., 1954-59; sr. lectr. U. Keele/U. Coll., North Staffordshire, 1959-61; Jowett fellow and tutor in philosophy Balliol Coll., Oxford, 1961-94; vis. prof. numerous instns., including McGill U., U. Montreal, U. Que., Can., 1969-76, various univs. India, 1987, Inst. Philosophy, Beijing, 1989, various instns. in Czechoslovakia and Romania, Middlesex U., 1997—; acad. visitor dept. philosophy London Sch. Econs., 1994-97; past gov. Froebel Coll. Edn.; mem. rsch. coms. Froebel Ednl. Inst.; pres. Weiner Libr., London, Forum for European Philosophy. Author: A Modern Introduction to Moral Philosophy, 1958; editor/contbr.: Neutrality and Objectivity - The University and Political Commitment, 1975; editor: Philosophy in France Today, 1983; joint editor: Goals, No-Goals and Own Goals, 1989, The Political Responsibility of Intellectuals, 1991, Integrity in the Public and Private Domains, 1999, others; contbr. numerous articles to profl. jours. and publs. Decorated Ordre du Mérite (France). Mem. Athenaeum Club. Home: 34 Scarsdale Villas, London W8 6PR, England

MONTEIRO, BRENDAN THOMAS, psychiatrist, consultant; b. Kalyan, India, Oct. 1, 1953; s. Constancio Ignatius and Celine (De Souza) M.; m. Margaret Bernadette Guider, Mar. 21, 1980; children: Rósín, Ravindra, Kieran, Sunil. MBBS, Grant Med. Coll., Bombay, 1978; Cert. Coun. for Advanced Comm. with Deaf, Eng., 1990. Med. degree; postgrad. psychiatry qualification. Registrar St. Davnets Hosp., Mohaghan, Ireland, 1979-81; sr. house officer Royal Manchester (Eng.) Children's Hosp., 1981-82; registrar Fife (Scotland) Health Bd., 1982-84; sr. registrar Manchester (Eng.) Rotation, 1984-86; cons. psychiatrist Whittingham Hosp., Preston, Eng., 1986-93, Nat. Ctr. Mental Health & Deafness, Manchester, Eng., 1993—; devel. cons. Forensic Svc. for Deaf People, 1997—; dir. eating disorder program Priory Hosp., Manchester, 1998—; hon. psychiatrist Brit. Deaf Assn., London, 1987—; chair congress European Soc. for Mental Health and Deafness, Europe, 1997—; immediate past inter-pres. Commn. on Mental Health-World Fedn. Deaf. Contbr. chpt. to book, articles to profl. jours. Past chair Sunil Appeal, Preston, Eng., 1992-96; trustee Age Concern, Manchester, 1996—. Mem. Royal Coll. Psychiatrists. Avocations: golf, travel, raising charity funds, music. Office: Nat Ctr M H Deafness, Bury New Rd, M25 3BR Manchester England

MONTEIRO, JOSÉ LUIZ FONTES, chemical engineering educator, researcher; b. Niteroi, Brazil, July 4, 1949; s. Augusto Araujo and Maria (Fontes) M.; m. Maria Del Carmen Quintas, Jul. 3, 1976 (div. 1992); 1 child: Andre Luis Quintas. MSc, Univ. Fed. Rio De Janeiro, 1973, DSc, 1980. Asst. lectr. Univ. Federal Rio de Janeiro, 1974-80, assoc. prof., 1981-92, head of dept., 1989-90, prof., 1993—; cons. Coppetec Found., 1980—; adjoint coord. NUCAT, Rio de Janeiro, 1995—; cons. Petrobras, 1996. Assoc. editor Brazilian Jour. Chem. Engring., 1999—; contbr. articles to profl. jours. Mem. Brazilian Assn. of Chemical Engrs. Avocations: diving, soccer, bike riding, jogging. Office: Coppe Univ Federal Rio de Janeiro, Centro De Tecnologia G 115, 21945970 Rio de Janeiro Brazil

MONTEIRO, JOSE MARIA PEREIRA, neurologist; b. Porto, Portugal, Jan. 2, 1945; s. Rodrigo Benito and Sara Gloria (Pereira) M.; m. Lidia Rodrigues Ferreira, May 16, 1971. MD, Faculty of Medicine U. Porto, 1971; PhD, Porto U., 1995. Neurologist, 1978; cons. neurology dept. neurology Hosp. Santo António, Porto, 1989—; asst. prof. neurology Inst. Ciencias Biomedicas, Abel Salazar Porto U., 1990—. Mem. Am. Acad. Neurology, Internat. Headache Soc., European Headache Fedn. Roman Catholic. Avocation: tennis. Office: Hosp Santo António, Largo Prof Abel Salazar, 4099-001 Porto Portugal

MONTEIRO, LUIZ FERNANDO, mathematician, researcher; b. Lisbon, Portugal, Oct. 5, 1936; arrived in Argentina, 1949; s. Antonio Aniceto and Lidia Marina (Torres) M.; m. Sara Esther Vincet, Sept. 9, 1961; children: Fernando Luis, Maria Fernanda, Maria Marcela. B in Math., Nat U. del Sur, Bahia Blanca, Argentina, 1961, D in Math., 1971. Asst. rschr. Inst. Math. Nat. U. del Sur, 1965, prof. Dept. Math., 1965-66, 83-00, rschr. Inst. Math., 1966-75, 88-97, chmn. Dept. Math., 1995—; chmn. Inst. Math. Bahia Blanca-CONICET-UNS, 1993-95, rschr., 1995-00; Editor: Revista de la Union Math. Argentina, 1989-95, 97—, Volumes de Homenaje, 1995, others. Mem. Union Math. Argentina. Avocations: model speed boats, paddle tennis, yew. Home: Rodriguez 1551, 8000 Bahia Blanca Argentina Office: Dept Math, Avda Alem 1253, 8000 Bahia Blanca Argentina

MONTEIRO, VICTOR JEROME, anatomy educator; b. Bombay, India, Jan. 19, 1936; s. Francis Xavier and Amelia (Fernandes) M.; m. Frida Ida Epifania Menezes-Souza, Jan. 6, 1974; children: Pearl Amelia, Jeanne Zara. MB BChir, Grant Med. Coll., Bombay, 1958, BSc in Anatomy, 1961, MSc in Medicine, 1963. Prof. anatomy Goa (India) Med. Coll., 1976-90, dean, 1990-94; ex-officio dean Goa Dental Coll., 1981-83; prof. anatomy Dy Patil Med. Coll., Kolhapur, India, 1994-95, SDM Coll. Dental Scis., Dharwad, India, 1995—; tech. expert Goa Pub. Svc. Commn., 1990, mem., 1995; tech. expert Union Pub. Svc. Commn., New Delhi, 1985; pres. Goa Med. Coun., 1993; mem. acad. ct. Goa U., 1990-94. Contbr. rsch. articles to profl. jours. Mem. Am. Assn. Anatomists, Anatom. Soc. India, N.Y. Acad. Scis., Goa Cancer Soc., Tagore Edn. Soc. Roman Catholic. Avocations: physical fitness, literature. Office: SDM Coll Dental Scis, Sattur Dharvad India

MONTEMAYOR, CARLOS RENE, advertising executive; b. San Antonio, Nov. 21, 1945; s. Raul Martin and Mary (Lyall) M.; m. Marina Cara Cook, Sep. 21, 1967 (div. Dec. 1978); m. Barbara Kay Volmer, Dec. 23, 1979; 1 child, Justin Norman. BBA in Mktg., U. Tex., 1967; MS in Journalism, Northwestern U., 1968. Account exec. Campbell-Ewald Co., Detroit and Cin., 1968-72, Ross Roy Inc., Detroit, 1972-74, Pitluk Group, San Antonio, 1974-76; v.p. GSD&M Advt., San Antonio, 1976-78; mktg. mgr. Church's Fried Chicken, San Antonio, 1978-81; v.p. Ed Yardang & Assocs., San

Antonio, 1981-83; pres. Montemayor y Asociados, San Antonio, 1983—; bd. dirs. USAA Fed. Savs. Bank, Witte Mus., sec., San Antonio Zoo; past pres. Fiesta San Antonio, Ray Feo XLVII Fiesta, 1995. 2d Lt. USAR, 1968-74. Mem. S.W. Found. Biomed. Rsch. (bd. govs.), Club Giraud, Argyle Club, Friends of McNay Club, Govs. Club. Republican. Roman Catholic. Avocations: collecting classic cars, traveling, racquet ball. Home: 5 Bitterblue Ln San Antonio TX 78218-1790 Office: Montemayor y Asociados Inc 70 NE Loop 410 San Antonio TX 78216-5849

MONTENEGRO-FERRÃO, AURA, psychologist, researcher; b. Vila Nova de Poiares, Coimbra, Portugal, June 28, 1925; d. Horácio Artur and Matilde Augusta (dos Santos) M. MA, U. Coimbra, 1949; PhD, St. Paul (Brazil) U., 1972. Lic. psychologist. Asst. Faculty of Letters U. Coimbra, 1952-72, rschr. Psychopedagogic Ctr., 1975-94, prof., 1975, mem. Scientific Coun. Faculty of Letters, 1976-83, founder, dir. Dept. Psychological Assessment and Rehab., Faculty of Psychology, 1982-95, full prof., 1983, head Scientific Coun. and Assembly of Reps., Faculty of Psychology, 1986-88, coord. Erasmus and Tempus Programs, 1987-95, prof. emeritus, 1995—; intern psychologist Laboratory Psychology Catholic U., Milan, 1953-54; clinical psychologist Ctr. Child Mental Health, U. Coimbra, 1959-67, 75-77, Ctr. Blind Children, 1969-70, Ctr. Deaf Children, 1960-82, trainer, supr., 1980-95. Editor Portuguese Pedagogic Jour., 1980-96; Translator: De l'Infinito, Universo e Mondi, 1968. Recipient Superior Course Lit. Philosophy and Art award, U. Perugia, 1950, Advanced Studies in Psychology award, French Govt., U. Paris, Sorbonne, 1956, Life time career achievement award, Portughese Psychol. Assn., 1997. Mem. Portuguese Psychology Soc. (pres. fiscal coun. 1976-96), Internat. Coun. Psychologists (life), Internat. Assn. Applied Psychology. Roman Catholic. Avocations: poetry, journalism, gymnastics, swimming, classical music. Home: Rua Gil Vicente 2, 3000202 Coimbra Portugal Office: Fac Psychology and Edn Scis, College Novo St-Ap 6153, 3001802 Coimbra Portugal

MONTENS, SERGE, civil engineer; b. St. Cloud, France, Sept. 8, 1956; s. Jean Montens and Colette Chretien; m. Benedicte Creancier, July 24, 1993. B in Econs., U. Paris, 1977; engr., Spl. Sch. Pub. Works, Paris, 1978, CHEBAP, Paris, 1979. Engr. Sogelerg, Rungis, France, 1981-86; bridge engr. Figg & Muller Engrs., La Defense, France, 1986-88; dir. tech. Jean Muller Internat., Guyancourt, France, 1988-99; expert engr. SYSTRA, Paris, 1999—. Contbr. articles to profl. jours. Mem. French Assn. for Civil Engring., French Assn. for Earthquake Engring., Internat. Assn. for Bridges and Structural Engring. Avocations: genealogy research, music. Home: 117 Elysee 2, 78170 La Celle St Cloud France

MONTERO, ANALIA HAIDEE, accountant, educator, consultant; b. Santa Rosa, La Pampa, Argentina, Dec. 28, 1956; d. Osvaldo and Maria del Carmen (Castro) M.; m. Arturo Ignacio Kehr, Mar. 21, 1986; 1 child, Ursula. Degree in pub. accountancy, U. Nat. La Pampa, 1982, degree in mgmt., 1987. Acct. Gente de la Pampa, Sirosa, 1982-86; cons. Ahmontero, 1986-99; dir. UCP, Corlienz, 1997, UTN-FRR, Resistencia, 1997—; cons. Jud. Br., 1989-90, San Juan Hosp., La Plata, 1989; dir. UCP, Corrientes, 1997, UTN FRR, Resistencia, 1997-99. Office: AH Montero, 9 de Julio 1331 P2 DTO 2, 3400 Corrientes Argentina

MONTERO, ANTONIO, internist, researcher; b. Rosario, Santa Fe, Argentina, Mar. 1, 1959; s. Antonio and Elvia del Carten (Nieva) M.; m. Adria Gabriela Giovannoni, Sept. 26, 1997; 1 child, Lucia Antonella. B.Econometrics, Superior of Commerce, Rosario, 1975; MD. Resident in internal medicine Clemente Alvarez Hosp., Rosario, 1984-87; rsch. fellow Academia Nacional de Medicina, Buenos Aires, 1987-88; asst. rschr. Rsch. Coun. of Nat. U. Rosario, 1992-96, assoc. rschr., 1996-99; ind. rschr. Rosario, 1999—; chmn. acad. expansion of infectious diseases Med. Sch. of Nat. U. Rosario, 1997—; AIDS cons. Emergency Hosp., Rosario, 1988-99; dir. med. area Ctr. for Advanced Studies in AIDs, Rosario, 1993-99; nat. cons. for AIDS Nat. System of Med. Cons., Argentina, 1998. Contbr. articles to profl. jours. Mcpl. rep. Com. for Prevention of AIDS, Rosario, 1990-92. Home: Dorrego 156-5A, 2000 Rosario Argentina

MONTES, JORGE ARAMAYO, consulting company executive; b. La Paz, Bolivia, Sept. 18, 1931; married; 2 children. BS in Mech. Engr., Okla. State U., 1956, MS in Petroleum Engring., 1957; degree in bus. adminstrn., Inst. Mex. Adminstrn. Negot., La Paz, 1961; postgrad., Syracuse U., 1968. Supr. constrn. of pipeline from Sica-Sica to Arica Yacimentos Petroliferos Fiscales Bolivianos, Cochabamba, Bolivia, 1958-59; dir. engring. divsn. pipelines and refineries Yacimentos Petroliferos Fiscales Bolivianos, Cochabamba, 1959-63; v.p. Instituto Tecnologico Boliviano, La Paz, 1963-65; mgr. dir. indsl. YPFB, La Paz, 1965-70, petrochem. dir., 1970-80; undersec. hydrocarbons Min. of Energy and Hydrocarbons, La Paz, 1980-83; chief negotiator YFPB, La Paz, 1989-93, rep. at Houston, 1993-94; exec. pres. Plis Plas, 1994-97; pres. A&Z, 1997-98, Econogas Bolivia, 1998—; dean petroleum engring. Tech. U., La Paz, 1962-64, San Andres U. UMSA, La Paz, 1965-82. Contbr. articles to tech. publs.; patentee in plastic field. Pres. Jr. Chamber Internat., 1972, sen., 1972. Mem. ASME, Internat. Assn. Petroleum Negotiators, Soc. Engrs. and Geologists of Yacimentos Petroliferos Fiscales Bolivianos (founder, 1st pres.), Bolivian Soc. Engrs. (pres.), Bolivian Petroleum Inst., Am. Inst. Petroleum Engrs., Soc. Plastic Engrs., Houston Internat. C. of C., Club Hípico los Sargentos, La Paz Tennis Club (pres. 1974), Petroleum Club (pres. La Paz chpt. 1978), Club Promoción 50 (pres. 1971), Golf Club Mallasilla, Petroleum Club Houston, Univ. Club Houston, Chi Epsilon, Alpha Tau Omega.

MONTGOMERIE, COLIN, professional golfer; b. Glasgow, Troon, Ayrshire, Scotland, June 23, 1963; m. Eimear Montgomerie; children: Olivia Rose, Venetia, Cameron. Profl. golfer, 1987—; mem. Walker Cup Team, 1985, 87, Ryder Cup Team, 1991, 93, Dunhill Cup Team, 1988, 91, 92, World Cup Team, 1988, 91; 2d place winner U.S. Open, 1994, 8th place winner, 1994; 5th world rank, 1998; winner Volvo PGA, 1998. Decorated European Order of Merit; winner Scottish Stroke Play, 1985, Scottish Amateur Championship, 1987, European Tour Rookie of Yr., 1988, Portuguese Open, 1989, Scandinavian Masters, 1991, Heineken Dutch Open, 1993, Volvo Masters, 1993, Spanish Open, 1994, English Open, 1994, German Open, 1994, PGA Championship, 1998, Brit. Masters, 1998, German Masters, 1998, Benson & Hedges Internat. Open, 1999, Volvo PGA Championship, 1999, BMW Internat. Open, 1999, Std. Life Loch Lomond, 1999, Volvo PGA Championship, 2000, Novotel Perner Open de France, 2000, others; leader European Tour Merit, 1993. Avocations: music, cars. Office: PGA Am PO Box 109601 100 Avenue Of Champions Palm Beach Gardens FL 33410 also: PGA Tour PGA Blvd 112 Tpc Blvd Ponte Vedra Beach FL 32082*

MONTGOMERY, ANNA FRANCES, elementary school educator; b. Spokane, Wash., Nov. 5, 1945; d. Carl Jacob and Edna Frances (Evans) Kuipers; m. William Lee Montgomery Jr., Oct. 7, 1989. AA, Mid. Ga. Coll., 1965; BS in Elem. Edn., Woman's Coll. of Ga., 1966; MEd, Ga. Coll., 1969, specialist in edn., 1973. Cert. elem. tchr., Ga. Classroom tchr. Muscogee County Sch. Dist., Columbus, Ga., 1966—, reading tchr. Title 1 tutorial program, summer 1975, instr. staff devel. program, 1977-80; social sci. lead tchr. Wesley Heights Elem. Sch., Columbus, 1992—, chmn. mgmt. team, 1997-98; tennis and athletic instr. Camp Tegawitha, Tobyhanna, Pa., summer 1970; presenter workshop Chattahoochee Valley Coun. for Social Studies, 1977; mem. social studies textbook adoption com. Muscogee County Sch. Dist., 1977-78, 82-83, 98-99, mem. sick leave com., 1993-95; judge Columbus Regional Social Sci. Fair, 1977, 93-96; mem. basic skills program comprehensive planning task force Muscogee County Sch. Dist., 1995-96, mem. com. to revise the basic skills program in social studies, 1980; presenter in field. Editor: Muscogee County School District's Handbook for Beginning Teachers, 1979. Treas. Wesley Heights PTA, 1983-86; vol. Med. Ctr. Aux., Columbus, 1975-79; pres. pastor's Bible study class St. Luke United Meth. Ch., 1993-94, 96, 97, 98, mem. Sarah Cir. 11, sec., 1969-71, 78-80, co-chmn., 1974-76, chmn., 1976-78; mem. Bessie Howard Ward Handbells Choir; devel. chmn. Ga. state divsn. Centennial/fellowships com. AAUW, 1974-76. Recipient Valley Forge Tchrs. medal Freedoms Found. at Valley Forge, 1975, Outstanding Tchr. of Yr. award Wesley Hts. Elem. Sch., 1975, Muscogee County Sch. Dist., 1979; named Very Important Lady award Girl Scouts Am., Columbus, 1976, Outstanding Young Woman Am., 1982. Mem. AAUW (chmn. centennial fellowship com. Columbus br. 1973-75), Ga. PTA (hon. life), Profl. Assn. Ga. Educators (bldg. rep. Muscogee County chpt. 1983—, sec. 1992-94, treas. 1994-98, pres.-elect 1998-2000, Muscogee County's sys. rep. to the state 2000—), Nat. Coun. Social Studies (mem. hostess and registration coms. ann. meeting 1975), Ga. Coun. for Social Studies, Ga. Sci. Tchrs. Assn., Atlanta Alumni Club, Valley Area Sci. Tchrs. (corr. sec. 1996-98), Ga. Coll. Alumni Assn., Mid. Ga. Coll. Alumni Assn., Order of Amaranth (charity 1991-93, 95, truth 1994, assoc. conductress 1996, conductress 1997, assoc. matron 1998, royal matron 1999), Scottish Rite Ladies Aux., Alpha Delta Kappa (Rho chpt., sec. 1975-76, pres.-elect 1976-78, pres. 1978-80, chaplain, 1996-98), Delta Kappa Gamma (Beta Xi chpt., pres. 1980-82, chmn. pubs. and publicity 1976-78, chmn. profl. affairs 1978-80, nominations com. chair 1980-82, chmn. world fellowship and fund raising 1984-86, 96-2000, chmn. fin. 1990-92, chmn. membership 1994-96), Order Internat. Fellowship in Edn., Wesley Heights Elem. Sch. PTA, Phi Delta Kappa (Chattahoochee Valley Ga. chpt.). Avocations: reading, gardening, travel, fishing, playing clarinet and handbells. Home: 5134 Stone Gate Dr Columbus GA 31909-5573

MONTGOMERY, BRUCE STEWART, urological surgeon; b. Boston, July 1; arrived in Eng., 1958; s. Stephen Ross and Ann Margaret (Barlow) M.; m. Bridget Ann Fisher; children: Caroline, Lily, Paddy. BSc with honors, Univ. Coll., London, 1978, MB BS, 1981, MS, 1992. Cons. urologist Frimley Park, Surrey, Eng., 1994—; hon. cons. North Hampshire Hosp., Basingstoke, Eng., 1994—. Fellow Royal Coll Surgery (London), Royal Coll. Surgery (in Urology); mem. Physiol. Soc., Royal Soc. Medicine. Avocations: flyfishing, cooking. Home: Chaundlers Farm, Crondall, nr Farnham, Surrey GU10 5NX, England

MONTGOMERY, CHARLES HARVEY, lawyer; b. Spartanburg, S.C., Jan. 28, 1949; s. Dan Hugh and Ann Louise (Gasque) M.; m. Renée Jean Gubernot, Mar. 27, 1971; children: Charles Scott, Marie Renée. BA, Duke U., 1971; JD, Vanderbilt U., 1974. Bar: N.C. 1974, U.S. Dist. Ct. (ea. dist.) N.C. 1974, U.S. Supreme Ct. 1979, U.S. Dist. Ct. (mid. dist.) N.C. 1991; cert. family law specialist, N.C., 1995. Assoc. Jordan Morris & Hoke, Raleigh, N.C., 1974-75; atty. Wake County Legal Svcs., Raleigh, 1975-76; pvt. practice, Raleigh, 1977; ptnr. Montgomery & Montgomery, Cary, N.C., 1978-79, Sanford Adams McCullough & Beard, Raleigh, 1979-86, Adams McCullough & Beard, Raleigh, 1986-88, Toms Reagan & Montgomery, Cary, 1989-92, Toms & Montgomery, Cary, 1992-93; pvt. practice, Cary, 1993—; bd. dirs. Br. Bank and Trust, Cary; pres. Family Law Mediation, Inc. Councilman Town of Cary, 1977-81, 83-87; vice-chmn. Wake County Dem. party, Raleigh, 1991-92; commr. Wake County, Raleigh, 1992; bd. dirs. East Cen. Cmty. Legal Svcs., Inc., 1997—, State Capitol Found., 1994—. Mem. ABA, N.C. Bar Assn. (chmn. pub. info. com. 1994-96, dir. family law coun. 1994-97), N.C. Acad. Trial Lawyers (chair family law sect. 1996-98). Methodist. Avocation: sailing. Office: PO Box 1325 1135 Kildaire Farm Rd Ste 315 Cary NC 27511-4566

MONTGOMERY, CLEOTHUS, minister; b. Henderson, Tex., Dec. 6, 1926; s. Lewis and Amanda (Waters) M.; m. Emma Agusta Tinch (dec. Aug. 23, 1987); children: Michael Dennis, Debra Marie, Pamela Key, Diane Renea, Anthony Cleothus (dec.). BS in Drafting, Calif. Coll., 1951; B in Theology, Union Bapt. Theol. Sem., 1962; M in Theology, Inter Bapt. Theol. Sem., 1965, DD, 1973; D in Sacred Theol. (hon.), Mt. Hope Bible Coll., 1973; M in Ministry, Trinity Theol. Sem., 1990, D in Ministry, 1993. Cert. christian counselor, Tex. Minister Northside Missionary Bapt. Ch., Houston, 1962—; counselor Chemical Dependency, Houston, 1989-97, Internat. Christian Isnt., 1990-97; invited pastor by Campus for Christ to Israel, 1987, Africa, 1990, Russia, 1995-97. Pres. World Christian Tng. Ctr., Houston, 1985-90, Houston Minister Christian Fellowship, 1992-97; chmn. Minister Network Life Gift, Houston, 1988-90, Ministers Against Crime, Houston, 1989-97; treas. Life Investment for Tng., Houston, 1990-97; v.p. Ministerial Adv. to Mayor, Houston, 1995-97; trustee bd. of regency, adv. bd. Coll. of Biblical Studies. With U.S. Army, 1945-46. Mem. NAACP, Am. Assn. Christian Counselors (chemical dependency counselor 1993-97). Democrat. Baptist. Avocations: reading, devotional writings, bowling, traveling, jogging. Home: 1407 Laurentide St Houston TX 77029-3411 Office: Northside Missionary Bapt Ch 3202 Bennington St Houston TX 77093-9222

MONTGOMERY, HENRY IRVING, financial planner; b. Dec. 18, 1924; s. Harry Biggs and Martha Grace (Wilkinson) M.; m. Barbara Louise Hook, Aug. 14, 1948; children: Barbara Ruth, Michael Henry, Kelly Ann, Andrew Stuart. Student, U. Iowa, 1942-43, 47-48; BBA, Tulane U., 1952; postgrad., U. Minn., 1976. CFP, Colo. Field agt. OSS, SSU, CIG, CIA, Cen. Europe, 1945-47; pres. Nehi Bottling Co., Decorah, Iowa, 1952-64; prin. Montgomery Assocs., Mktg. Cons., Trieste, Italy and Iowa, 1965-72; pres. Planners Fin. Svcs., Inc., Mpls., 1972-95, chmn., 1992—; prin. Montgomery Investment Mgmt., 1992—. Author: Race Toward Berlin, 1945. With U.S. Army, 1943-46, ETO. Decorated Bronze Star; recipient P. Kemp Fain Profl. Svc. award, 1998. Mem. Inst. CFPs (bd. dirs. 1977-82, pres. 1980-81, chmn. 1981-82, CFP of Yr. 1984, chmn. fin. products stds. bd. 1984-88), Nat. Assn. Securities Dealers (mem. dist. 8 com. 1988-91, vice chmn. 1990), Internat. Assn. Fin. Planning (internat. dir. 1976-81), Mpls. Estate Planning Coun., Met. Tax Planning Group (pres. 1984-87), Twin City Fin. Planners (pres. 1976-78), Twin Cities Soc. of Inst. CFPs, Am. Legion, Elks (Decorah), Beta Gamma Sigma. Avocations: Italian and German languages. Office: Planners Fin Svcs Inc 7710 Computer Ave Ste 100 Minneapolis MN 55435-5417

MONTGOMERY, JAMES FISCHER, savings and loan association executive; b. Topeka, Nov. 30, 1934; s. James Maurice and Frieda Ellen (Fischer) M.; m. Diane Dealey; children: Michael James, Jeffrey Allen, Andrew Steven, John Gregory. BA in Acctg., UCLA, 1957. With Price, Waterhouse & Co., C.P.A.'s, Los Angeles, 1957-60; controller Conejo Valley Devel. Co., Thousand Oaks, Calif., 1960; asst. to pres. Gt. Western Fin. Corp., Beverly Hills, Calif., 1960-64; pres. United Financial Corp of Calif., Los Angeles, 1964-75; chmn., CEO Great Western Financial Corp., Chatsworth, Calif., 1975-96; now chmn. bd. dirs. Great Western Financial Corp., Chatsworth, Calif., 1996-97; chmn., CEO Frontier Bank, Park City, Utah, 1997—; fin. v.p., treas. United Fin. Corp., Los Angeles, 1964-69, exec. v.p., 1969-74, pres., 1975; pres. Citizens Savs. & Loan Assn., Los Angeles, 1970-75. Served with AUS, 1958-60. Office: Frontier Bank 5217 Allott Ave Sherman Oaks CA 91401-5902

MONTGOMERY, JOHN CHARLES, biology educator; b. Auckland, New Zealand, Nov. 26, 1952; s. Henry Edward and Kathleen Moya (O'Hara) M.; m. Christina Roberts (div.); children: Gabriella, Charles. BSc with honors, Otago U., Dunedin, 1974; PhD, Bristol (U.K.) U., 1978, DSc, 1989. Assoc. prof. biology U. Auckland, 1978-98, prof. biology, 1998—. Contbr. articles to profl. publs. Fulbright Found. scholar, 1988. Fellow Royal Soc. New Zealand. Office: U Auckland, Sch Biol Scis, Auckland New Zealand

MONTGOMERY, JOHN WARWICK, law educator, theologian; b. Warsaw, N.Y., Oct. 18, 1931; s. Maurice Warwick and Harriet (Smith) M.; m. Joyce Ann Bailer, Aug. 14, 1954; children: Elizabeth Ann, Catherine Ann; m. Lanalee de Kant, Aug. 26, 1988; 1 adopted child, Jean-Marie. Baron of Kiltartan and Lord of Morris. AB in Philosophy with distinction, Cornell U., 1952; BLS, U. Calif., Berkeley, 1954, MA, 1958; BD, Wittenberg U., 1958, MST, 1960; PhD, U. Chgo., 1962; Docteur de l'Université, mention Théologie Protestante, U. Strasbourg, France, 1964; LLB, LaSalle Extension U., 1977; diplôme cum laude, Internat. Inst. Human Rights, Strasbourg, 1978; MPhil in Law, U. Essex, Eng., 1983; D in Civil and Canon Law (hon.), Inst. Religion and Law, Moscow, 1999; LLM, Cardiff U., Wales, 2000. Bar: Va. 1978, Calif. 1979, D.C. 1985, Wash. 1990, U.S. Supreme Ct. 1981, Eng. 1984; lic. real estate broker Calif.; cert. law librarian; diplomate Med. Library Assn.; ordained to ministry Luth. Ch., 1958. Librarian, gen. reference service U. Calif. Library, Berkeley, 1954-55; instr. Bibl. Hebrew, Hellenistic Greek, Medieval Latin Wittenberg U., Springfield, Ohio, 1956-59; head librarian Swift Libr. div. and Philosophy, mem. federated theol. faculty U. Chgo., 1959-60; assoc. prof., chmn. dept. history Wilfred Laurier U. (formerly Waterloo Luth. U.), Ont., Can., 1960-64; prof., chmn. div. ch. history, history of Christian thought, dir. European Seminar program Trinity Evang. Div. Sch., Deerfield, Ill., 1964-74; prof. law and theology George Mason U. Sch. Law (formerly Internat. Sch. of Law), Arlington, Va., 1974-75; theol. cons. Christian Legal Soc., 1975-76; dir. studies Internat. Inst. Human Rights, Strasbourg, France, 1979-81; founding dean, prof. jurisprudence, dir. European program Simon Greenleaf U. Sch. Law, Anaheim, Calif., 1980-88; lic. disting. prof. theology and law, dir. European program Faith Evang. Luth. Sem., Tacoma, Wash., 1989-91; from prin. lectr. to reader in law Luton U., Eng., 1991-93, prof. law and humanities, dir. Ctr. Human Rights, 1993-97, emeritus prof., 1997—; disting. prof. apologetics, law, and history of Christian thought, v.p. acad. affairs U.K. and Europe Trinity Coll. and Theol. Sem., Newburgh, Ind., 1997—; disting. prof. law Regent U., Va., 1997-99; sr. counsel European Ctr. Law and Justice, 1997—; vis. prof. Concordia Theol. Sem., Springfield, Ill., 1964-67, DePaul U., Chgo., 1967-70; hon. fellow Revelle Coll., U. Calif., San Diego, 1970; rector Freie Fakultaten Hamburg, Fed. Republic Germany, 1981-82; lectr. Rsch. Scientists Christian Fellowship Conf. St. Catherines Coll., Oxford U., 1985, Internat. Anti-Corruption Conf., Beijing, China, 1995; Pascal lectr. on Christianity and the Univ., U. Waterloo, Ont., Can., 1987; A. Kurt Weiss lectr. biomed. ethics U. Okla., 1997; adj. prof. Puget Sound U. Sch. Law, Tacoma, 1990-91; Worldwide Adv. Conf. lectr. Inns of Ct. Sch. Law, London, 1998; law and religion colloquium lectr. U. Coll. London, 2000; numerous other invitational functions. Author: The Writing of Research Papers in Theology, 1959; A Union List of Serial Publications in Chicago Area Protestant Theological Libraries, 1960; A Seventeenth-Century View of European Libraries, 1962; Chytraeus on Sacrifice: A Reformation Treatise in Biblical Theology, 1962; The Shape of the Past: An Introduction to Philosophical Historiography, 1962, rev. edition, 1975; The Is God Dead Controversy, 1966; (with Thomas J.J. Altizer) The Altizer-Montgomery Dialogue, 1967; Crisis in Lutheran Theology, 2 vols., 1967, rev. edit., 1973; Es confiable el Christianismo?, 1968; Ecumenicity, Evangelicals, and Rome, 1969; Where is History Going?, 1969; History and Christianity, 1970; Damned Through the Church, 1970; The Suicide of Christian Theology, 1970; Computers, Cultural Change and the Christ, 1970; In Defense of Martin Luther, 1970; La Mort de Dieu, 1971; (with Joseph Fletcher) Situation Ethics: True or False?, 1972; The Quest for Noah's Ark, 1972, rev. edit., 1974; Verdammt durch die Kirche, 1973; Christianity for the Toughminded, 1973; Cross and Crucible, 2 vols., 1973; Principalities and Powers: The World of the Occult, 1973, rev. edit., 1975; How Do We Know There is a God?, 1973; Myth, Allegory and Gospel, 1974; God's Inerrant Word, 1974; Jurisprudence: A Book of Readings, 1974, 4th edit., 1992; The Law Above the Law, 1975; Cómo Sabemos Que Hay un Dios?, 1975; Demon Possession, 1975; The Shaping of America, 1976; Faith Founded on Fact, 1978; Law and Gospel: A Study for Integrating Faith and Practice, 1978, 3rd edit., 1994; Slaughter of the Innocents, 1981; The Marxist Approach to Human Rights: Analysis & Critique, 1984; Human Rights and Human Dignity, 1987; Wohin marschiert China?, 1991; Evidence for Faith: Deciding the God Question, 1991; Giant in Chains: China Today and Tomorrow, 1994; Law and Morality: Friends or Foes?, 1994; Jésus: La Raison Rejoint L'Histoire, 1995; (with C.E.B. Cranfield and David Kilgour) Christians in the Public Square, 1996; Conflicts of Law, 1997; The Transcendental Holmes, 2000, The Repression of Evangelism in Greece, 2000; editor: Lippincott's Evangelical Perspectives, 7 vols., 1970-72; International Scholars Directory, 1973; Simon Greenleaf Law Rev., 7 vols., 1981-88; Global Jour. Classical Theology, 1998—; contbg. editor: Christianity Today, 1965-84, New Oxford Review, 1993-95; films: Is Christianity Credible?, 1968; In Search of Noah's Ark, 1977; Defending the Biblical Gospel, 1985 (11 videocassette series); (TV series) Christianity on Trial, 1987-93; contbr. articles to acad., theol., legal encys. and jours., chpts. to books. Nat. Luth. Ednl. Conf. fellow, 1959-60; Can. Council postdoctoral sr. research fellow, 1963-64; Am. Assn. Theol. Schs. faculty fellow, 1967-68; recipient Angel award Nat. Religious Broadcasters, 1989, 90, 92; named Lord of Morris. Fellow Trinity Coll. (Newburgh, Ind.), Royal Soc. Arts (Eng.), Victoria Inst. (London), Acad. Internat. des Gourmets et des Traditions Gastronomiques (Paris), Am. Sci. Affiliation (nat. philosophy sci. and history sci. commn. 1966-70); mem. ALA, European Acad. Arts, Scis. and Humanities (corr. mem., Paris), Acad. Lit. France (titulary mem.), Lawyers' Christian Fellowship (hon. v.p. 1995—), Nat. Conf. U. Profs., Calif. bar Assn. (human rights commn. 1980-83), Internat. Bar Assn., World Assn. Law Profs., Mid. Temple and Lincoln's Inn (barrister mem.), Am. Soc. Internat. Law, Union Internat. des Avocats, Nat. Assn. Realtors, Tolkien Soc. Am., N.Y. C.S. Lewis Soc., Am. Hist. Assn., Soc. Reformation Rsch., Creation Rsch. Soc., Tyndale Fellowship (Eng.), Stair Soc. (Scotland), Presbyn. Hist. Soc. (North Ireland), Am. Theol. Libr. Assn., Bibliog. Soc. U. Va., Evang. Theol. Soc., Internat. Wine and Food Soc., Soc. des Amis des Arts (Strasbourg), Chaîne des Rôtisseurs (commandeur), Athenaeum (London), Wig and Pen (London), Players' Theatre Club (London), Sherlock Holmes Soc. London, Soc. Sherlock Holmes de France (hon.), Club des Casseroles Lasserre (Paris), Ordre des chevaliers du Saint-Sepulcre Byzantin (commandeur), Phi Beta Kappa, Phi Kappa Phi, Beta Phi Mu. E-mail: 106612.1066@compuserve.com. Office: Church Lane Cottage 3-5 High St, Lidlington Bedfordshire MK43 0RN, England also: 2 rue de Rome, 67000 Strasbourg France

MONTGOMERY, JOSEPH WILLIAM, finance company executive. BBA, Coll. William and Mary, 1974. Cert. fin. planner; cert. portfolio mgr. Account exec. Wheat, First Securities, Inc., Lynchburg, Va., 1975-79; account exec. Wheat, First Securities, Inc., Williamsburg, Va., 1979-81, v.p., investment officer, 1981-82, sr. v.p., investment officer, 1982-90; mng. dir. First Union Securities, Williamsburg, Va., 1990—. Mem. nat. nominating com. Outstanding Young Am. Program, 1998; bd. dirs. Future Hampton Roads, Inc., 1995—; mem. nat. campaign steering com. Campaign of 4th Century, William & Mary, 1992, bd. vis., 1995-99; mem. commn. tercentenary observanced Coll. William & Mary, 1992; mem. adv. coun. Peninsula White Sox, 1986; bd. dirs. Nat. Conf. Christians & Jews, peninsula chpt., 1986-91; mem. Williamsburg Cmty. Health Found., 1998; dir., treas. Franklin & Gladys Clark Found. Named Top 300 Fin. Advisors in Country, Worth Mag., 1998, The Chancellor's Circle, Coll. William and Mary, 1998, Broker Hall Fame, Rsch. mag., 1996, Top 250 Fin. Advisors, Worth Mag., 1999. Mem. Internat. Assn. Fin. Planning, Inst. Cert. Fin. Planners, Investment Mgmt. Cons. Found., 1998, Soc. of Alumni William & Mary (pres. 1992, treas. 1991, sec. 1990, bd. dirs. 1989, Alumni Medallion 1996). Office: First Union Securities PO Box W Williamsburg VA 23187-3716

MONTGOMERY, LYNN MARIE, professional association executive; b. Faribault, Minn., July 13, 1955; d. Wilford C. and Marian Margaret Campbell; m. Daniel Dale Montgomery, June 12, 1976; children: Kristi Lynn, Ryan Lee. BS, Coll. of St. Benedict, St. Joseph, Minn., 1976; MA, U. St. Thomas, St. Paul, 1994. Elem. tchr. Anoka-Hennepin # 11, Coon Rapids, Minn., 1977-98; exec. dir. Assn. Tchr. Educators, Reston, Va., 1998—. Greater Minn. facilitator Destination Imagination, 1999-2000, Odyssey of the Mind, 1986-98; chair Adams Environ. Edn. Com., Minn., 1994—. Mem. AAUW, ASCD, Assn. Tchr. Educators (pres. 1998-99, Disting. Clinician 1995, Pres.'s Svc. award 1997), Minn. Assn. Tchr. Educators (bd. dirs. 1990-2000), Anoka-Hennepin Edn. Found. (bd. dirs. 1995-2000). Office: Assn Tchr Educators 1900 Association Dr Reston VA 20191-1502

MONTGOMERY, MAUREEN ELIZABETH, American studies educator; b. London, Eng., Mar. 16, 1956; arrived in New Zealand, 1986; d. Joseph and Mary (Roche) M.; m. Rodney Foster, Dec. 14, 1985. BA with honors, U. Warwick, Eng., 1978; PhD, U. East Anglia, Eng., 1983. Lectr. West London Inst. Higher Edn., 1984-85; lectr. U. Canterbury, Christchurch, New Zealand, 1986-92, sr. lectr., 1993—, head Am. Studies dept., 1996—; rsch. resident State Libr., Albany, 1990-91. Author: Gilded Prostitution: Status, Money & Transatlantic Marriage, 1870-1914, 1989, Displaying Women: Spectacles of Leisure in Edith Wharton's New York, 1998 (Spl. award N.Y. Soc. Libr. 1998, Outstanding Book award Choice 1999); mem. editl. bd. Am. Studies, 1999—; mem. fgn. bd. advisors Jour. Women's History, 1989—. Br. pres. Assn. Univ. Staff, Canterbury, 1999—. Fellow Rockefeller Found., 1999, Henry Francis DuPont Winterthur Mus., 1992. Mem. Am. Studies Assn. (chair internat. com. 1998—), Australian and New Zealand Am. Studies Assn. (v.p. New Zealand chpt. 1990-96). E-mail: m.montgomery@amst.canterbury.ac.nz. Office: U Canterbury/Am Studies, Pvt Bag 4800, Christchurch New Zealand

MONTGOMERY-DAVIS, JOSEPH, osteopathic physician; b. Annapolis, Md., Aug. 27, 1940; s. John and Flonila Alice (Sutphin) Swontek. Student, U. Wis., Milw., 1967-70; DO, Chgo. Coll. Osteo. Medicine, 1974. Diplomate Nat. Bd. Examiners for Osteo. Physicians and Surgeons; cert. family practice & osteo. manipulative treatment. Chief technologist nuclear medicine dept. Columbia Hosp., Milw., 1964-70; intern Richmond Heights (Ohio) Gen. Hosp., 1974-75; pvt. practice Raymondville, Tex., 1975—; med. care adv. com. Tex. Dept. Human Svcs., Austin, 1983-86, 90-94, physician payment adv. com., 1991-95; cons. health care issues Tex. Osteo. Med. Assn., 1991—;

health officer Willacy County Health Authority, Raymondville, 1984—; med. care adv. com. Tex. Workers' Compensation Commn., 1997—. Contbr. articles to profl. jours. With USAF, 1959-63. Mem. Am. Osteo. Assn., Am. Coll. Osteo. Family Physiacins (spl. Recognition award 1995), Tex. Soc. Am. Coll. Osteo. Family Physicians (pres. 1985-86, Physician of Yr. award 1989, T.R. Sharp Meritorious Svc. award 1999), Tex. Med. Found., Tex. Osteo. Med. Assn. (pres. 1989-90), Tex. Coll. Osteo. Medicine Alumni Assn., Phi Eta Sigma, Sigma Sigma Phi. Office: Neighborhood Dr 525 S 10th St Raymondville TX 78580-2593

MONTIEL, EDUARDO LUIS, business and economics educator, consultant; b. Managua, Nicaragua, Dec. 31, 1949; arrived in Costa Rica, 1983; s. Eduardo Montiel A. and Maria Lydia Morales; m. Eugenia Argenal; children: Alexandra, Eduardo. Student, Williams Coll., 1967-69; BSE, U. Mich., 1971; MS, MIT, 1974; DBA, Harvard U., 1983. Rschr. Harvard U., Cambridge, Mass., 1978-81, Inst. Centroamericano de Aminstrn. de Empresas, Managua, 1973-76; dir. banking and fin. program INCAE, San Jose, Costa Rica, 1983-88, prof. bus. and econs., 1983—; dir., editor-in-chief Revista INCAE, Alajeula, Costa Rica, 1986-98; dean INCAE, San Jose, Costa Rica, 1990-95; strategy cons., 1975—. Co-author: Strategic Planning, 1991; contbr. articles on bus. and econs. to profl. jours. Recipient Disting. Faculty award INCAE, 1986; grantee OAS, 1976. Mem. Am. Econ. Assn., Tau Beta Pi, Alpha Pi Mu. Roman Catholic. Office: Apartado 2485, INCAE, Managua Nicaragua

MONTIES, JEAN-RAOUL EMILE, cardiac surgeon, educator; b. Marseille, France, Jan. 7, 1934; s. Jean and Jeanne Noelle (Bicheron) M.; m. Hilke Leonore Sanders, June 11, 1976; m. Micheline Helen Allegre, June 25, 1957 (div. 1970); children: Veronique, Jean-Paul, Sophie. MD, Faculty Medicine, Marseille, 1960. Assoc. surgeon Marseille U. Hosp., 1962-66, assoc. prof., 1966-74, prof., chmn., 1974—; head cardiac surgery Marseille U., 1972—; chmn. cardiac surgery and surgical rsch. Marseille U., 1974—; mem. bd. U. Marseille, 1994—; rschr. on artifical heart. Contbr. articles to profl. jours. Lt. French Mil., 1960-62. Recipient Officer Dans L'Ordre Nat. du Merite, 1979, 98. Mem. Lions Club. Roman Catholic. Avocations: music, painting. Home: 18 Les Helianthes, F13390 Auriol France Office: LHMCV Faculty Medicine, 28 Ave Jean Moulin, 13385 Marseille O5, France

MONTORO, CRISTOBAL, federal official. Min. of fin. Office: Ministry of Econ and Fin, Alcala 9, 28014 Madrid Spain*

MONYA, NOBUO, law educator, arbitrator; b. Minato-ku, Tokyo, Aug. 21, 1936; s. Tohjiro and Hiro (Nakajima) M.; m. Makiko Kubota, Mar. 26, 1968; children: Takatoshi, Masanori. LLB, Tokyo U., 1960, 62, LLM, 1964, JD, 1967. Assoc. prof. law Seikei U., Tokyo, 1967-75, prof. law, 1975—; lectr. law Tohoku U., Sendai, Japan, 1979-89, Tokyo U., 1977, 79, Hokkaido U., Sapporo, Japan, 1986, 89, Keio U., Tokyo, 1993—; mem. legal deposit sys. coun. Nat. Diet Libr., 1997—; mem. experts group for environ. safety of genetically modified organisms Min. Agr., Forestry and Fishery, 2000—. Author: (book) Outline of Industrial Property Right Laws, 1976; editor: (book) Commentary Patent Law, 1986; co-author: (book) New Technology Development and Law, 1993; co-editor: (book) The Know-how of Copyright Law, 1982. Mem. exam. com. Com. of Patent Attys. Exam. Bd., The Patent Agy., 1978-85, mem. Indsl. Property Coun., The Patent Agy., 1979-87; mem. Agrl. Material Coun., Ministry of Agr., Forestry and Fishery, 1985-93, 2000—; mem. Copyright Coun., Ministry of Edn., 1993—, Legal Deposit Sys. Coun., Nat. Diet Libr., 1997—. Mem. Japan Assn. Econ. Jurisprudence (dir. 1984—), Japan Assn. Indsl. Property Law (dir. 1974—), Copyright Law Assn. Japan (dir. 1987—), Japan Assn. Internat. Econ. Law (dir. 1991—), Brazil Pub. Info. Union (hon.). Avocations: mountain climbing, scuba diving. Home: Honkomagome 3-9-14, 113-0021 Bunkyo-ku Tokyo, Japan Office: Seikei U, Kichijoji Kitamachi 3-3-1, 180-0001 Musashino Tokyo, Japan

MONYEKI, KOTSEDI DANIEL, education educator; b. Vaalwater, South Africa, Sept. 28, 1962; s. Lennpenne Judas and Mmalodi Annie M.; m. Mafoloa Susan Masekoamens; children: Neo, Moses, Judas. MA, South Africa, 1995. Asst. tchr. Makonkweklov Sch., South Africa, 1985-86, Modimolle H.S., South Africa, 1990; tutor U. of the North, South Africa, 1990-95, lectr., 1996—. Rsch. grant South African Ctr. for Sci. and Devel., 1997, U. Rsch., 1998. Mem. AAPHERD (exec. com.), TSAK, SAASS (exec. com.). Home: Mokolo Str 342 Peniner Ext, 0700 Roetersburg South Africa Office: Univ of the North, Kineisiology & Phys Edn, 0727 Sovegna South Africa

MONYPENY, DAVID MURRAY, lawyer; b. Jackson, Tenn., Apr. 29, 1957; s. Kent Brooks Monypeny and Kathryn (Warner) Sadowski. BBA, U. Okla., 1980; JD, U. Memphis, 1983. Bar: Tenn. 1983; CPA, Tenn. Assoc. Glankler, Brown et al, Memphis, 1983-85; acct. Frazer, Thomas & Tate, Memphis, 1985-87; ptnr. Diamond, Finklestein, Monypeny, Memphis, 1987-88, Lowrance & Monypeny, Memphis, 1988-94, Monypeny, Simpson Walker & Schatz, Memphis, 1994-97; sole practice Law Offices of David Monypeny, PLLC, 1997—; tax atty., cons. to nat. entertainers and celebrities. Author: (video) Wiping Out Tax Debt You Can't Afford To Pay, 1993. Mem. Bellevue Ch., Memphis, 1983—; campaign fin. chair Neil Small Chancellor, Memphis, 1990. Featured on TV, in mags. and newspapers for his client's tax settlements. Republican. Baptist. Avocations: music, video. Office: Law Offices of David Monypeny M PLLC 5100 Poplar Ave Ste 2700 Memphis TN 38137-2701

MONZEL, CATHERINE LUISE, international agency administrator; b. Washington, Aug. 16, 1960; d. Lionel Vincent and Edith Annaluise (Adam) Monzel; m. Harold Keane, Mar. 17, 1984 (div. 1987). BS in Fgn. Svc., Georgetown U., 1982; MA in Internat. Affairs, George Washington U., 1990. Staff asst. office internat. affairs U.S. Dept. Energy, Washington, 1982-90; mgr. govt. affairs, lobbyist Williams Cos., Inc., Washington, 1990-93; mgmt. analyst Internat. Atomic Energy Agy., Vienna, Austria, 1993-96; head office of mgmt. svcs. Internat. Atomic Energy Agy., Vienna, 1996—. Mem. Women in Govt. Rels. Office: Internat Atomic Energy Agy, PO Box 100 Wagramerstrasse 5, A-1400 Vienna Austria

MOO, HENG, fire protection equipment company executive; b. Kuala Lumpur, Malaysia, Oct. 13, 1955; s. Kwee and Sat Ying (Puk) M.; m. Keok Fong Choong, Sept. 28, 1979; children: Meng Huey, Meng Chyi. BSc with honors, Bolton (Eng.) Inst. Tech., 1979. Cert. electronic engr. Test engr. RCA, Kuala Lumpur, Malaysia, 1979-80; tech. svcs. engr. Malaysia Airlines Sys., Kuala Lumpur, 1980-81; mktg. mgr. Powermatic Sdn Bhd, Kuala Lumpur, 1981-91; gen. mgr. Sysscan (Malaysia) Sdn Bhd, Kuala Lumpur, 1991-92, Steel Recon Industries Sdn Bhd, Kuala Lumpur, 1992—. Office: Steel Recon Industries, 53 PWB 3 Wangsa Baiduri, 47500 Subang Jaya Malaysia

MOODIE, GRAEME COCHRANE, political science educator; b. Dundee, Scotland, Aug. 27, 1924; s. Alexander Reid and Emily Susan Herald (Cochrane) M.; m. Kathleen Marion Cremin, Apr. 28, 1956 (dec. 1985); children: Jennifer, Herald, Daniel, Mark; m. Andrea Joan Russell, Aug. 15, 1997. MA, St. Andrew's (Scotland) U., 1943; MA with honors, The Queen's Coll., Oxford, Eng., 1946. Lectr. polit. sci. St. Andrew's (Scotland) U., 1947-53; lectr. polit. sci. U. Glasgow, Scotland, 1953-61, sr. lectr., 1961-63; vis. assoc. prof. Princeton (N.J.) U., 1962-63; prof. politics U. York, Eng., 1963-88, emeritus prof. politics, 1988—; vis. hon. prof. U. Witwatersrand, Johannesburg, South Africa, 1991; dep. chmn. So. African Studies Trust, York, 1971-89, chmn., 1989-94; rsch. assoc. Ctr. for Studies in Higher Edn., U. Calif., Berkeley, 1985, 93. Author: The Government of Great Britain, 1961, Power and Authority in British Universities, 1974, Standards and Criteria in Higher Education, 1986; contbr. numerous articles to profl. jours. Parliamentary candidate Labour Party, Dumfriesshire, Scotland, 1959; chmn. Heslington Village Trust, York, 1975-98; chmn. York Older People's Forum, 1998—. Rsch. grantee Gulbenkian Found., U.K., 1966, Spencer Found., 1991-93; fellow Commonwealth Fund, 1949-51. Fellow Soc. for Rsch. in Higher Edn. (chmn. 1968-71), Polit. Studies Assn. (v.p., chmn. 1969-72), Royal Photographic Soc. Liberal Democrat. Avocation: photography. Home: 2 The Outgang Heslington, York YO1O 5EW, England

MOODIE, JANICE, golfer; b. Glasgow, Scotland, May 31, 1973. Degree in psychology, San Jose State U., 1997. Winner Scottish Ladies title, 1992; mem. team Great Britain, 1994, Ireland Curtis Cup, 1996; turned profl., 1996. Avocations: fitness, movies. Office: PGA 100 International Golf Dr Daytona Beach FL 32124-1092*

MOODLEY KUNNIE, THILO, psychologist, educator; b. Johannesburg, Gauteng, South Africa, Aug. 24, 1955; s. Bv. and Rajes (Pillay) Moodley; m. Lionel Kunnie, Nov. 5, 1983; children: Chiaca, Yastil. Bachelors, U. Durban, South Africa, 1978; bachelors with honors, U. Durban, 1979, magister in clin. psychology, 1987, PhD, 1995. Found., team mem. Devel. Assess Univ., South Africa, 1983-86; clin. psychology/lectr. Faculty of Medicine U. Natal, South Africa, 1982-88, sr. clin. lectr., 1988-89; clin. psychologist, also bd. dirs. Nelands Park Rehab. Ctr., South Africa, 1992-95; clin. supr. to degree students U. Natal, South Africa, 1992-95; clin., adminstrv. dir. Meyrick Bennett Child Guidance, Durban, 1992—; nat. supervisory psychologist Mensa, South Africa, 1997—; mem. Child Abuse in Indian Cmty., South Africa, 1982-86, Child Abuse, KE Hosp., South Africa, 1982-86; trust bd. mem. Assessment and Health Ctr., South Africa, 1991-92; dir. Meyrick Bennett Child Guidance Ctr., 1992—; fellow Children's Hosp., Mass., 1991-92. Author: Applications of Clinical Health Psychology to Paediatrics, 1990; contbr. articles to profl. jours. Harvard fellowship Harvard U., 1991-92. Mem. Profl. Bd. for Tech., British Psychol. Soc., Am. Psychol. Assn., South Africa Assn. of Child Psychiatry and Allied Discipline. Avocations: travelling, classical music (playing and listening), reading. Home: PO Box 1975 Tongaat, Durban 4400, South Africa

MOODY, ANTHONY DAVID, literature educator; b. Shannon, Manawatu, N.Z., Jan. 21, 1932; s. Edward Tabrum and Nora (Gordon) M. BA, U. N.Z., 1951, MA with 1st honors, 1952; BA with 1st class honors, Oxford U., 1955, MA, 1962. Lectr. in English Melbourne U., Australia, 1958-63, sr. lectr. in English, 1964-65; lectr. in English U. York, Eng., 1966-72, sr. lectr. in English, 1972-80, reader in English, 1980-84, prof. lit., 1984-99, emeritus prof. lit., 2000—; vis. prof. U. Toledo, fall 1988, Brit. Acad., 1988. Author: Virginia Woolf, 1963, The Merchant of Venice, 1964, T.S. Eliot: Poet, 1979, At the Antipodes, 1982, The El Salvador Sequence, 1984, Tracing T.S. Eliot's Spirit: Essays, 1996. U. N.Z. Shirtcliffe fellow, 1953-55, Nuffield Found. travelling fellow, 1965. Fellow English Assn.; mem. Assn. U. Tchrs., Nat. Poetry Found., T.S. Eliot Soc. (hon.). Avocations: publishing, tennis, walking. Office: U York Dept English, Heslington, York YO1 5DD, England

MOODY, EVELYN WILIE, consulting geologist, educator, artist; b. Waco, Tex.; d. William Braden and Enid Eva (Holt) Wilie; children: John D., Melissa L., Jennifer A. Student, Baylor U., 1934-35; BA with honors in Geology and Edn. U. Tex., 1938, MA with honors in geology, 1940. Cert. profl. geologist; cert. permanent tchr., Tex. Geologist Ark. Fuel Oil Co., Shreveport, La., New Orleans and Houston, 1942-45; teaching asst. Colo. Sch. Mines, Golden, 1946-47; exploration cons. geologist Gen. Crude Oil Co., Houston, 1975-77; ind. cons. geologist, Houston, 1977—; exploration cons. geologist Shell Oil Co., Houston, 1979-81; faculty dept. continuing edn. Rice U., Houston, 1978. Contbr. articles to profl. jours.; editor: The Manual for Independents, 1983, The Business of Being a Petroleum Independent (A Road Map for the Self Employed), 1987; co-author: How (to Try) To Find An Oil Field, 1981. Mem. Am. Assn. Petroleum Geologists (del. Houston chpt. 1986-89, 89-91, 91-94, 94—), Soc. Ind. Profl. Earth Scientists (hon. Houston chpt., sec. 1978-79, vice chmn. 1979-80, chpt. chmn. 1980-81, nat. dir. 1982-85, chpt. award for Outstanding Svc. 1986, editor SIPES Bull., 1983-85, treas. SIPES Found. 1984, pres. 1985, Nat. award for Outstanding Svc. 1988, SIPES Found. award 1994, hon. mem. in SIPES Houston chpt., 1994), Geol. Soc. Am., Watercolor Soc. Houston, Art Students League N.Y.C., Art Assn., Am. Inst. Profl. Geologists, Houston Geol. Soc. (chmn. libr. com. 1978—), Soc. Econ. Paleontologists and Mineralogists, Pi Beta Phi (nat. officer 1958-60, 66-68), Pi Lambda Theta. Republican. Presbyterian.

MOODY, MILES PHILLIPS, electrical engineer and educator; b. Melbourne, Australia, Oct. 2, 1943; s. Frank James and Eileen Elizabeth (Phillips) M.; m. Lynne Meredith Moody, Feb. 7, 1970; children: James Bradfield, Caroline Robin Victoria. B.Engring., U. Queensland, Brisbane, Australia, 1965, M.Engring. Sci., 1968, BA, 1974, PhD, 1985. Chartered profl. engr.; registered profl. engr., Queensland. Engr. Dept. Civil Aviation, Brisbane, 1966-67; lectr. U. Queensland, Brisbane, 1967-69; lectr. Queensland U. Tech., Brisbane, 1970-79, sr. lectr., 1980-84, head of sch., prof. elec. engring., 1985-98, mgr. Coop. Rsch. Ctr. for Satellite Sys., 1998—; rsch. engr. Standard Electrik Lorenz, Stuttgart, Germany, 1975, 83, 89; bd. dirs. Space Industry Devel. Ctr., Brisbane, St. Margarets AGS Coun., Voxson Ltd., Brisbane; forensic cons. law enforcement agencies, 1982—; external examiner Singapore Poly., 1991-97. Contbr. over 60 tech. papers to profl. jours. Mem. Nat. Com. on Space Engring., Canberra, 1992—; chmn. Profl. Engring. Wk., Brisbane, 1991, Internat. Space U. Affiliate Campus, Australia, 1989—. Rotary Group Study Exch. fellow, 1970. Fellow Instn. Engrs. Australia, Instn. Radio and Electronics Engrs. (sec.-treas.); mem. IEEE (sr., inaugural chmn.), Australian Coll. Edn., Audio Engrs. Soc., Australian Speech Sci. and Tech. Assn., Royal Queensland Golf Club, Rotary. Avocations: tennis, golf, model railways, languages. Home: 12 Jolimont Ave Ascot, Brisbane QLD 4007, Australia Office: Sch EESE Queensland Univ of Tech, 2 George St, Brisbane QLD 4000, Australia

MOODY, RON, actor, writer; b. London, Jan. 8, 1924; s. Bernard and Kate (Ogus) Moodnick. BSc in Econs., U. London, 1953. Appeared in plays: 6 Years Revue, 1959, Candide, 1960, Oliver, as Shylock in Merchant of Venice, 1967, as Polinius in Hamlet, 1972, as Richard in Richard III, 1978, Iago in Othello, 1981, as Harpagon in Moliere's The Miser, Peter Pan, 2000; (films) Oliver, 1967, Twelve Chairs, 1970, Dogpound Shuffle, 1973, Wrong is Right, 1981, Where is Parsifal?, 1983, Ghost in Monte Carlo, 1989, Kid at King Arthur's Court, 1995, The Three Kings, 1999, Paradise Grove, 1999, Chopsticks, 2000, Steps, 2000; stage musicals: USA tour HMS Pinafore, 1987, Sherlock Holmes, 1989, Streets of Dublin, 1992, Bertie, 1993, Peter Pan, 1995, The Canterville Ghost, 1998; on TV as Inspector Hart in Nobody's Perfect, ABC-TV, 1980, Dial M for Murder, 1981; dir. (play) Kafka In Love, 1991; author-composer musical comedies Joey, 1966, Saturnalia, 1970, Move Along Sideways, 1971, The Showman, 1976, Nine Lives, 1991; touring Move Along Sideways, 1991; author: (books) The Devil You Don't, 1980, Very Very Slightly Imperfect, Off the Cuff, 1987, The Soul of Leonardo, 1991, The Amazon Box, 1998. Served with RAF, 1943-48. Recipient Golden Globe award, 1968, Moscow Golden Bear award as best actor, 1970, Coco Trophy award, Clowns Internat., 1999; nominated Oscar, 1968. Mem. Am. Acad. Motion Picture Arts and Scis., Variety Club of Great Brit., Actors Equity, Screen Actors Guild, Clowns Internat. (pres. 1984), Performing Rights Soc. Writers, Soc. Authors. Home: Ingleside 41 The Green, Southgate London N14 6EN, England Office: Eric Glass Ltd, 28 Berkeley Sq, London W1, England also: care Barry Freed 2040 Ave Of Stars Ste 400 Los Angeles CA 90067-4703

MOODY, WILLARD JAMES, SR., lawyer; b. Franklin, Va., June 16, 1924; s. Willie James and Mary (Bryant) M.; m. Betty Glenn Covert, Aug. 21, 1948; children: Sharon Paige Moody Edwards, Willard J. Jr., Paul Glenn. AB, Old Dominion U., 1946; LLB, U. Richmond, 1952. Bar: Va. 1952. Pres. Moody, Strople & Kloeppel Ltd., Portsmouth, Va., 1952—; commr. Chancery, Portsmouth, 1960—, Accounts, 1960—. Del. Va. Ho. of Reps., Portsmouth, 1956-68; senator State of Va., 1968-83; chmn. Portsmouth Dems., 1983—. Recipient Friend of Edn. award Portsmouth Edn. Assn., 1981. Mem. ABA, Va. Bar Assn., Portsmouth Bar Assn. (pres. 1960-61, lectr. seminars), Va. Trial Lawyers Assn. (pres. 1968-69), Hampton Roads C. of C. (bd. dirs. 1983-86), Portsmouth C. of C. (bd. dirs. 1960-61), Inner Circle Advs., VFW, Cosmopolitan Club, Moose. Home: 120 River Point Cres Portsmouth VA 23707-1028 Office: Moody Strople & Kloeppel Ltd 500 Crawford St Portsmouth VA 23704-3844

MOODY-STUART, MARK, oil company executive; b. Tomlinsons, Antigua, Sept. 15, 1940; s. Alexander and Judith (Henzell) M.-S.; m. Judith Christine McLeavy, Sept. 19, 1964; children: Alexander, Douglas, Thomas, Elizabeth. MA, St. John's Coll., U. Cambridge, England, 1965, PhD, 1966; DBA (hon.), Robert Gordon U. Aberdeen. Geologist Shell, Spain, Oman and Brunei, 1966-72; chief geologist Shell, Australia, 1972-76; dir. North Sea Exploration Teams Shell, London, 1976-78; svcs. mgr. Shell, Brunei, 1978-79; mgr. we. divsn. Shell, Nigeria, 1979-82; gen. mgr. Shell, Turkey, 1982-86; chmn., CEO Shell, Malaysia, 1986-90; group exploration and prodn. coord. Shell, The Netherlands, 1990-94; chmn., grp. mng. dir Royal Dutch/Shell, The Hague, 1998—; dir. Shell Internat. Ltd., London, 1995—; mng. dir. Shell Transport & Trading Co., London, 1991—, chmn. 1997—; chmn. com. mng. dirs. Royal Dutch/Shell Group, 1998—. Contbr. numerous articles to profl. jours. Named knight comdr. St. Michael and St. George. Fellow Geological Sco. London, Royal Geographical Soc.; mem. The Travellers Club, Cruising Assn., Royal Yachting Assn. Avocations: sailing, travel. Office: Royal Dutch/Shell Group Cos, Shell Ctr, SE1 7NA London England

MOOK, SARAH, retired chemist; b. Bklyn., Oct. 29, 1929; d. Wong and Lie Won (Woo) M. BA, Hunter Coll., 1952; postgrad., Columbia U., 1954-57, 62-65, U. Hartford, 1958-59. Cartographic aide U.S. Geol. Survey Dept. of Interior, Washington, 1952-54; rsch. asst. Mineral Beneficiation Lab. Columbia U., N.Y.C., 1954-57; analytical chemist nuclera divsn. Combustion Engring., Inc., Windsor, Conn., 1957-59; rsch. scientist Radiations Applications Inc., Long Island City, N.Y., 1959-62; chemist Marks Polarized Corp., Whitestone, N.Y., 1962-64; sr. chemist NRA Inc. subs. Nuclear Rsch. Assoc., Inc., New Hyde Park, N.Y., 1964-75; clin. chemist Coney Island Hosp., Bklyn., 1974-84; cmty. bd. Coney Island Hosp., 1978-80; assoc. chemist Bellevue Hosp. Ctr., 1984-89, prin. chemist, 1989-95; ret., 1995. Contbr. articles to profl. jours. mem. adv. com. to state assemblyman State of N.Y., 1970-72; trustee park aVenue Christian Ch., 1973-82, sec., 1973-80, vice-chair, 1980-81, chair bd. trustees, 1981-82, pres. Christian Women's Fellowship, 1962-65, elder, 1982—; mem. Neighborhood Adv. Bd. for Cmty. Devel., 1996— (sec. 1996-99, chair 2000-02). Mem. Am. Assn. Clin. Chemistry (sec. N.Y. Met. sect. 1999—), AAAS, Am. Chem. Soc., N.Y. Acad. Scis., Van Slyke Soc. Republican. Home: 2042 E 14th St Brooklyn NY 11229-3314

MOOLLA, ZULKER NAIN, accountant; b. Johannesburg, South Africa, Dec. 2, 1961; s. Abdul Rashid and Aisa (Patel) M.; m. Najma Desai; children: Zaahida, Muhammad, Aslam, Zainab. BCompt, U. South Africa, Pretoria, 1985, BCompt with honors, 1987, cert. in theory of accountancy, 1987; CFA, Inst. Comml. and Fin. Accts. of So. Africa, Johannesburg, 1992. Chartered acct., South Africa. Sr. credit contr. Nedfin Bank Ltd., Johannesburg, 1980-85; clk. Cajee & Takolia, Johannesburg, 1986-87; chartered acct. Deloitte & Touche, Johannesburg, 1987-92; mgmt. cons. M-Net TV, Johannesburg, 1993-95; CEO Moolla Assocs. Chartered Accts., Johannesburg, 1996—; exec. cons. Deloitte & Touche, Johannesburg, 1993—, Goldclass Investments, Johannesburg, 1996—, Goldworths Investment Holdings, Johannesburg, 1997—, 786 Investment Holdings, Johannesburg, 1997—; group sec. Imperial Holdings, Ltd. Author: (manual) M-Net Internal Controls, 1995, (prospectus) Goldclass Profile, 1996, (books) Doing Business in South Africa, 1997, Small Business Handbook, 1997. Bd. dirs. Gauteng Tourism Bd., Johannesburg, 1997—, chmn. fin. com., 1997, chmn. audit com., 1997, mem. internat. exhbns. and trade shows com., 1997; spl. advisor to Dir. of Tourism Gauteng, Johannesburg, 1997. Mem. South African Inst. Chartered Accts. (chartered), Gauteng Soc. Chartered Accts., Ind. Mediation Svc. of South Africa (panelist 1994—, acctg. disclosure award 1994). Mem. African National Congress. Avocations: travel, game watching, squash, tennis, reading. Address: PO Box 2735, Houghton 2041, Republic of South Africa Home: 111 Albatross St, Johannesburg 1820, Republic of South Africa Office: Moolla Assocs Chartered Accts, 28 Osborn Rd Houghton, Johannesburg 2198, Republic of South Africa

MOON, AREE, biochemist, researcher; b. Seoul, Korea, Oct. 31, 1960; d. Kwan-Sup Moon and Kui-Kyung Lee; m. Nae-Kyung Sung, Apr. 2, 1983; children: Min-Young, Min-Ji. BS, Seoul National U., Korea, 1983; PhD, Iowa State U., Ames, 1989. Rsch. asst. Iowa State U., Ames, 1985-89; postdoctoral fellow Genetic Engring. Rsch. Inst., Seoul, Korea, 1989-90; sr. scientist Korea FDA, Seoul, 1991-95; asst. prof. Duksung Women's U., Seoul, 1995-99, assoc. prof., 1999—; mem. Drug Adverse Reaction Monitoring Com., 1992; attendee WHO Internat. Drug Adverse Reaction Monitoring Conf., Ottawa, Canada, 1992. Contbr. numerous articles to profl jours. WHO fellow NIBSC, 1994; recipient Dean's award Seoul National U., Coll. Pharmacy, 1983. Mem. Pharm. Soc. Korea, Biochemical Soc. Rep. Korea, Korean Soc. Molecular Biology. Home: Dae-Rim Apt #6-901, Song-Pa-Ku Bang-E-Dong, Seoul Korea Office: Duksung Women's U., 419 Ssang-Mun Dong, 132-714 Tobong-Ku Seoul Korea

MOON, BYEONG-JOON, economist, educator; b. Taegu, South Korea, Aug. 8, 1958; s. Hak-Joo Moon and Nam-Sook Im; m. Myeong-Hyeon Lee, Mar. 3, 1985; children: Jaewon, Soon-Hong. BBA, Seoul Nat. U., 1981, MBA, 1988; PhD, U. Conn., 1997. Economist Bank of Korea, Seoul, 1982-88; chief economist 1st Econ. Rsch. Inst., Seoul, 1988-93; instr. U. Conn., Storrs, 1994-97; prof. Internat. U. Japan, Niigata, 1997-98, Kyung-Hee U., Seoul, 1998—; dir. Indsl. Policy Studies Kyung-Hee U., 1999, advisor Mktg. Club, 1999. 1st lt. Korean air force, 1982-85. Mem. Global Mktg. Assn. (pres. 1999), Assn. Consumer Rsch., Korean Mktg. Assn., Korean Acad. Soc. Bus. Adminstrn., Korean Acad. Internat. Bus., Korean Internet Bus. Assn. Avocations: golf, mountain climbing, classical music, painting. Office: KyungHee U, Sch Internat Mgmt, Yongin City South Korea 449-701

MOON, GUN-WOO, researcher; b. Pusan, KyungNam, Korea, Oct. 3, 1966; parents Yung-Dal Moon and Ja-Nae Kweon; married; 1 child, Ji-Hean. PhD, KAIST, Taejon, Korea, 1996. Rschr. KEPRI, Taejon, 1996—. Recipient KIEE Paper award, 1995. Fax: 8242-865-5404. Office: KEPRI, Munji-Dong 103-16, Taejon 305-380, Korea

MOON, HEEJANG, aerospace engineer; b. Seoul, Oct. 1, 1963; s. Chongok and Yunsoo (Park) M.; m. Kyung-Ae (Sohn) M., Feb. 18, 1995; children: June-Young, Chung-Won. BS, U. Inha, 1987; DEA, U. de Rouen, 1988, doctorat N.R., 1991. Rschr. Complexe de Recherche Interprofl. en Aerothermochimie, Rouen, France, 1988-91; lectr. U. Inha, Inchon, Korea, 1993; sr. engr. Korea Inst. of Aeronautical Tech., Korean Air, Seoul, 1994-2000; asst. prof. Hankuk Aviation U., 2000—; def. tech. advisor Agy. for Def. Devel., Daejon, Korea, 1998, advisor for dual-use tech. Dept. of Def., 1998. Author: From Molecular Dynamics to Combustion Chemistry, 1992; contbr. articles to profl. jours. Mem. The Combustion Inst., Korean Soc. of Mech. Engr., Korean Soc. of Aeronautical and Space Sci. Avocations: movies, golf, sightseeing. E-mail: hjm@mail.hangkong.ac.kr. Home: 108-1604 Hangang-Daewoo Apt 415, Dongbu-ichon-dong Yonsan-Gu Seoul 140 031, Korea

MOON, IL SOO, medical educator; b. Kyungpook, Korea, Aug. 9, 1959; s. Kyungpook and Hanhyun (Park) M.; m. Myunghee Tak, Nov. 17, 1985; children: Julie, Eugene. BS, Kyungpook Nat. U., 1981; MS, Seoul Nat. U., 1983; PhD, U. N.B., 1991; post-doctoral, Calif. Inst. Tech., 1994. Rschr. Rsch. Inst. Pacific Chemicals, Seoul, 1984-85; asst. prof. Dongguk Med. Sch., Kyongju, Korea, 1994—; chair Dept. Premedicine Dongguk Med. Sch., 1996—; adv. com. Biochem. Soc. of the Republic of Korea. Author rsch. papers. Recipient KOSEF grants, 1995, 1996, KSEF grants, 1996, 1997. Mem. Soc. for Neurosci. (fgn.), Korean Soc. for Molecular Biology. Avocations: camping, photography. E-mail: moonis@mail.dongguk.ac.kr. Office: Sch of Medicine, 707 Sukjang, Kyongju 780-714, Korea

MOON, PETER GEOFFREY, investment executive; b. Southampton, England, Nov. 4, 1949; s. Roland Charles and Constance Bernice (Fudge) M.; m. Susan Elizabeth Williams, May 31, 1975; children: Richard, Katherine, Simon. BS in Econs. with honors, U. Coll. London, 1972. Investment analyst Ctrl. Bd. Fin. Ch. of England, London, 1972-75, Slater Walker Securities, London, 1975-78; overseas equities mgr. Nat. Provident Instn., London, 1978-85; investment mgr. British Airways Pensions, London, 1985-92; chief investment officer Univ. Super-Annvation Scheme, London, 1992—; investment advisor Teesside Super-Annvation Scheme, 1987—, Lincolnshire County Coun. Pension Fund, 1996—. Avocations: sailing, skiing, restaurant owner. Home: Hartnup House, Smarden TN27 8QB, England Office: USS Ltd, USS Ltd, 11th fl 1 Angel Ct, London EC2R 7EQ, England

MOON, RONALD LESLIE, materials scientist; b. July 15, 1939; s. Leslie H. and LaVonne Moon; 1 child, Gregory D. BS in Chem. Engring., U. Calif., Berkeley, 1962, MS in Chem. Engring., 1963, PhD in Materials Sci., 1967. Cert. gemologist. Rsch. fellow Imperial Coll., London, 1967-69; rsch. engr. Varian Assn., Palo Alto, Calif., 1969-79; rsch. scientist, project mgr., dept. mgr. Hewlett-Packard, Palo Alto, Calif., 1979-2000; dept. mgr. mater-

ials tech. dept. Agilent Labs., 2000—; contbr. to devel. of photocathodes, growth techs., LEDs, lasers, organic LEDs; chmn., com. various confs. Contbr. articles on solar cells, semiconductors, crystal growth and organic LEDs to various publs.; patentee in field. Mem. AIME, IEEE, Materials Rsch. Soc., Sigma Xi. Home: 152 Selby Ln Menlo Park CA 94027-3960 Office: Agilent Labs 3500 Deer Creek Rd Palo Alto CA 94304-1317

MOON, SANG-EUN, dermatologist, educator; b. Pusan, Korea, Mar. 29, 1960; s. Jae-koo and Mee-Ae (Choi) M.; m. Ae-Kyung Jun, Jan. 28, 1986; children: Young-Joo, Da-Young. PhD, Seoul Nat. U., 1998. Contbr. articles to profl. jours. including Brit. Jour. Dermatology, Dermatologic Surgery, Jour. Am. Acad. Dermatology. Mem. Internat. Soc. for Dermatologic Surgery, Korean Dermatol. Assn. Avocations: travel, swimming, skiing. Office: Seoul City Boramae Hosp, Dept Derm 395 Shindaebang 2-dong, Dongjak-ku Seoul 156-012, Korea

MOON, WILLIAM ARTHUR, JR., petroleum geologist, consultant; b. St. Louis, Oct. 20, 1932; s. William Arthur and Frances Anderson (Gannaway) M.; m. Marlene Joan Johnson, June 27, 1959 (dec. Mar. 1976) 1 adopted child, Arland David; m. Erika Cameron, Feb. 9, 1997. BSc in Geology, Va. Polytech. Inst., 1956, MSc in Geology, 1961. Field geologist Minerals Devel. Corp. subs. Norfolk and Western Rlwy., Pearisburg, Va., 1961-64; petroleum geologist offshore divsn. Texaco, New Orleans, 1964-70; staff geologist New Orleans divsn. Texaco, 1970; asst. dist. geologist Texaco, Houma, La., 1970-72; sr. geologist Texaco Ltd., London, 1972-75, advanced exploration geologist, 1975-77, sr. geol. supr., 1977-81, mgr. geol. ops., 1981-85, mgr. exploration ops., 1985-90, mgr. exploration, 1990-93, cons. geoscientist, 1993-97, ret., 1997. 1st lt. USAF, 1956-59. Decorated honorary officer of the most excellent Order of the Brit. Empire, 1998. Mem. Am. Assn. Petroleum Geologists, Geol. Soc. Am., Petroleum Exploration Soc. Gt. Britain, Sigma Xi, Sigma Gamma Epsilon. Republican. Avocations: golf, walking, chess, pistols, sports cars. Home: 1602 Scott Dr Farmville VA 23901-2584

MOONEY, HAROLD ALFRED, plant ecologist; b. Santa Rosa, Calif., June 1, 1932; s. Harold Walter and Sylvia Anita Stefany; m. Sherry Lynn Gulmon, Aug. 15, 1974; children—Adria, Alyssa, Arica. AB, U. Calif., Santa Barbara, 1957; MA, Duke U., 1958, PhD, 1960. From instr. to assoc. prof. UCLA, 1960-68; assoc. prof. Stanford U., 1968-73, prof. biology, 1975—, Paul S. Achilles prof. environ. biology, 1976—. Author: Mediterranean-type Ecosystems, 1973, Convergent Evolution in Chile and California, 1977, Components of Productivity of Mediterranean Climate Regions, 1981, Disturbance in Ecosystems, 1983, Physiological of Plants in the Wet Tropics, 1984, Physiological Ecology of North American Plant Communities, 1985, Ecology of Biological Invasions of North America and Hawaii, 1986, Biological Invasions, A Global Perspective, 1989, Biodiversity and Ecosystem Function, 1993, Seasonally Dry Tropical Forests, 1995, CO2 and Terrestrial Ecosystems, 1995, Functional Roles of Biodiversity, 1996. Served with AUS, 1953-55. Recipient Humboldt award, 1989, Max Planck Forscgungs Preis award Alexander von Humboldt Soc., 1992; Inst. Ecology prize, 1990; Guggenheim fellow, 1974; Nat. Acad. Scis. fellow, 1982. Fellow AAAS, Am. Acad. Arts and Scis., Am. Philos. Soc.; mem. Ecol. Soc. Am. (pres. 1988-89, Mercer award 1961, Eminent Ecologist 1996), Brit. Ecol. Soc. (hon. mem.), Am. Inst. Biol. Scis. (pres. 1994), Internat. Coun. Sci. Unions (sec. gen. 1996—). Home: 2625 Ramona St Palo Alto CA 94306-2315 Office: Stanford U Dept Biol Sci 477 Herrin Lab Stanford CA 94305

MOONEY, JAMES HUGH, newspaper editor; b. Pitts., Aug. 18, 1929; s. James H. and Kathryn A. (Hall) M.; m. Eileen Jane Casey, July 30, 1960; children: Mark Hall, Sean Francis, Annina Marie, James Matthew, Lorelei Jane, Paul Adam, Kathryn Celeste. B.A. in Journalism, Duquesne U., Pitts., 1957. With advt. dept., then editorial dept. Pitts. Post-Gazette, 1953-61; writer-editor Nat. Observer, 1961-77, Nat. Geographic, 1977-79; editor Found. News mag., Washington, 1979-81; press sec. Congressman Mickey Edwards of Okla., Washington, 1982; asst. nat. editor Washington Times, 1982-83; editor Status Report, 1983-92; dir. info. resources Ins. Inst. for Hwy. Safety, 1992-93; editor Western Pa. Medicine, Johnstown, 1993-95, Embassy Flash, Aspen Hill, Md., 1995-96. Mem. editorial adv. bd. Nat. Study Ctr. Trauma and Emergency Med. Systems. Served with AUS, 1951-53. Mem. European Assn. Sci. Editors, Washington Automotive Press Assn., Nat. Press Club. Home: 13820 N Gate Dr Silver Spring MD 20906-2215

MOONEY, LORI, county official; b. Atlantic City, Aug. 22, 1929; d. Joseph Aloysius and Alice Marie Inemer; m. Charles H. Calvi (div.); children: Joseph P., Stephen C., Christina L.; m. Thomas Christopher Mooney; children: Thomas C., Timothy C. Svc. rep. Bell Telephone Co., Atlantic City, 1950-58; sr. evaluator U.S. Census Bur., N.J., 1960-63; coord. Nat. Sml. Bus. Com. for Johnson and Humphrey, Washington, 1964; owner, mgr. Lori Mooney & Co., Realtors, Atlantic County, N.J., 1965-77; commr. Atlantic County Bd. Elections, 1970—, also chmn., 5 yrs; county clk. County of Atlantic, Mays Landing, 1978-96; mem. Active Corps Execs., Nat. SBA; chmn. county clk. liaison com. N.J. Supreme Ct., 1984-86. Del. Dem. Nat. Conv., 1972, 76, 84, 88, 96; mem. congl. liaison com. Acad. for State and Local Govts., 1989—; mem. U.S. Senator Bill Bradley's Citizen Adv. Com. Del. Dem. Nat. Conv., 1976, 84, 88, 92, 96, 2000. Recipient Woman of Achievement award N.J. Fedn. Bus. and Profl. Women, 1985, Role Model award The Sun Newspaper, 1989; inducted into Atlantic County Women's Hall of Fame, 2000, Holy Spirit H.S. Inaugural Hall of Fame, 2000. Mem. Internat. Assn. Clks., Recorders, Election Ofcls. and Treas. (N.J. dir. 1988—), Atlantic County Realtors Assn., Bus. and Profl. Women Atlantic County (scholarship chmn. 1982-85), County Officers Assn. N.J. (bd. dirs. 1978-96, pres. 1991-92, 92-93), N.J. Assn. County Clks. (chmn. 1984-86), N.J. Assn. Realtors, Nat. Assn. Realtors, Nat. Assn. Counties, N.J. League Municipalities, Assn. Records Mgrs. and Administrs., Atlantic City Women's C. of C. Home: 100 Carol Rd Linwood NJ 08221-2502 Office: Atlantic County Clks Office Main St Mays Landing NJ 08330-1702

MOONEY, THOMAS ROBERT, lawyer; b. Montclair, N.J., June 16, 1933; s. Thomas Edward and Ruth Evelyn (Meurling) M.; m. Mary Frances Davis, Aug. 23, 1958; children: Terrance Kevin, Rebecca Lee Poyner, Thomas Edward. BA in Econs., Fla. So. Coll., Lakeland, 1956; LLB, Stetson U., St. Petersburg, Fla., 1961, JD, 1961. BAr: Fla. 1961, Ga. 1962, U.S. Dist. Ct. (mid. dist.) 1964, U.S. Supreme Ct. 1965. Claims adjuster State Farm Mut. Ins. Co., Atlanta, 1961-63; atty. Maguire, Voorhis & Wells, P.A., Orlando, Fla., 1963-64, Meyers & Mooney, P.A., Orlando, 1964-94, Meyers, Mooney Stanley & Hollingsworth, Orlando, 1994—; chair Workers Compensation Ednl. Conf., Fla., 1980-81. Chmn. bd. dirs. Epilepsy Assn. Ctrl. Fla., Orlando, 1964-67; bd. dirs. Children's Home Soc., Orlando, 1970-75, chmn., 1970-72. 1st lt. U.S. Army, 1956-58, Korea. Mem. ATLA, ABA, Fla. Bar Assn., Ga. Bar Assn., Acad. Fla. Trial Lawyers (chair workers compensation sect. 1985), Fla. Workers Advocates (bd. dirs. 1992—). Democrat. Methodist. Avocations: skiing, golf, travel, hiking, rafting. Office: Meyers Mooney Stanley & Hollingsworth P A 17 Lake Ave Orlando FL 32801-2730

MOONIE, LIANA MARIA, artist; b. Trieste, Italy, Mar. 22, 1922; came to U.S., 1947; d. Angelo and Maria (Canciani) Gabrielli; m. Clyde W. Moonie, June 18, 1949; children: Gregory J., Barbara M. Tchrs. cert., U. Trieste, 1945. Chair, editor Beaux Arts Mag., 1978-79; exhibited in group exhbns. at Nat. Acad. Design, N.Y.C., Salmagundi Club, N.Y.C., Hudson River Mus., N.Y., Gallery Hastings, N.Y., Stamford (Conn.) Mus., Discovery Mus., Conn., Islip (N.Y.) Art Mus., Bergen Mus. Art and Sci., N.J., Monmouth Art Mus. of South, Mobile, Ala., Chattanooga Ctr., Oklahoma City, others; represented in permanent collection Palm Beach Internat. Airport; contbr. articles to profl. jours. Vol. Bruce Mus., Greenwich, Conn., 1997—; former pres. Mamaroneck Artists Guild, Hudson River Contemporary Artists; former bd. dirs. Am. Soc. Contemporary Artists, Scarsdale Art Assn.; former chmn. Beaux Arts Project in Westchester, N.Y. Recipient Emily Lowe award Allied Artists Am., 1985, Mary B. Hathaway award Scarsdale Art Assn., 1989, Therese Langhorne Duble award Hurlbutt Gallery, 1990, Quinn's award Greenwich Arts Ctr. Gallery, 1992, Jane Peterson Meml. award Allied Artists Am., 1992, Pres.' award Bush Holley Hist. House, 1995, F. Brooks award for graphic, Hurlbutt Gallery, 1998. Mem. Greenwich Art Soc. (bd. dirs. 1990—, pres. 1990-92, Pres.' award 1994, Mary B. Hathaway award 1993), Nat. Assn. Women Artists (pres. 1986-88, perm. adv. 1988—, chair Collection 1992-98, founder permanent collection 1992, founder Fla. chpt. 1995, Doris Kreindler award 1984, Elizabeth Morse Genius Found. award 1987, Ada Cecere Meml. award 1988, Myra Biggerstaff award 1995, Miriam E. Halpern Meml. award). Home: 4 Lafayette Ct Ph Greenwich CT 06830-5320 Studio: 89 Maple Ave Greenwich CT 06830-5621

MOORE, AUSTEN PETER, neurologist, educator; b. Hull, Yorkshire, Eng., Dec. 4, 1952; s. Austen Joseph and Patricia Theresa (Ferraro) M.; m. Julia Kay Wadham, June 20, 1981. MB ChB, Birmingham (Eng.) U., 1975, MD, 1987. House officer Birmingham Hosp., 1975-76; sr. house officer gen. medicine Leeds (Eng.) Hosp., 1977-79; registrar in gen. medicine Hallamshire Hosp., Sheffield, Eng., 1979-81; registrar in neurology Queen Elizabeth Hosp., Birmingham, 1981-83, Inst. Neurol. Scis., Glasgow, Scotland, 1983-87; lectr. in neurology Walton Ctr. for Neurology and Neurosurgery, Liverpool, Eng., 1987-94, assoc. specialist in neurology, 1994-96, sr. lectr., cons. neurologist, 1996—. Editor: Handbook of Botulinum Toxin Treatment, 1995; editor movement disorders sect. Cochrane Collaboration; contbr. articles to profl. jours., chpt. to book. Fellow Royal Coll. Physicians, Assn. Brit. Neurologists, Movement Disorder Soc. Avocations: mountaineering, sailing. Office: Walton Ctr Neurology, Lower Ln, Liverpool L9 7LJ, England

MOORE, BEATRICE, religious organization administrator; b. Somerville, Mass., Oct. 6, 1928; d. George and Christina Turner; m. Wendell Moore, May 9, 1953; children: Karl C., Linda Moore Flewelling, Diane Pearl, Larry. BS in Theology and English, Berkshire Christian Coll., Lenox, Mass., 1950. Pres. The Woman's Home and Foreign Mission Society, Loudon, N.H.; nat. pres. The Woman's Home and Foreign Mission Society, Charlotte, N.C.; chmn. Nat. Spiritual Life. Sunday sch. tchr., deaconess Loudon Ridge Family Bible Ch.; active Women's Home and Fgn. Mission Soc., Loudon, past pres. N.H. Soc., past pres. ea. region; hostess, contact chmn., prayer adv., Bible club guide Stonecroft Ministries, Friendship Bible Study Guide; past leader 4-H Club. Office: Woman's Home & Foreign Mission 845 Loudon Ridge Rd Loudon NH 03307-1712

MOORE, BOB STAHLY, communications executive; b. Pasadena, Calif., July 3, 1936; s. Norman Hastings and Mary Augusta (Stahly) M. Student, U. Mo., 1954-58, MIT, 1958-62. News dir. WPEO, Peoria, Ill., 1958-60, KSST, Davenport, Iowa, 1960-62, WIRE, Indpls., 1962-64, WCFL, Chgo., 1964-67; White House corr. Metromedia, Inc., Washington, 1967-71; news dir. Gateway Communications, Altoona, Pa., 1972-74; Washington Bur. chief MBS, 1974-76; v.p. news MBS, Arlington, Va., 1976-78; White House corr. MBS, 1978-81; dir. communications Fed. Home Loan Bank Bd., Washington, 1981-85; spl. asst. to bd. govs. Fed. Res. System, Washington, 1985—. Active ARC. Served with USAF, 1961-63. Recipient profl. awards Ind. News Broadcasters, 1963, Ill. News Broadcasters, 1965, UPI, 1960, 63, 65, AP, 1956, 58, 61, 65, 67, Mo. News Broadcasters, 1956, 61. Mem. Radio and Television News Dirs. Assn. (Profl. award), White House Corrs. Assn., State Dept. Corrs. Assn., Radio-Television Corrs. Gallery (U.S. Capitol), Chgo. Council on Fgn. Relations, Pub. Relations Soc. Am., Nat., Washington, Chgo. press clubs, U.S. Jr., Mo., Ill. chambers commerce, Sigma Delta Chi. Presbyterian. Home: 817 Crescent Dr Alexandria VA 22302-2214 Office: 20th And Constitution NW Washington DC 20551-0001

MOORE, BRIAN CECIL JOSEPH, auditory researcher; b. London, Feb. 10, 1946; s. Cecil George and Maria Anna Moore. BA, Cambridge (Eng.) U., 1968, PhD, 1971. Lectr. U. Reading, Eng., 1971-73, 1974-77; lectr. U. Cambridge, 1977-89, reader, 1989-95; prof. U. Cambridge, Eng., 1995—; vis. prof. Bklyn. Coll., 1973-74, U. Calif. Berkeley, 1990, U. Ulster North Ireland, 1991-94; sci. adv. bd. Resound Corp., Redwood City, Calif., 1988—. Author: An Introduction to the Psychology of Hearing, 1977, 83, 89, 97 (Littler prize 1983), Perceptual Consequences of Cochlear Damage, 1995, Cochlear Hearing Loss, 1998; contbr. articles to profl. jours. Fellow Acoustical Soc. Am., Belgian Soc. Audiology (hon.), Brit. Soc. Hearing Aid Audiologists (hon.). Avocations: music, playing jazz, collecting musical instruments. Office: U Cambridge Dept Exptl Psychology, Downing St, Cambridge CB2 3EB, England

MOORE, BRIAN CLIVE, actuary; b. Everett, Wash., Sept. 7, 1945; s. Frederic E. and Kathleen E. (Miller) M.; m. Lorraine Campbell, Feb. 11, 1946; children: Timothy, Jonathan. BA in Math., Yale U., 1970; MA in Math., U. Calif., 1971. Actuarial assoc. INA, Phila., 1971-73; asst. actuary Reliance Ins. Group, Phila., 1973-77, asst. sec., 1977-78, sec., 1978-80, asst. v.p., 1980-84, v.p., 1984-86, sr. v.p., 1986-99; asst. v.p. AIG Mktg., Wilmington, Del., 2000—. With U.S. Army, 1966-68. Fellow Casualty Actuarial Soc.; mem. Am. Acad. Actuaries. Office: AIG Mktg Inc 505 Carr Rd Wilmington DE 19809-2865

MOORE, CAROLE IRENE, librarian; b. Berkeley, Calif., Aug. 15, 1944. AB, Stanford U., 1966; MLS, Columbia U., 1967. Reference libr. Columbia U., N.Y.C., 1967-68; reference libr. U. Toronto, Can., 1968-80, head cataloging, 1980-85, assoc. libr., 1985-86, chief libr., 1986—; mem. nat. adv. bd. Nat. Libr. Can., Ottawa, 1991-94; bd. dirs. Rsch. Librs. Group. 1994-2000, U. Toronto Press, 1994—. Recipient Disting. Alumni award Columbia U., 1989. Mem. ALA, Can. Libr. Assn., Can. Assn. Rsch. Librs. (pres. 1989-91, bd. dirs. 1996-98). Avocation: gardening. Office: U Toronto Libr, 130 Saint George St, Toronto, ON Canada M5S 1A5

MOORE, CHRISTOPHER MINOR, lawyer; b. L.A., Oct. 12, 1938; s. Prentiss Elder and Josephine (French) M.; m. Gillian Reed, Sept. 29, 1965; children: Stephanie Kia Conn, Carrie Christine McKay. AB, Stanford U., 1961; JD, Harvard U., 1964. Dep. county counsel Los Angeles County Counsel, 1965-66; ptnr. Moore & Lindelof, L.A., 1966-69, Burkley & Moore, Torrance, Calif., 1969-74; pvt. practice Law Offices of Christopher Moore, Torrance, 1974-81; ptnr. Burkley, Moore, Greenberg & Lyman, Torrance, 1981-90; prin. Christopher M. Moore & Assoc., Torrance, 1990—. Mem. bd. edn. Palos Verdes (Calif.) Peninsula Unified Sch. Dist., 1972-77. Fellow Am. Coll. Trust and Estate Counsel, Am. Acad. Matrimonial Lawyers; mem. L.A. Yacht Club. Avocations: sailing, golf. Office: Christopher Moore & Assoc 21515 Hawthorne Blvd Ste 490 Torrance CA 90503-6525

MOORE, DAHLIA, psychologist, educator; b. Tel Aviv, July 7, 1953; d. David and Rebecca (Abramowitz) Benberry; m. Abraham Moore, Oct. 12, 1978; childen: Jonathan, Daniel. BA, Tel Aviv U., 1980, MA, 1984, PhD, 1988. Instr. Tel Aviv U., 1980-88; sr. rschr. Inst. Technol. Analysis, Tel Aviv, 1988-90; lectr. Hebrew U., Jerusalem, 1989-94, 96; sr. lectr. Coll. Mgmt., Tel Aviv, 1997—; cons. Israeli Bur. Stats., Jerusalem, 1991-93; advisor Israeli Parliament, Jerusalem, 1995—; disting. vis. prof. U. Calif., Davis, 1995-98; sr. lectr., The Sch. of Social Work, The Hebrew Univ., 1998—. Author: Segmentation of the Labor Market, 1992; contbr. articles to profl. jours. Party mem. Meretz, Israel, 1995—; elected coun. mem. Meretz-Jerusalem, 1996. Office: Coll Mgmt, 9 Shoshana Persitz St, 61480 Tel Aviv Israel

MOORE, DAN STERLING, insurance executive, sales trainer; b. Lincoln, Nebr., June 27, 1956; s. Jack Leroy and Carolyn Marie (Bachman) M.; m. Marla Janine Collister, June 2, 1979; children: Tyler David, Anna Rose. Student, Red Rocks Coll., 1977. Lic. ins. exec. Asst. mgr. European Health Spa, Englewood, Colo., 1975-78; sales mgr. Colo. Nat. Homes, Westminster, 1979-80; sales assoc. Dale Carnegie, Denver, 1981; sales mgr. Paramount Fabrics, Denver, 1981-84; sales assoc. Mighty Distbg., Arvada, Colo., 1984-87; divsn. mgr. Nat. Assn. for Self Employed/United Group Assn., Englewood, Colo., 1987—; divsn. mgr. Communicating for Agr. Assn., 1993-98, Am. Bus. Coalition, 1997-2000, Am. for Financial Security, 1999—. Leader, trainer Alpine Rescue Team, Evergreen, Colo., 1971-74; minister Jehovah's Witnesses, 1972—. Avocations: golf, skiing, backpacking, scuba diving, tennis. Home: 892 Nob Hill Trl Franktown CO 80116-7917 Office: Nat Assn Self Employed/United Group 10579 W Bradford Rd Ste 100 Littleton CO 80127-4247

MOORE, DANIEL EDMUND, psychologist, educator, retired educational administrator; b. Pitts., Dec. 31, 1926; s. John Daniel and Alma Helen (Goehring) M.; m. Rose Marie Blunkosky, Nov. 11, 1949; children: Catherine Chiodo, Claire Marie Moore Caveney, Mary Moore Brilmyer, Suzanne Moore Gray, Elizabeth Moore Sullivan. BSEd, Duquesne U., 1949, MEd, 1952; postgrad., California (Pa.) State Coll., 1954-56, U. Pitts., 1958-59, Mt. Mercy Coll., 1959-60, Cath. U. Am., 1966, W.Va. U., 1970-72. Lic. psychologist; cert. sch. psychologist. Tchr. math. Cecil Twp. Sch. Dist., McDonald, Pa., 1949-52, Pitts. Public Schs., 1952-53; with Mt. Lebanon Twp. (Pa.) Sch. Dist., 1953-88, psychologist, 1954-71, dir. pupil personnel svcs., 1988; psychol cons. Peters Twp. Sch. Dist., McMurray, Pa., 1961-88, Blackhawk Sch. Dist., Beaver, Pa., 1989—, Quaker Valley Sch. Dist., Sewickley, Pa., 1989-90; lectr., supr. Grad. and Undergrad. Sch. Edn. Duquesne U.; psychologist DePaul Inst., Pitts., 1992—; lectr. ednl. psychology Grad. Sch. Edn., Duquesne U., 1957-92, supr. student tchrs., 1989-92; ednl. cons. St. Francis Schs. Nursing, New Castle and Pitts., 1959-91; mem. test adv. bd. Ednl. Records Bur., 1976-86; hearing officer Right to Edn. Office, Dept. Edn., Harrisburg, Pa., 1975—; in-svc. adv. bd. Pa. Dept. Edn. Hearing Officers. Mem. Chartiers Valley Sch. Dist. Bd., 1963-94, pres., 1971, v.p., 1991; mem. Pkwy. West Tech. Sch. Bd. 1965-67; bd. dirs. secondary sch. rsch. program Ednl. Testing Svc., Princeton, 1971-85; bd. dirs. Robert E. Ward Home for Children, 1975-87, St. Agatha Parish Coun., 1988—, Pathfinder Sch., 1989, v.p., 1990-94, pres. sch. bd., 1991-92; vol. Bridgeville Area Food Bank, 1988—; chairperson Parish 100 Jubilee Ceremony, Goodwill Villa Bd., Goodwill Plaza, Inc., Goodwill Villa Bd. of Incorporators, 1992—; pres. bd. dirs. Goodwill Plaza, 1992—; jubilee chairperson St. Agatha's, Bridgeville, Pa. With USNR, 1945-48. Henry C. Frick grantee, 1970, 73; named Jaycee Educator of Yr. for South Hills Area, Ward Home Outstanding Community Leader, 1984, Outstanding Cmty. Leader, Chartiers Valley Human Rels. Coun., 1998; recipient Human Rels. award Chartiers Valley Inter-relationships Soc., 1998. Mem. Am., Pa. psychol. assns., Coun. Exceptional Children (pres. 1957), Phi Delta Kappa (pres. chpt. 1974-75, chmn. lay awards com. 1979—, Svc. Key award 1985). Roman Catholic. Home: 213 Station St Bridgeville PA 15017-1806

MOORE, DANIEL KEITH, scientific society executive, earth scientist; b. Provo, Utah, Dec. 3, 1966; s. Garry Keith and LaNell (Lines) M.; m. DaLynn N. Moore, Dec. 17, 1988; children: Ashton Tyler, Tanner Keith, Hunter Ryan, Atalie, Mason Talmage, Taylor David, McKay Reed. BS, Brigham Young U., Provo, 1991, MS, 1993; PhD, Rensselaer Poly. Inst., Troy, N.Y., 1997. Asst. to exec. dir. Am. Geophys. Union, Washington, 1997-98, mgr. spl. projects, 1998, mgr. adminstrn., 1998-2000, sys. devel. mgr., 2000—. Bishops counselor Ch. of Jesus Christ of Latter-Day Saints, Troy, N.Y., 1996-97, Waldorf, Md., 1998—, high councilor, Troy, 1995-96. Mem. Am. Geophys. Union. Avocations: family, learning, basketball, outdoors. Office: Am Geophys Union 2000 Florida Ave NW Washington DC 20009-1231

MOORE, DEMI (DEMI GUYNES), actress; b. Roswell, N.Mex., Nov. 11, 1962; d. Danny and Virginia Guynes; m. Bruce Willis, Nov. 21, 1987; 3 daughters: Rumer Glenn, Scout LaRue, Tallulah Belle. Studies with Zina Provendie. Actress: (feature films) Choices, 1981, Parasite, 1981, Young Doctors in Love, 1982, Blame it on Rio, 1984, No Small Affair, 1984, St. Elmo's Fire, 1985, About Last Night..., 1986, Wisdom, 1986, One Crazy Summer, 1987, The Seventh Sign, 1988, We're No Angels, 1989, Ghost, 1990, Mortal Thoughts, 1991 (also co-producer), The Butcher's Wife, 1991, Nothing But Trouble, 1991, A Few Good Men, 1992, Indecent Proposal, 1993, Disclosure, 1994, The Scarlet Letter, 1995, Now and Then, 1995 (also prodr.), Undisclosed, 1996, Striptease, 1996, The Juror, 1996; (TV series) General Hospital, 1982-83; (TV movies) If These Walls Could Talk, 1996 (also exec. prodr.); (voice) The Hunchback of Notre Dame, 1996, G.I. Jane, 1997, Deconstructing Harry, 1997, Austin Powers: International Man of Mystery, 1997. Office: Creative Artists Agy Inc 9830 Wilshire Blvd Beverly Hills CA 90212-1825

MOORE, DENNIS DUANE, English educator; b. Greenville, S.C., Oct. 25, 1949; s. Marvin R. Moore and Mildred E. Brown. BA, Clemson U., 1970; MA, U. N.C., 1971, PhD, 1990. Instr. English Greenville (S.C.) Tech. Coll., 1980-82, Clemson (S.C.) U., 1982-84; asst. prof. English U. Tex., El Paso, 1990-91; asst. prof. English Fla. State U., Tallahassee, 1991-95, assoc. prof. English, 1995—; dir. Bryan Hall Learning Cmty., 2000—. Editor: More Letters from the American Farmer: An Edition of Essays in English Left Unpublished by Crevecoeur, 1995; contbr. articles to profl. jours. V.p., program chair Friends of Fla. State U. Librs., 1995—; mem. Friends of Black History Archives, Tallahassee, Fla. History Assocs., Mus. Fla. History, Tallahassee. C. Hugh Holman fellow U. N.C. Dept. English, 1989; Rsch. grantee NEH, 1991, 92; fellow in Early Am. History and Culture, Libr. Co. Phila. and Hist. Soc. Pa., jointly, 1988. Mem. Am. Studies Assn. (life mem.), Am. Soc. Eighteenth-Century Studies (life mem.), Soc. Early Americanists, Toni Morrison Soc. (charter and life mem.), Internat. Iris Murdoch Soc. (founding mem., life mem., sec.), St. Marks Nat. Wildlife Refuge Assn. (life), Phi Theta Kappa (hon.). Democrat. Unitarian. Avocations: fly-fishing, birding, canoeing, traveling, films. E-mail: dmoore@english.fsu.edu. Office: Dept English Fla State U Tallahassee FL 32306-1580

MOORE, DONALD WALTER, academic administrator, school librarian; b. Culver City, Calif., June 9, 1942; s. Raymond Owen and Jewel Elizabeth (Young) M.; m. Dagmar Ulbrich, Mar. 28, 1968; 1 child, Michael. AA, L.A. Valley Coll., 1967; BA in History, Calif. State U., Northridge, 1970; MA in Learning Disability, Calif. State U., 1973; MLS, U. So. Calif., 1974. Part time librarian L.A. Pierce Coll., Woodland Hills, Calif., 1974—; instr. reading L.A. Trade Tech. Coll., 1978-80, pres.'s staff asst., 1983-87; instr. learning skills L.A. City Coll., 1987-88, dir. amnesty edn., 1988-92, dir. Citizenship Ctr., 1992—; adj. instr. computer sci. L.A. Trade-Tech. Coll., 1983—. Author: A Guidebook to U.S. Army Dress Helmets, 2000; contbr. fiction, articles, revs. to various publs. Mem. Ednl. Writers Am., Co. Mil. Historians, Edpress, Little Big Horn Assn., Planetary Soc. Republican. Roman Catholic. Avocations: writing, collecting U.S. frontier military memorabilia, computing. Office: LA City Coll Citizenship Program 855 N Vermont Ave Los Angeles CA 90029-3516

MOORE, DUDLEY STUART JOHN, actor, musician; b. Dagenham, Essex, Eng., Apr. 19, 1935; s. John and Ada Francis (Hughes) M.; m. Suzy Kendall, 1966 (div.); m. Tuesday Weld, 1975 (div.); 1 child: Patrick; m. Brogan Lane (Denise Brogan), Feb. 21, 1988 (div.); m. Nicole Rothschild, April 16, 1994. Student, Guildhall Sch. Music; BA, Oxford (Eng.) U., 1957, MusB, 1958. Author: Dud and Pete: The Dagenham Dialogues, 1971; stage debut with Oxford U. Drama Soc., 1955; other stage appearances include Beyond the Fringe, London, 1960-62, Broadway, 1962-64, Play It Again Sam, 1970, Good Evening, 1973-75; appeared with Vic Lewis, John Dankworth Jazz Band, 1959-60; composed incidental music Royal Ct. Theatre, 1958-60; appeared in own BBC-TV series with Peter Cook Not only...but also, 1964, 66, 70; Royal Command Performance, ITV, 1965, Goodbye Again, ITV, 1968; appeared on BBC-TV series It's Lulu, not to mention Dudley Moore, 1972, Dudley, 1993, Daddy's Girls, 1994—; toured U.S., 1975; appeared on various TV and radio shows with jazz piano trio; actor (films) The Wrong Box, 30 is a Dangerous Age, Cynthia, Alice in Wonderland, Those Daring Young Men in their Jaunty Jalopies, Bedazzled, The Bed Sitting Room, The Hound of the Baskervilles, Foul Play, 10, Wholly Moses, Arthur (Golden Globe award 1983, Acad. award nomination 1983), Six Weeks, Lovesick, Romantic Comedy, Unfaithfully Yours, Best Defense, Mickey & Maude (Golden Globe award 1985), Santa Claus The Movie, Like Father, Like Son, Arthur on the Rocks, (voice over) The Adventures of Milo and Otis, 1989, Crazy People, 1990, Blame it on the Bellboy, 1991, A Weekend in the Country, The Pickle, 1994, Parallel Lives, 1994, The Disappearance of Kevin Johnson, 1996, Respect, 1998, (voice) The Mighty Kong, 1998; (TV) Daddy's Girls, 1995, A Weekend in the Country, 1996; also various TV shows.; composer (film music) 30 is a Dangerous Age, Cynthia, Inadmissible Evidence, The Staircase, Six Weeks; rec. artist (albums) The Other Side of Dudley Moore, Today, Genuine Dud, Derek and Clive - Live, Beyond the Fringe and All That Jazz, Dudley Moore Trio - Down Under, Bedazzled, Songs Without Words, 1992, others. Named Male Star of Yr. N.A.T.O., 1983; Organ scholar Oxford U., 1958. Mem. St. James's Club, Annabel's Club, Harry's Bar, Tramp Club. Office: ICM care Duncan Heath 8942 Wilshire Blvd Beverly Hills CA 90211-1934 Home: PO Box 9 Fanwood NJ 07023-0009

MOORE, EDWARD WARREN, lawyer; b. Odessa, Tex., July 21, 1959; s. Edward Warren and Gloria (Schroeter) M.; m. JoAnne Bisso; children: Peggy, Barbara. BS in Econs., Princeton U., 1981; JD, So. Meth. U., 1984. Bar: Tex. 1984, U.S. Dist. Ct. (no. dist.) Tex. 1984, U.S. Ct. Appeals (5th cir.) 1984, U.S. Ct. Appeals (10th cir.) 1985. Assoc. Ravkind, Kuehne &

Biesel, Dallas, 1984-85; ptnr. Kuehne & Moore, Dallas, 1984-96; pvt. practice, 1996—. Vol. Park Cities YMCA. Mem. AAAS, ABA (litigation sect., trial practice sect. and com., product liability, antitrust, intellectual property sect.), ATLA (toxic, environ. and pharm. litigation sect., comml. litigation sect.), State Bar Tex., Dallas Bar Assn., Tex. Trial Lawyers Assn., Dallas Country Club. Methodist. E-mail: eddymoor@sprynet.com. Home: 3832 Villanova St Dallas TX 75225-5219

MOORE, EVERETT LEROY, library administrator; b. Eugene, Oreg., May 24, 1918; s. Clinton L. Moore and Elsie LaVerne (Crowder) Morgan; m. Fern Irene Owen, July 13, 1942; children: David LeRoy, Richard Eugene, Patricia Elaine. BA, Wheaton Coll., 1949; MA, Pasadena Coll., 1954; MA in Libr. Sci., Vanderbilt U., 1960; PhD, U. So. Calif., 1973. Cert. C.C. chief adminstrv. officer, Calif. Libr. Evangel Coll., Springfield, Mo., 1955-57; head tech. svcs. North Coastal Regional Libr., Tillamook, Oreg., 1957-60; head social sci. and bus. libr. Calif. State U., Chico, 1960-62; dir. libr. svcs. Coll. of the Desert, Palm Desert, Calif., 1962-75; dir. univ. libr. Am. U. Cairo, 1970-72; dir. libr. svcs. Woodbury U., L.A., 1976-87, dir. libr. svcs., prof. emeritus, 1987—; pres. so. region Jr. Coll. Round Table, Calif. Libr. Assn., Sacramento, 1965-66; chair tech. svcs. com. Calif. C.C. Libr. Coop., 1968-70, chmn. Desert area, 1974-75. Contbr. to profl. jours. Avocations: reading, computers, politics. Home: 1322 E Avenue Q12 Palmdale CA 93550-5168

MOORE, FLORIAN HOWARD, electronics engineer; b. Shelby, Ohio, Aug. 23, 1929; s. Carl Leslie and Mona Pearl (Dearth) M.; m. Dorothy Elizabeth Morse, Dec. 19, 1950. AA, Harvard U., 1974. Cert. indsl. maint. electrician; tchg. cert. indsl. electricity, indsl. electronics. With Diebold Inc., Boston, 1955-56; mem. electronics R & D staff Radio Corp. Am., Burlington, Mass., 1956-59; mem. electronics/mech. R & D staff MIT, Cambridge, 1959-74; mem. electricity/electronics/electromech. R & D staff Charles Stark Draper Labs., Cambridge, 1974-76; tchr. indsl. electronics Ashland County Joint Vocat. Sch., Ashland, Ohio, 1976-78; buyer Autocall divsn. Fed. Signal Corp., Shelby, 1978-79; journeyman electrician Excel Wire & Cable divsn. United Tech., Tiffin, Ohio, 1980-86; tchr. indsl. electricity Madison Comprehensive H.S., Mansfield, Ohio, 1986-88; pres., CEO Florian H. Moore & Assocs., Shelby, 1988—. Vol. Ohio Geneal. Libr., Mansfield; foster parent Commonwealth of Mass., 1962-82 (38 children). With USAF, 1948-52. Fellow Internat. Biog. Assn. (dep. dir. gen.); mem. Ohio Geneal. Soc. (v.p. Richland-Shelby gen. chpt. 1993-95, pres. 1995-97), Royal Lincolnshire Regtl. Assn. (life; Am. contingent, 10th foot), DAV (life), Order Internat. Fellowship (charter, U.S. rep. 1995), Masons (32 degree), Kappa Delta Phi (life). Avocations: history, snow skiing, sky diving, computer programming. Home: 22A Commandery Ct Springfield OH 45504-5601

MOORE, HELEN LUCILLE, recruiting company executive; b. Watseka, Ill., July 24, 1930; d. John Kenneth and Thelma Mae (Wollschlaeger) Weidert; m. Harold Junior Gossett, June 24, 1948 (div. May 1971); children: Steven, Joyce, Gary, Ricky, Kenny, Jane; m. Herff Leo Moore, Jr., Nov. 24, 1991. AS in Mgmt., Kankakee (Ill.) Jr. Coll., 1969. Sr. sec. Nimz Transp., Watseka, 1948-57; tchg. aide Glenn Raymond H.S., Watseka, 1964-71; asst. pers. and safety mgr. Gt. Plains Bag Co., Jacksonville, Ark., 1971-81; sr. human resources rep. Maybelline Products Co., Inc. divsn. L'Oreal, North Little Rock, Ark., 1981-2000; recruiting dir. StaffMark, Little Rock, 2000—; chmn. Ark. Human Resource Conf., Hot Springs, 1991-92. Contbr. articles to profl. publs. Bd. dirs. Ark. Urban League, Little Rock, 1985-93; co-founder, exec. bd. dirs. Workforce Alliance for Growth in Economy, 1993—; mem. exec. com. Ark. Gov.'s Workforce Investment Bd., 1999—. Recipient Outstanding Ark. Human Resources Profl. award Ark. Human Resources Coun., 1994; named Sr. Inspirational Employee of Yr., ABLE (Ability Based on Long Experience), 1997. Mem. Nat. Employer Coun. (Ark. chmn. local employer adv. couns. 1989—, sch.-to-work com., focus group 1998, Star Performer award 1999), Soc. for Human Resource Mgmt. (profl.), Ark. Human Resources Assn. (profl., bd. dirs. 1988-90, Outstanding Profl. Mem. award 1989), Ctrl. Ark. Mfg. Pers. Assn. (co-founder, chmn. 1990-2000), Am. Legion Aux. (life). Office: StaffMark 2024 Arkansas Valley Dr Little Rock AR 72212-4166

MOORE, HERFF LEO, JR., management educator; b. San Antonio, Jan. 24, 1937; s. Herff Leo Moore Sr. and Constance (Benesh) Wold; m. Helen Lucille Weidert, Nov. 1991; children by previous marriage: Terri Lynne, Christopher Scott, Kimberly Anne. BSBA, The Ohio State U., 1964; MBA, U. Tex., 1968; MS in Community Svcs., U. Rochester, 1976; PhD, U. Tex. at Arlington, 1980. Cert. sr. profl. in human resources (life). Prodn. mgmt., quality assurance officer Sacramento (Calif.) Air Logistics Ctr. USAF, 1964-67; personnel mgmt., adminstrv. cons. Aero. Systems Div. Wright-Patterson AFB, Dayton, Ohio, 1968-73; pers. mgmt. and quality assurance cons. Defense Contract Adminstrv. Svcs. Dist. Hdqrs., Rochester, N.Y., 1973-76; lectr. in mgmt. and doctoral student The Univ. of Tex. at Arlington, 1976-79; asst. prof. bus. adminstrn. Ea. Ky. U., Richmond, 1979-81; assoc. prof. mgmt. East Tex. State U. at Texarkana, 1981-83, Saint John Fisher Coll., Rochester, 1983-85; assoc. prof. mgmt. U. Cen. Ark., Conway, 1985-99, ret., 1999; pres. H.M.C.C. Mgmt. Group, Conway, 1988—; participant Leadership Texarkana Leadership Tng., 1981-82; mgmt. cons., Calif., N.Y., Ark., Ohio, N.J., Fla., Ga., Tex., 1964—. Author: (with others) Language, Customs and Protocol: A Guidebook for International Students and Employees, 1992; contbr. numerous articles to profl. jours. Capt. USAF, 1964-76. Recipient Significant Performance Contbr. award Def. Supply Agy., 1975; Nat. scholar Phi Kappa Phi, 1968; named Honor Grad. USAF Officers Tng. Sch., 1964. Mem. Soc. for Human Resource Mgmt. (tng. and devel. com. 1989-94, select panel on edn. 1989-91, coll. rels. com. 1989-92, bd. dirs. area IV 1987-91, sec., treas. Ark. coun. 1986-87), Ark. Human Resources Assn. (pres. 1991-92, bd. dirs. 1991-93), Acad. Mgmt., Soc. Human Resource Mgmt. (superior merit awards student chpt. U. Ctrl. Ark. 1985-90, 93), Alpha Kappa Psi, Phi Kappa Phi, Sigma Iota Epsilon. Mem. Assembly of God Ch. Avocations: chess playing, political button collecting. Home: 1910 Amelia Dr Conway AR 72032-3315

MOORE, HUGH JACOB, JR., lawyer; b. Norfolk, Va., June 29, 1944; s. Hugh Jacob and Ina Ruth (Hall) M.; m. Jean Garnett, June 10, 1972; children: Lela Miller, Sarah Garnett. BA, Vanderbilt U., 1966; LLB, Yale U., 1969. Bar: Tenn. 1970, U.S. Dist. Ct. (mid. dist.) Tenn. 1970, U.S. Supreme Ct. 1973, U.S. Ct. Appeals (6th cir.) 1973, U.S. Dist. Ct. (ea. dist.) Tenn. 1973, U.S. Dist. Ct. (we. dist.) Tenn. 1982, U.S. Ct. Claims 1993. Law clk. U.S. Dist. Ct. (mid. dist.) Tenn., Nashville, 1969-70; trial atty. civil rights divsn. U.S. Dept. Justice, Washington, 1970-73; asst. U.S. atty. Eastern Dist. of Tenn., Chattanooga, 1973-76; assoc. Witt, Gaither & Whitaker, P.C., Chattanooga, 1976-77, shareholder, 1977—, also bd. dirs.; mem. Commn. Women and Minorities Profession Law; mem. hearing com. Bd. Profl. Responsibility Supreme Ct. Tenn.; mem. mediation panel U.S. Dist. Ct. (ea. dist.) Tenn.; cert. arbitrator, cert. mediator Tenn. Rule 31 Nat. Assn. Securities Dealers; cert. arbitrator N.Y. Stock Exch., Nat. Arbitration Forum; mem. adv. commn. on rules of civil and appellate procedure Tenn. Supreme Ct., chmn., 1999—. Contbr. articles to profl. jours. Bd. dirs. Adult Edn. Coun., Chattanooga, 1976-81, pres., 1977-79; bd. dirs. Chattanooga Symphony and Opera Assn., 1981-87, Riverbend Festival, 1983-85, 91—, pres., 1995-97, Landmarks Chattanooga, 1983-84, Cornerstones, 1995-98, Orange Grove Sch., 1996—; mem. alumni coun. McCallie Sch., 1980-85; trustee St. Nicholas Sch., 1983-89, chmn., 1986-88. Fellow Am. Coll. Trial Lawyers, Tenn. State Com., Tenn. Bar Found., Chattanooga Bar Found.; mem. ABA (mem. bd. editors jour. Litigation News 1983-90), Tenn. Bar Assn., Chattanooga Bar Assn. (mem. bd. govs. 1985-87), Mountain City Club, Rotary. Methodist. Home: 101 Ridgeside Rd Chattanooga TN 37411-1830 Office: Witt Gaither & Whitaker 1100 SunTrust Bank Bldg Chattanooga TN 37402

MOORE, JEANNETTE AILEEN, animal nutrition educator; b. Bellflower, Calif., Jan. 6, 1957; d. Harry Joseph Jr. and Alba Aurora (Celaya) M.; m. Matthew Henry Poore, Oct. 2, 1982. BS in Animal Scis., Calif. State Polytechnic U., 1980; MS in Animal Scis., U. Ariz., 1983, PhD in Nutritional Scis., 1987. Cert. nutrition specialist. Postdoctoral rsch. assoc. U. Ariz., Tucson, 1988-90; postdoctoral rsch. assoc. N.C. State U., Raleigh, 1990-92, coord. Spend-A-Day-At-State program, 1994-97, chair dept. info. tech. com., 1996-97, mem. coll. acad. computing adv. com., 1996—, undergrad. tchg. coord. dept. animal sci., 1997—; vis. asst. prof. N.C. State U., Raleigh, 1992-98, asst. prof., 1998—, faculty advisor Animal Sci. Club, 1992—, advisor Acad. Quadrathlon Team, 1993-94, advisor Rodeo Club, 1994—, World Wide web coord. Dept. Animal Sci., 1994—. Author: (computer spreadsheet) Ruminant Animal Diet Evaluator, 1993; mem. editl. bd. Jour. Animal Sci., 1995—. Supt. jr. ewe show, N.C. State Fair, Raleigh, 1992-98; vol. N.C. Sci. and Math Partnership, Wake county, N.C., 1991—. Mem. Am. Soc. Nutritional Scis., Am. Soc. Animal Sci., Am. Dairy Sci. Assn., Am. Coll. Nutrition, Nat. Assn. Colls. and Tchrs. Agr., Coun. Agrl. Sci. and Tech., Alpha Zeta. Avocations: horseback riding, aerobics, reading, travel. Office: NC State U Dept Animal Sci PO Box 7621 Raleigh NC 27695-0001

MOORE, JOHN COLINTON, Australian government official; b. Rockhampton, Qld., Australia, Nov. 16, 1936; s. Thomas Roy and Doris (Alford) M.; m. Jacqualyn McDonald, Jan. 28, 1980; children: Simon, Sarah, Andrew. BCom, U. Queensland, Brisbane. Prin. John Moore Co., Stockbrokers, Brisbane, 1964-73; mem. Australian Parliament, Canberra, 1975—, min. for bus. and consumer affairs, 1980-82, shadow min. for no. devel. and local govt., now min. for def. Pres. Liberal Party Australia, 1973-76, Queensland divsn., 1984—. Mem. Queensland Club, Commonwealth Club. Home: 17 Ningana St, Fig Tree Pocket Brisbane Australia*

MOORE, JOHN CORDELL, retired lawyer; b. Winchester, Ill., July 20, 1912; s. John Clayton and Winifred (Peak) M.; m. Pauline Ruyle, July 29, 1939 (dec. 1979); m. Wilma K. Smith Jackson, Aug. 1981. A.B., Ill. Coll., 1936, LL.D., 1967; LL.B., Georgetown U., 1949, J.D., 1967; postgrad. in geology, Am. U., 1955-57. Bar: Tenn., U.S. Supreme Ct. Rep. Universal Credit Co., St. Louis, 1937-39; tchr. Capitol Page Sch.; also clk. to mem. Ho. of Reps., 1939-41; examiner Metals Res. Co., 1941-42; exec. dir. Fgn. Liquidation Commn. for S. and C. Am., Balboa, C.Z., 1946-47; with Office Alien Property, Dept. Justice, 1947-50; asst. dir. property mgmt. Interior Dept., 1950-52, dir. security for dept., 1952-61; adminstr. Oil Import Adminstrn., 1961-65, asst. sec. for mineral resources, 1965-69; ret.; U.S. rep. oil and energy com. OECD, Paris, 1965-69; former dir. Clark Oil, Milw. Served to comdr. USNR, 1942-46; capt. Res. Mem. Am. Legion, Scott County (Winchester, Ill.) Hist. Soc. (life), Delta Theta Phi, Elks, Army-Navy Club, Jacksonville Country Club.

MOORE, JOHN STERLING, JR., minister; b. Memphis, Aug. 25, 1918; s. John Sterling and Lorena (Bounds) M.; m. Martha Louise Paulette, July 6, 1944; children: Sterling Hale, John Marshall, Carolyn Paulette. Student, Auburn U., 1936-37; AB, Samford U., 1940; ThM, So. Bapt. Theol. Sem., 1944. Ordained to ministry So. Bapt. Conv., 1942. Pastor chs. Pamplin, Va., 1944-48, Amherst, Va., 1949-57; pastor Manly Meml. Bapt. Ch., Lexington, Va., 1957-84, pastor emeritus, 1984—; mem. Hist. Commn., So. Bapt. Conv., 1968-75; pres. Va. Bapt. Pastor's Conf., 1963. Author: History of Broad Run Baptist Church, 1762-1987, 1987, The History of Second Baptist Church Richmond Virginia, 1998; co-author: Meaningful Moments in Virginia Baptist Life, 1715-1972, 1973; editor Va. Bapt. Register, 1972—; contbr. articles to profl. jours. Chmn. Lexington Mayor's Com. on Race Rels., 1962-65; bd. dirs. Stonewall Jackson Hosp., 1967-72, pres., 1969-71; treas. Rockbridge Mental Health Clinic, 1971-84. Recipient Disting. Svc. award Hist. Commn., So. Bapt. Conv., 1988. Mem. Am. Soc. Ch. History, So. Bapt. Hist. Soc. (bd. dirs. 1972-91, pres. 1975-76, sec. 1977-85), Va. Bapt. Hist. Soc. (exec. com. 1963—, pres. 1984-85), Va. Hist. Soc., Masons. Home: 1900 Lauderdale Dr Apt D-115 Richmond VA 23233-3918

MOORE, JOYCE KRISTINA, financial planner; b. Phila., June 19, 1955; d. Oscar Herbert Hariu and Virginia Wilson (Guss) Leas ; m. William Burns Moore, June 20, 1980 (div. 1990); children: William Patrick, Kristofer Sean. Student, Beloit Coll., 1973-74, U. Pa., 1974-75, Lafayette Coll., 1984-88, Am. Coll., 1991—. Photographer Clair Pruett Studios, Drexel Hill, Pa., 1977-80; photographic cons. Dan's Camera City, Allentown, Pa., 1980-81; contr., co-founder BioService, Inc., Bethlehem, Pa., 1985-89; contr. Mega Video Inc., Easton, Pa., 1989-91; spl. rep. John Hancock Fin. Svcs., Allentown, Pa., 1990-93; prin. J.K. Moore Fins. Svcs., Easton, Pa., 1993—. Former mem. Warren County Dem. Com., Phillipsburg, N.J., 1981-83; overseer Religious Soc. Friends, 1986-92; bd. dirs. Spring Garden Children's Sch., Easton, Pa.; den leader Cub Scout Pack 31, Williams Twp., Pa., 1991-95, scout leader, 1995-97; councilwoman Glendon Borough, 1992-97, coun. v.p. 1996-97. Mem. LWV (bd. dirs. Easton area 1987-91, pres. 1989-90), Am. Soc. CLUs & ChFCs, Nat. Assn. Ins. and Fin. Advisors, Nat. Assn. Ins. and Fin. Advisors of Lehigh Valley (bd. dirs. 1995—, pres. 2000—). Avocations: needlework, hot air balloon piloting, scuba diving, folk music, canoeing. E-mail: JMFS@aol.com. Office: Joyce Moore Fin Svc PO Box 175 Macungie PA 18062-0175

MOORE, JUSTIN EDWARD, data processing executive; b. West Hartford, Conn., June 17, 1952; s. Walter Joseph and Victoria Mary (Calcagni) M. BS in Mgmt. Sci., Fla. Inst. Tech., 1974. Systems assoc. Travelers Ins., Hartford, Conn., 1974-77; data processing programmer R.J. Reynolds Inc., Winston-Salem, N.C., 1977-78; programmer/analyst Sea-Land Svc., Elizabeth, N.J., 1978-79; mgr. market analysis Sea-Land Svc., Oakland, Calif., 1979-82; asst. v.p., dir. application systems Fox Capital Mgmt. Corp., Foster City, Calif., 1982-86; mgr. bus. svcs. dept mktg. and pricing Am. Pres. Cos., Ltd., Oakland, 1987-88, dir. mktg. and pricing systems, 1988-89; dir. systems devel. The Office Club, Concord, Calif., 1989-91; dir. MIS Revo, Inc., Mountain View, Calif., 1992-93; account mgr. Imrex Computer Systems, Inc., South San Francisco, 1993-94; project mgr. Exigent Computer Group, Inc., San Ramon, Calif., 1994—. Democrat. Roman Catholic. Avocations: golf, personal computing, investment mgmt. Home: 5214 Jomar Dr Concord CA 94521-2343 Office: Exigent Computer Group Inc 4000 Executive Pky San Ramon CA 94583-4257

MOORE, KAREN CELYN, systems analyst; b. Waco, Tex., Jan. 7, 1964; d. Royce Kirby and Dorothy Ann (Schaefer) M. BBA, S.W. Tex. State U., 1986, MBA, 1993. Computer inventory assurance specialist Vogel Furniture Co., Lockhart, Tex., 1985-87; systems analyst III, programmer Tex. Dept. Transp., Austin, 1987-98; sys. analyst Coastal Oil and Gas, Houston, Tex., 1998-99; contract analyst Dynamics/COAD Solutions, Austin, Tex., 1999; cons. analyst Epic Edge, Austin, Tex., 1999—. Mem. Exec. Women in Tex. Govt., Women's Info. Network. Avocations: fashion designing, remodeling.

MOORE, LESTER LELAND, clergy, financial consultant; b. Troy, Iowa; s. Forest Allen and Ida May (Freeman) M.; m. Ruth Ellen Stremlow, Dec. 1, 1946 (dec. Jan. 31, 1990); children: David, Jeffrey, Jane, Randall. AB, Simpson Coll., 1949; STB, Boston U., 1953, STM, 1954; DD, Iowa Wesleyan Coll., 1988. Pastor North Meth. Parish, Muscatine, Iowa, 1953-57, Manning (Iowa)-Dedham Parish, 1957-65; adminstrv. asst. U.S. Congress, Washington, 1965-66; pastor Corning (Iowa) Parish, 1966-72; pastor, dir. Collegiate/Wesley Found., Ames, Iowa, 1972-83; dist. supr. Muscatine (Iowa) Dist., 1983-89; pastor Perry (Iowa) Parish, 1989-91; interm pastor St. Luke's Parish, Dubuque, Iowa, 1995, 1st United Meth. Ch., Anchorage, Alaska, 1996; ch. cons. Iowa United Meth. Found., Des Moines, 1997-00; trustee Iowa Wesleyan Coll., 1983-00, mem. exec. com. Scriptwriter: Maybe We Can Do Something, 1979, How Are We Doing, 1987, Believe It or Not, 1992; contbr. articles to mags. Mem. Iowa Annual Conf. United Meth. Ch., 1952, mem. Gen. Conf., 1960-92; del. Dem. county and dist. and state convs., 1954-80; candidate State Legis., Iowa, 1954; chair people of faith com. State of Iowa, 1994; mem. exec. com. Child Safe, 1994-99; served on gov.'s com. for alcoholism, juvenile problems, UN and civil rights. Sgt. U.S. Army, 1944-46, ETO. Mem. Interfaith Alliance (chair organizing 1994), Democrat. Avocations: photography, stamps, postcards, travel. Home: 2003 Cessna St Ames IA 50014-7026

MOORE, LINDA KATHLEEN, personnel agency executive; b. San Antonio, Tex., Feb. 18, 1944; d. Frank Edward and Louise Marie (Powell) Horton; m. Mack B. Taplin, May 25, 1963 (div. Feb. 1967); 1 child, Mack B.; m. William J. Moore, Mar. 8, 1967 (div. Nov. 1973). Student, Tex. A&I Coll., 1962-63. Co-owner S.R.O. Internat., Dallas, 1967-70; mgr. Exec. Girls Pers. & Modeling Svcs., Dallas, 1970-72, Gen. Employment Enterprises, Atlanta, 1972-88; owner, mgr. More Pers. Svcs., Inc., Atlanta, 1988-94, pres., chmn. bd., 1994—; Contbr. short story to Writer's Digest. Mem. NAFE, Nat. Fedn. Bus. and Profl. Women, Am. Soc. Profl. and Exec. Women, Women Bus. Owners, Nat. Assn. Women Cons., Nat. Assn. Personnel Svcs., Ga. Assn. Personnel Svcs., Women's Clubs, Atlanta C. of C. (speaker's bur.), Better Bus. Bur., Cobb County C. of C. Office: More Pers Svcs Inc 3016 Spring Hill Pkwy SE Apt D Smyrna GA 30080-4712

MOORE, MALCOLM FREDERICK, manufacturing executive; b. Kankakee, Ill., Sept. 19, 1950; s. Robert Dunham and Josephine Frances (Jones) M.; m. Patricia Claudine Bennert, June 13, 1971; children: Michael Dunham, Emily Suzanne, Marjorie Nicoll. BSBA, Am. U., 1972; M of Mgmt., Northwestern U., 1982. Internat. mktg. mgr., product mgr. FMC Corp., Chgo., 1973-84, mktg. and engring. mgr., 1985-90; cons. Frank Lynn & Assoc., Chgo., 1984-85; v.p., gen. mgr. Lindberg unit of Gen. Signal, Watertown, Wis., 1990-93; pres. Abar Ipsen Industries, Inc., Bensalem, Pa., 1993-96, Centorr Vacuum Industries, Nashua, N.H., 1993-96, Linac Holdings, Inc., Rockford, Ill., 1994-96; pres., CEO Pangborn Corp., Hagerstown, Md., 1996-98; exec. v.p., COO Gehl Co., West Bend, Wis., 1999—. Inventor material handling equipment. Episcopalian.

MOORE, MARIANNA GAY, law librarian, consultant; b. La Grange, Ga., Sept. 12, 1939; d. James Henry and Avanelle (Gay) M. AB in French, English, U. Ga., 1961; MLS, Emory U., 1964; postgrad., U. Ga., 1965-66, U. Ill., 1967-68. Asst. law libr. U. Ga., Athens, 1964-66; asst. libr. Yavapai Coll. Libr., Prescott, Ariz., 1969-72; libr. U. Ill. Law Libr., Urbana, 1966-68; law libr. Leva, Hawes, Symington, Washington, 1972-75; libr. project coord. Wash. Occupational Info. Svc., Olympia, 1976-80, Wash. State Health Facilities Assn., Olympia, 1981-82; mgr. Wash. State Ret. Tchrs. Assn., Olympia, 1982-83, exec. dir., 1984-89; exec. dir. Wash. State Retired Tchrs. Found., Olympia, 1986-89; law libr. Solano County Law Libr., Fairfield, Calif., 1989—; libr. LIBRARY/USA N.Y. World's Fair, N.Y.C., 1965; consulting law libr. Dobbins, Weir, Thompson & Stephenson, Vacaville, Calif., 1989—; law libr. cons. Coconino County Law Libr., Flagstaff, Ariz., 1968-70. Author: Guide to Fin. Aid for Wash. State Students, 1979; tng. package to introduce librs. to Wash. State Info. Svc., 1980; indexer for Calif. Coun. of County Law Libr.'s publ. For Your Information, 1999—; contbg. author Solano County Bar Assn. pub. VOIR DIRE. Bd. dirs. Thurston County Sr. Ctr., Olympia, 1976-84, Thurston-Mason Nutrition Program, Olympia, 1977-79, Wash. Soc. Assn. Execs., Edmonds, 1987-89. Mem. Am. Assn. Law Librs., No. Calif. Assn. Law Librs., Calif. Coun. of County Law Librs. Avocations: reading, tatting, travel, music, calligraphy, cats. E-mail: mmoore@solanocounty.com. Office: Solano County Law Libr Hall of Justice 600 Union Ave Fairfield CA 94533-6324

MOORE, MARY FRENCH (MUFFY MOORE), potter, community activist; b. N.Y.C., Feb. 25, 1938; d. John and Rhoda (Teagle) Walker French; m. Alan Baird Minier, Oct. 9, 1982; children: Jonathan Corbet, Jennifer Corbet, Michael Corbet. BA cum laude, Colo. U., 1964. Ceramics mfg. Wilson, Wyo., 1969-82, Cheyenne, Wyo., 1982—; commr. County Teton (Wyo.), 1976-83, chmn. bd. commrs., 1981, 83, mem. dept. pub. assistance and social svc., 1976-82, mem. recreation bd., 1978-81, water quality adv. bd., 1976-82. Bd. dirs. Teton Sci. Sch., 1968-83, vice chmn., 1979-81, chmn., 1982; bd. dirs. Grand Teton Music Festival, 1963-68, Teton Energy Coun., 1978-83, Whitney Gallery of Western Art, Cody, Wyo., 1995—, Opera Colo., 1998—; mem. water quality adv. bd. Wyo. Dept. Environ. Quality, 1979-83; Dem. precinct committeewoman, 1978-81; mem. Wyo. Dem. Ctrl. Com., 1981-83; vice chmn. Laramie County Dem. Ctrl. Com., 1983-84, Wyo. Dem. nat. committeewoman, 1984-87; chmn. Wyo. Dem. Party, 1987-89; del. Dem. Nat. Conv., 1984, 88, mem. fairness commn. Dem. Nat. Com., 1985, vice-chairwoman western caucus, 1986-89; chmn. platform com. Wyo. Dem. Conv., 1982; mem. Wyo. Dept. Environ. Quality Land Quality Adv. Bd., 1983-86; mem. Gov.'s Steering Com. on Troubled Youth, 1982, dem. nat. com. Compliance Assistance Commn., 1986-87; exec. com. Assn. of State Dem. Chairs, 1989; mem. Wyo. Coun. on the Arts, 1989-95, chmn., 1994-95, Dem. Nat. Com. Jud. Coun., 1989—; legis. aide for Gov. Wyo., 1985, 86; project coord. Gov.'s Com. on Childrens' Svcs., 1985-86; bd. dirs. Wyo. Outdoor Coun., 1984-85; polit. dir., dep. mgr. Schuster for Congress, 1994-95; pres.' adv. com. on the performing arts John F. Kennedy Ctr. for the Performing Arts, 1999—. Recipient Woman of Yr. award Jackson Hole Bus. and Profl. Women, 1981, Dem. of Yr. Nellie Tayloe Ross award Wyo. Dems., 1990. Mem. Alden Kindred of Am., Jackson Hole Art Assn. (bd. dirs., vice chmn. 1981, chmn. 1982), Assn. State Dem. Chairs, Soc. Mayflower Descendents, Pi Sigma Alpha. Home: 8907 Cowpoke Rd Cheyenne WY 82009-1234

MOORE, MARY JULIA, educator; b. Pitts., Oct. 10, 1949; d. Edward Henry and Julia Ann (Polkabla) Sauer; 1 child, Jason Michael Sauer; m. John Harold Moore, Oct. 27, 1990; 1 adopted child, Jocelyn Quan. BS in Art Edn., Edinboro State Coll., 1971; MS in Spl. Edn., Clarion State Coll., 1980; postgrad, U. Pitts., 1988—. Cert. art tchr., spl. edn. tchr. for mentally retarded. Tchr. Polk (Pa.) State Sch. & Hosp., 1971-72; vol. VISTA, Bath, N.Y., 1972-73; tchr. Polk Ctr., 1973-80, program specialist, 1980-92; residential svc. supr., qualified mental retardation profl. Polk (Pa.) Ctr., 1992—; lectr., speaker, video on local TV on history of Polk Ctr., 1987. Patentee beer bottle shaped cake pan; cakes displayed in TV videos and in various mags.; creator history video Polk Ctr., Some Leaky Boot Statues, Polk Center--100 Years. Democrat. Roman Catholic. Avocations: cake decorating, reading, maintaining 5 rental houses. Home: RR 3 Box 232-ai Franklin PA 16323-9803

MOORE, MATTHEW SCOTT, publisher, deaf advocate, author; b. Indpls., Dec. 31, 1958; s. Scott Moore and JoNelle (Painter) Giegerich. BA in Social Work, Rochester Inst. Tech., 1983. Founder, pres. MSM Prodns., Ltd., Rochester, N.Y., 1984—; pub., co-editor-in-chief Deaf Life, Rochester, 1986—. Co-author: For Hearing People Only, 1992, Great Deaf Americans, 2nd edit., 1996; launched several websites; lectr., spkr. in field; conf. organizer. Founder Deaf Rochesterians' Cmty. Ctr. Core Team, 1992; chmn. Third N.Y. State Conf. for Sign-Lang. Instrs., Rochester, 1992; coord. Am. Sign-Lang. Tchrs. Assn. 1st Nat. Profl. Devel. Conf., Rochester, N.Y., 1999. Recipient Recognition cert. World Recreation Assn. of Deaf, 1990, Humanitarian award Delta Sigma Phi, 1991, Pres. award Am. Sign Lang. Tchrs. Assn. Lilac chpt., 1993, Outstanding Alumni award NTID, 1993, Tex. Deaf Caucus award, 1993, Alice Cogswell award Gallaudet U., 1994, Printing Week award, 1995, Disting. Alumni Modern Era award Ind. Sch. Deaf, 1997, Georgianna Elliott award Dallas Deaf Celebration, 1998. Avocations: writing, performing, theater, collecting birdhouses. Office: MSM Prodns Ltd PO Box 23380 Rochester NY 14692-3380

MOORE, MELANIE, sociology educator; b. Norfolk, Va., Mar. 23, 1960; d. James and Jane (Juengst) M. BA, Pa. State U., 1981; MA, U. Ga., 1983; PhD, U. Wash., 1991. Instr. U. Wash., Seattle, 1984-91; postdoctoral fellow Ind. U., Bloomington, 1991-93; assoc. prof. sociology U. No. Colo., Greeley, 1993—; mem. faculty rsch. and publs. bd., U. No. Colo., 1999—, chair acad. policies com., 1998-99, faculty senator, 1996-99, mem. exec. com., 1998-99. Contbr. Ency. Criminology, 2000; contbr. articles to profl. jours. Bd. mem. Boulder (Colo.) Pride, 1999—; cmty. resource connection Gay and Lesbian Ctr., Denver, 1998-99, support staff Denver Women's Chorus, 1994-97; domestic violence advocate Middle Way Ho., Bloomington, 1991-93. Mem. Am. Sociol. Assn. (membership com. 1986—), Nat. Women's Studies Assn., Am. Ednlo. Rsch. Assn. Democrat. Avocations: photography, running, writing, tennis. E-mail: mmoore@bentley.unco.edu. Office: U No Colo Dept Sociology Greeley CO 80639-0001

MOORE, MICHAEL KENNETH, international organization executive. Min. recreation and sport, tourism New Zealand, 1984-87, min. overseas trade, 1984-88, min. external rels. and trade, 1988-90, prime minister, 1990; leader of opposition, 1990-93; opposition spokesperson on fgn. affairs and overseas trade Govt. of New Zealand, 1993-99; dir. gen. World Trade Orgn., Geneva, Switzerland, 1999—. Author: On Balance, 1980, Beyond Today, 1981, A Pacific Environment, 1982, The Added Value of Economy, 1984, Hard Labour, 1987, Fighting for New Zealand, 1993. Office: WTO Director General, rue de Lausanne 154, Geneva 21 CH-1211, Switzerland

MOORE, MICHAEL WATSON, musician, educator; b. Cin., May 16, 1945; s. Clarence Watson and Jeannette Elizabeth (Gardner) M.; m. Renee Allyn White, Oct. 23, 1993; children: Benjamin Butler, Matthew Satyavan. Attended, Cin. Coll. Conservatory of Music, 1964-65. Bass instr. Summer Stage Bank Clinic, 1969, Eastman Sch. of Music, Rochester, N.Y., 1974-87, U. Bridgeport, Bridgeport, Conn., 1981-83, L.I. U., Bklyn., 1993-96, William Patterson U., Wayne, N.J., 1994-95. String bass player with Cal

Collins Trio, Cin., 1965, Woody Evans Trio, Cin., 1965, Woody Herman Band, USO, Africa, Ea. Europe, 1966-67, Marion McPartland Trio, N.Y.C., 1968, Freddie Hubbard Quintet, N.Y.C., 1969-70, Jack Wilkins Trio, N.Y.C., 1971, Chet Baker Quartet, N.Y.C., 1972-73, Phil Woods Quartet, N.Y.C., 1972, Gene Bertoncini Duo, N.Y.C., 1972—, Stan Getz Quartet, N.Y.C., 1973, Tony Bennett, N.Y.C., 1973, Ruby Braff, George Barnes Quartet, N.Y.C., 1973-75, Gerry Mulligan Quartet, N.Y.C., 1974, Benny Goodman Sextet, N.Y.C., 1974-76, Lee Konitz Quartet, N.Y.C., 1975, Teddy Wilson Duo, N.Y.C., 1977, Jim Hall Trio, N.Y.C., 1977, Bill Evans Trio, N.Y.C., 1978, Bob Brookmeyer Quintet, N.Y.C., 1978, Mike Abene, Michael Moore Quintet, N.Y.C., 1978, Zoot Sims Quartet, N.Y.C., 1979, Gary Burton Quartet, N.Y.C., 1981-82, Louis Belson Quartet, N.Y.C., 1982, Roger Kellaway Duo and Trio, N.Y.C., 1980s, Jimmy Rowles Duo, N.Y.C., 1980s, Jon Scoffield Duo and Quartet, N.Y.C., 1980s, Lew Tabackin Trio, N.Y.C., 1980s, Hank Jones Trio, N.Y.C., 1980s, Shelly Mann Trio, N.Y.C., 1980s, Pepper Adams Quartet, N.Y.C., 1980s, Lou Levy Duo, N.Y.C., 1980s, Al Cohen Trio, N.Y.C., 1980s, Jake Hanna Quartet, N.Y.C., 1980s, Rosemary Clooney, N.Y.C., 1987-88, Louis Stewart Trio, Ireland and U.K., 1990, Howard Alden Trio, N.Y.C., 1990s, Warren Vache Trio, N.Y.C., 1990s, Harry Allen Trio, N.Y.C., 1990s, Ken Peplowski Trio, N.Y.C., 1990s, Charlie Byrd Quartet, N.Y.C., 1990s; co-leader duo with Rufus Reid, 1995, with Chris Potter, 1995; leader duo with Bill Charlap, 1995; tour Japan with Harry Allen, 1997; leader trio with Ken Peplowski and Tom Melito, 1998-2000; composer: Rio Pindare, 1986, Wake Me When It's Over, 1988, The Lilter, 1989, The Old New Waltz, 1992, Zoot's Suite, 1995, Just Me, Just Me, 1995, When I Wage Battle Next, 1999, Moon Dog, 1999; recs. Michael Moore Trio Plays Gershwin, 1993, Michael Moore/Bill Charlap, 1995 (One of the Best Jazz CDs of 95, The New Yorker, 1996), Michael Moore/Rufus Reid Doublebass Delights, 1996 (One of the Best Jazz CDs of 96, The New Yorker, 1997), Michael Moore/Rufus Reid The Intimacy of the Bass, 1999, Michael Moore and His Trio The History of Jazz: Vol. 1, 2000, Video with Rufus Reid, 1998; author: Melodic Improvising in the Thumb Position: Method for Improvisation for the String Bass, 1986; performer: (with Weslia Whitfield) The White House, 1996. Councilman Borough of Bangor, Pa., 1987-88. Mem. ASCAP. Avocation: piano. Home and Office: 5 E 22d St Apt 15M New York NY 10010-5325

MOORE, NANCY FISCHER, elementary school educator; b. Milw., Nov. 26, 1937; d. Herbert Conrad and Erma Emma (Schroeder) Fischer; m. William Stang Moore (dec.). BS, U. Wis., Milw., 1958; MS, U. So. Calif., 1969; cert. in reading edn., U. Ga., 1973, cert. in gerontology edn., 1983, postgrad., 1982-91. Tchr. Grand Rapids (Mich.) Bd. Edn., 1958-61; tchr. U.S. Dept. Def. Overseas Schs., Nfld., Can., 1961-62, Bermuda, 1962-64, Japan, 1964-66; dir. handicapped day camp, tchr. 1st grade/trainable MR U.S. Dept. Def. Overseas Schs., Fed. Republic of Germany, 1966-70, Japan, 1970-71; classrm. tchr. Richmond County Bd. Edn., Augusta, Ga., 1971-95, tchr. remedial reading, 1973-77, 78-79, Title I resource tchr., 1977-78; pres. Cen. Savannah River Area Reading Coun., Augusta, 1977-78; instr. Art in the Elem. Sch. Workshop, Augusta, 1979-80; tchr. conversational English to architecture students, Japan, 1964-66, to co. employees, Japan, 1966; instr. Augusta State U., 1995-98; test adminstr. Human Resources Rsch. Orgn., 1999—. Active Ft. Gordon Retiree Coun., 1991—; vol. Ombudsman, Augusta, 1982-83, Shelter for Abused Children; vol. Retiree Svcs. Office, Ft. Gordon, 1998—, Augusta State U. Literacy Ctr. Named Vol. of the Month, Ft. Gordon, 2000. Mem. NEA, Ga. Assn. Educators, Richmond County Assn. Educators (pres. 1976-77, membership chairperson 1972-74, bldg. rep.), Richmond County Retired Educators Assn. (pres. 1998-99), Nat. Mil. Family Assn. (rep. for Ft. Gordon 1999—). Avocations: crafts, children's art activities and games, travel. Home: 2346 New Mcduffie Rd Augusta GA 30906-9026

MOORE, NICHOLAS DELAFON, pharmacologist, educator; b. N.Y.C., Nov. 25, 1953; s. Richard Henry and Beatrice (Delafon) M.; m. Michele Garrigues, Jan. 29, 1977; children: Matthias, Lucie, Alexandre. MD, Rouen (France) U., 1982, PhD, 1989. Intern Rouen U. Hosp., 1978-82, asst. pharmacology, 1982-86, assoc. prof., 1986-96; prof. Bordeaux (France) U. Hosp., 1996—; rep. France-ENS/CARE, WHO-EU, 1992-95, Demp program EU, 1994-95; v.p. Assn. Pharmacovig Ctr., France, 1989-96. Contbr. over 400 articles to profl. publs. Office: U Victor Segalen, Dept Pharmacology, 33076 Bordeaux 1, France

MOORE, OMAR KHAYYAM, experimental sociologist; b. Helper, Utah, Feb. 11, 1920; s. John Gustav and Mary Jo (Crowley) M.; m. Ruth Garnand, Nov. 19, 1942; 1 child, Venn. BA, Doane Coll., 1942; MA, Washington U., St. Louis, 1946, PhD, 1949. Instr. Washington U., St. Louis, 1949-52; teaching assoc. Northwestern U., Evanston, Ill., 1950-51; rsch. asst., prof. sociology Tufts Coll., Medford, Mass., 1952-53; researcher Naval Rsch. Lab., Washington, 1953-54; asst. prof. sociology Yale U., New Haven, 1954-57, assoc. prof. sociology, 1957-63; prof. psychology Rutgers U., New Brunswick, N.J., 1963-65; prof. social psychology, sociology U. Pitts., 1965-71, prof. sociology, 1971-89, prof. emeritus, 1989—; scholar-in-residence Nat. Learning Ctr.'s Capital Children's Mus., Washington, 1989-90; pres. Responsive Environ. Found., Inc., Estes Park, Colo., 1962—; assessor of rsch. projects The Social Scis. and Humanities Rsch. Coun. Can., 1982—; adj. prof. U. Colo., Boulder, 1992—. Contbg. editor Educational Technology; contbr. numerous articles to profl. jours.; patentee in field; motion picture producer and director. Recipient Award The Nat. Soc. for Programmed Instruction, 1965, Award Doane Coll Builder Award, 1967, Ednl. Award Urban Youth Action, Inc., 1969, Award House of Culture, 1975, Cert. of Appreciation, 1986, Cert. of Appreciation D.C. Pub. Schs., 1987, da Vinci Award Inst. for the Achievement of Human Potential, 1988, Cert. of Appreciation Capital Children's Museum, 1988, award Jack & Jill of America Found., 1988, Cert. of Appreciation U.S. Dept. of Edn., 1988, Cert. of Appreciation D.C. Pub. Schs., 1990, Person of Yr. in Ednl. Tech. award Ednl. Tech. mag., 1990. Mem. AAAS, Am. Math. Soc., Am. Psychol. Assn., Internat. Sociol. Assn., Am. Sociol. Assn., Assn. for Symbolic Logic, Assn. for Anthrop. Study of Play, Philosophy Sci. Assn., Psychonomics Soc., Soc. for Applied Sociology, Soc. for Exact Philosophy, Math. Assn. Am. Republican. Avocation: mountaineering. Home and Office: 2341 Upper High Dr PO Box 1673 Estes Park CO 80517-1673

MOORE, PATRICIA CHANDLER, hair stylist; b. Fair Lawn, N.J., Mar. 28, 1956; d. Edward and Billie (Mullins) Olko; m. Charles Thomas Atwater, Oct. 13, 1978 (dec. Feb. 1979); 1 child, John David Chandler Joseph Atwater; m. Jeffrey Edwin Moore, Dec. 29, 1984; 1 child, Rose Theresa Patricia. Cosmetology cert., Ctrl. Fla. Coll., 1980; massage/esitican/aromotherapy cert., Aveda Design Sch., 1989. Hair stylist Sergio Franco Corp., Beverly Hills, Calif., 1980—; personal asst., hair stylist N.J. Films, 1980—; hair designer, make-up Jack Nicholson, 1986—; wardrobe, P.A., massage, hair stylist Al Pacino, 1990—; P.A., hair stylist Danny DeVito, 1989—; hair stylist Dennis Miller HBO, 1998—; personal asst. Joe Pesci, 1998—, Robert DeNiro, 1998—; haistylist Counting Crows Band summer tour, 1998. Author: Rejuvenation of and for Life, 1990, Personal Wellness through Aromatherapy, Ancient Oils and Massage, 1998. Massage therapist, hair stylist Spouse Abuse Shelter, Ocala, 1995-98. Mem. Screen Actors Guild, Massage Therapist Assn., Cosmetologist Assn. Democrat. Roman Catholic. Avocations: working out, swimming, hydrotherapy, reading, movies. Home and Office: PO Box 1420 Dunnellon FL 34430-1420

MOORE, PETER DAVID, finance director, accountant; b. Southport, Lancashire, Eng., June 5, 1945; s. Frederich Cecil and Joan Lambert (Wilkham) M.; m. Susan Janet Ure, Apr. 1973; children: Philippa Jane, Stepen David. Articled clk. Grant Thornton, Liverpool, Eng., 1963-69; audit sr. Arthur Andersen, London, 1969-72; Sterling money dealer Bankers Trust Co., London, 1972-73; acct. Martin Brokers Group Ltd., London, 1973—; co. sec. Martin Bierbaum Group Ltd., London; fin. dir. Trio Holdings Plc, London, 1996—. Mem. Inst. Chartered Accts. in Eng. and Wales. Avocations: sports, theatre.

MOORE, PHILIP JOHN, organist, artistic director, conductor, composer; b. London, Sept. 30, 1943; s. Cecil and Marjorie (Brewer) M.; divorced; children: Sophie, Bianca, Thomas. BMus, Durham U. Music master Eton Coll., 1966-68; asst. organist Canterbury Cathedral, 1968-74; organist, master of the choristers Guildford Cathedral, 1974-82; organist, master of music York Minster, 1983—. Fellow Royal Coll. Music, Royal Coll. Organists. Anglican. Home: 1 Minster Ct, York YO1 7JJ, England

MOORE, RAY, endocrinologist; b. Whitehaven, Cumbria, Eng., Dec. 21, 1947; arrived in South Africa, 1981; s. George and Nora (Kelley) M.; m. Ann Dorothy Clark, May 22, 1971; children: Claire Elizabeth, James Nicholas. MB BS, U. London, 1971. House physician St. Mary's Hosp., London, 1971; house surgeon King Edward VIII Hosp., Windsor, Eng., 1972; sr. house officer St. Peter's Hosp., Chertsey, Eng., 1972-73; med. registrar St. Peter's Hosp., Chertsey, 1973-75, St. George's Hosp., London, 1973-75; sr. med. registrar, sr. lectr. Addenbrookes Hosp., Cambridge, Eng., 1975-81; dir. endocrine unit King Edward VIII Hosp., Durban, South Africa, 1981-83; pvt. practice specialist endocrinologist, diabetologist Durban, 1983—; pres. Soc. for Diabetes, Endocrinology & Diabetes of So. Africa, 1992-94. Mem. Royal Coll. Physicians, Natal Philatelic Soc. (pres. 1996-97). Avocations: philately, photography, collecting and tasting red wine. Home: 6 Cheswold Close, Country Club 2 PO Box 2023, Country Club 4301, South Africa Office: Umhlanga Hosp, K2N Umhlonga Rocks South Africa

MOORE, RICHARD CARROLL, JR., family physician; b. Balt., Nov. 24, 1946; s. Richard Carroll and Virginia Mae (Clark) M.; m. Jeremy Pierson, Jan. 27, 1973; children: Peter Gregory, Laura Alexandra. BA, Johns Hopkins U., 1968, MPH, 1981; MD, UCLA, 1972. Diplomate Am. Bd. Family Practice. Intern South Balt. Gen. Hosp., 1972-73; commd. med. officer USPHS, 1976, ret., 1997; chief med. div. USCG Aviation Tng. Ctr., Mobile, Ala., 1976-80; chief med. ops. USCG, Washington, 1981-86; sr. med. officer USCG Yard, Curtis Bay, Md., 1986-88; dir. Health Unit # 1, USPHS, 1988-97; staff physician Piedmont Prime Care, Danville, Va., 1997-98; med. dir. Carilion Occupl. Medicin, Roanoke-Salem Ctr., 1999—; clin. asst. prof. family medicine U. Va., 1999—; mem. exec. bd. Emergency Med. Svcs. Coun., Mobile County, 1979, Med. and Chirurg. Faculty Md. Mem. editl. bd. MD Med. Jour., 1995-97. Bd. dirs. Midway Fed. Credit Union, 1989-96, pres., 1991-96. With USN, 1973-76. Mem. Aerospace Med. Assn., So. Med. Assn, Soc. U.S. Naval Flight Surgeons, Johns Hopkins U. Alumni Assn., Commd. Officers Assn. USPHS, UCLA Alumni Assn., Alpha Omega Alpha, Sigma Phi Epsilon. Republican. Home: 100 Kimball Ave Apt C27 Salem VA 24153-6718 Office: Carilion Occupational Medicine 1314 Peters Creek Rd NW Roanoke VA 24017-2500

MOORE, RICHARD LAWRENCE, structural engineer, consultant; b. Rocky Ford, Colo., Feb. 7, 1934; s. Lawrence and Margaret Kathryn (Bolling) M.; m. Donna St. Clair, Mar. 26, 1972 (div. 1983); 1 child, Andrew Trousdale; m. Margaret Ann Guthrie, May 4, 1984. BSCE, U. Colo., 1957; MS, Princeton U., 1963; PhD, Calif. Western U., Santa Ana, 1975. Registered profl. engr., Mass., Maine, Colo., Pa., Iowa, Nebr., N.Mex., Wyo., Ill., Ark., Mo., N.D., Mich., Okla., Mont. Structural engr. Cameron Engrs., Denver, 1964-66; v.p. Moore Internat., Jeddah, Saudi Arabia, 1967-78; asst. to pres. C.H. Guernsey Co., Oklahoma City, 1979-82; pres. R.L. Moore Co., Boston, 1983—; v.p., dir. Isolink Ing., Basel, Switzerland, 1990—; nat. chmn. Roof Cons. Inst., Raleigh, N.C., 1988-92; prof. Episcopal Sch. Theology, Denver, 1967-71. Patentee in field. Member Mound City (Mo.) Libr. Bd., 1963-64; pres. Dist. Rep. Party, Boston, 1988—; sr. warden St. John Chrysostom Epis. Ch., Denver, 1966-71. Danforth Found. scholar, 1962. Mem. ASCE, NSPE, Am. Concrete Inst., Nat. Forensic Ctr. Avocations: golf, travel, antique pocket watch collecting. Home and Office: RL Moore Co 534 E Broadway Boston MA 02127-4407

MOORE, RICHARD THOMAS, state legislator; b. Milford, Mass., Aug. 7, 1943; s. Thomas James and Helen Eliza (Andrew) M.; m. Joanne Bednarz, May 26, 1979. BA in History, Clark U., 1966; MA in Student Pers., Colgate U., 1967; postgrad., Clark U., 1967-70, U. Mass., 1981-85. Cert. tchr. secondary level social studies. Assoc. dean students Assumption Coll., Worcester, Mass., 1967-69; asst. to pres. Bentley Coll., Waltham, Mass., 1969-77; mem. Mass. Ho. of Reps., Boston, 1977-94; assoc. dir. mitigation Fed. Emergency Mgmt. Agy., Washington, 1994-96; senator Mass. Senate, Boston, 1996—, chmn. senate com. on pub. svc., 1997-98, chmn. senate com. healthcare, 1999—; pres. Mass. Selectmen's Assn., Boston, 1975-76; chmn. House Com. on Election Laws, Boston, 1992-94, House Com. on Taxation, Boston, 1983-85, House Com. on State Adminstrn., Boston, 1983. Chmn. Blackstone Nat. Heritage Corridor Commn., Uxbridge, Mass., 1988-90; presdl. elector Mass. Electoral Coll., Boston, 1992; chmn. Mass. Dem. Leadership Coun., Boston, 1990-93; bd. trustee Nichols Coll., 1997—. Named Outstanding Legislator Mass. Town Clks. Assn., Boston, 1993, New Dem. of Yr. Mass. Dem. Leadership Coun., Boston, 1994; recipient Disting. Svc. award Fed. Emergency Mgmt. Agy., 1996. Mem. ASPA (bd. dirs. Mass. chpt. 1981-85, chpt. v.p. 1999-2000, pres.-elect 2000—, Disting. Pub. Adminstrn. award 1997, Coun. State Govt.'s 2000 Toll fellow), Nat. Emergency Mgmt. Assn. Roman Catholic. Avocations: politics, collecting political items. Office: State House Rm 312D Boston MA 02133

MOORE, ROBERT HENRY, insurance company executive; b. Madisonville, Ky., Sept. 16, 1940; s. William Lee Moore and Robbie (Pritchett) Ruby; m. Diana Churchill, Aug. 17, 1963 (div. 1978); children: Randall Lee, Robin Churchill; m. Patricia Mary George, Oct. 4, 1981; 1 child, Christopher Robert. BA, Davidson (N.C.) Coll., 1962; MA, U. N.C., 1964; PhD, U. Wis., 1972. Asst. dir. admissions Davidson Coll., 1963-64; teaching asst. U. Wis., Madison, 1965-68; staff and faculty U.S. Mil. Acad., West Point, N.Y., 1968-70; lectr., asst. prof. U. Md., College Park, 1970-76, assoc. prof., 1976; cons. U.S. Congress, Washington, 1976-77; emerging issues coordinator The Conf. Bd., N.Y.C., 1977-79; dir. govt. relations Benefacts, Inc., Washington, 1977-78; v.p. Alexander & Alexander, Inc., Washington, 1978-81; v.p. Alexander & Alexander Svcs. Inc., N.Y.C., Washington, 1981-85, sr. v.p. corp. rels., 1985-95, sr. v.p. (inactive), 1995-97; chmn., pres. A & A Govt. and Industry Affairs Inc., Washington, 1990-94, Aon Corp., Vienna, Va., 1997—; del. Nat. Security Affairs Conf., Washington, 1978-82; mem. adv. bd. Career Opportunities Inst., U. Va., Charlottesville, 1982-86, Ctr. for New Am. Work Force, 1992-96; mem. corp. adv. bd. Queens Coll., CUNY, 1985-96; mem. V.P.'s Forum, 1989-94; mem. coun. Conf. Bd. Corp. Comm. Execs., 1990-94; mem. Pub. Rels. Sem., 1993-97; editl. advisor Ctr. for Mind-Body Medicine, Washington, 1998-2000; adv. coun. Mindfulness Practice Ctr. of Fairfax, 1998—; lectr. Shepherd's Ctr., 1999—; bd. visitors Dictionary of Am. Regional English, 1999—. Co-author: (with others) School for Soldiers: West Point and the Profession of Arms, 1974 (NYT award 1974); contbr. articles to profl. jours.; contbr. interviews to nat. mags., newspapers, radio and TV. Mem. kitchen cabinet Points of Light Found., 1991-95. With U.S. Army, 1968-70, capt. USAR, 1970-72. Ops. Crossroads Africa fellow, 1960; U. Md. rsch. grantee, 1972, 76. Mem. Nat. Assn. Ins. Brokers (exec. com., bd. dirs., pres. 1985-86, chmn. past presidents adv. coun. 1989-93).

MOORE, RODNEY GREGORY, lawyer; b. Birmingham, Ala., Sept. 1, 1960; s. Jethroe and Tommie (Feagin) M.; m. Yalsyn Moore; children: Nyosha, Rodney II, Imari. BA, U. Wash., 1982; JD, Santa Clara (Calif.) U., 1985. Bar: Calif. 1987, Ga. Concert promoter Clanagan & Moore/Class "A", Seattle and San Jose, Calif., 1984-87; ptnr. Williams, Robinson & Moore, San Jose, 1987-89; prin. Moore Law Firm, San Jose, 1989-97; gen. counsel East Side Union H.S. Dist., San Jose, 1997-2000, Atlanta Pub. Schs., 2000—; disc jockey Sta. KCMU, Seattle, 1980-82; gen. counsel Roy Ayers Ubiquity, 1994—; assoc. prof. contract law Lincoln Law Sch., 1992-94. Assoc. editor S.C. U. Computer Law Jour., 1984-85. Mem. sch. bd. East Side Union High Sch. Dist. S.C. U. scholar, 1982-85. Mem. Nat. Bar Assn. (chpt. pres. 1989, gen. counsel 1997-99), S.C. County Bar Assn. (trustee 1990), Assn. Trial Lawyers Am., N.Y. Sports and Entertainment Soc., S.C. County Black Lawyers Assn. (pres. San Jose chpt. 1989-90), Calif. Assn. Black Lawyers (pres. 1993-94, Loren Miller Atty. of Yr., 1997), Calif. Sch. Lawyers Assn., Ga. Sch. Lawyers Assn., Nat. Alliance Black Sch. Educators, Nat. Coun. Sch. Attys. Office: 210 Pryor St SW Atlanta GA 30303-3624

MOORE, RUTH LAMBERT BROMBERG, retired clinical psychologist; b. Lowell, Mass., Jan. 17, 1913; d. John Henry and Mabel F. (Forrest) Lambert; m. Georg Bromberg (dec.); children: Susan Lambert, Peter deForest, Jane Parker, Keith Emmons; m. Richard Warren Moore (dec.). BA, Conn. Coll., 1935; MA in Psychology, Boston U., 1938; postgrad., Chgo. Inst. Psychoanalysis, Boston U. Diplomate (emeritus) Am. Bd. Profl. Psychology. Clin. psychologist, rsch. asst. Commonwealth of Mass., Boston, 1935-39; psychology intern U. Ill. Med. Sch., Chgo., 1939-41; clin. psychologist, instr. U. Chgo. Med. Sch., 1941-51; chief psychology (joint appointments psychiatry/pediat.) U. Ill. Med. Sch. Neuropsychiatric Inst., Chgo., 1945-52; assoc. prof. Northwestern Med. Sch., Chgo., 1955-72; pvt. practice, Ill., 1952-72, Mass., 1972-93; examiner Am. Bd. Profl. Psychology, Chgo., 1956-72. Bd. dirs. Highland Park Family Svc.; pres., bd. dirs. Lake Forest-Lake Bluff Family Svcs. Rsch. fellow Chgo. Inst. Psychoanalysis. Mem. APA, Mass. Psychol. Assn., Charles Menninger Soc. Episcopalian. Avocations: music, art appreciation, archeology.

MOORE, SANDY, architect, environmental designer, urban strategist; b. Charleston, S.C., June 30, 1945. BA in Architecture, Tuskegee Inst., 1967; M in Environ. Design, Yale U., 1973; PhD, Harvard U., 1982. Architect Clauss and Nolan, Architects, Planners, Trenton, N.J., 1968-72; founder, exec. dir. Trenton Design Ctr., 1970-73; asst. prof. Schs. Architecture and Edn., U. Wis.-Milw., 1973-75; dir. ctrs. for environ. edn. Edn. Devel. Ctr., Cambridge, Mass., 1975-76; asst. prof. environ. design Mass. Coll. Art, Boston, 1975-76; assoc. Alexander Cooper & Assocs., N.Y.C., 1976; adminstr. Dept. Housing Preservation and Devel., N.Y.C., 1978-79; asst. prof., asst. dean Sch. Architecture, Fla. A&M U., Tallahassee, 1979-82; assoc. prof., assoc. dean Sch. Architecture, N.J. Inst. Tech., Newark, 1982-83, assoc. prof., 1983—; chmn. housing task force mayoral transition team City of Newark, 1986-87; community advisor, Newark, 1987—. Co-editor Many Faces of Architecture, 1988; prodr. video documentary "Work-in-Progress", Black Women in Architecture: A Sense of Place, 1992. Mem. policy panels Nat. Endowment for Arts, Nat. League Cities; cons. design arts program N.J. State Council on the Arts, 1987—; mem. Nat. Def. Exec; mem. architecture adv. commn. Mercer County Community Coll., 1987—; mem. community reinvestment act adv. bd. Midlantic Nat. Bank, Edison, N.J., 1987—. Recipient Pub. and Inst. Svc. award N.J. Inst. Tech., 1989; named Alumnus of Yr. Tuskegee U. Dept. Architecture, 1987; Nat. Endowment Arts fellow, 1984, 85. Mem. N.J. Soc. Architects (bd. dirs., citation award 1983).

MOORE, TIMOTHY MICHAEL, physiologist; b. Wiesbaden, Germany, Oct. 17, 1968; (parents Am. citizens); s. Terry Michael and Judith Manning Moore; m. LaDonna Latham, July 13, 1991; children: Abigail Fallin, Ashley Carolyn, Austin Michael. BS in Zoology, Auburn U., 1991; PhD in Basic Med. Sci., U. S. Ala., 1996, postgrad. Rsch. fellow Am. Heart Assn., Mobile, Ala., 1996-99; rsch. assoc. U. S. Ala., Mobile, 1999—. Peer reviewer Clin. Sci., Inflammation, Am. Jour. Physiology; contbr. articles to profl. jours. Recipient Proctor & Gamble award Am. Physiol. Soc., 1995. Mem. Student sect. AMA, Am. Thoracic Soc., Am. Heart Assn. (mem. caripulmonary coun. 1998—, Rsch. fellow 1997-99), Am. Fedn. Med. Rsch. (Henry Christian award 1999). Republican. Baptist. Office: U S Ala Coll Medicine MSB 3024 307 University Blvd N Mobile AL 36688-3053

MOORE, WILLIAM BLACK, JR., retired aluminum company executive; b. Jackson, Miss., Sept. 18, 1924; s. William Black and May Isom (Whitten) M.; m. Lillian Wells, Sept. 14, 1946; children: Kathryn Ramsey Moore Dannels, William Black III, Bethany Moore Richmond. BSChemE, U. Louisville, 1945, MSChemE, 1947. Registered profl. engr., Ky. Chem. engr. U. Louisville Rsch. Inst., 1947-49; mktg. mgr. Reynolds Metals, Louisville, 1949-58; dir. mktg. Reynolds Metals, Richmond, Va., 1958-61; regional gen. mgr. Reynolds Metals, St. Louis, 1961-69; v.p. Reynolds Metals, Richmond, 1969-80; ret.; mem. adv. bd. Bay Trust Co. Author: Letters to Rebecca; contbr. articles to profl. jours. Pres. bd. dirs. Rappahannock Found.; pres. Laguiapoe Found.; dir. adv. bd. Bay Trust Co., Kilmarnock, Va. Serves to lt. USNR, 1943-47. Mem. AIA (hon.), Indian Creek Club (Kilmarnock, Va.), Country Club of Va. (Richmond). Baptist. Avocations: fishing, farming, genealogy. Home: PO Box 1300 Kilmarnock VA 22482-1300

MOORE, WILLIAM CULLEN, retired electronics company executive; b. Portland, Oreg., Nov. 17, 1912; s. William Cullen and Lillian (Rodé) M.; m. Helen Hays Edgar, Aug. 8, 1936; children: Shirley Carol, Ronald Cullen, Paul Alan, Katherine Leone. BA in Physics, Reed Coll., Portland, 1936; MA in Physics, Boston U., 1949. Electronics engr. United Airlines, Chgo., 1937-38; project leader Motorola, Inc., Chgo., 1938-47; sect. head govt. electronics group Motorola, Inc., Scottsdale, Ariz., 1958-78; ret.; project supr./instr. Upper Air Lab., Boston U., 1947-51; chief engr. Tracerlab, Inc., Boston, 1951-53; engring. mgr. Boonton (N.J.) Radio Corp., 1953-58; cons./facilitator (space) Motorola Mus. of Electronics, Schaumburg, Ill., 1987-90; investigator Apollo comms. NASA, Madrid, Spain, 1971. Contbr. articles to profl. jours. Mem. sch. bd. Lombard (Ill.) Sch. Dist., 1946-47, Mountain Lakes (N.J.) Sch. Dist., 1956-58; mem. allocations panels United Way, 1977-94. Fellow AIAA (assoc.; sect. chair 1963-64); mem. IEEE (sr.; sect. chair 1940—). Achievements include patents on coupling transformer; coded range signal responsive system (aviation); low level bridge discriminator; transponder for moving vehicle tracking system (space). Home: 10015 W Royal Oak Rd Apt 346 Sun City AZ 85351-6100

MOORE, WILLIAM GROVER, JR., management consultant, former air freight executive, former air force officer; b. Waco, Tex., May 18; s. William Grover and Annie Elizabeth (Pickens) M.; student Kilgore (Tex.) Coll., 1937-39, Sacramento State Coll., 1951, George Washington U., 1962; grad. Air War Coll., Air U., 1957, Nat. War Coll., 1962; m. Marjorie Y. Gardella, Jan. 18, 1943; 1 dau., Allyson. Enlisted U.S. Army Air Force, 1940, commd. 2d lt., 1941, advanced through grades to gen., 1977; comdr. 777th Squadron, 15th AF, Italy, 1944-45, 3535th Maintenance and Supply Group, Mather AFB, Calif., 1951, 3d Bomb Group, Korea, 1952; chief bases and units div. Hdqrs. USAF, 1952-56; asst. dep. chief of staff ops. Hdqrs. USAF Europe, 1957-61; comdr. 314th Troop Carrier Wing, Sewart AFB, Tenn., 1962-63, 839th Air Div., 1963-65; asst. J3 U.S. Strike Command, 1965-66; comdr. 834th Air Div., Vietnam, 1966-67; dir. operational requirements Hdqrs. USAF, 1967-70; comdr. 22d AF, 1970-73, 13th AF, 1973; chief of staff Pacific Command, 1973-76; asst. vice chief of staff Hdqrs. USAF, 1976-77; comdr. in chief Mil. Air Lift Command, 1977-79; ret., 1979; pres., chief operating officer Emery Air Freight Corp., Wilton, Conn., 1981-83; bus. cons., 1983—; pres. Met. Nashville Airport Authority, 1984—. Decorated Def. D.S.M., Air Force D.S.M. with 2 oak leaf clusters, Legion of Merit with 4 oak leaf clusters, Silver Star, D.F.C. with oak leaf cluster, Air medal with 9 oak leaf clusters, AF Commendation medal with 10 oak leaf clusters (U.S.); Croix de Guerre with palm (France); Armed Forces Honor medal 1st class (Vietnam); Republic of China Cloud and Banner; Legion of Honor (Republic of Philippines); recipient L. Mendel Rivers award of excellence; Jimmy Doolittle fellow in aerospace edn., 1978; named to Minuteman Hall of Fame, 1979. Mem. Air Force Assn., Nat. Def. Transp. Assn., Am. Ordnance Assn. Home: 932 W Main St Franklin TN 37064-2730 Office: Nashville Internat Airport 1 Terminal Dr Ste 501 Nashville TN 37214-4110

MOORE, WISTAR, cardiovascular surgeon; b. Feb. 16, 1959. BA, U. N.C., 1981, MD, 1985. Bd. cert. gen. surgery, thoracic surgery. Gen. surgery resident Mass. Gen. Hosp., 1985-90; cardiothoracic resident The Emory Clinic, 1990-93; cardiovasc. surgeon Watson Clinic, Lakeland, Fla., 1993-2000; chief divsn. cardiovasc. thoracic surgery Lakeland Regional Med. Ctr., 1996-2000; cardiovasc. surgeon Cardiovasc. Surgeons, Orlando, Fla., 2000—. Fellow ACS, Am. Coll. Chest Physicians; mem. Fla. Soc. Thoracic and Cardiovasc. Surgeons, So. Thoracic Surg. Assn., Soc. Thoracic Surgeons. Office: 217 Hillcrest St Orlando FL 32801-1211

MOORE, WOODVALL RAY, librarian; b. Flatwoods, Ky., May 19, 1942; s. Clyde Raymond and Erma (Gallion) M.; m. Sarah Ellen Markham, Dec. 14, 1963; children: Tamra Sheri Harris, Woodvall Allen. AA, So. Bible Coll., Houston, 1963, BS, 1965; MSLS, U. Ky., 1972. Ordained to ministry Assemblies of God Ch., 1969. Dir. libr. So. Bible Coll., 1968-76; dir. libr. svcs. Evangel Coll., Springfield, Mo., 1976—; past pres. adv. coun. Southwestern Mo. Libr. Network; chaplain Greene County Sheriff Dept.; past presenter Assemblies of God Marriage Encounter Inc. Precinct chmn. Rep. Party, Houston, 1972-76; bd. dirs. Orion/Internet Sys., 1994—. Mem. ALA, Mo. Libr. Assn. (computer and info. tech. com.), Assn. Christian Librs. (bd. dirs. 1979—, pres. 1983-84, dir. pub. rels. 1988-92, conf. dir. 1995—), Springfield Librs. Assn. Republican. E-mail: woodie@mail.orion.org. Office: 1111 N Glenstone Ave Springfield MO 65802-2125*

MOORES, PETER, retired banker; b. Formby near Liverpool, Lancashire, Eng., Apr. 9, 1932; s. John and Ruby (Knowles) M.; m. Luciana Pinto, Feb. 27, 1960 (div. 1982); children: Donatella, Alexis. Student, Oxford U., 1952-54; MA, Christ Ch. - Oxford, 1975. Dir. The Littlewoods Orgn., Liverpool, Eng., 1957-93, Singer & Friedlander, London, 1972-92. Trustee Tate Gallery, London, 1978-85; gov. Brit. Broadcasting Corp., London, 1982-83; founder Peter Moores Found. Decorated medaglia d'oro (Italy); comdr. Brit. Empire.

MOORHEAD, JOHN ANTHONY, historian; b. Grafton, Australia, Dec. 7, 1948; s. John Irvine and Pauline Evelyn (Taylor) M. BA, U. New England, Armidale, Australia, 1971; PhD, U. Liverpool, England, 1974. Tutor history U. Tasmania, Hobart, Australia, 1975-76; lectr. history U. Queensland, Brisbane, Australia, 1976-82, sr. lectr. history, 1983-93, reader history, 1994-99, prof. history, 2000—. Author: History of the Vandal Persecution, 1992, Theoderic in Italy, 1992, Justinian, 1994, Ambrose, 1999; co-author: Suger's Deeds of Louis the Fat, 1992. Fellow Royal Hist. Soc.; mem. Clare Hall (life). Avocations: travel, vegetarian food. Office: U Queensland, Dept History, Saint Lucia 4072, Australia

MOORHEAD, ROLANDE ANNETTE REVERDY, artist, educator; b. Périgueux, France; d. RémyJean and Andrée Marcelle (Lavollée) Reverdy; m. Elliott Swift Moorhead, III, Sept. 30, 1960; children: Edward Marc, Roland Elliott, Rémy Bruce. Liberal arts degree, Coll. Technique, Nice, France, 1954. Bi-lingual sec. France, 1957-58, French Embassy, Washington, 1959-60, 68-70; chmn. exhibit com. Lauderdale-By-The-Sea Art Guild, Ft. Lauderdale, Fla., 1972-75, v.p., 1972-74, founder group 5 women artists; mem. exhibit com. Broward Art Guild, Ft. Lauderdale, Fla., 1976; treas., dir. Alliance Francaise, Miami, Fla., 1973-75; juror, lectr. in field; invited guest artist Franco-Am. Art Show, Ceremonte, France, 1996, 97. One-woman shows include numerous banks, Ft. Lauderdale area, 1971—, Ocean Club Art Gallery, Ft. Lauderdale, 1971-74, Pier 65 Gallery, Ft. Lauderdale, 1973, 75, 76, Ft. Lauderdale City Hall, 1974, 77-78, 81-88, 91-94, St. Basil Orthodox Ch., North Miami Beach, 1977, Galerie Vallombreuse, Biarritz, France, 1977, Gallerie du Palais des Fêtes, Périgueux, 1978, 88, Le Club Internat., Ft. Lauderdale, 1979, Leonard Gallery, Ft. Lauderdale, 1990-92, Tallahassee (Fla.) Capitol Bldg., 1990, Lighthouse Pt. (Fla.) Gallery, 1990, Hollywood (Fla.) Art and Cultural Ctr., 1987, 89, 90, 91, 93, 95, Ft. Lauderdale Arts Inst., 1991, 93-95, Dover Gallery, Boca Raton, Fla., 1992; exhibited in group shows: Broward Art Guild, 1971, 73, 74, Point of Am. Gallery, Ft. Lauderdale, 1971, 73, Internat. Festival, Miami, 1976, Internat. Salon, Biarritz, 1977, Internat. Summer Salon, Paris, 1977, Fine Art Gallery Show and Competition, Long Galleries, Ft. Lauderdale, 1979, Pembroke Pines (Fla.) City Hall, 1982, Hollywood City Libr., 1982, also area banks, chs. and librs., numerous local art festivals, Schacknow Mus. Plantation, Fla., 2000; represented in permanent collections: Fr. Lauderdale City Hall, DAV Hdqrs., Washington, Associated Aircraft Co., March of Dimes Bldg. (both Ft. Lauderdale), Oakland Park Libr., Fla., St. Josephs Convent, St. Augustine, Fla., U.S. Air Force Mus., Ohio, Main Line Fleets, Inc., Palm Beach, Fla., Creditreform, Dusseldorf, Germany, St. Front Cathedral, Périgueux, St. Sacerdoce, Sarlat, France, Club Med, Fla. and Caribbean, also numerous pvt. collections U.S. and Europe; author art manual for Broward Arts Coun., Fla., 1986. Recipient Best in Show award Internat. Salon, Biarritz, 1977; named artist in residence Broward County Sch., 1985. Mem. Am. Soc. Portrait Artists, Nat. Assn. Women Artists, Fla. Watercolor Soc., Palm Beach Watercolor Soc., Nat. League Am. Penwomen, Art 24, Périgueux, Internat. Soc. Marine Painters, Am. Watercolor Soc., Nat. Mus. Women in Arts, Nat. Mus. Am. Indian, Gold Coast Water Color Soc. (pres. 1984-87), 2 The Artist's Orgn., Union des Francais de l'Etranger. Office: PO Box 8692 Fort Lauderdale FL 33310-8692

MOORING, F. PAUL, physics editor; b. Pitt County, N.C., Feb. 6, 1921; s. Benjamin Arthur and Amanda Elizabeth (Congleton) M.; m. Jean Louise Carpenter, Aug. 28, 1948; children: Cecily Hamm, Carol Larson, Margaret. BA, Duke U., 1944; PhD, U. Wis., 1951. Instr. Duke U., Durham, N.C., 1943-46; teaching asst. U. Wis., Madison, 1946-50, rsch. asst., 1950-51; physicist Argonne (Ill.) Nat. Lab., 1951-83; editor, cons. Am. Inst. Physics, Argonne, 1983—; adj. prof. St. Louis U., 1966-83. Contbr. articles to profl. jours. Pres. The Ill. Prairie Path, Wheaton, Ill., 1971-93, Ill. Audubon Soc., Wayne, Ill., 1978-81. Fulbright Rsch. fellow U. Helsinki, 1962-63. Mem. AAAS, Am. Phys. Soc. Democrat. Home: 295 Abbotsford Ct Glen Ellyn IL 60137-4803

MOORO, HISHAM A.W., surgeon, educator; b. Cairo, Egypt, Sept. 16, 1930; s. Abdel-Wahab and Fatheya A. (Abdel-Khalek) M.; m. Fatima M. Sobhy, Jan. 16, 1955; children: Abdel-Wahab, Tarek. MB BCh, Cairo U., 1954, diploma of surgery, 1957, MCh, 1958. Prof. surgery Cairo U. Hosp., 1972—, house officer, 1955-56, surgical registrar, 1955-56, clin. demonstrator of surgery, 1956-58, lectr. surgery, asst. prof. surg.

MOOSA, ALLIE, pediatrics and pediatric neurology educator; b. Cape Town, South Africa, Nov. 23, 1939; s. Adam and Bibi Moosa; m. Mymoona Ederies, Feb. 7, 1965; children: Muhammed Irshad, Muhammed Shiraz, Tasnim. MB, BChir, U. Cape Town, 1963; MD, U. Sheffield, Eng., 1971. Rsch. fellow U. Sheffield, 1968-71; lectr. U. London, 1972-76; sr. lectr. U. Cape Town, 1976-78; prof., head dept. pediat. U. Natal, Durban, South Africa, 1978-88; prof., head dept. pediat. U. Kuwait, 1989-99, prof., 1999—; cons. neonatalogist Somerset Hosp., Cape Town, 1976-78; cons. pediatrician King Edward VIII Hosp., Durban, 1978-88; cons. neurologist Mubarak Al Kabir Hosp., Kuwait, 1989—; vis. prof. U. London, 1986, 98. contbr. chpts. to books and articles to profl. jours. Active Shawco Student Coun., Cape Town, 1961-64, Cmty. Rsch. Unit, 1982-88; chmn. Health Workers Orgn., Durban, 1982-88; pres. Islamic Med. Assn., South Africa, 1985-88. Entrance scholar U. Cape Town, 1958, Morris Mauberger scholar U. Cape Town, 1961-63. Fellow Am. Acad. Pediat., Royal Coll. Pediat. and Child Health, Royal Coll. Physicians. Islam. Avocations: reading, politics, social welfare, education.

MOOY, ADRIANUS, bank executive; b. 1936. MSc, U. Wis., 1960, PhD in Econs., 1966. Mem. rsch. staff Nat. Econ. Rsch. Inst., 1956-67; asst. lectr. faculty econs. Gajah Mada U., Yogyakarta, 1958-59, lectr., 1965-66; lectr. faculty econs. U. Indonesia, Jakarta, 1966-69; mem. staff Min. Econ., Fin. and Devel. Affairs, 1967; head bur. domestic financing Nat. Devel. Planning Agy., 1968-69; econ. ofcl. UN-ECAFE, Bangkok, 1969-73; dep. chmn. fiscal and monetary affairs Nat. Devel. Planning Agy., 1973-88; asst. Coordinating Min. Econ., Fin. and Indsl. Affairs in Monetary Affairs, 1978-83, State Min. Nat. Devel. Planning in Devel. Financing, 1985-88; prof. U. Indonesia, 1987—; gov. Bank Indonesia, 1988-99; exec. sec. Econ. and Social Commn. for Asia and Pacific, Bangkok; mem. Com. 11, 1982, Com. 9, 1987; exec. sec. Monetary Coun., 1983-88; mem. working com. People's Consultative Assembly, 1987—. Office: United Nations Bldg, Rajadamnern Ave, Bangkok 10200, Thailand*

MORA, JUAN CARLOS, telecommunications planning engineer; b. Palmira, Valle, Colombia, July 5, 1965; s. German and Celmira (Nakamura) M.; m. Ada Carmenza Yascual, Dec. 2, 1989. Electronics Engr. with hons., U. del Cauca, Popayan Cauca, 1989, telecomm. specialist, 1989, internat. econ. specialist, 1998. Instr. in computer Univ. Cauca, Popayan Cauca, 1988; software engr. Fujitsu Ltd., Medellin, Antioquia, 1989-94; planning specialist Empresa Publicas de Medellin, Medellin, 1995—, bus. specialist, 1998—. Mem. IEEE, Cooperative Medica del Valle (assoc.). Avocations: swimming, dancing, jogging, investigation. Home: Carrera 25A 40-28, Medellin Antioqia, Colombia Office: Empresas Publicas Medellin, Carrera 58 42-125, Medellin Colombia

MORA, PHILIPPE, screenwriter, producer, director, painter; b. Paris, Aug. 8, 1949; s. Georges and Mirka Madeleine (Zelik) M.; m. Pamela Mai Krause, Aug. 1, 1980; children: Madeleine Mai, Georges Ritchie Maximillian, Dominic Marceau. Student, La Trobe U., Melbourne, Australia, 1967. Screenwriter, dir., producer, 1969—; founder Cinema Papers mag., Melbourne, 1967. Dir., writer, prodr. (films) Trouble in Molopolis, 1969, The Howling III: The Marsupials, 1987, Snide and Prejudice, 1997, According to Occam's Razor, 1999; co-writer (film) Double Headed Eagle, 1971; dir., writer: (films) Swastika, 1972 (Blue Ribbon award 1974), Brother Can You Spare a Dime, 1975, Mad Dog, 1976 (John Ford Meml. award 1976), According to Occam's Razor, 2000; dir.: (films) The Beast Within, 1980, The Return of Captain Invincible, 1981, A Breed Apart, 1983, The Howling II, 1984, Death of a Soldier, 1985, Back in Business, 1996; dir. prodr.: Communion, 1990, Art Deco Detective, 1994, Pterodactyl Woman from Beverly Hills, 1994, Precious Find, 1995, Burning Down the House, 1996, Thick and Thin, 1997, Joseph's Gift, 1999; painter exhibited in group shows at Argys Gallery, Melbourne, 1967, Clytie Jessop Gallery, London, 1968-71, Sigi Krauss Gallery, London, 1970-71, Camden Arts Centre, London, 1970, Richard Demarco Gallery, Edinburgh, 1971, Tolarno Gallery, Melbourne, 1971, Watters Gallery, Sydney, Australia, 1972, William Mora Gallery, Melbourne, 1987, Caz Gallery, L.A., 1990; represented in permanent collection Nat. Gallery Collection, Canberra, Australia, 1982; English Lit. exhibition Victorian Edn. Authority, Victoria, Australia, 1966. Mem. Dirs. Guild Am., Acad. Motion Picture Arts and Scis., Australian Film Dirs. Assn. Office: Michael Blaha Esq 2530 Wilshire Blvd Santa Monica CA 90403-4616

MORABITO, ROBERTO, chemist; b. Rome, Feb. 8, 1957; s. Stefano and Sara (Biancolella) M. Degree in chemistry, U. Rome, 1982, PhD in Analytical Chemistry, 1987. Rschr. Italian Agy. for New Technology, Energy and the Environment, Rome, 1987—, head lab., 1994-95; contracting prof. environ. analytical chemistry U. Rome La Sapienza, 1995—; invited spkr. over 20 internat. confs.; leader several European environ. analytical chemistry projects, 1995—; mem. V.2. Internat. Union of Pure and Applied Chemistry Commn., 1998—; chmn. Italian Inst. for Water Rsch. Commn. for quality of analytical data, 1998—. Assoc. editor Annali di Chimica-Internat. Jour. Analytical and Environ. Chemistry, 1996—; contbr. over 70 articles to profl. jours. and books in field. Lt. Engr. Corps, Italian armed forces, 1982-83. Mem. Italian Chemistry Soc. Avocations: football, reading, theater, cinema. Office: Italian Agy New Technology Energy & Environment, Via Anguillarese 301, 00060 Rome Italy

MORAGA (MOREGA), ALEXANDRU MIHAIL, engineering educator; b. Bucharest, Romania, May 24, 1955; s. Ion and Ileana (Dobrescu) M.; m. Miheala Rizeanu, June 6; 1 child, Ion Alexand. MSEE, Polytech. U. Bucharest, Romania, 1980, PhD in Elec. Engring., 1987; PhD in Mech. Engring., Duke U., 1993. From asst. prof. to assoc. prof. Polytech. U. Bucharest, Romania, 1983-98; assoc. prof. dept. mech. engring. Tokiwadai, Ube, Japan, 1995-96; sr. rschr. Inst. Applied Math., Romanian Acad. Sci., Bucharest, 1995—; prof. dept. elec. engring. Polytech. U. Bucharest, 1998—; reviewer Romanian Acad., Bucharest, 1993—, Royal Soc., London, 2000—. Author: Numerical Models for Engineering, 1998; contbr. articles to profl. jour.; inventor in field. Mem. Neighborhood Cmty., Bucharest, 1984—. Rsch. grantee IBM & N.C. Computing Ctr., 1992-94. Mem. ASME, IEEE, Duke Alumni Assn. Avocations: history, literature, music, travel. Office: Polytech U Bucharest, 313 Splaiul Ind, 77206 Bucharest Romania

MORAIS, ALCINA MARIA M. BERNARDO, food science educator and researcher; b. Porto, Portugal, June 30, 1962; d. Jose Fernando Morais Bernardo and Maria Amavel Silva Miranda; m. Rui Manuel Santos Costa Morais, Feb. 9, 1991; children: Rui Pedro Bernardo Morais, Joana Maria B. Morais. Degree in Chem. Engring., U. Porto, 1985; MSc, ENSIA, Massy, France, 1986; PhD, ENSIA, France, 1990. Tchg. asst. ESB-UCP, Porto, 1985-89; rschr. Sucre R & D, Paris, 1986-89; asst. prof. ESB-UCP, Porto, 1990—; pres.'s coun. U. Fla., 1993—. Contbr. articles to profl. jours. Avocations: swimming, chess, puzzle solving. E-mail: amorais@esb.ucp.pt. Office: ESB-UCP, Rua Dr A Bernardino Almeida, 4200-072 Porto Portugal

MORAITIS, MICHAEL, information systems analyst; b. Athens, Greece, May 3, 1965; s. Mathew and Maria (Stamatoglou) M. BA, Am. Coll. of Greece, 1988; MS, Am. U., 1990; postgrad., Heriot-Watt U., Edinburgh, Scotland, 1993—. Sci. assoc. clin. info. systems Evangelismos Hosp., Athens, 1990-92; sci. assoc. bd. edn. U. Athens Med. Sch., 1990-92; bus. & info. tech. cons. Arthur Andersen & Co., Athens, 1992-94; info. sys. & bus. cons. Olympos, Nyarlorinc, Hungary, 1995—; dir. info. systems & procedures directorate Diagnostic & Therapeutic Ctr. Athens, Hygeia Hosp., 1994-98; mgr. mgmt. consulting svcs. divsn. Ernst & Young S.E. Europe and Hellas S.A., Athens, 1998-99; dir. pvt. sector INFORMER S.A. Mgmt., Athens, 1999—; prof. U. Plymouth, Athens, 1992-94; instr. at Inst. of Technol. Rsch., 1991; presenter confs. in field. Author: Computer Aided Software Engineering, 1990, Computer Aided Software Engineering Annotated Bibliography 1986-90, 1990, Medical Applications and Network Development, 1991. Sgt. Hellenic Army Corps of Engrs., 1990-92. Tchg. fellow Am. U., 1989-90. Mem. Assn. Computing Machinery, Hellenic Inst. of Info. Mgmt., Pan Hellenic Assn. Med. Informatics, Hellenic Common Interest Group, Acad. Soc. Computer Info. Systems, Hilton Club (co-founder). Avocations: volleyball, woodcarving, poetry. Home: 5 Gelonos St, 11521 Athens Greece Office: Diagnostic and Therapeutic Ctr of Athens, Kifissias & Erythrou, Stavrou 4, 15123 Athens Greece

MORAKINYO, OLUFEMI, psychiatrist, educator; b. Ijebu-Ode, Nigeria, Aug. 24, 1939; s. Erastus Akinboade and Alice Aderemi (Ola) M. MBBS, London U., 1964; MS in Medicine, U. Edinburgh, 1971. Resident U. Coll. Hosp., Nigeria, 1965-67; registrar, clin. asst. Royal Edinburgh Hosp., Scotland, 1967-69; rsch. fellow psychophysiology unit dept. psychiatry U. Edinburgh, 1969-72; lectr. U. Ife, Ile-Ife, Nigeria, 1972-74, sr. lectr., 1974-83, prof. mental health and psychiatry, 1983—; cons. psychiatrist Obafemi Awolowo U. Tchg. Hosps., 1972—, head dept., 1990—; psychiatrist Douglas Hos. Ctr., Montreal, 1980; head dpet. chem. pathology Obaf Awo Tchg. Hosp., 1987-89; dean Faculty Health Scis., Obafemi Awo U., 1991-92. Contbr. articles to profl. jours.; co-author: African Traditional Medicine and Pharmacopoeia, 1991, 92. Hon. chieftaincy Ijebu-jesa Town, Nigeria, 1991, Ola Town, Nigeria, 1992; Justice of the Peace, Osun State Govt., 1994. Scholar Fed. Govt. Ny, 1958; traveling fellow WHO, 1975, 78; study fellow Rockefeller Found., Edinburgh, 1967. Fellow West African Coll. Physicians; mem. Royal Coll. Psychiatrists U.K., Assn. Psychiatrists Nigeria, World Psychiatric Assn. (mem. transcultural psychiatry sect.). Avocations: swimming, angling, fishing, table tennis. Office: Obafemi Awolow U, Coll Health Scis Mental Hlt, Ile-Ife Nigeria

MORAL, EMRAH, dentist; b. Izmir, Europa, Turkey, Dec. 21, 1968; s. Memhet Irfan and Vesile (Gülümser) M.; m. Meltem Alkap, Dec. 19, 1992; children: Irfan Mete, M. Alkas. M in Dentistry, Ege U., Izmir, Turkey, 1991. Dentist Manisa, 1992-93, Erzurum, 1995-97, Izmir, 1997—. With Turkish mil., 1993-94. Avocations: painting, trekking, indoor hobbies.

MORALES, ENRIQUE C. MIGUEL, engineering educator; b. Alcazar de S. Juan, Ciudad Real, Spain, Nov. 11, 1949; s. Licinio and Antonia (Campo) M.; m. Debra Collins, Nov. 1972 (div. 1981); 1 child, Coral Sue; m. Dineke Brandsma, Nov. 1990, 1 child, Nathalie Marlene. BS in Petroleum Engring. with honors, U. Tulsa, 1972; MS in Petroleum Engring., Stanford U., 1975, MS in Ops. Rsch., 1976; Petroleum Engr. (reval.), Central U. Venezuela, 1979. Well site engr. Shell Venezuela, Lagunillas, 1972-73, heavy oil reservoir engr., 1973-74; rsch. engr. Chevron, La Habra, Calif., 1976-77; sr. reservoir engr. Shell Internat./Maraven, Caracas, Venezuela, The Hague, Holland, 1977-81, head of short term planning, Caracas, 1982-83, project leader, The Hague, 1983-86; head onshore oil reservoir engring., NAM, Holland, 1986-90; head reservoir engring. Al Furat Petroleum Co., Syria, 1991-94; mgr. gas devel. Woodside Offshore Petroleum, Perth, Australia, 1995-98; mgr. bus. devel. Latin Am. and Caribbean, 1998-99; vp. gas and power bus. devel. for Latin Am. and Caribbean, Shell Internat. Gas., 1999—; asst. prof. Calif. State U.-Fullerton, 1976-77, Cen. Univ. Grad. Div., Caracas, 1978-80. Shell Oil Co. scholar, 1968-72, 74-76. Mem. Soc. Petroleum Engrs. Roman Catholic. Avocations: sailing, tennis, stamp collecting, horseback riding. Home and Office: Shell Internat Gas, Shell Centre, London SE1 7NA, England

MORALES, GUSTAVO ADOLFO, business executive; b. Tela, Honduras, Apr. 19, 1950; s. Gustavo and Maria de los Angeles (Galindo) M.; m. Estela Ondina Interiano, June 7, 1974; children: Aldo, Gustavo Adolfo, Alejandro, Andres. Agronomist Diploma, Escuela Agricola Panamericana, Honduras, 1970; BS in Forestry, Stephen F. Austin State U., 1973; MS, U. Wash., 1983. Forester Corp. Hondurena de Desarrollo Forestal, Comayagua, Honduras, 1973-74; forest dist. mgr. Corp. Hondurena de Desarrollo Forestal, San Pedro Sula, Honduras, 1974-78; project mgr., tech. advisor Corp. Hondurena de Desarrollo Forestal, Tegucigalpa, Honduras, 1983-90; forest opers. mgr. Forestal Indsl. Agua Fria, S.A., Yoro, Honduras, 1978-79; dir. Escuela Nat. de Ciencias Forestales, Siguatepeque, Honduras, 1990-91; gen. mgr. Venepal-Ston Forestal S.A., Caracas, 1991-95; pres., gen. mgr. Ston Forestal S.A., San Jose, Costa Rica, 1995—; cons. Zobel Forestry Assocs., Inc., Cary, N.C.; dir. Ston Forestal S.A., San Jose. Mem. LDS Ch. Avocations: racuqetball, deep sea fishing. E-mail: gmoralesg@hotmail.com.

MORALES FLOREZ, MARTIN CARLOS, philosophy educator; b. El Socorro, Santander, Colombia, Jan. 10, 1920; s. Rodolfo Morales Villarreal and Concepcion Flórez de Morales. Lic. Philosophy, Cath. U., Lille, France, 1951, PhD, 1961. Provincial Provincialship La Salle, Bogotá, Colombia, 1962-65; founder Univ. de la Salle, Bogotá, 1964; dir. Tech. Inst., Bucaramanga, Colombia, 1969-70, Inst. de la Salle, Bogotá, 1971; dean philosophy U. de la Salle, Bogotá, 1972-75; dean, dir. Magister in Philosophy, Bogota, 1976-81; rschr. Stadt U., Tübingen, Germany, 1982, Freiburg, Germany, 1983; rschr. philosophy U. de la Salle, Bogota, 1984-88, rshcr. sociology, 1989—; dir. Cátedra Abierta: Filosofia Francesa Contemporánea, 1994-97. Author: Historia de Colombia, 1966, Curso de Logica, 1968, Filosofia de la Educacion, 1986, La Pobreza en Colombia, 1989, Historia de la Universidad de la Salle, 1993, Vision Filosófica del Mundo, del Hombre y de Dios, 1996, Filosofia del Pensamiento, 1998, Filosofia de la Acción, 2000. Recipient Orden Francisco de P. Santander, Gobierno de Colombia, 1981, Orden Francisco de Miranda, Gobierno de Venezuela, 1984. Roman Catholic. Avocations: promenade, swimming, music, poetry, meditation. Office: U de la Salle Carrera 2a, No 10-70, Apartado Aereo 28638, Bogota Colombia

MORALES-PERALTA, ESTELA, clinical geneticist, educator; b. Guanabacoa, Cuba, Nov. 12, 1957; d. Amado Oscar Morales-Perez and Juana Josefa Peralta-Santana; m. Miguel Alfonso Alvarez-Fornaris; children: Estela Maria Alvarez-Morales, Miguel Antonio Alvarez-Morales. MD, Higher Inst. Med. Sci., Havana, Cuba, 1983. MD, 1st and 2d degree specialist clin. genetics. Resident clin. genetics Nat. Ctr. Med. Genetics, Havana, Cuba, 1983-86, clin. geneticist, 1986—, prof. clin. genetics, 1990—; clin. geneticist Ctr. Havana Pediat. Univ. Hosp., 1986—; advisor Nat. Adv. Commn. Rsch. in Stomatology, Havana, 1990—. Contbr. numerous articles to profl. jours. Mem. Cuban Soc. Genetics (founder), Cuban Soc. Health Sci. Profs. (founder), Soc. Genetics (Jalisco, Mex.). Avocations: reading, philately, camping. Home: PO Box 5092, 10500 Havana Cuba Office: Nat Ctr Med Genetics, Med Sch Victoria de Giron, 11600 Playa Cuba

MORAL-LOPEZ, PEDRO, international civil servant; b. La Roda, Spain, Mar. 14, 1919; s. Antonio Moral and Remedios Lopez; m. Hilda Lopez-Vallarino, Jan. 17, 1953; children: Pedro-Antonio, Macarena, Juan-Ramon, Hilda-Teresa. Pub. svc. diploma, Inst. Polit. Studies, Paris, 1948; diploma, Inst. de Droit Comparé, Paris, 1949; LLD, The Sorbonne, Paris, 1951. Chief agrarian law sect. FAO of the UN, Rome, 1952-64; chief agrarian law dept. Land Reform Inst. FAO of the UN, Santiago, Chile, 1964-69, dep. regional rep., 1969-76, asst. dir.-gen., 1976-82; prof. Land Reform Inst., Santiago, 1964-69; vis. prof. Inst. Agr. U. Minn., 1968; lectr. Internat. Devel. Law Inst., Rome, 1987. Author: Legal Aspects of Land Reform and Development, 1968. Recipient Grand Cross Civil Order of Merit H.M. The King of Spain, 1983. Mem. Internat. Soc. Devel. (pres. Chile chpt. 1992—), Coll. of Lawyers (Madrid), Country Club Santiago. Avocations: golf, chess. Home: Avda Los Leones 1770, Casilla 5 Correo 29, Santiago Chile

MORAN, CHRISTA ILSE MERKEL, investor, linguist, educator; b. Leipzig, Saxony, Germany, Jan. 5, 1946; came to U.S., 1968; d. Erich Harry and Ilse Dora (Waehnert) Merkel; m. William Joseph Moran, May 5, 1967 (dec. Mar. 4, 1979); children: Leslie Paige, Linda Christa. BA, U. Tuebingen, 1968; postgrad., U. Alaska, 1968-69. Cert. in German linguistics. Clk. Anchorage Westward Hotel, 1969-71; sales mgr. Windsor Park Hotel, Washington, 1971-75; linguist, instr. Def. Lang. Inst., Dept. Def., Washington, 1975-79; investor in real estate, sports cars Atlanta, Atlanta, 1979—; cons. Dept. Def., 1976-79; real estate agt., Northside Realty Co., Atlanta, 1992—. Author: Die Millie Miglia, 1969, Der Nuerburgring, 1975, German Culture, 1977. Chairperson For a United Germany Com., Washington, Atlanta, Leipzig chpts.; fundraiser UNICEF. Named Sportswriter of Yr. ADAC of Germany, 1977. Democrat. Home: PO Box 34165 Pensacola FL 32507-4165 Office: Buckhead Brokers 5395 Roswell Rd NE Atlanta GA 30342-1976 Address: PO Box 71411 Marietta GA 30007-1411

MORAN, ELIZABETH AMES, library director; b. Camden, Maine, June 22, 1940; d. Robie Frank and Dorothy Dyer Ames; m. Andrew Jackson Moran, Dec. 3, 1966; children: Heather Elizabeth, Melissa Ames. BA, U. Maine, 1962; MA in Law & Diplomacy, Fletcher Sch. LAw & Diplomacy, 1964; MLS, U. S.C., 1997. Intelligence officer CIA, Washington, 1964-68; sch. libr. Fairfax (Va.) County Schs., 1981-87; libr. Camden (Maine) Pub. Libr., 1988-90, libr. dir., 1990—. Bd. dirs. Camden Tech. Conf., 1997-98. Mem. ALA, Maine Libr. Assn. (pres. 1998-2000, commn. chair 2000—), Pub. Libr. Assn., Small Pub. Libr. Assn., Camden Garden Club, Phi Beta Kappa. Republican. Episcopalian. Avocations: sailing, needlework. Home: 32 Atlantic Hwy Northport ME 04849-3010 Office: Camden Pub Libr 55 Main St Camden ME 04843-1794

MORAN, JAMES D., III, child development educator; b. Bklyn., Mar. 2, 1951; s. James D. and Monica (Scherzinger) M.; m. Laurette Virginia Miller, Aug. 11, 1973; children: Ryan, Mollie. BA magna cum laude, Duke U., 1973; MS, U. Okla., 1975; PhD, Okla. State U., 1978. Asst. prof. U. Okla., Norman, 1978-80; asst. prof. Va. Poly. Inst. and State U., Blacksburg, 1980-83, assoc. prof., asst. head dept. family and child devel., 1983-85; prof., head dept. family rels. and child devel. Okla. State U., Stillwater, 1985-89; assoc. dean coll. human ecology U. Tenn., 1989-98, dean, 1998—; v.p. U. Tenn. Rsch. Corp.; mng. dir. Tande Tech. Licensing. Mem. editl. bd. Home Econs. Rsch. Jour., 1983-85, Family Rels., 1985-91, Creativity Rsch. Jour., 1988-90, Home Econs. Forum, 1990-91, Jour. Family and Consumer Scis., 1993-95. Recipient Outstanding Rsch. award Va. Home Econs. Assn., 1982. Mem. Am. Assn. Family and Consumer Scis. (vice chmn. family rels. and child devel. sect. 1985-86, chmn. nomating com. 1987, chair coun. for accreditation 1989, 91, chair strategic planning com. 1989, chair collegiate assembly 1995-97, vice chair bd. on human scis. 1999, named among New Faces to Watch 1984, Leadership award 1986), Nat. Assn. for Edn. Young Children, Soc. for Rsch. in Child Devel., Licensing Exec. Soc., Kappa Omicron Nu, Phi Kappa Phi. Democrat. Roman Catholic. Avocation: golf. Home: 824 Andover Blvd Knoxville TN 37922-1532 Office: U Tenn Coll Human Ecology Knoxville TN 37996-0001

MORAN, MICHAEL EDWARD, automotive company executive; b. London, Feb. 16, 1960; s. Edward Joseph and Iris Jean (Munn) M.; m. Sonya Caroline Hambly, Dec. 8, 1984 (div. 1999); children: Oliver, Rebecca, Gabriella; m. Janet Mary Brown, Apr. 15, 2000. BA in Bus. with honors, Ealing Coll., London, 1982. Customer rels. exec. Ford Motor Co. Ltd., Brentwood, Essex, Eng., 1982-84, area svc. mgr., 1984-86, area sales mgr., 1986-87, mgmt. lectr., 1987-88, gen. field mgr., 1988-90, mgr. fleet sales and mktg., 1992-93; mgr. tng. Ford Mktg. Inst., Brussels, 1988-90; dir. field sales ops. Ford Motor Co., Madrid, 1993-96; mktg. dir. Toyota (GB) Ltd., Redhill, Surrey, Eng., 1996-99; comml. dir. Toyota (GB) PLC, Redhill, 1999-2000, mktg. dir., 2000—. Mem. Soc. Motor Mfrs. and Traders (chmn. exhbns. com. 1999—), Inc. Soc. Brit. Advertisers (dep. chmn. exec. com. 1999—). Avocations: golf, walking, wine, languages. Office: Toyota (GB) PLC, Station Rd, Surrey Redhill RH1 1PX, England

MORAN, PAUL JAMES, journalist, columnist; b. Buffalo, July 20, 1947; s. Paul James and Frances (Sciortino) M.; m. Kim Maldiner, Mar. 17, 1975 (div. July 1979); m. Colette Stass (div. Jan. 1997); 1 child, Heather. Student, SUNY, Buffalo, 1965-67, Millard Fillmore Coll., 1971-73. Sports editor Tonawanda News, North Tonawanda, N.Y., 1972-75; writer/columnist Fort Lauderdale (Fla.) News/Sun Sentinel, 1975-85, N.Y. Newsday, Melville, 1985—; cons. Green Country Racing Assn., Tulsa, 1983-85. Author: (with others) Crown Jewels of Thoroughbred Racing; contbr. articles to mags. and newspapers. Sgt. USAF, 1967-71. Recipient Eclipse award Thoroughbred Racing Assn., 1985, 90, Disting. Writing award Am. Soc. Newspaper Editors, 1990, Deadline Writing award Soc. Silurians, 1990, Deadline Reporting award L.I. Press Club, 1991, Disting. Sports Writing award N.Y. Newspaper Pubs. Assn., 1992, (with others) Journalism collection Best Newspaper Writing 1991, Media award L.I. Vet. Med. Assn., 1997, excellence in continuing feature Fla. Mag. Assn., 1999. Mem. N.Y. Turf Writers' Assn. (pres. 1990-92, sec.-treas. 1992-94), Nat. Turf Writers' Assn. (bd. dirs. 1987-90). Republican. Avocations: photography, art collecting. Home: 40 Carnation Ave Floral Park NY 11001-1730 Office: Newsday 235 Pinelawn Rd Melville NY 11747-4250

MORAN, RONALD WESSON, retired English educator, dean, writer; b. Phila., Sept. 9, 1936; s. Ronald Wesson and Julia Marie (Hagymasi) M.; m. Jane Edith Hetzler, Jan. 31, 1959; (twins) Sally and Ronald Wesson

III. BA, Colby Coll., 1958; MA, La. State U., 1962, PhD, 1966. Instr. English La. State U., Baton Rouge, 1963-66; asst. prof. English U. N.C., Chapel Hill, 1966-69, assoc. prof., 1969-75; prof. English Clemson (S.C.) U., 1975-99, head dept. English, 1975-80, asst. dean, 1986-91, assoc. dean, 1991-99, interim dean Coll. Arch., Arts and Humanities, 1999-2000; ret., 2000; arts and scis. adv. bd. Greenville (S.C.) Tech. Coll., 1986-89; Fulbright lectr., Würzburg, Germany, 1969-70. Author: So Simply Means the Rain, 1965, Louis Simpson, 1972, Life on the Rim, 1988, Sudden Fictions, 1994, Getting the Body to Dance Again, 1995, Fish Out of Water, 2000; co-author: Four Poets and the Emotive Imagination, 1976; assoc. editor South Atlantic Bull., 1975-77; adv. bd. S.C. Rev., 1980—. Recipient Nat. Looking Glass Poetry Chapbook award, 1994. Mem. Assn. Acad. Affairs Adminstrs.-Southeastern Region (bd. officers 1989-93). Methodist. Home: 114 Princess Ln Clemson SC 29631-2120

MORAN, SIEGFRIED, mathematics educator; b. Berlin, Sept. 7, 1930; m. Ruth Elisabeth Vogelberg, Dec. 16, 1960; children: Simon Gavin, Matthias Franklin, Anna Catherine, Ellaine Roberta. BSc, U. London, 1951, MSc, 1952, PhD, 1954. Lectr. Allahabad (India) U., 1955-57; rsch. fellow Glasgow (Scotland) U., 1958-59, lectr., 1959-64; mem. Inst. for Advanced Stidy, Princeton, N.J., 1962-63; lectr. Bristol (Eng.) U., 1964-65; sr. lectr. math. U. Kent, Canterbury, Eng., 1965-66; reader in pure math. U. Kent, Canberbury, Eng., 1966-96; vis. prof. U. Calif., Berkeley, U. Göttingen, Fed. Republic Germany, Queen's U., Kingston, Ont., Can.; spkr. in field. Author: The Mathematical Theory of Knots and Braids, 1983; also numerous articles. A founder Home for Vagrant Boys, Allahabad, 1957. Fulbright scholar, 1962-65. Avocations: weaving, book binding, silversmithing, gardening, antiques. Office: U Kent Dept Math, Canterbury England

MORANG, DIANE JUDY, writer, television producer, business entrepreneur; b. Chgo., Apr. 28, 1942; d. Anthony Thomas Morang and Laura Ann Andrzejczak. Student, Stevens Finishing Sch., Chgo., 1956, Fox Bus. Coll., 1959-60, UCLA, 1967-69. Mem. staff Chgo. Sun Times, Daily News, 1957—, Drury Ln. Theatre, Chgo., 1961-62, AM Show ABC-TV, Hollywood, Calif., 1970-71; chair, mem. judging panel Regional Emmy awards, 1989, judge 2 categories, 1985. Author: How to Get into the Movies, 1978; author, creator: The Rainbow Keyboard, 1991, The Translation of the Code of Music into Mathematics; creator: The Best Kids' Show in the World; contbr. numerous articles to newspapers, mags. Bd. dirs., mem. scholarship com. Ariz. Bruins UCLA Alumni Assn.; mem. Nat. Mus. Women in the Arts, Washington. Mem. NATAS (mem. Hollywood Emmy-award winning team Hollywood, Calif. 1971), Nat. Women's Hall of Fame, Seneca Falls, N.Y., Ariz. Authors Assn. (bd. dirs.), Women of the West Mus. Roman Catholic.

MORANO, GERARD JOHN, marketing executive; b. Mount Vernon, N.Y., Oct. 23, 1944; s. Gerard Anthony and Pauline (Ungaro) M.; m. Allison Lenore Folz, June 28, 1975; 1 child, Steven Christopher. BS in Fin., CUNY, 1974; BA in Mktg., Pace U., Pleasantville, N.Y., 1981; MBA, Pace U., White Plains, N.Y., 1982. Fin. planner ITT Continental, Rye, N.Y., 1968-74, product mgr., 1974-80, mgr. sales promotion, 1980-84; dir. mktg. Quality Bakers Am., Greenwich, Conn., 1984-88, v.p. mktg. and sales, 1988-96, sr. v.p. mktg. and comm., 1996—; exec. v.p. QBA, Advt., Inc., Greenwich, Conn., 1992—. Alumni mentor Pace U., 1988—; fund raiser Vietnam Vets. Meml. Com., Washington, 1980-82, alumni mentor Pace U., 1988—. Served with U.S. Army, 1966-68, Vietnam. Decorated Bronze Star, 4 Battle Stars; recipient Valorous Unit award, 1968, Presdl. Citation, 1968. Mem. Am. Film Inst., Promotional Mktg. Assn., ABA (mem. mktg. com.), Wildlife Conservation Soc., Vietnam Vets. Am., Ellis Island Found., 199th Inf. Assn. Avocations: photography, videography. Office: Quality Bakers Am 70 Riverdale Ave Greenwich CT 06831-5030

MORAWITZ, HANS, physicist; b. Wiener Neustadt, Austria, Feb. 6, 1935; came to U.S., 1955; s. Johann and Josephine (Dinda) M.; m. Terry Lynn Langhorne, July 27, 1963; children: Werner, Peter, Dana. BS summa cum laude, Stanford U., 1956, PhD, 1963. Sr. lectr. Monash U., Melbourne, Australia, 1965-66; rsch. assoc. U. Vienna, Austria, 1966-67; staff mem. IBM Rsch. Div., San Jose, Calif., 1963-65, 67—; vis. prof. dept. physics Ulm (Fed. Rep. of Germany) U., 1982, 91, 92, 96, 98, 99, 2000, Inst. for Advanced Study, Nat. U., Canberra, Australia, 1984, Bayreuth(Fed. Rep. of Germany) U., 1986. Co-author: Mechanisms of Conventional and High Temperature Superconductivity, 1993; co-editor: Vibrations at Surfaces, 1982; contbr. over 80 articles to profl. jours. Pres., bd. dirs. Ladera (Calif.) Community Assn., 1976-79, Ladera Recreation Dist., 1980-88, Com. for Green Foothills, Palo Alto, Calif. 1985—. NATO sr. fellow, 1993-97; Fulbright scholar, 1956; recipient award Dept. Supply, Canberra, 1965. Mem. Am. Phys. Soc., European Phys. Soc. Democrat. Achievements include development of quantum-electrodynamics near metal surfaces, of theory of photochemical holeburning in polymers; proposition of orientational peierls transition in organic conductors, of strong coupling phonon and layer plasmon pairing as explanation for the high superconducting transition temperatures in the cuprate superconductors. E-mail: morawitz@almaden.ibm.com. Home: 715 B Quetta Ave Sunnyvale CA 94087-1249 Office: IBM Almaden Rsch Ctr 650 Harry Rd San Jose CA 95120-6001

MORAY, NEVILLE, psychology educator; b. London, May 27, 1935; s. Peter Moray and Georgette (Campbell-Buller) Howson; children: Nerissa, Clea. BA, Oxford U., 1957, PhD, 1960. Cert. human factors profl. Asst. lectr. U. Hull, Eng., 1959-60; sr. lectr. U. Sheffield, Eng., 1960-70; prof. U. Toronto, Ont., Eng., 1970-74, 80-87, U. Stirling, Eng., 1974-80, U. Ill., Urbana, 1987-95; assoc. prof. U. Valenciennes, France, 1995-97; prof. psychology U. Surrey, Guildford, Eng., 1997—; pres. Technosophy, Inc., Urbana, 1988-97. Author: Attention, 1979, Cybernetics, 1963, Human Error, 1989; editor: Mental Workload, 1979, Robotics and Society, 1989; contbr. articles to profl. jours. Grantee U.K. Govt. Funding Agys., NSF, Dept. of Energy, Nuclear Regulatory Commn., NASA, Can. Govt. Funding Agys., 1959-97. Fellow Human Factors and Ergonomics Soc., Ergonomics Soc. Avocations: sailing, painting, reading, writing, singing. E-mail: nmoray@globalnet.co.uk. Home: 10A Hampstead Hill Gardens, London NW3 2PL, England Office: U Surrey, Dept Psychology, Guildford GU2 5XH, England

MORA Y ARAUJO, MANUEL J., political sociologist, researcher; b. Buenos Aires, Sept. 30, 1937; s. Juan B. Mora y Araujo and Dolores Comas; m. Carmen D. Kenning; children: Marcela, Juan Manuel, Ramiro, Jimena. MA in Sociology, FLACSO, Chile, 1963. Dir. dept. sociology Fundacion Bariloche, Argentina, 1967-72; dir. Ctr. for Social Rsch. Inst. Torcuato di Tella, Argentina, 1980-84; ptnr. Comunicacion Institucional, Argentina, 1990-95, Mora y Araujo & Assocs., Argentina, 1982—. Author: Ensayo y Error, 1991, Liberalismo y Democracia, 1989; editor: Politica Tecnoogica y Paises en Desarrollo, 1982; author/editor: El Voto Peronista, 1978. Pres. Fundacion Compromiso, Buenos Aires, 1994-99, bd. dirs.; v.p. Fundacion Poder Ciudadano, Buenos Aires, 1990-99; congl. candidate UCEDE Party, Buenos Aires, 1987; bd. mem. U. Torcuato di Tella, 1995; pres. acad. com. Argentine Commn. for Rsch. Nazi Activities, 1997-99. Mem. World Assn. for Pub. Opinion Rsch. E-mail: mmora@morayaraujo.com.ar. Home: Posadas 1120, 1011 Buenos Aires Argentina Office: Mora y Araujo Assoc, Ave Leandro N Alem 1050, 1001 Buenos Aires Argentina

MORCHIO, RENZO GIULIO, biophysicist, researcher, educator; b. Genoa, Italy, Dec. 7, 1924; s. Rocco and Leontina (Vildosi) M.; m. Ada Mussi, May 3, 1952. D in Scis., U. Genoa, 1947; PhD, U. Rome, 1971. Trainee Inst. Zoology U. Genoa, 1948-49, trainee Inst. Theoretic Physics, 1959, asst. prof., 1960, prof., 1962-97; ret., 1997; guest Harvard U., Boston, 1956-57; pres. Comitate Nazionale U. Genoa, 1970-84; pres. Commn. of the Faculty, U. Genoa, 1977-78. Author: Fondamenti Della Biofisica, 1982, others; mem. adv. bd. Rivista di Biologia/Biology Forum, 1997, asst. editor, 1999-2000, co-editor, 2000; contbr. nearly 6 articles to profl. jours. Mem. N.Y. Acad. Scis. Avocations: music, astronomy. Home: Via Canevari 24, 16137 Genoa Italy Office: Dept Physics Univ, Via Dodecaneso 33, 16146 Genoa Italy

MORD, IRVING CONRAD, II, lawyer; b. Mar. 22, 1950; s. Irving Conrad and Lillie Viva (Chapman) M.; m. Julia Ann Russell, Aug. 22, 1970 (div. Apr. 1980); children: Russell Conrad, Emily Ann; m. Kay E. McDaniel, Aug. 31, 1985; children: Kurt August, Clayton Troy. BS, Miss. State U., 1972; JD, U. Miss., 1974. Bar: Miss. 1974, U.S. Dist. Ct. (no. dist.) Miss. 1974, U.S. Dist. Ct. (so. dist.) Miss. 1984. Counsel to bd. suprs. Noxubee County, Miss., 1976-80, Walthall County, Miss., 1980—, Bd. Edn., Walthall County, 1982—; county pros. atty. Noxubee County, Miss., Macon, 1974-80, Walthall County, Tylertown, 1982-88, 91-96. Bd. dirs. East Miss. Coun., Meridian, 1978-80, Trustmark Nat. Bank, Tylertown, 1986—; v.p. Macon coun. Boy Scouts Am., 1978, mem. coun., 1979; county crusade chmn. Am. Cancer Soc., Macon, 1976-78, county pres., 1979; chmn. fund dr. fine arts complex Miss. State U., Macon, 1979; Walthall County family master, 1996—, Walthall County Youth referee, 1996—. Recipient Youth Leadership award Miss. Econ. Coun., 1976. Mem. ATLA, Miss. Prosecutors Assn., Miss. Assn. Bd. Attys. (v.p. 1985, pres. 1986), Miss. Assn. Sch. Bd. Attys., Miss. State Bar, Am. Judicature Soc. (Torts award 1972), Miss. Criminal Justice Planning Commn., Nat. Fed. Ind. Bus., Miss. State U. Alumni Assn., Macon-Noxubee County C. of C., Phi Kappa Tau (bd. govs. 1976-80, grad. coun. 1972—, pres. grad. coun. 1977-80, pres. house corp. 1977-80, Alumnus of Yr. Alpha Chi chpt. 1979), Rotary (sec.-treas. 1977, v.p. 1978, pres. Macon 1979, pres. Tylertown club 1986-87), Phi Delta Phi. Office: 729 Beulah Ave Tylertown MS 39667-2709

MORDECAI, DAVID K.A., financial economist, journal editor; b. N.Y.C., Oct. 18, 1961; s. Kenneth and Vinette Mordecai; m. Samantha Kappagoda, July 18, 1996. BA, Kings Coll., Briarcliff Manor, N.Y., 1983; MBA in Fin., NYU, N.Y.C., 1987; PhD in Fin. Econs., U. Chgo., 2000. Dir. comml. asset backed group Fitch IBCA, N.Y.C., 1997-98; v.p. fin. engring. AIG Risk Fin., N.Y.C., 1998-2000; v.p. fin. engring. and prin. fin. AIG Global Investments, N.Y.C., 2000—; mem. instnl. investment mgmt. adv. com. N.Y. Mercantile Exch., N.Y.C., 1998—. Editor in chief Jour. Risk Fin., 1999—. Mem. Internat. Assn. Fin. Engrs., Global Assn. Risk Profls., Am. Econ. Assn., Am. Fin. Assn. E-mail: dkmordecai@aol.com.

MORDEN, JOHN REID, security-business intelligence company executive; b. Hamilton, Ont., Canada, June 17, 1941; s. Warren Wilbert and Isabelle Gemmell (Reid) M.; m. Margaret Keens, June 27, 1964; children: Michael, Geoffrey. BA, Dalhousie U., 1962; postgrad., Dalhousie Law Sch., 1962-63. With Can. Dept. External Affairs, various worldwide cities, 1963-84; asst. dep. min. dept. native claims Dept. Indian & Northern Devel., Can., 1984-85; trade and econ. policy Can. Dept. External Affairs, 1985-86; asst. sec. to cabinet Fgn. and Def. Affairs, Can., 1986-87; dir. Can. Security Intelligence Svc., 1987-91; dep. min. fgn. affairs Govt. Can., 1991-94; pres, CEO, Atomic Energy of Can., Ltd., Ottawa, Ont., 1994-98; mng. dir. Kroll Asocs. Can., Toronto, Ont., 1999-2000; bd. dirs. Edn. Inst. Internat. Affairs, Toronto Symphony Orchestra; mem. adv. bd. Imagis Tech., Inst. for Study Violence and Terrorism; bd. govs. Trent U. Mem. internat. adv. coun. York U.; mem. Can. com. Coun. for Security and Cooperation in Asia and Pacific. Recipient Ian L. Macrae award, 1998. Mem. Royal Can. Yacht Club, Order of Can., Order of the So. Cross (Brazil), Toronto Hunt. Avocations: photography, music, ballet, reading. Office: Reid Morden & Assoc, 16 Duggan NE, Toronto, ON Canada M4V 1Y2

MORDLER, JOHN MICHAEL, opera manager, artistic consultant, recording producer; b. London, Nov. 8, 1938; s. Marcel and Olga Maria (Gaster) M. Student, H.E.C. Acad. Commerciale, Paris, 1958; MA, St. Andrews U., 1961. Recording producer Decca Records, London, 1963-73; mgr. artist devel., sr. producer EMI Angel Records, London, 1973-83; gen. mgr. Monte Carlo (Monaco) Opera, 1984—; artistic cons. Orch. Porto, Portugal, 1989-91; dir. Beacon Sound Internat., 1989—; jury mem. (singing competitions) Toti dal Monte, Treviso, Italy, , 95, Belvedere, Vienna, Madame Butterfly, Tokyo, Grand Prix Lyrique, Monte Carlo. Bd. dirs. French Nat. Opera Sch., Marseille, 1990—. Decorated officier de l'Ordre du Mérite Culturel. Avocations: squash, skiing. Home: 7 Ave St Roman, Monte-Carlo Monaco Office: Opera de Monte-Carlo, Place du Casino, Monte Carlo Monaco

MORDVINOV, VIATCHESLAV ALEKSEYEVICH, molecular biologist; b. Novosibirsk, Russia, Sept. 17, 1952; s. Aleksey Vassilevich Mordvinov and Ljudmila Nikolaevna Lapshina; m. Euguenia Anatoleivena Orlovskaya, Nov. 1, 1973. MD, Med. U., Novosibirsk, 1976; PhD, Inst. Molecular Biology, Kiev, Ukraine, 1986. Rschr., sr. rschr. Inst. Molecular Biology, 1976-87; sr. rschr. Inst. Clin. Immunology, Novosibirsk, 1987-93; rschr. officer U. Louis Pasteur, Illkirch, France, 1993-94; sr. rsch. officer Inst. Child Health Rsch., Perth, Australia, 1994-98; rsch. fellow Curtin U., Perth, 1998—. Author: Interleukin-5 From Molecule to Drug Target for Asthma, 1999; contbr. articles to profl. jours. Mem. Biochem. Soc. U.K. Avocation: snorkeling. Office: WA Inst Med Rsch Level 5, MRF Bldg Rear 50 Murray St, Perth 6000 WA, Australia

MORE, PHILIP HARVEY BIRNBAUM, business administration educator; b. San Diego, Jan. 21, 1944; s. Louis and Ruth Laureen (Bay) B.; m. Marlin Sue Van Every, Dec. 26, 1964; 1 child, Brian Philip. BA, U. Calif., Berkeley, 1965; PhD, U. Wash., 1975. Analyst Los Angeles County Civil Svc. Commn., 1965-67; tchg. assoc. U. Wash., Seattle, 1972-74; asst. prof. bus. adminstrn. Ind. U., Bloomington, 1975-80, assoc. prof., 1980-85, prof., 1986—; resident dir. J.F.K. Int., Tiburg U., The Netherlands; vis. scholar Polish Aca. Scis., Tokyo U., SDA Bocconi, Milan, Italy, Seoul Nat. U., Korea, Dartmouth Coll. Co-author: Organization Theory: Structural and Behavioral Analysis, Modern Management Techniques for Engineers and Scientists, International Research Management: Studies in Interdisciplinary Methods From Business, Government and Academics, 1990; assoc. editor IEEE Transaction on Engring. Mgmt. jour.; contbr. articles to profl. jours., book revs., sects. to books, invited papers Germany, Poland, Eng., Can., Thailand, Hong Kong, Korea. With USAF, 1967-71. NSF fellow, 1974-75, N.Y. Acad. Scis. fellow, 1981; U. Hong Kong Sr. Fulbright scholar, 1981-82. Mem. Acad. Mgmt. (pres. tech. and innovation mgmt. divsn. 1989-90), Engring. Mgmt. Soc., Inst. Ops. Rsch. and Mgmt. Scis., Internat. Assn. for Study of Interdisciplinary Rsch., Beta Gamma Sigma, Beta Alpha Psi, Sigma Iota Epsilon, Sigma Chi. Methodist. Office: Univ So Calif Marshall Sch Bus Los Angeles CA 90089-0001

MORE, RANJIT SINGH, cardiologist, consultant. BSc with honors, Manchester U., U.K., 1983, MB ChB, 1986; MRCP, Edinburgh U., U.K., 1989. Rsch. registrar Glenfield Hosp., Leicester, U.K., 1991-94; lectr. cardiology St.Mary's Hosp., London, 1994-97; cons. cardiologist St.Mary's Hosp., Portsmouth, U.K., 1997—. Jr. fellow Brit. Heart Found., Leicester, 1991. Mem. Royal Coll. Physicians, Brit. Cardiac Soc., Brit. Soc. Echocardiography. Avocations: swimming, squash, jogging. Office: Dept Cardiology, Milton Rd, Portsmouth PO3 6AD, England

MOREAU, CLAUDE OLIVIER, retired aircraft industry executive; b. St.-Bonnet-de-Bellac, France, Oct. 2, 1927; s. Jean and Annie (Lavaud) M.; m. Nicole Delmée, Oct. 11, 1952; children: Michel, Carole. Baccalaureat, Lycee Constantine, 1946; postgrad., Lycee Alger, 1946-49, E.N.S. Aeronautique, Paris, 1949-52, Ecole Chef Entreprises, Paris, 1966; Laureat (hon.), Dale Carnegie Sch., Paris, 1967-68. With design office Dassault, Paris, 1953-63, with equipment divsn., 1963-71; plant mgr. Dassault, Biarritz, France, 1972-76; gen. mgr. supplies Dassault, Paris, 1976-81, internat. coop. gen. mgr., 1981-85; gen. mgr. Air Materiel, Paris, 1985-88; ret., 1988; organizer travel groups. Creator, dir. jour. Le Rhomboedre, Annuaire des Anciens Eleves. Lt. French Air Force, 1952-53. Mem. Anciens Eleves (treas. 1996-99), N.Y. Acad. Scis. Avocations: computer programming, economics. Home: 122 rue de Vaugirard, 75006 Paris France

MOREAU, JEAN CLAUDE, astrophysician; b. Paris, Oct. 20, 1942; children: Anne Gaël, Joan Bertrand. MD, Nat Conserv. Arts et Metiers, Paris, 1976; degree in astrophysics, U. Orsay, France, 1997. Technician Thomson CSF, Malakoff, France, 1961-64; mgr. Electronic Lab., INSERM, Paris, 1965-78; dir. Ctr. Tech. Biomed., INSERM, St. Maurice, France, 1978-88; pres., mgr. Handisoft S.A., Vert St. Denis, France, 1980-90; R&D cons. JCM Consulting, Le Tallud, France, 1990—; pedagogic mgr. Inst. Lavoisier, Parthenay, France, 1994-95; pres. Ctr. Rsch. Arabel, France. Editor Internat. Jour. Rehab. Medicine, Internat. Jour. Astrophysics. Grantee in field, France, 1982; recipient Larriviere phys. prize, France, 1976, Innovation in Medicine award, France, 1990. Mem. N.Y. Acad. Scis., Soc. Française Physique, Memoire et Vie, Nouveaux Droits de l'Homme, Nouvelle Economie Fraternelle. E-mail: Jcmoreau@aol.com. Home and Office: La Grande Chaboissière, 79200 Le Tallud France

MOREAU, JEAN-PIERRE, history educator; b. Limoges, France, May 31, 1940; s. Paul and Germaine (Aubry) M. PhD, Sorbonne, Paris, 1980. Asst. U. Poitiers (France) Faculty of Lit., 1970-86; prof. U. Limoges (France) Faculty of Letters, 1986—. Author: Rome ou l'Angleterre?, 1984, Henry VIII et le Schisme Anglican, 1994; editor (jour.) L'Époque Conradienne, 1991—, L'Angleterre des Tudors, 1485-1603, 2000. Named Chevalier, Palmes Académiques, 1994. Fellow Royal Hist. Soc. (Eng.); mem. French Conrad Soc. (treas. 1991—). Office: Faculté des Lettres, 39 rue Camille-Guerin, F-87036 Limoges Cedex, France

MOREAU, PATRICK MARCEL, thoracic and vascular surgeon; b. Perpignan, France, Sept. 5, 1948; s. Marcel Jules and Yvonne Henriette (Delaunay) M.; m. Jacqueline Françoise Marulier, July 8, 1972; children: Dominique, Magali, Eric, Charles. MD, U. Montpellier, France, 1972. Intern Hosp. of Montpellier, 1974-79; hosp. asst. (the former) Clnique Mutualise de Beziers, France, 1979-82; resident in gen. surgery Paris, 1981, resident in vascular surgery, 1982, resident in thoracic surgery, 1982; pvt. practice thoracic and vascular surgery Béziers, France, 1982—. Contbr. articles to med. jours. Capt. French Navy, 1975-76. Recipient Lauréat de la Faculté de Médecine de Montpellier, 1982. Mem. Internat. Soc. for Cardiovascular Surgery, Soc. Chirurgie Thoracique et Cardiovasculaire, soc. Chirurgie Vasculaire. Republican. Roman Catholic. Avocations: hiking, cycling. Office: Ctr Med du Trencavel, 16 Ave Jean Moulin, 34500 Beziers France

MORECKI, ADAM, educator; b. Cracow, Poland, Sept. 5, 1929; s. Rafa and Henryka (Krygier) M.; m. Zofia Gajewska, July 8, 1954; 1 child, Elizabeth. MS, Acad. Mining, Cracow, Poland, 1951; PhD, Electrotech. U., Moscow, 1955; Doctorate (hon.), Acad. Mining & Metallurgy, Cracow, 1999. Asst. Acad. Mining, Cracow, Poland, 1949-51, older asst., 1951-52; asst. prof. Warsaw U. Tech., Poland, 1968-74, full prof., 1974—. Contbr. numerous articles to profl. jours., 38 books. Mem.. IFtoMM (sec. gen. 1976-83, pres. 1992-95, past pres. 1995-99). Avocations: hobby, car, bonsai. Home: Wolska 111/2, 01-235 Warsaw Poland Office: Warsaw U Tech, Nowowiejska 24, 00-665 Warsaw Poland

MOREHEAD, ANNETTE MARIE, disabled children's facility administrator, child advocate; b. San Diego; d. Michael Peter and Katherine Helen (Keegan) Russomondo; m. Peter James Morehead; children: Bradley Michael Caloca, Katherine Dana. AS in Acctg., Normandale C.C., Bloomington, Minn., 2000. Dir. Rayito Day Care Ctr., San Diego, 1981-85; instrnl. asst. for children with disabilities San Diego City Schools, 1985-88; owner, operator Scripps Ranch Childcare Ctr. for Disabled Children, San Diego, 1990—; child advocate; speaker San Diego Bd. Edn., 1986, News Eight Local TV News, 1989, Miramar Coll., 1991, Scottish Rite Charities, 1992, U. Calif., San Diego, 1992, Exceptional Parents Found., 1993. Vol. Schweitzer Ctr. for Disabled Children, San Diego, 1985, Stein Edn. Ctr. for Autistic Children, San Diego, 1987-88; bd. dirs. San Diego Autism Soc., 1989. Mem. Mensa. Democrat. Avocations: home, fine architecture.

MOREHOUSE, LAWRENCE GLEN, veterinarian, educator; b. Manchester, Kans., July 21, 1925; s. Edwy Owen and Ethel Merle (Glenn) M.; m. Georgia Ann Lewis, Oct. 6, 1956; children: Timothy Lawrence, Glenn Ellen. BS in Biol. Sci., Kans. State U., 1952, DVM, 1952; MS in Animal Pathology, Purdue U., 1956, PhD, 1960. Lic. vet. medicine. Veterinarian County Animal Hosp., Des Peres, Mo., 1952-53; supr. Brucellosis labs. Purdue U., West Lafayette, Ind., 1953-60; staff veterinarian lab. svcs. USDA, Washington, 1960-61; discipline leader in pathology and toxicology, animal health divsn. USDA Nat. Animal Disease Lab., Ames, Iowa, 1961-64; prof., chmn. dept. veterinary pathology U. Mo. Coll. Vet. Medicine, Columbia, 1964-69, 84-86, dir. Vet. Med. Diagnostic Labr., 1968-88, prof. emeritus, 1986—; cons. USDA, to comdg. gen. U.S. Army R & D Command, Am. Inst. Biol. Scis., NAS, Miss. State U., St. Louis Zoo Residency Tng. Program, Miss. Vet. Med. Assn., Okla. State U., Pa. Dept. Agr., Ohio Dept. Agr. Co-editor: Mycotoxic Fungi, Mycotoxins, Mycotoxicoses: An Encyclopedic Handbook , 3 vols., 1977; contbr. numerous articles on diseases of animals to profl. jours. Active Trinity Presbyn. Ch., Columbia, 1989-92; bd. dirs. Mo. Symphony Soc., Columbia, 1989-92. Pharmacists mate second class USNR, 1943-46, PTO; 2d. lt. U.S. Army, 1952-56. Recipient Outstanding Svc. award USDA, 1959, merit cert., 1963, 64, Disting. Svc. award U. Mo. Coll. Vet. Medicine, 1987, Dean's Impact award, 1996. Fellow Royal Soc. Health London; mem. Am. Assn. Vet. Lab. Diagnosticians (E.P. Pope award 1976, chmn. lab. accreditation bd. 1972-79, 87-90, pres. 1979-80, sec.-treas. 1983-87), World Assn. Vet. Lab. Diagnosticians (bd. dirs. 1984-94, dir. emeritus 1994—), N.Y. Acad. Sci., U. S. Animal Health Assn., Am. Assn. Lab. Animal Sci., Mo. Soc. Microbiology, Am. Assn. Avian Pathologists, N.Am. Conf. Rsch. Workers in Animal Diseases, Mo. Univ. Retirees Assn. (v.p. 1996-98, pres. 1998-99). Presbyterian. Avocations: classic cars, boating, genealogy. Home: 916 Danforth Dr Columbia MO 65201-6164 Office: U Mo Vet Med Diagnostic Lab PO Box 6023 Columbia MO 65205-6023

MOREHOUSE, VALERIE JEANNE, librarian; b. Taft, Calif., Jan. 30, 1947; d. Gordon Stanley and Cloe Ozelle (Reed) Hogue; m. Keith Herbert Morehouse, Aug. 22, 1968 (div. 1994); 1 child, Gordon. AA, Taft Coll., 1966; AB in English, U. Calif., Berkeley, 1968; MSLS, Simmons Grad. Sch. Libr. Sci., 1977. Cert. profl. librarian, Mass. Asst. libr. dir. Plymouth (Mass.) Pub. Librs., 1977-82; asst. exec. dir. Southeastern Librs. Coop., Rochester, Minn., 1982-84; libr. automation cons. N.D. State Libr., Bismarck, 1984-89; dist. libr. media dir. Bismarck Pub. Sch. Dist., 1989-97; sys. adminstr. MARINet, San Rafael, Calif., 1997—; adv. panelist for literature Mass. Coun. on Arts and Humanities, Boston, 1980-82. Editor, writer Libr. A Word to the Wise, 1995-97; author: Anthology: A Collection of Cape Cod Poets, 1974. Legis. chair, membership chair N.D. Libr. Assn., 1987-93; mem. N.D. Gov.'s Adv. Libr. Vision 2004 Com., Bismarck, 1995-96; mem. Ctrl. Dakota Libr. Network Bd., Bismarck, 1992—. Recipient Capewide 1st prize for poetry Provincetown Assn. for Living Arts, 1972, Spl. Recognition award COSMEP, 1977, Pres.' award for svc. to librs. N.D. Libr. Assn., 1994. Mem. ALA (chair publs. com. 1985-87, columnist, reviewer The Book List 1977-79), Calif. Libr. Assn., Beta Phi Mu. Avocations: gardening, travel. Office: MARINet 3501 Civic Center Dr Rm 414 San Rafael CA 94903-4189

MOREIRA, ALBERTO, electrical engineer, researcher; b. São José de Campos, Brazil, June 29, 1962; s. Luiz Erasmo and Isis (Costa Mendes) M.; m. Maria de Andrade Perocco, Nov. 14, 1992; children: Merina, Lucas. BSEE, Inst. Aero. Technol., São José dos Campos, 1984, MSEE, 1986; PhD summa cum laude, Tech. U., Munich, 1993. Scientist German Aerospace Rsch. Establishment, Munich, 1986-93, group leader, 1993-95, dept. leader, 1995—; rsch. asst., cons. ITA, São José dos Campos, 1984-86. Author: (chpt.) Synthetic Aperture Radar, 1997; contbr. articles to IEEE Transactions Geosci. Remote Sensing, Jour. Electromagnetic Waves Propagation, Internat. Jour. Elec. Comm. Recipient Sci. award German Aerospace Ctr., 1995, Young Engr. of the Yr. award IEEE Aerospace and Electronic Sys. Soc., Radar Sys. Panel, 1999. Mem. IEEE (sr., prize paper award Geosci. Remote Sensing Soc. 1996), Electromagnetics Acad. Roman Catholic. Achievements include 9 patents in field of synthetic aperture radar; development of innovative algorithms for the processing of synthetic aperture radars. Office: DLR HR, Münchenerstrasse 20, 82234 Wessling Bavaria, Germany

MOREIRA, MARCIO MARTINS, advertising executive; b. Sao Paulo, Brazil, Nov. 20, 1947; came to U.S. 1980; naturalized, 1990; s. Guido Martins and Maria Rosa (Macrine) M.; children from previous marriage: Joaquim Pedro Rezende Martins Moreira; m. Maria Auxiliadora Godinho, Oct. 18, 1981; children: Eliana Maria Godinho Martins Moreira. Ed., U. Sao Paulo, Brazil, 1970. TV producer-copywriter McCann-Erickson, Sao Paulo, Brazil, 1967-71; creative dir. McCann-Erickson, Sao Paulo, 1974-77; group creative dir. McCann-Erickson, London, Lisbon and Frankfurt, 1971-74; executive creative dir. McCann-Erickson, Latin America, 1977-80; internat. creative dir. McCann-Erickson, N.Y.C., 1980-88; vice chmn., chief creative officer McCann Erickson Worldwide, N.Y.C., 1988—; vice chmn., regional dir. Asia-Pacific McCann-Erickson Worldwide, N.Y.C., 1995-99, chief creative officer, dir. global brands, 1999—; lectr. various univs.

Author: Terraplenagem, 1968 Liquidacao, 1979; lyricist, 1968—; contbr. articles to profl. jours. U.S. judge, pres. jury Cannes Film Festival, 1989; chmn. bd. judges The New York Festivals. Recipient 5 Clio awards, 1976-89, Gold Lion, Silver Lion, Bronze Lion awards, Cannes, France, H.K. McCann award, Brazil, 1977, Paul Foley award Interpub. Group of Cos., 1983, Terence Cardinal Cooke medal for Disting. Svc. in Health Care, N.Y. Med. Coll., 1994. Mem. Brazilian-Am. C. of C. (bd. dir.). Republican. Roman Catholic. Avocations: cinema, songwriting, cars, speedwalking. Office: McCann-Erickson Worldwide 750 3rd Ave Fl 21 New York NY 10017-2703

MOREIRA, MILTON BAGGIO, neurologist, researcher; b. Curitiba, Paraná, Brazil, July 29, 1923; s. Carlos Estrella and Veronica Baggio Moreira; m. Alice Andrigo, Dec. 15, 1964; children: Elizabeth, Lilian, Viviane. Physician Fed. U. Parana, Curitiba, 1942-47, adj. prof., 1973-87, doctor, 1976—, prof., 1976-87; neurologist Particular, Curitiba, 1952—, Evang. Hosp., Curitiba, 1952-92; chair, prof. Evang. Sch. Medicine, Curitiba, 1972-90; dir. FEMPAR, Curitiba, 1975-92. Contbr. articles to profl. jours. Mem. AAAS, Neurology Acad. Brazilian, N.Y. Acad. Sci. Presbyterian. Avocation: soccer. Home: r Pedro N Pizzatto, 928 Bigorrilho, 80710120 Curitiba Parana, Brazil Office: Consultation Rm 2nd Fl, Av Luiz Xavier 68 218 Ctr, Curitiba Parana, Brazil

MOREIRA, ROSANA, food engineer, educator; b. Sorocaba, Brazil, Nov. 1, 1956; d. lenin and Odette Galves M. BS in Agrl. Engring., Campinas (Brazila) State U., 1980; MS in Agrl. Engring., Mich. State U., 1983, PhD in Agrl. Engring., 1989. From vis. prof. to assoc. prof. Tex. A&M U., College Station, 1990-98, assoc. prof., 1998—; cons. FAO, Italy, 1993, Rich-Seapack, Ga., 1997, Frito-Lay Elma Chips, Dallas, Brazil, 1998-99. Author: Deep-Fat Frying Fundamentals and Applications, 1999; editor EJournal of CIGR, 1998—; patentee in field. Grantee Advanced Rsch. Program, Austin, 1993, 99. Mem. Inst. Food Technologists, Am. Soc. Agrl. Engrs. Avocations: reading, skiing, cooking, theater, music. E-mail: mroreira@agen.tamu.edu. Office: Texas A&M Univ College Station TX 77843-2117

MOREL, MARY-ANNICK THÉRÈSE, educator; b. Saint Aignana, France, Sept. 29, 1944; d. Jean André and Geneviève (Martinet) Magnon; m. Jean Paul Morel, Dec. 23, 1968; children: Lise, Pascal, Diane, Aude. Agrégation de Grammaire, France, 1967; D, U. Paris III, 1980. Prof. agrégé Lycée de Troyes, France, 1967-69, Lycée Bergson, Paris, 1969-72; asst. U. Paris III, 1972-77, maitre de conférence, 1977-83, prof., 1983—. Coeditor Faits de Langues, 1993; author: La Concession en Français, 1996; co-author: Grammaire de l'intonation. L'exemple du Français, 1998. Mem. Soc. Linguistique de Paris (pres. 1999—). Home: 16 Rue Marx Dormoy, 92260 Fontenay-Aux Roses France Office: U Paris III, 13 Rue Santeuil, 75006 Paris France

MORELLI, ANTHONY FRANK, pediatric dentist; b. Chgo., Aug. 10, 1956; s. Frank A. and Josephine M. (Cerniglia) M.; m. Tina Makris, July 24, 1982; children: Deanna Nicole, Michelle Tina. BS, Loyola U., Chgo., 1976; DDS, Loyola U., Maywood, Ill., 1984, postgrad., 1986. Cert. specialist pediatric dentistry, Ill; Diplomate Am. Bd. Pediatric Dentistry. Pediatric dentist Infant Welfare Soc. Chgo., 1984-90; chief resident dept. pediatric dentistry sch. dentistry Loyola U., Maywood, 1985-86, assoc. prof. pediatric dentistry, 1986-91; pvt. practice La Grange, Ill., 1988—; mem. staff Children's Meml. Hosp., Chgo. and Westchester, Ill., MacNeal Hosp., Chgo. Mem. ADA, Chgo. Dental Soc., Am. Soc. Dentistry Children, Am. Acad. Pediatric Dentistry, Am. Bd. Pediatric Dentistry (diplomate), Ill. Soc. Pediatric Dentistry. Home: 6448 Cambridge Rd Hinsdale IL 60521-5402 Office: 4727 Willow Springs Rd La Grange IL 60525-6140

MORELLO, DANIEL CONWAY, plastic surgeon; b. Vineland, N.J., Nov. 12, 1943; s. John B. and Mina M. (Conway) M.; m. Mona L. Comras; children: Amy, Elise, Kate. BS, U. Notre Dame, 1965; MD, Georgetown U., 1969. Diplomate Am. Bd. Plastic Surgery, Am. Bd. Surgery, Nat. Bd. Med. Examiners. Intern Hahnemann Med. Coll. Hosp., Phila., 1969-70; surgery resident to chief resident Hahnemann Med. Coll. Hosp., 1970-74; plastic surgery resident to chief resident NYU Med. Ctr. Inst. for Reconstructive Plastic Surgery, N.Y.C., 1974-76; attending surgeon White Plains (N.Y.) Hosp. Med. Ctr., 1976—, chief of plastic surgery, 1992-98; pvt. practice in plastic surgery White Plains, 1976—; emeritus chief, 1998—; asst. attending surgeon Bellevue Hosp., Manhattan VA Hosp., Manhattan Eye, Ear and Throat Hosp. (all N.Y.C.), 1976-85; attending surgeon Northern Westchester (N.Y.) Hosp. Ctr., 1976—; United Hosp., Port Chester, N.Y., 1976—; cons. Burke Rehab. Ctr., 1977-81; asst. instr. surgery, Hahnemann Med. Coll., 1973-74, clin. instr. plastic surgery, NYU Sch. Medicine, 1974-78, clin. asst. prof. plastic surgery, 1978-86. Contbr. numerous articles to profl. jours., chpts. to books; presenter in field, including co-chair symposia 1993, 95. Bd. dirs., golf chmn. Whippoorwill Club, 1989-95, extensive com. work 1988-95. Fellow ACS; mem. Am. Soc. for Aesthetic Plastic Surgery (ofcl. spokesperson 1988—, bd. dirs. 1991—, treas. 1995-98, v.p. 1998-99, 1999-2000, pres. 2000—, chair pub. edn. com. and internat. task force 1994-97, other offices and coms.), Am. Soc. of Plastic and Reconstructive Surgeons (ofcl. spokesperson 1992—, pub. edn. com. and sci. program subcom. 1994-99, also other coms.), Am. Assn. for Accreditation of Ambulatory Surgery Facilities (pres. 1994-98, bd. dirs. 1989—, mem. strategic planning com. 1991—, other offices, coms.), N.Y. Regional Soc. Plastic Surgery (bd. dirs. 1988-91, chair program com. 1987-88, membership com. 1978-80, sec. 1988-90), Med. Soc. State of N.Y., Westchester County Med. Soc. (bd. dirs. 1986-88, extensive com. work, including med.-legal rels. com. 1986—). Avocations: golf, travel, reading. Home: 9 Hidden Pond Dr Rye Brook NY 10573-1942 Office: 10 Chester Ave White Plains NY 10601-5112 also: 91 Smith Ave Mount Kisco NY 10549-2810

MORELOS-ZARAGOZA, ROBERT HENRY, communications engineer; b. Houma, La., May 16, 1959; s. Jorge Rafael and Sandra Lola (Ascanio) Morelos-Z.; m. Naoko Tawara; children: Kai, Len. BSEE, Nat. Autonomous U. of Mexico, 1985, MSEE, 1987; PhD in Elec. Engring., U. Hawaii, 1992. Cons. engr. Tevescom, Mexico City, 1987-88; rsch. asst. U. Hawaii, Honolulu, 1988-92; asst. prof. Tec. Monterrey, Mexico, 1992-93; rsch. assoc. Osaka U., Japan, 1993-94; rsch. fellow Nara Inst. of Sci. and Technology, Japan, 1994-95; rsch. assoc. U. Tokyo, 1995-97; staff engr. LSI Logic Corp., Milpitas, Calif., 1997—; vis. rsch. assoc. Osaka U., Japan, 1993-94; rsch. asst. U. Hawaii, Manoa, 1988-92, tchg. asst., 1986-87. Contbr. articles to profl. jours. Mem. IEEE (sr.), Eta Kappa Nu. Office: Sony Computer Sci Labs Inc, 3-14-13 Higashi-Gotanda, Shinagawa-ku Tokyo 141-0022, Japan

MORENO, ANA MARIA, software engineer, researcher; b. Madrid, Jan. 6, 1970; d. Miguel Angel Moreno and Ana Maria Sanchez-Capuchino. B in Computer Sci., Tech. U., Madrid, 1994, M in Software Engring., 1995, D in Computer Scis., 1997. Rsch. asst. Tech. U. Madrid, 1995-97, asst. prof., 1998-99, assoc. prof., 1999—; cons. Spanish Telecom., Madrid, 1994-95, Spanish Ministry Adminstrn., Madrid, 1998—. Editor: Differnt Approximations for Software Engineering, 1999. Named Woman of the Yr. IBI, 1999; grantee Spanish Govt., 1995-99. Mem. IEEE, ACM, NYAC. Office: Tech U Madrid, Campus De Montegancedo, 28660 Boadilla Del Monte Spain

MORENO, FIDELA LLORCA, physician, medical educator; b. San Fernando, The Philippines, May 22, 1949; came to the U.S., 1987; d. Florencio Manalon Moreno and Rosario Soliven Llorca; m. Arthur Moreno, May 21, 1991. BS, U. Santo Tomas, Manila, 1969, MD, 1973. Internal medicine resident VA Hosp., Quezon City, The Philippines, 1974-78; cardiology fellow Philippine Heart Ctr., Quezon City, 1978-81, U. Utah, Salt Lake City, 1981-83; cons., vis. staff Philippine Heart Ctr. for Asia and St. Luke's Hosp., Quezon City, 1984-86; chief hypertension sect. Philippine Heart Ctr. for Asia, Quezon City, 1985-86; rsch. assoc. physician LDS Hosp., Salt Lake City, 1987-93; assoc. dir. clin. rsch. Prizer Inc., Groton, Conn., 1993-96; sr. assoc. dir. for Asia, Pzifer Pharms. Group, N.Y.C., 1996-99; dir. internat. clin. rsch. group Pfizer Ind., N.Y.C., 1999—; v.p. clin. rsch. Pfizer India, 1999—; presenter in field.; instr. medicine U. Utah Med. Sch., Salt Lake City, 1990-91, asst. prof., 1991-93. Contbr. chpts. to books and articles to profl. jours. Fellow Philippine Heart Assn. (assoc.); mem. Assocs. Clin. Pharmacology, Am. Heart Assn. (Utah chpt.). Democrat. Roman Catholic. Avocations: reading, theatre, symphony, ballet. Office: Pfizer Inc 60 E 42d St PMB 1166 New York NY 10165-0006

MORENO-ARIAS, GERARDO ANTONIO, dermatologist; b. San Cristobal, Venezuela, Dec. 12, 1963; arrived in Spain, 1997; s. Luis Fernando and Ana Teresa (Arias) Moreno; m. Maria Yolanda Lopez Vargas; 1 child, Laura; m. Mercedes Vazquez-Barrero, Dec. 5, 1997; 1 child, Sofia. MD, Javeriana U., Bogota, Colombia, 1989, U. Barcelona, 1997. Gen. practice Hosp. Regional, Tame, Colombia, 1990-91, Hosp. Padre Justo Arias, Rubio, Venezuela, 1991-92; fellow in dermatology UNIFESP-Escola Paulista Medicina, São Paulo, Brazil, 1993-97; fellow mohs micrographic surgery Hosp. Gen. de Catalunya, Barcelona, Spain, 1997-99; fellow in dermatol. surgery Hosp. Clinic, Barcelona, 1997-99; cons. dermatologist Hosp. Comarcal, Vielha, Spain, 1999—; cons. dermatologist Amecon, São Paulo, 1995-97. Mem. editl. com., articles reviewer Lasers in Surgery and Medicine, 1999; contbr. articles to profl. jours. Mem. Brazilian Soc. Dermatology. Home: Villarroel, 172-174, 2d-la-izq, 08036 Barcelona Spain Office: Hosp Clinic Dermatology, Villarroel 170, 08036 Barcelona Spain

MORENO-CABRAL, CARLOS EDUARDO, cardiac surgeon; b. Zacatecas, Mex., Nov. 4, 1951; s. Manuel Julio Moreno and Dominga Cabral; children: Rodrigo, Iza, Daniel. MD, Nat. U. Mex., 1976. Diplomate Am. Bd. Thoracic Surgery. Resident in gen. surgery U. Hawaii, 1977-80, Mich. State U., 1980-82; fellow in cardiac surgery Stanford (Calif.) U., 1982-84, 86-88; tng. in thoracic surgery SUNY, Bklyn., 1984-86; dir. cardiac transplant program St. Francis Hosp., Honolulu, 1989—. Author: Postoperative Management in Adult Cardiac Surgery, 1988. Fellow ACS; mem. Soc. Thoracic Surgeons. Avocation: photography. Office: 1380 Lusitana St Ste 912 Honolulu HI 96813-2448

MORENO-DAVILA, HERMAN WILLIAM, neurology educator; b. Pereira, Colombia, Dec. 8, 1963; s. Uriel Moreno and Isabel Davila; m. Gloria Escobar (div.). MD, U. de Caldas, Manizales, Colombia, 1988; PhD, NYU, 1996; postgrad., SUNY, N.Y.C. Prof. Nat. U., Bogota, Colombia, 1988-96, Rosario U., Bogota, 1988-96; asst. rsch. scientist NYU, N.Y.C., 1994-96, asst. prof., 1996-99; clin. instr. neurology SUNY, N.Y.C., 2000—; advisor Colombian Ctr. Devel. Sci., Bogota, 1996-2000. Cons. editor Neurosci. Jour., 1996-98; contbr. articles to profl. jours. Mem. Neurosci. Soc., Biophys. Soc., Latin Am. Biophys. Soc. Avocations: tennis, squash, poetry. E-mail: morenoherman@hotmail.com. Home: 176 13th St Brooklyn NY 11215-4703

MORENON, JEAN, psychiatrist; b. Marseilles, France, Aug. 26, 1930; s. Charles and Melanie (Mirapel) M.; m. Angèle Salle, July 5, 1954 (div. 1976); children: Jean-Pierre, Françoise; m. Martine Roguet, Nov. 8, 1980; children: Nathalie, Raphael. Grad. in Biology, Faculty Scis. de Marseilles, France, 1948; MD, Med. Sch. de Marseilles, France, 1960. Resident Hosp., Montfavet, France, 1957-61; head dept. Hosp., Montfavet, 1961-68, Bassens-Chambery, France, 1969-85, Montperrin, France, 1985—; tchr. psychology Coll. Chambery, 1970-85; chief dept. Med. Sch. Grenoble, 1970-80. Author: Alcoul-Alibis et Solitudes, 1997; contbr. articles to profl. jours. 2d lt., 1952-59. Mem. French Soc. Alcoologie, N.Y. Acad. Scis. Home: 8 rue des tanneurs, F-04500 Riez France Office: Centre Hosp Montperrin, Chemin du petit Barthelemy, 13617 Aix-en-Provence France

MORERO, ROBERTO DIONISIO, biochemistry educator; b. Esmeralda, Santa Fe, Argentina, May 31, 1945; s. Juan Roberto and Enedina Ana Morero; m. Eddy Marta Massa, Mar. 2, 1973 (div. June 1986); children: Matias, Pablo; m. Luisa Ester Peralta, Dec. 21, 1988. B, San Martin, San Francisco, 1962; Biochemistry Degree, Nat. U. Cordoba, Argentina, 1969; PhD in Biochemistry, Nat. U. Tucuman, Argentina, 1974. Teaching staff Nat. U. Tucuman, San Miguel, 1971-78, initial prof., 1978-81, assoc. prof., 1981-87, prof. biochemistry, 1987—; ind. researcher Consejo Nat. de Investigaciones, Buenos Aires, 1978-91. Contbr. articles to profl. jours. Initial fellow NRC, Nat. U. Cordoba, 1969; perfecting fellow NRC, Nat. U. Tucuman, 1971; internat. fellow NIH, U. Ill., 1976. Avocations: tennis, soccer. Home: Cariola 799, 4107 Yerba Buena Tucuman, Argentina Office: Nat U Tucuman, Chacabuco 461, 4000 San Miguel Tucuman Argentina

MORETON, THOMAS HUGH, minister; b. Shanghai, China, Dec. 2, 1917; came to U.S., 1946; s. Hugh and Tsuru M; m. Olive Mae Rives, Apr. 1, 1947 (dec. Apr. 1986); children: Ann Rives Moreton Smith, Andrew Hugh, Margaret Evelyn Moreton Hamar; m. Selma Littig, June 7, 1986. LLB, 1939, BD, 1942, PhD, 1946; ThD, Trinity Sem., 1948; LittD, 1949. Ordained to ministry Bapt. Ch., Glasgow, Scotland, 1942. Min. various chs., also tchr. Seaford Coll. Eng., 1945-46; tchr. coll. and sem. level. divsn. courses various schs., Atlanta, Oklahoma City, 1946-51; founder Tokyo Gospel Mission, Inc., House of Hope, Inc., Tokyo, 1951—; also World Gospel Fellowship, Inc., Norman, Okla., 1967—; pastor chs., Moore, Okla., Shawnee, Okla., Ada., Okla., Del City, Okla., Tahlequah, Okla. and Oklahoma City, 1968—; preacher numerous fgn. countries; internat. tour dir., radio broadcaster. Contbr. articles to religious jours. Charter mem. Am.-Japan Com. for Assisting Japanese-Am. Orphans. Chaplain AUS, 1952-63. Recipient various awards Japanese govt. Fellow Royal Geog. Soc., Philos. Soc.; mem. Royal Soc. Lit., Am.-Japan Soc., Israel-Japan Soc.

MORETTI, LUCIA HELENA TIOSSO, psychologist, educator; b. Osvaldocruz, Brazil, July 6, 1951; d. Isaltino and Iraci (Miranda) Tiosso; m. Itagiba Geraldo Moretti, July 6, 1993. Degree in psychology, FEB, Bauru, Brazil, 1975; PhD, U. Saõ Paulo, Brazil, 1989; postdoctorate, La Sapienza, Rome, 1993. Instr. State U. Londrina, Brazil, 1976-77, asst. prof., 1977-81, adj. prof., 1982-85, prof. DC IV, 1986-97, assoc. prof., 1998-99, head prof. Ctr. Higher Learning, 1999—. Contbr. articles to profl. jours. Fellow APA, SB Psychology, SBNP. Roman Catholic. Avocations: swimming, walking, reading, travel. Home: 1012 Nilson Ribas St, Londrina 86062090, Brazil Office: State U Londrina, Dept Psychology, Londrina 86051970, Brazil

MORETTI, NANNI, film director; b. Brunico, Bolzano, Italy, Aug. 19, 1953. films directed include: Come Parli, Frate?, 1974, Io Sono un Autarchico, 1976, Ecce Bombo, 1978, Sogni d'Oro, 1981, Bianca, 1984, La Messa e' Finita, 1985, Palombella Rossa, 1989, Caro Diario, 1994 (Cannes Internat. Film Festival Best Dir.), The SEcond Time, 1995, Opening Day of Close-Up, 1996, Aprile, 1998, La Stanza del figlio, 2000. *

MOREWITZ, STEPHEN JOHN, behavioral scientist, consultant, educator; b. Newport News, Va., May 14, 1954; s. Burt M. and Ruth (August) M., Lora Friedman (stepmother). BA, Coll. William and Mary, 1975, MA, 1978; PhD, U. Chgo., 1983. Rsch. asst. Michael Reese Hosp., Chgo., 1979-84; asst. social scientist Argonne (Ill.) Nat. Lab., 1984-85; asst. to dean, asst. prof. U. Ill., Chgo., 1988-92, sr. rsch. splst., 1991-92; vol. rsch. staff San Francisco Gen. Hosp., 1993-97; pres. S. Morewitz, PhD & Assocs., Chgo. and Buffalo Grove, Ill., 1988—, San Francisco, 1992—; part-time sociology faculty DePaul U., Chgo., 1985—; mem. faculty St. Elizabeth's Hosp., Chgo., 1987-88; assoc. prof. Calif. Coll. Podiatric Medicine, 1997—; cons. in field. Author: (monograph) Sexual Harassment, 1996; co-author: Medical Malpractice, 1996; contbr. articles to profl. jour., chpt. to book. Vol. docent Garfield Farm Mus., LaFox, Ill., 1979—; curator The Saving of S.S. Quanza, Chgo., 1991—. Mem. Am. Pub. Health Assn., Am. Diabetes Assn. (profl. sect.), Assn. for Behavioral Scis. and Med. Edn., Am. Sociol. Assn. (cert., nat. finalist med. sociology), Soc. Behavioral Medicine, Generalist in Med. Edn., Sociol. Practice Assn. Avocations: theatre, museum design, swimming, environmental preservation. Office: S Morewitz PhD & Assocs PMB M858 601 S Lasalle St Fl 6 Chicago IL 60605-1700

MOREY, CHARLES LEONARD, III, theatrical director; b. Oakland, Calif., June 23, 1947; s. Charles Leonard Jr. and Mozelle Kathleen (Milliken) M.; m. Mary Carolyn Donnet, June 10, 1973 (div. 1975); m. Joyce Miriam Schilke, May 29, 1982; 1 child, William. AB, Dartmouth Coll., 1969; MFA, Columbia U., 1971. Artistic dir. Peterborough (N.H.) Players, 1977-88, Pioneer Theatre Co., Salt Lake City, 1984—. Actor: N.Y. Shakespeare Festival, Playwrights Horizons, New Dramatists, ARK Theatre Co., Ensemble Studio Theatre, Cubiculo, Folger Theatre, Syracuse Repertory Theatre, Theatre by Sea, others; over 150 plays acted in or directed; guest dir. Ensemble Studio Theatre, ArK Theatre, Am. Stage Festivel, McCarter Theatre, Pioneer Theatre Co., PCPA Theatrefest, The Repertory Theater of St. Louis, Meadow Brook Theatre, Utah Shakespearean Festival; author new adaptations Alexander Dumas' The Three Musketeers, Bram Stoker's Dracula, Charles Dickens' A Tale of Two Cities, Victor Hugo's The Hunchback of Notre Dame, Alexandre Dumas' The Count of Monte Cristo. Trustee Utah Arts Endowment, Inc.; panelist Nat. Endowment for Arts. Mem. Soc. Stage Dirs. and Choreographers, AEA, SAG, AFTRA, Salt Lake City C. of C. (Honors in the Arts award 1991), Utah Assn. Gifted Children (Community Svc. award 1991), Peterborough Players (Edith Bond Stearns award 1990). Democrat. Episcopalian. Office: Pioneer Theatre Co 300 S 1400 E Salt Lake City UT 84112-0660

MOREY, JEAN W., artist; d. Carl Adolf Wuerfel and Lillian Florence Brown; m. William Joseph Morey., June 19, 1948; children: Susan, Nancy, Kenneth, David, Peter. Student, Art Inst. Chgo., DePauw U. Artist, illustrator Consolidated Publ. Co., Chgo., The Fair Store, Chgo.; co-founder Sci. Hall and Jr. Mus., Bradenton, Fla.; illustrator children's books Rand McNally, Children's Press, Ency. Britannica, Bonific Press; guest instr. Wheaton (Ill.) Coll.; lectr. in field. Illustrator 19 books, 6 readers, 3 childrens books. Deaconess Fox Valley Presbyn. Ch., Geneva, Ill., 1969-76. Mem. Nat. Women's Book Assn., Fla. Watercolor Soc., Citrus Water Color Club, Citrus County Art League, Nature Coast Painters. Avocations: archaeology, painting, softsculpture, boating, swimming. Home: 3590 N Wagon Pt Beverly Hills FL 34465-4484

MOREY, JERI LYNN SNYDER, architect; b. Midland, Tex., Sept. 7, 1943; d. Jerome R. and Doris (Prichard) Snyder; m. Philip Stockton Morey Jr., Sept. 5, 1964; children: W. Philip, Christopher J. BArch with honors, U. Tex., 1967; postgrad., Fla. Atlantic U., 1977-79. Registered architect, Tex. Draftsman William B. Stalter, Architect, Corpus Christi, Tex., 1968-69, Richard Colley, Architect, Corpus Christi, 1969-70; project architect Wisznia & Peterson Architects, Corpus Christi, 1971-76, Bennett, Martin & Solka, Corpus Christi, 1976-77, P.S.P. Profl. Corp., Corpus Christi, 1979, Mabrey Designs, Corpus Christi, 1979-80; owner, mgr. Jeri L.S. Morey Architect, Corpus Christi, 1980—. Mem., chair Kingsville Planning and Zoning Commn., 1983-88; campaign worker various local polit. races, Kingsville, 1985, 89; com. mem. Kingsville Action Network-Opera House Com., 1986-88. Mem. AIA (treas. Corpus Christi chpt. 1995), Tex. Soc. Architects (mem. profl. devel. com. 1985-86, conv. program com. 1991), Soroptimist Internat. (treas. 1984-86, pres. elect 1986). Democrat. Episcopalian. Avocations: gardening, hiking through national parks. Office: Am Bank Plz 711 N Carancahua St Ste 518 Corpus Christi TX 78475-0008

MOREY, PHILIP STOCKTON, JR., mathematics educator; b. Houston, July 11, 1937; s. Philip Stockton and Helen Holmes (Wolcott) M.; m. Jeri Lynn Snyder, Sept. 5, 1964; children: William Philip, Christopher Jerome. BA, U. Tex., 1959, Ma, 1961, PhD, 1967. Asst. prof. math. U. Nebr., Omaha, 1967-68; assoc. prof. Tex. A&I U., Kingsville, 1968-76; prof. Tex. A&M U., Kingsville, 1976—; lectr. U. Tokyo, 1976, U. Hokkaido, 1977, 88. Contbr. articles to Tensor N.S., Internat. Jour. Engring. Sci, Tex. Jour. Sci. Recipient Researcher of Yr. awrd Tex. A&I Alumni Assn., 1985. Mem. Tex. Acad. Sci. (chmn. math. sect. 1982, 85, 99), Am. Math. Soc., Tensor Soc., (Japan). Achievements include research in extensor analysis, tensor analysis, differential geometry, mathematical physics. Home: 1514 Lackey St Kingsville TX 78363-3199 Office: Tex A&M Univ Dept Math Kingsville TX 78362

MORGADO, WELLES A.M., physicist; b. Rio de Janeiro, Oct. 22, 1965; s. Welles Dos Santos Morgado and Aurora Martinez. BS, U. Fed. Rio De Janeiro, 1988; MSc, Ctr. Brasileiro Pesquisas Fis., Rio De Janeiro, 1991; PhD, MIT, 1997. Postdoctoral fellow U. Fed. Rio De Janeiro, 1997-99; prof. Pont. Univ. Cat.-RJ, Brazil, 2000—. Mem. Am. Phys. Soc., Brazilian Phys. Soc., Sigma Xi. Avocations: sports, minorities education, volunteering. Office: PUC-RJ Dept Phys, Cx PO 38071, 22452970 Rio De Janeiro Brazil

MORGAN, ALAN VIVIAN, geologist, educator; b. Barry, Glamorgan, Wales, Jan. 29, 1943; emigrated to Can., 1964, naturalized, 1977; s. George Vivian Williams and Sylvia Nesta (Atkinson) M.; m. Marion Anne Medhurst, June 14, 1966; children: Siân Kristina, Alexis John. B.Sc. with honors in Geology and Geography, U. Leicester, Eng., 1964; M.Sc. in Geography, U. Alta., Calgary, Can., 1966; Ph.D. in Geology, U. Birmingham, Eng., 1970. Postdoctoral fellow U. Western Ont. and U. Waterloo, Ont., Can., 1970-71; asst. prof. earth scis. and man-environ. studies U. Waterloo, 1971-78, assoc. prof. earth scis., 1978-85, prof., 1985—; assoc. dir. Quaternary Scis. Inst. U. Waterloo, Ont., Can., 1992-97; dir. Quaternary Scis. Inst. U. Waterloo, Can., 1997—; mem. Brit. Schs. Exploring Soc. Ctrl. Iceland Expdn., 1960; rep. Can. Geosci. Coun., 1977-83, exec. dir., 1988-94, adminstrv. dir., 1996—; mem. com. on global change Royal Soc. Can., 1988-91, mem. com. on pub. wareness of sci., 1989-94; coord. global change Geol. Survey Can.a, 1990-92. Author 6 field guides; editor newsletter OYEZ, 1990-94; contbr. articles to numerous profl. publs.; dir., prodr. documentary film The Heimaey Eruption, 1974. Recipient award for MS thesis Can. Assn. Petroleum Geologists, 1967, Bancroft award Royal Soc. Can., 1994, John H. Moss award Nat. Assn. Geology Tchrs., 1995, J. Willis Ambrose medal Geol. Assn. Can., 1997. E.R.W. Neale medal Geol. Assn. Canada, 1998; Charles Lapworth scholar, 1970; Nat. Scis. and Engring. Rsch. Coun. Can. grantee, 1971—;. Fellow Geol. Assn. Can. (hon. life, sec.-treas. 1975-83, disting. fellow), Geol. Soc. Am.; mem. Am. Quaternary Assn. (pres. 1990-92), Can. Quaternary Assn. (pres. 1987-89), Brit. Quaternary Research Assn., Internat. Union Quaternary Research (sec. gen. XII congress 1983-87). Office: U Waterloo, Dept Earth Scis, Waterloo, ON Canada N2L 3G1

MORGAN, ALAN WILLIAM, management consultant; b. Bristol, U.K., Oct. 4, 1951; s. Alfred Charles and Eliza Dora (Sproul-Cran) M.; m. Janet Cullis Connolly, Oct. 17, 1981; children: Campbell, Edward, Georgina. BA in Jurisprudence, Oxford (Eng.) U., 1973, MA in Jurisprudence, 1976; MBA, Harvard U., 1978. Cert. barrister, Eng., 1974. With Brandts, London, 1974-76; mgr. corp. banking Grindlays Bank, London, 1976; with McKinsey & Co., London, 1978—, prin., 1984—, dir., 1991—, head U.K. & European fin. instns. practice; adv. task force Lloyd's of London, 1990-91. Mem. Pres.'s com. Campaign for Oxford, 1989-94, mem. Oxford U. Campaign City com., 1992-94. Mem. R.A.C. Club, Oxford & Cambridge Club, Harvard Club of N.Y.C., Hurlingham Club, Ascot Race Course. Avocations: walking, swimming, theater, books, horseracing. Office: McKinsey and Co, 1 Jermyn St, London SW1, England

MORGAN, ANNE MARGARET BARCLAY, artist, author, ambassador; b. Washington, June 20, 1952; d. George A. and Margaret R. (Taylor) M. PhD in Psychology, U. Vienna, Austria, 1977; MA in Art History, U. Fla., 1990. lectr. on contemporary art; design cons. for serene environments. Prodr., dir., writer art documentaries, including Video Art to Virtual Reality, 1992; works exhibited in U.S. and Europe; contbr. over 220 articles and revs. to profl. jours., and books, including Art in America, Art News Sculpture, Garden Design, Camera Austria; contbr. articles to profl. jours. Bd. dirs., new art examiner Fla. Media Arts Ctr. Mem. Am. Assn. Mus., Coll. Art Assn., Internat. Assn. Art Critics (southeastern rep.). Office: 1119 NW 36th Dr Gainesville FL 32605-4944

MORGAN, ANTHONY JOHN, health, safety and environmental executive; b. Sydney, NSW, Australia, Dec. 7, 1937; s. Harold Eric and Hazel Gladys (Roadknight) M.; m. Florence Patricia Nightingale; children: Sally Adele, Richard Charles, Rebecca Kate, Megan Amanda. Cert. in accident control, Nat. Safety Coun. Australia, 1972; diploma in applied chemistry, Royal Melbourne Inst. Tech., 1973; diploma in occupaional hygiene, Deakin U., 1978; diploma in indsl. hygiene, Am. Bd. Indsl. Hygiene, 1982; M Applied Sci. in Toxicology, Royal Melbourne Inst. Tech., 1988. Chemist, quality and prodn. supr. CSR Co. Ltd., Sydney, Melbourne, Fiji, 1956-67; chem. supt., chem. hazards officer Kodak Australia, Melbourne, 1967-78; prin. occupational hygienist Telecom Australia, Melbourne, 1979-84, mgr. work environ., 1984-88, mgr. health and safety, 1988-90; mgr. health, safety and environ. Telstra Corp. (formerly Telecom Australia), 1990-97; mng. dir. Burgundy Crest Pty. Ltd., 1997-2000; prin. cons. Indsl. Hygiene Svcs.; employers rep. Comcare Joint Working Party on Stds., Codes of Practice, 1990-97; lectr. Royal Melbourne Inst. Tech. Univ., Deakin U., Box Hill TAFE; safety inst. rep. Stds. Australia Com. on Handcleaners; chmn. Commonwealth Employers Tech. Group, Canberra, Australia, 1992-97. Editor Jour. Occupational Health Soc. Australia, 1980-85. Ch. warden, mem. vestry St. Hilary's

Anglican Ch., Kew, 1965-94, 95-2000, chmn. camping com., 1970-78; synod rep. Anglican Diocese of Melbourne; chmn. mgmt. com. Camp Cormorant, 1975-90; pres. Occupational Health Soc. of Australia, 1979-85. Sgt. Australian Citizen Mil. Force, 1957-59. Mem. Australian Inst. Occupational Hygiene, Royal Australian Chem. Inst. (rep. stds. Australia com. on classification of hazardous areas), Australian Inst. Risk Mgmt., Am. Acad. Indsl. Hygiene, Am. Conf. Govtl. Indsl. Hygienists, Am. Indsl. Hygiene Assn., Australian Soc. Clin. and Exptl. Pharmacologists and Toxicologists, Brit. Occupational Hygiene Assn., Internat. Occupational Hygiene Assn., Internat. Comm. Occupational Health, Nat. Environ. Law Assn., Safety Inst. Australia (rep. com. 1979-2000). Anglican. Avocations: bushwalking, cycling, stamps, woodworking. Home: 3 Talbot St Lwr Templestowe, Victoria Australia Office: Burgundy Crest Pty Ltd, PO Box 2087 Templestowe Hts, LPO Victoria 3107, Australia

MORGAN, AVANELLE PROCTOR, physician; b. Yonkers, N.Y., Mar. 26, 1945; d. Egbert Purdy and Avanelle Major (Proctor) M. AB cum laude, Cornell U., Ithaca, 1967; MD, SUNY, 1971; AAS in Computer Info. Svcs., Cayuga C.C., Auburn, N.Y., 1996. Bd. cert. family practice. R-2 intern Cleve. Metro Gen. Hosp., 1971-72; resident family practice Resident-Maine Med. Ctr., Portland, 1972-75; pvt. practice Union Springs, N.Y., 1978-89; physician Health Svcs. of Ctrl. N.Y., Lafayette, 1989-95, Finger Lakes Family Medicine, Scipio, N.Y., 1996—; dept. head Auburn (N.Y.) Meml. Hosp., 1980-82, bd. trustees, 1985-89. Contbr. article to profl. jour. Physician USPHS, 1975-78. Recipient Commendation medal USPHS-Nat. Health Svc. Corps, 1978. Fellow Am. Acad. Family Physicians; mem. Cayuga County Med. Soc. (sec. 1985-86), Am. Acad. Family Practice. Presbyterian. Avocations: needlework, music, reading, sports, attending college. Home: 5207 Ridge Rd Union Springs NY 13160-9719 Office: Finger Lakes Family Medicine Center Rd Scipio Center NY 13147

MORGAN, CLYDE NATHANIEL, dermatologist; b. Bell County, Tex., Nov. 2, 1923; s. Xenophen William and Rhoda Ella (Deck) M.; m. Birdie Joyce Rich, Mar. 3, 1951; children: Clyde Nathaniel Jr., Reinette Jean, Nancy Elaine. BS, Abilene Christian Coll., 1948; MD, U. Tex. Galveston, 1953. Assoc. prof. biology Abilene (Tex.) Christian Coll., 1954-56; pvt. practice Abilene, 1954-67, dermatologist, 1969—. Contbr. articles to profl. jours. Mem. AMA, SAR (chpt. pres. 1997-99, award 1995), Am. Coll. Cryosurgery, Internat. Soc. Cryosurgery, Tex. Med. Assn., Tex. Dermatologic Soc., Taylor-Jones-Haskell County Med. Soc. Republican. Mem. Ch. of Christ. Avocations: golf, fishing, hunting, cryogenics research. Home: 1718 Cedar Crest Dr Abilene TX 79601-3228 Office: 1166 Merchant St Abilene TX 79603-5014

MORGAN, CONSTANCE LOUISE, real estate executive; b. Denver, July 24, 1941; d. Willis Stephen and Evelyn (Rutar) Claus; m. Robert M. Morgan, Jan. 3, 1963; children: Stephen, Melayne. BS, U. N. Mex., 1963. Lic. real estate broker; Fla. master gardener, 1996. Realtor, assoc. Investors Realty, Tallahassee, 1980-82, br. mgr., 1982-83; pres., broker Connie Morgan Realty, Inc., Tallahassee, 1983-96, Constance L. Morgan, Broker, Tallahassee, 1996—; founder Network for Ind. Brokers, 1989-93. Chmn. docents Fla. Gov.'s Mansion, Tallahassee, 1979-80; pres. Newcomers-Univ. Women, Tallahassee, 1968, Hunters Crossing Homeowners Assn., 1998-99; bd. dirs. Tallahassee Symphony Orch., 1990-96; bd. dirs. Rotary Youth Camp, Inc., 1995—, Tallahassee United Way. Mem. Nat. Assn. Realtors, Fla. Assn. Realtors, Tallahassee Bd. Realtors (chmn. Multiple Listing Svc. 1984, 94), Tallahassee Cmty. Realty Group, Tallahassee C. of C. (bd. dirs. 1984-86, 89-92), Rotary, Chi Omega (treas. 1962), Phi Gamma Nu (pres. 1962). Home and Office: 3322 Remington Run Tallahassee FL 32312-1462

MORGAN, DAHLIA, museum director. BA, McGill U., Montreal, 1958; postgrad., Sir George Williams U., Montreal, 1968-69, U. Miami, Fla., 1974. Lectr. Mus. of Fine Arts, Montreal, 1965-70; lectr./rschr. Sir George Williams U., Montreal, 1968-70; grad. asst. dept. art and art history U. Miami, Fla., 1971-74; adj. prof. visual arts dept. Fla. Internat. U., Miami, 1975-77, vis. rof. visual arts dept., 1978-79, faculty visual arts dept., 1979—, dir. Art in State Bldgs. Program, 1984—, dir. Art Mus., 1980—; lectr. in field; curator numerous exhbns.; panelist NEA Mus. Grants, 1993, Cultural Advancement Grants, 1992, 90; cons. Fed. Gen. Svcs. Adminstrn., 1992, Metro-Dade Art in Pub. Places Program, 1992. Prodr. numerous catalogues to exhbns. Juror South Miami Art Fair Photo Group; bd. dirs. Nat. Found. for Advancement in the Arts, 1984—; founder Friends of the Art Mus. Support Group at Fla. Internat. U., 1984—; chmn. State of Fla. Art in Bldgs., 1984—; chmn. Art in Pub. Places, Dade County, Fla., 1980-84. Recipient 3d Ann. MAXIE award Miami Arts Exchange, 1990; grantee Fla. Endowment for Humanities, 1986, Metro Dade County Cultural Affairs Coun., 1986, Fla. Internat. U., 1990, 91; U. Miami-Coral Gables merit scholar, fed. scholar. Mem. Assn. Coll. and Univ. Mus. and Galleries, Am. Assn. Mus., Coll. Art Assn. Am., Fla. Mus. Dirs. Assn., Fla. Higher Edn. Arts Network, Internat. Coun. Mus. (fine arts com.), Miami Cultural execs. Coun., Southeastern Mus. Assn., Fla. Cultural Action Alliance, Phi Kappa Phi. Office: Art Mus at Fla Internat U University Park Pc # 110 Miami FL 33199-0001

MORGAN, DAVID GETHIN, county treasurer; b. Swansea, Glamorgan, Wales, June 30, 1929; s. Edgar Llewellyn and Ethel (Jones) M.; m. Marion Morgan, Aug. 13, 1955. MA, Jesus Coll., Oxford, Eng., 1952; MA (hon.), U. W. England, 1994. Grad. acct. Staffordshire County Coun., Stafford, Eng., 1952-58; O&M officer Cheshire County Coun., Chester, Eng., 1958-62; county mgmt. svc. officer Durham (Eng.) County Coun., 1962-65; asst. county treas. Leicestershire County Coun., Leicester, 1965-68, dep. county treas., 1968-73; county treas. Avon County Coun., Bristol, Eng., 1973-94. Editor: (manual) O&M in Local Government, 1970. Sgt. Edn. Corps, Royal Army, 1947-49. Fellow Inst. Adminstrv. Mgmt. (regional chmn. 1970-93); mem. Brit. Inst. Mgmt., Chartered Inst. Pub. Fin. and Acctg. (vice chmn. local govt. com. 1990-94), Local Govt. Execs. (chmn. 1988-93), Soc. County Treas. (pres., treas. 1988-94), Avon Assn. Civic Treas. (chmn., sec. 1973-94), Avon Enterprise Fund (bd. dirs. 1985-94), Victory Svcs. Club. Anglican. Avocations: local history and architecture, French.

MORGAN, DIRCK, broadcast journalist; b. L.A., Feb. 3, 1954; s. Phillip Barton and Katherine (Ramirez) Segall; m. Ellen Tomoye Matsumoto, Dec. 1, 1993; 1 child, Makena Sunao. AA, Pierce Coll., 1973. Assignment editor KFWB/Group W. Westinghouse, L.A., 1972-74; corp. comm. specialist Northrop Corp., L.A., 1975-78; news dir. Stas. KARM, KFIG, Fresno, Calif., 1978-84; editor, anchor Sta. KGIL, L.A., 1984-85; fin. anchor Sta. KWHY-TV, L.A., 1985-87; cmty. resources specialist Optimist Boys Home, L.A., 1985-87; reporter Sta. KFWB, CBS, L.A., 1988—; media crisis mgmt. instr. L.A. County Fire Dept., 1990—, L.A. Police Dept., 1991—, LAUSD, 1996, Calif. State Mil. Res., L.A., 1990-95. Helicopter airborne reporter Sta. KFWB, 1988-91, broadcast series on L.A. riots, 1992 (L.A. Press Club award), L.A. Police Dept. Ballistics, 1994 (L.A. Press Club award), Radio TV News Assn. Instr., announcer Kenkojuku World Karate, L.A., 1984-92; host Nissei Week, L.A., 1990-98. Recipient 18 Golden Mike awards Radio and TV News Assn. Mem. L.A. Police Protective League (hon. life). Avocations: karate, Japanese koi fish, firearms, classic cars. Office: KFWB/CBS 6230 Yucca St Los Angeles CA 90028-5295

MORGAN, EDWIN (GEORGE), poet, writer; b. Glasgow, Scotland, Apr. 27, 1920; s. Stanley Lawrence and Margaret McKillop (Arnott) M. MA, U. Glasgow, 1947; DLitt, Loughborough U., 1981, U. Glasgow, 1990, U. Edinburgh, 1991, U. St. Andrews, 2000, Heriot-Watt U., 2000; D. Univ., Stirling U., 1989, U. Waikato, 1992; M. Univ., Open U., 1992. Asst. lectr. U. Glasgow, Scotland, 1947-50, lectr., 1950-65, sr. lectr., 1965-71, reader, 1971-75, titular prof. English, 1975-80, prof. emeritus, 1980—; vis. prof. Strathclyde U., 1987-90. Author: (poems) The Vision of Cathkin Braes and Other Poems, 1952, The Cape of Good Hope, 1955, Scotch Mist, 1965, Starryveldt, 1965, Sealwear, 1966, Emergent Poems, 1967, The Second Life, 1968, Gnomes, 1968, Proverbfolder, 1969, The Horseman's Word: A Sequence of Concrete Poems, 1970, Twelve Songs, 1970, The Dolphin's Song, 1971, Glasgow Sonnets, 1972, Instamatic Poems, 1972, The Whittrick: A Poem in Eight Dialogues...1955-61, 1973, From Glasgow to Saturn, 1973, !?:. Nuspeak 8, being a visual poem, 1973, The New Divan, 1977, Colour Poems, 1978, Star Gate: Science Fiction Poems, 1979, Poems of Thirty Years, 1982, Grafts/Takes, 1983, 4 Glasgow Subway Poems, 1983, Sonnets from Scotland, 1984, Selected Poems, 1985, From the Video Box, 1986, Newspoems, Wacy!, 1987, Themes on a Variation, 1988, Tales from Limerick Zoo, 1988, Collected Poems, 1990, Hold Hands among the Atoms, 1991, Sweeping Out the Dark, 1994, Virtual and Other Realities, 1997, Demon, 1999, New Selected Poems, 2000, (with others) Penguin Modern Poets 15, 1969, Three Scottish Poets, 1992, (nonfiction) Essays, 1974, Hugh MacDiarmid, 1976, East European Poets, 1976, Provenance and Problematics of "Sublime and Alarming Images" in Poetry, 1977, Edwin Morgan: An Interview, 1977, Twentieth-Century Scottish Classics, 1987, Crossing the Border: Essays on Scottish Literature, 1990, Nothing Not Giving Messages: Reflections on His Work and Life, 1990, Language, Poetry and Language Poetry, 1990, Evening Will Come They Will Sew the Blue Sail, 1991, (recordings) Selected Poems, 1987, 17 Poems of Edwin Morgan, 1987; editor: Collins Albatross Book of Longer Poems: English and American Poetry from the 14th Century to the Present Day, 1963, New English Dramatists 14, 1970, Scottish Satirical Verse, 1980, (with others) Scottish Poetry, vols. I-VI, 1966-72, Roadworks: Song Lyrics for Wildcat, 1987, New Writing Scotland, vols. 5-6, 1987-88, New Writing Scotland, vol. 7, 1989; translator: Beowulf: A Verse Translation into Modern English, 1952, Poems from Eugenio Montale, 1959, Sovpoems: Brecht, Neruda, Pasternak, Tsvetayeva, Mayakovsky, Martynov, Yevtushenko, 1961, Selected Poems: Sandor Weores, 1970, Wi the Haill Voice: 25 Poems by Vladimir Mayakovsky, 1972, Fifty Renascence Love-Poems, 1975, Rites of Passage: Translations, 1976, August Graf von Platen-Hallermuende, Selected Poems, 1978, The Apple-Tree: A Medieval Dutch Play in a Version by Edwin Morgan, 1982, Master Peter Pathelin, 1983, Cyrano de Bergerac (Edmond Rostand) 1992, (with others) Sandor Weores, Eternal Moment: Selected Poems, 1988, Collected Translations, 1996, St. Columba, The Maker on High, 1997, Phaedra (Racine), 2000; composer (opera librettos) The Charcoal-Burner, 1969, Valentine, 1976, Columba, 1976, Spell, 1979; contbr. essays, poems and translations to periodicals. With Royal Army Med. Corps, 1940-46. Decorated officer Order of the British Empire; recipient Cholmondeley award, 1968, Scottish Arts Coun. award, 1969, 73, 75, 78, 83, 84, 91, 92, Meml. award Hungarian PEN, 1972, Book of Yr. award Royal Bank of Scotland, 1983, Soros Transl. award Columbia U. Transl. Ctr., 1985, Order of Merit, Republic of Hungary, Stakis prize for Scottish Writer of the Yr., 1998, Queen's Gold Medal for Poetry, 2000; named hon. prof. U. Ctrl. Wales, 1991, Poet Laureate Glasgow, 1999. Avocations: photography, scrapbooks, walking. Home: 19 Whittingehame Ct, Glasgow G12 0BG, Scotland

MORGAN, EVAN, chemist; b. Spokane, Wash., Feb. 26, 1930; s. Evan and Emma Anne (Klobucher) M.; m. Johnnie Lu Dickson, Feb. 14, 1959; 1 child, James. BS, Gonzaga U., 1952; MS, U. Wash., 1954, PhD, 1956. Staff chemist IBM Corp., Poughkeepsie, N.Y., 1956-60; group supr. Olin Mathieson Co., New Haven, 1960-64; assoc. prof. chemistry High Point (N.C.) Coll., 1964-65; sr. rsch. chemist Reynolds Metals Co., Richmond, Va., 1965-72; chemist Babcock & Wilcox, Lynchburg, Va., 1972-95, Lynchburg Tree Steward, Lynchburg, 1995—. Mem. Am. Chem. Soc. Home: 5128 Wedgewood Rd Lynchburg VA 24503-4208

MORGAN, FRANK T., business educator, consultant; b. Shamokin, Pa., July 8, 1944; s. Burgess Sherman and Marion Regina (Lewis) M.; m. Nancy Ida Bishop, May 30, 1970; children: Elizabeth Marion, Douglas Bishop. AB, Princeton U., 1966; MS, Pa. State U., 1967; postgrad., Stevens Inst. Tech., Hoboken, N.J., 1976-79; PhD, Calif. Coast U., 1983. Cert. sr. profl. in human resources. Plant pers. mgr. Gen. Foods, Jacksonville, Fla., 1967-69; assoc. placement mgr. Gen. Foods, White Plains, N.Y., 1969-70; mgr. sales devel. Gen. Foods, 1970-71; mgr. orgn. devel. Berol Corp., Daubury, Conn., 1971-73; v.p. human resources Berol Corp., 1973-78, sr. grop v.p. internat., 1978-87; prof., dir. exec. edn. U. Va. Darden Grad. Sch. Bus., Charlottesville, 1987-94; global dir. exec. edn. U. N.C., Chapel Hill, 1994-99; dir. exec. devel. The Dow Chem. Co., Midland, Mich., 1999—; bd. dirs. Danbury Med. Ctr., 1977-85; chmn. Danbury Edn. Adv. Coun., 1978-86; pres. Morgan Assocs., Charlottesville, 1987—. Contbr. articles to publs. Mem. Am. Psychol. Assn., Am. Soc. for Tng. and Devel., Soc. for Pers. and Human Resources (chair), Consortium for Exec. Edn. Republican. Episcopalian. Avocations: sailing, tennis, history. Office: The Dow Chem Co Edc Midland MI 48674-0001

MORGAN, GARY CORDELL, market research company executive; b. Melbourne, Australia, Dec. 8, 1941; s. Roy Edward and Marie Emma (Plant) M.; m. Genevieve Joan Edwards, Oct. 27, 1977; children: Blayney, Xenia, Portia, Monte. BComm, Melbourne U., 1968. Exec. chmn. Roy Morgan Rsch., Melbourne, 1985—; chmn. Kitchener Mining, 1990-96, Haoma Mining, 1992—, Elazac Mining, 1993—. Fellow Australian Inst. Co. Dirs. (found.), Mktg. Assn. Australia and New Zealand, Sch. Behavioral Sci., U. Melbourne (hon.); mem. Am. Mktg. Assn., European Soc. Opinion and Market Rsch. Avocations: collecting Australian furniture, pottery and doors, skiing. Office: Roy Morgan Rsch, 411 Collins St, Melbourne Vic 3000, Australia

MORGAN, GARY LORIN, biophysicist, inventor; b. Balt., Oct. 23, 1948; s. Lorin C. and Pearl C. (Dise) M.; m. Kathleen Marie Lamm Morgan, Dec. 6, 1986; children: Ashley, Lauren. BS in Engring. Sci., Johns Hopkins U., 1975. Rsch. assoc. Johns Hopkins U., Balt., 1966-75; sr. rsch. scientist Pfizer Med. Systems, Columbia, Md., 1976-84; quality assurance mgr. U.S. Design Corps., Lanham, Md., 1984-88; dir. R&D Pacific Sci. Co., Silver Spring, Md., 1988-93; chief rsch. scientist Triton Thalassic Tech., Lusby, Md., 1994—. Contbr. articles to profl. jours. Pres., dir. Marshallee Civic Assn. Mem. Water Environment Fedn. Achievements include patents for Particle Detecting Instrument with Sapphire Detecting Cell, Particle Measurement System with Sonically Measured Flow Rate, Sterilization of Opaque Liquids with Ultraviolet Radiation, Lamp for Generating High Power Ultraviolet Radiation. Avocations: boating, marine sci. Office: Ship Point Rsch Lab 13325 Rousby Hall Rd Lusby MD 20657-2772

MORGAN, GWYN, oil and gas executive; b. Didsbury, Alta., Can., Nov. 4, 1945; s. Ian and Margaret (Hergenhein) M. BSc in Mech. Engring., U. Alta., 1967; postgrad., U. Calgary, Cornell U. Petroleum engr. Alta. Energy Resources Conservation Bd.; mgr. ops. and engring. Consolidated Natural Gas Ltd., Consolidated Pipelines Ltd., Norlands Petroleums Ltd.; with Alta. Energy Co., Ltd., Calgary, 1975—, pres., CEO; bd. dirs. HSBC-Bank Can. Dir. Bus. Coun. on Nat. Issues; trustee Fraser Inst.; hon. col. 410 Tactical Fighter Squadron, Can. Forces. Mem. Can. Assn. Petroleum Prodrs. Avocations: sailing, hiking, skiing, physical fitness, cycling. Office: Alberta Energy Co Ltd, 3900 421 7th Ave SW, Calgary, AB Canada T2P 4K9

MORGAN, IWAN WYN, political history educator; b. Gorseinon, Dyfed, U.K., June 11, 1949; s. David and May Margaret (Price) M.; m. Theresa Mary Ball, Apr. 9, 1977; children: Humphrey Alun, Eleanor Josie. BA with honors in History, Univ. Coll. Wales, Aberystwyth, 1970; Ph.D. in History, U. London, 1975. Lectr. in politics City of London Poly. (London Guildhall U.), 1973-84; acting head dep. politics and govt., 1984-94, head dept. politics and modern history, 1994—, apptd. head Am. history, 1997; exch. prof. Ind. U.-Purdue U., Ft. Wayne, 1979-80. Author: Eisenhower Versus "The Spenders", 1990, Beyond the Liberal Consensus, 1994, Deficit Government, 1995; contbr. articles to profl. jours. Mem. Orgn. Am. Historians, Brit. Assn. Am. Studies, Polit. Studies Assn. Avocations: squash, films, hill walking. Office: London Guildhall U, Oldcastle St, London E1 7NT, E1 7NT, England

MORGAN, JOHN PHILLIP, rail transportation executive; b. Durban, South Africa, July 18, 1939; s. Charles Allen and Dorothy Ann (Stark) M.; m. Barbara Ann Wayne, Sept. 9, 1963; 1 child, Louella Kalan. BS in Engring., U. Natal, Durban, South Africa, 1961. Engr. Robertson & Hitchins, Durban, South Africa, 1962-70, ptnr., 1971-79; ptnr. Robertson & Hitchins, Johannesburg, South Africa, 1980-88, mng. ptnr., 1989-97, sr. ptnr., 1998—; mem. adv. bd. Railway Engring. U. Pretoria, South Africa, 1996—. Fellow South African Inst. Civil Engrs.; mem. South African Assn. Cons. Engrs. (coun. mem. 1982-95, pres. 1990-91), Durban Country Club, Wanderers Club. Avocations: fly fishing, boardsailing, golf. Office: Robertson & Hitchins, R&H House 3 Seddon St, Randburg 2194, South Africa

MORGAN, KENNETH SMITH, retired editor; b. Bristol, Eng., Aug. 6, 1925; s. Edward Henry and Florence May (Wheeler) M.; m. Patrica Eva Hunt, Nov. 1, 1952; 2 children. Reporter for various weekly newspapers Nottingham, Eng., 1947-51; reporter Derby (Eng.) Telegraph, 1951-52, Reuters, London, 1952-54; reporter Hansard, Westminster, Eng., 1954-78, dep. editor, 1978-79, editor, 1979-89; ret., 1989; pres., founder Commonwealth Hansard Editors Assn., 1984-89. Author: Falklands Campaign. Lt. Royal West Kent Regiment, 1944-47. Avocation: Napoleonic history.

MORGAN, KERMIT JOHNSON, lawyer; b. Henderson, Iowa, Feb. 13, 1914; s. Samuel Jr. and Jennie Amelia Morgan; m. Georgina R. Morgan, Oct. 12, 1940 (dec. 1958); children: Georgina Morgan Street, Wilson S.; m. Ortrud Impol, Dec. 9, 1960. BA, U. Iowa, 1935; JD, U. So. Calif., 1937. Bar: Calif. 1939. Pvt. practice, L.A., 1940-45, 71-80; ptnr. McBain & Morgan, L.A., 1945-65, McBain, Morgan & Roper, L.A., 1965-71, Morgan & Armbrister, L.A., 1980-91; pvt. practice, Santa Monica, Calif., 1991—. Mem. ABA, Am. Bd. Trial Advs. (diplomate, nat. pres. 1973, pres. L.A. 1972, 77), Assn. Def. Trial Attys. (bd. dirs. 1982-85), Internat. Assn. Ins. Counsel, Calif. State Bar, Assn. Def. Trial Attys., Assn. So. Calif. Def. Counsel (bd. dirs. 1966-67), L.A. Bar Assn., Wilshire Bar Assn. Republican. Congregationalist. Avocation: golf. Home: 2108 Stradella Rd Los Angeles CA 90077-2325 Office: 2850 Ocean Park Bld Santa Monica CA 90405

MORGAN, LESLIE TALBOT, English language educator; b. Radford, Va., Nov. 2, 1968; d. David Conrad and Wilna Faye (Buckingham) M. BA, U. Mich., 1991; MA, U. Tex., 1994. Vice-chief instr. GEOS, Shiki, Japan, 1994-97; instr. Bunkyo Univ. Women's Coll., Chigasaki, Japan, 1997-2000, The Internat. Sch. Choueifat, Cairo, 2000—. Mem. Phi Kappa Phi. Avocations: hiking, art. Home: 204 Rockingham Dr Columbia MO 65203-1645 Office: Internat Sch Choueifat-Cairo, PO Box 2760, Al Horreya Heliopolis, Egypt

MORGAN, LESLIE YARBOROUGH, physician; b. New Orleans, Sept. 15, 1956; s. Ira Lee and Lucy Lynn (Strain) M.; m. Cynthia Louise Cook, Dec. 20, 1980; children: Laura Westbrook, Everett Scarborough, Grady Stewart. BA, Colby Coll., 1978; MD, La. State U., 1982; M.T.S., Harvard U., 1984; MPH, Johns Hopkins U., 1988. Cert. Am. Bd. Internal Medicine. Intern, resident La. State U. Med. Ctr., Shreveport, 1984-87; missionary coworker Presbyn. Ch. (U.S.A., Louisville), Bangladesh, 1989—; adv. for health programs Ch. of Bangladesh, 1993—. Contbr. sci. rsch. articles to profl. jours. Avocation: classical guitar. Home: 236 Gladstone Blvd Shreveport LA 71104-4511 Office: Christian Mission Hosp, GPO Box 25, Rajshahi 6000, Bangladesh

MORGAN, LINDA GAIL, theater producer; b. Tallahassee, May 14, 1952; d. Thomas Mitchell Morgan Sr. and Helen Frances (Rives) Stokes. BS, Fla. State U., 1974. Prodn. mgr. Valley Forge Ballet-5th World Peace Youth Culture Festival, Honolulu, 1985, Salute to Lady Liberty, Madison Square Gardens, 1986, U.S. Constn. 200 Yr. Anniversary Parade, Phila., 1986-89, Columbus Day Parade, N.Y.C., 1988, Gift of the White Bird Parade-Landmark Entertainment, Oita, Japan, 1990-91, 1996 Olympic Opening and Closing Ceremonies-Centenniel Events, Inc., Olympic Stadium, Atlanta, 1996, Super Bowl XXXI Half Time Show, New Orleans, 1997, N.Y. Jets Halftime Show, Meadowlands Stadium, N.J., 1997; prodn. state mgr. Walt Disney Bus. Prodns., 1998; coordinating prodr. (musical) This Is America, The New World, Freedom Music, Santa Monica, Calif., 1989, California Traditional Music Festival, Human Rights Lectr. Series, Soka U. Am., L.A., 1992-95, The Genius and the Great, L.A., 1993, Every Child Deserves a Chance, L.A., 1994, A Tribute to Burt Reynolds, L.A., 1994, Celebrate the Garnet and Gold IV Honoring Charles Nelson Reilly, L.A., 1995, Leisure Quest Internat./Entertainment Devel. Group, Burbank, Calif., 1997; artist agt., co. gen. mgr. Zoli Mgmt., Inc., N.Y.C., 1986-89; orch. prodn. mgr. All Am. Gen. Meeting, Spectrum, Phila., 1987; asst. prodn. mgr. 8th World Peace Culture Festival, Fukuoka, Japan, 1987, This Is America, Madison Square Gardens, 1988, 1991 Olympic Festival Opening Ceremonies Radio City Spl. Events, Dodger Stadium, L.A., 1991; prodn. staff Inauguration Mayor of Atlanta, Civic Ctr., Atlanta, 1998; event mgr. Coke on Ice World of Coca Cola, Atlanta, 1997-98, Disney Events Productions, 1998—. Mem. Soka Gakkai Internat. (arts divsn. culture dept. 1995-99), Fla. State U. So. Calif. Alumni Assn. (bd. dirs. 1991-95, Garnet/Gold award 1995), Internat. Spl. Event Soc., Alpha Chi Omega. Democrat. Buddhist. Avocations: arts, needlepoint, antiques, piano, gardening. Office: 1503 Live Oak Lane Lake Buena Vista FL 32830

MORGAN, MARIANNE, corporate professional; b. Muncie, Ind., Oct. 13, 1940; d. Clarence Wilson and Mary Estle (Shafer) M. BA, Calif. State U., Long Beach, 1962; MS, U. So. Calif., 1968. Lic. real estate salesperson, Fla. Lab. technician Ball Meml. Hosp. Pathology Lab, Muncie, 1956-61; sr. libr. asst. Anaheim (Calif.) Pub. Libr., 1963-68; coll. libr. Orange Coast Coll., Costa Mesa, Calif., 1968-73; exec. v.p. Brady Products, Inc., Clearwater, Fla., 1973—; bd. dirs. Brady Products, Inc., Clearwater, Suncoast Fluid Power, Inc., Clearwater. Fiction book reviewer, Libr. Jour., 1969-73; photography pub. in Irvine mag., 1973. Named Alice Miriam Kitselman Scholar, Kitselman Estate, Muncie, 1958. Mem. Nat. Water Well Assn., Boat Owners of the U.S., U.S. Tennis Assn., Sea Ray Boat Owners Club, RVing Women, Carefree Club. Republican. Avocations: boating, tennis, photography, travel, raising AKC Bulldogs.

MORGAN, MARY LOU, retired education educator, civic worker; b. Chgo., Mar. 5, 1938; d. William Nicholas and Esther Lucille (Galbraith) Wanmer; m. James Edward Morgan, May 30, 1963. BA in Bus. Edn. and Econs., Wichita State U., 1971, MEd in Student Pers. and Guidance, 1974; postgrad., Kans. State U., 1986. Cert. bus. tchr., Kans. Reservationist Braniff, Wichita, Kans., 1961-62; stenographer, fin. analyst, clk.-typist Boeing Co., Wichita, 1962-68, tng., pers. and records positions, 1979-93; pers. cons. Rita Pers. Svc., Wichita, 1974-75; adminstrv. aide, manpower specialist, job developer City of Wichita, 1975-76; account exec., employment counselor Mgmt. Recruiters, 1976-77; pers. mgr., patient cons. Women's Clinic, 1977; vocat. rehab. counselor State of Kans., Parsons, 1977-79; pvt. detective Investigation Svcs., Wichita, 1981-84; instr. career devel. Wichita State U., 1988-90; paralegal asst. Turner & Hensley, Wichita, 1975. Precinct committeewoman Wichita Dem. Com., 1992-94; founder, 1st pres., v.p. program chmn. NOW, Wichita, 1969-93, asst. state coord. polit. action com., Wichita, 1993-95, at-large state bd., Joplin, 1994-95, 97-98, 99-00; pres. Jasper County-Newton County Dems., 1998; coord. funding Women's Crisis Ctr., Wichita, 1975; docent Carver Mus., Hoover Mus.; bd. dirs. for City of Wichita, Wichita Commn. on Status of Women, 1988-91; vice chmn. Hist. Preservation Commn.; founder, coord. Ann. Women's Chautauqua. Mem. AAUW (bd. dirs. edn., equity, women's issues 1999—), LWV (v.p. issues study Joplin area chpt., 1998—), AARP, NOW, Am. Bus. Women's Assn. Avocations: water skiing, boating, collecting Victorian clothing, travel.

MORGAN, MARY LOUISE FITZSIMMONS, fund raising executive, lobbyist; b. N.Y.C., July 22, 1946; d. Robert John and Mary Louise (Gordon) Fitzsimmons; m. David William Morgan, Aug. 7, 1971; children: Mallory Siobhan, David William. BA, Marquette U., 1964; MA, Catholic U., Wash., 1966. Asst. prof. Monmouth Coll., West Long Branch, N.J., 1966-69; campaign dir. United Way, N.Y.C., 1969-80; pres. Morgan Communications, N.Y.C., 1980-82; capital campaign dir. YMCA of Greater N.Y., 1982-85; dir. devel. N.Y. Med. Coll., Valhalla, 1985-88; counsel Challenger Ctr., Va., 1988-89; v.p. Ctr. Molecular Medicine & Immunology, Newark, 1989-92, Garden State Cancer Ctr., Newark, 1989-92; chief devel. and pub. affairs officer Mental Health Assn., White Plains, N.Y., 1993-95; dir. external affairs St. Vincents Svcs., 1996—; adj. prof. Iona Coll., New Rochelle, N.Y., 1994-95; dir. Meth Ch. Home for Aged, Riverdale, N.Y., Casita Maria Inc., N.Y.C., 1975-95; pres., founding dir. Achievement Rewards for Coll. Scientists Inc., 1978-80. Sec. Darien (Conn.) Dem. Town Com., 1984—, vice chmn. Darien nominating com. 1986—. Recipient 50th Anniversary award Casita Maria Inc., N.Y.C., 1984, Iris award Bus. Communicators of Am., 1991, Nat. Depression Awareness Campaign award NMHA, 1994. Mem. Nat. Soc. Fund Raising Execs., Nat. Soc. Hosp. Adminstrn., Spring Lake (N.J.) Bath and Tennis Club. Democrat. Roman Catholic. Avocations: golf, gardening, tennis. Office: 66 Boerum Pl Brooklyn NY 11201-5705

MORGAN, MICHAEL JAMES, medical research administrator; b. Rhondda, Wales, Apr. 30, 1942; s. William H. and Elsie C. (Duffield) M.; m. Janice Treble (div.); m. Pelin Faik; children: Nadiye Gemma, Selen Michelle. BA, Dublin U., 1965; PhD, Leicester U., 1969. Rsch. fellow U. Calif., San Diego, 1969-70, U. Conn., Storrs, 1970-71; lectr., sr. lectr. Leicester U.,

1971-86; program dir. The Wellcome Trust, London, 1986—; hon. sr. lectr. div. biochemistry United Med. and Dental Schs. of Guy's and St. Thomas Hosps., London, 1986—. Contbr. articles to profl. jours. Harkness Found. fellow, 1969. Fellow Royal Soc. Medicine; mem. Biochem. Soc., Brit. Soc. Cell Biology, Human Genome Orgn. (trustee). Avocations: photography, reading, theatre. Office: The Wellcome Trust, 183 Euston Rd, London NW1 2BE, England

MORGAN, PETER WILLIAM LLOYD, technology company executive; b. Neath, Wales, May 9, 1936; s. Matthew and Margaret Gwynneth (Lloyd) M.; m. Elisabeth Susanne Davis, Apr. 18, 1964; children: Justine, Penelope, Gabrielle. MA, Cambridge (Eng.) U., 1959. Staff IBM U.K., London, 1959-73, dir., 1973-74, 80-89; group dir. IBM Europe, Paris, 1975-80; dir. gen. Inst. of Dirs., London, 1989-94; chmn. NPI, London, 1996-99, Pace Microtechnology plc, Saltaire, Eng., 1996-2000; dir., chmn. Swalec, Cardiff, Wales, 1989-96; dir. Firth Holdings plc, London, 1994—, ALM Ltd., London, 1997—; dir. Zergo Holdings plc (now Balt. Techs.), London, 1994-98, dep. chmn., 1998—; chmn. Kingston-SCL Ltd. (now KSCL), 1999-2000, Oxford (Eng.) Instruments plc, 2000—; coun. mem. Lloyds of London, 2000—. Mem. Eurpean Cmty. Econ. and Social Com., Brussels, 1994—. Conservative. Church of England. Avocations: skiing, dog walking, history, wine, opera. Office: 40 Catherine Pl, London SW1E 6HL, England

MORGAN, RICHARD GREER, lawyer; b. Houston, Dec. 23, 1943; s. John Benjamin (stepfather) and Audrey Valley (Brickwede) Haus; children: Richard Greer, Jonathan Roberts. AB in History, Princeton U., 1966; JD, U. Tex., 1969. Bar: Tex. 1969, D.C. 1970, Minn. 1976, U.S. Ct. Appeals (D.C. cir.) 1970, U.S. Ct. Appeals (5th and 9th cirs., temporary emergency ct. appeals) 1976. Atty., advisor to commr. Lawrence J. O'Connor, Jr. Fed. Power Commn., Washington, 1969-71; assoc. Morgan, Lewis & Bockius, Washington, 1971-75; ptnr. O'Connor & Hannan, Washington, 1975-89, Lane & Mittendorf, Washington, 1989-97; mng. ptnr. Shook, Hardy & Bacon, L.L.P., Houston, 1997—; bd. dirs. Hexagon, Inc.; instr. law seminars; lectr. in field. Author: Gas Lease and Royalty Issues, Natural Gas Yearbook, 1989, 90, 91, 92; contbr. articles on energy law to profl. jours. Bd. dirs. Mighty Spl. Music Makers, U. Tex. Law Sch. Found. Mem. ABA, Fed. Bar Assn., Energy Bar Assn. (bd. dirs.), D.C. Bar Assn., Princeton Alumni Coun., Princeton Alumni Assn. Houston, Energy Law Found. (pres.). Office: Shook Hardy and Bacon LLP 600 Travis St Ste 1600 Houston TX 77002-2911

MORGAN, ROBERT EDWARD, marketing and strategic management educator, consultant; b. Carmarthen, Wales, U.K., Oct. 24, 1967; s. David Clive and Eleanor (Davies) M.; m. Tracey Helen Ryan, Jan. 12, 1991; 1 child, Cian Padrig Ryan-Morgan. BS, U. Wales, Cardiff, 1989, PhD, 1996. Rschr. Cardiff Bus. Sch., U. Wales, 1989-91, lectr., 1991-97, sr. rsch. fellow, 1997-99; prof. U. Wales, Aberystwyth, 1999—; prin. Talis Partnership, Carmarthen, U.K., 1997—. Sch. gov. Ysgol Gymrael Treganna, Cardiff, 1997-98. Fellow Acad. Mktg. Sci.; mem. Am. Mktg. Assn., Chartered Inst. Mktg. Avocations: golf, wine. E-mail: robert.morgan@aber.ac.uk. FAX: 44(0)1970 622740. Office: Univ Wales Sch Mgmt and Bus, Cledwyn Bldg., Penglais, Aberystwyth Wales SY23 3DD, United Kingdom

MORGAN, ROBERT MILES, paramedic, educator; b. Memphis, Oct. 5, 1971; s. Charles Oscar Morgan and Maria T. (Tartaglia) Parton. Tech. Cert. Paramedicine, Shelby State Coll., Memphis; Tech. Cert. CCEMT-P, U. Md., Balt. EMS Southaven (Miss.) Emergency Med. Svc., 1991-92; EMT Mid-South Emergency Med. Svc., Southaven, 1992; EMT - intermediate Desoto County Emergency Med. Svc., Walls, Miss., 1992-95, paramedic, 1995—. Named EMT of the Yr., Desoto County Emergency Med. Svc., 1993, 94, Paramedic of the Yr., 1995. Mem. Nat. Assn. EMTs, Nat. Registry EMTs. (cert.), Nat. Flight Paramedics Assn., Miss. EMT Assn. Baptist. Avocations: scuba diving, travel, water sports. Home: 258 Malone Rd N Hernando MS 38632-7140 Office: Desoto County Emergency Med Svc 5876 Highway 301 Walls MS 38680-9785

MORGAN, WILLIAM J., accounting company executive; b. Bklyn., Jan. 12, 1947; s. William J. and Emma T. (Kraft) M.; m. Patricia A. Maltz, Mar. 23, 1968; children: Michele, Jennifer. BS, St. John's U., 1968. CPA, N.Y. Conn., N.J. Mng. ptnr. Stamford office, audit staff KPMG Peat Marwick, N.Y.C., 1968-72, audit supr., 1972-74, audit mgr., 1974-77, ptnr.-in-charge pvt. bus. adv. service, 1977-79; nat. office, ptnr.-in-charge recruiting KPMG Peat Marwick, 1979-82; ptnr. comml. health care practice KPMG Peat Marwick, Short Hills, 1982-91; ptnr.-in-charge N.J. audit practice KPMG Peat Marwick, 1989-91, mng. ptnr. Fairfield/Westchester counties practice, 1991-94, ptnr. in charge global accts., 1993-96, 1996-98; mem. Bus. Unit Planning Task Force, 1987-90, mem. compensation com., 1990-91, bd. dirs., 1991—, chmn. profit distbn. com., 1991-95, mem. future direction com., 1991-93, pension task force, 1991-92, chmn. compensation com., mem. bd. process com., 1997—. Acctg. adv. bd. Grad. Sch. Bus. Fordham U., 1979-82, mem. standardization com. Nat. Retail Mchts. Assn., 1979; trustee Tri County Sholarship Fund, 1984-91; v.p., exec. com., adv. bd. Fairfield coun. Boy Scouts Am., 1993-95; bd. dirs. Stamford Symphony, 1995-99; bd. dirs., chmn. bus. ops. com. heritage affiliate Am. Heart Assn.; chmn. Fairfield County Info. Exchange, 1992-94; bd. dirs. S.W. Area Commerce and Industry Assn., 1994—, Inroads Fairfield amd Westchesteer County chpt., 1992-95; active Bus. Execs. for Nat. Security, 1995-99, Ambs. Roundtable, 1995-99; exec. com. Conn. Policy and Econs Coun. Mem. Am. Inst. CPA's (small bus. devel. com. 1979-81, acctg. lit. awards com. 1983-86), N.J. Soc. CPA's (chmn. acctg. and auditing stds. com. 1988-90, trustee 1990-92, pub. rels. task force, 1987, subcom. health care acctg. 1983-86), N.Y. State CPA's (retail acctg. com. 1975-78, com. on edn. in coll. and univs. 1978-82), Nat. Assn. Accts. (dir. manuscripts 1975-77, v.p. N.Y. chpt. 1977-81, pres. N.Y. chpt. 1981-82, nat. publs. com. 1982-83, com. acad. relations 1983-84, nat. dir. 1983-86, Disting. Service award 1975), Health Care Fin. Mgmt. Assn. (N.J. chpt. chmn. auditing com. 1982-83, legis. task force com. 1985-86, chmn. joint ventures com., 1987-88), Fairmount Country Club (bd. govs., treas. 1987-90), Woodway Country Club, Conn. Golf Club, Landmark Club. Roman Catholic. Home: 14 Talmadge Hill Rd Darien CT 06820-2125 Office: KPMG LLP 3001 Summer St Stamford CT 06905-4317

MORGAN, WILLIAM P., JR., financial planning and investment firm executive; b. Statesville, N.C., Sept. 8, 1963; s. William Paul Sr. and Dorothy Mae (Law) M.; m. Tina Lynn Laws, Nov. 25, 1987; 1 child, Margaret Wells. BA in English, Wake Forest U., 1985. Registered investment advisor. Prime agt. Aetna Life & Casualty, Charlotte and Statesville, N.C., 1985-87; v.p. Webb Fin. Svcs., Statesville, 1987-91; pres., CEO Capital Mgmt. Group of the Carolinas, Inc., Statesville, 1991—, CMG Investment Adv., Inc., Statesville, 1991—; fin. svc. cons. Davidson Savs. Bank, Statesville, 1992-94. Author newspaper articles. Chmn. bd. ARC, Statesville, 1989-96; bd. dirs. Am. Heart Assn., Statesville, 1987-89; mem. pres.'s club. Statesville C. of C., 1986-91. Mem. Nat. Assn. Philanthropic Planners, Internat. Assn. Fin. Planning, Am. League Fin. Instns. (mem. adult care home adv. com.). Republican. Presbyterian. Avocations: golf, hiking, gardening, reading. Office: Capital Mgmt Group PO Box 5039 Statesville NC 28687-5039

MORGANROTH, FRED, lawyer; b. Detroit, Mar. 26, 1938; s. Ben and Grace (Greenfield) M.; m. Janice Marilyn Cohn, June 23, 1963; children: Greg, Candi, Erik. BA, Wayne State U., 1959, JD with distinction, 1961. Bar: Mich. 1961, U.S. Dist. Ct. (ea. dist.) Mich. 1961, U.S. Ct. Claims 1967, U.S. Supreme Ct. 1966; trained matrimonial arbitrator. Ptnr. Greenbaum, Greenbaum & Morganroth, Detroit, 1963-68, Lebenbom, Handler, Brody & Morganroth, Detroit, 1968-70, Lebenbom, Morganroth & Stern, Southfield, Mich., 1971-78; pvt. practice, Southfield, 1979-83; ptnr. Morganroth & Morganroth P.C., Southfield, 1983-94, Morganroth, Morganroth, Alexander & Nye, P.C., Birmingham, Mich., 1994-98, Morganroth, Morganroth, Jackman & Kasody, PC, Birmingham, 1999—. Mem. ABA (family law sect. 1987—), Mich. Bar Assn. (hearing panelist grievance bd. 1975—, Oakland County family law com. 1988—, vice chmn. 1992-93, chair 1993—), State Bar Mich. (mem. family law coun. of family law sect. 1990—, treas. 1993-94, chmn.-elect 1994-95, chmn. 1995-96), Detroit Bar Assn., Oakland Bar Assn. (cir. ct. mediator 1984—), Am. Arbitration Assn. (Oakland County family law com. 1985—, vice chmn. 1992-93, chmn. 1993-94, trained matrimonial arbitrator), Detroit Tennis Club (Farmington, Mich., pres. 1978-82), Charlevoix Country Club. Jewish. Avocations: comml. pilot, golfing. Home: 30920 Woodcrest Ct Franklin MI 48025-1435 Office: 300 Park St Ste 410 Birmingham MI 48009-3482

MORGENROTH, EARL EUGENE, entrepreneur; b. Sidney, Mont., May 7, 1936; s. Frank and Leona (Ellison) M.; m. Noella Nichols, Aug. 2, 1958; children: Dolores Roxanna, David Jonathan, Denise Christine. BS, U. Mont., 1961. From salesman to gen. mgr. Sta. KGVO-AM Radio, Missoula, Mont., 1958-65; sales mgr. Stas. KGVO-TV, KTVM-TV and KCFW-TV, Missoula, Butte, Kalispell, Mont., 1965-66, gen. mgr., 1966-68; gen. mgr. Sta. KCOY-TV, Santa Maria, Calif., 1968-69; v.p., gen. mgr. Western Broadcasting Co., Missoula, 1966-69, gen. mgr., pres., 1969-81; gen. mgr., pres. numerous cos., Mont., Calif. Idaho, P.R., Ga., 1966-84; pres., chmn. Western Broadcasting Co., Missoula, 1981-84, Western Communications, Inc., Reno, 1984-90; prin. Western Investments, Reno, 1984—; chmn. Western Fin., Inc., Morgenroth Music Ctrs., Inc., Mont., Mont. Band Instruments, Inc.; chmn. E & B Music Inc., Times Square, Inc., Rio de Plumas Ranches, LLC. Mem. Mont. Bank Bd., Helena; commencement spkr. U. Mont., 1988; bd. dirs. U. Mont. Found., 1985-95. With U.S. Army, 1954-57. Named Boss of Yr. Santa Maria Valley J.C.s, 1968, Alumnus of the Yr., U. Mont. Bus. Sch., 1998. Mem. U. Mont. Century Club (pres.), Missoula C. of C. (pres.), Rocky Mountain Broadcasters Assn. (pres.), Craighead Wildlife-Wildlands Inst. (bd. dirs. 1991-97), Boone and Crockett Club (pres.-elect), Grizzly Riders Internat. (bd. dirs., v.p.), Bldg. A Scholastic Heritage (bd. dirs. 1987-97). Republican. Methodist.

MORGENSTEIN, WILLIAM, shoe company executive; b. Bklyn., Jan. 11, 1933; s. Samuel and Jeanne Marie (Mittentag) M.; m. Sylvia Dove, June 8, 1952; children: Lee Brian, David Barry. BS in Fin., U. Ala., 1955. Salesman Greenwald Shoe Co., Birmingham, Ala., 1954-56; sr. buyer Melville Shoe Corp., N.Y.C., 1958-67; pres. Kitty Kelly Shoe Co., N.Y.C., 1967-70; exec. v.p. A.S. Beck Shoes, N.Y.C., 1970-71, Sandia Internat., Englewood Cliffs, N.J., 1971-75; pres., chief exec. officer Marquesa Internat. Corp., Englewood, N.J., 1975-95; sr. acct. mgr. Signature Group divsn. Montgomery Ward, 1995-99; regional dir., v.p. Advanceme.com Inc., 1999—; internat. cons. footwear exporting, 1965—. Served with U.S. Army, 1956-58. Mem. Footwear Distbrs. and Retailers Am. (vice chmn., bd. dirs., exec. com.), Internat. Footwear Assn. (chmn. 1989—, vice chmn. 1986—, exec. com. 1986—), 210 Assn. (Pres.' Circle 1987), Toastmasters (past pres. Teaneck, N.J. chpt.). Republican. Jewish. Avocations: history, golf.

MORGENSTERN, MATTHEW, computer scientist; b. N.Y.C.. BSEE, Columbia U., 1968, MSEE and Computer Sci., 1970; MS in Computer Sci. and Mgmt., MIT, 1975, PhD in Computer Sci., 1976. Asst. prof. computer sci. Rutgers U., New Brunswick, N.J., 1976-82; research computer scientist Info. Scis. Inst., U. So. Calif., Los Angeles, 1982-84; sr. computer scientist SRI Internat., Menlo Park, Calif., 1984-90; dir. R & D programs advt. info. tech. divsn. Xerox, Cambridge, Mass., 1990-92; prin. scientist Xerox Design Rsch. Inst./Cornell U., Ithaca, N.Y., 1992—; cons. Hewlett-Packard Corp., Palo Alto, Calif., 1990, Cornell U., 1996—; prin. investigator U.S. Govt. DARPA projects on heterogeneous databases and metadata repositories, 1992—. Co-author: Database Security VIII, 1994; contbr. articles to profl. jours. Mem. IEEE, Am. Assn. Artificial Intelligence, Assn. Computing Machinery, Sigma Xi, Tau Beta Pi, Eta Kappa Nu. E-mail: mmorgen@alum.mit.edu. Office: Xerox Design Research Inst Cornell Univ 603 Rhodes Hall Theory Ctr Ithaca NY 14853-3801

MORI, AKIO, immunologist, researcher; b. Tokushima, Japan, May 25, 1959; s. Hisao and Ikuko (Miki) M.; m. Fumiko Hazeyama, Nov. 17, 1991; children: Yuka, Noriyuki. MD, U. Tokyo, 1984, PhD, 1997. Resident U. Tokyo, 1984-86, rsch. fellow, 1986-89, rsch. assoc., 1992-98; rsch. fellow Johns Hopkins U., Balt., 1989, La Jolla (Calif.) Inst. for Allergy and Immunology, 1989-92; rsch. scientist Nat. Sagamihara (Japan) Hosp., 1998—. Contbr. articles to sci. jours., including Jour. Immunology. Astra rsch. grantee, 1997, rsch. grantee Japanese Respiratory Soc., 1998. Mem. Collegium Internat. Allergologicum. Avocation: golf. Office: Nat Sagamihara Hosp Clin, Rsch Ctr, 18-1 Sakuradai, Kanagawa Sagamihara 228-8522, Japan

MORI, KINJI, computer science educator; b. Tokyo, Jan. 3, 1947; s. Tokuzo and Masa (Suzuki) M.; m. Kazuyo Nozawa, Oct. 19, 1974; children: Masahiro, Chieko. BS, Waseda U., Tokyo, 1969, MS, 1971, PhD, 1974. Rschr. Hitachi Ltd., Tokyo, 1974-84, sr. rschr., 1984-93, dept. gen. mgr., 1993-95, chief rschr., 1995-97; prof. Tokyo Inst. Tech., 1997—, chair dept. computer sci., 1999—. Editor IEEE Transaction on Computers, 1993-96, Very Large Scale Integrated Circuit Signal Processing, 1989-96; holder more than 330 patents, including autonomous decentralized sys. (Sci. and Tech. Min.'s Patent award 1988, Japan Patent award 1990). Mem. Autonomous Decentralized Sys. Project by Ministry of Edn., 1990-93. Recipient Excellence Tech. Achievement Spl. prize, Ichimura Found., 1994, Min.'s Outstanding Achievement Rsch. award, Japanese Govt., 1994. Fellow IEEE (program com. internat. conf. on distributed computing sys. 1992-94, standing com. and program com. computer software and applications conf. 1993—, program com., founder, exec. sec. and gen. chair internat. symposium on autonomous decentralized sys. 1993—, program com. workshop on future trends of distbd. computing 1995—, founder and steering com. chair internat. workshop on distributed computing, comm. and applications; Best Paper award Computer Soc. internat. conf. 1984), Inst. Elec. Engrs. of Japan, Soc. of Instrument and Control Engrs. of Japan, Info. Processing Soc. Japan, N.Y. Acad. Sci. Avocations: swimming, music. Office: Tokyo Inst Tech, 2-12-1 Ookayana Meguro, Tokyo 152-8552, Japan

MORI, NOZOMU, medical educator; b. Osaka, Kinki, Japan, Feb. 19, 1950; s. Saburo and Isa Mori; m. Machiko Asano, Mar. 5, 1975; children: Wataru, Aya. MD, Osaka U., 1974, D of Med. Sci., 1986. Resident Osaka U. Med. Sch., 1974-75, Kansai Rosai Hosp., Amagasaki, Hyogo, Japan, 1975-78; asst. Nara (Japan) Med. U., Kashihara, 1978-81, Düsseldorf (Germany) U., 1981-83, Nara Med. U., 1983-85, Osaka U. Med. Sch., 1985-87; asst. prof. Kagawa (Miki, Japan) Med. Sch., 1987-95, prof., 1995. Contbr. articles to profl. jours. Recipient Rsch. Promotion award Nara Med. Soc., 1984; rsch. grantee Ministry of Edn., Sci. and Culture of Japan, 1991-97. Mem. AAAS, Japanese Soc. Otolaryngology (specialist 1983—), Japanese Audiol. Soc., Japanese Soc. Otology (mem. exec. com. 1978—), Japan Soc. Head and Neck Cancer, Assn. for Rsch. in Otolaryngology, N.Y. Acad. Sci. Buddhist. Avocations: listening to music, golf. Fax: 087-891-2215. Office: Kagawa Med Sch Dept Otolary, 1750-1 Ikenobe, Miki Kagawa 761-0793, Japan

MORI, WATARU, academic administrator, educator; b. Tokyo, Jan. 10, 1926; s. Keiji Inoue and Mume Mori; m. Hiroko Yoshino, May 6, 1955; children: Natsuko Ito, Junko Yoshida. MD, U. Tokyo, 1951, D of Med. Sci., 1957. Lic. med. practice; bd. cert. pathologist. Prof., chmn. pathology faculty medicine U. Tokyo, 1973-85, dean faculty medicine, 1981-83, v.p., 1983-85, pres., 1985-89, prof. emeritus, 1989—; exec. mem. coun. for sci. and tech. Prime Min.'s Office, Tokyo, 1989-98; mem. Sci. Coun. Japan, Tokyo, 1988-91; chmn. med. ethics coun. Ministry of Health and Welfare, Tokyo, 1989—; chmn. com. on policy matters Coun. for Sci. and Tech., Tokyo, 1990-98; prof. distinguido La Univ. Externado Colombia, Bogota, 1992; chmn. The Tobacco Industries Coun., Ministry of Fin., Tokyo, 1997—; chmn. Coun. for Relocation of the Diet and other Orgns. Nat. Land Agy., Tokyo, 1998—. Author: Science Advisors to Presidents and Prime Ministers, Vol. II, 1999; contbr. articles to profl. jours. Rep. Small Kindness Movement, Tokyo, 1993—; pres. 200th Yr. Jenner's Commemoration Events, Tokyo, 1996. Recipient Eleanor Roosevelt Internat. Cancer Fellowship award Internat. Union Against Cancer, 1996-97, Hon. Conferment Das gorsse Verdienstkreutz mit Stern und Schulterband, 1997; designated Person of Cultural Merits, 1998. Fellow Royal Coll. Pathologists (hon.); mem. NAS (fgn. assoc. mem. Inst. Medicine), Internat. Coun. of Socs. of Pathology (pres. 1992-96), Internat. Assn. Univs. (pres. 1995—), Japanese Assn. Med. Scis. (pres. 1992—), Japanese Pathol. Soc. (sec.-gen. 1983-89), Japan Acad., Am. Philos. Soc. (fgn. mem.). Avocation: gardening. Home: 2-20-13 Sengoku Bunkyo-ku, Tokyo 112-0011, Japan Office: Japanese Assn Med Scis, 2-28-16 Honkomagome, Bunkyo-ku Tokyo 113-8621, Japan

MORI, YOSHIRO, government official; b. Neagari, Ishikawa, July 14, 1937; m. Chieko Maki; children: Yuki, Yoko. Grad., Waseda (Japan) U., 1960. With Sankei Newspapers, Tokyo, 1960-62; rep. Ishikawa Prefecture Dist. 1 Ho. of Reps., Tokyo, 1969-96, rep. Ishikawa Prefecture Dist. 2, 1996—; dep. dir. gen. Prime Min.'s Office, Miki Cabinet, Tokyo, 1975-76; dep. chief cabinet sec. Fukuda Cabinet, Tokyo, 1977-78; dir. edn. divsn. Policy Rsch. Coun. Liberal Dem. Party, Tokyo, 1978-81, dep. sec.-gen., 1978-79, 84-85; chmn. standing com. on fin. Ho. of reps., Tokyo, 1981-82; min. of edn. Nakasone Cabinet, Tokyo, 1983-84; chmn. spl. com. on edn. reform Policy Rsch. Coun. Liberal Dem. Party, Tokyo, 1984-87, acting chmn. Policy Rsch. Coun., 1986, acting chmn. gen. coun., 1986-87, chmn. Nat. Orgn. com., 1987-88, chmn. rsch. commn. on edn. sys. Policy Rsch. Coun., 1989-91; chmn. standing com. on rules and adminstrn. Ho. of reps., Tokyo, 1991; prime minister Japan, Tokyo; chmn. Policy Rsch. Coun., 1991-92; min. internat. trade and industry Miyazawa Cabinet, 1992-93; sec.-gen. Liberal Dem. Party, Tokyo, 1993-95; min. constrn. Murayama Cabinet, Tokyo, 1995-96; chmn. gen. coun. Liberal Dem. Party, 1996-98, sec.-gen., 1998-2000. Avocations: rugby, golf. Office: Liberal Democratic Party, 1-11-23 Nagata-cho Chiyoda, Tokyo 100, Japan Office: Office of the Prime Minister, 1-6-1 Nagata-cho 1, Chiyoda-ku Tokyo 100, Japan

MORIARTY, JOHN KLINGE, electronics engineer, consultant; b. Washington, Feb. 6, 1956; s. John Klinge and Mary (Cozart) M.; m. Elizabeth Rouse, Dec. 31, 1987; children: Maire Elizabeth, John Lank, Harris James. BS in Physics, Va. Poly. Inst. and State U., 1981; M of Engring. in Elec. Engring., Clemson U., 1996. Project engr. Delco Electronics divsn. G.M.C., Kokomo, Ind., 1981-84; staff engr. Hekimian Labs., Gaithersburg, Md., 1984-85; sr. LSI design engr. Case Comms., Inc., Columbia, Md., 1985-86; ind. electronics cons. Gaithersburg, 1986-88; mem. tech. staff Bell Labs., Reading, Pa., 1988-97; ind. electronics cons. Reading, 1997—; cons. Squire Comms., Miami, Fla., 1986, Delco Electronics Corp., Kokomo, 1986-88, Mfg. Networks Inc., San Francisco, CPClare Corp., Beverly, Mass., Wireless Sys. Techs., Inc., San Jose, Calif.; tutorial presenter West Med. Design and Mfg. Conf., Anaheim, Calif., 1991, East Med. Design and Mfg. Conf., N.Y.C., 1991. Contbr. articles to profl. jours. including IEEE Jour. Solid State Cirs., Procs. IEEE Custom Integrated Cirs., Cancer Treatment Reports. Recipient Supplier Recognition award Hughes Aircraft Corp., 1992. Mem. IEEE, IEEE Electron Device Soc., IEEE Solid State Cirs. Soc., IEEE Cirs. and Sys. Soc. Achievements include patents in field. Home: 2557 River Rd Reading PA 19605-2840

MORICE, PETER BEAUMONT, civil engineer, educator; b. Farnham, Eng., May 15, 1926; s. Charles Henry and Mabel Stephanie (Horspool) M.; m. Rita Corless, Oct. 15, 1986. BS, U. Bristol, Eng., 1947; PhD, U. London, 1952, DS, 1958. Asst. engr. Surrey (Eng.) County Coun., 1947-48; rsch. engr. Cement and Concrete Assn., Bucks, Eng., 1948-51, head of structures rsch., 1951-57; prof. civil engring. Southampton (Eng.) U., 1957-91, prof. emeritus, 1991—; vis. prof. ENPC, Paris, 1980—; mem. found. com. Sultan Qaboos U., Oman, 1980—. Author: Prestressed Concrete, 1958, Linear Structural Analysis, 1959. Fellow Royal Acad. Engring., 1989. Fellow Instn. Civil Engrs., Instn. Structural Engrs. Avocations: painting, pottery, gardening, sailing. Home: 12 Abbotts Way Highfield, Southampton SO17 1QT, England

MORICE, WILLIAM DANIEL, business and tax counselor; b. May 6, 1946; s. John Lowry and Evelyn Mae (Brown) M.; m. Kay Iris Mason, June 14, 1975; children: Elizabeth Anne, Charlotte Katherine, Michelle Alexandra. BSEE, U. Md., 1973; MBA, Emory U., 1976. CPA, Md. Tech. rep. Xerox Corp., Washington, 1965-66, So. Ry., Atlanta, 1973; cons. Mantech of N.J., Washington, 1975, Peat Marwick Mitchell & Co., Washington, 1976-82; prin. Booz Allen & Hamilton, Inc., Bethesda, Md., 1982-84; owner Gen. Bus. Services, Bethesda, 1985-98; CEO Gen. Tax Svcs., Inc., 1996-98; v.p. Century Small Bus. Solutions, Inc., 1998—; pres. Apple Limousine Inc., 1988—, Morice and Blohm LLC, 1995-98. Asst. precinct chmn., 1971, chmn. 1980—; election judge, 1972, bd. dirs., treas. Nat. Pbt. Bus. Polit. Fund. With U.S. Army, 1966-69. Mem. Md. Assn. Accts., Delta Nu Alpha, Beta Gamma Sigma, Tau Kappa Epsilon, Terrapin Club, Friends of Kennedy Ctr. (founding mem.), River Hill Music Boosters (founder). Republican. Episcopalian. Office: Century Small Business Solutions Inc 7160 Columbia Gateway Dr Columbia MD 21046-2132

MORIHARA, KAZUYUKI, biochemist, researcher; b. Ondo-cho, Hiroshima, Japan, Nov. 12, 1926; s. Uichi and Hisano (Takamatsu) M.; m. Junko Ogata, May 1, 1954; children: Akiko, Tomoko, Hisashi. B of Agr., Kyoto (Japan) U., 1948, D of Agr., 1960. Cert. in biotech. Asst. Kagoshima (Japan) U., 1948-52, Kyoto U., 1952-53; rschr., head, dep. chief Shionogi Pharm. Co. Rsch. Labs., Osaka, Japan, 1953-84; dir. Toho Pharm. Co. Rsch. Labs., Kyoto, 1984-88; prof. Grad. Sch. U. of East Asia, Shimonoseki, Japan, 1989-2000. Author: (book) Methods in Enzymology, 1995; rschr.: (inventions) Pseudomonas vaccine, 1977, enzymatic semisynthesis of human insulin, 1979; editor: Jour. Molecular Recognition, 1988-91. Team leader Japan Internat. Coop. Agy., Kuala Lumpur, Malaysia, 1991-92. Recipient Encouragement award Japan Soc. for Biosci., Biotech. and Agrochemistry, 1966, Tech. award, 1986. Liberal. Buddhist. Avocation: golf. Home: Kita-Ondo 1-7-14 Ondo Cho, Aki-gun Hiroshima Japan

MORIKAWA, TOSHIO, bank executive; b. Mar. 3, 1933; m. Sawako Morikawa. Student, Tokyo U., 1955. Joined Sumitomo Bank Ltd., Tokyo, 1955, various mgmt. positions, including mng. dir., dep. pres., pres., 1993-97, chmn., 1997—. Avocations: golf, reading. Office: Sumitomo Bank Ltd, 6-5 Kitahama 4-chome, Chuo-k Tokyo 541-0041, Japan*

MORIMOTO, MASANORI, science educator, researcher; b. Hirakata, Osaka, Japan, Feb. 3, 1971; s. Masaki and Ayako Morimoto; m. Kayoko Morimoto; children: Sumire, Sho, Ai. BS, Kinki U., Nara, Japan, 1993, MS, 1995. Asst. rsch. agrl. chemistry Kinki U., 1995—. Mem. Weed Sci. Soc. Japan, Japan Soc. Biosci., Biotech. and Agrochemistry, Pesticide Sci. Soc. Japan. Office: Kinki U, Nara 3327-204, Japan

MORIMOTO, MASAO, education educator; b. Sapporo, Hokkaido, Japan, Oct. 3, 1931; s. Iwata and Setsu (Tanaka) M.; m. Setsuko Nasuno, Jan. 24, 1959; children: Miyuki, Ichiro. B Econs., Hokkai-Gakuen U., 1955; M Agr., Hokkaido U., Sapporo, Japan, 1957; LLD (hon.), U. Lethbridge, Can., 1989; Hon. prof., The Mongolian Tech. U., Ulaanbaatar, Mongolia, 1992. Asst. prof. Faculty of Econs. Hokkai-Gakuen U., Sapporo, 1965-70, prof. grad. sch., 1970—, dep. chmn. bd. govs., 1971-75, chmn. bd. govs., 1976—; pres. Hokkai-Gakuen Women's Jr. Coll. of Kitami, Japan, 1990-91, Hokkai-Gakuen U. of Kitami, 1991—; v.p. Japan Pvt. U. Assn., Tokyo, 1988—; chmn. Hokkaido Coun. of Japan Pvt. Univs. Assn., 1988—; commr. The Pvt. U. Coun., Tokyo, 1984-87, The Coun. for the Establishment of Univs. and the Incorporating of Schs., 1987-95; panelist in field. Co-author: (book) Transportation and Regional Development Research and Science Fund by the Ministry of Education, 1968; co-editor/author: (book) Theory of Modern Japanese Economics, 1980. Chmn. Sapporo Rev. Bd. on Bldgs., 1973-97, Sapporo City Coun. for Spl. Scholarships, 1984-96, The Coun. for the Establishment and Operation of the Sapporo Cen. Wholesale Market, 1988-97, The Sapporo Housing Devel. Coun., 1990-98, Sapporo Devel. Reviewing Com., 1972—; hon. consul Mongolia in Sapporo, 1999—. Recipient The Blue Ribbon medal The Imperial Palace, 1995, Disting. Svc. award Min. of Edn., 1988, 97, Hokkaido award for Contbns. to Soc., Hokkaido Govt., 1944. Mem. The Hokkaido Soc. (chmn. 1982—), Rotary Internat. (gov. dist. 2510 1999-2000). Avocations: fishing, travel. Office: Hokkai-Gakuen, 4-1-40 Asahimachi/Toyohira, 062-8605 Sapporo Hokkaido, Japan

MORIMOTO, TOYOTOMI, humanities educator; b. Tokyo, Oct. 10, 1956; s. Yutaka and TomikoM.; m. Machiko Suda, June 8, 1988; children: Daniel Tatsuru, Amie. BA, Nihon U., Tokyo, 1979; MA, UCLA, 1983, PhD, 1989. Asst. prof. Surugadai U., Hanno, Saitama, Japan, 1990-93, assoc. prof., 1993-97; assoc. prof. Waseda U., Tokorozawa, Japan, 1997-99, prof., 1999—; mem. steering com. Japanese Assn. Migration Studies, 1999. Author: Japanese Americans and Cultural Continuity, 1997; translator: The American South, 1995; editor-in-chief Ann. Rev. of Migration Studies, 1999—. Sec. Intercultural Edn. Soc., Japan, 1999. Mem. Comparative Edn. Soc., Am. Studies Assn. Avocation: golf. Office: Waseda U Sch Human Scis, 2-579-15 Mikajima, Tokorozawa 359-1192, Japan

MORIMOTO, YOSHIHARU, systems engineering educator; b. Osaka, Japan, Feb. 11, 1944; m. Shizuko Morimoto, Oct. 25, 1975; children: Yoshihiro, Hiroshi, Yuko. BS in Engring., Osaka U., 1966, MS in Engring.,

1968, Dr. in Engring., 1981. Rsch. engr. Komatsu Mfg. Ltd., Kawasaki, Japan, 1968-74; rsch. assoc. Osaka U., 1974-81, asst. prof., 1981-85, assoc. prof., 1985-93, prof. mech. engring., 1993-94; prof. indsl. engring. Wakayama (Japan) U., 1993-95, prof. sys. engring., 1995—; vis. prof. Va. Poly. Inst. and State U., Blacksburg, 1989-90. Author: Image Processing, 1984; editor: Handbook on Image Processing, 1988; contbr. articles to profl. jours. Home: 5-17-4-056 Rinku-Port-Kita, Tajiri-cho Sennan-gun, Osaka 598-0093, Japan Office: Wakayama U, Faculty Sys Engring, Sakaedani Wakayama 640-8510, Japan

MORIOKA, YASUO, electrical engineer, energy company engineer; b. Shiki dist., Nara pref., Japan, Oct. 9, 1954; s. Syoichiro and Chikako (Kotake) M.; m. Kazuko Takemura, Apr. 11, 1982; 1 child, Eriko. B in Engring., Kyoto (Japan) Inst. Tech., 1977, D in Engring., 1994. Cert. 1st class engr. in radio comm., 1st class programmer, chief preventive engr. environ. pollution, Japan. Sr. rsch. engr. The Kansai Elec. Power Co., Osaka, Japan, 1977—; mem. com. Devel. Interconnected Bulk Power Transmission System, Tokyo, 1994-97; chmn. Symposium on Power System Simulator, Osaka, Japan, 1996; mem. com. Bldg. Std. Power Sys. Model of Japan, 1997—. Inventor: identification system for hydraulic characteristics of a hydraulic power plant, 1990, control system for a generator, 1992. Mem. IEEE, Inst. Elec. Engrs. of Japan, Soc. Instrument and Control Engrs. of Japan. Buddhist. Avocations: chorus, travel, hiking. Office: Kansai Elec Power Co Inc, 11-20 Nakoji 3-chome, Amagasaki 661-0974 Hyogo, Japan

MORISHITA, TETSUO, physician, researcher in medical science; b. Shizuoka-shi, Japan, Mar. 8, 1947; s. Yoshiro and Umeko (Unno) M. MD, Keio U., Tokyo, 1971, PhD, 1977. Lic. physician, Japan. Instr. Keio U., 1975-84; rsch. fellow UCLA, 1984-86; asst. prof. Tokai U., Isehara-shi, Japan, 1986-87; dir. internal medicine Shizuoka Red Cross Hosp., 1987—; prof. titular Bolivian Christian U., Santa Cruz, Bolivia, 1993—; vis. rschr. San Lazaro Hosp., Manila, 1974; vis. rschr. Internat. Ctr. for Diarrhoeal Disease Rsch., Dacca, Bangladesh, 1980; dir. Health Care Ctr., Shizuoka-shi, 1993—. Author: Enfermedades Digestivas-Tracto Gastrointestinal, 1990, Enfermedades Digestivas-Higado, Vias Biliares y Pancreas, 1993; also sci. papers. Chmn. com. for vol. activity Red Cross, Shizuoka, 1989. Recipient Rsch. award Red Cross, Shizuoka, 1990; named Hon. Citizen, Santa Cruz City, Bolivia, 1988, Sucre City, Bolivia, 1993, La Paz City, Bolivia, 1995. Mem. AAAS, Japanese Soc. Gastroenterology, N.Y. Acad. Scis. Avocations: swimming, volleyball, singing. Office: Shizuoka Red Cross Hosp Internal Medicine Dept, 8-2 Ohtemachi, 420-0853 Shizuokashi shi, Japan

MORISHITA, YOICHI, electronics company executive. Pres.and ceo Matsushita Elec. Indsl. Co., Ltd., Osaka, Japan. Office: Matsushita Electric Indsl Co Ltd, 1006 Oaza Kadoma, Kadoma Osaka 571-8506, Japan*

MORISON, NIALL MACLAINE, business executive; b. Oakham, Rutland, Eng., May 3, 1944; s. Niel and Dorothy Marion Symington (Smith) M.; m. Alison Linda Hill, Feb. 22, 1948; children: Ruairiadh, Ludovic, Madeleine, Lachlan. Edinburgh (Scotland) Acad. Articled clk. Bird & Bird, London, 1963-66; exec. Kidsons, London, 1967-70; asst. sec. Retail Distbrs. Assn., London, 1970-74; asst. sec. Gen. Coun. of the Bar, London, 1974-85, dep. sec., 1985-86, dep. chief exec., 1986—. Gov. Stonegate (Eng.) Primary Sch., 1995-96. Home: Bramdean Cottage, Stonegate TN5 7EP, England Office: Gen Coun of the Bar, 3 Bedford Row, London WC1R 4DB, England

MORITA, MASATO, physicist; b. Sasebo, Japan, Nov. 22, 1927; m. Reiko Saito, Dec. 3, 1956; 1 child, Eugene Hayato. BSc, U. Tokyo, 1952, DSc, 1956. Rsch. assoc. Kobayashi Inst. Physics, Tokyo, 1954-56; rsch. assoc., asst. prof. physics Columbia U., N.Y.C., 1956-62; assoc. prof. physics Kyoto (Japan) U., 1962-66; prof. physics Osaka (Japan) U., Toyonaka, 1966-91; prof. math. Josai U., Sakado, Saitama, Japan, 1991-92; prof. physics Josai Internat. U., Gumyo, Togane, Japan, 1992—. Author: Beta Decay and Muon Capture, 1973; contbr. articles to Progress of Theoretical Physics, Phys. Rev. Recipient Yukawa-Yomiuri award for particle physics Yomiuri News, 1952, 53, 55, Ernest Kempton Adams award for physics Columbia U., 1958, prize for sci. and tech. TORAY Sci. Found., 1988. Mem. Phys. Soc. Japan (chmn. Osaka br. 1978-79, 81-82, 86-87, 88-89), Am. Phys. Soc. Home: 4-17-2 Asahiga-Oka, Yotsukaido 284-0024, Japan Office: Josai Internat U, 1 Gumyo, Togane Chiba 283-8555, Japan

MORITA, TOMIJIRO, insurance company executive. CEO The Dai-ichi Mut. Life Ins. Co., Tokyo. Office: Dai-ichi Mut Life Ins Co, 1-13-1 Yurakucho, Chiyodku Tokyo 100-8411, Japan*

MORITZ, HELMUT, geophysicist, educator; b. 1933. Prof. geodesy dept. Technische Universitat Berlin, 1964-71; prof. theoretical geodesy Technische Universitä Graz, 1971—; rsch. assoc. geodesy dept. Ohio State U., 1962-63, adj. prof., 1969—; lectr. geodesy dept. Technische Hochschule Graz, 1960-62, Technische Hochschule Hannover, 1964. Author: Physical Geodesy, 1967, Advanced Physical Geodesy, 1980, Earth Rotation, 1987, The Figure of the Earth, 1990. Mem. Royal Spanish Acad. Scis., Royal Swedish Acad. Engring. Scis., Hungarian Acad. Scis., Internat. Assn. Geodesy (hon. pres. 1983—), Finnish Acad. Scis., Accademia Nazionale dei Lincei, Osterreichische Akademie der Wissenschaften, Am. Geophys. Union, Akademie der Naturforscher Leopoldina, Polish Acad. Scis., Chinese Acad. Scis., Royal Astron. Soc., Internat. Union Geodesy and Geophysics (past pres.), Internat. League of Humanists (pres.). Office: Inst Theoretical Geodesy, Tech U Steyrergasse 30, A-8010 Graz Austria

MORITZ, TIMOTHY BOVIE, psychiatrist; b. Portsmouth, Ohio, July 26, 1936; s. Charles Raymond and Elisabeth Bovie (Morgan) M.; m. Joyce Elizabeth Rasmussen, Oct. 13, 1962 (div. Sept. 1969); children: Elizabeth Wynne, Laura Morgan; m. Antoinette Tanasichuk, Oct. 31, 1981; children: David Michael, Stephanie Lysbeth. BA, Ohio State U., 1959; MD, Cornell U., 1963. Diplomate Am. Bd. Psychiatry and Neurology. Intern in medicine N.Y. Hosp., N.Y.C., 1963-64, resident in psychiatry, 1964-67; spl. asst. to dir. NIMH, Bethesda, Md., 1967-69; dir. Community Mental Health Ctr., Rockland County, N.Y., 1970-74, Ohio Dept. Mental Health, Columbus, Ohio, 1975-81; med. dir. psychiatry Miami Valley Hosp., Dayton, Ohio, 1981-82; med. dir. N.E. Ga. Community Mental Health Ctr., Athens, Ga., 1982-83, Charter Vista Hosp., Fayetteville, Ark., 1983-87; clin. dir. adult psychiatry Charter Hosp., Las Vegas, Nev., 1987-94; pvt. practice psychiatry Las Vegas, Nev., 1987—; prof. Wright State U., Dayton, Ohio, 1981-82; asst. prof. Cornell U., N.Y.C., 1970-73; cons. NIMH, Rockville, Md., 1973-83. Author: (chpt.) Rehabilitation Medicine and Psychiatry, 1976; mem. editorial bd. Directions in Psychiatry, 1981—. Dir. dept. mental health and mental retardation Gov.'s Cabinet, State of Ohio, Columbus, 1975-81. Recipient Svc. award Ohio Senate, 1981, Svc. Achievement award Ohio Gov., 1981. Fellow Am. Psychiat. Assn. (Disting. Svc. award 1981); mem. AMA, Nev. Assn. Psychiat. Physicians, Nev. State Med. Assn., Clark County Med. Soc., Cornell U. Med. Coll. Alumni Assn. Office: 1640 Alta Dr Ste 11 Las Vegas NV 89106-4165

MORIUCHI, TAKAHIKO, electronic insulation company executive; b. Amagasaki, Hyogo, Japan, Sept. 27, 1939; s. Kofumi (Fukumura) M.; m. Akiko Sumino, Feb. 17, 1969; children: Shintarou, Kenjirou, Sayuri. BS, Osaka U., 1962, MS, 1966, PhD, 1984. Rschr. Nitto Denko Corp., Osaka, 1967—, chief rschr., 1976—, gen. mgr. electech. rsch. lab., 1986-88, gen. mgr. ctrl. rsch. lab., 1988-93, gen. mgr. devel. ctr. elec. and electronics products sect., 1993-94, gen. mgr. microelectronics divsn., 1994-98, gen. mgr. mrh sect., printed circuits sector, 1999; pre-venture sec. Japan Sci. and Tech. Corp., Osaka, 2000—. Recipient award Sec. Ministry Sci. and Tech. Japan, 1991. Mem. IEEE, Inst. Elec. Engrs. Japan, CIGRE SC-15. Home: I-904 2-7 Tennou, Ibaraki Osaka 567-0876, Japan Office: Japan Sci and Tech Corp, 1-14-14 Miyahara, Yodogawa Osaka 532 0003, Japan

MORIURA, SHIGEAKI, surgeon; b. Nagoya, Japan, Mar. 4, 1955; s. Showzabro and Miwako (Tanaka) M.; m. Yuko Hayashi, Mar. 16, 1980; 2 children. MD, Nagoya (Japan) U., 1979, DMS, 1990. Surgeon Toyohashi (Japan) Mcpl. Hosp., 1979-84; resident Nat. Cancer Ctr. Hosp., Tokyo, 1984-87; surgeon, rschr. surgery 1 Nagoya U., 1987-89; surgeon Aichi Prefectural Owari Hosp., Ichinomiya, Japan, 1989-94, Nagoya Posts and Telecomms. Hosp., 1995-97; chief dept. surgery Yachiyo Hosp., Anjo, Japan, 1997—. Contbr. papers to profl. jours. Mem., mgr. Fushimi Classical Music Assn., Nagoya, 1995. Mem. Japanese Soc. Gastroenterol. Surgery, Japanese Surg. Soc., Japanese Assn. for Thoracic Surgery, Japan Surg. Assn. (bd. dirs. 1998—). Avocations: skiing, tennis, classical music, jazz, cooking. Home: 3-32 Hakuryu-cho Mizuho-ku, Nagoya 467 0826, Japan Office: Yachiyo Hosp, 1-10-13 Toei-cho, Anjo 446-8510, Japan

MORIYA, TOSHIKAZU, accountant; b. Takato, Nagano, Japan, Aug. 18, 1953; s. Takehiko and Shigeko (Akiyama) M. BSc in Econ., Nihon U., Tokyo, 1976; student, U. London, 1994, U. Cambridge, Eng., 1994, London Guildhall U., 1994. With cost control dept. Kimuraya, Saitama, Japan, 1976-87; market analyst Kimuraya, Tokyo, 1987-89, with corp. fin. dept., 1989-93; fin. analyst Okura Shoji, Tokyo, 1995-98; acct. Nihon Chutetsukan, Tokyo, 1998-99; mem. maintenance staff Internat. Sch. Sacred Heart, Tokyo, 1999—. Mem. Nat. Liberal Club London. Avocations: gardening, architecture. Home: 1-10-71 Nodamachi, Saitama Kawagoe 350-1115, Japan Office: Internat Sch Sacred Heart, 4-3-1 Hiroo, Shbya-ku Tokyo 150-0012, Japan

MORIYAMA, HIROYOSHI, technical institute administrator; b. Tokyo, Aug. 13, 1955; s. Harumichi Takano and Nobuko Moriyama; m. Mariko Hinaga, Feb. 29, 1988; children: Atsue, Takanobu. BS, U. San Francisco, 1978; MS, San Jose State U., 1979. Marketer Japan Travenol Ltd., Tokyo, 1980-83; assoc. product Avon Products Co., Tokyo, 1983-84; cons., product mgr. Bayer Japan Ltd., Tokyo, 1984-87; mktg. supr. Amway Japn Ltd., Tokyo, 1987-92; pres. Moriyama Tech. Inst., Tokyo, 1992—; researcher Teikyo U. Hosp. Pharmacy, Tokyo, 1984-95. Contbr. articles to profl. jours.; patentee in field. Recipient Internat. Student scholarship U. San Francisco, 1976-78. Mem. Am. Chem. Soc. Avocations: chess, billiards, tennis, hiking, jogging. Office: Moriyama Tech Inst, 4-1-5 Hatanodai, Shinagawa-ku Tokyo 142, Japan

MORK, GORDON ROBERT, historian, educator; b. St. Cloud, Minn., May 6, 1938; s. Gordon Matthew and Agnes (Gibb) M.; m. Dianne Jeannette Muetzel, Aug. 11, 1963; children: Robert, Kristiana, Elizabeth. Instr. history U. Minn., Mpls., 1966; lectr., asst. prof. U. Calif., Davis, 1966-70; mem. faculty Purdue U., West Lafayette, Ind., 1970—, assoc. prof., 1973-94, prof. history, 1994—, dir. honors program in the humanities, 1985-87, dir grad. studies in history, Am. studies, 1987-93, mem. Jewish studies com., 1980—; head dept. history Purdue U., West Lafayette, 1998—; resident dir. Purdue U.-Ind. U. Program, Hamburg, Fed. Republic Germany, 1975-76; rsch. fellow in humanities U. Wis., Madison, 1969-70; mem. test devel. com., advanced placement European history Ednl. Testing Svc., 1993-99, chair, 1995-99. Author: Modern Western Civilization: A Concise History, 3d edit., 1994; editor: The Homes of Ober-Ammergau, 2000; mem. adv. bd. Teaching History, 1983—, History Tchr., 1986—. Mem. citizens task force Lafayette Sch. Corp., 1978-79; bd. dirs. Ind. Humanities Coun., 1986-89; bd. dirs., sec. Murdock-Sunnyside Bldg. Corp., 1980—; elder Cen. Presbyn. Ch., Lafayette, 1973-75, deacon, 1996-99. Mem. Internat. Soc. History Didactics (v.p. 1991-95, 96-00), Am. Hist. Assn., Conf. Group on Ctrl. European History, Soc. History Edn., Com. for History in the Classroom (treas. 1990-93), Phi Beta Kappa. Home: 1521 Cason St Lafayette IN 47904-2642 Office: Purdue U Dept of History West Lafayette IN 47907-1358

MORKIN, CLAIRE D., singer, actress; b. Waukesha, Wis., Nov. 1, 1959; d. Killian Thomas Morkin and Diane Sue Genrich. Writer, performer, prodr. one-woman show Hildgarde, 2000; appeared in off Broadway musical Zombies From the Beyond, 1995.

MORLEY, HARRY THOMAS, JR., real estate executive; b. St. Louis, Aug. 13, 1930; s. Harry Thomas and Celeste Elizabeth (Davies) M.; m. Nelda Lee Mulholland, Sept. 3, 1960; children: Lisa, Mark, Marci. BA, U. Mo., 1955; MA, U. Denver, 1959. Dir. men's student activities Iowa State Tchrs. Coll., 1955-57; dir. student housing U. Denver, 1957-60; pvt. practice psychol. consulting St. Louis, 1960-63; dir. adminstrn. County of St. Louis, Mo., 1963-70; regional dir. HUD, Kansas City, Mo., 1970-71; asst. sec. adminstrn. HUD, 1971-73; pres. St. Louis Regional Commerce and Growth Assn., 1973-78, Taylor, Morley, Inc., St. Louis, 1978—; teaching cons.-lectr. Washington U., St. Louis, 1962-70; bd. dirs. Mid-Am. Alliance Corp. and Life Ins. Co. Bd. dirs., mem. exec. com. St. Louis Coll. Pharmacy; past chmn. Better Bus. Bur.; chmn. Mo. Indsl. Devel. Bd., Mo. State Hwy. Commn.; bd. dirs. St. Luke's Hosps., St. Johns Hosp., Downtown St. Louis, Inc., Laclede's Landing Redevel. Corp. Served with USN, 1951-53. Mem. Am. C. of C. Execs., Nat. Assn. Homebuilders, St. Louis Homebuilders Assn. (pres.), St. Louis Advt. Club, Mo. Athletic Club, St. Louis Club, Noonday Club, Castle Oak Country Club, Round Table Club, Sunset Country Club. Republican. Methodist. Home: 14238 Forest Crest Dr Chesterfield MO 63017-2818 Office: 1224 Fern Ridge Pky Saint Louis MO 63141-4451

MORLEY, ROGER HUBERT, company executive, consultant; b. Cleve., June 21, 1931; s. Hubert Patrick and Ayleen Marie (Mosier) M. BS in Indsl. Engring., Ohio U., 1953; MBA, Harvard U., 1957. Contr. Stromberg-Carlson, Rochester, N.Y., 1957-60; v.p., gen. mgr. GATX, Chgo., 1960-67; gen. mgr. Burndy Corp., Norwalk, Conn., 1967-68; exec. v.p., CFO, Gould Inc., Chgo., 1968-74; pres., vice chmn. Am. Express, N.Y.C., 1974-80; co-mng. dir. R&R Inventions, Eng., 1986—; adv. bd. Bank of Am.-Ill., Biogen, Inc., Cambridge, Mass., Blyth Industries Inc., Artal SA, Luxembourg, 1987-97, Iris India Fund, Luxembourg, Blyth Industries, Greenwich, Conn.; assoc. lectr. U. Rochester, 1958-60; mem. U.S. adv. bd. European Inst. Bus. Adminstrn., 1975-81. Bd. dirs., mem. exec. com. Lincoln Ctr. for Performing Arts, 1974-81, chmn. consol. corp. fund drive, 1975-81; bd. dirs. Vis. Nurse Svc. N.Y., 1974-81. Sunny Bank Anglo-Am. Hosp., Cannes, France, 1985-87; trustee Darwin Trust Edinburgh, Scotland, 1991—; trustee, chmn. fin. com. Barnard Coll., 1976-80; v.p. Schiller Internat. U., Heidelburg, Germany, 1982—; mem. Com. de Jumelage, Ville de Grasse, 1983-87. Capt. USAF, 1953-55. Mem. Nat. Assn. Securities Dealers (gov.-at-large 1975-77), Grasse Country Club (France), Links (N.Y.C.), Harvard Club N.Y.C., Univ. Club (Chgo.). Republican. Avocations: golf, tennis, travel, reading. Home and Office: L'Horizon, Clos Barnier Spéracèdes, 06530 Alpes Maritimes France

MORLEY, SHERIDAN ROBERT, film critic, author, journalist, broadcaster; b. Ascot, Eng., Dec. 5, 1941; s. Robert and Joan (Buckmaster) M.; m. Margaret Gudejko, July 18, 1965 (div. 1990); children: Hugo, Alexis, Juliet; m. Ruth Leon, June 7, 1995. MA in Modern Langs. with honors, Oxford (Eng.) U., 1963; postgrad., U. Hawaii, 1963-64. Newscaster, reporter, scriptwriter ITN, London, 1964-67; interviewer Late Night Line Up BBC-TV, London, 1967-73, presenter Film Night, 1972; dep. features editor, asst. editor The Times, London, 1973-75, arts diarist, TV critic, 1989-90; arts editor and drama critic Punch, London, 1975-88; London drama critic Internat. Herald Tribune, 1979—, Spectator, 1992—; film critic Sunday Express, London, 1992-94, Arts Diarist Punch, 1997—; mem. drama panel Brit. Coun., 1982-89; presenter Kaleidoscope, Meridian; radio and TV broadcasts on performing arts, Arts Programme, Sheridan Morley Meets. . ., BBC Radio 2 Arts Programme, 1990—; host Theatreland, 1995-96. Author: A Talent to Amuse: the Life of Noel Coward, 1969, Oscar Wilde, 1976, Sybil Thorndike, 1977, Marlene Dietrich, 1977, Gladys Cooper, 1979, (with Cole Lesley and Graham Payn) Noel Coward and his Friends, 1979, The Stephen Sondheim Songbook, 1979, Gertrude Lawrence, 1981, Tales from the Hollywood Raj, 1983, Shooting Stars, 1983, The Theatregoers' Quiz Book, 1983, Katharine Hepburn, 1984, The Other Side of the Moon, 1985, Ingrid Bergman, 1985, The Great Stage Stars, 1986, Spread a Little Happiness, 1986, Out in the Midday Sun, 1988, Elizabeth Taylor, 1988, Odd Man Out: the life of James Mason, 1989, Our Theatres in the Eighties, 1990, Robert My Father, 1993, Audrey Hepburn, 1993, Ginger Rogers, 1995, (with Ruth Leon) Gene Kelly, 1996, Marilyn Monroe, 1996, Hey Mr. Producer: The Musicals of Sir Cameron Mackintosh, 1998; editor: (with Graham Payn) The Noel Coward Diaries, 1982, Bull's Eyes, 1985; editor Hutchinson Theatre Annuals, 1969-73, Studio Vista Film Studies, Punch at the Theatre, 1980, Methuen Book of Theatrical Short Stories, 1992, Methuen Book of Movie Stories, 1993, Rank Outsider, The Life of Dirk Bogarde, 1996, (with Ruth Leon) Gene Kelly, 1997, Marilyn Monroe, 1998, Hey Mr. Producer!, 1999, Chronicle of Theater, 1999, Beyond the Rainbow—Judy Garland, 1999, Private Lives, 1999, Companion to Noel Coward, 1999, John G: The Authorized Biography, 2000; dir. Song at Twilight, 1999; Noel and Gertie (writer and dir.), 1997,98, contbr. numerous articles to various mags. and jours. Named BP Journalist of Yr., 1989. Mem. Garrick Club. Avocations: talking, swimming, eating. Home: 7 Ivory Sq, Plantation Wharf, London SW11 OUF, England Office: care Curtis Brown Ltd, 28/29 Haymarket, London SW1Y 4SP, England

MORLEY-BALL, JOYCE ANN, psychotherapist, speaker, educational consultant; b. Ft. Lauderdale, Fla., Mar. 12, 1952; d. Theophilus and Lucille (McSmith) Morley; children: Yolanda Watson, Teknaya Watson, Natasha Ball. B of Elem. Edn., SUNY, Geneseo, 1973; M in Counseling, SUNY, Brockport, 1977, specialist degree in ednl. adminstrn., 1983, specialist degree in counseling, 1984; EdD in Counseling, Family Worklife, U. Rochester, 1991. Lic. profl. counselor, Ga.; cert. sch. counselor, sch. adminstr., Ga., N.Y.; cert. elem. tchr. Cons., trainer Profl. Counseling/Cons. Svc., Rochester, N.Y., 1974—; assoc. prof. Clark Atlanta U. radio talk show host. Bd. dirs. Rochester Mental Health, 1987-90, Westside Health Svc., Rochester, 1986-90, Jeannett Rankin Found.; trustee Zion Hill Missionary Bapt. Ch., Rochester, 1983-89; mem. Urban League of Rochester, 1983-90. Mem. AAUW (pres. Atlanta br.), Am. Assn. for Counseling and Devel. (nat. cert. counselor, nat. cert. sch. counselor trainer), Assn. for Multicultural Counseling and Devel., Nat. Coun. Negro Woman Inc., Am. Assn. for Marriage and Family Therapy (approved supr.). Democrat. African-Methodist Episcopal. Avocations: poetry writing, teaching, sewing.

MORNET, DOMINIQUE JEAN-MARIE, biochemist; b. Paris, Oct. 7, 1948; s. Jean Paul Louis and Paulette Emilienne (Chenu) M.; m. Daniele Olga Male, June 30, 1979; children: Alexandre, Pauline. DSc, U. VI, Paris, 1980. Technician CRBM, Montpellier, France, 1976-80; CR 1 in CNRS CRBM, Montpellier, 1980-82, 84-87, head of rsch. team, 1988-89; head rsch. team muscles and pathologies INSERM, Montpellier, 1989—; fellow U. Calif. San Francisco, 1982-84; asst. Coll. France, Paris, 1974-76. Fellowship NATO, 1982, 83-84, MDA, 1983-84, EMBO, 1987. Mem. Biophys. Soc., French Soc. of Biochemistry and Molecular Biology, World Muscle Soc. Home: 275 rue du Mas de Perrette, 34070 Montpellier France Office: Inserm U 128, 778 rue de law Croix Verle, 34196 Montpellier Cedex 5, France

MORO, BENIAMINO, economist; b. Tiana, Italy, Mar. 5, 1945; s. Salvatore and Priama (Marcello) M.; m. Maria Pasqua Deidda, Sept. 29, 1974; 1 child, Alessio. Degree in econs., U. Cagliari, 1969. From asst. prof. to prof. U. Cagliari, Italy, 1971—; prof. Northeastern U., Boston, 1997; dir. dept. econs. U. Cagliari, 1991—. Author: Linear Macroeconomics, 1990, Natural Capital and Environment, 1997, Economic Development and Employment, 1998; co-author: (with Modigliani, Fitoussi, Snower, Solow, Steinherr and Sylos Labini) An Economists' Manifesto on Unemployment in the European Union, BNL Quar. Rev., 1998; contbr. articles to profl. jours. Mem. Italian Soc. Econs., Rotary (fellow 1996—). Avocation: swimming. Home: Viale Merello 29, 09123 Cagliari Sardinia, Italy Office: Faculty Econs, Viale Sant'Ignazio 17, 09123 Cagliari Sardinia, Italy

MORODER, BERNARDO CORNELIO, chorus conductor; b. Reit im Winkl, Bayern, Germany, May 14, 1943; arrived in Argentina, 1949; s. Walter Maximin Otto and Judit Ana Cornelia (Dellai) M.; m. Graciela del Carmen Pedro, May 17, 1968; children: Ana Cecilia, Guillermina. Perito Mercantil, Escuela Nat. Comercio, Tandil, Argentina, 1960. Condr. Conjunto Vocal de Cámara, Tandil, 1965-69; condr., founder Coro Mpcl., Benito Juarez, Argentina, 1973-78, coro Estable de Tandil, 1972—, Coro Universitario, Tandil, 1977—; dir., founder Festival de Coros, Tandil, 1974—; music tchr. Centro Polivalente Arte, Tandil, 1978—; radio commentator FM Galáctica, Tandil, 1994-95; musical selector Escenas de la Redención, Tandil, 1963-96. Choral arranger, 1985. Sec. Fundación de Actores y C. de Semana Santa, Tandil, 1991-96. Mem. Internat. Fedn. for Choral Music. Avocations: organizing musical activities and concert tours. Home: Lamadrid 631, 7000 Tandil Argentina Office: Coro Estable de Tandil, CC 180, 7000 Tandil Argentina

MOROIANU, ANDREI M., mathematician; b. Bucharest, Romania, Mar. 9, 1971; s. Mihnea M. and Adelina (Georgescu) M.; m. Anne Yvonne Marie Langlois, Aug. 27, 1994; children: Alexandre, Constance. MS, U. Paris 11, 1993; PhD, Ecole Polytechnique, Palaiseau, France, 1996. Asst. U. Paris 9, 1995-96; rschr. Humboldt U., Berlin, 1996-97, CNRS, Palaiseau, 1997—. Contbr. articles to profl. jours. Recipient Peccot prize Coll. de France, Paris, 1997. Office: CMAT Ecole Polytechnique, Palaiseau 91128, France

MOROKOV, YURI NIKOLAEVICH, physicist; b. Cheliabinsk, Russia, Jan. 26, 1950; s. Nikolai and Alexandra (Korchagina) M.; m. Elena Vasilyevna, Sept. 14, 1978; children: Natalia, Anton. MSc, Novosibirsk State U., Russia, 1972, postgrad., 1974-77; PhD, Inst. Semicondr. Physics, Novosibirsk, 1981. Rsch. fellow Novosibirsk State U., 1972-74, assoc. prof., 1993—; rsch. scientist Inst. Theoretical and Applied Mechanics Russian Acad. Scis., Novosibirsk, 1977-81, sr. rsch. scientist, 1981-93, sr. rsch. scientist Inst. Computational Techs., 1993—; hon. assoc. prof. Internat. Soros. Sci. Ednl. Program, 1998. Contbr. articles to profl. jours. Office: Inst Computational Techs, Lavrentjev Ave 6, Novosibirsk Russia 630090

MORONEY, JOHN RODGERS, economist, educator; b. Dallas, Jan. 29, 1939; s. John Rodgers and Irene (Lewis) M.; m. Margaret Cecil Kearny, May 30, 1959; children: John Rodgers, Stephen Kearny, Helen, Michael Edward; m. Carmen Lambert, May 22, 1993. B.A., So. Meth. U., 1960; Ph.D., Duke, 1964. Asst. prof. econs. Fla. State U., 1964-66; asso. prof. econs. Mich. State U., 1966-69; mem. exec. com. Inst. Pub. Utilities, 1968-69; prof. econs., chmn. dept. Tulane U., New Orleans, 1969-81; prof., head dept. econs. Tex. A&M U., College Station, 1981—; vis. prof. econs. M.I.T., 1975-76; Schmidt internat. prof. A.B. Freeman Sch. Bus., Tulane U., New Orleans, 1998—; pres. Moroney Econ. Rsch. Assocs., 1992—. Author: The Structure of Production in American Manufacturing, 1972, Exploration, Development, and Production: Texas Oil and Gas, 1997; editor, contbr.: Income Inequality: Trends and Internat. Comparisons, 1979, Economic Aspects of New Technology, 1980, Formal Energy and Resource Models, 1982; editor: Econometric Models of the Demand for Energy, 1984; editor, contbr.: Energy, Capital, and Technological Change, 1987, Energy, Growth, and the Environment, 1992, Energy Prices and Production, 1994, Sustainable Economic Growth, 1995, Energy Supply and Demand, 1997, Fuels for the Future, 1999; mem. editl. bd. Bus. Topics, 1968-69, So. Econ. Jour, 1975—. Social Sci. Research Council faculty research fellow, 1969; NSF research fellow, 1975-76, 77-79. Mem. Am. Econ. Assn., So. Econ. Assn. (exec. com. 1975—, v.p. 1980), Royal Econ. Assn., Econometric Soc., Phi Beta Kappa. Home: 210 Fireside Cir College Station TX 77840-1877 Office: Dept Econs Tex A&M U College Station TX 77843-4228

MORONEY, MICHAEL JOHN, lawyer; b. Jamaica, N.Y., Nov. 8, 1940; s. Everard Vincent and Margaret Olga (Olson) M.; children: Sean, Megan, Matthew. BS in Polit. Sci., Villanova U., 1962; JD, Fordham U., 1965; Police Sci. (hon.), U. Guam, 1976. Bar: Hawaii 1974, U.S. Dist. Ct. Hawaii 1974, U.S. Ct. Appeals (9th cir.) 1974, Guam 1976, U.S. Dist. Ct. (Guam dist.) 1976, U.S. Ct. Claims 1976, U.S. Tax Ct. 1976, U.S. Ct. Mil. Appeals 1977, U.S. Supreme Ct. 1977, High Ct. Trust Ters. 1977, U.S. Dist. Ct. (No. Mariana Islands) 1983. Spl. agt. FBI, Memphis and Nashville, 1965-67, Cleve. and Elyria, Ohio, 1967-71; spl. agt., prin. legal advisor FBI, U.S. Dept. Justice, Honolulu, 1971-97; v.p. Merrill Corp., Honolulu, 1997—; bar examiner and applications rev. com. Supreme Ct. Hawaii, 1980—; pres. Hawaii State Law Enforcement Assn., 1985-86; mem. and del. to congress Gov.'s Task Force on Hawaii's Internat. Role, 1988; commr. Charter Commn., City and County of Honolulu, 1998—; mem. Consular Corps of Hawaii, 1997—. Mem. gov.'s task force, del. gov.'s congress on Hawaii's Internat. Role, 1988—; apptd. hon. consul gen. Republic of Palau, Pres. Kunio Nakamura, 1999. Recipient Govs. Award for Outstanding Contbns. to Law Enforcement, Gov. of Guam, 1974, 76, cert. of appreciation Supreme Ct. Hawaii, 1981, cert. of appreciation Honolulu Police Commn., 1984, 86; named Fed. Law Enforcement Officer of Yr., State of Hawaii, 1992, Outstanding Career award in Law Enforcement and Commitment to Hawaii State Law Enforcement Ofcls. Assn., 1998. Mem. ABA, Hawaii Bar Assn., Guam Bar Assn., Assn. Trial Lawyers Am., Inst. Jud. Adminstrn., Hawaii State Law Enforcement Ofcls. Assn., Hilo Yacht Club, Oahu Country Club, Plaza Club. Fax: 808-531-5354. E-mail: mmoro007@aol.com. Address: 7858 Makaaoa Pl Honolulu HI 96825-2848 Office: Merrill Corp 1154 Fort Street Mall Ste 300 Honolulu HI 96813-2712

MOROOKA, HIROSHI, neurosurgeon; b. Kurashiki, Okayama, Japan, Aug. 28, 1946; s. Shigeru and Akiko (Kobayashi) M.; m. Michiko Ninomiya, June 6, 1976; children: Takatoshi, Hanako, Teruko. MD, U. Okayama, 1971, D Med. Sci., 1978. Diplomate Japanese Bd. Neurol. Surgery. Clin. asst. neurosurgery U. Okayama Med. Sch., 1972-77, instr. neurosurgery, 1980-83, asst. prof. neurosurgery, 1984-86; rsch. assoc. neurology U. Miami (Fla.) Med. Sch., 1977-79; chief neurosurgery Okayama Rousai Hosp., 1987-92, Bizen City Hosp., 1993-95, Okayama Saidaiji Hosp., 1996—. Author: Cytoprotection & Cytobiology, 1995-97, Medical Biochemical & Chemical Aspects of Free Radicals, 1989, Intracranial Pressure VII, 1989, Brain Edema IX, 1993. Recipient Nat. Rsch. grant, 1981. Mem. Japan Neurol. Soc., Societas Neurologica Japonica, N.Y. Acad. Scis., Am. Heart Assn. Liberal Dem. Christian. Avocation: golf, the game of Go (7th degree). E-mail: morooka@okym.enjoy.ne.jp. Home: 880-165 Minato, 703 8266 Okayama Japan Office: Okayama Saidaiji Hosp, 8-41 Saidaiji Nakano, Honmachi Okayama 704-8192, Japan Office: Okayama Saidaiji Hosp, 8-41 Saidaiji Nakano, Honmachi Okayama 704 8192, Japan

MOROSANI, GEORGE WARRINGTON, real estate developer, realtor; b. Cin., July 20, 1941; s. Remy Edmond and Virginia Caroline (Warrington) M.; m. Judith Clontz, July 3, 1980; children by previous marriage: Katherine Carmichael, Elizabeth Warrington. BA, Rollins Coll., 1964, MBA, 1965. Fin. mgr. Lunar Orbitor and Minuteman Programs, Boeing Co., Cape Canaveral, Fla., 1965-68; controller Equitable Leasing Co., Asheville, N.C., 1968-69; founder, pres., treas. Western Carolina Warehousing Co., Asheville, 1969-87; co-founder, pres. Asheville Jaycee Housing, Inc., 1971-77; founder, pres., treas. A Mini Storage Co. (dba George's Stor-Mor), Asheville, N.C., 1976—; co-founder, treas. Accent on Living Co., Asheville, 1978-81; founder, pres., treas. G.M. Leasing, Asheville, N.C. 1986—, The Kingswood Co., Fletcher, N.C., 1986—; gen. partner Pine Needle Apts., Arden, N.C., 1978—, Pine Ridge Apts., Skyland, N.C., 1980—, Morganton Heights Apts., Morganton, N.C., 1981—, Maiden (N.C.) Apts., 1981—, Valley View Shopping Ctr., Candler, N.C., 1982-86, Meadow Garden Apts., Hendersonville, N.C., 1983—, Drexel Apts., N.C., 1983—, Heritage Hill Apts., Marion, N.C., 1983—, Cavalier Arms Apts., Waynesville, N.C., 1986—, Gwenmont Arms Apts., Murphy, N.C., 1986—, Nicol Arms Apts., Sylva, N.C., 1986—, Meadowwood Arms Apts., Gray, Tenn., 1986—, 4 Seasons Apts., Erwin, Tenn., 1986—, M. Realty LP, Asheville, 1986—, Woods Edge Apts., North Wilksboro, N.C., 1987—, Pond and Assocs., Asheville, 1992-94, Deer Park Apts., Cleve., N.C., 1987—; ptnr. Laurel Ridge Realty, Litchfield, Conn., 1973—, Laurel Properties, Rochester, Vt., 1978-94, Ashland Assocs., Asheville, N.C., 1985-88, Airport Assocs., Asheville, 1986-87; founder, owner George W. Morosani & Assocs., Asheville, 1981—, George's Rent-All, Asheville, N.C., 1988—; mgr. FI Realty I LLC, 1993—, Western Realty LLC, Asheville, 1994—, M Realty I LLC, 1994—, Sweeten Creek Realty LLC, 1994—, FI Realty I, LLC, 1994—, Patton Ave, LLC, 1995—, 3M Realty, LLC, 1995—, 3883 Sweeten Creek, LLC, 1997—. Bd. dirs. Jr. Achievement Greater Asheville Area, 1977—; mem. Regional Housing Adv. Com., 1981-86, Land-of-Sky Regional Coun., 1981-86, bd. dirs, 1990—; mem. Council Rural Housing and Devel., 1982-86, N.C. Real Estate Licensing Bd., S.C. Real Estate Commn., Tenn. Real Estate Commn., Ga. Real Estate Licensing Bd., Asheville Multiple Listing Svc., Hendersonville Multiple Listing Svc.; co-founder, treas. N.C. Council Rural Rental Housing, 1985—, sec., 1986-91; mem. Buncombe County Bd. Adjustment, 1988—, vice chmn., 1991—. Named Man of Yr., Asheville Jaycees, 1976. Mem. Sales and Mktg. Execs. Asheville (dir. 1974-76, 1982-84. chmn. membership com. 1976-77), Asheville Bd. Realtors, Hendersonville Bd. Realtors, Nat. Assn. Realtors, N.C. Assn. Realtors (property mgmt. div.). Mem. Asheville Comml. and Investment Realty Assn. (v.p. programs 1986-87, sec.-treas. 1987-92, 94—, pres., 1993), Nat. Mini-Storage Inst., W.N.C. Exchangers, Greater Asheville Apt. Assn. (chmn. membership com. 1988-89), Council Ind. Bus. Owners, Better Bus. Bur. Asheville/Western N.C. (dir. 1987—, second vice chmn. 1990, first vice chmn. 1991, chmn., 1992, chmn. nominating com., 1993), Econ. Devel. Assn. Western N.C., Self-Service Storage Assn., Asheville Area C. of C. (chmn. indsl. relations 1978-79), Hendersonville C. of C. Episcopalian. Clubs: Biltmore Forest Country. Lodge: Civitan (dir. 1975-77). Office: 932 Hendersonville Rd Asheville NC 28803-1733

MOROSANU, ION-CHRISTIAN, management executive; b. Piatra Neamt, Romania, Sept. 24, 1957; s. Ion and Elvira (Cotfas) M.; m. Daniela Moraru, July 1, 1982; children: Roxana, Dragos-Ioan. Engr., Poly. Inst. Mechanics Faculty, Iasi, Romania, 1982; postgrad., Poly. Inst, Bucharest, Romania, 1989, 97—. Diplomate in engring. Technologist, engr. Synthetic Fibres Works, Savinesti, Romania, 1982-90, prin. engr., 1990-91; office chief S.C. Comes S.A., Savinesti, 1991-92, dept. chief, 1992-94, pers. mgr., 1994-97; gen. mgr. State Ownership Fund County Neamt Br., Piatra Neamt, 1997-99, S.C. Bus. Consulting, SRL, Piatra Neamt, 2000—, Judiciary Clearancer. Patentee in field. Mem. com. The Civic Alliance, Piatra Neamt, 1991; pres. County Neamt br. World Union of Free Romanians, 1992; com. mem. County Neamt br. Romanian Dem. Conv., 1992; mem. Nat. Peasant Christian Dem. Party, 1996; pres. County Heamt Club Pro-Democratia Assn. Mem. Engrs. Gen. Assn. from Romania (sec. County Neamt br. 1992-98, pres. county Neamt br., nat. coun. mem.), Nat. Assn. Specialists in Human Resources Mgmt., Nat. Union Practitioners in Reorganization and Clearance (discipline superior coun. 2000). Avocations: politics, reading, sports, driving, music. Home: Sq M Kogalniceanu nr 8, BL 13 ScA ap 6, 5600 Piatra Neamt Romania Office: Comercial Tribunal, Bdul Republicii NR 16, 5600 Piatra Neamt Romania

MOROSETTI, ROBERTA, hematologist, researcher; b. Rome, Nov. 1, 1963; d. Maurizio and Simonetta (Bianconi) M.; m. Massimiliano Mirabella, Oct. 10, 1996; 1 child, Matteo. Med. degree with honors, Cath. U. Rome, 1988, specialized in hematology with honors, 1992. Bd. cert. in medicine and surgery, Italy; bd. cert. hematologist, Italy. Attending physician divsn. hematology Cath. U. Rome, 1988-91, attending physician dept. apheresis, 1992-93; rsch. fellow divsn. hematology-oncology UCLA Sch. Medicine, L.A., 1993-96; rschr. Istituto Di Semeiotica Medica Cath. U. Rome, 1996—. Author: (book chpt.) Vitamin D, 1997; contbr. papers to med. jours. Fellow Ministero Universita e Ricerca Sci. Tech., Rome, 1988, UCLA, 1993. Mem. Am. Assn. for Cancer Rsch., Am. Soc. Hematology. Avocations: tennis, skiing, swimming, gardening, music. Home: Via Mar Rosso 323, 00122 Rome Italy Office: U Sacred Heart, Largo Gemelli 8, 00168 Rome Italy

MOROZ, ALEXANDR GRIGORJEVICH, iron ore raw material company executive; b. Dneprodzerzhinsk, Ukraine, Feb. 12, 1959; s. Grigory Fyodorovich and Anna Vasiljevna (Olejnik) M.; m. Elena Alexejevna Alexejenko, Mar. 21, 1981; children: Oksana, Ekaterina. Engr., High Engr. Naval Sch., Odessa, Ukraine, 1981; postgrad., High Comml. Sch., Ukraine, 1989. Mechanic Steamship Line, Batumi, Georgia, 1981-82; fitter Poltavsky Gok, Komsomolsk, Ukraine, 1982-86, asst. of trade union chmn., 1986-88, asst. gen. dir., 1988-91, gen. dir., 1991—, mem. observing bd., 1998—; pres. Fgn. Trade Enterprise Mag., Komsomolsk, 1997—. People's dep. Town Soviet, Komsomolsk, 1986-90; mem. com. Regional Com. Komsomol, Poltava, 1984-86. Sr. lt. Ukraine Navy, 1981-82. Recipient torch award Internat. Acad. Leadership in Bus. and Adminstrn., Birmingham, Ala., 1995, diploma for Golden Book of Ukrainian Bus. Organising Com., Kiev, 1999. Avocation: sport fishing. Office: Slavutich-Ruda-Ukraine Ltd, 24 Mir St, 39800 Komsomolsk Poltava, Ukraine

MOROZIK, YURI, chemist, researcher, consultant; b. Magadan, Russia, July 2, 1946; s. Ivan and Zinaida (Matveyeva) M.; m. Lydia Guseva, Nov. 12, 1976; children: Elisaveta, Nina. BS, Lensoviet Coll. Chemistry and Tech., St. Petersburg, Russia, 1968; PhD, Lensoviet Tech. Inst., St. Petersburg, 1980. Rsch. scientist Inst. Tech. of Organic Synthesis, Volsk, Russia, 1968-80; sr. rsch. scientist Inst. Tech. of Organic Synthesis, Volsk, 1980-89, head of rsch. group, 1989—. Contbr. articles to profl. jours. Mem. N.Y. Acad. Scis. Russian Orthodox. Avocation: gardening.

MOROZKINA, EUGENIA ALEXANDROVNA, philology educator, consultant; b. Ufa, Russia, Nov. 28, 1953; d. Alexander Feodorovich and Angelina Alexandrovna (Sannikhova) Bashkatov; m. Nickolay Danilovich Morozkin, May 6, 1978; children: Yuri Nickolaevich, Nickita Nickolaevich. MA in Lit., Leningrad (Russia) State U., 1977, PhD in Philology, 1982, D in Philology, 1996. Asst. Bashkir State U., Ufa, 1983-87, prof. asst., 1987-96, prof. philology, 1996—; cons. prof. English Birsk (Russia) Pedagogical Inst., 1996—, Russian Inst. Fin. and Economy, Ufa, 1996—; cons. prof. Russian Emory and Henry Coll., Emory, Va., 1993; cons. prof. English Ufa State Pub. Sch. #3, 1998—; cons. prof. English, Bashkir Acad. of Complex Def., 2000—. Author: Theodore Dreiser and Literary Development of the USA at the Turn of the XIX-XXth Centuries, 1994, The Formation of the Southern Novel in the USA Literary Process: Novels of W.G. Simms, 1997, others; translator: The Writers of the USA About Literature, 1982. Grantee USIA, 1997. Mem. Am. Studies Assn., Australian and New Zealand Am. Studies Assn., Russian Assn. Am. Culture Studies, Russian Acad. Scis. Avocations: arts, literature. E-mail: MorozkinND@bsu.bashedu.ru. Home: Bakalinskaya St 68/6 Apt 45, 450022 Ufa Russia Office: Bashkir State U, Frunze St 32, 450074 Ufa Russia

MOROZOV, ANDREI NICOLAEVICH, physicist, researcher, educator; b. Moscow, June 17, 1959; s. Nicolai Andreevich and Galina Grigorevna (Lebedeva) M.; m. Lidia Aleksandrovna Tchertkova, Nov. 9, 1996. PhD, Bauman Moscow State Tech. U., 1986, DSc in Physics and Math. Scis., 1995, prof., 1997. Engr. Bauman Moscow State Tech. U., 1985-87, asst. prof., 1987-95, prof., 1995-98, head dept. physics, 1998—; gen. dir. Ctr. Applied Physics, Bauman Moscow State Tech. U., 1991—. Author: Theory of Brownian Motion, 1993, Irreversible Processes in Multibeam Fabry-Perot Interferometer, 1996, Irreversible Processes and Brownian Motion: The Physical-Technical Problems, 1997. Grantee Soros Fund, Moscow, 1993, Pres. Russia, 1996. Mem. Phys. Soc. Russia. Avocation: travel. Home: 14/16, 167 Zemlyanoy val St, 103064 Moscow Russia Office: Bauman Moscow State Tech U, 5 2d Baumanskaya St, 107005 Moscow Russia

MOROZOV, OLEG GENNADYEVICH, radio engineer, researcher; b. Kazan, Tatarstan, Russia, Oct. 30, 1960; s. Gennady Alexandrovich and Rimma Rinovna (Bagautdinova; m. Natalya Anatolievna Mashchenko, June 26, 1981; 1 child, Ekatherina. Engr. in Radiotechnics, Aviation Inst., Kazan, Russia, 1983; PhD in Technics, Tupolev Aviation Inst., Kazan, 1987. Rsch. scientist Tupolev Aviation Inst., Kazan, 1983-89, head R & D Lab., 1989-93; assoc. prof. Tupolev State Tech. U., Kazan, 1993—; mem. radiotech. faculty Tupolev Aviation Inst., Kazan, 1983-93; leading rsch. scientist Applied Electrodynamics Ctr., Kazan, 1993-99. Contbr. articles to profl. jours. Mem. faculty com. Communist Youth Union, Kazan, 1980-83; mem. faculty bur. Communist Party of Soviet Union, Kazan, 1983-91. Grantee Ministry of Edn., Moscow, 1993, 99. Mem. Popov Soc., SPIE. Avocations: postage stamps, books, philophonist, tourism, football. Office: State Tech U, K Marx St 10, 420111 Kazan Russia

MOROZOV, SERGUEI IVANOVICH, physicist, researcher, educator; b. Moscow, Feb. 24, 1951; s. Ivan Georgievich and Galina Gavrilovna (Kareva) M.; m. Tatiana Borisovna Tymosh, May 5, 1973; 1 child, Alexey Sergeevich. Engr.-Physicist, Moscow Engring./Physics Inst., Obninsk, USSR, 1974; Candidat Phys. and Math. Scis., Joint Inst. Nuclear Rsch., Dubna, USSR, 1989. Jr. scientist Inst. Physics and Power Engring., Obninsk, USSR, 1974-77; scientist Inst. Physics and Power Engring., Obninsk, 1977-87, sr. scientist, 1987—; sr. lectr. Inst. Nuclear and Power Engring., Obninsk, Russia, 1997—. Contbr. articles to profl. jours. Grantee Internat. Sci. Found., 1993, Russian Based Rsch. Found., 1995. Mem. Obninsk Club Scientists. Avocations: lawn tennis, downhill skiing, windsurfing. Office: Inst Physics and Power Engr, Bondarenko sq 1, 249020 Obninsk Kaluga, Russia

MOROZOV, VLADIMIR P., communications professional; b. Krestsy, Russia, Apr. 1, 1929; s. Pyotr Yefimovich Morozov and Irina Ivanovna Rodionova; m. Natalia Pavlovna Podkuitchenko, July 22, 1961; children: Andrei, Irina, Pyotr. Grad., Leningrad State U., 1955, Cand. of Scis. in Biology, 1962; DS in Biology, Pavlov Inst. of Physiology, USSR Acad. Scis., 1982; Prof. (hon.), Sechenov Inst. Evolutionary, Physiology/USSR Acad. Scis., 1982. Lab. asst. to head Bio-acoustics Lab./Inst. Evolution Phys. USSR Acad. Scis., Leningrad, 1959-87; head Lab. for Non-Verbal Comm. Inst. Psychology, Moscow, 1987—; head of Lab. for Psycho-Physiology of Singing, Leningrad Conservatoire, 1960-68; prof. Moscow Conservatorie, 1988—; head Interdisciplinary Ctr. of Art and Sci., Moscow, 1988—. Author: (monographs) Vocal Hearing and Voice, 1965, Biophysical Fundamentals of Vocal Speech, 1977, Art and Science of Intercourse: Non-Verbal Communication, 1988, Amazing Bio-Acoustics, 1983 (1st prize all-USSR contest sci. and progress 1983); author/editor: Perception of Speech: Questions of Functional Brain Asymmetry, others; contbr. articles to numerous scientific publs. Mem. Acad. of Art/Moscow, N.Y. Acad. of Scis. Avocation: singing. E-mail: nonverbal@psychol.ras.ru. Office: Inst Psychology/Russis Acad, Scis/13 Yaroslavskaya St, Moscow 129366, Russia

MOROZOV, VYACHESLAV GRIGORIEVICH, immunologist, researcher; b. Saint Petersburg, Russia, Nov. 17, 1946; m. Irena Petrovna Rudenko, Aug. 17, 1971; 1 child, Olga. MD, Mil. Med. Acad., Saint Petersburg, 1971, DSc in Immunology, 1990; PhD in Immunology, Rsch. Inst. Exptl. Medicine, Saint Petersburg, 1979. Microbiologist Med. Svc. of the Army, 1971-77; rschr. Mil. Med. Acad., 1977-88, chief immunology rsch. dept., 1988-93; sci. dir. Inst. Bioregulation and Gerontology, 1993—. Author: Peptide Bioregulation, 1996, Cytomedines, 1998; contbr. articles to profl. jours.; patentee in field. Recipient prize Coun. of Ministers, USSR, 1989. Mem. European Cytokine Soc., Internat. Cytokine Soc., Soc. for Leukocyte Biology, N.Y. Acad. Scis. Avocation: sports. Office: Inst Bioreg & Gerontology, Dynamo Prospect 3, 197110 Saint Petersburg Russia

MOROZOV, YURY GEORGIEVICH, physicist, researcher; b. Ussurijsk, USSR, June 21, 1948; s. Georgij Vasiljevich and Vera Ustinovna (Oreshkina) M.; m. Valentina Grigorjevna Zueva, Feb. 13, 1971; 1 child, Marina. PhD, Inst. Chem. Physics, Moscow, 1980. Rsch. scientist Inst. Chem. Physics, Chernogolovka, USSR, 1971-83; sr. rschr. Inst. Solid State Physics, Chernogolovka, 1984-87, Inst. Structural Macrokinetics, Chernogolovka, 1988-99; head lab. Inst. Structural Macrokinetics and Materials Sci., Chernogolovka, 1999—. Contbr. articles to profl. jours. Recipient SHS award William and Mary Greve Found., Inc., 1994. Office: Inst Structural, Macrokinetics/Material Sci, 142432 Chernogolovka Russia

MOROZOVSKY, NICHOLAS VLADIMIROVICH, physicist, researcher; b. Kiev, Ukraine, Dec. 22, 1949; s. Vladimir Antovich and Fira Davidovna Morozovsky: m. Svetlana Leonidovna Bravina; 1 child, Anna Nicholaevna. MS, Nat. U., Kiev, Ukraine, 1976; PhD, Inst. Semiconductors NASU, Kiev, Ukraine, 1983; DSc, Inst. Material Sci., Kiev, Ukraine, 1996. Engr. Inst. Physics Nat. Acad. Sci. of Ukraine, Kiev, 1974-76; sr. engr. Inst. Phys. NASU, Kiev, Ukraine, 1976-83, fr. rsch. scientist, 1983-87, rsch. scientist, 1987-90, sr. rsch. scientist, 1990-2000; leading rsch. scientist Inst. Phys. NASU, Kiev, 2000—; cons. Inst. Info. Sci., Kiev, Ukraine, 1992-93, Energoproject, Kiev, Ukarine, 1993-95; mem. Ukranian Adv. Commn. on Ferroelectricity. Patent: Memory Element, 1986, Converter of Temperature into frequency, 1988; contbr. more than 100 articles to profl. jours. Deputy chmn. Regional Election Commn, Kiev, Ukraine, 1991, 93, 98, 99. With USSR Army, 1968-70. Grantee Ukraine State Com. of Sci., Kiev, 1993, 94, 96, State Bur. of Fgn. Experts of China, 1997. Mem. Internat. Soc. for Optical Engring. Avocations: radioelectronics, fine arts, skiing, badminton. Home: 45th Fl, Strategicheskoe Shosse 15, 03028 Kiev Ukraine Office: Inst Physics NASU, Prospect Nauki 46, 03028 Kiev Ukraine

MORPETH, IAIN CARDEAN SPOTTISWOODE, solicitor; b. Edinburgh, Scotland, Dec. 28, 1953; s. Douglas Spottiswoode and Anne Rutherford (Bell) M.; m. Angela Susan Devitt, June 30, 1979; children: Richard, Duncan, Catherine, James. LLB, Bristol U., Eng., 1974. Ptnr. Clifford Chance, U.K., 1988—. Mem. Law Soc., City of London Solicitors Co. Office: Clifford Chance, 200 Aldersgate St, London EC1A 4JJ, England

MORPHONIOS, DEAN B., lawyer; b. Miami, Fla., Apr. 27, 1956; s. Alexander George and Ellen (James) M.; m. Joan Julien, Aug 7, 1982; children: Kimberly Anne, Matthew James. BA, Fla. Internat. U., Miami, 1979; JD, Fla. State U., 1983. Bar: Fla. 1983, U.S. Dist. Ct. (so. dist.) Fla. 1985, U.S. Dist. Ct. (mid. and no. dists.) 1988, U.S. Ct. Appeals, U.S. Supreme Ct. 1989. Assoc. gen. counsel Fla. Police Benevolent Assn., Tallahassee, 1983-84; sole practitioner Miami, 1984-86; asst. state atty. State Attys. Office/2d Jud. Cir., Tallahassee, 1986-88; assoc. Kitchen Judkins Simpson & High, Tallahassee, 1988-97; sole practitioner Tallahassee, 1997—; mem. Bench Bar Com., Tallahassee, 1996—, Conflict Rev. Com., Tallahassee, 1996—. Mem. Fla. Assn. Criminal Defendant Attys. (pres. Tallahassee chpt. 1994-95). Democrat. Christian. Office: 610 N Duval St Tallahassee FL 32301-1135

MORPURGO, JACK ERIC, author, broadcaster; b. Tottenham, Eng., Apr. 26, 1918; s. Mark and Nancy (Cook) M.; m. Catherine Noel Kippe Cammaerts (dec. 1993); children: Pieter, Michael, Mark, Katharine. BA, Coll. of William and Mary, 1938, LHD (hon.), 1970; postgrad., Inst. Hist. Rsch., London; LittD (hon.), Ricker Coll., 1962; DLit (hon.), Elmira Coll., 1964; D in Humanities (hon.), Coll. Idaho, 1983; ArtsD (hon.), Rocky Mountain Coll., 1995. Editor Penguin Books Ltd., London, 1945-47; asst. dir. Nuffield Found., London, 1950-54; dir.-gen. Nat. Book League, London, 1955-69; prof. Am. lit. U. Leeds, Eng., 1970-83, prof. emeritus, 1983—; vis. prof. Mich. State U., 1949, Free U., Berlin, 1958, George Washington U., Washington, 1973, Vanderbilt U., 1981; prof. Am. studies U. Geneva, 1967-69; dir. UNESCO Seminar on Reading Materials, Rangoon, Burma, 1957, Madras, India, 1959; vis. fellow Australian Nat. U., 1975, Bergmann Coll., 1977; scholar-in-residence Rockefeller Rsch. Ctr., Italy, 1974, Coll. of Idaho, 1986; mng. dir. Sexton Agy. and Press Ltd., P. and M. Youngman Carter Ltd. Author: American Excursion, 1949 (with Russell B. Nye) A History of the United States, 2 vols., 1955, rev. edits. 1969, 76, (with Kenneth Pelmear) Rugby Football: An Anthology, 1958, Paper Backs Across Frontiers, 1960, The Road to Athens, 1963, Venice, 1964, Book and Journal Services for Doctors and Nurses, 1966, Barnes Wallis: A Biography, 1972, Their Majesties' Royall College, 1976, Treason at West Point, 1976, Allen Lane: King Penguin, 1979, Verses Humorous and Post-Humorous, 1981, Christ's Hospital 1984, Christ's Hospital: An Introductory History, 1991, Master of None: An Autobiography, 1990; editor: Charles Lamb and Elia, 1948, 93, Edward the Second (Christopher Marlow), 1949, Life Under the Tudors, 1949, The Autobiography of Leigh Hunt, 1949, Life Under the Stuarts, 1950, The Humorous Verses of Lewis Carroll, 1950, The Last Days of Shelley and Byron (Edward John Trelawny), John Keats: A Selection of His Poetry, 1953, 85, Cobbett: A Year's Residence in the USA, 1964, Cooper: The Spy, 1968, Cobbett's America, 1985, The Return of Mr. Campion (Margery Allingham), 1989; gen. editor Penguin History of England, Penguin History of the World, 1947-69. Almoner Christ's Hosp., 1972-89, also dep. chmn., 1984; chmn. Working Party on Med. Librs.; dir. William and Mary Hist. Project, 1970-76. Served Brit. Army, Royal Arty., 1939-46. Recipient Yorkshire Post Spl. Lit. award, 1980; named hon. fellow Coll. William and Mary, 1949. Mem. Soc. Bookmen, Army and Navy Club, Pilgrims, Phi Beta Kappa. Home: 12 Laurence Mews Askew Rd, London W12 9AT, England

MORREALE, JOSEPH CONSTANTINO, higher education administrator, public administration educator, economic and financial consultant; b. Bronx, N.Y., Oct. 26, 1944; s. Joseph Vincent Morreale and Grace (Soricelli); m. Barbara McAdorey; children: Gwenn F., Margaret I., Adam J. BA, Queens Coll. CUNY, 1967; MA, SUNY, Buffalo, 1969, PhD in Econs., 1972; MS in Higher Ednl. Adminstrn., SUNY, Albany, 1989. Asst. prof. econs. Western Mich. U., Kalamazoo, 1970-74; rsch. assoc. U. Wis., Madison, 1974-75; asst. to assoc. prof. health svcs. adminstrn., econs. Grad. Sch. Pub. Health U. Pitts., 1975-79; assoc. to prof. econs., environ. studies Bard Coll., Annandale-On-Hudson, N.Y., 1979-88; vis. rsch. fellow Grad. Sch. Edn., H.E. Adminstrn. SUNY, Albany, 1988-89; prof., chmn. dept. pub. adminstrn. Grad. Sch. Pace U., White Plains, N.Y., 1989-96; vice provost for planning assessment and instnl. rsch. Pace U., N.Y.C., Westchester, 1996-98, v.p. planning, assessment, rsch. and acad. support, 1998—; health care and govt. fin. cons. to fed. agencies, state and local govts., pvt. firms, 1979—; adj. prof. law Pace U., 1990-96; adj. prof. pub. adminstrn. Grad. Sch. Pub. Affairs, SUNY-Albany, 1990-96; vis. prof. U. Lancaster, Eng., 1984-85; rsch. assoc., bd. dirs. Hudsonia Environ. Rsch., Annandale, 1985-95; fin. planner Prudential Fin. Svcs., Newburgh, N.Y., 1987-89. Author: Health Care Economics, 1977, Policies, Practices, Precautions, 1997; editor: The U.S. Medical Care Industry, 1974; contbr. articles to profl. jours. Appoint pub. rep. Westchester County Deferred Compensation Bd. Recipient NDEA fellowship, 1967-70, Pharm. Mfg. Assn. fellowship, 1969-70, post-doctoral fellowship Health Econ. Rsch. Ctr. U. Wis., 1974-75, rsch. fellowship Grad. Sch. Edn. SUNY-Albany, 1988-89, ACE fellowship UNC, Charlotte, 1995-96, sr. rsch. fellow Harvard IEM Inst., 2000. Mem. Am. Soc. for Pub. Adminstrn., Am. Econ. Assn., Am. Ednl. Fin. Assn., Assn. Instl. Rsch., Am. Assn. Higher Edn., Am. Coun. Edn. (fellow 1995-96), N.Y. State Govt. Fin. Officers Assn. (bd. dirs. 1990-95). Mem. Soc. of Friends. Avocations: photography, tennis, music, environ. concerns. Office: Pace U VP 1 Pace Plz New York NY 10038-1598

MORREAU, JACQUELINE, artist; b. Milw., Oct. 18, 1929; arrived in Eng., 1972; d. Eugene Richard and Jenny Segall; m. Theodore Kompanetz, Aug. 20, 1950 (div. 1954); 1 child, Arvad; m. Patrick Mark Morreau, Oct. 31, 1959; children: Mark, Cecilia, Andrea. Student, Chouinard Art Inst., L.A., 1945-49, Jepson Art Inst., L.A., 1945-49; diploma med. illustration, U. Calif., San Francisco, 1958. Artist, 1958—; prof. art Regent's Coll., London, 1990—; vis. lectr. Oxford Brookes U., 1990—, Royal Coll. Art, London. Exhibited in group shows including Women in War and Peace, Houston, 1986, Victoria and Albert Mus., 1989, Mus. Modern Art, Oxford, 1991; one-woman shows include Art Space, London, 1986, 88, Ferens Art Galery, 1988, 96, Odette Gilbert, London, 1989-90; represented in pub. collections including Victoria and Albert Mus., Cleve. Mus., Middlesborough, Ferrens Art Gallery, Rochdale Art Gallery, Nuffield Coll. Oxford, Open U., British Mus.; co-editor: (with Sarah Kent) Womens Images of Men, 1985, 90; editor: Drawings & Graphics Series, 1985-86; print comms. include U. Northumbria Press, Cargo Press, U.K. Trustee Rootstein-Hopkins Found., 1992—. Recipient Purchase award Arts Coun. Great Britain, 1984. Mem. Women Artists Slide Libr., Visual Arts and Galleries Assn.

MORREL, WILLIAM GRIFFIN, JR., banker; b. Lynchburg, Va., Aug 25, 1933; s. William Griffin and Virginia Louise (Baldwin) M.; m. Sandra Virginia Coats, Jan. 31, 1959; children: William Griffin, John Coats, Elisabeth White, Jere Coleman. BS, Yale U., 1955; postgrad. Rutgers U., 1965-67. With Md. Nat. Bank, Balt., 1955-84, asst. v.p., 1959, v.p., 1964, sr. v.p., 1975-84, mgmt. com. 1979-84, chmn. three lending coms., others; pres., bd. dirs. Md. Nat. Overseas Investment Corp.; chmn. bd. London Interstate Bank Ltd.; chmn. bd. dirs. Md. Internat. Bank; sr. v.p., chief operating officer Abu Dhabi Internat. Bank, Inc., 1984-86, pres., chief exec. officer Heritage Internat. Bank, 1986-89; dir., pres., CEO Madison Fin. Group, 1989-97, chmn., 1997—; CEO, chmn. The Valley Fin. Group, Balt., 1989—; pres., chief exec. officer Summit Bancorp, Balt., 1990-92; consul of the Netherlands at Balt., 1978-84. Mem. Balt. Consular Corps, 1978-84; chmn. Md. World Trade Efforts Commn., 1983-84; mem. Md. Trade Policy Council, 1985-88; vice chmn. Dist. Export Council, 1983—. Contbr. articles to profl. jours. Sr. fellow Ctr. for Internat. Banking Studies, Darden Grad. Bus. Sch. U. Va., 1978-91. Served with U.S. Army, 1956-58. Mem. Bankers Assn. for Fgn. Trade (bd. dirs. 1975-78), Robert Morris Assocs. (nat. bd. dirs. 1984-88), Internat. Lending Council (bd. dirs., chmn., 1978-80), Md. Hist. Soc. (trustee), Balt. Council Fgn. Relations (trustee), Econ. Devel. Council. Republican. Presbyterian. Clubs: Yale, Farmington Country, Elkridge, Md. Club. Home: 6 Beechdale Rd Baltimore MD 21210-2207 Office: The Madison Fin Group Inc PO Box 16265 Baltimore MD 21210-0265

MORRELL, DAVID CAMERON, medical practice educator; b. London, Nov. 6, 1929; s. William Escourt and Violet (Cameron) M.; m. Alison Joyce Eaton-Taylor, May 30, 1953; children: Margaret, William, Anthony, Thomas, Elizabeth. MBBS, London Univ., 1952; Fellow, Faculty Pub. Health Medicine, London, 1986. FRCP, FRCGP; diplomate Royal Coll. Obstet. Physician Royal Air Force Med. Br., Eng., 1954-57; prin. in gen. practice Hoddesdon, Eng., 1957-63; clin. asst. neurology St. Mary Hosp., London, 1960-63; lectr. in gen. practice Univ. Edinburg, 1963-67; sr. lectr. in gen. practice U. London, 1967-74, prof. gen. practice, 1974-93; sub dean St. Thomas' Hosp. Med. Sch., London, 1984-89; chmn. dep. gen. practice United Med. and Dental Schs., London, 1988-93. Author: Art of General Practice, 4 edits. 1966-91; editorial bd.: Practice, Clinical Management in General Practice, 1976, Teaching General Practice, 1981; editor: Epidemiology in General Practice, 1988. Squadron leader Royal Air Force, 1954-57. Officer of the Order of the Brit. Empire, 1982, Knight of St. Gregory The Great, 1982. Mem. Brit. Med. Assn. (pres. 1994). Roman Catholic. Avocations: gardening, hiking. Home: 14 Higher Green, KT173BA Epsom England

MORRELL, JACK BOWES, science history educator; b. Bradford, Eng., Nov. 24, 1933; s. Lewis and Caroline Annie (Bowes) M.; m. Janet Yorke, Dec. 29, 1962; children: Elizabeth, Margaret Jane. BSc, U. Birmingham, 1954; MA, Oxford U., 1957; Cert. Edn., U. Bristol, 1958. Schoolmaster Haberdashers Aske's Sch., London, 1958-59, Queen Elizabeth Grammar Sch., Wakfield, Eng., 1959-63; lectr. history of sci. U. Bradford, Yorkshire, Eng., 1964-83; reader U. Bradford, Yorkshire, 1983-94; vis. prof. U. Pa., 1970. Author: (with A.W. Thackray) Gentlemen of Science, 1981, (with I. Inkster) Metropolis and Province, 1983, Science at oxford 1914-1939, 1997; contbr. articles to profl. jours. Fellow Royal Hist. Soc.; mem. Brit. Soc. History of Sci. (pres. 1982-84). Avocations: music, mountain climbing.

MORRILL, PENNY CHITTIM, art historian; b. San Antonio, Feb. 4, 1947; d. Jack Robert and Dorothy Born (Sutherland) Chittim; m. James Agrippa Morrill, July 12, 1969; children: Jackson Forrest, Julia Chiltipin. BA with honors, Tulane U., 1969; MA, U. Pa., 1971; postgrad., U. Md., 1996—. Program coord. Cancer Rsch. Found. Am., Alexandria, Va., 1990-95; intern Nat. Gallery Art, Washington, summer 1997; tchg. asst. U. Md., College Park, 1997—; curator and traveling exhbn. on Mex. silver San Antonio Mus. of Art., 1998—. Author: Silver Masters of Mexico, 1996, Mexican Silver, 1994; contbr. articles to profl. jours. Vol. teen pregnancy prevention Nat. ARC, Washington, 1986-98; participant Coro Women in Leadership, Washington, 1988; adv. com. Betty Ford Breast Health Ctr., Washington, 1997-98; adv. com. Nat. Rehab. Hosp., Washington, 1991—; mem., v.p. Newcomb Coll./Tulane U. Alumnae Bd., 1990-94; mem., pres. Lyceum Mus., Alexandria, 1992-97; mem., editor, pres. Hist. Alexandria Found., 1980-89; curator exhbn. Carlyle House Mus., Alexandria, 1980. Recipient Achievement award Jr. League of Phila., 1985, Award for RAP and AMAZE, Nat. ARC, 1988, Spirit of Volunteerism award Jr. League of Washington, 1992, Recognition award Nat. Rehab. Hosp., 1997. Mem. Coll. Art Assn., Am. Soc. Jewelry Historians. Episcopalian. Avocations: knitting, gardening.

MORRIONE, MELCHIOR S., management consultant, accountant; b. Bklyn., Dec. 31, 1937; s. Charles and Dionisia (Eletto) M.; m. Joan Finnerty, June 22, 1968; children: Karyn Morrione Frick, Nicole. BBA magna cum laude, St. John's U., 1959. CPA, N.J., N.Y. Tax ptnr. Arthur Andersen & Co., N.Y.C., 1959-91; mng. dir. MSM Consulting LLC, Woodcliff Lake, N.J., 1992—; lectr. in field. Contbr. articles to profl. jours. With U.S. Army, 1960-61. Mem. CPAs, N.Y. State Soc. CPAs, N.J. Soc. CPAs, Internat. Fiscal Assn., Internat. Tax Assn., Ridgewood Country Club. Republican. Roman Catholic. Avocations: golf, tennis. E-mail: morrione@idt.net. Office: MSM Consulting LLC 11 Ginny Dr Woodcliff Lk NJ 07677-8115

MORRIS, ALEXANDER WILLIAM, physicist, manager; b. Hanover, Germany, June 1, 1959; s. Rowland George and Ann D'Orville (Morse) M.; m. Joy Mary Lecky-Thompson, Mar. 31, 1986. BA in Physics with honors, U. Oxford, Eng., 1980, MSc in Plasma Physics, 1981, DPhil, 1985. Jr. rsch. fellow Balliol Coll., Oxford U., 1983-88; vis. scientist Princeton (N.J.) U., 1985-87; rsch. physicist UKAEA Fusion, Culham, Eng., 1987—, programme mgr., 1993—. Contbr. articles to profl. jours. Recipient Scott prize Oxford U., 1980; Merton Coll. Oxford scholar, 1977. Mem. Inst. Phys., Am. Phys. Soc. Office: UKAEA Fusion, Culham Sci Ctr, Abingdon OX14 3DB, England

MORRIS, BRIAN JAMES, physiologist, educator; b. Adelaide, Australia, July 14, 1950; s. Harry Claude and Betty Aileen (Porter) M.; m. Julie Anne Robinson, May 3, 1975 (div. July 1978); m. Lilian Jean Mijatovic, Feb. 14, 1993. BS, U. Adelaide, South Australia, 1972; PhD, Monash U., Melbourne, Australia, 1975; DSc, U. Sydney, Australia, 1993. C.J. Martin fellow Nat. Health and Med. Rsch. coun., U. Mo., Columbia, 1975-76; C.J. Martin fellow Nat. Health and Med. Rsch. Ctr. U. Calif., San Francisco, 1976-77; Calif. Heart Adv. fellow Am. Heart Assn., San Francisco, 1977-78; lectr. U. Sydney, 1978-82, sr. lectr., 1982-88, reader, 1988-98, prof., 1999—. Contbr. over 180 articles to profl. jours. Recipient Edgeworth David medal Royal Soc. NSW, 1985. Mem. Internat. Soc. Hypertension, High Blood Pressure Rsch. Coun. Australia (exec. com.), Australian Soc. for Med. Rsch., Endocrine Soc. Australia. Achievements include cloning genes for hypertension, finding genes for cardiovascular disease, test for detection of human papillomavirus using polymerase chain reaction (virus that causes cervical cancer); patent in field. Office: Univ Sydney, Dept Physiology Bldg F13, Sydney 2006, Australia

MORRIS, CALVIN CURTIS, architect; b. Champaign, Ill., Mar. 5, 1955; s. Charles Calvin Morris and Audrey Jane (Carr) Johnson; m. Monica Lynn Greco, May 16, 1987; children: Amanda Pauline, Leah Marie. BS in Archtl. Studies, U. Ill., Champaign, 1978. Registered architect, Ill., Mo.; cert. NCARB. Draftsman Archtl. Assocs. Inc., Collinsville, Ill., 1977-78; v.p. Archtl. Assocs. Inc., Collinsville, 1978-88, exec. v.p., 1988-89; prin. AAI/Campbell, Inc., 1990-95, AAIC Inc., 1996—. Mem. Planning Commn., Collinsville, 1982-88, vice chmn., 1986-88, planning commn., Maryville, 1999—; bd. dirs. Collinsville United Way, 1988-92, Downtown Devel. Commn., 1993-94; mem. Collinsville Econ. Devel. Commn., 1996-97, Southwestern Ill. Leadership Coun., 1996—. Named one of Outstanding Young Men of Am. U.S. Jaycees, 1981; bd. dirs. Whitey Herzog Youth Found., 1996—. Mem. AIA, Nat. Coun. Archtl. Registration Bds., Nat. Trust for Historic Preservation, Soc. Am. Mil. Engrs., Collinsville C. of C. (bd. dirs. 1989-96), Collinsville Kiwanis Club (pres. 1983-85). Democrat. Lutheran. Avocations: camping, fishing, skiing, golf. Office: AAIC Inc 1 Design Mesa Collinsville IL 62234-4639

MORRIS, CHRISTOPHER DAVID, archaeology educator; b. Preston, U.K., Apr. 14, 1946; s. David Richard and Ethel Margaret (Back) M.; m. Vivienne Claire Wilkinson, July 7, 1968 (div. 1979); m. Colleen Elizabeth Batey, July 21, 1981. BA with honors, U. Durham, 1967; diploma in edn., U. Oxford, 1968. Asst. lectr. in history and archeology Hockerill Coll. of Edn., Bishops Stortford, 1968-72; lectr. in archaeology U. Durham, Eng., 1972-81, sr. lectr. in archaeology, 1981-88; reader in viking archaeology U. Durham, 1989-90; prof. archaeology U. Glasgow, Scotland, 1990—, vice prin., 2000—. Mem. Ancient Monuments Bd. for Scotland, 1990—; royal commr. Ancient and Hist. Monuments Scotland, 1999—. Fellow Royal Hist. Soc., Soc. Antiquaries of Scotland, Soc. of Antiquaries of London, Royal Soc. Edinburgh, Royal Soc. Arts; mem. Inst. Field Archaeologists. Avocations: opera, music, walking, gardening. Office: U Glasgow Archaeology Dept, Gregory Bldg Lilybank Gar, Glasgow G12 8QQ, Scotland

MORRIS, DAVID, retired electrical engineer; b. N.Y.C., July 18, 1924; s. Morris Elia and Esther (Kohn) M.; m. Minnie Kramer, Feb. 2, 1957. BEE, CCNY, 1947, MEE, 1954. Elec. engr. Magnetic Amplifiers Inc., L.I., N.Y., 1951-53; chief engr. Square Root Mfg. Corp., Yonkers, N.Y., 1953-56; sect. head Poly. R&D, Bklyn., 1956-58; chief engr. Brach div. Gen. Bronze Corp., Newark, N.J., 1958-62; unit head Kearfott div. Singer Corp., Little Falls, N.J., 1962-70; group leader Monroe div. Litton Industries, Orange, N.J., 1970-72; sr. mem. tech. staff Lepel High Frequency Labs., Maspeth, N.Y., 1972-80, I.T.T. Avionics, Nutley, N.J., 1980-89; ret., 1989. Contbr. articles to profl. jours.; 7 patents in field. Mem. IEEE (life). Achievements include development of off line transistor switching regulator; radiation hardened hybrid electro-magnetic device for protection of semiconductor circuits; multi-winding power inductor; design of magnetic amplifiers for servo mechanisms used in the Ballistic Missile early warning system; power systems for N.Y. Fire Dept., T.F.X. fighter aircraft, AH64 Apaache helicopter. Avocations: experimental physics, classical music, chess. Home: 806 Maple Hill Dr Woodbridge NJ 07095-4109

MORRIS, DAVID MICHAEL, insurance executive, lawyer; b. San Juan, P.R., Dec. 8, 1948; s. Edwin Thaddeus and Winifred Isabel (Walsh) M.; m. Carol Anderson Worden, Aug. 7, 1971; children: Laura H., John C. BA, U. Md., 1971; JD, U. Balt., 1975. Bar: Md. 1976, U.S. Dist. Ct. Md. 1976; CLU. Ptnr. Franklin/Morris Assocs., Balt., 1976—. Columnist legal newspaper Daily Record, 1985-87. Pres., trustee 2d Presbyn. Ch., Balt., 1980-86, elder, 1988—; vice chmn. Balt. div. United Way, 1981-84; fund raiser Johns Hopkins Children's Ctr., Balt., 1984-88; trustee Roland Park Country Sch., 1988-89, 90-98; mem. exec. com. Gilman Sch. Parents Assn., 1989-91; grad. Leadership Md., 1998. Mem. ABA, Md. Bar Assn., Balt. Bar Assn., Assn. Advanced Life Underwriting, Balt. Life Underwriters Assn. (chmn. ethics 1977-80, bd. dirs. 1982-85, bd. dirs. Charitable Found., 1998—), Balt. Soc. CLUs and Chartered Fin. Cons. (chmn. ethical guidance com., bd. dirs.), Million Dollar Round Table (life), Md. Club, Balt. Country Club, Leadership Maryland. Avocations: squash, tennis, golf, wine. Home: 205 Paddington Rd Baltimore MD 21212-3438 Office: Franklin/Morris Assocs 7 E Redwood St Ste 1900 Baltimore MD 21202-1113

MORRIS, DOROTHY KAY, writer; b. Charleston, S.C., Dec. 25, 1935; d. Robert Oliver and Desma Lee (Rudd) M.; m. Andre Marechal, Aug. 20, 1955 (div. July 1965); children: Désirée Katherine Araeipour, Suzette Maréchal. Pvt. coach competitive horseback riding, 1972-92; credit professional Internat. Credit Unocal Corp., Brea, Calif., 1985-99; ret., 1999. Author: Secret Sins of the Mothers, 1999; contbr. articles to horsemanship mags. Vol. English tchr., tutor Thai Community, L.A., 1986-91. Libertarian. Buddhist. Avocations: geneaology, languages.

MORRIS, EARLE ELIAS, JR., retired state official, business executive; b. Greenville, S.C., July 14, 1928; s. Earle Elias and Bernice (Carey) M.; m. Jane L. Boroughs, Apr. 12, 1958; children: Lynda Lewis, Carey Mauldin, Elizabeth McDaniel, Earle Elias III; m. Carol Telford, Oct. 4, 1972; 1 son, David Earle. BS, Clemson Coll., 1949, LLD; D.Pub. Svc. (hon.), U. S.C., 1980, S.C. State Coll., 1990; Dr. Med. Sci., U. S.C.; LLD (hon.), The Citadel, Cen. Wesleyan Coll.; HHD (hon.), Lander Coll., Francis Marion Coll., 1984, U. Charleston, 1992; DHL, Winthrop U., 1996. Pres., chmn. bd. Morris & Co., Inc. (wholesale grocers), Pickens, S.C.; v.p., dir. Pickens Bank, 1956-69, Bankers Trust S.C., Pickens, 1968-75; pres. Gen. Ins. Agy., Pickens, 1970—; chmn. bd. dirs. Carolina Investors, Inc., chmn., 1993—; ptnr. Morris Realty Co., Pickens; mem. S.C. Ho. of Reps., 1950-54, S.C. Senate, 1954-70; lt. gov. State of S.C., 1971-75, comptr. gen., 1976-99; chmn. bd. Santee Cooper Fisheries (Far East) Ltd., Hong Kong, Tai Pan Technologies, Ltd., Hong Kong; dir. Brunswick Worsted Mills, S.C. Devel. Corp., Pickens Savs. & Loan Assn.; hon. consul Govt. Korea. Pres. Clemson U. Found., 1984-85; state dir. Selective Svc. Sys. Served to brig. gen. S.C. N.G., maj. gen. S.C. S.G. Decorated Legion of Merit, Meritorious Svc. medals; recipient Algernon Sydney Sullivan award, 1980, Donald L. Scantlebury award, 1985, Nations Most Valuable Pub. Ofcl. award, 1993, Pub. Svc. award Am. Legion, 1993, Living Legend award S.C. Hist. Found., 1997, Clemson Medallion award 1997; named Disting. Alumnus, Clemson Coll. Mem. Nat. Assn. State Comptrollers (pres. 1982), Nat. Assn. State Auditors, Comptrollers and Treasurers (pres. 1988-89), S.C. Nat. Guard Assn. (pres. 1980-81), S.C. Jr. C. of C., S.C. Rehab. Assn. (v.p.), Govtl. Acctg. Standards Adv. Coun. (chmn. 1989-96), Fin. Acctg. Found. (trustee 1985-88, 96—), S.C. Retirees Assn. (pres.), Blue Key, Palmetto Club, Faculty Club (Columbia), Poinsett Club (Greenville), Masons, Shriners, Lions, Order of Saint Stanislas (grand chancellor, Knight Grand Cross), Order of white Eagle of Saint Stanislas, Sovereign Mil. Order Swabia, Order of Polonia Restituta (knight comdr., 2d class), Knights of Malta. Presbyterian (elder, former deacon, synod trustee). Home: 159 Lake Murray Ter Lexington SC 29072-9103

MORRIS, EDWIN ROBERT, chemistry educator, researcher; b. Dunfermline, Fife, Scotland, Apr. 15, 1944; s. Clarence and Elizabeth (MacDonald) M.; m. Paula Claire Marshall, Apr. 17, 1971; children: Robert, Peter, Jennifer. BSc, Edinburgh U., 1966, PhD, 1970. Chartered chemist. Rsch. scientist Unilever Rsch., Bedford, Eng., 1970-82, Med. Rsch. Coun., London, 1982-84; prof. Cranfield Inst. Tech., Silsoe Coll., Bedford, 1984-99; prof. food chemistry Univ. Coll., Cork, Ireland, 1999—. Contbr. over 200 articles to profl. jours. Fellow Royal Soc. Chemistry (Carbohydrate Chemistry award 1980), Inst. of Food Sci. and Tech. Office: Cranfield Inst Tech, Univ Coll Cork, Cork Ireland

MORRIS, ELIZABETH TREAT, physical therapist; b. Harford, Conn., Feb. 20, 1936; d. Charles Wells and Marion Louise (Case) Treat; m. David Breck Morris, July 10, 1961; children: Russell Charles, Jeffrey David. BS in Phys. Therapy, U. Conn., 1960. Phys. therapist Crippled Children's Clinic No. Va., Arlington, 1960-62, Shriners Hosp. Crippled Children, Salt Lake City, 1970-74; pvt. practice phys. therapy Salt Lake City, 1975—. Mem. nominating com. YMCA, Salt Lake City. Mem. AAHPERD, Am. Phys. Therapy Assn., Am. Congress Rehab. Medicine, Nat. Spkrs. Assn., Utah Spkrs. Assn., Salt Lake Area C. of C., Friendship Force Utah, U.S. Figure Skating Assn., Toastmasters Internat., Internat. Assn. for the Study Pain, Internat. Platform Assn., World Confederation Phys. Therapy, Medart Internat. Home: 4177 Mathews Way Salt Lake City UT 84124-4021 Office: PO Box 526186 Salt Lake City UT 84152-6186

MORRIS, FREDERICK WILLIAM (FRED WILLIAM MORRIS), technology management executive; b. L.A., Feb. 28, 1922; s. Fred William and Harriet Janet Morris; m. Nancy Renee Thompson, Oct. 21, 1949. BSEE, Calif. Inst. Tech., 1944; postgrad., Occidental Coll., 1946-48, Stanford U., 1947, George Washington U., 1966; DSc (hon.), Capitol Inst. Tech., 1975. Registered profl. engr., Calif. Engr., scientist U.S. Dept. Def., Washington, 1948-54; chmn., CEO, Tele-Scis. Assocs., Pebble Beach, Calif., 1954—; cons. Exec. Office of Pres., White House, Washington, 1960-64; dep. spl. asst. to pres., assoc. dir. telecomm. mgmt. White House, Washington, 1964-67; founder, exec. v.p., dir. Electromagnetic Tech. Corp., Palo Alto, Calif., 1962-64; v.p. Harris Corp., Washington, 1967-69; pres., CEO TRT Telecomms. Corp., Washington, 1972-75; v.p., dir., cons. COMSAT Corp., Washington, 1975-77; asst. prof. elec. engrng. U. So. Calif., 1947-50. Author numerous publs. in comms. and electronics. 1st lt. U.S. Army, WWII, 1944-48. Named Officier de l'Ordre Grand-ducal de la Couronne de Chéne, Luxembourg. Fellow AIAA (assoc.), East-West Ctr.; mem. Assocs. of Calif. Inst. Tech., IEEE (sr. life), Armed Forces Comms. and Electronics Assn. (life), Calif. Inst. Tech. Alumni Assn. (life), Stanford U. Alumni Assn. (life), Pres.' Cir. Calif. Inst. Tech., Pres.' Club Hillsdale Coll., Telephone Pioneers Assn., Missile, Space and Range Pioneers (founding mem.). Achievements include pioneer work in space communications. Avocations: travel, philately, classical music. Office: Tele-Scis Assocs PO Box 626 Pebble Beach CA 93953-0626

MORRIS, GARY WAYNE, lawyer; b. El Paso, Tex., Jan. 14, 1945; s. Harold W. and Ruth (Ingram) M.; m. Janet S. Young; children: Patricia Woodbury, Jennifer, Michael, John. BA, Point Loma Nazarene U., Pasadena, 1967; JD, U. Loyola, 1970. Assoc. Hart & Mieras, L.A., 1971-74, ptnr., 1974-96; ptnr. Hart, Mieras, Morris & Peale, Pasadena, Calif., 1996—. Presenter (audio cassette) Living Trust, 1992. Sec. L.A. Dist. Adv. Bd., Pasadena, 1976—; trustee Point Loma Nazarene U., San Diego, 1994—. Recipient Pres.'s award Optimist Club, 1975, Alumnus award Point Loma Nazarene U. Pasadena, 1980. Mem. State Bar Calif., Christian Legal Soc., L.A. County Bar Assn. Republican. Avocations: sandrail, fishing, tennis. Office: Hart Mieras Morris & Peale PO Box 662140 Arcadia CA 91066-2140

MORRIS, HENRY ALLEN, JR., publisher; b. Moncks Corner, S.C., Feb. 9, 1940; s. Henry Allen Sr. and Edith Luther (Wall) M.; divorced; 1 child, Anthony Duane Allen. A in Acctg., Palmer Jr. Coll., Charleston, S.C., 1959; BA in English cum laude, Belmont Abbey Coll., N.C., 1974. Office mgr. Gas Engine and Electric Co., Charleston, 1959; cargo coord. S.C. State Ports Authority, Charleston, 1959-70; headmaster St. Stephen Acad., S.C., 1973-77; gen. mgr. The Berkeley Democrat, Moncks Corner, 1977-86, owner, 1989—; pub., editor Berkeley Ind., Moncks Corner, 1987—; pres. Berkeley Pub. Inc., Moncks Corner, 1987—. Author: (short story) The Easter Gift, 1973. Bd. dirs. Council of Govts. Regional Forum, Charleston, 1987, Winthrop Coll., 1983, Moncks Corner Downtown, Inc., 1986-87; mem. Moncks Corner City Council, 1983-88; mayor pro tem, 1986-88; commr. S.C. Vocat. Rehab. Agy.; treas. bd. dirs. Berkeley County YMCA; founder Charleston Opera Corp.; past pres., bd. mem. Berkeley County Vol. Action Com.; former mem. parents' and cmty. leaders' focus group Berkeley County Sch. Dists. Strategic Planning Com.; founder, bd. mem. Lord Berkeley Conservation Trust; bd. mem., chmn. pub. rels. com. Berkeley H.S. Acad. Booster Club; bd. mem. Berkeley Trident United Way Adv. Bd.; lay reader, choir mem., Christian edn. com. and tchr. Ch. of the Holy Family; active Moncks Corner Planning and Zoning Commn.; bd. mem., spl. events chmn., exec. bd. sec. Moncks Corner Merchants Assn.; bd. mem., chmn. pub. rels. com. Kids Voting Berkeley. Recipient Pres. award Berkeley Arts Council, 1985, Charleston Jaycees, 1971, Friend of Edn. award Berkeley County Sch. System, 1991; named Handicapped Man of Yr., Moncks Corner's Mayor's Com., 1990. Mem. Nat. Newspaper Assn. (state meetings chmn., congl. action team), Low County Soc. Profl. Journalists (pres.), S.C. Mcpl. Assn. (lesis. com.), Berkeley C. of C. (eco-tourism com.), Moncks Corner Bus. Assn., Trident United Way (mem. exec. bd. 1983-91), Trident C. of C. (bd. dirs.), Rotary (past pres.), Moncks Corner Rotary Club (chmn. pub. rels. com.). Episcopalian. Avocations: reading, painting, collecting art. Home: 117 Merrimack Dr Moncks Corner SC 29461-3580

MORRIS, JAMES MALACHY, lawyer; b. Champaign, Ill., June 5, 1952; s. Walter Michael and Ellen Frances (Solon) M.; m. Mary Delilah Baker, Oct. 17, 1987; children: James Malachy Jr., Elliot Rice Baker, Walter Michael, Nicholas Aidan. Student, Oxford U. (Eng.), 1972; BA, Brown U., 1974; JD, U. Pa., 1977. Bar: N.Y. 1978, U.S. Dist. Ct. (so. and ea. dists.) N.Y. 1978, Ill. 1980, U.S. Tax Ct. 1982, U.S. Supreme Ct. 1983; admitted to Barristers Chambers, Manchester, Eng., 1987. Assoc. Reid & Priest, N.Y.C., 1977-80; sr. law clk. Supreme Ct. Ill., Springfield, 1980-81; assoc. Carter, Ledyard & Milburn, N.Y.C., 1981-83; sole practice N.Y.C., 1983-87; counsel FCA, Washington, 1987—; acting sec., gen. counsel FCS Ins. Corp., McLean, Va., 1990-98; cons. Internat. Awards Found., Zurich, 1981—, Pritzker Architecture Prize Found., N.Y.C., 1981—, Herbert Oppenheimer, Nathan & VanDyck, London, 1985—. Contbr. articles to profl. jours. Mem. ABA, Ill. Bar Assn., N.Y. State Bar Assn., N.Y. County Lawyers Assn., Assn. Bar City N.Y., Brit. Inst. Internat. and Comparative Law, Lansdowne Club (London), Casanova (Va.) Hunt Club. Office: PO Box 1407 Mc Lean VA 22101-1407

MORRIS, JAMES W., retired metallurgist; b. Lafayette, Ky., June 2, 1934; s. Bouldin and Irene M.; m. Thelma Roberta, Nov. 26, 1959 (dec. Apr. 1996); children: James, Jr., Jennifer. BS, U. Ky., 1957. Jr. metallurgist NASA, Cleve., 1957; 2d lt. USAR, Aberdeen, Md., 1958; ret. USAR; metallurgist, supr. design metallurgy Pratt & Whitney Aircraft, West Palm Beach, Fla., 1958-92. Lutheran. Avocations: choir, teaching Bible class, travel.

MORRIS, JAN, writer; b. Oct. 2, 1926. MA, Oxon U.; LittD (hon.), U. Wales, U. Wales, U. Glamorgan. Mem. editl. staff The Times, 1951-56, The Guardian, 1957-62. Author: (as James or Jan Morris) Coast to Coast, 1956, Sultan inOman, 1957, The Market of Seleukia, 1957, Coronation Everest, 1958, South African Winter, 1958, The Hashemite Kings, 1959, Venice, 1960, The Upstairs Donkey (for children), 1962, The Road to Huddersfield, 1963, Cities, 1963, The Presence of Spain, 1964, Oxford, 1965, Pax Britannica, 1968, The Great Port, 1970, Places,1972, Heaven's Command, 1973, Farewell the Trumpets, 1978, Conundrum, 1974, Travels, 1976, The Oxford Book of Oxford, 1978, Spain, 1979, Destinations, 1980, The Venetian Empire, 1980, The Small Oxford Book of Wales, 1982, The Spectacle of Empire, 1982, Stones of Empire, 1983, Journeys, 1984, The Matter of Wales, 1984, Among the Cities, 1985, Last Letters from Hav, 1985, Manhattan '45, 1987, Hong Kong, 1988, Pleasures of a Tangled Life, 1989, O Canada, 1991, Sydney, 1992, Locations, 1992, Travels with Virginia Woolf, 1993, A Machynlleth Triad, 1994, Fisher's Face, 1995, Fifty Years of Europe: An Album, 1997, Lincoln: A Foreigner's Quest, 1999. Decorated comdr. Order Brit. Empire. Fellow Royal Soc. Lit., U. Coll. of Wales (hon.), Royal Inst. Brit. Archs. (hon.), Acad. Gymreig; mem. Gorsedd of Bards, Nat. Eisteddfod of Wales.

MORRIS, JOHN CARL, neurologist, educator, researcher; b. Cleve., Feb. 13, 1948; s. Edward Francis and Eleanor Caroline (Pongratz) M.; m. Lucy Laub Babcox, Apr. 14, 1979; children: Carrie Laub, Edward Babcox, Mary Pongratz. BA, Ohio Wesleyan U., 1970; MD, U. Rochester Sch. Medicine and Dentistry, 1974. Diplomate Am. Bd. Internal Medicine, Am. Bd. Psychiatry and Neurology; cert. Nat. Bd. Med. Examiners. Intern San Francisco Gen. Hosp., 1974-75; pvt. practice Fairbanks (Alaska) Clinic, 1975-76, Carlsbad (N.Mex.) Regional Med. Ctr., 1976-77; asst. resident and sr. resident in medicine Akron (Ohio) Gen. Med. Ctr., 1977-79; asst. resident and sr. resident in neurology Cleve. Met. Gen. Hosp., 1979-81, resident in neuropathology, 1981-82; fellow in neuropharmacology Washington Univ. Sch. Medicine, St. Louis, 1982-85, rsch. instr. pharmacology, 1982-84, instr. neurology, 1983-85, asst. prof. neurology and neuropathology, 1985-91, asst. prof. pathology and immunology, 1989—, assoc. prof. neurology, 1991-97; Friedman prof. neurology Alzheimers Disease Rsch. Ctr., 1998—; dir. Memory Diagnostic Ctr. Barnes-Jewish Hosp. St. Louis, 1989—, dir. Alzheimer Treatment Unit, 1995—; bd. dirs. Alzheimer Assn., Chgo., 1998—; adv. bd. mem. St. Louis chap. Alzheimer's Assn.; lectr. in field. Editl. bd. mem. The Neurologist, 1992—, Alzheimer's Disease and Associated Disorders: An International Jour., 1994—; ad hoc reviewer and contbr. articles, chaps. to numerous profl. jours. Recipient Disting. Achievement Citation Ohio Wesleyan U., 2000. Fellow ACP, Am. Acad. Neurology (chair clin. practice com., mem. exec. com. geriatric neurology section, mem. commn. subspecialty cert.); mem. Am. Geriatrics Soc., Ctrl. Soc. for Neurological Rsch. (pres. 1995-96), Soc. for Neuroscience, So. for Exptl. Neuropathology, Am. Neurological Assn., Mo. State Neurological Assn., Am. Soc. Exptl. Neurotherapeutics. Office: Wash U Sch Medicine Dept Neurol Campus Box 8111-ADRC 660 S Euclid Ave Saint Louis MO 63110-1010

MORRIS, JOHN THEODORE, planning official; b. Denver, Jan. 18, 1929; s. Theodore Ora and Daisy Allison (McDonald) M.; BFA, Denver U., 1955; m. Dolores Irene Seaman, June 21, 1951; children: Holly Lee, Heather Ann, Heidi Jo, Douglas Fraser. Apprentice landscape architect S.R. DeBoer & Co., Denver, summer 1949, planning technician (part-time), 1954-55; sr. planner and assoc. Trafton Bean & Assocs., Boulder, Colo., 1955-62; prin. Land Planning Assocs., planning cons., Boulder, 1962-65; planning dir. and park coord. Boulder County, 1965-67; sch. planner Boulder Valley Sch. Dist., 1967-84, also dir. planning and engring., 1967-84, supr. facility improvement program, 1969-84; pvt. sch. planning cons., 1984—; cons. U. Colo. Bur. Ednl. Field Svcs., 1974. Bd. dirs. Historic Boulder, 1974-76; mem. parks and recreation adv. com. Denver Regional Coun. Govts., 1975-84. Served with USCG, 1950-53. Mem. Am. Inst. Cert. Planners, Am. Planning Assn., Longmont Artist Guild. Home and Office: 7647 32nd St Boulder CO 80302-9327

MORRIS, JOSEPH RAYMOND, business and economics educator; b. Stuckey, Ga., May 29, 1939; s. Joseph Alton and Ora Lou (Hinson) M.; m. Joyce Marilyn Speiller, Mar. 17, 1984; children from previous marriage: Theresa, Marianne, Jennifer. BA, Nova U., 1986, M of Internat. Bus. Adminstrn., 1988. Sales profl. Dixie Pllywood Corp. Inc., Miami, Fla., 1964-68; sales mgr. Bradley Plywood Corp. Inc., Savannah, Ga., 1968-73; mgr. City Motel Inc., Franklin, N.C., 1973-78; pres., owner Coweee Gem Shop, Franklin, 1973-78; with Eastern Airlines Inc., Miami, 1978-90; adj. prof., then full-time/part-time prof. Broward C.C., Ft. Lauderdale, Fla., 1989—; adj. prof. Palm Beach C.C., Boca Raton, Fla., 1995, Fla. Internat. U., Miami,1990—, Lynn U., Boca Raton, 1998—; instr. part-time Nova Southeastern U., Ft. Lauderdale, 1996—, Johnson & Wales U., 2000—. With USN, 1956-64. Recipient Enterpreneurship Inst. Svc. award, 1998, Fla. Inernat. U. Cmty. Svc. award, 1997. Mem. Am. Inst. Econ. Rsch., Acad. Internat. Bus., Franklin Gem and Mineral Soc., , Lions (pres. Franklin chpt. 1976-77, v.p. 1973-75, chmn. western counties 1977-78), Civitans (treas. 1982-83), Toastmasters, Masons, Shriners. Republican. Baptist. Avocations: golf, swimming, community service, time with students. Home and Office: PO Box 292104 Davie FL 33329-2104

MORRIS, NORMA, research scientist; b. London, Eng., Apr. 17, 1935; d. Henry Albert and Lilian Eliza (Flexon) Bevis; m. Samuel Francis Morris; children: Jane Albertine, John Stephen, Anne Caroline. BA, U. Coll. London, 1956, MA, 1960. Sci. adminstr. Med. Rsch. Coun., 1960-95; rsch. fellow U. Coll. London, 1995—; chmn. Gen. Chiropractic Coun., 1998. Contbr. articles to profl. jours. including Rsch. Policy, Sci. and Pub. Policy. Fellow Royal Soc. Medicine. Avocations: canoeing, opera. Office: U Coll London STS Dept, Gower St, London WC1E 6BT, England

MORRIS, NORMAN FREDERICK, gynecologist; b. Luton, U.K., Feb. 26, 1920; s. Frederick and Evelyn (Biggs) Morris; m. Lucy Xenia Rivlin, June 2, 1944; children: David, Jacqueline, Nicholas, Vanessa. MB, BS, London (U.K.) U., 1943, MD, 1959. Sr. lectr. U. Coll. Hosp., London, 1952-56; reader, dep. prof. Royal Postgrad. Hosp., London, 1956-58; prof. Charing Cross Hosp. Med. Sch., London, 1958-85; dean faculty of medicine London (Eng.) U., 1971-76; dep. chmn. N.W. Thames Health Authority, London,

1974-80; dep. vice chancellor London (Eng.) U., 1976-80; cons. gynecologist Cromwell Hosp., London, 1986—, dir. postgrad. med. dept.; chmn. Commonwealth Health Devel. Program, London, 1990; chmn. sci. com. Little found., London, 1993—; sec. gen. Commonwealth Health Found., London, 1994—. Contbr. articles to profl. jours. Named Hon. fellow Family Planning and Reproductive Faculty of the Royal Coll. Ob-Gyn. Fellow Royal Coll. Gynecology, Med. Soc. London. Home: Flat 3 13 Eton Ave, London NW3 3EL, England Office: Cromwell Hosp, Cromwell Rd, London SW5 07U, England

MORRIS, RAYMOND GREGORY, pharmacology scientist; b. Adelaide, Australia, May 30, 1953; s. Harry Claude and Betty Aileen (Porter) M.; m. Helen Latchford, Dec. 6, 1974; children: Rebecca Katherine, Samuel Ryan, Jacob Andrew. BS, U. Adelaide, 1975, PhD, 1982. Rsch. asst. U. Adelaide, 1975-82, affiliate sr. lectr., 1991—; sr. hosp. scientist The Queen Elizabeth Hosp., Woodville, Australia, 1982-87, chief hosp. scientist, 1987—. Contbr. over 75 articles to profl. jours. Mem. Internat. Assn. Therapeutic Drug Monitoring (dir. edn., chair awards com. 1999—). Avocations: family, basketball, fishing, kid's sports, travel. Office: Queen Elizabeth Hosp, 28 Woodville Rd, Woodville 5011, Australia

MORRIS, ROBERT, educator; b. Akron, Ohio, Nov. 21, 1910; s. Joseph and Katherine (Spielberger) Schmaltz; m. Sara Goldman, Dec. 20, 1940. AB, U. Akron, 1931; MSc, Western Res. U., 1935; DSW, Columbia U. Sch. Social Work, 1959; D of Humane Letters (hon.), Brandeis U., 1984. Prin. welfare officer UNRRA, 1945; regional dir. social services VA, Chgo., 1946-48; social planning cons. Council Jewish Fedns. and Welfare Funds, N.Y.C., 1948-58; prof. social planning Brandeis U., Waltham, Mass., 1959-68, Kirstein prof. planning, 1968-83; Cardinal Medeiros lectr. U. Mass., Boston, 1983—, lectr. Harvard U. Sch. Pub Health, 1974-88; prof. Inst. Health Professions, Mass. Gen. Hosp., 1980-83; mem. adv. com. Aging Rsch., U.S. Dept. Health, Edn. and Welfare, 1971, Helen Keller Internat. Found. on the Overseas Blind, 1971-74; mem. spl. med. adv. group VA, Washington, 1969-71; cons. on Geriatric Rsch., Nat. VA, 1974-78, U.S. Office of Human Devel. Svcs., 1978-79; v.p. Vis. Nurses Assn., Boston, 1979-92; mem. Fed. Adv. Coun. on Aging Rsch., Mass. State Health Coord. Coun., 1984-85; vice chmn. Mass. Health Data Consortium, 1979-89; chmn. Internat. Rev. Com. Brookdale Inst. for Gerontology and Adult Human Devel., Israel, 1982-83, cons., 1984-85; chmn. Am. Found. for the Blind Com. on Geriatric Blindness, 1969-74; adv. com. Md. Dept. Health & Mental Health, 1993-95; pub. policy com. Nat. Coun. on the Aging, 1993-95. Author: Feasible Planning for Social Change, 1966, Urban Planning and Social Policy, 1968, Centrally Planned Change, 1964, Trends and Issues in Jewish Social Welfare in the U.S., 1966, Encyclopedia Social Work and Social Welfare, 1971, Toward a Caring Society, 1974, Centrally Planned Change: A Re-Examination of Theories and Concepts, 1974, Social Policy of the American Welfare State, 1979, 2d edit., 1985, Allocating Resources for the Aged and Disabled, 1981, Rethinking Social Welfare: Why Care for the Stranger, 1986, Retirement Reconsidered, 1988, Economic Roles for the Elderly, 1987, Testing the Limits of Social Welfare; International Perspectives on Policy Changes in Nine Countries, 1988, International Perspectives on State and Family Support for the Elderly, 1993, The National Government and Social Welfare, 1997, Personal Assistance: The Future of Home Care, 1998, Welfare Reform 1996-2000: Is There a Safety Net, 1999, Social Work at the Millenum, 2000; editor-in-chief Jour. of Social Work, 1960-72; editor Jour. Aging and Social Policy, 1983—. Cons. NIMH, 1964-70; chmn. adv. bd. Mass. Dept. Welfare, 1968-69; profl. adv. com. Easter Seal Soc., 1971-80; mem. Mass. Gov.'s Commn. on Nursing Homes, 1962-67, on Aging, 1962-67, on Hosp. Costs, 1967, Mass. Soc. Prevention Blindness, 1971-75; organizer Odyssey Forum on Federal Social Policy, 1995—. With AUS, 1943-44. Fulbright award, Italy, 1965-66, 68, Ford Found. fellow U.K., 1969-70; recipient rsch. awards Ford Found., 1960-65, Treuhaft Found., 1964, 72, Max and Anna Levinson Fund, 1970, 72, U.S. Pub. Health Svcs., 1957, 59, 65, NSF, 1975-78, W.K. Kellog Found., 1997, Retirement Rsch. Found., 1998, Louis Lowy award Mass. Gerontology Soc., 1994. Fellow AAAS, APHA, Gerontol. Soc. Am. (Kent award 1988, Maxwell Pollack award 1992, pres. 1966-67), Mass. Pub. Health Assn. (Lemuel Shattuck medal 1976), Ctr. for Applied Gerontology (Heritage award 1987), Commonwealth of Mass. and Assn. for Gerontology in Higher Edn. (Spl. Recognition award 1987), Columbia U. Sch. Social Wor (centennial award for leadership in edn.). Home: 830 W 40th St Apt 604 Baltimore MD 21211-2164 Office: Univ Mass Boston MA 02125

MORRIS, ROBERT JOHN, retired insurance company executive; b. London, Jan. 22, 1934; arrived in Philippines, 1965; s. E. Hugh F. and Muriel Pamela (Cashmore) M.; divorced; children: Maria Pamela, William Henry A.T.; m. Helen Lim; children: Alexandria, Anna, Hugh Robert, Helen Rachael, Harold Richard. Salesman Mfrs. Life Ins. Co., Malaya, 1957-59, dist. mgr., 1959-62; life underwriter Mfrs. Life Ins. Co., London, 1962-65; mgr. for the Philippines Mfrs. Life Ins. Co., Manila, 1965-83; exec. v.p. Pioneer Life Assurance Corp., Manila, 1983-89, pres., 1989-97; ret., 1997; pres. All Asiaasset Mgmt., Inc., 1999—; bd. dirs. Papa Securities Corp. Mem. Casino Espanol de Cebu Club, Ins. Inst. Asia and Pacific (treas.). Avocations: badminton, computers. Fax: 63-2-8297054. Office: All Asia Captial Ctr, 105 Paseo de Roxas, Makati City 1200, Philippines

MORRIS, ROY LESLIE, lawyer, electrical engineer, venture capitalist; b. N.Y.C.. BE, SUNY, Stony Brook, 1975; EE, MIT, 1978, SM, 1978; JD, George Washington U., 1984; MBA, Wharton U., 1995. Bar: D.C. 1984, U.S. Patent Office. Mem. tech. staff Bell Telephone Labs., Holmdel, N.J., 1978-80; sr. staff engr. FCC, Washington, 1981-83; assoc. regulatory counsel MCI Communications, Washington, 1983-87; dep. gen. counsel Allnet Comms., Washington, 1988-95; dir. pub. policy and regulatory affairs Allnet/Frontier Comms., Washington, 1989-96; mng. ptnr. RoyLyn L.L.C., Arlington, Va., 1996—; v.p. govt. affairs and revenue devel. US ONE Comms., McLean, Va., 1996-97; mng. ptnr. Strategic Tech. Investors LLC, Arlington, Va., 1998—; pres. MIT Enterprise Forum, Washington/Balt., 1998—; ednl. counselor MIT; adj. prof. Capitol Coll., Laurel, Md., 1998—. Contbr. numerous articles to profl. publs. Mem. ABA, IEEE, MIT Enterprise Forum, Sigma Xi, Tau Beta Pi. Address: Strategic Tech Investors LLC 4001 9th St N Ste 306 Arlington VA 22203-1957

MORRIS, STEPHANIE ANN, chemist, educator; b. Norfolk, Va., Oct. 5, 1958; d. Billy Charles and Barbara Ann Howard; m. David Glenn Morris, Dec. 28, 1979; children: Ian Charles, Piper Ann. BS in Chemistry, Fla. State U., 1979; MS in Chemistry, U. Tenn., Knoxville, 1981. Rsch. asst. U. Tenn., Knoxville, 1980-81, Oak Ridge (Tenn.) Nat. Lab., 1981-82; instr. to asst. prof. Roane State C.C., Harriman, Tenn., 1983-88; asst. prof. to assoc. prof. chemistry Pellissippi State Tech. C.C., Knoxville, 1988—, instr. "Chemistry Magic" Knoxville Talented and Gifted, 1994-95, 98—, organizer, instr. Coll. for a Day, 1995, 97. Author, editor: (lab notebooks/manuals) Chemistry 1010 Laboratory Manual, 1999, Chemistry 1020 Laboratory Manual, 1999. Recipient Sarah Ellen Benroth Outstanding Faculty award Roane State C.C., 1987-88, Excellence in Tchg. award Pellissippi State Tech. C.C., 1997-98, Catalyst award Regional award for Excellence in Sci. Tchg., Chem. Mfrs. Assn., 1998; named Tenn. Prof. of the Yr., Carnegie Found. for Advancement of Tchg. and Coun. for Advancement and Support of Edn., 1998. Mem. AAUP, Am. Chem. Soc. (chmn. edn. divsn.), Alpha Chi Sigma. Republican. Methodist. Avocation: tennis. Home: 716 Lago Cir Knoxville TN 37922-4100 Office: Pellissippi State Tech Cmty Coll 10915 Hardin Valley Rd Knoxville TN 37932-1412

MORRIS, STEVEN LYNN, engineering specialist, retired career officer; b. Dallas, Dec. 7, 1952; s. William Ira and Alta Faye (McCarley) M.; m. Jacqueline Ann Fenter, July 30, 1977; children: Steven Sean, Michael Wayne. BS in Engring. Scis., USAF Acad., 1975; MS in Aero. Engring, Air Force Inst. Tech., 1980; PhD in Aerospace Engring., Tex. A&M U., 1989. Commd. 2d lt. USAF, 1975, advanced through grades to lt. col., 1991, ret., 1999; assoc. prof., dep. head dept. aeronautics USAF Acad., Colo., 1989-99; engring. specialist SRS Techs., Colorado Springs, Colo., 1999—. Named Outstanding Young Man Am., Jaycees, 1981. Fellow AIAA (assoc., sr. flight mechanics tech. com. 1991-94, 98—, dep. dir. for edn. region V 1992-94, dep. dir. for precoll. outreach region V 1998—); mem. USAF Acad. Assn. Grads., Am. Soc. for Engring. Edn., Air Force Assn., Tex. A&M U. Assn. Former Students, Tau Beta Pi, Sigma Gamma Tau. Baptist. Avocations: running, photography, hiking. Home: 6935 Snowbird Dr Colorado Springs CO 80918-1309 Office: SRS Techs 1915 Aerotech Dr Ste D Colorado Springs CO 80916-4222

MORRIS, TREVOR RAYMOND, biology educator; b. Tetbury, U.K., Apr. 11, 1930; s. Ivor Raymond and Dorothy May (Parker) M.; m. Elisabeth Jean Warren, Apr. 17, 1954 (dec. Apr. 1992); children: Stephen Peter, Wendy Ann, Jonathan Michael, Andrew Anthony, Virginia Caroline; m. Mary Newbery, Mar. 4, 1994. BSc in Agr., U. Reading, U.K., 1951, PhD, 1966, DSc, 1980. Asst. lectr. U. Reading, 1952-57, lectr., 1957-69, reader, 1969-81, prof. animal prodn., 1981—. Editor Jour. Agrl. Sci.; contbr. over 200 articles to sci. jours. Fellow Inst. Biology; mem. World's Poultry Sci. Assn. (v.p. 1986—). Home: Rowan Trees, Beech Rd Tokers Green, Oxfordshire RG4 9EH, England

MORRIS, WILLIAM THOMAS, general and vascular surgeon, researcher; b. Wolverhampton, Eng., Nov. 14, 1936; arrived in new Zealand, 1974; s. William Thomas and Elsie (Biffin) M.; m. Barbara Mary Braddon, June 21, 1959; children: Michael Charles, Mary Cecilia; m. Ann May Warlow, July 3, 1989. MB ChB, U. Bristol, Eng., 1961; PhD, U. Sheffield, Eng., 1973. Jr. lectr. in anatomy U. Sheffield, 1964-68; registrar Aberdare & Merthyr Hosp., 1968-70; registrar, sr. registrar Hammersmith Hosp., Eng., 1970-73; sr. lectr. in surgery U. Auckland, New Zealand, 1974-90; gen. and vascular surgeon in pvt. practice, Auckland, 1990—; chmn. Auckland Varicose Veins and Leg Ulcer Rsch. Trust, Auckland, 1980—. Contbr. chpts. to books, articles to profl. jours. Chmn. Nat. Alternative Party, 1977. Fellow Royal Coll. Surgeons; mem. N.Y. Acad. of Sci., Assn. of Surgeons New Zealand, Brit. Assn. Clin. Anatomists, Free China Soc. (v.p.). Avocations: sailing, gardening, carpentry, billiards, sharemarket speculation. Home and Office: 41 Margot St, Epsom Auckland New Zealand

MORRISON, ANN MARIE, information systems specialist; b. Grants Pass, Oreg., Mar. 29, 1944; d. Wilbur Lill and Esther Elaine Groner; m. Robert Thornton Morrison, Apr. 14, 1996; children: David William Hess, William Albert Hess. BSEE, BS in Math., Oregon State U., 1968. Engr. Lawrence Livermore Lab., Livermore, Calif., 1968-69; mgr., owner RBR Scales, Inc., Anaheim, Calif., 1969-84; lead engr. Rockwell Internat., Seal Beach, Calif., 1984-86, '87-88; software engr. Hughes Aircraft Co., Fullerton, Calif., 1986-87; sr. engr. Logican Eagle Tech., Inc., Eatontown, N.J., 1988-91; owner Holistic Eclectic Software Svc., Orange, Calif., 1991-93; database adminstr. Jacobs Engring Group, 1993—. Active Calif. Master Chorale, Santa Ana, 1990-92. Mem. Am. Soc. Quality Control, Phi Kappa Phi, Eta Kappa Nu, Tau Beta Pi, Sigma Beta Delta. Lutheran. Avocations: singing, art, gardening. Office: JEG/WSSRAP 7295 S Highway 94 Saint Charles MO 63304-2203

MORRISON, BARBARA SHEFFIELD, Japanese translator and interpreter, consultant, educator; b. Morristown, N.J., Dec. 22, 1958; d. Barclay Morrison and Pauline Morison O'Gorman; m. Michael Missiras, Nov. 2, 1991. BA, Wesleyan U., 1980; MA in Japanese Lit., Columbia U., 1998. Real estate salesperson Huberth & Peters, Inc., N.Y.C., 1986-88, Joseph Hilton & Assoc., N.Y.C., 1989; real estate systems rsch. cons. N.Y.C., 1989-92; pres. Redgate, N.Y.C., 1990—; tchr. The Bus. English Ctr., Tokyo, 1980-83; bilingual adminstrv. asst. The Chiba Bank, Ltd., N.Y.C., 1985-86; adj. instr. langs. dept. Minn. State U., 1999. Translator: Coltrane: A Player's Guide to His Harmony, 1994, American House Styles: A Concise Guide, 1997, Abstracts for the Shinto Dictionary, 1999. Avocation: painting, gardening. Home and Office: 703 5th St S Moorhead MN 56560-3403

MORRISON, FRANCINE DARLENE, psychiatrist, massage therapist, herbal simplist; b. Newburgh, N.Y., Dec. 9, 1950; d. Frank Burke and Gladys (Morrison) Singleton. BA, Mt. St. Mary's Coll., Newburgh, 1980; MD, N.Y. Med. Coll., Valhalla, 1986; massage therapist, Blue Cliff Sch. Massage, Kenner, La., 1996. Resident, intern Lincoln Hosp., Bronx, N.Y., 1986-90; fellow in psychiatry Met. Hosp., N.Y.C., 1990-91; attending psychiatrist Med. Ctr. La., New Orleans, 1991-95; dir. neurobehavioral unit The Greenery, Slidell, La., 1992-94, cons. psychiatrist, 1994-95; attending psychiatrist East La. State Hosp., Jackson, 1995—; Reiki Master tchr. Contbr. articles to profl. jours. Mem. Am. Oriental Bodywork Therapists Assn. (nat. and La. chpts.), Am. Coll. Forensic Examiners, Bi-Parish Med. Soc. Office: East La State Hosp CV I Hwy 10 Jackson LA 70748

MORRISON, GEORGE CHALMERS, physics educator; b. Glasgow, Scotland, May 14, 1930; s. Donald Crerar and Annie Sibbald (Johnston) M.; m. Prudence Knowers, Oct. 7, 1961; children: Leslie, Vanessa, Nicola. BSc with honors, Glasgow (Scotland) U., 1951, PhD, 1957. Rsch. fellow AERE, Harwell, Oxford, Eng., 1954-57; prin. sci. officer AERE, Harwell, Oxford, 1961-65; rsch. assoc. U. Chgo., 1957-60; rsch. scientist Argonne Nat. Lab., Ill., 1965-73; vis. scientist CEA, Saclay, Paris, 1971-72; prof. nuclear structure U. Birmingham, Eng., 1973-97; prof. emeritus, 1997—; dep. dean Faculty of Sci., Birmingham, 1985-88, dean, 1988-91; head Sch. of Physics & Space Rsch., Birmingham, 1990-97; del., individual ordinary mem. European Phys. Soc. Coun., 1991-98, exec. com., 1993; mem. nuclear structure com., 1974-78, 82-86, 91-92, chmn., 1992-94, nuclear physics bd., 1984-87, physics com., 1984-87, SERC, Swindon, Eng.; mem. working group on nuclear physics European Sci. Found., Strasbourg, France, 1981-84. Contbr. articles to profl. jours. Fellow Inst. of Physics, Am. Phys. Soc.; mem. European Phys. Soc. (bd. nuclear physics div. 1984-92). Avocations: golf, walking, philately. Office: U Birmingham, Sch Physics & Astronomy, Birmingham B15 2TT, England

MORRISON, GLENN LESLIE, minister; b. Cortez, Colo., Feb. 26, 1929; s. Ward Carl Morrison and Alma Irene (Butler) Anderson; m. Beverely Joanne Buck, Aug. 26, 1949; children: David Mark, Betty Jo Morrison Mullen, Gary Alan, Judith Lynn Morrison Oltmann, Stephen Scott. Student, San Diego State U., 1948-49, Chabot Coll., 1968-69. Ordained to ministry Evang. Ch. Alliance, 1961. Dir. counseling and follow-up Oakland (Calif.) Youth for Christ, 1954-56; pres. Follow Up Ministries, Inc., Castro Valley, Calif., 1956—; assoc. pastor 1st Covenant Ch., Oakland, 1956-58; exec. dir. East Bay Youth for Christ, Oakland, 1960-66; supervising chaplain Alameda County (Calif.) Probation Dept., 1971-90; vol. chaplain Alameda County Sheriff's Dept., 1971—; seminar leader Calif. Dept. Corrections, Sacramento, 1978—, mem. chaplains coordinating com., 1988—; founder, dir. God Squad Vol. Program for Prison Workers, 1972—. Author: Scripture Investigation Course, 1956. Mem. Am. Correctional Assn., Am. Protestant Correctional Chaplains Assn. (regional pres., sec. 1980-86, nat. sec. 1986-88, nat. 2nd v.p. 1996-98). Office: Follow Up Ministries Inc PO Box 2514 Castro Valley CA 94546-0514

MORRISON, GORDON MACKAY, JR., investment company executive; b. Boston, Jan. 18, 1930; s. Gordon Mackay and Alice (Blodgett) M.; m. Barbara J. Lee, June 15, 1954; children: Lee, Leighton, Faith. AB, Harvard U., 1952, MBA, 1954. Regional mgr. Bankers Leasing Corp., Boston, 1965-68; portfolio mgr. Loomis, Sayles and Co., Boston, 1969-71; sr. v.p. Ft. Hill Investors Mgmt., Boston, 1972-75; chmn. bd. Bradford Gordon, Inc., Boston, 1976—; trustee East Boston Savs. Bank, 1962-91, Meridian Fin. Svcs., Inc., 1991—. Bd. dirs. The New Eng. Hosp., 1961-96, emeritus, 1996—. Republican. Congl. Club: Harvard. Lodge: Masons. Home: 5 Neptune Ln Biddeford ME 04005-9594 Office: Bradford Gordon Inc 50 Congress St Ste 642 Boston MA 02109-4027

MORRISON, H. ROBERT, writer, editor, politician; b. Pitts., Apr. 7, 1938; s. Hugh and Gertrude Mary (Gehenio) M.; m. Meredith Wollenberg, Dec. 8, 1979; children: Hugh Robert Jr., Justin William, Elizabeth Jeanne. BA in English, Howard U., 1969. Cert. govtl. treas. Writer Nat. Geog. Soc., Washington, 1969-73, editor ednl. filmstrips, 1973-77, sr. writer, 1977-88, mng. editor nat. geography bee, 1988-89; elected treas. City of Falls Church, Va., 1993—; pres. Morrison & Reeve Sys., Inc., 1996—; bd. dirs. Falls Church Cable Access Corp., pres. 1990-93; bd. dirs. Tinner Hill Heritage Found.; bd. dirs., pres. Morrison & Reeve Systems, Inc., 1996—. Contbg. author to numerous books including America's Seashore Wonderlands, 1985, America's Wild Woodlands, 1985, Exploring America's Valleys, 1984, America's Hidden Corners, 1983, America's Magnificent Mountains, 1980, America's Majestic Canyons, 1979, Mysteries of the Ancient World, 1979, The Ocean Realm, 1978, As We Live and Breathe, 1971; co-author: America's Atlantic Isles, 1981. Vice chmn. Falls Church (Va.) Dem. Com., 1988-89, 98-99; treas. City of Falls Church, 1994—; mem. Galloway United Meth. Ch., Falls Church. With U.S. Army, 1961-64. Mem. NAACP, Mcpl. Treas.' Assn. U.S. and Can., Treas.' Assn. Va. (bd. dirs. 1996-97), Clan Morrison N.Am. (life), St. Andrew's Soc. Washington. Avocations: reading, personal computing, photography, TV production, historic preservation. Home: Bonnie Briar 502 Walden Ct Falls Church VA 22046-2628 Office: City Hall 300 Park Ave Falls Church VA 22046-3332

MORRISON, JOHN MARTIN, lawyer; b. McCook, Nebr., June 18, 1961; s. Frank Brennor and Sharon Romain (McDonald) M.; m. Catherine Helen Wright, Aug. 17, 1991; children: Allison Kay, Amanda Grace. BA, Whitman Coll., 1983; JD, U. Denver, 1986. Bar: Mont. 1987, U.S. Dist. Ct. Mont. 1988, U.S. Ct. Appeals (9th cir.) 1989, U.S. Supreme Ct., 1996. Legis. asst., legal counsel U.S. Senate, Washington, 1987-88; ptnr. Morrison Law Offices, Helena, Mont., 1988-93, Meloy & Morrison, Helena, 1994—; Dem. nominee Mont. State Auditor, 2000. Author: Mavericks: The Lives and Battles of Montana's Political Legends, 1997; contbr. articles to profl. jours. Alt. del. Dem. Nat. Conv., N.Y.C., 1980; del. Dem. Nat. Platform Com., 1992. Recipient Lewis F. Powell/ACTL/Bur. of Nat. Affairs Advocacy awards, 1986. Mem. ATLA, Mont. Bar Assn., Mont. Trial Lawyers Assn. (past pres., bd. dirs. 1991—), Western Trial Lawyers Assn. (bd. govs. 1990-95), Trial Lawyers Pub. Justice (chair 1989-90). Avocations: skiing, fly fishing, mountain climbing, river rafting, running. Office: Meloy & Morrison 80 S Warren St Helena MT 59601-5700

MORRISON, KEITH ROBERT BARCLAY, education educator, consultant; b. Wolverhampton, Eng., Sept. 27, 1948; s. William and Mary (Sutton) M.; m. Ann Patricia Wareham, Dec. 27, 1971 (div. Feb. 1997); children: Thomas, Peter, Stuart; m. Tang Fun Hei, Feb. 2000. BEd, U. Liverpool, 1971; MEd, U. Newcastle-Upon-Tyne, 1982; PhD, U. Durham, Eng., 1995. Tchr. Mid. Sch., Birkenhead, 1971-72; music tchr. Gateshead, 1972-76, Primary Sch., 1976-83; sr. lectr. North Riding Coll., Scarborough, 1983-85; univ. lectr. Durham U., 1986-96, sr. lectr.; 1996—; prof. edn. Inter-U. Inst. Macau, 2000—; cons. Ministry of Edn., Malaysia, 1997; vis. lectr., Malaysia, 1997. Co-author: A Guide to Teaching Practice, 4th edit., 1996, Planning and Accomplishing School-Centered Evaluation, 1993, Implementing Cross-Curricular Themes, 1994;, Management Theories for Educational Change, 1998, Research Methods in EDucation, 5th edit., 2000; editor Evaluation and Research in Education, 1995-00. Course convenor Brit. Coun., Czech Republic, 1994, Ministry of Edn., Malaysia, 1996. Rsch. grantee U. Grants Coun., 1988, Book Pub., 1990. Fellow Royal Soc. Arts. Labour. Avocations: pianoforte playing, clavichord playing, music, management studies. Office: Inter-U Inst Macau NAPE, Lote 18 Rua de Londres P, Macau Macau

MORRISON, MARGARET L., artist, educator, consultant; b. Atlanta, Oct. 6; d. Watson Russell Sr. and Eva (Darnell) Morrison. BS in Edn., U. Ga., 1970. Cert. tchr., Ga. Supr. KPMG Peat Marwick, Atlanta, 1971-97; art tchr. Decatur (Ga.) City Schs., Decatur, Ga., 1997-99; cons. art Decatur City Schs., 1997—. Exhbns. include Coastal Ctr. for the Arts, St. Simons Island, Ga., Gallery One, St. Simons Island, Decatur Arts Alliance, Acad. Midi, Paris, The Glynn County Art Assn., Jekyll Island, Ga., L'Orangerie Mus., Paris. Royal patron Hutt River Province, Queensland, Australia, 1995; active High Mus. Art, Atlanta, 1989—; bd. govs. Internat. Biog. Ctr.; adv. bd. Am. Biog. Inst. Fellow Acad. Midi (hon.); mem. DAR, NAFE, AAUW, Internat. Platform Assn., Nat. Mus. Women in Arts, Allied Artists of Ga., Pen and Ink, U. Ga. Alumni Soc. Home and Office: PO Box 2590 Decatur GA 30031-2590

MORRISON, MICHAEL DEAN, lawyer, law educator. BA with high honors, Okla. U., 1971, JD, 1974. Bar: Okla. 1975, Kans. 1975, Tex. 1981, U.S. Ct. Appeals (5th cir.) 1980, U.S. Dist. Ct. (ea., no. and so. dists.) Tex. 1983, U.S. Dist. Ct. (we. dist.) Tex. 1980, U.S. Dist. Ct. (we. dist.) Okla. 1975, U.S. Supreme Ct. 1979. Pvt. practice Wichita, Kans., 1974-75; asst. dir. Law Ctr. Okla. U., 1975-77, asst. prof., 1977-80, assoc. prof., 1980-82, prof. law, 1982-90, William J. Boswell chair of law, 1990—; mediator Atty.-Mediators Inst., Inc., 1993; trainer Am. Arbitration Assn., 1992; presenter Tex. A&M U., 1990, Tex. Apellate Cts. Chief Justices Meeting, 1990, Baylor U., 1990, 92, Nat. League of Cities Congress of Cities and Exposition, San Antonio, 1996, Assn. Mayors, Waco, 1997, among others. Contbr. articles to profl. publs. Mem. 1st Presbyn. Ch. Waco, ordained elder, stated clk. of session, 1996—; chair Waco/McLennan County Met. Planning Orgn., 1997—; elder, mem. session, 1995—; mayor City of Waco, 1996—; mem. Waco City Coun. for Dist. III, 1994-96; chmn. Cmty. of Cities, 1996—; chair Waco/McLennan County Met. Planning Orgn., 1996—; mem. Tex. Atty. Gen.'s Mcpl. Adv. Com., 1996-97; bd. dirs. Econ. Opportunities Advancement Corp., Planning Region XI, 1994-95, Waco Symphony Assn., 1988-91, exec. com., 1989-90; bd. dirs. Waco Montessori Sch., 1993-94, Cmtys. in Schs., McClennan County Youth Collaboration Inc., 1997—, Heart of Tex. Coun. Govts., 1995—; mem. adv. coun. Local Leaders of Tex. State Tech. Coll., Waco, 1995—, Salvation Army, 1997—; chair Waco Charter Commn., 1986; mem. Waco-McLenna County Task Force on AIDS, 1988-89; vol. Toys for Tots, 1990—. Recipient Comty. Builder award Masonic Grand Lodge of Tex., Disting. Achievement award VFW Post 2983, 1998. Mem. Rotary (Waco Downtown club 1984-96), Order of Coif, Phi Beta Kappa. Office: PO Box 97288 Waco TX 76798-7288

MORRISON, MICHAEL GORDON, university president, clergyman, history educator; b. Green Bay, Wis., Mar. 9, 1937; s. Gordon John and Gertrude (Crilly) M. A.B., St. Louis U., 1960, M.A., 1965, Ph.L., 1965, S.T.L., 1969; Ph.D., U. Wis., 1971. Ordained priest Roman Catholic Ch., 1968. Joined S.J., 1955; asst. v.p. acad. affairs Marquette U., Milw., 1974-77; v.p. acad. affairs Creighton U., Omaha, 1977-81, acting pres., 1981, pres., 1981-2000, dir.; mem. governing bd. Creighton Prep. Sch., 1993-99. Bd. dirs. Health Future Found., 1983-2000, Xavier U., 1992-98; mem. cons. com. SAC, 1988-99; mem. adv. bd. Salvation Army, 1992-2000; trustee Duchesne Acad. of Sacred Heart, 1995-2000; bd. dirs. Red Cloud Indian Sch., 1997-2000; bd. trustees, Loyola U., Chgo., 1998-2000. Recipient Human Rights award Anti-Defamation League, 1982, Humanitarian award Nat. Conf. Christians and Jews, 1989. Mem. Assn. Jesuit Colls. and Univs. (bd. dirs.), Assn. Ind. Colls. and Univs. Nebr. (bd. dirs. 1981-2000), Nat. Assn. Ind. Colls. and Univs. (bd. dirs. 1993-2000), Greater Omaha C. of C. (bd. dirs. 1993-2000), Alpha Sigma Nu, Beta Alpha Psi. Office: Creighton U 2500 California Plz Omaha NE 68178-0001

MORRISON, MURDO DONALD, architect; b. Feb. 21, 1919; s. Alexander and Johanna (Macaulay) M.; m. Judy D. Morrison (dec. May 1999); children from previous marriage: Paula L., Reed A., Anne H. BArch, Lawrence Tech. U., 1943. Individual practice arch. Detroit, 1949, Klamath Falls, Oreg., 1949-65, Oakland, Calif., 1965-78; prin. Morrison Assocs., San Francisco, 1978-85, Burlingame, Calif., 1985-89, Redwood City, Calif., 1989—; v.p. Lakeridge Corp., 1968—, Oreg. Bd. Archtl. Examiners, 1961-65, chmn., 1964. Architect: Gilliam County Courthouse, 1955 (Progressive Arch. Design award), Chiloquin (Oreg.) Elem. Sch., 1963, Lakeridge Office Bldg., Reno, 1984, Provident Cen. Credit Union Bldg., Monterey, Calif., 1986, Embarcadero Fed. Credit Union, San Francisco, 1991, Warrick Residence, The Sea Ranch, Calif., 1996, Spectre Industries Office Bldg., Milpitas, Calif., 1997, Rosenbaum Residency, Los Altos Hills, Calif., 1998, McCabe Residence, Los Altos Hills, 2000, others; master planner, Lakeridge, a 945-acre cmty. in Reno, v.p. devel., 1963—. Mem. Town Coun. Klamath Falls, 1955-57; co-chmn. Oakland Pride Com., 1968-77; mem. Redwood City Gen. Plan Com., 1986, Redwood City Design Rev. Com., 1991—, Emerald Hills Design Rev. Bd., 1990-97. With USN, 1943-46. Recipient Progressive Arch. award, 1955, Alumni of Yr. award Lawrence Inst., 1965. Mem. AIA (treas. East Bay, chmn. Oakland chpt., dir. San Mateo County chpt. 1996—). Presbyterian. Home and Office: 3645 Jefferson Ave Redwood City CA 94062-3149

MORRISON, NIGEL ALEXANDER, molecular biologist; b. Bulolo, Papua New Guinea, Feb. 1, 1959; s. Leo John and Joan Esme Louisa (Philp) M.; m. Christine Maree Bates, Dec. 3, 1983; children: Bronwyn, Rachel S. BS, U. Queensland, Brisbane, Australia, 1980, BS with honors, 1981; PhD, Australian Nat. U., Canberra, 1984. Rsch. fellow McGill U., 1984-86; Australia sr. rsch. fellow Garvan Inst. Med. Rsch., Sydney, 1986-96; Nat. Health and Med. Rsch. Coun. sr. rsch. fellow Genomics Rsch. Ctr., Griffith U., Australia, 1996—; cons. Gemini Rsch. Ltd., Cambridge, Eng., 1996—; dir. GeneNexus Pty. Ltd., Australia, 1996—. Patentee in field; contbr. articles to

profl. jours.; also book chpts. Competitive sci. grant NIH, 1990, Sci. Rsch. grant Cancer Coun., 1990; Commonwealth scholar, 1972-75. Mem. Am. Soc. for Bone and Mineral Rsch. Avocations: sailing, surfing, biology. Fax: 61-7-55976220. Home: 9 Aberdeen Ave, 4217 Benowa Waters Australia Office: Griffith U Genomics Rsch Ctr, Gold Coast Campus, PMB50 Gold Coast Australia

MORRISON, ROGER BARRON, geologist; b. Madison, Wis., Mar. 26, 1914; s. Frank Barron and Elsie Rhea (Bullard) M.; m. Harriet Louise Williams, Apr. 7, 1941 (dec. Feb. 1991); children: John Christopher, Peter Hallock and Craig Brewster (twins). BA, Cornell U., 1933, MS, 1934; postgrad., U. Calif., Berkeley, 1934-35, Stanford U., 1935-38; PhD, U. Nev., 1964. Registered profl. geologist, Wyo. Geologist U.S. Geol. Survey, 1939-76; vis. adj. prof. dept. geoscis. U. Ariz., 1976-81, Mackay Sch. Mines, U. Nev., Reno, 1984-86; cons. geologist; pres. Morrison and Assocs., Ltd., 1978—; prin. investigator 2 Landsat-1 and 2 Skylab earth resources investigation projects NASA, 1972-75. Author 3 books; co-author 1 book; co-editor 2 books; editor Quaternary Nonglacial Geology, Conterminous U.S., Geol. Soc. Am. Centennial Series, vol. K-2, 1991; mem. editl. bd. Catena, 1973-88; contbr. over 250 articles to profl. jours. Fellow Geol. Soc. Am.; mem. AAAS, Internat. Union Quaternary Rsch. (mem. Holocene and paleopedology commns., chmn. work group on pedostratigraphy), Am. Soc. Photogrammetry and Remote Sensing, Internat. Soil Sci. Soc., Am. Quaternary Assn., Colo. Sci. Soc., Geol. Soc. Nev. Achievements include research on Quaternary geolgoy and geomorphology, hydrogeology, environmental geology, neotectonics, remote sensing of Earth resources, paleoclimatology, pedostratigraphy; pioneer technology for converting waste wood, garbage, municipal solid waste, natural gas, landfill gas, etc. to mixed-alcholh motor fuel; development of forest and range land and a new town in western Praaguay. Office: 13150 W 9th Ave Golden CO 80401-4201

MORRISON, SAMUEL F., library administrator, chief librarian; b. Flagstaff, Ariz., Dec. 19, 1936; s. Travis B. and Esther (Polk) M. AA, Compton Jr. Coll., 1955; BA in English, Calif. State U., 1971; MLS, U. Ill., 1972; DHL (hon.), St. Thomas U., 1998. Dir. Frostproof (Fla.) Living/Learning Library, 1972-74; adminstrv. asst. Broward County Library System, Ft. Lauderdale, Fla., 1974-76, dep. dir., 1976-87; first dep. commr., chief librarian Chgo. Pub. Library/Chgo. Library System, 1987-90; dir. Broward County Libr. System, Ft. Lauderdale, Fla., 1990—; asst. librarian USAF, Morocco, 1956-58; instr. Inst. Multicultural Librarianship, U. Mich. Bd. dirs. Fla. Humanities Coun., United Way, Urban League, Ft. Lauderdale (Diversity Champion award 1998), Bonnet House, Ft. Lauderdale, Nat. Conf. Cmty. and Justice, Youth Orch. Fla., Tower Forum, Solinet, Broward County Special Olympics, Broward Partnership for Homeless, Broward Pub. Libr. Found., Kids Voting Broward, Old Dillard Found., SEFLIN, Sickle Cell Assn., Broward, S. Fla. Annenberg Challenge, Trejo Foster Found.; parliamentarian Area Agy. on Aging of Broward County, Ft. Lauderdale; pres. Gold Coast Jazz Soc., Ft. Lauderdale. Recipient HEW Title II fellowship U. Ill. Library Sch., Champaign, Faculty award U. Ill. Library Sch., Champaign, Freeman Bradley award NAACP, Silver Medallion Brotherhood award Nat. Conf., Pillar award The Links, Inc., 1998; named Advocate of Yr., Broward County Adv. Bd. for Persons with Disabilities, Achiever Emeritus, In Focus mag., 1998. Mem. ALA, NAACP, Fla. Libr. Assn., Nat. Assn. Black Pub. Adminstrs., Urban Librs. Coun., S.E. Libr. Assn., Pub. Libr. Assn., Broward County Libr. Assn. Office: Broward County Divsn Librs 100 S Andrews Ave Fort Lauderdale FL 33301-1830

MORRISON, SARAH LYDDON, author; b. Rochester, N.Y., May 19, 1939; d. Paul William and Winifred (Cowles) Lyddon. BA, U. Vt., 1961. Sec. asst. Glamour mag., N.Y.C., 1961-63, Vogue mag., N.Y.C., 1963-65; asst. editor Venture mag., N.Y.C., 1966-71; dir. pub. rels. for tourism Commonwealth of P.R., N.Y.C., 1971-75; asst. Am. Legion, Washington, 1988-98; owner Sarah Lyddon Morrison Pub. Rels., Washington, 1999—. Author: The Modern Witch's Spellbook, 1971, Book II, 1983, The Modern Witch's Dream Book, 1985, The Modern Witch's Book of Home Remedies, 1988, The Modern Witch's Book of Healing, 1991, The Modern Witch's Book of Symbols, 1997, Modern Witch's Guide to Magic and Spells, 1998. Mem. Washington Club, Nat. Press Club. Mem. Nat. League Am. Penwomen (rec. sec. 1993), DAR (dir. pub. rels. Emily Nelson chpt. 1999, 2000), Colonial Dames XVII. Avocations: travel, reading, swimming, rock music, cooking.

MORRISON, TONI (CHLOE ANTHONY MORRISON), novelist; b. Lorain, Ohio, Feb. 18, 1931; d. George and Ella Ramah (Willis) Wofford; m. Harold Morrison, 1958 (div. 1964); children: Harold Ford, Slade Kevin. B.A., Howard U., 1953; M.A., Cornell U., 1955. Tchr. English and humanities Tex. So. U., 1955-57, Howard U., 1957-64; editor Random House, N.Y.C., 1965—; assoc. prof. English SUNY, Purchase, NY, 1971-72; Schweitzer Prof. of the Humanities SUNY, Albany, NY, 1984-89; Robert F. Goheen Prof. of the Humanities Princeton Univ., Princeton, NJ, 1989—; Visiting prof., Yale Univ., 1976-77, Bard Coll., 1986-88. Author: The Bluest Eye, 1969, Sula, 1973 (National Book award nomination 1975, Ohioana Book award 1975), Song of Solomon, 1977 (National Book Critics Circle award 1977, American Acad. and Inst. of Arts and Letters award 1977), Tar Baby, 1981, (play) Dreaming Emmett, 1986, Beloved, 1987 (Pulitzer Prize for fiction 1988, Robert F. Kennedy Book award 1988, Melcher Book award Unitarian Universalist Assn. 1988, National Book award nomination 1987, National Book Critics Circle award nomination 1987), Jazz, 1992, Playing in the Dark: Whiteness and the Literary Imagination, 1992, Nobel Prize Speech, 1994, Birth of a Nation'hood: Gaze, Script & Spectacle in the O.J. Simpson Trial, 1997; editor: The Black Book, 1974, Race-ing Justice, En-Gendering Power: Essays on Anita Hill, Clarence Thomas, and the Construction of Social Reality, 1992; lyricist: Honey and Rue, 1992. Recipient New York State Governor's Art award, 1986; Washington College Literary award, 1987; Elizabeth Cady Stanton award National Organization for Women; Nobel prize in Literature Nobel Foundation, 1993. Mem. Author's Guild (council). Office: Princeton U Writing Program 185 Nassau St Princeton NJ 08544-2003 also: Internat Creative Mgmt 40 W 57th St New York NY 10019-4001

MORRISSEY, HELENA LOUISE, fund manager; b. Bowden, Cheshire, Eng., Mar. 22, 1966; d. Anthony and Jacqueline (Scott) Atkins; m. Richard Joseph Morrissey, Dec. 15, 1990; children: Fitzroy, Florence, Thomas, Amelia. MA in Philosophy, Cambridge (Eng.) U., 1987. Global bond analyst Schroder Capital Mgmt. Internat., N.Y.C., 1988-89; fund mgr. Schroder Investment Mgmt., London, 1990-93; fund mgr., dir. Newton Investment Mgmt., London, 1994—, also bd. dirs., head fixed income, 1999—. Editor: International Securitisation, 1992, (jour.) Internat. Securitisation Report, 1993—. Named Global Bond Fund Mgr. of the Yr. Investment Week, 1998, 99. Mem. Oxford Analytica. Avocation: playing piano. Office: Newton Investment Mgmt, 71 Queen Victoria St, London EC4V 4DR, England

MORRISSEY, JOSEPH JAMES, biologist; b. Wayne, Mich., Oct. 1, 1963; s. John Richard and Rosalie Catherine M.; m. Linda Kay, Oct. 25, 1997; 1 child, Nicolas. BS, U. So. Fla., 1985, MS, 1987; PhD, Stanford Med. Sch., 1993. Sr. scientist Motorola, Ft. Lauderdale, Fla., 1993—; review com. IEEE, ANSI. Mem. Bioelectromagnetics Soc. Roman Catholic. E-mail: ajm037@ewail.mot.com. Home: 9107 Vineyard Lake Dr Fort Lauderdale FL 33324-1110 Office: Motorola 8000 W Sunrise Blvd Fort Lauderdale FL 33322-4170

MORRISSEY, KIM, playwright, poet; d. Leslie Dales; m. Leroy John Morrissey (dec. June 1987); stepchildren: Timothy Edward, Kathleen, Sean Henry. BA in English, U. Saskatoon, Canada, 1979. Pvt. practice London, 1979—; lectr. Rose Bruford Drama Coll., London, 1995-96. Author: Batoche, 1989, Poems for Men Who Dream of Lolita, 1992, Dora: A Case of Hysteria, 1994, Clever as Paint: The Rossettis in Love, 1998; contbr.: Mythic Women/Real Women, 2000. Mem. Soc. Authors, Poetry Soc. London, Playwrights Union Canada. E-mail: cdplays@interlog.com. Address: c/o Coteau Books, 401-2206 Dewdney Ave, Regina, SK Canada 24R 1H3

MORRISS-KAY, GILLIAN MARY, embryologist; b. Redhill, Surrey, Eng., July 1, 1942; d. Edgar Stuart and Violet Jones (Walker) Morriss; m. Robert Henry Kay, Sept. 22, 1979 (dec. July 1994); 1 child, Matthew Roy. BSc in Zoology with 1st class honors, U. Durham, Eng., 1964; PhD, U. Cambridge, Eng., 1972; DSc, U. Oxford, 1995. Jr. lectr. zoology Massey U., New Zealand, 1965-67; rsch. officer teratology Reproductive Studies Sect. Huntingdon Rsch. Ctr., Eng., 1968; Wellcome Trust postdoctoral rsch. asst. dept. anatomy U. Cambridge, 1971-73; Tucker-Price jr. rsch. fellow Girton Coll., Cambridge, 1971-74; univ. demonstrator anatomy Cambridge, 1973-76; fellow, lectr. anatomy Newnham Coll., Cambridge, 1974-76; vis. fellow Lab. Devel. Biology and Anomalies Nat. Inst. Dental Health, Bethesda, Md., 1975; sr. rsch. fellow Balliol Coll., Oxford, Eng., 1976-90; lectr. devel. biology Balliol Coll., Oxford, 1990-92; univ. lectr. human anatomy U. Oxford, 1976—, prof. devel. anatomy, 1996—; mem. internat. adv. bd. on retinoids F. Hoffman LaRoche, Basel, Switzerland, 1990—; cons. embryologist, Squibb, U.S., 1983; spl. lectr. U. Oxford, 1994-95, acting head dept. human anatomy, spring 1995. Editor: Retinoids in Normal Development and Teratogenesis, 1992; contbr. articles to profl. jours. including Jour. Anatomy, Devel., Devel. Biology, Am. Jour. Human Genetics, Devel. Dynamics. Rsch. grantee Med. Rsch. Coun., Biotechnology and Biol. Scis. Rsch. Coun., Action Rsch., others, 1975—. Fellow Royal Microscopic Soc.; mem. Brit. Soc. for Devel. Biology (com. mem. 1977-81), Brit. Soc. for Cell Biology, Anatomical Soc. Gt. Britain and Ireland (coun. mem. 1996—, hon. sec. 1999—), Devel. Pathology Soc. (asst. sec., com. mem. 1976-80), Soc. for Devel. Biology, Inc. (U.S.). Office: U Oxford Dept Human Anatomy, S Parks Rd, Oxford OX1 3QX, England

MORROW, DEBBIE MARIE, continuity director, broadcast engineer; b. Schenectady, N.Y., July 12, 1962; d. James Donald and Marcia Marie (Petricca) M. AAS, SUNY, Morrisville, 1982; BA, SUNY, Albany, 1984; cert. in broadcasting, New Sch. Contemporary Radio, Albany, 1985; MEd, Coll. St. Rose, Albany, N.Y., 1994. Lic. gen. class radio broadcaster, N.Y. Assoc. dir., prodn. asst. Sta. WRGB-TV, Schenectady, 1983; with backstage securit/pub. relations Pyramid Security, Saratoga (N.Y.) Performing Arts Ctr., 1984; with pub. relations dept. Saratoga Performing Arts Ctr., 1984; salesperson Record Town, Schenectady, 1984-85; announcer, disc jockey Sta. WBEC, Pittsfield, Mass., 1985, Sta. WMVQ-FM, Amsterdam, N.Y., 1985-86; sec., asst. radio bd. operator Sta. WMHT-FM, Schenectady, 1986; sec. Sta. WXXA-TV, Albany, 1985-87, broadcast engr., 1985-94, 95, 97, cameraperson, 1987-94; sec. St. Clare's Hosp., Schenectady, N.Y., 1994-99; tutor, tchr. WSWHE BOCES, Saratoga Springs, N.Y.; tchr. Burnt Hills-Ballston Lake Schs., Scotia, N.Y., 1996-99. Editor various campus pubs., 1980-82. Roman Catholic. Avocations: photography, piano, writing, reading. Home: 23 Eagle St Schenectady NY 12302-1809 Office: Sta WXXA-TV 815 Central Pky Niskayuna NY 12309-6052

MORROW, LANCE THOMAS, journalist, educator, writer; b. Phila., Sept. 21, 1939; s. Hugh M. and Elise Vickers; m. Brooke Wayne, May 23, 1968 (div. Sept. 1983); children: James Michael, Justin Thomas; m. Susan Brind, Oct. 29, 1988. BA, Harvard U., 1963. Reporter Washington Star, 1964-65; writer, essayist Time Mag., N.Y.C., 1965—; univ. prof. Boston U., 1996—; mem. usage panel Am. Heritage Dictionary. Author: The Chief, 1988, Fishing in the Tiber, 1988, America, A Rediscovery, 1989, Safari, 1992, Heart, 1995. Recipient Nat. Mag. award Columbia U., 1981. Mem. Harvard Club (N.Y., Boston). E-mail: lmorrow1@aol.com. Office: Time Time-Life Bldg Rockefeller Plz New York NY 10020-2002

MORROW, MARTINA A., educator, cultural organization administrator; b. Portland, Maine, Aug. 20, 1975; d. Steven William and Catherine Martina M. B, Bowdoin Coll., 1997. Intern Yale U. Press, New Haven, 1997; interpreter Nantucket (Mass.) Hist. Assn., 1998-99, docent coord., 1999—; head tchr. Nantucket New Sch., 1997—; tutor Nantucket, 1997—; judge Nantucket Short Play Competition, 1998—. Mem. Actor's Theatre Workshop. Avocations: acting, volunteering.

MORROW, MONTY RAMSEY, marketing and advertising executive; b. Dallas, Mar. 14, 1952; s. William Lee and Doris Dale Morrow; m. Nancy Jean Babb, May 17, 1973 (div. July 1976). AA, Mountain View C.C., 1972; BA, So. Meth. U., 1975. Registered rep. Nat. Assn. Securities Dealers and SEC, 14 states. Tech. sales rep., parts mktg. analyst Frigiking Inc., Dallas, 1973-82; account exec. Advo Sys., Dallas, 1982-88, Lee Data Mail, Dallas, 1988-93, Texakoma Fin., Dallas, 1993-96; dir. mktg. and advt. Damark Svc. Co., Round Rock, Tex., 1996—. Mem. Austin C. of C. (Tex.). Avocations: travel, deep sea sport fishing, boating, golf. E-mail: mmorrow@dscine.com. Office: Damark Svc Co 200A Parker Dr Ste 480 Austin TX 78728-1228

MORROW, STEVEN ROGER, computer scientist; b. Sioux Falls, S.D., Sept. 20, 1963; s. Roger Lee and Rose Mary (Cooper) M.; m. Kerri Rene Verburg, Dec. 28, 1991; children: Melody Rene, Stephany Rose. BS, U. S.D., 1986, MA, 1988; MBA, Mankato State U., 1993. From programmer analyst to sr. software developer Clear with Computers, Inc., Mankato, Minn., 1988-98; data repository specialist Immanuel-St. Joseph's-Mayo Health Sys., Mankato, Minn., 1999—. County conv. del. Rep. County Conv., Mankato, 1996—; baritone player Mankato State U. Cmty. Symphonic Band, 1989—; mem. Hope Bapt. Ch., Mankato, 1990—, mem. leadership team, 1998—. Mem. IEEE, Assn. Computing Machinery. Baptist. Avocations: running, Bible study, collecting stamps & coins, sports. Home: 213 James Ct Eagle Lake MN 56024-9600 Office: Immanuel-St Josephs Mayo Health Sys 1025 Marsh St Mankato MN 56001-4752

MORROW, WALTER EUGENE, philosophy educator; b. Pretoria, Gauteng, S. Africa, July 15, 1939; s. Frederick Victor and Eugenie Leonie (Blake) M.; m. Diana Joan Baty, Aug. 14, 1970; children: Michael, Carl, Alice, Steven. BA, Witwatersrand, Johannesburg, 1961; BA with honors, U. S. Africa, Pretoria, 1964; MA, London U., 1968, PhD, 1982. Tchr. Secondary Schs., Johannesburg, 1962-65; lectr. U. Riyadh, Saudi Arabia, 1965-66, Maria Grey Coll., London, 1969-72; lectr. to sr. lectr. U. Witwatersrand, Johannesburg, 1972-84; dean of edn. U. Western Cape, Cape Town, S. Africa, 1991-96, prof. philosophy of edn., 1985-99; dean edn. U. Port Elizabeth, South Africa, 1999—; convenor Internat. Network of Philosophers of Edn., 1992-96. Author: (book) Chains of Thought, 1989; editor: (book) Problems of Pedagogics, 1981, (with K. King) Vision and Reality, 1998; founder/editor: Perspectives in Edn. jour., 1976-86; contbr. articles to profl. jours. Convenor Nat. Edn. Policy Initiative, 1994; coord. tchr. edn. group Nat. Commn. on Higher Edn., 1995, mem. task group, 1995-96. Avocations: endurance running, cycling, orienteering. Office: U Port Elizabeth, PO Box 1600, Port Elizabeth 6000, South Africa

MORSE, BRENTON TUPPER, JR., retired engineer, planner; b. Bklyn., June 2, 1925; s. Brenton T. Sr. and Lilian Milicent (Wilkinson) M.; m. Isabel Maria Peraza; children: Lilian Fidelina (dec.), Joseph Robert, Mariela Isabel Morse Saucier. BCE, Lehigh U., 1946. Profl. engr., land surveyor.; cert. profl. estimator. Trainee L.I. R.R. Co., Jamaica, N.Y., 1946-47; design engr. Rust Engring. Co., Pitts., 1947; field engr. Sanderson & Porter, Parkersburg, W.Va., 1947-48; design engr. Arthur G. McKee & Co., Elizabeth, N.J., 1948-50; office engr. Creole Petroleum Corp., Caracas, Venezuela, 1950-57; coordinating engr. J. Ray McDermott & Co., Inc., Maracaibo, Venezuela, Lagos, Nigeria, and New Orleans, 1957-71; estimating engr. Ingram Corp., New Orleans, 1971-72; resident engr. Community Improvement Agy., New Orleans, 1972-73; chief planning, permits mgr. Port of New Orleans, 1973-97; ret., 1997. With USMCR, 1943-45. Fellow ASCE (hon., Outstanding Civil Engr. Govt. New Orleans and State of La. 1995); mem. ASCE, Am. Soc. Profl. Estimators, Am. Planning Assn., Am. Concrete Inst., Soc. Am. Mil. Engrs., La. Engring. Soc. Roman Catholic. Avocations: swimming, tennis, skiing, softball, line, round, square, Cajun and ballroom dancing. Home: 6309 Cartier Dr New Orleans LA 70122-2227

MORSE, CHRISTOPHER GEORGE JOHN, law educator; b. Swansea, Wales, June 28, 1947; s. John and Margaret Gwenllian (Maliphant) M.; m. Louise Angela Stott, Mar. 26, 1983; 1 child, Richard. BA, Oxford (Eng.) U., 1969, B in Civil Law, 1970. Cert. barrister. Lectr. in law King's Coll., London, 1971-87, reader in law, 1987-92, prof. law, 1992—; vis. prof. John Marshall Law Sch., Chgo., 1979-80, KU Leuven, Belgium, 1982; head, dean Sch. Law, King's Coll., London, 1992-93, 97—. Author: Torts in Private International Law, 1978; co-author: Dicey and Morris on the Conflict of Laws, 11th edit., 1987, 13th edit., 2000, Benjamin's Sale of Goods, 3d edit., 1987, 4th edit., 1992, 5th edit., 1997, Chitty on Contracts, 28th edit., 1999. Office: King's Coll London, Sch of Law Strand, London WC2 R2LS, England

MORSE, JEAN AVNET, higher education administrator, lawyer; b. N.Y.C., Jan. 2, 1947; d. Samuel and Helen (Hershfield) Avnet; m. Stephen John Morse, Dec. 26, 1966; 1 child, Elisabeth Avnet Morse. BA in History with high honors, Wellesley Coll., 1968; JD cum laude, Harvard U., 1971. Bar: Mass. 1971, Calif. 1974, U.S. Dist. Ct. Mass. 1972, U.S. Dist. Ct. (ctrl. dist.) Calif. 1974. Law clk. Superior Ct. Commonwealth of Mass., Boston, 1971-72; atty. Palmer & Dodge, Boston, 1972-74; assoc. to ptnr. Kaplan, Livingston, Goodwin, Berkowitz & Selvin, Beverly Hills, Calif., 1974-81; ptnr. Hufstedler & Kaus, L.A., 1981-87, of counsel, 1988; dep. assoc. dean, dir. coll. office, Sch. Arts and Scis. U. Pa., Phila., 1989-93; lectr. sociology, ind. study supr. U. Pa. Sch. Arts and Scis., Phila., 1991; acting asst. provost U. Pa., Phila., 1991-92, dean's acad. planning cons., 1992-93; assoc. dean for adminstrn. NYU Sch. Law, N.Y.C., 1993-94; dep. to pres. U. Pa., 1994-95; exec. dir. Commn. on Higher Edn. Middle States Assn. of Colls. and Schs., Phila., 1996—. Bd. govs. Greater Phila. Philosophy Consortium, 1990-93; bd. dirs. Women in Bus., 1985-88, The Women's Bldg., 1985-86; chair individual rights sect. L.A. County Bar Assn., 1985-86, vice-chair, 1986-88, exec. com. mem., 1985-88.

MORSE, M. HOWARD, lawyer; b. Louisville, Ky., May 30, 1959; s. Marvin Henry and Betty Anne (Hess) M.; m. Laura E. Loeb, Apr. 17, 1988; children: Elizabeth Loeb, Marni Loeb. AB summa cum laude, Dartmouth Coll., 1981; JD cum laude, Harvard U., 1984. Bar: D.C. 1984, U.S. Ct. of Internat. Trade 1985, U.S. Ct. Appeals (fed. cir.) 1985, U.S. Dist. Ct. D.C. 1986, U.S. Ct. Appeals (D.C. cir.) 1986, U.S. Ct. Appeals (4th cir.) 1987. Assoc. Arnold & Porter, Washington, 1984-88; atty. FTC Bur. Competition, Washington, 1988-91; dep. asst. dir. for policy FTC Bur. Competition, 1991-93, asst. dir. for merger litigation, 1993-97; ptnr. Drinker, Biddle & Reath, Washington, 1998—; adj. prof. law Georgetown Law Ctr., Washington, 1995—. Mem. ABA (mem. antitrust sect., chair computer industry com. 1996-99, chair antitrust issues in high-tech industries program 1999, chair intellectual property com. 1999—, chair antitrust and intellectuall property: The Crossroads program 2000), FBA, D.C. Bar Assn., Phi Beta Kappa. E-mail: morsemh@dbr.com. Office: Drinker Biddle & Reath 1500 K St NW Ste 1100 Washington DC 20005-1209

MORSE, MARTIN A., surgeon; b. Louisville, June 25, 1957; s. Marvin Henry and Betty Anne (Hess) M. BS in Zoology with distinction, Duke U., 1979, MD, 1983. Diplomate Nat. Bd. Med. Examiners. Intern, jr. resident in surgery Barnes Hosp./Washington U., St. Louis, 1983-85; rsch. fellow dept. pediat. surgery Children's Hosp./Harvard Med. Sch., Boston, 1985-87; sr. resident in surgery U. Rochester, N.Y., 1987-89, chief resident, 1989-90; rsch./clin. fellow in transplantation dept. pediatric surg. Children's Hosp. Med. Ctr., Cin., 1990-92; clin. fellow hand and upper extremity surgery dept. orthopedic surgery U. Pitts. Med. Ctr., 1992-93; fellow in plastic and reconstructive surgery, dept. surgery U. Fla. Coll. Medicine, Gainesville, 1993-95; clin. staff Georgetown U., Washington, 1995—; pvt. practice plastic and reconstructive surgery McLean and Reston, Va., 1995-98; prin., owner The Great Falls (Va.) Plastic Surgery Ctr., 1999—; lab. investigator Lab. Exptl. Pathology divsn. cancer cause and prevention Nat. Cancer Inst./NIH, Rockville, Md., summer 1974-80; invited prof. dept. grad. nursing Simmons Coll., Boston, 1986-87; NASA flight surgeon, 1994—; adj. clinical staff Duke Univ. Medical Ctr., Durham, N.C., 1999—. Contbr. articles to profl. jours. Vol. Cystic Fibrosis, Am. Cancer Soc., Am. Heart Assn., March of Dimes, Am. Lung Assn.; founding mem. Statue of Liberty/Ellis Isle Found., N.Y.C., 1985, JFK Libr. Found., Boston, 1987, Challenger Ctr. for Space Sci. Edn., Washington, 1987, U.S. Naval Meml. Found., Washington, 1990; active Friends Nat. Libr. Medicine, Col. Williamsburg Found., Met. Mus. Art, Boston Mus. Fine Arts, Carnegie Mellon Mus.; patron The John F. Kennedy Ctr. for the Performing Arts, Wolf Trap, Friends of the Nat. Zoo, Nat. Audobon Soc., World Wildlife Fund, U.S. Holocaust Mus.; vol. surgeons overseas medical Missions, 1998—; vol. physician Wolf Trap Farm Park, Nat Park Svc., Vienna, Va., 1998—. Farley Found. fellow Children's Hosp., Harvard Med. Sch., 1986; recipient Outstanding Svc. award Nat. Cancer Inst., NIH, 1977, Nat. Def. medal. Fellow ACS (assoc.); mem. AMA (Physician's Recognition award 1984, 87, 90, 93, 96, 99), AAAS, Am. Soc. Plastic Surgeons, Soc. Laparoendoscopic Surgeons, Am. Soc. Artificial Internal Organs, Am. Trauma Soc., Fla. State Med. Soc., Assn. for Acad. Surgery, Surg. Infection Soc., Aerospace Med. Assn., Assn. Mil. Surgeons U.S., Am. Soc. Cell Biology and Tissue Culture Assn., Southeastern Soc. Plastic and Reconstructive Surgeons (candidate), So. Med. Assn., Physicians for Social Responsibility, Rochester Surg. Soc., N.Y. Acad. Scis., Fairfax County Med. Soc., Fla. State Med. Soc., Fla. Hand Soc., Va. State Med. Soc., Am. Legion, Naval Res. Assn., Res. Officers Assn., Phi Beta Kappa, Alpha Omega Alpha, Phi Lambda Epsilon. Achievements include patent for Controlled Cellular Implantation Using Artificial Matrices; first to describe long-term growth of established human extrahepatic biliary epithelial cells in culture; first to describe a specific chemoattractant neutral proteinase in whole human skin, fibroblasts, lymphocytes, and granulocytes.

MORSE, ROBERT PARKER, investment company executive; b. Nyack, N.Y., May 8, 1945; s. Robert Willard Parker and Julia (Larson) M.; m. Sarah Morgan Cumings, Sept. 23, 1978; children: Robert Bradley St. Clair, Parker Morgan, Sarah Spencer. BS in Econs., U. Pa., 1967; student in advanced currency theory, Adelphi Suffolk U., 1970-71. V.p. Am. Express/W.H. Morton Divsn., N.Y.C., 1970-74; sr. v.p., ptnr. William G. Campbell & Co., Inc., N.Y.C., 1975-80; pres. Morse, Williams & Co., Inc., N.Y.C., 1981—. Gov. Soc. Mayflower Descendents, N.Y., 1993-98; trustee Plymouth Plantation, Mass., 1994—, Bermuda Biol. Sta. Rsch., 1983-2000, Gen. Svc. Bd., N.Y., 1981-93, trustee English Speaking Union, 1998—; bd. assocs. The Whitehead Inst., MIT, 1996—; chmn. bd. The Wall Street Fund, 1984—. Lt. USNR, 1967-78. Mem. Bond Club N.Y., U.S. Naval Inst. Episcopalian. Avocations: sailing, skiing, reading, golf, tennis, squash. Office: Morse Williams & Co Inc 230 Park Ave Rm 1635 New York NY 10169-1602

MORSE, SCOTT DAVID, international trade research executive, consultant, publisher; b. Sacramento, Dec. 6, 1950; s. David Comestock and Jane Berenice (Derr) M. BSFS in Internat. Econs., Georgetown U., 1974, MSFS in Internat. Trade, 1983. Adminstrv. asst. nat. security coun. Exec. Office of The Pres. of U.S., Washington, 1972-73; internat. trade policy analyst Calif. Farm Bur. Fedn., Berkeley, Calif., 1975-76; mgr. commodity svc. divsn. Calif. Farm Bur. Fedn., 1977-81; agrl. trade regulation analyst Patton, Boggs & Blow, Washington, 1983; v.p. agribus. BankAm. World Trade Corp., San Francisco, 1984-85; pres. Morse Mcht. Agribus., San Francisco, 1985-90, Morse Agri-Energy Assocs., San Francisco, 1990-91, World Tariff Ltd. (subs. FedEx Trade), San Francisco, 1991-2000, FedEx Trade Network, Inc., 2000—; cons. European Commn. DG-Trade, 1996—, others. Contbr. over 12 articles to profl. jours. Avocations: playing guitar, tennis, snow skiing. Office: World Tariff Ltd 220 Montgomery St Ste 448 San Francisco CA 94104-3410

MORSE, STEPHEN, agronomist; b. Newport, England, Jan. 25, 1957; s. Clfford and Margaret (Whelan) M.; m. Maura Bridget (O'Mahoney) Morse, Aug. 14, 1985; children: LLewellyn Anthony, Rhianna Maria. BS in Applied Biology, UWist, Cardiff, Wales, 1978; MS in Crop Protection, U. Reading, England, 1979; PhD, U. Reading, 1989, U. Southampton, England, 1990. Entomologist Agrl. Devel. Adv. Svc., Cambridge, England, 1979; tech. officer Stokes Bamford, Soham, England, 1979-80; extension officer World Bank, Nigeria, 1980-82; agronomist Diocesan Devel. Svcs., Nigeria, 1982-87; lectr. U. East Anglia, Norwich, England, 1990-98; sr. lectr. U. East Anglia, 1998; reader Reading (Eng.) U., 1999—; cons. Overseas Devel. Group, Norwich, England, 1990—. Author: Integrated Pest Management, 1997, Developing On-Farm Rsch., 1996, Developing Financial Services, 1998, Measuring the Immeasurable, 1998, Visions of Sustainability, 2000; editor: People and Environment, 1995. Mem. Inst. Biology, Assn. Applied Biologists. Avocation: soccer. Office: Intern Devel Ctr U Reading, PO Box 239 Earley Gate, Reading RG6 6AU, England

MORSE, SUSAN EDWINA, film editor; b. Bklyn., Mar. 4, 1952; d. Rogers Watrous and Marian Edwina (Davis) M.; m. Jack Carter Richardson, July 11, 1987; 1 child, Dwight Rogers Richardson. BA, Yale U., 1974. Film editor Rollins & Joffe Prodns., N.Y.C., 1976-93, Sweetheart Prodns., N.Y.C., 1994-98, Sandrew Prodns., N.Y.C., 1998—. Editor (films) Manhattan, 1979 (Brit. Acad. Award Nomination), Stardust Memories, 1980, Arthur, 1981, A Midsummer Night's Sex Comedy, 1982, Zelig, 1983 (Brit. Acad. Award Nomination), Broadway Danny Rose, 1984, The Purple Rose of Cairo, 1984,

Hannah and Her Sisters, 1985 (Brit. Acad. Award Nomination, Oscar Nomination), Radio Days, 1986 (Brit. Acad. Award Nomination), September, 1987, Another Woman, 1988, New York Stories (Oedipus Wrecks), 1989, Crimes and Misdemeanors, 1989 (Brit. Acad. Award Nomination), Alice, 1990, Shadows and Fog, 1991, Husbands and Wives, 1992, Manhattan Murder Mystery, 1993, Bullets Over Broadway, 1994, Mighty Aphrodite, 1995, Everyone Says I Love You, 1996, Deconstructing Harry, 1997, Celebrity, 1998, (TV films) The Greatest Man in the World, 1978, Don't Drink the Water, 1994; co-editor (with Dennis Virkler) Miracles, 1985; assoc. editor (with David Holden) The Warriors, 1978, (with Thelma Schoonmaker) Raging Bull, 1979. Coach youth baseball team, coach youth baketball team; referee youth soccer team. Mem. Acad. Motion Picture Arts and Scis., Am. Cinema Editors. Avocations: field hockey, music, theatre.

MORSE-MCNEELY, PATRICIA, poet, writer, retired middle school educator; b. Galveston, Tex., Apr. 2, 1923; d. Bleecker Lansing Sr. and Annie Maud (Pillow) Morse; m. Chalmers Rankin McNeely, Mar. 22, 1949 (div. Aug. 1959); children: David Lansing McNeely, Timothy Ann McNeely Caldwell, Patricia Grace McNeely Dragon, Abigail Rankin McNeely. BS in Edn., U. Tex., 1972; MA in Ednl. Psychology, Spl. Edn. LLD, U. Tex., San Antonio, 1976, MA in Ednl. Psychology-Spl. Edn. Counseling, 1981. Cert. tchr., Tex., profl. counselor. Sec./adminstrv. sec. various cos., Galveston & Austin, Tex., 1945-49, 60-70; dep. clk. Ct. of Civil Appeals, Galveston, 1947-48; police stenographer Austin Police Dept., 1970-74; history and spl. edn. tchr. N.E. Ind. Sch. Dist., San Antonio, 1974-76; spl. edn. tchr. S.W. Ind. Sch. Dist., San Antonio, 1978-81; vocat. adjustment coord. East Ctrl. Ind. Sch. Dist., San Antonio, 1981-82; counselor, tchr. Stockdale (Tex.) Ind. Sch. Dist., 1982-84; clinic sec. Humana Hosp., Dallas, 1985-87; tchr. history and spl. edn. Dallas Ind. Sch. Dist., 1987-2000; ret., 2000; CTD/TSTA/NEA assn. rep. Hill Mid. Sch., Dallas, 1988-89, E.B. Comstock Mid. Sch., Dallas, 1991-2000. Author: (poetry) Texas City, 1947, A Gift of Love, 1978, The Key, 1991, The House (1st prize) 1993, various anthologies; contbr. articles to newsletters and co. publs. V.p. zone, sec., libr., com. mem. Parents Without Ptnrs., Inc., Austin, 1965-72, chmn. internat. ad hoc com. for writing leadership tng. program, 1968, newsletter editor, 1967-72; trustee Nat. Trust for Edn. First recipient Bernice Milburn Moore scholarship award U. Tex. Austin Alumni Assn., 1972. Mem. AARP, ASCD, NAFE, Assn. Am. Poets, Internat. Lib. Poetry (Hall of Fame 1997) Internat. Soc. Poets, Classroom Tchrs. of Dallas (del. to Tex. State Tchrs. Assn. Conf. 1978-81, 91-97), U. Tex. Austin Alumni Assn., U. Tex. San Antonio Alumni Assn. Episcopalian. Avocations: writing, reading, music, sewing/handicrafts, book collector.

MORSIANI, EUGENIO ANTONIO, surgeon; b. Ferrara, Italy, Jan. 16, 1953; came to U.S., 1993; s. Mario and Carla (Bonsetti) M.; m. Alessandra Fiocca, July 15, 1977; children: Giovanna, Francesco. MD, U. Ferrara, 1978. Med. licensure, Italy. Asst. resident dept. surgery Sant'Anna Gen. Hosp., Ferrara, 1980-85, attending surgeon dept. surgery, 1989-92; assoc. surgeon-in-chief Sant'Anna Gen. Hosp, Ferrara, 1995—; clin. fellow dept. surgery Deutsche Klinik fur Diagnostik, Wiesbaden, Germany, 1986; clin. fellow dept. pathology Oncological Tng. Program, Ferrara, 1987-88; prof. surgery U. Ferrara, 1989-93; rsch. scientist II Cedars-Sinai Med. Ctr., L.A., 1993-95; cons. divsn. surg. rsch. Cedars-Sinai Med. Ctr., L.A., 1995-96, Hesperia Hosp., Modena, Italy, 1995-96; vis. scientist dept. pathology Washington U., St. Louis, 1988, dept. surgery Lund (Sweden) U., 1988-89; vis. scholar Sch. Medicine UCLA, 1993-95; vis. physician dept. surg. oncology Washngton Hosp. Ctr., 1999; mem. editl. bd. CRC Press Inc., Times Mirror Books, Boca Raton, Fla., 1985—; editor liver assist device sect. Internat. Jour. Artificial Organs, 2000. G. Medini Best Doctoral Thesis scholar, 1978; G. Fornasini Rsch. Found. scholar, 1981; Eli Lilly scholar, 1988; Microsurgery Rsch. award Fidia Rsch. Labs., 1985. Mem. Am. Assn. Study Liver Diseases (corres.), N.Y. Acad. Scis., European Soc. Surg. Rsch., Cell Transplant Soc., European Soc. Artificial Organs, Italian Soc. Surgery, Internat. Soc. Regional Cancer Therapy, Am. Diabetes Assn. Achievements include patent for automated, large scale production of porcine hepatocytes for bioartifical liver support (in U.S., Europe, Japan); patent pending for radial-flow bioreactor for hepatocyte perfusion. Home: Via Caneva 5, 44100 Ferrara Italy Office: Sant'Anna Gen Hosp Dept Surgery, 203 Corso Giovecca, 44100 Ferrara Italy

MORT, ANTHONY GORDON, international trade consultant, business executive; b. Castletown, Isle of Man, Mar. 22, 1949; s. Reginald Gordon and Doris Eileen (Dodd) M.; m. Suzanne Zona Berry, Dec. 6, 1969; children: Donna Marie, Andrew Gordon, Brenden Anthony, Christopher Paul, Angela Rachel. Student, Hastings (N.Z.) Boys H.S. With New Zealand Customs Dept., Wellington, 1967-91, sr. sales tax auditor, 1977-82, sr. systems planner, 1982-83, applications devel. mgr., 1983-85, dir. systems, 1985-87, gen. mgr. info. tech., 1987-91; trade and transport mktg. mgr. GE Info. Svcs., Sydney, Australia, 1991—; electronic trading cons. Soc. Internat. Télécomm., Aeronautique, Sydney, 1992-93; owner Dorimor Mgmt. Svcs. Pty. Ltd., Lower Hutt, New Zealand, 1993—; vice-chmn. ADP subcom. World Customs Org., Brussels, 1990-91; mem. Australia/New Zealand EDIFACT Bd., Wellington, 1989-91; cons. in field. Launch master Wellington Coastguard, 1977-91. With New Zealand Navy res., 1968-73. Mem. New Zealand Inst. Pub. Adminstrn., New Zealand Inst. Mgmt., Internat. Narcotics Enforcement Officers Assn., New Zealand Inst. Logistics Mgmt., Electronic Data Interchange Assn. (chmn. edn. com. 1990), C. of C. Mem Ch. of England. Office: PO Box 30046, Lower Hutt New Zealand

MORTENSEN, CHRISTIAN EDWARD, philosopher; b. Rockhampton, Queensland, Australia, Apr. 25, 1945; s. Percival and Marjory (Percy) M.; m. Catherine Margaret Speck, May 5, 1972; children: Edith, Jesse. BA, U. Queensland, 1967; PhD, U. Adelaide, 1976. Postdoctoral fellow Australian Nat. U., Canberra, 1977; lectr. U. Adelaide, Australia, 1978-79; rsch. fellow Australian Nat. U., 1980-82; from lectr. to hughes prof. U. Adelaide, 1982—. Author: Inconsistent Mathematics, 1995; contbr. articles to profl. jours. Fellow Australian Acad. of the Humanities; mem. Australasian Assn. Logic (pres. 1993-94, gen. sec. 1995—), Australasian Assn. Philosophy (pres. 1999-00). Avocations: tennis, martial arts. Office: U Adelaide, Dept Philosophy, 5005 Adelaide Australia

MORTENSON, THOMAS THEODORE, medical products executive, management consultant; b. Hallock, Minn., Dec. 18, 1934; s. Theodore William and Esther (Hanson) M.; m. Alice L. Girdvain, June 27, 1958; children: Kim M., Laura Dee Mortenson Pavlides. BSBA, U. N.D., 1956, postgrad., 1957-58. Sales rep. Johnson & Johnson, Detroit, 1960-66; tng. and product dir. Johnson & Johnson, New Brunswick, N.J., 1967-72; dir. market devel. C.R. Bard, Murray Hill, N.J., 1973-75; gen. mgr. MacBick, Murray Hill, 1976-78; dir. mktg. Bard Med. Systems, Murray Hill, 1979-81; dir. sales, 1982; dir. sales/mktg., bd. dirs. Bac-Data Med. Info. Systems, Totowa, N.J., 1983-84; v.p. mktg. and sales United Med. Corp., Haddenfield, N.J., 1985-86; exec. v.p. Daltex Med. Scis., West Orange, N.J., 1987-92; assoc. ConMed Corp., Utica, N.Y., 1993—; guest lectr. Am. Mgmt. Assn., 1971, Mktg. Scis. Inc., N.Y.C., 1978, Internat. Novel Drug Delivery Techs., Tustin, Calif., 1987. With U.S. Army, 1957-58. Mem. Am. Mgmt. Assn. (instr. 1971), Berkeley Swim Club (Berkeley Heights, N.J.) (pres. 1979-82, bd. dirs. 1974-84). Avocations: woodworking, golf, volleyball, auto restoration. Home: 44 Ironwood Rd New Hartford NY 13413-3906 Office: 310 Broad St Utica NY 13501-1203

MORTIMER, ANITA LOUISE, minister; b. Jefferson City, Mo., July 2, 1950; m. Ross Maitland Snell and Viola Alice (Leigh) M.; children: Caleb Ross, Hannah Erin (dec.). BA, Graceland Coll., 1973; JD, Washburn U., 1976; MA in Religion with honors, Park Coll., 1992. Bar: Kans. 1976, U.S. Dist. Ct. Kans. 1976, Mo. 1980, U.S. Dist. Ct. (we. dist.) Mo. 1980, U.S. Ct. Appeals (8th cir.) 1980, U.S. Supreme Ct. 1980; ordained to ministry Reorganized Ch. of Jesus Christ of Latter-day Saints, 1993. Tng. cons. Orgn. to Counter Sexual Assault, Mo., Iowa, Kans., Ill., 1979-80; asst. dist. atty. Wyandotte County, Kansas City, Kans., 1976-80; asst. U.S. atty. U.S. Dept. Justice, Kansas City, Mo., 1980-97; min. Reorganized Ch. of Jesus Christ Latter-day Saints Ch., 1998—; appointee Organized Crime and Drug Enforcement Task Force, 1988; cons. Govs. Task Force on Rape Prevention, Mo., 1979-80; instr. Nat. Coll. Dist. Attys., 1980, various camps and retreats, family-related topics, various seminars for fed. agts.; bd. dirs. SHARE, Inc. Contbr. articles to profl. jours. Bd. dirs. Met. Orgn. to Counter Sexual Assault, Kansas City, 1976-80, Outreach Internat., 1995-99; apptd. to Presdl. Com. on Status of Women, 1979-80; trustee Independence (Mo.) Regional Health Ctr., 1990-94; mem. Ctr. Stake Strategic Planning Commn. RLDS, 1989-90; apptd. chair World Ch. Task Force on Singles' Ministry RLDS, 1990—; chair del. caucus RLDS World Conf., 1992, 94, 96, 98, 00; trustee Graceland Coll., 1994-2000, chair, 1998-2000; mem. Friends of the Zoo. Named to Honorable Order of Ky. Cols., Gov., 1980. Mem. ABA, Mo. Bar Assn., Assn. Women Lawyers, Kansas City Met. Bar Assn.; Alumni Assn. Graceland Coll. (bd. dirs. 1987, pres. 1988), John Whitmer Hist. Soc. Clubs: MOCSA (Kansas City), Friends of Art. Office: Peace and Justice Ministries Community of Christ PO Box 1059 Independence MO 64051-0559

MORTIMER, ANN MARGARET, psychiatrist, educator, consultant; b. Batley, Yorkshire, Eng., May 11, 1957; d. Harry and Muriel (Wood) M. BSc, U. Leicester, 1978, MB ChB, 1981; M in Med. Sci., U. Leeds, 1987. Lectr. U. Leeds, 1986-88; cons. psychiatrist Huddersfield Health Authority, 1988-91; sr. lectr. psychiatry Charing Cross and Westminster Med. Sch., London, 1991-95; prof., found. chair psychiatry U. Hull, 1995—; mem. Novartis U.K. Adv. Bd., Frimley, Surrey, 1993—; examiner in medicine U. London, U. Sheffield, U. Leeds, U. Manchester, 1993—. Editor: Psychopathology, 1991. Recipient faculty award U. Leicester, 1980, Young Investigator award Internat. Congress on Schizophrenia, 1992. Fellow Royal Coll. Psychiatrists (media experts 1991—, examiner 1995—). Office: U Hull Dept Psy East Riding, Campus Beverley Rd Willerby, Hull HU10 6NS, England

MORTIMER, JAMES WINSLOW, analytical chemist; b. Mt. Kisco, N.Y., Mar. 11, 1955; s. James Winslow and Eileen Ruth (Cutting) M.; m. Dawn Romay Kania, Apr. 30, 1977. BA, Washington and Jefferson U., 1976. Tech. sales rep. Waters Assocs., Milford, Mass., 1978-82; dir. nat. accounts Zymark Corp., Hopkinton, Mass., 1982-89; v.p. Microflex Tech., Triadelphia, W.Va., 1989-90; mgr. mktg. Berthold Systems, Inc., Aliquippa, Pa., 1990-95; dir. life sci. and chems. Fisher Sci., Pitts., 1995—; speaker at profl. confs. Author: Laboratory Robotics, 1987; cons. editor Lab. Robotics Jour., Hershey, Pa., 1990—; assoc. editor Lab. Robotics and Automation, 1988, 90; contbr. articles to tech. publs. Mem. TAPPI, Soc. Analytical Chemists (speaker 1978, 87), Masons. Achievements include development of cleavastat surgical instrument, beaker that will not cause vortexing action. Home: 113 Little John Dr Mc Murray PA 15317-2542 Office: Fisher Scientific 2000 Park Lane Dr Ste 2 Pittsburgh PA 15275-1104

MORTIMER, ROBERT AMSDEN, political science educator; b. N.Y.C., Oct. 16, 1938; s. James Sinclair and Ivy (Amsden) M.; m. Mildred Palmer, June 9, 1962; children: Anne-Michele, Janine, Sylvie, Denise. BA, Wesleyan U., Middletown, Conn., 1960; MA, Columbia U., N.Y.C., 1963, PhD, 1968. Asst. prof. Haverford (Pa.) Coll., 1966-72, assoc. prof., 1972-80, prof. polit. sci., 1980—; Fulbright prof. U. Algiers, Algeria, 1974-75, U. Dakar, Senegal, 1991-92; Aspinall lectr. Mesa Coll., Grand Junction, Colo., 1986; dir. West African Rsch. Ctr. Dakar, 1998. Author: The Third World Coalition, 1980, 84, Politics and Society in Contemporary Africa, 1988, 92, 99 (Best Book award 1988); contbr. articles to profl. jours. Mem. bd. trustees Wesleyan U., 1999—. Fulbright scholar, France, Senegal, 1960, 69, Woodrow Wilson fellow, 1961, 64. Mem. Internat. Studies Assn., Am. Polit. Sci. Assn., African Studies Assn. Democrat. Avocations: running, skiing, tennis. E-Mail:rmortime@haverford.edu. Office: Haverford Coll Haverford PA 19041

MORTIMER, WENDELL REED, JR., judge; b. Alhambra, Calif., Apr. 7, 1937; s. Wendell Reed and Blanche (Wilson) M.; m. Cecilia Vick, Aug. 11, 1962; children: Michelle Dawn, Kimberly Grace. AB, Occidental Coll., 1958; JD, U. So. Calif., L.A., 1965. Bar: Calif. 1966. Trial atty. Legal div. State of Calif., L.A., 1965-73; assoc. Thelen, Marrin, Johnson & Bridges, L.A., 1973-76, ptnr., 1976-93; pvt. practice San Marino, Calif., 1994-95; judge L.A. Superior Ct., 1995—. With U.S. Army, 1960-62. Mem. ABA, Internat. Acad. Trial Judges, Los Angeles County Bar Assn., Calif. Judges Assn., Am. Judicature Soc., Am. Judges Assn., Legion Lex., ABOTA, San Marino City Club, Pasadena Bar Assn., Balboa Yacht Club. Home: 1420 San Marino Ave San Marino CA 91108-2042

MORTIMORE, PETER JOHN, university administrator, education educator; b. Twickenham, Middlesex, Eng., Jan. 17, 1942; s. Claude and Rose (Townsend) M.; m. Jo Hargaden, Apr. 19, 1965; children: Joanna, Rebecca, Claudia. B in Psychology, U. London, 1973, M in Ednl. Psychology, 1974, D Psychology, 1978; LittD (hon.), Heriot-Watt U., Edinburgh, Scotland, 1998. Cert. edn., ednl. psychologist. Tchr. Inner London Edn. Authority, 1964-74; rsch. officer Inst. Psychiatry, U. London, 1975-78; sch. inspector Her Majesty's Inspectorate, London, 1978-79; dir. rsch. and stats. Inner London Edn. Authority, 1979-85; asst. edn. officer Inner London Edn. Authority, London, 1985-88; prof. edn., dir. Sch. Edn. U. Lancaster, Eng., 1988-90; prof. emeritus; dep. dir., dir. Inst. Edn. U. London, 1990-2000, pro vice-chancellor, 1999-2000; cons. Orgn. for Econ. Cooperation and Devel., Paris, 1990—, Govt. Mauritius, 1996, U. Toronto, 1995, U.K. Govt. Edn. and Tng. Mission, Brazil and Argentina, 1995. Co-author: 15,000 Hours, 1979, School Matters, 1988, The Primary Head, 1991, The Secondary Head, 1991, Managing Associate Staff, 1994, Planning Matters, 1995, Living Education, 1997, Forging Links, 1997, The Road to Improvement, 1998, Understanding Pedagogy, 1999, The Culture of Change, 2000. Gov. Sch. Oriental and African Studies, 1991-98, Birkbeck Coll., 1998-2000; trustee Vol. Svc. Overseas, London, 1992—; conf. chair Orgn. for Econ. Cooperation and Devel., London and Toronto, 1995, 97; U.K. coord. edn. UNESCO, London, 1997; mem. U.K. UNESCO Commn., 2000—. Named Officer of Order of Brit. Empire, 1993; fellow Brit. Psychol. Soc., 1989, Coll. Precepters, London, 1994. Mem. Am. Ednl. Rsch. Assn., Internat. Congress Sch. Effectiveness and Sch. Improvement (com. mem. 1988), Assn. Child Psychiatrists and Child Psychologists, Brit. Ednl. Rsch. Assn. (pres. 1999—). Avocations: music, theatre, art, walking. Office: Inst Edn, Inst Edn 20 Bedford Way, London WC1H OAL, England

MORTON, SIR ALASTAIR, business executive; b. Jan. 11, 1938; s. Harry Newton Morton and Elizabeth Martino; m. Sara Bridget Stephens, 1964; 2 children. BA, Witwatersrand U., South Africa; MA, Oxford (Eng.) U.; postgrad., MIT, 1964; LLD (hon.), U. Bath, Eng., 1990, U. Kent, Eng., 1992; D (hon.), U. Brunel, Eng., 1992; DSc (hon.), U. Warwick, Eng., 1994, U. Cranfield, Eng., 1996. With Anglo Am. Corp. of South Africa, London and Cen. Africa, 1959-63, Internat. Fin. Corp., Washington, 1964-67, Indsl. Reorgn. Corp., London, 1967-70; dir., chmn. Draymont Securities, London, 1970-76; mng. dir. Brit. Nat. Oil Corp., London, 1976-80; CEO Guinness Peat Group, London, 1982-87, chmn., 1987; co-chmn. The Eurotunnel Group, London, 1987-96, hon. chmn., 1997—; chmn. bd. Brit. Railways and Shadow Strategic Rail Authority, 1999—; chmn. Kent TEC, 1990-95, Chancellor's Pvt. Fin. Panel, 1993-95, Chartered Inst. Transport, 1992-94. Mem. coun. Royal Inst. Internat. Affairs, 1990-96; chmn. Nat. Youth Orch. of Great Britain, 1994—. Named Knight, 1991, Comdr. de la Légion d'Honneur, France, 1994; gold medalist Instn. of Civil Engrs., 1994. Mem. Univ. Club (N.Y.C.), Itchenor Sailing Club, Country Club (Johannesburg, South Africa). Avocations: sailing, walking, touring.

MORTON, ANDREW CLIFFORD, geologist; b. Hull, Great Britain, Feb. 2, 1954; s. Frederick and Joan (Wallace) M.; m. Anne Johnson, June 18, 1977 (div. 1993); children: Owen, Elizabeth. BA, U. Oxford, 1975, MA, 1979. Geologist Br. Geol. Survey, Leeds, England, 1976-89; project mgr. Br. Geol. Survey, Nottingham, England, 1989—; sr. lectr. U. Aberdeen, Scotland, 1998—. Editor: Developments in Sedimentary Provenance Studies, 1991, Geology of the Brent Group, 1992; contbr. articles to profl. jours. Fellow Geol. Soc. London. Office: Br Geol Survey, Keyworth, Nottingham NG12 5GG, UK

MORTON, ANNE JENNIFER, neuroscientist; b. Kawakawa, New Zealand, June 6, 1957; arrived in U.K., 1984; d. Alistair Steven and Shirley Grace (Macdonald) M.; m. John Michael Edwardson, May 18, 1985; children: Oliver, Matthew (twins). BS, U. Otago, 1978, PhD, 1983. From postdoctoral rsch. asst. to postdoctoral rsch. assoc. U. Cambridge, U.K., 1984-88; sr. scientific officer Inst. Animal Physiology & Genetics Rsch., Cambridge, 1988-91; lectr. U. Cambridge, 1991—; fellow Nennham Coll., Cambridge, 1991—. Recipient Riker prize in endocrinology Australian/New Zealand Soc. Endocrinology, 1982. Office: U Cambridge Dept Pharmacology, Tennis Ct Rd, Cambridge England

MORTON, CRAIG RICHARD, real estate investor; b. Mpls., Dec. 8, 1942; s. William Charles and Patricia Louise (Hare) M.; m. Barbara Jean Larsen, 1998; children: Kelly McCall, Bradley Winslow. Student, U. Philippines, Quezon City, 1961-62; BA in Geography of Southeast Asia, U. Minn., 1966; postgrad., St. John's Coll., Annapolis, 1966. Vol. U.S. Peace Corps, Philippines, 1966-68; v.p. Rent Mgmt., Inc., Mpls., 1970-80; pres. Diversified Hawaiian Investments, Inc., Mpls., 1981—, Craig R. Morton & Assoc., Inc., Mpls., 1980—; founder 49 real estate ltd. partnerships, Minn., N.Mex., Hawaii, Tex.; real estate developer Enchanted Lakes, Minn., 1990; pres. Am. Forex Corp., 1995. Am. Field Svc. scholar to Pakistan, 1960. Mem. Soc. Mayflower Descs., Jaguar Club Minn., Country Classics Car Club, Rotary (Paul Harris fellow), Order of DeMolay, Boy Scouts Order of Arrow, Loyal Order of Moose. Republican. Lutheran. Avocations: tree farming, reading, stamp collecting, woodsmanship, raising Arabian horses. Home: RR 8 Box 605 Aitkin MN 56431-8723

MORTON, DAVID, retired aluminum company executive; b. Devonport, Eng., Oct. 31, 1929; s. Leslie and Mary Morton; m. Bess Townsend, July 24, 1954; children: Sarah, James. MA, Pembroke Coll., Cambridge U., 1954; postgrad., Centre d'Etudes Industrielles, Geneva, 1960-61. Various mgmt. and staff positions Alcan Aluminum, Ltd., U.K., 1954-74; mng. dir. Alcan Booth Industries Ltd., U.K., 1974-77; v.p. corp. planning Alcan Aluminium Ltd., Montreal, Que., Can., 1977-79; mng. dir., CEO Alcan Aluminium (U.K.) Ltd., London, 1979-81; pres., CEO Aluminium Co. Can., Ltd., Montreal, 1981-84; exec. v.p. N.Am. and S.Am. ops. Alcan Aluminium Ltd., Montreal, 1984-87; also bd. dirs. Alcan Aluminium Ltd., 1985-95, pres., COO, 1987-89, chmn., CEO, 1989-93, chmn. bd. dirs., 1993-95, ret., 1995; bd. dirs. McCain Foods Ltd., Methanex Corp. Inc., Canadian Overseas Packaging Industries, Ltd., The Laird Group PLC; mem. internat. adv. bd. Lafarge; former chmn. Internat. Primary Aluminum Inst. Former gov. McGill U.

MORTON, ERIC, liberal arts educator; b. Detroit, Feb. 24, 1934; s. Lee Jack and Theresa Magdalen (Leonard) M.; children: Tracey Lynn, Theresa Dallas; m. Virgie Tillman, Sept. 27, 1997. AA, Merritt Coll., 1992; BA, U. Calif., Berkeley, 1992; M of Profl. Studies, Cornell U., 1994; MA, SUNY, Binghamton, 1998, PhD, 1999. Internat. organizer Am. Fedn. of State, County, Mcpl. Employees, Calif., 1970-73; field rep. State Senator Nicholas Petris, Oakland, Calif., 1973-75; mktg. adminstr. Safegate Aviation Systems, Oakland, 1975-80; asst. to dir. recreational sports U. Calif., 1980-92; grad. tchg. asst. Africana Studies and Rsch. Ctr., Cornell U., 1992-94; adj. lectr., rschr., tchr. SUNY, Binghamton, 1994-2000; assoc. prof. philosophy Fort Valley (Ga.) State U., 2000—; mem., multicultural core group Cornell U., 1992-94; lectr., rschr., tchr. SUNY Binghamton, 1994-2000; assoc. prof. philosophy Fort Valley State U., Ga., 2000—. Compiler (book) Mississippi Black Paper, 1965; contbr. articles to profl. jours. Active polit. campaigns; project mgr. Ctr. for Ind. Living, Berkeley, 1975-77. With U.S. Army, 1951-54. Recipient Award Met. Trans. Commn., 1973. Avocations: photography, reading. Home: 612 W Seminole Dr Byron GA 31008-4114

MORTON, LEE JACK, JR., graphic artist, designer, art educator; b. Detroit, Apr. 20, 1928; s. Lee Jack Sr. and Theresa (Leonard) M.; m. Carlene Hatcher, Feb. 18, 1950 (div. Mar. 1960); 1 child, Glynda Leslie; m. Vivian Louise Shepherd, Aug. 25, 1962; children: Jill Lei, Lee Jack III. BFA, Wayne State U., 1954; Corp. Pub. Rels. Mgmt. Cert., Am. Mgmt. Assn., 1969; Color Stripping Cert., Rochester Inst. Tech., 1990. Display designer Detroit Hist. Mus., 1954-57; graphic designer Herbert/Morris Advt., N.Y.C., 1957-60; prodn. mgr. Temco Press, N.Y.C., 1960-63; art instr. Harlem Commonwealth Coun., N.Y.C., 1966-72; pub. rels. dir. Haryou-Act, N.Y.C., 1972-78; art dir. City of Newark, 1979-96. Illustrator (children's books) The Freedom Ship of Robert Smalls, 1970, Birthday Present for Kathy Kenyatta, 1971, Leroy, Oops!, 1972, Animal Stories from Africa, 1973. Field sec., English tchr. Coun. of Federated Orgns., Jackson, Miss., 1964-65. With USN, 1947-49. Recipient Illustrator of Yr. award Highlights For Children, 1984, Disting. Svc. award UN Assn./USA, 1986, Outstanding Svc. award Nat. Coun. Women, 1991, Graphic Design award of excellence Comm. Concepts, 1992. Mem. Am. Inst. Graphic Artists. Democrat. Mem. AME Ch. Avocation: model building. Home: 209 Prospect St Apt 403 East Orange NJ 07017-2720

MORTON, MICHAEL JAMES, software engineer; b. Long Beach, Calif., Apr. 15, 1969; s. Thomas James and Carol Ann Morton. B in Computer Sci., U. Calif., Irvine, 1994. Photo finisher One Hour Moto Photo, Lake Forest, Calif., 1988-94; software engr. Quarterdeck Corp., Marina Del Rey, Calif., 1994-96, Connect-3, Los Alamitos, Calif., 1996-97, Beckman Instruments, Fullerton, Calif., 1997—; co-founder Tru Justice LLC, Claremont, Calif., 1996—. Mem. Phi Beta Kappa (sponsor, contbr.). Libertarian. Avocations: automobiles, electronics/circuit design, photography, aviation, horology. E-mail: morton555@worldnet.att.net. Home: 6260 E Via Ribazo Anaheim CA 92807-2334 Office: Beckman Instruments 4300 N Harbor Blvd Fullerton CA 92834

MORTON, RICHARD HUGH, statistician, educator; b. Grahamstown, South Africa, Sept. 16, 1946; arrived in New Zealand, 1981; s. Dan M. and Margaret I. (Hemming) M.; m. Colleen Ann Cavanagh, Apr. 11, 1974; children: Sarah, Penelope. BS, Rhodes Coll., Grahamstown, South Africa, 1968; MSc, U. Wales, Aberystwyth, 1970; MA, Cambridge (Eng.) U., 1976; PhD, Massey U., Palmerston North, New Zealand, 1985. Chartered statistician. Lectr. U. Canberra (Australia), 1974-80; assoc. prof. Massey U., 1981—. Editor (jour.) The New Zealand Statistician, 1990-96; assoc. editor (jour.) Sports Medicine, Training and Rehabilitation, 1995—, The Statistician, 1997—; mem. editorial bd. Jour. of Sports Scis., 1996—. Douglas Smith scholar St. Johns Coll., Cambridge, 1970-72; Sir Allan Sewell fellow Griffith U., 1995, Fulbright fellow New Zealand-U.S. Ednl. Found., 1996. Fellow Inst. Statisticians; mem. Assn. Track and Field Statisticians, New Zealand Statis. Assn. (com. mem. 1990-96). Avocations: bridge player, aviation interest. E-mail: h.morton@massey.ac.nz. Office: Massey U Inst Food Nutrit-, Human Health Pvt Bag 11-222, Palmerston North New Zealand

MORTON, RONALD LEE, pharmacist; b. Winter Haven, Fla., May 14, 1953; s. Paul Vane and Bobbie Christine (Warren) M. AA, Polk C.C., Winter Haven, 1973; BS, U. Fla., 1976. Registered pharmacist, Fla. Staff pharmacist Eckerd Drugs, Lake Wales, Avon Park, Auburndale, Bartow, Winter Haven, Fla., 1977-84; pharmacy mgr. Eckerd Drugs, Winter Haven, 1984-99, Auburndale, 1999—. Mem. Am. Pharmacy Assn., Fla. Pharmacy Assn., Polk County Pharmacy Assn., Auburndale Civitan Club. Republican. Baptist. Avocations: gardening, golf, skiing. Home: 110 Sevilla St Auburndale FL 33823-2518 Office: Eckerd Drugs # 0278 99 Magnolia Ave Auburndale FL 33823-4301

MÖRX, ALFRED FRANZ, technical physicist, consultant; b. Vienna, Austria, Oct. 21, 1958; s. Alfred and Karoline Mörx; m. Renate Hejkrlik, Feb. 7, 1986; children: Bernhard, Karin. Diploma in engring., Tech. U. Vienna, 1985. Trainer Tech. U. Vienna, 1984-85; project mgr. Sci. Rsch. Inst. Edn., Vienna, 1985-86; head tech. dept. Fed. Guild Elec. Contractors, Vienna, 1986-91; head product mgr. EH-Schrack Components Ltd., Vienna, 1991-93, tech. mgr., 1993-94; tech. dir. Felten a. Guilleaume plc, Vienna, 1994—; sci. cons. engr., tech. physicist, Vienna, 1991—; project mgr. rsch. Pvt. Rsch. Inst., 1988-95. Author: Electrical Installation in Buildings, Vol. I, 1991, Vol. II, 1994, Protection against Electric Shock, 1991; contbr. articles to Elec. Contractor's Jour., Technik für Praktiker. Mem. IEEE, Verband Deutscher Elektrotechniker, N.Y. Acad. Scis. Avocation: tennis.

MORYS, JANUSZ, neuroanatomist, educator; b. Gdansk, Poland, Jan. 20, 1958; s. Maciej and Anna (Kawczynska) M.; m. Jwona Małecka, Jan. 6, 1983 (div. Arp. 1995). MD, Med. U. Gdansk, Poland, 1983, PhD, 1985. Pre-registration house officer Med. U. Gdansk, 1982-83, asst., 1983-84, sr. asst., 1984-87, 88-91, assoc. prof., 1991-96; rsch. scientist Inst. for Basic Rsch., N.Y., 1987-88, 91-92; prof., head dept. anatomy, dean med. faculty Med. U. Gdansk, 1996—. Contbr. over 150 sci. papers to profl. publs. Recipient award Polish Acad. Sci., 1987. Mem. Polish Anatomical Soc., Polish Neurosci. Soc., Polish Alzhemier Soc., Polish Acad. Health. Roman Catholic. Avocations: music, soccer. Home: 6 Bema St Apt 5, 81-386 Gdynia Poland Office: Med U Gdansk Dept Anatomy Neurobiology, 1 Debinki St, 80-211 Gdansk Poland

MOSA, ALI ABDULLAH, dean, education educator; b. Abha, Assir, Saudi Arabia, Dec. 31, 1959; s. Abdullah Yehya Mosa and Jumaah Mohammed Sultan. BA in coll. edn., King Saud U., Abha, Saudi Arabia, 1986; MS in coll. edn., Ind. U., Bloomington, 1990; grad. sch. edn., SUNY, Buffalo, 1995. Tchr. Ministry Edn., Abha, Saudi Arabia, 1978-86, SUNY, Buffalo, 1991-92; asst. prof. coll. of Edn. King Saud U., Abha, 1995-99; assoc. prof. of Edn. King Khalid U., Abha, 1999—, chmn. dept. edn. coll. edn., 1996-99, dean coll. edn., 1999—; specialized in internat. and comparative edn.; tchr. comparative edn., econ. edn., ednl. found., ednl. adminstrn. and guidance, ednl. policy and ednl. rsch.; coordinator, organizer, active different programs various instns. edn. nationally and internationally; participant many profl. confs. nationally and internationally. Writer and translator books, active rschr.; contbr. articles to profl. jours. Coord. programs various nat. and internat. ednl. instns. Recipient British Aerospace award Brit. Coun., Riyadh, 1996, several certs. and medals acad. and social svcs.; scholar King Saud U., 1987-95. Mem. Am. Ednl. Rsch. Assn., Internat. and Compartive Edn. Soc., Saudi Ednl. and Psychol. Assn., Saudi Family Tchrs. Preparation, Arab Insts. Tchrs. Preparation (founding mem. 1999), Colls. Edn. Assn. (founding mem. 1999). Avocations: poetry, reading, writing, traveling, various sports activities. Fax: 966 7 224 9647. E-mail: aamosa@hotmail.com. Office: PO Box 9090, Abha Saudi Arabia

MOSBACH, KLAUS HERMANN, biochemistry educator; b. Leipzig, Germany, Nov. 26, 1932; arrived in Sweden, 1950; s. Hermann Theodor and Katharine Therese (Stolle) M.; m. May Eivor Roslund, Aug. 31, 1963; children: Petra, Katja, Vanja. MSc, Lund (Sweden) U., 1956, PhD, 1960. Prof. biochemistry, chmn. dept. Lund U., 1970—; Humboldt asst. prof. Max Planck Inst., Munich, 1967; vis. prof. Weizmann Inst. Sci., Rehovot, Israel, 1970; vis. prof., Dallas, 1973, Japanese Soc. for Promotion Sci., 1978, U. Bath, Eng., 1996—, Cath. U. Louvain, Belgium, 1996—; prof. biotech. Swiss Fed. Inst. Tech., Zurich, 1982-85; mem. sci. bd. biotech. cos., including Biogen and Hybritech, also involved with start-up of new cos. Editor: Immobilized Enzymes and Cells, Vols. 44, 135-37; mem. editl. and adv. bd. numerous biotech. or biochem. jours.; contbr. over 450 articles to sci. jours.; over 50 patents in biotech. and biochemistry field, especially affinity chromatography, immobilized enzymes, biosensors, and molecular imprinting. Recipient Arrhenius medal, 1983, gold medal Royal Swedish Acad. Engring. Scis., 1990, rsch. prize Swedish Fund for Rsch. with Animal Expts., 1993; Internat. prize Enzyme Engring. Found., 1985, Internat. prize Orgn. Affinity Chromatography., 1985. Fellow Internat. Inst. Biotech.; mem. European Molecular Biology Orgn., Am. Soc. Biol. Chemists (hon.). Office: Ctr Chemistry Chem Engring, PO Box 124, S-221 00 Lund Sweden

MOSBACHER, ROBERT ADAM, oil and gas industry executive, political organization executive; b. Mt. Vernon, N.Y., Mar. 11, 1927; s. Emil and Gertrude (Schwartz) M.; children—Diane, Robert, Kathryn, Lisa Mosbacher Mears. BS, Washington and Lee U., 1947, LLD (hon.), 1984. Independent oil and gas producer, 1948—; former sec. Dept. of Commerce, Washington, 1989-92; gen. chmn. Pres. Bush's re-election campaign, 1992; gen. chmn. fin. Rep. Nat. Com., Washington, 1992; chmn. Mosbacher Energy Co., Houston, Mosbacher Power Group, Houston, 1995—. Former bd. dirs. Choate Sch., Wallingford, Conn.; dir. emeritus Aspen Inst., Ctr. for Strategic and Internat. Studies; chmn. bd. visitors M.D. Anderson Hosp.; nat. fin. chmn. George Bush for Pres.; chmn. Pres. Ford Fin. Com.; co-chmn. Republican Nat. Fin. Com.; dir. Tex. Heart Inst.; pres. Odyssey Acad., Galveston, 1998—. Mem. Am. Petroleum Inst. (dir., exec. com.), Nat. Petroleum Coun. (past chmn.), All Am. Wildcatters Assn. (past chmn.), Am. Assn. Petroleum Landmen (past pres.). Presbyterian. Address: Mosbacher Energy Corp 712 Main St Ste 2200 Houston TX 77002-3206

MOSBAUGH, PHILLIP GEORGE, urologist, educator; b. Noblesville, Ind., Jan. 15, 1938; s.Ward C. and Frances J. Mosbaugh; m. Vera A. Deganutti Green, Jan. 21, 1963; children: Anne R. Mosbaugh Knapp, Virginia G. AB, Ind. U., Bloomington, 1959; MD, Ind. U., Indpls., 1963. Diplomate Am. Bd. Urology. Intern Orange County Hosp., Orange, Calif., 1963-64; resident in gen. surgery and urology Ind. U. Med. Ctr., Indpls., 1964-68; pvt. practice, Indpls., 1970—; asst. clin. prof. urology Ind. U. Sch. Medicine, 1975—; mem. med. adv. bd. on interstitial cystitis ALZA Pharms., 1988—, mem. spkr.'s bur., 1998—. Contbr. articles to med. jours., including Jour. Urology. Capt. M.C., USNR, 1968-70. Fellow ACS; mem. Interstitial Cystitis Assn. (med. advisor Ind. chpt. 1987—). Republican. Roman Catholic. Avocations: golf, travel, reading, crosswords. Home: 623 Round Hill Rd Indianapolis IN 46260-2915 Office: Urology of Ind LLC 1801 Senate Blvd Ste 655 Indianapolis IN 46202-1259

MOSBECH, HOLGER, allergist, educator; b. Copenhagen, Apr. 20, 1951; s. Johannes and Margrethe (Jespersen) M.; m. Eva Hammershaimb, Oct. 18, 1980. MD, U. Copenhagen, 1977, DMS, 1991. Cert. specialist gen. medicine, allergology, respiratory medicine. Resident Copenhagen U. Hosps., 1977-83, 87-93; rsch. fellow allergy unit Nat. U. Hosp., Copenhagen, 1983-87; cons., head allergy unit Frederiksberg U. Hosp., Copenhagen, 1994—; cons. Gentofte (Denmark) U. Hosp., 1994; lectr. med. faculty Copenhagen U., 1996-99, assoc. prof., 1999—. Mem. editl. bd. Danish Asthma-Allergy Jour., 1993-98; contbr. chpts. in books, articles to profl. jours. Mem. European Acad. Allergology and Clin. Immunology (sec. subcom. Insect Venom Allergy 1988-98, chmn. interest group 1998—), Danish Soc. Allergology (officer, Honour prize 1990), Orgn. Med. Allergologists Denmark (vice chmn. 1992-2000), Soc. Med. Allergologists (chmn. 1999—). Office: Frederiksberg U Hosp Allergy Unit, Ndr Fasanvej, DK-2000 Copenhagen Denmark Home: Skovdiget 44, DK 2880 Bagsvard Denmark

MOSCHOVITIS, JASON P., journalist; b. Athens, Greece, July 17, 1932. Mem. Nat. Coun. for Radio and TV, 1994—. Mem. Internat. Fedn. Journalism, Union Journalists. Office: N C R T, 6 Pindarou St, Athens Greece

MOSCOVICH, HILA, dentist, dental researcher; b. Tel-Aviv, June 23, 1967; arrived in The Netherlands, 1993; d. Ivan and Anitta (Danziger) M.; m. Jeroen Lucianus Maria Haans, Oct. 9, 1998; 1 child, Emilia. Student, Tel-Aviv U., 1986-88; B in Dental Sci., U. Manchester, Eng., 1992; PhD, U. Nijmegen, The Netherlands, 1999. rschr. Nijmegen U., 1993—. Contbr. articles to profl. jours. Mem. Internat. Assn. Dental Rsch. Achievements include pioneer in Natural-Inlay, the novel technique of using extracted teeth as a dental restorative material. Office: U Nijmegen Dental Sch, PO Box 9101, 6500 HB Nijmegen The Netherlands

MOSCOVICI, PIERRE, government official; b. Sept. 16, 1957. Grad., Inst. Polit. Studies, Paris, Nat. Sch. Adminstrn., Paris. With Auditor Gen.'s Dept., 1984-88; advisor Min. Nat. Edn., 1988, spl. advisor, 1990; nat. sec. PS, 1990-92, 95-97, nat. treas., 1992-94; mem. Doubs Gen. Coun., 1994; mcpl. councilor Montbeliard, France, 1995; nat. assembly deputy Douds, 1997; min. del. Responsibility for European Affairs, Paris, 1997—. Office: Min Fgn Affairs, 37 quai d'Orsay, 75700 Paris France

MOSCOWITZ, JOYCE MARLA, elementary school educator; b. Bklyn., Apr. 6, 1961; d. Leonard and Arleen Bandler; m. Lou Moskowitz, Dec. 12, 1994 (div. Dec. 1997); children: Harrison Evan, Jessica Sara. AA, Fashion Inst. Tech., N.Y.C., 1980; BA, Bklyn. Coll., 1983. Cert. tchr., Fla. Photography/art tchr. Boyd Anderson H.S., Lauderdale Lakes, Fla., 1989-96; tchr. art Plantation (Fla.) Elem. Sch., 1997-98, Eagle Point Elem. Sch., Weston, Fla., 1998—. Author: Hooked on Feeling Bad, 2000; contbr. articles to profl. jours. Mem. Eagle Point Elem. PTA, 1998—; co-leader chavurch Temple Ramat Shalom, Plantation, 1998-99. Mem. Broward Tchrs. Art Guild, Broward Tchrs. Union. Avocations: photography, computers, art projects. Home: 11912 SW 9th Ct Davie FL 33325-3847

MOSEKILDE, LEIF, endocrinologist, educator; b. Aarhus, Denmark, Sept. 24, 1942; Eyvind and Vibeke (Freund) M.; m. Eydna Joensen, Nov. 12, 1971; children: Rune, Anna-Maria, Jacob. GCE sci., Aarhus (Denmark) Kathedral Sch., 1961; MD, Aarhus U., 1968, DMS, 1979; specialist in internal medicine and endocrinology. Cert. specialist in internal medicine and endocrinology. Registrar Aarhus County Hosp., 1968-72, spl. edn. positions, 1972-73, registrar, sr. registrar, 1973-77, chief physician, 1980—, med. dir., 1990-95, prof. osteoporosis and metabolic bone disease, 1995—, mem. rsch. coun.; sr. registrar Randers (Denmark) Ctrl. Sys., 1977-79; chief physician King Fahd Ctrl. Hosp., Gizan, Saudi Arabia, 1985-86; chmn. Med. Soc. Jutland, Aarhus, 1984-90, 93—, Internat. Congress XXIVth symposium, 1995, Baltic Bone and Cartilage Conf., 1997, 98, 99; bd. dirs. European Soc. Calcified Tissues, 1987-97, European Osteoporosis Found., 1991-94, Danish Nutritional Bd., Copenhagen, 1995-98; chmn. Danish Osteoporosis Study, 1999—; mem. bibliometry group Danish Rsch. Agy., 2000—. Lt. Navy, Faroe Islands, 1979-80. Recipient Hagedorn prize Danish Med. Soc., 1990, Gert Espersens prize Jutland Soc. Medicine, 1991. Mem. Danish Bone and Tooth Soc. (chmn. 1986-92), Danish Soc. Internal Medicine, Danish Med. Soc. Rsch. Coun. Avocations: sailing, photography, diving, skiing, traveling. Home: Skolebakken 11th, DK 8000 Aarhus Denmark Office: Aarhus Amtssygehus, Tage Hansensgade 2, DK 8000 Arhus Denmark

MOSEL, ULRICH BERND, physics educator; b. Hannover, Fed. Republic Germany, Feb. 8, 1943; s. Hermann and Elfriede (Börner) M.; m. Sigrun K. Schneider, Dec. 12, 1969; children: Christoph, Stephan, Michael. Diploma in physics, U. Frankfurt, Fed. Republic Germany, 1968, PhD, 1969. Rsch. assoc. U. Tenn., Knoxville, 1970-71; cons. Oak Ridge (Tenn.) Nat. Lab., 1970-72; rsch. assoc. U. Wash., Seattle, 1971-72; prof. physics U. Giessen, Fed. Republic Germany, 1972—, chmn. dept. physics, 1980-81, 93-94. Author: Fields, Symmetrics and Quarks, 1989, 99. Fellow Am. Phys. Soc.; mem. German Phys. Soc. (chmn. Nuclear Physics Sect. 1989-92). Avocations: sailing, mountaineering. Office: Inst fur Theoretische, Physik Heinrich-Buff-Ring16, D 35392 Giessen Germany

MOSELEY, IVAN FREDERICK, neuroradiologist; b. Isleworth, Middlesex, Eng., May 29, 1940; s. Frederick Clarence and Edith Sophia (Smith) M.; m. Mary Cheyne Thomson Malcolm, Apr. 22, 1967; children: Hannah, James. BSc in Physiology, U. London, 1962, MB, BS, 1965, MD, 1978; PhD in Philosophy, U. Coll. Swansea, 1996. House physician St. Mary's Hosp., London, 1965-66; house physician neurosurgery Whittington Hosp., London, 1966; registrar radiology St. Bartholomew's Hosp., London, 1968-72; fellow radiology Mt. Zion Hosp., San Francisco, 1972-73; sr. registrar radiology Nat. Hosp. Neurology & Neurosurgery, London, 1973-75, dir. radiology, 1994—; sec. XIV Symposium Neuroradiologicum, London, 1986-90; treas. Symposia Neuroradiologica Ltd., London, 1990—; nat. rep. European Union Med. Specialists, Brussels, 1988—. Editor: The First European Seminar on CAT in Clinical Practice, 1977; author: Computerized Tomography in Neuro-Ophthalmology, 1982, Diagnostic Imaging in Neurological Disease, 1986, Magnetic Resonance Imaging in Diseases of the Nervous System, 1988. Recipient scholarship in physiology St. Mary's Hosp. Med. Sch., London, 1961-62, vis. scholarship CIBA/INSERM, Paris, 1974, Ann. prize European Soc. Neuroradiology, Dijon, 1976. Fellow Royal Coll. Radiologists, Royal Coll. Physicians; mem. Royal Soc. Medicine (pres. sect. clin. neuroscis. 1999—), Brit. Soc. Neuroradiologists (pres. 1998—), Club Taurino London (pres. 1990—), European Soc. Neuroradiology (chmn. nat. dels. 1996—). Mem. Labour party. Avocations: bullfighting, music, graphic arts, wine. Home: 65 St Marys Grove, London W4 3LW, England Office: Nat Hosp Neur & Neurosurg, Lysholm Radio Dept Queen Sq, London WCIN 3BG, England

MOSELEY, KAREN FRANCES FLANIGAN, retired school system administrator, educator; b. Oneonta, N.Y., Sept. 18, 1944; d. Albert Francis and Dorothy (Brown) Flanigan; m. David Michael McLaud, Sept. 8, 1962 (div. Dec. 1966); m. Harry R. Lasalle, Dec. 24, 1970 (dec. Feb. 1990); 1 child, Christopher Michael; m. Kel Moseley, Jan. 22, 1994. BA, SUNY, Oneonta, 1969; MS, Hockerill Coll., Eng., 1970. Cert. secondary edn. tchr., Fla., Mass., N.Y. Tchr. Hanover (Mass.) Pub. Schs., 1970-80; lobbyist Mass. Fed. Nursing Homes, Boston, 1980-84; tchr., dept. chair Palm Beach County Schs., Jupiter, Fla., 1985-95; ret., 1996; chair of accredidation Jupiter H.S., 1990-91; Fulbright tchr., Denmark, 1994-95. Author: How to Teach About King, 1978, 10 Year Study, 1991. Del. Dem. Conv., Mass., 1976-84; campaign mgr. Kennedy for Senate, N.Y., 1966, Tsongas for Senate, Boston, 1978; dir. Plymouth County Dems., Marshfield, Mass., 1978-84; Sch. Accountability Com., 1991-95; polit. cons. Paul Tsongas U.S. Senate, Boston, 1978-84, Michael Dukakis for Gov., Boston, 1978-84; mem. PBC chpt. ARC; disaster team vol. Palm Beach County Red Cross. Mem. AAUW (No. Palm Beach county), NEA (lifetime mem.), Nat. Honor Soc. Polit. Scientists, Classroom Tchrs. Assn., Palm Beach County Classroom Tchrs. Assn., Mass. Coun. Social Studies (bd. dirs. Boston chpt. 1970-80), Mass. Tchrs. Assn. (chair human rels. com. Boston chpt. 1976-80), Plymouth County Social Studies (bd. dirs. 1970-80), Mass. Hosp. Assn. (bd. dirs. Boston chpt. 1980-84), Nat. Coun. for Social Studies, Fulbright Alumni Assn., Prologue Soc., Lyceum Soc., Fla. History Ctr. Roman Catholic. Avocations: reading, fishing, traveling, art collector, boating. Home: 369 River Edge Rd Jupiter FL 33477-9350

MOSELEY, KEITH ANTONY, physicist, geologist, educator; b. Birmingham, Eng., Feb. 27, 1956; s. John Harold and Jean (Twyford) M.; m. Paula Mary Brunsdon, Oct. 21, 1996; 1 child, Matthew. BSc with honors, Birmingham U., 1977, PhD, 1982; Postgrad. Cert. of Edn., Keele U., 1983. Chartered physicist, Eng. Physics tchr. Monmouth Sch., 1983-85, head of geology, 1985-95, head of physics, 1995—; assoc. lectr. The Open U., Milton Keynes, 1988—; continuing edn. lectr. Cardiff U., 1995—; cons. Nuffield Found., London, 1990-93. Co-author: (textbooks) An Introduction to Geological Structures and Maps, 6th edit., 1997, Nuffield Year 7 Science, 1991, Nuffield Year 9 Science, 1990, Nuffield: Pathways Through Science, 1994, Nuffield: Earth and Space, 1992, Nuffield Coordinated Sciences, 1992; columnist Tchg. Earth Sci. jour., 1993-99. Mem. Inst. Physics, Inst. Materials, Monmouth Astron. Soc. Avocations: photography, astronomy, computing. E-mail: keith moseley@monmouth.monm.sch.uk. Office: Monmouth Sch, Almshouse St, Monmouth NP25 3XP, England

MOSENSON, STEVEN HARRIS, lawyer; b. Phila., Dec. 3, 1956. BS, NYU, 1978, M of Pub. Adminstrn., 1979; JD, Yeshiva U., 1982. Bar: N.Y. 1983, U.S. Ct. Appeals (2d cir.) 1983, U.S. Dist. Ct. (so. and ea. dists.) N.Y. 1983, U.S. Ct. Internat. Trade 1985, U.S. Supreme Ct. 1986. Assoc. Baden Kramer Huffman & Brodsky, N.Y.C., 1982-85; asst. corp. counsel N.Y.C. Law Dept., 1985-89; gen. counsel United Cerebral Palsy Assns. of N.Y. State, Inc., N.Y.C., 1989—. Pres. bd. dirs. Bklyn. Heights Ctr. for Counseling, Inc., 1992—; bd. dirs. Walden, N.Y. Local Devel. Corp., 1998—; mem. Walden Cmty. Coun., 1998—. Mem. N.Y. State Bar Assn. (chmn. com. on issues affecting people 1997—), Guardianship Assn. of N.Y. State, Inc. (v.p. 1995—). Fax: 212-356-0746. E-mail: mosenson@aol.com. Office: United Cerebral Palsy Assns of NY 330 W 34th St Fl 13 New York NY 10001-2488

MOSER, EWALD VALENTIN, physicist, educator; b. Villach, Carinthia, Austria, Aug. 23, 1952; s. Valentin and Maria (Scholin) M. Diploma in engring., U. Tech., Graz, Austria, 1978; PhD, U. Tech., Vienna, Austria, 1981. Rsch. asst. U. Geneva, 1981-82, U. Tech., Graz, 1982; lectr., rsch. asst. U. Vienna, 1982-88, asst. prof. med. physics, 1988-92, assoc. prof., sr. lectr., 1992-97, prof. med. physics and biophysics, 1997—; rsch. asst. U. Pa., Phila., 1988, U. Oxford, Eng., 1989—; head NMR group dept. med. physics U. Va., 1989—, dept. head Inst. Med. Physics, 1991-99. Contbr. articles to profl. jours. With Austrian Mil., 1970-71. Austrian Rsch. Found. fellow, 1988; rsch. grantee Bundeswirtschaftskammer, Vienna, 1981. Mem. N.Y. Acad. Scis., European Soc. Rsch. Med. Biology, Internat. Soc. Med. Rsch. Avocations: jogging, skiing, reading, music. Office: Inst Med Physics U Vienna, Waehringerstrasse 13, A-1090 Vienna Austria

MOSER, GREGG ANTHONY, retired career officer; b. Holton, Kans., Aug. 6, 1954; s. Paul Robert and Ila Rose (Jenkins) M.; m. Shari Ann Larson, Nov. 3, 1984 (div. Apr. 1999). BS in Constrn. Sci., Kans. State U., 1979; MS in Safety, Ctrl. Mo. State U., 1984. Commd. 2d lt. USAF, 1980, advanced through grades to maj., 1991; ret., 2000. Mem. Air Force Assn. (pres. Lt. Erwin R. Bleckley chpt. 1992-93, Medal of Merit 1994), Lions (pres. Wichita Flying Lions chpt. 1992-93, zone 1 chmn. dist. 17-SE region II 1993-94, dir. Scott Comty. Lions Club 1994-95, v.p. Scott Comty. Lions Club 1995-96). Republican. Methodist. Avocations: photography, reading. Home: 617 West Fifth St Holton KS 66436-1406

MOSER, JEFFERY RICHARD, state agency administrator, public affairs and public management executive, artist, writer, former state official; b. Miller, S.D., Feb. 8, 1961; s. Richard and Ardessa Joan (Yost) M. Student, U. Minn., 1979-84, Duke U., 1995, Northwestern U., 1997. Cert. lay minister; cert. in pub. policy and pub. fin.; cert. CPR, Am. Red Cross. Lab asst., intern U. Minn. Dept. Limnology, Mpls., 1980-81; exec. intern pub. affairs dept. Target Corp., Mpls., 1982; Nat. Farmers Union, Nat. Youth Adv. Coun., Denver, 1980-81; intern/asst. for legis. and policy Minn. Agri-Growth Coun., Bloomington, 1984-85; field office asst. U.S. Congressman Thomas A. Daschle, Aberdeen, S.D., 1986; pvt. cons. to non-profit orgns., 1986-89; notary pub. State of S.D., 1986-99; acting camp dir. S.D. Farmers Union Edn. Program, 1987-88; small bus. owner, 1986—; exec. dir. S.D. Assn. Towns and Twps., 1990-95; dep. state treas. to treas. Richard D. Butler State of S.D., Pierre, 1995-99; dir. econ. & co-op devel. Nat. Farmer's Union, Aurora, Colo., 1999—; participant 4-H/UN/USAID Presdl. young adult exch. program to Kenya and Botswana, Africa, summer 1985. Vol. U. Minn. Hosps., 1979-83, U. Minn. Dept. Minn. Unions, Mpls., 1983-84; gen. election poll watcher Hand County Rural precincts, 1988; past mem. Beadle County Dems., Hand County Dems., Brown County Dems., Hughes County Dems., v.p., 1997-98, Arapahoe County Dems., 1999—; del. State Dem. Conv., 1990, 92, 94; alt. del. Nat. Dem. Conv., Chgo., 1996, Clinton for Pres., 1992; nom. dem. candidate State Auditor, 1994, U.S. House, 1998; donor S.D. Dems., Dem. Nat. Com.; Dem. Nat. Senate Task Force; Dem. Congl. Campaign Com.; chair, del. Selection/Affirmative Action Com., 1996; Clinton-Gore, mem. State Adv. Com., 1996; at. del. Dem. Nat. Conv., 1996; mem. Hughes County Steering Com. to Re-Elect Senator Tom Daschle, 1997-98; dem. candidate S.D. at-large dist. U.S. Ho. of Rep., 1998; vol. leader, advisor, and state fair judge S.D. 4-H Program, 1981-94; bd. dirs. S.D. Rural Devel. Coun., 1993-95, S.D. State Adv. Com. for Green Thumb, Inc., 1993-95; mem. task force Nat. Urban Comparative Risk Environ., 1994, Common Cause S.D., 1991-94; dist. edn. dir. S.D. Farmers Union, 1988-93; dir. Minn. Union Coordinating Bd., U. Minn., 1982-84; bd. dirs. Golden Razor Hair Salon, Inc., Mpls., 1983-84, bd. dirs. Internat. Study & Travel Assn., Mpls., 1982-83; mem. Rose Hill Presbyn. Ch., Clan Campbell Soc. (N.Am.), E. River Sierra Club, Rocky Mountains/Hi Plains Group Sierra Club, S.D. AG Heritage Mus., S.D. Com. for World Food Day, S.D. Bread for the World, Dakota Rural Action, S.D. Project Prosperity Coalition, S.D. Farmers Union, S.D. Horticulture Soc., Dakota Rural Action, South Dakotans For the Arts, Wilson Ctr., Am. Mus. Nat. Hist., Smithsonian Assocs., Lib. Congress, Oscar Howe Art Ctr., Siouxland chpt. Alzheimer's Assn., S.D. Health Care Reform Coalition, S.D. Artists Network, S.D. Hist. Soc., Colo. Pub. Radio (donor), 9th Jud. Circuit Ct. Soc., Nat. Resource Defense Coun., Nat. Audubon Soc., Internat. 4-H Programs; host family Botswana Agr. Exch. Program, 1992; Presbytery of S.D., sec. Congl. Devel. Ministry, 1988-91, Advocacy Devel. Ministry unit, 1992-93, ch. camp dean, moderator Soc. Witness and Action Com., 1995-99, mem. com. representation, 1995-99, mem. com. Self-Devel. People, 1995-99; exec. Presbytery Search com., 1995-96, active Am. Heart Assn. Pierre Area Heart Walk, 1995, 97; vol. coord. Bread for the World Hunger Awareness event, Huron, 1993; mem. planning com. 1993 Regional 4-H Leaders Forum, Sioux Falls; past del. rep. S.D. Nat. 4-H Congress, 1981; past del. rep. Nat. Farmers Union Nat. conf., Presbyn. Ch. USA Gen. Assembly, Presbyn. Ch. USA Consultation on Sustainable Devel., 1995, Nat. 4-H Coun. Master Communicators Conf., Albuquerque, Presbyn. Ch. USA Synod Lakes and Prairies Workshop on Representation and Nominations, Rochester, Minn., 1997, Common Cause Nat. Leadership conf., Washington, 1993, Sharing Global Harvests Nat. Tng., Nat. Assn. Towns and Twps. Am.'s Town Meeting, Washington, 1992, strategic leadership for state execs. course Duke U., 1995, Inst. Pub. Fin. Northwestern U., 1997; bd. co-chair Huron Postal Customer Adv. Bd., 1993-95; bd. dirs. S.D. Peace and Justice Ctr., sec.-treas., 1994, v.p., 1995, dir. 1994-97; copywriter Minn. Ag. Manual, 1985; active Fed. Credit Union. Mem. Nat. Audubon Soc., S.D. Hort. Soc., Phi Beta Kappa, Omicron Delta Kappa, Mortar Bd., Golden Key. Democrat. Office: 11900 E Cornell Ave Aurora CO 80014-3194 also: PO Box 1682 Aurora CO 80040-1682

MOSER, KATHLEEN ANNE, systems analyst and data modeling educator, consultant; b. Sept. 18, 1957. BSc, DeVry Inst. Tech., Phoenix, 1985; MSc, Ariz. State U., 1989, PhD, 1991. Instr. Ariz. State U., Tempe, 1988-90; asst. prof. Iowa State U., Ames, 1991-98; assoc. prof. No. Ariz. U., Flagstaff, 1998—; cons. Heartland, Ft. Dodge, Iowa. Contbr. articles to profl. jours. Mem. Assn. Info. Sys., Decision Scis. Inst. Fax: 520-523-7331. E-mail: kam@nau.edu. Office: No Ariz U PO Box 15066 Flagstaff AZ 86011-0001

MOSER, MICHAEL JOSEPH, lawyer; b. N.Y.C., Aug. 31, 1950; s. Joseph Georg and Patricia Ann (Robertson) M.; m. Yvonne Yi-Feng Wei, Aug. 17, 1973; children: Yeone, Anna-Sieglinde, Christa Isolde. BSFS, Georgetown U., 1972; MA, Columbia U., 1974, PhD, 1981; JD, Harvard U., 1980. Bar: N.Y. 1981, D.C. 1989. Vis. scholar Academia Sinica, Taiwan, Republic of China, 1974-76; rsch. assoc. Kyoto Comparative Law Ctr., Doshisha U., Japan, 1978-79; assoc. Coudert Bros., Hong Kong, 1980-82, Peking, People's Republic of China, 1982-83; assoc. Baker and McKenzie, 1983-85; ptnr. Baker and McKenzie, Hong Kong, Beijing, 1985-99, Freshfields, Bruckhaus & Deringer, Hong Kong, 2000—; prof. law Peking U.; arbitrator Chinese Securities Regulatory Commn., Beijing. Author: Law and Social Change in a Chinese Community, 1982, Business Strategies in the People's Republic of China, 1986, (with others) China Tax Guide, 1987, 93, 99; editor: (book) Foreign Trade, Investment and the Law in the People's Republic of China, 1984, 87, China Business Law Guide, 1990, Foreigners Within the Gates: The Legations at Peking, 1993, Hong Kong and China Arbitration, 1994, International Arbitration in the People's Republic of China, 1995, 2000; bd. advisors World Arbitration and Mediation Report. V.p. Am. C. of C., Peking, 1983. Fellow Chartered Inst. Arbitrators London (arbitrator), Hong Kong Inst. Arbitrators Ltd. (arbitrator), Royal Geog. Soc.; mem. ABA, N.Y. State Bar Assn., D.C. Bar Assn., Internat. Bar Assn., Am. Bar Assn. (arbitrator), China Internat. Econ. and Trade Arbitration Commn. (Peking) (arbitrator), Hong Kong Internat. Arbitration Ctr. (arbitrator, governing coun., mgmt.), UN Working Group on Ofcl. Translation of Chinese Fgn. Investment Legislation, Hong Kong Arbitration Ordinance Review Com., China Securities Regulatory Com., Peking (arbitrator), Singapore Internat. Arbitration Ctr. (arbitrator), Australian Ctr. Internat. Commercial Arbitration (arbitrator), B.C. Internat. Comml. Arbitration Ctr. (arbitrator), The Indian Coun. Arbitration (arbitrator), WIPO Arbitration Ctr. (arbitrator), MCCI Permanent Ct. of Comml. Arbitration (arbitrator), Cairo Regional Ctr. for Internat. Comml. Arbitration (arbitrator), Royal Hong Kong Yacht Club, The Hong Kong Club, Aberdeen Marina Club, Harvard Club N.Y. Roman Catholic. Avocations: opera, poetry, sports. Office: Freshfields 12/F 2 Exch Sq, 8 Connaught Pl Central, Central Hong Kong also: Freshfields, 2 Dong San Huan Bei Lu, Chaoyang Beijing 100027, China

MOSER, ROYCE, JR., physician, medical educator; b. Versailles, Mo., Aug. 21, 1935; s. Royce and Russie Frances (Stringer) M.; m. Lois Anne Hunter, June 14, 1958; children: Beth Anne Moser McLean, Donald Royce. BA, Harvard U., 1957, MD, 1961; MPH, Harvard Sch. Pub. Health, Boston, 1965. Diplomate Am. Bd. Preventive Medicine (trustee 1989-98), Am. Bd. Family Practice. Commd. officer USAF, 1962, advanced through grades to col., 1974; resident in aerospace medicine USAF Sch. Aerospace Medicine, Brooks AFB, Tex., 1965-67; chief aerospace medicine Aerospace Def. Command, Colorado Springs, Colo., 1967-70; comdr. 35th USAF Dispensary Phan Rang, Vietnam, 1970-71; chief aerospace medicine br. USAF Sch. Aerospace Medicine, Brooks AFB, 1971-77; comdr. USAF Hosp., Tyndall AFB, Fla., 1977-79; chief clin. scis. div. USAF Sch. Aerospace Medicine, Brooks AFB, 1979-81, chief edn. div., 1981-83, sch. comdr., 1983-85; ret., 1985; prof. dept. family and preventive medicine U. Utah Sch. Medicine, Salt Lake City, 1985—, vice chmn. dept., 1985-95; dir. Rocky Mountain Ctr. for Occupl. and Environ. Health, Salt Lake City, 1987—; cons. in occupational, environ. and aerospace medicine, Salt Lake City, 1985—; presenter nat. and internat. med. meetings. Author: Effective Management of Occupational and Environmental Health and Safety Programs, 1992, 2d edit. 1999; contbr. book chpts. and articles to profl. jours. Mem., past pres. 1st Bapt. Ch. Found., Salt Lake City, 1987-89; mem., chmn. numerous univ. coms., Salt Lake City, 1985—; bd. dirs. Hanford Environ. Health Found., 1990-92; mem. preventive medicine residency rev. com. Accreditation Coun. Grad. Med. Edn., 1991-97; mem. ednl. adv. bd. USAF Human Sys. Ctr., 1991-96; chmn. long-range planning com. Am. Bd. Preventive Medicine, 1992-95. Decorated Legion of Merit (2); recipient Harriet Hardy award New England Coll. Occupl. and Environ. Medicine, 1998. Fellow Aerospace Med. Assn. (pres. 1989-90, chair fellows group 1994-97, Harry G. Mosely award 1981, Theodore C. Lyster award 1988), Am. Coll. Preventive Medicine (regent 1981-82), Am. Coll. Occupl. and Environ. Medicine (v.p. med. affairs 1995-97, Robert A. Kehoe award 1996), Am. Acad. Family Physicians; mem. Internat. Acad. Aviation and Space Medicine (selector 1989-94, chancellor 1994-98), Soc. of USAF Flight Surgeons (pres. 1978-79, George E. Schafer award 1982), Phi Beta Kappa. Avocations: photography, fishing. Home: 664 Aloha Rd Salt Lake City UT

84103-3329 Office: Rocky Mountain Ctr Occupl & Environ Health 75 S 2000 E Salt Lake City UT 84112-8930

MOSES, CLAIRE GOLDBERG, history educator; b. Hartford, Conn., June 22, 1941; d. Albraham Raymond and Pauline Horwich Goldberg; m. Arnold Moses, Sept. 11, 1966; children: Lisa Moses Leff, Leslie. AB, Smith Coll., 1963; MPhil, George Washington U., 1972, PhD, 1978. Prof. U. Md., College Park, 1977—. Author: French Feminism in the 19th Century, 1984, Feminism, Socialism & French Romanticism, 1993; editor: U.S. Women in Struggle, 1994. Named honoreé3 Women Legislators of the State Md., 1986. Mem. Am. Hist. Assn. (profl. divsn. 1997-98, program com. chair 2000, Joan Kelly Meml. prize 1985), Nat. Women's Studies Assn. (program adminstrs. adv. com. 1999-2000), Conf. Group for Women in History (pres. 1987-90), World Wide Orgn. for Women's Studies (exec. com. 1995-99), Soc. for French Hist. Studies, Phi Beta Kappa (pres. Gamma chpt. 1985-86). E-mail: cm45@umail.umd.edu. Office: Univ Md College Park MD 20742-0001

MOSES, ED, Olympic athlete; b. Burke, Va., June 7, 1980. Recipient Gold medal 4 x 100-meter medley (team) Sydney Olympics, 2000, Gold medal 100-meter backstroke Pan Am. Games, 1999; 3d pl. 100-meter breaststroke spring nats., 1998, 1st pl. 100-meter breaststroke summer nats., 1999. Office: USA Swimming 1 Olympic Plz Colorado Springs CO 80909-5746*

MOSES, HAMILTON, III, medical educator, hospital executive, management consultant; b. Chgo., Apr. 29, 1950; s. Hamilton Jr. and Betty Anne (Theurer) M.; m. Elizabeth Lawrence Hormel, 1977 (dec. 1988); m. Alexandra McCullough Gibson, 1992. BA in Psychology, U. Pa., 1972; MD, Rush Med. Coll., Chgo., 1975. Clk. Nat. Hosp. for Nervous Diseases, London, 1974; intern in medicine Johns Hopkins Hosp., Balt., 1976-77, resident in neurology, 1977-79, chief resident, 1979-80, assoc. prof. neurology, 1986-94, vice chmn. neurology and neurosurgery, 1980-88, v.p., 1988-94, dir. Parkinson's Ctr., 1984-94; dir. neurol. inst., prof. neurology and neurosurgery and mgmt. U. Va., Charlottesville, 1994-97; sr. advisor Boston Cons. Group, 1995—; prof. Darden Sch. Bus. U. Va., Charlottesville, 1994-98; mem. staff Mass. Gen. Hosp., Boston, 1997—; vis. prof. neurology and psychiatry Harvard U. Sch. Medicine, Boston, 1997-99; staff mem. Mass. Gen. Hosp., 1997—; prof. neurology and neurosurgery Johns Hopkins, Balt., 2000—; founder several tech. bus.'; sr. advisor Ptnrs. Healthcare, Boston; spl. advisor Nat. Health Svc., Eng., 1988-91. Editor, major author: Principles of Medicine, 1985-96; editor newsletter Johns Hopkins Health, 1988-94; contbr. numerous articles to med. jours. Mem. com. on med. ministries Episcopal Diocese Md., Balt., 1987; bd. dirs. Valleys Planning Ct.; trustee McLean Hosp., Belmont, Mass., 1997—. Fellow Am. Acad. Neurology (sec. 1989-91), Royal Soc. Medicine (U.K.) (overseas fellow 2000—); mem. Am. Neurol. Assn., Md. Neurol. Soc. (pres. 1984-86), Movement Disorders Soc., Md. Club, Green Spring Valley Hunt Club (Garrison, Md.). Republican. Avocations: landscape photography, sailing. Office: PO Box 150 North Garden VA 22959-0150 also: 4800 Hampden Ln Bethesda MD 20814-2930

MOSES, MIRIAM ISREAL, composer; b. N.Y.C., Aug. 11, 1950; d. hasday Yaakov Moché and Lena Eskenazi. BA, Hunter Coll., 1993; MBA, So. Calif. U., 1993. Sales rep. Merrill Lynch, N.Y.C., 1972-73; consumer mktg. rep. The New York Times, N.Y.C., 1973-80; mktg. cons. Seattle, 1980-86; composer/lyricist Rising Phoenix Inc., Seattle, 1986—; pub. works investigator Rebound, Seattle Bldg. and Constrn. Trades Coun., 1988-89; indsl. statistician, program mgr. State of Wash. Dept. Labor and Industries, Seattle, 1989-93; hearing examiner City of Seattle, 1993-96. Author: (poetry) Arabesque, 1996, (novella) Survivors and Pieces of Glass, 2000; author, composer, lyricist (mus. revue) Intimate Friends, 1986, (musical play) Reflections, 1972. Mem. Am. Arbitration Assn., The Dramatist Guild, The Authors League, African-Am. Jewish Coalition for Justice, Seattle Mgmt. Assn. Office: City of Seattle Civil Svc Commn 700 3d Ave Ste #360 Seattle WA 98122

MOSETTI, ANDY CHRIS, communications executive; b. Zurich, Switzerland, June 22, 1970; s. Giuseppe and Hildegard (Muller) M. Diploma, Zurich Bus. Sch., 1989. Clk. Bank Sparhaen, Zurich, 1986-88; travel cons. Northwest Airlines, Zurich, 1988-91, acct. mgr., 1991-93; country mgr. Worldspan, Zurich, 1993—; radio host, DJ Radio Z, Zurich, 1984-96; editor, prodr. Night Bird radio spl., 1984-96; editor, host Pink Elephant TV lifestyle show, 1994-97. Avocations: travel, telecommunications, networking, computer, Internet. Home: Gloriastreet 58, CH-8044 Zurich Switzerland

MOSETTIG, MICHAEL DAVID, television producer, writer; b. Washington, July 21, 1942; s. Erich and Ann (Nelson) M.; m. Anne L. Groer. Student, Ind. U., 1960-61; BA in Polit. Sci., George Washington U., 1964; MA in European History, Georgetown U., 1968. Reporter Leslie E. Carpenter News Bur., Washington, 1961-65, Newhouse Nat. News Svc., Washington, 1965-69, UPI, London and Brussels, 1969-70; editor, reporter Nat. Jour., Washington, 1970-71; producer NBC News, Washington and N.Y.C., 1971-79; assoc. Grad. Sch. Journalism Columbia U., N.Y.C., 1979-83; prodr. MacNeil/Lehrer News Hour, 1983-85, sr. prodr. fgn. affairs and def., 1985-95; sr. prodr. fgn. affairs and def. News Hour with Jim Lehrer, 1995—; mem. Internat. Inst. for Strategic Studies, London, Coun. Fgn. Rels., N.Y. Author: DeGaulle and His Anglo-Saxon Allies, 1968, (with Ronald Müller) Revitalizing America, 1980. With USCGR, 1966-68, USNR, 1968-78. Herman Lowe Meml. scholar Washington chpt. Sigma Delta Chi; Joan Barone award Radio-TV Corrs. Assn., Nat. Emmy award, 1997. Mem. Overseas Writers, Cosmos Club. Home: 3340 Northampton St NW Washington DC 20015-1653

MOSHMAN, DAVID STEWART, educational psychology educator; b. Bklyn., May 9, 1951; s. Howard and Ruth (Silver) M.; m. Sara Anderson, Sept. 26, 1987; children: Eric Schroeder, Michael. BA, Lehigh U., 1971; PhD, Rutgers U., 1977. Asst. prof. ednl. psychology U. Nebr., Lincoln, 1977-82, assoc. prof., 1982-89, prof., 1989—, chmn. ednl. psychology dept., 1994-97; mem. exec. com. Acad. Freedom Coalition Nebr., 1988—, pres., 1993. Author: Developmental Psychology, 1987, Children, Education and the First Amendment, 1989, Adolescent Psychological Development, 1999; editor: (book) Children's Intellectual Rights, 1986; mem. editl. bd. Devel. Rev. Jour. 1996—. Bd. dirs. ACLU Nebr., 1982—, pres., 1987-89, 93-95. Mem. APA, Soc. Rsch. Child Devel., Soc. Rsch. Adolescence, Jean Piaget Soc. (bd. dirs. 1995-99, v.p. 1998-99). Democrat. Home: 1901 Pepper Ave Lincoln NE 68502-3044 Office: U Nebr Dept Ednl Psychology Lincoln NE 68588-0345

MOSISILI, PAKALITHA, prime minister of Lesotho. Min. edn. and tng., sports culture and youth affairs Govt. of Lesotho, 1993-95, dep. prime min., min. home affairs, local govt., rural and urban devel., 1995-98, prime min., min. def., 1998—. Office: Office of Prime Min, PO Box 527, Maseru 100, Lesotho*

MOSK, RICHARD MITCHELL, lawyer; b. L.A., May 18, 1939; s. Stanley and Edna M.; m. Sandra Lee Budnitz, Mar. 21, 1964; children: Julie, Matthew. AB with great distinction, Stanford U., 1960; JD cum laude, Harvard U., 1963. Bar: Calif. 1964, U.S. Supreme Ct. 1970, U.S. Ct. Mil. Appeals 1970, U.S. Dist. Ct. (no., so., ea., and cen. dists.) Calif 1964, U.S. Ct. Appeals (9th dist.) 1964. Staff Pres.'s Commn. on Assassination Pres. Kennedy, 1964; rsch. clk. Calif. Supreme Ct., 1964-65; ptnr. Mitchell, Silberberg & Knupp, L.A., 1965-87; prin. Sanders, Barnet, Goldman, Simons & Mosk, PC, L.A., 1987-2000; spl. dep. Fed. Pub. Defender, L.A., 1975-76; instr. U. So. Calif. Law Sch., 1978; judge Iran-U.S. Claims Tribunal, 1981-84, 97—, substitute arbitrator, 1984-97; mem. L.A. County Jud. Procedures Commn., 1973-82, chmn., 1978; co-chmn. Motion Picture Assn. Classification and Rating Adminstrn., 1994-2000; mem. panel Ct. Arbitration for Sport-Geneva. Contbr. articles to profl. jours. Mem. L.A. City-County Inquiry on Brush Fires, 1970; bd. dirs. Calif. Mus. Sci. and Industry, 1979-82, Vista Del Mar Child Ctr., 1979-82; trustee L.A. County Law Libr., 1985-86; bd. govs. Town Hall Calif., 1986-91; mem. Christopher Commn. on L.A. Police Dept., 1991; mem. Stanford U. Athletic Bd., 1991-95. With USNR, 1964-75. Hon. Woodrow Wilson fellow, 1960; recipient Roscoe Pound prize, 1961. Fellow Am. Bar Found.; mem. ABA (coun. internat. law sect. 1986-90), FBA (pres. L.A. chpt. 1972), L.A. County Bar Assn., Beverly Hills Bar Assn., Internat. Bar Assn., Am. Arbitration Assn. (comml. panel, large complex case panel, Asia/Pacific panel), Hong Kong Internat. Arbitration Ctr. (mem. panel 1986—), Am. Film Mktg. Assn. (arbitration panel), B.C. Internat. Arbitration Ctr. (mem. panel), World Intellectual Property Orgn. (mem. arbitration panel), Ctr. Pub. Resources (mem. arbitration panel), Ct. Arbitration Sport-Gengua (mem. arbitration panel), Phi Beta Kappa. Office: Sanders Barnet Goldman Simons & Mosk PC Ste 850 1901 Avenue Of The Stars Los Angeles CA 90067-6078

MOSK, STANLEY, state supreme court justice; b. San Antonio, TX, Sept. 4, 1912; s. Paul and Minna (Perl) M.; m. Edna Mitchell, Sept. 27, 1937 (dec.); 1 child, Richard Mitchell; m. Susan Hines, Aug. 27, 1982 (div.); m. Kaygey Kash, Jan. 15, 1995. Student, U. Tex., 1931; PhB, U. Chgo., 1933; postgrad., U. Chgo. Law Sch., 1934; JD, Southwestern U., 1935; postgrad., The Hague Acad. Internat. Law, 1970, U. Pacific, 1970; LLD, U. San Diego, 1971, U. Santa Clara, 1976, Calif. Western U., 1984, Whittier Coll. Law, 1993, Pepperdine U., 1995, Western State U., San Diego, 1995. Bar: Calif. 1935, U.S. Supreme Ct. 1956. Practiced in Los Angeles, until 1939; exec. sec. to gov. Calif., 1939-42; judge Superior Ct. Los Angeles County, 1943-58; pro tem justice Dist. Ct. Appeal, Calif., 1954; atty. gen. Calif., also head state dept., justice, 1959-64; justice Supreme Ct. Calif., 1964—; mem. Jud. Coun. Calif., 1973-75, Internat. Commn. Jurists. Author: Democracy in America-Day by Day, 1995. Chmn. San Francisco Internat. Film Festival, 1967; mem. Dem. Nat. Com, Calif., 1960-64; mem. bd. regents U. Calif., 1940; pres. Vista Del Mar Child Care Svc., 1954-58; bd. dirs. San Francisco Law Sch., 1971-73, San Francisco Regional Cancer Found., 1980-83. With AUS, WWII. Recipient Disting. Alumnus award U. Chgo., 1958, 93. Mem. ABA, Nat. Assn. Attys. Gen. (exec. bd. 1964), Western Assn. Attys. Gen. (pres. 1963), L.A. Bar Assn., San Francisco Bar Assn., Am. Legion, Manuscript Soc., Calif. Hist. Soc., Am. Judicature Soc., Inst. Jud. Adminstrn., U. Chgo. Alumni Assn. No. Calif. (pres. 1957-58, 67), Order of Coif (hon.), B'nai B'rith, Hillcrest Country Club (L.A.), Commonwealth Club, Beverly Hills Tennis Club. Office: Supreme Ct Calif 350 Mcallister St San Francisco CA 94102-4712

MOSKAL, ANTHONY JOHN, former dean, professor, management and education consultant; b. South Amboy, N.J., May 31, 1946; s. Anthony Joseph and Jennie (Salamon) M.; m. Kathryn Jean Coakley, July 8, 1978; 1 child, Nicole Elizabeth. AB, Villanova (Pa.) U., 1968, MA, 1972; MEd, Ga. State U., 1974; PhD, Columbia Pacific U., San Rafael, Calif., 1987. Prin. instr. U.S. Army, Ft. Benning, Ga., 1969-71; research mgr. Blue Cross and Blue Shield, Columbus, Ga., 1972-74; sales rep. J.C. Penney Co., Parlin, N.J., 1974-76; dean of students Alliance Coll., Cambridge Springs, Pa., 1976-77; tchr. Sayreville (N.J.) pub. schs., 1977-79; county 4-H agt. Rutgers U., New Brunswick, 1979-86; pres. Eagle Assocs., South Amboy, N.J., 1985—; adj. faculty Georgian Ct. Coll., Lakewood, N.J., 1987—, U.S. Army Command and Gen. Staff Coll., Ft. Leavenworth, Kans., 1989—, Nat. Def. U., Washington, 1991; cons. dir. Union County Ednl. Svcs. Commn., 2000—; cons. in mgmt., leadership, edn., volunteerism, youth programs, career planning; spl. liason to Mcpl. Bd. Edn., Sayreville, 1991-95; area admissions rep. U.S. Mil. Acad., 1984-91; cons. dir. Union County Ednl. Svcs. Commn., 2000—. Contbr. articles to profl. jours. Mem. Boy Scouts Am.; dir. religious edn. Sacred Heart Parish, South Amboy, N.J., 1988-91; counselor, mem. dist. com. Ctrl. N.J. Coun. Boy Scouts Am., 1982—; pres., bd. dirs. Vol. Action Ctr., Middlesex County, N.J., 1979-87; pres. Sayreville (N.J.) War Meml. H.S. Band Parents Assn., 1994-96; county committeeman, Middlesex County, N.J., 1990-94. With U.S. Army, 1969-71, 90-92, lt. col. USAR. Decorated Meritorious Svc. medal, Army Commendation medal (2), Mil. Outstanding Vol. Svc. medal; recipient Order of the Arrow award Boy Scouts Am., 1960, 20th Century award of Achievement, Nat. Assn. Chiefs of Police, Desert Shield/Desert Storm medal State of N.J., Disting. Svc. medal State of N.J.; United Way of Ctrl. Jersey grantee, 1984, others. Mem. ASCD, Nat. Infantry Assn., Nat. Eagle Scout Assn., N.J. Assn. 4-H Agts. (pres. 1985-86, outstanding svc. citation 1981, 87), Nat. Assn. Extension 4-H Agts. (regional contact 1981-83, cert. appreciation 1983), Am. Fedn. Police (award of merit 1989, legion of honor 1990, St. Michael the Archangel award 1992, patriotism award 1993, J. Edgar Hoover meml. medal 1991), Res. Officers Assn., Mil. Police Regtl. Assn., U.S. Army Officer Candidate Alumni Assn., Vietnam Vets. of Am. (life, recording sec., honor guard), Holy Name Soc., Kiwanis, K. of C. (officer, youth dir., vol. coord. fife and drums corps, Knight of the Month, 4th degree color corps, Family of the Month), Am. Legion, U.S. Army Officer Candidate Alumni, Nat. Infantry Assn. (life), Alpha Phi Omega, Epsilon Sigma Phi, Pi Gamma Mu. Republican. Roman Catholic. Avocations: reading, music, recreational camping, travel, woodworking. Office: Eagle Assocs 166 Luke St South Amboy NJ 08879-2231

MOSKALENKO, IGOR VLADIMIROVICH, physicist, astrophysicist; b. Moscow, May 4, 1962; s. Vladimir Anatolievich and Galina Petrovna (Kuznetsova) M.; m. Irina Viktorovna Surikova, July 12, 1984 (div. May 1992); 1 child, Maria; m. Irina Vladimirovna Malkova, June 10, 1994. MS, M.V. Lomonosov Moscow State U., 1985, PhD in Physics, 1990. Guest scientist U. Łodz (Poland) Inst. Physics, 1990-91; rschr. Moscow State U. Inst. Nuc. Physics, 1991-93, sr. scientist, 1993—; sr. rsch. assoc. Lab. for High Energy Astrophysics NASA/Goddard Space Flight Ctr., Greenbelt, Md., 1999—; guest scientist Ctr. d'Etude Spatiale des Rayonnements, CRNS, Toulouse, France, 1994-95, Max-Planck-Inst. für Extraterrestrische Physik, Garching, Germany, 1996-99. Contbr. numerous articles to profl. jours. and conf. procs. Grantee Am. Astron. Soc., 1992, Am. Phys. Soc., 1992, Soros Found., Moscow, 1993; Max Planck fellowship Max Planck Soc., 1996-99; sr. associateship Nat. Rsch. Coun./Nat. Acad. Scis., 1999—. Mem. N.Y. Acad. Scis., Russian Astron. Soc. Russian Orthodox. Avocations: tennis, skiing, swimming, travel. Home: 21 Parkway Apt F Greenbelt MD 20770-1866 Office: Lab for High Energy Astrophysics NASA/Goddard Space Flight Ctr Code 660 Ctr Greenbelt MD 20771-0001

MOSKALENKO, YURI EUGENIJ, human physiologist; b. Leningrad, June 28, 1932; s. Eugenij Alexander and Yanina Stanislaw (Radzikovskaja) M.; m. Kiza Michael Warshauskaja, Oct. 11, 1956 (wid. 1981); m. Anna Nicolaj Markovetz, Dec. 25, 1982; 1 child, Alexander. PhD, Pavlov Physiol. Inst., Leningrad, 1962; DS, Inst. Med. Biology Problems, Moscow, 1969. Jr. rsch. worker Inst. Evolutionary Physiology/USSR Acad. Scis., Leningrad, 1957-62, head of lab., 1962-82, head of dept., 1982-91; head of dept. Inst. Evolutionary Physiology/Russian Acad. Scis., St. Petersburg, 1991—. Author: CBF Under Space Conditions, 1957, Biophysical Aspects of Cerebral Circulation, 1980, Cerebral Circulation: Physical and Chemical Principles of the Study, 1989, others. Dep. chmn. Problem Commn. of Russian Acad. Scis., 1975-89, supr. spl. commn. of multidisciplinary cerebral blood flow studies, 1980-95. Recipient three government medals, 1970, 77, 83; named Hon. Scientist of Russian Fedn., 1998, Academician of Internat. Astronautics Acad., 1985. Avocations: classical music, bicycling. Home: Svetlanovsky prosp 19, Apt 13, 194223 Saint Petersburg Russia Office: Inst Evolutionary Phys, Russian Acad Scis, 194223 Saint Petersburg Russia

MOSKOS, CHARLES C., sociology educator; b. Chgo., May 20, 1934; s. Charles and Rita (Shukas) M.; m. Ilca Hohn, July 3, 1966; children—Andrew, Peter. BA cum laude, Princeton, 1956; MA, UCLA, 1961, PhD, 1963; LHD (hon.), Norwich U., 1992. Asst. prof. U. Mich., Ann Arbor, 1964-66; assoc. prof. sociology Northwestern U., Evanston, Ill., 1966-70, prof., 1970—; fellow Progressive Policy Inst., 1992—; mem. Presdl. Commn. on Women in the Mil., 1992. Author: The Sociology of Political Independence, 1967, The American Enlisted Man, 1970, Public Opinion and the Military Establishment, 1971, Peace Soldiers, 1976, Fuerzas Armadas y Sociedad, 1984, The Military--More Than Just A Job?, 1988, A Call to Civil Service, 1988, Greek Americans, 1989, Soldiers and Sociology, 1989, New Directions in Greek American Studies, 1991, The New Conscientious Objection, 1993, All That We Can Be, 1996, Reporting War When There Is No War, 1996, The Media and the Military, 2000, The Postmodern Military, 2000. Mem. bd. advisors Dem. Leadership Coun., 1989—; chmn. Theodore Saloutos Meml. Fund; mem. Archdiocesean Commn. Third Millenium, 1982-88; mem adv. bd. Vets. for Am., 1997—; mem. Congl. Commn. on Mil. Tng. and Gender-Related Issues, 1998-99, Nat. Security Study Group, 1998—. Served with AUS, 1956-58. Decorated D.S.M., Fondation pour les Etudes de Def. Nat. (France), S.M.K. (The Netherlands); named to Marshall rsch. chair ARI, 1987-88, 95-96; Ford. Found. faculty fellow, 1969-70; fellow Wilson Ctr., 1980-81, guest scholar, 1991; fellow Rockefeller Found. Humanities, 1983-84, Guggenheim fellow, 1992-93, fellow Annenberg Washington Program, 1995; grantee 20th Century Fund, 1983-87, 92-94, Ford Found., 1989-90; recipient Nat. Educator Leadership award Todd Found., 1997, Book award Washington Monthly, 1997, Honored Patriot award Selective Svc. Sys., 1998. Mem. Am. Sociol. Assn., Internat. Sociol. Assn. (pres. rsch. com. on armed forces and conflict resolution 1982-86), Am. Polit. Sci. Assn., Inter-Univ. Seminar on Armed Forces and Soc. (chmn. 1987-99), Am. Acad. Arts and Scis. Greek Orthodox. Home: 2440 Asbury Ave Evanston IL 60201-2307

MOSKOVITZ, JIM, radio, television and film producer, writer; b. L.A., Aug. 14, 1958; s. Mayer and Charlotte (Creamer) M.; m. Joyce Ferro, Nov. 25, 1989. BA in Pol. Sci., Stanford U., 1980. Pres. JMJ Films, Inc., N.Y.C., 1991—, JJMI, Inc., N.Y.C., 1985—, Marathon Sports Group, Inc., 1998—; writer/prodr. Pat Summerall's Sports in Am., N.Y.C., 1990-97, Instant Replay with R. MacLean, Toronto, 1992-97, Dr. Ferdie Pacheco Network Radio, N.Y.C., 1997—, McCarver One on One with Talking Sports with Tim McCarver, 1998—; prodr. The Boys of Summer, N.Y.C., 1994—. Author: Pat Summerall's Sports in America, 1997; writer, dir., prodr. (television special) Grand Slam!, 1989. Recipient Sports Video of Yr. award Video Magazine, N.Y.C., 1989, Video Review, N.Y.C., 1990, silver medal Internat. Radio Awards, N.Y.C., 1996; named finalist Internat. Radio Awards, N.Y.C., 1994. Mem. Nat. Assn. Radio Talk Show Hosts, Writers Guild Am., Assn., Composers, Authors, Producers, Stanford Alumni Assn. Avocations: baseball, history, politics. Fax: 212-724-7712. Office: JJMI Inc 11 W 84th St Apt 4 New York NY 10024-4761

MOSKOWITZ, ESTELLE WITZLING, freelance writer, retired clinical psychologist, editor. B, Hunter Coll.; M, Columbia U.; D, NYU. Tchr. N.Y.C. Bd. Edn., chmn. English dept., examiner, supr. speech vocat. h.s. divsn.; instr. NYU; chief dept. psychology United Cerebral Palsy Miami; psychologist Jackson Meml. Hosp., U. Miami (Fla.) Med. Coll., N.Y. Med. Coll., Flower Fifth Ave. Hosp.; pvt. practice, ret.; radio cons., Miami. Editor-in-chief Phoenix Forever; founder, co-editor Connections Elderly at Home, Phoenix Stay-At-Home Elders; contbg. editor, cons. Mother's Manual; contbr. articles to profl. jours. Bd. examiners N.Y.C. Bd. Edn. Named Outstanding Older Am. Elders divsn. HRS, 1988; May 6-May 12 proclaimed Dr. Estelle Witzling-Moskowitz Week, 1990; recipient Super Sr. award Fla. Coun. Aging, 1994; elected to Hall of Fame Hunter Coll. Alumni Assn., 1999. Home: 2121 N Bayshore Dr Miami FL 33137-5123

MOSKOWITZ, KARLA, lawyer, judge; b. N.Y.C., June 8, 1941. BA cum laude, Alfred U., 1963; JD, Columbia U., 1966. Bar: N.Y. 1966. Atty. N.Y. State Atty. Gen.'s Office, N.Y.C., 1966-70; assoc. counsel N.Y.C. Human Resources Adminstrn., 1970-74, N.Y. Health and Hosp. Corp., N.Y.C., 1974-75; of counsel Moskowitz and Moll, N.Y.C., 1975-80; adminstrv. law judge N.Y. State Dept. Health, N.Y.C., 1978-81; judge Civil Ct. City N.Y., 1982-91, acting justice Supreme Ct. Civil Term, 1986-91, justice Supreme Ct., 1992—. Pres. Judges and Lawyers Breast Cancer Alert, 1995-97; co.-pres. Supreme Ct. N.Y. County Civil Term Anti-Bias com., 1992-95; mem. State Ct. Civil Law Curriculum Devel. com., 1998—. Mem. Nat. Assn. Women Judges (dir. dist. 2 1990-91, 95-97, treas. 1999, vice pres. 2000), N.Y. State Assn. Women Judges (pres. 1997-99), N.Y. County Lawyers Assn. (Supreme Ct. com., 1997-99), Assn. of Bar of City of N.Y. (med. malpractice com.), Women's Bar Assn. N.Y. State (bd. dirs. 1988-90), N.Y. Women's Bar Assn. (pres. 1981, adv. coun.), Met. Women's Bar Assn. (bd. dirs.), Women's City Club. Office: Supreme Ct City NY Civil Term 60 Centre St New York NY 10007-1402

MOSKOWITZ, MICHAEL ARTHUR, neuroscientist, neurologist; b. N.Y.C., May 26, 1942; s. Irving Lawrence and Clara (Dranoff) M.; m. Mary Henderson, May 18, 1991; 1 child, Jenna Rachel. AB, Johns Hopkins U., 1964; MD, Tufts U., 1968; MSc (hon.), Harvard U., 1992. Diplomate Am. Bd. Psychiaty and Neurology, Am. Bd. Internal Medicine. Intern Yale U. Dept. Medicine, 1968-69, resident, 1969-71; resident in neurology Peter Bent Brigham Children Hosp., 1971-74; asst. prof. Med. Sch., Harvard U., Boston, 1975-79, assoc. prof., 1979-92; prof. divsn. health sci. and tech. Harvard-MIT, Boston, 1992—; established investigator Am. Heart Assn., 1980-85; neurophysiologist and assoc. neurologist Mass. Gen. Hosp., Boston, 1981—; H.J. Barnett lectr. Canadian Heart Assn., Queens U., Kingston, Ont., 1993—, Witter lectr. U. Calif., San Francisco, 1994—, Barraquer-LaFora lectr. Spanish Neurol. Soc., Barcelona, Spain, 1994—, Decade of the Brain lectr. Am. Acad. Neurology, 1995, Briggs lecture dept. pharmacology U. Tex., San Antonio, 1995, Richardson lectr. Canadian Neurol. Assn., 1998, John Graham lectr. Am. Assn. Study Headache; chmn. sci. adv. bd. Max Plank Inst., KÖn; program project dir. stroke and migraine NIH program projects, NIH rev. study sect. mem. 1982-85, 88-91, 97—; 2nd internat. hon. lectureship European Stroke Conf., 1997; cons. pharm. industry; chmn. sci. adv. bd. Max Planck Inst., U. of Ottawa, Can., Queen's Neuroscience Inst.; scientific adv. bd. Queen's Med. Ctr., Honolulu, U. Ottawa. Editl. bd. Stroke, Acta Neurol. Scandinavica Cephalalgia, Jour. Cerebral Blood Flow & Metabolism, Cerebrovascular Disease; editor: Animal Models of Headache, 1996; basic sci. editor Stroke (AHA jour.); contbr. numerous articles to profl. jours; patentee in field. MIT postdoctoral fellow, 1974-76, Alfred Sloan Found. fellow, 1978-80; recipient Enrico Greppi award Italian Neurology Soc., 1986, 88, Tchr.-Investigator award Nat. Inst. Neurol. Disease and Stroke, 1975-80, Zülch prize Max-Planck Soc./Inst., 1996, John Graham award AASH, 1998; rsch. grantee Bristol-Myers Squibb, 1993—, MGH Interdepartmental Stroke Ctr. Mem. Am. Heart Assn. (nat. rsch. com. 1991-96, exec. com. stroke coun. 1991-96), Am. Neurol. Assn., Am. Heart and Stroke Assn. (program com.), Am. Acad. Neurology, Am. Pain Soc., Soc. Neurosci., Internat. Soc. for Cerebral Blood Flow and Metabolism (bd. dirs.), Internat. Symposium Pharm. of Cerebral Ischemia, Can. Neurol. Soc. (hon.). Achievements include research in neuroscientific, neurology literature including stroke and migraine. Office: Mass Gen Hosp Charleston Navy Yard 149 13th St Charlestown MA 02129-2020

MOSKVITIN, VLADIMIR IVANOVICH, physical-chemical science educator; b. Moscow, Mar. 23, 1937; s. Ivan Nikolayevich and Evdokiya Prokhorovna (Bolshakova) M.; m. Emilia Andreevna Ershova, Jan. 30, 1963; 1 daughter. B in Engring., Moscow Inst. Metals & Gold, 1959; PhD, Inst. Rare Metals, Moscow, 1968. Engr. Inst. Rare Metals (GIREDMET), Moscow, 1960-61, scientific collaborator, 1962-70; asst. prof. Moscow Inst. Steel and Alloys, 1970-72, assoc. prof., 1972-94, prof., 1994—. Author: (textbook) Theory and Technology of the Electrometallurgical Processes, 1994, Metallurgy of Light Metals, 1997; chief cons. ednl. film The Electrochemical Production of Aluminum, 1979. Avocations: sports, travel. Home: Frunzenskaya Nab 50-587, 119270 Moscow Russia Office: Moscow Steel & Alloys Inst, Leninskiy pro 4, 117936 Moscow Russia

MOSLER, JOHN, retired financial planner; b. N.Y.C., Sept. 24, 1922; s. Edwin H. and Irma M.; children: Bruce Elliot, John Edwin, Michele Andree. Student, Philips Exeter Acad., 1938-41, Princeton U., 1941-43; L.H.D., Fordham U., 1965; D.C.S., Duquesne U., 1968. With Mosler Safe Co., 1945-67, exec. v.p., 1948-61, pres., 1961-66, chmn., 1966-67; pres., dir. Mosler Lock Co., 1953-67, Mosler de Mexico S.A., 1953-67; exec. v.p., dir. Mosler Research Products, Inc., 1956-67; dir. 1st Caribbean Mainland Capital Co., Inc., 1962-68, chmn. bd., 1963-68, pres., 1966-68; v.p., dir. Am. Standard Inc., 1967-68; chmn. bd., dir., chief exec. officer Holmes Protection, Inc., 1968-73, Holmes Protection Services Corp., 1968-73; chmn. bd. Hidromex, S.A. de C.V., Mex., 1968—, Mosler N.V., Europe, 1973—; chmn. bd. Internat. Controls Corp., 1973-87, resigned, 1987; past chmn. bd. Royal Bus. Funds Inc.; pres. Mosler Investments. Mem. Mayor's Com. on Judiciary; pres. Am.-Romanian Flood Relief Com.; past dir. Jr. Achievement N.Y.; spl. U.S. amb. to Mauritius, to Zambia's Indpendence ceremony; vice chmn. N.Y. Rep. County Com.; chmn. John Mosler Found.; trustee, dir. Nat. Urban League; trustee Appeal of Conscience Found., Linden Hall Sch. for Girls, Lititz, Pa.; hon. trustee, past pres. N.Y. Urban League; founder Harlem Prep. Sch. With CIC, AUS, 1943-46. Decorated knight comdr. Ordo Supremus Militaris A. Lilio Regni Navarrae; Sovereign Order Hospitallers St. John of Jerusalem, Knights of Malta; comdt. L'Ordre Senegal; recipient Man of Conscience award Appeal of Conscience Found., 1969. Mem. Young Pres.'s Orgn. (past pres.), U.S. C. of C., N.Y. World Bus. Coun., Bankers of Mex. Club (Mex.)., Princeton U. (N.Y.), Confrerie des Chevaliers du Tastevin, Manhattan, Real Nautico de Barcelona (Spain), Sag Harbor Yacht, Univ. Club, Wall St. Club. *

MOSLEY, DAVID P., school system administrator; b. Decatur, Tex., Apr. 16, 1951; s. Glenn Owen and Rosa Lee M.; m. Cheryl Anne, July 29, 1977; children: Scott, Bart, Lindsey. BS in Edn., U. North Tex., MEd. Tchr.

Decatur Ind. Sch. Dist., 1975-86; asst. prin. Decatur Mid. Sch., 1986-88; prin. Decatur Intermediate Sch., 1988-90, Decatur Mid. Sch., 1990-99; dir. personnel/maintenance Decatur Ind. Sch. Dist., 1999—. Mem. Tex. Assn. Personnel Dirs., Decatur C. of C. (bd. dirs. 1988-91). Baptist. Avocations: woodworking, golf, reading, travel. Office: Decatur ISD 501 E Collins St Decatur TX 76234-2360

MOSLEY, DEREK JOHN, classicist, retired educator; b. Kingston-upon-Hill, Eng., Nov. 11, 1934; s. Frederick and Louisa Ellen (Wallis) M.; m. Margot Firth, Dec. 29, 1962; children: Karen Angela, Nicole Andrea. BA, Durham (Eng.) U., 1956, Cambridge (Eng.) U., 1959; MA, PhD, Cambridge (Eng.) U., 1965. Lectr. Sheffield (Eng.) U., 1959-68, sr. lectr., 1968-75, prof., 1975-88, dep. dean, dean of arts, 1985-88; prof., now emeritus Warwick U., Coventry, Eng., 1988—; vis. lectr. U. Mich., Ann Arbor, 1965-66; mem. exam. coun. Matriculation Bd., Manchester, Eng., 1974-87; sch. gov. Leicester County (Eng.) Coun., 1995—. Co-author: Diplomacy in Ancient Greece, 1975, Antike Diplomatie, 1979; editl. advisor (book) A History of Ancient Greece, 1966. Mem. Parish Coun., Burbage, Eng., 1991-95, chmn. planning, 1994-95; exec. Conservative Assn., Bosworth, Eng., 1995—. Mem. Assn. Univ. Tchrs. (pres. 1980-82), Ernst Kirsten Assn. (mem. editl. bd. 1990—), Hinckley Philatelic Soc. (chmn. 1994-95), Vancouver Island Classical Assn., Friends Royal B.C. Mus. Avocations: hiking, music, travel, philately, local politics.

MOSLEY, SHELLEY ELIZABETH, library administrator; b. Baxter Springs, Kans., Sept. 8, 1950; d. Billy Ralph and Jennie Naomi Burrell; m. David Ray Mosley, Mar. 26, 1971; children: Andrew Scott, Jessica Rae. BS in Edn., Grand Canyon U., 1971; MLS, U. Ariz., 1977. Instr. Grad. Libr. Sch. U. Ariz., Tucson, 1976-78, 92; sch. libr. Tucson Unified, 1977-78, Glendale (Ariz.) Elem. Sch., 1978-79; libr. Glendale Pub. Libr., 1979-85, libr. mgr., 1985—. Author: Talk About Love, 1999, It's in His Kiss, 1999, One Starry Night, 2000, My Favorite Flavor, 2000; columnist Glendale Star, 1999—; tech. editor: Selecting Library Furniture, 1989; contbr. articles to profl. jours. including Libr. Jour., Wilson Libr. Bull., Romance Writer's Report. Chair benchmarking team City of Glendale, 1993-95, co-chair diversity task force, 1999—, mem. diversity task force, 1996—, visionary Magnetic Mile Project, 1990; co-founder Show Them a Better Way, Glendale, 1993-95; bd. dirs. Mayor's Alliance for Youth, Glendale, 1994—; adult participant Youth Town Hall, Glendale, 1994—; mem. gifted edn. task force Glendale Elem. Schs., 1991-93, mem. textbook adoption com., 1989; soprano First United Meth. Ch., 1997—; mem. Friends of the Glendale Libr., 1985—. Mem. Ariz. State Libr. Assn. (conf. co-chair 1988, sec.-treas. pub. libr. divsn. 1980—), Maricopa Assn. Govts. (prevention/intervention task force 1996—), Romance Writers Am. (program chair Valley of the Sun chpt. 1998—), Soc. Children's Book Writers and Illustrators, Alpha Lambda Delta, Alpha Chi Omega, Beta Phi Mu. Democrat. Methodist. Avocations: writing lyrics, writing limericks, playing the piano, singing, reading. Home: 8619 N 53rd Dr Glendale AZ 85302-4847 Office: Velma Teague Libr 7010 N 58th Ave Glendale AZ 85301-2425

MOSLI, HISHAM AHMED, urologist; b. Makkah, Saudi Arabia, Mar. 6, 1954; s. Ahmed Mohammed and Nazek Abdullah M.; m. Faten Salah Gazzaz, May 5, 1978; children: Hala, Mahmoud, Mohammed, Yasmin, Rana, Rayan. MBBCh, Cairo U., 1977; FRCS, Ottawa U., 1983. Diplomate Am. Bd. Urology. Demonstrator King Abdulaziz U., Jeddah, Saudi Arabia, 1979-86, asst. prof., 1986-92, assoc. prof., 1992-97, prof., 1997—, chmn. dept., 1997—. Fellow Royal Coll Phys. and Surgeons of Can.; mem. Am. Urol. Assn., European Soc. Urology, Brit. Urology Soc. Office: King Abdulaziz Univ Hosp, PO Box 6615, 21452 Jeddah Saudi Arabia

MOSOLOLI, THAGO FELIX, accountant; b. Johannesburg, South Africa, Sept. 12, 1969; s. Mothuoa Joel and Masingoaneng Ceasarine (Mothibeu) M. B Commerce, Western Cape U., South Africa, 1989, postgrad. degree in acctg. with honors, 1990. Chartered acct., South Africa. Acct. KPMG, Johannesburg, 1991-94, mgr., 1995; pvt. practice cons. South Africa, 1996; ptnr. Gobodo Inc., Johannesburg, 1996—; treas. ABASA, Johannesburg, 1995—; mem. Insider Trading Directorate FSB, South Africa, 1999. Avocations: tennis, gtolf, reading, off road adventure. Office: Gobodo Inc 1st Fl Block B, 55 Empire Rd, Johannesburg 2041, South Africa

MOSON, PETER, mathematician, educator; b. Budapest, Hungary, Sept. 23, 1949; s. Ferenc Moson and Irén (Csaba) M.; m. Piroska Csörgö, Dec. 12, 1974 (div. 1980); children: László, Agnes; m. Ilona Gerzsenyi, Nov. 17, 1986. Math diploma, Lenningrad State U., 1973; PhD, Eötvös U., 1978; postgrad., Hungarian Acad. Scis., 1985. Prof. math. Budapest U. Tech. and Econs., 1974—, vice dean faculty mech. engring., 1994-96, vice dir. Inst. of Math., 1996—. Mem. Hungarian Nat. Coun. for Distance Edn., Budapest, 1996—. Recipient Prize Ministry of Edn., 1981; named Excellent worker Coun. of Ministries, 1982. Mem. J. Bolyai Math. Soc. (Farkas Gyula Meml. prize 1982). Avocations: soccer, basketball, swimming, tourism. Office: Budapest U Tech and Econs, Müegyetem Rkp 1-3, H-1521 Budapest Hungary

MOSQUEDA-GARCIA, A. ROGELIO, physician; b. Mexico City; s. Rogelio and Martha Mosqueda; m. Roxana Fernandez-Violante; children: Sara Ximena, Arantxa Gabriela, Rogelio Sebestian. MD, Nat. U. Mex., Mexico City, 1982; PhD, McGill U., Montreal, Que., Can., 1987. Fellow Vanderbilt U., Nashville, 1990, instr. divsn. clin. pharmacology, 1990-92, asst. prof. dept. medicine, 1992-98; dir. syncope unit Vanderbilt Hosp., Nashville, 1995-98; dir. divsn. clin. pharmacology DuPont Pharms., Wilmington, Del., 1998. Contbr. articles to profl. jours. Recipient Marion Merrell Dow Hypertension award Am. Hypertension Assn., 1990, Predl. award Am. Autonomic Soc., 1996; rsch. grantee NIH, 1988-98. Fax: 302-992-4890. Office: DuPont Pharms 974 Centre Rd Wilmington DE 19805-1269

MOSQUERA-LOSADA, MARÍA ROSA, agricultural/forestry science researcher, educator; b. Caracas, Venezuela, Sept. 26; arrived in Spain, 1974; d. Luis Mosquera-Rodríguez and Elena Losada-Fernández; m. Jose Javier Santiago-Freijanes, Aug. 28, 1993; 1 child, Elena Santiago-Mosquera. BSc, Inst. Alvaro Cunqueiro, Vigo, Spain, 1983; degree in biology, U. Santiago Compostela, Spain, 1988, PhD in Biology, 1993. Rschr. CIAM Agr. Ministry, A Coruña, Spain, 1988-93, European Union/U. Sheffield, Eng., 1993-94; rschr., tchr. U. Santiago Compostela, 1994—; expert for sci. project evaluation European Union, Brussels, 1999—. Author: Ecologia y Manejo de Praderas, 1999; contbr. articles to profl. jours. Postdoctoral grantee European Union, 1993-94, doctoral grantee Agr. Ministry, Coruña, 1989-93. Mem. Soc. Española Para El Estudio de los Pastos, Soc. Española Ciencias Forestales, Colegio Oficial de Biólogos Europa, Grassland Fedn. Office: Escuela Politec Superior, U Santiago Compostela, 27002 Lugo Spain

MOSS, BILL RALPH, lawyer; b. Amarillo, Tex., Sept. 27, 1950; s. Ralph Voniver and Virginia May (Atkins) M.; 1 child, Brandon Price. BS with spl. honors, West Tex. State U., 1972, MA, 1974; JD, Baylor U., 1976; cert. regulatory studies program, Mich. State U., 1981. Bar: Tex. 1976, U.S. Dist. Ct. (no. dist.) 1976, U.S. Tax Ct. 1979, U.S. Ct. Appeals (5th cir.) 1983. Briefing atty. Ct. Appeals 7th Supreme Jud. Dist. Tex., Amarillo, 1976-77; assoc. Culton, Morgan, Britain & White, Amarillo, 1977-80; hearings examiner Pub. Utility Commn. Tex., Austin, 1981-83; asst. gen. counsel State Bar Tex., Austin, 1983-87; founder, owner Price & Co. Publs., Austin, 1987-97; asst. gen. counsel Tex. Ethics Commn., Austin, 1997—; instr., lectr. West Tex. State U., Canyon, Ea. N.Mex. U., Portales, 1977-80. Active St. Matthew's Episcopal Ch.; election inspector State of Tex., 1998—. Mem. ABA, Tex. Bar Assn. (speaker profl. devel. programs 1983—), Nat. Orgn. Bar Counsel, Internat. Platform Assn., Alpha Chi, Lambda Chi Alpha, Omicron Delta Epsilon, Phi Alpha Delta, Sigma Tau Delta, Pi Gamma Mu. Home: 506 Explorer St Lakeway TX 78734-3447 Office: Sam Houston Bldg 201 E 14th St Fl 10 Austin TX 78701

MOSS, ELIZABETH LUCILLE (BETTY MOSS), transportation company executive; b. Ironton, Mo., Feb. 13, 1939; d. James Leon and Dorothy Lucille (Russell) Rollen; m. Elliott Theodore Moss, Nov. 10, 1963 (div. Jan. 1984); children: Robert Belmont, Wendy Rollen. BA in Econs. and Bus. Adminstrn., Drury Coll., 1960. Registrar, transp. mgr. Cheley Colo. Camps, Inc., Denver and Estes Park, 1960-61; office mgr. Washington Nat. Ins. Co., Denver, 1960-61; sec. White House Decorating, Denver, 1961-62; with Ringsby Truck Lines, Denver, Oakland, Calif., and L.A., 1962-67, System 99 Freight Lines, L.A., 1967-69; terminal mgr. System 99 Freight Lines, Stockton, Calif., 1981-84; with Yellow Freight System, L.A., 1969-74, Hayward, Calif., 1974-77; ops. mgr. Yellow Freight System, Urbana, Ill., 1977-80; sales rep. Calif. Motor Express, San Jose, 1981; regional sales mgr. Schneider Nat. Carriers, Inc., No. Calif., 1984-86; account exec. TNT-Can., Nev. and Cen. Calif., 1986-88; mgr. Interstate-Intermodal Divs. HVH Transp., Denver, 1988-89; regional sales mgr. MNX, Inc., Northern Calif., 1989-91; dir. sales Mountain Valley Express, Manteca, Calif., 1992—; chmn. op. coun. for San Joaquin and Stanislaus Counties Calif. Trucking Assn., 1983-84, Truck Accident Reduction Projects, San Joaquin County, 1987-88. Mem. Econ. Devel. Coun. Stockton C. of C., 1985-86; active Edison High Sch. Boosters, 1982-88. Mem. Nat. Def. Transp. Assn. (bd. dirs. 1986-87), Stockton Traffic Club (bd. dirs. 1982-84, Trucker of Yr.), Ctrl. Valley Traffic Club, Oakland Traffic Club, Delta Nu Alpha (bd. dirs. Region 1 1982-84, v.p. chpt. 103 1984-85, pres. 1985-86, chmn. bd. 1985-87, regional sec. 1987-88, Outstanding Achievement award 1986, 88), Coun. Logistics Mgmt., So. Calif. Roundtable (bd. dirs. 1993—). Methodist. Avocations: reading. Home: 2805 E 3d St # 9 Long Beach CA 90814

MOSS, JOSEPH EDWARD, JR., poet; b. Birmingham, Ala., Nov. 25, 1946; s. Joseph E. and Annie Pearl (Black) M.; m. Gloria Stallworth; children: Carlton Graves, Joann, Morgan, Makenzie. Grad., Overbrook H.S., Phila., 1965. Clk. U.S. Postal Svc., Detroit, 1977—. Author: Graveyard Moss is Still Alive, 1986, Diamonds on Paper, 1994, I Do "Jah Rasta Farri" Dambalah is My Pet, 1999. Mem. Masons. Home: 8566 Prest St Detroit MI 48228-2231

MOSS, KATE, model; b. Croydon, England, Jan. 16, 1974. With Storm Agy., England, Women Model Mgmt., N.Y.; model Calvin Klein Jeans. Appeared in films Unzipped, 1995, Catwalk, 1995, Beautopia, 1998, Blackadder Back and Forth, 1999, Original Copies, 1999, (TV films) Inferno, 1992, Naomi Conquers Africa, 1998, (TV series) French and Saunders, 1987. Office: Storm Model Mgmt, 5 Jubilee Pl 1st Fl, London SW3 3TD, England*

MOSS, MALCOLM DOUGLAS, member parliament; b. Audenshaw, Manchester, Eng., Mar. 6, 1943; s. Norman and Annie (Gay) M.; m. Vivien Lorraine Peake, Nov. 14, 1942 (dec. 1997); children: Alison Claire, Sarah Nicole; m. Sonya Alexandra McFarlin, May 12, 2000. BA, Cambridge U., 1965, MA, 1967, cert. edn., 1966. Head geography dept. Blundell's Sch., Tiverton, Eng., 1966-71; ins. cons. Barwick Assocs. Ltd., Wisbech, Eng., 1971-72, gen. mgr., 1972-74; dir. Mandrake Assocs. Ltd., Wisbech, 1974-86, chmn., 1986-92, non exec. dir., 1992—; mem. Ho. of Commons, London, 1987—. Councilor Wisbech Town Coun., 1979-86, mayor, 1983; councilor Fenland Dist. Coun., 1983-87, Cambridgeshire County Coun., 1985-88. Conservative. Mem. Ch. of Eng. Avocations: gardening, tennis, skiing, music.

MOSS, NORMAN BERNARD, author, journalist, broadcaster; b. London, Eng., Sept. 30, 1928; s. Benjamin and Lydia Frances (Nathan) M.; m. Hilary Sesta, July 21, 1963; children: Paul Nathanael, Antony Jason. Ed. schs., N.Y.C.; student, Hamilton Coll., Clinton, N.Y., 1946-47. Journalist Continental Daily Mail, Reuters, A.P., Radio Press Internat., 1950-66; chief European corr. Metromedia Radio News, 1968-71; contbr. various mags.; Mem. Internat. Inst. Strategic Studies. Author: Men Who Play God: The Story of the Hydrogen Bomb, 1969, What's the Difference? A British/American Dictionary, 1973, rev. edits., 1978, 84, 90, The Pleasures of Deception, 1977, The Politics of Uranium, 1982, Klaus Fuchs: The Man Who Stole the Atom Bomb, 1987, Managing the Planet: the Politics of the New Millenium, 2000, monograph The Politics of Global Warming, 1992; contbr. to Freedom of Dilemma, 1971. Home: 21 Rylett Crescent, London W12 9RP, England

MOSS, STEPHEN J., neuroscience and pharmacology educator; b. Liverpool, Eng., May 8, 1962; s. Stephen Richard and Margaret Kathleen (Brazendale) M.; m. Kathryn Jane Walke, June 13, 1989 (div. Jan. 1999). BSc with honors, U. Bath, Eng., 1984; PhD, U. London, 1989. With Johns Hopkins U., Balt., 1989-92; lectr. Univ. Coll., London, 1992-96, reader, 1996-99, prof., 2000—; cons. SmithKline Beecham, U.K., 1998—. Contbr. articles to profl. jours. Med. Rsch. Coun. sr. fellow, 1993, program grantee, 1997, Wellcome Trust grantee, 1995, 99. Mem. Soc. Neurosci., Brit. Pharmacol. Soc. Avocations: fishing, hiking, European history, rugby, football, skiing. E-Mail: steve.moss@ucl.ac.uk. Office: Univ Coll Med Rsch Coun, Lab Molec Cell Bio Gower St, London England

MOSS, VERONICA ANN, palliative care physician; b. Nagpur, Madhya Pradesh, India, Nov. 24, 1943; d. Clement F. and Agnes Ingegerd (Iwarsson) M. MBBS, London U., 1970, diploma in Tropical Medicine and Hygeine, 1972, diploma in Obstetrics, 1974, diploma in Child Health, 1975. Intern Nat. Health Svc., U.K., London, 1970-71, sr. house officer in obstetrics, 1973-74, sr. house officer in pediatrics, 1974-75, gen. practitioner to nursing staff St. Bartholomew's Hosp., 1978-80; sr. house surgeon Padhar (India) Hosp., Madhya Pradesh, 1971; asst. med. supt., dir. Community Health & Devel. Project, Madhya Pradesh, 1975-77; gen. practitioner, ptnr. Gen. Practitioner Health Ctr., Bedford, U.K., 1980-86; med. dir. Mildmay Mission Hosp., London, 1986—; dir. Mildmay Trust, London, 1987—; bd. dirs. Interhealth, London, 1988—; med. adviser Ch. Missionary Soc., London, 1980-86. Author: Healthmanual: Self Help Guide, 1985, Terminal Care for People with AIDS, 1991, 2d edit., 1995; co-author: (with others) Prepared to Serve, 1991, HIV/AIDS in Women, 1993, Palliative Care for the Terminally Ill, 1993, Palliative Day Care, 1996. Fellow Royal Soc. Tropical Medicine and Hygiene; mem. Royal Soc. Medicine, Royal Coll. Physicians (award), Brit. Med. Assn., Assn. Palliative Medicine, European Assn. Palliative Medicine, Internat. Assn. for the Study of Pain. Baptist. Avocation: travel, reading, birdwatching, painting, embroidery. Office: Mildmay Mission Hosp, Hackney Rd, London E2 7NA, England

MÖSSBAUER, RUDOLF LUDWIG, physicist, educator; b. Munich, Jan. 31, 1929; s. Ludwig and Erna M.; 3 children. Ed., Technische Hochschule, Munich; DSc (hon.), Gustaphus Adolphus Coll., 1963, U. Lille, France, 1963, Oxford U., 1973, U. Leicester, Eng., 1975; Dr. honoris causa, U. Grenoble, France, 1974, U. Madrid, 1975, U. Leuven, 1976, U. Saarbrücken, 1985, Eötvös Loránd U., Budapest, Hungary, 1989, U. Montreal, 1989, U. Birmingham, U.K., 1998. Research asst. Max-Planck Inst., Heidelberg, Fed. Republic Germany, 1955-57; research fellow Technische Hochschule, Munich, 1958-60; research fellow Calif. Inst. Tech., 1960, sr. research fellow, 1961, prof. physics, 1961; prof. exptl. physics Tech. U. Munich, 1964-72, 77-97, prof. emeritus, 1997—; dir. Inst. Max von Laue, Grenoble, France and German-French-Brit. High Flux Reactor, 1972-77. Author publs. on recoilless nuclear resonance absorption and neutrino physics. Decorated Order for Merit for Scis. and Arts (Germany); recipient Research Corp. award, 1961, Röntgen prize U. Giessen, 1961, Elliott Cresson medal Franklin Inst., Phila., 1961, Nobel prize for physics, 1961, Guthrie medal Inst. Physics (London), 1974, Lomonossov medal Acad. Sci. USSR, 1984, Einstein medal Albert Einstein Soc., Bern, 1986; named to Order of Merit for Arts and Scis., Bonn, Germany, 1996. Fellow Franklin Inst. (life); mem. Deutsche Physikalische Gesellschaft, Deutsche Gesellschaft der Naturforscher und Aerzte, Deutsche Akademie der Naturforscher Leopoldina, Am. Phys. Soc., European Phys. Soc., Indian Acad. Scis., Am. Acad. Sci. (fgn.), Am. Acad. Arts Scis. (fgn), Nat. Acad. Scis. (fgn. assoc.), Bavarian Acad. Scis., Academia Nazionale dei XL Roma, Pontifical Acad. Scis., Acad. Sci. USSR (fgn.), Acad. European Scis. Arts des Letters France, Hungarian Acad. of Scis., Internat. Acad. Scis., Internat. Acad. of Science, Munich, Acad. Europe U.K., French Phys. Soc. (hon.), Brit. Inst. Physics (hon.)., Academia Scientiarum et Artium Europaea. Office: Tech U Munich, Dept Physics E15, 85748 Garching Germany

MOSSELMANS, CAREL MAURITS, investment banker; b. East Knoyle, Wiltshire, Eng., Mar. 9, 1929; s. Adriaan Willem and Nancy Henriette (Van der Wyck) M.; m. Prudence Fiona McCorquodale, Jan. 4, 1962; children: Michael Lodowick Stewart, Julian Frederick Willem. MA, Trinity Coll., Cambridge, Eng., 1952. With Sedgwick Collins & Co., 1952-63; dir. Sedgwick Collins & Co. Ltd., 1963-71; dir., mng. dir. Sedgwick Collins (Underwriting) Ltd., 1971, 72-73; chmn. Sedgwick Lloyd's Underwriting Agts., 1974-89, Sedgwick Forbes Marine Ltd., 1974-78, Sedgwick Forbes Svcs. Ltd., 1978-81, Sedgwick Ltd., 1981-84, Sedgwick Group Plc., 1984-89, The Sumitomo Marine & Fire Ins. Co. (Europe) Ltd., 1981-90; Coutts & Co., 1981-95; chmn. Rothschild Asset Mgmt. Ltd., 1989-99, Rothschild Int. Asset Mgmt., 1989-96; chmn. Exco Plc, 1991-96, Janson Green Holdings Spl. Trust Ltd., 1993-96, Rothschild Fund Mgmt. Ltd., 1990-96; chmn. Janson Green Ltd., 1993-96, non-exec. dir., 1997-98; bd. dirs. Rothschild Continuation Ltd. Avocations: shooting, fishing, music, golf. Home: 15 Chelsea Sq, London SW3 6LF, England

MOSSINGHOFF, GERALD JOSEPH, patent lawyer, educator; b. St. Louis, Sept. 30, 1935; m. Jeanne Carole Jack, Dec. 29, 1958; children: Pamela Ann Jennings, Gregory Joseph, Melissa M. Ronayne. BSEE, St. Louis U., 1957; JD with honors, George Washington U., 1961. Bar: Mo. 1961, D.C. 1965, Va. 1981. Project engr. Sachs Electric Corp., 1954-57; dir. congl. liaison NASA, Washington, 1967-73, dep. gen. counsel, 1976-81; asst. Sec. Commerce, commr. patents and trademarks U.S. Patent Office, 1981-85; pres. Pharm. Rsch. and Mfrs. Am., Washington, 1985-96; Cifelli prof. intellectual property law George Washington U., Washington, 1996—; sr. counsel Oblon, Spivak, McClelland, Maier & Neustadt, Arlington, Va., 1997—; amb. Paris Conv. Diplomatic Conf.; adj. prof. George Mason U. Law Sch. Recipient Exceptional Svc. medal NASA, 1971, Disting. Svc. medal, 1980, Outstanding Leadership medal, 1981, Disting. Alumnus George Washington U., 1996; granted presdl. rank of meritorious exec., 1980; Disting. Pub. Svc. award Sec. of Commerce, 1983. Fellow Am. Acad. Pub. Adminstrn.; mem. Reagan Alumni Assn. (bd. dirs.), Cosmos Club, Knights of Malta, Order of Coif, Eta Kappa Nu, Pi Mu Epsilon. Home: 1530 Key Blvd Penthouse 28 Arlington VA 22209-1532 Office: Oblon Spivak McClelland Maier & Neustadt 1755 Jefferson Davis Hwy Fl 4 Arlington VA 22202-3509

MOSTAFA, BADR ELDIN, otolaryngologist, educator; b. Beyrouth, Lebanon, May 30, 1958; s. Badr Eldin Ahmed and Faiza Hassan (Khaled) M.; m. Lobna Mohammed El Fiky, Jan. 29, 1993; children: Badr Eldin, Omar, Mostafa, Ali. MB BCh, Ain-Shams Faculty Medicine, 1981, MS, 1985, MD, 1989. Resident Faculty of Medicine Ain-Shams U., Cairo, 1982-85, asst. lectr., 1985-89, lectr., 1989-94, asst. prof. ear, nose, throat-head, neck surgery, 1994-99, prof., 1999—; cons. ENT-HNS Nat. Health Svc., Cairo, 1991—, cons. vestibular disease, 1993—; cons. ENT-HNS Health Assn. Read Crescent Hosp., Cairo, 1996—; cons. ENT-HNS Medina Nat. Hosp., Saudi-Arabia, 1994-95. Contbr. articles to profl. jours. Recipient Distinctive Svc. award Med. Syndicate, 1983, 97. Mem. Egyptian Soc. of the UN (youth rep. 1984—), African Assn. (youth rep. 1987—), Soc. d'Otologie Pratique, European Laryngologic Soc., Egyptian Soc. of Otolaryngology. Avocations: squash, scuba diving, photography. Home: 48 Ibn El Nafees St, Cairo 11371, Egypt Office: Faculty of Medicine, Ain Shams U POB 38, Cairo 11381, Egypt

MOSTAFA, JAVED, information scientist, edcuator; b. Chittagong, Bangladesh, July 31, 1966; came to U.S., 1984; s. Ghulam Mustafa and Jobeda Khatun; m. Sigma Salahuddin, June 7, 1991. BSc magna cum laude, N.W. Okla. State U., 1987; MA, Ohio State U., 1990; PhD, U. Tex., 1994. Dir. info. processing lab U. Tex., Austin, 1991-92; asst. prof. Ind. U., Bloomington, 1994—, Victor Yngve asst. prof., 1998—; adj. asst. prof. computer sci. dept. Ind. U., Inpls., 1996—, rschr. web lab., 1996-97; vis. scholar sys. engrng. dept. Chinese U. Hong Kong, 1998. Author: Easy Internet Handbook, 1994; contbr. articles to profl. jours. Grantee NSF, 1999, Eli Lilly & Co., 1999. Fellow Ctr. Social Informatics; mem. Am. Soc. Info. Sci., Assn. Computing Machinery, Phi Kappa Phi. Avocations: reading, traveling, jogging, racquetball. Home: 1041 Knollwood Cir Bloomington IN 47401-4561 Office: Ind U SLIS # 025 10th & Jordan Ave Bloomington IN 47405-1801

MOSTAFA, NAGAT ABDALLA, chemical engineering educator, researcher; b. Alexandria, Egypt, Aug. 19, 1956; d. Abdalla Mostafa El Sordy and Hanem Hassan Ebrahiem; m. Farouk Shehata Ali, Feb. 1, 1982; children: Mohamed, Ahmed, Taha, Yassen, El-Mostafa, Abd Alla. BSc in Chem. Engring., U. Alexandria, 1979; MSc in Chem. Engring., El Minia U., 1984, PhD in Chem. Engring., 1990. Demonstrator El Minia U. Faculty Engring., 1979-85, tchg. asst., 1985-90, instr. chem. engring., 1991-95, assoc. prof., 1995—. Contbr. articles to sci. jours., including Jour. Energy Conversion and Mgmt., Jour. Biomass and Bioenergy. Office: El Minia U, Faculty Engring, El Minia 61111, Egypt

MOST-LEVIN, CAROL LYNN, physician, geriatrician; b. Long Island, N.Y., Sept. 1, 1959; d. Herbert Jules and Jean (Friedman) Most; m. Ronald Mitchell Levin, June 17, 1979; children: Jay Samuel, Marc Andrew, Eric Brian. BA, La Salle Coll., Phila., 1981; MD, Med. Coll. Pa., 1985. Diplomate Nat. Bd. Med. Examiners, Am. Bd. Internal Medicine. Intern and resident Abington (Pa.) Meml. Hosp., 1985-88; pvt. practice, 1988-95; internist Abington Meml. Hosp., 1995—, mem.-at-large med. exec. com., 1999—; med. dir. U.S. Homecare, Phila., 1991-94; clin. instr. Temple U., Phila., 1995-96; instr. Jefferson U., 1996—; med. sch. interviewer Alleghany U., 1996—; spkr. in field. Contbr. articles to mag., jours. Recipient First prize Eleanor Dixon Writing/Rsch. Competition, 1988. Fellow ACP; mem. AMA (Physician's Recognition award 1991, 94, 97), Am. Geriatrics Soc., Pa. Med. Soc., Montgomery County Med. Soc. Avocations: traveling, cooking, decorating. Office: 7848 Old York Rd Ste 104 Elkins Park PA 19027-2541

MOSTOFI, FATHOLLAH KESHVAR, pathologist, educator, consultant; b. Teheran, Iran, Aug. 10, 1911; came to U.S., 1931; s. Farajullah Khan and Kursum (Khanum) M.; m. Dorothy Ida Krock, June 20, 1940; 1 child, Keith. AB, BSc, U. Nebr., 1935; MD, Harvard U., 1939, grad. Kennedy Sch. Govt., 1982. Diplomate Am. Bd. Pathology. Intern St. Luke's Hosp., Bethlehem, Pa., 1939-40; house officer Peter Bent Brigham Hosp., Boston, 1940-41; resident in pathology Boston Lying-In Hosp. and Free Hosp. for Women, 1941-42, Children's Hosp., Boston, 1942-43; asst. pathologist Mass. Gen. Hosp., Boston, 1943-44; rsch. fellow Nat. Cancer Inst., Bethesda, Md., 1947-48; pathologist, spl. asst. VA Cen. Lab. Anat. Pathology Armed Forces Inst. Path., Washington, 1948-62; chmn. dept. genitourinary pathology Armed Forces Inst. Pathology, Washington, 1962—; sci. dir. Am. Registry Pathology, 1957-59; clin. assoc. prof. pathology Johns Hopkins U., Balt., 1960—; clin. prof. pathology Georgetown U., 1961—, U. Md., 1968—, Uniformed Svcs. U. Health Scis., Bethesda, Md., 1970—; head Collaborating Ctr. for Histological Classification of Tumors in Urinary Tract and Male Genital Sys., WHO, Geneva, 1963—; hon. prof. Chinese Peoples Liberation Army Gen. Hosp. Postgrad. Med. Sch., Beijing, 1988—; registrar Am. Urol. Assn., Washington, 1949—; hon fellow Royal Coll. Pathologists, 1990. Co-author: Tumors of the Male Genital System, 1973, International Histological Classification of Bladder Tumors, 1974, of Testes Tumors, 1977, of Prostatic Tumore, 1980, of Kidney Tumors, 1981, Atlas of Kidney Biopsies, 1980; four books transl. into Russian, French, Spanish; editor: Bilharziasis Proc., 1976; co-editor: The Kidney, 1966, The Skin, 1971, The Platelet, 1972, The Liver, 1973, Striated Muscle, 1973, Kidney Disease: Present Status, 1979. Maj. M.C., U.S. Army, 1944-47. Recipient Presdl. Rank of Disting. Exec. Svc., 1982, Ferdinand C. Valentine award N.Y. Acad. Medicine, John Shaw Billings Lifetime Achievement award DOD-AFIP, ARP, 1995; 2 books dedicated to him. Mem. Internat. Acad. Pathology (sec.-treas. 1952-70, pres. 1972-76), Internat. Soc. Pathology, U.S.-Can. Acad. Pathology (pres. 1972-73, gold medal 1974, ann. F.K. Mostofi award for disting. svc. to pathology established in his name), Internat. Coun. Socs. Pathology (sec.-treas. 1970—), Acad. Medicine (pres. 1992—), Cosmos Club, Harvard Club. Republican. Islam. Avocation: photography. Home: 7001 Georgia St Chevy Chase MD 20815-4135 Office: Armed Forces Inst Pathology 147th And Alaska Ave NW Washington DC 20306-0001

MOSTOVAYA, IRINA VLADIMIROVNA, science administrator; b. Rostov-on-Don, USSR, Apr. 1, 1965; d. Vladimir Ivanovich Kozhin and Nina Fiodorovna Kozhina; m. Igor Mechislavovich Mostovoy, Nov. 6, 1986. Diploma in econs., philosophy, Rostov State U., Rostov-on-Don, 1990, D in Sociology, 1995. Lectr. Inst. Advanced Humanities & Social Studies Rostov State U., Rostov-on-Don, 1990-92, assoc. dir. sci. Inst. Advanced Humanities & Studies, 1992—; supr., cons. Rostov State U., Rostov-on-Don, 1994—, S.-Russian State Tech. U., Rostov-on-Don, 1994—, Donskoy Law Inst., Rostov-on-Don, 1994—. Author: Social Stratification: the Simbolic World of Methagame, 1996. Grantee Soros Found., 1994, 96, Russia Found. Fundamental Rsch., 1997, 98. Fellow Russian Acad. Humanities, Pub. Def. Coun. Rostov State U. (exec. sec. 1996—, v.p. 1998—), Pub. Def. Coun. Rostov State Econs. Acad. Avocations: planting, swimming, reading, computer. Home: Tovarishcheskaya Str 2a, 344101

Rostov-on-Don Russia Office: Inst Advanced Humanties Social Studies, Pushkinskaya Str., 160, 34406 Rostov-on-Don Russia

MOSTOW, GEORGE DANIEL, mathematics educator; b. Boston, July 4, 1923; s. Isaac J. and Ida (Rotman) M.; m. Evelyn Davidoff, Sept. 1, 1947; children: Mark Alan, David Jechiel, Carol Held, Jonathan Carl. B.A., Harvard U., 1943, M.A., 1946, Ph.D., 1948; DSc (hon.), U. Ill., Chgo., 1989. Instr. math. Princeton U., 1947-48; mem. Inst. Advanced Study, 1947-49, 56-57, 75, trustee, 1982-92; asst. prof. Syracuse U., 1949-52; asst. prof. math. Johns Hopkins U., 1952-53, assoc. prof., 1954-56, prof., 1957-61; prof. math. Yale U., 1961-66, James E. English prof. math., 1966-81, Henry Ford II prof. math., 1981—, chmn., 1971-74; vis. prof. Conselho Nat. des Pesquisas, Inst. de Matematica, Rio de Janiero, Brazil, 1953-54, 91, U. Paris, 1966-67, Hebrew U., Jerusalem, 1967, Tata Inst. Fundamental Rsch., Bombay, 1970, Inst. des Hautes Etudes Scientifiques, Bures-Sur-Yvette, 1966, 71, 75, Japan Soc. for Promotion of Sci., 1985, Eidgenossische Technische Hochschule, Switzerland, 1986; chmn. U.S. Nat. Com. for Math , 1971-73, 83-85, Office Math. Scis., NRC, 1975-78; mem. sci. adv. coun. Math. Scis. Rsch. Inst., Berkeley, Calif., 1988-91; mem. sci. adv. com., bd. govs. Weizmann Inst., Israel, 1987—; bd. govs. Tel Aviv U., 1990-2000; mem. vis. com. dept. math. Harvard U., 1975-81, MIT, 1981-94; Ritt lectr. Columbia U., 1982, Bergman lectr. Stanford U., 1983, Sachar lectr. Tel Aviv U., 1985, Karcher lectr. U. Okla., 1986, Markert lectr. Pa. State U., 1993. Assoc. editor Annals of Math, 1957-64, Trans. Am. Math. Soc, 1958-65, Am. Scientist, 1970-82, Geometrica Dedicata, 1985-90; bd. cons. Jour. D'Analyse Mathématique, 1994—; editor Am. Jour. Math, 1965-69, assoc. editor, 1969-79; author rsch. articles. Fulbright rsch. scholar, Utrecht U., The Netherlands; Guggenheim fellow, 1957-58. Mem. AAAS, NAS (chmn. sect. math. 1982-84), Am. Math. Soc. (pres. 1987-88, Steele prize for paper of lasting importance 1993), Internat. Math. Union (chmn. U.S. del. to gen. assembly Warsaw 1982, exec. com. 1983-86), Phi Beta Kappa, Sigma Xi. E-mail: george.mostow@yale.edu. Home: 25 Beechwood Rd Woodbridge CT 06525-1309 Office: Yale Univ Dept Mathematics New Haven CT 06520

MOSTOW, JONATHAN CARL, film director; b. New Haven, Nov. 28, 1961. BA, Harvard U., 1983. Film dir. Hess-Kalberg Assocs., Santa Monica, Calif. Dir., writer (motion picture) Flight of Black Angel, 1991. Office: Hess-Kalberg Assoc 3000 Airport Ave # A Santa Monica CA 90405-6111

MOSZCZYŃSKI, PAULIN, hematologist; b. Janów Lubelski, Lublin, Poland, Jan. 3, 1936; s. Paulin and Bronisława (Malawska) M.; m. Maria Leokadia Otto, Feb. 11, 1961; children: Paulin, Anna. Degree, Univ. Med. Sch., Cracow, Poland, 1960, MD, 1968; postgrad. in hematology, Med. Postgrad. Ctr., Warsaw, Poland, 1975; hon. degree, State Med. U., Odessa, Ukraine, 1997. Asst. dept. med. physics Univ. Med. Sch., Cracow, 1960-63; registrar dept. medicine L. Rydygier Hosp., Brzesko, Poland, 1963-76, cons. hematologist, 1975—, chief med. outpatient clinic, 1975—, head dept. medicine, 1976—; lectr. Open Tech. U., Cracow, 1995—; vice dir. Health Care Complex, Brzesko, 1975-78; head Province Immunol. Lab., Brzesko, 1978—; cons. immunologist L. Rydygier Hosp., 1978—; pres. Internat. Inst. Universalistic Medicine, Tarnów, Poland, 1996—. Contbr. over 600 popular-sci. articles to various mags. Chmn. Internat. Fair of Health Life and Food, Tarnów, 1992-95. Recipient 2d prize Ministry of Health and Social Welfare, Poland, 1989, Individual prize Ministry of Health and Social Welfare, 1995, Golden medal Albert Schweitzer World Acad. Medicine, 1996, 99. Mem. Polish Med. Assn. (Gloria Medicinae medal 1994), Polish Soc. of Health Life and Food Promotion (mem. physicians' coun. 1992—, Golden medal 1995), Polish Acad. Medicine (Golden medal 1996), N.Y. Acad. Scis. Roman Catholic. Avocations: theater, tennis, travel. Home: Wyzwolenia 7, 32-800 Brzesko Poland Office: Rydygier Hosp, Kosciuszki 68, 32-800 Brzesko Poland

MOSZKOWICZ, VIRGINIA MARIE, quality administrator; b. Uniontown, Pa., July 6, 1952; d. Edward Louis and Theresa Elizabeth (Congelio) Olsavicky; m. Michael John Moszkowicz, Sept. 29, 1979. BA in Chemistry, Thiel Coll., 1974; MS in Organic Chemistry, Duquesne U., 1978; MS in Mgmt. Tech., MIT, 1987. Devel. chemist PPG Inds., Pitts., 1974-75; analytical chemist Bayer/Mobay Chem. Corp., Pitts., 1975-78; chem testing leader sensitized goods mfg. divsn. Eastman Kodak Co., Rochester, 1978-80, devel. engr. sensitized goods mfg. divsn., 1980-84, product mgr. motion picture film, 1984-86, unit dir., quality assurance orgn. mfg. supply & distbn., 1987-91; mid. mgr. quality and indsl. engring. Equipment Mfg. Divsn., Ro, 1991-94, quality leader mechanical products, 1995-96; project mgr. consumer cameras Eastman Kodak Co., Rochester, 1996; quality mgr. mfg. Xerox Corp., 1996-2000; quality dir. logistics R.R. Donnelly & Sons, Chgo., 2000—. Past bd. dirs. Lifetime Assistance Inc. Mme. Am. Soc. Quality Control, Toastmasters Internat. (dist. gov. 1991, club pres. 1994, Toastmaster of Yr. 1981, Disting. Toastmaster 1987). Avocations: skiing, golf, travel, French and German langs.

MOSZKOWSKI, LENA IGGERS, secondary school educator; b. Hamburg, Mar. 8, 1930; d. Alfred G. and Lizzie (Minden) M.; m. Steven Alexander, Aug. 29, 1952 (div. Oct. 1977); children: Benjamin Charles, Richard David (dec. 1995), Ronald Bertram. BS, U. Richmond, 1948; MS, U. Chgo., 1953; postgrad., UCLA, 1958. Tchr. Lab. asst. U. Chgo. Ben May Cancer Research Lab., Chgo., 1951-53; biology, sci. tchrs. Bishop Conaty High Sch., Los Angeles, 1967-68; chemistry, sci. tchr. St. Paul High Sch., Santa Fe Springs, Calif., 1968-69; chemistry, human ecology tchr. Marlborough Sch., Los Angeles, 1969-71; tchr. biology and sci. ecology L.A. Unified Sch. Dist., 1971—. Author: Termite Taxonomy Cryptotermes Haviland and C. Krybi, Madagascar, 1955, Ecology and Man, 1971, Parallels in Human and Biological Ecology, 1977, American Public Education, An Inside Journey, 1991-92. Founder, adminstr., com. mem. UCLA Student (and Practical Assistance Cooperative Furniture), Los Angeles, 1963-67; active participant UCLA Earth Day Program, Los Angeles, 1970. Recipient Va. Sci. Talent Search Winner Va. Acad. of Sci., 1946; Push Vol. Tchr. award John C. Fremont High Sch., Los Angeles, 1978. Mem. Calif. Tchrs. Assn., United Tchrs. L.A., Balt. Coun. on Fgn. Affairs, Sierra Club. Democrat. Jewish. Avocations: civil rights, workers rights, redirecting public education, photography, animals. Home: 3301 Shelburne Rd Baltimore MD 21208-5626

MOTA, OSCAR DAVID SANTOS, engineering educator, researcher; b. Gondomar, Porto, Portugal, Apr. 30, 1960; s. Jose De Oliveira and Laurinda Dos Santos (Azevedo) M.; m. Anabela Almendra Dias Antunes, Dec. 19, 1987. MS in Thermal Engring., Oporto U., Portugal, 1987, PhD Mech. Engring., 1997. Univ. lectr. Oporto U., Portugal, 1983-98. Contbr. articles to profl. jours. Cadet Naval Acad., Lisbon, 1978-81. Mem. Ordem Dos Engenheiros. Avocations: reading, crafts, cross-country, cycling, tennis. Office: Faculdade Engenharia Demergi-SFC, R Dos Bragas, 4050-123 Porto Portugal

MOTCHALOV, IGOR VALENTINOVICH, optical engineer, educator; b. Leningrad, Russia, Aug. 12, 1949; s. Valentin Iosifovich and Merry Issakovna (Nalyubitskaya) M.; m. Elena Anatolievna Vlasova, July 26, 1972 (div. Feb. 1979); 1 child, Karina; m. Elena Vasilievna Bazhenova, May 25, 1988; 1 child, Sternik Denis. MS, Moscow Chem. Tech. Inst., 1972; PhD, Vavilov's State Optical Inst., Leningrad, 1979. Rsch. scientist Vavilov's State Optical Inst., Leningrad, 1973-79, sr. rsch. scientist, 1979-84, prin. rsch. scientist, 1984-89; gen. dir. Ctr. Tech. Optical Materials, St. Petersburg, 1989—; prof. St. Petersburg Inst. Fine Mechanics and Optics, 1994—; cons. Vavilov's State Optical Inst., St. Petersburg, 1989—. Contbr. articles to profl. jours. including Optical Engring., Jour. Optical Tech., others. Mem. Optical Soc. Am., N.Y. Acad. Scis., Internat. Soc. Optical Engring., The Planetary Soc., Nat. Geog. Soc. Avocations: music, theater, travel. Fax: 7 812 2737660. E-mail: mochalov@mail.line.ru. Home: Mokhovaya Str 43 Apt 12, 193028 Saint Petersburg Russia Office: Ctr Tech Optical Materials, N 36/1 Bubushkina Str, 193171 Saint Petersburg Russia

MOTES, MICHAEL ALLEN, psychologist; b. Yuma, Ariz., Aug. 21, 1970; s. Larry Franklin and Cecilia Mary (Langford) M.; m. Kendra Rose Hensley-Motes, Jan. 1, 1996. AA, Fla. C.C., Jacksonville, 1993; BA in Psychology, U. N.Fla., 1995, MA in Gen. Psychology, 1996. Grad. student tchg. asst. U. N. Fla., Jacksonville, 1995-96, Tex. Christian U., Ft. Worth, 1998—; vis. instr. dept. psychology, U. N. Fla., Jacksonville, 1996-98. Contbr. articles to profl. jours. Mem. Fla. Coun. of Sexual Abuse Svcs., Inc., 1994-96. Recipient scholarship Humana Found., 1990-94. Mem. Am. Psychol. Soc., Southwestern Psychol. Assn., Southeastern Psychol. Assn. Libertarian. Avocations: computer programming, skiing, surfing. E-mail: mmotes@netzero.net. Office: Tex Christian U/Dept Psyc PO Box 298920 Fort Worth TX 76129-0001

MOTLATLE, RESHOKETSWE MARIA, human resources executive, psychologist; b. Johannesburg, South Africa, Nov. 1, 1957; d. Joel Felix and Kabesabe Elizabeth (Galobetse) M. BA with honors, U. of the North, Pietersburg, South Africa, 1982, BA, 1982; MA, U. Oreg., 1989. Registered counselling psychologist. Sr. counsellor U. of the North, 1989-91; student counsellor Witwatersrand Technikon, Johannesburg, 1991-92; sr. psychologist Telkom, Randburg, South AFrica, 1992-93, mgr. affirmative action, 1993-96; sr. human resources cons. Telkom, Pretoria, South AFrica, 1996-97, exec. in human resources, 1997—; tech. asst. Aurora Assocs., Johannesburg, 1995-96; cons. Children and Violence Trust, Johannesburg, 1992-94; trainer peer counseling Vista U., Soweto, 1991-95; trainer tchr. upgrading project Sweetwaters Squatting Camp, 1993-96. Inst. Internat. Edn. scholar, 1987; Ctr. for Study of Women in Society grantee, 1989. Mem. Psychol. Soc. South Africa (treas. 1997—). Mem. ANC Party. Lutheran. Avocations: reading, theater, game viewing, sports. Home: PO Box 1476, 2185 Olivedale South Africa

MOTOKAWA, TATSUO, biology educator; b. Sendai, Miyagi, Japan, Apr. 9, 1948; s. Koiti and Miyo (Wakida) M.; m. Kyoko Motokawa, Dec. 7, 1980; children: Namiko, Toyoko, Kyuri. BS in Zoology, U. Tokyo, 1971, MS in Zoology, 1973, DSc, 1985. Asst. prof. U. Tokyo, 1975-78; lectr. U. Ryukyus, Nishihara, Japan, 1978-85, assoc. prof., 1985-91; prof. Tokyo Inst. Tech., 1991—; vis. assoc. prof. Duke U., Durham, N.C., 1986-88. Author: Coral Reef Animals, 1985, The Time of an Elephant, the Time of a Mouse, 1992 (award 1993), Biology by Singing, 1993, Time, 1996, Organisms are Cylindrical, 1998. Home: Tsuchihashi 7-28-5 Miyamae, Kawasaki 216-0005, Japan Office: Tokyo Inst Tech Dept Biol, O-okayama 2-12-1, Meguro Tokyo 152-8551, Japan

MOTOKI, KEN, education educator; b. Tokyo, Mar. 31, 1930; s. Mamoru and Ruriko (Takiguchi) M.; m. Sumie Mizusaki, 1955; children: Tsuyoshi, Tomoko Makita. B degree, Tokyo U., 1953, M degree, 1955; PhD, Nagoya U., 1993. Rsch. mem. Nat. Inst. Ednl. Rsch., Tokyo, 1955-67; assoc. prof. Osaka (Japan) U., 1967-74, prof., 1974-93, prof. emeritus, 1993—; prof. Kawamura Gakuen Women's U., 1993—, dean faculty edn., 1995-98, vice-chancellor, 1998—; guest prof. Osaka U. Econs. and Law, 1993-2000; bd. dirs. Nat. Fedn. of Social Edn. Japan. Author: Methodology of Technical Education, 1963, Social Studies as a Study of Human, 1966, Human Rights and Education, 1989, Technology and Human Formation, 1990. Mem. Japanese Soc. for Study of Adult Edn. (v.p. 1983-87, 91-93), Japan Soc. for Study of Indsl. Edn. (bd. dirs. 1970—), East Asia Forum for Adult Edn. (chmn. 1995-99, hon. chmn. 1999—). Avocations: fine arts, traveling. Home: Higashi-ashiya-cho, 17-23-206, Ashiya-shi 659-0095, Japan Office: Kawamura Gakuen Womens Univ, Sageto 1133, Abiko-shi 270-1138, Japan

MOTONAKA, JUNKO, educator; b. Tokushima, Japan, Jan. 13, 1945; d. Tamotu and Chiyoko (Hayabuchi) Hirata; m. Hiroshi Motonaka, Oct. 13, 1973; 1 child, Kimiko. B of Pharmacy, Mukogawa Womens U., 1967; M of Pharmacy, U. Tokushima, 1969; EdD in Sci., Tohuku U., 1981. Rsch. assoc. tech. coll. U. Tokushima (Japan), 1969-93, rsch. assoc. faculty engring., 1993-94, assoc. prof., 1994-99, prof., 1999—. Chair The Women's Com. for Loss of Weight in Dust, Tokushima, 1990-91; vice chair Tokushima Civic Com. of Dust, 1992-93; mem. Tokushima Water and Green Forward Coun., 1993—. Mem. Am. Chem. Soc., Chem. Soc. Japan, Japan Soc. Analytical Chemistry (sec. 1995—). Buddhist. Avocations: flower arrangement, tea ceremony, Japanese dance. Home: Sumiyoshi 3-9-12, Tokushima 770-0861, Japan Office: U Tokushima Faculty Engring, U Tokushima Faculty Engring, Minamijosanjima 2-1, Tokushima 770-8506, Japan

MOTOORI, SHIGEATSU, physician, researcher; b. Japan, July 13, 1967. Chief physician Namazu City (Japan) Hosp., 1994-98; resident Nat. Inst. Radiol. Scis., Chiba City, Japan, 1999—. Office: Nat Inst Radiol Scis, 4-9-1 Anagawa, Inage Ward, Chiba City 263-8555, Japan

MOTOYAMA, SATORU, medical educator; b. Oga, Japan, Nov. 26, 1965; s. Hifumi and Terumi (Suzuki) M.; m. Yumiko Suzuki, July 10, 1992; children: Yuki, Yukari. MD, PhD, Akita U., Japan, 1997. Asst. prof. Akita U., Japan, 1997-98, asst. prof. 2d dept. surgery, 1999—. Office: Akita U Sch Medicine, 1-1-1 Hondo, 010-8543 Akita City Japan

MOTREANU, DUMITRU, mathematics educator; b. Tîrgu-Ocna, Bacău, Romania, Jan. 30, 1949; s. Dumitru and Venera Cleopatra (Teoharescu) M.; m. Mariana Claudia Gavrilas, Jan. 24, 1975; 1 child, Viorica-Venera. Diploma in math., U. Iasi, Romania, 1972, PhD in Math., 1978. From asst. prof. to assoc. prof. U. Iasi, 1978-95, prof., 1996—; vis. prof. U. Pau, France, 1994, U. Athens, Ohio, 1997, U. La Réunion, France, 1998, U. Catania, Italy, 1999. Author: (books) Minimax Theorems and Qualitative Properties of the Solutions of Hemivariational Ineqalities, 1999, Tangency, Flow for Differential Equations and Optimization Problems, 1999; editor: Jour. Global Optimization, 1999-00; reviewer: Zentralblat für Mathematik; contbr. rsch. articles to profl. jours. Recipient Simion Stoilov award Romanian Acad., 1981. Mem. Internat. Fedn. Nonlinear Analysts, Am. Math. Soc. Orthodox. Home: Bl Y2 Et 8 Ap 39, Bd Alexandru cel Bun 51, RO-6600 Iasi Romania Office: Al i Cuza U, Dept Math, RO-6600 Iasi Romania

MOTSON, ROGER WINGFIELD, surgeon; b. London, Nov. 14, 1946; s. Norman W. and Sylvia B.I. (Hagedorn) M.; m. Janet Anne Bradwell, Oct. 7, 1972; children: Simon, Toby, Alexander. M.B.B.S., U. London, 1971, MS, 1980. Intern Charing Cross Hosp., London, 1971-72; resident fellow U. Calif., San Francisco, 1975-76; registrar Norfolk & Norwich Hosp., 1976-77; sr. registrar London Hosp., 1977-84; cons. surgeon Colchester Gen. Hosp., 1984—; surgeon The Oaks Hosp., Colchester; vis. prof. Alexandria Armed Forces Hosp., Alexandria Egypt, 1998, U. Calif., San Francisco, 2000; Simpson-Smith Meml. lectr. Charing Cross Hosp., London, 1986. Editor: Retained Common Duct Stones - Prevention and Treatment, 1985. Fellow Royal Coll. Surgeons Eng., Assn. Endoscopic Surgeons Gt. Britain and Ireland (hon. sec. 1997-99, pres. 1999—), Royal Soc. Medicine (hon. sec. 1994-96, v.p. sect. coloproctology 1996-98), Assn. Surgeons Gt. Britain and Ireland (coun. 1996—), Assn. Coloproctology of Gt. Britain and Ireland (coun. 1992-98). Office: The Oaks Hosp, Oaks Pl, Colchester CO4 5XR, United Kingdom

MOTT, JUNE MARJORIE, school system administrator; b. Faribault, Minn., Mar. 8, 1920; d. David C. and Tillie W. (Nelson) Shifflett; m. Elwood Knight Mott, Oct. 18, 1958. BS, U. Minn., 1943, MA, 1948. Tchr. high schs. in Minn., 1943-46, 48-53, 54-57; script writer, Hollywood, Calif., 1953-54; tchr. English, creative writing and journalism Mt. Miguel High Sch., Spring Valley, Calif., 1957-86, chmn. English dept., 1964-71, chmn. Dist. English council, 1967-68; mem. Press Bur., Grossmont (Calif.) High Sch. Dist., 1958-86; elected to Grossmont Union High Sch. Governing Bd., 1986—, clk. sch. bd., 1989, v.p. governing bd., 1989-90, 93, pres. sch. bd., 1991-92, v.p., 1992-93, pres. governing bd., 1993-94, v.p., 1998; scriptwriter TV prodn. Lamp Unto My Feet, Jam Dandy Corp.; free-lance writer, cons. travel writer, photographer; editor, publ Listening Heart, 1989. Author, editor in field. Vice chmn. polit. action San Diego County Regional Resource Ctr., 1980-81; mem. S.D. Bd. of Alcohol and Drug Abuse Prevention, 1990—, Curriculum Com. Grossmont Dist., 1990—, Site Facilities Com., Master Planning Com., 1992—, East County Issues and Mgmt. Com., 1990—, East County Women in Edn.; apptd. del. Calif. Sch. Bds. Assn., 1992—, del. assembly, 1992—, apptd. to Race/Human Rels. Com., 1992—, elected to region 17 del. assembly, 1993—; v.p., pub. rels. chmn. Lemon Grove Luth. Ch., 1962-78, 89—, v.p., 1993, pres. 1994, chair concert series, 1997—. Writing project fellow U. Calif., San Diego, 1978; named Outstanding Journalism Tchr., State of Calif., Outstanding Humanities Tchr., San Diego County, Tchr. of Yr. for San Diego County, 1978; U. Cambridge scholar, 1982; Woman of Yr. Lemon Grove Soroptimists, 1990. Mem. ASCD, NEA, AAUW, Nat. Council Tchrs. English, Nat. Journalism Assn., Calif. Assn. Tchrs. English, Calif. Tchrs. Assn., So. Calif. Journalism Assn., Calif. Sch. Bds. Assn. (elected del. region 17, del. assembly 1993—), Calif. Elected Women's Assn. for Edn. Rsch. (ednl. cons. 1990), Lemon Grove C. of C., 1996—, San Diego County Journalism Educators Assn. (pres. 1975-76), Grossmont Edn. Assn. (pres. 1978-80), Greater San Diego Council Tchrs. English, Nat. Writers Club, Am. Guild Theatre Organists, Am. Guild Organists, Am. Poets, L.G. Friends of the Libr., Libr. Congress, Palomar Chpt. Organ Soc., San Diego Mus. of Art, Lemon Grove Hist. Soc., Lemon Grove Friends of Libr., Spreckels Organ Soc., Calif. Retired Tchrs. Assn. (membership chairwoman 1986-89, pres. chpt. # 69 1989-94, parlimentarian 1992-93, chair bylaws 1996—), Lemon Grove C. of C. (mem. econ. devel. com. 1994—), Nat. Sch. Bds. Assn., Order Ea. Star, Kiwanis (pres. elect Lemon grove chpt. 1992, program chmn., pres. 1993-94), Sigma Delta Chi, Delta Kappa Gamma (pres. Theta Gamma chpt. 1993—). Democrat. Home and Office: 2885 New Jersey Ave Lemon Grove CA 91945-2826

MOTT, ROBERT LEWIS, writer, sound effects artist; b. Nyack, N.Y.; s. Morgan Edward and Grace (Groben) M.; m. Catherine O'Keefe, June 28, 1947 (div. 1974); children: Susan Patricia, Gail Ann, Cathee Caron, Nancy Jean; m. Cinda M. Yank, Dec. 28, 1985. Grad., NYU, 1947-50. Freelance writer, 1951—; sound effects artist CBS, N.Y.C., 1951-69, NBC, Burbank, Calif., 1970-89. Writer (children's record) Rocket to Mars, 1954, (cartoon series) Cool McCool, 1956, (Broadway mus.) Girls Against the Boys, 1958; comedy writer The Ed Sullivan Show, Garry Moore Show, Andy Williams Show, Dick Van Dyke Show, Red Skelton Show; author: Sound Effects: Radio, TV and Film, 1988, Sound Effects: Who Did It and How, in the Era of Live Broadcasting, 1993 (Best Lit. List, Choice Mag. 1993), Radio Live! Television Live! When Horses Were Coconuts!, 2000, Served with USMC, 1943-45, ETO. Decorated 4 campaign battle stars; recipient 3 Emmy award nominations Acad. TV Arts and Scis., 1986, 87, Byron Kane award, Lifetime achievement award Soc. to Preserve and Encourage Radio Drama, Variety and Comedy. Mem. Writers Guild Am., Pacific Pioneer Broadcasters. Home: 396 Miller Way Arroyo Grande CA 93420-2004

MOTTALEB, MOHAMMAD, ABDUL, chemistry educator; b. Rangpur, Bangladesh, Jan. 2, 1963; s. Mohammad Fazlar and Tobeza (Khatun) M.; m. Jutika Parveen, May 3, 1990; children: Zubayed Muhi, Mosavvir Arafat. BS with hons., U. Rajshahi, Bangladesh, 1986; MS, U. Rajshahi, 1987; PhD, U. Strathclyde, U.K., 1996. Rsch. fellow Ministry of Edn., Bangladesh, 1989; scientific officer Atomic Energy Commn., Bangladesh, 1989-91; lectr. Shahjalal U. Sci. & Tech., Bangladesh, 1991-92; rsch. student U. Strathclyde, U.K., 1992-96; asst. prof. U. Rajshahai, Bangladesh, 1996-98, assoc. prof., 1998—; project dir. Ministry Sci. & Tech., 1997-98, U. Rajshahi, 1998—; asst. proctor U. Rajshahi, 1997—. Recipient Overseas Rsch. Award, com. principal, U.K., 1992; chancellor award, Bangladesh, 1987. Mem. Nat. Heart Found. Avocations: travel, fishing, inventing. Office: Dept Chemistry, U Rajshahi, 6205 Rajshahi Bangladesh

MOTTE, PETER, translator; b. Geraardsbergen, Flanders, Belgium, Mar. 31, 1966; s. Roger Alfons and Monique (Vander Poorten) M. Lic. in letters and lang., U. Gent, Belgium, 1990, spl. lic. in lit. scis., 1991. Pvt. practice translator Geraardsbergen, 1992-93; tchr. Royal Inst., Brussels, 1996-97, Aloysius Coll., Ninove, Belgium, 1996; copywriter, tchr. Students Tech. Inst., Aalter, Belgium, 1996; pvt. practice translator, 1997—. Author: Twee Molens, 1984, Aan De Oevers Van De Nacht: Een Bijdrage Tot Een Overzicht Van De Nederlandstalige Science Fiction Van 1976 Tot 1987, 1990, Een Benadering Tot The Satanic Verses Van Salman Rushdie: De Rushdie-Crisis Na 28 April 1990 En Een Structurele Benadering Van The Satanic Verses, 1990, 4th edit., 1993, Inleiding Tot Tolkien, Zijn Werk En Zijn Fandom, 1994, Hij Van Donatia, 1998, Een collectie, 2000; editor De Tijdlijn, 1992—; contbr. articles to profl. jours. Jury mem. Literair Beproefd-CSC, Geraardsbergen, 1997. Recipient European Encouragement award, 1992. Mem. Van Pion tot Dame, Onderzoekscentrum Johan Daisne, Belgische Kamer voor Vertalers, Vriendenkring Jean Ray/John Flanders, Louis Paul Boonkring, Cyril Buysse Genootschap, Vlaamse Diabetesvereniging, Volkssterrenwacht Mira. Avocations: literature, physics, chess. Home: Abdijstraat 33, B-9500 Geraardsbergen Belgium

MOTTER, GREGG A., electrical engineer, consultant; b. Flint, Mich., May 25, 1951; s. Rex A. and Evelette Jo Motter; m. Amy Lou M., Oct. 6, 1973; children: Eric A., Ryan D. BS in Elec. Engring., Mich. State U., 1973, MS in Systems Engring., 1980. Sr. engr., prodn. mgr., project mgr. Dow Chem., Midland, Mich., 1973-87, mkt. devel. mgr., 1987-89, project mgr., 1989-96, application devel. scientist, 1992-96, global elec. scientist, 1996—; adv. bd. Mich. State U. Coll. Engring., East Lansing, 1990—, mem. ANSI Z21 std. com., 1992—; invited spkr. industry and univs., 1992—. Patentee in field. Mem. IEEE, SAE. Avocations: sailing, woodworking, gardening, kayaking, golf. E-mail: gmotter@dow.com. Home: 1401 Sylvan Ln Midland MI 48640-7208 Office: Dow Chemical Bldg 1702 Midland MI 48674-0001

MOTTER, THOMAS FRANKLIN, medical products executive; b. Modesto, Calif., June 27, 1948; s. Thomas Dean and Beverley June (Mosier) M.; m. Wanda Lenice Parker, Feb. 9, 1968 (div. Jan. 1972); children: Eric Franklin, Katrina Lenice; m. Jerry Ann Averill, Oct. 24, 1976; children: Heidi Marika, Courtney Averill. AA, Cabrillo Jr. Coll., Santa Cruz, Calif., 1968; BA, Stephens Coll., 1970; MBA, Pepperdine U., 1975. Social worker County of Santa Cruz and Amador, 1970-77; nat. dir. mktg. Humphrey Instruments/SmithKline, San Leandro, Calif., 1978-88; internat. gen. mgr. HGM Med. Lasers, Salt Lake City, 1988-89; pres., CEO Paradigm Med. Industries Inc., Salt Lake City, 1989—. Mem. Nat. Ski Patrol, Stockton, 1973-79; v.p. Sandy (Utah) Pony Baseball, 1994-95; coach Kearns (Utah) Am. Legion Baseball, 1995-96. Capt. U.S. Army, 1970-76. Named. Mem. Nat. Adult Baseball Assn. (mem. Nat. Championship team), Am. Legion, Sons of the Am. Revolution Utah State Chpt., Knight Orthodox Order of the Knights of the Hosp. of St. John of Jerusalem. Episcopalian. Avocations: skiing, hardball baseball, coaching, fly fishing, hunting. Office: Paradigm Med Industries Inc 2355 S 1070 W Salt Lake City UT 84119-1552

MOTTLEY, MIA A., Barbadian government official, minister of education, youth affairs and culture; b. Oct. 1, 1965; single. Student, Queen's Coll., 1977-83, UN Internat. Sch., 1976; B of Law, London Sch. Econs., 1986; Holborn Tutors, 1986-87; pupilage, No 2 Harcourt Bldg, London, 1987. Barrister Bar of Eng. and Wales. With Nat. Cultural Found., 1983-85; pvt. law practice, 1987-94; min. edn., youth affairs and culture Govt. of Barbados, St. Michael, 1994—; bus. mgr. SYGNACHA reggae band, Barbados, 1990-94; co-founder Manic Riddims Inc., Rawriddim Assocs. Inc., 1992. Mem. Labor Party. Office: Ministry Edn Youth Affairs, Jemmott's Ln, Saint Michael Barbados*

MOU, THOMAS WILLIAM, physician, medical educator and consultant; b. Phila., May 17, 1920; s. Thomas Simonsen and Ellen Marie (Mathiesen) M.; m. Marie Elizabeth Hartmann, Dec. 29, 1945 (div. Oct. 1976); children: Susan, Roberta; m. M. Delma Jane Schreiber, Nov. 11, 1976. BSc in Bacteriology, Phila. Coll. Pharm & Sci., 1941; MD, U. Rochester, 1950. Diplomate Nat. Bd. Med. Examiners. Instr. medicine and bacteriology U. Rochester (N.Y.) Sch. of Medicine, 1954-56; asst. prof. preventive medicine to prof. cmty. medicine SUNY at Syracuse, 1956-70; exec. dean to assoc chancellor health sci. SUNY Ctrl. Adminstrn., Albany, 1970-77; dean clin. campus W. Va. U., Charleston, 1977-85; pres. Ednl. Commn. for Fgn. Med. Grads., Phila., 1986-88; dean emeritus W. Va. U. Med. Ctr., Morgantown, 1986—; geriatric practice Adult Medicine Specialists, Pueblo, Colo., 1990-2000; cons. Carnegie Commn. for Advancement of Tchg., Princeton, N.J., 1987-88, Charles A. Dana Found., N.Y.C., 1988, Geriatric Pharmacy Inst. of Phila. Coll. of Pharmacy and Sci., 1988. Contbr. 36 article or presentations to profl. jours or sci. confs. Trustee Phila. Coll. Pharmacy and Sci., 1972-81. Capt. Sanitary Corps, 1941-45. Recipient Disting. Alumnus award Phila. Coll. Pharmacy and Sci., 1975, award of distinction and honor Ben Franklin Soc. SUNY, N.Y.C., 1975, Koch medal Am. Optometric Soc., N.Y.C., 1976; T.W. Mou Endowed Lectureship W. Va. U., Charleston, 1985. Fellow Am. Coll. Physicians, Am. Coll. Preventive Medicine, Phila. Coll. Physicians, Infectious Diseases Soc. Am. (founding fellow). Avocations: violin, travel. Home: 3050 Valleybrook Ln Colorado Springs CO 80904-1154 Office: Adult Medicine Specialists 314 W 16th St Pueblo CO 81003-2728

MOUAZEN, ABDUL MOUNEM, agricultural studies educator; b. Aleppo, Syria, Feb. 3, 1966; s. Abdul Daim Mouazen and Sanaa Dabagh; m. Khawwlah Alazwar, May 6, 1993; 2 children. Lic. in agrl. scis., U. Aleppo,

1988, diplomate in horticulture, 1989; PhD in Agrl. Engring., Hungarian Acad. Scis., Budapest, 1999. Sci. asst. U. Aleppo, 1991-93; univ. lectr. Pannon Agrl. U., Mosonmagyarovar, Hungary, 1999—; postdoctoral fellow Ku Leuven, Belgium, 1999. Contbr. chpts. to books. Avocations: botany, forestry, fishing, modelling. Office: U Aleppo Fac Agrl, PO Box 12214, Aleppo Syria

MOUCHATY, SUZETTE KAY, biologist; b. Morenci, Mich., Jan. 7, 1965; d. Ray Allen Durall and Janet Sue (Gould) Fretz; m. Georges Mouchaty, Mar. 16, 1994. AS, San Juan Coll., 1986; BS, U. Alaska, 1990, MS in Biology, 1993; PhD in Genetics, Lund (Sweden) U., 1999. Fire patrol officer U.S. Forest Svc.-Sawtooth Nat. Forest, 1989; vol. interpreter U.S. Nat. Park Svc.-Tusayan Mus., Grand Canyon Nat. Park, winter 1989-90; curatorial asst. U. Alaska Mus., Fairbanks, 1990; tchg. asst. U. Alaska, Fairbanks, 1991-92, Tex. A&M U., College Station, 1993-95; Fulbright fellow Genetics Inst., U. Lund, Sweden, 1996-97; sr. projects coord. Baylor Coll. Medicine Human Genome Sequencing Ctr., Houston, 2000—; planner, author (mus. exhibit) Systematics Rsch., U. Alaska Mus., 1993. Mem. AAAS, Soc. for Study Evolution, Am. Soc. Mammalogists. E-mail: smouchaty@bcm.tmc.edu. Office: 1 Baylor Plz Houston TX 77030-3411

MOUDATSOU, ARGIRO, statistician; b. Heraklion, Greece, Oct. 8, 1957; s. Konstantinos and Stiliani (Nikolai-di) M.; m. Dimitrios Vernardos, Apr. 15, 1985 (div. 1995); 1 child. Diploma in econs., U. Athens, 1981; MA in Econs., Athens Sch. Econs. Bus. Sci., 1983; PhD, Technische U., Berlin, 1999. Lectr. Heraklion Inst. Tech., 1984-95; info. officer C. of C., Heraklion, 1993-94, head statistics office, 1994—. Mem. String Orch. Municipality of Heraklion. Avocations: playing violin, swimming. Home: M Avgeri 3, 71202 Heraklion Greece Office: Heraklion C of C & Industry, Heraklion C of C & Industry, Koroneou 9 Str, 71202 Heraklion Greece

MOUELLE, ALEXIS DIPANDA, judge. Pres. Supreme Ct. Cameroon, Yaoundé. *

MOUGRABI, MOHAMMED MOSTAFA, cardiologist; b. Beirut, Oct. 5, 1961; s. Mostafa Hussien Mougrabi and Muzian Mussa Khadorah; m. Sammar Mohammed Labadidi, Apr. 9, 1993; children: Majid, Meerva. MD, King Faisal U., Dammam, Saudi Arabia, 1983; D of Cardiology, Pierre & Marie Curie U., Paris, 1996; Doctoral in-depth tng. in cardiology, Val-de-Marne U., Paris, 1996, fellowship interventional cardiology, 1997. Cert. cons.-interventional cardiologist. Med. resident Al-Shaty Hosp., Jeddah, Saudi Arabia, 1984-85; cardiology resident King Fahad Hosp., Jeddah, 1985-86, sr. cardiology resident, 1987-90, coronary care sr. resident, 1991-93; med. trainee State of N.Y. U., 1986-87; hypertension and cardiology fellowship fellow U. Calif., Irvine, 1990-91; dir. Al-Naeem Med. Ctr., Jeddah, 1992-93; sr./supr. critical care unit Armed Forces Hosp., Jeddah, 1993; chief cardiac unit King Abdulaziz Hosp., Jeddah, 1998—; dir. Salama Med. Ctr., Jeddah, 1987-88. Contbr. rsch. articles to profl. jours.; inventor in field. Educator King Abdulaziz Hosp., Jeddah, 1999. Fellow French Cardiologists; mem. Saudi Heart Assn., N.Y. Acad. Sci. Muslim. Avocations: chess, reading, jogging, music, computer. Fax: 009662 682 1924. Home: PO Box 6449, 21442 Jeddah Saudi Arabia

MOUKARZEL, JUAN CARLOS, internist; b. Buenos Aires, Feb. 2, 1950; s. Juan and May (Klater) M.; m. Myrna Liliana Frem Bestani, Dec. 30, 1981; children: Maria Josefina, Juan Alberto, María, Myrna Verónica. Grad., Cardenal Newman Coll., Buenos Aires, 1967; MD, U. Buenos Aires, 1974. Med. Diplomate. Resident internal medicine Hosp. Rawson, Buenos Aires, 1974-77, resident, instr., 1977-78; instr. internal medicine Hosp. Escuela y Clinica Jose de San Martin, Buenos Aires, 1978-80, staff internal medicine, 1978-82, staff allergy and immunology, 1982-85; staff ambulatory medicine Pvt. Hosp.-CIM, Buenos Aires, 1983-87, Suizo-Argentina Clinic-CIM, Buenos Aires, 1990-99; staff internal medicine Hosp. Escuela y de Clínicas José de San Martín, Buenos Aires, 1999—. Contbr. articles to profl. jours. Mem. family br. Apostolic Movement of Schoenstatt, Buenos Aires, 1990—. Fellow Interam. Coll. Physicians and Surgeons; mem. Assn. Argentina de Medicina Familiar. Roman Catholic. Avocations: numismatics, swimming, soccer, football, ping pong. Home: Melian 2321 Piso 12 Dep 1, 1430 Buenos Aires Argentina Office: La Pampa 2643 Piso 2 Dep 21, Buenos Aires Argentina

MOUL, JUDD WENDELL, urologist, surgeon; b. York, Pa., Feb. 8, 1957; s. George William and Dorothy Dodd (Firebaugh) M.; m. Ellen R. Jablonski, Oct. 3, 1981. BS summa cum laude, Pa. State U., 1979; MD, Jefferson Med. Coll. of Phila., 1982. Diplomate Am. Bd. Urology. Commd. 2d lt. Med. Corps U.S. Army, 1982, advanced through grades to col., 2000; intern, resident Walter Reed Army Med. Ctr., Washington, 1982-87, attending urologist Army Med. Corps, 1987—; urologic oncology fellow Duke U., Durham, N.C., 1988-89; asst. prof. surgery Uniformed Svcs. U. of Health Scis., Bethesda, Md., 1989-93, assoc. prof. surgery, 1993-99; prof. Uniformed Svcs. U. of Health Scis., Bethesda, 1999—; dir. Dept. of Def. Ctr. for Prostate Disease Rsch., H.M. Jackson Found., Rockville, Md., 1992—; nat. cons. "Us-Too" Prostate Cancer Support Group Hinsdale, Ill., and Nat. Assn. for Continence, Union, S.C., 1992—. Contbr. over 200 articles to profl. jours.; mem. editl. bd. numerous profl. jours. U.S. Army Med. Rsch. and Materiel Comd. Rsch. grantee, 1992—. Fellow ACS; mem. AMA (Cmty. Svc. award 1995), Am. Urol. Assn. (tech. assessment com., meeting essay prizes 1986, 89, Gold Cystoscope award 1997), Soc. Urologic Oncology, Am. Assn. Cancer Rsch. (Meeting prize 1995), Soc. Univ. Urologists, Assn. Mil. Surgeons of the U.S. (History of Med. Mil. History award 1992, Sir Henry Wellcome medal and prize 1996), Phi Beta Kappa, Alpha Omega Alpha, Phi Kappa Phi, Alpha Epsilon Delta. Home: 8917 Holly Leaf Ln Bethesda MD 20817-2654 Office: CPDR 1530 E Jefferson St Rockville MD 20852-1501

MOULAERT, JACQUES, banker; b. Ostend, Belgium, Oct. 23, 1930; s. Albert Moulaert and Marie de Neckere; m. Christiane Lalous, 1957; 4 children. Student, St. Barbaraa Coll., Ghent, Belgium, U. Ghent, Harvard U. Gen. sec. Aleurope S.A., 1961-67; asst. mgr. Compagnie Lambert, 1967-72; mgr. Compagnie Bruxelles Lambert, 1972-79; mng. dir. Groupe Bruxelles Lambert, 1979-93; chmn. bd. Bank Brussels Lambert, 1993—. Office: Bank Brussels Lambert, 24 Ave Marnix, B-1040 Brussels Belgium*

MOULANA, ABDULRAHEEM, nephrologist; b. Hyderabad, India, Oct. 2, 1946; arrived in Saudi Arabia, 1975; s. Mohammed Bhikku and Kulsum Mohammed Moulana; m. Arifunnisa Abdulaleem Hyder, Apr. 1972; children: Arjumand, Ashraf, Amena, Hanan. MB BS, Osmania Med. Coll., Hyderabad, 1972, MS in Gen. Surgery, 1976; DM in Nephrology, U. Vienna, Austria, 1986. Registered med. practitioner Gen. Med. Coun.-U.K., Indian Med. Coun. Resident nephrology King Abdul Aziz Hosp., Makkah, Saudi Arabia, 1975-85; nephrologist King Abdul Aziz Hosp., Makkah, 1986-90, head nephrology, 1990—, cons. nephrologist, 1990—; resident nephrology 1st U. Med. Clinic, Vienna, 1985-86; head Kidney Ctr., Makkah, 1990—. Contbr. articles to profl. jours. Mem. Internat. Soc. Nephrology, European Dialysis and Transplant Soc. (assoc.), Arab Soc. Dialysis and Transplant. Islamic. Avocation: computer programming. Achievements include devel. of database patient mgmt. program; translating the meaning of holy Qu'ran into Telugu. Home: PO Box 2043, Holy Makkah Saudi Arabia Office: King Abdul Aziz Hosp, Zahir, Holy Makkah Saudi Arabia

MOULDER, DAVID STEPHEN, information scientist, librarian; b. Stourbridge, Eng., Dec. 27, 1944; s. Maurice Phillip and Jenny (Dale) M.; m. Christine Heather Downes, July 13, 1968; children: Justin Bryce, Russell Paul. BSc, London U., 1967. Info. scientist Metal Box Co., London, 1967-70, Marine Biol. Assn., Plymouth, Eng., 1970-92; head Nat. Marine Biol. Libr. Plymouth Marine Lab./Marine Biol. Assn., 1992-97; libr. World Maritime U., 1998—; cons. UN Environ. Programme, Geneva, 1986; Internat. Maritime Orgn., London, 1990. Author: (with C. McFadden, P. Pissierssens, P. Reyniers) Standard Directory Record Structure for Organizations, Individuals and Their Research Interests, 1994, (with K. Djørup, S. Heath) Proceedings of the Sixth Meeting of the European Association of Aquatic Sciences Libraries and Information Centres, 1997, Standard Library Directory Record Structure, 1999; editor: Directory of European Aquatic Sciences Libraries and Information Centres, 1991, 94, Aquatic Sciences and Fisheries Information System Geographic Authority List, 1992. Devel. treas. Ivybridge (Eng.) Meth. Ch., 1994-97. Mem. European Assn. Aquatic Scis. Librs. and Info. Ctrs. (pres. 1992-96), Internat. Assn. Aquatic and Marine Scis. Librs. and Info. Ctrs. (regional bd. dirs. 1992-96), Inst. Info. Scientists. Avocations: gardening, walking, reading. Fax: 46 40 12 84 42. E-mail: david.moulder@wmu.se. Office: World Maritime Univ, Citadellsvägen 29 Box 500, S-20124 Malmö Sweden

MOULDER, T. EARLINE, musician; b. Buffalo, Mo., Oct. 11; d. Earl Young and Ruby M. (Philipot) M.; m. R. David Plank, Dec. 21, 1980; children: Jeannine Stanton, Jon Stanton, Timothy Stanton. AB in Biology and French, Drury Coll., 1973; studied piano with Soulima Stravinsky, 1961; M in Music magna cum laude, Ind. U., 1963; D in Musical Arts, U. Kansas, 1991; pvt. organ study, Andre Marchal, Paris, France, 1971. Organist St. Paul Meth. Ch., Springfield, Mo., 1961-81; concert organist U.S., Europe, Middle East, Australia, 1964—; exec. editor Drury Coll. Mirror, Springfield, Mo., 1971-73; rschr. Am. U., Beirut, 1973; journalist U.S. Naval Res., Springfield and Treasure Island, Calif., 1975-77; organist King's Way Meth. Ch., Springfield, Mo., 1983-93; chair organ dept. Drury U., Springfield, Mo., 1968—, univ. organist, 1991—; lectr. recitals on Jewish music, 1991—; translator, Profl. documents, 1990—. Author: Organ Works of Elsa Barraine, 1995, Music of Alice Jordan, 1998; composer organ composition The Crucifixion, 1995; contbr. articles to profl. jours. Charter mem. Nat. Mus. Am. Indian, 1994—. Recipient Teaching fellow U. Kans., Drury Mirror award Rank I Mo. Coll. Newspaper Assn. Mem. Mortar Bd., Sigma Alpha Iota, Alpha Lambda Delta, Pi Delta Phi, Beta Beta Beta, Pi Kappa Lambda, Organ Hist. Soc., Am. Guild Organist. Home: 3563 E Linwood Dr Springfield MO 65809-2131 Office: Drury Univ 900 N Benton Ave Springfield MO 65802-3712

MOULIJN, JACOB ADRIANUS, chemical technology educator; b. Harlingen, Friesland, The Netherlands, Mar. 13, 1942. D, U. Amsterdam, The Netherlands, 1967, Lab. Chem. Tech., The Netherlands, 1974. Asst. prof. U. Amsterdam, 1972-86, prof. chem. tech., 1986-90; prof. chem. tech. Tech. U. Delft, The Netherlands, 1990—; chief tech. advisor in China, 1995-99. Mem. editl. bd. Fuel, 1982, Fuel Processing Tech.; editor 6 books; contbr. over 400 articles to profl. jours. Recipient Nat. BP Energy prize, 1982, Simon Stevin Meester, 2000. Mem. AICE, ACS, Royal Chem. Soc. (The Netherlands). Achievements include patents in catalysis, zeolite-based membrane monolithic reactors; research in monolithic reactors, catalytic reactors, petroleum conversion, exhaust gas catalysis, mass transfer in porous materials, catalytic reactors, catalytic testing, process development. Office: U Delft, Julianalaan 136, 2628 BL Delft The Netherlands

MOULIN, JANE ANN FREEMAN, ethnomusicology educator, researcher; b. Oak Park, Ill., Mar. 4, 1946; d. James Frederic and Georgia Charlotte (Rahn) Freeman; m. Jacques Edouard Moulin, Apr. 26, 1975; children: Jean-Philippe Keala, Marie-Chantal Mahala. BA in Music cum laude, U. Hawaii, 1969; MA in Music, UCLA, 1971; PhD in Music, U. Calif., Santa Barbara, 1991. Libr. Music Libr UCLA, 1970-71; tchr. English Companions, Osaka, Japan, 1972; dancer Te Maeva and Tahiti Nui, Papeete, Tahiti, 1973-76; rsch. fellow U. Auckland, New Zealand, 1989; fellow East-West Ctr., Honolulu, 1984-85, 91; assoc. prof. Hawaii Loa Coll., Kaneohe, 1980-92; prof. U. Hawaii, Honolulu, 1992—; dir. Europa Early Music Consort, Honolulu, 1981—; primary rschr. field work in French Polynesia, 1973-77, 85, 89, 95, 98, 2000, Territorial Survey Oceanic Music, Marquesas Islands, 1989; cons. Video series Dancing, WNET Channel 13, N.Y.C., 1989-92. Author: The Dance of Tahiti, 1979, Music of the Southern Marquesas Islands, 1994, (audio catalog) Music of the Southern Marquesas Islands, 1991, ency. and jour. articles on Tahitian and Marquesan performing arts, field recordings of Tahitian and Marquesan music; editl. bd. Jour. Perfect Beat, 1993—, Pacific Islands Monograph Series, 1997—; bd. dirs. Hawaii Assn. Music Socs., Honolulu, 1983-88. Bd. dirs. Tahiti-USA Assn., Honolulu, 1997-2000; mem. adv. bd. folk arts State Found. Culture and Arts, Honolulu, 1985-87. Recipient Regents' fellowship U. Calif., 1970-71, 88-89, rsch. grant UNESCO/Archives of Maori and Pacific Music, Auckland, 1989, regents' award for excellence in tchg. U. Hawaii, Honolulu, 1997, First Prize Thèse-Pac Assn. Competition, New Caledonia, 1994. Mem. Soc. Ethomusicology (mem. coun. 1995-97), Internat. Coun. Traditional Music, Polynesia Soc., Pacific Arts Assn., Viola da Gamba Soc. Am. Avocations: Tahitian dance, hula, consort playing. Office: U Hawaii Music Dept 2411 Dole St Honolulu HI 96822-2329

MOULINES, CARLOS ULISES, philosopher, educator; b. Caracas, Venezuela, Oct. 26, 1946; arrived in Germany, 1984; s. Lino and Otilia (Castellví) M.; m. Adriana Valadés, Feb. 10, 1981. MA, U. Barcelona, Spain, 1971; PhD, U. Munich, Germany, 1975. Rschr. Deutsche Forschungsgemeinschaft, Germany, 1972-75; asst. U. Munich, 1975-76; prof. Nat. U. Mexico, Mexico City, 1976-84, U. Bielefeld, Germany, 1984-88, U. Berlin, 1988-93; chmn. U. Munich, 1993—. Author: La estructura del mundo sensible, 1973, Exploraciones metacientíficas, 1982, Pluralidad y recursión, 1991, Antes del olvido, 1996; co-author: An Architectonic for Science, 1987, Fundamentos de Filosofía de la Ciencia, 1997; co-editor: Structuralist Theory of Science, 1996, Structuralist Knowledge Representation, 2000. Recipient Nat. Prize Mexican Acad. Scis., Mexico City, 1983. Mem. German Soc. Analytical Philosophy (pres. 1997—), German Soc. Philosophy, Humboldt-Gesellschaft, N.Y. Acad. Scis., Academie Internationale de Philosophie des Scis. Office: Seminar Philosophie Logik & Wissenschaftstheorie, Ludwig Strasse 31, 80539 Munich Bavaria, Germany

MOULTON, JONATHAN PAUL, venture capitalist; b. Stoke-on-Trent, England, Oct. 15, 1950; s. Douglas Cecil and Elsi Tuner (Pointon) M.; m. Pauline Dunn, Aug. 13, 1972; Rebecca Clare, Spencer Jonathan. BA, Lancaster U., 1971. Mgr. Coopers & Lybrand, 1973-80; dir. Citicorp Venture Capital, 1980-83, gen. mgr., 1983-85; mng. ptnr. Schroder Ventures, London, 1985-95; dir. Apax Ventures, London, 1995—; non-exec. Hornby Hobbies Plc, Margate, Kent, Eng., 1981-87, Halls Homes & Gardens Plc, Tonbridge, Kent, 1982-92, Haden Macllellan Holdings Plc, Egham, Surrey, Eng., 1987—, Interconnection Sys. Ltd., Tyne, Wear, Newcastle, Eng., 1987-91, Ushers Holdings Plc, 1991—, Parker Pen Ltd., 1986-92, Prestige Holdings Ltd., 1995—, Unicorn Holdings Plc, 1995—, United Texon Plc, 1995—, Brit. Fuels Ltd., 1995—. Fellow Inst. Chartered Accts. in England & Wales. Avocations: chess, fishing. Office: Apax Ventures, 20 Bedfordbury, London WC2N 4BL, England

MOUNAYER, JOSEPH AYOUB, archbishop; b. Katana, Syria, June 6, 1925; s. Ayoub Mounayer and Abila Fakhoury. D of Canon Law, U. Lateran, Rome, 1953. Ordained priest Roman Cath. Ch., 1949, ordained bishop, 1971. Archbishop Damascus Syria, 1978—; created ctr. for handicapped children, Damascus, 1979, home for elderly, Damascus, 1985, sheltered workshop for handicapped youth, Damascus, 1990. Author: Les Synodes Syriens Jacobites, 1963; dir. rev. Al Karma; translator Ishhim, 1965, 2d edit., 1994, Saint Ephrem & the Syriac Church, 1983; contbr. articles and revs. to profl. jours. Fax: 00963-11-5434009. Home and Office: Archevêché Syrien Cth, PO Box 2129 Rue Bab-Charki, Damascus Syria

MOUNLA-HAYDAR, NASRAT, judge; b. Deir-ez-Zor, Furat, Syria, July 28, 1930; s. Saleh Mounla-Haydar and Salema Tcherkesse; m. Jihan Habbak, July 29, 1982. Licentiate of law, Damascus U., Syria, 1950, Diploma of High Studies in Pvt. Law, 1951. Cert. Judge of Peace Aleppo 1954-1955-1956; Judge of Criminal Instruction Hama 1955, Aleppo 1959. Avocat stagiaire Ct. of Appeal, Aleppo, 1950, master adv., 1952; dir. Cabinet of Justice Min., 1959; mem. Legis. Dept., 1962, dir., 1968; judge Supreme Constnl. Ct., 1973-86, chief justice, 1986—; legal advisor to the presidency, 1962—; lectr. license sect. faculty of law Damascus U., 1963-67, mem. high studies sect., 1972-74, 82-84; gen. sec. Ministry of Justice, 1973. Sr. mem. Syrian Del. to Madrid Peace Conf. on Middle East, 1991. Home: Mezze, Damascus Syria Office: Supreme Constl Ct, Rawda Quar Kassem Amin St, Damascus Syria*

MOUNSEY, JOSEPH BACKHOUSE, investment consultant; b. Lisburn, Northern Ireland, Mar. 27, 1949; arrived in Can., 1994; s. Colin Anthony and Helen (Roake) M.; m. Josephine Jennifer Gough, July 6, 1995; 1 child, Elizabeth Helen. MA with honors, Oxford (Eng.) U., 1970. Sr. v.p. Internat. Investments Manulife Fin., 1991-94; chmn. Western Trust and Savings Ltd., 1991-94; sr. v.p. investments Manulife Fin., Toronto, Ont., Can., 1994-97; cons., 1998—. Mem. Inst. Investment, Mgmt. and Rsch. (cert.). Home: 218 Blythwood Rd, Toronto, Canada M4N 1A6

MOUNT, CHRISTOPHER JOHN, solicitor; b. London, Dec. 14, 1913; s. Francis and Gladys (Llewelyn) M.; m. Audrey Mabel Clarke, Feb. 6, 1947; children: David, Antony. MA, Oxford U., 1937. Lic. solicitor. Solicitor asst. Maidenhead, Eng., 1967-69; solicitor, ptnr. C.R. Thomas, Maidenhead, 1969-79; cons. Wrights Soliakon, Ascot Berks, Eng., 1978; dep. lt. Berkshire, Eng., 1984-93. With RAF Aux., 1935-38, Air Cadre, RAF, 1938-66. Decorated DFC, Disting. Svc. Order, Comdr. Brit. Empire. Anglican. Address: Garden House Bagshot Rd, Sunninghill Ascot SL5 9JL, England

MOUNTCASTLE, KENNETH FRANKLIN, JR., retired stockbroker; b. Winston-Salem, N.C., Oct. 8, 1928; s. Kenneth Franklin and May M.; m. Mary Katharine Babcock, Sept. 1, 1951; children: Mary Babcock, Laura Lewis, Kenneth Franklin, Katharine Reynolds. BS in Commerce, U. N.C., 1950. With Mountcastle Knitting Co., Lexington, N.C., 1952-55, Reynolds & Co., N.Y.C., 1955-71, Reynolds Securities Inc. (formerly Reynolds and Co.), N.Y.C., 1971-95; sr. v.p. Reynolds Securities Inc., N.Y.C., 1974-78, Dean Witter Reynolds (formerly Reynolds Securities Inc.), N.Y.C., 1978-95; ret., 1995. Trustee New Canaan (Conn.) Country Sch., 1962-68, Ethel Walker Sch., Simsbury, Conn., 1973-85, Coro Found., 1980—, nat. chmn., 1986-89; past bd. dirs., past pres. Mary Reynolds Babcock Found., Winston-Salem; former bd. visitors U. N.C., Chapel Hill,; bd. dirs. Inform, N.Y.C., Fresh Air Fund, N.Y.C., The Giraffe Project Friends of 13, Bus. Execs. Nat. Security. Served with U.S. Army, 1950-52. Mem. Country Club of New Canaan, Wee Burn Country Club (Darien, Conn.), Old Town Club (Winston-Salem), Racquet and Tennis Club, Ocean Forest Golf Club (Sea Island, Ga.), Sea Island Club, Pine Valley Golf Club, Bond Club, Stock Exch. Luncheon Club, The Down Town Assn. (N.Y.C.). Office: 49 Locust Ave Ste 104 New Canaan CT 06840-4764

MOUNTFORT, DOUGLAS OPIE, biochemist, researcher; b. Taupo, New Zealand, Aug. 25, 1946; s. Hugh Vaughan and Joan (Opie) M.; m. Gaye Coila Armitage, Dec. 14, 1974; children: Jane, Richard, Thomas. BS in Biochemistry, Massey U., Palmerston, New Zealand, 1969, MS in Biochemistry with honors, 1972; PhD in Biochemistry, U. Auckland, New Zealand. Jr. lectr. biochemistry U. Auckland, 1973-75; rsch. asst. dept. dairy sci. U. Ill., Urbana-Champaign, Ill., 1981-82; biochemist Cawthron Inst., Nelson, New Zealand, 1976-81, microbial biochemist, 1982-84, sr. scientist, 1986—, rsch. chmn., 1994-2000; mem. rev. panel com. Found. for Rsch. Sci. and Tech., New Zealand, 1996-97, programme mgr., 1993—. Co-editor: (book) Anaerobic Fungi, 1994; contbr. over 60 articles to sci. jours. Postdoctoral rsch. fellow, U. Ill., 1981-82, Humboldt fellow dept. microbiology, Phillips U., Marburg, Germany, 1984-86; Marsden grantee Royal Soc. New Zealand, 1997. Mem. New Zealand Microbiol. Soc. (mem. com. 1992-94), Internat. Soc. Study of Harmful Algae. Anglican. Avocations: hiking, gardening. Home: 33 Maitland Ave, Nelson New Zealand Office: Cawthron Inst, 92 A Halifax St, Nelson New Zealand

MOUNTZ, LOUISE CARSON SMITH, retired librarian; b. Fond Du Lac, Wis., Oct. 20, 1911; d. Roy Carson and Charlotte Louise (Scheurs) Smith; m. George Edward Mountz, May 4, 1935 (dec. Oct. 3 1951); children: Peter Carson, Pamela Teeters Mountz McDonald. Student, Western Coll. for Women, 1929-31; AB, The Ohio State U., 1933; MA, Ball State U., 1962; postgrad., Manchester Coll., 1954, Ind. U., 1960-61. Cert. tchr., Ind. Tchr. Monroeville (Ind.) High Sch., 1953-54, Riverdale High Sch., St. Joe, Ind., 1954-55; libr. High Sch., Avilla, Ind., 1955-58; head libr. Penn High Sch., Mishawaka, Ind., 1958-67, Northwood Jr. High Sch., Ft. Wayne, Ind., 1967-69, McIntosh Jr. High Sch., Auburn, Ind., 1969-74; dir. Media Ctr. DeKalb Jr. High Sch., Auburn, Ind., 1974-78; ret., 1978; cons. media ctr. planning Penn-Harris-Madison Sch. Corp., Mishawaka, 1966-67. Author: Biographies for Junior High Schools and Correlated Audio-Visual Materials, 1970; contbr. articles to profl. jours. Bd. dirs. DeKalb County chpt. ARC, 1938-42, 51-53, DeKalb County Heart Assn., 1946-52, DeKalb County Cmty. Concert Assn., 1946-58, Am. Field Svc. Mishawaka chpt., 1960-67; mem. Ft. Wayne Philharmonic Orch. Assn., Ft. Wayne Art Mus., DeKalb County Hist. Soc., Garrett Hist. Soc., DeKalb County Genealogy Soc., Acres Landtrust, Preservation of DeKalb County Heritage Assn., DeKalb Meml. Hosp. Women's Guild, also life mem. Mem. Ind. Sch. Librarians Assn. (dir. 1963-67), Internat. Assn. Sch. Librarianship, Ind. Assn. Ednl. Communication and Tech., Assn. Ind. Media Educators, Nat. Ret. Tchrs. Assns., Nat. Trust Hist. Preservation, Hist. Landmarks Found. Ind., Delta Kappa Gamma (charter mem., Beta Beta chpt.), Kappa Kappa Kappa (pr. officer 1941-45, pres. Alpha Chi chpt. 1938-40, organizer Garrett Assoc. chpt. pres. Garrett Assoc. chpt. 1971-73), Delta Delta Delta (house pres.). Methodist. Lodge: Order Ea. Star. Clubs: Greenhurst Country, Ft. Wayne Women's, Athena Lit. (hon. mem.), Ladies Lit. of Auburn. Home: 19 Castle Ct Auburn IN 46706-1439

MOURAD, JEAN-JACQUES, physician, researcher; b. Ajaltoun, Lebanon, Apr. 26, 1966; s. Joseph Nicolas and Eliane Mourad; m. Isabelle Thauvin, Dec. 3, 1988; children: Nicolas, Clarisse, Romain. Asst. Broussais Hosp., Paris, 1996-98; chief dept. Saint-Michel Hosp., Paris, 1999—; cons. Institut Cardio-Vasculaire, Paris, 1998—. Editor-in-chief Jour. de L'Interniste. Mem. French Soc. Internal Medicine, French Soc. Hypertension. Office: Hopital Saint Michel, 33 Rue Olivier de Serres, 75730 Cedex 15 Paris, France

MOURAD, MAMDOUH YOUSSEF, chemist, educator; b. Cairo, Mar. 4, 1946; s. Yossef Mourad El Sayed and Raisa El Sayed Agmy; m. Samia Abd El Hamid Hassan, June 9, 1976; children: Ahmed, Hesham, Hatem. BS in Chemistry and Physics, Cairo U., 1966; MS in Chemistry, Al Azhar U., 1971; PhD of Phys. Chemistry, Erlangen-Nürnberg U., 1976. Demonstrator, lectr. Al Azhar U., Cairo, 1966-82, asst. prof., 1982-83; asst. prof., prof. Qatar U., Doha, 1983-2000; expert dept. curriculum and textbooks Ministry Edn. and higher Edn., Doha, 2000—. Author, editor Chemistry Books for Secondary Sch. Edn., 1990-95. Mem. Egyptian Soc. Corrosion. Moslem. Office: Curriculum & Textbook Dept, PO Box 80, Doha Qatar

MOURAD, WALID A., pathologist; b. Cairo, July 8, 1955; s. Aly A. Mourad and Atteyat Hamed; m. Hala Mourad; children: Youssef, Moustafa, Adam, Marian, Ismail. MB BChir, Ain-Shams Sch. Medicine, Cairo, 1979. Cert. in anatomic and clin. pathology and cytopathology Am. Bd. Pathology. Resident U. South Fla., Tampa, 1985-89, fellow, 1990; fellow Rosewell Parl Meml. Inst., Buffalo, N.Y., 1984-85, U. Tex. M.D. Anderson Cancer Ctr., Houston, 1990-92; from asst. prof. to assoc. prof. U. Alta., Edmonton, Can., 1992-96; cons. pathologist King Faisal Specialist Hosp. and Rsch. Ctr., Riyadh, Saudi Arabia. Office: MBC10 PO Box 3354, 11211 Riyadh Saudi Arabia

MOURADIAN, ZADIG, astrophysicist; b. Bucharest, Romania, July 10, 1930; arrived in France, 1958; s. Hampartzoum and Mariam (Chevorkian) M.; m. Aida Marie Basmadjian, July 12, 1974; children: Van, Taline. BS, U. Bucharest, 1954; PhD, U Paris, 1965. Lab. chief Vulcan Factory, Bucharest, 1955-57; sci. investigator Astron. Inst., Bucharest, 1957-58; sci. investigator Paris Obs., 1959—, sr. scientist, 1993—; dir., procs. editor NATO workshop, 1997; lectr. Bucharest U., 1998—. Co-author: Solar Interior and Atmosphere, 1991; editor: Synoptic Maps of Solar Activity; contbr. articles to profl. jours. Mem. Internat. Astron. Union. Christian Ch. Avocations: opera, pre-Columbian art, modern painting, history of architecture. Office: Obs de Paris-Meudon, 5 Place Jules Janssen, 92195 Meudon Prin Cedex, France

MOURÃO, PAULO DE SALLES, retired civil engineer, programmer; b. Belo Horizonte, Brazil, May 1, 1924; s. Paulo Krüger and Maria Efigenia (de Salles) M.; m. Lucia Vianna, Mar. 19, 1948; children: Ana Lucia, Junia, Paulo, Suzana, Rodrigo. Degree in civil engring., Fed. U. Rio de Janeiro, 1946, postgrad., 1986. Contracts ruler Belo Horizonte City Hall, 1947-49, dir. hwys., 1949-53, chief resident, 1953-56, mcpl. plan supr., 1957-76, designer, programmer, 1976-99, ret., 1999; mem. CEPA, Palacio das Artes Found., Belo Horizonte, 1952-53; programmer Hewlett-Packard User's Libr., U.S., 1980-83; prof. Kennedy Sch. Engring., Belo Horizonte, 1966-67. Author: Reinforced Concrete Draftsman Manual, 1962, Reinforced Concrete by Electronic Computation, 1979, Structural Engineering Programs, 1989. Reciient medal Minas Gerais Coun., 1953. Mem. Minas Engring. Soc. (tech. councilor 1948—), N.Y. Acad. Scis. Roman Catholic. Avocations: swim-

ming, playing violin, classical music, theatre, Internet. Home and Office: Rua Engenheiro Amaro Lanari, 110/201, 30310580 Belo Horizonte Brazil

MOURA-RELVAS, JOAQUIM M.M.A., electrical engineer, educator; b. Aveiro, Portugal, May 9, 1926; s. Joaquim Moura and Maria Emilia Albuquerque (Branco de Melo) Relvas; m. Maria Alice Barata Portugal, May 9, 1953; children: Jose Pedro, Joao Paulo, Luis Filipe, Joaquim Jose, Francisco Manuel, Maria Isabel. Degree in Elec. Engr., U. Porto, Portugal, 1951. Asst. engr. CTT (State Telecomms.), Lisbon, Portugal, 1951-53; design engr. UEP (Elec. Power Co.), Porto, 1953-73; prof. U. Coimbra, Portugal, 1973-81; chief engr. EDP (Electricidade de Portugal), Lisbon, 1981-88; prof. Poly. Inst. of Gaya, Vila Nova de Gaia, Portugal, 1988—. Author: Introduction to Digital Electronics, 1971, Introduction to Microcomputers, 1981, Digital Electronics, 1986. Mem. AAAS, N.Y. Acad. Scis., Ordem dos Engenheiros, Planetary Soc. Avocations: swimming, walking, photography, home movies, historical books. Home: Av da Republica 1815, Vila Nova de Gaia 4430-206, Portugal Office: ISP Gaya, R Antonio R da Rocha 341, Vila Nova de Gaia 4430-206, Portugal

MOURASHKIN, BORIS, composer, educator, sound therapist, poet, performer, producer; b. Kemerovo, Siberia, Feb. 27, 1949. BA in Musical Theory and Composition, Novosibirsk Mus. Coll., 1972; postgrad., M.I. Glinka Conservatory, 1972-76. Head rsch. lab. (Bio-Energetic Music) for Bio-Energetic and Ecology of Consciousness Russian Fedn., Inst. Human Ecology, Acad. Tech. Scis., Moscow, 1993—. Prof., composer various styles of music including choir music, piano composition, compositions for string orchs., incidental music, musical scores for films and plays;compositions include Jungle Passion, Odd & Even, Two-Step for Lovers, The Stirrings of Love, Blizzard Dance, Without End..., others; music editor Novosibirsk-Telefilm, 1980-83; rec. engr., composer, film actor TV, 1980-90; composer: This Is Us, O Lord!, 1991, Kama Sutra, 1991, Points of Light, 1994, Healing Music, 1994, Bio-Energetic Psychotropic Music, Touching the Mystical of Outer Space (dedicated to Steven Spielberg, Jeffrey Katzenberg and David Geffen), Night of Open Doors, 1995, author: (poetry and prose) The Existence of Man Begins with Protest (a tribute to V.M. Schukschin), The Broom's Solo, God Loves the Righteous; Cds include Howl of the Siberian Wolf, 2000, Tribute to the East, 2000; inventor, founder Bio-Enegetic Psychotropic Music, Healing Power of Music, 1983; founder, dir., prodr. Golden Fund of Documentary Films (extraordinary Russian-Americans); contbr. various articles to newspapers and mags. Vol. Siberian Orphanage, 1972-89, Siberian Prison, 1976-89, St. Christopher-Ottilie Home, Bio-Energetic Psychotropic Music Therapy Workshops for mentally and retarded children, Sea Cliff, N.Y., 1992-94, Gift of Life, Inc., 1993, Manhattan Psychiat. Ctr. workshops with Bio-Energetic, Psychotropic Music with mentally disordered people, Wards Island, N.Y., 1997; bd. dirs., mem. adv. bd. Tchertkoff Meml. & Cultural Found.; hon. mem. operation kids program Nat. Police Def. Found., 1999. Named Famous Poet, Famous Poets Soc., 1998, One of Best Poets of 2000 Internat. Libr. Poetry, 2000; recipient award of recognition Famous Poets Soc., 1998, Poet of the Yr. medallion Famous Poets Soc., 1999, Diamond Homer trophy Famous Poets Soc., 1999, Internat. Poet of Merit award medallion Internat. Soc. Poets, 1999, Pres. Recognition Lit. Excellence The Drifting Sands, Nat. Libr. Poetry, 1999. Fellow Internat. Informatization Acad. UN (academician, prof., PhD Art of Music Alternative Music Therapy, PhD Art of Science Practical Elaboration and Expertise BioSound Therapy Tech. and Soundpsycho-neuro-reflective immunotherapy); mem. Internat. Union Info., World Assn. Edn. Worlddidac, Nat. Acad. Rec. Art & Scis. Inc., Internat. Soc. Poets (disting., Internat. Poet of Merit award medallion 1999, Poet of Yr. 1999), Broadcast Music, Inc., Cinematographer's Union of Russian Fedn., Nat. Authors Registry. E-mail: godforus@earthlink.net. Home: 165 Brown St Sea Cliff NY 11579-1601

MOURATIDIS, PAVLOS I., chemical company executive, chemical engineer; b. Thessaloniki, Greece, Feb. 23, 1961; s. Ioannis P. and Eleni I. (Skenderoglou) M.; m. Stavroula C. Argyriou, Oct. 18, 1992; children: Ioannis, Christos. Degree in chem. engring., Aristotle's U. Thessaloniki, 1984; degree in polymer tech., Helsinki (Finland) U. Tech., 1991. Registered profl. engr., Tech. Chamber Greece, 1984. Trainee Esso-Pappas S.A., Thessaloniki, 1982; adminstrv. staff Nat. Bank Greece, Thessaloniki, 1984-87; tech. svc. rep. Marlit Ltd., Thessaloniki, 1987-89; R & D mgr. A.R.I. Ltd., Thessaloniki, 1989—; tech. mgr. Marlit Ltd., 1993-97; asst. head R & D A.C.M. Wood Chem. Ltd., Fribourg, Switzerland, 1989—. Inventor in field. Gen. sec. Christian Students Assn., Thessaloniki, 1980-83. Recipient scholarships Greek Ministry Edn., 1980, 82, 83, Finnish Govt., 1990-91, Danish Govt., 1987. Mem. Profl. Chem. Engrs. Assn., Tech. Chamber Greece, Forest Products Rsch. Soc. Avocations: computers, chess, travel, cycling, playing music. Home: Zoumetikou 42, GR-54249 Thessaloniki Greece Office: A R I Ltd, Soufouli 88, GR-55131 Kalamaria Greece

MOURAVIEFF-APOSTOL, ANDREW, association executive; b. Cannes, France, Feb. 7, 1913; s. Wladimir and Nadine (Tereschenko) M.-A.; m. Mary C. Hall-Caine, Nov. 10, 1938; m. 2d, Ellen Marion Rothschild, Nov. 12, 1956; children: Michael, Nicholas, Christopher A. BS, Geneva U., 1935; Dr (hon.), Tumen U. Paris and Berlin corr. London Daily Telegraph, 1936-40; columnist Evening Standard, London, 1940-48; resettlement officer UN High Commn. for Refugees, Geneva, 1949-67; hon. pres. Internat. Fedn. Social Workers; dir. info. P.C./UNESCO, London, 1946-48; UN advisor to Govt. Peru, 1951-52. Decorated Bailiff Grand Cross Order of St. John of Jerusalem; Grand Cross Order of St. Saba; Order Homayun (Iran); Order of Merit (Chile). Mem. Russian Acad. of Learning, Royal Soc. St. George (life gov.), Naval and Military Club (London). Mem. Anglican Church. Home: 31 Rue de l'Athenee, 1206 Geneva Switzerland

MOURE, NANCY DUSTIN WALL, art historian; b. Dayton, Ohio, Feb. 26, 1943; d. Clayton Edgar and Bernis (Willigar) Wall; m. Joseph Laurence Moure, June 19, 1970 (div. 1982). BA in Art, San Diego State Coll., 1965; MA in Art History, UCLA, 1968. Asst. curator L.A. County Mus. Art, 1968-83; art cons. Jonathan Club, L.A., 1985-88; freelance art cons., 1989—; cons. Trust Co. of West, L.A. Author: Dictionary of Art and Artists in Southern California Before 1930, 1975, Index to Reproductions of American Paintings in Books, 1977, William Louis Sonntag, 1822-1900, 1980, Painting and Sculpture in Los Angeles, 1900-1945, 1980, Drawings and Illustrations by Southern California Artists Before 1950, 1982, Loners, Mavericks and Dreamers: Art in Los Angeles Before 1900, 1994, California Art: 450 Years of Painting and Other Media, 1998 and numerous others. Mem. Hist. Collections Coun. (editor newsletter 1986—). E-mail: nancymoure@earthlink.net. Home: 935 W Mountain St Glendale CA 91202-1045

MOURGUE D'ALGUE, PIERRE ANDRE, finance company executive; b. Geneva, Aug. 25, 1960; s. Georges Emile and Pierrette Micheline (Wyss) M.D. BS, L.I. U., 1982; MBA, Columbia U., 1984. Account officer Citicorp NA, N.Y.C., 1984-85; v.p. Hoare Govett Inc., N.Y.C., 1985-88; dir. Schroder Securities Ltd., London, 1988-91; mng. dir. BBV Latinvest Securities Ltd., London, 1992-97; dir. Galdessa Safaris Ltd., Nairobi, Kenya, 1991—, Galdessa Camps Ltd., Nairobi, 1991—; dir. La Regie Fonciere SA, Geneva, 1995—; trustee The Tusk Trust, London, 1994—; bd. dirs. Liability Solutions Ltd., London, 1999—. Fellow Royal Geographic Soc.; mem. Securities Inst. Avocations: conservation, skiing, scuba diving, traveling. Office: Liability Solutions Ltd, 17C Curzon St, London W1J 5HS, England

MOURNING, ALONZO, professional basketball player; b. Chesapeake, Va., Feb. 8, 1970. Student, Georgetown U. Center Charlotte Hornets, 1992-95; player Miami Heat, 1995—; player All-Star Game, 1994. Named to NBA All-Rookie First Team, 1993, Dream Team II, 1994. Office: Miami Heat SunTrust Int'l Ctr One SE 3rd Ave Ste 2300 Miami FL 33131

MOUROKH, LEV GRIGORIEVICH, physicist, educator; b. Nizhny Novgorod, Russia, Mar. 23, 1968; came to U.S., 1998.; s. Grigory Lvovich and Serafima Maksovna (Mil'ner) M. Diploma in Engring., N. Lobachevsky State U., Nizhny Novgorod, 1991, PhD, 1996. Engr. Tech. Rsch. Inst., Nizhny Novgorod, 1991-92; asst. prof. physics N. Lobachevsky State U., 1995-98; vis. asst. prof. physics City Coll. of CUNY, 1998-99, vis. rsch. asst. prof. physics, Stevens Inst. Tech., Hoboken, N.J., 1998—, rsch. scientist, Brooklyn Coll. of CUNY, 1999—. Contbr. articles to profl. jours. Swedish Roy. Acad. Sci. fellow, 1995. Mem. N.Y. Acad. Scis., Am. Physical Soc. Home: 1751 67th St Apt E11 Brooklyn NY 11204-4361 Office: Bklyn Coll CUNY Dept Physics 2900 Bedford Ave Brooklyn NY 11210-2814

MOURTADA, FIRAS, physicist, researcher; b. Damascus, Syria, July 17, 1970; came to U.S., 1988; s. Abdul Al-Ghani and Jumanah Mourtada. BS in Biomedical Engring., Mercer U., 1992; MS in Biomedical Engring., Johns Hopkins U., 1994, PhD in Environ. Health, 1998. Rsch. assoc. Nat. Inst. Stds. and Tech., Gaithersburg, Md., 1997-98; R&D med. physicist Guidant Vascular Intervention Corp., Houston, 1998—. Contbr. articles to profl. jours. Whitaker Found. fellow Johns Hopkins U., 1992-94. Mem. Am. Assn. Physicists Medicine, Health Physics Soc., Blue Key, Phi Kappa Phi. Avocations: golfing, fishing. Address: 402 N Elder Grove Dr Pearland TX 77584-7764 Office: Guidant Vascular Intervention Corp 8934 Kirby Dr Houston TX 77054-2829

MOUSA, AMANY MOHAMED, statistics educator, consultant, researcher; b. Shebin El Kom, Egypt, Jan. 28, 1948; s. Mousa Mohamed Mousa and Hanem Mohamed Mahmoud; m. Atef Mohamed Abdel Moneim, Aug. 31, 1974. BSc, Cairo U., 1969, MSc, 1974; MSc, Fla. State U., 1976, PhD, 1981. Asst. rschr. INP, Cairo, 1969-70; asst. lectr. Cairo U., 1974-76, prof., 1992—; lectr. Fla. State U., Tallahassee, 1976-80; asst. prof. U. Greece, Athens, 1980-81; assoc. prof. King Saud U., Riyadh, Saudi Arabia, 1986-91; cons. CDC, Cairo, 1992—. E-mail: atefmo@starnet.com.eg. Home: Cairo U Inst Stat Study & rsch, 5 Thrawt St, Giza Cairo 2613, Egypt Office: Cairo U ISSR, 5 Tharwat St, Cairo Giza, Egypt

MOUSEL, CRAIG LAWRENCE, lawyer; b. St. Louis, July 22, 1947; s. George William and Charlotte (Howard) M.; m. Polly Deane Burkett, Dec. 21, 1974; children: Donna, Dennis, D'Arcy. AB, U. So. Calif., 1969; JD, Ariz. State U., 1972. Bar: Ariz. 1973, U.S. Dist. Ct. Ariz. 1973, U.S. Ct. Appeals (9th cir.) 1973, U.S. Dist. Ct. (cen. dist.) Calif. 1984, Colo. 1993; registered lobbyist, Ariz. Adminstrv. asst. to Hon. Sandra O'Connor Ariz. State Senate, Phoenix, 1971-72; asst. atty. gen. Ariz. Atty. Gen.'s Office, Phoenix, 1973-75; ptnr. Sundberg & Mousel, Phoenix, 1975—; spl. counsel City of Chandler, 1991. Hearing officer Ariz. State Personnel Bd., 1976-80, spl. appeals counsel, 1978—; hearing officer Ariz. Outdoor Recreation Coordinating Commn., 1975; dep. state land commr. Ariz. State Land Dept., 1978; precinct capt. Rep. Com.; mem. Ariz. Kidney Found., Orpheum Theatre Found., Phoenix Zoo Curators Club; sponsor Phoenix Art Mus.; varsity baseball coach Valley Luth. H.S., 1995-97, St. Mary's H.S., 2000; asst. baseball coach St. Mary's H.S., 1997-99. Fellow Ariz. Bar Found.; mem. ABA, ATLA, Ariz. Bar Assn., Maricopa County Bar Assn., Sports Lawyers Assn., Internat. Platform Assn., Ariz. Club, Am. Baseball Coaches Assn., Nat. High Sch. Baseball Coaches Assn., Ariz. Baseball Coaches Assn., USC Ptnrs. Alumni Group, U. So. Calif. Alumni Assn., Ariz. State U. Alumni Assn., Ariz. State Coll. Law Alumni Assn. Office: Sundberg & Mousel 934 W Mcdowell Rd Phoenix AZ 85007-1730

MOUSLEY, JUDITH ANNE, educator; b. Melbourne, Australia, Sept. 18, 1945; d. Oscar Crarnet and Vera May (McKenzie) LeMaistre; m. Selwyn Mousley, Aug. 10, 1968; children: Peter Dean, Christopher. BEd (hon.), Deakin U., MEd. Tchr. various schs., Australia, 1964-82; sr. lectr. Deakin U., Australia, 1982—; v.p. Internat. Group for the Psychology of Math. Edn., 1997—, Math. Edn. Group of Australasia, Australia, 1997—. Author: (CD-ROM) Learning About Teaching, 1996; editor: Developing Practice, 1997. Recipient awd. for Disting. Univ. Teaching, WJC Banks. Office: Faculty of Edn, Deakin Univ, Geelong 3217, Australia

MOUSSA, AMRE MAHMOUD, Egyptian government official; b. 1936. LLB, Cairo U., 1957. Min. Ministry Fgn. Affairs, 1958—; amb. of Egypt Switzerland, India, 1982-86; head internat. orgns. dept. Ministry Fgn. Affairs, 1986-89; perm. chief rep. of Egypt UN, 1989-91; min. fgn. affairs Arab Republic of Egypt. Office: Ministry Fgn Affairs, Tahrir Sq Kournish al-Nile, Maspiro Cairo Egypt*

MOUSSA, MOHAMED AHMED AMIN, biostatistics educator, consultant; b. Abu-Kebir, Sharkia, Egypt, Dec. 10, 1939; s. Ahmed Amin and Fatma Mohamed (Abbas) M.; m. Mervat Rashad Mahmoud Meheisen, July 20, 1949; children: Osama, Nesreen, Nermeen. BS in Pharmacy, Alexandria (Egypt) U., 1960; diploma, Cairo U., 1970, MSc, 1972; PhD, Edinburgh U., 1976. Asst. prof. Al-Fateh U., Tripoli, Libya, 1977-78; assoc. prof. King Saud U., Riyadh, Saudi Arabia, 1990-91; asst. prof. Kuwait U., 1978-81, assoc. prof., 1981-90, 91-93, prof. biostats., 1994—; cons. Ministry of Health, Kuwait, 1993—. Contbr. articles to The Statistician, Stats. in Medicine, Internat. Jour. Obesity, Genus, Clin. Epidemiology, Metabolism, Internat. Jour. Epidemiology. Fellow Royal Statis. Soc., Am. Statis. Assn.; mem. Internat. Statis. Inst., Biometric Soc. Avocations: swimming, bowling. Office: Kuwait U, Faculty of Medicine, 24923 Safat 13110, Kuwait

MOUSSA, NABIL MOHAMED AHMED, engineering educator, mathematician; b. Cairo, Jan. 19, 1945; s. Mohamed and Atiat (Mansi) M.; m. Ulrike Schmidt, July 8, 1972 (div. Nov. 1992); children: Daina, Sandra. BSc in Engring., Ain-Shams, Cairo, 1965, BSc in Math., 1967; D of Natural Scis., Leipzig U., Germany, 1971. Lectr. Azhar U., Cairo, 1972-76; asst. prof. math. Fateh U., Tripolis, Libya, 1976-77; tchr. Holzheim (Germany) Gymnasium, 1977-79; rschr., head software Essen (Germany) U., 1979-83; asst. prof. math. Bahrain U., 1983-87; assoc. prof. math. Am. U., Cairo, 1987-88, 95-97, head math. unit, 1988-95, 98—, prof., 1997—; tchg. asst. Azhar U., Cairo, 1965-68; lectr. Poly., Koeln, Germany, 1977-81, Md. U., Bahrain, 1985-87. Contbr. articles to profl. jours. Recipient numerous rsch. grants, 1976—. Mem. Am. Math. Soc., Soc. Indsl. & Applied Math., Egyptian Math. Soc. Avocations: sports, music, dancing. Office: The Am Univ, PO Box 2511, 2511 Cairo Egypt

MOUSSA, PIERRE LOUIS, banker; b. Lyon, Rhône, France, Mar. 5, 1922; arrived in Eng. 1984; m. Anne-Marie Denise Trousseau, Aug. 14, 1957. Student, Ecole Normale Supérieure, Paris, 1940-43, 45-46, Agrégé des Lettres, Paris, 1943. Various positions in French adminstrn., 1949-54; dir. of Cabinet of the Minister French overseas territories, 1954, under-sec. for econ. affairs and planification, 1954-59; dir. civil aviation, 1959-62; dir. dept. ops., Africa The World Bank, 1962-64; chmn. Fedn. French Ins. Cos., 1965-69; sr. exec. v.p. to chmn., CEO Paribas Group, 1969-81; chmn. Fin. and Devel., Inc., 1982-87, Pallas Holdings (formerly Pallas Group), Luxembourg, 1984-92, Pallas Invest, Luxembourg, 1989-90, Strand Assocs., Guernsey, U.K., 1990—; chmn. West Africa Growth Fund, Luxembourg, Fondation pour l'Entreprise Africaine, Paris, Ciris Investment Mgrs. Ltd., Mauritius; bd. dirs. Alliance Francaise France; past prof. Inst. Polit. Studies of Paris, Nat. Sch. Adminstrn. Author: Les chances économiques de la Communauté franco-africaine, 1957, Les nations prolétaires, 1959, l'économie de la zone franc, 1960, Les Etats-Unis et les nations prolétaires, 1965, La roue de la fortune, Souvenirs d'un financier, 1989, Prix Européen des Affaires du Livre, 1989; contbr. articles to profl. jours. Decorated Officier de la Légion d'Honneur, France, 1976, Officier de l'Ordre Nat. du Mérite, France, 1966, Médaille Aéronautique, France, 1962, Commdr. de l'Ordre Nat. Mauritanien, 1965, Commdr. de l'Ordre Nat. de L'Etoile Equatoriale, Gabon, 1972, Commdr. de l'Ordre Nat. du Lion, Senegal, 1975, Chevalier de l'Etoile Noire du Bénin, others.

MOUSSEAU, TIMOTHY ALEXANDER, biology educator; b. Marville, France, Oct. 10, 1958; came to U.S., 1988; BSc, U. Ottawa, 1980; MSc, U. Toronto, 1983; PhD, McGill U., 1988. Postdoctoral fellow U. Calif., Davis, 1988-90; asst. prof. biology U. S.C., Columbia, 1991-97, assoc. prof., 1997—; program dir. NSF, 1997-98. Mem. Soc. for Study of Evolution, Am. Soc. Naturalists, Entomological Soc. Am., Sigma Xi. Office: U SC Dept Biol Scis Columbia SC 29208-0001

MOUSSEUX, RENATE, language educator; b. Stuttgart, Germany, Oct. 27, 1942; came to U.S., 1964; d. Emile and Gertrud Muller; m. Patrick Mousseux, Dec. 12, 1974; 1 child, Marc. BA, Padagogische Hochschule, Germany; MA, Grand Canyon U.; BL French, German, ESL, Phoenix U. Cert. French, German, psychology, bilingual French, ESL, secondary grades 7-12, Ariz., Calif. Prof. German Berlitz Sch. Lang., Sherman Oaks, Calif., 1966-67, Thunderbird Grad. Sch. Internat. Mgmt., Glendale, Ariz., 1968-72; prof. German and French Scottsdale Dist. H.S., 1980—; prof. French and German Rio Salado C.C., 1976-86; prof. French Scottsdale C.C., 1990-96, U. Phoenix, 1991—, 1991—; lit. and talent agt., co-prodr. for film and lit., 1991—, editor, pub. poetry books, 1991—; distbr. Native Am. Music; bus. lang. trainer, course developer various corps.; trainer student tchrs. Ariz. State U., Ottawa U. Author: Accellerated French (Vive le Francais), 1989, Accellerated German (Willkommen Deutsch), 1990, Accellerated Spanish (Viva el Espanol), 1991, Accellerated Japanese (Moshi Moshi), 1991, Accellerated English (Hello English), 1992. With Essential Skills Com. Ariz. State Bd. Edn. Recipient Ariz. Fgn. Lang. Tchr. of Yr. award Ariz. Assn. Fgn. Lang. Tchrs., 1986, Exceptional Mentorship Skills award Ariz. State U., 1994, Excellence in Mentorship cert. Ariz. State U., 1995; named Tchr. of Yr., U.S. West Outstanding Tchr. Program, 1989, Nat. Day of Excellence award 1996, award in leadership and quality in edn. ASCD, 1990. Mem. NEA, Nat. Geographic Soc., Am. Assn. Tchrs. German, Alliance Francaise, French Tchrs. Assn., Cultural Heritage Alliance, Ariz. Fgn. Lang. Assn., Scottsdale Edn. Assn. Avocation: reading, writing, psychology, anthropology. Home: 15611 N Boulder Dr Fountain Hls AZ 85268-1814 Office: Chaparral High School 6935 E Gold Dust Ave Scottsdale AZ 85253-1484

MOUSTACCHI, ETHEL E., geneticist; b. Cairo, Aug. 21, 1933; d. Felix P. and Flora (Revi) M. BA, Lycee du Caire, Egypt, 1951; BS in Chemistry, Coll. of Chemistry, Paris, 1955; Lic. Scis., Sorbonne, Paris, 1958, PhD, 1964. Fellowship Anti-Cancer League, Paris, 1957-59; rsch. staff asst. CNRS, Paris, 1959-60, rsch. staff, 1960-64; postdoctoral fellow NATO, Seattle, 1964-66; asst. prof. rsch. CNRS, Paris, 1964-69, head of rsch., 1969-84, dir. first rank, 1984-92, dir. exceptional rank, 1992-99, dir. emeritus, 1999—; asst. dir. Inst. Curie, Orsay, France, 1974-77, head of dept., 1977-91; head of unit, CNRS, Paris, 1984-99; scientific councilor Dir. Life Sci. French Atomic Energy Commn., 1999—. Assoc. editor: Mutation Rsch. jour., 1970—, Mutagenesis, 1986-95, Jour. of Photochemistry and Photobiology, 1989-94; contbr. over 200 articles to profl. jours. and books. Mem. French Nat. Sci. Com., Paris, 1985-89, 92-95. Decorated Chevalier Légion d'Honneur., officer Nat. Order Merit; recipient award Anti-Cancer League, French Acad. of Sci., Femme d'Europe-France, 1996, French Acad. Medicine, 1997, Frits Sobels prize, 1999 for major achievements in the field of environ. mutagenesis. Mem. French Genetic Soc. (pres. 1988-92), European Environ. Mutagen Soc. (pres. 1991-93). Avocations: swimming, music, plastic arts. Office: Inst Curie-Recherche, 26 Rue D'ulm, 75248 Paris Cedex 5 France

MOUSTAFA, ABDALLA BAKR, chemistry and technology of plastics educator; b. Minshat Kassem, Sharkeia, Egypt, Jan. 9, 1925; s. Soliman Bakr and Azisa Abdou (Mohammed) B.; m. Bousaina Abdelfattah Ayoub, June 15, 1949. BSc in Tech., Farouk U., Alexandria, Egypt, 1948; MS in Chem. Engring., Alexandria U., 1955; DrRerNat, Tech. U. Munich, 1966. Tchr. chemistry and physics Ministry of Edn., Alexandria, 1948-56; tchr. sci. Syria Secondary Schs., 1956-61; sr. master of sci. Kafr Eldawar, Egypt, 1961-63; mem. Mission to West Germany, 1963-66; rschr. Nat. Rsch. Ctr., Cairo, 1966-72, assoc. prof. applied chemistry, 1972-77, prof. chemistry and tech. of plastics, 1977-85, prof. emeritus, 1985—; cons. Ministry of Industry, 1967-85; vis. prof. Tohoku Faculty Engring, Sendai, Japan, 1972; prof. gen. chemistry Mil. Tech. Coll., 1973-74; prof. chem. and tech. of plastics Suez Canal U., 1977-90. Referee Jour. Applied Polymer Sci., Egyptian Chem. Jour., Engring. Jour. Saudi Arabia, Katter Jour. Chemistry; contbr. articles to profl. jours. Recipient 1st Honour State prize for Sci. and Art 1st class, 1972, State prize in chemistry, 1976, Republic prize 2d class, 1982, 85, Einstein Diploma Cultural Sci., 1986, Distinction in Chem. Sci. prize Nat. Rsch. Ctr., 1988. Mem. Chemistry and Tech. of Polymers Orgn. (coun.), Engring. Chem. Soc., Egyptian Chem. Soc., Am. Chem. Soc., Am. Soc. Promotion Sci. Moslem. Home: Post Code 12311, 1 Ibraheem Khater St, Giza, Agouza Egypt Office: Nat Rsch Ctr, Tahreer St, 12622 Giza Dokki Egypt

MOUSTAFA, MAHMOUD MOHAMED, civil engineer, researcher; b. Cairo, Oct. 20, 1961; s. Mohamed Moustafa Mohamed and Enayat Zaki Ahmed; m. Amal Ahmed El-Samadwny, Aug. 25, 1989; children: Ahmed Mahmoud, Nada Mahmoud, Omar Mahmoud. BSc in Civil Engring., Cairo U., Giza, Egypt, 1984, MSc in Civil Engring., 1994; diploma in hydraulic, Internat. Inst. Hydraulic & Environ. Engring., Delft, The Netherlands, 1988; diploma in irrigation, Mediterranean Agronomic Inst., Bari, Italy, 1991; PhD in Civil Engring., Okayama (Japan) U., 1999. Civil engr. Can. Project Egyptian Pub. Authority for Drainage Projects, Mansoura, Egypt, 1986-87; civil engr. for drainage projects Egyptian Pub. Authority for Drainage Projects, Giza, 1986-94, head operational rsch. unit, 1992-95, asst. dir., 1994—, head rsch. unit, 1999—; mem. steering com. Japanese-Egyptian Environ. Project, Giza, 1993-95; mem. Can.-Egyptian Steering Com. for Water Mgmt. Projects, Ottawa, Can., 1994; gen. coord. Refresher Couse on Land Drainage in Egypt, Qanater, 1994; lectr. Nat. Water Rsch. Ctr., Qalubia, Egypt, 1994; vis. rschr. RWS-Directorate Flevoland, Lelystad, The Netherlands, 1995; Egyptian del. UN Conv. to Combat Desertification, 1999. Editor (sci. newsletter) The Netherlands-Egyptian Drainage Exec. Mgmt. Project, 1991-94; contbr. articles to profl. jours. Scholar Okayama (Japan) U., 1995; fellow Internat. Inst. for Hydraulic and Environ. Engring., Delft, The Netherlands, 1987, Mediterranean Agronomic Inst., Bari, 1990. Mem. Egyptian Syndicate Engrs., Arab Contractor Club. Avocations: reading, table tennis, football. Home: Flat 4 2nd Fl, Saudi Bldgs 39/2, New El-Maadi Cairo, Egypt

MOUSTAKIS, VASSILIS S., engineering educator; b. Athens, Attiki, Greece, Oct. 15, 1955; s. Stylianos V. and Helen S. (Kazazi) M.; m. Helen V. Costaridou, Aug. 21, 1980 (div. Mar. 1993); 1 child, Melenia; m. Dimitra E. Athenaki, May 28, 1993; children: Stylianos, Katerina. Diploma in Mech. Engring., U. Patras, Greece, 1978; M Engring. Adminstrn., George Washington U., Washington, 1980, DSc, 1984. Cert. mech. engring. Asst. rsch. prof. George Washington U., Washington, 1984-85; adj. asst. prof. Tech. U. Crete, Chania, 1986-88, asst. prof., 1989-94, assoc. prof., 1995—, chmn. dept. prodn. and mgmt. engring., 1997-99; rschr. Forth, Heraklion, Greece, 1987; self-employed cons., Chania, 1986—. Contbr. articles to profl. jours. With Greek mil., 1986-87. Recipient scholarships Am. Assn. Cost Engrs., 1979, 80. Mem. Soc. Logistics Engrs., Greek Chamber Engrs. Christian Orthodox. Avocations: hiking, swimming.

MOUTAFCHIEV, DIMITER ANDONOV, biologist, biochemistry researcher; b. Sofia, Bulgaria, Jan. 9, 1936; s. Andon Mitsov and Raina Georgieva (Papakotcheva) M.; m. Victorina Valentinovna Vassileva, Feb. 11, 1986; 1 child, Andon. Student, Coll. Med. Tech., Sofia, 1955; degree in biology, U. Sofia, 1966, PhD in Biology, 1982. Med. lab. asst. Inst. Pediatrics Coll. Med. Tech., 1955-66, biochem. scientist Inst. Pediatrics, 1967-81; biochem. scientist dept. biochemistry Med. Acad., Sofia, 1982-99. Contbr. articles to profl. jours. Mem. Am. Geog. Soc. Home: Quarter Droujba 1 Blk 49/4, 1592 Sofia Bulgaria

MOUTSELOS, EUTHIMIOS CRISTOS, information scientist; b. Athens, Attiki, Greece, June 25, 1968; s. Cristos E. and Maria N. (Mantzoufa) M. Elec. engr., I.T.S., Xania, Greece, 1990; MSc, Bradford U., 1991. Technician R&D Marac SA, Athens, Greece, 1990-91; engr. R&D Pan Drive SA, Athens, 1994-95; mgr. info. tech. Violex Bic SA, Athens, 1995-98, Novo Nordisk Hellas Ltd., Athens, 1998—; tech. mgr. Silkom Sys., Athens, 1996—; cons. Athens, 1996—. Author: Stand Alone Intelligent Modems, 1990, High Speed Date Capture Systems, 1991. With Greek Info. Tech. Svc., 1992-94. Mem. IEEE (Comm. sect., Control Sys. sect., Computer sect.). Avocations: wind surfing, basketball, automotives, music. Home: Pierrakou 46-48, 15771 Athens Greece Office: Novo Nordisk Hellas Ltd, 518 Messoghiou Ave, GR-15342 Athens Greece

MOUTZOUKIS, CHRIS, psychologist; b. Drama, Greece, Mar. 24, 1946; s. Anastasios and Maria M.; m. Jean Bailey, Oct. 7, 1972; 1 child, Maria. BS, London U., 1983; MS, Miss. State U., 1985. Clin. psychologist, Greece. Clin. psychologist Psychiat. Hosp. of Thessaloniki, 1985-86, Manchester Health Area/Withington Hosp., Eng., 1987-89, Min. of Health, Thessaloniki, 1989-90; clin. psychologist, pvt. practice Thessaloniki, 1990-91; clin. psychologist EPSYCA/Min. of Health, Thessaloniki, 1991—; clin. psychologist/scientific collaborator Aristotle U., Thessaloniki, 1997—; clin. tutor Aristotle U. of Thessaloniki, 1997—; dir. of rehab. unit EPSYCA, 1991—. Author/translator: Translation and Standardisation for the Greek Population, 1990; translator: Love is Never Engouh, 1996. 2d lt. Grecian inf., 1966-69. Mem. Greek Assn. for Cognitive and Behavioural Psychotherapies (pres. 1994-97). Avocations: reading, driving, music. Office: 63 Egnatia Str, 54631 Thessaloniki Greece

MOUZAKIDIS, CHRISTOS ALEXANDER, physical education educator, basketball coach; b. Thessaloniki, Greece, Apr. 12, 1963; s. Alexander Spyros

and Crystallia (Andreas) M. Diploma in Phys. Edn., U. Thessaloniki, 1990, Diploma in Basketball Coaching, 1990; MSc in Exercise and Dementia, U. Komotini, 1997. Basketball coach basketball teams, Thessaloniki, 1990—; tchr. phys. edn. local authorities, Thessaloniki, 1995—; fitness instr. for mental health patients Municipality of Thessaloniki, 1995-2000, Municipality of Neapoli, 1998-2000; fitness instr. for disabled people Neapoli, 1999-2000. Editor jour. Comm. for Alzheimer's Disease, 1999—; contbr. chpt. to book, article to profl. jours. Served with Signal Corps, Greek Army, 1991-92. Grantee European Commn., Luxembourg, 1997, Ministry Edn. and European Commn., 1999. Mem. Greek Basketball Coaches Assn., Kentavroi Sports Club (exec. com.), Greek Assn. Alzheimer's Disease and Related Disorders (exec. com.). Avocations: music, sports. E-mail: evita@psy.auth.gr. Home: 40 Mikras Asias Str, Thessaloniki Greece 551 32 Office: Greek Assn Alzheimer's, 92 Egnatia Str, Thessaloniki Greece

MOVSISYAN, YURI, mathematics educator; b. Nagorni Karabach, Armenia, Apr. 11, 1949; s. Movses and Izabela (Avakyan) M.; m. Gayane Melkonyan, June 10, 1978; children: Movses, Tatevik. MS in Math., Yerevan (Armenia) State U., 1971; PhD in Math., Kishinev (Moldova) State U., 1974; DSc in Math., St. Petersburg State U., Russia, 1992. Asst. prof. math. Yerevan State U., 1974-76, assoc. prof., 1976-85, prof., head dept. algebra and geometry, 1985—. Author: Higher Algebra, 1983, Introduction to the Theory of Algebras with Hyperidentities, 1986, Hyperidentities and Hypervarieties in Algebras, 1990; mem. editorial bd. Jour. Math., 1980—; also articles. Mem. Armenian Math. Soc. Office: Yerevan State U Dept Math, Alex Manoukyan 1, 375049 Yerevan Armenia

MOW, VAN C., engineering educator, researcher; b. Chengdu, China, Jan. 10, 1939. B. Aero. Engring., Rensselaer Poly. Inst., 1962, Ph.D., 1966. Mem. tech. staff Bell Telephone Labs., Whippany, N.J., 1968-69; assoc. prof. mechanics Rensselaer Poly. Inst., Troy, N.Y., 1969-76, prof. mechanics and biomed. engring., 1976-82, John A. Clark and Edward T. Crossan prof. engring., 1982-86; prof. mechanical engring. and orthopedic bioengring. Columbia U., N.Y.C., 1986—; dir. Orthopedic Research Lab., Columbia-Presbyn. Med. Ctr., N.Y.C., 1986—; Stanley Dicker prof. of biomed. engring. Orthopedic Research Lab., Columbia-Presbyn. Med. Ctr., 1998—; vis. mem. Courant Inst. Math. Sci., NYU, 1967-68; vis. prof. Harvard U., Boston, 1976-77; chmn. orthopaedics and musculoskeletal study sect. NIH, Bethesda, Md., 1982-84; hon. prof. Chengdu U. Sci. Tech., 1981, Shanghai Jiao Tong U., 1987; mem. grants rev. bd. Orthopaedic Rsch. Edn. Found., 1992-96; bd. dirs. Hoar Rsch. Found., 1993—; chmn. adv. com. divsn. Med. Engring. Rsch. Nat. Health Rsch. Inst., Taiwan, 1999—; cons. in field. Assoc. editor Jour. Biomechanics, 1981—, Jour. Biomech. Engring., 1979-86; chmn. editorial adv. bd. Jour. Orthopedic Rsch., 1983-90; adv. editor Clin. Orthopedic Rel. Rsch., 1993—; contbr. numerous articles to profl. jours. Founder Gordon Research Conf. on Bioengring. and Orthopedic Sci., 1980. NATO sr. fellow, 1978; recipient William H. Wiley Disting. Faculty award Rensselaer Poly. Inst., 1981; Japan Soc. for Promotion Sci. Fellow, 1986, Fogarty Sr. Internat. fellow, 1987; Alza disting. lectr. Biomed. Engring. Soc., 1987; H.R. Lissner award ASME, 1987, Kappa Delta award AAOS, 1980, Giovani Borelli award, 1991. Fellow ASME (chmn. biomechanics divsn. 1984-85, Melville medal 1982), Am. Inst. Med. Biol. Engring.; mem. NAE, Orthopaedic Rsch. Soc. (pres. 1982-83), Am. Soc. Biomechanics (founding), Internat. Soc. Biorheology, U.S. Nat. Com. on Biomechanics (sec.-treas. 1985-90, chmn. 1991-94), Inst. of Medicine, Nat. Acad. Sci. Office: Columbia-Presbyn Med Ctr 630 W 168th St # Bb-1412 New York NY 10032-3702

MOW, WAI HO, communications engineer, lecturer, researcher; b. Hong Kong, June 12, 1966; s. Ming and Kum Oy (Wong) M. BSc, Chinese U. Hong Kong, 1989, MPhil, 1991, PhD, 1993. Lectr. info. engring. Chinese U. Hong Kong, 1993-94; postdoctoral fellow dept. elect. and computer engring. U. Waterloo, Ont., Can., 1995; postdoctoral fellow dept. comm. engring. Tech. U. Munich, Germany, 1996; asst. prof. Sch. EEE, Nanyang Tech. U., Singapore, 1997-99; asst. prof. dept. EEE Hong Kong Univ. Sch. & Tech., 2000—. Author: Sequence Design for Spread Spectrum, 1995; contbr. numerous papers to field. Recipient Young Scholar Dissertation award, 1993; named Humboldt Rsch. fellow, 1996, Croucher Found. fellow, 1995; Ho Tim scholar Chinese U. Hong Kong, 1985, Dr. Kikai Tchang Meml. scholar, 1986; recipient Outstanding PhD Thesis in Engring. award, 1993; fellow Telecommunications Advancement Rsch., 2000. Mem. IEEE (sr.). Office: Hong Kong U Sci Tech Dept EEE, Clearwater Bay, Hong Kong China

MOWAIYE-FAGBEMI, OLUFUNMILAYO JULIAN, educator; b. Iyah, Nigeria, Oct. 4, 1963; d. Femi Zach and Ebun Victoria (Makanjuola) M.; m. Taiye Moses Fagbemi, July 8, 1995; 1 child, Olutobi. BA in Edn. & History, U. Ilorin, Nigeria, 1985, MEd in Psychology, 1990, PhD in Psychology, 1995. Tutor Polytech. & School, Ilorin, Nigeria, 1987-91; asst. lectr. U. Ilorin, Nigeria, 1992-94, lectr. II, 1994-96, lectr. I, 1996-98, sr. lectr., 1998—; cons. in field. Author: The Psychology of Women in Education, 1998, Key Success Points in History for O' Levels, 1995. Mem. Internat. Assn. Cross Cultural Psychology, Counseling Assn. Nigeria, Hist. Soc. Nigeria, Reading Assn. Nigeria. Baptist. Avocations: reading, writing. Office: U Ilorin, Univ Campus Box 5047, Ilorin Nigeria

MOWAT, FARLEY MCGILL, writer; b. Belleville, Ont., Can., May 12, 1921; s. Angus McGill and Helen (Thomson) M.; m. Frances Elizabeth Thornhill, Dec. 21, 1947; children: Robert Alexander, David Peter; m. Claire Angel Wheeler, 1965. BA, U. Toronto, 1949, LLD, 1973; DLitt (hon.), Laurentian U., 1970; LLD, U. Lethbridge, Alta., 1973, U. P.E.I., 1979; DLitt, U. Victoria, B.C., 1982, Lakehead U., Thunder Bay, Ont., 1986; LHD (hon.), McMaster U., Hamilton, Ont., 1994; LLD (hon.), Queen's Univ., Kingston, Ont., 1995; DLitt (hon.), U. Coll. of Cape Breton, Sydney, Nova Scotia, 1996. Arctic exploration, sci. work, 1947-48, writer, 1950—. Author: People of the Deer, 1952, The Regiment, 1955, Lost in the Barrens, 1956, The Dog Who Wouldn't Be, 1957, Coppermine Journey, 1958, The Grey Seas Under, 1958, The Desperate People, 1959, Ordeal By Ice, 1960, Owls in the Family, 1961, The Serpent's Coil, 1961, The Black Joke, 1962, Never Cry Wolf, 1963, Westviking, 1965, The Curse of the Viking Grave, 1966, Canada North, 1967, The Polar Passion, 1967 (with John de Visser) This Rock Within the Sea, 1968, The Boat Who Wouldn't Float, 1969, The Siberians, 1971, A Whale for the Killing, 1972, Tundra, 1973, (with David Blackwood) Wake of the Great Sealers, 1973, The Snow Walker, 1975, Canada North Now, 1976, And No Birds Sang, 1979, The World of Farley Mowat, 1980, Sea of Slaughter, 1984, My Discovery of America, 1985, Woman in the Mist, 1987, The New Founde Land, 1989, Rescue the Earth, 1990, My Father's Son, 1992, Born Naked, 1993, Aftermath, 1995, The Farfarers, 1998, Goodbye Ohoto, 2000; author documentary script The New North (Gemini award 1989); film Sea of Slaughter (Conservation Film of Yr. award 1990, ACE award finalist 1990, award of Excellence Atlantic Film Festival 1990). Served to capt. inf. Canadian Army, 1939-45. Recipient Pres. Medal Univ. Western Ont., 1952, Anisfield Wolfe award, 1954, Gov. Gen.'s medal, 1957, Book of Yr. Medal Can. Library Assn., 1958, Hans Christian Anderson Internat. award, 1958, 65, Can. Women's Clubs award, 1958, Boys Clubs Am. award, 1962, Nat. Assn. Ind. Schs. award, 1963, Can. Centennial medal, 1967, Stephen Leacock medal for humor, 1970, Leacock Medal for Humour, 1970, Vicky Metcalf award, 1970, Mark Twain award, 1971, Book of Yr. award, 1976, Curran award, 1977, Queen Elizabeth II Jubilee medal, 1978, Knight of Mark Twain, 1980, Can. Author's award, 1981, 85, Can. Author of Year award, 1988, Can. Book of Yr. award, 1988, Torgi Can. Talking Book of Yr. award, 1989, Can. Achievers award Toshiba Can., 1990, Take Back the Nation award Coun. Cans., 1991, Authors award, Author of Yr. Found. for Advancement of Can. Letters, 1993, Nat. prize for fgn. lit. books Beiyue Lit. and Art Pub. House, Taiyuan, China, 1999; decorated officer Order of Can., 1981, L'Etoile de la Mer, 1972. Address: c/o Writers Union Can, 24 Ryerson Ave, Toronto, ON Canada M4T 2P3

MOWAT, MAGNUS CHARLES, company executive; b. Sheffield, Yorkshire, U.K., Apr. 5, 1940; s. John Frederick and Elizabeth Rebecca (Murray) M.; m. Mary Lynette Stoddart, Apr. 27, 1968; children: Charles, Alexander, Hugh. Ptnr. Illingworth & Henriques, Manchester, U.K., 1970-83; dir. Barclays de Zoete Wedd Ltd., London, 1983-91; non-exec. dir. Allen plc, Ryalux Carpets Ltd., other cos., U.K., 1991—. Chmn. Manchester (U.K.) YMCA, 1983-97, Booths Charities, Manchester, 1985—, Manchester Br. of Inst. Dirs., 1993-97. Fellow Inst. Chartered Accts.; mem. East India Club (London). Avocations: gardening, music, economic history. Home: Westcott Farm, Brompton Ralph, Taunton Somerset TA4 2SF, England

MOWBRAY, CAROL BEATRICE THIESSEN, mental health researcher, social work educator; b. Boston, Aug. 20, 1948; d. Peter Isaac and Jessamine Beatrice (Olpin) Thiessen; m. Charles Sherman Mowbray, June 1, 1970; children: Orion, Nicholas. BS, Tufts U., 1970, MS, 1971; PhD, U. Mich., 1975. Lectr. dept. psychology Mich. State U., East Lansing, 1974-75; social rsch. analyst Mich. Dept. Mental Health, Lansing, 1975-76, dir. spl. analytical studies, 1976-77, exec. asst. to dir., 1977-78, dir., program and grants coord., 1978-80, dir. rsch., evaluation and demonstration, 1980-90; assoc. prof. social work Wayne State U., Detroit, 1990-94; assoc. prof. social work U. Mich., Ann Arbor, 1994-2000, prof., 2000—, faculty assoc. Poverty Risk and Mental Health Rsch. Ctr., 1995—, assoc. dean rsch., 1996—; cons. grant rev. substance abuse mental health svcs. adminstrn. Ctr. for Mental Health Svcs. and NIMH, Rockville, Md., 1981—. Author: Women and Mental Health, 1984; co-editor: Consumers as Providers in Psychiatric Rehabilitation, 1997, Supported Education: Models & Methods, 2000; mem. editl. bd. Evaluation and Program Planning, Rsch. in Social Work Practice, Am. Jour. Evaluation, Psychiat. Rehab. Jour.; consulting editor: Social Work Jour.; contbr. articles to profl. jours. Rsch. grantee dual diagnosis NIMH, 1989-95, supported edn. grantee Ctr. for Mental Health Svcs., Substance Abuse-Mental Health Svcs. Adminstrn., 1992-97, mentally ill mothers grantee NIMH, 1994—; cmty. action grantee Ctr. for Mental Health Svcs./Substance Abuse Mental Health Svc. Adminstrn., 1997-2000. Fellow APA (sect. chmn. 1990-92, Disting. Svc. award div. 18 1988); mem. NASW, CSWE, Internat. Assn. Psychosocial Rehab. Svcs. (rsch. com. 1994—, rsch. com. chair 1998—, Armin Loeb award 1998), Am. Evaluation Assn., Midwest Psychol. Assn., Soc. Social Work Rsch. (Oustanding Rsch. Article award 2000). Avocations: needlework, gardening, piano, jazz/blues music. Home: 5460 Prairie Vw Brighton MI 48116-7715 Office: U Mich Sch Social Work 1080 S University Ave Ann Arbor MI 48109-1106

MOWBRAY, JOHN, biochemistry educator; b. Stirling, Scotland, Sept. 12, 1942; s. William Craig and Martha Roy (Crawford) M.; m. Sylvia Laureen Glover, Apr. 1, 1967 (dec. Sept. 1996); children: Donald Crawford, Christine Knox, Gordon Craig. BSc in Biochemistry with honors, U. Edinburgh, Scotland, 1964; PhD in Biochemistry, U. Edinburgh, 1969. Demonstrator U. Edinburgh, 1965-69; postdoctoral fellow, external tutor in biochemistry U. Calif., Berkeley, 1969-71; lectr. in biochemistry Univ. Coll. London, 1971-86, reader in biochemistry, 1986—; prin. investigator Brit. Heart Found., Wellcome Trust, Med. Rsch. Coun., 1977—. Contbg. author: Current Topics in Cellular Regulation, Advances in Enzyme Regulation: Short-Term Control of Liver Metabolism, others, 1977—; contbr. articles to profl. jours.; editor, referee jours. in field. Prize rsch. scholar U. Edinburgh, 1964, sr. scholar Carnegie Trust, Berkeley, Calif., 1969; recipient Allan Souttar Meml. award Univ. Coll. London, 1989. Mem. Fedn. European Biochem. Socs. (asst. treas. 1986-90, treas. 1991—), The Biochem. Soc. (exec. com. 1978-82, group sec. Regulation in Metabolism Group 1978-82, chmn. 1982-84), Brit. Soc. Cardiovascular Rsch. (founder), The Metabolic Discussion Group (chmn. 1976—). Avocations: classical music, camping, sailing, gardening, cooking. Office: Univ Coll London, Gower St Dept Biochem & Molecular Bio, London WC1E 6BT, England

MOWBRAY, ROBERT NORMAN, natural resource management consultant, ecologist; b. Warren, Pa., Feb. 26, 1935; s. Leonard Kelly and Jean Elizabeth (Lowes) M.; m. Sonia de los Angeles Baquerizo, June 7, 1969; children: Norma Mercedes, Elizabeth Laning. BA, Dartmouth Coll., 1957; M of Forestry, Yale U., 1963; postgrad., Duke U., 1966-70. Rsch. asst. forest ecology Duke U., Panama, 1967, Ecuador, 1968-70; rsch. asst. forest ecology U. Tenn., Knoxville, 1970-71; rsch. asst. ecology Oak Ridge (Tenn.) Nat. Labs., 1971-72; reclamation crew chief Tenn. Mountain Mgmt., Knoxville, 1972; assoc. dir. Peace Corps, Asunción, Paraguay, 1972-78; agrl. devel. officer U.S. Agy. for Internat. Devel., San Jose, Costa Rica, 1978-80; agrl. devel. officer U.S. AID, Kingston, Jamaica, 1980-83, Washington, 1983-88, 90-91; forestry devel. officer U.S. AID, Quito, Ecuador, 1988-90; sr. forest ecologist, natural resource mgmt. specialist U.S. AID, Washington, 1991-94; internat. natural resource mgmt. cons., Reston, Va., 1994—; forestry vol. Peace Corps, Ecuador, 1963-66, editor tech. newsletter, 1964-66. Author: (with others) Natural Resource Management and Conservation of Biodiversity and Tropical Forests in Ecuador-A Strategy for USAID, 1989; editor (spl. issues) NicAvance, 1995-96; contbr. articles to profl. jours. Botany vol. The Nature Conservancy, 1997-98; mem. Reston Environment and Ecology Adv. Com., Watershed Subcom. 1st lt. USMC, 1958-61. Recipient U.S. Forest Svc. Chief's Internat. Forestry award, 1994. Mem. World Wildlife Fund, Nature Conservancy, Assn. for Tropical Biology, Internat. Soc. Tropical Foresters, Friends of the Nat. Zoo, Nat. Coun. Returned Peace Corps Vols., Soc. Conservation Biology. Avocations: gardening, photography. Home and Office: 2218 Wheelwright Ct Reston VA 20191-2313

MOWERY, GERALD EUGENE, publisher, writer; b. Buena, Wash., Mar. 7, 1927; s. Jennings Bryan and Opal Mae Mowery; children: Colleen, Theresa, Rhonda, Laura, Victoria, Charles, Peggy. Degree in bus., Kinmen's U. Lic. pub. acct., Wash. Supr. Boeing Airplane Co., Seattle, 1968-78; owner Jerry's Coin, Book and Frame Shops, Puyallup, Wash., 1978-85, Rudolph Maurer Pub., Puyallup, Wash., Tampa, Fla., 1985—. Author and pub. more than 131 books including All Matter Originates from Electrons and Positrons, 1981, E=GM Squared, 1994, The Revised Periodic Table of Elements, The .000249031 Atomic Mass Particle, 1998, The Four Unacknowledged Elements, 1999; co-author with Gene Buck: The Entrepreneurs Favorite Short Stories, Favorite Poems, Favorite Facts and Stuff; author, publ. Adjusted Periodic Table of Elements, 1982, 93, 97, 98; author children's books The Adventures of Alexander Smiriotes series including Alexander Smiriotes Rides his Alligator Through Tampa, Alexander Visits Athens, Greece. Achievements include defining the atomic mass make up of sub atomic particles and their relationship to carbon 12, defining light as a .0001245445 atomic mass particle and heat as a .000249089 atomic mass particle; prepared (atomic mass) sub atomic particle table. Avocations: philosophical thinking, bridge, stamp collecting, writing stories and poems. Office: Rudolph Maurer Publishing 8311 54th Ave South Seattle WA 98118-4702 Office: Rudolph Publishing 8212 110th St E Puyallup WA 98373-3941

MOWERY, J. RONALD, geologist, physicist, educator; b. Princeton, N.J., Nov. 2, 1939; s. J. Harry and Dorothy E. (Miller) M.; m. Nancy J. Bricker, Aug. 10, 1963 (div. Jan. 10, 1990); children: Stephen A., Karen L.; m. Judy A. Bauer, Dec. 27, 1992. BS, Shippensburg State U., 1964; MS, U. S.D., 1969. Tchr., dept. chmn. Pen Argyl (Pa.) Area H.S., 1964-68; prof. geology and physics Harrisburg (Pa.) Area C.C., 1969—; cons. Personal Profl. Svc., Harrisburg, 1980—; cons. Dunn Geosci., Harrisburg, 1977, R.E. Wright & Assocs., Harrisburg, 1980-82. Author: Physical Science Laboratory Manual, 1973; editor: Geology & Hydrology of Delaware River Basin, 1982, (field guidebook) Susquehanna River Valley, 1983; developer/producer phys. sci. video course for coll. freshman, 1996. Cubmaster Boy Scouts Am., 1973-76; commr. Susquehanna Twp. Bd. Commn., 1984-89. With USN, 1958-63. NSF rsch. grantee, 1973, 92; recipient NISOD award 1996. Mem. AAAS, Harrisburg Area Geol. Soc. (pres. 1970), Nat. Assn. Geology Tchrs. Republican. Avocation: mineral and fossil collecting. Home: 2301 Oakwood Rd Harrisburg PA 17104-1427 Office: Harrisburg Area CC 1 Hacc Dr Harrisburg PA 17110-2903

MOWLAM, MARJORIE, minister; b. Sept. 18, 1949; married; 2 stepchildren. BA in Social Anthropology, Durham U., 1971; MA, Iowa U., PhD, 1978. Lectr. Fla. State U., 1977-78, Newcastle upon Tyne (Eng.) U., 1979-83; adminstr. Northern Coll., Barnsley, Eng., 1984-87; mem. Parliament for Redcar, 1987—; opposition frontbench spokesman on No. Ireland Brit. Parliament, 1988-89, spokesman on city and corp. affairs, 1989-92, spokesman on citizen's charter and women, 1992-93, spokesman on nat. heritage, 1993-94, spokesman on No. Ireland, 1994-97; mem. Shadow Cabinet, 1992-97, NEC, 1995—; sec. of state for No. Ireland, 1997-99; min. Cabinet Office, London, 1999—. Avocations: travelling, swimming, jigsaws. Office: Cabinet Office, 70 Whitehall, Whitehall London SW1A 2AS, England

MOXEY-INGRAHAM, THERESA, government official; b. Oct. 15, 1950; 1 child. BA in English, McMaster U., Can., 1976; MA in Edn., U. Miami, Fla., 1982. Tchr. high sch. until 1982; tchr. Bahamas Bus. Coll., Hotel Tng. Coll., Inst. Acctg. and Fin.; asst. dir., then food mgr. Resorts Internat. Corp., 1983-87; v.p. Women's Assn. of Bahamas; apptd. senator Govt. of Bahamas, 1987, opposition leader, 1988-92; mem. Golden Gates Ho. of Assembly, Nassau, 1992—; min. transport and comm. Govt. Bahamas, Nassau, 1992-94, min. social devel. and nat. ins., 1994-95, min. health and environment, 1995-97, min. labor, immigration & tng., 1997—, min. agr., commerce and industry. Mem. Free Nat. Movement. Office: Min Labor Immigration Tng, PO Box N-4891, Nassau Bahamas Address: East Bay St, PO Box N-3028, Nassau Bahamas*

MOXON-BROWNE, EDWARD PHILIP, educator; b. Halifax, Can., Jan. 28, 1944; s. Kendal and Sheila (Weatherbe) M. MA, St. Andrews, Scotland, 1967, U. Pa., 1973. Lectr. U.S. Intenat. U., 1971-72; reader Queens U., Belfast, Ireland, 1973-91; prof. U. Limerick, Ireland, 1992—. Author: Nation, Class and Creed in Northern Ireland, 1983, Political Change in Spain, 1989; editor: European Terrorism, 1994, A Future for Peacekeeping?, 1997. Kennedy grantee, Wesleyan U., 1989; rsch. fellow U. Pa., 1970; Thouron scholar U. Pa., 1967, Fulbright scholar Hollins Coll., Va., 1997. Mem. royal Inst. Internat. Affairs, Inst. European Affairs, Mensa. Office: U Limerick, Ctr European Studies, Limerick Ireland

MOY, HELEN KWONG, accountant; b. Taipei, Taiwan, Nov. 28, 1971; d. Paul Shao Zeng and Linda Hsiao Ling Wong K.; m. Reginald Moy, Dec. 12, 1994. BSBA, Calif. State Polytechnic U., 1994. CPA, Nev. Sr. acct. Rich, Wightman & Co., CPAs, Las Vegas, 1995-99; sr. tax cons. Deloitte & Touche, LLP, Las Vegas, 1999-2000; with Tang Industries, Las Vegas, 2000—; propr. Helen K. Moy, CPA, 2000—. Vol. income tax asst. IRS, Hacienda Heights, Calif., 1994. Mem. Nev. Soc. CPAs, AICPAs. Republican. Avocations: reading fin./investment materials, movies, talk radio, bus. law knowledge. E-mail: bog5cpa@prodigy.net. Office: Tang Industries 3773 Howard Hughes Pkwy Las Vegas NV 89109-5948

MOY, RONALD LEONARD, dermatologist, surgeon; b. Stuttgart, Germany, June 10, 1957; s. Howard Leonard Stephen and Jenny (Yee) M.; m. Lisa Wing Lan Lin, Aug. 10, 1986; children: Lauren, Erin. Grad., Rensselaer Poly. Inst., 1977, Albany Med. Coll., 1981. Dir. Mohs micrographic surgery div. dermatology UCLA, 1988-93, dir. dermatologic surgery div. dermatology, 1988-93, co-chief div. dermatology, 1992-93; chief dermatologic surgery VA-West Los Angeles Med. Ctr., 1988—; gov. apptd. Med. Bd. Calif. Author: Atlas of Cutaneous Flaps and Grafts, 1990; editor: Principle and Practice of Dermatologic Surgery, 1993; editor-in-chief: Dermatologic Surgery, 1997—; contbr. articles to profl. jours. Bd. dirs. L.A. Costal unit Am. Cancer Soc., 1988. Recipient J. Lewis Pipkin award in dermatology Nat. Student Rsch. Forum, 1981, Henry Christian award Am. Fedn. Clin. Rsch., T-cell and Cytokine Patterns in Skin Cancer award NIH, 1992. Fellow Am. Acad. Dermatology (Gold award 1986); mem. Am. Soc. Dermatologic Surgery (bd. dirs. 1993-96), Am. Coll. Mohs Micrographic Surgery and Cutaneous Oncology (bd. dirs. 1992-95), Assn. Acad. Dermatologic Surgeons (bd. dirs. 1992-95), L.A. County Med. Assn. (pres. Bay dist. 1997-98). Roman Catholic. Office: 100 Ucla Medical Plz Ste 590 Los Angeles CA 90024-6992

MOYA, CARLOS, professional tennis player; b. Palma de Mallorca, Spain, Aug. 27, 1976. Winner Buenos Aires, 1995, Umag, 1996, L.I., 1996, U.S. Open, 1997, 18 European singles and doubles titles. Avocations: video games, music, soccer. Office: c/o ATP Tour Internat Hdqrs 201 Atp Tour Blvd Ponte Vedra Beach FL 32082*

MOYA, DIMAS EDUARDO, plastics company executive; b. Guayaquil, Guayas, Ecuador, May 22, 1962; arrived in Honduras, 1968; s. Eduardo G. and Maria A. (Sanchez) M.; m. Aminta J. Gomez, Mar. 24, 1984; children: Christian, Daniel, Gerardo. BS in Indsl. Engring., U. San Pedro Sula (Honduras), 1987, MBA, 1995. Prodn. supr. Clover Brand, San Pedro Sula, 1985-87; prodn. mgr. Maprica/Hondulit, San Pedro Sula, 1987-89, Gamoz, San Pedro Sula, 1989-91; owner, gen. mgr. Vanguardia, San Pedro Sula, 1991-94, Proteca, San Pedro Sula, 1994—; tech. cons. Plastesa, San Pedro Sula, 1985-92. Mem. Club Honduras A., Colegio de Ing. Ind. Conservative. Roman Catholic. Home: Col Trejo 9 Y 10 CII, 19 Ave # 97, San Pedro Sula Honduras Office: Proteca, PO Box 3763, San Pedro Sula Honduras

MOYA, OLGA LYDIA, law educator; b. Weslaco, Tex., Dec. 27, 1959; d. Leonel V. and Genoveva (Tamez) M.; children: Leanessa Geneva Byrd, Taylor Moya Byrd. BA, U. Tex., 1981, JD, 1984. Bar: Tex. 1984. Legis. atty. Tex. Ho. of Reps., Austin, 1985; atty. Tex. Dept. Agr., Austin, 1985-90; asst. regional counsel U.S. EPA, Dallas, 1990-91; from asst. prof. to assoc. prof. South Tex. Coll. of Law, Houston, 1992-97; prof. law South Tex. Coll. Law, Houston, 1997—. Author: (with Andrew L. Fono) Federal Environmental Law: The User's Guide, 1997. Bd. dirs. Hermann Children's Hosp., Houston, 1993-97; mem. Leadership Tex., Austin, 1991—; bd. trustees Meml. Hermann Healthcare Sys. Found., 1997-99; bd. dirs. Tex. Clean Water Coun., Austin, 1992, Met. Transit Authority of Harris County, 1999—; U.S. del. to UN Conf. on the Environ. for Latin Am. and the Caribbean, San Juan, P.R., 1995. Recipient Nat. Top 12 Hispanics in Law, Miller Brewing Co., 1996; Vol. of Yr. award George H. Hermann Soc., 1995, Hispanic Law Prof. of Yr. Hispanic Nat. Bar Assn., 1995. Mem. ABA (environ. law sect.), Hispanic Bar Assn. (bd. dirs. 1992—, Excellence award 1995, 96), Mex.-Am. Bar Assn. Office: South Tex Coll of Law 1303 San Jacinto St Houston TX 77002-7013

MOYÉ, DEAN, lighting design professional; b. Phila., Jan. 7, 1969. Tech. dir. Stratford Playhouse, Houston, 1984-90, Country Playhouse Theatre, Houston, 1986-91, Aloha Showroom, 1991; asst. lighting designer Theatre Under The Stars, 1989-92; lighting dir., asst. prodn. mgr. Neil Diamond World Tour, 1991-93; lighting dir. Tom Collins Tour of World Figure Skating Champions, 1992—; lighting designer Lido de Paris Tour of South America, 1995, Lido de Paris, 1994; asst. lighting designer Ann Margret Tour, Phantom Tour, 1991; lighting dir. George Lucas Superlive Adventure Japan Tour; resident lighting designer Cleve. Ballet, San Jose Ballet; asst. lighting designer Blue Suede Shoes Nat. Tour. asst. lighting designer (mus. theatre) Mame (nat. tour), 1990, The Unsinkable Molly Brown, 1989, Ain't Misbehavin', 1989-90; lighting designer/prodn. mgr. Kalapana (Calif. tour), 1988; lighting designer (musical) Merrily We Roll Along, 1985, Barnum, 1986, Company, 1988 (Best Lighting Design award), Little Shop of Horrors, 1987-88 (Best Lighting Design award), Side By Side by Sondheim, 1988, A...My Name Is Alice, 1988, Peter Pan, 1989, Annie, 1989, Into The Woods, 1991. Recipient Orchid award Country Playhouse, 1987-90, Ruby award Country Playhouse, 1987-90, Dean Moyé Honor award Stratford Playhouse, 1987, Gov. of Hawaii Clothing Design award, 1991, Best Lighting Design award for stage mus. Best Little Whorehouse in Tex. Avocations: photography, film, computers, video. Office: Empire State Bldg 350 5th Ave Ste 3304 New York NY 10118-3399

MOYER, F. STANTON, financial executive, advisor; b. Phila., June 7, 1929; s. Edward T. and Beatrice (Stanton) M.; m. Ann P. Stovell, May 16, 1953; 1 child, Alice E. B.S. in Econs., U. Pa., 1951. Registered rep. Smith, Barney & Co., Phila., 1951-54, Kidder, Peabody & Co., Phila., 1954-60; mgr. corp. dept. Blyth Eastman Dillon & Co., Inc. (formerly Eastman Dillon, Union Securities & Co.), Phila., 1960-65; instl. sales mgr. Blyth Eastman Dillon & Co., Inc. (formerly Eastman Dillon, Union Securities & Co.), 1965-67, gen. partner, 1967-71, 1st v.p., 1971-74, sr. v.p., 1974-80; v.p., resident officer Kidder, Peabody & Co. Inc., Phila., 1980-86; chmn. Pa. Mcht. Group Ltd., Radnor, 1987-88; exec. v.p. Rorer Asset Mgmt., Phila., 1990-92; chmn. Mercer Capital Mgmt., 1992-93, Global Mgmt. Group, Inc., 1993-95; mng. dir. Avonwood Capital Corp., 1995-97; chmn. Main Line Capital Ptnrs. Inc., 1997—. Trustee U. Pa., 1978-83, Hosp. of U. Pa., 1978-87; bd. dirs. Atwater Kent Mus., Phila., 1983—. Mem. Racquet Club (Phila.), St. Anthony Club (Phila.), Merion Cricket Club (Haverford, Pa.), Gulph Mills Golf Club (King of Prussia, Pa.), Gulf Stream Golf Club (Fla.), Gulf Stream Bath and Tennis Club, The Little Club (Gulf Stream), Delta Psi. Republican. Episcopalian. Home: 445 Caversham Rd Bryn Mawr PA 19010-2901

MOYER, JACK THOMSON, science administrator, ecologist, writer, consultant; b. Topeka, Mar. 7, 1929; arrived in Japan Aug. 1951.; s. Frank Henry and Edith Evelin (Connell) M.; m. Lorna Misa Paragsa, Feb. 3, 1987; 2 children: Jack Thomson Jr., Leona Lorenza. BS, Colgate U., 1952; MA, U. Mich., 1961; DSc, U. Tokyo, 1984. Tchr. Miyake-Jima Pub. Schs., Izu

Islands, Japan, 1957-58; tchr., adminstr. Am. Sch. in Japan, Tokyo, 1963-84; dir., chief scientist Tatsuo Tanaka Meml. Biol. Sta., Izu Islands, 1970-99; advisor in environ. edn. Govt. of Miyake-Mura, Izu Islands, 1993—; sci. cons. Toba (Japan) Aquarium, Japan Underwater Films, Ltd., Tokyo, 1988—; environ. cons. Govt. of Bais City, Negros, The Philippines, 1996—; ednl. cons. Am. Sch. in Japan, Tokyo, 1984—; ecotour cons. Co-X/Japan R.R. East, Tokyo, 1997—; sci. cons. Profl. Assn. Cetacean Interpreters, 2000—. Author: (books) Miyake-jima Naturalist, 1993, The Joy of the Ocean, 1994, A View of Japan from Southern Islands, 1994, Discoveries of an Underwater Naturalist, 1995, The Mikura-jima Dolphins, 1997, Our Coral Seas, 1998, Jack Moyer's Ocean Adventures, 1999, The Dolphin Interpreter's Handbook, 2000, Dr. Moyer's Ocean Friends I: The Bottlenose Dolphin, 2000, Dr. Moyer's Ocean Friends II: The Community of the Striped Cowfish, 2000, (CD) Papa Jack Moyer: To the Children of the Earth, 2000; editor: Japanese Jour. of Ichthyology, 1975-84, Japanese Jour. Ethology, 1982-84; contbr. numerous papers to sci. jours. Sgt. USAF, 1951-54. Recipient Conservation award Wild Bird Soc. of Japan, 1953, Govt. of Miyake-mura, 1959, Japan Environ. Agy., 1974, World Wildlife Fund, 1995, 1st Ocean award for environ. edn. Asahi Newspapers, 1996, Omega award for Continuing Contbn. in Marine Ecology, 1998; named Hon. Citizen Miyake-jima. Mem. Ichthyol. Soc. Japan (bd. trustees, editor 1976-90), Am. Soc. Ichthyologists and Herpitologists, Animal Behavior Soc. Avocations: jazz, blues, classical music, baseball, basketball. Home: 919 Ako Miyake-mura, Tokyo 100-1212, Japan Office: Miyake-jima Nature Ctr, Tsubota Miyake-Mura, Tokyo 100-1211, Japan

MOYERS, SYLVIA DEAN, retired medical record librarian; b. Independence, W.Va., Oct. 22, 1936; d. Wilkie Russell and Ina Laura (Watkins) Collins; m. Paul Franklin Moyers, June 29, 1957; children: Tammy Jeanne, Thomas Paul, Tara Sue. Student, Am. Med. Record Assn., 1977-79. Sec. Teets Lumber Co., Terra Alta, W.Va., 1954-58, Preston County News, Terra Alta, 1958-60; med. record clk. med. record dept. Hopemont (W.Va.) Hosp., 1960-75, dir., 1975-88; sec. The Terra Alta Bank, W.Va., 1990-95; ret., 1995. Charter mem., past mother advisor Terra Alta Assembly No. 26, Order of Rainbow for Girls, past grand editor Mountain Echoes; vol. Preston Meml. Hosp., ARC, Salvation Army, Am. Cancer Soc. Mem. Kingwood Civic Club. Republican. Methodist. Home: 120 Miller Rd Kingwood WV 26537-1321

MOYES, PATRICIA (HASZARD MOYES), mystery writer; b. Bray, Ireland, Jan. 19, 1923; d. Ernst and Marion (Boyd) Pakenham-Walsh; m. John Moyes, 1951 (div. 1959); m. John S. Haszard, Oct. 13, 1962. Writer, sec. Peter Ustinov Prodns., Ltd., London, 1947-53; asst. editor Vogue, London, 1954-58. Author: Dead Men Don't Ski, 1959, Down Among the Dead Men, 1961, Death on the Agenda, 1962, Murder a la Mode, 1963, Falling Star, 1964, Johnny under Ground, 1965, Murder by 3's, 1965, Murder Fantastical, 1967, Death and the Dutch Uncle, 1968, Helter-Skelter, 1968, Many Deadly Returns, 1970 (Edgar Allan Poe award Mystery Writers of Am. 1970), Seasons of Snows and Sins, 1971, The Curious Affair of the Third Dog, 1973, After All, They're Only Cats, 1973, Black Widower, 1975, The Coconut Killings, 1977, How to Talk to Your Cat, 1978, Who Is Simon Warwick, 1978, Angel Death, 1980, A Six-Letter Word for Death, 1983, Night Ferry to Death, 1985, Black Girl, White Girl, 1989, Twice in or Blue Moon, 1993, Who Killed Father Christmas, 1996, (play) Time Remembered, 1954, (screenplay with Peter Ustinov and Hal E. Chester) School for Scoundrels, 1960; contbr. short stories, articles to Women's Mirror, Evening News (London), Writer, Ellery Queen's Mystery Mag., others. With British Women's Auxiliary Air Force, 1940-45. Church of England. Avocations: skiing, sailing, good food and wine, travel. Home: PO Box 1, Virgin Gorda British Virgin Islands Office: care Curtis Brown Ltd, Haymarket House 28/29 Haymarket, London SW1Y 4SP, England also: The Karpfinger Agy 357 W 20th St New York NY 10011-3379

MOYLE, GRAEME JOHN, physician; b. Mildura, Victoria, Australia, June 1, 1963; arrived in U.K., 1987; s. Jack Dudley and Audrey Mary (Craddock) M.; m. Christine Baldwin. MD, Adelaide (Australia) U., 1986, PhD, 1996; diploma in Genitourinary Medicine, Soc. Apothecaries, U.K., 1989. Sr. house officer St. Stephen's Hosp., London, 1988-90, rsch. fellow, 1990-92; internat. med. mgr. F. Hoffmann LaRoche, Basel, Switzerland, 1992-94; rsch. fellow Chelsea & Westminster Hosp., London, 1994-95, sr. rsch. fellow, 1995-98, assoc. dir. HIV rsch., 1999—; med. advisor AIDS Treatment Project, 1996—; med. advisor Nat. AIDS Manual, U.K., 1996—. Author: Resistance to Antiretroviral Compounds, 1994, Medical Treatment of HIV Disease, 1992, 95, 96, What we Should All Know About HIV, 1995, Virus Load and AIDS, 1997; editor (HIV sect.) Current Opinion in Infectiouis Disease, 1999—. Mem. Australian Coll. Venereologists, Med. Soc. for Study Venereal Diseases. Avocations: travel, photography, squash, food and wine. Office: Chelsea & Westminster Hosp, 369 Fulham Rd, London SW10 9TH, England

MOYLE, ROBERT JOHN, forensic psychiatrist; b. Auckland, New Zealand, Feb. 13, 1952; s. Alfred Nicholas and Florence Kezia (Rowlands) M.; m. Wendy Tremaine, Mar. 11, 1978; children: Peter, Dylan. MB, BChir, U. Otago, 1976. House surgeon Otago Hosp. Bd., Dunedin, New Zealand, 1976-78, registrar in psychol. medicine, 1978-83; registrar in psychiatry Glenside Hosp., Adelaide, Australia, 1983; psychiatrist Hillcrest Hosp. and Northfield Security Hosp., Adelaide, Australia, 1984-88; sr. psychiatrist Hillcrest Hosp., Adelaide, Australia, 1988-90; dir. forensic psychiatry Queensland Health (now Royal Brisbane Hosp. and Dist.), Brisbane, Australia, 1990-2000; dir. forensic psychiatry Royal Brisbane Hosp. and Dist., 1992-2000. Mem. editl. bd. Psychiatry Psychol. and Law, Brisbane, 1995—. Fellow Royal Australian and New Zealand Coll. Psychiatrists (mem. 1984-86, treas. forensic sect. 1993—, chair Queensland br. forensic sect. 1992—, sec. social and cultural sect. 1985-89, sec. South Australian and br. com. 1986-87), Australian and New Zealand Assn. of Psychiatry Psychology and Law (asst. sec. 1994—). Avocations: reading, TV, scuba diving, theatre. Office: 101 Wickham Tce, Silverton Pl Ste 58, Spring Hill QLD 4000, Australia

MOYLES, PHILIP VINCENT, JR., financial services company executive; b. N.Y.C., July 14, 1964; s. Philip Vincent and Anne Kane Moyles; m. Beth O'Connor. BA in History, Kenyon Coll., 1986; postgrad., Dartmouth Coll., 2000. Mgmt. trainee Rollins Burdick Hunter Co., Chgo., 1986-87; assoc. Johnson & Higgins, N.Y.C., 1987-90; sr. acct. rep. Marsh & McLennan Inc., N.Y.C., 1990-91, asst. v.p., 1991-93, v.p., 1993-95, sr. v.p., 1995-96; mng. dir., practice leader mergers and acquisitions Marsh Inc., N.Y.C., 1996—. Mem. Union League Club N.Y., Allegheny Country Club (Sewickley, Pa.). Republican. Roman Catholic. Office: Marsh Inc 1166 Ave of Americas New York NY 10036

MOYNIHAN, GARY PETER, industrial engineering educator; b. Little Falls, N.Y., Mar. 5, 1956; s. Peter H. and Frances S. (Ferjanec) M.; m. Eleanor T. McCusker, Mar. 10, 1984; children: Andrew Ross, Keith Patrick. BS in Chemistry, Rensselaer Polytech. Inst., 1978, MBA in Opsl. Mgmt., 1980; PhD in Indsl. Engring., U. Ctrl. Fla., 1990. Prodn. supr. Am. Cyanamid, Bound Brook, N.J., 1978-79, Nat. Micronetics, Kingston, N.Y., 1980-81; assoc. mfg. engr. Martin Marietta Aerospace, Orlando, Fla., 1981-82, indsl. engr., 1982-85, sr. indsl. engr., 1985-87, group indsl. engr., 1987-90; asst. prof. indsl. engring. U. Ala., Tuscaloosa, 1990-96, assoc. prof., 1996—; cons. in field. Contbr. articles to profl. jours. Regents scholar N.Y. State Bd. Regents, 1974-78; rsch. fellow NASA, 1992-93, 98-99; rsch. grant Bell-South Telecomm., 1994-96; recipient Outstanding Tchg. award AMOCO Found., 1993-94, Ralph R. Teetor Engring. Educator award Soc. Automotive Engrs, 2000. Mem. IEEE, Inst. Indsl. Engrs. (sr. mem., chpt. dir. 1991-95, chpt. pres. 1996-97), Aerospace & Def. Soc. (v.p. fin. and adminstrn. 1994-97). Achievements include design and development of information systems applications for the aerospace and foundry industries; 2 software copyrights in field of measurement and prediction of on-line information system failure costs. Office: U Ala Dept Indsl Engring Tuscaloosa AL 35487-0001

MOYNIHAN, JOHN BIGNELL, lawyer; b. N.Y.C., July 25, 1933; s. Jerome J. and Stephanie (Bignell) M.; m. Odilia Marie Jacques, Nov. 13, 1965; children: Blair, Dana. BS, Fordham U., 1955; JD, St. John's U., N.Y.C., 1958. Bar: Tex. 1961, U.S. Supreme Ct. 1965, U.S. Dist. Ct. (we. dist.) Tex. 1968, U.S. Ct. Appeals (5th cir.) 1973. Sole practice Brownsville, Tex., 1961-62; asst. city atty. City of San Antonio, 1962-63; sole practice San Antonio, 1963-65; estate tax atty. IRS, San Antonio, 1965-73; dist. counsel EEOC, San Antonio, 1974-79; asst. U.S. atty. Office U.S. Atty., San Antonio, 1980-87, sr. litigation counsel, 1987-94; sole practice San Antonio, 1995-98; ret., 1998. Chmn. reform and renewal com., San Antonio Roman Cath. Archdiocese, 1968. Served with U.S. Army, 1958-60; lt. col. USAFR (ret.), 1986. Mem. San Antonio Bar Assn. (chmn. state and nat. legis. com. 1972-73, Meritorious Svc. award 1968), Fed. Bar Assn. (bd. dirs. San Antonio chpt. 1983—, pres. elect 1986, pres. 1987), KC (pres. 1967). Home: 11011 Whispering Wind St San Antonio TX 78230-3746

MOYSSIDES, PAUL GREGORY, physicist, educator, researcher; b. Athens, Greece, Jan. 6, 1946; s. Gregory Paul and Elpis Andrew (Karydides) M.; m. Myrsine Eleftherios Kakouri, Jan. 8, 1989. BS, Aristoteleian U. Thessaloniki, 1969; PhD of Physics, Imperial Coll. Sci. and Tech., 1977; diploma, Imperial Coll. Physics, 1977. Prof. physics Anargyrios and Korgialenios Sch. Spetses, 1978-79; lectr. physics Nat. Tech. U. Athens, 1979-91, asst. prof., 1992—. Mem. Hellenic Astron. Soc., Am. Inst. Physics, Inst. Physics, European Phys. Soc., Hellenic Soc. for the Study of High Energy Physics. Avocations: electronics, computers. Office: Nat Tech Univ Athens, Zografou Campus, 15780 Zografou Greece

MOZHAROV, OLEG TIKHON, geneticist; b. Dushambe, Tadjkikistan,, Russia, June 5, 1940; m. Vera Paley, Sept. 18, 1944; 1 child, Nadja, June 29, 1972. PhD, Microbe Inst., Saratov, Russia, 1983. Geneticist, rschr. Med. Inst., Dushambe, 1971-73; sr. rschr. Microbe Inst., Saratov, 1974-96; geneticist, rschr., cons. Regional Children Hosp., Saratov, 1996—, prof., regional base med. coll., 1999—. Author: Molecular Genetics and DNA-Diagnostics of the Human Hereditary Diseases, 2000; inventor in field; contbr. more than 80 articles to profl. jours. Vice-pres. Mid. and Lower Volga br. All-Union Vavilov's Soc. of Genetists and Selectioners, 1984-93; counsellor/biologist dist. Ct. of Law, Saratov, 1990—. Mem. N.J. Acad. of Scis., Planetar Assn. of Scientists, Nat. Geograph. Soc. Avocations: reading, walking in the woods. Office: Volskaja str 6, 410028 Saratov Russia

MÓZSIK, GYULA, internist, gastroenterologist, educator; b. Dancsháza, Hungary, June 7, 1938; s. Károly Mózsik and Mária Pozsár; m. Ilona Vizi; 1 child, Andrea. MD, U. Debrecen, Hungary, 1962. Asst. to 2d dept. medicine Med. U., Debrecen, 1962-67, asst. prof. medicine, 1967—; assoc. prof. medicine U. Pécs, Hungary, 1975, prof. medicine, 1989—, head 1st dept. medicine, 1993, vice-dean clin. matters, 1996—; vis. scientist Dept. Pharmacology, Oslo, Norway, 1968-69; vis. scientist chem. pathology lab. Harvard Med. Sch., Boston, 1985. Contbr. over 150 chpts. to books, over 230 articles to profl. jours.; editor numerous textbooks. Mem. Am. Gastroenterol. Assn., Internat. Soc. Internal Medicine, Nat. Inst. Dietetics (adv. bd.), Hungarian Ministry of Health (adv. bd.), European Soc. Clin. Investigation, Hungarian Soc. Physiology, Hungarian Soc. Pharmacology, Hungarian Soc. Nutrition (medal József SOS 1984), Hungarian Soc. Gastroenterology (Pro Optimo Merito medal 1989), Internat. Brain-Gut Soc. (diplome, winner Széchenyi scolarship for prof. 1999—), Internat. Soc. Internal Medicine, Internat. Soc. Metabolic Therapy, N.Y. Acad. Scis. Home: Angster József 12, H-7624 Pécs Hungary Office: First Dept Medicine, U Med Sch, H-7643 Pécs Hungary

MPASU, SAMUEL JOHN, government of Malawi minister; b. Ntcheu, Malawi, Sept. 17, 1945; married; 7 children. BA in Econs. and English, U. Malawi, 1969. Gen. mgr. Assn. Chambers of Commerce and Industry of Malawi, 1988-90; sales and mktg. mgr. Xerographics, 1991-94; mem. underground exec. com. United Dem. Front, 1991; editor-in-chief United Dem. Front News, 1992; mem. Nat. Referendum Commn., 1993; mem. Malawi Parliament, Ntcheu Ctrl., 1994—, govt. whip, 1994—; min. edn., sci. and tech. Govt. of Malawi, 1994—, min. health and population; min. info., broadcasting, posts and telecomm.; sec.-gen. United Dem. Front, Limbe; mem. Pres. Com. on Poverty Alleviation, 1994—, Cabinet Com. on Economy, 1994—. Mem. United Democratic Front Party. Office: Spkr/Nat Assembly, P/Bag B 362, Lilongwe 3 Malawi

MRÁČEK, ZDENĚK, entomologist; b. Pardubice, Czech Republic, Apr. 7, 1950; s. Zdeněk and Dagmar (Robova) M.; 1 child, Zuzana. MS, Charles U., 1975; PhD, Inst. Entomology, 1982. Postdoctoral rschr. Inst. Entomology, C. Budejovice, Czech Republic, 1982-85, scientist, 1985-95; vis. prof. Simon Fraser U., Burnaby, Canada, 1991. Co-author: Insect Nematodes, 1988; contbr. articles and revs. to profl. jours. Investor water revitalization project Czech Ministry of Environment, 1993-96. Recipient Internat. Exch. award Natural Scis. and Engring. Rsch. Coun., 1991. Mem. Soc. Invertebrate Pathology, European Soc. Nematology, EC COST 819 Mgmt. Com., Hunting Soc. (head 1993—). Avocations: hunting, entomological expeditions in Central Asia mountains. Office: Acad Sci, Branisovska 31, 37005 Ceske Budejovice Czech Republic

MRAČEK, ZDENĚK, neurosurgeon, educator; b. Pilsen, Czech Republic, Jan. 6, 1930; s. Jan and Zdeňka (Smolová) M.; m. Eva Marcelliová, Sept. 18, 1970; children: Jan, Eva. MD, Charles U., Pilsen, Czech Republic, 1957. Resident U. Hosp., Pilsen, 1957-63; clin. asst. Mil. and Univ. Hosp., Prague, Czech Republic, 1964-66; head divsn. neurosurgery U. Hosp., Pilsen, 1966-82, chief dept. neurosurgery, 1982-95; cons. prof. U. Hosp., 5, 1995—; corr. mem. Societa Italiana de Neurochirurgia, 1972, Nordisk Neurokirurgisk Forening, 1973; assoc. prof. Charles U., Pilsen, 1990-92, univ. prof., 1992—; presenter in field. Author: Frontobasal Injuries, 1980, Craniocerebral Traumatology, 1988; contbr. articles to profl. jours. Mem. City Coun., Pilsen, 1990; lord mayor City of Pilsen, 1990-94. Mem. Czech Neurosurg. Soc. (pres. 1990-94), European Soc. for Pediat. Neurosurgery, Rotary Club, Becher Club. Avocations: basketball, literature. Home: K Světlé 1, 323 18 Plzeň Czech Republic Office: Univ Hosp, Ed Beneše 13, 305 99 Plzeň Czech Republic

MRACKY, RONALD SYDNEY, marketing and promotion executive, travel consultant; b. Sydney, Australia, Oct. 22, 1932; came to U.S., 1947, naturalized, 1957; s. Joseph and Anna (Janousek) M.; m. Sylvia Frommer, Jan. 1, 1960; children: Enid Hillevi, Jason Adam. Student, English Inst., Prague, Czechoslovakia, 1943-47; grad., Parsons Sch. Design, N.Y.C., 1950-53; postgrad., NYU, 1953-54. Designer D. Deskey Assocs., N.Y.C., 1952-53; art dir., designer ABC-TV, Hollywood, Calif., 1956-57; creative dir. Neal Advt. Assocs., L.A., 1957-59; pres. Richter & Mracky Design Assocs., L.A., 1959-68; pres., CEO Richter & Mracky-Bates divsn. Ted Bates & Co., L.A., 1968-73, Regency Fin., Internat. Fin. Svcs., Beverly Hills, Calif., 1974-76; sr. ptnr. Sylron Internat., L.A., 1973—, mgmt. dir. for N.Am. Standard Advt.-Tokyo, 1978-91; CEO Standard/Worldwide Cons. Group, L.A., Tokyo, 1981-87; officer, bd. dirs. Theme Resorts, Inc., Denver, 1979—; prin., officer Prodn. Travel & Tours, Universal City, 1981—; Eques Ltd., L.A., 1988—; mng. ptnr. GO! Pubs., 1993—; cons. in field; exec. dir. Inst. for Internat. Studies and Devel. L.A., 1976-77; mng. ptnr. Africa Consult Group, 1998—. Contbr. articles to profl. jours.; mem. editl. bd., mktg. dir. The African Times and Africa Quar., 1990—. With U.S. Army, 1954-56. Recipient nat. and internat. awards design and mktg. Mem. Am. Mktg. Assn., African Travel Assn. (amb.-at-large, pres. So. Calif. chpt.), L.A. Publicity Club, Pacific Asia Travel Assn., S.Am. Travel Assn., Am. Soc. Travel Agents. Office: 10554 Riverside Dr Toluca Lake CA 91602-2441

MRAMOR, JAMES PLUMMER, security consultant; b. Cleve., Feb. 10, 1943; s. Frank James and Lucille (Cannon) M.; m. Dolores Dergance, Oct. 17, 1964 (div. June 1974); m. Patricia Ann Taddeo, June 12, 1976; children: Michael, Wendy, Allison. B in Criminal Justice, Youngstown State U., 1999; postgrad., Cleve. State U., 1999—. Police lt. East Cleve. (Ohio) Police Dept., 1964-79; v.p., security Centran Corp./ Central Bank, Cleve., 1979-86, Soc. Nat. Bank, Cleve., 1986; security dir. Cleve. Mus. Art, 1987—; cons. Topwatch Corp., Cleve., 1986; adj. instr. Case Western Reserve U., Cleve., 1979. With U.S. Army, 1961-64. Mem. Ohio State Bar Assn. (student mem.), Cugahoya County Bar Assn. (student mem.), Cleve. Bar Assn. (student mem.). Democrat. Avocations: gourmet cooking, travel, sports. E-mail: mramor@hotmail.com. Home: 3070 Nantucket Dr Willoughby OH 44094-7679

MRAZEK, DAVID ALLEN, pediatric psychiatrist; b. Ft. Riley, Kans., Oct. 1, 1947; s. Rudolph George and Hazel Ruth (Schayes) M.; m. Patricia Jean, Sept. 2, 1978; children: Nicola, Matthew, Michael, Alissa. AB in Genetics, Cornell U., 1969; MD, Wake Forest U., 1973. Lic. psychiatrist, child psychiatrist, N.C., Ohio, Colo., D.C., Va., Md.; med. lic. N.C., Ohio, D.C., Va., Md. Lectr. child psychiatry Inst. of Psychiatry, London, 1977-79; dir. pediatric psychiatry Nat. Jewish Ctr. for Immunology and Respiratory Medicine, Denver, 1979-91; chmn. psychiatry Children's Nat. Med. Ctr., Washington, 1991-98; chair psychiatry and behavioral scis. George Washington U. Sch. Medicine, 1996-2000; dir. Children's Rsch. Inst. Neurosci., 1995-98; chair psychiatry and psychology Mayo Clinic, Rochester, Minn., 2000—; prof. psychiatry and psychology Mayo Sch. Medicine, Rochester, 2000—; asst. prof. psychiatry U. Colo. Sch. Medicine, 1979-83, assoc. prof. psychiatry and pediatrics, 1984-89, prof., 1990-91; prof. psychiatry and pediatrics George Washington U. Sch. Medicine, 1991—, Leon Yochelson prof. psychiatry and behavioral scis. Contbr. articles and book chpts. on child devel. and asthma to profl. publs. Recipient Rsch. Scientist Devel. awards NIMH, 1983-88, 88-91, Irving Phillips Meml. award for outstanding rsch. in prevention Acad. Child and Adolescent Psychiatry, 2000. Fellow Am. Acad. Child Psychiatry, Royal Soc. Medicine, Am. Psychiat. Assn. (Blanche F. Ittleson award 1996, Agnes Purcell McGavin award 1999), Royal Coll. Psychiatrists; mem. Am. Coll. Psychiatrists, Group for the Advancement of Psychiatry, Colo. Child and Adolescent Psychiatry Soc. (pres. 1984). Office: Mayo Clinic Dept Psychiatry/Pschology 200 1st St SW Rochester MN 55905

MRAZEK, THELMA STEVENS, writer; b. Macon, Ga., Sept. 22, 1930; d. Samuel Levi and Vivian (Pierce) Stevens; m. James Edward Mrazek, Nov. 28, 1970. BA, Duke U., 1952; MA, U. Pa., 1954. Editorial asst. Fgn. Policy Assn., N.Y.C., 1954-60; rsch. editor Time-Life Books, Time, Inc., N.Y.C., 1960-66; editor Pres.' Commn. on Adminstrn. of Justice, Washington, 1966-67; dir. tech info. svcs. Appalachian Regional Commn., Washington, 1967-71; dir. communications Mech. Contractors Assn. Am., Bethesda, 1972-85; pres. Mrazek Communications, Bethesda, 1985—; sec.-treas. Constrn. Writers Assn., Chevy Chase, Md., 1990—. Recipient 2 1st Prize awards Fed. Editors Assn., 1969-70. Mem. Nat. Press Club, Washington Ind. Writers, Constrn. Writers Assn. Office: Constrn Writers Assn PO Box 70835 Bethesda MD 20813-0835

MRIDHA, SHAHJAHAN, materials engineering educator; b. Rajapur, Jhalakati, Bangladesh, Oct. 31, 1948; s. Mohammad Ali Mridha and Noor Banu; m. Fatema Begum, May 17, 1981; chldren: Sachi Arafat, Shefa Jahan. BSc in Engring., Bangladesh U. Engring./Tech., Dhaka, 1970, MSc in Engring., 1976; PhD, U. Leeds, Eng., 1980. Lectr. Bangladesh U. Engring. and Tech., Dhaka, 1972-76, asst. prof., 1977-83, assoc. prof., 1983-86, prof., 1986-89, head dept. metall. engring., 1988-89; sr. rsch. fellow Strathclyde U., Glasgow, Scotland, 1989-94; sr. lectr. Nanyang Tech. U., Singapore, 1994-98, assoc. prof., 1999—; cons. Teesta Barrage, Rangpur, Bangladesh, 1985-86, Chem. Industries Corp., Dhaka, 1987, Chittagong Steel Mills, Bangladesh, 1987-89. Contbr. chpts. in books, articles to profl. jours. Gen. sec. World Univ. Svcs., Bangladesh, 1985; advisor Sport Coun., Bangladesh, 1981-89. Fellow Inst. of Engrs. (life); mem. Inst. of Materials (U.K.), Am. Soc. Materials, Heat Treatment Soc. Avocations: swimming, badminton. Office: Nanyang Tech U/Mats Engring, Nanyang Ave, Singapore 639798, Singapore

MRINAL, NIHAR RANJAN, psychologist, psychotherapist; b. Agra, India, July 8, 1947; s. Jai Ram and Krishna Devi Mahaur; m. Uma Singhal, Sept. 21, 1980; children: Nimisha, Nishant. BA, Agra Coll., 1970, MA, 1972; MPhil in Clin. Psychology, Ctrl. Inst. Psychiatry, Ranchi, India, 1975; PhD, Indian Inst. Tech., 1980. Cert. clin. psychologist. Rsch. assoc. IIndian Inst. Tech., Kanpur, 1978-80; lectr. Nagpur (India) U., 1980-85, lectr. sr. grade, 1985-93, reader in psychology, 1993—; cons. Ketki Rsch. Inst. Med. Scis., Nagpur, 1997—; hon. dir. Psychology Study Cir., Nagpur, 1994—. Contbr. articles to profl. jours., chpts. to books. Ctrl. Govt. Health Svcs., Govt. of India scholar, 1973-75; Indian Inst. Tech. fellow, 1975-80. Fellow Indian Assn. Clin. Psychology (life), Indian Sci. Congress (life), Indian Psychol. Assn. (life), Indian Soc. Clin. and Exptl. Hypnosis (life), Psycholinguistic Assn. India (life), Assn. Psychocultural Dimensions (life). Avocations: psychotherapy, helping others. E-mail: nmrinal@yahoo.com. Office: Nagpur U Dept Psychology, Amravati Rd, Nagpur India

MRÓZ, JAN KAZIMIERZ, physician; b. Rdziostów, Nowy Sacz, Poland, Feb. 19, 1942; s. Jan and Julia (Sutkowska) M.; m. Helena Grzegorzek, July 11, 1970; children: Krzysztof, Krystyna, Marek, Małgorzata, Jan (dec.), Helena. MD, Med. Acad. Cracow, 1967. Intern Provincial Hosp., Nowy Sacz, Poland, 1967-69; physician, chief Rural Health Svc. Ctr., Kruzlowa, Poland, 1969, Podegrodzie, Poland, 1969-71, Brzezna, Poland, 1971-73, Lukowica, Poland, 1973-76, Golkowice Górne, Poland, 1976—. Pres. United Peasant's Party, Med. Acad., Cracow, 1960-67, mem., Nowy Sacz, 1967-71. Mem. Chamber of Physicians. Avocations: languages, hiking, table tennis, bridge, volleyball. E-mail: JanKazimie.686519@pharmanet.com. Home: Golkowice Górne 124, 33-388 Golkowice Poland Office: Wojewódzki Szpital Zespolony, Golkowice Gorne 119, 33-388 Golkowice Gorne, Poland

MROZIEWICZ, BOHDAN, electrical engineer, researcher; b. Piastów, Warsaw, Poland, Sept. 6, 1933; s. Piotr and Zofia (Semenowicz) M.; m. Eulalia Haniewicz, July 31, 1959; 1 child, Joanna. BSc, Warsaw U. Tech., 1955, MSc, 1957, DSc, 1972; PhD, Inst. Fundamental Tech. Problems, Warsaw, 1964; diploma, London U., 1960. Engr. Inst. Fundamental Tech. Problems, Warsaw, 1956-57, sr. asst., 1957-59, asst. prof., 1959-73; assoc. prof. Inst. Electron Tech. (formerly Inst. Fundamental Tech. Probl), Warsaw, 1973-84, prof., 1984—; postdoctoral fellow U. So. Calif., L.A., 1969-70; head of lab. Inst. Electron Tech., 1966-71, dep. dir., 1971-90, dir. rsch., 1992-94; advisor to dir. Inst. Electronic Materials, Warsaw, 1996—. Author: Semiconductor Lasers, 1967; co-author: Junction Lasers, 1985, Physics of Semiconductor Lasers, 1991; contbr. over 130 articles to profl. jours.; patentee in field. Recipient State award Com. of State Awards, Warsaw, 1964, awards Minister of Edn., Warsaw, 1977, 80, State Distinctions, medals, crosses, Warsaw, 1969, 73, 74, 78, Hon. medal Polish Elec. Soc., 1992. Mem. IEEE (exec. com. Poland sect. 1974—), Internat. Union Radio Sci. (chmn. Commn. D), Warsaw Sci. Soc. Avocation: gardening. Home: ul Neseberska 1 m 7, 02-758 Warsaw Poland Office: Inst Electron Tech, Al Lotników 32/46, 02-668 Warsaw Poland

MROZIŃSKA, TERESA MARIA, botany educator; b. Pszczyna, Silesia, Poland, Apr. 9, 1931; d. Wacław and Maria (Wojnowska) Mroziński; m. Bolesław Broda, May 1979 (dec. 1999); m. Harold Harvey Webb, Jan. 1960; 1 child, Maria Webb-Janich. MS, Jagiellonian U., Poland, 1956, D Habilitation, 1978; DS, Polish Acad. Sci., 1958. Asst. Inst. Botany, Polish Acad. Sci., Cracow, 1955-58, adj., 1958-78, docent, 1978-92; prof. botany Pedagogical U., Kielce, Poland, 1992—; sec. bot. com. Polish Acad. Sci., Warsaw, 1987-90, mem., 1990-93. Author: Chlorophyta VI Oedogoniophyceae, 1985 (award Polish Acad. Sci. 1987), Oedogoniales.Süsswasserflora von Mitteleuropa, 14; contbr. articles to profl. jours. Recipient medal Polish Acad. Sci., 1984. Mem. Polish bot. Assn., N.Y. Acad. Scis. Avocations: skiing, tennis, driving, piano, travel. Home: Gońaška St, 30-619 Cracow Poland Office: Pedagogical U, Konipnicka 15, 25-406 Kielce Poland

MSWATI, HIS MAJESTY III, King of Swaziland; b. Apr. 19, 1968; s. King Sobhuza II and Ntombi. Ed., Sherborne Sch., Dorset, Eng. Installed as King of Swaziland, 1986—. Office: Office of H M The King, PO Box 1, Lobamba Swaziland also: Univ of Swaziland, Private Bag 4, Kwaluseni Swaziland*

MTHEMBI-MAHANYELE, SANKIE DOLLY, government official; b. Sophiatown, South Africa, Mar. 23, 1951. Diploma in tchg., U. of the North, 1973, BA, 1976; postgrad., Sch. of Solidarity, Germany, 1978, U. Zambia, 1982. Radio journalist Dar-as-Salaam, Tanzania, 1977; radio journalist African Nat. Congress, 1977-81, editor Voice of Women jour., 1979-81, mem. NEC and Coun. for Women's Study Sect., 1979-92, adminstrv. sec. mission in Sweden, 1982-84, adminstrv. sec. mission for Nigeria and West Africa, 1986-89, chief rep. for Germany and Austrai, 1989-93, dep. head dept. internat. affairs, 1993-94; dep. welfare South African Govt. of Nat. Unity, 1994-95; min. housing South African Ministry of Housing, Capetown, 1995—; mem. numerous congresses in field; rschr. Eduardo Mondlane Inst. Mozambique, 1980. Author: (anthology) Flames of Fury, 1990; contbr. poetry, short stories to lit. publs.; editor Voice of Women jour., 1979-81. Radio journalist Radio Freedom, Lusaka, Zambia, 1979.

Avocations: writing poetry, reading. Office: Ministry of Housing, Pretoria South Africa

MTHOKO, NOVEMBER ANANIAS, adult education educator; b. Onyaanya, Oshikoto, Namibia, Nov. 22, 1943; s. Ananias Shikongo Mthoko and Hilma Nuukwawo Festus; m. Ndahambelela Frederica Nepando, July 27, 1982; 3 children. BA in Adult Education with honors, U. Lagos, Nigeria, 1981. Tchr. Govt., Zambia, 1971-73; tchr. Swapo, Nyango, 1976-77, Kwanza-sul, 1980-81; dir. Namibian Extension Unit, Lusaka, Zambia, 1981-90, Govt., Namibia, 1990—. Co-author: (textbook series) Basic Agriculture, 1984, (textbooks) English Course, 1980, Primary Health Care, 1985, Junior Secondary Geography, 1990. Scholar European Cmty., Brussels, 1977-80. Mem. Internat. Diabetic Fedn. (Belgium), N.Y. Acad. Sci., Nat. Geog. Soc. Active Swapo Party of Namibia. Evangelical Lutheran. Avocations: photography, reading non-fiction, writing, exercises, site-seeing. Home and Office: PO Box 776, 89 Bach Strasse Windhoek West, Windhoek 9000, Namibia

MU, CHUNDI, control theory educator, researcher; b. Qingdao, China, June 9, 1946; d. Keqin and Fuan (Yang) M.; m. Lizhu Zhou, Jan. 1, 1974; 1 child, Zhou Hualiang. BS, Tsinghua U., Beijing, China, 1970; MS, Pa. State U. Asst. prof. Tsinghua U., Beijing, China, 1978-83; lectr. Tsinghua U., Beijing, 1983-92, assoc. prof., 1992-99, prof., 1999—; dir. of control theory group, Tsinghua U., 1994-99. Co-author: Automatic Control Principles, 1990; translator: Feedback Control Theory, 1993; contbr. articles to profl. jours. Mem. IEEE (sr.). Avocations: swimming, basketball, running. Office: Dept of Automation, Tsinghua University, Beijing 100084, China

MU, GUOGUANG, former university president, educator. Prof. Chinese U.; pres. Nankai U.; dir. Inst. of Modern Optics, Nankai U.; v.p. Internat. Commn. Optics. Fellow Third World Acad. Scis., mem. Chinese Sci. Acad., Chinese Optical Soc. (pres.), Tianjin Assn. of Sci. and Tech. (pres.). Office: Nankai U Inst Modern Optics, 94 Weijin Rd, Tianjin 300071, China

MU, MU, geophysicist; b. Dingyuan, Anhui, China, Aug. 31, 1954; s. Yaoxue Mu and Xialing Dai; m. Fanghua Ge, May 1, 1981; 1 child, Ting. BS, Anhui U., Hefei, China, 1978, MS, 1982; PhD, Fudan U., Shanghai, 1985. Asst. lectr. Anhui U., 1981-82; lectr. Shanghai Jiao Tong U., 1985-87; postdoctoral fellow Chinese Acad. Scis., Beijing, 1987-89, assoc. prof., 1989-92, prof., 1993—; mem. Acad. Commn., Inst. of Atmospheric Physics, 1994—; reviewer Math. Reviews, 1994—; doctoral tutor Chinese Acad. Scis., 1993—. Editor: Chinese Jour. Atmospheric Scis., 1994—; contbr. articles to profl. jours. Recipient Youth prize China Assn. for Sci. and Technology, 1990, Young Scientist prize Chinese Acad. Scis., 1992, prize for Young Scientists, All-China Youth Fedn., 1994, Guoshi Postdoctoral award China Postdoctoral Sci. Found., 1995. Mem. China Meterol. Soc., Soc. of Chinese Young Scientists (bd. dirs. 1993—), Am. Math. Soc. Office: Inst Atmospheric Physics, Chinese Acad Scis, 100029 Beijing China

MU, YONGKE, research scientist; b. Shouguang, Shandong, China, Dec. 13, 1962; came to the U.S., 1994; s. Diqi Mu and Sulan Liou; m. Hui Zheng, June 7, 1989. BS, Shandong U., Jinan, China, 1985, MS, 1988; PhD, U. Del., 1998. Asst. prof. Shandong U., Jinan, 1988-94; rsch. asst. U. Del., Newark, 1996-98, postdoctoral fellow Coll. Marine Studies, 1998-99, rsch. scientist Coll. Marine Studies, 1999—. Contbr. articles to profl. jours. Mem. Am. Geophys. Union (sr.), Soc. Exploration Geophysicists (sr.), Acoustic Soc. Am. (assoc.). Avocations: travel, fishing, field exploring. E-mail: yongkee@udel.edu. Home: 2828 Egypt Rd Apt B201 Audubon PA 19403-2151 Office: Univ Del Grad Sch Marine Studies Ocean Acoust Lab Newark DE 19716

MUAMMAR, ABDALLAH BIN ABD AL-AZIZ, federal official; b. 1950. BA in Econs., Internat. Am. U., 1976, MBA in Adminstrn., Devel. Orgn., 1978; MA in Social Sci., U. Calif., Irvine, 1981, PhD in Social Sci., 1983. Dir. dept. rsch. and studies Gen. Secretariat of Labor Force, 1983; cons. Min. of Agr., 1988; dep. min. Ministry Agr. and Water, Riyadh, Saudi Arabia, 1988; min. Ministry Agr. and Water, Riyadh, 1995—. Office: Min Agr and Water, Airport Rd, Riyadh 1195, Saudi Arabia*

MUANGMAN, DEBHANOM, public health physician, administrator, researcher; b. Bangkok, Sept. 18, 1935; s. Pyn and Chamnong Muangman; m. Chayaporn Muangman, June 9, 1962; children: Suphichaya, Pimporn; daughter in law, Thanthip. BA, Grinnell Coll., 1958; MD, Jefferson Med. Coll., 1962; MPH, Harvard U., 1965, DrPH, 1968; DSc (hon.), Thomas Jefferson U., 1995. Diplomate Am. Bd. Med. Examiners; med. lic. Thailand. Lectr. Faculty Pub. Health Mahidol U., Bangkok, 1968-72, chmn. dept. pub. health adminstrn., 1972-76, dean Faculty Pub. Health, 1976-92; dean Faculty Environment Resource Studies Mahidol U., Nakornpathom Province, Thailand, 1992-95; dir. Harvard-Rangsit U. Med. Program; adviser to Min. Pub. Health, Thailand, 1980-96, Min. Sci. and Environment; dir. HFA Leadership Ctr., WHO, S.E. Asia, 1988-95; environ. adviser Parliament Thailand, 1992-96; adviser Bangkok Gov., 1992-2000. Author 10 textbooks, 200 sci. papers; editor Thai Jour. Pub. Health, 1968-90. Chair Nat. Family Planning Evaluation Com., Thailand, 1975-91; dir. Slum Devel. Project, Bangkok, 1982-94; AIDS advisor to Prime Min. Thailand, 1992; advisor Dem. Party Thailand, 1982-94. Named Outstanding Health Educator, Health Edn. Assn., 1985; recipient Nat. Rsch. award NRC Thailand, 1991, Health Leadership award Asia Pacific Pub. Health Consortium, 1992, Harvard scholarship, 1964-68, Outstanding Health Adminstr. award Found. Thai Soc., 1999, Outstanding Contbr. to Mental Health Devel. award Buddhist Coun. of Thailand, 2000. Mem. Fertility Rsch. Assn. (bd. dirs., pres. 1983-87), AIDS Prevention Assn. (bd. dirs., pres. 1992-96), Thai Med. Assn. (bd. dirs., v.p. 1990-92), Nat. Soc. Welfare (bd. dirs., exec. 1990-93), Life and Environment Co. (chmn. 1991—). Buddhist. Fax: 662-2759777. E-mail: debhanom@bkk.a-net.net.th. Home: Soi-8, 69/1 Vibhavadi Rangsit, Bangkok 10400, Thailand

MUBARAK, MUHAMMAD HOSNI, president of Egypt; b. Kafre al-Musailha, Minufiya, Egypt, May 4, 1928; m. Susan Sabet; 2 sons. Grad., Mil. Acad. Egypt, 1949, Air Acad. Egypt, 1950. Head mil. del. to USSR, 1964-65; sta. comdr. Egyptian Air Force, Cairo West Airfield, 1966, chief staff, 1969-72, air vice marshal, 1969-74, air marshal, 1974—, commdr., 1972-75; apptd. dep. minister war Govt. of Egypt, Cairo West Airfield, 1972, maj. gen., 1973-75, v.p., 1975-81, pres., 1981—; dir. gen. Egyptian Arms Procurement Agy., 1975—; chmn. Orgn. African Unity, 1990. Vice chmn. Nat. Democratic Party, 1980—, sec. gen., 1980-82, chmn., 1982—. Decorated Medal of Mil. Duty 2d class, Honour Star, Medal of Tng., Medal of Long Svc. and Good Example, Collar of the Republic, Sinai Star 1st class, Mil. Star, Mil. Medal of the Republic 1st class, Mil. Medal of Courage 1st class, Medal of Mil. Duty 1st class (Egypt); Order of the Republic 1st class, Supreme Class of 7th Sept. Order of Republic of Tunisia (Tunisia); Order of King Abdel Aziz Supreme class (Saudi Arabia); Order of Homayoun 2d class (Iran); Grand Cordon of Order of Kuwait, Collar of Great Mubarak (Kuwait); Grand Cross of Nat. Order of Merit (France); Grand Cordon of Golden Order of Honour (Austria); Mex. Order of Aguila Azteca; Grand Cordon of Order of Honour, Grand Cordon of Order of Redeemer (Greece); Order of Ma'reb Dam 2d class, Order of Republic (Yemen); Order of Oman 2d class; Order of Ommia with braid (Syria); Grand Cordon of Order of Isabel la Catolica, Collar of Isabel la Catolica (Spain); Grand Cross of Nat. Order of Merit (Togo); Order of Republic of Indonesia Adipradana; Trishakti Patta 1st class (Nepal); Grand Cross of Nat. Order of Legion of Honour (France); Grand Cordon of Grand Cross Order (Italy); Collar of Order of Infante Don Henrique, Grand Cross of Order of Christ (Portugal); Grand Cordon of Supreme Order of Chrysanthemum (Japan); Order of Nat. Flag 1st class (Republic of Korea); Grand Cordon of Nat. Order of Niger; Grand Cordon of Nat. Order of Leopard (Zaire); Grand Cross of Nat. Order of Mali; Grand Collar of Cen. African Republic; Collar of Al-Hussein Bin Ali (Jordan); Order of Yugoslavia; Collar from HRM the Sultan of Brunei Darussalam; Mil. Order of Oman 1st class; Grand Cross of Order of Merit of Fed. Republic Germany supreme class; Order of the Elephant (Denmark); Order of the Seraphim (Sweden); Collar of Honour (Sudan); extraordinary supreme class of Order of Congress (Colombia); Order of Champion of Dem. People's Republic of Korea; The Most Honourable Order of Bath (U.K.); Grand Collar of Libertarian Gen. San Martin (Argentina); recipient Collar of Nile award, Grand Cordon of Nile, Order of Republic 1st class, Order of Merit 1st class, Order of Labour 1st class, Order of Scis. and Arts 1st class, Order of Sports 1st class, Medal of Distinction 1st class, Medal of Merit 1st class (Egypt); Louise Michel prize for Human Rights, Democracy, Dialogue and Peace, 1990. Mem. Higher Council Nuclear Energy. Office: Office of the President, Heliopolis Al-Etehadia Bldg, Abdeen Cairo Egypt*

MUBARAK, UMID MIDHAT, Iraq minister of health, internist; b. Suleimania, Iraq, 1939; m.; 4 children. BA in Medicine, Ankara U., Turkey, 1962. Internal Medicine specialization, 1972. Physician, dir. hosps. Baghdad, Iraq, 1977—; chief of health Baghdad, adviser to pres., 1987; minister of health Govt. of Iraq, Baghdad, Iraq. mem. regional coun. Arab Baath Socialist Party, Suleimania Province, 1980; chief of Ongoing Assistance for Religious Endowments, Chief of Health, Social and Religious Affairs, Sulaimania Province two terms; mem. Nat. Coun. Arab Ba'ath Socialist Party 1984. *

MUCCI, GARY LOUIS, lawyer; b. Buffalo, Nov. 12, 1946; s. Guy Charles and Sally Rose (Battaglia) M.; m. Carolyn Belle Taylor, May 4, 1991. BA cum laude, St. John Fisher Coll., 1968; JD, Cath. U., 1972. Bar: N.Y. 1972. Law clk. to Hon. John T. Curtin U.S. Dist. Ct., Buffalo, 1972-74; assoc. atty. Donovan Leisure Newton & Irvine, N.Y.C., 1974-75; assoc. atty. Saperston & Day P.C., Buffalo, 1975-80, sr. ptnr., 1980—. Chmn. bd. Buffalo Philharm. Orch., 1985-86; pres. Hospice Buffalo, 1986-87; mem. N.Y. State Coun. on the Arts, 1987; chmn. Citizens Com. on Cultural Aid, Buffalo, 1992—; trustee St. John Fisher Coll. Recipient Brotherhood award NCCJ, Buffalo, 1983; named Man of Yr. William Paca Soc., 1984. Mem. Erie County Bar Assn., N.Y. State Bar Assn. Home: 27 Tudor Pl Buffalo NY 14222-1615 Office: Saperston & Day PC 3 Fountain Plz Ste 1100 Buffalo NY 14203-1486

MUCCI, LOUIE (LOUIS DAVID MUCCIOLO), music composer, producer; b. Jamaica, N.Y., Apr. 16, 1958; s. Louis Cosmo and Mary Michelina (Galante) M.; m. Lindsey Anne Howes, Sept. 16, 1990; 1 child, Evan. BA, CUNY, Flushing, 1980. Musical dir., performer N.Y. Rhythm, Glendale, 1981-91; disc jockey U.R.S.DJ's, Flushing, N.Y., 1986—; owner GAL Pub., Flushing, 1990—; pub. Active Nature, G-n-A, Flushing, 1989—. Music producer, composer, performer: (TV show soundtrack) Nothing Upstairs, 1990, (short film soundtracks) How to Be An American, 1993, Sleep, 1994, (TV comml.) Private Eyes, 1989; composer: (song) G-n-A TV Appearance, 1991, (musical) A Dream You Can Feel, 1996-99; prodr. Biofeedback Exercise Tape, 1992; co-composer album Active Nature, 1995. Mem. ASCAP, Nat. Music Pubs. Assn. Democrat. Roman Catholic. Avocations: record and disc collecting, travelling, sports viewing and playing, photography. Home and Office: GAL Pub ASCAP 43-21 189th St Flushing NY 11358-3423

MUCCINI, GIANNI, communications executive; b. Verona, Italy, Nov. 1, 1938; s. Massimo and Lina (Pedrotti) M.; m. Laura Pellegrini, Sept. 9, 1969; 1 child, Marco. LLD, U. Florence, Italy, 1964. Trainee Lintas, Milan, Italy; acct. dir. YeR, Milan, 1964-69; chmn. OeM, Milan, 1969-72, Italia/BBDO, Milan, 1972-92, ORMA e INTEMA, Milan and Florence, 1992—; editl. cons., pub. Flor/Media, Milan. Pub. Musica Viva, 1974-94, Nuova Cucina, 1975-94, Pubblico, 1975—. Electoral cons. Forza Italia, 1999. Avocations: classical music, wine, art deco. Office: Flor/Media, Via Torino 64, 20121 Milan Italy

MUCHA, JANUSZ LESZEK, sociologist, social anthropologist; b. Cracow, Poland, July 18, 1949; s. Władysław and Janina (Oparska) M. MA in Sociology, Jagiellonian U., Poland, 1972, MA in Philosophy, 1973, PhD in Sociology, 1976, Habilitation, 1986. Tchg. asst. Jagiellonian U., 1972-76, asst. prof., 1976-86, assoc. prof., 1986-90; vis. prof. Ind. U., 1990-91; prof. Nicholas Copernicus U., Poland, 1991—. Author: Conflict and Society, 1978, Critical Functions of Sociology, 1986, Cooley, 1922, Everyday Life and Festivity, 1996. Recipient 5 award Min. Edn., Poland. 010Mem. Polish Sociol. Assn. (bd. dirs. 1993—), European Sociol. Assn. (bd. dirs. 1995-97).

MUCHEMBLED, ROBERT PIERRE, historian, educator; b. Liévin, France, Mar. 4, 1944; s. Marcel Muchembled and Marie-Louise Dubois; 1 child. Degree, U. Paris, 1986, PhD, 1974. Asst. then master conf. U. Lille, France, 1969-86; prof. U. Paris-Nord, 1987—, dir. dept. history, 1990-95, dir. Doctoral Sch. Letters, 2000—; cons. Conseil Recherches Social Scis. Humanities, Can., 1983—, Meertens Inst., The Netherlands, 1995—. Author: L'Invention de L'Homme Moderne, 1988, La Violence au Village, 1989, Politesse et politique, 1998, Une Histoire du Diable, 2000; mem. editl. bd. Tijdschrift voor Geschiedenis, 1985—. Recipient Descartes-Huygens prize, 1997. Fellow Soc. Histoire Moderne, Soc. Histoire Moderne Contemporaine, Commission Historique Nord. E-mail: r.muchembled@wanadoo.fr. Office: U Paris Nord UFR Lettres, Av JB Clément, 93430 Villetaneuse France

MUCHIRI, MARY NYAMBURA, linguist, educator; b. Nairobi, Kenya, Aug. 1, 1943; d. Jimnah Muthuita and Josephine Wambui Kimori; m. Humphrey Wamai Muciiri, Dec. 20, 1969; 1 child, Timothy Wamai Muciiri. BA with honors, U. Nairobi, 1969, postgrad. diploma, 1970; MEd, Manchester (Eng.) U., 1981; PhD in Linguistics, Lancaster (Eng.) U., 1993. Head of dept. Kenyatta U., Nairobi, 1990-91, lectr., 1994-95; head of dept. Daystar U., Nairobi, 1996-98, dean of arts, 1998-2000, acting dep. vice chancellor, 1998-99; ext. examiner, Daressalaam, Tanzania, 1995-97, Egerton, Kenya, 1996-98, Moi, Kenya, 1997-2000; rschr. Inst. Devel. Studies, Nairobi, 1997-98. Author: Communication Skills, 1993; contbr. (books) Society and the Language Classroom, 1996, On Writing Research, 1999; contbr. articles to profl. jours. Editor ch. mag., Nairobi, 1998-2000. Mem. Internat. Assn. for the Promotion Christian Higher Edn. Avocations: reading, writing, swimming, farming. Office: Daystar U, PO Box 44400, Nairobi Kenya

MUCHNICK, RICHARD STUART, ophthalmologist; b. Bklyn., June 21, 1942; s. Max and Rae (Kozinsky) M.; BA with honors, Cornell U., 1963, MD, 1967; m. Felice Dee Greenberg, Oct. 29, 1978; 1 child, Amanda Michelle. Intern in medicine N.Y. Hosp., N.Y.C., 1967-68, now assoc. attending ophthalmologist, chief Pediatric Ophthalmology Clinic; resident in ophthalmology, 1970-73; practice medicine, specializing in ophthalmology, notably strabismus and ophthalmic plastic surgery N.Y.C., 1974—; attending surgeon, chief Ocular Motility Clinic, Manhattan Eye, Ear and Throat Hosp., N.Y.C.; clin. assoc. prof. ophthalmology Cornell U., N.Y.C., 1984—. Served with USPHS, 1968-70. Recipient Coryell Prize Surgery Cornell U. Med. Coll., 1967. Diplomate Am. Bd. Ophthalmology, Nat. Bd. Med. Examiners. Fellow A.C.S., Am. Acad. Ophthalmology; mem. Am. Soc. Ophthalmic Plastic and Reconstructive Surgery, Am. Assn. Pediatric Ophthalmology and Strabismus, Internat. Strabismological Assn., N.Y. Soc. Clin. Ophthalmology, AMA, N.Y. Acad. Medicine, Greater N.Y. Soc. for Pediat. Ophthalmology and Strabismus (pres.), Manhattan Ophthal. Soc., Alpha Omega Alpha, Alpha Epsilon Delta. Clubs: Lotos, 7th Regt. Tennis. Clin. researcher strabismus, ophthalmic plastic surgery, 1973—. Office: 69 E 71st St New York NY 10021-4213

MUCHNIK, ROSA, chemistry educator, researcher; b. Buenos Aires, Jan. 12, 1932; d. Miguel and Soulamit (Ravitz) M.; m. Jehoszua Mosze Lederkremer, Mar. 27, 1955; children: Gerardo, Miguel, Javier. Lic. in chemistry, U. Buenos Aires, 1954, D in Chemistry, 1956. Prof. U. Buenos Aires, 1982—; mem. com. Nat. Rsch. Coun., Buenos Aires, 1967—; vis. prof. São Paulo U., 1975-77; rsch. assoc. Ohio State U., Columbus, 1962-65. Author: Hidratos de Carbono, 1988; contbr. articles to profl. jours. including Jour. Biol. Chemistry and Jour. Organic Chemistry. Grantee Fundacion Konex, 1983, Liga Argentina Lucha Contra el Cancer, 1988, Academia Nacional Ciencias Exactas, 1990. Mem. Am. Chem. Soc., Asociacion Quimica Argentina, Sociedad Argentina Investigacion Bioquimica. Jewish. Achievements include first report of galactofuranose in a trypanosomatid. Home: Colombres 1372, 1238 Buenos Aires Argentina Office: Fac de Ciencias Exactas y Naturales, Pabellon 2 Cuidad Univ, 1428 Buenos Aires Argentina

MUCK, ALEXANDER, chemist, educator; b. Pécs, Hungary, June 2, 1937; s. Alexander and Eugenia (Draskóczy) M.; m. Marie Mácza, Feb. 25, 1967; children: Alexander, Marta. Grad., Charles U., 1961, Dr. RN, 1968; PhD, Inst. Chem. Tech. Prague, 1968. Sci. worker, sr. lectr. Inst. Chem. Tech. Prague, Czech Republic, 1967-90, assoc. prof. inorganic chemistry, 1991—; sci. sec. Inorganic sect. Czech. Chem. Soc., 1972-90. Author: Symmetry of Crystals and Vibrational Spectra, 1987 (Polish, 1992); contbr. articles to profl. jours. Named Knight of Magistral Grace of Sovereign Mil. Hosp. Order of St. John of Malta, 1990. Avocations: order and decoration collecting, antiquity, playing piano. Office: Inst Chem Tech, Technicka 5, 166 28 Praha 6 Czech Republic

MUCKE, HERMANN ALOIS MARTIN, consultant; b. Vienna, Austria, Sept. 4, 1955; s. Hermann B.W. and Elfriede (Jourez) M.; m. Mag Eva Grabler, Feb. 28, 1981; children: Peter, Melanie, Georg. MS, U. Vienna, 1980, DSc, 1983. Rsch. asst. U. Vienna, 1983-86; rsch. fellow Sandoz, Vienna, 1986-87; R&D lab. dir. Waldheim Pharma, Neufeld, Austria, 1987-89; mng. dir. Waldheim Pharma, Vienna, 1989-98; v.p. R&D Sanochemia AG, Vienna, 1994-99; v.p. R&D Viral Testing Sys. Corp., Houston, 1992-93; mem. evaluator panel Current Drugs Ltd., 1997—, Prous Sci. Pubs., 1998—, Decision Resources, Inc., 1998—. Mem. editl. staff European Affairs, Pharm. News, 1998—; contbr. articles to profl. jours. Chmn. Sci. Students' Coun., Vienna, 1976-77. With Austrian Army Res., 1995. Mem. AAAS, N.Y. Acad. Scis., Austrian Biochem. Soc., Austrian Soc. for Gene Tech., Austrian Chem. Soc. Avocations: family, science fiction, photography, computers and electronic communication. Home and Office: Enenkelstrasse 28/32, A-1160 Wien Austria

MUCKLE, DAVID SUTHERLAND, surgeon, educator; b. Weardale, Durham, Eng., Aug. 30, 1939; s. John L. and Ruth J. (Sutherland) M.; m. Christine Haymonds; children: Carolyn Jane, Deborah Christine. BMed, U. Durham, 1963, BSurgery, 1963, MD, 1981, MSurgery, 1971; hon. diploma sports medicine, Scottish Royal Colls. Surgeon Oxford, 1970-77, South Cleveland Hosp., 1977—; cons. orthopedic surgeon, 1977—; med. advisor Fédération Internationale de Football Assn., Switzerland, 1977—; surgeon, dep. chmn. med. com. Football Assn., 1983-98; surgeon Nuffield Hosp., Cleveland, 1981-98; med. com. Union Des Assns. Européennes de Football, 1990-98, Switzerland; vis. prof. U. Teesside, 1994-95. Author: Femoral Neck Fracture, 1977; Injuries in Sport, 1982; An Outline of Fractures, 1985, An Outline of Orthopedic Practice, 1986. Recipient Championship medal European Nations Cup Final, 1992, 96. Fellow Brit. Orthopedic Assn. (rsch. scholarship com. 1990—), Brit. Orthopedic Rsch. (com. mem. 1979, Pres. Orthopedic Rsch. prize 1973), Royal Coll. Surgeons (Eng. and Edinburg), Royal Geog. Soc. Home: Redcroft 72 The Grove, Marton Middlesbrough TS7 8AJ, England Office: Middlesbrough Gen Hosp, Ward 14, Middlesbrough TS4 2NS, England

MUDAG, SALIC CADAR, civil engineer; b. Taraka, Philippines, Feb. 1, 1958; arrived in Saudi Arabia, 1983; s. Sirad Liwalug and Maimona (Cadar) M.; m. Rohanie Sampao Rasul, May 7, 1987; children: Haifa, Hanadi, Reemah, Mohammad, Najma, Hanan, Khairan, Abdulhalim; m. Sophia T. Mamaluba, May 17, 1988 (dec. May 1994); 1 child, Salic Jr. BSCE, Mindanao State U., Marawi City, Philippines, 1980, postgrad., 1982; grad. mgmt. advancement program, fin. and acctg. program, AHI. Registered civil engr., and geodetic engr. Project engr. Trans-Amanah Constrn. Internat., Ltd., Marawi City, 1980-83; site inspector, surveyor A.M.R. Cons. Engrs., Jeddah, Saudi Arabia, 1983-89; site engr. Zuhair Fayez Partnership, Jeddah, 1989—; gen. mgr., owner S.M. Surveying Office, Marawi City, 1980-83. Press rels. officer Ninoy Aquino Movement, Jeddah, 1986; v.p. Tugayans Islamic Found. Internat., Jeddah, 1994. Consistent Acad. scholar Mindanao State U., 1975-80. Mem. Soc. Am. Mil. Engrs., Philippine Inst. Civil Engrs., Insan Islamic Assembly (chmn. 1994—, lectr. on Islamic economy 1988), Am. Biograph. Inst. (rsch. bd. advisors). Islam. Avocations: praying, bowling, swimming, chess, reading. Office: Zuhair Fayez Ptnrship, PO Box 5445, Jeddah 21422, Saudi Arabia

MUDENGE, STANISLAUS, Zimbabwean government official; b. Dec. 17, 1941; married; 3 children. Student, U. Coll. Rhodesia & Nyasaland, 1965-66, U. York, Eng., 1967-68, U. London, 1968-71. Sr. lectr. history Sierra Leone, 1971-73; lectr. history Botswana, Lesotho, Swaziland, 1973-75; dean faculty humanities, acting pro-vice chancellor Nat. U. Lesotho, 1978; permanent sec. Ministry Fgn. Affairs Govt. of Zimbabwe, 1980; min. fgn. affairs Govt. of Zimbabwe, Harare. Office: Ministry Fgn Affairs Munhumutapa Bldg, PO Box 4240 Samora Machel Ave, Causeway Harare Zimbabwe*

MUDGE, DAVID CLAYTON, archaeologist; b. Mt. Holly, N.J., May 11, 1951; s. Clayton Ray and Phyllis Crystal (Michie) M.; m. Patricia Eva Conway, Sept. 3, 1983; 1 child, Sumner William. AB, U. Pa., 1973; MA, Temple U., 2000. Archaeologist N.J. Dept. Transp., Trenton, 1982—. Sci. advisor: (TV documentary) The Turtle Stone, 1994-95 (Regional Emmys 1995); (guide) Teacher's Guide to the Turtle Stone, 1996 (Hist. Preservation award 1996). Vice chmn. Environ. Commn., Florence Twp., N.J., 1994—; chmn. com. W. Jersey Mission, Haddon Heights, 1999—. Lt. USN, 1973-78. Mem. Ea. States Archeol. Fedn. (state rep. 1885—), Mid. Atlantic Archeol. Conf. (mem.-at-large bd. dirs. 1997—), Archeol. Soc. N.J. (life, v.p. 1984-92, Achievement award 1992). Presbyterian. Avocations: gunsmithing, watch repair. E-mail: arkydave@aol.com. Home: 2021 Old York Rd Burlington NJ 08016-9738 Office: NJ Dept Transp 1065 Parkway Ave Trenton NJ 08628-3003

MUDRY, MICHAEL, pension and benefit consultant; b. Lucina, Czechoslovakia, Dec. 5, 1926; (parents Am. citizens); s. John Zaleta and Helen (Molchan) M.; m. Kendall Archer, June 17, 1960; children: F. Goodrich Archer, Benjamin Kendall. BA, U. Conn., 1951. Sr. v.p. Hay/Huggins Co. Inc., Phila., 1956-93; self-employed pension and benefit cons. Wayne, Pa., 1994—; former actuary Ch. Pensions Conf. Contbr. articles to profl. jours. Bd. mem., actuary Am. Coun. on Gift Annuities, Indpls., 1978—. Served with U.S. Army, 1945-46. Fellow Soc. Actuaries, Conf. Cons. Actuaries; mem. Am. Acad. Actuaries, Internat. Actuarial Assn., Internat. Assn. Cons. Actuaries.

MUEHLBACH, GUENTER W., mathematics educator; b. Breslau, Germany, Jan. 5, 1941; s. Alois J. and Klara (Koch) M.; m. Barbara M. Steins, Apr. 28, 1967; children: Martina, Cornelia. Diploma, U. Hannover, Germany, 1966, Dr.rer.nat., 1969, Dr.habil., 1971. Asst. prof. Inst. Math. U. Hannover, Germany, 1966-73, dozent Inst. Math., 1973-75, prof. math., 1975—. Author: Repetitorium der Ingenieurmathematik III, 1988, Mathematik fur Wirtschaftswissenschaftler, 1993; co-author: Repetitorium der Ingenieurmathematik I, 1972; co-editor: Numerical Algorithms, 1994. Mem. Deutsche Mathematiker Vereinigung. Office: Inst Angewandte Math, U Hannover, 30167 Hannover Germany

MUEHLEMANN, ROLF, electrical engineer; b. Zurich, Switzerland, Apr. 5, 1959; s. Albert and Susann (Eggerling) M. Diploma in elec. engring., Swis Fed. Inst. Tech., Zurich, 1986. Product mgr. Philips Med. Sys. AG, Zurich, 1986-89; mgr. Engring. & Test Svcs. AG, Baden, Switzerland, 1989-91; cons. Mühlemann & Ptnr., Wallisellen, Switzerland, 1991—. Lt. Swiss Army, 1980-87. Mem. IEEE, Swiss Soc. Engrs. and Archs., Swiss Assn. Electricians. Home and Office: Obere Kirchstrasse 22, 8304 Wallisellen Switzerland

MUELLBACHER, WOLF, neurologist; b. Vienna, Austria, Mar. 8, 1961; s. Horst Helmut and Karin Margarethe (Schmidinger) M. MD, U. Vienna, 1989. Med. asst. U. Vienna, 1985-89, sci. asst., 1985-89; resident U. Bern, Switzerland, 1989-91, U. Vienna, 1991-92, NRR, Vienna, 1992-96; grantee NIH/NINDS, Bethesda, Md., 1998-99; sr. neurologist NKR, Vienna, 1996—; dir. PN, Vienna. Contbr. articles to profl. jours. Grantee Max-Kade Found., 1998-99, Bürgermeister-Fonds, Vienna, 1995-96, BMWF, Vienna, 1989-91. Mem. OGNP, OGCNP. Avocations: swimming, windsurfing, downhill skiing. Office: Neurol Hosp Vienna, Riedelgasse 5, A-1130 Vienna Austria

MUELLBAUER, JOHN NORBERT JOSEPH, economist, educator; b. Kempten, Germany, July 17, 1944; arrived in Eng., 1953; s. Norbert Joseph and Edith (Heinz) M. BA, King's Coll., Cambridge, Eng., 1965; PhD, U. Calif., Berkeley, 1969. Lectr. U. Warwick, Eng., 1969-72; lectr. Birkbeck Coll., London, 1972-75, reader, 1975-77, prof. econs., 1977-81; ofcl. fellow Nuffield Coll., Oxford, Eng., 1981—; investment bursar Nuffield Coll., Oxford, 1984-85, prof. econs., 1998—. Author: Economics and Consumer Behavior, 1980; contbr. articles to profl. jours. Econ. and Social Rsch.

Coun. grantee, London, 1974—. Fellow Econometric Soc., Brit. Acad. Avocation: skiing. Office: Nuffield Coll,, New Road,, Oxford OX1 1NF, England

MUELLEMAN, ROBERT LEO, physician, researcher medical educator; b. Omaha, July 4, 1957; s. Joseph John and Virginia Lee (Fromm) M.; m. Diane Marie Schekirke, June 18, 1982; children: Therese, Thomas, Daniel, Robert. BS cum laude, U. Nebr., Omaha, 1979, MD with honors, 1984. Diplomate Am. Bd. Emergency Medicine. Emergency medicine resident Truman Med. Ctr., Kansas City, Mo., 1984-87; rsch. fellowship Truman Med. Ctr., Kansas City, 1987-88; asst. prof. U. Nebr. Med. Ctr., Omaha, 1988-93; assoc. prof. U. Mo., Kansas City, 1993-98; med. dir. Dept. Emergency Medicine Nebr. Health Sys., 1998—; sect. chief emergency medicine U. Nebr. Med. Ctr., Omaha, 1998—, assoc. prof., 1998-2000, prof., 2000—; mem. injury control adv. com. Mo. Dept. Health, Jefferson City, 1994-98, co-dir. rsch. Dept. Emergency Medicine, 1993-98; mem. motor vehicle safety rsch. adv. com. Nat. Hwy. Traffic Safety Adminstrn., 1995—; mem. nat. occupant protection program adv. com. Nat. Rural Health Assn., 1996—. Contbr. chpt. to book and articles to profl. jours. Fellow Am. Coll. Emergency Physicians (trauma care and injury control com. 1996-98); mem. Soc. Acad. Emergency Medicine, Alpha Omega Alpha. Democrat. Roman Catholic. Avocations: family, reading, outdoors. Office: Nebr Med Ctr Emergency Dept 981150 Nebr Med Ctr Omaha NE 68198-0001

MUELLER, CHARLES BARBER, surgeon, educator; b. Carlinville, Ill., Jan. 22, 1917; s. Gustav Henry and Myrtle May (Barber) M.; m. Jean Mahaffey, Sept. 7, 1940; children: Frances Ann, John Barber, Richard Carl, William Gustav. A.B., U. Ill., 1938; M.D., Washington U., St. Louis, 1942; LHD (honoris causa), Blackburn Coll., 1987. Intern, then resident in surgery Barnes Hosp., St. Louis, 1942-43, 46-51; asst. prof. Washington U. Med. Sch., 1951-56; prof. surgery, chmn. dept. State U. N.Y. Med. Sch., Syracuse, 1956-67; prof. surgery McMaster U. Med. Sch., Hamilton, Ont., Can., 1967—; chmn. dept. McMaster U. Med. Sch., 1967-72. Contbr. articles to med. jours. Served with USNR, 1943-46. Decorated Purple Heart with 2 oak leaf clusters, Bronze Star; recipient Favorite Son award So. Ill. Med. Soc., 1996; Jackson Johnson fellow, 1938-42; Rockefeller postwar asst., 1946-49; Markle scholar, 1949-54. Mem. ACS (v.p. 1987-88, Disting. Svc. award 1984), Am. Surg. Assn., Ctrl. Surg. Assn., Soc. Univ. Surgeons, Assn. Acad. Surgery, Royal Coll. Physicians and Surgeons (Duncan Graham Disting. Svc. award 1992), Phi Beta Kappa, Sigma Xi, Alpha Omega Alpha, Phi Kappa Phi. Home: 139 Dalewood Crescent, Hamilton, ON Canada L8S 4B8 Office: McMaster U, 1200 Main St W, Hamilton, ON Canada L8N 3Z5

MUELLER, HERWART, surgeon; b. Giessen, Hessen, Germany, July 22, 1957; s. Rudolf and Gerda Mueller; m. Jasmin Aull, July 7, 1989; children: Anja, Mark. Diploma, Justus-Liebig-U., Giessen, 1983, MD, 1988. Resident Dist. Hosp., Achern, Germany, 1984, Justus-Liebig-U., Geissen, 1985-86; resident Dist. Hosp., Trostberg, Germany, 1986-87, sr. physician, 1987-91; leading sr. physician dept. oncologic surgery Paulinenstift, Wiesbaden, Germany, 1992-94; sr. cons. dept. oncology surgery Carl von Hess Hosp., Hammelburg, Germany, 1994—. Author: Malignant Melanoma, 1994. Home: Karlsbaderstrasse 20, 97762 Hammelburg Germany Office: Carl von Hess Hosp, Ofenthaler Weg 20, 97762 Hammelburg Germany

MUELLER, I. LYNN, strategic planning and communications consultant; b. Cin., Feb. 2, 1941; s. Irwin Ludwig and Helen Marie (Bloomfield) M.; m. Maria Rose Cavallino; children: Adria Whitney, Shallah Whitney. BBA, U. Cin., 1964, MBA, 1966; postgrad., George Washington U., 1966-68. V.p., founder Robert-Lynn Assoc., Ltd., Washington, 1968-72; spl. asst. N.Y. State Assembly Spkr., Albany, 1971-74; v.p. adminstrn. and fin. Epsilon Data Mgmt., Boston, 1974-75; founder, sr. v.p. First Tuesday Comms., Buffalo, N.Y., 1974-78; v.p. cmty. affairs Gardenway Mgmt., Troy, N.Y., 1976; pres. ILM Enterprises, Old Chatham, N.Y., 1977-91; exec. dir. Minority Leader, N.Y. State Assembly, Albany, 1983-91; founder Decision Strategies Group, Albany, 1991—. Contbr. chpt. to book. Trustee Chatham (N.Y.) Meth. Ch., 1992-94; mem. Chatham Sch. Bd., 1990-93; Cons. to Gov. George Pataki Transition Com., 1994; advisor Morris Meml. Bd., Chatham, 1984-98; alumni rep. George Washington U., Albany, 1993—. Mem. Nat. Space Soc., Planetary Soc., Cin. Soc. (pres. 1961-62), McMicken Soc., Sigma Sigma, Omicron Delta Kappa, Alpha Kappa Psi, Beta Alpha Psi. Republican. Presbyterian. Avocations: basketball, tennis, sailing, bridge, reading non-fiction. Office: Decision Strategies Group Ste 2001 One Commerce Plz Albany NY 12210

MUELLER, JOAQUIN PABLO, agricultural engineer, researcher; b. Buenos Aires, Argentina, Oct. 15, 1950; s. Horst and Rosemarie (Wortmann) M.; m. Silvia Beatriz Ingianna, Sept. 3, 1976; children: Pablo, Tomas, Mariana, Martin. Degree in agrl. engring., U. Buenos Aires, 1975; PhD in Animal Breeding, U. NSW, Australia, 1983. Rsch. fellow Instituto Nacional Tecnologia Agropecuaria, Bariloche, 1976-78, rsch. scientist, 1979—, vice dir., 1985—, mem. regional adv. bd., 1988-90, coord. dept. animal prodn., 1989-91, small ruminant nat. rsch. coord., 1991—; mem. genetics adv. group Mercosur, 1996—; invited prof. numerous univs.; reviewer sci. jours. Editor: Third World Sheep and Wool Congress Proceedings, 1992; contbr. articles to profl. jours. including Jour. Animal Breeding, Theoretical Applied Genetics, among others. Recipient San Isidro Labrador award Sociedad Rural Argentina, 1994, prize Assn. Argentina Criad. Merino, 1995, Animal Breed award, 1995. Mem. AAAS, Asociacion Argentina Prodn. Animal, Sociedad Argentina Genetica, Australian Assn. Animal Breeding and Genetics. Avocations: mountain climbing, soccer, music. Office: Inst Nac Tec Agropecuaria, CC 277, 8400 Bariloche Argentina

MUELLER, JOHN ERNEST, political science educator, dance critic and historian; b. St. Paul, June 21, 1937; s. Ernst A. and Elsie E. (Schleh) M.; m. Judy A. Reader, Sept. 6, 1960; children: Karl, Karen, Susan. AB, U. Chgo., 1960; MA, UCLA, 1963, PhD, 1965. Asst. prof. polit. sci. U. Rochester, N.Y., 1965-69, assoc. prof., 1969-72, prof., 1972-2000, prof. film studies, 1983-2000, founder, dir. Dance Film Archive, 1973—; prof. polit. sci. Ohio State U., 2000—; lectr. on dance in U.S., Europe, Australia, 1973—; OP-ED columnist Wall St. Jour., 1984—, L.A., Times, 1988—, N.Y. Times, 1990—; mem. dance panel NEA, 1983-85; columnist Dance Mag., 1974-82; dance critic Rochester Dem. and Chronicle, 1974-82; mem. adv. bd. Dance in Am., PBS, 1975. Author: War, Presidents and Public Opinion, 1973 (book selected as one of Fifty Books That Significantly Shaped Public Opinion Rsch. 1946-95 Am. Assn. Pub. Opinion Rsch. 1995), Dance Film Directory, 1979, Astaire Dancing: The Musical Films, 1985 (de la Torre Bueno prize 1983), Retreat From Doomsday: The Obsolescence of Major War, 1989, Policy and Opinion in the Gulf War, 1994, Quiet Cataclysm: Reflections on the Recent Transformation of World Politics, 1995, Capitalism, Democracy, and Ralph's Pretty Good Grocery, 1999; co-author: Trends in Public Opinion: A Compendium of Survey Data, 1989; editor: Approaches to Measurement, 1969, Peace, Prosperity, and Politics, 2000; co-editor Jour. Policy Analysis and Mgmt., 1985-89; mem. editl. bd. Pub. Opinion Quar., 1988-91, Jour. Cold War Studies, 1999—; prodr. 12 dance films/recorded commentator on 2nd soundtrack of laser disc edit. Swing Time, 1986; coadapter (musical) A Foggy Day, 1998; prodr. Shaw Festival Niagara-on-the-Lake, Ont., 1998, 99. Grantee NSF, 1967-70, 74-75, NEH, 1972-73, 74-75, 77-78, 79-81; Guggenheim fellow, 1988. Mem. Am. Acad. Arts and Scis., Am. Polit. Sci. Assn., Dance Critics Assn. (bd. dirs. 1983-85), Am. Assn. for Public Policy and Mgmt. (mem. editl. bd. 1985-89). Home: 420 W 5th Ave Columbus OH 43201-3159 Office: Ohio State U Polit Sci Dept Columbus OH 43210-1373

MUELLER, LISA MARIA, chemical engineer; b. Bedford, Ohio, Aug. 29, 1966; d. Dieter Hermann and Hannelore (Habeck) M. BSChemE, U. Akron, Ohio, 1988, postgrad., 1988-89; postgrad., Kent State U., 1993; MEChemE, Lamar U., 1999. Devel. engr. Goodyear Chem. Divsn., Akron, 1988-90; process devel. engr. AcroMed Corp., Cleve., 1990; process design engr. Norton Co., Akron, 1991-93; process engr. BF Goodrich Co., Akron, 1994-95; sr. process engr. Mobil, Beaumont, Tex., 1996-97; co-author paper Food Engring. Ann. Nat. Meeting, Chgo., 1993. Mem. Tau Beta Pi. Avocations: music, computers, stamps.

MUELLER, OTHMAR, forensic expert; b. Budapest, Hungary, Mar. 15, 1932; s. Félix and Félixné (Daniels) M.; m. Othmárné Toldi, Jan. 25, 1958; 1 child, Othmar Jr. Diploma in Bldg. Engring., Tech. U. Budapest, 1954, First DrTechn, 1955, Diploma in Econ. Engring., 1961; DEng, U. Safety in Labour, Budapest, 1965, PhD, 1995. Registered profl. engr. Bldg. site leader County Bldg. Co., Esztergom, Hungary, 1954-55; chief engr. then chief of sect. Bldg. authority Dept., Coun. of Budapest, 1955-77; pres. Bldg. Co. Aprilis 4, Budapest, 1977-80; dir. Forensic Tech. Expert Inst. Hungary, Budapest, 1981-95. Author: Modern Demolition, 1965, 2d edit., 1985, Protection of Buildings Against Bombings, 1990, Bomb Threats, 1991, Home Made Explosives And Their Suppression, 1995; contbr. articles to profl. jours. Chmn. Com. for Explosives and Blasting Techniques, 1972—; founder, chief Libr. for Explosives and Blasting Techniques, Budapest, 1980—. Lt. Hungarian Army, 1955. Mem. Hungarian Soc. Forensic Experts, Trade Union. Roman Catholic. Avocations: gardening, reading, touring.

MUELLER, PAUL HENRY, retired banker; b. N.Y.C., June 24, 1917; s. Paul Herbert and Helen (Cantwell) M.; m. Jean Bonnel Vreeland, Sept. 10, 1949; 1 child, Donald Vreeland. BS, NYU, 1940; AB, Princeton U., 1941; LittD (hon.), Heriot-Watt U., Edinburgh, Scotland, 1981; LHD (hon.), Bloomfield Coll., 1991. Page Citibank N.A., 1934; on leave, 1939-46, asst. cashier, 1947-52, asst. v.p., 1952-58, v.p., 1958-65, sr. v.p., 1965-74, chmn. credit policy com., 1974-82; chmn. Saab-Scania Am. Inc., 1982-90, Atlas Copco N.Am. Inc., 1975-93; dir. Atlas Copco AB, Stockholm, 1982-91, Skandinaviska Enskilda Banken Corp., 1983-93, Ericsson N.Am., Inc., 1986-91; entered U.S. Fgn. Svc., served in Panama, Cairo, Washington, 1941-43; asst. adminstrv. sec. UN Montary and Fin. Conf., Bretton Woods, N.H., 1944; divisional asst. Dept. State, 1946; sec. West Indian Conf., 2d session, St. Thomas, V.I., 1946; vis. lectr. U. Va., 1980—; founding chmn., sr. fellow Ctr. Internat. Banking Studies, 1977-91. Contbg. author: Offshore Lending by U.S. Commercial Banks, 1975, 81, Bank Credit, 1981, Classics in Commercial Bank Lending, 1981, Vol. II, 1985, Loan Portfolio Management, 1988, Credit Culture, 1994, Credit Risk Management, 1995; author: (with Leif H. Olsen) Credit and the Business Cycle, 1979, Learning from Lending, 1979, Credit Doctrine for Lending Officers, 1976, 81, 97, Credit Endpapers, 1982, Perspective on Credit Risk, 1988, In a Nutshell, 1999; contbr. articles to profl. jours. Trustee Bloomfield Coll., N.J., 1983-91, vice chmn., 1987-88, chmn., 1988-91, trustee emeritus; treas. Marcus Wallenberg Found. (U.S.), 1984—. Served from 2d lt. to capt. USMCR, 1944-45. Decorated Royal Order Polar Star (Sweden); recipient Alumni award Grad. Sch. Credit and Fin. Mgmt., Dartmouth Coll., Disting. Svc. award Robert Morris Assocs., award for journalistic excellence, 1991. Mem. Bankers Assn. Fgn. Trade (hon., v.p. 1976), Pilgrims, SAR, Swedish-Am. C. of C. USA (chmn. 1989-90, hon. dir.), Royal Econ. Soc. (U.K.), Univ. Club (N.Y.C.), Beta Gamma Sigma. Republican. Presbyterian. Home: 75 Rotary Dr Summit NJ 07901-3131

MUELLER, SHIRLEY ANNE, lawyer, real estate broker; b. Miami, Fla., Aug. 25, 1950; d. Robert Peter and Arvella Gertrude (Feldkamp) M.; divorced; children: Peter, Tybe, Samantha. AA in Journalism, Miami Dade Jr. Coll., 1970; BA in Philosophy, U. Calif., Berkeley, 1972; JD, Benjamin Cardozo Sch. Law, N.Y.C., 1982. Dir. children's advt. div. Coun. Better Bus. Bur., N.Y.C., 1973-79; assoc. Cutner & Rathkopf, N.Y.C., 1983-87; pres. Uncommon Properties, Inc., N.Y.C., 1990-94; pvt. practice N.Y.C., 1994—. Fundraising com. Children's Air Ctr., N.Y. Hosp., N.Y.C., 1988—, Nightingale Bamford Sch., N.Y.C., 1987-98. Roman Catholic. Avocations: reading, music, travel, dancing. Home and Office: 1000 Park Ave Apt 3B New York NY 10028-0934

MUELLER, WALTER E., pharmacologist, educator; b. Worms, Germany, Oct. 22, 1947; s. E. and G. Mueller; m. Heidrun E. Becker, Mar. 24, 1972; children: Helge F., Ulf J., Juliane K. Degree in pharmacy, U. Frankfurt/Main, Germany, 1971; PhD, U. Mainz, Germany, 1974. Cert. pharmacist. Asst. dept. pharmacology U. Mainz, 1972-83; prof. psychopharmacology Cen. Inst. Mental Health, Mannheim, Germany, 1983-97; dir. dept. pharmacology Biocenter U., Frankfurt/Main, Germany, 1997—. Author: The Benzodiazepine Receptor, 1987; contbr. articles to profl. jours. Recipient Fritz-Külz award German Pharmacol. Soc., 1974, Organon award German Soc. Biol. Psychiatry, 1994. Mem. Rotary. Office: Biocenter U Frankfurt/Main, Dept Pharmacology, D-60439 Frankfurt am Main Germany

MUELLER, WERNER, government official. Min. of economy Govt. of Germany. Office: Fed Ministry of Economy, Fed Ministry Econ Affairs/, and Tech, 11019 Berlin Germany*

MUELLER, WILLIAM GLENNON, JR., recruiting company executive; b. St. Louis, Jan. 19, 1971; s. William Glennon and Janet Marie M.; m. Michelle Christine Flatken, July 11, 1998. BS in Comms., U. Mo., 1995. Cert. personnel cons. Nat. Assn. Personnel Svcs. Exec. recruiter, team leader Mgmt. Recruiters, St. Louis, 1995-97; divsn. mgr. NOLL Inc., St. Louis, 1997—. Mem. St. John Bosco Men's Club, Concord Village Lions Club. Roman Catholic. Avocations: golf, snow skiing, reading, public speaking, family activities. Office: NOLL Inc 55 Westport Plz Ste 575 Saint Louis MO 63146-3195

MUELLER-HEUBACH, EBERHARD, medical educator; b. Berlin, Germany, Feb. 24, 1942; came to U.S., 1968; s. Heinrich Gustav and Elisabeth (Heubach) M.; m. Cornelia Rosemarie Uffmann, Sept. 6, 1941; 1 child, Oliver Maximilian. MD, U. Koeln, 1966. Intern U. Koeln (Germany) Women's Hosp., 1967-68, Middlesex Gen. Hosp., New Brunswick, N.J., 1968-69; resident Columbia-Presbyn. Med. Ctr., N.Y.C., 1971-74, chief resident, 1974-75; asst. prof. Magee-Women's Hosp. U. Pitts., 1975-81, assoc. prof. Magee-Women's Hosp., 1981-89; prof., chmn. ob-gyn. Sch. Medicine Wake Forest U., Winston-Salem, N.C., 1989—. Mem. Am. Gyn.-Ob Soc. (asst. sec. 1999—), Soc. Gynecol. Investigation, The Perinatal Rsch. Soc., Coun. Univ. Chairs Ob-Gyn. (pres. 1998-2000). Avocations: horses, travel, arts. Office: Wake Forest U Bapt Med Ctr Medical Center Blvd Winston Salem NC 27157-0001

MUELLER-HEUMANN, GUENTHER, emeritus educator, business advisor; b. Nuremberg, Germany, Nov. 3, 1941; s. Georg and Anna Katharina (Adler) Mueller; m. Ursula Romanino, May 23, 1969; children: Michael Ariki, Thomas Teina. Diplom., U. Erlangen-Nuremberg, Germany, 1968, DrRerPol, 1972. Asst. U. Erlangen-Nuremberg, 1968-74; sr. lectr. Victoria U., Wellington, New Zealand, 1975-76; Found. prof. mktg. U. Otago, Dunedin, New Zealand, 1976-95, emeritus prof., 1995—; vis. prof. mgmt. Cranfield Sch. Bus., U.K., 1983; vis. prof. mktg. U. Otaru, Japan, 1983, U. South Australia, 1991; bd. dirs. Top Mark Ltd., Auckland, 1973—. Author gen. mktg. books; author lifestyle studies of New Zealanders, mktg. mgmt. studies of New Zealand; contbr. more than 80 articles to bus. and mktg. mags. PRD scholar, 1970. Mem. Am. Mktg. Assn., Rotary Internat. (dir., convenor). Avocations: Dixieland jazz, duckhunting, flyfishing, sheep farming. Office: Middlemarch, Pinnack Hill Rd RD1, Bombay-Auckland 1851, New Zealand

MUELLER-KOHLENBERG, HILDEGARD, social education educator, researcher; b. Limburg, Hessen, Germany, Jan. 11, 1940; d. Friedrich and Maria-Theresia (Reusch)K.; m. Lothan Mueller, Aug. 28, 1968; 1 child, Paul Joscha. Psychology diploma, U. Marburg, 1965, D in Pedagogy, 1969. Rsch. asst. U. Marburg, Germany, 1965-71, asst. prof., 1971-74; prof. social edn. U. Osnabrück, Germany, 1974—. Contbr. articles to profl. jours., including Zeitschrift fuer Paedagogik, Argument, Sozialpaedagogik, Recht der Jugend und des Bildungswesens, Social Extra, Diakonie. Mem. German Soc. for Psychology, German Soc. for Edn. Sci., German Soc. for Evaluation (bd. mem.). Office: U Osnabrück, Heger-Tor-Wall 9, 49069 Osnabrück Germany

MUELLER-SCHIMPFLE, MARKUS PETER, radiologist; b. Elz, Hesse, Germany, Dec. 16, 1962; s. Paul Georg and Klara Franziska (Michel) Mueller; m. Gudrun Ursula Schimpfle, Oct. 21, 1989; children: Lukas Paul, Elias Vinzenz Cyrill, Amelie Dorothea Klara. Med. Diplomate, U. Tuebingen, Germany, 1990. Med. diplomate, bd. cert. asst. and rsch. fellow German Cancer Rsch. Ctr., Heidelberg, 1990-92; sci. asst. U. Tuebingen, Germany, 1992-98; asst. prof. U. Tuebingen, 1998—. Contbr. articles to profl. jours. Roman Catholic. Avocations: photography, tennis, classical music. Office: Univ Tuebingen, Hoppe-Seyler-Str 3, 72076 Tübingen Germany

MUENSTER, ARNO FRANZ, chemistry educator; b. Voehringen, Bavaria, Germany, June 8, 1962; s. Franz and Erika M. (Gaisbauer) M.; m. Barbara Labusiak, Oct. 4, 1991; children: Katharina, Nicolas. M in chemistry, U. Wuerzburg, 1989, D natural scis., 1992, D natural scis. edn., 1998. Cert. phys. chemist. Lectr. U. Wuerzburg, 1993-97, asst. prof., 1998, assoc. prof., 1998—. Author: Nichtlineare Dynamik in der Chemie, 1996. Recipient grant Studienstiftung des Deutschen Volkes, 1986, German Sci. Found., 1992, 1995. Evangelical Lutheran. E-mail: phch030@phys-chemie.uni-wuerzburg.de. Home: Am Ring 4, Werneck 97440, Germany Office: U Wuerzburg, Am Hubland, Würzburg 97074, Germany

MUFAMADI, SYDNEY FHOLISANI, South African federal official; b. Johannesburg, South Africa, Feb. 28, 1959; s. Masindi and Reuben M.; m. Nomsa Mufamadi; 3 children. Tchr. Lamula Secondary Sch., Soweto, South Africa, 1980-81; messanger law firm; gen. sec. Gen. and Allied Workers Union, 1982-85; transvaal publicity sec. United Dem. Front, 1984-90; asst. gen. sec. Congress of South African Trade Unions, 1985-91; mem. interim leadership group South African Communist Party, 1990, mem. ctrl. com., 1991; mem. nat. exec. com. African Nat. Congress, 1991—; min. of safety & security South Africa, 1994—, min. provincial and local govt.; vol. Gen. and Allied Workers Union; mem. working com. NEC; South African Communist Party del. to working group Conv. Dem. South Africa; African Nat. Congress rep. Nat. Peace Com. Active Congress South African Students. Office: Ministry Safety and Security, Private Bag X463, Pretoria 0001, South Africa Address: 260 Walker St, Pvt Bag 802, Pretoria 0001, South Africa*

MUFFATTO, MORENO, technology educator; b. Mirano, Italy, Mar. 5, 1958. MSME, U. Padua, Italy, 1982, PhD in Mgmt. of Innovation, 1987. Rsch. asst. U. Padua, 1987-90, asst. prof., 1990-92, assoc. prof., 1992—; mem. internat. adv. com. Internat. Symposium on Mfg. Strategy, 1997—, Internat. Symposium on Logistics, 1993—, Internat. Conf. on Prodn. Rsch., 1995—. Editor: Procs. 3d Internat. Symposium on Logistics, 1997, 4th Internat. Symposium on Logistics, 1999; mem. editl. adv. bd. Internat. Jour. Logistics, 1997—. Fellow Japan Found., 1994. Mem. Project Mgmt. Inst. (pres. No. Italy chpt. 1996—), Product Devel. Mgmt. Assn., Prodn. and Ops. Mgmt. Soc. Office: U Padua DIMEG, Via Venezia 1, 35131 Padua Italy

MUFFOLETTO, BARRY CHARLES, engineering executive; b. Buffalo, N.Y., Oct. 19, 1950; s. Vincent Hugo and Lucille Elva (Sorge) M.; m. Michelle Louise Pariso, June 16, 1978; children: Daniel, Mark. AS in Elec. Tech., Erie Cmty. Coll., Buffalo, N.Y., 1975; BET in Elec. Engring., SUNY, 1983. Prodn. supr. Wilson Greatbatch Ltd., Clarence, N.Y., 1975-76; asst. prodn. mgr., 1976-77, project engr., 1977-79, process control engr., 1979-81, mgr. Welding Tech., 1981-82, dir. Battery Engring., 1982-94, dir. Capacitor Products, 1994—. Mem. IEEE, Am. Welding Soc., Am. Soc. Metals. Avocations: golf, fishing. Office: Wilson Greatbatch Ltd 10000 Wehrle Dr Clarence NY 14031-2090

MUGABE, ROBERT GABRIEL, president of Zimbabwe; b. Kutama, Feb. 21, 1924; m. Sarah Hayfron (dec.); 1 son (dec.). B.A., Ft. Hare U., Republic of South Africa, 1951, B.Ed.; B.Sc. (Econ.), U. London, B.Admin., LL.B., LL.M.; hon. Dr., Ahmadu Bello U. Tchr. Driefontein Roman Cath. Sch., Umvuma, 1952; now pres. Govt. of Zimbabwe, Harare; Salisbury S. Primary Sch., 1953, Gwelo, 1954, Chalimbana Tchr. Tng. Coll., Zambia, 1955-58, St. Mary's Tchr. Tng. Coll., Takoradi, Ghana, 1958-60; publicity sec. Nat. Democratic Party, 1960-61; publicity sec. Zimbabwe African People's Union, 1961-62; detained, 1962, 63, escaped to Tanzania, 1963; co-founder Zimbabwe African Nat. Union, 1963, sec.-gen., 1963, pres., 1977—; detained in Rhodesia, 1964-74; joint leader Patriotic Front (with Joshua Nkomo), 1976-80; leader Zimbabwe African Nat. Union del. Geneva Constl. Conf. on Rhodesia, 1976, Malta Conf., 1978, Lancaster House Conf., 1979-80; prime minister Zimbabwe, 1980-87, minister of def., 1980-87, exec. pres., 1988—; chmn. Frontline States, 1992—. Recipient Newsmaker of Yr. award S. African Soc. Journalism, Internat. Human Rights award Howard U., Africa Prize, 1988. Address: Munhumupaga Bldg, Pvt Bag 7700 Samora Machel Ave, Causeway Harare Zimbabwe*

MUGANGA, ALBERT, business executive; b. Rutova, Burundi, June 18, 1945; s. Zacharie Barandiye and Anastasie Mtibankiza; m. Idith Kitifu-Muganga, Dec. 2, 1972; children: Aimé-Désiré, Fabrice, Nadia, Martine. BA in Econs., Cath. U. Leuven, Belgium, 1970. Rschr. Ctrl. Bank Burundi, 1971-74; vice chancellor U. Burundi, 1974-76; minister fgn. affairs Burundi, 1976-78, minister commerce and industry, 1978-87; bd. dirs. SOMEBU, 1975-76. First v.p. 33d session UN, 1978; pres. African Mins. Fgn. Affairs, OAU, 1978; pres. non-alined group ministers, 1978; pres. OAU Mins. of Industry, 1986-87; pres. PTA's Coun. of Mins., 1984-86. Decorated officer Royal Crown of Belgium. Mem. Rotary Club, Tennis Club of Bujumbura. Roman Catholic. Avocations: football, tennis, chess, jogging. Home: Ave Nzero No 1, BP262 Bujumbura Burundi Office: Performance, BP 1160 Bujumbura Burundi

MUGARRA, PEDRO M., engineering professional; b. Erandio-Bilbao, Bizkaia, Spain, Apr. 18, 1945; s. Pedro and Maria (Arieta-araunabena) M.; m. Adele Aristi, Nov. 20, 1971; children: Ainhoa, Ane. Mech. Engr., ETS de Ingenieros Industriales, Bilbao, Spain, 1969. Project mgr. OCINCO, Bilbao, Spain, 1969-74; grad. engr. LAING, London, 1969-70; project mgr. SENER, Bilbao, 1974-86, head quality assurance, 1992—; dir. industry Basque Govt., Gasteiz, Spain, 1986-87, dir. telecomms., 1987-92. Mem. Assn. Mech. Engrs. Roman Catholic. Avocations: music, photography, computing. Office: SENER Ingenieria y Sistemas, Avda Zugatzarte 56 L Arenas, 48930 Getxo Euskadi, Spain

MUGGLESTONE, CHRISTOPHER JOHN, health facility executive; b. Chesterfield, Eng., May 17, 1939; s. John Joseph and Winifred (Buckley) M.; m. Elizabeth Roberts (wid. Feb. 1967); children: Jayne Suzanne, Robert James; m. Linda Margaret Oliver, Aug. 7, 1967; children: Paula Ann, Kay Julia. MBChB, Birmingham U. Med. Sch., 1962; Fellow Faculty Pharm. Medicine, Royal Coll. Phys., U.K., 1989. House phys. NHS, Walsall, Eng., 1962-63; SHO NHS, Shrewsbury, Eng., 1963-64; trainee gen. practitioner NHS, Derbyshire, Eng., 1964-65; jr. ptnr., gen. practitioner NHS, Droitwich, Eng., 1965-68; ptnr., gen. practitioner NHS, Wellington, Eng., 1968-74; med. adviser, head med. dept. Organon Labs., London, 1974-77; head clin. rsch. Schering Health Care, Burgess Hill, Eng., 1977-82; med., tech. dir. Brocades, London, 1982-86; chief exec. CJM Med. Ltd., London, 1986—; hon. cons. in andrology NHS, Haywards Heath, Eng., 1977-93; chmn. Medisite Mgmt. Ltd., 1999—. Contbr. articles to profl. jours. Fellow Royal Soc. Medicine; mem. Brit. Med. Assn., Brit. Andrology Soc. (mem. com. 1990-93). Avocations: gardening and horticulture, walking. Home: 233 Banstead Rd, SM7 1RB Banstead Surrey, England Office: CJM Med Ltd/Salatin House, 19 Cedar Rd, SM2 5JG Sutton Surrey, England

MUGGLETON, STEPHEN HOWARD, computer scientist, educator; b. Harare, Zimbabwe, Dec. 6, 1959; arrived in U.K., 1961; s. Louis Miles and Alice Sylvia (Loftie-Eaton) M.; m. Thirza Ana Castello-Cortes, May 15, 1988; 1 child, Clare Eloise. BSc with honors, U. Edinburgh, 1982, PhD, 1986; MA (hon.), U. Oxford, 1993. Serc postdoctoral fellow Turing Inst., Glasgow, U.K., 1990-92, non-exec. dir., 1992; EPSRC advanced rsch. fellow Oxford U. Computing Lab., 1993-98, reader in machine learning, 1997; prof. machine learning U. York, U.K., 1997—; vis. assoc. prof., Fujitsu chair U. Tokyo, 1993; cons. Knowledgelink, Glasgow, 1988, Pfizer Ltd., Sandwich, U.K., 1994, British Telecom. Labs., Martlesham Health, U.K., 1995, Smith Inst., Guildford, U.K., 1997. Author: Inductive Acquisition of Expert Knowledge, 1989; editor: Inductive Logic Programming, 1992, Machine Intelligence 13, 1994, Machine Intelligence 14, 1995; mem. editl. bd. Artificial Intelligence Jour., 1996, Jour. Logic Programming, 1996, ACM Trans. on Computational Logic, 1999; editor-in-chief Machine Intelligence series, 2000. Rsch. fellow Wolfson Coll., Oxford, 1993-97. Avocations: reading, chess, Go. Office: U York Computer Sci Dept, Heslington, York Y01 5DD, England

MUGLER, JOSEF ALOIS, education educator; b. Vienna, Austria, Jan. 26, 1948; s. Josef and Hedwig (Moser) M.; m. Elisabeth Maria Polt, Apr. 19, 1974; 1 child, Andreas. Diploma, U. Econs., Vienna, 1969; D Comm., U. Econs., 1972. Civil servant City of Vienna, 1970-71; asst. prof. U. Econs., 1971-82, prof., 1982—; vis. prof. U. Innbruck, Austria, 1980-81. Author:

Risk Management in der Unternehmung, 1979 (Kardinal Innitzer Preis award 1979), Betriebswirtschaftslehre der Klein und Mittelbetriebe, 3rd edit., 1998. Rudolf Sallinger Ehrenpreis award, Vienna, 1987. Mem. European Coun. for Sml. Bus. (pres. 1989-91). Avocations: opera, tennis. Office: Univ Econs Vienna, Augasse 2-6, A-1090 Vienna Austria

MUGRIDGE, DAVID RAYMOND, lawyer, educator, writer; b. Detroit, Aug. 6, 1949; s. Harry Raymond and Elizabeth Lou (Aldrich) M.; m. Sandra Lee Jackson, June 25, 1988; children: James Raymond, Sarah Lorraine. BA, U. of Ams., Puebla, Mex., 1970; MA, Santa Clara U., 1973; JD, San Joaquin Coll. of Law, 1985. Bar: Calif. 1986, U.S. Dist. Ct. (ea. dist.) Calif. 1986, U.S. Ct. Appeals (9th cir.) 1987, U.S. Supreme Ct. 1996; cert. specialist in criminal law. Staff atty. to presiding justice 5th Dist. Ct. Appeals, Fresno, Calif., 1985-87; assoc. Law Office of Nuttall, Berman, Magill, Fresno, 1987-88; pvt. practice Fresno, 1988—; tchr. Fresno City Coll., 1988-96; tchr. Spanish for legal profession, Fresno, 1994; tchr. Fresno Pacific U., 1997—; arbitrator Fresno County Bar Assn., 1988—; judge pro-tem juvenile, traffic and small claims Fresno County Superior Ct., 1988—. Contbg. author: Practical Real Estate Law, 1995,99. Mem. ABA, NACDL, Calif. Attys. for Criminal Justice, Calif. Trial Lawyers Assn. (cert. specialist in criminal law). Republican. Roman Catholic. Avocations: fishing, travel, photography, hiking.

MUGUTI, GODFREY IGNATIUS, surgeon, consultant; b. Masvingo, Zimbabwe, Aug. 30, 1952; s. Ignatius and Joan (Mukaro) M.; m. Martha Raiza Macheka, Sept. 9, 1977; children: Nyaradzo Jane, Chiedza Janet, Kudakwashe Godfrey. MB ChB, Univ. Zimbabwe, 1978; MS, U. Sydney, 1996. Intern Mpilo Hosp., Bulawayo, Zimbabwe, 1979, sr. house officer, 1980-81, registrar, 1982-84, cons. surgeon, 1985—, head dept. surgery, 1986-95; assoc. prof. Univ. Zimbabwe Medical Sch., 1995-99; rsch. fellow Univ. Sydney, Sydney, 1991; prof. U. Zimbabwe, 2000—; chmn. postgrad. edn. Mpilo Hosp., 1984-89; coun. mem. Assn. Surgeons of East Africa, 1988-90; appt. commr. Zimbabwe Health Review Commn., 1997. Contbr. articles to profl. jours. Active mem. Roman Catholic Ch., Bulawayo, 1979-95. Recipient Beit scholarship Beit Trust, 1968, British Coun. scholarship, 1981, ROwan Nicks scholarship Royal Australasian Coll. Surgeons, 1990. Fellow Assn. of Surgeons of East Africa, Royal Coll. Surgeons of Edinburgh, Royal Coll. Surgeons Eng. (hon.), Order of Internat. Fellowship, Internat. Biog. Assn., Am. Biog. Inst.; mem. Surgical Soc. Zimbabwe (pres. 1994), N.Y. Acad. Scis. Avocations: reading, writing, jogging. Home: PO Box Cy 3014 Causeway, 60 Baines Ave, Harare Zimbabwe Office: Univ Zimbabwe Dept Surgery, Mazowe St PO Box A178, Avondale Harare Zimbabwe

MÜHLANGER, ERICH, ski manufacturing company executive; b. Liezen, Austria, Aug. 26, 1941; came to U.S., 1971, naturalized, 1975; s. Alois and Maria (Stückelschweiger) M.; m. Gilda V. Oliver, July 13, 1973; 1 child, Erich. Assoc. Engring., Murau Berufsschule Spl. Trade, Austria, 1959; student Inst. Tech. and Engring., Weiler Im Allgau, Germany, 1963-65. Salesman, Olin Ski Co. (Olin-Authier), Switzerland, 1965-67, mem. mktg. dept., 1967-69, svc. and mfg., 1969-71, quality control insp., Middletown, Conn., 1971-77, supr., 1977-78, gen. foreman, 1978-83, process control mgr., 1983-88; dir. mfg. Entech Corp., 1988-89; prodn. mgr. Metallizing div. Risden Corp., Thomaston, Conn., 1989-94, quality process engr., 1994—. ; pres. Bus. Consolidating Svcs. Internat., Rocky Hill, Conn., 1989—, quality control technician, 1990—; quality process request divsn., fragrance divsn., 1993—; pres. Consulting Svcs. Internat. Charter mem. Presdl. Task Force, trustee; preferred mem. of U.S. Senatorial Club. Served to cpl. Austrian Air Force, 1959-60. Mem. Screenprinting Assn. Am., Am. Mgmt. Assn., Am. Soc. for Qualtiy Control, Mgmt. Club. Roman Catholic. Home: 13 Clemens Ct Rocky Hill CT 06067-3218 Office: 60 Electric Ave Thomaston CT 06787-1617 also: Bus Consolidating Svcs Internat Rocky Hill CT 06067

MUHLEMANN, LUKAS, financial executive. MBA, Harvard U. Systems engr. IBM; mgmt. cons. McKinsey, 1977-94; chief exec. Swiss Re, 1994; CEO Credit Suisse Group, chmn., CEO, 2000—. Office: Credit Suisse Group, Paradeplatz 8, 8001 Zurich Switzerland*

MUHLENBRUCH, CARL W., civil engineer; b. Decatur, Ill., Nov. 21, 1915; s. Carl William and Clara (Theobald) M.; m. Agnes M. Kringel, Nov. 22, 1939; children: Phyllis Elaine (Mrs. Richard B. Wallace), Joan Carol (Mrs. Frederick W. Wenk). BCE, U. Ill., 1937, CE, 1945; MCE, Carnegie Inst. Tech., 1943; LLD, Concordia U., River Forest, Ill., 1955. Research engineer Aluminum Research Labs., Pitts., 1937-39; cons. engring., 1939-50; mem. faculty Carnegie Inst. Tech., 1939-48; assoc. prof. civil engring. Northwestern U., 1948-54; pres. TEC-SEARCH, Inc. (formerly Ednl. and Tech. Consultants Inc.), 1954-67, chmn. bd., 1967—; lect. in Civil Engring. Northwestern U., 1998—; Pres. Profl. Centers Bldg. Corp., 1961-77; lectr. civil engring., 1997—. Author: Experimental Mechanics and Properties of Materials; Contbr. articles engring. publs. Treas., bd. dirs. Concordia Coll. Found.; dir. Mo. Lutheran Synod, 1965-77, vice chmn. 1977-79. Recipient Stanford E. Thompson award, 1945. Mem. Am. Econ. Devel. Coun. (cert. econ. developer), Am. Soc. Engring. Edn. (editor Ednl. Aids in Engring.), NSPE, ASCE, Sigma Xi, Tau Beta Phi, Omicron Delta Kappa. Club: University (Evanston). Lodge: Rotary (dist. gov. 1980-81, dir. service projects Ghana and the Bahamas). Home and Office: Tec-Search Inc 4071 Fairway Dr Wilmette IL 60091-1005

MUHRA, ALI A., economist, diplomat, researcher, consultant; b. Damascus, Syria, Apr. 21, 1959; came to U.S., 1996; s. Abdel Gani Muhra and Hend Hamad; m. Ghosoun Jouma'a, July 12, 1998; 1 child, Hend. BS in Econs., U. Damascus, 1986, MS in Banking, 1991, PhD in Econs., 1996. Dir. developing countries sect. Ministry of Economy and Fgn. Trade, Damascus, 1986-94; prof. Damascus U., 1993-94; dir. diplomat sect. Ministry Fgn. Affairs, 1994-96; in charge of econ. and cultural affairs Embassy of Syria, Washington, 1996—; econ. advisor ann. meetings IMF and World Bank, Washington, 1996—; econ. advisor Internat. Cotton Adv. Com., Washington, 1996—. Author: Saving and its Role in Development, 1992, International Information Periodical, 1996. Mem. Econ. Scis. Assn. Avocations: travel, reading, swimming, basketball, table tennis. Home: 5505 Seminary Rd Falls Church VA 22041-3500 Office: Embassy of the Syrian Arab Republic 2215 Wyoming Ave NW Washington DC 20008-3991

MUI, PIU CHEUNG, internist; b. Hong Kong, Hong Kong, Apr. 22, 1952; s. Lit Yuen and Yuet Ngan (Fung) M.; m. Shau Wen Chung, Oct. 24, 1981; 1 child, Hoi-Sze. MD, China Med. Coll., Taiwan, 1980. Rsch. fellow Vet. Gen. Hosp., Taichung, Taiwan; ho. physician Mennonite Christian Hosp., Huacien, Taiwan, 1980-84, staff physician, 1984-86, chief sect. gastroenterology, 1989-92, dir. edn., 1992-94, chief dept. internal medicine, 1994—. Trustee Agapa Ho., Hualien, Taiwan, 1994-97; organizer, tech. support cons. Hualien Children's Drama Group, 1992-95; planner, med. support cons. YWCA, Hualien, 1991-97; mem. bd. govs. Meilung Bapt. Ch., Hualien, 1989-91. Fellow Soc. Gastroenterology, Digestive Endoscopy Soc.; mem. N.Y. Acad. Scis., Am. Gastroenterology Assn., Am. Soc. Gastrointestinal Endoscopy. Avocations: collecting stamps, bicycling, table tennis. Home: 17 Chung-Mei 12th St, Hualien 97047, Taiwan Office: Mennonite Christian Hosp, 44 Min-Cheng Rd, Hualien 97047, Taiwan

MUIĆ, VLADIMIR, microbiologist, parasitologist, researcher; b. Zagreb, Croatia, Oct. 27, 1936; s. Nikola Muić and Mira Zidovec; m. Zlata Momić, Jan. 31, 1965. MD, U. Zagreb, 1963, B in Med. Scis., 1970, D in Med. Scis., 1978; Diploma in External Lab. Proficiency Testing, European Com. External Quality Assessment Organizers, Budapest, 1992. Intern Gen. Hosp., Zagreb, 1963-64; head gen. practice med. surgery Primary Health Care Ctr., Konjice, Slovenia, 1965-67; inter Pub. Health Inst. Croatia, Zagreb, 1967-70, head immunology dept., 1970-92, head referal v.cholerae lab., 1976-92, head referal streptoccus lab, 1980-92, head ctrl. diagnostic bacteriology and parasitology, 1984-92, head sci. rsch. program, 1974—; sci. collaborator Faculty Medicine, Zagreb, 1974, higher sci. collaborator, 1979, sci. advisor, 1984; cons. pub. health labs. svc., Croatia, 1994; rep. Croatian med. microbiologists European Com. External Quality Assessment Organizers, Budapest, Hungary, 1993. Author: Quality Control in Microbiology, 1993; contbr. articles to profl. jours. Recipient primateship in medicine Nat. Dept. Health and Social Welfare, Zagreb, 1982. Mem. Croatian Acad. of Med. Scis. Achievements include interpretation of medical microbiological laboratory results. Home: Medvescak 51, 10 000 Zagreb Croatia

MUIR, JOHN ROBERT, cardiologist; b. London, July 30, 1936; s. Edward Grainger and Estelle (Russell) M.; m. Susan Mary Rudland, 1965 (div. 1982); children: Edward Robert, Elizabeth. BA with honors, Oxford U., 1958, MB BCh, 1961, D.M., 1968. House surgeon surg. unit Middlesex Hosp., 1961-62; house physician Leicester Royal Infirmary, 1962, London Chest Hosp., 1962-63; sr. house officer Cen. Middlesex Hosp., 1963; med. registrar profl. med. unit U. Birmingham, Birmingham, Eng., 1964-66; sr. registrar Nat. Heart Hosp., London, 1966-70; USPHS postdoctoral rsch. fellow dept. biochemistry, St. Louis U., 1968; prof., chmn. dept. cardiology Welsh Nat. Sch. Medicine, Cardiff, 1970-78; med. dir. Allied Med. Group, Riyadh, Saudi Arabia, 1978-80; chmn. cardiac dept. Armed Forces Hosp., Riyadh, 1980-83; pvt. practice London, 1983—; Editor: Advanced Medicine, 1979; editor Saudi Med. Jour., 1980-83; contbr. articles and chapts. to med. publs. Fellow Royal Soc. Medicine, Royal Coll. Physicians London, Assn. Physicians Gt. Britain and Ireland; mem. Brit. Cardiac Soc., Med. Rsch. Soc. Mem. Ch. of Scotland. Avocations: skiing, collecting carpets. Office: 21 Devonshire Pl, London W1N 1PD, England

MUIR, PATRICIA ALLEN, professional association administrator; b. Dallas, Nov. 4, 1929; d. Jack Charleton Allen and Anna Patricia (Hovis) Allen Atchison; m. Lester Doyle Rader, Jr., Aug. 4, 1950 (dec. Sept. 1950); 1 child, Lester Doyle III; m. Perren James Muir, June 2, 1956 (div.); children: Edward John, Patricia Jane. Grad., Our Lady of Victory Coll., 1948; student, George Washington U., 1948-49, Washington Sch. for Secs., 1949-50. Traffic mgr. Am. Storage Co., Washington, 1960-69; asst. sec. Ind. Telephone Pioneer Assn., Washington, 1969-76; adminstrv. asst. ALA, Washington, 1977-98, staff liaison to Fed. Librs. Round Table, 1991-98, staff liaison to Armed Forces Librs. Round Table, 1991-98, staff liaison to Govt. Documents Round Table, 1991-98; office mgr. Fed. Documents Clearing House, Washington, 1998—. Columnist, contbr. The Ind. Pioneer, 1969-76. V.p. Friendship House Child Devel. Ctr. Parents, Washington, 1978, pres., 1979-83; mem. parish coun. St. Peter's Cath. Ch., 1987-91, mem. edn. and spiritual devel. com., 1986—, chair, 1988-91, coord. Bible study, 1999—. Mem. Ladies Ancient Order of Hibernians (state pres. 1991-97, nat. budget com. 1996-98, nat. elections com. 1998—, nat. constn. com. 1998—, nat. rules of order com. 2000—). Avocations: travel, genealogy, reading, writing. Home: 343 11th St SE Washington DC 20003-2105 Office: Fed Documents Clearing House 209 Pennsylvania Ave SE Washington DC 20003-1107

MUIR, WILLIAM LLOYD, III, academic administrator; b. Norton, Kans., Mar. 20, 1948; s. John Thomas and Rosalie June (Benton) M. BBA, Kans. State U., 1977. Asst. sec. of state State of Kans., Topeka, 1971-72, fin. adminstr. atty. gen. office, 1972-79, comptr. Office of Gov., 1979-87; dir. econ. devel. Kans. State U., Manhattan, 1987-91; sec. of cabinet State of Kans., Topeka, 1979-87, asst. sec. adminstrn., 1986-87; asst. to v.p., dir. cmty. rels. Kans. State U., Manhattan, 1991—, faculty rep., senator Student Governing Assn., 1992—, mem. union governing bd., 1997—. Bd. dirs. United Way of Riley County, 1989-99, chair, 1992; mem. housing appeals bd. City of Manhattan, 1996—, mem.econ. devel. adv. bd., 1999—; trustee Kans. State U. Found., 1993—; mem. Leadership Kans., 1989; state officer Native Sons and Daus. Mem. Friends of Cedar Crest Assn., Nat. Geog. Soc., Sierra Club, Masons (Scottish rite), Blue Key, Alpha Tau Omega (nat. officer), Alpha Kappa Psi. Episcopalian. Avocations: travel, volunteer work, advising. Home: 2040 Shirley Ln Manhattan KS 66502-2059 Office: Kansas State U 122 Anderson Hall Manhattan KS 66506-0100

MUIRDEN, GEOFFREY WILLIAM ADELAIDE, institute assistant director; b. Melbourne, Australia, Feb. 10, 1941; s. Angus Wallace and Norma Constance (Whittle) M.; m. Helen Marguerite Giles, aug. 20, 1977 (div. 1986). BA, Melbourne U., 1965; EdB, Monash U., Clayton, Australia, 1979. Tchr., libr. Edn. Dept., Victoria, Australia, 1971-82; sec. Australian Civil Liberties Union, 1988-98; acting dir. Adelaide Inst., 1999—. Author book revs., 1969—. Recipient C.E. Watson Meml. award Wesley Coll, Prahran, Victoria, Australia, 1960. Avocations: films, books.

MUJA, KATHLEEN ANN, state official, consultant; b. Denver, June 24, 1965; d. Thomas Raymond and Bridget Catherine (Hirschfeld) Cramer; m. Adrian Constantin Muja, June 4, 1988 (div. Apr. 1991); 1 child, Thomas Constantin. BBA, U. Denver, 1995. Employment specialist Dept. of Labor and Employment, Colo., 1991-98; office mgr. Colo. Dept. Labor, Denver, 1999—. Contbr. poems to various publs. Vol. Mus. Natural History, Denver, 1987—; home visitor Cmty. Caring Project, Denver, 1996—. Mem. AAUW, U. Denver Alumni Assn. Democrat. Roman Catholic. Avocations: hiking, biking, canvas cross-stitch, writing, reading. Home: 460 Washington St Denver CO 80203-3810 Office: Colo Dept Labor 1515 Arapahoe St Ste 400 Denver CO 80202-2104

MUJEEB, SYED ABUDL, pathologist; b. Shikarpur, Sindh, Pakistan, Feb. 12, 1957; s. Syed Mohummad Saleem and Asia Khatoom Asia. MB BChir, LMC, Hyderabad, 1983; MPhil, BMSI/JPMC, Karachi, Pakistan, 1992. Asst. prof. AIDS Surveillance Ctr., Blood Transfusion Svcs. JPMC, Karachi, 1986—; cons. UNAIDS, Pakistan, 1999, Sindh AIDS Control Program, Karachi, 1992—. Author: (book) Blood Transfusion Technical and Clinical Care, 1999; contbr. sci. papers to profl. jours. E-mail: smujeeb@super.net.pk. Office: JPMC, AIDS Surveillance Ctr, Karachi Sindh, Pakistan

MUJICA, MAURO E., architect; b. Antofagasta, Chile, Apr. 20, 1941; came to U.S., 1965, naturalized, 1970; s. Mauro Raul and Graciela (Parodi-Blayfus) M.; m. Barbara Louise Kaminar, Dec. 26, 1966; children: Lillian Louise, Mariana Ximena, Mauro Eduardo Ignacio III. BArch, MArch, Columbia U., 1971. Head designer Columbia U. Office Archtl. Planning, N.Y.C., 1966-71; project mgr. Walker, Sander, Ford & Kerr, Architects, Princeton, N.J., 1971-72; prin. Mauro E. Mujica, Architect, N.Y.C., 1972-74; dir. internat. div. Greenhorne & O'Mara, Inc., Riverdale, Md., 1974-78; ptnr. Mujica & Reddy Architects, Washington, 1978-80; prin. Mauro E. Mujica, Architect, Washington, 1980-81; ptnr. Mujica & Berlin Investment Bankers, Washington, 1982-85, Mujica Keppie Henderson Internat., Washington and Glasgow, Scotland, 1981-83, Mujica-Seifert Architects, Washington and London, 1983-87; pres., chief exec. officer The Pace Group, Washington, 1987-91; ptnr. PACE/WALSHE Internat., London and Washington. Chmn. bd. and CEO U.S. English Found., Washington, 1993—; hon. mem. Emmanuel Coll. Cambridge U., Eng., 1995; mem. adv. bd. U.S.-U.K. Fulbright Commn.

MUJUMDAR, ARUN S., chemical engineering educator, consultant; b. Karwar, India, Jan. 14, 1945; arrived in Can., 1971; s. Sadashiv V. and Ramabai (Divekar) M.; m. Purnima Wagle; children: Anita, Amit. BChem Engring., Bombay U., 1965; MEngring., McGill U., Montreal, 1968, PhD, 1971. Rsch. engr. Carrier Corp., Syracuse, N.Y., 1969-71; rsch. asst. McGill U., 1965-69, rsch. assoc., 1971-75, asst. prof., 1975-78, assoc. prof., 1978-86, prof. chem. engring., 1986-2000; prof. mech. engring. Nat. U. Singapore, 2000—; pres. Exergex Corp., Brossard, Can., 1989-2000; program chair Internat. Drying Symposia, 1978—; hon. prof. East China U. Tech., Shanghai, 1993—; vis. prof. numerous univs. worldwide; cons. in field; mem. numerous organizing and scientific adv. panels for five maj. internat. confs., currently including IDS'2000, CHISA'2000, 50th CSChE Conf., others. Editor/co-editor of 50 hardcover books since 1978, including, editor: Handbook of Industrial Drying, 2d edit., 1995, Mathematical Modeling and Numerical Techniques in Drying Technology, 1997, Handbook of Postharvest Technology, 1988—; editor Drying Tech.-An Internat. Jour., 1988—; editor collections of monographs; numerous other publs. Recipient Innovation in Drying award Hemisphere, 1986, Outstanding Contbns. to Chem. Engring. award Czech Acad. Scis., 1990, Disting. Contbns. to Internat. Chem. Engring., Polish Acad. Scis., 1996; Japan Soc. Promotion of Sci. sr. fellow, 1988, 96. Fellow ASME, Chem. Soc. Can.; mem. AIChE, Japan Soc. for Promotion of Sci. (sr. fellowship 1988, 96). Avocations: photography, travel, tennis. E-mail: arun mujumdar@hotmail.com. Office: Nat U Singapore, Mech Prod Engring, Singapore 119260, Singapore

MUJUMDAR, VIKAS SITARAM, engineering and construction management consultant; b. Indore, M.P., India, Aug. 8, 1954; s. Sitaram Mhalsakant and Kamla (Kulkarni) M.; m. Vanita Wadwekar, June 9, 1979. BSc, U. Indore, India, 1972, BS in Engring., 1977. Constrn. engr. Hydle Constrn. Ltd., Delhi, India, 1977-81, sr. constrn. engr., 1981-83; engr. EIL, New Delhi, 1983-87, sr. engr., 1987-91, dep. mgr., 1991-95; mgr. EIL, 1995-97; constrn. mgr. Vanir Constn. Mgmt. Inc., L.A.; group leader for petrochems. mega project of IPCL, EIL, Dahej, Gujarat, India, 1993-97. Merit scholar Govt. of M.P., 1972-77. Mem. Inst. Engrs. (constrn. mgr., registered chartered engr.). Avocation: sports. Home: 150 S Magnolia Ave Apt 277 Anaheim CA 92804-2164 Office: Vanir Constrn Mgmt Inc Ste 2050 3435 Wilshire Blvd Los Angeles CA 90010-1981

MUKAI, HISAKAZU, electronics executive; b. Shizuoka shi, Japan, Sept. 3, 1932; s. Toshitsugu and Tokiwa (Uematsu) M.; m. Junko Tada, May 27, 1964. B in Engring., U. Tokyo, 1957, PhD, 1988. Dir. memory integrated cir. lab. Nippon Telegraph and Tel. Corp., Musashino-shi, Japan, 1981-82, dir. integrated cir. process lab., 1982-83; dir. integrated cir. lab. Nippon Telegraph and Tel. Corp., Atsugi-shi, Japan, 1983-86, mgr. Atsugi Elec. Comm. Labs., 1986-88, mgr. Atsugi Elec. Comm. Labs, 1986-88, exec. mgr. large scale integration labs, 1988-90; dir. OKI Electric Industry Co., Ltd., Tokyo, 1990-93, fellow, 1993—; vis. lectr. U. Tokyo, 1972-76; spkr. in field. Inventor in field. Mem. IEEE, Inst. Electronics, Info., Comm. Engrs. Japan (Inada award 1960, Outstanding Achievement award 1972, 80), Inst. Elec. Engrs. Japan. Avocations: golf, karaoke, photography. Office: OKI Electric Industry Co, 550 1 Higashiasakawa-cho, Hachioji-shi Tokyo 193-8550, Japan

MUKAI, MINORU, oncologist; b. Ryugasaki, Japan, July 28, 1947; s. Masu Makai and Jun Sakurai; m. Takako Mukai; children: Tomomi, Manami. MD, Chiba (Japan) U., 1972, PhD, 1985. Resident Chiba U., 1972-77; chief surgeon Shioya Hosp., Tochigi, Japan, 1978-79, Naruto Hosp., Chiba, 1980-83; asst. prof., surg. oncologist 2d dept. surgry Chiba U., 1984-86; chief oncologist Nat. Inst. Radiol. Sci., Chiba, 1987-97; dir. Kamogawa City Hosp., Chiba, 1997-99, Shioya Gen. Hosp., Tochigi, 2000—. *A new combination therapy of radiation and local administration of OK-432 which is one of biologic response modifiers was developed by Minoru Mukai and applied for esophageal cancer patients since 1987. The 5-year survival rate and local control rate of esophageal cancer patients by this combination therapy were almost two times higher than those of conventional radiotherapy. He proposed the basic theory that "the attacker" and "the sweeper" are necessary on cancer treatments.* Mem. Japan Soc. Clin. Oncology, Japan Radiol. Soc., Japan. Soc. Radiol. Oncology, Japan Surg. Soc., Order International. Fellowship. Avocations: golf, tennis, driving, hiking. Office: Shioya Gen Hosp, 77 Tomita, Yaita 329-2145, Japan

MUKAMAL, DAVID SAMIER, sign manufacturing company executive; b. Baghdad, Iraq, Oct. 6, 1944; came to U.S., 1950; s. Abraham Sassoon and Mary (Murad) M.; m. Anitamarie Costa, July 31, 1970; children: Adam Scott, Rebecca Kate. BBA in Econs. with honors, Bryant Coll., 1970; MBA in Fin. Mgmt., Iona Coll., 1975. Budget analyst USV Pharm./Revlon, Inc., Tuckahoe, N.Y., 1970-72; sr. budget officer Met. Transp. Authority, N.Y.C., 1972-74; sr. fin. analyst Am. Airlines, Inc., Dallas, 1974-82; chmn. DSM Industries Inc.; pres. All State Signs, Richardson, Tex., 1982—, Framed Enterprises, Inc., Irving, Tex., 1995—. With USN, 1965-66. Recipient Jerremiah Clarke Barber award Bryant Coll., 1970. Mem. Dallas Apt. Assn., Tex. Sign Mfrs. Assn., Internat. Sign Assn., La Cima Club (bd. dirs.), Omicron Delta Epsilon. Republican. Jewish.

MUKANGA, PAUL MAMBE, bishop; b. Omana, Zaire, Apr. 13, 1929; s. Andre Okasa and Henriette Koyenyi. Grad. in philosophie, Grand Seminaire, Kabwe, Zaire, 1952, grad. in theologie, 1957; grad. in economie, Univ. Cath., Louvain, Belgium, 1966. Dir. Ecole Primaire, Omendjadi, Zaire, 1958; prof. Petit Seminaire, Onema-Ototo, Zaire, 1958-60, dir., 1961-62; prof. Coll. St. Augustin, Lodja, Zaire, 1966-68; asst. Univ. Lovanium, Zaire, 1969-72; chet des travaux Univ. Nationale de Zaire, Kiushasa, 1977-79; sec. adminstrn. Faculte de Theologie Cath., Kinshasa, 1977-79; bishop Diocese de Kindu, Zaire, 1979—. Author: (with El Boustani) L'Enseignement au Congo, 1969; contbr. articles to profl. jours. Pres. Soc. Civile du Maniema, Kindu, 1994—. Home: Ave de L'Eveché 1, Kindu Zaire Office: Diocese de Kindu, BP 18, Kindu Zaire*

MUKASYAN, ALEXANDER SERGEEVICH, science administrator; b. Samara, Russia, Jan. 17, 1956; came to U.S., 1995; s. Sergey Papchanovich Mukasyan and Victorina Alexandrovna Bessonova; m. Alla Gennadievna Klimova, Aug. 12, 1976; children: Vasiliy, Alexander. MS, Phys. Engring. Inst., Moscow, 1980; PhD, Russian Acad. Scis., Moscow, 1986; DSc, Russian Acad. Scis., Chernogolovka, Russia, 1994. Scientist Russian Acad. Scis., Inst. Chem. Physics, Moscow, 1980-88; sr. scientist Russian Acad. Scis., Inst. Structural Macrokinetics, Chernogolovka, 1989-93, head lab., 1993-96; mgr. lab. dept. chem. engring. U. Notre Dame, Ind., 1996-2000; prof. U. Notre Dame, 2000—; mem. sci. bd. Inst. Structural Macrokinetics, Chernogolovka; vice-chmn. Internat. Symposium, Wuhan, China, 1995. Mem. editl. bd. Internat. Jour. Self-Propagating High-Temperature Synthesis. Recipient medal Exhbn. Inds. Achievements, Moscow, 1986. Mem. AIChE, Am. Chem. Soc., Internat. Combustion Inst. Achievements include invention of methods for production of ceramics. Avocations: soccer, volleyball, history. E-mail: amoukasi@nd.edu. Fax: 219-631-8366. Home: 4005 Parkwood Cir Mishawaka IN 46545-2648 Office: Dept Chem Engring Univ Notre Dame Notre Dame IN 46556-7878

MUKERJEE, DEBDAS, environmental health scientist, educator; b. Darjeeling, India; came to U.S., 1959.; s. Suresh Chandra and Budyutlata Mukerjee; m. Bhaisa Freny Dee, July 15, 1959; 1 child, Shaibal. BSc with honors, Calcutta (India) U., 1954, MSc, 1957; PhD, U. Ky., 1962. Rsch. prof. pathology Jefferson Med. Coll., Thomas Jefferson U., Phila., 1974-80; sr. sci. advisor, environ. health scientist U.S. EPA Environ. Criteria Assessment Office, Cin., 1980-91; environ. health scientist U.S. EPA Nat. Ctr. for Environtl. Assessment, Cin., 1991—; adj. prof. toxicology Inst. Toxicology, U. Kiel (Germany) Med. Sch., 1990—; adj. prof. environ. toxicology Ohio No. U., Ada, 1998—; assoc. prof. pathology, dir. divsn. basic rsch. U. Tex. Med. Br., Galveston, 1969-74; asst. prof. biology M.D. Anderson Hosp. & Tumor Inst., U. Tex. Cancer Ctr., Houston, 1966-69; mem. NATO/Com. Challenges of Modern Soc. Study on Internat. Info. Exch. of Dioxins and Related Compounds, 1985-88. Contbr. articles to profl. jours., chpts. to books. Sir J.C. Bose rsch. scholar Bose Inst., Calcutta, 1958; recipient cert. of appreciation for contbn. to devel. of guidelines for health risk chem. mixtures, 1996; recipient medal for commendable svc. to EPA, 1980. Mem. AAAS, World Affairs Coun. Greater Cin., N.Y. Acad. Scis. Achievements include pioneering in risk assessment of dioxins, pcbs, children's risk from multimedia exposures to environmental pollutants, methodology of risk assessment, in vitro transformation of cells from cancer genetic susceptible persons, human secondary trisomy chromosome, transclocation between sex and somatic chromosomes; avocations: comparative religion, philosophy of life, reading, writing. E-mail: mukerjee.debdas@epa.gov. Office: US EPA Nat Ctr Environ Assessment Cincinnati OH 45268-0001

MUKERJI, TAPAN, geophysicist, researcher; b. Varanasi, India, May 3, 1965; came to U.S., 1989; s. Girija Prasad and Manju (Banerjee) M. BSc in Physics, Banaras Hindu U., Varanasi, India, 1986, MSc in Geophysics, 1989; PhD in Geophysics, Stanford U., 1995. Rsch. and tchg. asst. Stanford U., 1990-95, rschr., 1995—. Co-author: The Rock Physics Handbook; contbr.

articles to profl. jours. Fellow Coun. Sci. and Indsl. Rsch., India, 1989, Green fellow Stanford U., 1989-90, Haider fellow Stanford U., 1997. Mem. IEEE, Am. Geophys. Union, Am. Phys. Soc., Soc. Exploration Geophysicists (Karcher award 2000). Achievements include work with new theoretical model for estimating velocity dispersion in anisotropic rock; scale dependent wave propagation in heterogeneous media; new strategies for quantifying uncertainty in rock physics; multi-disciplinary time lapse seismic monitoring. Avocations: science, music. Office: Rock Physics Lab Geophysics Dept Stanford U Stanford CA 94305

MUKHERJEE, AMALENDU, mechanical engineering educator; b. Bikaner, Rajasthan, India, May 29, 1946; s. Tarak Das and Ananda Rani (Chatterjee) M.; m. Nita Chowdhury; 1 child, Abhro. B Engring., U. Rojasthan, Jodhpur, India, 1967; M Tech., Indian Inst. Tech., Kharagpur, 1969, PhD, 1976. Lectr. Indian Inst. Tech., Kharagpur, 1970-76, asst. prof., 1976-85, prof., 1985—. Creator: The Software Symbols, 1990; author: (video course) Modelling and Simutation of Dynamic Systems, 1996. Bd. govs. Indian Inst. Tech., Kharagpur, 1998. Recipient gold medal IETE, 1996, fellowship Alexander von Humbodt, Germany, 1980. Fellow Indian Nat. Acad. Engrs. Avocation: music. Home: Indian Inst Tech, Qtrs No B-207, 721302 Kharagpur West Bengal, India Office: Indian Inst Tech, 721302 Kharagpur West Bengal, India

MUKHERJEE, SHIB PRASAD, engineering executive; b. Muzaffarpur, Bihar, India, Jan. 3, 1945; s. Late Sanat Kumar and Latika M.; m. Aparna, Nov. 24, 1969. BME with honors, Jadavpur U., India, 1964; MSME, U. Colo., 1968; MBA, U. Ill., 1972. Design engr. CBI Sys. Engring. Divsn., 1968-71; project engr. Corp. HQ- Nuc. Reactor Design and Devel., 1971-76; chief and sr. mech. engr. Walker Process Corp. subs. CBI, 1976-80; sr. project mgr. Chgo. Bridge & Iron Industries, 1980-85; gen. mgr. Balmer Lawrie & Co. Ltd., India, 1985-90; gen. mgr. to mng. dir. Biecco Lawrie Ltd., India, 1991-92, mng. dir., 1993—. Recipient Udyog Rattan award Inst. Econ. Studies, India, 1998. Fellow Inst. Engr.; mem. Inst. Dirs., Corp. Mgmt. Coun., Nat. Found. Indian Engrs.(named Best Chief Exec. of the year 1998). Developer Indirect-direct Freeze Exch. Concentrator and method. Avocations: tennis, cricket, table tennis, surfing through internet. Fax: 91-33-44959388. E-mail: spmALbieccomb@giascl01.vsnl.net.in. Home: P-553 Hemanto Mukhergee, Saroni Flat 3B, 700 029 West Bengal West Bengal, India Office: Biecco Lawrie Ltd, 6 Mayurbhanj Rd, 700023 Calcutta West Bengal, India

MUKHERJI, DEBASHIS, materials scientist; b. Bankura, India, July 3, 1953; s. Bidhan and Ruby (Chatterji) M.; m. Arundhati Chatterji, July 28, 1980; children: Alekhya, Debarati. B in Technology, Indian Inst. Technology, Kharagpur, 1976, PhD, 1987. Scientist Def. Metallurgical Rsch. Lab., Hyderabad, India, 1976-88, 90-93; guest scientist Hahn-Meitner-Inst., Berlin, 1988-90, scientist, 1993-96; scientist Technische Universitat, Berlin, 1997-98, Tech. U., Braunschweig, 1998—; expert group chmn. Kaveri Engine Devel. Program, 1991-93, project mgmt. bd., 1991-93. Mem. Deutsche Gesellschaft fur Materialkunde. Home: Kröppel Str 2, 38100 Braunschweig Germany Office: Inst Werkstaffe Tech U, Braunschweig Langer Kamp 8, 38106 Braunschweig Germany

MUKHERJI, MRIDUL, biotechnologist, educator; b. Allahabad, India, June 25, 1972; s. Mukul and Mitali Mukherji. Grad., U. Allahabad, 1993; post graduate studies, U. Calicut, 1997; DPhil, Oxford (Eng.) U., 1998. Mgmt. trainee Roys Electronics, Allahabad, 1993-95; rsch. asst., supr. Internat. Centre for Genetic Engring. and Biotech., Delhi, 1997-98. Contbr. articles to profl. jours. Mem. Oxonford, Oxford, 1999—, Oxford U. Student Union, 1998—. Recipient Felix scholarship Oxford U., 1998—. Mem. Am. Oil Chemists Soc., Chemistry and Industry, Acad. Pharm. Scientists Gt. Brit. Avocations: cricket, tennis, travel, reading. Office: Oxford U, Dyson Perrine Lab, Oxford OX1 3QY, England

MUKHIA, HARBANS, educator; b. Village Allah, India, Feb. 1, 1939; s. Deshraj and Rampiari (Malhotra) M.; m. Banani Majumdar, Sept. 28, 1966; children: Sudeep, Neelanjana. BA with honors, Kirori Mal Coll., Delhi, 1958; MA, Delhi U., 1960, PhD, 1970. Lectr. Kirori Mal Coll., Delhi, 1960-63, Rajdhani Coll., Delhi, 1964-69, Hindu Coll., Delhi, 1967-70; assoc. prof. Jawaharlal Nehru U., New Delhi, 1971-83, prof., 1983—; vis. prof. Ecole des Hautes Etudes en Scis. Sociales, Paris, 1980—, Brit. Acad., London, 1993; mem. bd. studies Kashmir U., 1996-97; mem. acad. coun. Jawaharlal Nehru U., New Delhi, 1997—, rector 1999—. Author: Historians and Historiography During the Reign of Akbar, 1976, Perspectives on Medieval History, 1993; co-editor: Feudalism and Non-European Societies, 1985, French Studies in History, 2 vols., 1988-90; editor The Medieval History Jour., The Feudalism Debate, 1999. Activist Communist Party India, Delhi, 1959-64, Communist Party India-Marxist, Delhi, 1964-73; cons. People's Union Civil Liberties and Dem. Rights, Delhi, 1985, Andhra Pradesh Civil Liberties com., Hyderabad, India, 1986-87. Nat. Lectr. U. Grants Commn., New Delhi, 1985-86; nat. fellow U. Grants Commn., New Delhi, 1991-93; sr. vis. fellow Internat. Inst. Asian Studies, Leiden, 1997, fellow Homi Bhabha Coun., Bombay, 1979-81. Mem. Indian Nat. Scis. Acad. (com. on history of sci. tech. 1994—). Avocations: computers, classical Indian music, poetry. Home: 24 New Campus JNU, New Delhi 110067, India Office: Ctr for Hist Studies, Jawaharlal Nehru Univ, New Delhi 110067, India

MUKHOMOROV, VLADIMIR KOSTANTINOVITCH, physicist, researcher; b. Leepeck, Russia, July 10, 1943; s. Konstantin Ivanovitch and Lubov Ivanovna (Ganshina) M.; m. Elena Konstantinovna Kraiukhina, Dec. 27, 1968; children: Konstantin, Alexander. Degree in Engring. and Physics, Poly. Inst., St. Petersburg, Russia, 1965, Dr. of Physics and Math. Sci., 1974. Sr. rschr. State Optical Inst., St. Petersburg, 1970-79, Inst. Mil. Medicine, St. Petersburg, 1979-88; chief rschr. Agrophysical Inst., St. Petersburg, 1988—; asst. prof. Leningrad U., St. Petersburg, 1988-90. Contbr. articles to profl. jours. Recipient Vet. of Labour medal, Moscow, 1987; grantee Internat. Sci. Found., Washington, 1995. Mem. Soc. Toxicology, N.Y. Acad. Scis. Avocations: sports, classic literature, classical music, history. Home: Apt 466, 58 Rustavely, 195299 St Petersburg Russia Office: Agrophys Inst, 14 Grazhdansky Prospect, 195220 St Petersburg Russia

MUKHOPADHYAY, ARNAB, biologist; b. Calcutta, India, July 20, 1972; s. Arun and Nanda Mukherjee. BS, Presidency Coll., Calcutta, 1995; MS, U. Delhi, New Delhi, 1997. Jr. rsch. fellow U. Delhi, New Delhi, 1997—; sr. rsch. fellow Coun. Sci. and Indsl. Rsch., 1999. Recipient medal of merit, Botanical Soc. India, 1995; jr. rsch. fellowship, Coun. Sci. and Indsl. Rsch., 1997. Hindu. Avocations: reading, football, cricket, gardening, painting. Home: 56 Anjuman Ara Begum Row, 700033 Calcutta India Office: U Delhi Plant/Molecular Bio, Benito Juarez Rd, 110021 New Delhi India

MUKHOPADHYAY, RABINDRA, engineering executive, researcher; b. Old Kharagpur, India, Nov. 25, 1947; s. Bamandas and Saraswati (Chakravarty) M.; m. Nibha Ghatak Mukhopadhyay, July 5, 1981; children: Anshuman, Dhritiman. BS, Calcutta U., India, 1967; MS in Chemistry, IIT, Kharagpur, India, 1975; PhD in Rubber Tech., 1978. Mem. faculty Rubber Tech. Ctr., Kharagpur, India, 1971-78; tech. svc. officer Bayer Ltd., Bombay, India, 1979-85, tech. mgr., 1985-97; chief scientist Hasetri, Kankroli, India, 1987-91; v.p. J.K. Tyre, Kankroli, 1992-98, dir. R&D, 1999—; dir., chief exec. Hasetri, Kankroli, India, 1995—; vis. prof. IIT, Kharagpur, India, 1984-87, M.S. U., Udaipur, India, 1989—; chmn. Indian Rubber Inst., Rajasthan, India, 1988—; dir. Hasetri, Kankroli, India, 1995—; covenor PCD 13.9 Bur. Indian Standards, Delhi, India, 1996. Editor: IRC'93 Procs., 1993, others; author: Progress in Rubber and Plastic Technology Vol. 10, 1994; patentee New Test Method Development Polymer Testing, 1994, Green Tyre Lubricant, 1994. mem. governing coun. Indian Rubber Inst., Calcutta, India, 1992; mem. Nat. Space Def. Com. CII, New Delhi, India, 1995; life mem. Indian Soc. Analytical Scientists, Bombay, India, 1996; governing coun. The Instn. of Engrs., Udaipur, India, 1996. Recipient Vijay Shree award India Internat. Friendship Soc., New Delhi, India, 1996, Award for Excellence Rubber Plus '93, Bombay, India, 1993. Mem. N.Y. Acad. Scis., Am. Chem. Soc., All India Rubber Ind. Assn. Avocations: reading, touring, football, cricket. Home: PO Tyre Factory, A2 Jaykaygram, Kankroli 313342, India Office: Hari Shankar Singhania Elas, PO Tyre Factory, Kankroli 313342, India

MUKHOPADHYAY, SATYA NARAYAN, mathematician, educator; b. Burdwan, India, Dec. 8, 1934; s. Ram and Renu (Bandyopadhyay) M.; m. Pratibha Bandyopadhyay, Apr. 30, 1968; 1 child, Shyamasree. BA, U. Calcutta, 1957, U. Calcutta, 1960; MA, U. Burdwan, 1962; PhD, U. Calcutta, 1967. From lectr. to prof. U. Burdwan, 1963—; asst. prof. U. B.C., Can., 1971-73, vis. prof., 1986-87. Mem. West Bengal Acad. Sci. & Tech., Am. Math. Soc., Calcutta Math. Soc. Hindu. Avocation: books on mathematics. Home: Univ Tchrs Housing, Krishnapur Rd Keshabganj, Burdwan 713104, India Office: U Burdwan, Dept Maths, Burdwan 713104, India

MUKHOPADHYAY, SIDDHARTHA, electrical engineering educator, researcher; b. Calcutta, India, May 27, 1964; s. Sunil Chandra and Manju (Bhattacharya) M.; m. Damayanti Basu, Jan. 29, 1988; 1 child, Sharanya. B Tech. with honours, Indian Inst. Tech., Kharagpur, 1985, MTech., 1988, PhD, 1991. Sys. control engr. CESC (I) Ltd., Calcutta, 1985-86; lectr. elec. engring. Indian Inst. Tech., 1990-93, asst. prof., 1994-98, assoc. prof., 1998—; assoc. coord. Tech. Devel. Mission on Comm. Networking and Intelligent Automation, Indian Inst. Tech., 1993-95; ptnr. Control & Automation Techs., Sys. and Software, tech. devel. and cons. co., Kharagpur, 1996—. Contbr. articles to sci. jours., including IEEE Trans., IEE Procs., Internat. Jour. Control, Procs. Nat. Sys. Conf. Recipient young tchr.'s career award Univ. Grants Commn., 1993, young scientist medal Indian Nat. Sci. Acad., 1996, Young Engr. award Indian Nat. Acad. Engring., 1999. Mem. IEEE, Sys. Soc. India. Hindu. Avocations: vocal music, creative writing, reading, travel. Office: Indian Inst Tech, Dept Elec Engring, Kharagpur 721302, India

MUKHOPADHYAY, SUMIT, chemical engineering researcher; b. Calcutta, India, Aug. 1, 1966; s. Sushil K. and Sabita Mukhopadhyay. BSChemE, Jadavpur U., Caltutta, 1987; PhD in Chem. Engring., U. So. Calif., 1995. Asst. dir. reservoir engring. Oil and Natural Gas Commn. India, 1988-89; grad. asst, U. So. Calif., L.A., 1990-94; rsch. assoc. Purdue U., West Lafayette, Ind., 1995-97; scientist Lawrence Berkeley (Calif.) Nat. Lab., 1998—; cons. Dept. Energy, Berkeley. Contbr. articles to sci. jours., including Phys. Rev. E, Transport in Porous Media, Chem. Engring. Sci., Jour. Statis. Physics. Nat. scholar Govt. of India, New Delhi, 1981-87, John J. Watumul scholar U. So. Calif., 1994. Mem. AIChE, Am. Chem. Soc., Am. Geophys. Soc., Sigma Xi. Avocations: music, writing, reading. Fax: 510-486-5686. E-mail: sumit mukhopa@hotmail.com. Home: 3375 Carlson Blvd Apt 11 El Cerrito CA 94530-3942 Office: Lawrence Berkeley Nat Lab 1 Cyclotron Rd Ms 90 1116 Berkeley CA 94720-0001

MUKHOPADHYAY, UTPAL KANTI, textiles executive; b. Murshidabad, India, Apr. 3, 1967; s. Nandadulal and Nibedita Mukhopadhyay; m. Madhumita Thakur, Feb. 11, 1993; 1 child, Soham. BSc in Tech., U. Calcutta, India, 1988, MSc in Tech., 1996; PGDPM, NIPM, Calcutta, 1996. Trainee engr. Jayashree Textiles, India, 1988-90; shift-in-charge Mayurakshi Cotton Mills, India, 1990-91; textile supr. Kalyani Spinning Mills, India, 1993-96, 98—. Nat. Merit scholar Ministry Edn., Govt. India, 1982. Avocation: reading magazines. Home: 13/1 Shyama Charan Maitra Ln, 36 Calcutta West Bengal, India Office: Kalyani Spinning Mills, Unit 2, Ashoknagar DT-24PGS, India

MUKHOTI, BELA BANERJEE, economics educator; b. Vikrampur, Bengal, India, Mar. 1, 1932; came to U.S., 1965; d. Priyanath and Labanya (Ganguli) B.; m. Santi Ranjan Mukhoti, Dec. 14, 1957 (dec. 1988); children: Jayati, Mona. BA in Econs. with honors, Calcutta U., 1950, MA in Econs., 1953; PhD in Econs., London Sch. Econs., 1964. Rsch. specialist U. Ky., Lexington, 1965-66; assoc. prof. Memphis State U., 1966-68, U. No. Iowa, Cedar Falls, 1972-74; asst. prof. Lakehead U., Ont., Can., 1968-69; rsch. officer Planning Commn. Govt. of India, New Delhi, 1969-71; agrl. economist Econ. Rsch. Svc., USDA, Washington, 1979-86; prof. econs. Rowan U., Glassboro, N.J., 1987—. Author: Agriculture and Employment in Developing Countries--Strategy for Effective Rural Development, 1985; Measures of Development, 1986, International Monetary Fund and Low-Income Countries, 1986, Impact of Agricultural Growth Patterns on Import Demand for Food and Agricultural Commodities, 1983; contbr. articles to profl. jours. Recipient Rhoda Freeman recognition award N.J. Coll. and Univ. Coalition for Women's Edn., 1988, merit award Rowan U., 1989; Sr. Ernest Cassels Trust grantee, 1962-63, Brit. Univ. and Coll. Tchr.'s Assn. grantee, 1964, also various univs. and colls., 1965—. Mem. Am. Econ. Assn., Ea. Econ. Assn., Internat. Assn. Agrl. Econs., Assn. Indian Econ. Studies (exec. com. 1990—), Congress Econ. and Polit. Democracy Internat. (program com. 1990), Am. Friends London Sch. Econs., Assn. Indians in Am., Sanskriti (exec. com. 1985, pres. 1990). Hindu. Avocations: horticulture, cooking, photography, travel. Home: 49 E Holly Ave Sewell NJ 08080-2603 Office: Rowan U Dept Econs Bunce Hall Glassboro NJ 08028

MUKKAI, LALITHA KESAVAN, microbiology educator, consultant, researcher; b. Palghat, Kerala, India, Mar. 11, 1946; d. Ramaswamy Kesavan M. and Jayalakshmi Subramaniam; m. Balasubramaniam Neelakantan, Oct. 20, 1969; children: Arun, Anand, Anuradha. MBBS, Med. Coll. Calicut, 1969; MD in Microbiology, Christian Med. Coll., Madras, India, 1975. Demonstrator in microbiology Christian Med. Coll., Vellore, India, 1972-75, jr. lectr., 1975-76, sr. lectr., 1976-79, reader, 1979-82, assoc. prof. microbiology, 1982-84, prof. microbiology, 1984—, head microbiology, 1995—; acting head dept. microbiology Christian Med. Coll. Hosp., Vellore, India, 1982-84, head microbiology unit, 1987-95, acting head microbiology, virology, 1991-92, head dept. clin. microbiology, 1995—. Editor: Indian Jour. Med. Microbiologists; contbr. about 75 articles to profl. jours. Past mem. round table Vellore (Indian) br. Inner Circle. Fellow Indian Assn. Pathologists; mem. Indian Assn. Med. Microbiologists, Am. Soc. Microbiologists, European Soc. Microbiologists and Infectious Diseases, Hosp. Infection Soc. India. Avocations: music, gardening, writing, interior decoration. Office: Christian Med Coll Hosp, Dept Clin Microbiology, 632 004 Vellore Tamil Nadu, India

MULADI, H., university rector. Rector U. Diponegoro, Semarang, Indonesia. Office: Jl Iman Barjo, Sh 1-3 POB 270, Semarang 50241, Indonesia*

MULCAHY, NOEL WILLIAM, consultant; b. Limerick, Ireland, Dec. 25, 1930; s. William and Eileen (MacMahon) M.; m. Caroline Philomena Buckley, Apr. 4, 1959; children: Daragh, Colm, Aisling, Garech. B in Engring., U. Coll., Dublin, 1952, M in Electronics, 1958; LLD (hon.), Nat. Coun. for Ednl. Awards, Dublin, 1993. Devel. engr. STC Co., London; broadcasting engr. Radio Eireann TV, Dublin; divsn. mgr. SPS Technologies Inc., Shannon; dep. dir. gen. Trish Mgmt. Inst., Dublin; pvt. cons. Dublin; prof. insdl. strategy, dean engring. sch. U. Limerick, Ireland, exec. v.p.; ret., 1996; chmn. bd. com. McInerney Properties Ltd., Dublin, chmn. nat. coun.; edn. awards WCEA, Dublin, 1975-76; chmn. Innovation, Nat. Technol. Park, Limerick, 1984—; chmn. Adv. Com. on Stats. for Sci. and Tech.; chmn. Nat. Construction Industry Tng. Com., Nat. Com. on Outreach Higher Edn., Mktg. Support Solutions, Ltd. Author: Planning Your Business, 1966. Senator Irish Senate, Dublin, 1977-81; chmn. econ. affairs Joint Secondary Legis. Com. EEC, Dublin, 1977-81. Fellow Inst. of Engrs., Irish Mgmt. Inst. (chmn. nat. sci. tech. and innovation stats. com.); mem. Acad. Engrs. Roman Catholic. Avocations: golf, boating, swimming, singing. Office: U Limerick, Limerick Ireland

MULCHANDANI, KISHANCHAND BALCHAND, mechanical and industrial engineering educator, researcher; b. Jabalpur, India, Feb. 1, 1951; s. Balchand Kalyandas and Lachhmi (Bai) M.; m. Beena Chandwani, July 24, 1981; children: Neha, Hema, Vinay. B in Engring., Jabalpur U., 1972, M in Engring., 1976; PhD, Roorkee U., 1993. Trainee Bharat Heavy Elec., Bhopal, 1973; sr. rsch. fellow U. Grants Commn., 1976-78; lectr. U. Roorkee, 1978-85, reader, 1995-96, assoc. prof., 1996—. Contbr. articles to profl. jours. including Jour. Instn. Engrs. and Jour. Strain Analysis. Grantee Coun. Sci. and Indsl. Rsch., 1988, CSIR, 1996. Fellow Instn. Engrs. (Sir R.N. Mookerjee Meml. award 1995). Avocations: music, reading Hindi story books. Office: U Roorkee, Roorkee 247667, India

MULCKHUYSE, JACOB JOHN, energy conservation and environmental consultant; b. Utrecht, The Netherlands, July 21, 1922; came to U.S., 1982; s. Lambertus D. and Aagje (Van Geyn) M.; m. Cornelia Jacoba Wentink, Jan. 17, 1953; children: Jacobien, Hans, Dieuwke, Linda, Marlies. MSc, U. Amsterdam (the Netherlands), 1952, PhD, 1960. Dir. Chemisch-Farmaceutische Fabriek Hamu, the Netherlands, 1951-57; tech. asst. mgr. Polak & Schwarz (now IFF), the Netherlands, 1957-60; asst. tech. mgr. Albatros Superphosphate Fabrieken, the Netherlands, 1960-61; tech. mgr. for overseas subsidiaries Verenigde Kunstmestfabrieken, the Netherlands, 1961-64, gen. mgr. process engring. dept., 1964-70; dept. head process engring. dept. Unie van Kunstmestfabrieken, the Netherlands, 1970-82; sr. chem. engr. World Bank, Washington, 1982-83, sr. cons. chem. engr., 1983-87; ind. cons. environ. engring. World Bank and several cons. firms, 1987-97. Author: (with Heath and Venkataraman) The Potential for Energy Efficiency in the Fertilizer Industry, 1985, (with Gamba and Caplin) Industrial Energy Rationalization in Developing Countries and Constraints in Energy Conservation, 1990, Process Safety Analysis: Incentive for the Identification of Inherent Process Hazards, 1985, Energy Efficiency and Conservation in the Developing World, 1992; editor: Environmental Balance of the Netherlands, 1972. Mem. AIChE, Royal Dutch Chem. Soc., Fertilizer Soc. (pres. 1969-70), Internat. Inst. for Energy Conservation (bd. dirs. 1990-93), N.Y. Acad. Scis., Rotary. Avocations: philosophy, tennis, advising developing countries. Home: Watersedge 5 Broken Island Rd Palmyra VA 22963-2064

MULDER, PATRICIA MARIE, education educator; b. South Bend, Ind., Dec. 28, 1944; d. Ervin James and Carmen Virginia (Sheeley) Anderson; m. James R. Mulder, Dec. 27, 1964; children: Todd Alan, Scott Robert. BA, Western Mich. U., 1967. Freelance writer, photographer Berrien Springs, Mich., 1980—; tchr. Eau Claire (Mich.) Pub. Schs., 1969-70; staff writer, sales rep. Jour. Era, Berrien Springs, 1979-81; sales rep. Berrien County Record, Buchana, Mich., 1981-82; account exec. WHFB Radio Palladium Pub. Co., St. Joseph, Mich., 1982-86; substitute tchr. Berrien County Intermediate Dist., 1986-89; instr. Southwestern Mich. Coll., Dowagiac, 1989-96; cons. Writing Ctr. Southwestern Mich. Coll., 1996—; corp. trainer, 2000—. Editor The Positive Image newsletter, 1980—, The F Stop, 1982-90; author: Poetry Anthologies, 1989—; staff writer Decision Point, 1988-89; newsletter editor Fernwood Nature Photographers, 1980—. Ofcl. photographer Ind. and Internat. Spl. Olympics, Notre Dame, 1986. Named Emerging Artist Ind. Coun. for the Arts, 1989, Honor award Southwestern Coun. of Camera Clubs, 1988, Photographer of the Yr. Berrien County Photographic Artists, 1987, 90. Mem. AAUW, Nat. Authors Registry, Meth. Profl. Women (sec. 1990—), Berrien County Artists (v.p. 1986), Berrien County Photographic Artists (v.p. 1984), Southwestern Mich. Coun. Camera Clubs, Berrien Springs Camrea Club (v.p. 1980—). Methodist. Avocations: writing, photography, oil painting, watercolor painting. Home: 10252 Castner Dr Berrien Springs MI 49103-9602 Office: Southwestern Mich Coll 58900 Cherry Grove Rd # 316L Dowagiac MI 49047-9726

MULDOON, FRANCIS CREIGHTON, Canadian federal judge; b. Winnipeg, Manitoba, Canada, Aug. 3, 1930; s. William John and Laura Grace (Meredith) M.; m. M. Lucille Shirtliff, Aug. 6, 1955; 2 children. BA, U. Manitoba, 1952, LLB, 1956. Cert. barrister, solicitor, notary pub. Lawyer Monnin, Grafton, Deniset & Co., Winnipeg, Man., 1956-70; chmn. Manitoba Law Reform Commn., Winnipeg, 1970-77; v.p. Law Reform Commn. Can., Ottawa, 1977-78, pres., 1978-83; judge Fed. Ct. Can., Ottawa, 1983—, Ct. Martial Appeal Ct., Ottawa, 1983—; Bencher Law Soc. Manitoba, Winnipeg, 1968-71. Contbr. articles to profl. jours. President Children Aid Soc. Winnipeg, 1969-70, Manitoba Medico-Legal Soc., Winnipeg, 1973-77. Lt. Can. Army, 1952-60. Disting. Svc. Manitoba Bar Assn., 1987; hon. mem. Bar U.S. Ct. Milit. Appeals, 1991. Mem. Med. Legal Soc. Ottawa-Carleton (co-founder), St. Paul's Coll. (hon.). Roman Catholic. Avocations: reading, bicycling, public speaking. Office: Fed Ct Can, Kent & Wellington Sts, Ottawa, ON Canada K1A 0H9

MULDOWNEY, MICHAEL PATRICK, finance executive; b. Chgo., Oct. 8, 1963; s. James Joseph and Clare (Sexton) M.; m. Daniela Nicoletta Pernis, Apr. 25, 1992; children: Michael James, Patrick Nicholas. BA, St. Ambrose U., 1985. CPA, Ill., Mass. Acctg. mgr. Fletcher Engring., Des Plaines, Ill., 1985; asst. auditor Marsh & McLennan Cos., Chgo., 1986; auditor Marsh & McLennan Cos., London, 1987; sr. auditor Marsh & McLennan Cos., N.Y.C., 1988; asst. corp. contr. Temple, Barker & Sloane, Lexington, Mass., 1989; regional contr. Temple, Barker & Sloane/Strategic Planning Assocs., Lexington, 1990; dir. fin. and adminstrn. Mercer Mgmt. Consulting, Lexington, 1991; corp. contr. Mercer Mgmt. Consulting, N.Y.C., 1992-97; v.p. fin. Nextera Enterprises, Lexington, 1997-98, CFO, 1998—; mem. Boston mgmt. com. Mercer Mgmt., Lexington, 1994-96; chmn. Fin. Execs. Mgmt. Consulting Firm, Boston, 1995. Chmn. United Way fundraiser Mercer Mgmt. Consulting, Lexington, 1992, chmn. co. fundraiser, 1993; trustee Meadowbrook Water Trust, Dover, Mass., 1993-97. Mem. AICPA, Ill. Soc. CPA's, Mass. Soc. CPA's, Fin. Execs. Inst., Wellesley Country Club (Tennis champion 1995-98). Avocation: tennis. Office: Nextera Enterprises LLC 1 Cranberry Hl Ste 9 Lexington MA 02421-7321

MULEJ, MATJAZ ZORAN, systems educator; b. Maribor, Yugoslavia, Jan. 20, 1941; s. Zoran Anton and Kosara Franc (Tomazin) M.; m. Ivka Ivan Smrk, Mar. 23, 1962; children: Matjaz Jr., Nastja. BA in Econ., U. Ljubljana, 1967; MA in Econ. Devel., U. Beograd, 1973; PhD in Sys. Theory in Econ., U. Zagreb, 1977. Instr. English, various primary schs., Maribor, 1955-59; clk. Coll. Bus. & Econ., Maribor, 1962-65, tchr., rsch. asst., 1968-71, lectr., sr. lectr., 1971-77; adv. to vicechair Fed. Govt., Beograd, 1979, prof. sys. and innovation theory, 1977—; sci. cons. Inst. Econ. Ctr., Maribor, 1973-88; internat. tech. asst. Govt. Angola, 1979. Author: Creative Work and Dialectical Systems Theory, 1979; co-author: Innovative Business, 1987, Self-Transformation of the Forgotten Four-Fifths, 1998; guest editor Systems Rsch., 1994; contbr. articles to profl. jours. Sec. Tennis Club Branik, Maribor, 1956-91; pres. Inventors Assn., Solvenia, 1985-2000. With Slovenia mil., 1967-68. Recipient Innovator's Golden medal Socialist Federative Rep. Yugoslavia, 1989; named Innovator of Yr., Socialist Rep. Slovenia, 1987. Mem. Inst. Sys. Rsch. (head ISRUM 1994—), Internat. Orgnl. Devel. Assn., Orgnl. Devel. Inst., Sys. Rsch. Soc. Slovenia (pres. 1994), N.Y. Acad. Scis. Avocations: tennis, skiing. Home: Gregorciceva 27, SI 2000 Maribor Slovenia Office: UNI Maribor Sch Bus & Econ, Razlagova 14, SI 2000 Maribor Slovenia

MULEKAR, MANOHAR KRISHNAJI, chemist; b. Mumbai, India, Dec. 23, 1945; s. Krishnaji Narhar and Mandakini Krishnaji (Vatsala Vasudev Railkar) M.; m. Mira Manohar Havnurkar (Godse) Mira Vasudev, Sept. 2, 1973; 1 child, Mandar Manohar. BSc, S.S.C., Mumbai, 1967. Cert. chemist, 1968, 73. Chemist Wadhus India, Mumbai, 1968; supr. Swastik Oils Ltd., Maharashtra, India, 1968-69; lab. chemist, supr. IndoFil Chem. Ltd., Thane, India, 1969-71; lab. chemist Nirlon Chems. and Synthetic Fibres, Ltd., Mumbai, 1971-73, Inchage Sonawala Industries Pvt. Ltd., Thane, 1973; scientist Hindustan Composite Ltd., Mumbai, 1974; sole distbr. Kaizen Properties Pvt. Ltd., Mumbai; field officer M/S Pearl Agro Trees, Ltd., Maharashtra; pres. Ferodo Dyandeep Mandel, Mumbai, 1979-84; adult edn. tchr. Dyandeep Mahasangh, Mumbai, 1978-84. Writer (TV serials), 1979-80. Elected mng. com. mem. Hindustan Ferodo Coop. Credit Soc., Ltd., 1978-81, Marathi Scientific Coun., Mumbai, 1990-96, Deshast Rigvedi Brahmin Sangh, Mumbai, 1981-97; ind. candidate in contested election Maharashtra Legis. Coun., Greater Bombay Grad. Constituency, 1982. Cadet, N.C.C., 1964-66, Mumbai. Mem. Hindustan Ferodo Ltd. Recreation Club (sec. chess 1977-78, sec. cricket 1980-87), Lions Club. Office: M/S Pearl Agro Trees Ltd, 8 Paradise House, Thane Maharashtra India

MULFORD, RAND PERRY, business executive; b. Denver, Sept. 30, 1943; s. Roger Wayne and Ann Louise (Perry) M.; 1 child, Conrad Perry; m. Paula Marie Skelley, 1987. BS in Basic Engring., Princeton U., 1965; MBA, Harvard U., 1972. Mgmt. cons. McKinsey & Co. Inc., Chgo., 1972-80; v.p. planning and control splty. chem. group Occidental Chem. Co., Houston, 1980-82; pres. Technivest Inc., Houston, 1982-85; exec. dir. corp. planning Merck & Co., Inc., Rahway, N.J., 1985-88; v.p. fin. Advanced Tissue Scis., Inc., La Jolla, Calif., 1989-90; CEO Chiron Mimotopes Peptide Systems, San Diego, Calif., 1991-94; COO Xytronyx, Inc., San Diego, 1994-95; chmn. of bd. Medication Delivery Devices, San Diego, 1991-95; CEO World Blood, Inc., 1997-99; mng. dir. bus strategy Spencer Trask, Inc.; bd. dirs. ZymeTx, Inc., Oklahoma City, Diamonex Inc., Allentown, Pa. Lt. USN, 1965-70. Home: 2178 Caminito Del Barco Del Mar CA 92014-3619

MULFORD, RICHARD ALBERT, mechanical engineer; b. Phila., Dec. 13, 1930; s. William Abernathy and Jeanne Ann (Roy) M. BSME, U. Pa., 1952, MS in Mech. Engring., 1957; Diploma in Bus., Dartmouth Coll., 1985. Registered profl. engr., Pa. Engr. Phila. Elec. Co., 1952-64, sr. engr., 1964-67, project mgr., 1967-85, staff engr., 1985-91; exec. dir. Engrs. Club of Phila., 1991—. Patentee in field. Vol. Paoli Meml. Hosp., Pa., 1991—; donor Phila. Orchestra Assn., 1980—; treas./donor Phila. Engring. Found., 1991—. Recipient Disting. Svc. award Pa. Soc. of Profl. Engrs., Harrisburg, 1991, 98, Alumni award of merit U. Pa., Phila., 1993, George Washington medal Engrs. Club of Phila., 1988. Fellow Engrs. Club of Phila. (sec./treas. 1953—); mem. NSPE, Union League Phila. (scholarship trustee 1963—), Racquet Club of Phila. Republican. Presbyterian. Avocations: classical music, antique cars, home and lawn maintenance. Home: 1231 Wisteria Dr Malvern PA 19355-9736 Office: Engrs Club of Phila 215 S 16th St Ste 36 Philadelphia PA 19102-3349

MULFORD, WILLIAM RICHARD, education educator; b. Bishops Stortford Herts, Eng., Nov. 27, 1941; s. Albert Walter and Ursula Mary (Clayden) M.; m. Therese Odile Gallays, Feb. 21, 1969; children: Jonathan, Alice. BA in Edn. with great dist., U. Sask., Can., 1968, MEdn, 1969; PhD, U. Alta., Edmonton, Can., 1971. Tchr.-in-charge NSW Dept. Edn., Australia, 1961-64; tchr. various, U.K., 1965-66; prin. Eastern Sch. Dist., Frobisher, Can., 1966-67; acting asst. dir. PNG Dept. Edn., Port Moresby, 1972-74; acting principal lectr. Canberra CAE, Australia, 1974-87; prof., dean U. Tasmania, Launceton, Australia, 1987—; sr. fellow OECD, Paris, 1978; cons. Singapore Min. Edn., 1980-97, Asia Devel. Bank, 1995, UNESCO/Commonwealth Coun. Ednl. Adminstrn., 1975—. Author: Structured Experiences and Group Development, 1981, Indicators of School Effectiveness, 1987, Shaping Tommorow's Schools, 1994, Organisational Learning and Educational Change, 1998. Australian Coun. Ednl. Adminstrn. fellow, 1982, CCEA fellow, 1992. Mem. Australian Coun. for Ednl. Adminstrn., Commonwealth Coun. for Ednl. Adminstrn. Avocations: golf, gardening. Office: Fac Edn U Tasmania, Locked Bag 1-308, Launceston, Tasmania 7250, Australia

MULHOLLAND, BERNARD JAMES, engineer; b. Hamburg, Germany, May 18, 1957; s. William James and Waltraud (Giesecke) M. BA in Environ. Scis. 1st class honors, Queen's U., Belfast, No. Ireland, 2000. Engr., 1975—. Editor jour. Poli-Ticks, 1995-96. Mem. AAAS, No. Ireland Master Plumbers Assn., N.Y. Acad. Scis., Brit. Assn., Brit. Mensa, Royal Overseas League. Avocations: adventurer, creative thinking, reading, writing. Home: 3 Killicomain Rd, Portadown BT63 5BT, Northern Ireland

MULIC, HAZIM A., neurology and psychiatry educator; b. Livno, Bosnia, May 16, 1941; arrived in Croatia, 1988; s. Abdullah O. and Fehima I. (Dendo) M.; m. Dragica Gasparovic, Nov. 30, 1964; children: Arlenka, Alma. MD, Med. Faculty, Zagreb, Croatia, 1966, neuropsychiatrist, 1973; Magister of Medicine, Med. Faculty, Tulza, Bosnia, 1982, PhD, 1987. Med. diplomate. Dir. Univ. Med. Ctr., Tuzla, 1975-78, Neuropsychiat. Clinic, Tuzla, 1979-80; head Dept. Cerebrovascular Disease, Tuzla, 1981-82; chmn. Neurology and Psychiat. Med. Faculty, Tuzla, 1983-87; head Neuropsychiat. Svc. Mil. Hosp., Pula, Croatia, 1988-91; pvt. practice Pula, 1992—; Co-author: Touristic Medicine, 1993; contbr. articles to profl. jours. Recipient Plaque, Med. Assn. Bosnia-Herzeg Sarajevo, 1975. Mem. Am. Acad. Neurology, Am. Heart Assn., N.Y. Acad. Sci., Acology Assn., Internt. Acad. for Whole Medicine of Vienna, Med. Assn. Croatia. Atheist. Avocations: traveling, sports. Home: Jeretova 20, 52000 Pula Croatia Office: Pvt Neuropsychiat Ordin, Rimske centurijacije 16, 52000 Pula Croatia

MULJADI, PAULUS BENJAMIN, electrical engineer, webmaster; b. Jakarta, Indonesia, Mar. 28, 1964; came to U.S., 1977; s. Daniel and Emelia Muljadi. BS, U. Tex., San Antonio, 1987; postgrad., U. Tex., Austin, 1987-89, So. Meth. U., 1991. Registered profl. engr., Tex.; cert. computing profl. Grad. rsch. asst. U. Tex., San Antonio and Austin, 1987-89; tech. asst. U. Tex., Austin, 1989; devel. engr. Motorola, Inc., Ft. Worth, 1990-93; elec. engr. K.M. Ng & Assocs., San Antonio, 1993—; co-founder 4JavaWeb, Austin, 1996, Giftware, Etc., San Antonio, 1995; founder GiftLite, San Antonio, 1995, PBM, Ft. Worth, 1990. webmaster, coord. ednl. website, 1995; author, pub.: (computer software) Giftware, 1995; contbr. articles to profl. jours. Mentor San Antonio BEST, 1995-98; computer cons. Youth Orch., San Antonio, 1994; vol. Compumentor, Ft. Worth, 1992. Rsch. grantee MBRS, San Antonio, 1987-88. Mem. IEEE, NSPE, Tex. Soc. Profl. Engrs., Lightning Protection Inst. Unitarian. Achievements include development of novel peak-to-peak detection using DSPs. E-mail: paul@muljadi.com. Address: PO Box 100393 San Antonio TX 78201-1693

MULL, GALE W., lawyer; b. Hillsdale, Mich., Sept. 8, 1945; s. Wayne E. and Vivian M. (Bavin) M.; m. Holly Ann Allen, Aug. 2, 1969 (div. Nov. 1983); 1 child, Carter B.; m. Jeanne Anne Haughey, Aug. 18, 1985. BA, Mich. State U., 1967; MA in Sociology, Ind. U., 1969; JD, Emory U., 1972. Bar: Ga. 1972, U.S. Dist. Ct. (no. dist.) Ga. 1972, U.S. Ct. Appeals (5th cir.) 1973, U.S. Ct. Appeals (11th cir.) 1981. Instr. sociology Clemson (S.C.) U., 1968-69, Spelman Coll., Atlanta, 1969-70; pvt. practice, Atlanta, 1972-75; ptnr. Mull & Sweet, Atlanta, 1975-81; pres. Gale W. Mull, P.C., Atlanta, 1981—; bd. dirs. BOND Community Fed. Credit Union, Atlanta, 1975-81; directing atty. Emory Student Legal Services, Atlanta, 1975-91; Sociology instr. Clemson U., Clemson, S.C., 1968-69, Spelman Coll., Atlanta, Ga., 1969-70. Pres. Inman Park Restoration, Inc., Atlanta, 1972-74, BASS Orgn. for Neighborhood Devel., Inc., 1974-78; mem. Housing Appeals Bd., Atlanta, 1982-88; mem. Mayor's Task Force on Prostitution, 1984-86; bd. dirs. ACLU Ga., 1981-92, sec. bd. dirs., 1983-85, cooperating atty., 1972—; vestry St. John's Episcopal Ch., 1992-99, sr. warden, 1998-99; bd. dirs. St. John's Episcopal Day Sch., 1992-97, Bethlehem Ministries, 1997—, Trinity Towers, Inc., 1999-2000. Mem. ABA, Ga. Bar Assn., Atlanta Bar Assn., Lawyers Club Atlanta. Club: Quail Unltd. (bd. dirs., sec. 1984-86). Office: 990 Edgewood Ave NE Atlanta GA 30307-2581

MULLAJANOV, FAIZULLA MAKHSUTJANOVICH, bank executive; b. Pobeda, Uzbekistan, Mar. 10, 1950; s. Makhsutjan Mullajanovich and Ibodat Samsakbayevna (Ruzimbayeva) M.; m. Mekhry Nisogiyezovna Ruzimbayeva; children: Abdumajid, Ozoda, Khikoyat, Abdukakhor, Abdujabbor. Grad., Inst. Nat. Economy, Tashkent, Uzbekistan, 1971. Sec. of bd. Collective farm "Pobeda", Syrdaria, Uzbekistan, 1966-67; credit inspector Syrdaria Br. of State Bank, Gulistan, Uzbekistan, 1971, sr. credit inspector, 1971-72; head credit dept. Verknevolynsk (Uzbekistan) Br. of State Bank, 1972-73; mgr. Krestiyanski (Uzbekistan) Br. of State Bank, 1973-76, Golodnostepski Br. of State Bank, Yangiyer, Uzbekistan, 1976-86; dep. mgr. Syrdaria Regional Office of State Bank, Gulistan, 1986-87, mgr., 1987; head Syrdaria Regional Bd. Agroprombank, Jizak, Uzbekistan, 1988-90, Syrdaria Regional Bd. State Bank, Gulistan, 1990-91; chmn. Bd. of Ctrl. Bank of Republic of Uzbekistan, Tashkent, 1991—. Dep. Oliy Majlis (Supreme Soviet), Tashkent, 1991. People's Democratic Party of Uzbekistan. Muslem. Avocations: books, theatre, hunting. Office: Ctrl Bank Rep Uzbekistan, 6 Uzbekistansky Av, 700001 Tashkent Uzbekistan*

MULLALLY, PIERCE HARRY, retired steel company executive; b. Cleve., Oct. 6, 1918; s. Pierce Harry and Laura (Lynch) M.; m. Mary Eileen Murphy, Feb. 22, 1943; children: Mary Kathleen, Pierce Harry. Student, U. Western Ont., 1935; BS, John Carroll U., 1939; MD, St. Louis U., 1943. Diplomate Am. Bd. Surgery. Intern St. Vincent Charity Hosp., Cleve., 1943, resident in surgery, 1944, 47-50, staff surgeon, 1951-62, head peripheral vascular surgery, 1963-76, dir. med. edn., 1967-73, dir. dept. surgery, 1968-75, trustee, 1977-86; plant physician Rep. Steel Corp., Cleve., 1952-68, med. dir., 1968-76, corp. dir. occupl. medicine, 1976-84; cons. LTV Steel Co., 1984-86; med. dir., chmn. med. adv. bd. Ohio Health Choice Plan Inc. Vice-chmn. Cleve. Clinic-Charity Hosp. Com. Surg. Residency Tng., 1970-78; health com. Bituminous Coal Operators Assn.; trustee Wood Hudson Cancer Research Labs., Inc., 1984—; bd. dirs. Phoenix Theatre Ensemble, 1982-86; foreman grand jury Cuyahoga County, 1986. Capt. U.S. Army, 1944-46; PTO. Fellow ACS, Am. Coll. Angiology; mem. Am. Iron and Steel Inst. (chmn. health com. 1977-79), Am. Acad. Occupl. Medicine, Am. Occupl. Med. Assn., Ohio Occupl. Med. Assn., Acad. Medicine Cleve. (dir. 1969-72), Cleve. Surg. Soc., Western Res. Med. Dirs., Soc. Clin. Vascular Surgery, Cleve. Skating Club, Cleve. Playhouse Club, Serra Club. Roman Catholic. Home: 1890 E 107th St Apt 905 Cleveland OH 44106-2252

MULLAN, HOMI P.R., banker; b. Bombay, India, Feb. 22, 1948; s. Phiroz and Gool Mullan; m. Usha Kalsia, Feb. 22, 1978. B of Commerce, U. Bombay; MBA, Cranfield Sch. of Mgmt. Articled clk. Coopers & Lybrand, London, 1968-72; mgr. corp. fin. BOC Internat. Plc, London, 1974-80; asst. group treas. Burmah-Castrol Plc, Swindon, U.K., 1980-84; mng. dir. Chase Manhattan Bank, London, 1984—. Fellow Inst. of Chartered Accts. Home: 23 Harley House, London NW1 5HE, England Office: The Chase Manhattan Bank, 125 London Wall, London EC2Y 5AJ, England

MULLANE, DENIS FRANCIS, insurance executive; b. Astoria, N.Y., Aug. 28, 1930; s. Patrick F. and Margaret (O'Neill) M.; m. Kathryn Mullman, June 28, 1952; children: Gerard, Kevin, Denise. BS in Mil. Engring, U.S. Mil. Acad., 1952; LHD (hon.), U. Conn., 1988, St. Joseph's Coll., 1990; LLD (hon.), U. Hartford, 1993, Trinity Coll., Hartford, Conn., 1995; MS in Fin. Svcs., The Am. Coll., Bryn Mawr, Pa., 1995. CLU. With Conn. Mut. Life Ins. Co., Hartford, 1956—, v.p., 1969-72, sr. v.p., 1972-74, exec. v.p., 1974-76, pres., 1977—, chief exec. officer, 1983-85, chmn., chief exec. officer, 1985-90; chief exec. officer, pres. Conn. Mut. Life Ins. Co., 1990-93; chmn. Mulane Enterprises, Inc., Hartford, Conn., 1994—; with Mullane Enterprises, West Hartford, Conn., 1994—; bd. dirs. Conn. Natural Gas Co.; chmn. The Am. Coll., Bryn Mawr, Pa., 1993-96; chmn. joint planning com. Am. Coll. and Soc. Fin. Svcs. Profls., 1996-99. Dir. U.S. Chamber, 1991-95. 1st lt. C.E., U.S. Army, 1952-56. Recipient John Newton Russell award, 1987, Knight of St. Gregory award. Mem. Am. Soc. Corp. Execs., Nat. Assn. Life Underwriters, Assn. Grads. U.S. Mil. Acad. (pres. 1989-93). Republican. Roman Catholic. Office: Mullane Enterprises Inc 29 S Main St Hartford CT 06107-2449

MULLEN, ANDREA MARIE, insurance agent; b. Pottstown, Pa., July 30; d. Edward Donald and Virginia Mae Beckwith; m. James Allen Mullen, Sr., Apr. 21, 1996; children: James Allen Jr., Jordan Thomas. A in Bus. Mgmt., Lansdale Sch. Bus., 1996. Lic. property and casualty agt. CSR Evans, Hauseman and Richard, Inc., Pottstown, 1995—. Mem. Nat. Assn. Ins. Women. Democrat. Office: Evans Hauseman and Richard Inc 343 High St Pottstown PA 19464

MULLEN, ROD, nonprofit organization executive; b. Puyallup, Wash., Aug. 2, 1943; s. Charles Rodney and Grace Violet (Fritsch) M.; m. Lois Fern Tobiska, May 3, 1963 (div. Jan. 1977); children: Cristina, Charles, Moneka; m. Naya Arbiter, Oct. 17, 1977. Student, U. Idaho, 1961-63; AB in Polit. Sci., U. Calif., Berkeley, 1966; postgrad., San Francisco Art Inst., 1968. Dir. Oakland (Calif.) facility Synanon Found., Inc., 1971-72, dir. San Francisco facility, 1972-73, dir. Tomales Bay (Calif.) facility, 1976-78, dir. Synanon edn. programs, 1973-76; treatment dir. nat. programs Vision Quest, Inc., Tucson, 1981-82; dir. resources and devel. Amity, Inc., Tucson, 1982-84, exec. dir., 1984-95; founder, pres., CEO, Amity Found. of Calif., Porterville, Calif., 1995—; mem. Nat. Adv. Com. on Substance Abuse Prevention, 1990-92, 93-96; mem. sci. adv. bd. Ctr. for Therapeutic Cmty. Rsch., Nat. Devel. and Rsch. Insts., N.Y.C., 1991—; cons. Calif. Office Criminal Justice Planning, Sacramento, 1993; prin. investigator program Nat. Inst. on Drug Abuse, 1990-93. Contbr. numerous articles to profl. publs., chpts. to books. Mem. Am. Correctional Assn., Therapeutic Coms. of Am., Calif. Assn. of Therapeutic Comtys. (sec.). Fax: (209) 783-2846. E-mail: rodm@amityfound.com. Office: Amity Found Calif PO Box 713 Porterville CA 93258-0713

MULLEN, TERRI ANN, special education educator; b. St. Louis, Apr. 1; d. William Earl and Sophia Kinniff; m. Thomas Patrick Mullen; children: David, Mark, Debi. BS in Edn., S.E. Mo. State U.; M in Sch. Adminstrn., Calif. State U., 1978, M in Spl. Edn., 1981; EdD in Institutional Mgmt., Pepperdine U., 1985. Cert. spl. edn., std. sec., std. elem., adminstrv. svc. K-12, cmty. coll. instr. Tchr. Irvine (Calif.) Unified Sch. Dist., 1972-84; lectr., spl. edn. Calif. State U., Fullerton, 1989-90; asst. prin. Moreno Valley (Calif.) Unified Sch. Dist., 1984-85; adminstr. of spl. svcs. Centralia Sch. Dist., Buena Park, Calif., 1984-89; elem. prin. Capistrano Unified Sch. Dist., San Juan Capistrano, 1989-93; spl. edn. tchr., dept. chair Moreno Valley (Calif.) Unified Sch. Dist., 1993—; chair, cmty. staff ednl. planning com. Santiago Elem. Sch., Irvine Unified Sch. Dist., 1981; dir., staff devel. for spl. programs pers. Centralia Sch. Dist., Buena Park, 1984-89; workshop presenter Assn. of Calif. Sch. Adminstrs. Conf., San Francisco, 1983. Author: Resource Book of Classroom Interventions for the Collaborative Teaching Model, 1994, Tips of the Trade for the Classroom Aide, 1984; contbr. articles to profl. jours. Adv. bd. for sp. edn. Calif. State U. Fullerton, 1988-89. Recipient Cmty. Svc. award Disneyland, 1992, 93; named Outstanding Educator of Yr. Rotary Club, 1983. Mem. Coun. for Exceptional Children, Kappa Delta Pi, Phi Kappa Phi. Avocations: roller skating, fashion design, interior design, computer applications, writing. Office: Valley View High Sch 13135 Nason St Moreno Valley CA 92555-4504

MULLENDORE, MARK EDWARD, internist, educator; b. Richland Center, Wis., May 15, 1960; s. Daniel Wertz and Catherine (Spangler) M.; m. Regina Ann Kovach, May 29, 1977 (div. 1984); 1 child, Laura Kathryn; m. Michelle Bohlen, 1985 (div. 1989); m. Paula Marie Payne, Mar. 5, 1990 (div. 1994); 1 child, Danielle Marie. BS, U. Ill., Urbana, 1973; MD, U. Ill., Chgo., 1977. Resident in internal medicine So. Ill. U., Springfield, 1977-80; pvt. practice, Springfield, 1980—; mem. clin. faculty So. Ill. U. Sch. Medicine, 1980—. Mem. AMA, Am. Soc. Internal Medicine, Ill. Soc. Internal Medicine, Sangamon County Med. Soc. Republican. Methodist. Avocations: diving, gardening, woodworking. Office: Physicians Group Assocs 2305 W Monroe St Springfield IL 62704-1401

MÜLLER, ACHIM, chemistry educator; b. Detmold, Germany, Feb. 14, 1938. PhD in Natural Scis., U. Göttingen, Germany, 1965; Dr honoris causa, U. Wroclaw, Poland, 1997. Lectr. U. Göttingen, 1967-71; assoc. prof. U. Dortmund (Germany), 1971-77; full prof. U. Bielefeld (Germany), 1977—; v.p. European Congress on Molecular Spectroscopy, 1980—. Editor: (with others) Spectroscopy in Chemistry and Physics, 1980, Transition Metal Chemistry, 1981, Electron and Proton Transfer in Chemistry and Biology, 1992, Matrix Isolation Spectroscopy, 1981, Nitrogen Fixation: The Chemical-Biochemical-Genetic Interface, 1982, Sulfur, Its Significance for Chemistry, for the Geo- and Bio- and Cosmosphere and Technology, 1984, Polyoxometalates: From Platonic Solids to Anti-Retroviral Activity, 1994, From Simplicity to Complexity in Chemistry—and Beyond, Part I, 1996, From Simplicity to Complexity: Information, Interaction, Emergence, Part II, 1998. Recipietn Alfred Stock award German Chem. Soc., 2000. Mem. Academia Europaea, Nat. Acad. Exact, Phys. and Natural Scis. (Argentina), European Acad. (Paris), Polish Acad. Sci., Deutsche Akademie Leopoldina, Chem. Rsch. Soc. India (hon.). Achievements include research on transition metal sulfur clusters, on new class of metal oxides. Office: Lehrstuhl F Anorg Chemie, Univ Postfach 100131, Bielefeld D-33501, Germany

MÜLLER, BEATE SUSANNE, German language and literature educator; b. Hagen, Germany, Jan. 7, 1963; came to Great Britain, 1992; MPhil, U. Bochum, Germany, 1988, PhD, 1993. Jr. asst. Bochum chair for Anglistik I U. Bochum, 1988-92; German lektorin Sidney Sussex Coll., Cambridge, Eng., 1992-95; asst. prof. Flensburg (Germany) U., 1995-97; lectr. modern German lit. U. Newcastle, Eng., 1997—. Author: Komische Intertextualität: Die Literarische Parodie, 1994; editor: Parody: Dimensions and Perspectives, 1997. Office: Sch Modern Langs, Univ Newcastle, Newcastle NE1 7RU, England

MÜLLER, DANIEL, geologist, educator, consultant; b. Frankfurt, Hessen, Germany, Nov. 6, 1962; s. Herbert and Margot (Nitz) M. MSc, Johannes Gutenberg U., Mainz, Germany, 1990; PhD in Sci., U. Western Australia, Perth, 1994. Geologist Placer Dome Exploration, Santiago, Chile, 1994-95, North Mining Ltd., Parkes, Australia, 1995-96; mine geologist North Mining Ltd., Kalgoorlie, Australia, 1996-97; project geologist North Mining Ltd., Jakarta, Indonesia, 1997-98, Kalgoorlie, Australia, 1998-99; lectr. Mining-Acad., Freiberg, Germany, 1999—. 1st author: (textbook) Potassic Igneous Rocks and Associated Gold-Copper Mineralization, 3rd edit., 2000; contbr. sci. papers to profl. jours. 1st lt. German Air Force Res., 1982-85. Recipient Postgrad. award Hesperian Press, 1992, Western Mining Postgrad. award, 1993. Mem. Assn. Exploration Geochemists, Soc. Econ. Geologists. Avocations: flying, cycling. Fax: 0049-3731-392610.

MULLER, DANIEL JEAN, aeronautical engineer, experimental test pilot; b. Sierre, Valais, Switzerland, Jan. 30, 1946; s. Jacques and Ida (Cina) M.; m. Lisa Hofer, Jan. 21, 1972; 1 child, Diane. Degree in aero. engring., Eidgen Tech. Hochschule, Zurich, 1970; postgrad., Ecole Personal Navigant Essais, Istres, France, 1989. Lic. test pilot. Structure engr. Flug-und Fahrzeugwerke Altenrhein, Switzerland, 1971-72; aero. engr. Avions Pierre Robin, Darois, France, 1972-75, chief engring. office, 1975-81, dir. R & D, 1981—, experimental test pilot, 1983—. Recipient French Aero. medal, 1995. Mem. Soc. Exptl. Test Pilots (assoc. fellow 2000—). Avocations: ice hockey, acrobatics, history. Home: 22 Boulevard de Brosses, 21000 Dijon France Office: Robin Aviation, 1 Rte de Troyes, 21121 Darois France

MÜLLER, DETLEF HORST, mathematician, educator; b. Dissen, Germany, June 13, 1954; s. Alfred Horst and Helga Lydia (Ottke) M.; m. Gisela Teske; children: Helen, Daphne, Norman. Dr. math., U. Bielefeld, Germany, 1981; habilitation, U. Bielefeld, 1984. Hochschulassistent U. Bielefeld, Germany, 1982-88; Heisenberg scholarship DFG, Bielefeld, 1988-92; prof. U. Louis Pasteur, Strasbourg, France, 1992-94, U. Kiel, Germany, 1994—; vis. asst. prof. La. State U., Baton Rouge, 1982-83; mem. Inst. for Advanced Study, Princeton, N.J., 1991; editor Mathematische Zeitschrift. Office: Christian Albrechts U, Ludewig Meyn Strasse 4, 24098 Kiel Germany

MÜLLER, FRANK ROBERT, pharmacologist; b. Pretoria, South Africa, Jan. 20, 1969; s. Frank Otto and Friedegund Gertrud (Krueger) M. B Medicine B Surgery, U. Orange Free State, Bloemfontein, South Africa, 1992, M Med. Sci. in Pharmacology, 1995. Dir. clin. trials Farmovs, Bloemfontein, 1995-97; dir. Zauberkraut, George, South Africa, 1997—; cons. South Africa Clin. Trials, George, 1997-99. Travelling sec. Christian Med. Fellowship, South Africa, 1994-96; nat. coord. Christian Worldview Network, South Africa, 1998—. Mem. South African Med. Assn., Health Professions Coun. South Africa, Christian Med. Fellowship South Africa, N.Y. Acad. Scis. Mem. Anglican Ch. Avocations: photography, travel, medicinal plants, agriculture. E-mail: fm18@pixie.co.za. Office: Po Box 4075, 6539 George East South Africa

MULLER, FREDERIK ARCHIBALD, philosopher, physicist, writer; b. Amsterdam, Holland, Jan. 30, 1962; s. Jan Frederik and Petronella Marinus (Wilhelm) M.; m. Memia Bint-Abdelkader Ghedamsi, Aug. 21, 1990; children: Suleyman, Faysal, Olfa. Student, Vrje Leergangen, Amsterdam, 1983; DRS, Univ. Amsterdam, 1989, PhD, 1998. Temp. assoc. Utrecht Univ., Holland, 1990-96; postdoctoral rschr. Utrecht Univ., 2000—. Contbr. articles to profl. jours. Mem. Dutch Physical Soc., Philosophy of Sci. Assn., Duhh Orgn. for Philosophy Of Sci. Avocations: music, literature, reading, writing, painting. E-mail: f.a.muller@phys.uu.nl. Office: Utrecht Univ, PO Box 80 000, 3508 TA Utrecht Holland

MÜLLER, GERHARD, bishop; b. Marburg/Lahn, May 10, 1929; s. Karl and Elisabeth Landau M.; m. Ursula Herboth, 1957; 2 children. Attended, Marburg, Göttingen and Tübingen. Priest Hanau/Main, 1956-57; scholar Deutsche Forschungsgemeinschaft, Italy, 1957-59; asst. Ecumenical Sem. U. Marburg, 1959-61; docent Faculty Theology, 1961-66; guest lectr. German Hist. Inst., Rome, 1966-67; prof. hist. theol., modern church history U. Erlangen, 1967-82; Evangelical-Lutheran bishop of Brunswick, 1982-94; hon. prof. U. Göttingen, 1983—. Author: Franz Lambert von Avignon und die Reformation in Hessen, 1958, Nuntiaturberichte aus Deutschland 1530-1532 (2 vols.) 1963, 69, Die römische Kurie und die Reformation, 1969, Die Rechtfertigungslehre, 1977, Reformation und Stadt, 1981, Zwischen Reformation und Gegenwart, 1983, II, 1988, Causa Reformationis, 1989, Die Mystik oder das Wort?, 2000; editor: Kirche, Frömmigkeit und Theologie im 12. Jahrhundert, 1996, Handbuch der feschichte der evangelischen Kindre in Bayern II, 2000, works of Andreas Osiander and a 31 vol. theol. ency. Home: 91056 Erlangen, Sperlingstr 59, Germany

MULLER, JOHAN TOBIAS, investment company executive; b. Kroonstad, South Africa, Sept. 16, 1969; s. Jan Chriostphel and Lynette Juliana (Laubscher) N,. Businessman diploma, Damelin, Johannesburg, South Africa, 1991. Mktg. dir. I.C.E., Cape Town, South Africa, 1993-95; mng. dir. I.C.E., Cape Town, 1995—, I.I.C., Cape Town, 1995-98, Roebcon Investment Holdings Ltd., Cape Town, 1996—. Lt. inf. South African Army, 1988-90. Mem. Health and Racquet Club. Avocation: chess, gym, pool, squash, photography. Office: Robecon Investment Holdings, PO Box 50803, Waterfront, Cape Town WC 8002, South Africa

MULLER, JOHN BARTLETT, university president; b. Port Jefferson, N.Y., Nov. 8, 1940; s. Frederick Henry and Estelle May (Reeve) M.; m. Barbara Ann Schmidt, May 30, 1964 (dec. 1972); m. Lynn Anne Spongberg, Oct. 10, 1987. AB in Polit. Sci., U. Rochester, 1962; postgrad. in apologetics, Westminster Sem., Phila., 1962-63; MS in Psychology, Purdue U., 1968, PhD in Psychology, 1975. Asst. prof. psychology Roberts Wesleyan Coll., Rochester, N.Y., 1964-66, acting chmn. div. behavioral sci., dir. instl. research, 1967-70; vis. asst. prof. psychology Wabash Coll., Crawfordsville, Ind., 1970-71; research assoc. Ind. U.-Purdue U., Indpls., 1971-72; prof. psychology, v.p. for acad. affairs Hillsdale (Mich.) Coll., 1972-85; pres. BMW Assocs., Osseo, Mich., 1984-85, Bellevue (Nebr.) U., 1985—; bd. dirs. Nebr. Ind. Coll. Found., Omaha, Assn. Ind. Colls. Nebr., Lincoln; bd. advisors Wells Fargo Bank of Omaha, Applied Info. Mgmt. Inst., Am. Nat. Bank. Contbr. articles to profl. jours. and textbooks. Bd. govs. Boys Club of Omaha. Nat. Inst. Mental Health fellowship Purdue U., 1963, Nat. Tchg. fellowship Fed. Govt., 1967, Townsend fellowship U. Rochester, 1962. Mem. APA, Bellevue C. of C. (bd. dirs. 1989-95), Phi Beta Kappa, Phi Kappa Phi. Republican. Home: 13303 Lochmoor Cir Bellevue NE 68123-3770 Office: Bellevue U Office of the Pres 1000 Galvin Rd S Bellevue NE 68005-3098

MULLER, JON, archaeologist, educator; b. Salina, Kans., Oct. 23, 1941. BA, U. Kans., 1963; PhD, Harvard U., 1967. Tchg. fellow Harvard U., Cambridge, Mass., 1965-66; prof. dept. anthropology So. Ill. U., Carbondale, 1966—, assoc. dean Coll. Liberal Arts, 1997-99. Author: Archaeology of Lower Ohio River Valley, 1986 (Delta award 1987), Mississippian Political Economy, 1997 (Soc. Am. Archaeology Book award 1999). Chmn. adv. bd. Ill. Historic Sites, Springfield, 1983-89. Office: Southern Illinois Univ Dept Anthropology 4502 Carbondale IL 62901

MÜLLER, KARL ALEXANDER, retired physicist, researcher; b. Apr. 20, 1927. PhD in Physics, Swiss Fed. Inst. Tech., 1958; DSc (hon.), U. Geneva, 1987, Tech. U. Munich, 1987, U. Studi di Pavia, Italy, 1987. Project mgr. Battelle Inst., Geneva, 1958-63; lectr., titular prof., prof. U. Zurich, Switzerland, 1962-70, 1970-87, 1987—; researcher solid-state physics IBM Zurich Research Lab., Rüschlikon, Switzerland, 1963-73, mgr. dept. physics, 1973-82, fellow, 1982-85; researcher Switzerland, 1985—. Contbr. over 200 articles to tech. publs. Recipient Marcel-Benoist Found. prize, 1986, Nobel prize in physics, 1987, (with J. Georg Bednorz) Fritz London Meml. award, 1987, Dannie Heineman prize Acad. Scis. Göttingen, Fed. Republic of Germany, 1987, Robert Wichard Pohl prize German Phys. Soc., 1987, Europhysics prize Hewlett-Packard Co., 1988. Fellow Am. Phys. Soc. (Internat. prize for new materials research 1988); mem. European Phys. Soc. (mem. ferroelectricity group), Swiss Phys. Soc., Zurich Phys. Soc. (pres. 1968-69), Groupement Ampère, Nat. Acad. Scis. (fgn. assoc.). Office: IBM Zurich Rsch Lab, Saumerstrasse 4, Ruschlikon Zurich CH8803, Switzerland*

MÜLLER, KLAUS-JÜRGEN, advertising executive; b. Munich, Jan. 4, 1943; s. Albert and Elisabeth (Ertl) M.; m. Sybill Maubach, Apr. 30, 1979; children: Sophie, Sissy. Degree in econs., U. Berlin, 1968. Account mgr. O&M, Frankfurt, Germany, 1968-70, BBDO, Frankfurt, 1970; account dir. Team/BBDO, Düsseldorf, Germany, 1971-72, mgmt. supr., 1973-76; mgmt. trainee BBDO, N.Y.C., 1972-73; mgmt. ptnr., stockholder BMZ, Düsseldorf, 1976-90, mng. dir., 1990-93; chmn. Düsseldorf and Europe BMZ! FCA Europe, Düsseldorf and Paris, 1994—. Office: BMZ! FCA, PO Box 101454/Schirmer Str 72, 40211 Dusseldorf Germany

MÜLLER, MARIA BEATRIZ, psychologist; b. Santa Fe, Argentina, Dec. 9, 1950; d. Juan Antonio and Beatriz (Urondo) M.; m. Francisco Maria Amato, July 10, 1971; children: German, Maria Paola, Maria Cecilia, Maria Micaela, Lucas, Francisco. Psychologist, U. Buenos Aires, 1990. Tchr. Sch.

#30, Merlo, Argentina, 1969-72; prin. Kindergarden #15, Merlo, 1973-89; dir. Ctr. Investigacion y Asistencia Psicosomatica, Buenos Aires, 1989—; prof. U. Buenos Aires, 1995—, Meth. U., Belo Horizonte, 1997. Contbr. articles to profl. jours. Mem. APA, Soc. InterAm. Psychology, Internat. Assn. Applied Psychology. Avocations: reading, travel, flying. Home: Jujuy 326, 1722 Merlo Argentina Office: Ctr Investigation Psychosomatic, Rio Bamba 186, 1722 Merlo Argentina

MULLER, PATRICIA ANN, nursing administrator, educator; b. N.Y.C., July 22, 1943; d. Joseph H. and Rosanne (Bautz) Felter; m. David G. Smith, Mar. 19, 1988; children: Frank M. Muller III, Kimberly M. Muller. BSN, Georgetown U., 1965; MA, U. Tulsa, 1978, EdD, 1983. RN. Staff devel. coord. St. Francis Hosp., Tulsa, 1978-79, asst. dir. for nursing svc., nursing edn., 1979-82, dir. dept. edn., 1982-98; dir. dept. edn. St. Francis Health System, 1998—; mem. faculty Okla. U., Northeastern U., Tulsa U.; presenter at confs. and convs. Contbg. editor JOPAN, 1992—; contbr. articles to profl. jours. Mem. Leadership Tulsa, 1991; bd. dirs. Am. Heart Assn., Ronald McDonald House. Mem. ANA, Nat. League for Nursing, Am. Soc. for Nursing Svc. Adminstrs., Am. Soc. for Health Manpower Edn. and Tng., Okla. Nurses Assn., Okla. Orgn. of Nurse Execs. (pres. 1992-93), Sigma Theta Tau. Office: Saint Francis Hosp 6161 S Yale Ave Tulsa OK 74136-1992

MULLER, SIEGFRIED WOLFGANG, export executive; b. Essen, Germany, May 9, 1942; came to France, 1968; s. Eduard and Juliane (Grahli) M.; m. Maria Ines Munoz Gomez, Dec. 14, 1979; children: Juliana, Klaus. BS, Calif. Coast U., 1985. Programmer Eurocomp, Minden, Germany, 1963-65; sales engr. CAE, Frankfurt, Germany, 1965-68; area mgr. export Telemecanique, Rueil, France, 1968-76, SEMS, Louveciennes, France, 1976-81; export mgr. Orega, Auxonne, France, 1981-87, Videocolor, Paris, 1987-91; v.p. Valtimet, Boulogne, France, 1991—. Home: 2 Rue des Pepinieres, 92330 Sceaux France Office: Valtimet, 130 rue de Silly, 92103 Boulogne France

MÜLLER, STEPHAN GEORG, materials scientist, physicist, engineer; b. Nürnberg, Germany, May 25, 1967; s. Georg and Annelore (Herbst) M. Diploma in physics, U. Erlangen-Nürnberg, 1993, PhD in Materials Sci., 1998. Sci. employee U. Erlangen, 1993-98; crystal growth scientist CREE Inc., Durham, N.C., 1998—. Author: Production of Silicon Carbide by the Sublimation Method, 1998; contbr. articles to profl. jours. With Bundeswehr, Germany, 1986-87. Mem. Deutsche Physikalische Gesellschaft. Office: CREE Rsch Inc 4600 Silicon Dr Durham NC 27703-8475

MULLER, STEVEN, international studies educator, retired university president; b. Hamburg, Germany, Nov. 22, 1927; came to U.S., 1940, naturalized, 1949; 0. Werner Adolph and Marianne (Hartstein) M.; m. Margie Hellman, June 19, 1951 (dec. July 1999); children: Julie, Elizabeth; m. Jill E. McGovern, Feb. 5, 2000. BA, UCLA, 1948; BLitt (Rhodes scholar), Oxford (Eng.) U., 1951; PhD, Cornell U., 1958. Asst. prof. Haverford (Pa.) Coll., 1956-58; mem. faculty and adminstrn. Cornell U., 1958-71, dir. Ctr. Internat. Studies, 1961-66, v.p. pub. affairs, 1966-71; provost Johns Hopkins U., 1971-72, pres., 1972-90, pres. emeritus, 1990—, fellow Fgn. Policy Inst., disting. lectr., 1993—; cons. Dept. Def., 1962-67, ACDA, 1967-77; bd. dirs. Orgn. Resources Counselors, Inc., Law-Gibb Inc., Atlantic Coun. of the U.S. Author: Documents on European Government, 1963; co-editor: From Occupation to Cooperation, 1992, In Search of Germany, 1996; editor: Universities in the Twenty First Century, 1996. Trustee, chmn. St. Mary's Coll.; trustee German Marshall Fund of the U.S. Decorated comdr. Order of Merit (Fed. Republic of Germany), commendatore Republic of Italy. Mem. Am. Inst. Contemporary German Studies (co-chmn.), Coun. Fgn. Rels., Am. Polit. Sci. Assn., Internat. Inst. Strategic Studies, Am. Assn. Rhodes Scholars, Phi Beta Kappa, Cosmos Club (Washington). Office: Johns Hopkins U Sch Advanced Internat Studies 1619 Massachusetts Ave NW Washington DC 20036-2213

MULLER, THOMAS EDWARD, social scientist, writer; b. Nairobi, Kenya, Dec. 13, 1939; arrived in Australia, 1994; s. Bohuslav and Marie Claire (De La Reina) M.; m. Edith Berta Saatkamp, Nov. 22, 1966 (div. June 1994); 1 child, Monica Silvie; m. Miyuki Tajiri, Mar. 21, 1997; 1 child, Tommi von Manner. Licentiate, Nat. Coll. Rubber Tech., London, 1960, Instn. Rubber Industry, London, 1960; MBA, Simon Fraser U., Vancouver, Can., 1975; PhD, U. B.C., Vancouver, Can., 1982. Mng. dir. Festa Co. Ltd., Tehran, Iran, 1963-71; sr. market analyst Esso Petroleum, Vancouver, 1973-75; asst. prof. mktg. Concordia U., Montreal, Can., 1979-84; assoc. prof. mktg. U. Guelph, Can., 1984-86; from assoc. prof. to prof. mktg. McMaster U., Hamilton, Can., 1987-94; prof., found. chair in mktg. Griffith U., Gold Coast, Australia, 1994-2000, head Sch. Mktg. and Mgmt., 1994-98, adj. prof., 2000—; divsn. chmn. mktg. Adminstrv. Scis. Assn. Can., 1986-87; bd. dirs. Internat. Soc. for Quality-of-Life Studies, Blacksburg, Va., 1994-98; expert commentator on aging baby boomers on network TV, radio and print, Australia, Can., U.S.A., 1980—. Author: (with M. Laroche and G.S. Kindra) Consumer Behaviour in Canada, 1989 (Can. Studies Writing award Sec. State Can. 1986, 87), 2d edit., 1994, French edit., 1991, 2d French edit., 1996; editor: Marketing, vol. 7, 1986; co-editor: Asia Pacific Advances in Consumer Research, vol. 4, 2000; contbr. numerous articles to profl. jours. Chairperson Seminar on Consumer Issues for Older People, Govt. Queensland, Office Aging, Southport, Australia, 1997. Recipient Outstanding Mktg. Tchr. award Acad. Mktg. Sci., 2000. Fellow Australian Inst. Mgmt., Australian Mktg. Inst. (councilor Queensland br. 1994-96); mem. World Future Soc. (profl.). Avocations: learning languages, dancing, alpine skiing, scuba diving, traveling. E-mail: T.muller@mailbox.gu.edu.au. Home: PO Box 905, Runaway Bay QLD 4216, Australia

MÜLLER, TORSTEN, soil scientist, educator; b. Hesse, Germany, July 12, 1961; s. Herbert and Helga Müller; m. Marianne Brunke, Mar. 10, 1995. Degree as Agrl. Engr., Georg-August U., Goettingen, Germany, 1989, Dr of Agrl. Sci. in Soil Sci., 1992. Rsch. asst. Inst. Soil Scis., Georg-August U., 1989-92; asst. rsch. prof. sect. soil water and plant nutrition Royal Vet. and Agrl. U., Copenhagen, Denmark, 1993-96, assoc. rsch. prof. plant nutrition and soil fertility lab., 1996-98, assoc. prof., 1998—. Mem. German Soil Sci. Soc., Danish Soil Sci. Soc., Internat. Union Soil Scis., Nordic Assn. Agrl. Scis. Reformed Protestant Christian. E-mail: tm@kvl.dk. Office: Royal Vet U/Plant Nutrition, Thorvaldsenvej 40, DK-1871 Copenhagen Denmark

MÜLLER, ULRICH, chemistry educator; b. Bogota, Colombia, July 6, 1940; s. Fritz and Maria (Hell) M.; m. Elke Bayer; children: Antje, Jan, Marcel. Diploma in chemistry, U. Stuttgart, 1963, PhD, 1967; postgrad., Purdue U., 1964-65. Sci. asst. U. Karlsruhe, 1967-70; sci. asst. U. Marburg, 1970-72, prof. chemistry, 1972-92, 2000—; prof. chemistry U. Kassel, 1992-99; vis. prof. U. Costa Rica, 1975-77, lectr., 1974, 79; lectr. U. de Santa Maria, 1982, U. de Conception, Chile, 1986. Translator: Chemistry, 1986; author: Inorganic Structural Chemistry, 1991 (German Lit. prize 1992); co-author: Schwingungsspektroskopie, 1982, Schwingungsfrequenzen I, 1982, II, 1986. Mem. Gesellschaft Deutscher Chemiker, Deutsche Gesellschaft für Kristallographie. Office: U Marburg, Fachbereich of Chemie, 35032 Marburg Germany

MULLER, WILLIAM ALBERT, III, library director; b. Savannah, Ga., Jan. 1, 1943; s. William Albert Jr. and Julia Catherine (Cleary) M.; m. Claudya Barbara Burkett, Dec. 12, 1965 (div. 1986); 1 child, Martha Genevieve; m. Pamala Qualls, Apr. 9, 1988; 1 child, Tabitha Wade. BA, Ga. So. Coll., 1966; MLS, Emory U., 1969. Dir. War Woman Regional Libr., Elberton, Ga., 1969-73; rsch. libr. City of Savannah, 1973-75; dir. Mason County Pub. Libr., Point Pleasant, W.Va., 1976-78; pub. rels. cons. Eastern Shore Regional Libr., Salisbury, Md., 1978-81; dir. Brooke County Pub. Libr., Wellsburg, W.Va., 1982-84, McDowell Pub. Libr., Welch, W.Va., 1984-88, Bristol (Va.) Pub. Libr., 1988—; sec. So. W.Va. Libr. Automation Corp., Beckley, 1984-87, pres. 1987-88, S.W. Info. Network Group, Abingdon, Va., 1990-91, treas. (swing) 1993—. Fundraiser Paramount Fund, Bristol, 1989; acct. exec. United Way Fund of Bristol, 1991; bd. dirs. Mid-Atlantic Chamber Orch., Bristol, 1988-92, treas., 1992; bd. dirs. Bristol Preservation Soc., 1988-98, Nat. Ctr. for Quality, 1992-98, Main St. Bristol, 1991-95, treas., 1994; bd. dirs. Jr. Achievement, 1992-99, pres., 1997-99; bd. dirs. Vol. Bristol, 1998—; bd. dirs., vol. chair Racefest 98, 99. Mem. ALA, Southeastern Libr. Assn., Va. Libr. Assn., Rotary Internat. (club pres. 1980-81). Democrat. Avocations: gardening, cabinetry, photography, traveling, model railroads. Home: 706 Piedmont Ave Bristol VA 24201-3446 Office: Bristol Pub Libr 701 Goode St Bristol VA 24201-4199

MÜLLER, WOLFGANG HELMUT, engineering educator, researcher; b. Wiesbaden, Germany, Apr. 13, 1959; s. Helmut August and Angela Klara (Gerwald) M. Diploma in Physics, Tech. U. of Berlin, 1982, Dr. rer. nat., 1986. Teaching asst. Tech. U. of Berlin, 1982-86; devel. engr. Siemens, Munich, Germany, 1986-88; rsch. asst. HFI-Berlin, 1988-90; vis. scholar Stanford U., Stanford, Calif., 1990; guest researcher U. Calif., Santa Barbara, 1990-91; sr. engr. Failure Analysis Assocs., Inc., Menlo Park, Calif., 1991-93; lectr. U. Paderborn (Germany), 1993; reader Heriot-Watt U., Edinburgh, Eng., 1993-99; prof. Heriot-Watt U., Edinburgh, 1999—; cons. Siemens-Berlin. Recipient Jean Mandel award Nat. Ctr. Sci. Rsch., Paris, 1985, Joachim Tiburtius award Senate of Berlin, 1987; Max-Kade Found. grantee, 1990-91. Mem. ASME, ASTM, Gesellschaft für Angewandte Mathematik und Mechanik, SMTA, DHV. Office: U Heriot-Watt U, Dept Mech and Chem, Edinburgh EH14 4AS, Scotland

MÜLLER-MERBACH, HEINER ERICH, educator; b. Hamburg, Fed. Republic Germany, June 28, 1936; s. Erich Müller and Gertrud Müller-Merbach; m. Uta Schade, May 16, 1969; children: Jens, Mareile. Diploma Wirtschaftsingenieur, Technische U. Darmstadt, Fed. Republic Germany, 1960, PhD, 1962. Prof. U. Mainz, Fed. Republic of Germany, 1967-71, Technische U. Darmstadt, 1971-83, U. Kaiserslautern, Fed. Republic of Germany, 1983—; hon. prof. Tongji U., Shanghai, Peoples Republic of China, 1986. Author: Operations Research, 1969; editor-in-chief (jour.): Technologie & Management, 1985-97; also author of over 380 sci. publs., including 14 books. Mem. Internat. Fedn. Operational Research Socs. (v.p. 1974-76, pres. 1983-85, past pres. 1986-88), Inst. Mgmt. Scis. (council mem. 1986-88), Verband Deutscher Wirtschaftsingenieure (pres. 1985-87), Tech. Coun. of State Adminstrn. (co-chmn. 1986—). Home: Am Löwentor 11, D-64287 Darmstadt Germany Office: U Kaiserslautern, PO Box 3049, D-67653 Kaiserslautern Germany

MÜLLER-SCHIMPFLE, MARKUS PETER, radiologist, researcher; b. Elz, Hesse, Germany, Dec. 16, 1962; s. Paul Georg and Klara Franziska (Michel) M.; m. Gudrun Ursula Schimpfle, Oct. 21, 1989; children: Lukas Paul, Elias Vinzenz Cyrill. MD, Dr, U. Tübingen, Germany, 1990. Cert. radiologist, Germany. Resident fellow German Cancer Rsch. Ctr., Heidelberg, 1990-92; sci. asst. dept. diagnostic radiology U. Tübingen, 1992-98, assoc. prof. dept. diagnostic radiology, 1998—. Contbr. articles to med. jours., including Radiology, Am. Jour. Roentgenology, Jour. MRI. Grantee European Congress Radiology, Vienna, Austria, 1997. Mem. German Roentgen Soc., Internat. Soc. Magnetic Resonance Medicine, German Soc. Senology. Roman Catholic. Avocations Ludwig van Beethoven, Photography. Office: U Tübingen, Hoppe Seyler Strasse 3, 72076 Tübingen Germany

MÜLLER-SCHWEINITZER, ELSE ELISE, pharmacologist, researcher; b. Berlin, Mar. 30, 1936; arrived in Switzerland, 1971; d. Arthur and Else (Wollgast) Schweinitzer; m. Hans Martin Müller, Dec. 23, 1969 (dec. 1983); 1 child, Sandra. MD, Free U. Berlin, 1965, postgrad. in orthopedics, 1970. Asst. physician Hosp., Berlin, 1965-70; rschr. Sandoz Pharma Ltd., Basel, Switzerland, 1971-94; rschr. clin. pharmacology U. Hosp., Basel, Switzerland, 1995-00, rschr. cardiovasc. surgery, 2000—. Contbr. chpts. to books; numerous articles to profl. publs. Recipient award for alternative methods to reduce use of animals in pharmacol. rsch. German Ministry of Family and Health, 1986. Mem. German Pharmacol. Soc., Soc. for Cryobiology. Avocations: skiing, photography, electronics, woodworking, painting. Home: Eimattstrasse 28, CH-4436 Oberdorf BL, Switzerland

MULLERY, GEOFFREY PATRICK, computer consultant; b. Shepperton, Middlesex, Eng., Feb. 16, 1942; s. Austin and Rose Elizabeth (Bosley) M.; m. Margaret Patricia Bowdery, Jan. 25, 1969; children: Teresa, Timothy. BSc with spl. honors, Bristol (Eng.) U., 1964. Sci. officer Royal Aircraft Establishment, Farnborough, Eng., 1964-69; systems engr. Easams, Camberley, Eng., 1969-70, Scicon, London, 1970-72; sr. group leader Ferranti, Bracknell, Eng., 1972-77; cons. Sys. Designers Ltd., Camberley, 1977-83; mng. dir. Systemic Methods Ltd, Farnborough, 1983—; com. mem. European Workshop on Indsl. Computing Sys., Brussels, 1982-83, Dept. of Industry Starts Initiative, London, 1983-84. Co-author: Distributed Systems: Methods & Tools for Specification, 1984. Office: Systemic Methods Ltd, 12 Firs Close, Farnborough Hampshire, England GU14 6SR

MULLEY, ROBERT CLAUDE, agricultural studies educator, researcher; b. Camden, NSW, Australia, Oct. 10, 1951; s. Albert Graham and Daphne Jean (Smart) M.; m. Dianne Cheryl Tildsley, Oct. 9, 1976; children: Paul, Adam. BA, MacQuarie U., Sydney, 1977; MSc in Agr., Sydney U., 1983, PhD, 1989. Tech. officer Sydney U., 1970-91; sr. lectr., rschr., cons., dir. undergrad. studies U. Western Sydney, Hawkesbury, NSW, 1991—, dean faculty environ. mgmt. and agr., 1998—; rschr. U. Sydney, 1970-91. Eleanor Sophia Wood Traveling fellow U. Sydney, 1990, life membership NSW Deer Farmers Assn., 1989. Mem. Australian Inst. Biologists, Camden A H & I Soc., Australian Soc. Animal Prodn., New Zealand Vet. Assn. (deer br.), Rotary (pres. Camden club 1997-98). Avocations: shooting, fishing, camping. Office: U Western Sydney, Bourke St, Richmond NSW 2753, Australia

MULLIGAN, MARK, geographer, educator; b. Nuneaton, Warwicksh, Eng., May 30, 1970; s. David Charles and Filomena Bambina (De Paola) M. BSc in Geography with honors, U. Bristol, Eng., 1991; PhD in Geography, King's Coll., London, 1996. Lectr. in geography King's Coll., London, 1994—. Contbr. articles to profl. jours., chpts. to books. Recipient numerous rsch. grants. Mem. Brit. Ecol. Soc., Internat. Soc. Ecol. Modeling. Office: King's College of London, Dept Geography, London WC2R 2LS, England

MULLIGAN, TIMOTHY HAYDEN, public relations executive, writer; b. Wilkes-Barre, Pa., May 21, 1938; s. Edward Bowman and Celia Hayden (Rhoads) M. BA, Yale U., 1962. Sr. editor Good Housekeeping, N.Y.C., 1966-75; mng. editor Family Weekly, N.Y.C., 1975-85; writer N.Y.C., 1985-88; sr. press officer Met. Mus. Art, N.Y.C., 1988-90; dir. comm. N.Y. State Coun. on the Arts, N.Y.C., 1990-95; dir. external affairs The Bard Grad. Ctr. for Studies in Decorative Arts, Design & Culture, 1995—. Author: Travelers Guide to the Hudson River Valley, 1985, 91, 95, 99, Virginia: A History Guide, 1986, Travelers Guide to Western New England and the Connecticut River Valley, 1994. Office: The Bard Grad Ctr 18 W 86th St New York NY 10024-3602

MULLIN, LEO FRANCIS, airline executive; b. Concord, Mass., Jan. 26, 1943; s. Leo F. and Alice L. (Fearns) M.; m. Leah J. Malmberg, Sept. 10, 1966; children: Jessica, Matthew. AB, Harvard U., 1964, MS, 1965, MBA, 1967. Assoc. McKinsey & Co., Washington, 1967-73, prin., 1973-76; sr. v.p. strategic planning Consol. Rail Corp., Phila., 1976-78; sr. v.p. 1st Chgo. Corp., 1981-84, exec. v.p., 1984-91; chmn. Am. Nat. Bank and Trust Co. Chgo. subs. 1st Chgo., Chgo., 1991-93; pres., COO 1st Chgo. Corp., Chgo., 1993-95; vice chmn. Unicom/Commonwealth Edison, Chgo., 1995—; CEO, pres., now chmn. Delta Airlines, Atlanta, 1997—; bd. dirs. Pittway Corp., Inland Steel Industries, Inc. Vice chmn. Chgo. Urban League, 1993—; chmn. bd. trustees Field Mus. Natural History, 1994—; bd. dirs. Chgo. chpt. Juvenile Diabetes Found., 1985—, Met. Planning Coun., 1983—, Children's Meml. Hosp., Chgo., 1989—, Chgo. Coun. Fgn. Rels., 1994—; mem. Chgo. Econ. Devel. Commn., 1992-95; trustee Northwestern U., 1992—. Mem. Chgo. Club, Harvard Club of Chgo., Econ. Club of Chgo. Office: Delta Air Lines Inc Office of Pres 1030 Delta Blvd Dept 940 Atlanta GA 30354-1989

MULLIN, TOM, physics educator; b. Broxburn, Scotland, Sept. 5, 1949; s. Joseph Michael and Elsie Mullin; m. Sylvia Janet Wernick, Nov. 26, 1970; children: Zoe, Graham. Grad. Inst. Physics, Napier U., Edinburgh, Scotland, 1975; PhD, Edinburgh U., 1978. Rsch. fellow Oxford (Eng.) U., 1980-91, lectr., 1991-96; prof. physics Manchester (Eng.) U., 1996—; cons. DeBeers, Eng. Editor: Nature of Chaos, 1993. Avocations: cycling, walking, opera, music.

MULLINGS, ANTHONY MORTIMER ALEXANDER, medical educator, consultant; b. Mt. Carey, St. James, Jamaica, July 3, 1946; s. George Samuel Agustus and Eunice Coreen (Smith) M.; m. Dorothy Mirelda Patrick, Jan. 6, 1979; children: David, Robert, Shannon. MBBS, U. W. Indies, Kingston, Jamaica, 1977, DM in Ob-Gyn, 1984; MPH, U. Miami, 1998. Lectr. U. W.I., Kingston, Jamaica, 1984-97, sr. lectr., 1997—; cons. U. Hosp. W. Indies, Kingston, 1984—, head dept. Ob-Gyn, divsn. Ob-Gyn, 1991-96. Contbr. articles to med. jours., med. manual. Dir. Jamaica Cancer Soc., Kingston, 1984—, editor, publ. newsletter, 1987—; mem. mgmt. Ch. of the Ascension, Kingston, 1976-82, vol. dr., 1982-89. Fellow UNICEF, 1993. Fellow Am. Coll. Ob-Gyn; mem. Am. Soc. Colposcopy and Cervical Pathology, Am. Inst. Ultrasound in Medicine. Anglican. Avocations: reading, driving, gardening. Office: U W Indies, Mona, Kingston 7, Jamaica

MULLINGS, SEYMOUR, Jamaican government official; b. Cave Valley, St. Ann, May 12, 1931; married; 1 child. Student, Jamaica Coll. Commd. land surveyor Survey Dept. Govt. of Jamaica, 1955-58; mem. nat. exec. coun. People's Nat. Party, 1967—; mem. for S.E. St. Ann Parliament, 1969-83, 89—; min. of agr. and pub. works, min. of local govt., min. of health and social svcs., min. in charge of electoral affairs Govt. of Jamaica, 1970s, shadow min. of fin., 1980-88; v.p. People's Nat. Party, 1982—; min. of pub. svc. Govt. of Jamaica, 1989-90, min. of fin., 1990, min. of agr., 1990—; leader govt. bus. Ho. of Reps., 1991—; dep. prime min. Govt. of Jamaica, 1993—; min. fgn. affairs and fgn. trade Govt. of Jamaica, Kingston, min. land and the environment. Office: Ministry of Fgn Affairs and Fgn Trade, POB 624, 21 Dominica Drive, Kingston 5, Jamaica Address: 2 Hagley Pk Rd, Kingston 10, Jamaica*

MULLINS, OBERA, retired microbiologist; b. Egypt, Miss., Feb. 15, 1927; d. Willie Ree and Maggie Sue (Orr) Gunn; m. Charles Leroy Mullins, Nov. 2, 1952; children: Mary Artavia, Arthur Curtis, Charles Leroy, Charlester Teresa, William Hellman. BS, Chgo. State U., 1974; MS in Health Sci. Edn., Governors State U., 1981. Med. technician, microbiologist Chgo. Health Dept., Chgo., 1976—, now pers. asst. III, to 1999; ret., 1999. Mem. AAUW, Am. Soc. Clin. Pathologists (cert. med. lab. technician), Ill. Soc. Lab. Technicians. Roman Catholic. Home: 9325 S Marquette Ave Chicago IL 60617-4131

MULLINS, W. STAN, artist, cultural ambassador; b. Cherry Point, N.C., July 1, 1964; s. Robert R. and Carolyn Hankins Mullins. BFA, U. Ga., 1987, MFA, 1989. Internat. artist Stan Mullins, Inc.; cultural amb. various orgns.; exec. dir. Athens (Ga.) Ctr. for Internat. Arts; freelance artist, assoc. adminstr. Waters Design Group, N.Y.C.; developer, mem. Mus. Modern Art, N.Y.C. Exhibited in one-man shows: Galleria Del Sole, Perugia, Italy, 1991, Candide Gallery, Atlanta, 1992, The Athens Coffee House, Athens, Ga., 1993, French Cultural Ctr., Kigali, Rwanda, 1994, The Main Gallery, U. Ga., Athens, Ga., 1994, The King Plow Arts Ctr., Atlanta, 1995, Alliance Francaise d'Atlanta, 1995, The Renaissance Gallery, Washington, DC, 1995, Eklektikos Gallery, Washington, DC, 1996, The Athens Classic Ctr., 1996, La Boulangere, N.Y.C., 1997, Hearon-Hempenstall Gallery, Jersey City, 1997, Jersey City City Hall, 1998, Galleria d'Arte G. Severini, Cortona, Italy, 1999, East/West Bistro, Athens, 1999, Classic Ctr. Main Ballroom, Athens, 1999, Belenky Gallery, N.Y.C., 2000, State Botanical Garden of Ga., Athens, 2000; exhibited in group shows: Galleria Renata, Chgo., 1990, Provincia di Perugia, Italy, 1991, Coll. Square, Athens, 1994, Mus. Contemporary Art, Washington, DC., 1995, Kearon-Hempenstall Gallery, Jersey City, 1997, Georgetown Hilton, Washington, DC., 1997, The Sharjah Art Mus., United Arab Emirates, 2000, Firehall Gallery, Athens, 2000; Artist (children's book) Under the Back Yard Sky, 1995. Recipient Le Depozitione, The Ch. of the Holy Spirit, Cortona, Italy, 1989; named Featured Artist, CNN, 1992, 93, 94, N.Y. Times, N.Y.C., 1999, Majii with the Mountain Gorillas of Rowanda, 2000; exhbns. include French Cultural Ctr., Kigali, Rwanda, King Plow Arts Ctr., Atlanta, La Rocca Paolina, Perugia, Italia, Belenky Gallery, N.Y.C. E-mail: stanarts@aol.com. Home: 650 Pulaski St Athens GA 30601-2349

MULLIS, KARY BANKS, biochemist; b. Lenoir, N.C., Dec. 28, 1944; s. Cecil Banks Mullis and Bernice Alberta (Barker) Fredericks; children: Christopher, Jeremy, Louise. BS in Chemistry, Ga. Inst. Tech, 1966; PhD in Biochemistry, U. Calif., Berkeley, 1973; DSc (hon.), U. S.C., 1994. Lectr. biochemistry U. Calif., Berkeley, 1972; postdoctoral fellow U. Calif., San Francisco, 1977-79, U. Kans. Med. Sch., Kansas City, 1973-76; scientist Cetus Corp., Emeryville, Calif., 1979-86; dir. molecular biology Xytronyx, Inc., San Diego, 1986-88; cons. Specialty Labs. Inc., Amersham, Inc., Chiron Inc. and various others, Calif., 1988-96; chmn. StarGene, Inc., San Rafael, Calif.; v.p. Histotec, Inc., Cedar Rapids, Iowa; v.p. molecular biology chemistry Vyrex Inc., La Jolla, Calif.; Disting. vis. prof. U. S.C. Coll. of Sci. and Math. Contbr. articles to profl. jours.; patentee in field. Recipient Preis Biochemische Analytik award German Soc. Clin. Chem., 1990, Allan award Am. Soc. of Human Genetics, 1990, award Gairdner Found. Internat., 1991, Nat. Biotech. award, 1991, Robert Koch award, 1992, Chiron Corp. Biotechnology Rsch. award Am. Soc. Microbiology, 1992, Japan prize Sci. and Tech. Found. Japan, 1993, Nobel Prize in Chemistry, Nobel Foundation, 1993; named Calif. Scientist of Yr., 1992, Scientist of Yr., R&D Mag., 1991. Mem. Am. Chem. Soc., Am. Acad. Achievement, Inst. Further Study (dir. 1983—). Achievements include invention of Polymerase Chain Reaction (PCR). Office: PO Box 333 A Encinitas CA 92024*

MULONDO, LARRY YAWE, management consultant, educator, researcher; b. Kampala, Buganda, Uganda, Jan. 18, 1943; s. James Kidza and Ida Joan (Nakaketo) Mukasa; m. Jane Frances Nandaula, Jan. 5, 1967; children: Florence, Richard, Georgina, Carol, Eddie. BS in Econs., U. Hull, Eng., 1963; postgrad. diploma mgmt., Glasgow (Eng.) U., 1967; MA in Devel. Econs., Inst. for Econ. Devel. Studies, Naples, Italy, 1986. Cert. export promotion, indsl. project planning. Sec. Uganda Govt., Kampala, 1963-64, East African Community, Nairobi, Kenya, 1964-65; corp. exec. Uganda Devel. Corp., Kampala, 1967, head div., 1970-73, asst. mgr., 1974-75; gen. mgr. several cos. Kampala, 1976-84; mktg. mgr. Gava Property Agy., Kampala, 1984-85; prin. cons. M&M Consultancy, Kampala, 1987—; part-time lectr. various instns., Kampala, 1974—; bd. dirs. numerous cos., 1969—. Author study manuals in econs. and bus. adminstrn.; mem. editorial bds.; mem. jour. adv. bds. Chmn. Internat. Confederation of Christian Family Movement, Uganda; adv. several ch. bodies and couns. Mem. Brit. Inst. Mgmt., Uganda Econ. Assn., East African Econ. Assn. Avocations: gardening, social work, reading, writing, travel. Home: PO Box 8240, Kampala Uganda

MULRONEY, BRIAN (MARTIN BRIAN MULRONEY), former prime minister of Canada; b. Baie Comeau, Que., Can., Mar. 20, 1939; s. Benjamin and Irene (O'Shea) M.; m. Mila Pivnicki, 1973; 4 children. BA, St. Francis Xavier U., LLD, 1979; LLL, U. Laval, Que.; LLD, Meml. U. Nfld., Nfld., 1980, U. W.I., 1993, Tel Aviv U., 1994, Ctrl. Conn. State U., 1994, Barry U., 1995. Ptnr. Ogilvy Renault, Montreal, 1965-76; exec. v.p. Iron Ore Co. Can., Montreal, 1977-83, Iron Ore Co. of Can., Montreal, Que., 1976-77; pres. Iron Ore Co. Can., Montreal, 1977-83; mem. Parliament Can. from Ctrl. N.S., Ottawa, Ont., 1983-84; mem. Parliament Can. from Manicouagan, 1984-88, mem. Parliament Can. from Charlevoix, 1988-93, leader of Her Majesty's Loyal Opposition, 1983-84; prime minister Can., 1984-93; royal commr. Cliche Commn. investigating violence in Que. constrn. industry, 1974; sr. ptnr. Ogilvy Renault, Montreal, 1993—; chmn. internat. adv. bd. Barrick Gold Corp., The Chase Manhattan Corp.; mem. internat. adv. coun. Power Corp. Can.; mem. adv. bd. The China Internat. Trust and Investment Corp.; mem. Bombadier/Aerospace Group N.Am., Violy Ptnrs. and Assocs., US&A Comm. Ptnrs. III, L.P., Hicks Muse Tate & Furst Ind. Newspapers, PLC, Sun Media Corp.; trustee Freedom Forum; mem. internat. adv. coun. Inst. Internat. Studies; bd. dirs. Archer Daniels Midland Co., Barrick Gold Corp., Chase Manhattan Corp. N.Y., The Trizec Hahn Corp., Power Corp., Quebecor World Inc., Quebecor Inc., Telesys., Inc., Cognicase; chmn. Forbes Global (N.Y.C.). Author: Where I Stand, 1983. Trustee Montreal Heart Inst., Freedom Forum, George Bush Presdl. Libr.; mem. internat. adv. coun. Les Hautes Etudes Commerciales l'Université de Montréal, Inst. Internat. Studies, Stanford U., First Amendment Ctr. Vanderbilt U., Ctr. Strategic and Internat. Studies, Washington. Recipient Companion of the Order of Can. Office: Ogilvy Renault, 1981 McGill College Ave Ste 1100, Montreal, PQ Canada H3A 3C1

MULROY, THOMAS ROBERT, JR., lawyer; b. Evanston, Ill., June 26, 1946; s. Thomas Robert and Dorothy (Reiner) M.; m. Elaine Mazzone, Aug.

16, 1969. Student, Loyola U., Rome, 1966; BA, U. Santa Clara, Calif., 1968; JD, Loyola U., Chgo., 1972. Bar: Ill. 1973, U.S. Dist. Ct. (no. dist.) Ill. 1973, U.S. Ct. Appeals (7th cir.) 1973. Asst. U.S. atty. No. Dist. Ill., Chgo., 1972-76; ptnr. Jenner & Block, Chgo. 1976—, chmn. products liability group; adj. prof. Northwestern U. Sch. Law, Chgo., 1978-85, Loyola U. Sch. Law, 1983—, DePaul U. Sch. Law, Chgo., Nova U. Ctr. for Study of Law. Editor: Annotated Guide to Illinois Rules of Professional Conduct; contbr. articles to profl. jours.; bd. dirs. Loyola U. Trial Advocacy Workshop, 1982—, Legal Assistance Found., Ill. Inst. for Continued Legal Edn.; chmn. inquiry panel Ill. Atty. Registration and Disciplinary Commn., spl. counsel, 1989—. Mem. Chgo. Crime Commn., 1978—. Mem. ABA, (torts and ins. pratcie, chmn. rules and evidence com.), Am. Judicature Soc., Fed. Trial Bar, Legal Club Chgo., Law Club, 7th Fed. Cir. Bar Assn., Chgo. Bar Assn., Ill. Assn. Def. Trial Counsel, Ill. Bar Assn. Clubs: Univ., Execs. of Chgo., Union League. Office: Jenner & Block 1 E Ibm Plz Fl 42 Chicago IL 60611-3586*

MULTHAUP, MERREL KEYES, artist; b. Cedar Rapids, Iowa, Sept. 27, 1922; d. Stephen Dows and Edna Gertrude (Gard) Keyes; m. Robert Hansen Multhaup, Apr. 7, 1944; children: Eric Stephen, Robert Bruce. Student, State U. Iowa, 1942-43, Rice U., 1971. Tchg. faculty Summit (N.J.) Art Assn., 1956-60; art instr. studio classes Springfield, N.J., 1954-55, Bloomfield (N.J.) Art Group, 1955-56, Westport, Conn., 1962-63; tchg. faculty Hunterdon Art Ctr., Clinton, N.J., 1985-92. One-woman shows include Coriell Gallery, 1995; exhibited in group shows at Nat. Assn. Women Artists, N.Y.C., 1957-2000 (awards in figure painting), Hartford (Conn.) Athanaeum Mus., 1961 (1st prize), Highgate Gallery, N.Y.C., Waverly Gallery, N.Y.C., Leicester Gallery, London, Silvermine Gallery, Conn., Pendut Gallery, Tex., Benedict Gallery, Sidney Rothman Gallery, N.J., Stamford (Conn.) Mus., Bridgeport (Conn.) Mus., Montclair (N.J.) Mus., Newark Mus., Coriell Gallery, Albuquerque; (traveling exhibit) Nat. Assn. Women Artists, 1996—, Travel USA, 1999, New World Art Ctr., N.Y.C., 1998-99, Gallery Art 54, N.Y.C., 1997, Atelier 14 Gallery, N.Y.C., 2000; also numerous commd. portraits. Bd. dirs., exhbn. chmn. Summit Art Assn., 1950-60, Silvermine Guild of Art, New Canaan, Conn., 1960-64; bd. dirs. Artist's Equity of N.J., 1977-84, chmn. state-wide event, 1983, 86; artist's adv. coun. Hunterdon Art Ctr., Clinton, 1988-92; pres. Four Hills Neighbors, 1998-2000. Recipient awards in juried exhbns. in Iowa, Pa., N.J., Conn., N.Y.C. Mem. Nat. Mus. for Women in Arts (charter mem.), Nat. Assn. Women Artists Inc. (awards for figure painting 1957, 80-89). Avocations: entertaining, sewing, singing, playing the piano, reading. Home and Studio: 1321 Stagecoach Rd SE Albuquerque NM 87123-4320

MULTON, FRANCK, computer scientist; b. Chatellerault, France, Oct. 15, 1971; s. Multon Richard and Daniele (Muller) M.; m. Gwenaelle Le Buzulier, Oct. 24, 1998. Grad. in computer sci., U. Poitiers, 1991; DSc, U. Rennes, 1994, PhD, 1998. Asst. prof. U. Rennes, France, 1998—. Mem. Internat. Soc. Biomechs. in Sport. Office: U Rennes 2 UFRAPS, Av Charles Tillon, Rennes France 35044

MULUZI, BAKILI, Malawian government official; b. Mar. 17, 1943. Regional sec., then branch sec. Malawi Congress Party, 1959-60, sec. gen., adminstrv. sec.; elected M.P., 1975; parliamentary sec. Ministry of Youth and Culture, 1976; min. edn. Republic of Malawi, Lilongwe, 1976-77, min. without portfolio, 1977-82, min. transport and comm., 1982, pres., 1994—; prin. Nasawa Tech. Coll., 1973-75; mem. Commonwealth Parliamentary Assn., 1975. Mem. United Dem. Front (pres. 1992—). Mem. United Democratic Front. Office: Office Pres. Private Bag 301, Capital City Lilongwe 3, Malawi*

MULVEY, CHRISTOPHER JOHN, mathematics educator, researcher; b. Bristol, Eng., Sept. 4, 1946; s. John Allen and Marjory Irene Maud (Anderson) M.; m. Jean Frances Uzzell, Nov. 23, 1968; children: Sarah Louise, James Alexander. BA, Cambridge (Eng.) U., 1967, MA, 1970; MSc, U. Sheffield, Eng., 1968; DPhil, U Sussex, Brighton, Eng., 1970. Lectr. math. U. Sussex, 1970—; vis. asst. prof. McGill U., Montreal, Que., Can., 1972-73; vis. assoc. prof. Columbia U., N.Y.C., 1975-76, vis. prof., 1980-81; vis. prof. Cath. U. Louvain, Belgium, 1983-86; bd. dirs. LMS Pub. Ltd.; project coodr. Euromath. project European Commn., Brussels, 1986; sec. Com. Heads Univ. Depts. Math., U.K., 1986-88. Editor: Applications of Sheaves, 1979, Jour. Pure and Applied Algebra, 1976-96; also numerous articles. Scholar Trevelyan Trust, 1964-67; grantee Sci. and Engring. Rsch. Coun., Royal Soc., Brit. Coun., NSF, NATO, European Commn. Mem. London Math. Soc. (gen. sec. 1983-89, coun. 1983-91), European Math. Soc. (coun. 1990-97), European Math. Trust (exec. sec. 1987-91). Avocations: family, music, travel, walking. Home: Aldsworth, Lewes Rd, East Sussex, Ringmer BN8 5ER, England Office: U Sussex Sch Math Scis, Falmer, Brighton BN1 9QH, England

MULVEY, GERALD JOHN, telecommunication engineering administrator, meteorologist educator; b. Cambria Heights, N.Y., Dec. 20, 1949; s. George Patrick and Estelle Florence M.; m. Katherine Louise Strick, July 7, 1973. BS in Physics, York Coll., Jamaica, N.Y., 1971; MS in Atmospheric Sci., SUNY, Albany, 1973; PhD in Atmospheric Sci., Colo. State U., 1977. Cert. cons. meteorologist, CCM. Rsch. assoc. dept. atmospheric sci. Colo. State U., 1977-78; mgr. dept. atmospheric physics Meteorology Rsch., Inc., Altadena, Calif., 1978-80; sr. rsch. engr. Lockheed Martin Missiles and Space, Sunnyvale, Calif., 1980-97; advanced programs mgr. Lockheed Martin Western Devel. Labs., 1997-98; lectr. dept. geoscis. San Francisco State U., 1995-98; advanced programs mgr. Lockheed Martin Global Telecomm., Sunnyvale, Calif., 1998-99; prin. sys. engr. DIVA Sys. Corp., Redwood City, Calif., 1999—. Co-author: Environmental Impacts of Artificial Ice Nucleating Agents, 1978; contbr. articles to profl. jours. including Analytical Chemistry and Jour. Applied Meteorology. Commr. Cupertino (Calif.) Libr. Commn., 1989-93; v.p. bd. dirs. Cupertino Libr. Found., 2000—. Mem. AAAS, Am. Meteorological Soc., Internat. Soc. Measurement and Control (v.p. Santa Clara valley 1996-97), Sigma Xi. Roman Catholic. Achievements include development of long range transport of active cloud nucleating agents. Office: DIVA Sys Corp 800 Saginaw Dr Redwood City CA 94063-4740

MULVEY, LAURA MARY ALICE, film studies educator; b. Oxford, Eng., Aug. 15, 1941; d. Charles Docherty and Sylvia Mary Alice (Lucas) M.; m. Peter Wollen; 1 child, Chad Stephen Khalid. BA in History with honors, Oxford U., 1963. Lectr. Bulmershe Coll., Reading, Eng., 1979-84; sr. lectr. London Inst., 1984-90; lectr. English and Am. studies U. East Anglia, Norwich, Eng., 1992-94; prof. film and visual media U. London, 1999—; vis. prof. Cornell U., U. Calif., Davis, also others; postgrad. coord. Brit. Film Inst., London, 1994. Author: Visual and Other Pleasures, 1989, Citizen Kane, 1992, Fetishism and Curiosity, 1996. Mem. Amnesty Internat. Mem. Labour Party. Office: Birkbeck Coll U London, 43 Gordon Sq, London WCH 0PD, England

MULVEY-ROBERTS, MARIE ELIZABETH, English educator; b. Ruthin, N. Wales, U.K., Aug. 21, 1955; d. Samuel Emrys and Catherine Teresa (Mulvey) R. BA, Manchester U., 1977, MA, 1979, PhD, 1987. Lectr. Open U., Manchester, England, 1980-90; lectr. Manchester U., 1986-87, N. Staffordshire Poly., Stafford, England, 1987-88, Bristol Poly., Bristol, England, 1988-92, U. West England, Bristol, England, 92—. Author: British Poets and Secret Societies, 1986, Gothic Immortals, 1990; editor: Explorations in Medicine, 1987, Literature and Medicine During the Eighteenth Century, 1993, Appeal of One Half of the Human Race, Women, Against the Other Half, Men, 1994, A Blighted Life, 1994, Out of the Night: Writings from Death Row, 1994, Shells from the Sands of Time, 1995, Sources, Perspectives and Controversies in the History of British Feminism, 1993-95, Secret Texts: The Literature of Secret Societies, 1995, Pleasure in the 18th Century, 1996, The Handbook to Gothic Literature, 1998, Sex and Sexuality, 1640-1940: Literary, Medical and Sociological Perspectives, 1998; reviews editor, over-seas advisor, mem. editorial bd. Cauda Pavonis: Studies in Hermeticism, 1989—. Roman Catholic. Office: U West of England, Faculty Humanities, St Matthias Fishpond Bristol, England BS162JP

MULVIHILL, PETER JAMES, fire protection engineer; b. Honolulu, Jan. 24, 1956; s. James H. and Jane A. (Norton) M. BSCE, Worcester (Mass.) Poly. Inst., 1978. Registered profl. engr. Fire Protection, Nev. Sr. engr. Indsl. Risk Insurers, San Francisco, 1978-84; fire protection engr. Aerojet Gen. Corp., Sacramento, 1984-87, Reno Fire Dept., 1987-93; bn. chief Boise (Idaho) Fire Dept., 1993-95; cons. Rolf Jensen & Assocs., Inc., Lehi, Utah, 1995-96; fire protection engr. Rolf Jensen & Assocs., Inc., Las Vegas, Nev., 1996-99; mgr. western region Fire Protection Mgmt., Inc., 1999—; part-time instr. univ. extension U. Calif., Davis, 1993-95, Truckee Meadows Community Coll., Reno, 1988-93. Commr. Gov.'s Blue Ribbon Commn. to Study Adequacy of State Regulations Concerning Highly Combustible Materials, Carson City, Nev., 1988. Mem. Soc. Fire Protection Engrs., No. Nev. Fire Marshals Assn. (pres. 1992-93), Nat. Fire Protection Assn. (alt. mem. com. air conditioning and profl. qualifications for fire insps.), Internat. Assn. Fire Chiefs, Utah Fire Marshals Assn. Office: 101 Convention Center Dr Ste 650 101 Convention Center Dr Las Vegas NV 89109-2000

MUMCUOGLU, KOSTA YANI, medical entomologist; b. Istanbul; s. Dimosthenis and Eleni (Hiotopulos) M.; m. Madeleine Bliah, July 6, 1975; 1 child. BSc, Basel U., 1972, PhD, 1975. Vis. scientist Hebrew U., Jerusalem, 1975-76; rsch. biologist Dept. Dermatology, U. Basel, Switzerland, 1975-80; vis. scientist Agrl. Coll., Teheran, 1978; rsch. biologist Dept. Parasitology, U. Zurich, Switzerland, 1980-83; rsch. biologist dept. zoology Hebrew U., Jerusalem, 1983-85, sr. rsch. asst. dept. parasitology, 1985—; mem. Nat. Com. on Allergy and Clin. Immunology, sect. Indoor Allergies, 1994—. Author: Dermatological Entomology, 1982; contbr. articles to profl. jours. Recipient Wilhelm-Lutz award Swiss Soc. of Dermatology and Venerology. Mem. Israel Soc. for Parasitology (sec. 1990-94), Israel Soc. for Protozoology (sec. 1994-96), Internat. Biotherapy Soc. (steering com. 1996—, pres. 1999—), Entomological Soc. of Am., Entomological Soc. of Israel, Israel Soc. for Skin Rsch. Greek Orthodox. Avocations: folk dancing, squash, photography, computers. Office: Dept Parasitology Hebrew U, Hadassah Med Sch POB 12272, 91120 Jerusalem Israel

MUMENTHALER, MARCO, neurologist, educator; b. Bern, Switzerland, July 23, 1925; s. Giovanni Jakob Mumenthaler and Lydia Giannina Piccoli; m. Livia Maria Morandini, Nov. 19,1949 (div. 1991); children: Maia, Manuela, Isabel; m. Regula Christine Dejung Hausammann, Feb. 4, 1992; 1 child, Sofia Rebecca. Degree in medicine, U. Basle, Switzerland, 1950; MD, U. Zurich, Switzerland, 1951. Intern various clinics, Switzerland, 1951-60; asst. étranger Hôp. Paris, 1952; vis. assoc. NIH, Bethesda, Md., 1961; asst. prof. neurology Berne U., Switzerland, 1962-66, prof. neurology, head dept., 1966-90, univ. pres., 1989-91; pvt. practice specialized in neurology Zürich. Author: Ulnarislähmungen, 1961,Klinische Neurologie ein Lernbuch, 1973, Der Schulter-Arm-Schmerz, 2d edit., 1982, Synkopen, 1984, Atlas der Klinischen Neurologie, 2nd edit., 1987, Der Kopfschmerz, 1990, Neuromuskuläre Erkrankungen, 1992, Pratique de Neurologie Clinique, 2d edit., 1995, Basiswissen Neurologie, 1996, Neurologie, 10th edit., 1997, Neurologische Differentialdiagnostik, 4th edit., 1997, Läsionen peripherer Nerven, 7th edit., 1998, (CD Rom) Neurologie Internaktiv, 1998. Mem. Internat. Com. Red Cross, Geneva, 1990-94. Maj. Med. Corps Swiss Army. Mem. Swiss Neurol. Soc. (former pres., hon. pres.), German Neurol. Soc. (hon.), French Neurol. Soc. (hon.), Italian Neurol. Soc. (hon.), Belgian Neurol. Soc. (hon.), Polish Neurol. Soc. (hon.), Austrian Neurol. Soc. (hon.), European Neurol. Soc. (hon.), Am. Neurol. Assn. (hon.), European Neurol. Soc. (hon.), Acad. Scis. Leopoldina Halle (ancient senator), Royal Brit. Soc. Medicine (affiliate). Avocations: literature, photography. Office: Witikonerstrasse 326, CH-8053 Zurich Switzerland

MUMICK, INDERPAL SINGH, computer scientist, engineer; b. New Delhi, Dec. 26, 1963; came to U.S., 1986; s. Ichhpal Singh and Narinder Kaur (Batra) M.; m. Ravneet Kaur Sodhi, Dec. 21, 1989; children: Kieraj Singh, Ruhani Kaur, Saran Singh. B Tech. in Computer Sci. and Engring., Indian Inst. Tech., New Delhi, 1986; PhD in Computer Sci., Stanford U., 1991. Rsch. student assoc. IBM Rsch., San Jose, Calif., 1988-91; tech. staff AT&T Bell Labs., Murray Hill, N.J., 1991-96; prin. tech. staff AT&T Labs., Murray Hill, 1996-97; CEO, pres., COO, chief tech. officer Savera Systems, Murray Hill, N.J., 1997—; gen. co-chair Internat. Conf. on Very Large Databases, N.Y.C., 1998. Editor: Proceedings of ACM-Sigmod Conference, 1996, Materialized Views, 1996; contbr. articles to profl. jours. Recipient India Gold medal Govt. of India, 1986, Gold medal in math. Ctrl. Bd. Secondary Edn., Govt. of India, 1982. Mem. IEEE, Assn. Computing Machinery. Sikh. Achievements include several patents. Office: Savera Systems 535 Mountain Ave New Providence NJ 07974-2006

MUMOLO, ENZO, computer science educator, researcher; b. Udine, Italy, May 4, 1956; s. Francesco Mumolo and Attilia Alessandris; m. Carla Broccaioli, May 12, 1984; 1 child, Matteo. Degree in electronics, Tech. Inst., Udine, 1975; D Engring., U. Trieste, Italy, 1982. Rschr. U. Trieste, 1982-84, asst. prof., 1992—; vis. rschr. ITT Defense Commn. Divsn., San Diego, 1984-85; rsch. engr. ITT/FACE, Rome, 1985-87; rsch. mgr. Alcatel/FACE, Rome, 1987-90; head Sincrotrone Spa, Trieste, 1990-91; cons. U. Trieste, 1982. Contbr. articles to profl. jours.; inventor in field. Recipient Zoldan Gold medal Associazione Elettrotecnica Italiana, 1983. Mem. IEEE, Assn. Computing Machinery. Avocations: amateur radio, collecting minerals, guitar. Home: Sistiana 34/D, 34019 Duino-Arisina Italy Office: U Trieste DEEI, Via Valerio 10, 34127 Trieste Italy

MUNAS, FIL A., psychiatric physician; b. Colombo, Sri Lanka, Aug. 30, 1946; came to U.S., 1972; s. M.H.M. and C.P. M. MBBS, MD, Christian Med. Coll., Vellore, India, 1971. Diplomate Am. Bd. Psychiatry and Neurology. Dir. geropsychiatry Trinity Meml. Hosp., Cudahy, Wis., 1991-95; dir. clin. svcs./chief of staff De Paul Hosp., Milw., 1996-97; dir. behavioral medicine VA Med. Ctr., Marion, Ill., 1998—; assoc. clinical prof. of psychiatry S.I.U. Sch. Medicine, Springfield, Ill., 1998—; pres. Extended Family Svcs. Corp., Big Bend, Wis., 1989-97; assoc. clin. prof. psychiatry So. Ill. U. Sch. Medicine, Springfield, 1998-2000. E-mail: filmunas@midamev.net. Home: 23107 Galatia Post Rd Pittsburg IL 62974-1832 Office: VA Med Ctr 2401 W Main St Marion IL 62959-1188

MUNASINGHE, MOHAN, development economist; b. Colombo, Sri Lanka, July 25, 1945; s. Peter Munasinghe and Flower Wickramasinghe; m. Sria Gooneratne, May 8, 1970; children: Anusha, Ranjiva. BA with honors, Cambridge (Eng.) U., 1967, MA, 1968; SM, MIT, 1969, EE, 1970; PhD in EE, McGill U., Montreal, Can., 1973; MA in Econs., Concordia U., 1975. Sr. advisor World Bank, Washington, 1996—; vis. prof. Am. U., Washington, 1977-81, Inst. Tech. Policy in Devel., SUNY, 1982-88, Energy Ctr. U. Pa., Phila., 1988-94, UN U./Inst. for Advanced Studies, 1997—; disting. vis. prof. of environ. mgmt. Colo. U., Sri Lanka, 1995—; vice chair intergovernmental panel on climate change, Geneva, 1997—; sr. advisor Min. of Environment, Sri Lanka, 1995—; pres. Lanka Internat. Forum Environ. & Sustainable Devel., Sri Lanka, 1996—; sr. advisor to pres. Office of Pres. of Sri Lanka, Colombo, 1982-87, chmn. computer and info. tech. coun., 1983-86; divsn. chief World Bank, Washington, 1987-96; sr. rsch. fellow Ctr. Internat. Devel. and Conflict Mgmt. U. Md., College Park, 1987-90; pres.-emeritus Sri Lanka Energy Mgmt. Assn., Colombo, 1985—, pres. 1983-85; advisor U.S. Pres.'s Coun. on Environ. Quality, 1990-92; chancellor Internat. Water Acad., Norway, 1999—; chmn. Munasinghe Inst. Devel., 1999—. Author: 65 books including Economics of Power System Reliability and Planning, 1979, Energy Economics, Demand Management and Pricing, 1983, Rural Electrification for Development, 1987, Integrated National Energy Planning and Management, 1988, Computers and Informatics in Developing Countries, 1989, Energy Analysis and Policy, 1990, Electric Power Economics, 1990, Water Supply and Environmental Management, 1992, Energy Modelling and Policy, 1992, Environmental Economics & Sustainable Development, 1993, Economywide Policies and the Environment, 1994, Protected Area Economics & Policy, 1994, Defining & Measuring Sustainability, 1995, Natural Disasters & Environment, 1995, Property Rights in Social and Ecological Context, 1995, Environmental Impacts of Macroeconomic Policies, 1997, Climate Change Policy, 1998, Sustainomics, 1999; author over 300 tech. papers; mem. editl. bd. Energy Jour., Environ. and Devel. Econ., Environ. Econ. and Policy Studies, Internat. Jour. Elec. Power and Energy Systems, Open Economics Review, Pacific and Asian Jour. of Energy, Utilities Policy. Recipient Award for Outstanding Contbns. World Water Congress, 1995, Prize for Outstanding Achievement Latin Am. and Caribbean Energy Conf., 1988, Exceptional Contbns. award Internat. Assn. Energy Econs., 1987, Outstanding Scientists Gold medal Lions Internat., 1985, Global Green award Internat. Fedn. Environ. Journalists, 1998; Grass fellow MIT, 1968, fellow Beijer Internat. Inst.-Royal Swedish Acad. Scis. Fellow Nat. Acad. Scis. (Sri Lanka), Third World Acad. Scis. (Italy), World Water Acad. (Norway), Royal Soc. Arts, (U.K.) Inst. Elec. Engrs. (U.K., Beauchamp prize 1967), Inst. Engrs. (Sri Lanka); mem. IEEE, Am. Econ. Assn., Am. Phys. Soc., Sri Lanka Assn. Adv. Sci., Sri Lanka Econ. Assn. Home: 4201 E West Hwy Bethesda MD 20815-5910 Office: World Bank 1818 H St NW Washington DC 20433-0001

MUNAVVAR, MOHAMMED, Maldivian government official. Atty. gen. Govt. Maldives, Malé. Office: Office Atty Gen, Huravee Bldg, Malé 20-05, Maldives*

MUNDA, IVKA MARIA, marine biologist, phycologist, researcher; b. Ljubljana, Slovenia, July 7, 1927; d. August Franz and Marija (Arselin) M. Dr., Univ. Ljubljana (Slovenia), 1963, U. Gothenborg (Sweden), 1963. Asst. Biol. Inst. Med. Faculty U., Ljubljana, Slovenia, 1955-60; rsch. fellow Norwegian Inst. Algological Rsch., Trondheim, 1960-63; scientific official Hydrobiologish Inst., Yerseke, Holland, 1963-65; rsch. asst. Inst. Food Tech. Ljubljana (Slovenia) U., 1965-66; assoc. researcher Biol. Inst. Slovene Acad. Sci. and Arts, Ljubljana, 1966-83, scienific official Ctr. Scientific Rsch., 1983—. Contbr. 120 articles to scientific jours., on topics of ecology of benthic marine algae from Iceland and North Adriatic, and pollution problems. Rsch. grantee Norwegian Found. Natural Scis., 1958-62, Icelandic Rsch. Found., 1963-80, Alexander von Humboldt Found., 1975, 76, 78. Mem. Brit. Phycol. Soc., Internat. Phycol. Soc., Phycol. Soc. Am., N.Y. Acad. Scis., Internat. Commn. Scientific Exploration of the Mediterranean Sea (CIESM) (Monaco), European Cooperation in Field of Scientific and Tech. Rsch. (COST), German Bot. Soc., The Planetary Soc., Internat. Govs. Club. Christian Democrat. Roman Catholic. Avocations: watercolor painting. Office: Ctr Scientific Rsch Slovene, Acad Sci & Arts Gosposka 13, 1000 Ljubljana Slovenia

MUNDELL, ROBERT ALEXANDER, economics educator; b. Kingston, Ont., Can., Oct. 24, 1932; s. William C. and Lila (Knifton) M.; m. Barbara Sheff, Oct. 14, 1957 (div. 1972); children: Paul Alexander, William Andrew, Robyn Leslie; m. Valerie Sophia Natsios, Nov. 10, 1998; 1 child, Nicholas Robert. BA, U. B.C., Can., 1953; postgrad., U. Wash., 1953-54, London Sch. Econs. and Polit. Sci., 1955-56; PhD, MIT, 1956; postdoc., U. Chgo., 1956-57; PhD (hon.), Renmin U. China, 1985, U. Paris, 1992. Instr. econs. U. B.C., Vancouver, Can., 1957-58; acting asst. prof. econs. Stanford U., Calif., 1958-59; vis. prof. econs. Sch. Advanced Internat. Studies, Johns Hopkins U. Ctr., Bologna, Italy, 1959-61; sr. economist research dept. IMF, Washington, 1961-63; vis. prof. econs. McGill U., Montreal, Que., Can., 1963-64; Rockefeller vis. research prof. internat. econs. Brookings Instn., Washington, 1964-65; prof. Grad. Inst. Internat. Studies, Geneva, summers 1965-75; Ford Found. vis. research prof. econs. U. Chgo., 1965-66, prof., 1966-71; prof. econs., chmn. dept. U. Waterloo, Ont., Can., 1972-74; prof. econs. Columbia U., N.Y.C., 1974—; economist Can. Royal Commn. on Price Spreads on Food Products, summer 1957; mem. joint fiscal mission to Peru OAS and Inter-Am. Devel. Bank, summer 1964; cons. FRS, IBRD, 1966—, U.S. Treasury Dept., 1969-74, EEC, 1970-73, UN, Govt. Panama; organizer, participant internat. confs., lectr. numerous univs. and profl. orgn. meetings; hon. prof. Renmin U. China, Beijing. Author: The International Monetary System--Conflict and Reform, 1965, Man and Economics, 1968, International Economics, 1968, Monetary Theory--Interest, Inflation and Growth in the World Economy, 1971; contbr. sects. to books, encys., U.S. Congl. Hearings, numerous articles to profl. jours.; co-editor, contbr.: Monetary Problems of the International Economy, 1969, Trade, Balance of Payments and Growth, 1971; co-editor: The New International Monetary System, 1977; editor: Jour. Polit. Economy, 1966-70, Global Disequilibrium in the World Economy, 1989, 92, Building the New Europe, 1991, Debt, Deficit and Economic Importance, 1990, Inflation and Growth in China, 1996. Recipient Jacques Rueff Prize medal, 1983; NSF rsch. grantee, 1967-70; Guggenheim fellow, 1970-71; Marshall lectr. Cambridge U., 1974, Nobel Prize in Economics, 1999. Mem. Am. Econ. Assn. (Disting. fellow 1997). Office: Dept Econs Columbia U 1031 Internat Affairs 420 W 118th St # Mc3308 New York NY 10027-7213

MUNDHEIM, ROBERT HARRY, law educator; b. Hamburg, Germany, Feb. 24, 1933; m. Guna Smitchens; children: Susan, Peter. BA, Harvard U., 1954, LLB, 1957; MA (hon.), U. Pa., 1971. Bar: N.Y. 1958, Pa. 1979. Assoc. Shearman & Sterling, N.Y.C., 1958-61; spl. counsel to SEC Washington, 1962-63; vis. prof. Duke Law Sch., Durham, N.C., 1964; prof. law U. Pa., Phila., 1965—; univ. prof. law and fin., 1980-93, dean, 1982-89, Bernard G. Segal prof. law, 1987-89; co-chmn. Fried, Frank, Harris, Shriver & Jacobson, N.Y.C., 1990-92; exec. v.p., gen. counsel Salomon Inc., 1992-97; sr. exec. v.p., gen. counsel Salomon Smith Barney Holdings, Inc., 1997-98; of counsel Shearman & Sterling, 1999—; gen. counsel U.S. Dept. Treasury, Washington, 1977-80; dir. Ctr. for Study of Fin. Instns., U. Pa.; pres. Appleseed Found.; trustee New Sch. U.; bd. dirs. Salzburg Seminar, The Kitchen, Benjamin Moore & Co.; gen. counsel Chrysler Loan Guarantee Bd., 1980; mng. dir., mem. mgmt. bd. Salomon Bros. Inc., N.Y.C., 1992-97. Author: Outside Director of the Publicity Held Corporation, 1976; American Attitudes Toward Foreign Direct Investment in the United States, 1979; Conflict of Interest and the Former Government Employee: Re-thinking the Revolving Door, 1981; chmn. adv. bd. Jour. Internat. Econ. Law, 1996-97. With USAF, 1961-62. Recipient Alexander Hamilton award U.S. Dept. Treasury, 1980, Harold P. Seligson award Practicing Law Inst., 1988, Francis J. Rawle award, ABA-ALI, 1992, Anti-Defamation League Human Rels. award, 1999. Mem. Am. Law Inst. (mem. coun., mem. exec. com.), Nat. Assn. Securities Dealers (gov.-at-large, vice-chmn.), San Diego Securities Regulation Inst. (chmn.), Am. Acad. in Berlin (pres. 2000—). Office: Shearman & Sterling 599 Lexington Ave Fl 16 New York NY 10022-6069

MUNDSCHENK, MARK, photographer; b. Hamburg, Germany, Apr. 2, 1961; s. Egon and Rosemarie (Stuedemann) M.; m. Stephanie Jaqueline Krugmann, June 7, 1991; children: Alexander Raphael, Maxim Constantin, Niklas Leon. Cert. import-export merchant Hamburg C. of C. Jr. chief Mundschenk Wine Import Co., Hamburg, 1983-87; freelance photographer Krugmann-Mundschenk Photodesign, Hamburg, 1987—; co-founder advt. agy. TIC-The Image Co. Photographer, author: Cocktail Visions, 1989. Mem. Young Liberals, Hamburg, 1976-81. Mem. Planetary Soc.

MUNE, MASATOSHI, medical educator; b. Awajishima, Hyogo, Japan, Nov. 7, 1948; s. Yasuo and Yoshiko (Masuda) M.; m. Etsuko Kashihara, Nov. 10, 1974; 1 child, Sachiko. MD, Wakayama (Japan) Med. Coll., 1974, PhD, 1986. Lectr. Wakayama Med. Coll., 1979-87, asst. prof., 1987-90, 91-98, assoc. prof., 1998—; chief physician Tanabe (Japan) Nat. Hosp., 1990-91; vis. scientist Tufts U., Boston, 1993-94; sec. gen. Internat. Symposium on Lipids and Renal Disease, Shima, Japan, 1997-98. Editor jour. Kidney Internat., 1999. Grantee Japanese Ministry of Edn., 1994, Japanese Ministry of Health and Welfare, 1997. Fellow Japanese Soc. Nephrology; mem. Am. Soc. Nephrology. Buddhist. Avocations: music, golf, driving. Office: Wakayama Med Coll, 811-1 Kimiidera, Wakayama 641-0012, Japan

MUNE, OLE, physician, rheumatologist, physiologist; b. Lundby, Zealand, Denmark, Sept. 24, 1928; s. Niels Frederik Mune and Karen Margrethe Fischer-Nielsen; children: Lars, Peter. MD, U. Copenhagen, 1956; postgrad., Acad. Tech. Scis., Copenhagen, 1960, Danish Med. Assn., 1966; Ph.D.med.doctor, Danish Soc. Phys. Medicine, 1967; postgrad., Leyden U., Holland, 1968. Asst. doctor Copenhagen County Hosp., Gentofte; from second asst. to asst. internal medicine, pediatrics Frederiksberg Hosp., State Hosp., Arhus Hosp.; asst. orthopedic surgery Orthopedic Hosp., Copenhagen; asst. psychiatry Frösö Sjukhus, Östersund, Sverige; practitioner Copenhagen; chief physician Kolding Ctrl. Hosp., Denmark, 1966-92, supt. dept. phys. medicine, rehab., rheumatology, 1966-92; chief cons., supt. Queen Alexandrines Sanatorium of Rheumatic Diseases, Middelfart, Denmark, 1968—; pvt. practice rheumatology, 1971—; 2790. internat. med. summer sch., Copenhagen, 1961, internat. course on rehabilitation WHO, 1963, 67, postgrad. courses; v.p. Internat. Coll. Angiology, 1966; journalist, reporter Nordisk Medicin, 1966; cons. Fredericia Hosp., 1966-68; mem. Medico-Tech. Com., County Health Svc., 1970; mem. planning com. county hosps., 1967, European Soc. for Clin. Investigation, 1968; specialistboard rep. physs. medicine and rehab. for nat. health authorities; chmn. art com., Kolding Hosp., Denmark; mem. study tour Eng., 1961, Göteborg, 1962, Pavia, 1962, Oslo, 1963, Poland, 1968, Hong Kong, 1973, Osaka, Japan, 1973. Author: (monograph) Clinical Plethysmography of the Forefoot in Arteriosclerosis Obliterans, 1967; author: (film) Reconstruction and Rehabilitation of Upper

Extremity After Traumatic Amputation, 1963, supplement, 1970; contbr. articles, reviews to profl. jours. Recipient numerous grants. Mem. Danish Soc. Phys. Medicine (mem. postgrad. com. 1967, planning com. 1968-70, chmn. rheumatic com. 1972), Danish Soc. Phys. Medicine and Rehab. (pres. 1971), Internat. College Angiology (v.p. 1966). Avocations: Japanese garden, painting and sculpture in censored exhbn. Home and Office: Nordvang 17, Jutland Kolding 6000, Denmark

MUNEKATA, EISUKE, biochemistry educator; b. Tokyo, Feb. 25, 1940; d. Eiji and Miyoko M.; m. Yasuko Takeda, Nov. 15, 1969; children: Yuko, Hideaki, Yasuaki. DSc, U. Osaka, 1972. Lectr. Max-Planck Inst. for Med. Sci., Heidelberg, Germany, 1974; Prof. Inst. of Applied Biochemistry U. Tsukuba, 1978. Home: Higashi 2-22-1, 305 Tsukuba Japan Office: Inst Applied Biochemistry, U Tsukuba, 305 Tsukuba Japan

MUNETAKE, TANAKA, computer engineer, consultant; b. Tokyo, Feb. 10, 1940; s. Kaku and Masae Tanaka; m. Toshiko Tanaka, Feb. 19, 1967; children: Tomoko, Atsuko. LLB, Rikkyo U., Tokyo, 1964. Stock dealer Daiwa Security Corp., Tokyo, 1964-68; system engr. System Devel. div., Tokyo, 1968-85; mgr. edn. divsn. NEC, Tokyo, 1985-87; sr. mgr. Govtl. Found., Tokyo, 1987-89; mgr. PC mktg. divsn. NEC, Tokyo, 1989-91, sr. mgr. C&C planning divsn., 1991-2000; pres. Sabi Consulting Co., Tokyo, 2000—; rep. of Japanese Govt., COCOM Internat. Meeting, 1990-93; planner and rep. of Japanese Govt., ODA. Avocations: translation from English to Japanese, tennis, skiing, golf. Home: Narita Higashi 5-13-3, Suginami Tokyo 166, Japan Office: Sabi Consulting Co, Akasaka 2-21-2 30/ Minato, Tokyo 107, Japan

MUNGAN, NECMETTIN AYDIN, urologist; b. Ankara, Turkey, Mar. 24, 1965; s. Selahattin and Hasene Sevim (Oktu) M.; m. Ayca Gorkem Kir, Sept. 18, 1990; children: Gokhan, Dogukan. MD, U. Ankara, 1989; specialist in urology, Ankara Numune Edn./Rsch. Hosp., 1995; PhD in Superficial Bladder Cancer, Nijmegen (The Netherlands) U., 2000. Resident urology Ankara Numune Edn. and Rsch. Hosp., 1991-95, specialist, trainer in urology, 2000—; fellow urology Baylor Coll., Tex., 1997. Active Turkish Mil., 1993. Recipient 1st prize Netherlands Higher Edn. Internat., 1997. Mem. Internat. Assn. Andrology, European Assn. Urology, Turkish Assn. Urology. Avocations: scuba diving, stamp and money collecting. Home: A Kemal Mah Baris Sitesi, 74 Sok 29 Eskisehiryolu, 06530 Ankara Turkey Office: Ankara Numune Edn & Rsch, Urology Dept Samanpazari, Ankara Turkey

MUNGER, ELMER LEWIS, civil engineer, educator; b. Manhattan, Kans., Jan. 4, 1915; s. Harold Hawley and Jane (Green) M.; m. Vivian Marie Bloomfield, Dec. 28, 1939; children: John Thomas, Harold Hawley II, Jane Marie. BS, Kans. State U., 1936, MS, 1938; PhD, Iowa State U., 1957. Registered profl. engr., Nebr., Kans., Iowa, Vt.; registered pvt. land surveyor Republic of The Philippines. Rodman St. Louis-Southwestern Ry., Ark., Mo., 1937-38; engr. U.S. Engr. Dept., Ohio, Nebr., 1938-46; missionary engr. Philippine Episcopal Ch., 1946-48; engr. Wilson & Co., Salina, Kans., 1948; tchr. Iowa State U., 1948-51, 54-58; engr. C.E., U.S. Army, Alaska, 1951-54; from tchr. to dean Norwich U., Northfield, Vt., 1958-69; prof. gen. engring. U. P.R., Mayagüez, 1969-75; prof. civil engring. Mich. Tech. U., 1975-80; ret.; mem. spl. com. on engring. Inter-Am. Devel. Bank, U. W.I., 1971. Author: (with Clarence J. Douglas) Construction Management, 1970. Fellow ASCE; mem. NSPE, Vt. Soc. Profl. Engrs., Am. Soc. Engring. Edn., Phi Kappa Phi, Sigma Tau, Tau Beta Pi, Chi Epsilon. Episcopalian. Clubs: Masons, Shriners. Home: 21260 Brinson Ave Apt 311 Pt Charlotte FL 33952-5005

MUNGER, PAUL DAVID, company executive, educational administrator; b. Selma, Ala., Oct. 12, 1945; s. Paul Francis and Arlene Lorraine (McFillen) M.; m. Paula Jean Dominici, May 30, 1969; children: Kimberley Beth, Christopher David. AB in Philosophy, Kenyon Coll., 1967; MA in Govt., Ind. U., 1969. Commd. 2d lt. USAF, 1969, advanced through grades to capt., resigned, 1978; asst. dir. faculty devel. Ind. U., Bloomington, 1974-77; from asst. dean to dean continuing studies Am. U., Washington, 1980-83, asst. provost acad. devel., 1983-84; dir. Commn. on Future Acad. Leadership, Washington, 1984-86; v.p. Acad. Strategies, Washington, 1986-88; pres. Strategic Edn. Svcs. Inc., Sterling, Va., 1988—; bd. dirs. Munger Acad. Bd. advisors Madeira Sch., McLean, Va., 1993-96; treas. Bus.-Higher Edn. Fedn., Washington, 1992—; asst. scoutmaster Boy Scouts Am., 1991-93, scoutmaster, 1994-97; dir. Czech-am. LaCrosse Found., 1996—; bd. dirs. Thomas Jefferson H.S. for Sci. and Tech. Found., 1999—, PTSA, 1996-98, chair bus. rels. com., 1996-98. Mem. Am. Soc. Tng. & Devel. (chmn. strategic planning com. 1993-95, continuing profl. edn. electronic forum coord. 1995-97), Assn. Continuing Higher Edn., Am. Soc. Curriculum Devel. Office: Strategic Education Services Inc 624 W Church Rd Sterling VA 20164-4608

MUNGIA, SALVADOR ALEJO, JR., lawyer; b. Tacoma, Feb. 19, 1959; s. Salvador Alejo Sr. and Susie (Tamaki) M. BA, Pacific Luth. U., 1981; JD, Georgetown U., 1984. Bar: Wash. 1984, U.S. Dist. Ct. (we. dist.) Wash. 1985, U.S. Ct. Appeals (9th cir.) 1986, U.S. Supreme Ct. 1992. Law clk. to Justice Fred Dore Wash. State Supreme Ct., Olympia, 1984-85; law clerk to Hon. Carolyn R. Dimmick U.S. Dist. Ct. (we. dist.) Wash., Seattle, 1985-86; assoc. Gordon, Thomas, Honeywell, Malanca, Peterson & Daheim, Tacoma, 1986-91, ptnr., 1991—; adj. prof. Pacific Luth. U., 1993-94. Vol. atty. ACLU, Tacoma, 1986—, bd. dirs., 1987-92; commr. Tacoma Human Rights Commn., 1990-96; bd. dirs. Legal Aid for Washington, 1992-96, life bd. dirs., 1997—. Mem. ABA, Wash. State Bar Assn., Fed. Bar Assn. Western Wash., Tacoma-Pierce County Bar Assn. (pres. 1999), Pierce County Young Lawyers Assn. (trustee 1988-90), Wash. Alpine Club, Tacoma Lawn Tennis Club, Tacoma Club. Avocations: mountain climbing, skiing, tennis, running. Home: 615 N C St Tacoma WA 98403-2810 Office: Gordon Thomas Honeywell Malance Peterson & Daheim PO Box 1157 Tacoma WA 98401-1157

MUNGIU, OSTIN COSTEL, medical educator; b. Iasi, Romania, Oct. 16, 1941; s. Teodosie and Tatiana (Liurca) M.; m. Maria Elena Ionascu, Dec. 14, 1961; children: Tatiana-Alina, Cristian. MD, U. Medicine, Iasi, 1963, PhD, 1971. Asst. prof. U. Medicine, Iasi, 1965-74, assoc. prof., 1974-92, prof., 1993—; vis. scholar Roswell Pk. Meml. Inst., Buffalo, 1971-72, cancer rsch. scientist, 1972; vice dean Faculty of Medicine, Iasi, 1983-90, head of dept., 1993—; dir. Drug Testing Lab., Iasi, 1986—. Author: (handbooks) Biochemical Pharmacology, 1974, Medical Pharmacology, 1977, Practical Pharmacology, 1980, Clinical Pharmacology, Vol. I, 1981, Vol. II, 1985, Elements of Fundamental Pharmacology, 1996, Elements of Pharmacology and Drug Testing, 1996, General Algesiology, 1999; co-author: (book) (with I. Triandaf) New Data in Clinics and Pharmacology, 1981, (handbooks) (with S. Dumitrescu) and V. Bobulescu) Handbook of Pharmcology, Vol. I, 1981, Vol. II, 1985, (with P.P. Vancea and D. Chiselita) Drug Ophthalmic Therapy, 1987; author, editor: Medicine Day, 1996, Biochemical Pharmacology, 2000, Special Algesiology, 2000. Mem. Romanian Assn. for Study of Pain (v.p. 1993-98, pres. 1999—), Internat. Assn. for Study of Pain (councilor European Fedn. 1998—), European Assn. Clin. Pharmacology and Therapeutics. Eastern Orthodox. Avocation: collecting pottery. Home: Stradela Sararie 6, 6600 Iasi Romania Office: U Medicine and Pharmacy, Universitatii 16, 6600 Iasi Romania

MUNGRA, SOEBHAS CHANDRA, Surinamese government official; b. Paramaribo, Sept. 2, 1945. Statistics asst. Nat. Planning Office, 1968; tchg. asst. U. Amsterdam, 1971-72; with dept. econ. affairs Ministry of Finance, 1973-80, dep. dir., 1980, acting dir., 1980-81; lectr. Anton De Kom U., Suriname, 1976-86; min. finance Govt. of Suriname, Paramaribo, 1986-90, min. fgn. affairs, 1991-97; now permanent rep. to UN N.Y.C., 1997—; bd. chmn. Nat. Cardboard Industry, 1985-86; vice chmn. Centre for Devel. of Industry Joint Governing Bd., Brussels, 1986, chmn., 1988-90; bd. chmn. Nat. Devel. Bank, 1981-82, dir., 1983-84. Office: Permanent Mission of Suriname 866 U N Plz Rm 320 New York NY 10017-1822*

MUNIAIN, JAVIER P., computer software company executive, theoretical physicist, researcher; b. Madrid, Apr. 4, 1966; came to U.S., 1989.; s. Luis Perez De Muniain y Leal and Crescencia Mohedano Hernandez. BSc, U. Complutense of Madrid, 1990; M. in Physics, U. Calif., Riverside, 1992, PhD in Theoretical Physics, 1996. Rsch., tchg. asst. U. Calif., Riverside, 1992-96; pres., founder Surfernet, San Diego, 1996—, Madrid, Spain, 1996; exec. pres., CEO Surfernet, Spain, 1997; CEO, co-founder Adventureland.com, San Diego, 1997; co-founder J&R Global, Ltd., Naples, Fla., 1997. Author: Gauge Fields, Knots and Gravity, 1994; contbr. articles to profl. jours. Mem. Am. Phys. Soc., Riverside Wine Tasing Soc. (co-founder 1994). Avocations: classic cars, chess, surfing, antiques, architecture. Home: Avenida General Mola 36, 11 Pozuelo de Alarcou, Madrid 28224, Spain

MUNIC, RACHELLE ETHEL, health services administrator; b. Hartford, Conn., Apr. 15, 1953; d. Abe and Sara (Levenberg) M. BS in Med. Tech. summa cum laude, U. Bridgeport, 1975; physician asst. cert., Yale U., 1979; MBA in Health & Med. Svcs. Adminstrn., Widener U., 1991. Med. technologist St. Francis Hosp., Hartford, 1975-77; physician asst. Fox Chase Cancer Ctr., Phila., 1979-85; clin. dir. Fox Chase Network, Phila., 1986-92; adminstrv. dir., oncology Cooper Hosp., U. Med. Ctr., Camden, N.J., 1992-96, healthcare cons., 1996—; corp. mgr. cancer svcs. Grad. Health Sys., Phila., 1996—; cancer svc. line adminstr. Albert Einstein Med. Ctr., Phila., 1996-99; adminstrv. dir. divsn. med. oncology, hematology & genetics Jefferson U., Phila., 1999—; mem. Cancer Prevention and Control Adv. Group to N.J. Commn. on Cancer Rsch., New Brunswick, N.J., 1993-96; mem. program com. Greater Phila. Health Assembly, 1996; presenter in field. Dana scholar U. Bridgeport, 1972; recipient Foster G. McGaw Scholarship award Assn. Univ. Programs in Health Adminstrn., 1990, Student award Hosp. Assn. Pa., 1992; Breast Cancer project grantee The Susan G. Komen Breast Cancer Found., Dallas, 1995. Mem. Am. Hosp. Assn., Am. Cancer Soc. (Camden County), Assn. Cancer Execs., Soc. Radiation Oncology Adminstrs., Assn. Cmty. Cancer Ctrs. (del.), Widener Alumni Assn. (pres. 1995), U. Bridgeport Asteria Honor Soc. Avocations: softball, golf, swimming, cross-country skiing, reading.

MUNIR, JAMSHED AQIL, retired educator; b. Badayun, India, Dec. 15, 1927; s. Syed Mohammad and Intikhab (Nayab Bano) M.; m. Akhtar Jamshed Munir, June 1955 (div. 1977); children: Jahangir, Farha. BSEE, Z.H. Coll. Engring. and Tech., Aligarh, India, 1947, BSME, 1948; MS in Indsl. Engring., U. So. Calif., 1962. Lectr. Z.H. Coll. Engring. and Tech., Aligarh Muslim U., 1948-58, reader in mech. engr., 1958-67, prof. mech. and indsl. engring., 1967-89; head dept. mech. engring., 1968-84, dean faculty engring., 1976-79; ret., 1989; vis. lectr. U. So. Calif., L.A., 1961-62. Inventor in field. Avocation: photography. Home: Kothi Judge Munir, Sir Syed Nagar, Aligarh UP 202001, India

MUNIRUZZAMAN, MD, pharmaceutical scientist; b. Chandpur, Bangladesh, Feb. 1, 1962; s. Abdur Rauf and Azizun Nesa Begum. B Pharmacy, Dhaka U., Bangladesh, 1987; M Pharmacy, Dhaka U., 1988; M in Engring., Kyoto U., Japan, 1997; PhD, Kyoto U., 2000. Cert. pharmacist. Prodn. officer Acme Labs., Ltd., Dhaka, 1989-94. Mem. Old Rajshahi Cadets Assn., 1981—. Recipient scholarship, Bd. Intermediate and Secondary Edn., 1981, Japanese Govt., 1994. Mem. Bangladesh Pharmaceutical Soc., Am. Assn. Pharm. Scientists, Am. Chemical Soc. Avocations: reading, movies, music, sports. Home: House #465, Rd # 8 DOHS Baridhara, Dhaka 1206, Bangladesh

MUNISAMY, THULASIMANI, pharmacologist, consultant; b. Pondicherry, Union Territory of Pondicherry India, India, Apr. 25, 1949; s. Iyyasami and Irichammal M.; m. Selliammal Thulasimani, Apr. 5, 1987. Cert. in French, U. Madras, India, 1969, bachelor in Medicine and Surgery, 1974, MD, 1979. Med. Diplomate. Jr. resident Jawaharlal Inst. Postgrad. Med. Edn. and Rsch., Pondicherry, 1976-79; med. officer Dept. Health, Pondicherry, 1980-87, chief govt. pharmacy, 1988-93, sr. med. officer, 1994-96; head dept. pharmacology Mahatma Gandhi Dental Coll. and Hosp., Pondicherry, 1997—; Mem. bd. med. edn. Dept. Health, Pondicherry, 1990—, drug insp., 1992-95. Author: Textbook of Pharmacology in Tamil (award Govt. Tamilnadu 1985), 1985, Ancient Indian Medicine; contbr. articles to profl. jours. Recipient Honor for contbn. to medicine Tamil U., 1996; grantee Tamil U., 1983. Mem. Indian Pharmacological Soc. (assoc. editor jour. 1992-94), Toxicological Soc. India, Nature Soc., Navadharshan Film Soc. (life mem.). Avocations: writing medical articles, giving talks on health education, reading novels about social problems. Home: 250 Lal Bahadhur St. Pondicherry 605 001, India Office: Mahatma Gandhi Dental Coll and Hosp, Pondicherry 605 001, India

MUNIZ, JAVIER, physician; b. La Coruna, Spain, May 17, 1959; s. Jose Luis and Emilia (Garcia) M.; m. Pino Saenz Diez, Aug. 4, 1990; children: Javier, Pino. MS in Epidemiology, Sch. Pub. Health, 1987; MD, Santiago, Spain, 1982, PhD, 1996. Emergency physician Sanatorio Medelo, A Coruna, Spain, 1983-86; gen. sec. BIOMEGA, A Coruna, Spain, 1988—; sec. Inst. Univ. Ciencias, A Coruna, Spain, 1996—; dir. ODDS SL, A Coruna, Spain, 1997—. Corr. fellow Real Acad. Med. Galicia, 1997. Fellow Coun. Epidemiology, Am. Heart Assn.; mem. Soc. Espanola Arteriosclerosis Vocal, Soc. Espanola Cardiologia. Avocation: golf. Fax: 981-21-75-39. Office: ODDS SL, c/Emilia Bardo Bazan 8 1, 15005 A Curuna Spain

MUNK, PETER, mining executive; b. Budapest, Hungary, Nov. 8, 1927; arrived in Can., 1948; s. Louis L. and Katherine (Adler) M.; m. Linda Gutterson; children: Anthony, Nina; m. Melanie Jane Bosanquet, 1973; children: Natalie, Cheyne, Marc David. BASc in Elec. Engring., U. Toronto, Ont., Can., 1953, LLD, 1995; LLD, Upsala Coll., N.J., 1991, U. Toronto, Que., Can., 1995, Bishops Coll., Que., Can., 1995, Concordia U., Montreal, Que., 1999. Chmn., chief exec. officer So. Pacific Hotel Corp., Sydney, Australia, 1969-81; chmn. Barrick Resources, Toronto, 1981-83, Am. Barrick Resources Corp. (now Barrick Gold Corp.), Toronto, 1983—, The Horsham Corp., Toronto, 1987-96; CEO Trizec Hahn Corp., Toronto; bd. dirs. Trizec Hahn Corp. Ltd., World Gold Coun., Geneva. Trustee Toronto Hosp.; bd. dirs. U. Toronto Found. Decorated officer Order of Can. Office: Trizec Hahn Corporation, 181 Bay Street Ste 3900, Toronto, ON Canada M5J 2T3

MUNK, ZEV MOSHE, allergist, researcher; b. Stockholm, July 14, 1950; m. Susan Deitcher; 4 children. BS, McGill U., 1972; MD, C.M., 1974. Licentiate Med. Coun. Can.; diplomate Am. Bd. Internal Medicine, Am. Bd. Allergy and Clin. Immunology. Intern Royal Victoria Hosp., Montreal, 1974-75, resident, 1975-76; resident in clin. immunology and allergy Montreal Gen. Hosp., 1976-78; practice medicine specializing in allergy/clin. immunology Houston, 1978—; founder, CEO Europe, Latin Am., U.S., CIS ops. Pharm-Olam Internat. Inc.; mem. staff Meml. City Med. Ctr., Meml. S.W., Spring Branch Meml., Cy-Fair hosps. (all Houston); clin. instr. allergy and clin. immunology Baylor Coll. Medicine, 1979—, U. Tex.-Houston, 1979—; pres. Breco Rsch. Contbr. articles to med. jours. Pres. Young Israel Synagogue of Houston, 1994-96; founder Allergy Ctr., Inc., Houston, Clin. Rsch. Ctr., Houston; founder, pres. Torah and Outreach Resource Ctr. of Houston. McGill U. scholar, 1968-74. Fellow Am. Acad. Allergy, Am. Coll. Allergy and Immunogy, Royal Coll. Physician (Can.); mem. ACP, Am. Assn. Pharm. Physicians, Tex. Med. Assn., Que. Med. Assn., Am. Acad. Allergy, Tex. Allergy Soc., Harris County Med. Soc., Houston Allergy Soc. Office: 902 Frostwood Dr Ste 222 Houston TX 77024-2402

MUNKER, REINHOLD, physician; b. Nürnberg, Germany, Apr. 17, 1953; s. Heinrich and Berta (Bö) M.; m. Mirsinoula Kamaterou; children: Stefan, Dieter. MD, Med. Sch., Erlangen, Germany, 1979. Clin. trainee U. Essen, Germany, 1979-80; rsch. scientist GSF Inst. Hematology, Munich, 1980-84; rsch. fellow dept. hematology UCLA, 1984-86; physician Med. Klinik III, Uniklinikum Grosshadern der LMU, Munich, 1986-99; attending physician Städt Kraukenhaus Harlaching, 1999—; vis. scientist M.D. Anderson Cancer Ctr., Houston, 1994-96; vis. scientist UCLA, 1996. Co-author: Leitfaden der Hämatologie, 1994; contbr. articles to profl. publs. Mem. European Group for Blood and Marrow Transplantation, Am. Assn. Cancer Rsch., Am. Soc. Clin. Oncology, Am. Soc. Hematology, Deutsche Gesellschaft für Hämatologie and Onkologie, Deutsche Gesellschaft für Innere Medizin. Home: Hartliebstr 2, D-80637 Munich Germany Office: Med Abteilung, Städt Krankenhause Harlaching, D-81545 Munich Germany

MUNKHOLT, PEER, fund executive; b. Saltum, Denmark, Apr. 11, 1955; s. Hans and Inger (Vejby Noergaard) M.; m. Cherine Weliwita-Gunaratne, May 9, 1984; children: Nina, Martin. M of Econs., U. Copenhagen, 1981. Economist Danish Employers Confedn., Copenhagen, 1981-82; rsch. fellow Internat. Inst. for Strategic Studies, London, 1982-84; economist Internat. Textile Mfrs. Fedn., Zurich, Switzerland, 1984-91, dep. dir., 1991-97; chief sect. Russian Fedn., Investment Fund for Ctrl. and Ea. Europe, Copenhagen, 1997—; Bd. dirs. CJSC Dronningborg Ukraine, ZAO St. Petersburg Taxophones, Sadolin Properties A/S, Harry's Russia A/S, SIA Kaas Steel, OOO Sadolin Sestroretsk, TK Devel. Pushkin A/S. Author: Defence and Economics in the USSR, 1984, The Soviet Economy: Protection of the Military Sector in Case of a Protracted Deterioration, 1985; contbr. articles to profl. jours. Lt. Danish Air Force, 1976-80. Recipient N.A.T.O. Sci. fellow., 1982. Liberal. Lutheran. E-mail: munkholt@mail.tele.dk. Office: IO, Bremerholm 4, 1069 Copenhagen Denmark

MUNK OLSEN, BIRGER, medieval philology and culture educator; b. Copenhagen, June 26, 1935; s. Rudolf and Ida (Soerensen) M.; m. Annalise Bliddal, Apr. 4, 1964 (div. 1987); children: Birgitte, Helene; m. Gudrun Kannik Christensen, Oct. 15, 1995. D in Lit., Sorbonne, Paris, 1963; diploma, Pontificia U. Gregoriana, Rome, 1965. Asst. prof. U. Copenhagen, Denmark, 1961-64, 66-68, prof., 1974—; vice dir. Accademia di Danimarca, Rome, 1964-66; lectr. U. Paris, Sorbonne, 1968-74; dean faculty of humanities U. Copenhagen, 1979-80; chmn. Nat. Rsch. Coun. for the Humanities, Denmark, 1987-90; mem. Danish Nat. Coun. for Rsch. Planning and Policy, Denmark, 1987-89; mem. standing com. for the humanities European Sci. Found., Strasburg, 1988-92; mem. exec. coun., 1991-92, chmn. ESF Network, 1991-97; mem. European Sci. and Tech. Assembly, Brussels, 1997—. Author: L'étude des auteurs classiques latins aux XI et XII siècles, Vol 1-4, 1982-89, I classici nel canone scolastico altomedievale, 1991, L'atteggiamento medievale di fronte alla cultura classica, 1994, Le réception de la littérature classique au Moyen Age, 1995. Decorated knight Order of Dannebrog (Denmark); officer Nat. Order of Merit (France), comdr. Nat. Order of Merit, Romania. Mem. Soc. Internat. de Bibliographie Classique (v.p. 1994-99, pres. 1999—), Academia Europea (founder, exec. coun. 1989-92), Acad. des Inscriptions et Belles-Lettres (corr. mem. 1996-98, mem. 1998—, Prix Brunet 1984), Royal Danish Acad. of Scis. and Letters (v.p. chmn. humanities class 1989-95, pres. of the acad. 1996—), Romanian Acad. (hon.). Home: Ny Kongensgade 20, 1557 Copenhagen V, Denmark Office: Inst for Greek and Latin, U Copenhagen Njalsgade 90, 2300 Copenhagen S, Denmark

MUNKSGAARD, JESPER, government studies educator; b. Copenhagen, July 2, 1957; s. Alf Munksgaard and Kirsten Kamper; m. Birgitte Tranum, Nov. 21, 1993; children: Gustav, Anne, Mette. MA in Econs., U. Copenhagen, 1983, PhD in Econs., 1987. Jr. rschr. Risoe Nat. Lab., Denmark, 1983-87; energy economist COWIconsult, Denmark, 1987-88; economist Komgas, Denmark, 1988-92, Danish Natural Gas A/S, Denmark, 1992-94; sr. rschr. Inst. Local Govt. Studies Amterhes Kummuruhes Forstkingsinstitut, Copenhagen, 1994-99, assoc. prof. Inst. Local Govt. Studies, 1999—. Contbr. articles to profl. jours. Home: Sonnerupvej 4, DK-2700 Brønshøi Denmark Office: AKF Inst Local Govt Studies, Nyropsgade 37, DK-1602 Copenhagen V, Denmark

MUNLU, KAMIL CEMAL, educator; b. Istanbul, Turkey, July 14, 1954; came to U.S., 1981; s. Adnan and Jale Sidika (Konari) M. BA in Econs., Calif. State U., Long Beach, 1983; MBA in Bus. Adminstrn., Nat. U., San Diego, 1986, MS in Logistics, 1988; M in Internat. Bus. Adminstrn., U.S. Internat. U., San Diego, 1990; DPA, U. La Verne, Calif., 1995. Adj. prof. Woodbury U., Burbank, Calif., 1998—; adj. prof. Nat. U., San Diego, 1999, U. La Verne, Calif., 2000. Mem. Turkish Army, 1984-85. Avocations: art, boating, golfing, reading, travel.

MUNOA, JOSÉ L., ophthalmologist, medical educator; b. San Sebastian, Spain, Feb. 14, 1926; s. Claudio and Purificacion (Roiz) M.; m. Maria P. Salvador; children: Laura, Nelida. Degree in medicine, U. Complutense, Madrid, 1951; MD, U. Salamanca, 1964. Resident in ophthalmology Hosp. Clinic U. San Carlos, Madrid, 1951-54, St. Clare's Hosp., N.Y.C., 1955-56; pvt. practice ophthalmology Policlinica Guipuzcoa, San Sebastian, 1958—; chief surgeon dept. ophthalmology Hosp. Cruz Roja Espanola, San Sebastian, Spain, 1970-75; head dept. ophthalmology Hosp. N.S. Aranzazu, San Sebastian, 1975-85; prof. ophthalmology U. Basque Country, San Sebastian, 1977-91, prof. history of medicine, 1977-87, prof. med. ethics, deontology, 1990-95, emeritus prof., 1995—. Author: Fractures of the Orbit, 1984; co-author: History of Medicine, 1964, Neuro-Ophthalmology, 1985, History of Spanish Ophthalmology, 1993. Recipient First prize Jorn. Internat. Cine Medico, 1971, Gold Hipocrates award Stampa Medica, 1984. Fellow Internat. Coll. Surgeons, Royal Coll. Ophthalmologists; mem. Sociedad Española Oftalmologia (Premio Arruga 1965), Premio Castroveijo, Societe Française D'Ophtalmologie, Am. Acad. Ophthalmology, Sociedad Española Historia de la Medicina. Office: Policlinica Guipuzcoa, Paseo Miramon 174, 20014 San Sebastian Spain

MUÑOZ, CARLOS RAMÓN, bank executive; b. N.Y.C., Dec. 8, 1935; s. Alejandro and Gladys Helena (Judah) M.; m. Wilhelmina Elaine North, June 8, 1957 (div. 1993); children: Carla Christine, Kyle Alexander. BA, Columbia U., 1957, MA, 1961. Insp., ofcl. asst. Citibank N.A., N.Y.C., 1959-64; from asst. mgr. to mgr. Dominican Republic, P.R. Citibank N.A., 1965-70; asst. v.p. Citibank N.A., N.Y.C., 1971-72, v.p., dept. head, 1972-78; sr. v.p., regional mgr. and dir. Citicorp USA, San Francisco, 1978-81, sr. v.p. mem. credit policy com., 1982-95; exec. v.p., chief credit and risk mgmt. officer Dime Savings Bank, N.Y.C., 1995—; adv. coun. Credit Rsch. Ctr., 1994—; bd. dirs. N. Am. Mortgage Corp., 1998—. Bd. dirs. Episcopal Mission Soc., N.Y.C., 1974—, v.p. 1995—; bd. dirs. Inner City Scholarship Fund, 1984-95; trustee Episcopal Diocese of N.Y., 1994—; trustee Cathedral of St. John the Divine, 1998—. 1st lt. USAR 1958-64. Recipient Productivity award State Senator Diane Watson, L.A., 1981; named Fairfield County Alumnus of Yr., 1989-90. Mem. Columbia Coll. Alumni Assn. (bd. dirs., treas. 1988-92, v.p., 1992-93, 1st v.p. 1994-96, pres. 1996-98, Alumni medal 1998), Univ. Club (N.Y.C.), Columbia Club. Republican.

MUNOZ, MARIO ALEJANDRO, civil engineer, retired consultant; b. Havana, Cuba, Feb. 27, 1928; came to U.S., 1961, naturalized, 1968; s. Ramón and Concepción (Bermudo) M.; m. Julia Josephine Garrofe, Jan. 17, 1970. M.Arch., U. Havana, 1954; postgrad., City Colls., Chgo., 1974, U. Wis., 1974. Owner Muñoz Burmudo-Construcciones, Havana, 1954-61; designer various cos. Chgo., 1961-65, designer Chgo. Transit Authority, Mdse. Mart, 1965-69; civil engr. Dept. Water and Sewers, City of Chgo., 1969-79; supervising engr. Dept. of Sewers, 1979-85, coordinating engr., 1985-88, asst. chief engr., 1988-93; mem. ctrl. area subway sys. utilities com. City of Chgo., 1974-93, mem. computer graphics com., 1977-78. Mem. Am. Pub. Works Assn., Western Soc. Engrs., Chgo. Architecture Found., Theodore Thomas Soc. Chgo. Symphony, Chgo. Coun. Fgn. Rels., Am. Mgmt. Assn., Ground Hog Club, Execs. Club (speaker's table com.), Polo and Equestrian Club of Oak Brook. Roman Catholic. Home: 5455 N Sheridan Rd Apt 1912 Chicago IL 60640-1933

MUÑOZ, RICARDO, pediatrician, educator, researcher; b. Sabinas, Coahuila, Mex., June 17, 1941; s. Ricardo and Virgnia (Arizpe) M.; m. Marisela Esquivel, Mar. 5, 1966; children: Marisela, Ricardo, Abelardo. MD, Med. Sch. Mex., 1966. Prof. Hosp. Infatil Mex., Mexico City, 1975-86, 91-00; assoc. prof. Albany (N.Y.) Med. Ctr., 1986-90; pres. Med. Assn. Hosp. Infantil Mex., Mexico City, 1993-94, Inst. Med. Rsch., Mexico City, 1997.

MUÑOZ, ROMEO SOLANO, audio visual curator, educator; b. Daraga, Philippines, July 2, 1933; s. Maximo M. and Fe (Solano) M.; m. Soledad Roselada, Jan. 2, 1964; children: Francis Vincent, Theresa Lourdes, Romualdo Romeo, Maria Cecilia, Anafe, Stephen Ignatius. BA in Psychology, Letran Coll., Manila, 1965; MS, Ea. Ill. U., 1968; MA, Gov's. State U., 1989; EdD, No. Ill. U., 1995. Audio visual curator Ateneo U., Quezon City, Philippines, 1962-67; audio visual dir. Olive-Harvey Coll., Chgo., 1969—; assoc. prof. City Coll. Chgo., 1969—; cons. adminstrv. svcs., fin. City Coll. Bd. Trustees, Chgo., 1988—; v.p. Gov.'s State U., Univ. Park, Ill. Del. AFL/CIO, Chgo., 1989, 90; deacon Archdiocese Chgo. Roman Cath. Ch., 1976—, Professed Secular Franciscan; trustee Calumet City Libr., 1993. Recipient fellowship Ea. Ill. U., Charleston, 1967-68, So. Ill. U., Carbondale, 1968-70, Gov.'s State U., Univ. Park, Ill., 1981-2000. Mem. ALA, Gov.'s State U. Alumni (bd. dirs.), Philippine Profls. Assn. (pres.), Nat. Fedn. of Filipino-Am. Orgns., Philippine Hist. Soc., Phi Delta Kappa (v.p. 1992-2000, pres. 2000). Avocation: physical fitness. E-mail: munoz8@aol.com. or

rmunoz@ccc.edu. Home: 383 Hoxie Ave Calumet City IL 60409-2330 Office: Olive-Harvey Coll 10001 S Woodlawn Ave Chicago IL 60628-1645

MUÑOZ, VICTOR EMILIO, chemist, biochemist, educator; b. Liege, Belgium, Nov. 26, 1965; came to the U.S., 1996; s. Emilio Muñoz and Maria Ángeles Van-den-Eynde. B in Biology, U. Alcala de Henares, 1989; M in Biochemistry, Autonomous U., Madrid, 1991, PhD in Biophys. Chemistry, 1995. With European Molecular Biology Lab., Heidelberg, Germany, 1992-96; postdoctoral fellow NIH, Bethesda, Md., 1996-2000; asst. prof. U. Md., College Park, 2000—. Postdoctoral fellow Human Frontiers Sci. Program, Strasbourg, France, 1996, European Molecular Biology Orgn., Heidelberg, 1996. E-mail: vmunoz@helix.nih.gov. Office: Dept Chemistry/Biochemistry Univ Md College Park MD 20742-0001

MUÑOZ-HOYOS, ANTONIO, pediatrics educator; b. Malaga, Andalucia, Spain, Nov. 30, 1950; s. Diego Muqoz-Doblas and Ascension Hoyos-Sevillano; m. May 14, 1978; children: Antonio, Domingo, Maria de Los Angeles, Ignacio. Maestro de Primera Enseñanza, Ministerio de Edn. y Ciencia, Malaga, 1972; Licenciado en Medicina y Cirugia, U. de Granada, Spain, 1976, Especialista en Pediatria y Puericultura, 1981. Asst. prof. U. Granada, 1980-85, titular prof. pediat., 1985—; Editor: Aspectos Morfofuncionales y Fisiopatologicos de la Glandula Pineal: Consideraciones de Interes Pediatrico, 1994. Mem. Assn. Española de Pediatria, Sociedad Espaqola de Pediatria Social, Medicus Mundi. Roman Catholic. Avocations: European football, sports. E-mail: amunozh@goliat.ugr.es. Fax: 34958244051. Office: U Granada Faculty Medicine, Avda de Madrid 12, 18012 Granada Spain

MUNOZ NUNEZ, RAFAEL, bishop; b. Vista Hermosa, Mex., Jan. 14, 1925; s. Francisco and Sara Munoz Nunez. Student, Seminario Conciliar de Guadalajara, Mex., Seminario Interdiocesano de Montezuma, N.Mex. Ordained priest Roman Cath. Ch., 1951. Nat. asst. Accion Catolica Mexicana; sec. Apostolic Del. in Mex.; consecrated bishop of Zacatecas Mex., 1972; bishop Diocese of Aguascalientes, Mex., 1984-98.

MUÑOZ-SOLÁ, HAYDEÉ SOCORRO, library administrator; b. Caguas, P.R., Dec. 27, 1943; d. Gilberto Muñoz and Carmen Haydeé (Solá) de Muñoz; m. Juan M. Masini-Soler, Jan. 8, 1966 (div. 1979); children: Juan Martín Masini-Muñoz, Haydeé Milagros Masini-Muñoz. BA in Psychology, U. P.R., Río Piedras, 1965, MLS, 1970; D in Libr. Sci., Columbia U., 1985. Asst. libr. U. P.R., Río Piedras, 1964-67; dir. libr. Interam. U., Aguadilla, P.R., 1974-75; head svcs. to pub. U. P.R., Aguadilla, 1975-76; cataloguer Cath. U., Ponce, P.R., 1976-79; cataloguer U. P.R., Río Piedras, 1982-84, head libr. and info. sci. libr., 1984-85, prof. grad. libr. sch., 1986, 99, dir. libr. sys., 1986-93, coord. external resources libr. sys., 1994-97; dir. of libr. U. P.R., Ponce, P.R., 1997; collection devel. officer U. P.R., Rio Piedras, 1998-2000, sabbatical leave, 2000-01; dir. P.R. Newspaper Project, Río Piedras, 1986-90; mem. Adv. Com. on Pub. Librs., San Juan, 1987-93; proposal reviewer NEH, 1990—; chmn. Puerto Rican Del. to Nat. White House Conf. on Libr. and Info. Svcs., 1991. Author: La Información y la Documentación Educativa/Informe Sobre la Situación Actual en Puerto Rico, 1991, Memorias: Segunda Pre-Conferencia de Casa Blanca Sobre Bibliotecas y Servicios de Información en Puerto Rico, 1991, Lineamientos para Colecciones Bibliograficas Nacionales, 1997, Premio por Excelencia en Investigación Aplicada y Publicación, 1997; compiler, editor ann. Puerto Rican Bibliography, 1999—; contbr. articles to profl. jours. Mem. Ponce Sport Club, 1976-83, ARC, Ponce, 1978. Recipient plaque White House Pre-Conf. on Libr. and Info. Scis., 1990, others; French Alps Study Tour scholar Assn. Caribbean Univ. Rsch. and Instl. Librs., 1989, Germany Study Tour scholar Fgn. Rels. Office, Germany, 1991. Mem. ALA, Am. Mgmt. Assn., Grad. Sch. Libr. and Info. Sci. Alumni Assn. (pres. 1988-90), Seminar for Acquisitions L.Am. Libr. Materials, Iberoamerican Nat. Librs. Assn. (pres. 1992-93), Puerto Rican Librs. Soc. (coord. So. area 1974, Lauro award 1989, Rsch. and Pub. award 1998), Assn. Caribbean U. Rsch. and Instnl. Librs. (Parchment award 1988), Asoc. para las Comunicaciones y Tecnología Educativa, Mid. States Assn. Colls. and Schs. (collaborator), Am. Women Assn., Nat. Commn. P.R. Women, Phi Delta Kappa (chair P.R. com. 1988-90, Kappan of Yr. 1990), Eta Gamma Delta. Roman Catholic. Avocations: reading, crewel work, embroidery, knitting, movies.

MUNRO, ALICE, author; b. Wingham, Ont., Can., July 10, 1931; d. Robert Eric and Anne Clarke (Chamney) Laidlaw; m. James Armstrong Munro, 1951 (div. 1976); children: Sheila, Jenny, Andrea; m. Gerald Fremlin, 1976. BA, U. Western Ont., 1952, DLitt (hon.), 1976. Author: (short stories) Dance of the Happy Shades, 1968 (Gov.-Gen.'s Lit. award 1969), A Place for Everything, 1970, Lives of Girls and Women, 1971 (Can. Booksellers award, 1972), (short stories) Something I've Been Meaning To Tell You, 1974, Who Do You Think You Are?, 1979 (pub. in U.S. as Beggar Maid: Stories of Flo and Rose, 1984, Gov.-Gen.'s Lit. award 1978), The Moons of Jupiter, 1982, The Progress of Love, 1986 (Gov. Gens. Lit. award 1987), Friend of My Youth, 1990, (short stories) Open Secrets, 1994, A Wilderness Station, 1994, Selected Stories, 1996, The Love of a Good Woman, 1998 (Fiction prize Nat. Book Critics Circle 1999); TV scripts: A Trip to the Coast, 1973, Thanks For The Ride, 1973, How I Met My Husband, 1974, 1847: The Irish, 1978. Recipient Can.-Australia Lit. Prize 1994, Marian Engel award, 1986. Office: The Writers Shop 101 5th Ave New York NY 10003-1008

MUNRO, DONALD, psychology educator; b. Torbeck, Sutherland, Scotland, Oct. 16, 1940; arrived in Australia, 1984; s. Donald and Catherine (Matheson) M.; m. Irene Adams Henderson, Sept. 3, 1964; children: Karen Imanda, Lisa Jane. BA in Psychology with honors, Manchester (Eng.) U., 1965, MA in Psychology, 1967; PhD in Psychology, London U., 1973. Registered psychologist NSW, Australia and Zimbabwe. Rsch. fellow U. Zambia, 1965-69; lectr., sr. lectr. U. Rhodesia, 1970-78, prof. psychology, 1978-84, head psychology dept., 1974-82; sr. lectr. U. Newcastle, Australia, 1984—; head psychology dept. U. Newcastle, 1994-96. Co-author: Heterogeneity in Cross-cultural Psychology, 1989; contbr. articles to profl. jours. Fellow Zimbabwe Psychol. Assn. (life); mem. Internat. Soc. Study of Individual Differences, Internat. Assn. Applied Psychology, Australian Psychol. Assn., Coll. Organizational Psychologists. Avocation: photography. Office: Psychology Dept, Univ Newcastle, Newcastle NSW 2308, Australia

MUNRO, DONALD SINCLAIR, endocrinologist, educator; b. London, Feb. 14, 1925; m. Helen Reid Phemister, Dec. 28, 1951; children: Alistair, Janet, Duncan, Elizabeth. MBChB, Med. Sch., Aberdeen, 1947, MD, 1957. House physician Royal Infirmary, Aberdeen, 1947; asst. lect. Materia Medica, Aberdeen U., 1948-49; med. registrar Tchg. Hosps., Aberdeen, 1951-53; lectr. therapeutics Sheffield U., 1953-59, sr. lectr., 1959-65, reader clin. endocrine, 1965-67, prof. clin. endocrine, 1967-73, Sir Arthur Hall prof. medicine, 1973-90; ret., 1990; hon. cons. Sheffield Health Authority, 1959-90. Mem. editl. bd. Jour. Endocrinology, 1963-75, Clin. Endocrinology, 1978-80; contbr. articles to profl. jours. Served with RAMC, 1949-51. Rsch. fellow New Eng. Med. Ctr., 1957-58. Mem. Assn. Physicians Great Britain and Ireland, Royal Soc. Medicine, Soc. Endocrinology, Am. Thyroid Assn. (assoc.), Med. Rsch. Soc. Home: 26 Endcliffe Grove Ave,, Sheffield, South Yorkshire S10 3EJ, England

MUNROE, PAUL RICHARD, electron microscopy educator; b. Marton, Eng., Apr. 14, 1963; arrived in Australia, 1990; s. Henry and Pauline Valerie (Lamb) M.; m. Gillian Carmichael, Feb. 13, 1993. BSc in Metallurgy, U. Birmingham, Eng., 1984; PhD in Metallurgy, U. Birmingham, 1987. Rsch. asst. prof. Dartmouth Coll., Hanover, N.H., 1987-90; dir. electron microscopy U. New South Wales, Sydney, Australia, 1990—. Contbr. more than 125 articles to profl. jours. Recipient Philips Cowley-Moodie award Australian Electron Microscopy Soc., 1996. Avocations: opera, cricket.

MUNSHI, AZIZ A., minister of law. Jr. in legal practice Offices of I.I. Chundrigar, Karachi, Pakistan, 1955-60; atty. gen. Pakistan, 1985-86, 88, 1990-93, min. of law; vice chmn. Asian African Legal Consultative conf., 1991; defended dissolution of Nat. Assembly. Author constnl. legislation. Office: Ministry of Law, Pakistan Secretariat Blk R, Islamabad Pakistan*

MUNSHI, PRABHAT, engineering educator, researcher; b. Kanpur, U.P., India, Mar. 7, 1956; s. Brij Krishna and Asha (Zutshi) M.; m. Sangita Bahadur. B Tech., Indian Inst. Tech., Kanpur, 1977, PhD, 1989; MS, Ohio State U., 1979. Engr. Commonwealth Edison, Chgo., 1979-82; lectr. Indian Inst. Tech., Kanpur, 1983-89, asst. prof., 1989-94, assoc. prof., 1994-96, prof., 1997—. Contbr. article to profl. jour. Mem. Indian Nuclear Soc., Assn. Med. Physicists India. Office: IIT, Dept Nuclear and Mechanical Engrng, 208-016 Kanpur Uttar Pradesh, India

MUNSLOW, ALUN, historiographer, educator; b. Connah's Quay, Wales, Dec. 15, 1947; s. Wallace Samuel and Beatrice (Walker) M.; m. Carolyn Jane Rideout, Sept. 29, 1973. BSc in Social Sci., U. Bradford, Wales, 1970; PhD, U. Wales, 1979. Lectr. Staffordshire Poly., Stafford, Eng., 1974-80, sr. lectr., 1980-91; prin. lectr., prof. of History and Hist. Theory Staffordshire U., 1991—. Author: Discourse and Culture, 1992, Deconstructing History, 1997, (with O.R. Ashton) Our American Cousins, 1992, (with O.R. Ashton) H.D. Lloyd's Critiques of American Capitalism, 1995, The Routledge Companion to Historical Studies, 2000; U.K. editor: Rethinking History: The Journal of Theory and Practice. Mem. Brit. Assn. for Am. Studies (treas. 1991-96), Am. Hist. Assn., Hist. Assn. Avocations: classical music, crosswords, golf. Office: Staffordshire U, Staffordshire U, Dept History & Politics, Stoke-on-Trent ST4 2DE, England

MUNSON, JANIS ELIZABETH TREMBLAY, engineering company executive; b. Beverly, Mass., Dec. 17, 1948; d. Louis Story Tremblay and Doroth Ellen (Burnham) Tonkin; divorced. BS in Geology summa cum laude, Boston U., 1976, M in Urban Planning, 1982. Tech. libr. United Engrs. & Constructors, Boston, 1971-73, land use planner, 1973-76, lead land use planner, 1976-80, supervising lic. engr., 1980—, environ./scientific cons., 1980-85, head mktg. analysis svcs. group power div., 1987-89, mgr. land use planning group, 1989-92, sr. ptnr., 1992—. Bd. dirs. Ctr. City Residents Assn., Phila., 1986; mem. Multiple Sclerosis Soc.; vol. for disabled. Mem. Internat. Platform Assn., Internat. Biog. Inst., Am. Planning Assn., Am. Inst. Cert. Planners (assoc.), World Affairs Coun., Smithsonian Assn. Republican. Congregationalist. Achievements include research on transmission line site selection process, on crime control through environmental design, on emotion exercise and nutrition fro those labeled chronic/progressive. Home: 2401 Pennsylvania Ave Apt 30-50 Philadelphia PA 19130-3010 Office: United Engrs and Constructors 30 S 17th St Philadelphia PA 19103-4001

MUNSON, NANCY KAY, lawyer; b. Huntington, N.Y., June 22, 1936; d. Howard H. and Edna M. (Keenan) Munson. Student, Hofstra U., 1959-62; JD, Bklyn. Law Sch., 1965. Bar: N.Y. 1966, U.S. Supreme Ct. 1970, U.S. Ct. Appeals (2d cir.) 1971, U.S. Dist. Ct. (ea. and so. dists.) N.Y. 1968. Law clk. to E. Merritt Weidner Huntington, 1959-66, sole practice, 1966—; mem. legal adv. bd. Chgo. Title Ins. Co., Riverhead, N.Y., 1981—; bd. dirs., legal officer Thomas Munson Found. Arustee Huntington Fire Dept. Death Benefit Fund; pres., trustee, chmn. bd. Bklyn. Home Aged Men Found.; bd. dirs. Elderly Day Svcs. on the Sound, Huntington Rural Cemetery Assn., Inc. Mem. ABA, N.Y. State Bar Assn., Suffolk County Bar Assn., Bklyn. Bar Assn., NRA, DAR, Soroptimists (past pres.). Republican. Christian Scientist. Office: 197 New York Ave Huntington NY 11743-2711

MUNSON, PAUL LEWIS, pharmacologist; b. Washta, Iowa, Aug. 21, 1910; s. Lewis Sylvester and Alice E. (Orser) M.; m. Aileen Geisinger, Mar. 7, 1931 (div. 1948); 1 dau., Abigail (Mrs. Mark Krumel); m. Mary Ellen Jones, Aug. 15, 1948 (div. 1971); children: Ethan Vincent, Catherine Laura; m. Yu Chen, Feb. 27, 1987; 1 stepchild, Ming An Chen. B.A., Antioch Coll., 1933; M.A., U. Wis., 1937; Ph.D., U. Chgo., 1942; M.A. (hon.), Harvard, 1955. Fellow, asst. biochemistry U. Chgo., 1939-42; research biochemist William S. Merrell Co., Cin., 1942-43; research biochemist, head endocrinology research Armour Labs., Chgo., 1943-48; research asst., then research asso. Yale Sch. Medicine, 1948-50; asst. prof., asso. prof. pharmacology, then prof. Harvard Sch. Dental Medicine, 1950-65; prof. pharmacology, chmn. dept. U. N.C. Sch. Medicine, 1965-77, Sarah Graham Kenan prof., 1970—; Mem. U.S. Pharmacopeia Panel on Corticotropin, 1951-55; mem. pharmacology test com. Nat. Bd. Med. Examiners, 1966-71; mem. gen. medicine B study section NIH, 1966-70, chmn., 1969-70, mem. pharmacology-toxicology rev. com., 1972-76. Author numerous articles on hormones; co-editor: Vitamins and Hormones, 1968-82; editl. bd. Endocrinology, 1957-63, Jour. Pharmacology and Exptl. Therapeutics, 1959-65, Jour. Dental Rsch., 1962-64, Biochem. Medicine, 1967-84, Am. Jour. Chinese Medicine, 1973-79, 99—, Pharmacol. Revs., 1967-70, editor-in-chief, 1977-81; editor-in-chief: Principles of Pharmacology, 1981-94. Fellow AAAS, Am. Acad. Arts and Scis.; mem. Am. Soc. Pharmacology and Exptl. Therapeutics (council 1970-73, sec.-treas. 1971-72), Am. Soc. Biol. Chemists, Endocrine Soc. (council 1963-65, Fred Conrad Koch award 1976), Am. Soc. Bone and Mineral Research (William F. Neuman award 1982), Am. Chem. Soc., Biometrics Soc., Internat. Assn. Dental Research (councillor 1957-59), AAUP, ACLU (mem. internat. confs. on calcium regulating hormones, Elsevier Sci. Pubs. award 1989), Assn. Med. Sch. Pharmacology (council 1971-73, sec. 1972-73, pres. 1974-76), Am. Thyroid Assn. (nominating com. 1973), Sigma Xi. Dem. Socialist. Unitarian. Home and Office: 1520 Taylor Ave Parkville MD 21234-5241

MUNSON, VIRGINIA ALDRICH, interior designer, decorator; b. Evanston, Ill., Oct. 10, 1932; d. Jefferson Elliott and Catherine (Stinson) Aldrich; m. John Chester Munson, Feb. 4, 1956; children: Catherine, John Jr., Laura. AA, Bennett Junior Coll., 1952. Owner, pres. Virginia Munson Interiors, Lake Forest, Ill., 1967—. Mem. Lake Forest Ctr. Infant Welfare Soc., 1957-93, pres., 1976-78; active com. candidates caucus, Lake Forest, 1984-87; mem. women's bd. Lake Forest Hosp., 1977—, Guild of Chgo. Hist. Soc., 1990—; bd. dirs. Infant Welfare Soc. Chgo., 1967-93, Ill. Regent Gunston Hall, 1988-96, Altar Guild, Ch. of the Holy Spirit, 1980—; bd. trustees St. Mary's Svcs., 1998—. Mem. Am. Soc. Interior Designers (Allied 1989—), Nat. Soc. Colonial Dames Am. (pres. State of Ill. br. 1982-84), Soc. Mayflower Descendants, Contemporary Club, Onwentsia Club, Winter Club. Republican. Episcopalian. Avocations: tennis, needlepoint. E-mail: Ginmunson@aol.com.

MÜNSTER, GERNOT, theoretical physicist, educator; b. Elmshorn, Germany, Oct. 11, 1952; m. Ulrike Aude; children: Clemens, Christoph. Diploma in Physics, U. Hamburg, 1978, PhD in Theoretical Physics, 1980. Prof. theoretical physics U. Münster, Germany, 1990—. Co-author: Quantum Fields on a Lattice, 1994. Office: U Münster, Wilhelm-Klemm Str 9, D-48149 Münster Germany

MUNTANER, CARLES, social epidemiologist, researcher, educator; s. Juan and Carmen Bonet Muntaner; m. Patricia O'Campo, Aug. 19, 1991. BS, Lycee Francais, Toulouse, France, 1975; MD, U. Barcelona, 1982, PhD, 1986. Asst. prof. U. Autonoma of Barcelona, 1982-86, W.Va. U., Morgantown, 1996-99; assoc. prof. U. Md., Balt., 2000—; vis. fellow Nat. Inst. Drug Abuse, Balt., 1986-89; Fulbright fellow Johns Hopkins U., Balt., 1989-91; vis. assoc. Nat. Inst. Mental Health, Bethesda, Md., 1991-96. Author: (with others) ILO Encyclopedia, 1998, Sociology of Mental Disorders, 1999; contbr. articles to profl. jours. including Am. Jour. Epidemiology and Social Sci. Medicine. Office: U Md 655 W Lombard St Baltimore MD 21201-1512

MUNTASSER, MOHAMED ABDULLA, engineering educator; b. Souk Guma, Libya, Jan. 21, 1945; s. Mohamed Abdalla and Fatma Ali (ElZwawi) M.; m. Fawzia Mustaffa Farres, Sept. 9, 1970; children: Shada, Zeiad, Deigh Adean, Talal, Nada. Issra. BS, Faculty Engrng., Tripoli, Libya, 1969; MS, Purdue U., 1972; PhD, N.C. State U., 1978. Head grad. studies dept. Faculty Engrng., Tripoli, Libya, 1980-82, head asroengrng. dept., 1982-84, head solar lab., 1984-89, assoc. dean, 1986-87, chmn. mech. engrng. dept., 1987-89, lectr., 1989—; gen. mgr. Shara Engrng. Consultancy Office, Tripoli; pres. IEF, Tripoli, 1989—; com. mem. numerous internat. conf., Libyan U., Teaching Union. Contbr. more than 60 articles to profl. jours. Mem. ASME, Am. Soc. Engrng. Edn., Libyan Engrng. Union, Libyan Univ. Teaching Union, Arab Engrng. Union, Internat. Soc. Solar Energy. E-mail: iefmuntasser@hotmail.com; Fax: á-21-3331831. Office: Internat Energy Found, PO Box 83617, Tripoli Libya

MUNTEANU, FLORIN, aerodynamicist, researcher; b. Oravita, Romania, Feb. 23, 1946; s. Diomid Munteanu and Antonia Levandovski; m. Viorica Vlad, Nov. 11, 1971; children: Emilia-Diana, Anca-Magdalena. Diploma in engrng., Politechnical Inst., Bucharest, Romania, 1968; PhD, Nat. Inst. Sci. Tech. Creation, Bucharest, 1980. Cert. scientifical rschr. 1st class. Scientifical rschr. Inst. Fluid Mechanics and Aerospace Constrns., Bucharest, 1973-78; scientifical rschr. 3d class Nat. Inst. Sci. Tech. Creation, Bucharest, 1978-90; scientifical rschr. 1st class Inst. Aviation, Bucharest, 1990-91; lab. head Trisonic Wind Tunnel Nat. Inst. Aerospace Rsch., Bucharest, 1991—; assoc. prof. Mil. Tech. Acad., Bucharest, 1989. Contbr. articles to profl. jours. Sub-lt. Romanian Air Force, 1968-69. Mem. Romanian Orthodox. Achievements include patents in Aerodynamic Balance Calibration Rig. Fax: 401-413-0690. Office: Nat Inst Aerospace Rsch, Bd Iuliu Maniu 220 Sector 6, 77538 Bucharest Romania

MUNTON, CHARLES GREGORY, consultant ophthamalic surgeon; b. Smethwick, Eng., Mar. 11, 1933; s. Francis Thomas and Winifred (McCann) M.; m. June Veronica Hall, Aug. 15, 1960; children: Dominic, Timothy, Rachel, Christopher. MB, ChB, U. Birmingham, Eng., 1960. Registered Med. Practitioner, U.K. House surgeon Royal Hosp., Wolverhampton, Eng., 1960; house physician Gen. Hosp., Birmingham, Eng., 1961; sr. house surgeon County Hosp., York, Eng., 1961-63; registrar Midland Counties Eye Infirmary, Wolverhampton, Eng., 1963-65; sr. registrar Eye and Ear Hosp., Shrewsbury, Eng., 1965-67; cons. ophthalmic surgeon Kent County Ophthalmic and Aural Hosp., Maidstone, Eng., 1967-96, St. Bartholomew's Hosp., Rochester, Eng., 1967-96; pvt. practice ophthalmic surgery Maidstone, Eng., 1967—; chmn. visual stds. com. Coll. Ophthamology, London, 1989-95; chmn. med. adv. com. Somerfield Hosp., Maidstone. Author: Regional Strategy for Ophthalmology, 1993; contbr. articles to profl. jours., including Brit. Jour. Ophthalmology, Am. Intraocular Implant Soc. Jour., European Jour. Implant and Refractive Surgery, also chpts. to books. Mem. S.E. Thames Regional Health Authority, 1988-94, chmn. ophthalmology specialist adv. com.; nat. del. Ophthamology, European Union of Med. Specialists, 1988-96. Fellow Royal Coll. Surgeons Eng., Royal Coll. Ophthamologists (coun. mem. 1988-94); mem. Faculty Ophthamologists (coun. mem. 1985-88)), Royal Soc. Medicine, Oxford Ophthalmol. Congress (dept. master 1992), Radio Soc. Great Britain. Roman Catholic. Avocations: amateur radio, photography, optical-laser physics, music. Home: 86 Amsbury Rd, Kent, ME15OQH Maidstone England Office: 36 Marsham St, Kent, ME141HG Maidstone England

MUNZ, DIANA, Olympic athlete; b. Cleve., Jan. 19, 1982; d. Robert and Carol Munz. Recipient Gold medal 4 x 200-meter freestyle Sydney Olympics, 2000, Silver medal 800-meter freestyle World Championships, 1998; winner 800-meter freestyle, non-Olympic 1500-meter freestyle nat. championships, spring and summer 1998, spring 1999, 400-meter freestyle nat. championships, spring 1999. Office: USA Swimming 1 Olympic Plz Colorado Springs CO 80909-5746*

MUNZ, DIETER LUDWIG, nuclear medicine physician; b. Schwäbisch Gmünd, Germany, Feb. 9, 1952; s. Ludwig and Martha Maria Munz; m. Christine Sabine Haug, Oct. 26, 1979; children: Florian Dieter, Sebastian Manuel. MD, U. Ulm, Germany, 1979; PhD, U. Frankfurt, Germany, 1984. Med. diplomate. Intern anatomy, pathology and medicine U. Ulm, 1978-79; resident nuclear medicine U. Düsseldorf and Frankfurt, 1979-81; fellow, asst. chief nuclear medicine U. Frankfurt, 1981-84; Heisenberg stipend Deutsche Forschungsgemeinschaft, Wistar Inst. & Hosp. U. Pa., Phila., M.D., 1984-86, Nat. Inst. Health, Bethesda, M.D., 1984-86; assoc. prof. nuclear medicine, dep. chief dept. U. Göttingen, Germany, 1986-94; prof., chmn. nuclear medicine, dir. Clinic Nuclear Medicine Charité, Humboldt U., Berlin, 1994—; adj. assoc. prof. radiology U. Pa., Phila., 1986-94, adj. prof. radiology, 1995—. Mem. editl. bd. several med. jours.; editor: Immunoscintigraphy: Facts and Fiction, 1990; contbr. articles to profl. jours. Recipient prizes Acad. Soc. of U. of Ulm, Germany, 1982, Med. Faculty of U. Frankfurt, Germany, 1983, Fiebiger professorship award Ministry of Sci. and Rsch. of State of Lower Saxony, Germany, 1988. Mem. AAAS, Soc. Nuclear Medicine, N.Y. Acad. Scis., others. Avocations: classical and modern music, soccer, tennis, theatre, opera. Home: Berliner Str 102, D-14169 Berlin Germany Office: Humboldt U Klinik f Nuklearmedizin, Schumannstr 20/21, D-10098 Berlin Germany

MUNZINGER, LUDWIG WERNER, editor; b. Weingarten, Germany, Feb. 24, 1921; s. Ludwig and Cora (Hartenstein) M.; m. Maria Johanna Rülke, June 9, 1951; children: Ernst, Anne, Cornelia, Ina. Law exam., U. Tübingen, 1952; 2d law exam., State Baden-Württemberg, 1955; JD, U. Tübingen, 1956. Lawyer Ravensburg, Germany, 1955-70; editor Munzinger-Archiv GmbH, Ravensburg, 1957—. Author: Rechtlicher Schutz der Nachricht; author, editor: (periodicals) Internat. Biographisches Archiv, 1955—, Internat. Handbuch—Länder aktuell, 1955—. Town councillor Stadtrat, Ravensburg, 1963-65. Recipient Medal of Merit, Land Baden-Württemberg, 1992. Mem. Rotary Club Ravensburg. Christlich-Demokratische Union. Avocations: tennis, history. Office: Munzinger-Archiv GmbH, Albersfelder Strasse 34, D-88213 Ravensburg Germany

MUPANEMUNDA, RICHARD HENRY J., pediatrician; b. Harare, Zimbabwe, Aug. 12, 1955; s. Emerson Ophard and Grace Clara (Mutseriwa) M.; m. Ratidzo Florence Danha, July 23, 1994; children: Grace, Shauna. BSc with honors, Liverpool (Eng.) U., 1979; B Medicine, Southampton U., Eng., 1983. Sr. house officer pediatric cardiology Hosp. Sick Children, London, 1987; sr. house officer pediatrics St. Marys Hosp., London, 1988-89; pediatric registrar York Hill Hosp. Sick children, Glasgow, Scotland, 1989; resident U. Western Ont., London, Can., 1989-90; sr. clin. fellow Hosp. for Sick Children, Toronto, 1990-91; pediatrician Hammersmith Hosp., London, 1991—; vice-chair London Borough of Fulham & Hammersmith Area Child Protection Com., London, 1992—; mem. Brit. Pediatric Assn. Working Party on Pediatric Exams., London, 1995—. Author: Preterm Labor, 1996; contbr. articles to profl. jours. Project grantee Royal Soc. London, 1993, Hammersmith Spl. Trustees, London, 1996. Mem. Royal Coll. Physicians, Brit. Med. Assn. (H.C. Roscoe fellowship 1994), Brit. Pediatric Assn., Am. Thoracic Soc. Labour party. Avocations: long distance running, travel, scuba diving, computing. Office: Hammersmith Hosp, Du Cane Rd, London W12 ONN, England

MURA, GÉRARD PAUL PACIFIQUE, company executive; b. Ambleny, France, Mar. 24, 1946; s. Paul and Odette (Cezin) M.; m. Corazon Cruz, June 5, 1971; children: Christophe, Florence. Degree in Engrng., Ecole Nat. Superieur Arts métiers, Lille, France, 1969; MSEE, Carnegie-Mellon U., 1970. Gen. mgr. SCPB and ISBA subs. of VALEO, Paris, 1981-85; mng. dir. trucks clutch divsn. VALEO, Paris, 1985-89, mng. dir. friction materials divsn., 1989-90; CEO Bendix Friction Materials (AlliedSignal Group), Paris, 1990-94, Bendix Europe (AlliedSignal Group), Paris, 1992-94; gen. mgr., then CEO, exec. pres. AFE Group, Paris, 1995—. Mem. Automobile Club France. Avocations: golf, opera. Office: AFE, 15-17 Bd du Gen de Gaulle, 92120 Montrouge France

MURA, PATRICK, toxicologist, researcher; b. Casablanca, Morocco, Oct. 4, 1948; s. Raymond and Reine (Lehideux) M.; m. Sylvette Eyrignou, Sept. 3, 1975; children: Virginie, Francois. D in Pharmaceuticals, Univ., Poitiers, France, 1977; degree in Med. Pathology, Univ., Linoges, France, 1980; degree in Toxicology, Univ., Paris, 1983. Lab. mgr. U. Hosp., Poitiers, France, 1984—; cons. Syva-Behring, Paris, 1995-98. Author: Therapeutique Psychiatrique, 1997, Toxicologie et Pharmacologie, 1998, Dictionnaire des Drogues, 1999; editor: Alcool, Medicaments, Stupefiants et Conduite, 1999. Fellow CNBE; mem. French Soc. Toxicology (Poitier chpt. v.p. 1996—). Avocations: tennis, fishing, hunting. Home: 15th rue des Tamoris, 86580 Vouneuil France Office: Toxicology Lab, C H U, 86021 Poitiers France

MURAD, ENVER, mineralogist; b. Berlin, June 9, 1941; s. Fehmi and Rosa (Spiro) M.; m. Gerda Maria Kleffmann, Sept. 26, 1969; children: Nadja Simone Andrea, Nicole Daniela. Mineralogist, Tech. Hochschule Darmstadt, 1967; dr. phil. nat., U. Frankfurt, 1970; dr. rer. nat. habil., Tech. Univ. Munich, 1986. Rschr. U. Tubingen, Germany, 1970-75, Tech. U. Munich, Germany, 1975-93; sect. head Bayerisches Geologisches Landesamt, Bamberg, Germany, 1993—. Assoc. editor Jour. European Clay Groups, 1997—; contbr. chpts. in books and articles to profl. jours. Fellow Mineral. Soc. Britain; mem. Mineral. Soc. Germany, Mineral. Soc. Am., Am. Geophys. Union, Geochem. Soc., Clay Minerals Soc. Avocations: travel, photography, rock hounding. Office: Bayerisches Geol Landesamt, Leopoldstrasse 30, D-95615 Marktredwitz Germany

MURAD, FERID, physician; b. Whiting, Ind., Sept. 14, 1936; s. John and Josephine Murad; m. Carol Ann Leopold, June 21, 1958; children: Christine, Marianne, Carrie, Julie, Joseph. BA, DePauw U., 1958; MD, Case Western Res. U., 1965, PhD, 1965. Diplomate Nat. Bd. Med. Examiners. Intern and resident Mass. Gen. Hosp., Boston, 1965-67; clin. assoc. NIH, Bethesda, Md., 1967-70; from assoc. prof. to prof. U. Va., Charlottesville, 1970-81, dir. clin. research ctr., 1971-81, dir. clin. pharmacology, 1973-81; prof. Stanford (Calif.) U., 1981-88, assoc. to acting chmn. dept. medicine, 1984-88; chief of medicine VA Med. Ctr., Palo Alto, Calif., 1981-88; v.p. pharm. divsn. Abbott Labs., 1988-92, CEO, pres. molecular geriatrics, 1993-95; prof. dept. medicine, chmn. dept. integrative biology and pharmacology U. Tex., Houston, 1997—, dir. Inst. Molecular Medicine, 1999—. Co-editor The Pharmacological Basis of Therapeutics, 7th edit., 1985; patentee in field; contbr articles to profl. jours. Recipient Lasker award, 1996, Nobel prize for medicine, 1998, others. Mem. NAS, Inst. Medicine, Am. Acad. Arts & Scis., Am. Soc. for Pharmacology and Exptl. Therapeutics, Am. Soc. Biol. Chemists, Am. Soc. Physiology, Am. Soc. Clin. Investigation, Assn. Am. Physicians, Western Assn. Physicians (Ciba award 1988, Lasker award 1996). Office: U Tex Med Sch Dept Integrative Biology/Pharmacology PO Box 20708 Houston TX 77225-0708

MURADOV, SAKHAT NEPESOVICH, Turkmen government official, educator; b. Ivanovo, Russia, May 7, 1932; s. Nepes Muradov and Nursoltan Muradova; m. Sona Höwme, Apr. 24, 1954; children: Murad, Serdar, Maya. Diploma high edn., Turkmen Agrl. Inst., Ashgabat, Turkmenistan, 1956; diploma candidate of sci., Acad. Scis. Turkmenistan, Ashgabat, 1962, DSc, 1991. Sr. lab asst. Agrl. Inst., Ashgabat, 1956-57; jr. rsch. worker, head dept. rsch. inst. Acad. of Scis., Ashgabat, 1960-65, dep. chmn. Coun. for Coordination of Rsch., 1965-70; rector Turkmen State U., Ashgabat, 1970-79, prof., 1977—; min. Ministry for Higher Edn., Ashgabat, 1979-85; rector Turkmen Polytechnic U., Ashgabat, 1985-90; 1st dep. chmn. Supreme Soviet of Turkmenistan, Ashgabat, 1990-92; chmn. Mejlis of Turkmenistan, Ashgabat, 1992—. Author 3 books; contbr. 51 articles to profl. manuals. Chmn. Solidarity Com. for African Asian Nations, Ashgabat, 1971-93, Turkmen-Indian Friendship Soc., Ashgabat, 1973-83, Ashgabat City Soc. of Knowledge, 1970-90; dep. chmn. Turkmenistan Rep. Soc. Knowledge, 1983-90. Decorated (2) Order of Red Banner of Labour (Supreme Soviet of USSR), Star of Pres. (Turkmenistan). Avocations: sports, tourism, literature. Office: Mejlis of Turkmenistan, 17 Bitarap Turkmenistan St, 744000 Ashgabat Turkmenistan

MURAGE, STANLEY KARUTHAI, quantity surveyor; b. Kirinyaga District, Kenya, May 18, 1950; s. Karuthai Ngunga and Zipporah Waruguru (Koigi) Karuthai; m. Monica Nyambura Mbuthia. BA in Quality Surveying with honors, U. Nairobi, Kenya, 1974. Asst. quantity surveyor Govt. Kenya, Nairobi, 1974-76, quantity surveyor, 1976-77; quantity surveyor ArmstronG & Duncan, Chartered Quantity Surveyors, Nairobi, 1977-78; ptnr. Armstron & Duncan, Chartered Quantity Surveyors, Nairobi, 1978—; permanent sec. Govt. Kenya, Nairobi, 1994—. Fellow Archtl. Assn. Kenya; mem. Chartered Inst. Arbitrators, Surveyor's Inst. Zambia. Office: Armstrong & Duncan Adak Ho, Milimani Rd PO Box 40426, Nairobi Kenya

MURAI, RENE VICENTE, lawyer; b. Havana, Cuba, Mar. 11, 1945; came to the U.S., 1960; s. Andres and Silvia (Muñiz) M.; m. Luisa Botifoll, June 12, 1970; 1 child, Elisa. BA, Brown U., 1966; JD cum laude, Columbia U., 1969. Bar: Fla. 1970, N.Y. 1972, U.S. Supreme Ct. 1977. Atty. Reginald Heber Smith Fellow Legal Svcs. Greater Miami, Fla., 1969-71; assoc. Willkie, Farr & Gallagher, N.Y.C., 1971-73; ptnr. Paul, Landy & Beiley, Miami, 1973-79; shareholder Murai, Wald, Biondo & Moreno, Miami, 1979—; acting chmn. bd. dirs. PanAm. Bank, Miami; dir. Cuban Am. Bar Assn., 1982-96, pres., 1985; vice chmn., lectr. Internat. Conf. for Lawyers of the Ams., 1982, chmn. and lectr., 1984; mem. panel grievance com. Fla. Bar, 1983-86. Mng. editor Columbia Law Rev., 1967-69. Bd. dirs., sec. Archtl. Club of Miami, 1978-86; bd. dirs. Dade Heritage Trust, 1979-82, Facts About Cuban Exiles, Inc., 1982—, pres., 1989, Legal Svcs. of Greater Miami, Inc., 1980-90, pres. 1986-88, ARC, 1984-90, exec. com., 1988-90, Mercy Hosp. Found., 1985-91, United Way, 1989-95, dir. Dade Cmty. Found., 1988-93, chair grants com., 1991-93; chmn. adminstrn. of justice com. Fla. Bar Found., 1996-98, bd. dirs., 1991-2000, chmn. audit and fin. com., 1993-98, sec., 1997-98, pres. 1999-2000; mem. task force leadership Dade County Ptnrs. for Safe Neighborhoods, 1994-95, Code Enforcement Bd. City of Coral Gables, 1982-86, Bd. Adjustment, 1987-89, city mgr. selection com., 1987, charter rev. commn., 1980; trustee U. Miami, 1994-96; bd. dirs. Miami Children's Hosp., 1999—. Mem. ABA, Cuban-Am. Bar Assn., Dade County Bar Assn. (dir. 1987-88), Greater Miami C. of C., Spain-U.S. C. of C., Miami City Club (bd. dirs. 1997—, pres. 2000—). Democrat. Roman Catholic. Avocation: sports. Home: 3833 Alhambra Ct Coral Gables FL 33134-6229 Office: Murai Wald Biondo & Moreno PA 25 SE 2nd Ave Ste 900 Miami FL 33131-1600

MURAKAMI, EDAHIKO, chemistry educator; b. Kyoto, Japan, Jan. 11, 1922; s. Sanji and Nobuko M.; m. Hiroko, Aug. 28, 1949; children: Akihiko, Jiro. BS, Nagoya Imperial U., 1944; PhD, Nagoya U., 1947; PhD (hon.), Aichi Kyoiku U., 1965. Asst. Nagoya Imperial U., Japan, 1944-49; asst. prof. Aichi Kyoiku U., Japan, 1950-68, prof., 1968-85, honored prof., 1985-98; prof. Nagoya Women's Jr. Coll. of Commerce, Japan, 1985-99; mgr. Japanese Study Group for Tryptophan Rsch., 1974-93. Author: Kagaku Koyomi, Numon Seikagaku, 1977, Seikagaku Numon, 1989, Jinbutsu Kagakushi Jiten, 1994. Recipient Award for Disting. Svc., Assn. of the Sci. Edn., 1985, award Internat. Peace Artist, 1994. Avocations: painting. Home: 3-13 Kamioka Cho Meito-ku, Nagoya 465, Japan

MURAKAMI, MASAHIDE, mechanical engineer; b. Sapporo, Japan, June 26, 1946; s. Masao and Kimiko (Miyazawa) M.; Mitsuko Iwasawa, Oct. 1, 1972; two children. BS, U. Tokyo, 1969, MS, 1971, DSc, 1974. Assoc. NASA Ames Rsch. Ctr., 1974-76; lectr. U. Tokyo, 1977-80; from lectr. to prof. U. Tsukuba, Japan, 1980—. Author: Heat Pipe Engineering, 1979. Recipient Ooyama prize Cryogenic Soc. Japan, 1996. Home: Koyadai 3 14-10, Tsukuba 305-0074, Japan Office: U Tsukuba, Tennodai 1-1-1, Tsukuba 305-8573, Japan

MURAKAMI, MASATO, engineering educator, researcher; b. Morioka, Japan, Feb. 13, 1955; s. Matsuo and Sachiko (Kasahara) M.; m. Yukiko Tsushima, May 11, 1985; 1 child, Shiori. Bachelor, Tokyo U., 1979, Master, 1981, DEng, 1984. Rsch. scientist Nippon Steel, Japan, 1984-94; sr. rschr. Superconductivity Rsch. Lab., Tokyo, 1994-95, dir., 1995—; guest prof. Nagoya U., 1996-98, Iwate U., 1998—. Editor, author: Melt Processed HTSC, 1991, Advances in Superconductivity, 1997, Processing and Applications of (RE) BCO, 1998. Recipient NBP prize Nikkei, Tokyo, 1989, World Congress Superconductivity award of Excellence, 1991, Iwate Press Culture prize, 1996; named Man of Yr. Iwate Prefecture Assn., Tokyo, 1993. Avocations: skiing, tennis, golf, guitar. Office: Superconductivity Rsch Lab, 1-16-25 Shibaura/Minato-ku, Tokyo 105-0023, Japan

MURAKAMI, YOSHIO, educator, editor; b. Toyama-shi, Japan, Mar. 14, 1946; s. Ryoichi and Misao (Sakuho) M.; m. Mariko Mori, June 20, 1976; children: Ryohei, Momoko, Kohei. BL, Tokyo U., 1969; BA, San-iku Gakuin Coll., Chiba, Japan, 1972; MA, Andrews U., 1978; PhD, Drew U., 1994. Ordained minister Seventh-day Adventist Ch., Japan, 1983—. Editor Japan Pub. House, Yokohama, 1972-80, editor-in-chief, 1981-87, 94-96; instr. Hokuriku U., Kanazawa, Japan, 1987-91; prof. history & religion Hokuriku U., Kanazawa, 1996—; editl. advisor Japan Pub. House, 1987-91. Author: I Saw a New Heaven and a New Earth, 1987, How to Read the Bible, 1997, Eschatology, Prophecy and the Sabbath, 1998. Mem. Am. Acad. Religion, Soc. Bibl. Lit., Japanese Assn. for Am. Studies. Home: 2-30-3 Kodatsuno, Kanazawa 920-0942, Japan Office: Hokuriku U, 1-1 Taiyogaoka, Kanazawa 920-1180, Japan

MURAKI, MASATAKE, retired linguistics educator, researcher; b. Ryuyocho, Shizuoka, Japan, Jan. 26, 1923; s. Yoshitaro and Chie (Suzuki) M.; m. Keiko Honma, Dec. 1, 1955; 1 child, Kyoji. BA, Keio U., Tokyo, 1946; MA, Internat. Christian U., Tokyo, 1963; PhD, U. Tex., Austin, 1970. Tchr. Tokyo H.S., 1946-63; asst. prof. Internat. Christian U., Tokyo, 1963-88; prof. Dokkyo U., Sōka, Japan, 1988-93, Kanda U. Internat. Studies, Chiba, Japan, 1993-98; vis. prof. U. Brit. Columbia, Vancouver, Can., 1979-80; specialist mem. Acad. Terminology Commn., Ministry Edn., 1986-88. Author: (book) Presupposition and Thematisation, 1974; contbr. (book) Problems in Japanese Syntax and Semantics, 1978. Fulbright exchange tchr., San Francisco State U., 1961-62, Fulbright Rsch. scholar U. Tex., Austin, 1967-70. Mem. Linguitic Soc. Japan, English Linguistic Soc. Japan (editor 1983-87, chmn. editl. com. 1989-91), English Literary Soc. Japan (editor 1975-79). Home: 5-8-4 Mejiro Toshimaku, Tokyo 171-0031, Japan

MURALI, KRISHNAMURTHY, research scientist; b. Kulithalai, Tamilnadu, India, July 22, 1965; s. Sanjeevi Krishnamurthy and Krishnamurthy Dhanalakshmi; m. Priya Murali. BSc in Physics, Bharathidasan U., Tiruchirapalli, India, 1985, MSc in Physics, 1987, MPhil in Physics, 1988, PhD in Physics, 1995. Rsch. fellow Bharathidasan U., Tiruchirapalli, 1989-94, vis. scientist, 1994-95, scientist, 1995-98; lectr. physics Anna U., Chennai, India, 1998—. Co-author: Chaos in Nonlinear Oscillators - Controlling and Synchronization, 1996; contbr. articles to profl. jours. Dr. K.S. Krishnan Rsch. fellow Dept. Atomic Energy, Govt. India, 1989-94. Avocations: photography, painting. E-mail: kmurali@ns.annauniv.edu. Home: 116 Nakkeeran St, Cauvery Nagar, Kulithalai 639 104, India Office: Dept Physics, Anna Univ, Chennai 600 025, India

MURALIDHARA, BILIKALLAHALLI KRISHNAMURTHY, protein biochemist, researcher; b. Bilikallahalli, India, July 28, 1966; s. Bilikallahalli Lakshme Gowda Krishnamurthy and Bilikallahalli Muddappa Gowramma; m. Selanere Lingegowda Shobha, Nov. 20, 1994; 1 child, Gokul Muralidhar. BSc, U. Mysore, India, 1988, MSc, 1990, PhD in Biochemistry, 1997. Jr. rsch. fellow Ctrl. Food Technol. Rsch. Inst./U. Mysore, India, 1991-93, sr. rsch. fellow, 1993-96, rsch. assoc., 1996-97, scientist, 2000—; Japan Soc. for the Promotion of Sci. postdoctoral fellow Rsch. Inst. for Food Sci., Kyoto (Japan) U., 1998-00. Contbr. articles to profl. jours. Cadet officer Nat. Cadet Corps, New Delhi, 1987-90. Nat. Merit scholar Govt. of India, 1990; Coun. Sci. Indsl. Rsch. fellow, 1996, rsch. assoc., 1997. Mem. Soc. Biol. Chemists India (exec mem.), Indian Biophys. Soc., Nutrition Soc. India, Assn. Food Scientists and Technologists (life). Avocations: badminton, music, creative writing. Office: Dept Protein Chem & Tech, Ctrl Food Tech Rsch Inst, Mysore 570013, India

MURALIKRISHNA, POLINAYA, physicist; b. Kottachery, India, Sept. 8, 1947; arrived in Brazil, 1983; s. Polinaya and Saraswati Srinivasarao; m. Vijayavani Mallara, June 24, 1977; children: Amita, Aasita, Anoopa. BSc, Govt. Coll., Kasaragod, India, 1967; MSc, Union Christian Coll., Alwaye, India, 1969; PhD, Physical Rsch. Lab., Ahmedabad, India, 1975. Vis. scientist Physical Rsch. Lab., Ahmedabad, India, 1975-76, rsch. assoc., 1977-80, fellow, 1980-83; vis. fellow Max Planck Inst. Extraterrestrial Physics, Garching, Germany, 1976-77; from rsch. assoc. to sr. scientist Nat. Inst. Space Rsch., Sao Paulo, Brazil, 1983-94, sr. scientist, 1994—; post-graduate council Nat. Inst. Space Rsch., Sao Paulo, Brazil, 1993-97; project leader Nat. Inst. Space Rsch., 1983—; speaker in field. Contbr. over 30 articles to profl. jours. Recipient Best Student in Physics award Kerala U., India, 1966-69. Mem. Brazilian Geophysical Soc. (regional com. mem. 1994-98), Am. Geophysical Union, Indian Physics Assn. Hindu. Avocations: Indian music, jogging, shuttle badminton, swimming. E-mail: murali@dae.inpe.br. Fax: 55 12 3456990. Home: Blvd Villa Lobos 56 Apt 161, 12242-020 São José dos Campos Brazil Office: Inst Nac Pesquisas Esapciai, Av dos Astronautas 1758, 12227010 São Paulo Brazil

MURALI KRISHNA, SRIKANTESWARA SHARMA, mechanical engineering educator; b. Mysore, Karnataka, India, Oct. 15, 1960; s. Ramaswamy Handanhal and Padmini Mysore Srikanteswara; m. Sharma Sushma, Apr. 24, 1995; 1 child, Shvetha. B Mech. Engrng., Sri Jayacham. Coll. Engrng., Mysore, 1982; M Tech. in Mech. Engrng., Indian Inst. Tech., Madras, 1984, PhD, 1991. Lectr. Pondicherry (India) Engrng. Coll., 1989-92; asst. prof. Anjuman Engrng. Coll., Bhatkal, India, 1992-97; prof., head dept. Sri Ramakrishna Engrng. Coll., Coimbatore, India, 1997—; chief cons. Puduvai Bricks, Pondicherry, 1989-92, Climate Controls, Hyderabad, India, 1989-90, So. Group, Madras, 1990-97; cons. TVS-Whirlpool, Pondicherry, 1990-92. Author: Signal Data Simulation, 1995 (Best paper award), Emerging Trends in Design, 1997 (Advanced Tech. award). Mem. Citizens' Forum, Mysore, 1980, Sankethi Sanga, Mysore, 1994, Local Assn., Coimbatore, 1998, Staff Fund, Coimbatore, 1998. Recipient Vikas Rattan award India Internat. Friendship Soc., 1998, Bharat Gaurav award Indsl. Econ. Forum, 1998. Mem. Indian Soc. for Tech. Edn., Instn. Engrs., Inst. Std. Engrs. Avocations: swimming, chess, soft toys, toy circuits, cricket. Home: 4 Sridevinagar, 641006 Coimbatore Tamilnadu India Office: Sri Ramakrishna Engr Coll, NGGO Colony Post, 641022 Coimbatore Tamilnadu India

MURANAKA, HIDEO, artist, educator; b. Mitaka, Tokyo, Japan, Feb. 4, 1946; s. Nobukichi and Hisae M. BFA, Tokyo Nat. U. of Fine Arts, 1970, MFA, 1972. Calif. Community Coll.- Instr. Cred. Drawing accepted for The Pacific Coast States Collection from the v.p. house, Washington, 1980, Nat. Mus. Art, Bklyn. Mus., Achenbach Found., Calif. Palace of Legion of Hon., Yergeau-Musee Internat. d'Art (Can.). Mem. Democratic Nat. Comm., Wash., 1985—. Recipient second prize Iternat. Art Exhbn. Museo Hosio, Italy, 1984, V.J.'s Artist award Palm Springs Desert Mus., 1995; named to Hist. Preservation Am. Hall of Fame. Mem. Oakland Mus. Assn., The Fine Arts Mus. San Francisco, Lepidopterist's Soc. Avocations: collecting butterflies, music. Home: 179 Oak St Apt W San Francisco CA 94102-5948

MURANAKA, KEN-ICHIRO, biophysicist, columnist; b. Nagoya, Japan, Sept. 7, 1958; s. Megumi and Takeko (Ohtsuka) M.; m. Yumie Amatsu, May 12, 1997; 1 child, Fuyuko. BS in Math., U. Ill., Chgo., 1982; MS in Biophysics, U. Ill., Urbana, 1985. Teaching asst. U. Ill., Chgo., 1982-83, rsch. asst., summer 1983; teaching asst. U. Ill., Urbana, fall 1984, rsch. asst., 1984-85; grad. teaching assoc. Ohio State U., Columbus, 1985-87; coop. editor in patent svcs. Chem. Abstracts Svc., Columbus, 1986-87; quantitative rsch. analyst The Yasuda Trust and Banking, Tokyo, 1987-91; rsch. asst. prof. Aichi-Mizuho U., Nagoya, Japan, 1991-93; sr. rsch. scientist, chief R&D, Drug Discovery Inst. Nippon Shinyaku Pharm. Co., Kyoto, Japan, 1993—. Author: (in Japanese) Introduction to Theory of Financial Options, 1988. Edmund James scholar U. Ill. at Chgo. Mem. N.Y. Acad. Scis., Biophys. Soc. (U.S.), Am. Chem. Soc., Japan Soc. for Simulation Tech., Soc. for Econ. Studies of Securities, Chem. Soc. Japan, Phi Eta Sigma, Alpha Lambda Delta. Roman Catholic. Avocation: classical guitar.

MURANAKA, TORU, radiologist; b. Fukuoka, Japan, June 22, 1949; s. Masao and Kazuko (Kaneko) M.; m. Mikako Tahara, Apr. 3, 1988; children: Kodai, Sayaka. MD, Kyushu U., Fukuoka, 1976, DMS, 1992. Mem. staff Kyushu U., 1976-80, asst. prof., 1981-86; chief radiologist Nat. Fukuoka Ctrl. Hosp., 1987-94; chief radiologist, chief clin. rsch. med. imaging br. Nat. Kyushu Med. Ctr., Fukuoka, 1994—, dir. radiology, 1995—; organizer Pancreatic Rsch. Conf., Fukuoka, 1985; vis. lectr. Kyushu U., 1998—. Contbr. articles to Digestive Diseases and Scis., Diseases of Colon and Rectum, Am. Jour. Roentgenology, European Radiology. Recipient Irie Meml. award, 1993, winner's award ECR 95 (film reading session), 1995, Cert. of Merit ECR '97; grantee Japanese Ministry Welfare, 1985, 86, 90, 91, 92, 93, 95. Fellow Japanese Coll Radiology, Japan Pancreas Assn. (Kyushu br. organizer), Japan Radiol. Assn., Japanese Soc. Gastroenterology (coun. 1992—); mem. AAAS, Japanese Soc. Gastrointestinal Endoscopy (coun. 1992—), Japanese Assn. Tomegra (organizer), Kyushu Hyperthermia Soc. (organizer), Fukuoka Cancer Prevention Assn. (expert), Fukuoka Med. Assn. (cons. physician), Japan Cath. Med. Assn., Orgn. Mondiale de Gastro-Enterology, European Assn. Gastroenterology and Endoscopy, European Congress Radiology, Japan Radiologist Assn. (mng. dir. 1996—). Avocations: golf, classical music. Office: Nat Kyushu Med Ctr, 1-8-1 Jigyohama, Chuo-ku, Fukuoka 810, Japan

MURANOV, YURI VLADIMIROVICH, mathematics educator, researcher; b. Lachinovo, USSR, Aug. 23, 1957; s. Vladimir Antonovich and Anna Davidovna (Kirillova) M.; m. Irina Nikolaevna Stecjuc, Dec. 17, 1977 (dec. Nov. 20, 1986); children: Aleksej, Alexandr; m. Elena Nikolaevna Slizhevskaja, Jan. 8, 1988; 1 child, Anna. Candidate degree, U. Moscow, 1987; Docent, Tech. Inst. Vitebsk, Belarus', USSR, 1991, doctorate, 1996. Engr. Machine Works, Uzgorod, Ukraine, 1979-81; sci. rschr. Solid Inst., Vitebsk, 1984-88; educator Tech. Inst., Vitebsk, 1988-92; doctorant Mian, Moscow, 1992-95; educator Vitebsk U. State Tech. Inst., 1988-92; docent Vitebsk U. State Tech. U., 1995—; prof. in math. State Tech. U., Vladimir, Russia, 1996-98; head dept. theoret. and applied math. Vitebsk State Tech. U., Belarus', 1998—. Contbr. articles to profl. jours. Mem. Am. Math. Soc., Moscow Math. Soc. Home: Stroitelei 12, 1, 167, Vitebsk 210022, Belarus Office: VSTU, Moskovskij 72, Vitebsk 210028, Belarus

MURANTY, WOJCIECH, pastor, youth group administrator; b. Bydgoszcz, Poland, Feb. 3, 1967; s. Jan and Genowefa (Dębosz) M.; m. Iwona Foks, June 30, 1990; 1 child, Damian. Tech. diploma, Tech. Coll., Poland, 1987; grad., Christian Acad. Theology, Warsaw, Poland, 1990, Bethel Sem., St. Paul, Minn. Dir. youth dept. Evang. Christian Ch., Poland, 1989—, pastor, 1996—; dir. Scripture Union, Poland, 1991-96; chmn. to gen. sec. Youth Coordinating Com., Poland, 1989—; leader nat. and internat. pastoral and youth ministry. Co-author: (book) Tylko dla Boga, 1996—; contbr. articles to mags.; exec. editor: Glos Ewangelii, 1996-99. Recipient Master of Technics award State Office, 1987. Mem. Towarzystwo Ewangeliczne, Youth Forum (nat. bd. 1995—). Mem. Free Evang. Ch. of Poland. Avocations: swimming, billiards, table tennis, camping, reading. E-mail: wojtasdn@wa.onet.pl. Office: Kosciol Ewangelicznych Chrzescijan, ul Czerwonego Krzyza 46, 85-338 Bydgoszcz Poland

MURAO, SATOSHI, geologist; b. Hiroshima, Japan, Feb. 1, 1959. DSc, Hiroshima U., 1988. Cert. A-class proficiency in English, UN. Geologist Geol. Survey Japan, 1987-92, sr. geologist, 1992—, asst. officer in charge of internat. affairs, 1998; cons. Mines & Geoscis. Bur., The Philippines, 1987, Mongolian Geol. Survey Bur., 1991, 97; leader Pixe Com. for Exploration, Tokyo, 1996—; collaborator Chinese Acad. Geol. Scis., 1997. Contbr. articles to profls. jours. Active Helpers for Victims of the Toroku Mine Pollution, Miyazaki, 1987-93, Amnesty Internat., Tokyo, 1987-92, Sierra Leone Friends, Tokyo, 1987—. Ditard grantee Australian Govt., Sydney, 1994; fellow Commonwealth Scientific & Indsl. Rsch. Orgn., Australia, 1994-95. Mem. Soc. Resource Geology (Arai grantee 1993), Global Ednl. Assocs. Office: Geol Survey Japan, 1-1-3 Higashi, Tsukuba 305-8567, Japan

MURAOKA, OSAMU, organic chemist, consultant; b. Wakayama, Kansai, Japan, Jan. 7, 1950; s. Tsuyoshi and Kayako (Nishioka) M.; m. Fusako Ogata, July 4, 1981; children: Yuko, Satoshi. BS, Gifu (Japan) Pharm. U., 1973; MS, Osaka (Japan) U., 1975, PhD, 1978. Fellow U. N.C., Chapel Hill, 1978-80; asst. Kinki (Japan) U., 1980-84, asst. prof., 1984-89, assoc. prof., 1989-99, prof., 1999—; cons. Maruho Co., Ltd., Osaka, 1989—, Seiwa Kasei Co., Ltd., Higashiosaka, Japan, 1990—, Towa Co., Ltd., Osaka, 1991—; bd. dirs. Koshimune Hosp., Osaka. Author: Radiochemistry for Pharmaceutical Students, 1986; contbr. articles to profl. jours. Mem. Japan Pharm. Soc., Am. Chem. Soc., Am. Pharm. Assn. Avocations: flying as pvt. pilot, mountaineering, watching movies, classical music. Home: Nova Hishiyanishi 205, 1-4-25 Hishiyanishi, Higashiosaka Osaka 577, Japan Office: Faculty Pharm Scis Kinki U, 3-4-1 Kowakae, Higashiosaka Osaka 577, Japan

MURARIU, DUMITRU TOADER, biologist, zoologist, researcher; b. Ungureni-Botosani, Romania, Sept. 21, 1940; s. Toader A. and Elena D. (Amortitoaie) M.; m. Angela Al. Vasiliu, July 28, 1966; children: Mihail, Magdalena. Grad., Faculty of Biology, Iasi, Romania, 1966; PhD, Faculty of Biology, Bucharest, Romania, 1975. Tchr. Gymnasium, Ungureni-Botosani, Romania, 1957-58; biologist Tuberculozis Hosp., Bucharest, 1966-69; museologist Mus. Natural History, Bucharest, 1969-76, head sect., 1976-88, sr. rschr., 1991—; dir. Mus. Natural History, 1988; tchr. museology Ministry of Culture, Bucharest, 1982-94; sr. rschr. Faculty of Biology, Bucharest, 1995; mem. adv. com. EUROBATS, 1998—. Author: On the Life of Mammals, vol. I, 1989, vol. II, 1993, vol. III, 1998; editor-in-chief Travaux du Museum H.N., 1991-2000. With Romanian mil., 1958-61. Recipient Fulbright grant Am. Coun. Edn., 1975-76; expdn. grant to Indonesia, 1991 and Brazil, 1994, Romanian Ministry of Edn. Mem. Am. Soc. Mammalogists (life), Romanian Soc. Biology, Romanian Assn. Museologists, Romanian Assn. Scientists, Soc. for Conservation of Bats in Europe. Avocations: gardening, music, reading, trips. Home: Amman 20A Sectorul 1, 71228 Bucharest Romania Office: Grigore Antipa Mus Natural History, Sos Kisseleff No 1, 79744 Bucharest Romania

MURARKA, SHYAM PRASAD, science and engineering educator, administrator; b. Jaynagar, Bihar, India, Mar. 13, 1940; came to U.S., 1966; s. Bihari L. and Suti Murarka; m. Saroj Murarka, May 21, 1962; children: Sumeet, Amal. BS in Chemistry with honors, Bihar U., Muzaffarpur, 1958, MS in Chemistry, 1960; PhD in Chemistry, Agra (India) U., 1970; PhD in Materials Sci. and Metals, U. Minn., 1970. Lectr., rsch. assoc. Bihar U., 1960-61; trainee Atomic Energy Est., Trombay, Maharastra, 1961-62, sci. officer, 1962-66; rsch. asst. U. Minn., Mpls., 1966-70, rsch. assoc., 1970-72; mem. tech. staff, supr. Bell Labs., Murray Hill, N.J., 1972-84; prof. Rensselaer Poly. Inst., Troy, N.Y., 1984—, dir. Ctr. for Integrated Electronics and Electronics Mfg., 1994-96, dir. Ctr. for Advanced Interconnect Sci. and Tech., 1996—, dir. Sematech Ctr. of Excellence, 1989-96; cons. Bell Labs., Murray Hill, N.J., 1984-89, Applied Materials, Santa Clara, Calif., 1997—. Author: Silicides for VLSI Applications, 1983, Metallization Theory and Practice for VLSI and ULSI, 1993; (with others) Electronic Materials Science and Technology, 1989, Chemical Mechanical Planarization of Microelectronic Materials, 1997, Copper Fundamental Mechanisms for Microelectronic Applications, 2000; co-editor: Advanced Metallizations in Microelectronics, 1990, Advanced Metallization and Processing for Semiconductor Devices and Circuits II, 1992, Interface Control of Electrical, Chemical, and Mechanical Properties, 1994, Advaned Metallization for Devices and Circuits, 1994, Microelectronics Technology and Process Integration, 1994, Low Dielectric Constant Materials Synthesis in Microelectronics, 1995; contbr. book chpt. Transition Metal Silicides, 1983. Mem. Tri-City India Assn.'s Indian Comty. Support Group, Albany, 1996. Univ. Grants Commn. scholar, 1961. Fellow IEEE, Am. Vacuum Soc., Am. Soc. Metals and Electrochem. Soc. (Thomas Callinan award 1987); mem. Materials Rsch Soc. and TMS, Bihar U. Chem. Soc. (hon. life). Achievements include 11 patents in field, over 500 rsch. papers and talks. Office: CIEEM Materials Engring Dept 110 8th St Troy NY 12180-3522

MURASHIMA, YOSHIYA LUCA, psychiatrist, neuroscientist; b. Osaka, Japan, Dec. 30, 1954; s. Zensaku and Nobuko Maria (Sugimoto) M.; m. Ryoko Noeala Maeda, Aug. 1986; children: Yoshiko Angelica, Eiko Maria del Fiore, Koya Marco del Aurelio, Naoya Tomaso del Aquini. MD, Tokyo U., 1980, PhD, 1984. Med. diplomate and sci. rsch. Intern Murakami Mental Hosp., Tokyo, 1980-82, resident, 1982-84; chief Tokyo Inst. Psychiatry, 1984-91, dir., 1991—. Avocations: classical music and arts, European travel, scuba diving. Home: 5-12-2-202 Kamikitazawa, Setagaya-Ku, Tokyo MZ 156-0057, Japan Office: Tokyo Inst Psychiatry, 2-1-8 Kamikitazawa, Tokyo MZ 156-8585, Japan

MURASKI, ANTHONY AUGUSTUS, lawyer; b. Cohoes, N.Y., July 28, 1946; s. Adam Joseph and Angeline Mary (Vozzy) M.; children: Adam Peter, Emily Jo. BA, MA in Speech/Hearing, Sacramento State Coll., 1970; PhD in Audiology/ Hearing Sci., U. Mich., 1977; JD, Detroit Coll. Law, 1979. Bar: Mich. 1980, U.S. Dist. Ct. (ea. dist.) Mich. 1981, U.S. Ct. Appeals (6th cir.) 1982, U.S. Claims Ct. 1989, U.S. Supreme Ct. 1990, Pa. 1990. Asst. Kresge Hearing Research Inst. U. Mich., Ann Arbor, 1971-77; asst. prof. Wayne State U. Med. Sch., Detroit, 1979-82; assoc. Kitch, Suhrheinrich, Saurbier & Drutchas, Detroit, 1982-83; assoc. prof. Detroit Coll. Law, 1983-85; mng. ptnr. Muraski & Sikorski, Ann Arbor, 1985—; cons. audiology Ministry of Environment, Ont., Can., 1980-81; trustee Deaf, Speech and Hearing Ctr., Detroit, 1981—; legal adv. on air WWJ Radio, Detroit, 1984—; mem. mental health adv. bd. on deafness Dept. Mental Health, 1984, vis. com. U. Mich. Sch. Edn., 1986—. Author: Legal Aspects of Audiological Practice, 1982, Hearing Conservation in Industry: Licensure, Liability and Forensics, 1985. Mem. ABA, Mich. Bar Assn., Washtenaw County Bar Assn., Am. Speech-Lang.-Hearing Assn. (sci. merit award, 1981), Ann Arbor C. of C. Avocations: photography, running. Home: 1603 Westminster Pl Ann Arbor MI 48104-4358

MURATA, AKIRA, nutrition educator; b. Shimonoseki, Japan, Aug. 2, 1935; s. Sunao and Yoshiko (Ueno) M.; m. Yuko Fujita; children: Hiroko, Shuichi. BS, Kyushu U., Fukuoka, Japan, 1958; MS, Kyushu U., 1960, PhD, 1964. Assoc. prof. Saga (Japan) U., 1966-79, prof. vitaminology, 1979—. Author 36 books on vitamin C; translator 5 books including those

by Linus Pauling. Home: 17-19 Isemachi, Saga 840, Japan Office: Saga U, 1 Honjomachi, Saga 840, Japan

MURATA, ITARU, international relations educator; b. Tokyo, Nov. 22, 1928; s. Tangue and Hatsuko (Hama) M. Student, Tokyo U. Fgn. Studies, 1945-48. Officer-in-charge of liaison with Supreme Cmdr. Allied Force Ministry Fgn. Affairs, Tokyo, 1948-54, politico-mil. officer-in-charge U.S.-Japan security treaty, 1955-58, asst. to dep. chief of protocol, 1964-65, asst. dir. nat. security affairs divsn. N.Am. affairs bur., 1966-69, dep. dir. 2d internat. econ. affairs divsn., 1971-72, dep. dir. nat. security affairs divsn., 1980-89; rschr. Ministry of Fgn. Affairs, Tokyo, 1992—; attache politico-mil. arrairs Embassy of Japan, Washington, 1959-64, 2d sec., Caracas, Venazuela, 1969-71, 1st consul-gen., Kansas City, Mo., 1979-80, sr. consul, dir. politico-mil. affairs, N.Y.C., 1990-92; prof. internat. rels., polit. sci. Yamamura Women's Coll. Active Mus. Modern Art, Solomon R. Guggenheim Mus., Phillips Meml. Gallery, Corcoran Gallery Art. Mem. Japan Soc., Asia Soc., Japan-Am. Soc. Kansas City (hon.), Japan-Am. Soc. St. Louis (hon.), U.S. Strategic Inst., Rsch. Inst. for Peace and Security, Japan Inst. Internat. Affairs, Japan Acad. Internat. Polit. Sci., Japan Ground Warfare Acad., Acad. Polit. Sci. N.Y.C. Buddhist. Home: 1-1-22-505 Seishin-cho, Edogawa-ku, Tokyo 134-0087, Japan Office: Ministry Fgn Affairs Chiyoda-ku, 2-2-1 Kasumigaseki Chiyoda, Tokyo 100-8919, Japan

MURATA, KATSUMI, physician; b. Mito, Japan; s. Noboru Suzuki and Fumi M.; m. Atsuko Takeuchi; children: Kato Eriko, Miyamori Yuriko. MD, U. Tokyo, 1954; PhD, Postdoc. Univ. Tokyo, 1960. Asst. sch. medicine U. Tokyo, 1960-61, instr., 1968-88; asst. sch. medicine Washington U., St. Louis, 1961-62; prof. Nat. U. Fine Art Music, Tokyo, 1988-97; vis. prof. dept. nutrition Tokyo Agr. U., 1997—; vis. asst. prof. Loma Linda U. Sch. Medicine, L.A., 1962-68. Author: Werner's Syndrome and Human Aging, 1982, Acidic Glycosaminoglycans in Human Kidney, 1982, Arterial Glycosaminoglycans with Advance of Atherosclerosis, 1989, Enzymic Analysis of Glycosaminoglycans, 1994; editor: Degenerative Diseases of Connective Tissue and Aging, 1985; contbr. over 240 articles to profl. jours. Articular Rsch. award Articular Rsch. Found., 1980. Mem. Japanese Soc. Internal Medicine, Japanese Soc. Gerontology, Japanese Soc. Rheumatology, Japanese Connective Tissue Soc. (gen. sec. 1968-95, emeritus 1995—), European Connective Tissue Soc. (contact man 1974-94). Buddhist. Avocations: oil painting, water color painting. Home: 2-45-14 Kitamagome Ota-ku, Tokyo 143-0021, Japan Office: U Tokyo Dept Medicine, 7-3-1 Hongo Bunkyo-ku, Tokyo 113, Japan

MURATA, MASARU, oral surgeon, educator; b. Nagano, Japan, May 11, 1961; s. Hiroshi and Kazuko Murata; m. Kyoko Sawatari, 1989; children: Daichi, Yuudai, Koudai. DDS, Hokkaido (Japan) U., 1988, PhD, 1993. Asst. Okayama (Japan) U., 1994-97; fellow L. Pasteur U., Strasbourg, France, 1996-97; asst. Health Scis. U. Hokkaido, 1997-99, assoc. prof., 1999—; guest lectr. Soc. Hard Tissue Biology, Tokyo, 1995; symposist Japanese Soc. Oral Maxillofacial Surgeons, Niigata, 1998. Author: The Bone-Biomaterials Interface, 1990, New Technology of Morphogenesis Research, 1998, Mechanism of Odontogenesis, 1999. Recipient disting. article prizes Japanese Soc. Oral Implant, 1995, Soc. Hard Tissue Biology, 1999, grant-in-aid for sci. rsch., Japan, 1999—. Mem. Internat. Assn. Dental Rsch., Soc. Hard Tissue Biology (dir. 1994—), Japanese Stomatology Soc. Avocations: camping, mountain climbing. Home: 4-4-1-12 Ainosato, Sapporo 002-8074, Japan Office: Health Scis U Hokkaido, 1757 Kanazawa, Tobetsu 061-0293, Japan

MURATA, SATORU, radiologist, researcher; b. Ogawa-Machi, Saitama, Japan, Apr. 17, 1960; s. Taiichi and Minako (Sekine) M.; m. Masako Yoshino, Sept. 8, 1996; 1 child, Munetomo. Student, Kagoshima (Japan) U., 1983-89; MD, Ministry of Health and Welfare, Japan; PhD, Tsukuba (Japan) U. Resident Kagoshima U., 1989-91; fellow Kyushu U., Fukuoka, Japan, 1991-93; fellow Tsukuba U., 1993-95, rschr., 1996; chief Naka-Chuo Gen. Hosp., Naka, Japan, 1996; rschr. Lund U., Malmö, Sweden, 1997—. Contbr. articles to profl. jours. Recipient cert. of appreciation 9th European Congress of Radiology, Vienna, 1995, Magna Cum Laude award 10th European Congress of Radiology, Vienna, 1997. Roman Catholic. Avocations: karate, judo, movies. Home: Sankt Johannes gatan 6, 211-46 Malmö Sweden Office: Dept Diagnostic Radiology, Lund U Malmö Hosp, S-205 02 Malmö Sweden

MURATA, TATSUO, humanities educator; b. Otsu, Japan, Jan. 25, 1928; s. Denjiro and Tsune (Hirata) M.; m. Toshiko Akamatsu, May 27, 1959; children: Atsushi, Oba Yukiko. BA, Doshisha U., 1952, MA, 1965. Tchr. English Zeze H.S., Otsu, 1952-65; lectr. Baika Women's Coll., Osaka, 1966-69; asst. prof. Baika Women's Coll., 1969-76, prof., 1976-98, emeritus prof., 1998—; curator Baika Women's Coll. Libr., 1984-85; dean Baika Women's Coll., 1985-90. Author: Mind-Scape, 1974, I Am a Cormorant, 1991, T.S. Eliot, and Indo-Buddhism; translator several books of T.S. Eliot, Philip Larkin, Seamus Heaney. Trustee Baika Ednl. Inst., Osaka, 1980-98. Mem. Japan T.S. Eliot Soc. (gen. sec. 1988-95, v.p. 1996-99, pres. 2000), Japan Poets' Club, English Literary Soc. Japan, Rotary. Avocations: noh-chorus, tea ceremony. Home: 20 6 Takasago cho, Otsu 520 005, Japan Office: Baika Women's Coll Fac Lit, Shukunosho, Ibaraki, Osaka 567 8578, Japan

MURATA, YASUO, economics educator; b. Osaka, Japan, Jan. 26, 1931; s. Masao and Sadae (Morii) M.; m. Hiroko Sakurai, Feb. 7, 1960; 1 child, Akiko. BA, Kobe U. (Japan), 1953, MA, 1955, DEcons, 1970; PhD, Stanford U., 1965. Lectr., Kobe U. Commerce, 1958-60, assoc. prof., 1960-68, prof., 1968-71; prof. Dalhousie U., Halifax, N.S., Can., 1971-74; prof. econs. Nagoya City U. (Japan) 1974-86. Author: (with Michio Morishima) Working of Econometric Models, 1972; Mathematics for Stability and Optimization of Economic Systems, 1977; Optimal Control Methods for Discrete-Time Economic System, 1982; Modern Macroeconomics (in Japanese), 1984; Finance, Exchange, Prices and Investment (in Japanese), 1992, Introductory Macroeconomics (in Japanese), 1996, Optimal Control of Dynamic Economic Systems (in Japanese), 1998; mem. editl. bd. Optimal Control Applications and Methods, 1984-96. Grantee Fulbright Commn., 1962, Japan Econ. Research Found., 1979, Mishima Meml. Found., 1982. Mem. Econometric Soc., Japan Assn. Econs. and Econometrics (trustee 1980-95), Japan Assn. Automatic Control. Home: 1-16-17 Karatodai Kitaku, Kobe 651-1332, Japan Office: Kansai U, Dept Econs, Suita 564-8680, Japan

MURATIKOV, KYRILL L'VOVICH, physicist; b. St. Petersburg, Russia, Aug. 8, 1949; s. Lev Nikolaevich and Vera Alexjeevna (Smirnova) M. MS, St. Petersburg State U., Russia, 1972; PhD, Ioffe Phys. Tech. Inst., St. Petersburg, 1983. Rsch. asst. Ioffe Phys. Tech. Inst., St. Petersburg, Russia, 1972-74, jr. rschr., 1974-83, rschr., 1983-87, sr. rschr., 1987—; invited rschr. Friedrich-Schiller U., Jena, Germany, 1993; cons. in field. Co-author: (with S.B. Gurevich) Photothermoacoustics, 1990; contbr. articles to profl. jours.; inventor in field. Mem. IEEE. Avocations: travel, history. E-mail: klm.holo.ioffe.rssi.ru. Office: AF Ioffe Phys Tech Inst, Polytechnicheskaya 26, 194021 Saint Petersburg Russia

MURATOVIC, HASAN, diplomat; b. Olovo, Bosnia and Herzegovinia, 1940; children: Amir, Faruk. PhD in Orgn. Scis., U. Belgrade, Yugoslavia, 1981. Prof. orgn. theory and systems, econs. and electrotechnics U. Sarajevo; dir. rsch. and planning Famos Sarajevo, 1966-74; tech. dir. United Bus Co. Zambia, 1974-78; sci. cons. Inst. Orgn. and Econs., Sarajevo, 1978-88; dir. Inst. for R&D UPI, Sarajevo, 1988-90, BHM Cons. Co., 1990-92; min. forestry and industry wood processing Govt. of Bosnia-Herzegovina, Sarajevo, 1992-93, min. without portfolio rels. with UN, 1993-96, prime min., 1996-97, min. fgn. trade and econ. rels., 1997-98, ambassador to Croatia, 1998—. Author of four books including How to Manage Crisis in Company, 1999; contbr. over 80 articles to profl. jours. Pres. Chess Olympic Com., Bosnia and Hevzegovlrus. Recipient Silver medal Rep. Yugoslavia, 1989, Award Town of Sarajevo for Sci., 1989, Presidency of FR Yugoslavia, 1985. Office: Amb Bosnia-Herzegovina, Torbarova 9, 71000 Zagreb Croatia

MURATSUGU, MAKOTO, bioanalytical chemist, researcher; b. Hirakata, Japan, July 11, 1950; s. Jyozo Toki and Mariko Muratsugu; m. Chiemi Shirakawa, Oct. 25, 1980; children: Satoshi, Atsushi. B in Pharmacy, Hokkaido U., Sapporo, Japan, 1973, M in Pharmacy, 1976, PhD, 1979. Pharm. diplomate, 1st class radiation protection supr. diplomate. Instr. Asahikawa Med. Coll., Japan, 1979-94; assoc. prof. Osaka Prefecture Coll. Health Scis., Habikino, Japan, 1994—; vice-chief practical radiation adminstrn. Asahikawa Med. Coll., 1991-94; vis. prof. U. Toronto, Can., 1995-96; inventor in field. Encouragement Young Scientists grantee Min. Edn., Sci., Sports and Culture, Tokyo, 1985, 86, Sci. Rsch. grantee, 1993. Mem. Pharm. Soc. Japan, Japan Soc. Analytical Chemistry, Japanese Biochem. Soc., N.Y. Acad. Sci. Office: Osaka Prefectural Coll, Health Scis, 7-30 3-chome Habikino Osaka 583-8555, Japan

MURAVSKAYA, GALINA VLADIMIROVNA, radiologist, oncologist; b. Tver, Russia; d. Vladimir Alexandrovich and Lidiya Grigoryevna (Savelyeva) Zyubko; m. Vladimir Antonovich Muravsky (div. June 1987); children: Oleg Vladimirovich, Igor Vladimirovich. Cand.Sc., Rsch. Inst. Oncology, Moscow, 1971; MD, Roentegen Radiology Rsch. Inst, Moscow, 1986. Jr. rsch. assoc. Rsch. Inst. Oncology, Moscow, 1969-70; jr. rsch. assoc. Rsch. Inst. Oncology & Med. Radiology, Minsk, Belarus, 1971-72, sr. rsch. assoc., 1972-73, head high energies dept., 1973-90, head dept. radiodiagnosis & radiotherapy, 1990—; mem. Expert Coun. Higher Attesting Comnm., Minsk, 1993—; cons. in field. COntbr. articles to profl. jours.; inventor in field. Recipient Bronze medal USSR Exhbn. Econ. Achievements, 1979. Mem. Byelorussian Soc. Therapeutic Radiologists-Oncologists (chair 1977), Assn. Radiation Diagnosticians and Therapeutists (v.p. 1989). Avocations: chess, swimming, theatre. Office: Rsch Inst Oncology & Med Radiology, PO Lesnoy 2, 223 052 Minsk Belarus

MURAVSKY, LEONID, research scientist, lecturer; b. Turijsk, Volyn, USSR, May 2, 1953; s. Igor Muravksy and Nadiya Muravska; m. Lilliya Andreichyn, June 17, 1995; 1 child, Bogdana. Diploma in physics, Franko Lviv (USSR) Nat. U., 1975; PhD in Tech. Scis., Nat. Acad. Sci., Lviv, 1989. Rschr. Karpenko Inst. Physics and Mechanics Nat. Acad. Scis., Lviv, 1980-90, sr. rschr. Karpenko Inst. Physics and Mechanics, 1990-98, acting head dept. Karpenko Inst. Physics and Mechanics, 1998-99; lectr. electrophysical dept. State U. Livivska Poly., Lviv, 1996-98, head bd. examiners, 1999. Author: binary PHase Image Processing in Optical and Optial/Digital Correlation Systems, 1999; contbr. articles to profl. jours. Mem. Internat. Soc. Optical Engring. Russian Orthodox. Avocations: skiing, swimming. Fax: 380-322-649427. Office: Nat Acad Scis, 5, Naukova, 79601 Lviv Ukraine

MURAVYOV, SERGEY VASILYEVICH, research scientist, educator; b. Kineshma, Ivanovo, Russia, Dec. 27, 1954; s. Vasiliy Fyodorovich and Zinaida Mikhailovna (Bogomolova) M.; m. Olga Nikolaevna Bukharina; children: Valerija, Anton. Engr., Tomsk Polytech. U., 1977, Candidate of Scis., 1984, DSc, 1998. Engr., rschr. Tomsk (Russia) Polytech. U., 1977-91, assoc. prof., 1992-99, prof., dept. head, 1999—. Author: Programming for Measurement Information Systems, 1998; patentee in field; contbr. articles to profl. jours. Fellow U. Jyvaskyla, 1991, 95, 97, 98, 2000; grantee Acad. Finland, 1997, 98, 2000, Ministry Higher Edn. Moscow, 1994. Avocations: gardening, wood carving. Home: Pr Mira 35 cv 95, 634027 Tomsk Russia Office: Tomsk Poly U Comp Meas Sys, Lenina 30, Tomsk 634034, Russia

MURAYAMA, MAKIO, biochemist; b. San Francisco, Aug. 10, 1912; s. Hakuyo and Namiye (Miyasaka) M.; children: Gibbs Soga, Alice Myra. B.A., U. Calif., Berkeley, 1938, M.A., 1940; Ph.D. (NIH fellow), U. Mich., 1953; ScD honoris causa, Open Internat. U., Sri Lanka, 1994. Rsch. biochemist Children's Hosp. of Mich., Detroit, 1943, 45-48, Bellevue Hosp., N.Y.C., 1943-45; Research biochemist Harper Hosp., Detroit, 1949-54; research fellow in chemistry Calif. Inst. Tech., Pasadena, 1954-56; research asso. in biochemistry Grad. Sch. Medicine, U. Pa., Phila., 1956-58; spl. research fellow Nat. Cancer Inst. at Cavendish Lab., Cambridge, Eng., 1958; sr. research biochemist NIH, Bethesda, Md., 1958-93. Author: (with Robert M. Nalbandian) Sickle Cell Hemoglobin, 1973; discovered DIPA (decompression-inducible platelet aggregation), 1975; discovered DIPA causes vascular occlusion in both acute mountain sickness and diver's syndrome. Fellow Am. Inst. Chemists; mem. AAAS, Am. Chem. Soc., Am. Soc. Biol. Chemists, Assn. Clin. Scientists, Undersea and Hyperbaric Med. Soc., Aerospace Med. Assn., Internat. Platform Assn., West African Soc. Pharmacology (hon.), N.Y. Acad. Sci., Sigma Xi. Achievements include patent for automatic amperometric titration apparatus; development of molecular mechanism of human red cell sickling and prevention of sickle cell crisis by oral prophylactic carbamide; discovery of decompression inducible platelet aggregation by means of simulation of decompression-inducible platelet aggregation of diving in frogs and mice that diver's disease and acute mountain sickness could be alleviated by piracetam and thymol, antiplatelet agents. Home: 5010 Benton Ave Bethesda MD 20814-2804

MURAYAMA, MICHIKO, executive; b. Aug. 16, 1920. Owner Asahi Shimbun, Chuo-ku, Japan. Office: Asahi Shimbun, 5-3-2 Tsukiji, Chuo-ku 104-11, Japan*

MURAYAMA, MISAO, statistical researcher; b. Kasaoka, Japan, Feb. 23, 1911; s. Shogo and Asa Murayama; married; 1 chid, Mary. PhD, Honolulu U., 1996. Adviser on history Nat. Policy Rsch. Assn. Japan, 1942-47; dir., editor Coop. Assn., Tokyo, 1946-57; ofcl. scholar Ministry Fgn. Affairs, Japan, 1952-62; rep. Civilization Laws Assn., Japan, 1965—; adviser Coop. party, Japan, 1947-48. Author: A Study on Civilization, 1975, World Civilization on Progress, 1980, Theory of Life and Civilization in Cosmos, 1992, Civilization Notes, 1985—, World Civilizations under the Undulation, 1995; contbr. weekly items to Mainichi Press, 1951-62, Nihon Keizai Press, Tokyo, 1951-64. Home: 2-19-43 Hiyoshi Kohoku-ku, 223 Yokohama Japan

MURAYAMA, TADASHI, automotive engineer, educator; b. Takizawa, Iwate, Japan, July 25, 1931; s. Yutaka and Hanako (Uno) M.; m. Tomoko Tozu, Dec. 9, 1959; 3 children. BS, Hokkaido U., Sapporo, Japan, 1953, MS, 1955, DEng, 1970. Registered profl. automotive engr. Engr. Prince Motors Co., Tokyo, 1955-60, jr. group leader, 1961-62; assoc. prof. engring. Hokkaido U., Sapporo, 1962-71, prof. engring., 1971-95, prof. engring. emeritus, 1995—; vis. prof. U. Wis., Madison, 1977-78, Jeonbog Nat. U., Jeonsu, Korea, 1981; cons. prof. Xi'an Jiaotong U., China, 1986, Shanghai Jiaotong U., China, 1993; chmn. internat. rels. Hokkaido U., 1990-95; vice-chmn. Petroleum Energy Ctr., Tokyo, 1986-95. Councilor Hokkaido YMCA, Sapporo, 1980—. Fellow Soc. Automotive Engrs.; mem. Japan Soc. Mech. Engring. (chmn. of div. 1990-91, medal for an excellent paper 1977, Engine Systems Meml. award 1997), Japan Soc. Automotive Engrs. (chmn. of div. 1990-91, Sci. Contbns. award 1993), Sapporo Rotary Club. Mem. Japanese Dem. Party. Methodist. Avocations: traveling, reading, physical fitness. Fax: 001-81-11-621-8055. E-mail: tadastmu@poppy.ocn.ne.jp. Home: 8-6-1 Maruyama-Nishimachi, 064-0944 Sapporo Hokkaido, Japan Office: Hokkaido Auto Engring Coll, 2-6 Nakanoshima Toyohira-ku, 062 Sapporo Hokkaido, Japan

MURAYAMA, TOMOYA, correspondent; b. Tokyo, Feb. 25, 1963; came to U.S., 1996; s. Tomiya and Toshiko (Ishizuka) M. BA, Tokyo U., 1985. Reporter, corr. NHK Japan Broadcasting Co., Tokushima, Tokyo, 1985-96; corr. NHK Japan Broadcasting Co., N.Y.C., 1996-97; corr. for South Am. NHK, Rio de Janeiro, Brazil, 1998—. corr. (TV documentary) High-Technology Aircraft, 1994, NASA, After the Cold War Era, 1996, Hostage Crisis in Peru, 1997, Environmental Crisis in Indonesia, 1997, Economic Crisis in Brazil, 1998, NHK Japan Broadcasting Co., Rio de Janeiro, Brazil. Office: care NHK Rio de Janeiro, Ave Nilo Pecanha 50 Gp 1208, Rio de Janeiro CEP20044-900, Brazil

MURAYAMA, YOSHIMASA, materials science educator; b. Seoul, Korea, Aug. 2, 1936; s. Saburo and Mitsu (Kojima) M.; m. Naoko Watanabe, Mar. 21, 1963 (dec. Apr. 1981); children: Hitoshi, Nozomi; m. Yasuko Hirase, July 26, 1981. B, U. Tokyo, 1959, MS, 1961; DSc, Waseda U., Tokyo, 1990. Cert. sci./physics. Rsch. scientist Ctrl. Rsch. Lab. Hitachi, Ltd., Tokyo, 1961-70, sr. rsch. scientist, 1970-89; chief staff rsch. scientist Advanced Rsch. Lab. Hitachi, Ltd., Saitama, Japan, 1989-96; lectr. Saitama U., 1995-97; exec., cons. ProTech, Ltd., Tokyo, 1996-97; prof. materials sci. Niigata (Japan) U., 1997—; rschr. Ctrl. Rsch. Lab., Hitachi, Ltd., Tokyo, 1961-89, rsch. group leader, 1989-96; com. mem. Com. for Electronics Materials, Tokyo, 1971-74. Editor Procs. Internat. Symposium on Founds. of Quantum Mechanics, 1984, 2nd Internat. Symposium, 1987, 3rd Internat. Symposium, 1990, Quantum Control and Measurement, 1993, Founds. Quantum Mechanics in the Light of New Tech., 1996; author: Quantum Mechanics (in Japanese), 1996; editl. cons.: Encyclopedia of Applied Physics, 1990—; contbr. articles to profl. jours.; patentee in field. Mem. AAAS, Phys. Soc. Japan, Japan Soc. Applied Physics. Home: Maehara-cho 4-2-1-320, Koganei-shi Tokyo 184-0013, Japan

MURCH, GRAEME ELLIOTT, materials science educator; b. Adelaide, Australia, Feb. 2, 1948; s. Thomas Richard and Ida Bidmead (Lokan) M.; m. Christine Margaret Bruff, Aug. 15, 1970; children: Stuart, Craig. BSc with honors, Flinders U., Adelaide, Australia, 1970, PhD, 1974, DSc, 1982; D Engring., U. Newcastle, Australia, 1991. Chartered engr., Australia. Rsch. fellow Flinders U., 1973-75; scientist Argonne (Ill.) Nat. Lab., 1975-85; prin. rsch. scientist ICI-Australia, Melbourne, 1985-86; assoc. prof. U. Newcastle, 1986-93, prof. materials engring., pers. chair, 1993—; lectr. at internat. confs., 1980—. Editor jour. Diffusion and Defect Data (pts. A and B.), 1982—; founding editor internat. jour. Materials Sci. Forum, 1984—; contbr. numerous articles to profl. jours., chpts. to books. Fellow Instn. Engrs. Australia; mem. Am. Soc. for Metals Internat. Avocation: piano performance. Office: U Newcastle Dept Mech Engrg, University Dr, Callaghan NSW 2308, Australia

MURCH, SIMON HARRY, pediatric gastroenterologist; b. Liverpool, Eng., June 29, 1956; s. Henry Osborne and Anne Margaret (Godfrey) M.; m. Fiona Margaret King, July 12, 1980; 1 child, Rosalind. MBBS, U. London, 1980, PhD, 1995. Lectr. child health St. Bartholomew's Hosp., London, 1988-91; sr. lectr. Royal Free Hosp., London, 1995—; action rsch. fellow St. Bartholomew's Hosp., London, 1992-93, lectr. pediatric gastroenterology, 1993-94, sr. lectr., 1995; sr. lectr. Royal Free Hosp., London, 1995—; Mem. Royal Coll. Physicians, U.K., 1984. Contbr. articles to profl. jours. Project grantee Action Rsch., Eng., 1992-93, Project Grantee, MAFF, 1996—. Fellow Royal Coll. Pediat. and Child Health, Royal Soc. Medicine, Royal Coll. Physicians (London); mem. Brit. Soc. Immunology, The Neonatal Soc., Brit. Soc. for Pediatric Gastroenterology and Nutrition, European Soc. Pediatric Gastroenterology and Nutrition, Soc., for Mucosal Immunology, Harveian Soc. Avocations: running, cycling, music. Office: Univ Dept Pediat Gastroenterology, Royal Free Hosp Bond St, London NW3 2QG, England

MURCHISON, DAVID CLAUDIUS, lawyer; b. N.Y.C., Aug. 19, 1923; s. Claudius Temple and Constance (Waterman) M.; m. June Margaret Guilfoyle, Dec. 19, 1946; children: David Roderick, Brian, Courtney, Bradley, Stacy. AA, George Washington U., 1947, BA, 1949, JD with honors, 1949. Bar: D.C. 1949, Supreme Ct. 1955. Assoc. Dorr, Hand & Dawson, N.Y.C., 1949-50; founding ptnr. Howrey & Simon, Washington, 1956-90; counsel Howrey & Simon, 1990—; legal asst. under sec. army, 1949-51; counsel motor vehicle, textile, aircraft, ordinance and shipbldg. divsns. Nat. Prodn. Authority, 1951-52; assoc. gen. counsel Small Def. Plants Adminstrn., 1952-53; legal adv. and asst. to chmn. FTC, 1953-55. Chmn. So. Africa Wildlife Trust. With AUS, 1943-45, ETO. Mem. ABA (chmn. com. internat. restrictive bus. practices sect. antitrust law 1954-55, sect. adminstrv. law, sect. litigation), FBA, D.C. Bar Assn., N.Y. State Bar Assn., Order of Coif, Met. Club, Chevy Chase Club, Talbot Country Club. Republican.

MURCIA LORA, JOSE MARIA, obstetrician/gynecologist, consultant; b. Bogota, Colombia, Jan. 9, 1965; arrived in Spain, 1992; s. Jorge Enrique Murcia and Maria Socorro Lora. MD, Javeriana U., Bogota, 1989; diplomate in ob-gyn., Navarra U., Pamplona, Spain, 1995, PhD, 1996. Gen. med. physician Ministry of Health, Bogota, 1990-91; resident Clinic Universitary, Pamplona, 1992-95; rschr. Navarra U., 1994-96; pvt. practice Pamplona, 1997—; fertility and endocrinology/gynecology cons. Unity (Logruño); minimal access surgery cons. Unity (Logroño). Colombian Inst. Educative Credit and Tech. Studies in Exterior fellow, 1992, IEISA Found. rsch. fellow, 1994. Roman Catholic. Avocations: squash, tennis. E-mail: jmmurcia@edunet.es. Home: Gran Via 4, Entreplanta, CP 26002 Logroño Spain

MURDOCH, BRIAN OLIVER, German language educator; b. London, June 26, 1944; s. Cecil Oliver and Jane Amelia (Rowe) M.; m. Ursula Irene Riffer, Mar. 25, 1967; children: Adrian, Ilona. BA, Exeter U., Eng., 1965; PhD, Jesus Coll., Cambridge, Eng., 1967; LittD, Jesus Coll., 1991. Lectr. German Glasgow U., Scotland, 1968-70; asst. prof. U. Ill., Chgo., 1970-72; from lectr. to prof. German Stirling U., Scotland, 1972—; vis. fellow Trinity Hall Cambridge (Eng.) U., 1989, Hulsean vis. lectr. in divinity, 1997-98; vis. fellow, Waynflete lectr. Magdalen Coll., Oxford U., Eng., 1994. Editor: School Edits. Remarque, Zweig; author many books on medieval literature and war literature; translator various modern and medieval works; contbr. articles to profl. jours. Fellow Royal Hist. Soc. Avocations: books, music. Office: Stirling U German Dept, Stirling FK9 4LA, Scotland

MURDOCH, KEITH MICHAEL, physicist; b. Auckland, New Zealand, Jan. 12, 1968; s. Neil W. and Noelene A. (Charlton) M. BSc with honors, U. Canterbury, Christchurch, New Zealand, 1990, PhD in Physics, 1994. Postdoctoral fellow Lawrence Berkeley (Calif.) Nat. Lab., 1994-96; rsch. asst. U. Oxford, Eng., 1996-97; rsch. assoc. U. Wis., Madison, 1997—. Contbr. articles to profl. jours. Charles Cook Warwick House Meml. scholar, U. Canterbury, 1990-91, Australian Nat. U. Vacation scholar, Canberra, Australia, 1989; Grad. Rsch. Los Alamos Nat. Lab., N.Mex., 1991. Mem. AAAS, Royal Soc. New Zealand, Royal Astron. Soc. New Zealand, New Zealand Inst. Physics, Am. Phys. Soc. Avocations: astronomy, travel, hiking, reading, current affairs. Office: U Wis Dept Chemistry 1101 University Ave Madison WI 53706-1322

MURDOCH, LACHLAN KEITH, publishing executive; b. Sept. 8, 1971; s. Keith Rupert Murdoch and Anna Maria Torv. Student, Princeton U. Former reporter San Antonio Express News, The Times, U.K.; former sub-editor The Sun, U.K.; gen. mgr. Queensland Newspapers Pty. Ltd., 1994-95; exec. dir. News Ltd., 1995; dir. Beijing PDN Xinren Info. Tech. Co. Ltd., 1995—; dep. chair Star TV, 1995—; dep. CEO News Ltd., 1995—, chair, 1997—; CEO, chmn. New Ltd. Australian subs. News Corp.; sr. v.p. News Corp. Avocations: Greek philosophy, ancient history, rock climbing. Office: News Corp 3rd Fl 1211 Ave of the Americas New York NY 10036*

MURDOCH, RUPERT (KEITH RUPERT MURDOCH), publisher; b. Melbourne, Australia, Mar. 11, 1931; came to U.S., 1974, naturalized, 1985; s. Keith and Elisabeth Joy (Greene) M.; m. Anna Maria Torv, Apr. 28, 1967 (div.); children: Prudence, Elisabeth, Lachlan, James; m. Wendi Deng, June 25, 1999. M.A., Worcester Coll., Oxford, Eng., 1953. Chmn. bd. dirs. News Corp., 1979—, chief exec., 1979—; dir. BSkyB, 1990—; CEO Fox Entertainment Group, 1995—; chair., pres. New York Post, N.Y.C.; dir. Phillip Morris Cos., Inc., 1989—; owner, pub. numerous newspapers, mags. and TV stas. in U.S.A., Australia, U.K., Asia. Office: The News Corp Ltd 3rd Fl 1211 Avenue Of The Americas New York NY 10036

MURDOCK, ROBERT MCCLELLAN, air force officer; b. Montclair, N.J., Sept. 27, 1947; s. George Rutherford and Mary (Newell) M.; m. Ann Marie Wingo, Aug. 20, 1977; 1 child, Kristen. BA, Davis and Elkins Coll., 1969; MA, Ctrl. Mich. U., 1979; postgrad., Armed Forces Staff Coll., 1983, U.S. Army War Coll., 1988. Lic. command pilot, USAF. Aide, chief of staff The Pentagon, Washington, 1980-82; ops. officer 22 Airlift Squadron, Travis AFB, Calif., 1984, comdr., 1985-87; dep. inspector gen. Hdqs. European Command, Stuttgart, Germany, 1988-90; vice comdr. 436 Airlift Wing, Dover AFB, Del., 1990-92; nat. def. fellow The Atlantic Coun., Washington, 1992-93; comdr. Air Force Inspection Agy., Kirtland AFB, N.Mex., 1993-96; dep. U.S. Mil. Rep. to NATO Brussels, Belgium, 1996-98; vice comdr. San Antonio Air Logistics Ctr., Kelly AFB, Tex., 1998-2000; comdr. San Antonio Air Logistics Ctr., Kelly AFB, 2000—. Decorated D.F.C., Air medal, Legion of Merit, Def. Superior Svc. medal. Mem. Air Force Assn., The Airlift and Tanker Assn., Order of Daedalians. Methodist. Avocations: skiing, golf, travel. Address: 108 Robins Dr San Antonio TX 78226-1814 Office: San Antonio Air Logistics Ctr Kelly A F B TX 78241

MURDOLO, FRANK JOSEPH, pharmaceutical company executive; b. Summit, N.J., Nov. 21, 1946; s. Joseph and Rose Murdolo; m. Nancy Lynn Vinci, Jan. 25, 1970; children: Kimberly L., Tracy L., Christy L. BS in Econs./Fin., Fairleigh Dickinson U., Madison, N.J., 1977, postgrad., 1978-79. Mgr. fin. planning Monroe Bus. Sys., Morris Plains, N.J., 1970-77; sr. fin. analyst Schering-Plough Rsch., Kenilworth, N.J., 1977-79; mgr. budgets & analysis Schering-Plough Corp., Madison, N.J., 1979-83, dir. investor rels.,

1991-97; mgr. capital planning Schering-Plough Internat., Kenilworth, N.J., 1983-87; dir. fin. reporting Schering-Plough Corp., Madison, N.J., 1987-91; v.p., dir. investor rels. Glaxo Wellcome, plc, N.Y.C., 1997—; lectr. MBA program for investor rels. Fairleigh Dickinson U., Madison, N.J., 1993—; exec. advisor exec. scholars program Fairleigh Dickinson U., Madison, N.J., 1993—. Mem. Nat. Investor Rels. Inst. (bd. dirs. N.Y.C. chpt.), Inst. Mgmt. Accts. Avocation: bicycling. Office: Glaxo Wellcome plc 499 Park Ave New York NY 10022-1240

MURETTO, PIETRO AURELIO, pathologist; b. Sermide, Mantova, Italy, Feb. 18, 1941; s. Giovanni Maria Muretto and Emma Fiorenza; m. Franca Maria Giorgioni; 1 child, Francesca. Degree in Medicine, U. Sassari, Italy, 1968; Degree in Hematology, U. Genova, Italy, 1970; Degree in Pathology, Cath. U., Rome, 1976, Degree in Oncology, 1979. Asst. U. Sassari, 1968-69; gen. practitioner Civic, Torpe, Italy, 1971; asst. pathologist Hosp., Faenza, Italy, 1973-79; chief pathologist Hosp., Pesaro, Italy, 1980-99. Contbr. articles to profl. jours. Lt. Italian Mil., 1969-70. Mem. Lions. Roman Catholic. Avocations: bicycling, running, swimming. Home: Via Cesare Lombroso 26A, 61100 Pesaro Italy

MUREZ, JOHN, music education director, educator; b. Paterson, N.J., Feb. 14, 1943; s. John Sr. and Sophie A. Murez; m. Dorothy L. Pohlman, May 29, 1971; 1 child, Daniel C. BA in Elem. Edn., William Paterson U., 1963; MAT, Seton Hall U., 1966; MusM., Montclair State U., 1976; postgrad., Drew U. Cert. tchr., N.J. Tchr. Paterson (N.J.) Pub. Schs., 1963-68; asst. prof. William Paterson Coll., Wayne, N.J., 1968-70; tchr. Tenafly (N.J.) Pub. Schs., 1970-80; prof. Luther Coll., Teaneck, N.J., 1976-79; dir. Office of Music Edn. Newark Pub. Schs., 1988-98; dist. supr. fine and performing arts Paterson Pub. Schs., 1998—; music min. Mt. Carmel R.C. Ch., Montclair, N.J., 1998—; organ design cons. various chs., North Jersey, 1976—; cons. music workshops Diocese of Paterson, 1984—. Mem. Newark Teen Arts Festival Com., 1988-98. Mem. N.J. Music Adminstrs., Music Educators Nat. Conf., Paterson Adminstrs. Assn. Home: 2 Berkeley Pl Montclair NJ 07042-2303 Office: Paterson Pub Schs 137 Ellison St Paterson NJ 07505-1308

MURFET, IAN CAMPBELL, retired botany educator; b. Launceston, Tasmania, Australia, Apr. 2, 1934; s. Campbell Vernon and Pretoria Clara (Rutherford) M.; m. Barbara Janet Forward, Feb. 1, 1958; children: Gregory, Andrew, Robyn. BSc, U. Tasmania, Hobart, 1957, BSc with first class honors, 1958, PhD, 1971. Temporary lectr. botany U. Tasmania, Hobart, 1961, lectr. botany, 1962-70, sr. lectr. botany, 1971-76, sub dean faculty sci., 1976-79, reader in botany, 1977-91, head dept. plant sci., 1989, assoc. prof. plant sci., 1992-93, prof. plant sci., 1994-97; ret., 1997; emeritus prof. plant sci. U. Tasmania, Hobart, 1998—; vis. fellow Cornell U., Ithaca, N.Y., 1974-75, 78. Editor Pisum Genetics, 1989-98; contbr. articles to profl. jours., chpts. to books. Mem. Australian Soc. Plant Physiologists, Scandinavian Soc. Plant Physiology, Internat. Working Group on Flowering, Pisum Genetics Assn. (mem. coordinating com. 1975—, chmn. 1989-98). Avocations: tennis, swimming, choral singing, bush walking. Office: U Tasmania Dept Plant Sci, Hobart TAS 7001, Australia

MURGU, ALEXANDRU N., engineering educator; b. Fintina-Dsca, Mehedinti, Romania, Aug. 1, 1962; s. Nicolae C. and Maria A. (Maciuca) M. MSc, Polytech. Inst. Bucharest, Romania, 1987; PhL, U. Jyväskylä, Finland, 1993, PhD, 1995. Rsch. engr. IIRUC, Bucharest, 1987-91; rsch. asst. Poly. Inst. Bucharest, 1987-92; rsch. asst. U. Jyväskylä, 1992-95, asst. prof. engring., 1995—, dir. rsch., 1996—; cons. Nokia telecom., Finland, 1997—; referee IEEE AC conf., 1996, Internat. Inst. Informatics and Systemics conf., Orlando, Fla., 1996—; co-chair symposium 9th Internat. Conf. Systems Rsch. Informatics and Cybernetics, Baden-Baden, Germany, 1997, 11th Internat. Conf., 1999; organizer, chair mini-symposium 3d European Conf. Numerical Math. and Advanced Applications, Jyväskylä, Finland, 1999. Author: Neural Networks for Planning and Control in Communication Networks, 1995, Learning and Optimal Decision with Dynamic Programming and Neural Networks, 1993. Lt. Romanian Mil., 1981-82. Recipient Outstanding Scholarly award Internat. Inst. for Advanced Studies in Sys. Rsch. and Cybernetics, Windsor, Can., 1996, 97; U. Jyväskylä scholar, 1995, docent telecomm. dept. math., 1998; Fellow of the Inst. award Internat. Inst. Advanced Studies in Sys. Rsch. and Cybernetics, Windsor, Can., 1999, Millennium award of excellence, 2000. Fellow Internat. Inst. Advanced Studies in Sys. Rsch. and Cybernetics; mem. IEEE (Comm. Soc., Info. Theory Soc., Systems, Man and Cybernetics Soc.), N.Y. Acad. Sci., Internat. Neural Network Soc., Nat. Geographic Soc. Avocations: study of ancient Greek and Roman comparative history, classic and modern Italian architecture, classic literature, symphonic music, fishing. Home: Pohjanaho 1 C 19, 40520 Jyväskylä Finland Office: Univ Jyväskylä, Dept Math Info Tech, 40351 Jyväskylä Finland

MURIÁ, JOSÉ MARÍA, academic administrator, researcher; b. Guadalajara, Jalisco, Mex., Aug. 17, 1942; s. Josep Maria MuriÁ Romani and Ana Rouret Callol. Bachelor's degree, U. Guadalajara, 1960, Master's degree, 1966; PhD in History, Coll. of Mex., Mexico City, 1969. Editor-in-chief of mag. U. Guadalajara, 1965-66; rsch. and divulgation dept. chief Pub. Edn. Dept., Guadalajara, 1971-72; prin. Enrique Díaz de León H.S., Guadalajara, 1971-73; researching coord. Nat. Inst. Anthropology and History, Guadalajara, 1973-81; archives and libr. gen. dir. External Affairs Office, Mexico City, 1981-88; dir. Estudios Jaliscienses program Govt. and Univ. of the State, Guadalajara, 1989-91; pres. Coll. of Jalisco, Zapopan, 1991—; mem. consultative coun. Pub. Adminstrn. Inst. of State, Guadalajara, 1992-95; emeritus tchr. Instituto Alfonso Reyes, 1993. Author: (books) History of Territorial Divisions of Jalisco, 1976, A Thumbnail History of Guadalajara, 1982, Brief History of Jalisco, 1988, Tequila: Historical Sketch of an Industry, 1990, Jalisco: An Historical Review, 1993, Historical Brief of Jalisco, 1996, (pamphlets) Jalisco: A Glance At Its History, 1993, Jalisco Today, 1994; co-editor: (sci. mag.) Estudios Jaliscienses, 1990—; dir. History of Jalisco, 1980-82. Mem. Culture and Arts State Found., Guadalajara, 1990-91. Recipient award for best article published in sci. mag. Consejo Mexicano de Ciencias Históricas, 1979, Hist. Mention medal Acero Capitán Alonso de León, Sociedad Nuevoleonesa de Historia, Geografía y Estadística, 1984, Literacy Mention award Libreros de Guadalajara, 1993, Joan B. Cendrós prize Omnium Cultural, 1996. Mem. Academia Mexicana de la Historia (numerary mem.), Nat. Rschrs. Sys. (level III). Office: El Colegio de Jalisco, 5 de Mayo 321, 44660 Zapopan Jalisco, Mexico

MURISON, ROBERT CHARLES CARISBROOKE, psychologist, educator; b. Llandrindod Wells, Powys, U.K., Oct. 20, 1951; arrived in Norway, 1978; s. John Charles Carisbrooke and Margaret Anne Hamilton (Dicker) M.; m. June Ward; children: Michael Charles, Nicholas John. BSc in Psychology, U. St. Andrews, 1974; PhD of Psychology, U. Leicester, 1978. Rsch. fellow, assoc. prof. U. Bergen, Norway, 1977-93; prof. biol. psychology U. Bergen, 1993—; prof. psychology U. Trondheim, Norway, 1995—. Editl. bd. mem. Psychoneuroendocrinology, 1990—, Stress, 1995—. Mem. Internat. Soc. Psychoneuroendocrinology (treas. 1987-93, bd. dirs.), Pavlovian Soc., Scandinavian Fed. Lab. Animal Sci. (v.p. 1992-95). Office: Univ Bergen Biol/Med Dept, Årstadveien 21, 5009 Bergen Norway

MURKES, JAKOB, research engineer; b. Lodz, Poland, Feb. 10, 1920; s. Israel and Rosa (Dlugacz) M.; m. Felicja Birnbaum, July 20, 1946 (dec. Aug. 1988); children: Anita Cecilia, Daniel Ivar. Lic es Scis., Nancy, France, 1939; MSc in Engring., Royal Inst. Tech., Stockholm, 1956. Rsch. engr. Swedish Ironmasters Assn., 1949-56, AB Separator, 1957-63; mgr. separation rsch. dept. Alfa-Laval AB, Stockholm, 1963-80; cons. separation tech. Stockholm, 1980—. Author: Crossflow Filtration, 1989; author novel, 1995; contbr. numerous articles to profl. jours.; patentee in field. Mem. Filtration Soc. (Gold medal 1967), European Fedn. Chem. Engrs., Assn. Swedish Grad. Engrs. Avocations: literature, music. Home: Linnégatan 48B, 11454 Stockholm Sweden

MUROBUSE, FUMIRO, publishing company executive; b. Kawasaki, Kanagawa, Japan, Apr. 1, 1925; s. Hidehira and Miki (Yajima) M.; m. Fuyumi Nakazato, Nov. 7, 1960. M in Econs., Tokyo U., 1949. Editor Nihon Keizai Shimbun, Inc., Tokyo, 1949-57; corr. N.Y.C., 1957-60; chief editor econ. dept. Osaka, Japan, 1960-63; gen. sec. Japan Econ. Research Ctr., Tokyo, 1964-68; dir. Nikkei Bus. Publs. Inc., Tokyo, 1969-90; pres. Tokyo, 1980-90, sr. mgmt. cons., 1990—; mgmt. advisor Nihon Keizai Shimbun, Tokyo, 1985-90. Co-author: Japan's Economy in 1985, 1964; translator: New Business Journalism, 1981. Grantee Ford Found., N.Y.C., 1968. Mem. Japan Futurology Assn. Buddhist. Clubs: New Otani Spa (Tokyo); Kawagoe (Saitama). Avocation: painting. Home: Apt 1303, 2-3-1 Ohtsuka, Bunkyo-ku, Tokyo 112-0012, Japan Office: Nikkei Bus Publs Inc, 2-7-6 Hirakawacho Chiyodaku, Tokyo 102-8622, Japan

MUROFF, LAWRENCE ROSS, nuclear medicine physician, educator; b. Phila., Dec. 26, 1942; s. John M. and Carolyn (Kramer) M.; m. Carol R. Savoy, July 12, 1969; children: Michael Bruce, Julie Anne. AB cum laude, Dartmouth Coll., 1964, B of Med. Sci., 1965; MD cum laude, Harvard U., 1967. Diplomate Am. Bd. Radiology, Am. Bd. Nuclear Medicine. Intern Boston City Hosp., Harvard, 1968; resident in radiology Columbia-Presbyn. Med. Ctr., N.Y.C., 1970-73, chief resident, 1973; instr. dept. radiology, asst. radiologist Columbia U. Med. Ctr., N.Y.C., 1973-74; dir. dept. nuc. medicine, computed tomography and MRI Univ. Cmty. Hosp., Tampa, Fla., 1974-94, H. Lee Moffitt Cancer Hosp., Tampa, 1994—; pres. Edn. Symposia Inc., Tampa, 1975—, Imaging Cons. Inc., Tampa, 1994—; chmn. bd. Am. Phys. Ptnrs. Inc., Dallas, 1996-98; clin. asst. prof. radiology U. South Fla., 1974-78, clin. assoc. prof., 1978-82, clin. prof., 1982—; clin. prof. U. Fla., 1988—. Contbr. articles to profl. jours. Lt. comdr. USPHS, 1968-70. Fellow Am. Coll. Nuclear Medicine (disting. fellow., Fla. del.), Am. Coll. Nuclear Physicians (regents 1976-78, pres.-elect 1978, pres. 1979, fellow 1980), Am. Coll. Radiology (councilor 1979-80, 91-96, chancellor 1981-87, chmn. commn. on nuclear medicine 1981-87, fellow 1981); mem. Am. Assn. Acad. Chief Residents Radiology (chmn. 1973), AMA, Boylston Soc., Fla. Assn. Nuclear Physician (pres. 1976), Fla. Med. Assn., Hillsborough County Med. Assn., Radiol. Soc. N.Am., Soc. Nuclear Medicine (coun. 1975-90, trustee 1980-84, 86-89, pres. Southeastern chpt. 1983, vice chmn. correlative imaging coun. 1983), Fla. Radiol. Soc. (exec. com. 1976-91, treas. 1984, sec. 1985, v.p. 1986, pres. elect 1987, pres. 1988, gold medal 1995), West Coast Radiol. Soc., Soc. Mag. resonance Imaging (bd. dirs. 1988-91, chmn. ednl. program 1989, chmn. membership com. 1989-93), Clinical Magnetic Resonance Soc. (pres. elect 1995-98, pres. 1998-2000). Office: 4515 George Rd Ste 355 Tampa FL 33634-7300

MUROFUSHI, MINORU, import and export company executive. BA, Tokyo U., 1956. With Itochu Corp. (formerly C. Itoh & Co.), Tokyo, 1956—; gen. mgr. coal dept. Itochu Corp. (formerly C. Itoh & Co.), N.Y., 1963-71; v.p. Am. divsn. Itochu Corp. (formerly C. Itoh & Co.), 1971, bd. dirs., 1985, chief exec., 1990—, now chmn. bd., pres., chmn. bd.; chmn. Japan Fgn. Trade Coun., Japan Reps. APEC Bus. Adv. Coun. Office: Itochu Corp, 5-1 Kita-Aoyama 2-chome, Minato-ku Osaka 107-8077, Japan*

MUROMACHI, KANEO, bank executive. Pres., CEO The Sanwa Bank, Ltd., Osaka, Japan. Office: The Sanwa Bank Ltd, 5-6 Fushimimachi 3-chome, Osaka 541-8530, Japan*

MUROMTSEV, JURI LEONIDOVICH, engineering educator; b. Novokuznetsk, Kemerovo, Russia, Nov. 7, 1934; s. Leonid Ivanovich and Valentina Nikolaevna (Rossova) M.; m. Galina Vasiljevna Jasakova, Aug. 25, 1973; 1 child, Dmitri. Degree in Engring., Minsk (Russia) High Mil. Sch., 1956; postgrad., Moscow Inst. Chem. Engring., 1963-67. Cert. engring. mil. Asst. Kuzbass Poly. Inst., Kemerovo, Russia, 1957-63; dr. tech. Moscow Inst. Chem. Engring., Kemerovo, 1968; docent chair for automation Kuzbass Poly. Inst., Kemerovo, 1968-71; chair radioelectronic and microprocessing constructing Tambov (Russia) State Tech. U., 1971—; full prof. Tambov State Te. U., 1982—; sr. dir. tech. D.I. Mendeleev Moscow Chem.-Tech. Inst., 1981. Author: Chemical Factories Without Breakdown, 1990; patentee in field. Dep. Town Coun., Tambov, 1992, 93; holder ecology com. Tambov Region Adminstrn., 1994, 95; chmn. Town Duma at City Adminstrns., Tambov, 1993-95. Recipient Order Sign of Honor, Presidium of Supreme Soviet, 1986, Well-earned Figure of Sci. and Tech. award Pres. Russia Fedn., 1994. Mem. Internat. Acad. for Info., Russian Acad. Natural Scis., N.Y. Acad. Scis. Avocation: tourism. E-mail: crems@crems.jesby.t-stu.ru. Home: 24/2 16 Naberezhnaya Str, 392002 Tambov Russia Office: Tambov State Tech Univ, 106 Soviet Str, 392000 Tambov Russia

MURPHREE, HENRY BERNARD SCOTT, psychiatry and pharmacology educator, consultant; b. Decatur, Ala., Aug. 11, 1927; s. Henry Bernard and Nancy Mae (Burrus) M.; m. Dorothy Elaine Simmons, Nov. 14, 1953 (dec.); children: Julie Elizabeth, Susan Louise, Jefferson Van; m. Dorothy Elizabeth Olson, Sept. 23, 1993. Student, MIT, 1944-45; BA, Yale U., 1950; MD, Emory U., 1959. Intern internal medicine, fellow clin. pharmacology, instr. Emory U., 1959-61; resident psychiatry Med. Sch. Rutgers U., 1972-76, mem. grad. faculty psychology, 1972-97; rsch. asst. Johns Hopkins U., Balt., 1950; asst. chief neuropharmacology Bur. Rsch., Princeton, N.J., 1961-68; from assoc prof. to prof. Univ. of Medicine and Dentistry Robert Wood Johnson Med. Sch., Piscataway, N.J., 1968-97, assoc. dean acad. affairs Univ. Medicine and Dentistry, 1977-81, chmn. psychiatry Univ. Medicine and Dentistry, 1977-91; cons. medicinal chemistry and pharmacology FMC Chem. R&D Ctr., Princeton, N.J., 1962-68, Roche Labs., Nutley and Verona, N.J., 1968-77. Author bylaws Rutgers Med. Sch.; contbr. articles to profl. jours. Founding mem. Somerset Coun. Alcoholism, Somerville, N.J., 1974-77; founding cons. Impaired Physicians Com. Med. Soc. N.J.; mem. Sci. Adv. Com., State of N.J., 1981-97; bd. trustees Carrier Found., Belle Mead, N.J., 1981-95, vice chmn. bd., chmn. exec. com., 1989-95. Aviation cadet USNR, 1945-46; lt. MSC USN, 1951-55. Mem. Am. Soc. for Pharmacology and Exptl. Therapeutics, Am. Psychiat. Assn., Soc. Biol. Psychiatry, Am. Coll. Neuropsychopharmacology, Sigma Xi, Alpha Omega Alpha. Avocations: music, electronics. Home: 467 Ridge Rd Watchung NJ 07069-5433

MURPHY, ALEXANDER BAILEY, geography educator; b. Washington, July 10, 1954; s. Richard Ernest and Esther Bailey M.; m. Susan Nannette Gary, Aug. 15, 1981; children: Richard Holland, George Robinson. BA, Yale U., 1977; JD, Columbia U., 1981; PhD, U. Chgo., 1987. Bar: Ill. 1981. Lawyer Katten, Muchin and Zavis, Chgo., 1981-83; from asst. prof. to prof. geography U. Oreg., Eugene, 1987-96, prof., 1996—, Rippey chair liberal arts scis., 1998—; chair advanced placement geography devel. com. Coll. Bd., N.Y.C., 1996—; spkr. in field. Author: The Regional Dynamics of Language Differentiation in Belgium, 1988; co-author: Human Geography: Culture, Society and Space, 1998; editor Progress Human Geography, 1995—; contbr. chpts. to books, articles to profl. publs. Pres. Land County UN Assn., Eugene, 1989-91; mem. acad. coun. UN Sys. Recipient Presl. Young Investigator's award NSF, 1991-97; Deutscher Akademischer Austauschdienst grantee, 1977-78, Fulbright-Hays Rsch. grantee, 1985-86. Mem. Am. Geog. Soc. (v.p., coun. 1997—), Assn. Am. Geographers (councillor 1997—), Nat. Coun. Geog. Edn. Avocations: traveling, hiking, skiing. Fax: 541-346-2067. E-mail: abmurphy@oregon.uoregon.edu. Home: 2275 Potter St Eugene OR 97405-3065 Office: Dept Geography U Oreg Eugene OR 97403

MURPHY, BRUCE ALLEN, government and law educator, author; b. Abington, Mass., Sept. 30, 1951; m. Carol Lynn Wright, June 14, 1975; children: Emily, Geoffrey. BA, U. Mass., 1973; PhD, U. Va., 1978. Fred Morgan Kirby prof. civil rights Lafayette Coll., Easton, Pa. Author: The Brandeis/Frankfurter Connection: The Secret Political Activities of Two Supreme Court Justices, 1982, Fortas: The Rise and Ruin of a Supreme Court Justice, 1988, (with Larry Berman) Approaching Democracy, 1996, 99. Avocations: fishing, reading, sports. E-mail: murphyb@lafayette.edu. Office: Lafayette Coll Dept Govt and Law 200 Kirby Hall Civil Rights Easton PA 18042

MURPHY, DANIEL IGNATIUS, lawyer; b. Phila., Mar. 14, 1927; s. John Anthony Murphy and Irene Cooper Thorn; m. Jeanne B. Genetti, July 28, 1956 (div. Aug. 1978); children: Jewel A., Daniel I. Jr.; m. Barbara Ann Uncles, Jan. 1, 1979. BS in Econs., U. Pa., 1950; LLB, Yale U., 1953. Bar: Pa. 1954, U.S. Dist Ct. (ea. dist.) Pa. 1954, U.S. Ct. Appeals (3d cir.) 1954, U.S. Tax Ct. 1956, U.S. Supreme Ct. 1959. Assoc. Evans, Bayard & Frick, Phila., 1953-55; asst. city solicitor City of Phila., Pa., 1956-59; ptnr. Cavanaugh, Murphy & Kalodner, Phila., 1958-64, Shapiro, Stalberg, Cook, Murphy & Kalodner, Phila., 1964-66, Takiff, Bolger & Murphy, Phila., 1966-72, Waters, Gallagher, Collins & Masterson, Phila., 1972-80; ptnr. Stradley, Ronon, Stevens & Young, Phila., 1980-92, ret., of counsel, 1993; tchr. Am. Soc. CLUs, Villanova, Pa., 1956-57; mem. exec. com. Phila. Estate Planning Coun., 1958-60; lectr. Pa. Bar Inst., Harrisburg, 1974-92, Pa. Coll. Orphans Ct. Judges, Harrisburg, 1978, Pitts., 1991; apptd. spl. master for trial mgmt. of complex litigation Phila. County Ct. Common Pleas, 1994—. Editor: Phila. Bar Assn. Mag. The Shingle, 1958-67; contbr. chpts. to manuals and articles to profl. jours. Chmn. Phila. Chpt. Am. Cancer Soc., 1956-63; mem. Com. of 70, Phila., 1968—, chmn., 1972-74; trustee Hahnemann U., Phila., 1983-86. With USN, 1945-46. Fellow Pa. Bar Found. (life); mem. ABA, Pa. Bar Assn., Phila. Bar Assn. (vice-chmn. com. censors 1971), Union League Phila., Soc. Colonial Wars, Phila. Country Club, Pa. Soc. S.R., Colonial Soc. of Pa. Democrat. Roman Catholic. Avocation: U.S. Civil War history. Office: 2600 One Commerce Sq Philadelphia PA 19103

MURPHY, DANIEL J., lawyer; b. North Adams, Mass., Dec. 5, 1955; s. John A. and Carol E. M.; m. Charlotte S. Murphy, July 6, 1985; children: Daniel, Brianne, John. BA, North Adams State Coll., 1979; JD, Northeastern U., Boston, 1986. Congrl. aid U.S. Rep. Byron Dorgan, Washington, 1981-83; lawyer McCabe Gordon, Boston, 1986-87, Brown, Rudnick, Freed & Gesmer, Boston, 1987-89, Gordon & Wise, Boston, 1989-92; founding ptnr. Murphy, MacKenzie, Michaels, & Sullivan, Boston, 1992—. Dir. North Andover Boosters, 1997—; bd. dirs. Jerry Moses Major League Baseball Players Alumni Golf Tournament, Ipswich, Mass., 1994—; founding mem. 406 Club, Boston, 1995—; mem. North Andover Sch. Com. Recipient Major League Baseball Alumni/Cystic Fibrosis award Ipswich, 1997, Andover, Maine, 1998. Mem. N. Andover Country Club, Lanam Club. Roman Catholic. Office: Murphy MacKenzie Michaels & Sullivan LLP One Liberty Square Boston MA 02109-4825

MURPHY, DEBORAH JANE, lawyer; b. Clinton, Tenn., Dec. 19, 1955; d. Robert C. and Mary R. (Melton) M. BS, U. Tenn., 1977; JD, Nashville Sch. Law, 1987. Bar: Tenn. 1987, U.S. Dist. Ct. (D.C. dist.) 1988, U.S. Dist. Ct. (6th cir.) 1988. Estate tax atty. U.S. Dept. Treasury, Knoxville, Tenn., 1987—; mcpl. judge Lake City, Tenn., 1997—; bd. dirs. Tenn. Lawyers Assn. Women, Nashville, 1987—. Mem. cmty. adv. bd. East Tenn. Children's Hosp., 1998—. Mem. ABA, Tenn. Bar Assn., Estate Planning Counsel, Club LeConte. Dem. Methodist. Avocations: dog training, golf, travel. Home: PO Box 510 Clinton TN 37717-0510 Office: IRS 710 Locust St Fl 4 Knoxville TN 37902-2540

MURPHY, DENNIS PATRICK, hotel business entrepreneur; b. Buffalo, N.Y., Jan. 12, 1958; s. Dennis Charles and Dorothy E. Murphy; m. Carol Ann Klocke. B in Hospitality Mgmt., Fla. Internat. U., 1980. Cert. hotel exec. Mgr. hotel ops. Marriott Corp., Washington, 1979-80; dir. food and beverage Mariner Corp., Houston, 1980-83; corp. dir. Innco Hospitality, Wichita, Kans., 1984-86; ops. exec. Clubhouse Inns of Am., 1986-88; chmn. JLH Lodge Corp., Amherst, N.Y., 1988—, also bd. dirs.; founding pres. InnVest Lodging Svcs. Inc., 1990—; bd. dirs. Hotel Baronette, Inc., Genoa Lodging, LLC, Suzuki & Son Ltd., Penn Investors IV LLC; nominated Esquire mag. register, 1985; chair project devel. com., exec. lodging coun. Am. Hotel/Motel Assn., 1990; dep. chair World U. Games, 1990-93; treas. World Vets. Games, L/O/C Buffalo, 1994-96, Greater Buffalo Conv. and Visitors Bur., 1992—, chmn. 1999; mem. exec. com. Buffalo Niagara Partnership, 1999—; trustee Gates Found., 1998—. recipient Elsworth Statler award The Statler Found., 1978-79, Eugene Fitzsimmons award Internat. Assn. Hospitality Accts., 1980. Mem. Soc. Wine Educators (pubs. com. 1977-79), Am. Hotel Motel Assn., The Buffalo Club, The Buffalo Launch Club. Home: 227 Dan Troy Dr Buffalo NY 14221-3545 Office: 300 Pearl St Ste 200 Buffalo NY 14202-2510

MURPHY, EDWARD STACK, pathologist; b. Utica, N.Y., June 8, 1923; arrived in Mexico, 1958; s. Edward Simon Murphy and Elizabeth Stack; m. Consuelo Pérez Arteaga, Aug. 6, 1953; children: Eduardo, Tomás, Roberto, Andrés, Juan Pablo. BA, U. Mich., 1945, MD, 1946. Diplomate Am. Bd. Pathology, Mexican Bd. Pathology. Intern St. Anthony Hosp., Denver, 1947; gen. practice Grand Lake, Colo., 1948; resident St. Luke's Hosp. & Denver Children's Ctr., 1949-52; Barth fellow in pathology Nat. Inst. Cardiology, Mexico City, 1952-53; chief pathologist U.S. Army Hosp., Osaka, Japan, 1953-55, Atomic Bomb Casualty Commn., Hiroshima, Japan, 1955-57, Hosp. Francés, Mexico City, 1958-61; asst. to chief pathology Nutritional Disease Hosp., Mexico City, 1958-59; chief pathologist Hosp. Santelena, Mexico City, 1962—; founder Mexican Bd. Pathology, 1963, Mexican Soc. Nuc. Medicine, 1965, Mexican Bd. Nuc. Medicine, 1973. Author: El Linfoma, 1964; contbr. articles to profl. jours. Capt. U.S. Army Med. Corps, 1953-55, PTO. Roman Catholic. Home: Corregidora 110, 10200 Mexico City Mexico Office: Hosp Santelema, Queretaro 58, 06700 Mexico City Mexico

MURPHY, EVELYN FRANCES, economist; b. Panama Canal Zone, Panama Canal Zone, May 14, 1940; d. Clement Bernard and Dorothy Eloise (Jackson) M. AB, Duke U., 1961, PhD, 1965; MA, Columbia U., 1963; hon. degrees, Regis Coll., 1978, Curry Coll., Northeastern U., Simmons Coll., Wheaton Coll., Anna Maria Coll., Bridgewater State Coll., Salem State Coll., Emmanuel Coll.; hon. degree, Suffolk U. Pres. Ancon Assocs., Boston, 1971-72; ptnr. Llewelyn-Davies, Weeks, Forrester-Walker & Bor, London, 1973-74; sec. environ. affairs Commonwealth of Mass., Boston, 1975-79, sec. econ. affairs, 1983-86, lt. gov., 1987-91; mng. dir. Brown Rudnick Freed and Gesmer, Boston, 1991-93; exec. v.p. Blue Cross/Blue Shield of Mass., Boston, 1994-98; also bd. dirs. Blue Cross Blue Shield Mass., Boston; vis. pub. policy scholar Radcliffe Coll., 1991; vice chmn./chmn. Nat. Adv. Com. on Oceans and Atmosphere (Presdl. apptd.), 1979-80; bd. dirs. Fleet Credit Card Corp., Savs. Bank Mut. Life Ins. N.Y., Citizens Energy Corp., SBLI USA Mut. Life Ins., The Commonwealth Inst., Nat. Ctr. on Women and Aging, chair; pres. Health Care and Policy Inst., 1997-98; resident scholar Brandeis U., 1998—. Recipient Dist. Svc. award New Eng. Coun., 1996, Nat. Sierra Club, 1978, Nat. Bd. Govs. Assn., 1978, Outstanding Citizen award Mass. Audobon Soc., 1978; Harvard U. fellow, 1979-80. Mem. Women Execs. in State Govt. (chair 1987), Internat. Women's Forum, 1993—. Democrat. Avocation: jogging. Office: 225 Franklin St Ste 2700 Boston MA 02110-2804

MURPHY, FRANCIS SEWARD, journalist; b. Portland, Oreg., Sept. 9, 1914; s. Francis H. and Blanche (Livesay) M.; m. Clare Eastham Cooke, Sept. 20, 1974 (dec. Apr. 1990). BA, Reed Coll., 1936. With The Oregonian, Portland, 1936-79, TV editor, Behind the Mike columnist, 1952-79; archeol. explorer Mayan ruins, Yucatan, Mex., 1950-87, mem. Am. Quintana Roo Expdn., 1965, 66, 68. Author: Dragon Mask Temples in Central Yucatan, 1988. With U.S. Army, 1942-46. Mem. Am. Philat. Soc. (life), Royal Asiatic Soc., City Club, Am. Club of Hong Kong, Explorer's Club, Oreg. Hist. Soc., Soc. Am. Archaeology, Hong Kong Philat Soc., World Wide Fund Nature, Hong Kong Jockey Club. Democrat. Congregationalist. Home: 4213 NE 32nd Ave Portland OR 97211-7149

MURPHY, GEORGE FRANCIS, pathologist, dermatologist, oncologist, educator; b. Natick, Mass., Feb. 12, 1950; s. George Francis and Barbara Elizabeth Murphy; m. Sharon Elizabeth Murphy, Aug. 26, 1972; children: Erin Elizabeth, Emily Elise. BA, U. Pa., 1972; MD, U. Vt., 1976. Diplomate Nat. Bd. Med. Examiners, Am. Bd. Pathology, Am. Bd. Pathology and Dermatology. Resident, fellow Harvard Med. Sch., Mass. Gen. Hosp., Boston, 1977-81; assoc. prof. pathology Harvard Med. Sch., Boston, 1982-87; prof. dermatology and pathology U. Pa. Sch. Medicine, Phila., 1987-97, Herman Beerman endowed chair dermatology, 1991-97; prof. pathology, dermatology and oncology Johns Hopkins U. Sch. Medicine, Balt., 2000—; pres., chmn. bd. dirs. Am. Soc. for Dermatopathology, 1997-98. Author: Fasicles in Skin Pathology, 1991, Dermatopathology, 1995; contbr. numerous articles to profl. jours. Mem. Am. Soc. for Clin. Investigation.

MURPHY, GRAEME, artistic director. Artistic dir. Sydney Dance Co. Office: Sydney Dance Co, Pier 4/5 Hickson Rd, Sydney NSW 2000, Australia*

MURPHY, JAMES RODNEY, playwright; b. Kenton, Ohio, Mar. 23, 1933; m. Teruko Murakami, 1958; children: Cynthia, Laurel. BS in Bus. Adminstrn., U. Tenn., Knoxville, 1962; MS in Edn., U. So. Calif., 1967, MS in Sys. Mgmt., 1983; PhD in Aerospace Studies, Union Inst., Cin., 1990; Air Command and Staff Coll. Diploma, Air U., Maxwell AFB, Ala., 1987, Air War Coll. Diploma, 1988. Enlisted USAF, 1951, advanced through grades to capt., 1968; transp. combat adv., 1968-69; transp. analyst, def. transp. policy coun. advisor Ctr. for Studies and Analyses, Hdqrs. USAF, Washington, 1989-92; hazardous cargo and packaging policy specialist Directorate

of Transp., Hdqrs. U.S. Air Force, Washington, 1992-95; ret. USAF, 1995—; playwright/poet, lyricist/librettist Plays Around, Colorado Springs, Colo., 1995—. Author: (musical) Truck Stop, 1994, (opera) Luke and Sarah, (musical) Member of the Team, 1996, (biography) Peon to Pentagon, 1999, also numerous poetry, lyrics and short stories. Founder, chmn. Am. Nat. Opera, 2000. Decorated Meritorious Svc. medal, Bronze Star medal, others. Mem. Nat. Def. Transp. Assn., Coun. Logistics Mgmt., Soc. Logistics Engrs., Nat. Panel Consumer Arbitrators, Better Bus. Bur., Masons, Internat. Soc. Poets, Rockford Writers Guild, Wyo. Players, Opera Am., Dramatists Guild, Writers Guild, Songwriters Assn. Washington, Washington Area Music Assn., Nashville Songwriters Assn. Internat., Am. Soc. Composers, Authors and Pubs., Drama League, Theatre Comms. Group, Colo. Opera Festival Guild, Phi Kappa Phi, Beta Gamma Sigma, Delta Nu Alpha, Delta Sigma Pi. Address: 4745 Purcell Dr Colorado Springs CO 80922-1615

MURPHY, JOHN ARTHUR, tobacco, food and brewing company executive; b. N.Y.C., Dec. 15, 1929; s. John A. and Mary J. (Touhy) M.; m. Carole Ann Paul, June 28, 1952; children: John A., Kevin P., Timothy M., Kellyann, Robert B., Kathleen. B.S., Villanova U., 1951; J.D., Columbia U., 1954. Bar: N.Y. 1954. Since practiced in N.Y.C.; ptnr. firm Conboy Hewitt O'Brien & Boardman, 1954-62; asst. gen. counsel Philip Morris Co. Inc., N.Y.C., 1962-66, v.p., 1967-76, exec. v.p., 1976-78, group exec. v.p., 1978-84, pres., 1984-91, vice chmn., 1991-92, also bd. dirs.; asst. to pres. Philip Morris Internat., 1966-67, exec. v.p., 1967-71; pres., chief exec. officer Miller Brewing Co., Milw., 1971-78, chmn. bd., chief exec. officer, 1978-84. Trustee North Shore Univ. Hosp., Marquette U., 1973-91; mem. exec. com. Keep Am. Beautiful, Inc.; mem. bd. consultors Sch. Law Villanova U.; mem. bus. com. Met. Mus. Art. Decorated Knight of Malta. Mem. ABA, N.Y. State Bar Assn. Office: Philip Morris Cos Inc 100 Park Ave New York NY 10017-5516

MURPHY, JOHN JOSEPH, educator in English literature, critic, editor; b. N.Y.C., Apr. 3, 1933; s. John and Margaret B. (Shadegg) M.; m. Sarah Marie McMahon, June 30, 1962; children: Sarah, Joseph, Willa, John, Emily. BA, St. John's U., N.Y.C., 1956, MA, 1961. Instr. English Lit. Coll. of St. Teresa, Winona, Minn., 1960-65; asst. prof. English Lit. Merrimack Coll., No. Andover, Mass., 1965-68; assoc. prof. Merrimack Coll., No. Andover, 1969-84; prof. English Lit. Brigham Young U., Provo, Utah, 1984—; chmn. dept. English, Merrimack Coll., N. Andover, Mass., 1974-76, 79-82; organizer and dir. Willa Cather and Nebr. 1st Internat. U. of Nebr. Cather Seminar, Hastings and Red Cloud, Nebr., June 14-20, 1981; bd. govs. Willa Cather Meml.; mem. editl. adv. bd. Western Am. Lit., 1985—; mem. editl. bd. Willa Cather Scholarly Edition, U. Nebr. Press, 1986—; chair Am. Lit. sect. English Dept., Brigham Young U., 1986-89, English Dept. Profl. Devel. Com., 1989-92; assoc. dir. BYU's Ctr. for Study Christian Values in Lit., 1994—. Author: My Antonia: The Road Home, 1989; editor: Critical Essays on Willa Cather, 1984, Willa Cather: Family, Community, History, 1990, Penguin My Antonia, 1994, Death Comes for the Archbishop, 1999; co-editor Lit. and Belief, 1994—; contbr. chpts. to numerous books and over 60 articles to lit. jours. including Am. Lit., Twentieth Century Lit., Thought, Religion and Lit.; prepared and presented (TV Series) KTCA TV, Great Ladies of the Am. Novel, 1963, Nathaniel Hawthorne, An Am. Realist, 1964; also presentations to scholarly symposiums and seminars in U.S. and abroad. With U.S. Army, 1958-60. Recipient NEH fellowship for Coll. Tchrs, 1982. Home: 8707 Hidden Oak Dr Salt Lake City UT 84121-6128 Office: Brigham Young U English Dept 3171 JKHB Provo UT 84602

MURPHY, JULIE ANN, zookeeper, consultant, educator, zoologist; b. Melbourne, Victoria, Australia, Aug. 6, 1965. BS hons, U. Melbourne, 1988, MSc, 1991; cert. zookeeping, Box Hill Inst. Tech & Further Edn., Australia, 1996. Jr. tech. asst. Microbiological Diagnostic Unit, Melbourne, 1984; demonstrator in biology U. Melbourne, 1989, rsch. asst. in zoology, 1990; conservation biologist, 1991; zookeeper Healesville Sanctuary, Melbourne, 1994—; cons. lectr. Royal Guide Dogs Assns. Australia, 1990-98, Box Hill Inst. Tech. & Further Edn., Melbourne, 1998, 2000—; freelance journalist, 2000—. Contbr. articles to profl. jours. and popular mags. Recipient Commonwealth Postgrad. Rsch. award Commonwealth Australia, 1989-91. Mem. Fellowship Australian Writers, Australasian Soc. Zookeepers (conservation grant 1996). Avocations: writing, travel. Office: Healesville Sanctuary, PO Box 248, Healesville 3777, Australia

MURPHY, MARGARET A., nursing educator, adult nurse practitioner; b. N.Y.C., Apr. 4, 1934; d. William J. and Margaret (Burchill) Allen; m. Raymond L.H. Murphy, Jr., July 12, 1958; children: Raymond L.H. III, Michael W., Ann Murphy Postell, Maureen D. Murphy Olsen, Alice M., Matthew D. BSN, St. Joseph Coll., West Hartford, Conn., 1955; MS, NYU, 1957; PhD, Boston Coll., Chestnut Hill, Mass., 1987. RN, Mass.; cert. adult nurse practitioner. Instr. Boston U. Sch. Nursing, 1971-72; pulmonary clin. nurse specialist Pulmonary Assocs., Boston, 1972-73; pulmonary nurse clinician Tufts U., Medford, Mass., 1973-76; asst. prof. Boston Coll., 1982-87, instr. prof. nursing, 1976-82, asst. prof., 1982-87, assoc. prof. nursing, 1987—, chmn. adult health nursing, 1988-92, dir. adult nurse practitioners program, 1987—, dir. Kennedy Audio Visual Resource Ctr., 1991-95, coord. MBA-MSN program, 1993-99; rschr. in lung sound patterns in health and disease, women's attitudes toward menopause. Co-editor: Pharmacotherapeutics and Advanced Nursing Practice, 1998; contbr. articles to profl. jours. Fellow USPHS, 1957-58; grantee Uniformed Svcs. U. Health Scis., 1995-96, Boston Coll., 1997-98. Fellow Am. Coll. Nurse Practitioners; mem. ANA, Mass. Nurses Assn. (co-chmn. cabinet on legis. 1985-88), Am. Thoracic Soc., Mass. Thoracic Soc. (chmn. com. on nursing practice, counselor 1989-91), Sigma Theta Tau (chmn. awards and scholarships com. Alpha Chi chpt. 1994-96, pres. 1996-98).

MURPHY, MARY ANN, human services administrator; b. Salt Lake City, Feb. 13, 1943; d. Wallace L. and Irene (Hummer) Matlock; m. Robert A. Glatzer, Dec. 31, 1977; children: Gabriela, Jessica, Nicholas. BA, U. Wash., 1964; MS, Ea. Wash. U., 1975. House counselor Ryther Child Ctr., Seattle, 1966-67; tchr. presch. Head Start, L.A. and Seattle, 1967-70, Children's Orthopedic Hosp., Seattle, 1970-72; faculty Ea. Wash. U., Cheney, 1973-82; exec. dir. Youth Help Assn., Spokane, Wash., 1983-88; mgr. regional ctr. for child abuse and neglect Deaconess Med. Ctr., Spokane, 1988-97; dir. Casey Family Ptnrs., Spokane, 1997—; pres. Wash. State Alliance for Children, Youth and Families, Seattle, 1985-87; chairperson Gov.'s Juvenile Justice Adv. Commn., Olympia, Wash., 1987—. Mem. Nat. Coun. on Juvenile Justice, 1994-98. Recipient Alumni Achievement award Ea. Wash. U., 1994; named Outstanding Women Leader in Health Care YWCA, 1992, Outstanding Children's Advocate, Wash. State Children's Alliance, 1996. Avocations: reading, swimming, backpacking. Home: 1950 W Clarke Ave Spokane WA 99201-1306 Office: Casey Family Ptnrs 613 S Washington St Spokane WA 99204-2535

MURPHY, PAT GORDON, aviation educator; b. Walla Walla, Wash., Oct. 1, 1950; s. Glenn Harwood and Mary L. Ausmus; m. Victoria Ann Wallace, July 28, 1984; children: Sara, Laura, Emily. ME, U. Pitts., 1978; BS, Pacific Union Coll., 1977. Aircraft mechanic Frakes Aviation, Angwin, Calif., 1970-72; chief mechanic Loma Linda U., La Sierra, Calif., 1972-74; instr. Pitts. Inst. of Tech., 1977-79; shop mgr. Cessna Aircraft Sales, Pitts., 1979-80, Beech Airo, Pitts., 1980-82; instr. Lane C.C., Eugene, Oreg., 1982-84, Everett (Wash.) C.C., 1984—; cons. LASTIC, Inc., Seattle, 1996—; dir. of maintainence U. Wash. Atmos. Aircraft, Everett, 1996—. Author/photographer: (tng. film) Sand Castings, 1977; photographer: (photo show) Black and White Works, 1975 (1st place). Democrat. Seventh Day Adventist. Avocations: flying, photography, prop making, sailing. Office: Everett CC 2000 Tower St Everett WA 98201-1352

MURPHY, PATRICK GREGORY, real estate company executive; b. Salina, Kans., May 21, 1947; s. Jorel Edward and Geneva Gail (Jordan) M. Student, Tulsa U., 1971-72; cert. grad. realtors inst., Okla. State U., 1977. Lic. real estate broker. V.p. Profl. Home Finder, Tulsa, 1972-77, Sunshine Properties, Tulsa, 1977-81, Robert A. McNeil Corp., Phoenix, 1981-85, Resources Property Mgmt. div. Integrated Resources, Houston, 1985-88; sr. asset mgr. G.A.C. Consultants, Atlanta and Tulsa, 1988—. Co-author: Todays Real Estate, 1979. Mem. real estate com. Tulsa Jr. Coll., 1977-81; bd. dirs. Trinity Episcopal Ch., Tulsa, 1972-81; founder Greater Atlanta Bus. Coalition, 1993, pres., 1993-96. Served with USN, 1965-70. Mem. Nat. Assn. Realtors (cert. residential specialist and broker), Inst. Real Estate Mgmt. (cert. property mgr., edn. com. Houston chpt. 1987, bd. dirs. Fla. chpt. 1989-91, pres. Fla. chpt. 1991), Nat. Apt. Assn. (cert. apt. property supr.), Tex. Apt. Assn., Houston Apt. Assn. (steering com. 1986-87), Internat. Real Estate Inst. (registered property mgr.). Democrat. Episcopalian. Avocations: travel, bridge, reading. Office: GAC Cons 7357 S Sleepy Hollow Dr Tulsa OK 74136-5918

MURPHY, RANDALL KENT, training consultant; b. Laramie, Wyo., Nov. 8, 1943; s. Robert Joseph and Sally (McConnell) M.; student U. Wyo., 1961-65; MBA, So. Meth. U., 1983; m. Cynthia Laura Hillhouse, Dec. 29, 1978; children: Caroline, Scott, Emily. Dir. mktg. Wycoa, Inc., Denver, 1967-70; dir. Communications Resource Inst., Dallas, 1971-72; account exec. Xerox Learning Systems, Dallas, 1973-74; regional mgr. Systema Corp., Dallas, 1975; pres. Performance Assocs.; pres., dir. Acclivus Corp., Dallas, 1976—; founder, chmn. Acclivus Inst., 1982—. Active, Dallas Mus. Fine Arts, Dallas Hist. Soc., Dallas Symphony Assn.; vice chmn. bd. trustees The Winston Sch., 1994-96, chmn. of the bd. of trustees, 1997—; ; mem. adv. bd. The Women's Ctr. of Dallas, 1995-98. Served with AUS, 1966. Mem. Am. Soc. Tng. and Devel., Sales and Mktg. Execs. Internat., Inst. Mgmt. Scis., Soc. Applied Learning Tech., Nat. Soc. Performance and Instrn., , Assn. Mgmt. Cons., Am. Assn. Higher Edn., World Future Soc., Soc. for Intercultural Edn., Tng. and Rsch., Internat. Fedn. Tng. and Devel. Orgns., Inst. Noetic Scis., Nat. Peace Inst., Amnesty Internat. The Acad. Pol. Sci., The Nature Conservancy, Children's Arts & Ideas Found., So. Meth. U. Alumni Assn. U. Wyo. Alumni Assn. Roman Catholic. Author: Performance Management of the Selling Process, 1979; Coaching and Counseling for Performance, 1980; Managing Development and Performance, 1982; Acclivus Performance Planning System, 1983; (with others) BASE for Sales Performance, 1983, Acclivus Coaching, 1984, Acclivus Sales Negotiation, 1985; R3 Service, 1997; BASE for Effective Presentations, 1987, BASE for Strategic Sales Presentations, 1988, The New BASE for Sales Excellence, 1988, Major Account Planning and Strategy, 1989, Strategic Management of the Selling Process, 1989, Building on the BASE, 1992, Negotiation Mastery, 1995; R3 Service, 1997, co-inventor The Randy-Band, multi-purpose apparel accessory, 1968. Home: 9323 Preston Rd Dallas TX 75225-1642

MURPHY, RICARDO, neuroscientist, plant physiologist; b. London, Aug. 15, 1957; came to U.S., 1993; s. Martin Murphy and Lillian Blackwell. BSc, U. E. Anglia, Norwich, Eng., 1978, PhD, 1984. Rsch. fellow Trinity Coll., Dublin, Ireland, 1984-87; rsch. assoc. U. Edinburgh, Scotland, 1987-90; rsch. fellow U. Oxford, Eng., 1990-93; rsch. assoc. U. Colo., Denver, 1993-96, U. Del., Lewes, 1996-98, Northeastern U., Boston, 1998—; lectr., tutor, 1984-96. Peer reviewer sci. jours., 1987—; contbr. articles to profl. jours. Rsch. fellow Dept. Edn., 1984, Glasstone fellow U. Oxford, 1990, Linacre fellow Linacre Coll., 1991. Mem. Soc. Neuroscience, Phi Beta Delta. Office: Northeastern U MU312 360 Huntington Ave Boston MA 02115-5000

MURPHY, ROBERT, search firm executive; b. Davenport, Iowa; s. James and Patricia (Cahill) M.; children: Lisa, Todd, Kyle; B.S., U. Ill. Med. Ctr.-Chgo., 1963. Founder, chrmn. Murphy Partners Intl., Americas, Asia, Europe, 1992—; registered pharmacist, Ill.; with Coopers & Lybrand, Chgo., 1973-92; U.S. ptnr.-in-charge exec. Search, Chgo. The Walgreen Co., Chgo., 1963-73; Corp. Mgr. of Coll. Relations and Recruiting, Corp., Mgr. Manpower Planning, Corp., Dir. Orgn. and Human Resource Planning and Devel. Mem. Intl. Human Resource Assn., Soc. Human Resource Managers, Intl. Consultants Assn., Am. Soc. Personnel Adminstrs., Soc. of Human Resource Profls., Young Execs., Kappa Psi. Republican. Contbr. articles to profl. jours. including Wall St Jour., AMA, Newsweek. Office: 956 Shoreline Rd Barrington IL 60010-3815

MURPHY, ROBERT BLAIR, management consulting company executive; b. Phila., Jan. 19, 1931; s. William Beverly and Helen Marie (Brennan) M.; children: Stephen, Emily, Julia, David, Catherine. BS, Yale, 1953. Indsl. engr. DuPont Corp., Aiken, S.C., 1953-55; mgr. sales can divsn. Reynolds Metals Co., Richmond, Va., 1955-69; gen. mgr. corrugated divsn. Continental Can Co., N.Y.C., 1969-73; v.p. and gen. mgr. beverage divsn. Am. Can Co., Greenwich, Conn., 1973-75; assoc. Heidrick & Struggles, Inc., N.Y.C., 1976-78, v.p., 1978; v.p., mng. dir. Stamford office Spencer Stuart & Assocs., 1978-84, ptnr., 1982-84; co-founder Sullivan-Murphy Assocs., 1984—; dir. Digital Phone USA, Stamford. Mem. Riverside Yacht Club (Greenwich), Yale Club (N.Y.C.), Merion Cricket Club (Haverford, Pa.), Bucks Harbor Yacht Club (Brooksville, Maine). Home: 11 Indian Mill Rd Cos Cob CT 06807-1315

MURPHY, ROBERT PATRICK, physician, ophthalmic researcher; b. Aug. 11, 1943; m. Emily Ying Chew, Oct. 11, 1986; children: Alison Anne Chew Murphy, Emma Elizabeth Ying Murphy, Erica Lynn Chew Murphy. BS, St. Louis U., 1965; MD, Northwestern U., 1969. Intern Milw. County Gen. Hosp., 1969-70; resident internal medicine U. Calif., Irvine, 1972-75; resident ophthalmology Stanford (Calif.) U. Med. Ctr., 1975-78; assoc. prof. Sch. of Medicine Johns Hopkins U., Balt., 1984-91; pvt. practice Glaser Murphy Retina Treatment Ctr., Balt., 1991—. Mem. AMA, Am. Acad. Ophthalmology, Assn. Rsch. in Vision and Ophthalmology, Macula Soc., Retina Soc., Pan-Am. Assn. Ophthalmology, Md. Soc. Eye Physicians and Surgeons, Balt. City Med. Soc., Chirurgical Faculty Md., Atlantic Coast Retina Club, Club Jules Gonin, Johns Hopkins U. Alumni Assn. Office: Glaser Murphy Retinal Treatment Ctr 5530 Wisconsin Ave Ste 835 Chevy Chase MD 20815-4401

MURPHY, THOMAS MICHAEL, civil engineer; b. Hubbard, Ohio, Mar. 26, 1963; s. Michael F. Jr. and Gratia Marie (Henry) M.; m. Regina Marie Quinn, Mar. 28, 1992; 1 child, Caitlin Marie. BS, Youngstown State U., 1988. Cert. asst. team leader N.Y.C. Dept. Transp., N.Y. State Dept. Transp., N.Y. State Thruway Authority. Structural engr. Marsico & Assocs., Youngstown, Ohio, 1987; constrn. inspector Adlaka & Assocs., Boardman, Ohio, 1987, Marsico & Assocs., Youngstown, 1987; structural engr. Hardesty & Hanover, N.Y.C., 1988-94, A&H Engrs., N.Y.C., 1994, Ammann & Whitney, N.Y.C., 1995-96, M.S. Cons., Youngstown, 1996; quality assurance/quality control engr. Star Aluminum Extrusions, Canfield, Ohio, 1997-99; civil engr. PSI Inc., Pitts., 1999-2000, Youngstown, Ohio, 2000—. Mem. ASCE (affiliate mem. N.Y. met. chpt. and Youngstown State U. chpt.) Am. Soc. Cert. Engring. Technicians (mem., sec.-tres. Youngstown State U. Steel Valley chpt. 1985-86), KC (3d and 4th degree). Democrat. Roman Catholic. Avocations: photography, new technology in bridge design and construction. Home: 210 Christian Ave Hubbard OH 44425-2010 Office: PSI 1057 Trumbull Ave Youngstown OH 44505

MURPHY, THOMAS MILES, pediatrician; b. Sioux City, Iowa, Dec. 5, 1945; s. Charles Thomas and Madeline Elizabeth (McGovern) M.; m. Priscilla Rollin Coit, Oct. 4, 1969; 1 child, Nicholas Charles. AB in Math., Harvard Coll., 1969; MD, U. Rochester, 1973. Diplomate Am. Bd. Med. Examiners, Am. Bd. Internal Medicine, Am. Bd. Pediatrics, subbd. pulmonology; lic. physician, N.C. Intern Georgetown U. Med. Divsn., D.C. Gen. Hosp., Washington, 1973-74; resident in internal medicine Georgetown U. Med. Ctr., Washington, 1974-76, fellow pediat. pulmonary medicine, 1976-78; asst. prof. pediat. Georgetown U. Sch. Medicine, Washington, 1979-80, asst. prof. clin. pediat., 1980-85; asst. prof. clin. pediat. U. Chgo., 1985-87, asst. prof. pediat. and medicine, 1990-93; asst. prof. pediat. U. Chgo. Pritzker Sch. Medicine, 1987-90, chief sect. pulmonary medicine dept. pediat., 1992-93; assoc. prof., chief divsn. pediat. pulmonary diseases Duke U., Durham, N.C., 1993—; assoc. dir. Pediatric Pulmonary and Cystic Fibrosis Ctr., Georgetown U., 1978-80; asst. prof. child health and devel. George Washington U. Sch. Medicine and Health Scis., Washington, 1980-85; assoc. chmn. dept. pulmonary medicine, co-dir. Cystic Fibrosis Ctr. for Care, Teaching and Rsch., Children's Hosp. Nat. Med. Ctr., Washington, 1980-85; dir. pediatric pulmonary fellowship tng. program U. Chgo., 1990-93, dir. Cystic Fibrosis Ctr., 1991-93, assoc. chief sect. allergy, immunology and pulmonology, dept. pediatrics, 1991-92; editor ATS Pediat. Assembly Website, 2000—. Contbr. articles to profl. jours., chpts. to books; cons. referee editor New Eng. Jour. Medicine, 1989, Am. Rev. Respiratory Disease, 1989—, Am. Jour. Physiology: Lung Cellular and Molecular Physiology, 1990—, Pediatric Rsch., 1991—, Jour. Applied Physiology, 1991—, Pediat. Pulmonology, 1993—, mem. editl. bd., 1996—; contbg. editor The Hudson Monitor. Mem. ctr. com. Cystic Fibrosis Found., 1992-97, 2000-2002; chmn. childhood lung disease com. D.C. Lung Assn., 1980-83, lung disease com., 1984; mem. adv. coun. D.C. Sudden Infant Death Syndrome, 1981-83, chmn. med. adv. com., 1982-83. Recipient Cmty. Svc. award So. Md. Lung Assn., 1980, Media award Am. Acad. Pediatrics, 1980, Svc. award homicide br. Met. Police Dept. D.C., 1983, Svc. award Met. D.C. chpt. Cystic Fibrosis Foun., Washington, 1985, Nat. Cystic Fibrosis Found., 1997; Rsch. grantee Am. Lung Assn., N.Y.C., 1992, NIH, Bethesda, Md., 1993, 98. Mem. AAAS, Soc. Pediatric Rsch., Am. Physiol. Soc., N.Y. Acad. Scis., Am. Thoracic Soc. (program com. assembly on respiratory structure and function 1993-96, chair long range planning com. 2000-2002, chair subcom. on physician scientists, pediat. assembly 1997—). Avocations: refereeing soccer, jazz. Office: Duke U Med Ctr PO Box 2994 Durham NC 27715-2994

MURPHY, TIMOTHY FRANCIS, physician, scientist; b. Chgo., Aug. 21, 1950; s. Thomas Edward and Patricia Elizabeth (Manning) M.; m. Vicki Adee, Apr. 21, 1979; children: Brendan Thomas, Sean Alexander. BS, NYU, 1972; MD, Tufts U., 1976. Diplomate Am. Bd. Internal Medicine, Diplomate Infectious Diseases Subspecialty. Intern N.Y. Hosp. Cornell Med. Ctr., N.Y.C., 1976-77, med. resident, 1977-79; infectious disease fellow Tufts New Eng. Med. Ctr., Boston, 1979-81; faculty, prof. medicine and microbiology SUNY, Buffalo, 1981—, chief infectious diseases, 1990—. Contbr. articles to Jour. Infection and Immunity, Jour. Clin. Investigation, Jour. Infectious Diseases, Revs. of Infectious Diseases. Recipient Sinscheimer Scholar award 1982; named Niagara Frontier Inventor of Yr., 1992, 98. Fellow ACP, Infectious Disease Soc. Am.; mem. Am. Soc. Microbiology, Am. Fedn. Clin. Rsch. (Eastern Young Investigator award 1994), Am. Soc. for Clin. Investigation, Alpha Omega Alpha. Achievements include discovery of P6 protein as possible vaccine for nontypeable haemophilus influenzae; research on outer membrane proteins of branhamella catarrhalis. Office: Buffalo VA Med Ctr 3495 Bailey Ave Buffalo NY 14215-1129

MURPHY COLUCCI, MARION, writer, poet; b. Queens, N.Y., Mar. 6, 1940; s. Frank and Ida (Giotta) Colucci; children: Carrie, Maureen, Raygen, Erin. free-lance profl. painter, N.Y., 1950's-80's; freelance costume mask designer, N.Y., 1969-78. Writer numerous poems; lyric recs. Petunia Revival, D.O.A. Dog, 1998, Fun Baby, Up Shoes, 1999. Mem. Internat. Soc. Poets, Songwriters Guild Am., Internat. Poetry Hall Fame. Avocations: solitude, music, innovating, walking and loving God's creations.

MURPHY-O'CONNOR, CORMAC, archbishop; b. Aug. 24, 1932; s. Patrick George and Ellen Theresa (Cuddigan) M.-O'C. PhL, Gregorian U., Rome, 1956; STL, Venerable English Coll., Rome, 1956; DD, Archbishop of Canterbury, 1999. Ordained priest Roman Cath. Ch., 1956. Asst. priest Corpus Christi Parish, Portsmouth, 1956-63, Sacred Heart Parish, Fareham, 1963-66; pvt. sec., chaplain to bishop Portsmouth, 1966-70; priest Parish of the Immaculate Conception, Southampton, Eng., 1970-71; rector sem. Venerable English Coll., 1971-77; bishop of Arundel and Brighton, West Sussex, Eng., 1977-2000; archbishop of Westminster Eng., 2000—; 1st chmn. Bishops' Com. for Europe, 1978-83; chmn. Com. for Christian Unity, 1983-99; co-chmn. 2d Anglican-Roman Cath. Internat. Commn., 1983-99; chmn. Bishops' Dept. for Mission and Unity, 1993—. Author: The Family of the Church, 1984. Home and Office: Archbishop's House, Ambrosden Ave Westminster, London SW1P 1QJ, England

MURRAY, ALAN, engineering executive; b. Newcastle upon Tyne, Eng., Aug. 21, 1949; s. Gavin Murray and Hilda Brook; m. Marie Jane Walker, Mar. 8, 1973; children: Lloyd Kennedy, Aidan Taylor. Higher Nat. Cert. Mech., Newcastle Poly., Newcastle upon Tyne, 1970; Nat. Cert. Bus. Studies, Coll. Art and Tech., Newcastle upon Tyne, 1985. Draughtsman design Sir Howard Grubb Parsons & Co. Ltd., Newcastle upon Tyne, 1966-75, C.A. Parsons & Co. Ltd., Newcastle upon Tyne, 1975-77, Grubb Parsons & Co. Ltd., Newcastle upon Tyne, 1977-78, Am. Air Filters, Cramlington, Eng., 1978, Winthrop Labs. Ltd., Newcastle upon Tyne, 1978; mfg. liaison engr. on line inspection Brit. Gas Corp., Cramlington, 1978-80; engr. product design and devel. Elmwood Sensors Ltd., Tyne, Eng., 1980-85, mgr. product engring., 1985-89; tech. dir. Jonas Woodhead Ltd., 1989—. Patentee in field. Fellow Inst. Bus. and Tech. Mgmt.; mem. Brit. Inst. Mgmt. (assoc.). Avocations: motor sports, personal computers, family activities. Home: 46 Roast Calf Ln, Bishop Middleham, County Durham DL17 9AT, England Office: Krupp Hoesch Woodmead Ltd, 177 Kirkstall Rd, Leeds LS4 2AQ, England

MURRAY, BARBARA OLIVIA, writer, retired psychologist; b. Summit, N.J., July 8, 1947; d. Archibald and Anna Cutler (Mattison) M. Student, Inst. d'Etudes Francaises Pour trangers, France, 1965, U. de Grenoble, France, 1968; BA in Psychology, Lake Erie Coll., 1969; MA in Clin. Psychology, Cleve. State U., 1971; postgrad., Gestalt Inst. Cleve., 1971-73; PhD in Clin. Psychology, Calif. Sch. Profl. Psychology, Fresno, 1976. Lic. psychologist, Calif. Mental health worker Cleve. Clinic Hosp., 1970-71, assoc. psychologist, 1971-73; psychiat. intake worker Cleve. Free Clinic, 1971, group leader, 1972; cons. St. John's Coll., Cleve., 1972-73; psychology intern Fresno County Dept. Health, 1973-75, student profl. worker, 1974; mem. faculty Calif. Sch. Profl. Psychology, Fresno, 1974; psychology intern Calif. State U., Fresno, 1975, lectr., 1975-77; treatment program dir. E. Ross Clark Home for Children, Inc., Modesto, Calif., 1976-77; clin. psychologist Santa Cruz County (Calif.) Cmty. Mental Health Svcs., 1977-79, dir. psychol. svcs., 1979-83; pvt. practice psychotherapy Soquel, Calif., 1979-98; oral commr. Calif. State Psychology Licensing Exam, 1988-98; designated expert for Med. Bd. Calif., 1991-98; mem. med. staff Dominican Hosp., 1983-93, vice-chmn. dept. psychiatry/psychology, 1985-87, acting chair, 1987-88; mem. Citizens Involvement Assocs., 1984-87; adj. faculty Pacific Grad. Sch. Psychology, 1984-89; mem. faculty San Francisco State U., 1987; cons. NOW, 1973-76, Cmty. Hosp., Fresno, 1974; expert witness Santa Cruz, Monterey, Santa Clara and San Francisco counties, 1979-98, law and ethics workshop, 1984, CPI-MMPI workshop, 1986, child sexual assault asst. workshop, 1986, The Role of the Profl. in Complex Custody Disputes, 1993. Contbr. articles to jours. in psychology. Mem. Women's Studies Adv. Bd., Fresno, 1975-76. Recipient Disting. Psychologist award Calif. State Psychol. Assn., 1982, recognition for contbns. to the field of psychology and Mid-Coast Psychol. Assn., 1996; Hill scholar, 1968, Smith scholar, 1969, Fritz Perls scholar, 1970. Mem. APA, Calif. Psychol. Assn. (bd. dirs. Observer 1981-83), Mid-Coast Psychol. Assn. (pres. 1981, forensic chmn. 1983-96), Psychol. Inst., Forensic Mental Health Assn., No. Calif. Psychologists for Social Responsibility, Laurel Soc., Psi Chi (v.p. 1968-69), Kappa Alpha Sigma, Cotuit Mosquito Yacht Club, Mt. Women Investment Club. Home and Office: 4595 Fairway Dr Soquel CA 95073-3010

MURRAY, BRIAN VICTOR, investment banker; b. Teaneck, N.J., Oct. 17, 1947; s. Harry Lawrence and Marie Antoinette (Brizzi) M.; m. Dec. 14, 1974; children: B. Patrick, Megan, Sean, Matthew. BS in Econs., Villanova U., 1970; MBA with hons., U. Chgo., 1975. Ptnr. H.C. Wainwright & Co., N.Y.C., Boston, 1974-78; sr. mng. dir. Bear, Stearns & Co., N.Y.C., 1978-96; pres. B.V. Murray & Co., Englewood Cliffs, N.J., 1996—; chmn. First Hungary Fund, Isle of Jersey, 1996—, Carlson Bolivia Fund, 1997—; bd. dirs. 4 Front Tech., Del., U.S., 1996—, Renal Tech. DVT. N.Y.C., 1998—; founder, bd. dirs. Ascent/Meredith Asset Mgmt., N.Y.C., 1998—. Trustee, mem. exec. com. Elizabeth Morrow Sch., Englewood, N.J., 1991—. Lt. U.S. Navy, 1970. Named Internat. Dealer of Yr., Instnl. Investment Mag., 1989. Mem. Union League (N.Y.), Inst. of Chartered Fin. Analysts (chartered). Avocation: judging horses (recognized judge Am. Horse Show Assn.). E-mail: Bvm@bvmurray.com. Office: BV Murray & Co Inc 560 Sylvan Ave Englewd Clfs NJ 07632-3104

MURRAY, BRUCE ALAN, reading educator; b. Quincy, Ill., Sept. 10, 1951; s. Richard Charles and Mary Evelyn (Broyles) M.; m. Geralyn Genevieve Naylor Murray, June 15, 1975; children: Douglas Joseph, Ellen Cecilia, Paul Nicholas, Jack Christopher. BA in Philosophy, Quincy (Ill.) Coll., 1973, BA in Psychology, 1973; MS in Sch. Adminstrn., Southwest Mo. State U., Springfield, 1981, MS in Reading Edn., 1990; PhD in Reading Edn., U. Ga., Athens, 1995. Cert. in elem. and secondary edn., Mo. Elem. tchr. St. Joseph Sch., Springfield, Mo., 1975-78, Licking (Mo.) Elem. Sch., 1978-90; asst. prof. Marquette U., Milw., 1995-96; asst. prof. reading edn. Auburn (Ala.) U., 1996—; cons. Ala. Reading Initiative, Montgomery; edtl. review bd. Jour. of Literacy Rsch., Athens, Ga. Contbr. articles to profl. jours. Named Finalist Student Rsch. award, Nat. Reading Conf., 1994, 95; recipient Elmer Jackson Carson Meml scholarship U. Ga., Athens, 1993-94, Grad. Sch. Assistantship U. Ga., Athens, 1992-95. Mem. Internat. Reading Assn., Nat. Reading Conf. Republican. Roman Catholic. Avocations:

church musician, editoralist. E-mail address: murraba@auburn.edu. Fax: 334-844-6789. Office: Dept Curriculum and Teaching 5040 Haley Ctr Auburn AL 36830

MURRAY, CAROLINE FISH, psychologist; b. Buenos Aires, Argentina, Mar. 28, 1920; came to U.S., 1924; d. Alfred Dupont and Caroline Johnston (Ramsay) Chandler; m. Henry A. Murray, May 17, 1969; children by previous marriages: Caroline D. Janover, Alexander M. Davis, Ann Kelso D. McLaughlin, Quita D. Palmer, Maude I. Fish. AB magna cum laude, Smith Coll., 1942; MEd, U. N.H., 1962; EdD, Boston U., 1967. Exec. sec. to dir. Alfred I. duPont Inst., Wilmington, Del., 1953-55; tchr. Kingston (N.H.) Pub. Schs., 1962-63; instr. Boston U., 1966-67, asst. prof. psychology, 1967-71, co-dir. psycho-educational clinic, 1966-70, coord. headstart evaluation and rsch. ctr., 1966-69, cons., 1969-83; mem. clin. staff Mass. Mental Health Ctr., Boston, 1983-90; lectr. psychology dept. psychiatry Harvard Med. Sch., 1983-91; cons. Indochinese Psychiatry Clinic, Brighton, Mass., 1987—, sch. consultation and treatment team Mass. Mental Health Ctr., 1987-90; mem. profl. adv. com. Mass. Dept. Mental Health, 1983-85, adolescent planning subcom., 1990-92. Corporator Nantucket Cottage Hosp., 1993—, trustee, 1997-2000; bd. dirs. Friends Nantucket Pub. Schs., 1993-98, Wediko Children's Svcs., 1975-85, Shaker Village, Hancock, Mass., Douglas A. Thom Clinic, Boston, 1974-77, pres., 1977; chmn. bd. Ariel Chamber Music, Cambridge, 1979, Mass. Children's Lobby, 1978-82, pres. 1979-82, Nantucket Edn. Trust, 1990—, Friends of Nantucket Atheneum, 1990-2000, pres., 2000—, trustee; chmn. statewide adv. coun. Office for Children, 1980-82. Mem. APA, Am. Assn. Advancement Psychology, Mass. Pschol. Assn., Eastern Pschol. Assn., N.Y. Acad. Scis., Fedn. Am. Sci., Jean Piaget Soc., Pi Lambda Theta. Democrat. Home: 11 Lincoln Ave Nantucket MA 02554-3412

MURRAY, CHARLES NICHOLAS, chemical oceanographer; b. Warrington, Eng., Sept. 5, 1943; s. Charles Angelo and Alice Eunice Myfannwy (Nicholas) M.; m. Ghislaine Estelle Benayoun, May 19, 1982. BSc in Physics and Chemistry, U. Liverpool, 1966, MSc in Oceanography, 1968, PhD in Chem. Oceanography, 1970, DSc in Environ. Nuclear Waste Protection, 1988. Asst. officer Internat. Atomic Energy Agy., Monaco, 1971-75; head environ. transuranic sect. German Hydrographic Inst., Hamburg, 1975-77; scientific officer Commn. European Cmtys., Ispra, Italy, 1977—; co-internat. coord. Internat. Sub-Seabed Program, Nuclear Energy Agy. OECD, Paris, 1983-88; sci. and tech. asst. to dir. Inst. for Remote Sensing Applications, Ispra, 1988-91; sci. officer Environment Inst., Ispra, 1997—. Editl. bd. Jour. Marine Models Online, 1997—; contbr. over 130 articles to profl. jours.; patentee in field. Avocations: languages, golf, travel, gardening. Office: Environment Inst, Joint Rsch Ctr, 21020 Ispra Italy

MURRAY, DANIEL RICHARD, lawyer; b. Mar. 23, 1946; s. Alfred W. and Gloria D. Murray. AB, U. Notre Dame, 1967; JD, Harvard U., 1970. Bar: Ill. 1970, U.S. Dist. Ct. (no. dist.) Ill. 1970, U.S. Ct. Appeals (7th cir.) 1971, U.S. Supreme Ct. 1974. Ptnr. Jenner & Block, Chgo., 1970—; trustee Chgo. Mo. and Western Rlwy. Co., 1988-97; adj. prof. U. Notre Dame, 1997—. Co-author: Secured Transactions, 1978, Illinois Practice: Uniform Commercial Code with Illinois Code Comments, 1997. Bd. regents Big Shoulders Fund, Archdiocese of Chgo., Bernadin Ctr., Cath. Theol. Union. Mem. Am. Bankruptcy Inst., Am. Law Inst., Am. Coll. Comml. Fin. Lawyers (bd. regents), Transp. Lawyers Assn., Assn. Transp. Practitioners, Cath. Lawyers Guild (bd. dirs.), Law Club, Legal Club. Roman Catholic. Home: 1307 N Sutton Pl Chicago IL 60610-2007 Office: Jenner & Block One IBM Plz Chicago IL 60611-3605

MURRAY, GRAEME DOUGLAS, travel company executive; b. Temuka, Canterbury, New Zealand, Dec. 20, 1943; s. James Edward and Ellen Elizabeth (Anderson) M.; m. Carolyn Jean Mathieson, Feb. 5, 1975; children: Jessica, James, David, Rebecca. Mgr. Dalgety Travel, Timaru, New Zealand, 1963-74; gen. mgr. Lynn River Products Ltd., Geraldine, New Zealand, 1974-77; mng. dir. sales/adminstrn. Air Safaris, Lake Tekapo, New Zealand, 1977—. Bd. dirs. Mackenzie Tourism & Devel. Bd., Fairlie, 1995—, Tourism and Hospitality divsn. Aoraki Poly., Timar, 1994—; justice of the peace, Lake Tekapo, 1989—; marriage celebrant Lake Tekapo, 1989—. Mem. N.Z. Inst. Travel, Rotary (hon.). Presbyterian. Avocation: outdoor sports. Home: 3 Sealy St, Lake Tekapo New Zealand Office: Air Safaris & Svcs (NZ) Ltd, Main Hwy, Lake Tekapo New Zealand

MURRAY, IAIN HAMISH, clergy member; b. Liverpool, Eng., Apr. 19, 1931; s. James and Emily Florence (Copland) M.; m. Jean Ann Walters, Apr. 23, 1955; children: Stephen, David, Deborah, Jonathan, Andrew, James. BA, Durham U., 1954. Editor Banner of Truth, Eng., 1955-87; founder, editl. bd. dir. Banner of Truth Trust, London, Edinburgh, 1957-96; min. Grove Chapel, London, 1961-69, St. Giles, Sydney, 1981-84. Author: D. Martyn Lloyd-Jones, 2 Vols., 1982, 90, Jonathan Edwards: A New Biography, 1987, Revival and Revivalism: The Making and Marring of American Evangelicalism, 1750-1858, 1994, The Forgotten Spurgeon, 1996, Evangelicalism Divided, 2000. Lt. Scottish Rifles, 1950-51. Avocations: gardening, swimming, tennis, family activities. Office: Banner of Truth Trust, 3 Murrayfield Rd, Edinburgh Scotland

MURRAY, JOEL N., English educator; b. Chester, S.C., Mar. 17, 1973; s. Dennis James and Lois Whitman M.; m. Sherry Lynn, July 25, 1997; children: Philip, Chris, Matt. BA, St. Leo U., 1995; MA, Lancaster U., 1996. English tchr. West Hernando Christian Sch., Hernando Beach, Fla., 1996-97; instr. English composition St. Leo U., St. Leo, Fla., 1997-98, St. Leo U. Weekend Writing Program, 1998—; English tchr. Hudson (Fla.) H.S., 1998—. Author: Simple Machine, 1994. Mem. Underground Poets Soc., Sigma Tau Delta. Avocations: reading, writing, flute, guitar. E-mail: coffindodger@hotmail.com. Home: 8606 Arrow Head Dr Bayonet Point FL 34667-2521

MURRAY, JOHN FREDERIC, physician, educator; b. Mineola, N.Y., June 8, 1927; s. Frederic S. and Dorothy Murray; m. Diane Lain, Nov. 30, 1968; children—James R., Douglas S., Elizabeth. A.B., Stanford, 1949, M.D., 1953; D.Sc. (hon.), U. Paris, 1983. From instr. to asso. prof. medicine U. Calif. at Los Angeles, 1957-66; mem. sr. staff Cardiovascular Research Inst., U. Calif., San Francisco, 1966-94; asso. prof. medicine Cardiovascular Research Inst., U. Calif. (Sch. Medicine), 1966-69, prof., 1969-94; chief chest service San Francisco Gen. Hosp., 1966-89; Vis. prof. Brompton Inst. for Diseases of the Chest, London, 1972-73; Macy faculty scholar Inst. Nat. de la Santé et de la Recherche Medicale, Paris, 1979-80; mem. adv. council and pulmonary disease adv. com. Nat. Heart, Lung and Blood Inst.; mem. clin. studies panel NRC.; bd. govs. Am. Bd. Internal Medicine, Am. Bd. Emergency Medicine. Author: The Normal Lung, 1976, 2d edit., 1986; co-author: Diseases of the Chest, 5th edit., 1980; co-editor: Textbook of Respiratory Medicine, 1988, 2d edit., 1994, 3rd edit., 2000; editor: Am. Rev. Respiratory Disease, 1973-79; contbr. articles to profl. jours. Chmn. Internat. Union Against Tb and Lung Disease. Served with USNR, 1945-46. Sr. Internat. fellow Fogarty Inst.; recipient Pres.'s award European Respiratory Soc., 1996. Fellow Royal Coll. Physicians; mem. Assn. Am. Physicians, Am. Soc. Clin. Investigation, Am. Physiol. Soc., Western Soc. Clin. Research, Western Assn. Physicians, Am. Thoracic Soc. (pres. 1981-82, Trudeau medal 1994), Académie Nationale de Médecine Francaise. Home: 24 Edith St San Francisco CA 94133-2913 Office: U Calif PO Box 841 San Francisco CA 94143-0001

MURRAY, JOHN JOSEPH, dentistry educator, academic dean; b. Bradford, U.K., Dec. 28, 1941; s. John Gerald and Margaret Sheila (Parle) M.; m. Valerie Allen, Mar. 28, 1967; children: Mark Robert, Christopher James. BChD, U. Leeds, 1966, MChD, 1968, PhD, 1970. Rsch. fellow in children's and preventive dentistry Leeds U., 1966-70, sr. lectr. in children's dentistry, 1970-75; reader Inst. of Dental Surgery, London, 1975-77; prof. child dental health U. Newcastle Upon Tyne, 1977-92, postbrad. sub-dean, 1982-92, dean of dentistry, The Dental Sch., 1992—; chmn. clin. standards; mem. adv. group com. on cleft lip and palate, Dept. of Health, London. Author: Fluoride in Caries Prevention, 1991, The Prevention of Oral Disease, 1997. Fellow Acad. Med. Sci; mem. Internat. Assn. Paediatric Dentistry (chmn. organizig com. 1999), Pub. Health Medicine (hon.), Gen. Dental Coun. (chmn. edn. com. 1999—). Roman Catholic. Avocations: golf, photography. Office: U Newcastle The Dental Sch, Office Dean Framlington Pl, Newcastle upon Tyne NE2 4BW, England

MURRAY, JOHN LOYOLA, judge; b. Limerick, Ireland, June 27, 1943; arrived in Luxembourg, 1991; s. John Cecil and Catherine Mary (Casey) M.; m. Gabrielle Mary Walsh, May 25, 1969; children: Catriona Joanne, Brian Conor. Barrister-at-law, King's Inns, Dublin, 1967, sr. counsel, 1981; LLD (hon.), U. Limerick, Ireland, 1992. Pvt. practice Ireland, 1967-81, 83-87; atty. Gen. of Ireland, Dublin, 1982, 87-91; mem. Coun. of State, Ireland, 1987-91; judge Ct. of Justice, EEC, Luxembourg, from 1991; now mem. anti-fraud com. ECB; judge Supreme Ct. Ireland, Dublin; vis. prof. law U. Catholique de Louvain, 1997—. Trustee Rotunda Hosp. Tchg. Trust. Mem. King's Inns (bencher), Fitzwilliam Lawn Tennis Club, Royal Irish Yacht Club, Stephen's Green Club. Avocations: yachting, swimming, art, traveling. Office: Supreme Ct Ireland, Four Cts, Morgan Pl, Dublin 7, Ireland*

MURRAY, JOSEPH EDWARD, retired plastic surgeon; b. Milford, Mass., Apr. 1, 1919; s. William Andrew and Mary (DePasquale) M.; m. Virginia Link, June 2, 1945; children: Virginia, Margaret, Joseph Link, Katharine, Thomas, Richard. AB, Holy Cross Coll., 1940, DSc, 1965; MD, Harvard, 1943; DSc, Rockford (Ill.) Coll., 1966, Roger Williams Coll., 1986; D (hon.), Anna Marie Coll., 1993, SUNY, Albany, 1993, U. Suffolk, 1993, Magill U., Montreal, 1996. Diplomate: Am. Bd. Surgery, Am. Bd. Plastic Surgery (chmn. 1969). Chief plastic surgeon Peter Bent Brigham Hosp., Boston, 1951-86, chief plastic surgeon emeritus, 1986—; chief plastic surgeon Children's Hosp. Med. Center, Boston, 1972-85, emeritus, 1985; prof. surgery Harvard Med. Sch., 1970-86; ret., 1986. Served to maj. M.C. AUS, 1944-47. Recipient Gold medal Internat. Soc. Surgeons, 1963, hon. award Am. Acad. Arts and Sci., 1962, Nobel prize for medicine or physiology, 1990, Sabin award 1994, Lifetime Achievement award Mass. Med. Soc., 1998. Fellow AAAS (hon.), AMA, Royal Australasian Coll. Surgeons, Royal Coll. Surgeons of Eng., Royal Coll. Surgeons Ireland, Royal Coll. Surgeons Edinburgh; mem. ACS (regent 1970-79, v.p. 1983), NAS, Am. Surg. Assn. (v.p. 1979), New Eng. Surg. Assn. (pres. 1986-87), Boston Surg. Soc. (pres. 1975), Soc. U. Surgeons, Am. Assn. Plastic Surgeons (hon. award 1969, pres. 1964-65), Am. Acad. Arts and Scis., Harvard Med. Sch. Alumni Coun. (pres. 1984), Badminton and Tennis Club, Wellesley Country Club, Tavern Club (Boston), Alpha Omega Alpha. Home: 108 Abbott Rd Wellesley MA 02481-6104

MURRAY, JULIA KAORU (MRS. JOSEPH E. MURRAY), occupational therapist; b. Wahiawa, Oahu, Hawaii, 1934; d. Gijun and Edna Tsuruko (Taba) Funakoshi; m. Joseph Edward Murray, 1961; children: Michael, Susan, Leslie. BA, U. Hawaii, 1956; cert. occupational therapy, U. Puget Sound, 1958. Therapist Inst. Logopedics, Wichita, Kans., 1958; sr. therapist Hawaii State Hosp., Kaneohe, 1959; part-time therapist Centre County Ctr. for Crippled Children and Adults, State College, Pa., 1963; vice chmn. adv. bd. Hosp. Improvement Program East Oreg. State Hosp., Pendleton, 1974; v.p. Ind. Living, Inc., 1976-79; job search instr.; mem. adv. com. Oreg. Ednl. Coordinating Commn., 1979-82; mem. Oreg. Bd. Engring. Examiners, 1979-87; supr., occupational therapist Fairview Tng. Ctr., Salem, Oreg., 1984-94; occupational therapist U.S. Naval Hosp., Okinawa, Japan, 1994—. Rep. from Umatilla County Commrs. to Blue Mountain Econ. Devel. Council, 1976-78; mem. Ashland Park and Recreation Bd., 1972-73; vice chmn. adv. bd. LINC, 1978; mem. exec. bd. Liberty-Boone Neighborhood Assn., 1979-83. Mem. Am. Occupational Therapy Assn., Oreg. Occupational Therapy Assn., Hawaii Occupational Therapy Assn. (sec. 1960, LWV (bd. dirs. Pendleton 1974, 77-78, pres. 1975-77; bd. dirs. Oreg. 1979-81, Ashland, Wis., 1967-71, Wis. v.p. 1970). Office: Ednl & Developmental Svcs, US Naval Hosp, APO AP Tokyo 96326, Japan also: Ednl & Develmntl Intervention Svcs, Naval Hosp, Yokosuka Japan

MURRAY, KATHLEEN, municipal official; b. Phillipsburg, N.J., Nov. 1, 1960; d. Joseph A. and Joann P. (Sepple) M. BS, Rosemont Coll., 1983. Legis. asst. Office of Anna C. Verna, Phila., 1983-86, aide to fin. com., 1989-94, chief of staff, 1994—; head of circulation Haverford (Pa.) Coll., 1987-88; asst. dir. Outreach Coord. Ctr., Phila., 1988-89; staff mem. select com. of fiscal stability, Phila., 1992-94; mem. pub. affairs com. Local Emergency Planning Commn., Phila., 1995—; staff Mayor's Commn. of Phila. Naval Base, 1997; mem. Mayor's Commn. on Homelessness, Phila., 1993-96. Bd. dirs. Southwest Task Force, Inc., Phila., 1983-86, Voyage House Inc., Phila., 1991-96, PrideFest Am., 1998; mem. Police Commrs. Gay and Lesbian Liaison Com., 1998—; bd. mem. POPEC, 1999—. Democrat. Episcopalian. Avocations: tennis, golf, reading, U.S. history. Office: Office of Pres 494 City Hall Philadelphia PA 19107-3201

MURRAY, KATHLEEN, research psychologist; b. Peterculter, Scotland, May 6, 1932; d. William Alexander and Kate Sim (Riddell) Craib; m. Robert Ian Murray, Sept. 14, 1962. MA, U. Aberdeen, 1953, MEd, 1958. Chartered psychologist. Tchr. Edn. Dept., Dumfries, 1954-56; ednl. psychologist Child Guidance, Bristol, 1958-62; clin. psychologist Health Bd., Glasgow, Scotland, 1962-70; lectr. U. Glasgow, 1970-83, rsch. fellow, 1983-90; sr. rsch. fellow, 1990—; coun. mem. Barnardo's, London, 1982-98; dir. Nat. Children's Bur., London, 1986-92. Editor: Children's Hearings, 1976, The Scottish Juvenile Justice System, 1983, Intervening in Child Sexual Abuse, 1991; co-author: Children Out of Court, 1981; author: Live Television Link-An Evaluation of its Use in Scottish Criminal Courts, 1995, Preparing Child Witnesses for Court, 1997. Fellow Brit. Psychol. Soc. (assoc.). Avocations: gardening, skiing. E-mail: kaymurray@excite.co.uk.

MURRAY, LAWRENCE, management consultant; b. N.Y.C., May 10, 1939; s. Gilbert and Edna (Blatt) M.; children: Robert, Stacy, David, Daniel, Abigail. BA, Cornell U., 1961; MBA, U. Okla., 1966; PhD, Pacific Western Univ., 1993. Cert. Pa. Food Mgmt.; Microsoft cert. sys. engr., Cisco cert. network assoc. Account exec. Merrill Lynch, Paramus, N.J., 1965-69; chmn., pres. Murray, Lind & Co., Inc., Jersey City, 1969-72; dir. investor rels. IU Internat. Corp., Phila., 1972-73, dir. spl. projects, 1974-75; dir. fin. com., mem. exec. staff, chmn. bd. ARA Svcs., Inc., Phila., 1975-78; chmn., chief exec. officer Century Mgmt. and affiliated cos., West Chester, Pa., 1976-82, Creative Mgmt. Corp., Bala Cynwyd and West Chester, Pa., 1982-87, Fin. Mgmt. Profl. Corp., West Chester, 1983-89; chmn. bd. dirs. Venture Frontiers Co., Denver, 1984-89; chmn. bd., CEO Fin. Intelligence Corp., West Chester, 1989-95; lectr. bus. orgn. and mgmt. Bergen Cmty. Coll., 1971-72; chmn. bd. dirs. Med. Intelligence Corp., West Chester, 1993-95, Healthy Living Ctrs., 1996—, Miramax Corp. Author: The Organized Stockbroker, 1970; A New Era in Mergers and Acquisitions, 1974; Communications: Management's Newest Marketing Skill, 1976, Powerful Tax-Saving Strategies for Honest People, 1992, Dr. Murray's Smart, Easy Formula for Fast, All-Natural Weight Loss for a Longer Healthier Life Without Dieting, 1999, Teach Your Children How to Eat Properly and Add 20 Years to Their Lives, 1999; contbr. articles to profl. jours. Pres., Congregation Beth Israel, Media, Pa., 1977-78, Parents Without Partners, Valley Forge, Pa., 1982-83; v.p. Cornell U. Class of 1961, 1981-86; mem. White House Conf. on Bus. Ethics in Am., 1986. Served to 1st lt. arty., U.S. Army, 1963-64. Decorated U.S. Army Commendation medal. Mem. Nat. Investor Rels. Inst. (pres. Phila. chpt. 1976-78), Internat. Coun. Shopping Ctrs., Am. Health Info. Mgmt. Assn., C. of C. of Greater West Chester, Rotary. Home: 924 Hollyview Ln West Chester PA 19380-1376

MURRAY, MUZ, metaphysician, artist, writer; b. Nuneaton, Eng., Mar. 15, 1940; arrived in France, 1980; s. Gilbert Edwin and Hilda (Boff) Winfield. Student, Coventry (Eng.) Coll. Art, 1951-56; diploma in psychotherapy, Churchill Ctr., London, 1980. Advt. designer Cogent Advt., Coventry, 1957-58; scenic artist Coventry Theatre, 1958-60, Samuel Bronston Films, Madrid, 1960-61, BBC-TV, London, 1962-63, 67, Habima Nat. Theatre, Tel Aviv, 1963; head designer Egyptian TV, Cairo, 1964-65; tchr. art Kenya Girl's H.S., Nairobi, 1964; designer, scenic artist Donovan Maule Theatre, Nairobi, 1964; costume and scenery designer Brian Brooke Theatre, Johannesburg, South Africa, 1965; founder-dir., spiritual head, creator/artist, editor mag. Gandalf's Garden Mystical Cmty., London, 1968-71; mendicant monk India and Iran, 1972-75; co-founder, psychotherapist Open Ctr., Cmty. Health Found., London, 1977-80; founder-dir., spiritual therapist Inner Garden Retreat Ctr., Bury St. Edmunds, Suffolk, Eng., 1977-80; ind. tchr. spiritual evolution through various practices Eng., 1967-98; founder-dir. Inner Garden Ctr., Six Fours les Plages, France, 1994-96; art dir. South Africa Films, Jamie Uys Film Co., Johannesburg, 1965. Author: Seeking the Master—A Guide to the Ashrams and Monasteries of India and Nepal, 1980, Sharing the Quest—The Way of Sunconsciousness, 1986, Segrete del Anima, 1999; mem. modern art group Surrealismo Cadaques, 1961; designer Hasslauer Display stands for Royal Trade Fair, Nairobi, 1964; columnist Yoga Today mag., 1981-86; contbr. articles to various publs.; composer/singer (audio cassettes) Willow in the Wind, 1982, The Sound of Silence, Songs of Silence, Yoganidra, (compact disk) Mantra-il souono dell'energia vitale, 1997, Chanting the Chakras (CD), 1999; actor, singer, dancer, performances including (film) The Second Sin, (theatre) Auntie Mame, (mus. theatre) The Beggar's Opera, (comedy) Pranks a Million; appeared in various U.K. radio and TV documentaries, 1968-71. Dir. Seed-Crystal Trust Charity, London, 1968-96; del. Yoga For Peace in the Middle East Conf., Jerusalem, 1995; internat. lectr. therapy through vocalized sound. Avocations: Mantra yoga, writing fairytales, spiritual aid, gardening, artwork. Home and Office: Aelfylon, 179 Montee du Levant, 30820 Caveirac France

MURRAY, NEIL VINCENT, computer science educator; b. Schenectady, N.Y., July 14, 1948; s. Robert Emslie and Eileen Marie (Milano) M. BS in Engring. Physics, Cornell U., 1970; MS in Computer and Info. Sci., Syracuse U., 1974, PhD in Computer and Info. Sci., 1979. Rsch. asst. Syracuse (N.Y.) U., 1977-78; instr. computer sci. dept. LeMoyne Coll., Syracuse, 1978-79, asst. prof., 1979-82; asst. prof. computer sci. SUNY, Albany, 1982-87, assoc. prof., 1987-97, prof., 1997—, dept. chair, 1999—; Treas. CADE, Inc., Assn. Automated Reasoning; presenter in field. Contbr. articles to profl. jours. Mem. IEEE Computer Soc., Am. Assn. Artificial Intelligence, Assn. Automated Reasoning, Assn. Computing Machinery. Home: 1125 Glenmeadow Ct Niskayuna NY 12309-2511 Office: SUNY Dept Computer Sci L1 67A Albany NY 12222-0001

MURRAY, NICHOLAS JOSEPH, councillor, compliance officer; b. Gateshead, England, Apr. 1, 1954; s. James and Patricia Frances Joan (Downie) M.; m. Joyce Diane Reed, May 31, 1980; children: Ruth Louise, Luke Jerome, Abigail Rose Georgina, Jacob Oliver Nicholas. BA in Geography, U. Birmingham, Eng., 1975; postgrad. diploma in Bus. Computing, Gateshead Coll., 1986. Reg. Mgr. & Securities Rep., Eng., 1993. Grad. trainee British Gas, Enfield, Middlesex, Eng., 1976-79; database adminstr. Project North East, Newcastle Upon Tyne, Eng., 1986-89; client svcs. mgr. Wise Speke Ltd., Newcastle Upon Tyne, Eng., 1989-93; compliance officer Wise Speke Ltd., 1993-2000; asst. compliance dir. Brewin Dolphin Securities Ltd.; compliance dir. Stocktrade, 2000—; dir. Tyne & Wear Devel. Co., Eng., 1990—, Washington Self-Help Initiative Project, Eng., 1992-95. Mem. Local Govt. Assn. Edn. Com., Nat. Drugs and Forum Edn. Body for Drug Awareness; sch. gov. Sunderland LEA Lambton Primary Sch., 1985-94, Oxclose Cmty. Secondary Sch., 1989-99; councillor City of Sunderland Local Authority, 1990-98; vice-chmn. Edn. Com. City of Sunderland LEA, 1994-98. Mem. Tyneside Irish Club, Manors Social Club, No. Constl. Club (mem. exec. com. 1995—); assoc. mem. Securities Inst. Mem. Labour Party. Roman Cath. Avocations: football, the arts, literature, cricket. E-mail: nick.murray@stocktrade.co.uk.

MURRAY, RODERICK CHARLES, manufacturing executive; b. Johannesburg, S. Africa, Jan. 29, 1945; came to U.S., 1987; s. Charles Victor Murray and Yvonne Margaret Sherriffs; m. Yvonne Edna Bennett, Feb. 26, 1966; children: Sandra Leigh, Stuart Charles. BS, Witwatersrand U., Johannesburg, 1967; MBA, MCC, 1990. Qualtiy assurance S. African Breweries, Johannesburg, 1971-75; tech. mgr. Hens Paper, Eerbeek, Holland, 1975-80; dir. mktg. and sales Metal Box, Barlow Rand, Johannesburg, 1980-87; v.p. mktg. ARPAC L.P., Chgo., 1987-89; pres. BMI Machinery, Milw., 1990-96; CEO PPi Tech., Sarasota, Fla., 1996—; v.p. Klockner Packaging, 1996—. Author: Label Paper Technology, 1976, Brand Introductions, 1989; contbr. articles to profl. jours. Fellow British Bottlers; mem. Inst. Packaging Profls. (chmn. 1976), Internat. Beverage Tech. (vice chmn. 1978). Republican. Anglican. Avocations: golf, tennis, boating, travelling. E-mail: RCMPP@AOL.COM. Office: PPi Tech 4378 Longchamp Dr Sarasota FL 34235-3637

MURRAY, SANDRA ANN, biology research scientist, educator; b. Chgo., Oct. 7, 1947; d. Charles William and Muggie (Wise) M. BS, U. Ill., 1970; MS, Tex. So. U., 1973; PhD, U. Iowa, 1980. Instr. biology Tex. So. U., Houston, 1972-73; NIH rsch. fellow U. Calif., Riverside, 1980-82; asst. prof. anatomy U. Pitts., 1982-89, prof. cell biology and physiology, 1989—; prof. Health Officers Inst. Office Def., Addis Ababa, Ethiopia, 1996—; vis. scientist Scripps Rsch. Inst., La Jolla, Calif., 1991-92, INSERM-INRA Hosp. Debrousse, Lyon, France, 1995; cons. NIH, NSF; vis. sci. cons. Fedn. Am. Soc. Exptl. Biology; invited internat. rsch. lectr. at sci. confs. Contbr. articles to Jour. Cell Biology, Anat. Records, Endocrinology, Am. Jour. Anatomy, Molecular and Cellular Endocrinology, Cancer Rsch. Bd. dirs. NAACP, Riverside, 1980-81. Ford Found. fellow, 1978; Rsch. grantee NSF, 1984—, Beta Kappa Chi, Tri Beta Biol. Soc.; recipient Outstanding Achievment award in Sci., Omega Psi Chi; recipient Faculty award Student Nat. Med. Assn. Mem. Am. Soc. Cell Biology (mem. minority affairs com. 1980—, rsch. award to marine biol. lab. 1986, 87, 88, 89, rsch. presentation travel award 1984, mem. coun. 1999), Am. Soc. Biol. Chemists (rsch. presentation travel award 1985), Am. Assn. Anatomists, Tissue Culture Assn. (chairperson internat. sci. com. 1982), Endocrine Soc. (student affairs com.). Office: U Pitts Scaife Hall 864A Pittsburgh PA 15261-0001

MURRAY, STEPHEN JAMES, lawyer; b. Phila., Jan. 27, 1943; s. Paul Martin and Hannah (Smith) M.; m. Linda Sanders, June 20, 1970; children: Gordon Joshua, Cara Sanders. AB cum laude, Brown U., 1963; LLB, Harvard U., 1966; LLM, George Washington U., 1967. Bar: N.Y. 1968, U.S. Ct. Appeals (2nd cir.) 1971, U.S. Ct. Appeals (fed. cir.) 1998, U.S. Dist. Ct. (so. and ea. dists.) N.Y. 1972, U.S. Ct. Claims 1974, U.S. Supreme Ct. 1975, Conn. 1988, U.S. Dist. Ct. Conn. 1988, U.S. Ct. Internat. Trade 1998. Spl. asst. SEC, Washington, 1966-67, Maritime Adminstrn., Washington, 1967-68; assoc. Hill, Betts & Nash, N.Y.C., 1970-76; transp. atty. Union Carbide Corp., N.Y.C., 1976-78, sr. transp. atty., 1978-85; chief transp. counsel Union Carbide Corp., Danbury, Conn., 1985—, group counsel, 1986—, real estate counsel, 1992—, comml. counsel, 1993—, customs and internat. trade counsel, 1997—; spkr. in field. Contbr. articles to profl. jours. Lt. JAGC, USN, 1968-70. Mem. ABA, Conn. State Bar, U.S. Naval Inst., Navy League of U.S., Maritime Law Assn., U.S. Transp. Lawyers Assn., N.Y. State Bar Assn., Am. Corp. Counsel Assn. (co-chair real estate com. Westchester-So. Conn. chpt.), Conn. Maritime Assn., Harvard Club, Brown Club (co-pres.), Brown Faculty Club, Brown Alumni Schs. Commn. (chmn. Fairfield County), Brown Alumni Assn. (bd. govs.). Home: 14 Pilgrim Ln Weston CT 06883-2412 Office: Union Carbide Corp Law Dept 39 Old Ridgebury Rd Danbury CT 06817-0001

MURRAY, TERRENCE, banker; b. Woonsocket, R.I., July 11, 1939; s. Joseph W. and Florence (Blackburn) M.; m. Suzanne Young, Jan. 24, 1960; children: Colleen, Paula, Terrence, Christopher, Megan. B.A., Harvard U., 1962. With Fleet Nat. Bank, Providence, 1962—, pres., 1978-86; with Fleet Fin. Group Inc., Providence, 1969—, pres., 1978—, chmn., pres., chief exec. officer, 1982-88, pres., 1988, chmn., pres., chief exec. officer, 1988-97; also bd. dirs. Fleet Fin. Group Inc., Boston; chmn. & CEO FleetBoston Fin. Corp., Boston; bd. dirs. Fleet Nat. Bank, A.T. Cross Co., State Mut. Assurance Co. Am., Fed. Res. Bank Boston, Stop & Shop Cos. Inc. Trustee R.I. Sch. of Design, Brown U. Recipient Outstanding Bus. Leader award Northwood Inst., 1986, Humanitarian award Nat. Jewish Ctr. for Immunology and Respiratory Medicine, 1988, Never Again award Jewish Fedn., 1989, New Englander of Yr. award New England Coun., 1990, New England Businessperson of Yr. award New England Bus. Mag., 1991, Humanitarian award Fogarty Found., 1991. Mem. Am. Bankers Assn. (bd. dirs.), Assn. of Res. City Bankers (bd. dirs.), Harvard Alumni Assn. (bd. dirs.). Office: Fleet Fin Group 1 Federal St Fl 36 Boston MA 02110-2003

MURRAY, THOMAS JAMES, financial planner, publisher; b. Jamestown, R.I., Mar. 26, 1924; s. Daniel Peter and Margaret (McPartland) M.; m. Jean Shaw, July 2, 1948 (dec. June 1985); children: Thomas, Carolyn, Elizabeth, John, Peter; m. Evelyn Ayers, Apr. 19, 1986. Student, Brown U., 1942-44; BA in Social Sci., George Washington U., 1964. Commissioned ensign U.S. Navy, 1944, advanced through ranks to lt. comdr., 1964, ret., 1964; sales rep. J.D. Marsh & Assoc., Washington, 1964-78; pres. TJM Securities Inc., Chevy Chase, Md., 1978—, Thomas Murray Assocs. Inc., Chevy Chase, Md., 1978—, TMA Ins., Chevy Chase, Md., 1978—; pub. Social List Washington Inc., Kensington, 1985—. Mem. Am. Legion (comdr. Thad Dulin post 1975-76), Rotary (pres. Wheaton Kensington chpt. 1966-67), Knights of Malta, St. Andrew's Soc. (Washington)(pres. 1997-99). Roman Catholic.

Home: 10500 Rockville Pike Apt 1702 N Bethesda MD 20852-3356 Office: Social List Washington 9620 E Bexhill Dr Kensington MD 20895-3103 also: Thomas Murray Assocs 6935 Wisconsin Ave Chevy Chase MD 20815-6109

MURRAY, WALLACE SHORDON, publisher, educator; b. Dorchester, Mass., May 9, 1921; s. Wallace Jennings and Ina (Shordon) M.; m. Eleanor Muriel Grandy, Oct. 30, 1948; children: Patricia Ann, William Howard. B.S., MIT, 1942; M.Ed., Boston U., 1949; Litt.D. (hon.), Western New Eng. Coll., 1965. Tchr. Bolles Sch., Jacksonville, Fla., 1945-46; head math. dept., asst. prin. Bolles Sch., 1946-49; headmaster Berwick Acad., South Berwick, Maine, 1949-50; sales rep. D.C. Heath & Co., Boston, 1950-52; editor D.C. Heath & Co., 1952-53, head elementary editorial dept., 1953-55, editor in chief, 1955-66, v.p., 1962-66, dir., 1956-66, sec. of corp., 1957-66; dir. Erica Corp., 1956-66; exec. v.p. Heath de Rochemont Corp., 1960-66, dir., 1960-66; editor-in-chief, mgr. materials devel. dept. Raytheon Edn. Co., 1966-68; v.p., editorial dir. domestic and internat. ops. Grolier Inc., 1968-80, dir., 1969-82, cons., 1980-82; dir. Grolier Edn. Corp., 1968-80, Scarecrow Press Inc., 1969-80; Chmn. elementary and high sch. research com. Am. Ednl. Pubs. Inst., 1966-68, chmn. elem. and high sch. sect., 1968-69. Lay leader Boston dist. Meth. Ch., 1952-56; mem. adv. bd. Boston U. Student Christian Assn., 1954-62, treas., 1957-59, chmn., 1959-61; mem. president's adv. council St. Joseph's Coll., North Windham, Maine, 1973-88; mem. corp. New Eng. Deaconess Assn., 1965-95, exec. com., 1965-68; mem. corp. New Eng. Deaconess Hosp., 1967-93; dir. Japan America Soc. of Maine, 1981-91, pres., 1984-86; merit badge counselor Pine Tree Coun., Boy Scouts Am., 1984-95; dir. Children's Mus. of Maine, 1987-89; dir. Leisure Ctr. for the Handicapped, Inc., Portland, Maine, 1987-93, treas. 1988-93; mem. adv. council So. Maine Retired Sr. Vol. Program, 1987-90, chmn. fin. com., 1987-89; mem. Foster Care Case Review Panel Maine Dept. Human Services, 1987-91; dir. Foreside Common Condominium Assn., Falmouth, Maine, 1986-89, 1991-92, pres., 1987-89; vol. staff mem. Vol. Lawyers Project of Maine, 1987-90; vol. math. instr. Adult Basic Learning Exchange, Portland, 1987-91. Served to capt. AUS, 1942-46, to maj. USAR. Mem. Newcomen Soc., Masons, Shriners, Phi Delta Kappa. Republican. Episcopalian. Home: PO Box 17 Sebago Lake ME 04075-0017

MURRAY-HARVEY, ROSALIND, education educator; b. Melbourne, Australia, Nov. 25, 1948; d. John Joseph and Nehama Miriam (Amitai) Stewart; m. Peter Nigel Murray-Harvey, Oct. 4, 1969 (div. 1988); 1 child, Alexandra. BE, U. Sydney (Australia), 1970; ME, Flinders U. South Australia, Adelaide, 1990, PhD in Edn., 1994. Registered tchr., South Australia. Tchr. various elem. schs. Australia, 1970-80; lectr. Flinders U., 1980-94, sr. lectr., 1994—; co-dir. Child Adolescent Psychol. and Ednl. Resources, Adelaide, 1997. Co-author: Assessment for Learning, 1996; co-rschr., writer, creator (video discussion package) Stressed Out & Coping in Families, 1997. Bd. dirs. Sr. Secondary Assessment Bd., Adelaide, 1997—; bd. mgmt. The Flinders U. Inst. Internat. Edn. Nat. Staff Devel. Fund scholar, 1992. Mem. Am. Ednl. Rsch. Assn., Australian Assn. Rsch. in Edn., Higher Edn. Rsch. and Devel. Soc. Australasia.

MURRAY-LYON, IAIN MALCOLM, gastroenterologist; b. Edinburgh, Scotland, U.K., Aug. 28, 1940; s. Ranald Malcolm and Jennipher Helen (Dryburgh) Murray-L.; m. Teresa Elvira Gonzalez Montero, Nov. 7, 1981; children: Caroline Claire, Andrew Malcolm. BSc, U. Edinburgh, 1962, MBChB, 1964, MD, 1973. Med. registrar Royal Infirmary, Edinburgh, 1967-68; sr. med. registrar liver unit Kings Coll. Hosp., London, 1968-72; hon. sr. lectr. liver unit Kings Coll. Hosp., 1972-74; gastroenterologist Charing Cross Hosp., London, 1974—, Chelsea Westminster Hosp., 1993; cons. physician Hosp. St. John & Elizabeth, London, 1976—, King Edward VII Hosp. for Officers, London, 1991—. NIH fellow, 1972. Fellow Royal Coll. Physicians (London), Royal Coll. Physicians (Edinburgh); mem. British Assn. for Study of Liver (sec. 1985-86), British Soc. Gastroenterology (chmn. liver sect. 1989-90). Mem. Ch. Scotland. Avocations: skiing, tennis, fishing, golf. Home: 12 St James Gardens, London W11 4RD, England Office: 149 Harley St, London WIN 2DE, England

MURRAY-PARKER, KAREN S., journalist, newspaper editor; b. Tampa, Fla., Dec. 5, 1953; d. Jack Vernon and Jacqueline Louise (Holder) Murray; m. William L. Parker, Apr. 21, 1978 (div. Apr. 1982); m. Katharine Crystal Willow. BA in Journalism, U. South Fla., 1975, BS in Pre-disciplinary Sci., 1975. Lic. capt, USCG; lic. airplane pilot, FAA. Journalist, photographer Oracle, Tampa, Fla., 1972-75; art specialist Dept. Recreation City of Tampa, 1976-80; journalist Tampa Tribune, 1980-82; editor, assoc. pub. Roofer Mag., Ft. Myers, Fla., 1982-85; owner, designer Oceanographics Design, Boca Grande, Fla., 1986-87; journalist Ft. Myers (Fla.) News-Press, 1987-88, Boca Beacon Newspaper, Boca Grande, 1988-96; editor, gen. mgr. Gasparilla Gazette Newspaper, Boca Grande, 1996—, exec. editor, gen. mgr., 1996—; exec. editor, gen. mgr. Gasparilla Mag. and Island Angler Mag., Boca Grande, 1996—. Actress, set. designer Royal Palm Player Inc., Boca Grande, 1987—; exhibiting artist Boca Grande Art Alliance, 1986—; editor (mags.) History of Boca Grande, 1996, First Drift, 1997. Sec., treas. Barrier Island Pks. Soc., Boca Grande, 1990—. Recipient 21 awards for editl. content Fla. Mag. Assn., Orlando, 1982-85; named one of 85 Most Interesting People in Fla., Gulfshore Life Mag., Naples, 1985. Mem. Fla. Press Assn. (18 writing awards 1988—). Democrat. Roman Catholic. Avocations: painting, sailing, writing, scuba diving, flying. Home: PO Box 1258 Boca Grande FL 33921-1258 Office: Gasparilla Gazette PO Box 929 Boca Grande FL 33921-0929

MURRAY-SMITH, DAVID JAMES, engineering educator; b. Aberdeen, Scotland, Oct. 20, 1941; s. William and Katherine Brenda (Trail) Murray-Smith; m. Effie MacPhail Smith, Aug. 9, 1966; children: Roderick, Gordon. BSc in Engring., U. Aberdeen, Scotland, 1963, MSc, 1964, PhD, 1970. Chartered engr. Engr. Ferranti Ltd., Edinburgh, Scotland, 1964-65; asst. U. Glasgow, 1965-67, lectr., 1967-77, sr. lectr., 1977-83, reader, 1983-85, prof., 1983—, dean engring., 1997—; vis. rschr. U. So. Calif., 1976, 79, Technical U. Vienna, Austria, 1991. Author: Proceedings 1984 UKSC Conference on Computer Simulation, 1984, Proceedings 3rd European Simulation Congress, 1989, Continuous System Simulation, 1995; assoc. editor Math. and Computer Modelling of Dynamical Systems. Fellow Instn. Elec. Engrs.; mem. Inst. Measurement and Control, U.K. Simulation Soc. (chmn. 1989-90). Avocations: hill walking, photography, railways. Home: 25 Heather Ave Bearsden, Glasgow G61 3JD, Scotland Office: U Glasgow Rankine Bldg, Oakfield Ave, Glasgow G12 8LT, Scotland

MURRELLE, RONALD KEMP, architectural firm executive; b. Greensboro, N.C., Aug. 14, 1940; s. George Kemp and Marian (Lewis) M.; m. Betsy Blackburn Stevens, Oct. 1960 (div. Aug. 1982); children: Brett Stevens, Mary Anna. Student, N.C. State Sch. Design, 1958-60. Dept. mgr. Kirkman and Koury, Inc., Greensboro, 1961-70; v.p. Wm. B. Owen Constrn. Co. Inc., Banner Elk, N.C., 1970-76, M and B Constrn. Inc., Vansant, Va., 1976-77; multifamily dept. mgr. Harmon Assoc., Greensboro, 1978-80; pres. Diversified Residential Svcs., Inc., Banner Elk, 1980-82; project designer Harmn Assoc., Greensboro, 1984-85; with Hotel Designs, 1986-88, Nu-Stone Surfacing, Orlando, Fla., 1989, Fellowship Facilities Designs, Orlando, Myrtle Beach, 1990, Fulfilled Mansions, Greensboro, 1991—; pres. Diversified Residential Svcs., Greensboro, 1998. Author: His Father's Temple, 1994, God Experience, 1996, Recovery Words with Definitions, 1996. Founder Fulfilled Mansions. Avocations: chess, golf. Address: PO Box 66055 Greensboro NC 27403-6055

MURRENHOFF, HUBERTUS JOSEF, research institute executive; b. Gladbeck, NRW, Germany, Aug. 13, 1953; s. Bernhard and Agnes (Breick) M.; m. Anne Niemer, June 15, 1979; children: Sarah, Manuel. Diploma in engring., Rheinisch-Westfaelische Tech., Aachen, Germany, 1978, Dr. of Engring., 1983. V.p. HSC Controls Inc., Buffalo, 1987-91; geschäftsführer Magnet-Schultz GmbH, Memmingen, Germany, 1991-94; exec. dir., prof. Inst. Fluidpower, RWTH, Aachen, 1994—; cons. Fluidton GmbH, Aachen, 1995—; self-employed cons., Aachen, 1994—. Editor Vereinigte Fachverlage, Mainz, Germany, 1994—, Oelhydraulik and Pneumatik. Mem. SAE, Verein Deutscher Ingenieure. Roman Catholic. Avocations: reading, travel, bicycling, crafting. Home: Wildbachstr 59, D-52074 Aachen NRW, Germany Office: Inst Fluidpower, Steinbachstr 53, D-52074 Aachen NRW, Germany

MURRIN, DENIS ROLAND, aviation consultant; b. Bromley, Kent, Eng., Aug. 27, 1925; s. Edmunt and Julie Edith (Symes) M.; m. Daphne June Martin, May 14, 1930; children: David Paul, Ian Patrick. Higher nat. cert. in aero. engring.; chartered engr. Student apprentice Handley Page, London, 1942-47, flight test engr., 1947-48; surveyor Air Registration Bd., London, 1948-72; dep. dir. Civil Aviation Authority, Redhill, Eng., 1972-85; mng. dir. Globeair Ltd., Farnham, Eng., 1985—. Fellow Royal Aero. Soc.; mem. Brit. Acad. Experts, Brit. Assn. Aviation Cons. Avocation: sailing. Office: Globeair Ltd, 33 Dene Ln Farnham, Surrey GU10 3RH, England

MURRY, HAROLD DAVID, JR., lawyer; b. Holdenville, Okla., June 30, 1943; s. Harold David Sr. and Willie Elizabeth (Dees) M.; m. Ann Moore Earnhardt, Nov. 1, 1975; children: Elizabeth Ann, Sarah Bryant. BA, Okla. U., 1965, JD, 1968. Bar: Okla. 1968, D.C. 1974. Asst. to v.p. U. Okla., Norman, 1968-71, legal counsel Research Inst., 1969-71; atty. U.S. Dept. Justice, Washington, 1971-74; spl. asst. U.S. Atty., Washington, 1972; assoc. Clifford & Warnke, Washington, 1974-78, ptnr., 1978-91; ptnr. Howrey & Simon, Washington, 1991-98, Baker Botts LLP, Washington, 1998—. Mem. ABA, Okla. Bar Assn., D.C. Bar Assn., Fed. Bar Assn., Met. Club (Washington), Chevy Chase Club (Md.), Phi Alpha Delta. Democrat. Home: 8931 Bel Air Pl Potomac MD 20854-1606 Office: Baker Botts LLP Ste 1300 1299 Pennsylvania Ave NW Washington DC 20004-2408

MURSHID, WALEED RIDA, neurosurgery educator; b. Medinah, Saudi Arabia, Dec. 19, 1960; s. Rida Abdulla and Marriyum Abdulhay (Abu Khdair) M.; m. Baida Abdul Gadder Hussien, Jan. 20, 1990; children: Naif, Ahmed. B Medicine and Surgery, King Saud U., Riyadh, Saudi Arabia, 1984. Demonstrator neurosurgery King Saud U., Riyadh, 1985-88, asst. prof. neurosurgery, 1989-96; resident surgery King Khalid U. Hosp., Riyadh, 1985-88, registrar neurosurgery, 1988-91, cons. neurosurgery, 1994—; sr. registrar Frenchay Hosp., Bristol, Eng., 1991-93; assoc. prof. neurosurgery, 1996—; mem. Riyadh Neurosci. Club Joint Bd. Postgrad. Med., 1984—, mem. health edn. com.; mem. med. records com. King Khalid U. Hosp., Riyadh, 1994—. Fellow ACS, Royal Coll. Surgeons Edinburgh, Royal Coll. Surgeons in Surg. Neurology, Internat. Coll. Surgeons; mem. Congress Neurol. Surgeons. Office: King Saud U Dept Neurosurgery, PO Box 7805, Riyadh 11472, Saudi Arabia

MURTAGH, JOHN EDWARD, alcohol production consultant; b. Wallington, Surrey, Eng., Sept. 12, 1936; came to U.S., 1982; s. Thomas Henry and Elsie (Kershaw Paterson) M.; m. Eithne Anne Fawsitt, July 18, 1959; children: Catherine, Rhoda, Sean, Aidan, Doreen. BSc, U. Wales, 1959, MSc, 1970, PhD, 1972. Rsch. coord. House of Seagram, Long Pond, Jamaica, 1959-63; whisky distillery mgr. House of Seagram, Beaupre, Que., Can., 1963-65; rum distillery mgr. House of Seagram, Richibucto, N.B., Can., 1965-68; rsch. mgr. House of Seagram, Montreal, Que., 1968-70; alcohol prodn. cons. Murtagh & Assocs., Buttevant, Ireland, 1972-77, 79-82, Winchester, Va., 1982—; vodka distillery mgr. Iran Beverages, Tehran, 1977-79; ethanol tech. cons., adv. bd. Info. Resources, Inc., Washington, 1988—; lectr. Alltech Ann. Alcohol Sch., Lexington, Ky., 1982—; chmn. World Ethanol Conf., London, 1998, 99, 2000. Author: Glossary of Fuel-Ethanol Terms, 1990; co-author, editor: The Alcohol Textbook, 1995; editor: Worldwide Directory of Distilleries, 1996; contbr. articles to profl. jours. Adv. bd. Byrd Sch. Bus., Shenandoah U., Winchester, Va., 1989-95. Recipient Millers Mutual prize, U. Wales, 1959. Fellow Am. Inst. Chemists, Inst. Chemistry of Ireland, Inst. Food Sci. and Tech. of Ireland; mem. Royal Soc. Chemistry (chartered), Am. Arbitration Assn. (arbitrator nat. comml. panel 1990—). Achievements include development of proprietary process for production of ethanol from cheese whey and the design of whey-ethanol production plants. Home and Office: 160 Bay Ct Winchester VA 22602-4700

MURTAUGH, JOHN PATRICK, lawyer; b. Orrville, Ohio, Feb. 23, 1952; s. Bernard Francis and Helen Jane (Ellsworth) M.; m. Elaine Zack, Aug. 12, 1989. BA summa cum laude, U. Notre Dame, 1974; JD magna cum laude, U. Mich., 1978; BA summa cum laude, Case Western Reserve U., 1989. Bar: Ohio 1981, U.S. Dist. Ct. (no. dist.) Ohio 1981, U.S. Ct. Appeals (D.C. cir.) 1979, U.S. Ct. Appeals (6th cir.) 1982, U.S. Ct. Appeals (fed. cir.) 1989; registered to practice before U.S. Patent and Trademark Office. Law clk. to judge U.S. Ct. Appeals (D.C. cir.), Washington, 1978-79; assoc. Orrick, Herrington, Rowley & Sutcliffe, San Francisco, 1979-80, Calfee, Halter & Griswold, Cleve., 1980-89; assoc. Pearne, Gordon, McCoy & Granger, Cleve., 1989-90, ptnr., 1991—. Assoc. editor U. Mich. Law Rev., 1976-77, sr. editor, 1977-78; co-author: Baldwin's Ohio Civil Practice,. Mem. Am. Intellectual Property Law Assn., Cleve. Intellectual Property Law Assn., Notre Dame Club Cleve., Phi Beta Kappa. Roman Catholic. Avocations: sailing, camping, skiing. Home: 25200 S Woodland Rd Cleveland OH 44122-3342

MURTHY, HANUMAPPA SHIVANANDA, aquaculture educator, researcher, consultant; b. Chitradurga, India, Apr. 6, 1957; s. Kenchadyamappa Hannmappa and Thippamma; m. Sujatha Hucchavvanahally Rangaiah, Aug. 27, 1981; children: Lavanya, Vikram. B in Fisheries Sci., Coll. Fisheries, Mangalore, India, 1979, M in Fisheries Sci., 1989; PhD of Aquaculture, U. Agrl. Sci., Bangalore, India1993. Rsch. asst. Regional Rsch. Sta., Dharwad, India, 1980-82; instr. Coll. Fisheries, 1982-84, asst. prof. aquaculture, 1984-94, assoc. prof. aquaculture, 1994—; tech. advisor Zee Sea Foods Ltd., Bangalore, 1993-98; mem. rsch. bd. advisors Am. Biographical Inst. Contbr. over 100 articles to profl. jours. Recipient Rsch. and Travel grants Internat. Found. Scis., Stockholm, Sweden, 1992-96, Jawaharalal Nehru Rsch. award Indian Coun. Agr. Rsch., Govt. of India, 1996, Best Rsch. award U. Agrl. Sci., Bangalore, 1997, Sir C.V. Raman award Govt. Karnataka, 1998. Mem. Asian Fisheries Soc., Network Tropical Aquaculture Scientists Philippines, Fed. India Fisheries Grads. Assn. (founding pres. 1997—), Assn. Brit. Scholars (sec. Coastal Karnataka chpt. 1999—), Kaikunje Welfare Assn. (pres. 1999—). Avocations: reading, driving, sports. Fax: 91-824 438366. Home: Lavanya Kaikunje, BC Rd DK Dist, Karnataka 574219, India Office: Dept Aquaculture, Coll Fisheries, Mangalore 575002, India

MURTHY, NARAYANA N.R., software company executive; b. Sid Laghatta, Karnataka, India, Aug. 20, 1946; s. Nagavara Ramarao and Padmavathamma Rao; m. Sudha Kulkarni, Feb. 10, 1978; children: Akshata, Rohan. BEE, U. Mysore (India), 1967; M in Tech., Indian Inst. Tech., Kanpur, 1969. Chief syss. programmer Indian Inst. Mgmt., Ahmedabad, India, 1969-71; syss. engr. SESA, Paris, 1972-74; project leader Syss. Rsch. Inst., Pune, India, 1975-77; head software group Patni Computer Syss., Mumbai, India, 1977-81; chmn., ceo Infosys Techs. Ltd., Bangalore, India, 1982—; mem. govning. coun. Nat. Ctrl. Software Tech., Mumbai, India, Ctr. Mathemat. Modelling and Computer Simulation, Bangalore, India; dir. Software Syss. Support and Edn. Ctr. Ltd., Bangalore. Named Best Entrepreneur Rotary Club, 1994-95, IT Man of Yr. Dataquest, 1996; recipient Vocat. Excellence award Rotary Club, 1995, Award of Excellence Karnataka State Fin. Corp., 1995, Rotary Club, 1996. Fellow Computer Soc. India; mem. ACM, Confedn. Indian Industry, Nat. Assn. Software and Svcs. (pres. 1992-94). Avocations: reading, listening to Western and Indian classical music. Office: Infosys Techs Ltd 3rd Cross, Hosur Rd Electronic City, 561 229 Bangalore India

MURTHY, PRAKHYA BALAKRISHNA, geneticist, toxicologist, researcher; b. Bapatla, A.P., India, Aug. 1, 1953; s. Anjaneya Sarma and Sita Mahalakshmi P.; m. Nagalakshmi Veerubhotla, Dec. 12, 1980; 2 children. BSc in Chemistry, Botany, Zoology, Andhra U., Bapatla, India, 1973; MSc in Human Genetics, Phys. Anthropology, Andhra U., Waltair AP, India, 1975; PhD, Managlore (India) U., 1982; DSc, Madras (India) U., 2000. Project assoc. chromosomes and criminality All India Inst. Med. Scis., New Delhi, India, 1976-77, JIPMER, Pondicherry, India, 1977-78; asst. rsch. officer genetic toxicology, malnutrition Nat. Inst. Nutrition, Hyderabad, India, 1978-82; post-doctoral fellow cancer and molecular genetics Hiroshima (Japan) U., 1982-84; dir., head toxicology dept. Frederick Inst. Plant Protection & Toxicology, Padappai, Tamil Nadu, India, 1984—; mem. adv. bd. Faculty Biomed. Sci. Tamil Nadu, Dr. M.G.R. Med. U., Ctrl. Insecticides Bd. Faridabad, India; PhD thesis adjudicator for U. Madras, India, Calcutta (India) U., Osmania U., Hyderabad AP, India. Contbr. over 38 articles to profl. jours.; mem. editl. bd. Indian Jour. Toxicology, Indian Jour. Pharmacology; presenter at sci. confs. and instns. nationally and internationally. Recipient Young Scientist award, 1979. Mem. Toxicology Soc. of India (life), Environmental Mutagen Soc. of India, (life), Assn. Environ. Biologists of India (life), Indian Assn. Aquatic Biologists (life), Indian Sci. Congress (life), Indian Pharmacolog. Soc. (life), Nat. Environ., Sci. Acad. (life). Home: 14 Laxmi Nagar, Seliyur, Chennai 600073, India Office: Dir Fredrick Inst Plant, Protection & Toxicology, Padappai 601301 Tamil Nadu, India

MURTI, MULAKALURI SRIMANNARAYANA, sanskritist, linguist, educator, researcher; b. Guntur, India, June 19, 1941; s. Mulakaluri Veerabhadraiah and Mulakaluri Alamelu Mangamma; m. Mulakaluri Sitalakshmi, Feb. 7, 1969; children: M.V. Vijayakumar, M. Srividya. MA, Sri Venkateswara U., Tirupati, India, 1963, PhD, 1971. Rsch. asst. Sri Venkateswara U. Rsch. Inst., Tirupati, 1964-72, lectr. in Sanskrit, 1972-74, prof., dir., 1989—; lectr. in Sanskrit SVU Coll., Tirupati, 1974-79, reader in Sanskrit, 1979-87, prof. of Sanskrit, 1987-89; wissenschaftlicher angestellt Inst. of Indology U., Köln, Germany, 1973-74, 83-84; head, dept. Sanskrit Sri Venkateswara U. Coll., 1985-87; dir. Sri Venkateswara U. Oriental Rsch. Inst., 1989—. Author: An Introduction to Sanskrit Linguistics, 1984, Methodology in Indological Research, 1991, Bhartrihari, 1997; editor: (book) Vallabhadeva's Kommentar Zum Kumarasambhava Des Kalidasa, 1980, (periodical) Sri Venkateswara University Oriental Journal, 1989—. Home: 18-3-24 Santi Nagar K.T. Rd, Tirupati 517 507 India Office: SVU Oriental Rsch Insts, 517 502 Andhra Pradesh India

MURTIYOSO, SUTRÍSNO, architect; b. Parakan, Java, Indonesia, Apr. 11, 1955; s. Hardjono and Indriani Murtiyoso; m. Indrayani Natawardaya, Apr. 24, 1983; 1 child, Arnadi Dhestaratri. Degree in Engring., Cath. U. Parahyangan, Bandung, Indonesia, 1985. Pres. Atelier Megatruh, Bandung, 1986-96; ptnr. Kompanima, Jakarta, Indonesia, 1990-91; pres. Megatruh Internet Svcs., Bandung, 1996—. Caption author: Islamic Spirit in Indonesian Culture, 1991; author, editor: Historical Mosques in Indonesia, 1994; contbg. editor: Indonesian Heritage Series: Architecture, 1998; dir. computer animation Development of Bandung, 1991. Mem. Lembaga Sejarah Arsitektur Indonesia (gen. sec. 1989—), Ikatan Arsitek Indonesia (head info. sys. 1995-99), Internat. Coun. Monuments and Sites, Bandung Heritage Soc. Avocations: travel, reading.

MURTY, HEMA S., aerospace engineer, researcher; b. Calcutta, India, Apr. 5, 1960; arrived in Can., 1962; d. Nirmalamba (Maddali) M. B of Engring., Carleton U., Ottawa, Ont., Can., 1982; MASc, U. Toronto, 1983, PhD in Aerospace Engring., 1992. Rsch. asst. U. Toronto, 1982-90; engring. contractor NRC of Can., Ottawa, 1990-94; rsch. assoc. Rensselaer Poly. Inst., Troy, N.Y., 1994-96; sr. aerodynamicist Sikorsky Aircraft, Stratford, Conn., 1996—; bd. dirs. South Shore Music. Contbr. articles to profl. jours. Mem. AIAA, Am. Helicopter Soc. (pres. Stratford chpt.), ASME, Can. Aeronautics and Space Inst. Avocations: singing East Indian classical music, East Indian classical dancing, classical piano, tennis. Office: Sikorsky Aircraft Corp PO Box 9729 6900 Main St M/S S317A5 Stratford CT 06497-9129

MURUGAVEL, S., medical researcher, consultant, anesthesiologist; b. Vellore, India, June 22, 1942; s. D. Shanmugam and S. Vittobai. BSc, U. Madras, India, 1969; MD, Free Univ., Berlin, Germany, 1985. Registered profl. nurse. Intern, resident West End Hosp., Free U. Berlin Hosp.; mem. staff Madras Port Trust, 1966-69; vol. Ev-Hohannesstift, Berlin, 1969-71; nurse Govt. Hosp., Berlin, 1974-79; physician West End Hosp. Free Univ., Berlin, 1985, Hosp. Neukoelln, Berlin, 1986—; rsch. fellow Western Gen. Hosp. U. Edinburgh, Scotland, 1997-98. Contbr. articles to profl. jours.; patentee in field. Sec. Svc. Civil Internat., Madras, 1967, com. mem. 1968-69. Mem. Soc. Neurosurgical Anesthesiology and Critical Care, N.Y. Acad. Scis. Home: Riehlstr 6, 14057 Berlin Germany

MUSA, ABDUL ABDULKADIR, diplomat; b. Kano, Nigeria, Jan. 10, 1958; s. Musa-Fari and Aishat Abdulkadir; m. Sakina Derhei, June 8, 1982; children: Faizah, Jamila, Aishat, Hadiza. BS in Polit. Sci., Ahamdu Bello U., Zaria, Nigeria, 1979; MA in Internat. Rels., U. Kent-Canterbury (Eng.), 1992. Cert. Fgn. Svc. Acad. Nigeria. Head chancery Nigerian Emb., Jakarta, Indonesia, 1982-85; head consular and immigration Nigerian Emb., Washington, 1998—; personal asst. hon. min. Ministry Fgn. Affairs, Nigeria, 1985-88; spl. asst. dep. dir.'s office Ministry Fgn. Affairs, 1993-98; counsellor Nigeria High Commn. to St. James, London, 1989-92; del. various bilateral/multilateral UN, 1985-88; sr. cousellor various bus. groups in Nigeria, 1998—. Mem. Fgn. Svc. Acad., Fed. Civil Svc. Club. Avocations: soccer, art, drawing, music, reading. Office: Emb Nigeria 2201 M St NW Washington DC 20037-1416

MUSAEV, MUSA ABDURAKHMAN OGLU, science association director; b. Gyanja, Azerbaijan, Dec. 27, 1921; s. Abdurakhman Musa oglu and Raziya Mamed kyzy Pishnamasov; m. Azara Kafar kyzy Gassanova, Apr. 2, 1953: children: Zaur Musa oglu Musaev, Zakir Musa oglu Musaev. MS, Azerbaijanian Inst. Agrl., 1945; PhD in Vet. Medicine, Moscow Acad. Vet. Medicine, 1948, DSc in Vet. Medicine, 1956. Cert. Vet. Asst. prof. Moscow Acad. Vet. Medicine, USSR, 1946-48; rsch. fellow Inst. Zoology, Acad. Sci. of Azerbaijan, Baku, Azerbaijan, 1949-56, head lab., 1957-87, dir., 1960—; chmn. Council on the defence of theses Inst. Zoology, 1962-92, commn. of experts awarding scientific degrees and titles, Supreme Certification Commn. of Azerbaijan, 1992—; asst. academic sec. biology dept. Acad. Sci. of Azerbaijan, 1980-91. Mem. editorial bd. Izvestiya A N Azerbaijana Seriya Biologicheskikhnauk Jour., 1961-87, Parazitologia Jour., 1967-87; author: (books) Serological Diagnostics of Animal Leptospirosis, 1950, Leptospirosis of Cattle, 1959, Coccidia of Rodents in USSR, 1965, The Parasitofauna of the Common Vole and structure of its Parasitocenosis. 1969, Biochemical Aspects of Hostparasite Relationship in Domestic Bird Coccidiosis, 1977 (State prize of Azerbaijan 1991), Parasitocenosis and Deseases of Nutria, 1987; editor: Zoology of Invertebrates, 1988, Zoology, 1993, The Animal World of Azerbaijan, 1994. co-author 5 inventions. Named Honored Scientist Supreme Coun. Azerbaijan, 1974, Order Badge of Honor, 1976, Order Labour Red Banner, 1980; recipient medal of Valiant Labour in the Great Patriotic War 1941-44 Presidium Supreme Coun. USSR, 1945. Mem. Azerbaijanian Soc. for Nature Protection (mem. ctrl. com. 1970—), Azerbaijanian Soc. Protozoologists, All Union Soc. of Protozoologists. Avocations: reading fiction, music. Home: ul M A Alieva d 231 kv 35, Baku 370014, Azerbaijan Office: Inst Zoology, Proyezd 1128 Kvartal 504, Baku 370602, Azerbaijan

MUSALIMOV, VICTOR MICHAEL, mechanical engineer, researcher, educator; b. Prokopyevsk, USSR, May 24, 1939; s. Michael Vasily and Galina Peter (Shmotchenko) M.; m. Ludmila Nicholas Medvedeva, Mar. 17, 1963; children: Julia, Anastasia. B in Enging., Indsl. Coll., Leningrad, USSR, 1960; MSc, U. Leningrad-Sverdlovsk, 1969; DSc, Mining Inst. Acad. Scis., Novosibirsk, USSR, 1972; PhD, U. Tomsk, USSR, 1986. Indsl. engr. Prokopyevsk, 1963-64; rschr., head computing machine lab. Mining Inst., Prokopyevsk, 1964-72; lectr. Civil Engring. Inst., Tomsk, 1972-89; rschr., head anisotropic body lab. Inst. Physics Strength, Tomsk, 1987-89; lectr. mechatronics dept. U. Fine Mechanics and Optics, St. Petersburg, Russia, 1989—; rschr., prof. Inst. Mech. Engring. Problem, St. Petersburg, 1998—; cons. Cabel Plants, Tomsk, Moscow, 1975-89, Ctrl. Inst. Aircraft Engring., Moscow, 1980-85, Optico-Mech. Firm, St. Petersburg, 1998—, Observatory, St. Petersburg, 1993—. Author: Mechanical Tests of Flexible Cables, 1984, Elastic Frictional Interaction Between Elements of Some Flexible Cable Constructions, 1986, Algebra of Socio-Bio-Catastrophe, 1998, Fundamental Problem of Precision and Quality Machines and Instruments, 1999; editor-in-chief Tomsk U. Sci. Papers. Recipient medal Ministry Higher Edn., 1988. Mem. Ctr. Precision of Russian Acad., N.Y. Acad. Scis. Orthodox Christian. Achievements include 10 patents. Avocations: stamp collecting, fencing, skiing, dancing, traveling. Home: Narodnogo Opolchenijia, Ave 77, Apt 21, 198215 Saint Petersburg Russia Office: U Fine Mechanics and Optics, Sablinskaya 14, 197101 Saint Petersburg Russia

MUSCARELLA, CHRISTOPHER JAMES, finance educator; b. New Brunswick, N.J., Aug. 30, 1952; s. Mark Benjamin and Virginia (Pickert) M.; m. Bobbie Jean Weidner, June 1, 1985; children: Sarah Anne, Aaron Matthew,. BSEE, U. Notre Dame, 1974, MBA, 1976, PhD, Purdue U., 1983. Asst. prof. So. Meth. U., Dallas, 1984-90; sr. fin. economist U.S. Securities & Exch. Commn., Washington, 1990-91; prof., L.W. Roy and

Mary Lois Clark tchg. fellow Pa. State U., University Park, 1991—; vis. asst. prof. U. Notre Dame (Ind.), 1979, U. Oreg., Eugene, 1980-82, U. Utah, Sale Lake City, 1982-84; Dale S. Coenen vis. prof. free enterprise, Darden Grad. Sch. Bus. Adminstrn., U. Va., 2000. Assoc. editor Jour. Fin. Rsch., 1993—. Mem. Am. Fin. Assn., Fin. Mgmt. Assn. (northeast regional dir. 1994-96), European Fin. Assn. Avocations: genealogy. Office: Coll Bus Adminstrn 609 BAB University Park PA 16802

MUSCATELLO, GARY, veterinary surgeon; b. Melbourne, Victoria, Australia, Jan. 12, 1974; s. Giuseppe and Raffaella (Todarello) M. B of Vet. Sci., U. Melbourne, 1997, postgrad., 2000—. Vet. surgeon, cons. Animal Welfare League of Victoria, Melbourne, 1997—. Contbr. articles to profl. publs. Mem. AAAS, Australia Vet. Assn., Assn. of Profl. Engrs., Scientist and Mgrs. Australia, Assn. of Small Animal Vets. of Australia. Roman Catholic. Avocations: sports, fine food, information technology. Home: 9 Martin St, Sunshine VIC 3020, Australia Office: Lort Smith Animal Hosp, 24 Villiers St, North Melbourne VIC 3051, Australia also: Vet Preclin Ctr U Melbourne, Flemington Rd and Park Dr, Parkville, Victoria 305Z, Australia

MUSCATO, GIOVANNI, engineering educator; b. Catania, Italy, Sept. 2, 1965; s. Giuseppe and Carmela (Carbone) M.; m. Carmela Ballati, Dec. 7, 1996. MS, Leonardo da Vinci, Catania, 1983; degree in elect. engring., U. di Catania, 1988. Asst. prof. U. Catania, 1990-98, assoc. prof., 1998—. Author: Robust Control for Unstructured Perturbations, 1992, Neural Networks in Miltidimensional Domains, 1998. Served with Italian mil., 1989-90. Mem. IEEE. Avocations: windsurfing, photography, bricolage. Office: Univ di Catania, Viale A Doria 6, 95125 Catania Italy

MUSCHIOLIK, GERALD FRANZ WILHELM, food technologist; b. Cottbus, Germany, May 7, 1941; s. Julius and Hildegard (Herrmann) M.; m. Ursula John, Mar. 1, 1969; 1 child, Bert. Diploma in engring., Humboldt U. Berlin, 1966, D Agr., 1972, DSc, 1980; Dr.rer.nat.habil., Tech. U., Dresden, Germany, 1994. Head food control canning factory, Potsdam, Germany, 1966-71; scientist Ctrl. Inst. Nutrition, Potsdam-Rehbrücke, Germany, 1971-92, head food chemistry and tech. divsn., 1987-90; head rsch. group U. Potsdam, 1992-97; head rsch. group Potsdam-Rehbrücke German Inst. Food Tech., 1997-98; prof. food tech. Inst. Nutrition Friedrich-Schiller U., Jena, Germany, 1998—. Inventor new protein foods (medal Inst. of Nutrition 1979). Recipient Fichte award Humboldt U., Berlin, 1967. Mem. Soc. Engrs. and Economists, Soc. German Food Technologists. Avocations: men's choir, piano, gardening. E-mail: b6muge@tz.uni-jena.de. Office: Friedrich-Schiller U Jena, Dornburger Str 29 Inst Nut, D-07743 Jena Germany

MUSCOLINO EMANUELE, GIUSEPPE, thoracic surgeon; b. Casalvecchio, Messina, Italy, Sept. 29, 1943; s. Giacomo and Rosa (Emanuele) M.; m. Carla Vanni di San Vincenzo; children: Marcello, Rosa Maria Carolina. Degree in Med. and Surg. Sci., U. Palermo, Italy, 1968. Asst. surgery Ospedale Saronno, 1970-75; asst. thoracic surgery Istituto Nazionale Tumori, Milan, 1975-80, cons. in thoracic surgery, 1980—; chief gen. and throacic surgery Ospedale Cannizzaro, Catania, 1999—. Contbr. articles to profl. jours. Mem. Directory of Liberal Youth in Palermo, 1966-70, Milan, 1970-74. With Italian Mil., 1969-70. Named Hon. Citizen by Lega Nazionale Tumori, 1989, Univ. Lectr. in Thoracic Surgery Honoris Causa, Constantinian U. Cranston, 1998. Mem. AAAS, N.Y. Acad. Sci., European Soc. Surg. Oncology. Avocations: bridge, antiques, contemporary art. Home: Via Giacinta Pezzana 25, Acicastello Catania Italy Office: Galleria Strasburgo 1, 20122 Milan Italy

MUSEKAMP, LINDA NOE, television producer, volunteer; b. Campbellsville, Ky., July 31, 1951; d. Charles Simpson and Audrey Ethel (Akin) Noe; m. George Justin Musekamp, Sept. 8, 1979 (dec.); children: George Brookshire, Charles Oliver Justin. Cert. exec. sec., Patricia Stevens Coll., Tampa, Fla., 1970. Cert. property mgr. Exec. sec. Sta. WLWT-TV, Cin., 1975-77, talent coord., 1977-80; prodr. Musekamp Prodns., Cin., 1980-83, cons., 1983-85; chmn., vol. Am. Cancer Soc., Cin., 1992—, bd. dirs., 1993—; pres., vol. PTO, Cin., 1992—; publicity chmn. Kindervelt, Cin., 1993—; real estate agt., 1994-96. Prodr.: (TV show) Real Cincinnati, 1996—. Republican. Baptist. Avocations: tennis, piano.

MUSEVENI, YOWERI KAGUTA, president of Uganda; b. 1944; married; 4 children. Grad. in econs. and polit. sci., Univ. Coll. Dar es Salaam, Tanzania, 1970. Former tchr. Tech. Coll., then rsch. officer of intelligence unit; polit. exile Tanzania, 1971-79; creator, head guerilla forces Front for Nat. Salvation; min. def. Govt. of Uganda, 1979-80, 86—; guerilla leader, 1981-86; pres. Govt. of Uganda, Kampala, 1986—. Author: What is Africa's Problem--A Collection of Speeches, 1992, Sowing the Mustard Seed--The Struggle for Freedom and Democracy in Uganda--An Autobiography, 1997. Office: Office of the Pres, Parliament Bldgs POB 7168, Kampala Uganda*

MUSGRAVE, CATHERINE, nurse educator; b. Mpls., June 13, 1946; arrived in Israel, 1982; d. Ann and William E. Musgrave. BSc, Hunter Bellevue Sch. Nursing, N.Y.C., 1979; MA, Columbia U., 1982; postgrad., Cath. U. Am., 2000—. RN, N.Y. Staff nurse Mount Sinai Hosp., N.Y.C., 1979-82; coord. oncology curriculum Hadassah Hebrew U. Sch. Nursing, Jerusalem, 1983—; presenter in field. Contbr. articles to profl. jours. Grantee Ministry of Health, Israel, 1996. Home: PO Box 12072, IL 91120 Jerusalem Israel Office: Hadassah-Hebrew U Sch Nurse, Kiryat Hadassah, IL 91120 Jerusalem Israel

MUSGRAVE, THEA, composer, conductor; b. Edinburgh, Scotland, May 27, 1928; m. Peter Mark, 1971. Ed., Edinburgh U., Paris Conservatory; Mus.D. (hon.). Composer: (opera) The Abbot of Drimock, 1955, The Decision, 1964-65, The Voice of Ariadne, 1972-73, Mary, Queen of Scots, 1975-77, (first performed Scottish Opera) A Christmas Carol, 1978-79 (first performed Va. Opera Assn., 1979), An Occurrence at Owl Creek Bridge, 1981, Harriet, The Woman Called Moses, 1981-84 (first performed Va. Opera 1985) Simon Bolivar, (ballet) Beauty and the Beast, 1969, (symphony and orchestral music) Obliques, 1958, Nocturnes and Arias, 1966, Concerto for Orch., 1967, Clarinet Concerto, 1968, Night Music, 1969, Scottish Dance Suite, 1969, Memento Vitae, 1969-70, Orfeo II, 1975, Soliloquy II and III, 1980, From One to Another, 1980, Peripeteia, 1981, The Seasons, 1988, (marimba concerto) Journey through a Japanese Landscape, (bass-clarinet concerto) Autumn Sonata, (oboe concerto) Helios, Phoenix Rising, 1997, (chamber and instrumental music) String Quartet, 1958, Trio for flute, oboe and piano, 1960, Monologue, 1960, Serenade, 1961, Chamber concerto No. 1, 1962, Chamber Concerto No. 2, 1966, Chamber Concerto No. 3, 1966, Music for horn and piano, 1967, Impromptu No. 1, 1967, Soliloquy I, 1969, Elegy, 1970, Impromptu No. 2, 1970, Space Play, 1974, Orfeo I, 1975, Fanfare, 1982, Pierrot, 1985, Narcissus, 1987, Niobe, 1987, (vocal and choral music) Two Songs, 1951, Four Madrigals, 1953, Six Songs: Two Early English Poems, 1953, A Suite O'Bairnsangs, 1953, Cantata for a Summer's Day, 1954, Song of the Burn, 1954, Five Love Songs, 1955, Four Portraits, 1956, A Song for Christmas, 1958, Triptych, 1959, Sir Patrick Spens, 1961, Make Ye Merry for Him That Is to Come, 1962, Two Christmas Carols in Traditional Style, 1963, John Cook, 1963, Five Ages of Man, 1963-64, Memento Creatoris, 1967, Primavera, 1971, Rorate Coeli, 1973, Monologues of Mary, Queen of Scots, 1977-86, O Caro M'e Il Sonno, 1978, The Last Twilight, 1980, Black Tambourine, 1985, For the Time Being, 1986, Echoes Through Time, 1988, Wild Winter for Viols & Voices, 1993, On the Underground Sets 1, 2 & 3, 1994, 95, (Robert Burns' poems for soprano & orch.) Songs for a Winter's Evening, 1995, Phoenix Rising for orchestra, 1996-97, Voices from the Ancient World for 3 flutes and percussion, 1998, Celebration Day for chorus and orchestra, 1998-99, Lamenting With Ariadne for 8 instruments, 1999. Office: VA Opera Assn PO Box 2580 Norfolk VA 23501-2580

MUSHARRAF, PERVEZ, military officer; b. New Delhi, India, 1943; arrived in Pakistan, 1947.; married; one son, one daughter. Studied, Mil. Acad. of Kakul. Career soldier Pakistani Army, 1964—, promoted through ranks to commdr., 1971-75; comdr. of Mangla Punjab, 1995; apptd. head of army, 1998—. medal for gallantry, 1965. *

MUSICH, ROBERT LORIN, motivational speaker; b. Glendale, Calif., Feb. 15, 1969; s. Richard and Zola (Nickel) M. MBA, La Salle U., M. Sr. asst. mgr. Am. Gen. Fin., Upland, Calif., 1988-89; mgmt./corp. trainer Mortgage Link, Pasadena, 1989-94; mgr. AT&T, L.A., 1994-96; owner Musich & Assocs., West Covina, Calif., 1989—. Singer (tenor) So. Calif. Mormon Choir, 1994—; cand. Calif. State Assembly, 59th Dist., 1995; vol. Am. Cancer Soc., 1994-96; coach Youth League Football, 1987-92; elder's quorum pres. LDS Ch., sec., 1992-93, 2d and 1st counselor, 1995-96, mem. stake single adult com., 1993-95, mem. regional single adult com. bi-regional chmn., 1993-95. Republican. Avocations: singing, dancing, theatre, volleyball, football. Office: Musich and Associates 3447 E Hillhaven Dr West Covina CA 91791-1718

MUSIKER, REUBEN, library director; b. Johannesburg, South Africa, Jan. 12, 1931; s. Judel and Sarah Musiker; m. Naomi Measroch, Apr. 9, 1961; children: Judith, Arnon, Carmel. BSc, U. Witwatersrand, Johannesburg, 1954; MA, U. Pretoria, South Africa, 1968. Dep. univ. libr. Rhodes U., Grahamstown, South Africa, 1962-72; univ. libr. U. Witwatersrand, Johannesburg, 1973-91, prof. librarianship and bibliography, 1975-91; dir. librs. United Jewish Orgsn., Johannesburg, 1999—. Recipient Sailis award for bibliography, 1986. Fellow South African Inst. Librarianship (life). Avocations: music, collecting books.

MUSIL, FRANTIŠEK, clinical chemist; b. Plzeň, Czech Republic, July 28, 1957; s. František and Žofie (Nejmanová) M.; m. Jana Járová, Dec. 18, 1982; children: František, Jiří. MD, Charles U., Prague, Czech Republic, 1982, Anesthesiology, 1986, Clin. Chemistry, 1991. Lic. physician. Resident in anesthesiology Dist. Hosp., Klatovy, 1986-88, resident in clin. chemistry, 1991; anesthesiologist U. Hosp., Plzeň, Czech Republic, 1982-83; anesthesiologist Dist. Hosp., Klatovy, Czech Republic, 1983-86, cons. anesthesiologist, 1986-88, clin. chemist, 1988-91, dep. cons. clin. chemist, 1991-92, cons. clin. chemist, 1991—; head pvt. med. lab. BioLab Ltd, Klatovy, 1992—. Mem. Czech Anesthesiology and Critical Care Assn., Czech Clin. Chemistry Assn., Czech Parenteral and Enteral Nutrition Assn., Czech Med. Chamber. Avocations: football, skiing, modern music, travel. Home: Purkyňova 740/II, 339 01 Klatovy Czech Republic Office: BioLab Ltd Pvt Med Lab, Nadrazni 844/II, 339 01 Klatovy Czech Republic

MUSIL, JAN, manufacturing executive; b. Domažlice, Czech Republic, May 26, 1959; s. Jan Musil and Zdeňka Barochová Musilová; m. Ilona Křičková, June 1, 1986; 1 child, Daniel. Diploma in mech. engring., U. West Bohemia, 1983, PhD, 1991. Rschr., UTAM Czechoslovak Acad. Scis., Praha, 1983-85; head, dept. plasma processes, Inst. Tech. Czechoslovak Acad. Scis., Plzeň, 1985-92, scientific sec., Inst. Tech., 1985-92; vice dir., mgr. R&D Plasmacentrum Ltd., Praha, 1992-94; mgr. materials and tech. rsch. Škoda Rsch., Plzeň, 1994-96; physics tchr. U. West Bohemia, 1994-97; exec. v.p. Škoda A.S. Co., Plzeň, 1996—. Contbr. articles to profl. jours.; spkr., patentee in field. Recipient grants from Czech Acad. Scis., 1990-92, from Grant Agy., Praha, 1994, 95, from European Union, Brussels, 1995, 96. Avocations: family, soccer, windsurfing. Office: Škoda A S, Tylova 57, Plzeň Czech Republic

MUSIL, ROBERT KIRKLAND, professional society administrator; b. N.Y.C., Oct. 27, 1943; s. Ralph A. and Margaret Hooker (Kirkland) M.; m. Caryn Lynne McTighe, June 15, 1968; children: Rebecca McTighe, Emily Kirkland. BA, Yale U., 1964; MA, Northwestern U., 1966, PhD, 1970. Instr. Def. Info. Sch., Ft. Benjamin Harrison, Ind., 1969-71; co-dir. CCCO/An Agy. for Mil. and Draft Counseling, Phila., 1971-74; dir. mil. affairs project Ctr. for Nat. Security Studies, Washington, 1974-75; asst. prof. English and Am. studies Temple U., Phila., 1976-78; prodr., host Consider the Alternatives Radio, Phila., 1978-92; exec. dir. SANE Edn. Fund, Phila. and Washington, 1984-88, Profls. Coalition for Nuclear Arms Control, Washington, 1988-92; dir. policy and programs Physicians for Social Responsibility, Washington, 1992-95, exec. dir., CEO, 1995—; adj. prof. Sch. of Internat. Svc. Am. U., 1997—. Prodr.: (documentary series) Shadows of the Nuclear Age: American Culture and the Bomb, 1980 (NEH grantee). Bd. dirs. Scoville Fellowships, Washington, 1989-92, 95—, SANE, 1978-84. Capt. U.S. Army, 1969-71. Recipient Maj. Armstrong award for radio Armstrong Found., Columbia U., N.Y.C., 1988, 89. Mem. United Ch. of Christ. Home: 8600 Irvington Ave Bethesda MD 20817-3604 Office: Physicians for Social Resp 1101 14th St NW Ste 700 Washington DC 20005-5601

MUSIL, VLADISLAV, electrical engineering educator; b. Boskovice, Czech Republic, Apr. 27, 1953; s. Miloslav and Františka (Špačková) M.; m. Ilona Prokešová, Mar. 15, 1986, 1 child, Vladislav. MSEE, Tech. U. Brno, Czech Republic, 1977, PhD, 1981. Rschr. Metra, Brno, Czech Republic, 1977-78; lectr. Tech. U. Brno, Czech Republic, 1981-87; assoc. prof. elec. engring. Tech. U. Brno., 1987-1999, prof. elec. engring, 1999—; gen. chmn. Electronic Devices and Systems, '98 Conf., Brno. Author: (books in Czech.) Switched-current Circuits, Statistical Design of Electronic Circuits. Mem. IEEE, N.Y. Acad. Scis. Avocations: electronics, photography. Office: Tech U Brno, Údolní 53, CS-60200 Brno Czech Republic

MUSKETT, DAVID, engineer, project management consultant; b. Llunneli, Wales, Eng., May 25, 1953; s. David William and Amila (Pasko) M. BSc in Engring., Hamilton U., 1982. Accredited expert witness/cons. Site rep. Lankro Chems., Kent, 1975-77; project engr. Shell Expo U.K., London, 1977-82; responsible for audits to determine safety sys. W.H. Smith Offshore, Aberdeen, Scotland, 1982-83; lead project constrn. engr. control and safety sys. Dansk Boreselskab A/S (now Maersk Oil and Gas A/S), Denmark, 1983-84; responsible for tech. and progress audits on safety sys. Brit. Gas, Barrow, U.K., 1984-85; lead instrument engr. Maersk Oil & Gas A/S, Copenhagen, 1985-87; lead project engr. Brit. Gas Ltd., London, 1987-89; specialist team engring. dept. Single Buoy Moorings Inc., Monaco, 1989-90; control sys. supr. Brit. Gas Ltd., London, 1990-91; responsible for upgrades to safety sys. Maersk Oil & Gas A/S, Denmark, 1991-94; control sys. project mgr. Astilleros Espanoles, Ferrol, Spain, 1994-96; engring. design mgr. Astilleros Espanoles, Cadiz, Spain, 1996-97; design evaluation/implementation of upgrades to safety sys. Esso Norge, Stavanger, Norway, 1997-99; instigator and implementor project mgmt. sys. EEMA Engring. S.A., 1999—. Mem. Inst. Petroleum, Soc. Naval Archs. and Marine Engrs., Project Mgmt. Inst. Avocations: golf, skiing. Home: care Fontaina 29-31/LA, 15404 Ferrol Spain Office: 27 Old Gloucester St, London WC1N 3AF, England

MUSKÓ, ILONA B., biologist, researcher; b. Szeged, Hungary, Mar. 12, 1947; d. István and Istvánné Ilona Gajdács; m. Mihály Bede, Oct. 30, 1965; children: Péter, Tamás. MS, A. József U., Szeged, 1970; PhD, 1984. Asst. rsch. worker Biol. Rsch. Inst. Hungarian Acad. Sci., Tihany, Hungary, 1970-78; rsch. scientist, 1978-94; sr. rsch. scientist Balaton Limnol. Rsch. Inst. Hungarian Acad. Sci., 1995—. Contbr. 35 articles to scientific jours. Mem. Hungarian Hydrological Soc., Budapest, 1985—, Soc. Hungarian Electron Microscopy, Budapest, 1973—, Ecological Group of Acad. Com., Veszprem, 1985—. Roman Catholic. Home: Furdotelepi Str 18, H-8237 Tihany Hungary Office: Balaton Limnol Rsch Inst, Hungarian Acad Sci PO Box 35, H-8237 Tihany Hungary

MUSLIMOV, RENAT KHALIULLOVICH, state administrator, scientist, educator; b. Kazan, Tatarstan, Russia, Oct. 31, 1934; s. Khalil Sibgatullovich Muslimov and Assia Akhmetzianovna Akhmerova; m. Rimma Salimovna Khusnutdinova, Nov. 6, 1956 (div. June 1976); children: Sadeeva Zoulfia Renatovna, Shakirova Lutsia Renatovna; m. Shakira Nigmatullovna Nafikova, Oct. 8, 1976; children:. Geologist, oil industry worker, Kazan (Russia) State U., 1957; Candidate of Geol.-Mineral. Sci., Bashkir Sci.-Rsch. and Design Inst. of Petroleum Industry, Ufa, Russia, 1975; D of Geol.-Mineral. Sci., All-Russia Petroleum Rsch. Geol. Exploration Inst., St. Petersburg, Russia, 1997. Geologist oil and gas prodn. dept. Leningorskneft, Leningorsk, Russia, 1957-60; head geologist, dep. chief oil and gas prodn. dept. Indsl. Joining Up "Tatneft", Almetyevsk, Russia, 1960-66, chief geologist, vice-dir. gen., 1966-97; state advisor Pres.'s Office of Republic of Tatarstan, 1998—; mem., expert Cen. Commn. on Oil and Gas Fields Devel. of Ministry of Fuel Energy, Moscow, 1999—. Author: (books) Influence of Geological Structure Features on the Development of Romashkinskoye Oil Field, 1979, Perfection of the Development of Tataria's Hard-Recoverable Oil Reservoirs, 1983, Efficiency Increasing of the Exploitation of Tataria's Oil Fields, 1985, (textbook) Planning of the Supplementary Oil Production and Evaluation of the Efficiency of Methods for Oil Recovery Increase, 1999; co-author: (books) Intensification of the Oil Fields Development, 1968, Geology, Development and Exploitation of Romashkinskoye Oil Field, 1995, Geology and Development of the Largest and Unique Oil and Oil and Gas Fields of Russia, 1996, Geological Structure and Development of Bavlinskoye Oil Field, 1996, Experience of Thermal Methods Application to Oil Fields Development, 2000; mem. editl. bd. Oil Economy mag., 1996—; contbr. numerous sci. articles and monographs to profl. publs.; inventor and patentee in field. Mem. Acad. Coun. on Acad. Degrees Conferrment. Recipient USSR State Prize Laureate, Presidium of Supreme Soviet of the USSR, 1982, Jubilee medal for labor valor in commemoration of V.I. Lenin Centenary, 1970, Order of the Red Banner of Labor, 1971, 81, Order of the Friendship of Peoples, 1994, Medal for Vet. of Labor, 1987, Laureate of the I.M. Gubkin prize, 1977, 82, Laureate of Ministry of Oil and Gas Industry, Ministry of Oil and Gas Industry of USSR, 1989, 91, Russian Fedn. Govt. Prize Laureate, Govt. Russian Fedn., 1996, Tatarstan Republic State Prize Laureate, Pres. of Tatarstan Republic, 1995, Tatarstan Republic diploma, 1998; named Excellent Worker of Oil Industry, 1983, Honor Oil Industry Worker, 1984, Honored Geologist of Russian Fedn., Presidium of Supreme Soviet of Russian Fedn., 1989, Honored Geologist of Tatarstan Republic, Pres. of Tatarstan Republic, 1995. Mem. Russian Acad. Natural Scis., Acad. Mining Scis., Acad. Mineral Scis., Acad. Scis. of Tatarstan Republic (corr. mem. 1995—, pres. Ctr. of Hard Recoverable Oil and Natural Bitumen Res. 1995—), Rusian Acad. Natural Scis. (pres. Volga-Kama dept. 1994—), Russian Acad. Scis. (mem. sci. coun. of nuclear physics 1995—), Acad. Mining Scis. (mem. So.-Ural dept. 1996—). Avocations: gardening, reading, skiing.

MUSMANN, KLAUS, librarian; b. Magdeburg, Germany, June 27, 1935; came to U.S., 1957; s. Ernst Hans and Eva (Grunow) M.; m. Gladys H. Arakawa, June 15, 1963 (div. 1973); children: Carlton, Michelle; m. Lois Geneva Steele, Dec. 27, 1986. BA, Wayne State U., 1962; MALS, U. Mich., 1963; MA, Mich. State U., 1967; PhD, U. So. Calif., 1981. Libr. Detroit Pub. Libr., 1962-65; asst. serials libr. Mich. State U., East Lansing, 1965-67; head of acquisitions Los Angeles County Law Libr., L.A., 1968-84; coll. devel. libr. U. Redlands, Calif., 1984—, acting dir., 1994-96, dir., 1996—. Author: Helen and Vernon Farquhar Collection: A Bibliography, 1987, Diffusion of Innovations, 1989, Technological Innovations in Libraries, 1850-1950, 1993; contbr. articles to profl. jours. Grantee Coun. on Libr. Resources, 1990. Mem. ALA, Assn. Coll. and Rsch. Librs., Soc. for History of Tech., Fortnightly Club. Avocations: photography, travel. Home: 220 W Highland Ave Redlands CA 92373-6768 Office: U Redlands Redlands CA 92374

MUSONGE, PETER MAFANY, government official. Gen. mgr. Cameroon Devel. Corp.; prime min. Govt. Cameroon, 1996—. Office: Office Prime Min, Yaoundé Cameroon*

MUSSELL, JOHN WILLIAM, editor; b. Salisbury, Wiltshire, Eng., July 9, 1942; s. Ronald James and Iris (Humby) M.; m. Mary Rose Moody, May 18, 1964 (div. 1990); children: Philip Charles, Nicholas John; m. Carol Ann Hartman, July 5, 1996. Mktg. mgr. H.R. Harmer Ltd., London, 1964-83; mng. editor, dir. Token Pub. Ltd., Honiton, Eng., 1983—. Editor Coin News, Medal News, Coin Yearbook, 1993—, Medal Yearbook, 1993—. Fellow Royal Numismatic Soc.; mem. Am. Numismatic Assn., Numismatic Lit. Guild. Avocations: walking, reading, driving. Office: 1 Orchard House Duchy Rd, Heathpark Devon EX14 8YT, England

MUSSHOFF, FRANK, forensic toxicologist, researcher; b. Luedinghausen, Germany, Aug. 4, 1964; s. Hans and Ilse (Mueller) M.; m. Reinhild M. Schulze, Feb. 6, 1998; 1 child, Sarah. Degree in Biology, Heinrich-Heine U., Düsseldorf, Germany, 1990. Asst. Inst. Legal Medicine, Düsseldorf, 1990-96; chief toxicologist Inst. Legal Medicine, Bonn, Germany, 1996—; presenter in field. Authro: Formaldehyde-Neuroamine Condensation Products in Chronic Alcoholics, 1995. Recipient Young Investigators award Internat. Assn. Forensic Scientists, Tokyo, 1996. Mem. Gesellschaft für Toxikologische and Forensische Chemie (Young Investigator award 1997, Forensic Toxicologist 1997), German Assn. Legal Medicine, Internat. Assn. Forensic Toxicologists. Avocations: soccer, ice hockey, cycling. Home: Weiherstr 31, D-53111 Bonn Germany Office: Inst Legal Medicine, Stiftsplatz 12, 53111 Bonn Germany

MUSSI, ALESSANDRO, painter, writer; b. Milan, May 31, 1945. Grad. secondary sch., Milan, 1959. Author: The Second Christ, 1967; author of numerous short stories; exhbns. in Milan, Rome, Florence, Paris, London. Mem. Grande Oriente d'Italia. Avocation: philosophic and esoteric studies. E-mail: maestro@alessandromussi.it. Home: via delle Betulle 1, 20152 Milan Italy

MUSSO, LOUIS ALBERT, librarian, bibliographer; b. Montevideo, Uruguay, Nov. 20, 1918; s. Roberto and Mary Louise (Ambrosi) M.; m. Emerald Iris Espiga, Aug. 24, 1942; children: Emerald Louise, Louise Graciela. Cert. libr., U. de la Republica, Argentina, 1946; cert. archivist, U. Nacional de Cordoba, Argentina, 1976. Subdir. Gen. Parliament Libr., 1936-76; dir. Gen. Nat. Libr., 1989-90, 95-00; indice gen. del diario El Dia, 1997—. Author: Bibliografia Bibliotecologica Uruguay, 1964, Anales del Senado Uruguay, 1970, Uruguay-Brasil y Sus Medallas, 1976, El Rio de la Plata en Archivo Indias, 1976, Bibliografia de Bibliografias Uruguay, 1964, Colonizacion Canaria, 1997, De Libros Y Lectores, 2000, Artigas en la Medalla Inventario de Una Coleccion, 2000. Recipient silver medal Sociedades Barsileira de Educacao, Preio Club Brasileiro, 1999. Mem. Inst. Historico y Geografico Uruguay, Real Academia de Historia Espana, Asociacion de Bibliotecarios del Uruguay (founder), Instituto Uruguayo de Numismatica (hon.), Asociacion Archivistica Argentina (corr.), Sociedad de Estudios Bibliograficos Argentinos (hon.), Pan-Am. Inst. Geography and History (corr.), Commn. Asesora de Billetes y Monedas del Banco Cen. del Uruguay, Comisiín de vocabulario técnico de la Academia Nacional de Letras. Roman Catholic. Avocations: numismatics, photography, drawing. Home: 1666 Cerro Largo, 11200 Montevideo Uruguay Office: Nat Libr, Av 18 de Julio Nro 1790, Montevideo Uruguay

MUSSURAKIS, STAVROS, radiologist, researcher; b. Heraklion, Crete, Greece, Aug. 25, 1961; s. Constantine and Alice (Taptopoulou) M.; m. Eleftheria Symeonidi, Aug. 26, 1993; children: Constantine, Gabriella. MD, Athens (Greece) Med. Sch., 1986; doctorate, U. Athens, 1990. Diploma in med. radiodiagnosis, London; cert. specialist in radiology, Greece, U.K. Resident in radiology Hippokration Hosp., Athens, 1987-90; resident in internal medicine U. Athens, 1990; registrar in radiology Sheffield (Eng.) Hosps., 1990-93; clin. rsch. fellow U. Sheffield, 1993-94; clin. lectr. in magnetic resonance imaging U. Hull, Eng., 1994-97; sci. dir. x-ray dept. Mitera Kritis, Iraklion, 1997—; peer reviewer Investigative Radiology, 1995—, Jour. Computer Assisted Tomography, 1997—, Jour. Magnetic Resonance Imaging, 1997—, European Radiology, 1998—. Mem. editl. bd. Hellenic Radiology, 1988-90; contbr. articles to med. jours., including Clin. Radiology, Brit. Jour. Radiology, Radiology. Postgrad. grantee NATO, 1989, Brit. Coun., 1990, postdoctoral rsch. grantee European Cmty., 1993; recipient clin. MRI prize BIR, 1996, editor's medal Clin. Radiology, 1997. Fellow Royal Coll. Radiologists (London); mem. Radiol. Soc. N.Am., Am. Roentgen Ray Soc. Avocations: long distance running, chess, computing. Home: Athenas 2, 71306 Heraklion Crete, Greece Office: Mitera Kritis, Arh Makariou-S Venizelou, 71202 Heraklion Crete, Greece

MUSTAFA, SEHAM M. DARWISH, pharmacist, educator; b. Cairo, Jan. 23, 1954; d. Mohammed Darwish Mustafa and Horiya Salama Hassan; m. Nabil Fathy Ismael, Aug. 20, 1979; children: Hussam, Hisham, Dalya. B in Pharmacy, Cairo U., 1977; MSc, Kuwait U., 1986; PhD, U. Bath, U.K., 1997. Pharm. analyst CID Drug Co., Cairo, 1977-84; rsch. asst. faculty medicine Kuwait U., 1984-86, asst. lectr. faculty medicine, 1986—. Contbr. articles to profl. jours. Mem. Profl. Soc. Pharmacists Egypt, Profl. Soc. Pharmacists. Avocations: chess, tennis, swimming. Office: Faculty medicine, Kuwait Univ, Kuwait Jabrya, Kuwait

MUSTAFA, SHAWKAT ISSA, government executive; b. Qalandia, Jerusalem, Palestine, May 20, 1948; s. Issa Abdelmajeed and Aysa Said (Hamad) M.; m. Samia Soubhi Jarbouh, Nov. 10, 1954; children: Feras, Raya. German diploma, U. Leipzig, Germany, 1976, D in Econs., 1991. Advisor PLO, Beirut, Lebanon, 1976-80; spl. invoy, chmn. PLO, Rome, 1981-94; gen. dir. of office of pres. Yasser Arafat Palestinian Nat. Authority, Gaza, 1995—. Avocations: reading, classical music, nature, gardening.

Home: via Giannutri 2, 00141 Rome Italy Office: Palestinian Nat Authority, Al-Rashid str, Gaza Palestine

MUSTAPHA, BASIRAT ADETOUN, environmental scientist; b. Ibadan, Nigeria, June 8, 1969; d. Ganiyu Adebisi and Amudat Ojuolape (Akinsanya) M. BSc with honors in microbiology, U. Lagos, Nigeria, 1990, MSc in Med. Microbiology, 1992; MPH, U. Wales, Cardiff, 1999. Grad. asst., asst. lectr. U. Ilorin and Cosit U. Lagos, 1990-92; rsch. asst. wins Tufts U./U. Lagos, 1993; mgmt. trainee Ladgroup Ltd., Lagos, 1993-94; environ. adviser Shell Petroleum Devel. Co., Nigeria, 1994-98; guest lectr. U. Wales Inst., Cardiff, 1999; pub. health adviser Shell Petroleum Devel. Co., Warri, Nigeria, 1999—. Contbr. articles to profl. jours. Recipient univ. scholarship U. Lagos, 1988-89, fed. govt. scholarship Nigerian Govt., 1991-92, Cheuening scholarship Brit. Govt., Nigeria, 1998-99. Fellow Nigerian Conservation Found.; mem. Internat. Soc. Environ. Epidemiology (mem. ethics com. 1999—), Inst. Petroleum U.K. Mem. Pentecostal Ch. Avocations: reading, writing, travel, cooking, engaging in Christian activities. Home: 8 Jaginrin St, GPO Box 285, Ijebu-Ode Ogun, Nigeria Office: Shell Petroleum Devel Co, Cmty Hlth Team GPO Box 230, Warri Delta, Nigeria

MUSTE, MARIAN, civil engineer; b. Reghin, Romania, Mar. 14, 1955; s. Traian and Maria M.; m. Gabriela, Apr. 26, 1980; 1 child, Vlad. MSc, Inst. Poly. Cluj, Romania, 1980, U. Iowa, 1993; PhD, U. Iowa, 1995. Profl. engr. heavy machine co., Cluj, 1980-82; from asst. prof. to assoc. prof. Inst. Poly., Cluj, 1983-91; rsch. engr. Iowa Inst. Hydraulic Rsch., Iowa City, 1991—. Mem. Am. Soc. Civil Engring., Internat. Assn. Hydraulic Rsch., Internat. Assn., Hydrol. Scis. Avocations: soccer, tennis, music, violin. Office: Iowa Inst Hydraulic Rsch 404 Hydraulic Lab Iowa City IA 42242

MUSTI, NARASIMHA MURTY, computer science educator; b. Visakhapatnam, India, Dec. 21, 1954; s. Chitti Babu and Appala Narasamma (Kota) M.; m. Lakshmi Kota, June 19, 1983; 1 child, Virinchi. BSc, Andhra U., Visakhapatnam, 1972; BEE, Indian Inst. Sci., Bangalore, 1975, MEE, 1978, PhD, 1982. Project leader Processor Sys. India, Bangalore, 1982-83; rsch. assoc. Indian Inst. Sci., 1983-84, asst. prof., 1984-90, assoc. prof., 1990-96, prof., 1996—; cons. Novell Software Devel., Bangalore, 1997-98, Advanced Synergic Micro Sys. Ltd., Bangalore, 1997; vis. scientist Mich. State U., East Lansing, 1995. Author: Pattern Recognition, 1997; contbr. articles to sci. jours.; editor Vivek Jour., Mumbai, India, 1990-96. Indo-U.S. project grantee NSF, Indian Inst. Sci. and Mich. State U., 1995-97. Mem. Internat. Assn. for Pattern Recognition. Avocations: English literature, Indian music, cricket. Office: Indian Inst Sci, Dept Computer Sci, Bangalore 560 012, India

MUSTILA, ANU KRISTIINA, physician; b. Valkeakoski, Finland, Sept. 21, 1971; d. Vaino Olavi and Pirjo Marjatta (Eerola) Mattila; m. Simo Juhani Mustila, June 15, 1996; 1 child, Arttu Simo Juhani. MD, U. Tampere, Finland, 1996; PhD, U. Tampere, 2000. Resident dept. clin. microbiology Tampere U. Hosp., 1996, 99—; gen. practitioner Health Care Ctr. of Lempaala, Finland, 1997-98. Contbr. articles to profl. jours. Grantee Emil Aaltonen Found., 1995, Med. Rsch. Fund of Tampere U. Hosp., 1996. Lutheran. Avocations: jogging, skiing, piano playing. Home: Kajanteentie 6, 37500 Lempäälä Finland Office: Tampere U Hosp Ctr Lab Med, Teiskontie 35, 33521 Tampere Finland

MUSTONEN, EILA MARJA AULIKKI, neuro-ophthalmologist; b. Juva, Finland, July 21, 1941; s. Olavi and Lyyli (Haataja) M. B of Medicine, U. Turku, Finland, 1962; Licentiate in Medicine, U. Oulu, Finland, 1966, MD, 1966, PhD, 1984. Intern Oulu Provincial Hosp., Finland, 1963-67; resident dept. ophthalmology, dept. neurology Oulu U. Hosp., Finland, 1967-72; fellow in neuro-ophthalmology Johns Hopkins Hosp., Balt., 1972-73; chief neuro-ophthalmology unit, dept. ophthalmology Oulu U. Hosp., 1973—; docent in ophthalmology Oulu U., 1984—. Contbr. articles to ophthal. jours. Fellow Internat. Neuro-Ophthalmology Soc., European Neuro-Ophthalmology Soc. (provisional com.). Avocations: literature, classical music, summer cottage. Home: Syrjakatu 2 B 12, 90100 Oulu Finland Office: Oulu U Hosp Dept Ophthalmology, Kajaanintie 50, Oulu 90220, Finland

MUSUDA, WATARU, mechanical engineering educator; b. Sumoto, Hyogo, Japan, Feb. 13, 1948; s. Minoru and Sumiko (Nakamura) M.; m. Shigemi Ideno, Feb. 8, 1981; children: Haruka, Susumu. BS, Kyoto Inst. Tech., 1970, MS, 1972; Dr.Engring., U. Tokyo, 1975. Rschr. Ishikawajima-Harima Heavy Industries, Co., Ltd., Tokyo, 1975-81; assoc. prof. Nagaoka (Japan) U. Tech., 1981-92, prof. dept. mech. engring., 1992—; courtesy prof. Fla. State U., Tallahassee, 1993-94. Contbr. articles to profl. jours. Mem. Japan Soc. Mech. Engring., Japan Soc. Aerospace Sci. Avocation: ceramic art.

MUSZYŃSKI, ROBERT, engineering educator; b. Pabianice, Mazowsze, Poland, June 4, 1967; s. Jan and Teresa (Grzegorzewska) M. MSc, Wrocław U. Tech., Poland, 1992, PhD, 1996. Registered profl. engr. Invited rschr. J. Kepler U., Linz, Austria, 1994-96; asst. prof. engring. cybernetics Wrocław U. Tech., Poland, 1997—. Contbr. articles to profl. jours. Recipient Primus Inter Pares' award Found. for Young Talents Promotion, Warsaw, Poland, 1991. Mem. World Exclusive Minolta Club. Home: Bardowskiego 5/18, 95-200 Pabianice Mazowsze, Poland Office: Wrocław Univ Tech, Janiszewskiego 11/17, 50-372 Wrocław Poland

MUT, JOSEP, conductor; b. Benegida, Valencia, Spain, Nov. 13, 1947; s. Josep Mut and Herminia Benavent; m. Heleno Bosque, Nov. 2, 1977; children: María, José Ramón, Clara. Solista Banda Municipal, Barcelona, 1969-81, subdir., 1981-93, dir., 1993—; solista Liceo (Gran Teatro), Barna, 1969-90; pres. Liceo (Gran Teatro) Barcelona, 1975-85. Avocations: football, tennis. Home: Can Guitart C/Sport 20, 08758 Cervelló Spain Office: Banda Municipal, Palav Vivreina Rambla 99, Barcelona Spain

MUTA, TAIZO, academic administrator; b. Kurume, Fukuoka, Japan, June 1, 1937; s. Tadashi and Kozue (Koga) M.; m. Takako Noda, July 15, 1965; children: Hidemasa, Takefumi. BS, Kyushu U., Fukuoka, 1960; MS, U. Tokyo, 1962, DSc, 1965. Rsch. assoc. Kyoto U., 1965-71, assoc. prof., 1971-82; prof. Hiroshima U., 1982—; dean of sci. Hiroshima (Japan) U., 1995-99, v.p., 1999—. Author: Foundations of Quantum Chromodynamics, 1987. Mem. Japan Phys. Soc. Buddhist. Avocation: fishing. Home: Saijo-Chuo 3-36-17, Higashi Hiroshima 739-0025, Japan Office: Hiroshima Univ, Kagamiyama 1-3-2, Higashi Hiroshima 739-8511, Japan

MUTAFOV, CHRISTO GEORGIEV, medical information specialist; b. Sofia, Bulgaria, Jan. 27, 1936; s. Georgi Christov and Sophie Leopold (Lindbichler) M.; m. Ubavka Jordanova Jakovtsheva, June 2, 1937; children: Jordan Christov, Sophie Christova. Diploma in stomatology, Med. U., Sofia, 1960; diploma in sci. info., U. Sofia, 1968; DSc in Philosophy, Bulgarian Acad. Scis., 1991. Stomatologist Med. Svc., Montana, Bulgaria, 1960-70; with Med. Info. Ctr., Sofia, 1971—, chief of dept., 1974-91, dir., 1991—, team work leader drug info. sys., 1994—, team work leader Bulgarian Index of Citations, 1996—; dep. dir. Ctrl. Med. Libr., Sofia, 1993—; main expert Coun. Ministers, Sofia, 1989-91; expert High Attestation Commn., Sofia, 1983-90; mem. editl. bds. Modern Medicine, Med. Rsch., Acta Medica Bulgarica, Pub. Health Care, Med. Rev., The World, Ex-Libris, Medicus, Internal Diseases, Gen. Medicine, 1993—; prof. theory sci. info. Med. U., Sofia, 1995—. Leader author's team (book) Index Pharmacorum Bulgaricus, 1994—. Capt. Bulgarian Army, 1990-94. Mem. European Assn. for Health Info. and Librs., Union Scientists, Libr. Info. Union, Assn. Touristic Telemation (mng. com. 1994—), Bulgarian Nat. Acad. Medicine, N.Y. Acad. Sci., Atlanto-Euro-Mediterranean Acad. Med. Scis., Assn. Info. World-2000 (mng. com. 1998—). Avocations: reading, hiking, music, traveling. E-mail: mutafov@sun.medun.acad.bg. Office: Med Info Ctr, 1 G Sofijski Str, 1431 Sofia Bulgaria

MUTAWALLI, HISHAM, bank executive. Gov. Ctrl. Bank of Syria, Damascus. Office: Ctrl Bank Syria POB 2254, Altarjrida Al Mughrabia Sq, Damascus Syria*

MUTEMBEREZI, FRANCOIS, bank executive. Gov. Ctrl. Bank of Rwanda. Office: Banque Nat du Rwanda, BP 531, Kigali Rwanda*

MUTHANA, DECHU PALECANDA, structured finance analyst; b. Bangalore, Karnataka, India, Nov. 21, 1967; Came to U.S., 1987; s. Palecanda P. and Bojie Palecanda Muthana. BBA, Hofstra U., 1991, MBA, 1993. Dir. Shak T LLC, N.Y.C., 1997—; sr. cons. PricewaterhouseCoopers LLC, Arlington, VA., 1998-2000; v.p. Bondglobe Inc., N.Y.C., 2000—. Mem. Internat. Assn. Fin. Engrs., Global Assn. Risk Profls. Office: Bondglobe Inc One World Trade Ctr New York NY 10048

MUTHIRENTHY, VARKEY JOSEPH, physical oceanographer; b. Kerala, India, Nov. 30, 1945; s. Joseph Varkey and Aley Joseph Muthirenthical; m. Aniamma Varkey Karanthanam, May 20, 1979; children: Elizabeth Maya, Joseph Robin. BSc, S.H. Coll., Cochin, India, 1965; MSc, Dept. Marine Scis., Cochin, 1967; PhD, Nat. Inst. Oceanography, India, 1989. Diplomate oceanography for marine civil engring. The Norwegian Inst. of Tech., Trondheim, Norway. Jr. sci. asst. N.P.O.L., India, 1969-71; sr. sci. asst. Nat. Inst. Oceanography, Dona Paula, India, 1971-73, scientist B, 1973-78, scientist C, 1978-85, scientist E1, 1985-91, scientist E2, 1991-97; scientist F, 1997—. First author: Wave Atlas for Arabian Sea and Bay of Bengal, 1982. Mem. Indian Sci. Congress Assn., Indian Meteorol. Soc. Avocations: popular science writing, photography, gardening. Office: Nat Inst Oceanography, Dona Paula 403004, India

MUTHUKUMAR, GANAPATHY, biochemist; b. Namakkal, Tamilnadu, India, Feb. 17, 1955; came to U.S., 1982; s. Ganapathy and Sethurama Lakshmi (Arumugam) G.; m. Alahari Arunakumari, Apr. 17, 1982; children: Madhukiran, Manoja. BSc, Madurai-Kamaraj U., Tamilnadu, India, 1974; MSc, Andhra U., Guntur, A.P., India, 1976; PhD, U. Madras, India, 1981. Postdoctoral fellow U. Nebr., Lincoln, 1982-85; vis. scientist Mich. State U., East Lansing, 1986-88; instr. R.W.J. Med. Sch., Piscataway, N.J., 1988-91; scientist I Enzon, Inc., Piscataway, 1992-93, scientist II, 1993-94, assoc. dir., head bioprocess devel., 1995-96; sr. scientist Neorx Corp., Seattle, 1996-97; rsch. leader Roche Molecular Sys., Somerville, N.J., 1997—. Contbr. articles to profl. jours. Mem. AAAS, Am. Soc. Microbiology (referee 1986-88). Democrat. Hindu. Home: One Beechwood Dr Pennington NJ 08534 Office: Roche Molecular Sys 1080 Us Highway 202 S Somerville NJ 08876-3733

MUTHUKUMAR, NATARAJAN, neurosurgeon; b. Madras, Tamil Nadu, India, Apr. 13, 1959; s. Murugesan and Sivanantham Natarajan; m. Suganthy Muthukrishnan, June 3, 1984; 1 child, Prasanna Kumar. MB BChir, Madurai Med. Coll., Tamil Nadu, 1982, MCh in Neurosurgery, 1988. Scientist pool officer CSIR Sri Chithra Thirunal Inst. Med. Scis. and Tech., Thiruvananthapuram, 1988-89; tutor in neurosurgery Govt. Royapettah Hosp., Madras, 1989; asst. prof. neurosurgery Madurai Med. Coll., 1989—. Sugita scholar dept. neurosurgery Nagoya (Japan) U. Sch. Medicine, 1992; skull base surgery fellow Osaka City U. Med. Sch., Japan, 1994. Fellow Congress Neurol. Surgeons (internat. fellow); mem. ACS, Internat. Coll. Surgeons, Internat. Brain Rsch. Orgn. Hindu. Fax: 91-452-531056. E-mail: natmuthu@vsnl.com. Home: Muruganagam 138 Anna Nagar, Madurai 625 020, India Office: Govt Rajaji Hosp, Dept Neurosurgery, Madurai 625 020, India

MUTI, PAOLA CORNELIA, physician, educator; b. Milan, Italy, July 3, 1956; came to US, 1994; d. Paolo Muti and Rosalba Rossi; m. Paolo Carpi de Restini, Dec. 13, 1984 (div. Apr. 1996); m. Holger J. Schünemann, Aug. 31, 1996; children: Gretia, Giovanna Muti Schünemann. MD, U. Pisa (Italy), 1984; MS, SUNY, Buffalo, 1991. Sr. researcher Nat. Cancer Inst., Milan, 1986-99; assoc. prof. SUNY, Buffalo, 1999—. Buswell fellow SUNY, 1996-99; recipient Young Investigator award AHA, 1995. Mem. Am. Assn. Cancer Rsch., Europ Assn. Cancer Rsch., Soc. Epidemiology Rsch. Office: SUNY 3435 Main St Buffalo NY 14214-3099

MUTIHAC, LUCIA, chemistry educator, researcher; b. Olanesti, Valcea, Romania, Apr. 15, 1951; d. Nicolae and Eleonora (Dobriceanu) Diaconu; m. Radu Mutihac, Aug. 21, 1977; children: Radu Cristian, Ruxandra. B, U. Bucharest, Romania, 1974; MSc, U. Politechnica, Bucharest, 1975; PhD, Bucharest, Romania, 1990. Diplomate in Inst. Phys. Chemistry, Romanian Acad., Bucharest, 1990. Diplomate in chemistry. Chemist Ctr. of Chem. Rsch., Valcea, 1975-78; chemist rschr. Inst. Phys. Chemistry, Bucharest, 1978-89, sr. rschr., 1989-91; lectr. U. Bucharest, 1991-97, assoc. prof., 1997-99, prof., 2000—; exec. sec. Rev. of Romanian Chemistry, Romanian Acad., Bucharest, 1986-95; Romanian rep. Global Supramolecular Chemistry Network, 1996—. Author: Chemometrics, 1997, Separation of Chemical and Biological Species Through Membranes and Membrane Processes, 1998; co-author: Transport Mechanisms Through Liquid Membranes, 1997, Chemometrics: Principles and Applications, 2000; patentee in field. Recipient various awards. Mem. European Membrane Soc., Romanian Soc. Analytical Chemistry, Romanian Soc. Chemistry. Orthodox Christian. Avocations: classical music, literature, travel. Home: Blvd Jon Mihalache 64, Bl 41 Ap 12, 78215 Bucharest 1, Romania Office: U Bucharest Fac Chemistry, Blvd Regina Elisabeta 4-12, 703461 Bucharest Romania

MUTIKAINEN, RISTO HEIKKI, physicist; b. Espoo, Finland, Sept. 19, 1961; s. Heikki Ilmari and Kerttu Mirjami (Kiiski) M. MSc, Helsinki U. Tech., 1985, DSc, 1995. Rsch. scientist Tech. Rsch. Ctr. Finland, Espoo, 1985-87; vis. scientist U. Calif., Berkeley, 1987-88; rsch. scientist Tech. Rsch. Ctr. Finland, 1988-94, VTT Electronics, Espoo, 1995-96; process physicist VTI Hamlin, Vantaa, Finland, 1996-99, process devel. mgr., 1999—. Avocations: paddling, choir singing. Home: Rantaraitti 5 A 2, 02230 Espoo Finland Office: VTI Hamlin, PL 27, 01621 Vantaa Finland

MUTINGA, MUTUKU JOHN, university president, parasitologist, entomologist; b. Machakos, Kenya, Feb. 19, 1939; s. John Mutinga Kiamba and Alice Kaindwa (Kyai) M.; m. Gloria Jean Friday, Feb. 4, 1968; children: Muthoka, Nzisa, Mueni. BA, Union Coll., Lincoln, Nebr., 1965; MSc, U. Mo., 1968; PhD, U. Nairobi, Kenya, 1972. Med. entomologist Ministry of Health, Nairobi, 1968-73; sr. lectr. U. Nairobi, 1973-79; prin. rsch. scientist ICIPE, Nairobi, 1979-86, dep. dir., 1986-87, sr. prin. rsch. scientist, 1986-94; prof. zoology Jomo Kenyatta U., Nairobi, 1995; vice-chancellor U. Ea. Africa, Baraton, Kenya, 1996—; commr. Commn. for Higher Edn., Nairobi, 1996—. Contbr. over 100 articles to sci. jours.; inventor MBU cloth for killing mosquitos, 1990; discoverer insect disease cycles, Kenya, 1969, 85. Fellow African Acad. Scis., N.Y. Acad. Scis., Kenya Nat. Acad. Avocations: reading, tennis, swimming, gardening, bird watching. Home: PO Box 43904, Nairobi Kenya Office: U Ea Africa, PO Box 2500, Eldoret Kenya

MUTISO, SAMUEL KITUKU, physical and human geography educator, consultant; b. Nairobi, Kenya, Jan. 21, 1947; s. Mutiso and Martha Kavenge Mutiso; m. Wanja Janet Mburugu, 1974; 6 children. BEd with honors, U. Nairobi, 1977; postgrad., Giessen U., Montreal, Can., 1977-78, McGill U., 1980-81; MA, U. Nairobi, 1983; PhD, U. Reading, U.K., 1988. Cert. in remote sensing of environment, McGill U., 1980-81. Tchg. asst. McGill U.; grad. asst. U. Nairobi, 1981-82, tutorial fellow, 1983-86, from asst. lectr. to lectr., 1986-93, sr. lectr., 1990-99, assoc. prof., 1999—; vice-chmn. com. on sci. and tech. UN Conv. to Combat Desertification, Geneva, Switzerland, 1998-99; mem. nat. task force on desertification Ministry of Environment and Natural Resources, Nairobi, 1993-94; team leader social econ. indications of land degradation UNEP, Nairobi, 1994-96; dir. WHO family planning aerial mapping of homesteads Dept. of Ob-Gyn., U. Nairobi, Matungulu, 1984. Chmn. bd. govs. Mitaboni A.B.C. Girls, 1992-95; bd. govs. Tala (Kenya) H.S., 1994—; chmn. interministerial com. on environment, subcom. on desertification and drought Ministry of Environment Conservation, Nairobi, 1995—. Mem. Kenya Rain Water Harvesting Assn. (founder). Avocations: reading, climbing, swimming, singing. Office: U Nairobi Dept Geography, PO Box 30197, Nairobi Kenya

MUTO, TETSUJI, geologist; b. Hamamatsu, Japan, June 17, 1959; m. Tomiko, May 29, 1988; children: Noruji, Natsumi. BS, Shizuoka U., 1982; MS, Kyoto U., 1984, DSc, 1987. Postdoctoral fellow Kyushu U., Fukuoka, Japan, 1989-91, U. Bergen, Norway, 1991-92; from lectr. to assoc. prof. Nagasaki U., Nagasaki, Japan, 1992—. Office: Nagasaki U Faculty Environ, 1-14 Bunkyomachi, 852-8521 Nagasaki Japan

MUTOH, TATSURO, neurologist, molecular neurochemist; b. Kanazawa City, Japan, Sept. 30, 1953; s. Akira and Itsuko (Yamashiro) M.; m. Etsuko Kosugi Mutoh; children: Eri, Manabu Cedric, Osamu, Marie. MD, Nagoya U. Sch. Medicine, Japan, 1980; PhD, Nagoya U. Postgrad. Sch. Med., Japan, 1986. Asst. prof. Fukui (Japan) Med. Sch., 1986-95, assoc. prof., 1995—; vis. fellow Nat. Inst. Health, Bethesda, 1987-90. Recipient Profl. Contract Svc. award NIH, Bethesda, Md., 1992, 94; grant for Experiments Abroad Japanese Found. for Health and Aging, Tokyo, 1993. Mem. N.Y. Acad. Scis., Am. Acad. Neurology. Home: 13-1-46 Wakamiya Sakai-cho, Fukui 919 0515, Japan Office: Fukui Med U, 23 Shimoaizuk Matsuoka-cho, Fukui 910 1193, Japan

MUTOLA, MARIA, Olympic athlete; b. Maputo, Mozambique, Oct. 27, 1972. Winner World Championship, 1993; winner Bronze medal 800 meter race Atlanta, 1996; winner Bronze medal 800 meter race World Championship, 1997; winner 800 meter IAAF World Cup Johannesburg, Sounth Africa, 1998; winner Silver medal 800 meter race World Championships, 1999; winner Gold medal Sydney, 2000. Office: Fed Moçambicana Atletismo, CP 1094, Maputo Mozambique*

MUTOMBO, DIKEMBE (DIKEMBE MUTOMBO MPOLONDO MUKAMBA JEAN JACQUE WAMUTOMBO), professional basketball player; b. Kinshasa, Zaire, June 25, 1966. Grad., Georgetown U., 1991. Ctr. Denver Nuggets, 1991-96, Atlanta Hawks, 1996—. NBA All-Star, 1992; NBA All-Rookie Team, 1992; NBA Defensive Player of Year, 1995, 97. Office: Atlanta Hawks One CNN Ctr Ste 405 S Tower Atlanta GA 30303

MUTSCHLER, HANS-DIETER, philosophy educator; b. Stuttgart, Germany, Sept. 11, 1946; s. Alfred and Mariliese (Probst) M.; m. Monika Gotschol, Nov. 27, 1991; 1 child, Sophia. Diploma in theology, Theology Hochschule, Germany, 1979; Staatsexamen in Physics, Physics Inst., 1983; PhD, Philosophy Inst., 1989. Tchr. Technikfolgen Forschung, Germany, 1987—; faculty Theol. Hochschule, Frankfurt, Germany, 1991—, Innsbruck, Austria, 1995—; faculty Philosophy Hochschule, Frankfurt, 1989—; with Hessischer Rundfunk, 1992—, Frankfurter Allgemeine Zeitung, 1993—. Author: Spekulative und Empirische Physik, 1990, Physik-Religion-New Age, 1991, Zur Person und Theologie Karl Rahners, 1994, Die Virtualisierung der Realitaet, 1996. Organist St. Ignatiuskirche Frankfurt. Roman Catholic. Office: Philosophisdies Inst, Dantestrasse 4-6, 60054 Frankfurt Hessen, Germany

MUTSCHLER, HERBERT FREDERICK, retired librarian; b. Eureka, S.D., Nov. 28, 1919; s. Frederick and Helena (Oster) M.; m. Lucille I. Gross, Aug. 18, 1945; 1 dau., Linda M. B.A., Jamestown Coll., 1947; M.A., Western Res. U., 1949, M.S., 1952. Tchr. history high sch. Lemmon, S.D., 1947-48; asst. librarian Royal Oak (Mich.) Libr., 1952-55; head librarian Hamtramck (Mich.) Libr., 1955-56; head public svcs. Wayne County Libr. System, Wayne, Mich., 1956-59; asst. county librarian Wayne County Libr. System, 1960-62; dir. King County Libr. System, Seattle, 1963-89; library bldg. cons. Wayne County Libr., 1956-62, Wash. State Libr., 1966—; cons. Salt Lake County Libr., Pierce County Libr., North Olympic Libr.; lectr. U. Wash. Sch. Librarianship, 1970-71; bldg. cons. Hoquiam (Wash.) Libr., Olympic (Wash.) Regional Libr., Camas (Wash.) Pub. Libr., N. Cen. (Wash.) Regional Libr., Spokane (Wash.) County Libr., Enumclaw (Wash.) Libr., Puyallup (Wash.) Pub. Libr., Kennewick (Wash.) Pub. Libr., Lopez Island (Wash.) Libr. Contbr. articles profl. jours. Mem. Foss Home and Village Bd. Trustees, 1989-98; bd. dirs. King County Libr. Sys. Found., 1990—. With AUS, 1941-45; to capt. 1950-52. Decorated Silver Star, Bronze Star with cluster, Purple Heart, Presdl. Unit Citation. Mem. ALA (councilor at large 1965-69, chpt. councilor 1971-75, pres. library adminstrv. div. 1974-75), Pacific N.W. Library Assn., Wash. Library Assn. (exec. bd. 1964-65, 69-71, pres. 1967-69), Enological Soc. N.W. Seattle (bd. dirs. 1988—). Republican. Lutheran. Club: City, Municipal League. Lodge: Kiwanis. Home: 5300 128th Ave SE Bellevue WA 98006-2952

MUTTER, DIDIER, surgeon, educator, researcher; b. Luxembourg, Mar. 15, 1959; s. Jean Marie and Nicole (Rieger) M.; m. Catherine Schmidt, June 6, 1992; children: Louis, Laure, Colas. MD, Strasbourg (France) Med. U., 1990; PhD, Louis Pasteur U., Strasbourg, 1996. Intern Hopitaux U., Strasbourg, 1985-90, chief resident, 1990-92, cons. surgeon, 1992—, prof. surgery. Contbr. articles to profl. jours. Mem. European Assn. Endoscopic Surgery, Soc. Française Chirurgie Digestive, Assn., Française Chirurgie, Inst. Rsch. Cancers Appareil Digestif, European Sch. TelesSurgery, Assn. Francophone Chirurgie Endocrinienne, Internat. Assn. Endocrine Surgeon, Internat. Soc. Surgery. Office: Chirurgie A Hopital Civil, 1 Place Hopital, 67091 Strasbourg France

MUTWALLY, HAMED MOHAMMED A., science educator; b. Makkah, Saudi Arabia, Oct. 13, 1962; s. Mohammed Abd Alqadir Mutwally and Rahma Salem Zeiter; m. Hasnaa Ahmed Akram, Mar. 15, 1987; children: Lubabah, Lujain, Mohammed, Ahmed. BSc in Edn. and Biology, Umm Alqura U., Makkah, Saudi Arabia, 1982; MPhil, Lancaster (Eng.) U., 1986, PhD, 1990. Demonstrator biology dept. Umm Alqura U., Makkah, 1983-84, asst. prof. biology dept., 1990-95, assoc. prof. biology dept., 1995-2000, prof., 2000—. Contbr. articles to profl. jours. Scholar Lancaster U., 1991—, Odense (Denmark) U., 1997—. Mem. Biol. Soc., N.Y. Acad. Sci., Saudi Biol. Soc., Med. Herb Soc., Saudi Environ. Soc. Muslim. Avocations: reading, football, traveling, swimming, riding horses. Fax: 092-550100 (6069-6071). E-mail: hamed@uqu.edu.sa. Home: Alaziziah St, PO Box 6215, Makkah 6215, Saudi Arabia Office: Umm Alqura Univ Biology, Alaziziah St, Makkah 3711, Saudi Arabia

MUTZIGER, JOHN CHARLES, physician; b. Natchez, Miss., June 23, 1949; s. Dudley Henson and Marie Louise (Eyrich) M.; m. Sarah Edwards Meyer, Nov. 17, 1973 (div. Apr. 1979, remarried Oct., 1995); m. Janis Merle Averyt, Sept. 13, 1980 (div. Apr. 1995); children: John Charles Jr., William Westley. BS in Anthropology with honors, Tulane U., 1971; DO, U. Health and Sci., 1982. Diplomate Am. Coll. Family Practitioners, Am. Soc. Addiction Medicine. Pvt. practice, Philadelphia, Miss., 1983-90, Decatur, Miss., 1990-91, Meridian, Miss., 1992—; emergency room dir. Laird Hosp., Union, 1990-92; med. dir. Weems Life Care, 1992—, Magnolia Med. Group, 1998-99, Queen City Nursing Home, 1998—, Okatibbee Family Med. Clinic, 1999. Mem. Rotary, Phila., 1983-89; bd. dirs. Meridian Symphony Orch., 1992. Mem. AMA (Phys. recognition award 1991), Am. Coll. Family Practitioners, Am. Osteo. Assn., Am. Osteo. Acad. Addictionology (charter mem. 1986—), Am. Soc. Addiction Medicine, Miss. Med. Assn., Miss. Osteo. Med. Assn. (pres. 1986-87, program chmn. ann. coast conv. 1986-95), So. Med. Assn. Republican. Presbyterian. Avocations: golf, tennis, sailing, gourmet cooking, bridge. Home: 5503 13th Pl Meridian MS 39305-1446 Office: Okatibbee Family Med Clinic 9097 Collinsville Rd Collinsville MS 39325-9779

MUYEMBE, VICTOR MWANZI, surgeon, consultant; b. Karamega, Kenya; s. John Mahindu and Ceacilia M'mbali M.; m. Joyce Katdu Mukui, May 30, 1997; children: David Murunga, Daisyanne Aliela, Diana M'mbali. MBBS, U. Nairobi (Kenya), 1986, M in Medicine in Gen. Surgery, 1992. Intern Ministry of Health, Kenya, 1986-87, med. officer, 1987-89; surg. registrar Aga Khan Hosp., Nairobi, 1993-94; gen. surgeon Ministry of Health, Nyeri, Kenya, 1994—; cons. in-charge dept. surgery, 1998—; sr. house officer Kenyatta Nat. Hosp., Kenya, 1989-92. Contbr. articles to med. jours. Mem. Kenya Med. Asn., Assn. Surgeons East and Ctrl. Africa. Roman Catholic. Avocations: chess, body building, football. Home: Box 124-85, Nyeri Kenya Office: Ministry of Health, Box 27, Nyeri Kenya

MUYSSON, PHIL, book publisher; b. Rotterdam, The Netherlands, Dec. 23, 1949; s. Willem and Suze (v.d. Horst) M.; m. Karin Hasselo, July 29, 1994. Bacalaureat, Social Acad., The Hague. Dir. Uitgeverij BZZTOH, The Hague. Avocation: travel. Office: Uitgeverij BZZTOH, Laan van Meerdervoort 10, 2517 AJ The Hague The Netherlands

MUZENDA, SIMON VENGAI, vice president of Zimbabwe; b. Gutu, Masvingo Province, Zimbabwe, Oct. 28, 1922; m. Maude Muzenda; 8 children. Diploma in carpentry, Marianhill Coll., South Africa, 1948. Instr. Mazenod Sch., Mayville, South Africa, 1948-50; carpenter, Bulawayo twp. of Barbourfields, from 1953, also Umvuma; co-founder Barbourfields Tenants Assn.; co-founder Nat. Democratic Party; chmn. Umvuma br., organizing

sec. for Masvingo province, 1960-61, party banned, 1962; adminstrv. sec. Masvingo, Zimbabwe African People's Union, 1962, dep. organizing sec. 1st Congress Zimbabwe African Nat. Union; dep. adminstrv. sec. Zambia, 1975-76, minister fgn. affairs, 1980-81; with Zimbabwe African Nat. Liberation Army, 1977-80; dep. prime minister Republic of Zimbabwe, 1980-88, v.p., 1988—. Office: Office VP Munhumutapa Bldg, Samora Machel Ave Bag 7700, Harare Zimbabwe*

MUZIKANTE, INTA, physicist; b. Valmiera, Latvia, Jan. 8, 1951; d. Janis and Irena (Spure) M.; m. Egils Fonavs, Jan. 11, 1985. MS, U. Latvia, 1974, Dr. habil. phys., 1998; D of Physics, Inst. Physics Latvia, 1983. Sci. worker Inst. Phys. Energetics, Riga, Latvia, 1982-94; leading sci. worker Inst. Phys. Energetics, Riga, 1994—. Contbr. articles to profl. jours. Grantee Latvian Coun. Sci., 1997—; recipient E. Silinsh's prize of Latvian Acad. of Scis. in Physics, 1999. Mem. Physics Soc. Latvia, N.Y. Acad. of Scis. Avocations: weaving, floriculture, wash-drawing. E-mail: intam@edi.lv. Home: 12-15 Stadiona Str, LV3018 Ozolnieki Jelgava, Latvia Office: Inst Phys Energetics, 21 Aizkraukles Str, LV1006 Riga Latvia

MUZYCHENKO, LEONID A., laboratory director; b. Baku, Azerbaijan, Dec. 22, 1932; s. Aphanasy P. and Olga E. (Kjunda) M.; m. Lucy I. Morugova, Mar. 4, 1960; 1 child, Maxim. Degree in Chem. Engring., Chem. Tech. Inst., Moscow, 1955, Candidate in Tech. Scis., 1962; D in Tech. Scis., Sci. Consul Biotechnology, Moscow, 1982; prof., Chem. and Mech. Inst., Moscow, 1995. Cert. chem. tech. engr., indsl. microbiology sr. rschr. Jr. rschr. Chem. Tech. Inst., Moscow, 1955-62; sr. rschr. Phys. and Chem. Inst., Moscow, 1963-71; head lab. dept. Indsl. Microoramisms Genetic Inst., Moscow, 1971-84; head dept. Biotech. Rsch. Inst., Moscow, 1985-89; head lab. Protein Substances Biosynthesis Rsch. Inst., Moscow, 1990—; chmn. Amicor Ltd., Moscow, 1992-98; sci. dir. PCF Bigor, Moscow, 1999—. Recipient Premium award Coun. Mins. USSR, Moscow, 1990. Mem. Microbial Soc. USSR (dep. head math. modeling sect. 1971-85), Scientists House. Avocation: reading. Office: Gos NIISynthesbelok, B Communisticheskaya St 27, 109004 Moscow Russia

MUZYKA, JENNIFER LOUISE, chemist, educator; b. Fredericksburg, Va., Nov. 9, 1963; d. Kie Muzyka and Jo Anne (Martin) Cepeda; m. Mark Stephan Meier, June 4, 1994; 1 child, Maxwell Stephan Meier. BS in Chemistry, U. Dallas, 1985; PhD in Organic Chemistry, U. Tex., 1990. Asst. prof. Roanoke Coll., Salem, Va., 1990-94; asst. prof. Centre Coll., Danville, Ky., 1994-98, assoc. prof., 1998—; Petroleum Rsch. Fund summer faculty fellow U. Ky., 1992. Contbr. articles to profl. jours. Grantee NSF, 2000, Ky. NSF EPSCOR, 1995, Petroleum Rsch. Fund, 1992; Engrs. Club Dallascholar, 1981-82. Mem. AAUP, Am. Chem. Soc. (chair-elect Lexington sect. 1995-96, chair 1996-97, sec. Va. Blue Ridge sect. 1993-94), Ky. Acad. Sci. (Marcia Athey Rsch. grantee 1995), Coun. Undergrad. Rsch., Iota Sigma Pi (sec. Argentum chpt. 1993-94). Avocations: scuba diving, cross stitch, hiking. Office: Centre Coll Chemistry Dept 600 W Walnut St Danville KY 40422-1309

MWAKAWAGO, DAUDI NGELAUTWA, diplomat; b. 1939. Student, Makerere U., Uganda, Victoria U., Manchester, Eng. Tutor Kivukoni Coll., Dar es Salaam, 1965-72, vice-prin., 1970, prin., 1971, 77; nat. mem. Parliament, 1970-75; min. for info. and broadcasting Govt. of Tanzania, 1972-77; constituent mem. Parliament, 1975; mem. Party of Constitution Com., 1976, Constituent Assembly, 1977; mem. cen. com. Chama cha Mapinduzi, 1977—; min. of info. and culture Govt. of Tanzania, 1982-84, min. of labour and manpower devel., 1984-86, min. of industries and trade, 1986-88; now permanent rep. United Republic Tanzania UN, N.Y.C. Former mem. Income Tax Local Com., Nat. Adv. Coun. on Edn.; past bd. dirs. Inst. of Adult Edn., Nat. Mus.; chair Wildlife Corp., 1979—; vice-chair Co-op. Coll., Moshi. Mem. TIRDO. Office: Permanent Mission of the United Republic of Tanzania to the UN 205 E 42nd St Fl 13 New York NY 10017-5706*

MWAMBA, CHARLES KENNEDY, soil scientist; b. Chinsali, Zambia, Jan. 2, 1949; s. Benson Mwamba and Kafula Estele; m. Drevine Longe, Jan. 1, 1972; children: Evans, Eunice, Aaron, Charity, Patricia. Diploma in forestry, Kitwe, Zambia, 1972; BSc in Forestry, Australian Nat. U., Canberra, Australia, 1980; MSc in Soil Sci., State U. Ghent, Belgium, 1983. Cert. soil physics and chemistry. Forester Forest Rsch., Kitwe, 1972-73; tech. officer Sci. Rsch., Zambia, 1973-79, sci. officer, 1980-83, sr. sci. officer, 1983-92, prin. sci. officer, 1992-96, sec. gen., 1996-98; agr. dir. Sci. Rsch., 1999—; also bd. dirs. Sci. Rsch., Zambia; nat. coord. Internat. Atomic Energy Agy., Zambia, 1996-98; cons. Food and Agrl. Orgn./Internat. Union for Nature Conservation/Commonwealth Sci. Coun., U.K., 1998. Contbr. articles to profl. jours. Recipient Study award Australia Overseas Devel., Canberra, 1975, Study award Belgian Overseas Devel., Brussels, 1981. Mem. Internat. Union for Forestry Rsch. Orgn. (Travel award 1991), Internat. Ctr. for Rsch. in Agroforestry (chmn. 1996-98), Commonwealth Sci. Coun. Mem. Pentecostal Assemblies of God Church. Avocation: football. Office: Nat Inst Sci & Indsl Rsch, PO Box 310158, 15302 Chelston Lusaka, Zambia

MWANGI, EVANS MUNGAI, conservation biologist, consultant; b. Muranga, Kenya, Aug. 30, 1961; s. Daniel Mwangi and Susan (Nyambura) Mwangi; m. Esterline Wanjiru Mungai; children: Andrew, Nyambura. BSc, U. Nairobi, Kenya, 1985, MSc, 1989, PhD in Conservation Biology, 1995. Biologist Dept. Resource Surveys and Remote Sensing, Nairobi, 1988-89; lectr. Jomo Kenyatta U. Agr. and Tech., Nairobi, 1989-97; cons. Kenya Wildlife Svc., Nairobi, 1993-96, scientist, 1997-99; program officer UN Environ. Program, Nairobi, 1999; regional adviser UN Econ. Commn. Africa, Addia Ababa, Ethopia, 1999—; cons. African Devel. Bank, Abidjan, Ivory Coast, 1996-97; trustee Mpala Rsch. Ctr., Nanyuki, Kenya, 1997-99; mem. World Conservation Union-Species Servival Commn. Author: East African Ecosystems and Their Conservation, 1996; contbr. articles to profl. jours., including Bustard Studies, Biodiversity and Conservation, African Jour. Ecology. Recipient ecology award Peregrine Fund, 1992; rsch. fellow Wildlife Conservation Soc., 1991-94. Mem. Nature Kenya. Anglican. Avocations: travel, reading. Home: Econ Comms for Africa, FSSDD/PO Box 3005, Addis Ababa Ethiopia Office: UN Econ Commn Africa, PO Box 3001, Addis Ababa Ethopia

MWANZA, FREDERICK KAMNONGONA, management consultant; b. Petauke, Zambia, Sept. 20, 1936; s. Kamnongona Lufeo and Lozi Margerita (Zulu) M.; m. Stella Kelie Lungu, Oct. 25, 1973; children: Paul, Chinyimbiri, Lozi, Margaret, Mphasa, Nyakwazi, Malili, Ntumpha, Nukwase, Kaya. Co. sectl. asst. Rhodesian Selection Trust Ltd., Zimbabwe and Zambia, 1963-66; asst. acct. Indeco Ltd., Lusaka, Zambia, 1966-67, co. sec., 1968-70; mng. dir. Niec Ltd., Lusaka, Zambia, 1971-74; gen. mgr. UBZ Ltd., Lusaka, Zambia, 1974-75; mgmt. cons. MFK Mgmt. Consultancy Svcs., Lusaka, Zambia, 1975—; bd. dirs., chmn. ZCBC Ltd., Lusaka, 1971-74, Mwaiseni Stores Ltd., Lusaka, 1971-74, Niec Stores Ltd., Lusaka, 1971-74, ZNWM Co., Ltd., Lusaka, 1971-74. Author: Chasins the Winds and Dependency Syndrome on Political Economy; newspaper writer on contemporary social, economic, polit. and religious human conditions. Mem., vice chmn. St. Ignatius Parish Com. of the Cath. Commn. for Justice and Peace in Zambia, Lusaka; mem. United Nat. Independence Party, Lusaka. Mem. Inst. Chartered Secs. and Adminstrs. Roman Catholic. Avocation: reading. Home: 38 Ome lo Mumba Rd Rhodes P, PO Box 31411, Lusaka Zambia Office: MFK Mgmt Consultancy Svcs, Cairo Rd Box 31411, Lusaka Zambia

MWANZA, JACOB M., bank executive. Gov. Bank of Zambia. Office: Bank Zambia, PO Box 30080 Cairo Rd, Lusaka 10101, Zambia*

MWATHA, WANJIRU ELIZABETH, microbiologist, educator; b. Nyeri, Kenya, Jan. 28, 1954; d. James and Damaris Wangechi (Benson) Kiama; children: Ken, James Kiama. BSc, U. Nairobi, Kenya, 1977, MSc, 1981; PhD, Leicester U., U.K., 1992. Rsch. officer Ministry Agr., Nairobi, 1977-78; grad. asst. Kenyatta U., Nairobi, 1980-82, tutorial fellow, 1982-88, lectr., 1988-95, sr. lectr., 1995—; biodiversity cons. Gov. Kenya/Overseas Devel. Assistance/UN Environ. Programme, 1991; coord. Microbial Strain Data Network, U.K. and Kenya, 1995-96; biodiversity cons. UN Environ. Programme/Global Environ. Facility, Kenya, 1996-98. Inventor in field. Mem. Kenya Soc. Microbiology (chmn. 1996-98), Kenya Assn. Women Scientists and Engrs. (com. mem. 1995-98), Nat. Biosafety Com., Cath. Women Assn., Kenya Assn. Univ. Women, East African Natural History Soc. Avocations: squash playing, reading. Home: PO Box 39542, Nairobi Kenya Office: Kenyatta U, PO Box 43844, Nairobi Kenya

MWELWA, JERRY BALDWIN, bank executive; b. Mwense, Zambia, Dec. 14, 1957; s. Kasonde Leonard and Magdalene Ntenda (Chitembo) M.; m. Ruth Kakaya, June 12, 1998; children: Daisy, Felicitus, Theresa, Jerry Jr. MA in Edn., U. Zambia, 1979. Lectr. Canisius Coll., Zambia, 1978-83; internat. banking mgr. ZNCB Ltd., Zambia, 1984-86; trade attache French Embassy, Zambia, 1986-88; dir. Aquarian Impex Ltd., Zambia, 1989—; chmn. Bankers' Union Zambia, 1985-86. Life mem. Internat. Shalom Club; pres. Zambia chpt. Movement for Multiparty Democracy. Roman Catholic. Avocations: reading, swimming, weight lifting, tennis, fishing.

MWENDA, KENNETH KAOMA, legal consultant, educator. LLB, U. Zambia, 1990; Gr.Dip, LCCI, U.K, 1991; DMS, IoC, U.K, 1992; BCL, MPhil, U. Oxford, U.K., 1994, MPhil, 1994; MBA, U. Hull, U.K, 1995; DBA, Pacific Western U., L.A., 1996, PhD in Publs., 1999; PhD, U. Warwick, U.K., 2000, Pacific Western U., L.A., 1999. Cert. Bar, Zambia, 1991; cert. post-cumpolsory edn., devels. in comml. securities, intellectual property law. Worked in trust funds and co-financing dept. Vice-Presidency of World Bank, Washington, 1998-99, worked in poverty reduction, mgmt. and pub. sector reform unit, 1999; worked in adv. unit legal dept. World Bank, Washington, 1999—, counsel in legal dept., 2000—; vis. prof. U. Miskolc Sch. Law, Hungary, 1996; speaker and presenter in field. Author: Legal Aspects of Corporate Capital and Finance, 1999, Contemporary Issues In Corporate Finance and Investment Law, 2000, Contemporary Issues in Banking Supervision and Systemic Bank Restructuring, 2000; contbr. articles to numerous profl. jours. tutor U. Zambia Law Sch., 1991-95. Staff Devel. fellow in law U. Zambia, 1991, U. Yale Law Faculty fellow, 1998; Rhodes scholar U. Zambia, 1992, U. Oxford, 1992-94, U. Hull, 1994-95. Fellow Royal Soc. Arts. of England, Inst. Commerce of England; mem. Internat. Bar Assn., Law Assn. of Zambia, Brit. Assn. Lawyers for Def. of Unborn. Office: The World Bank 1818 H St NW Washington DC 20433-0001

MWENDWA, KYALE, educational services executive; b. Kitui, Kenya, May 23, 1926; s. Mwendwa and Damaris Kathuka (Mumo) M.; m. Susan Nthenya Masila, Aug. 28, 1954; children: Mumo Ikui, Vonza Kavila, Suki Kaloo Kathuka, Nzambu Mulaimu. Diploma in edn., Makerere U., 1948; BA, Rhodes U., South Africa, 1951; MA, Mich. State U., 1961. Edn. officer Ministry of Edn., Kenya, 1952-62, dir. edn., 1963-70; exec. chmn. Riverside Investments, Kenya, 1973—, Muvokanza Ltd., Kenya, 1974—, Acad. Svcs. Ltd., Nairobi, Kenya, 1976—; bd. dirs. Ctrl. Tobacco Distbrs. Ltd., Kenya, Gateway Ins. Co. Ltd., Kenya; deputy chmn. African Med. & Rsch. Found., 1974-99; exec. chmn. Ednl. Svcs. Found., Kenya, 1990—; exec. chmn. Nasela Svcs. Ltd., Kenya, 1993—; chmn. Acad. Profl. Studies, Kenya, 1993—. Contbr. foreword to: New Directions in Teacher Education, 1969; contbr. articles on edn., employment and rural devel. to various publs. Mem. Parliament, Kenya, 1985-92, cabinet min., 1986-88; chmn. Kitui br. Dem. Party Kenya, 1992—. Named Elder, Order of Golden Heart, Govt. of Kenya, 1986. Fellow Kenya Inst. Mgmt.; mem. Am. Mgmt. Assn., Mombasa Club, Outward Bound Trust (chmn.). Avocations: tennis, hunting, walking, reading. Home and Office: Acad Svcs Ltd, PO Box 46274, Nairobi Kenya

MWETHERA, PETER GICHUHI, research scientist; b. Nyeri, Kenya, Apr. 10, 1964; s. Johnstone and Florence Wacu (Githua) M.; m. Mary Mutitu Muriuki, May 25, 1966; children: Lilian Wacu, Barbara Mukami. BSc with honors, Kenyatta U., Nairobi, Kenya, 1989; PhD in Molecular Reprodn., Bristol (Eng.) U., 1995. Asst. rsch. scientist Internat. Ctr. of Insect Physiology and Ecology, Kenya, 1989-90; asst. rsch. scientist Inst. Primate Rsch., Nairobi, 1990-95, sr. rsch. scientist, 1995—; hon. lectr. U. Nairobi, 1995. Author: Male Fertility Regulation, 1993; contbr. articles to profl. jours. Recipient Govt. scholarship Kenya Govt., 1989, PhD scholarship WHO, 1992. Mem. Brit. Fertility Soc. Roman Catholic. Avocations: swimming, soccer, volleyball, boxing. Home: Box 11706, Nairobi Kenya Office: Inst Primate Rsch, Bo 24481, Karen, Nairobi Kenya

MWORIA, STEVE KYARA, information technology executive; b. Moshi, Tanzania, Oct. 7, 1944; s. Teweli Francis and Nkaleni Helena (Mworota) Lobo; m. Christine Steve Massawe, Jan. 11, 1975; children: Teweli Kyara Teweli, Nkaleni, Amani, Manka, Lobo. Grad. Air Traffic Control, Sch. of Aviation, Nairobi, Kenya, 1967. Cert. air traffic contr. Air traffic contr. East African Cmty., Mombasa, Kenya, 1967-70, air traffic contr. approach control, 1970-72; air traffic contr. area control East African Cmty., Nairobi, 1972-75, chief air traffic contrs., 1975-77. V.p. Tanzania C. of C., Industry and Agr., 1993—; mem. World Econ. Forum, 1994—; dir. Parastatal Pension Fund, Tanzania, 1996—, Tanzania-Zambia Railway Authority, 1995—; promoter, dir. Akiba Comml. Bank Ltd., Royal and SunAlliance Ins. (Tanzania) Ltd., 1999—; adv. coun. Internat. Inst. Comm. and Devel.; adv. com. African. Devel. Forum UN Econ. Commn. Africa. Mem. Internat. Fedn. Air Traffic Contrs. Assns. (v.p. 1986-90), Tanzania Air Traffic Contrs. Assn. (patron, chmn. 1982-91). Avocations: golf, reading. Home: Corridor Area PO Box 117, Arusha Tanzania Office: Computer Corp Tanzania, Ohio St PO Box 1583, Dar es Salaam Tanzania

MYERS, ADELE ANNA, artist, educator, nun; b. Bklyn., Oct. 4, 1925; d. Everett Ecil and Anna Maria (Menig) M. Student, U. Notre Dame; BS in Edn., Fordham U., 1956; MA in Fine Arts, Villa Schifanoia, Florence, Italy, 1962; postgrad., NYU, Pratt Graphics Ctr., Columbia U. Cert. permanent tchr. art, grades K-12, N.Y.; joined Sparkill Dominican Sisters, Roman Cath. Ch., 1944. Tchr. art Monsignor Scanlon H.S., Bronx, N.Y., 1956-60, Albertus Magnus H.S., Bardonia, N.Y., 1961-62; founder, dir. Thorpe Intermedia Gallery, Sparkill, N.Y., 1976-91; prof., chairperson art dept. St. Thomas Aquinas Coll., Sparkill, 1962-78, adj. prof., 1978-99; design cons. sr. housing devels. Thorpe Village and Dowling Gardens, Sparkill, N.Y., 1981—; mem. adv. bd. Bogliasco Found., N.Y.C. and Italy, 1997—; free-lance curator contemporary art exhbns., 1986—. Commd. works include cross in fresco and cement St. Peter's Ch., Yonkers, N.Y., 1990, outdoor sidewalk mosaic Thorpe Village, 1997, stained glass windows for meditation rm. Dowling Gardens, 1996; exhibited sculpture in fresco and cement, most recently at ArtBldrs. Gallery, Jersey City, 1994-95, Rockland Ctr. for Arts, 1995, 96, 99, St. John's Chapel Gallery, Newark, 1996, Piermont Flywheel Gallery, N.Y., 1999; one-woman shows include Hopper Ho. Art Ctr., Nyack, 1992, Piermont Flywheel Gallery, 1996, 98, 2000, ArtBldrs. Gallery, 1996, Old Ch. Cultural Ctr. Gallery, Demarest, N.J., 1997; represented in pub. and pvt. collections; works and exhibits reviewed in various publs., including N.Y. Times, Star Ledger, Suburban People, Arts Happenings; featured on cable TV program, N.J., 1988. Apptd. art in pub. places com. Rockland County, 1987-92; founding bd. dirs. Arts Fund Rockland, 1989-91. Post-grad. studies scholar Villa Schifanoia, 1960; Sister Adele Myers Scholarship established in her name St. Thomas Aquinas Coll., 1986; recipient award for Outstanding Contbn. in Field of Art, Rockland County Women's Network, Rockland C.C., Suffern, N.Y., 1980, 1st Ann. Arts award Rockland County Execs., 1987. Mem. Nat. Mus. Women in Arts, Internat. Sculpture Ctr., Christians in Visual Arts. Democrat. Avocations: reading, travel, visiting places of historical interest. Home and Studio: Dominican Convent 175 Route 340 Sparkill NY 10976-1041

MYERS, ALLAN ARTHUR, physician; b. Townsville, Queensland, Australia, Sept. 29, 1937; s. Arthur Mervyn and Marjorie Allan (Strachan) M.; m. Mary Seamark, Sept. 20, 1963; children: Jane Elizabeth, Anne Mary, Sarah Kate Allan; m. Joy Quarrel, Jan. 8, 1977; 1 stepdaughter: Lisa Nicole. MBBS, Adelaide U., 1963. FRACGP, Australia. Resident med. officer Queen Elizabeth Hosp., Adelaide, 1963-64; dist. med. officer Tasmania Health Svc., 1964; 2d yr. resident med. officer Ballarat Base, Victoria, 1965; pvt. gen. practitioner Port Adelaide, Australia, 1966-73; community med. officer Melba Canberra, 1974; family physician Western Region Health Ctr., Footscray, Australia, 1975-76, 78-81; dir. med. officer Risdon Tasmania, 1977; sr. med. officer Victorian Prison Health Svcs./Pentridge Prison, Victoria, 1981-96; pvt. practice Melbourne, 1996—; sessional med. practitioner, Western Gen. Hosp., Footscray, 1977-90; clin. asst. medicine, Queen Victoria Med. Ctr., 1977; assoc. hon. physician Med. Western Gen. Hosp., 1978-81; instr. gen. practice, Monash U., Victoria, 1978-81; clin. asst. med. outpatients, St. Vincent's Hosp., Melbourne, 1982-91. Recipient cert. and medal Dept. Justice, Pentridge Prison, 1992, G.P. Menzor award Royal Coll. Australian Gen. Practitioners, 1996. Mem. Australian Med. Assn., Northwest Med. Assn., Carlton Football Club. Avocations: computers, swimming, football, stamp collecting. E0mail: aamyers@ozemail.com.au. Home: 33 Pegasus Dr, Victoria 3040 Dromedary, Tasmania 7030, Australia Office: Hughes Parade Med Ctr, 147 Hughes Parade, 3073 North Reservoir Australia

MYERS, ANTHONY CHARLES, accountant; b. London, Oct. 30, 1933; s. John Walter and Barbara Catherine M.; m. Marion Elizabeth Little; children: Philippa, Camilla, Christopher. Student, Uppingham Sch., Rutland, Eng., 1947-51. Chartered acct. Articled clk. and sr. Whinney Smith & Whinney, London, 1954-62; supr. and mgr. Ernst & Whinney, Liberia, Hamburg, Chgo., and Zurich, 1962-67; ptnr. Ernst & Whinney (now Ernst & Young), Paris, 1968-75, Ernst & Whinney, Brussels, 1975-85; dir. The Conf. Bd. Europe, Brussels, 1986-96; gen. commr. income tax Dorset, 1997—. Contbr. articles to profl. jours. Br. chmn. The Conservation Assn., Bradford Abbas, U.K., 1997, The Nat. Decorative and Fine Arts Soc., Belgium, 1988-90; br. treas. The Sail Tng. Assn., Belgium, 1987-93, Ambulance Assn., Sherborne, U.K., 1997. Fellow Inst. Chartered Accts. in Eng. and Wales; mem. Hon. Artillery Co., Marylebone Cricket Club. Roman Catholic. Avocations: mountain trekking, skiing, tennis, bridge, politics.

MYERS, BERNARD IAN, merchant banker; b. London, Apr. 2, 1944; s. Edward Nathan and Isobel Violet (Myers) M.; m. Sandra Hannah Barc, Sept. 17, 1967; children: Lara Yvonne, Andrew Leon, Lyndsey Claire. BSc in Econs., London Sch. Econs., 1965. Mgr. Arthur Andersen & Co., London, 1965-72; mng. dir. internat. and group fin. N.M. Rothschild & Sons, Ltd., London, 1972-96, also bd. dirs.; bd. dirs. Rothschilds Continuation Ltd., Rothschild Bank A.G. Fellow Inst. Chartered Accts. in Eng. and Wales. Avocations: opera, golf, theatre. Office: NM Rothschild & Sons Ltd, New Ct St Swithins Ln, London EC4 P4DU, England

MYERS, CAROL MCCLARY, retired sales administrator, editor; b. Dawson, N.Mex.; d. Joseph Franklin and Alberta Lenore (McGarvey) McClary; m. Dwight Andrew Myers, Sept. 16, 1950 (dec. Sept. 1995); children: Robert Andrew, Debra Ann, James Allen. MusB, U. Redlands, 1950. Cert. tchr., Calif. Tchr. music Barstow (Calif.) Pub. Schs., 1950-52; sec., acct. U.S. Army, Columbus, Ga., 1952-54; part-time sec. Robert Lafollette, Atty., Albuquerque, 1954-57; sec., acct. Midland Specialty Co., Albuquerque, 1957-60; pvt. tchr. piano Oakland, N.J., 1960-70; organist, choir dir., ch. sec. Ramapo Valley Bapt., Oakland, N.J., 1965-70; order fulfillment/invoicing U. N.Mex. Press, Albuquerque, 1974-76, sales mgr., 1976-88; ret., 1988. Editor (mag.) Book Talk, 1971-2000; (7 books) In Celebration of the Book: Literary New Mexico, 1982, Literary New Mexico: Essays From Book Talk, 1998. Recipient Edgar Lee Hewett award Hist. Soc. N.Mex., 1985, Paso Por Aquí award Rio Grande Hist. Collections, 1990. Mem. N.Mex. Libr. Assn. (hon. life, treas. 1989-91, bd. dirs. 1992-94), Rocky Mountain Book Pubs. Assn. (Jack D. Rittenhouse award 1994), Mountains and Plains Booksellers Assn. Republican. Avocations: piano playing, New Mexico Book League (vol. editor). Home: 8632 Horacio Pl NE Albuquerque NM 87111-3218

MYERS, EDDIE EARL, clinical psychologist; b. Ardmore, Okla., Nov. 24, 1937; s. Finis Weldon and Fern Durrell (Johnson) M.; m. Ineta June Moore, July 2, 1955 (div. Mar. 1988); children: Richard Weldon, Ronald Leland, Marilyn June, Rebecca Jean; m. Ann Clymer Taylor, July 15, 1988 (div. May 1996); Clark Clymer Taylor, Katy Ann Taylor; m. Katherine Call Emch, Dec. 28, 1996. BSEd, Tex. Christian U., 1958, MEd, U. N. Tex., 1967, EdD, 1969. Lic. psychologist, Ohio; Nat. Drug Edn. Leadership Tng. Adelphi U., 1970. Machinist Chance Vaught Aircraft, Grand Prairie, Tex., 1957-58; 5th grade tchr., jr. high coach Ft. Worth Christian Schs., 1958-59; 6th grade tchr., jr. high coach Corpus Christi (Tex.) Ind. Sch. Dist., 1959-60; youth, music, ednl. min. Norton St. Ch. Christ, Corpus Christi, 1960-61, Procter St. Ch. Christ, Port Arthur, Tex., 1963-65; min. Cameron (Tex.) Ch. Christ, 1961-63; high sch. English tchr. Christian Schs., Inc., Dallas, 1965-66; psychology instr. Tex. Women's U., Denton, 1968-69; sr. rsch. assoc., dir. psychology dept. Ednl. Rsch. Coun. Am., Cleve., 1969-78; clin. psychologist pvt. practice Cleve., 1978—; faculty dept. guidance anc counseling U. Oreg. Workshop, Frankfurt, German, 1972; Ea. U.S. drug abuse task force Am. Soc. Health Assn., N.Y.C., 1971-73; chmn. drug abuse and alcoholism task force Fedn. Cmty. Planning, Cleve., 1970-71; adv. bd. Freedom House Rehab. Ctr., Cleve., 1993—; adj. assoc. prof. ednl. specialists Cleve. State U., 1970-74; mem. med. staff St. John Westshore Hosp., West Lake, Ohio, Fairview Hosp., Cleve. Author: Social Isolation and Personality, 1973, Handy Asks the Psychologist, 1974, (tchr. manual) Human Persons and Use of Psychoactive Agents, 1974; co-author: (tchr. manual) New Model Me: Operator's Guide to Coping with Aggression, 1974; contbr. articles to profl. jours. R & D grantee NIMH, Washington, 1974-78, Nat. Def. Edn. Rsch. Tng. grantee U.S. Dept. Edn., Washington, 1965-69. Mem. APA, Cleve. Psychol. Assn. (bd. trustees 1981-85), Cleve. Acad. Consulting Psychologists (pres. 1984-86), Ohio Psychol. Assn. (bd. trustees 1978—), Phi Delta Kappa. Avocations: computers, golf, jet boating. Office: 3865 Rocky River Dr Ste 2 Cleveland OH 44111-4114

MYERS, ELISSA MATULIS, publisher, association executive; b. Munich, Aug. 4, 1950; (parents Am. citizens); d. Raymond George and Anne Constance (Moley) Matulis; m. John Wake Myers, Sept. 13, 1967 (div. 1972); 1 child, Jennifer Anne Myers Bick. BA in English Lit., George Mason U., 1972, MA in English Lit., 1982. Dir. rsch. and info. Am. Soc. Assn. Execs., Washington, 1972-80, dir. mem. svcs., 1980-88, v.p., pub. Assn. Mgmt. mag., 1988-97; pres., CEO Nat. Informercial Mktg. Assn., Washington, 1997—, Electronic Retailing Assn., Washington, 1998—. Pub. Principles of Association Management, 1976, 3d edit., 1996; columnist Footnotes, 1988-97. Bd. dirs. Ethics Resource Ctr., Washington, 1982-86; mem. Universal Postal Union Adv. Group 2000; mem. Fed. Adv. Commn. on e-commerce. Mem. Am. Soc. Assn. Execs. (cert.), Assn. Conv. Mktg. Execs., Greater Washington Soc. Assn. Execs. (bd. dirs. 2000—), Nat. Assn. Hispanic Mktg. Profls. (adv. bd.), Soc. Nat. Assn. Publs., Com. of 100 U.S. C. of C., Soc. Scholarly Pubs. Roman Catholic. Avocations: running, scuba diving. Home: 5315 Moultrie Rd Springfield VA 22151-1915 Office: Electronic Retailing Assn 2101 Wilson Blvd Arlington VA 22201-3062

MYERS, ELMER, social worker, psychiatrist; b. Blackwell, Ark., Nov. 12, 1926; s. Chester Elmer Myers and Irene (Davenport) Lewis; widowed; children: Elmer Jr., Keith, Kevin. BA, U. Kans., 1951, MA, 1962; student, U. Calif., Santa Barbara, 1977-78. Lic. clin. social worker; C.C. counselor credentials. Psychiat. social worker Hastings (Nebr.) State Hosp., 1960-62, State of Calif. Bur. Social Tng. Com., Sacramento, 1962-75; supr. psychiat. social worker State of Calif., Sacramento, 1975-80, Alta Calif. Regional Ctr., Sacramento, 1980-85; exec. dir. Tri-County Family Services, Yuba City, Calif., 1966-69; cons. to 3 convalescent Hosps., Marysville, Calif., 1969-71; lectr. Yuba Coll., Marysville, 1971-76; assoc. prof. Calif. State U., Chico, 1972-73; cons. in field, Marysville, 1985—; group therapist Depot Homeless Shelter, 1996—, counselor 1995—; cons., therapist New Millennium Group Home, 2000. Juror Yuba County Grand Jury, Marysville, 1965, 87-88; sec. Y's Men's Club, Yuba City, 1964-65; chmn. Tri-County Home Health Agy., Yuba City, 1974-76; vice-chmn. Gateway Projects, Inc., Yuba City, 1974-75; bd. dirs. Christian Assistance Network, 1993, Habitat for Humanity, 1993, Yuba County Truancy Bd., Marysville, 1964-67, Golden Empire Health Sys. Agy., Sacramento, 1972-76, Youth Svcs. Bur., Yuba City, 1967, Bi-County Mental Retardation Planning Bd., Yuba City, 1972, Yuba County Juvenile Justice Commn., Marysville, 1982-90, Am. Cancer Soc., Marysville, 1985-92, Yuba County Rep. Ctrl. Com., 1983-90, Salvation Army, 1990—, facilittor care project, 1992; asst. dir. Marysville Adult Activity Ctr., 1990—; active Yuba-Sutter United Way, 1971-73, 91-92, Tri-County Ethnic Forum, sec., 1991-1993;steering com. Yuba County Sr. Ctr. Assn., 1992, 95—; chmn. Yuba County Cmty. Svcs. Commn., 1997-99, Yuba-Sutter Gleaners, 1997—, Yuba-Sutter Commn. on Aging, 1996, H.E.L.P. Working Group, HIV prevention, 2000. Recipient Cert. Spl. Recognition, Calif. Rehab. Planning Project, 1969, Cert. Spl. Recognition, State of Calif., 1967, Cert. Spl. Recognition, Alta Calif. Regional Ctrs., 1985; named Vol. of Week, Appeal Dem. newspaper, 1999. Mem. Nat. Assn. Social Workers (cert.), Kern County Mental Health Assn. (chmn. 1978-79). Lodge: Rotary (bd. dirs. Marysville club 1975-76). Avocations: fgn. lang. study, gardening, reading, computers. Home and Office: 3920 State Hwy 20 Marysville CA 95901-9003

MYERS, EUGENE EKANDER, art consultant; b. Grand Forks, N.D., May 5, 1914; s. John Q. and Hattye Jane (Ekander) M.; m. Florence Hutchinson Ritchie, Sept. 9, 1974. BS in Edn., U. N.D., 1936, MS in Edn., 1938; postgrad., U. Oreg., 1937; MA, Northwestern U., 1940, Columbia U., 1947; grad., Advanced Mgmt. Program, Harvard U., 1953; cert., Cambridge (Eng.) U., 1958; postgrad., U. Md., 1958-61, Oxford (Eng.) U., 1964; diploma, various mil. schs. Student asst. U. N.D., 1935-36, instr. summer sessions, 1936, 37, asst., 1936-37; prof., head dept. N.D. Tchrs. Coll., 1938-40; instr. Columbia U. Tchrs. Coll., 1940-41; vis. prof. U. Vt., summers, 1941, 42; commd. 1st lt. USAAF, 1942, advanced through grades to col., 1951; dir. personnel plans and tng. Hdqrs. Air Force Systems Command Washington, 1959-60; dir. personnel research and long-range plans Hdqrs. Air Force Systems Command, 1960-62; head dept. internat. relations Air War Coll., Air U. Maxwell AFB, Ala., 1962-63; dir. curriculum, dean (Air War Coll., Air U.), 1963-65; dir. res. affairs Hdqrs. Air Res. Personnel Center Denver, 1965-66; ret., 1966; dean Corcoran Sch. Art, Washington, 1966-70; founder Corcoran Sch. Art Abroad, Leeds, Eng., 1967; v.p. mgmt. Corcoran Gallery Art, Washington, 1970-72; vis. art dir. Washington, also Palm Beach, Fla.; art cons., 1972—; adv. Washington chpt. Nat. Soc. Arts and Letters.; bd. assos. Artists Equity. Author: (with Paul E. Barr) Creative Lettering, 1938, (with others) The Subject Fields in General Education, 1939, Applied Psychology, 1940; contbr. articles, reports to mags. and profl. publs. bd. dirs. Columbia (Md.) Inst. Art, World Arts Found., N.Y., Court Art Center, Montgomery, Ala. and Palm Beach, Fla., Order of Lafayette, Boston, English-Speaking Union, Palm Beach; mem. Hamilton St. Vol. Fire Dept. and Lit. Soc., Balt., Pundits, Palm Beach. Recipient Sioux award U. N.D., 1978. Mem. Internat. Communication Assn. (hon.), U. N.D. Alumni Assn. (pres. Washington chpt. 1959), Mil. Classics Soc., Titanic Soc., Mil. Order Carabao, Order of St. John of Jerusalem, Knightly Assn. St. George the Martyr, Co. Mil. Historians, Mil. Order World Wars, Ancient Order United Workmen, Saint Andrews Soc., Clan Donnachaidh (Perthshire, Scotland), Soc. Friends St. Andrews (Scotland) U., Delta Omicron Epsilon, Lambda Chi Alpha, Delta Phi Delta, Phi Delta Kappa, Phi Alpha Theta. Republican. Presbyterian. Clubs: Union (Manchester, Eng.) (hon.); Royal Scottish Automobile (Glasgow, Scotland); Royal Overseas (London); New (Edinburgh, Scotland) (assoc.); Army and Navy (Washington), Nat. Aviation (Washington), City Tavern (Washington), Harvard Business School (Washington); Army and Navy Country (Arlington, Va.); Metropolitan (N.Y.C.), Wings (N.Y.C.), Explorers (N.Y.C.) (fellow), Harvard (N.Y.C.); Minneapolis; Everglades (Palm Beach, Fla.), Beach (Palm Beach, Fla.), Sailfish of Fla. (Palm Beach, Fla.); Liitle (Gulf Stream, Fla.); Fairmont (W.Va.) Field Country, Lions. Home: 1 Royal Palm Way Palm Beach FL 33480-4213 also: 3320 Volta Pl NW Washington DC 20007-2733 also: 721 Mount Vernon Ave Fairmont WV 26554-2522

MYERS, HAROLD MATHEWS, academic administrator; b. Doylestown, Pa., Apr. 13, 1915; s. Carl and Alice W. Myers; m. Margaret F. Smith, July 19, 1946 (dec. Sept. 1963); children: Donald Smith, Dean Chappell, Deborah Kay; m. L. Marjorie Bellau, Nov. 28, 1964. BS in Commerce, Drexel Inst. Tech., 1938, DSc in Commerce (hon.), 1983; postgrad., Temple U., 1940-41, U. Omaha, summer 1957. Instr. coop. edn., dir. grad. placement Drexel U., Phila., 1938-46, asst. dean men, dir. student bldgs., adj. instr. labor econs., 1946-52, dean of men, 1952-55, treas., 1955-57, v.p., treas., 1957-80, sr. v.p., 1980-82, sr. v.p. emeritus, 1982-87, interim pres., 1987-88, pres. emeritus, 1988—, life trustee, 1986—; regional dir. First Pa. Banking and Trust Co., 1959-76; dir. Sadtler Rsch. Labs., Inc., 1963-69, Almo Indsl. Elecs., Inc., 1966-68; dir., treas. Uni-Coll Corp., 1974-81; bd. dirs. Beulah Cemetary Assn., asst. treas., 1984-89, treas., 1989-90, v.p. and treas., 1980—; bd. dirs., mem. exec. com. Univ. City Sci. Ctr., 1974-90, dir. emeritus, 1991—, chmn. fin. com., 1976-88, vice chmn., 1988-90. Contbr. articles to profl. jours. Bd. dirs. Internat. House of Phila. Inc., 1954-81, exec. com., 1972-81; active Phila. coun. Boy Scouts Am., 1953—, hon. chmn., 1985-97, pres., 1982, 83; mem. citizens fire prevention com. Phila. Fire Dept., 1970-86; bd. dirs. United Fund Greater Phila., 1983-87, Luth. Ch. of Am. Common Investing Fund, 1976-82, NCCJ, Inc., Phila. and S. Jersey region NCCJ, 1959-65; dir. Phila. Coun. of Chs., 1954-61; bd. dirs., pres. Ea. Assn. Coll. and Univ. Bus. Officers, 1971-72; treas. Lambda Chi Alpha Found., 1970-84, dir. emeritus, 1984—; pres. Broadmoor Pines Home Owners Assn., 1993-94; dir. PalmAire Comty. Action Coun., Inc., 1993-95, chmn. security, 1995—. Served to comdr. USNR, ret. Recipient Silver Beaver award Boy Scouts Am., 1963, Mary M. Hart award Phila. coun. Boy Scouts Am., 1986, Drexel Alumni Varsity Club award, 1966, Drexel U. Evening Coll. Alumni Assn. award, 1973, Drexel U. Anthony J. Drexel Paul award, 1988, Dept. of Army Cert. of Appreciation for Patriotic Civilian Svc., 1979, Disting. Bus. Officer award Nat. Assn. Coll. and Bus. Officers, 1989, Disting. Svc. in Trusteeship award Assn. Governing Bd. Univs. and Colls., 1989; named Educator of Yr., Phila. coun. Boy Scouts Am., 1989; named to Legion of Honor, Chapel of Four Chaplins; Drexel U. student dormitory named Myers Hall in his honor, 1984; 1 of 100 alumni honored Centennial of Drexel U., 1992. Mem. AARP, Am. Legion, Mil. Order World Wars (perpetual, comdr. Phila. chpt. 1958-59), Ret. Officers Assn. (life), Swedish Colonial Soc. Phila. (sec. 1968), Welsh Soc. Phila. (life), Internat. Frat. Lambda Chi Alpha (pres. 1966-70), Vet. Corps 1st Regiment Infantry, N.G.P. (hon.), Penn Club, Union League Phila. (pres. 1980-81), Sarasota Yacht Club, Masons, Rotary (Paul Harris fellow), Gulf Coast Corvair Club.

MYERS, HENRY, playwright; b. Slough, Eng., Dec. 4, 1940; s. Edward Isaac and Sophie (Goodrich) M.; m. Lisbet Clasen, 1965; 2 children; m. Lone Davidsen, 1978; 1 child. MA, Cambridge (Eng.) U., 1974; BA in Drama, U. Århus, Denmark, 1989. Office boy, clk. Daily Mirror newspaper, London, 1956-58; agrl. laborer, factory, worker, 1958-66; tchr. high sch., Denmark, 1974-87; playwright, Denmark, 1982—; dir. profl. and non-profl. theatre coprodns., Denmark, 1992—. Author: (stage play) Kiss Me, I'm Jewish, 1984; (radio plays) Sam, 1987 (Best European Radio Script award European Broadcasting Union 1987), Thy Neighbor's Love, 1990 (best European Script award European Broadcasting Union 1990), The Slap (Nat. Children's Theatre Frstival), 2000, other plays for stage, radio and TV; editor, contbr. (anthology) The Jewbird, 1981. Bd. dirs. Hald Cultural Ctr., Denmark, 1987-95. Travel grant Ministry Culture, Denmark, 1992, Study grant, 1995; manuscript grant Nat. Arts Coun., Denmark, 1994, 97. Mem. Assn. Danish Playwrights (bd. dirs. 1993—). Home: Sct Mogensgade 26, 8800 Viborg Denmark

MYERS, JACK ELLIOTT, English educator, poet; b. Lynn, Mass., Nov. 29, 1941; s. Alvin George and Ruth Libby (Cohen) M.; m. Willa Naomi Robins, Aug. 15, 1981 (div. Oct. 1992); children: Jacob, Jessica; children from previous marriage: Benjamin, Seth; m. Thea Temple, Sept. 25, 1993. BA, U. Mass., 1970; MFA, U. Iowa, 1972. Prof. English So. Meth. U., Dallas, 1975—; disting. vis. writer U. Idaho, 1993, Wichita State U., 1994, Old Dominion U., 1998. Author: (poetry) The Family War, 1978, I'm Amazed That You're Still Singing, 1981, As Long As You're Happy, 1985 (Nat. Poetry Series selection), Blindsided, 1993, One On One, 1999, The Glowing River: New and Selected Poems, 2000; editor: A Trout in the Milk: on Richard Hugo; co-editor: A Longman Dictionary of Poetic Terms, 1989, A Profile of 20th-Century American Poetry, 1991, New American Poets of the 90's, 1991. Bd. dirs. The Writer's Garret, Dallas, 1993—. NEA fellow, 1983, 86; recipient award in poetry Tex. Inst. Letters, 1978, 94. Mem. PEN, Assoc. Writing Programs (v.p. 1994, cons. 1995), Writer's Garret (bd. dirs. 1993—). Democrat. Avocation: pocket billiards. Office: So Meth U Dept English Dallas TX 75275-0001

MYERS, KENNETH ARTHUR, vascular surgeon, antique dealer; b. Melbourne, Victoria, Australia, Feb. 14, 1935; s. Robert James and Edith Mabel (Hunt) M.; m. Barbara Anne Dickason; children: Susan, Kim, Andrew, Tracey. MB BS, U. Melbourne, 1957, MS, 1967. Surg. fellow St. Mary's Hosp., 1964-65, U. Ill., 1966; surgeon Royal Melbourne Hosp., 1966-71, Prince Henry's Hosp., 1971-91; head dept. vasc. surgery Monash Med. Ctr., 1991-98; vasc. surgeon Epworth Hosp., 1980—; mem. bd. mgmt. Prince Henry's Hosp., 1984-89, dean clin. sch., 1987-89. Author: Principles of Pathology in Surgical Practice, 1990, Lower Limb Ischaemia, 1997. Fellow Royal Australian Coll. Surgeons, ACS; mem. Internat. Soc. Cardiovasc. Surgery, European Soc. Vasc. Surgery. Avocation: antiques. Office: 173 Lennox St, Richmond Melbourne VIC 3121, Australia

MYERS, KENNETH L(EROY), secondary education educator; b. Auburn, Nebr., Oct. 5, 1954; s. Kenneth E. and Erma F. (Hardwick) M.; m. Willo Kay Dykstra, July 1, 1995; children: Kendra, Kayla. BS in Edn., Peru State Coll., 1985, mid. sch. endorsement, 1990, MS in Edn., 1992. Cert. tchr., Nebr., Mo., Iowa. Tchr. math., coach Nodaway-Holt High Sch., Graham, Mo., 1985-87, Nebraska City (Nebr.) Lourdes High Sch., 1987-89; tchr. math., social studies, coach Newcastle (Nebr.) High Sch., 1989-97; tchr. math., coach Schaller/Crestland H.S., Early, Iowa, 1997—; chair Newcastle Math. Curriculum Team, 1991-97; master tchr. N.E. Nebr. Masters Tchrs. Project, 1991-97; past mem. N.E. Nebr. Math. Cadre. Mem. Iowa Coaches Assn., Newcastle Faculty Orgn. (pres. 1992-95). Office: Schaller Crestland HS Early IA 50535

MYERS, KIMBERLY ANN, mathematics educator; b. Glasgow, Ky., Aug. 16, 1962; d. Edward Botts and Betty Jo Myers. BA in Math., Western Ky. U., 1984, MS in Math., 1987; PhD in Curriculum and Instrn., U. Cin., 1998. Tchr., coach Warren County Pub. Schs., Bowling Green, Ky., 1984-88; programmer, analyst for market rsch. Fruit of the Loom, Bowling Green, 1988-89; instr. math. Western Ky. U., Bowling Green, 1989-91, Wright State U., Dayton, Ohio, 1991-92; assoc. prof. math., dept. head U. Cin., 1992—; faculty senator U. Cin., 1996-98; conf. co-chair Ohio Coun. Tchrs. Math., Cin., 1996; invited panelist Greater Cin. Software Assn., 1999, Ohio Info. Tech. Task Force, Columbus, 1999; presenter in field. Editor: Putting Theory into Practice: Studies in Curriculum and Instruction, 1997. Tech. prep compentency profile com. Greater Cin. Tech. Prep Consortium, 1995-96. Mem. Am. Math. Assn. Two-Yr. Colls. (cons. for traveling tech. workshops 1992—), Ohio Coun. Tchrs. Math. (conf. co-chair 1996). Avocations: boating, spending time with friends. E-mail: kim.myers@uc.edu. Fax: 513-556-4878. Office: Univ Cin 2220 Victory Pkwy Cincinnati OH 45206-2822

MYERS, LIBBY ANN, retired nurse; b. Hutchinson, Kans., July 22, 1936; d. Edwin Eugene and Verna Maxine (Craig) Schroëder; m. William Wayne Osborne, Apr. 1950 (div. 1960); m. William Andrew Myers III, June 21, 1962; children: Linda Kay, Lloyd Lee, Diana Gaye, Joe Lyle, Delbert Matthew. MSN, Okla. Bapt. U., 1958. RN, Okla. Nurse Bapt. Meml. Hosp., Oklahoma City, 1967-70, Doctors Gen. Hosp., Oklahoma City, 1970-73, Mercy Hosp., Oklahoma City, 1973-79; nurse, team leader PICU Hutchinson (Kans.) Hosp., 1979-87; pvt. practice pvt. duty nurse Oklahoma City, 1987-93; ret., 1993; owner, operator Day Care Facility, Oklahoma City, 1977-79. Precinct poll inspector Precinct 238 Oklahoma City Election Bd., 1988-96, precinct com. chair Precinct 238 Oklahoma City Rep., 1992-96; exec. com. Oklahoma County Rep. Hdqrs., Oklahoma City, 1994-96; pres., former block capt. Epworth Neighborhood Assn., Oklahoma City, 1991-96; counselor Homicide Survivors Support Group, Oklahoma City, 1991-96, lobbyist for victims bills, 1992-96; Sunday sch. tchr., Bible sch. tchr. Crestwood Bapt. Ch., Oklahoma City; rescue worker during Oklahoma City bombing aftermath, also mem. survivor notifcation team, 1st Christian Ch., and victim advocate, Save Haven, Oklahoma City, during trials; candidate for Okla. Ho. of Reps., Dist. 88, 1998. Mem. Tri-City Rep. Women, Bapt. Women. Avocations: reading, poetry writing, watching ball games, cooking, crafts.

MYERS, MARY A., public relations executive, consultant; b. Waukesha, Wis., July 28, 1936; d. Willard R. and Ruth Hardaker Evans; m. Ralph Payton Myers, June 14, 1958 (dec. Sept. 1969); children: Marsha Ruth, Evan Scott. BS, Northwe. U., 1957; MBA, De Paul U., 1984. Mng. editor Pioneer Press, Wilmette, Ill., 1969-73; dep. bus. editor Chgo. Sun-Times, 1973-84; v.p. Hill & Knowlton, Chgo., 1984-86; dep. bus. editor The Washington Post, 1986-88; sr. v.p. Hill & Knowlton, 1988-92; dir. Burson-Marsteller, Chgo., 1992-96, mng. dir., chair Midwest corp. practice, 1996—. Mem. Soc. Profl. Journalists, Chgo. Headline Club, Exec. Club Chgo., Univ. Club. Presbyterian. Office: Burson-Marsteller 233 N Michigan Ave Chicago IL 60601-5519

MYERS, NORMAN LEWIS, fund development consultant; b. Xenia, Ohio, Oct. 21, 1932; s. Norman Theodore and Effie Marie (DeLawder) M.; m. Sue Anne Hanlon, Nov. 7, 1953; children: John Norman, Jeffrey Alan, Joseph Brian. Stuent, U.S. Armed Forces Inst., 1956. Chief dep. clk. Ohio Supreme Ct., Columbus, 1957-66; divsn. dir. United Way, Columbus, 1966-69; sr. assoc. dir. Children's Hosp. Found., Columbus, 1970-94; cons. Arnold Palmer Children's Hosp., Orlando, Fla., 1995, Orland Amateur Athletic Assn., Orlando, 1996. Author: The Buck Starts Here, 1999. Bd. dirs. various ch. and civic assns.; trustee Children's Miracle Network, 1983-85. Served with USN and USNR, 1952-76, comdg. Naval Res. unit, Zanesville, Ohio. Recipient Best Total Devel. award Nat. Assn. for Hosp. Devel., 1977; Norman L. Myers Staff award for support of devel. of volunteerism named in his honor, 1994. Fellow Assn. Healthcare Philanthropy (Harold J. Seymour honors award 1991); mem. Univ. Club (Winter Park, Fla.) (2d vice chair 1998—), Sigma Phi Epsilon (hon.). Methodist. Avocations: golf, genealogy. Home: 1500 Gay Rd Apt 20B Winter Park FL 32789-2962

MYERS, RICHARD KELLEY, family physician; b. Decatur, Ga., Dec. 26, 1968; s. Charles Hugh Myers and Judy Thomas. AA, Gainesville Coll., 1989; BS, U. Ga., 1993; MD in Microbiology and Psychology, Med. Coll. Ga., 1997. House officer Self Meml. Hosp., Greenwood, S.C., 1997-98; emergency rm. physician Abbeyville (S.C.) Hosp., 1998—; family physician Montgomery Ctr. for Family Medicine, Greenwood, 1998—; physician Nat. Health Care Nursing Home, Greenwood, 1997—. Scholar Ty Cobb Ednl. Found., 1993-97, Dan Printup Meml. Trust, 1993-97, Sch. Med., 1993-94, Gainesville Coll. Found. Mem. AMA, Am. Acad. Family Physicians, Gideons Internat., Phi Beta Kappa, Phi Kappa Phi, Alpha Epsilon Delta, Beta Beta Beta, Psi Chi, Golden Key Honor Soc. Address: 112 Robusta Ct Harlingen TX 78552-6634

MYERS, ROBERT EUGENE, writer, educator; b. Los Angeles, CA, Jan. 15, 1924; s. Harold Eugene and Margaret (Anawalt) M.; m. Joyce E. Daily, 1946 (div. 1949); 1 child, Kathleen; m. Patricia A. Tazer, Aug. 17, 1956; children: Edward E., Margaret A., Hal R., Karen I. AB, U. Calif., Berkeley, 1955; MA (Crown-Zellerbach fellow), Reed Coll., 1960; EdD, U. Ga., 1968. Employed in phonograph record bus., 1946-54; tchr. elem. sch. Calif., Oreg., Minn., 1954-61; rsch. asst. U. Minn., 1961-62; asst. prof. Augsburg Coll., 1962-63, U. Oreg., 1963-66; elem. tchr. Eugene, Oreg., 1966-67; assoc. prof. U. Victoria, 1968-70; assoc. rsch. prof. Oreg. System of Higher Edn., 1970-73; film maker, producer ednl. filmstrips, books, recs., 1973-77; learning resources specialist Oreg. Dept. Edn., Salem, 1977-81; with Linn-Benton Edn. Svc. Dist., Albany, Oreg., 1982-87; ret., 1987. Author: (with E. Paul Torrance) Creative Learning and Teaching (Pi Lambda Theta award 1971), 1970, La Ensenanza Creativa, 1970, Can You Imagine?, 1965, Invitations to Thinking and Doing, 1964, Invitations to Speaking and Writing Creatively, 1965, Plots, Puzzles, and Ploys, 1966, For Those Who Wonder, 1966, Timberwood Tales, Vol. II, 1977, Wondering, 1984, Imagining, 1985, What Next?, 1994, Facing the Issues, 1995, Cognitive Connections, 1996, Mind Sparklers, 1997, Multiple Ways of Thinking with Social Studies, 1997, Character Matters, 1999, A Matter of Respect, 2000, It's Your Attitude That Counts, 2000; films: Feather (CINE Golden Eagle award), 1972, The Magic Net, 1972, Elephants, 1973. Mem. exec. bd. Nat. Assn. Gifted Children, 1974-77. With U.S. Mcht. Marine, 1944-45. Recipient CINE Golden Eagle award Coun. Internat. Non-theatrical Events, 1973. Mem. Internat. Reading Assn. Democrat. Home: 1357 Meadow Ct Healdsburg CA 95448-3347

MYERS, ROBERT GEAROLD, developmental test executive, flight test engineer; b. Santa Fe, Mar. 12, 1935; s. Franklin Gearold and Nadine Cathrine (Torrey) M.; children: Paul Wayne, Laura Ellen; m. Sherry Kay Myers, Jan. 31, 1998. BSME, N.Mex. State U., 1958; MBA, Golden Gate U., 1972. Engrng. officer Air Force Res., 1959-86; engrng. mgr. Boeing Devel. Projects, Seattle, 1958-84; B-1B sys. engrng. mgr., base mgr. Boeing Mojave Test Ctr., Edwards AFB, Calif., 1984-88, base mgr., 1989-91; v.p. B2 Flight Test and Test Labs. Mil. Aircraft Sys. divsn. Northrop Grumman, Edwards AFB, Calif., 1991-98; ret. Northrop Grumman, Century City, Calif., 1999. Recipient Tech. Laureatte Aviation Week and Space Tech., 1997. Fellow ASME; mem. AIAA (sr.). Avocations: softball, skiing, backpacking, hunting. Home: PO Box 1659 Tehachapi CA 93581-1659

MYERS, RODMAN NATHANIEL, lawyer; b. Detroit, Oct. 27, 1920; s. Isaac Rodman and Fredericka (Hirschman) M.; m. Jeanette Polisei, Mar. 19, 1957 (dec. 1996); children: Jennifer Sue, Rodman Jay. BA, Wayne State U., 1941; LLB, U. Mich., 1943. Bar: Mich. 1943, U.S. Supreme Ct. 1962. Agt. IRS, Detroit, 1943; from assoc. to ptnr. Butzel, Keidan, Simon, Myers & Graham, Detroit, 1943-90; of counsel Honigman Miller Schwartz and Cohn, Detroit, 1991—. Bd. dirs. United Cmty. Svcs. of Met. Detroit, 1978-85, v.p., 1981-85, chmn. social svcs. divsn., 1982-85; bd. dirs. Children's Ctr. of Wayne County (Mich.), 1963—, pres., 1969-72; mem. blue ribbon task force Mich. Dept. Edn., 1988-89; founding mem., trustee Detroit Sci. Ctr.; trustee Mich. chpt. Leukemia Soc. Am., founding pres., 1984-86, nat. trustee, 1984—; commr. Detroit Mcpl. Parking Authority, 1963-71; trustee Temple Beth El, Bloomfield Hills, Mich., Bloomfield Twp. Pub. Libr. Mem. ABA, State Bar Mich. (chmn. atty. discipline panel, past vice chmn. unauthorized practice of law com., past mem. character and fitness com.). Home: 3833 Lakeland Ln Bloomfield Hills MI 48302-1328 Office: 2290 1st National Bldg Detroit MI 48226

MYERS, SIDNEY ALBERT, lawyer; b. London, May 21, 1958; s. Gordon David and Leonora Isabelle (Wilson) M.; m. Lorraine Rosine Viner, Apr. 2, 1995; children: Rosine Alex, Samuel Edward. BA with honors, Worcester Coll., Oxford, Eng., 1980. Articled clk. Allen & Overy, London, 1982-84, asst. solicitor, 1984-90, ptnr., 1991-94; ptnr. Allen & Overy, Hong Kong, 1994-96, London, 1996—. Mem. Law Soc., Marylebone Cricket Club. Jewish. Avocations: cricket, golf. Office: Allen & Overy, One New Change, London EC4M 9QQ, England

MYERS, WILLIAM OSGOOD, thoracic and cardiovascular surgeon; b. Hastings, Nebr., Aug. 19, 1929; s. Joy Uberto and Lena C. (Osgood) M.; m. Lois Mae Payne, Dec. 26, 1952; children: Jessica, Wendell, Inez, John, Michael. BA, Hastings Coll., 1951; MD, Northwestern U., 1955. Diplomate Am. Bd. Surgery, Am. Bd. Thoracic Surgery. Intern City Detroit Receiving Hosp., 1955-56, resident in anesthesiology, 1956-57; gen. practice medicine Blue Hill, Nebr., 1959-62; surg. resident Sacred Heart Hosp., Yankton, S.D., 1962-65; instr. anatomy U. S.D. Med. Sch., Vermillion, S.D., 1963-65; resident in gen. surgery U. Kans. Med. Ctr., Kansas City, 1965-66, resident in thoracic and cardiovascular surgery, 1966-68; cardiovascular surgeon Marshfield Clinic, Marshfield, Wis.; and St. Joseph's Hosp., Marshfield, 1968—, chmn. sect. thoracic and cardiovascular surgery, 1972-76, chmn. dept. surgery, 1974-79; clin. assoc. prof. surgery U. Wis., 1996—; prin. investigator Coronary Artery Surgery Study, Nat. Heart, Lung and Blood Inst., 1973—; bd. dirs. Marshfield Med. Found., 1978-84. Contbr. articles to profl. jours. Chmn. rsch. com. Marshfield Med. Found., 1985-2000; mem. coun. Wis. Surg. Soc. Coun., pres. 1993, Wis. Chpt. ACS, 1986-89; coun. on Cardiovascular Surgery AHA. Served with USAF, 1957-59. Mem. Wis., Wood County Med. Socs., AMA, Wis. Surg. Soc., ACS (credentials com. 1988—), Wis. Heart Assn. (bd. dirs.), Am. Coll. Cardiology, Am. Thoracic Soc., Am. Assn. Thoracic Surgery, Frederick A. Coller Surg. Soc. (pres. 1998-99), Ctrl. Surg. Assn., Western Surg. Assn. Home: 1110 N Balsam Ave Marshfield WI 54449-1361 Office: 1000 N Oak Ave Marshfield WI 54449-5703

MYERSON, KEITH ROGER, anesthesia and intensive care medicine consultant; b. Eng., Feb. 1, 1950. MB, ChB, U. Liverpool, Eng., 1973. Registrar U. Southampton, Wessex, Eng., 1979-81; sr. register S.W. Regional Health Authority, Eng., 1981-86, Flinders Med. Ctr., South Australia, Australia, 1982-83; cons. Eastbourne (Eng.) Hosps. Nat. Health Svc. Trust, 1987—; dep. regional advisor, South Thames, Eng., 1988—, regional assessment coord., 1996—. Fellow Royal Coll. Anesthesiologists (examiner final fellowship 1997—).

MYGIND, JESPER, physicist, educator; b. Copenhagen, Mar. 21, 1942; s. Troels and Gunvor Mygind; m. Annette Holtoft, Aug. 17, 1968; children: Thomas, Jacob. MSc in Elec. Engring., Tech. U. Denmark, Copenhagen, 1966; PhD in Physics, Tech. U. Denmark, Lyngby, 1972. Mem. Danish Def. Rsch. Coun., 1966-68; asst. prof. physics lab. Tech. U. Denmark, Lyngby, 1970-72, assoc. prof., 1972-86, 89-90; prof. Tech. U. Denmark, 1990—; rsch. staff Danish Inst. Fundamental Metrology, 1986-89; tech. assessor Dansk Akkrediterings Ordning; mem. steering bd. MIDIT, Ctr. for Nonlinear Studies. Contbr. over 60 articles to profl. jours.; referee Phys. Rev. Letters, Phys. Rev., Jour. Applied Physics, Applied Physics Letters, Physica Scripta, IEEE Transaction Instrumentation Measurement, IEEE Transactions Microwave Theory Tech., Chem. Engring. Sci., Superconductor Sci. and Tech., Jour. Phys. Conductor Material, Physica D. Mem. Danish Acad. Natural Scis., Danish Inst. for Fundamental Metrology (cons.). Office: Tech Univ Denmark Dept Physics, Anker Engelundsvej 1, DK-2800 Lyngby Denmark

MYHAND, WANDA RESHEL, paralegal, legal assistant; b. Detroit, Aug. 15, 1963; d. Ralph and Geraldine (Leavell) M. Office mgr./adminstrv. asst. Gregory Terrell & Co., CPA, Detroit, 1987-90; legal sec. Ford Motor Co., Detroit, 1990-91; office mgr. M.G. Christian Builders, Inc., Detroit, 1991; paralegal, legal asst. Law Office of Karri Mitchell, Detroit, 1991-98; legal sec., paralegal The KPM Group, Southfield, Mich., 1998—. Vol. UNCF Telethon Detroit, 1988. Mem. NAFE. Avocations: crossword puzzles, travel, theatre and concerts.

MYHRE, HANS OLAV, vascular surgeon, educator; b. Grimstad, Norway, Oct. 19, 1939; s. Olav and Ella (Hansen) M.; m. Else Marie Johnsen, June 29, 1963; children: Anne, Olav, Christine. MD, U. Oslo, 1964, PhD, 1975, specialist degree in gen. surgery, 1974, specialist degree in thoracic surgery, 1982, specialist degree in vascular surgery, 1986. Intern Aust-Agder Gen. Hosp., Arendal, Norway, 1964-65; resident in gen., vascular surgery, cons. vascular surgery Aker Hosp. U. Oslo, 1967-76, head dept. vascular surgery, 1977-81; fellow in cardiovascular surgery Baylor Coll. Medicine, Houston, 1978-79; prof., chief dept. surgery U. Hosp. Trondheim, Norway, 1982-92; med. dir. U. Hosp. Trondheim, 1992-93, dir. surgery, 1993-96, 98—. Author: Ultrasound in the Examination of the Peripheral Circulation, 1979 (HM King Olav V Gold medal for rsch. 1979), (poetry) Preparations for a Journey, 1996; co-author: (with A. Kroese) Atherosclerosis, Cardiac and Vascular Diseases, 1982, Scandinavian texbbook on vascular surgery, 1997; contbr. over 200 articles to profl. jours. Capt. Norwegian Army, 1966-85. Recipient Best Sci. Work award European Soc. Vascular Surgery, 1989, Acrel medal for sci. work Swedish Surg. Soc., 1991, award for best sci. work Norwegian Surg. Soc. Vascular Surgery Sect., 1988, 92, 96. Mem. European Soc. Vascular Surgery (pres. 1987-88), Scandinavian Surg. Soc. (chmn. sect. vascular surgery 1987-90), Norwegian Soc. Thoracic and Vascular Surgery (v.p. 1981-84), Michael E. DeBakey Internat. Surg. Soc., Union European Med. Specialists (Norwegian rep., bd. dirs. vascular surgery divsn.). Lutheran. Avocations: painting, poetry, fishing, cross-country running, music. Home: Valkendorfs gt 21, 7030 Trondheim Norway Office: Dept Surgery, U Hosp Trondheim, 7006 Trondheim Norway

MYKHALEVYCH, VOLODYMYR MARKUSOVYCH, mathematics educator, researcher; b. Yinnytsia, Ukraine, Apr. 11, 1953; s. Marquss Lyovich Ziydler and Maja Averkievna Mykhalevych; m. Tetyana Vadimovna Kyrylenko, June 20, 1989; 1 child, Oleksiy. Grad. in mech. engring., Machine Bldg. Faculty, Vinnytsia, 1975; postgrad., Ctrl. Inst. Tech. Mech. Eng., Moscow, 1980-83; Candidate Sci., Tech. Inst., Moscow, 1986; DSc, Inst. for Problems of Strength, Kiev, Ukraine, 1996. Jr. instr. Vinnytsia State Tech. U., 1976-80, lectr. math., 1986-96, prof., 1996-98, mng. prof., 1998—. Author: Tensor Models of Damage Accumulation, 1998; contbr. articles to sci. jours. Rsch. fellow Ctrl. Inst. on Tech. of Mech. Engring., Volgodonsk, Russia, 1983-86. Mem. Nat. Com. Ukraine on Theoretical and Applied Mechanics, N.Y. Acad. Scis. Achievements include mode forgings of bar and pressing; research in field of mechanics of deformable solids. Avocation: computers. Home: 15/9 Kwyateka St, 286029 Vinnytsia Ukraine

MYKLEBUST, EGIL, chemical executive; b. Uskedal Kvinnherad, Norway, June 9, 1942; s. Einar and Else M.; m. Anne Helene Kvikne; 2 children. Degree, Real Artium, Bergen, 1961; JD, Oslo U., 1967. Cons. Nat. Ins. Adminstrn., Oslo, 1967-71; various positions Norsk Hydro, Oslo, 1971; dir. gen. Norwegian Employers' Orgn., 1987, Naeringslivets Hovedorganisasjon, Oslo, 1989-91; pres., CEO Norsk Hydro. Office: Norsk Hydro A/S, Bygdoy Alle 2, N-0240 Oslo 2, Norway*

MYLER, COLIN, editor. Editor Sunday Mirror, Canary Wharf, England. Office: Sunday Mirror, 1 Canada Sq, Canary Wharf E14 5AP, England*

MYLER, STEPHEN FRANCIS, psychologist, consultant; b. Leicester, Eng., May 3, 1955; s. Patrick and Anastasia (Coleman) M.; m. Margaret

Louise Sutton, June 14, 1975 (div. Feb. 1986); children: Kerry Sara, Josie Claire; m. Judith Ann Bishop, June 14, 1986. MSc in Psychology, Knightsbridge U., Copenhagen, 1994, PhD in Psychology, 1995; BSc in Psychology with honours, Open U., Milton Keynes, Eng., 1997; diploma in therapeutic counseling, Internat. Corr. Schs., Eng., 1998. Lic. in consumer credit, in data protection. Ptnr. Myler Fin. Planning, Leicester, Eng., 1984-92; exec. dir. The Baron Health Group Plc, Leicester, 1984-94; lectr. Grantham (Eng.) Coll., 1994-95; sr. lectr. New Parks C.C., Leicester, 1994—; head tng. IPC Tng. Partnership, Leicester, 1996—; cons. psychologist Myler Psychometric Testing Co., Leicester, 1995-99; dir. studies Brooke House Internat. Coll., Leicester, 1999—; dir. M&S Contrs. Ltd., Leicester, 1984-93, St. Stephen's Nursing Home Ltd., Derby, Eng., 1990-93, Blockmerit Ltd., 1990-93, Coolteam Ltd. T/A The Leicester Stress Clinic, Gravure Products Ltd.; br. mgr., ptnr. Myler Fin. Planning (Fimbra), Can. Life Assurance Co. (Lautro), Am. Life Assurance Co. (Lautro), Allied Dunbar Plc (Lautro); part-time lectr. South Fields Coll.; lectr. in field; personal tutor. Editor The Braunstone Life, 1982-86. Local candidate Liberal Dems., Markfield, Leicester, 1987, supporter, 1989—. With Coldstream Guards, 1971-73. Fellow Inst. Dirs., Inst. Ins. Cons.; mem. East Midlands Assn. for Psychotherapy and Counseling, Assn. Stress Cons., Brit. Psychol. Soc., Inst. Employment Cons., Leicester Jr. Chamber (past pres.), Life Ins. Assn. (assoc.), Leicester Bus. Club (life v.p., past chmn.). Mem. Liberal Dem. Party, Buddhist. Avocations: reading, volunteer for homeless. Fax: 44 1858 462487. E-mail: drmyler@myler.fsnet.co.uk. Home: care JA Bishop, PO Box 494, Leicester LE5 5ZW, England Office: Brooke House, Leicester Rd Mkt Harborough, Leicester LE16 7AU, England

MYLES, LYNDA ROBBIE, film producer; b. Arbroath, Angus, Scotland, May 2, 1947; d. Alexander Watt and Kathleen Kilgour (Polson) M.; m. David Will, Dec. 6, 1972 (div. 1978). MA in Mental Philosophy with honors, U. Edinburgh, Scotland, 1970. Dir. Edinburgh Internat. Film Festival, 1973-80, Pacific Film Archive, Berkeley, Calif., 1980-82; film cons. Channel Four, London, 1982-83; prodr. Enigma Films, London, 1983-85; sr. v.p. Columbia Pictures, London, 1986-88; commissioning editor for drama BBC, London, 1988-91; ind. film prodr., 1991—; bd. dirs. ACE, Paris, 1995—; co-exec. dir. East-West Prodrs.' Seminar, London, 1990-95; cons. European Script Fund, London, 1993-96. Co-author: The Movie Brats, 1979; prodr. feature films: Defence of the Realm, 1986, (with others) The Commitments, 1990 (Best Film Bafta awards), The Snapper, 1993 (Premio Goya award Banff Festival), The Van, 1995, When Brendan Met Trudy, 1999. Bd. dirs. Roundhouse Trust, London, 1998—. Recipient award for svcs. Brit. Film Inst., 1982. Mem. Am. Acad. Motion Picture Scis., European Film Acad., Groucho Club. Avocations: opera, visual arts. Office: Pandora Prodns Ltd, 48 Dean St, London W1V 5HL, England

MYLES, TRAVIS OLEN, JR., lawyer; b. Louisville, July 28, 1972; s. Travis Olen Myles Sr. and Linda Kay Mahaffey; m. Kimberly McIver, June 11, 1994. AA, U. Louisville, 1993, BA, 1994; JD, Brandeis U., 1998. Bar: Ky. 1998. Paralegal Lorch & Naville, Attys., New Albany, Ind., 1991-93, Chi-Chi's, Inc., Louisville, 1993-94, Sidney Hanish, P.S.C., Louisville, 1994-98; ptnr. Hanish & Myles, Attys., Louisville, 1998—. Mem. ABA, Ky. Bar Assn., Louisville Bar Assn. (section chair 1999, 00), Am. Trial Lawyer's Assn., Ky. Acad. Trial Lawyers, Nat. Org. Social Security Claimant's Reps. Republican. Baptist. Avocations: poetry, aspiring novelist. E-mail: tkmyles@worldnet.att.net. Home: 102 Alvina Way Louisville KY 40214-3702 Office: Hanish & Myles Attys 835 W Jefferson St Ste 200 Louisville KY 40202-2639

MYLLYKANGAS-LUOSUJARVI, RIITTA ANNELI, rheumatologist; b. Kuopio, Finland, Aug. 23, 1951; d. Luja Ludvig and Anna-Liisa (Tuppurainen) Miettinen; m. Juha Tapio Myllykangas, Aug. 12, 1972 (div. May 1997); m. Tuomo Tapio Lousujärvi, Aug. 4, 1990; children: Tiia Maaria, Kimmo Tapio, Päivi Anneli. MD, U. Oulu, Finland, 1976; diploma in rheumatology, U. Tampere, Finland, 1995. Asst. physician Oulu U. Hosp., 1976-78, Mikkeli (Finland) Ctrl. Hosp., 1979-80, Lahti (Finland) Ctrl. Hosp., 1984-85; gen. practitioner Kangasniem (Finland) Hosp., 1978-79, 80-81, Asikkala Hosp., Vääksy, Finland, 1981-84; cons. rheumagolotist Rheumatism Found. Hosp., Heinola, Finland, 1986-95; rheumagolotist Kuopio (Finland) U. Hosp., 1995—; cons. musculoskeletal ultrasound examiner Rheumatism Found. Hosp., 1986-95; tchr. med. sch. cons. musculoskeletal ultrasound examiner Kuopio U. Hosp., 1995—; cons. rheumatologist Kuopio U. Hosp., 1995—. Contbr. numerous articles, abstracts to profl. jours. Mem. Finnish Med. Assn., Musculoskeletal Ultrasound Soc., N.Y. Acad. Scis. Avocations: reading, music, theater, concerts. Home: Kauppakatu 3A8, 70100 Kuopio Finland Office: Kuopio U Hosp, PO Box 1777, 70211 Kuopio Finland

MYLLYLÄ, VILHO VALDEMAR, neurologist, educator; b. Oulu, Finland, Sept. 5, 1943; s. Juho Ilmari and Johanna Valpuri (Kuurola) M.; m. Raili Mirja Heleena Allila, Jan. 6, 1968; children: Mikko, Markus. MD, U. Oulu, 1971, PhD, 1976. Lic. physician, Finland. Acting resident Oulu Univ. Hosp., 1968-72, resident in neurology, 1973, lectr. neurology, 1974-77, acting assoc. prof. neurology, 1977-81, assoc. prof., 1981-97, prof., 1998—, acting prof., head neurology dept., 1987-91; vis. scientist Thomas Jefferson U., Phila., 1990; active participant 56 internat. congresses; nat. examiner in neurology U. Oulu, 1987-89, dean med. faculty, 1997—, mem. faculty of council, 1994—, mem. senate, 1997—; permanent expert in neurology, mem. adv. bd. Nat. Bd. Health, 1988-92, Ministry of Social Affairs and Health, Nat. Rsch. and Devel. Ctr. for Welfare and Health, 1992—, Nat. Bd. Medicolegal Affairs, 1992—, Nat. Agy. for Medicines, 1993—. Contbr. over 100 articles to profl. jours.; adv. bd. Cephalalgia, Internat. Jour. Headache, 1981-90, editl. bd., 1990-94. Mng. bd. Finnish Neurology Found., 1982-89, 92—. 2d lt. Finnish Army, 1963-64. Mem. Finnish Neurol. Assn. (exec. com. 1978-86, 88-90, dep. pres. 1980-82, pres. 1982-84), Finnish Med. Assn. (exec. com. 1985-87), Scandinavian Migraine Soc. (sec. 1981-83), World Fedn. Neurology (rsch. group intensive mgmt. in neurology). Avocations: travel, reading, skiing, slalom, tennis. E-mail: vilho.myllyla@oulu.fi. Office: Univ of Oulu Dept Neurology, Kajaanintie 50, 90220 Oulu Finland

MYLLYNEN, OLLI-PEKKA, lawyer, Finnish government official; b. Oulu, Finland, Dec. 15, 1962; s. Pertti Olavi and Arja Marjatta Myllynen; m. Leena Riittaliisa Kylliainen, July 25, 1992; children: Matti, Helena, Emma. LLM, U. Helsinki, 1995. Bar: Finland 1995. Radio editor Radio City, Helsinki, 1986-90, YLE, Helsinki, 1990; producing editor Yleisradio, Helsinki, 1990-91; legal counsel APM-tieto Oy, Helsinki, 1995-96; sec. gen. Supervisory Commn. for Mktg. Medicinal Products, Helsinki, 1996—; mgr. legal affairs Pharma Industry Finland, Helsinki, 1996—; dep. judge Market Ct. Finland, 1998—; country coord. for Estonia, Latvia and Lithuania, European Fedn. Pharm. Industries and Assns. European Union Enlargement Priority Action Team, Brussels, 1998—; spkr. IBC Conf. on European Union Data Protection Directive, 1999; editor radio talk show series. Mem. Finnish Confedn. Industries and Employers (Intellectual Property legal group). Avocations: family life, yachting, history. Fax: 358 9 5842 4728. E-mail: olli.myllynen@pif.fi. Office: Pharma Industry Finland, Somaisten Rantatie, POB 108, 00501 Helsinki Finland

MYLLYNIEMI, SEPPO JUHANI, historian; b. Nakkila, Finland, Oct. 25, 1937; s. Kalle and Anna Maria (Salokangas) M.; m. Irja Eeva-Tuulikki Nummi, June 13, 1965; 1 child, Elina. MA, U. Helsinki, Finland, 1964, PhD, 1973. Archivist Provincial Archives, Hämeenlinna, Finland, 1964-73, dir., 1973-2000, ret., 2000; docent gen. history U. Tampere, Finland, 1974—. Author: The New Order in the Baltic Countries 1941-1944, 1973, The Baltic Crisis 1938-1941, 1979, Finland in War 1939-1945, 1982; contbr. articles to profl. jours. Mem. Finnish Hist. Soc., Baltische Hist. Commn. E-mail: s.myllyniemi@mail.htk.fi. Office: Provincial Archives of Hämeenlinna, Arvi Kariston katu 2A, 13100 Hämeenlinna Finland

MYLONAS, THEODOROS P., bank officer; b. Athens, Greece, Nov. 19, 1947; s. Pavlos and Helen (Antoniou) M.; m. Nikoletta Ioakim, June 23, 1982. BA in Polit. Sci., U. Athens, 1973, BA in Pub. Adminstrn., 1982. With P. Mylonas & Co., Athens, 1961-63; messenger Am. Express Bank, Athens, 1963-65, deposit clk., 1965-67, loan clk., 1969-70; asst. head deposits dept. Am. Express Bank, 1970-72, asst. head loans dept., 1972-74, head loans dept., 1974-78, asst. br. mgr., 1978-79, corp. account officer, 1979-81, br. mgr., sr. corp. account officer, 1981-91, mgr. retail banking, br. adminstr., 1992; mgr. network Piraeus Bank SA, Athens, 1992-95, dep. gen. mgr., 1995-98, gen. mgr., 1998—. Served with Greek mil., 1967-69. Scholar State Found., 1972, Ministry of Labor, 1972. Club: Marine (Piraeus). Home: 5 Irodotou Str, 16674 Glyfada Greece Office: Piraeus Bank SA, 5 Souri St 20 Amalias Ave, Athens 10557, Greece

MYNARSKI, STEFAN A., economics educator, researcher; b. Stara Wies, Poland, Dec. 1, 1935; s. Jan and Maria (Foksinski) M.; m. Helena Gasior, Nov. 4, 1935; 1 child, Beata. Master, Cracow (Poland) Acad. Econs., 1960; PhD, Cracow Acad. Econs., 1966; Habilitation, Wroclaw (Poland) Acad. Econs., 1971. Asst. Cracow Acad. Econs., 1960-61, sr. asst., 1961-66, asst. prof., 1966-74, head dept., 1964-84, V-dir. inst., 1984-86, dir. inst., 1986-88, pro-rector, 1988-90, head chair, 1988—; vis. scholar U. Calif., Berkeley, 1968, U. Pa., Phila., 1969, Northwestern U., Chgo., 1969; pres. bd. doctoral studies Cracow Acad. Econs., 1994—, pres. bd. libr. coun., 1996—. Author: Cybernetic Aspects of Market Analysis, 1973, Market Analysis, 1973, Elements of System Theory and Cybernetics, 1979, Modelling of Market in System Approach, 1979, Methods of Marketing Research, 1990, Market Research in Competitive Conditions, 1992; co-author: Marketing research, Methods and Computer Programming, 1992. Mem. Commn. of Trade, Cracow, 1976-80, Com. of Sci. Rsch., Warsaw, 1995—, Ctrl. Commn. Sci. Degrees, Warsaw, 1995—. Recipient Sci. award Ministry Edn., Warsaw, 1993, 96. Mem. European Soc. Opinion and Mktg. Rsch., Polish Acad. Scis. (econ. commn. 1976—, mgmt. commn. 1977—, sec. editl. com. 1980-88, O. Lange award 1976), Polish Cybernetic Soc. (mgmt. coun. 1976—). Roman Catholic. Avocations: swimming, rowing, philately. Office: Cracow Acad Econs, Rakovicka 27, 30-510 Cracow Poland

MYNICK, HARRY ELLIOT, physicist; b. Phila., Aug. 9, 1950; s. David D. and Virginia (Haskins) M.; m. Alison Anne Wholey, May 30, 1979; children: Daniel E., Anna R. BS, Yale U., 1972; MS, U. Calif., Berkeley, 1974, PhD, 1978. Tchg. and rsch. asst. U. Calif., Berkeley, 1972-78; asst. scientist U. Wis., Madison, 1981-83; postdoctoral rsch. assoc. plasma physics lab. Princeton (N.J.) U., 1979-81, rsch. physicist II plasma physics lab., 1983-86, rsch. physicist plasma physics lab., 1986-92, rsch. physicist Ctr. for Energy and Environ. Studies, 1990-91, prin. rsch. physicist plasma physics lab., 1992—; tchr., thesis supr. plasma physics lab. Princeton U., 1987—, energy and environ. tech. assessment, 1990-91; mem. fusion chart com. Contemporary Physics Edn. Project, Pitts., 1994-95. Contbr. physics rsch. papers to Physics of Fluids, Nuclear Fusion, Phys. Rev. Letters, Plasma Physics,; energy and environ. papers to Nature, Sci. and Global Security. Mem. Princeton Cmty. Dem. Orgn., 1983—. Hewlett fellow Princeton U., 1990-91. Fellow Am. Phys. Soc. Avocations: languages, travel, artificial intelligence, water sports, history. Office: Princeton U Theory Divsn Plasma Physics Lab Princeton NJ 08543

MYO-KHIN, physician, researcher; b. Rangoon, Myanmar, Mar. 12, 1953; s. Kyi-Khin and Nyunt-Nyunt-Tin; m. Khin-May-Oo, Nov. 18, 1979; children: Thurein-Myo-Khin, Khine-Sandar-Myo-Khin, Eindra-Myo-Khin. MBBS, Inst. of Medicine 2, Rangoon, 1976; DCH, Inst. of Medicine 1, Rangoon, 1986; MD, U. New South Wales, Sydney, Australia, 1998. Rsch. officer Dept. Med. Rsch., Rangoon, 1981-90, sr. rsch. officer, 1990-92, rsch. scientist, head, 1992-98, dep. dir., head, 1998—. Office: Dept Med Rsch/Div Exper Med, 5 Ziwaka Rd, Rangoon 11191, Myanmar

MYRBERG, ARTHUR AUGUST, JR., marine biological sciences educator; b. Chicago Heights, Ill., June 28, 1933; s. Arthur August and Helen Katherine (Stelle) M.; divorced; children—Arthur August III, Beverly Priscilla. A.B., Ripon Coll., 1954; M.S., U. Ill., 1958; Ph.D. (NIH fellow), UCLA, 1961. Research asst. Ill. Natural History Survey, Champaign-Urbana, 1957; mem. faculty U. Miami, Fla., 1964—; assoc. prof. Sch. Marine and Atmospheric Sci., 1967-72, prof., 1972—; chmn. div. marine biology and fisheries U. Miami, Fla., 1991, academic chmn. div. marine biology and fisheries, 1991-93. Contbr. articles to profl. jours., chpts. to books; assoc. editor Bull. Marine Sci, 1964-73. Mem. Khoury League, 1967-75. Served to 1st lt., inf. U.S. Army, 1954-57. Recipient Disting. Alumni award Ripon Coll., 1991; NIH postdoctoral fellow Max Planck Inst. Behavioral Physiology, Seewiesen, Germany, 1961-64. Fellow Animal Behavior Soc. (Disting. Fellow Lecture award 1993), Am. Inst. Fishery Rsch. Biologists; mem. Am. Soc. Ichthyologists and Herpetologists, Am. Soc. Zoologists, Ecol. Soc. Am., Am. Inst. Biol. Scis., N.Y. Acad. Scis., Internat. Assn. Fish Ethologists, Am. Elasmobranch Soc. (gov. 1985-90), Sigma Xi (nat. lectr. 1980-81), Phi Sigma, Omicron Delta Kappa. Achievements include demonstration of the importance of sound production and hearing for survival and reproduction in fishes, that sharks are attracted to and repelled by specific types of underwater sound; reported on the social behavior of sharks and bony fishes. Home: 6001 SW 65th Ave Miami FL 33143-2031

MYRICK, BISMARCK, diplomat; b. Portsmouth, Va., Dec. 23, 1940; children: Bismarck, Jr., Wesley Todd, Allison Elizabeth. BA, U. Tampa, 1972; MA, Syracuse U., 1973, postgrad., 1979-80. Enlisted U.S. Army, 1959; desk officer for Somalia, U.S. Dept. State, Washington, 1980-82; advanced through grades to maj., 1975, ret., 1979; polit. officer Am. Embassy, Monrovia, Liberia, 1982-84; action officer office strategic nuclear policy bur. politico-milit. affairs U.S. Dept. State, 1985-87, dep. dir. policy plans and coordination bur. inter-Am. affairs, 1987-89, Una Chapman Cox fellow US-African Policy, 1988-90; consul gen. Am. Consulate Gen., Durban, South Africa, 1990-93, Capetown, South Africa, 1993-95; amb. to Lesotho, Am. Embassy, Maseru, 1995-98; diplomat-in-residence Atlanta U. Ctr. at Spelman Coll., 1998-99; U.S. amb. to Liberia Dept. of State, Monrovia, Liberia, 1999—. Author: Three Aspects of Crisis in Colonial Kenya, 1975. Decorated Silver Star, Purple Heart, 4 Bronze Stars; inducted into U.S. Army Hall of Fame, 1996; named Ambassador Bismarck Myrick Days, City of Portsmouth, Va., 2000. Address: Dept State Monrovia Washington DC 20521

MYRSTAD, TROND, chemical engineer; b. Hamar, Norway, Apr. 30, 1961; s. Ivar and Tea Johanne M.; m. Hege Malin Engan; 1 child, Håkon. MS, U. Trondheim, Norway, 1984. Engr. Statoil, Stavanger, Norway, 1985-90; sr. engr. Statoil, Trondheim, Norway, 1990-93; staff engr. Statoil, Trondheim, 1994—. Contbr. articles to profl. jours.; patantee in field. Office: Statoil, Postuttak, 7005 Trondheim Norway

MYRUP, BJARNE, internist; b. Randers, Denmark, Nov. 20, 1957; s. Robert and Else (Lassen) M.; m. Britt Lind Pedersen, Aug. 234, 1997; children: Line, Peter, Kristine. MD, U. Copenhagen, 1986. Registrar Frederiksberg Hosp., Denmark, 1986-92; rsch. fellow Steno Diabetes Ctr., Gentofte, Denmark, 1992-94; registrar Rigshospitalet, Copenhagen, 1994-96; sr. registrar Holbek Centralsygehüs, Denmark, 1996-98, Bispebjerg Hosp., Copenhagen, 1998—. Home: Matthaeusgade 12A 1TV, DK1666 Copenhagen Denmark Office: Bispebjerg Hosp, Bispebjerg Bakke, DK-2400 Copenhagen Denmark

MYSHLAYEV, LEONID PAVLOVICH, research administrator; b. Ayaguz, Russia, Jan. 5, 1948; s. Pavel Vasilyevich and Valentina Vasilyevna Myshlayeva; m. Nina Stepanovna Myshlayeva; 1 child, Julia Leonidovna. Student, Siberian Inst. Metallurgy, Novokuznetsk, 1967-72, Candidate's degree, 1972-75; Doctorate, Moscow Inst. Steel & Alloys, 1991. Cert. automation prodn. and rsch. engr. Head of complex automation lab. State Cen. Inst., Novokuznetsk, 1976-86; rschr. Siberian Inst. Metallurgy, Novokuznetsk, 1975-76, prin. lectr., 1986-90, prof. dept. automation of prodn. and rsch., 1990-96; asst. dir. Novokuznetsk Inst. br. State U. Kemerovo, 1997—; sci. sec. br. Russian Engring. Acad., Kuzbass, 1993-95; v.p. Kuzbass Sci. Ctr., Acad. Engring. Russian Fedn., 1993-97; advisor CASM devel. West-Siberian Steel Combine, 1995-96; mem. thesis coun. SibGIU, Novokuznetsk, 1983-99; mem. sci. coun. State U. Kemerovo, 1997-98; mgr. Soros Grant for Novokuznetsk, Univ. Internet nets, 1999. Author: (book) Production and Research Systems with Multivariant Structure, 1992, Methods of the Material Masses Calculation, 1994; contbr. numerous papers to profl. jours.; patentee in field; dep. editor-in-chief Math. and Econ. Models digest, 1996-99. Recipient USSR Coun. Mins. Prize laureate in field of sci. and engring., 1981, 89; named honored inventor of Russian Fedn., 1989. Mem. Acad. Engring. Sci. Russian Fedn., Russian Acad. Natural Scis. (corr. mem.), N.Y. Acad. Scis. Avocation: aquatic touring. Home: 5-45 Frankfurt St, Novokuznetsk 654080, Russia Office: 23 Tsiolkovsky St, Novokuznetsk 654041, Russia

MYSLINSKI, NORBERT RAYMOND, medical educator; b. Buffalo, Apr. 14, 1947; s. Bernard and Amelia Joan (Lesniak) M.; m. Patricia Ann Byrne, June 19, 1970 (dec. 1980); m. René Carter, Nov. 21, 1993; children: Matthew Ryan, Kelly Lynn. BS in Biology, Canisius Coll., Buffalo, 1965-69; PhD in Pharmacology, U. Ill., Chgo., 1973. Rsch. assoc. Tufts U., Boston, 1973-75; asst. prof. U. Md., Balt., 1975-80; assoc. prof. physiology U. Md., 1980—, co-dir. Facial Pain Clinic, 1980-84, instr. nursing, 1982-84; rsch. fellow U. Bristol, Eng., 1984-85; adj. assoc. prof. U. Md. Sch. Nursing, 1997—; instr. C.C. Balt., 1980-82; dir. grad. program dept. physiology U. Md., 1981-97; founder, dir. Patricia Byrne Nursing Scholarship Fund Trocaire Coll., Buffalo, 19805; dir. NIH Minority Rsch. Apprentice Program Balt. Coll. Dental Surgery, 19885; faculty Marine-Estuarine Environ. Scis. grad program U. Md., 1988-97; grant rev. com. Nat. Inst. Nursing Rsch., 1993-94; grant reviewer Dept. of Health and Human Svcs., 1993-94; cons. in field; appeared in more than 20 live TV and radio programs. Editor newsletters Med. Soc. Med. Rsch., 1977-82, Brain Storm, 19995; author book chpts., revs. and numerous abstracts on pharmacology and neurosci.; inventor in field; reviewer 7 jours. Rep. task force on aging U. Md., 1979-84; instr. Am. Heart Assn., Balt., 19785, ARC, Balt., 1977-83; eucharistic min., pastoral visitor Cath. Ch., 1983-93; dir. Brain Awareness Week, 19965; founder, bd. dirs. Nat. Brain Bee, 19985. Capt. U.S. Army 1969-77. Grantee NIH, various drug cos. and founds.; USPHS fellow, 1969-73; recipient Alumni of Yr. award St. Mary's H.S., Lancaster, N.Y., 1996, Disting. Alumni award for outstanding career Canisius Coll., Buffalo, 1997, Time to Care Cmty. Svc. award U. Md., 1998, Founders Day Pub. Svc. award U. Md., 2000. Mem. European Brain and Behavior Soc. (hon.), Internat. Brain Rsch. Orgn., Md. Soc. Med. Rsch. (exec. com., bd. dirs. 1978-86), Internat. Assn. Dental Rsch. (advisor 1980-81), Am. Physiol. Soc., Soc. for Neurosci. (pres. Balt. chpt. 1990-92, editor newsletter 1990-97), Am. Soc. Pharmacology and Exptl. Therapeutics, Soc. for Neurosci. (neurosci. literacy com. 19975). Republican. Fax: (410) 706-0193. E-mail: nrm001@dental.umaryland.edu. Home: 9395 Carrie Way Ellicott City MD 21042-1701 Office: U Md OCBS Dept 666 W Baltimore St Baltimore MD 21201-1510

MYSOREKAR, VISWANATH RAMRAO, anatomist, educator, researcher; b. Mysore, Karnataka, India, Dec. 13, 1931; s. Mysore Sreenivasrao Venkataramarao and Mysore Ramalakshamma; m. Sharada Viswanath, Jan. 18, 1961; children: Sudha, Vijaya, Mohan. BSc with honors, Sir Parashurambhau Coll., Pune, India, 1949; MB, BChir, Byramjee Jeejeebhoy Med. Coll., Pune, India, 1954, MSc, 1962, PhD in Anatomy, 1972. Med. diplomate. Lectr. in anatomy Byramjee Jeejeebhoy Med. Coll., Pune, 1956-62, asst. prof., 1962-71; prof., head Miraj (India) Med. Coll., 1971-73, Armed Forces Med. Coll., Pune, 1973-87, M.S. Ramaiah Med. Coll., Bangalore, India, 1988-95, Krishnadevaraya Coll. Dental Scis., Bangalore, 1995-97; prof. Sri Devaraj Urs Med. Coll., Karnataka, India, 1997-98; fellow WHO, Newcastle-Upon-Tyne, Eng., 1967-68. Contbr. 57 articles to profl. jours. Recipient Commendation medal Chief of Army Staff, New Delhi, 1981, Dr. B.C. Roy Nat. award Med. Coun. India, New Delhi, 1983. Avocations: sports, music. Home: 55-55A AECS Layout, 60 Feet Rd Corner RMV Ext, Bangalore 560 094, India

NA, MAN-GYUN, nuclear engineering educator; b. Seocheon, Chungnam, Korea, Feb. 17, 1963; s. Chong-Yoon Na and Soon-Yeh Seo; m. Byung-Sun Lee, Apr. 15, 1990; children: Yoon-Ho, Yeh-Seul. BS, Seoul Nat. U., 1986; MS, Korea Advanced Inst. Sci/Tech., Taejon, 1988, PhD, 1992. Instr. nuclear engring. Chosun U., Kwangju, Korea, 1992-94, asst. prof., 1994-98, assoc. prof., 1998—, dept. head, 1993-94; vis. scholar U. Tenn., Knxoville, 1996-97. Contbr. articles to sci. jours., including Nuclear Sci. and Engring., IEEE Transactions on Nuclear Sci., Annals Nuclear Energy, Jour. Korean Nuclear Soc., others; mem. editl. bd. Jour. Korean Nuc. Soc., 1997—. Mem. Korean Nuclear Soc., Korean Soc. Mech. Engrs., N.Y. Acad. Scis., Am. Nuclear Soc. Avocations: tennis, golf. Office: Chosun U Dept Nuclear Engr, 375 Seosuk-dong, Dong-gu, Kwangju 501-759, Republic of Korea

NA, SUCK-JOO, mechanical engineer, educator; b. Naju, Republic of Korea, Jan. 10, 1952; s. Seung-Oen and Aeng-Rim (Yoon) Na; m. Il-Hee Suh, Feb. 16, 1979; children: Byoung-Joon, Byoung-Kuk. BSc, Seoul Nat. U., Republic of Korea, 1975; MSc, Korea Advanced Inst. Sci. Tech., Taejon, 1977; D of Engring., Tech. U., Braunschweig, Germany, 1983. Asst. Korean Advanced Inst. Sci. and Tech., Taejon, 1977-78, prof., 1983—; rschr. Tech. U., Braunschweig, 1978-83; vis. prof. Tech. U., Braunschweig, 1989-90, U. Wollongong, Australia, 1997-98; tech. advisor Choongwon Machinery Co., Seoul, 1990-92; com. mem. KOPEC, Seoul, 1993-96; adv. mem. City of Seoul, 1994—; chmn. mech. engring. subcom. Korea-Germany coop. KOSEF, Taejon, 1995-97. Contbr. articles to profl. jours. Rsch. fellow Alexander von Humboldt Stiftung, 1988, Internat. rsch. fellow DEETYA, Australia, 1997. Mem. Korean Welding Soc. (editor 1991-98, dir. gen. affairs 1999—), Am. Welding Soc., Deutscher Verband fuer Schweissen und verwandte Verfahren. Avocations: tennis, swimming, golf, gardening. Office: Dept Mech Engring KAIST, Kusong dong 373-1 Yusonggu, Taejon Republic of Korea

NA, TSUNG SHUN (TERRY NA), Chinese studies educator, writer; b. Beijing, Nov. 3, 1932; came to U.S., 1964; s. Chi-L and Hui (Hu) N.; m. Yen Yen Chao, 1964. BA, Taiwan Normal U., 1956; MA, U. B.C., 1970; PhD, U. Minn., 1978. Assoc. prof. Taipei Normal Coll., Taiwan, Republic of China, 1956-64; vis. lectr. Ind. U., Bloomington, 1964-66; asst. prof. U. Minn., Mpls., 1970-80; vis. prof. Sun Yat-sen U., Taiwan, 1981-84; prof., dir. Am. Inst. Chinese Studies, Charles Town, W.Va., 1985—. Author: (English books) A Linguistic Study of P'i-pa Chi, 1969, Studies on Dream of the Red Chamber: A Selected and Classified Bibliography, 1979, Supplement, 1981, Taiwan Studies on Dream of the Red Chamber: A Selected and Classified Bibliography, 1983, Chinese Studies in English: A Selected Bibliography, 1991, (Chinese) Mandarin Pronunciation, 1966, Teaching Chinese in the U.S.A., 1983, Studies on Chinese Classical Novels, 1985, A Collection of Short Stories, 1987; contbr. numerous articles, short stories, and research essays to jours. and newspapers in U.S., Taiwan, ROC, and China. Mem. MLA, Assn. Asian Studies. Office: Am Inst Chinese Studies PO Box 453 Charles Town WV 25414-0453

NAAMAN, NAJI, publisher, poet, writer prose; b. Harissa, Kesrouan, Lebanon, May 19, 1954; s. Mitri and Angélique (Bacha) N.; m. Fadia El-Hawa, July 19, 1981; children: Hanane, Marwan, Rayyan. Lic. in law, Lebanese U., Beirut, 1979; lic. in comml. scis., U.S.E.K., Lebanon, 1979, lic. in history, 1979; DEA in History, U. Nantes, France, 1980. Dir. Al Manchourat Al-Arabiyya, Beirut, 1978-79; prof. econs. and mgmt. Beirut, 1978-85; owner Dar Naaman Lith-Thaqafa, Jounieh, Lebanon, 1979—, Galerie d'Art Naaman, Jounieh, 1987—, Naaman Translation Office, Jounieh, 1991—, Naaman Biographical Ctr., Jounieh, 1997—; founder Markaz At-Tarbiya At-Tiqaniyya, Ajaltoun, Lebanon, 1987. Editor: Politics and Strategy, 1981—, The Arab World (in English), 1985—, Press and Information, 1987, 2000 Prominent Arabs of the 20th Century (in English), 1999, World of Arabs (in English), 2000; editor, prin. author: Ency. of Contemporary Arab World, 1983—, Informative and Biographical Directory of the Arab World, 1985, 90, Arab Press Directory, 1988, Ethnic and Confessional Groups of the Arab World, 1990, One Hundred Arab Figures in a Century, 1993, The Arab World at the Threshold of the 21st Century, 1993, One Hundred Arab Events in a Century, 1996, the Independence of the Arab World, 1996, Encyclopedia of Arab Events, 2000; contbr. articles to profl. jours.; translator various publs. from French to Arabic; founder free book series: Ath Thaqafa bil Majjan min Dar Naaman lith Thaqafa, 1991—; author, pub. Khamson wa 'Ishrun, 1979, Anti wal Watan, 1980, Ar-Rasa'il, 1995, 96, Al Mun'atiq, 1997, Al-Mundamij, 1999, Az-Ziqra, 1999, Adabiyyatul Alfith Thani, 1999, Al-Halim, 2000. Founder Humanitarian Movement, 1971, Universal Unity of Man, 1976. Mem. Lebanese Pubs. Assn. Avocations: painting, films, music, swimming, sports. Home: New Shaileh, Main St, Kesrouan Lebanon Office: Dar Naaman Lith Thaqafa, PO Box 567, Jounieh Kesrouan, Lebanon

NAAR, HARRY I., fine arts educator, artist; b. New Brunswick, N.J., July 28, 1946; s. Isidore B. and Dorothy Naar; m. Barbara Jean Naar, June 25, 1972; children: Devin, Aaron. BFA, Phila. Coll. Art, 1968; MFA, Ind. U., 1970; pvt. study, Jean Helion, Paris, 1970-71. Tchg. assoc. Ind. U., Bloomington, 1968-70; instr. Middlesex County Coll., Edison, N.J., 1972-77, Beaver Coll., Glenside, Pa., 1975-78, Moore Coll. Art, Phila., 1978, Rutgers U., Newark, 1979-80; instr. fine arts Rider Coll., Lawrenceville, N.J., 1980-

93, assoc. prof., 1993, prof., 1993—; tchr. Gill-St. Bernard's Upper Sch., Gladstone, N.J., 1972-74, Princeton (N.J.) Art Assn., 1974-76, Art Ctr. No. N.J., Tenafly, 1975-76, Princeton Adult Sch., 1976, Somerset Art Assn., Bernardsville, N.J., 1977-78; vis. artist, instr. Phila. Coll. Art, 1978, 84; juror numerous shows, latest being Ellarslie Open XVII, Trenton (N.J.) City Mus., 1999; guest lectr. Westminster Coll., New Wilmington, Pa., 1976; mem. symposium panel Montgomery Coll., Rockville, Md., 1983; lectr. Kean Coll., Newark, 1988, Western Carolina U., Cullowhee, N.C., 1989, Somerset Art Assn., Far Hills, N.J., Rider U., 1998, Trenton (N.J.) City Mus., 1999, also others; vis. artist-juror Princeton Regional H.S., 1991. Numerous one-man shows, 1968—, including N.J. State Mus., Trenton, 1977, Princeton Gallery Fine Art, 1979, Rider Coll., 1980, 93, Western Carolina U., 1989, NIH Clin. Ctr. Galleries, Bethesda, Md., 1992, Rowan Coll., Glasboro, N.J., 1994, Gallery South Orange, N.J., 1995, Les Malaut Art Gallery, Union, N.J., 1999; 2-man show Rider U., 1997; exhibited in numerous group exhbns., 1967—, including Indpls. Mus. Art, 1970, Corcoran Gallery Art, 1970, N.J. State Mus., Trenton, 1974, 75, 79, Rider Coll., 1974, 99, Hunterdon Art Ctr., Clinton, N.J., 1977, 86, 87, 90, Barbara Glaberson Gallery, New Brunswick, N.J., 1981, More Gallery, Phila., 1982, Carimor Galleries, N.Y.C., 1984, David Adamson Gallery, Washington, 1984, Bergen (N.J.) Mus. Art and Sci., 1987, Boca Raton Mus. Art, 1987, Princeton Gallery Fine Arts, 1988, Western Carolina U., 1989, USSR Artists Union Gallery, Moscow, 1990, Trenton City Mus., 1991, 92, Scanticon, Princeton, 1992, 93, 95, Hardcastle Gallery, Wilmington, Del., 1997, Coll. of N.J., Trenton, 2000; represented in permanent collections Ind. U., Morris Mus. Art and Scis., Morristown, N.J. State Mus., Jane Voorhees Zimmerli Art Mus., Rutgers U., New Brunswick, also corp. collections; work reviewed in numerous articles and interviews and represented in catalogs. Recipient Dorothy Malloy Meml. award for painting Trenton City Mus., 1992; fellow Ind. U., 1968-69; rsch. grantee Rider Coll., summers 1982, 88, grantee TAWA-Soviet Exch. Program summer 1990. Mem. Printmaking Coun. N.J. (bd. dirs. 1984-86), Assoc. Artists N.J. Home: 4 Tracey Dr Lawrenceville NJ 08648-1543 Office: Rider Coll Fine Arts Dept Lawrenceville NJ 08648

NAARALA, JONNE TAPIO, cell biologist, educator; b. Oulainen, Finland, Mar. 6, 1968; s. Tapio I. and Leena M. (Mämmelä) N. BS, U. Jyväskylä, Finland, 1991, MS, 1993, PhD, 1997. Vis. trainee Mitsubishi Kasei Inst. Life Sci., Japan, 1989; rschr. U. Kuopio, Finland, 1992; rsch. asst. Nat. Pub. Health Inst., Kuopio, Finland, 1992, rschr., 1992-94; scientist Acad. of Finland, 1994—; vis. scientist U. Munich, 1997-98; asst. prof. U. Kuopio, 1998—. Editor: The Cell Biologist (In Finnish), 1995—. Mem. Finnish Soc. for Cell Biology (councillor 1992—, v.p. 1998-99), Finnish Soc. Toxicology, Soc. for Neurosci. (fgn. mem.), Oxygen Soc. Avocations: kayaking, martial arts, cycling. Home: Satamakatu 7 A2, FIN70100 Kuopio Finland Office: U Kuopio Dept Environ Sci, PO Box 1627, FIN70211 Kuopio Finland

NAASANI, IMAD, pharmacist, medical researcher; b. Damascus, Syria, Oct. 19, 1965; s. Abdulkader Naasani and Fatima Hamwee. BSc, Damascus U., 1988, diploma pharm. tech., 1990, Master's degree, 1993, PhD, 1996. Cert. cmty. pharmacist. Pharmacy mgr. Cmty. Pharmacy, Damascus, 1988-90; postdoctoral fellow Cancer Chemotherapy Ctr., Tokyo, 1996-98; rsch. scientist Tokyo U., 1998—; R&D cons. Adamco Pharms., Damascus, 1996-97. Contbr. articles to profl. jours.; patentee in field. Mem. Am. Assn. for Cancer Rsch. (assoc. mem., Young Investigator award 1998), Japanese Cancer Rsch. Assn., Syrian Pharm. Assn. Muslim. Avocations: sports, aviation, touring. Home: Kassa George Khouri Sq, Damascus Syria Office: Cancer Chemotherapy Ctr, Kami-Ikebukuro, 170-8455 Tokyo Japan

NABAE, TOSHINAGA, surgeon; b. Fukuoka, Japan, Dec. 19, 1966; s. Ichizo and Masumi N.; m. Kinuko, Dec. 19, 1997; 1 child, Kazutoshi. Grad., Kyushu U., Fukuoka, Japan, 1992. Fellow Kyushu U., Faculty Medicine, Fukuoka, Japan, 1992—. Office: Kyushu U Faculty Medicine, Maidoshi 3-1-1, Fukuoka 812-8582, Japan

NABER, DIETER HELMUT, psychiatrist; b. Oldenburg, Germany, Sept. 9, 1947; s. Helmut and Inge (Andreae) N.; m. Monika Bullinger, Apr. 7, 1983; children: Jan, Nora, Adam. MD, U. Bonn, 1976. Physician Psychiatric State Hosp., Bonn, Germany, 1975-76, Munich, Germany, 1977-78, 80-83; rschr. NIH, Bethesda, Md., 1978-80, NIMH, Elizabeth Hosp., Bethesda, Md., 1983-84; assoc. prof. psychiatry U. Munich, 1984-95; chmn. Psychiat. Hosp. U. Hamburg, Germany, 1995—. Contbr. articles to profl. jours. Recipient A.E. Bennet Neuropsychiat. Rsch. Found. award, 1982, 1st Plotzitzko prize for rsch. on endogenous psychosis, 1983, Best Poster award AGNP, 1991. Mem. Internat. Soc. Psychoneuroendocrinology, Arbeitsgemeinschaft für Neuropsychopharmakologie, Deutsche Gesellschaft für Neurologie und Psychiatrie, Deutsche Gesellschaft für Biologische Psychiatrie, European Coll. Neuropsychopharmacology, Arbeitsgemeinschaft Europaischer Psychiater. Achievements include rsch. in endorphins in endogenous psychoses, long-term effects of neuroleptic treatment, biol. mechanisms of addiction, psychoses after open-heart surgery, efficacy and adverse effects of clozapine, psychiat. aspects of HIV-infection, psychiat. symptoms in endocrinopathies, subjective effects of neuroleptics, methadone treatment, and quality of life in psychiat. patients. Office: U Hamburg Dept Psychiatry, Martinstr 52, 20246 Hamburg Germany

NABERS, CLAUDE LOWREY, retired periodontist, writer; b. Vernon, Tex., Mar. 29, 1924; s. John Bradford and Mae (Moore) N.; m. Blanche Lillian Eaton, Sept. 28, 1951; children: Marquis Eaton, Bradford Claude. DDS, U. Tex., 1946; MS in Dentistry, Northwestern U., Chgo., 1949. Diplomate Am. Bd. Periodontology (bd. dirs. 1965-71, chmn. 1971). Civilian cons. Brook Army Hosp., 1958-84, Lackland Air Force Hosp., 1958-75, Sch. Aerospace Medicine, 1975-80; pres. Nabers Eaton Properties, San Antonio, 1983—; nat. cons. Surgeon Gen. USAF, 1969-71; mem. ADA Coun. on Dental Rsch., Chgo., 1983-87; lectr. in field worldwide. Author: (in Japanese) Periodontal Therapy, 1980; co-author: Periodontal Therapy, 1990; originator procedures in field. Mem. devel. bd. U. Tex. Health Sci. Ctr., San Antonio, 1989-94; trustee Cancer Therapy and Rsch. Ctr. Found. Bd., San Antonio, 1998—; elder 1st Presbyn. Ch., San Antonio, 1960; v.p. Alamo Kiwanis, San Antonio, 1990-91; bd. dirs. The 100 Club, San Antonio, 1993-96, McFarland Tennis Found., San Antonio, 1994-97, San Antonio Salvation Army, 1998—; bd. govs. Cancer Therapy and Rsch. Ctr., San Antonio, 1999—. Capt. U.S. Army, 1946-48. Recipient 1st Holler's Disting. Lectureship award, San Antonio, 1984; recipient Outstanding Civilian Svc. medal Dept. of the Army, 1978, 1st Meml. G.R. Landquist Lectureship Northwestern U., 1979. Fellow Am. Coll. Dentists, Am. Acad. Periodontology (pres. 1972-73, exec. coun. 1962-74, Gold medal 1978, Master Clinician award 1990), Acad. Internat. Dentistry; mem. S.W. Soc. Periodontists (pres. 1961), San Antonio Country Club, Town Club, Argyle, European Acad. Dentistry (hon.), South African Soc. Periodontology (hon.), Omicron Kappa Upsilon (hon.). Republican. Avocations: tennis, golf, hunting, bridge, travel.

NABEYA, SEIJI, education educator; b. Tokyo, Oct. 12, 1925. Bachelor Degree, Tokyo Imperial U., 1947; Doctoral Degree, Hitotsubashi U., 1988. Rschr. Inst. of Statis. Math., Tokyo, 1947-53; tech. officer Bur. of Statistics, Tokyo, 1953-56; lectr. Hitotsubashi U., Tokyo, 1956-59, assoc. prof., 1959-65, prof., 1965-89, prof. emeritus, 1989—; prof. Tokyo Internat. U., Kawagoe, 1989-99. Author: Mathematical Statistics, 1978; contbr. articles to profl. jours. Home: 3-13-16 Maehara Koganei, Tokyo 184-0013, Japan

NABI, SYED RASHIDUN, physicist, educator, researcher; b. Bashirhat, India; arrived in Bangladesh, 1950; s. Syed Abdul Badii and Musammat Akbari Khanam; m. Salma Mussamat Umme, Jan. 20, 1973; children: Samin, Humaira, Munaim. BSc with honors, U. Dhaka, Bangladesh, 1963, MSc, 1964; MSc in Applied Acoustics, U. London, 1970. Rsch. physicist Bcsir, Dhaka, 1966-67; ast. prof. dept. physics Chittagong (Bangladesh) U., 1973-78, assoc. prof., 1978-89, prof., 1989—. Author: Translation of Variation of Meson Components of Cosmic Rays, 1964 (Devel. Bd. of Bengali award). Active Bangladesh Tablig Orgn., Dhaka, Sri Lanka, Afganistan and Pakistan, 1963—. Mem. Bangladesh Electronic Soc., Bangladesh Phys. Soc. (life), Bangladesh Assn. for Advancement of Sci. Islamic. Avocations: reading religious books, chess, gardening. Home: 80 Miapara Rd, Khulna 9100, Bangladesh Office: Dept Physics, Chittagong U, Hathazary, 4133 Chittagong Bangladesh

NABIL, MOHAMED, computer company executive, legal consultant; b. Casablanca, Morocco, June 18, 1945; s. Zitouni and Hadda (Alouani) N.; m. Graziella Amand, July 21, 1975; children: Karim, Samia. Degree in elec. engring., I.N.S.A, Lyon, France, 1968; degree in computers, European Sys Rsch. Inst., Geneva, Switzerland, 1974; LLM, U. Casablanca, 1984; PhD in Law, U. Perpignan, 1999. Cert. computer engr.; cert. legal cons. Cons. IBM, Morocco and France, 1968-85; pres. First Informatique, Casablanca, 1985—, Processing Techs., Casablanca; legal cons. Dept. Justice, 1982—. Author: Computers and Copyright, 1984. Mem. A.P.E.B.I. (hon. pres.), Lions Clubs Internat. (gov. 1994-95, forum chmn. 1996, Ext. award 1995, Leadership award 1996), Churchill Club. Avocation: golf. Office: First Informatique Tour Atlas, 1 Place Zellaqa, 20000 Casablanca Morocco

NACHEMSON, ANN KERSTIN, hand surgeon; b. Goteborg, Sweden, Apr. 18, 1948; d. Sten and Kersin Johannesson; m. Alf Louis Nachemson, Oct. 16, 1978; 1 child, Louise. MD, Goteborg U., 1975, PhD in Hand Surgery, 1988. Vis. scientist U. Wash., Seattle, 1980-81, sr. registrar hand surgery, 1982-91; vis. scientist NIH, Bethesda, Md., 1990-91; hand surgeon Goteborg U., Sweden, 1991—. Mem. Swedish Hand Soc. (bd. dirs. 1993-98), Fedn. European Socs. Hand Surgery (bd. dirs. 1996—). Home: 3A Geijersgat, S-41134 Goteborg Sweden Office: Sahlgren Univ Hosp, Dept Hand Surgery, S-41345 Goteborg Sweden

NACHWALTER, MICHAEL, lawyer; b. N.Y.C., Aug. 31, 1940; s. Samuel J. Nachwalter; m. Irene, Aug. 15, 1965; children: Helynn, Robert. BS, Bucknell U., 1962; MS, L.I. U., 1967; JD cum laude, U. Miami, 1967; LLM, Yale U., 1968. Bar: Fla. 1967, D.C. 1979, U.S. Dist. Ct. (so. dist.) Fla. 1967, U.S. Dist. Ct. (mid. dist.) Fla. 1982, U.S. Ct. Appeals (5th and 11th cirs.) 1967, U.S. Supreme Ct. 1975. Law clk. to judge U.S. Dist. Ct. (so. dist.) Fla.; shareholder Kelly, Black, Black & Kenny; now shareholder Kenny Nachwalter Seymour Critchlow & Spector, P.A., Miami; lectr. Law Sch. U. Miami. Editor-in-chief U. Miami Law Rev., 1966-67. Fellow Am. Coll. Trial Lawyers (vice-chair Jud. Qualifications Commn.); mem. ABA, FBA, Am. Bd. Trial Advs., Fla. Bar Assn. (bd. govs. 1982-90), Internat. Soc. Barristers (dir.), Dade County Bar Assn., Iron Arrow, Soc. Wig and Robe, Omicron Delta Kappa, Phi Kappa Phi, Phi Delta Phi. Office: Kenny Nachwalter Seymour Arnold Critchlow & Spector PA 201 S Biscayne Blvd Ste 1100 Miami FL 33131-4327

NACK, CLAIRE DURANI, artist, author; b. N.Y.C.; d. Myron Irving and Rachel Rita Adele (Feldman) N. Student, NYU, 1975, Sculpture Ctr., N.Y.C., 1975; Arts Student League. Pres., owner, founder Claire Durani Nack Corp. subs. Princess Enterprs./Durani Co., N.Y.C., 1993; pres. Books of Poetry by Claire Durani Nack, Mystery Stories by Claire Durani Nack, Books of Science Fiction by Claire Durani Nack, Works of Art by Claire Durani Nack, C.D.N. Co.; prof. N.Y. State Mus., Albany, 1992, Hudson Valley C.C., 1986-92, Schenectady (N.Y.) Mus.; lectr. Troy Arts League, 1989. Artist sketchbooks; author/artist: Something Happened in the Kitchen, 1981, European Journey, Book II, 1981, Cat Book, 1994, Diary, 2, 1980, Diary, Vol. 4, 1994, Vol. 5, 1994, The Journals of Claire Durani Nack, 1994, Art Book 1, 1982, Art Book 2, 1982, My World, 1999, Blue Book, Upwards Bent (books 1-5), 1993-94, Spiders Web Unspun, 1994, An Unfamiliar Place, 1993, The Adventures of Cora, 1994 (books 1-5), Cahiers de Dessins de Paris, 1994, Big City Lights, 1991, Something Happened in the Bathroom, 1981, Something Happened in the Living Room, 1981, Children's Coloring Book, 1995, Animal Book, 1995, The Adventures of Cora, Plot, Counterplot, Plot, 1997, All About Life, Sorrow and Joy, Essays and Soliliquis, Stoolie the Ghoulie, The Small Book of Art, The Gold Book, 1997, The Book of Art, 1997, Conversations with Myself, 1997, Facts, Fools and Ghools, 1997, All About Life, 1997, Sorrow and Joy, 1997, The Silver Book, 1997, A Light's Work, 1997, Being C, 1997, Alive, 1998, The Cheerful Book, 1998, Essays and Soliloquis, 1998, Questions and Answers, 1998, The Prosecuting Lawyer, 1998, Life's a Theatre, 1999, The Cheetah, 1999, Toulouse Lautrec and Claire Durani Nack, 1999, The Scrapbook of Claire Durani Nack, 1998, The Album of Claire Durani Nack, 1999, Life's a Theatre, 1999, The Portfolio of Claire Durani Nack in Paris, 1999. Recipient poetry award Nat. Libr. of Poetry, Calif., 1991; scholar Art Students League, 1985. Mem. Nat. Mus. of Women in the Arts (charter mem.), Art Students League (life), N.Y. State Mus. Avocations: travel, collecting model airplanes, collecting hats, art and art books, jewelry, real estate. Office: 416 East St Rensselaer NY 12144-2303

NACOL, MAE, lawyer; b. Beaumont, Tex., June 15, 1944; d. William Samuel and Ethel (Bowman) N.; children: Shawn Alexander Nacol, Catherine Regina Nacol. BA, Rice U., 1965; postgrad., South Tex. Coll. Law, 1966-68. Bar: Tex. 1969, U.S. Dist. Ct. (so. dist.) Tex. 1969. Diamond buyer/appraiser Nacol's Jewelry, Houston, 1961—; pvt. practice law Houston, 1969—. Author, editor ednl. materials on multiple sclerosis, 1981-85. Nat. dir. A.R.M.S. of Am. Ltd., Houston, 1984-85. Recipient Mayor's Recognition award City of Houston, 1972; Ford Found. fellow So. Tex. Coll. Law, Houston, 1964. Mem. Houston Bar Assn. (chmn. candidate com. 1970, chmn. membership com. 1971, chmn. lawyers referral com. 1972), Assn. Trial Lawyers Am., Tex. Trial Lawyers Assn., Am. Judicature Soc. (sustaining), Houston Fin. Coun. Women, Houston Trial Lawyers Assn. Presbyterian. Office: 600 Jefferson St Ste 750 Houston TX 77002-7326

NACUL, LUIS CARLOS, epidemiologist; b. Porto Alegre, Brazil, July 13, 1959; s. Jacob Augusto Moojen and Lilian Ruhling N. MSc with distinction, London Sch. Hygiene and Tropical Medicine, 1989, PhD, 1997. Resident U. Sao Paulo, Brazil, 1984-85; physician Orgn. Saude de Goias, Mambai, Brazil, 1985-87, Secretaria de Saude, Olinda, Brazil, 1988-91; epidemiologist IMIP, Recife, Brazil, 1991-92; prof. U. Fed. Pernambuco, Recife, 1993—; dir. Mcpl. Hosp. Mambai, 1986-87. Mem. Am. Assn. Chronic Fatigue Syndrome. Roman Catholic. Avocations: reading, chess, yoga. Home: 4971 ap 302, Av Bernardo Vieira de Melo, 54450020 Jaboatao Brazil

NADAGOUDAR, BABAGOUDA SHANKARAGOUDA, forestry researcher, educator; b. Bagalkot, Karnataka, India, Feb. 28, 1946; s. S. B. and M. S. N.; m. G. N. Patil, May 9, 1971; 1 child. BS in Agr., U. Agrl. Scis., Bangalore, India, 1967, MS in Agr., 1970; PhD, Karnatak U., Dharwad, India, 1995; MS in Forestry, Oxford U., Eng., 1986. Instr. U. Agrl. Scis., Dharwad, Karnataka, 1970-73; jr. agronomist U. Agrl. Scis., Dharwad, 1972-77, agronomist, 1977-87, sr. scientist agroforestry, 1987-96, 97-98, 1999—, assoc. dir. rsch., 1996-97, prof. agronomy, tech. advisor, 1998-99, dir. ext., 1999. Author: Sugarcane Cultivation, 1983 (State Level First Prize 1986); inventor in field. Recipient Australian Bicentennary award, 1988, award Nat. Level (India) 1994. Mem. Indian Soc. Tree Scientists, Alumni Assn. Coll. Agr. Avocations: reading and writing scientific articles, field visits. Office: U Agrl Scis, Dharwad 580005 Karnataka, India

NADAR, THANKAYYAN SANKARAN, physician, researcher; b. Trivandrum, Kerala, India, Oct. 27, 1940; s. Kochummini Madan and Chellamma Mariamma Nadar; m. Nandini Nadar, Feb. 22, 1972; children: T.N. Sajilal, T.N. Lajimol, T.N. Ajilal. BSc in Zoology, Mahatma Gandhi Coll., Trivandrum, 1962; B Medicine B Surgery, Med. Coll. Trivandrum, 1971. Tchr. New H.S., Trivandrum, 1962-63; asst. surgeon Kerala Health Svcs., Trivandrum, 1972-73; tutor Med. Coll. Hosp., Kozhikode, India, 1973-74; tutor Med. Coll. Hosp., Trivandrum, 1974-80, asst. prof. anesthesia, 1980-85, prof., 1990-92; mng. dir. Dr. T.N. Internat. Inst. Med. Sci. Rsch., Trivandrum, 1992—; chief med. officer Devi Hosp., Trivandrum, 1998—. Developer med. equipment herbo diabetase, keloid scar injector. Recipient med. award Padmasree Dr. K.H. Pai, 1995, Satyan film star, 1998. Mem. Lions Club (bd. dirs. 1995-99, Puraskar award for med. inventions 1996). E-mail: cybernet@techpark.net. Home: Sastra Bhavan Nalanchira, Trivandrum Kerala 695015, India Office: Devi Hosp/Scan's Pvt Ltd, Sreekaryam, Trivandrum Kerala India

NADARAJAH, CHITHRANJAN, mechanical engineer, consultant; b. Colombo, Sri Lanka, Jan. 15, 1964; s. Nadarajah and Maheswari Comaraswamy; ; m. Suchitra Kumarapathy, Aug. 20, 1999; children: Sajanee Sankari, Haran Krishan. B in Mech. Engring. 1st class honors, U. Strathclyde, Glasgow, Scotland, 1989, PhD in Mech. Engring., 1993. Rsch. fellow Nanyang Technol. U., Singapore, 1993-95; sr. engr. Exxon Engring. Asia Pacific, Singapore, 1995—; cons. Esso Refinery, Antwerp, Belgium, Esso Singapore Refinery. Contbr. articles to profl. jours. Cpl. Singapore Mil., 1984-86. Mem. ASME, Inst. Mech. Engrs. U.K. Avocations: computing, jogging, swimming, reading. E-mail: cranjan@pacific.net.sg. Fax: 4381335. Office: Exxon Engring Asia Pacific, 3 Phillip St Commerce Point, Singapore 048693, Singapore

NADARZINSKI, KLAUS, materials scientist; b. Hilden, Germany, Apr. 5, 1968; s. Werner Walter and Monika (Szag) N.; m. Liane Wunschel, Aug. 14, 1993; children: Daniel, Patrick. Diplom-Ing., U. Erlangen, Germany, 1992; PhD, Max-Planck Inst. Material Sci., Stuttgart, Germany, 1995. Application specialist Philips Electron Optics, Eindhoven, The Netherlands, 1995-99; material engr. quartz Infineon Techs. AG, Munich, Germany, 1999—. Mem. Verein Deutscher Ingenieure. E-mail: klaus.nadarzinski@infineon.com. Office: Infineon Techs AG SIPM2, Rosenheimer Str 1166, 81609 Muenchen Germany

NADAS, JOHN ADALBERT, psychiatrist; b. Innsbruck, Austria, Mar. 14, 1949; came to U.S., 1950; s. Julius Zoltan and Ibolya Erzsebet (Szöllösy) N.; m. Gabriella Ilona Ormay, Apr. 11, 1981; children: János, Miklós, István. BA, Case Western Res. U., Cleve., 1970; MD, Duke U., Durham, N.C., 1974. Diplomate Am. Bd. Psychiatry and Neurology. Resident in psychiatry U. Chgo., 1974-77; pvt. practice Munster, Ind., 1977-84, Canton, 1984—; instr. psychiatry Northeastern Ohio U. Coll. Medicine, Rootstown, 1985-86; coord. psychiat. edn. Mercy Med. Ctr., Canton, Ohio, 1985-87; clin. dir. psychiat. svcs. Mercy Med. Ctr., Canton, 1990-91; asst. prof. Northeast Ohio U. Coll. Medicine, Rootstown, 1986—; cons. Crisis Ctr., Canton, 1985-92. Author: Philosophical Basis of Depth Psychotherapy, 1983, Journey Toward Energy, 1995, Transformation, 1999. Trustee Sisters of Charity Found., Canton, 1996—. NCAA nat. collegiate epee champion, 1970; mem. All-Am. Fencing Team, 1969, 70. Mem. AMA, Am. Psychiat. Assn. Roman Catholic. Avocations: basketball, computer programming. Office: 1330 Mercy Dr NW Ste 320 Canton OH 44708-2624

NADASEN, SUNDRASAGARAN, law educator; b. Germiston, Gauteng, South Africa, Aug. 15, 1954; s. Velaitham and Panjalli (Nair) Perumal; m. Krishnavelli Kathleen Naidoo, Apr. 9, 1977. BA in Law, U. Durban-Westville, South Africa, 1976, LLB, 1978; JD/LLD, U. Leiden, The Netherlands, 1988—. Bar: South Africa, Natal Provincial Divsn. Lab. asst. S.A. Glazing, Benoni, South Africa, 1972; dispatch clk. Eclipse Engring., Benoni, 1973; candidate atty. M.J. Naidoo & Co., Durban, 1979-80; atty. S. Nadasen & Co., Durban, 1981-84; sr. lectr. U. Durban-Westville, 1992-94, assoc. prof. law, 1995—, prof. of pub. law, coord. pub. health law; cons. human rights edn. project Western Cape Province Coun. of Chs., Cape Town, 1995; cons. atty. Siven Samuels & Assocs., Durban, 1996—. Contbr. articles to profl. jours. Mem. exec. com. Nat. Assn. Dem. Lawyers, Durban, 1992; legal cons. Crisis Care, Durban, 1993, Children's Rights Ministries, Durban, 1993; sec. to and mem. bd. trustees Asoka Adult Basic Edn., Durban, 1996—. Ecumenical Scholarships Programme scholar, Germany, 1985-91; Brit. Coun. grantee, 1996; recipient Med. Rsch. Coun. Overseas scholarship, 1999. Mem. Natal Law Soc. Avocations: reading, sports, music. Office: Univ of Durban-Westville, Post Bag X54001, Durban 4001, South Africa

NADEL, DANIEL, archaeologist; b. Tiberias, Israel, Jan. 18, 1955; married; 2 children. BA, Hebrew U., Jerusalem, 1985, MA, 1988, PhD, 1997. Curator Mus. Prehistory, Haifa, Israel, 1990-95; tchr. U. Haifa, 1993—; speaker in field. Contbr. articles to profl. jours. Grantee Leakey Found., 1990, 99, Care Archaeol. Found., 1990-98, Jerusalem Ctr. Anthrop. Studies, 1990-98, Nat. Geog., 1999. Mem. Israel Prehist. Soc. (chmn. 1991-93. Office: U Haifa, Zinman Inst Archaeology, 31905 Haifa Israel

NÁDENÍK, ZBYNĚK, mathematician; b. Markvartovice, Opava, Czech Republic, Nov. 21, 1925; s. Rudolf and Františka (Hlávková) N.; m. Marie Kirbisová, Jan. 26, 1956; children: Zbyněk, Ladislav. D in Natural Scis., Charles U., Prague, 1950; DSc, Acad. Sci., Prague, 1969. Asst. Tech. U., Prague, 1950-57, assoc. prof., 1957-77, prof., 1977—; mem. Sci. Coun. Rsch. Inst. Geodesy, Prague, 1990—, Commn. for DSc Math., Czech Acad. Scis., Prague, 1975—, Commn. for DSc Geodesy, 1988—. Contbr. more than 100 articles to profl. jours. including Czech Math. Jour., Mathematica Bohemica, among others. Mem. Union of Czech Mathematicians and Physicists, Am. Math. Soc. Avocations: geometry, arts. Home: Libocká 262-14, 162 00 Prague Praha 6, Czech Republic

NADER, NADER DJALAL, anesthesiologist, health science researcher; b. Tabriz, Iran; s. Mohmad Ali and Zerrin Taj (Khodadel) N.; m. Faranack Ahmadpuwr Benz, Mar. 18, 1980; children: Camelia D., Heerbode D. MD, Tabriz U.; MA, SUNY, Buffalo, PhD. Diplomate Am. Bd. Anesthesiology. Fellow in cardiothoracic surgery Toronto (Ont., Can.) U., 1990-91; resident in surgery Easton (Pa.) Hosp., 1991-92; resident in anesthesia SUNY, 1992-95, fellow in cardiac anesthesiology, 1995-96, asst. prof. anesthesiology, 1996-99, dir. rsch. dept. anesthesia, 1997-99; chief anesthesiologist VA Med. Ctr.-U. Ark., Little Rock, 1999—; assoc. prof. anesthesiology and physiology U. Ark. for Med. Scis., 2000—; mem. editl. adf. bd. Jour. Immunological Investigation, 1999—. Recipient Paul R. Knight award NIH, 1996; grantee Buffalo Gen. Found., 1993, SUNY, 1998. Mem. Am. Coll. Chest Physicians, N.Y. Acad. Scis. E-mail:nnader@med.va.gov. Office: CAVHS 4300 W 7th St Little Rock AR 72205-5484

NADEZHDINSKII, ALEXANDER, physicist; b. Moscow, Sept. 29, 1947; s. Ivan and Ekaterina (Kuptsova) V.; m. Irina Kochetova, July 19, 1969; children: Marie, Elizabeth. MS, Inst. for Physics and Tech., Moscow, 1972; PhD, P.N. Lebedev Phys. Inst., Moscow, 1978; DS in Laser Physics, GPI, Moscow, 1987. Rschr. P.N. Lebedev Phys. Inst., Moscow, 1972-81, sr. rschr., 1981-83; sr. rschr. Gen. Physics Inst., Moscow, 1983-89, head lab., 1989-93, head dept., 1993—. Editor spl. issue Tunable Diode Laser Applications, 1992; contbr. over 150 articles to profl. jours. Recipient State prize in sci. USSR Govt., 1985. Mem. IEEE, Optical Soc. Am., Internat. Soc. Optical Engring., Spectroscopy Assn. Moscow (mem. coun. 1993), Am. Physics Soc. Home: Profsouznaya 43-2-638, 117420 Moscow Russia Office: Russian Acad Sci, Gen Physics Inst Vavilova 38, 117942 Moscow Russia

NADIG, GERALD GEORGE, manufacturing executive; b. Astoria, N.Y., May 9, 1945; s. Charles Edwin and Louise (Hahn) N.; m. Nancy Hanford Stewart, June 20, 1970; children: Sara Hanford, Jennifer Stewart. AB cum laude, Harvard Coll., 1967, MBA, 1974. Fin. mgr. Rockwell Internat., Hopedale, Mass., 1974-76; materials mgr. Rockwell Internat., Oshkosh, Wis., 1976-78, Marysville, Ohio, 1978-79; ops. mgr. Rockwell Internat., Marysville, 1979-80, plant mgr., 1980-82; regional mgr. Rockwell Internat., Atlanta, 1984-85; mng. dir. Rockwell Maudslay Ltd., Great Alne, Eng., 1982-84; dir. mfg. Toyoda Machinery USA, Arlington Heights, Ill., 1985-87; v.p., gen. mgr. Toyoda Machinery USA, Arlington Heights, 1987-88; v.p., gen. mgr. Littell div. Allied Products Corp., Chgo., 1988-89; exec. v.p. pre finish metals Material Scis. Corp., 1989-90; pres. Pre Finish Metals Materials Scis. Corp., 1990-91; pres., chief oper. officer Material Scis. Corp., Chgo., 1991-96, pres., CEO, 1997—, chmn. bd. dirs., 1998—. Trustee Village of Lake Barrington, 1989-91. With U.S. Army, 1966-70. Mem. Soc. Mfg. Engrs. (sr.), Biltmore Country Club. Avocations: golf, tennis, game theory. Home: 24354 N Grandview Dr Barrington IL 60010-6218 Office: Material Scis Corp 2200 Pratt Blvd Elk Grove Village IL 60007-5917

NADLER, ARIE, psychologist, educator, researcher; b. Munich, Germany, May 10, 1947; arrived in Israel, 1947; s. Isak and Miriam (Frucht) N.; m. Etta Grinstein, July 27, 1969; children: Keren, Gil. BA, Bar-Ilan U., Ramat-Gan, Israel, 1970; MA, Purdue U., 1973, PhD, 1975. Registered expert Israeli Ministry Health. Lectr. in psychology Tel-Aviv U., Ramat-Aviv, Israel, 1976-80, sr. lectr., 1981-84, assoc. prof., 1985-88, head dept. psychology, 1985-89, prof. psychology, 1988—, dean Faculty Social Scis., 1993-98, head Peres Inst. Diplomacy Regional Cooperation, 1998—; vis. prof. CUNY Grad. Ctr., N.Y.C., U. Wash., Seattle; cons. Intel Electronics, israel, 1990—, Israeli Govt., including Ministry of Treasury, 1984—, Open U., Israel, 1985—. Editor: New Directions in Helping, 3 vols., 1983. Chair exec. coun. Internat. Edn. Found., Tel Aviv/N.Y.C., 1994—; chmn. bd. Orgn. for Child Placement, Tel Aviv, 1996. Grantee Bi-NSF, 1981-84, 86-89, Lion Found., Konstanz, Germany, 1990, 92, 94. Fellow APA, Am. Psychol. Soc.; mem. Soc. Exptl. Social Psychology. Jewish. Office: Tel Aviv U Fac Scis, Office of the Dean, 69978 Ramat Aviv Israel

NADYKTO, BORIS ANDREEVICH, physicist, researcher; b. Odoev, Tula, Russia, Mar. 13, 1939; s. Andrey Korneevich and Alexandra Sergeevna (Dugina) N.; m. Nelli Ivanovna Zarikhina, July 6, 1963; children: Aleksei, Olga. Physicist, Moscow U., 1962; PhD, VNIIEF, Arzamas-16, 1972, DSc, 1995. Engr. VNIIEF, Arzamas-16, USSR, 1962-65, sr. engr., 1965-70, head lab., 1970-73; head dept. VNIIEF, Arzamas-16, Russia, 1973—. Contbr. articles to profl. jours. Recipient State Prize USSR Govt. of USSR, 1975. Mem. N.Y. Acad. Scis. Home: 5-25 Dzerzhinsky st, 607190 Arzamas-16 Russia Office: RFNC-VNIIEF, 37 Mir Ave, 607190 Arzamas-16 Russia

NAEF, PAUL ANDREAS, thoracic surgeon; b. Leipzig, Germany, July 21, 1916; s. Martin Ernst and Charlotte Marie (Abraham-Collin) N.; m. France Grety Blum, 1955 (div. 1997); children: Claude, Bernard. MD, U. Med. Sch., Zurich, 1941. Intern then resident U. Hosp., Lausanne, Switzerland, 1943-49; thoracic surgeon Clinic La Source, Lausanne, Switzerland, 1950-64; chief of surgery Yverdon Hosp., Switzerland, 1964-80; ret.; invited prof. Mayo Clinic, various Am. univs., 1973-74. Author: Permanentes Lernen in der Medizin, 1986, Chirurgie thoracique, 1987, The Story of Thoracic Surgery, 1990, De la tuberculose a la greffe du coeur, 1940-90, 1995; contbr. chpts. to books and articles to profl. jours. Mem. Soc. of Thoracic Surgeons, So. Thoracic Surg. Assn. (hon.), Am. Assn. for Thoracic Surgery (hon.), many others. Avocations: history of medicine, tennis, mountain hiking. Home: 12 av Villardin, CH-1009 Pully Switzerland

NAEGELE, ELIZABETH MARIE, musician, educator; b. Minot, N.D., July 17, 1951; d. George Eugene and Margaret Lenora (Wiens) Faul; m. Michael Dean Naegele, June 17, 1972; children: Heidi Marie, Nicholas Michael. Diploma, Moody Bible Inst., 1972; MusB, Mich. State U., 1975, MusM, 1976; MusD, Northwestern U., Evanston, Ill., 1989. Prof. music Moody Bible Inst., Chgo., 1976—. Organ recitalist, Ill., Mich. Dir. music Eastminster Presbyn. Ch., East Lansing, Mich., 1975-76, Carter Westminster Presbyn., Skokie, Ill., 1976-82, 1st Presbyn. Ch., Waukegan, Ill., 1990—; organist Winnetka (Ill.) Bible Ch., 1982-89. Mem. Assn. Am. Guild Organists (bd. dirs. Chgo. chpt. 1977-79, 88-91, 96—), Chgo. Club Woman Organists (bd. dirs. 1986-94), Phi Kappa Phi. Avocation: word games. Home: 2516 Edina Blvd Zion IL 60099-2702 Office: Moody Bible Inst 820 N La Salle Dr Chicago IL 60610-3263

NAEGLE, MADELINE ANNE, mental health nurse, educator; b. Penn Yan, N.Y., Feb. 2, 1942; d. Lester Lawrence and Nona Caroline (Muir) N.; m. James Michael McGowan, Aug. 6, 1966 (div. 1984); children: Amanda Allen, Benjamin Logan. BS, Nazareth Coll. Rochester, 1964; MA, NYU, 1967, PhD, 1980. Staff nurse Syracuse (N.Y.) Meml. Hosp., summer 1964; staff nurse, asst. head nurse Payne Whitney Clinic, N.Y.C., 1964-65; instr. nursing Herbert H. Lehman Coll., Bronx, N.Y., 1972-75, part-time instr. nursing, 1975-78; asst. clin. prof. Sch. Nursing U. Pa., Phila., 1979-83; pvt. practice N.Y.C., 1980—; assoc. prof. Leinhard Sch. Nursing Pace U., Pleasantville, N.Y., 1983-85; assoc. prof. div. nursing NYU, N.Y.C., 1985—; cons. The Day Sch., 1980-84; mem. N.Y. State Gov.'s Health Care Adv. Bd., 1991-94. Author: Nursing Process with Clients Using Drugs, 1993, Patterns of Substance Abuse, 1996; author, editor: (model curriculum) Substance Abuse Education in Nursing, 1991; editor Addictions Nursing, 1988-98; contbr. articles to profl. jours. Recipient Presdl. Citation award N.Y. County RN Assn., 1986, Amanda Silver Disting. Svc. award N.Y. County RN Assn., 1994; inducted into Acad. Women Achievers, YWCA, 1991; USPHS fellow, 1978-79, Pres.'s award Nat. Nurses Soc. on Addiction; grantee Nat. Inst. Alcohol Abuse and Alcoholism, Nat. Inst. Drug Abuse, 1989-90, Ctr. for Substance Abuse Prevention, 1990-95, U.S. Human Resources Adminstrn., 1999; Fulbright scholar U. Malta, 1995. Fellow Am. Acad. of Nursing; mem. ANA (com. chair 1987-89, com. on addiction 1990, nominating com. 1996-2000), N.Y. State Nurses Assn. (chair com. on impaired nursing practice 1986-88, pres. elect. 1987-89, pres. 1989-91), Assn. Med. Educators and Rschrs. in Substance Abuse, Sigma Theta Tau (Upsilon chpt.). Democrat. Avocations: hiking, running, dancing, theatre, music. Office: NYU Div Nursing 50 W 4th St New York NY 10012-1156

NAESER, MARGARET ANN, linguist, medical researcher; b. Washington, June 22, 1944; d. Charles Rudolph and Elma Mathilda (Meyer) N. BA in German, Smith Coll., 1966; PhD in Linguistics, U. Wis., 1970. Chief speech pathology sect. Martinez (Calif.) VA Med. Ctr., 1972-74, Palo Alta (Calif.) VA Med. Ctr., 1974-77; rsch. linguist Boston VA Med. Ctr., 1977—; dir. CT scan/MRI scan Aphasia rsch. sect. Boston U. Aphasia Rsch. Ctr., Boston U. Sch. Medicine, asst. rsch. prof. neurology, 1978-84, assoc. rsch. prof., 1984-97, rsch. prof., 1997—; mem. adv. bd. CT scan/aphasia VA Nat. Task Force, Washington, 1990-91; panel mem. Office Alternative Medicine NIH, 1994, NIH sponsored conf. Acupuncture: A Consensus Devel. Conf., 1997. Contbr. articles to Neurology, Archives of Neurology, Brain; author: Outline Guide to Chinese Herbal Patent Medicines in Pill Form, 1990, Laser Acupuncture: An Introductory Textbook, 1994, Naeser Laser Home Treatment Program for the Hand- An Alternative Treatment for Carpal Tunnel Syndrome and Repetitive Strain Injury, 1996. NDEA fellow, 1967, AAUW fellow, 1970. Mem. Acoustical Soc. Am., Am. Speech, Lang., Hearing Assn., Acad. Aphasia, AAAS, Am. Assn. Oriental Medicine. Office: Boston VA Med Ctr 150 S Huntington Ave Boston MA 02130-4817

NAESS, PETTER, urban planning researcher; b. Bodø, Norway, July 9, 1951; s. Gunnar and Solveig (Schrøder) N.; m. Nina Kirkevold, Apr. 7, 1982; 1 child, Sigurd. Degree in Civil Architecture, Norwegian Inst. Tech., Trondheim, 1976, D in Engring., 1995. Arch. Eriksen & Knutsen, Oslo, 1977-82; sr. arch., cons. Ministry Environment, Oslo, 1982-88; rschr. Norwegian Inst. for Urban and Regional Rsch., Oslo, 1988, rsch. mgr., head divsn. for environ. planning rsch., 1989-92, 95-98, rschr., 1993-94; prof. dept. devel. and planning Aalborg U., 1998—. Author of textbook on phys. planning and energy use; contbr. articles to sci. jours. Pvt. Norwegian Infantry, 1970-71. Mem. Norwegian Soc. Housing and Urban Planning, Assn. Norwegian Non-Fiction Writers, Assn. Danish Urban Planners, Assn. Danish Archs. Home: Kronosvej 159, DK-9210 Ålborg Denmark Office: Aalborg U Dept Devel & Plan, Fibigerstrade 11, DK-9220 Ålborg Denmark

NAEVEKE, ROLF J. F., science educator; b. Dresden, Germany, Feb. 17, 1928; s. Friedrich and Grete (Braack) N.; m. Sabine Schmidtke; children: Martina, Philip, Cornelius. Diploma in biology, U. Hamburg, Germany, 1954, D of Natural Scis., 1957; prof., Tech. U. Braunschweig, Germany, 1971. Prof. emeritus Inst. for Microbiology Tech. U. Braunschweig, 1996—. Mem. Am. Soc. for Microbiology, Vereinigung fur Allgemeine und Angewandte Mikrobiologie. E-mail: r.naeveke@tu-bs.de. Office: Tech U Braunschweig, Spielmannstr 7, 38106 Braunschweig Germany

NAFALSKI, ANDRZEJ (ANDREW NAFALSKI), electrical engineering educator, administrator; b. Lublin, Poland, Oct. 26, 1948; arrived in Australia, 1992; s. Ryszard and Maria (Kalinowska) N. BEng, Lublin Poly., Poland, 1970; MEng, Warsaw Tech. U., 1972, PhD, 1978, DSc, 1989. Cert. elec. engr., tech. translator. Asst. prof. Lublin Tech. U., 1970-89, assoc. prof., prof., 1989-90, prof., dept. chair, 1990-91; sr. lectr. Curtin U., Australia, 1992-93; prof. U. South Australia, 1993—, head of school, 1994—; dir. computer ctr. Lublin Tech. U., 1988-89; dir. Magnetics Tech. Group, Adelaide, Australia, 1994—; lectr. in field. Author 12 books, 5 software sets; contbr. articles to profl. jours.; patentee (10) in field. Recipient Excellence in Teaching award U. South Australia, Adelaide, 1997, 1999. Fellow Inst. of Engrs. Australia (Nat. Engring. Excellence award 1998), IEEE (U.K.); mem. IEEE (sr.). Avocations: photography, gym, choir and solo singing. Office: Univ S Australia, The Levels, Adelaide 5095, Australia

NAFE, REINHOLD, neuropathologist; b. Mainz, Germany, July 14, 1959; s. Reinhold and Elfriede (Henrici) N. MD, Gutenberg U., 1985. Mil. physician NATO, Tongeren, Belgium, 1986-87; rschr. dept. urology Duren Hosp., Germany, 1987-88; rschr. dept. pathology U. Hannover Med. Sch., Germany, 1989-96, rsch. dept. neuropathology, 1996-97; rsch. dept. neuropathology Univ. Clinics, Frankfurt, Germany, 1997—. Mem. German Soc. Cytology, European Soc. Pathology, German Soc. Pathology, German Soc. Neuropathology. Office: Univ Clins Dept Neuropath, Deutschordenstrasse 46, 60528 Frankfurt Main, Germany

NAFEH, MOHAMAD ADAWY, gastroenterologist, educator; b. El-edwah, El-minya, Egypt, Apr. 6, 1937; s. Mahmoud Adawy N.; m. Nabila Mohamad Rashwan, Sept. 16, 1944; children: Hanan, Amani, Ayman. Diploma of Medicine, Assiut Univ., 1967; Diploma of Tropical Medicine, Cairo Univ., 1963; Diploma of Med. Sci., Assiut Univ., 1966, PhD in Medicine, 1971. Resident Assiut (Egypt) U., 1961-63, demonstrator in medicine, 1963-70, lectr. in medicine, 1971-75, asst. prof., 1975-80, prof. gastroenterology, 1981-97, hosp. dir., 1971-75, head spl. medicine Faculty of Medicine, 1984-87; physician Mabarra, Assiut, 1964. Author, editor: Fevers, 1981, Selections in Gastroenterology, 1982; co-author, editor: Principles of Gastroenterology, 1993. Decorated Bronz Medal of Mil. Svc. Med. Syndicate, 1973, First Class Armour Med. Syndicate, 1993. Mem. Assiut U. Club, Soc. Prevention of Hepatitis. Home: Assiut Staff Bldg, Assiut Egypt Office: Assiut U, Faculty Medicine, Assiut Egypt

NAFORNITA, IOAN LUCIAN, electronics educator; b. Lipova, Arad, Romania, July 12, 1945; s. Ioan and Juliana (Henc) N.; m. Monica Miranda Tautan, Mar. 18, 1971; children: Monica-Codruth, Corina-Alda. Engr., U. Politechnica, Timisoara, Romania, 1968, PhD, 1980. Asst. prof. U. Politechnica, Timisoara, 1968-91, prof., 1991—; expert Nat. Coun. of Sci., Bucharest, 1995—. Mem. IEEE. Roman Catholic. Office: Univ Politehnica Timisoara, BD Parvan No 2, 1900 Timisoara Romania

NAFTALIN, RICHARD JULIAN, physiologist, educator; b. Glasgow, Scotland, Feb. 11, 1939; s. Simon S. and Marjorie M. (Jacobs) N.; m. Barbara Rose Landman, Sept. 8, 1968; children: James, Alison, Guy. MB, ChB, Glasgow U., 1962, DSc, 1990; MSc, U. Coll., London, 1965; PhD, Nat. Inst. Med. Rsch., London, 1969. Registered med. practitioner. Jr. house officer Glasgow Royal Infirmary, 1962-63; fellow Nat. Inst. Med. Rsch., London, 1965-68; lectr. physiology U. Leicester, Eng., 1968-75; sr. lectr. physiology King's Coll. London, 1975-80, reader physiology, 1980-92, prof. physiology, 1992—. Contbr. articles to profl. jours. Mem. Physiol. Soc., Biochem. Soc. Avocations: music, reading, computers, modeling. Office: Kings Coll London, Kings Coll London, Guy's Campus, London SE1 1UL, England

NAFTALIS, GARY PHILIP, lawyer, educator; b. Newark, Nov. 23, 1941; s. Gilbert and Bertha Beatrice Naftalis; m. Donna Arditi, June 30, 1974; children: Benjamin, Joshua, Daniel, Sarah. AB, Rutgers U., 1963; AM, Brown U., 1965; LLB, Columbia U., 1967. Bar: N.Y. 1967, U.S. Dist. Ct. (so. dist.) N.Y. 1969, U.S. Ct. Appeals (2d cir.) 1968, U.S. Ct. Appeals (3d cir.) 1973, U.S. Ct. Appeals (D.C. cir.) 1993, U.S. Supreme Ct. 1974. Law clk. to judge U.S. Dist. Ct. So. Dist. N.Y., 1967-68; asst. U.S. atty. So. Dist. N.Y., 1968-74, asst. chief criminal divsn., 1972-74; spl. asst. U.S. atty. for V.I., 1972-73; spl. counsel U.S. Senate Subcom. on Long Term Care, 1975, N.Y. State Temp. Commn. on Living Costs and the Economy, 1975; ptnr. Orans, Elsen, Polstein & Naftalis, N.Y.C., 1974-81, Kramer, Levin, Naftalis & Frankel, N.Y.C., 1981—; lectr. Law Sch. Columbia U., 1976-88; vis. lectr. Law Sch. Harvard U., 1979; mem. deptl. disciplinary com. Appellate div. 1st Dept., 1980-86. Author: (with Marvin E. Frankel) The Grand Jury: An Institution on Trial, 1977, Considerations in Representing Attorneys in Civil and Criminal Enforcement Proceedings, 1981, Sentencing: Helping Judges Do Their Jobs, 1986, SEC Actions Seeking to Bar Securities Professionals, 1995, SEC Cease and Desist Powers Limited, 1997, The Foreign Corrupt Practices Act, 1997, Prosecuting Lawyers Who Defend Clients in SEC Actions, 1998, Obtaining Reports from a Credit Bureau for Litigation May be a Crime, 1999; editor: White Collar Crimes, 1980. Trustee Boys Brotherhood Rep., 1978—, Blueberry Treatment Ctr., 1981-91, Joseph Haggerty Children's Fund, 1991—; bd. dirs. The Legal Aid Soc., 2000—. Fellow Am. Coll. Trial Lawyers; mem. ABA (white collar crime com. criminal justice sect. 1985—), Assn. of Bar of City of N.Y. (com. criminal cts. 1980-83, com. judiciary 1984-87, com. on criminal law 1987-90, 97—, coun. criminal justice 1985-88), Fed. Bar Coun. (com. cts. 2d cir. 1974-77), N.Y. Bar Assn. (com. state legis. 1974-76, exec. com. comml. and fed. litigation sect.), Internat. Bar Assn. (bus. crimes com. 1988—). Home: 1125 Park Ave Apt 7B New York NY 10128-1243 Office: Kramer Levin Naftalis & Frankel 919 3rd Ave New York NY 10022-3902

NAG, RAJENDRA GOPAL, aerospace technology and managemenet adviser; b. Aligarh, India, July 1, 1937; s. Sham Gopal and Shibban (Rani) N.; m. Sarvesh Mathur, Jan. 22, 1963; children: Pankul, Atul, Mukul; m. Ratna Nag, Sept. 24, 1990; m. Sangeeta K. Nag, Sept 23, 1990; children: Sidhant, Saevia, Vedant, Kaeya; m. Juhi Nag, Mar. 10, 1997. BSc, Agra U., Aligarh, 1955; MSc, Aligarh Muslim U., 1957. Jr. sci. officer DRDO/DLJ, Jodhpur, India, 1959-62; sr. sci. officer GDE II/SSO GDE I AF, Delhi, India, 1962-73; sci. advisor AOC-in-C HQ WAC, Delhi, 1973-77; head weapons evaluation group DRDO/ISSA, Delhi, 1977-86; joint dir. Office of SA to CAS, Delhi, 1986-92; sci. adviser to chief of air staff DRDO/AF, Delhi, 1992-97; cons. HQWAC, Air Force, Delhi, 1962-77, DRDO/ISSA, 1977-86, Air HQ Air Force, 1986-97. Contbr. articles to profl. jours. Decorated Poorvi Star, Paschmi Star, Sangram medal, others. Fellow Aero. Soc. India (mem. coun., hon. treas.), Indian Soc. Advancement of Materials and Process Engring. (profl.). Avocations: non-classical music, photography. Home: F-5 Vikas Puri, 110018 New Delhi India

NAG, TAPAN KUMAR, electronic controls company executive; b. Sambalpur, Orissa, India, Aug. 27, 1945; s. Bibhuti Bhushan and Subala (Roy) N.; m. Shuvra Dasgupta, Apr. 17, 1974; 1 child, Swarnali. MSc, Birla Inst. Tech. & Sci., Pilani, India, 1966. Cert. physicist, specialization in electronics, lead assessor. Design engr. Bharat Heavy Elecs. Ltd., Bhopal, India, 1970-76; dy. mgr. BHEL, Bangalore, India, 1977-82, mgr., sr. mgr., 1982-87, 91, dy. gen. mgr., 1992-95, addl. gen. mgr., 1995—, design engr., 1970-83, head R&D, 1983-94, head R&D, engring., prodn., 1994-95, head quality, 1995—; trainee on project engring. Brown Boveri, Switzerland, 1976-77, 78; v.p. Bhel Officer's Club, Bangalore, 1991-92, pres., 1996-97. Editor Newsletter on Material Infomat, 1992. Mem. IEEE. Avocations: reading books on spiritual sciences, holistic approach to health and fitness, cooking, listening to music. Office: BHEL Electronics Divsn, Mysore Rd, Bangalore 560026, India

NAGAE, MOICHIRO, physicist, educator; b. Kyoto, Japan, Mar. 15, 1925; s. Isaburo and Fumi Nagae; m. Yae Ataka, Nov. 17, 1958; 1 child, Yohko. BS, Kyoto (Japan) U., 1953, DSc, 1966. Assoc. prof. Nat. Def. Acad., Yokosuka, Japan, 1963-73, prof., 1973-90, prof. emeritus, 1990—; tech. adviser New Medics Synthetic Inst. Ltd., Tokyo, 1991-96. Recipient The Order of the Rising Sun Gold Rays with Neck Ribbon, 1995. Mem. Phys. Soc. Japan, Am. Phys. Soc. Avocations: music, computers. Home: 12-5 Futaba 2, Yokosuka 239-0814, Japan

NAGAI, TSUNEJI, pharmaceutics educator; b. Shikishima, Gumma, Japan, June 10, 1933; s. Ushinosuke and Take (Kogure) N.; m. Kiyoko Usui, May 5, 1964. BS, U. of Tokyo, 1956, MS, 1958, PhD, 1961; D (hon.), Hacettepe U., Ankara, Turkey, 1996. Lic. pharmacist. Rsch. and teaching assoc. U. of Tokyo, 1961-71; postdoct. fellow Columbia U., N.Y.C., 1965-66, U. Mich., Ann Arbor, 1966-67; prof. pharmaceutics Hoshi U., Tokyo, 1971-99, prof. emeritus, 1999—; Chmn. bd. trustees The Nagai Found., Tokyo, 1986—; dir. FIP Found. for Edn. and Rsch., The Hague, The Netherlands, 1983-97, Iwaki Found., Tokyo, 1985—; pres. Fedn. Asian Pharm. Assns. Coll. Pharmacy, Bangkok, 1997—. Author numerous books, papers and articles in field; holder 61 patents. Trustee Hoshi U., Tokyo, 1979-91; mem. adv. com. Ministry of Health and Welfare, Tokyo, 1967-83, Ministry of Fgn. Affairs, Tokyo, 1981-87, Ministry of Edn. Culture and Sci., Tokyo, 1981-83; spl. mem. Japan Accredidation Assn., Tokyo, 1981-99. Decorated Imperial medal of Purple Ribbon (Japan), 1999; recipient Japan Invention prize Japan Invention Assn., Tokyo, 1984, Most Prestigious Rsch. prize Pharm. Soc. Japan, Tokyo, 1987, Rsch. Achievement award in pharmaceutics and drug delivery Am. Assn. Pharm. Scientists, 1999; William Evans fellow U. Otago, Duneden, New Zealand, 1993. Mem. Acad. Pharm. Sci. and Tech. (founding pres. 1985-87), Internat. Pharm. Fedn. (v.p. 1986-94, Host-Madsen medal 1986, Millennial Pharm. Scientist award 2000), Controlled Release Soc. (pres. 1996-97), Japan Soc. Drug Delivery (pres., chmn. bd. dirs. 1994-97), Soc. of Cyclodextrins Japan (founding pres.), Internat. House of Japan. Avocations: kabuki, music, antiques. Home: 1-23-10-103 Hon-Komagome, Bunkyo-ku Tokyo 113, Japan Office: Hoshi U Dept Pharmaceutics, 2-4-41 Ebara Shinagawa-ku, Tokyo 142, Japan

NAGAI, YOSHIO, economist, educator; b. Tsushima City, Japan, Nov. 25, 1931; s. Tadaichi and Tome (Ozeki) N.; m. Machiko Matsushima, Mar. 18, 1958; 1 child, Jun. BA, Nagoya U., 1954, M in Economics, 1956, Doctor of Economics, 1963. Rsch. asst. Nagoya U., Japan, 1959-61; from lectr. to assoc. prof. Nagoya Women's Coll., 1961-65; assoc. prof. to prof. Kamazawa U., 1965-81; prof. Nagoya U., 1981-90, Hitotsubashi U., Tokyo, 1990-95, Kanta Gakuin U., Yokohama, 1995—. Author: (books) Studies on the English Radicalism, 1962, Essays on Robert Owen, 1974, Bentham, 1982, Robert Owen and the Modern Socialism, 1993. Mem. Internat. Soc. Utilitarian Studies (v.p.), Internat. Bentham Soc. (v.p.), Japanese Soc. Utilitarian Studies (chairperson). Avocations: cello, skiing, tennis. Office: Kanto Gakuin U, 4834 Mutsuura-cho Kanazawa, 236-8501 Yokohama Japan

NAGALINGAM, SEV VERL, mechanical engineer, consultant; b. Batticaloa, Sri Lanka, May 26, 1964; arrived in Australia, 1994; s. Nalathamby and Kamaleswary (Ganeshamudaly) N. BEng with honors, U. Peradeniya, Sri Lanka, 1990; PhD In Engring., U. South Australia, 1999. Assoc. lectr. Faculty of Engring., U. Peradeniya, 1990-92; sr. exec. Air Lank Ltd., Colombo, Sri Lanka, 1992-94; rsch. engr. Ctr. Advanced Mfg. Rsch., South Australia, 1998—. Author: CIM Justification and Optimisation; contbr. articles to profl. jours. Colombo Dock Yard scholar U. Peradeniya, 1989, Postgrad. scholar U. South Australia, 1994. Avocations: badminton, reading, cycling, swimming. Home: TVIR Smart Rd, Midbury SA 5092, Australia Office: Ctr Advanced Mfg Rsch, Mawson Lakes Blvd, Mawson Lakes SA 5095, Australia

NAGAMI, HIROSHI, chemist, researcher; b. Iwami, Tottori, Japan, Feb. 27, 1957; s. Tadakatsu and Chiyoko (Nakajima) N.; children: Tatsuya, Kayoko, Tomoya. PhD, Kyoto U., 1999. Rschr. in chemistry Nara Pref. Inst. Pub. Health, Nara, Japan, 1984-96; rschr. in chemistry Nara Pref. Inst. Sci. & Tech., 1996-99, with dept. environ. mgmt., 1999—. Contbr. articles to profl. jours. Home: 437-21 Kujoh, Yamatokohriyama 639-1001, Japan Office: Nara Pref Dept Environ Mgmt, 30 Noboriohji, Nara 630-8501, Japan

NAGANAGOWDA, GOWDA AJJAPPA, research scientist; b. Musandihal, Karnataka, India, July 23, 1961; s. Gowda and Susheelamma Ajjappa; m. Gowda Nagana Taramani, June 4, 1992; 1 child, Yashas. Lectr. D.R.M. Sci. Coll., Davangere, India, 1985-86; scientist Indian Inst. Sci., Bangalore, 1986—; postdoct. fellow SUNY, Buffalo, 1996-98. Contbr. articles to profl. jours. Named Young Scientist Bruker India, 1993. Mem. Magnetic Resonance Soc. India (life). Hindu. Home: 3/A Krishnappa Layout, Nagasetty Hally, Bangalore Karnataka, India Office: Indian Inst Sci, Sophisticated Instr Faculty, 560012 Bangalore India

NAGAO, MAKOTO, academic administrator, engineering educator; b. Ise City, Japan, Oct. 4, 1936; s. Kaoru and Yukie Nagao; m. Mikiko Nagao, Dec. 5, 1964; children: Noriko, Fumiko, Takashi. BS, Kyoto U., Japan, 1959, MS, 1961, D in Engring., 1965; DSc (hon.), Nottingham U., Eng., 1999. Asst. prof. elec. engring. Kyoto U., 1961-68, assoc. prof. elec. engring., 1968-73, prof. elec. engring., 1973-97, v.p., 1996-97, dir. libr., 1995-97, dean faculty engring., 1997, pres., 1997—; prof. Nat. Mus. Ethnology, Osaka, Japan, 1976-94. Author: Knowledge and Inference, 1988, English transl., 1990, Machine Translation, 1986, English transl., 1990; editor Ency. Computer Sci., 1990, Multimedia Digital Libr., 1994, Natural Language Processing, 1996, Basis of Multimedia Information Processing, 1999. Recipient IEEE Emanuel R. Piore award, 1993, Medal with Purple Ribbon Japan Govt., 1997. Fellow IEEE (Emanuel R. Piore award 1993); mem. Inst. Elect. Info. Comm. Engring. Japan (v.p. 1993-98, pres. 1998-99), Internat. Assn. Machine Translation (pres. 1991-93), Cognitive Sci. Soc. Japan (pres. 1988-90), Internat. Assn. Pattern Recognition (v.p. 1986-88), Info. Processing Soc. Japan (pres. 1999—), Assn. Natural Lang. Processing (pres. 1994-96). Avocations: reading, golf, swimming, classical music, walking. Home: 19-106 Nishihimurocho, Kamitakano Sakyo, Kyoto 606-0095, Japan Office: Kyoto U Office of Pres, Yoshida-Hon Machi Sakyo-Ku, Kyoto 606-8501, Japan

NAGAOKA, SHINICHI, chemistry educator; b. Kyoto, Japan, Jan. 1, 1956; s. Choji and Ichiko (Matsuda) N.; m. Yumiko Okada, Oct. 19, 1985. BS, Kyoto U., 1978, MS, 1980, DS, 1983. Rsch. asst. Hokkaido U., Sapporo, Japan, 1983-85, Inst. for Molecular Sci., Okazaki, Japan, 1985-89; assoc. prof. Ehime U., Matsuyama, Japan, 1989-99, Inst. Molecular Sci., Okazaki, Japan, 1999—; vis. prof. U. Minn., Mpls., 1994-95; vis. rschr. Horishima U., Higashi-Hiroshima, 1999—. Contbr. articles to profl. jours. Mem. Chem. Soc. of Japan (Chem. Frontier VII award 1990, Young Scholar Lectr. award 1991), Vitamin Soc. of Japan, N.Y. Acad. Sci. Avocation: calligraphy. Office: Inst Molecular Sci, Okazaki 444-8585, Japan

NAGARAJA, S.K., electrical engineer; b. Anekal/Bangalore, Karnataka, India, May 1, 1955; s. Suda Krishnappa and S.K. Chinnamma; m. S.N. Gayathri, May 27, 1982; children: S.N. Prashanth, S.N. Prathibha. BEE, UVCE Bangalore, 1976; M in Tech., Indian Inst. Tech., 1978. Sr. engr. Best & Crompton, Madras, India, 1978-83; divsn. mgr. NGEF Ltd., Bangalore, 1983—. Contbr. articles to profl. jours. Avocations: reading, playing chess, table tennis. Office: Systems Engring Divsn, PO Box 3876, Bangalore 560 038, India

NAGARAJAN, BALASUBRAMANYAM, microbiologist; b. Madras, India, July 13, 1937; s. Balasubramanyam and Parvati B.; m. Thirunagavalli Nagarajan, July 1959; children: Ramesh, Satya. BS with honors, Annamalai U., 1958; MS, Madras U., 1960; PhD, Vanderbilt U., 1970. Biochemist Cancer Inst., Madras, 1960-64, head of lab., 1970-80, prof., chmn., 1980—; rsch. asst. Vanderbilt Med. Sch., Nashville, 1964-69, rsch. assoc., 1969-70; guest scientist Fed. Govt. of Germany, 1992-97; fellow Internat. Union Against Cancer, 1993; mem. expert com. Union pub. Svc. Com., Govt. India, med. rsch. com. CSIR, Govt. India, bd. rsch. Med. Univ., Madras; vis. scientist Govt. of France, 1999—. Prin. investigator numerous refereed jours.; contbr. 170 scientific articles to profl. jours. Recipient B.C. Roy Nat. award Med. Coun. of India, 1996; doctoral fellow U.S. Pub. Health Svc., 1964-70; merit scholar Annamalai U., 1953-58. Mem. Environ. Mutagen Soc./India (life), Soc. Biology Chemists (life). Home: 17 12th Cross St, Indiranagar/Chennai 600 020, India Office: Cancer Inst, Chennai 600 020, India

NAGARAJAN, LAXMI PRIYADHARSHINI, dietitian; b. Thirunelveli, Tamil Nadu, India, Apr. 10; d. Nagarajan Sivalingam and Kalaivani (Ramanan) Nagarajan. BSc, P.S.G. Coll. Arts & Sci., Coimbatore, India, 1996; CNSD, Tamil Nad Hosp., Chennai, India, 1997; MSc, Tamil Nadu Agrl. Coll. & Rsch., Madurai, India, 1999. Dietitian Apollo Speciality Hosp., Chennai, 1999—. Mem. N.Y. Acad. Scis. Avocations: compereing, traveling, interior decorating, stamp collecting, listening to music. Home: A-36 Ground Fl I St, Secretariat Colony Kellys, Chennai 600010, India

NAGARSENKER, MANGAL SHAILESH, pharmaceutical technologist; b. Rajapur, India, Nov. 5, 1957; d. Anant and Nalini Shikhare; m. Shailesh Nagarsenker, May 9, 1983; two children. B in Pharm. Sci., Mumbai U., 1978, M in Pharm. Sci., 1981; PhD, Bombay Coll. Pharmacy, 1989. Pharmacist Nicholas (I) Ltd., Mumbai, India, 1980-81; from lectr. to prof. Bombay Coll. Pharmacy, India, 1982—. Author: Hospital and Clinical Pharmacy, 1997, Biopharmaceutics and Pharmacokinetics, 1999; contbr. articles to profl. jours. Mem. Indian Pharm. Assn., Controlled Release Soc. Office: Bombay Coll Pharmacy, Kalina Santacruz, Mumbai 400 098, India

NAGASAKA, FRANCIS GENICHIRO, retired philosophy educator; b. Yamagata-shi, Japan, Dec. 7, 1921; s. Ryiochi Francis and Shiu Mary (Kunii) N.; m. Akiko Elizabeth Itoho, Sept. 22, 1938; children: Michiko Korine, Naoko Sorial, Kiyoshi, Etsuko Molka, Itaru, Susumu. B in Engring., Keio U., Tokyo, 1945; BS, U. Tokyo, 1949; PhD, U. Notre Dame, 1956. Instr. Nanzan U., Nagoya, Japan, 1950-59; assoc. prof. Nanzan U., Nagoya, 1959-75, prof., 1972-90, dean gen. edn., 1972—, v.p., 1973-85, dean fgn. affairs, 1982-85; rsch. assoc. U. Notre Dame, South Bend, Ind., 1953-55, Boston U., 1971-72. Author: Problems of Scientific Explanation, 1973, Boston Studies in the Philosophy of Science, 1972; editor: Life Science and Religion, 1983, Japanese Studies in the Philosophy of Science, 1998, Memory of Father John Hirschmeier, 1999. Recipient Imperial Honor for Achievements in Rsch. and Edn., Govt. of Japan, Tokyo, 1997. Mem. Philosophy Sci. Soc., Soc. for Asian and Comparative Philosophy, Brit. Soc. for

Philosophy of Sci., Ctr. for Process Studies. Home: 33-103 Dialand Kanami-cho, Tagata-gun Shizu-ken 419-0106, Japan

NAGASE, FUMIHIKO, immunologist, researcher; b. Kani, Gifu, Japan, July 8, 1945; s. Yoshimi and Satsuki (Sone) N. B in Engring., Nagoya U., Japan, 1970, M in Engring., 1972, DMS, 1978. Rsch. assoc. Nagoya U. Sch. Medicine, Japan, 1976-82, asst. prof., 1982-86, assoc. prof., 1986; prof. Nagoya U. Coll. Med. Tech., Japan, 1986-97, Nagoya U. Sch. Health Scis., Japan, 1997—. Contbr. articles to profl. jours. Postdoctoral fellow NYU Med. Ctr., 1981-83. Mem. Japanese Soc. for Immunology, Japanese Soc. for Bacteriology, Japanese Cancer Assn. Home: Suimei-biru 602, 12 Gokisodori 1-chome Showa-ku, Aichi Nagoya 466-0015, Japan Office: Nagoya Univ Sch Health Scis, 1-20 Daikominami-1-chome, Higashi-ku Nagoya 461-8673, Japan

NAGASE, SOHJI, medical educator; b. Mitsukaido, Ibaraki, Japan, May 23, 1954; s. Senpei and Kikue (Iizumi) N.; m. Etsuko Ishitsuka, Apr. 2, 1978; children: Chihiro, Rei, Yui. MD, Yamagata U., Japan, 1979; PhD, U. Tsukuba, Ibaraki, Japan, 1985. Resident internal medicine U. Tsukuba, Japan, 1979-85, asst. prof., 1986-97, assoc. prof., 1997—; clin. fellow Tsukuba Gakuen Hosp., Japan, 1985-86; rsch. fellow Albert Einstein Med. Coll., N.Y., 1989-90. Contbr. articles to profl. jours. Mem. Am. Soc. Nephrology, European Dialysis and Transplant Assn. Avocations: car, audio, Japanese soba making. Home: 486 Kou Moriya, Moriya Ibaraki 302-0115, Japan Office: U Tsukuba Inst Clin Med, 1-1-1 Ten-nodai, Tsukuba Ibaraki 305-8575, Japan

NAGASHIMA, HIDEYO, electronics educator; b. Sagamihara, Kanagawa, Japan, Jan. 1, 1941; s. Sadatoshi and Momoe (Kojima) N.; m. Shizuyo Kitagawa, Sept. 29, 1971; children: Hideyuki, Hidekazu. B of Engring., Kogakuin U., Japan, 1964, M of Engring., 1966; D of Engring., Tokyo Inst. of Tech., 1973. Asst. Tokyo Inst. Tech., 1966-69; from lectr. to assoc. prof. Kogakuin U., Tokyo, 1970-82, prof., 1982—, also bd. dirs.; v.p. Kogakuin U., Tokyo, 1999—. Author: Numerical Method, 1979 (Maki award 1979). Avocations: golf, bowling, igo, Japanese chess. Office: Kogakuin U, 1-24-2 Nishi Shinjuku, 7160 Tokyo Japan

NAGASHIMA, RYU, film research company executive; b. Musashino, Japan, Nov. 5, 1957; s. Shinsak and Shizu (Ito) N. B Commerce, Takachiho Coll. Commerce, Tokyo, 1980. Gen. mgr. Film Rsch. Ltd., Tokyo, 1980—. Avocations: films, television. Home: Musashino-shi 1-20-10, Kitamachi, Kichijoji Tokyo 180-0001, Japan Office: Film Rsch Ltd, Musashino-shi 1-20-10 Kita, Kichijoji Tokyo 180-0001, Japan

NAGASHIMA, TAKASHI, retired mathematician, educator; b. Tokyo, Jan. 21, 1935; s. Kichitaro John and Amy Margaret (Kitashima) N.; m. Noriko Iochi, Mar. 30, 1967. BS, Tokyo U. Edn., 1960, MS, 1962. Asst. Tokyo U. Edn., 1963-67; instr. dept. math. Hitotsubashi U., Kunitachi, Japan, 1967-70, assoc. prof., 1970-78, prof., 1978-98, prof. emeritus, 1998—. Contbr. articles to profl. jours. Mem. Math. Soc. Japan. E-mail: nagasimat@mta.biglobe.ne.jp.

NAGATA, SHOICHI, engineering educator, researcher; b. Koshoku-shi, Nagano-ken, Japan, July 4, 1945; s. Kazuo and Masako (Aoki) N.; m. Noriko Haga, Mar. 14, 1975; 1 child, Fumi. BS, Kanazawa (Japan) U., 1968; MS, Hokkaido U., Sapporo, Japan, 1970, PhD, 1975. Postdoctoral assoc. Purdue U., West Lafayette, Ind., 1977-80; rsch. assoc. Ames Lab. Iowa State U., 1980-82; assoc. prof. Muroran (Japan) Inst. Tech., 1982-91, prof. engring., 1991—. Avocations: skiing, golf. Fax: 81 143 46 5612. Home: Sakuragi-cho 12-86, 5-chome, Noboribetsu-shi Hokkaido 059-0023, Japan Office: Muroran Inst Tech, Mizumoto-cho 27-1, Muroran Hokkaido 050-8585, Japan

NAGATA, TETSUJI, anatomist, biology educator; b. Suwa, Nagano, Japan, Feb. 5, 1931; s. Kamashige and Haruko (Takeuchi) N.; m. Kyoko Nakamura, Mar. 15, 1962; children: Seiji, Hiroko. BSc, Shinshu U., Matsumoto, Japan, 1951, MD, 1955, PhD, 1962. Instr. in anatomy Shinshu U., Matsumoto, 1956-58, asst. prof. anatomy, 1958-59, assoc. prof. anatomy, 1959-62, asoc. prof. anatomy, 1964-74, prof., chmn. anatomy, 1974-96, prof. emeritus, 1996—, dean sch. of medicine, 1990-92; rsch. assoc. in physiology U. Ill., 1962-64; prof. emeritus Hebei Med. U., China, 1987; pres. emeritus Hebei Med. Coll., China, 1991—; prof. anatomy & physiology Nagano Women's Jr. Coll., 1997—; pres. 4th Japan-U.S. Joint Congress Histochemistry and Cytochemistry, 1994, 4th Internat. Symposium Radioautography, 1993; vis. prof. Nat. U. Singapore, Singapore, 1995—, U. Sau Paulo, Brazil, 1989—, U. Campinas, Brazil, 1995—; prof. emeritus ChangDe Med. U., ChengDe, China, 1999—. Assoc. editor Cellular and Molecular Biology, 1989—. Hon. pres. 5th Internat. Symposium Radioautography, 1997. Mem. Japanese Assn. Anatomists (bd. dirs. 1988-95, hon. dir. 1996—), Japan Soc. Histochemistry and Cytochemistry (bd. dirs. 1989-96, hon. dir. 1999—, pres. 1994, 4th Japan-U.S. congress 1994), Clin. Electron Microscopy Soc. Japan (pres. 1992-93, bd. dirs. 1988-99, hon. dir. 1999—), World Soc. Cellular and Molecular Biology (v.p. 1991-96, pres. 1996—), N.Y. Acad. Sci., Sigma Xi. Home: 1361 Matsuoka Okada, Matumoto 3900313, Japan Office: Dept Anatomy Cell Biology, Shinshu U Sch Med 3-1-1 Asahi, Matsumoto 390-8621, Japan

NAGATA, YOSHIAKI, phsychology educator; b. Tokyo, Dec. 2, 1935; s. Yasukichi and Kura (Kuki) N.; m. Teruko Hatano, June 23, 1963; 2 children. BA, Kyoto (Japan) U., 1959, MA, 1961, PhD, 1985. Rsch. asst. Kyoto U., 1966-69; assoc. prof. Osaka (Japan) Women's Coll., 1969-73; assoc. prof. Gakushuin U., Tokyo, 1973-79, prof., 1979—; mem. liaison coms. Sci. Coun. Japan, Tokyo, 1985-87, 93—; mem. specialized rev. subcoms. Japanese U. Acreditation Assn., 1988-89. Author, editor: Psychology of Group Behavior, 1986, Development of Social Psychology, 1987. Mem. Japanese Soc. Social Psychology (pres. 1999-2001), Japanese Psychol. Assn. Office: Gakushuin U, 1-5-1 Mejiro, Toshimaku 171-8588, Japan

NAGATANI, TAKESHI, aircraft engineer; b. Yamaguchi, Japan, May 5, 1948; s. Nobuo and Sumiko (Nawata) N. Grad., Nagasaki (Japan) Naval-Architecture Coll., 1971. Chief engr. Asahi Airlines Co., Ltd., Osaka, Japan, 1971—. Mem. Japan Aero. Engrs. Assn., Internal Cons. Assn. Avocations: travel, driving, movies. Home: Sanhaitsu Yaominami I-505, 6-57-1 Minami-Kinomoto, Yao City Osaka 581, Japan Office: Asahi Airlines Co Ltd, Kuko 2-12, Yao City Osaka 581, Japan

NAGATOMI, AKIRA, entomologist, educator; b. Kita-Kyushu, Japan, Dec. 10, 1928; s. Kiyomi and Masu Nagatomi; m. Miyo Maruyama, May 28, 1953; children: Noriko, Hisako. BS, Kyushu U., Fukuoka, Japan, 1951, PhD, 1961. Instr. Hyogo U. Agr., Sasyama-Cho, Japan, 1951-60; instr. Kagoshima (Japan) U., 1960-67, assoc. prof., 1967-69, prof. entomology, 1969-94, prof. emeritus, 1994—. Contbr. articles to sci. jours. Avocations: garden seeing, traveling over hill and dale. Home: 4-30-7 Murasaki-Baru, Kyushu Kagoshima 890-0082, Japan

NAGATSU, MASAYOSHI, cardiothoracic surgeon, researcher; b. Tokyo, Apr. 15, 1957; s. Hiroshi and Reiko (Komatsu) N.; m. Yuko Komatsu, Dec. 18, 1988; children: Kazuki, Naoki, Koki. MD, Tsukuba U., 1983. Intern, resident Heart Inst. Japan, Tokyo Women's Med. Coll., 1983-91; postdoctoral fellow, rsch. fellow Gazes Cardiac Rsch. Inst. Med. U. S.C., 1991-93; asst. in pediat. cardiovasc. surgery Heart Inst. Japan Tokyo Women's Med. Coll., 1993-97; chief in pediat. cardiac surgery Gifu Prefecture Hosp., Japan, 1997—. Mem. Japan Surg. Soc., Japan Assn. for Thoracic Surgery (surg. instr. 1996—), Am. Heart Assn., Asian Soc. for Cardiovasc. Surgery. Avocations: guitar synthesizer, medical multimedia. Office: Gifu Prefecture Hosp, 4-6-1 Noishiki, Gifu-shi Gifu 500-8717, Japan

NAGATSUMA, TADAO, electrical engineer, researcher; b. Hamada, Shimane, Japan, Dec. 10, 1958; s. Takao and Katsuko (Nakamura) N.; m. Naoko Omachi, Apr. 28, 1984; children: Nanako, Yukiko. BS, Kyushu U., Fukuoka, Japan, 1981, MS, 1983, PhD, 1986. Engr. Nippon Telegraph and Tel. Corp., Atsugi Electrocomm. Labs., Kanagawa, Japan, 1986-89; sr. rsch. engr. Nippon Telegraph and Tel. Corp., LSI Labs., Kanagawa, 1990-95; sr. rsch. engr. supr. Nippon Telegraph and Tel. Corp., Sys. Electronics Lab., Kanagawa, Japan, 1996-98; dist. tech. mem. sr. rsch. scientist, supervisor Nippon Telegraph & Tel. Corp. Telecomms. Energy Labs., Kanagawa, 1999—. Guest editor Optical and Quantum Electronics, 1996. Recipient Okochi Meml. award, 1998, Japan Microwave Prize, 1998, Min.'s award Sci. and Tech. Agy., 2000. Mem. IEEE (A.R. Chi. Best Paper award Instrumentation and Measurement Soc. 1993), Inst. Electronics, Info. and Comm. Engrs. of Japan, (Young Engrs. award 1989), Optical Soc. Am., Japan Soc. Applied Physics. Avocations: tennis, table tennis, badminton, painting. Home: 2232-1-701 Kamitsuruma, Sagamihara, Kanagawa 228-0802, Japan Office: Nippon Tel/Telecoms Energy, Lab 3-1 Morinosato Wakamiya, Kanagawa 243-0198, Japan

NAGAYAMA, KUNIAKI, biophysics educator; b. Gumma, Japan, July 22, 1945; s. Masaji and Tomi (Furuichi) N.; m. Sachiko Tanabe, Mar. 28, 1948; children: Yuko, Taichi, Noriko. BS, U. Tokyo, Japan, 1968, MS in Physics, 1970, PhD in Physics, 1974. Rsch. assoc. U. Tokyo, Japan, 1973-83; gen. mgr. Jeol Ltd., Tokyo, 1983-88, dir., 1988-93; prof. U. Tokyo, Japan, 1993-97, Nat. Inst. Physiol. Soc., Okazaki, 1997—; rsch. assoc. Eidgenosische Technische Hochschule-Zürich, Switzerland, 1976-79; dir. Exploratory Rsch. for Advanced Tech. Protein Array Project, Japan Corp. Sci. Tech., Tokyo, 1990-95; mem. Rev. Com. of Human Frontier Sci. Program, Strasbourg, 1993-98; Faraday lectr. Royal Inst. G.B., 1997. Contbr. 250 articles to profl. jours. Mem. Japan Soc. Physics, Japan Soc. Chemistry, Japan Soc. Biophysics. Achievements include patents in representation of 2D NMR spectrum; protein 2D crystal on mercury; lateral capillary force; digital coloring; monoparticle films; color ellipsoscope; complex electron microscopy; electron phasemicroscopy. Office: Nat Inst Physiol Scis, Okazaki 444-8585, Japan

NAGAYAMA, MASAO, neurologist, neuroscientist, educator; b. Yokohama, Japan, Nov. 13, 1958; s. Masami and Aya (Arima) N.; m. Tomiko Nagai, Mar. 18, 1991; 1 child, Masami. MD, Tokai U., Isehara, Kanagawa, Japan, 1983, PhD, 1992. Diplomate in medicine. Jr. resident Tokai U. Hosp., Isehara, 1983-85, sr. resident, 1985-88; mem. staff 2d Tokyo Nat. Hosp. (now Nat. Tokyo Med. Ctr.), 1987-89; asst. prof. Tokai U. Sch. Medicine, Isehara, 1988-99, lectr., 1999—; vis. scientist U. Minn. Med. Sch., Mpls., 1996-98. Ad hoc reviewer Preventive Medicine, 1994, Stroke, 1996; contbr. articles to profl. jours. Recipient Excellent Paper award Japanese Cerebrovascular Disease Soc., 1987, 96; Ministry of Edn., Sci. and Culture Japan grantee, 1991, 92, 95, 99. Fellow Am. Acad. Neurology (corr.), Japanese Soc. Internal Medicine; mem. Soc. for Neuroscience, Japan Stroke Soc. (councilor 1999), Japanese Soc. Neurology (councilor 2000). Avocations: music, histories of Japan and the West, reading. Home: 3-10-5 Isogo, Isogo-ku, 235-0016 Yokohama Japan Office: Tokai U Sch Med Dept Neur, Bohseidai, 259-1193 Isehara Kanagawa, Japan

NAGAZUMI, YASUO, electronics researcher, software company executive; b. Tokyo, Japan, Feb. 18, 1945; s. Torahiko Ohsako and Sumiko Nagazumi; m. Nariko Kuroki, May 4, 1972; 2 children. B of Engring., Waseda U., Tokyo, 1967, M of Engring., 1969. Engr. Nissan Motor Co. Ltd., Tokyo, 1969-80; pres. G.D.S. Inc., Tokyo, 1983—; cons. T.R.L., Tokyo, 1980-82, G.R.E., Tokyo, 1983. Contbr. articles to profl. jours.; patentee in field. Mem. IEEE, IEICE. Buddhist. Avocations: skiing, playing banjo, gardening, painting. Office: GDS Inc 3-12-17 Mita, Minato-ku, Tokyo 108 0073, Japan

NAGDA, KANTI, advice services administrator; b. May 1, 1946; s, Vershi Bhoja and Zaviben N.; m. Bhagwati Desai, Nov. 9, 1972; children: Dipen, Rupen. Student, Coll. Future Edn., Chipenham, U.K., 1967, East African U., Kampala, Uganda, 1969. Tchr. City H.S., Kampala, 1969-72; acct. Hollander Hyams Ltd., London, 1972-82; mgr. Cmty. Ctr., Harrow, U.K., 1982-97; dir. Anglo-Indian Circle, Harrow, 1974-97. Author: Muratiyo Ke Nokar, 1967; hon. editl. cons. Internat. Asian Guide and Who's Who, U.K., 1975; contbr. articles in field to profl. jours. and newspapers. Sec. gen. Confederation Indian Orgns. U.K., 1975-98; mem. Harrow Crime Prevention Panel, U.K., 1983-96. Mem. Indian Nat. Club, Lions (pres. Greenford Willow Tree chpt. 1988—). Home: 170 Tolcarne Dr, Pinner, Middlesex HA5 2DR, England Office: London Borough Harrow, Station Rd, Harrow Middlesex HA1 2UL, England

NAGEL, IVAN, theater administrator; b. Budapest, Hungary, June 28, 1931; arrived in Germany, 1951; s. Ignac and Yolanda (Guttmann) N. Artistic advisor Münchner Kammerspiele, Munich, 1962-69; theater critic Süddeutsche Zeitung, Munich, 1969-71; theater mgr. Deutsches Schauspielhaus, Hamburg, Germany, 1972-79; cultural arts corr. Frankfurter Allgemeine, N.Y., 1981-83; theater mgr. Staatsschauspiel, Stuttgart, Germany, 1985-88; prof. Hochschule der Künste, Berlin, 1988-96; mgr. drama sect. Salzburg Festival, 1997-99; pres. Theater der Nationen, Hamburg, 1979, Theater der Welt, Cologne, Stuttgart, Hamburg, 1981, 87, 89; fellow Wissenschaftskolleg, Berlin, 1984, 89. Author: Autonomie und Gnade, 1985 (Merck prize 1988), Autonomy & Mercy. On Mozart's Operas, 1991, Gedankengange als Lebensläufe, 1987, Danneckers "Ariadne," 1993, Der Kunstler als Kuppler, 1997. V.p. Acad. for Lang. and Poetry, 1989-96; mem. Acad. Künste, 1991—. Recipient Merck prize, 1988, Kortner prize, 1999, Mendelssohn prize, 2000. Home: Keithstr 10, 10787 Berlin Germany

NAGELE, SUSAN LYNN, physician; b. Rantoul, Ill., Dec. 24, 1955; d. Thomas Eugene and Lenore Irene (Loess) N. BS, U. Ill., 1978; MD, So. Ill. U., 1981. Diplomate Am. Bd. Family Physicians. Residency in family practice Carbondale Mem. Hosp., Ill., 1981-84; med. officer Maryknoll Mission Assn., Diocese of Musoma, Kowak, Tanzania, 1985-91, Torit, Sudan, 1991-92, Nimule, Sudan, 1992-97, Lotimor, Sudan, 1997—; mem. TB task force Operation Lifeline Sudan, 1993-94. Named Alumna of Yr., So. Ill. U. Sch. Medicine, Springfield, 1996. Mem. Am. Acad. Family Physicians. Roman Catholic. Office: Diocese of Torit c/o NCA, Box 52802, Nairobi Kenya

NAGEM, TANUS JORGE, organic chemist, educator; b. S. domanhuaçú, Brazil, Sept. 6, 1944; s. Salim and Nazha Mansur Nagem; m. Sonia Murta, Aug. 15, 1946; children: Tanise Murta, Carine Murta. Sci. degree, Colegio Anchieta, Belo Horizonte, Brazil, 1962. Cert. in pharm. biochemistry. Adj. prof. U. Minas Gerais, Belo Horizonte, 1970-93; titular prof. U. Viçosa, Brazil, 1993-95; adj. prof. U. Ouro Preto, Brazil, 1995—; cons. Fapemig, Belo Horizonte, 1993-97. Office: Instituto Ciencias Exatas, Campus Morro Do Cruzeiro, 35400000 Ouro Preto Brazil

NAGESH, K.S., oral surgeon; b. May 23, 1947. B Dental Surgery, Bangalore U., 1969, M Dental Surgery, 1975. Dental surgeon Rural Health Tng. Ctr., Nanjungud, 1970-73, Govt. Hosp., Hospet, 1975-76; lectr. Govt. Dental Coll., Bangalore, 1976-82, asst. prof., 1982-92; prof., head dept. oral medicine diagnosis & radiology, prin. R.V. Dental Coll., Jayanagar, Bangalore; mem. Karnataka State Dental Coun., 1984-91; condr. various workshops; mem. bd. studiees Bangalore U., 1989-90, 93-94, 94-97, Mysore U., 1992, Andhra Pradesh Health U. Vijayawada, 1996-99; mem. faculty medicine Bangalore U., 1995-99; mem. bd. studies Rajiv Gandhi U. Health Scis., Bangalore, 1997—, mem. faculty dentistry, 1997—. Contbr. articles to profl. jours. Mem. Indian Dental Assn., Intian Acad. Oral Medicine (gen. sec. 1988-90, 90-91, 91-92, 92-93), Indian Acad. Oral Medicine and Radiology (life, pres. 1993-94), Indian Soc. Dental Rsch. (life), Karnataka Medico-Legal Soc. (life), Indian Soc. Oral Implantologist (life), S.E. Asia Assn. Dental Edn. (India sect.), Internat. Assn. Dento Maxillofacial Radiology (regional dir.), N.Y. Acad. Scis. Office: RV Dental Coll, IV Block, Jayanagar 560 011, Bangalore

NAGI, CATHERINE RASEH, retired educational administrator, financial planner; b. Bklyn., Oct. 13, 1940; d. Massed and Catherine (Irato) N. BS, Bklyn. Coll., 1962, MS, 1964, postgrad., 1965-67, 76; postgrad., Hofstra U., 1967-76, St. Johns U., Queens, N.Y., 1976-78. Cert. dist. sch. adminstr., supr., prin., asst. prin., tchr. health/phys. edn., N.Y.; CFP. Tchr. health/phys. edn. Jr. High Sch. 211-Dist. 18, Bklyn., 1962, Bay Ridge High Sch., Bklyn., 1962-63; tchr., acting chair Jr. High Sch. 78-Dist. 22, Bklyn., 1963-70; acting asst. prin. Intermediate Sch. 302-Dist. 19, Bklyn., 1970-71; narcotics edn. tchr. trainer Dist. 19 Bd. of Edn., Bklyn., 1971-73, supr. health/drug edn./svcs., 1973-75; supr. reimbursable programs Dist. 22 Bd. of Edn., Bklyn., 1975-79, supr. comprehensive planning, 1979-84, dep. supt., 1984-90; acting prin. Pub. Sch. 217-Dist. 22, Bklyn., 1980; sch. supt. Dist. 28 Bd. of Edn., Queens, N.Y., 1990-97; ret., 1997; tchr. Adult Edn./Community Ctrs., N.Y.C., 1959-65; presenter N.Y.C. and N.Y. State Ednl. Confs., Univs.; grant writer N.Y.C. Bd. Edn., 1973—. Co-author, cons. (math. workbook) Get Ahead in Math, 1985; creator, editor (ednl. mag.) Gateways to Learning, 1977-90; creator, ednl. data system, 1976; developer first N.Y.C./N.Y. State early identification learning disabilities program, 1975. Named Educator of Yr. Assn. Tchrs. N.Y., 1980; recipient City Coun. Proclamation N.Y.C. Coun., 1991, 97, Legis. resolution N.Y. State Assembly/Senate, 1991, 97, Congl. Record recognition U.S. Congress, 1991, 97, Recognition award Forestdale Foster and Adoptive Parents Assn., Queens, 1992, Queensboro Pres. Proclamation, Supts.' Network Recognition, Fordham U., N.Y.C., Recognition, 112 Pct. Cmty. Coun. Mem. ASCD, Am. Assn. Sch. Adminstrs., N.Y.C. Assn. Supts., N.Y.C. Adminstrv. Women in Edn., Bklyn./N.Y. State Reading Coun./Assn., Thomas Jefferson Dem. Club, Kings County Dem. Com. Avocations: languages, sports, singing, gourmet cooking, collecting stamps, coins and pens. Office: 122 Crispell Rd Krumville NY 12461-5408

NAGIB, NABIL NAEEM, physicist; b. Cairo, Egypt, June 1, 1945; s. Naeem and Lily (Fahmy) Hanna; m. Manal Zaky, Jan. 7, 1979; two children. BSc, Ain Shams U., 1967; MSc, Am. U. Cairo, 1979; PhD, Moscow State U., 1988. Physicist Acad. Scientific Rsch. & Technology, Cairo, 1967-80; from asst. rschr. to rschr. Nat. Inst. Standards, Cairo, 1980-95; asst. prof. Nat. Inst. Standards, Giza, 1995—. Mem. Optical Soc. Am., Am. Inst. Physics. Office: Nat Inst Standards, Tersa St PO Box 136, Giza 12211, Egypt

NAGISETTY, IRENA ALDONA, technical specialist; b. Ionishkis, Lithuania, Aug. 9, 1941; d. Adomas Gulbinas and Ona Chepaite Gulbiniene; m. Rao Venkateshwara Nagisetty, Jan. 23, 1969; children: Ramune, Vytas. MS in Physics, Moscow State U., 1969; MSEE, U. Toledo, 1978; MS in Computer Sci., Wayne State U., 1990. Tchg. instr. nonlinear physics U. Vilnius, Lithuania, 1965-67; tech. transl. U. Madison, 1973-75; grad. asst. Engring. Coll. U. Toledo, 1977-78; real-time applications engr. Schindler Elevator Co., Toledo, 1978-83; mfg. engr. Ford Motor Co., Detroit, 1984-89, mfg. engr. expert sys. devel. & replication, 1989-92, tech. specialist intelligent plant/product ops. control, 1992-99, tech. specialist ops. engring., 1999—; advisor Berkeley (Calif.) Initiative for Soft Computing; organizer, chair Internat. Symposium for Automotive Applications Tech. and Automation, Croydon, Eng. Assoc. editor: REVIEWS iNtELLIGENT Automation and Soft Computing, 1995—; reviewer books on fuzzy logic and intelligent control, 1996—. Mem. IEEE, Soc. Automotive Engrs. (internat. automotive mfg.). Avocations: skiing, gardening. Fax: (313) 592-2388. E-mail: inagiset@ford.com. Home: 2807 Barrington Dr Toledo OH 43606-3004 Office: Ford Motor Co 24500 Glendale Detroit MI 48239-2698

NAGISETTY, LAKSHMI NARAYANA, geophysicist, engineering executive; b. Thurimella, India, Aug. 30, 1957; s. Rangaiah Venkata and Achhamma Nagisetty; m. Venkata Lakshmi; children: Bhuvanesh Kumar, Lokhesh Kumar. BSc, Silver Jubilee Govt. Coll., Kurnool, India, 1979; MSc, Ctr. Exploration Geophysics, Hyderabad, India, 1982; postgrad. diploma, Productivity Coun., 1995. Jr. rsch. fellow Ctr. Exploration Geophysics, Hyderabad, 1982-83; geophysicist Directorate of Geology and Mining, Govt. Gujarat, Ahmedabad, India, 1983-85; sr. geophysicist Mineral Exploration Corp. Ltd., Nagpur, India, 1985—. Mem. Assn. Exploration Geophysicists, Indian Assn. Hydrogeologists, Indian Assn. Environ. Mgmt. Avocations: trekking, mountaineering, earth science education. Home: 18-33/16, Mak Towers, Opp. Survey of India, Andhra Pradesh 500 039, India Office: MECL, Seminary Hills, Utiliy Complex, Nagpur 440 006, India

NAGL-DOCEKAL, HERTA, philosopher; b. Wels, Austria, May 29, 1944; d. Friedrich and Anna (Kirchmayr) Docekal; m. Ludwig Nagl. PhD, U. Vienna, 1967, Habil., 1981. Asst. prof. U. Vienna, 1968-85, Univ. prof., 1985—; vis. prof. U. Utrecht, Netherlands, 1990, U. Frankfurt, Germany, 1991-92, U. Konstanz, Germany, 1993, Freie U. Berlin, 1995; vis. fellow Inst. fuer die Wissenschaften vom Menschen, Vienna, 1995; speaker in field. Author: Die Objektivitaet der Geschichtswissenschaft, 1982, Feministische Philosophie, Ergebnisse, Probleme, Perspektiven, 2000; editor: Feministische Philosophie, 1990, 94, Der Sinn des Historischen, 1996; co-editor: Jenseits der Geschlechtermoral, 1993; co-editor Politische Theorie. Differenz und Lebensqualitaet, 1996, Deutsche Zeitschrift fuer Philosophie, 1993—. Mem. Fedn. Internat. Soc. Philosophy (steering com. 1999—), Austrian Acad. Scis. (corr.), Allgemeine Gesellschaft fuer Philosophie in Deutschland (bd. dirs. 1994-99). Office: U Vienna Dept Philosophy, Universitaetsstr 7, A-1010 Vienna Austria

NAGLE, MARK EARL, lawyer; b. Dearborn, Mich., Aug. 7, 1954; s. Earl C. and Mildred K. Nagle. BA, Emory U., 1976; JD, Georgetown U., 1979. Bar: Va. 1980, D.C. 1988, Pa. 1997. Assoc. Moorcones Firm, Leesburg, Va., 1979-82; atty. Dept. Justice, Washington, 1982-85; asst. U.S. atty. U.S. Atty.'s Office, Washington, 1985-97, chief civil divsn., 1998—; assoc. Leboeuf, Lamb, Pitts., 1997-98. Home: 4675 Kirkpatrick Ln Alexandria VA 22311-4914 Office: US Attys Office 555 4th St NW Washington DC 20001-2733

NAGOTHU, DUAYA SEKHAR, forester, researcher; b. Guntur, India, Apr. 21, 1962; s. Rayanna Choudhary and Kamala (Uppalapati) N.; m. Shanthi Yerram, Feb. 8, 1989. MSc in Agr., Andhra Pradesh Agrl. U., Hyderabad, India, 1985; diploma in forestry, Nat. Forest Acad., Dehradun, India, 1989; MSc in Natural Resource Mgmt., Agrl. U. Norway, Aas, 1995; PhD in Devel. Studies, Noragric Agrl. U. Norway, Aas, 1999. Rschr. A.P. Agrl. U., Hyderabad, India, 1986-87; probationer Nat. Forest Acad., Dehradun, India, 1987-89; asst. conservator Forest Dept., Rajasthan, India, 1989-91, dist. forest officer, 1991-93; rsch. fellow Noragric/NLH, Aas, 1993-99, guest rschr., 1999—; cons. Norad Project, Aas, 1998, Undpproject, Dehradun, India, 1993. Contbr. articles to profl. jours. Sec. Nature Club, Nat. Adminstrv. Acad., Mussoorie, India, 1989, Dist. Environ. Soc., Bharatpur, India, 1991-93. Norad fellow Norwegian Govt., 1993-95, 95-99. Mem. Internat. Assn. for Study of Common Property, Indian Inst. Pub. Adminstrn. (life), Dryland Network Group. Avocations: bird watching, swimming. Home: Hasselbakken 20, 1430 Aas Norway Office: Ctr Internat Environ and, Devel Studies, 1432 Aas Norway

NAGPURKAR, AJIT DATTATREYA, management consultant; b. Dhule, Maharashtr, India, Jan. 7, 1948; s. Dattatreya Appaji and Nalini Dattatreya (Agnihotri) N.; m. Suniti Ajit Bokil; children: Manjusri, Veda. B Com with hons., VWS Coll., 1970; Diploma in Bus. Mgmt., Davars Coll. Mgmt., Mumbai, India, 1971, Diploma in Import Export Mgmt., 1980; M Com with hons., Univ. Pune, India, 1974. Asst. mgr. Surjit Motors Pvt. Ltd., Dhule, India, 1965-67; statistician Maharashtra State Road Transport Corp., India, 1968-70; fin. cons. Datamatics Corp., Mumbai, 1970-75; fin. and project exec. Garware Group Cos., Mumbai, 1975-82; CEO, v.p. Double Cola Mfg. Co. I. P. Ltd., Mumbai, 1982-89; mng. dir. Timely Assocs., Mumbai, 1989-99; dir. Timely Mgmt. Con.Ser.P.Ltd., Mumbai, 1993-2000, Dwijvihar Agro Horti, Mumbai; indsl. expert M.J. C. of C. and Industry, 1995-98; mktg. cons. Inst. of Chartered Fin. Analysts of India, 1995-98; rep. The McGraw-Hill Cos. Resident editor: Banking Fin. mag.; author: So. Economist mag., Banking Fin. mag., Business Econs (book). Hon. sec. Swastik Minaxi Co.Op Sty, Mumbai, 1984-2000. Fellow Inst. of Dirs.; mem. Maharashtra C. of C. and Industry, Maharashtra Econ. Devel. Coun. Avocations: drawing, sculpture, writing, classical music. Home: ST Rd Chembur, Minaxi Swastik Park, 400071 Mumbai India Office: Timely Mgmt Cons Svcs, Pvt Ltd 15/4 Shivpuri Colon, 400071 Chembur/Maharashtra India

NAGUIB, RAOUF GORGUI, electrical engineering educator, researcher; b. Cairo, Oct. 26, 1956; s. Naguib Gorgui Naguib and Aida Kamel Ghobrial; m. May Salah Shaker, Aug. 30, 1987; children: Nadine, Hannah. BSc, Cairo U., 1979; Diploma, U. London, 1982, MSc with distinction, 1983, PhD in Elec. and Electronic Engring., 1986. Rsch. asst. U. London, 1986-87; Brit. Telecom. lectr. U. Newcastle, Newcastle Upon Tyne, Eng., 1987-89, lectr. data comm. sys., 1989-98; prof. biomed. computing, mem. biomed. computing rsch. group Coventry (Eng.) U., 1998—. Co-author: Digital Filtering in One and Two Dimensions, 1989; contbr. articles to sci. jours., including Procs. Instn. Elec. Engrs., Can. Jour. Elec. Engring., IEEE Trans. on Computers, Info. Tech. in Biomedicine, European Urology, Brit. Jour. Urology, Pathobiology, Analytical and Quantitative Cytology and Histology, Brit. Jour. Cancer, Anticancer Rsch., Physiol. Measurement, Neurocomputing, Neural Networks. Scholar U. London, 1983, Com. Vice Chancellors and Prins. U.K. Univs., 1983; cancer rsch. fellow Fulbright Commn., Hawaii,

1995. Mem. IEEE (sr.), Brit. Engring. Coun., Instn. Elec. Engrs., N.Y. Acad. Scis., Am. Assn. for Cancer Rsch., Inst. Physics and Engring. in Medicine. Avocations: scuba diving, flying, training German shepherd dogs, squash, golf. Office: Coventry U BIOCORE, Sch Math and Info Scis, Coventry CV1 5FB, England

NAGUMO, MICHIHIKO, materials science and engineering educator; b. Sapporo, Hokkaido, Japan, Apr. 2, 1932; s. Junji and Ryoko (Yamaguchi) N.; m. Yasuko Tamama, Oct. 3, 1959. BS, U. Tokyo, 1955, MS, 1957, DrSci, 1960. Rschr. Nippon Steel Corp., Tokyo, 1960-88, dir. R&D Lab. 1, 1985-87, exec. councillor, 1987-88; prof. materials sci. and engring. Waseda U., Tokyo, 1988—, dir. materials sci. tech. dept., 2000—. Contbr. articles to profl. jours. Recipient Allan Dove award Wire Assn. Internat., 1983, Honorable Mention award, 1984. Mem. Japan Inst. Metals, Iron and Steel Inst. Japan (Nishiyama Meml. prize 1983), Phys. Soc. Japan, TMS, MRS. Office: Waseda U Dept Mat Sci/Engr, Okubo 3-4-1, Shinjuku Tokyo 169-0072, Japan

NAGY, ÁRPÁD ZOLTÁN, physicist; b. Debrecen, Hajdu, Hungary, June 24, 1931; s. Sándor Macsingo Mohácsi and Julianna D. Nagy; m. Árpádné Marta Szappanos, Jan. 16, 1955 (dec. Mar. 1997); children: Márta, Zoltán. Student, Kossuth Lajos U., Debrecen, Hungary, 1950-52; MS in physics, Eötvös Lóránd U., Budapet, 1954, Diplomate, 1955, PhD in Neutron Physics, 1972. Cert. applied neutron physicist. Applied rsch. physicist, project leader Ctrl. Rsch. Inst. Physics, Hungarian Acad. Scis., Budapest, 1954-80; postdoctoral fellow, project leader Joint Inst. Nuclear Rsch., Dubna, Former Soviet Union, 1972-75, Inst. Laue-Langevin, Grenoble, France, 1976; prof. physics Gödöllö (Hungary) U. Agrl. Scis., 1980—; sr. adviser energy prodn. and environ. consequences Hungarian Power Cos. Ltd., Budapes, 1980-92, pub. rels. office, 1996—. Editor-in-chief Jour. Internat, Agrophysics, 1984—, Electronic Bull. of SUSDEV, 1993—; author 6 books; contbr. numerous articles to profl. jours.; patentee in field. Lt. Hungarian Artillery, 1950-55. Mem. Hungarian Acad. Scis. (chmn. agrophysics and food physics nat. com. 1988-92, radiation protection end envrion. physics nat. com. 1993—), Eötvös Lóránd Phys. Soc. (county pres. 1980—). Avocations: camping, swimming, sailing. Home: Eötvös ut 53/B, 1121 Budapest Hungary

NAGY, ATTILA, mathematician; b. Nyiregyháza, Hungary, June 15, 1952; parents: Gusztáv Nagy and Julianna Horváth. Degree in math., Kossuth Lajos U., Debrecen, Hungary, 1976. Asst. prof. math. Tech. U. Budapest, Hungary, 1976-80, 1st asst. prof., 1980—. Mem. Am. Math. Soc. Office: Tech U Budapest, Muegyetem rkp 9, Budapest 1111, Hungary

NAGY, BALINT, biologist; b. Szabadszallas, Hungary, Feb. 29, 1956; came to U.S., 1991; s. Balint and Julia (Bajnoczi) N.; m. Maria Vegh, Jan. 30, 1982; children: Balint Miklos, Balazs Gabor. MS, Attila Jozsef U., 1980; PhD, Semmelweis Med. U. Sch., 1986. Biologist Human Inst. for Serobact Prodn., Budapest, 1980-85; rsch. assoc. Semmelweis U. Med. Sch., Budapest, 1986—, head molecular diagnostics lab., 1998—; vis. fellow NIH Clin. Ctr., Bethesda, Md., 1992-96, vis. researcher CMG Lab. U. Helsinki, Finland, 1999—. Contbr. articles to profl. jours. Recipient Young Investigator awrd Acad. for Clin. Physicians and Scientists, 1995. Mem. Am. Assn. Clin. Chemistry, N.Y. Acad. Scis., Assn. Hungarian Ob.-Gyn., Assn. Hungarian Microbiologists, Acad. Clin. Lab. Physicians and Scientists. Achievements include research in downward transfer of proteins, pulsed field electrophoresis applicable for proteins; applying fluorescent PCR in the detection of most common trisomies, cystic fibrosis; using molecular biological methods in diagnosis and detection of cardiovascular disease; detection of chimenism in leukemic patients. Home: Liljasaarentie 3A2, 00340 Helsinki Finland Office: U Helsinki Dept Med Genetics, Haartmaninkatu 3, 00029 Helsinki Finland

NAGY, BOLDIZSÁR, lawyer, educator; b. Budapest, Hungary, Oct. 22, 1953; s. László and Anna (Hrabovszky) N.; m. Ágnes Ambrus, Apr., 1984 (div. 1996); 1 child, Benedek. Diploma, Johns Hopkins, Bologna, Italy, 1984; JD, Eötvös U., Budapest, 1977, MA in Philosophy, 1987. Postgrad. fellow Eötvös U., Budapest, 1977-79; asst. prof. EötvÖs U., Budapest, 1979-83, assoc. prof., 1983—; cons., counsel Hungarian Govt., Budapest, 1989—; mem. expert group UN, Geneva, 1995; legal expert Coun. Europe, 1995, 98, 99, 2000; cons. UN High Commr. for Refugees, Budapest, 1994—; vis. prof. Ctrl. European U., 1999—. V.p. Menedék, Budapest, 1995—; founder Environ. Rsch. Inst., Budapest, 1990. Recipient 1st prize Hungarian Lawyers Assn., Budapest, 1980. Mem. Internat. Law Assn., Hungarian Soc. for Fgn. Politics, Hungarian Polit. Sci. Assn., Am. Soc. Internat. Law. Avocation: writing essays. Office: Eötvös Loránd U, Egyetem tér 1-3 POB 109, 1364 Budapest Hungary

NAGY, DÉNES LAJOS, physicist; b. Budapest, Hungary, Sept. 9, 1944; s. István György and Magdolna (Dénes) N.; m. Katalin Kulcsár, Aug. 30, 1969; children: Gábor, Balázs. MSc, Eötvös U., 1967; DSc, Hungarian Acad. Scis., Budapest, 1988; D in Habilitation, Eötvös U., 1996. From jr. mem. to sr. me. Ctrl. Rsch. Inst. Physics, Budapest, 1967-89; scientific counselor KFKI Rsch. Inst. Particle and Nuclear Physics, Budapest, 1989—; guest prof. U. Erlangen-Nürnberg, Germany, 1990-91; scientific counselor KFKI Rsch. Inst. Particle and Nuclear Physics, 1989—, head dept. solid state and molecule spectrometry, 1993-95, head dept. nuclear physics, 1995—; scientific counsellor Eötvös U., 1995-98, prof., 1998—; head dept. nuclear physics Ctrl. Rsch. Inst. Physics, 1979-88, dep. dir., 1988-91; pres. Hungarian Synchrotron Com., 1998—. Co-author, co-editor: Mössbauer Spectroscopy of Frozen Solutions, 1990; contbr. articles to profl. jours. Mem. Roland Eötvös Phys. Soc. (Gyulai prize 1985, chmn. revision com. 1993-96, sec. gen. 1996-99, v.p. 1999—), European Phys. Soc., Fedn. Sci. and Tech. Assns. (v.p. 1998—), vice pres., Federation of Scientific and Technical Assns. (Hungary), 1998—. Mem. Hungarian Socialist Party. Home: Lidérc u 40-42, H-1121 Budapest Hungary Office: KFKI Rsch Inst Particle &, Nuclear Physics PO Box 49, 1525 Budapest Hungary

NAGY, ENDRE ANDREW, microbiologist, consultant, researcher; b. Sekic, Yugoslavia, Aug. 15, 1929; arrived in Hungary, 1944; s, Endre Andreas and Rose Lidia (Kelemen) N.; m. Klara Maria Csatary Nagy, Aug. 14, 1964; children: Liliana, Emese. 1st class student, Med. U. Szeged, Hungary, 1955. Medical diplomate. Externist U. Med. Sch. Dept. Microbiology, Szeged, Hungary, 1952-55; asst., 1956-59, adjunct, 1959-60; chief med. officer Hosp. Hodmezovasarhely, 1961-66, Hosp. Kalocsa, 1966-69, Teaching Hosp., Vac, Hungary, 1970—; mem. residency Hungarian Soc. for Clin. Lab., 1965-96, Hungarian Soc. Clin. Microbiology, 1970-96, Hungarian Soc. Chemotherapy, 1978-96. Editor: Hungarian Laboratory Digest. Avocation: diagnostic microbiology. Office: Tchg Hosp, Argenti Square 3, H-2601 Vac Hungary

NAGY, ENDRE LÁSZLÓ, electrical engineer, researcher, educator; b. Terehegy, Baranya, Hungary, Dec. 25, 1942; arrived in Japan, 1984; s. Sándor and Irén (Fekete) N.; m. Ritsuko Mine, Aug. 1, 1978. Diploma in Elec. Engring., Tech. U. Budapest, Hungary, 1966; PhD, Hungarian Acad. Scis., 1973. Sci. assoc. Rsch. Inst. Electric Energy Industry, Budapest, 1966-70, 73-74; assoc. prof. Kandó Kálmán Coll. Elec. Engring., Budapest, 1974-84; guest rschr. Chuo U., Tokyo, 1984-86; chief rschr. Birds Info. Sci. Rsch. Inst., Tokyo, 1987-89; head dept. Sanrura Corp., Tokyo and Yokohama, Japan, 1990-93; lectr. U. Horticulture, Budapest, 1971-72; licence application evaluator Howa Licence Tech. Office, Tokyo, 1994-96. Inventor adaptive sampling circuit arrangement, 1979; innovator variable sampling interval control system, 1993; contbr. articles to profl. jours. Recipient diploma prize Electrotech. Soc., Budapest, 1966; rsch. scholar Imperial Coll., London, 1972, Tech. U. Dresden, Germany, 1973. Mem. Soc. Instrument and Control Engrs. Avocations: nature observation, bird watching, exhibitions, concerts, theater.

NAGY, GÁBOR, dentist, educator; b. Debrecen, Hungary, Mar. 16, 1957; s. Imre Nagy and Ilona Kovács; m. Melinda Madlèna, July 14, 1984. MD, U. Medicine, Debrecen, 1981; PhD, Hungarian Sci. Acad., Budapest, Hungary, 1995. Asst. lectr. Sch. Dentistry U. Medicine, Debrecen, 1981-84, lectr. Sch. Dentistry, 1984-90, sr. lectr. Sch. Dentistry, 1990-96, assoc. prof., 1996—. Contbr. articles to profl. jours.; patentee in field. Fellow Hungarian Periodontal Assn. (directory bd. 1995—); mem. Hungarian Dental Assn. (Körmöczy award 1987, bd. dirs. 1996—). Avocation: hunting. Home: Blaháné u 18, 4024 Debrecen Hungary Office: U Medicine Sch Dentistry, Univ Debreun, Nagyerdei krt 98, 4012 Debrecen Hungary

NAGY, IMRE V., civil engineer, educator; b. Fuzesgyarmat, Hungary, Nov. 2, 1927; s. Istvan V. Nagy and Eszter Dajka; m. Imrene Szucs Jolan; children: Imre, Laszlo, Edina, Zoltan. MS in Civil Engring., Tech. U., Budapest, 1952, PhD in Civil Engring., 1956; DSC, Hungarian Acad. Scis., Budapest, 1963. Head Dept. foe Edn. Tech. U., Budapest, 1952-53; prin. investigator U. Moscow, 1953-56; cons. engr. Design Office, Budapest, 1957-58; vice dir. Rsch. Inst., Budapest, 1958-64; dep. head Tech. U., Budapest, 1964—. Author: (book) Hydrology, 1965, Probability and Statistics in Hydrology, 1984, Internat. Trade in Hazardous Wastes, 1996. Sec. gen. Comm. of Hydr. Science, Budapest, 1958-63; sec. Hung Hydrological Soc., 1960-62; chmn. Nat. Comm. for Environment Protection, 1964-92. Recipient Order of Labour award Hungarian Govt., 1984. Mem. Hungarian Acad. (mem. water resources com. 1957—), Hungarian Soc. Environ. Protection (chmn. 1964—). Home: Etele U 19, H-1119 Budapest Hungary Office: Technical U, Budafoki U 4 Kmf 8, H1111 Budapest Hungary

NAGY, ISTVÁN, engineering educator; b. Budapest, Hungary, Aug. 12, 1931; s. Károly and Károlyné (Lehner) N.; m. Istvánné Tassy, June 10, 1958; 1 child, Andrea. MSc, Tech. U., Budapest, 1953, Univ. Dr., 1960; MS in Tech., Hungarian Acad. Scis., Budapest, 1959, Dr of Tech. Sci., 1975. Chief rschr. Computation and Automation Inst., Budapest, 1967-70, head dept., 1970-90; rsch. Tech. U., 1957-65, head dept., 1976-96, head group, 1996—; part-time project engr. Ganz Electric Work, Budapest, 1960-74; vis. prof. U. Madison (Wis.), 1991, U. Tokyo, 1994. Author: (textbook) Fundamentals of Elec. Circuit, 1963; contbr. articles to profl. jours.; patentee in field (Golden award for Disting. Inventions, 1975, 78, 84). Postdoctorate fellow U. Toronto, 1965-67, Erskine fellow U. Canterbury, Christ Church, New Zealand, 1989. Fellow IEEE; mem. Hungarian Electrotech. Assn. (Zipernowsky award 1963, Csáki award 1992), Hungarian Acad. Scis. (acad. award 1974, chmn. elec. engring. com. 1990-96), European Power Elec. Assn. (exec. coun. 1993—), Power Elec. and Motion Control (coun. 1996—). Avocations: literature, tennis. Home: Tigris u 12, 1016 Budapest Hungary Office: Tech U Budapest, Budafoki ut 8 F ep II lpcs, 1111 Budapest Hungary

NAGY, JANOS, agricultural sciences educator; b. Hajdunanas, Hungary, July 13, 1951; s. Janos and Erzsebet (Beres) N.; m. Judit, Jan. 9, 1988; children: Attila, Orsolya. BSc, U. Debrecen, 1975; PhD, U. Budapest, 1987, DSc, 1997. Rsch. scientist Agrl. U., Debrecen, 1975-77; from asst. to assoc. prof. U. Agrl. Scis., Debrecen, 1977-96; prof. U. Agrl. Sci., 1996—, vice rector, 1998-2000. Author: Crop Production, 1992, Land Use, 1994; contbr. articles to profl. jours. Mem. Internat. Soil Tillage Rsch. Orgn., European Soc. for Agronomy, Am. Soc. for Agronomy. Home: Borbiro ter 8, H-4032 Debrecen Hungary Office: U Agrl Scis, Boszormenyi ut 138, H-4032 Debrecen Hungary

NAGY, JÓZSEF, horticulture educator; b. Ecséd, Hungary, Mar. 12, 1938; s. Mihály and Rozália (Bubórék) N.; m. Zsófia Tőkés, Aug. 3, 1963; children: György, Gyöngyi. Cert. agrl. engr., U. Horticulture, Budapest, 1961; D Horticulture, U. Horticulture, 1965; candidate in Agrl. Studies, Hungarian Acad. Scis. and Arts, 1982. Jr. mem. Hort. Rsch. Inst., Budapest, 1961-68, rsch. worker, 1968-71; asst. prof. U Szent István Faculty Hort., Budapest, 1971-80, assoc. prof., 1980—. Author: Melons, 1994, Cucurbits: Melons, Cucumbers, Squash, 1997, Vegetable Growing, 1999; editor jour., 1988—; patentee in field. Mem. Hungarian Acad. Sci. (hort. com. 1990—), Hungarian Soc. Agrl. Sci. (com. mem. 1990-99, mem. governing body 1999—, pres. plastics in agr. sect. 1990—), Internat. Plastics in Agr. Commn. (coun. mem. 1990-99). Roman Catholic. Avocations: gardening, rose breeding. Home: Lehel u 11, 1224 Budapest Hungary Office: U Szent István Fac Hort, Ménesi ut 44, 1118 Budapest Hungary

NAGY, PHYLLIS, playwright; b. N.Y.C., Nov. 7, 1962; d. Peter Thomas and Virginia Marie (Sottile) N. BFA, NYU, 1986. panelist N.C. Arts Coun. Playwriting Fellowships, 1991, N.Y. Found. for the Arts Playwriting Fellowships, 1991; writer in residence Royal Court Theatre, 1994-95. Author: (play) Butterfly Kiss, 1988, Plaza Delores, 1988, Girl Bar, 1989-90, Awake, 1990-91, Disappeared, 1991, Weldon Rising, 1992, Entering Queens, 1993, Trip's Cinch, 1994, The Scarlet Letter, 1994, The Strip, 1995, Never Land, 1998, The Talented Mr. Ripley, 1998. Fellow NEA Playwrights, 1989-90, 93-95, N.Y. Found. for the Arts Playwrights, 1989-90, McKnight fellow, Mpls., 1991; recipient Mobil Playwriting prize, 1992, Writers Guild Gt. Brit. prize, 1995, Susan Smith Blackburn prize, 1995, Eileen Anderson award, 1995. Mem. Writers Guild Gt. Brit., Pen Am. Ctr., Dramatists Guild. Democrat. Roman Catholic. Avocations: collecting baseball cards, rare books, records. Office: c/o Casarotto Ramsay Ltd, 60-66 Wardour St, London W1V 4ND, England

NAGY, TAMAS, automotive company executive; b. Csorna, Hungary, Mar. 11, 1957; s. Gyula and Etelka (Bereczki) N.; m. Zsuzsanna Sarai, July 12, 1980; children: Zoltan, Mate. Grad. in Mech. Engring., Tech. U. Heavy Industry, Miskolc, Hungary, 1980; grad. in Info. with distinction, Eötvös Loránd U., Budapest, Hungary, 1983; BA in Internat. Mktg., Fgn. Trade H.S., Budapest, Hungary, 1994. Tech. informator Raba, Györ, Hungary, 1980-90, mgr. tech. info. dept., 1990-91, innovation mgr., 1991-94, strategy mktg. exec., 1994-2000, info. tech. mgr., 2000—. Office: Raba Rio, Budai u 1, H-9027 Gyor Hungary

NAH, FIONA FUI-HOON, infomation technology educator, researcher. BSc, Nat. U. Singapore, 1988, BSc with honors, 1989, MSc, 1992; PhD, U. B.C., 1997. Asst. prof. Purdue U., West Lafayette, Ind., 1996-98, U. Nebr., Lincoln, 1998—. Contbr. articles to profl. jours. E-mail: fnah2@unl.edu.

NAH, SEUNG-YEOL, veterinary medicine educator, neuroscientist; b. Seoul, Feb. 11, 1961; s. Sang-Sun Nah and Chang-Hwan Goo; m. Eun-Sook Yoon, Sept. 12, 1987; 3 children. BA, Kon-Kuk U., Seoul, 1983, MS, 1985; PhD, Weizmann Inst., Rehovot, Israel, 1993. Postdoctoral fellow Washington U., St. Louis, 1992-93, Vollum Inst. U. Oreg., 1993-95; asst. prof. Chonnam Nat. U., Kwangju, Korea, 1995—; expert in ginseng rsch. Contbr. articles to profl. jours.; mem. editl. bd. Korean Jour. Lab. Animal Sci., 1999. 2nd lt. Korean Army, 1985-86. Mem. Korean Ginseng Soc. (councilor 1999). Avocations: mountain climbing, fishing. Office: Chonnam Nat. U Dept Physio, Coll Veterinary Medicine, Kwangju 500-757, Korea

NAHAL, ARASHMID, physicist, optics educator, consultant; b. Tehran, Iran, June 14, 1966; s. Manouchehr and Shokouh (Shahabi) N. BSc, U. Tehran, 1989; MSc, Kharkov State U., Ukraine, 1996, PhD, 1999. Cert. in Russian lang. Kiev State U., Ukraine, 1994. Rsch. asst. mgr. Azad U., Iran, 1991-92; instr. Omid Computer Tng. Ctr., Iran, 1992-93; engr. Nat. Cadaster Project, Iran, 1993; rsch. asst. Kharkov State U., 1997-2000; asst. prof. optics., cons. Inst. for Advanced Studies in Basic Scis., Physics Dept., Zanjan, Iran, 2000—. Contbr. sci. articles to profl. jours. Mem. Phys. Soc. Iran. Muslim. Avocations: drawing, sports, expeditions. Home: 20 Block B YAS Apts, Debaji Shomali St, 19537 Tehran Iran

NAHAR, NAVRATNA MAL, solar energy scientist, researcher; b. Jhalara, India, Mar. 1, 1952; s. Chandan Mal and Bhanwari Devi (Bumb) N.; m. Indu Lodha, Apr. 27, 1980; children: Aakanksha, Ankit. BS, U. Udaipur, India, 1972, MS, 1974; PhD, U. Jodhpur, India, 1989. Jr. rsch. fellow U. Delhi, 1974-76; officer Bank of Rajasthan, Jaipur, India, 1976-77; scientist S-1 Ctrl. Arid Zone Rsch. Inst. Jodhpur, 1977-82; scientist S-2 Azri Jodhpur, 1983-85, sr. scientist, 1986—. Contbr. over 100 articles to profl. jours. Sec. Nahar Brotherhood, Jodhpur, 1995-98. Recipient Indo Am. fellowship Coun. Internat. Exch. Scholars, Washington DC, 1985, Kheti award Indian Coun. Agrl. Rsch., New Delhi, 1985-86, Outstanding Young Person award Raj. State Jaycees, Jaipur, 1988, Postdoctoral fellowship Commn. of European Communities, Cardiff, U.K., 1992, Abhimanyu Purushkar for the Yr. award Bharat Ednl. and Welfare Trust, West Bengal, India, 1999. Mem. Arad Zone Rsch. Assn. India (life, exec. mem. 1996-98), Agrl. Rsch. Svc. Scientist's Forum (life, Jodhpur sec. 1996-98), Solar Energy Soc. India (life), Semiconductor Soc. India (life). Avocations: social work, reading. Home: 34 Durga Vihar, Pal Link Rd, Jodhpur 342 008, India Office: Ctrl Arid Zone Rsch Inst, Jodhpur 342 003, India

NAHAT, DENNIS F., artistic director, choreographer; b. Detroit, Feb. 20, 1946; s. Fred H. and Linda M. (Haddad) N. Hon. degree, Juilliard Sch. Music, 1965. Prin. dancer Joffrey Ballet, N.Y.C., 1965-66; prin. dancer Am. Ballet Theatre, N.Y.C., 1968-79; co-founder Cleve. Ballet, 1976, Sch. of Cleve. Ballet, 1972; founder, artistic dir. San Jose Cleve. Ballet, 1985, Sch. Cleve. San Jose Ballet, 1996; founder New Sch. of Cleve. San Jose Ballet, 1996—; co-chair Artists Round Table Dance USA, 1991; trustee Cecchetti Coun. Am., 1991; mem. adv. bd. Ohio Dance Regional Dance Am. Prin. performer Broadway show Sweet Charity, 1966-67; choreographer Two Gentlemen of Verona (Tony award 1972), 1969-70; (ballet) Celebrations and Ode (resolution award 1985), 1985, Green Table, Three Virgins and a Devil (Isadora Duncan award 1985); conceived, directed, choreographed Blue Suede Shoes, PBS, 1997-98. Grantee Nat. Endowment Arts, 1978, Andrew Mellow Found., 1985; recipient Outstanding Achievement award Am. Dance Guild, 1995, 96, 2000-2001. Avocation: master chef. Office: Cleve San Jose Ballet 3615 Euclid Ave Ste 1A Cleveland OH 44115-2527 also: Cleve San Jose Ballet PO Box 1666 San Jose CA 95109-1666 also: San Jose Cleve Ballet 40 N 1st St San Jose CA 95113-1200

NAHMAN, NORRIS STANLEY, electrical engineer; b. San Francisco, Nov. 9, 1925; s. Hyman Cohen and Rae (Levin) N.; m. Shirley D. Maxwell, July 20, 1968; children: Norris Stanley, Vicki L., Vance W., Scott T. B.S. in Electronics Engring, Calif. Poly. State U., 1951; M.S.E.E., Stanford U., 1952; Ph.D. in Elec. Engring, U. Kans., 1961. Registered profl. engr., Colo. Electronic scientist Nat. Security Agy., Washington, 1955-56; prof. elec. engring., dir. electronics rsch. lab. U. Kans., Lawrence, 1955-66; sci. cons., chief pulse and time domain sect. Nat. Bur. Standards, Boulder, Colo., 1966-73; chief time domain metrology, sr. scientist Nat. Bur. Standards, 1975-83, group leader field characterization group, 1984-85; v.p. Picosecond Pulse Labs, Inc., Boulder, 1986-90, scientific advisor, co-chair tech. adv. bd., 1990—; cons. elec. engr., 1990—; prof., chmn. dept. elec. engring. U. Toledo, 1973-75;; prof. elec. engring. U. Colo., Boulder, 1966—; affiliate staff Los Alamos (N.Mex.) Nat. Lab., 1990—; Disting. lectr., prin. prof. Ctr. Nat. d'Etude des Telecomm. Summer Sch., Lannion France, 1978; disting. lectr. Harbin Inst. Tech., Peoples Republic China, summer 1982; mem. faculty NATO Advanced Study Inst., Castelvecchio, Italy, 1983, Internat. Radio Sci. Union/NRC; chmn. Internat. Intercomm. Group Waveform Measurements, 1981-90, chmn. Commn. A, 1985-86. Contbr. rsch. articles profl. jours.; patentee in field. Asst. scoutmaster Longs Peak coun. Boy Scouts Am., 1970-73, 75-89. With U.S. Mcht. Marine, 1943-46, U.S. Army, 1952-55. Ford Found. faculty fellow MIT, 1962; Nat. Bur. Standards sr. staff fellow, 1978-79; recipient Disting. Alumnus award Calif. Poly. State U., 1972, Order of Arrow Boy Scouts Am., 1976. Fellow IEEE (life), Internat. Sci. Radio Union; mem. Instrumentation and Measurement Soc. of IEEE (admstrv. com. 1982-84, editorial bd. Trans., 1982-86, Andrew H. chi Best Tech. Paper award 1984, Tech. Leadership and Achievement award 1987), Am. Assn. Engring. Edn., U.S. Mcht. Marine Veterans World War II, Am. Legion, Calif. Poly. State U. Alumni Assn. (life), Stanford U. (life), U. Kans. (life), Am. Radio Relay League Club (life), Sigma Pi Sigma, Tau Beta Pi, Eta Kappa Nu, Sigma Tau, Sigma Xi.

NAIDITCH, LARISSA, linguistics educator; b. Leningrad, Russia, Mar. 13, 1947; arrived in Israel, 1993; d. Erik Ezrovich and Lidia Mikhailovna (Lotman) N.; m. Lev Palatnik, Mar. 25, 1966 (div. Oct. 1993); children: Michael, Alexander. MA with honors in German Philology, Philology U., Leningrad, 1970; PhD in German Philology, Acad. Scis., Leningrad, 1978. Translator Inst. Geology of Oceans, Leningrad, 1970-88; rsch. scientist Inst. Linguistics, Leningrad, 1988-92; lectr. dept. linguistics Hebrew U. Jerusalem, 1992—. Author: Trace on the Sand (in Russian), 1995, Deutsche Bauern bei St. Petersburg-Leningrad, 1997. Grantee Deutscher Akademischer Austauschdienst, Germany, 1995, Ministry Sci. and Arts, Israel, 1996, 97. Mem. Societas Linguistica Europaea, Internat. Assn. for Germanic Studies, Internat. Soc. Dialetologists and Geolinguists, Internat. Gesellschaft für Dialektologie des Deutschen. Office: Hebrew U Jerusalem, Mount Scopus Dept Linguist, 91905 Jerusalem Israel

NAIDOO, DATSHANA PRAKESH, cardiologist, researcher; b. Durban, Natal, South Africa, Feb. 21, 1952; s. Venkatasamy and Lutchmi Naidoo; m. Kamsila Naidoo, Feb. 28, 1985; 1 child, Kumari. MB BChir, U. Natal, Durban, 1974; Diploma in child health, Coll. Medicine, Cape Town, South Africa, 1977. Registrar U. Natal, Duban, 1976-81; lectr. U. Natal, Durban, 1982-86, sr. specialist, 1987-90, sr. lectr., 1990-92, prin. specialist, 1992—; head cardiac unit King Edward VIII Hosp., Durban, 1992-99; sec. 20th Congress South African Cardiac Soc., Durban, 1995-96; rsch. fellow Western Gen. Hosp., Edinburgh, Scotland, 1991; exec. mem. faculty bd., 1994-95; mem. curriculum reform group; designer cardiovasc. module for med. students, 1996-99. Reviewer: Cardiovasc. Jour. South Africa, 1994-96; mem. editl. bd.: Specialist Medicine, 1994-96; contbr. rsch. papers to profl. jours. Mem. Cato Manor Residents Assn., Mayville, 1980-96. Beriberi heart failure rsch. grantee Med. Rsch. Coun., Durban, 1990, Hypertension rsch. grantee U. Natal, 1992, Hypertension Soc. Astra grantee, 1999, Coronary Risk Factor rsch. grantee MRC, 1995. Fellow, mem. Coll. Medicine, Royal Coll. Physicians London; mem. South African Hypertension Soc. (exec. mem. 1995-99, pres. 1997-99), South African Heart Assn., Hypertension Soc. South Africa (pres. 1997-99, chmn. 11th Cong.). African Nat. Congress. Hindu. Avocations: antique furniture, coins, gardening. Home: #2 Jubilee Crescent, Mayville Durban 4058, South Africa Office: U Natal Dept Medicine, Private Bag x7, 4013 Congella Natal, South Africa

NAIDOO, PRAGALATHAN DHANAPALAN, engineering executive; b. Durban, South Africa, Apr. 30, 1958; s. Dhanapalan Gonarathnam an dDoorgamah N.; m. Jacqueline Lutchmi Padayachy, Apr. 24, 1982; children: Prinita, Mervyn. BSCE with honors, U. London, 1981. Trainee engr. W.S. Atkins, England, 1979-80; grad. engr. Anglo Am., South Africa, 1981-83, divsn. engr., 1983-87, mgmt. trainee, 1987-90; personal asst. De Beers, South Africa, 1990-92; corp. mgr. Anglo Am., South Africa, 1992-93, mktg. mgr., 1993-96; chmn., CEO P.D. Naidoo & Assocs., South Africa, 1996—. UNESCO scholar, London, 1976-81. Mem. SAACE, SABMC, SAICE, MICE. Avocations: reading, golf, community. Office: P D Naidoo & Assocs, 25 Owl St, Johannesburg 2092, South Africa

NAIDU, KAMATHAM AKHILENDER, scientist, researcher; b. Anantapur, India, May 29, 1956; s. Kamatham Vanamala and Kamatham Sumithra Naidu; m. Saraswathi Praveena Naidu, July 27, 1989; children: Kamtham Aashish, Kamtham Abhinav. BS, Andhra U., Waltair, India, 1976, MS, 1978; PhD, S.V. U., Tirupati, India, 1982; postgrad., U. South Fla., 1989-91. Jr. rsch. fellow S.V. U., Tirupati, 1979-80, sr. rsch. fellow, 1980-82, rsch. assoc., 1982-84; scientist B Ctrl. Food Technol. Rsch. Inst., Mysore, India, 1984-90; scientist C Ctrl. Food Technol. Rsch. Inst., Mysore, 1990-95, scientist EI, 1995—. Co-editor Jour. MATSYA, 1987-89. Mem. Soc. Biol. Chemists, Assn. Food Scientists and Technologists, Assn. Microbiologists India. Avocations: cricket, tennis, reading. Home: 7 Abhishek, 1st Main Rd, South Kumbarkoppal 570 002, India Office: Ctrl Food Technol Rsch Inst, Cheluvamba Mansion, Mysore 570 013, India

NAIK, NAGARAJA, chemistry educator; b. Bendekatte Tanda, Karnataka, India, Sept. 11, 1962; s. Sakrya Naik and Dargi Bai; m. M. Sujatha Naik, Mar. 15, 1998. BSc, Sahyadri Coll. Shimoga, India, 1983; MSc, U. Mysore, India, 1985, PhD, 1997. Govt. Karnataka lectr. Govt. Sci. Coll. Tumkur, India, 1985-87, Kalpataru Sci. Coll., India, 1987-92; sr. lectr. U. Mysore, 1992-96, reader, 1996—. Contbr. articles to sci. jours. Mem. Indian Chem. Soc. (life), Assn. Microbiologists of India (life), Analytical Chemists of India (life). Home: L-29 9th Cross, Manasagangotri, 57 0006 Mysore India Office: U Mysore Dept Chemistry, Manasa Gangotri, 57 0006 Mysore India

NAIK, PRASAD ANAND, marketing educator; b. Bombay, July 15, 1962; came to the U.S., 1991; BSChemE, U. Bombay, 1984; MBA, Indian Inst. Mgmt., 1987; PhD, U. Fla., 1996. Sales exec. Dorr Oliver, Bombay, 1984-85; brand exec. SmithKline Beecham, Delhi, India, 1987-91; asst. prof. mktg. U. Calif., Davis, 1996—. Contbr. articles to profl. jours. Recipient Frank Bass award Inst. Ops. Rsch., 1999. Mem. Am. Mktg. Assn., Assn. Consumer Rsch., Inst. for Ops. Rsch. and Mgmt. Scis. Office: U Calif One Shields Ave Davis CA 95616

NAIMARK, GEORGE MODELL, marketing and management consultant; b. N.Y.C., Feb. 5, 1925; s. Myron S. and Mary (Modell) N.; m. Helen Anne

Wythes, June 24, 1946; children: Ann, Richard, Jane. BS, Bucknell U., 1947, MS, 1948; PhD, U. Del., 1951. Rsch. biochemist Brush Devel. Co., Cleve., 1951; dir. quality control Strong, Cobb & Co., Inc., Cleve., 1951-54; dir. sci. svcs. White Labs., Inc., Kenilworth, N.J., 1954-60; v.p. Burdick Assocs., Inc., N.Y.C., 1960-66; pres. Rajah Press, Summit, N.J., 1963—, Naimark and Barba, Inc., Florham Park, N.J., 1966—, Naimark & Assocs., Inc., Florham Park, N.J., 1994—; dir. Alteon, Inc., 2000—; bd. dirs. Alteon Inc., Ramsey, N.J. Author: A Patent Manual for Scientists and Engineers, 1961, Communications on Communication, 1971, 3d edit., 1987, A Man Called Skeeter, 1996; patentee in field; contbr. articles in profl. jours. With USNR, 1944-46. Fellow AAAS, Am. Inst. Chemists; mem. Am. Chem. Soc., N.Y. Acad. Scis., Am. Mktg. Assn. Home: 87 Canoe Brook Pky Summit NJ 07901-1404 Office: Naimark & Barba Inc 248 Columbia Tpke Ste 1 Florham Park NJ 07932-1210

NAIMI, SHAPUR, cardiologist, educator; b. Tehran, Iran, Mar. 28, 1928; s. Mohsen and Mahbuba (Naim) N.; came to U.S., 1959; MB, ChB, Birmingham (Eng.) U., 1953; m. Amy Cabot Simonds, May 11, 1963; children: Timothy Simonds, Susan Lyman, Cameron Lowell. House physician Royal Postgrad Med. Sch. London, 1955; sr. house officer Inst. Diseases of the Chest, London, 1956; fellow in grad. tng. New Eng. Med. Center and Mass. Inst. Tech., 1961-64; cardiologist Tufts New Eng. Med. Center, Boston, 1966—, dir. intensive cardiac care unit, 1973—, assoc. prof. 1970-93, prof. 1993—. Recipient Distinguished Instr. award, 1972, Teaching citation, 1976, Excellence in Teaching award, 1982 (all Tufts Med. Sch.); diplomate Royal Coll. Physicians London, Royal Coll. Physicians Edinburgh, Am. Bd. Internal Medicine (subsplty. bd. cardiovascular disease). Fellow Royal Coll. Physicians (Edinburgh), A.C.P., Am. Coll. Cardiology; mem. Am. Soc. Exptl. Biology and Medicine, Am. Heart Assn., Mass. Med. Soc. Clubs: Country Brookline; Cohasset Yacht. Contbr. to profl. jours. Home: 265 Woodland Rd Chestnut Hill MA 02467-2204 also: 55 Lothrop Ln Cohasset MA 02025-1425 Office: 750 Washington St Boston MA 02111-1526

NAIPAUL, VIDIADHAR SURAJPRASAD, author; b. Trinidad, Aug. 17, 1932. Student, Queen's Royal Coll., Trinidad, 1943-48; B.A., University Coll., Oxford, Eng., 1953; D.Litt. (hon.), St. Andrews Coll., Scotland, 1979, Columbia U., 1981, Cambridge U., 1983, London U., 1988; DLitt (hon.), Oxford U., 1992. Author: Miguel Street, 1959, A House for Mr. Biswas, 1961, An Area of Darkness, 1964, In a Free State, 1971, Guerrillas, 1975, India: A Wounded Civilization, 1977, A Bend in the River, 1979, Among the Believers, 1981, The Enigma of Arrival, 1987, A Turn in the South, 1989, India: A Million Mutinies Now, 1990, A Way in the World, 1994, Beyond Belief, 1997, Between Father and Son: Family Letters, 2000, Reading & Writing: A Personal Account, 2000. Office: Aitken & Stone Ltd, 29 Fernshaw Rd, London SW10 0TG, England

NAIR, GOPAKUMAR GOPALAN, chemical company executive; b. Chathannoor, Kerala, India, June 11, 1941; s. Gopalan M. and Pankajakshy P. (Amma) N.; m. Jayashree G. Parmeswar (Nair), Aug. 18, 1966; children: Karthink, Pimmima, Laxmi. Organic chemist ITT, Bombay, 1977; organic chemist BDH Industries Ltd., Bombay, 1977-92, chmn., 1990—; organic chemist Bombay Drugs, 1992—; Indian del. chem. session ILO, Geneva, 1995. Editor: Indian Pharma Sourcing Directory, 1996; contbr. rsch. articles to profl. publs.; asst. editor Idnian Drugs, 1980—. Pres. Karthika Nair Smarak Samithi and Rehab. Ctr. for Physically Handicapped. Mem. Indian Drug Mfrs. Assn. (hon. sec. gen., v.p. 1981-83, 83-85, 95—, editor bull. 1980—), Bharat Edn. Soc. (v.p. 1969-90, pres. 1990—), INdian Pharm. Assn. (life), Balkan-ji-Bari, Indo Am. Soc. Office: Bombay Drugs & Pharms P Ltd, Akurli Rd, Mumbai Kandivli East 400101, India

NAIR, KRISHNADAS C.G., aerospace company executive; b. Alwaye, Kerala, India, Aug. 17, 1941; s. Ed Krishnan Nambooripad and Chandrathil Gowriamma; m. Tara Krishnadas Nair; children: Anita Shet, Aparna. B in Tech., IIT, Madras, India, 1984; MS in Engring., U. Sask., Can., 1966, PhD in Engring., 1968. Asst. prof. Karnataka Regional Engring. Coll., India, 1968-69; vis. scientist U. Sheffield, U.K., 1969-71; materials specialist helicopter divsn. Hindustan Aeronautics Ltd., Bangalore, India, 1971-72; mng. dir. Hindustan Aeronautics Ltd., Bangalore, 1988-96, chmn., 1997—; mem., coord. Aeronautics R&D Bd., India, 1986; mem. standing sci. adv. com. dept. steel and mines GOI, India, 1986-92; mem. rsch. coun. Nat. Aerospace Lab., India, 1990—; mem. governing coun. Jawaharlal Nehru R&D Ctr., India. Author: Aircraft Materials, 1976, Cost Reduction Thro' Value Engineering, 1980, Research Management and Technology Utilization, 1980, Advanced Technology of Aerospace, 1993. Recipient Nat. Metalurist award Govt. of India, 1975, Fie Found. award for tech. devel. and bus. mgmt. P.M. Govt. of India, 1991, Indira Gandhi Priyadashini award Govt. of India, 1997. Fellow Royal Aero. Soc. London, Indian Nat. Acad. Engring., Aero. Soc. India (hon., pres. 1995-97). Office: Hindustan Aeronautics Ltd, 15/1 Cubbon Rd, Bangalore 560001, India

NAIR, KRISHNAKUMAR R., software engineer, researcher; b. Trivandrum, Kerala, India; s. Raghavan N.S. and Vijayamma R. Nair; m. Shyama R. Nair; 1 child, Srijith K. BS, U. Kerala, 1980; MTech, Cochin U. Sci & Tech., 1988; MS, U. Ill., Chgo., 1994. Mem. rsch. and devel. group Ctrl. Elecrochem. Rsch. Inst., Karaikudi, 1983-90; computer cons. U. Ill., Chgo., 1990-95; engring. intern Motorola, Inc., Boynton, Fla., 1995; mem. tech. staff Lucent Technolgies, Naperville, Ill., 1996; software engr. Motorola, Inc., Boynton Beach, 1996-98, sr. software engr., 1998-99, lead/staff software engr., 1999—; referee, reviewer tech. articles to Motorola, jours., and confs. Contbr. more than 30 articles to profl. jours. Mem. IEEE (sr.), AAAS, Assn. Computing Machinery, Inst. Engrs. (India). Avocations: reading, sports, numismatics. Home: 4327 Juniper Ter Boynton Beach FL 33436-3024 Office: Motorola Inc 3301 Quantum Blvd # Q10C Boynton Beach FL 33426-8622

NAIR, M.P.K., banker; b. Wadakaneheri, India, Sept. 13, 1932; s. Nair Parangat Parameswaran and Malmal Pattiath Sarada; m. Manickath Lakshmi, Nov. 28, 1960; children: Usha, Sunil, Anil. Degree in banking, U. Wash., 1993. From br. mgr. to dep. gen. mgr. Union Bank of India, 1964-87; chmn. Fed. Bank Aluva, India, 1988-95, WTC Ltd., Cochim, India, 1996; dir. Shogui Group Cos., 1996, Mather Projects & Constrn., 1996—, Asianet Comm. Ltd., Chennai, 1999—. Mem. Lions. Home: Triveni G-196 P'Nagar, 682036 Kochi Kerala, India Office: World Trade Ctr, Asianet Comm Ltd, 3 Nungombakkam High Rd, 600034 Chennai Kerala, India

NAIR, MURALI, software engineering consultant; b. Singapore, Apr. 5, 1965; s. Narayanan and Santha (Thankappan) N.; m. Prasana Sankarapillai, June 1, 1997. B Engring., Nanyang Tech. U., Singapore, 1990; MS in Software Engring., Andrews U., 1997. Systems engr. Singapore Techs. Computer Systems Ltd., 1990-92, systems specialist, 1992-96, systems cons., project team leader, 1996-97; sr. cons. Object Oriented Pte Ltd., Singapore, 1997-2000; sr. server engr. Organic Inc., Singapore, 2000—. Sgt. Singapore Armed Forces, 1983-99. Affiliate mem. IEEE Computer Soc. Avocations: swimming, karate black belt, badminton, squash.

NAIR, SHAMILA, research scientist, consultant; b. Ladysmith, S. Africa, July 4, 1960; arrived to France, 1992; s. Soobramoney and Mariamma (Chetty) N.; m. Hugues Bedouelle, Sept. 4, 1995. PhD, U. Capetown, S. Africa, 1992. Postdoctoral Inst. Pasteur, Paris, 1992-94; rsch. scientist Cubist Pharm., Boston, 1994-95, Inserm, Paris, 1995—; cons. World Bank, Unexo. Contbr. articles to profl. jours. Mem. ASM. Office: Inserm, 156 Rue De Vaugirard, 75730 Paris France

NAIR, VELAYUDHAN, pharmacologist, medical educator; b. India, Dec. 29, 1928; came to U.S., 1956, naturalized, 1963; s. Parameswaran and Ammini N.; m. Jo Ann Burke, Nov. 30, 1957; children: David, Larry, Sharon. Ph.D. in Medicine, U. London, 1956, D.Sc., 1976. Research assoc. U. Ill. Coll. Medicine, 1956-58; asst. prof. U. Chgo. Sch. Medicine, 1958-63; dir. lab. neuropharmacology and biochemistry Michael Reese Hosp. and Med. Center, Chgo., 1963-68; dir. therapeutic research Michael Reese Hosp. and Med. Center, 1968-71; vis. assoc. prof. pharmacology FUHS/Chgo. Med. Sch., 1963-68, vis. prof., 1968-71, prof. pharmacology, 1971—, vice chmn. dept. pharmacology and therapeutics, 1971-76, dean Sch. Grad. and Postdoctoral Studies, 1976—, v.p. for rsch., 1999—; v.is. prof. Harvard U., 1994, Johns Hopkins Sch. Medicine, 1995. Contbr. articles to profl. publs. Recipient Morris Parker award U. Health Scis./Chgo. Med. Sch., 1972. Fellow AAAS, N.Y. Acad. Scis., Am. Coll. Clin. Pharmacology; mem. AAUP, Internat. Brain Rsch. Orgn., Internat. Soc. Biochem. Pharmacology, Am. Soc. Pharmacology & Exptl. Therapeutics, Am. Soc. Clin. Pharmacology & Therapeutics, Radiation Rsch. Soc., Soc. Toxicology, Am. Chem. Soc., Brit. Chem. Soc., Royal Inst. Chemistry (London), Pan Am. Med. Assn. (council on toxicology), Soc. Exptl. Biology & Medicine, Soc. Neurosci., Internat. Soc. Chronobiology, Am. Coll. Toxicology, Internat. Soc. Developmental Neurosci., Sigma Xi, Alpha Omega Alpha. Club: Cosmos (Washington). Office: FUHS Chgo Med Sch 3333 Green Bay Rd North Chicago IL 60064-3037

NAIR GOVINDAPILLAI, ACHUTHAN, biologist, ecologist; b. Thiruvananthapuram, India, Feb. 17, 1946; s. P. Govinda Pillai and Parvathy Gourikutty Amma; m. Parvathi Lakshmi Devi, May 13, 1975; children: L. Deepthi Nair, L. Aarathi Nair, A. Aditya Nair. BSc, Kerala U., Trivandrum, India, 1965, PhD, 1981; MSc, Birla Inst. Tech. and Sci., Pilani, India, 1969. Sr. rsch. assoc. Madurai (India) U., 1974-76; sr. and postdoctoral fellow Kerala U., Trivandrum, 1979-84, rsch. assoc. dept. ocean devel., 1984-86; asst. prof. zoology U. Garyounis, Benghazi, Libya, 1987-89, assoc. prof. zoology, 1990-95; prin. rschr. Environ. Resources Rsch. Ctr., Trivandrum, 1996-99; prin. investigator Min. of Higher Edn. Govt. of Libya, Benghazi, 1990-95; project dir. Min. of Def. Govt. of India, 1997-98. Joint editor Aquatic Biology jour., 1983-86; author: Biology of Terrestrial Isopoda, 1984, Terrestrial Molluscs as Crop Pests, 1998; mem. editl. bds. various jours., 1996—; contbr. over 80 articles to profl. jours. Fellow Linnean Soc. London; mem. Inst. Biology, N.Y. Acad. Scis. Hindu. Avocations: stamp and butterfly collecting, travel, reading, cricket, tennis. Home: Easwari Vilas, Sasthamangalam, Thiruvananthapuram 695 010, India Office: Ctr Highrange Welfare, Via Vandanmettu Idukki, 685 551 Kerala India

NAITO, HIROYOSHI, physicist, educator; b. Akashi, Hyogo, Japan, Oct. 18, 1956; s. Takeo and Toyo (Ishino) N.; m. Masako Kimura, July 1, 1990; children: Tomomi, Shun-ichiro. BEng, Osaka (Japan) Prefecture U., 1979, MEng, 1981, DEng, 1984. Asst. prof. Osaka Prefecture U., 1984-91, lectr., 1991, assoc. prof., 1991—. Contbr. articles to profl. jours. including Phys. Rev. Letters. Grantee Selenium-Tellurium Devel. Assn., 1990. Mem. Soc. Electrography Japan (mem. com. 1985—, mem. tech. com. 1994—), Inst. Electronics, Info. and Comm. Engrs. (sec. gen. affairs), Am. Phys. Soc., Japanese Phys. Soc., N.Y. Acad. Scis. Democrat. Buddhist. Avocations: amateur radio, music. Office: Osaka Prefecture U, 1 1 Gakuen-cho, Sakai 599-8531, Japan

NAITO, KENSEI, otolaryngologist, researcher; b. Nagoya, Aichi, Japan, June 12, 1953; s. Kazumi and Emiko (Nagata) N.; m. Kazuyo Yamada, May 12, 1979; children: Goki, Daisuke, Anne-Lee. DrMedSci, Fujita Health U., Toyoake, Japan, 1986. Cert. specialist in otolaryngology, broncho-esophagology, allergology, Japan. Head and neck surgeon-in-chief Aichi Hosp., Okazaki, Japan, 1981-83; asst. Fujita Health U., Toyoake, 1984-86; otolaryngology-in-chief Daido Hosp., Nagoya, Japan, 1986; clin. fellow U. Toronto, 1986-88; otolaryngologist in chief Shinshiro (Japan) City Hosp., 1988-91; asst. prof. Fujita Health U., 1991-99. Contbr. articles to profl. jours. Fujita Health U. grantee, 1995, 96, 97. Mem. Otolaryngic Allergy Soc. Japan (coun. 1992-94), Japan Allergol. Soc. (coun. 1991—), Internat. Com. Rhinomanometry, Wild Bird Soc. Japan, World Wildlife Found. Japan, World Wildlife Found. Can. Office: Fujita Health U/Otolaryngol, 1-98 Kutsukake, Aichi Toyoake 470-1192, Japan

NAITO, MASAHITO, cardiologist; b. Yokohama, Japan, June 8, 1946; s. Yoshiaki and Mitsu (Suzuki) N.; m. Noriko Kamachi, Apr. 12, 1975; children: Kotaro, Mari. MD, Keio U., 1971, PhD, 1976. Chief Nat. Tokyo Med. Ctr., 1976-78, 81-94; rsch. assoc. Thomas Jefferson Med. U., Phila., 1978-81; dir. The Naito Clinic, Yokohama, Japan, 1994—. Author: Cardiovascular Roentgenology, 1982, Medical Essays, 1990. Mem. Japan Med. Assn. Home: 8-5 Isogodai Isogo-ku, 235-0019, Yokohama Kanagawa, Japan Office: The Naito Clinic 2-20-2, Minamisaiwai Nishi-ku, 220-0005 Yokohama Japan

NAITO, MASATOSHI, orthopedic surgeon, educator; b. Fukuoka, Japan, May 5, 1950; m. Kiyoko Morifuku, July 22, 1980; children: Reiko, Michiko. MD, Kagoshima U., 1977; D in Med. Sci., Kyushu U., 1992. Tng. orthopaedic surgery Kyushu U., 1977-82, asst., 1990-91; chief orthopaedic surgery Saiseikai Yahata Hosp., 1982-88, 89-90; rsch. fellow Washington U. Sch. Medicine, St. Louis, 1988-89; chief Yamaguchi Rosai Hosp., 1991-92; assoc. prof. Fukuoka U., 1992-99, prof., chmn., 1999—; lectr. Kyushu U., 1991—. Contbr. artilces to profl. jours. Mem. Japanese Orthopaedic Assn., Orthopaedic Rsch. Soc. (U.S.A.), Societe Internationale de Recherche Orthopedique et de Traumatologie, Societe Internationale de Chirurgie Orthopedique et de Traumatologie. Office: Fukuoka U Sch Dept Orthop, 7 45 1 Nanakuma, Jonan-ku, Fukuoka 814 0180, Japan

NAITO, TAKASHI, psychology educator; b. Yokohama, Kanagawa, Japan, Apr. 22, 1950; s. Masayuki and Hanae (Shinbori) N.; m. Ryoko Takahashi, Mar. 8, 1998. BA, Keio U., Tokyo, 1973, MA, 1975, PhD, 1998. Instr. Keio U., Tokyo, 1978-83; assoc. prof. Ochanomizu U., Tokyo, 1986-94, prof., 1994—; vis. prof. U. Minn., Mpls., 1999—; vis. prof. U. Minn., Mpls., 1999-2000. Author: Children, Society and Culture, 1991; contbr. articles to profl. jours. Inst. Civic Edn. Ctr., Setagaya, Tokyo, 1992; adviser Chiba Edn. Ctr., 1998-99. Mem. Japanese Assn. of Ednl. Psychology (dir. 1998—), Japanese Assn. of Psychology (dir. 1998—), Japanese Assn. of Ednl. Psychology (editl. bd. 1998—), Assn. of Moral Edn., Soc. for Cross-Cultural Rsch. Avocations: playing guitar, listening to ethnic music, traveling. Home: 3-5-1 Shimokodanaka, Nakaharaku, Kawasaki 211-0041, Japan Office: Ochanomizu U, 2-1-1 Otsuka Bunkyoku, Tokyo 112-8610, Japan

NAITOH, KEN, scientist, researcher; b. Kawasaki-shi, Kanagawa, Japan, Nov. 20, 1961; s. Kazuo and Yoshiko (Nakajima) N.; m. Atsuko Sakai, March 6, 1988; children: Shun, Ushio. B, Waseda U., Tokyo, 1985, M, 1987, D, 1992. Rschr. Nissan Rsch. Ctr., Kanagawa, Japan, 1987-93, Inst. Space and Astronautical Sci., Kanagawa, Japan, 1988-89; invited rschr. RWTH Aachen, Germany, 1994; sr. engr. Nissan Rsch. Ctr., Kanagawa, 1994—. Contbr. articles to profl. jours.; editor: Design Optimization, 1998—. Mem. Internat. Inst. Advanced Studies (rsch. mem. 1995-97), Japan Marine Sci. and Tech. Ctr. (rsch. mem. 1988—), Japan Soc. Indsl. and Applied Maths. (editor 1995—), Japan Soc. Automotive Engrs. (Best Paper award 1992), Japan Soc. Mech. Engrs. (Best Paper award 1993). Avocations: tennis, painting, windsurfing, hiking. Office: Nissan Rsch Ctr, 1 Natsushima-cho, Yokosuka-shi 237, Japan

NAJAFI, S. IRAJ, optical engineering executive; b. Tabriz, Iran, Mar. 2, 1953; arrived in Can., 1996; s. S. Hedayat Najafi and Hekmat Dargahi; m. Zohreh Tabaeizadeh, June 5, 1953; 1 child, Shahrzad. BSc, Shiraz (Iran) U., 1976, MSc, 1979; PhD, Ecole Ctrl., Paris, 1983. Postdoctoral fellow Ecole Ctrl., Paris, 1983-84, U. Fla., Gainesville, 1984-86; rsch. scientist Ecole Poly., Montreal, Can., 1986-90; asst. prof. Ecole Poly., Montreal, 1990-93, assoc. prof., 1993-98, grad. studies coord., 1994-97; pres., CEO Lumenon Innovative Lightware Tech., Inc., 1998—; cons. in field. Editor: Introduction to Glass Integrated Optics, 1992, Sol-Gel Photonics, 1998; contbr. articles to profl. jours.; patentee in field. Fellow Internat. Soc. for Optical Engring.; mem. IEEE, Optical Soc. Am. Avocation: tennis. Office: Lumenon, 8851 Trans-Canada Hwy, Saint Laurent, PQ Canada H9P 2M8

NAJAR, JERZY, engineering educator; b. Warsaw, Aug. 19, 1936; arrived in Germany, 1981; s. Marian and Ruta (Koenigsberg) N.; m. Julianne Short, Oct. 28, 1976; children: Christine, Caroline, John. D Engring., Polish Acad. Scis., Warsaw, 1968; Doctor habil., U. Technology, Munich, 1986, Prof. Mechanics, 1992. Testing engr. Automotive Industry, Warsaw, 1960-63; docent prof. U. Technology, Kielce, Poland, 1974-77; sr. rsch. fellow U. Technology, Munich, 1981—; adj. prof. Polish Acad. Scis., 1968-74, 77-79; vis. prof. U. Notre Dame, 1979-80; vis. rschr. Soviet Acad. Scis., USSR, 1969-70; mng. editor Archive of Applied Mechanics, Springer Verlag, Germany, 1993—. Author: (book) Continuous Damage of Elastic-Brittle Materials (German edit.), 1988; editor: (books) Advances in Continuum Mechanics, 1991, Proceedings 9 Dymatn, 1995; co-editor: Physico Chemical Mechanics of Materials, Materials Science, 1994—; contbr. articles to profl. jours. and publs. Fellow A.V. Humboldt Found., Germany, 1976, 81; grantee Deutsche Forschungsgemeinschaft, Germany, 1991-96. Mem. Gesellschaft Angewandte Mathematik und Mechanik, Euromech. Office: Technische Univ Munich, Technische Univ Munich, Boltzmounstr 15 Garching, D-85747 Munich Germany

NAJARIAN, BETTY JO, music educator; b. Samson, Ala., Nov. 6, 1929; d. Edward Bryan and Ida (Cox) Murdock; m. Zovak Najarian, July 25, 1953; children: Pamela Najarian Whitehead, Brian Keith Najarian. BA in Music Edn., Troy (Ala.) State U., 1951; student, Fla. State U., Tallahassee, 1952, Auburn U., 1956. Ind. music tchr., ch. musician Destin, Fla., 1955-99; pres. Okaloosa County Music. Tchrs., Ft. Walton Beach, Fla., 1987-89, Fla. State Music Tchrs. Assn. Dist. I, Ft. Walton Beach, Fla., 1993-95; pres. Choctaw Bay Music Club, Ft. Walton Beach, 1983-85, Niceville, 1993-95; pres. Fla. Fedn. Music Capital Dist., Destin, 1985-87, 95-97, Fla. Fedn. Music Clubs, Destin, 1997-99. Composer: The Auxiliary Song, 1987. Pres. Am. Legion Aux #296, Destin, Fla., 1958; mem. Sarasota Music Archives, 1997-98. Named Tchr. of Yr., Destin Elem. Sch., Okaloosa County Sch. Bd., Destin, Fla., 1956-57. Mem. Am. Coll. Musicians, Music Tchrs. Nat. Assn., Nat. Fedn. Music Clubs (chmn. 1999—), Am. Folk Music (chmn. 1999—), Fla. State Music. Tchrs. Assn., Okaloosa County Music Tchrs. Assn., Choctaw Bay Music CLub, Fla. Fedn. of Music Clubs. (state pres., 1997-99, chmn. coun. dist. and club presidents 1999—). Democrat. Presbyterian. Avocations: collecting old music and hymn books, collecting music boxes, collecting glass bluebirds, collecting baskets, word games, crossword puzzles. Home: 130 Calhoun Ave Destin FL 32541-1504

NAJARIAN, JACK GEORGE, investment banker; b. Beirut, Lebanon, Jan. 11, 1956; came to U.S., 1970, naturalized, 1976; s. George O. Najarian and Marie Keuftejian; m. Victoria A. Dickson, Oct. 6, 1984; 1 child, Emily Jane Marie. BBA in Pub. Acctg., Bernard Baruch Coll., 1976; JD, Hofstra U., 1979. Internat. tax cons. Arthur Andersen & Co., N.Y.C., 1979-81; internat. banking cons. Deloitte & Touche, N.Y.C., 1981-82; v.p. internat. treasury and capital markets Societe Generale, N.Y.C., 1982-94; acting treas. treasury and capital markets Nat. Australia Bank, N.Y.C., 1994-96; chmn. Griffin Securities, Inc., N.Y.C., 1997-99; pres. Weatherly Securities Corp., N.Y.C., 1999—; chmn. acctg., fin. and taxation dept. World Trade Inst.; mem. Securities Ins. Protection Corp.; bd. dirs. Uni-Marts, Inc., Weatherly Internat. Plc. Mem. Securities Industry Assn. (bd. dirs. 1997—), Nat. Assn. Securities Dealers. Home: 219 W 81st St Apt 12D New York NY 10024-5826 Office: Weatherly Securities Corp Two World Trade Ctr New York NY 10048

NAJM, RIYADH KAMAL, broadcast executive; b. Riyadh, Saudi Arabia, July 17, 1956; s. Kamal K. and Imtithal Najm; m. May Reda Halawani, July 5, 1984; children: Najla, Sarah, Muhammed. BS, U. Calif., Berkeley, 1978, MS, 1980; PhD, Liverpool (Eng.) U., 1992. Sr. engr. Saudi TV, Riyadh, 1980-84; dir. engring. north Min. of Info., Medina, Saudi Arabia, 1984-85; dir. tech. dept. Saudi TV, Riyadh, 1985-95, TV chief engr., 1995—; tech. advisor Gulfvision, Riyadh, 1984-88; chair tech. com. Arab States Broadcasting Union, 1995—. Author: Principles of TV System, 1993; contbr. articles to profl. jours. Mem. IEEE, Saudi Computer Soc. Avocation: reading. Office: Saudi TV, PO Box 10152, Riyadh 11433, Saudi Arabia

NAKABAYASHI, NICHOLAS TAKATERU, retired retail executive; b. Honolulu, Feb. 25, 1920; s. Denji and Ume (Teraoka) N. BS, Utah State U., 1949; MS, U. Ill., 1953, PhD, 1959. Rsch. asst. U. Ill., Urbana, 1953-59; jr. rsch. physiologist UCLA, 1959-61, asst. rsch. physiologist, 1961-64; rsch. fellow Calif. Inst. Tech., Pasadena, 1961-64; sec.-treas. Underwater Rsch. Corp., L.A., 1962-64; rsch. asst. dept. ob/gyn U. Mich. Med. Ctr., Ann Arbor, 1964-70; biologist VA Hosp., Wadsworth, 1971-72; instr. San Gabriel Adult Sch., Calif., 1971-78; supr. serology VA Hosp., Long Beach, Calif., 1972-74; owner Regent Liquor Store, L.A., 1974-79; pres., treas. Regent Liquor, Inc., L.A., 1979-85; ret.; tutor Waikiki Lifelong Learning Ctr. Kapiolani C.C., Honolulu, 1993—. NIH grantee, 1967, 69. Mem. N.Y. Acad. Sci., 100th Inf. Battalion Vets. Club. Avocations: calligraphy, Hawaiiana. Home: 516 Kamoku St Apt 302 Honolulu HI 96826-5101 Office: Waikiki Lifelong Learning Ctr Kapiolani C C 2301 Kuhio Ave Ste 212 Honolulu HI 96815-2970

NAKADA, ISAO, metal research company executive; b. Kyoto, Japan, Nov. 29, 1937; s. Akira and Ayako (Iwasaki) N.; m. Mizuko Koizumi, Jan. 15, 1964 (div. Sept. 1994); children: Atsuko, Tai.; m. Keiko Miyata. B Econs., Keio U., Tokyo, 1962. Mgr. corp. planning Kobe Steel Ltd., Tokyo, 1975-83, gen. mgr. of sales adminstrn., 1983-87; gen. mgr. of sales Kobe Steel Ltd., Osaka, Japan, 1987-89; pres. Nalk Corp., Tokyo, 1989—. Editor: Nalk Report, 1990—, Japan Metal Bulletin, 1993—. Avocations: golf, piano, gardening. Office: Nalk Corp Rm 615/Grand Pal, Tamachi/ 4-9-18 Shibaura, 108-0023 Tokyo Japan

NAKAE, HIDEO, metallurgical engineering educator, researcher; b. Tokyo, Sept. 11, 1941; s. Nobutaro and Sumiko (Sugiyama) Nakae; m. Komumi Yuhki, Dec. 8, 1970. B of Engring., Waseda U., Tokyo, 1964, M of Engring., 1966, D of Engring. (hon.), 1970. Rschr. Hitachi Ltd., Ibaragi, Japan, 1971-77, sr. rschr., 1977-83; prof. Waseda U., Tokyo, 1983—, rsch. fellow Lab. for MS&T, 1984—. Author: Solidification Processing, 1987, Casting Technology, 1995, Crystal Growth and Solidification, 1998; editor Jour. Japan Foundrymen's Soc., 1992-94; co-editor Trans. Japan Inst. Metals, 1991-93, 95—. Mem. com. Bur. of Jour. Indsl. Std., Tokyo, 1987—; mem. liason com. Sci. Coun. Japan, 1994-2000. Avocations: travel, photography, golf. Home: 3-3-3-214 Hikarigaoka Nerima, Tokyo 179, Japan Office: Waseda U Dept Material Sci & Engring, 3-4-1 Okubo Shinjuku, Tokyo 169, Japan

NAKAGAMI, TOMOKO, internist, researcher; b. Tokyo, Feb. 1, 1962. MD, Tokyo Women's Med. U., 1987, PhD, 1991. Med. asst. Diabetes Ctr. Tokyo Women's Med. U., 1991—; postdoctoral rsch. fellow Steno Diabetes Ctr., Denmark, 1998—. Scholar Shisei-kai Overseas Rsch. Found., 1998; grantee Itoe Okamoto Internat. Exch. Found., 1998. Mem. Am. Diabetes Assn., Internat. Diabetes Fedn., Japan Diabetese Soc., Japanese Soc. Internal Medicine. Office: Steno Diabetes Ctr, Niels Steensens Vej 2, 2820 Gentofte Denmark

NAKAGAWA, ALLEN DONALD, radiologic technologist; b. N.Y.C., Mar. 14, 1955; s. Walter Tsunehiko and Alyce Tsuneko (Kinoshita) N. BS in Environ. Studies, St. John's U., Jamaica, N.Y., 1977; MS in Marine Biology, C.W. Post Coll., 1980. Cert. radiologic technologist, in fluoroscopy, Calif.; cert. Am. Registry Radiol. Technologists. Research asst. environ. studies St. John's U., 1976-78; lab. asst. Bur. Water Surveillance, Nassau Co. of Health Dept., Wantaugh, N.Y., 1978; clin. endocrinology asst. U. Calif. VA Hosp., San Francisco, 1981-83; student technologist St. Mary's Hosp., San Francisco, 1985-86; radiologic technologist Mt. Zion Hosp., San Francisco, 1986-88; sr. radiologic technologist U. Calif., San Francisco, 1989—, urosurg. radiologic technologists, 1988-89; attendee U. Calif. San Francisco Trauma and Emergency Radiology Conf., 1995, U. Calif. San Francisco Musculoskeletal MRI Conf., 1996, PACS for Hour Hosp., 1998, Breast Imaging for Technologists and Health Care Providers, U. Calif. Stanford Health Care, 1999. Mem. AAAS, ACLU, Calif. Soc. Radiologic Technologists, Calif. Acad. Scis., Japanese-Am. Nat. Mus., Sigma Xi. Democrat. Methodist. Avocations: photography, music, computer illustration, studying advanced technology. E-mail: gadgets@hotmail.com.

NAKAGAWA, HIDEKI, computer science educator; b. Otake-Si, Japan, Feb. 5, 1961; s. Seiri and Masako (Fujimura) N. BS, Hiroshima (Japan) U., 1984; MS, Hokkaido U., Sapporo, Japan, 1986, PhD, 1990. Rsch. fellow Japan Soc. for Promotion of Sci., Sapporo, 1989-91; postdoctoral fellow U. Calif., Davis, 1991-92; asst. prof. Kyushu Inst. Tech., Iizuka, Japan, 1992-2000, assoc. prof., 2000—. Contbr. articles to profl. jours. Mem. Zool. Soc. Japan, Japanese Soc. for Comparative Physiology and Biochemistry (councilor, Yoshida prize for young rschrs. 1999), Internat. Soc. for Neuroethology. Avocations: hill walking, birding. Office: Kyushu Inst Tech/Comp Sci, Kawazu 680-4, Iizuka-si, Fukuoka 820-8502, Japan

NAKAGAWA, HIDEMITSU, neurosurgeon, researcher; b. Kumatori-Cho, Osaka, Japan, Mar. 7, 1949; s. Eiichi and Hisako (Nagai) N.; m. Noriko Minamigawa, Feb. 19, 1977; 2 children. MD, Tottori U., Yonago, Japan, 1974; PhD, Osaka U., 1982. Diplomate in neurosurgery. Resident dept.

neurosurgery Osaka U. Med. Sch., 1974-80; rsch. fellow Cancer Inst., Osaka U. Med. Sch., 1975-82; mem. dept. neurosurgery Toyonaka (Japan) Mcpl. Hosp., 1980-82; vis. fellow Cancer Inst./NIH, Bethesda, Md., 1982-84; chief resident dept. neurosurgery Osaka Med. Ctr. for Cancer and Cardiovasc. Diseases, 1984-90, dir. dept. neurosurgery, 1990—. Contbr. articles to profl. jours. Recipient Olga Sain award 6th Intenrat. Congress on Anti-Cancer Treatment, 1996. Mem. Japan Neurosurg. Soc. (Galenus award 1985), Japanese Cancer Assn., Japan Soc. Clin. Oncology, Am. Soc. Clin. Oncology, Am. Assn. Cancer Rsch., N.Y. Acad. Scis. Avocations: painting, personal computer, travel. Home: 9-28 Gomon-Nishi 2 Chome, Kumatori-Cho Sennan Gun, Osaka 590-0411, Japan Office: Osaka Med Ctr/Cancer Cardiovasc Dis, 3 Nakamichi 1-chome, Higashinari-ku Osaka 537-8511, Japan

NAKAGAWA, ICHIRO, science educator, consultant; b. Nara, Japan, Feb. 8, 1932; s. Yasaburo and Tomie Nakagawa; m. Keiko Fujimori, Oct. 4, 1959. BS, Kyoto (Japan) U., 1954, MS, 1956, DS, 1962. Rsch. assoc. disaster prevention rsch. inst. Kyoto U., 1958-60, rsch. assoc. faculty of sci., 1960-63, lectr. faculty of sci., 1963-65, assoc. prof. faculty of sci., 1965-88, prof. faculty of sci., 1988-95, dir. Beppu geophys. rsch. lab., 1990-94, dir. Aso volcanol. lab., 1990-95, prof. emeritus, 1995—; tech. adviser Daiichi Fukken Engring. Co., Ltd., 1995—. Fellow Internat. Assn. Geodesy; mem. Japanese Assn. Surveyors (pres. 1999—), Geodetic Soc. Japan (pres. 1991-95), Japan Fedn. Surveyors (pres. 1999—). Avocations: photography, classical music, travel. Home: Nango 4-11-14, Otsu Shiga 520-0865, Japan

NAKAGAWA, KOJI, endocrinologist, educator; b. Sapporo, Hokkaido, Japan, June 5, 1932; s. Satosu and Michi (Yokoyama) N.; m. Keiko Hirato, Oct. 20, 1962; children: Shin, Tamao Yamaguchi. MD, Hokkaido U., 1957, PhD, 1962. Lic. endocrinologist, Japan. Staff scientist Worcester Found. for Experimental Biology, Shrewsbury, Mass., 1964-65; rsch. staff Syntex Rsch. Ctr., Palo Alto, Calif., 1965; rsch. fellow U. Utah Med. Ctr., Salt Lake City, 1965-66; rsch. assoc. 2d dept. medicine Hokkaido U. Sch. Medicine, Sapporo, 1967-83, asst. prof., 1983-89; prof. Health Adminstrn. Ctr., Hokkaido U. Edn., Sapporo, 1989-96, dir. Health Adminstrn. Ctr., 1990-96; prof. dept. nutrition Tenshi Coll., Sapporo, 2000—. Contbr. articles to profl. jours. Fellow Japan Endocrine Soc.; mem. Endocrine Soc., Japanese Soc. Internal Medicine, Japan Diabetes Soc. Home: 2-8 4-chome Yamanote 1-jo, Nishi-ku Sapporo 063-0001, Japan Office: Tenshi Coll, North 13 East 3, Higashi-Ku Sapporo 065-0013, Japan

NAKAGAWA, TAKEO RYUSUI, science educator, poet, writer, priest; b. Shinshiro, Aichi, Japan, May 25, 1945; s. Yoichi and Suyo (Sakai) N.; m. Reiko Suzuki, Oct. 27, 1972. BS, Nat. Def. Acad., Yokosuka, Japan, 1969; MS, Nat. Def. Acad., 1975; PhD, Monash U., 1981. Rsch. scientist Japan Def. Agy., Tokyo, 1975-77; rsch. fellow Melbourne (Australia) U., 1979; rsch. assoc. Nagoya (Japan) U., 1980-81; prof. Kanazawa (Japan) Inst. Tech., 1984-99, Wales (U.K.) U., 1999-2000; vis. prof. Max Planck Inst. Strömung, Göttingen, Germany, 1984-85; vis. fellow U. Karlsruhe, Germany, 1989; dir. Shisei Inst. Innovative Sci., Ishikawa, Japan, 1992—; course dir. Dept. of Environtl. Mgmt., U. Wales, Aberystwyth, U.K., 1999-2000; dean Faculty of Human Environ. Creation Iond U., Honolulu, 2000—; mem. expert investigation com. Komatsu-Tenmangu Shrine and Kakehashi River, 1984-86. Author: Graceful Japanese Souls, 1996, The Tatsumi Canal, 1997, Theory of Meanders, 2000; author, editor: Philosophy of Flow, 1996; translator: What is the Relativity Theory?, 1996. Pres. Soc. for Protection of Kenrokuen Garden and Tatsumi Canal, and Against Dam Constrn., Kanazawa, 1994-99, Hakusan Soccer Club, Ishikawa, 1988—. Lt. Japanese Navy, 1969-77. Fellow Minna-James-Heineman Found., 1984, German Rsch. Exch. Svc., 1989; recipient Shibuya Cultural award Shibuya Found., 1992, 93. Mem. Japan Soc. Heat and Fluid Engring. (councilor). Avocations: walking, travel, reading, soccer, music. Home: 2-14 Meiko, Tsurugi Ishikawa 920-2152, Japan Office: Kanazawa Inst Tech, Iond U Otemachi Build 4F, 1-3 Mikage, Otemachi Kanazawa 920-0912, Japan

NAKAGAWA, TOHRU, electronic company researcher; b. Toyama, Japan, May 23, 1957; s. Yukio and Suiko (Fujinaga) N.; m. Chiaki Nakano, Apr. 26, 1992; children: Takashi, Akito. BS, Hokkaido U., Sapporo, Japan, 1983, MS, 1985; DEng, Osaka (Japan) U., 1998. Semiconductor rschr. Komatsu Ltd., Kanagawa, Japan, 1985-90; molecular electronic rschr. Matsushita Electric Indsl. Co., Ltd., Osaka, 1990—. Contbr. articles to sci. jours. Recipient Technique prize Surface Finishing Soc. Japan, 1995. Mem. Japan Soc. Applied Physics, Phys. Soc. Japan. Avocations: mountain climbing, playing the okarina. Office: Human Environ Devel Ctr, 3-1-1 Yagumo-Nakamachi, Morigchi Osaka 570-8501, Japan

NAKAGAWA, YASUAKI, orthopaedic surgeon, educator; b. Kaizuka, Osaka, Japan, July 20, 1956; s. Haruo Sakaguchi and Hideko Nakagawa; m. Harumi Ichihara, Feb. 16, 1992; 1 child, Shinnosuke. MD, Kyoto (Japan) U., 1982, PhD, Kyoto (Japan) U., 1994. Resident dept. orthopedics Kyoto U., 1982-83, asst. prof. dept. orthopedics, 1996—; resident dept. orthopedics Kyoto City Hosp., 1983-85; orthopedic surgeon Fukui (Japan) Red Cross Hosp., 1985-88, Tamatsukuri Koseinenkin Hosp., Shimane, Japan, 1992-95, Kishiwada (Japan) City Hosp., 1995-96; med. staff Internat. Sumo Fedn., Tokyo, 1993-2000, Japanese Olympic Com., Tokyo, 1998-2000. Contbr. articles to profl. jours. Ofcl. referee Japanese Sumo Fedn. Office: Kyoto U Dept Ortho Surg, 54 Kawahara-cho, Shogoin Sakyo-ku Kyoto 606-8507, Japan

NAKAGAWA, YASUYOSHI, microbiologist, researcher; b. Osaka, Japan, Jan. 26, 1965; s. Shoichi and Hiroko Nakagawa; m. Hiroko Kawasaki, June 1, 1996. BSc, Shizuoka (Japan) U., 1988, MSc, 1990; PhD, U. Tokyo, 1993. Rschr. Inst. for Fermentation, Osaka, 1993-97, rsch. head, 1997—. Mem. Am. Soc. Microbiology, Soc. for Gen. Microbiology, Internat. Com. on Systematic Bacteriology (subcom. on taxonomy of flavobacterium and cytophaga-like bacteria). Office: Inst for Fermentation Osaka, 17-85 Juso-honmachi 2-chome, Yodogawa-ku, Osaka 532-8686, Japan

NAKAGOE, TOHRU, surgeon, researcher; b. Uwajima-City, Japan, Sept. 26, 1949; s. Matao and Sumie (Utsunomiya) N.; m. Yuko Taguchi, Feb. 12, 1977; 2 children. MB, Nagasaki (Japan) U., 1975. Resident Nagasaki U. Hosp., 1975-78, 83-86; surgeon Ohmura (Japan) Mcpl. Hosp., 1978-83; asst. prof. Nagasaki U. Sch. Medicine, 1986—. Contbr. articles to profl. jours. Home: 12-3-701 Bunkyou-machi, Nagasaki 852, Japan Office: Dept of Surgery I, 1-7-1 Sakamoto, Nagasaki 852, Japan

NAKAGO-MATSUO, CHIE, orthodontist; b. Nishinomiya, Hyogo, Japan, Jan. 8, 1962; d. Tadao and Fusako (Kitagawa) N.; m. Toshihiko Matsuo. DDS, Osaka (Japan) Dental U., 1987; PhD, Okayama (Japan) U. Dental Sch., 1996. Resident Okayama (Japan) U. Dental Sch., 1987-90, clin. fellow, 1995-96; orthodontist Kyoyama Dental Clinic, Okayama City, 1997—. Avocations: skiing, diving, hiking. Home: 4-8-48-202 Ifukucho, Okayama 700, Japan Office: Kyoyama Dental Clinic, 2-22-13 Ishimacho, Okayama 700, Japan

NAKAHAMA, HAJIME, physician, educator; b. Ikeda, Osaka, Japan, Feb. 11, 1954; s. Hiromu and Teru (Enza) N.; m. Noriko Chujo, May 4, 1988. MD, Osaka U., 1980, PhD, 1989. Diplomate in internal medicine, nephrology, dialysis therapy, pulmonology, primary care medicine, industrial medicine. Clin. fellow Osaka U. Hosp., 1980-81; internist Osaka Koseinenkin Hosp., 1982-83; clin. fellow Osaka U. Hosp., 1984-90; prin. internist Kansairosai Hosp., Amagasaki, Japan, 1990-92; asst. prof. Hyogo Coll. Medicine, Nishinomiya, Japan, 1992-93, 94-99; rsch. fellow Emory U., Atlanta, 1993-94; vice dir. Nat. Cardiovascular Ctr., Fujishirodai, Japan, 1999—; lectr. Osaka U., Suita, Japan, 1992-98. Author/co-author 12 med. textbooks; contbr. articles to med. jours.; mem. internat. editl. bd. Renal Failure, 1988—. Mem. Internat. Soc. Nephrology, European Renal Assn., Am. Soc. Nephrology, Am. Thoracic Soc., European Respiratory Soc., Am. Heart Assn. Home: Tsukushigaoka 5-14-8 Kitaku, Kobe Hyogo 651-1212, Japan Office: Nat Cardiovascular Ctr, Fujishirodai 5-7-1, Suita 565-8565, Japan

NAKAHIRA, HIROYUKI, chemistry researcher; b. Kochi, Japan, Sept. 5, 1963; s. Satoru and Eiko Nakahira; m. Mayumi Oguchi, Apr. 5, 1992; children: Marika, Sakurao. Bachelor, Tokyo U. Agrl. and Tech., 1986; master, Ehime (Japan) U., 1988; PhD, Osaka (Japan) U., 1991. Asst. rsch. mgr. Sumitomo Pharms., Osaka, 1996—; vis. scholar Stanford (Calif.) U., 1994-96. Contbr. articles to profl. publs. Mem. Am. Chem. Soc. Avocations: listening to classical music, fishing, gardening. Office: 1-98 Kasugadenaka 3-chome, Konohanaku, Osaka 554-0022, Japan

NAKAHORI, ICHIRO, research and development executive; b. Kyoto, Japan, Aug. 24, 1941; s. Takashi and Taeko (Sugie) N.; m. Junko Kato, July 22, 1941. BS, Kyoto U., 1965, MS, 1967, D of Engring., 1976. Mgr. Mitsubishi Electric PISC, Kobe, Japan, 1986-90; mgr. Mitsubishi IESL, Amagasaki, Japan, 1990-95; gen. mgr. Mitsubishi IESL, Amagasaki, 1995-99; asst. dir. Mitsubishi Corp. R&D, Amagasaki, 1999—; pres. Schatsu Sys. Lab. Inc., Kobe, 2000—. Mem. IEEE. Home: 5-13-27 Kitaochiai Suma-ku, Kobe Hyogo 654-0151, Japan Office: Mitsubishi Electric Co IESL, 8-1-1 Tsukaguchi Honmachi, Amagasaki Japan

NAKAI, HIROSHI, civil engineering educator; b. Mitsukaido, Japan, Dec. 14, 1935; s. Ichiro and Kikue (Yoshida) N.; m. Yoshiko Sawa, Oct. 26, 1968; children: Fuyuko, Makiko. BS in Engring., Osaka City U., 1959, MS, 1961; D in Engring., Osaka U., 1972. Rsch. assoc. Osaka City (Japan) U., 1961-66, asst. prof., 1966-70, assoc. prof., 1970-73, prof., 1973-99; prof. Fukui (Japan) U. Tech., 1999—; vis. prof. U. Md., College Park, 1976, San Paulo (Brazil) U., 1983, Imperial Coll. Sci. and Tech., London, 1984; acad. advisor Hanshin Expy. Pub. Corp., Osaka, 1969—, Osaka Mcpl. Office, 1977—; dir. Found. Disaster Sci., Osaka, 1988—. Co-author: Analysis and Design of Curved Steel Bridges, 1988. Mem. ASCE, Internat. Assn. Bridge and Structural Engring., Japanese Soc. Civil Engring. (Tech. Paper prize 1966, Tanaka's prize 1984), Japanese Soc. Steel Constrn. Avocations: farming, fishing, traveling. Office: Fukui U Tech Dept Civil Engring, 3-6-1 Gakuen, Fukui 910-8505, Japan

NAKAI, SADAO, engineering educator; b. Osaka, Japan, June 4, 1938; s. Kunitaro and Naragiku Nakai; m. Yasuko Matsunaga, June 5, 1966; children: Kumiyo, Mikiharu, Keiko. B in Engring., Osaka U., 1961, M in Engring., 1963, D in Engring., 1966. Rsch. assoc. engring. Osaka U., 1966-68, engring. lectr., 1968-71, assoc. prof. engring., 1971-78, prof., 1978—, dir. Inst. Laser Engring., 1987-95, mem. univ. coun., 1994-95, dir. Inst. Free Electron Laser, 2000—; mem. profl. com. on nuclear fusion Atomic Energy Commn. Japan, 1992—. Editor: Physics of High Power Laser Matter-Interaction, 1992, Laser Interaction and Related Plasma Phenomena, I, II, 1996; mem. editl. bd. Nuclear Fusion Jour., IAEA, Plasma Physics and Controlled Fusion, Laser and Particle Beams; contbr. articles to profl. jours. Recipient Max-Planck-Forschungspreis, 1992, Edward Teller award, 1993, The Daiwa-Anglo-Japanese Found. Daiwa awards, 1994. Fellow Am. Phys. Soc.; mem. Laser Soc. Japan (dean 1986—, v.p. 1997—), Japan Soc. Plasma Sci. and Nuclear Fusion Rsch. (dean 1986-92, v.p. 1995-97), IEE Japan (dean 1985-87, chmn. tech. com. opto-quantum device 1994-2000), Senri Rotary Club, Osaka U. Judo Club (pres.). Avocations: judo, golf. E-mail: nakai@ile.osaka-u.ac.jp. Home: Kitakasuga-oka 3-6-45, Ibaraki Osaka 567-0048, Japan Office: Osaka U Inst Laser Engr, Yamada-oka 2-6, Suita Osaka 565-0871, Japan

NAKAI, YUICHIRO, obstetrician and gynecologist; b. Takatsuki, Osaka, Japan, Mar. 10, 1961; s. Keiji (Mori) and Misao (Nakai) M.; m. Katsuko Kita, Aug. 4, 1988 (div. 1990); m. Ayako Higashi, June 10, 1995; children: Akiyuki, Shuhei. MD, Kobe U., 1986. Intern Amagasaki (Hyogo, Japan) Med. Coop Hosp., 1986-88; resident Osaka City Perinatal Ctr., 1988-89; chief obstetrician dept. ob-gyn. Amagasaki Med. Coop. Hosp., 1991-93, Nachi-Katsuura Mcpl. Hosp., 1993-94; rsch. assoc. dept. ob-gyn. Sch. of Medicine Osaka City U., 1994—. Contbr. articles to profl. jours. Avocations: driving, collecting CDs of old conductors. Home: 4-11-18-707 Matsugaoka, Matsubara 580, Japan Office: Osaka City U Sch Medicine, 1-4-3 Asahi-Machi, Abeno Osaka 545-8585, Japan

NAKAJIMA, KENJI, biochemist, researcher, educator; b. Kyoto, Japan, June 29, 1941; s. Ennosuke and Sumi (Saito) N.; m. Junko Ohgushi, June 7, 1975; children: Hironori, Yoshiki. Grad., Kyoto U., 1966, postgrad., 1968, Doctor, 1971, PhD, 1972. Lectr. Kyoto U., 1971-77; lectr. Koshien U., Takarazuka, Japan, 1973-79, assoc. prof., 1979-87, prof., 1987—; co-rschr. Biwa Lake Rsch. Inst., Shiga, Japan, 1988—. Author: Data Book of Biochemistry, 1979, Methods in Enzymology, vol. 62, 66, 1979, 80, Vitaminolog II, 1980, Chemical Stimulants for Feeding Behavior of Fish and Shellfish, 1994, Biology Environ. Chem. of DMSP and Related Sulfonium Comp., 1995, Biochemistry, 2000. Recipient Acad. award The Vitamin Soc. of Japan, 1971, Outstanding Achievement award, 2000. Mem. Agrl. Chem. Soc. of Japan, Japan Vitamin Soc. (coun. 1996—), Japan Nutrition Food (coun. 1997—), Japan Fish Sci. Soc., Senescene-Accelerated Mouse Soc. (coun. 1997—), Japan Diabetes Soc. Avocations: painting, reading novels, music, cars, yacht. Office: Koshien U, 10-1 Momijigaoka, Hyogo Takarazuka 665-0006, Japan

NAKAJIMA, OSAMU, physician, cardiologist; b. Osaka, Japan, Aug. 1, 1962; s. Takao and Kiyoe (Yasui) N.; m. Chise Sagawa, Sept. 29, 1996; children: Yuka, Eri. MD, Osaka Med. Coll., Takatsuki, Japan, 1989. House staff Osaka Med. Coll., Takatsuki, Japan, 1989-90; resident Mishima Criticla Care Ctr., Takatsuki, Japan, 1990-92; chief Nissay Hosp., Osaka, Japan, 1993—. Recipient Nissay Med. award, 1997. Mem. Japanese Soc. Internal Medicine, Japanese Circulation Soc., Japanese Assn. for Acute Medicine, Japanese Endocrinological Soc., Japan Med.-Dental Assn. Tobacco Control. Office: Nissay Hosp, 6-3-8 Itachibori, Nishi-ku Osaka 550-0012, Japan

NAKAJIMA, SUMIO, physician, researcher; b. Tateshina, Nagano, Japan, Jan. 24, 1939; s. Kazutoshi and Sakuyo (Musha) N.; m. Midori Senba, Feb. 25, 1967; children: Morio, Atsuo. MD, Nagyoa U., 1964, PhD, 1973. Rsch. fellow Creighton U., Omaha, 1967, vis. instr., 1968; fellow U. Ala., Birmingham, 1969-70, vis. instr., 1970-71; asst. prof. Fujita Health U., Toyoake, Japan, 1977-89, prof., 1989—, assoc. dean, 1989-98, dean, 1998—. Author: Comprehensive and Practical Respiratory, Metabolic and Endocrinal Disea es, 1999; contbr. articles to med. jours., including Gut, Archives Internal Medicine. Mem. Japan Gastroenterol. Assn. (mem. coun.), Japanese Soc. Internal Medicine, Internat. Diabetes Fedn. (life). Avocations: skiing, gardening. Home: 1-174 Kaminokura Midori-Ku, Aichi Nagoya 458-0812, Japan Office: Fujita Health U, 1-98 Dengakugakubo, Aichi Toyoake 470-1192, Japan

NAKAJIMA, TOSHINORI, physics educator; b. Chiryu-shi, Japan, 1943; m. Hiroko Nakajima. B in Engring., U. Tokyo, 1966; M in Engring., 1968, D in Engring., 1976. Rsch. scientist Inst. Phys. and Chem. Rsch., Wako, Japan, 1968-96; rsch. fellow Alexander von Humboldt Found., Bonn, Germany, 1978-79; prof. Bunkyo U., Koshigaya, Japan, 1996—; lectr. Toyo U., Kawagoe, Japan, 1986-98; sr. rsch. scientist U. Sci. and Tech. of China, Hefei, 1988. Recipient The Optics Prize for Excellent Papers Japan Soc. Applied Physics, Tokyo, 1975. Home: 2-27-20-306 Hasune, Itabashi-ku Tokyo 174-0046, Japan Office: Bunkyo U, 3337 Minami-Ogishima, Koshigaya-shi Saitama 343-8511, Japan

NAKAMORI, SEIICHI, electrical engineering educator; b. Kagoshima, Japan, Mar. 9, 1951; s. Shigeru and Toshie (Torii) N.; m. Akiko Fukudome, Nov. 28, 1952; 3 children. B of Engring., Kagoshima (Japan) U., 1974; D of Engring., Kyoto (Japan) U., 1982. Asst. faculty engring. Ohita (Japan) U., 1974-85, lectr. faculty engring. & applied math., 1985-87; assoc. prof. dept. tech. edn. Kagoshima (Japan) U., 1987-94, prof. dept. tech. edn., 1994—. Author: (with others) Fundamental Electric and Electronic Engineering (in Japanese), 1994; contbr. articles to profl. jours. Home: 1947-5, Miyanoura, Yoshida Town, Kagoshima 891-1305, Japan Office: Kagoshima U Dept Tech Faculty Edn, Kagoshima U Dept Tech Edn, 1-20-6 Kohrimoto, Kagoshima 890 0065, Japan

NAKAMOTO, MITSU-HARU KOSEI, religious studies educator; b. Tokyo, Sept. 18, 1926; s. Yoshi-haru and Miyo-ko (Wada) N. BDiv, St. Pauls U., Tokyo; M. of Lit., U. Tokyo, 1963; postgrad., U. Cambridge, Eng., 1963-66. Lectr. Luth. Sem., Japan, 1966-76; prof. religious studies Societas Summae Mentis, Mobara-shi, Japan, 1977—, theol. cons., 1982—. Author: The Fundamental Principles of Christianity, 1982. Mem. Asiatic Soc. Japan, Cambridge and Oxford Soc. Avocations: fine art, tea ceremonies. Home: Koh-164 Noi Shiroyama, Aino-cho 854-0301, Japan

NAKAMURA, HIDEHO, medical publication editor; b. Osaka, Sept. 3, 1938; s. Satoru and Shizuko (Mimata) N.; m. Yumiko Naito, Feb. 22, 1947. BS, Waseda U., 1961. V.p. Igaku-Shoin, Tokyo, 1961—. Avocation: travel. Home: 2-20-2-1002 Shin-Oohashi, Kohto-ku, 135-0007 Tokyo Japan Office: Igaku-Shoin, 5-24-3 Hongo Bunkyo-ku, 113-8719 Tokyo Japan

NAKAMURA, HIROSHI, urology educator; b. Tokyo, Mar. 22, 1933; s. Yataroh and Hideko (Tanaka) N.; m. Miyoko Kodachi, Aug. 13, 1966. MD, Keio U., Tokyo, 1960; PhD, Grad. Sch. Medicine, Keio U., 1966. Med. diplomate. Asst. resident Mt. Sinai Hosp., N.Y.C., 1962-63; rsch. fellow Cornell U. Med. Coll., N.Y.C., 1966-68; asst. Sch. Medicine Keio U., Tokyo, 1968-70; chmn. urology dept. Tokyo Elec. Power Hosp., 1970-73; vis. asst. prof. surgery Cornell U. Med. Coll., N.Y.C., 1973; chmn. urology Kitasato Inst. Hosp., Tokyo, 1973-77; chmn. dept., prof. urology Nat. Def. Med. Coll., Tokorozawa, Saitama, Japan, 1977-98, dir. dept. acad. affairs, 1994-96, prof. emeritus, 1999—; emeritus dir. Tokorozawa Ishikawa Clinic, 1998—. Author: Bedside Urology, 1991, Modern Clinical Point-Urology, 1993; editor: Up-to-date Urology, 1983, Medical Ethics Q&A, 1998, Caveats & Pitfalls in Clinical Urology, 1999. Recipient Tamura award Keio U. Sch. Medicine, 1967, All-around Med. award, Igaku-Shoin, Ltd., Tokyo, 1967. Buddhist. Avocations: jazz, audiophile, travel, fishing, baseball. Home: 11-1-1204 Higashicho, Tokorozawa Saitama 359-1116, Japan Office: Ishikawa Clin Iseki Bldg 4F, 9-22 Hiyoshicho, Tokorozawa Saitama 359-1123, Japan

NAKAMURA, HIROYUKI, chemistry educator; b. Kobe, Hyogo, Japan, Aug. 2, 1967; s. Yuzo and Tatsuko (Sadamoto) N.; m. Makiko Akashi, Mar. 3, 1969; 1 child, Kouki. BSc, Tohoku U., Sendai, Japan, 1991, MS, 1993, PhD, 1996. Cert. govt. ofcl. Japanese Soc. for Promotion of Sci. fellow Japanese Jr. Scientists, 1993-95; rsch. instr. Tohoku U., Sendai, 1995, 97—, Kyushu U., Fukuoka, Japan, 1995-97. Contbr. articles to profl. jours. Recipient Award of Chem. Soc. of Japan for Young Chemists, 1999. Mem. Internat. Soc. for Neutron Capture Therapy, Am. Chem. Soc., Japan Chem. Soc. (award for young chemist 1999). Home: 35-1-206 Kawauchi Moto, Hasekura Aoba, Taihaku-ku Sendai 980-0861, Japan Office: Tohoku U Faculty of Sci, Dept Chemistry, Sendai 980-8578, Japan

NAKAMURA, ISAO, acoustician, researcher; b. Ookuwa, Nagano, Japan, Sept. 19, 1925; m. Yuriko Taniyama, Apr. 3, 1952. BS, Tohoku U., Sendai, Japan, 1950, D Engring., 1981. Tech. ofcl. Meteorol. Agy., Japan, 1950-61; assoc. prof. Shizuoka U., Hamamatsu, Japan, 1962-81, prof., 1981-84; prof. U. Electro-Communications, Chofu, Japan, 1984-91, Teikyo U. Tech., Ichihara, Japan, 1991-95, Teikyo Heisei U., Ichihara, 1995-98; dir. Athena Co., Tokyo, 1998—; chmn. organizing com. Internat. Symposium on Mus. Acoustics, Tokyo, 1992, mem. sci. com., Dourdan, France, 1995, Edinburgh, U.K., 1997, mem. Internat. Sci. Adv. Bd., Leavenworth, Wash., 1998; chmn. (Japan side) organizing com. Japan-China Joint Meeting on Mus. Acoustics, Beijing, 1994, chmn. adv. com., Chofu, Tokyo, 1997. Author: Computer and Electronics Terms Dictionary, 1977; contbr. articles to profl. jours. Mem. Inst. Electronics Info. and Comm. (life), Acoustical Soc. Japan (chmn. tech. com. on mus. acoustics 1982-86, Sato prize for outstanding papers 1982, prize for disting. achievement in acoustics 1996), Catgut Acoustical Soc. (v.p. internat. com. 1995—). Avocation: travel. Home: 1-33-25 Kokuryo, Chofu 182-0022, Japan

NAKAMURA, KEIJIRO, company executive; b. Hita City, Japan, Aug. 27, 1935; s. Sukezo and Yoshi Anai; m. Kinue Asakura, Nov. 14, 1959; children: Kenyu, Rie, Yoshihiro. BArch, U. Fukuoka, Japan, 1957. Rep. Towa Hakko Shokuhin, Kogyo, Japan, 1961-67, Orient Green Co., Ltd., Tachikawa, Japan, 1991—; cons. Matsushita Electrical Indsl. Co., Ltd., 1999—, Asahl Glass Co., Ltd., 1999—, Mcpl. Disposal Plant, Saijo City, Japan, 1998, Yahatahama City, 1998—, Shinjo City, 1996—, Taiwan, 1998—, purification of gen. exhaust and conversion of exhaust soil into fertile soil, China, 2000—. Patentee method of converting seawater into fresh water and method for converting depleted soils into fertile soils. Buddhist. Avocation: playing Igo. Home and Office: 10-138 Minamidairo 1-chome, Hino-shi, Tokyo 191-0041, Japan

NAKAMURA, KENICHI, engineering educator; b. Otahara, Tochigi, Japan, Nov. 4, 1925; s. Tahei and Haru (Sekiya) N.; m. Aiko Tonomura, Feb. 14, 1958; children: Tetsuya, Yoshimi. BS, Tokyo U., 1948, DrEngr, 1960. Asst. Tokyo U., 1950-54; asst. prof. Shizuoka (Japan) U., 1954-57, assoc. prof., 1957-59; assoc. prof. engring. Waseda U., Tokyo, 1959-65, prof., 1965-96, emeritus prof., 1996—; trustee SICE, Tokyo, 1970-72. Author: Elementary Physics, 1972; editor Japan Soc. Applied Physics, 1982-83; contbr. articles to profl. jours. Recipient Disting. Svc. award Soc. Electrophotography of Japan, 1996. Mem. Soc. Electrophotography Japan (disting. svc. award 1996). Home and Office: 4-6-5 Shimoigusa, Suginami, Tokyo 167-0022, Japan

NAKAMURA, KUMI, anesthesiologist; b. Tokyo, Sept. 28, 1949; d. Shosuke and Utako (Abe) Okamoto; m. Takashi Nakamura, May 7, 1974; 2 children. MD, Kyoto (Japan) U., 1974. Resident in anesthesiology Kyoto U. Hosp., 1974-76, fellow in anesthesiology, 1983-85, lectr., 1987-92, assoc. prof., 1992-97; staff anesthesiologist Kyoto City Hosp., 1976-83, chief anesthesiologist, 1997—; rsch. fellow McMaster U., Hamilton, Ont., Can., 1986. Grantee Ministry of Edn., Sci. and Culture, Tokyo, 1995-97, Fujiwara Found., Kyoto, Japan, 1995, Esso-Sekiyu, Tokyo, 1994. Mem. Japanese Soc. Anesthesiologists (councilor 1995-99), Japan Soc. Circuation Control in Medicine (councilor 1994—). Home: 36-13 Saiin-Shuneicho, Ukyo-ku Kyoto 615, Japan Office: Kyoto City Hosp, Kyoto 604, Japan

NAKAMURA, KUNIO, electronics company executive; b. Shiga, Japan, July 5, 1939. Grad. econs., Osaka U., 1962. With Matsushita Elec. Indsl. Co. Ltd., 1962—, dir. Tokyo spl. sales office, corp. consumer sales divsn., pres. Panasonic Co., pres. Panasonic U.K. Ltd., mng. dir., sr. mng. dir., pres. AVC co., pres., 2000—; dir., bd. dirs, corp. mgmt. divsn. Ams.; chmn. bd. Matsushita Elec. Corp. of Am., 1993. Office: Matsushita Elec Indsl Co, 1006 Oaza Kadona, Kadoma City 571 8501, Japan*

NAKAMURA, KUNIWO, president of Palau. Pres. Govt. of Palau, Koror. Office: Office of Pres PO Box 100 Palau PW 96940-0100*

NAKAMURA, MAKOTO, manufacturing company executive; b. Sapporo, Japan, May 31, 1946; came to U.S., 1989; s. Naohiko and Hideko Nakamura; m. Sachiko Nakamura, Oct. 30, 1971; 1 child, Yutaka. BS, U. Tokyo, 1969; M of Indsl. Adminstrn., Carnegie-Mellon U., 1978. Sr. advisor Komatsu Dresser Co., Chattanooga, 1989-90; asst. contr. Komatsu Dresser Co., Lincolnshire, Ill., 1990-94; treas. Komatsu Am. Internat., Lincolnshire, 1994-97; pres., COO Komatsu Am. Corp., Vernon Hills, Ill., 1997—. Home: 1471 N Pinehurst Dr Vernon Hills IL 60061-1230 Office: Komatsu Am Corp 440 N Fairway Dr Vernon Hills IL 60061-1836

NAKAMURA, MASAMI, internist; b. Yokohama, Japan, Nov. 18, 1934; s. Seiichi and Wasako Nakamura; m. Yuriko Yamashita, Jan. 26, 1963; children: Mari, Hiromi. MD, Tokyo U., 1959, D of Med. Scis., 1965. Mem. med. staff Tokyo U., 1965-66, 69-70; rsch. fellow U. Minn., Austin, 1966-69; dir. Nakamura Clinic, Yokohama, 1972—; auditor The Kanagawa-ku Med. Assn., Yokohama, Japan, 1979—; rep. The Yokohama Med. Assn., 1990—. Mem. Japanese Soc. Internal Medicine, Japanese Soc. Gastroenterology, Japanese Soc. Alcohol Studies, N.Y. Acad. Scis., Kanagawa-East Rotary Club. Home: 59-8 Sawatari Kanagawa-Ku, Yokohama 221-0844, Japan Office: Nakamura Clinic, 2-16 Kamitanmachi, Yokohama 221-0831, Japan

NAKAMURA, YASHUHIDE, community health educator; b. Tanabe City, Japan, Feb. 18, 1952; s. Hiroshi and Yoko (Yamakawa) N.; m. Mariko Morii, Aug. 21, 1986; children: Fumi, Yuto. MD, U. Tokyo, 1977, PhD, 1993. Med. diplomate. Med. staff Metro. Fuchu (Japan) Hosp., 1978-85; expert of JICA North Sumatra Health Project, Medan, Indonesia, 1986-89; health officer UNHCR, Islamabad, Pakistan, 1990-91; asst. prof. U. Tokyo, 1992-95, assoc. prof., 1997-99; prof. Osaka U., 1999—. Author: The Handicapped Baby, 1986; co-editor: Textbook of Maternal and Child Health

Community Care, 1994; editor: International Health for High School Children, 1995. Pres. Shishinoko Camp, Fuchu, Japan, 1982-86; chmn. Tokyo Internat. Soc. for Child Health, 1993—, HANDS. Fellow Harvard Sch. Pub. Health; mem. Japan Assn. for Internat. Health, Japan Child Health Assn., Japan Primary Care Assn. Avocations: travel, music, Noh play. Home: # 404 4-37-12 Nishiogi-kita, Suginami-ku, Tokyo 167, Japan Office: Faculty Human Scis Osaka U, 1-2 Yamadaoka Suita City, Osaka 565-0871, Japan

NAKAMURA, YASUAKI, electronics engineer, educator; b. Numakuma, Japan, Mar. 30, 1955; s. Hiromu and Etsuko Nakamura; m. Kana Nakano, Nov. 23, 1979; children: Yuka, Ayaka, Keishi. B in Engring., Osaka U., 1977, M in Engring., 1979; PhD, U. Tokyo, 1991. From rschr. to mgr. Mitsubishi Elec. Corp., Amagasaki, Japan, 1979-94; prof. Hiroshima City U., Japan, 1994—. patentee in field. Mem. IEEE, Inst. Elec., Info. & Comm. Engrs. Avocations: tennis, skiing, fishing. Home: 16-53-202 Hijiyama-honmachi, Minami-ku, Hiroshima 732-0816, Japan Office: Hiroshima City U, 3-4-1 Asa-minmi-ku, 731-31 Hiroshima Japan

NAKANE, YOSHIBUMI, psychiatry educator; b. Korea, Jan. 1, 1938; came to Japan, 1945; s. Akira and Masae Nakane; m. Motoko Imamura, June 30, 1962; children: Hideyuki, Eiji, Shunya. B, Nagasaki (Japan) U., 1963, DMS, 1968. Lic. physician. Assoc. prof. Nagasaki Sch. Medicine, 1981-84, prof. psychiatry, 1984—; dir. WHO Collaborating Ctr. for Rsch. and Tng. in Mental Health, Nagasaki, 1984—; mem. adv. com. WHO Expert Adv. Panel on Mental Health, Geneva, 1984—. Author: Mental Illness in General Health Care, 1995, Nagasaki Symposium: Radiation and Human Health, 1996, Radiation Dose and Health Effects, 1997. Fellow Pacific Rim Coll. Psychiatrist, Collegium Internat. Neuro-Psychopharmacology. Home: 3-9-904 Sumiyoshi-machi, Nagasaki 852-8154, Japan Office: Nagasaki U Sch Medicine, 1-7-1 Sakamoto, Nagasaki 852-8501, Japan

NAKANISHI, OSAMU, historian; b. Osaka, Japan, Dec. 30, 1932; s. Arajiro and Suzue (Abe) N.; m. Setsuko Takebe, Mar. 24, 1957; children: Nobuki, Tomoki. BA, Osaka U. Fgn. Studies, 1956; MA, U. Tokyo, 1963. Lectr. Hosei U., Tokyo, 1966-74; assoc. prof. U. Kanagawa, Yokohama, Japan, 1974-77; prof. faculty letters Soka U., Tokyo, 1977—, dean faculty of letters, 1994—, dep. v.p., 1998—; vis. prof. Moscow U., 1992-93, Wuhan (China) U., 1994, 97—; vis. scholar Columbia U., N.Y.C., 1996; cons. prof. Shanghai Normal U., 1995—. Author: China and the Soviet Union, 1979, Soviet Society and Soviet Diplomacy, 1986, International Relations, 1990, From the Soviet Union to the CIS, 1992, New International Relations, 1999. Mem. Japanese Assn. for Russian and East European Studies (gen. sec. 1991-97, mem. standing com. 1988—). Home: 1-9-3 Yokodai Isogoku, Yokohama Kanagawa 235-0045, Japan Office: Soka U, 1-236 Tangicho, Hachioji Tokyo 192-8577, Japan

NAKANISHI, TSUTOMU, pharmaceutical science educator; b. Osaka, Japan, Mar. 4, 1939; s. Noboru and Shizuko (Kurata) N.; m. Naoko Nishihara, May 3, 1969; children: Wataru N., Nozomi N., Hiromu N. Diploma in pharm. scis., Osaka U., 1961, PhD, 1968; diploma in organic chemistry, Imperial Coll., London. Lectr. pharm. scis. Osaka U., 1970-78, assoc. prof., 1978-83; prof. faculty pharm. sci. Setsunan U., Osaka, 1983—; rsch. fellow in organic chemistry, Imperial Coll., London, 1973-74. Author; contbr. articles to English and Japanese lang. sci. publs. Mem. Pharm. Soc. Japan, Chem. Soc. Japan, Royal Soc. Chemistry. Office: Pharm Scis Setsunan U, 45-1 Nagaotoge cho, Hirakata 573-01, Japan

NAKANO, ISAO, accounting educator; b. Sakai, Japan, Oct. 24, 1937; s. Tomekichi and Hagino (Nakagawa) N.; m. Keiko Miki; 1 child, Takeshi. BBA, Kobe U., 1960, MBA, 1962, DBA, 1977. Asst. prof. rsch. inst. for econs. and bus. adminstrn. Kobe (Japan) U., 1967-79, prof., 1979-89, dir., 1989-91, prof., leader info. systems study, 1991—. Editor: Business Behavior and Information, 1992; contbr. articles to profl. jours. Recipient Ohta prize Japan Acctg. Assn., 1972. Home: Tsukimigaoka 7-13 Nigawa, Takarazuka 665-0067, Japan Office: Himeji Dokkyo U, Kamiohno 7-2-1, Himeji 670-0896, Japan

NAKANO, MASAHIRO, pharmacist; b. Kikugawa, Japan, Nov. 20, 1937; s. Sadaichi and Saki (Kuroda) N.; m. Naomi Ishizaki, Aug. 22, 1964; children: Masako Pamela, Takahiro Edwin. BS in Pharmacy, Kyoto U., 1960, MS in Pharmacy, 1962; PhD in Pharmacy, U. Wis., 1967. Instr. pharmacy Kyoto U., 1967-68; rsch. assoc. U. Alberta, Edmonton, Canada, 1968-69; rsch. pharmacist Food & Drug Directorate, Ottawa, Canada, 1969-70; sr. rsch. scientist Alza Inst., Lawrence, Kans., 1970-72; assoc. prof. pharmacy Hokkaido U., Sapporo, Japan, 1972-80; prof. pharmacy Kumamoto Univ. Hosp., Japan, 1980—; dir. gen. Japanese Soc. for Therapeutic Drug Monitoring, 1998—, dir. Japanese Soc. Clinical Pharmacology and Therapeutics, 1999—. Fellow Am. Assn. Pharm. Scientists. Avocations: softball, photography. Home: 2243-197 Shimosuzurikawa-machi, Kumamoto 861-5522, Japan Office: Kumamoto U Hosp, 1-1-1 Honjo, Kumamoto 860-8556, Japan

NAKANO, MASAYUKI, drug company executive; b. Kanzaki-gun, Saga, Japan, July 16, 1945; s. Tetsusaburo and Chizu (Baba) N.; m. Etsuko Hasegawa, Nov. 28, 1971; children: Yoshiko, Yuko. PhD, Kushu U., Fukuoka, Japan, 1981. Rschr. Shionogi & Co. Ltd., Osaka, Japan, 1971-81, 88-91, dep. mgr., 1991—; postdoctoral fellow U. Toronto, Ont., 1982-84. Contbr. articles to profl. jours. Office: Shionogi Co Ltd Clin Rsch, 12-4 Sagisu 5-chome, Osaka 553-0002, Japan

NAKANO, MINEO, plastic surgeon; b. Onomichi, Hiroshima, Japan, July 12, 1956; s. Isamu and Kinue (Kaneshima) N.; m. Mieko Chou, Apr. 8, 1984; children: Go, Ray. MD, Nat. Def. Med. Coll., Tokorozawa, Japan, 1982; PhD, Hokkaido U., Sapporo, Japan, 1990. Resident dept. plastic reconstructive surgery Nat. Def. Med. Coll., Tokorozawa, 1982-90; rsch. fellow Roger Williams Med. Ctr., Providence, 1990-91, R.I. Hosp., Providence, 1991-92; head physician dept. plastic surgery Nakano Gen. Hosp., Tokyo, 1992-94; lectr. dept. plastic reconstructive surgery Saitama Med. Sch., Moroyoma, Japan, 1994-99; assoc. prof. unit plastic reconstructive surgery Internat. U. Health & Welfare Med. Ctr., Nishinasuno, Japan, 1999—. Contbr. articles to profl. jours. Capt. Japanese Army, 1982-90. Avocations: tennis, golf, travel, classical music. Office: Internat U Health & Welfare, Med Ctr 537-3 Iguchi, Nishinasuno 329-2763, Japan

NAKANO, SHINJI, race car driver; b. Osaka, Japan, Apr. 1, 1971. Japanese karting champion Formula 3, Japan, 1984-89; race care driver Brit. Formula Vauxhall, 1990-92, All-Japan Formula 3 & Formula Nippo Championship, Japan, 1992-97, Prost Team, Europe, 1997-98; profl. race car driver Minardi Team, 1998—. Champion Kansai Kartland All Class, 1984, 85, 2d pl. All Japan Kart Championship, 1987, champion Internat. Hong Kong Kart Grand Prix, 1987, 1st pl. Japan Kart Grand Prix, 1987, 3d pl. All Japan Formula 3 Championship, 1994. Office: Minardi Team Spa, Via Spallanzani 21, I-48018 Faenta Ravenna, Italy*

NAKAO, MITSUHIRO, mathematician, educator; b. Awaji, Hyogo, Japan, Oct. 17, 1944; s. Masamichi and Kiyoko (Kawakami) N.; m. Jinko Suenobu, Nov. 15, 1970; 1 child, Maki. BS, Kyoto (Japan) U., 1968; MS, Kyushu U., Fukuoka, Japan, 1970, DSc, 1977. Rsch. asst. Kyushu U., Fukuoka, 1972-76, assoc. prof., 1976-90, prof., 1990—. Contbr. articles to profl. jours. Elder Nagaoka Ch., Fukuoka, 1993—. Grantee Matsunaga Found., Tokyo, 1978. Office: Kyushu U Grad Sch Math, Ropponmatsu, Fukuoka 810-8560, Japan

NAKAO, TOSHIHIKO, veterinary medicine educator; b. Ohshima-qun, Japan, Jan. 14, 1947; s. Kinzo and Chieko (Nishimoto) N.; m. Toyoko Machida; 1 child, Keiichiro. DVM, Obihiro U. Agrl. Vet. Medicine, Japan, 1969, MSc, 1976; PhD, Hokkaido U., Sapporo, Japan, 1981. Cert. vet. surgeon Ministry of Agrl., Japan. Vet. surgeon Japan Overseas Coop. Vols., Punjab, India, 1970-72; lectr. vet. medicine Rakuno Gakuen U., Ebetsu, Japan, 1975-78, asst. prof., 1978-84, assoc. prof., 1984-93, prof., 1993-99; prof. animal reproduction Hiroshima U., 1999—; mem. Nat. Vet. Coun., Ministry of Agrl., Forestry and Fishery, Tokyo, 1995—. Contbr. articles to med. jours. v.p. Ebetsu UNESCO, 1997—. Rsch. fellow Alexander von Humbolt Found., Hannover, 1980. Mem. Japanese Soc. Farm Animal Vet. Medicine (bd. dirs. 1995—), Japanese Soc. Animal Reproduction (bd. dirs. 1997—, SATO award 1980), Japanese Soc. Vet. Sci. (mem. jour. editl. bd. 1995—), Soc. Theriogenology, Am. Dairy Sci. Assn., Am. Assn. Bovine Practitioners. Avocations: jogging, gardening, swimming. Office: Hiroshima U, IDEC, Higashi-Hiroshima 739-8529, Japan

NAKARAI, CHARLES FREDERICK TOYOZO, music educator, adjudicator; b. Indpls., Apr. 25, 1936; s. Toyozo Wada and Frances Aileen N. B.A. cum laude, Butler U., 1958, Mus.M., 1967; postgrad., U. N.C., 1967-70. Organist, dir. choirs Northwood Christian Ch., Indpls., 1954-57; minister music Allisonville Christian Ch., Indpls., 1957-58; asst. prof. music Milligan Coll., Tenn., 1970-72; pvt. instr. organ, piano Durham, 1972—; mem. faculty piano camp U. N.C.-Greensboro, 1996, 97, 2000; adjudicator N.C. Fedn. Music Clubs, Raleigh Music Tchrs. Assn., Charlotte Piano Tchrs. Forum, Chapel Hill Music Tchrs. Assn. Composer: Three Movements for Chorus, 1971, Bluesy, 1979. Served with USAF, 1958-64. Mem. Am. Musicol. Soc., Coll. Music Soc., Am. Guild Organists, Music Tchrs. Nat. Assn., Music Library Assn., N.C. Music Tchrs. Assn. (chair student activities, vice chair piano sect.), Organ Hist. Soc., Durham Music Tchrs. Assn. (chair student activities), Triangle Guitar Soc. Address: 3520 Mayfair St Apt 205 Durham NC 27707-2673

NAKASHIMA, NOBUAKI, chemistry educator; b. Kinosaki-Gun, Hyogo, Japan, Oct. 4, 1946; s. Junichi and Shigeno Nakashima; m. Mieko Nakamura, May 23, 1975; children: Kumiko, Mitsuaki. B in Tech., Osaka (Japan) U., 1969, M in Tech., 1971, D in Tech., 1974. Rsch. scholar Japanese Sci. Promotion Soc., Osaka, 1974-76; rsch. assoc. Inst. for Molecular Sci., Okazaki, Aichi, Japan, 1976-87; vis. scientist Royal Instn., London, 1981; assoc. prof. chemistry Inst. Laser Engring., Osaka U., 1987-96; prof. chemistry Grad. Sch. Sci. Osaka City U., 1996—. Contbr. numerous articles to profl. publs. Mem. Chem. Soc. Japan (Progress prize 1981), Laser Soc. Japan (Progress prize 1983), Japanese Photochem. Assn. (award 1993), Am. Chem. Soc. Avocations: skiing, jogging, gardening. Home: 2-20-502 Takezono Senriyama, Suita Osaka 565-0852, Japan Office: Osaka City U Grad Sch Sci, 3-3-138 Sugimoto Sumiyoshi, Osaka 558-8585, Japan

NAKATA, GARY KENJI, lawyer; b. Okinawa, Japan, Nov. 13, 1964; came to the U.S., 1971; s. Hiroshi Nakata and Miwako Kin; m. Jo Ann Akiko Tengan, Aug. 22, 1998. BBA in Fin., U. Hawaii, 1988; JD with distinction, U. of the Pacific, 1995. Bar: Hawaii 1996, Calif. 1996, U.S. Dist. Ct. Hawaii, 1996; cert. mgmt. acct.; cert. fin. mgr.; cert. grad. Am. Banker's Assn. Nat. Sch. Regulatory Compliance. Credit analyst Bank of Hawaii, Honolulu, 1988-90, sr. credit analyst, 1990-92; law clk. Hawaii Atty. Gen. Tax Divsn., Honolulu, 1994; sr. assoc. Kobayashi, Sugita & Goda, Honolulu, 1995—; mem. new product devel. adv. bd. Warren Gorham & Lamont, N.Y.C., 1997-98. Editor-in-chief: The Transnational Lawyer, 1994, 95. pres., enlisted adv. coun. Hawaii Air Nat. Guard, Honolulu, 1986-92; mem. ex officio alumni coun., mem. membership com., mem. membership benefits subcom. U. Hawaii Alumni Assn., Honolulu, 1990-91; mem. fin. com. and bylaws subcom. Soc. Coll. Bus. Alumni and Friends, U. Hawaii Coll. Bus. Adminstrn. Alumni Affairs, Honolulu, 1990-91, founding mem., treas., 1990-91, mem. steering com. to form alumni orgn., 1997-98, pres., 1998-2000; at-large rep., treas., legis. liaison Neighborhood Bd., Kaneohe, Hawaii, 1991-92. Mem. ABA (bus. law sect., comml. fin. svcs. com., electronic commerce com., consumer fin. svcs. com., comml. loan documentation sub-com., comml. loan workout subcom. 1997—), Hawaii State Bar Assn. (mem. real property and fin. svcs. sect. 1997—), Calif. State Bar Assn., Inst. Cert. Mgmt. Accts. (bd. dirs. 1998-2000, dir. mem. acquistion 1998-2000), Hawaii Fin. Regulatory Compliance Assn. (bd. dirs. 1997—, chairperson fair credit reporting act regulatory update com. 1998—), Hawaii Bus. Jaycees (charter mem. 1991—, charter pres. 1991-92, chmn. bd. 1992-93, R. Allen Watkins Outstanding Chpt. Pres. award 1992, Hampton Whetsell award 1992, Clarence Howard award 1992), Hawaiian Jaycees (legal counsel 2000). Office: Kobayashi Sugita & Goda 999 Bishop St Ste 2600 Honolulu HI 96813-4430

NAKATA, YOSHIKI, electrical engineering researcher; b. Iuzuka, Fukuoka, Japan, Aug. 19, 1968; s. Takeshi and Mizuho (Kanamaru) N. BEE, Kyushu U., Fukuoka, 1992, MEE, 1994, D of Engring., 1996. Rschr. Japan Soc. for the Promotion of Sci., Tokyo, 1996; rsch. assoc. Kyushu U., 1996—. Contbr. articles to profl. jours. including Applied Surface Sci., Jour. Applied Physics. Rsch. scholar Japan Soc. for Promotion of Sci., 1996. Mem. Japanese Soc. Applied Physics, Inst. Elec. Engring. Japan, Laser Soc. Japan. Avocations: travel, reading, skiing. Office: Kyushu U, Hakozaki 6-10-1, Fukuoka 812-8581, Japan

NAKATANI, HIROSHI, biophysical chemist; b. Osaka, Osaka, Japan, Dec. 17, 1941; s. Naomasa and Shizue (Nishida) N.; m. Setsuko Sugai, 1976; children: Kazumi, Fumiko. BSc, Kyoto (Japan) U., 1966, MSc, 1968, DSc, 1974. Instr. faculty agr. Kyoto U., 1971—. Mem. AAAS, Japanese Biochem. Soc., Biophysical Soc. Japan. Home: Sakyou-ku, Yoshida Nakaojichou 31-66, Kyoto 606-8313, Japan Office: Kyoto U, Faculty Agr, Kyoto 606-8224, Japan

NAKATANI, IWAO, economist, educator; b. Osaka, Japan, Jan. 22, 1942; m. Tomoko Muramatsu, Nov. 3, 1966; children: Kentaro, Yujiro, Saeko. BA, Hitotsubashi U., Tokyo, 1965; MA, Harvard U., 1971, PhD, 1973. Staff Nissan Motor Co., Tokyo, 1965-69; lectr. dept. econs., rsch. fellow Harvard U., Cambridge, 1973-74; assoc. prof. econs. Osaka U., 1974-84, prof. econs., 1984-91; prof. econs. Hitotsubashi U., Tokyo, 1991-99, Tama U., Tokyo, 1999—; dir. Sony Corp., 1999—; pres. SRIC Corp., 2000—. Author: Borderless Economy, 1987, The Transition of the Japanese Firm, 1987, Historical Transformation of the Japanese Economy, 1996, The IT Power, 2000. Home: 1-14-5-4-2 Akasaka, Minato-ku, Tokyo 107-0052, Japan Office: 11-7 Shinbashi 1-Chome, Minato-ku, Tokyo 105-8631, Japan

NAKATANI, SATOSHI, cardiologist; b. Himeji City, Japan, Sept. 13, 1957; s. Kazuo and Yasuyo (Ohashi) N.; m. Akiko Ogasawara, Oct. 29, 1988; children: Hiroko, Susumu. MD, Osaka U. Med. Sch., 1983, PhD, 1989. Staff Osaka U. Hosp., 1985; cardiologist Osaka Police Hosp., 1986-87; from staff researcher to staff cardiologist Nat. Cardiovascular Ctr., Suita, Japan, 1987-93, 95—; rsch. assoc. The Cleve. Clinic Found., 1993-95; dir. echocardiography rsch. Nat. Cardiovascular Ctr., 1995—. Author: Advances in Echo-Contrast, 1993; contbr. articles to profl. jours. Uehara Meml. Found. fellow, 1993. Fellow Am. Coll. Cardiology; mem. Am. Heart Assn., Japanese Soc. Internal Medicine, Japanese Circulation Soc. Avocations: skiing. Office: Nat Cardivasc Ctr Cardi Div, 5-7-1 Fujishiro-dai, Suita 565, Japan

NAKATSU, RYOHEI, research company executive; b. Himeji, Japan, Oct. 19, 1946; s. Sadamu and Masako (Fujita) N.; m. Yukiko Katoh Nakatsu, Feb. 10, 1975; 1 child, Rie. BS, Kyoto (Japan) U., 1969; MS, 1971, PhD, 1982. Researcher Nippon Telephone & Telegraph, Musashino, Japan, 1971-78; sr. researcher, 1978-87; group leader Nippon Telephone & Telegraph Human Interface Rsch. Labs., Yokosuka, Japan, 1987-90; exec. mgr. Nippon Telephone & Telegraph Basic Rsch. Labs., Musaschino, Japan, 1990-91; dir., 1991-94; pres. ATR Media Integration & Comms. Rsch. Labs., Kyoto, 1994—; vis. prof. Seikei U., Musashino, Japan, 1993—, Sophia U., Tokyo, 1996—, Doshisha U., Kyoto, Japan, 1996—, Kobe U., Japan, 1999—; vis. rschr. U. Tokyo, 1998—. Contbr. several papers in field. Dir. Musashino (Japan) Internat. Assn., 1990-94. Recipient Best Paper award Annual Meeting IEICE, 1978, Internat. Conf. on Multinmedia Computing and Systems, 1996, Inst. Image Info. and TV Engrs., 1999, Virtual Reality Soc. Japan, 1999, Japanese Soc. Artificial Intelligence, 2000, NTT Pres. award Automatic Answering Svc. for Elec. Request, 1980, L'Oreal prize Art and Sci. Found., 1997. Mem. IEEE, Japan Soc. for Archaeol. Info. (dir.), Japanese Soc. for Artificial Intelligence (dir.), Inst. of Image Electronics Engr. of Japan (dir.), Virtual Reality Soc. of Japan (vice chmn.). Avocation: golf, tennis, skiing. Office: ATR Media Int & Comms Rsch, 2-2 Hikaridai, Seika-cho Kyoto 619-0288, Japan

NAKATSUJI, TADAKO, medical researcher, educator; b. Kochi-ken, Takaoka-gun, Nakatosa-cho, Kaminokae, Japan, Mar. 30, 1947; s. Kanoo and Yoshiko Nakatsuji. MD, Yamaguchi U., 1974, DS, 1980. Clin. tng. Yamaguchi U. Hosp., Japan, 1974-75, 76, Osaka U. Hosp., Japan, 1975-76; asst. Sch. Medicine Yamaguchi U., Japan, 1976-79; asst. U. Tokyo, 1979-81; asst. prof. Med. Coll. Ga., 1981-85; asst. prof., assoc. dir. dept. transfusion Hamamatsu U. Sch. Medicine, 1986—. Contbr. articles to profl. jours. Mem. Japanese Soc. Transfusion (councilor 1992, qualifying doctor 1993). Avocation: drawing. Home: Idaishukusha E-222, 3776 Handa-cho, Hamamatsu City 431-3124, Japan Office: Hamamatsu U Sch Medicine, 3600 Handa-cho, Hamamatsu 431-3192, Japan

NAKAUCHI, ISAO, retail executive; b. Osaka, Japan, Aug. 2, 1922. Student, Kobe (Japan) Coll. of Commerce, 1941. Pres. Daiei Pharm. Industry Co., Kobe, 1957-82; chmn., CEO The Daiei, Inc., Kobe, 1982—. Author: Waga Yasuuri Tetsugaku, 1969. Recipient Grand Cordon of Order of Scared Treasure Japanese Govt., 1993, A Chevalier de la Legion d'Honneur France, French Govt., 1984, Prince Henrik's medal of honor and Diploma of Denmark, 1990, Insignia of Comdr. of Order of Leopold of Belgium, 1996. Avocations: reading, golf. Office: Daiei Inc, 4-1-1 Minatojima-Nakamachi, Chuo-ku Kobe 650-0046, Japan*

NAKAYA, RINTARO, microbiologist, consultant; b. Ohno, Japan, Nov. 10, 1924; s. Rinzaemon and Tomi (Kurota) N.; m. Yukie Tanaka, Nov. 22, 1951; children: Saeko Nakaya Fujino, Mizuho. MD, U. Tokyo, 1947, DMS, 1958. Cert. med. practitioner Min. of Health and Welfare, Japanese Govt. Chief labs. NIH, Tokyo, 1948-68; dir. dept. Nat. Inst. Pub. Health, Tokyo, 1968-73; prof. microbiology Tokyo Med. and Dental U., 1973-90, prof. emeritus, 1990—; prof. Sch. Home Econs. Japan Women's U., Tokyo, 1990-93; adviser Japan Bifidus Found., Tokyo, 1999—; dir. Kurozumi Med. Rsch. Found., Tokyo, 1999—. Author: Drug Resistance, 1976; author, editor: Infectious Enteritis in Japan, 1986; editor Infectious Enteritis in Japan II, 1997. Rsch. fellow Rockefeller Found., 1957-58, U. Wis., 1967-68. Mem. AAAS, Am. Soc. Microbiology (emeritus), Japanese Soc. Bacteriology (hon.), Japanese Assn. for Infectious Diseases (hon.). Buddhist. Avocations: Kendo, swimming, fishing, reading novels. Home: 2-21-16 Kitashinjuku, Shinjuku-Ku, Tokyo 169-0074, Japan

NAKAYAMA, HIDEAKI, academic administrator; b. Kitakyushu, Fukuoka, Japan, Oct. 31, 1946; s. Sunao and Hisako (Yoshida) N.; m. Akiko Oka, Oct. 14, 1975; children: Kazumichi, Hiroshi. B in Engring., Ritsumeikan U., Kyoto, Japan, 1970, M in Engring., 1972, D in Engring., 1975. Cert. mech. engring. and material sci. Lectr. Osaka (Japan) Sangyo Univ., 1975-76, assoc. prof., 1976-84, prof., 1984—, dept. dir., 1990-93, mng. trustee, dir. exec. office head quarter Sch. Ju. Person, 1993—. Author: Introduction to Fracture Mechanics, 1979, Handbook of Fatigue Crack Propagation in Metallic Structures, 1994, Current Japanese Materials Research Vol. 14 Cyclic Fatigue in Ceramics, 1995; editor: Data Book of Fatigue Strength of Metallic Materials, 1982, Ceramics Strength Database, 1996, Database on Mechanial Properties of Powder Metallurgical Materials, 1997, Fatigue Strength Reliability Design Handbook for Metallic Materials, 1998. Mem. Japan Soc. Mech. Engring., Soc. Materials Sci. Japan, Japan Friction Welding Assn. (dir. 1988—). Avocations: golf, tennis, reading. Home: 1-12 Miyanoshita-cho, Hirakata Osaka 5730046, Japan Office: Osaka Sangyo Univ, 3-1-1 Nakagaito, Daito Osaka 5748530, Japan

NAKAYAMA, HIDEO, dermatologist, allergist; b. Nagoya, Aichi, Japan, Jan. 11, 1936; s. Jiro and Yoko (Asano) N.; m. Yoshiko Yoshiike, Nov. 7, 1963; children: Masako, Hiroshi. MD, Keio U., Tokyo, 1961. Dermatologist Keio U. Hosp., 1962-63, 64-68, Keiyu Hosp., Yokohama, Japan, 1963-64, Kawasaki (Japan) City Hosp., 1968-70; chief dermatologist Saiseikai Ctrl. Hosp., Tokyo, 1970-95; lectr. Sch. Medicine Keio U., 1973-95; chief physician Nakayama Dermatology Clinic, Tokyo, 1995—; chief Project E-88, Tokyo, 1970-77; adviser Project Dental Metal Eruption, Tokyo, 1988-94; mgr. Project E-360, U.S., Japan, Germany, Denmark, Switzerland and Sweden, 1991-95; chief Allergen Control Sys. Rsch. Group, Tokyo, 1970—. Mem. editl. bd. Am. Jour. Contact Dermatitis; patentee allergen control system for treatment of allergic contact dermatitis; non allergenic fragrant materials; instant patch test allergens to detect contact allergens. Recipient Nippikyo prize, 1988. Mem. Japan Fire Retardant Assn. (safety com. 1974—). Avocation: aviation history. Home: 6-1-4 Hatanodai Shinagawa, Tokyo 142-0064, Japan Office: Nakayama Dermatology Clinic, 3-3-5 Shinagawa-ku, Tokyo 141-0021, Japan

NAKAYAMA, MASAYUKI, electronics company executive, lecturer; b. Ishikawa, Japan, Jan. 30, 1939; s. Zuigaku and Tori (Mori) N.; m. Akiko Sugiura, Apr. 3, 1967; children: Ken-ichi, Shin-ichi, Jun-ichi. BE, Tohoku U., Sendai, Japan, 1962, M Elec. Comm. Engring., 1964; Doctor, Tokyo U., 1996. Mem. Sony Ctrl. Rsch. Lab., Tokyo, 1964-69, leader VTR devel. team, 1970-77, mgr. sys. devel. divsn., 1978-87, gen. mgr. magnetic head bus. divsn., Sendai, 1988-92, gen. mgr. R&D divsn., 1987-92, tech. cons. R&D divsn., 1993-98; lectr. Shohoku Coll., Tokyo Inst. Tech., 1996—; prof. Daichi U, Kagoshima, Japan, 1999—. Author: Information Storage and Printing Devices, 1995, The Nature of Technical Knowledge, 1996. Fellow IEEE (sr.); mem. IEICE, MSJ, Internat. Disk Drive Equipment and Material Assn. (bd. dirs. 1996—). Home: 4-37-5 Tamagawa, 158-0094 Setagaya-ku, Tokyo Japan Office: Dai-ichi U, 1-10-2 Chuuo Kokubu-shi, Kagoshima 899-4395, Japan

NAKAYAMA, MASHO, diplomat. Rep. UN, N.Y.C. Office: UN 820 2d Ave Ste 204 New York NY 10017

NAKAYAMA, OSAMU, education educator; b. Yokkaichi, Japan, Sept. 14, 1952; s. Yoshio and Sugako (Hayashi) N.; m. Junko Yamada Nakayama, Oct. 30, 1986; children: Satoshi, Yuri. BA, Reitaku U., Kashiwa, Japan, 1976; MA, Sophia Grad. Sch., Tokyo, 1978, student, 1981. Lectr. Reitaku U., Kashiwa, Japan, 1984-88, assoc. prof., 1988-95, prof., 1995—. Translator: The Dictionary of Animals in the Bible, 1992, The Dictionary of Symbols in Christian Arts, 1997, The Macmillan Good English Handbook, 1998; author: Provoking Milton-Paradise Lost and Contemporary Criticism, 1995, Reading the Structure of Feelings of " Life and Death" in Literature, 2000. Avocations: Shorinjikempo, oil painting. Home: Nakashinjiku 2-16-9, Kashiwa 277-0066, Japan Office: Reitaku U, Hikarigaoka 2-1-1, Kashiwa 277, Japan

NAKAYAMA, TAKEO, epidemiologist; b. Tokyo, Japan, July 19, 1961; s. Keizo and Mitsuko Nakayama; m. Erika; children: Kaho, Kentaro. MD, Tokyo Med. and Dental U., 1987, PhD, 1997. Resident Tokyo Kosei-Nenkin Hosp., 1987-89; asst. prof. Tokyo Med. and Dental U., 1998—; postdoctoral fellow UCLA, 1998-99; sect. head Nat. Cancer Rsch. Inst., Japan, 1999—; councillor Japan Epidemiological Assn., Japanese Soc. Hygiene, 1998—; review bd. Am. Pub. Health Assn., Washington, 1999—; cons. City of Shibata, Niigata, Japan, 1993-98. Mem. rev. bd. Japanese Jour. Pub. Health, 2000—; contbr. articles to profl. jours. Recipient Young Investigators award Japan Heart Found., Tokyo, 1993; grantee Ministry of Edn., Tokyo, 1995; fellow Japan Found. Aging and Health, Tokyo, 1998; Ministry of Health and Welfare grantee, 1999-2000. Fellow Internat. Coll. Angiology; mem. Internat. Epidemiologic Assn., Internat. Soc. Behavioral Medicine. Avocation: art appreciation, scuba diving. E-mail: takeo18@ibm.net. Home: 1-39-21-502 Hikari Cho, Kokubunji-shi Tokyo 185-0034, Japan Office: Nat Cancer Ctr Rsch Inst, 5-1-1 Tsukiji, Chuo-Ku Tokyo 104 0045, Japan

NAKAYAMA, TOMOHIRO, internist, molecular biologist; b. Mie, Japan, Apr. 22, 1963; s. Toshitaka and Toshiko (Nakano) N. MD, Nihon U., 1988, PhD, 1994. Internist Nihon U., Tokyo, 1988-90, rschr. in physiology, 1991, rschr. Med. Rsch. Inst., 1993-94. Mem. AAAS, Am. Diabetes Assn., Am. Heart Assn. (sci. coun. 2000—), N.Y. Acad. Sci., Japan Endocrine Soc. (councilor 1997—), Japan Pathophysiology Soc. (councilor 1998—), Japan Hypertension Soc. (councilor 2000—), Japan Circulation Soc., Japan Nephrology Soc., Japan Cardiovascular Endocrinology and Metabolism Soc. (councilor 1999—), Japan Soc. Gene Diagnosis and Therapy (coun. 2000—), Japan Soc. Internal Medicine, Japan Soc. Atherosclerosis, Japan Soc. Molecular Biology, Japan Soc. Physiology, Japan Soc. Geriatrics. Avocations: soft tennis, photography, astronomical observation. Office: Nihon U Sch Medicine, Ooyaguchi Kamiamchi 30-1, 173-8610 Itabashi Tokyo, Japan

NAKAZATO, HIROSHI, molecular biologist; b. Osaka, Japan, July 25, 1941; s. Goro and Yaye (Kijima) N.; m. Michiyo Matsuda; children: Mari,

Yuri. BS, Tokyo U., 1965, MS, 1967, PhD, 1970. Postdoctoral fellow U. Pitts., 1970-74, rsch. assoc., 1974-76; cancer expert NCI, Bethesda, Md., 1976-80; molecular biologist Suntory Inst. for Biomed. Rsch., Osaka, Japan, 1981—; gen. mgr. divsn. pharms. Suntory, Ltd., Tokyo, 1997-98; vis. scientist Butantan Inst., São Paulo, Brazil, 1999—. Contbr. articles to profl. jours. Recipient ISOBM Abbott award, 1999. Mem. AAAS, Japanese Cancer Assn., Conf. on Proteases and Inhibitors in Pathophysiology and Therapeutics, Japanese Soc. Immunology, Molecular Biology Soc. Japan, Japanese Biochem. Soc., Marine Biotech. Soc. Avocations: fishing, bonsai, gardening. Home: 0372-3 Yachimata-shi, Chiba 289-1115, Japan Office: Inst Butantan, Avenida Vital Brazil 1500, 05503-900 São Paulo SP, Brazil

NAKAZAWA, TAKAO, marketing professional; b. Tokyo, Nov. 12, 1964. LLB in Polit. Sci., Keio U., Tokyo, 1987. Officer gen. affairs divsn. Japan Regional Devel. Corp., Tokyo, 1987-90, officer estate adminstrn. divsn., 1990-91, officer planning & coord. divsn., 1991-92; chief credit adminstrn. divsn. Kyushu br. Japan Regional Devel. Corp., Fukuoka, Japan, 1992-95; chief sales promotion divsn. Japan Regional Devel. Corp., Tokyo, 1995-97, sr. adviser location promotion, 1997-99, mgr. dept. regional industries activation, 1999—; dep. mgr. internat. exch. Japan External Trade Orgn., Tokyo, 1995-96, expert promoting fgn. direct investment, London, 1996-97. Avocations: scuba-diving, writing. Home: 40-10 Gamo-Akane-cho, 343-0843 Koshigaya-shi Saitama, Japan Office: Japan Regional Devel Corp, 8-1 3-chome Kasumigaseki, 100-8906 Chiyoda-ku Japan

NAKHODKIN, MYKOLA GRIGOROVICH (MYKOLA NIKOLAY NAKHODKIN), physicist, educator, researcher; b. Prochorovka, Ukraine, Jan. 25, 1925; s. Grigoriy Pavlovich and Tatiana Yurievna (Michnovskaiy) N.; m. Valentina Zacharovna Turbovets, Nov. 7, 1950; 1 child, Taras Nikolaevich (dec. 1996). Grad., T. Shevchenko Nat. U., Kiev, 1950, Cand. Physics-Math., 1954, PhD in Physics and Math., 1969. Reader in physics T. Shevchenko Nat. U., 1951-69, prof., 1969—, chiar cryogenic and microelectronics, 1971, dean radiophys. dept., 1972-90; chmn. Nat. coun. Ukraine on Sci. and Tech., 1991-95; mem. Glavnogo Soviet Visshey Atestacionnoy Komisiy Ukraine, 1993; mem. Internat. Union of Radio Sci., Ukraine, pres., 1994-96. Author, editor: The Laser in Criminalist and Legal Examination, 1986, Atlas of Ionization Spectra, 1989, Ionization Spectroscopy, 1992, Vyshcha shkola, 1992; contbr. more than 300 articles to profl. jours. Decorated Order of Symbol of Honor (USSR); recipient State prize Govt. of Ukraine, 1970, 97, Charter of honor Verchovnogo Soveta of Ukraine, 1984. Mem. Nat. Acad. Sci. Ukraine (academician), Ukrainian Soc. Znaniye, Ukrainian Popov Soc. (mem. coun.), Ukrainian Phys. Soc., othres. Avocation: history of Kiev. Home: 24 Gorkogo St Ap 5, 252005 Kiev Ukraine Office: T Shevchenko Nat U, 64 Vladimirskaya St, 252601 Kiev 17, Ukraine

NAKRA, BAHADUR CHAND, mechanical engineering educator; b. Mianwali, Punjab, India, Mar. 31, 1939; s. Nota Ram and Lila Wati (Bajaj) N.; m. Sharda Vasudeva, May 12, 1943; children: Mohit, Tarun. BSc in Engring., Punjab U., India, 1959; M in Tech., Indian Inst. Tech., Kharagpur, India, 1961; PhD, Imperial Coll. Sci. & Tech., London, 1966. Cert. engring. Lectr. Indian Inst. Tech., Delhi, 1962-66, asst. prof., 1966-71, prof., 1971—, head mech. engring. dept., 1975-78, dean U.G. studies, 1982-83, head indsl. tribology, machine dynamics & maintenance engr., 1983-87, dep. dir. faculty, 1991-94, dir. officiating, 1994-95, chair prof., 1998—. Author: Instrumentation, Measurement and Analysis, 1985, Theory and Applications of Automatic Controls, 1998; contbr. articles to rsch. and profl. jours. House master Karakoram & Shivak Halls, Indian Inst. Tech., Delhi, 1975-78, chmn. Campus Consultative Com., 1994-95. Fellow Indian Nat. Sci. Acad., Indian Nat. Acad. Engring., Instn. Engrs. India, Acoustical Soc. India, Indian Nat. Sci. Acad. (treas.); mem. Internat. Union Theoretical and Applied Mechanics (congress com. 1995—). Avocations: reading fiction, games, yoga, theatre. Office: Indian Inst Tech, Mech Engring Haux Khas, New Delhi 110016, India

NALETOV, ALEXEJ YURIEVICH, chemical technology educator, researcher; b. Moscow, Russia, Apr. 29, 1948; s. Maya Vladimirovna (Tichonravova) N.; m. Bella Romanovna Mushailova, Apr. 12, 1985; children: Ksenia, Vladislav. MSc with honours, Bauman State Tech. U., Moscow, 1973; CandSci, Mendeleev U. Chem Tech., Moscow, 1983, Doctorate, 1994. Engr. Rsch. Inst. Chem. Engring., Moscow, 1973-76; jr. rschr. Mendeleev U. Chem. Tech., Moscow, 1976-83, sr. rschr., 1983-88, sr. lectr., 1988-94, prof., 1994—, dir. energy office, 1998—; leading mgr. projects Ministry Nature and Environ. Security, Moscow, 1992-95, Ministry Sci. and Engring., Moscow, 1995—; exec. dir. Technopark of Mendeleef U., 1996—. Author: Information and Thermodynamic Principle of Analysis of Power-Technological Processes, 1986, Principles of designing. Theory and computation of technological apparatus, 1993, also articles. Grantee State Com. on Sci. and Engring., 1990-91, Ministry Nature and Environ. Security, 1992-95, Ministry Sci. and Engring., 1995—. Avocations: fiction, world history, fishing and hunting. E-mail: ksushavlad@mtu-net.ru. Home: fl 131, Bld 36/1, Rublevskoe shosse, 121609 Moscow Russia Office: Mendeleev U Chem Tech, 9 Miusskaya Pl, 125190 Moscow Russia

NALLY, EDWARD, solicitor; b. Salford, Lancashire, Eng., Jan. 18, 1956; s. Edward and Sarah (Durkin) N.; m. Julie Fagan, July 23, 1977; children: Kieran, Carmel. Student, De La Salle Coll., Salford, 1963-74; LLB with honors, Nottingham U., 1977. Solicitor, ptnr. Fieldings, Solicitors, Bolton, Eng., 1980—; diocesan solicitor Salford (Eng.) Roman Cath. Diocese, 1983—; exec. mem. Bolton (Eng.) Family Health Svcs., 1985—; coun. mem. Law Soc., London, 1993. Chmn. govs. Pendleton Sixth Form Coll. Roman Catholic. Avocations: golf, football. Office: Fieldings Porter Silverwell House, Silverwell St, Bolton BL1 1PT, England

NALWA, VANIT, management consultant, educator, hypnotherapist, neuropsychologist; b. New Delhi, Mar. 31, 1957; d. Amarjit Singh and Gulabi (Bhandary) N. BA with honors, Indraprastha Coll., Delhi, India, 1977, MA, 1979; MPhil, U. Delhi, 1980, PhD, 1984. Sr. lectr. in psychology Kamala Nehru Coll. U. Delhi, New Delhi, 1983-93, counsellor, 1983-92; postdoctoral U. Oxford, Eng., 1986-87, NIH, Bethesda, Md., 1990-91; assoc. prof. Assumption Bus. Sch., Bangkok, 1993-96; dir. Empower, New Delhi, 1996—; cons. ABAC, Bangkok, 1992-95, Tata Energy Rsch. Inst., New Delhi, 1997—, Indo Mobil, New Delhi, 1997—, corp. Coop., New Delhi, 1999—. Author: The ABCs of Research, 1992; co-author: The ABCs of the Internet, 1994. Commonwealth scholar, Oxford, 1986-87; Fulbright scholar, Washington, 1990-91. Mem. APA (fgn. affiliate), Assn. Pharmacologists and Physiologists India, Indian Sci. Congress. Avocations: creating public awareness through writing, traveling, music. Home and Office: Empower, S-64 Panch Shila Park, New Delhi 110 017, India

NAM, CHARLES BENJAMIN, sociologist, demographer, educator; b. Lynbrook, N.Y., Mar. 25, 1926; s. Samuel and Yetta (Huff) N.; m. Marjorie Lee Tallant, Jan. 1, 1956; children: David Wallace, Rebecca Jane. BA, NYU, 1950; MA, U. N.C., 1957, PhD, 1959. Statistician U.S. Bur. Census, Washington, 1950-53; chief edn. and social stratification br. U.S. Bur. Census, 1957-64; statistician USAF, Montgomery, Ala., 1953-54; rsch. asst. U. N.C., Chapel Hill, 1954-57; prof. sociology Fla. State U., Tallahassee, 1964-96; chmn. dept. sociology Fla. State U., 1968-71; dir. Center for Study of Population, 1967-82; disting. rsch. prof. Fla. State U., Tallahassee, 1994-96, disting. rsch. prof. emeritus, 1996—; mem. population adv. com. U.S. Bur. Census, 1978-81; cons. population divsn. Orgn. for Econ. Coop. and Devel., 1968-70, UNESCO, 1978-83, Indonesian Ministry of Population and Environment, Jakarta, 1988-90; Social Sci. Rsch. Coun., 1981-88. Author: (with John K. Folger) Education of the American Population, 1967, Population and Society, 1968, (with Susan Gustavus) Population: The Dynamics of Demographic Change, 1976, Nationality Groups and Social Stratification, 1981, (with Susan Philliber) Population: A Basic Orientation, 1983, (with Mary Powers) The Socioeconomic Approach to Status Measurement, 1983, Our Population: The Face of America, 1988, Understanding Population Change, 1994, (with Richard Rogers and Robert Hummer) Living and Dying in the USA, 1999; editor: Demography, 1972-75; co-editor: (with David Sly, William Serow) International Handbook of Internal Migration, 1990, Handbook of International Migration, 1990; assoc. editor jour. Population Research and Policy Review, 1993-94. Mem. Am. Sociol. Assn. (chmn. sect. on population 1976-78), Population Assn. Am. (pres. 1979), Internat. Union for Sci. Study Population, Am. Statis. Assn. (chmn. social statistics sect. 1974), So. Sociol. Soc. (pres. 1981-82), So. Regional Demographic Group (vice chmn. 1974-75), Soc. Study Social Biology (bd. dirs. 1996—, exec. com. 1998-99). Home: 820 Live Oak Plantation Rd Tallahassee FL 32312-2413

NAM, HYOUNG GIN, electrical engineering educator; b. Seoul, Nov. 13, 1956; s. Kyo Mock and Soon Jae (Lee) N. BSEE, U. Tex., 1984, MSE, 1986, PhD, 1991. Sr. rschr. Electronic and Telecomms. Inst., Korea, 1992-95; asst. prof. Sun Moon U., Korea, 1995—. Contbr. articles to profl. jours. Sgt. Republic of Korea Army, 1977-80. Rsch. grant Ministry of Info. and Comm., 1996—, Electronic Telecomm. Inst., 1995-96, Next Co., 1997. Mem. Material Rsch. Soc., Korean Inst. of Telematics and Electronics. Home: Mido Apt 203-107, Daechi-dong Kangnam-ku, 135-282 Seoul Korea Office: Sun Moon Univ, Asan-si Choongnam, 336-840 Seoul Korea

NAM, MYEONG-JIN, philosophy educator; b. Taejon, South Korea, Nov. 5, 1943; s. Kyo-kwan and Sam-kyo (Kwon) N.; m. Song Suk; children: Soo-joong, Soo-jeong, Hyo-jeong, Soo-hyeon. BA, Chungnam Nat. U., Taejon, Korea, 1967, MA, 1971; PhD, Chinese Culture U., Taipei, Taiwan, 1985. From instr. to assoc. prof. philosophy Chungnam U., Taejon, 1981-90, prof., 1991—, chmn. dept. philosophy, 1999—, grad. sch. chmn. dept. philosophy, 1999—, vice dean Coll. Humanities, 1985-86, vice dir. Sae Maul Rsch. Inst., 1988-89, vice dir. Paekche Rsch. Inst., 1990-91; dir. Confucianism Rsch. Inst., 1997; exch. prof. Nat. Taiwan Normal U., 1988-89, Jilin U., Changchun, China, 1995-96. Co-author: I-Ching and Philosophy, 1993, New Research of Korean Philosophers, 1993, Biographical Confucianism History of Korea, 1996; editor Korean Nat. Spirit (Kyeoreol), 1997—, Studies in Confucianism, 1997—; contbr. articles to profl. jours. Mem. Korean Philos. Soc. (vice-chmn. 1995-96, chmn. 2000—), Korean Soc. for Philosophy East-West (vice-chmn. 1995-99, chmn. 2000—), Korea Soc. of the I-Ching (vice-chmn. 1990-97, chmn. 2000—), Korean Philos. Assn. (trustee 1999—), Internat. Confucian Assn. (trustee 1999—). Fax: 042-823-2881. E-mail: mjnam@hanbat.chungnam.ac.kr. Home: 33-16 Nae-dong Seo-gu, Daejon 302-181, Korea Office: Chungnam Nat U, 220 Kung-dong Yusong-gu, Daejon 305-764, Korea

NAMBA, KANJI, mathematics educator; b. Sojya, Okayama, Japan, Apr. 12, 1939; s. Shigeyo and Takeo (Maruyama) N.; m. Toshiko Hosoya, Mar. 20, 1967; children: Akira, Osamu. BS, Okayama U., 1962; MS, Tokyo U. Edn., 1964, DrSci, 1968. Asst. Tokyo U. Edn., 1964-66, lectr., 1967-69; assoc. prof. Nagoya (Japan) U., 1970-78; assoc. prof. Tokyo U., 1979-85, prof. math., 1986-2000, prof. emeritus, 2000. Author: Calculus, 1977, Linear Algebra, 1976, Axiomatic Set Theory, 1985. Mem. Japan Assn. Philos. Sci. (bd. dirs.), Math. Soc. Japan, Am. Math. Soc., assn. Symbolic Logic. Avocations: reading, travel. Home: 463-3 Kitamizote, Sojya, Okayama 719-1117, Japan Office: U Tokyo Grad Sch Math Scis, Komaba Meguro, Tokyo 153-8914, Japan

NAMBA, KEIICHI, biophysical research scientist; b. Amagasaki, Hyogo, Japan, Mar. 7, 1952; s. Tsuneo and Toshiko (Furutsuka) N.; m. Mieko Kashiwai, Feb. 22, 1992. B in Engring. Sci., Osaka U., 1974, M in Engring. Sci., 1976, PhD, 1980. Postdoctoral fellow Japan Soc. for the Promotion of Sci., Toyonaka, 1980-81; rsch. assoc. Brandeis U., Waltham, Mass., 1981-84, sr. rsch. assoc., 1986; rsch. assoc. Vanderbilt U., Nashville, 1984-85, rsch. instr., 1985-86; group leader ERATO Molecular Dynamic Assembly Project, Tsukuba, 1986-91; rsch. dir. Internat. Inst. for Advanced Rsch. Matsushita Electric Indsl. Co., Ltd., Seika, 1992-99, project dir. Protonic NanoMachine Project, ERATO, JST, 1997—; rsch. dir. Adavanced Tech. Rsch. Labs., Matsushita Electric Indls. Co., Ltd., Seika, 1999—. Mem. Biophys. Soc., Biophys. Soc. of Japan, Molecular Biology Soc. Japan. Office: Matsushita Elec Indsl Co, Advanced Tech Rsch Labs 3-4 Hikaridai, Seika Kyoto 619-0237, Japan

NAMBURI, ESWARA PRASAD, materials scientist, researcher; b. Eluru, India, Aug. 5, 1962; s. Vishnuvardhana Rao and Santa Mahalakshmi (Grandhi) N.; m. Swarna Latha Rayikanti, Mar. 6, 1988; 1 child Shanti Ravali. B Tech. in Metall. Engring., Banaras Hindu U., Varanasi, India, 1985, PhD in Metall. Engring., 1993. Scientist B Def. Metall. Rsch. Lab., Hyderabad, India, 1985-89, scientist C, 1989-94, scientist D, 1994—; external rsch. scholar Banaras Hindu U., Varanasi, 1988-93; presenter lectures, seminars and confs. in field. Contbr. articles to profl. jours. Rsch. fellow Alexander von Humboldt Found., Bonn. Mem. Materials Rsch. Soc. India (founder life), Indian Sci. Congress Assn. (life, Young Scientist award 1991), Indian Inst. Metals (assoc., Young Metallurgist's award 1994). Avocations: Indian mythology, sports, games. Office: Def Metall Rsch Lab, PO Kanchanbagh, Hyderabad 500058, India

NAMEDA, NAOYOSHI, engineering educator; b. Maebashi, Gumma, Japan, Feb. 11, 1936; s. Eichiro and Shinobu (Suzuki) N.; m. Kyoko Yamamoto, Mar. 15, 1960; 1 child. B in Engring., Gumma U., 1958; M in Engring., Waseda U., 1985, D in Engring., 1988. Rschr. Toshiba Corp., 1958-70, mgr., 1970; prof. Kagoshima U., 1990—; prof. Gastwissenschaftler der Univ., Münster, Germany, 1998. Author: (book) Vision and Image (Japanese), 1994; also articles to profl. jours. Recipient OHM Tech. award, Tokyo, 1966. Fellow Inst. Illuminating Engring.. Home: 1-51 Kinkodai, Kagoshima City 891-0145, Japan Office: 1-21-40 Korimoto, Kagoshima City 890-0084, Japan

NAMGUNG, IHN, engineer; b. Heong-Song, Kang-Won, Republic of Korea, Aug. 27, 1959; s. Kyun and Imwha (Jung) N.; m. Yonok Yoon K., May 4, 1988; children: Eugene, Yun. BS, Ajou U., Korea, 1981, MS, 1983; PhD, U. Fla., 1989. Cert. profl. engr., Conn. Sr. rschr. Korea Atomic Energy Rsch. Inst., Taejon, 1990-96; supervising rschr. Korea Power Engring., Taejon, 1997—. Contbr. profl. publs. 2d. lt. Korean Army, 1983-84. Avocation: golf. Office: Korea Power Engring, Yusong-ku Dukjin-dong 150, Taejon 305-353, Republic of Korea

NAMI, HUGO GABRIEL, archaeologist, researcher; b. Buenos Aires, Argentina, Mar. 23, 1957; s. Arturo and Irene (Bassi) N. Lic. in Anthrop. Philosophy and Lit., Buenos Aires U., Argentina, 1983; postgrad., Buenos Aires U., 1990—. Fellow Nat. Coun. Sci. Rsch., Buenos Aires, 1984-90, asst. rschr., 1990-93, adj. rschr., 1993—; adj. prof. social scis. Nat. U. of Jujuy, Argentina, 1993-94; rschr. dept. geol. scis. FCEFN, U. Buenos Aires, 1996—; vis. scholar Ctr. for Study of First Americans, Orono, Maine, 1988, various Canadian Instns.: Royal Ontario Mus., Canadian Mus. of Civilization, Univs. of Alberta and Edmonton, 1992; predoctoral fellow Wenner-Gren Found. for Anthropol. Rsch., 1989-92, rsch. fellow Smithsonian Instn., Washington, 1994-95; vis. rschr. Banco Ctrl. Mus., Quito, Ecuador, U. Magallanes, Chile, 1985-93, Canelones Mus., Uruguay, 1999; archaeologist coord. Climate and Human Change in Latin Am., NAS, 1999—. Contbr. articles to profl. jours., chpt. to book. Fulbright fellow 1988, Can. Embassy fellow Argentina, 1992; grantee Sigma Xi, 1988, 89, Japanese Ministry Justice and Culture, 1992, Nat. Geog. Soc., 1996-97, Am. Mus. Natural History, 1992, 98, CONICET, 1997, 98, 99; recipient Inter-Am. Inst. Support award NAS, 1999—. Mem. Argentine Soc. Anthropology, Plains Anthrop. Soc., Soc. Am. Archeology, Soc. Chilena Arqueologia, Sigma Xi. Avocation: Soo Bahk Do, Mu Duk Kwan. Home: Larrea 2033, 1752 Lomas del Mirador Bs Aires, Argentina Office: PREP-CONICET, B Mitre 1970 Piso 5 "A", 1039 Buenos Aires Argentina

NAMIESNIK, JACEK, chemistry educator, researcher; b. Mogilno, Poland, Dec. 10, 1949; s. Tadeusz and Jadwiga (Jóźwiak) N.; m. Krystyna Jucha, June 4, 1976; children: Katarzyna, Justyna. MSc, Tech. U., Gdansk, Poland, 1972, PhD, 1978, DSc, 1985. Asst. Chem. Faculty Tech. U., 1972-78, tutor, 1979-85, asst. prof., 1986-95, prof., 1996—, dean, 1996—; vis. prof. ENSCT, Toulouse, France, 1988, 92, 95, 97, Roskilde Univ. Ctr., Denmark, 1993. Co-author, editor: Handling Environmental Samples, 1995, Principles of Ecotoxicology, 1995, Physiochemical Methods of Control of Environmental Pollutants, 1998; co-author: Secondary Effects and Pollutants of the Environment, 1993, Pretreatment of Environmental Samples for Analysis, 2000. Mem. Polish Soc. Chemistry, Polish Acad. of Scis. (vice chmn. com. analytical chemistry 1996—), Romanian Soc. Analytical Chemistry, Assn. Chemistry. Avocation: French history. Home: 16 Posejdon Str, 80-299 Gdańsk Poland Office: Chemi Faculty Tech U, 11/12 G Narutowicz Str, 80-952 Gdańsk Poland

NAMIN, MONA LIZA CALADIAO, banker; b. Manila, July 4, 1964; adopted d. Maria Hipolito Caladiao (dec.) and Amelia Dayao Hipolito; m. Gregorio Gequiliana Namin, July 7, 1990; children: Gregg Kristian C. Namin, Gregg Nicklaus C. Namin. BSBA in Mgmt., PSBA, Quezon City, 1986. Cashierclerk trainee Shoe Mart, Inc., Makati City, Philippines, 1986-87; posting clk. Real Savs. & Loan Assn., Cainta, Rizal, Philippines, 1987-91, teller, 1991-92, br. cashier trainee, 1992-93, br. cashier, money custodian, 1994-95, officer-in-charge, 1995; br. mgr. AMA Bank, Marikina City, Philippines, 1996—. Mem. Marikina Central Lions Club (asst. treas., 1997, club sec., 1998, re-elected club sec., 1999), Marikina Bankers Assn. Office: Ventures Bank, 279 Shoe Ave Sto Nino, 1800 Marikina City Philippines

NÁNAI, LÁSZLÓ, physics educator, principal; b. Csopak, Veszprem, Hungary, Apr. 19, 1948; s. László Nánai and Gizella Hoffmann; m. Mária Takács, Oct. 6, 1973; children: László, Mária, Katalin. MSc, U. St. Petersburg, Russia, 1972; PhD, U. Szeged, Hungary, 1975; Candidate of Scis., Acad. Inst., Moscow, 1982. Asst. U. Szeged, 1972-84, assoc. prof., 1984—; prin. H.S., Békéscsaba, Hungary, 1993—. Contbr. articles to profl. jours. Recipient Vedres award Tech. State Com., Szeged, Hungary. Mem. European Physical Soc., Hungarian Physical Soc., Internat. Soc. Optical Engring. Lutheran. Avocations: theatre, swimming. Home: Hajós 18, H-6720 Szeged Hungary Office: Univ Szeged, Dom t 9, H-6720 Szeged Hungary

NÁNÁSI, PÁL, biochemist; b. Debrecen, Hungary, Sept. 17, 1923; s. Vilmos and Anna (Csapo) N.; m. Éva Nemes, Sept. 10, 1949 (dec. Oct. 1976); 1 child, Peter; m. Hajnalka Derzsy, Dec. 15, 1984. M, L. Kossuth U., Debrecen, 1945, PhD, 1956; DSc, Acad. Scis., Budapest, 1966. Vol. Inst. Chemistry Med. Sch., Debrecen, 1943-47; asst. prof. Inst. Organic Chemistry, Debrecen U., 1948-51, 1st asst., 1952-57, assoc. prof., 1958-66; prof. Inst. Biochemistry L. Kossuth U., Debrecen, 1967-94, prof. emeritus, 1995—, head, 1970-88; dean faculty sci. Lajos Kossuth U., Debrecen, 1980-83; mem. com. organic chemistry Hungarian Acad. Sci., Budapest, 1960—, mem. com. biopolymer chemistry, 1975-85, pres. com. of chemistry local group, 1980-92. Author: Novel Results in Chemistry, 1975; contbr. articles to profl. jours.; patentee in field. Mem. World Fedn. Hungarians. Recipient prize Ministry of Edn., Budapest, 1975, Gold prize of work State, Budapest, 1981, Bocskai prize medal County Debrecen, 1993. Avocations: history of arts, tourism. Office: Inst Biochemistry, Egyetem tér 1, 4010 Debrecen Hungary

NÁNÁSI, PÉTER PÁL, physiologist; b. Debrecen, Hungary, Aug. 20, 1956; s. Pál and Éva (Nemes) N.; m. Asztalos Borbála, June 15, 1985; 1 child, Péter Pál Jr. MD, U. Med. Sch. of Debrecen, 1980; PhD, Hungarian Acad. of Sci., 1992, DSc, 1999. Scientific officer Dept. Physiology, U. Med. Sch. of Debrecen, 1980-85, asst. lectr., 1986-91, asst. prof., 1992-94, assoc. prof., 1994—. Contbr. articles to profl. jours. Mem. Hungarian Physiol. Soc., N.Y. Acad. Scis., Hungarian Med. Assn., Hungarian Soc. Cardiology, Hungarian Biophys. Soc. Avocations: fishing, science fiction, bridge. Home: Bolyai St 38, 4032 Debrecen Hungary Office: U Med Sch Debrecen Dept Physiology, Nagyerdei krt 98 POB 22, 4012 Debrecen Hungary

NANCE, JOHN JOSEPH, lawyer, writer, air safety analyst, broadcaster, consultant; b. Dallas, July 5, 1946; s. Joseph Turner and Margrette (Grubbs) N.; m. Benita Ann Priest, July 26, 1968; children: Dawn Michelle, Bridgitte Cathleen, Christopher Sean. BA, So. Meth. U., 1968, JD, 1969; grad., USAF Undergrad. Pilot Tng., Williams AFB, Ariz., 1971. Bar: Tex. 1970, U.S. Ct. Appeals (fed. cir.), 1994. News reporter, broadcaster, newsman various papers and stas. Honolulu and Dallas, 1957-66; radio news anchorman Sta. WFAA-AM, Dallas, 1966-70; newsman including on camera Sta. WFAA-TV, Dallas; pvt. practice law Dallas, 1970—; news dir. Newscom Network, Dallas, 1970; airline pilot Braniff Internat. Airways, Dallas, 1975-82, Alaska Airlines, Inc., Seattle, 1985—; chmn., pres. Exec. Transport, Inc., Tacoma, 1979-85; chmn., chief exec. officer EMEX Corp., Kent, Wash., 1987—; mng. ptnr. Phoenix Ptnrs., Ltd., Tacoma, Wash., 1995—; project devel. assoc. Columbia Tristar TV, 1997—; with Nance & Carmichael, PLLC, Austin, Tex., 1997—; profl. speaker Human Mgmt., 1984—, Teamwork and Comms. in the Med. Profession; airline safety, advocate Ind. Cons., earthquake preparedness spokesman Ind. Cons.; dir. steering com. Found. for Issues Resolution in Sci. Tech., Seattle, 1987-89; speaker Northwestern Transp. Ctr. Deregulation and Safety Conf., 1987; cons. NOVA Why Planes Crash, PBS, 1987, ABC World News Tonight Crash of US AIR 427, 1994; aviation analyst ABC-TV and radio, 1995—; aviation editor: ABC Good Morning Am., 1995—; broadcast analyst, 1986—; spkr. in field. Author: Splash of Colors, 1984, Blind Trust, 1986 (Wash. Gov.'s award 1987), On Shaky Ground, 1988, Final Approach, 1990, What Goes Up, 1991, Scorpion Strike, 1982, Operating Handbook USAF Air Carrier Safety and Inspection Office, 1991, Phoenix Rising, 1994, Pandora's Clock, 1995, Medusa's Child, 1997, The Last Hostage, 1998, Blackout, 2000; contbr. to Transportation Deregulation in the U.S., 1988; appeared in Sheep on the Runway Tacoma Little Theater, 1975; tech. advisor, actor Pandora's Clock NBC mini-series, 1996; appeared in Medusa's Child, ABC Mini-series, 1997; prodr., writer, dir. USAF Video Prodns.: ANG Introduction to CRM, 1992, USAF SOC CRM Program, 1992, Test and Evaluation CRM, 1993, The Teamwork Connection, 1996. Prs. Fox Glen Homeowners Assn., Tacoma, 1974-77; cons. Congl. Office Tech. Assessment, Tacoma, 1987; witness numerous air safety hearings U.S. Congress, Washington, 1986-88; bd. dirs. St. Charles Borromeo Sch., Tacoma, 1975-78, Nat. Patient Safety Found. of AMA, 1997—; mem. Mayor's Vets. Task Force, Tacoma, 1991; bd. advisors Jour. Air Law and Commerce So. Meth. Sch. Law, 1995—, exec. bd. Sch. of Law, 1998—; bd. advisors Pacific Northwest Writer's Conf., 1994—; mem. adv. bd. supply and logistics mgmt. program Portland State U., 1997-98. Capt. USAFR, 1975-94; lt. col. Persian Gulf. Decorated Merit Svc. medal; named Airline Safety Man of Year Wash. State Div. of Aeronautics, 1987. Fellow Chartered Inst. Transport (Canberra, Australia); mem. ABA, SAG, Tex. Bar Assn., Author's Guild Am., Res. Officers Assn. (life), Aircraft Owners' and Pilots' Assn., Phi Alpha Delta, Delta Chi. Home and Office: John Nance Prodns 4512 87th Ave W Tacoma WA 98466-1920 Office: Phoenix Ptnrs Ltd PO Box 24465 Federal Way WA 98093-1465

NANCE, RETHA HARDISON, reading specialist; b. Athens, Ala., July 18, 1952; d. Roy King and Bertie Mae (Pettus) McLemore; m. Amos Wayne Hardison, July 23, 1971 (dec. Mar. 1983); children: Genoa, Karol, Nancy; m. Robert Arthur Nance, May 30, 1984. BS in Edn., U. Ctrl. Okla., 1987, MEd summa cum laude, 1988; postgrad., U. Va., Charlottesville, 1994. Cert. tchr. reading, Okla. Reading specialist Moore (Okla.) Pub. Schs., 1987—; officer Moore Sch. dist. Profl. Devel. Com., 1990-98, chair, 1997, 98; mem. Moore Pub. Schs. Supts. Adv. Com., 1996-99; participant Ann. Monticello-Stratford Hall Summer Seminar for Tchrs., U. Va., Charlottesville, 1994, Colonial Williamsburg Summer Tchg. Inst., 1995. Co-founder We the People Living Memls., Oklahoma City, 1987—; tchr. Great Expectations, 1998—; mem. Okla. City Fire Dept. Citizens' Academy, 1999, Okla. City Police Dept. Citizen Acad., 2000, Multi-Cultural Commn., 1999—, SAFE Sch. Commn., 1999—. Recipient Liberty award Downtown Oklahoma City, 1990. Mem. Internat. Reading Assn., Assn. Profl. Okla. Educators (state treas. 2000—), Okla. Reading Assn., Ctrl. Okla. Reading Coun. (pres. 1992). Avocations: reading, cross stitching, traveling, sewing. Home: PO Box 405 Wheatland OK 73097-0405

NANCE, RICHARD EARLE, computer science educator; b. Raleigh, N.C., July 22, 1940; s. Walter Ethridge and Shirley Elizabeth (Doyle) N.; m. Ann Henderson Middleton, June 9, 1962 (div. Apr. 1992); children: Richard Fleming, Adriann Arrington. BS Indsl. Engring., N.C. State U., 1962, MS Indsl. Engring., 1966; PhD Indsl. Engring., Purdue U., 1968. Mgmt. staff Procter & Gamble Co., Cin., 1962-64; grad. asst. N.C. State U., Raleigh, 1964-66; grad. rsch. instr. Purdue U., West Lafayette, Ind., 1966-68; asst. prof. computer sci. So. Meth. U., Dallas, 1968-72, assoc. prof. of computer sci., 1972-73; assoc. prof. and head, computer sci. Va. Polytechnic Inst. and State U., Blacksburg, Va., 1973-77; prof. computer scis. Va. Polytechnic Inst. and State U., Blacksburg, 1977-83, prof. computer sci., dir. Systems Rsch. Ctr., 1984—, John A. Dahlgren Prof. computer sci., 1989—; vis. rsch. fellow Imperial Coll., London, 1980; computer scientist Naval Surface Warfare Ctr., Dahlgren, 1979-80; U.S. rep. to Internat. Fedn. for Info. Processing. Contbg. author: Studies in Applied Probability, 1994, History of Programming Languages II, 1995; contbr. articles to profl. jours. Recipient Disting. Svc. award Coll. on Simulation/Inst. Mgmt. Scis., 1987, Outstanding Svc.

award Naval Surface Warfare Ctr., 1980. Fellow Assn. for Computing Machinery (chmn. SIGIR 1970-71, chmn. SIGSIM 1983-85, founding editor-in-chief TOMACS 1990-95, Outstanding Svc. award 1995); mem. Inst. Indsl. Engrs., Inst. for Ops. Rsch. and Mgmt. Sci., Sigma Xi. Avocation: restoration of antique automobiles. E-mail: nance@vt.edu. Office: Va Tech Systems Rsch Ctr (0251) Blacksburg VA 24061

NANDAN, SATYA NAND, ecological organization executive; b. Suva, Fiji, July 10, 1936; s. Shiu and Rajkuar Nandan; m. Sreekumari Nandan, 1966 (dec. 1971); m. Zarine Merchant, 1976; 1 child. Student, Dayanand Anglo-Vedic Coll., Suva, John McGlashan Coll., Dunedin, New Zealand; degree, U. London; LLD (hon.), U. Newfoundland, 1995; D (hon.), U. South Pacific, 1996. Bar: Lincoln's Inn, London, 1965; barrister and solicitor Supreme Ct. of Fiji, 1966—. Pvt. practice Suva, 1965-70; from counsellor to am. Permanent Mission of Fiji to UN, 1970-76; mem. UN Gen. Assembly, 1970-76, 92-96, Permanent Mission of Fiji to UN, 1993—; amb. EEC, 1976-80; perm sec. for fgn. affairs Govt. Fiji, 1981-83; under-sec.-gen. for ocean affairs and law of the sea UN, 1983-92, spl. rep. of sec.-gen. for law of the sea, 1983-92; sec.-gen. Internat. Seabed Authority; leader Fiji del. to 3d UN Conf. on Law of Sea, 1973-82; chair Conf. on Straddling Fish Stocks and Highly Migratory Fish Stocks UN, 1993-95; rep. of Fiji to Internat. Seabed Authority, 1994-95; internat. law advisor to Govt. of Fiji, 1994-95; del. numerous internat. confs.; vis. lectr. NYU, U. Va.; sr. vis. fellow U.S. Inst. Peace, 1992. Editor Commentary on 1982 UN Conv. on Law of Sea, 7 vols.; contbr. articles to profl. jours. Decorated Commander of the Order of the British Empire, 1978, Grand Cross of Order of Merit Fed. Rep. of Germany, 1996, Companion of Order of Fiji, 1999. Avocations: reading, swimming, watching sports. Home: 301 E 48th St New York NY 10017-1748 also: Internat Seabed Auth, 14-20 Port Royal St, Kingston Jamaica

NANDI, ARUN KUMAR, chemist, physicist, educator; b. Bankura, India, Feb. 21, 1955; s. Anath Bandhu and Asha Lata (Patra) N.; m. Bithika Atta, Feb. 18, 1987; children: Amrit, Debosmita. BSc with honors, Bankura (India) Christian Coll, 1975; MSc, U. Burdwan, India, 1977; PhD, Indian Assn. Cultivation Sci., Calcutta, 1986. Lectr. Sripat Singh Coll., Murshidabad, India, 1984-86, North Bengal U., Darjeeling, India, 1986-92; vis. scientist Fla. State U., Tallahassee, 1988-89; sr. lectr. Indian Assn. Cultivation Sci., 1992-96, reader, 1997—. Patentee in field. Nat. scholar Govt. West Bengal, 1976-77. Mem. Soc. Polymer Sci. (India chpt.), Indian Assn. for Cultivation of Sci. Hindu. Avocation: reading. Office: Indian Assn Cultivation Sci, 2A&B Raja SC Mullick Rd, Calcutta 700032, India

NANDI, OWI IVAR, botanist, quality control professional; b. Wettingen, Aargau, Switzerland, Aug. 31, 1966; s. Nandadulal and Christine (Rieder) N.; m. Annette Ines Koch, Sept. 30, 1995. Diploma, U. Zurich, Switzerland, 1992, PhD, 1999. Head of quality control Sinecura Analysen Aarau, Switzerland, 1995—; postdoctoral in phytochemistry U. Zurich, Switzerland, 1998—. Author: Seesommer, 1999; contbr. articles to profl. jours. Recipient Lyric award Nat. Acad. of German Lyrics, 1998. Office: Inst Systematic Botany, Zollikerstrasse 107, 8008 Zurich Switzerland

NANDI, TAPASVI SHAMBHUCHANDRA, language educator; b. Kaira, Gujarat, India, Sept. 22, 1933; s. Shambhuchandra Ramchandra and Madhumati (Shambhuchandra) N.; m. Harsha A. Gharekhan, Dec. 8, 1956; 1 child, Chinmayee M. Rali. MA, Gujarat U., Ahmedabad, 1955, PhD, 1967. Lectr., prof. H.K. Arts Coll., Ahmedabad, 1955-64, lectr. dept. Sanskrit Sch. Langs., 1964-80, reader dept. Sanskrit Sch. Langs., 1980-88, prof., head dept. Sanskrit Sch. Langs., 1988-93; prof. emeritus Univ. Grants Commn., New Delhi, India, 1995. Author: Principles of Literary Criticism in Sanskrit, 1974, Sanskrit Drama, 1974, 15 others; contbr. 100 articles to profl. jours. Recipient Pres.'s Cert. of Merit Pres. of India, 1990, Sâhitya-Chudamani Rashtriya Sanskrit Samsthan, 1994. Avocations: chess, viewing cricket. Home: 4 Professors' Colony, Navrangpura, 380009 Ahmedabad Gujarat, India

NANDIBEWOOR, SHARANAPPA THOTAPPA, chemist educator, researcher; b. Hirehadagali, Karnataka, India, July 1, 1953; s. Thotappa Sangappa and Sundravva Thotappa (Simpiger) N.; m. Aruna Sharanappa Javali, May 9, 1980; children: Archana, Amaresh. BSc, S.A. Coll. Naregal, India, 1972; MSc, Karnatak U., Dharwad, India, 1974, PhD, 1979. Lectr. Karnatak U., Dharwad, 1978-87, reader, 1987-95, prof., 1995—; pres. Shreenagar Assn., Dharwad, 1983-93; sec. Indian Coun. of Chemists, Agra, 1996—; reviewer of PhD and M.Phil theses at various univs.; reviewer Jour. Indian Chem. Soc., Asian Jour. Chem.; vis. prof. Lajos Kossuth U., Debrecen, Hungary, 1998, Ctrl. Rsch. Inst. for Chemistry, Budapest, Hungary, 1998, Josef Attila U., Szeged, Hungary, 1998; vis. Cambridge U., Eng., 1999. Inventor in field of reaction kinetics and catalysis; contbr. articles to profl. jours. CSIR fellow in rsch., New Delhi, 1974-78. Fellow Indian Chem. Soc. (life), Indian Coun. Chemists (life), Assn. Kineticists of India (life); mem. Tchrs. Assn. Dharwad (exec. mem. 1997). Avocations: reading, yoga, playing games, debating, social work. Office: Dept Chemistry, Karnatak Univ, 580 003 Dharwad India

NANDURY, SATYANARAYANA VENKATA, researcher; b. Guntur, Andhra Pradesh, India, Oct. 24, 1961; s. Murali Krishna and Meenakshi (Bhavaraju) Nandury; m. Sunita Jonnalagadda, Nov. 19, 1993; 1 child, Vishnu. BSc, Osmania U., Hyderabad, India, 1982; MSc in Tech., Sri Venkateswara U., Tirupati, India, 1986; MBA, Xaviour's Labour Rels. Inst., Jamshedpur, India, 1994. Lectr. Sri Sant Gajanan Maharaj Coll. Engring., Shegaon, India, 1986-89; scientist B Nat. Metall. Lab., Jamshedpur, India, 1989-92, scientist C, 1992-97; scientist E1 Nat. Metall. Lab., Jamshedpur, 1997—; mem. 17th Indian Nat. Sci. Expdn. to Antartica, 1997-98. Contbr. articles to profl. jours.; author, editor procs. Mem. Inst. Electronic & Telecom. Engrs., Computer Soc. India, Instrument Soc. India. Avocations: trekking, biking, sports. E-mail: nvs@csnml.men.nic.in. Office: Nat Metall Lab, Burma Mines Area, Jamshedpur Bihar 831 007, India

NANGJU, DIMYATI, agronomist, banker; b. Pagaralam, Sumatra, Indonesia, Mar. 14, 1941; s. Haji Asyik and Nyemas (Mascik) N.; m. Nora Alagao, Dec. 5, 1970; children: Daleel, Norma. B in Rural Sci., U. New Eng., Armidale, Australia, 1967; MS, U. Philippines, Los Banos, 1969; PhD, U. Hawaii, 1972. Tchr. English Lang. Inst., Palembang, Indonesia, 1960-62; lectr. U. Sriwijaya, Palambang, Indonesia, 1960-69; rsch. asst. U. Hawaii, Honolulu, 1970-72; head of agronomy divsn. Internat. Inst. Tropical Agr., Ibadan, Nigeria, 1972-78; lead agronomist Asian Devel. Bank, Manila, 1978—. Author: Rice Production and Integrated Pest Management, 1969; contbr. articles to profl. jours. including Weed Sci. Jour., Agronomy Jour., Jour. Agrl. Scis., among others. Recipient scholarship Am. Field Svc., 1959, Colombo Plan, 1962-67, Rockefeller Found., 1967-69. Mem. World Assn. of Soil and Water Conservation (v.p. 1988—), Agronomy Soc. Am., Indonesian Moslem Intellectual's Assn. (pres. 1993—), Gamma Sigma Delta. Avocations: badminton, bridge, ping pong. Office: Asian Devel Bank, 6 Asian Devel Bank Ave, Mandaluyong 0980, The Philippines

NAN-YA, SHOJIRO, rail transportation executive; b. Aichi, Japan, July 2, 1941. B of Econs., U. Tokyo, 1964. With Japanese Nat. Rys., 1964-87, chief labor rels. divsn., 1985-87; dir. West Japan Ry. Co. (JR-WEST), 1987—; pres. Japan Ry. Co. (JR-WEST), 1997—. Fax: 81-6-63758919. Office: West Japan Rlwy Co, 2-4-24 Shibata Kita-ku, Osaka 530-8341, Japan

NAOR, DANIEL, management consultant; b. Paris, July 1, 1960; s. Shlomo and Sarah (Puderbeutel) N.; m. Michal Ben Moshe (Jan. 1, 1997); 1 child, Nathalie. BS in Elec. Engring., MIT, 1981, MS in Elec. Engring. and Computer Sci., 1981; MBA, INSEAD, 1990. Cert. engr. Project mgr. ELOP, Rehovot, Israel, 1985-87, mktg. mgr., 1988-89; assoc. McKinsey & Co., Paris, 1990-95, prin., 1995-98; prin. McKinsey & Co., Dallas, 1998—. Contbr. articles to profl. jours. Active Dallas Theater Ctr. Bd., 1999—, Variety, 1997—. Capt. Israeli Air Force, 1981-85. Mem. IEEE, Tau Beta Pi, Sigma Xi (assoc.). Jewish. Avocations: ballroom dancing, cinema, theater, philately. Office: McKinsey & Co 2200 Ross Ave Ste 5200 Dallas TX 75201-2793

NAOR, GIDEON, retired executive, developer; b. Varnsdorf, Sudeten, Czechoslovakia, Apr. 9, 1929; arrived in Israel, 1939; s. Ernst and Lilly (Scheuer) Nassau; m. Devorah Romano, Feb. 28, 1950; children: Ofer, Tamar. MA, Claremont Grad. Sch., 1967; PhD, Syracuse U., 1969. Mgr. dairy farm, gen. sec. Kibbutz Gevim, Israel, 1947-58; chmn. rural coun., Shaar Hanegev, Israel, 1955-57; first mayor Town of Kiriat-Gat, Israel, 1958-65; dep. dir. gen. Israeli Ministry Labor, Jerusalem, 1971-73; dir. gen. Israel Export Inst., Tel Aviv, 1974-76; dir. gen. mktg. mgr., mgr. various cos., Israel and U.S., 1976-88; sec. gen. subsidiary company of Ctr. for Internat. Cooperation Ministry Fgn. Affairs, Jerusalem, 1988-98; tchg. fellow U. Tel Aviv, U. Haifa; v.p. Galillee Coll., Tivon; dir. Union Local Authorities, Israel, 1960-65; chmn. bd. Hameshakem, Israel, 1971-73, Inst. for Labor Safety, Israel, 1971-73, Circom. Tel Aviv, 1971-73. Mem. Ctr. of Labor Party, Tel Aviv, 1960-71; sec. gen. OISCA, Israel, 1989-97. Sgt. comdr. Israel Def. Forces, 1947-49. Named hon. citizen City of Jacksonville, Fla., 1961, City of Detroit, 1961, City of Enschede, The Netherlands, 1961, City of Claremont, Calif., 1966. Fellow Israel Mgmt. Ctr.; mem. Soc. for Internat. Devel. (sec.-treas. Israel br. 1990-94, governing coun. Rome 1994—). Mem. Israel Labor Party. Avocations: swimming, classical music, computers. Home: 46 Ben-Gurion St, 47321 Ramat Hasharon Israel

NAOR, MORDECAI, author, historian; b. Tel Aviv, Israel, Aug. 19, 1934; s. Meshulam and Tova Levinhertz; m. Lea Mishkowski, Oct. 25, 1955; children: Neta, Amir, Yael. BA, Hebrew U., Jerusalem, Israel, 1963, MA, 1970; PhD, Tel Aviv U., Israel, 1984. Editor Min. of Defense, Israel, 1961-71; dir. gen. Galei Zahal Radio Sta., Israel, 1974-78; editor-in-chief Min. of Defense Pub. House, Israel, 1978-81; editor Qesher, Tel Aviv U., 1987—. Author 40 books including Tales From My Beloved Country, 1979, The Western Wall, 1981, English edit. 1983, German edit. 1989, Please Meet Israel, 1983, Emergence of a Leader-Pinhas Sapir, 1987, Laskov, 1988, The Good Old Days of Eretz Israel, 1989, Eretz Israel in the 20th Century, 1990, The Aliya Book, 1991, The Twentieth Century in Eretz Israel-A Pictorial History, 1996, English edit., 1998, German edit., 1998, Jerusalem, City of Hope, 1996. Home: 51 Azmaut St, Herzliyya 46381, Israel

NAPAU, IOAN, mechanical engineer, mathematician, researcher; b. Baia de Aries, Alba, Romania, Dec. 11, 1959; s. Ioan and Ileana (Cuc) N.; m. Maria Negoita, Aug. 16, 1986; children: Anca, Maria. Engr. degree, Tech. U., Cluj-Napoca, Romania, 1984, D in Engrng., 1999; math. degree, Babes-Boyai U., Cluj-Napoca, Romania, 1994. Engr. Mech. Enterprise, Oradea, Romania, 1984-86; design engr. Mech. Enterprise, Ougir, Romania, 1986-94, chief tech. dept., 1994-99, technol. chief engr., 1999—; assoc. prof. Tech. U., 1989-99. Contbr. over 30 articles to profl. publs.; patentee in field. Grant scholarship Tech. U., 1999. Fellow Gen. Assn. of Romanian Engrs. Avocations: mathematics, football. Home: 4/38 Stefan cel Mare St, 2566 Cugir Alba, Romania Office: Uzina Mecanica Cugir, 1 21 December 1989 Str, 2566 Cugir Alba, Romania

NAPIER, PETER CHARLES, manufacturing company consultant; b. Bryn Mawr, Pa., July 5, 1936; s. Charles Campbell and Violet Burnie Napier; m. Elena Nikolaeva, Oct. 5, 1996; children: Arianne, Tanya, Anna, Lydia. BA, BS, Swarthmore Coll., 1958; MS, Technische Hochschule, Munich, Germany, 1959. Dir. ops. The Gillette Co., London, 1968-81, Schering-Plough Inc., London, 1981-87; pres. Advent Mfg. Internat., 1987-90; v.p. internat. ops. Tambrands Inc., White Plains, N.Y., 1990-96; dir. internat. ops. Am. Saw, East Longmeadow, Mass., 1997—; part-time lectr. Ashridge Coll., Berkhamstead, Eng., 1985-87. Mem. Hurlingham Club. Avocations: skiing, motorcycling, traveling. Home: 42 Pinckney St Boston MA 02114-4800

NAPIER AND ETTRICK, LORD (KNIGHT COMDR.), member Royal household; b. Dec. 5, 1930; m. Delia Mary Pearson, 1958; 4 children. Student, Eton; RMA, Sandhurst; LittD (hon.), Napier U., Edinburgh, Scotland, 1992. Mem. Queens Bodyguard for Scotland, Royal Co. of Archers, 1953—; M.P. Ho. of Lords, Eng., 1954-99, conservative whip, 1970-71; equerry Prince Henry, Duke of Gloucester, 1958-60; dep. ceremonial, protocol sec. Commonwealth Rels. Office, 1962-66; pvt. sec. comptr. Princess Margaret of Eng., Countess of Snowdon, 1973-98; treas., 1973-98; liveryman Grocers Co.; freeman City of London; knight commdr. Royal Victorian Order. Mem. exec. com. Standing Coun. of the Baronetage, 1985-2000; past pres. London (Prin ce of Wales's) Dist. of St. John Ambulance Brigade, 1975-83; mem. standing coun. Scottish Chiefs. Knight of Justice of Order of St. John, 1991; Purple Staff Officer at State Funeral of Sir Winston Churchill. Mem. Pratt's Club, Turf Club, Royal Caldeonian Hunt Club, Pitt Club. Office: Nottingham Cottage, Down House, Wylye, Wiltshire BA12 OQN, England

NAPOLITANO, GIORGIO, Italian government official; b. Naples, Italy, June 29, 1925. LLD, U. Naples, Italy, 1946. Former sec. Communist Fedns. of Naples and Caserta; dep. Naples-Caserta Partito Comunista Italiano, 1953—, mem. Com. from 8th Congress, pres. parliamentary group, 1981-86, mem. Leadership from 10th Congress, head cultural com. Ctrl. Com.; M.P. European Parliament, 1989-92; mem. Partito Democratico della Sinistra, 1990—; pres. Chamber of Deps., 1992-94; mem. European Parliament, Brussels, Belgium; mem. com. fgn. and cmty. affairs; chmn. spl. com. for re-organizing Radio-TV sector, 1994—. Office: Camera dei Deputati, Piazza Montecitorio, I-00186 Rome Italy*

NAPP, GUDRUN F., artist; b. Kiel, Germany, Aug. 14, 1929; came to the U.S., 1986; d. Walter Alexander and Erika Elisabeth (Burchard) Rode; m. Edmund Carl Napp, Dec. 29, 1951; children: Helenita F., Johann Christian, Anneke J., Florian D. Student, Art Sch., Kiel, 1949, Escuela Artes Plastias, Caracas, Venezuela, 1950, Toronto (Can.) Coll. Art, 1950-51. assoc. dir. One Ear Soc., 1999. Exhibited in group shows at Miami Beach Conv. Ctr., 1997, Art Expo L.A., 1997, 98, Art Expo N.Y., 1998, Art Expo Fla., 2000; one-woman shows include Art Am., 1997. Recipient cert. of excellence Art Horizon, N.Y.C., 1988, hon. mention Royal Poinciana Fiesta, Miami, 1993, The Fla. Mus. of Hispanic and L.Am. Art, Miami, 1994, Miami Watercolor Soc. exhibit, 1999, One Ear Soc. exhibit. Mem. Nat. Collage Soc., Fla. Watercolor Soc., Internat. Soc. Exptl. Artists (signature mem.), Miami Watercolor Soc. (pres. 1995, 96, trustee 1997, publicity chair 1998-99, 3rd place 1990), Art Expo Fla. Lutheran. Avocations: exercising, painting. Home: 155 Ocean Lane Dr Apt 1100 Key Biscayne FL 33149-1468 Studio: Studio Gallery Napp Inc 260 Crandon Blvd Ste 18 Key Biscayne FL 33149-1537

NAPPI, GIUSEPPE, neurology educator; b. Naples, Italy, Oct. 23, 1939; m. Emilia Sangermano; 2 children. Degree in medicine and surgery, U. Pavia, 1969. Founder Ctr. Study Headache and Cerebral Circulation U. Pavia (Italy), 1970-80, asst. prof. dept. neurology, 1981-85, asoc. prof., rschr. extrapyramidal diseases, 1985—, prof. neurology, chair neurology dept., 1986—; dir. 3d neurology divsn. Casimiro Mondino Inst., U. Pavia, 1989—, scientific dir., 1987—. Co-editor over 25 volumes including Chronobiological Correlates of Headache, 1983, Headache-Diagnostic System and Taxonomic Criteria, 1985, Migraine Versus Transient Cerebral Ischemia, 1985, Stress and Aging Brain, 1990, Stress and Related Disorders, 1991, Textbook of Headache, 1995; contbr. over 1000 articles to profl. jours. Mem. Italian Soc. Cardioneurology (past pres.), Italian Soc. Neurovegetative Rsch. (pres.), Italian Soc. Neurology (pres.), Neuropharmacology (pres.), Chronobiology and the Study of Headache (pres.), World Fedn. Neurology, Royal Soc. Medicine, Acad. Sci. San Marino, Italian League for Fight Against Parkinson's Disease, European Headache Fedn. (founder, pres. 1994-96), Assn. Scientific Insts. Neurosci. (pres.), Collegium Italian IRCCS Scientific Dirs. (pres. 1995—). Office: C Mondino Found, Via Palestro 3, I-27100 Pavia Italy

NAPUK, KERRY F., management executive; b. Great Falls, Mont., Oct. 5, 1939; s. David and Bernice (Manheim) N.; m. Angela Mary Bryant, July 31, 1970; children: Sarah, David. BS, U. Calif., 1961, MA, 1963. Intern AFL-CIO, Washington, 1963-64; rsch. dir. packinghouse workers AFL-CIO, Chgo., 1964-68; project mgr. SAC, San Francisco, 1968-72; non exec. dir. group of cos., Edinburgh, Scotland, 1973—; dir. Open Futures Ltd., Scottis Dir. Centre. Author: The Strategy Led Business, 1993. Fellow Inst. Dirs. (London). Office: NAP Assocs Ltd, 10 W Savile Rd, Edinburgh EH16 5NG, Scotland

NAQI, ABDULRAHAMAN, journalist, academic administrator; b. Ras Alkhaimah, United Arab Emirates, Dec. 31, 1963; s. Abdallah and Maryam (Al Ali) N.; m. Khadeeja Ahmed Bani Hammad, Dec. 1, 1988; children: Bader, Noura, Maryam, Mohammed. BA in Mass Comm. and Sociology, United Arab Emirates U., 1986. Student social advisor Min. Edn., Ras Al Kahaimah, 1986-90, vice prin., 1990-91, pub. and media rels. specialist, 1991-97; dir. office Al-Ittihad Press, Ras Al Kahaimah, 1997—; anchorman radio and TV, Abu Dhabi, United Arab Emirates, 1990-95; cons. Red Crescent Soc., Abu Dhabi. Author: United Arab Emirates Annual Educational Directory, 1989 (ann. award). Recipient AlOwas Cultural prize AlOwas Cultural Orgn., 1990, Art Exhbn. award United Arab Emirates Art Assn., 1990. Muslim. Avocations: photography, travel. Fax: 00971-7-2331717. E-mail: naqipres@emirates.net.ae. Home: PO Box 808, Ras Alkhaimah United Arab Emirates Office: Emirates Media, pO Box 5443, Ras Al Kahaimah United Arab Emirates

NAQSHBAND, GHULAM, travel and tourism company executive; b. Kasur, Punjab, Pakistan, Feb. 2, 1921; s. Nabi Bakhsh and Bakhtawar Begum. BA, Islamic Coll., Lahore, Pakistan, 1941. Pub. rels. officer Ministry of Def., New Delhi, 1941-48; sec. to Ambassador Embassy of Iraq, New Delhi, 1949-58; exec. dir. Saha & Rai Travels, New Delhi, 1958-65; exec. dir. SITA World Travel, New Delhi, 1966—, mng. dir., 1979, dep. chmn., 1994—; mng. dir. Indrama Pvt. Ltd., New Delhi, 1970-82. Editor: INDRAMA Mag., 1976—. Mem. Delhi Music Soc. (pres. 1998—), Alliance Francaise de Delhi (hon. sec. 1952-60), Internat. Congress and Conv. Assn. (v.p. 1992-93), Indian Heritage Soc. (v.p. 1986—), Nat. Skal Com. India (hon., chmn. 1987, 96), Indo-Am. Commerce and Industry, Press Club of India, Rotary. Avocations: community service, gardening, reading. Home: 17 Feroz Gandhi Rd, New Delhi 110021, India Office: SITA Wrold Travel India, 4 Malcha Marg Shopping Ctr, 110-021 New Delhi India

NAQUIN, PATRICIA ELIZABETH, employee assistance consultant; b. Houston, Jan. 28, 1943; d. Louie Dee and Etha Beatrice (English) Price; m. Hollis James Naquin, Mar. 23, 1961; children: Price Naquin, Holli Campbell. BS, U. Houston, 1969, MS, 1982; PhD, Tex. Woman's U., 1988. Lic. profl. counselor; lic. chem. dependency counselor; nat. cert. counselor; cert. chem. dependency specialist; cert. employee assistance profl. Purchasing agt. Internat. Affairs U. Houston, 1966-68; elem. sch. tchr. Pasadena (Tex.) Ind. Sch. Dist., 1969-82; spl. edn. counselor Alvin (Tex.) Ind. Sch. Dist., 1982-85, drug-free schs. coord., 1988-92; marriage and family therapist Lifespan Counseling, Pasadena, 1985-92; employee assistance cons. DuPont, LaPorte, Tex., 1992—; adv. com. mem. Sam Houston U., Huntsville, Tex., 1983; trainer and instr. Bay Area Coun. on Drugs and Alcohol, Houston, 1988-92; cons. Alvin Ind. Sch. Dist., 1989-92, DuPont Valuing People Core Team, 1993—; supr. State Bd. of Profl. Counselors, Houston, 1988—. Co-author: Life is for Everyone Manual, 1990. Com. co-chair Alvin S.A.P. Task Force, 1988-92; com. mem. Tri-Dist. Task Force, Alvin, 1990-91; com. chmn. Alvin Bus./Edn. Partnership, 1992; bd. dirs. Brazoria (Tex.) County Coun. Drugs and Alcohol, 1991. Mem. Am. Assn. Marriage and Family Therapists, Tex. Assn. Counselors of Alcohol and Drug Abuse, Am. Counseling Assn., Employee Assistance Program Assn., Nat. Disting. Svc. Registry/Libr. of Congress, Phi Delta Kappa. Republican. Methodist. Avocations: quilting, playing piano, playing with grandchildren, computer games.

NARAIN, PREM, agricultural scientist, educator, researcher; b. Lucknow, India, Jan. 3, 1934; s. Govind Narain Verma and Lalli Devi; m. Krishna Srivastava, June 14, 1955; 1 child, Dhirendra Verma. BSc (hons.), Lucknow U., 1953, MSc, 1954; PhD, Edinburgh (Scotland) U., 1969, DSc, 1984. Stats. investigator Ministry of Transport, New Delhi, 1955-58; asst. rsch. officer Indian Vet. Rsch. Inst., Izatnagar, 1958-61; asst. prof. Indian Agrl. Rsch. Stats., New Delhi, 1961-70, from prof. to sr. prof., 1970-78; joint dir. Indian Agrl. Stats. Rsch. Inst., New Delhi, 1978-81, dir., 1981-92; prin. scientist Indian Agrl. Rsch. Inst., New Delhi, 1992-93, dean, joint dir., 1993-94, prof. emeritus, 1994—. Author: Statistical Genetics, 1990; editor, chair Indian Soc. Agrl. Stats. Jour., 1983, Impact Of P.V. Sukhatme On Agricultural Statistics And Nutrition, 1984. Recipient Rafi Ahmad Kidwai prize Indian Coun. Agrl. Rsch., 1977, Sankhyiki Bhushan award Indian Soc. Agrl. Stats., 1991, O.P. Bhasin Found. award, 1992, Dr. M.S. Randhawa Meml. medal, Nat. Acad. Agrl. Sci., 1999. Fellow Indian Nat. Sci. Acad. (G.P. Chatterji Meml. prize 1987), Indian Acad. Sci.; mem. Nat. Acad. Agrl. Sci. (founding), Internat. Statis. Inst. (mem. coun. 1989-93), Internat. Biometric Soc. (mem. coun. 1988-91). Home: B-3/27 A Lawrence Rd, New Delhi 110035, India Office: Indian Agrl Rsch Inst, Director's Office, New Delhi 110012, India

NARANG, ANIL, neonatologist; b. Sargodha, India, May 4, 1945; s. Ram and Sumitra (Luthra) N.; m. Rupinder Kaur Tangri, May 23, 1976; two children. MBBS, Med. Coll. Rohtak, India, 1967, MD, PGI, Chandigarh, India, 1973. From registrar pediats. to lectr. pediats. PGI, 1972-79; sr. registrar John Radcliffe Hosp., Oxford, England, 1979-80; from asst. prof. to prof. pediats. PGI, 1980—; cons. Govt. India, 1976-79; chief neonatal svcs. PGI, 1995—; pres. Nat. Neonatology Forum, India, 1996—. Editor: Primary Care of Newborn, 1990, Neonatal Ventilation, 1992. WHO fellow in neonatology, 1974, Commonwealth Med. fellow, 1979. Fellow Nat. Acad. Med. Scis., Indian Acad. Pediats.; mem. Neonatal Soc. England, Indian Med. Assn. Avocations: badminton, cricket, computers, travel, music. Home: 1032 Sector 24, 160023 Chandigarh India Office: PGIMER, Dept Pediats Sector 12, 160012 Chandigarh India

NARANG, CHANDER KUMAR, chemist, educator, researcher; b. Rawalpindi, Pakistan, Feb. 28, 1933; arrived in India, 1947; s. Dass and Devi (Kaushlia) N.; m. Mohini Paruthi, May 11, 1962; children: Avinash, Vandana, Neeraj. BSc, Khalsa Coll., Amritsar, India, 1953; MSc, Holkar Coll., Indore, India, 1959; PhD, U. Jodhpur, India, 1966. Lectr. Govt. Coll., Ratlam, India, 1959-60, Lohia Coll., Churu, India, 1960-62; lectr. U. Jodhpur, 1962-80, reader, 1985-93, prof. chemistry, 1993—; scientist Danish Inst. Protein Chemistry, Horsholm, 1975-77; R&D chemist Biosyntech GmbH, Hamburg, Germany, 1982-84. Author: Determination of Organic Compounds Using N-Bromosuccinimide, 1975, Polymers as Aids in Organic Chemistry, 1980; contbg. author: Solid-phase Synthesis of Oligo-nucleotides Using the Phosphite Method, 1982; referee Indian Jour. Chemistry, 1985—. Mem. N.Y. Acad. Scis. Avocation: gardening. Home: G-139 Shastri Nagar, Jodhpur 342003, India

NARASIMHAM, PRABHALA LAKSHMI, civil engineering and management consultant; b. Draksharama, India, Jan. 8, 1941; s. Prabhala Subbarao and Prabhala Sitadevi Challa; m. Prabhala Laxmi Addanki, June 26, 1967; children: Anupama Prabhala Kapse, Madhav Prabhala. B of Engring. with honors, Andhra U., Visakhapatnam, India, 1961; M of Engring., Indian Inst. Sci., Bangalore, 1962; Diploma of Imperial Coll., U. London, 1970. Cert. specialist course in foundation engring., U. Roorkee, India, 1966; cert. in Urdu, Urdu Acad., Delhi, India, 1994; cert. proficiency in carnatic music Sangeeta Janakulam, 2000; registered individual cons. Asian Devel. Bank. Extra asst. dir. Ctrl. Water & Power Commn., Govt. India, New Delhi, 1963-64, asst. dir., 1964-75, dep. dir., 1975-76; sr. engr. Howe (India) Pvt. Ltd., New Delhi, 1977-87, sr. cons., 1987-94, dep. chief, project mgmt., 1994-2000; civil engring. and mgmt. cons., 2000—; asst. in tech. capacity various adv. coms., Govt. of India, New Delhi, 1963-76; advisor in formulation of design stds. for dams, Indian Stds. Instn., New Delhi, 1963-76; organizer rsch. activities for R & D in the irrigation sector all centrally-funded rsch. orgns./labs. in India, including the premier hydraulic rsch. inst. The Ctrl. Water & Power Rsch. Sta., Pune, 1975-76. Contbr. articles to profl. jours. and conf. procs. V.p. Residents' Welfare Assn., Sector-26, Noida, India, 1984-85, 86-87. Hindu. Avocations: Hindu philosophy, religion and theosophy, languages, journalism and literary pursuits, reading. Home: A-149/Sector 26, Noida 201301, India

NARASIMHAMOORTHY, LALITHA, oncologist, consultant, medical researcher; b. Bangalore, India, June 7, 1936; d. Venkatanarasiah and Visalakshamma N. MBBS, Mysore (India) Med. Coll., 1958; MD, Bangalore Med. Coll., 1965; cert. in nutrition, Nat. Inst. Nutrition, Hydrabad, India, 1971. Intern Bangalore Med. Coll. Hosps., Bangalore, 1958; resident in internal medicine Bangalore Med. Coll. (Victoria Hosp.), 1962-65; asst. surgeon Govt. of Karnataka, India, 1959-66; asst. prof. internal medicine Karnataka State Govt. Med. Colls., India, 1966-73; assoc. prof. med. and pediat. oncology Kidwai Meml. Inst. of Oncology, Bangalore, 1973-75, prof., head dept., 1975-94, med. supt., dean, 1990-94; freelance med. oncologist Bangalore, 1994—. Contbr. articles to med. jours. Mem. Indian Soc.

Oncology (mem. exec. com. 1986—), Indian Soc. Med. and Pediat. Oncology (life, Dr. Subodhmitra oration 1995, mem. exec. com. 1986—), Indian Assn. Physicians, N.Y. Acad. Scis. Fellow WHO, U.K. and Germany, 1977-78; rsch. grantee NIH, Bangalore and Bethesda, Md., 1993-98. Avocations: scientific reading and writing, music, painting, gardening. Home: No 52 S End Rd Basavanagudi, KRN Bangalore 560 004, India

NARASIMHAN, NURANI SIVARAMAKRISHNA, chemistry educator, researcher; b. Palakkad, Kerala, India, Nov. 11, 1928; s. Nurani Narasimha Sivaramakrishma Tyerand Nurani Seshadri Apeethakuchambal.; m. Trichur Venkareswara Subbalakshmi, 1957; children: Sivaramakrishnan, Rajalakshmi, Lakshmi. BSc, Presidency Coll., Madras, India, 1948, MA, 1950, PhD, 1954. Nat. postdoctoral rsch. fellow Govt. of India, Delhi, 1955-58; reader in chemistry U. Pune, 1958-77, prof. chemistry, 1977-89, emeritus prof., 1989—; sr. scientist Indian Nat. Sci. Acad., Delhi, 1989-92; dir. Spic Sci. Found., Madras, 1994-97; nat. lectr. U. Grants, Delhi, 1985-86; rsch. assoc. U. Zurich, 1971-72; vis. prof. U. Alberta, Can., 1980, So. Meth. U., Dallas, 1988. Contbr. articles to profl. jours. Fellow Indian Acad. Scis., Indian Nat. Sci. Acad. Avocation: music appreciation. Home: 22 Niyoshi Park II Aundh, Pune Maharashtra 411007, India Office: U Pune, Dept Chemistry, Pune Maharashtra 411007, India

NARATH, ALBERT, retired laboratory administrator; b. Berlin, Mar. 5, 1933; came to U.S., 1947; s. Albert Narath and Johanna Agnes Anna (Brueggemann) Bruckmann; m. Worth Haines Scattergood (div. 1976); children: Tanya, Lise, Yvette; m. Barbara Dean Camp (div. 1983); 1 child, Albert; m. Shanna S. Lindeman. BS in Chemistry, U. Cin., 1955; PhD in Phys. Chemistry, U. Calif., Berkeley, 1959. Mem. tech. staff, mgr. phys. sci. Sandia Nat. Labs., Albuquerque, 1959-68, dir. solid state sci., 1968-71, mng. dir. phys. sci., 1971-73, v.p. rsch., 1973-82, exec. v.p. rsch. and adv. weapons sys., 1982-84, pres., 1989-95; pres. energy and environ. sect. Lockheed Martin Corp., Albuquerque, 1995-98; ret., 1998. Contbr. sci. articles to profl. jours. Fellow AAAS, Am. Phys. Soc. (George E. Pake prize 1991); mem. NAE.

NARAYAN, BEVERLY ELAINE, lawyer; b. Berkeley, Calif., June 19, 1961; d. Jagjiwan and Alexandra (Mataras) N.; m. James Dean Schmidt, Jan. 7, 1989; children: Sasha Karan, Kaiya Maria. Student, San Francisco State U., 1979-80; BA, U. Calif., Berkeley, 1983; JD, U. Calif., San Francisco, 1987. Bar: Calif. 1987, U.S. Dist. Ct. (no. dist.) Calif. 1987, U.S. Dist. Ct. (ctrl. dist.) 1988. Atty. Daniels Barratta & Fine, L.A., 1988-89, Kornblum Ferry & Frye, L.A., 1990-91, Clapp Moroney Bellagamba Davis & Vucinich, Menlo Park, Calif., 1991-93, pvt. practice, Burlingame, Calif., 1993—; mng. dir. KarmaTek, Burlingame, Calif., 1999—; arbitrator Nat. Assn. Securities Dealers, San Francisco, 1987—, Pacific Stock Exch., San Francisco, 1994—; mediator Peninsula Conflict Resolution Ctr., San Mateo, Calif., 1995—; judge pro tem San Mateo Superior Ct., Redwood City, Calif., 1994—. Candidate Sch. Bd. San Mateo (Calif.) Unified Sch. Dist., 1993; mem. San Mateo County Task Force Violence Against Women. Recipient U. Calif. Hastings Coll. Law Achievement award, 1986; named Barrister of Yr., San Mateo County, 1996. Mem. ABA, San Mateo County Bar Assn. (co-chair women lawyers 1995, bd. dirs. 1994-96), South Asian Bar Assn., Nat. Women's Polit. Caucus (bd. dirs., diversity chair 1993-96), San Mateo County Barristers Club (bd. dirs. 1993-99, child watch chair 1995-99). Avocations: baking, cooking, reading, travel, motorcycles, family. Office: 1508 Howard Ave Burlingame CA 94010-5216

NARAYAN, SHASHI PRAKASH, research scientist; b. Bhagalpur, India, Sept. 3, 1953; s. Harihar and Jagrani (Devi) N.; m. Jhunjhun Bala Sinha, June 20, 1983; children: Abhineet Prakash, Abhijeet Prakash. BS with honors, U. Bihar, India, 1971; B of Engring., Indian Inst. Metals, 1980; MS in Engring., Regional Inst. Tech., Jamshedpur, India, 1989; PhD in Engring., Indian Inst. Sci., 1998. Sr. lab. asst. Nat. Metall. Lab., Jamshedpur, 1974-80; sr. tech. asst. Ctrl. U., Hyderabad, India, 1980-81; asst. supt. Tube Products of India, Madras, 1981-83; supt. Tin Plate Co. of India, Jamshedpur, 1983-87; sr. scientist Regional Rsch. Lab., Bhopal, India, 1987—; vis. scientist Naval Rsch. Lab., Washington, 1994, collaborating scientist, 1995—; rsch. scholar Indian Inst. Sci., Banglore, 1990; lectr. in field; expert in magnetic materials field. Contbr. articles to profl. jours.; patentee in field. Recipient fellowship Acad. Ednl. Devel., 1993, grant Office of Naval Rsch. USN, 1995. Mem. IEEE, Indian Inst. Metals (life), Materials Rsch. Soc. India (life), Sci. and Workers' Assn. (treas. 1988, 96), Inst. Stds. Engrs. (joint sec. 1991-93, exec. mem. 1991-93), Magnetics Soc. India (exec. mem. 1993—). Avocations: tourism, cooking, badminton, writing. Home: 14/6 Geetanjali Complex, Bhopal 462003, India Office: Regional Rsch Lab, Hosangabad Rd, Bhopal 462026, India

NARAYANAN, ARUMUGAKANNU, plant physiologist, educator, researcher; b. Nagercoil, Tamil Nadu, India, Dec. 31, 1938; m. Kamala Devi, Jan. 24, 1972; children: Suresh, Sudha, Satish. BSc, Kerala U., 1955; BSc in Agr., Madras U., Coimbatore, India, 1958; MSc, Indian Agrl. Rsch. Inst., New Delhi, 1961, PhD, 1966. Attaché de recherche CNRS, Paris, 1970-74; plant physiologist ICRISAT, Hyderabad, India, 1974-76; prof., univ. head ANGR Agrl. U. Hyderabad, 1976-98; prin. Agrl. Coll., Bapatla, 1986-89. Mem. editl. bd. Annals of Plant Physiology; contbr. articles to profl. jours. Recipient Agrl. Sci. award Assn. for Acad. Agrl. Scis., 1990. Fellow Indian Soc. Plant Physiology; mem. Plant Physiology Club (patron), Organic Agr. Sci. Soc. for Integrated Svcs. (sec.). Avocations: photography, stamps. Office: 8/5A Maharani Ave, Vadavalli Coimbatore 641041, India

NARAYANAN, KOCHERIL RAMAN, president of India; b. Ozhavoor, Kerala, Feb. 4, 1921; s. Raman Vaidyan; m. Usha Ma Tint Tint, 1951; 2 children. Student, Travancore U., London Sch. Econs. U. London; DSc (hon.), 1987. Lectr. in English literature Travacore U., 1943; with editl. dept. of Hindu newspaper Madras, 1944-45; reporter Times of India, 1945; London corr. social welfare Bombay, 1945-48; with Fgn. Svc., 1949; joint dir. orientation ctr. for fgn. technicians Delhi Sch. of Econs., 1954-55; served in Rangoon, Tokyo, London and in ministry external affairs, 1949-60; acting high commr. Australia, 1961-62; consul-gen. Hanoi, 1962-63; dir. China divsn. Ministry External Affairs, 1963-67; ambassador to Thailand, 1967-69, joint sec. for policy planning in ministry, 1969-70, Jawaharlal Nehru fellow, 1970-72; hon. prof. Jawaharlal Nerhu U., 1970-72; ambassador to Turkey, 1973-75, additional sec. for policy planning divsn. of ministry, 1975-76; sec. for the east Ministry External Affairs, 1976; ambassador to People's Republic of China, 1976-78, ambassador to U.S., 1980-83; min. state for planning Govt. of India, 1984-85, min. state for external affairs, 1985-86, min. for atomic energy, space, electronics and ocean devel., 1986-87, min. for sci. and tech., 1986-89, v.p., 1992-97, pres., 1997—; mem. Indian del. to UN Gen. Assembly, 1979, Lok Sabha for Ottapalath, Kerala, 1984—, Indian Coun. for Social Sci. Rsch., New Delhi, Inst. of Defence Studies an d Analysis, Indian Assn. Social Sci. Inst.; v.p. Coun. Scientific and Industrial Rsch., 1986—; fellow Jawaharlal Nehru U., 1970-72, hon. prof., 1970-71, vice-chancellor, 1979-80; co-chmn. Indo-U.S. Sub-com. on Edn. and Culture, 1980. Author: (with K.P. Mishra) India and America—Essays in Understanding, Images, and Insights, Non-Alignment in Contemporary International Relations, and others. Mem. Exec. Coun. Children's Book Trust. Fellow L.S.E. (hon.). Avocations: literature, philosophy. Office: Office of President, Rashtrapati Bhavan, New Delhi 110004, India Address: 81 Lodhi Estate, New Delhi 110003, India*

NARAYANAN, RAMASWAMY, biomedical engineer; b. Mohanur, India, Mar. 15, 1952; s. Anandhachari and Jayalakshmi R.; m. Jeanine Bouchard, Apr. 29, 1982, 1 child, Anndal. BS in Chemistry and Physics, Bombay U., 1972, MS in Clin. Biochemistry, 1974; PhD in Biochemistry, U. Coll., Dublin, 1980. Teaching asst., jr. lectr. U. Bombay, 1972-75; med. coord. Themis Pharm. Co., Bombay, 1975-76; teaching asst. dept. biochemistry Univ. Coll. of Dublin, 1977-80; vis. fellow Lab. Viral Carcinogenesis/Cellular Molecular Bio Nat. Cancer Inst. NIH, Bethesda, Md., 1981-83; vis. scientist AIDS Rsch. Lab. Ctrs. for Disease Control, Atlanta, 1983-85; assoc. rsch. scientist dept. pharmacology Sch. Medicine Yale U., New Haven, 1985-87; asst. lab. mem. Meml. Sloan-Kettering Inst., N.Y.C., 1987-88, adj. asst. mem., 1988-94; rsch. investigator dept. molecular genetics Hoffmann-La Roche, Inc., Nutley, N.J., 1988-94; rsch. leader divsn. oncology Hoffmann-LaRoche Inc., Nutley, N.J., 1994-98; prof. dept. biol. scis. Fla. Atlantic U., Boca Raton, Fla., 1998—; assoc. dir. Ctr. for Molecular Biology and Biotech. Fla. Atlantic U., Boca Raton, 1998—; vis. prof. Rutgers U., New Brunswick, N.J., 1993-98. Mem. editorial bd. Antisense Rsch. Devel., 1994—, In Vivo, 1995—, Anticancer Rsch., 1996—; contbr. numerous chpts. to books, articles to profl. jours. Bd. Advisors Am. Biographic Inst., 1996—; panel mem. NCI study sect., 1995—, Dept. Def. Breast Cancer Rsch., 1995—. Fellow Med. Rsch. Coun. Ireland, 1980; grantee Am. Cancer Soc., 1986. Mem. AAAS, Am. Assn. Advancement Cancer Rsch., Am. Soc. Microbiology, Am. Soc. Hematology, N.Y. Acad. Scis., Internat. Soc. Hematology, Internat. Soc. Comparative Oncology. Office: 777 Glades Rd Boca Raton FL 33431-6424

NARAYANAN, SHRIDHAR, pharmacology educator; b. Mumbai, May 20, 1969; s. Narayanan Sundaraja Kizhanatham and Andal Srinivasa Narayanana. B of Pharm. Sci., U. Bombay, 1990; PhD, Ohio State U., 1996. Postdoctoral rschr. UCLA, 1996-97; asst. prof. K.M.Kundnani Coll. Pharmacy, Mumbai, 1997—. Recipient Excellence in Rsch. award Sigma Xi, 1996; rsch. grantee All India Coun. Tech. Edn., 1998. Mem. Indian Pharmacol. Soc. (life), Soc. Neurosci., N.Y. Acad. Scis. Avocations: music, philately, reading, trekking. Home: UCLA-NPI 760 Westwood Plz # 77 Los Angeles CA 90095-8353

NA'RAY-SZABÓ, GÁBOR, chemist; b. Budapest, Hungary, Mar. 11, 1943; s. Istvan and Dorottya (Dobay) N.S.; m. Zsuzsanna Szirmay, Apr. 2, 1949; children: Márton, A'gnes. Diploma in chemistry, Lorand Eötvös U., Budapest, 1967; postgrad., Tech. U. Budapest, 1968-70. Rsch. fellow Chinoin Pharm. Works, Budapest, 1967-78, head sci. info. dept., 1978-90; mng. dir. Bionavion Biochem. R&D Ltd., Budapest, 1990; prof. chemistry dept. theoretical chemistry Lorand Eötvös U., 1991-96; dep. sec. gen. Hungarian Acad. Scis., Budapest, 1996-99; head dept. sci. affairs Ministry of Edn., Budapest, 1999—; Alexander von Humboldt fellow Göttingen (Germany) U., 1971, 73; vis. scientist chemistry dept. U. So. Calif., L.A., 1988. Co-author: Applied Quantum Chemistry, 1986; mem. editl. bd. Jour. Molecular Graphics, 1985—, Jour. Molecular Structure Theochem, 1987—; Chem. Design Automation News, 1993—, Curr. Prot. Peptide Sci., 2000—; contbr. articles to profl. publs. Mem. Hungarian Acad. Engring., Hungarian Acad. Scis., Acad. European Art, Sci. and Letters (titular mem.), Hungarian Chem. Soc. (sec. gen. 1983-90, pres. 1990-97), Fedn. Tech. and Sci. Socs. (pres. 1990-94). Home: Ulászló 24, H-1114 Budapest Hungary

NARBUTAS, AMALIJUS STEPONAS, publisher, editor, artist; b. Klaipeda, Lithuania, July 10, 1934; s. Vladislovas and Stefanija (Budrevičiute) N.; m. Stase Momkute (div. 1980); children: Vaiva, Teisius; m. Dangute Vaidilaite, Apr. 25, 1986. Grad. in engring. technology, Vilnius Tech. Coll., 1958; grad. in mech. engring., Kaunas Higher Politech. U., 1969. Engr.-technologist Machine-Tool Plant, Šiauliai, Lithuania, 1959-67; gen. technologist Machine Plant, Šiauliai, 1967-70; sr. lectr. Higher Poly. Sch., Šiauliai, 1970-84; painter Šiauliai, 1984-89; publ. A.S. Narbuto Leidykla (publishing house), Šiauliai, Lithuania, 1989—. Author: Seriously and Otherwise, 1995; contbr., editor: (jour.) Titnagas, 1989. Mem. Folk Art Union Lithuania, Journalists Soc. Lithuania, Nobility Union Lithuania. Roman Catholic. Avocations: visual arts, graphics, cartoonist. Office: AS Narbuto leidykla, Klevu 9, 5400 Šiauliai Lithuania

NARDA, NARINDER KRISHAN, agricultural engineering studies educator; b. Nangal, Punjab, India, Jan. 1, 1945; s. Amar Nath and Devki Devi N.; m. chhaya Rani Shoree, Jan. 16, 1971; children: Sanjay, Poonam. BS, Punjab U., Chandigarh, India, 1965; B Tech, Punjab Agr. U., Ludhiana, India, 1969; MS, Ohio State U., 1975, PhD, 1979. Rsch. asst. in agrl. engring. Punjab Agr. U., Ludhiana, 1969-71, rsch. asst. in agrl. engring. and water mgmt., 1971-72, subject matter specialist, 1972-74, asst. prof., 1979-82, assoc. prof., 1982-88, prof., 1988—; grad. tchg. assoc. Ohio State U., Columbus, 1974-79. Pres. Hathi Compl. Residents' Welfare Assn., Ludhiana, 1991-93, 95—. Recipient Best Tchr. award P.A.U. Tchr.'s Assn., Ludhiana, 1982, Disting. Alumnus award Coll. of Agr. Engring., Ludhiana, 1989. Mem. Indian Soc. Agr. Engring. (vice-chmn. Punjab chpt. 1991-93, Best Tchr. award 1982, Jain Irrigation award), Indian Soc. Tech. Edn., Alumni Assn. Coll. Agr. Engring. Punjab Agr. U. (pres. 1990—, chief editor 1986—). Avocations: social activities, music, alumni association activities, watching movies. Office: Dept Soil and Water Engring, Punjab Agrl Univ, 141004 Ludhiana/Punjab India

NARIN'YANI, ALEXANDER SEMYONOVICH, artificial intelligence researcher; b. Moscow, Nov. 2, 1937; s. Semyon Davydovich and Natalya Pavlovna (Gercenberg) N.; m. Galina Ivanovna Bykova, Mar. 11, 1968; children: Alexander, Michail. D of Physics-Math Sci., USSR Acad. of Scis., 1971. Rschr. Computer Sci. Ctr. of Siberian divsn. USSR Acad. of Scis., Novosibirsk, 1962-72, head rsch. group, 1972-78, head AI lab., 1978-88; gen. dir. Intelligent Tech., Moscow, Novosibirsk, 1988-91; dir. Russian Rsch. Inst. of Artifical Intelligence, Moscow, Novosibirsk, 1992—; mem. program coms. internat. confs. Editl. bd. Applied Artificial Intelligence, 1995-97; contbr. numerous articles to profl. publs. Mem. AI Assn. (v.p. 1989-90, coordination com. 1994-95). Avocations: tourism, photography. E-Mail: narin@aha.ru. Fax: 7-095-158 9430. Office: Russian Rsch Inst, PO Box 111, 103001 Moscow Russia

NARITA, KAZUAKI, mathematical physicist, consultant; b. Seoul, Korea, Mar. 3, 1941; s. Fujio and Kikue (Okamoto) N.; m. Kazuko Kashima, July 3, 1977. B in Engring., Kyoto (Japan) U., 1964, MS, 1966, PhD in Sci., 1989. Cons. Wakatake Sch., Kobe, Japan, 1972—. Contbr. articles to scientific jours. Mem. N.Y. Acad. Scis. Avocation: drawing. Home and Office: B1010 CI Heights, 1-31 Yamada-Nishi, Osaka Suita 565-0824, Japan

NARITA, MITSUO, pediatrician, microbiologist; b. Otaru, Japan, Apr. 12, 1957; s. Tomio and Masuho (Takaoka) N.; m. Yuko Fukao, Sept. 23, 1984; children: Rina, Kenji. MD, Hokkaido U., Sapporo, Japan, 1982, PhD, 1993. Physician Hokkaido U., 1982-86, 88-96, Tetsudo Hosp., Sapporo, 1997—; rschr. Sapporo Med. Coll., 1987; cons. Japan Soc. Mycoplasmology, 1996—, Japan Soc. CNS Infection, 1997—. Contbr. articles to profl. jours. Rsch. grantee Sapporo Med. Soc., 1997. Mem. Am. Soc. Microbiology, Internat. Orgn. Mycoplasmology. Avocation: running marathons. Home: Chuo-ku Odori W-26 3-5-601, Hokkaido Sapporo 064-0820, Japan Office: Sapporo Tetsudo Hosp, Chuo-ku N-3 E-1, Hokkaido Sapporo 060-0033, Japan

NARITA, TADASHI, science educator; b. Nishikasugai-gun, Aichi Prefecture, Japan, Aug. 7, 1939; s. Tokiji and Asako (Fukuta) N.; m. Mieko Hori, April 29, 1969; children: Mamiko, Masako, Naomi. BS, Yokohama (Japan) Nat. U., 1963; MS, U. Tokyo, 1965, PhD, 1970. Tech. ofcl. U. Tokyo, 1968-73, asst., 1973-76; assoc. prof. Saitama Inst. of Tech., Okabe, Japan, 1976-83, prof., 1983—. Contbr. articles to books and profl. jours.; patentee in field. Postdoctoral fellow U. Md., 1974-75. Office: Saitama Inst of Tech, Saitama Inst Tech, 1690, Okabe Saitama 369-0293, Japan

NARITA, YUTAKA, advertising executive; b. Japan, Sept. 19, 1929; s. Kiyoomi and Some Narita; m. Michi Narita; children: Chiaki, Akira. BA in Law, U. Tokyo, 1953. Exec. dir. Dentsu Inc., Tokyo, 1981-83, mng. dir., 1983-89, sr. mng. dir., 1989-93, pres., 1993—. Office: Dentsu Inc, 1-11 Tsukiji Chuo-ku, Tokyo 104, Japan*

NARITOMI, KENJI, pediatrician, clinical geneticist, educator; b. Tosu, Saga, Japan, Jan. 12, 1949; s. Tateki and Momoe (Uchida) N.; m. Mariko Kanoh, Dec. 8, 1979; children: Masako, Kenta. MD, Kagoshima (Japan) U., 1974, PhD, 1982. Lic. physician, med. geneticist. Intern Kagoshima U. Hosp., 1974-75, resident, 1976-81; instr. Kagoshima U., 1982-85; assoc. prof. dept. pediatrics Ryukyu U., Nishihara, Japan, 1985-99; prof. dept. med. genetics Ryukyu U., Nishihara, 1999—. Author: Congenital Malformation and Databook, 1994, Congenital Malformation and Databook 2d edit., 1996. Mem. AAAS, N.Y. Acad. Sci. Avocations: baseball, golf, movies, television. Home: 3-22-22 Maehara, Ginowan 901-2215, Japan Office: U Ryukyus Dept Med Genetics, 207 Uehara, Nishihara 903-0215, Japan

NARMONT, JOHN STEPHEN, lawyer; b. Auburn, Ill., June 24, 1942; s. Stephen and Luriel (Welle) N.; m. Sondra J. Nicholls, Feb. 12, 1978. BBA magna cum laude, U. Notre Dame, 1964; JD, U. Ill., Champaign, 1967. ar: Ill. 1967, U.S. Dist. Ct. (so. dist.) Ill. 1967, U.S. Ct. Appeals (7th cir.) 1967, U.S. Tax Ct. 1978, U.S. Supreme Ct. 1973. Pvt. practice Springfield, Ill.; founder, pres., owner Richland Ranch, Inc., Auburn; originator, pres. The Solid Gold Futurity, Ltd. Mem. Sangamon Valley Estate Planning Coun. Mem. ABA, Sangamon County Bar Assn., Ill. State Bar Assn., Assn. Trial Lawyer Am., Am. Agrl. Law Assn., Ill. Inst. for Continuing Legal Edn., Internat. Livestock Exposition (pres., founder). Office: 209 N Bruns Ln Springfield IL 62702-4612

NARRAMORE, CHRISTOPHER LLEWELLYN, orthopaedic surgeon; b. Port Elizabeth, South Africa, Oct. 11, 1953; s. Ralph Llewellyn and Cecelia Wilhelmina (Ferrera) N.; m. Deborah Naish, Apr. 25, 1980; children: Luke, Mark. BSc, U. Cape Town, South Africa, 1974, M.B.Ch.B., 1979. Resident dept. orthop. Groote Schull Hosp., Cape Town; pvt. practice Cape Town; cons., orthop. surgeon Groote Schull Hosp., Cape Town, 1994; part-time cons. Victoria Hosp., Wynberg, Cape Town. Fellow South African Coll. Surgeons. Office: 207 Constantiabera Mediclinic, Burnham Rd, Plumstead Capetown 7800, South Africa

NARTEY, EBENEZER JACKSON, accountant, finance manager; b. Accra, Ghana, Mar. 21, 1951; s. Joseph Nartey and Lydia (Seka) Devia; m. Juliet Joyce Ntim, May 14, 1976; children: Michael, Juliet, Joyce, Andrew. ACCA, U. Ghana, 1973; MBA, Open U., U.K., 1995. Sr. acct. Accra (Ghana) Polytechnil, 1973-80; port acct. Port Authority, Ghana, 1980-85; fin. mgr. Anglo Continental Consultants Ltd., London, 1990—; mgmt. cons. ACL, London, 1995-96. Author: (book) Ghana Ports Financial Manager, 1983. Financier UNC, Accra, 1978. Fellow Royal Soc. Arts, London. Fellow Royal Soc. Arts; mem. AMBAS. Avocations: reading, cleaning, dancing, business research. Home: 5 Bredgar House, Westwall Close, Orpington BR5 4QP, England Office: Anglo Continental Cons Ltd, 119-123 Hackford Rd, Wandsworth Stockwell London SW9 0QT, England

NARUKAWA, KIMIAKI, mathematician, educator, researcher; b. Komatsushima, Japan, Dec. 6, 1950; s. Ryutatsu and Teruko (Yuasa) N.; m. Kazuyo Sano, Jan. 13, 1956; children: Satoshi, Yuka. BS, Kyoto (Japan) U., 1974; MS, Hiroshima (Japan) U., 1976, DSc, 1982. Rsch. assoc. Hiroshima U., 1978-85; assoc. prof. math. Naruto (Japan) U. Edn., 1985-97, prof. math., 1997—. Contbr. articles to profl. jours., including SIAM Jour. on Control and Optimization, Applied Math. and Optimization, Pacific Jour. Math., Bull. Italian Math. Union. Grantee Japanese Ministry Edn., 1994, 96, 97, 2000. Fellow Math. Soc. Japan (councilor 1997-98), Italian Math. Union. Avocations: walking, jogging. Home: Muya-cho, Ohkuwajima Ebisuyama 88-2, Naruto 772-0011, Japan Office: Naruto U Edn, Naruto-cho, Takashima, Naruto 772-8502, Japan

NARULA, PORNTHEP, network technology researcher; b. Bangkok, Mar. 4, 1972; s. Navaraj and Ratana (Sajdev) N. B in Computer Engring., King Mongkut's Inst. Tech., Ladkrabang, Bangkok, 1994; TRLabs Scholarship Stud. in Elec. and Comp. Engrg. Grad. Sch., Univ. Manitoba, Canada. Rschr. NECTEC, Bangkok, 1994-99; R&D chief Govt. IT Svcs., 1998-99; Cache BOF chmn. APNG, Asia-Pacific region, 1997; adv. Embeded Sys. Lab., King Mongkut's Inst. Tech. Ladkrabang, Bangkok, 1998—, adj. instr. computer engring, 1998-99; seasonal instr. dept. computer sci. U. Manitoba, Can., 2000. Engring. Project Mgr.; Internet for Ministers, 1997, Golden Jubilee Network, 1997. Mem. IEEE. Office: TR Labs, 10-75 Scurfield Blvd, Winnipeg, MB Canada R3Y 1P6

NARUMI, HIDEYUKI, secondary education educator; b. Sapporo, Japan, 1940. D of Natural Scis., U. Zagreb, Croatia, 1993; D of Environ. Earth Scis., Hokkaido U., Sapporo, Japan, 1997. Tchr. Hokkaido Tech. H.S., Sapporo, 1974—. Author: Old Japanese and Old Chinese, 1996, The Origin of Japanese and English Languages, 1997, The Ainu Language and the Indo-European Protolanguage, 1999.

NARUSE, TOMONORI, retired bank executive; b. Kofu, Japan, July 26, 1933; came to Eng., 1989; d. Yoshitaka and Yoshiko (Saegusa) N.; m. Fujiko Naruse, Mar. 18, 1960 (dec. Apr. 1997); children: Mana, Yuzuru. B in Gen. Arts, Tokyo U., 1958. With The Bank of Tokyo, Ltd., 1976, dept. gen. mgr. Singapore office, 1976-81, gen. mgr. Internat. Project Fin. Dept., 1981-83, gen. mgr. Jakarta (Indonesia) Office, 1983-84, gen. mgr. and agt. N.Y. agy., 1984; pres. The Bank of Tokyo Trust Co., N.Y.C., 1986-88; dir. The Bank of Tokyo Ltd., 1988-89, mng. dir., 1989, resident mng. dir. in Europe, 1989-94, also bd. dirs.; sr. mng. dir. The Bank of Tokyo Ltd., Tokyo, 1992-94; chmn. Bank of Tokyo Internat. Ltd., London, Bank of Tokyo Capital Markets, London; dep. pres. Japan l'Devel. Corp. (JAIDO), 1994; advisor Japan Asia Investment Co. (JAIC), 1996. Mem. Japan C. of C. London (vice-chmn.), Nippon Club (pres.).

NARUSZEWICZ, MAREK ALEKSY, biochemistry educator; b. Warsaw, Poland, Sept. 6, 1947; s. Józef Naruszewicz and Janina Guzek; m. Krystyna Bednarska, May 22, 1971; children: Beata, Katarzyna. MSc in Pharmacy, U. Sch. Medicine, Warsaw, 1972, PhD, 1979, assoc. prof., 1982; prof., U. Sch. Medicine, Szczecin, Poland, 1992. Sr. rsch. asst. Food and Nutrition Inst., Warsaw, 1976-79, head lipid lab., 1979-83, head pathophysiology dept., 1985-89; vis. prof. Clin. Rsch. Inst., Montreal, Can., 1990-92; prof., head clin. biochemistry dept. Univ. Sch. Medicine, Szczecin, 1992—; pres. Polish Atherosclerosis Soc., 1993; chmn. organizing com. Cardiol. Family Prevention Program Szczecin 2000, 1994—. Editor Risk Factors, 1993. Recipient awards Polish Acad. Scis., Warsaw, 1992, Polish Ministry Health, Szczecin, 1995; postdoctoral fellow Fogarty Internat. Ctr., NIH, Bethesda, Md., 1983-84. Fellow Am. Heart Assn.; mem. Internat. Atherosclerosis Soc., European Atherosclerosis Soc. Avocations: walking in the forest with pet dogs, traveling, music, books, theater. Home: Zaczarowanej Róży, 05-540 Zalesie Górne Poland Office: Univ Sch Medicine, Powstańców Wlkp, 70-111 Szczecin Poland

NARVESON, JOYCE ANN, public services administrator; b. Madison, Wis., Mar. 22, 1942; d. Oscar N. and Ada S. Narveson. BS, U. Wis., 1964; MBA, No. Ill. U., 1976. Mgmt. info. specialist dept. health and social svcs. State of Wis., Madison, 1982-85, fin. officer dept. industry labor and human rels., 1985-86; adminstr. adminstrv. svcs. Pub. Svc. Commn. Wis., Madison, 1986-93, adminstr. water and consumer affairs, 1993—; fiscal mgr. for child support Dept. Workforce Devel., Madison; sec., vice chair, then chair Wis. Adminstrv. Officers Coun., 1989-91. Bd. dirs., fin. chair Black Hawk coun. Girl Scouts U.S., 1985-87; mem. pers. com. Lake Edge Luth. Ch., 1999—. Mem. Phi Beta Kappa, Phi Kappa Gamma, Beta Gamma Sigma. Avocations: antiques, cross-country skiing, golf, U. Wis. sports, Green Bay Packers football. E-mail: narvejo@dwd.state.wi.us. Home: 905 Birch Haven Cir Monona WI 53716-3001 Office: Dept Workforce Devel PO Box 7935 201 E Washington Ave Madison WI 53707-7935

NARWAL, RAM PHAL, soil scientist, researcher; b. Banwasa, Haryana, India, May 6, 1952; s. Rattan Singh and Panmeshri Devi (Malik) N.; m. Nirmal Dahiya, June 18, 1978; children: Preeti, Shweta, Abhimanyu. BSc in Agr. with honors, Haryana Agrl. U., 1973, MSc in Soil Sci., 1976, PhD in Soil Sci., 1986. Rsch. assoc. Haryana Agrl. U., 1976-79, asst. prof., 1979-88, assoc. prof., 1988-96, prof., 1996—; vis. sci. fellow Rsch. Coun. Norway, Agrl. U. Norway, 1993-95. Indian Coun. Rsch. fellow Govt. of India, 1968, Norwegian Agy. Internat. Devel. fellow Agrl. U. Norway, 1980-82. Avocations: reading, music, kitchen gardening, television. Home: 118-PLA Sector 15, Hisar Haryana 125001, India Office: CCSHAU, Dept Soil Sci, Hisar Haryana 125004, India

NARY, JOHN HENRY, interior designer; b. Rochester, N.Y., Oct. 14, 1948; s. Robert John and Edna Gertrude (Gessner) N.; A.A., Erie County Community Coll., 1974; m. Jacqueline Marie Steiger, Jan. 13, 1970. Staff artist, regional mgr. The Birge Co., Buffalo, 1969-71; v.p. Heinzelman Interiors, Inc., Buffalo, 1971-72; dir. design McMullen Dental, Buffalo, 1972-80; v.p. design and sales William H. Prentice, Inc., Buffalo, 1980-91; pres. Corning (N.Y.) Office Interiors, Inc., 1991—; guest lectr. Sch. Dentistry SUNY, Buffalo. Bd. dirs. S.E. Steuben County Habitat for Humanity, 1993-94, v.p., 1995, pres. 1997; mem. Community Services Pilot Program, 1982. Cert., Nat. Council Interior Design Qualification. Mem. Am. Soc. Interior Designers (past pres. N.Y. Upstate/Can. East chpt., bd. dirs., nat. ethics com. 1987, 88, assessment task force 1990, nominating com. 1994, dealer adv. team 1997—), Corning Country Club, Corning Rotary Club. Author:

Dental Office Design, 1974. Home: 109 W Hill Ter Painted Post NY 14870-1001 Office: 19 Denison Pkwy Ste 100 Corning NY 14830

NASAR, A. SULTAN, chemist; b. Kakkoor, Tamil Nadu, India, June 2, 1964; s. M. Abdul and A. Fathima (Beevi) Salam; m. S. Nazimunisha; 1 child, S. Aysha Barsana. BSc, Madurai (India) Kamaraj U., 1985; MSc, Anna U., Chennai, India, 1988; PhD, U. Madras, Chennai, India, 1993. Sr. rschr. U. Madras, Chennai, 1992-93; rsch. assoc. Cen. Leather Rsch. Inst., Chennai, 1994—; fellow U. So. Miss., Hattiesburg, 1995; cons. Anabond Pvt. Ltd., Chennai, 1996-97. Contbr. articles to profl. jours. Fellow Japan Soc. Promotion Sci. Avocations: international issues, reading, theatre, folk dance, music. Home: Kakkoor Post, Ramanathapuram Dist, 623711 Mudukulathur Taluk India Office: Cen Leather Rsch Inst, Patel Rd, 600 020 Chennai India

NASCIMENTO, JOSÉ PEDRO, communications company executive; b. Lisboa, Portugal, May 14, 1966; s. José Augusto and Maria Delfina (Barreiros) N.; m. Teresa Maria Neto, Aug. 15, 1992 (div. 1998); children: Catarina, Henrique. Degree in Engring., Inst. Superior Tecinio, Lisboa, Portugal, 1989. Registered profl. engr. Maths monitor Inst. Superior Tecinio, Lisboa, 1987-89; telecomms. engr. Marconi, Lisboa, 1989-93; from telecomm. engr. to Global Sys. Mobility design dir. Telecel, Lisboa, 1993-99; network dir. Jazztel Portugal, 1999—; cons. Lucent, Chgo., 1996. 2d. Lt. Portugese Army, 1990-91. Mem. Ordem Dos Engenheiros. Roman Cath. Avocations: swimming, body board. Office: Jazztel, Doca de Alcantara, 1350 Lisboa Portugal

NASH, ALICIA, computer programmer, physicist; b. San Salvador, Jan. 1, 1933; came to U.S., 1944; d. Carlos Roberto and Alicia (Lopez-Harrison) Larde; m. John Forbes Nash, Jr., Feb. 16, 1957; children: John Charles Martin. BS in Physics, MIT, 1955, postgrad., 1959. Physicist Nuclear Devel. Corp. of Am., White Plains, N.Y., 1956-57, Tech. Ops., Burlington, Mass., 1957-58; rsch. assoc. MIT Computation Ctr., Cambridge, Mass., 1958-59; physicist, aerospace engr. R.C.A. Astro Divsn., Hightstown, N.J., 1960-66; programmer, analyst Mgmt. Data Processing, N.Y.C., 1972-74, Con Edison, N.Y.C., 1974-80, Blue Cross Blue Shield of N.Y., N.Y.C., 1980-82; systems/analyst programmer specialist N.J. Transit, Newark, 1983—. Mem. AAUW, MIT Club of Princeton (past pres., bd. dirs.), Soc. of Women Engring. Home: 932 Alexander Rd Princeton Junction NJ 08550-1002 Office: NJ Transit One Penn Plaza East Newark NJ 07105

NASH, JAMES LEE, poet, security official; b. Lynchburg, Va., Oct. 1, 1957; s. James Belvy and Marjorie Lea Glden (Campbell) N. Grad., Brookville H.S., Lynchburg, 1977. VIP transp.-info. aide de camp Greater Ft. Lauderdale Broward County Conv. Ctr.; with Brookville H.S., Lynchburg, 1977. Author: (poetry) Casus Belli, 1993, Enduring Significance, 1996; contbg. author: T.P.O.A., 1994, Treasure the Moment, 1996, A Shadow in the Light, 1999, Love and Other Observations, 1999, Melodies and Madness, 1999, Explanations, 2000, Other Planets are Places Too, 2000. Mem. at large Dem. Exec. Com., Broward County, Fla., 1997—; mem. Croissant Park Civic Assn., Ft. Lauderdale, Fla., 1997—. Mem. Titanic Hist. Soc., Soc. Am. Magicians. Avocations: playing piano, juggling. Home: 1114 F St NE # 108 Washington DC 20002

NASH, JOHN FORBES, JR., research mathematician; b. Bluefield, W.Va., 1928. BS in Math., Carnegie-Mellon U., 1945, MS, 1948, PhD (hon.); PhD, Princeton U., 1950; PhD (hon.), U. Athens. Rsch. asst., instr. Princeton (N.J.) U., 1950-51; Moore instr. MIT, 1951-53, asst. prof., 1953-57, assoc. prof., 1957-59; sr. rsch. mathematician Princeton U.; cons. RAND Corp., summers 1950, 52, 54; vis. mem. Inst. Advanced Study, Princeton, 1956-57, 61-62, 63-64; rsch. assoc. math. MIT, 1966-67. Co-recipient Nobel Prize in Econ. Scis., 1994, Bus. Week award Erasmus U., Rotterdam, 1998, Leroy P. Steele prize in math., 1999; recipient von Neumann Theory prize Ops. Rsch. Soc. Am., Pres.'s award Nat. Alliance for the Mentally Ill, 1999; Sloan fellow, NSF fellow; Westinghouse scholar. Fellow Econometric Soc., Am. Acad. Arts and Scis.; mem. NAS. Office: Princeton U Fine Hall Math Dept Princeton NJ 08544-0001

NASH, JOHN J(OSEPH), real estate manager, computer programmer; b. Des Moines; s. Donald Harry and Dortha Darlene Nash. BA, Iowa State U., 1992, MBA, 1999; AAS in Computer Programming, Des Moines Area C.C., 1999. Cert. secondary tchr., Iowa. Office mgr. JDJ Investments, Ankeny, Iowa, 1988-94, real estate mgr., 1994—; tchr. sci. Hubbard (Iowa) Cmty. Sch. Dist., 1992-93, Urbandale (Iowa) Cmty. Sch. Dist., 1994-95, Twin Cedars Cmty. Sch. Dist., Bussey, Iowa, 1995-96; sys. programmer Am. Republic Ins., Des Moines, 1999—; adj. instr. computer programming Des Moines Area C.C., 1998. Author: (textbook) Simply Chemistry, 1993. Mem. U.S. Chess Fedn. (life; cert. local tournament dir. 1990—), Iowa State Chess Assn. (bd. dirs. 1994-99, Svc. award 1990, editor 1996—). Democrat. Methodist. Avocation: wood carving.

NASH, RICHARD EUGENE, aerospace engineer; b. San Diego, Feb. 18, 1954; s. Clifford Arthur Jr. and Dorothy Fay (Johnson) N.; m. Lynn Elora Martin, Aug. 5, 1978. BSCE, U. Ky., 1981; MSCE, U. So. Calif., 1988; MSEM, West Coast U., 1995; postgrad., LeVern U. Registered profl. civil engr., Calif.; cert. profl. mgr. Mem. tech. staff Boeing, Downey, Calif., 1982, lead engr. space shuttle propulsion systems, 1986-88; engr. Nat. Aero-Space Plane, Long Beach, Calif., 1988-89, space shuttle orbiter project engr., 1989-95; project mgr. problem action ctr., product mgr., problem reporting and corrective action, orbiter shuttle program Boeing, Huntington Beach, Calif., 1995—; pvt. practice civil engring., Calif., 1985-87. Scoutmaster Boy Scouts Am., Covington, Ky., 1972-74, Williamstown, Ky., 1976-82, asst. scoutmaster, Ft. Hood, Tex., 1975-76. Sgt. U.S. Army, 1976. Decorated Nat. Def. Svc. medal, Armed Forces Expeditionary medal; recipient Quality Spotlight award, 1971, Space Flight Awareness award, 1992, 95, Manned Space Flight Awareness award 1996, NASA Group Achievement award, 1997, Sustained Superior Performance award, 1985, Divsn. Quality award, 1997; named to Hon. Order of Ky. Cols., 1985. Mem. Nat. Mgmt. Assn. (series facilities), Nat. Eagle Scout Assn. (advisor 1983), Masons (32 degree, sr. warden), Chi Epsilon. Republican. Avocations: backpacking, scouting. Office: Boeing Reusable Space Sys 5301 Bolsa Ave MC H017-D414 Huntington Beach CA 92647-2099

NASH, ROBERT JOHN, materials educator; b. Coventry, Eng., Jan. 10, 1944. BSc with honors in Chemistry, St. Andrews U., Scotland, 1966; PhD in Crystallography, Dundee U., Scotland, 1969. Sr. rsch. assoc. Newcastle (Eng.) U., 1969-70; sr. scientist Sandvik Hard Materials, Coventry, 1970-85; mktg. officer Sanovik Hard Materials, Coventry, 1985-91; sr. lectr. Faculty Computing Scis. and Engring., De Montfort U., Leicester, Eng., 1992—; cons. Indsl. Carbides Ltd., Bromsgrove, Eng., 1991—; tutor Open U., Milton Keynes, Eng., 1971—. Gov. Lyng Hall and Woodway Park schs., Coventry. Fellow Royal Astron. Soc.; mem. Royal Soc. Chemistry, Radio Soc. Great Britain. Avocations: ham radio, rugby football, astronomy, computing. Home: 135 Farren Rd, Coventry CV2 5EH, England Office: De Montfort U, Queens Bldg, Leicester LE1 9BH, England

NASH, WARREN LESLIE, banker; b. Jackson, Miss., Aug. 26, 1955; s. Henry Warren and Frances Lora (Venters) N.; m. Valerie Ann Roberts, Nov. 22, 1980; children: John Wilson, Warren Graham, William Dixon. Student, U.S. Naval Acad., 1973-75; BS in Banking and Fin., Miss. State U., Starkville, 1978; MBA, U. Ala., Birmingham, 1982; profl. cert., Stonier Grad. Sch. Banking, Newark, Del., 1987. Asst. br. mgr. 1st Nat. Bank of Birmingham, Ala., 1978-80, br. officer, 1980-81, asst. v.p., 1981-84; v.p. AmSouth Bank, N.A., Birmingham, 1984-86; v.p., regional retail banking mgr. AmSouth Bank, N.A., Montgomery, Ala., 1986-89; sr. v.p. AmSouth Bank, Montgomery, 1989-91; sr. v.p. consumer banking AmSouth Bank, N.A., Birmingham, 1991-93; v.p. productivity AmSouth Bank, Birmingham, 1993-94, sr. v.p. tech., 1994-95, sr. v.p. retail delivery, 1995-98; pres. Retail BancAssocs., LLC, Birmingham, 1998—; instr. fin. Samford U., Birmingham, 1982-84; v.p., Ala. Automated Clearing house, 1983-84. Counselor Jr. Achievement, Birmingham, 1980-82; loaned exec. United Way, Birmingham, 1980; com. chmn. Birmingham Festival Arts, 1985-86. Named one of Outstanding Young Men of Am., 1984, 85, 86. Mem. Am. Mktg. Assn. (bd. dirs. 1983-84), Am. Inst. Banking, Birmingham C. of C. (dept. coord. 1985), Newcomen Soc., Young Montgomerians Bus. Club, Summit Club, Kiwanis (local pres. 1985-86), Alpha Kappa Psi, Beta Gamma Sigma. Republican. Methodist. Home: 3772 Rockhill Rd Birmingham AL 35223-1560 Office: Retail BancAssocs 2100 Southbridge Pkwy Birmingham AL 35209-1310

NASH, WILLIAM LEWIS, III, retired music education educator; b. Kingston, Pa., July 5, 1946; s. Ray S. and Margaret (Zimmerman) N.; m. Janet Nossal, Dec. 29, 1979; children: Adrienne, William James. B of Music Edn., Westminster Choir Coll., 1968; MA in Music Performance, Trenton State Coll., 1970; PhD, Columbia State U., 1997. Cert. elementary and secondary edn. educator. Music tchr. Milford Mid. Sch. Quakertown (Pa.) Cmty. Sch. Dist., 1968-98; coord. of music Quakertown Cmty. sch. dist., 1974-98. Organist, choirmaster St. John's Luth. Ch., Boyertown, Pa., 1968-87; organist, music dir., dir. concert series Emmanuel Luth. Ch., Pottstown, Pa., 1987—; organist Am. Legion Baseball World Series, Boyertown, Pa., 1990—; organist St. David's Soc., 1998—, v.p., 2000. Mem. Bucks County Music Educators Assn. (pres. 1978-80), Antique Classic Boat Soc. (N.E. chpt. founder, bd. dirs., pres. 1991-94), Pa. Music Educators Assn. (Citation of Excellence, 1997, bd dirs 1992—). Republican. Avocations: restoration of antique cars, boats, antique furniture; painting, fishing gardening, cooking, composing music. Home: 285 E Moyer Rd Pottstown PA 19464-1534 Office: Emmanuel Lutheran Ch Hanover and Walnut Sts Pottstown PA 19464

NASHAWI, IBRAHIM SAMI, engineering educator; b. Aleppo, Syria, Nov. 3, 1956; s. Sami Ahmad Nashawi and Fatima Abdul-Kader Antakli; m. Maha Taha Nashawi, Oct. 21, 1982; children: Houda I., Rima I., Salam I. BSc in Petroleum Engring., La. Tech. U., 1981, MSc in Petroleum Engring./Applied Math., 1987, PhD in Petroleum Engring., 1989. Cert. Syrian Engrs. Soc. Asst. engr. Tapline Refinery, Sidoun, Lebanon, 1977-78; grad. tchr./rsch. asst. La. Tech. U., Ruston, 1982-89; instr. United Arab Emirates U., Al-Ain, 1989-94; asst. prof. Kuwait U., Kuwait, 1994-99, assoc. prof., 1999—; cons. in field. Contbr. articles to profl. jours. Grantee Kuwait U. Rsch. Coun., 1996-98. Mem. Soc. Petroleum Engrs., La. Tech. Alumni Assn., Petroleum Engrs. HOnor Soc., Math. Honor Soc. Avocations: swimming, tennis, reading, research. Fax: (865) 4849558. E-mail: nashawi@kuc01.kuniv.edu.kw. Office: Kuwait U Coll Engring, PO Box 5969, Safat 13060, Kuwait

NASHIDA, ATSUHIRO, astronautical science administrator. Dir. gen. Inst. of Space and Astronautical Sci., Sagamihara, Japan. Office: 3-1-1 Yoshinodai Sagamihara, Kanagawa 229, Japan*

NASIM, YOUSAF, executive; b. Pakistan, Apr. 26, 1953; s. Yusaf Mohammed Khan and Masuda Uisaf, Ambereen; children: Mehreen, Zain, Myra. BA, Punjab U., Pakistan. Co-pres. Manhattan Traders, Pakistan, 1979-89; pres. Internat. Bus. Bur., Pakistan, 1979-80; owner AMZ World Trade Venue, 1995—; bd. dirs. Pakistan Comml. exporters Towels Assn., vice chmn., 1988-89, mem. ctrl. exec. com., 1987-88, textile quota com., 1987-88. Avocations: swimming, walking.

NASIR, MOHAMMED, retired educator and diplomat; b. Basra, Iraq, Dec. 20, 1913; s. Nasir and Saliha Al-Othman; m. Laila Al-Alousy, Jan. 12, 1940 (dec. Nov. 1990); children: Aseel, Ali, Faisal, Farouk. BSc, Columbia U., 1936, MA, 1937, EdD, 1955. Tchr. Ministry of Edn., Baghdad, Iraq, 1937-45; cultural attache, permanent cultural rep. Iraqi Embassy and Arab League, Cairo, 1945-48; cultural attache Iraqi Consulate and Embassy, N.Y.C. and Washington, 1948-54; vis. prof. UCLA, 1954-55; prof. edn. Baghdad U., 1955-64; min. of edn. Baghdad, 1964; Iraqi amb. Moscow, 1964-65; min. of culture Baghdad, 1965-66; prof., chmn. dept. edn. Kuwait U., 1967-90; Iraqu i. Co-author: Civic Education, 1940; editor: Readings in Educational Thought, vol. 1, 1973, Readings in Arab Islamic Educational Thought, 1977; contbr. numerous articles in Arabic and English to various jours. Founding mem. Baghdad U., 1957-58; rep. of Iraq at numerous internat. confs., including UNESCO, ALECSO, UN; pres. Iraqi Tchrs. Union, 1961-62, 64; alt. del. UN Gen. Assembly, 1949. Muslim. Avocation: photography. Home: PO Box 6549 Mansur 12605, Baghdad Iraq

NASIRULLAH, MOHAMMED, port executive; b. Chittagong, Bangladesh, Jan. 18, 1945; s. Mohammed Salamatullah and Rezia (Begum) S.; m. Nazma Sultana, July 11, 1976; children: Rebecca, Monica, Farhana, Tamanna. HSC, Chittagong Coll., 1963; BS in Engring., Hiroshima U., 1969, MS in Engring., 1971. Profl. cert. ofcl., Japan; cert. quality control mgr., Japan. Lectr. Bangadesh U. of Engring. and Tech., Dhaka, 1972-73; factory engr. Glaxo, Chittagong, 1973; cons. A.K. Dockyard, Chittagong, 1974-75; adminstrv. officer Japan Drilling Co., Chittagong, 1975-76; supt. marine engr. Chittagong Port Authority, 1976-82, dep. chief engr. (marine), 1982—. Adviser Tritorongo, Chittagong, 1990—; v.p. Port Schs., 1995—. Recipient 3rd prize Internat. Speech Contest, Tokyo, 1965. Mem. Instn. Engrs., Chittagong Club, Assn. for Overseas Tech. Scholarship/Japan Alumni Soc. (v.p. 1995-97). Avocations: rsch. in towing tanks, ship design, gardening. Home: Bungalow #3 Officers Colony, Chittagong Port Authority, Chittagong Bangladesh Office: Dep Chief Engr/Marine, Chittagong Port Auth, Chittagong Bangladesh

NASKAR, SYAMAL, scientist; b. Calcutta, W Bengal, India, Oct. 2, 1967; s. Chandra Kanta and Phalguni N.; m. Shampa (Bag) Naskar, Oct. 28, 1999. B in Vet. Sc., BCKVV, 1990; MSC, NDRI, 1992, PhD, 1995. Scientist I.C.A.R., India, 1996—. Contbr. articles in profl. jours. Avocations: listening to Indian classical music. Office: ICAR Rsch Complex, Shampa Bag (Naskar), 793103 Shillong India

NASLEDOV, GRIGORY ALEXANDROVICH, laboratory administrator, muscle physiologist, educator; b. Leningrad, Russia, Oct. 11, 1928; s. Alexandr Nikolaevich and Lidia Grigorievna (Dain) N.; Nina Ivanovna Evsyunina, 1956 (div. 1959); 1 child, Alexandra Dubovskaja; m. Natalja Federovna Skorobovichuk, Dec. 26, 1961; 1 child, Dmitry. Grad., Leningrad U., St. Petersburg, Russia, 1951; Candidate, Pavlov Physiol. Inst., St. Petersburg, Russia, 1962; DSc, Cytological Inst., St. Petersburg, Russia, 1972. Lab. asst. Inst. Exptl. Medicine, St. Petersburg, 1951-53; aspirant Inst. Dentistry, St. Petersburg, 1953-55; rschr. Sechenov Inst. Evolutionary Physiology and Biochemistry, St. Petersburg, 1955-71, head lab. neuroregulation of muscle function, 1971—; mem. coun. for sci. degree awards Pavlov Physiol. Inst., 1979-85, Sechenov Inst. Evolution Physiology and Biochemistry, 1998—. Author, editor: The Development of Contractile Function in Muscles, 1974; author: Tonic Muscle System in Vertebrates, 1981. Recipient grant George Soros Found., Russia, 1994, 95. Mem. Russian Physiol. Soc. E-mail: nasledov@nasl.ief.spb.su. Office: Sechenov Inst Evol Phys/Bio, Thorez av 44, 194223 Saint Petersburg Russia

NÄSLUND, INGEMAR, fish biologist, researcher; b. Åsele, Lapland, Sweden, Sept. 3, 1957; s. Karl Lennart and Irma Aurora (Nilsson) N.; m. Kristina Maria Ericsson, July 11, 1987; children: Hanna, Johan, Per. MS, U. Umeå, 1981; PhD, Swedish U. Agrl. Scis., Umeå, 1991. Rsch. scientist U. Umeå, 1982-87; environ. adviser County Adminstrn., Östersund, 1987-88; rsch. scientist Nat. Bd. Fisheries, Kälarne, 1988-99; lectr. Mid-Sweden U., Östersund, 1997-99; environ. advisor County Adminstrn. Bd. Jamtland, Ostersund, Sweden, 1999—. Author: Modern Fiskevård, 1995; co-author: Ekologisk Fiskevård; editor: Fiske, Skogsbruk och Vattendrag; contbr. articles to profl. jours. Recipient scholarship Swedish Inst., 1989. Mem. Frösö Idrottsförening, Östersunds Flugfiskesällskap, Åsele Sportfiskeklubb. Avocations: sport fishing, skiing, sailing. Office: County Administrv, Bd Jamtland, SE 83186 Ostersund Sweden

NASO, VALERIE JOAN, automobile dealership executive, travel company operator, artist, photographer, writer; b. Stockton, Calif., Aug. 19, 1941; d. Alan Robert and Natalie Grace (Gardner) McKittrick Naso; m. Peter Joralemon, May 31, 1971 (div.). Student pub. schs., Piedmont, Calif. Cert. graphoanalyst. Pres., Naso Motor Co. (formerly Broadway Cadillacs, Oakland, Calif.) Bishop, Calif., 1964—; freelance artist, 1965—; owner, operator Wooden Horse Antiques, Bishop, 1970-82; editor, writer, photographer Sierra Life Mag., Bishop, 1980-83; freelance writer, photographer, 1972—; owner, operator Boredom Tours, Bishop, 1981—; owner, sole photographer, Renaissance Photography, N.Y.C. and Bishop, Calif., 1982—, Keyboard Colors, 1986; cons. graphoanalyst, 1976—. Fiction, non-fiction work pub. in Horse and Horseman, Am. Horseman, Horse & Rider Mag., Cameo Mag., Desert Mag., Sierra Life Mag. Mem. Nat. Assn. Female Execs., Authors Guild, Inc., Authors League Am., Am. Film Inst., Archives of Am. Art, Lalique Soc. Am., Musical Box Soc. Internat., Alliance Francaise (N.Y. chpt.), Bishop C. of C., Victorian Soc. Am., Nat. Trust for Hist. Preservation, Am. Craft Coun., Nat. Rifle Assn. Clubs: Cadillac LaSalle (nat. and so. calif. chpts.); Wagner Soc. (N.Y.C.). Office: 783 N Main St Bishop CA 93514-2427 also: PO Box 1625 Bishop CA 93515-1625

NASRI, AHMAD HACHEM, computer science educator, consultant, researcher; b. Talbibe, Lebanon, Dec. 15, 1956; s. Hachem A. and Jamile Y. (Chakouf) N.; m. Khalida A. Iali Nasri, Aug. 14, 1981; children: Souha, Hachem. BS, Lebanese U., Beirut, 1978; PhD, U. E. Anglia, Norwich, U.K., 1985. Asst. prof. Lebanese U., Lebanon, 1985-87, United Arab Emirates U., Al-Ain, 1987-92; asst. prof. Am. U. Beirut, Lebanon, 1992-97, assoc. prof., 1997—; rsch. engr. MIT, Boston, 1993; vis. rschr. Bremen (Germany) U., 1990; vis. prof. Ariz. State U., Tempe, 1994; vis. faculty Cambridge U., 1996. Contbr. rsch. articles to profl. jours. Recipient PhD scholarship Lebanese U., 1978, Educator's grant, ACM Siggraph, L.A., 1997, Educator's grant workshop, NSF, Atlanta, 1997. Mem. ACM, ACM Siggraph. Avocations: music, swimming, chess. Office: Am U Beirut, Bliss St, Beirut 11-236, Lebanon

NASSAR, AMIN, judge; s. Fares Nassar. Pres. Appeal Ct. of Mount Lebanon, Beirut. Named comdr. Patriarchal Cross of St. Peter the Apostle. Office: Cour de Cassation, Palais de Justice, Beirut Lebanon*

NASSAR, FARIS MICHAEL, physician, researcher; b. Nazareth, Galilee, Israel, Dec. 15, 1947; s. Michael Shafic and Naife Farah (Bishara) N.; m. Hala Elias Bathish, Feb. 12, 1978; children: Adi, Ala, Rima. MD summa cum laude, Sackler's Med. Sch., Tel Aviv, 1976. Intern Rambam U. Hosp., Haifa, Israel, 1972-73; resident dept. medicine Ctrl. Emek Hosp., Afula, Israel, 1973-78, sr. physician, 1979-84, dep. chief, 1984-92, 1st dep. chief, 1992-96, acting chief, 1996-98; chief dept. medicine Western Galilee Hosp., Nahariya, Israel; fellow Stanford U., 1992-94. Dep. Nazareth Med. Assn., 1989-92. Mem. Am. Soc. Microbiology. Achievements include research in human cytokines, anti-microbiological agent and chemotherapy and cellular immunology. Office: Western Galilee Hosp, Dept Medicine H, 22100 Nahariya Israel

NASSAR, MUNIR EMILE, retired cardiovascular physician; b. Lebanon, June 21, 1934; s. Emile G. and Hanai'l Nassar; m. Leila George, June 17, 1959; children: Ramzi, Rania. BSc, Am. U. Beirut, 1955, MD, 1959. Diplomate Am. Bd. Tropical Medicine, Am. Bd. Ambulatory Medicine. Pvt. practice cardiology and internal medicine, Beirut, 1966-75; assoc. cardiologist Am. U. Hosp. Med. Ctr. Faculty Medicine, Beirut, 1967-75; pvt. practice cardiology and internal medicine, Albion, N.Y., 1975-76, 78-86; cardiologist and internist VA Salisbury (N.C.) Med. Ctr., 1986-87, VA Western N.Y. Healthcare Network, Batavia and Rochester, 1987-98; ret., 1998; attending physician Arnold Gregory Hosp., Albion, 1975-76, 78-86. Author: The Stethoscopeless Cardiologist, 1988; also articles. Maj. USAFR, 1976-78. Fellow ACP; mem. AMA, Am. Coll. Cardiology, Royal Soc. Medicine. Presbyterian. Avocations: tennis, bridge, classical music, writing medical papers and poetry.

NASSAR, WILLIAM MICHAEL, lawyer; b. Methuen, Mass., June 5, 1958; s. William M. and Catherine M. Nassar; m. Ermelinda Amezcua, June 26, 1982; children: Brandon Michael, Elyse Renae. AAS, R.I. C.C., 1978; BSBA, U. Redlands, 1980; JD, Western State Coll. of Law, 1986. Legal adminstr. Bourns Inc., Riverside, Calif., 1988-90, dir. worldwide contracts adminstr., 1990-94, dir. worldwide contracts/legal counsel, 1994-97, sr. legal counsel, 1997-2000; v.p., gen. counsel Standard MEMS, Inc., Burlington, Mass., 1999—; bd. dirs. Advanced Med. Inc., Riverside, Calif., Global Pathways Inc., Riverside; v.p. Bourns Employees Fed. Credit Union, bd. dirs. Adv. bd. Ronald McDonald House, Loma Linda, Calif., 1994-98. Roman Catholic. Avocations: sailing, boating, skiing, reading. Home: 13015 Burns Ln Redlands CA 92373-7415 Office: 673 S Waterman Ave San Bernardino CA 92408-2329

NASSEHI, VAHID, chemical engineer, educator; b. Tabriz, Iran, Feb. 9, 1950; arrived in Wales, 1976; s. Karim Nassehi and Tahereh Farid; m. Kereshmeh Shahbandi, Dec. 2, 1975; 1 child, Roshanak Nassehi. MSc in Chem. Engring., Tehran (Iran) U., 1974; MSc, U. Wales, Swansea, 1978, PhD, 1981. Rsch. officer Oil Svc. Co. Iran, Ahwaz, 1976; sr. rsch. asst. U. Swansea, Swansea, 1981-86; sr. lectr. U. Tesside, Cleveland, 1986-89, Loughrorough (Eng.) U., 1989—; cons. UN, N.Y.C., 1992; sci. advisor Polymer Rsch. Ctr. Iran, Tehran, 1993—. Contbr. articles to profl. jours. Home: 11 Oakland Ave, Loughborough LE11 3JF, England Office: Loughborough U, Ashby Rd, Loughborough LE11 3TU, England

NASSER, JACQUES, automotive company executive; b. Dec. 12, 1947; Australian citizen; Degree in Bus. Studies, Royal Melbourne Inst. Tech. With Ford of Australia, 1968-73; mem. fin. staff N.Am. Truck ops. Ford Motor Co., 1973; mgr. profit analysis, mgr. product programming Ford Motor Co., Australia, 1973-75; various positions Internat. Automotive ops. Ford Motor Co., from 1975, with Asia-Pacific and Latin-Am. ops., 1970s and 80s; dir., vp.. fin. and adminstrn. Autolatina joint venture Brazil and Argentina, 1987-90; pres., CEO Ford of Australia, 1990-93; chmn. Ford of Europe Fort Motor Co., 1993-96; v.p Ford Motor Co., 1993-96, chmn. Ford of Europe, pres. Fort Automotive ops., exec. v.p., 1996—; pres., CEO Ford Motor Co., Detroit, 1999—. Office: Ford Motor Co American Rd Dearborn MI 48121-1899

NASSER, MAHMOOD MOHAMMED KHALIL, electrical engineer, researcher; b. Manama, Bahrain, Aug. 15, 1968; s. Mohammed Khalil and Zainab Yaqoub (Al-Basri) N.; m. Yoko Sayed Mahmood, Niov. 16, 1998. BSc in Elec. Engring., Bahrain U., 1994; MSc in Elec. Engring., Saga (Japan) U., 1997, PhD in Elec. Engring., 1997—. Trainee engr. Min. of Power and Work, Bahrain, 1992, Yokogawa, Tokyo, 1993; engr. Batelco, Manama, 1994-95; part-time rsch. assoc. Saga U., 1997-2000, profl. rsch. assoc. dept. elec. engring., 2000—. Contbr. articles to profl. jours.; inventor in field. Banigas grantee, 1992; recipient Young Sci. prize Japan Soc. Applied Physics, 2000. Mem. Am. Phys. Soc., Soc. Applied Physics Japan (Young Scientist prize 2000), Inst. Elec. Engrs. Japan. Avocations: reading, fishing, music, travel. Office: Saga Univ, Honjo Machi 1, Saga 840-8502, Japan

NASSER, MOES ROSHANALI, optometrist; b. Sumve, Mwanza, Tanzania, Jan. 20, 1956; came to U.S., 1976; s. Roshanali Hassanali and Rehmat (Kara) N.; m. Anar Hemnani, Dec. 20, 1979; children: Faria, Sarah. BS in Optometry, U. Houston, 1980, OD, 1982. Cons., mgr. optometric practice Houston, 1984—; mem. adv. bd. Houston Eye Assocs.; cons. in field. Vol. Agakhan Ch., Tanzania, 1966-71; sec. Agakhan Ch. health com., 1976-82, mem. ch. coun., Houston, 1981-82, mem. coun. for S.W., 1987-90, chmn. edn. bd. for Southwest, 1987-90, Agakhan Found.; hon. sec. Shia Imami Ismaili Tarigah and Religious Edn. Bd. U.S., 1990-93, chmn. Southwestern U.S., 1996—; convenor S.W. U.S.A. for Inst. of Ismaili Studies, London. Mem. Harris County Optometric Soc., Tex. Optometric Assn., Tex. Assn. for Optometrists, Am. Optometric Assn., Alta. Optometric Assn., Can. Assn. Optometrists. Avocations: tennis, volleyball, reading. Office: 1524 Willowbrook Mall Houston TX 77070-5715

NASSERI, SIMIN, researcher; b. Kerman, Iran, Feb. 12, 1963; d. Masha-Alah and Aghdass (Kamalian) N.; m. Mohammad Jonaidi, Nov. 14, 1986; 1 child, Yassaman. BSc in mech. engring., Iran Univ. Sc. & Tech., Tehran, Iran, 1987, MSc in mech. engring., 1992; PhD in mech. engring., Sydney Univ., Sydney, Australia, 1997. Die designer Universal Factory, Tehran, 1987-89; design engr. Mahab Ghodss/Acres Gen. Partnership Cons. Engr. Co., Tehran, 1992-93; project mgr. Mahab Ghodss Acres Co., Tehran, 1992-93; post doctoral fellow Sydney U., 1997—; die mfg. controller Universal Co., Tehran, 1987-88. Contbr. articles to profl. jours. Recipient Australian Rsch. grant Sydney Univ., 1995. Mem. ASME. Avocations: painting, sculpture, reading books. Office: Mech and Mechatronic Engring Dept Sydney Univ, 2006 Sydney Australia

NASSIM, MICHAEL ARNOLD, clinical pharmacologist; b. London, Dec. 10, 1942; s. Joseph Reginald and Dorothy MacLeod (Manning) N.; m. Delia

Mary Glasgow, Oct. 9, 1971. BSc in Physiology, Oxford U., MA in Physiology, BM BCh. Lectr. nephrology Inst. Urology, London, 1977-81; sr. clin. pharmacologist Fisons PLC, Eng., 1982-95, Astra Charnwood Pharms., Loughborough, Eng., 1995—. Inventor/patentee in field; contbr. articles to profl. jours. Mem. Royal Coll. Physicians, Assn. Human Pharmacology. Avocations: music, antique restoration.

NAST, DIANNE MARTHA, lawyer; b. Mount Holly, N.J., Jan. 30, 1948; d. Henry Daniel and Anastasia (Lovenduski) N.; m. Joseph Francis Roda, Aug. 23, 1980; children: Michael, Daniel, Joseph, Joshua, Anastasia. BA, Pa. State U.; JD, Rutgers U., 1976. Bar: Pa. 1976, U.S. Dist. Ct. Pa. 1976, N.J. 1976, U.S. Dist. Ct. N.J. 1976, U.S. Ct. Appeals (3d, 5th, 6th, 7th, 8th and 11th cirs.) 1976, U.S. Supreme Ct. 1982, U.S. Dist. Ct. Ariz. 1985. Dir., v.p. Kohn, Nast & Graf, P.C., Phila., 1976-95, Roda & Nast, P.C., Lancaster, Pa., 1995—; mem. lawyers adv. com. U.S. Ct. Appeals (3d cir.), 1982-84, chmn., 1983-84, mem. com. on revision jud. conf. conduct rules, 1982-84; mem. U.S. Ct. Appeals for the 3d Cir. Jud. Conf. Permanent Planning Com., 1983-90; bd. dirs. 3d Cir. Hist. Soc., 1993—; bd. dirs. Phila. Pub. Def., 1980-89; dir. U.S. Fed. Judicial Ctr. Found., 1991—, chair, 1996—; chmn. lawyers adv. com. U.S. Dist. Ct. (ea. dist.) Pa., 1982-90. Pres. Hist. Soc., 1988-91. Fellow ABA (coun. litigation sect. 1986-89, co-chmn. anti-trust com. litigation sect. 1984-86, div. dir. 1990-91, practical litigation editl. bd. 1989—, ho. of dels. 1992-94, mem. task force state justice initiatives, mem. task force state of justice system. 1993, mem. task force long range planning com. 1994), Am. Law Inst. (chair internat. professionalism com. 1991-94, civil justice task force 1993-95), Am. Arbitration Assn. (bd. dirs., mem. alt. dispute resolution and mass torts task force), Am. Judicature Soc., Pa. Bar Assn. (bd. of dels. 1983-95), N.J. Bar Assn., Pa. Trial Lawyers Assn., Phila. Bar Assn. (bd. govs. 1985-87, chmn., bicentennial com. 1986-87, chmn. bench bar conf. 1988-89), Lancaster Bar Assn. (co-chair civil litigation and rules com. trial law sect.), Rutgers Law Sch. Alumni Assn. Home: 1059 Sylvan Rd Lancaster PA 17601-1923 Office: Roda & Nast PC 801 Estelle Dr Lancaster PA 17601-2130

NAST, EDWARD PAUL, cardiac surgeon; b. Balt., Dec. 13, 1958; s. Richard Cecil and Lenora (Heilig) N.; m. Sandye Hammerman, June 3, 1984; 1 child, Bennett Ross. BS, Emory U., 1979; MD, U. Md., 1984. Diplomate Am. Bd. Thoracic Surgery, Am. Bd. Surgery. Intern Georgetown U. Med. Ctr., Washington, 1984-85, resident in gen. surgery, 1985-86, 88-91; resident in thoracic and cardiovascular surgery U. Md. Med. Sys., Balt., 1991-93; fellow in cardiac surgery NIH, Bethesda, Md., 1986-88; cardiac surgeon St. Joseph's Cardiac Surgery Assocs., P.C., Syracuse, N.Y., 1993—. Contbr. articles to profl. jours. Named one of Outstanding Young Men of Am., 1996, 98. Fellow ACS, Am. Coll. Cardiology, Am. Coll. Chest Physicians; mem. AMA, Med. Soc. State N.Y., Soc. Thoracic Surgeons, Phi Beta Kappa. Office: St Josephs Cardiac Surgery 101 Union Ave # 813 Syracuse NY 13203-2761

NASTAC, LAURENTIU, materials and metallurgy engineer; b. Bucharest, Romania; came to US, 1991; m. Mihaela Nicoleta Nastac; children: Gabriel Cristian, Michael Lucian. Diploma in engrnig., U. Poly., Bucharest, 1985; MS in Metall. and Materials Engring., U. Ala., 1993, PhD in Metall. and Materials Engring., 1995. Project mgmt. cert. Concurrent Techs. Corp. Plant metall. engr. Fine Mechanisms Unit, Spl. Foundry, Sinaia, Romania, 1985-87; jr. rschr. Inst. for Hot Processes, Bucharest, 1987-89, sr. rschr., 1989-90; asst. prof. dept. metall. and materials engring. U. Poly., Bucharest, 1990-91; grad. rsch. asst. dept. metall. and materials engring. U. Ala. Solidification Lab., Tuscaloosa, 1991-94; cons., co-investigator Automated Techs. Corp., Peoria, Ill., 1991-94, project engr., 1994-96; sr. tech. staff Concurrent Techs. Corp., Johnstown, Pa., 1996-99, prin. process modeling engr., 1999—; cons. Caterpillar, Inc., Peoria; co-investigator NASA, Huntsville, Ala. Contbr. articles to profl. jours. Recipient Bunshah Best Paper award Am. Vacuum Soc. Vacuum Metallurgy Divsn., Santa Fe, 1999; Spain-Hickman scholar Rotary Internat., Tuscaloosa, 1993; Sullivan, Long and Hagerty Endowed fellow U. Ala., Tuscaloosa, 1993. Mem. Am. Foundrymen's Soc., The Materials Soc., Am. Soc. Metals, Sigma Xi. Achievements include patent in field. Avocations: skiing, chess, traveling, tennis. E-mail: nastac@hotmail.com and nastac@ctc.com. Fax: (412) 577-2660. Home: 1006 Arbutus Vlg Apt C26 Johnstown PA 15904-3743 Office: Concurrent Techs Corp Royal Enterprise Tower 425 6th Ave 28th Fl Pittsburgh PA 15219

NASU, KENICHI, engineering educator; b. Fukui, Japan, Aug. 29, 1949; s. Shinichiro and Tazuko Nasu; m. Kyoko Iwata, Jan. 10, 1984; children: Kento, Masato, Erika. Bachelor degree, U. Tokyo, 1973, M of Engring., 1976, D of Engring., 1983. Engr. Fujitsu Ltd., Tokyo, 1976-80; sr. rsch. assoc. Nat. Rsch. Coun. NASA Ames Rsch. Ctr., Mountain View, Calif., 1984-86; rsch. engr. Sigma Optical Co., Saitama, Japan, 1988, Rsch. Ctr. Computational Mechanics, Tokyo, 1988-90; assoc. prof. U. Ryukyus, Okinawa, Japan, 1990—. Mem. ASME, AIAA, Japan Soc. Aero. and Space Scis., Japan Soc. Mech. Engrs. Avocations: skiing, swimming, jogging. Home: 1-141-1-202 Shuri-Yamagawa Naha, Okinawa 903-0825, Japan Office: U Ryukyus, Senbaru 1, Nishihara Okinawa 903-0213, Japan

NASU, SHOICHI, electrical engineering educator; b. Sendai-Shi, Miyagi-Ken, Japan, July 10, 1933; s. Nobuyuki and Yuri N.; m. Masako Hoshinami, Oct. 8, 1967; children: Masayuki, Akiko. BS, Kyoto U., Japan, 1959, DSc, 1967. Chief fuel property lab. Japan Atomic Energy Rsch. Inst., Tokai, Ibaraki, Japan, 1960-81; rsch. assoc. U. Pitts., 1969-70; exec. dir., gen. mgr. rsch. and devel. Ushio Inc., Tokyo, 1981-91, cons., 1991; prof. divsn. materials sci. Kanazawa Inst. Tech., Japan, 1992—, dir. Advanced Optical Electro Magnetic Fild Sci. Lab., 1999—; mem. internat. adv. com. Internat. Symposium in Electronic Structure of Actinides, Argonne, Ill., 1973-74; Japanese del. IAEA Advising Group, Vienna, Austria, 1979. Japanese compiler of Actinides News Letters, 1976-80; contbr. revs., handbooks and articles to profl. jours.; patentee in field. Mem. AAAS, Am. Phys. Soc. (life), Am. Assn. Physics Tchrs., Planetary Soc., Atomic Energy Soc. Japan (life), Laser Soc. Japan, Japan Soc. Applied Physics. Avocations: jogging, swimming, mountain climbing, golf. Home: Eminensu Kohto 301, Saiwai-cho 3-28, Kanazawa-shi 920-0968, Japan Office: Ohgigaoka 7-1 Nonoichi, Kanazawa Minami-kyoku, Ishikawa 921-8501, Japan

NASU, YUKIO, business educator; b. Nagoya, Aichi, Japan, Jan. 24, 1946; s. Sonosuke Kato and Sachiko Nasu; m. Kumiko Someno, Dec. 6, 1980 (div. June 1981). BA, Keio U., Tokyo, 1968, MA, 1970. Staff Mitsubishi Rsch. Inst., Inc., Tokyo, 1971-76, staff rschr., 1976-83, sr. staff rschr., 1983-93; prof. Nippon Bunri U., Oita, Japan, 1988—; database searcher 2d class Info. Sci. and Tech. Assn., Tokyo, 1985-87, database searcher 1st class, 1987—, tng. committeeman, 1987-88; committeeman Agrl. Goods Distbn. Com., Oita City, 1995-98. Author: Corporate Charm Management, 1996, Current Marketing, 1998, City Retailing Activities, 1999; contbr. articles to profl. jours. Rsch. grantee Shimabara Sci. Promotion Found., 1988, 91, Acad. Bus. and Econs., Nippon Bunri U., 1992. Mem. Am. Mktg. Assn., Am. Soc. Info. Sci., Acad. Mgmt. Philosophy (internat. dir. 1990-96), Creative Tech. Study Assn. (chair Oita chpt. 1990—), Oita C. of C. and Industry (com. vice-chmn. bus. activating com. 1997-98), Oita Y's Mens Club (acct. 1993-98, chair 2000—). Rinzai Shu in Buddhism. Avocations: telecommunications, singing songs, collecting coins and Japanese swords, reading historical books. Home: 271-8 Senzai Takajou, Oita-ken Oita 870-0132, Japan Office: Nippon Bunri U, 1727-162 Ichigi Oaza, Oita Oita-ken 870-0397, Japan

NÁSZ, ISTVÁN, microbiologist, educator, researcher; b. Turkeve, Hungary, Mar. 3, 1927; s. István and Julianna (Szabó) N.; m. Sarolta Albrecht, Aug. 2, 1954; 1 child, Ildikó. MD, Semmelweis U., Budapest, Hungary, 1951, PhD, 1955, DMS, 1964; D (hon.), Marquis Giuseppe Scicluna Internat. U., Miss., 1988. Mem. Inst. Microbiology, Semmelweis U. Med. Sch., 1948—, assoc. prof., 1961-69, prof. microbiology, 1969—, dir., 1974-94, prof. microbiology, 1994—; dep. dean Semmelweis U. Med. Sch., 1970-73, vice rector, 1973-79. Author: Adenoviruses and Their Pathogenic Role, 1967 (Nivo prize 1972), Microbiology, 1974, Medical Microbiology, Immunology and Parasitology, 1978, 2d edit., 1983, Microbiology and Immunology, 1982, Clinical Microbiology, 1988, Medical Microbiology, 1993; mem. editl. bd. Acta Virologica, Orvosi Hetilap, Internat. Adenovirus Study Group, Internat. Com. Taxonomy of Viruses, European Group for Rapid Viral Diagnosis; contbr. over 300 articles to profl. jours. Mem. Metchnicoff Microbiol. Soc. Russia (hon.), Hungarian Acad. Scis. (med. sect. v.p. 1980-90, pres. microbiol. com., editor-in-chief Acta Microbiologica et Immunologica, 1980—, Manninger medal 1982, Markusovszki prize 1998, Szechenyi prize 1998, Man of the Yr. 1997). Avocation: viniculture. Home: Eromu u 8, H-1117 Budapest Hungary Office: Microbiol Inst, Nagyvarad ter 4, H-1089 Budapest Hungary

NASZÁLYI, BARON PHILIPPE JACQUES, economics educator, publication director; b. Savigny, Orge, France, Apr. 7, 1955; s. François and Monique (Moine) N. BA in History, Sorbonne U., Paris, 1976, MA in History, 1977, BA in Lit., 1978, PhD in History, 1982. Cert. tchr. capes and agregation. Tchr. St. Charles Coll., Athis-Mons, France, 1981-93; dep. dir. Jeanne d'Arc Sch., Bretigny, France, 1983-84; lectr. Justice Ministry, Paris, 1988-92; prof. C. of C. EGC, Evry, France, 1994-95; prof. econs. U. Evry, Telecomms. Nat. Inst., 1995—; dir. mgmt. master dept. CFA U. Evry; dir. Direction et Gestion La Revue des Scis. de Gestion, Epinay sur Orge, France, 1990—; v.p. Credit Mutuel Bank, Epinay Sur Orge, 1981-86, chmn. bd., 1986-89, 92-93, fed. adminstr., 1986-89; mgmt. Nat. Inst. Telecoms. Evry. Author: Computers for Everyone, 1985, Guide du Pélerin de Compostelle, 1989, L'Euro, APE, PUF, 1997, L'Hôpital et la Santé publique, APE, 1998, Investment in China, AFPA, 1999, editor-in-chief Politique et Technologies, Paris, 1986-89. Councillor City Coun., Epinay Sur Orge, 1983-95. Recipient 2nd prize on French revolution Regional Coun. of Ile de France, 1989; Bronze Medal of Essonne, 1989, Mot d'or du Français des Affaires, 1996. Mem. Syndicate of Econ. Press (exec. com. 1992—), Fedn. of Press (exec. com. 1992—), Assn. Press et Enseignement (asst. gen. sec. 1996), Malta Order, Computer Mgmt. Assn. (founding pres. 1980-93), Alumni Club (pres. 1978-89, 92-93). Roman Catholic. Avocation: resting in the country. Home: 31 Rue de L'Esplanade, F 91360 Epinay Sur Orge France Office: Direction et Gestion, BP 49, F 91360 Epinay Sur Orge France

NASZLADY, ATTILA JANOS, physician, educator; b. Budapest, Hungary, Nov. 4, 1931; s. Janos and Maria (Piroska Karacsony) N.; m. Eva Csuros, Aug. 27, 1960; children: Agnes, Janos, Geraldin. MD, Semmelweis U., Budapest, 1958; PhD, Hungarian Acad. Scis., Budapest, 1967, D, 1979. Diplomate in medicine and cardiology; cert. spl. expert in computer application. Resident physician Mcpl. Hosp., Esztergom, Hungary, 1958-60; rsch. fellow Nat. Inst. Cardiology, Budapest, 1960-64; asst. prof. 4th Med. Clinic of Semmelweis U., Budapest, 1964-70; hon. prof. 4th Med Clinic of Semmelweis U., Budapest, 1980; head cardiopulmonary dept. Nat. Inst. Pulmonology, Budapest, 1970-96, ctrl. dir., 1992-95; med. gen. dir. Malthese Charity Svc. Hungary, Budapest, 1996—; ctrl. dir. Hospitaller Bros. of St. John of God Polyclinic, Budapest, 2000—; cons. Coll. Cardiology Hungary, 1985—, Coll. Pulmonology Hungary, 1990-96, Coll. Med. Informatics Hungary, 1990—; nat. rep. Internat. Measurement Confedn., 1985—. Co-author: Diagnostics in Medicine, 1983, 89, Textbook of Internal Medicine, 1986, Congenital Heart Diseases, 1983, 96, also monographs; editor: Health Care Informatics in Hungary, 1985; editor-in-chief Cardiologia Hungarica; mem. editorial bd. Medicina Thoracalis, 1985—; contbr. more than 120 articles to internat. and domestic jours.; patentee Saninform Memory Chip System. Ministerial commr. Ministry of Welfare, Hungary, 1992; rep. Social Security, 1993—. Recipient Acad. prize Hungarian Acad. Scis., 1974, 78; named Eminent Physician, Ministry of Welfare, Hungary, 1991, Eminent Univ. Tchr., 1988; WHO fellow, 1969, 80-90; knighted Ordo Equestris Sancti Sepulchri Hierosolymitani, 1993. Mem. Hungarian Soc. Cardiologists (bd. dirs. 1984—), Hungarian Soc. Pulmonologists (bd. dirs. 1980-96), J. von Neumann Soc. for Computer Scis. (pres. biomed. sect.), European Fedn. for Med. Informatics (v.p. 1996—, pres. 1998-2000), Internat. Med. Informatics Assn. (v.p. 2000—), Pontificia Acad. Tiberina, Ctrl. Sport Office Club. Avocations: tennis, table tennis, sculpturing.

NATALONI, ANDREW HECTOR, obstetrician, gynecologist; b. Bologna, Italy, Feb. 24, 1955; s. Marino and Faustina (Minarelli) N.; m. Zeinab Fathel-Bab. MD, U. Bologna, 1981. Intern Flushing Hosp. and Med. Ctr., N.Y.C., 1981-82, resident in ob-gyn., 1982-85, chief resident in ob-gyn., 1984-85; full attending staff Ctrl. Suffolk Hosp., Riverhead, N.Y., 1985—, chmn. dept. ob-gyn., 1991—, also bd. dirs.; bd. dirs. Peconic Health Corp., Riverhead. Mem. AAAS, N.Y. State Med. Soc., N.Y. State Soc. Ob-Gyn., N.Y. Acad. Scis., Suffolk County Med. Soc. Office: Central Suffolk Hosp 1333 Roanoke Ave Riverhead NY 11901-2029

NATARAJAN, ARUNA, physician, educator, researcher; b. Madras, Tamilnadu, India, Nov. 5, 1960; came to U.S., 1994; d. R. and Bama N.; m. Rajiv N. Sheth, July 12, 1998. BS, MB, Armed Forces Med. Coll., Poona, Maharashtra, India, 1984. Diplomate Am. Bd. Pediatrics. Chief resident, instr. Dartmouth Med. Sch., Hanover, N.H., 1995-96; fellow pediat. intensive care U. Tex. Southwestern Med. Ctr., Dallas, 1996-99; asst. prof. pediat. Georgetown U. Med. Ctr., Washington, 1999—. Contbr. author: Clinics in Primary Care, 1995. Mem. Soc. Critical Care Medicine. Avocations: reading, writing, listening to Indian classical music. E-mail: AN5@gunet.georgetown.edu. Office: Georgetown U Med Ctr CCC Bldg Rm 5414 #800 Reservior Rd Washington DC 20007

NATCHEFF, NATCHO DONKOFF, physiologist; b. Sofia, Bulgaria, May 2, 1922; s. Josifoff Donko Natcheff and Tina Diankova (Kovatcheva) Natcheva; m. Milka Todorva Angelova, Mar. 5, 1950; 1 child, Doriana. MD, Univ. Med. Faculty, 1947; PhD, Med. Faculty Med. Acad., 1961. Asst. prof. Dept. Physiology, Med. Faculty, Sofia, Bulgaria, 1947-61, assoc. prof., 1961-69, prof., 1969—, head dept. physiology, med. faculty, 1965-81; head of sect. Dept. Physiology, Med. Faculty, Sofia, 1965-88, cons. prof., 1988—; dep. dir. Medico-Biol. Inst., Sofia, 1975-77, dep. rector Higher Med. Inst., Sofia, 1981-86; mem. exec. com. Bulgarian Soc. Physiology, 1965-72. Editor/author: Kidney and Body Fluids, 1968 (Award 1969), Hypothalamus, 1990, Physiology Regul. of the Basic Life Processes, 1987, Physiology for Medical Students, 1985 (Award 1986). Grant State Dept., 1966. Mem. Hungarian Soc. of Physiology (hon. mem.), German Soc. of Nephrology, Union of Scientific Med. Socs. of Bulgaria (hon. pres.), Exec. Com. Internat. Organ. Med. Sci., Bulgarian League Hypertension, Bulgarian Acad. Medicine. Orthodox. Avocation: amateur photography. Home: Svilenitza 14/G, 1463 Sofia Bulgaria Office: Dept Physiology Med Faculty, 1431 Sofia Bulgaria

NATELLO, GREGORY WILLIAM, cardiologist, educator; b. Phila., Mar. 30, 1954; s. Americo Vespucci and Catherine (Logan) N.; m. Judy Marie Cutcliffe; children: Logan Angelina, Connolly Claire. AB in Biology, Gettysburg COll., 1976; DO, Phila. Coll. Osteo. Medicine, 1980. Diplomate Nat. Bd. Examiners, in internal medicine, geriatric medicine, cardiovascular disease, interventional cardiology Am. Bd. Internal Medicine. Intern Detroit Osteo. Hosp., 1980-81; gen. practice medicine Pennsauken, N.J., 1981-82; resident in internal medicine Cleve. Clinic Found., 1982-85; fellow in geriatrics Case Western Res. U., Cleve., 1985-86; assoc. in cardiovascular disease U. Ala., Birmingham, 1986-89; fellow in interventional cardiology Thomas Jefferson U., Phila., 1989-91; instr. phys. diagnosis Case Western Res. U., 1984-85; asst. prof. medicine, dir. labs. cardiac catheterization U. Mo., Columbia, 1991-93; asst. prof. medicine U. Tenn., Chattanooga, 1993-96; assoc. West Fla. Med. Ctr. Clinc, P.A., 1996-99, CardioVascular Assocs., P.C., Birmingham, Ala., 1999—; cardiology cons. Dept. athletics U. Mo.-Columbia, 1991-93, U. Tenn., Chattanooga, 1993-96, co-leader heart failure continuous quality improvement team, 1995-96; mem. sleep disorders com. and quality assurance com. W. Fla. Med. Ctr. Clinic, 1997-99; bd. dirs. Prin. Healthcare Fla., 1997-99. Contbr. articles to profl. jours. Recipient award of Merit for Outstanding Achievement, Detroit Osteo. Hosp., 1981, Disting. Sr. Resident award Cleve. Clinic Found., 1985. Fellow Am. Coll. Cardiology; mem. AMA, Am. Heart Assn. (bd. dirs. Escambia unit 1997-99), Phila. Coll. Osteo. Medicine Alumni Assn. (life), Eisenhower Soc. Gettysburg, Fla. Osteo. Med. Assn. (pres. dist. I 1997-99), Jefferson Med. Coll. Alumni Assn., Phi Kappa Psi. Republican. Episcopalian. Fax: 205-425-0118.

NATH, KAMALA KANTA, meteorologist, researcher, educator; b. Jorhat, Assam, India, Mar. 1, 1952; s. Phanidhar and Faguni N.; m. Swapna Jyoti Devi, May 6, 1985; 2 children. BS, Dibrugar (India) U., 1971; MS, Gauhati (India) U., 1973; Post Grad. Diploma Instrument, Kurukshetra (India) U., 1979; PhD, Indian Agrl. Rsch. Inst., New Delhi, 1986. Lectr. Assam Agrl. U., Jorhat, India, 1974-75, asst. prof., 1975-86, assoc. prof., 1986-95, prof., 1995—. Avocations: reading and writing scientific articles, attending religious functions. Home: No-1 Sonarigaon Tarajan, 785001 Jorhat Assam, India Office: Assam Agrl U, 785013 Jorhat Assam, India

NATH, NARENDRA, physics educator; b. Lahore, India, Dec. 13, 1932; s. Raghbir Sahai and Shanti (Devi) Mathur; m. Pratibha Mathur, Feb. 15, 1966; children: Charu, Ruchi. BSc with Honors, U. Delhi, 1951, MSc, 1953, PhD, 1961. Bartol fellow Franklin Inst. Bartol Rsch. Found., Swarthmore, Pa., 1957-59; rsch. assoc. La. State U., Baton Rouge, 1959-60, U.K. Atomic Energy Rsch. Establishment, Harwell, Eng., 1962-64; reader in physics Banaras Hindu U., Varanasi, India, 1964-70; sr. fgn. scientist U.S. Nat. Sci. Found., Washington, 1971-72; prof. physics Kurukshetra (India) U., 1970-92; emeritus fellow U. Grants Commn., New Delhi, 1993-95; guest faculty U. Hyderabad, India, 1996; pool officer Coun. of Scientific and Indsl. Rsch., New Delhi, 1961-62; vis. prof. Brigham Young U., Provo, 1971-72; head of physics dept., dean faculty sci. Kurukshetra U., 1970-71, 72-82, 73-76. Editor: Horizons of Physics, 1996; contbr. numerous articles to profl. jours.; patentee in field. Mem. Internat. Radiation Physics Soc., Instruments Soc. of India (life), Indian Soc. of Radiation Physics (v.p.), Sigma Pi Sigma. Hindu. Avocations: writing articles, walking, meditation, traveling. Home: 259 Sector 7 Urban Estate, Kurukshetra 136118, India Office: Nuclear Sci Ctr, Aruna Asaf Ali Marg, New Delhi 110067, India

NATH, RAVI, lawyer; b. New Delhi, Dec. 16, 1944; s. Rameshwar and Vidyawati; m. Madhu Sogani, Nov. 30; children: Nikhil, Chaiara. B Commerce with honors, Delhi (India) U., LLB, 1966; postgrad., Kings Coll., London, 1967; PIL, Harvard U., 1979. Bar: India. Trainee Sinclair, Roche & Temperly, London; assoc. Rajinder Narain & Co., New Delhi, 1967, ptnr., sr. ptnr. Co-author: Aircraft Finance and Securitisation; contbr. articles to profl. jours. Mem. Coun. Representing India, 1996-99; pres. Delhi Midtown Rotary Club, New Delhi, 1993-94. Mem. World Trade Law Assn. (mem. governing coun.), Internat. Bar Assn., Supreme Ct. Bar Assn. India, India Internat. Ctr., Delhi Golf Club, Polo Club New Delhi, Oriental Club. Avocations: golf, reading, squash, horseback riding. Home: Maulseri House, 7 Kapashera Estate, New Delhi 1100037, India Office: 14 F Connaught Pl, New Delhi India

NATHAN, LAURA E., sociology educator; b. L.A., Oct. 28, 1951; d. Monroe and Sheila (Solomon) Engelberg; m. Mark D. Nathan, April 9, 1978; children: Justin, Michael. BA in Sociology, U. Calif., Santa Barbara, 1973; MA in Sociology, U. Calif., L.A., 1975, PhD in Sociology, 1981. Teaching assoc. in sociology Univ. Calif., L.A., 1975-76; acting asst. prof. sociology Calif. State Univ., Fullerton, Calif., 1977-81; coord., instr. Univ. Calif., L.A., 1979-80; assoc. prof. sociology and psychology Antelope Valley Coll., Lancaster, Calif., 1981-82; asst. prof. sociology Mills Coll., Oakland, Calif., 1982-87; assoc. prof. sociology Mills Coll., Oakland, 1987-93; prof. of sociology Mills Coll., Oakland, Calif., 1993—, Robert J. and Ann B. Wert prof. of sociology, 1993-96; lectr. in sociology and womens studies Calif. State Univ., Long Beach, 1978; program evaluator U.S. Dept. Health, Edn. and Welfare, L.A., 1974-75, program dir. 1975-76; mem. conf. planning com. Womens Leadership Conf., Mills Coll., also com. chair, 1992-93; bd. dirs. Am. Cancer Soc., Alameda County, Calif., 1985—. Author: (with others) Secondary Analysis of Survey Data, 1985; contbr. chpts. to books. Regents Rsch. grantee, 1979, Mellon Found. grantee, 1983, Faculty Devel. Rsch. grantee Mills. Coll., 1985, 86, 87, 90, 91, 94, 95l W.K. Kellogg Nat. fellow, 1988, Thornton Bradshaw Humanities fellow Claremont Grad. Sch., 1990, Graduate Leadership Am., 1997; recipient Disting. Leadership award Am. Cancer Soc., 1995, ten Broek Soc. award for Excellence in Teaching, 1996. Mem. Pacific Sociol. Assn. (mem. nominating com. 1985-88, mem. program com. 1995-96, exec. coun., 1997-99), Am. Sociol. Assn. (membership com. 1988-92, com. soc. and persons with disabilities 1997-99, chair), Soc. for the Study of Social Problems (chmn. poverty, class inequality div. 1987-88). Jewish. Avocations: traveling, mysteries, vol. work. Office: Mills Coll 5000 Macarthur Blvd Oakland CA 94613-1301

NATHAN, PHIL OVE, physicist; b. Copenhagen, Jan. 12, 1926; s. Frits and Amelie (Friedmann) N.; m. Marianne Wandall, Apr. 1956; children: Marietta, Camilla. MS, Tech. U. of Copenhagen, 1952; DSc, U. Copenhagen, 1964. Full prof. The Niels Bohr Inst. U. Copenhagen, 1970, inst. dir., 1971-75, 80-82; pres., rector The U. Copenhagen, 1982-93; prof. physics The Niels Bohr Inst., Copenhagen, 1994-96; chmn. The Danish UNESCO Commn., 1996-99. Editor: Taenk Ogvaelg, 1980, The Challenge of Nuclear Armanments, 1986, The Challenge of An Open World, 1989, Rescue 43-Xenophobia and Exile, 1993, (autobiography) My Own Ways, 1998, (with Henrik Smith) The Harmonic Enthusiasm, 1999, The Pow Einstein, 2000. Recipient E.E.C. Gad prize, 1969, Rosenkjaer prize Danish State Broadcasting System, 1974, Oersted medal, 1999; Niels Bohr grantee, 1969, Joergen Vedel Petersen grantee, 1987. Mem. Royal Danish Acad. Scis. and Letters, Danish Acad. Tech. Scis. Avocations: gardening, mathematics, theatre. Home: 144 Bernstorffsvej, 2900 Hellerup Denmark Office: The Niels Bohr Inst, 17 Blegdamsvej, 2100 Copenhagen Denmark

NATHAN, ROBERT BURTON, life insurance agent; b. Chgo., Aug. 7, 1917; s. Louis and Della (Lustgarden) N.; m. Shirley Caplan, Dec. 24, 1939; children: Richard A., Jill S., Lisbeth M. BS, Northwestern U., 1939. Founder, chmn. bd. Presdl. Life Ins. Co., 1959-65; pres. Consolidated Funding Corp., Chgo., 1968-82, Consolidated Assocs. Inc., Chgo., 1968-82; agt. Equitable Life Assurance Soc., Chgo., 1940-63, 70—; nat. sales cons. Equitable Life Assurance Soc., N.Y.C., 1970-74; co-founder, pres. Robert B. Nathan Assocs. Inc., Chgo., 1966—; pres. NEFS, Inc., Chgo., 1980—, also chmn. bd. dirs.; pres. SCN Inc., Chgo., 1981—, also chmn. bd. dirs. Author: (with others) Encyclopedia of Tax Procedure, 1956; contbr. articles to profl. jours. 1st lt., MAC, 1943-46. Mem. NALU, Assn. Advanced Life Underwriters, Anti-defamation League, Chgo. Assn. Life Underwriters, Million Dollar Round Table, Northmoor Country Club, The Standard Club. Avocation: tennis. Office: 600 Central Ave Ste 320 Highland Park IL 60035-5605

NATHAN, RODERIC JOHN, hydrologist, consultant; b. Melbourne, Australia, June 22, 1958; s. Jonathon and Joan Rewa (Crosswell) N.; m. Julienne Patricia Kinna, May 20, 1988; children: Daniel, Therese. Bachelor of Engring., U. Melbourne, 1980, PhD, 1990; diploma of Imperial Coll., U. London, 1985, MS, 1985. Engr. Cementation Internat. Engring. Ltd., London, 1981-84; hydrologist Gutteridge Haskins and Davey Pty Ltd., Melbourne, 1986-87; rsch. fellow U. Melbourne, 1987-90; sr. hydrologist Rural Water Commn., Melbourne, 1990-95; prin. hydrologist Sinclair Knight Merz, Melbourne, 1995—. Contbr. articles to profl. publs. including Australian Jour. Water Resources (G.N. Alexander medal 1992, 98), Instn. Engrs., Civil Engring. Transactions (W.H. Warren medal 1997), others. Fellow (hon.) U. Melbourne, 1999—. Mem. Instn. Engrs. Australia (sr., cert.), River Basin Mgmt. Soc. Home: 8 Pascoe Ave, VIC Bentleigh 3204, Australia Office: Sinclair Knight Merz, 590 Orrong Rd, Armdale VIC 3143, Australia

NATHAN, SAMANDAM SHANMUGA, principal, educational consultant; b. Trivandrum, Kerela, India, Jan. 24, 1958; s. Thiyakaraja Samandam and Shanmuga Sundari (Doraiswamy) Murthy; m. Sudarsana Rajagopal Nathan, Sept. 15, 1967; 1 child, Satvika. BA, Madras Christian Coll., Chennai, India, 1980; MA, Presidency Coll., Chennai, 1982; BEd, Madurai (India) Kamaraj U., 1988; MEd, Madras U., Chennai, 1998. Tchg. asst. NSS Schs., Tambaram, India, 1978-80; lectr. City Coll., Chennad, 1980-82; sub-editor Emerald Pubs., Chennai, 1983-84; vice prin. Durga Pub. Sch., Dachepalle, India, 1984-86, Bala Brindavan Sch., Chennai, 1986-88; prin. Vidya Mandir Adyar Sch., Chennai, 1988—; head examiner English Ctrl. Bd. Secondary Edn., New Delhi, 1992—; adv. mem. Gen. Vocat. Course, New Delhi, 1997—; cons. Resource Mgmt. in Schs., India, 1999; edn. cons. RVS Schs., Sholingur, India, 1999—, SRM Sch. Chennai, 1997—, Viuekanana Vidynaya, Tambaram, India, 1996—. Editor: An Anthology of Indo-Anglian Poetry. Recipient Pres. award for scouting Pres. India, 1976, Best Prin. award Nat. Inst. Info. Tech., 1998. Mem. Indian Soc. Applied Behavioral Scientists, Adminstrv. Staff Coll. India, Assn. Pvt. Schs. Conf. (v.p.). Hindu. Avocations: reading, gardening, carpentry, interior design. Home: 28/2 Thirumurthy St, Chennai 600017, India Office: Vidya Mandir Adayar, IV Main Rd, Chennai 600020, India

NATHANAEL, MUTHU PAUL, police officer; b. New Delhi, Sept. 16, 1951; s. Muthu and Raham (Reddy) Swamy; m. Snehlata Herbert, Dec. 27, 1979; children: Heber, Peter. BA, Delhi U., 1971. From dep. supt. police to

commandant Ctrl. Res. Police Force, Manipur, India, 1972-98; group comdr. Nat. Security Guard, Gurgaon, India, 1998—; pub. rels. officer Ctrl. Res. Police Force, 1985-90. Avocations: writing, reading, photography, travel, tourism.

NATHANSON, LINDA SUE, publisher, author, technical writer; b. Washington, Aug. 11, 1946; d. Nat and Edith (Weinstein) N.; m. James F. Barrett. BS, U. Md., 1969; MA, UCLA, 1970, PhD, 1975. Tng. dir. Rockland Research Inst., Orangeburg, N.Y., 1975-77; asst. prof. psychology SUNY, 1978-79; pres. Cabri Prodns., Inc., Ft. Lee, N.J., 1979-81; rsch. supr. Darcy, McManus & Masius, St. Louis, 1981-83; mgr. software tng., documentation On-Line Software Internat., Ft. Lee, 1983-85; pvt. practice Ft. Lee, 1985-87; founder, exec. dir. The Edin. Group, Inc., Gillette, N.J., 1987-98; founder, pres. Edin Books, Inc., Gillette, N.J., 1994—. Author: (with others) Psychological Testing: An Introduction to Tests and Measurements, 1988; (with S.J. Thayer) Interview with an Angel, 1997; (with S.J. Thayer) The Heart of Interview with an Angel, 1998; publ. A Funny Thing Happened at the Interview (G.F. Farrell), 1996, Angel Talk (R. Crystal), 1996; (audiobook with W. Barnes) I Built the Titanic: Past-Life Memories of a Master Shipbuilder, 1999, Thomas Andrews, Voyage into History, 2000; (audio book with W. Barnes and F. Baranowski) A Past-Life Interview with Titanic's Designer, 1999. Recipient Rsch. Svc. award 1978; Albert Einstein Coll. Medicine Research fellow, 1978-79. Jewish. Home and Office: 102 Sunrise Dr Gillette NJ 07933-1944

NATHOO, NARENDRA, neurosurgeon, consultant; b. Port Elizabeth, South Africa, June 11, 1965; s. Brijlall and Cecelia (Kathan) N.; m. Vimila Omagesvarie Athiemoolam, June 26, 1992; 1 child, Tayla. MBChB, Natal Med. Sch., Durban, South Africa, 1989. Intern Livingstone Hosp., Port Elizabeth, 1990, med. officer, 1991; registrar King Edward VIII, Durban, 1992; registrar Wentworth Hosp., Durban, 1992-97, cons., 1997—; mem. Prenatal Task Group, 1997. Contbr. articles to profl. jours. Recipient Rsch. grant Med. Rsch. Coun. South Africa, 1996, U. Natal, 1995. Fellow Coll. Surgeons South Africa; mem. Soc. Neurosurgeons South Africa, Pan African Assn. Neurological Socs., Pan African Assn. Neurol. Socs. (asst. treas.). Avocations: reading, squash, watching movies. Fax: 27 (31) 4612897. E-mail: nathoo@wwh.und.ac.za. Office: Dept Neurological Surgery, PO Jacobs, Durban 4026, South Africa

NATION, EARL KELVIN, mechanical engineer; b. Black River, Jamaica, Apr. 15, 1946; s. Roy Walter and Kathleen (Salmon) N.; m. Lorna Mae Morgan, June 2, 1984; children: Michael, Mark. Cert. in mech. engring., U. Tech., Jamaica, 1980. Millwright Alcan, Jamaica, 1965-71, technician, 1971-76, technician engr., 1976-88, rotary kiln maintenance specialist, 1976—, mech. engr., 1988—; mem. internat. skills group, Alcan, Jamaica, 1990—, internat. alumina plant start-up team, 1995; mem. plant audit team Alcan Internat. Alumina, Alunorte, Brazil, 1997. Author: Design & Maintenance of a Lime Plant, 1975. Mem. ASME. Avocations: reading, listening to music, driving, fishing, farming. Office: Alcan Jamaica Co PO, Kirkvine Jamaica

NATIONS, HOWARD LYNN, lawyer; b. Dalton, Ga., Jan. 9, 1938; s. Howard Lynn and Eva Earline (Armstrong) Lamb; m. Ella Lois Johnson, June 4, 1960 (div. Nov. 1976); children: Cynthia Lynn Nations Garcia, Angela Jean Gordon. BA, Florida State U., 1963; JD, Fla. State U., 1966. Bar: Tex. 1966; cert. trial atty. Tex. Bd. Legal Specialization. Assoc. Butler, Rice Cook & Knapp, Houston, 1966-71; pres. Nations & Cross, Houston, 1971—; v.p., dir., co-founder Ins. Corp. Am., Houston, 1972—; pres. Caplinger & Nations Galleries, Houston, 1973—, Nations Investment Corp., Houston, 1975—, NCM Trade Corp., Houston, 1975; v.p. Delher Am. Inc., Houston, 1975—; pres. Howard L. Nations, PC, Houston, 1971—, Trial Focus, Inc., 1995—; founder Nations Found.; adj. prof. So. Tex. Coll. Law, Houston, 1967—; speaker in field. Author: Structuring Settlements, 1987; co-author: Texas Workers' Compensation, 1988, (with others) The Anatomy of a Personal Injury Lawsuit, 3rd rev. edit. 1991; editor: Maximizing Damages in Wrongful Death and Personal Injury Litigation, 1985; contbr. articles to profl. jours. Chmn., trustee Nat. Coll. Advocacy, Washington, 1985-92. With M.I. Corps, U.S. Army, 1957-60. Fellow Tex. Bar Found., Houston Bar Found. (life); mem. ATLA (exec. com. 1991-95), Nat. Bd. Trial Advocacy (diplomate civil trial advocacy), So. Trial Lawyers Assn. (pres. 1994-95), Tex. Trial Lawyers Assn. (pres. 1992-93). Office: The Sterling Mansion 4515 Yoakum Blvd Houston TX 77006-5821

NATIVI, CRISTINA, chemist, educator; b. Florence, Italy, Apr. 10, 1961; d. Sergio Nativi and Rosalia Zanetti. BA in Chemistry, U. Florence, 1985, D in Chemistry, 1986. Postdoctoral rschr. U. Lausanne, Switzerland, 1986-89; rschr. CNR, Florence, 1989-92, U. Montreal, Can., 1992-93; rsch. scientist U. Florence, 1993—. Author: Synthesis of Sulfones, Sulfoxides and Related Cyclic Sulfides, 1994, O-glycosides in Medicinal Chemistry, 1998. Mem. ACS, Italian Chem. Soc. Avocations: traveling, reading. Office: U Florence, via Gino Capponi 9, I-50121 Florence Italy

NATORI, JEFFREY KAZUO, lawyer; b. Honolulu, Aug. 15, 1958; s. Shigeo and Gertrude Keiko (Miyamoto) N.; m. Eriko Sudo, June 24, 1989; children: Gemma Reina, Justin Kirika, Amy Julie. BA, Am. U., 1980; JD, Del. Law Sch., 1983; MBA, Drexel U., 1987; cert. completion, Japan-Am. Inst. Mgmt. Sci., Honolulu and Tokyo, 1986-87. Bar: Pa. 1983, U.S. Dist. Ct. (ea. dist) Pa. 1983, Hawaii, 1987, Japan 1999. Pvt. practice law Jeffrey K. Natori, Esquire, Phila., 1983-86; intern Seiko Instruments Inc., Tokyo, 1987; in-house counsel Chiyoda Corp., Yokohama, Japan, 1988-92; assoc. Cades Schutte Fleming & Wright, Honolulu, 1993-96; in-house counsel Chiyoda Corp., Tokyo, 1996-98; fgn. assoc. Takaishi Law Office, Tokyo, 1998; assoc. White & Case, Tokyo, 1998—. Mem. ABA (speaker, Hawaii state chair, regions divsn., Fidelity and Surety law com., tort and ins. practice sect. 1994-96), Internat. Bar Assn. (speaker), Inter-Pacific Bar Assn. (vice chair com. on internat. constrn. projects 1991-93, chair, 1993-95, com. coord. 1995-97), Lawasia (spkr.). Office: White & Case, 1-19-1 Kanda-Nishikicho, Chiyoda-ku Tokyo 101-0054, Japan

NATZKE, KIRK ROLAND, poet, author; b. Cedar Falls, Iowa, Sept. 13, 1943; s. Roland Felton Lange Natzke and Mae Clark Arnold; m. Vicki Gritton, June 30, 1973 (div. Oct. 1979). Student, U. No. Iowa, Cedar Falls, 1967-68, Elmhurst (Ill.) Coll., 1968-69, Hawkeye C.C., Waterloo, Iowa, 1969-70. Laborer John Deere Co., Waterloo, 1972-95; ret. Columnist Common Ground, 1999; editor Post-Modern Art, 1999—; author poetry: Human Spirituality, 1965-90; actor stage musical: "Hero," A Funny Thing, 1968. Charter dir. Cedar Falls Cmty. Playhouse, 1978-80, also budget dir. With U.S. Army, 1964-66. Christian Existentialist. Avocations: folk music, jazz, coffee. Home: 418 Cutler St Waterloo IA 50703-2452

NAU, WERNER MICHAEL, chemist; b. Fulda, Germany, May 22, 1968; s. Karl and Wilhelmine (Lotz) N.; m. Kerstin Staudt, Aug. 5, 1994; children: Merlin, Julia. MS, St. Francis Xavier U., Antigonish, Can., 1992; D, U. Wuerzburg, Germany, 1994. Rsch. assoc. U. Wuerzburg, Germany, 1992-94, U. Ottawa, Can., 1994-95; rschr. U. Basel, Switzerland, 1996-2000, prof., 2000—. Contbr. articles to profl. jours. Kekule fellow, 1992-94, Can. Internat. fellow, 1994-95, Liebig fellow, 1996-98, Profil fellow, 1998-2000; named James Chair Prof. St. Francis Xavier U., 1998; recipient Internat. Grammaticakis-Neumann prize, 1999. Mem. Assn. Deutscher Chem., European Photochemistry Assn., New Swiss Chem. Soc. Office: Inst Phys Chemistry, Klingelbergstrasse 80, CH-4056 Basel Switzerland

NAUCK, MATTHIAS ALEXANDER, internist; b. Köln, Germany, Oct. 20, 1961; s. Joachim and Gundela (Beyer) N.; m. Verena Marion Hahn, Mar. 16, 1990; children: Christian, Stephanie, Tobias. Degree, U. Freiburg, Karlsruhe, Germany, 1989, U. Freiburg, Karlsruhe, Germany, 1992. Specialist for lab. medicine, 1997. Asst. U. Freiburg, 1989-90, Ludwig-Maximilians U., München, 1990-91, Medizinisch Diegnotisches Institut, Freiburg, 1991-93; asst. in internal medicine U. Freiburg, 1993-94, asst. dept. clin. chemistry, 1991-99, asst. med. dir. dept. clin. chemistry, 1999—; vis. prof. Children's Hosp./Harvard Med. Sch., Boston, 1999; cons. Lab Consult GmbH, Denzlingen, Germany, 1998—. Contbr. articles to profl. jours. inventor in field. Mem. Deutsch Gesellschaft für Arteriosklerosforschung, German Soc. for Clin. Chemistry, German Soc. for Lab. Medicine, GTH (congress com. 1999—). Avocations: music, hiking, theatre, bicycling, skiing. Office: University Hosp Freiburg, Hugstetter Str 55, 79106 Freiburg Germany

NAUDZIUS, ALDONA KANAUKA, pianist, music educator; b. Kaunas, Lithuania, Sept. 18, 1933; came to U.S., 1949; d. Vincas and Ona (Razmaite) Kanauka; m. Victor K. Naudzius, Dec. 1961; children: Ingrid Aldona, Renata Victoria. BA, Bennington Coll., 1955; MA, Columbia U., 1957; EdD, U. Ill., 1983. Cert. music tchr., Ill., Ind., N.Y., Mass., social studies tchr., Ill., N.Y. Tchr. music Pub. Schs., N.Y., 1958-59, N.Y.C., 1959-62, East Chicago, Ind., 1963-67; tchr. piano Morton East H.S., Cicero, Ill., 1985-86; tchr. music De Lourdes Coll., Des Plaines, Ill., 1986, Chgo. Pub. Elem. Schs., 1989-94, Near North Metro H.S., Chgo., 1994-96, William Taft H.S., Chgo., 1996-98; pvt. piano tchr., 1998—; participant internat. piano seminars Graz, Austria, 1992, Lyon, France, 1994. Performer Nelita True's Master Class, Graz; piano soloist various cmty. functions, N.Y., Chgo. Mem. Am.-Lithuanian Cmty., Lithuanian Scouts Assn. (collegiate divsn.), Am.-Lithuanian Music Soc., Wagner Music Soc. Roman Catholic. Home: 5733 N Sheridan Rd Chicago IL 60660-4758

NAUGLE, CHARLOTTE JUNE, principal, educator; b. Long Beach, Calif., June 1, 1938; d. Robert F. and Florence A. (Smith) Ballenger; children: Roberta Lynn, Marina Rae. AA, San Bernardino Valley Coll., 1959; BA, Calif. State U., 1966, MA, 1978. Tchr. Barstow (Calif.) Sch. Dist., 1966, U.S. Dependent Sch., Kenitra, Morocco, 1967-69; tchr., bilingual coord., state demonstration tchr. Colton (Calif.) Sch. Dist., 1970-81, state compensation project dir., 1981-83; prin. Smith Demonstration Sch., Bloomington, Calif., 1984-87, Walter Zimmerman Sch., Bloomington, 1987-94, Wilson Elem. Sch., Colton, Calif., 1994-97; tech. dir. PeaceBuilders, Inland Agy., Riverside, Calif., 1998—; ednl. cons.; extension instr. U. Calif., Riverside, 1975-77. Pub. edn. chmn. San Bernardino-Riverside Counties, Am. Cancer Soc., 1979-81; bd. dirs. Cedar House Rehab. Ctr. Mem. steering com. Island Empire Quality Improvement Network. Recipient Able Toastmasters award, 1982; named Outstanding Tchr. of Writing award Inland Area Writing Project, U. Calif., Riverside, 1980. Mem. ASCD, Nat. Assn. Exec. Women, Mgmt. Assn. Colton Educators (pres. 1990), Assn. Calif. Sch. Adminstrs. (sec. region 12 1992-93), Toastmasters (internat. pres. 1980, div. ednl. v.p. 1981), Phi Delta Kappa. Republican. Home: 25590 Prospect Ave Apt 41E Loma Linda CA 92354-3154 Office: Inland Agy 6235 River Crest Dr Ste P Riverside CA 92507-0758

NAUGLE, KIM ALAN, counseling psychologist, educator; b. Salem, Ind., Sept. 12, 1954; s. Everett Dossey and Dorothy Marie (Durham) N.; m. Lottie Rebecca Barnett, Sept. 2, 1972; 1 child, Ryan Jerel. BA, Ind. U. S.E., New Albany, 1981, MS in Counseling and Guidance, 1983; PhD, Ind. U., 1991. Lic. psychologist, Ind. and Ky; cert. profl. counselor, Ky. Therapist Family Svc. Assn. Monroe County, Bloomington, Ind., 1985-86; counseling psychology intern U. Louisville, 1986-87, psychol. counselor, 1990-91; psychol. So. Hills Counseling Ctr., Jasper, Ind., 1991-95; mgr. mental health ctr. River Valley Behavioral Health, Owensboro, Ky., 1995-96; prof. counselor edn. Ea. Ky. U., Richmond, Ky., 1996—; adj. instr. U. Louisville, 1987, 1990-91, Ind. U., 1988-89; counselor in pvt. practice Psychol. Consultation Assocs., Inc., Salem, 1990-91; presenter internat. and state confs. Contbr. articles to profl. jours. Bd. dirs., v.p. Washington County Park and Recreation Bd., 1988-91. Mem. Am. Psychol. Assn., Am. Counseling Assn., Ky. Counseling Assn. (bd. dirs., 1998—), Ky. Mental Health Counselors Assn. (past pres. 1998-2000), Assn. Assessment Counseling, 2000. Home: 296 Jacks Creek Rd Richmond KY 40475-8454 Office: Ea Ky U 406 Bert Combs Bldg. Richmond KY 40475

NAUMANN, GOTTFRIED OTTO HELMUT, ophthalmology educator; b. Wiesbaden, Hessen, Germany, Apr. 25, 1935; s. Otto and Margarete (Fuerer) N.; m. Lieselotte Regine Mueller, Nov. 27, 1964; children: Uta-Rike, Maike-Liesel, Doerte-Iris, Frauke-Elke. MD, U. Leipzig, Germany, 1957; D (honoris causa), Semmelweis U., Budapest, Hungary, 2000. Diplomate Am. Bd. Ophthalmology. Intern Ventnor Found., Atlantic City, 1959-60; resident dept. ophthalmology U. Hamburg, Germany, 1961-64, instr. dept. ophthalmology, 1967, assoc. prof. ophthalmology, 1968-74; fellow Armed Forces Inst. Pathology, Washington, 1965-66; internat. vis. prof. Assoc. Univ. Profl. Ophthalmology, Balt., 1972; prof., chmn. dept. ophthalmology U. Tübingen, Germany, 1975-80, U. Erlangen, Germany, 1980—; co-founder European Bd. Ophthalmology, London, 1992, pres., 1996-98; 7th Harvard lectr. ophthalmology, Boston, 1994; 30th Bjerrum lectr. Danish Ophthal. Soc., 1995; 11th European guest lectr. Oxford intern Congress, 1996; spl. lectr. Internat. Acad. Ophthalmology, Chgo., 1996. Prin. author: Pathology of the Eye, German edit., 1980, 97 (2 vols.), English edit., 1986, Japanese edits., 1987, 2000; co-editor: Wound Healing of the Eye, 1979, Klin. Monatsblätter Augenheilkunde, 1980; co-founder Jour. Ophthal. Rsch., 1970; mem. editl. bd. Am. Jour. Ophthalmology, Japanese Jour. Ophthalmology, others. Mem. Founding Coun. Univ., Dresden, Germany, 1992-94; reviewer WHO, Geneva, 1972-95; co-founder German-Speaking Ophthal. Pathologists, Hamburg, 1972, European Univ. Prof. Ophthalmology, Nijmegen, The Netherlands, 1986. Recipient William Mackenzie medal U. Glasgow, Scotland, 1991, T. Krwawicz Gold medal Polish Ophthal. Soc., 1993, 56 Bowman medal Royal Coll. Ophthalmology, London, 1994, Alcon Rsch. Inst. award, 1996, German Fed. award of Merit, 1st class, 1996, Dr. Frank Claffy medal U. Sydney, 2000. Fellow German Ophthal. Soc. (councillor 1970-75, 78-85), Am. Acad. Ophthalmologica (honor award 1992); mem. Italian Ophthal. Soc. (hon.), Hungarian Ophthal. Soc. (hon.), Assn. Rsch. in Vision and Ophthalmology (life), Acad. Ophthalmology Internat. (spl. lectr. Chgo. 1996), Internat. Coun. Ophthalmology (pres. 1998-2002), Internat. Agy. Prevention Blindness (v.p. 1998-2002), European Ophthalmology Soc. (gen. sec. 1976, 6th Charamis medal 1995), German Univ. Profs. Ophthalmology (pres. 1985-88), European Ophthal. Path. Soc. (pres. 1990-93), Rotary. Lutheran. Office: Univ-Augenklinik, Schwabachanlage 6, 91054 Erlangen Germany

NAUMANN, HANS J., manufacturing company executive; b. Germany, May 5, 1935; came to U.S., 1960; s. Herbert and Elfriede (Heydenreich) N.; m. Edith Huempel; children: Irene, Michelle, Jacqueline, John. MME, U. Hamburg, Fed. Rep. Germany, 1960; MBA, Rochester (N.Y.) U., 1965. Registered profl. engr., N.Y. Mgr. engring. Farrell Corp., Rochester, 1961-66; exec. v.p. Hegenscheidt Corp., Troy, Mich., 1966-70; pres., chief exec. officer, stockholder Hegenscheidt GmbH, Erkelenz, Fed. Republic Germany, 1970-82; chmn., chief exec. officer Internat. Knife Corp., Erlanger, Ky., 1982-84; chmn. bd., chief exec. officer, stockholder Simmons Machine Tool Corp., Albany, N.Y., 1984—; chmn., CEO, stockholder Niles-Simmons Industrieanlagen, GmbH, Chemnitz, Germany, 1992—; chmn. bd. dirs., CEO Constant Velocity Systems, Inc., Ballston Spa, N.Y., 1993—. Author: Tool and Manufacturing Engineering Handbook, 1976; patentee roller finishing and deep rolling. Bd. dirs. U. Albany Fund, Inc., 1986—. Mem. ASME, SAE, Am. Inst. Mgmt. (pres.'s coun.), Am. Mgmt. Assn., Am. Pub. Transit Assn., Verein Deutscher Ingenieure, Soc. Mech. Engrs., Capital Region Tech. Devel. Coun., Capital Region World Trade Coun., Assn. for Mfg. Tech. (formerly Nat. Machine Tool Builders Assn.), Albany Colonie Regional C. of C., Rwy. Supply Assn., N.Y. R.R. Club Inc., Lions (past pres.). Avocations: sailing, tennis, golf, skiing. Home: 26 Folmsbee Dr Albany NY 12204-1206 Office: Simmons Machine Tool Corp 1700 Broadway Albany NY 12204-2701 also: Niles-Simmons Industrieanlagen, Zwickauer Str 355, 09117 Chemnitz Germany

NAUMANN, HORST BRUNO, linguist; b. Grimmma, Germany, Nov. 20, 1925; s. Bruno Otto and Hertha Minna (Jahn) N.; m. Margarethe Johanna Poitzsch, Dec. 31, 1950; children: Sabine, Ute. PhD, U. Leipzig, 1959, DPhil, 1968. H.S. tchr. Grimma, 1953-57; from asst. to scientific rschr. U. Leipzig, 1956-62; from asst. prof. to prof. Tchr. Tng. Coll., Zwickau, 1962-90; editl. adv. coun. U. Leipzig, 1978-94; dean Tchr. Tng. Coll., 1975-81, editor-in-chief, 1964-89. Author: Nativinstructions and Onomastics, 1961, Placenames and Fieldnames in the Region Grimma and Wurzen, 1962, German Rural Microtoponymics in the Area of Meissen, 1972, Streetnames of the Town of Grimma, 1997; editor: Early Printings at Zwickau from 1523-1666, 1977, First Names Today, 1977, Little Book of First Names, 1978, Book of First Names, 1988, Book of Last Names, 1987, 2d edit., 1989, The Great Book of Last Names, 1994, 2d edit., 1996, 3d edit., 1999. Mem. Soc. for German Lang., Soc. for Names. Avocations: music, bicycling, gardening. Home: Göschenstr 13, D-04668 Grimma Saxony, Germany

NAUMANN ZU KÖNIGSBRÜCK, CLAS MICHAEL, museum director, zoology educator; b. Dresden, Sachsen, Germany, June 26, 1939; s. Eberhard Bruno and Freda Irene (Hannemann) Naumann zu Königsbrück; m. Storai Nawabi, Dec. 17, 1974; children: Alexander Eberhard, Roxana Jamila. Dr.rer.nat., U. Bonn, Germany, 1970, Dr.rer.nat.habil., U. Munich, 1977. Tchr. U. Kabul, Afghanistan, 1970-72; sci. asst. U. Bonn, 1973-74, U. Munich, 1975-77; prof. U. Bielefeld, Germany, 1977-89, U. Bonn, Germany, 1989—; dir. Zoologisches Forschungsinstitut und Museum Alexander Koenig, Bonn, 1989—; mem. presidium Arbeitsgem. Afghanistan, Germany, 1985—; cons. referee Deutsche Forschungs Gemeinschaft, Germany, 1992-99; mem. sci. adv. bd. WWF Germany, 1992-95; mem. German Nat. Com. for Unesco Programm-Man and Biosphere, 1992-95; vice chmn. UNESCO program, Diversitas Deutschland, 1997—. Author: Die Kirghisen des Afghanistan Pamir, 1977; editor-in-chief: Zoologischer Anzeiger, 1994—, Entomologische Zeitschrift, 1999—; mng. editor Handbook of Palaearctic Macrolepidoptera, 1991—. Fellow Rotary. Avocations: travel, books, entomology, photography, music. Office: Zoologisches Forschungsinstitut, Mus A Koenig Adenauerallee 160, 53113 Bonn Germany

NAUMOV, GENNADI IVANOVICH, biologist, geneticist; b. Krasnojarsk, Russia, July 8, 1944; s. Ivan Petrovich and Anna Petrovna (Motry) N.; m. Taisia Ivanovna Boiko N., Aug. 10, 1965 (div. Sept. 1983); children: Pavel, Daniil; m. Elena Sergeevna Mashkina N., Nov. 26, 1983. Diploma, Moscow State U., 1966, PhD, 1969; DS, Inst. of Genetics Microorgs., Moscow, 1978. Staff rsch. scientist Inst. of Genetics of Microorganisms, Moscow, 1969-73, sr. investigator, 1973-79, chief of lab. of yeast genetics, 1979—; vis. scientist Rsch. Labs. of Finnish State Alcohol Co., Helsinki, 1989, 90-91, Inst. of Molecular Medicine, Oxford, U.K., 1994, molecular genetics lab. Queens Coll. CUNY, 1990, Lab. Genetics, Grignon, France, 1991-92, Ctr. for Microbial Ecology, East Lansing, Mich., 1995, Tech. U. Denmark, Copenhagen, 1997, U. Pa., 1997, U. Bordeaux2, France, 1998, Centraalbureau voor Schimmelcultures, Baarn, The Netherlands, 1998, U. Agrl. Sci., Uppsula, 2000, others. Contbr. articles to profl. jours. Recipient Kapitza fellowship Royal Soc., 1994; Finnish grantee Found. for Biotechnol. and Indsl. Fermentation Rsch., 1995, others. Mem. Russian Soc. Geneticists and Breeders, Russian Microbiol. Soc., Moscow Soc. Natural Explorers. Avocations: Philately, birds, aquarium fish, mushrooms, travel. Office: Inst Genetics Microorganism, I Dorozhnyj 1, 113545 Moscow Russia

NAUMOVICH, EVGENY NIKOLAYEVICH, chemist, researcher; b. Minsk, Belarus, Aug. 9, 1964; s. Nikolay Valentinovich and Tamara Mitrofanovna (Nikolayenko) N.; m. Tatyana Fedorovna Poltoran, Feb. 1, 1986; 1 child, Elena. Grad., Sch. N 88, Minsk, Belarus, 1981, Byelarussian State U., Minsk, Belarus, 1986; PhD, Byelarussian State U., Minsk, Belarus, 1991. Cert. chemist. Engr. Rsch. Inst. for Phisico-Chem. Problems Byelarussian State U., Minsk, Belarus, 1986-87, jr. rschr. Rsch. Inst. for Phisico-Chem. Problems, 1987-92, rschr. Rsch. Inst. for Phisico-Chem. Problems, 1992-94, maj. rschr. Rsch. Inst. for Phisico-Chem. Problems, 1994—. Contbr. articles to profl. jours. Avocation: bridge. Office: Rsch Inst Physico-Chem Prob, 14 Leningradskaya St, Minsk 220080, Belarus

NAUROSCHAT, JUERGEN THOMAS, biosystems researcher, mathematician, educator; b. Cologne, Germany, Sept. 10, 1964; s. Guenther Fritz and Helga Wilhelmine (Schneider) N. BS, U. Cologne, 1988, MS, 1993. Tchr. adult edn. program Cologne, 1989—; sci. collaborator U. Witten/Herdecke, Germany, 1993—; tchr. U. Witten/Herdecke, 1994—. Contbr. articles to profl. jours, and books. Rsch. fellow German Soc. Advancement of Scientific Rsch., 1993, 96. Mem. Soc. for Simulation in Engring. and Natural Sci., European Soc. for Math. and Theoretical Biology, N.Y. Acad. Sci., Internat. Biographical Ctr. (adv. coun.), Am. Biog. Inst. (bd. advisors). Roman Catholic. Avocations: sports, fishing, friends. Home: Ostring 75, 50259 Pulheim Germany Office: U Witten/Herdecke Math Dept, Stockumer Str 10, 58448 Witten Germany

NAUŠ, ANTONIN, occupational health educator; b. Tisovec, Slovak Republic, Jan. 9, 1925; s. Antonin and Božena (Vitek) N.; m. Zdenka Sazama, July 21, 1958; children: Alice, Marketa. MD, Charles U., 1952, PhD, 1962, DSc, 1980. Head occupl. health Hygiene Epidemiology Sta., Jihlava, Czech Republic, 1952-53; asst. prof. to prof. U. Charles, Prague, Czech Republic, 1953—; expert WHO, Kabul, Afghanistan, 1984. Author: The Olphactoric Properties of Industrial Matters, 1976 (Golden medal 1978); contbr. numerous articles to profl. jours. Recipient J. Kaplan prize Internat. Assn. Occupational Health, J.E. Purkyne prize Czech Med. Assn., 1982. Mem. Czech Soc. of Occupl. Health, Czech Med. Bd., Soc. Aerosols in Medicine. Avocations: chess, travel, correspondence. Home: Nam Sv Cecha 11, 10100 Prague 10 Czech Republic Office: Univ Hosp, Srobarova 50, 10034 Prague Czech Republic

NAUTH, PETER MATTHIAS, information technology educator; b. Mainz, Germany, June 23, 1956; s. Gerhard and Gabriele Sofia (Pohl) N.; m. Anna Kristina Blumers, Apr. 12, 1986; children: Alexander, Manuel, Julian. MSEE, U. Darmstadt, Germany, 1981; PhD in Biology, U. Mainz, 1985. Scientist Deutsche Klinik Diagnostik, Wiesbaden, Germany, 1981-87; project mgr. FIBH GmbH, Hannover, Germany, 1987-88; vis. scientist U. Rochester, N.Y., 1988-89; project mgr. Romaco-Laetus GmbH, Alsbach, Germany, 1990-91, R & D mgr., 1991-94, sys. integration mgr., 1994-97; prof. info. tech. U. of Applied Scis., Frankfurt, Germany, 1998—. Editor: Bildverarbeitung und Dokumentation in der Medizin, 1987. Mem. IEEE Computer Soc. Roman Catholic. Avocation: swimming. Home: Starkenburgring 32a, 64665 Alsbach Germany Office: U of Applied Scis, Kleiststrasse 3, 60318 Frankfurt Germany

NAVARA, MIRKO, mathematician, educator; b. Ledec nad Sazavou, Czech Republic, Apr. 11, 1959; s. Vaclav and Jaroslava (Chudackova) N.; m. Lia Brezikova, Aug. 22, 1981; children: David, Filip. Diploma in engring., Czech Tech. U., Prague, 1983, PhD, 1988. From asst. prof. to assoc. prof. Czech Tech. U., Prague, 1987—. Mem. Am. Math. Soc., Internat. Quantum Structures Assn. (Sci. Achievement prize 1996), Union Czech Maths. and Physicists. Avocation: canoeing. Home: Hornocholupicka 34, 143 00 Prague Czech Republic Office: Czech Tech U Faculty Elec Engring, Technicka 2, 166 27 Prague Czech Republic

NAVARATNAM, VISVANATHAN, medical educator; b. Colombo, Sri Lanka, June 30, 1933; arrived in England, 1967; s. Samuel and Katie (Ratnam) N.; m. Sundari Kamalini Rasaretnam, Oct. 6, 1933; children: Prethiva, Keshini. MB BS, U. Ceylon, Colombo, Sri Lanka, 1957; PhD, U. Cambridge, England, 1964. Houseman Ceylon Med. Svc., Kandy, Sri Lanka, 1957-59; lectr. U. Ceylon, Colombo, Sri Lanka, 1959-67; lectr. U. Cambridge, England, 1967-2000, dir. med. studies Christ's Coll., 1971-2000. Author: Progress in Anatomy, vols. 1-3, 1981-83, The Human Heart and Circulation, 1975, Heart Muscle Ultrastructural Studies, 1987. Mem. Anatomical Soc. Great Britain. Avocations: bridge, rugby, cricket. E-mail: vn@mole.bio.cam.ac.uk. Office: U Cambridge Dept Anatomy, Downing St, Cambridge CB2 3DY, England

NAVARRA, GIUSEPPE, surgeon, educator; b. Catania, Sicily, Italy, July 22, 1965; s. Salvatore and Serafina (Macaione) N. Grad. in medicine and surgery, U. Messina, Italy, 1988, bd. cert. in gen. surgery, 1993; postgrad. in coloproctology, St. Mark's Hosp., London, 1996; bd. cert. in vascular surgery, U. Ferrara, 1998. Lectr. U. Ferrara, Italy, 1990-93, sr. lectr., 1993-2000; assoc. prof. endoscopic surgery U. Sassari, Italy, 2000—; chief outpatients coloproctology U. Ferrara, 1996-2000. Author 15 videos; contbr. over 200 articles to profl. jours. Recipient grant Ente Nazionale Previdenza-Assistenza Sociale, 1982-83, 83-84, 84-85, grant Opera Universiaria, 1985-86, 86-87, 87-88, U. Bonino and M.S. Pulejo Found. grants, 1988. Mem. Italian Soc. Surgery (Premio Giovani award 1992), Italian Soc. Young Surgeons, Coll. Med. Drs., N.Y. Acad. Scis. Avocations: tennis, soccer, skiing, classical lecturer, visual art. Home: Via Cammello 10/A, 44100 Ferrara Italy Office: U Sassari Patologia Chirurg, V S Pietro 42, 07100 Sassari Italy

NAVARRO, CASAS JAIME, architect, educator; b. Seville, Spain, June 8, 1952; s. Galafate Antonio Navarro and Sainz Maria Luz Casas; m. Fort Paloma Osta, Oct. 20, 1975; children: Jacobo, Jose, Antonio. BS, Claret U., Spain, 1969; PhD in Arch., U. de Sevilla, 1980. Asst. prof. U. Seville, 1977-81, prof., 1981-87, chair, 1987-97, dir. dept., 1997—, dir. inst., 1997—; cons. in field; architect Sapain, 1977—. Author: About Daylighting in Architec-

ture, 1991; co-author: Computational Acoustics, 1999; prin. works include rural houses project (Nat. award of arch.). Recipient award for painting Seville govt., 1976, Regional Mention for sculpture Assn. Nat. U. Españolas, 1979, Nat. Mention award Toledo Found., 1992. Mem. Acoustic Soc. Am., Commn. Española de Iluminacion, Architech's Assn. (officer 1985-91). Office: U Seville, Reina Mercedes N1-2, 41012 Seville Spain

NAVARRO, FERNANDO A., medical translator, pharmacologist; b. Granada, Spain, Sept. 14, 1962; arrived in Switzerland, 1992; s. Alberto Navarro-González and María Pilar González-Velasco; m. Lydia Rodríguez-Villanueva, May 21, 1988; children: Antonio, Alvaro, Isabel, Miguel. MD, U. Salamanca, Spain, 1986; med. specialist, U. Cantabria, Santander, Spain, 1991. Resident clin. pharmacology Marqués Valdecilla U. Hosp., Santander, Spain, 1988-91; rschr. human pharmacology Sandoz, Basle, Switzerland, 1992; med. translator F. Hoffmann-La Roche & Co., Basle, 1993—. Author: English-Spanish Medical Dictionary of Translation Difficulties, 2000, Medical Language and Translation, 1997; translator: Sleep in Art, 1994, The Pharmacy-Windows on History, 1994; mem. editl. bd. Medicina Clínica, 1994—, Actas Dermo-Sifiliográficas, 1997; contbr. over 150 articles to profl. jours. Mem. Swiss Soc. Translators Interpreters, Spanish Soc. Physician-Writers. Office: F Hoffmann La Roche & Co, CH 4070 Basel Switzerland

NAVARRO, HECTOR ALEJANDRO, veterinarian; b. Mexico City, Jan. 25, 1963; s. Hector A. Navarro and Rosalva N. Gonzalez. Veterinarian, Nat. Autonomous U. Mex., Mexico City, 1987; diploma in philosophy, Iberoamerican U., Mexico City, 1998. Tech. dir. Sistemas Pecuarios, Guadalajara, Mex., 1987-89; asst. animal nutrition dir. Am. Soybean Assn., Mexico City, 1989-93, animal nutrition dir., 1993—. Mem. Mex. Poultry Specialists Assn. (scientific com. 1997), Mex. Animal Nutrition Specialists Assn. (scientific com. 1993—, Best Paper 1992, 96). Roman Catholic. Avocation: ecology. E-mail: asamexna@mail.internet.com.mx. Home: Plateros #76-603 Col, San Jose Insurgentes, 03900 Mexico City DF, Mexico Office: American Soybean Assn, Jaime Balmes #8 2do Piso Cl, Los Morales Ploanco Mexico City CP 11510, Mexico

NAVARRO, JOSE TOMAS, physician, researcher; b. Aldaia, Valencia, Spain, Mar. 28, 1964; s. Tomas Navarro and Elisa Ferrando. MD, U. Valencia (Spain), 1988; Hematologist, Hosp. Can Ruti, Barcelona, Spain, 1995. Med. diplomate, hematology diplomate. Hematologist Hosp. Grandollers, Spain, 1996, Hosp. Can Ruti, Barcelona, Spain, 1996—. Author: Manual del SIDA, 1997, 99, Schalm's Veterinary Hematology, 5th edit., 2000. Avocations: classical music. Office: Hosp Germans Trias i Pujol, Carretera del Canyet s/n, 08916 Badalona Barcelona, Spain

NAVARRO, JUAN JESÚS MORENO, foreign language educator; b. Santa Brigida Las Palmas, Spain, May 4, 1937; arrived in Japan, 1964; s. Manuel Navarro González and Heriberta Moreno Rodríguez; m. Noriko Yabe, Nov. 18, 1992. MA in Philosphy, Facultdad de Filosfía, Alcalá de Henares, Spain, 1962; MA in Theology, Sophia U., Tokyo, 1968. Part-time prof. Waseda U., Tokyo, 1966—; prof. Inst. for Internat. Studies and Trade, Fujinomiya, Japan, 1970-72, Takushoku U., Tokyo, 1972—; cons. editor PHP (Spanish), Tokyo, 1981—. Office: Takushoku Univ, 815-1 Tatemachi, Hachioji-Shi Tokyo 193, Japan

NAVARRO DURÁN, ROSA, philology educator; b. Figueres, Girona, Spain, Nov. 16, 1947; d. Manuel Navarro and Margarita Durán. D Hispanic Philology, U. Barcelona, Spain, 1981. Tchr. U. Barcelona, 1969-90, prof., 1990—, dir. Spanish philology dept., 1991-97. Author: La Mirada al Texto (The Look at the Text), 1995, Por Qué Hay Que Leer Los Clásicos? (Why We May Read the Classic Writers?), 1996, Cómo Leer un Poema (How to Read a Poem), 1998; editor: Libro de las Suertes, 1986, Diálogo de Mercurio Y Carón, 1999; contbr. articles to profl. publs. Office: U Barcelona Dept Philology, Gran Via 585, 08071 Barcelona Spain

NAVICKAS, JOHN, fluid dynamics engineer, researcher, consultant; b. Raseiniai, Lithuania, Nov. 26, 1933; came to U.S., 1949; s. John and Ona (Remeikis) N.; m. Marija D. Masionis Navickas, Sept. 1, 1985; children: Rima, Rymante, Tadas, Dalia. BS, UCLA, 1957; MS, 1961. Tech. fellow The Boeing Co., Huntington Beach, Calif., 1957—; cons. Lloyd's Registry of Shipping, Eng., 1982, Am. Bur. Shipping, 1992, Nippon Kokan, Japan, 1979-82, Lithuania Acad. Sci., 1978, 82. Editor: Conference Proceedings Computational Experiments, 1989; author more than 40 articles on multiphase fluid dynamics, computational methods and space systems. Com. mem. Lithuanian Childrens Hope, L.A., 1992—. Capt. U.S. Army, 1957-65. Mem. ASME, AIAA.

NAVON, LIORA, anthropologist, researcher; b. Tel Aviv, Israel, Apr. 19, 1957; d. Moshe and Berta (Eisenberger) Meisels; m. David Navon, Oct. 5, 1980. PhD summa cum laude, Tel Aviv U., 1992. Field psychologist Israel Defense Forces, Israel, 1978-81; instr. Tel Aviv U., Israel, 1986-90, vis. lectr., 1991-95, head rsch unit, Sch. Health Professions, 1991—, lectr., 1995—. Contbr. articles to profl. jours. Lt. Israel Defense Forces, Israel, 1978-81. Grantee Rothschild Fellow, 1983, Leprosy Relief Work Emmaus, Switzerland, 1984, Israel Founds. Trustees, 1987. Mem. IDEA. Jewish. Avocations: archeology, numismatics. Office: Tel Aviv U, Faculty Medicine Dept Nursing, 69978 Tel Aviv Israel

NAVRAT, PAVOL, software engineer, educator; b. Bratislava, Slovakia, Jan. 20, 1952; parents: Rudolf and Kristina (Zubkova) N.; m. Darina (Kubackova) Navratova, July 7, 1979, children: Matus, Julia, Lucia. MSc, Slovak U. Tech., Bratislava, 1975, PhD, 1984, docent habilitation, 1993. CEng. Engrg. Counc., U.K. Rsch. asst. Slovak U. Tech., Bratislava, 1975-92; assoc. prof. Kuwait U., Kuwait, 1992-94; prof. Slovak U. Tech., Bratislava, 1996—; vice chmn., Accreditation Commn. of Govt. of Republic of Slovakia, Bratislava, 1999—, country's rep., Counc. of Europe, Comm. on Higher Edn. and Rsch., Strassbourg, 1999—. Co-author: Micro-computers, Computers, People, 1996, Programming in Lisp (scientific monograph), 1998; editor and co-author: (sci. monograph) Knowledge-based Software Engineering, 1998; author: Contribution to Methods of Building and Applying of Computing Tools, 1987; contbg. author: Great Slovakian Encyclopedia Beliana, 1999—. Chmn., Slovakia Ctr. of the Inst. of Elc. Engrs., 1997—; comm. mem., Christian Democratic Union Educators, 1997—; mem., Slovak Foreign Policy Assn., 1995—. Fell., Inst. Elec. Engrs., 1998, sr. mem., Inst. Elec. and Electronic Engrs., 1996, mem., Assn. of Computing Machinery, Amer. Assn., for Artificial Intelligence, 1995. Avocations: foreign policy, tennis, guitar. E-mail: navrat@elf.stuba.sk. Fax: 421765420587. Office: Slovak U Tech, Ilkovicova 3, SK-81219 Britislava Slovakia

NAVRÁTIL, LEOŠ, radiobiologist; b. Prague, Czech Repubic, Aug. 7, 1954; s. Josef and Věra (Bílová) N.; m. Blanka (Chemišincová), June 16, 1979; 1 child, Václav. MD, Charles U., Prague, Czechoslovakia, 1978, PhD, 1984. Chief Inst. Biophysics, com. postgrad. edn. biophysics Charles U.; asst. prof. Mil. Med. Acad., Hradec Králové, 1997. Author: Prostaglandins in Clinical Medicine, 1989, Clinical Radiobiology, 1990, Lasers and Pulse Magnets in Therapy, 1994, Non Invasive Laser Therapy, 1997, Contemporary Phototherapy and Lasertherapy, 2000. Mem. European Soc. Radiobiology, Soc. Radiobiology of Czech Med. Soc. Jana Evangelisty Purkyně (chmn. 1992). E-mail: leos.navratil@lf1.cuni.cz. Office: Charles Univ Inst Biophysics 1st Med Fac, Salmovská 1, 120 00 Prague 2, Czech Republic

NAVRÁTIL, OLDŘICH, chemistry educator; b. Senice, Olomouc, Czech Republic, Dec. 26, 1930; s. Josef and Alžběta (Nováková) N.; m. Anna Strnadová, Jan. 26, 1955 (dec. June 1996); children: Oldřich, Petr. CSc, Masaryk U., Brno, Czech Republic, 1965, RNDr, 1966, DSc, 1979. Chemist ZPS, Zlin, Czech Republic, 1953-54; from asst. prof. to prof. br. nuclear chemistry Masaryk U., Brno, 1959-90, dept. head, 1973-89; prof. Mil. U., Vyškov, Czech Republic, 1991—; prof. postgrad. studies Nat. Rsch. Inst., Risø, Denmark, 1968; postdoctoral fellow Dalhousie U., Halifax, N.S., Can., 1969-70. Chief co-author: Nuclear Chemistry, 1985; co-author: Nuclear Chemistry, 1990. Mem. Czech Chem. Soc. Avocation: mountain climbing. Office: Mil Coll Ground Forces, 68203 Vyškov Czech Republic

NAVRATILOVA, MARTINA, former professional tennis player; b. Prague, Czech Republic, Oct. 18, 1956; came to U.S., 1975, naturalized, 1981; d. Miroslav Navratil and Jana Navratilova. Student, schs. in Czechoslovakia; Hon. doctorate, George Washington U., 1996. Profl. tennis player, 1973-94; tennis commentator/broadcaster HBO Sports, 1995-99; spkr. in field. Author: (with George Vecsey) Martina, 1985, (with Liz Nickles) The Total Zone, 1995, (with Liz Nickels) The Breaking Point, (with Liz Nickles) 1996, Killer Instinct, 1997; columnist. Co-founder Rainbow Card. Winner Czechoslovak Nat. singles, 1972-74, U.S. Open singles, 1983, 84, 86, 87, U.S. Open doubles, 1977, 78, 80, 83, 84, 87, 90, U.S. Open mixed doubles, 1987, Va. Slims Tournament, 1978, 83, 84, 85, 86, Va. Slims doubles, 1991, Wimbledon singles, 1978, 79, 82, 83, 84, 85, 86, 87, 90, Wimbledon women's doubles, 1976, 79, 81, 82, 83, 84, 86, Wimbledon mixed doubles, 1985, 94, 95, French Open singles, 1982, 84, Australian Open singles, 1981, 83, 85, Australian Doubles (with Nagelsen) 1980, (with Shriver), 1982, 84, 85, 87, 88, 89, Roland Garros (with Shriver), 1985, 87, 89, Italian Open doubles (with Sabatini), 1987, (with Shriver) COREL WTA Tour doubles team of yr., 1981-89, triple Crown at U.S. Open, 1987; recipient Women's Sports Found. Flo Hyman award, 1987; named Female Athlete of the Decade (1980s) The Nat. Sports Review, UPI, and AP, WTA Player of Yr., 1978-79, 82-86, Women's Sports Found. Sportswoman of Yr., 1982-84, Hon. Citizen of Dallas, AP Female Athlete of Yr., 1983, Chgo. Hall of Fame, 1994; Martina Navratilova Day proclaimed in Chgo., 1992. Mem. Women's Tennis Assn. (dir., exec. com., pres.), Women's Tennis Assn. Tour Player's Assn. (pres. 1979-80, 83-84, 94-95). Achievements include being the holder of 168 singles titles and 165 doubles titles; holder of record of singles-match wins which is 1,309, 1991. *

NAWAR, NAGWA ABD EL-ALL, chemist, educator; b. Mansoura, Egypt, Aug. 7, 1957; d. Abd El-All Nawar and Fatina Hamoda; m. Hamad Helmy Yehia; children: Hani Hamad Yehia, Magid Hamad Yehia. BSc, Mansoura (Egypt) U., 1979, MSc, 1983; PhD, Liverpool (Eng.) U., 1989. Demonstrator Mansoura U., 1979-83, asst. lectr., 1983-85, lectr. inorganic chemistry, 1989-95, assoc. prof. inorganic chemistry, 1995—; vis. fellow British Coun., Liverpool, 1991, 95; vis. asst. rsch. scientist Tex. A&M U., College Station, 1996. Contbr. articles to profl. jours. Fulbright rsch. grantee, 1995-96; recipient Shoman prize (Jordan), 1996. Mem. Am. Chem. Soc., Egyptian Chem. Soc., Women in Sci. and Engrng. Avocations: leading social and recreation activities. Office: Faculty Sci Dept Chemistry, Mansoura U PO Box 79, Mansoura 35516, Egypt

NAWRAT, ZBIGNIEW, physicist, researcher; b. Zabrze, Silesia, Poland, Apr. 28, 1960; s. Zygmunt and Bronisława (Zok) N.; m. Halina Arszułowicz, Feb. 13, 1985; children: Szymon, Alicja. M Physics, Silesian U., Katowice, Poland, 1984; D, Silesian Med. U., Zabrze, Poland, 1996. Asst. dept. biophysics Silesian Med. U., Zabrze, 1984-89, specialist Artificial Heart Lab., 1988—; head Found. Cardiac Surgery Devel. Bioflolab Inst. Heart Prostheses, Zabrze, 1995-98, head Biocybernetics Lab., 1998—, sci. dir., 1998—. Contbr. articles to profl. jours. Grantee Polish Artificial Heart, 1991-94, Biol. Heart Prostheses, 1992-98, Cardiac Surgery Simulation Devel., 1998—, Cardio-Robots, 2000—. Office: Found Cardiac Surg Devel, Wolności St 345A, 41-800 Zabrze Poland

NAWY, EDWARD GEORGE, civil engineer, educator; b. Baghdad, Iraq, Dec. 21, 1926; came to U.S., 1957, naturalized, 1966; s. George M. and Ava (Marshall) N.; m. Rachel E. Shebbath, Mar. 23, 1949; children: Ava Margaret, Robert M. DIC, Imperial Coll. Sci. and Tech., London, 1951; CE, MIT, 1959; D of Engring., U. Pisa, Italy, 1967. Registered profl. engr. N.J., N.Y., Pa., Calif., Fla. Head structures Israel Water Planning Authority, Tel-Aviv, 1952-57; faculty Rutgers U., New Brunswick, N.J., 1959—; grad. faculty Rutgers U., 1961—, prof. civil engring., 1966-72, Distinguished prof. (prof. II), 1972—, chmn. dept. civil and environ. engring., dir. grad. programs, 1980-86; chmn. Coll. Engring. Del. Assembly, 1969-72; mem. Univ. Senate, 1973-80, exec. com., faculty rep., bd. govs., trustee; guest prof. Nat. U. Tucaman, Argentina, summer 1963, Imperial Coll. Sci. and Tech., summer 1964; vis. prof. Stevens Inst. Tech., Hoboken, N.J., 1968-72; hon. prof. Nanjing Inst. Tech., China, 1987; mem. N.J. Chancellor Higher Edn. for Higher Edn. Master Plan; mem. Rutgers U. rep. Transp. Rsch. Bd. Bridge Com., chmn. com. on concrete materials; cons. to industry; U.S. mem. commn. on cracking Comitè EuroInternat. du Beton; mem. Civil Engring. Tech. Adv. Coun. N.J., 1966-72; concrete sys. cons. FAA, Washington; cons. energy divsn. U.S. Gen. Acctg. Office, Washington; gen. chmn. Internat. Symposium on Slabs and Plates, 1971; hon. presidium internat. conf. Reunion Internat. des Lab. d'Essais et de Rsch. sur Les Materiaux et les Constructions, Budapest, 1977; mem. Accreditation Bd. Engring. and Tech. Author: Reinforced Concrete, 4th edit., 2000, Simplified Reinforced Concrete, 1986, Prestressed Concrete, 3d edit., 2000, High Performance Concrete, 1996; author, editor-in-chief: Concrete Construction Engineering Handbook, 1998; contbr. over 160 articles to profl. jours. V.p. Berkeley Twp. Taxpayers Assn., Ocean City, N.J., 1966-70. Recipient Merit citation and award N.J. Concrete Assn., 1966; C. Gulbenkian Found. fellow, 1972. Fellow ASCE (mem. joint com. on slabs), Instn. Civil Engrs. (London), Am. Concrete Inst. (pres. N.J. chpt. 1966, 77-78, chmn. nat. com. on cracking 1966-73, bd. com. chpts. 1969-72, ACI rep. internat. commn. fractures, H.L. Kenneday award 1972, award of recognition N.J. chpt. 1972, chpt. activities award 1978, chmn. nat. com. on deflection 1989-96); mem. NSPE, AAUP (chmn. budget and priorities com. Rutgers U. chpt. 1972), Am. Soc. Engring. Edn., Prestressed Concrete Inst. (Bridge Competition award 1971, mem. tech. activities com.), N.Y. Acad. Scis., Tall Bldgs. Coun., N.J. Contractors Assn. (cons. ednl. com., tall bldgs. coun.), Rotary, Sigma Xi, Tau Beta Pi, Chi Epsilon (hon.).

NAYAK, GANGA DHARA, science educator, researcher; b. Hinjilicut, Orissa, India, Mar. 5, 1962; s. Nityananda and Chandrama (Palo) N.; m. Aditi Bala Panda, Feb. 23, 1993; 1 child. B in Vet. Sci. and Animal Husbandry, Vet. Coll., Bhubaneswar, India, 1985, M in Vet. Sci., 1987; PhD, G.B. Panth U. Agrl. Tech., Panthnagar, India, 1999. Jr. vet. officer Govt. Orissa, Mathalput, India, 1987-89; jr. scientist Orissa U. Agr. and Tech., Bhubaneswar, India, 1989—. Contbr. articles to profl. jours. Mem. Indian Soc. for Sheep and Goat Prodn. and Utilization, Ctrl. Sheep Wool Rsch. Inst. Avocation: writing short stories. Home: Regidee St, Hinjilicut 761102, India Office: Regional Rsch & Tech Trans, Srirampada, G Udayagiri 762100, India

NAYAK, JAYANTA KUMAR, physicist, educator, researcher; b. Chilima, India, Apr. 3, 1950; s. B.C. and K. (Jena) N.; m. P. Mahapatra, May 27, 1976; 1 child, A. Nayak. BSc, Utkal (India) U., 1970; MSc, Delhi (India) U., 1972; PhD, Indian Inst. Tech., Delhi, 1980. Lectr. Govt. Coll., Orissa, India, 1972-81; sr. scientific officer grade I Indian Inst. Tech., Delhi, 1981-82; lectr. Indian Inst. Tech., Bombay, 1982-86, asst. prof., 1986-90, assoc. prof., 1990-98, prof., 1998—. Co-author books; contbr. approximately 40 articles to profl. jours. Recipient Shri Hari Om Ashram Prerit s.S. Bhatnagar endowment award, 1978. Mem. Internat. Solar Energy Soc., Solar Energy Soc. of India. Avocation: outdoor sports. Home: B51, IIT Powai, Bombay 400 076, India Office: IIT, Powai, Dept Mech Engring, Bombay 400076, India

NAYAK, RAJENDRA KUMAR, lawyer; b. Jabalpur, Madhya Pra, India, Dec. 3, 1932; s. Gulab Chand and Rajrani N.; m. Sheela Johari, June 21, 1965; children: Shruti, Arinjay. MA, U. Jabalpur, 1957, LLB, 1959; MSLI, U. Wis., 1961; LLM, NYU, 1963; LLD, World Devel. Parliament, India, 1987. Rsch. prof. Indian Law Inst., India, 1965-92, mem. governing coun., 1998-2000; exec. chmn. The Environ. and Consumer Protection Found., New Delhi, 1994—; sec. gen. Internat. Confs. viz. Children, Environment and Human Health, India, 1994, Global AIDS Law, India, 1995, Global Drugs Law, India, 1997; chief monitor Global Health Law, India, 1997. Author: (book) Consumer Protection Law in India, 1991; chief editor: (book) Children, Environment and Human Health, 1997, Global Health Law, 1999; editor: (book) Global Drugs Law, 1997. Mem. All-India Congress Com., Indian Nat. Congress, 1972-92. Mem. India Habitat Ctr. (assoc.). Mem. Indian Nat. Congress. Avocations: reading books, attending internat. confs., religious music. Home: J-92 South Extension Part-I, 110049 New Delhi India Office: Indian Law Inst, Bhagwandas Rd, 110 001 New Delhi India

NAYAK, SHAILESH RAMESHCHANDRA, remote sensing scientist; b. Billimora, India, Aug. 21, 1953; s. Rameshchandra Dahyabhai Naik; m. Prity Shailesh Patel, Dec. 27, 1975; 1 child, Aesha. BS, U. Baroda, Vadodara, India, 1973, MS, 1975, PhD, 1980. Sr. sci. asst. Guarat Engring. Rsch. Inst., Vadodara, India, 1977; from sci. asst. C to scientist SF Space Applications Ctr., Ahmedabad, India, 1978-98, scientist SG, 1998—; project mgr. Space Applications Ctr., 1986-98, prin. investigator, 1985-89, 95-98, head marine and water resources divsn. Contbr. articles to profl. jours. Mem. Indian Soc. Remote Sensing (treas. 1984-86, sec. 1986-89, 92-96), Geology Soc. India, Managroye Soc. India (coun. mem. 1990). Avocations: swimming, music, travel. Home: 3/17 Ashraya Apts, Satyagrah Rd, Ahmedabad 380 015, India Office: Space Applications Ctr, Jodhpur Tekra, Ahmedabad 380 015, India

NAYAR, CHEMMANGOT VELAYUDHAN, electrical engineering educator; b. Calicut, Kerala, India, Apr. 2, 1946; s. Gopalan Nair and Meenakshi Chemmangot; m. Ambika Ponnamma; children: Lakshmi, Sujith. BS in Engring., REC, Calicut, India, 1969; MS, Indian Inst. Tech., Kanpur, India, 1977; PhD, U. W. Australia, Perth, 1985. Lectr. REC, Calicut, India, 1969-82, Singapore Polytech. U., 1984-86; from lectr. to prof. Curtin U., Perth, Australia, 1986—; dir. Cresta, Perth, 1996—; head Power Elec. Reg. Unit, Perth, 1989-96; dir. Athreyenix, Bangalore, India, 1994—, Ausindia, Perth, 1994-97. Contbr. articles to profl. jours. Mem. IEEE, IEE, IE Australia. Avocations: movies, swimming. Home: 23 Darian Dr, Willetton WA6155, Australia Office: CRESTA Curtin U Tech, Bentley 6102, Australia

NAYLOR, JOHN THOMAS, telephone company executive; b. Orillia, Ont., Can., Jan. 30, 1913; s. Fred Addison and Ethel (Thompson) N.; m. Ruth Louisa Tissot, Dec. 21, 1934; children: Joan Crosby, Carol Manka. BSEE, Oreg. State U., 1934. Registered profl. engr., Calif., Oreg., Wash. Chief accountant McKesson & Robbins, Inc., Portland, Oreg., 1934-38; engr. Pub. Service Commn. Oreg., 1938-41; v.p. Gen. Telephone Co. Calif., 1941-50; v.p., gen. mgr. Philippine Long Distance Telephone Co., Manila, 1950-56; also dir.; v.p. United Utilities, Inc., 1956-59; pres., dir. United Telephone Co.; v.p. Internat. Tel. & Tel. Corp., N.Y.C., 1959-61; pres., dir. Telectronic Systems, Inc., Manila, Philippines, 1962-73; cons., 1973—. Author articles on engring., finance, mgmt., pub. service. Active Boy Scouts Am., YMCA; pres. Am. Sch., Manila; mem. coun. regents Oreg. State U., 1981—. Mem. IEEE, NSPE, Philippine Assn. Mech. and Elec. Engrs., Phi Kappa Phi, Tau Beta Pi, Eta Kappa Nu. Club: Army and Navy. Address: 1451 NE Meier Dr Grants Pass OR 97526-3805

NAYLOR, PAUL DONALD, lawyer; b. St. Bernard, Ohio, May 28, 1925; s. David Frederick and Erna Helen (Miller) N.; m. Geraldine L. Lacy, Jan. 20, 1945; children: Linda S., Paul Scott, Todd L. JD, U. Cin., 1948. Bar: Ohio 1948. Ptnr. Pulse & Naylor, Cin., 1949-65; pvt. practice Cin., 1965—. Mem. Nat. Rep. Com. Lt. (j.g.) USN, 1943-46. Recipient Svc. to Mankind award Sertoma Internat. Mem. Cin. Bar Assn. (real property com. 1966-86), Ohio Bar Assn., Cin. Lawyers Club (pres. 1955), Order of the Coif. Office: 30 E Central Pky Ste 210 Cincinnati OH 45202-1118

NAYLOR, RUSSELL, insurance brokerage company executive; b. Aquetong, Pa., Feb. 13, 1941; s. Charles Ross and Helen Courtney N.; m. Suzanne C., Aug. 2, 1941; children: Elizabeth, Christopher, Matthew, William. BSBA, Pa. State U., 1963. Asst. mgr. group dept. The Travelers Ins. Co., Phila., 1964-70; pres. Group Benefit Adminstrs. Pa., Media, 1970-73; regional mgr. State Mus. Ins. Co., Phila., 1973-75; pres., chmn. Comprehensive Benefits Svcs., Inc., Newton Square, Pa., 1975-86, Elite Brokerage Svcs. Ltd., Exxon, Pa., 1986—; bd. dirs. Stirling Benefits Corp. Mem. Stonewall Golf Club, Stone Harbor Golf Club, Sandbarons Golf Club. Republican. Avocations: fishing, golf.

NAZ, MUGHAL MUHAMMAD YOUSIF, hospital administrator; b. Lahore, Punjab, Pakistan, Feb. 11, 1927; s. Ghulam Nabi Mughal and Ghulam Fathima Mughal; m. Arifa Sultana Mughal, Oct. 15, 1954; children: Rehana Khalid, Rukhsana Foozan. MBA, Columbia Pacific U., 1980, PhD in Hosp. Adminstrn., 1982. Accts. rev. clk. Arabian Am. Oil Co., Abqaiq, 1952-61; biostatistician Arabian Am. Oil Co., Dhahran, 1962-65, planning and programming analyst, 1965-76, contract analyst, 1976-78; fin. contr. Ash-Sharq Hosp., Al-Khobar, Saudi Arabia, 1979-81; vice chmn. contr. gen. Mohammad Dossary Hosp., Al-Khobar, 1982—. Founder, owner social activity group for aid to needy, Lahore, Pakistan. Avocations: supporting mosques, reading, travel, social group activities. Fax: (966 3) 895 0735. Home and Office: Mohammad Dossary Hosp, PO Box 335, Al-Khobar Saudi Arabia Address: 10-A Rachna Block, Allama Iqbal Town, Lahore Pakistan

NAZAIRE, MICHEL HARRY, physician; b. Jérémie, Haiti, Sept. 29, 1939; s. Joseph and Hermance N.; m. Nicole Lamarque, Dec. 28, 1968; children: Hannick and Carline (twins). Grad., Coll. St. Louis de Gonzague, A. Petion, 1959; MD Faculty of Medicine and Pharmacology, State U. Haiti, 1966. Intern State U. Hosp., Port-Au-Prince, Haiti, 1965-66; resident physician Sanitarium, Port-Au-Prince, Haiti, 1966-68; practice medicine specializing in pneumology, 1966-68; practice medicine specializing in pneumo-physiology Port-Au-Prince, 1966—; physician fellow Klinik Havelhohe and Heckeshorn, Berlin, 1969-70, 89-91; attending physician Sanitarium, Port-Au-Prince, 1976-91; Dep. mem. Internat. Parliament for Safety and Peace, envoy-at-large Internat. State Parliament, mem. global environ. technol. newtwork Who. Contbr. articles to Jour. Indsl. Hygiene, Pneumology and Respiratory Protection. Fellow Internat. Soc. for Respiratory Protection, Am. Coll. Chest Physicians (assoc.), mem. Am. Pub. Health Assn., Am. Conf. Govtl. Indsl. Hygienists, Internat. Union Against Tuberculosis, Internat. Platform Assn., Physicians for Social Responsibility. Address: 2455 F St SE Apt 57 Auburn WA 98002-7662 also: 1115-25 Dorchester Rd #3C Brooklyn NY 11218

NAZARBAYEV, NURSULTAN ABISHEVICH, president of Kazakhstan; b. Kazakhstan, June 6, 1940. Grad., Higher Tech. Ednl. Inst. of Karaganda Metall. Combine, 1967; cert. in Econ. Sci., Moscow Acad. of Social Scis., 1990. Worker Karaganda Metall. Plant, 1960-69; now pres. Govt. of Kazakhstan, Almaty; 1st sec. of Temir-Tau City Com. Komsomol, 1969-71; 2d sec. of Temir-Tau City Com. Kazakh Communist Party, 1971-73; sec. of party com. of Karaganda Metall. Combine, 1973-77; sec. 2nd sec. of Karaganda Oblast Com. Kazakh Communist Party, 1977-79; sec. of cen. com. and mem. bur. cen. com. Kazakh Communist Party, 1979-84, leader, 1989—, chmn. Kazakh SSR Council of Ministers, 1984-89; 1st sec. cen. com. Communist Party Kazakhstan, 1989-91; chmn. Kazakh SSR Supreme Soviet, 1990; pres. Republic Kazakhstan, 1990—. Office: Office Pres, 11 Beibitshilik St, Astana 473000, Kazakhstan*

NAZARENKO, SERGEY ANDREEVICH, biologist, researcher; b. Dushanbe, Tadjikistan, Nov. 20, 1949; s. Andrey Demjanovich Nazarenko and Marija Petrovna Nikolaeva; m. Ludmila Pavlovna Druchevskaja, July 15, 1977; 1 child, Marija Sergeevna. MS, Tadjik State U., Dushanbe, Russia, 1971; PhD in Med. Genetics, Inst. Med. Genetics, Moscow, 1977; DSc in Clin. Cytogenetics, Ctr. Med. Genetics, Moscow, 1993. Sr. technician State Inst. Medicine, Dushanbe, 1971-74; sr. scientist Kirghiz Inst. Cardiology, Frunze, Russia, 1977-81, Inst. Oncology, Tomsk, Russia, 1981-86; head of lab. Inst. Med. Genetics, Tomsk, 1987—; asst. prof. State Med. Inst., Tomsk, 1989-95; prof. Siberian Med. U., Tomsk, 1995—; expert sci. program Health of Russian People, Moscow. Author: Clinical and Genetic Study of Indigenous Populations of West Siberia, 1987, Chromosomal Polymorphism and Human Development, 1993; contbr. articles to profl. jours. Grantee Human Genome, 1992, Russian Found. Fundamental Investigations, 1996. Mem. Acad. Natural Scis., Soc. Med. Genetics, Am. Soc. Human Genetics. Office: Inst Med Genetics, Ushaika 10, 634050 Tomsk Russia

NAZARENO, JULIO, judge. Pres. Supreme Ct. Argentina. Office: Supreme Ct Talcahuano 550, Office 4113 4th Fl, 1013 Buenos Aires Argentina*

NAZARETH, IRWIN DARRYL WILFRED, general practitioner, educator; b. Bombay, India, Oct. 12, 1958; s. Ignatius Xavier and Maria Carolina Clothilda (Rodrigues) N. MBBS, Topiwala Nat. Med. Sch., Bombay, 1984. Lic. Scottish Triple Qualification Com., 1986. Rsch. fellow Univ. Coll. London Med. Sch., 1989-95, lectr. in primary care medicine, 1995—; sr. lectr. in primary care medicine, 1995—; part time gen. practitioner The Keats

Group Practice, London, 1995—. Contbr. articles to profl. publs. Mem. Royal Coll. Gynecologists, Royal Coll. Gen. Practitioners. Office: U Coll London/Whittington, Dept Primary Health Care, London N19 5NF, England also: The Keats Group Practice, 1B Downshire Hill, London NW3 2NR, England

NAZARIAN, ASHOT, chemical physicist, consultant, researcher; b. Yerevan, Armenia, Jan. 3, 1955; came to U.S., 1992; s. Hoctemberic and Flora (Pashinian) N.; m. Karine Roushanian, Dec. 16, 1991; children: Alexander, Michael; children from previous marriage: David, Narine. BS, Yerevan State U., 1977; MS, Kurchatov Inst., Moscow, 1982, PhD, 1985. Scientist Kurchatov Inst., 1980-86; chief scientist Laser Technique Inst., Yerevan, 1986-88; dir. lab. Yerevan State U., 1988-90; dir. Ctr. for Applied Environ. Rsch., Yerevan, 1990-92; guest rschr. Nat. Inst. Standards and Tech., Gaithersburg, Md., 1992—; CRADA prin. investigator Nat. Inst. Standards, 1993-95; IR&D prin. investigator Sci. Applications Internat. Corp., Germantown, Md., 1993—, sr. scientist, project dir., 1992—. Contbr. numerous articles to profl. jours.; patentee in field. Recipient prize of Kurchatov, Kurchatov Inst., 1984; NRC grantee, 1996. Mem. Tech. Transfer Soc., Am. Pys. Soc. Avocations: music, travel, photography. Home: 110 Watch Hill Ln Gaithersburg MD 20878-2859 Office: Sci Applications Internat Corp 20201 Century Blvd Germantown MD 20874-1113

NAZÁRIO DA LIMA, RONALDO LUIZ See RONALDO

NAZAROV, PETER GRIGORIEVICH, immunologist; b. Novogeorgievsk, USSR, July 20, 1945; s. Grigory Dmitrievich and Anna Trophimovna (Stelmaschuk) N.; m. Margaret Golubeva, Jan. 25, 1978; 1 child, Marina. Diploma physician, First Leningrad Med. Inst., USSR, 1968; Doctor Med. Sci., Inst. Exptl. Medicine, Leningrad, 1988. Cytogeneticist City Cen. Med. Genetics, Leningrad, USSR, 1968-70; postgrad. fellow Inst. Exptl. Medicine, Leningrad, 1971-73; jr. rschr. Inst. Exptl. Medicine, 1974-78, sr. rschr., 1979-90, head lab. gen. immunology, 1990—; prof. immunology 3rd Med. Coll., Leningrad, 1997-99; lectr. Leningrad State U., 1979-80, Med. Acad. Postgrad. Edn., 1997-99. Author: V.I. Joffe in the Institute of Experimental Medicine, 1998, Reactants of Acute Phase of Inflammation, 2000. Recipient pres. stipend, Govt. Russia, 1997—; grantee Russian Found. Fundamental Rsch., 1998—. Mem. Russian Immunological Soc., Internat. Atherosclerosis Soc., Internat. Cytokine Soc. Avocations: reading, painting, historical studies. Home: Briusovskaya Str 12-75, 195271 Saint Petersburg Russia Office: Inst Exptl Medicine RAMS, 12 Academy Pavlov St, 197376 Saint Petersburg Russia

NAZAROV, TALBAK, Tajik government official; b. Dangara, Tadzhik, USSR, Mar. 15, 1938; s. Nazar Khodzhayev and Khnaifa (Ismailova) N.; m. Tatiana Grigorievna Teodorovich; children: Dmitry, Khanifa. Grad., Fin. Econ. Inst., Leningrad, USSR, 1960, DSc, 1965. Cert. economist, educator. Lectr. Lenin State U., Dushanbe, USSR, 1960-62; sr. lectr. Tadzhik Lenin State U., Dushanbe, 1965-80, rector, 1982-88, prof., head specialized sci. coun. on thesis; chmn., dean, head of coun. on productive forces Acad. Scis., Tadzhik SSR, Dushanbe, 1980-82; min. edn. Ministry of Edn., Tadzhik SSR, 1988-90; 1st dep. chmn. Coun. of Mins. of Tadzhik SSR, 1990-91; v.p. Presidium of Tadzhik Republic Acad. Scis., 1991—; now min. fgn. affairs Republic of Tajikistan, Dushanbe; Author: The Problems of Economic Industrial Stimulation, 1972, Financial Credit Methods of the Efficiency of Capital Investments, 1982; contbr. articles and essays to profl. jours. The people's dep. Supreme Soviet of Tadzhik SSR, Dushanbe, 1980—, Supreme Soviet of USSR, Moscow, 1989—. Recipient medal for Valiant Labour Supreme Soviet of USSR, 1970, Order of Honour, 1976, Academician Vavilov medal All-Union Soc., 1986. Mem. Communist Party. Avocations: reading, books. Office: Min Fgn Affairs, pr Rudaki 42, Dushanbe 734051, Tajikistan*

NAZAROVA, TAMARA B., English educator; b. Russia, Mar. 14, 1958. BA, Moscow State U., 1980, MA, 1984, PhD, 1990. Sr. lectr. dept. English, Moscow State U., 1983-90, asst. prof. dept. English,, 1990-94, prof. dept. English,, 1994—; dir./coord. internat. debate exch. program Nat. Comm. Assn., 1990—. Asst. editor Internat. Jour. Forensics, 1999—; mem. editl. bd. ESP Russia Newsletter, 1996-98; contbr. numerous articles to profl. jours. Mem. Internat. Assn. Tchrs. English as Fgn. Lang. (editor-in-chief newsletter 1990-95, br. sec. 1993-96), Linguistic Assn. Tchrs. English at U. Moscow (editor-in-chief newsletter 1990-95, pres. 1993-96, v.p. 1996-97), Bus. English Spl. Interest Group, Bus. English Spl. Interest Group Russia, Internat. Assn. Semiotic Studies, Semiotic Soc. Am., Nat. Comm. Assn. USA (dir./coord. internat. debate exch. program 1990—), Internat. Pub. Debate Assn., Libr. Congress USA, Smithsonian Nat. Assocs./Smithsonian Instn. E-mail: tnazarov@ozelle.com. Fax: 210 690-3015.

NAZAR-STEWART, VALLE, epidemiologist, educator; b. Cambridge, Mass., June 6, 1956; d. Jack and Vera Elizabeth (Schuett) Nazar; m. Brian Kirk Stewart, Nov. 30, 1991; 1 child, Zachary Lee Stewart. BA in Biology, Cornell U., 1978; MS in Health Policy and Mgmt., Harvard U., 1982; PhD in Epidemiology, U. Wash., Seattle, 1991. Policy analyst Office of Policy and Resource Mgmt., U.S. EPA, Washington, 1982-83, Office of Air and Radiation, U.S. EPA, Washington, 1983-86; asst. mem. Fred Hutchinson Cancer Rsch. Ctr., Seattle, 1992-00; asst. prof. epidemiology U. Wash., Seattle, 1992-96; asst. prof. epidemiology U. Pitts., 1996—, mem. Cancer Inst., 1996—; asst. staff scientist Ctr. Rsch. Occpl./Environ. Toxicology Oreg. Health Scis. U., Portland, 2000—. Home: 3033 NW Colonial Dr Bend OR 97701-5447 Office: CROET OHSU L 606 3181 SW Sam Jackson Park Rd Portland OR 97201-3011

NAZARYK, PAUL ALAN, lawyer, environmental consultant; b. Denver; s. Milton Paul and Margaret Ann Nazaryk; m. Jennifer Phillips, June 16, 1990; children: Krista Brooke, Carly Rebekah. BA, U. No. Colo., 1976; MA, Colo. State U., 1979; JD, U. Denver, 1986. Bar: Colo. 1987, Mont. 2000. Legis. intern Rep. James P. Johnson Ho. Reps., Washington, 1976; policy analyst U.S. Water Resources Coun., Washington, 1979, water policy specialist, 1979-81; environ. policy specialist, atty. Colo. Dept. Pub. Health and Environment, Denver, 1981-90; regulatory specialist ERM-Rocky Mountain Inc., Englewood, Colo., 1990-96; regulatory specialist, in-house atty. Harding Lawson Assocs., Denver, 1996-2000; regulatory specialist ERM-Rocky Mountain Inc., Greenwood Village, Colo., 2000—; adj. faculty, U. Denver. Contbr. articles to profl. jours. Mem. Mont. Bar Assn. (natural resources and environ. law sect. 2000—), Colo. Bar Assn. (environ. law sect. 1987—), Denver C. of C. (environ. com. 1997-98). Democrat. Episcopalian. Avocations: western history, camping, cycling, skiing. Office: ERM-Rocky Mountain cs 5950 S Willow Dr Greenwood Vlg CO 80111-5170

NAZEM, FEREYDOUN F., venture capitalist, financier; b. Tehran, Iran, Dec. 29, 1940; came to U.S., 1960; naturalized, 1976; s. Hassan and Afsar N.; m. Susie Gharib, Jan. 20, 1973; children: Alexander, Taraneh. BS, Ohio State U., 1964; MSc, U. Cin., 1967; MBA, Columbia U., 1971. Sr. rsch. chemist Matheson Coleman & Bell, Norwood, Ohio, 1967-68; asst. v.p., investment analyst Irving Trust Co., N.Y.C., 1969-74; v.p., venture capital officer Charter N.Y., N.Y.C., 1974-75; mng. dir. Collier Enterprises, N.Y.C., 1976-81; mng. ptnr. Nazem & Co., N.Y.C., 1981—, Explorer Fund, N.Y.C., 1997—, Transatlantic Venture Fund; bd. dirs. Tegal Corp., Petaluma, Calif., Spatial Tech. Inc., Boulder, Colo., Genetix Corp., Boston, IQ Systems, Newtown, Conn., Mastercare Corp., Cranford, N.J., Oxford Health, Norwalk, Conn., iwin.com, L.A., Mediconsult.com, N.Y.C., breathnet.com., Inc. Author: The Chemical Industry and Energy Shortage. Mem. N.Y. Soc. Security Analysts, N.Y. Venture Capital Forum. Office: Nazem & Co 645 Madison Ave New York NY 10022-1010

NAZINA, TAMARA NIKOLAEVNA, microbiologist, researcher; b. Chernogorsk, Russia, Mar. 17, 1953; d. Nikolay Ulianovich and Aleksandra Mikhailovna (Burmakina) N.; m. Andrew Borisovich Poltaraus, July 12, 1974; children: Mikhail, Vassily. MSc in Biochemistry, Moscow State U. M.V. Lomonosov, 1975; PhD in Microbiology, Russian Acad. Scis., Moscow, 1983. Rsch. probationer Inst. Microbiology, Russian Acad. Scis., 1975-77, rsch. scientist, 1977-87, sr. rsch. scientist, 1987—. Author: (with S.I. Kuznetsov and A.I. Saralov) Microbiological Processes of Carbon and Nitrogen Cycle in Lakes, 1985; contbr. over 50 articles to sci. jours., including Geomicrobiology Jour., Microbiology; co-patentee in field. Named Laureate in field sci. and techniques Premium of Russian Govt., 1995; grantee Internat. Sci. Found., 1993, 94, travel grantee, 1996. Fellow Russian Soc. Microbiology. Avocations: travel, fishing. Fax: (7-095) 135-6530. E-mail: Nazina@inmi.host.ru. Home: Krupskaya 15, 53, 117331 Moscow Russia Office: Russian Acad Scis Inst Micr, Prosp 60-Let Oktyabrya 7/2, 117811 Moscow Russia

NAZLI, CEM, physician, educator; b. Izmir, Turkey, Aug. 27, 1970; s. Birol and Emine (Sunmak) N. MD, Hacettepe U., Ankara, Turkey, 1994. Resident in cardiology Dokuz Eylul U., Izmir, 1994-99; assoc. prof. Suleyman Demirel U., Isparta, Turkey, 1999—. Contbr. articles to profl. jours. Mem. Am. Soc. Echocardiography, Turkish Soc. Cardiology (Young Scientist award 1999). Avocations: computers, Internet, political history. Home: Mustafa Bey Cad No 12/6, Alsancak Izmir 35220, Turkey

NDAM, SHADRACK NJAH, United Nations official, adviser; b. Mundum I., Mezam, Cameroon, May 18, 1942; arrived in Austria, 1969; s. Marcus Tebo and Magdalena Ngum Ndam; m. Phebe Ngum; children: Marilyn Bih, Kingsley Nibahfor, Carlson Njih, Shirley Ngum, Kasama Mancho. BS in Chem. Engring., U. R.I., 1968, MS in Chem. Engring., 1969. Registered profl. engr. Prodn. and process control officer Cameroon Devel. Corp., Bota/Tiko, 1969; indsl. devel. officer UN Indsl. Devel. Orgn., Vienna, 1969-75, spl. asst. to dir. Indsl. Tech. Divsn., 1979-80; chief, coord. unit Indsl. Devel. Decade for Africa, 1983—, tech. asst. to dep. exec. dir., 1980-90; adviser to Orgn. of African Unity UN Indsl. Devel. Orgn., Addis Ababa, Ethiopia, 1980-82; head/dir. African Programme/Bur. UN Indsl. Devel. Orgn., 1990-96, dir. Human Resources Devel. Programme, 1996-98, sr. advisor, investment promotion and internat. capacity/bdg, 1996-99; rep. for the Sudan, Yemen, 1999—; Editor: Industrial Research Institutes: Organization for Effective Research, Technical and Commercial Services; Programme for the IDDA, 1982; Development of Industrial and Technological Manpower in Africa, 1984; cons. Lagos Plan of Action and Final Act of Lagos, 1980. Editor: Reports on 3d world industrialization and Africa. Scoutmaster World Scout Assn., Owerri, Nigeria, 1961-62. Mem. Am. Inst. Chem. Engring. (vice-chmn. chpt. 1968-69), Cameroon Nat. Union, Lions Club, Tau Beta Pi. E-mail: snndam@hotmail.com. Home: Grossbauerstrasse 83, A-1210 Vienna Austria Office: UN Industrial Devel Orgn, Wagrammerstrasse 5, A-1220 Vienna Austria also Address: UNDP, PO Box 913, Khartoum Sudam

NDEGE, MAURICE MBEDA, utilities executive, researcher; b. Kisumu, Nyanza, Kenya, Jan. 3, 1955; s. Alphonce John and Philipina Ajuan'g (Ahenda) N.; m. Maria Gorzkowska Mbeda, Apr. 29, 1983; children. Diploma, Kraków (Poland) Agrl. U., 1983, Norwegian Inst. Tech., Trondheim, 1990. Engr. Ministry Water Resources, Nairobi, Kenya, 1973-89; lectr. U. Nairobi, 1990-98; exec. dir. Africa Water Network, Nairobi, 1993—. Mem. Internat. Hydraulic Rsch. Assn., Internat. Water Resources Assn., Internat. Assn. Water Quality. Roman Catholic. Avocations: table tennis, football, dancing, fishing, reading. Home: PO Box 51004, Peponi Rd, 51004 Nairobi Kenya Office: Africa Water Network, Meilili Rd, PO Box 10538, Nairobi Kenya

NDIAYE, YOUSSOUPHA, judge. Pres. Constl. Ct. of Senegal, Dakar. Office: Conseil Constitutional, Dakar Senegal*

NDJOUNTCHE, TERTULIEN, engineer; b. Bangwa, Cameroon, Nov. 7, 1968; s. Michel and Emilienne (Happi) Tchikangoua. MS, Yaounde U., Cameroon, 1992; PhD, Erlangen-Nuremberg U., Germany, 1999. Rsch. engr. Yaounde U., Cameroon, 1992-96; rsch. asst. Erlangen-Nuremberg U., Germany, 1996—; cons. in field. Author: Dynamic Analog Circuit Techniques for Real-Time Adaptive Networks, 2000; co-author: Artificial Neural Nets and Genetic Algorithms, 1999; inventor in field. Mem. IEEE. Avocations: basketball, cycling, chess, electronic games. Office: LATE/Erlangen-Nuremberg U, Cauerstr 7, 91058 Erlangen Germany

NDON, BASSEY ASUQUO, agronomist, educator; b. Ita Uruan, Akwa Ibom, Nigeria, Sept. 28, 1946; m. Eno Okon Inyang; children: Ifiok, Mbuotidem, Imaobong, Sana, Edikan. BSc in Agr., Obafemi Awolowo U., Ife, Nigeria, 1973; MS in Agronomy, U. Wis., 1977, PhD in Agronomy, 1980. Sr. tutor Luth. H.S., Uyo, Nigeria, 1968-70; asst. chief rsch. agronomist/physiologist Nigerian Inst. for Oil Palm Rsch., Benin City, 1973-84, acting head plant physiology divsn., 1980-82; sr. lectr. U. Cross River State, Uyo, 1984-90, acting head dept. agr., 1984-85, acting dean faculty agr. Okuku campus, 1989, dept. agronomy Okuku campus, 1989-90; sr. lectr. dept. agronomy U. Uyo, 1992-94, head dept. agronomy, 1992-94; vis. prof. agronomy Coll. Agr., Pt. Antonio, Portland, Jamaica, 1990-91; cons. agronomist/dir. Jerpro (Nigeria) Ltd. Co., 1992—; external examiner diploma exam. Sch. Agr., Akampa, Cross River State, 1990; external examiner dept. agronomy U. Calabar, 1993-98. Contbr. numerous articles to profl. jours. Apptd. mem. Akwa Ibom State Local Govt. Svc. Commn., 1994-99. Mem. Am. Soc. Agronomy, Am. Soc. Crop Sci., Nigerian Soc. of Agr., Weed Sci. Soc. Nigeria. Home: 7 Jerusalem St, Mbiabong PO Box 243, Ikot Essien Uyo Nigeria Office: U Uyo Dept Agronomy, PMB 1017, Uyo Nigeria

NDON, UDEME JAMES, civil engineering educator; b. Ukanafun, Akwaibom, Nigeria, Oct. 12, 1958; came to the U.S., 1981; s. James Udo and Marit James Ndon; m. Tersie Udeme, Oct. 20, 1980; children: Ediomo U., Sifon U., Idara U., Anietie U. BS, Harding U., 1984; MS, Western Ill. U., 1987; BS in Civil Engring., Iowa State U., 1990, MS in Civil Engring., 1990, PhD, 1995. Tchg. asst. Western Ill. U., Macomb, 1985-86, instr., 1986-87; instr. Iowa State U., Ames, 1987-88, 90, rsch. asst., 1987-94; process/rsch. engr. McClure Engring. Co., Ft. Dodge, Iowa, 1994-95; instr., rsch. assoc. U. Ctrl. Fla., Orlando, 1995-96; asst. prof. San Jose (Calif.) State U., 1996—; mem. organizing com. Environ. Conf., Boston, 1998. Contbr. articles to profl. jours. Recipient Rsch. Presentation award Purdue U., West Lafayette, Ind., 1993, Environ. Edn. award Silicon Valley Joint Venture, San Jose, 1997. Mem. ASCE (com. mem.), Assn. Environ. Profs. (com. chair), Am. Water Works Assn., Nat. Environ. Health Assn., Internat. Assn. on Water Quality, Water Environment Fedn. Office: San Jose State Univ One Washington Sq San Jose CA 95192

NDUKUBA, PATRICK IFEANYICHUKWU, physiologist, biomedical researcher; b. Aba, Abia, Nigeria, Apr. 12, 1950; s. Sampson Chukwueke and Margaret (Nwaulari) N. BSc, N.C. State U., 1979; MSc, U. Baroda, India, 1983, PhD, 1991. Diploma in chem. tech., Baroda, 1981. Sr. lectr., head dept. human physiology Abia State U., Uturu, Nigeria, 1992—; coord. Sch. Basic Med. Scis. Abia State U., Uturu, 1992-94; external examiner Nnamdi Azukiwe U. Coll. Medicine, Nnewi, 1997—, Ebonyi State U. Coll. Medicine, Abakaliki, 1997—; mem. Abia State U. Senate, 1992—. Author: Artificial Kidney and Clinical Problems of Uremia, 1996, Renal and Cardiovascular Physiology, 1997, Physiological Electrocardiography, 1998, History and Philosophy of Science: From 5th Century B.C. to 20th Century A.D., 1998, Fundamentals of Human Physiology, 1999; contbr. articles to profl. jours. Recipient first prize Hari Ohm Ashram Prerit Shri Bhaikaka Inter-Univ. Smarak Trust, India, 1991, Econ. commn. Africa internat. Orgn. Migration Sponsored Return of Skills Programme, 1991. Mem. Indian Soc. for Reproductive Biology and Comparative Endocrinology, Physiol. Soc. Nigeria, N.Y. Acad. Scis. Roman Catholic. Avocations: footballl, lawn tennis, table tennis, reading novels, movies. Office: Abia State U Coll Medicine, PMB 2000, Uturu Abia, Nigeria

NEAGU, GABRIEL, research scientist; b. Bucharest, Romania, Nov. 1, 1949; s. Nicolae and Elena (Oprisan) N.; m. Dorela Harsulescu, Aug. 31, 1985; children: Andrei, Ana Flavia. Student, Politehnica U., Bucharest, 1969, PhD, 1998; BSc in Info. Systems, Inst. of Energetics, Moscow, 1974. Programmer Ctrl. Inst. for Mgmt. and Informatics, Bucharest, 1974-79, rschr., 1979-83, sr. rschr., 1983-85, head R&D lab., 1984-85; head rsch. lab. Rsch. Inst. for Informatics, Bucharest, 1985-93, sr. rschr., 1985-95, advisor, 1993—, rsch. scientist, 1995-; rep. of the Romanian party Tech. Com. for Indsl. Info. Systems, Intergovt. Commn. of Ea. European Countries for Computers and Informatics, 1980-87; assoc. prof. Human Resources Training Ctr., (HRTC), Tng. Ctr. for MSc students Politehnica U., Bucharest, 1996—, head, Rschr. Lab., 1999—; local mgr. European rsch. projects, 1995-97, assoc. prof. Nat. Inst. for Econ. Devel. and Valahia U., 1999—, expert evaluator, EC Espirit Projs., 1998—. Contbr. contbr. articles to profl. publs.. Lt. Comms., 1975. Grantee CEPIA, 1985, IREX (N.. Inst. of Tech. and Carnegie Melon U., 1993), Ministry of Rsch. and Tech., 1996, Romanian Acad., 1997-98. Mem. Romanian Soc. on Concurrent Engring. (founder mem.), N.Y. Acad. Scis. (hon.), Romanian Soc. for Automation and Tech. Informatics, Romanian Soc. for Simulation, IFAC (tech. com. on social impact of automatic control, tech. com. on advanced mfg. techniques). Avocations: classical music, theatre, travel. E-Mail: gneagu@ici.ro. Fax: 40 1 224 05 39. Office: Nat Inst R&D in Informatics, Averescu Av 8-10 sector 1, Bucharest Romania

NEAGU, STEFAN ILIE, surgeon, educator; b. Bucharest, Romania, Sept. 13, 1949; s. Valentin and Natalia (Stoenescu) N.; m. Eugenia Cristina Marin, Oct. 15, 1972; 1 child, Manuela Stefana. MD, Faculty Medicine Bucharest, 1974, PhD, 1984; dipl. cancer surgery, Cancer Inst. Bucharest, 1982; dipl. transplantation surgery, Strasbourg U., 1992, dipl. visceral surgery, 1994. Asst. prof. surgery Faculty Medicine Bucharest, 1976-79, asst. prof. titular, 1980-93, assoc. prof. surgery, 1993—; head 2nd. dept. surgery U. Hosp., Bucharest, 1998—; pres. "Alexis Carrel" Found. Med. Rsch., 2000. Author: Renal Preservation by Cold Storage, 1990, Surgery, 2 vols., 1992, 94; inventor in field. Fellow Roman Soc. Surgery, French Assn. Surgery, Internat. Assn. Pancreatology, Jockey Club Romania, European Digestive Surgery; mem. N.Y. Acad. Scis. Avocations: fencing, gardening, history. Home: str Viitorului 22, 70 266 Bucharest Romania Office: Univ Hosp Dept Surgery, Splaiul Independentei 169, Bucharest Romania

NEAL, ANTHONY JAMES, oncologist; b. London, Oct. 18, 1961. MB, BS, St. Thomas' Hosp., London, 1985; MD, Inst. Cancer Rsch., Sutton, Eng., 1995. Registrar Royal London Hosp., 1988-92; clin. rsch. fellow Inst. Cancer Rsch., Sutton, 1993-94; sr. registrar Royal Marsden Nat. Health Svc. Trust, London and Sutton, 1994-95; cons. oncologist Royal Marsden NHS Trust, Sutton, 1996-2000; cons. oncologist St. Luke's Cancer Ctr. Royal Surrey County Hosp., Guildford, Eng., 2000—. Author: Clinical Oncology: A Textbook for Students, 1994, 2d edit., 1997; contbr. articles to profl. jours. Formerly Recognized Tchr. and Hon. Sr. Lectr., U. London/Inst. Cancer Rsch., 1996. Fellow Royal Coll. Radiologists; mem. Royal Coll. Physicians (U.K.), Brit. Med. Assn., Brit. Oncol. Assn. (Amgen-Roche Jr. Investigator award 1994), European Soc. Therapeutic Radiology (Estro-Varian Physics Rsch. award 1994, Estro-Philips Traveling fellow 1994). Office: Royal Marsden NHS Trust, Royal Surrey County Hosp, Saint Lukes Cancer Ctr, Guildford Surrey GU2 5XX, England

NEAL, JOSEPH LEE, vocational school educator; b. Memphis, Feb. 17, 1948; s. James Henry and Minnie Rue (Waldrop) N.; children: Janice Celeste Neal, Mary Joanne; m. Lou Alice Smith, Apr. 10, 1999. AAS, N.W. C.C., Senatobia, Miss., 1979, AS in Bus., 1980; BS, U. S. Miss., 1984, MS, 1986. Cert. tchr. Miss. Police officer City of W. Memphis, Ark., 1970-72; customer svc. rep. Biomed. Labs., Little Rock, Ark., 1972-75; sales, svc. rep Moore Ford Co., N. Little Rock, 1975-77; electronics technician N.W. Miss. C.C., Senatobia, 1979-82, electronics inst., 1982-83; electronics engr. U. So. Miss., Hattiesburg, 1983-85; electronics instr. Tex. State Tech. Inst., Sweetwater, 1985-87, De Soto County Vo-Tech. Ctr., Southaven, Miss., 1988-97, South Panola H.S., Batesville, Miss., 1997—; cons. engr. various radio ops., Hattiesburg, 1982-85; mem. curriculum com. De Soto County Schs., 1990-95; steering com. N.W. Miss. Tech. Prep., Senatobia, 1992-95, participant in Learn to Work Workshop Miss. St. U. and Pealey Electronics, 1997, tchr. trainer for Tech. Discovery, 1998, 99. Bd. dirs. Optimist Club, Sweetwater, Tex., 1987. Named Outstanding Tchr., Horn Lake So. C. of C., 1992. Mem. Am. Vocat. Assn., Miss. Trade and Tech. Assn. (v.p. 1994-95, pres. 1995-96), Miss. Assn. Vocat. Educators (pres. dist. 1 1991-92, 95-96, bd. dirs. 1991-92, 95-96, sec. dist. 1 1993-94, v.p. 1994-95), Vocat.-Indsl. Clubs of Am. (100% Advisor 1990, 91, 92, VICA state advisor of yr. 1993), N.Am. Hunting Club (life). Baptist. Avocations: hunting, fishing, pub. speaking. Home: PO Box 172 1578 Freeman Rd Como MS 38619 Office: South Panola HS Batesville MS 38606

NEAL, LEORA LOUISE HASKETT, social services administrator; b. N.Y.C., Feb. 23, 1943; d. Melvin Elias and Miriam Emily (Johnson) Haskett; m. Robert A. Neal, Apr. 23, 1966; children: Marla Patrice, Johnathan Robert. BA in Psychology and Sociology, City Coll. N.Y., 1965; MS in Social Work, Columbia U., 1970, cert. adoption specialist, 1977; IBM cert. community exec. tng. program, N.Y., 1982. Cert. social worker N.Y. Caseworker N.Y.C. Dept. Social Service, 1965-67, Windham Child Care, N.Y.C., 1967-73; exec. dir., founder Assn. Black Social Workers Child Adoption Counseling and Referral Service, N.Y.C., 1975-96; adoption tng. specialist Ctr. for Devel. Human Svcs., SUNY-N.Y. State Office Children and Family Svcs., Yonkers, 1996—; cons. in field; founder Haskett-Neal Publs., Bronx, N.Y., 1993. Co-author: Transracial Adoptive Parenting: A Black/White Community Issue, 1993; contbr. articles to profl. jours. Pres. bd. dirs. Fountain Ave. Cmty. Devel. Corp. Child Welfare League Am. fellow, 1976; recipient cert. No Time to Lose cert. N.Y. State Dept. Social Svcs., 1989. Mem. NAFE, Nat. Assn. Black Social Workers, Columbia U. Alumni Assn., CCNY Alumni Assn., Missionary Com. Revival Team (outreach chair 1982-88). Democrat. Avocations: writing, history and religious studies, travel, cultural activities. Office: NY State Office of Children and Family Svcs SUNY 525 Nepperhan Ave Yonkers NY 10703-2857

NEAL, LESLIE ROBERT, computer science educator; b. Northampton, Eng., Dec. 28, 1941; m. Christine Hill, Apr. 12, 1966; children: Simon, Louise, Robert. BSc, U. Nottingham, Eng., 1963, PhD, 1970. Chartered engr. Lectr. Brunel U., Uxbridge, Eng., 1966-78, sr. lectr., 1978—. Fellow Brit. Computer Soc., Inst. of Math. U.K. Avocations: golf, tennis, badminton. Home: 1 Thrushe Close, Booker, High Wycombe HP12 4RJ, England Office: Dept Computer Sci, Brunel U, Uxbridge UB8 3PH, England

NEAL, MARGARET SHERRILL, writer, editor; b. Memphis, Apr. 13, 1950; d. Wilburn Franklin and Merle Aileen (Willis) N. BA, Memphis State U., 1972, postgrad., 1973; MS, Columbia Pacific U., 1984. Air traffic contr. FAA, Memphis, 1974-76, New Bern, N.C., 1976-81, Vero Beach, Fla., 1981-83; detection sys. specialist U.S. Customs Svc., Miami, 1983-87, intelligence rsch. specialist, 1987-89; ret., 1989. Sec. Pompano Beach Highlands Civic Improvement Assn., 1998; mem. Highlands Neighborhood Watch. Mem. NOW, Smithsonian Instn., Mensa, Nat. Trust Hist. Preservation, Greenpeace, Clan Macneil Soc., Nature Conservancy, Lighthouse Point Writers' Workshops, Save the Manatee Club, learning partner tutor Norcrest Elem. Sch. Democrat. Presbyterian. Avocations: genealogy, needlework, traveling, sketching, growing orchids.

NEAL, MICHAEL DEWAYNE, company executive; b. Memphis, Apr. 7, 1968; s. Bessie Neal and Margie Etta Malone; children: Brittany, Ashley. BBA in Fin., U. Memphis, 1996, MA in Econs., 1998. Mgr. FedEx Properties MIS, Memphis; bd. dirs. Fogleman Coll. Bus. and Econs. Alumni Assn., Memphis. E-mail: mdneal1@fedex.com.

NEAL, (TIMOTHY) RUFUS, editor; b. Ashbourne, Derbyshire, Eng., Sept. 23, 1954; s. Richard Crawley and Elizabeth (Caiger) N.; m. J. Valerie Oppenheim, Mar. 2, 1979; children: Rebecca Tarn, Jennifer Cerian. BSc with honors, U. Sussex, Eng., 1976. With Cambridge (Eng.) U. Press, 1976—, commissioning editor phys. scis., 1993—, sr. commissioning editor phys. scis., 1996—, mgr. digital bus. coordination, 1999—. Mem. Am. Phys. Soc. Avocations: making things, music. Office: Cambridge U Press, Shaftesbury Rd, Cambridge CB2 2RU, England

NEALE, FRANK LESLIE GEORGE, venture capitalist; b. Coventry, Eng., Aug. 25, 1950; s. Hugh and Mona (Clarkson) N.; m. Helen Veronica Carter, June 16, 1975; children: Michael, Jeremy, Rory. BA in Econs., St. John's Coll., Cambridge, 1971; MBA, U. Manchester, 1973. Cons. Economist Intelligence Unit, London, 1973-77; sr. cons. PA Mgmt. Cons., London, 1977-80; gen. mgr. PA Devel., London, 1980-83; dir. Citicorp Venture Capital, London, 1983-88; ptnr. Phildrew Ventures, London, 1988—; non-exec. dir. HR Holdings, Surrey, Locum Group, Essex, Parkhill Pub., London, No. 2 Venture Capital Trust, Newcastle; former vice chmn. Brit. Venture Capitol Assocs. Avocations: ballet, reading, swimming, football. Office: Phildrew Ventures, 100 Liverpool St, London EC2M 2RH, England EC2A1BD

NEALE, GAIL LOVEJOY, non-profit organization management consultant; b. Detroit, Feb. 8, 1935; d. Elijah Parish and Jane Appleton

(Howell) Lovejoy; m. Richard Potter (div.); m. Anthony Astrachan (div.); children: Owen Lovejoy Astrachan, Joshua Howell Astrachan; m. Robert Edward Neale, June 23, 1984. Rsch. aide, dir. devel., corp. sec., v.p. Hudson Inst., Inc., Croton on Hudson, N.Y., 1962-76; v.p. Aspen Inst., N.Y.C., 1976-78; dir. external affairs Middlebury (Vt.) Coll., 1978-80; pres. Hudson Inst., Croton on Hudson, 1980-82; corp. sec. Commonwealth Fund, N.Y.C., 1983-86; project adminstr. Mt. Holyoke Coll., South Hadley, Mass., 1986-88; dir. devel. Hampshire Coll., Amherst, Mass., 1988-91; exec. v.p., COO Salzburg Seminar, Middlebury, Vt., 1991-96; pres., founder The Lovejoy Consulting Group, Inc., Burlington, Vt., 1997—; trustee JL Found., L.A.; bd. dirs. Capital Income Builder, L.A., Capital World Growth and Income Fund, L.A., Fundamental Investors, L.A., Growth Fund Am., Vera Inst. for Justice, N.Y.C.; trustee Endowments, Inc., L.A.; dir., chair campaign Shelburne Farms, 1997-2000; dir. Circus Smirkus. Bd. dirs. Conern for Dying, N.Y.C., 1986-90; dir. Frances Clark Ctr. for Keyboard Pedagogy, 1997-2000; mem. Preservation Land Trust Vt., Mozart Festival Vt., Flynn Theatre. Mem. Origami U.S.A. Democrat. Episcopalian. Avocations: reading, cooking, knitting, origami, magic. Fax: 802-658-6189. E-mail: neale@together.net. Office: The Lovejoy Consulting Group Inc 154 Prospect Pkwy Burlington VT 05401-4148

NEALE, MICHAEL JOHN, engineering company executive; b. Hampstead, London, Eng., Dec. 14, 1926; s. Harold Arthur and Patricia Kathleen (McMahon) N.; life ptnr.: Ian Peter Lansley. BSc in Engring., U. London, 1948; DIC, Imperial Coll. London, 1955. Apprentice Rolls Royce, Derby, Eng., 1944-49; rsch. mgr. Glacier Metal Co., London, 1956-59, mgr. customer tech. support, 1959-62; cons. engr. Michael Neale & Assocs., Farnham, 1962-92; chmn. Neale Cons. Engrs., Ltd., Farnham, 1992—. Editor/author: The Tribology Handbook, 1973, 2d edit., 1995; author: Guide to the Condition Monitoring of Machinery, 1979; co-author: Couplings and Shaft Alignment, 1991. Decorated Order Brit. Empire, Queen of Eng., 1984. Fellow Royal Acad. Engring., Instn. Mech. Engrs., City and Guilds Inst., Instn. Mech. Engrs. (pres. 1990-91), Assn. Cons. Scientists (pres. 1996—), Athenaeum Club London. Labour Party. Avocation: restoration old houses and steam machines. Home: Chalkdell, Herriard RG25 2PR, England Office: Neale Cons Engrs Ltd, 43 Downing St, Farnham Surrey GU9 7PH, England

NEALL, VINCENT ERNEST, earth science educator; b. Bristol, Eng., June 17, 1947; s. Kenneth William and Betty Eileen (Beard) N.; m. Annabel Margaret Hurford, Feb. 12, 1972; children: Susan Esther, Malcolm Vernon Kenneth. BSc, Victoria U. Wellington, New Zealand, 1967, BSc with honours, 1968, PhD in Geology, 1973. Scientist Antarctic divsn. Dept. Sci. and Indsl. Rsch., New Zealand, 1967-68; jr. lectr. Victoria U. Wellington, 1968-73; from lectr. to assoc. prof. soil sci. Massey U., Palmerston North, New Zealand, 1973—; chmn. Nat. CD Volcanic Hazards Working Group, 1989-99; chmn. nat. com. New Zealand Internat. Geol. Correlation Programme, 1992—; mem. earth sci. com. New Zealand Found. for Rsch., Sci. and Tech., 1993-99; dep. chmn. New Zealand sci. subcommn. UNESCO, 1996-99. Mem. adv. com. to Robert Bruce Trust, Palmerston North, 1988—; chmn. Camellia Meml. Trust, Palmerston North, 1994—; pres. Sci. Ctr. Inc. (Soc.), Palmerston North, 1995-97. Recipient environ. award Taranaki Regional Coun., 1997, New Zealand Sci. and Tech. medal Royal Soc. New Zealand, 1998. Fellow Geol. Soc. Am., Soil Sci. Soc. New Zealand; mem. Geol. Soc. New Zealand (pres. 1981-83, McKay Hammer award 1981, Hochstetter lectr. 1981). Office: Massey U Inst Natural Res, Pvt Bag 11-222, Palmerston North New Zealand

NEAL-PARKER, SHIRLEY ANITA, obstetrician and gynecologist; b. Washington, Aug. 28, 1949; d. Leon Walker and Pearl Anita (Shelton) Neal; m. Andre Cowan Dasent, June 21, 1971 (div. Feb. 1978); 1 child, Erika Michelle Dasent; m. James Carl Parker, Feb. 11, 1979; 1 child, Amirah Nabeehah. BS in Biology, Am. U., 1971; MD, Hahnemann U., 1979. Med. lic. Md., W.Va., Calif., Wash. Intern Howard U. Hosp., 1979-80, resident, 1980-84; physician Nat. Health Svc. Corp., Charleston, W. Va., 1984-86; clin. instr. W. Va. U., Charleston, 1985-86; pvt. practice ob./gyn. Sacramento, 1986-95; pvt. practice Chehalis, Wash., 1995—; chair dept. perinatology Providence Centralia Hosp., 1999—. Bd. dirs. Ruth Rosenberg Dance Ensemble, Sacramento, 1992-95, Human Response Network, Chehalis, 1995-97. Mem. Am. Assn. Gynecologic Laparoscopists, Am. Productive Health Profls., Nat. Med. Assn., Am. Med. Women's Assn. (comty. svc. award Mother Hale br. 1994), Nat. Assn. Gynecol. Laparoscopists, Nat. Assn. Reproductive Profls., Wash. State Med. Assn., Lewis County Med. Soc., Soroptomist Internat. Avocations: traveling, reading, crocheting, collecting ethnic dolls, magnets. Home: 221 Vista Rd Chehalis WA 98532-8766 Office: PO Box 997 Chehalis WA 98532-0997

NEARY, VINCENT SINCLAIR, engineering educator; b. Vineland, N.J., May 20, 1964; s. James Vincent Neary and Carol Lucille Sinclair; m. Jessica Graydon Taylor, June 23, 1990; 1 child, Liam James. BS in Agrl. Engring., Rutgers U., 1987; MS, Univ. Iowa, 1992, PhD, 1995. Cert. profl. engr., Tenn. Engr.-in-tng. Sadat Assocs., Inc., Princeton, N.J., 1987-88, Post, Buckley, Schuh & Jernigan, Inc., Princeton, 1988-89; sr. assoc. Philip Williams & Assocs., Ltd., San Francisco, 1996-97; asst. prof. dept. civil and environ. engring. Tenn. Technol., Cookeville, Tenn., 1997—; advisor Napa-Sonoma Marsh Restoration Com., San Francisco, 1996-97; sec. Environ. Hydraulics Tech. Com., Am. Soc. Civil Engrs., Washington, 1999—. Contbr. articles to profl. jours. Founder, coord. Ralston Creek Watershed Ptnrship, Iowa City, 1995. Recipient Ralph E. Power Jr. Faculty Enhancement award in Engring., Oak Ridge Assoc. Univs., 1999, Iowa Engring. Dean's scholarship U. Iowa, 1990. Mem. Am. Soc. Civil Engrs., Internat. Assn. of Hydraulic Rsch. Democrat. Avocations: soccer, cooking, reading, gardening. Office: Tenn Tech Univ PO Box 5015 Cookeville TN 38505-0001

NEAVE, GUY RICHARD, education educator; b. lyndhurst, England, Dec. 27, 1941; s. Arundel and Barbara (Liardet) N.; m. Martine Herlant, Dec. 6, 1986; children: Joel, Magali (twins). BA, London U., 1964, PhD, 1967. Lectr. U. Wales, Bangor, 1967-69; rsch. fellow Leicester U., England, 1969-72, Edinburgh U., Scotland, 1973-75; maitre de recherche European Inst. Edn. & Social Policy, Paris, 1975-85; prof. Inst. Edn. London U., 1985-90; dir. rsch. Internat. Assn. Univs., Paris, 1990—; prof. Ctr. for Higher Edn. Policy Studies, U. Twente, Netherlands, 2000—. Mem. Nat. Acad. Edn. U.S. (fgn. assoc.). Office: Internat Assn Univs, 1 rue Miollis, F75732 Paris Cedex 15, France also: PO 217, 7500HE Enschede Netherlands

NEAVE, HENRY ROBERT, mathematician, statistician, management consultant; b. Norwich, Norfolk, Eng., July 14, 1942; s. George Robert and Hettie Rose (Woodhouse) N.; m. Bette Jane Cox, July 4, 1970 (div. Feb. 1976). BSc, U. Nottingham, Eng., 1963, PhD, 1967. Tutorial asst. U. Nottingham, 1963-66, asst. lectr. math. statistics, 1966-67, lectr., 1968-96; prin. lectr. mgmt. Trent U., Nottingham, 1996-98, W. Edwards Deming prof. mgmt., 1998—; asst. prof. U. Wis., Madison, 1967-68; rsch. fellow McGill U., Montreal, Que., Can., 1970; founder and ednl. advisor Brit. Deming Assn., 1987-2000; statis. quality cons. Nashua Corp., Bracknell, Berkshire, Eng., 1981-83, PPG Industries, France, 1984-92. Author: (with E. Foxley) Programming in Algol 60, 1968, Statistics Tables, 1978, Elementary Statistics Tables, 1981; (with P.L.B. Worthington) Distribution-Free Tests, 1988, The Deming Dimension, 1990; contbr. articles to profl. jours. Mus. dir. Beeston Operatic Soc., Nottingham, 1976-83, West Bridgford Operatic Soc., Nottingham, 1983-85. Fellow Royal Statis. Soc. (sec. East Midlands br. 1972-74, vice-chmn. 1974-87); mem. Inst. Math. Statistics, Am. Statis. Assn., Am. Soc. for Quality. Home: 168 Melton Rd, West Bridgford, Nottingham NG2 6FJ, England

NEBENZAHL, ISRAEL D., marketing and business educator; b. Ramat-Gan, Israel, Sept. 19, 1940; s. Menashe J. and Nina (Lustig) N.; m. Ora Soffer, Aug. 16, 1964; children: Lemore Allal, Daniel, Menash J. BS in Econs., Columbia U., 1965, MBA, 1967; PhD in Mktg. and Ops. Rsch., NYU, 1974. Analyst Sinclair Oil, N.Y.C., 1967-69; mgr. direct mktg. svcs. divsn. CBS, N.Y.C., 1969-71; asst. prof. mgmt. scis. Sch. Bus. Rider Coll., Trenton, N.J., 1971-76; lectr. mktg. dept. econs. and bus. adminstrn. Bar-Ilan U., Ramat-Gan, 1976-86, lectr. mgmt. tng. ctr., 1978-89, sr. lectr., 1986-98, assoc. prof., 1998—; dir. departmental microcomputers lab. Bar Ilan U., 1984-94, vice chmn. dept., head MBA program, 1987-89, dep. head, grad. Sch. Bus. Adminstrn., 1992-94, head mktg. area, 1997—, active various coms.; part-time adj. asst. prof. Touro Coll., N.Y.C., 1975-76; part-time adj. lectr. Faculty Indsl. Mgmt., Ben Gurion U., Israel, 1976-78, Grad. Sch. Bus., Tel Aviv U., 1978-79; acad. advisor Coll. Bus. Adminstrn., Tel Aviv, 1978-83, part-time lectr., 1978-88, dean students, 1984-88, adj. sr. lectr., 1988-89; part-time adj. sr. lectr. mktg. Sch. Bus. Adminstrn., Hebrew U., 1994-96; vis. assoc. prof. Baruch Coll., CUNY, 1989-90; inventor Karisma Tech. Ltd., Israel, 1997—, also bd. dirs.; pres. Shillan, Cons. and Bus. Adminstrn., Ltd., Israel, 1983-96; acad. advisor in bus. games Israel Mgmt. Ctr., 1980-89; bd. dirs. Bar Ilan R & D Co.; presenter in field, most recently including Assn. for Consumer Rsch., Stockholm, 1997, European Bus. Ethics Network, Prague, Czech Republic, 1997. Mem. editl. bd. Indsl. Mktg. Mgmt. jour., 1995—; contbr. chpt. to: (with J.K. Johansson) Advances in International Marketing, 1987, Dimensions of International Business, 1991, (with E.D. Jaffe) Product-Country Images: Impact and Role in International Marketing, 1993 (2 chpts.); contbr. or co-contbr. over 30 articles to profl. publs.; patentee configurable keyboard, U.S., Israel, India, Europe. Lt. Israeli Mil., 1958-61. Recipient Segal Rsch. prize Tel Aviv U., 1982. Mem. Am. Mktg. Assn., Assn. Bus. Simulation and Exptl. Learning, European Internat. Bus. Acad. (chairperson program com. ann. conf. 1998). Jewish. Office: Bar-Ilan U, Grad Sch Bus, 52900 Ramat Gan Israel

NECCO, E(DNA) JOANNE, school psychologist; b. Klamath Falls, Oreg., June 23, 1941; d. Joseph Rogers and Lillian Laura (Owings) Painter; m. Jon F. Puryear, Aug. 25, 1963 (div. Oct. 1987); children: Laura L., Douglas F.; m. A. David Necco, July 1, 1989. BS, Cen. State U., 1978, MEd, 1985; PhD in Applied Behavioral Studies, Okla. State U., 1993. Med.-surg. asst. Oklahoma City Clinic, 1961-68; spl. edn. tchr. Oklahoma City Pub. Schs., 1978-79, Edmond (Okla.) Pub. Schs., 1979-83; co-founder, owner Learning Devel. Clinic, Edmond, 1983-93; asst. prof. profl. tchr. edn. U. Ctrl. Okla., Edmond, 1993-97; assoc. prof., profl. tchr. edn. U. Ctr. Okla., Edmond, 1998—; adj. instr. Ctrl. State U., Edmond, 1989-93, Oklahoma City U., 1991-93; mem. rsch. group Okla. State U., Stillwater, 1991-93; presenter in field. Contbr. articles to profl. jours. Com. mem. Boy Scouts Am., SCUBA Post 604, Oklahoma City, 1981-86; mem. Edmon TAsk Force for Youth, 1983-87, Edmond C. of C., 1984-87; presenter internat. conf. Okla. Ctr. for Neurosci., 1996; evaluator for Even Start Literacy Program, 1994-96, reviewer Okla. Even Start applicants, 1997, presenter internat. conf., Singapore, 1996, Alta., Can., 1996, 98. Mem. ASCD, PEO, Nat. Assn. for Sch. Psychologists, Am. Bus Women's Assn., Coun. for Exceptional Children, Learning Disabilities Assn., Am. Assn. for Gifted Underachieving Students, Am. Tchr. Educators, Okla. Learning Disabilities Assn., Okla. Ctr. Neurosci., Okla. Assn. for Counseling and Devel., Okla. Psychol. Soc., Golden Key Nat. Honor Soc., Internat. Soc. for Scientific Study of Subjectivity, Am. Coun. on Rural Spl. Edn., Ctrl State U. (Okla., life), Phi Delta Kappa. Republican. Avocations: scuba diving, underwater photography, water skiing, travel, golf. Home: 3624 Equestrian Ct Edmond OK 73034-5871 Office: U Ctrl Okla Coll Edn 100 N University Dr Edmond OK 73034-5207

NECHAEV, ILYA ALEXANDROVICH, physicist, educator; b. Kostroma, Russia, Jan. 24, 1972; s. Alexander Vladimirovich and Irina Alexandrovna (Ivanova) N.; m. Natalia Bronislavovna Skosyrskaya, July 8, 1995. First-class diploma, Tomsk (Russia) State U., 1994, candidate of sci. diploma, 1997. Jr. rsch. worker Siberian Physico-Tech. Inst., Tomsk, Russia, 1997-98; sr. tchr. Tomsk State U., 1998—; sr. rsch. worker Siberian Phys. and Tech. Inst. Contbr. articles to profl. publs. Avocations: reading books, traveling, photography. Office: Siberian Phys Tech Inst, Sq Novosobornaya 1, 634050 Tomsk Russia

NECHAEV, YURI SERGEEVICH, metallurgist; b. Voronezh, Russia, Aug. 4, 1939; s. Sergei and Zinaida (Burjan) N.; m. Galina Grigorjevna Mackarova, June 16, 1962; 1 child. BSc, Moscow Steel and Alloys U., 1962, PhD, 1968, DSc, 1982. Rschr. All Union Rsch. Inst. Aviation Materials, Moscow, 1962-68; assoc. prof. Moscow Steel and alloys U., 1968-89; from head dept. materials sci. to chief rschr. Karaganda Metallurgical U., Kazakhstan, Karaganda, 1989-95; chief rschr. A.A. Baikov Inst. Metallurgy Russian Acad. Scis., Moscow, 1996-98, I.P. Bardin Ctrl. Rsch. Inst. for Iron and Steel Industry, Moscow, 1998—. Mem. N.Y. Acad. Scis. E-mail: netch-aev@online.ru. Home: 32 Block 25/1, Bolshaja Naberezhnaja, 123362 Moscow Russia

NECHITAILENKO, VITALY A., geophysicist, researcher; b. Vesely Village, USSR, Jan. 10, 1937; s. Andrey M. and Anna D. (Shianova) N.; m. Violetta N. Ermakova, Nov. 12, 1976; 1 child, Dmitry. Degree in engring., Polytech. Inst., Kharkov, 1962, PhD, 1970. Engring. head of lab. Polytech. Inst., Kharkov, 1962-71; head of lab. Inst. Radioelectronics, Kharkov, 1971-77, Soyuzgasautomat, Moscow, 1977-83; head of lab., dep. chair Soviet Geophys. Com., Moscow, 1983-92; dep. dir. Geophys. Ctr., Moscow, 1992-95, leading scientist, head of group, 1995—; head of radar group Equatorial Expdn., Mogadishu, Somalia, 1968-69. Author: Radio Meteor Research of Upper Atmosphere, 1974, Meteor Wind Selectivity Factors, 1977, Statistical Theory of Meteor Winds, 1979; editor: Proceedings of Workshop on Geophysical Informatics, 1991; mem. press. Internat. Coun. Sci. Unions. Sec. Internat. Globmet Com., Paris, 1981-90; mem. Internat. Coun. of Sci. Unions panel on World Data Ctrs., 1989-97, Nat. Codata Commn., Moscow, 1994—. Sgt. USSR Mil., 1957-59. Recipient silver medal USSR State Exbhn., 1970, Moscow-850 medal Pres. of Russia, 1997. Mem. Am. Geophys. Union (rep. 1992—). Avocation: amateur movie making. Office: Geophys Ctr RAS, 3 Molodezhnaya Str, 117296 Moscow Russia

NECHUSHTAI, RACHEL, biochemist; b. Haifa, Israel, Aug. 24, 1956; d. Haim and Sosi (Fonia) Regenshtrich; m. Shai Shmuel, Sept. 18, 1975; 3 children. BSc, Technion U., 1980, DSc, 1984. Postdoctoral fellow UCLA, 1984-87; sr. lectr. The Hebrew U., Jerusalem, 1987-92, assoc. prof., 1992-98, prof. botany, 1998—, assoc. chair tchg. Life Sci. Inst., 1995-97, dep. dean for rsch. Faculty of Scis., 1997—; mem. Israel Nat. Coun. for Rsch. Devel., 1995—; chairperson Da'at Consortium, Israel, 1996—. Editl. bd. Photosynthesis Rsch., 1995—; contbr. articles to profl. jours. Corporal Air Force-IDF, 1974-75. Mem. Israel Soc. for Molecular Biology, Internat. Soc. of Photosynthesis. Avocations: reading, traveling. Home: 16 Harimon St, 90820 Motza Illit Israel Office: Hebrew U of Jerusalem, Givat Ram, 91904 Jerusalem Israel

NECK, REINHARD, economics educator; b. Vienna, Austria, May 19, 1951; s. Rudolf and Irmingard N.; m. Elisabeth Schaukowitsch, Dec. 22, 1986. MA, U. Vienna, Austria, 1974, PhD, 1975. Rsch. and teaching asst. U. Vienna, 1975-86; vis. asst. prof. U. Ill., Urbana, 1976; rschr. U. Fribourg, Switzerland, 1974-77; asst. prof. Vienna U. of Econs. and Bus. Adminstrn., 1977-91, assoc. prof., 1991-92; Joseph Schumpeter rsch. fellow Harvard U., Cambridge, Mass., 1991-92; prof. U. Bielefeld, Germany, 1992-95, U. Osnabrueck, Germany, 1995-97, U. Klagenfurt, Austria, 1997—; dir. rsch. projects, Vienna, 1975—; reviewer, referee, editorial bd. mem. several internat. jours., 1977—; lectr. U. Vienna, 1981-84; speaker, lectr., panelist at numerous scientific meetings. With Austrian Army, 1969-70. Recipient Wilfling Rsch. award, Vienna U. of Econs. & Bus. Adminstrn., 1988, Best Paper award European Meeting of Cybernetics and Systems Rsch., 1988; grantee Austrian Nat. Sci. Found. and several other Austrian sci. orgns., 1978—. Mem. approximately 20 sci., profl. orgns. Avocations: theater, concerts, travel. Home: Josefstaedter Str 87-2-34, A-1080 Vienna Austria Office: U Klagenfurt, Dept Econs, A-9020 Klagenfurt Austria

NECKÁŘ, BOHUSLAV, textile science educator, researcher; b. Jihlava, Moravia, Czech Republic, June 17, 1943; s. Bohuslav and Anna (Havlíková) N.; m. Hana Voňková, Oct. 10, 1970; children: Pavel, Jan. MSc, Tech. U., Liberec, Czech Republic, 1967, PhD, 1975, DSc, 1991. Rschr. State Textile Rsch. Inst., Liberec, 1967-75, sr. rschr., 1975-90; assoc. prof. Tech. U., Liberec, 1990-93, prof., 1993—; vice head dept. State Textile Rsch. Inst., Liberec, 1978-90; vice dean textile faculty Tech. U., Liberec, 1991-94, head dept. spinning, 1991-97, head dept. textile structures, 1997—. Author: Yarns-Building, Structure, Properties, 1990, Morphology and Structural Mechanics of Fiber Assemblies, 1998; contbr. articles to profl. jours. Avocations: music, tourism. Office: Tech U Liberec, Hálkova 6, 46117 Liberec Czech Republic

NECSOIU, TEODOR E., atomic physics institute administrator, researcher; b. Pojogeni/Gorj, Romania, Aug. 4, 1939; s. Eugeniu and Ana (Toma) N.; m. Ana V. Pirta, July 11, 1964; children: Marius Sorel, Daniela. Engr., Tech. Mil. Acad., Bucharest, Romania, 1972; DSc, U. Bucharest, 1979, Prof., 1980. Engr. Inst. Atomic Physics, Bucharest, 1972-77; sr. engr. Inst. R&D for Laser, Plasma and Radiation Physics, Bucharest, 1977-83, vice dir., 1983-90, gen. mgr., 1991-92; gen. mgr. Inst. of Optoelectronics, Bucharest, 1992—, Inst. Atomic Physics, Bucharest, 1995-97; expert-evaluator European Commn., Brussels, 1998—; assoc. prof. U. Bucharest, 1993—, U. Hyperion, Bucharest, 1993—. Author: Modern Methods of the Optics for Optical Systems Calculus of the Night Vision Devices, 1998, also articles. Col., Ministry of Def., 1964-95. Mem. Assn. European Sensing Labs., European Optical Soc., SPIE-Romania, Romanian Soc. Physics. Avocations: mathematics, physics, computers. Office: Inst of Optoelectronics, 111 Atomistilor Str, 76900 Bucharest-Magurele Romania

NEDERMARK, RIKKE, mechanical engineer; b. Copenhagen, Jan. 12, 1966; d. Frantz and Karen (Christensen) N.; m. Carl-Christian Munk-Nielsen, Dec. 1, 1990; children: Jacob, Ida. MSc, Aalborg U., 1989. Engr. Aalborg Marine Boilers, Aalborg, Denmark, 1989-91; from cons. to specialist Bang & Olufsen, Struer, Denmark, 1991—; participant Environ. Design Indsl. Products project Danish Environ. Protection Agy., 1991-97. Home: Gjelleroddeved 36, 7620 Lemvig Denmark Office: Bang & Olufsen, Peter Bangsvej 15, 7600 Struer Denmark

NEDILKO, SERGYI GERASIMOVICH, physicist, researcher; b. Voznesensk, Ukraine, Sept. 10, 1950; s. Gerasim Ivanovich and Eugenia Anisimovna (Radkevich) N.; m. Irina Mikolaivna Panjuta, Jan. 12, 1973; children: Maksim, Hanna. MS, Kyiv (Ukraine) U., 1972, PhD in Physics, 1979, MD in Physics, 1999. Engr. Kyiv U., 1976-79, jr. scientist, 1979-86, asst. prof. physics, 1982-84, head of lab., 1992—, dep. dean physics faculty, 1999—; asst. prof. physics, Agr. U., Kyiv, 1988-94. Contbr. articles to profl. jours. Grantee Soros Found., Kyiv, 1995, Internat. Assn. for the Promotion of Cooperation with Scientists from the New Ind. States of the Former Soviet Union Program, The Netherlands, 1997. Mem. Am. Phys. Soc., Ukrainian Phys. Soc. (bookkeeper 1990-97, chmn. 1998—). Home: Yakuba Kolasa 6 B fl 117, 03146 Kyiv Ukraine Office: Kyiv U Faculty Physics, 6 Acad Glushkova Ave, 01680 Kyiv Ukraine

NEDOLYA, ANATOLIY VASYLYOVYCH, physicist; b. Uman, Ukraine, Apr. 18, 1963; s. Vasyliy and Elena (Lytsenko) N.; m. Julia Prokopenko, Aug. 18, 1990; 1 child, Dmitry. MSc, T.G. Shevchenko State U., 1985; PhD, Zaporizhya State U., 1996. Engr. Metal Physics Inst., Kiev, Ukraine, 1985-88, 90-91; from asst. prof. to sr. lectr. Zaporizhya State U., Ukraine, 1991—. Sr. lt. Ukraine armed svcs., 1988-90. Grantee Renaissance Found., 1995, 96, Eurasia Found., 1996. Mem. Ukrainian Physics Soc., Polish Synchrotron Radiation Soc., Internat. Union Crystallography, European Synchrotron Radiation Soc. Avocations: guitar, classical music, travel. Office: Zaporizhya State U, Zhukovsky Str 66, Zaporizhzhya Ukraine 330600

NEDVECKAITE, TATJANA, physicist, researcher; b. Kaunas, Lithuania, June 16, 1934; d. Nikalojus and Elena (Afanasjeva) N.; m. Petras Rovda, Apr. 21, 1962; 1 child, Olegas Rovda. Grad. in Physics, Vilnius (Lithuania) U., 1958, D of Natural Scis., 1967. Sci. worker Inst. Physics, Vilnius, 1958-70, sr. sci. worker, 1970-86; head radiation protection dept. Inst. Physics, 1986—; consulting expert in radiation protection Min. of Health, Lithuania, 1994. Author: Iodine Isotopes and Radiation Protection, 1992, Radiation Protection in Lithuania, 1995. Mem. N.Y. Acad. Scis. Avocations: music, playing pian. Home: Moniuskos 42, 2004 Vilnius Lithuania Office: Inst Physics, Savanoriu av 231, 2028 Vilnius Lithuania

NEDVĚD, RUDOLF, retired building engineer, scientist; b. Kralupy-on-Vltava near Prague, Bohemia, Nov. 4, 1908; s. Rudolf and Emily (Jenč) N.; m. Ludmila Deutch, Nov. 7, 1931 (div. 1954); children: Ludmila, Rudolph Nedwed; m. Margaret Hanjalka Laupal, Mar. 13, 1954. MSc in Civil Engring., Tech. U., Prague, ČSR, 1931; PhD in Tech. Scis., Tech. U., Brno, ČSR, 1946. Designer pvt. practice, Pilsen, ČSR, 1931-33; head bldg. dept. City of Slany, ČSR, 1933-37; pvt. practice ČSR, 1937-38; designer of r.r. stas. Brno, ČSR, 1938-78; lectr. r.r. stas. Tech. U., Brno, 1954-75; mfg. slide rules Brno, ČSR, 1948-51. Author: (books) Theory of Relativity on the Basis of Classic Physics, 1964; Mercury's Anomaly (German), 1966, Physics of Motion, 1983, The 2v Law, 1986; contbr. numerous articles to Toth-Maatian Rev. and others, 1978-94. Mem. Social Dem. Party, Pilsen, 1933-34, Slany, 1934-37, Brno, 1937-48, Communist Party, 1948-68 (expelled 1969).

NEDVÍDEK, JOSEF, biologist, educator; b. Lanžov, Czech Republic, Mar. 12, 1934; s. Josef and Marie (Šedivková) N.; m. Jara Urbánková, June 23, 1963; 1 child, Jan. Diploma in biology, Charles U., Prague, Czech Republic, 1958, PhD, 1968. Asst. prof. Charles U., 1958-90, prof. biology, 1990—. Author: Methods in Experimental Embryology, 1974, Plasma Membrane in Signa Transduction, 1975, General Biology, 1985. Mem. Czech Histochem. Cytochem. Soc. Avocations: history, nature, gardening. Office: Charles U Faculty Sci, Viničná 7, 128 00 Prague 2 Czech Republic

NEE, MICHAEL H., botanist; b. Richland Center, Wis., Mar. 25, 1947; s. Harry J. and Freda Marie N. BA, U. Wis., 1970, PhD, 1979. Asst. curator N.Y. Botanical Garden, Bronx, 1984-91, neotropical collections specialist, 1991-95, assoc. curator, 1995—; vis. asst. curator Field Mus. Natural History, Chgo., 1980-84. Co-editor: Solanaceae III, Solanaceae IV. Mem. Am. Soc. Plant Taxonomists. Democrat. Office: NY Botanical Garden Bronx NY 10458

NEECE, OLIVIA HELENE ERNST, investment company executive, consultant; b. L.A., Jan. 3, 1948; d. Robert and Beatrice Pearl Ernst; m. Huntley Lee Bluestein, 1967 (div. 1974); children: Melissa Dawn, Brendon Wade; m. Anthony Ray Neece, Mar. 20, 1976. Cert. interior design, UCLA, 1972-75; BSBA, U. So. Calif., 1990; MBA, UCLA, 1993; postgrad., Claremont U., 1998—. Cert. interior designer Calif. Coun. for Interior Design; lic. gen. contractor, real estate broker, Calif. Staff designer Frances Lux Designs, L.A., 1974; project designer Yates Silverman Inc., L.A., 1974-77; owner Olivia Neece Planning & Design, Tarzana, Calif., 1977-86; v.p. project devel. Design Services/Aircoa, Englewood, Colo., 1986-87; v.p. project adminstrn. Hirsch-Bedner Assoc., Santa Monica, Calif., 1987-88; treas.-sec. EON Corp., L.A., 1980—; owner Olivia Neece Planning & Design, Tarzana, 1988-93; dir. ops. The Ernst Group, L.A., 1980—; prof. Calif. State U., Northridge, part-time, 1994-99; spkr. in field; instr. ext. program UCLA, 1981-83; acad. rschr. Jet Propulsion Lab., 2000—. Co-author: A Step by Step Approach to Hotel Development, 1988; contbr. articles to profl. jours. Bd. dirs., chmn. advt. L.A. Music Ctr. Opera League; co-chair L.A. Master Chorale Gala; founder, mem. Performing Arts Ctr. L.A.; mem. Performing Arts Ctr. L.A. County, Gold Guild of Ctr. Theatre Group/Ahmanson of Performing Arts Ctr. L.A., Hollywood Bowl Soc.; charter mem. Los Angeles County Mus. Art; vol. restoration of San Diego R.R. Mus., 1985-92; founder L.A. Music Ctr. Recipient Holiday Inn Devel. award, Foster City, Calif., 1986, Warwick, R.I., 1988, 1st and 2d place awards Lodging Hospitality Designers Circle, 1987, Gold Key award Russell St. Inn, 1986. Mem. Am. Soc. Interior Designers (1st pl. portfolio competition 1974), Acad. Mgmt., Fin. Mgmt. Assn., Internat. Inst. Designers & Arch. (profl., v.p., bd. dirs.), Nat. Restaurant Assn., We. Acad. Mgmt. Office: Neece Assoc 18200 Rosita St Tarzana CA 91356-4622

NEEL, ELISABETH, company director; b. Copenhagen, May 2, 1954; d. Ole and Tove (Torrild) N. BA, Copenhagen U., 1976; MA, Odense (Denmark) U., 1981. Cert. tchr. h.s. Tchr. h.s. Odense, 1981-82; rschr. Landsarkivet, Odense, 1983-84, Meteorol. Inst., Copenhagen, 1986-92, Rigsarkivet, Copenhagen, 1986-92; lit. agt. Rights Promotion, Copenhagen, 1993—, dir., 1994—. Home and Office: Øresundsvej 22, 2300 Copenhagen S, Denmark

NEEL, LOUIS EUGENE FELIX, physicist; b. Lyons, France, Nov. 22, 1904; s. Louis Antoine and Marie Antoinette (Hartmayer) N.; m. Hélène Hourticq, Sept. 14, 1931; children: Marie-Francoise, Marguerite Guély, Pierre. Agrégé de l'Université, Ecole Normale Supérieure, 1928; Docteur ès-Sciences, Strasbourg, France, 1932. With Faculté des Sciences, Strasbourg, 1928-45, prof., 1937-45; prof. Faculté des Sciences Grenoble, France, 1945-76; dir. Lab. Electrostatics and Physics of Metal, 1940-71; pres. Institut Nat. Polytechnique, Grenoble, 1970-76; dir. Centre d'Etudes Nucléaires, Grenoble, 1957-71; French rep. sci. council NATO, 1960-82; pres. Conseil Sup.

Sûreté nucléaire, 1973-86. Decorated grand croix Legion of Honor, Gold medal Nat. Center Sci. Research; Nobel prize in physics, 1970. Mem. French Acad. Sci., acads. sci. Moscow, Halle, Royal Soc. London, Romanian Acad., Royal Netherlands Acad. Scis., Am. Acad. Arts and Scis., French Soc. Physics (hon. pres.), Internat. Union Pure and Applied Physics (hon. pres.). Achievements include research and numerous publs. on magnetic properties of solids; introduced sci. ideas of ferrimagnetism and antiferromagnetism; discoveries of certain magnetic properties of fine grains and crystals, directional order of magnetism, magnetic after effect. Home: 41 rue Pierre Benoit, 19100 Brive France

NEELAM, VENKATARAMANA KRISHNAN, neurosurgeon, consultant; b. Tirupathi, Pradesh, India, Feb. 27, 1958; s. Krishnan and Susheela Neelam; m. Shobha Ramachandra, Oct. 30, 1995; 1 child, Bhargavi. MBBS, Sri Venkateswara Med. Coll., Tirupati, 1980; MCh in Neurosurgery, 1986. Sr. resident Nat. Inst. Mental Health and Neuroscis., Bangalore, India, 1981-87, asst. prof. neurosurgery, 1987-91; cons. neurosurgeon Manipal Hosp., Bangalore, 1991—; cons. Elbit Diagnostics, Bangalore, 1997—; acad. coord. Manipal Hosp., Bangalore, 1994-99, mem. pharmacy com., 1995-99, mem. operation theater users com., 1996-99, project coord. Comprehensive Trauma Consortium, Bangalore City. Contbr. articles to profl. publs. Mem. Internat. Soc. Pediat. Neurosurgery, Neurol. Soc. of India, Bangalore Neurol. Soc. (sec.), Indian Soc. of Pediatric Neurosurgery, N.Y. Acad. Sci., Indian Soc. for Stereotactic and Functional Neurosurgery, Nat. Geographic Soc., Asian Congress of Neurol. Surgeons. Avocations: music, reading, photography, literature. Home: 105 Surya Apts, Airport Road, Bangalore 560017, India Office: Manipal Hosp Neurol Surgery, Airport Rd, Bangalore 560017, India

NEELEY, JAMES KAME, credit agency executive; b. Visalia, Calif., Dec. 4, 1955; s. James M. and Dorothy Neeley; m. Lynn Travioli, Aug. 13, 1977; children: Janessa, Jimmy. BS in Bus. Adminstrn., Calif. State U., Fresno, 1978. Lic. personal property appraiser. Loan officer Visalia Prodn. Credit Assn., Tipton, Calif., 1978-82; asst. br. mgr. Visalia (Calif.) Prodn. Credit Assn., 1982-83; v.p., br. mgr. Valley Prodn. Credit Assn., Visalia, 1983-91, Valley Farm Credit, Visalia, 1991—; advisor Redwood Future Farmers of Am., Visalia, 1988-90; advisor computer software devel. Western Farm Credit Bank, Sacramento, 1990-91; mem., advisor Kit Fox Adv. Com., Visalia, 1995-96. Mem. Ctrl. Dem. Com., Visalia, 1975-77; soccer coach Am. Youth Soccer Orgn., Tulare, Calif., 1990-96, 99; coach Tulare Little League, 1996-97; parent vol. St. Alyosios Sch., Tulare, 1993-96; mem. coun. on fin., head audit com. Calif./Nev. United Meth., 1990-96; layleader Tulare United Meth. Ch., 1994-96, mem. adminstrv. bd., 1996-97. Scholar So. Calif. Edn., 1974. Fellow Calif. Agrl. Leadership Program; mem. Tulare Host Lions Club (pres. 1982-83), Phi Kappa Phi. Avocations: collecting old and rare books, soccer, basketball, skiing. Office: Valley Farm Credit Svcs PO Box 4379 Visalia CA 93278-4379

NEELY, MARION VICTORIA, community volunteer; b. Prescott, Mich., Apr. 5, 1937; d. Robert John and Marie Caroline (Koch) Fabera; divorced; children: Rebekah, Nathan, Sally. Student, Lake Superior State Coll., Sault Ste. Marie, Mich., 1954-56, Lincoln U., 1981-85. Lab. tech., acctg. clk., prodn. worker Chesebrough Ponds, Inc., Jefferson City, 1967-86; supr. for telephone book delivery Directory Distributing Assocs., Inc., St. Louis, 1986-95; innovative recycler, Holts Summit, 1997—. Editor: (newsletter) Another Look Unltd., Holts Summit, 1992—; contbg. author: (anthology) The Simple Life, 1998; designer: Memory Quilts, 1993—, Broken Levees Sample Quilt (1993 Flood Memoir) 1994, Miniature Books, 1999, others; contbr. articles to mags. Quilt donation to Habitat for Humanity, Jefferson City, Mo., 1998, Fulton, Mo., 1995; active cmty. recycling projects. Mem. Co-op Am., Phi Alpha Theta. Avocations: piecing quilt tops, writing, travel, community volunteerism.

NEETER, HENRY, financial analyst; b. Amsterdam, The Netherlands, July 20, 1939; s. Emanuel and Anna Maria Johanna (Harms) N.; m. Sonja Ingrid Vennik, Aug. 27, 1977. Engring. degree, Hogere Technische Sch. Mr. Koetsier, Amsterdam, 1961. Cert. securities and futures broker, U.S. Product group mgr. Benelux Rowntree Mackintosh, The Netherlands, 1969-72; self-employed, 1972-82; fin. advisor Merrill Lynch & Co., Manila, 1982-87; fund mgr. Optimix Stockbrokers, Amsterdam, 1987-89, Bank Insinger de Beaufort, Amsterdam, 1989-91; dir. Stocktimer, Amsterdam, 1990-98, Waterscape, Amstelveen, The Netherlands, 1990—; bd. dirs. Internat. Fedn. Tech. Analysts, N.Y.; vice-chmn. Vereniging Technische Analisten, The Netherlands, 1989-93, chmn., 1993-95; vice chmn. Makati Toastmasters, Manila, 1986-87. Co-author: Koersstrateeg, 1988; author: (weekly column) Beleggers Belangen, 1993-96, (monthly column) Fondsdata Charts, 1992—; editor IFTA Jour., 1995-97; contbr. articles to profl. publs. including Money, Nautique, Zeilen, Fin. and Yachting mags. Avocation: sailing. Office: Waterscape, Schoener 188, 1186 VN Amstelveen The Netherlands

NEETESON, JACQUES J., agronomist; b. Utrecht, The Netherlands, June 17, 1954; s. François Adriaan and Jellina Johanna (Groen) N.; m. Anne-Marie Apollonia Van Nieuwenhoven, Aug. 8, 1980; children: Arthur, Constantijn. MSc, Agrl. U. Wageningen, 1981, PhD, 1989. Soil scientist, dept. head, acting dir. IB-DLO, Haren, The Netherlands, 1981-93; dep. dir. AB-DLO, Haren, 1994-95; interim mgr. LNV, The Hague, The Netherlands, 1996-97; rsch. mgr. AB, Wageningen, 1997-99; bus. unit mgr. Plant Rsch. Internat., Wageningen, 2000—. Author: Assessment of Fertilizer Nitrogen Requirement of Potatoes and Sugar Beet, 1989, Nitrogen Mineralization in Agricultural Soils, 1994; editor-in-chief Netherlands Jour. Agrl. Sci., 1993—; cons. editor Plant and Soil, 1989—; editor spl. issue European Jour. Agronomy, 1994. Mem. Dutch Soil Sci. Soc. (bd. dirs.), Groningen Knowledge Ctr. (bd. dirs.), European Soc. Agronomy (nat. rep. 1998—). Avocation: photography. Home: Benedendorpsweg 98, NL-6862 WL Oosterbeek The Netherlands Office: Plant Rsch Internat, PO Box 16, NL-6700 AA Wageningen The Netherlands

NEFEDIEVA, ELENA EDWARDOVNA, plant physiologist, educator; b. Volgograd, Russia, Aug. 2, 1972; d. Edward Sergeevich and Galina Nikolaevna (Skakunova) Atroschenko; m. Alexei Ivanovich Nefediev, July 12, 1997. D in Tchg. Biology and Chemistry, State Pegagogical U., Penza, Russia, 1994; Candidate in Biol. Scis., Agr. Acad., Moscow, 1997. Tchr. biology Secondary Sch. No. 49, Penza, 1993-94; sr. lectr. State Pedagogical U., Penza, 1997—; lab. asst. State Pedagogical U., Penza, 1996-98; pedagogue of additional edn. Town Ctr. Tech. Creation, Zarechny, Penza, 1999—; sci. cons. Secondary Sch. 222, Zarechny, 1999-2000. Contbr. articles to profl. jours. Leader student's sci. work faculty natural history and geography State Pedagogical U., Penza, 1999. Mem. Russian Soc. Plant Physiologists (sec. Penza br. 1994—). Achievements include patent for method of pre-sowing treatment of seeds. Avocations: music, theatre, tennis, applied arts. Home: 25 House 5 Slava St, 440600 Penza Russia Office: Penza State Pedag U Botany, 37 Lermontova ul, 440026 Penza Russia

NEFF, FRED LEONARD, lawyer; b. St. Paul, Nov. 1, 1948; s. Elliott Ira and Mollie (Poboisk) N.; m. Christa Ruth Powell, Sept. 10, 1989. BS with high distinction, U. Minn., 1970; JD, William Mitchell Coll. Law, 1976. Bar: Minn. 1976, N.D. 1994, U.S. Dist. Ct. Minn. 1977, U.S. Ct. Appeals (8th cir.) 1985, U.S. Supreme Ct. 1985, Wis. 1986, U.S. Dist. Ct. (ea. and we. dists.) Wis. 1992. Tchr. Hopkins (Minn.) Pub. Schs., 1970-72; instr. U. Minn., Mpls., 1974-76; pvt. practice Mpls., 1976-79; asst. county atty. Sibley County, Gaylord, Minn., 1979-80; mng. atty. Hyatt Legal Svcs., St. Paul, 1981-83, regional ptnr., 1983-85, profl. devel. ptnr., 1985-86; pres. Neff Law Firm, PA, Mpls., 1986—; CEO Profl. Devel. Inst. Inc., Edina, Minn., 1994—, also bd. dirs.; instr. Inver Hills Coll., 1973-77; counsel Am. Tool Supply Co., St. Paul, 1976-78; cons. Nat. Detective Agy., Inc., St. Paul, 1980-83; CEO A Basic Legal Svc., Bloomington, 1990—; CEO, bd. dirs. Profl. Devel. Inst., Inc., Edina, Minn., 1994—; lectr., guest instr. U. Wis., River Falls, 1976-77; spl. instr. Hamline U., St. Paul, 1977; vis. lectr. Coll. St. Scholastica, Duluth, Minn., 1977; program. faculty, cons. Employment Law Seminar for Colo., Fla., La., Oreg., Employment and Labor Law Seminar for Ala., Alaska, Calif., Conn., Ind., N.C., Ohio, Va., N.C. Safety and Health at the Workplace, S.C. Labor Law, Ohio Safety at the Workplace; bd. dirs. Acceptance Ins. Holdings, Inc., Omaha; active Internat. Confederation Jurists, 1993; mem. faculty sem. Ariz. Safety at Workplace, Hawaii Employment & Labor, Miss. Employment & Labor Law, Del. Employment & Labor, Alaska Employment and Labor Law, Ga. Employment & Labor Law, N.J. Employment & Labor, Wash. Employment Law, Mass. Employment & Labor Law, 1995—, Ark. Employment and Labor Law, Mo. Employment and Labor Law, Iowa Employment and Labor Law, Utah Employment and Labor Law; pres. Martial Arts Bookstore Internat., Inc., 1998; pres. Endless Fist Soc., Inc., 1998. Author: Fred Neff's Self-Defense Library, 1976, Everybody's Self-Defense Book, 1978, Karate Is for Me, 1980, Running Is for Me, 1980, Lessons from the Samurai, 1986, Lessons from the Art of Kempo, 1986, Lessons from the Western Warriors, 1986, Lessons from the Fighting Commandos, 1990, Lessons from the Ancient Japanese Masters of Self-Defense, 1990, Lessons from the Eastern Warrors, 1990, Mysterious Persons of the Past, 1991, Great Mysteries of Crime, 1991; host TV series Great Puzzles In History; co-host TV series Great Unsolved Crimes, Minn.; asst. editor: Hennepic County Lawyer, 1992—. Advisor to bd. Sibley County Commrs., 1979-80; speaker civic groups, 1976-82; mem. Hennepin County Juvenile Justice Panel, 1980-82, Hennepin County (Minn.) Pub. Def. Conflict Panel, 1980-82, 86—, Hennepin County Bar Assn. Advice Panel Law Day, 1987, mem. dist. ethics com., 1990—; mem. Panel Union Privilege Legal Svcs. div. AFL-CIO, 1986—, Montgomery Wards Legal Svcs. Panel, 1986—, Edina Hist. Soc., Decathlon Athletic Club; charter mem. Commn. for the Battle of Normandy Mus.; founding sponsor Civil Justice Found., 1986—; mem. com. for publ. Hennepin County Lawyer, 1992; pres. Endless Fist Soc., Inc., 1998. Recipient Outstanding Tchr. award Inver Hills Coll. Student Body, 1973, St. Paul Citizen of Month award Citizens Group, 1975, Kempo Club award U. Minn., 1975, U. Minn. Student Appreciation award Kempo Club, 1978, Sibley County Atty. Commendation award, 1980, Good Neighbor award WCCO Radio, 1985, Lamp of Knowledge award Twin Cities Lawyers Guild, 1986, N.W. Cmty. TV Commendation award, 1989-91, Presdl. Merit medal Pres. George Bush, 1990, N.W. Cmty. TV award, 1991, HLS Leadership award, 1984, Mng. Attys. Guidance award, 1985, Creative Thinker award Regional Staff, 1986, HLS Justice award, 1986, Honors cert. for Authors, Childrens Reading Round Table of Chgo., 1988, Wisdom Soc. Wisdom award, 1998. Fellow Roscoe Pound Found., Nat. Dist. Attys. Assn.; mem. ABA, ATLA, Minn. Bar Assn. (com. on ethics 1994—, com. on alternative dispute resolution 1994—), Minn. Trial Lawyers Assn., Hennepin County Bar Assn. (dist. ethics com. 1990—), Wis. Bar Assn., Ramsey County Bar Assn., Am. Judicature Soc., Internat. Platform Assn., Am. Arbitration Assn. (panel of arbitrators 1992), Minn. Martial Arts Assn. (pres. 1974-78, Outstanding Instr. award 1973), Nippon Kobudo Rengokai (bd. dirs. North Ctrl. States 1972-76, regional dir. 1972-76), Endless Fist Soc. (pres. 1998), Internat. Confedn. Jurists, Edina C. of C., Southview Country Club, Masons, Kiwanis, Scottish Rite, Sigma Alpha Mu. Avocations: reading, Far Eastern and Oriental studies, civic activities, physical conditioning, gardening. Home: 4515 Andover Rd Minneapolis MN 55435-4031 Office: 5930 Brooklyn Blvd Ste 206 Brooklyn Center MN 55429-2518 also: 1711 County Road B W Ste 340N Roseville MN 55113-4077 also: Minn Ctr 7760 France Ave S Ste 720 Bloomington MN 55435-5921

NEFF, MICHAEL, prosecutor; b. Queens, N.Y., May 13, 1968; s. H. Alton and Anita (Liotta) N. BBA, George Wash. U., 1990; JD, Pa. State U., 1993. Bar: Ga., N.J., U.S. District Ct. Ga. (no. dist.). Atty. Anita Liotta Law Office, Brick, N.J., 1993-95; intern to judge Superior Ct., Ocean County, N.J., 1994; atty. Smelzik & Shapiro, P.A., Atlanta, 1995-96; pvt. practie Atlanta, 1996—; of counsel Lefco & Blumenthal, P.C., Atlanta, 1997—; city atty. City of Greenville, GA, Greenville, Calif., 1998—. Contbr. article to profl. jour. Mem. Atlanta Jr. C. of C. (bd. dirs. 1995—). Avocations: running, baseball. Office: 4651 Roswell Rd NE Ste G602 Atlanta GA 30342-3049

NEFF, P. SHERRILL, health care executive; b. Balt., Dec. 18, 1951; s. Paul Heston and Mary (Poulnot) N.; m. Sarah B. Barrett, June 20, 1976 (div. 1985); 1 child, Jacob Colin; m. Alicia Phyll Felton, May 26, 1988; children: Michael Felton, Jonathan Felton. BA, Wesleyan U., 1974; JD magna cum laude, U. Mich., 1980. Bar: Pa. 1980. Atty. Morgan Lewis & Bockius, Phila., 1980-84; investment banker Alex Brown & Sons, Inc., Balt., 1984-93, mng. dir., 1992-93; sr. v.p. corp. devel. U.S. Healthcare, Blue Bell, Pa., 1993-94; pres., CFO Neose Techs., Inc., Horsham, Pa., 1994—, also bd. dirs., pres., COO, 2000—; bd. dirs. Jeff Banks, Inc., Phila., Resource America, Inc., Phila., Bancorp.com., Inc., Phila., Prima Facie, Inc., King of Prussia, Biotechnology Inst. Trustee Zero Moving Dance Co., Phila., 1984-93; bd. dirs. Univ. City Sci. Ctr., 1998—. Mem. Pa. Biotech. Assn. (bd. dirs. 1996—, pres.-elect 1997-98, pres. 1998-99). Democrat. Jewish. Home: 619 Revere Rd Merion Station PA 19066-1007 Office: Neose Techs Inc PO Box 1109 102 Witmer Rd Horsham PA 19044-2211

NEFF, ROBERT CLARK, SR., lawyer; b. St. Marys, Ohio, Feb. 11, 1921; s. Homer Armstrong and Irene (McCulloch) N.; m. Betty Baker, July 3, 1954 (dec.); children: Cynthia Lee Neff Schifer, Robert Clark Jr., Abigail Lynn (dec.); m. Helen Picking, July 24, 1975. BA, Coll. Wooster, 1943; postgrad., U. Mich., 1946-47; LLB, Ohio No. U., 1950. Bar: Ohio 1950, U.S. Dist. Ct. (no. dist.) Ohio, 1978. Pvt. practice Bucyrus, Ohio, 1950—; ptnr. Neff Law Firm Ltd.; law dir. City of Bucyrus, 1962-95. Chmn. blood program Crawford County (Ohio) unit ARC, 1955-89; life mem. adv. bd. Salvation Army, 1962—; clk. of session 1st Presbyn. Ch., Bucyrus, 1958-96; bd. dirs. Bucyrus Area Cmty. Found., Crawford County Bd. Mental Retardation and Devel. Disabilities, 1977-82. With USNR, WWII; comdr. Res. ret. Recipient "Others" plaque for 30 yrs. adv. bd. svc. Salvation Army, Ohio No. U. Coll. Law Alumni award for cmty. svc., 1996; inducted Ohio Vets. Hall Fame, Columbus, 1996. Mem. Ohio Bar Assn., Crawford County Bar Assn., Naval Res. Assn., Ret. Officers Assn., Am. Legion, Bucyrus Area C. of C. (past bd. dirs., Outstanding Citizen award, 1973, Bucyrus Citizen of Yr. 1981), Kiwanis (life mem., past pres.), Masons. Republican. Fax: 419-562-1660. Home: 1085 Mary Ann Ln Bucyrus OH 44820-3145 Office: 840 S Sandusky Ave PO Box 406 Bucyrus OH 44820-0406

NEFF, THOMAS JOSEPH, executive search firm executive; b. Easton, Pa., Oct. 2, 1937; s. John Wallace and Elizabeth Ann (Dougherty) N.; m. Susan Culver Paull, Nov. 26, 1971 (dec.); children: David Andrew, Mark Gregory, Scott Dougherty; m. Sarah Brown Hallingby, Jan. 20, 1989; stepchildren: Brooke, Bailey. BS in Indsl. Engring., Lafayette Coll., 1959; MBA, Lehigh U., 1961. Assoc. McKinsey & Co., Inc., N.Y.C. and Australia, 1963-66; dir. mktg. planning Trans-World Airlines, N.Y.C., 1966-69; pres. Hosp. Data Scis., Inc., N.Y.C., 1969-74; prin. Booz, Allen & Hamilton, Inc., N.Y.C., 1974-76; regional ptnr. Spencer Stuart, Inc., N.Y.C., N.Am., 1976-79; bd. dirs. Spencer Stuart & Assocs., N.Y.C., 1976-79, pres., 1979-96, also bd. dirs., chmn. U.S., 1996—; bd. dirs. Lord Abbett Mut. Funds, Ace Ltd. Exult, Inc.; chmn. Brunswick Sch., 1991-95. Trustee, exec. com. Lafayette Coll. 1st lt. U.S. Army, 1961-63. Mem. Links Club, Sky Club, Blind Brook Club, Quogue (N.Y.) Beach Club, Quogue Field Club, Round Hill Club, Belle Haven Club, Coral Beach Club, Quantuck Beach Club, Nat. Golf Links, Lost Tree Club. Republican. Roman Catholic. Home: 144 Peckslan Rd Greenwich CT 06831-3652 Office: Spencer Stuart & Assocs 277 Park Ave Fl 29 New York NY 10172-2998

NEFT BYERS, SUZI TERRY, television producer; b. Pitts., Sept. 17, 1957; d. Harris Rosenberg and Fannie Rachel Neft; m. Paul Alan Byers, June 14, 1986 (div. 2000); 1 child, Charles Alexander II. BA in Journalism and Comm., Point Park Coll., 1979. Announcer, writer WNUF-FM, Millvale, Pa., 1979-80; news reporter WESA-AM, Charleroi, Pa., 1980-81; ops. coord. WQED-TV, WQEX-TV, WQED-FM, Pitts., 1981-87; location prodn. mgr. You TV Cable Network, Pitts., 1988; tv prodr. The Mercy Hosp., Pitts., 1992-93; dir. internship devel., sr. tv prodr. Reliance Tng. Networks, Pitts., 1996-2000; freelance TV prodr., writer, pub. rels./mktg. profl., 1977—. Assoc. prodr. KDKA/Children's Hospital Free Care Fund Benefit Show, 1994, 95, Lucille's Car Care Clinic, 1994; prodr. HealthVision, 1998—. Mem. publicity com., music tchr. kindergarten-grade 3, intergenerational choir Temple Sinai. Recipient Emmy Mid-Atlantic Region Best Live Show, Acad. TV Arts and Scis., 1991, 1st pl. best tv comml. Women in Comm., 1994, 1st pl. spl. events promo under $20,000 Women in Comm., 1995, 1st pl. spl. events budgets under $20,000 Women in Comm., 1996. Mem. Am. Women in Radio and TV (pres. chpt. 1995-97), Soc. Profl. Journalists, Pitts. Radio and TV Club, Press Club Western Pa. (bd. dirs. 1994-95). Home and Office: 633 Montclair St Pittsburgh PA 15217-2808

NEFYODOV, IGOR YURIEVICH, radiobiologist, researcher; b. Samara, Russia, May 29, 1964; s. Yuri Mihailovich and Galina Grigorievna 9Komleva) N.; m. Irina Yurievna Suzdaltseva, Aug. 10, 1989. MD, Med. Inst. Samara, 1987; PhD in Radiobiology, Russian Acad. Med. Sci., 1993, ScD, 1998. Asst. Med. Inst. Samara, 1987-89; rschr. Med. Radiol. Rsch. Ctr., Obninsk, Russia, 1989-95, sr. rschr., 1995—. Contbr. articles to profl. jours. Grantee WHO, 1997, John D. and Catherine T. MacArthur Found., Chgo., 1997, Russian Rsch. Fundamental Found., 1994, 97. Avocation: tennis. Office: Med Radiol Rsch Ctr, Koroliov Str 4, 249020 Obninsk Russia

NEGASSO, GIDADA, president of Ethiopia; b. Dembi Dolo, 1944; married; 3 children. BA in History and Libr. Sci., Haile Selassie First U., Ethiopia; MA in Ethnology and Social Psychology, Johan Wolfgang Goethe U., Germany, 1978, PhD in Ethnology, 1984. Prof. history Addis Ababa U.; mem. Oromo Liberation Front, Ethiopian Discussion Forum; min. labor and social affairs, min. info. in transitional govt. Govt. of Ethiopia, 1991, min. of labor and social affairs, 1991-93, min. of info., 1993-95, pres., 1995—; chmn. Assn. Oromo Students in Germany; dir. Third World Ctr., Frankfurt, 1985. Avocations: reading, collecting oral literature, walking, gymnastics, table tennis. Office: Office of the President, PO Box 1031, Addis Ababa Ethiopia*

NEGEM, HELMI M., accountant, lawyer; b. Fakos, Egypt, 1950. B in Comm., Cairo U., 1972, JD, 2000. With Bright Star Cons., 1973. Author 5 books; contbr. articles to profl. jours. Founder Negem Found. Avocations: travel, reading, sports. Home: 196 Sudan St, Cairo Egypt Office: 196A Sudan St, Giza Cairo Egypt

NEGI, ROHIT, researcher; b. Bombay; came to U.S., 1995; p. B.S. and D. Negi. B in Tech., Indian Inst. Tech., Bombay, 1995; MSEE, Stanford U., 1996, postgrad., 1996—. Rsch. asst. Stanford U., Palo Alto, Calif., 1996—. Contbr. articles to profl. jours. Adult literacy vol. Nat. Social Svc. India, Bombay, 1995-97. Grantee Tex. Instruments, Inc., 1997—; Stanford Engring. fellow Stanford U., 1995-96. Mem. IEEE (student), The Indus Entrepreneur (student). Avocations: tennis, portrait sketching. E-mail: negi@isl.stanford.edu. Fax: 650-723-9251. Office: Stanford Univ 350 Serra St Rm 360 Stanford CA 94305-4020

NEGLEN, NILS PETER, surgeon; b. Helsingborg, Sweden, July 30, 1948; came to U.S., 1996; s. Malte and Ewy Ingeborg (Karlsson) N.; m. Linda Pamela Ohnell, July 19, 1975; children: Niclas Peter, Nils Pontus. MD, U. Lund, Sweden, 1974, PhD in Surgery, 1980, Docent, 1988. Rotating intern Danderyd, Sweden, 1974-76; resident Helsingborg/Lund, Sweden, 1976-81; clin. rsch. fellow Duke U., N.C., 1981-82; cons. surgeon Helsingborg, 1982-83; asst. prof. Kuwait U., 1983-88, assoc. prof., 1988-90; prof. United Arab Emirates U., Al Ain, 1991-96; sr. resident Temple U., Phila., 1996-97; attending vascular surgeon River Oaks Hosp., Jackson, Miss., 1997—; vis. prof. U. Miss. Med. Ctr., Jackson, 1990-91. Contbr. chpts. to books and articles to profl. jours. Mem. Am. Venous Forum, Internat. Soc. Surgery, European Soc. Vascular Surgery, Internat. Cardiovascular Soc. Avocations: tennis, horseback riding. Office: 1020 River Oaks Dr Ste 480 Jackson MS 39208-9536

NEGLEY, FLOYD ROLLIN, genealogist, retired army officer and civilian military employee; b. Ashland, Nebr., Apr. 26, 1924; s. Floyd Carroll and Margaret Negley; m. Teresa Mitsuko, Mar. 12, 1954; children: Teresa Kei, Caroline Yumi. Japanese lang. student, U.S. Army Lang. Sch., Monterey, Calif., 1956-57; student in computer scis., U. Ariz., 1959-61; BS in Econs., Sophia U., Tokyo, 1965. Intelligence analyst U.S. Army, Tokyo, Okinawa, Japan, 1949-59; automated comm. maintenance officer U.S. Army, various cities, 1960-69; automated comm. analyst U.S. Army, Ft. Huachua, Ariz., 1970-92; genealogist Tucson, 1970—; advisor Armed Forces Comm.-Electronics Assn., Tokyo/Ft. Huachuca, 1961-92; computer advisor Japanese Army/Air Force, Tokyo, 1963-67; owner Japan Food Mart, Tucson, 1971-80; owner, property mgr. Negley Svcs., Tucson, 1970—; indexer mortality/natality for Pima County, Ariz., 1987-97. Author: Negley USA, History and Genealogy, The Hans Rudolph Line, 1986, Negley USA, History and Genealogy, The Baltazar Negley Line, 1987, Negley USA, History and Genealogy, The John Leonhardt Line, 1987, Negley USA, History and Genealogy, The Other Negley Lines, 1988, Arizona Death Records, Pima County 1989-1990, 1991, Arizona Territorial Marriages, Pima County 1871-1912, 1994, Arizona Marriages, Pima County Marriage Books 6-10, February 1912-December 1926, 1997; author, indexer 2 books, 1994-96; translator (Japanese fiction) A Bamboo Doll, 1967. Pres. Pima-Cochise Commuters, Inc., Tucson, 1988, advisor, 1971-91; various offices Aztec Toastmasters, Tucson, 1992—, Thunder Mountain Toastmasters, Ft. Huachuca, 1982-91. Named Disting. Toastmaster, Toastmasters Internat., 1995, state 4-H champion, Nebr. 4-H Clubs, Lincoln, 1943. Mem. SAR, Ariz. Geneal. Soc. (pres. 1985-87, editor Copper State Bull. 1987—). Avocations: indexing, swimming, travel, gardening. Home: 2726 E Waverly St Tucson AZ 85716-3083

NEGNEVITSKY, MICHAEL, electrical engineer; b. Minsk, Belarus, Sept. 14, 1956; arrived in Australia, 1991; s. Vladimir and Bella (Kugelman) N.; m. Svetlana Feldman, Aug. 2, 1986; 1 child, Vladimir. BEE, Byelorussian U. Tech., Minsk, USSR, 1978, PhD, 1983; MBA, Ctrl. Inst. for the Further Tng. Managerial Staff and Nat. Econ. Specialists in the Field of Patenting, Moscow, 1988. Chartered profl. engr. Elec. engr. Byelorussian Elec. Maintenance Constrn. Commissioning Co., Minsk, 1978-80, rsch. fellow, lectr., 1983-84, sr. rsch. fellow, sr. lectr., 1984-91; sr. rsch. assoc. Monash U., Melbourne, Australia, 1992; sr. lectr. U. Tasmania, Hobart, Australia, 1993—; rsch. project mgr., chief investigator Byelorussian U. Tech., 1983-91; head rsch. lab. Energy Systems Rsch. Co., Minsk, 1989-91; rsch. project mgr., chief investigator U. Tasmania, Hobart, 1994—. Co-author: Reliability Assessment of Large Electric Power Systems: Controllability, 1988, Reliability Assessment of Large Electric Power Systems: Concepts and Techniques, 1990, Restoration of Power Systems After Large Blackouts, 1991, Applications of Artificial Intelligence in Engineering XI, 1996, XII, 1997, XIII, 1998; patentee in field; contbr. over 150 articles to profl. jours. Mem. IEEE, Instn. Engrs. Australia (sr.), N.Y. Acad. Scis. Office: U Tasmania Dept EE Engring, GPO Box 252-65, Hobart 7001, Australia

NEGOITA, CONSTANTIN VIRGIL, educator; b. Bucharest, Romania, Feb. 3, 1936; s. Athanasie Negoita and Ileana Popescu; m. Seta Shishmanian, Mar. 10, 1986. PhD, Poly. U., Bucharest, 1969. Rschr. City U. Inst. Informatics, Bucharest, 1972-82; prof. Hunter Coll., CUNY, N.Y.C., 1983—; chmn. 8th Internat. Congress Cybernetics and Sys., N.Y., 1990. Author: Expert Systems and Fuzzy Systems, 1985 (award IEEE 1985), Cybernetic Conspiracy, 1988; editor Kybernetes, 1972—, The Jour. of Fuzzy Sets and Systems, 1978-96. E-mail: cnegoita@shiva.hunter.cuny.edu. Fax: 212-772-5219. Office: Hunter Coll 695 Park Ave New York NY 10021-5024

NEGOITA, NICOLAE VASILE, chemist, educator, researcher; b. Buzau, Romania, Oct. 20, 1939; s. Gheorghe and Stana (Stefan) N.; m. Angela Manole, Feb. 29, 1964; children: Julia, Lavinia-Nicoleta. Degree in chemistry, U. Bucharest, 1963; PhD in Chemistry, U. Iassy, Romania, 1974. Rschr. Nat. Inst. R&D for Phys. and Nuclear Engring., Bucharest, Romania, 1963-74, sr. rschr., 1974—, head of organic labelled compounds lab., 1980-90, head radiopharm. lab., 1990-00. Contbr. more than 30 articles to profl. jours. including Tetrahedron, Jour. Magnetic Resonance, Chemistry Jour. Physics Letters, Jour. Chem. Soc., among others. Recipient Nicolae Teclu award Romanian Acad., 1991. Home: Aleea Padurea Craiului, NR 2 BL H2 Apt 13 Sec 3, Bucharest Romania

NEGRO, PAOLO, civil engineer; b. Treviso, Italy, July 11, 1959; s. Fermo and Dina (Varroto) N.; m. Morena Abiti, June 9, 1990; children: Jacopo, Anna. Degree in civil engring., U. Padua, Italy, 1985; MS in Earthquake Engring., U. Calif., Berkeley, 1987; PhDCE, U. Wales, Swansea, 1997. Structural designer Polytecna Harris, Milan, 1987-88; head design office Agribeton Spa, Treviso, Italy, 1989-91; engr. Joint Rsch. Ctr. European Commn., Ispra, Italy, 1991—; mem. faculty PhD program on earthquake engring. Poly. Milan, 1998—; rep. European Network for Prenormative Rsch. in Support of EuroCode 8, 1993-97; rep. European Assn. Structural Mechanics Labs., 1993—, European Union-Japan Collaboration on Earthquake Engring., 1995—, European Union-U.S. Collaboration on Earthquake Engring., 1998—; responsible European Union-Japan Collaboration on

Earthquake Engring. Contbr. articles to profl. jours. Fulbright scholar U. Calif., Berkeley, 1986. Mem. Seismic Isolation Working Group. Home: via Canova 12, 31100 Treviso Italy Office: Joint Rsch Ctr, TP 480, 21020 Ispra Italy

NEGRON, JAIME, performing arts center sales director; b. San Juan, P.R., Dec. 23, 1939; came to U.S., 1952; s. Rito and Tomasa (Otero) N.; m. Barbara Charlotte Stovall, Nov. 5, 1959; children: Jeannette Michelle, Victoria Frances. BA in Econs., Howard U., 1987. Lic. realtor. Chief receiving & shipping Am. Univ., Washington, 1960-62; book dept. mgr. Am. U., Washington, 1968-71; bookstore mgr. Follett Corp., Chgo., 1962-68, Cath. U., Washington, 1971-74; dir. Howard U. stores Howard Univ., Washington, 1974-87; dir. aux. enterprises Howard U., Washington, 1987-91; real estate agt. Weichert Referral Assocs., Vienna, Va., 1993—; asst. dir. aux. enterprises DeKalb Coll., Atlanta, 1992-96; dir. retail operations J.F. Kennedy Ctr. for Performing Arts, Washington, 1997—; cons. U. Del., Newark, 1988, Wesley Sem., Washington, 1984, R.R. Moton Meml. Inst., N.Y.C., 1974-79. Active Vienna Jaycees, 1970-80. With USN, 1958-60. Mem. Middle Atlantic Coll. Stores (pres. 1984), Nat. Assn. Coll. Stores, Nat. Bd. Realtors, Va. Bd. Realtors. Episcopalian. Avocation: dancing. Office: JFK Ctr Performing Arts 2700 F St NW Washington DC 20566-0002

NEGROPONTE, JOHN DIMITRI, publishing company official, former diplomat; b. London, July 21, 1939; s. Dimitri John and Catherine (Coumantaros) N.; m. Diana Mary Villiers, Dec. 14, 1976; children: Marina, Alexandra, John, George, Sophia. BA, Yale U., 1960. Commd. fgn. svc. officer U.S. Dept. of State, 1960; vice consul Hong Kong, 1961-63; 2nd sec. Saigon, 1964-68; mem. U.S. Del. to Paris Peace Talks on Viet-Nam, 1968-69; mem. staff NSC, 1970-73; polit. counselor Quito, Ecuador, 1973-75; consul gen. Thessaloniki, Greece, 1975-77; dep. asst. sec. of state for oceans and fisheries affairs Washington, 1977-79; dep. asst. sec. for East Asian and Pacific affairs U.S. Dept. State, Washington, 1980-81; U.S. amb. to Honduras, 1981-85, asst. sec. for oceans and internat. environ. and sci. affairs, 1985-87; dep. asst. Pres. for Nat. Security Affairs, 1987-89; U.S. amb. to Mexico, 1989-93, U.S. amb. to The Philippines, 1993-96, spl. coord. for post-1999 U.S. presence in Panama, 1996-97; exec. v.p. global markets McGraw-Hill Cos., N.Y.C., 1997—; co-pres. U.S./Mexico Commn. for Ednl. and Cultural Exch., 1997—; chmn. The French-Am. Found., 1998—; mem. exec. com. U.S. Coun. for Internat. Bus., 1998—. Mem. Am. Fgn. Svc. Assn., Coun. on Fgn. Rels., Am. Acad. Diplomacy, Fgn. Policy Assn. Greek Orthodox. Home: 4936 Lowell St NW Washington DC 20016-2604 Office: McGraw-Hill Cos 49th Fl 1221 Ave of Americas New York NY 10020

NEGROTTI, MASSIMO, social sciences educator; b. Lovere, Bergamo, Italy, Sept. 25, 1944; s. Aldo and Vittoria Sorlini; m. Cristina Cigoli, Aug. 12, 1971; 1 child, Ilaria. Laurea in Sociology, U. Trento, 1970. Cert. methodologist of social scis. Rschr. U. Parma, Italy, 1970-72, asst. prof., 1973-79; prof. U. Genova, Italy, 1980-86; prof. methodology of social scis. U. Urbino, Italy, 1980—, prof., chair, 1987—. Author: (book) The Theory of the Artificial, 1999; editor: (book) Understanding the Artificial, 1991; contbr. articles to sci. publs. Avocations: music composition, electronics. E-mail: maxnegro@synet.it. Home: Bandini 7, 43100 Parma Italy Office: IMES Inst Method Econ Stats, Saffi 15, 61029 Urbino Italy

NEGRU, TRAIAN, pathophysiology educator, physician; b. Roman, Neamt, Romania, July 11, 1932; s. Dumitru and Eugenia (Stefanescu) N.; m. Aneta Vasilescu, Dec. 14, 1972; 1 child, Traian. Carol davila, U. Medicine and Pharmacy, Bucharest, 1957. Univ. asst. Dr. Alexandru Obregia, Bucharest, 1959-74, univ. lectr., 1974-90, univ. conf., 1990-93; univ. prof., chief of pathophysiology Cathedra, Bucharest, 1993—; medic sef de judge Zimnicea Romania, 1957-59; chief of staff Zimnicea, 1957-59. Author: Special Pathophisiology, 1973, Psychosomatic Medicine, 1969, General Pathophisiology, 1969, Experimental Allergic Encephalita, 1965 (Medicine award 1965). Lt. col. Bucharest, 1952-81. Mem. Romanian Soc. of Pathophisiology, European Fedn. of Physiologic Sci. Socs., Med. Sci. Acad. Avocation: philately. Home: Dr Alexandru Vitzu St, Nr 13, 76226 Bucharest Romania

NEHER, BOBIJEAN CESNIK, merchandiser; b. Dec. 28, 1948; d. Rudy L. and Iris V. (Norton) Cesnik; m. Joseph Allen Neher, 1967 (div. 1976); 1 son, Eric Simon. Student, Ind. U.-Purdue U., Indpls., 1970-93, Butler U., 1979-80; Assoc. in Comm., Ind. U., 1992. Sec.-treas. Heat-Cool Sales & Svc., Inc., Danville, Ind., 1971-76; travel dept. coord. Ambassadair, Inc., Indpls., 1976-78; asst. cmty. affairs dir. WISH-TV, Indpls.; prodr. Indy Today, 1978-80; host prodr. Community, 1978-80; prodr. PM Mag. WTHI-TV, Terre Haute, Ind., 1980-81; mgr. aircraft scheduling Am. Trans Air, Indpls., 1981-90, acosta sales & mktg., 1999-2000; acosta sales & mktg. Brann Nat. Regail Svcs., 2000—. Fax: 317 238-9430. E-mail: mother411@surfree.com. Home: 1157 Spruce St Indianapolis IN 46203-2055

NEHER, ERWIN, biophysicist; b. Landsberg, Bavaria, Germany, Mar. 20, 1944; s. Franz Xaver and Elisabeth (Pfeiffer) N.; m. Eva-Maria Ruhr, Dec. 26, 1978; children: Richard, Benjamin, Carola, Sigmund, Margret. MS, U. Wis., 1967; PhD, Tech. U., Munich, 1970. Rsch. assoc. Max Planck Inst. for Psychiatry, Munich, 1970-72; rsch. assoc. Max Planck Inst. for Biophys. Chemistry, Göttingen, 1972-75, 1976-83, rsch. dir., 1983—; rsch. assoc. Yale U., 1975-76; Fairchild Scholar, Calif. Inst. of Tech., 1988-89. Author: Elektronische Messtechnik, 1974; editor: Single Channel Recording, 1983; contbr. articles to profl. jours. Co-recipient Nobel Prize physiology or medicine, 1991; recipient Louisa Gross-Horwitz award Columbia U., N.Y.C., 1986, Leibniz award Deutsche Forschungsgemeinschaft, Bonn, 1986, Gairdner Found. award, 1989. Mem. NAS (fgn. assoc.), Royal Soc. (fgn. mem.), Bavarian Acad. Scis. (corr.), Academia Europea, Acad. d. Wissensch. zu Goettingen, Ukrainian Acad. Sci. (fgn.), Leopoldina Halle. Roman Catholic. Office: Max Planck Inst Biophys Chemistry, Am Fassberg, 37070 Göttingen Germany*

NEHER, LESLIE IRWIN, engineer, former air force officer; b. Marion, Ind., Mar. 15, 1906; s. Irvin Warner and Lelia Myrtle (Irwin) N.; m. Lucy Marion Price; 1 child, David Price; married, June 14, 1956. BSEE, Purdue U., 1930. Registered profl. engr., Ind., N.Mex. Engr. high voltage rsch., 1930-32; engr. U.S. Army, Phila., 1933-37; heating engr. gas utility, 1937-40; commd. 2d lt. U.S. Army, 1929, advanced through grades to col., 1947; dir. tng. Tng. Command, Heavy Bombardment, Amarillo AFB, Tex., 1942-44; dir. mgmt. tng. 15th AF, Colorado Springs, Colo., 1945-46; mgr. Korea Electric Power Co., Seoul, 1946-47, ret., 1960; engr. Neher Engring. Co., Gas City Ind., 1960—; rschr. volcanic materials, 1948-49; chmn. Midwest Indsl. Gas Coun., 1969; historian Grant County, Ind., 1982-95. Named Outstanding Liaison Officer Air Force Acad., 1959; Amb. for Peace, Republic of Korea, 1977; recipient Republic of Korea Svc. medal, 1977. Mem. Ind. Soc. Profl. Engrs. (Outstanding Engr. 1982, Engr. of Yr. Ind. 1986), Nat. Soc. Profl. Engrs., Midwest Indsl. Gas Assn. (chmn. 1969), AARP (pres. Grant County chpt. 1986, 87, 89, 90, dir. dist. 5 1992-93), NAUS (pres. Grissom chpt. 1992—), Kiwanis (Disting. sect. 1979-85, lt. gov. 1964, Disting. Svc. award 1962). Republican. Methodist. Address: 801 Huntington Ave Warren IN 46792-9402

NEHMZOW, ULRICH D.F., electrical engineer, educator; b. Kulmbach, Germany, Sept. 18, 1961; arrived in Great Britain, 1989; s. Hartmut and Fritzi-Maria (Liecks) N.; m. Claudia Alsdorf, 1991; 1 child. Diploma in elec. engring. and info. sci., Tech. U. Munich, 1988; PhD in Artificial Intelligence, Edinburgh (Scotland) U., 1992. Rsch. asst. Edinburgh U., 1989-91, postdoc. rsch. asst., 1992-94; lectr., head robotics rsch. group dept. computer sci. Manchester (Eng.) U., 1994—. Author: Mobile Robotics: A Practical Introduction, 2000; contbr. articles to profl. jours. With German Armed Forces, 1980-82. Royal Soc./STA rsch. fellow Electrotech. Lab. (Japan), 1998. Mem. Internat. Soc. for Adaptive Behavior, Instn. Elec. Engrs. (info. tech. engring. and control 1995—, vice chmn. 1996, chmn. 1997, N.W. Ctr. com.), Soc. Artificial Intelligence and Simulation of Behaviour. Avocations: amateur radio, hillwalking. Office: U Manchester Dept Computer Sci, Oxford Rd, Manchester M13 9PL, England

NEHRA, SANJEEV, consulting company executive; b. Ambala, Haryana, India, Aug. 4, 1961; s. Baldev Swarup and Surender (Sood) N. BComm, Govt. Coll. Chandigarh (India), 1981; MA in Econs., Punjab U., Chandigarh, 1985, Advanced Postgrad. Taxation Diploma, 1986; Computer Degree, NICI, Chandigarh, 1987. Liaison mgr. Ansal Group of Industries, Chandigarh, 1982-84; devel. officer Life Ins. Corp. of India, Chandigarh, 1984-85; mgmt. trainee LML Ltd., Chandigarh, 1986-89; comm. officer Punjab Electro Optics Ltd., Mohali, India, 1989-92; dir. Nehre Con Ser "P" Ltd., Chandigarh, 1992—. Event mgr. Youth Hostel, Chandigarh, 1997. Mem. Youth Travel Assn. (founder, sec. 1996-97, hon. sec. 1997-99). Mem. Congress Party. Avocations: music, nature trekking, advanture sports. Home: The Shelter 2237, Sector 15-C, Chandigarh 160015, India Office: Nehra Cons Svcs P Ltd, The Shelter Com Complex 2237 Sector 15-C, Chandigarh 160015, India

NEIDHARDT, FREDERICK CARL, microbiologist; b. Phila., May 12, 1931; s. Adam Fred and Carrie (Fry) N.; m. Elizabeth Robinson, June 9, 1956 (div. Sept. 1977); children: Richard Frederick, Jane Elizabeth; m. Germaine Chipault, Dec. 3, 1977; 1 son, Marc Frederick. BA, Kenyon Coll., 1952, DSc (hon.), 1976; PhD, Harvard U., 1956; DSc (hon.), Purdue U., 1988, Umea U., 1994. Research fellow Pasteur Inst., Paris, 1956-57; H.C. Ernst research fellow Harvard Med. Sch., 1957-58, instr., then assoc., 1958-61; mem. faculty Purdue U., 1961-70, assoc. prof, then prof., assoc. head dept. biol. scis., 1965-70; mem. faculty U. Mich., Ann Arbor, 1970—, chmn. dept. microbiology and immunology, 1970-82, F.G. Novy disting. univ. prof., 1989-99, F.G. Novy disting. univ. prof. emeritus, 2000—, assoc. dean faculty affairs, 1990-93, assoc. v.p. for rsch., 1993-96, acting v.p. for rsch., 1996-97, interim v.p. for rsch., 1997, v.p. for rsch., 1998; cons. Dept. Agr., 1964-65; mem. grant study panel NIH, 1965-69, 88-92; mem. commn. scholars Ill. Bd. Higher Edn., 1973-79; mem. test com. for microbiology Nat. Bd. Med. Examiners, 1975-79, chmn., 1979-83; mem. sci. adv. com. Neogen Corp., 1982-92; mem. basic energy scis. adv. com. U.S. Dept. Energy, 1994-98; Wellcome vis. prof. in microbiology U. Ky., 1986. Author books and papers in field; mem. editorial bd. profl. jours. Recipient award bacteriology and immunology Eli Lilly and Co., 1966; Alexander von Humboldt Found. award for U.S. sr. scientist, 1979; NSF sr. fellow U. Copenhagen, 1968-69. Mem. Am. Soc. Microbiology (pres. 1981-82), Am. Acad. Arts and Scis., Am. Soc. Biochemistry and Molecular Biology, Am. Inst. Biol. Scis., Genetics Soc. Am., Soc. Gen. Physiology, Waksman Found. for Microbiology (bd. dirs. 1996—, pres.-elect 1999—), Phi Beta Kappa, Sigma Xi. Office: U Mich Med Sch Dept Microbiology and Immunology Ann Arbor MI 48109-0620

NEIDITZ, ANDREW E., city administrator; b. Glen Cove, N.Y., June 21, 1953; s. Victor and Marie C. Neiditz; m. Marie Alice Yount, Aug. 30, 1980; children: Nicole, Elliot. BS in Social Work, Stockton State Coll., 1975; MS in Pub. Adminstrn., U. Oreg., 1977. Cert. sr. exec. program state and local govt. Kennedy Sch., Harvard, 1993. Dep. county exec. Pierce County, Tacoma, 1985-93, exec. dir. pub. safety, 1993-96; dep. city mgr. City of Lakewood, Wash., 1996-99; city adminstr. City of Sumner, Wash., 1999—. Mem., com. chair Tacoma Rotary, 1986-96, Lakewood Rotary, 1997-99; bd. mem. Tacoma Zoo Soc., 1992-94. Recipient Liberty Bell award Tacoma Bar Assn., 1992. Mem. Safe Sts. Bd. Dirs. (chair 1989-92). Roman Catholic. E-mail: aneiditz@ci.sumner.wa.us. Home: 4936 N Lexington St Tacoma WA 98407-1326 Office: 1104 Maple St Sumner WA 98390-1423

NEILD, ROBERT RALPH, economist, educator; b. Peterborough, U.K., Sept. 10, 1924; s. Ralph and Josephine Neild; m. Elizabeth W. Griffiths (div.); 5 children. Ed. Charterhouse and Trinity Coll., Cambridge. Sec. UN Econ. Commn. for Europe, Geneva, 1947-51; mem. staff econ. sect. Cabinet Office (later Treasury), 1951-56; lectr. econs., fellow Trinity Coll., Cambridge U., 1956-58, prof. econs., 1971-84; mem. staff Nat. Inst. Econ. and Social Research, 1958-64; econ. adviser to Treasury, 1964-67; mem. Fulton Com. on Civil Service, 1966-68; dir. Stockholm Internat. Peace Research Inst., 1967-71, mem. governing bd., 1972-82; lectr. in field. Author: Pricing and Employment in the Trade Cycle, 1964; The Measurement and Reform of Budgetary Policy (with T.S. Ward), 1978; How to Make Up Your Mind About the Bomb, 1981, An Essay on Strategy, 1990; co-editor: The Foundations of Defensive Defense, 1990, The English, The French and the Oyster, 1995. Mem. governing body Queen Elizabeth Coll., Oxford, 1978-86. Served with RAF, 1943-45.

NEILL, SIR (FRANCIS) PATRICK, lawyer, educator, college administrator; b. Eng., Aug. 8, 1926; s. Sir Thomas and Lady Annie Strachan (Bishop) N.; m. Lady Caroline Susan, 1954; children: Timothy, Robin, Jonathan, Harriet, Matthew, Emma. Ed., Highgate Sch.; BA, Oxford (Eng.) U., 1950, BCL, 1951, MA, 1972, DCL (hon.), 1987; LLD, U. Hull, Eng., 1978, U. Buckingham, Eng., 1995. Called to the Bar, Gray's INn, 1951, bencher, 1971; Queen's Cousnel, 1966. Fellow All Souls Coll., Oxford U., 1950-77, sub-warden, 1972-74, warden, 1977-95, univ. vice chancellor, 1985-89, hon. fellow, 1995—; leading counsel; recorder of Crown Ct., 1975-78; judge Cts. of Appeal of Jersey and Guernsey, 1977-94; chmn. Justice All Souls Com. for Rev. Adminstrv. Law, 1978-87, Press Coun., 1978-83, Coun. for Securities Industry, 1978-85, treas., 1990; chmn. Dept. Trade and Industry com. of inquiry into regulatory arrangement Lloyd's of London, 1986-87, chmn. Feltrim Loss Rev. Com., 1991-92; ind. nat. dir. Times Newspaper Holdings, 1988—; lectr. in air law, London Sch. Econs., 1955-58; mem. Bar Coun., 1967-71, vice chmn. 1973-74, chmn. 1974-75; chmn. Senate of Inns of Ct. and the Bar, 1974-75; hon. prof. legal ethics Birmingham U., 1983-84. Served with Rifle Brigade, 1944-47, GSO, III (Tng.) Brit. Troops Egypt, 1947. Gibbs Law scholar, 1949, Eldon Law scholar, 1950. Mem. Athenaeum Club, Garrick Club, Beefstake Club. Office: 1 Hare Ct Temple, London EC4Y 7BE, England

NEILL, ROBERT D., engineering executive; b. Fredericton, N.B., Can., Aug. 8, 1932; s. Wallace Raymond and Marjorie Haines (Fletcher) N.; m. Joey J. Coates, June 25, 1954; children: Katherine Josephine, Kimberly Robert. BS, U. N.B., 1954, DSc (hon.), 1985. Design engr. N.B. Power, 1954-56, sr. mech. engr., 1957-61, chief design engr., 1962-64; exec. v.p. Neill and Gunter Ltd., Fredericton, N.B., 1964-78, pres., CEO, 1979-84, chmn., CEO, 1984-93, chmn., 1993—; chmn. Neill Gunter, Inc., 1990—; bd. dirs. N.B. Rsch. and Productivity Coun., Neill & Gunter Inc., Beaverbrook Art Gallery. Mem. ASME, Assn. Profl. Engrs. of N.B., Can. Coun. Profl. Engrs. (dir. gold medal 1991), Forest Product Rsch. Soc., Fredericton Garrison Club, Fredericton Golf and Curling Club. Home: 505 Golf Club Rd, Fredericton, NB Canada E3B 5Z5 Office: Neill & Gunter Ltd, PO Box 713, Fredericton, NB Canada E3B 5B4*

NEILSON, CHARLES BIENVENU, education executive; b. Abbeville, La., Oct. 23, 1948; s. William Barry and Lillian Anne (Bienvenu) N.; m. Maria Elizabeth Hallak, Dec. 15, 1979; children: Marc Lucas, John Peter. BA, La. State U., 1970; MBA, Fundacao Getulio Vargas, Sao Paulo, Brazil, 1989. Dir. John Somers & CIA Ltd., Sao Joao del Rei, Brazil, 1972-78, Audio Visual Systems Ltd., Sao Joao del Rei, 1979-85; exec. dir. Assn. Alumni, Sao Paulo, 1985-96; pres. Bus. Sch. Sao Paulo, 1996—; vol. U.S. Peace Corps, Recife, Brazil, 1970-71. Vol. U.S. Peace Corps, Recife, Brazil, 1970-71; treas. Am. Soc., Sao Paulo, 1986-90; bd. dirs. Jr. Achievement, Brazil, 1989-97, Fernand Braudel Inst. World Econs., 1999—; vice-chmn. Reps. Abroad, Brazil, 1990-94. Home: Rua Peixoto Gomide, 1014 Apt 15A, Sáo Paulo 01409000, Brazil Office: Bus Sch Sao Paulo, Rua Alexandre Dumas 2100-15, São Paulo 04717004, Brazil

NEILSON, ROY, agriculturist, researcher; b. St. Andrews, Fife, Scotland, Jan. 29, 1964; s. Robert Alexander and Mary Jack (Farmer) N.; m. Sharon Jean Johnston, Oct. 4, 1996; 1 child, Kirstin. MSc, U. Dundee (Scotland), 1993, PhD, 1999. Rsch. scientist Scottish Crop Rsch. Inst., Dundee, 1982—. Asst. chief editor Russian Jour. Nematology, 1997—; referee sci. publs. in numerous jours.; contbr. articles to profl. jours. Mem. British Ecol. Soc., European Soc. Nematologists, Russian Soc. Nematologists, Radio Soc. Gt. Britain. Avocations: amateur radio, computing, motorsport, cricket, gardening. Office: Scottish Crop Rsch Inst, Mylnefield Invergowrie, Dundee DD2 5DA, Scotland

NEIMAN, JACK, neurologist, psychiatrist; b. Rakvere, Estonia, Jan. 8, 1948; arrived in Sweden, 1976; MD, Tartu U., 1972; PhD, Karolinska Inst., 1987. Assoc. prof. Karolinska Inst., Stockholm, 1990; asst. chief physician Magnus Huss Clinic, Karolinska Hosp., Stockholm, 1989-95; head unit for treatment of drug dependence Danderyd (Sweden) Hosp., 1995-97, head, clinic for treatment of alcohol and drug dependence, 1997-2000; head tchg. & profl. tng. unit No. Stockholm Ctr. Treatment Drug & Alcohol Dependence, 2000—. Contbr. numerous articles to profl. jours., chpts. to textbooks. Mem. AAAS, Swedish Med. Assn., Swedish Psychiat. Assn., N.Y. Acad. Scis. Office: Magnus Huss Clin, Karolinska Hosp, 171 29 Stockholm Sweden

NEIMAN, LEROY, artist; b. St. Paul, June 8, 1927; s. Charles and Lydia (Serline) Runquist; m. Janet Byrne, June 22, 1957. Student, Sch. Art Inst., Chgo., 1946-50, U. Ill., 1951, DePaul U., 1951; LittD (hon.), Franklin Pierce Coll., 1976; D (hon.), St. John's U., 1980, Iona Coll., 1985, Hofstra U., 1997, St. Francis Coll., 1998, St. Bonaventure U., 1999. Instr. Sch. Art Inst. Chgo., 1950-60, Saugatuck (Mich.) Summer Sch. Painting, 1957-58, 63, Sch. Arts and Crafts, Winston-Salem, N.C., 1963; instr. painting Atlanta Youth Council, 1968-69; printmaker-graphics, 1971—; artist Olympics, ABC-TV, Munich, 1972; ofcl. artist Olympics, ABC-TV, Montreal, 1976, U.S. Olympics, 1980, 84; computer artist CBS-TV (Superbowl), New Orleans, 1978; ofcl. artist Goodwill Games CNN-TV, Moscow, USSR, 1986; 1st ofcl. artist Ky. Derby, Louisville, 1997; mem. adv. com. LeRoy Neiman Ctr. for Print Studies Sch. of the Arts Columbia U., 1995; mem. adv. com. for N.Y.C. Commn. for Cultural Affairs, 1995, UCLA LeRoy Neiman Ctr. for Study of Am. Soc. and Culture, 1998; establisher LeRoy Neiman Art Ctr. for Youth, San Francisco, 2000. Exhibited one-man shows: Oehlschlaeger Gallery, Chgo., 1959, 61, O'Hana Gallery, London, Gallerie O. Bosc, Paris, 1962, Hammer Gallery, N.Y.C., 1963, 65, 67, 70, 72, 76, 78, 79, 81-83, 85-87, 89, 92, 94, 97, 2000, Huntington-Hartford Gallery Modern Art, N.Y.C., 1967, Heath Gallery, Atlanta, 1969, Abbey Theatre, Dublin, Ireland, 1970, Museo de Bellas Artes, Caracas, Indpls. Inst. Arts, 1972, Hermitage Mus., Leningrad, Tobu Gallery, Tokyo, 1974, Springfield (Mass.) Mus. Fine Arts, 1974, 84, Knoedler Gallery, London, 1976, Casa gratica, Helsinki, 1977, Renée Victor, Stockholm, 1977, Okla. Art Ctr., Oklahoma City, 1981, Harrod's, London, 1982; retrospective show, Minn. Mus. Art, St. Paul, 1975, Meredith Long Galleries, Houston, 1978, Hanae Mori Gallery, Tokyo, 1988, New State Tretyakov Mus., 1988, Butler Inst., Youngstown, Ohio, 1990, Galerie Marcel Bernheim, Paris, 1993, Ky. Derby Mus., Louisville, 1995, 1997; two-man show, Neiman-Warhol, Los Angeles Inst. Contemporary Art, 1981; exhibited in group shows, Art Inst. Chgo., 1954-60, Carnegie Internat., 1956, Corcoran Gallery Am., Washington, Walker Art Center, Mpls., 1957, Ringling Mus., Sarasota, Fla., 1959, Salon d'Art Mus., Paris, 1961, Nat. Gallery Portraiture, Smithsonian Instn., Washington, Minn. Mus. Art, 1969, Rotunda Della Basana, Milan, Italy, 1971, Royal Coll. Art, London, 1971, Minn. Mus. Art Nat. Tour, 1976-77, Whitney Mus., 1985 ; Master Prints of 19th and 20th Centuries, Hammer Galls., N.Y., 1987, Salon d'Automne, Paris, 1992, 93; represented in permanent collections, Mpls. Inst. Arts, Ill. State Mus., Springfield, Joslyn Mus., Omaha, Wodham Coll., Oxford, Eng., Nat. Art Mus. Sport, N.Y.C., Museo De Ballas Artes Caracas, Hermitage Mus., Indpls. Inst. Arts, U. Ill., Balt. Mus. Fine Art, The Armand Hammer Collection, Los Angeles, Edwin & Ruth Kennedy Mus. of Am. Art at Ohio U.; executed murals at, Merc. Nat. Bank, Hammond, Ind., Continental Hotel, Chgo., Swedish Lloyd Ship S.S. Patricia, Stockholm, ceramic tile mural, Sportsmans Park, Chgo.; author: LeRoy Neiman—Art and Life Style, 1974, Horses, 1979, LeRoy Neiman. Posters, 1980, LeRoy Neiman. Catalogue Raisonné, 1980, Carnaval, 1981, LeRoy Neiman: Winners, 1983, Japanese translation, 1985, LeRoy Neiman, Monte Carlo Chase, 1988, The Prints of LeRoy Neiman, 1980-90, Big Time Golf, 1992, LeRoy Neiman, An American in Paris, 1994, LeRoy Neiman on Safari, 1997, The Prints of LeRoy Neiman 1991-2000; illustrator: 12 paintings deluxe edit. Moby Dick, 1975, 35 charcoal drawings deluxe edit. Casey at the Bat, 2000. Served with AUS, 1942-46. Recipient 1st prize Twin City Show, 1953, 2d prize Minn. State Show, 1954, Clark Meml. prize Chgo. Show, 1957, Hamilton-Graham prize Ball State Coll., 1958, Municipal prize Chgo. Show, 1958, Purchase prize Miss. Valley Show, 1959, Gold medal Salon d'Art Modern Paris, 1961; award of merit as nation's outstanding sports artist AAU, 1976; Olympic Artist of Century award, 1979, Gold Medal award St. John's U., 1985. Address: 1 W 67th St New York NY 10023-6200

NEIMAN, NORMAN, aerospace business and marketing executive; b. Phila., May 23, 1935; s. Harry and Clara (Schuller) N.; m. Sandra Elaine Berk (dec. 1989); children: Nadene Lori Eisaman, Andrea Neiman-Pearce, David Michael; m. Bonnie Gail McCoy, Sept. 5, 1990. BSME, U. Miami, 1957; postgrad., Alexander Hamilton Inst., N.Y.C., 1959; postgrad. real estate law, Brevard C.C., Cocoa, Fla., 1973. Lic. real estate broker, Fla.; lic. fed. firearms dealer. Engr. Sperry Gyroscope Corp., Gt. Neck, N.Y., 1957-59; lead mech. engr. Convair Aerospace Co., Cape Canaveral, Fla., 1959-62; engring. scientist Douglas Aircraft Corp., Cape Canaveral, 1962-65; chief support engr. Grumman Aerospace Corp., Kennedy Space Center, Fla., 1965-73; mgr. Cocoa Beach (Fla.) ops. Grumman Aerospace Corp., 1973-74, mgr. Orlando (Fla.) ops., 1974-79; pres. Neiman and Co., Inc., Orlando, 1980—; COO Neiman and Assocs., Inc., Orlando, 2000—; pres. Sunshine State Realty, Inc., Cocoa Beach, 1972-76; v.p. Vitality Workshop, Inc., Orlando, 1978-80, Reconnaissance Techs., Arlington, Va., 1985-89; U.S. Govt. sales agt. Calico Light Weapon Systems, 1989-91; dir. program devel. NYMA Inc., Cocoa Beach, 1990-97, Fed. Data Corp., Orlando, Fla., 1998-2000, Neiman & Assocs., Inc., 2000—. Patentee waveguide disconnect. Mem. NRA, AIAA, Tech. Mktg. Soc., Range, Missile and Space Pioneers (life), Am. Meteorol. Soc., Am. Numismatic Assn., Air Force Assn., Mensa, Intertel. Republican. Jewish. Avocations: shooting, model railroading, coin collecting, foreign travel. Office: Neiman and Co Inc PO Box 140094 Orlando FL 32814-0094

NEIMARK, JURI ISAAKOVICH (YURI NEIMARK), mathematician; b. Amur-Nizhne-Dneprovsk, Russia, Nov. 24, 1920; s. Isaak Hustavovich and Lena Nikolaevna (Perfil'eva) N.; m. Valentina Vasil'evna Ushakova, Nov. 9, 1946; children: Tatjana, Alexandr. D of Engring. Scis., Inst. Control Scis., Moscow, 1958. Asst. prof. Nizhni Novgorod State U., Russia, 1944-46, assoc. prof., 1946-58, head of chair control theory & dynamics of machines, 1958-91, prof., 1991—; head dpet. dynamics & control Applied Maths. & Cybernetics TRsch., Nizhi Novgorod, 1964—. Author: The Method of Point Mapping in the Theory of Nonlinear Oscillations, 1972, Dynamical Systems and Processes of Control, 1978, (with N.A. Fufaev) Dynamics of Nonholonomic Systems, 1972, (with P.S. Landa) Stochastic and Chaotic Oscillations, 1992. Recipient A.A. Andronov award USSR Acad. Scis., 1989. Mem. Russian Acad. Natural Scis. (Norbert Wiener award 1993), Internat. Sci. Found. Office: Nizhni Novgorod State U, Gagarin Ave 23, 603600 Nizhni Novgorod Russia

NEIMARK, MIKHAIL IZRAILEVICH, anesthesiologist; b. St. Petersburg, Russia, Feb. 21, 1951; s. Izrail Isayevich Neimark and Valentina Alexayevna Arabei; m. Tamara Simonovna Volpe, Apr. 12, 1992; children: Eugeny, Dmitry. MD cum laude, Altai Med. U., Barnaul, Russia, 1974. Docent, chair anesthesiology and reanimatology Altai Med. U., Barnaul, 1989-90, prof. anesthesiology and reanimatology, 1990-92, chair dep. anesthesiology and reanimatology, 1992—; chief anesthesiologist, reanimatologist, Altai Region, Russia, 1995—. Author: Intensive Therapy of the Post Operative Thyrotoxic Storm, 1980, Anesthesia and Intensive Therapy in the Endocrinological Surgery, 1995. Mem. Regional Sci. Soc. of Anesthesiologists and Reanimatologists, Coun. of Fedn. of Anesthesiologists and Reanimatologists, Acad. Natural History. Avocation: swimming. Home: Lenina 53-10, 656099 Barnaul Russia

NEIRA ARCHILA, LUIS CARLOS, legal consultant, accountant; b. Bogotá, Colombia, Jan. 3, 1924; s. Luis Carlos Neira Cadena and Maria Del Carmen Archila; m. Ruth Mejia, Sept. 18, 1946; children: Patricia, Margarita Maria, Luis Carlos, Maria Jose. Diploma in law, U. Javeriana, Bogotá, 1946; cert. in acctg., Junta Ctrl. de Contadores, Bogotá, 1962. Lawyer Superintendency of Corps., Bogotá, 1946-50, del. supt., 1952-56; prof. fin. analysis U. Javeriana, 1955-60, prof. comml. law, 1960-90; ptnr., lawyer Holguín Neira y Pombo, Bogotá, 1957—; lectr. comml. law various forums, various cities, 1971—; arbitrator, Bogotá, 1979—; mem. Commerce Code Revision Commn., Ministry of Justice, Bogotá, 1970-71, 73-74; bd. mem. Grancolombiana Fin. Corp., Bogotá, 1976-84. Co-author: Accounting, Theory and Operation, 1959; contbr. articles to profl. jours., chpts. to books. Pres. Abogados Javerianos 1945, Bogotá, 1970-90; dir. Colegio Abogados Javerianos, 1982-94; v.p. Inst. Nacional de Contadores, Bogotá, 1955-57. Recipient Santiago Pérez award Ministry of Justice, 1951, Félix Restrepo award U. Javeriana, 1995, Disting. Prof. award, 1980. Mem. Coll. Comml. Lawyers (hon.), Nat. Accts. Assn., Arbitrators Settlement Assn., (founding mem.), U. Javeriana Law Sch. 1945 Grads. Assn., U. Javeriana Law Sch. Grads. Assn. Roman Catholic. Avocations: golf, bridge, reading, classical

music. Office: Holguin Neira y Pombos Abo, Carrera 7 #71-52 Of 1502, Torre B Bogotá Colombia

NEIRYNCK, JACQUES JULIEN, electrical engineering educator, writer; b. Uccle, Belgium, Aug. 17, 1931; arrived in Switzerland, 1972; s. Joseph Emile and Cecile Augusta (Dubrulle) N.; m. Georgette Marie Werbrouck, May 5, 1955 (div. July 1976); children: Anne, Isabelle, Stephane, Cecile; m. Marie-Annick Françoise Roy, Dec. 17, 1977; 1 child, Julien. EE, U. Louvain, Belgium, 1954, PhD, 1958. Engr. Foraky, Belgium, 1954-57; prof. U. Lovanium, Kinshasa, Zaire, 1957-63; dep. dir. Philips, Brussels, 1963-72; prof. U. Louvain, 1965-72; prof. elec. engring. Swiss Fed. Inst. Tech., Lausanne, 1972—, head dept., 1983-85, 91-96; pres. Presses Polytechniques Universitaires Romanoes, Lausanne, 1980-92; chmn. bd. dirs. Testachat, Brussels, 1968-74. Author: Manuscrit du Saint Sepulcre, 1994 (Prix Oulmont 1995), Le Huitieme Jour de la Creation, 1996, Le Siege de Bruxelles, 1996; assoc. editor Jour. Franklin Inst., Phila., 1970-96; editor series Traite d'Electricite, 22 books, 1986. Fellow IEEE (edul. activities award 1994); Swiss Fed. Parliament. Roman Catholic. Home: Ormet 17b, CH-1024 Ecublens Vaud, Switzerland Office: Swiss Fed Inst Tech, Dept Elec Engring, CH-1015 Lausanne Switzerland

NEIS, ARNOLD HAYWARD, pharmaceutical company executive; b. N.Y.C., Feb. 13, 1938; s. Harry H. and Mary Ruth (Bishop) N.; m. Lucy de Puig, Dec. 8, 1989; children by previous marriage: Nancy R., Robert C. BS cum laude, Columbia U., 1959; MBA, NYU, 1967. With Scott Chem. Co., 1959-64; v.p. mktg., then v.p. Odell, Inc., N.Y.C., 1964-71, pres. Thayer Knomark div., 1969-71; pres., chief exec. officer E.T. Browne Drug Co., Inc., Englewood Cliffs, N.J., 1971—; dir. Esquire A.B. Stockholm, Knomark Can. Ltd., E.T. Browne Internat. Fellow Royal Soc. Chemists, Royal Geog. Soc., Am. Inst. Chemists, N.Y. Acad. Scis.; mem. AAAS, Am. Chem. Soc., Am. Pharm. Assn., New Eng. Soc. (bd. dirs.), Explorers Club (v.p., bd. dirs., Sweeney medal 1997), Chemists Club, Lotos Club, Soldiers, Sailors and Airmans Club (bd. dirs.), St. Georges Soc., Ch. Club, Pilgrims of the U.S. Episcopalian. Home: 898 Park Ave New York NY 10021-0234 Office: PO Box 1613 440 Sylvan Ave Englewood NJ 07632-2700

NEISEN, HANS JOSEF, management consultant; b. Frechen, Germany, Oct. 28, 1946; s. Josef and Klara Agnes (Hoffzimmer) N.; m. Melanie Wilma Maria Thull, Aug. 9, 1974; children: Uta Clara Maria, Sigrun Vera Ricarda. Diploma, U. Cologne, Germany, 1973. Asst. prof. U. Cologne, 1973-75; project mgr. Battelle Inst., Frankfurt, Germany, 1975-77; economic advisor European Investment Bank, Luxembourg, 1977-80; internat. mktg. dir. C.A. Weidmüller GMBH, Detmold, Germany, 1980-85; mng. dir. Kienbaum, Düsseldorf, Germany, 1985-89; pres. Neisen & Ptnr., Gummersbach, Germany, 1989—, TelMark Mgmt. Cons. GMBH, Gummersbach, Germany, 1992—; chmn. bd. dirs. TelMark Internat. Mgmt. Cons., Inc., Lower Gwynedd, Pa. Contbr. articles to profl. pubs. Mem. Rotary. Roman Catholic. Avocations: history (stone age), horseback riding. Office: Telmark GmbH, Auf der Vosswiese 2, 51643 Gummersbach Germany also: 1-323 Towyn Ct Lower Gwynedd PA 19002

NEISER, BRENT ALLEN, public affairs and personal finance consultant, speaker; b. Cin., Sept. 16, 1954; s. Rodger and Hazel Neiser; m. Marion, Apr. 1, 1978; children: Christy Jean, Steven José, April Reneé. BA in Pub. Affairs, George Washington U., 1976; MA in Urban Studies, Occidental Coll., 1978; MBA, U. Louisville, 1979; postgrad. in internat. affairs, U. Denver, 1987-90. Cert. fin. planner, 1985; cert. assn. exec., 1994; chartered mut. fund counselor, 1996; accredited asset mgmt. specialist, 1998. Project mgr., analyst Legis. Research Com., Frankfort, Ky., 1978-84; pres. Moneyminder, Denver and Frankfort, 1983-91; dir. edn., govt. affairs and ethics Inst. Cert. Fin. Planners, Denver, 1985-91, exec. dir., 1991-94; pub. affairs, govt. rels. bus. strategies cons. The Brent Neiser Co., Englewood, Colo., 1994—; dir. Nat. Endowment for Fin. Edn., 1995—; mng. dir. Fin. Products Stds. Bd., Denver, 1985-91; co-creator Personal Econ. Summit '93, Washington; adv. bd. MoneyForMail.Com. Author: EPCOT/World Showcase External Directions, Walt Disney Imagineering, 1977, Personal Management, 1996; co-inventor: Trivia Express (game) Denver, 1986. Vol., v.p. Big Bros./Big Sisters, Frankfort, 1982; del. Colo. Model Constrnl. Conv., 1987; mem. citizens budget rev. com. Greenwood Village; parent trainer The Adoption Exch., Denver, 1988, mem. long range planning com., 1992-93, bd. dirs., 1993-99; polit. action dir. Frankfort NAACP, 1983, legis. chmn. state conf., 1984; troop com. mem., asst. scoutmaster Boy Scouts Am., Englewood, 1993-99; bd. dirs. Young Ams. Bank Edn. Found., 1993—, chair edn. coun.; bd. dirs. Leadership Denver, 1993; vol. host com. Denver Summit of the Eight, 1997; nat. spokesperson Protect our Children Campaign, 1996; active Annie E. Casey Found.: Nat. Foster Care Awareness Project, 1999-2000; citizen's panelist News Hour with Jim Lehrer (PBS), 1998—; founding ptnr. Social Venture Ptnrs., Denver. Lt. (j.g.) USNR, 1985-92. Recipient Assn. Advance Am. award Excellence, 1996, 98; named Man of Yr., Frankfort NAACP, 1983; Pub. Affairs fellow Coro Found., 1976-77. Mem. Investors Edn. Assn. Colo. (bd. dirs.), Nat. Assns. in Colo., Denver C. of C. (pub. affairs coun.), Adoptive Families of Am., Assn. for Fin. Counseling and Planning Edn., Am. Soc. Assn. Execs., Inst. Mgmt. Cons., N.Am. Securities Adminstrs. Assn. (investment adviser and fin. planner adv. com.), Nat. Soc. Compliance Profls. (bd. dirs. 1987-89), Am. Film Inst. (writers workshop), Fin. Planning Assn. Ind. Sector. Office: 5860 Big Canyon Dr Englewood CO 80111-3516

NEISLER, OTHERINE JOHNSON, education educator, consultant; b. St. Louis, Apr. 27, 1954; d. Robert Louis and Ruth (Wilson) Johnson; m. Anton Ross Neisler, Sr. (div. 1988); children: Maiya Rose Neisler Benda, Anton Ross Jr. BA, Brandeis U., 1972; MA, Fairfield U., 1991; PhD, Syracuse U., 1994. Tchr. social studies Warren H.S., Newton, Mass., 1974-76; mktg. mgr./analyst IBM, White Plains, N.Y., 1976-88; asst. prof. Boston Coll., Chestnut Hill, Mass., 1994-2000; assoc. dir. tchr. preparation program Yale U., New Haven, 2000—; curriculum cons. numerous schs., 1994—. Contbr. articles to profl. jours. Pres. bd. dirs. Erie County (Pa.) Domestic Abuse Agy., 1978-80; bd. dirs. The Multicultural Resource Ctr., Phila., 1996—, Primary Source, Inc., Boston, 1996-98. Mem. ASCD, Am. Edn. Rsch. Assn. (equity com. 1992—), Nat. Coun. Social Studies (citizenship com. 1992—), Links, Inc. Avocations: hiking, tennis. E-mail: otherine.neisler@yale.edu. Office: Yale Univ PO Box 208241 New Haven CT 06520-8241

NEISS, HUBERT, international banking executive; b. Taiskirchen, Austria, Jan. 29, 1935; m. Susanne Neiss; three children. M in Econs., U. Kans.; PhD in Econs. and Bus., Hochschule fur Welthandel, Vienna. Economist IMF, Washington, 1967-73, chief South Pacific Divsn., 1973; resident rep., dep. dir. Asian dept. IMF in Indonesia, 1980-91; dir. Asia and Pacific dept. IMF, Washington, 1991—. Office: Internat Monetary Fund 700 19th St NW Washington DC 20431-0001*

NEITZEL, LISA ANN, newscaster, reporter; b. Watertown, Wis., Jan. 5, 1970; d. Deane Allen and Ruth Emma (Johnson) N. BA in Broadcast Journalism, U. Wis., 1993, BA in Polit. Sci., 1993. News reporter, anchor WBKB-TV (CBS), Alpena, Mich., 1994-95; reporter, weathercaster WDIO-TV (ABC), Duluth, Minn., 1995—. Mem. Soc. Profl. Journalists, Women in Comms, Inc. Avocations: skiing, mountain biking, reading, swimming.

NEITZEL, SOENKE, historian; b. Hamburg, Germany, June 26, 1968; s. Gunther and Elke (Klingenberg) N. Abitur, Claus-von-Stauffenberg-Schule, Dudenhofen, 1987; PhD, U. Mainz, Germany, 1994. Cons. Second German TV, Mainz, Germany, 1994—; univ. asst. Historisches Seminar U., Mainz, 1994-98; lectr. modern hist. U. Mainz, 1998—. Author: (books) The German U-Boat-plus, 1991, The Operations fo the Luftwaffe over the Atlantic and the North Sea 1939-45, 1995 (recipient prize of the Werner-Hahlweg Mil. History, 1996), World Power or Ruin, The Theory of World Power in the Period of Imperialism, 2000. Avocation: diving. Office: Johannes Gutenberg Univ, Hist Sem Abt IV Saarstr 21, D-55099 Mainz Germany

NEIVA, ANA MARGARIDA RIBEIRO, geochemistry educator; b. Oporto, Portugal, May 7, 1941; d. João Manuel Cotelo and Margarida Mendes Ribeiro Neiva. BSc, Coimbra (Portugal) U., 1963, DSc, 1984; PhD, Cambridge (Eng.) U., 1971. Rschr. Mineralogy Geol. Mus., Coimbra, 1971-72; lectr. Coimbra U., 1972-75, 76-77, reader, 1983-85, prof., 1985—; lectr. Brasilia (Brasil) U., 1975-76; lectr. Oporto U., 1977-79, reader, 1979-83. Contbr. numerous articles to profl. jours. Mem. N.Y. Acad. Scis., Geochem. Soc. Columbus, Geol. Soc. London, European Assn. Geochemistry, Mineral Soc. London, Soc. Française Mineral. Cristallographie, Geol. Soc. Lisbon, Soc. Geology Applied to Mineral Deposits, Internat. Assn. Genesis Ore Deposits, Lisbon Acad. Scis., Internat. Mineral Assn., Brazilian Acad. Scis. Roman Catholic. Avocations: reading, listening classic music, theater, cooking, table tennis. Home: R do Telegrafo 78, 3000 Coimbra Portugal Office: U Coimbra, Dept Earth Scis, 3000 Coimbra Portugal

NEJAD-HOSEINIAN, MOHAMMAD HADI, diplomat; b. Karbala, Iraq, Feb. 1, 1947; came to U.S., 1997; s. Hossein and Razie (Haj Tarkhani) N.; m. Fatemeh Tadbir; children: Seyed Hamed, Vahid, Zahra, Seyedeh Hoda. MS, Tehran U., Iran, 1970, George Washington U., 1978. Deputy Plan & Budget Orgn., Tehran, Iran, 1980-81; min. Ministry Road Transp., Tehran, Iran, 1981-85; deputy min. Ministry of Oil, Tehran, Iran, 1985-89, 94-97; min. Ministry Heavy Industry, Tehran, Iran, 1989-94; ambassador, permanent rep. Mission Iran, N.Y.C., 1997—. Office: Mission of Iran to UN 622 3rd Ave Fl Dave34 New York NY 10017-6707

NEJEDLI, SREBRENKA, veterinarian, researcher; b. Zagreb, Croatia, Nov. 29, 1965; d. Jakov and Dragica (Badovinac) Kaufman; m. Damir Nejedli, May 27, 1995; 1 child, Marina. DVM, U. Zagreb, 1991, MS, 1994, PhD, 1999. Rschr., sci. asst. vet. faculty U. Zagreb, 1992-99; performance project Vet. Faculty, Zagreb, 1998. Mem. Croatian Anat., Histological and Embriological Soc. Avocation: numismatics. Office: Zagreb U, Veterinary Faculty, 10 000 Zagreb Croatia

NEKI, SAICHI, marketing educator; b. Tokyo, June 15, 1949; s. Sukeaki and Eiko (Takano) N.; m. Takako Nakajima, Oct. 14, 1996. Bachelor's degree, Keio U. Commerce, Tokyo, 1971; Master's degree, Chuo U. Commerce, Tokyo, 1974, PhD, 1980; Master's degree, Kokushikan Econ., Tokyo, 1983. Asst. prof. Toyama (Japan) Women Coll., 1981-84; prof. Shoin Women Coll., Kanagawa, Japan, 1984-90, Tokai U., Kanagawa, Japan, 1990—. Avocations: basketball coach, golf. Home: Kashiwagi mansion # 201, 4-9-18 Kitashinjuku, Tokyo 169-0074, Japan

NEKMAN, DONALD JOHN, communications company executive; b. Edinburgh, Scotland, July 23, 1942; arrived in Denmark, 1947; s. Bent and Margaret (Sloan) N.; m. Birthe Hoiland Andersen (div. 1982); children: John, Bettina. MS in Mktg., Copenhagen Bus. Sch., 1968, MS in Orgn., 1974. Account dir. Eberlin, Copenhagen, 1965-74; dep. mgr. Foote, Cone & Belding, Copenhagen, 1974-80; ptnr. EURORSCG, Copenhagen, 1980—. Mem. Internat. Advt. Assn. (headmaster diploma edn. 1994—, pres. 1997—, The Columbus Egg award 1999), Danish Mktg. assn. (chmn. supervisory bd. 1996—). Avocations: wine, traveling, film, theatre. Home: Frederikkevej 2A, DK-2900 Hellerup Denmark Office: EURO RSCG, Vangehusvej 19, DK-2100 Copenhagen Denmark

NEL, ETIENNE LOUIS, geography educator; b. Ndola, Zambia, Oct. 19, 1962; arrived in South Africa, 1980; s. Vernon Eslie and Dina Maria (Roux) N.; m. Noleen Taylor, Dec. 7, 1985; children: Catherine, Amy. BA with honors, Rhodes U., Grahamstown, South Africa, 1984, edn. diploma, 1986, PhD, 1997; MA, U. Witwatersrand, Johannesburg, South Africa, 1991. Tchr. Estcourt (South Africa) High, 1986-87; lectr. U. Transkei, Butterworth, South Africa, 1988-89; sr. lectr. Gyani (South Africa) Coll., 1989, Rhodes U., Grahamstown, 1990—; cons. UN Ctr. for Regional Devel., 1990—; rschr. in field. Author: Regional and Local Economic Development in South Africa, 1999; contbr. chpts. to books and articles to profl. jours. Mem. tech. adv. com. Ministry Econ. Affairs Easter Cape Province, 1994; mgmt. com. Eastern Cape Agrl. Rsch. Project, 1998—; mem. local econ. devel. unit com. Grahamstown City Coun., 1999—. Mem. Assn. Am. Geographers, Devel. Soc. Presbyterian. Fax: 46-6361199. Office: Rhodes U Dept Geography, PO Box 94, Grahamstown 6140, South Africa

NEL, IDA JOHANNA WILHELMINA, import/export company executive; b. Boksburg, Transvaal, South Africa, Apr. 1, 1954; d. Cornelius Johannes and Ida Johanna (Jooste) Venter; m. Lukas Cornelius Nel, Feb. 3, 1973 (dec. Aug. 1994); 1 child, Johannes. Student, Rand African Univ., Johannesburg, South Africa, 1972-73. Dir., owner Film Fun, Nelspruit, South Africa, 1973-74; dir., owner S.N.I.E. S.A., Mayotte Island, France, 1980-90, mng. dir., 1991-94, chmn., 1995—; dir. subsidiary companies (all in Mayotte): Mayotte Motor Corp., 1986, Somadis, 1984, Transit SARL, 1990, Transnie EURL, 1988, SCI Z.I. Nel, 1995, BDM, SA, 1998, UTV, SA, 1996. Mem. Rotary Innerwheel (founder). Protestant. Avocations: reading, architecture. Home: Estate Pt Hamaha, 97600 Mamoudzou Mayotte Office: SNIE, Z I Kaweni, B P159 Mamoudzou Mayotte

NEL, MAGDALENA, scientist, physicist, finance company administrator; b. Calitzdorp, South Africa, May 11, 1960; d. Johannes Gerhardus and Susan (Calitz) N. BS, U. Port Elizabeth, South Africa, 1982, BSc with honors in Physics, 1983, MS cum laude, 1986, PhD, 1989; diploma in Prodn. Mgmt., Damelin, Johannesburg, South Africa, 1993; diploma in fin. mgmt., UNISA, RSA, 1998. Cert. natural scientist South African Coun. Sci. Professions. Student asst. physics U. Port Elizabeth, 1983-86, rsch. asst. dept. physics, 1984-88; optical engr. ELOPTRO, ARMSCOR, Kemptonpark, South Africa, 1989-91; sr. scientist ELOPTRO, DENEL, KemptOnpark, South Africa, 1991-92; process sustaining engr. SAMES, Pretoria, South Africa, 1993-96; dir. Vanzylsdamme, Ladismith WC, South Africa, 1996—; dir. Ladismith Landbou Kooperasie, South Africa, 1996—, Gellman Seeds, Outdshoorn, South Africa, 1996—, Vanzylsdamme Edns.Bpk., Ladismith, 1996—; mem. Lusern Seed Forum, Outsdhoorn, South Africa, 1997—; bd. dirs. Lusern Social Produsente Orgn., Reinders Garage Edms Bpk. Contbr. articles to profl. jours. Mem. Ladismith Landelihe Forum, 1996. Mem. Dendrological Soc. (sec. 1988), We. Cape Farmers Assn. Avocations: collecting first day covers, stamp collecting, Bonzai trees, tennis. Home: Vanzylsamme PO Box 6, 6655 Ladismith South Africa Office: Vanzylsdamme, 6655 Ladismith South Africa

NEL, PIETER BARENDSE, armaments company executive; b. Steynsburg, South Africa, Dec. 20, 1946; s. Philip Daniëel and Sarah Alice (Botha) N.; m. Janie Adriana Raubenheimer, Dec. 9, 1950; children: Philip, Corlie, Sulice. BSc, Potchefstroom U., South Africa, 1968, Potchefstroom U., South Africa, 1969; MSc, Potchefstroom U., South Africa, 1970; PhD, U. South Africa, South Africa, 1974. Scientist Atomic Energy Bd., Pretoria, South Africa, 1972-74; sr. lectr. Ft. Hare U., South Africa, 1974-77; rschr. U. Pretoria, 1977-81; quality assurance rep. Armscor, South Africa, 1981-83; projects mgr. Armscor, 1983-89, mgr., program mgr., 1989—; chmn. South African Ballistics Orgn., 1995—, Explosives Bd., South Africa, 1987—; mem. Internat. Ballistics Com., South Africa, 1995—, sec. exec. bd., 1999—. Chmn. Tennis Club, Pretoria, 1997. Avocations: tennis, reading, gardening. Office: Armscor, P/Bag X337, 0001 Pretoria South Africa

NELDER, JOHN ASHWORTH, statistician; b. Dulverton, England, Oct. 8, 1924; s. Reginald Charles and Edith May Ashworth (Briggs) N.; m. Mary Hawkes, Jan. 13, 1955; children: Jan Richard, Rosalind May. MA, Cambridge (Eng.) U., 1948; DSc, U. Birmingham, Eng., 1968, U. Paul Sabatier, Toulouse, France, 1980. Head stats. sect. Nat. Vegetable Rsch. Sta., Wellesbourne, Eng., 1950-68; head stats. dept. Rothamsted Exptl. Sta., Harpenden, Eng., 1968-84; vis. prof. Imperial Coll. of Sci., Tech. and Medicine, London, 1984—. Author (with P. McCullagh): Generalized Linear Models, 1989; contbr. numerous sci. papers to profl. publs.; originator computer packages Genstat and GLIM. Sgt. RAF, 1943-46, S.Africa. Fellow Royal Soc., Royal Statis. Soc. (pres. 1985-86, Silver medal), Internat. Statis. Inst.; mem. Internat. Biometric Soc. (pres. 1978-79). Avocation: ornithology, piano. Office: Dept Math, Imperial Coll, 180 Queen's Gate, London SW7 2BZ, England

NELIPOVICH, SANDRA GRASSI, artist; b. Oak Park, Ill., Nov. 22, 1939; d. Alessandro and Lena Mary (Ascareggi) Grassi; m. John Nelipovich Jr., Aug. 19, 1973. BFA in Art Edn., U. Ill., 1961; postgrad., Northwestern U., 1963, Gonzaga U., Florence, Italy, 1966, Art Inst. Chgo., 1968; diploma, Accademia Universale Alessandro Magno, Prato, Italy, 1983. Tchr. art Edgewood Jr. High Sch., Highland Park, Ill., 1961-62, Emerson Sch. Jr. High Sch., Oak Park, 1962-77; batik artist Calif., 1977—; illustrator Jolly Robin Publ. Co., Anaheim, Calif., 1988—, Assistance League of Anaheim, Calif., 2000—; supr. student tchrs., Oak Park, 1970-75; adult edn. tchr. ESL, ceramics, Medinah, Ill., 1974; mem. curriculum action group on human dignity, EEO workshop demonstration, Oak Park, 1975-76; guest lectr. Muckenthaler Ctr., Fullerton, Calif., 1980, 92, Niguel Art Group, Dana Point, Calif., 1989, Carlsbad A.A., 1990, ARt League, Oceanside Art Group, 1992; 2d v.p. Anaheim Hills Women's Club, 1990-91, rec. sec. 1991-92; fabric designer for fashion designer Barbara Jax, 1987; illustrator Assistance League Anaheim (Calif.), 2000—. One-Woman shows include Lawry's Calif. Ctr., L.A., 1981-83, Whittier (Calif.) Mus., 1985-86, Anaheim Cultural Ctr., 1986-88, Ill. Inst. Tech., Chgo., 1989, Muckenthaler Cultural Ctr., Fullerton, 1990; also gallery exhibits in Oak Brook, 1982, La Habra, Calif., 1983, Millard Sheets Gallery, Pomona, Calif., 1996; represented in permanent collections McDonald's Corp., Oak Brook, Glenkirk Sch., Deerfield, Ill., Emerson Sch., Oak Park, Calif.; poster designer Saratoga Fine Arts. Active Assistance League, Anaheim, Calif., 1992—, 2d v.p. ways and means com., 1995-96, 97-98. Recipient numerous awards, purchase prizes, 1979—; featured in Calif. Art Rev., Artists of So. Calif., Vol. II, Nat. Artists' Network, 1992. Mem. AAUW (hospitality chmn. 1984-85), Soc. Children's Book Writers and Illustrators, Assistance League Anaheim, Orange Art Assn. (jury chmn. 1980). Roman Catholic. Avocations: cooking, gardening, travel. Home and Office: 5922 E Calle Cedro Anaheim CA 92807-3207

NELISSEN, ROELOF JOHANNUS, bank executive; b. Hoofdplaat, The Netherlands, Apr. 4, 1931. MA in Law, Cath. U., Nijmegen, The Netherlands, 1956. Mem. Sociaal Fonds Bouwnijverheid, Amsterdam, 1956; various positions for small and medium sized bus., 1956-69; mem. lower house Dutch parliament, 1963-70; min. Econ. Affairs, 1970-71; vice premier, min. fin., 1971-73; adviser bd. mng. dirs. Amsterdam-Rotterdam Bank N.V., 1973, mem. bd. mng. dirs., 1974, vice chmn. bd. mng. dirs., 1979, chmn. bd. mng. dirs., 1983; chmn. bd. mng. dirs. ABN AMRO Bank N.V., 1991; vice chmn. Royal Ahold N.V., Zaandam; mem. supervisory bd. ABN AMRO Holding N.V., Elsevier N.V., Koninklyke Ahold N.V., Internat. Flavors and Fragrances; chmn. supervisory bd. N.V. Luchthaven Schiphol, Koninklyke Ten Cate, Koninklyke Boskalis Westminster, Stichting Singer Meml. Found., Mercedes Nederland BV; chmn. bd. trustees Sara Lee/DE N.V.; chmn. supervisory bd. Schiphol Area Devel. Co. N.V. Decorated condr. Order of Orange Nassau, grand cross Order Crown of Belgium. Office: Albert Heijnweg 1, 1500 HB Zaandam The Netherlands Office: PO Box 552, 1250 AN Laren The Netherlands*

NELL, VICTOR, neuropsychologist, educator; b. Kwe-Kwe, Zimbabwe, Sept. 15, 1935; s. Sam and Dinnie (Topic) N.; m. Myrna Grace Loon, July 4, 1982; children: Adi, Elli. BA, U. Cape Town, Capetown, 1956; MA, U. Port Elizabeth, 1974; PhD, U. South Africa, Port Elizabeth, 1983. Lic. clin. psychologist. Prof. Inst. Social and Health Scis. U. South Africa; dir. Nat. Rsch. Found. Health Psychology Unit; head WHO Collaborating Ctr. Injury and Violence Prevention. Author: Lost in a Book, 1988, Cross-Cultural Neuropsychological Assessment, 2000. Fellow APA. Jewish. Office: PO Box 84320, Greenside, Johannesburg 2034, South Africa

NELLIGAN, KATE (PATRICIA COLLEEN NELLIGAN), actress; b. London, Ont., Can., Mar. 16, 1951; d. Patrick Joseph and Alice (Dier) N. Attended, York U., Toronto, Ctrl. Sch. Speech and Drama, London. Appeared in plays in Bristol, London, and New York: Barefoot in the Park, 1972, Misalliance, A Streetcar Named Desire, The Playboy of the Western World, London Assurance, Lulu, Private Lives, Knuckle, 1974, Heartbreak House, 1975, Plenty, 1975, As You Like It, A Moon for the Misbegotten, 1984, Virginia, 1985, Serious Money, 1988, Spoils of War, 1988, Bad Habits; films include: The Count of Monte Cristo, 1979, The Romantic Englishwoman, 1979, Dracula, 1979, Mr. Patman, 1980, Eye of the Needle, 1980, Agent, 1980, Without a Trace, 1983, Eleni, 1985, White Room, 1990, Bethune: The Making of a Hero, 1990, Frankie and Johnnie, 1991, The Prince of Tides, 1991, Shadows and Fog, 1992, Fatal Instinct, 1993, Wolf, 1994, Into the Deep, 1994, How to Make an American Quilt, 1995, Margaret's Museum, 1995, Up Close and Personal, 1996, U.S. Marshals, 1998, (voice) Stolen Moments, 1998 Boy Meets Girl, 1998, The Cider House Rules, 1999; TV appearances include: The Arcata Promise, 1974, The Onedin Line, The Lady of the Camellias, Licking Hitler, Measure for Measure, Therese Raquin, 1980, Forgive Our Foolish Ways, 1980, Kojak: The Price of Justice, 1987, Control, 1987, Love and Hate: A Marriage Made in Hell, 1990, Terror Strikes the Class Reunion, 1992, The Diamond Fleece, 1992, Liar Liar, 1993, Shattered Trust: The Shari Karney Story, 1993, Spoils of War, 1994, Million Dollar Babies, 1994, A Mother's Prayer, 1995, Captive Heart: The James Mink Story, 1996, Calm at Sunset, Calm at Dawn, 1996, Love Is Strange, 1998, Swing Vote, 1999; TV guest appearance Road to Avonlea, 1990. Recipient Best Actress award Evening Standard, 1978. Avocations: reading, cooking. Office: Innovative Artists Ste 2850 1999 Avenue Of The Stars Los Angeles CA 90067-4612

NELLIGAN, MAURICE JOHN, psychologist; b. Phila., Dec. 11, 1926; arrived in Mexico, 1960; s. Maurice and Helen Louise (Provost) N.; m. Ramona Angelica Loza-Medina, June 5, 1964; 1 child, Maurice. BA, Boston Coll., 1950, MA, Boston U., 1957; D Psychology, Nat. U. Mexico, Mexico City, 1965. Diplomate psychology; lic. psychology. Prof., coord. psychology dept. Monterrey (Mexico) Inst. Tech., 1965-70; owner, dir. Human Devel. Ctr., Mexico City, 1971-82; program dir. Yalentay, Cuernavaca, Mexico, 1983-89; chief counselor Pizarro Clinic, L.A., 1990-92; owner, dir. Stress Mgmt., Mexico City, 1993-97; prof., tech., cons. Cisle, Mexico City, 1996—; pres., owner Inst. of Motivation and Leadership, Mexico City, 1999—; cons. Productivity Ctr., Monterrey, 1965-70, Channel-13 TV, Mexico City, 1971-82, Radio Centro, Mexico City, 1975-82, Inst. Latin Am. Integration, Mexico City, 1973-76. Author: The Art of Reading, 1976, The Other Side of Machismo, 1982, A Guide to Good Living, 1995 (gold medal 1996), The Funny Mexican, 1996, 9 others. Bd. dirs. Juvenile Ctrs., Mexico CIty, 1978-82; bd. dir. Inst. Latin Am. Integration, Mexico City, 1994-96; active Families Against Drugs, Mexico City, 1993-97. Lt. USCG, 1952-54. Recipient gold medal Assn. Authors and Composers, Mexico City, 1985, diploma Mexican Psychol. Assn., Mexico City, 1981. Mem. APA, Univ. Club Mexico. Republican. Avocations: music, organ, piano. Home: Col Malinche, Norte 92 # 4229, 07899 Mexico City Mexico

NELSEN-CUDDEIRO, JEFFREY CHARLES, leadership consultant; b. Elgin, Ill., Dec. 8, 1949; s. Robert Louis and Audrey Florence Nelsen; m. Amalia Cudeiro, Dec. 3, 1997; 1 child, Lauren Elizabeth Demestre. BA in Music, Calif. State U., Chico, 1971; MA in Ednl. Adminstrn., Calif. Luth. U., 1980; PhD in Orgn. and Policy, U. Calif., Santa Barbara, 1986. Tchr. credential, K-12 adminstrv. svcs. credential, Calif. Tchr. Ventura (Calif.) Unified Schs., 1972-78, prin., 1978-93; vis. prof. UCLA, 1993-96; internat. leadership cons., Narshfield, Mass., 1996—; sr. ptnr. Focus on Results, 1998—. Recipient hon. and continuing svc. awards PTA, Ventura, 1978, 86, Golden Bell award Calif. Sch. Bd. Assn., 1990, Alternative H.S. Educator award L.A. Unified Sch. Dist., 1995. Mem. ASCD. Avocations: reading, sailing, walking. E-mail: nelsen143@earthlink.net. Home and Office: 100 Earldor Cir Marshfield MA 02050-2002

NELSON, ALLEN F., proxy solicitation company executive; b. Portland, Oreg., Oct. 17, 1943; s. Roy August and MIldred Mary (Jensen) N.; m. Johanna Molenaar, Dec. 8, 1973. BS, U. Iowa, 1965, MA, 1968. V.p. Shareholder Comm. Corp., N.Y.C., 1970-72; v.p. Trafalgar Capital Corp., N.Y.C., 1973; pres. Nelson, Lasky & Co., Inc., N.Y.C., 1974-76; account exec. Corp. Comm., Inc., Seattle, 1976-77; pres. Allen Nelson & Co., Inc., Seattle, 1977—. Mem. Fin. Analysts Fedn., Nat. Investor Rels. Inst., Nat. Security Traders Assn., Practicing Law Inst., Pub. Rels. Soc. Am., Am. Soc. Corp. Secs., Can Corp. Shareholder Svcs. Assn., Ranier Club, Montana Club, Vancouver Club. Home: 4400 Beach Dr SW Seattle WA 98116-3937 Office: Allen Nelson & Co Inc PO Box 16157 Seattle WA 98116-0157

NELSON, ARTHUR HUNT, real estate management development company executive; b. Kansas City, Mo., May 21, 1923; s. Carl Ferdinand and Hearty (Brown) N.; m. Eleanor Thomas, Dec. 27, 1954; children: Carl F., Frances, Pamela. AB, U. Kans., 1943; JD, Harvard U., 1949. Bar: Mass. 1949. Staff radiation lab. MIT, 1943-44; sr. engr., cons. Raytheon Mfg. Co., Boston, 1948-52; pvt. practice Boston, 1949; v.p., treas., dir. Gen. Electronic Labs., Inc., Cambridge, Mass., 1951-64, chmn. bd., 1959-63; treas., dir. Sci. Electronics, Inc., Cambridge, 1955-64; treas., dir. Assocs. for Internat. Rsch., Inc., Cambridge, 1954—, pres., 1968—; treas., dir. Victor Realty Devel.,

Inc., Cambridge, 1959-76, pres., 1972-76, gen. ptnr., 1976—; gen. ptnr. Prospect Hill Exec. Office Park, Waltham, Mass., 1977—; chmn. Nelson Cos., 1990—, Cambridge Devel. Lab., 1994—; Bd. dirs. Internat. Data Group, Inc., Sterling Bank; chmn. Cambridge Devel. Lab., Inc., 1994—. Pres., trustee Tech. Edn. Rsch. Ctrs., Inc., 1965—; trustee Winsor Sch., Boston, 1978-88, treas., 1978-82; bd. dirs. Charles River Mus. Industry, Waltham, 1986—, pres. 1994—, pres., dir. 128 Bus. Coun. Inc., 1987—, Hist. Waltham Inc., 1996—, Am. Computer Fedn. Inc., 1996—, Charles River Pub. Internet Ctr. Inc., 1996—. Ensign USNR, 1944-46. Recipient Ernst & Young New Eng. Master Entrepreneur of Yr. award, 1999. Mem. ABA, Mass. Bar Assn., Boston Bar Assn., Boston Computer Soc. (bd. dirs. 1985-97, chmn. 1994-97), Greater Boston C. of C., Harvard Club Boston, Beta Theta Pi, Phi Beta Kappa, Sigma Xi. Home: 75 Robin Rd Weston MA 02493-2436 Office: care The Nelson Cos Prospect Place 230 3rd Ave Waltham MA 02451-7528

NELSON, CAREY BOONE, sculptor; b. Lexington, Mo.; d. William M. and Carey (Butler) Boone; m. Kenneth Warwick Nelson; children: Caren, Kenneth Warwick II, Kimberley, Keith, Kyle, Craig. Student, U. Mo.; BA, Wellesley Coll.; MS in Edn., Wagner Coll. Cert. tchr., N.Y.C., N.Y. State. Tchr. N.Y.C. Pub. Schs.; instr. sculpture Snug Harbor Cultural Ctr., N.Y.C., 1982-84; per diem col., artist USAF, 1974—; artist USCG, 1974—. One-women shows Pietrantonio Galleries, N.Y.C., St. Bartholomew's, N.Y.C., Salmagundi Club, N.Y.C., Poly. Prep. Country Day Sch., Bklyn., Shug Harbor Cultural Ctr., N.Y.C., Epiphany Libr., N.Y.C.; exhibited in group shows Internat. Art Exchange, Monte Carlo, Paris, Cannes, Athens, Victoria Mus. Libr., Melbourne, Australia, numerous others; represented in permanent collections Victoria Libr. Mus., Australia, Sheldon Swope Mus., Terre Haute, Ind., Esperanza, Antarctica, 1988, Durban (Republic South Africa) Mus., also others; sculptures commd. for Am.-Israel Friendship House, Mildred McAffee Horton, Wellesley Coll., Everett Barnes, Colgate U., Chuck Yeager for USAF, Daniel Boone for Rotunda of Mo. State Capitol, Jimmie Doolittle for USAF, Franklin (N.J.) Mineral Mus., 1980, Munro Monument USCG, 1989, Zinc Miner Monument, Col. Vaughn, Coll. Aeronautics, LaGuardia Airport, N.Y.C., 1991, James Madison Monument, Montpellier, Va., 1992, Subway Riders, Internat. Mus. Cartoon Art, 1996. Bd. dirs. Cerebral Palsy Assn., S.I., N.Y., Vis. Nurse Assn., S.I. Named Woman of Achievement Wagner Coll., 1978, Hon. Life Artist Catharine Lorillard Wolfe Art Club, 1990; recipient awards Salmagundi, 1995, 96, 97, 98, 99, Anna Hyatt Huntington award, Catharine Lorillard Wolfe Art Club, Horsehead Trophy, 1980, Coun. of Am. Artists award Hudson Valley, 1996, Medal of Achievement, USCG, 1991, Nat. Arts Club Award, 1998, Salmagundi Peter Helch Award, 1998, 1st Pl. Sculpture award, 1999, M. Soroka Meml. award, 1999, Cert. of Appreciation, USCG, 1999, George Gray award, 1999. Fellow Am. Artists Profl. League (cert. of appreciation 1999); mem. Nat. Arts Club (life, award 1998), Royal Soc. Arts (London, life), Composers, Authors and Artists Am. (nat. bd. dirs. 1981-90, 1st pl. award 1982, 84, 86), Soc. Illustrators, Burr Artists (bd. dirs.), Catharine Lorillard Wolfe Art Club (pres. 1978-81, bd. dirs., sculpture chmn., Creative Hands award 1987, Artist of Yr. 1985, tour U.S. Mus., Colls., 1996—), Nat. League Am. Pen Women (pres. N.Y.C. br. 1981-84, Manhattan, N.Y.C. br. 1990-94, 96-98, Woman of Achievement award 1988), Wellesley Coll. Club (pres. S.I.), Kappa Kappa Gamma (Woman of Achievement award 1978). Episcopalian. Avocations: jewelry design, snorkeling, travel. Home: 282 Douglas Rd Staten Island NY 10304-1526

NELSON, CHARLES ARTHUR, publisher, author; b. Berwyn, Ill., Dec. 21, 1922; s. Arthur A.R. and Florence Dorothy (Lagergren) N.; m. Anne Ballou Higgins, July 1946; children: Christopher, Janet, Colin, Edward. BA, St. John's Coll., Annapolis, Md., 1947. Dir. liberal arts program, humanities lectr. U. Chgo., 1947-52; exec. dir. Am. Found. For Polit. Edn., Chgo., 1947-56; sr. cons. Cresap, McCormick & Paget, N.Y.C., 1956-58; pres. Nelson Assocs., N.Y.C., 1958-68; prin. Peat Marwick Mitchell & co., N.Y.C., 1968-83; pub. Croton-Cortlandt Gazette, Croton-on-Hudson, 1986—. Author: Developing Responsible Public Leaders, 1963; co-author: The University, The Citizen, & World Affairs, 1956, Financial Management for the Arts, 1975, Ratio Analysis in Higher Education, 1980, Ethics, Leadership and the Bottom Line, 1991, Scott Buchanan: A Centennial Appreciation of His Life and Work, 1995, Stringfellow Barr: A Centennial Appreciation of His Life and Work, 1997; contbr. articles to jours. Chmn. bd. Exec. Council on Fgn. Diplomats, N.Y.C.; trustee St. John's Coll., Annapolis, Md., Santa Fe, 1952-91, chmn. bd., 1978-83. Mem. Asian and Western Studies Initiative (pres. 1997-99). Democrat. Home and Office: PO Box 247 Croton On Hudson NY 10520-0247

NELSON, DENNIS GEORGE ANTHONY, dental researcher, life scientist; b. New Plymouth, New Zealand, Dec. 25, 1954; came to U.S., 1983; s. Hugo and Johanna Katherina (Dekker) N.; m. Joanne Elizabeth Dick; children: Kathryn Sarah, John Clifford. BS with honors, Victoria U., Wellington, New Zealand, 1977, PhD, 1981. Postdoctoral fellow Med. Rsch. Coun. of New Zealand, Wellington, 1981-82; rsch. assoc. Materia Technica Rijksuniversiteit, Groningen, Netherlands, 1982-83; Fogarty Internat. fellow Eastman Dental Ctr., Rochester, N.Y., 1983-85; sr. fellow Med. Rsch. Coun. of New Zealand, Wellington, 1985-88; staff scientist Procter & Gamble Co., Cin., 1988-94; assoc. dir. rsch. and devel. Pfizer Inc., Parsippany, N.J., 1994—; rev. cons. NIH, Washington, 1991—; sci. reviewer for various jours., 1983—. Contbr. articles to profl. jours. Recipient Colgate-Palmolive Travel award Internat. Assn. for Dental Rsch., 1980, Colgate-Palmolive prize Internat. Assn. for Dental Rsch., 1980, Edward H. Hatton award, 1981, Hamilton Meml. prize Royal Soc. of New Zealand, 1983. Mem. AAAS, Internat. Assn. for Dental Rsch., European Orgn. for Caries Rsch. Achievements include patents in field and patents pending; rsch. in high resolution TEM of hydroxyapatites; rsch. in interaction of laser radiation with dental enamel; rsch. in elucidation of fluoridation mechanisms of dental enamel and apatites; formulation of consumer products. Office: Pfizer Inc Consumer Health Care Group 400 Webro Rd Parsippany NJ 07054-2894

NELSON, DENNIS LEE, finance educator; b. Randall, Minn., Nov. 4, 1929; s. George Otto and Emma Ida (Schwanke) N.; m. Joyce Marie Prozinski, Aug. 25, 1956; children: Constance, Kristin, Norma Joan. BS, St. Cloud State U., 1954; MA, U. Minn., 1964, PhD in Econs., 1970. Prof. econs. U. Minn., Duluth, 1964—, dir. ctr. for econ. edn., 1967-71, grad. faculty, 1970—, head dept. econs., 1971-77, assoc. chancellor, 1977-88, vice chancellor fin. ops., 1987-88; mem. faculty Westhill Coll., U. Birmingham, Eng., 1997-98; instnl. rep. for adminstrs. on Nat. Collegiate Athletic Assn., 1978-87; adminstr., vis. faculty Oxford U., Eng., 1997, Yonsei U., Seoul, 1988, Moscow U., 1978, 84. Author econ. textbooks. Recipient Disting. Alumnus award U. Minn. Mem. Duluth Blueline Club, Duluth Quarterback Club, UMD Rasmussen Fund, UMD Hoop Club, Pres. Club U. Minn. Lutheran. Avocations: gardening, writing, reading, woodworking, bridge. Home: On the Lake 21190 Forest Rd Little Falls MN 56345-4065 Office: U Minn 10 University Dr Duluth MN 55812-2403

NELSON, ED, medical educator, research scientist; b. Nov. 1950; m. Anke Wiesmann, Aug. 1986; children: Shirley, Scott. BSc, U. Med. Sci., 1975; MSc, East Tenn. U., 1980; ScD, Essen U., 1986. Lab. asst. East Tenn. State U., 1979-80; from lab. asst. to assoc. prof. Essen (Germany) U. Med. Sch., 1982-98, prof., 1998—; cons. in field. Contbr. articles to profl. jours. Mem. Am. Assn. Cancer Rsch., European Soc. Toxicology (specialty sec. chmn. 1995-99), Am. Acad. Clin. Toxicology, Soc. Toxicology. Avocations: computers, videography. E-mail: ednelso@aol.com. Office: Essen U Sch Medicine, Hufelandstr 55 Toxicology, D-45147 Essen Germany

NELSON, ELIZABETH HAWKINS, public association administrator; b. Rockville Centre, N.Y., N.Y., Jan. 27, 1931; arrived in Eng., 1951; d. Harry Dadmun and Gretchen (Hawkins) N.; m. Ivan Piercy, Dec. 7, 1960 (div. 1972); children: Catherine, Christopher, Nicholas; m. Claude Jacob Esterson, July 26, 1975 (div. 1998). BA, Middlebury Coll., 1951; PhD, U. London, 1953; D (hon.), City U., London, 1994. Rsch. psychologist Mars Ltd., London, 1954-55; dir., mng. dir. rsch. unit Benton & Bowles, London, 1955-64; dir. Mass Observation Ltd., London, 1964-65; founder dir., chmn. Taylor Nelson/Sofres plc, London, 1965-92; chief exec. The Princess Royal Trust for Carers, London, 1992-95; chair coun. U. Surrey Roehampton, 1995—; chmn. South West London Cmty. NHS Trust, 1997—; non-exec. dir. Royal Bank Scotland, Edinburgh, 1988-97; chmn. bd. UK Ecolabelling, 1992-98; pres. World Assn. Pub. Opinion Rsch., 1990-92; strategic dir. Online Rsch. Agy. Mem. Doctors and Dentists Pay Rev. Bd., London, 1992-97; vice chair coun. Open U., Milton Keynes, Eng., 1991; dir. U.S. Open U., 1998—. Decorated Order Brit. Empire; City & Guilds hon. fellow, 1993. Fellow Royal Soc Arts, Market Rsch. Soc. (hon., gold medal 1993); mem. Forum U.K., Freedom City of London. Avocations: choral singing, opera, bridge. Home: 57 Home Park Rd London SW19 7HS, England Office: SW London Cmty Trust Clare, House Blackshaw Rd, London SW17 0QT, England

NELSON, ERIC VICTOR, retired diplomat; b. Faversham, Kent, Eng., Jan. 11, 1927; s. Victor Henry Horatio and Emily Vera Barton (Collingwood) N.; m. Maria Teresa Paul, Sept. 5, 1960; children: Amanda Christina (dec.), Linda Susan. Student, George Washington U., 1943-45. Cost acct. Electrical & Musical Industries Ltd., London, 1948-49; exec. officer Bd. of Trade, London, 1949-50; acct. Brit. Embassy, Athens, Greece, 1950-53; third sec. (info.) Brit. Embassy, Belgrade, Yugoslavia, 1953-55; second sec. (info.) Brit. Embassy, Caracas, Venezuela, 1959-62; first sec. (info.) Brit. Embassy, Saigon, Vietnam, 1962-64; first sec., head of chancery and consul Brit. Embassy, Bujumbura, Burundi, Kigali, Rwanda, 1964-67, Asuncion, Paraguay, 1971-74; first sec. (info.) Brit. Embassy, Mexico City, 1974-79; second sec. Fgn. Office, London, 1955-57, first sec., 1967-71, 79-81; vice-consul Brit. Vice-Consulate, Haiphong, North Vietnam, 1957-59; spl. adviser to His Majesty the Sultan of Brunei Dept. Fgn. Affairs, Bandar Seri Begawan, Negara Brunei Darussalaam, 1981-84; consul-gen. Brit. Consulate-Gen., Bordeaux, France, 1984-87; ret., 1987. With Royal Air Force, Eng., 1945-48. Decorated lt. Royal Victorian Order (Eng.), Insignia of the Order of The Aztec Eagle (Mex.). Mem. Nat. Trust (life), Friends of the Royal Acad., Brit. Mus. Soc. Avocations: travel, photography, lecturing, cartooning, sculpture. Home: 8 Purberry Grove, Ewell Surrey, England KT17 1LU

NELSON, GEORGE DRIVER, astronomy and education educator, former astronaut; b. Charles City, Iowa, July 13, 1950; s. George Vernon and Evelyn Elenor (Driver) N.; m. Susan Lynn Howard, June 19, 1971; children: Aimee Tess, Marti Ann. BS, Harvey Mudd Coll., 1972; MS, U. Wash., 1974, PhD, 1978; DSc honoris causa, U. Colo., 2000. Astronaut NASA, Houston, 1978-89; mission specialist Space Shuttle flight, 1984, 86, 88; assoc. vice provost for rsch., assoc. prof. astronomy U. Wash., Seattle, 1989-96; dir. project 2061, AAAS, Washington, 1996—; adj. assoc. prof. edn. U. Wash., 1989-96. Recipient Haley Space Flight award AIAA, 1989. Unitarian. Avocations: reading; athletics; guitar. Office: AAAS Project 2061 1333 H St NW Washington DC 20005-4707

NELSON, GORDON LEIGH, chemist, educator; b. Palo Alto, Calif., May 27, 1943; s. Nels Folke and Alice Virginia (Fredrickson) N. BS in Chemistry, U. Nev., 1965; MS, Yale U., 1967, PhD, 1970; DSc (hon.), William Carey Coll., 1988. Staff research chemist corp. research and devel. Gen. Electric Co., Schenectady, N.Y., 1970-74; mgr. combustibility tech. plastics div. Gen. Electric Co., Pittsfield, Mass., 1974-79, mgr. environ. protection plastics div., 1979-82; v.p. materials sci. and tech. Springborn Labs. Inc., Enfield, Conn., 1982-83; prof., chmn. dept. polymer sci. U. So. Miss., Hattiesburg, 1983-89; dean Coll. Sci. and Liberal Arts, prof. chemistry Fla. Inst. Tech., Melbourne, 1989—, mem. coun. sci., soc. pres., sec., 1989-90, chair-elect, 1991, chair, 1992; cons. in field. Author: Carbon-13 Nuclear Magnetic Resonance for Organic Chemists, 1972, 2d edit., 1980; co-author: Polymeric Materials--Chemistry for the Future, 1989,Carbon Monoxide and Human Lethality, 1993; editor: Fire and Polymers--Hazard Identification and Prevention, 1990; editor: Fire and Polymers II-Materials and Tests for Hazard Prevention, 1995; editor books on coating sci. tech.; contbr. articles to profl. jours. Mem. ASTM (E5 cert. of appreciation 1985, D1, 1997), Am. Inst. Chemists (Mems. and Fellows Lectr. award 1989), Am. Chem. Soc. (pres. 1988, bd. dirs. 1977-85, 87-89, 92-94, Henry Hill award 1986, 1st Nelson award Orlando sect., 1996, Charles Holmes Herty medal Ga. sect. 1998), Info. Tech. Industry coun. (chmn. plastics task group), Ctr. Sci., Tech. and the Media (bd. dirs. 1991-94), So. Soc. for Coatings Tech., Internat. Electrotech. Commn. (U.S. tech. adv. group on info. processing equipment), Soc. of Plastics Industry (structural plastics divsn., Man of Yr. 1979), Coun. Colls. Arts and Scis., Yale Chemists Assn. (pres. 1981—), Nev. Hist. Soc., Sigma Xi. Republican. Presbyterian. Avocations: travel, western U.S. history. Office: Fla Inst Tech Coll Sci & Liberal Arts 150 W University Blvd Melbourne FL 32901-6975

NELSON, JAMES ALAN, publishing executive; b. Pitts., Dec. 4, 1941; s. Frederick Emil and Gladys (Laughner) N. AA, Compton Jr. Coll., 1963; BA, Calif. State U., Long Beach, 1966. CEO Pit Stop Automotive Svcs., Berlin, 1971-82; pub., prin. Strategic Direction Pubs. Ltd., Zürich, Switzerland, 1983—. Pub.: (books) International Business Strategy Resource Book, 1989, 90, International Technology Strategy Resource Book, 1990, International Manufacturing Strategy Resource Book, 1991; pub., editl. dir.: (books) Marketing Strategy Resource Book, 1993, Strategic Marketing for Service Industries in the 1990s, 1993, Total Quality Handbook, 1993, Total Quality in Action, 1993, Continuous Quality Improvement, 1993, The Company Audit Guide, 1994, The Company Audit Portfolio, 1994, The Re-engineering Handbook, 1994, Tactical Re-engineering for Rapid Results, 1994, Corporate Re-engineering in Action, 1994, Re-engineering from the Board's Perspective, 1994, Re-engineering from the Project Team's Perspective, 1994, The Critical Success Factors for Effective Re-engineering, 1994, The Benchmarking Handbook, 1994, The Benchmarking Project Control Handbook, 1994, Benchmarking in Action, 1994, Critical Success Factors for Effective Benchmarking, 1994, The Team-Based Organization Handbook, 1995, Creating High-Performance Work Teams, 1995, Team-Based Top Management, 1995, The Portfolio of Marketing Audits, 1998, The Company Policy Manual for Electronic Communications, 2000, The Company Policy Manual for Defending Against Competitor Intelligence, 2000; founder, pub. jours. Strategic Direction, 1985, Technology Strategies, 1985, Marketing Strategy, 1991. 1st lt. U.S. Army, 1966-69. Recipient Defender of Freedom award U.S. Mil. Command, Berlin, 1969. Avocations: reading, languages, tennis, jogging, mountain climbing. Home: Dohnenstieg 8a, 14195 Berlin Germany Office: Strategic Direction Publishers Ltd, Puendt Stasse 11, 8610 Uster Zürich, Switzerland

NELSON, JAMES HAROLD, health sciences administrator; b. Gosnell, Ark., Apr. 26, 1936; s. J.D. and Louise (Gann) N.; m. Betty Sue Leonard, Sept. 21, 1974; children: Amelia Rebecca, Rachel Louise. BS, Ark. State U., 1961, MS, 1969; PhD, Okla. State U., 1972. Br. chief U.S. Army Environ. Hygiene Agy., Edgewood, Md., 1972-76; from rsch. area mgr. to div. chief U.S. Army Biomed. R & D Lab., Frederick, Md., 1976-92; project mgr. applied med. systems U.S. Army Med. Materiel Devel. Activity, Fort Derick, Md., 1992-96, dir., 1996—; mem. Fed. Work Group Pest Mgmt., Washington, 1977-81; chmn. equipment com. Armed Forces Pest Mgmt. Bd., Washington, 1979-83; cons. dir. engrs. Ft. Detrick, Frederick, 1976—; guest lectr. Acad. Health Scis., U.S. Army, Ft. Sam Houston, Tex., 1986-88. Contbr. articles to profl. jours.; assoc. editor: Jour. Am. Mosquito Control Assn., 1982-88; chmn. editorial bd.: Equipment & Insecticides-Mosquito Control, 1989. With USN, 1954-58. Recipient numerous commendations U.S. Army, Ft. Detrick, 1981-93, R&D Achievement award Asst. Sec. of the Army, 1988, Order of Mil. Med. Merit, 1992. Mem. AAAS, AMVETS, Am. Pub. Health Assn., Assn. Mil. Surgeons U.S., Am. Legion, Internat. Platform Assn., N.Y. Acad. Scis., Sigma Xi (pres. 1987-88). Presbyterian. Achievements include patent for far-forward surgical table. Home: 2419 Tabor Dr Middletown MD 21769-9006 Office: US Army Med Materiel Devel Activity Fort Detrick Frederick MD 21702

NELSON, JOYCE SUE, insurance agency executive; b. Davenport, Iowa, Mar. 4, 1953; d. Samuel Winfield and Irene E. Yocum; m. Jack Lynn Nelson, Sept. 21, 1979; children: Ryan Lynn, Anthony Kurt. AA, Clinton Cmty. Coll., 1973. Underwriting asst. Iowa Mutual Ins., Dewitt, Iowa, 1973-76; customer svc. IPS, Inc., Bemidji, Minn., 1976-78, Neubauer Darr Agy., Clinton, Iowa, 1978-94, Trissel, Graham & Toole, Davenport, Iowa, 1994—, dir., v.p. Concerned DeWitt (Iowa) Citizens, 1992-97. Mem. Quad City Ins. Assn. (mem. com. 1997-99), Ctrl. Cmty. PTA (sec. 1990-92). Methodist. Avocations: singing, community theater, children's activities. E-mail: jnelson@tgt-insurance.com. Home: 204 8th Ave De Witt IA 52742-1930 Office: Trissel Graham & Toole 220 Emerson Pl Davenport IA 52801-1633

NELSON, K. BONITA, literary agent; b. Austin, Minn., July 5, 1945; d. Wallace Arthur and Opal Rebecca (Lustine) N.; m. John W. Benson, Jan. 5, 1980. BA, Hunter Coll., 1969; B in laws, LaSalle U., 1982. Literary agent trainee Am. Play Co., Inc., N.Y., 1970-75; legal sec., reviewer Eastman & DaSilva, Esqs., N.Y., 1975-79; founder, pres. BK Nelson Literary Agy., N.Y., 1983—, BK Nelson Lect. Bureau, N.Y., 1988—, BK Nelson Word-processing, Pleasantville, N.Y., 1994—; pres., publ. Internat. Media Comm., Inc., 1998; bd. dirs. Dynaray, N.Y.; founder BK Nelson, Inc., 1995, BJ Book Prodrs., 1996, Nelson Am. Movies Ptnrs., 1997. Collaborator: Looking for Canterbury, 1994; author: My Literary Agent, 1998, (on tape) Tape Your Own Talk Show, 1999; exec. prodr. (movie) Paradise FOUND. Mem. Authors Guild (assoc.), NAFE (assoc.), Nat. Assn. Campus Activities (assoc.), AAUW, (assoc.), Dramatists Guild (assoc.), Am. Booksellers Assn. (assoc.), Minority and Woman Owned Businesses. Avocations: aerobics, yoga, needlepoint, stamp collecting. Home and Office: 84 Woodland Rd Pleasantville NY 10570-1322 also: 139 S Beverly Dr Beverly Hills CA 90212-3032 also: 1565 Paseo Vida Palm Springs CA 92264-9508

NELSON, LARRY DEAN, telecommunications and computer systems company executive, consultant; b. Newton, Kans., Aug. 5, 1937; s. Carl Aaron and Leta V. (Van Eaton) N.; m. Linda Hawkins, June 2, 1972. BA, Phillips U., 1959; MS, Kans. State U., 1962; PhD, Ohio State U., 1965. From rsch. asst. to rsch. assoc. Rsch. Found., Ohio State U., Columbus, 1962-65; mathematician II Batelle Meml. Inst., Columbus, 1962-65; from mem. tech. staff to supr. math. dept., data sys. devel. Bellcomm, Inc., Washington, 1965-72; supr. mgmt. info. sys. dept. Bell Telephone Labs., Murray Hill, N.J., 1972-77; supr. rate and tariff planning divsn. AT&T, N.Y.C., 1977-79; dep. adminstr. rsch. and spl. programs adminstrn. U.S. Dept. Transp., Washington, 1979-81; pres. MCS, Inc., Washington, 1981—; supr. govt. comm. ctr. AT&T Bell Labs., 1985-89; mgr. govt. mktg. AT&T Network Sys., 1989-90, supr. secure info. sys. engring., 1990-94, disting. mem. tech. staff, secure sys. engring., 1995-96; tech. cons. AT&T Labs, Info. Security Ctr., AT&T, 1996-98; cons. Contel Info. Sys., Denver, 1982-85, Martin Marietta Corp., Denver, 1982-85; mem. info. assurance task force, info infrastructure group, intrusion detection task force, cybercrime subgroup Nat. Security Telecomms. Advisory Com. Contbr. articles to profl. jours. Organizer, sponsor Odd Jobs Club, Washington, 1967-72; pres. Mountain County Condominiums Assn., Dillon, Colo., 1975-83, 85—; treas. Chris' Landing Condominium Assn., 1986-90; mem. Am. del. 5th Meeting of U.S.-USSR Working Group on Transp., Moscow, 1979; head Am. del. 5th Meeting of U.S.-USSR Working Group on Transport of Future, Moscow, 1979; head meeting Am. Del. to ISO/IEC TCI/SC27 Working Group 1 of Info. Tech. Security Methodology Stds., editor Intrusion Detection Project, Germany 1997, Kista, Sweden, 1998, Rio De Janeiro, 1998, Spain, 1999, Brazil, 1999, U.S., 1999, England, 2000; internat. rep. Am. Stds. Inst.-Tech. Com. on Info. Tech. Security Methodology. Mem. ABA (assoc., info. security com.), Am. Nat. Stds. Inst. (info. tech. security tech. stds. com., internat. rep. tech. com. on info. tech. security mgmt.), IEEE (sec. D.C. sect. 1982, cert. appreciation 1968), Sys., Man and Cybernetics Soc. (sec. 1981, v.p. 1982-83), Math. Programming Soc, Am. Math Soc., N.Y. Acad. Scis., Assn. Computing Machinery, Sigma Xi, Phi Kappa Phi, Pi Mu Epsilon. Democrat. Mem. Disciples of Christ. Current work: information systems, networks and network management, digital signature, public key infrastructure, and electronic commerce technology. Subspecialties: secure information technology systems and networks; systems engineering. Office: MCS Inc 440 New Jersey Ave SE Washington DC 20003-4008

NELSON, MARY ELLEN DICKSON, retired actuary; b. Mpls., Mar. 24, 1933; d. William Alexander and Laura Winona (Baxter) Dickson; m. David Aldrich Nelson, Aug. 25, 1956; children: Frederick Dickson Nelson, Claudia Baxter Nelson, Caleb Edward Nelson. BA, Vassar Coll., 1954; postgrad., Cambridge (Eng.) U., 1954-55. Enrolled actuary under program adminstr. by joint bd. Dept. Labor and Dept. Treas. Rsch. assoc. N.Am. Life & Casualty Co., Mpls., 1955-56; actuarial asst. John Hancock Mut. Life Ins. Co., Boston, 1956-58; actuary David R. Kass & Assocs., Cleve., 1973-74; pres. Nelson & Co., Cleve., 1975, Conrad, Nelson & Co., Cleve., 1975-81, Nelson & Co., Cleve./Cin., 1981-99; bd. dirs. Blount Internat., Inc., and its subsidiary, Blount, Inc., Montgomery, Ala., 1986-99; bd. dirs. Broadwing, Inc., Union Ctrl. Life Ins. Co., Cin. Fulbright scholar, 1954-55. Fellow Soc. Actuaries, Phi Beta Kappa; mem. Am. Acad. Actuaries, Cin. Actuaries Club, Midwest Benefits Conf. (chair 1991). Republican.

NELSON, MERLIN EDWARD, international business consultant, company director; b. Fargo, N.D., Jan. 30, 1922; s. Theodore G. and Eva C. (Hultgren) N.; m. Nancy Ellen Craig, June 1952 (div. June 1962); children: Craig Edward, Brian Anthony; m. Janet April Pope, Aug. 30, 1963; children: Claudia Jane, Rolf Merlin. BS in Polit. Sci., U. Oreg., 1943; postgrad., Fordham U., 1943-44; JD, Yale U., 1948. Bar: Oreg. 1948, N.Y. 1954, U.S. Dist. Ct. D.C. 1954. Atty. Office Gen. Counsel, ECA, Washington and Paris, 1949-52; assoc. Davis, Polk, Wardwell, Sunderland & Kiendl, 1952-59; exec. asst. to v.p. AMF, Inc., N.Y.C., 1960-62; chmn., mng. dir. AMF Internat., Ltd., London, 1962-63; v.p., group exec. AMF, Inc., 1963-70, exec. v.p., vice chmn., dir., 1970-84, now cons., 1984—; ret., 1984; bd. dirs. Indsl. Bank Japan Trust Co., Derby Internat. Corp., S.A., Exeter Internat. Corp., S.A., Mitsui Found., IBJ Found.; chmn., pres. Tuckernuck Land Trust. Mem. Coun. Fgn. Rels., Overseas Devel. Coun.; mem. nat. adv. coun. Trust for Pub. Land. Decorated Purple Heart. Mem. Phi Beta Kappa. Home and Office: 16 W 77th St Apt 12E New York NY 10024-5126

NELSON, PAUL NETELENBOS, soil scientist; b. Adelaide, SA, Australia, Apr. 17, 1963; s. Bernard Gerardus and Anna (Noomen) N. B in Agrl. Sci., U. Adelaide, 1987, PhD, 1997. Rsch. officer U. Adelaide, 1987-90; rsch. asst. Swedish U. Agrl. Scis., Uppsala, 1991; rsch. officer Inst. Nat. de la Recherche Agronomique, Dijon, France, 1991-92, Bureau of Sugar Experiment Stations, Ayr, Australia, 1996-99; rsch. scientist CSIRO, Townsville, 1997-99. Author: (with others) Handbook of Soil Science, 1999, Sodic Soils, 1998; contbr. articles to profl. jours. Recipient Harold Woolhouse award U. Adelaide, 1998. Mem. Australian Soc. Soil Sci., Australian Soc. Sugar Cane Technologists, Soil Sci. Soc. Am. Office: CSIRO Land and Water, University Dr, Aitkenvale 4814 QLD, Australia

NELSON, PHILIP ARTHUR, engineering educator; b. Bishops Stortford, Hertfordshire, Eng., June 22, 1952; s. David and Brenda Marion (Sneath) N.; m. Jennifer Patricia Mills, Aug. 4, 1979; children: Benjamin, Samuel. BS in Mech. Engring., U. Southampton, Eng., 1974, PhD in Sound and Vibration Studies, 1981. Chartered engr. R&D engr. Sound Attenuators Ltd., Colchester, Essex, Eng., 1978-82; lectr. U. Southampton, 1982-88, sr. lectr., 1988-94, prof., 1994—; bd. dirs. Adaptive Control Ltd., Southampton. Co-author: Active Control of Sound, 1991, Active Control of Vibration, 1996; patentee in field; contbr. articles to profl. jours. Recipient rsch. grants U.K. Dept. of Trade & Industry, 1983, 86, 89, Sci. & Engring. Rsch. Coun., 1984, 86, Ministry of Defense, 1985. Mem. Inst. Acoustics (coun. mem. 1991—), Hockley Golf Club. Home: 3 Montfort Hts, Romsey, Southampton SO51 9LP, England Office: Univ Southampton, Highfield, Southampton SO9 5NH, England

NELSON, PHILIP HUMPHREY HARDWICK, oil and gas industry consultant; b. Liverpool, U.K., Jan. 23, 1938; s. Humphrey Gordon and Margaret Eleanor (Hardwick) N.; m. Mary Cecilia Roberts, May 6, 1966; children: James Philip, Lucy Elizabeth. BSc in Geology, U. Manchester, 1959; PhD in Geology, U. Birmingham, 1965. Sr. explorationist Pakistan Shell, Karachi, 1979-80; head land and west offshore exploration Shell U.K., London, 1981-83, geophys. advisor, 1992-93; team leader north sea/mid-Norway A/S Norske Shell, Stavanger, Norway, 1984-87; geophys. advisor Shell Internat., The Hague, Netherlands, 1988-92; cons. Philms Internat., Sevenoaks, U.K., 1994—; vis. prof. Imperial Coll., London, 1994-96. Joint editor: Geology of the Norwegian Oil and Gas Fields, 1987, Habitat of Hydrocarbons on the Norwegian Continental Shelf, 1986; contbr. articles to profl. jours. Recipient Polar medal Her Majesty Queen Elizabeth II, 1967. Fellow Inst. of Petroleum; mem. Am. Assn. of Petroleum Geologists, Soc. of Exploration Geophysicists. Avocations: photography, skiing, windsurfing. Office: Philms Internat, 3 High St, Sevenoaks TN13 1HY, United Kingdom

NELSON, RANDY J., psychology educator; b. Detroit, Mich., Jan. 13, 1954; s. Ralph Edward and Ada B. Nelson; m. Anne Courtney DeVries. AB in Psychology with honors, U. Calif., Berkeley, 1978, MA in Psychology,

1980, PhD in Psychology, 1983, PhD in Endocrinology, 1984. Rsch. asst. Dr. F.A. Beach U. Calif., Berkeley, 1978, Dr. I Zucker U. Calif., Berkeley, 1978-84; post doctoral fellow U. Tex., Austin, 1984-86; asst. prof. psychology The Johns Hopkins Univ., Balt., 1986-91, assoc. prof. psychology, 1991-96, assoc. prof. population dynamics, 1991-96, prof. psychology, neurosci., population dynamics, 1996—; grant application reviewer NIH, 1986-87, 95—, NSF, 1986—, NSF program officer, 1995-96, 97-98; jour. reviewer Animal Behavior, Brain Rsch., Biology of Reproduction, Jour. Biol. Rhythms, Jour. Comparative Neurology, Jour. Comparative Psychology, Jour. Mammology, Jour. of Reproduction & Fertility, Jour. Exptl. Psychology, Jour. Reproduction, Fertility & Devel., Jour. Pineal Rsch., Neuroendocrine Letters, Nature, Neurobehavioral Toxicology and Teratology, Neuroendocrinology, Physiology and Behavior, Sci., Procs. of NAS. Author: An Introduction to Behavioral Endocrinology, 1995; contbr. numerous articles to profl. jours. including Nature, Jour. of Nervous and Mental Disease, Jour. Comparative Psychology, Jour. Exptl. Zoology, Biology of Reproduction, Jour. of Urology, Physiology and Behavior, Am. Jour. Physiology, Physiological Zoology, Behavioral and Brain Scis., Can. Jour. Zoology, others; mem. editorial bd. Behavioral Neuroscience, J. Pineal Rsch. Recipient post-doctoral fellowship NIH, 1984-86, James A. Shannon award Nat. Cancer Inst., 1992-94. Mem. Soc. for Neurosci., Am. Soc. Mammalogists, Animal Behavior Soc., Soc. for Study of Biolog. Rhythyms, Soc. for the Study of Reproduction (mem. edn. com. 1982-83, 85-86, chairperson edn. com. 1986-87, editor newsletter 1986-88, membership com. 1990-94), Phi Beta Kappa, Sigma Chi, Psi Chi. Office: Johns Hopkins Univ Dept Psychology Behavioral Neuroendo Group Baltimore MD 21218

NELSON, RICHARD HENRY, manufacturing company executive; b. Norfolk, Va., May 24, 1939; s. Irvin Joseph and Ethel Blair (Levy) N.; m. Carole Ellen Rosen, Mar. 12, 1966; children: Christopher, Karin. BA, Princeton U., 1961; postgrad., Georgetown U., 1962-63. Spl. asst. to dir. Peace Corps, Washington, 1961-62; mil. aide to U.S. v.p. Office of the V.P., Washington, 1962-63; asst. to U.S. Pres. Office of the Pres., Washington, 1963-66; spl. asst. to sec. HUD, Washington, 1966-68; v.p. Am. Internat. Bank, N.Y.C., 1968-70, Studebaker-Worthington, N.Y.C., 1970-73; pres. Sartex Corp., N.Y.C., 1973-80; pres., CEO Cogenic Energy Systems, Inc., N.Y.C., 1981-91; CEO U.S. Energy Systems, Inc., West Palm Beach, Fla., 1992—; bd. dirs. Nelco Corp., Laurel, Md.; chmn. bd. Powersave, Inc., N.Y.C., 1984-92. Bd. dirs. Nat. Hypertension Assn., N.Y.C., 1982-90; exec. com. Southampton Assn., N.Y., 1983—. 1st lt. U.S. Army, 1962-64. Recipient Presdl. Medal Office of Pres. of U.S., 1965. Mem. Nev. Geothermal Industry Coun., Nat. Sporting Clays Assn., Amateur Trap Assn., U.S. Polo Assn., Princeton Club, Southampton Hunt and Polo Club, Palm Beach Polo and Country Club, Meadow Club, Palm Beach Yacht Club. Democrat. Avocations: horseback riding, trap and skeet shooting. Home: 12012 Longwood Green Dr West Palm Beach FL 33414-7070 Office: US Energy Systems Inc 515 N Flagler Dr Ste 702 West Palm Beach FL 33401-4324

NELSON, ROBERT EDDINGER, management and development consultant; b. Mentone, Ind., Mar. 2, 1928; s. Arthur Irven and Tural Cecile (Eddinger) N.; m. Carol J., Nov. 24, 1951; children: Janet K., Eric P. BA, Northwestern U., 1949; LHD, Iowa Wesleyan Coll., 1969, North Ctrl. Coll., 1987. Asst. dir. alumni rels. Northwestern U., Evanston, Ill., 1950-51; v.p., dir. pub. rels. Iowa Wesleyan Coll., Mt. Pleasant, 1955-58; vice chancellor for devel. U. Kansas City, 1959-61; v.p. instl. devel. Ill. Inst. Tech., Chgo., 1961-68; pres. Robert Johnston Corp., Oak Brook, Ill., 1968-69, Robert E. Nelson Assocs., Inc., Oak Brook, 1969—; bd. dirs. Chautauqua Workshop in Fund Raising and Instl. Relations, Continental Bank of Oak Brook Terr., The Sun Cos.; nat. conf. chmn. and program dir. Am. Coll. Pub. Relations Assn., 1961; trustee, Iowa Wesleyan Coll., 1962-68; faculty mem. Ind. U. Workshops on Coll. and Univ. Devel., 1963-65, Lorretto Heights Summer Inst. for Fund Raising and Pub. Relations, 1964-68; mem. Pub. Review Panel for Grants Programs, Lilly Endowment, Inc., 1975. Contbr. chpt. to Handbook of College and University Administration, 1970. With U.S. Army, 1951-54. Mem. Coun. on Fin. Aid to Edn. (bd. dirs. 1957-63), Pub. Rels. Soc. Am., Nat. Soc. Fund Raisers, Nat. Small Bus. Assn., Chgo. Soc. Fund Raising Execs., Blue Key, Execs. Club, Econ. Club, Union League, DuPage Club, Masons, Delta Tau Delta. Methodist. Home and Office: 5 Oakbrook Club Dr # 101 Oak Brook IL 60523-1348

NELSON, ROBERT LOUIS, lawyer; b. Dover, N.H., Aug. 10, 1931; s. Albert Louis and Alice (Rogers) N.; m. Rita Jean Hutchins, June 11, 1955; children: Karen, Robin Andrea. BA, Bates Coll., Lewiston, Maine, 1956; LLB, Georgetown U., 1959. Bar: D.C. 1960. With U.S. Commn. Civil Rights, 1958-63, AID, 1963-66; program sec. U.S. Mission to Brazil, 1965-66; exec. dir. Lawyers Com. Civil Rights Under Law, 1966-70; dep. campaign mgr. Muskie for Pres., 1970-72; v.p. Perpetual Corp., Houston, 1972-74; sr. v.p., gen. counsel Washington Star, 1974-76; pres. broadcast div. Washington Star Communications, Inc., 1976-77; asst. sec. of army U.S. Dept. Def., 1977-79; spl. advisor to chief N.G. Bur., Dept. Def., 1980-85; pres., dir. Mid-Md. Communications Corp., 1981-85; ptnr. Verner, Liipfert, Bernhard, McPherson and Hand,, 1979-87; gen. counsel Paralyzed Vets. Am., 1988-99, sr. counsel, 2000—. Vice chmn. D.C. Redevel. Land Agy., 1976-77; bd. dirs. Community Found. Greater Washington, 1977-78 ; bd. dirs. Friends of Nat. Zoo, 1975—, pres., 1982-84; bd. dirs. Downtown Progress, 1976-77, Fed. City Council, 1976-77, 83-87, Pennsylvania Ave. Devel. Corp., 1976-77. Served with AUS, 1953-54. Mem. ABA, D.C. Bar Assn., Army Navy Club (Washington). Democrat. Episcopalian. Home: Robins Nest PO Box 52 Orrs Island ME 04066-0052 Office: 801 18th St NW Washington DC 20006-3517

NELSON, ROY HUGH, JR., lawyer, mediator, arbitrator; b. St. Paul, May 13, 1955; s. Roy H. and Helen S. Nelson; m. MaryJean G. Froehlich, Aug. 13, 1994; children: Benjamin, Calla. BS, U. Wis., Milw., 1979, MS, 1985; JD, U. Wis., 1988. Bar: Wis. 1988, U.S. Dist. Ct. (ea. and we. dists.) Wis. 1988, U.S. Dist. Ct. (ea. dist.) Mich. 1991, U.S. Ct. Appeals (7th cir.) 1988, U.S. Ct. Appeals (fed. cir.) 1996, U.S. Supreme Ct. 1999. Police officer City of Brookfield, Wis., 1978-88; assoc. Borgelt, Powell, Peterson & Frauen, Milw., 1988-92; shareholder, dir. Petrie & Stocking SC, Milw., 1992—; mediator, arbitrator, dir. Conflict Resolution Svcs., Milw., 1997—; exec. dir. Conflict Mgmt. Edn. Project, 1999; chair adv. bd. Mediation Ministries, Sun Prairie, Wis., 1998—. Mem. ABA, Wis. Bar Assn., Milw. Bar Assn., Christian Legal Soc., Acad. Family Mediators, Alliance Advancement Profl. Mediation, Bus. Network Internat., Am. Arbitration Assn., Am. Intellectual Property Law Assn., Wis. Intellectual Property Law Assn., Wis. Assn. Mediators. Lutheran. Office: Petrie & Stocking SC 111 E Wisconsin Ave Ste 1500 Milwaukee WI 53202-4808 also: Conflict Resolution Svcs 756 N Milwaukee St Ste 310 Milwaukee WI 53202-3719

NELSON, STEPHEN GLEN, biologist, researcher; b. Frederick, Okla., July 22, 1947; s. Eddie Glen And Wilna Lee (Phipps) N.; m. Feng Jyu Tang, June 30, 1989. BS in Biology, San Diego State U., 1970, MS in Zoology, 1975; PhD in Ecology, U. Calif., Davis, 1976. Post-doctoral water scientist U. Calif., Davis, 1976-77; asst. prof. to prof. U. Guam, Mangilao, 1977-97; sr. rsch. scientist U. Ariz., Tucson, 1998—. Mem. Ecol. Assn. Am., World Aquaculture Soc., Am. Assn. for Advancement of Sci. E-mail: nsteve@ag.arizona.edu. Office: Environ Rsch Lab 2601 E Airport Dr Tucson AZ 85706-6905

NELSON, STEVEN DWAYNE, lawyer; b. Austin, Minn., Jan. 30, 1950; s. Dwayne Ronald and Verna Nathelle (Larick) N.; m. Vicky L. Staab, July 6, 1990. BA in English, SUNY, Buffalo, 1972; JD, U. Mont., 1978. Bar: Mont. 1978, U.S. Dist. Ct. Mont. 1978. Sole practice Bozeman, Mont., 1978—; city prosecutor City of Bozeman, 1979-82; city atty. City of Ennis (Mont.), 1980-82; prof. U. Great Falls, Mont., 1990—, mediator, 1998—. Mem. ABA, Mont. State Bar Assn., Phi Delta Phi. Avocations: fishing, skiing, hiking. Home and Office: 4590 Maiden Rock Rd Bozeman MT 59715-7769

NELSON, THOMAS RICHARD (BOB), broadcasting executive; b. Ilford, Eng., Mar. 25, 1949; m. Paula Frances Noble; children: Thomas, Christina, Caroline. BSc in Econs., London U., 1970; MA, Birbeck Coll., 1977. Pers. officer Brit. Overseas Airways Corp., London, 1970-75; head manpower planning British Airways, London, 1975-83, bus. strategist, 1983-85, head devel., 1985-87, chmn. Chartride Ctr. Ltd., 1985-87; cons. London, 1987-88; head corp. devel. mgmt. BBC, London, 1988-95, head mgmt. and orgnl. devel., 1995-96, dir. tng., contr. devel. and tng., 1996—; bd. dirs. Roffey Park Inst., Horsham, Sussex, Eng., Skillset Ltd., London; dir. World Svc. Tng. Trust Co. Chmn. nat. pers. com. YMCA, London, 1990—; councillor Penn Parish, Bucks, Eng. Fellow Royal Soc. for Encouragement Arts, Manufactures and Commerce, Bradford U. Mgmt. Ctr. (assoc., adv. bd.). E-mail: Bob.Nelson@bbc.co.uk. Office: BBC, 16 Langham St, London W1A 1AA, England

NELSON, WALTER HENRY, communications consultant, author; b. Munich, Mar. 23, 1928; parents Am. citizens; s. Casimir Thaddeus and Eugenie (Simon) Zawadzki; m. Rose Marie Carson, Mar. 4, 1950; children: Roger Stuart, Gregory Eugene, Victoria Eugenie; 2d marriage to Rita L. Christoffersen, June 30, 1962; 1 child, Samantha Christine. Student, NYU, 1944, Norwich U., 1944-46, Columbia U., 1949-50. News editor, info. analyst Radio Free Europe, N.Y.C., Munich, 1950-53; dir. mag. info. Am. Heritage Found., N.Y.C., 1953-55; mag. pub. dir., editor quar. Am. Petroleum Inst., 1955-57; dir. pub. rels. Reach, McClinton & Co., Inc., N.Y.C., 1957-59; v.p., gen. mgr. Candygram, Inc., Chgo., 1959-60; asst. to pres. Stevens Candy Kitchens, Inc., Chgo., 1960-61; assoc. in pub. rels. Fred Rosen Assocs., Inc., 1961-62; ptnr. Prittie and Nelson Internat. Pub. Rels., London, 1975-81; chmn. Nelson Assocs. Ltd., London, 1981-93; freelance author and comms. cons., 1993—; Pub. rels. dir. William H. Rentschler for U.S. Senator, 1959-60. Author: Small Wonder: The Amazing Story of the Volkswagen Beetle, 1965, rev., 1998, German edit., 1966, Br. edit., 1967, rev., 1971, Dutch edit., 1968, Spanish edit., 1974, revised edit., 1998, The Great Discount Delusion, 1965, The Berliners: Their City and Their Saga, 1969, Br. edit., 1969, The Soldier Kings: The House of Hohenzollern, 1970, Br. and Italian edits., 1971, German edit., 1972, Ernest Hemingway, 1971, Germany Rearmed, 1972, The Londoners: Life in A Civilized City, 1974, Br. edit., 1975, Japanese edit., 1976, 77, (with Terence Prittie) Economic War Against the Jews, 1977, Br. Edit., 1978, the Siege of Buckingham Palace, 1980, The Minstrel Code, 1979, Spanish edit., 1982, Gautama Buddha: His life and his Teaching, U.K. edit., 1998, Buddha: Life & Teaching, U.S. edit., 2000; contbr. articles to popular mags., newspapers. Served in U.S. Army, 1946-49. Address: 23 Clifford Ave, London SW14 7BT, England

NELSON, WILLIAM EUGENE, lawyer; b. Roland, Iowa, Sept. 23, 1927; s. Sam J. and Katherine A. (Coffey) N.; m. Sherlee M. Stanford, July 11, 1959; children: Anne, Kristin, William. BA, U. Iowa, 1950; JD, Drake U., 1957. Bar: Iowa 1957, D.C. 1965, Md. 1976. Trial atty. civil divsn. U.S. Dept. Justice, 1957-65, asst. chief tort sect., 1966-70, chief r.r. reorgn. unit, 1970-71; gen. counsel Cost of Living Coun. Phase I, 1971, chief econ. stblzn. sect., 1971-74; ptnr. Nelson and Nelson, LLP, Washington, Bethesda, Md., 1975—; gen. counsel the Communicators, Inc., Myersville, Md. Assoc. editor Drake Law Rev., 1955-57. With USN, 1945-46. Recipient Atty. Gen.'s Disting. Svc. award, 1972. Mem. Order of Coif, Omicron Delta Kappa. Home: RR 5 Box 48A Hedgesville WV 25427-9201 Office: Nelson & Nelson LLP 3 Bethesda Metro Ctr Ste 700 Bethesda MD 20814-6300

NELSON, WILLIAM JOSEPH, oncological and community health nurse; b. Plainfield, N.J., June 14, 1950; s. William Cornelius III and Margaret Elizabeth Nelson. BSN, Seattle U., 1975; BA in Philosophy, Dominican Sch. Philosophy and Theology, 1979; postgrad., San Francisco State U. Cert. pub. health nurse. Staff nurse, rschr. San Francisco Gen. Hosp., 1984-87; adminstrv. nurse U. Calif., San Francisco, 1986-87, health facilities evaluator nurse, 1990—; health facilities evaluator nurse Dept. Health Svcs., Licensing and Cert., State of Calif., Berkeley. Contbr. chpts. on AIDS to profl. publs. Mem. Am. Pub. Health Assn., Assn. Practitioners of Infection Control and Epidemiology, Soc. Nursing Profls., Alpha Sigma Nu. Home: 1852 Key Blvd El Cerrito CA 94530-1928

NELSON, WINIFRED HARRISON, singer, actress, computer programmer; b. Oak Park, Ill., Dec. 29, 1924; d. Fred Harrison; m. Robert Hartley Nelson, May 5, 1945 (dec. Feb. 24, 1994); children: Richard, Wendy, Steven (dec.), Jonathan, Elizabeth. BA, Knox Coll., 1945; MusM, Northwestern U., 1970. Tchr. voice, 1972-78, Chgo., 1976-80; computer programmer U. Ill., Champaign, 1978-82, Tex. A&M U., College Station, 1982-90; mem. Chgo. Symphony Chorus, 1972-80. Mem. Briarcrest Country Club. Presbyterian. Avocations: community theater, music, golf. Home: 2505 Oak Cir Bryan TX 77802-2009

NELSON-THORPE, CARLON JUSTINE, engineering and operations executive; b. Siloam Springs, Ark., May 26, 1960; d. Robert F. and Jean (Caroom) Toenges. BS in Indsl. Engring., U. Ark., 1982; MBA, Houston Bapt. U., 1988. Registered profl. engr., Tex. Supr. codes and regulatory compliance Tex. Ea., Houston, 1982-85, supr. ops. spl. projects, 1985-87, mgr. project devel., 1987-90; dir. spl. projects, tech. asst. to pres. Enron, Houston, 1990-91, dir. throughput engring., 1991-92, project dir., 1992-95; v.p. engring. So. Union Gas Co., Austin, Tex., 1995-96; v.p. ops. Mo. Gas Energy, Kansas City, Mo., 1996-99; gen. mgr. Shell Tech. Ventures, Houston, Tex., 1999—. Mem. NSPE, Tex. Soc. Profl. Engrs. Home: 5334 Indian Shores Ln Houston TX 77041-4298 Office: 200 N Dairy Ashford St Houston TX 77079-1101

NELSON-WALKER, ROBERTA, management software company executive; b. N.Y.C., Sept. 1, 1936; d. Richard E. and Esther (McBride) Martin; m. Robert L. Nelson, July 20, 1957 (div.); children: Carol, Craig, Robert H.; m. Dan Walker, Nov. 1978 (div.). BA, DePaul U., 1976, MS in Mgmt. with distinction, 1977. Dir. devel. Ray Graham Assocs., Elmhurst, Ill., 1970-76; dir. human resources Nat. Easter Seal Soc., Chgo., 1979-81; v.p. Butler Walker Inc., Oak Brook, Ill., 1981-85; pres. CNR, Inc., Oak Brook, Ill., 1985-91; spl. agt. Prudential Ins., Oak Brook, Ill., 1991-95; mng. dir. Visimark L.L.C., Oak Brook, Ill., 1995—. Author: Creating Acceptance for Handicapped People, 1975, Creating, Planning, and Financial Housing for Handicapped People, 1979. Founder, organizer Found. for Handicapped, 1970-76,; pres. DuPage County Pub. Health Coun., 1974; bd. dirs. DuPage County Mental Health Assocs., 1970, Forest Found. DuPage County, 1976-86, Shakespeare Globe, London and Chgo., 1982—; mem. DuPage County Bd. Health, 1975, Ill. Gov.'s Com. for Handicapped, 1976, women's coun. Chgo. Heart Assn., 1979—. Recipient Meritorious Svc. award, Chgo. Heart Assn., 1968, 70, Fond du Coer award AHA, 1968, Cursade of Mercy Achievement awards, 1974-76, State of Ill. procalmation by Gov. James Thompson, Ill. Epilepsy Assn., 1978.

NELTNER, MICHAEL MARTIN, lawyer; b. Cin., July 31, 1959; s. Harold John and Joyce Ann Neltner; m. Barbara Ann Phair, July 9, 1988; children: Brandon August, Alexandra Nicole. BA, Mercy Coll., 1981; MA, Athenaeum of Ohio, 1987; JD, U. Cin., 1994. Bar: Ohio 1994, U.S. Dist. Ct. (so. dist.) Ohio 1995. Tchr. Elder H.S., Cin., 1985-91; ins. agt. Ky. Ctrl., Cin., 1987-91; mediator City of Cin., 1992-94; tchg. asst. Ohio Gov.'s Inst., Cin., 1992; legal extern to Chief Justice Thomas Moyer Ohio Supreme Ct., 1993; assoc. Eagen, Wykoff & Healy, LPA, Cin., 1994-99, Thompson Hine & Flory, Cin., 1999—. Editor-in-chief Mercy Coll. Lit. Mag., 1980-81, U. Cin. Law Rev., 1993-94. Campaign coord. Rep. Orgn. Detroit, 1980. Recipient Merit scholarship Cin. Enquirer, 1977-81, Sage scholarship Mercy Coll., 1980, Am. Jurisprudence award Lawyers Coop. Publishing, 1994. Mem ABA, Ohio Bar Assn., Cin. Bar Assn. (mem. acad. medicine com. 1995—, chair Ct. Appeals com. 1998—). Home: 3344 Milverton Ct Cincinnati OH 45248-2865 Office: Thompson Hine & Flory LLP 312 Walnut St Cincinnati OH 45202-4089

NELZÉN, OLLE PER, vascular surgeon; b. Stockholm, Sweden, Apr. 2, 1952; s. Karl-Vilhelm Per and Margit Elsa (Norell) N.; m. Yvonne Margareta Wester, July 9, 1983; children: Oskar, Elias, Sofia. MD, Karolinska Inst., Stockholm, 1978; D of Med. Sci., 1997. Lic. med. doctor; qualified gen. surgeon. Gen. surgeon Ctrl. Hosp., Skövde, Sweden, 1985-91, cons. vascular surgeon, 1992—; vascular surgeon U. Hosp., Malmö, Sweden, 1991-92; dir. Uppsala U. Wound Ctr., 1998-99; dir. leg ulcer rsch. Skaraborg Leg Ulcer Ctr., 1999—; mem. Internat. Com. on Wound Mgmt., 1992—, European Panel on Endoscopic Vein Surgery, 1995—. Author: Patients with Chronic Leg Ulcer, 1997; contbr. articles to profl. jours. Mem. Swedish Med. Assn., Swedish Soc. Surgery and Vascular Surgery (Swedish Vascular award 1992), Soc. Phlebologica Scandinavica (bd. dirs. 1996-2000, chmn. 2000—, Gunnar Bauer prize 1994). Avocations: cross-country running, downhill skiing. Home: Vårvägen 25, S-541 33 Skövde Sweden Office: Skaraborg Hosp, Leg Ulcer Ctr, S-54185 Skovde Sweden

NEMCHINOV, SERGEI, hockey player; b. Moscow, Jan. 14, 1964; married. Hockey player SOVI/USSR, 1981-82, 85-91, CSKA/USSR, 1982-85, NYRA/NHL, 1991-97, VANC/NHL, 1996-97, N.Y. Islanders/NHL, 1997-98, 98-99, N.J. Devils/NHL, 1998-2000; mem. Russian Olympic Hockey Team, 1998-99. Recipient ice hockey Silver medal Olympic Games, Nagano, Japan, 1998. Office: NJ Devils PO Box 504 East Rutherford NJ 07073-0504 also: Continental Airlines Arena 50 Route 120 North East Rutherford NJ 07073*

NĚMCOVÁ, IRENA MARIE, chemistry educator, researcher; b. Pilsen, Czechoslovakia, June 5, 1940; d. Frantisek Josef and Marie Ruzena Bucil; m. Ivan Frantisek Nemec, Sept. 21, 1963; children: Ivan, Petr. MS, Charles U., Prague, Czechoslovakia, 1958, PhD, 1966. Rschr. dept. analytical chemistry Charles U., 1966-87, sr. rschr. dept. analytical chemistry, 1988-90, assoc. prof. dept. analytical chemistry, 1991—; mem. Czech Pharmacopoeial Commn., Prague, 1995—. Co-author: Handbook of Triarylmethane and Xanthene Dyes: Spectrophotometric Determination of Metals, 1985, Instrumentation in Analytical Chemistry, 1994, Spectrophotometric Reactions, 1996; contbr. articles to profl. jours. Recipient Rsch. grant Charles U., 1996-98, 99—. Avocations: music, literature, sports. Office: Charles Univ, Dept Analytical Chemistry, Prague Czech Republic

NEMCSICS, ANTAL KÁROLY, architect, artist, educator; b. Pápa, Hungary, June 9, 1927; s. Elek Nemcsics and Mária Széptóth; m. Magdolna Takács, Aug. 14, 1951; children: Csongor, Ákos, Endre. BSc, Hungarian Acad. Fine Arts, Budapest, 1950; DTech, Tech. U. Budapest, 1966; PhD, Hungarian Acad. Scis., Budapest, 1980, DSc, 1985. Asst. Tech. U. Budapest, 1951-60, sr. asst., 1960-74, assoc. prof., 1974-87, prof. colordynamics, 1987—; leading color designer Internat. Study Group Environ. Color Design, Budapest, Zurich, Switzerland, 1965—; chmn. Hungarian Nat. Color Com., 1969—; leading rschr. Inst. Color and Color Sys., 1980—. Author: Coloroid Colour System, 1982 (sci. prize 1982), Coloroid Colour Atlas, 1985 (rsch. prize 1989), Colour Dynamics, 1990 (pub. prize 1995), Axial and Coaxial Orders, 1993 (arts prize), 1996, Colorland's Laws, 1996. Recipient Giorgione prize Internat. Assn. Arts, 1963, Internat. Color Design prize Farb-Design Internat., 1984, Alpar Ignac medal Scientific Soc. Bldg., 1995, Cross of the Order of Merit of Hungarian State, 1996; named Fresman of a City Budapest, 1997. Mem. Assn. Hungarian Artists (murals painter 1955—), Hungarian Acad. Scis. (chmn. com. colorscis. 1982—), Internat. Color Assn. (bd. dirs. 1990-94), Internat. Color Light Found. (chmn. 1992—), Internat. Acad. Colorscis. (v.p. 1986—, prof. colorscis. 1987—), N.Y. Acad. Scis. Roman Catholic. Home: Ungvár u 42, 1185 Budapest Hungary Office: Tech U Budapest, Müegyetem rkp 3, 1111 Budapest Hungary

NÊME, JACQUES, economist; b. St. Laurent de Maroni, France, June 13, 1930; s. Marcel Pierre and Aimée Jeanne (Janin) N.; m. Marine Collignon, Jan. 29, 1957 (div. 1958); children: Jean Pol, Richard, Sylvie; m. Colette Jeanne Cordebas, Aug. 30, 1963; children: Christiane, Charles Henri, Isabelle, Vincent Neme-Peyron. Diploma, Inst. Etudes Polit., Paris, 1951; lic. en droit, Faculte de Droit, Paris, 1952. Chief svc. economist soc. Gen. de Presse, Paris, 1951-58; dir. Europe Svc., Paris, 1958-80, Afrique Svc., Paris, 1960-80; sec. gen. for econs. Soc. Generale de Presse, Paris, 1980-92; lectr. Inst. du Commerce Internat., 1959-79, U. Paris II, 1973—, U. Paris IX Dauphine, 1992-95, Ecole de Guerre, 1979; cons. Syndicat de la Margarine, Paris, 1970, Assn. Francaise des Banques, 1979. Author: European Economies, 1970, International Economic Organizations, 1972, Compared Economic Policies, 1977, 2d edit., 1989, (with C. Nême) The European Economic Community, 1992, European Union Economics: Analysis of an Integration Process, 1994; contbr. articles to profl. jours. With French Air Force, 1954-55. Recipient Officer award Order of Merit, 1988, Laureat de l'Institut de France, 1972. Roman Catholic. Avocation: gardening. Home: 83 Rue de Rome, 75017 Paris France

NEMEC, MARIJA, veterinarian; b. Ljubljana, Slovenia, Aug. 6, 1960; d. Rafael Nemec and Marija Golobič. D in Vet. Medicine, Vet. Faculty, Ljubljana, 1986; MSc, Vet. Faculty, 1989. Rschr. Vet. Faculty, Ljubljana, 1986-90, tech. co-worker, 1991-92, sr. specialist adviser, 1993—; head lab. for clin. biochemistry, quality mgr. Clinic for Ruminants, Ljubljana, 1997—. Contbr. articles to profl. jours. Mem. Assn. Buiatrics Slovenia, World Assn. Buiatrics, Internat. Soc. Animal Cli n. Biochemistry, European Soc. of Vet. Clin. Pathology, Soc. of European Soc. of Internal Medicine. Avocations: gardening. Office: Vet Faculty Clin Ruminants, p p 3425, 1115 Ljubljana Slovenia

NEMECEK, EDUARD, bank educator; b. Hradec Králové, Czech Republic, July 2, 1927; s. Eduard and Míla (Halberstadtová) N.; m. Hana Stychová, Mar. 22, 1975; children: Eduard, Radim. JUDr, Charles U., 1950; CSc in Econs., Acad. of Sci., Prague, 1961. Mem. dept. econs. Law Faculty of Charles U., Prague, 1950-90, head pub. fin. and banking dept., 1990—; fgn. exch. policy advisor State Bank of Czechoslovakia, Prague, 1968-81; counsel Burns Schwartz-Barristers and Solicitors, Prague, 1991—. Author: Introduction in Financial Science and Czech Financial Law, 1994, Introduction in the Financial Policy, 1987, (monographs) International Monetary System, 1996, Theory of Exchange Rates, 1967, The International Monetary System (The Issue of Convertibility, Stability and Liquidity), 2000. Mem. Network of Insts. and Schs. in Pub. Adminstrn. in Ctrl. and Eastern Europe. Avocations: riding horses, fishing. Office: Charles Univ Law Faculty, Nam Curieovych 7, 110 00 Prague 1, Czech Republic

NEMENYI, BEN, aerospace marketing company executive; b. Subotica, Serbia, Yugoslavia, Dec. 24, 1946; s. George and Anna (Hudushka) N.; m. Sally Ann Simon, July 1978; children: Adam, Daniel. BA, Middlesex U., London, 1976. Qualified aircraft engr., avionics and electronic equipment. Dir. mtkg. CMBI, Hamburg, Germany, 1986-89; mng. dir. Aerospheres (UK) Ltd., London, 1990—. Avocation: philately. Office: Aerospheres (UK) Ltd, Aerospace House 2A Tudor Rd, Harrow Middlesex HA3 5PE, England

NEMES, LÁSZLÓ, research chemist; b. Budapest, Hungary, Jan. 4, 1936; s. Dénes Aladár and Ibolya (Eiler) N.; m. Klára Tóth-Sarudy; 1 child, András. Diploma in Chem. Engring., Polytech U., Budapest, Hungary, 1959; PhD in Chem. Scis., Hungarian Acad. Scis., Budapest, 1967, D in Chem. Scis., 1982; D habil., Polytech. U., Budapest, 1995. Rsch. assoc. Pharm. Rsch. Inst., Budapest, 1959-61; rsch. worker Instrument Svcs. Hungarian Acad. Scis., Budapest, 1961-65; sr. rsch. worker Ctrl. Rsch. Inst. Chem. Hungarian Acad. Scis., Budapest, 1965-80; sci. advisor Rsch. Lab. Inorganic Chemistry Hungarian Acad. Scis., Budapest, 1980-98; sci. adviser Rsch. Lab. Materials & Environ. Chemistry, Hungarian Acad. Scis., Budapest, 1998—; rsch. assoc. U. Coll. Wales, 1964-65; Alexander von Humboldt fellow, Kiel, Germany, 1972-73; vis. prof. Tech. and Sci. U., Lille, France, 1986; vis. scientist U. Mich., Ann Arbor, U.S., 1990-91; rsch. prof. Acad. Sinica, Taiwan, 1993-95; W.F. James prof. pure and applied scis. St. Francis Xavier U., Antigonish, Can., 1996. Author: (book) Molecular Geometry and Rotational Spectra, 1980; contbr. chptrs. to Vibrational Spectra and Structure, 1981, rev. edit. '84; contbr. over 70 articles to profl. jours.; mem. editorial bd. Fullerene Sci. and Tech. Mem. Hungarian Chem. Soc., Alumni Assn. Chemistry Dept. U. Mich., Internat. Soc.for Optical Engring., Hungarian Humboldt Assn. Mem. Evangelical Ch. Avocations: classical music, reading, personal computers, swimming, gardening. Home: IIIem12, Kárpát utca 22, H-1133 Budapest Hungary Office: Rsch Lab Materials & Environ Chemistry, Pusztaszeri ut 59-67, H-1025 Budapest Hungary

NEMESIO, ALDO SEVERINO, linguist, humanities educator; b. Turin, Italy, Jan. 20, 1952; s. Giovanni and Elsa (Stellino) Nemesio. LLM, U. Turin, 1974; MA, U. Va., 1977. Fulbright fellow U. Va., 1974-75; lectr. Bryn Mawr Coll., 1975-76; prof. Sarah Lawrence Coll., 1976-77; lectr. U. Kent, England, 1978-81, U. Liege, Belgium, 1983-85; prof. U. Torino, Italy, 1985—.

NÉMETH, KÁROLY, chemistry educator; b. Sopron, Hungary, Aug. 5, 1934; s. Károly and Mária (Lobenwein) N.; m. Sarolta Sasfalvi; children:

Ervin, Eszter. Diploma chem. engring., U. Veszprém, Hungary, 1957; D in Tech., U. Miskolc, Hungary, 1961; CSc, Hungarian Sci. Acad., Budapest, 1972, DSc, 1989. Rschr. U. Sopron, 1957-59, asst. prof., 1963-68, assoc. prof., 1968-89, full prof., 1989—; rschr. U. Mikolc, 1959-61; head chem. lab. Sugarfactory, Petohaza, Hungary, 1961-63. Author: Wood Chemistry, 1997, Wood Degradation, 1998, Adhesion of Wood, 1998. Recipient prize Min. of Agriculture, prize Min. of Edn. Mem. Corp. Hungarian Sci. Acad., Soc. Hungarian Chem. (regional pres. 1972, regional award). Avocations: history, do it yourself projects. Home: Kossuth L u 15, H-9400 Sopron Hungary Office: U Sopron Inst Chem, Ady E 5, H-9400 Sopron Hungary Address: Inst Chem, H-9401 Sopron Hungary

NEMETH, MIKLOS, politician; b. Monok, Hungary, Jan. 24, 1948; married; 2 children. Grad., Karl Marx U. Economics, Budapest, Hungary, 1971. Teaching asst. Karl Marx U., Budapest, asst. prof., 1971-77; dep. head dept. Nat. Planning Office, Budapest, 1977-81; mem. staff econ. policy Hungarian Socialist Worker's Party Cen. Com., Budapest, 1981-88, head, 1986-87, mem., sec., 1987; mem. Politburo, Budapest, 1988, Parliament, Budapest, 1988-90; pres. Coun. Ministers, Budapest, 1988-90; appointed to four mem. Presidium of the Hungarian Socialist Workers Party, Budapest, 1990-91; ind. mem. Parliament Budapest, 1990-91; v.p. European Bank for Reconstrn. and Devel., London, 1991-2000.

NEMETZ MILLS, PATRICIA LOUISE, engineer, educator; b. Bethlehem, Pa., June 10, 1956; d. Stephen Andrew N. and Anna Julia Schadl; m. Alyn James Mills, June 18, 1983; 1 child, Andrea. BS in Mech. Engring., Pa. State U., 1979; MBA, Gonzaga U., 1985; PhD in Bus. Adminstrn., U. Wash., 1989. Project engr. Air Products and Chems., Trexlertown, Pa., 1979-83; instr. Gonzaga U., Spokane, Wash., 1984-85; prof. Ea. Washington U., Spokane, 1989—; cons. Spokane Auto Transport, Auburn, Wash., 1985-95, Boeing, Seatle, 1988-89, Eldec, Seattle, 1988; instr., seminar leader Bulgaria, 1990, EWU/Montenegro U., 1991. Contbr. articles to profl. jours. Office: Ea Washington U 668 N Riverpoint Blvd Ste A Spokane WA 99202-1677

NEMFAKOS, CHARLES PANAGIOTIS, government official; b. Athens, Greece, Oct. 21, 1942; s. Panagiotis Soterios and Mirka (Kyriakakis) N.; children: Mirka Leigh, Charles Jr., Alexandra Kaitlyn; m. Pamela Durrant. BA, Pan Am. U., 1964; MA, Georgetown U., 1982. Cert. in nat. security. Health advisor USPHS, Washington, 1965-66; fed. mgmt. intern Dept. Navy, Washington, 1966-67; budget analyst Naval Ordnance Systems Command, Washington, 1967-71; supervisory budget analyst Naval Ship Systems Command, Washington, 1971-73; sr. budget analyst Office of Sec. of Def., Washington, 1973-75; divsn. dir. Office Budget and Reports, Dept. Navy, Washington, 1975-76, assoc. dir., 1976-93, dep. asst. sec., 1994-95, dep. under sec., 1995—, sr. civilian official for fin. mgmt., comptr., 1998—; lectr. Naval Postgrad. Sch., Monterey, Calif., 1984—, Georgetown U., Washington, 1987—; mem. base structure com. Dept. Navy, Washington, 1990-91, mem. sr. advisors group, 1991-92, vice-chmn. base structure com., 1992-95; mem. gen. adminstrn. bd. USDA Grad. Sch., 2000—. Contbr. articles to profl. jours. Coach McLean (Va.) Youth Soccer, 1978-93, chmn., 1982-85; bd. dirs. McLean Youth, Inc., 1980-84; registrar Va. Youth Soccer Assn., 1984-86. Recipient Dept. Navy Superior Civilian Svc. award Asst. Sec. of Navy, 1980, Dept. Navy Disting. Civilian Svc. award Sec. of Navy, 1985, 87, 93, Dept. Def. Disting. Civilian Svc. award Sec. of Def., 1990, Dept. Navy Disting. Pub. Svc. award Sec. of Navy, 1995, Roger W. Jones award exec. leadership Am. U., 2000; named to Rank of Disting. Exec. Pres. of U.S., 1986, 95, to Rank of Meritorious Exec., Pres. of U.S., 1981, 91. Mem. Am. Assn. Budget and Program Analysis (dir.-at-large 1980-83), Am. Soc. of Mil. Comptrs. (v.p. 1988-90), Fed. Execs. Inst. Alumni Assn., Tau Kappa Epsilon (chpt. pres. 1964-65). Greek Orthodox. Avocations: golf, tennis, coaching soccer. Office: Under Sec of Navy Pentagon 4E 775 Washington DC 20350-0001

NEMICKAS, RIMGAUDAS, cardiologist, educator; b. Kaunas, Lithuania, Mar. 10, 1938; came to U.S., 1949; s. Romualdas and Elena (Saulyte) N.; m. Joan A. McLee, Feb. 16, 1965; children: Rimas Jonas, Kristina Nemickas Tomlinson, Tomas Edward, Nikolas. Student, Ind. U., 1954-57; MD magna cum laude, Loyola U., 1961; MD (hon.), Kaunas Med. Acad., 1993. Diplomate in internal medicine and cardiovascular diseases Am. Bd. Internal Medicine; lic. physician, Ill., Ind. Intern U. Chgo. Clinics, 1961-62; resident inmedicine U. Ill. Rsch. and Edn. Hosps., 1966-67; fellow in cardiology Cook County Hosp., Chgo., 1962-63, U. Chgo. Hosp., 1967-69; assoc. chief cardiology Loyola U., Maywood, Ill., 1972-77, clin. prof. medicine, 1979—; dir. cardiology Ill. Masonic Med. Ctr., Chgo., 1980—. Mem. Task Force for Health Care Reform, Ministry of Health, Vilnius, Lithuania, 1994-97. Capt. USAF, 1963-66. Fellow ACP, Am. Coll. Cardiology, Am. Coll. Chest Physicians; mem. Am. Heart Assn., Chgo. Soc. Internal Medicine, Chgo. Cardiology Group. Republican. Roman Catholic. Avocations: walking, travel, fishing, collecting art. Office: Ill Masonic Med Ctr 3000 N Halsted St Chicago IL 60657-5188

NEMILOV, SERGEI VLADIMIROVICH, chemist; b. Moscow, Jan. 3, 1939; s. Vladimir and Tatiana (Belousova) N.; m. Nadezhda Zotina, Nov. 27, 1965. MSc, Vavilov State Optical Inst., 1965; PhD, Acad. Sci. USSR, 1972. From jr. rschr. to prin. rschr., prof. Vavilov State Optical Inst., Leningrad, 1964—. Author: Thermodynamic and Kinetic Aspects of Vitreous State, 1995; contbr. articles to profl. jours. Recipient Grebenschikov prize in chemistry Russian Acad. Scis., 1997. Fellow Mendeleev All-Russian Chem. Soc., Rozhdestvensky All-Russian Optical Soc. Home: 995 ap 14-1 Podvoiskogo str, 193 318 Saint Petersburg Russia

NEMIRO, BEVERLY MIRIUM ANDERSON, author, educator; b. St. Paul, May 29, 1925; d. Martin and Anna Mae Anderson; m. Jerome Morton Nemiro, Feb. 10, 1951 (div. May 1975); children: Guy Samuel, Lee Anna, Dee Martin. Student, Reed Coll., 1943-44; BA, U. Colo., 1947; postgrad., U. Denver. Tchr. Seattle Pub. Schs., 1945-46; fashion coord., dir. Denver Dry Goods Co., 1948-51; fashion dir. Denver Market Week Assn., 1952-53; free-lance writer Denver, 1958—; moderator TV program Your Presch. Child, Denver, 1955-56; instr. writing and comm. U. Colo. Denver Ctr., 1970—, U. Calif., San Diego, 1976-78, Met. State Coll., 1985; dir. pub. rels. Fairmont Hotel, Denver, 1979-80; freelance fashion and TV model. Author, co-author: The Complete Book of High Altitude Baking, 1961, Colorado a la Carte, 1963, Colorado a la Carte, Series II, 1966, (with Donna Hamilton) The High Altitude Cookbook, 1969, The Busy People's Cookbook, 1971 (Better Homes and Gardens Book Club selection 1971), Where to Eat in Colorado, 1967, Lunch Box Cookbook, 1965, Complete Book of High Altitude Baking, 1961, (under name Beverly Anderson) Single After 50, 1978, The New High Altitude Cookbook, 1980. Co-founder, pres. Jr. Symphony Guild, Denver, 1959-60; active Friends of Denver Libr., Opera Colo.; mem. Friends of Painting and Sculpture, Denver Art Mus. Recipient Top Hand award Colo. Authors' League, 1969, 72, 79-82, 100 Best Books of Yr. award N.Y. Times, 1969, 71; named one of Colo.'s Women of Yr., Denver Post, 1964. Mem. Am. Soc. Journalists and Authors, Colo. Authors League (dir. 1969-79), Authors Guild, Authors League Am., Friends Denver Libr., Opera Colo. Guild, Denver Women's Press Club, Rotary, Kappa Alpha Theta. Address: Park Towers 1299 Gilpin St Apt 15W Denver CO 80218-2556

NEMIROFF, MAXINE CELIA, art educator, gallery owner, consultant; b. Chgo., Feb. 11, 1935; d. Oscar Bernard and Martha (Mann) Kessler; m. Paul Rubenstein, June 26, 1955 (div. 1974); children: Daniel, Peter, Anthony; m. Allan Nemiroff, Dec. 24, 1979. BA, U. So. Calif., 1955; MA, UCLA, 1974. Sr. instr. UCLA, 1974-92; dir., curator art gallery Doolittle Theater, Los Angeles, 1985-86; owner Nemiroff Deutsch Fine Art, Santa Monica, Calif.; leader of worldwide art tours; cons. L'Ermitage Hotel Group, Beverly Hills, Calif., 1982—, Broadway Dept. Stores, So. Calif., 1979—, Security Pacific Bank, Calif., 1978—, Am. Airlines, Calif. Pizza Kitchen Restaurants; art chmn. UCLA Thieves Market, Century City, 1960—, L.A. Music Ctr. Mercado, 1982—; lectr. in field. Apptd. bd. dirs. Dublin (Calif.) Fine Arts Found., 1989; mem. Calif. Govs. Adv. Coun. for Women, 1992; mem. art selection com. Calif. State Office Bldgs., 1997—. Named Woman of Yr. UCLA Panhellenic Council, 1982, Instr. of Yr. UCLA Dept. Arts, 1984; elected to Fashion Circle of the Costume Coun., L.A. County Mus. Art, 1997—. Mem. L.A. County Mus. Art Coun., UCLA Art Coun., UCLA Art Coun. Docents, Alpha Epsilon Phi (alumnus of yr. 1983). Avocations: tennis, horseback riding, skiing, piano and guitar.

NEMNYUGIN, SERGEI ANDREEVICH, physics educator, researcher; b. Astrakhan, Russia, June 20, 1959; s. Andrei Vasilievich and Maria Dmitrievna (Prokofieva) N.; m. Olga Aleksandrovna Bondarenko, Dec. 15, 1983; children: Anton, Stanislaw. MSc, Saint Petersburg State U., 1982, PhD, 1992. Rschr. Inst. Electrophys. Equipment, St. Petersburg, 1982-86; rschr. St. Petersburg State U., 1986-90, asst. prof., 1990-96, assoc. prof., 1996—, referee Ctr. Grants, 1995; cons. Tutkemuskestus Vinko oy Yuvaskila, Finland, 1996-97; reviewer Math. Rev., Am. Math. Soc., Ann Arbor, 1996—. Translator: Scientific Pascal, 1997. Grantee Am. Phys. Soc., 1993, Soros Found., 1994, 95. Mem. Am. Math. Soc., N.Y. Acad. Scis. Avocation: music. Home: ul Oleko Dunditch 36/1 #359, 192289 Saint Petersburg Russia Office: St Petersburg State U Phys, Ulyanovskaya 1, 198904 Saint Petersburg Russia

NEMOTO, SHOJIRO, engineering educator; b. Nagoya, Aichi, Japan, Mar. 9, 1944; s. Kinoji and Akie (Nakajima) N.; m. Hiroko Muratsu, July 29, 1973; 1 child, Yumiko. B of Engring., Osaka U., 1966, M of Engring., 1968, D of Engring., 1972. Rsch. assoc. Osaka U., 1971-80; postdoctoral rsch. fellow McGill U., Montreal, Can., 1973-75; assoc. prof. U. Tsukuba, Japan, 1980-94, prof., 1994—; mem. domestic com. Internat. Orgn. for Standardization, Tokyo, 1994—. Contbr. articles to profl. jours. Mem. Inst. of Electronics, Info. and Comm. Engrs., Optical Soc. of Am. (reviewer), N.Y. Acad. Scis. Home: 2-9-12 Sengen, Tsukuba 305-0047, Japan Office: U Tsukuba Inst Info Scis & Electron, 1-1-1 Tennohdai, Tsukuba 305-8573, Japan

NEMOV, ALEXI, Olympic athlete; b. Barashevo, Russia, May 28, 1976. Recipient 2 Gold medals, 1 Silver medal, 3 Bronze medals in Men's Gymnastics, Olympic Games, Atlanta, 1996.

NEMOV, VICTOR VADIMOVICH, physicist, researcher; b. Krasnodar, Russia, Dec. 13, 1930; s. Vadim Georgievich and Anna Afanasievna (Smola) N.; m. Zoya Vladimirovna Vyshemirskaya, Dec. 9, 1954; 1 child, Konstantin. Degree in Elec. Engring., Odessa (Ukraine) Poly. Inst., 1954; Degree in Physics, Kharkov (Ukraine) State U., 1966, DSc, 1994; PhD in Physics and Math., Donetsk State U., Ukraine, 1972. Cert. sci. rschr. in the field of plasma physics and controlled nuclear fusion. Elec. engr. Industry, Kirov, Russia, 1954-56; engr. investigator Kharkov Electromechanical Plant, 1956-59; sci. rschr. All-Union Electrodevice Rsch. Inst., Kharkov, 1959-66; rsch. assoc. Kharkov Inst. Physics and Tech., 1966-77, sr. rsch. staff, 1977-96, leading rsch. staff, 1996—. Contbr. articles to profl. jours. Mem. Ukrainian Phys. Soc. Avocations: classical music, vegetable gardening. Office: Nat Sci Ctr, Akademicheskaya Str 1, 61108 Kharkov Ukraine

NEMTSEVICH, LYUDMILA VASILEVNA, physicist, researcher; b. Orekhovsk, Vitebskaya, Byelarus, Nov. 10, 1955; arrived in Can.; d. Vasilii Dmitrievich and Nina Alexandrovna (Shaduikis) Brukshtin; m. Mikhail Petrovich Nemtsevich, Oct. 2, 1987. Degree, Pedagogical Inst., Minsk, Byelarus, 1977; MS, Inst. Solid and Semiconductor Physics, Minsk, Byelarus, 1983. Tchr. Secondary H.S. Gen. Edn., Gorbazevichy, Byelarus, 1977-80; postgrad. fellow Inst. Solid State Physics, Minsk, 1980-83, scientist, 1983—. Contbr. articles to Physics State Solid, Jour. Magnetism and Magnetic Materials, Crystal Rsch. Tech., Russian Jour. Electrochemistry. Mem. Trade Union. Achievements include patents for formation of amorphous soft magnetic alloys and materials for magnetic record. Office: Inst Solid State Physics, P Brovki 17, 220072 Minsk Belarus

NENCIU, GHEORGHE, physics educator, researcher; b. Moeciul de Jos, Transilvania, Romania, June 28, 1944; s. Ioan and Ana (Pintea) N.; m. Alexandrina Chiculita, July 15, 1976; 1 child, Irina. PhD, Inst. Atomic Physics, Bucharest, Romania, 1973. Cert. physicist. Sci. rsch. Inst. Atomic Physics, Bucharest, Romania, 1967-90; prof. theoretical physics U. Bucharest, Romania, 1990—; sr. rschr. Inst. Math. Romanian Acad., Bucharest, 1993—; vis. prof. E.T.H., Zürich, Switzerland, 1992, U. Paris Nord, 1996; dir., rschr. CNRS, Paris, 1994. Co-editor: Recent Developments in Quantum Mechanics, 1991; contbr. articles to profl. jours. Recipient D. Hurmuzescu prize Romanian Acad., Bucharest, 1972. Romanian Orthodox. Home: 31A Henri Coandă, Bucharest Romania Office: Univ Bucharest, Dept Theoretical Physics, 76900 Bucharest Romania

NENE, PRABHAKAR LAXMAN, utility executive; b. Gwalior, India, Nov. 6, 1934; s. Laxman Ganesh and Laxmi (Barve) N.; m. Jyotsna Prabhakar Ranade, June 6, 1961; children: Shubhangi, Kishore. BSc in Engring., Banaras Hindu U., Varanasi, India, 1955; postgrad., U. Roorkee, India, Indo French Collaboration, France, 1968, Indian Inst. Mgmt., Ahmedabad, 1987, Ashridge Coll. Mgmt., U.K., 1987. Cert. in advance power sector mgmt. Ctrl. Electricity Generating Bd., U.K. Middle level exec. Madhya Pradesh Electricity Bd., Indore, Bhopal, Raipur, Bhilai, India, 1955-73; sr. level exec. Madhya Pradesh Electricity Bd., Jabalpur, India, 1973-85, sec., 1985-87, mem. transmission and distbn. divsn., 1987-90, chmn., 1990-93; mng. dir. Jyotsna Engrs. & Cons., India, 1994—; bd. dirs. Modern Malleables Ltd., India, M.P. Elecs. Ltd., India, R.T.S. Power Ltd., India, Monnet Power Ltd.; chmn. Western Regional Electriciay Bd., India, 1990-91; cons. in field. Editor Jour. Nat. Inst. Industry Forum of Energy, 1996—, Approach to Power Problems in M.P., 1996-97. Pres. Rotary Club-South, Jabalpur, India, 1991-92; advisor All India Mfrs. Assn., Indore, India, 1995—; mem. power think tank Surya Found., New Delhi, India, 1999—; advisor Nat. Inst. Industry Forum for Energy, Indore, 1996—. Recipient Best Power Man Excellence award Nat. Found. Indian Engrs., 1992, Best Energy Mgmt. of Yr. award IBPL Urja Rsch. Found., 1992, award for outstanding svc. achievements and contbns. India Internat. Friendship Soc., 1997. Fellow Instn. Engrs. india (chmn. Jabalpur ctr. 1991-93), Soc. Power Engrs. (chmn. Jabalpur Ctr. 1992), Indian Soc. Lighting Engrs. (chmn. Indore ctr. 1996-97); mem. All India Mgmt. Assn. (chmn. Jabalpur Ctr. 1991-93, life), Internat. Assn. Energy Econs. (chmn. 1991—), Indian Soc. Tng. and Devel. (chmn. 1990-93, life). Avocations: reading, drama club, sports, writing articles.

NENNIGER, PETER, education educator; b. Bienne, Berne, Switzerland, May 29, 1944; s. Paul and Maria (Waelti) N.; m. Margot Bader, Aug. 1, 1973; 1 child, Markus. Diploma in Psychology, U. Mannheim, Germany, 1970; postgrad., U. Mannheim; PhD, U. Provence, Aix-en-Provence, France, 1977; Habil., U. Freiburg, Germany, 1984. Rsch. asst. Univs. Freiburg and Mannheim, 1971-77; asst. prof. U. Freiburg, 1977-85; assoc. prof. U. Kiel, Germany, 1985-92; vis. prof. U. Basel, Switzerland, from 1985; prof. U. Koblenz-Landau, Landau, Germany, 1992—; dir. Inst. for Pedagogics, Ctr. Ednl. Rsch. U. Koblenz-Landau, 1992—; spokesman for U. Basel at Commn. du 3 cycle des sciences en edn. de la Suisse Romande, Geneva, from 1994. Author and editor several books in edn.; editor, cons. to sci. jours., 1987—; coord. Jour. Empirische Paedagogik/Current Empirische Paedagogik, 1994—; contbr. articles to profl. jours. Mem. Commn. of the Parliament of the German State of Schleswig Holstein, 1989-93. Recipient medal IFAK-Inst., Germany, 1971, U. Zagazig, Egypt, 1995. Mem. Humboldt Acad. (life; mem. acad. coun.), Acad. di Studi Merano Italy (hon.), N.Y. Acad. Scis. Roman Catholic. Avocations: playing piano and organ, collecting lyrics. Home: Muenzbergweg 7, 76829 Landau Germany Office: Ctr Ednl Rsch U Koblenz-Landau, Friedrich-Ebert-Str 12, 76829 Landau Germany

NENSTIEL, SUSAN KISTHART, fundraising professional; b. Hazleton, Pa., Aug. 21, 1951; d. Frank W. and Mary A. (Price) Kisthart. BS, Pa. State U., 1973; MBA, Wilkes (Pa.) Coll., 1982. Control mgr. Barrett, Haentjens & Co., Hazleton, 1973-79, export mgr., 1979-86; exec. dir. Leadership Hazleton, 1986-87; devel. officer Planned Parenthood of NE Pa., Wilkes-Barre, 1986-87; ins. broker, office mgr. Nenstiel & Nenstiel, West Hazleton, Pa., 1988-96; assoc. dir. devel. Hospice St. John, 1996-97; devel. assoc. Luth. Svcs. N.E., 1997-98, reg. dir. devel., 1998-2000; exec. dir. LWV of Pa., 2000—. Pres. YWCA, Hazleton, 1983-85, Women's Coalition of Greater Hazleton, 1987-91; sec. Govt. Study Commn., Hazleton, 1986; trustee Hazleton Area Pub. Libr., sec., 1987-89, v.p., 1990-91, pres., 1991-93; chmn. Luzerne County Commn. for Women, 1988-91; mem., chmn. Hazleton City Zoning Bd., 1988-92; treas. Pa. Women's Campaign Fund, 1987-91, pres., 1991-92; mem. Leadership Hazleton Adv. Coun., 1988-92; mem. Pa. Pub. Libr. Project, 1992-94; bd. dirs. Hazleton Health Care Found., 1992-2000, chairperson, 1994-99, Cmty. Banks, Inc., 1996-2000; mem. Greater Hazleton Health Alliance Bd., 1995-2000, sec., 2000; mem. Luzerne County Regional Bd. Cmty. Banks, N.A., 1993-2000, YWCA adv. coun., 1998-2000. Named one of Outstanding Women Penns Woods Coun. Girl Scouts USA, 1977, Outstanding Young Women in Am., 1985, Woman of Yr. Soroptimist Internat., 1984, Greater Hazleton Jaycee Disting. Svc. award, 1990; recipient Luzerne County Pathfinder's award, 1990, Hon. P.E.A.R.L. award YWCA, 1996; named to Pa. Honor Roll of Women, 1996. Mem. AAUW (br. pres. 1977-79, 97-2000, state sec. 1981-83, state treas. 1983-85, state pres. 1992-96, Br. Outstanding Woman of Yr. 1980, assn. program com. 1995-97, ednl. found. bd. dirs. 1999—), Nat. Soc. Fund Raising Execs., Assn. Luth. Devel. Execs., Greater Hazleton C. of C. (bd. dirs. 1995-2000, treas. 1998-2000). Home: 6130 Springford Dr Apt E-3 Harrisburg PA 17111-6871

NENTWICH, MICHAEL ANDREAS ERHART, educator, consultant; b. Prague, Czech Republic, Sept. 6, 1941; came to U.S., 1994; s. Walter Joseph and Charlotte Rosina (Hawle) N. Student, Nuremberg (Germany) U., 1960-64; postgrad., Heidelberg (Germany) U., 1965-69, PhD, 1973. English lectr. Mannheim (Germany) U., 1969-75; vis. lectr. in German, Chinese U. Hong Kong, 1975-80; rsch. scholar in English Tech. U. Berlin, 1980-81; educator, cons. Goethe-Inst., Bremen, Germany, 1982, Madrid, 1983-85, Düsseldorf, Germany, 1985-88, São Paulo, 1988-92, Munich, 1992-94, N.Y.C., 1994-2000; exec. dir. Goethe-Inst., Atlanta, 2000—; Werbemappe advocacy binder Tchrs. of German in the USA, 1999. Author: Der schottische Shaw, 1973; editor Contemporary German Modern Germany Update; contbr. articles to profl. jours. Recipient Sophie Bernsthen scholarship U. Heidelberg, 1968. Avocations: music, painting, travel, theatre. Office: Goethe-Inst Atlanta Colony Sq Plaza Level 1197 Peachtree St NE Atlanta GA 30361-3502

NEOCLEOUS, KYRIAKOS, school principal, writer; b. Limassol, Cyprus, Dec. 11, 1922; s. Neocles Constantinou and Augusta (Papatheodorou) N.; m. Elsie Gaston Mavroides, Nov. 2, 1947; children: Nelson, Hermes, Gaston, Chris, Elmos. Shorthand tchrs. cert. (corr.), Pitman's Coll., London, 1944; diploma in administrn., Northwestern U., 1964; diploma in edn., Leeds (Eng.) U., 1969. Tutor pvt. inst., Nicosia, Cyprus, 1943-47; tchr. Samuel Comml. Sch., Nicosia, Cyprus, 1947-50, Pancyprian Acad., Nicosia, Cyprus, 1947-50; prin. Pancyprian Econ. Lyceum, Nicosia, Cyprus, 1950-83; pres. Cyprus Sport Orgn., Nicosia, 1983-88; state examiner Ministry Edn., Nicosia, 1960—; founder Pancyprian Econ. Lyceum, 1950; cons. Ministry Edn., Nicosia, 1983-88. author: International Typewriting, 1947 (still in print), The Headmaster in Cyprus, 1969, Golden Key to Classical Wisdom, 1971, School Pulses, 1972, Education in Yorkshire, 1973; co-author (with Nelson Neocleous): Political Economy (Elements), 1976, Chronicle of Sport in Cyprus, Centennial edit., 1986, The Computer Processor, 1986. Founder 40th Scouts Group, Nicosia, 1952, Neocleous' Evening Sch., Nicosia, 1953. Fulbright scholar, Northwestern U., 1964; recipient Commonwealth Bursary scholarship, Leeds U., 1969; recipient award for contbn. to advancement of sport, Pres. Republic Cyprus, 1988; recipient Authors' award Ayios Dometios Cooperative Soc., Nicosia, 1995; recipient award Greek Literary Soc., Athens, 1995. Fellow Royal Soc. Arts (London), Inst. Bus. Adminstrn. (London); mem. City and Guilds of London Inst. (hon.). Greek Orthodox. Avocations: sports, classical music, reading, crossword puzzles. Home: 24 Smyrnis St, 2401 Engomi Nicosia Cyprus

NEOPHYTOU, PAVLOS IOANNI, molecular geneticist; b. Nicosia, Cyprus, July 29, 1967; s. John P. and Elpiniki N. (Papadopoulou) N. BA with honors, U. Cambridge, England, 1990, MA, 1994, PhD, 1995. Dir. Pavlos Neophytou Molecular Diagnosis, Ltd., Nicosia, Cyprus, 1997; founder, chmn. Mendel Ctr. for Biomed. Scis., Nicosia, Cyprus, 1998; gen. organising sec. Biol. Soc. of Cyprus, 1998—. Contbr. articles to profl. jours.; inventer/developer T-cell epitope analysis using subtracted expression libraries method for identification of novel vaccine components. With Cyprus Army, 1985-87. Rsch. grantee Cyprus Found. for Rsch. Promotion, Mendel Ctr. for Biomed. Scis., 1999—, Nat. Multiple Sclerosis Soc., Mendel Ctr. for Biomed. Scis., 1998—, Middle East Cancer Consortium, Mendel Ctr. for Biomed. Scis., 1999—; Fulbright fellow Colo. and N.Y., 1997; recipient Commonwealth scholarship Brit. Coun., U. Cambridge, 1987-90. Mem. Biol. Soc. Cyprus (gen. organising sec. 1997—), Cyprus Acad. Scis., Hellenic Assn. Med. Geneticists, Cyprus Assn. Dirs. of Clin. Labs. Achievements include invention/development of the method TEASEL (T-cell Epitope Analysis using Subtracted Expression Libraries) for the identification of novel vaccine components (antigens). E-mail: pneophyt@logos.cy.net. Office: Mendel Ctr Biomed Scis, 5 Kimonos/Egkomi, 2406 Nicosia Cyprus

NEOPTOLEMOS, JOHN PHYTHOHIANNIS, surgeon, educator; b. Pandozodhia, Cyprus, June 30, 1951; arrived in Eng., 1955.; m. Linda Joan Blaylock, 1975; children: Ptolemy, Eleni. BA, Cambridge (Eng.) U., 1973, MB BChir, 1976, MA, 1977; MD, Leicester (Eng.) U., 1985. Sr. registrar U. Leicester, 1982-87; rsch. fellow U. Calif., San Diego, 1984-85; sr. lectr. surgery U. Birmingham, Eng., 1987-90; reader in surgery U. Birmingham, 1990-94, prof. surgery, 1994—; head of dept. U. Liverpool, Eng., 1996—. Co-editor: (textbook) The Pancreas, 2 vols., 1998, (sci. book) Pancreatic Cancer: Molecular and Clinical Advances, 1996. Recipient Rodney Smith prize Pancreatic Soc. Gt. Britain and Ireland, 1987. Fellow Royal Coll. Surgeons Eng. (Hunterian prof. 1987); mem. United European Gastroenterology Fedn. (coun. mem. 1998-02), Internat. Assn. Pancreatology (coun. mem. 1996—), European Digestive Surgery (treas. 1995—), South African Gastroenterology Soc. (hon. mem.), European Pancreatic Club (sec. 1997-02). Avocations: squash, football. Office: Royal Liverpool U Hosp, Dept Surgery Daulby St, Liverpool L69 3GA, England

NEPALIA, VIRENDRA, agriculture educator; b. Chittorgarh, Rajasthan, India, Aug. 13, 1958; s. Ganpat Lal and Chatar Devi (Chatar) Mathur; m. Kirti Mathur, Mar. 12, 1986; children: Raghav, Madhav. BSc in Agr., Udaipur U., India, 1981; MSc in Agr., Sukhadia U., Udaipur, 1984; PhD in Agr., Rajasthan Agrl. U., Bikaner, India, 1997. Agr. officer Bank of Rajasthan, Bhadsora, India, 1983-86; dist. agr. officer Govt. of Rajasthan, Udaipur, 1986-89; asst. prof. Agrl. U., Udaipur, India, 1989—. Contbr. articles to profl. jours. Recipient Gold medal Sukhadia U., Udaipur, 1984. E-mail: vnepalia@usa.net. Home: 161 Road No 11 Ashok Nagar, Udaipur 313 001, India Office: Agr Univ, Rajasthan Coll Agr, Udaipur 313 001, India

NEPERSHIN, ROSTISLAV, mechanical engineering educator, researcher; b. Rastorguevo, Russia, July 28, 1938; s. Ivan Vasilevich Nepershin and Mariya Petrovna Pahvitsevich; m. Nataliya Borisovna Levina, Jan. 13, 1967 (div. June 1983); children: Leonid, Anton, Mariya. Degree in mech. engring., Moscow Tech. U., 1962; D of Engring. Sci.-Inst. Machine Rsch., Russian Acad. Scis., Moscow, 1977. Engr. Automotive Tech. Rsch. Inst., Moscow, 1962-65; rsch. scientist Inst. Machine Rsch., 1965-91; prof. Moscow State Acad. Instrument Engring. and Informatics, Moscow, 1991—; vis. rsch. scientist Alcoa Tech. Ctr., U.S., 1996, 98, 99; mem. hon. com. 1st Internat. Conf. of Technology of Plasticity, Tokyo, 1984. Co-author: (with B. Druyanov) Theory of Technological Plasticity, 1990, Problems of Technological Plasticity, 1994; contbr. articles to profl. jours. Mem. Sci. Coun. Russian People's Friendship U. Christian Orthodox. Avocations: skiing, swimming, running, church, classical music. E-mail: vep@oktava.msk.su. Office: Acad Instrument Engr Info, Stromynka Str 20, 107846 Moscow Russia

NERDAL, WILLY, chemistry educator, researcher; b. Bergen, Norway, Sept. 28, 1954; s. Ludvik Bernhard and Inga Johanne (Svardal) N.; m. Signe Steinkopf, Oct. 16, 1993; children: Steffen Steinkopf Nerdal, Jon Steinkopf Nerdal. Cand. Sci., U. Bergen, 1985, PhD, 1990. Fellow Royal Norwegian Coun. Scientific and Indsl. Rsch., Seattle, Wash., 1985-88; fellow U. Bergen, 1988-92, rsch. assoc. dept. chemistry, 1992-93, asst. prof., 1993-96, assoc. prof., 1996—. Contbr. articles to profl. jours. Mem. Am. Chem. Soc., Norwegian Chem. Soc. Avocations: mountaineering, sport fishing, sailing. Office: Univ Bergen, Dept Chemistry Allegaten 41, Bergen Norway

NERGIZ, IBRAHIM, dentist; b. Trabzon, Blacksea, Turkey, June 25, 1958; arrived in Germany, 1981; s. Bahattin Nergiz and Sevim (Surmen) Uzel; m. Nilufer Nilgun Akin, Mar. 10, 1993; 1 child, Omer Berk. DDS, U. Ankara, Turkey, 1981; Doctorate, U. Ankara, 1996; Dr. Med. Dentistry, U. Erlangen, Germany, 1989. Assoc. prof., rschr. U. Erlangen, 1983-86, U. Hamburg, 1988-93, U. Cologne, 1993-97, U. Hamburg, 1998—. Contbr. articles to profl. jours. With Turkish Army, 1991. Recipient awards for Best Poster Presentations, Deutsche Gesellschaft fur Zahnerhaltung,

Germany, 1996, Deutsche Gesellschaft fur Prothetik, Germany, 1997. Islamic. Avocations: diving, swimming, travel. Office: U Hamburg, Martinistrasse 52, 20246 Hamburg Germany

NERMUT, MILAN VLADIMIR, biomedical scientist, researcher; b. Kyjov, Czechoslovakia, Mar. 19, 1924; arrived in Eng., 1971; s. Vladimir and Marie (Suchomelová) N.; m. Kveta Kumrova, Oct. 20, 1945 (div. Mar. 1989); children: Jana, Magda, Irena, Hana. Student, Masaryk U., Brno, Czechoslovakia, 1950, PhD, 1955, docent, 1965; prof., Med. Rsch. Coun., London, 1982; DSci (hon.), Slovak Acad. Sci., 1995. Asst. lectr. Masaryk U., Brno, 1950-62; rsch. scientist Czech Acad. Sci., Prague, 1962-65; head of rsch. group Czech Acad. Sci., Bratislava, Czechoslovakia, 1965-70; rsch. scientist Max Planck Inst., Tübingen, Germany, 1970-71; group leader Nat. Inst. Med. Rsch., London, 1971-89; retired scientist U. Autonoma, Madrid, 1990-91; grantee MRC Nat. Inst. Biolog. Standards and Control, London, 1991—. Editor: (book) Animal Virus Structure, 1987; contbr. numerous papers to profl. jours. and sci. meetings, 14 chpts. to sci. books; editor Intervirology (U.S.), 1975-79; editl. bd. Micron, 1989—, Microscopy and Analysis, 1990—, Czech Vet. Medicine, 1994—. Recipient Hlavka medal Czechoslovak Acad. Sci., 1993, Purkyne gold medal Med. Faculty Masaryk U., Brno, 1993. Mem. Royal Microscopical Soc., Soc. of Gen. Microbiology, Brit. Soc. for Cell Biology. Achievements include disclosing the mechanism of action of penicillin; discovering the fine structure of leukemia viruses, the molecular organization of HIV new model. Home: 12 Milton Rd, London NW7 4AX, England Office: Nat Inst Biol Stds & Contrl, South Mimms Potters Bar, Hertfordshire EN6 3QG, England

NERMUTH, MANFRED, economics educator; b. Vienna, Austria, Mar. 5, 1948; s. Josef and Helene (Brandes) N. PhD in Math., U. Vienna, 1973, postgrad., 1981. Rsch. student Cambridge U., Eng., 1974-75; asst. prof. U. Bonn, Federal Republic of Germany, 1975-76, U. Catholique de Louvain, Belgium, 1976-77; asst. prof. U. Vienna, 1977-80, univ.-dozent, 1981-85, prof. econs., 1989—; assoc. prof. Cornell U., Ithaca, N.Y., 1980-81; prof. econs. U. Bielefeld, Federal Republic of Germany, 1985-89. Author: Information Structures in Economics, 1982; contbr. articles to profl. jours. Office: U Vienna Dept Econs, Hohenstaufengasse 9, 1010 Vienna 1010, Austria

NERNEY, AMANDA ELIZABETH, management trainer and coach; b. Manchester, Eng., July 3, 1969; d. James Joseph and Dorothy Bernadette (Bebbington) N. Cert. in tng. and devel., 1991; diploma in tng. mgmt., 1992, in counseling, 1996. Jr. Frankeuk Sales, Manchester, Eng., 1985-87; sales exec. Best Western Hotels, Manchester, Eng., 1987-90; sales mgr. Copthorne Hotels, Manchester, Eng., 1990-91; asst. account mgr. Tyndall & Co. Bankers, Bristol, Eng., 1990-91; trainer, adminstr. H.A.T.S., Manchester, Eng., 1991-92; mng. cons. Optimum Tng. Consultancy, Manchester, Eng., 1992—; br. sec., com. mem. Inst. of Tng. & Devel., Eng., 1992-94. Author: First Aid at Work Manual, 1994, revised edit., 1998, First Aid 2000 plus, 2000. Vol. Brit. Territorial Army, 1988-95, Stroke Assn., 1992-93. Mem. Inst. of Personnel and Devel. (diploma). Roman Catholic. Avocations: scuba diving, skiing, adventure travel. Office: Optimum Tng Consultancy, 15 Castle St, Ashton-U-Lyne Chester Cheshire CH1 2DS, England

NERUKH, ALEXANDER GEORGIEVICH, mathematics educator, researcher; b. Akhtyrka, Sumy, Ukraine, June 3, 1944; s. Georgy Timofeevich Nerukh and Polina Andreevna Pilipko; m. Helen Alexandrovna Novoselova, Mar. 22, 1968; children: Dmitry, Daria. Grad. in radiophysics, U. Kharkov, Ukraine, 1968, Cand Sci, 1975, DSc, 1991. Engr. State U., Kharkov, 1968-71; rsch. worker State U., 1974-77; assoc. prof. math. Inst. Radioelectronics, Tech. U. Radioelectronics, Kharkov, 1977-91, prof., 1991—, head dept., 1994—. Grantee Internat. Soros Found., 1993, Internat. Soros Sci. Edn. Program, 1996. Mem. IEEE, Trans Black Sea Regional Sci. Union, N.Y. Acad. Scis. Office: Kharkov Tech U Radioelec, Lenin Ave 14, 61166 Kharkov Ukraine

NERY, EDUARDO, painter; b. Figueira da Foz, Portugal, Sept. 2, 1938; s. Sebastiao Jose and Maria Elisa (Nery) Oliveira; m. Ana Maria Pacheco Vieira, Nov. 22, 1965 (div. 1981); children: Miguel, Paula; m. Maria da Graca Marques Maia, Dec. 17, 1988. Diploma in painting, Fine Arts Acad. Lisbon, 1969; student under painter Jean Lurcat, Saint-Cere, France, 1960-61. instr. Instituto de Artes Visuais e Design SA, Lisbon, 1970-72, ARCO Centro de Arte e Comunicacão Visual, Lisbon, 1973-75; lectr. on art themes and guide on visits to art mus. Artist numerous various projects for mural paintings, ceramic tile panels including Internat. Airport Macao in China, mural reliefs, stained glasses, interior and exterior walls and one cupola in mosaic, metallic railing designs, large paving designs in two colors of stone in big squares, the decoration of a new underground station in Lisbon, in two new railway stations in Oporto and in Lisbon; author several studies and projects of color for facades in bldgs. and for housing devels., in which it is included the environ. color planning of two new Portuguese towns; one-man shows Portugal, Centre Culturel Portugais, Paris, 1973, Wenger Gallery, San Diego, 1983, The Judge Gallery, Washington, 1984; group shows with paintings, drawings, prints, photography, tapestry, and ceramics in more than 200 shows in Portugal, U.S., France, Eng., Italy, Spain, Belgium, Germany, Sweden, Switerland, Poland, Hungary, Finland, Monaco, Japan, Brazil, Colombia, Can., South Africa, Taiwan, among others; represented in Everson Mus. Art, Syracuse, N.Y., Taipei Fine Arts Mus., Taiwan, 16 Portuguese art mus., including Centro de Arte Moderna, Calouste Gulbenkian Found., Lisbon, Serralves Found., Oporto. Mem. Comissão Nacional de Socorro aos Presos Politicos, 1969-74. Recipient Soquil 69, Portuguese Art Critique prize, 1969, II Palme d'Or des Beaux-Arts, Internat. Arts Guild, 1969, Mobil Arte, 1970, I Bienal Internat. de Obidos, 1987, silver and gold medals Tommaso Campanella Acad. Rome, 1970, 72, medal of artistic merit Govt. Macao, 1996, 4 Lisbon Mcpl. prizes in ceramic tiles, 1987, 91, 92, 95, prize Bordalo/Art '95, Portuguese Press Prize, 1996, I Biennale Internat. de Arte Contemporaneo Europeo, Sta Margherita Ligure, 1975, Lombardia 75 Milan, 1975, IV Giacinto Gigante 76, 1976, San Marco 76, 1976, V Giacinto Gigante 77, 1977, photography prize III Bienal Internat. de Arte de Cerveira, 1982. Mem. Sociedade Nacional de Belas Artes, Associacao Nacional dos Artistas Plasticos. Avocation: photography. Home: Rua S Bernardo, 102 2o, 1200-826 Lisbon Portugal Studio: Rua Coelho da Rocha 69, Atelier 15, 1350 Lisbon Portugal

NES, DAVID GULICK, retired diplomat; b. York, Pa., Feb. 17, 1917; s. Charles Motier and Ethel (Billmeyer) N.; m. Elizabeth Taylor Houghton, Dec. 7, 1946; children: Victoria, Nancy, Margaret, Audrey, Wendy. AB in History with hons., Princeton U., 1939; postgrad., Harvard U., 1939-40. With Balt. Sun, 1940-41; div. asst. Dept. State, Washington, 1941-42; fgn. svc. officer Dept. State, 1946-68, assigned to Washington, 1952-54, 56-59; vice consul Am. Consulate, Glasgow, Scotland, 1946-49; 2d sec. Am. Embassy, Paris, 1949-52; dep. chief mission, counselor Tripoli, 1954-56, Rabat, 1959-62; dep. chief mission min. Saigon, Vietnam, 1963-64, Cairo, 1965-67; ret., 1968; columnist, lectr. in field, 1968—. Capt. AUS, 1942-46, CBI. Decorated Bronze Star. Mem. Chevy Chase Golf Club, Green Spring Valley Hunt Club, West River Sailing Club, N.Y. Yacht Club. Home: 15 Crestline Ct Owings Mills MD 21117-4336

NESBIT, GARY MERLIN, neuroradiologist, educator. Student, Winona State U., 1978-79; BA in Chemistry, St. Olaf Coll., 1982; MD, U. Minn., 1986. Diplomate Am. Bd. Radiology added qualification in neuroradiology, Nat. Bd. Med. Examiners. Radiology resident Mayo Grad. Sch. Medicine, Rochester, Minn., 1986-90; neuroradiology fellow Mayo Grad. Sch. Medicine, Rochester, 1990-91; asst. clin. prof. U. Calif. Sch. Medicine, San Diego, 1992-94; dir. neuroradiology and spl. studies U.S. Naval Med. Ctr., San Diego, 1993-94; interventional neuroradiology fellow Oreg. Health Scis. U., Dotter Interventional Inst., Portland, Oreg., 1994-96; instr. Oreg. Health Scis. U., Dotter Interventional Inst., Portland, 1994-95, asst. prof., 1995-99, assoc. prof., 1999—; interim chief neuroradiology and MRI Oreg. Health Scis. U., Portland, 1995-96, chief neuroradiology and MRI, 1996—; assoc. cons. neuroradiology Mayo Clinic, Rochester, 1991; presenter in field. Manuscript reviewer Am. Jour. Neuroradiology, 1994—; guest editor Neuroimaging Clinics of North America, 1999. Mem. Am. Soc. Neuroradiology (sr. mem. 1992—, mem./chmn. sci. exhibits com. 1998—), Radiol. Soc. N.Am., Western Neuroradiol. Soc. (chmn. membership com. 1997-98), Soc. Cardiovascular and Interventional Radiology, Am. Soc. Interventional and Therapeutic Neuroradiology, Alpha Omega Alpha. E-mail: nesbitg@ohsu.edu. Fax: 503-494-7129. Office: Oreg Health Scis Univ CR 135 3181 SW Sam Jackson Park Rd Portland OR 97201-3011

NESBITT, ROBERT EDWARD LEE, JR., physician, educator, scientific researcher, writer, poet; b. Albany, Ga., Aug. 21, 1924; s. Robert E.L. and Anne Louise (Hill) N.; m. Ellen Therese Morrissey. BA, Vanderbilt U., 1944, MD, 1947. Diplomate: Am. Bd. Ob-Gyn (asso. examiner). Asst. prof. Johns Hopkins U., 1954-56, chief obstetric pathology lab., acting chief obstetrics, 1955-56; prof., chmn. dept. ob-gyn Albany (N.Y.) Med. Coll., Union U., 1956-61; prof., chmn. dept. ob-gyn SUNY Health Sci. Ctr., Syracuse, 1961-81, dir. gen. gynecology service, 1982-84, prof. and chmn. emeritus dept. ob-gyn; obstetrician-gynecologist-in-chief Albany Hosp., 1956-61; obstetrician, gynecologist-in-chief Syracuse Meml. Hosp., 1961-65; obstetrician-gynecologist-in-chief Crouse-Irving Hosp., 1963-70, attending staff, 1970-84; chief prof. surgery U. South Fla., Tampa, 1988-92, prof. ob.-gyn., 1988-92; chief ob-gyn State U. Hosp., 1964-81, chmn. med. staff and med. bd., 1964-66; attending staff St. Joseph's Hosp.; cons., chief gynecology sect. surg. service Syracuse VA Hosp., 1984-88; chief gynecology sect., asst. chief surgery, dir. uro-gynecology VA Med. Ctr., Bay Pines, Fla., 1988-92, acting chief of staff, 1990, interim chief surgery, 1991-92, chmn. O.R. com. surg. svc., 1988-92, chmn. patient care evaluation com., 1989-90, chmn. clin. exec. bd., 1990, chmn. drug usage evaluation com., 1990-91, chmn. profl. standards bd., 1990; cons. Syracuse Psychiat. Inst.; mem. cancer tng. grants and edn. com. Nat. Cancer Insts.; mem. adv. com. Bur. Maternal and Child Health, N.Y. State Dept. Health, 1957-61; nat. adviser to Children, publ. of Children's Bur., HEW, 1959-63; cons. Children's Bur., 1959-62; mem. prenatal care guide subcom. Am. Pub. Health Assn., 1962-64; cons. to regional adviser in maternal and child health Pan Am. San. Bur., WHO, 1963-65; numerous guest professorships including univs. in Mex., Chile, Uruguay, Colombia, St. Vincent (W.I.), Venezuela, People's Republic of China, Western Europe, Panama, Australia, Canada; numerous guest professorships including univs. in others. Author: Perinatal Loss in Modern Obstetrics, 1957, Last Twig on the Bush?, 1999, In the Fullness of Time, 1999, (poetry collections) Chorales for Arid Souls, 1999, The Fullness Search, 2000, Visions Shared, 2000, Daily Relevance, 2000; also poems in numerous anthologies; sect. on ob-gyn in Rypin's Med. Licensure Exams; co-author: Infant, Perinatal, Maternal and Childhood Mortality in U.S. 1968; editor: sect. on obstetrics and gynecology Stedman's Medical Dictionary, 1958-64, sect. on fetus Funk and Wagnalls Universal Std. Ency., 1959; 1st guest editor: sect. on fetus Clinics in Perinatology, 1974; 1st editor: sect. on fetus Clinical Diagnosis Quiz for Obstetrics and Gynecology, 1976, Clini-Pearls in Obstetrics and Gynecology, 1977; contbr.: sect. on fetus Attorneys' Textbook of Medicine. Capt. M.C., U.S. Army, 1952-54. Named One of Ten Outstanding Young Men in Am., U.S. Jr. C. of C., 1957; Robert E.L. Nesbitt Jr. scholarship, Sr. Resident in Ob-Gyn, and Robert E.L. Nesbitt Jr. student scholarship established in his honor, SUNY Health Sci. Ctr. at Syracuse, 1987. Fellow Am. Assn. Maternal and Child Health, Am. Coll. Obstetricians and Gynecologists (chmn. com. mental retardation and perinatal health 1966), A.C.S. (com. forum fundamental surg. problems 1962-67), Venezuelan Obstetrics-Gynecol. Soc. (hon.), N.Y. Acad. Scis.; mem. AMA (mem. residency accreditation com., site visit team mem.), Soc. for Gynecol. Investigation (council), Pan Am. Med. Assn. (med. ambassador goodwill, life mem. sect. on cancer), Med. Soc. N.Y. State (regional obstetrics chmn., subcom. Maternal and Child Welfare), Onondaga County Med. Soc., Am. Soc. Cytology, Pub. Health Council N.Y. State, Internat. Soc. Poets, Alpha Omega Alpha; hon. mem. Southwest, Fla. obstet. and gynecol. socs., others. Achievements include research and 230 publications on cytologic, cytochemical and histochemical study of early cervical cancer, perinatal and placental pathology, cytologic and hormonal studies in normal and high-risk obstetrics patients, experimental production of abruptio placentae, reproductive endocrinology, animal experimentation, induced endocrine insults upon pregnant and nonpregnant ewes and hormonal influence on placentation, invitro placenta perfusion, fetal growth and development, female urology, surgical techniques for restoration of female pelvic floor integrity; human spirituality; inspirational poetry. Home: 11639 Grove St North Seminole FL 33772-7137

NESBITT, VERONICA A., management executive; b. Henderson, Tenn., June 10, 1959; d. Hiawatha Daniel and Laura Mae (Green) Thompson; divorced; children: Shemenya A. Davis, Maleka L. Cert. stenographer, Miller-Hawkins B. Coll., 1979; Cert. data transcriber, IRS, Memphis, Tenn., 1981; Cert. computer operator, U.S. Army, Newport News, Va., 1985, Cert. computer programmer, 1987; postgrad., Columbia Coll., 1990. Cert. computer opr. Stenographer Memphis & Shelby County Health Dept., Memphis, 1979-80; cash clk./data transcriber IRS, Memphis, 1980-82; data transcriber U.S. Army, Fort Sheridan, Ill., 1982-83; work order clk. U.S. Army, Fort Sheridan, 1984-85, quality control clk., 1985-89; mgmt. asst. HQ USAREC, Fort Sheridan, Ill., 1989-92; data transcriber Selective Svc., North Chicago, Ill., 1983-84; telemarketer Allstate Ins. Co., Northbrook, Ill., 1986-88; unit supr. Allstate Ins. Co., Glenview, Ill., 1988-92; employee coun., 1994; total quality facilitator Allstate Ins. Co., Glenview, Ill., 1992; mgmt. asst. Hdqs. US Army Recruiting Command, Ft. Knox, Ky., 1992-94, 233d Base Support Bn., Darmstadt, Germany, 1994-97; staffing specialist Snelling Staffing Network, Columbia, Md., 1997-99; exec. adminstrv. asst. GSE Sys., Inc., Columbia, Md., 1999; mgmt. analyst Navy Internat. Programs/INS, Inc., 1999—; mgmt. analyst, INS, Inc., Washington, 1999—; chmn. task force Allstate, Glenview, 1990; interviewer Mathematica Policy Rsch., Inc., Columbia, Md., 1998-99, supr., 1999—. Mem. Am. Heart Disease Found., 1991-92, Easter Seal Soc., 1991-92, March of Dimes, 1991—, Nat. Heart Rsch., 1991-95; mem. Nat. Cancer Rsch., 1991-95, fed. women's program mgr., 1995-97; treas. Second Glance Thrift Store, 1996-97; welfare com., continuing edn. grants Darmstadt Women's Club, 1995-96, chmn. Second Glance Thrift Store; counselor Equal Employment Opportunity, 1995-97; mem. Equal Opportunity Adv. Action Team, 1995-97; assoc. matron Everlasting Light #28, Order Ea. Star, Prince Hall Affiliated, 1997. Mem. NAFE, Am. Cancer Soc., Am. Heart Disease Prevention Found., Jack Anderson Internat. Platform Assn. Baptist. Avocations: reading, knitting, drama, bicycling, sewing. Office: Navy Internat Programs Office Nebraska Ave Complex 4255 Mt Vernon Dr Ste 17100 Washington DC 20393-5445

NESETRIL, JAROSLAV, mathematics educator; b. Brno, Czech Republic, Mar. 13, 1946; s. Otakar and Blazena (Vackova) N.; m. Helena Bustova, 1970; 1 child, Jakub. BS, McMaster U., Hamilton, Ont., 1969; RNDR, Charles U., Prague, 1970; CSc., Charles U., 1975, DSc, 1988. Asst. prof. Charles U., Prague, 1970-88; assoc. prof., 1988-92, prof., 1992—; dir. Dimatia Ctr., Prague, 1996. Author: Mathematics of Ramsey Theory, 1992, Mathematics of Paul Erdös, 1997, Invitation to Discrete Mathematics, 1998, Anthropogeometry (2 vols.), 1999. Recipient State Prize Czechoslovakia, 1985. Mem. Nordrhein-Westphalia Acad. Scis. (fgn.). Home: Cechova 587, CZ-25263 Roztoky Czech Republic Office: Charles U, Malostranské Nám 25, CZ11800 Prague Czech Republic

NESHYBA, VICTOR PETER, retired aerophysics engineer; b. New Ulm, Tex., Oct. 8, 1922; s. Peter and Anna (Zietz) N.; m. Mary Cecilia Gwazdacz, Jan. 6, 1945; children: Victor Jr., Ronald, Janice, Mary Lee, Valiant, Michele, Dolores, Keith, David. BSEE, U. Calif., 1949; diploma, Mass. Inst. Tech., 1968, Naval Intelligence Sch., 1950. Registered profl. engr., Tex. Commd. 2d lt. USMC, 1942-47, advance through grades to col., 1970; aerophysics engr. Gen. Dynamics, Ft. Worth, Tex., 1957-62; data transmission and interface mgr. Gemini and Shuttle programs NASA, Houston, 1962-73; pres. Ener-G-Eco, Inc., Dickinson, Tex., 1974-80; owner, gen. mgr. Star Square Ranches, Wilson, Galveston, Colorado counties, Tex., 1980—; dir. Rabbit Hill Sch. Charity Found. Precinct chmn. Rep. Party, Galveston, Tex., 1974-76; sch. bd. Cath. Diocesan Schs., 1968. Decorated Medal of Honor by Shah of Iran, 1952; recipient Mgmt. award U.S. pres., 1970; Hugh W. Dryden fellow NASA, 1967, 68. Mem. Profl. Engrs. of Tex., Marine Corps. Res. Officers Assn., Former Marines of Tex. Assn. (life), Rep. Senatorial Club, VFW, Knights of Columbus (4th degree), Min. of the Word, Shrine of True Cross. Roman Catholic. Avocations: reading, research.

NESIS, KIR NAZIMOVICH, marine biologist; b. Moscow, Jan. 9, 1934; s. Nazim Zinovievich and Sofia Josifovna (Rozova) N.; m. Tatjana Nikolaevna Semenova, May 25, 1963; 1 child, Anna Kirovna Nessis. DS in Marine Biology. Marine biologist Polar Inst. Marine Fisheries and Oceanography, 1956-60, 63-66; jr. rsch. scientist, sr. rsch. scientist, head lab. P.P. Shishov Inst. Oceanology (Now Russian Acad. Scis.), 1967—. Editor-in-chief Ruthenica: Russian Malacological Jour.; mem. editl. bd. Okeanologiya, Biologiya morya, Priroda; contbr. articles to profl. jours. Mem. Malacological Soc. Russia (v.p.), Plenum Ichthyological Commn. Avocation: reading. Office: PP Shirshov Inst Oceanology, 36 Nakhimov Ave, 117218 Moscow Russia

NESLAND, JAMES EDWARD, lawyer; b. Mobridge, S.D., Aug. 13, 1944; s. Virgil Robert and Thelma Loretta Nesland; m. Carol Ann Ide, Nov. 9, 1946; children: Matthew James, John Edward. BA, U. Denver, 1966; JD, George Washington U., 1970. Bar: N.Y. 1971, U.S. Dist. Ct. (so. dist.) N.Y. 1971, U.S. Ct. Appeals (2nd cir.) 1971, U.S. D.C. Colo. 1976, U.S. Ct. Appeals (10th cir.) 1976, Colo. 1977, U.S. Supreme Ct. 1988. Assoc. Donovan Leisure Newton & Irvine, N.Y.C., 1970-73; asst. U.S. atty. U.S. Atty.'s Office, N.Y.C., 1973-76, Denver, 1977-78; assoc., ptnr. Ireland, Stapleton LLC, Denver, 1978-94; ptnr. Cooley Godward LLP, Denver, 1994—; assoc. spl. coun. Pres. Jimmy Carter Warehouse Inv., 1979. Author: Federal Criminal Law, 1988. Mem. ABA, Colo. Bar Assn., Denver Bar Assn. Home: 14252 E Caley Ave Aurora CO 80016-1090 Office: Cooley Godward LLP 1200 17th St Ste 2100 Denver CO 80202-5821

NESMELOVA, IRINA VLADISLAVOVNA, research scientist, physicist; b. Kazan, Russia, Sept. 8, 1968; d. Vladislav Nikolaevich and Tamara Alexandrovna (Frolova) Serebrennikov; m. Yuriy Eugenévich Nesmelov, Aug. 10, 1990; 1 child, Andrei. BS, Kazan State U., 1990, PhD, 1998. Jr. rsch. scientist Kazan Med. Inst., 1990-92, Kazan Biol. Inst. and State U., 1995-98; postdoctoral assoc. U. Minn., Mpls., 1999—. Kazan Inst. Biology grant, 1997-98.

NESMITH, KIMBLIN EUGENE, law educator; b. Jacksonville, Fla., Sept. 19, 1963; s. James and Elizabeth (Crawley) N.; m. Lisa Jeanette Brown, Jan. 1, 1994 (div. Jan. 3, 1997); 1 child, Lana Imani Jene'. BS in Experimental Psychology, Morehouse Coll., Atlanta, 1985; JD in Corp. Bus. Transactions, U. Miami Law Sch., 1991; postgrad., Yale U., 1987-89, Northwestern U., 1994. Adj. prof. U. North Fla. Coll. Bus., Jacksonville, 1992-94; assoc. prof. Edward Waters Coll., Jacksonville, 1993—; asst. prof., chmn. Divsn. Criminal Justice, Jacksonville, 1993—; adjunct prof. Webster U., Jacksonville, 1996; exec. dir. Ctr. for Commerce and Trade at Edwards Waters Coll., Jacksonville, 1996—, Inst. for Global Entrepreneurship at Edwards Waters Coll., Jacksonville, 1996—; v.p. Henry Roberts Gourmet Food Co., Jacksonville, 1998—; faculty rep., mem. Bd. Trustees Edward Waters Coll., Jacksonville, 1996—; vice chmn. Cmty. Alliance Devel. Corp., Jacksonville, 1996—. mem. Jacksonville Chpt. NAACP. Recipient Outstanding Achievement, William R. Raines Sr. H.S., Jacksonville, 1998, Recognition of Disting. Accomplishment Boys & Girls, Inc., Jacksonville Housing Authority and The Tenant Adv., Jakcsonville, 1998, Outstanding Accomplishment, S.P. Livingston Elem., Jacksonville, 1998; named Outstanding Guest Spke., Fla. C.C. of Jacksonville, Downtown Campus, 1998. Mem. Daniel Webster Perkins Bar Assn., First Coast Micro Loan Program, First Coast African-Am. C. of C., Morehouse Coll. Alumni Assn. Avocations: writing and reading books and articles on wealth, lecturing on entrepreneurship, exercising. E-mail address: kenesmith@lib.ewc.edu. Fax: 904-366-2723. Home: 6161 Pettiford Dr W Jacksonville FL 32209-1843 Office: Edward Waters Coll 1658 Kings Rd Jacksonville FL 32209-6167

NESOFF, ROBERT, newspaper publisher; b. Bronx, N.Y., July 6, 1938; s. Hyman and Sally Leah (Reznikoff) N.; m. Sandra Roberta Levine, June 27, 1965; children: Wendy Naimaister, Barbara Thorson, Karen Nesoff. Editor Country Wide Publs., N.Y.C., 1964-65; reporter The Record, Hackensack, N.J., 1965-66, Newark News, 1966-72; pub. Metro Publs. Group/Metro Feature Syndicate, Oradell, N.J., 1972—, Palisadian Newspaper, East Bergen, N.J., 1984—; pub. rels. cons. U.S. Homes Corp., 1973, Best Western Internat. Hotels, 1979, tourism ministries Republics of Guatemala, 1979-80, Panama, 1979-81, Kenya, 1985; former N.Y. State pub. rels. dir. Common Cause, N.Y.C. Mcpl. Svcs. Adminstrn., 1974-75; pub. rels. dir. N.J. State Assn. Chiefs of Police, Bergen County Police Chiefs Assn.; com. dir. Bergen County Sheriff's Dept., 2000—; instr. police-press rels. Bergen County Police Acad., 1970-75; nat. rep., spokesman Fed. Criminal Investigators Assn., 1974-85; mem. Stein Commn., N.Y. State Commn., dir. info. and investigations.; dir. investigations into funeral home abuses; expert witness FTC, 1975; appeared on numerous radio and TV shows including 20/20, Sta. KABC, L.A., Sta. WABC Radio, N.Y., Eleanor Guggenheim Consumer show on Channel 5, Richard Bey, Jackie Mason shows on Sta. WWOR-TV; sgt. Bergen County SPCA Law Enforcement Agy., 1997—. Author: Never a Doubt, 1996; contbg. editor Lifestyles mag., 1997—; columnist Metro Feature Svc., 1972—; radio and TV appearances. Pres. sch. bd. New Milford, N.J., 1983-90, Ctrl. Bergen Crime Stoppers Orgn.; councilman City of New Milford, 1990-99, pres. coun., 1996-98, 99; pres. New Milford Jewish Ctr., 1991-92, past bd. dirs.; past trustee New Milford Swim Club, past sec., v.p., 1980-83; former coach Princess League Softball, 1983; scoutmaster Boy Scouts Am., New Milford; mem. N.J. Dem. State Com., 1997—, Dem. County Com., 1998—, Bergen County Task Force on Youth Violence, Bias Crimes sub-com., 1994, Bergen County Bicentennial Com., 1976, Family Life Curriculum Com.; commr. New Bridge Landing Pk. Commn., 1996-98. Sgt. U.S. Army 11th Spl. Forces Group (Green Berets), 1962-64. Recipient Heroism award N.Y.C. Police Dept., cert. of recognition Newark Police Dept., Voice of Democracy award VFW, cert. of appreciation NCCJ, Citizenship award Am. Legion, cert. of appreciation Kiwanis, Pax Et Justicia plaque Royal St. Vincent Police Force, Grenadine Islands, 30 awards from various press assns.; named hon. mem. Fed. Criminal Investigators Assn., Leonia (N.J.) Police Dept. SWAT Team. Mem. N.Am. Travel Journalists Assn. (pres. 1989-96, Best Profile Feature, 1996, other awards), Working press Assn. N.J. (pres. 1987-90, Best Edtl. Writer 1985-86, 90-91, 93, 95, Best Column 1990, Best Critical Rev. 1991-95, Gold Medal award), North Jersey Press Assn. (pres. 1972-73, 76-77, 81-83), N. Am. Ski Journalists Assn., Ea. Ski Writers Assn. (bd. dirs. 1998—), Jewish War Vets. (comdr. Wallach-Gold-Moses Post #773 1996-97). Democrat. Jewish. Avocations: skiing, scuba diving. Office: Metro Publs Group/Metro Feature Syndicate PO Box 104 Oradell NJ 07649-0104

NESS, ALBERT KENNETH, artist; b. St. Ignace, Mich., June 21, 1903; s. Albert Klingberg and Violet Matilda (Sutherland); m. Lenore Consuelo Chrisman, Aug. 4, 1926; children: Peter, James Kenneth, Jane Lenore. Student U. Detroit, 1923-24, Detroit Sch. of Applied Art, 1924-26, Wicker Sch. of Fine Art, 1926-28; Diploma, Sch. of Art Inst., 1932. Show-card writer, window display man S.S. Kresge Co., Detroit, 1923-24; artist poster and advt. Cunningham Drugs, Detroit, 1924-26; artist layout lettering and design W.L. Flemming Studios, Detroit, 1926-28, McAleer Displays, Chgo., 1929-32; artist, design asst. Layman-Whitney Assocs., 1933 World's Fair, Chgo.; layout artist, poster designer Elevated Advt. Co., Chgo., 1934-37; instr., art dir. Sch. of Applied Art, Chgo., 1938-40; Carnegie resident artist U. N.C., Chapel Hill, 1941-43, dir. War Art Ctr., 1942-43, resident artist, assoc. prof. art, 1943-49, acting head, dept. art, acting dir. Person Hall Art Gallery, 1944-45, resident artist, prof. art, 1949-73, acting head dept. of art, acting dir. Person Hall Art Gallery, 1955, 57-58, resident artist, prof. emeritus, 1973—. One man shows include: Chester Johnson Galleries, Chgo., 1932, Evanston Art Ctr., Ill., 1940, Person Hall Art Gallery, 1941, N.C. Art Soc. Gallery, Raleigh, 1942, Duke U. Art Gallery, Durham, N.C., 1955, Louisburg Coll. Gallery, N.C., 1964, Ackland Art Mus., U.N.C. Chapel Hill, 1973; Internat. Water Color Exhbn. Chgo. Art Inst., 1934-39; Golden Gate Internat. Exposition, San Francisco, 1939, exhibited in group shows: Whitney Mus., N.Y.C., 1933, U. Chattanooga, Tenn., 1946, Centennial Exhbn. U. Fla., Gainesville, 1953, Jacksonville Art Mus, Fla., 1960; exhibited nationally Am. Artists' Anns., Chgo. Art Inst., 1935-37, Butler Art Inst., Youngstown, Ohio, 1951, Pa. Acad. Am. Annuals, Phila., 1953-54, Optique Gallery, Lambertville, N.J., 1991—, Ross-Constantine Gallery, N.Y.C., 1991—, others; works in pub. collections include: N.C. Mus., Raleigh, Ackland Art Mus., Reynolds Found., Winston Salem, Duke U. Art Mus., Durham. Contbr. to local and state newspapers. Editor, designer, photographer: A brochure on art study, 1964. Recipient Jenkins Meml. prize 38th Ann. Chgo. Artists' Exhbn., 1934, Purchase award N.C. Artists' Ann., Raleigh, 1953; 2-Star award Movie Maker Competition, London, 1970, N.C. award in Fine Arts, 1973, Purchase award Reynolds Competition, Winston Salem, 1977. Home: PO Box 14 Chapel Hill NC 27514-0014

NESSA, JOHN NIKOLAUS, physician; b. Hjelmeland, Rogaland, Norway, Mar. 10, 1949; s. Lars and Doris (Staurland) N.; m. Kirsti Flato, Oct. 14, 1979; children: Lars, Kyrre, Dyre. MD, U. Oslo, 1979; PhD, U. Bergen, 1999. Cert. specialist gen. practice. Physician Psychiatric Ward, Stavanger,

Norway, 1982-84; pvt. practice Gloppen, Norway, 1984-85, Hjelmeland, 1985—. Contbr. articles to profl. jours. Officer Norwegian mil., 1981-83. Mem. Norwegian Med. Assn., Royal Coll. Gen. Practitioners. Lutheran. Avocations: philosphy, farming. Home: Bratthetland, 4139 Fister Rogaland, Norway Office: Community, 4130 Hjelmeland Norway

NESTERENKO, YEVGENIY YEVGENIYEVICH, singer, vocal art educator; b. Moscow, Jan. 8, 1938; s. Yevgeniy Nikiforovich Nesterenko and Velta Woldemarovna Baumann; m. Yekaterina Dmitrievna Alexeyeva; 1 child, Maxim Yevgeniyevich. Diploma in engring., Engring and Bldg. Inst., Leningrad, USSR, 1961; grad., Rimsky-Korsakov Conservatoire, Leningrad, 1965. Engr. Lensovnarkhoz, Leningrad, 1961-62; soloist Maly Theatre Opera and Ballet, Leningrad, 1963-67, Kirov Theatre Opera and Ballet, Leningrad, 1967-71, Bolshoi Theatre, Moscow, 1971—; vocal tchr. Leningrad Conservatoire, 1967-72, Musical-Pedagogical Inst. Gnessin, Moscow, 1972-75; prof., chmn. vocal dept. Tchaikovsky Conservatoire, Moscow, 1975-93, prof. Konservatorium Der Stadt Wien, Austria, 1993—. Author: Thoughts on My Profession, 1985. Named People's Artist Govt. USSR, 1976, Hero of Labour Govt. USSR, 1988; recipient Lenin prize, 1982, Golden Disc, Melodia, USSR, 1984, Giovanni Zenatello prize City of Verona, Italy, 1986, Viotti d'Oro prize City of Vercelli, Italy, 1981, Wilhelm-Furtwängler-Preis City of Baden-Baden, Germany, 1992, Shaliapin prize City of Moscow, Russia, 1992, Titel Austrian Kammersänger, 1992. Mem. Acad. Creative Endeavors (Moscow). Home: Riemergasse 10/14, A-1010 Vienna Austria Office: Konservatorium Stadt Wien, Johannesgasse 4A, A-1010 Vienna Austria

NESTEROV, ALEXANDER ILYICH, physicist, researcher, educator; b. Krasnogorsk, Russia, June 22, 1950; s. Ilya Arkadievich and Maria Pavlovna (Ogloblina) N.; m. Elena Dmitrievna Pashennyh, May 12, 1972; children: Sergey, Ilya. PhD, Peoples' Friendship U., Moscow, 1976; DrSci, Krasnoyarsk (Russia) State U., 1989. Cert. prof., Moscow. Asst. prof. Krasnoyarsk State U., 1977-80, sr. lectr., 1980-84, assoc. prof., 1984-86, 88-90, sr. rschr., 1986-88, prof., 1990-97; vis. prof. Guadalajara (Mex.) U., 1993-94, prof., rschr., 1994—. Author: (with N.V. Mitskievich and A.P. Yefremov) Dynamics of Fields in General Relativity, 1985; contbr. articles to profl. jours. Recipient Honorable Mention awrd Gravity Rsch. Found., 1988; Internat. Sci. Found. grantee, 1993, Gravity Rsch. Found. grantee, 1994, 96. Mem. Russian Gravitational Soc., Mex. Phys. Soc., Am. Phys. Soc., Am. Math. Soc., Mex. Acad. of Sci. Avocation: bicycling. Home: Fray Antonio de Segovia 729, Guadalajara 44840, Mexico Office: Blvd M Garcia Barragan y Calz Olimpica, Olimpica Guadalajara 44460, Mexico

NESTEROV, YURII EUGENIEVICH, mathematician, researcher, educator; b. Moscow, Jan. 25, 1956; s. Eugenij F. and Olga D. (Frolova) N.; m. Svetlana Ivanovna Volkova, Dec. 25, 1982; children: André, Dimitri. MS, Moscow U., 1977; PhD in Math., Inst. Control Problems, Moscow, 1984. Rschr. Ctrl. Econ. and Math. Inst., Moscow, 1977-84, leading rschr., 1985-93; prof. math. Cath. U. Louvain, Belgium, 1993—. Author: Efficient Methods in Nonlinear Programming, 1989, Lectures on Convex Optimization, 1998; co-author: (with A. Nemirovskii): Interior-point Polynomial Algorithms in Convex Programming, 1994; contbr. articles to profl. jours. Recipient Dantzig prize Math. Programming Soc., 2000. Home: 42 rue Victor Horta, 1348 Louvain-la-Neuve Belgium Office: Cath U of Louvain/ CORE, 34 voie du Roman Pays, 1348 Louvain-la-Neuve Belgium

NESTOR CASTELLANO, BRENDA DIANA, real estate company executive; b. Palm Beach, Fla., Nov. 10, 1955; d. John Joseph and Marion O'Connor Nestor; m. Robert Castellano. Student, U. Miami, Fla., 1978. Lic. real estate broker, Fla. Salesman Oscar E Dooley, Inc., Miami, Fla., 1978-80; prin. Brenda Nestor Assocs, Inc., Miami Beach, Fla., 1980—; exec. v.p., bd. dirs. D.W.G. Corp., 1988-94, N.V.F. Corp., Salem Corp., 1988-97, Southeastern Pub. Svc., Graniteville Corp., 1988-94, Essex Ins., Chesapeake Ins.; exec. v.p., dir. Security Mgmt. Bd. dirs. Vizceyan Mus.; dir. Miami's Jackson Meml. Found. Named Ms. Charity, City of Miami, 1985, Lady Comdr., State of Fla. Mem. Miami Beach Bd. Realtors (bd. dirs. 1984—), Real Estate Securities and Exch. Com., Knights of Malta, Doubles Club (N.Y.C.), La Gorce Country Club, Fisher Island Club, Bath Club, Surf Club. Roman Catholic. Avocations: golf, tennis, boating, skiing. Home and Office: 6917 Collins Ave Miami FL 33141-3263

NESTURI, DIONIS, agronomist, educator. Grad., Agrl. U. Tirana, Albania, 1964. Agronomist, head of agronomists Farm of Thumana, Kruja, 1964-77; lectr. in chair field crops faculty agronomy Agrl. U. Tirana, 1977-85, chmn. field crops chair, 1985—, head dept. plant prodn., 1989-91, senate mem., 1998-99. Author: Phytotechnics, 1987, Field Crops, 1988, Forage Crops, 1989; contbr. chpts. to books and articles to profl. jours. Fax: 355 42 27804. Office: Faculty Agr Dept Crop Prodn, Agrl Univ Tirana, Tirana Albania

NESVIJSKI, EDOUARD G., materials engineer, educator, researcher; b. Livov, Ukraine, Jan. 2, 1948; s. Grigory I. and Nadezhda I. (Kulagina) N.; m. Tatiana E. Choutova, June 2, 1990. MS in Elec. and Underwater Acoustics, Kiev (Ukraine) Poly. U., 1972; PhD, Moscow State U. Civil Engring., 1984. Cert. sr. scientist USSR Coun. Mins. Sr. scientist Quality Testing Lab., Rsch. Inst. Concrete and Reinforced Concrete Structures, Moscow, 1987-91; cons. Protecs, Moscow, 1991-94; vis. prof. Ctr. of Tech., Fed. U. Santa Maria, Brazil, 1996—; cons. State Inst. Patents, Moscow, 1987-90, Zarubezhstroy, Moscow, 1990-92; organizer, co-chmn., spkr. Nondestructive Testing Infrastructure Safety Sys. Internat. Symposium, 1999. Vis. scholar Drexel U., Phila., 1993, 94; scholar Nat. Coun. Sci. and Tech. Devel., Brasilia, 1996-99. Mem. ASTM (mem. E-7 com. 1993—), Am. Soc. Nondestructive Testing, Acoustical Soc. Am. Avocations: jazz, classical music, judo, fishing, book reading. E-mail: edouard@infoway.com.br. Office: Ctr of Tech UFSM, Campus Univ, 97105900 Santa Maria RS, Brazil

NESVIZHEVSKY, VALERY VICTOROVICH, physicist; b. Leningrad, Russia, Sept. 2, 1963; arrived in France, 1995; s. Victor Evgenievich and Valentina Vassilievna (Nakhozheva) N.; m. Marina Alexandrovna Denissova; children: Anna, Natalia, Grigory. PhD with honors, Leningrad State U., 1986; DSc, Petersburg Nuclear Physics Inst., Russian Acad. Scis., 1992. Stagier, 1986-88, asst. scientist, 1988-90, rsch. scientist, 1990-93, sr. scientist, 1993-95; scientist European Neutron Ctr. Inst. Laue-Langevin, Grenoble, France, 1995-98; staff scientist European Neutron Ctr. Inst. Laue-Langevin, Grenoble, 1998—; responsible for beam facility and experiments with polarized cold neutrons European Neutron Ctr. Inst. Laue-Langevin, Nuclear and Particle Physics Coll., Grenoble, 1995—, coord. Russian experiments in fundamental neutron physics, 1995—, co-organizer of workshop PPSN-ILL, 1998; coord. INTAS grant, 2000-2002; lectr. in field. Co-editor: (spl. issue) Nuclear Methods and Instruments, 1998; contbr. numerous articles to profl. jours. Recipient Gold medal Ministry Edn., 1980; Soros fellow, 1994-95; grantee Russian Found. Fundamental Investigations, 1992-95. Avocations: traveling, poetry. Office: Inst Laue-Langevin, 6 rue Jules Horowitz, F-38042 Grenoble France

NETELENBOS, TINEKE, government official; b. Wromerveer, The Netherlands, Feb. 15, 1944. Tchr., instr., 1966-81; chair South Holland Labor Party Regional Com., 1977-81; mem. Labor Party Exec. Com., 1981-87, 2d sec., 1985-87; state A sec. Ministry Edn., Culture & Sci., 1994-98, Ministry Transport & Pub. Works, The Hague, The Netherlands, 1998—. Office: Ministry Transp & Pub Works, Plesmanweg 1-6, 2597 The Hague The Netherlands also: JG, PO Box 20901, 2500 EX The Hague The Netherlands*

NETEROWICZ, JÓZEF ANDRZEJ, executive director, metallurgist; b. Czarnków, Poland, Apr. 10, 1952; arrived in Sweden, 1976; s. Alojzy and Irena Wanda (Gruca) N.; m. Renata Maria; children: Philip, Nathalie, Madeleine, Martin. MSc, Acad. Mining and Metallurgy, Krakow, Poland, 1976. Constructor Knights Consomans, Sweden, 1978-84; project mgr. Semcon Engring., Sweden, 1978-88; cons. engr. SWECO, Sweden, 1989-93; sales mgr. Cetetherm AB, Sweden, 1993-94; exec. dir. Cetetherm Polska, Poland, 1994—. Roman Catholic. Home: Strandvagen 46, 72592 Vasterås Sweden Office: Cetetherm Polska, Piekna 68, 00672 Warszawa Poland

NETHERCOT, DAVID ARTHUR, civil engineering educator, consultant; b. London, Apr. 26, 1946; s. Arthur Owen Martin and Dorothy May (Bearman) N.; m. Hedd Dwynwen Evans, Aug. 3, 1968; children: Susanna Kate, Emily Victoria. BSc, U. Wales, Cardiff, 1967, PhD, 1970, DSc, 1993. Imperial Chemistry Industries fellow U. Wales, 1970-71; lectr. U. Sheffield, Eng., 1971-81, sr. lectr., 1981-86, reader, 1986-89; prof. civil engring. U. Nottingham, Eng., 1989-99, head dept., 1994-99; prof. civil engring., head dept. civil/environtl. engring. Imperial Coll., Eng., 1999—; vice-chmn. coun. Steel Constrn. Inst., Eng., 1999—; chmn. Joint Bd. Moderators, Eng., 1996-99; vice-chmn. Tech. Inst. Structural Engrs. 2000—, Internat. Assn. for Bridge and Structural Engring., 1996-99. Author: Design for Structural Stability, 1985, Limit States Design of Structural Steelwork, 1991; contbr. over 250 articles on structural engring. to profl. jours. Fellow Inst. Structural Engrs. (v.p. 2000—, Oscar Faber bronze medal 1989), Inst. Civil Engrs. (Telford premium prize 1991), Royal Acad. Engring. (standing com. for engrs. 1996-99, coun. 2000—). Avocation: sports. Fax: (0) 207 594 6049. Office: Imperial Coll Dept Civil/, Environ Engring, London SW7 2BV, England

NETI, SUDHAKAR, mechanical engineering educator; b. Bapatla, India, 1947; came to U.S., 1968, naturalized, 1977; s. Chiranjeeva Rao and Meenakshi Neti; BME, Osmania U., 1968; MS, U. Ky., 1970, PhD, 1977; m. Kathy Gibson, Jan. 11, 1974. Research asst. U. Ky., 1968-77; asst. prof. mech. engring. Lehigh U., Bethlehem, Pa., 1978-83, assoc. prof., 1983-92, prof., 1992—; vis. fellow Wolfson Coll., Oxford U., Eng.; vis. rsch. assoc. U.K. Atomic Energy Rsch. Establishment, Harwell, Eng.; fallout shelter analyst Fed. Emergency Mgmt. Adminstrn.; chair Mech. Engring. Thermal-Fluids Divsn., 1996—, mem. Lehigh Valley Planning Commn., 1996, 97; bd. dirs. ANS, PANE; cons. to industry. Summer faculty fellow NASA-Am. Soc. Engring. Edn., 1978; grantee Electric Power Research Inst., NSF, NRC. Mem. ASME, AAAS, Sigma Xi (chpt. treas. 1997—), Phi Beta Delta. Contbr. articles to profl. jours. Office: Lehigh U Mech Engring Dept 19 Memorial Dr W Bethlehem PA 18015-3006

NETO, FELIX FERNANDO, psychologist, educator; b. Mirandela, Portugal, Apr. 5, 1950; s. Tadeu Esteves and Albina Monteiro Neto; m. Maria Lurdes Sequeira, June 9, 1976; children: Andre, Joana. Diploma in psychology, U. Paris VII, 1975; D.E.A., Sch. of Social Scis., Paris, 1976, PhD, 1980; PhD, Faculty of Psychology, Portugal, 1985. Lic. psychologist, Portugal. Asst. Ctr. Social Psychology, Porto, Portugal, 1977-85, asst. prof., 1985-88, assoc. prof., 1988-93, prof. psychology, 1993—; dir.-master cultural rels. Open U., Porto, 1995—. Author: Psicologia da Migracao, 1993, Estudos de Psicologia Intercultural, 1997; contbr. articles to profl. jours. Mem. Internat. Assn. Cross-Cultural Psychology, Internat. Assn. Applied Psychology, Am. Psychol. Assn. Home: Rua Antonio Patricio 28 1o, 4150 Porto Portugal

NETO, LUCIANO MARTINS, engineering educator; b. Botucatu, Sao Paulo, Brazil, May 22, 1948; s. Alvaro and Iolanda (Soares) M.; m. Ana Maria Corrêa, Feb. 1, 1969; children: Franco André, Fábio Conrado. BSc in Engring., Sch. Engring. Lins, Brazil, 1971; MSc in Engring., U. São Paulo, São Carlos, Brazil, 1976, D Engring., 1980. Lectr. U. São Paulo, 1972-78, Sch. Engring. Bauru, Brazil, 1972-79; sr. lectr. Sch. Engring. Lins, Brazil, 1976-85, U. Uberlândia, Brazil, 1985—. Author: (CD-Rom) Grounding of Electrical Systems, 1988. Home: Rua Rio Preto No 390, 38400151 Uberlâandia MC, Brazil Office: U Uberlândia, Av Joã Naves Avila 2160, 38400902 Uberlândia MC, Brazil

NETO, LUIS MIGUEL, psychologist, educator; b. Lisbon, Portugal, July 22, 1958; s. Jose Luis and Maria Jose (Dos Santos) N.; m. Helena Maria Marujo; June 23, 1983; children: David A., Thomas A. PsyD, Faculdade Psicologia, Lisbon, 1982; MS, Med. Sch. Seville, Spain, 1995; EdD, U. Mass., Amherst, 1995. Cert. family therapist, Internat. Family Therapy Assn. Prof. U. Lisbon, Portugal, 1985-95; external examiner U. Luton, U.K., 1997—; full prof. U. Lisbon, Portugal, 1996—. Recipient Fullbright scholarship, U. Mass., 1988-95. Mem. APA, Internat. Family Therapy Assn. Avocations: running, kayaking. Office: Fac Psicologia ECE, Alameda Da Universidade, 1600 Lisbon Portugal

NETO, LUIZ GONÇALVES, electrical engineering educator, researcher; b. São Paulo, Aug. 16, 1962; s. Luiz Gonçalves Filho and Elza Negrã Gonçalves; m. Roseli Maria de C ampos, Dec. 26, 1991; children; Alessandra, Gabriela. Degree in engring., U. São Paulo, 1985, MSc in Physics, 1990; PhD in Physics, Laval U., Que., Can., 1996. Engr. U. Sã Paulo, 1986-87, rschr., 1996-97, assoc. prof., 1997—, cons., 1997—. Contbr. articles to profl. jours., chpt. to book. Grantee Fundacao de AMparo a pesquisa do Estado de Sao Paulo, 1997, Finaciadors de Estudos E Projetos Brazil, 1998, Motorola, Inc., 1999. Mem. Optical Soc. Am., Internat. Soc. Optical Engring. Sociedade Brasileira de Microondas & Optoeletronica Brazil. Avocations: sailing, motorcross, photography. Office: EESC-USP Dept Elec Engring, Av Dr Carlos Botelho 1465, 13590970 São Carlos Brazil

NETTELHORST, ROBIN PAUL, academic administrator, writer; b. Ohio, Mar. 14, 1957; s. Paul Merrit and Naomi Jean (Saylor) N.; m. Ruth Williamson, June 25, 1983; children: Vanessa Rachel, Nichole Antoinette, Sarah Brittany. BA, L.A. Bapt. Coll., 1979; MA, UCLA, 1983. Lectr. Christian Heritage Coll., El Cagon, Calif., 1984; lectr. old testament and bibl. langs. L.A. Bapt. Coll., 1984-87; novelist, 1987—; v.p. Quartz Hill (Calif.) Sch. Theology, 1992—; webmaster Quartz Hill Sch. Theology, 1996—. Editor Quartz Hill Jour. Theology, 1994-99; author short stories; contbr. articles to mags.; host (internet and FM Radio broadcast) Beyond the Box, 1999—; author: What Dreamers Be These Rocks: Tableland, Book I, 2000, Dreams of Nothingness: Tableland, Book II, 2000, Shut the Doors Behind: Tableland, Book III, 2000, The Wrong Side of Morning, 2000, With a Rod of Iron, 2000, Antediluvian, 2000, Somewhere Obscurely, 2000, Does God Have a Long Nose? vol. I, 2000, Does God Have a Long Nose? vol. 2, 2000. Ordained deacon Quartz Hill Cmty. Ch., 1989—. Mem. Am. Acad. Religion, Soc. Bibl. Lit. Baptist. Avocations: camping, reading, philately, numismatics. E-mail: robin@theology.edu. Office: Quartz Hill Sch Theology 43543 51st St W Quartz Hill CA 93536-5608

NETTER, PETRA SYLVIA, psychologist, physician, educator; b. Hamburg, Germany, Apr. 1, 1937; d. Werner Paul Albert and Greta (Hellmann) Munkelt; m. Karl Joachim Netter. MA in Psychology, U. Hamburg, Germany, 1960, PhD in Psychology, 1963, MD, 1970. Rsch. asst. U. Hamburg, 1966-67; intern U. Mainz, Germany, 1967-68, rsch. asst. stats., 1968-75, prof. med. psychology, 1977-79; prof. psychology U. Düsseldorf, Germany, 1975-77; prof. personality psychology U. Giessen, Germany, 1979—, dean of faculty, 1982-83, 94-95; drug evaluation com. Com. Fed. Health Dept., Berlin, 1978-94. Co-editor: Anxiety and Psychotropic Drugs, 1986. Mem. Inst. Psychobiology and Behavioral Medicine (co-dir. 1989—). Home: An den Brunnenröhren 14, D35037 Marburg Germany Office: Dept Psychology U Giessen, Otto Behaghelstrasse 10F, D35394 Giessen Hessia, Germany

NETTERS, JAMES LAVIRT, pastor; b. Aliceville, Ala., Sept. 10, 1927; s. James and Bessie N.; m. Leona Netters, Nov. 26, 1948; children: James L. Jr., Edwinta, Chandra. BA in Sociology, LeMoyne Owen Coll., 1963; M in Divinity, Memphis Theol., 1991, DD, 1994. Commr. Memphis Light, Gas & Water, Memphis; pastor Mt. Vernon Baptist Ch., Memphis; Evangilistic Com. Progressive Nat. Baptist, Washington D.C., Shelby County Mayors Adv. Bd., Memphis. Councilman, Memphis, 1968-71; Mayor's Adminstrn. asst., Memphis, 1972-75; bd. dirs., Goodwill Boys Club. Renaming of South Third Street (Hwy. 61) to Rev. James L. Netters Pkwy., State of Tenn., 1991. Mem. Omega Psi Phi.

NETTHEIM, NIGEL FELIX, musicologist; b. Sydney, Australia, Jan. 10, 1940; s. Ronald Felix and Viva Lily (Meyers) N.; m. Dawn Esther Kohlhagen, Jan. 9, 1987. BEc, Sydney U., 1961; MEc, Australian Nat. U., 1964; MS, Stanford U., 1965, PhD, 1966; BMus, NSW State Conservatorium, 1989; MLitt, U. New England, 1991; postgrad., U. NSW. Lectr. in statistics A.N.U., Canberra, Australia, 1967-68; math. statistician U.S. Bur. of the Census, Washington, 1969; piano faculty Royal Conservatory of Music, Toronto, Can., 1976-80; rsch. fellow NSW State Conservatorium of Music, Sydney, 1980-86; sr. rsch. assoc./vis. fellow U. N.S.W., Sydney, 1986-96; lectr. Australian Inst. of Music, Sydney, 1996-97. Contbr. articles to profl. jours. Travel grant Fulbright Found., 1963; rsch. grant Australian Rsch. Coun., 1993. Mem. Musicological Soc. of Australia, Ind. Scholars Assn. Australia. Avocation: chess. Home: 204A Beecroft Rd, Cheltenham NSW 2119, Australia

NETTLE, DANIEL, writer; b. London, Oct. 4, 1970; s. Keith Anthony N. and Gillian (Brand) Carter. BA, U. Oxford, England, 1993; PhD, U. Coll. London, 1996. Fellow Merton Coll., Oxford, England, 1996-99. Author: The Fyem Language of Northern Nigeria, 1998, Linguistic Diversity, 1999, Vanishing Voices. Recipient Wilde prize Philosophy, U. Oxford, 1993. Office: Merton Coll, Merton St, Oxford 0X1 4JD, England

NETTLES, JOHN BARNWELL, obstetrics and gynecology educator; b. Dover, N.C., May 19, 1922; s. Stephen A. and Estelle (Hendrix) N.; m. Eunice Anita Saugstad, Apr. 28, 1956; children: Eric, Robert, John Barnwell; m. 2d, Sandra Williams, Sept. 14, 1991; stepchildren: Steven Williams, Clayton Williams. B.S., U. S.C., 1941; M.D., Med. Coll. S.C., 1944. Diplomate: Am. Bd. Obstetrics and Gynecology. Intern Garfield Meml. Hosp., Washington, 1944-45; research fellow in pathology Med. Coll. Ga., Augusta, 1946-47; resident in ob-gyn. U. Ill. Rsch. and Ednl. Hosps., Chgo., 1947-51; instr. to asst. prof. ob-gyn. U. Ill. Coll. Medicine, Chgo., 1951-57; asst. prof., assoc. prof., prof. ob-gyn. U. Ark. Med. Ctr., Little Rock, 1957-69; dir. grad. edn. Hillcrest Med. Ctr., Tulsa, 1969-73; prof. ob-gyn Coll. Medicine, U. Okla., Oklahoma City, 1969-78; chmn. dept. ob-gyn. U. Okla.-Tulsa Med. Coll., 1975-80, prof., 1980—, mem. coun. on residency edn. in ob-gyn., 1974-79; dir. Tulsa Obstet. and Gynecol. Edn. Found., 1969-80; Coordinator med. edn. Nat. Def., Ark., 1961-69; mem. S.W. regional med. adv. com. Planned Parenthood Fedn. Am., 1974-78; mem. adv. com. Health Policy Agenda Am. People, 1982-85, rev. com. Accrediation Coun. for Continuing Med. Edn., 1987-92. Contbr. articles on uterine malignancy, kidney biopsy in pregnancy, perinatal morbidity and mortality, human sexuality sch. age pregnancy to profl. jours. Served as lt. (j.g.) M.C. USNR, 1945-46; as lt. 1953-54. Fellow Am. Coll. Obstetricians and Gynecologists (dist. sec.-treas. 1964-70, dist. chmn. exec. bd. 1970-73, v.p. 1977-78, Disting. Svc. award 1998), A.C.S. (bd. govs. 1969-71, program com. 1970-71, Surg. forum 1977-84, adv. com. gyn/ob 1985-92), Royal Soc. Health, Royal Soc. Medicine; mem. Ark. Obstet. and Gynecol. Soc. (exec. sec. 1959-69), Ctrl. Assn. Obstetrics and Gynecology (exec. com. 1966-69, pres. 1978-79), Internat. Soc. Advancement Humanistic Studies in Gynecology, Assn. Mil. Surgeons U.S., AMA (sect. coun. on obstetrics and gynecology 1975-96, chmn. 1982-96, del. from Am. Coll. Obstetricians and Gynecologists 1987—, Young at Heart award Young Physicians sect. 1994), Nurses Assn. Am. Coll. Obstetricians and Gynecologists (exec. bd. 1970-73, assoc. 1980-95), So. Med. Assn. (chmn. obstetrics 1973-74), Okla. Med. Soc., Tulsa County Med. Soc., Chgo. Med. Soc., Am. Assn. for Maternal and Infant Health, Assn. Am. Med. Colls., Am. Public Health Assn., Am. Assn. Sex Edn. Counselors and Therapists (S.W. regional bd. 1976-79), Soc. for Gynecol. Investigation, AAAS, Am. Soc. for Study Fertility and Sterility, Internat. Soc. Gen. Semantics, So. Gynecol. and Obstet. Soc. (pres. 1981-82), Am. Cancer Soc. (pres. Okla. div. 1979-83, St. George's medal 1991), Com. on In-Tng. Exam. in Obstetrics and Gynecology, Am. Coll. Nurse Midwives (governing bd. examiners 1979-83), Sigma Xi (pres. Tulsa chpt. 1992-93), Phi Rho Sigma. Lutheran. Office: U Okla Health Sci Ctr 1145 S Utica Ave Ste 600 Tulsa OK 74104-4070

NETZER, MOSHE Z, electrical engineer; b. Haifa, Israel, Dec. 11, 1950; s. Hanoch and Hindah (Rosentzweig) T.; m. Hanna L. Kalechaim, Mar. 13, 1973; children: Itamar, Osnat, Ayala. BSEE, Technion U., Haifa, 1976, postgrad., 1982—. Cert. electromagnetic compatibility engr. U.S. Nat. Assn. Radio and Telecomms. Engrs. Group leader Rafael, Haifa, 76-85, 86-89, 91-97, 98—; head EMP Lighting Lab. R & B Enterprises, Conshohocken, Pa., 1985-86; sr. engr. R & B Enterprises, 1990-91, 97-98, head engr., 1998—; head EMC engring. and tech. Rafael, 1979—, non-ionizing radiation safety engr., 1989—, cons. 1995—; founder EMC Engring. and Safety Co., 1998—; head Rafael's EMC Group. Author: (books) Hardening and Testing of EEDs, Initating Circuits and Ordnance, 1993, Electrostatic Discharge Safety Handbook, 1997; co-author: (book) EMP Testing Handbook, 1986; computer programmer scientific codes in field, 1997—. Cons. Environ. Office on Radiation Hazards, Israel, 1994-99. Maj. Israeli Def. Force Army Munition Corp, 1987—. Mem. IEEE (sr. mem., vice chair Israeli EMC chpt., First Paper award 1992), Assn. Engrs. and Architects in Israel. Jewish. Avocations: photography, computer programming. Email: netzerm@netvision.net.il. Home: 11 Avigail St, 34674 Haifa Israel Office: Rafael Dept 87, PO Box 2250, 31021 Haifa Israel

NETZER, WALTHER ALOIS JOHANN, civil engineer, educator, consultant, researcher; b. Vienna, Austria, May 22, 1936; m. Walter Alois Karl and Barbara (Holzer) N.; m. Christine Maria Wasle, Aug. 30, 1966; children: Alexandra, Katharina, Britta. Grad. in Engring., U. Agrl. Scis., Vienna, 1962, Doctors, 1968; Habilitation, U. Innsbruck, Austria, 1980. Asst. prof. U. Agrl. Scis., 1962-69; asst. prof. U. Innsbruck, 1969-80, assoc. prof., 1980—, Univ. prof., 1997—; mem. tech. com. Austrian Standardization Orgn., Vienna, 1983—, European Com. Standardization, Brussels, 1989—. Author: Structural Design of Buried Pipelines with Standardized Cross Sections, 1980; contbr. articles to profl. jours. Home: Hocheggweg 13, A-6020 Innsbruck Austria Office: Univ Innsbruck, Technikerstrasse 13, A-6020 Innsbruck Austria

NEU, CARL HERBERT, JR., management consultant; b. Miami Beach, Fla., Sept. 4, 1937; s. Carl Herbert and Catherine Mary (Miller) N.; BS, MIT, 1959; MBA, Harvard U., 1961; m. Carmen Mercedes Smith, Feb. 8, 1964; children—Carl Bartley, David Conrad. Cert. profl. mgmt. cons. Indsl. liaison officer MIT, Cambridge, 1967-69; coord. forward planning Gates Rubber Co., Denver, 1969-71; pres., co-founder Dyna-Com Resources, Lakewood, Colo., 1971-77; pres., founder Neu & Co., Lakewood, 1977—; mng. dir. Pro-Med Mgmt. Systems, Lakewood, 1981—; lectr. Grad. Sch. Pub. Affairs, U. Colo. Denver, 1982-84. Mem. exec. coun. Episcopal Diocese Colo., 1974; mem. Lakewood City Coun., 1975-80, pres., 1976; chmn. Lakewood City Charter Commn., 1982, Lakewood Civic Found., Inc., 1986-91; pres. Lakewood on Parade, 1978, bd. dirs., 1978-80; pres. Classic Chorale, Denver, 1979, bd. dirs., 1978-83; pres. Lakewood Pub. Bldg. Authority, 1983—; bd. dirs. Metro State Coll. of Denver Found., 1990—, treas., 1994-97; bd. dirs. Kaiser Permanente Health Adv. Com., 1990—, chair, 1997. With U.S. Army, 1961-67. Decorated Bronze Star medal, Army Commendation medal; recipient Arthur Page award AT&T, 1979; Kettering Found. grantee, 1979-80. Mem. Internat. City Mgrs. Assn., Lakewood-So. Jefferson County C. of C. (bd. dirs. 1983-89, chmn. 1988, chmn. 1987-88), Jefferson County C. of C. (chmn. 1988). Republican. Episcopalian. Contbr. articles to profl. jours. Home: 8169 W Baker Ave Denver CO 80227-3129

NEU, PETER, physicist, banker; b. Neunkirchen, Germany, Dec. 12, 1965; s. Bertold and Isolde N.; m. Maria Basler, July 5, 1996. Diploma, Imperial Coll. Sci. & Tech., London, 1990; diploma in Physics, U. Heidelberg,

Germany, 1991, PhD with hons. in Physics, 1994. Post-doctoral U. Heidelberg, Germany, 1994-95, MIT, Cambridge, 1995-97; risk mgr. Dresdner Bank, Frankfurt, Germany, 1997—. Contbr. articles to profl. jours. Avocations: sports, chess, reading, music. Office: Dresdner Bank AG, Jurgen-Ponto-Platz, D-60301 Frankfurt Germany

NEUBAUER, FRITZ, linguistics educator; b. Vienna, 1940; s. Thomas and Paula N.; m. Marilyn Schapiro; 1 child, Miranda. MA Ord., U. Edinburgh, 1972, MA with honors, 1974; PhD, U. Bielefeld, 1980. Sr. lectr. Faculty for Linguistics and Lit. U. Bielefeld, 1980—. Author: (book) Die Struktur der Explikationen in deutschen einsprachigen Wörterbüchern, 1980; co-editor: Informationen Deutsch als Fremdsprache; contbr. articles to profl. jours. Avocations: hiking, cycling. Home: Weststr 80, D-33615 Bielefeld Germany Office: Fakultät Linguistik/Lit, Univ Bielefeld/PB 100 131, D-33501 Bielefeld Germany

NEUBAUER, HUGO DUANE, JR., software engineer; b. Mankato, Minn., Oct. 31, 1959; s. Hugo Duane and Joan Marie (Habinger) N.; m. Susan A. May, July 7, 1990. Student, U. Miami, 1978-80; AA, U. Fla., 1981; AS, Santa Fe C.C., 1984; student, U. Fla., 1984—. Aquaculture specialist, technician Aqualife Rsch. Inc., 1979-80; automotive dept. K-Mart, 1981-82; electronic technician Synergetics, Inc., 1983-84; water resources equipment technician Environ. Sci. and Engring., Inc., Gainesville, Fla., 1984-89; tech. ops. equipment mgr. Environ. Sci. and Engring., Inc., Gainesville, 1990-91, geosciences divsn. equipment mgr., 1992-93, ctr. 3 equipment mgr., 1994-95; office mgr. Keck Instruments, Inc., Newberry, Fla., 1996-98; founder, owner, web master and designer Innovative Computer and Instrument Svcs., Alachua, Fla., 1996—; co-founder, co-owner Dances with Hooves, Alachua, Fla., 1997—; info. tech. systems adminstr. CPAmerica Internat. (formerly Acctg. Firms Associated Inc.), 1999—; cons. in field. Mem. IEEE, IEEE Computer Soc., NRA, HTML Writers Guild. Avocations: computer programming and Internet, horses, gun collecting and shooting, videography and photography (including underwater), scuba diving (cert. Profl. Assn. Diving Instrs.). Home and Office: 14108 NW 195th St Alachua FL 32615-8023

NEUBER, FRIEDEL, banker; b. Duisburg-Rheinhausen, Germany, July 10, 1935. Indsl. apprentice Fried. Krupp Huttenwerke A.G., Essen, Germany, 1953-61; chief exec. Bertha Hosp., Duisburg, 1961-69; pres. Rhineland Sparkassen and Giro Assn., Dusseldorf, Germany, 1969-81; chmn. mng. bd. Westdeutsche Landesbank, Dusseldorf, from 1981; now chmn. supervisory bd. RWE/VEW, Essen; dep. State Parliament North Rhine-Westphalia, 1962-75. *

NEUBERGER, HERMAN NAFTOLI, college president, rabbi; b. Germany, June 26, 1918; came to U.S., 1938, naturalized, 1945; s. Max and Bertha (Hiller) N.; m. Judith Kramer, Mar. 10, 1941 (dec. Aug. 1994); children: Sheftel M., Isaac M., Shrago S., Yaakov S., Ezra D. Student, Mir (Poland) Rabbinical Sem.; grad., Ner Israel Rabbinical Coll., 1943. Ordained rabbi, 1943. V.p., sec. bd. trustees Ner Israel Rabbinical Coll., Balt., 1943-87, pres., 1987—. Contbr. to Md. Law Rev. Mem. exec. bd. Balt. Youth Commn.; bd. dirs. Balt. Jewish Coun.; founder Coun. Orthodox Jewish Congregations of Balt. Mem. Assn. Advanced Rabbinical and Talmudic Schs. (founder, mem. exec. action com.). Home: 401 Yeshiva Ln Baltimore MD 21208-1117 Office: Ner Israel Rabbinical Coll 400 Mount Wilson Ln Baltimore MD 21208-1198

NEUBERGER, JAMES MAX, physician, consultant; b. London, Nov. 4, 1949; s. Albert and Lilian Neuberger; m. Belinda Keogh, Sept., 1989; children: Oliver, Francesca, Edmund, Octavia. DM, Oxford (Eng.) U., 1970, MA in Physiology, 1972, BM BCh, 1972. Sr. lectr. Kings Coll. Hosp., London, 1978-86; cons. physician Queen Elizabeth Hosp., Birmingham, Eng., 1989—. Editor: Immunology of Liver Transplantation, 1992, Practice of Liver Transplation, 1995. Fellow Royal Coll. Physicians. Avocation: fishing. Home: Moat House Radford Rd, Allechurch BU8 75T, England

NEUBERGER, MANFRED ARTHUR, medical educator, researcher; b. Vienna, Austria, Sept. 14, 1946; s. Arthur and Erika (Grimm) N.; m. Marion Binderberger, May 26, 1975; 1 child, Danja. MD, U. Vienna, 1971. Assoc. prof. Med. Sch. U. Vienna, 1971-80, prof., 1980—, dep. dir. Inst. Environ. Hygiene, 1980—, dep. dir. Inst. Environ. Medicine, 1989—, head dept. preventive medicine, 1992—; cons. Workers Compensation Bd., Vienna, 1980—, WHO-Internat. Program Chem. Safety, Geneva, 1992-93, 95-96, WHO-Europe, Copenhagen, 1979-84, UN Devel. Program, N.Y.C., 1986-87, ILO Delegation, Geneva, 1985-86. Author: New Approaches to Risk Estimation of Air Pollution, 1979 (U. Vienna award 1980), Prevention of Noise Induced Hearing Loss, 1989 (Austrian Soc. Occpl. Medicine award 1983); contbr. articles to profl. jours. Mem. planning commn. City of Vienna, 1993—. With Austrian Army, 1974. Grantee U. Vienna, 1982, 95, 91. Mem. Austrian Soc. Occpl. Medicine (bd. dirs. 1997—), Austrian Soc. Lung Diseases (bd. dirs. 1997—, chair working group 1997—), European Network for Smoking Prevention, Austrian Acad. Sci. (clean air com. 1993—), Austrian Soc. Ecology (sci. adv. bd. 1997—). Avocations: music, cycling, hiking, gardening. Office: U Vienna Dept Prev Medicine, Kinderspitalgasse 15, A-1095 Vienna Austria

NEUENSCHWANDER, ERWIN, science historian, mathematician, educator; b. Zürich, Switzerland, June 25, 1942; s. Gustav and Annie (Fischer) N. Diploma in Math., U. Zürich, 1969, PhD, 1972, habil., 1974. Asst. U. Zürich, Switzerland, 1970-79; investigator Volkswagen Found., Göttingen, Germany, 1982-85, Swiss Nat. Found., Zürich, 1986—; prof. U. Zürich, 1995—; vis. scholar U. Aarhus, Harvard U., CNRS, Paris, 1977-81; pres. Swiss Nat. Com., Internat. Union of History and Philosophy of Sci., 1989—, pres. joint commn. IUHPS/DHS-DLMPS, 1999—; cons. Historisches Lexikon der Schweiz, 1996—. Author: (with B.L. van der Waerden) Methods of Calculation, 1976, Riemann's Introduction to Complex Analysis, 1996; editor: Science, Society and Political Power, 1993; assoc. editor Lexikon des Mittelalters, 1975-98; contbr. over 40 sci. articles to profl. jours. Recipient Henry E. Sigerist prize Schweizerische Gesellschaft für Geschichte der Medizin und der Naturwissenschaften, 1974. Mem. Internat. Acad. History Sci., Swiss Acad. Scis., Gesellschaft für Wissenschaftsgeschichte, History of Sci. Soc. Office: Inst Math U Zürich, Winterthurerstr 190, 8057 Zürich Switzerland

NEUFANG, KARL FRIEDRICH RUDOLF, radiologist, educator; b. Cologne, Germany, Nov. 21, 1953; s. Karl Friedrich and Hedwig Johanna (Kopp) N.; m. Ursula Anna Mueller Neufang, Oct. 18, 1985; 1 child, Benedikt Johannes Cornelius. MD, U. Sch. Medicine, Cologne, Germany, 1978. Resident U. Hosp. Radiology, Cologne, Germany, 1979, 81-85; med. capt. Ctrl. Army Hosp. Koblenz, Germany, 1979-80; sr. officer, 1985-90, first sr. officer, 1990-92; asst. prof. U. Cologne, 1988-94, assoc. prof., 1994—; pvt. practice Inst. for Diagnostic Radiology and Nuclear Medicine, Euskirchen, Germany, 1992—. Co-author: Digital Subtraction Angiography, 1988, Degenerative Vascular Disease, 1992; co-editor: Vascular Stenting/Magnetic Resonance Angiography, 1991; assoc. editor: Aktuelle Radiologie, 1991-93; contbr. articles to profl. jours. Mem. Internat. Soc. for Magnetic Resonance in Medicine, Radiol. Soc. N.Am., Am. Roentgen Ray Soc., Deutsche Rontgengesellschaft, Gesellschaft Deutscher Naturforscher u Aerzte. Roman Catholic. Avocations: architecture, 19th and 20th century paintings, local and political history, photography, model railroading. Office: Praxis Radiologie, Nuklearmedizin, D-53879 Euskirchen Germany

NEUFELD, HOWARD B., foundation administrator; b. N.Y.C., Mar. 1, 1956; s. Helmuth and Nina N.; m. Joan Nina, Aug. 7, 1994; children: Elise Joy, Jennifer Michell. BA in Psychology, Queens Coll.; M, Yeshiva U., 1981. Pres. Young Israel of Coop., N.Y., 1987—; treas. BY Jewish Cmty. Coun., 1989—; pres. Coop. Jewish Cmty. Coun., 1990—; exec. dir. Chelsea Assisted Living, N.Y.C., 1998—; pres. Bronx (N.Y.) Jewish Home Care Agy., 1999—. Exec. v.p. Young Israel Ohab Zedek. Recipient cert. Nat. Coun. Sr. Citizens, 1992, proclamation City of N.Y., 1993, congressional record Ho. Reps., 1991. Mem. Gerontol. Soc. Am., Am. Assn. Counseling and Devel., Rotary. Jewish. Home: 12 Fanshaw Ave Yonkers NY 10705-3713

NEUGEBAUER, ROSAMUNDE See SCHULENBURG, ROSAMUNDE MARIA GRAEFIN VON DER

NEUHAUS, DAVID, structural biologist, researcher; b. Reading, Berkshire, Eng., Jan. 28, 1956; s. Max and Audrey (Chown) N.; m. Deirdre Mary Bernadette Hickey, May 7, 1988; children: James, Peter. BA, Oxford (Eng.) U., 1978; PhD, Imperial Coll. Sci. and Tech., London, 1982. Postdoctoral rsch. fellow Eidgenössiche Technische Hochschule, Zürich, Switzerland, 1983, Oxford U., 1984; rsch. assoc. Parke-Davis Rsch. Unit, Cambridge, Eng., 1985-88; staff scientist Med. Rsch. Coun. Lab. Molecular Biology, Cambridge, Eng., 1988—. Joint author: The Nuclear Overhauser Effect in Stereochemical and Conformational Analysis, 1989, 2nd edit., 2000; contbr. over 50 articles to profl. jours. Fellow Royal Soc. Chemistry. Avocation: classical music. Office: MRC Lab Molecular Biology, Hills Rd, Cambridge CB2 2QH, England

NEUHAUS, JOAN T., finance company executive, private investigator; b. Houston, Oct. 28, 1958; d. Philip Ross and Lacey (Thompson) N.; m. Daniel J. Schaan. BA, Williams Coll., 1980; MBA, Rice U., 1987. Registered rep., SEC. Mem. fixed income dept. Goldman, Sachs, N.Y.C., 1986; dir. tech. transfer Houston Area Rsch. Ctr., The Woodlands, 1988-89; v.p. Instl. Equity Sales Underwood, Neuhaus & Co., Inc., Houston, 1981-85, mem. corp. fin. dept., 1989; mktg. mgr. energy and fin. div. Westinghouse Credit Corp., Houston, 1989-91; pres. Neuhaus Capital Corp., Houston, 1991-93; pres., prin. Confidential Adv. Svcs., Inc., Houston, 1993—; appointee Tex. Commn. on Pvt. Security by Gov. George Bush, 1999—. Bd. dirs., treas. St. Joseph's Meca, Tex. Lyceum Assn., 1988-93; founding mem. Charity Players, Houston, 1982-89; bd. dirs., treas. Julia C. Hester House, 1994—; adv. bd. Southwest Bank Tex., Univ. Houston Sch. Architecture. With USNR, 1993—; apptd. Tex. Commn. on Pvt. Security by Gov. George W. Bush, 1999. Mem. Tex. Assn. Lic. Investigators, World Affairs Coun., Tex. Tech. Transfer Assn. (profl.), Williams Coll. Alumni Assn. (bd. dirs. 1984-86). Republican. Episcopalian. Address: Confidential Advisory Serv Inc 5615 Morningside Dr Houston TX 77005-3218

NEUKIRCHEN, KAJO, industry executive. Dr.rer.pol, Bonn U., 1973. With Kabelwerke Reinshagen GmbH, Wuppertal, 1973-77, Felten & Guilleaume Carlswerke AG, Cologne, 1977-81, SKF Kugellagerfabriken GmbH, Schweinfurt, 1981-87, KHD Aktiengesellschaft, Cologne, 1987-91; CEO Hoesch AG, Dortmund, 1991-92, mg technologies ag, Frankfurt, Germany, 1993—. Office: mg technologies ag, 60325 Frankfurt Germany

NEUMAN, MAXINE DARCY, cellist, educator; b. Phila., July 1, 1948; d. Marvin Memorial and Helga (Hennigson) N.; m. Reinhard Humburg, Oct. 16, 1987; children: Julia Vera Neuman, Mark Daniel Humburg. MusB, Manhattan Sch. Music, 1968, MusM, 1969. Cellist N.J. Symphony Orch., Newark, 1969-71; cellist with variety of groups including Mostly Mozart Festival, Am. Ballet Theatre, "Y" Chamber Symphony, Martha Graham, Dance Theatre of Harlem, Am. Composers Orch., N.Y.C., 1971-80; cellist Walden Trio (Vanguard Records), Leonia, N.J., 1972—, Contemporary Trio (Crest Records), N.Y.C., 1975-80; cellist U.S. and European tours Crescent Quartet (Leonarda Records) U.S. & European tours, N.Y.C., 1979—; cellist St. Luke's Chamber Ensemble (Angel, Mus. Heritage, CBS Records), N.Y.C., 1981—; prof. music Bennington (Vt.) Coll., Vermont, 1981-95, Williams Coll., Mass., 1994-95, 98—, Hawthorne Valley Sch., 1996—; mem. faculty Sch. for Strings, N.Y.C., 1996—; cellist Claremont Duo, Germany, 1998—; mem. faculty Chamber Music Conf. N.E. Bennington, 1982—, bd. dirs; chmn. dept. music Bennington Coll., 1985-86, 90-91; touring solo cellist yearly to Europe, Mex., S.Am., Japan, 1980—, Montreux Jazz Festival, 1993, 94, N.Y. Film Festival, 1995; founder Bennington Cello Quartet; panelist Chamber Music Am. Nat. conv., 2000. Rec. artist on Swiss, French, Australian, German, Italian, Ecuadorian, Colombian radio and TV, 1980—, also Columbia, Orion, CRI, Opus One, London Argo, Albany Records, Sony/Virgin, Koch Internat., CBS World, Nonesuch, AMC, Biddulph Records, B.E. Records, PBS Gt. Performers, 1995, 96, 97, Sat. Night Live, 1998, Metallica Concert, Madison Sq. Garden, 1999. Bd. dirs. Bronx (N.Y.) Opera Co., 1972-85. Recipient Double Award of Merit Nat. Fedn. Music Clubs, 1976, award Internat. Congress on Women in Music, UN, 1990, prize Am. Soc. for Jewish Music, 1998; Ford Found. grantee, 1971-72. Mem. Am. Fedn. Musicians, Chamber Music Conf. of the East (bd. dirs.), Kulturforum (artistic advisor). Avocations: photography, traveling, cooking, hiking. Home: 200 Claremont Ave Apt 52 New York NY 10027-4070 Office: Box 42 Park St North Bennington VT 05257

NEUMAN, ROBERT HAROLD, communication executive; b. Phila.; s. Otto and Bessie Neuman; m. Joan Elizabeth Huhn, June 3, 1978 (dec. Feb. 1996). Cert. sys. application, U. So. Calif., Arlington, Va., 1981; BA, U. Md., 1972; MLA, Johns Hopkins U., 1983, cert. advanced study, 1987. Photographer Photo Corp. Am., Rockville, Md., 1973; retail mgr. various firms, 1974-77; acct. rep. Kastle Security Inc., Arlington, Va., 1977-80; sr. data technician Mantech Internat. Corp., Rockville, 1981-82; computer programmer Harry Diamond Lab., Adelphi, Md., 1982-86; program analyst Lab. Command, Adelphi, 1986-88; analyst internat. programs Army Rsch. Lab., Adelphi, 1988-93; owner, mgr. Neu-Enterprise Prodns., Potomac, Md., 1993—; prodr., program dir. Laurel (Md.) Cable Network, 1990-98, bd. dirs. Vol. Hospice Caring, Inc., Gaithersburg, Md., 2000—; bd. dirs. Vistas Condominium, Laurel, Md., 1993-95. With U.S. Army, 1960-63. Mem. Alliance for Cmty. Media, Internat. TV Assn. Avocations: videographer, travel.

NEUMAN, WILLIAM LAWRENCE, JR., sociology educator; b. Phila., Oct. 1, 1950; s. William Lawrence and Elizabeth Ruth (Mearkle) N.; m. Diane Kathryn Mertens, June 16, 1984; m. Deanna Sue Livingstone, Aug. 18, 1970 (div. 1976). BA with honors, Ind. U., Bloomington, 1972; MS, U. Wis., Madison, 1975, PhD, 1982. Lectr. U. Wis., Madison, 1976-82; vis. asst. Oberlin Coll., 1983; prof. sociology U. Wis., Whitewater, 1983—, asst. dean, 1985-91; adminstrv. assoc. Office Acad. Affairs U. Wis. System, 1992; vis. prof. Tohoku U., Sendai, Japan, 1995-96; dir. Pacific Asia Ednl. Resource Ctr., 1999—. Grantee Fulbright Coun. for Exch. Internat. Scholars, 1995. Mem. Am. Sociol. Assn., Wis. Sociol. Assn. (pres. 1993-94), Midwest Sociol. Assn. (bd. dirs. 1995-97). Democrat. Unitarian. Home: 2935 Forest Down Madison WI 53711-5294

NEUMANN, ALFRED JOHN, music director; b. Bklyn., Dec. 15, 1928; s. Erich Paul and Elsa (Kleiber) N. BS, Davidson Coll., 1951; MMus, U. Mich., 1954. Asst. to music dir. Brevard (N.C.) Music Ctr., 1948-52; dir. of bands Furman U., Greenville, S.C., 1951-52; asst. instr. in music U. Mich., Ann Arbor, 1952-54; music dir. Nat. Conv. of United Ch. of Christ, Washington, 1976, Christ Congregational Ch., Silver Spring, Md., 1958-94; accompanist Washington Performing Arts Soc. Concerts in Schs., Washington, 1972-97, Todd Duncan Voice Studio, Washington, 1992-98; mem. adv. bd. to select the Bicentennial hymn, U.S. Army, Washington, 1976; student condr. U. Mich. Choirs, Ann Arbor, 1952-54; accompanist U. Mich. Opera Dept., Ann Arbor, 1952-54, The Mozart Trio, Washington, 1958-68. Composer: (church anthems) Truly, We Shall Be in Paradise, 1970, I Sing to Thee, 1983, (sacred opera) An Opera for Christmas, 1961, An Opera for Easter (both premiered on NBC-TV, Washington); contbr. articles to profl. jours. Organizer, dir. concerts to benefit AMA Colls., Washington, 1974, 75; music dir. Nat. Conv. of the United Ch. of Christ, Washington, 1976. Recipient Cert. commendation Can. Internat. Exhbn., Montreal, Can., 1967, Performance award WGMS Good Music Sta., Washington, 1980, 1981. Democrat. United Ch. of Christ. Home: Ste 1515 1400 E West Hwy Apt 1515 Silver Spring MD 20910-3264

NEUMANN, BERNHARD HERMANN, mathematician; b. Berlin-Charlottenburg, Germany, Oct. 15, 1909; s. Richard and Else (Aronstein) N.; m. Hanna von Caemmerer, Dec. 22, 1938 (dec. Nov. 1971); children: Irene Brown, Peter, Barbara Cullingworth, Walter, Daniel; m. Dorothea Zeim, Dec. 24, 1973. Student, U. Freiburg, Germany, 1928-29; Dr.phil., U. Berlin, 1932; PhD, Cambridge U., Eng., 1935; DSc, U. Manchester, Eng., 1954; DSc (hon.), U. Newcastle, Australia, 1974, Monash U., Australia, 1982, U. Western Australia, 1995, U. Hull, Eng., 1995; D.Math. (hon.), U. Waterloo, 1986; Dr.rer.nat. (hon.), Humboldt U., Berlin, 1992. Lectr. Univ. Coll., Hull, 1946-48; faculty U. Manchester, 1948-61; prof., head dept. math. Inst. Advanced Studies, Australian Nat. U., Canberra, 1962-74, hon. univ. fellow, 1975—; hon. rsch. fellow divsn. Math. and Info. Sci., Commonwealth Sci. and Indsl. Rsch. Orgn., Canberra, 1978—. Editor Houston Jour. Math., 1974—; editor, pub. IMU Canberra Circular, 1972-99, other editorships; contbr. numerous articles to math. jours. Served with Brit. Armed Forces, 1940-45. Decorated Companion Order of Australia, 1994; recipient prize Wiskundig Genootschap, Amsterdam, The Netherlands, 1949, Adams prize U. Cambridge, 1952-53. Fellow Royal Soc., Australian Acad. Sci. (v.p. 1969-71, Matthew Flinders lectr. 1984), Inst. Combinatorics and Its Applications (hon.), Australian Math. Soc. (hon., v.p. several terms, pres. 1964-66, hon. mem. 1981—, editor bull. 1969-79, hon. editor 1979—); mem. London Math. Soc. (v.p. 1959-61, editor proc. 1959-61), many other profl. orgns., also chess and musical clubs and socs. Avocations: classical music (cello), chess, cycling, camping. E-mail: bernhard.neumann@maths.anu.edu.au. Home: 20 Talbot St, Forrest ACT 2603, Australia Office: Australian Nat U, Canberra ACT 0200, Australia also: CSIRO-Divsn Math Info Scis, GPO Box 664, Canberra ACT 2601, Australia

NEUMANN, HANS-ADOLF, international governmental administrator; b. Berlin, Aug. 18, 1938; s. Erich and Hildegard (Winter) N.; m. Rosemarie Gebler, Mar. 8, 1968; children: Marie-Gabriele, Robert, Constanze, Corinna, Desiree. Student, U. Heidelberg, U. Berlin, U. Munich, 1959-62, Ministry of Justice, Munich, 1963-66; D. in Law, U. Munich, 1967. Cert. 2d state law exam. award, Munich, 1967. Lawyer Dr. Lois Erdl Law Firm, Munich, 1967-68; employee Kreditanstalt für Wiederaufbau, Frankfurt am Main, Fed. Republic Germany, 1968-71; prin. adminstr. DG for Credit & Investment EEC, Luxembourg, 1971-72, DG for External Rels. EEC, Brussels, 1972-74, DG for Fin. Control EEC, Brussels, 1974-81; head of div. DG for External Rels. EEC, Brussels, 1981-96; with export credit policy and export promotion, anti-dumping policy and measures, new instrument comml. policy, export regime EEC; dir. anti-dumping policy and measures, 1996—. Office: Commn European Cmtys, Rue de Loi 200, B-1049 Brussels Belgium

NEUMANN, HEINZ DIETER, occupational health engineer, researcher; b. Hemer, Germany, Aug. 2, 1951; s. Heinz and Irmgard (Satorius) N.; m. Christa Peika, Dec. 24, 1982; children:Christopher, Amelie. Diploma in Elect. Engring., University, Bochum, Germany, 1979; Doctor, University, Wuppertal, Germany, 1994. Cert. engr. 1. Systems engr. Rhode & Schwarz, Munich, 1979-80; devel. GUVV Westfalen-Lippe, Muenster, Germany, 1980-82; technical inspector Guvv Westfalen-Lippe, Muenster, Germany, 1982-85, group mgr., 1985-90, sect. mgr., 1990—. Author: (book) Health Risks at Work in Pathological Laboratories, 1994, Report: Dioxines in the Workplace, 1997, Occupational Health Risks Due To Microbial Exposition During Collection and Removal of Household Wastes, 2000; contbr. articles to profl. jours. Mem. Working Com. Hazardous Substances, Com. Ear Protection, N.Y. Acad. Scis. Roman Catholic. Avocations: family, sports, music, reading, journeys. Home: Im Turm 5, D-58675 Hemer Germany Office: GUVV Westfalen-Lippe, Salzmannstrasse 156, 48159 Münster Germany

NEUMANN, JEFFREY JAY, photographer, minister; b. Cleve., Aug. 6, 1948; s. Fred and LaVerne (Vavra) N.; m. Charlene Rose Sparrow, Apr. 21, 1968 (dec.); children: Stephan, Corene, Lara; m. Carolyn Hannah, Nov. 4, 1972; 1 son, Jeffrey. Ordained to ministry, 1962. Lithographer, camera operator Advertype, Inc., Cleve., 1972; lab. technician Vista Color Lab., Cleve., 1972-73; prodn. mgr. Mort Tucker Photography, Cleve., 1973-78; owner, photographer Photography by Jeffrey Neumann, Wadsworth, OH, 1978—. Author: Thirty Years as Jehovah's Slave, 2000, To Have and Remember the Perfect Wedding, 1997. Mem. Sm. Bus. Mgmt. Adv. Com., 1980-83. Mem. Internat. Platform Assn., Profl. Photographers Am. (awards), Wedding and Portrait Photographers Internat. (awards), Profl. Photographers Ohio (awards). Jehovah's Witness. Home and Office: 9960 Mount Eaton Rd Wadsworth OH 44281-9028

NEUMANN, KATHARINA, archaeobotanist; b. Munich, Germany, Oct. 15, 1953; d. Klaus and Marlise (Hoffmann) N.; 1 child, Ruth Marie. Diploma, U. Frankfurt, Germany, 1981, PhD, 1988. Rsch. asst. U. Cologne, Germany, 1984-88; rsch. asst. U. Frankfurt, 1988-93, rsch. fellow, 1994—. Mem. Soc. Africanist Archaeologists. Office: U Frankfurt, Robert-Mayer-Str 1, 60054 Frankfurt Germany

NEUMANN, LINDA KAY, marketing executive; b. Wyandotte, Mich., Feb. 5, 1959; d. Michael and Raelene Fern (Bongart) Goldman; m. David Dewain Neumann, Mar. 31, 1980; children: Rachel Anne, Kyle Wayne. Student, Mesa C.C., San Diego, 1976-86; grad. with honors, Bank Mktg. Sch., 1991. Mail clk., securities clk. Hawaiian Trust Co. Ltd., Honolulu, 1977-78, supr., 1979-81; securities vault clk., bank card clk. Union Bank Calif., San Diego, 1981-82, sales adminstrv. asst., 1983-86, mktg. adminstrv. asst., mktg. officer, 1986-88, from mktg. asst. v.p. to mktg. v.p., 1992-94, mktg. v.p., mgr., 1994-96, bus. and sales planning mgr., v.p., 1996—; chmn. San Diego Ednl. Coun. Am. Banking Assn. Am. Inst. Banking, 1996-97; owner Brilliant Mktg. Ideas, 1999—. Pres. Rolling Hills Elem. PTA, 1995-96; parliamentarian Deer Canyon Elem. PTA. Mem. Am. Soc. Autism, Direct Mktg. Assn., Advt. Club San Diego, San Diego Direct Mktg. Assn., Bank Mktg. Assn., Advt. Splty. Inst. Promotional Products Assns., Nat. Soc. Fundraising Execs., San Diego Employers Assn., Am. Soc. Autism. Office: Brilliant Marketing Ideas Ste 109 8340 Clairemont Mesa Blvd San Diego CA 92111-1320

NEUMANN, LISELOTTE, professional golfer; b. Finspang, Sweden, May 20, 1966. With LPGA, 1987—; mem. European Solheim Cup Team, 1990, 92, 94, 96, 98. Named Golf Digest Rolex Rookie of Year, 1988, Swedish Golfer of Year, 1994, GolfWorld's Most Improved Golfer, 1994. Achievements in LPGA victories include: U.S. Women's Open, 1988, Mazda Japan Classic, 1991, Minn. LPGA Classic, 1994, Weetabix Women's Brit. Open, 1994, GHP Heartland Classic, 1994, Chrysler-Plymouth Tournament of Champions, 1996, PING/Welch's Championship, 1996, First Bank-Edina Realty Classic, 1996, Welch's Champsionship, 1997, Toray Japan Queens Cup, 1997, Standard Register Ping, 1998, Chick-fil-A Charity Championship, 1998; other victories include: European Open, 1985, German Open, 1986-88, French Open, 1987, Solheim Cup, 1998. Office: LPGA 100 International Golf Dr Daytona Beach FL 32124-1092

NEUMANN, THOMAS WILLIAM, archaeologist; b. Cin., Aug. 30, 1951; s. William Henry and Virginia Marie (Walz) N.; m. Mary Louise Spink, Sept. 3, 1988. BA in Anthropology, U. Ky., 1973; PhD in Anthropology, U. Minn., 1979. Instr. U. Minn., Mpls., 1977-79; asst. prof. Syracuse U., 1979-86, dir. archaeology field program, 1979-86; sr. ptnr. Neumann & Sanford Cultural Resource Assessments, Syracuse, 1985-87; sr. scientist R. Christopher Goodwin & Assocs., Inc., Frederick, Md., 1987-92; rsch. assoc. Terrestrial Environ. Specialists, Phoenix, N.Y., 1980-83, SUNY Rsch. Found., Potsdam, 1985-87; external reviewer NSF, Washington, 1982-85; dir. Ctr. for Archaeol. Rsch. and Edn., Houston, Minn., 1982-84; vis. assoc. prof. Emory U., 1991-93, 96, 97—, U. Ga., 1997; ind. cons., 1991—. Author, co-author more than 80 monographs including 2 winners of the Anne Arundell County Hist. Preservation award; asst. editor Amanuensis, 1972-73; contbr. more than 40 articles to profl. jours. Nat. Trust Historic Preservation honor award. Recipient Oswald award U. Ky., 1973; co-recipient Vt. Gov.'s medal for Stonewalls and Cellarholes; grantee Am. Philos. Soc., 1981, Appleby-Mosher Found., 1983, Landmarks Assn. Ctrl. N.Y., 1984. Mem. AAAS, N.Y. Acad. Sci., Soc. for Am. Archaeology, Ea. States Archaeol. Fedn., Mid. Atlantic Archaeol. Conf., Ga. Coun. Profl. Archaeologists, Phi Beta Kappa. Roman Catholic. Achievements include development of use of vegetation successional stages for cultural resource assessments; identification of cause of passenger pigeon extinctions, microlithic compound tool industry in the eastern prehistoric U.S., contingency planning budget system for Archdiocese of Atlanta. Home and Office: Ind Archeol Cons 3859 Wentworth Ln SW Lilburn GA 30047-2260

NEUMAYR, GUENTHER, medical educator; b. Lienz, Austria, Sept. 5, 1964; s. Leo and Ingrid (Braunegger) N.; m. Sabine Lukasser, May 8, 1993; children: Mara, Lea. MD, U. Innsbruck, Austria, 1989. Asst. prof. dept. microbiology U. Innsbruck, Austria, 1990, asst. prof. pathology, 1991, asst. prof. internal medicine, 1992-98, asst. prof. dept. cardiology, 1998-99, asst. prof. dept. sports medicine, 1999—; cons. in field. Contbr. articles to profl. jours. Office: U Innsbruck, Anichstr 35, 6020 Innsbruck Austria

NEUMEIER, JOHN, choreographer, ballet company director; b. Milw., Feb. 24, 1942; s. Albert and Lucille N. BA, Marquette U., 1961, DFA (hon.), 1987; student, Stone-Camryn Ballet Sch., Chgo., 1957-62, Royal Ballet Sch., London, 1962-63; student of Vera Volkova, Copenhagen, 1962-63. Dancer Sybil Shearer Co., Chgo., 1960-62, Stuttgart (Fed. Republic Germany) Ballet, 1963-69; artistic dir. Frankfurt (Fed. Republic Germany) Opera Ballet, 1969-73, Hamburg (Fed. Republic Germany) State Opera Ballet, 1973—; prof. City of Hamburg, 1987; dir. Hamburg Ballet, 1996, ballettintendant, 1997—; found. ballet sch. Hamburg State Opera, 1978; found. ballet ctr. John Neumeier, ballet sch., Hamburg State Opera co. tng. under one roof., 1989. Guest choreographer for various cos. including Am. Ballet Theatre, Royal Ballet London, Royal Danish Ballet, Nat. Ballet Can., Royal Winnipeg Ballet, Stuttgart Ballet, Munich Opera, Vienna Opera, Ballet du XX siecle, Brussels, Opera de Paris, Opera of Stockholm; guest opera dir. Otello, Munich Opera, Hamburg State Opera; ballet dir. (films) Rondo, 1971 (Prix Italia 1972), Third Symphony of Gustav Mahler (Golden Camera award 1978), Legend of Joseph, Wendungen (String Quintet in C major by Schubert), 1979, Scenes of Childhood, The Lady of the Camellias, 1986, Othello, 1987; choreographer Romeo and Juliet, The Nutcracker, 1971, Daphnis and Chloé, 1972, Third Symphony of Gustav Mahler, 1975, Illusions-Like Swan Lake, 1976, A Midsummer Night's Dream, 1977, Sleeping Beauty, The Lady of the Camelias, 1978, Matthaeus-Passion, 1981, Giselle, 1983, Sixth Symphony of G. Mahler, 1984, Peer Gynt, 1989, Fifth Symphony of G. Mahler, 1989, Requiem, 1991, A Cinderella Story, 1992, Odyssee, 1995, Vivaldi Or What You Will, 1996, Sylvia, 1997, Images from Bartók, 1998, Messias, 1999, Nijinsky, 2000. Decorated knight's cross Danebrog Order (Denmark); recipient Dance mag. award, 1983, Fed. German Cross of Merit, 1987, German Dance prize, 1988; title of Prof. conferred by City of Hamburg, 1987, Deutscher Tanzpreis, Fed. Republic of Germany, 1988; recipient Prix Diaghilev award, France, 1988, Order Des Arts et des Lettres award French Minister Culture, 1991, Carina Ari award, Stockholm, 1994, Nijinsky medal Polish Minister Culture, 1996. Mem. Acad. der Kuenste Hamburg, Acad. der Kuenste Berlin. Roman Catholic. Office: Ballettzentrum Hamburg, Caspar-Voght-Strasse 54, D-20535 Hamburg Germany

NEUNDOERFER, BERNHARD, neurologist; b. Worms/Rhein, Germany, July 2, 1937; s. Carl and Leonie (Geiger) N.; m. Gerta Zirngibl, Jan. 7, 1966; children: Gabriele, Andreas. MD, U. Heidelberg, Germany, 1963, Dr.med.habil, 1972. Med. asst. Univ. Hosp., Heidelberg, 1966-69; cons. Univ. Hosp., Mannheim, Germany, 1969-78; chmn. neurol. dept. U. Lübeck, Germany, 1978-84, U. Erlangen, Germany, 1984—; prof. U. Heidelberg, 1974; prof. U. Lübeck, 1978. Author: Polyneuritiden und Polyneuropathien, 1987, EEG-Fibel, 4th edit., 1995; editor jour. Fortschritte Neurologie Psychiatrie, Internat. Archives of Occupl. Environ. Health. With res. Germany armed forces. Mem. Am. Acad. Neurology, European Neurol. Soc., Rotary. Home: Platenstr 56, 91054 Erlangen Germany Office: U Erlangen, Dept Neurology, Schwabachanlage 6, 91054 Erlangen Germany

NEUNZIG, HERBERT HENRY, entomologist, educator; b. N.Y.C., May 11, 1927; s. Henry Edward and Elsie Wilhelmina (Schwinn) N.; m. Carolyn Miller, May 28, 1955; children: Kurt Miller, Keith Weidler. BS cum laude, Cornell U., 1953, MS, 1955, PhD, 1957. From asst. prof. to prof. emeritus N.C. State U., Raleigh, 1957-92, prof. emeritus, 1992—, acting head dept. entomology, 1988-89, grad. adminstr. dept. entomology, 1990-92, curator insect collection, 1995-98; vis. scientist Smithsonian Instn., 1994; curator lepidoptera and megaloptera N.C. State U., 1997—. Author: Moths of America North of Mexico: Fascicle 15.2, 1986, Fascicle 15.3, 1990, Fascicle 15.4, 1997, The Phycitinae of Belize, 1993; contbr.: An Introduction to the Aquatic Insects of North America, 1978, 84, 96, Immature Insects, Vol. 1, 1987, Vol. 2, 1991. With USNR, 1945-46. Grantee USDA, 1967-70, 72-75. Mem. Entomol. Soc. Washington, Lepidopterists Soc., Assn. for Tropical Lepidoptera, Phi Kappa Phi, Sigma Xi. Lutheran. Avocations: gardening, photography, carpentry. Office: NC State U Dept Entomology Raleigh NC 27695-0001

NEURGAONKAR, MILIND MADHUKAR, information systems manager; b. Sholapur, Mah, India, May 30, 1963; parents Madhukar and Manda Neurgaonkar; m. Medha Neurgaonkar, Jan. 18, 1991; children: Rahul, Rohit. BS, Pune (India) U., 1981. Cert. postgrad. diploma in computers. Sys. analyst Tandon Data Sys. Ltd., Bombay, 1987-91; sys. mgr. Hindustan Ferodo Ltd., Bombay, 1991-93, Intech Tng. Ctr., Singapore, 1993-96; MIS mgr. Merck (S) Pte Ltd., Singapore, 1997—.

NEUSCHEL, ROBERT PERCY, management consultant, educator; b. Hamburg, N.Y., Mar. 13, 1919; s. Percy J. and Anna (Becker) N.; m. Dorothy Virginia Maxwell, Oct. 20, 1944; children—Kerr Anne Ziprick, Carla Becker Neuschel Wyckoff, Robert Friedrich (Fritz). BA, Denison U., 1941; MBA, Harvard U., 1947. Indsl. engr. Sylvania Elec. Products Co., Inc., 1947-49; with McKinsey & Co., Inc., 1950-79, sr. partner, dir., 1967-79; prof. corp. governance, assoc. dean J. L. Kellogg Grad. Sch. Mgmt.; former dir. Northwestern U., assoc. dean J.L. Kellogg Sch. Mgmt.; mem. exec. bd. Internat. Air Cargo Forum, 1988—; mem. com. study air passenger svc. and safety NRC, 1989—; bd. dirs. Butler Mfg. Co., Combined Ins. Co. Am., Templeton, Kenley & Co., U.S. Freightways Co.; lectr. in field; mem. McKinsey Found. Mgmt. Rsch., Inc.; transp. task force Reagan transition team; chmn. bd. dirs. Internat. Intermodal Expn. Atlanta. Author: The Servant Leader: Unleashing the Power of Your People, 1998; co-author: Emerging Issues in Corporate Governance, 1983; contbr. over 125 articles to profl. jours. Pres. Bd. Edn., Lake Forest, Ill., 1965-70; rep. Nat. council Boy Scouts Am., 1970—, mem. N.E. exec. coun., 1969—; chmn. bd. Lake Forest Symphony, 1973; bd. dirs. Loyola U., Chgo., Chgo. Boys' Club, Nat. Ctr. Voluntary Action, Inst. Mgmt. Consultants; trustee N. Suburban Mass Transit, 1972-73, Loyola Med. Ctr.; mem. adv. coun. Kellogg Grad. Sch. Mgmt., Northwestern U., White House conferee Drug Free Am.; mem. Nat. Petroleum Coun. Transp. and Supply Com. Served to capt. USAAF, World War II. Named Transporation Man of Yr. Chitransp. Assoc., 1994; recipient Salzberg medallion Syracuse U., 1999. Fellow Acad. Advancement Corp. Governance; mem. Transp. Assn. Am., Nat. Def. Transp. Assn. (subcom. transp. tech. agenda 1990—), Intermodal Assn. N.Am. (chmn. bd. dirs.). Presbyterian (ruling elder). Clubs: Harvard Bus. Sch. (pres. 1964-65), Economic, Executive, Chicago, Mid America, Mid-Day (Chgo.); Onwentsia (Lake Forest). Home: 101 Sunset Pl Lake Forest IL 60045-1834 Office: 1936 Sheridan Rd Evanston IL 60208-0849

NEUSS, RAIMUND, newspaper editor; b. Cologne, Germany, July 9, 1963; s. Franz-Josef and Helga (Huerter) N. Abitur, Apostel Gymnasium, Cologne, 1981; MA, U. Cologne, 1986, Dr.Phil., 1988. Editor Koelnische Rundschau, Cologne, 1989—; pub. SH. Verlag GmbH, Cologne, 1992—. Author: Tugend Und Toleranz, 1989, Anmerkungen zu Walter Flex, 1992, Menschen im Aufbruch, 1995; editor: Wien-Auschwitz-Wien, 1997; editor jour. Studenten-Kurier, 1986—. Mem. Cartellverband der Katholischen Deutschen Studentenverbindungen, Gemeinschaft fuer Deutsche Studentengeschichte. Home: Boisseréestrasse 4, 50674 Cologne Germany Office: Koelnische Rundschau, Stolkgasse 25/45, 50667 Cologne Germany

NEUTATZ, DIETMAR, historian; b. Bad Homburg, Germany, Apr. 13, 1964; s. Adolf and Margaretha (Filippi) N.; m. Nicole Neutatz, Dec. 6, 1996; children: Katharina, Reglindis. PhD, U. Salzburg, Austria, 1991. Asst. prof. U. Wien, Austria, 1991, Heinrich-Heine U., Dusseldorf, Germany, 1992—. Author: Die Deutsche Frage Im Schwarzmeergebiet und in Wolhynien, 1992; editor (with D. Brandes, M. Rhode) Veroeffentlichungen des Inst. fuer Kultur und Geschichte der Deutschen im Oestlichen Europa, 1993—; editor: (with D. Brandes, E. Barbashina) Die Russlanddeutschen in Russland und Deutschland, 2000; contbr. articles to profl. jours. Home: Emil-Barth-Strasse 107, D-40595 Düsseldorf Germany Office: Inst Kultur & Geschichte, Heinrich Heine U, Düsseldorf D-40225, Germany

NEUTRA, RAYMOND RICHARD, epidemiologist; b. L.A., Mar. 12, 1939; s. Richard Joseph and Dione Niederman Neutra; m. Marian Ruth Peterson, Dec. 10, 1964 (div. Aug. 1976); children: Justin, Matthew, Brendan; m. Penelope Der Yuen, June 12, 1977. BA, Pomona Coll., 1961; MD, McGill U., Montreal, Que., Can., 1965; MPH, Harvard U., 1968, PhD, 1974. Field health officer U.S. Indian Health Svc., Crown Point, N.Mex., 1966-68; asst. prof. U. del Valle, Cali, Colombia, 1970-73, Harvard Med. Sch., Harvard Sch. Pub. Health, Boston, 1973-77; assoc. prof. UCLA, 1977-80; epidemiologist, chief spl. epidemiology program Calif. Dept. Health Svcs., Berkeley, 1980-92, acting chief environ. health, 1992-96, chief divsn. environ. and occupl. disease control, 1996—. Co-author: Clinical Decision Analysis, 1980. Bd. mem. Happy Valley Found., Ojai, Calif., 1985—. Capt. USPHS, 1966-68. Mem. Internat. Soc. for Environ. Epidemiologyh (founding pres. 1990-93). Avocations: singing, hiking. E-mail: rneutra@dhs.ca.gov. Home: 956 Evelyn Ave Albany CA 94706-2014 Office: Calif Dept Health Svcs 17th Fl 1515 Clay St Fl 17 Oakland CA 94612-1499

NEUVO, YRJÖ AUNUS OLAVI, engineering educator; b. Turku, Finland, July 21, 1943; s. Olavi and Aune (Väisälä) N.; m. Tuula Halsas, Feb. 3, 1968; children: Niilo, Marja, Pekka. Diploma in engring., Helsinki (Finland) U. Tech., 1968, lic. tech., 1971; PhD, Cornell U., 1974. Teaching asst. Helsinki U. Tech., 1967-68, acting prof., 1975-76; rsch. asst. Acad. Finland, Tampere, 1969-71, rsch. assoc., 1974-75, sr. rsch. fellow, 1979-80, rsch. prof., 1984-94; rsch. asst. Cornell U., Ithaca, N.Y., 1971-74; prof. Tampere U. Tech., 1976-93; sr. v.p. technology Nokia Corp., Espoo, Finland, 1993-94; exec. v.p., chief tech. officer Nokia Mobile Phones, Espoo, 1994—; vis. prof. U. Calif., Santa Barbara, 1981-82; bd. dirs. Vaisala Oy, Nelsinki; mem. sci. adv. group ABB Strömberg, Helsinki. Contbr. over 300 articles to profl. publs.; patentee in field. Recipient Ann. prize Finnish Elec. and Electronics Industry Assn., 1988, Nokia Corp., 1989, Tekniikka and Talous prize, 1990; Fulbright Found. grantee, 1971-72. Fellow IEEE (chmn. internat. symposium circuits and systems 1988); mem. Finnish Acad. Tech. Scis. (bd. dirs. 1990—), Royal Swedish Acad. Engring., Nordisk Forksningspolitisk rad, Academiae Europaea, Soc. Electronics Engrs. (chmn. 1978-80), PHi Kappa Phi. Lutheran. Home: Kontionkuja 3, FIN02110 Espoo Finland Office: Nokia Mobile Phones, PO Box 100, FIN000Y5 Nokia Group Finland

NEUWALD, CHRISTINE ANGELA, physician; b. Vienna, Austria, Mar. 19, 1947; d. Rudolf and Auguste Karoline Landshut; m. Michael Neuwald, May 25, 1972; children: Alexander Claudius, Tanja Christina Sofia. MD, U. Vienna, 1972. Cert. gen. practitioner; cert. med. specialist of lab. diagnostics. Asst. med. dir. Kaiser Franz Joseph Hosp., Vienna, 1982—; dir. Med. Lab. of Dept. Justice, Goellersdorf, Austria, 1995—; chair Soc. of Physicians of Kaiser Franz Joseph Hosp., 1991-92. Contbr. articles to profl. jours. Mem. Austrian Soc. Lab. Medicine, Austrian Soc. Clin. Chemistry, Internat. Soc. Thrombosis and Haemostasis, Austrian Soc. Homeopathic Medicine. Avocations: Buddhist philosophy, skiing, mountain climbing, painting. E-mail: christine.neuwald@kfj.magwien.gv.at. Office: Kaiser Franz Joseph Spital, Kundratstrasse 3, Vienna A-1100, Austria

NEUWALD, VERA LITTMANN, association administrator; b. Berlin, Germany, May 22, 1931; arrived in Peru, 1938; d. Ewald and Gertrud (Littmann) N. Sec. E.G. Kleiber, Buenos Aires, 1944-50, adminstr., 1956-60; interpreter Porgy and Bess Co., 1955-56; asst. to the pre. Empresas Electricas Asociadas, Lima, 1960-64; owner Orgn. de Congresos, Lima, 1965-86; sec. gen. Internat. Orgn. Afida, Lima, 1985—. Office: AFIDA, PO Box 227, Lima 100, Peru

NEVANS, ROY NORMAN, food products executive, producer; b. N.Y.C., July 1, 1931; s. Al Nevans and Lillian (Schiff) Margolis; m. Virginia Place, Dec. 31, 1961; children: Lisa Ann, Laurel Sue, Judith Lynn. BS, U. Pa., 1953; MBA, Columbia U., 1957. Mgmt. trainee Henningsen Foods, Inc., N.Y.C., 1958-60, mgr. export sales div., 1960-65, mgr. nat. sales div., 1965-70; v.p. mktg. Henningsen Foods, Inc., White Plains, N.Y., 1970-90; mng. dir. Henningsen Van Den Burg, Waalyk, Holland, 1979-90, Henningsen Nederland B.V., Waalyk, 1984-90, Henningsen Foods Ltd., London, 1977-90; pres. Royco Internat. Inc., Stamford, Conn., 1991—; pres. Royal Prodns., Ltd., N.Y.C., 1968-73, Internat. TV Prodns., Ltd., London, 1978—; exec. prodr. NCM Entertainment, Inc., N.Y.C., 1982—; bd. dirs. Global Edn. Mgmt., Wall Street Inst., World Trade Club. Producer Broadway shows Gandhi, 1969, Solitaire Double Solitaire, 1972; producer TV series Juke box, 1978-79; exec. producer TV mini-series Roots of Rock and Roll, 1981. Lt. comdr. USN, 1953-56. Mem. NATAS, U.S. Naval War Coll., U.S. Naval Order, River Club, Jaguar Touring Club, U. Pa. Club. Avocations: classic car collector, boating, theatre. FAX: 203-321-1295. Home: 19 Roberta Ln Greenwich CT 06830-3953 Office: Royco Internat Inc 1177 High Ridge Rd Stamford CT 06905-1203

NEVEROV, VALERI VLADIMIROVICH, physicist, educator, researcher; b. Kirsanov, Tambovskaia, USSR, Aug. 3, 1939; p. Vladimir Ivanovich and Valentina Tichonovna (Orlova) N.; m. Galina Aleksandrovna Vachrusheva (dec. Jan. 1983); children: Dmitrii, Ilia; m. Tatiana Ivanovna Belskaia, Aug. 1992; 1 child, Vladimir. Engr., Siberia Metallurg. Inst., Novokuznetsk, USSR, 1962, PhD, 1968; D in Physics and Maths., Moscow State Inst. Steel and, Alloies, 1996. Engring.; cert. docent; cert. prof. Asst. physics chair Siberia Metall. Inst., Novokuznetsk, USSR, 1966-69; lectr. Siberia Metall. Inst., Novokuznetsk, 1969-72, docent, 1972-75; docent physics Novokuznetsk State Pedagogical Inst., Russia, 1975-93; prof. Novokuznetsk State Pedagogical Inst., 1993—, head physics chair, 1999—. Contbr. numerous articles to profl. jours. Mem. Mechanochemistry Assn. Russian Fedn., N.Y. Acad. Scis., Planetary Soc. Avocation: kitchen garden. Home: Post box 7451, 654027 Novokuznetsk Russia Office: Novokuznetsk State Ped Inst, Pionersky Prosp 13, 654027 Novokuznetsk Russia

NEVES, JAYME, medical educator, consultant, researcher; b. Diamantina, Brazil, Jan. 2, 1926; s. Nilo and Leticia (Teixeira) N.; m. Maria Flora Penna, Sept. 17, 1934; children: Mauro, Mario, Aloysio, Simone, Ronaldo. MD, Federal Univ. Minas Gerais, Belo Horizonte, Brazil, 1963, PhD, 1968. Rsch. dir. Carlos Chagas Hosp. UFMG, Belo Horizonte, 1964-80; prof. Tropical Medicine Federal Univ., Belo Horizonte, 1972, head prof. of tropical medicine, 1972-80; cons. WHO Infections Diseases PAHO, Ginebra, 1974, cons. Brazilian African Soc. Tropical Medicine, Recife, Brazil, 1974, cons. health & edn. ministries, Brazil, 1985-97; invited by Karolinska Inst. to propose candidate for Nobel Prize of Medicine, 1977. Author: Author of 19 books on medicine and literature plus Textbook of Tropical Medicine, 1978-83, Pediatric Infections Diseases, 1981; editor: Nosocomial Infections: Prevention, Diagnostic & Treatment, 1987; contbr. over 500 articles to profl. jours. and sci. publs. and chpts. to books. Mem. Brazilian Soc. Hosp. Adminstr., Rio de Janeiro, 1990-97, Brazilian Soc. Hosp. Adminstr., 1990-97, Acad. of Hosp. Adminstrn., 1991-97, Acad. of Medicine of M. Gerais, 1985-97, Nat. Acad. of Military Medicine, 1968-97. Recipient Prof. Pedreira de Freitas medal, 1968, Rhodia Chemistry medal, 1969, Carlos Chagas medal, 1979. Avocations: journal writer, painting, music, journalist. Home: Rua Claudio Manoel 5991001, 30140100 Belo Horizonte Brazil

NEVES, JOÃO ADAMOR DIAS, marketing educator, researcher; b. Tocantinópolis, Goiás, Brazil, Sept. 2, 1943; s. Luiz Gonçalves and Marcelina Dias Neves; m. Mirtes Ferreira Alves, Dec. 28, 1974; children: Atila, Alexandre. Grad. in sociology, Fed. U. Minas Gerais, Belo Horizonte, Brazil, 1972, MBA, 1977; PhD in Bus. and Mgmt., Stirling (Scotland) U., 1988. Tchr. langs. Don Orione H.S., Siderópolis, Brazil, 1965-66, Belo Horizonte, 1967-68; tchr. langs. Santos Dumont H.S., Belo Horizonte, 1969-72; head pers. tng. Mesbla S.A., dept. store, Belo Horizonte, 1976-78; mktg. cons. Lê Editora, book office, Belo Horizonte, 1977-78; lectr. mktg. Viçosa (Brazil) U., 1978-84; prof. mktg. Uberlândia (Brazil) U., 1989-91; rschr., lectr. mktg. Cath. U. Portugal, Lisbon, 1991-94, Inst. Novas Pofissões, Lisbon, 1992—; mktg. cons. Jocarmy Ltd., Lisbon, 1994. Author: Marketing in the Educational Sector, 1977, Human Resources and Training, 1988. Cons. Amnesty Internat., Lisbon, 1994. Grantee U.K. Univs. Assn., 1987. Mem. Portuguese Pers. Assn., Portuguese Mktg. Assn. Roman Catholic. Avocations: music, sports activities, computers, reading, walking. E-mail: joao adamor@yahoo.com. Home: Rua Julião Quintinha, 5-4 Esq, 1500-381 Lisbon Portugal Office: Inst Novas Profissões, Av Duque Loulè 47, 1050-086 Lisbon Portugal

NEVES, JOAQUIM JOSE, electrical engineer, educator; b. Guimaraes, Portugal, Mar. 5, 1961; s. Antonio de Abrev Neves and Cremilda Augusta Dos Santos Esteves. Lic., Porto U., 1985, PhD, 1996. Rsch. asst. INESC, Porto, Portugal, 1985-96; lectr., asst. prof. Minho U., Guimaraes, 1990—; associated CERN, Geneva, Switzerland, 1987; projects mgr. ENT, Maia, Portugal, 1996—. Inventor in field; contbr. articles to profl. jours. Mem. IEEE, Ordem Dos Engenheiros Portugal. Office: Campus de Azurem, Minho Univ, 4800 Guimaraes Portugal

NEVES, LUCAS MOREIRA CARDINAL, archbishop; b. Sao Joao del Rei, Brazil, Sept. 16, 1925. ordained priest Roman Cath. Ch., 1950, as titular bishop, 1967. V.p. Pontifical Commn. for Laity, 1974-79; archbishop, 1979; sec. Congregation for Bishops, 1979-87; titular see Vescovia, 1987; archbishop Sao Salvador da Bahia, 1987-88, cardinal, from 1988; now prefect Congregation of Bishops, Vatican City; titular ch. Sts. Boniface and Alexius; curial mem. Secretariat of State (2nd sect.), Doctrine of the Faith, Bishops (congregations), Family, Culture (couns.) Latin Am. (commn.). Office: Congregation of Bishops, 00120 Vatican City Vatican City*

NEVEUX, DENIS, marketing executive; b. Sedan, France, Mar. 9, 1949; s. Louis and Marcelle (Bourga) N.; m. Martine Manlhiot; children: Nathalie, Caroline, Nicolas. M in Pub. Law, Paris Law U., 1971; grad., Inst. Polit. Sci., Paris, 1971; Higher Edn. Diploma in Pub. Law, U. Paris, 1972. Chartered acct., statutory auditor. Credit mgr. Societe Gen. France, 1972-76; cons. KMPG, Paris, 1976-78, auditor, 1978-80; mgr. KPMG, Reims, France, 1980-84; ptnr. KPMG, Paris, 1984-89; ptnr. in charge of mktg. KPMG France, 1989—; lectr. in fin. Inst. Polit. Sci., Paris, 1984—. Author book and articles. Mem. Assn. Europe et Entreprizes (bd. dirs. 1989—). Roman Catholic. Home: 8 Av Daniel LeSueur, 75007 Paris France Office: KPMG, 2 bis rue de Villiers, 92309 Levallois-Perret France

NEVILL, ANDREW JOHN, biomedical engineer; b. Exeter, Eng., Jan. 8, 1966; s. Colin Edward and Gloria Vivian (Spooner) N.; m. Ruth Joanna Sayer, July 13, 1996; 1 child, Holly. BSc with honors, U. Kent, Canterbury, Eng., 1987, PhD in Biomed. Engring., 1991. Chartered engr. Rsch. fellow U. Dundee, Scotland, 1990-91; systems programmer Alpha-Numeric Devels. Ltd., Oxford, Eng., 1991-93; med. engr. Ministry of Health, Lilongwe, Malawi, 1993-96; clin. scientist North Staffordshire Hosp., Stoke on Trent, Eng., 1996—; head dept. clin. tech. North Staffordshire Hosp., Stoke on Trent, 1999—. Mem. Instn. Elec. Engrs. (corp. mem.), Instn. Physics and Engrng. in Medicine (clin. engrng. spl. interest group 1997—). Avocations: squash, walking, camping, do-it-yourself projects, mycology. Home: Oldway, 22 Bar Hill, Madeley, Crewe CW3 9QD, England

NEVILLE, ADAM MATTHEW, civil engineer, consultant, arbitrator; b. Feb. 5, 1923; m. Mary Hallam Cousins, Mar. 29, 1952. BSc, MSc, U. London, 1950, 51, PhD, DSc, 1958, 64; DSc, U. Leeds, Eng., 1978; LLD (hon.), St. Andrews U., Scotland, 1987, Dundee (Scotland) U., 1998; D in Applied Sci. (hon.), U. Sherbrooke. Chartered civil engr. Dean of engring. U. Calgary, Can., 1963-67; head dept. civil engring. U. Leeds, 1968-78; prin. U. Dundee, U.K., 1978-87; ptnr. A&M Neville Engring. U.K., London, 1975—. Author: Properties of Concrete, 1963, 4th edit., 1995, Creep of Concrete, 1970; co-author: Basic Statistical Methods, 1964, Structural Analysis, 1971, 4th edit., 1997, Creep of Plain and Structural Concrete, 1983. Maj. Royal Engrs. Decorated CBE; hon. fellow Queen Mary Coll., London U., 1997. Fellow Royal Acad. Engring. (v.p. 1992-95); mem. Am. Concrete Inst. (hon.), Athenaeum, New Club (Edinburgh). Avocations: skiing, travel. Office: 24 Gun Wharf, 130 Wapping High St, London E1W 2NH, England

NEVILLE, ALEXANDER MUNRO, pathologist; b. Glasgow, Scotland, Mar. 24, 1935; s. Alexander Munro and Georgina Neville; m. Anne Margaret Stroyan Black, Sept. 5, 1961; children: Judeth Anne, Alexander Munro. M.B. Ch.B, U. Glasgow, 1959, PhD, 1965, MD, 1969, DSc, 1985. Sr. lectr. pathology U. Glasgow, 1967-70; hon. cons. in pathology Royal Marsden Hosp., London, 1970-85; prof. pathology U. London, 1972-85; dir. Ludwig Inst. Cancer Rsch., London, 1975-85; assoc. dir., sci. sec. Ludwig Inst. Cancer Rsch., N.Y., London and Zurich, 1985—; prof. pathology Royal Postgrad. Med. Sch., London, 1992—. Author: the Human Adrenal Cortex, 1982; editor: Biopsy Pathology, 1975 (award); editor jour. Tumor Biology, 1978 (award). Fellow Royal Coll. Pathologists (hon. treas. 1993-98); mem. Athenaeum Club. Avocations: gardening, golf, history. Home: 6 Woodlands Park, Tadworth Surrey KT20 7JL, England Office: Ludwig Inst Cancer Rsch, Glen House Stag Pl Sixth Fl, London SW1E 5AG, England also: 605 3rd Ave New York NY 10158-0180

NEVILLE, JOHN, actor, director; b. London, May 2, 1925; s. Reginald and Mabel L. (Fry) Neville; m. Caroline Hooper, 1948; 6 children. Ed., Royal Acad. Dramatic Art; DFA (hon.), Lethbridge U., Alta., Can., 1979, N.S. Coll. Art and Design, 1981. With Lowestoft Repertory Co., Eng., 1948, Birmingham (Eng.) Repertory Co., 1949-50, Bristol Old Vic Co., London, 1953, Chichester Theatre Co., 1962; dir. Nottingham Playhouse, 1963-68, Newcastle Playhouse, 1967; hon. prof. drama Nottingham U., 1967—; drama adviser Howard and Wyndham, Ltd.; artistic dir. Citadel Theatre, Edmonton, Alta., Can., 1973-78, Neptune Theatre, Halifax, N.S., 1978-83; artistic dir., Stratford Shakespearean Festival, Stratford, Ont., Can., 1985-89. Actor (films) Mr. Topaz, Oscar Wilde, Billy Budd, The Unearthly Stanger, A Study in Terror, Adventures of Gerrard, lead role Adventures of Baron Munchausen, 1987, The Road to Wellville, 1994, Regeneration, The X-Files: Fight the Future, Little Women, High School High, Dangerous Minds, The Fifth Element, Sabotage; (prin. stage appearances) A Misummer Night's Dream, King John, (Broadway plays) Romeo and Juliet, 1956, Sherlock Holmes, 1975, (with Bristol Old Vic Co. Eng.) She Stoops to Conquer, Macbeth, Richard III, (with Nottingham Playhouse Co. Eng.) A Man for All Seasons, 1961, Death of a Salesman, Othello, others, (TV appearances) Henry V, Romeo and Juliet, Hamlet, The First Churchills, (TV series) Grand, 1990; dir. (plays) Heny V, 1960, Twelfth Night, 1962, The Importance of Being Earnest, 1963, Richard II, 1965, Saint Joan, 1966, The Rivals, 1972, The Seagull, 1978, Hamlet, 1986, Mother Courage, 1987, Othello, 1987, Three Sisters, 1989, School for Scandal, 1990, St John, 1993, The X-Files, others, (opera) Don Giovanni; prin. film major tours include U.S., 1956, 58-59, 70, Malta, 1961, West African cities, 1963;. With Royal Navy, World War II. Decorated knight Order Brit. Empire. Mem. Brit. Actor's Equity Assn. Home: 139 Winnett Ave, Toronto, ON Canada M6C 3L7

NEVILLE, THOMAS LEE, food service company executive; b. Columbus, Ind., Jan. 1, 1947; s. Frank Thomas and Esquline Coons (Davis) N.; m. Shavona Rose Lagneau, Aug. 10, 1966; children: Timothy David, Sherry Lynn. AAS, Austin Peay State U., Clarksville, Tenn., 1994. Cert. exec. chef; cert. food exec. Enlisted U.S. Army, 1966, apptd. WO1, 1976, commd. CW3, 1986; food advisor Army Food Rsch., Devel. and Engring. Ctr., Natick, Mass.; ret. U.S. Army, 1990; regional mgr. KCA Corp., Hopkinsville, Ky., 1990—; mem. Warrant Officers Assn., 1976-90. Mem. Ret. Officers Assn., Am. Soc. Quality Control, Am. Culinary Fedn., Am. Mgmt. Assn., Internat. Food Svc. Execs. Assn., Masons. Home: 1728 Clara Ct Clarksville TN 37040-7823 Office: KCA Corp PO Box 641 Hopkinsville KY 42241-0641

NEVINS, SHEILA, television programmer and producer; b. N.Y.C.; d. Benjamin and Stella Nevins; m. Sidney Koch; 1 child, David Andrew. BA, Barnard Coll.; MFA, Yale U. TV prodr. Great Am. Dream Machine, NET, 1971-73, The Reasoner Report, ABC, 1973, Feeling Good, Children's TV Workshop, 1975-76, Who's Who, CBS, 1977-78; dir. documentary and family programming HBO, N.Y.C., 1978-82; v.p. documentary programming Home Box Office, N.Y.C., 1986-95, sr. v.p. original programming, 1998-99; exec. v.p. original programming HBO, N.Y.C., 1999—. Bd. dirs. Women's Action Alliance. Recipient Peabody award, 1986, 92, 95, 96, 97, Acad. Award for Documentary, 1993, 96, 98, Emmy award, 1994, 95, 96, 97, 98, 99, 2000, Glaad Media award, 1998, Media award Mental Health Assn. N.Y.C., 1996, Three Arts award; named Woman of Achievement YMCA, 1991, Top 25 Women in TV, Emmy mag., 1996, Top 25 Smartest Women Am., Mirabella Mag., 1999. Mem. Writers Guild Am., N.Y. Women in Film (Muse award 1998), Internat. Documentary Assn. (Vision award 1998). *

NEVINS, WILLIAM J., oil and gas brokerage executive, consultant; b. Yonkers, N.Y., Sept. 16, 1952; s. Francis Robert and Alice Frances (Stager) N.; m. Joan Evelyn Leach, June 8, 1975 (div. June, 1980). BA in English Lit. and Fin., U. Miami, Coral Gables, Fla., 1974; postgrad. studies in Law, Western State U., Fullerton, Calif., 1974-75. CEO Nevins Enterprises Ltd., various cities, U.S., 1976—; CEO, pres. Century 21, Heritage Realty, Inc., North Miami, Fla., 1985-87, N&Z, Heritage Realty, Inc., Miami, 1987-96; sr. assoc., registered rep. Texakoma Fin. Oil and Gas, Dallas, 1996-98; v.p., oil and gas broker Western Am. Securities, Reef Exploration, Inc., Dallas, 1998—; v.p., bd. dirs. Pyramid Fin. Svcs., Inc. N. Miami Beach, Fla., 1983-84; cons. Park West Overtown Devel. Com., Miami, Fla., 1984-85, Miami

Beach Developers and Investors Conf., 1985-90. Vol. asst. mgr. John V. Lindsay Miami Dem. Primary Campaign. 1972; founder Universal Children's Found. Inc., 1995. Mem. Nat. Assn. Security Dealers (registered rep.). Roman Catholic. Avocations: game fishing, antique autos, coin collecting, travel, yachting. Office: Nevins Enterprises Ltd 13237 Montfort Dr Ste 438 Dallas TX 75240-1117

NEVIRKOVETS, IVAN PETROVICH, physicist; b. Rivne, Ukraine, Apr. 13, 1955; s. Petro Volodymyrovich and Galina Antonivna N. Student, Kiev (Ukraine) State U., 1972-77; PhD, Inst. Metal Physics, Kiev, 1985. Engr. Inst. Superhard Materials, Kiev, 1977-79; engr. Inst. Metal Physics, Kiev, 1979-82, jr. rschr., 1982-85, rschr., 1985-88, sr. rschr., 1988—; lectr. Kiev State U., 1996. Contbr. articles to profl. jours. German Acad. Exch. Svc. fellow, 1991, Royal Soc. Eng. fellow, 1993; grantee Internat. Sci. Found., 1994. Mem. Ukrainian Phys. Soc., Am. Phys. Soc. Office: Inst Metal Physics, 36 Vernadsky Blvd, UA252680 Kiev Ukraine

NEVIUS, RICHARD CASSELS, religious studies educator, priest; b. Washington, Apr. 6, 1936; arrived in Mex., 1990; s. Richard David and Laura Eva (Cassels) N.; m. Elizabeth Aline Quereau, June 13, 1959; children: Alistair Michael, Victoria Nevius Skoog, James Cassels. BA, Lafayette Coll., 1956; MDiv, Gen. Theol. Sem., N.Y.C., 1959; M of Letters, Oxford (Eng.) U., 1962; D in Ministry, Princeton (N.J.) Sem., 1987. Ordained priest Anglican Ch., 1961. Curate St. Paul's Parish, Washington, 1962-64; fellow, tutor Gen. Theol. Sem., N.Y.C., 1964-66; prof. theology St. Stephen's Sch., Rome, 1966-69; headmaster Heathwood Hall, Columbia, S.C., 1969-72; rector various parishes, U.S., Eng., Middle East, Mex., 1972-95; prof. New Testament St. Andrew's Sem., Manila, 1997—; sec. standing com. Diocese of Eau Claire, Wis., 1976-79; canon missioner Diocese of Utah, Salt Lake City, 1982—; lectr. Day Spring Westminster Coll., Salt Lake City, 1979-82; interim vicar Christ Ch. St. Kilda, Melbourne, Australia, 1996. Author: The Divine Names in St. Mark, Vol. XXV of Studies and Documents, 1964, The Divine Names in the Gospels, Vol. XXX of Studies and Documents, 1967; contbr. articles to profl. jours. Mem. Davis County Mental Health Bd., Farmington, Utah, 1979-82; spl. tchr. Canterbury Group, ARAMCO, Dhahran, Saudi Arabia, 1982-88; founder Leisure Learning, San Miguel de Allende, Mex., 1990—. Named Sr. Active Priest, Iglesia Anglicana de Mex., 1995. Mem. Soc. Internat. Papyrologues, Am. Soc. Papyrology, Soc. Biblical Lit./Am. Acad. Religion, N.Y. Acad. Sci. Democrat. Avocations: palaeography, oil painting, acting, sailing, travel. Home: Apartado 268, 37700 San Miguel de Allende, Estado de Guanjuato Mexico

NEVLING, HARRY REED, human resources consultant; b. Rochester, Minn., Sept. 15, 1946; s. Edwin Reid and Ruth Margaret (Mulvihill) N.; m. Joanne Carol Meyer, Nov. 26, 1976; 1 son, Terry John. AA, Rochester C.C., 1973; BA cum laude, U. Winona, 1974; MBA, U. Colo., 1990. Pers. rep. Rochester Meth. Hosp., 1974-75; dist. mgr. Internat. Dairy Queen Corp., 1975-76; with David Realty Corp. David Realty Corp., Littleton, Colo., 1976-83; v.p. David Realty Corp., Littleton, 1979-83, gen. mgr., 1981-83; gen. mgr. Longmont (Colo.) United Hosp., 1977-99, pers. dir., 1977-87, dir. human resources, 1988-95, v.p. human resources, 1995-99; prin. HR Cons., Longmont, 1999—, pres., 1999; cons. Front Range C.C. Denver, 1983-85; prin. Harry R. Nevling-Broker, 1983-85, 95-97; v.p. Realty Mart Internat., Inc., 1985-93, Dist. chmn. Am. party, 1973-74, St. Vrain Valley Sch. Dist., Health Occupations Adv. Com. 1977—, chmn. 1979-85, Vocat. Edn. Adv. Coun. 1986-91, pres. 1986-91; with Citizen Amb. People to People Program, Hungary, Czech Republic, Germany, 1991; mem. exec. com. Nat. Health Care Skills Stds. Project, 1993-95; spkr., presenter in field. Co-author: Healthcare Reform: The Human Resources Cornerstone to Successful Reform, 1992. Served to capt. U.S. Army, 1965-72; Vietnam. Decorated D.F.C., Bronze Star with oakleaf cluster, Air medal (22, valor device). Recipient Rescue citation for lifesaving Boeing Co., 1969, Helping Hand award United Way, 1974, Outstanding Svc. award, 1979, cert. of appreciation, 1982, Disting. Young Alumni award Winona State U., 1989. Mem. VFW (past post comdr.), Longmont Area Human Resources Assn., 1980-89, Boulder Area Human Resource Assn., 1978—, Mountain States VHA (pers. com. 1989-96, chmn. 1989-93), Colo. Healthcare Assn. for Human Resource Mgmt. (sec. 1980, pres. elect 1981, pres. 1981-82, exec. com. 1986—), Am. Soc. for Healthcare Human Resources Adminstrn. (ann. meeting chmn. 1985-86, regional dir. 1986-90, legis. and labor liaison 1988-90, chpt. rels. com. 1990-91, pres. elect 1991-92, pres. 1992-93, immediate past pres. 1993-95, exec. com. 1991-95, chmn. nominating com. 1994-95, chmn. conflict of interest com., 1994-95, nat. nominating com. 1996, Bylaws com. 1992-93, 96-99, Disting. Svc. award 1996), Soc. Human Resource Mgmt., Human Resource Cert. Inst. (sr. profl. in human resources), Vietnam Helicopter Pilots Assn.; bd. mem. Bus. Dependent Care Assn., 1995-99, pres. 1996. Home and Office: 2346 Eagleview Cir Longmont CO 80504-7797

NEVYJEL, ALEXANDER, scientist; b. Vienna, Austria, Jan. 17, 1949; s. Ferdinand and Eleonore (Herzog) N.; children: Katharina, Cornelia. PhD in Natural Scis., U. Vienna, 1972. Scientist Austrian Rsch. Ctr. Seibersdorf (Austria), 1972-83, dep. head dept. math., head libr., 1983-88, head dept. info. and documentation, 1989—. Contbr. articles to profl. jours. Mem. Austrian Assn. for Documentation and Info., Austrian Libr. Assn., Austrian Online User Group, Fachbeirat fur Info. and Documentation Systeme. Roman Catholic. Office: OFZS, A 2444 Seibersdorf Austria

NEW, ANNE LATROBE, public relations, fund raising executive; b. Evanston, Ill., May 10, 1910; d. Charles Edward and Agnes (Bateman) N.; m. John C. Timmerman, Sept. 30, 1933; 1 child, Jan LaTrobe. AB, U. S.C., 1930; postgrad., Hunter Coll., 1930-31, NYU, 1932-33. APR (Accredited Pub. Relations Practitioner). Editorial asst. Pictorial Review Mag., N.Y.C., 1930-32; copy asst. J. Walter Thompson Co., N.Y.C., 1932-33; sub editor Cosmopolitan Mag., N.Y.C., 1933-37; with Girl Scouts of the U.S., N.Y.C., 1937-57, chief pub. rels. officer, 1945-57; dir. pub. info. edn. Nat. Recreation and Park Assn., 1957-66; special asst. gen. dir. Internat. Social Svc. Am. Branch, N.Y.C., 1966-68; dir. devel. Nat. Accreditation Coun. for Agys. Serving Blind and Visually Handicapped, N.Y.C., 1969-78; pres. Timmerman & New Inc., Mamaroneck, N.Y., 1980—; cons. dept. pub. adminstrn. Baruch Coll., CUNY, 1987-94, Sch. Pub. Affairs, 1994-99. Author: Service For Givers, The Story of the National Information Bureau, 1983, Raise More Money for Your Nonprofit Organization, 1991; contbr. articles to profl. jours. Mem. Westchester Dem. Com. Westchester County, 1963-67, 89—; bd. dirs. Mamaroneck (N.Y.) United Fund, 1963-64; chair nominating com. LWV, Mamaroneck, 1988, chair by-law com., 1989; warden emerita, mem. fin. com. St. Thomas' Episc. Ch., Mamaroneck; dist. leader Village of Mamaroneck Dem. Com. Recipient Marzella Garland award for outstanding achievement in promotion of improved housing conditions in Mamaroneck Village, 1995. Mem. Pub. Rels. Soc. Am. (bd. dirs. N.Y. chpt. 1958-72), Women Execs. Pub. Rels. (sec. 1962-63), Nat. Soc. Fund Raising Execs. (bd. dirs. Greater N.Y. chpt. 1978-84), Phi Beta Kappa. Democrat. Avocations: tennis, dancing. Office: Timmerman & New Inc 235 S Barry Ave Mamaroneck NY 10543-4104

NEWBERRY, ELIZABETH CARTER, greenhouse and floral company owner; b. Blackwell, Tex., Nov. 25, 1921; m. Weldon Omar Newberry, Sept. 24, 1950 (dec. Nov. 1984); 1 child. Student Hardin Simmons U., 1938-39. Office mgr. F. W. Woolworth, Abilene, Tex., 1939-50; acct. Western Devel. & Investment Corp., Englewood, Colo., 1968-72; owner, operator Newberry Bros. Greenhouse and Florist, Denver, 1972—; bd. dirs. Western Devel. and Investment Corp. Englewood, Colo., 1979-87. Pres. Ellsworth Elem. Sch. PTA, Denver, 1961-62; v.p. Hill Jr. High Sch. PTA, Denver. Home: 201 Monroe St Denver CO 80206-5505 Office: Newberry Bros Greenhouse 201 Garfield St Denver CO 80206-5518

NEWBERY, DAVID MICHAEL GARROOD, economics educator; b. Fulmer Chase, Eng., June 1, 1943; s. Alan James and Betty Amelia (Roche) N.; m. Terry Eve Apter; children: Miranda, Julia M. Grad. in math., Cambridge U., 1963, grad. in econs., 1965, PhD in Econs., 1976. Economist Treasury of Tanzanian Govt., 1965-66; asst. lectr. econs. Cambridge (Eng.) U., 1966-71, Univ. lectr., 1971, reader, 1986, prof. applied econs., dir. dept., 1988—, fellow, dir. studies Churchill Coll., 1966-87, professorial fellow, 1988—; with Cowles Found., Yale U., 1969; assoc. prof. Stanford (Calif.) U., 1976; vis. prof. Princeton (N.J.) U., 1985; Ford vis. prof. U. Calif., Berkeley, 1987-88. Co-author: Theory of Commodity Price Stabilization, 1981; co-editor: Theory of Taxation for Developing Countries, 1987; assoc. editor Econ. Jour., 1977—, European Econ. Rev., 1989-93; contbr. articles to profl. jours., chpts. to books. British Acad. fellow, 1991. Fellow Ctr. for Econ. Policy Rsch.; mem. Royal Econ. Soc. (coun. 1984-89), European Econ. Assn. (pres. 1996). Office: Cambridge U Dept Appl Ec, Sidgwick Ave, Cambridge CB3 9DE, England

NEWBOULD, BRIAN RABY, musicologist; b. Kettering, Northants, Eng., Feb. 26, 1936; s. Harry Raby and Norah Millicent (Butler) N.; m. Anne Leicester, 1960 (div. 1971); children: Alison, Stephen; m. Ann Elizabeth Airton, July 27, 1976; 1 child, Fiona. BA, U. Bristol, Eng., 1957, BMus, 1958, MA, 1961. Lectr. Royal Scottish Acad. Music, Glasgow, 1960-65, U. Leeds, Eng., 1965-79; prof. music U. Hull, Eng., 1979—; chmn. Schubert Inst., Eng., 1994—. Author: Schubert and The Symphony: A New Perspective, 1992, Schubert: The Music and the Man, 1997; completer: Schubert: Symphony No. 7 in E, 1978, Schubert: Symphonies Nos. 8 and 10, 1980-82; editor Incorporated Soc. Musicians Jour., London, 1969-73, Schubert Studies, 1998. Fellow Royal Soc. Arts. Avocations: fell walking, crosswords. Office: U of Hull, Hull HU6 7RX, England

NEWBURG, ANDRE, lawyer; b. Berlin, Jan. 9, 1928; s. Hugo and Olga (Cherniak) N.; m. Ellen French Vanderbilt, Dec. 27, 1953 (div. 1996); children: Michael W., Anne C., Daniel F., Thomas H.; m. Susan Renwick Baring, June 26, 1997. AB, Harvard U., 1949, LLB, 1952. Bar: N.Y. 1952. Mem. Cleary, Gottlieb, Steen & Hamilton, N.Y.C., 1952-91, Paris, 1956-59, 74-76, Brussels, 1960-64, Hong Kong, 1980; ptnr. Cleary, Gottlieb, Steen & Hamilton, 1963-91, counsel, 1997—; gen. counsel European Bank for Reconstrn. and Devel., London, 1991-95, sr. adv., 1995-97. Mem. Coun. on Fgn. Rels., 1973—; trustee Am. Sch. Classical Studies at Athens, 1965-99, Gennadius Libr., Athens, 2000; bd. dirs. Small Enterprise Assistance Funds, 1999—. Decorated Order of Leopold II (Belgium). Mem. ABA, Am. Assn. Internat. Commn. Jurists (bd. dirs. 1971—, chmn. 1989-91), Internat. Bar Assn., Internat. Law Assn. (monetary law com.), Assn. Bar City N.Y. chmn. spl. com. on Soviet affairs 1989-91), London Ct. Internat. Arbitration (arbitrator), Royal Inst. Internat. Affairs, Century Assn., Brooks's, Polo Club (Paris). Office: Cleary Gottlieb Steen Hamilton, 55 Basinghall St, London EC2V 5EH, England

NEWBURGER, CARYN LASON, English educator; b. Chgo., Aug. 28, 1960; d. Marvin Mitchell and Sandra Woolman Lason; m. Manuel Harry Newburger, Aug. 14, 1983; children: Michael Jonathon, Joshua Ian. BA in English, U. Tex., 1982, postgrad., 1996-97, MEd in Ednl. Psychology, 1989. Cert. counselor; cert. tchr. Tex. Tchr. lang. arts Bastrop (Tex.) Ind. Sch. Dist., 1982-89; adj. instr., writing Austin C.C., 1989—; adj. rep. Austin C.C., Austin, 1996—; ednl. cons., writer Comms. Cons., Norman, Okla., 1989—. Student coun. advisor Bastrop Ind. Sch. Dist., 1983-86, mid. sch. gifted program coord., 1988-89; room parent St. Francis Sch., Austin, 1998—; ballet docent Ballet Austin, 1989-90. Recipient Tchg. Excellence award Nat. Inst. for Staff and Orgnl. Devel., 2000. Mem. MLA, Nat. Coun. of Tchrs. of English. Avocations: ballet dancing, writing, gardening. E-mail: carynn@austin.cc.tx.us. Office: Austin CC 5930 Middle Fiskville Rd Austin TX 78752-4341

NEWBURY, ANTHONY CHARLES, dental surgeon; b. Hobart, Tasmania, Australia, Jan. 19, 1940; s. Charles Renton and Isabella Dawson (Davie) N.; m. Delia Kate Frances Miles, Apr. 16, 1964 (div. 1984); children: Kim Frances, Andrew Charles; m. Brigitte Stevenson, Oct. 4, 1986. B Dental Sci., U. Melbourne, Australia, 1964, MDSc, 1969. Pvt. dental practice Melbourne, 1963-66, London, 1970-71; pvt. practice in orthodontia Melbourne, 1966-70; pvt. practice dental surgery London, 1971—; founding ptnr. Oral Hygiene Ctr., London, 1977—; sr. clin. demonstrator dept. restorative dentistry U. Melbourne, 1964-69, sr. lectr. dept. anatomy, 1964-69; presenter in field. Fellow Internat. Coll. Dentists; mem. ADA (assoc.), Royal Soc. Medicine, Brit. Dental Assn. (pres. Met. br. 1983, mem. rep. bd. 1975-81, former mem. dental health com.), Chgo. Dental Soc. (assoc.), European Orthodontic Soc., Brit. Orthodontic Soc., Cranio Group Brit., Dental Migraine Study Club, European Dental Soc. (founding mem.), Brit. Dental Soc. for Clin. Nutrition (founding mem.), Pierre Fauchard Soc., Internat. Acad. Oral Medicine and Toxicology (pres. 1994—), Brit. Soc. Restorative Dentistry, Brit. Soc. Periodontology. Avocations: tennis, golf, gardening, antiques, wine. Home: 5 Doria Rd, London SW6 4UF, England Office: 72 Harley St, London W1N 1AE, England

NEWBY, EARL FERNANDO, educator; b. Louisville, Apr. 14, 1948. BS, Tenn. State U., 1970; MA, U. Louisville, 1972; EdD, Spalding U., 1998. Cons., tchr. edn. Ky. Dept. Edn., Frankfort, 1970; tchr., prin. Jefferson County Schs., Louisville, 1971-75, Greater Clark County Schs., Jeffersonville, Ind., 1975-98; cons., computer tech. Newby & Assocs., Louisville, 1996—; asst. prof. Morehead (Ky.) State U., 1998—; adj. prof. Western Ky. U., Bowling Green, 1998; prof. Eastern Ky. U., 1999-2001; presenter Ky. Assn. Sch. Adminstrs., 1999, Pi Lamdba Theta Internat., 1999, , Nat. Assn. Elem. Sch. Prins., 2000, Nat. Assn. Black Sch. Educators, 2000, Nat. Coun. Profs. Ednl. Adminstrn., 2000, Ky. Assn. Sch. Adminstrs., 2000, So. Regional Coun. Ednl. Adminstrn., 2000. Contbr. articles to profl. publs. Named to Order Ky. Cols. Mem. Am. Assn. Sch. Adminstrs., NAESP, So. Regional Coun. Ednl. Adminstrs., Nat. Coun. Profs. Ednl. Adminstrn., Nat. Assn. Black Sch. Educators, Ky. Assn. Sch. Adminstrs., Ky. Assn. Black Sch. Educators, Lexington Assn. Black Sch. Educators, Kappa Alpha Psi, Phi Delta Kappa, Pi Lambda Theta, Sigma Rho Sigma. Democrat. Methodist. Avocations: tennis, basketball, reading, bowling, golf. Home: PO Box 211 Harrods Creek KY 40027-0211 Office: Eastern Ky U/Coll Edn Dept Adminstrn Counseling 521 Lancaster Ave Richmond KY 40475-3100

NEWBY, JOHN ROBERT, metallurgical engineer; b. Kansas City, Mo., Nov. 17, 1923; s. Merritt Owen and Gladys Mary (McCleery) N.; m. Audry Marie Loniker, Sept. 21, 1963 (div. 1980); children: Deborah A., Walter J., William F., Matthew O., Robert J. BA, U. Mo., Kansas City, 1947; BS in Metall. Engring., Colo. Sch. Mines, 1949; MS, U. Cin., 1963. Cert. profl. engr. Chemist Bar Rusto Plating Corp., Kansas City, 1949; supr. United Chromium, Ferndale, Mich., 1949-52; prin. rsch. metallurgist Armco Inc., Middletown, Ohio, 1952-85; prin. John Newby Cons., Middletown, 1985—; cons. Phoenix Cons., Inc., Cin., 1988—. Author, editor: Formability 2000, 1982, Metallic Materials, 1978, Sheet Metal Forming, 1976; editor: Mechanical Testing, Vol. 8, 9th edit., 1985. Scoutmaster Boy Scouts Am., Middletown, 1952-86, now asst. dist. commr.; chmn. Safety Coun., Middletown, 1978-80. Staff sgt. USAF, 1943-46, PTO. Fellow ASTM (chmn. 1963—, chmn. E-28 com. on mech. testing 1998—, Award of Merit 1984), ASM (sustaining mem., chpt. chmn. 1970, Award of Merit 1980); mem. SAE (sect. chmn. 1984). Democrat. Achievements include patent for high strength formable steel sheet; development of interstitial free steel, strain analysis process for metallic sheet formability. Home and Office: 100 Marymont Ct Middletown OH 45042-3735

NEWCOMBE, HANNA, chemistry educator, organization executive, editor; b. Prague, Czechoslovakia, Feb. 5, 1922; m. Alan George Newcombe, Sept. 8, 1946; 3 children. BA in Chemistry, McMaster U., Can., 1945; PhD in Chemistry, U. Toronto, Ont., Can., 1951. Lab. analyst Can. Packers, Toronto, 1943-44; rsch. Polymer Corp., Sarnia, Ont., Can., 1945; abstractor Chem. Abstracts, Hamilton, Ont., 1945-60; supr. Chem. Lab. of McMaster U., 1957-58; instr. Chem. Inst. Can., 1959-60; with Newcombe Assn., 1961-64; tchr. Ancaster (Ont.) H.S., 1961; lectr. in peace York U., Toronto, 1976-97, tutorial instr., 1977-85; pres. World Fed. Authority Com., Dundas, Ont., ., 1980—. Author: Alternative Approaches to World Government, 1967, National Patterns in International Organization, 1975, Reform of the UN Security Council, 1979, Approaches to a Nuclear-Free Future, 1982, Design for a Better World, 1983; editor Peace Rsch. Abstracts Jour., 1962—. Mem. Hamilton Mundialization Com., Dundas Mundialization Com. Recipient Lentz Internat. Peace Rsch. award, 1974, named Woman of Yr. for pub. affairs, Hamilton, Ont., 1985. Mem. Internat. Peace Rsch. Assn., Consortium on Peace Rsch., Edn. and Devel., Can. Voice of Women for Peace, Can. UN Assn. (Pearson Peace medal 1997), Can. Peace Rsch. and Edn. Assn. (award 1983), World Federalists of Can. (Peace award 1972). Mem. Soc. of Friends. Office: 25 Dundana Ave, Dundas, ON Canada L9H 4E5

NEWCOMB-HODGETTS, BARRY JOHN, media company executive; b. London, Sept. 4, 1953; s. Arthur Earnest and Audrey Olga (Butler) Hodgetts; m. Vaune Craig-Raymond, Sept. 1, 1977; 1 child, Chlor Olga. MA, Coll. Distributive Trade, 1972. Prodn. mgr. I.P.C., London, 1972-74; media planner, buyer Charles Barker, London, 1974-76; asst. media dir. Rickey Tibble, London, 1976-78; mng. dir. Blazelynn, London, 1978-84, Media Assocs., Hamphire, Eng., 1984—. Avocations: reading, writing, arts, social science, sports. Office: Media Assocs, Dower House Bramdean, Hampshire SO24OHP, England

NEWELL, ALAN FRANCIS, computing researcher, educator; b. Birmingham, Eng., Mar. 1, 1941; s. Frank and Lily M. (Taylor) N.; m. Margaret E. Morgan, July, 1965; children: Anna, Catherine, David. BSc, U. Birmingham, Eng., 1962, PhD, 1965. Chartered engr. Rsch. engr. Std. Telecomm. Labs., Eng., 1965-69; lectr. U. Southampton, Eng., 1970-79; prof. U. Dundee, Scotland, 1980—; dep. prin. U. Dundee, 1992-95, dean faculty engring. and applied sci., 1985-87, head dept. applied computing, 1998—; phonic ear disting. lectr. Internat. Soc. of Augmentative and Alternative Comms., 1991, Jansson Meml. lectr. The Coll. of Speech and Lang. Therapists, 1990. Contbr. over 100 articles to profl. jours., 16 chpts. to boks; patentee in field. Recipient Lloyd of Kilgerran prize Found. of Sci. and Tech., Eng., 1995, Franklin V. Taylor award IEEE, 1994; Winston Churchill Travel fellow Winston Church Meml. Trust, 1976. Fellow Brit. Computer Soc. (award for social benefit 1988), Instn. Elec. Engrs., Royal Soc. Edinburgh, Royal Coll. Speech & Lang. Therapists (hon.), Order of Brit. Empire. Avocations: sailing, skiing. Office: Dept Applied Computing, U Dundee, Dundee DD1 4HN, Scotland

NEWELL, BYRON BRUCE, JR., pastor; b. Long Beach, Calif., July 31, 1932; s. Byron Bruce and Eleanor Whitaker (Davis) N.; m. Ingrid Charlotte Asche, June 11, 1955 (dec. July 1989); children: Thomas, Susan, Robert, Michael; m. Theresa Ann Troncale, Sept. 1, 1990. Student, Wesleyan U., 1950-51; BS, U.S. Naval Acad., 1955; MSEE, U.S. Naval Postgrad. Sch. Monterey, 1962; postgrad. nuclear power tng., 1964-65; MDiv, Va. Theol. Sem., 1987. Ordained priest, Episcopal Ch., 1988. Commd. ensign U.S. Navy, 1955, advanced through grades to rear adm., 1980; weapons officer U.S.S. Lowry, Hull (destroyers), 1955-58; comdg. officer salvage ship, 1962-64, exec., comdg. officer nuclear cruisers, 1968-77, manpower/tng. surface ship personnel, 1977-79; with Nat. Mil. Command Center, Washington, 1979-80, chief navy info., 1980-82, chief navy legis. affairs, 1982-84; assoc. dean Trinity Episcopal Sch. for Ministry, Ambridge, Pa., 1990-96; chmn., trustee Breakthrough, Inc. Decorated Legion of Merit, D.S.M. Mem. Naval Inst., Naval Hist. Soc., Met. Club. Home: 256 Thorn St Sewickley PA 15143-1204

NEWELL, CHRISTOPHER JAMES, medical educator; b. Sydney, Australia, Mar. 2, 1964; s. Phillip Keith and Merle Edith (Callaghan) N.; m. Jill Collyer, June 25, 1994; 1 child, Christine. BA, Tasmanian State Inst. Tech., Lauceston, Australia, 1987; MA with honors, U. Wollongong, Australia, 1989; PhD, Deakin U., Geelong, Australia, 1994. Ordained to ministry Anglican Ch., 1996. Tutor Tasmanian State Inst. Tech., Lauceston, 1988-91; lectr. U. Tasmania Sch. Nursing, Australia, 1991-93; lectr. dept. cmty. health U. Tasmania, Australia, 1993-95; sr. lectr. U. Tasmania Sch. Medicine, Australia, 1995—; med. educator Royal Australian Coll. Gen. Practitioners, 1998—; Bishops advisor on ethical issues Anglican DIocese Tasmania, 1995—; dir. Disaled Peoples Internat. Ltd., 1990-96; mem. Australian Health Ethics Com., 1994—; cons. in field. Co-author: Managing Mortality: Euthanasia on Trial, 1996, Euthanasia, Death and Dying: An Anglican Resource, 1998; editor: What Is This Thing Called Bioethics?, 1999; mem. editl. bd. Health Forum, 1994—. Active Telstra Australian Consumer Consultative Com., 1989—, chair, 1998—; asst. St. Davids Anglican Cathedral, Hobart, Australia, 1996—; mgmt. com. Consumers Health Forum Australia, 1989—. Mem. Australian Coll. Edn., Australian Bioethics Assn. Anglican. Avocation: church music. Home: 8 Lawley Crescent, South Hobert 7004, Australia Office: Univ Tasmania Sch Medicine, GPO Box 252-33, Hobart TAS 7001, Australia

NEWELL, MIKE, film director; b. 1942. Films include: The Awakening, 1980, Bad Blood, 1983, Dance With a Stranger, 1985, The Good Father, 1986, Amazing Grace and Chuck, 1987, Soursweet, 1988, Enchanted April, 1991, Into the West, 1992, Four Weddings and a Funeral, 1994, An Awfully Big Adventure, 1995, Donnie Brasco, 1997, Pushing Tin, 1999, The Adventures of Young Indiana Jones: Masks of Evil, 1999; exec. prodr. (films) Photographing Fairies, 1997, 20 Cigarettes, 1999, Best Laid Plans, 1999, High Fidelity, 2000, Traffic, 2000; TV films include: Big Soft Nellie, Mrs. Mouse, Baa Baa Blacksheep, The Melancholy Hussar, Ready When You Are Mr. McGill, Destiny, The Man in the Iron Mask, 1977, The Gift of Friendship, Blood Feud, 1983, Common Ground, 1990. Office: Dogstar UK, 5 Sherwood St, London W1V 7RA, England Mailing: ICM Ste 219 8942 Wilshire Blvd Beverly Hills CA 90211*

NEWELL, SIMON JAMES, medical educator, consultant; b. London, Sept. 23, 1956; m. Debra Newell, June 26, 1982; children: Kathryn, Richard, Penelope. MBChB, Leeds U., 1980, MD, 1996. Lectr. paediatrics U. Birmingham, England, 1986-92; cons. in neonatal medicine and paediatrics Leeds United Tchg. Hosp. NHS Trust, 1992—; acad. sub-dean U. Leeds Sch. Medicine, 1996—. Author: Neonatology, 1996; contbr. articles to profl. jours., chpts. to books. Recipient various grants Action Rsch., Med. Rsch. Coun., Nutricia Found., SPARKS. Fellow Royal Coll. Physicians, Royal Coll. Paediatrics and Child Health (mem. acad. bd. and examinations com. 1995—); mem. Brit. Soc. Paediatric Gastroenterology and Nutrition, Paediatric Rsch. Soc. (com. mem. 1993-98), Neonatal Soc. Avocations: running, jazz saxophone. Fax: 0113-206-5405. E-mail: newells@sjuhn-nu.demon.co.uk. Office: St James U Hosp, Becket St, Leeds LS9 7TF, England

NEWELL, WILLIAM KEITH, neurobiological researcher; b. Buffalo, N.Y., Oct. 12, 1954; s. Frederick Dwelley Newell and Dian Sloan Randel; m. Joanne Marrie Hatch, Dec. 1979 (div. July 1983); 1 child, Arian Justine. BA in Psychology, SUNY, Binghamton, 1985. Rschr. assoc. U. Pitts., 1986-90, rsch. specialist, lab. mgr. dept. neurosci., 1990-95, rsch. specialist MRI rsch., MRI rsch. machinist, 1995-98. Democrat. Avocations: mural art, electronics.

NEWING, ANGELA, physics educator, medical physicist; b. London, Sept. 16, 1938; d. James and Mabel (Steel) Grainger. BSc in Physics, Bristol U., Eng., 1960; MSc in Math., 1984; PhD in Math., Columbia Pacific, 1985. Chartered physicist. Physicist Royal Sussex County Hosp., Brighton, Eng., 1960-65; tchr. Physics & Math. Chipping Campden Sch., Gloucestershire, 1966-68; sr. physicist Cheltenham Gen. Hosp., 1968-81; prin. physicist, 1981-89; dir. Med. Physics Gloucester, Eng., 1989—; prof. med. physics Cranfield U., Eng., 1994—. Author of three books of mathematical puzzles, 1978, 84; joint author: two books of puzzles, 1993, 94; contbr. 37 scientific papers to profl. jours. Justice of Peace Gloucestershire, 1978—. Fellow IEE, Inst. of Physics. Office: Medical Physics Dept, Gloucestershire Royal Hosp, Gloucester GL1 3NN, England

NEWKIRK, PEGGY ROSE WILLS, civic volunteer; b. Middletown, Ohio, Oct. 8, 1936; d. Hurby and Mirl Daisy (Amburgey) Wills; m. Raymond Daniel Spencer (div. 1972); children: Debra, Raymond II, Stephany; m. Donald Richard Newkirk, Dec. 9, 1976. BS in Edn., Ohio State U., 1984. Cert. tchr., Ohio. Exec. sec. Ohio Dominican Coll., Columbus, 1971-74; exec. asst. Ctrl. Ohio Reg. Coun. on Alcoholism, Columbus, 1974-76, Ohio Hosp. Assn., Columbus, 1976-77; cons. Mercy Hosp., Columbus, 1984; dir. human resources Hosp. Choice Health Plan, Columbus, 1984-86. Author: Wills Ancestry in America (From England to New Jersey, Kentucky, Ohio, California), 1997; contbr. stories to mags. Vol. Willowbrook Christian Nursing Home, Columbus, 1987; mem. Ohio Hist. Soc., Ky. Hist. Soc. Mem. DAR (vice regent 1992-94, regent 1994-96, chmn. mag. and advt. 1996-98, yearbook editor 1998—), Internat. Soc. for Brit. Genealogy and Family History, Nat. Soc. Colonial Dames XVII Century, Nat. Soc. Descendants of Early Quakers, 1999, Worthington Hist. Soc. (yearbook editor 1993—), Worthington Art Study (yearbook editor 1995—), Worthington Women's Club. Republican. Avocations: genealogy research, writing, flower gardening, music. Home: 6770 Masefield St Worthington OH 43085-3075

NEWKIRK, RAYMOND LESLIE, management consultant; b. Shreveport, La., July 13, 1944; s. Raymond Clay and Dorothy Emily (Parker) N.; m.

Felicisima Guese Calma, Jan. 19, 1985; 1 child, Maria Dorothy Alma. AA, Dayton Community Coll., 1973; BS in Behavioral Sci., N.Y. Inst. Tech., 1976; MS in Philosophy, Columbia Pacific U., 1980, PhD in Behavioral Sci., 1982; PhD in Human Sci., Saybrook Inst., 1992; MS in Clin. Psychology, Calif. Coast U., 1997. Clin. intern Fielding Inst., 1995; chief exec. officer, cons. Newkirk & Assocs., Ft. Lauderdale, Fla., 1980-84; head dept. ADP Royal Saudi Naval Forces, Jeddah, 1984-86; pres., cons. Internat. Assn. Info. Mgmt., Santa Clara, Calif., 1984; cert. quality analyst Quality Assurance Inst., Orlando, Fla., 1986—; prin. cons. Info. Impact Internat., Nashville, 1988—; pres., CEO Sys. Mgmt. Inst., Pleasant Hill, Calif., 1987; pres., COO P.Q. Info. Group, Egmont ann Hoeff, The Netherlands, 1992-94; pres., CEO Systems Mgmt. Inst., 1994—; chmn., CEO Bay U., 1999—; prin. Forum 2000, 1996—; dep. gov. Am. Biog. Inst., 1995. Author: Chronicles of the Making of A Philosopher, 1983; contbr. articles to profl. jours. Speaker, mem. Union for Concerned Scientists, San Francisco, 1988. Recipient Internat Order of Merit, 1999; Eminent Churchill fellow, Eminent Wisdom fellow. Fellow Brit. Inst. Mgmt., Internat. Biog. Assn.; mem. Assn. Systems Mgmt., Assn. Profl. Cons., Planetary Soc., Columbia Pacific Alumni Assn. (pres. Mid-east chpt. 1985, Internat. Order of Merit), Assn. Computing Machinery, IEEE Computer Soc., Am. Biograph. Inst. (dep. gov. 1995), Phi Theta Kappa (outstanding scholar award 1973), Confedn. of Chivalry (knight). Roman Catholic. Avocations: writing, classical guitar, tennis, weight lifting. Home: 95 Greenock Ln Pleasant Hill CA 94523-2083

NEWLAND, DAVID EDWARD, engineering educator; b. Knebworth, Eng., May 8, 1936; s. Robert William and Marion Amelia (Dearman) N.; m. Patricia Frances Mayne, July 18, 1959; children: Andrew David William, Richard David Philip. MA, Cambridge (Eng.) U., 1957, ScD, 1990; ScD, MIT, 1963; DEng (hon.), U. Sheffield, 1997. Various positions Eng. Electric Co., 1957-61; instr., asst. prof. mech. engring. MIT, Cambridge, Mass., 1961-64; lectr., sr. lectr. mech. engring. Imperial Coll. U. London, 1964-67; prof. mech. engring. Sheffield (Eng.) U., 1967-76; prof. engring. Cambridge (Eng.) U., 1976—, head dept. engring., 1996—, dep. vice-chancellor, 1999—; cons. numerous engring. cos. in the U.S. and Eng., 1963—; tech. witness Flixborough Inquiry and other cases, 1974—. Author: Mechanical Vibration Analysis and Computation, 1989, Random Vibration, Spectral and Wavelet Analysis, 3d edit., 1993. Mem. Royal Commn. Environ. Pollution, London, 1984-89; mem. coms. of Engring. Coun., Design Coun., Transport Rsch. Lab., Sci. and Engring. Rsch. Coun., Brit. Stds. Instn. Fellow Royal Acad. Engring. London (coun. 1985-87), Inst. Mech. Engrs. (London), Acoustical Soc. Am.; mem. ASME. Avocations: music, jogging, golf. Office: Cambridge U Dept Engring, Trumpington St, Cambridge CB2 1PZ, England

NEWLIN, GEORGE CHRISTIAN, writer; b. Bklyn., Feb. 14, 1931; s. Albert Chauncey and Janet Bethell Newlin; m. Janine Jordan, Dec. 23, 1967 (div. Apr. 1991); children: Jennifer Ruck, Pamela Williams Bowen, Ian Williams, Elizabeth Coker, Colin. AB, Princeton U., 1952; postgrad., Salzburg Mozarteum, 1954, Vienna Acad. Music, 1955-56; LLB, Yale U., 1955; MA in History, Trinity U., San Antonio, 1958. Legal assoc. Milbank, Tweed, Hadley & McCloy, N.Y.C., 1958-65; vp. corp. fin. Dominick & Dominick, Inc., N.Y.C., 1965-71; v.p. corp. fin. G. H. Walker & Co. Inc., N.Y.C., 1971-72; v.p., gen. counsel Faxon Comm. Inc., White Plains, N.Y., 1972-76; pres. Braintree Mgmt. Ltd., N.Y.C., 1976-88, Windows into Fiction, Somers, N.Y., 1988—; presenter, lectr. in field English lit., U.S., Can., Eng.; vis. lectr. Lycyle Hook series Barnard Coll., Calif. State U., Fullerton; lectr. Dickens Conf., U. Calif., Santa Cruz. Author: (anthologies) Everyone in Dickens, 3 vols., 1995, Every Thing in Dickens, 1996, (textbooks) Understanding A Tale of Two Cities, 1998, Understanding Great Expectations, 2000; former concert pianist N.Y. met. area; stage actor; trained with Shakespeare & Co., Lenox, Mass.; interviewee Can. Pub. Radio, ABC Radio, N.Y.; appeared in spl. TV broadcast on Great Expectations, Learning Channel. Past mem. planning bd., past chmn. conservation bd., New Castle, N.Y.; founder New Castle Glazier Arboretum; treas., bd. dirs. Koussevitzky Found. for Music, Robert Miller Fund for Music; past pres., past chmn. bd. dirs. Westchester Conservatory of Music; former trustee, mem. fin. com. Bagby Found. for Music; founding pres. then chmn. Coun. for Arts in Westchester (now Westchester Arts Coun.); trustee, asst. treas. Composers Conf. Wellesley Coll. Mem. The Century Assn. N.Y.C. E-mail: gcnewlin@aol.com. Home and Office: 428A Heritage Hls Somers NY 10589-1919

NEWLIN, LYMAN WILBUR, bookseller, consultant; b. Buda, Ill., May 26, 1910; s. Fred Matheny and Maude Lillian (Potter) N.; m. Evy Ottonia Magnusson, 1966; children: Fred M. II, Erik B.M. Student, Coll. Emporia, Kans., 1928-30, U. Chgo., 1930-32. Buyer, bus. mgr. Follett Book Co., Chgo., 1934-44; mgr. Minn. Book Store and Macalester Coll. Book Store, Mpls. and St. Paul, 1944-48; co-owner Broadwater Lodge, Hackensack, Minn., 1948-65; founder, owner Broadwater Books, Lewiston, N.Y., 1948—; buyer, dept. mgr. Kroch's & Brentano's Book Store, Chgo., 1951-65; regional mgr. Richard Abel and Co., Portland, Oreg. and Zion, Ill., 1966-69, asst. to pres., 1969-75; founder, prin. counselor Lyman W. Newlin Book Trade Counsellors, Lewiston, N.Y., 1975—; mdse. mgr. Coutts Library Services, Inc., Lewiston, 1976-90; pub. rels. advisor The Charleston (Coll. Libr.) Conf., 1985—; pub. liaison Book News, Inc., Portland, 1989—; program coord. Acad. of Scholarly Pub. seminar Coll. of Charleston, 1995—; cons. Rutgers U. Press, New Brunswick, N.J., 1975-81; panelist and lectr. to acad. libr. and schs., booksellers. Pub. Rev. Index Quar. Guide to Profl. Revs., 1941-43; pub. rels. advisor, contbr. Bi-Monthly Publ. Against the Grain, 1985—; contbr. articles to profl. jours. Founder, 1st pres. Boy River Chain of Lakes Improvement Assn., Cass County, Minn., 1961-65, Concerned Parents Orgn., Freehold, 1976-79; trustee, v.p., sec., chmn. new libr. bldg. com. Lewiston Pub. Libr., 1985—; committeeman Niagara County Dem. Party, 1987—, sec., 1988-90; mem. coun. Luth. Ch. Messiah, Lewiston, 1982-93, deacon, 1992-97; mem. Town of Lewiston Sr. Citizens Adv. Bd., 1992—; mem., com. person Zion Luth. Ch., Niagara Falls, N.Y., 1995—; pres. bd. trustees Lewiston Pub. Libr., 1998—. Mem. ALA, Assn. Book Travelers (50 Yr. award 1984), Am. Booksellers Assn. (50 yr. bronze plaque 1998), Soc. Scholarly Pub. (program com. 1985), Book Industry Study Group, Pi Kappa Delta. Lutheran. Democrat. Avocations: amateur ornithology, Am. folk music, New Orleans jazz, book collecting. Office: PO Box 278 Lewiston NY 14092-0278

NEWMAN, ANITA NADINE, surgeon; b. Honolulu, June 13, 1949; d. William Reece Elton and Margie Ruth (Pollard) Newman; m. Frank E.X. Ward, Sept. 9, 1995; children: Justin Ellis, Chelsea Newman, Andrew Frank, Tyler William. BA, Stanford U., 1971; MD, Dartmouth Coll., 1975. Diplomate Am. Bd. Otolaryngology. From intern to resident in gen. surgery Northwestern Meml. Hosp., Chgo., 1975-77, resident in otolaryngology, 1977-78; resident UCLA Hosp. and Clinics, 1979-82; assoc. prof. UCLA, 1982-96; rsch. fellow in neurotology, 1984-88; surgeon USC Head and Neck Group, 1997-2000; staff surgeon Wadsworth VA Hosp., L.A., 1982-84; pvt. practice L.A., 2000—. Contbr. articles to profl. jours. Mem. alumni admissions support com. Dartmouth Med. Sch. Alumni Coun., 1983-87. Fellow ACS; mem. Am. Acad. Otolaryngology, Am. Med. Women's Assn., L.A. County Med. Women's Assn., Assn. Rsch. Otolaryngology, Stanford Women's Honor Soc. Democrat. Office: 8631 W 3d St Ste 625E Los Angeles CA 90048

NEWMAN, BARRY MARC, pediatric surgeon; b. N.Y.C., Dec. 13, 1951; s. Sheldon and Miriam (Jasphy) N.; m. Jane Post, July 2, 1989; 1 child, Alexander Ross. BA, U. Pa., 1973; MD, SUNY, Stony Brook, 1976. Diplomate Nat. Bd. Med. Examiners, Am. Bd. Surgery, Am. Bd. Pediatric Surgery. Resident in surgery N.Y. Med. Coll., N.Y.C., 1976-78; sr. resident in surgery SUNY, Stony Brook, 1978-81; chief resident pediatric surgery Childrens Hosp. of Buffalo, 1981-83, fellow pediatric surgery and gastroenterology, 1983-84; asst. prof. surgery U. Va., Charlottesville, 1984-88, U. Ill., Chgo., 1988-93; dir. pediatric surgery Luth. Gen. Children's Hosp., Park Ridge, Ill., 1991-96; clin. assoc. prof. surgery U. Chgo., 1993-95; dir. pediatric surg. svcs. Loyola U. Med. Ctr., Maywood, Ill., 1996—, co-dir. surg. laparoscopy lab., 1996-97, assoc. prof. surgery and pediatrics, 1996—; instr. Adv. Trauma and Life Support, ACS, Chgo., 1984—. Contbr. articles to profl. jours., chpts. to books. NIH grantee, 1982-83, 87-88. Fellow Am. Acad. Pediatrics, ACS; mem. Am. Gastroenterol. Assn., Am. Pediatric Surg. Assn., Am. Coll. Physician Execs. Democrat. Jewish. Avocations: wine collecting, scuba diving, underwater photography, personal computing. Office: Loyola U Med Ctr Dept Surgery 2160 S 1st Ave Dept Surgery Maywood IL 60153-3304

NEWMAN, BRUCE ALLAN, political science educator; b. Wilmington, Del., Aug. 30, 1960; s. Thomas Allan and Ethel Mae (Stayton) N. BA, U. Del., 1986; MA, U. Dallas, 1990, PhD in Politics, 2000. Instr. in polit. sci. Western Okla. State Coll., Altus, 1991—. With U.S. Army, 1980-83. Earhart Found. fellow, 1987-88, 88-89. Mem. Am. Polit. Sci. Assn., Okla. Polit. Sci. Assn., Nat. Assn. Scholars. Republican. Avocations: reading, hiking, travel, movies. Home: 201 N Veterans Dr Apt 501 Altus OK 73521-5410 Office: Western Okla State Coll 2801 N Main St Altus OK 73521-1310

NEWMAN, CLAIRE POE, private investor; b. Jacksonville, Fla., Dec. 12, 1926; d. Leslie Ralph and Gertrude (Criswell) Poe; m. Robert Jacob Newman, July 3, 1948 (dec. 1994); children: Leslie Claire, Robert, Christoper David. Student, Fla. State Coll. for Women, 1944-45, Tulane U., 1971-73. Co-owner Vineyards in Burgundy, France. Mem. various coms. New Orleans Mus. Art; mem. women's com. New Orleans Philharmonic Symphony Assn., 1961—, chmn. orch. rels. com., 1961-63; chmn. New Orleans Easter Seal Drive, 1963; La. trustee Nat. Soc. Crippled Children and Adults, 1963-65. Featured on cover of Life mag., Sept. 25, 1944. Mem. Women's Aus. C. of C., New Orleans Soc. Archeol., Inst. Am. (v.p. 1972-74), Confrérie des Chevaliers du Tastevin, Sigma Kappa, Eichenheim Golf Club, Golden Skibook Club (Austria), Kitzbuhel Golf Club (Austria), Pass Christian Yacht Club (Miss.), Ski Club (Arlberg), Eichenheim Golf and Country Club. Address: Tiemberg, Kitzbuehel Austria Office: 240 Audubon St New Orleans LA 70118-4838

NEWMAN, FREDRIC ALAN, plastic surgeon, educator; b. Bklyn., Aug. 16, 1948; s. Harold Louis and Isabel (Seltzer) N.; m. Stacey Hope Clarfield, Nov. 27, 1983; children: Benjamin, Marissa, Alexandra. BA, Yale Coll., 1970; MD summa cum laude, SUNY Downstate, Bklyn., 1974. Bd. cert. Am. Bd. Plastic Surgery, Am. Bd. Surgery. Resident gen. surgery Beth Israel Hosp., Boston, 1974-77; resident and chief gen. surgery SUNY Downstate, Bklyn., 1977-79; fellow plastic surgery NYU/Inst. Reconstrv. Plastic Surgery, N.Y.C., 1979-81; fellow facial reconstruction Jackson Meml. Hosp., Miami, Fla., 1981-82; asst. clin. prof. dept. plastic surgery N.Y. Med. Coll., West, 1984-95, Columbia Coll. Physicians and Surgeons, N.Y.C., 1995—; chmn. bd. Cutting Edge Techs., Inc., N.Y.C., 1994-97; chmn. bd., CEO, pres. Endo Surg. Devices, Inc., Del., 1998—. Author: Aesthetic Plastic Surgery, 1984, Plastic Surgery, 1985; contbr. articles to profl. jours. Fellow ACS, Internat. Coll. Surgeons (regent 1990—); mem. Am. Soc. Plastic and Reconstructive Surgeons, Am. Soc. Aesthetic Plastic Surgery, Am. Cleft Palate Assn., N.Y. State Med. Soc. Avocations: sailing, skiing, reading, computers. Office: Two Overhill Rd Scarsdale NY 10583

NEWMAN, GERALDINE ANNE, advertising executive, inventor; b. Boston, Apr. 1; d. Joseph M. and Clara (Bistry) N. BS, UCLA; postgrad., Alliance Francaise, Paris, Los Angeles Sch. Fine Arts, NYU. Writer Tinker Dodge and Delano, N.Y.C., 1970-72, Ketchum Advt., N.Y.C., 1972-75, Advt. to Women, N.Y.C., 1975-78; v.p., creative supr. Young and Rubicam, N.Y.C., 1978-83; v.p., assoc. creative dir. Backer Spielvogel Bates Worldwide Internat. Div., N.Y.C., 1983-90; pres. Geraldine Newman Comm., Inc., N.Y.C., 1990—. County committeewoman Dem. Party, N.Y.C., 1972; advt. adviser Youth at Risk, Breakthrough Found., Food Bank, Food for All, Gifts that Give Back. Featured in Adweek mag., 1986; winner Andy award 1975, 78, 82, 84, Clio award 1982, ERA award, 1998, numerous others. Mem. Ad-net (bd. dirs. 1984-89, creative dir. 1986-89, Pres.'s award 1988), Electronic Retailing Assn., Ad Club N.Y. Avocations: painting, travel. Home and Office: 315 E 72nd St New York NY 10021-4625

NEWMAN, HUBERT NEIL, periodontist, researcher, educator; b. Dublin, Ireland, Sept. 13, 1943; s. Victor J. and Nettie (Jackson) N. BA, U. Dublin, 1964, BDentSc, 1967, MA, 1968, ScD, 1980; PhD, U. Bristol, 1973, MDS, 1976. House surgeon Dublin Dental Hosp., 1967-68, registrar in oral surgery, 1968-69; sci. asst. Med. Rsch. Coun. U.K., Bristol, Eng., 1969-76; lectr. in dental medicine U. Bristol, 1973-76; sr. lectr. periodontology Eastman Dental Inst., London, 1977-81, reader in periodontology, 1981-85, prof. periodontology and preventive dentistry, 1985—, head dept. periodontology, 1993-99, vice dean, 1984-87, vice dean for tchg., 1990-93, head electron microscopy unit, 1989-94; dir. Clin. Rsch. Ctr. Eastman Dental Inst., emeritus prof. periodontology and preventative dentistry, 1999—; prof. (hon.) Univ. Coll. London, 1999—; hon. cons. Eastman Dental Hosp., 1980-99, Internat. Ctr. for Excellence in Dentistry, U. Coll. London, 1999—. Contbr. more than 30 chpts. to books and over 200 articles to profl. jours. Recipient medal Paris Assn. Odontology, 1990, medal U. Athens, 1991, medal City of Paris, 1991. Fellow Royal Coll. Pathologists; mem. Internat. Acad. Periodontology (v.p., pres.-elect 1997-98, pres. 1999—, v.p., chmn. sci. com. 1996—, chmn. periodontal rsch. group 1982-84), Internat. Acad. Periodontology, Br. Soc. Periodontology (pres.-elect 1999—). Avocations: thinking, travel, gardening, music. E-mail: crc@eastman.ucl.ac.uk. Fax: 44 20 7905 1292. Office: Univ Coll London, 123 Grays Inn Rd, London WC1X 8TZ, England

NEWMAN, JAMES MICHAEL, judge, lawyer; b. Bklyn., Apr. 3, 1946; s. Sheldon and Ethel (Silverman) N.; m. Lee Galen; children: Danielle Cari, Matthew Evan, Merrie Lee, Cindy Joy, Bradley Curtis. BA, Queens Coll., 1966; JD, NYU, 1969, LLM, 1975. Bar: N.Y. 1970, N.J. 1977; cert. matrimonial atty., N.J. Assoc. Kramer, Marx, Greenlee & Backus, N.Y.C., 1970-73, Forsyth, Decker, Murray & Broderick, N.Y.C., 1973-74; ptnr. Tommaney & Newman, N.Y.C., 1975-82, Goldzweig, Reilly, Grossman & Newman, Marlboro, N.J., 1978-79, Canarick & Newman, Freehold, N.J., 1979-97, Newman, Scarola & Assocs., Freehold, 1998—; pub. defender Marlboro Twp. (N.J.), 1984-86; judge Marlboro Twp., 1986—, Englishtown Borough, 1990—, Farmingdale Borough, 1991—, Manalapan Township, 1993—, Borough Fair Haven, 1996—. Dep. mayor Marlboro Twp., 1975-79, dir. econ. devel., 1975-79, dir. commuter affairs, 1974; interim commr. Western Monmouth Utilities Authority, 1977; mem. Central N.J. Transp. Bd., 1974-76. Mem. N.J. Bar Assn., Monmouth County Bar Assn. (co-chairperson family law com. 1996-98, trustee 1999—), Monmouth County Judges Assn. (pres. 1995), Am. Judges Assn., Masons. Jewish. Office: 64 W Main St Freehold NJ 07728-2142

NEWMAN, JOCELYN, administrator; b. Melbourne, Australia, July 8, 1937; married; 2 children. Grad., Melbourne U. Elected Australian Senate, 1986; shadow portfolios Dept. Vets. Affairs, Def. Sci. & Personnel, Australia, 1993-97; min. Dept. Social Security, Australia, 1997-98, Dept. Family Svcs., Australia, 1998—. Office: Dept Family & Cmty Svcs, PO Box 7788 Canberra Mail Ctr, Canberra ACT 2610, Australia also: Dept Health & Family Svcs, Parliament House Ste MG48, Canberra ACT 2600, Australia*

NEWMAN, JUDITH ALICE, education educator; b. Preston, Eng., May 9, 1950; d. Ellis Edward and Alice Dorothy Elizabeth (Herringshaw) N.; m. Ian William Revie, Oct. 10, 1978; 1 child, James Michael Edward. MA in English, U. Edinburgh, Scotland, 1972, MA in French, 1974; PhD, U. Cambridge, Eng., 1982. Lectr. U. Metz, France, 1973-74; lectr. U. Newcastle, Eng., 1976-90, reader, 1990-95, prof. Am. and postcolonial lit., 1995-2000; prof. Am. studies U. Nottingham, Eng., 2000—. Author: Saul Bellow and History, 1984, John Updike, 1988, Nadine Gordimer, 1988, H.B. Stowe, Dred: A Tale of the Great Dismal Swamp, 1992, The Ballistic Bard: Postcolonial Fictions, 1994. Recipient Arthur Miller prize U. East Anglia, 1993. Mem. British Assn. Am. Studies (sec. 1993-95, chair 1995-98, chair rsch. assessment palen Am. studies 1999—). Mem. Labour Party. Avocations: family, gardening. Office: U Nottingham, Sch Am Studies, Nottingham NG7 2RI, Scotland

NEWMAN, LAWRENCE WALKER, lawyer; b. Boston, July 1, 1935; s. Leon Bettoney and Hazel W. (Walker) N.; children: Timothy D., Isabel B., Thomas H. A.B., Harvard U., 1957, LL.B., 1960. Bar: D.C. 1961, N.Y. 1965. Atty. U.S. Dept. Justice, 1960-61, Spl. Study of Securities Markets and Office Spl. Counsel on Investment Co. Act Matters, U.S. SEC, 1961-64; asst. U.S. atty. So. Dist. N.Y., 1964-69; assoc. Baker & McKenzie, N.Y.C., 1969-71, ptnr., 1971—; mem. internat. adv. coun. World Arbitration Inst., 1984-87; mem. adv. com. Asia Pacific Ctr. for Resolution of Internat. Trade Disputes, 1987—; mem. adv. bd. Inst. for Transnational Arbitration, 1988—; chmn. U.S. Iranian Claimants Com., 1982—; mem. adv. bd. World Arbitration and Mediation Report, 1993—; mem. bd. adv. to Corporate Counsel's Internat. Adviser, 1995—. Co-author: The Practice of Internat. Litigation, 1992, 93, 2nd edit. 1998, Litigating Internat. Commercial Disputes, 1996; columnist N.Y. Law Jour., 1982—; adv. bd. World Arbitration and Mediation Report; bd. advisors Corp. Counsel's Internat. Adviser; contbr. articles to profl. jours. and books on litigation and internat. arbitration; editor: Enforcement of Money Judgments, Attachment of Assets; chmn. editl. bd. Juris Pub., Inc.; co-editor: Revolutionary Days: The Iran Hostage Crisis and the Hague Claims Tribunal, A Look Back, 1999. Mem. ABA (internat. litigation com., internat. arbitration com.), Internat. Bar Assn. (com. dispute resolution, com. constrn. litigation), Inter-Am. Bar Assn., Fed. Bar Coun., Am. Fgn. Law Assn., Maritime Law Assn. U.S., Assn. Bar City N.Y. (com. on arbitration & alternative dispute resolution 1991-94), Am. Arbitration Assn. (corp. counsel com. 1987—, panel comml. arbitrators), U.S. Coun. Internat. Bus., Ct. Arbitration of Polish Chamber Fgn. Trade (panel of arbitrators), Brit. Col. Internat. Comml. Arbitration Ctr. Office: Baker & McKenzie 805 3rd Ave New York NY 10022-7513

NEWMAN, MICHAEL CHARLES, ecotoxicologist; b. Bridgeport, Conn., Feb. 21, 1951; s. Thomas Walter and Mary Catherine (Bowen) N.; m. Margaret Ellen Mulvey, May 24, 1980; children: Benjamin Sean, Ian Michael. BA, U. Conn., 1974, MS, 1978; MS, Rutgers, 1980, PhD, 1981. Postdoctoral rsch. fellow U. Ga.'s Savannah River Ecol. Lab, Aiken, S.C., 1981-82, rsch., asst. prof., 1983-90, rsch. assoc. prof., 1990-96; rsch. prof. U. Ga.'s Savannah River Ecol. Lab, Aiken, 1996-98; prof. Coll. of William and Mary, Gloucester Point, Va., 1998—; dean grad. studies Sch. Marine Sci. Coll. of William and Mary, Gloucester Point, 1999—. Author: Quantitative Methods in Aquatic Ecotoxicology, 1995, Fundamentals of Ecotoxicology, 1998; co-editor: Metal Ecotoxicology, 1991, Ecotoxicology, 1996, Risk Assessment, 1998; mem. editl. bd. Advances in Trace Substance Rsch., 1990—; editor Jour. Environ. Toxicol. Chem.; contbr. numerous articles to profl. jours. Rsch. grantee NATO, 1990. Mem. Soc. Environ. Toxicology and Chemistry (pres. Carolinas chpt. 1991), S.C. Lab. Mgmt. Soc. (v.p. 1988). Office: VA Inst Marine Scis Coll of William and Mary Gloucester Point VA 23062

NEWMAN, MICHAEL RODNEY, lawyer; b. N.Y.C., Oct. 2, 1945; s. Morris and Helen Gloria (Hendler) N.; m. Cheryl Jeanne Anker, June 11, 1967; children: Hillary Abra, Nicole Brooke. Student NASA Inst. Space Physics, Columbia U., 1964; BA, U. Denver, 1967; JD, U. Chgo., 1970. Bar: Calif. 1971, U.S. Dist. Ct. (cen. dist.) Calif. 1972, U.S. Ct. Appeals (9th cir.) 1974, U.S. Dist. Ct. (no. dist.) Calif. 1975, U.S. Supreme Ct. 1978, U.S. Dist. Ct. (so. dist.) Calif. 1979, U.S. Tax Ct. 1979, U.S. Dist. Ct. (ea. dist.) Calif. 1983. Assoc. David Daar, 1971-76; ptnr. Daar & Newman, 1976-78, Miller & Daar, 1978-88, Miller, Daar & Newman, 1988-89, Daar & Newman, 1989—; judge pro-tem L.A. Mcpl. Ct., 1982—, L.A. Superior Ct., 1988—; bd. govs. U. Haifa, Israel, mem. fin. and phys. devel. com.; bd. dirs. Consulegis EEIG; founder, facilitator First, Second and Third Ann. German-Am. Strategic Partnership Conf.; lectr. Ea. Claims Conf., Ea. Life Claims Conf., Nat. Health Care Anti-Fraud Assn., AIA Conf. on Ins. Fraud, Consulegis A.G.M.'s Paris, 1997, Madrid, 1998, Dublin, 1999; bd. gov.'s U. Haifa, Israel (mem. finance and physical devel. com.). mem. L.A. Citizens Organizing Com. for Olympic Summer Games, 1984, mem. govtl. liaison adv. commn., 1984; mem. So. Calif. Com. for Olympic Summer Games, 1984; cert. ofcl. Athletics Congress of U.S., co-chmn. legal com. S.P.A.-T.A.C., chief finish judge; trustee Massada lodge B'nai Brith. Recipient NYU Bronze medal in Physics, 1962, Maths. award USN Sci., 1963. Mem. ABA (multi-dist. litigation subcom., com. on class actions), L.A. County Bar Assn. (chmn. attys. errors and omissions prevention com., mem. cts. com. litigation sect.), Conf. Ins. Counsel, So. Pacific Assn., TAC (bd. dirs., Disting. Svc. award 1988), German Am. C. of C. (bd. dirs.), Porter Valley Country Club, Breakfast Club. Office: 865 S Figueroa St Ste 2500 Los Angeles CA 90017-2567

NEWMAN, PAUL JOSEPH, communications executive; b. Heston, Eng., Oct. 3, 1931; s. Cyril Alfred and Gladys Beatrice (Barrington) N.; m. Josephine Catherine Hardy, Apr. 4, 1959; children: Mark, Anne-Marie, Matthew. Student, St. Joseph's Coll., London, 1948. Cons. pub. rels. Picton & Turner, London, 1951-58; asst. editor Tin Pubs., London, 1958-67, editor, 1967-83; civil servant Internat. Tin Coun., London, 1983-88; exec. Newman Media, Gerrards Cross, Eng., 1988—. Author: Tin in your Industry, 1968, Tin in Indonesia, 1972; columnist Malaysian Bus., 1988-90, Bus. Times, Kuala Lumpur, 1988-98. Liberal Democrat. Roman Catholic. Avocations: tennis, football, swimming. Home and Office: 26 The Queensway, Gerrards Cross SL9 8NB, England

NEWMAN, PETER WILLIAM GEOFFREY, city policy educator; b. Perth, Australia, Aug. 20, 1945; s. Geoffrey Herbert and Betty (White) N.; m. Janice Beryl Hogan, Feb. 28, 1970; children: Christy, Renée, Samuel. BSc with honors, U. Western Australia, Perth, 1967, PhD, 1972; diploma, Delft (The Netherlands) U., 1973. Lectr. in environ. sci. Murdoch U., Perth, 1974-80, sr. lectr., 1980-86, assoc. prof., 1986-96, prof. city policy, 1996—; dir. environ. planning Office of Cabinet, Perth, 1989, Inst. for Sci. and Tech. Policy Murdoch U., 1989—; advisor minister for transport Western Australia Govt., Perth, 1986. Co-author: (with Jeff Kenworthy) Sustainable Cities: Overcoming Automobile Dependence, 1999, Winning Back the Cities, 1992. Councillor City of Fremantle, Perth, 1976-80. Anglican. Avocation: travel. Office: Inst for Sustainability & Tech Policy, Murdoch Univ, Perth 6150, Australia

NEWMAN, PHILIP ROBERT, psychologist; b. Dec. 17, 1942; s. Samuel M. and Sara Rose (Dumain) N.; m. Barbara Miller, June 12, 1966; children: Samuel Asher, Abraham Levy, Rachel Florence. AB with high distinction, U. Mich., 1964, PhD, 1971. Asst. prof. psychology U. Mich., Ann Arbor, 1971-72, Union Coll., Schenectady, N.Y., 1972-76; dir. human behavior curriculum project APA, Washington, 1977-81; pvt. practice psychology Columbus, Ohio, 1978-2000, South Kingston, R.I., 2000—; adj. prof., sr. rschr. young scholars program Ohio State U., 1990-98; adj. prof. human devel. and family studies U. R.I., 2000—; cons. Agy. Instrnl. TV, 1979. Author: (with B. Newman) Development through Life: A Psychosocial Approach, 1975, 7th edit., 1999; Infancy and Childhood Development and Its Context, 1978, An Introduction to the Psychology of Adolescence, 1979, Personality Development through the Life Span, 1980, Living: The Process of Adjustment, 1981, Understanding Adulthood, 1983, Principles of Psychology, 1983, Adolescent Development, 1986, When Kids Go to College: A Parents Guide to Changing Relationships, 1992, Childhood and Adolescence, 1997; editor: (with B. Newman) Development Through Life: A Case Study Approach, 1976. Woodrow Wilson fellow U. Mich., 1964, Univ. fellow, 1964-66, Horace H. Rackham Rsch. scholar, 1969-71. Mem. APA, APHA, Internat. Assn. Applied Psychology, Internat. Sociol. Assn., Soc. Psychol. Study Social Issues, Am. Sociol. Assn., Nat. Coun. Family Rels., Groves Conf. Marriage and Family, Ea. Psychol. Assn., Midwestern Psychol. Assn., Western Psychol. Assn., N.Y. Acad. Sci., Gerontol. Soc. Am., Am. Orthopsychiat. Assn., Am. Statis. Assn., Phi Beta Kappa, Sigma Xi, Phi Kappa Phi. Home and Office: 240 Broad Rock Rd S Kingstown RI 02879-1804

NEWMAN, RAYMOND MELVIN, biologist, educator; b. New Castle, Pa., June 10, 1956; s. Raymond Melvin and Sarah L. (Lawton) N.; m. Patricia Ann Scott, Nov. 22, 1989. BS in Biology, Slippery Rock (Pa.) U., 1978; MS, U. Minn., 1982, PhD in Fisheries, 1985. Grad. asst. U. Minn., St. Paul, 1979-84, rsch. specialist forest resources, 1985-86, asst. prof. fisheries, 1988-94; assoc. prof. fisheries, 1995—; fellow natural resources U. Conn., Storrs, 1986-88; investigator U. Mich. Biol. Sta., Pellston, 1987-88; exotics task force Nat. Sea Grant, Silver Spring, Md., 1991; mem. interagy. exotic species com. Minn. Dept. Natural Resources, St. Paul, 1992—; vis. scientist Inst. for Freshwater Ecology, River Lab., Dorset, U.K. Assoc. editor Jour. N.Am. Biol. Soc., 1994-98; mem. editl. bd. Ecology Freshwater Fish, 1992—; contbr. articles to profl. jours., chpts. to books. Bd. dirs. Twin Cities Trout Unltd., Mpls., 1982-87. Mem. Am. Fisheries Soc. (exec. com. Minn. chpt. 1992, 96), Am. Inst. Fishery Rsch. Biologists, Ecol. Soc. Am., North Am. Benthological Soc. Achievements include documentation of chemical defense from herbivory by aquatic plants; control of an exotic weed by native insects. Office: U Minn Fisheries Wildlife 1980 Folwell Ave Saint Paul MN 55108-1037

NEWMAN, RONALD CHARLES, physicist, educator; b. London, Dec. 10, 1931; s. Charles Henry and Margaret Victoria May (Cooper) N.; m. Jill Laura Weeks, Apr. 7, 1956; children: Susan Laura Newman Lee, Vivienne

Heather Newman Cadman. BSc, Imperial Coll., London, 1952, DIC, 1954, PhD, 1955; postgrad., Chelsea Poly., 1952-53. Rsch. scientist AEI Rsch. Lab., Aldermaston Court, U.K., 1955-63, sr. rsch. scientist, 1963-64; lectr. Reading (U.K.) U., 1964-69, reader in physics, 1969-75, prof. physics, 1975-89; assoc. dir. IRC Semicondr. Materials Lab. Imperial Coll., 1989-99, emeritus prof., sr. rsch. fellow, 1999—; prof. London U., 1989-99; 'is. prof. Reading U., 1989—, U. Manchester in Sci. and Tech., 2000—; cons., lectr. in field; vice chmn. Fachbeirat, Max-Planck Inst., Halle, 1995-98. Author: Infrared Studies of Crystal Defects, 1973; contbr. numerous articles, revs. to profl. publs.; mem. editl. bd. Jour. Physics C Solid State Physics, 1975-77. Fellow Royal Soc. Avocations: music, photography, foreign travel. Home: 23 Betchworth Ave, Reading Berkshire RG6 7RH, England Office: Ctr for Elec Materials & Devices, Physics Dept Prince Consort Rd, London SW7 2BZ, England

NEWMAN, STACEY CLARFIELD, artist, curator; b. N.Y.C., July 21, 1956; d. Wallace J. Clarfield and Elinor (Kandel) Clarfield-Toberoff; m. Fredric Alan Newman, Nov. 27, 1983; children: Benjamin Clarfield, Marissa Paige, Alexandra Brooke. Student, Franklin & Marshall, 1974-76; BS in Labor Rels. and Mgmt., U. Bridgeport, 1978. Dir. ops. Nat. Rec. and Video Studios, N.Y.C., 1978-80; dir. tech. ops. VCA/Teletronics, N.Y.C., 1980-82, cons., client rep./MTV, 1981-83, exec. prodr., 1982-84; artist, art curator Stacey Clarfield Newman Studios, Scarsdale, N.Y., 1986—; merchandise cons. Tahari Fashions, N.Y.C., 1985-86; artist mem., jury com. You Gotta Have Art program White Plains Hosp. Ctr., 1990-92; art tchr. collage Scarsdale (N.Y.) Adult Edn. Program, 1993-95; artist in residence Scarsdale Elem. Schs., 1995-97; art cons., curator Manhattan Transfer, Inc., N.Y.C., 1997—. One-person shows include Quogue (N.Y.) Gallery, 1986, Ch. St. Gallery, White Plains, N.Y., 1987, Greenburgh Nature Ctr., N.Y., 1988, Grinton I. Will Libr. Gallery, Yonkers, N.Y., 1988, Scarsdale (N.Y.) Nat. Bank Gallery, 1989, Bronxville (N.Y.) Libr. Gallery, 1991, Piermont (N.Y.) Fine Arts Gallery, 1997-98, Manhattan Transfer, Inc., 1997, Piermont Fine Arts Gallery, 1999, J&W Gallery, New Hope, Pa., 1999, Adele Greenberg Salon, Cambridge, Mass., 2000; exhibited in group shows: Anaya Gallery, Scarsdale, 1986, Katonah (N.Y.) Gallery, 1986, Gallery at Jamaica, Stratton Mountain, Vt., 1987, CDS Contemporary Art, Albuquerque, 1989, Mari Galleries, Mamaroneck, N.Y., 1992, Manhattan Transfer, Inc., 1993, 98, 93 South Gallery, Nyack, N.Y., 1998-99, Piermont Fine Arts Gallery, 1995, 96, 98, Bibro Fine Arts Gallery, Chelsea, N.Y., 1998, Weber Fine Art, Scarsdale, N.Y., 1998, 93 South Gallery, Nyack, N.Y., 1998, J&W Gallery, New Hope, Pa., 1998, 99, Studio 4 West, Piermont, N.Y., 1999, Hewlett Mus., 2000, Ambassador Gallery, Palm Beach, Fla., 2000, Viridian Gallery, N.Y.C., 2000; commd. Am. Soc. Plastic and Reconstructive Surgeons, L.A. Conv. Ctr., 1988, White Plains Hosp. Ctr., 1989, 90, Cystic Fibrosis Found., N.Y.C., 1990, Joan Kroc Found., Calif., 1989-91. Regional v.p. Am. Cancer Soc., White Plains, 1986-88; 1st v.p., bd. dirs. Internat. Coll. Surgeons Aux., Chgo., 1988-90; bd. dirs. White Plains Hosp. Ctr. Aux., 1995—; fund raiser, event planner Holocaust Commn., N.Y.C., 1998; mem. Juvenile Diabetes Found., Gala, 2000, Hewlett Mus., 2000, J&W Gallery, 2000, Piermont Fine Arts Gallery, 2000—. Mem. Internat. Platform Assn., Nat. Assn. Women Artists, Inc., Nat. Arts Club, Penumbra Soc. (artist mem.), Katonah Mus., Piermont Fine Arts Gallery (publicity chair). Avocations: piano, photography, tennis, skiing, sailing, cycling. Studio: 21 Wayside Ln Scarsdale NY 10583-2911

NEWMAN, STEVEN E., neurologist; b. Detroit, July 1, 1945; children: Nathan, Rachel, Emily, Benjamin, Daniel. BA, Albion Coll., 1966; MD, U. Mich., 1970. Diplomate Am. Bd. Psychiatry & Neurology, Am. Bd. Forensic Examiners, Am. Bd. Forensic Medicine, Am. Bd. of Clin. Neurophysiology, Am. Bd. of EEG. With dept. neurology Dept. Internal Medicine, Dept. Psychiatry U. Mich., 1971-77; with NIH, 1977-79, Detroit Inst. PM&R, 1979—; mem. Mich. Spinal Cord/Traumatic Brain Injury Adv. Com., 1994-97; mem. State of Mich. Adv. Coun. Traumatic Brain Injury Grant Com., 1999—. Author: Legal Medicine, 1995; contbr. articles to profl. jours. Fellow Am. Acad. Neurology; mem. Am. Coll. of Forensic Examiners, Mich. State Med. Soc., Oakland County Med. Soc. (pres. 2000-2001), Nat. Assn. Disability Evaluating Physicians, Am. Acad. Clin. Neurophysiology. Office: Detroit Inst Phys Med & Rehab 25811 W 12 Mile Rd Southfield MI 48034-1896

NEWMAN-TANCREDI, ADRIAN, research neuroscientist; b. Foggia, Italy, Sept. 14, 1964; s. Michele and Audrey Ruth (Newman) Tancredi; m. Susan Jacques, Aug. 6, 1988; children: Miriam Lydia, Katia Elizabeth. BS, U. Kent at Canterbury, Eng., 1988, PhD, 1992. arrived in France, 1993;. Postgrad. rschr. Wellcome Labs., Beckenham, U.K., 1990-91; rsch. fellow U. Kent at Canterbury, 1992-93; jr. rsch. scientist Inst. Recherches Servier, Paris, 1993-95, rsch. scientist, 1995-97, neuropharmacology group leader, 1997—; participant numerous internat. symposia. Manuscript reviewer neurosci. and pharmacology jours., 1995—; contbr. numerous rsch. articles to profl. jours.; patentee and inventor in field. Mem. leadership team Canterbury Evangel. Ch., 1989-92, Eglise Protestante Evangélique, Rueil-Malmaison, 1994—. Mem. Brit. Pharmacol. Soc., Soc. for Neurosci., Christians in Sci. Avocations: Citroën 2CV fan, pianoforte, influence of Christianity on history of science. Office: Inst Recherches Servier, 125 Chemin de Ronde, 78290 Croissy-Sur-Seine France

NEWMARK, MARILYN, sculptor; b. N.Y.C., July 20, 1928; d. Edward Ellis and Mabel (Davies) Newmark; m. Leonard J. Meiselman, Mar. 15, 1952. Student, Adelphi Coll., 1945-47, Alfred U., 1949. sculpture specializing in horses, equestrian figures, dogs in sports scenes. Exhibited in group shows; sculpture exhbn. Ky. Derby Mus., Fleischer Mus., Scottsdale, Leigh Yawkey Woodson Art Mus., Wis., Bennington Ctr. for Arts, Vt., Calif. Acad. Sci., NAD, N.Y.C., Nat. Arts Club, N.Y.C., Nat. Art Mus. Sport, N.Y.C., James Ford Bell Mus., Wis., Smithsonian Instn., Washington, Mus. of Horse, Ky., Phila. Acad. Natural Scis., Port of History Mus., Pa.; represented in permanent collections Nat. Mus. Racing, Saratoga, N.Y., Internat. Mus. Horse, Ky. Horse Park; pvt. collections Harvey Firestone, Whitney Stone, Ogden Phipps, A.B. Hancock Jr., Peggy Agustus, Morgan Firestone, A. Werk Cook. Recipient Anna Hyatt Huntington award, 1970, 71, 72, 75, 78, 80, 81, 82, 83, 86, 88, 90, 97, gold medal, 1973, award Coun. Am. Artists Socs., 1972, 73, 79, 80, Hudson Valley John Newington award, 1973, 77, gold medal, 1979, Elliot Liskin Meml. award, 1989, 96, Nat. Acad. Ellin P. Speyer award, 1974, 93, 99, Artist Fund award, 1982. Fellow Nat. Sculpture Soc. (coun. 1973-75, rec. sec. 1976, sec. 1977-79, coun. 1981-83, 92-97, Bronze medal 1986, Mildred Victor Meml. award 1996), Am. Artists Profl. League (Gold medal 1974, 77, medal of hon. 1987), Allied Artists Am. (Gold medal 1981, 93, In Memorium award 1994), Pen & Brush Club (Gold medal 1977, Salmagundi Club award 1982, 83, 91, C. Dunwiddie Meml. award 1999), Soc. Animal Artists (jury of admissions 1972-75, 90—, bd. dirs. 1991—, v.p. 1998—), Am. Acad. Equine Art (founding mem., dir. sculpture 1980—), Nassau Suffolk Horsemans Assn. (dir. 1968-82), Catherine Lorillard Wolfe Art Club, Smithtown Hunt Club, Meadowbrook Hunt Club. Address: 22 Woodhollow Rd Roslyn Heights NY 11577-2217

NEWMARK, RICHARD ALAN, chemist; b. Urbana, Ill., Nov. 11, 1940; s. Nathan M. and Anne Mae (Cohen) N.; m. Joan Friedman, July 4, 1965; children: David, Merel. AB, Harvard Coll., 1961; PhD, U. Calif., Berkeley, 1964. Postgrad. fellow Mass. Inst. Tech., Cambridge, 1964-66; asst. prof. U. Colo., Boulder, 1966-69; rsch. chemist 3M, St. Paul, 1969-72, rsch. specialist, 1972-76, sr. rsch. specialist, 1976-81, staff scientist, 1981-92, corp. scientist, 1992—; councilor Minn. section Am. Chem. Soc., Washington, 1992-94. Contbr. articles to profl. jours. Chair Dist. 1 Community Coun., St. Paul, 1984-88; co-chair St. Paul Sch. Bd. Commn. of Gifted and Talented, 1986-88. Recipient award 3M Carlton Soc., 1993, Minn. award Am. Chem. Soc., 2000. Mem. Phi Beta Kappa, Sigma Xi. Jewish. Avocations: skiing, bicycling. Office: 3M 201-bs 07 Saint Paul MN 55144-0001

NEWSOM, JAMES THOMAS, lawyer; b. Carrollton, Mo., Oct. 6, 1944; s. Thomas Edward and Hazel Love (Mitchell) N.; m. Sherry Elaine Retzloff, Aug. 9, 1986; stepchildren: Benjamin A. Bawden, Holly K. Bawden. AB, U. Mo., 1966, JD, 1968. Bar: Mo. 1968, U.S. Supreme Ct. 1971. Assoc. Shook, Hardy & Bacon, London and Kansas City, Mo., 1972, ptnr., 1976—. Mem. Mo. Law Rev., 1966-68. Lt. comdr. JAGC, USNR, 1968-72. Mem. ABA, Internat. Bar Assn., Kansas City Met. Bar Assn., Lawyers Assn. Kansas City, U. Mo. Law Sch. Law Soc., Kansas City Club, U. Mo. Jefferson Club, Order of Coif, Perry (Kans.) Yacht Club, Stone Horse Yacht Club (Harwich Port, Mass.). Avocations: skiing, sailing, car racing. Office: Shook Hardy & Bacon One Kansas City Pl 1200 Main St Ste 3100 Kansas City MO 64105-2139

NEWSOME, BURTON WHEELER, lawyer; b. Geneva, Ala., Sept. 4, 1966; s. Paul Wesley Jr. and Patricia (Harris) N. BS magna cum laude, Troy State U., 1988; JD, U. Ala., 1998. Bar: Ala. 1999; cert. bank auditor. Asst. auditor Region Bank, Montgomery, Ala., 1988-89; auditor Colonial Bank, Montgomery, 1989-93; asst. v.p. AmSouth Bank, Birmingham, Ala., 1993-99; lawyer Wolfe, Jones & Boswell, Huntsville, Ala., 2000—. Mem. Ala. Dem. Party. Mem. ABA (comml. law sect.), Ala. State Bar Assn. (bankruptcy sect.), Madison County Bar Assn., Phi Kappa Phi, Beta Upsilon Sigma. Episcopalian. E-mail: bnewsome@wjb-law.com. Home: 15020 Decatur Dr Huntsville AL 35803 Office: Wolfe, Jones & Boswell 905 Bob Wallace Ave SW Huntsville AL 35801-6504

NEWSOME, DAVID HAY, retired headmaster; b. Leamington Spa, England, June 15, 1929; s. Charles Todd and Elsie Mary (Hay) N.; m. Joan Florence Trist, Dec. 4, 1955 (dec. 1999); children: Clare, Janet, Louise, Cordelia. BA with double first class honors, Emmanuel Coll., Cambridge, 1954, MA, 1957, Litt.D., 1976. Head dept. history Wellington Coll., Crowthorne, England, 1954-59, Master, 1980-89; fellow Emmanuel Coll., Cambridge, England, 1959-70, sr. tutor, 1965-70; univ. lectr. in ecclesiastical history Cambridge U., 1961-70; headmaster Christ's Hosp., Horsham, England, 1970-79. Author: A History of Wellington College, 1959, Godliness and Good Learning, 1961, The Parting of Friends, 1966, Two Classes of Men, 1974, On the Edge of Paradise, 1980 (Whitbread prize for biography of yr.), Edwardian Excursions, 1982, The Convert Cardinals: Newman and Manning, 1993, The Victorian World Picture, 1998. Fellow Royal Hist. Soc., Royal Soc. Lit. Anglican. Home: The Retreat Thornthwaite, Keswick CA12 5SA, England

NEWSTEAD, CHARLES GEORGE, renal physician; b. London, Apr. 8, 1956; s. Charles Arthur and Clara Amelia (Forrest) N.; m. Catherine Lucy McEwen, Apr. 19, 1980; children: David, Douglas, George, Heather. BSc 1st class, U. London, 1978, M.B.B.S., 1981, MD, 1991. Accreditation in gen., internal and renal medicine. Sr. house officer/registrar London Hosp., 1982-86; lectr. renal medicine Royal London Hosp. Med. Coll., 1986-90; clin. lectr. medicine U. Manchester, 1990-93; cons. renal physician St. James's U. Hosp., Leeds, 1993—; mem. nat. com. on renal medicine and transplantation. Contbr. numerous articles to profl. jours. Grantee Med. Rsch. Coun., Nat. Kidney Rsch. Fund. Fellow Royal Coll. Physicians London; mem. Physiol. Soc., Internat. Soc. Nephrology, Transplantation Soc. Labour Party. Avocations: cycling, long-distance running, Scottish hill walking, orienteering. Office: St James's Univ Hosp, Renal Unit, Leeds LS9 7TF, England

NEWSTEAD, STEPHEN EDWARD, psychology educator; b. Scunthorpe, Lincolnsh., Eng., Dec. 27, 1946; s. Henry and Maria (Hookham) N.; m. Jane Elizab3th Smith, July 31, 1970; children: Beth Ann, Amy Jane. BA, Oxford (Eng.) U., 1969; PhD, Nottingham (Eng.) U., 1972. Lectr. psychology Bolton Inst. Higher Edn., Eng., 1972-73; sr. lectr. psychology U. Plymouth, Eng., 1973-83, head dept., 1983-91, prof., 1988—; course tutor Open U., Exeter, Eng., 1977-80; vis. prof. U. Fla., Gainesville, 1980-81. Editor acad. books; contbr. articles to profl. jours. Bd. govs. Ivybridge Comprehensive Sch., Devon, Eng., 1981-85; councillor Ivybridge Town Coun., 1983-86. Fellow Brit. Psychol. Soc. (award for disting. contbns. to tchg. psychology 1999); mem. Exptl. Psychology Soc., Assn. Heads Psychology Depts. (vice chmn. 1988-91), Coun. for Nat. Acad. Awards, Brit. Psychol. Soc. (dep. pres. 1991-94, pres. 1995-96), Ivybridge Constl. Club. Avocations: bridge, walking. Home: Ermeleigh Erme Rd, Ivybridge, Devon PL21 0AB, England Office: U Plymouth Dept Psychology, Drake Circus, Plymouth PL4 8AA, England

NEWTON, DAVID ALEXANDER, holding company executive; b. Westmoreland, Eng., 1942; m. Kathleen Mary Newton; 2 children. Attended, Wyvern Coll. Mgmt. trainee J. Bibby & Sons Ltd., Eng., 1964; area mgr. Cobb Breeding Co., 1967; gen. mgr., dir. Anglian Food Group, 1969; agrl. dir. Sovereign Chicken Ltd., 1972; ops. dir. Ross Poultry Ltd., 1982; CEO, dir. Buxted Poultry Ltd., 1984; chmn. Maple Leaf Mills Ltd., Toronto, 1987; pres., CEO Can. Packers Inc. (now Maple Leaf Foods Inc.), 1990-92; COO Hillsdown Holdings plc, London, 1992, CEO, 1993-96; chmn. Carr's Milling Industries, Carlisle, Eng., 1996—; bd. dirs. Bernard Matthews Plc, Bodfari Ltd., MRCT Ltd.; chmn. bd. dirs. Prism Rail Plc. Fellow Royal Soc. Arts, Inst. Dirs. U.K.; mem. Brit. Inst. Mgmt. (companion),. Avocations: golf, music, spectator sports. Office: Carrs Milling Industries, Old Croft, Stanwix Carlisle CA3 9BA, England

NEWTON, DAVID JAMES, biomedical research scientist; b. Hereford, Eng., June 17, 1970; s. Roger and Anita May (Watt) N. B of Electronic Engring., U. Reading, Eng., 1991; MSc in Biomed. Instrumentation Engring., U. Dundee, Scotland, 1992, PhD, 1999. Rsch. asst. U. Dundee, 1993—. Contbr. articles to profl. jours. Grantee Tenovus, Scotland, 1996, 99, Sir Jules Thorn Trust, 1997. Avocations: amateur musicals, guitar, cinema. Office: Ninewells Hosp U Dept Med, Sect Vascular Med and Biol, Dundee Tayside DD1 9SY, Scotland

NEWTON, HUGH C., public relations executive; b. N.Y.C., Oct. 17, 1930; s. Avery Curtis and Ruth (Juster) N.; m. Charlotte Eloise Wallin, Nov. 3, 1956 (div. 1968); 1 child, Margaret Wren Newton Rosello; m. Joanne Elaine Harding, Dec. 27, 1969; children: Matthew Curtis, Christopher Stuart, Kimberly Kelly. BA, Washington & Lee U., 1952. Reporter Danville (Va.) Bee, 1955; mgr. news Carnegie Inst. Tech., Pitts., 1956-57; staff writer Westinghouse Elec., Pitts., 1957; acct. exec. Burson Marsteller Assocs., Pitts., 1958-59; asst. dir. pub. rels. Rockwell Mfg., Pitts., 1959-61; mgr. spl. projects Reynolds Metals Co., Richmond, Va., 1961-64; dir. pub. rels. Nat. Right to Work Com., Washington, 1964-67, Air Transport Assn., Washington, 1967-68; pres. Hugh C. Newton & Assocs., Washington, 1968—; mem. Interstate Commn. on Potomac River Basin, Washington, 1982-89. Contbr. to Lesly's Public Relations Handbook, 1991. Bd. dirs. Friends of the Torpedo Factory Art Ctr., Alexandria, Va., 1987-91. Recipient Silver Anvil award Pub. Rels. Soc. Am., 1966, 85. Mem. Soc. Profl. Journalists, Nat. Press Club, Capitol Hill Club. Episcopalian. Avocations: skiing, boating, stamp collecting. Home: 629 S Fairfax St Alexandria VA 22314-3833 Office: Hugh C Newton & Assocs 214 Massachusetts Ave NE Washington DC 20002-4958

NEWTON, JONATHON TIMOTHY, psychologist, researcher; b. Middlesbrough, U.K., June 22, 1963; s. John Douglas and Ann Newton. BA, Liverpool (Eng.) U., 1984, PhD, 1992. Rsch. psychologist U. Liverpool, 1984-88, lectr., 1988-92; lectr. United Med. & Dental Schs., London, 1992—. Author: Careful Communication; editor European Eating Disorders Review; contbr. articles to profl. jours. Mem. British Psychol. Soc. Avocations: rowing, eating, cooking. Office: United Med & Dental Schs, Fl 21 Guy's Tower Guy's Hosp, London SE1 9RT, England

NEWTON, KENNETH KURT, physician, educator; b. Landsberg, Germany, May 18, 1927; came to U.S., 1946; s. Arthur Neuweg and Margaret Joan (Blume) Newton. BA, U. Buffalo, 1951; MD, Western Res. U., 1955; honor grad. U.S. Army, Command/Gen. Staff Coll., 1972; flight surgeon tng., U.S. Army Aviation Sch., Ft. Rucker, Ala., 1974. Med. lic. Ohio, Mich. Advanced through ranks to col. U. S. Army, 1946-97; intern Henry Ford Hosp., Detroit, 1955-56, resident in internal medicine, phys. medicine and rehab., 1956-60; preceptor, dept. family medicine Wayne State U., Mich. State U., U. Mich., 1960—; clin. assoc. prof. medicine Wayne State U., Detroit, 1995—; dir. med. edn. Holy Cross Hosp., Detroit, 1976-88, chief dept. medicine, 1977-79, 91, pres. of staff, 1982-83; departmental surgeon Reserve Officers Assn. of Mich., Detroit, 1988-98; pres. EKG Assocs., P.C., Detroit, 1990—; med. officer 107th med. battalion, Mich. Army N.G., 1955-57, divsn. artillery surgeon, 46th inf. divsn., 1957-59, command surgeon, 1959-75, state surgeon, 1975-85, post surgeon Camp Atterbury Res. Forces Tng. Area, 1985-89, divsn. surgeon 70th divsn., Livonia, Mich., 1989-92, flight surgeon U.S. Army 1993; instr., course dir. ACLS, Am. Heart Assn., 1977—, Acad. Health Scis., U.S. Army, Ft. Sam Houston, Tex., 1992—; mem. governing bd. Holy Cross Hosp. 1988-92, pres. 1990; tchr. U. Buffalo, N.Y., 1950-51, preceptor U. Essen, Germany, 1980, U. Göttingen, Germany, 1993, U. München, Germany, 1993, Humboldt U., Berlin, 1994; med. advisor to Selective Svcs. Sys., Washington, 1968-76; mem. ad hoc med. panel to Res. Forces Policy Bd., Dept. Army, Washington, 1972; mem. adv. group for Aerospace R&D, NATO, 1978; mem. med. evaluation bds. State of Mich., Lansing, 1975-85. Decorated Legion of Merit, 1977, 97; recipient cert. of pub. svc. State of N.Y., 1958, Disting. Svc. medal State of Mich. 1985, Spl. tribute State of Mich. Senate, 1985, Invitation Governing Mayor of Berlin, 1990, Conspicuous Svc. order, State of N.Y., 1997. Mem. (life) Sr. Army Reserve Comdrs. Assn., (life) Reserve Officers Assn. (nat. surgeon 1993), (life) Nat. Guard Assn. (dir. 1979-82), Am. Heart Assn. (course dir. 1980—), Soc. of Med. Consultants to the Armed Forces, Confedn. Interalliée des Officiers de Reserve NATO (del. 1973—, vice chief del. 1986). Avocations: travel, photography, music and the arts, national security. Office: 15252 Gratiot Ave Detroit MI 48205-1327

NEWTON, SARAH ELIZABETH, nursing researcher, educator; b. Ann Arbor, Mich., Aug. 31, 1960; d. Maynard A. and Margery (Kenvin) N.; m. David Howard Maas. BSN, U. Mich., 1982, MS Med.-Surg. Nursing (Transplantation), 1987, PhD in Nursing, 1997. RN, Mich. Clin. nurse U. Mich. Hosp., Ann Arbor, 1982-97; clin. instr. U. Mich. Sch. Nursing, Ann Arbor, 1987-91, grad. student instr., 1992-97; asst. prof. Oakland U. Sch. Nursing, Rochester, Mich., 1997—; rsch. asst. U. Mich. Sch. Nursing, Ann Arbor, 1993; U.S. govt. profl. nurse trainee, 1985-86, 91-92. Mem. ANA, Internat. Transplant Nurses Soc., Mich. Nurses Assn., U. Mich. Alumni Assn., U. Mich. Nurses Alumni Assn., Midwest Nursing Rsch. Soc., Sigma Theta Tau (Rho chpt., v.p. Theta Psi chpt.), Alpha Gamma Delta. Republican. Avocations: golf, needlepoint, cats, art.

NEXSEN, JULIAN JACOBS, JR., lawyer; b. Columbia, S.C., Sept. 22, 1954; s. Julian J. and Mary Elizabeth (McIntosh) N.; m. Christine Spigner Johnston, Feb. 25, 1984; children: Elizabeth Kincaid, Julian J. III, Sarah Ivey. BA, Washington and Lee U., 1976; JD, U. S.C., 1979. Bar: S.C. 1979, U.S. Ct. Appeals (4th cir.) 1982. Assoc. Nexsen, Pruet, Jacobs & Pollard, Columbia, S.C., 1979-84; assoc. in house counsel, asst. sec. Greenwood (S.C.) Mills, Inc., 1984-95, exec. v.p., 1999—; exec. v.p., COO Greenwood Devel. Corp., 1995-99, pres., CEO, 1999—; bd. dirs. The County Bank, Greenwood Mills, Inc., Greenwood Devel. Corp., Ctrl. Trust Co. Bd. visitors Lander Coll., 1985-87; bd. dirs. Edn. Enrichment Found., 1986-89, Greenwood United Way, 1989-92, Greenwood Community Theatre, 1989-93, Greenwood Uptown Devel. Corp., 1991-93; bd. deacons 1st Presbyn. Ch., 1990-93, session, 1993-96; trustee Self Meml. Hosp., 1992-98; bd. dirs. Partnership for a Greater Greenwood, 1999—, Greenwood County Econ. Alliance, 1999—. Mem. ABA, Am. Corp. Counsel Assn., S.C. Bar Assn., Forest Lake Club, Greenwood Country Club, Rotary, S.C. C. of C. (bd. dirs. 1990-93). Presbyterian. Home: 512 E Henrietta Ave Greenwood SC 29649-3142 Office: Greenwood Devel Corp PO Box 1017 Greenwood SC 29648-1017

NEYELOFF, ALEJO, travel agency executive; b. Buenos Aires, July 19, 1929; s. Vladimir and Valentina (Leontovitch) N.; Maria Gema Frugone, Nov. 27, 1951 (dec. 1968); m. Adriana Cecilia Lilliecreutz, June 11, 1993. Bus. adminstn. lic., Cath. U., Argentina, 1974. Mgr. Neyeloff y Barrandeguy, Montevideo, Uruguay, 1951-60; dir. mgr. Christophersen, S.A., Montevideo, 1960-64; mgr. Pisadal S.A., Buenos Aires, 1964-67, exec. pres., 1967—. Fellow Masons Argentina (grand master 1987-93, Supreme Coun. 33d degree, grand sec. 1996-98); mem. AVIABUE-Buenos Aires Travel Agys. Assn. (gen. mgr. 1994-97), Hogar Bernardino Rivadavia (exec. dir. 1997—), Costa Rica Grand Lodge (hon.), Uruguay Grand Lodge (hon.), Grande Loge France (hon.). Avocation: historian, philanthropic organizations. Home and Office: Pico 1701 P 7 A, 1429 Buenos Aires Argentina

NEYIN, ALEXANDER AKUMEME, petroleum engineer, educator; b. Ikpisan-Warri, Delta, Nigeria, Aug. 31, 1950; came to U.S., 1975; s. Neyin Siunuphro and Newe (Odumu) Neyin; m. Matilda Ugomma, Dec. 23, 1976; children: Walter O., Kingsley O., Constance N., Gregory S., Rosemary O. BSc in Petroleum Engring., Texas A&M U., 1977; MSc in Petroleum Engring., U. S.W. La., 1978. Reservoir prodn. engr. Gulf Oil Co., Houston, Lafayette, Lagos, Nigeria, 1977-80; engring. supr. Gulf Oil Co., Escravos, Lagos, Nigeria, 1980-88; from mem. staff to mgr. Chevron Oil Co. Nigeria LTD, Lagos and others, Nigeria, 1990-97; mgr. Chevron Oil Co. Nigeria LTD, Lagos, Nigeria, 1997—. Contbr. articles to profl. jours. Recipient First prize JFK Essay U.S. Embassy, Lagos, Nigeria, 1971. Mem. Soc. Petroleum Engrs. (section chmn. 1997), Nigerian Soc. Engrs., Council of Registered Engrs. Nigeria, Ikoyi Club. Office: Chevron Nigeria Ltd, 2 Chevron Dr, Lekki Lagos Nigeria

NEYKOV, IVAN, law educator; b. Haskovo, Bulgaria, Apr. 17, 1955; married; 2 children. LLM, Sofia U., 1978; posgrad., Internat. Inst. Histadrut, Israel, 1991, Friedrich Ebert Found., Germany, 1992-93. Insp. Nat. Labour Inspectorate, Sofia, 1981-90; head of legal divsn. Confedn. Ind. Trade Unions in Bulgaria, 1990-92, v.p., 1992-97; minister labor and social affairs Caretaker Cabinet, Sofia, 1997; minister labor and social policy Republic of Bulgaria, Sofia, 1997—; mem. Task Force on drafting Labour Code, 1985-87; mem. task force on amendments to Labour Code, 1992-93, others. Author publs. in ILO edits., publs. on Labor Code applications. Office: Min Labour/Social Policy, 2 Triaditsa Str, 1000 Sofia Bulgaria

NEYLAN, JOHN FRANCIS, III, nephrologist, educator; b. Chgo., Feb. 20, 1953; s. John Francis and Mary Alice (Coogan) N.; m. Cynthia Barnes, May 17, 1980; children: John Francis IV, Elizabeth Marie, James Christopher. BS, Duke U., 1975; MD, Rush Med. Coll., Chgo., 1979. Intern in medicine Vanderbilt U., Nashville, 1979-80, resident, 1980-82; fellow in nephrology Brigham and Women's Hosp., Boston, 1983-84; fellow in immunogenetics Harvard U. Med. Sch., Boston, 1984-86, clin. preceptor, 1986; asst. prof. medicine U. Calif., Davis, 1986-88; asst. prof. medicine Emory U., Atlanta, 1988-93, assoc. prof., 1993-98, prof., 1998—, med. dir. renal transplantation, 1988—; vis. cons. Wanless Hosp., Miraj, India, 1982-83; assoc. med. dir. Lifelink of Ga. Organ Procurement Orgn., Atlanta, 1989—; bd. govs. Lifelink Found., Tampa, Fla., 1988—. Editor: Am. Soc. Transplantation Newsletter, 1994-98; contbr. articles and abstracts to med. jours., chpts. to books. Vol. Nat. Kidney Found., N.Y.C., 1990—, ARC, Atlanta, 1991, Spl. Olympics, Atlanta, 1991—, Habitat for Humanity, 1993—; chmn. Nat. Kidney Found. Coun. on Transplantation, 1995-98; bd. dirs. United Network for Organ Sharing. Recipient Physician's Recognition award AMA, 1989. Mem. ACP, Am. Fedn. Clin. Rsch. (councillor 1988), Am. Soc. Transplantation (co-chmn. patient care com. 1988-90, chmn. 1991-93, councillor-at-large exec. coun. 1993-96, sec.-treas. 1996-97, pres.-elect 1997-98, pres. 1998—, editor newsletter), Am. Soc. Nephrology, Internat. Soc. Nephrology, Transplantation Soc., United Network for Organ Sharing, Circumnavigator Club, Alpha Omega Alpha. Avocations: windsurfing, tennis, cycling. Office: Emory U Hosp D240 1364 Clifton Rd NE Atlanta GA 30322-0001

NEYMEYER, VALERIE R., research scientist; b. Clinton, Iowa, Nov. 24, 1969; d. Calvin Eugene and Carol Dean N. BA, U. Iowa, 1991, MS, 1995; postgrad., Chgo-Kent Coll. Law, 1998—. Scientist Bio-Rsch. Products, Inc., Coralville, Iowa, 1996-97; rsch. assoc. II Chirm Corp., Emeryville, Calif., 1997-98. Mem. AAAS, ABA. E-mail: vneymeye@kentlaw.edu.

NEYT, PHILIP, pension fund executive; b. Sleidinge, Ghent, Belgium, Mar. 4, 1963; s. Willem Neyt and Maria Roegiers; m. Sien Vermoesen. M in Polit. Scis., U. Leuven, Belgium, 1988; MBA in Econs., U. Brussels, 1988. Advisor Belgian Assn. Pension Funds, Brussels, 1988-91, Belgian Sec. of State for Pensions, Brussels, 1989-91; lectr., asst. officer U. Antwerp, Belgium, 1989-95; mng. dir. Belgacom Pension Funds, Brussels, 1995—; advisor Min. in the Ctrl. and Flemish Govt., Brussels, 1991-96; dir. BELGACOM Svcs., Brussels Internat. Airport Co. Pension Fund. Contbr. articles to profl. jours. Recipient Laureat of the Ministry of Edn., 1989. Avocations: traveling, gardening, shopping, theatre, collecting stamps. Home: Kapitteldreef 75B, 9830 Sint Martens Latem Belgium Office: Belgacom, Blvd Roi Albert II 27, 1030 Brussels Belgium

NEZELOF, CHRISTIAN, retired pathologist, educator; b. Barrou, France, Jan. 19, 1922; s. Pierre and Irene (Bouttier) N.; m. Luce d'Amato, June 8, 1954; children: Pierre, Sylvie. Student, U. Paris, 1941-46. Intern Hosp. Paris, 1946-50; prof. agregé Med. Tours, France, 1951-60; prof. medicine U. Paris, 1960-91; ret., 1991. Achievements include description of Nezelof's

syndrome, identification of Langerhans cell origin of Histiocytosis X. Mem. Acad. Royale de Medicine Brussels, European Soc. Pathology (pres.), Internat. Acad. Pathology (v.p., pres. XIII congress 1980), Internat. Pediat. Pathology Assn. (pres.), Leopoldina. Avocation: sailing. Home: 27 rue Gazan, 75014 Paris France

NEZER, CARINE, animal geneticist; b. Brussels, Jan. 17, 1966; d. Jacques and Danielle (Jouret) Nezer. Degree in Vet. Medicine, U. Liege, Belgium, 1991, M in Animal Tech. Sic., 1995. Animal geneticist rschr. U. Liege, 1993—. Contbr. articles to profl. jours. Avocations: travel, horseback riding. E-mail: carine.nezer@ulg.ac.be. Office: U Liege, Bd de Colonster 20, Liege Belgium 4000

NG, BRUCE CHUNG DAN See **WU, BRUCE CHUNG DAN**

NG, CHI-SING, pathologist, consultant; b. Hong Kong; s. Pang and Yee (Chan) Ng; m. Yuen-Wah Yvonne Chan, Nov. 23, 1992; children: Pok-Hym, Paul. MBBS, U. Hong Kong, 1979. Resident Queen Elizabeth Hosp., Hong Kong, 1981-83; resident Prince of Wales Hosp., Hong Kong, 1983-86, cons., 1986-87; cons. Caritas Med. Ctr., 1987—; chief of svc. Caritas Med. Ctr., Hong Kong, 1991—; dir. Lion's Eye Bank, Hong Kong, 1995—; examiner Hong Kong Coll. of Pathologists, 1995—; lab. inspector Hong Kong Coll. of Pathologists, 1996—. Author: (book) Diagnostic Histopathology of Tumors, 1995; contbr. articles to profl. jours. Fellow Royal Coll. Pathologists, Hong Kong Coll. Pathologists, Hong Kong Acad. Medicine. E-mail: ngcs@ha.org.hk. Office: Caritas Med Ctr, 111 Wing Hong St, Kowloon Shamshuipo Hong Kong China

NG, ENG-HEN, surgeon; b. Singapore, Dec. 10, 1958; s. Kim-Leong Ng and Bee-Choo Tan; m. Ivy Swee-Lian Lim, Nov. 8, 1958; children: Jonathan, Jill, Joel, Jeanne. MB, BChir, Nat. U. Singapore, 1982, CM, 1987. Resident Ministry of Health, Singapore, 1987-89; rsch. fellow N.Y. Hosp., 1989-90; surg. oncology fellow MD Anderson Cancer Ctr., Houston, 1990-91; cons. surgeon Singapore Gen. Hosp., 1993—, dir. breast svc., 1996—; advisor Ho Chi Minh Cancer Ctr., Vietnam, 1993-95; sec. gen. 12th Asia Pacific Cancer Conf., 1995. Contbr. articles to profl. jours. Capt. Singapore Armed Forces, 1986-87. SmithKline Beecham Surg. scholar MD Anderson Cancer Ctr., Houston, 1991. Fellow Royal Coll. Surgeons Edinburgh; mem. Soc. Surg. Oncology, Acad. Medicine Singapore. Home: 38F Jervois Rd, Singapore 249036, Singapore Office: Mt Elizabeth Med Ctr, 3 Mt Elizabeth #07-09, Singapore 228510, Singapore

NG, HEUNG-TAT, obstetrics and gynecology educator, hospital official; b. Canton, China, Oct. 2, 1938; s. P.C. and H.R. (Cheng) N.; m. Kok-Choo Chen; children: Anne, Pei, Sally. BM, Nat. Defense Med. Sch., Taipei, Taiwan, 1963; MD, U. N.C., 1971. Resident ob-gyn. Vets. Gen. Hosp., Taipei, Taiwan, 1963-67; attending ob-gyn. physician Vets. Gen. Hosp., Taipei, 1967-75, chief divsn. obstetrics, 1975-78, head dept. ob-gyn., 1979-96, dep. dir., 1996—; prof. ob-gyn. Nat. Yang-Ming U., Taipei, 1979—; vis. prof. Pa. State U., 1989, L.I. Jewish Med. Ctr., 1991. Author: Color Atlas of Radical Hysterectomy with Pelvic Lymph Node Dissection, 1994; chief editor Jour. Ob-Gyn., Taipei, Taiwan, 1990-91; pres. Jour. Gynecologic Oncology, 1990-96; editor Chinese sect. Internat. Jour. Ob-Gyn., Tapei, 1990-94; contbr. more than 140 articles to profl. jours. Named 1 of ten top vets., Vet. Affairs Commn., Taipei, Taiwan, 1985, 1 of ten top govt. ofcls., Exec. Yuan, Taiwan, 1986, 8th ann. Alexander H. and Dorothy Rosenthal Lectr., Albert Einstein Coll. Medicine, N.Y.C., 1991. Mem. Soc. Gynencol. Oncology (pres. Taipei 1990-96, Hon. chmn. 1996), Female Cancer Found. (chmn. Taipei 1993—), Asian Oceania Fedn. Ob-Gyn., (chmn. ethics com. 1994). Avocations: swimming, sketching, collecting stamps. Office: Vets Gen Hosp Dept Ob-Gyn, 201 Shih-Pai Rd Sect 2, Taipei 11217, Taiwan

NG, HON WAH, physician; b. Hong Kong, Feb. 1, 1959; arrived in the U.K., 1977; s. Shing Wei and How Ying (Yu) N.; m. Nancy Hwang, Sept. 10, 1992; 1 child, Kieran Ghing Hai. MB, BChir, U. Sheffield, Eng., 1984; MD, U. Liverpool, Eng., 1994. Trained specialist in gen. medicine and clin. pharmacology; trained gen. practitioner; MRCP/U.K. Sr. house officer King Edward VII Hosp., Midhurst, Eng., 1985-86, Royal Liverpool Hosp., 1986-87; registrar Southport (Eng.) and Formby Dist. Hosp., 1987-89; rsch. fellow U. Liverpool, 1989-91, clin. lectr., 1991-94; gen. practitioner Scott Park Surgery, Southend-on-Sea, Eng., 1995—. Contbr. articles to profl. jours. Sponsor World Vision Charity, Eng., 1995—. Mem. Royal Coll. Physicians (U.K.), Brit. Med. Assn. Avocations: golf, badminton, ten-pin bowling, travel, cooking. Office: Scott Park Surgery, 205 Western Approaches, Southend-on-Sea Essex SS2 6XY, England

NG, KIM CHAI, electrical engineer; b. Johor Bahru, Johor, Malaysia, Feb. 26, 1971; s. Lai Hock Ng and Moy Tay. BS, U. Tenn., 1993, MS, 1995; PhD, U. Calif., San Diego, 2000. Registered engr.-in-tng., Tenn. Rsch. asst. Computer Vision and Robotics Rsch. Lab., Knoxville, Tenn., 1993-95; rsch. asst. Computer Vision and Robotics Rsch. Lab., San Diego, 1998-2000, sr. rsch. engr., 2000—. Recipient Col. Samuel H. Lockett Engring. scholarship U. Tenn., 1992, Arthur B. Wood Meml. scholarship U. Tenn., 1993. Mem. IEEE, Soc. Profl. Indsl. Engrs. Avocations: reading, movies, camping, traveling, guitar. E-mail: kimcng@hotmail.com. Office: 9500 Gilman Dr Dept 407 La Jolla CA 92093-0407

NG, KINGSLEY KING KAU, hospital pharmacy administrator, educator; b. Hong Kong, July 13, 1945; s. Kai Lam and Kwei Tsin (Tang) N.; m. Elizabeth Yueh-Ling Low; children: Olivia, Stefanie. B Pharmcy, U. Sydney, Australia, 1967, MSc, 1979; diploma in food and drug analysis, U. NSW, Australia, 1969, grad. mgmt. qualification, 1995. Administrator dept. pharmacy Westmead (Australia) Hosp.; clin. sr. lectr. U. Sydney, Australia. Mem. editl. com. Australian Pharmaceutical Formulary and Handbook, 13th edit., 1983, 14th edit., 1988; contbr. chpts. to books, articles to profl. publs. S.E. Wright Rsch. grantee Pharm. Soc. NSW, 1976. Fellow Soc. Hosp. Pharmacists of Australia (Abbot Bursary award 1975, Casemix Rsch. grantee 1995), Australian Inst. Pharmacy Mgmt., Australian Coll. Health Svcs. Execs.; mem. Australasian Soc. Clin. and Exptl. Pharmacologists, NSW Assn. Dirs. of Pharmacy, Univ. Tchg. Hosps. (chmn. 1990—), Health and Rsch. Employees' Assn. NSW (v.p. profl. officer's sub-br. 1983-96). Home: 31 Tomah St, Carlingford NSW 2118, Australia Office: Westmead Hosp Dept Pharmacy, Hawkesbury Rd, Westmead NSW 2145, Australia

NG, LORENZ K., neurologist, educator; b. Singapore, Aug. 6, 1940; came to U.S., 1958; s. Seak and Poh (Tan) N.; m. Roberta Melia, Dec. 7, 1981. BA, Stanford U., 1961; MD, Columbia U., 1965. Diplomate Am. Bd. Psychiatry and Neurology. Resident neurology U. Pa. Hosp., Phila., 1966-69; rsch. fellow NIMH, Bethesda, Md., 1969-72; spl. asst. to dir., chief rsch. lab., chief pain studies Nat. Inst. on Drug Abuse, Rockville, Md., 1972-81; dir. Washington Pain Ctr., 1986-91; med. dir. Chronic Pain program Nat. Rehab. Hosp., Washington, 1991-98; dir. med. & regulatory affairs, Greater China Eli Lilly & Co., Shanghai, 1998—; pres., med. dir. Washington Pain and Rehab. Ctr., Inc., 1986-91; clin. prof. dept. neurology George Washington U., Washington, 1995—; vis. lectr. dept. neurosurgery Johns Hopkins Med. Sch.; mem. adv. coun. Alternative Medicine Program NIH, Bethesda, 1996-98; spl. cons. Tan Tock Seng Hosp., Singapore, 1995-96; bd. dirs. Am. Acad. Pain Medicine, Chgo., 1990-93, Reflex Sympathetic Dystrophy Syndrome Assn., N.J., 1993-98; cons. Eli Lilly & Co., 1996-98, dir. greater China med. & regulatory affairs Eli Lilly Asia, Inc., 1998—; cons. Merck-Medco Managed Care, LLC, 1998. Author: (with S. Liao and M. Lee) Principles and Practice of Contemporary Acupuncture, 1994; editor: Alternatives to Violence, 1968, (with D. Davis) Strategies for Public Health, 1981, (with J. Bonica) Pain, Discomfort and Humanitarian Care, 1980, (with S. Mudd) Population Crisis: Implications and Plans for Action, 1965. Mem. bd. trustees Cosmos Club Found., Washington, 1993-98; mem. adv. coun. Third World Found., Md., 1994; pres. Am. divsn. World Acad. Art and Sci., 1982-93. Recipient S. Weir Mitchell award Am. Acad. Neurology, 1971, A.E. Bennett award Soc. Biol. Psychiatry, 1972, Commendation medal USPHS, 1981. Fellow Coll. of Physicians Phila., Am. Coll. Pain Medicine Chgo.; mem. Cosmos Club Washington, Am. Club Internat., The China Club (Beijing). E-mail: ng lorenz@lilly.com. Office: Harbor Ring Plaza 31st Fl, No 18 Xizang (M) Rd, Shanghai 200001, China

NG, MAN-LUN, psychiatrist, educator; b. Hong Kong; s. Fei-Yang and Wing-Hsia (Li) N.; m. May Sui; children: Luk-Pan, Luk-Ting. MB, BS, U. Hong Kong, 1971, MD, 1992. Med. officer Hong Kong Govt., 1972-73; lectr. psychiatry U. Hong Kong, 1971-81, sr. lectr. psychiatry, 1981-93, reader psychiatry, 1993-96, prof. psychiatry, 1996—; pres. 14th World Congress Sexology, Hong Kong, 1996-99. Co-author: Sexual Behavior in Modern China, 1992 (China Publs. award 1993); co-author, editor: Chinese Dictionary of Sexology, 1993; co-prodr. (TV sex edn. series) Incest, 1988 (Gold medal N.Y. Internat. TV and Film Festival 1989). Med. insp. Supreme Ct., Hong Kong, 1985—; mem. TV adv. panel Radio-TV Hong kong, 1993—; mem. mental health review tribunal Govt. Hong Kong, 1995—. Fellow Royal Coll. Psychiatrists, Australia and New Zealand Coll. Psychiatrists, Hong Kong Coll. Psychiatrists; mem. Hong Kong Edn. Assn. (pres. 1985-91), Asian Fedn. Sexology (pres. 1992-94), Hong Kong Family Planning Assn. (life). Avocations: music, computer. Office: Univ Hong Kong, Pokfulum Rd Dept Psychiatry, Hong Kong China

NG, SHU HANG, radiologist; b. Hong Kong, Aug. 30, 1955; arrived in Taiwan, 1976; s. Yuen Shing Ng and King Ying Leung; m. Hsiu Chen Lin, Feb. 9, 1985; children: Yi Wei, Ben Leung. B Medicine, Taipei (Taiwan) Med. Coll., 1983. Resident Chang Gung Meml. Hosp., Taipei, 1983-87, attending radiologist, 1987—, dept. chief, 1998—; lectr. Chang Gung U., Taipei, 1992-98, assoc. prof., 1998—. Contbr. articles to profl. jours. Recipient Best Article award Radiol. Soc. Republic of China, 1997, award Bracco Internat., 1999. Home: 6F 6 Lane 155, Tung Hwa North Rd, Taipei Taiwan Office: Dept Diagnostic Radiology, 222 Mai-Chin Rd, Keelung Taiwan

NG, TAI-KAI, physics educator; b. Hong Kong, Guandong, China, Apr. 29, 1959; p. Young-Pi Ng and Tze-Ling Wong. BS, U. Hong Kong, 1981; PhD in Physics, Northwestern U., 1987. Post-doctoral assoc. Mass. Inst. Tech., Cambridge, 1987-89, AT&T Bell Labs., Murray Hill, N.J., 1989-91; lectr. Hong Kong U. Sci. & Tech., 1991-96, assoc. prof., 1996—; cons. Lucent Techs., Murray Hill, 1996—; external examiner dept. physics Chinese U. Hong Kong, 1997—; mem. acad. com. Inst. Theoretical Physics, Academia Sinica, Beijing, 1999—. Contbr. articles to profl. jours. Recipient Outstanding Young Rschr. Hon. Mention, Oversea Chinese Physicists Assn., 1993. Mem. Phys. Soc. Hong Kong (chmn. 1999—), Am. Phys. Soc. Office: Dept Physics, Hong Kong U Sci & Tech, Hong Kong Hong Kong

NG, TIAN SENG, internal medicine consultant; b. Seremban, Malaysia, Sept. 26, 1943; s. Thong and Soon (Lim) Ng; m. Oi Mooi Yip, Jan. 22, 1979; children: Eleanor, Michelle, William. MBBS, U. Singapore, 1968. Cert. in internal medicine. Cons. in internal medicine District Hosp. Kuala Pilah, Malaysia, 1974-78, Gen. Hosp. Ipoh, Malaysia, 1978-83, Gen. Hosp. Alor Setar, Malaysia, 1983-91; sr. cons. in internal medicine Hosp. Sultanah Aminah, Johor Baru, Malaysia, 1991-98; lectr., coord. U. Kebangsaan Malaysia, Kuala Lumpur, 1993-98; supr. internal medicine U. Malaya, Kuala, 1996-98; assoc. prof. medicine U. Putra Malaysia, 1998—. Contbg. author: Lipids and Ischaemic Heart Disease, 1985; contbr. articles to profl. jours. Recipient Kesatria Mangku Negara award Fed. Govt., 1991, Johan Setia Mahkota, 1996. Fellow Royal Australasian Coll. Physicians; mem. Malaysian Med. Assn., Coll. Physicians U.K. Avocation: photography. Home: 20 Jalan Anggerik 5/2, Taman Anggerik, 81300 Johor Bahru Johor, Malaysia Office: 8th Fl, Grand Seasons Hotel, Kuala Lumpur Malaysia

NG, TUCK WAH, engineering educator; b. Ipoh, Perak, Malaysia, Apr. 7, 1964; parents Yew Kee Ng and Ah Kuan Lee; m. Peck Chin Hoh, June 4, 1994; 1 child, Enoch. B of Engring. with honors, Nat. U. Singapore, 1988, M of Engring., 1990, PhD, 1996. Profl. officer Nat. U. Singapore, 1990-96, asst. prof., 1996—; info. tech. coord. Bachelor of Tech. program Nat. U. Singapore, 1999—. Reviewer internat. jours. Mem. Internat. Soc. Optical Engring., Optical Soc. Am., Soc. for Exptl. Mechanics. Avocations: swimming, Bible study. Fax: 65-7773525. E-mail: engngtw@nus.edu.sg. Office: Nat U Singapore, EA-07-35 9 Engineering Dr 1, Singapore 117576, Singapore

NG, YING CHU, economics educator; b. Hong Kong, Dec. 19, 1963. BSc, U. S.C., 1987, MA, 1988, PhD, 1991. Cons. World Bank, Washington, 1991, 92; asst. prof. Hong Kong Bapt. U., 1991-97, assoc. prof., 1998—. Contbr. articles and book revs. to profl. jours. and chpt. to book. Recipient Outstanding Acad. Performance award U. S.C. Econs. Dept., 1991. Mem. Am. Econ. Assn., Hong Kong Exams. Authority, Econs. Subject Com., Com. on Status of Women in Econs. Profession, Soc. Labor Econs. Avocations: tennis, badminton, reading. Office: Hong Kong Bapt U, Dept Econs, Kowloon Tong Hong Kong

NGAI, YIN LEUNG STEPHEN, dermatologist; b. Hong Kong, June 24, 1949; s. Lam Sai and Pui Lan (Cheung) N.; m. Hei Pun, Aug. 30, 1982 (div. 1997); children: Yue Ching Eugene, Yue Yan Ian. MB, BS, U. Hong Kong, 1973; Diploma in Dermatology, U. London, 1979. Intern Queen Mary Hosp., Hong Kong, 1973-74; resident in gen. medicine and dermatology Auckland Hosp. Bd., New Zealand, 1974-78; practice medicine specializing in dermatology Hong Kong, 1979—; staff dermatologist St. Teresa's Hosp., Hong Kong, 1980-99; cons. dermatologist Fedn. Trade Unions, Hong Kong, 1984-90, Hong Kong Stockbrokers Assn., 1982—, Cathay Pacific Airways, 1980-99. Fellow Hong Kong Coll. Physicians, Hong Kong Acad. Medicine; mem. Royal Coll. Physicians (U.K.), Hong Kong Soc. Dermatology and Venereology (hon. sec. 1985-87, vice chmn. 1987-89, chmn. 1989-90), Asian Dermatol. Assn. (hon. sec. 1990-92). Office: Room 807 Hang Shing Bldg, 363 Nathan Rd, Kowloon Hong Kong

NGANG'A, PETER MACHARIA, orthodontist, consultant, researcher; b. Gilgil, Kenya, June 21, 1956; s. Samson Ngururu and Jane Wambui Ngang'a; m. Rose Njeri Kariuki, Dec. 31, 1993; children: Jane Wambui, Sami Ng'ang'a. B of Dental Surgery, U. Nairobi, Kenya, 1980; MSc in Dentistry, U. Oslo, Norway, 1991, PhD, 1996. Diplomate orthodontics. Rshc. asst. U. Nairobi, 1986-90, lectr., 1991-97, sr. lectr., 1997—; cons. Gertrude's Children's Hosp., Nairobi, 1997—; hon. cons. Kenyatta Hosp., Nairobi, 1995—; hon. lectr. Coll. Health Professions, Nairobi, 1989—. Contbr. articles to profl. jours. Commonwealth fellow British Govt., 1988, Norwegian fellow Norwegian Govt., Oslo, 1989-91, 95, 96. Mem. Kenya Rwy. Golf Club. Avocation: golf. Office: 4th Fl PO Box 38761, Kimathi St Kimathi House, Nairobi Kenya

NGCOBO, THEMBEKILE THELMA, human resources executive; b. Gauteng, South Africa, Apr. 5, 1949; d. Moli Caroline (Zitha) N.; 1 child, Musa Moses. BA in Social Scis., U. North, Pietersburg, South Africa, 1971; postgrad. diploma in mgmt., Witwatersrand U., 1989; PMD, diploma in Internat. Rels., Harvard B Sch., diploma in co. direction. Cmty. worker Christian Inst. South Africa, Johannesburg, 1972-75; rsch. officer Inst. Social and Econ. Rsch. Rhodes U., Grahamstown, South Africa, 1975-76; rsch. exec. Van Zijl and Schultze Lund & Tredoux Party Ltd., Johannesburg, 1976-78; sr. rsch. exec. B.B.D.O. SA, Johannesburg, 1978-80; rsch. exec. OK Bazaars Ltd., Johannesburg, 1980-85; planning mgr. dept. mktg. Johannesburg Consolidate Investment Co. Ltd., 1985-87, with indsl. rels. dept., 1988-92, indsl. rels. mgr., 1992-95, with transformation and human resources dept., 1995-96; ptnr. Tasa Internat. Ltd., Johannesburg, 1996-97; founder Thelma Ngcobo and Assocs., Johannesburg, 1997—; gen. mgr. South African Res. Bank, Pretoria, 1998—; apptd. advisor faculty of info. scis. Dept. Lang. Dynamics/Technikon Pretoria, 1999; bd. dirs. SC Johnson, Women Spearheading Investments Pty Ltd. Mem. Inst. Personal Mgmt., South African Bd. Personnel Practitioners, Black Mgmt. Forum (founder), Harvard Bus. Sch. Club South Africa. Roman Catholic. Avocations: reading, traveling, public speaking, gardening, jazz. Office: SA Res Bank, PO Box 427, 0001 Pretoria South Africa also: 111 Elevation Rd, Randjesfontein, Midrand South Africa

NGENY, NOAH KIPRONO, Olympic athlete; b. Eldoret, Kenya, Nov. 2, 1978. Winner Gold medal 1500 meter Sydney, 2000. Broke world jr. record for 1500 meters, 1997, record for 1500, 1999; set new Kenyan record for 1500 meters at World Championships, 1999. Office: Kenya Amateur Athletic Assn, Nyayo Nat Stadium PO Box 46722, Nairobi West Nairobi, Kenya*

NGIRAKLSONG, ARTHUR, judge. Chief justice Supreme Ct., Palau. Office: Supreme Ct Rep of Palau PO Box 248, Koror Palau PW 96940-0248*

NGO, NAM QUOC, electrical engineering educator; b. Phnom Penh, Cambodia, Oct. 28, 1969; arrived in Australia, 1983; s. Hung Van and Diep Kha (Te) N. BEng, Monash U., Melbourne, Australia, 1992, PhD in Engring., 1998. Salesman family bus., Saigon, Vietnam, 1975-80, Phnom Penh, 1981; rsch. engr. Monash U., 1992, rsch. asst., 1993-97; lectr. electronic engring. Griffith U., Nathan, Australia, 1997—; asst. prof. elec. & electronic engring. Nanyoung Technol. U., Singapore, 2000—. Contbr. articles to sci. jours., including IEEE Jour. Lightwave Tech., Microwave and Optical Tech. Letters, Applied Optics, Optics Comm., Fiber and Integrated Optics, IEE Procs. Optoelectronics, IEEE Jour. Quantum Electronics. Postgrad. scholar Monash U., 1994, Australian Govt., 1995-96; recipient Electrical Coll. Prize Inst. of Engrs., Australia, 1999. Mem. Chinese Fraternity Assn. of Queensland (pres. 1999—). Avocations: swimming, tennis, table tennis, badminton, volleyball. Office: Griffith U, Sch Microelectronic Engring, Nathan Qld 4111, Australia

NGOENMUN, SUTHAT, federal official; b. May 18, 1945; married. LLB, Thammasat U. Elected Ho. of Reps., 1975, 83, 88, 92, 95, 96, dep. min. of pub. health, 1988-90; dep. min. of agrl. and coops., 1990-91, dep. min. of interior, 1992-95, chmn. ho. of standing com. on justice and human rights, 1996-97, dep. leader of Democrat Party; min. of justice Ministry of Justice, Bangkok, 1997—. Democrat. Office: Ministry of Justice, 6 Thanon Rachini, 10200 Bangkok Thailand*

NGONGI, A. NAMANGA, federal agency administrator; b. Cameroon, Sept. 3, 1945; married; 3 children. BS in Agrl., Calif. State Polytech.; M in Agronomy, Cornell U., PhD. With World Food Programme; regional bur. mgr. Ea. and So. Africa Bur., with West and Ctrl. Africa Bur., dep. dir. external rels., assoc. dir. ops., dir. devel. ops., dep. exec. dir., 1994—; 1st sec. Cameroon Embassy, 1980, counsellor. Mem. Soc. for Internat. Devel. (former v.p. Rome Internat. chpt., ACC subcom. on nutrition). Office: Via Cesare Giulio Viola 68, Pasco de Medici, Rome 00148, Italy*

NGUGI, ELIZABETH NJERI, medical educator; b. Kenya, Oct. 10, 1937; d. Solomon Kariuki and Phylis Huro (Ngaku) Munyua; m. Leonard James Ngugi; 1 child, James Ngochi. BS, Columbia Pacific U., 1983, MA, 1985, PhD, 1989. RN; cert. nurse mgr., adminstr. Co-dir. Strengthening STD/HIV/AIDS, Uon, Kenya, 1990—; dir. Kenya Vol. Women Rehab. Ctr., 1991—; sr. lectr. U. Nairobi, Kenya, 1992; mem. Brit. Coun. Nairobi Initiative TOT, 1997; coord. Heart to Heart Found. Kenya, 1996; co-dir. STD/HIV/AIDS Project UoN, Kenya, 1990—; trainer/coord. Kenya Assn. of Profl. Counsellors, 1996—; developer peer edn. for comml. sex workers in Kenya. Co-author: Implications for Sexually Transmitted Diseases Transmission and Control, 1994; contbr. articles to profl. publs. Chmn. Soc. for Women and AIDS, Kenya, 1990—, Nat. Nurses Assn. of Kenya, 1980-82. Recipient cert. honor Kenya Red Cross Soc., 1979, Pub. Health award Kenyatta U., 1995. Mem. Nat. Nurses Assn. (life), Internat. Epidemiology Assn., Global Task Force on AIDS Edn. Roman Catholic. Avocations: watching environment, walking, reading, watching TV, relating with human being. Office: U Nairobi, PO Box 19676, Nairobi Kenya

NGULUBE, MATHEW M. S. W., judge. Chief justice Supreme Ct. of Zambia, Lusaka. Office: Supreme Ct of Zambia, Independence Ave PO Box 50067, Ridgeway Lusaka Zambia*

NGUYEN, ANN CAC KHUE, pharmaceutical and medicinal chemist; b. Kieu Moc, Sontay, Vietnam, Nov. 12, 1949; d. Nguyen Van Soan and Luu Thi Hieu. BS, U. Saigon, 1973; MS, San Francisco State U., 1978; PhD, U. Calif., San Francisco, 1983. Teaching and research asst. U. Calif., San Francisco, 1978-83, postdoctoral fellow, 1983-86; research scientist U. Calif., 1987—. Contbr. articles to profl. jours. Recipient Nat. Research Service award, NIH, 1981-83; Regents fellow U. Calif., San Francisco, 1978-81. Mem. AAAS, Am. Chem. Soc., N.Y. Acad. Scis., Bay Area Enzyme Mechanism Group, Am. Assn. Pharm. Scientists. Roman Catholic. Home: 1488 Portola Dr San Francisco CA 94127-1409 Office: U Calif PO Box 446 San Francisco CA 94143-0001

NGUYEN, CHINH MINH, computer vision scientist; b. Thaibinh, Vietnam, Sept. 17, 1960; d. Minh Nguyen Hung and Kieu Thi Pham; 1 child, Duc Chinh Nguyen. Diploma in elec. and info engring., U. Hanoi, 1982, diploma in Eng., 1986; Dr. Ing., Fed. Armed Forces U. Munich, 1999. Rschr. Nat. Ctr. Scis. Vietnam, Hanoi, 1989-91, Space Applications Ctr., Ahmedabad, India, 1988-89; rsch. assoc. Nat. Ctr. Natural Scis. & Technologies, Hanoi, 1990-91; rschr. Inst. Oceanorg Russia Sci. Acad., Moscow, 1992; Ctr. Natural Sci. & Tech., Vietnam, 1993; rschr. Fed. Armed Forces U. Munich, 1994-95, project mgr., 1996-99; sci. asst. faculty Inst. Informatics U. Munich, Germany, 2000—; chief bookkeeping and engring. Elec. and Optical Corp., Vietnam, 1989-93. Author: Vector Engine, 1989; contbr. articles to profl. jours. Recipient rsch. grants Gov. India, 1988-89, Gov. Germany, 1994-95, Boston Univ., 1998, Inst. Robotics and Automation Soc., 1999, 2000. Mem. IEEE, Robotics and Automation Soc., Imaging Sci. and Tech. IS&T, Internat. Soc. Optical Engring., SPIE. Avocations: reading, traveling, researching, sports, table ball. Office: Inst for Informatics IX, Tech U Munich Orleansstr 34, 81667 Munich Germany

NGUYEN, DINH LOC, Vietnamese government official. Min. of justice Govt. of Vietnam, Hanoi. Office: Ministry of Justice, 25 A Cat Linh St, Hanoi Vietnam*

NGUYEN, DUC DINH, physician; b. Hetay, Vietnam, Oct. 11, 1963; s. Thanh Dinh and Ky Thi (Luong) N.; m. Yen Tran, Nov. 12, 1992; children: Linh Jhanh, Khoa Donh. BS, Hanoi State U., Vietnam, 1984; PhD, Moscow State U., 1991; DS, Russian Acad. Scis., Moscow, 1997; M, Internat. Acad. Mktg. Mgmt., Moscow, 1996. Lectr. Hanoi State U., Vietnam, 1984-86; trainer Moscow State U., 1991-93; prof. Mech. Engring. Rsch. Inst., Moscow, 1998—; hon. prof. European U., 1999. Contbr. articles to profl. jours. Mem. Russian Acad. Scis., Internat. Acad. Authors Sci. Discoveries, N.Y. Acad. Scis. Avocations: sports, reading, travel.

NGUYEN, DUNG LUONG, mechanical and aeronautical engineer, researcher; b. Hanoi, Vietnam, Mar. 23, 1948; s. Tai Luong and Nguyen Loc Thi Tran Nguyen; m. Huong Tra Le-Nguyen, Oct. 30, 1993; 1 child, Viet Luong. Dipl.ing., U. Stuttgart, Germany, 1973; dr.-ing., U. Hanover, Germany, 1981. Rsch. assoc. U. Hanover, 1977-84; vis. postdoctoral fellow McMaster Univ., Hamilton, Can., 1982-83; sr. rsch. assoc. Tech. Univ. of Hamburg, 1984-89, habil. fellow, 1991-92; vis. prof. Ho-Chi-Minh-City U. Tech., Vietnam, 1990, 92—, dir. Centre of Computational Mechanics, 1992; vis. prof. German Acad. Exch. Svc., Ho-Chi-Minh-City, 1992-97. Author tech. books; contbr. articles on plasticity and finite element method to sci. jours. Mem. N.Y. Acad. Scis., German Soc. of Engrs. (Ring of Honor for Outstanding Scientific Work 1987), Soc. for Applied Math. and Mechanics. Avocations: downhill skiing, hiking, classical music. Home: 198/16 Huynh Van Banh, F11-QPN Ho Chi Minh City Vietnam Office: Ho-Chi-Minh City U Tech, 268 Ly Thuong Kiet Q10, Ho Chi Minh City Vietnam

NGUYEN, GIANG DAI (DAI-GIANG), artist, sculptor, graphic artist, muralist; b. Hanoi, Vietnam, May 21, 1944; came to U.S., 1992; s. Bui Dinh and Luan Thi (Le) N.; m. Thuy Bich Cao, Dec. 1976 (div. May 1985); children: Anh Nhat, Lan Thuy; m. Nguyen Tuoi Thi, Oct. 24, 1998. Grad. Sch. Art, Hanoi, 1965; AA, Coll. Art, Hanoi, 1968; BA, Coll. Art, Moscow, 1974. Supervisory artist advtg. and exhibiting co., Hanoi, 1975-78; lectr. Coll. Art, Hanoi, 1978-80; polit. prisoner Hanoi, 1980-87; polit. refugee Hong Kong, 1988-91; artist Seattle, 1992—. Pvt. collections in U.S., Japan, Can., Hong Kong, France; collection in Mus. of Art, Voronezh, Russia; murals include USA Today, Seattle, 1995, American Jazz, Seattle, 1994, Traditions of Vietnamese Culture, Seattle, 1992, Old Medicine of the Philippines, Battayon, 1991; exhbns. include Chinese Galley: Asian artists group show, Seattle, 1996, University Friends Ctr., Seattle, 1994, solo show at Pillar Point, Hong Kong, 1991, internat. group show at mus., Sophia, Bulgaria, 1977, group show Moscow, 1972; inventor of Upside Down art; author: Manifesto of Upside-Downism. Named Most Talented Artist of the World in internat. competition Stockholm, 1997; winner 3rd prize 1st Internat. Drawing Contest World of Art, 1997, 3rd prize Internat. Competi-

tion, Stockholm, 1997, 3rd prize Wash. State Conv. Ctr. group show, 1993, Best Contemporary Art CD-ROM--juried collection, 1996. Mem. Vietnamese Artist Assn. of N.W. U.S.A., S.E. Effective Devel., Inc. Home: 7416 Holly Park Dr S # 800 Seattle WA 98118-3720

NGUYEN, HAN VAN, mechanical engineer; b. Danang, Vietnam, June 10, 1956; came to U.S., 1974; s. Tien Van and Dieu Anh (Khoa) N.; m. Thien-Tam Trang, Jan. 7, 1995; children: Huy, Minh. BSME with distinction, Iowa State U., 1979; MSME, Purdue U., 1981, PhD, 1986. Registered profl. engr., Calif., Wash. Grad. rsch. asst. Purdue U., West Lafayette, 1979-83; sr. engr. Westinghouse Electric Corp., Sunnyvale, Calif., 1983-87; prin. engr., scientist The Boeing Co., Huntington Beach, Calif., 1987—; mem. adj. faculty Calif. State Poly. U., Pomona, 1995—. Contbr. articles to profl. jours. Mem. bd. dirs. L.A. Coun. Engrs. and Scientists. Recipient Cert. of Appreciation, Rockwell Internat. Corp., 1989, 94, Instant Compensation award Rockwell Internat. Corp., 1992, 94, NASA Group Achievement award, 1992; Iowa State U. scholar; Purdue U. fellow;. Fellow AIAA (assoc., liquid propulsion tech. com., 2000—, stds. reviewer), Inst. Advancement Engring.; mem. Golden Key, Sigma Xi, Phi Kappa Phi, Tau Beta Pi, Pi Tau Sigma, Eta Kappa Nu, Pi Mu Epsilon, Phi Eta Sigma. Achievements include development of numerous thermo-fluid models to evaluate the design and predict the performance of launch vehicle propulsion systems, and publications in space propulsion. Office: The Boeing Co 5301 Bolsa Ave # H013c322 Huntington Beach CA 92647-2048

NGUYEN, HIEU TRONG, physician; b. Saigon, Vietnam, July 10, 1956; arrived in France, 1974; s. Hoan Ngoc and Thin Thi (Pham) N. MD, U. Paris, 1983. Physician pvt. practice, Nanterre, France, 1985—; med. expert Gan Ins. Co., France, 1986—; sr. dr. emergency medicine Hosp. Lariboisepere, Paris, 1990—; ofcl. dr. French Fedn. Badminton, 1997—. With French Artillery Regiment, 1984. Mem. Med. Assn. Nanterre, Oriental Med. Assn. France., Med. Soccer Assn., Tennis Sport Assn., Multisport Assn. Buddhist. Avocations: travel, sports, humanitarian acts. Home: 49 Ave de Colmar, 92500 Rueil-Malmaison France Office: 2 Ave Felix Faure, 92000 Nanterre France

NGUYEN, HOE, physics researcher, educator; b. Hanoi, Vietnam, Dec. 12, 1933; arrived in France, 1956; s. Ba Nguyen and Qui Pham; m. Elisabeth Vaucourt, Jan. 25, 1936; children: Bertrand, Laurent, Corinne. BS, U. Sorbonne, Paris, 1957, PhD in Physics, 1966; Civil Engr. Degree, Nat. Sch. Engring., Paris, 1961. Asst. prof. Cath. Inst., Paris, 1958-61; engr. Atomic Energy Agy., Paris, 1962-64; rschr. Nat. Ctr. Rsch., France, 1964-72, sr. mem., 1972-84, dir. rsch., 1984—; mem. internat. com. Internat. Confs. on Spectral Line Shapes and Related Topics, 1980—; prof. U. Paris II, 1980—; head lab. gas and plasma spectroscopy Rsch. Dept. Physics, Paris, 1980-97. Contbr. articles to profl. jours. Mem. Civil Engr. Assn., French Assn. Physics. Avocations: Oriental and French cuisine, music. Office: U Paris VI DRP, 4 Place Jussieu, 75252 Paris France

NGUYEN, MANH CAM, Vietnamese government official; b. June 15, 1929. Revolutionary work Hung Dung Commune, Vietnam, 1945; mem. youth orgn. adminstrv. work Fourth Interzone, Vietnam, 1947; with various depts. Ministry of Fgn. Affairs, Vietnam, 1952; amb. to Hungary, Austria and Iran, 1973-77, amb. Federal Republic Germany, Austria, Iran, and Switzerland, 1977-81; vice min. Ministry of Fgn. Trade, Vietnam, 1981-87; amb. Soviet Union, 1987-91; min. fgn. affairs 9th Session Nat. Assembly Socialist Republic Vietnam (8th Legis.), Vietnam, 1991—; dep. prime min. Govt. Vietnam, Hanoi; mem. ctrl com. Communist Party Vietnam 6th Congress, 1986, 7th Congress, 1991; mem. Nat. Assembly Vietnam, 1992—; mem. Commn. for Nat. Defense and Security, 1992. Mem. Politbureau Cen. Com. Communist Party of Vietnam, 1994. Office: Office of Min Fgn Affairs, 1 Ton That Dam, Hanoi Vietnam Office: Office of the Prime Min, Hoang Hoa Thum St, Hanoi Vietnam*

NGUYEN, PHONG CHAU, biomathematics educator; b. Bach Hac, Vinh Yen, Vietnam, July 2, 1936; arrived in France, 1957; s. The Toan and Thi Riep (Nguyen) N.; m. Lien Tran, July 22, 1972; children: Helene, Pierre. MA, U. Paris, 1959, PhD, 1963. Rschr. Nat. Ctr. for Sci. Rsch., Paris, 1959-63; prof. U. St. Quentin-Amiens, France, 1964-90, U. Paris, 1990—; mem. French del. to UN Sci. Com. on Effects of Atomic Radiation, Vienna, Austria, 1989. Co-author: (books) Contribution to Nephrology, 1977, Néphrotoxicité et ototoxicité médicamenteuses, 1982, Heart Perfusion, Energetics and Ischemia, 1983, Hypertension: Physiopathology and Treatment, 2d edit., 1983, Computer Modelling of Complex Biological Systems, 1984, Giant Intracranial Aneurysms, Therapeutic Approaches, 1988, A Course on Theoretical Biology, 1998; contbr. numerous articles and reports to profl. jours. Mem. Internat. Soc. Hypertension, European Soc. Hypertension, French Soc. Math., Frenh Soc. Hypertension, French Soc. Theoretical Biology. Buddhist. Avocations: stone sculpture, pastels, tennis. E-mail: chau@urbb.jussieu.fr. Office: Ctr Bioinformatique, 2 Pl Jussieu Courrier 7113, 75251 Paris France

NGUYEN, THACH NGOC, cardiologist; b. Feb. 2, 1953; s. Sau Ngoc Nguyen and Hanh Hong Tran. Resident internal medicine Bklyn. Hosp., 1982-85, fellow cardiology, 1985-87; clin. asst. prof. medicine Ind. U. Sch. Medicine, 1992—; dir. cardiovascular rsch. St. Mary Med. Ctr., Hobart, Ind., 1997—, pres.-elect med. staff, 2000—; pvt. practice; chmn. Internat. Continuing Med. Edn. Com., 1995—; course dir., Cardiology Update, Siriraj Hosp., Bangkok, 1999; chmn. sci. com. 11th Great Wall Internat. Congress of Cardiology, Beijing, 2000. Editor: Cardiology Today, 1995, Advances and Challenges in Today's Cardiology, 1997, Management of Complex Cardiovascular Problems: The Consultant's Approach, 1999, Spanish edit., 2000, Vietnamese edit., 2000, Practical Handbook of Advanced Interventional Cardiology, 2000. Fellow ACP, Am. Coll. Cardiology, Soc. Cardiovascular Angiography and Intervention. Roman Catholic. Fax: 219-756-1410. E-mail: thachnguyen2000@yahoo.com. Address: 200 E 86th Pl Merrillville IN 46410-6258

NGUYEN, THANH HIÊN, biochemistry educator; b. Ha-Dông Quan, Vietnam, Sept. 17, 1947; arrived in France, 1963; d. Bich Mông and Lan (Vu) N.; m. Jean Claude Maziere, Dec. 22, 1975; children: Jean-Yves, Sylvie. PhD, Paris VI U., 1980. Sr. lectr. Paris VI U., 1977-97; sr. lectr. faculty medicine Hôpital Nord, Amiens, France, 1997—. Contbr. over 115 articles to profl. jours. Avocation: gardening. Home: Hôpital Nord, Place Victor Pauchet, 80054 Amiens France

NGUYEN, THE ANH, historian, educator; b. Thakhek, Laos, June 1, 1936; arrived in France, 1975; s. Nguyen Van Thuoc and Vu Thi Thuy; m. Constance Smith, Feb. 20, 1959; children: Andrew, Clifford, Claire, Catherine. Agrege d'Histoire, Sorbonne U., Paris, 1963; PhD, U. Toulouse, France, 1964; LittD, Sorbonne U., Paris, 1987. From dean to rector Faculty of Letters, U. Hue, Vietnam, 1964-69; dep. min. Ministry Edn., Saigon, Vietnam, 1969; dir. history dept. Saigon U., Vietnam, 1969-75; rschr. Ctr. Nat. Rsch. Sci., Paris, 1976-91; prof. Ecole Pratique des Hautes Etudes IVe sect., Paris, 1991—; cons. S.E. Asian program Ford Found., 1973-75, Asia com. European Sci. Found., 1995-97; vis. prof. Harvard U., Cambridge, Mass., 1978; dir. Lab. Peninsule Indochinoise, Paris, 1991—. Author: Bibliographie Critique sur les Relations Entre L'occident et le Vietnam, 1967, Vietnamese Economy and Society Under the Nguyen Dynasty, 1968, Monarchie et Fait Colonial Au Vietnam, 1992, L'Asia orientale et meridionale aux 19e et 20e siecles, 1999; editor: Notes sur la Culture et la Religion en Peninsule Indochinoise, 1995, War and Peace in Southeast Asia (14th-19th century), 1998, Trade and Navigation in Southeast Asia (14th-19th centuries), 1999, L'Asie orientale et meridionale aux 19 et20 Siecles, 1999; mem. editl. bd. Bull. Ecole Francaise d'Extreme Orient, 1991—, Jour. Asiatique, 1993—, Asia Jour. Nat. U. Seoul, 1995—. Decorated officier Ordre des Palmes Academiques (France); recipient Edn. medal Govt. Vietnam, 1973. Mem. Soc. Francaise Histoire D'Outremer, Soc. Asiatique. Office: Ecole Pratique des Hautes Etudes IV sect, 22 Ave Du President Wilson, 75116 Paris France

NGUYEN, THI BINH, Vietnamese government official; b. Vietnam, 1927. Min. fgn. affairs Provisional Revolutionary Govt. South Vietnam, Saigon, 1969-76; min. edn. Socialist Republic of Vietnam, 1976-87; v.p. Govt. of Vietnam, 1992—. Office: Office of Pres, Hoang Hoa Tham, Hanoi Vietnam also: Ministry of Edn, 21 Le Thanh Tong, Hanoi Vietnam*

NGUYEN, THIEN NGOC, science administrator; b. Pakse, Laos, July 10, 1959; arrived in France, 1978; s. Cuong Nguyen and Then Thi Tran; m. Anh Thi, July 15, 1989; children: Quang, Phuong, Mai Thi. BA in Math. and Physics, Barral, Castres, France, 1979; engr. in chemistry, Ecole Nat. Superieure Chem., Toulouse, France, 1984; PhD in Microbiology, Ctr. Nat. Rsch. Sci., Toulouse, France, 1987. Staff in microbiology Johns Hopkins U., Balt., 1987-89; staff in biotechnology Kungl Tekniska Hogskolan, Stockholm, 1989-90; head genetic engring. Ctr. Immunology Pierre Fabre, St. Julien en Genevois, 1990-98, head molecular scis., 1998—; project leader in vaccine rsch. Pierre Fabre, St. Julien, 1990—. Contbr. articles to profl. jours. Active French Air Army, 1985-86. Mem. Am. Soc. for Microbiology. Achievements include patents for recombinant DNA, recombinant subunit vaccine. Avocations: photography, playing guitar, computing, wine. E-mail: thien.nguyen@pierre-fabre.com. Fax: 33 4 50353590. Office: Pierre Fabre, 5 ave Napoleon 3, 74164 St Julien Genevois France

NGUYEN, TIEN MANH, physician; b. Nam Dinh, Vietnam, Sept. 20, 1948; arrived in Australia, 1980; s. Le Xuan and Cam Tu (Hoang) N.; m. Ai Minh Cao-Xuan, Nov. 7, 1981; children: Cybelle, Giselle, Arielle. MD, U. Saigon, 1973; MB BS, U. NSW, 1984; diploma in child health, U. Sydney, 1997. Head Tuberculosis Clinic, Binh Chanh, 1978-79; intern Wollongong Hosp., 1984-85; resident St. Joseph's Hops., 1985; registrar in psychiatry Cumberland Hosp., 1985-87; gen. practitioner Cabramatta, 1987—. Mng. bd. dirs. Svcs. for Treatment and Rehab. of Torture and Trauma Survivors, NSW, 1988-89. Lt. physician Armed Forces of the Republic of Vietnam, 1973-75. Recipient Austcare Paul Cullen award for Outstanding Svc. to Refugees, Austcare, 1997. Mem. Australian Vietnamese Health Profl. Assn. in NSW (gen. sec. 1997—), Coun. Vietnamese Refugees Supporting Orgns. in Australia (pres. 1994—), League of Vietnamese Ex-Polit. Prisoners in Australia (pres. 1993—). Avocations: reading, writing, fishing, tennis. Home: 6 Isobell Ave, West Pennant Hills NSW 2125, Australia Office: Rear 51 John St, Cabramatta NSW 2166, Australia

NGUYEN, UU VAN, lawyer, civil engineering consultant; b. Saigon, Vietnam, May 21, 1947; arrived in Australia, 1976; s. Uou Van nd Tam Thi (Pham) N.; m. Lan Thanh Le, Mar. 9, 1979; 1 child, Michael Leminh. B Engring. with 1st class honors, U. Auckland, New Zealand, 1970, PhD in Civil Engring., 1975; LLB, Macquarie, Sydney, 1991. Chartered engr., Australia. Planning chief Vietnam's Nat. Water Supply Agy., Saigon, 1974-75; civil engr. Ministry of Works & Devel., Wellington, New Zealand, 1975-76, Pub. Works Dept. New South Wales, Sydney, 1976-79; rsch. scientist CSIRO Geomechanics, Melbourne, Australia, 1979-81; geotech. cons. K. Robert Johnson Assocs., Sydney, 1982-83; sr. lectr. U. Wollongong, Sydney, 1983-90; prin. Warren Nguyen & Assocs., Sydney, 1991—; dir. Bankstown Cmty. Housing Coop. Ltd., Sydney, 1996—. Contbr. articles to internat. jours. Mem. ASCE, Law Soc. New South Wales Australia, New South Wales-Vietnam C. of C. (sec. 1996—). Office: Warren Nguyen & Assocs, 439 Sussex St Ste 510, Sydney NSW 2000, Australia

NGUYEN, X. NGUYEN, economist, writer; b. Da Nang, Vietnam, Apr. 15, 1958; came to U.S., 1975; m. Xuong Xuan and Nghiem Doan N.; m. Tram Quynh Tran, May 14, 1992; children: Adelaide, Teresa. MA, Trinity Coll., 1981, Am. U., 1982; PHD, George Mason U., 1990. Tchr. Arlington (Va.) Pub. Schs., 1981-84; economist Consolidated Cons. Group, Washington, 1985-87, U.S. Dept. Health & Human Svcs., Washington, 1988-91, U.S. Exec. Office of Pres., Washington, 1991-92; sr. economist U.S. Congress, Washington, 1992-93, The World Bank, Washington, 1993-96, Infrastructure Capital Group, Washington, 1996-97; sr. mgr. The Lewin Group, Fairfax, Va., 1997-99; prin. analyst/economist U.S. Congress, Washington, 1999—. Chair info. & liaison Interfaith Com. Refugee Concerns, Fairfax, 1988-90; policy bd. mem. Arlington-Trinity Tchr. Corps, 1979-81; faculty advisor Vietnamese Parent Assn. in Arlington, 1979-84. E-mail: nguyenxn@usa.net. Office: Congl Budget Office 2D D Sts SW Ofc Washington DC 20515-0001

NGUYEN, XUAN QUANG, chemist; b. Quang Binh, Vietnam, Jan. 15, 1957; s. Vinh Nguyen and Thi Phiet Truong; m. Thu Uyen Nguyen, Apr. 7, 1985; children: Bich, Xuan. Degree in chem. engring., Prague Inst. Chem. Technology, Czechoslovakia, 1983; PhD, Inst. Chem. Process Fund., Czechoslovakia, 1991—. Rschr. Vietnam Nat. Ctr. Sci. & Technology, 1984-87, 97—, Czechoslovak Acad. Scis., 1988-91, Ctr. Nat. Rsch. Sci., France, 1992-93, Prague Inst. Chem. Technology, 1994-96. Mem. N.Y. Acad. Scis. Achievements include quality improvement of gas separation membranes, design of instrument for study of gas-sweeping pervaporation membranes. Office: VNCT Inst Chemistry, Nghia Do Tu Liem, Hanoi Vietnam

NGUYEN-DUY, PHI, railway expert; b. Hanoi, Vietnam, May 29, 1930; arrived in France, 1949; s. Xan and Thuoc; m. Suzanne Huynh, Dec. 21, 1957. Grad. Engr., Ecole Centrale de Paris, 1955; grad., Inst. d'Adminstrn. Entreprises, France, 1961. Cert. engr. Engr. Cie Electro-Mecanique, France, 1955-73; tech. mgr. Traction CEM-Oerlikon, France, 1974-84; project mgr. Gec-Alsthom, France, 1984-87; cons. France, 1988—; patent mgr. Traction CEM-Oerlikon and Gec-Alsthom, France, 1974-87; rwy. expert Internat. C. of C., 1990—; rep. Internat. Electrotechnic Com., 1974-84. Patentee in field. Mem. Echanges et Consultations Techniques Internationaux, Assn. Ecole Centrale de Paris. Avocations: finance, travel. Home: 1 quai Aulagnier, 92600 Asnieres France Office: Nguyen Duy Phi, 9 Rue Leonard de Vinci, 92230 Gennevilliers France

NGUYEN-TRONG, HOANG, physician, consultant; b. Hue, Republic of Vietnam, Sept. 4, 1936; s. Nguyen-Trong Hiep and Nguyen-Phuoc Ton-nu-Thi Sung. B in Math., Lycée d'Etat Michel Montaigne, Bordeaux, 1956; state diploma of medicine, Sch. Medicine, Paris, 1966, also cert. aeronautical medicine and health and sanitation, 1965, diploma Health and Smoking, 1993; diploma post traumatic stress disorder, crises and disasters, The Am. U. and Centre Internat. de Scis. Criminelles de Paris, Washington, 1995. Resident surgeon Compiegne State Hosp., 1963-64, Meaux State Hosp., 1964-66, Lagny State Hosp., 1966; specialist in health and sanitation Paris Sch. Medicine, 1965—; specialist in family planning French Action of Family Planning, Paris, 1968—; practice medicine, Nanterre, France, 1969—; cons. physician various pharm. labs., Paris, 1987; investigator physician WHO regional office for Europe, 1991. Contbr. articles to profl. jours. Active mem. task force on tobacco dependency Biomed. Saints Péres Rsch. Unit, Paris, 1993, AIDS treatment assn. Le Val de Seine, 1993. Recipient World Decoration of Excellence, 1990, Commemorative Medal of Honor, 1990, Internat. Order of Merit, 1990. Mem. French Soc. Aviation and Space Physiology and Medicine (titulary, specialist in aviation medicine), Assn. Nanterre Physicians, Assn. Vietnamese Practitioners in France, Assn. Le Val de Seine, Chambre Syndicale des Medecins des Hauts de Seine, Ordre des Medecins des Hauts de Seine, Les Ex du XIV Shooting Club. Avocations: painting, poetry, classical and modern jazz music, riflery, martial arts. Home: 3 Rue Gazan, 75014 Paris France Office: Cabinet Med Privé, 38 Rue des Fontenelles, 92000 Nanterre France

NGUYEN-VAN-TAM, JONATHAN STAFFORD, public health educator; b. Boston, Eng., Feb. 2, 1964; s. Paul and Elizabeth Mary (Thompson) Nguyen-Van-Tam; m. Sarah Elizabeth Heaney, Oct. 3, 1992; 1 child, Erin. B Med. Sci., Nottingham (Eng.) U., 1985, B Medicine B Surgery, 1987. Lectr. U. Nottingham, 1991-97, sr. lectr., 1997-99; assoc. med. dir. SmithKline Beecham Pharms., 2000—; mem. faculty pub. health medicine Royal Coll. Physicians; sci. advisor Assn. for Influenza Monitoring and Surveillance, London, 1992-99; cons. regional epidemiologist Pub. Health Lab Svc., 1997-99. Contbr. articles to profl. jours. Maj. Royal Army Med. Corps, 1988-2000. Named to Order of Brit. Empire, Queen of Eng., 1998. Avocations: mountaineering, running, wine. Office: SmithKline Beecham, Welwyn Garden City AL7 1EY, England

NHA, IL-SEONG, astronomy educator; b. Songjin, Hambuk, Republic of Korea, Nov. 11, 1932; s. Byung-Gi and Muok (Hahn) Nha; m. Soon-Hee Lee, June 8, 1963; children: Kayoung, Sarah. BS, Yonsei U., Seoul, Republic of Korea, 1959, MS, 1961; PhD, U. Pa., Phila., 1971. Instr. physics Yonsei U., Seoul, 1961-63, prof. astronomy, 1974-98, dir. obs., 1981-89; prof. emeritus Yonsei U., Seoul, Pa., 1998—; rsch. assoc. Flower and Cook Obs., Marbern, Pa., 1972-74; dir. Nha Astron. Obs., 1993—; cons. Nat. Inst. Geodesy, Seoul, 1978—, Inamori Found., Kyoto, Japan, 1988. Author: Seong-do, 1979, Comet Halley, 1985, New Astronomy, 1987; co-editor: New Frontiers in Binary Star Research, 1991, Oriental Astronomy from Guo Shoujing to King Sejong, 1997. Mem. Korean History Sci. Soc. (v.p. 1983-85), Korean Space Sci. Soc. (pres. 1988-90), Korean Astron. Soc. (pres. 1975-77), Solar Energy Soc. Korea (editor jour. 1978-80), Am. Astron. Soc., Internat. Astron. Union (nat. rep. 18th and 20th gen. assemblies). Presbyterian. Home: 112-12 Yonhi-dong, Seoul 120 111, Republic of Korea Office: Yonsei U Nha Obs, San-133 Dokyul-ri Gamchon, Yechon Kyongbuk 757-910, Republic of Korea

NI, HAITAO, food products engineer, mechanical engineer; b. Hefei, Anhui, China, June 5, 1962; came to U.S., 1992; m. Hui Zhou; children: Teddy, Julie. BS, U. Sci. & Tech., Hefei, 1984, MS, 1987; PhD, Cornell U., 1996. Postdoctorate Cornell U., Ithaca, N.Y., 1997, Pa. State U., U. Pk., Pa., 1997; sr. food technologist Nabisco, Fair Lawn, N.J., 1997—. Office: Nabisco 21-11 Route 208 Fair Lawn NJ 07410-2694

NI, JIQIN, environmental scientist, researcher; b. Xiaoshan, Zhejiang, China, June 20, 1954; s. Wenhan and Lizhen (Shao) N.; m. Xiaoming Xu, Feb. 6, 1984; 1 child, Fangzhen. BA, Hangzhou (China) U., 1989; MS, Cath. U. Leuven, Belgium, 1991, PhD, 1998. Cert. engr. Dep. dir. Hangzhou Rural Energy Office, 1985-89; vis. scholar Cath. U. Leuven, 1991-92, rsch. engr., 1992-96; rsch. assoc. Purdue U., West Lafayette, Ind., 1997—. Author: Biomethanation: A Developing Technology in Latin America, 1993; contbr. articles to profl. jours. Recipient 2d prize of agrl. zoning rsch. achievement Zhejiang Province Agrl. Zoning Com., 1986, 88. Mem. Am. Soc. Agrl. Engrs., China Focal Point Expert Group, Internat. Found. Woodstove, Water Environment Fedn. E-mail: jiqin@ecn.purdue.edu. Office: Purdue U 114 6ABE Bldg West Lafayette IN 47907-1146

NI, XIONG, Olympic athlete; b. Changsha, China, Jan. 24, 1974. Winner Silver medal platform diving Seoul, 1988; winner Bronze medal platform diving Barcelona, 1992; winner Gold medal springboard diving Atlanta, 1996; winner 2 Gold medals springboard and synchronized 3 meter Sydney, 2000. Office: Swimming Assn People's Rep China, 9 Ti Yuguan Rd, Beijing 100061, China*

NI, YICHENG, radiologist, educator and researcher; b. Zhenjiang, Jiangsu, China, Mar. 31, 1957; s. Bin and Bingqing (Xu) N.; m. Jie Yu, Feb. 19, 1985; children: Xiaoxu, Bona, Boen. Diploma, Jiangsu Sch. Chinese Medicine, Nanjing, 1977; MD, Nanjing Med. U., 1983, MS, 1989; PhD, Cath. U. Leuven, Belgium, 1995. Med. diplomate. Practicioner Chinese medicine Yijiangmen Hosp., Nanjing, 1977-78; intern U. Hosp. Nanjing Med. U., 1982-83, surgeon, lectr., rschr., 1983-90; rschr. Cath. U. Leuven, Belgium, 1990-95, prof. dept. radiology, 1995—; invited spkr. in field. Mem. sci. editl bd. European Radiology, 1996—; reviewer, contbr. articles to internat. acad. jours.; patentee for cardiac infarct avid MRI contrast media and novel electrodes in radiofrequency tumor ablation; chair internat. congresses. Recipient Stauffer award Assn. Univ. Radiologists and Soc. Chmn. Acad. Radiology Dept., 1993, European Congress Radiology award, ECR Rsch. and Edn. Fund, 1997. Mem. Internat. Soc. Magnetic Resonance in Medicine, Belgian Royal Soc. Radiology. Avocations: sports, English-Chinese translation, helping others. Office: Univ Hosps Dept Radiology, Herestraat 49, B-3000 Leuven Brabant, Belgium

NIANE, MARY TEUW, mathematician; b. St. Louis, Senegal, July 15, 1954; d. Mamadou and Bigue (Sow) N.; m. Fatoumata Ndiaye, Sept. 11, 1985; children: Ngolo, Aissatou, Abdou. D, U. Dakar, 1990. Lectr. U. Dakar, Senegal, 1982-86; guest reader U. Paris, 1988-89, INSA, Rennes, France, 1989-90; reader U. St. Louis, Senegal, 1991-96, prof., 1996—. Mem. Math. Soc. Senegal (gen. sec. 1994). Muslim. Avocation: walking. Office: U St Louis, PO Box 234, Saint Louis Senegal

NIAZI, SHAHIDA BEGUM, chemistry educator; b. Multan, Punjab, Pakistan, Dec. 14, 1950; d. Bashir Ahmed Khan Niazi and Akbari Begum. BS in Chemistry, Coll. Women, Multan, 1971; MSc, Inst. Chemistry, Punjab U., Lahore, 1974; PhD, King's Coll., London U., 1982. Lectr. chemistry dept. Bahauddin Zakariya U., Multan, Pakistan, 1976-83, asst. prof., 1983-88, assoc. prof., 1988-95, prof., 1996—. Contbr. articles to profl. jours. Post Doctoral fellow Commonwealth U.K., 1992; recipient Star Women Internat. award in edn., Star Girls & Women Found., Pakistan, 1996. Mem. Chemistry Soc. Pakistan (life). Office: Bahauddin Zakariya U, Dept Chemistry, 60800 Multan Punjab, Pakistan

NICAUD, JEAN MARC JACQUES, microbiologist, researcher; b. Paris, June 4, 1956; s. Claude Jacques and Colette (Prevot) N.; children: Cecile, Victor. BAC, Paris, 1975; DEUG, U. Paris VII, 1978, maitise biology and biochemistry, 1979, DEA in Ecotoxicology, 1980; PhD, U. Compiegne, France, 1983, doctorat d'etat, 1986. Postdoctorate U. Leicester, Eng., 1984-86, Nat. Inst. Agronomy Paris-Grignon, Paris, 1986-88; rschr. Nat. Ctr. Sci. Rsch., Paris, 1988-92, Eurolysine, Orsay, France, 1992-93, Nat. Ctr. Sci. Rsch., Thiverval, France, 1993—. Mem. Soc. Francaise Microbiologie, Codesqy, Nat. Syndicate Sci. Rsch. Avocations: flying, squach. Office: INRA/CNRS Lab Gen Micro, CBAI, 78850 Thiverval-Grignon France

NICELY, ANDREW ABBOTT, lawyer; b. Rochester, N.Y.; s. William Abbott and Linda Brunjes Nicely. BA in Psychology, Bates Coll., 1990; MA in Clin. Psychology, SUNY, Buffalo, 1994; JD, U. Pa., 1997. Bar: Va. 1997, U.S. Ct. Appeals (4th cir.), 1997, D.C. 1998, Ill. 1998, U.S. Dist. Ct. (ea. dist.) Va. 1998, U.S. Dist. Ct. D.C. 1998, U.S. Ct. Appeals (6th, 8th and D.C. cirs.) 1998, U.S. Bankruptcy Ct. (ea. dist.) Va. 1999. Program counselor Alternatives Unlimited, Inc., Whitinsville, Mass., 1990-91; program mgr. Waltham (Mass.) Com., 1991-92; law clk. Office of Disciplinary Counsel, Phila., 1996-97; assoc. Mayer, Brown & Platt, Washington, 1997—. Mem. Va. Sta Bar Assn., D.C. Bar Assn., Ill. State Bar Assn., Order of Coif. Avocation: aviculture. Office: Mayer Brown & Platt 1909 K St NW Washington DC 20006-1152

NICHOLAS, ALISON, professional golfer; b. Gilbraltar, Mar. 6, 1962. Profl. golfer, 1989—. Winner LPGA Corning Classic, PING-AT&T Wireless Championship, 1995, U.S. Women Open, 1997; placed first Hawaiian Ladies Open, 1999. Office: LPGA 100 International Golf Dr Daytona Beach FL 32124-1092*

NICHOLAS, FREDERICK M., lawyer; b. N.Y.C., May 30, 1920; s. Benjamin L. and Rose F. (Nechols) N.; m. Eleanore Berman, Sept. 2, 1951 (div. 1963); children: Deborah, Jan, Tony; m. Joan Fields, Jan. 2, 1983. AB, U. So. Calif., 1947; postgrad., U. Chgo., 1949-50; JD, U. So. Calif., 1952. Bar: Calif. 1952, U.S. Dist. Ct. Calif. 1952, U.S. Ct. Appeals (9th cir.) 1952. Assoc. Loeb & Loeb, L.A., 1952-56; ptnr. Swerdlow, Glikbarg & Nicholas, Beverly Hills, Calif., 1956-62; pvt. practice Beverly Hills, 1962-80; pres., atty. Hapsmith Co., Beverly Hills, 1980—; bd. dirs. Malibu Grand Prix, L.A., 1982-90; gen. counsel Beverly Hills Realty Bd., 1971-79; founder, pres. Pub. Counsel, L.A., 1970-73. Author: Commercial Real Property Lease Practice, 1976. Chmn. Mus. Contemporary Art, L.A., 1987-93, chmn. com. Walt Disney Concert Hall, L.A., 1987-95; trustee Music Ctr. L.A. County, 1987-95, L.A. Philharm. Assn., 1987-95; chmn. Calif. Pub. Broadcasting Commn., Sacramento, 1972-78; pres. Maple Ctr., 1977-79. Recipient Citizen of Yr. award Beverly Hills Bd. Realtors, 1978, Man of Yr. award Maple Ctr., 1980, Pub. Svc. award Coro Found., 1988, The Medici award L.A. C. of C., 1990, Founders award Pub. Counsel, 1990, Trustees award Calif. Inst. Arts, 1993, City of Angels award L.A. Ctrl. Bus. Assn.; named Outstanding Founder in Philanthropy, Nat. Philanthropy Day Com., 1990. Mem. Beverly Hills Bar Assn. (bd. govs. 1970-76, Disting. Svc. award 1974, 81, Exceptional Svc. award 1986), Beverly Hills C. of C. (Man of Yr. 1983). Home: 1001 Maybrook Dr Beverly Hills CA 90210-2715 Office: Hapsmith Co 589 N Venice Blvd Venice CA 90291-4276

NICHOLAS, LESLIE STEPHEN, energy analyst; b. Morogoro, Tanzania; arrived in Eng., 1975; s. Mowbray Stephen and June (Robson) N. BSc in Econs. with honors, London U., 1990. Securities and futures authority qualification. Oil products editor London Oil Reports, 1991-94; energy/commodity analyst GNI Ltd., London, 1994-99; energy analyst, oil derivatives project mgr. Platt's, London, 1999—. Contbr. articles to profl. jours. Mem. Inst. Petroleum. E-mail: leslie nicholaw@standardandpoors.com.

Office: GNI Ltd, Platt's/Wimbledon Bridge Ho, 1 Hartfield Rd, London SW19 3RU, England

NICHOLAS, NICK SOTIRIOU, consultant obstetrician and gynecologist; b. London, June 23, 1953; s. Sotiris and Lucy (Plastiras) N.; m. Eve Aresti, June 7, 1980; children: Irenee, Sotiris, Katerina. BSc (hons.), Guys Hosp., London, 1974, MRCS, LRCS, 1977, MB, BS, 1977; MD, Univ. London, 1987. FRCOG. Sr. house officer in urology/gynecology Royal Marsden Hosp., Eng., 1979-80; sr. house officer in accident/ emergency Univ. Coll. Hosp., London, 1980-87; registrar in Ob-Gyn. Guys Hosp., London, 1981-83, Wellcome rsch. fellow, 1983-85; sr. registrar in ob-gyn Queen Charlotte Hosp., Eng., 1985-88; cons. obstetrician and gynecologist Hillingdon Hosp., 1988—; dist. tutor in Hillingdon Hosp., 1991—, clin. dir. women's svcs., 1994—; hon. clin. tchr. Middlesex UCH Hosp., 1992—; examiner MB, BS U. London, 1993—. Author: Immunosuppression in Pregnancy, 1987; co-author (with others) Human Fetal Allograft Survival, 1988, Immunology of Recurrent Miscarriage, 1994. Fellow Royal Coll. Gynecologists and Obstetricians; mem. Royal Soc. Medicine (coun., treas. 1992—). Democrat. Greek Orthodox. Avocations: computing, skiing, music, jogging. Office: Portland Hosp, 209 Gt Portland St, London WIN GAH, England

NICHOLLS, CHRISTINE STEPHANIE, writer, editor; b. Bury, Lancashire, Eng., Jan. 23, 1943; d. Christopher James and Olive (Kennedy) Metcalfe; m. Anthony James Nicholls, Mar. 12, 1966; children: Alexander, Caroline, Isabel. BA, Oxford (Eng.) U., 1964, MA, 1968, DPhil, 1968. Rsch. fellow London U., 1968-69; freelance writer BBC, London, 1970-74; rsch. asst. Oxford U., 1975-76; joint editor Dictionary of Nat. Biography, Oxford, 1977-89, editor, 1989-95; editor Hutchinson Ency. of Biography, 1995—. Author: The Swahili Coast, 1971, (with P. Awdry) Cataract, 1985; author, editor: The Dictionary of National Biography, 4 vols., 1981, 86, 90, 93, 96, Power: A Political History, 1990, David Livingstone, 1998, A History of St. Antony's College, Oxford 1950-2000, 2000. Avocation: playing the flute. Home: 27 Davenant Rd, Oxford OX2 8BU, England

NICHOLLS, DALE WILLIAM, lawyer; b. Hancock, Mich., Mar. 23, 1950; arrived in Australia, 1981; s. William Pollard and Ruth Luella (Morcom) N.; m. Linda Bardo Poor, Nov. 16, 1979; children: Dale Jr., Edward, Kathryn. BA, Yale U., 1972; JD, U. Mich., 1975; MBA, Harvard U., 1979; LLB, U. Melbourne, 1985. Bar: Mich. 1975, D.C. 1976, U.S. Supreme Ct. 1980, Victoria 1985, High Ct. Australia 1986, Western Australia 1997, NSW 1998, Queensland, 1999. Republican mem. subcom. coun. U.S. Ho. of Reps., Washington, 1975-77; asst. to pres. AMAX Copper Inc., N.Y.C., 1979-81; assoc. Arthur Robinson & Hedderwicks, Melbourne, 1982-88, ptnr., 1988—. Mem. Law Coun. Australia (internat. trade and bus. com. 1990—, banking finance and consumer credit com. 1985-96), Internat. Bar Assn. (sect. on energy and natural resources law 1991—), Australian Mining and Petroleum Law Assn., Yale Club N.Y.C., Australian Club. Home: 12 Wilks Ave, Malvern 3144, Australia Office: Arthur Robinson & Hedderwicks, 530 Collins St, Melbourne 3000, Australia

NICHOLLS, FRANK GORDON, computer scientist, consultant; b. Malvern, Victoria, Australia, Jan. 1, 1916; s. William David and Coral Daphne (Bailey) N.; m. Yvonne Isabel Miles, Jan. 20, 1940. BSc, U. Melbourne, Australia, 1936, MSc, 1938. Rschr. Radio Rsch. Bd. Coun. for Sci. and Indsl. Rsch., Melbourne, Australia, 1936-40; officer in charge Australian and New Zealand Sci. Liason Office, London, 1940-44; asst. sec., rsch. sec. gen. adminstrn. and sci. svcs. Coun. for Sci. and Indsl. Rsch. and succesor, Melbourne, Australia, 1944-63; spl. gov. Applied Sci. and Indsl. Rsch. Corp., Thailand, 1963-70; dep. dir. gen. Internat. Union for Conservation Nature and Natural Resource, Morges, Switzerland, 1970-78; mng. dir. Trans Knowledge Assocs. Pty. Ltd., Melbourne, 1978—; sec. Nat. Assn. Testing Authorities, Australia, 1949-60, Nat. Standards Commn., 1949-60, Radio Astronomy Trust, 1956-63; chmn. organizing com. Melbourne Film Festival, 1952-63, Melbourne Film Soc., 1956-60; chmn. of govs. Australian Film Inst., 1958-63; mem. Pakistan Sci. Commn., 1959; UN appraisal sci. activities expert advisor to Govt. Thailand, 1960-61; UN chief sci. advisor on applied rsch., Thailand, 1963-70. Decorated Cmmdr. Most Noble Order of the Crown of Thailand. Fellow Illuminating Engring. Socs. of Australia and New Zealand; mem. Royal Australian Chem. Inst. (chartered chemist), Australian and New Zealand Inst. of Physics, Pub. Rels. Inst. Australia (hon.), Internat. Coun. of Environ. Law, 20 Club. Avocations: reading, music, theatre, skin diving. Home: 61/4 Sydney St, Prahran 3181 Vic, Australia Office: Trans Knowledge Assocs Ltd, 2/1 Sydney St, Prahran 3181 Vic, Australia

NICHOLLS, JOHN ANTHONY, solicitor; b. London, Apr. 19, 1946; s. Frederick Ernest and Marjorie Enid (Lewisohn) N.; m. Patricia Anne Howes, Aug. 31, 1984; children: Timothy, Mark Anthony; stepchildren: Louise Frances, Claire. Law degree, Coll. of Law, London, 1968. Articled clk. W. Feldman, London, 1962-68, asst. solicitor, 1968-69, ptnr., 1969-81; ptnr. Feldman Nicholls and Co., London, 1981—. Mem. Law Soc., Chiswick & Brentford Rotary Club, Theatre West 4. Avocations: theatre, acting, stage directing, sports. Office: Feldman Nicholls and Co, 277/9 Chiswick High Rd, London W 44PY, England

NICHOLLS, MILES GRAFTON, business educator; m. Barbara J. Cargill, 2000. B in Econs. with honors, Monash U., Melbourne, Victoria, Australia, 1968, M in Econs., 1972, PhD, 1982. Ops. rsch. officer Shell Co. Australia, Melbourne, Victoria, Australia, 1969-71; sr. tchg. fellow Faculty Econs. and Politics, Monash U., Clayton, Victoria, 1971-72; lectr., then sr. lectr. quantitative methods Faculty Bus., Swinburne U. Tech., Hawthorn, Victoria, 1972-90, head bus. modelling, 1991, assoc. prof., 1991-94, sub-dean rsch., 1993-95, apptd. personal chair, 1994—; dir. rsch. Sch. Bus., Swinburne U. Tech., Hawthorn, 1998—, dir. Ctr. Bus. and Mgmt. Rsch., 1998; prin. cons. QMS Cons. Svcs., 1985-97; leader process modelling sect. Energy Sys. Engring. Ctr., 1992-95; assoc. Ctr. for Orgnl. and Strategic Studies; vis. prof. Lancaster (Eng.) U., 1993, 94, 96, Pa. State U., Harrisburg, 1994, 95, 96, Calif. Poly. State U., San Luis Obispo, 1994, 97, U. Strathclyde, Eng., 1995, 96, City U. Hong Kong, 1995, U. Linköping, Sweden, 1995, Kingston U., Kingston-on-Thames, Surrey, Eng., 1995, U. Birmingham, End., 1996, U. Southampton, Eng., 1996, U. Luton, Eng., 1997; presenter profl. confs., most recently in Australia, U.K., and the U.S., 16th Internat. Symposium on Math. Programming, Lausanne, Switzerland, 1997; mem. tech. program com. Asia Pacific Ops. Rsch. Conf., Melbourne, 1997; chairperson bi-level programming stream 15th Internat. Symposium on Math. Programming, U. Mich., 1994;; cons. various orgns., including Pilkington, U.K., Australia, Brit. Alcan Aluminium P.L.C., ALCOA, Lindemans Wines, Tandem Computers, Ajax Fasteners, Philip Morris Ltd., Comalco Smelting; participant rsch. teams at Pa. State U., Harrisburg, Calif. Poly. State U., others; advisor ednl. instns. Referee internat. jours., including Studies in Ednl. Evaluation, Israel, Internat. Transactions in Operational Rsch., Eng., Omega, Eng., Jour. of Operational Rsch. Soc., Eng., Jour. Bus. and Mgmt., European Jour. Operational Rsch.; contbr. chpt. to: The Economics of Education, 1993, Multilevel Optimization Algorithms and Applications, 1997; contbr. numerous articles to sci. jours. and conf. procs. ARC Collaborative Rsch. grantee, 1994-96; recipient other rsch. grants, scholarships. Mem. Decision Scis. Inst. (chairperson prodn. modelling and prodn. rationalisation streams 2nd internat. conf. 1993, co-program chairperson 4th internat. conf. 1997, referee conf., v.p. member svcs. 2000), Western Decision Scis. Inst. (internat. coord. Pacific Rim, track co-chmn., session chmn. 10 streams 1994-97, referee conf.), Inst. for Ops. Rsch. and Mgmt. Scis., Australian Coll. Edn., Australian Soc. for Ops. Rsch. Inc., Operational Rsch. Soc. (Eng.), Australia and New Zealand Acad. Mgmt. Office: Swinburne U Tech, PO Box 218, Victoria Hawthorn 3122, Australia

NICHOLS, ANTHONY HOWARD, bishop; b. Sheffield, Eng., Mar. 29, 1938; s. Howard and Alice Ellen (Hawkins) N.; m. Judith Margaret Ross, Dec. 14, 1968; children: Elizabeth Parker, Naomi Flavell, Daniel, John. BA, U. Sydney, 1959, MEd, 1972; BD with honors, U. London, Eng., 1966; MA with honors, Macquarie U., Sydney, 1982; PhD, U. Sheffield, 1997. Latin tchr. NSW Dept. Edn. Australia, 1960-61; high sch. tchr. Ch. Mission Soc. North Borneo, Sabah, 1962-63; asst. min. Anglican Diocese of Sydney, Drummoyne, 1967; lectr. Bibl. studies and exegisis Moore Coll., Sydney, 1968-72; lectr. Bibl. studies and edn., dean faculty of theology Satya Wacana Christian U., Indonesia, 1972-81, 76-79; prin. Nungalinya Coll., Darwin, Australia, 1982-87, St. Andrew's Hall, Melbourne, 1988-91; bishop North West Australia Geraldton, 1992—; mem. Commn. on Ministry and Tng., 1993—. Author: Mirror of the Soul: A Lenten Study Book on the Psalms, 1997; contbr. articles to profl. jours. including Jour. Christian Edn., Reformed Theol. Rev., Interchange, Colloquium, among others. Recipient Queen Scout award Australian Boy Scouts, 1954, John Forster New Testament Greek prize Australian Coll. Theology, 1967; Stephen Bayne scholar St. Augustine Found., U. Sheffield, 1985. Mem. South Am. Mission Soc. (v.p. 1995—), Ch. Mission Soc. (v.p. 1995—), Coun. Australian Coll. Theology (coun. 1993—). Anglican. Office: Anglican Diocese NW Austr, PO Box 140, Geraldton WA 6531, Australia

NICHOLS, C. WALTER, III, retired trust company executive; b. N.Y.C., Aug. 25, 1937; s. Charles Walter and Marjorie (Jones) N.; m. Anne Sharp, Aug. 8, 1959 (dec. Nov. 1996); children: Blair, Sandra, Walter, Hope. V.p. Citibank, N.Y.C., 1962-78, J.P. Morgan & Co., N.Y.C., 1979-93; 1st v.p. Republic Nat. Bank N.Y., N.Y.C., 1994. Bd. dirs. Nichols Found., Inc., Greenwich House, 1969-94, pres., 1984-90; trustee Choate Rosemary Hall, 1972-77, 82-89, Westover Sch., 1979-81, ea. N.Y. chpt. Nature Conservancy, 1978-87, hon. trustee, 1988—; trustee John Jay Homestead, 1980-2000, Nat. Audubon Soc., 1983-87; mem. adv. bd. Wildlife Conservation Soc. (Bronx Zoo), 1987-94. Served to 1st lt. U.S. Army, 1960-62. Decorated Army Commendation medal. Mem. Naturist Soc., Nat. Assn. Railroad Passengers (bd. dirs. 1996-98), Am. Sunbathing Assn., Pilgrims of U.S., Yale (N.Y.C.) Club.

NICHOLS, CLYDE RICHARD, clergyman, company executive; b. N.Y.C., Apr. 15, 1945; s. William and Novella Nichols; m. Marsha A. Wade, Oct. 11, 1986. BS, Met. State Coll., Denver, 1985; ThD, Berean Bible Coll., Dallas, 1994. Ordained pastor and bishop Fellowship of Deliverance Chs., Inc. Correction officer City and County Denver, 1981-92; sr. pastor Redeeming Love Ch., Denver; sr. dir. M&C Enterprises, Inc., Denver; dir. media Greater Metro Denver Ministers Alliance Orgn., Denver, 1997-99. Recipient award for outstanding cmty. work Cheyenne (Wyo.) br. NAACP, 1982, award for outstanding cmty. activities 24th Syl Morgan Acad. Arts, Denver, 1992. Avocations: travel, reading, computers. Home and Office: PO Box 31092 Aurora CO 80041-0092

NICHOLS, DINAH ALISON, environmental agency official; b. Leicester, Eng., Sept. 28, 1943; d. Sydney Hirst and Elsie Freda (Pratt) N. BA in History with honors, U. London, 1965. Prin. pvt. sec. to sec. of state for transport Dept. Transport, London, 1983-85; dir. adminstrv. resources Dept. Environ. and Transport, London, 1985-88; dir. water Dept. of Environ., London, 1988-91, dir. gen. property holdings, 1991-94, dep. sec. housing and constrn., 1994-96, dir. gen. environ. protection, 1996—; sec. of state's rep. Commonwealth War Graves Commn., U.K., 1993-96. Dir. Cities in Schs., London, 1995-00; bd. dirs. Toynbee Housing Assn., London, 1996—, Shiresmaller Cos., 1999—; chmn. Goldsmith's Choral Union, 1991-94. Reid Arts scholar London U., 1965; Winston Churchill travelling fellow, Japan, 1969; hon. fellow Royal Holloway Coll., London U., 1997. Mem. Royal Soc. Arts, Swiss Alpine Club. Avocations: hiking, choral singing, music, theatre, travel. Office: Dept Env Transport & Region, 123 Victoria St, London SW1E 6DE, England

NICHOLS, GEORGE LEON, JR., minister; b. Phila., Mar. 7, 1938; s. George Leon Sr. and Elva Grace (Berger) N.; m. K. Diane Hunt, Sept. 21, 1963; children: Katherine J., Stephen J. BS in Bible, Phila. Coll. Bible, 1961; postgrad., Reformed Episcopal Sem., Phila., 1961-63; DD, Fla. Bible Coll, Hollywood, 1976; D of Ministry, Luther Rice Sem., Jacksonville, Fla., 1979; MA, Liberty U., 1988. Ordained to ministry Bapt. Ch., 1961; cert. Christian counselor. Pastor Nicetown Bapt. Ch., Phila., 1961-64, 1st Bapt. Ch., Elmer, N.J., 1964-67; sr. pastor Pennsville Bapt. Ch., Mt. Pleasant, Pa., 1967-87, Faith Bapt. Ch., Wilmington, Del., 1987—; trustee Phila. Coll. Bible, Langhorne, Pa., 1987; trustee, v.p. Out-island Ministries, St. Petersburg, Fla., 1973; bd. dirs. Mil. Evangelism, Aberdeen, Md., Sandy Cove Ministries, N.E. Md. Mem. Am. Assn. Christian Counselors, United Assn. Christian Counselors (bd. dirs., pres. Harrisburg, Pa.), Bibl. Archeol. Soc., Evang. Theol. Soc. Home: 2707 Burnley Rd Wilmington DE 19808-3623 Office: Faith Bapt Ch 4210 Limestone Rd Wilmington DE 19808-2099

NICHOLS, GERALD, counselor, hypnotist; b. L.A., Dec. 30, 1934; s. Clyde William and Iva Margaret Nichols. AA, L.A. City Coll., 1968; BA, Calif. State U., L.A., 1970. Cert. profl. hypnotist. Counselor, v.p. Nat. League for Social Understanding, L.A.; cons. Internat. Gay and Lesbian Archives, L.A., Leathermasters Internat., L.A.; spkr. in field. Mem. Stonewall Dem. Club, L.A., 1989—; rev., life mem. Universal Ch. of the Master, 1969-99. Avocation: selling collectibles. E-mail: foncards@4link.net. Office: Nat League for Social Understanding Ste 293 4470 Sunset Blvd Los Angeles CA 90027-6305

NICHOLS, KATIE, investment company executive; b. Des Moines, May 19, 1940; d. Gardner "Mike" and Lois (Thornburg) Cowles; m. Julian Strauss, June 11, 1960 (div. 1971); children: Elizabeth Lois Strauss Grossi, Gwen Beatrix Strauss Jenkins, Kate Anne Strauss Long; m. Roger Marcus Nichols, Sept. 1, 1973 (div. 1981); m. H.E. Rummel, Mar. 27, 1983 (div. 1994). Student, Cornell U., 1957-61. Ptnr., v.p. The Rummel Group, Inc., St. Petersburg, Fla., 1985—; trustee Cowles Charitable Trust, N.Y.C., 1985—. Vol. Hosp. Albert Schweitzer, Deschapelles, Haiti, 1961-63; vice chmn. Fla. Human Rels. Commn., Tallahassee, 1974-75 (award of honor 1985); Dem. candidate Fla. Pub. Svc. Commn., 1976; commr. Fla. Pub. Svc. Commn., 1981-89, chmn., 1987-89; vice chmn. Fla. Corrections Commn., 1994-98; bd. dirs. Nat. Coun. on Crime and Delinquency, San Francisco, 1990—, chmn. 1997-98; bd. dirs. HAS2000 Campaign for Hosp. Albert Schweitzer, Haiti. Mem. NOW, Emily's List, League of Women Voters of Fla. Democrat. Episcopalian. Avocations: reading, needlepoint. Home: 1682 Oceanview Dr Tierra Verde FL 33715-2500 Office: The Rummel Group Inc 1641 1st Ave N Saint Petersburg FL 33713-8935

NICHOLS, LESLIE CAROL, music educator; b. Va., Dec. 6, 1970; d. Paul Andrew Sr. and Charlotte Golladay Nichols. BA, Mary Washington Coll., 1992; MusM, Bowling Green State U., 1995. Assoc. tchr. Keyboard Connection, Swanton, Ohio, 1993-95; piano instr. Appel Farm Arts & Music Ctr., Elmer, N.J., 1994, swimming instr., 1995-96; adminstrv. asst. Faith Mountain Co., Sperryville, Va., 1996-98, tng. coord., 1998; ind. piano tchr. Woodville, Va., 1998—; staff piano tchr. Wakefield Country Day Sch., Flint Hill, Va., 1999—; vis. artist Mary Washington Coll., Fredericksburg, Va., 1998, 99; accompanist Rappahannock County (Va.) C.C., 1996—. Register of the vestry, Trinity Episc. Ch., Washington, Va., 1999-00, mem. vestry, 1997-99. Recipient Sabetty Orch. award, Friends of Mary Washington Coll. Orch., 1990, Woodard Orch. scholarship, 1991-92. Mem. Music Tchrs. Nat. Assn., Va. Music Tchrs. Nat. Assn., Front Royal (Va.) Oratorio Soc. (bd. mem. 1997—). Episcopalian. Avocations: mountain biking, cross-country skiing, travel, swimming. Home: PO Box 62 Washington VA 22747-0062 Studio: 285 Rock Mills Rd Woodville VA 22749-1829

NICHOLS, MARCI LYNNE, gifted education coordinator, educator, consultant; b. Cin., July 7, 1948; m. James G. Nichols, June 19, 1970; children: Lisa, Jeannette. B in Arts and Sci., Miami U., Oxford, Ohio, 1970, MEd, 1990, PhD, 1997. Cert. Secondary English, elem. gifted edn., computer edn., Ohio. Secondary English tchr. West Clermont Local Schs., Cin., 1970-71; coord. gifted edn. and tchr. Batavia (Ohio) Local Schs., 1981—; spkr., cons. Local Gifted Orgns., Cin., 1988—; vis. instr. dept. ednl. psychology Miami U., Oxford, Ohio, 1991-98, assoc./adj. prof. 1998—; presenter Nat. Rsch. Symposium on Talent Devel., 1991. Author, presenter: (videotape series) Parenting the Gifted Parts I and II, 1992; columnist, contbr. Resources for Everyday Living; contbr. articles to profl. jours; creator attitude assessment instrument. Speaker Christian Women's Club, Ohio, Ind., Ky., W.Va., 1981—; deacon First Presbyn. Ch. of Batavia, Ohio, 1986-88; bd. trustee Super Saturday program gifted edn. com. Miami U., 1995—. Recipient Douglas Miller Rsch. award Miami U., 1991. Mem. ASCD, Am. Ednl. Rsch. Assn. (presenter 1997, 98), Nat. Assn. for Gifted Children, Consortium Ohio Coords. of Gifted, Parents Assn. for Gifted Edn. (trustee 1997), Midwest Ednl. Rsch. Assn. (presenter), Internat. Platform Assn., Mensa (ann. gathering presenter 1998), Phi Kappa Phi. Home: 110 Wood St Batavia OH 45103-2923 Office: Batavia Local Schs 800 Bauer Ave Batavia OH 45103-2837

NICHOLS, MARK WILLIAM, economist, educator; b. Daytona Beach, Fla., Oct. 14, 1966; s. William Barret and Marquerite Joann N.; m. Jody Ann, Aug. 17, 1991. BS in Econs., U. Ctrl. Fla., 1990; MA in Econs., Fla. State U., 1994, PhD in Econs., 1994. Asst. prof. econs. U. of the South, Sewanee, Tenn., 1994-96, U. Nev., Reno, 1996—; spkr. in field; cons. London Clubs, 1998; guest lectr. U. Salford, England, 1997—. Contbr. articles to profl. jours. Grantee U. Nev., 1998, Nat. Inst. Justice, Washington, 1999. Mem. Indsl. Organzation Soc., Am. Economic Assn. (western chpt.), Truckee River Fly Fishers. Presbyn. Avocations: fly fishing, playing saxophone, listening to jazz. E-mail: mnichols@unr.edu. Office: Dept of Economics Ms 030 Reno NV 89557-0001

NICHOLS, MICHAEL ADAIR, horticulture educator; b. London, May 13, 1934; s. Francis Langston and Eleanor Maude (Waldron) N.; m. Lindsay Betts, May 12, 1962; children: Jane, Tim, Catherine. BSc in Horticulture, U. Nottingham, U.K., 1957, MSc, 1965; PhD, Massey U., Palmerston North, New Zealand, 1970. Advisory officer Ministry of Agr., New Zealand, 1958-62; demonstrator in horticulture U. Nottingham, 1962-65; lectr. in horticulture Massey U., 1965-70, sr. lectr. in horticulture, 1970—; cons. FAO, World Bank, Pakistan, EEC, Thailand, Dole Foods, The Philippines. Contbr. articles to profl. jours. Mem. Internat. Soc. for Hort. Sci. (mem. coun. 1982-86, chair asparagus group, chair commn. for edn. 1986-88, chair sect. root, tuber crops 1998—), New Zealand Soc. for Hort. Sci. Avocation: gardening. Office: INR Massey U, Pvt Bag 11-222, Palmerston North New Zealand

NICHOLS, PETER (RICHARD), playwright; b. Bristol, Eng., July 31, 1927; s. Richard George and Violet Annie (Poole) N.; m. Thelma Reed, Dec. 26, 1959; children: Abigail (dec.), Louise, Daniel, Catherine. Student, Bristol Old Vic Theatre Sch., 1951-53, Trent Park Tchrs. Coll., 1958-60. Profl. actor, 1950-55, tchr., 1956-59; vis. playwright Guthrie Theatre, Mpls., 1976; writer in residence, Nan Yang Coll., Singapore, 1994. Writings include: (plays) Promenade, 1959, Ben Spray, 1961, The Hooded Terror, 1963, The Gorge, 1965, A Day in the Death of Joe Egg, 1967 (Best Play award Evening Std. 1967, Best Revival Play Tony award 1985), Daddy Kiss It Better, 1968, The National Health, 1969 (Best Play award Evening Std. 1969), Forget-Me-Not Lane, 1971, Neither Up Nor Down, 1972, Chez Nouz, 1974, The Freeway, 1974, Privates on Parade, 1977 (Ivor Novello Best Brit. Mus. award 1977, Best Comedy award Evening Std. 1978, Best Comedy award Soc. West End Theatres 1978), Harding's Luck, 1977, Born in the Gardens, 1979, Passion Play, 1981 (Best Play award Evening Std. 1981), Poppy, 1982 (Best Mus. award Soc. West End Theatres 1983), A Piece of My Mind, 1987, Blue Murder, 1995, So Long Life, 2000; (screenplays) Catch Us if You Can/ Having a Wild Weekend, 1965, Georgy Girl, 1966, Joe Egg, 1971, National Health, 1973, Privates on Parade, 1983; (other writings) Feeling You're Behind, 1984, Selected Diary, 2000. Bd. govs. Greenwich Theatre, 1971-75; mem. drama panel Arts Coun., 1973-76. Recipient John Whiting award, 1969. Fellow Royal Soc. Lit. Office: Alan Brodie Representation, 211 Piccadilly, London W1V 9LD, England

NICHOLS, RONALD LEE, surgeon, educator; b. Chgo., June 25, 1941; s. Peter Raymond and Jane Eleanor (Johnson) N.; m. Elsa Elaine Johnson, Dec. 4, 1964; children: Kimberly Jane, Matthew Bennett. MD, U. Ill., 1966, MS, 1970. Diplomate Am. Bd. Surgery (assoc. cert. examiner, New Orleans, 1991), Nat. Bd. Med. Examiners. Intern U. Ill. Hosp., Chgo., 1966-67, resident in surgery, 1967-72, instr. surgery, 1970-72, asst. prof. surgery, 1972-74; assoc. prof. surgery U. Health Scis. Chgo. Med. Sch., 1975-77, dir. surg. edn., 1975-77; William Henderson prof. surgery Tulane U. Sch. Medicine, New Orleans, 1977—, vice chmn. dept. surgery, 1982-91, staff surgeon, 1977—, prof. microbiology, immunology and surgery, 1979—; cons. surgeon VA Hosp., Alexandria, La., 1978-93, Huey P. Long Hosp., Pineville, La., 1978—, Lallie Kemp Charity Hosp., Independence, La., 1977-85, Touro Infirmary, New Orleans, Monmouth Med. Ctr., Long Branch, N.J., 1979-88; mem. VA Coop. Study Rev. Bd., 1978-81, VA Merit Rev. Bd. in Surgery, 1979-82; mem. sci. program com. 3d Internat. Conf. Nosocomial Infections, Ctr. Disease Control, mem. sci. program and fundraising com. 4th Internat. Conf.; bd. dirs. Nat. Found. Infectious Diseases, 1989—, v.p., 1994-97, pres.-elect., 1997-99, pres., 1999—; hon. fellow faculty Kasr El Aini Cairo U. Sch. Medicine, 1989; mem. adv. com. on infection control Ctrs. for Disease Control, 1991-97; disting. guest, vis. prof. Royal Coll. Surgeons Thailand 14th Ann. Clin. Congress, 1989, 17th Ann. Clin. Congress, 1992; mem. infectious diseases adv. bd. Roche Labs., 1988-95, Abbott Labs., 1990-92, Kimberly Clark Corp., 1990-99, SmithKline Beecham Labs., 1990-95, Fujisawa Pharm., chmn., 1990-99, Bayer Pharm., 1994—, Merck Sharpe Dohme, 1996, Depotech, 1996, Zeneca Pharm., 1997—, Rhone-Poulenc Rorer, 1997-99, Wyeth-Ayrest Labs., 1998—, Pfizer Pharm., 1999, Searle Pharm., 1999—, GlaxoWellcome, 1999, Aventis, 2000—, others; mem. study group Prophylaxis Antibiotic Project La. Health Care Rev., Inc., 1995—; lectr. Royal Coll. Physicians and Surgeons Can., 1998, Internat. Infectious Disease Soc. Ob-gyn., 1998, 20th N.Y. State Surg. Symposium, 1998, dept. surgery Dept. U. Ark., 1998; apptd. by gov. La. commn. HIV and AIDS, 1999—. Author: (with Gorbach, Bartlett and Nichols) Manual of Surgical Infection, 1984; author, guest editor: (with Nichols, Hyslop Jr. and Bartlett) Decision Mking in Surgical Sepsis, 1991; guest editor, author: Surgical Sepsis and Beyond, 1993; mem. editl. bd. Current Surgery, 1977—, Hosp. Physician, 1980—, Infection Control, 1980-86, Guidelines to Antibiotic Therapy, 1976-81, Am. Jour. Infection Control, 1981-99, Internat. Medicine, 1983—, Confronting Infection, 1983-86, Current Concepts in Clin. Surgery, 1984—, Fact Line, 1984-91, Host/Pathogen News, 1984—, Infectious Diseases in Clin. Practice, 1991—, surg. sect. editor, 1992—, Surg. Infections: Index and Revs., 1991—, So. Med. Jour., 1992-97, ANAEROBE, 1994—, Surg. Infections, 1998—, Clin. Infectious Diseases, 1999—; mem. adv. bd. Physician News Network, 1991-95; patentee (with S.G. schoenberger and W.R. Rank) Helical-Tipped Lesion Localization Needle Device; patentee in field. Elected faculty sponsor graduating class Tulane Med. Sch., 1979-80, 83, 85, 87, 88, 91-92. Maj. USAR, 1972-75. Recipient House Staff tchg. award U. Ill. Coll. Medicine, 1973, Rsch. award Bd. Trustees U. Health Scis.-Chgo. Med. Sch., 1977, Owl Club Tchg. award, 1980-86, 90; named Clin. Prof. of Yr. U. Health Scis., Chgo. Med. Sch., 1977, Clin. Prof. of Yr., Tulane U. Sch. Medicine, 1979; Douglas Stubbs Lectr. award Surg. Sect. Nat. Med. Assn., 1987, Prix d'Elegance award Men of Fashion, New Orleans, 1993; named Brit. Jour. of Surgery Lectr., 1997. Fellow Infectious Disease Soc. Am. (mem. FDA subcom. to develop guidelines in surg. prophylaxis 1989-93, co-recipient Joseph Susman Meml. award 1990), Am. Acad. Microbiology, Internat. Soc. Univ. Colon and Rectal Surgeons, ACS (mem. operating rm. environ. com. 1978-80, vice chair operating rm. environ. com. 1980-81, chmn. operating rm. environ. com. 1981-83, sr. mem. operating rm. environ. com. 1983-87, mem. internat. rels. com. 1987-93, sr. mem. internat. rels. com. 1993-97); mem. AMA, Nat. Found. for Infectious Diseases (bd. dirs.), Joint Commn. on Accreditation of Health Care Orgn. (Infection Control adv. group, 1988-98, sci. program com. 3d internat. conf. nosocomial infections CDC/Nat. Found. Infectious Diseases 1990, FDA Subcom. to Develop Guidelines in Surg. Prophylaxis, prophylactic antibiotic study group La. Health Care Rev. Inc. 1996—, AIDS commr. State of La. 1992-94, mem., La. Commn. HIV and AIDS, 1999—), 5th Nat. Forum on AIDS (sci. program com.), U.S. Pharmacopeial Convention Inc. (adv. panelsurg. drugs and devices 1995-2000, nominating com. The Heinz Awards 1995-96), Assn. Practitioners in Infection Control (physician adv. coun. 1991-98), Internat. Soc. Anaerobic Bacteria, So. Med. Assn. (vice chmn. sect. surgery 1980-81, chmn. 1982-83), Assn. Acad. Surgery, N.Y. Acad. Sci., Warren H. Cole Soc. (pres.-elect 1988, pres. 1989-90), Assn. VA Surgeons, Soc. Surgery Alimentary Tract, Inst. Medicine Chgo., Midwest Surg. Assn., Cen. Surg. Assn., Ill. Surg. Soc., European Soc. Surg. Rsch., Collegium Internationale Chirugiae Digestivae, Chgo. Surg. Soc. (hon.), New Orleans Surg. Soc. (bd. dirs. 1983-87), Soc. Univ. Surgeons, Surg. Soc. La., Southeastern Surg. Soc., Phoenix Surg. Soc. (hon.), Hellenic Surg. Soc. (hon.), Cen. N.Y. Surg. Soc. (hon.), Tulane Surg. Soc., Alton Ochsner Surg. Soc., Am. Soc. Microbiology, Soc. Internat. de Chirugie, Surg. Infection Soc. (sci. study com. 1982-83, fellowship com. 1985-87, ad hoc sci. liaison com. 1986-89, program com. 1986-87, chmn. ad hoc com. rels. with industry 1990-93, mem. sci. liaison com. 1995-96), Soc. for Intestinal Microbial Ecology and Disease, Soc. Critical Care Medicine, Am. Surg. Assn., Kansas City Surg. Soc., Bay Surg. Soc. (hon.), Cuban Surg. Soc. (hon.), Panhellenic Surg. Soc. (hon.), Tacoma Surg. Club (hon.), Sigma Xi, Alpha Omega Alpha. Episcopalian. Home: 1521 7th St New Orleans LA 70115-3322 Office: 1430 Tulane Ave New Orleans LA 70112-2699

NICHOLS, TRENT LEE, physician, physicist; b. Knoxville, Tenn., Apr. 4, 1954; s. Ted and Audrey Ruth (Owens) N.; m. Sally Ann Summers, Mar. 18,

1978; children: Theodore Franklin, Frances Ruth. BS, U. Tenn., 1976, MS, 1978, MD, 1986, postgrad. Diplomate Am. Bd. Internal Medicine. Intern U. Tenn. Meml. Rsch. Ctr. & Hosp., Knoxville, 1986-87, resident in internal medicine, 1987-89; internist Internal Medicine Assoc., Knoxville, 1989-92; asst. prof. medicine U. Tenn. Meml. Rsch. Ctr. and Hosp., Knoxville, 1992—, rschr., 1996—; bd. dirs. Univ. Physicians Assoc., Inc., Knoxville, pres., 1994-98, med. dir., 1998-99; bd. dirs. BioNeutrics, Inc., Knoxville. Contbr. over 35 articles to profl. jours. Asst. scoutmaster Boy Scouts of Am., Knoxville, 1991—, bd. dirs. Great Smoky Mountain Coun., 1994—. Recipient fellowship Niels Bohr Inst., Copenhagen, 1979, fellowship NIH, 1983, 84. Mem. AMA, Am. Phys. Soc., Am. Coll. Physicians, Sigma Pi Sigma. Achievements include developing new treatment planning techniques for boron neutron capture therapy for cancer. Avocations: astronomy, boy scouting. Office: Univ Tenn Meml Rsch Ctr and Hosp 1924 Alcoa Hwy Knoxville TN 37920-1511

NICHOLS, WILLIAM J., film studies educator; b. N.Y.C., Aug. 19, 1942; s. James William and Nellie Mae Nichols; m. Catherine M. Soussloff, June 24, 1994; 1 child, Eugenia Clark. BA, Duke U., 1964; MA, UCLA, 1972, PhD, 1978. Prof. Queen's U., Kingston, Ont., Can., 1978-87, chair, 1976-85; chair San Francisco State U., 1987-90, prof., 1987—; vis. assoc. scholar U. Calif., Santa Cruz, 1990-93; legal cons., L.A. and San Francisco, 1991—; critic Sta. KUSP-NPR Radio, Santa Cruz, 1990—. Author: (books) Movies and Methods, 2 vols., 1985, Representing Reality, 1991, Blurred Boundaries, 1994 (Critic's Choice award 1994). Getty assoc. chair Getty Mus., L.A., 1999-00. Office: San Francisco State U Cinema Dept 1600 Hathaway Ave San Francisco CA 94132

NICHOLSON, ELLEN ELLIS, clinical social worker; b. Boston, Apr. 1, 1940; d. George Letham and Mary Stirling (Money) McIver; divorced; 1 child, Matthew Norman Ellis. Dental Hygienist, Forsyth Coll., 1959; BS, Northeastern U., 1973, MEd in Counseling, 1974; MSW, Boston U., 1984. Registered dental hygienist, Mass. Dental hygienist, 1959-66; clin. coord., pvt. dental practice Forsyth Dental Ctr., Boston, 1966-70; dir. vol. counseling Solomon Mental Health Ctr., Lowell, Mass., 1974-75; social worker East Boston Social Ctrs., Inc., 1976-77, dir. youth family counseling, 1977-79; supr. family svc. Boston Housing Authority, 1979-81; social worker Mass. Soc. Prevention Cruelty to Children, Hyannis, 1984-86, supr., 1986-93, clinic dir., 1993-95; dir. profl. svcs. Child and Family Svc. of Cape Cod, Hyannis, 1995-98, dir., 1998—, dir. Abuse Prevention Svcs., 1995-96, dir., 1995—; psychotherapist Riverview Sch., Sandwich, Mass., 1989-93. Advisor youth group Christ Episcopal Ch., Needham, Mass., 1960-64, St. Paul's Ch., Newburyport, Mass., 1964-65; vol. counselor Solomon Mental Health Ctr., Lowell, 1972-74; chair Barnstable County Children's Task Force, 1994-96; chmn. adv. com. Barnstable County Sexual Abuse Intervention Network, 1994-96; mem. task force Barnstable County Juvenile Firesetters, 1995-96, mem. steering com., 1996—; mem. adv. bd. Cape and Islands Child Advocacy Ctr.; mem. Cape & Islands Domestic Violence Coun. Bd., 1998—. Mem. NASW, Am. Profl. Soc. on Abuse of Children, Assn. for Treatment of Sexual Abusers, Sigma Phi Alpha, Sigma Epsilon Rho, Kappa Delta Pi. Avocations: travel, ballroom dancing, skiing. Office: Child and Family Svc of Cape Cod 1019 Route 132 Hyannis MA 02601-1839

NICHOLSON, JACK, actor, director, producer; b. Neptune, N.J., Apr. 28, 1937; s. John and Ethel May N.; m. Sandra Knight, 1961 (div. 1966); children: Jennifer, Lorraine Broussard. Acting debut Hollywood stage prodn. Tea and Sympathy; films include Cry-Baby Killer, 1958, Studs Lonigan, 1960, Little Shop of Horrors, 1960, Ensign Pulver, 1964, The Trip, 1967, Easy Rider, (Acad. award nomination for best supporting actor), 1969, Five Easy Pieces, 1970, Carnal Knowledge, 1971, A Safe Place, 1971, The Last Detail, 1974 (Cannes Film Festival prize), Chinatown, 1974 (Acad. award nomination, N.Y. Film Critics Circle award), Tommy, The Passenger, 1975, The Fortune, 1975, One Flew Over the Cuckoo's Nest (Golden Globe award, Acad. award for best actor, N.Y. Film Critics Circle award), 1975, The Missouri Breaks, 1976, The Last Tycoon, 1976, The Shining, 1980, The Postman Always Rings Twice, 1981, Reds,1981 (Acad. award nomination for best supporting actor), The Border, 1982, Terms of Endearment (Acad. award for best supporting actor), 1983, Prizzi's Honor,1985 (Acad. award nomination for best actor), Heartburn, 1986, The Witches of Eastwick, 1987, Broadcast News, 1987, Ironweed, 1987 (Acad. award nomination for bestactor), Batman, 1989, Man Trouble, 1991, A Few Good Men, 1992, Hoffa, 1992, Wolf, 1994, The Crossing Guard, 1995, Mars Attacks!, 1996, The Evening Star, 1996, Blood and Wine, 1996, As Good As It Gets, 1997 (Acad. award best actor), A Salute to Dustin Hoffman; producer films Head, 1968, Ride the Whirlwind, The Shooting; dir. films Drive, He Said, 1971; dir., actor films Goin' South, 1978, The Two Jakes, 1990. Co-recipient (with Bobby McFerrin) Grammy award for best recording for children,1987. Office: Bresler Kelly & Assocs 11500 W Olympic Blvd Ste 510 Los Angeles CA 90064-1578*

NICHOLSON, NIGEL, business educator; b. Banbury, Eng., Jan. 1, 1944; s. Hubert Nicholson and Barbara Olive (Collard) Cropley; m. Jane Colquhon McVeigh, July 12, 1965; children: Alice, Nell; m. Veronica Mary McNamara, Nov. 20, 1971; children: Sam, Leo. BA in Psychology with honors, U. Coll., Cardiff, Wales, 1969, PhD in Occupl. Psychology, 1975. Chartered occupl. psychologist; lic. level B occupl. test. Rschr. Occupl. Psychology Unit, Cardiff, 1969-72; sr. rsch. fellow Sheffield (Eng.) U., 1972-90; prof. London Bus. Sch., 1990—; ptnr. Nicholson Ptnrs., Sheffield, 1991—; assoc. prof. U. Ill., 1980-81. Author: Executive Instinct, 2000, others; editor: Encyclopedic Dictionary of Organizational Behavior, 1995; editor 100 books; contbr. chpts. to books and articles to profl. jours. Fellow Brit. Psychol. Soc., Brit. Acad. Mgmt.; mem. APA. Avocations: jazz flute, opera, cycling, bird watching. Home: 27 Charlbert Ct/Charlbert S, London NW8 7BX, England Office: London Bus Sch, Sussex Pl Regents Park, London NW1 4SA, England

NICHOLSON, WILLIAM BATEMAN, insurance company executive; b. Tarboro, N.C., Feb. 17, 1957; s. Henry Gilliam and Gwendolyn Bateman Nicholson; m. Sharon Snow, Oct. 13, 1984; children: Bowman James, William Bateman Jr., Henry Gilliam, Nicholson II. BS, U. N.C., 1979. ChFC. Salesman McLean Trucking Co., Winston-Salem, N.C., 1979-82; assoc. W.L. Gore and Assocs., Elkton, Md., 1982-84; broker Dixon Comml. Properties, Inc., Raleigh, N.C., 1984-89, Insured Benefit Design, Inc., Raleigh, 1989-96; v.p. ins. Capital Investment Cos., Raleigh, 1996—. Advisor, H.S. tchr., children's min. St. Michaels Episcopal Ch., Raleigh, 1984—; bd. mem. WakeMedFound., Raleigh, 1999—. Mem. Sphinx Club. E-mail: bnicholson@capinvestco.com. Fax: 919-832-7928. Office: Capital Investment Cos 17 Glenwood Ave Raleigh NC 27603-1754

NICHOLSON, WILLIAM NOEL, clinical neuropsychologist; b. Detroit, Dec. 24, 1936; s. James Eardly and Hazel A. (Wagner) N.; m. Nancy Ann Marshall, June 15, 1957; children: Anne Marie, Kristin, Scott. AB, Wittenberg U., 1959; MDiv, Luth. Theol. Sem., Phila., 1962; PhD, Mich. State U., 1972. Diplomate Am. Bd. Forensic Examiners, Am. Bd. Med. Psychotherapists; lic. clin. psychologist, Mich.; ordained to ministry Luth. Ch., 1962; cert. Nat. Register health Care Providers in Psychology. Parish pastor Our Saviour Luth. Ch., Saginaw, Mich., 1962-69; intern in psychology Ingham Mental Health Bd., 1971-72; resident in psychology Bay-Arenac Mental Health Bd., 1972-74; dir., psychologist Riverside Ctr., Bay City, Mich., 1974-75; pastor, psychologist Psych Studies & Clergy Consultation of Mich., 1989—; pres. Bay Psychol. Assocs., P.C., Bay City, 1975—; cons. Gov.'s Office of Drug Abuse, 1972-74. Author: A Guttman Facet Analysis of Attitude-Behaviors Toward Drug Users by Heroin Addicts and Mental Health Therapists, 1972, An Episcopalian Guide to the Augsburg Confession, 1997; contbr. articles to profl. jours. Mem. APA, Mich. Psychol. Assn., Mental Health Assn. (pres. Bay-ARenac chpt. 1981), Bay City Yacht Club. Office: Behavioral Med Ctr 3442 Wilder Rd Bay City MI 48706-2331

NICKEL, KLAUS GEORG, mineralogy educator; b. Langen, Germany, June 29, 1953. Diploma geology, Johannes Gutenberg Univ., Mainz, Germany, 1979; PhD, Univ. Tasmania, Hobart, Australia, 1983. Scientist Max-Plank Inst, Mainz, 1983-86; sr. scientist Max-Planck Inst, Stuttgart, Germany, 1986-91; prof. Eberhard Karls Univ., Tuebingen, 1991—; vice-dir. mineralogy Univ. Tuebingen, 1996-98, dir. 1998—; vice dean Faculty of Geosci. Univ. Tuebingen, 1997-99, bd. curators Nat. and Med. Sci. Inst., Reutlingen, Germany, 1997—. Editor: Corrosion of Advanced Ceramics, 1994; inventor in field. Mem. Am. Ceramic Soc., German Ceramic Soc. (mem. coord. com. 1995—), German Soc. Materials Rsch. Office: Eberhard Karls Univ, Wilhelmstr 56, D 72074 Tübingen Germany

NICKELS, CHRISTOPHER, lawyer; b. Chgo., July 23, 1963; s. Joseph John and Dorothy Barbara Nickels; m. Kimarie Nagel, Sept. 7, 1992; children: Eric, Laura, Katherine. BS in Fin., Northern Ill. U., 1985, JD, 1988. Bar: N.Mex. 1988. Atty. Sturges, Houston & Johanson, P.C., Albuquerque, 1995—; prof. spkr., Albuquerque, 1988—, N.Mex. Def. Lawyers, Albuquerque, 2000. Author: Amicus Brief, 1993 (award NMDLA 1994). Baseball Mgr., coach Little League, 1992-98, basketball coach YMCA, 1992-98; republican candidate sch. bd. Albuquerque, 1994. Mem. N.Mex. Workers compensation Assn. Republican. Mem. Evangelic Ch. Avocations: sports, politics, computers. Fax: 505-888-8929. E-mail: cnickels@nm.net. Home: 7804 Hendrix Rd NE Albuquerque NM 87110-1522 Office: Sturges Houston & Johanson PC PO Box 36210 Albuquerque NM 87176-6210

NICKELS, MAVIS LANORE, secondary education education, farmer; b. Okeene, Okla., May 19, 1939; d. E. E. and Eleanor (Bingo) Woodson; m. J.D. Nickels, Sept. 27, 1958 (dec. May 1996); children: Kevin, Kyle, Kent, Allison. Student, Okla. State U., 1956-59; BS, Phillips U., 1966; postgrad., U. Okla., Oklahoma City, 1968-70, U. Oreg., Portland, 1970-72. Tchr. Moore (Okla.) Pub. Schs., 1966-68; contractor Nickels Constrn., Battle Ground, Wash., 1972-76; tchr. Battle Ground Pub. Schs., 1976-00; farmer Battle Ground, 1976—; adj. prof. Concordia U., Portland, 2000—; mem., writer Wash. Commn. Student Learning, Olympia, 1994-99; presiding cochair Program Delivery Coun., Brush Prairie, Wash., 1997-99; assessment coord. Prairie H.S., Brush Prairie, 1998-00; cons. Everett (Wash.) Pub. Schs., 2000. Fellow Okla. U. Sch. Medicine, 1968-70, U. Oreg. Sch. Medicine, 1970-72. Mem. AAUW (treas. Hudson's Bay Br.), NEA, Nat. Coun. Tchrs. Math., Wash. State Coun. Math Tchrs., Battle Ground Edn. Assn. (pres., sec.). Avocations: oil painting, gardening, sewing, crocheting, reading.

NICKELSEN, THOMAS NIKOLAUS, endocrinologist, internist, researcher; b. Frankfurt, Germany, June 22, 1954; s. Herbert H. and Ingeborg J. (Bessler) N.; m. Elzbieta M. Zajac, Dec. 23, 1980; 1 child, Lara. MD, Frankfurt (Germany) U., 1979, PhD, 1980. Bd. Cert. Internal Medicine, Endocrinology. Resident in radiology St. Joseph Hosp., Wiesbaden, Germany, 1979-82; resident in cardiology U. Hosp., Frankfurt, Germany, 1982-83, resident in internal medicine, 1983-88, sr. physician in endocrine dept., 1988-90; clin. rsch. physician Eli Lilly & Co., Bad Homburg, Germany, 1990-93, dept. head in endocrine rsch., 1991—; global clin. rsch. physician Eli Lilly & Co., Indpls., 1993-96; lectr., Frankfurt Med. Sch., 1990—, German Acad. Aviation Medicine, Frankfurt, 1992—. Contbr. articles to profl. jours. Capt. in German Army, 1981-82. Mem. Am. Soc. Bone and Mineral Rsch., German Soc. Endocrinology. Avocations: classical music, piano, languages, art. Office: Lilly Deutschland GMBH, Saalburgstrasse 153, 61350 Bad Homburg Germany

NICKERSON, RICHARD GORHAM, research company executive; b. Harwich, Mass., Nov. 20, 1927; s. Ephriam Gorham and Elizabeth (Wardle) N.; m. Eileen Florence Tressler, June 7, 1957 (dec. Apr. 1994); children: Holly Anne, Wendy Elyse, Susan Denise; m. Barbara Bernice Harper-Schofield, Aug. 14, 1999. BS cum laude, U. Mass., 1950; PhD, Northwestern U., 1955; postgrad., Poly. Inst. Bklyn., 1955-57; MBA cum laude, Boston U., 1983. Rsch. chemist DuPont, Cellophane Tech. Sect., Richmond, Va., 1954-55; rsch. chemist Dewey & Almy divsn. W.R. Grace Corp., Cambridge, Mass., 1957-60; v.p. R & D Electronautics Corp., Maynard, Mass., 1960-61; pres. Electronautics Corp., Maynard, 1961-63; project leader Polyco Borden Chem. divsn. Borden, Inc., Leominister, Mass., 1963-65, group leader, 1965-67, devel. mgr., 1967-81, lab. mgr., 1981-87; pres., mng. dir. Boston Profls. Internat., Inc., Hopkinton, Mass., 1987—. Patentee in field; designer, developer of water based polymers to meet specific performance requirement. With Chem. Corps, U.S. Army, 1955-57. Mem. Am. Chem. Soc., Soc. Plastics Engrs., Sigma Xi, Phi Lambda Upsilon, Alpha Chi Sigma. Avocations: sailing, photography, antique autos, classical music, dancing. Home: 9 Lyford Rd Hopkinton MA 01748-1581

NICKLAUS, JACK WILLIAM, professional golfer; b. Columbus, Ohio, Jan. 21, 1940; s. Louis Charles, Jr. and Helen (Schoener) N.; m. Barbara Bash, July 23, 1960; children: Jack William II, Steven Charles, Nancy Jean, Gary Thomas, Michael Scott. Student, Ohio State U., 1957-62, D of Athletic Arts (hon.), 1972; LLD (hon.), U. St. Andrews, 1984. Chmn., chief exec. officer Golden Bear Internat., Inc. Author: My 55 Ways to Lower Your Golf Score, 1964, Take a Tip From Me, 1968, The Greatest Game of All, 1969, Jack Nicklaus' Lesson Tee, 1972, Golf My Way, 1974, Jack Nicklaus' Playing Lessons, 1976, On and Off the Fairway, 1978, Play Better Golf, Vols. 1-3, 1980, 81, 83, The Full Swing, 1982, My Most Memorable Shots in the Majors, 1988. Chmn. Ohio div. Am. Cancer Soc., 1967; chmn. sports div. Nat. Easter Seal Soc., 1967. Named PGA Player of Year, 1967, 72, 73, 75, 76, Dunlop Profl. Athlete of Yr., 1972, Golfer of Year Profl. Golfers Assn., 1973, Byron Nelson award, 1964, 65, 72, 73, Bob Jones award, 1975; named Sportsman of Year, Sports Illus. mag., 1978; named to World Golf Hall of Fame; named Athlete of the Decade for 1970-79, 1979, Golfer of the '70s, 1979, Golfer of the Century, 1988. Mem. President's Club Ohio State U., Phi Gamma Delta. Achievements include playing on over 105 golf courses on 5 continents, 12 ranked in U.S. Top 100; hosted 185 profl. tournaments 1973—; won 71 tournaments including 20 maj. championships; maj. tournaments won include Tournament of Champions, 1963, 64, 71, 73, 77, U.S. Amateur, 1959, 61, U.S. Open, 1962, 67, 72, 80, U.S. Masters, 1963, 65, 66, 72, 75, 86, Brit. Open, 1966, 70, 78, PGA Championship, 1963, 71, 73, 75, 80, Internat. Pro-Amateur, 1973, Atlanta Golf Classic, 1973, Walt Disney World Golf Classic, 1971-73, 75, Hawaiian Open, 1974, Tournament Players Championship, 1974, 76, 78, Hawaiian Open, 1974, Doral-Eastern Open, 1975, Heritage Classic, 1975, Australian Open, 1964, 68, 71, 75, 76, 78, World Series of Golf, 1962, 63, 67, 70, 76, Gleason Inverrary Classic, 1976, 77, 78, Phila. Classic, 1965, 78, Colonial Nat. Invitational, 1982, PGA Seniors Championship, 1991, U.S. Senior Open, 1991, 93, Mercedes Sr. Championship, 1994, others.

NICKLE, DENNIS EDWIN, electronics engineer, church deacon; b. Sioux City, Iowa, Jan. 30, 1936; s. Harold Bateman and Helen Cecilia (Killackey) H. BS in Math., Fla. State U., 1961. Ordained deacon Roman Cath. Ch., 1979. Reliability mathematician Pratt & Whitney Aircraft Co., West Palm Beach, Fla., 1961-63; br. supr. Melpar Inc., Falls Church, Va., 1963-66; prin. mem. tech. staff Xerox Data Sys., Rockville, Md., 1966-70; sr. tech. officer WHO, Washington, 1970-76; software tech. mgr. Melpar divsn. E-Sys., Inc., Falls Church, 1976-95; software process improvement mgr. Bell Atlantic, Arlington, Va., 1996-97; sr. software mgr. Litton Denro, Gaithersburg, Md., 1997—; lectr. in field. Author: Stress in Adolescents, 1986; co-author: Handbook for Handling Non-Productive Stress in Adolescence, Standard for Software Life Cycle Processes, IMPEESA Junior Leader Training Guide, Standard for Software Quality Assurance, 1984-91, Standard for Developing Software Life Cycle Processes, Configuration Management Procedures, Software Quality Assurance Procedures, Software Development Procedures; contbr. to profl. jours. Chief judge for computers Fairfax County Regional Sci. Fair, 1964-88; scoutmaster, commr. Boy Scouts Am., 1957-92; youth custodian Fairfax County Juvenile Ct., 1973-87; chaplain No. Va. Regional Juvenile Detention Home, 1978-88; moderator Nocturnal Adoration Soc.; parochial St. Michael's Ch., Annandale, Va., 1979-89, Christ the Redeemer, Sterling, Va., 1990-93. With U.S. Army, 1958-60. Recipient Eagle award, Silver award, Silver Beaver award, other awards Boy Scouts Am.; Ad Altare Dei, St. George Emblem, Diocese of Richmond. Mem. Assn. Computing Machinery, Computer Soc., Am. Soc. for Quality Control, CODSIA (chmn. working groups), ORLANDO II (Govt./industry working group), Old Crows Assn., Rolm Mil-Spec Computer Users Group (internat. pres.), San Antonio I (select industry coord. group), Nat. Security Indsl. Assn. (conv. com. 1985-96, software quality assurance subcom., regional membership chmn. 1981-89, nat. exec. vice-chmn. 1989-94, chmn. 1994-96), Am. Security Coun., IEEE (sr., stds. working group in computers 1983—, Outstanding Vol. award 1993, Golden Core 1996), Def. Software Devel. Stds. Adv. Bd. (chmn. 1991-96), Soc. Software Quality, Hewlett-Packard Users Group, Smithsonian Assn., Internat. Platform Assn., NRA (endowment), Nat. Eagle Scout Assn. (life), KC (4 deg.), Alpha Phi Omega (life), Sigma Phi Epsilon. Office: 9318 Gaither Rd Gaithersburg MD 20877-1441

NICKLIN, GEORGE LESLIE, JR., psychoanalyst, educator, physician, author; b. Franklin, Pa., July 25, 1925; s. George Leslie and Emma (Reed) N.; m. Katherine Mildred Aronson, Sept. 30, 1950. BA, Haverford Coll., 1949; MD, Columbia U., 1951; cert. in psychoanalysis, William A. White Inst., N.Y.C., 1962. Diplomate Am. Bd. Psychiatry and Neurology. Resident, then chief resident Bellevue Psychiat. Hosp., N.Y.C., 1953-56; pvt. practice specializing in psychoanalytic psychiatry, 1956—; staff Bellevue Hosp., 1956—; asst. clin. prof. psychiatry NYU Med. Sch., 1962-70, assoc. clin. prof. psychiatry, 1970—; dir. L.I. Inst. Psychoanalysis, 1978-88, dir. emeritus, 1988—, dir. emeritus; mem. Com. to Award Martin Luther King Peace Prize. Author: Doctors In Peril, 2000. Trustee W.B. Foss Sch., 1958—; mem. Corp. Haverford Coll., 1949-98; trustee Westbury Friends Sch., 1957-98; founder Friends World Coll., 1958, trustee, 1968-89. With AUS, 1943-46, ETO. Decorated Purple Heart with oak leaf cluster, Bronze Star with oak leaf cluster and three battle stars. Fellow Am. Acad. Psychoanalysis, Am. Psychiat. Assn.; mem. AAAS, NAACP, Soc. Med. Psychoanalysts (pres. 1986-87), White Psychoanalytic Soc., Assn. for World Edn. (charter trustee, treas. 1970-78), 9th Inf. Divsn. Assn., Vets. of the Bulge, Mil. Order of the Purple Heart. Mem. Soc. of Friends. Clubs: Gardiner's Bay Country (Shelter Island, N.Y.); Penn (London). Home and Office: 6 Butler Pl Garden City NY 11530-4603

NICOLAE, PAUL, metallurgical engineer; b. Bucharest, Romania, Dec. 8, 1945; s. Ilie and Profira (Dumitrescu) N.; m. Veronica Stefan, Aug. 15, 1971; 1 child, Daniela. Grad., Polytech. Inst., Bucharest, 1968. From engr. to sr. scientist Metall. Rsch. Inst.-ICEM, Bucharest, 1968-94, councillor, 1994—; asst. assoc. prof. Polytech. Inst., Bucharest, 1975-83; pres. Romanian Tech. Com. for Metal Powders and Sintered Parts, Bucharest, 1991—. Patentee in field; contbr. articles to profl. jours. Recipient Aurel Vlaicu prize Romanian Acad., Bucharest, 1985, prize for metallurgy Gen. Assn. Engrs., Romania, 1999. Fellow Romanian Soc. for Metallurgy (1st prize 1995). Orthodox Christian. Avocations: Romanian literature, ernst hemingway, constantin Brâncusi, painting. Office: Metall Rsch Inst ICEM, 39 Mehadia St, 77769 Bucharest Romania

NICOLAÏ, JUDITHE, international business trade executive; b. Lawrence, Mass., Dec. 15, 1945; d. Victor and Evelyn (Otash) Abisalih; children: Michelle Marie, Monique Therese. Student in photography, L.A. City Coll., 1967, UCLA, 1971; AA in Fgn. Langs., Coll. of Marin, 1983; hon. degree, Culinary Inst., San Francisco, 1981. Photographer Scott Paper Co., N.Y.C., 1975; owner, operator restaurant The Raincheck Room, West Hollywood, Calif., 1976; prin., pres., chief exec. officer, photographer fashion Photographie sub. Nicolaï Internat. Svcs., Nice, France, 1977—; prin., pres., chief exec. officer, instr. catering and cooking Back to Basics sub. Nicolaï Internat. Svcs., San Francisco, 1980—; chief photographer exhibit and trade show, chief of staff food div. Agri-Bus. U.S.A., Moscow and Washington, 1983; head transp. U.S. Summer Olympics, L.A., 1984, interpreter for Spanish, French, Portuguese, and Italian, 1985; prin., pres., chief exec. officer, interpreter Intertrans subs. (Nicolaï Internat. Svcs.), San Francisco, 1985—; founder, pres. Nicolaï Internat. Svcs., San Francisco, 1985—; pres., CEO Cyprus Personal Care Products, Inc., 1994—; mem. Internat. Diplomacy Coun., 1997—. Contbr. column on food and nutrition to jour., 1983-84. Mem. NAFE, Internat. Diplomacy Coun., Alpha Gamma Sigma. Avocations: cooking, fencing, archery, golf, photography. Office: Nicolai Internat Svcs 1686 Union St Ste 237 PMB San Francisco CA 94123-4509 Address: 2269 Chestnut St PMB 237 San Francisco CA 94123-2600

NICOLAI, PAUL PETER, lawyer; b. Trenton, N.J., Jan. 22, 1953; s. Ernest and Preziosa E. (Cattani) N.; m. Anne Marie Elizabeth LaRochelle, May 14, 1976; children: Caroline Emma, Peter Ernest, Margaret Elizabeth, Alexandra Marie, Elizabeth Anne. BA, Am. Internat. Coll., 1975; JD, Western New Eng. Coll., 1979. Bar: Mass. 1979, U.S. Dist. Ct. Mass. 1980, U.S. Ct. Appeals (1st cir.) 1983, U.S. Supreme Ct. 1984, N.Y. 1987, Washington 1987, U.S. Ct. Appeals (Fed. cir.) 1990, U.S. Tax Ct. 1991. Legal asst. Friendly Ice Cream Corp., Wilbraham, Mass., 1976-79, staff counsel, 1979-81, co. counsel, 1981-88; pres. Nicolai Law Group, P.C., Springfield, Mass., 1984-97; bd. dirs. Video Comms., Inc., Springfield, Package Machinery Co., Inc., Prentice Reed Ltd.; pres., bd. dirs. Paugus TV, Inc., Manchester, N.H., 1995—, T-W Realty, Inc., Springfield, Mass., 1996—. Bd. dirs. Citizens for Ltd. Taxation, Mass., 1981-84, chmn., 1984-97; mem. we. Mass. exec. com. NCCJ, mem. we. Mass. and Conn. devel. com. 1995-99, nat. trustee, 1991-99; corporator Springfield Day Nursery, Inc., 1995—, mem. mktg. com., 1995-96, Springfield Libr. Mus. Assn., Inc., 1985—; bd. dirs. Pioneer Valley Montessori Soc., Inc., Springfield, 1985-93, v.p., 1988-92, pres., 1992-93; bd. dirs., chmn. Citizens Econs. Rsch. Found., Inc., Boston, 1984-97; mem. adv. bd. Springfield Enterprise Ctr., 1998—. Mem. ABA, Am. Arbitration Assn. (arbitration panel 1992—), Mass. Bar Assn. (fee arbitration panel 1997—, arbitration and mediation panel 1999—), Hampden County Bar Assn. (arbitration and mediation panel 1998—), Boston Bar Assn., Assn. Bar City N.Y., D.C. Bar Assn., Fed. Cir. Ct. Appeals Bar Assn., Am. Internat. Coll. Corp. (reunion com., 2000, venture forum, planning com., program com., mktg. com. chair, bus. plans review com., nat. bd. dirs., v.p. 1989-90, pres. 1990-91), Soc. Everett Barney Inc. (treas., clk. 1995-99, dir. 1995—, sec. 1996-99), Western Mass. Tech. Bus. Coun. (bd. dirs. 1998—, treas.). Roman Catholic. Avocation: reading. Home: 24 Venture Dr Springfield MA 01119-2727 Office: Nicolai Law Group PC 146 Chestnut St Ste 1 Springfield MA 01103-1539

NICOLAIDIS, STYLIANOS, neurosurgeon, institute director, former educator; b. Verria, Macedonia, Greece, Nov. 26, 1933; arrived in France, 1952; s. Dimitry and Kalypso (Sava) N.; m. José Clara Reinhardt, July 7, 1987; children: Kalypso Aude, Dimitri Yves. MD with honours, U. Paris, 1961; PhD, U. Paris Sorbonne, 1962. Cert. in neurosurgery. Resident, then neurosurgeon Hosp. La Salpetriere, Paris, 1960-72; vis. prof. Inst. Neurol. Sics., U. Pa., Phila., 1972-73; dir. neurosurgery Mont Louis Hosp., Paris, 1973-88; chair, prof. physiology and neurosurgery U. Calif., San Francisco, 1988-89; dir. Inst. of Biology, Coll. de France, Paris, 1989-97, CNRS European Inst. Scis. of Taste and Ingestion/U. Burgundy, France, 1997-99. Author 3 books; contbr. chpts. to books; contbr. more than 300 articles to internat. jours. Chmn. Internat. Union Physiol. Scis., 1982-86, 86-90; vice chmn. Greek Acads. of France, 1995—. Recipient prix Acad. of Scis., Paris, 1962; award Found. for Nutrition, Paris, 1986. Mem. Soc. Neurosurgery for French Lang., Soc. Physiologists, Soc. for Sci. of Ingestive Behavior (pres.-elect N.Y.). Avocations: music (classical and jazz piano), tennis, skiing. Home: 84 Blvd du Mal Joffre, 92340 Bourg La Reine France

NICOLAS, FRANÇOIS, biologist; b. Marseille, France, Sept. 30, 1965; s. Charles and Jacqueline (Maximin) N.; m. Odile Houdard, May 13, 1994; 1 child, Pierre. M in Biochemistry, U. Marseille, 1989, cert. extensive studies in nutrition, 1990, PhD in Biology with hons., 1994. Rsch. asst. Nat. Ctr. Sci. Rsch., Marseille, France, 1990-95; European product mgr. Edge Scientific Instrument, Santa Monica, Calif., 1995-97; mng. dir. Data Ptnrs., Marseille, 1997-98; engr. Beckman-Coulter France, 1998—. Co-Author: Le livre de l'annee 1995, 1994, Le livre de l'annee 1996, 1995, Le livre de l'annee 1997, 1996. Fellow Royal Microscopical Soc. London; mem. Soc. Française Microscopies, Dirigeants Commerçiaux France. Avocations: classical singing, music, history of sciences, skiing. Home: 33 Crs Jean Jaures, 30490 Montfrin France

NICOLAS, MARINA SAVVIDOU, architect; b. Nicosia, Cyprus, Sept. 1, 1960; d. Nicodemos and Maroulla (Papakyriacou) Savva; m. George Nicolas; children: Stephanie, Alexia. BA in Architecture with honors, Thames Polytech., London, 1982, Diploma in Architecture with honors, 1985. Pvt. practice architecture Nicosia, Cyprus, 1985—; with Al Harthy Icory Contracting, Oman, 1990-91. Recipient Distinction award World Competition for Young Architects, Bulgaria, 1987. Mem. The Cyprus Architects Assn., The Cyprus Architects and Civil Engrs. Assn., Council of Registration for Architects and Civil Engrs. Greek Orthodox. Avocations: icon painting, oil painting, wood engraving, batik art. Home and Office: PO Box 22268, Nicosia 1519, Cyprus

NICOLAU, RADU ALEXANDRU, distribution company executive; b. Bucharest, Romania, Feb. 25, 1957; s. Marius Eugeniu and Aneta Nicoleta (Tudose) N.; m. Oana Mihaela Filotti, Aug. 31, 1985; children: Smaranda, Mihnea. Grad. coll., Bucharest, 1976; civil engring. diploma, Civil Engring. U., Bucharest, 1982. Civil engr. CNE Cernavoda, Romania, 1982-83, CET

Giurgiu, Romania, 1983-84; civil engring. designer ISPE, Romania, 1984-90; editor, dep. chief editor Romanian TV, 1990-94; dep. gen. mgr. Tele 7abc, Romania, 1994-97; programming dir. Romanian TV, 1997-99; mng. dir. New Films Internat., Romania, 1999; asst. Civil Engring. U., Bucharest, 1988-90; trainee BBC, London, 1993, Phare-Tacis Program, Athens, Greece, 1995, NATO, Brussels, 1995. Reporter, anchor, prodr. TV documentaries (Best Documentary 1994, 95), TV talk show and current affairs programs (Best Talk Show 1997). internat. visitor U.S. Govt., 1993; spkr. Libertarian Internat. Conf., 1991. Lt. Romanian mil., 1976-77. Recipient prize for journalism dedicated to truth of Romanian Revolution, Asociatia 21, 1995. Mem. Uniunea Ziaristilor Profesionisti Din Romania, Profl. Journalists Orgn., Mental Health League. Avocations: jazz, mountain climbing, mountain biking, skiing. Home: #4 Bl 1 SC 3 Ap 79, Str Barbu Vacarescu, 71422 Bucharest Sector 2, Romania Office: New Films Internat Romania, Bvd Unirii # 27 Bl 15 Sc 3, 751012 Bucharest Sector 5, Romania

NICOLAUS, BRUNO J.R., chemistry educator, researcher; b. Naples, Italy, June 2, 1928; s. Oscar and Rosa (Bipper-De Bonito) N.; m. Lotte Gertrud Koechli-Alleman, Oct. 18, 1954; children: Patricia Jessica, Stephan Alexander. BS, Lic. Jacopo Sannazzaro, Naples, 1946; PhD in Organic Chemistry, U. Zurich, 1954; degree in chemistry, U. Bologna, Italy, 1979. Sr. rschr. Sandoz AG, Basel, 1954-60; dir. new products dept. Dow-Lepetit, Milan, Italy, 1960-68; dir. innovation ISF (Smithkline Beecham), Milan, Italy, 1969-91; dep. gen. mgr., v.p. bd. dirs. ISF (Smithkline Beecham), Milan, 1980-91; chmn. Mediator Pharma Consultants, Milan, 1991-96; freelance writer on history and scis. and future of medicine, 1996—; asst. to prof. Karrer, Nobel Prize Laureate, U. Zurich, 1949-52; lectr. in organic chemistry U. Milan, 1962-72; pharm. industry adviser UN, Mexico City, 1966; contract prof. pharm. chemistry U. Perugia, Italy, 1987-88. Author: Decision Making in Drug Design, 1983, L'Arca di Noe, 1996; contbr. more than 150 articles to profl. publs. including Jour. Organic Chemistry, Integrative Psychiatry, Gazzetta Chimica Italiana, Jour. Chromatography, among others. Mem. Pro Raetia, 1995—, Soc. Svizzera, Milan, 1985—. Fellow New Swiss Chem. Soc., Internat. Coll. Neuropsychopharmacology; mem. Accademia Pontaniana Napoli, Soc. Italiana di Scienze Farmaceutiche, Ordine dei Biologi, Internat. Coll. Neuropsychopharmacology, European Coll. Neuropsychopharmacology, Internat. Psychogeriat. Assn., Acad. Medicine et Psychiatriae Found., Associazione Italiana Malattia di Alzheimer, Soc. Lit. and Sci., Swiss Soc. History Medicine and Scis., Gruppo Nazionale di Fondamenti e Storia della Chimica, Chem. Heritage Found. Avocations: tennis, swimming, diving, skiing, golf. Home: Via Crescitelli 6, 20052 Monza Italy

NICOLESCU, VALERIU NOROCEL, engineering educator, researcher; b. Curtea de Arges, Romania, Apr. 26, 1961; s. Valeriu and Evghenia Nicolescu; m. Delia Larise Ritiu, Aug. 18, 1984; 1 child, Aurel. BSc, U. Brasov, Romania, 1986, PhD, 1997; MSc, U. Oxford, 1994. Forest planner Forest Rsch. and Mgmt. Inst., Brasov, Romania, 1986-88; dist. officer Sacueni (Romania) Forest Dist., 1988-89; asst. lectr. U. Transilvania, Brasov, 1989-95, lectr., 1995-2000, assoc. prof., 2000—; mem. Transilvania U. Senate, Brasov, 1996—. Co-author: Silvicultura I, 1996, Silvicultura II, 1998; author: Artificial Pruning-a Review, 1999. Dep. lt. Bat., 1986. Grantee European Union, 1991, 93, Soros Found., 1995, European Union, 1999. Fellow Romanian Forestry Soc. Avocations: reading, playing tennis and football. Home: Apt 1, Str Dr Ion Ratiu 19, 2200 Brasov Romania Office: U Transilvania Fac Silvicul, Sirul Beethoven 1, 2200 Brasov Romania

NICOLETTI, ROSARIO, research scientist; b. Naples, Campania, Italy, May 2, 1961; s. Giuseppe Nicoletti and Flora Pacini; m. Luisa Ambrosino, Apr. 9, 1996; 1 child, Simone. Degree in agrl. scis., Naples U., 1985. Cert. agronomist. Tchr. Ministry of Pub. Edn., Naples, 1986-88; rschr. Flower Crops Rsch. Inst., Sanremo, Italy, 1990, Olive-growing Rsch. Inst., Cosenza, Italy, 1990-92; asst. rschr. Tobacco Rsch. Inst., Scafati, Italy, 1988-89, rschr., 1992-98, sr. rschr., 1998—; cons. Agrl.-Indls. Rsch. Ctr., Piana di Verna, Italy, 1987. Contbr. articles to profl. jours., including Jour. Phytopathology, Phytochemistry; co-author CD-ROM: Crop Protection Compendium, 1999; patentee in field. Mem. Italian Soc. Plant Pathology, Order of Agronomists. Fax: 03039-081-8506206. E-mail: istab@uniserv.uniplan.it. Office: Tobacco Rsch Inst, Via Vitiello 66, 84018 Scafati Salerno, Italy

NICOLINI, CLAUDIO, biophysics researcher; b. Udine, Italy, Apr. 4, 1942; came to U.S., 1968, naturalized, 1982; married; 2 children. D.Physics, U. Padova, Italy, 1967. Cert. rschr. Nat. Inst. Nuclear Physics. Guest research assoc. Brookhaven Nat. Lab., L.I., N.Y., 1967-70; research assoc. dept. physics and lab. nuclear sci. MIT, Cambridge, Mass., 1968-70; asst. prof. theoretical physics U. Bari, Italy, 1970; assoc. prof. physics U. Bari (Italy), 1970-72; sr. fellow molecular pathology Temple U. Sch. Medicine, 1972-74, adj. assoc. prof. pathology, 1975-79, assoc. prof. biophysics and pysiology, 1974-76; prof. biophysics and physiology Temple U. Health Sci. Ctr., 1977—, chmn. com. biophysics and bioengring., 1974-76; research assoc. prof. pharm. chemistry Temple U. Sch. Pharmacy, 1976-77; head biophysics research div. Temple U., 1975—; prof. biophysics and physiology Temple U. Health Sci. Ctr., 1977-84; Disting. Prof. Biophysics Faculty of Medicine/Surgery U. Genoa, 1984—; sr. investigator NRC, Italy, 1980-81; dir. NATO Advanced Study Insts., 1978, 80, 81, 83, 84, 85, 86, 87, 88, 92; permanent dir. Internat. Sch. Pure and Applied Biostructure Ettore Majorana Ctr. for Sci. Culture, 1979—; spl. study sect. cell biology NIH Nat. Inst. Gen. Medicine, Bethesda, Md., 1976; mem. spl. study sect. biochemstry NIH Nat. Inst. Arthritis and Metabolic Diseases, Bethesda, 1977; sci. and tech. advisor Prime Minister Italy, 1984-86; mem. Nat. Sci. and Tech. Coun., 1990-98; reviewer Am. Cancer Soc.; reviewer Med. Research Council Can.; vis. prof. Stanford U., 1990-96; pres. Polo Nazionale Bioelettronica, Sci. Tech. Pk. Elba Island, 1990—; pres. Found. El.B.A., 1992—; cons. in field. Author: textbooks, most recent Biophysics and Cancer, 1984, Il Cancro, 1991, Biofisica o Tecnologic Biomediche, 1992, Molecular Bioelectronics, 1996; contbr. numerous articles to profl. jours; editor: Chromatin Structure and Function, 2 vols., 1979, Cell Growth, 1982, Chemical Carcinogenesis, 1982, Modeling and Analysis in Biomedicine, 1984, Bioscience at the Physical Science Frontier, Nobel Symposium, 1986, Molecular Manufacturing, 1995, Biophysics of Electron Transfer, 1998, From Neural Network and Biomolecular Engineering to Bioelectronics, 1994, Genome Structure and Function, 1992; editorial adv. bd., World Pub. Co., Singapore, 1983—; editor Cell Biophysics, 1990-98; editor 21 books in field. NIH research grantee, 1975-80; Internat. Sch. Subnuclear Physcis Ettore Majorana summer scholar, 1970; CERN Joint Inst. Nuclear Physics summer scholar, 1971. Mem. Biophys. Soc., Acad. Scis. and Arts (Bergamo, Italy) (hon.), AAAS, Cell Kinetic Soc. (founding), Analytical Cytology Soc. (founding), N.Y. Acad. Scis., Sigma Xi. Office: SEDE, Corso Europa 30, 35-16132 Genoa Italy

NICOLODI, MARIA, neuropharmacologist, medical researcher; b. Florence, Italy, June 2, 1955; d. Beniamino and Giovanna (Zicari) N. B in Medicine, U. Florence, 1984, MD, 1992; specialist in neurology, U. Pavia, Italy, 1994. Asst. prof. U. Catania, Italy, 1997-99; fellow U. Florence, 1990-93, asst. rsch. prof., 1999—; internat. cons. Med. Inst. Treatment of Pain, Santiago, Chile, 1997; asst. prof., rschr. U. Florence, Italy; gen. sec. Interuniv. Ctr. Neurochemistry and Clin. Pharmacology of Primary Headaches, Italy, 1997; asst. rschr. U. Florence, 1999. Contbr. over 200 articles to profl. med. jours. (Internat. Greppi Jr. prize, 1990, Sr. prize, 1995); editor 2 Congress Procs. books; inventor in fields of therapy for chronic headache and primary fibromyalgia; patentee in field; referee Jour. Internat. Headache Soc., 1993-97, Jour. Am. Assn. Headache, Scientific Cooperator Italian Soc. Study of Headache. Rsch. grantee Solvay-Pharma and Florence U., 1994, Nat. Coun. Rsch., Rome, 1995. Mem. Internat. Headache Soc., Internat. Club Functional Organic and Non-Organic Nociceptive Diseases (founder, mem. scientific bd. 1991). Avocations: gardening, painting. Office: Medical Association, Via Costa de' Magnoli 28, I-50125 Florence Italy

NICOLSON, JOHN ALICK, business executive; b. Inverness, Scotland, Sept. 26, 1945; s. Ewen and Janet (Macdonald) N.; m. Effie Bella Macphie, Oct. 3, 1971. Grad. high sch., Skye, United Kingdom. Civil servant D.A.F.S., Scotland; ins. rep. Prudential, Scotland; prin. Jansvans, Scotland; founder, chmn. Skye & Lochalsh Enterprise, 1992-94; chmn. Hie-Screen Ltd.; bd. dirs. Caledonian MacBrayne Ltd. Scottish commr. Clan Nicolson of Scorrybrear, 1992; trustee Urras Clan of Mhicneacail, 1992. Mem. Isle of Skye Round Table (chmn. 1976), Portree Dist. Rotary. Avocations: collecting vintage motor vehicles, computer programming. Home: Almond Bank Viewfield Rd, Portree Isle of Skye 1Y51 9EU, Scotland Office: Jansvans, 6 Broom Pl Dunvegan Rd, Portree Isle of Skye 1V51 9HD, Scotland

NICOPOULOU-KARAYIANNI, KETY, oral radiology educator; b. Athens, Greece, July 7, 1951; d. Panayiotis and Stamatia (Sycara) N.; m. Athanasios Karayiannis, June 24, 1976; children: Yiannis, Stamos. D of Dental Sci., U. Thessaloniki, Greece, 1975; D of Dentistry, Athens U., 1985; postgrad., Berne U., Switzerland, 1988-89. Asst. Athens U., 1976-85, lectr., 1985-89; asst. prof. U. Greece, 1989-99; assoc. prof. Athens U., 1999—. Contbr. rsch. articles to profl. jours. Scholar Papaveamidis Found., Berne U., 1988. Mem. Hellenic Soc. Dento-Maxillo-Facial Radiology (sec. 1998, 99, 00). Home: Uifisou 3A, 15234 Athens Greece

NIDA-RÜMELIN, JULIAN THOMAS, philosopher; b. Munich, Bavaria, Germany, Nov. 28, 1954; s. Rolf and Margret (Ploeger) Nida-Rümelin. PhD in Philosophy, U. Munich, 1983, Philosophy Habil., 1989. Asst. prof. U. Munich, 1984-89, vis. prof., 1989-90; vis. prof. U. Minn., 1991; prof. U. Tübingen, Germany, 1991-93; prof., chair U. Göttingen, Germany, 1993—; min. City Culture and Arts, Germany, 1998—. Author: Entscheidungstheorie und Ethik, 1987, Kritik des Konsequentialismus, 1993 (2d. edit. 1995), Economic Rationality and Practical Reason, 1997, Demokatie als Kooperation, 1999; co-author: Logik kollektiver Entscheidungen, 1994; editor and author: Angewandte Ethik, 1996. V.p. Kulturforum, Berlin, 1994—. Fellow European Acad. Scis. and Arts; mem. Soc. for Analytic Philosophy (pres. 1994-97), European Soc. for Analytic Philosophy (exec. com. 1996—), Am. Philos. Assn., German Soc. for the UN. Avocations: swimming, scuba diving. Home: An der Schanze 5, 81925 Munich Germany Office: U Göttingen, Humboldtallee 19, D-37073 Göttingen Germany also: Kulturralerat, Burgstr 4, D-80331 Munich Germany

NIDECKER, ANDREAS CORNELIS, radiologist, educator; b. Tiel, The Netherlands, Oct. 1, 1947; s. Hans Jakob and Rosemarie (Huggenberg) Nidecker; divorced; children: Florian, Maja, Eva. MD, U. Basel, Switzerland, 1973. Diplomate Am. Bd. Radiology. Asst. prof. radiology U. Basel, 1985-99, prof. radiology, 1999—; pvt. practice Basel, 1982—; mem. Arbeitsgruppe Knochentumoren, Deutsches Krebsforschungsfentrur; co-owner Roentgeninst./Inst. for MRI, Basel. Mem. exec. com., past pres. Internat. Physicians for Prevention of Nuc. War, 1982—, Found. SUNswitaerland; mem. constl. coun. Basel Canton, 1999—; pres. Basel Vocal Ensemble. Mem. Internat. Soc. Skeletal Radiology, Radiol. Soc. N.Am., Swiss Soc. Radiology. Avocations: driving electric car, hiking, skiing, travel, music. Office: Roentgeninstitute, Untere Rebgasse 18, 4058 Basel Switzerland

NI DHOMHNAILL, GRAINNE, psychology educator; b. Dublin, Ireland, Sept. 6, 1959; d. Kevin and Maureen (Farrell) O'Donnell. BEd, St. Patrick's Coll., Dublin, 1980; BA, U. Coll. Dublin, 1983, PhD, 1992, MEd, 1997; MSc, U. Coll. London, 1990. Cert. elem. tchr. Univ. lectr. U. Coll., Dublin, 1993—. Mem. The Psychol. Soc. of Ireland (pres. 1999-2000). Roman Catholic. Office: Univ Coll Dublin, Edn Dept, Dublin D 4 Belfield, Ireland

NIE, ZHONGNAN, research scientist; b. Qianjiang, Hubei, China, Aug. 31, 1962; arrived in New Zealand, 1993; s. Yipei Nie and Xinguo Zhang; m. Anli Zuo, Aur. 1, 1986; 1 child, Bruce. B Agrl. Sci., Hubei (China) Agrl. Coll., 1982; PhD, Massey U., New Zealand, 1998. Rsch. agronomist Hubei Inst. Animal Sci., Wuhan, 1982-85; rsch. leader Hongyan Pastoral Rsch. Sta., Yichang, China, 1986-88, 89-92; vis. scientist Pastoral Rsch. Inst., Victoria, Australia, 1988-89; feed cons. Wuhan Huamei Feed Co., Ltd., 1992-93; vis. academic Massey U., Palmerston North, New Zealand, 1993-97; rsch. fellow, program leader U. Melbourne, Australia, 1997—. Author: Development of Grassland in Sub-tropical Hill Country, 1992; contbr. rsch. papers to profl. jours. Recipient award Ministry of Agr., China, 1988; doctoral scholar Massey U., 1995. Mem. Royal Soc. New Zealand, New Zealand Grassland Soc., Grassland Soc. Victoria. Avocations: running, fishing, chess, reading, table tennis. Office: U Melbourne Glenormiston, PMB 6200, Terang Victoria 3264, Australia

NIEBRZYDOWSKI, LEON, psychologist researcher; b. Obrytki, Mazowsze, Poland, May 3, 1931; s. Stanislaw and Waleria (Dombroska) N.; m. Maria Chlopek (div. 1968); children: Jaroslaw, Marek, Eva; m. Jolanta Icha, 1978. Master, Catolik U., Lublin, Poland, 1956; PhD, U. M. Curie Skłodowskiej, Lublin, Poland, 1968; Dr. habil., U. Gdańsk, Poland, 1974; docent-prof., U. Gdańsk and Lodz, Poland, 1980—. Tchr., master Sch., Elk, Poland, 1951-52; tchr. H.S., Gdansk, 1956-62; tchr., master High Sch., Gdańsk, Poland, 1962-68; adj. U. Gdańsk, Poland, 1968-74; docent-prof. U. Lodz, Poland, 1980—; dir. dept. psychology U. Gdansk, 1974-80, U. Lodz, 1980-92; vis. prof. U. So. Calif., 1985, U. N.D., 1985, U. Grand Forks, N.D., 1986, Northwestern U., Evanston, Ill., 1987, U. Utah, 1984, Ariz. State U., Phoenix, 1988, U. Windsor, Can., 1988, Conn. U., 1991, York U., U.K., Justus Liebig U. Germany, Russian Acad. Sci., 1970, Oxford (Eng.) U., 1998, Bern (Switzerland) U., 1998; pres. Nat. Coun. for Self-Esteem, 1990—; co-editor European Jour. for High Ability, Hamburg, Germany, 1990—; mem. The Citizen Amb. program Dwight D. Eisenhower Found., 1995. Author: (book) Development of Self-evaluation During Adolescence, 1973, Self-Disclosure in Interpersonal Relationships, 1990, Self-Disclosure, Empathy and Sexual Satisfaction in Marriage, 1994, Friendship and Self-Disclosure in Interhuman Relationships, 1989, Educational and Social Psychology, 1995, New Challenges for Educational Psychology, 1997; contbr. over 150 sci. articles to profl. jours. Recipient Concordia U. award Ctr. for Rsch. in Human Devel., 1995, Brit. Coun. for Brit. and East European Coop. Psychology Group award, 1995, UNSCO award for participation on XXV Congress World Psychology, 1992, Washington U. award, 1995, Manitoba U. award, 1996, Daniels Pub. award, 1996, award U. Berne, 1998, Westminster Coll., 1998, patent and trademarks excellence in edn. award U.S. Dpet. Commerce. Mem. World Coun. Gifted and Talented Children, World Senate of Educators, Internat. Coun. for Self-Esteem, Nat. Coun. for Self-Esteem. Avocations: travels. Home: Mateusza 15, 91-613 Lodz Poland Office: U Łódź Dept of Psychology, Smugowa 10, 90-432 Lodz Poland

NIEBUHR, JOHANNES HEINRICH, physics educator; b. Otterstedt, Germany, June 11, 1924. Diploma in Physics, U. Erlangen, Germany, 1950, D of Natural Scis., 1952. Rschr. Elchem, Nuernberg, Germany, 1952-57; head dept. Ges.F.Elektrometallurgy, Nuernberg, 1957-61; rsch. assoc. dept. metallurgy MIT, Cambridge, 1961-62; rsch. assoc. MPI Metallkunde, Stuttgart, Germany, 1963-65; prof. physics Sch. Engring. Fachhochschule Ravensburg, Weingarten, Germany, 1965-88; ret., 1988. Co-author: Physical Measuring with Sensors, 5th edit., 2000; contbr. articles to profl. jours. Mem. Assn. German Engrs., Lions Club (Ravensburg pres. 1988-89), Sigma Xi. Home: Sandstr 20, D-79104 Freiburg Germany

NIECHOY, DETLEV HEINZ THOMAS, fiscal officer; b. Goettingen, Germany, Aug. 26, 1959; s. Siegfried Stefan and Lieselotte Lina Gertrud (Zornow) N.; m. Silvia Christa Grube, Dec. 30 1988; children: Jacqueline, Adriana; stepchildren: Melanie Schaefer, Nadine Schaefer. Founder, leader Astronomical Workgroup, Goettingen, 1978-86; leader, evelator Arbeitskreis Planetenbeobachter, Berlin, 1983—; coord. ashen light of Venus project UCLA, 1987-90; asst. lectr. Volkshochschule Goettingen, 1992—; coord. nightside of Venus project U. Western Ont., Can., 1994—; founder Mercury and Venus drawing Archive Goettingen, 1995—. Contbr. articles to profl. jours. Founder, exec. mem. Aktienfreunde 2000, 1999—. Fellow Brit. Astron. Assn., Swiss Astron. Soc., Vereinigung der Sternfreunde, Astron. Soc. Pacific, Astronomische Gesellschaft, Assn. Lunar and Planetary Observers, Planetary Soc., Internat. Amateur and Profl. Photoelectric Photometry Soc., Phoenix aus der Aktie GbR (founder, exec. mem. 1987-99).

NIEDERHAUSER, EMIL KÁROLY, history educator; b. Bratislava, Czechoslovakia, Nov. 16, 1923; s. Károly and Irén (Ponner) N. Teaching cert., U. Budapest, Hungary, 1948, PhD, 1959. Researcher Inst. History Hungarian Acad. Sci., Budapest, 1949-85, prof., 1984-93, scientific advisor, 1991—, prof. emeritus, 1994—; dep. dir. U. Budapest, 1986-90; assoc. prof. U. Debrecen, Hungary, 1953-73, prof., 1973-83. Author: A jobbágyfelszabaditás, 1962, The Rise of Nationality in Eastern Europe, 1982, Die Habsburger, 1983. Mem. Hungarian Acad. Scis. Roman Catholic. Office: Inst History Hung Acad Sci, Uri 53, 1014 Budapest Hungary

NIEDERMAN, JAMES CORSON, physician, educator; b. Hamilton, Ohio, Nov. 27, 1924; s. Clifford Frederick and Henrietta (Corson) N.; m. Miriam Camp, Dec. 12, 1951; children—Timothy Porter, Derrick Corson, Eliza Orton, Caroline Noble. Student, Kenyon Coll., 1942-45, D.Sc. (hon.), 1981; M.D., Johns Hopkins U., 1949. Intern Johns Hopkins Hosp., Balt., 1949-50; asst. resident in medicine Yale-New Haven Med. Center, 1950-51, assoc. resident, 1953-55; med. ctr. practice specializing in internal medicine, infectious disease and clin. epidemiology New Haven, 1955-97; instr. Yale U., 1955-58, asst. prof., 1958-66, assoc. prof., 1966-76, clin. prof. medicine and epidemiology, 1976-97, emeritus clin. prof. medicine and epidemiology, 1997—, clin. prof. emeritus epidemiology and pub. health, 1998; mem. Nat. Coun. for Johns Hopkins Medicine. Trustee Kenyon Coll., 1974-97, trustee emeritus, 1997—; bd. counselors Smith Coll., 1970-77; mem. Alumni Coun. Johns Hopkins U. Served to 1st lt. M.C. U.S. Army, 1951-53. Fellow Silliman Coll., Yale U. Fellow Am. Coll. Epidemiology; mem. Infectious Diseases Soc. Am., Am. Epidemiol. Soc., Johns Hopkins Med. and Surg. Assn.; trustee Assocs. of Cushing Whitney Med. Libr.; mem. The Kenyon Rev. Bd. Trustees, Conn. Soc. Arts and Scis. Democrat. Episcopalian. Clubs: Yale (N.Y.C.); New Haven Lawn. Achievements include research in clin. epidemiology. Fax: 203-393-1902. E-mail: dr.j.@cshore.com. Home: 429 Sperry Rd Bethany CT 06524-3544 Office: 60 College St New Haven CT 06510-3210

NIEDERMULLER, HANS, science educator; b. Klangenfurt, Austria, June 10, 1940; s. Gretl Niedermuller; m. Tanya Koppel, Oct. 6, 1978; children: Iris, Simone, Katharina. Degree in engring., Tech. U., Vienna, Austria, 1967, PhD in Natural Scis., 1972. Synthetical organic chemist Bender & Co., Ciby/Geigy, Vienna, 1967-68; asst. prof. U. Vet. Medicine, Vienna, 1968-78, prof., 1978—, head dept. exptl. gerontology, physiology, 1978—; dir. rsch. lab. Ludwig Boltzhann Soc., Vienna, 1992—. Editor procs. Advances in Experimental Gerongology, 1989; contbr. articles to profl. jours. Head mng. bd. Union Socialistic Univ. Tchrs., Austria, 1982—. Mem. various sci. assns. and socs. Avocations: philosophy, theory of knowledge, skiing, swimming, tennis. Home: Robert Lachgasse 50/19, A-1210 Vienna Austria Office: U Vet Medicine, Veterinärplatz 1, A-1210 Vienna Austria

NIEDERREITER, HARALD GUENTHER, mathematician, researcher; b. Vienna, June 7, 1944; s. Simon and Erna (Emig) N.; m. Gerlinde Hollweger, Aug. 30, 1969. PhD, U. Vienna, 1969. Asst. prof. So. Ill. U., Carbondale, 1969-72, assoc. prof., 1972-73; mem. Inst. Advanced Study, Princeton, N.J., 1973-75; vis. prof. UCLA, 1975-76; prof. U. Ill., Urbana, 1976-78, U. W.I., Kingston, Jamaica, 1978-81; rschr. Austrian Acad. Scis., Vienna, 1981-89, dir. Inst. Info. Processing, 1989-98, dir. Inst. Discrete Math., 1999—; math. & info. scis. panel TMR Tng. Grants EU Commn., Brussels, 1995-99, chmn., 1996-99, TMR Networks, 1995-99. Author: Uniform Distribution of Sequences, 1974, Russian transl., 1985, Finite Fields, 1983, Russian transl., 1988, Introduction to Finite Fields and Their Applications, 1986, rev. edit., 1994, Random Number Generation and Quasi-Monte Carlo Methods, 1992 (Outstanding Simulation Publ. award 1995), Monte Carlo and Quasi-Monte Carlo Methods in Scientific Computing, 1995, Finite Fields and Applications, 1996, Monte Carlo and Quasi-Monte Carlo Methods '96, 1997, Sequences and Their Applications, 1999, Monte Carlo and Quasi-Monte Carlo Methods, '98, 2000; contbr. numerous rsch. articles to math. jours.; editor Jour. Complexity, 1999—; assoc. editor Maths. of Computation, 1988—, ACM Trans. Modeling and Computer Simulation, 1990—, Fibonacci Quar., 1995—; mem. editl. bd. Caribbean Jour. Math., 1982—, Applicable Algebra, 1990—, Stochastic Optimization and Design, 1991-93, Jour. Ramanujan Math. Soc., 1991-96, Acta Arithmetica, 1992—, Monatshefte Math., 1993—, Finite Fields and Their Applications, 1993—, Jour. Info. and Optimization Scis., 1995—, Jour. Complexity, 1996-99. Named hon. prof. U. Vienna, 1986, Cardinal Innitzer prize for natural scis., 1998. Mem. Am. Math. Soc., Austrian Math. Soc., Austrian Acad. Scis., Internat. Assn. Cryptologic Rsch., Austrian Computer Soc., Assn. for Informatik, Soc. Indsl. Applied Math., German Acad. Natural Scientists Leopoldina (elected 1996, mem. presidium 1999), N.Y. Acad. Scis. Home: Sieveringer Str 41, A1190 Vienna Austria Office: Austrian Acad Scis, Sonnenfelsgasse 19, A1010 Vienna Austria

NIEFELD, JAYE SUTTER, advertising executive; b. Mpls., May 27, 1924; s. Julius and Sophia (Rosenfeld) N.; m. Piri Elizabeth Von Zabrana-Szilagy, July 5, 1947; 1 child, Peter Wendell. Cert., London U., 1945; B.A., U. Minn., 1948; B.S., Georgetown U., 1949; Ph.D., U. Vienna, 1951. Project dir. Bur. Social Sci. Research, Washington, 1952-54; research dir. McCann-Erickson, Inc., N.Y.C., 1954-57; v.p., dir. mktg. Keyes, Madden & Jones, Chgo., 1957-60; pres., dir. Niefeld, Paley & Kuhn, Inc., Chgo., 1961-71; exec. v.p. Bozell, Inc., Chgo., 1971-89; pres. The Georgetown Group, Inc., 1991—; cons. U.S. Dept. State, Commerce, HEW, also others; lectr. Columbia U., Northwestern U., U. Chgo., 1989-94; chmn. Ctr. Advanced Comm. Rsch.; owner Glencoe Angus Farms, Glencoe Arabians; ptnr. Sunny Valley Farm, Talcott-Fromkin Freehold Assocs., Neptune Realty, J&J Enterprises, The Georgetown Group Inc., 1991; bd. dirs. Mktg. Decisions, Inc., E. Morris Comms., Inc. Author: The Making of an Advertising Campaign, 1989; (with others) Marketing's Role in Scientific Management, 1957, Advertising and Marketing to Young People, 1965, The Ultimate Overseas Business Guide for Growing Companies, 1990; contbr. articles to profl. jours. Mem. adv. bd. Glencoe Family Svc.; bd. dirs. Big Bros. Met. Chgo.; exec. v.p. City of Hope; mem. Theodore Thomas Soc. Chgo. Symphony Orch., Overture Soc. Lyric Opera Chgo. Capt. AUS, 1942-46. Decorated Bronze Star. Mem. Am. Assn. Pub. Opinion Rsch., Am. Film Inst., Am. Mktg. Assn., Am. Sociol. Assn., Smithsonian Instn., The Caxton Club, Chgo. Horticultural Soc. (governing bd.), Chgo. Coun. on Fgn. Rels. Home: 1011 Bluff St Glencoe IL 60022-1120

NIEH, T. G., materials scientist, researcher; b. Hsinchu, Taiwan, Apr. 27, 1951; came to U.S., 1975; s. Haifan Nieh and Shu Chen; m. Chien-I Chang, Aug. 25, 1979; children: Bing, Grace, Joyce, Timothy. MS, U. Wash., 1976; PhD, Stanford U., 1980. Sr. fellow Lockheed Missiles and Space, Palo Alto, Calif., 1980-92; sr. scientist Lawrence Livermore (Calif.) Nat. Lab., 1992—. Author: Superplasticity in Metals and Ceramics, 1997. With Taiwan Army, 1973-75. Fellow ASM Internat. Office: Lawrence Livermore Nat Lab PO Box 808 Livermore CA 94551-0808

NIEHUSS, JOHN MARVIN, lawyer; b. Ann Arbor, Mich., Mar. 7, 1937; s. Marvin Lemmon Niehuss and Lois Celicia Markham; m. Rosemary Juliette Neaher, June 30, 1973 (div. Mar. 1991); children: Juliette, John. BA, Amherst Coll., 1958; JD, U. Mich., 1962. Assoc. atty. Sullivan & Cromwell, N.Y.C., 1966-69; legal advisor Govt. of Zambia, Lusaka, 1969-71; loan officer, dir. World Bank, Washington, 1971-73, 90-91; dep. asst. sec. U.S. Treasury Dept., Washington, 1974-77, 89-90; v.p. Merrill Lynch, N.Y.C., 1977-89; gen. counsel Inter-Am. Devel. Bank, Washington, 1992-99, Export-Import Bank U.S., Washington, 1999—; mem. adv. bd. Internat. Law Inst., Washington, 1977—. Mem. Coun. Fgn. Rels., Met. Club. Republican. Avocations: golf, hiking, fly fishing, whitewater rafting. Home: 3019 45th St NW Washington DC 20016-3523 Office: Export Import Bank US 811 Vermont Ave NW Washington DC 20571-0002

NIELSEN, BONNIE BELLE, secondary school educator; b. Temple, Tex., Nov. 18, 1945; d. Greig B. and Rita (Sowerby) Beeler; m. Joel Allan Battle III, Aug. 28, 1966 (div.); children: Joel Allan Battle IV, Brian Scott Battle, Ginger Marie Battle; m. Gary Edgar Nielsen, Feb. 26, 1987. Student, U. Hawaii, 1967-68; BS in Art Edn., U. Houston, 1970, cert. in math., 1973; cert. in tchg., U. Alta., Edmonton, Can., 1986. Cert. art and math. tchr., Tex. 7th and 8th grade art and math. tchr. Pearland (Tex.) Jr. H.S., 1970-74, 7th and 8th grade math. tchr., 1975-76; substitute tchr. Tyler (Tex.) Ind. Sch. Dist., 1974-75, Edmonton Pub. Schs., 1986-87; 7th and 8th grade math. tchr. Missouri City (Tex.) Jr. H.S., 1976-77; art and math. tchr. Pearland H.S., 1987—. mgr., proctor Am. H.S. Math. Exam., Pearland, 1992-98; cons. Tex. Assessment of Acad. Skills, Pearland, 1995—; sponsor Nat. Honor Soc., Pearland, 1995—, Adopt-A-Senior Program, Pearland, 1996-99. Named PISD Secondary Tchr. of Yr., 1996-97, Outstanding Educator award, 1999. Mem. NEA, ASCD, Nat. Assn. Student Activity Advisors, Nat. Coun. Tchrs. Math., Pearland/Friens Wood-Aggie Mom's Club (scholarship chmn. 1995-99. Avocationsz: shirt designs, painting, crafts, travel, grandchildren. Home: 2906 Saxton Ct Pearland TX 77581-4834

NIELSEN, CARL EBY, physicist, educator, consultant; b. Los Angeles County, Jan. 22, 1915; s. Charlie Harry and Josie Elizabeth (Musselman) N.; m. Imogene Herron, June 26, 1938; children: Paul Herron, Sylvia Jean, Robert Kent. AB, U. Calif., Berkeley, 1934, MA, 1940, PhD, 1941. Instr. physics U. Calif., Berkeley, 1941-45, lectr. physics, 1945-46; asst. prof. U. Denver, 1946-47; asst. prof. Ohio State U., Columbus, 1947-53, assoc. prof., 1953-64, prof., 1964-85, prof. emeritus, 1985—; vis. scientist Max Planck Inst. for Plasma Physics, Garching, Germany, summers, 1969, 70, 72-74, Culham Lab., U.K. Atomic Energy Auth., Culham, Eng., 1966; scientist Midwestern Univs. Rsch. Assn., Madison, Wis., 1960-61; fellow European Orgn. for Nuclear Rsch., Geneva, Switzerland, 1958-59; cons. Oak Ridge (Tenn.) Nat. Lab., 1961-70, Los Alamos (N.Mex.) Sci. Lab., 1971-75, Lawrence Livermore (Calif.) Lab., 1974-77, U. of Tex., El Paso, 1985—. Co-author (with J.R. Hull and P. Golding): Salinity-Gradient Solar Ponds, 1989; contbr. numerous papers and articles to sci. jours., publs. Mem. AAAS, Am. Phys. Soc., Am. Solar Energy Soc. (Charles Greeley Abbot award 1990), Internat. Solar Energy Soc., Phi Beta Kappa. Unitarian-Universalist. Avocations: history, philosophy. Office: Ohio State U Dept Physics 174 W 18th Ave Columbus OH 43210-1106

NIELSEN, FLEMMING, archivist; b. Vejen, Denmark, Mar. 29, 1955; s. Erik Emil and Dorrith Karen (Jessen) N.; m. Bente Lukman Christensen, May 17, 1986; 1 child, Emilie. Cand. mag., Aarhus U., Denmark, 1981. Tchr. Skive Gymnasium, Skive, Denmark, 1982; asst. archivist Danish Bus. Archives, Aarhus, 1983-84; project leader Local Archives Ribe County, Esbjerg, Denmark, 1984-85; archivist Bangsbo Mus. and Archives, Frederikshavn, Denmark, 1986-96, Aalborg City Archives, Aalborg, Denmark, 1996—; guest lectr. Aalborg U., 1998—; Chmn. bd. dirs. SLA Arkivsvc. APS, Denmark, 1990—; bd. dirs. Local Archives No. Jutland, Denmark, 1990—, Open U., Aalborg, 1996—. Author: Bønder: Farmers in Northeastern Vendsyssel Through 200 Years, 1988, Kirker I Frederikshavn Kommune, 1990, Et Handelshus i Frederikshavn, 1991, Foreningsarkiver Fra Ribe AMT, 1994, Popular University in Northern Jutland 1898-1998, 1998; editor: Lananyt, 1996—. Office: Aalborg City Archives, Arkivstraede 1, DK-9000 Ålborg Denmark

NIELSEN, FRANÇOIS, sociology educator; b. Brabant, Belgium, June 17, 1949; s. David B. Nielsen and Françoise Rolin; m. Maryse Posenaer, 1975 (div. 1979); m. Martha Diehl; children: Claire, Sam. BA in Sociology, U. Libre Brussels, 1972; PhD in Sociology, Stanford U., 1978. Asst. prof. McGill U., Montreal, Que., Can., 1977-78, U. Chgo., 1978-82; rsch. assoc. Nat. Opinion Rsch. Ctr., Chgo., 1978-82; from asst. prof. to prof. U. N.C., Chapel Hill, 1983—. Contbr. articles to profl. jours. Mem. Am. Sociol. Assn., So. Sociol. Soc., Human Behavior and Evolution Soc. Avocations: swing dancing, genealogical research, photography. Fax: :(919) 962-7568. E-mail: francois nielsen@unc.edu. Home: 414 Russells Ford Chapel Hill NC 27516 Office: U NC Dept Sociology Chapel Hill NC 27599-0001

NIELSEN, HANS MUNK, telecommunications executive; b. Odder, Denmark, Oct. 13, 1946; s. Vagn and Karen (Kaae) N.; m. Gitte Forsberg, May 17, 1997. M in Econs., U. Aarhus, 1973. Prin. Danish Min. Finance, Copenhagen, 1973-75; v.p. Den Dansk Bank, Copenhagen, 1975-83; chief fin. officer Carl Bro Gruppen, Copenhagen, 1983-87, Storebalt, Copenhagen, 1987-91, Tele Danmark, Copenhagen, 1991—. Office: Tele Danmark A/S, Noerregade 21, 0900 Copenhagen Denmark

NIELSEN, JENNIFER LEE, molecular ecologist, researcher; b. Balt., Mar. 21, 1946; d. Leo Jay and Mary Marriott (Mules) N.; divorced; children: Nadja Ochs, Allisha Ochs. MFA, Ecole des Beaux Arts, Paris, 1968; BS, Evergreen State Coll., 1987; MS, U. Calif., Berkeley, 1990, PhD, 1994. Artist Seattle, 1969-78; fish biologist Weyerhaeuser Co., Tacoma, Wash., 1978-89; resource cons. Berkeley, 1989-90; rsch. biologist USDA-Forest Svc., Albany, Calif., 1990-99; vis. scientist Stanford U., Pacific Grove, Calif., 1994-99; supr. fisheries Alaska Biol. Sci. Ctr., Anchorage, 1999—; rsch. assoc. Calif. State U. Mosslanding Marie Sta., 1995-99; adj. prof. integrated biology U. Calif., Berkeley, 1998; adj. prof. U. Alaska, Fairbanks, 1999—; supervisory rsch. fishery biologist U.S. Geol. Svc., Biol. Resources Divsn., Alaska Biol. Sci. Ctr., Anchorage, 1999—. Editor-in-chief: Reviews in Fish Biology and Fisheries, 1999—; editor: Evolution and the Aquatic Ecosystem, 1995, Environ. Biology of Fishes, 1998—; contbr. over 50 articles to profl. jours.; paintings exhibited at Metro. Mus. Modern Art, 1966; represented in numerous pvt. collections, U.S. and Europe. Mem. Am. Fisheries Soc. (pres. chpt. 1993-94, genetics sect. pres. 1999—), Molecular Marine Biology and Biotech. (regional editor 1995), Animal Behaviour Soc. (policy com. 1993-94). Avocations: painting, cooking, gardening, rock climbing, sailing. Office: USGS/BRD Alaska Biol Sci Ctr 1011 E Tudor Rd Anchorage AK 99503-6119

NIELSEN, JORGEN, air transportation executive; b. Sonderborg, Denmark, Oct. 3, 1957; s. Ingolf Lorenz and Marie Magrethe (Krog) N.; m. Stella Arpe, Sept. 2, 1978. Grad. h.s., Denmark, 1974. Engr. student Cimber Air, Sonderborg, 1975-77, dir. spl. projects, 1985-90, airport mgr., v.p. airline, 1990-94, pres., CEO, 1994—. Fighter pilot Royal Danish Air Force, 1979-85. Mem. Royal Air Force Club. Avocations: flying, hunting, golf. Office: Cimber Air A/S, Lufthaunsvej 2, 6400 Sonderborg Denmark

NIELSEN, LINDA, lawyer; b. Copenhagen, Jan. 2, 1952; d. Svend Erik and Tove Esther (Hansen) N.; ptnr. Kjeld Dele Eklund; children: Christoffer Eklund, Simon Eklund, Larke Eklund. Law degree, U. Copenhagen, 1976, JD, 1993. Civil servant Ministry of Housing, Denmark, 1976-79, vice head sect., 1982-84; rsch. fellow U. Copenhagen, 1979-82, asst. prof., 1985-88, assoc. prof., 1988-96, prof., 1996—; head inst. Faculty of Law, Copenhagen, 1989-92, head tchg. bd., 1992-94; expert in peer rev. evaluation European Union, 1996—; pres. Danish Coun. Ethics, 1997-2000; active various Law Reform Commns., 1984—; mem. European Standing Com. of Nat. Ethics Coms. Coun. of Europe, 1998; chmn. law reform commn. on pensions and divorce, 1998—; chair law reform commn. on children, 1996—; vice-chmn. electricity coun., 1997—, vice-chmn. adoption coun., 2000, law reform commn. on Danish Intellegence Svc., adv. commn. to advise Min. of Justice on rsch. Author: Familie Formueretten, 1993, Genetic Tests, Screening and Use of Genetic Data, 1994; mem. editl. adv. bd. Jour. Social Welfare and Family Law; contbr. articles to profl. jours. Traveling fellow Nat. Establishment, Denmark, 1995. Mem. Internat. Soc. Family Law (exec. coun.), Nordic Bioethics Com. (chmn.). Home: Dyrehavevej 35, DK-2930 Klampenborg Denmark Office: Faculty of Law, Studiestrade 6, DK-1455 Copenhagen Denmark

NIELSEN, LOUISA AUGUSTA, broadcast association executive; b. Balt., Dec. 14, 1950; d. William Alexander and Louisa Augusta N. BA, Coll. Notre Dame Md., Balt., 1972; MA, Antioch U., 1975. Coord. Assn. Ind. Md. Schools, 1972-75; chair theater dept. Maryvale Coll. Prep. Sch., 1972-75; coord. Balt. Cable Planning Ctr., 1974-75; proj. founder/dir. Mayor's Office Manpower Resources Sidewalk Theater, Balt., 1975; documentary dir. Wash. Cmty. Video Access Ctr., D.C., 1975; adj. asst. prof. Antioch Coll., Balt. and D.C., 1976-79; asst. prof. Howard U., D.C., 1976-77; dir. ednl. programming svcs. Nat. Publ. Radio, D.C., 1976-79; humanities adminstr. media programs Nat. Endowment Humanities, D.C., 1979-82; dir. cable TV, asst. dir. broadcast TV Nat. Captioning Inst., D.C., 1982-83; vis. asst. prof. George Wash. U., D.C., 1983-1985, dir., prodr. ednl. programming, 1985-87; exec. dir., CEO Broadcast Edn. Assn., D.C., 1987-96; pub. Jour. Broadcasting & Electronic Media, Feedback mag., others; spl. invitee/fellow, Harvard Law Sch., 1987—; trustee, Brit. Broadcasting Corp., Nat. Univ., 1999—; bd. dirs. George Foster Peabody Awards, Ohio State Awards; bd. advisors, FCC; video conf. moderator, Nat. U.; judge, ACE Awards, NCTA, Corp. Publ. Broadcasting Programming Awards; presenter, AT&T, Publ. Svc. Satellite Consortium; invited panelist, Internat. Inst. Astronautics, Annenberg Wash. HDTV workshop; reviewer, Annenberg/CPB Project prog. Editl. advisory bd. Simon & Schuster Communications Dictionary; appeared as guest, PBS Nat. Narrowcast Svc. Telecommunication and Distance Learning. Chair, Soc. Satellite Profls. Internat., mid-atlantic region. E-mail: lnielsen@nab.org. Office: Broadcast Education Assn World Hdqs 1771 N St NW Washington DC 20036-2812

NIELSEN, OLE LERBERG, veterinary surgeon, researcher; b. Saxild, Jutland, Denmark, Aug. 28, 1956; s. Christen Lerberg and Elisabeth (Refslund) N.; m. Karin Ellemose Hansen, Mar. 15, 1997; children: Nina, Jakob, Johanne. DVM, Royal Vet. & Agrl. U., Copenhagen, 1983, PhD, 1993. Vet. surgeon Herlufmagle Vet. Hosp., 1983-88; scholar Royal Vet. & Agrl. U., Copenhagen, 1988-91; rsch. officer Danish Vet. Lab., Aarhus, 1991-98; assoc. prof. Royal Vet. and Agrl. U., Copenhagen, 1998—. Contbr. articles to profl. jours. including Jour. Vet. Immunology and Immunopathology, Avian Pathology, Immunology. Travel grantee Danish Pasteur Soc., 1990. Avocation: angling. Home: Muldager 35, DK-3600 Frederikssund Denmark Office: Royal Vet & Agrl U, Ridebanevej 1, DK-1870 Frederiksberg C, Denmark

NIELSEN, PEDER BO, clinical microbiologist; b. Copenhagen, Sept. 27, 1945; s. Svend and Karla (Petersen) N.; m. Inger Lise Kristensen, July 3, 1971; children: Jens Bo, Morten Bo. MD, U. Copenhagen, 1974; postgrad., U. Claude Bernard, 1982-83; MSc in Communicable Disease Epidemiology, London Sch. Hygiene and Tropical Medicine, 1996. Registrar Hvidovre Hosp., Copenhagen, 1979-82; sr. registrar, registrar State Seruminstitute, Copenhagen, 1983-88; cons. WHO, Global Programme on AIDS, Geneva, 1988-90; sr. registrar Bispebjerg Hosp., Denmark, 1988-91; cons. Esberg Centralsygehus, Denmark, 1991-92; cons., head Armed Forces Hosp., Min. of Defense & Aviation, Khamis, Dhahran, Saudi Arabia, 1992-95; cons. Pub. Health Lab. Svcs., London, 1996-99; dir. Peterborough PHL, 1999—; chmn. Infection Control Coms., 1988-95; chmn., invited spkr. various symposiums; peer reviewer Internat. Sci. Found., Washington, 1994. Contbr. articles to profl. jours. Scholarship Municipality of Lyon. Mem. Danish Soc. for Clin. Microbiology, Am. Soc. for Microbiology, British Med. Coun., Educative Coun. under Danish Soc. for Clin. Microbiology, Bd. for Jr. Microbiologist. Home: 43 Vermont Grove, Peterborough, Cambridge PE3 6BN, England

NIELSEN, PHILIP EDWARD, physicist, research manager; b. Chgo., July 18, 1944; s. John Edward and Doris Anne (Roessler) N.; m. Mary Jane Hill, Aug. 21, 1971; children: Aaron P., June E., David C. BS in Physics, Ill. Inst. Tech., 1966; MS in Physics, Case Western Reserve U., 1968, PhD, 1970. Commd. 2d lt. USAF, 1970, advanced through ranks to col., 1988; ret., 1996; chief, interaction physics group AF Weapons Lab., Kirtland AFB, N.Mex., 1970-74; assoc. prof. physics AF Inst. Tech., Wright-Patterson AFB, Ohio, 1974-79; dep. dir. Directorate of Aerospace Studies, Kirtland AFB, 1980-84; dep. chief, missile divsn. AF Studies and Analyses, Pentagon, Washington, 1984-86, chief, force analyses divsn., 1986-87; dir. tech. Fgn. Tech. Divsn., Wright-Patterson AFB, 1988-92; chief, tech. requirements HQ AF Materiel Command, Wright-Patterson AFB, 1992-96; mgr. tech. ctr. MacAulay-Brown, Inc., Dayton, Ohio, 1996—. Author: Effects of Directed Energy Weapons, 2000. Pres. Shadowbrook Homeowners Assn., Mt. Vernon, Va., 1986-87. Recipient USAF R & D award, 1975, Supr. Rsch. award Air Command and Staff Coll., Montgomery, Ala., 1980, Disting. Govt. Svc. award Albuquerque-Santa Fe Fed. Exec. Bd., 1983, Devel. Planning cert. of merit AF Systems Command, Washington, 1983. Mem. AAAS, Am. Phys. Soc., Inst. Ops. Rsch. and Mgmt. Sci., Mil. Ops. Rsch. Soc. Achievements include co-discovery (with P.L. Taylor) of an effect in the low-temperature thermoelectric power of metals and alloys now known as the "Nielsen-Taylor" or "N-T" effect; resolution of many puzzling results in the laser-induced breakdown thresholds of clean and aerosol-laden atmospheres; analysis of solid response to laser radiation which provided insights needed to extrapolate small scale experiments to large scale applications. Home: 9138 Payne Farm Ln Dayton OH 45458-9388 Office: MacAulay-Brown Inc 4021 Executive Dr Dayton OH 45430-1062

NIELSEN, SOREN KRAG, software product development executive; b. Odense, Denmark, Aug. 27, 1963; s. Jorgen Krag Nielsen and Aase Agnete Mose Rasmussen-Nielsen; m. Berit Helsted, July 6, 1990; children: Robin Sebastian Helsted, Emilia Victoria Helsted. BSEE, Odense Teck., 1986. Software engr. CRI A/S/European Space Agy., Noordwijk, The Netherlands, 1986-90; analyst CRI A/S Matra Marconi Space, Toulouse, France, 1990; mgr. engring. CRI A/S, Leiden, The Netherlands, 1990-93, project mgr., 1993-97; devel. mgr. Compuware Europe BV, Amsterdam, The Netherlands, 1997, control and verification mgr., 1997-98; mgr. Nokia Telecom., Copenhagen, 1998-2000, Phone.com, Copenhagen, 2000—. Mem. Soc. Danish Engrs., European Fedn. of Nat. Engring. Assn. Office: Phone.com Denmark ApS, Klingseyvej 15, 2720 Vanløse Denmark

NIELSEN-JONES, IAN RICHARD, lottery and gaming executive; b. Winchester, England, Jan. 24, 1950; arrived in Can., 1950; came to U.S., 1995; s. Richard and Jean-Marie (Edwards) Nielsen-J.; m. Linda Ann George, June 10, 1972; children: Christopher James, Alison Leigh, Eric Philip. BA in Econs., Loyola Coll., 1971; MA in Econs., McMaster U., 1972. From investigator to dep. dir. investigation & rsch. Competition Bur., Ottawa, Ontario, Canada, 1972-89; pres. Ont. Lottery Corp., Toronto, Sault Ste. Marie, Can., 1989-93; mng. dir. nat. lottery Rank Orgn. Plc, London, 1993-94; pres. gaming and recreation Rank Canada Ltd., Toronto, 1994-95; pres., chief operating officer CUE Network Corp., Irvine, Calif., 1995-97; pres., CEO Online Internat. Corp., Smithtown, N.Y., 1997-99, Gaming Mgmt. Group, Del., 1999—; bd. dirs. Lotto4U.com, Calif., Computer Radio Network, Ltd., Toronto, LotCo Plc, London, Gamex Corp., Nev., Gaming Mgmt. Corp., Del. Hon. bd. dirs. Bushplane Mus., Sault Ste. Marie, Ont.; bd. dirs. Econ. Devel. Corp., Sault Ste. Marie, 1992-93, United Way, 1990-93, Plummer Hosp., 1991-93, Algoma Univ. Coll., 1991-93. Named newsmaker of yr. Gaming and Wagering Mag., 1992. Avocations: writing, music, running, coin collecting, traveling. Home: 18 Rippling Strm Irvine CA 92612-3421 Office: 5 Corporate Park Irvine CA 92606-5113

NIEMANN, HEINER JULIUS, reproductive biotechnologist, researcher; b. Muenster, Westfalen, Germany, Jan. 7, 1953; s. Julius and Angelika (Duesterhaus) N.; m. Annette Becker, Aug. 30, 1980; children: Hannah, Helen. DVM, Tieraerztliche Hochschule, Hannover, Germany, 1978; Dr.med.vet., Tieraerztliche Hochschule, 1980; habilitation, Tieraerztliche Hochschule, Hannover, Germany, 1989. Staff scientist Inst. for Tierzucht & Tierverhalten, Mariensee, Germany, 1980—; dept. head Inst. für Tierzucht & Tierverhalten, Mariensee, Germany, 1987—, sci. dir., 1990, dir., prof., 1991—; prof. reprodn. biology Tieraerztliche Hochschule, Hannover, Germany, 1994—; vis. scientist Vet. Coll. Tex. A&M U., College Station, 1985; cons. in goat embryo technologies, New Zealand, 1987; cons. in field. Author: Biotechnological Studies with Farm Animal Embryos, 1988; co-author: Embryo Transfer and Related Biotechniques in Farm Animals, 1993; mem. editl. bd. Theriogenology, 1987-95, 2000—, Cloning, 1999—; contbr. articles to profl. jours. Recipient Biotech. award H.W,. Schaumann Found., 1987. Mem. Internat. Embryo Transfer Soc. (pres. 1988, bd. govs. 1987-90, 94-96, program chmn. 1993), soc. Study of Reproduction, soc. Study of Fertility, German Embryo Transfer Assn. (v.p 1991-93, pres. 1993-95), German Primate Ctr. (mem. sci. adv. bd.), Bundesaerztekammer (mem. sci. adv. bd. xenotransplantation). Avocations: reading, biking, tennis, history. Fax: 49-5034-871-101.

NIEMANN-STIRNEMANN, GUNDA, speed skater; b. Sonderhausen, Germany, Sept. 7, 1966; married. Student, libr. sch. Libr.; mem. German Nat. Women's Speed Skating Team, 1985—. Recipient Silver medal women's speed skating 1500 meters, Olympic Games, Nagano, Japan, 1998, Gold medal women's speed skating 3000 meters, 1998, Silver medal women's speed skating 5000 meters, 1998, World Cup, 2000. Avocations: dancing, sports. Office: Nat Olympic Com for Germany, Postfach 71 02 63, 60492 Frankfurt am Main Germany*

NIEMANTSVERDRIET, JOHANNES WILLEM, chemistry educator; b. Amsterdam, The Netherlands, Oct. 15, 1951; s. Antonie and Niesje (Ros) N.; m. Marianne van Goudoever, May 25, 1979; children: Hanneke, Annemieke, Karin, Peter. MSc in Physics, Free U., Amsterdam, The Netherlands, 1978; D Tech. Scis., Delft U. Tech., 1983. Postdoctoral fellow Reactor Inst., Delft, The Netherlands, 1983-84; C. and C. Huygens fellow U. Munich, 1985-86, Fritz Haber Inst., Berlin, 1986-87; C. and C. Huygens fellow Eindhoven (The Netherlands) U. Tech., 1984-85, 86-89, assoc. prof. chemistry, 1989-99, prof. physical chem. of surfaces, 1999—. Author: Spectroscopy in Catalysis, 1993, (with R.A. van Santen) Chemical Kinetics and Catalysis, 1995; assoc. editor Jour. of Catalysis, 1996—; mng. editor: Catalysis Tech., 1996—; contbr. over 150 articles to profl. jours. Pionier fellow Netherlands Orgn. for Sci. Rsch., 1989. Mem. Am. Chem. Soc., N.Am. Catalysis Soc., Am. Vacuum Soc., Royal Dutch Chem. Soc., Dutch Phys. Soc., Netherlands Vacuum Soc. (pres. 1997), European Fed. of Catalysis Socs. (pres. 1999-2001). Avocations: music, playing guitar. Office: Eindhoven U Tech, PO Box 513, 5600 MB Eindhoven The Netherlands

NIEMEYER, ANTONIO BILISOLY, JR., school system administrator; b. Norfolk, Va., Apr. 13, 1928; s. Antonio Bilisoly Niemeyer and Lutie Stuart Spotts; m. Alice Virginia Berry, Nov. 20, 1965; children: William Frederic, Frank Berry, John Stuart. BS, Va. Mil. Inst., 1949; MEd, U. Va., 1955; cert. advanced study, Old Dominion U., 1973. Asst. prin. Portsmouth (Va.) Schs., 1966-67, supr. sci., 1967-77, prin. Churchland Jr., 1977-78, prin. Manor H.S., 1978-80, 86-88, dir. secondary edn., 1980-86, dir. personnel, 1988-91; dir. Va. Jr. Acad. Sci., 1979-81. Cons. Science Far and Near, Tchrs. edit., 1973. Pres. Tidewater Heart Assn., 1968. Recipient Disting. Svc. award Jr. C. of C., 1957; named Sci. Educator of Yr., Tidewater Sci. Congress, 1975; fellow Va. Acad. Sci. Mem. SAR. Episcopalian. Avocation: historical studies. Home: 4324 Greendell Rd Chesapeake VA 23321-5504

NIEMI, NIKO TIMO, entrepreneur; b. Vaasa, Finland, Mar. 2, 1949; s. Veikko Armas and Beata (Hrabie) N.; m. Sirkku Anneli Suopanki, June 24, 1978; children: Sade, Saku. Comml. Grad., Comml. Coll., Kouvola, 1970; Restauranteur, Hotel & Restaurant Inst., Helsinki, 1973. Pvt. entrepreneur Kouvola, 1970—. Mem. Mcpl. Coun. Kouvola, 1989—, bd. dirs., 1990-92; mem. Provincial Cons. Com., Kymi Province, 1990-93. With Finnish Army. Recipient Golden Badge Finnish Hotel, Restaurant and Cafeteria Assn., 1997, Finnish Bakery Assn., 1986, Confederation of Finnish Entrepreneurs, 1990. Mem. Hotel, Restaurant and Cafeteria Employers Assn. (bd. dirs. 1981-90), Jaycees of Finland (v.p. 1984-85, internat. senate 1989—), Rotary (pres. 1991-92). Mem. Nat. Coalition Party. Avocation: golf. Home: Koriankuja 7, Kouvola Finland 45130 Office: Hotel Turistihoviky, Valtakatu 23, Kouvola Finland 45100

NIEMIEC, WACŁAW STANISŁAW, mathematics educator; b. Nowy Sacz, Poland, May 13, 1951; s. Antoni and Stefania (Uruska) N. Master's degree, Silesian Tech. U., Gliwice, Poland, 1975, intramural doctoral studies, 1976-81, PhD, 1984; DSc, Polish Acad. Scis.-U. Miami, Fla., 1985. Prof. Ind. Inst.-Edn. Ctr. Knowledge-Sci., Nowy S—cz, 1986—, rector, dir., 1992—. Contbr. articles to profl. jours. Mem. NATO Sci. Affairs Divsn. Mem. ASIDIC, Internat. Fedn. Automatic Control, Electrochem. Soc., Inc. Minerals, Metals, Materials Soc., Am. Math. Soc., Am. Nuclear Soc. Roman Catholic. Avocation: classical dance. Office: Ind Inst-Edn Ctr Knowle-Sci, Ul Barska 33, PL-33300 Nowy Sacz Poland

NIEMISTÖ, KARI PERTTI HENRIK, investment company executive; b. Helsinki, Oct. 6, 1962; s. Pertti Väinö and Henna Sinikka (Seppälä) N.; m. Leena Katriina Lammenranta, 1989; 3 children. U. student, Sr. H.S., Töölö, Helsinki, 1983; M.Se. Sch. Econs., Helsinki, 1989, postgrad., 1989-91. Adminstrv. dir. Suunto Yhtymä Oy, Helsinki, 1992; mng. dir. Oy Selective Investor Ab, Helsinki, 1993—; bd. dirs. Hämeen Peruna Oy, Helsinki, Suunto Oy, Helsinki, Pertitet Oy, Helsinki, Decolletage AG, Grenchen, Switzerland, Oy Stockmann Ab, Tykkimiehet ry. Mem. Ars Fennica Found. (v.p.), Rotary Club-Munkkiniemi. Avocations: tennis, art, history of culture. Home: Hirvilahdenkuja 5 B, 00340 Helsinki Finland Office: Oy Selective Investor Ab, Laurinmäenkuja 3 B, 00440 Helsinki Finland

NIEMITZ, CARSTEN, zoologist and medical researcher; b. Dessau, Germany, Sept. 29, 1945; s. Johannes and Ruth (Voigt) N.; m. Sigrun Finke, Sept. 12, 1997; 1 child. BSc, U. Freiburg, 1968; MSc, U. Giessen, 1970, PhD, DSc. Jr. research mem. Max-Planck-Institut, Frankfurt, 1968-71; leader expedition Behavioral Field Research, Malaysia, 1971-73; research mem. Neurol. Ctr., Giessen, U., 1974; asst. prof. Anatomical Inst., U. Gottingen, 1975-78; prof., head div. human biology Free U. Berlin, 1978—; dir. Inst. Animal Physiology U. Berlin, 1992-94; apptd. dir. Duisburg Zoo; apptd. dir. zoology U. Essen, 1994—; primate expert Species Survival Commn., IUCN, Switzerland, 1988—; v.p. Urania Kulturgemeinschaft, 1992—; presdl. bd. Humboldt Gesellschaft, 1994—; guest prof. zoology U. Potsdam, 1998-99. Editor: Biology of Tarsiers, 1984, Heredity and Environment, 1987, 94, Gravity in Primates, 1990, The Rainforestbook, 1990, Genetics and Genetic Engineering, 1999; author: (film) Forging of a Ritual Knife in Bidayuh, 1972, Life History of Carrion Beetles, 1977, The Life of Tarsiers, 1987. Grantee, German Research Union, 1982-87. Fellow Borneo Rsch. Coun., Ency. Cinematographica; mem. German Soc. Mammalogy, Gesellschaft Anthropologie (pres. 1994-96, v.p. 1996—). Avocations: painting, lyrics. Office: Free Univ Berlin, Fabeckstr 15, D-14195 Berlin Germany

NIENHAUS, ADRIANUS GERARDUS, information technology company executive; b. Veghel, The Netherlands, May 6, 1971; arrived in Poland, 1999; s. Adrianus Johannes and Elly (van de Leijgraaf) N. BBA, Henley, Huis Ter Heide, The Netherlands, 1993; MBA, Cath. U., Nijmegen, The Netherlands, 1996. Cert. for medium knowledge of Polish lang, Internat. Lang. Ctr. Mktg. intern Unilever, Oss, The Netherlands, 1991, Monetar Sarl, Luxembourg, 1992-93; mktg. mgr. NCH Gmbh, Meppen, 1993-94; trainee Dataquest, San Jose, Calif., 1995; mktg. and sales mgr. MBC Europe b.v., Nijmegen, 1996-98; gen. mgr. ICS Polska Sp zoo, Poznań, Poland, 1998—; pres. Priapus, Zeist, The Netherlands, 1990—; bd. mem. Z.S.V. Istfiest, Zeist, 1992-93; mem. fin. com. NMHC, Nijmegen, 1997-98; spkr. in field. Mem. Lech Poznan, Poznań Internat. Club. Roman Catholic. Avocations: hockey, tennis, golf, skiing, sightseeing. Home: ul Sędziwoja 61/5, PL-61063 Poznń Poland Office: ICS Polska Sp zoo, ul Zb—szyńska 3, PL-60359 Poznań Poland

NIEPMANN, MICHAEL, molecular biologist; b. Niedersachsen, Germany, May 13, 1959. Diplom, U. Heidelberg, Germany, 1986, PhD, 1990. Scientist U. Heidelberg, 1986-90, U. Giessen, Germany, 1991—. Contbr. articles to profl. jours. E-mail: michael.niepmann@biochemie.med.uni-giessen.de. Office: Inst Biochemistry, Friedrichstrasse 24, Geissen 35392, Germany

NIERENBERG, NORMAN, urban land economist, retired state official; b. Chgo., May 8, 1919; s. Isadore Isaac and Sadie Sarah (Dorfman) N.; m. Nanette Joyce Fortgang, Feb. 9, 1950; children: Andrew Paul, Claudia Robin. AA, U. Chgo., 1939; AB, Calif. State Coll., L.A., 1952; MA, U. So. Calif., 1956. Lic. real estate broker, Calif.; cert. supr. and coll. instr., Calif. Right-of-way agt. Calif. Dept. Transp., L.A., 1951-61, 85-90; sr. agt. Calif. Dept. Transp., San Francisco, 1988-89; instr. UCLA, 1960-61, 67-75, 81-85; coord. continuing edn. in real estate U. Calif., Berkeley, 1961-64; coord. econ. benefits study Salton Sea, Calif. Dept. Water Resources, L.A., 1968-69; regional economist L.A. dist. CE, 1970-75, chief economist, 1981-85; regional economist Bd. Engrs. for Rivers and Harbors, Ft. Belvoir, Va., 1975-81; faculty resource person Oakland Project, Ford Found., U. Calif., Berkeley, 1962-64; project reviewer EPA, Washington, 1972-73. Editor: History of 82d Fighter Control Squadron, 1945; assoc. editor Right of Way Nat. Mag., 1952-55. Capt. USAAF, 1942-46, ETO, Lt. Col. USAFR ret. Mem. NEA, Am. Econ. Assn., Calif. Tchrs. Assn., Calif. Assn. Real Estate Tchrs. (bd. dirs. 1962), L.A. Coll. Tchrs. Assn., Ret. Officers Assn., Omicron Delta Epsilon. Democrat. Jewish. Home: Unit 4 21931 Burbank Blvd Woodland Hills CA 91367-6456

NIERENBERG, WILLIAM AARON, oceanography educator; b. N.Y.C., Feb. 13, 1919; s. Joseph and Minnie (Drucker) N.; m. Edith Meyerson, Nov. 21, 1941; children—Victoria Jean (Mrs. Tschinkel), Nicolas Clarke Eugene. Aaron Naumberg scholar, U. Paris, 1937-38; B.S., CCNY, 1939; M.A., Columbia U., 1942, Ph.D. (NRC predoctoral fellow), 1947. Tutor CCNY, 1939-42; sect. leader Manhattan Project, 1942-45; instr. physics Columbia U., 1946-48; asst. prof. physics U. Mich., 1948-50; assoc. prof. physics U. Calif. at Berkeley, 1950-53, prof., 1954-65; dir. Scripps Instn. Oceanography, 1965-86, dir. emeritus, 1986—; vice chancellor for marine scis. U. Calif. at San Diego, 1969-86; dir. Hudson Labs., Columbia, 1953-54; assoc. prof. U. Paris, 1960-62; asst. sec. gen. NATO for sci. affairs, 1960-62; spl. cons. Exec. Office Pres., 1958-60; sr. cons. White House Office Sci. and Tech. Policy, 1976-78. Contbr. papers to profl. jours. E.O. Lawrence lectr. Nat. Acad. Sci., 1958, Miller Found. fellow, 1957-59, Sloan Found. fellow, 1958, Fulbright fellow, 1960-61; mem. U.S. Nat. Commn. UNESCO, 1964-68, Calif. Adv. Com. on Marine and Coastal Resources, 1967-71; adviser-at-large U.S. Dept. State, 1968—; mem. Nat. Sci. Bd., 1972-78, 82-88, cons., 1988-89; chmn. USNC/PSA, NRC, 1988—; mem. Nat. Adv. Com. on Oceans and Atmosphere, 1971-77, chmn., 1971-75; mem. sci. and tech. adv.

Council Calif. Assembly; mem. adv. council NASA, 1978-83, chmn. adv. council, 1978-82. NATO Sr. Sci. fellow, 1969; Decorated officer Nat. Order of Merit France; recipient Golden Dolphin award Assn. Artistico Letteraria Internazionale, Disting. Pub. Service medal NASA, 1982, Delmer S. Fahrney medal The Franklin Inst., 1987, Compass award Marine Tech. Soc., 1975. Fellow Am. Phys. Soc. (coun., sec. Pacific Coast sect. 1955-64); mem. Am. Acad. Arts and Scis., NAE, NAS (coun. 1973—), Am. Philos. Soc., Sigma Xi (pres. 1981-82, Procter prize 1977). Home: 9494 La Jolla Farms Rd La Jolla CA 92037-1127 Office: U Calif Scripps Instn Oceanography 0221 La Jolla CA 92093-0221

NIERENGARTEN, JEAN-FRANÇOIS, chemist; b. Strasbourg, Alsace, France, Dec. 16, 1966; s. Jean-Marie and Violette (Lichtenauer) N.; m. Nathalié Solladié, July 19, 1996. Diploma in Biology, U. Louis Pasteur, Strasbourg, 1988, M in Biochemistry, 1990, PhD in Chemistry, 1994. Rschr. ETH-Zentrum, Zurich, 1994-96, IPCMS, Strasbourg, 1996—. Avocations: music, arts, sports, reading. Office: CNRS/IPCMS/GMO, 23 rue du Loess, Strasbourg 67037, France

NIESKENS, MART J., petroleum company official; b. Heerlen, Limburg, The Netherlands, Apr. 9, 1953; s. Gerard A. and Maria (Hundscheid) N.; m. Maria W. Bindels, Sept. 15, 1978. MSChemE, Tech. U., Eindhoven, The Netherlands, 1976. Sci. co-worker Inst. of Atomic and Molecular Physics, Amsterdam, The Netherlands, 1976-77; rsch. engr. Shell Rsch., Amsterdam, The Netherlands, 1977-87; sr. tech. svcs. engr. Shell Internat., The Hague, The Netherlands, 1987-91; sect. head process tech. Shell Singapore, 1991-95; tech. mgr. Equilon, Wood River, Ill., 1995-99; mgr. tech. svcs. Reliance Petroleum, Jamnagar, India, 1999-2000; bus. group mgr. Shell Global Solutions, Amsterdam, 2000—. Contbr. articles to profl. jours. Mem. Royal Dutch Inst. Engrs., Dutch Soc. Computers for Chem. Engrs. (sec.-treas. 1986-91). Roman Catholic. Avocations: cycling, swimming, scuba diving, tennis. Office: Shell Global Solutions, Badhuisweg 3, 1031 Amsterdam 361 140, The Netherlands

NIETO, JUAN MANUEL, emergency medicine physician; b. Alpine, Tex., Sept. 24, 1949; s. Edmundo Miguel and Socorro (Herrera) N.; BS, U. Notre Dame, 1970; MD, U. Colo., 1974; children: Ana Raquel, Cristina Marie. Intern, Los Angeles County, U. So. Calif. Med. Ctr., 1974-75; physician Community Health Found., Los Angeles, 1975-77, Emergency Dept. Physicians Med. Group, Marina Del Ray, Calif., 1977-78; resident in emergency medicine Denver Gen.-St. Anthony Hosp. Systems, 1978-80; mem. staff North Colo. Med. Center, Greeley, Colo., 1980-83; emergency physician, med. dir. emergency dept. Brackenridge Hosp., Austin, Tex., 1984-85; practice medicine, Austin, 1983—; emergency physician Emergency Physicians Affiliates, 1986-89; asst. prof. U. Tex. Health Sci. Ctr., San Antonio, 1994—; mem. planning com. Starflight Helicopter Air Transport, 1985; instr. advanced cardiac life support, 1977; bd. dirs. Nat. Chicano Health Orgn., 1971-74; advisor East Los Angeles Hypertension Screening Program, 1978; med. advisor Weld County Ambulance Service, 1980-83; med. dir. Air Life, 1980-83; med. dir. Alamo Heights Emergency Med. Svc., 1988-90, med. dir. AMR Ambulance, 1991-98. del. Colo. Med. Soc., 1983. Fellow Am. Coll. Emergency Physicians, Am. Acad. Emergency Medicine; mem. APHA, Am. Coll. Emergency Physicians, Tex. Med. Assn., Travis County Med. Soc., Nat. Hispanic Med. Assn., Amnesty Internat., Physicians for a Nat. Healthcare Program.

NIETO DIAZ, ANIBAL, obstetrician, gynecologist; b. Albacete, Spain, Jan. 24, 1959; s. Anibal and Nieves (Diaz) Nieto; m. MAria Serra, June 3, 1984; children: Laura, Anibal. MD, U. Murcia, Murcia, Spain, 1982; PhD, U. Alcala, Madrid, 1992. Med. resident Hosp. La Paz, Madrid, 1984-88; assoc. prof. U. Alcala, Alcala de Henares, Spain, 1990—; med. staff U. Hosp. Principe de Asturias, Madrid, Spain, 1988—. Contbr. articles to profl. jours. Recipient Laguna Serrano, Real Acad. Nat. de Medicina, Madrid, 1992, Marañon, Academia Medico Quirurgica Española, Madrid, 1992, F. Garcia Sicila, Revista Toko-Ginecologia Practica, Madrid, 1996. Mem. Sociedad Española de Ginecologia y Obstetricia (premio 1995), European Sch. Oncology, European Soc. Mastology. Roman Catholic. Avocations: travel, sports. Office: Hosp U Principe de Asturias, Ctra Alcala/Meco SN, 28805 Alcala de Henares Madrid, Spain

NIETO-GARCÍA, FERNANDO JAVIER, science educator; b. Linares, Spain, July 11, 1955; s. Fernando Nieto-Gutierrez and Isabel García-Muñoz; m. Mari Angeles Chacón-Guzmán, Nov. 13, 1982; children: Paula, Isabel. BSc, U. Granada, Spain, 1977, PhD, 1982. Cert. geologist. Tchr. Universitary Sch., Linares, 1977-78; fellow U. Granada, 1978-80, asst. lectr., 1981-86, lectr., 1986-2000, prof., 2000—. Referee: Internat. Mineral. Jour.; contbr. articles to profl. jours. Mem. Spanish Soc. Mineralogy, Geol. Soc. Spain, Sociedad Española de Arcillas. Avocations: reading, films, sports, traveling. Home: Av Andaluces 10 3 A, 18014 Granada Spain Office: Ins Andaluz Ciencias/Tierra, Av Fuentenueva s/n, 18002 Granada Spain

NIETO-ROIG, JUAN JOSE, mathematics educator; b. Madrid, Spain, Sept. 27, 1958; s. Ruperto Nieto and Maria Concepcion Roig; m. Angela Torres, July 13, 1985; children: Juan, Miriam, Miguel. MA, U. Santiago, Spain, 1980, PhD, 1983. Rsch. fellow U. Tex., Arlington, 1981-83; prof. U. Santiago, Spain, 1983-85, assoc. prof., 1985-90, prof., 1991—; mem. editl. bd. Nonlinear Studies and Differential Equations and Dynamical Systems. Office: U. Santiago de Compostela, Campus Sur, 15706 Santiago de C. Spain

NIEUW AMERONGEN, ARIE VAN, biochemist, educator, researcher; b. Veenendaal, Utrecht, The Netherlands, July 24, 1944; s. Gerrit Van and Hendrika Jacoba (Ee) N.; m. Cornelia Gerritje Van Den Dikkenberg, June 25, 1970; children: Gerard Peter, Cornelius Maarten, Hendrika Maria, Jannette Alinda, Gerdine Cornelia, Clara Cornelia, Matthilde Philippine, Jacobine Gertrude, Johanna Eleonora, Hendrik Johannes, Marinus Christian. MS, Vrije U., Amsterdam, The Netherlands, 1970, PhD, 1974. Asst. prof. Vrije U., Amsterdam, 1974-78, assoc. prof., 1978-90, prof. biochemistry, 1990—. Author: (monographs) Saliva and Salivary Glands, 1988, Saliva and Oral Health, 1994, Saliva and Dental Elements, 1999; contbr. numerous articles to profl. jours.; patentee on composition for protecting teeth, 1986, therapeutic composition for replacing and/or supplementing body fluids, 1995, antimicrobial peptides, 1999. Elder, Breukelen, The Netherlands, 1971—. Mem. Internat. Assn. for Dental Rsch., European Orgn. for Caries Rsch. Accord. Office: Free U Dept Oral Biochem, V D Boechorststraat 7, 1081 BT Amsterdam The Netherlands

NIEUWENHUYS, RUDOLF, retired neuroanatomy educator; b. Amsterdam, The Netherlands, June 11, 1927; s. Adam Hendrik and Marie Henriette (de Menthon Bake) N.; m. Aletta Maria Esselink, July 13, 1955; children: Elisabeth, Judith. MD, U. Amsterdam, 1955, PhD, 1960. Rsch. fellow Netherlands Inst. Brain Rsch., Amsterdam, 1954-68; reader in anatomy U. Nymegen, The Netherlands, 1968-69, prof. neuroanatomy, 1969-92, prof. emeritus, 1992—; rsch. assoc. dept. anatomy Case Western Res. U., Cleve., 1961-62. Author: Human Central Nervous System, 1978 (2 awards 1979), 3d edit., 1988, also Spanish, German, Chinese, Greek, Italian and Japanese edits., Chemoarchitecture of Brain, 1985, Central Nervous System of Vertebrates, 3 vols., 1998. 1st lt. M.C., Dutch Army, 1956-57. Named Knight Order of Dutch Lion, 1998; recipient medal Royal Netherlands Acad. Scis., 1998, C.U. Ariëns Kappers medal, 2000. Mem. Reformed Ch. Avocation: Roman and gothic art photography from the air. Home: Papehof 25, 1391 BD Abcoude The Netherlands

NIEUWSMA, MILTON JOHN, writer, journalist; b. Sioux Falls, S.D., Sept. 5, 1941; s. John and Jean (Potter) N.; BA, Hope Coll., Holland, Mich., 1963; postgrad. Wayne State U., 1963-65; MA, U. Ill., 1978; m. Marilee Gordon, Feb. 1, 1964; children: Jonathan, Gregory, Elizabeth. Pres. Trans Am. Syndicate, Inc., Chgo., 1988-97; vis. prof. Rutgers U., New Brunswick, N.J., 1990-95, St. Xavier U., Chgo., 1996-97. Author: Kinderlager, 1998; contbg. editor Chgo. Tribune, L.A. Times, others. Home: 2421 Central-Idlewood Beach Holland MI 49424-2277

NIEWIADOMSKA, EWA MARIA, plant physiologist, researcher; b. Cracow, Poland, Oct. 4, 1962; s. Zygmunt and Jadwiga N. MS, Agrl. Acad., Cracow, Poland, 1987; PhD, Inst. Botany, Polish Acad. Sci, Cracow, Poland, 1995. Asst. Dept. Plant Physiol., Polish Acad. Sci., Cracow, Poland, 1987-95, rschr., 1995—. Contbr. articles to profl. jours. Recipient Scholarship French Govt., 1996; Invited Royal Soc., Great Britain, 1995. Mem. Internat. Soc. for Free Radical Rsch. Avocations: travel, mountain climbing, skiing, music. E-mail address: E.Niewiadomska@zfr.pan.krakow.pl. Fax: (12)421-79-01. Home phone: (12)415-08-38. Office phone: (12)422-79-44. Office: Dept Plant Physiol, Slawkowska 17, Cracow 31-016, Poland

NIEWIAROWSKI, STEFAN, physiology educator, biomedical research scientist; b. Warsaw, Poland, Dec. 4, 1926; came to U.S., 1972, naturalized, 1978; s. Marian and Janina (Sledzinska) N.; m. Marta Ciswicka (div. 1974); children: Agata, Tomasz; m. Jeanette P. Nichols, June 1995. MD, Warsaw U., 1952, PhD, 1960, Dozent, 1961; Hon. Doctorate, Bialystok U. Med. Sch., Warsaw, Poland, 1993. Lic. physician, Pa.; cert. Ednl. Coun. Fgn. Med. Grads. Intern, med. resident Inst. Hematology, Warsaw, 1951-54; rsch. fellow, rsch. assoc. dept. physiol. chemistry Warsaw U. Med. Sch., 1948-54; rsch. assoc., sr. rsch. assoc. Lab. Clin. Biochemistry, Inst. Hematology, Warsaw, 1951-61; physician in charge Outpatient Dept. for Hemophiliacs, Warsaw, 1957-61; head dept., prof. physiol. chemistry Med. Sch., Bialystok, Poland, 1961-68; assoc. prof. pahtology dept. pathology McMaster U., Hamilton, Ont., Can., 1970-72; rsch. prof. medicine, head coagulation sect. Specialized Ctr. Thrombosis Rsch., Temple U. Sch. Medicine, Phila., 1972-78; prof. physiology Temple U. Sch. Medicine, Phila., 1975—, prof. physiology Thrombosis Rsch. Ctr., 1978—; cons. dept. infectious diseases Warsaw U. Med. Sch., 1954-60; vis. scientist Centre Nat. de Transfusion Sanguine, Paris, 1959; cons. dept. pediatrics Warsaw U. Med. Sch., 1961-65; vis. scientist Vascular Lab., Lemeul Shattuck Hosp., Boston, 1965, 68-70; vis. prof. medicine Tufts U. Sch. Medicine, Boston, 1968-70; dir. Blood Components Devel. Lab., Hamilton Red Cross and McMaster U., 1971-72; mem. sr. coun. Internat. Com. on Haemostatis and Thrombosis, 1973—; mem. NIH rsch. rev. coms., 1975—. Editor Thrombosis Rsch., 1972-80; mem. editl. com. Procs. of Soc. of Exptl. Biology and Medicine, 1980-82, mem. editl. bd., 1980—; reviewer Jour. Clin. Investigation, Jour. Lab. and Clin. Medicine, Blood, Biochimica et Biophysica Acta, Archives of Biochemistry and Biophysics, Jour. Biol. Chemistry, Am. Jour. Physiology; contbr. more than 300 articles in the field of blood coagulation, platelet physiology and cell adhesion. Ont. Heart Found. fellow, 1970-71; recipient Jurzykowski Found. award, 1990, rsch. awards NIH, 1972—. Mem. Internat. Soc. Hematology, Internat. Soc. Thrombosis and Hemostasis, Am. Physiology Soc., Am. Soc. Hematology, Coun. of Thrombosis of Am. Heart Assn., Soc. Exptl. Biology and Medicine, Polish Inst. Arts and Scis. in Am., Am. Soc. Exptl. Pathology, Polish Am. Med. Soc. (hon.). Achievements include patent for trigramin a platelet aggregation inhibiting polypeptide. Home: 445 S Woodbine Ave Narberth PA 19072-2027 Office: Temple U Sch Medicine 3400 N Broad St Philadelphia PA 19140-5104

NIGAM, PRAKASH KUMAR, historian, consultant; b. Bhainsdahi, India, Oct. 10, 1923; s. Har Prasad and Nanki Devi N.; m. Kanta Darbari, Feb. 16, 1953; children: Chitra, Ravi Kumar, Dilip Kumar. BS, Nagpur U., India, 1944; BS in Electrical Engring., U. Wisc., Madison, 1948. Cert. profl. engr. Electrical engr./asst. supr. Tata Electric, Bombay, India, 1950-60; chief power engr. H.E.C., Ranchi, India, 1960-68; electrical engr. various companies, U.S., 1968-81; cons. Acro Corp., Livonia, Mich., 1983—, ADSC, Ann Arbor, Mich., 1985—. Author: Reflections on The World History in the 20th Century, 2000. Recipient scholarship, J.N. Tata Endowment, India, 1946. Mem. Lions Club, Rotary Internat. Club. Avocations: reading, writing, public speaking, chess, bridge. Phone: 91 755-542805. Home: Lalghati, 43/44 Vijaynagar Colony, Lalghati Bhopal 462032, India

NIGGEBRUGGE, ARTHUR HENRI PHILIPS, surgeon; b. Amsterdam, Netherlands, Apr. 17, 1960; s. Philip Maurits Theodoor and Ria Petronella (Schouten) N.; m. Annemieke Janssen, June 3, 1987; children: Ruben, Sarah, David. MD, Leiden (Netherlands) U., 1989, PhD, 1999, Surgeon, 1996. Gen. surgeon Leyenburg Hosp., The Hague, 1993-96; trauma surgeon Leiden U. Med. Ctr., 1997-98; cons. Bronovo Hosp., The Hague, 1998—; trauma instr. ATLS, Tilburg, Netherlands, 1996—. Author: Abdominal Wound Closure, 1999, also articles. Lt. Dutch Air Force, 1979-82. Mem. Gastroenterology Surgery Soc., Trauma Surgery Soc., Lung Surgery Soc. Evangelical. Avocations: chess, squash, skiing, water sports. Home: Drontermeerlaan 25, 2317 GH Leiden Netherlands Office: Bronovo Hosp, Bronovolaan 5, 2597 AX The Hague Netherlands

NIGGEMAN, ELISABETH, library director; b. Dortmund, Germany, Apr. 2, 1954. Diploma in biology, Ruhr U., Bochum, 1978, diploma in English, 1985, PhD in Biology, 1982. Head acquisition dept. German Ctrl. Libr. for Medicine, Cologne, 1987-89; head cataloguing and subject indexing dept., subject special Univ. and State Libr. of Heinrich Heine U., Düsseldorf, 1989-94, dir., 1994-99; dir. gen. Nat. Libr. Germany, Frankfurt, 1999—; chair union conf. of univ. libr. ctr. of North Rhine Westfalia, Cologne, 1995-99, mem. libr. com. Deutsche Forschungsgemeinschaft, 1998—; initiator book sponsorship campaign, North Rhine Westfalia. Editor: Zeitschrift für Bibliothekswesen und Bibliographie, Libri: Internat. Jour. Librs. and Info. Scis. Mem. Conf. European Nat. Librs., Conf. Dirs. Nat. Librs., Libr. Adv. Bd. Stiftung Preussischer Kulturbesitz. Office: Die Deutsche Bibliothek, Adickesallee 1, D-60322 Frankfurt Germany

NIGHOSKAR, MAHESH VISHNU, language educator; b. Varanasi, India, July 1, 1942; s. Vishnu Laxman and Jayashree (Mahesh) N.; Jayashree V. Paturkar, Nov. 20, 1964; children: Madhavi, Manisha. BA, Harishchandra Degree Coll., Varanasi, 1961; MA, Banaras Hindu U., Varanasi, 1963; PhD, Bombay U., 1979. Read. C.S.'s Patkar Coll., Bombay, 1964—; mem. faculty arts Bombay U. Contbr. article to Bombay Hindi mag. Hindu. Avocations: travel, reading in Marathi, Hindi and English. Home: 22/27 Jawahar Nagar, Goregaon (West), Bombay 400 062, India Office: CS's Patkar Coll, SV Rd Goregaon (W), Bombay 62, India

NIGHTINGALE, STEPHEN JAMES, electronics engineer, consultant; b. Redhill, Surrey, Eng., May 7, 1949; s. Douglas Arthur and Margaret Elizabeth (Ballantyne) N.; m. Jill Elizabeth Harris, June 28, 1975; children: Julia Margaret, Philip James, Elizabeth Shirley Louise. Ordinary Nat. Cert., Redhill Tech. Coll., 1968; diploma in elec. engring., South Bank U., London, 1974; PhD, Kent U., Canterbury, Eng., 1980. Chartered engr. Engring. Coun. Eng., European engr. FEANI; chartered physicist Inst. Physics (London). Rsch. scientist Philips Rsch. Labs., Redhill, 1967-77, 78-82, Philips Rsch. Lab., Hamburg, Germany, 1977-78; sr. devel. engr., tech. mgr. GE, Syracuse, N.Y., 1982-86; tech. mgr., MMIC tech. cons. radar divsn. THORN EMI Electronics, Hayes, Eng., 1986-88; mgr. radiation dept., tech. mgr. THORN EMI Electronics, Hayes and Crawley, Eng., 1988-96; mgr. microwave dept., RF components dept. ERA Tech. Ltd., Leatherhead, Eng., 1996-98; sr. tech. exec., bus. devel. mgr. RF Tech. Leatherhead, England, 1998—; dir., European Microwave Assn., 1998—, vis. prof. dept electronic and elec. engring. U. Leeds, Eng., 1995—; indsl. adv. Elec. Engring. Lab., U. Kent, 1996—; peer reviwer, assessor Engring. and Phys. Scis. Rsch. Coun., Info. Tech.-Comm. Coll., 1997—; advisor to U.K. Dept. Trade and Industry Tech. Foresight Programme. Author: Millimetre Wave Radiometry, 1980, MMIC Design, 1995; contbr. over 45 sci. articles to numerous profl. pubs.; invited lectr. internat. confs. External examiner U. Leeds, U. Kent, King's Coll., London, 1991—; judge problem solving and young engrs. competitions, Greater London, 1991—; spkr. local secondary schs., Eng., 1986—; founder Redhill Redstone Rotary Club, 1990—. Redhill Tech. Coll. Feynman prize for physics, 1968, General Electric Inventors Awd. for patents, 1983, Recipient Chmn. of Judges award for excellence in engring. Standing Conf. on Schs., Sci. and Tech., London, 1995. Fellow Inst. Elec. Engrs. Eng. (chmn. bd. electronics & comm. divsn. 1997-98); mem. IEEE (sr.), European Microwave Assn. (dir. 1998—). Anglican. Achievements include patents in the field of microwave circuit and systems design; research and development in microwave theory and techniques, electron devices and millimeter wave devices; development and production of RF, microwave and optoelectronic components and subsystems for communications markets. Fax: 0 1372 367138. E-mail: steve.nightingale@era.co.uk. Home: Sandyhills, 131 Blackborough Rd, Reigate RH2 7DA, England Office: ERA Tech Ltd, Cleeve Rd, Leatherhead, Leatherhead Surrey KT22 7SA, England

NIGRO, GIOVANNI, physician, researcher, medical educator; b. Naples, Campania, Italy, Apr. 24, 1931; s. Vincenzo and Angela Maria (Ruggiero) N.; m. Maria Rosaria Colella. MD, U. Naples, 1954, Prof. Medicine, 1961; Prof. (hon.), U. Moscow, 1996, U. Cairo, 1997. Prof. U. Naples, 1969—, head dept., 1998—. Author: Lineamenti di Cardiomiologia, 1977, Ecocardiografia, 1981, Fisiopatologia e Clinica del Cuore, 1987. Recipient Gaetano Conte prize, 1993. Mem. Mediterranean Soc. Myology (pres. 1993), World Muscle Soc. (treas. 1995). Home: Viale dei Pini, 80131 Naples Campania, Italy Office: U Policlinico, P Miraglia 2, 80138 Naples Campania, Italy

NIHOUL, PAUL LOUIS, law educator; b. Brussels, Jan. 26, 1963; s. Jules and Anne-Marie (Henry) N.; m. Valerie Rosoux. Lic. in philosophy and letters, U. Catholique de Louvain, Belgium, 1984, lic. in law, 1988, LLD, 1998; LLM, Harvard U., 1989. Bar: N.Y. Atty., counselor at law Cleary Gottlieb Steen & Hamilton, N.Y., 1989-90; counselor Cabinet of Min. Fin., Brussels, Belgium, 1990-91; referendaire Ct. of Justice of European Cmtys., Luxembourg, 1991-95; dir. Telecom Unit, Belgium, 1995—; prof. law U. Catholique de Louvain, 1997—; bd. dirs. Info., U.K. Author: European Telecommunications Law, 1999; editor: Broadcasting and Telecommunications Networks Under European Law, 1999, The Convergence Between Telecommunications and Other Media, 1998; editor Jour. des Tribunaux Droit Europeen, 1998; editor-in-chief JTDE/Larcier, 1995—; assoc. editor Harvard Internat. Law Jour., 1988-89. Pres. Harvard Law Sch. Grad. Student Assn., 1988-89; founder, pres. Linkus, Brussels, 1997; founding mem., pres. Campagnol, Rixensart, Belgium, 1985-88. Fulbright scholar, 1988-90, Nijenrode fellow, 1989; recipient Salanang award Consejo Superior de Investigaciones Scientificas, Spain, 1985. Mem. Internat. Telecomms. Soc. Avocations: literature, music, trekking. Home: Rue Lannoy 15/4, 1050 Brussels Belgium Office: U Catholique de Louvain, Place Montesquieu 2, 1348 Louvain-La-Neuve Belgium

NIHOYANNOPOULOS, PETROS, cardiologist, consultant; b. Athens, Greece, Sept. 8, 1952; s. John and Myrto (Grigoriadou) N.; m. Gillian Clare Smith, Aug. 2, 1986; children: Leonidas, Alexander. Grad., Protypon Lykion Athinon, Athens, 1970; MD, Louis Pasteur U., Strasbourg, France, 1978. Med. diplomate 1978. Intern Naval & Vets. Hosp., Crete, Greece, 1980-81, Athens, 1981-82; rsch. fellow Hammersmith Hosp., London, 1982-84, cardiology registrar, 1984-86, sr. registrar, 1986-88, lectr., 1988-90; sr. lectr., cons. cardiologist, 1990-99, reader in cardiology, 1999—; Contbr. articles to profl. jours. Fellow Am. Coll. Cardiology, Am. Heart Assn., European Soc. Cardiology; mem. Helenic Soc. Cardiology, Brit. Cardiac Soc. Home: 18 Endlesham Rd, London SW12 8JU, England Office: Hammersmith Hosp Cardiology Dep, Du Cane Rd, London W12 0HS, England

NII, SHIRO, college executive, virology educator; b. Naruto, Tokushima, Japan, Jan. 12, 1932; parents Atsushi and Toyo (Toyota) N.; m. Etsuko Tada, Mar. 29, 1960; children: Satoshi, Keiko Maeda, Yoshiko Fujita. MD, Osaka (Japan) U., 1956, PhD, 1961. Lic. physician. Rsch. assoc. Rsch. Inst. for Microbial Diseases Osaka U., 1961-66, assoc. prof. Rsch. Inst. for Microbial Diseases, 1966-78; prof. Okayama (Japan) U. Med. Sch., 1978-97, dean, 1993-95; prof. Kawasaki Coll. Allied Health Professions, Kurashiki, Japan, 1997-98; pres. Niimi (Japan) Coll., 1998—; prof. emeritus Okayama U., 1997—; councilor Okayama U., 1990-92; hon. prof. Jiangxi (China) Med. Coll., 1993; guest prof. Dalian (China) Med. Coll., 1994; expert adviser Sci. and Tech. Com., 1994; pres. Univ. and Coll. Assn. Okayama Prefecture, 1995, 43d Ann. Meeting of Japanese Virologists, 1995. Co-author: (book) Virology, 1997; editor, co-author: (book) Essentials of Microbiology, 1983, 98; contbr. articles to sci. jours. Mem. Japanese Assn. for Infectious Diseases (auditor 1995-98), Niimi Rotary Club (hon.). Avocations: reading, baseball, walking. Home: 372-1-206 Hama, 703-8256 Okayama Japan Office: Niimi Coll, 1263-2 Nishigata, 718-8585 Niimi Okayama, Japan

NII-AMON-KOTEI, DAVID, medical educator, surgeon, consultant, dean; b. LA, Accra, Ghana, Jan. 1, 1939; s. Sampson Amon Kotey and Comfort Koteitso Dsane; m. Angelika Maria Schmitz; children: Flora, David Nii-quaye, Jean, Beatrice, Adei. MD, Friedrich Wilhelm U., Bonn, Germany, 1969, D in Medicine, 1970. Rsch. asst. Inst. Biophysics, U. Bonn, 1965-69; rsch. fellow Inst. Parasitology, U. Bonn, 1970-72; resident surgery Kreiskrankenhaus, Waldbrol, Germany, 1978-80; head dept. physiology UST SMS, Kumasi, Ghana, 1985-93; head dept. surgery UST SMS, Kumasi, 1993-96; dean Sch. Medicine and Health Scis., Tamale, Ghana, 1997—; assoc. prof. surgery Sch. Med. Sci. UST, Kumasi, 1996, Sch. Medicine and Health Sci., Tamale, 1997. Scholar DAAD, Bonn, 1963-69; fellow DAAD, Bonn, 1983; fellow Internat. Inst. for Theoretical Physics Triest. Fellow West African Coll. Surgeons; mem. German Assn. Tropical Surgery, Soc. Med. Physics (organizing sec. 1986), Ghana Surg. Rsch. Soc., Med. and Dental Coun. Avocation: oil painting. Home: UST Post Office, PO Box 615, Kumasi Ghana Office: Sch Medicine & Health Scis, Univ for Devel, Kumasi Ghana

NIINI, HEIKKI ILMARI, geologist, educator; b. Helsinki, Feb. 4, 1937; s. Eino M. and Aune (Kyöstilä) N.; m. Sirkka Pylvänäinen, 1961; children: Suvi, Ilkka, Yrjö. MS, U. Helsinki, 1961, PhD, 1968. Asst. Helsinki U. Tech., 1961-65, prof. econ. geology, head lab. engring. geology/geophysics, 1982-2000; geologist Nat. Bd. Pub. Rds. and Waterworks, Helsinki, 1965-69; sr. fellow Acad. Finland, Helsinki, 1969-75, prin. rsch. scientist, 1975-77; project leader Geol. Survey Finland, Espoo, 1977-81; cons. IAEA, 1978-82; project evaluator, chmn. Finnish Ministry for Fgn. Affairs, Nairobi, Kenya, 1987; project evaluator Nordic Coun. Mins., Copenhagen, 1991-95; engring. geology sect. head Rt. Selection of 120-km Bedrock Tunnel, Päijänne-Helsinki Water Supply Tunnel, 1965-69; chmn. local organizing com. of internat. conf. IAEA/OECD Underground Disposal of Radioactive Wastes, 1979. Co-editor: Earth and Rock Construction, 1976, (UNESCO Casebook) Methods of Computation of Quantitative Changes in the Hydrological Regime, 1980; contbr. more than 300 articles to profl. jours. Recipient Fountain Pen award Suomen Kuvalehti (Finnish mag.), 1955. Mem. Engring.-Geol. Soc. Finland (chmn. 1972-73, 79-81), Internat. Assn. Engring. Geology (exec. com. 1972-78), Geol. Soc. Finland (pres. 1990). Office: Engring Geology & Geophysic, PO Box 6200, FIN02015 Hut Finland

NIINILUOTO, ILKKA MAUNU OLAVI, philosophy educator; b. Helsinki, Finland, Mar. 12, 1946; s. Yrjö Eemil and Marja Annikki (Linturi) N.; m. Ritva Tuulikki Pelkonen, Jan. 11, 1973; children: Petro, Riikka-Maria, Atro. BS, U. Helsinki, 1967, MS, 1968, Lic. of Philosophy, 1971, PhD, 1974. Teaching asst. U. Helsinki, 1969-71, docent in philosophy, 1974-81, assoc. prof. math., 1975-81, prof. theoretical philosophy, 1981—; rsch. asst. Acad. Finland, Helsinki, 1971-73; mem. Rsch. Coun. for Humanities, Acad. Finland, 1974-79; dean Faculty of Arts U. Helsinki, 1990-91, 93-94, vice-rector, 1998—. Author: Theoretical Concepts and Hypothetico-Inductive Inference, 1973, Is Science Progressive?, 1984, Truthlikeness, 1987, Critical Scientific Realism, 1999; editor: Synthese, Dordrecht, Netherlands, 1977-79, Acta Philosophica Fennica, Helsinki, 1980—; contbr. articles to profl. jours. and textbooks. Mem. governing bd. Internat. Fedn. Philos. Socs., 1985-88, 98—, Finnish Cultural Found., Helsinki, 1985-94, chmn., 1992-94; pres. Finnish Soc. for Sci. Studies, 1985-86. Recipient Pub. Info. award, U. Helsinki, 1986, Chydenius award, Chydenius Found., Kokkola, Finland, 1990. Mem. Philos. Soc. Finland (pres. 1975—), Philosophy of Sci. Assn., Assn. for Symbolic Logic, Brit. Soc. for Philosophy of Sci., Charles Pierce Soc., Soc. for Social Study of Sci., Soc. for Philosophy and Tech. Home: Maria Jotunintie 6 A 2, 00400 Helsinki Finland Office: U Helsinki, Unioninkatu 40 B, 00170 Helsinki Finland

NIINISTÖ, SAULI, Finnish government official; b. Salo, Aug. 24, 1948; s. Väinö and Niinistö and Hilkka Helena Heimo; m. Marja-Leena Alanko, 1974 (dec. 1995); children: Nuutti, Matias. LLM, U. Turku, 1974. Sr. sec. Turku Ct. Appeal, 1976-87, appeal ct. justice, 1994-95; pvt. practice Salo, 1978-88; dep. prime min., 1995—, min. of justice, 1995-96; min. of fin. Govt. of Finland, Helsinki, 1996—; mem. Grand Com., 1987-90, Com. Constl. Law, 1987-90, 93-94, Finnish Delegation to Nordic Coun., 1989-93, Salo City Coun., 1977-92, City Bd., 1977-88; chmn. City Coun., 1989-92, Parliament Coun. Bank of Finland, 1995; parliamentary trustee Bank of Finland, 1995; mem. supervisory bd. Valmet Corp., 1993-94, Postipankki, 1991-93. Mem. exec. bd. Nat. Coalition Party, 1993-94; chmn. Kokoomus, 1994—. With Mil. Mem. European Dem. Union (chmn. 1998—). Office: Min of Finance, PO Box 28, FIN00023 Government Finland

NIIT, TOOMAS, psychologist, educator; b. Tartu, Estonia, June 7, 1953; s. Heldur and Ellen (Hiob) N.; m. Helle Kalliver, Dec. 15, 1973 (div. 1991); children: Kaisa-Kitri, Eeva-Liisa, Madli-Maria, Hanna-Maarja; m. Kadi

Liik, Aug. 1, 1991; 1 child, Öösike. Diploma in psychology, Tartu (Estonia) State U., 1976; MSc in Psychology, Tallinn (Estonia) U. of Ednl. Scis., 1993. Rsch. psychologist Inst. History Estonian Acad. Scis., Tallinn, 1976-88, rsch. psychologist Inst. Philosophy Sociology and Law, 1989-93; assoc. to prof. dept. psychology Tallinn U. Ednl. Scis., 1993—, assoc. dean, fac. of social scis., 1993-99, chmn. dept. psychology, 1994-99; assoc. prof. U. Tartu, 1994-98; project coord. European Commn. PHARE (Tempus). Author: Handbook of Environmental Psychology, 1987; editor, author: Environmental Conditions for Community Development, 1989, Identity, Freedom, Values & Memory: Proceedings of the 2d International Baltic Psychology Conf., 1996; editor: Environment & Social Development, 1991; mem. editl. bd. Jour. Environ. Psychology, 1981—, European Psychologist, 1996—. Nordic Coun. of Minsters scholar Danish Bldg. Rsch. Inst., 1991-92, U. Oslo, 1993, U. Tampere, Finland, 1993, European Coun. U. Kent, Canterbury, Eng., 1994, U. Iceland, 1995. Mem. APA (affiliate), Union Estonian Psychologists (v.p. 1990-94, 97—; pres. 1995-97), Internat. Assn. Applied Psychology, Internat. Assoc. for People - Environment Studies (bd. mem. 1994-96), Internat. Assn. for Cross-Cultural Psychology, Soc. for Personality and Social Psychology, European Network for Housing Rsch. Avocation: collecting beer cans and labels. Office: Tallinn U Ednl Scis, Narva Rd 25, EE-10120 Tallinn Estonia

NIJBOER, JOHANNES FREDRIKUS, law educator, judge; b. Ysselmuiden, The Netherlands, June 22, 1951; s. Albert and Johanna Elisa (Vosjan) N.; m. Janneke Eppinga (div. 1983); 1 child, Boudewijn; life ptnr. Katy De Kogel; 1 child, Anne. MA in Law, Free U., Amsterdam, The Netherlands; PhD in Law, U. Leiden, The Netherlands, 1982. Admitted to profl. bench 1988. Tchr. Coll. Calvyn, Kampen, 1973-76; asst. prof. U. Leiden, 1976-84, prof., 1984—; dir. Internat. Network for Rsch. on Evidence and Procedure, Amsterdam, 1992—; justice Ct. of Appeals, Amsterdam, 1988—; cons. Coun. Europe, Strassburg, 1992—. Author: Strafrechtelijk bewijsrecht, 1986, 97, Proof and Criminal Justice Systems, 1995, De doolhof van de Nederlandse strafwetgeving, 1987. Adv. bd. 21st Century Trust. Mem. Soc. for Reform of Criminal Law (dir. 1993—), Assn. Internat. de Droit Penal. Office: U Leiden, NL 2300 Leiden The Netherlands

NIJEVITCH, ALEXANDER ALBERTOVICH, pediatrician, researcher; b. Ufa, Bashkortostan, USSR, Sept. 15, 1962; s. Albert Vasiljevich and Zakhida Mullajarovna (Sufijarova) N.; m. Valentina Vladimirovna Loguinovskaja; 1 child, Natalia. Student, Bashkir State Med. Inst., Ufa, 1986, MD, 1996, PhD in Medicine, 1996. Physician Children's Rep. Hosp., Ufa, 1987; cons. Ufa Emergency Hosp., 1994-98. Patentee in field. Mem. Russian Helicobacter Pylori Study Group. Avocations: classical and jazz music. Home: PO Box 4894, 450057 Ufa Russia

NIJNENS, FRANS ANDREAS MARIA, marketing executive; b. Eindhoven, The Netherlands, Dec. 10, 1947; s. Frans C. and Madeleine H. (Spaninks) N.; m. Lies Roos, Sept. 14, 1974; children: Marjol, Xander. BA in Bus. Adminstrn., Nat. Inst. Bus., The Netherlands, 1972; MBA in Mktg., Netherlands Inst. for Mktg., 1976. Export mgr. Eurolicht, Utrecht, The Netherlands, 1972-75; mktg. mgr. Polar's Frutal Works, Amersfoort, The Netherlands, 1975-81; sales mgr. Internat. Flavors and Fragrances, Hilversum, The Netherlands, 1981-82; gen. mgr. Internat. Flavors and Fragrances, Jakarta, Indonesia, 1987-93; area mgr. Internat. Flavors and Fragrances, Singapore, 1993—. Avocations: tennis, hockey, running. Office: IFF Asia-Pacific LKN Bldg, 135 Cecil St #11-03, Singapore 069536, Singapore

NIKAIDO, HUKUKANE, economics researcher, educator; b. Tokyo, June 28, 1923; s. Michinosuke and Yone (Kanesaka) N.; m. Chisato Tange, Oct. 29, 1957; children: Masako, Kazuko. Bs, U. Tokyo, 1949, DSc, 1961. Asst., assoc. prof. Tokyo Coll. Sci., 1950-57; assoc. prof. to prof. Osaka U., Toyonaka, Japan, 1957-69; prof. Hitotsubashi U., Tokyo, 1969-83, prof. emeritus, 1998—; prof. U. Tsukuba, Japan, 1983-87; prof. Tokyo Internat. U., Kawagoe, Japan, 1987-97, prof. emeritus, 1997—. Author: Convex Structures and Economic Theory, 1968, Monopolistic Competition and Effective Demand, 1975, Prices, Cycles and Growth, 1996. Anti-aircraft artillery Japanese Army, 1945. Fellow Econometric Soc.; mem. Japan Econs. Assn. (pres. 1978-79). Home: 4-23-11 Nakaarai, Tokorozawa Saitama-ken 359-0041, Japan

NIKANDROV, VITALY NIKOLAEVICH, biochemist; b. Lyda, Grodno, Belarus, Aug. 4, 1949; s. Nicholas Simonovich and Tamara Gregorevna (Bogomolova) N.; m. Nelly Semyonovna Pyzhova, Dec. 10, 1977; children: Andrew, Nicholas. MDV, Vitebsk Acad. Vet. Medicine, 1971; PhD, Byelorussian Vet. Rsch. Inst., 1975; DSc (hon.), P. Lumumba U., 1989. Rschr. Byelorussian Resh. Inst. Epidemiology and Microbiology, Minsk, Belarus, 1975-78; head biochemistry lab. Byelorussian Resh. Inst. Epidemiology and Microbiology, Minsk, 1978—, assoc. prof., 1981-93, prof., 1993—; head lab. regulatory proteins and peptides Inst. Physiology Nat. Acad. Scis., Belarus, 1998—. Editor: Enzymology of Thrombolysis and Streptokinase, 1982; inventor in field; contbr. articles to profl. jours. Mem. Belorussian Biochem. Soc. (bd. dirs.), N.Y. Acad. Scis., European Peptide Soc., Belorussian Physiol. Soc. Office: Byelorussian Rsch Inst, K Zetkin str 4, 220050 Minsk Belarus

NIKHILESWARANANDA, SWAMI, editor; b. Rajkot, India, Sept. 9, 1948. B in Chem. Engring., Ravishanker U., 1970. From joint editor to editor Sri Ramakrishna Jyot-Math and Mission, Rajkot, India, 1989—. Avocations: lecturing, pen pals, counseling, serving the poor. Home: Ramakrishna Mission Vivekananda Meml, Opp. Duleep Cricket School, Swami Vivekananada Marg Porbandar 360 575, India Office: Ramakrishna Mission, PO Belur Math, Howrah 711 202, India

NIKIFOROV, ALEXANDER YURY, physicist, educator; b. Moscow, June 24, 1961; s. Yury and Margorita (Ershova) N.; m. Elena Kobiseva, Apr. 14, 1984; 1 child, Anna. BSc, Moscow Engring. Physics Inst., 1984, PhD, 1992. From engr. to assoc. prof. Moscow Engring. Physics Inst., 1984—; pres. SPELS, Moscow, 1992—. Co-author: Radiation Effects in CMOS IC; contbr. articles to profl. jours. Mem. (sr.) IEEE. Office: SPELS, 31 Kashirskoe Shosse, 115409 Moscow Russia

NIKIFOROV, ALEXEI SERGEEVICH, acoustician; b. Leningrad, USSR, Mar. 28, 1927; s. Sergei Alexeevich and Alexandra Vasilievna (Rogovastova) N.; m. Zoya Davidovna Bogen, Nov. 25, 1953; 1 child, Sergei Alexeevich. Technician, Shipbldg. Secondary Tech. Sch., Leningrad, 1947; engr., Electrotech. Inst., Leningrad, 1954; PhD, Krylov Rsch. Inst., Leningrad, 1962, DSc, 1971. Cert. in engring. Bookbinder Designers' Office, Kazan, USSR, 1942-43; technician Iceberg Designers' Office, Leningrad, 1947-48; engr. Krylov Rsch. Inst., Leningrad, 1954-61; head of lab. Krylov Rsch. Inst., St. Petersburg, 1961-92, prin. sci. worker, 1992—; prof. Marine Tech. U., Leningrad, 1968-75; expert Highest Certifying Commn. of USSR, Moscow, 1976-86; cons. SC High-Speed Rwys., St. Petersburg, 1995-97. Author: (books) Vibro-Isolation in Ships, 1975, Vibro-Damping in Ships, 1979, Acoustical Design of Ships, 1990; editor: (jour.) Tech. Acoustics, 1992—; contbr. articles to profl. jours. Decorated Order of Badge of Honor, Govt. of USSR, 1975, Order of Friendship Between Peoples, 1984. Mem. East-European Acoustical Assn. (pres. 1992—), Acoustical Soc. Am., Audio Engring. Soc., Acoustical Soc. Japan, Acoustical Soc. Russia. Avocation: collecting Mozart records. Home: Ave Kosmonavtov 19-2-93, 196211 Saint Petersburg Russia Office: Krylov Shipbldg Rsch Inst, Moscow Shosse 44, 196158 Saint Petersburg Russia

NIKIFOROV, VICTOR SERGEEVICH, museum director; b. Odessa, Ukraine, May 3, 1957; s. Sergei Petrovich and Tamara Nikolayvna (Pavlova) N.; m. Irina Anatolievna Kaminskaya, July 15, 1983; 1 child, Anastasia. Student, Odessa State U., 1974-79. Curator ancient art dept. Odessa Mus. Western & Eastern Art, 1979-85, dept. dir., 1987, dir., 1994—; inspector Dept. Culture Odessa Region, 1985-87. Co-author: Odessa Museum of Western and Oriental Art, 1988; editor: Odessa Museum of Western and Eastern Art, 1984; script writer Odessa Mus. Western and Eastern Art Video Film, 1998. Home: 17 Troitskaya, 65011 Odessa Ukraine Office: Mus Western & Eastern Art, 9 Pushkinskaya, 65026 Odessa Ukraine

NIKIFOROV, VICTOR VASILIEVICH, chemist, educator; b. Krasnaya Polyana, Russia, Jan. 15, 1948; s. Vasiliy Vasilievich and Clavdia Victorovna (Chebotaryova) N. Chemist, Saratov State Univ., Saratov, Russia, 1973; cand. of chemistry, Ural Univ., Ekaterinburg, Russia, 1993. Engr. Saratov State Univ., 1973, Chemical Plant, Balakovo, Russia, 1973-75, Geological Expedition 31, Kalach, Russia, 1975-76; rsch. worker Inst. of Tech., Balakovo, Russia, 1976—. Contbr. articles to profl. jours. Recipient grant Internat. Sci. Found., 1994. Mem. N.Y. Acad. Scis. Avocations: touring in mountains, photography. Office: Inst of Tech, Ul Chapayeva 140, 413800 Balakovo GSP Russia

NIKITA, KONSTANTINA S., electrical engineer, educator; b. Tripolis, Greece, Aug. 20, 1963; d. Spilios and Kostoula (Nikolopoulou) N.; m. Ilias A. Angelikas, July 20, 1995. PhD, Nat. Tech. U. Athens, 1990; MD, U. Athens, 1993. From researcher to asst. prof. Nat. Tech. U. Athens, 1990—. Mem. IEEE, Med. Assn. Athens, Hellenic Biomed. Engring. Soc., Tech. Chamber Greece. Avocations: concerts, movies, traveling, skiing. Office: Nat Tech U Athens, Iroon Polytechniou 9, 15773 Athens Greece

NIKITENKO, VLADIMIR ALEXANDROVICH, physics educator, researcher; b. Moscow, Jan. 28, 1946; s. Alexandr Sidorovich and Valentina Pavlovna (Gorianova) N.; m. Natalya Glebovna Stoyukhina, July 19, 1969; 1 child, Elena. Bachelor, Moscow Power Engring. Inst., 1970, Master Phys. and Math. Scis., 1975, D of Phys. and Math. Scis., 1988. Asst. Moscow Railway U. (MIIT), 1975-79, assoc. prof., 1979-88, prof., 1988-93, head dept. physics, 1993—. Author: Zinc Oxide. Production and Optical Properties, 1994, Theory and Decision of Physical Solution, 1993, Conceptions of Modern Natural Science, 1997, Visual Methods of Decision of Physical Solutions, 1997. Mem. N.Y. Acad. Scis. Avocations: travel, music. Home: Novopeschanaya str 14 Apt24, 125252 Moscow Russia Office: Moscow Railway U (MIIT), Obraztsova 15, 103055 Moscow Russia

NIKITIN, EUGUENI EUGUENI, chemistry educator, researcher; b. Saratov, USSR, May 9, 1933; s. Eugueni Kirill and Serafima Ivan (Spiridonova) N.; m. Elena Iliya Dashevskaya Nikitin, Dec. 11, 1971. MD, Saratov U., 1955; SDc, Inst. Chem. Physics, Moscow, 1958. Student dept. physics U. Saratov, 1950-55; jr. rschr. Inst. Chem. Physics, Moscow, 1958-65, sr. rschr., 1965-71, head of rsch., 1971-92; prof. chem. physics Physico Tech. Inst., Moscow, 1965-92; prof. phys. chemistry Technion, Haifa, Israel, 1992—. Author: Theory of Elementary Atom-Molecule Processes in Gases, 1971, Nonadiabatic Transitions in Slow Atomic Collisions, 1984, Chemical Processes in Gases, 1981, Adiabatic and Diabatic Collisions, 1996. Humboldt prof. Humboldt Found., 1991. Mem. Deutsche Academie Leopoldina, European Acad. Arts, Scis. and Humanities, Internat. Acad. Quant. Molecule Scis.

NIKITIN, EVGENY KIRILLOVICH, journalist; b. Karaulovo, Russia, Apr. 17, 1938; s. Kirill Mikhailovich Nikitin and Vera Dmitrievna Sushkina Nikitina; m. Tatyana Aleksandrovna Grechishkina, Sept. 9, 1958 (div. June 1978); children: Andrei, Mikhail; m. Tatyana Kuzminichna Dyakonova; children: Sergei, Kirill, Anna. Comms. Engr., Inst. St. Petersburg, 1963. Engr. Comm. Plant, Moscow, 1963-64; clk. Naval Attache Office Russian Embassy, London, 1964-69; pub. rels. officer Main Staff Navy, Moscow, 1969-82; head of dept. Red Star Newspaper, Moscow, 1983-86; head of fgn. dept. Morskoy Sbornik Mag., Moscow, 1986-90; corr. TTAR-TASS News Agy., Moscow, 1991—. Contbr. poetry to books, articles to profl. jours. Capt. Russian Navy, 1986-90. Mem. All Russian Union of Journalists, Moscow Union of Poets. Avocations: downhill skiing, wind surfing, poetry. Office: ITAR-TASS News Agy, Tverskoy Blvd 10-12, 103009 Moscow Russia

NIKITIN, KONSTANTIN LEONIDOVICH, physics educator; b. Moscow, Jan. 23, 1968; s. Leonid Petrovich and Tamara Alekseevna (Krasnoslobodzeva) N.; m. Olga Vladimirovna Zaginaiko, May 23, 1998; 1 child, Marina. Diploma in Engring., Moscow Engring. Physics Inst., 1993, Cert. Postgrad. Tng., 1996; postgrad., Tokyo Inst. Tech., 1998—. Rschr. Moscow Engring. Physics Inst., 1996-97; tchg. asst. Tokyo Inst. Tech., 1999—. Contbr. articles to profl. jours. With Soviet Army, 1986-88. Recipient scholarship Ministry Edn., Sci., Sports and Culture Japan, 1997—. Mem. Nuclear Soc. Japan. Avocations: family, soccer, computer. Home: Fujigaoka 2-46-651, Yokohama Kanagawa 227-0043, Japan Office: Tokyo Inst Tech, 2-12-1 O-okayama Meguro-ku, Tokyo 152, Japan

NIKITIN, SERGEI MICHAILOVICH, economics researcher, educator; b. Moscow, May 5, 1928; s. Michail Sergeyevich and Aleksandra Andreyevna (Tsenina) N.; m. Zoya Ivanovna Pekhtereva, Aug. 4, 1964; 1 child, Aleksandr. PhD, Moscow State U., 1958; D in Econs., Inst. World Economy and Internat. Relations in Acad., Moscow, 1966. Rschr. IMEMO AN, 1956-75, head dept., 1975—; tchr. Moscow State U., 1970-76, prof., 1976—. Co-author, co-editor: Political Economy of Current Monopol Capitalism, 1975 (USSR State prize 1977); co-author, editor: Modern Inflation: History, Causes, Paradoxes, 1980, Science in Current Capitalist Economy, 1987 (Nat. Economy Exhbn. silver medal 1988). Recipient Working Valor medal Supreme Soviet of USSR, Presidium, 1975, Friendship of Peoples Order, Supreme Soviet USSR, Presidium, 1986, Disting. scholar of Russia, Supreme Soviet Russian Union Rep., 1989, grant Tech. Assistance Commnowealth Ind. States-Action for Cooperation Econs., Brussels, 1995-96. Mem. N.Y. Acad. Scis. Avocations: history, fiction reading. Office: IMEMO RAN, Profsoyuznaya 23, 117859 Moscow Russia

NIKITIN, YAKOV YURIEVICH, statistics and probability educator, researcher; b. St. Petersburg, Russia, Jan. 10, 1947; s. Yuri Nikitin and Iraida Shokhor; m. Tatiana Kazakova, Dec. 26, 1969; 1 child, Ekaterina. Degree, St. Petersburg U., 1968, candidate of scis., 1973, DSc, 1987. Asst. prof. St. Petersburg U., 1968-77, assoc. prof., 1977-88, prof., 1988—; vis. prof. U. Paris-Sud, 1992, U. Milan, 1994, Rome U., 1996, 97, 98, 99, Lille (France) U., 1998, 2000, Naples (Italy) U., 1999; invited rschr. Ctr. de Rsch. en Economie et Statistique, Paris, 1993, 96. Author: Asymptotic Efficiency of Nonparametric Tests, 1995 (Best Sci. Work award St. Petersburg U. 1997); contbr. articles to profl. jours.; mem. editl. bd. Math. Methods of Statistics jour., 1992—, Metron jour., 1997—. State sci. grantee Russian Acad. Scis., Moscow, 1994, 97, 2000; named Soros Prof., Internat. Soros Sci. Edn. Program, Moscow, 1994, 97. Mem. Inst. Math. Statistics, Bernoulli Soc. Math. Statistics and Probability (European com. 1998—),. Home: PO Box 90 C-36, 193036 St Petersburg Russia Office: St Petersburg U, Bibliotechnaya Sq 2, 198904 St Petersburg Russia

NIKKEL, RONALD WILBERT, social services administrator; b. Lethbridge, Alta., Can., June 8, 1946; came to U.S., 1978; s. Henry Peter and Katharine (Penner) N.; m. Celeste Carisa Friesen, June 11, 1970. BA, U. Winnipeg (Can.), 1970; MPS, Loyola U., Chgo., 1983. Nat. dir. YFC/Youth Guidance, Toronto, Ont., Can., 1973-78, Chgo., 1978-82; field dir. Prison Fellowship Internat., Washington, 1982-84, v.p., 1984-88, pres., 1988—, CEO, 1996—. Editor: Guidelines for Volunteer Programs in Justice, 1988-95. Chmn. Non Govtl. Orgns. Alliance in Crime Prevention and Criminal Justice, N.Y.C., 1988-96; bd. dirs. Love and Action, Annapolis, Md., 1989—, Jericho Rd. Found., Chgo., 1992-96, Advocates Internat., 1993—. Mem. Acad. Criminal Justice Scis. Episcopalian. Avocations: photography, hiking, gardening, sailing. Office: Prison Fellowship Internat PO Box 17434 Washington DC 20041-0434

NIKKOLA, ANTTI SALOMONI, retired government official; b. Seinajoki, Finland, June 27, 1934; s. Niilo Salomon and Vieno Maria (Ketonen) N. MS, U. Minn., 1963; DAgr, U. Helsinki, Finland, 1968. Researcher Agrl. Econs. Rsch. Inst., Helsinki, 1960-68; dir. internat. affairs Ministry Agr. and Forestry, Helsinki, 1968-98. Contbr. articles to profl. jours. and books. Recipient Decoration of Knighthood of First Class, Order of Finnish White Rose, 1980. Mem. Finnish Soc. Agrl. Scis., Finnish Econ. Soc., Am. Agrl. Econs. Assn. Home: Niemistontie 7, 60420 Seinajoki Finland

NIKL, JÁNOS, neurologist; b. Paks, Tolna, Hungary, Jan. 18, 1953; s. Ferenc Nikl and Erzsébet Haaz; m. Sarolta Molnár, July 22, 1978; children: András, Sarolta. Physician, Med. U., Pécs, Hungary, 1977; psychiatrist, Postgrad. U., Budapest, 1981, neurologist, 1986, electrophysiologist, 1988. Cert. specialist of neurology, psychiatry, and electrophysiology. Head dept neurology County Hosp., Zalaegerszeg, Hungary, 1993-96; head neurology Vaszary Kolos County Hosp., Esztergom, Hungary, 1996—, County Hosp. Zala, Zalaegerszeg, 1998. Author: Liquor-Cytodiagnosis in Clinical Practice, 1993, Neurology, 1995; contbr. articles to profl. jours. V.p. Hungarian Med. Chamber, Zalaigerszeg, 1991-97. Lt. Hungarian Army, 1978-79. Mem. Hungarian Soc. Neurology and Psychiatry, Hungarian Soc. Electrophysiology. Roman Catholic. Avocations: sports, traveling, languages. Office: County Hosp Zala, Zrinyi U 1, H 8901 Zalaegersleg Hungary

NIK MOHAMED DIN, stock exchange executive; b. Kelantan, Malaysia, Feb. 16, 1943; s. Nik Yusoff and Nik Amnah; m. Zairin Ibrahim; children: Nik Mohamed Sharifidin, Nik Ahmad Zairidin, Nik Ibrahim, Nik Emir Din. Cert. barrister-at-law, Lincoln's Inn. Magistrate, dep. pub. prosecuter Malaysian Jud. & Legal Svc., 1968-69; sr. ptnr. Mah-Kok & Din, 1970-82; exec. chmn. Osk & Ptnrs. SDN BHD, 1982-88; chmn. Kuala Lumpur Stock Exch., Malaysia, 1986-88, exec. chmn., 1988-99; exec. chmn. Virtual Commerce Group, Malaysia, 1999—. Mem. Internat. Arbitration Ctr. (assoc.). Avocations: golf, squash, horse riding, swimming, badminton. Home: 48 Taman Hillview, 68000 Ampang Selangor, Malaysia Office: Virtual Commerce Group, PO Box 11821, 50758 Kuala Lumpur Malaysia*

NIKOEVSKI, NIKOLAI PENCHEV, neurologist, lecturer, consultant; b. Sofia, Bulgaria, Dec. 16, 1939; s. Pencho Kolev and Lilia Lyubomirova (Bogdanova) N.; m. Tzana Alexandrova Kyurkchiiska, Sept. 27, 1964; children: Pencho, Anna. MD, Med. U., Sofia, 1963, PhD, 1987, DSc, 1998. Gen. practitioner Dist. Physician, Selishte Village, Bulgaria, 1964-67; neurologist Second City Hosp., Sofia, 1967-72; asst. neurologist Med. U., 1972-90, assoc. prof. 1st Neurolog. Clinic, 1990—, head neurolog. dept. Mem. Soc. Electroencephalography, Electromyography and Clin. Neurophysiology (sec.), Soc. Neurology Bulgaria. Home: 20 Assen Zlatarov St, 1504 Sofia Bulgaria Office: 1st Neurolog Clinic, 1 G Sofiiski Blvd, 1431 Sofia Bulgaria

NIKOGIANNIS, NIKOLAS STYLIANOS, food company executive; b. Athens, Greece, Aug. 26, 1953; s. Stelios and Anna (Attart) N.; m. Vicky Pikoula, Dec. 15, 1980; children: Ellianna, Stelios. Diploma in engring., Nat. Tech. U., 1976; MS, U. Manchester, Eng., 1978. Dept. head Piraiki-Patraiki, Patras, Greece, 1980-82; project mgr. BIEX, Athens, 1982-86, Hellenic Shipyards, Athens, 1986-88; tech. mgr. Elite, Athens, 1988-93; prodn. mgr. Hellenic Biscuit Co., Chalkis, Greece, 1993-95, plant mgr., 1995—; cons. BIEX, Athens, 1982-84. Mem. Tech. Chamber of Greece. Christian Orthodox. Avocations: books, chess, cycling. Home: 34-40 Fokinou St, 11635 Athens Greece Office: Hellenic Biscuit Co, Glyla, 34100 Chalkis Greece

NIKOGOSIAN, IGOR KIMOVICH, geochemist, petrologist; b. Yerevan, Armenia, Apr. 2, 1959; s. Kim Surenovich and Nella(Petrovna) N.; m. Mariam Stepanovna Andranikyan, Dec. 1, 1985; children: Narek, Areg. BSc, MSc, Yerevan (Armenia) State U., 1981; PhD, Vernadsky Inst. Geochemistry, Moscow, 1990. Jr. scientist Geol. Inst., Yerevan, 1981-84; rsch. asst. Vernadsky Inst. Geochemistry, Moscow, 1984-86, scientist, 1990-94, sr. scientist, 1994-98; postdoctoral rschr. Vrije U., Amsterdam, The Netherlands, 1998—. Contbr. articles to profl. jours. Grantee Internat. Sci. Found., 1994-95, 97-2000, Russian Basic Rsch. Found., Netherland Sci. Found., 2000—. Mem. Am. Geophys. Union, N.Y. Acad. Scis. Avocations: music, sports, literature, history. Office: Vrije U Faculty Earth Sci, De Bolelaan 1085, 1981 HV Amsterdam The Netherlands

NIKOLAEV, ANDREI VLADIMIROVICH, chemistry researcher; b. Moscow, Aug. 22, 1952; s. Vladimir Alexandrovich and Lidiia Mikhailovna (Porozhniakova) N.; m. Olga Alexeevna Kost, June 29, 1974; 1 child, Nikolaeva Natalia Andreevna. Diploma in Chemistry, Lomonosov Moscow State U., 1974; PhD in Chemistry, Zelinskiy Inst. Organic Chem., Moscow, 1981. Jr. rschr. Zelinskiy Inst. Organic Chemistry, Moscow, 1974-81, rschr., 1981-92; sr. rschr. Inst. Food Substances, Moscow, 1992-96, Nesmeyanov Inst. Organo-Element Compounds, Moscow, 1996—. Contbr. articles to profl. jours. Recipient internat. rsch. fellowship The Wellcome Trust, U.K., 1992-94, internat. rsch. scholarship Howard Hughes Med. Inst., 1995-2000. Mem. Biochem. Soc. Avocations: swimming, playing badminton and table tennis, listening to classical music, playing guitar and singing. Office: Nesmeyanov Inst Organo-Element Compounds, Vavilova St 28, 117813 Moscow Russia

NIKOLAYEV, NIKOLAY NIKOLAYEVICH, bank executive; b. Haritonovo Village, Altai, Russia, Aug. 7, 1959; s. Nikolay Makarovich and Anna Tikhonovna Nikolayeva; m. Olga Gennadyevna Fedeneva, Aug. 30, 1980; children: Kseniya, Irina. Grad., Altai State U., Barnaul, Russia, 1981, Moscow Internat. Sch. Polit., 1997. Tchr., asst. prin. H.S. 2, Zaviyalovo Village, Altai, 1980-82; first sec. Zaviyalovo Dist. Com. All-Union Lenins Young Communists, 1982-86; sec., second sec. Altai Regional Com. All-Union Lenins Young Communists, Barnaul, 1986-91; v.p. Youth Affairs Com., Barnaul, 1991; dir. Altai State Social Youth Svc., Barnaul, 1991-92; pres., chmn. adminstrn. ZAO Comml. Bank Zernobank, Barnaul, 1992—; asst. prof. Altai State Agrl. U., Barnaul, 1998—; bd. dirs. ZAO Zernocenter, Barnaul, OAO The Ctrl. Co. Fin. Agrl. Indsl. Group, Barnaul. Advisor Barnaul City Mayor, 1998—. Mem. Altai Banks Union (v.p. 1994—) Coordinating Coun. Businessmen at the City Adminstrn., Chmn. of Regional Legis. Assembly and City Adminstrn. (Pub. Coun. on Small and Middle-Size Businesses). Avocation: soccer. E-mail: nnik@zerno.barrt.ru and office@zerno.barrt.ru. Fax: 7 3852 249490. Office: ABC Zernobank, ul Anatoliya 6, 656056 Barnaul Russia

NIKOLENKO, VLADIMIR NIKOLAEVICH, anatomist, dean, educator; b. Sett. Sharovo, Russia, Nov. 14, 1956; s. Nikolay Alexandrovich and Valentina Andreevna (Burae) N.; m. Svetlana Nikolaevnae Frolova, June 9, 1989; 1 child, Lilia. MD in Human Anatomy, Med. U. Saratov, Russia, 1997, prof. human anatomy, 1998. Asst. chair human anatomy Med. U. Saratov, 1983-90, reader chair human anatomy, 1990-96, head chair human anatomy, 1996—, dean physician, 1997—. Contbr. numerous sci. articles to profl. jours.; inventor in field. Avocations: books, photography, theater, fishing. Office: Med U, B Kazachia 112, 410610 Saratov Russia

NIKOLIC, NEBOJSA, physician, educator; b. Rijeka, Croatia, Mar. 9, 1957; s. Janko and Eleonora (Petrinov) N.; m. Violeta Muhic, Sept. 26, 1987; 1 child, Gala. MD, U. Rijeka, Croatia, 1980, MSc, 1995. Physician Cmty. Primary Health Care Ctr., Rovinj, Croatia, 1983, Rijeka, Croatia, 1983-98; lectr. maritime medicine Coll. of Maritime Studies, Rijeka, Croatia, 1997—; head chair maritime medicine Maritime Acad., Rijeka, Croatia, 1997—; physician in pvt. practice Rijeka, Croatia, 1998—. Author: Nova vitka linija, 1986, ANA medicinski prirucnik, 1994; contbr. articles to profl. jours. Recipient grant Open Soc. Croatia, 1993, ITF WHO, 1998. Mem. Internat. Soc. Travel Medicine, Internat. Maritime Health Assn., Royal Inst. Pub. Health, Soc. Pub. Health Hygiene. Avocation: sailing. Office: Ordinacija opce medicine, Riva Boduli 1, 51000 Rijeka Croatia Address: Fac Maritime Studies, Rastocine S-6, 51000 Rijeka Croatia

NIKOLIĆ, SONJA, chemist; b. Zagreb, Croatia, July 21, 1954; d. Sergije and Magarita (Miličić) N. BSc, U. Zagreb, 1978, MSc, 1983, PhD, 1988. Rsch. asst. Inst. R. Bošković, Zagreb, 1978-83, rsch. assoc., 1983-89, dozent, 1989-98, rsch. assoc. prof., 1998—; postdoctoral fellow Tex. A&M U., Galveston, 1988; vis. rsch. scientist U. Reading, Eng., 1989, U. Fla., Gainesville, 1990-97, Tech. U., Graz, 1995-96, Chem. Rsc h. Ctr., Hungarian Acad. Sci., Budapest, 1998—, U. Minn., Duluth, 1998—. Author: (with others) Computational Chemical Graph Theory: Characterization, Enumeration and Generation of Chemical Structures by Computer Methods, 1991; editor: (with J. Herak) Distinguished Croatian Scientists in America, 1997. Host Non-profit Art Gallery, Inst. R. Bošković, 1978—. Mem. N.Y. Acad. Scis., Croatian Chem. Soc., Matrix Croatica. Avocations: fine arts, theatre, literature, music, swimming. Office: Rugjer Bošković Inst, Bijenička 54 POB 80, HR-10002 Zagreb Croatia

NIKOLOPOULOS, THOMAS PANAYOTIS, physician, consultant; b. Athens, July 13, 1962; s. Panayotis and Stella (Hartocollis) N.; m. Irene Gamatsi, July 14, 1990; 1 child, Philippe. MD, U. Athens, 1987, PhD, 1993. Cert. E.N.T. Gen. practitioner Health Ctr., Siatista Kozani, 1988-89; sr. house officer 2d Surgery Dept. Athens U., 1989-90, pediatric Ear Nose and

Throat dept. Akyriakou Hosp., 1990-92; med. supr. Schering Plough, SA, Athens, 1992; clin. elective pediatric Ear, Nose and Throat dept. Columbia Med. Ctr., N.Y.C., 1992-93; vis. scholar pediatric Ear, Nose and Throat dept. Pitts. Children's Hosp., 1993; registrar Ear Nose and Throat dept. Athens Univ. Med. Ctr., 1993-95; with Ear, Nose and Throat Bds. Examinations, 1995; fellow Nottingham (U.K.) U. Hosp., 1995-98, lectr., 1998—; ear, nose and throat cons., 1995—. Contbr. articles to profl. jours. Recipient scholarship Varyka, Athens, 1983-87, EEC Rsch. scholar for cochlear implants, 1996—; Lectr. E.N.T. Dept. Nottingham U. Hosp., Eng., 1996-98; Brit. Skull Base Soc. fellow, 1999. Mem. Athens Med. Assn., Pan-Hellenic Med. Assn., Internat. Microsurg. Soc., N.Y. Acad. Scis. Mem. Greek Orthodox Ch. Fax: 115-9709748. Home: Michael Voda 120, Athens 104-46, Greece

NIKOLOV, BLAGOWEST ATANASSOV, physics educator, researcher; b. Russe, Bulgaria, Dec. 23, 1942; s. Atanas Kolev and Penka Ivanova Tzoneva (Atanassova) N.; m. Yordanka Ivanova Georgieva, Sept. 19, 1972 (div. July 1975); 1 child, Ivan; m. Penka Dimitrova Adjamova, Feb. 25, 1978; children: Petya, Natalia. MSc, Sofia (Bulgaria) U., 1970; PhD, Bulgarian Acad. Scis., Sofia, 1989. Asst. faculty br. Sofia U., 1970-74; asst. Tech. U., Russe, 1974-83; rschr. Ctrl. Lab. Space Rsch., St. Zagora, 1983-86; sr. asst. Shumen U., 1986-96, assoc. prof., 1996—. Author: Lectures on Quantum Mechanics, 1996; contbr. articles to profl. jours. including Phys. Rev. E and Founds. of Physics. 1st sgt. Bulgarian Army, 1960-62. Avocation: sports. Home: Simeon Veliki 19, en 2 Apt 43, 9704 Shumen Varna, Bulgaria Office: K Preslawski U, 9712 Shumen Varna, Bulgaria

NIKOLSKAYA, ELENA BORISOVNA, chemistry researcher, consultant; b. Leningrad, Russia, May 21, 1932; d. Boris Petrovich Nikolsky and Valentina Ivanovna Paramonova; m. Yury Vasilevich Ivanov, Sept. 29, 1930; children: Alexey, Sergey, Michail, Nikolay, Vasily. Diploma, Leningrad State U., 1954, DSc, 1988; PhD in Chemistry, Tech. Inst., Leningrad, 1960. Jr. scientist Tech. Inst., Leningrad, 1959-60; sr. lectr. Med. Inst., Leningrad, 1960-63; chief of chair of chemistry Vet. Inst., Leningrad, 1963-77; sr. scientist Sechenov Inst. Evolution Physiology & Biochemi Russian Acad. Sci., Leningrad, 1977-92, leading scientist, 1992—, prof. biochemistry, 2000—; prof., cons. State U., Kazan, 1991-94. Contbr. articles to profl. jours.; inventor in field. Recipient award Ministry of Sci., 1991-93, 94-96, Univs. of Russia, 1993-95. Mem. Mendeleev Chem. Assn., Assn. Biochemistry of Acad. Sci. of Russia. Avocations: poetry, dogs, books about animals. Office: Sechenov Inst Evol Phys Bioch, Pr Morisa Toreza 44, 194223 St Petersburg Russia

NIKOLSKII, IOURII GAVRILOV, engineering educator; b. Moscow, Russia, June 8, 1941; s. Nikolai Pavlovich and Varvara Aleksandrovna (Gavrilova) N.; m. Irina Sergeevna, Oct. 10, 1969 (div. Nov. 1996); m. Oktiabrina Sergeevna Bakhlaeva, Jan. 3, 1997; 1 child, Serge. Engr., Moscow Inst. Land Reclamation, 1964, PhD in Tech., 1968, D Sci., 1989. Rsch. engr. Moscow Inst. Land Reclamation, 1964-65, rsch. group leader, 1969-72; vis. scientist soil physics ARC, Cambridge, England, 1975-76; head dept. soil-water relations Moscow Inst. Land Reclamation, 1976-83; vis. prof. Post-Grad. Coll., Montecillo, Mexico, 1979-80; prof. Moscow Inst. Land Reclamation, 1983-91, Post-Grad. Coll., Montecillo, 1991—; cons. Expert Coun. at Planning Com. USSR, Moscow, 1988-91; v.p. agrl. drainage sect. Acad. Agrl. Scis., 1990-91. Author: (book) Nuevos Enfoques de Diseno y Optimizacion de Sistemas de Riego y Drenaje, 1991; co-author: (book) Optimization of Water, Heat and Fertilizer Regimes of Irrigated and Drained; (manual CD-ROM) Guia Computarizada del Drenaje Parcelario de Distritos de Riego, 1995, (manual) Manual de Diseno e Instalacion de Drenaje Parcelario en Zonas Aridas Y, 1998. Recipient Presidium award, Acad. Argl. Scis. USSR, 1970, Silver Medal Achievement award, Exposition of Acon. Progress USSR, 1988, 91. Orthodox. Avocations: fishing, tourism. E-mail: nikolski@colpos.colpos.mx. Office: Post Grad Coll, Km 36.5 Carretera Mexico, Montecillo 56230, Mexico

NIKONOROV, NIKOLAI VALENTINOVICH, physicist, educator; b. Leningrad, Russia, Dec. 18, 1952; s. Valentin Petrovich and Nina Vasiljevna (Romanova) N.; m. Natalia Nikolaevna Mikhailova, Apr. 30, 1977; 1 child, Nikonorova Anna Nikolaevna. MS in Quantum Electronics, Inst. Fine Mechanics & Optics, Leningrad, Russia, 1976; PhD in Optics, Vavilov State Optical Inst., St. Petersburg, Russia, 1986, DSc in Optics, 1996. Mechanic Vavilov State Optical Inst., Leningrad, 1970-72; technician Vavilov State Optical Inst., Leningrad, 1972-76, sr. rschr., 1976-95; head lab. Vavilov State Optical Inst., St. Petersburg, 1995-97; prof. optics Inst. Fine Mechanics and Optics, St. Petersburg, 1996—; rsch. group leader Corning Sci. Ctr., St. Petersburg, 1997—; vis. rsch. scientist Ctr. for Rsch. and Edn. in Optics and Lasers, U. Ctrl. Fla., Orlando, 1994;. Patentee in field. Honored inventor of Soviet Union, Moscow, 1985; recipient cert. for outstanding rsch. Ctr. for Rsch. and Edn. in Optics and Lasers, U. Ctrl. Fla., Orlando, 1994, cert. project mgmt. Ctr. for Bus. Skills Devel., Moscow, 1999. Mem. Internat. Soc. Optical Engring., Am. Ceramic Soc. Avocations: travel, heavy athletics. Home: Apt 15, 25 S'ezdovskaya Liniya, 199053 Saint Petersburg Russia Office: Corning Sci Ctr, 4 Birzhevaya Liniya, 199034 Saint Petersburg Russia

NIKOSHKOV, ANDREJ, biologist, researcher; b. Moscow, Oct. 2, 1956; arrived in Sweden, 1990; s. Boris Vladimirovich Nikoshkov and Dina Iosifovna Slutskovskaja; m. Peri Noori, Feb. 8, 1988; children: Diana, David. BS, Moscow Pedagogical U., 1978; PhD, Inst. Genetics and Selection Indsl. Microorganisms, Moscow, 1985. Jr. rschr. Inst. Gen. Genetics, Moscow, 1978-82, postdoctoral rsch. asst., 1985-90; postdoctoral rschr. dept. molecular medicine Karolinska Inst., Stockholm, 1991—. Contbr. articles to profl. jours. Mem. N.Y. Acad. Scis. Avocations: swimming, karate. Home: Storgatan 50, 17152 Stockholm Sweden

NIKULIN, ANDREI YURIEVICH, physicist, researcher; b. Oryol, Russia, Mar. 30, 1962; s. Yuri Pavlovich and Svetlana Petrovna (Belkina) N.; m. Elena Vladimirovna Kozlova, Mar. 7, 1987; 1 child, Dmitri Andreevich. BS with honors, Moscow Steel and Alloys Inst., 1984; PhD in Solid State Physics, USSR Acad. Scis., Moscow, 1990. Postdoctoral fellow Inst. Microelectronics Tech. Russian Acad. Scis., Moscow, 1984-92; postdoctoral fellow Tokyo Inst. Tech., 1992-93; rsch. fellow Melbourne (Australia) U., 1993-96; Monash Logal fellow Monash U., Melbourne, 1996—. Contbr. articles to profl. publs. Fellow Japanese Soc. for Promotion of Sci., Tokyo, 1991; Australian Rsch. Coun. rsch. grantee, 1995. Office: Monash U, Dept Physics, Clayton Vic 3168, Australia

NILIUS, BERND, physiologist, educator; b. Halle Saalel, Germany, July 16, 1945; s. Bernhard and Anneliese (Sander) N.; m. Eva Hoffmann, May 20, 1970; children: Niklas, Jakob. MD, Martin Luther U., Halle, 1970, M of Math., 1974, PhD, 1978. Rsch. asst. Martin Luther U., 1970-80, asst. prof., 1980-85, assoc. prof., 1985-90; prof. physiology Med. Acad., Erfart, Germany, 1990-92; prof. physiology, chmn. Max Planck Soc., Leuven, Germany, 1991-93; prof. Cath. U., Leuven, 1993—; leader Max Planck Rsch. Group, 1991-93; leader rsch. group Cath. U., 1997—. Mem. Soc. German Physiologists, Royal Acad. Med. Scis., Physiol. Soc. (U.K.), Am. Phys. Soc. Avocations: literature, music, painting, history. Home: Huldenberg Str 12, B-3040 St Agatha Rode Belgium Office: Cath U Campus Gasthuisberg, Physiol Lab Herestr 49, B-3000 Leuven Belgium

NILLES, JOHN MATHIAS (JACK NILLES), futurist; b. Evanston, Ill., Aug. 25, 1932; s. Elmer Edward and Hazel Evelyn Nilles; m. Laila Padorr, July 8, 1957. BA magna cum laude, Lawrence Coll., 1954; MS in Engring., UCLA, Los Angeles, 1964. Sr. engr. Raytheon Mfg. Co., Santa Barbara, Calif., 1956-58; section head. Ramo-Woodridge Corp., L.A., 1958-59; project engr. Space Technology Lab., L.A., 1960; dir. The Aerospace Corp., L.A., 1961-67; sr. systems engr. TRW Systems, L.A., 1967-69; assoc. group dir. The Aerospace Corp., L.A., 1969-72; dir. interdisciplinary programs U. So. Calif., L.A., 1972-81, dir. info. technology program, 1981-89; pres. JALA Internat. Inc., L.A., 1980—; coord. EC Telework Forum, Madrid, 1992—; dir. Telecommuting Adv. Coun., L.A., 1991-97, pres., 1993-94; chmn. Telecommuting Rsch. Inst., Inc., L.A., 1990—. Author: The Telecommunications Transportation Tradeoff, 1976, Japanese edit., 1977, Exploring the World of the Personal Computer, 1982, French edit., 1985, Micros and Modems, 1983, French edit., 1986, Making Telecommuting Happen, 1994, Portuguese edit., 1997, Managing Telework, 1998; mem. editl. bd. Revista Portuguesa de Gestao, 2000—. Capt. USAF, 1954-56. Recipient Rod Rose award Soc. Rsch. Adminstrs., 1976, Environ. Pride award L.A. Mag., 1993, Environ. Achievement award Renew Am., 1994-96, Commendation, L.A. County Bd. Suprs., 1997; inducted into Telework Hall of Fame, 1998. Mem. IEEE, IEEE Computer Soc., AAAS, Assn. Computing Machinery, Inst. Ops. Rsch. and Mgmt. Scis., World Future Soc., Calif. Yacht Club. Avocations: sailing, photography. E-mail: jnilles@jala.com. Office: JALA Internat Inc 971 Stonehill Ln Los Angeles CA 90049-1412

NILLES, LAILA PADORR, musician, record producer; b. Chgo., July 25, 1929; d. Abraham Leonard Ginsburg and Jeanette Padorr; m. Jack Mathias Nilles, July 8, 1957. MusB, Northwestern U., 1947, B of Music Edn., 1947, M of Music, 1949; postgrad., Julliard Sch. Music, 1950, 51, Ecoles d'Art Am. Fontainebleau, France, 1953. Founder, dir. Padorr Trio, Chgo. and Los Angeles, 1951-55, 56-72; dir. Concerts at the Mt., Los Angeles, 1958-60; mgr., dir. Concerts West, Los Angeles, 1965-75; freelance musician Los Angeles, 1975-77; asst. dir. Protone Records, Los Angeles, 1977-82, assoc. dir., 1982—; v.p. Jala Internat., Inc., Los Angeles, 1982—; dir. design for Sharing UCLA, L.A., 1984-89, Friends of Music U. So. Calif., 1984-90, Am. Youth Symphony, 1981-88. Soloist: (record) music for Flute and Piano by Four Americans, 1976; co-producer 42 records, cassettes and compact discs, 1977—. Recipient First prize Coleman Auditions, 1956, Young Artists League, 1956. Mem. Audio Engring. Soc., Nat. Acad. Recording Arts and Scis., Musicians Union Local 47. Club: Calif. Yacht (Marina Del Ray). Avocations: photography, sailing, astronomy. Home and Office: 971 Stonehill Ln Los Angeles CA 90049-1412

NILSMARK, CATRIN, professional golfer; b. Goteborg, Sweden, Aug. 30, 1967. Student, U. Fla. Profl. golfer, 1994; mem. European Solheim Cup Team, 1992, 94, 96, 98. Winner Ford Golf Classic, WPGET, 1994. Avocations: motorcycling, horseback riding, tennis. Office: LPGA 100 Intenational Golf Dr Daytona Beach FL 32124*

NILSSON, BENGT OLOF, physiologist; b. Hassleholm, Sweden, Jan. 18, 1961; s. Ove Ingvar and Sonja (Goransson) N.; m. Monika Inger Andersson, May 21, 1988; children: Henrik, Viktoria, Gustav. DDS, Lund U., 1986, PhD, 1991. Asst. prof. Lund U., Sweden, 1991—. Office: Lund U Dept Physiology, Solvegstan 19, S-223 62 Lund Sweden

NILSSON, BERNT OVE, human anatomy educator; b. Falun, Sweden, Jan. 8, 1929; s. Johan Bernhard and Gurli Elisabet (Hogman) N.; m. Irene Brann, Dec. 16, 1956; children: Sven Ludvig, Karin Elisabet, Ebba Agneta. MB, Karolinska Inst., Stockholm, 1953, DMS, 1959, MD, 1960. Instr. Karolinska Inst., 1951-60, lectr., 1961-62; assoc. prof. Uppsala (Sweden) U., 1963-68, prof. anatomy, 1969-93, chmn., 1969-93, vice dean med. faculty, 1975-77; active Swedish Med. Rsch. Coun. Stockholm, 1973-79. Author: Ljusmikroskopisk teknik, 1968, Elektronmikroskopisk teknik, 1972, Immunocontraception, 1995; mem. editl. bd. several jours.; contbr. articles to profl. jours. Decorated knight Royal Order Pole Star (Sweden). Fellow Royal Soc. Scis., Swedish Soc. Medicine; mem. Soc. for Study Reprodn., Am. Soc. for Reproductive Immunology, Internat. Com. on Morphological Scis., Scandinavian Soc. for Electron Microscopy. Home: Götgatan 12A, S-753 15 Uppsala Sweden Office: U Uppsala Dept Anatomy, Box 571 Biomedical Ctr, S-751 23 Uppsala Sweden

NILSSON, BO INGVAR, hematologist; b. Helsingborg, Sweden, Sept. 15, 1947; s. Jonny Ingvar and Sonja Eugenia (Akesson) N.; m. Elsa Sigbritt Warkander, Aug. 20, 1971; children: Victoria, Philip, Sofia. MD, U. Gothenburg, 1973; PhD, U. Lund, 1985. Lic. physician, 1973. Resident Dept. Radiology, Univ. Hosp., Gothenburg, 1973-74, Dept. Internal Medicine, County Hosp., Angelholm, 1974-76; resident Dept. Internal Medicine, Univ. Hosp. Lund, 1976-78, amanuensis, 1978-83; sr. house officer Dept. Internal Medicine, County Hosp., Helsingborg, 1983-86; med. dir. oncology Pharmacia Leo Therapeutics, Helsingborg, 1986-88; rsch. dir. oncology Pharmacia Leo Therapeutics, 1989-90; rsch. dir. oncology Kabi Pharmacia Therapeutics, 1991-92, dir. med. affairs, 1992-93; dir. oncology Pharmacia, Inc. (USA), 1993-95, med. dir. hematology, 1995-96; clin. drug devel. cons. Connector Med. AB, 1997—. Contbr. articles to profl. jours. U. Lund, Segerfalk Found. grantee, 1978-86. Mem. Am. Soc. Clin. Oncology, Am. Soc. Hematology, European Hematology Assn., Swedish Soc. Medicine, Swedish Soc. Hematology-Oncology (edn. com. 1985-89), European Soc. Med. Oncology, Oncology of So. Sweden (bd. dirs. 1980-83), Wig. Home and Office: Båthusgatan 1, SE-25267 Helsingborg Sweden

NILSSON, GERT E., biomedical engineer; b. Malmo, Skane, Sweden, June 12, 1947; s. Erik N. and Karla M. N.; m. Lena C. Gren, Sept. 4, 1945; children: Jenny, Annette, Ingela. MSEE, Lund (Sweden) U., 1972; PhD Biomed. Engring., Linkoping (Sweden) U., 1977. Assoc. prof. biomed. engring. Linkoping U., 1980-83, prof., 1987—; devel. mgr. Gambro Cardio AB, Lund, 1983-85; cons. Perimed AB, Lund, 1985-87; head of inst. Linkoping U., 1990-93, chmn. faculty com., 1993-96; dir. Lisca AB, Linkoping, 1991—; coord. EU project HIRELADO, 1996—. Contbr. articles to profl. jours.; co-inventor controlled heat ceiling, laser doppler perfusion monitor, laser doppler perfusion imager. Arnbergsk award Swedish Acad. Sci., 1986, Innovation award European Microcirculatory Soc., 1990. Mem. IEEE, Soc. for Optical Engring. Avocations: computing, travel. Office: Linkoping Univ, Dept Biomed Engring, S-58185 Linköping Sweden

NILSSON, HOLGER, physiology/pharmacology educator and researcher; b. Lund, Sweden, Sept. 12, 1956; s. Nils Johan and Hildegard (Holland) N. MD, U. Göteborg, Sweden, 1980, PhD, 1985. Postdoctoral rsch. assoc. U. Vt., Burlington, 1985-86; rsch. assoc. U. Göteborg, 1986-90; intern Sahlgren's Hosp., Göteborg, 1990-91; rsch. assoc. U. Aarhus, Denmark, 1991-93, lectr., 1993—; guest prof. U. Lund (Sweden), 1998—. Contbr. articles to profl. jours.; editor: Brit. Jour. Pharmacology. Mem. Scandinavian Physiol. Soc., Danish Pharmacological Soc., British Pharmacological Soc., N.Y. Acad. Scis., Assn. Computers Machinery. Avocations: veteran and sports cars, computing. Home: Horsensgade 3 1tv, DK-8000 Århus C, Denmark Office: Dept Physiology U Aarhus, Universitets Parken 160, DK-8000 Århus C, Denmark

NILSSON, NILS JOHNNY, aviation executive; b. Dorotea, Sweden, Dec. 16, 1942; s. N. Axel and Karin (Adén) N.; m. K. Ann-Christine Nilsson, Sept. 6, 1976; children: N. Daniel, Lisa M., K. Martin. Grad., Air Traffic Contr. Acad., Stockholm, 1966. Lic. pvt. pilot, Sweden. Air traffic control officer Swedish Civil Aviation Adminstrn., Stockholm, 1963-70, sr. air traffic control officer ATC Acad., 1970-72, sr. air traffic control officer planning dept., 1972-76, exec. sec. Satellite Policy Group, 1993—; exec. sec. gen. aviation, domestic comml. air transport Ministry of Transport and Comm., Stockholm, 1976-81; asst. mng. dir. Swedair AB, Stockholm, 1981-82; dir. Swedavia AB, Norrköping, Sweden, 1982—; lectr. in field to various workshops/confs.; mgr. CEC funded projects on CNS/ATM systems; chmn. Eurocae WG-51 SG-2; part-time tchr. flying schs. Stockholm, Uppsala, Norrtälje, 1967-71. Author/pub. (textbook): Air Radio Communication and Aviation English, 1971; contbr. numerous articles to profl. jours. With Swedish Air Force, 1961-62. Mem. Swedish Soc. Aeronautics and Astronautics, Am. Inst. Aeronautics and Astronautics. Avocations: tennis, skiing. Office: Swedavia AB, S-60179 Norrkoping Sweden

NILSSON, OVE, biologist; b. Bjornekulla, Sweden, Dec. 13, 1964; s. Bo and Solveig (Andersson) N. BS, U. Umea, Sweden, 1988; PhD, Swedish U. Agrl. Scis., 1995. Postdoctoral rschr. The Salk Inst., La Jolla, Calif., 1995-97; asst. prof. SLU, Umea, Sweden, 1997-99, assoc. prof., 1999—. Contbr. articles to profl. jours. Human Frontiers of Sci. Progran Orgn. fellow, 1995. Avocations: singing, backpacking, wine, music. Office: Swedish U Agrl Scis, Dept Plant Phys, 90183 Umea Sweden

NILSSON, PER GUSTAN RAGNAR, business executive, management consultant; b. Luleå, Norrbotten, Sweden, Oct. 1, 1955; s. Arne V.H. and Ingegard (Petterson) N.; m. Barbara Teresa Bobrowska, Nov. 6, 1951; children: Eva Emilia, Emil Eduard. BS, Stockholm U., 1986, postgrad., 1986-88. Sr. cons. Swedish Mgmt. Group, Stockholm, 1985-88; MD Resco Ptnr., Stockholm, 1988-91; CEO Radius Holdings, Marsta Stockholm, 1991-96; MD AssiDoman Sacks, Aylesford, U.K., 1996-98, Scania Russia, Moscow, 1998—; sr. advisor Polish Ministry Industry, Warsaw, Poland, 1991-92; rector, co-founder Wysza Szkola Biznesu, Nowy Sacz, 1991-92; vis. prof. Higher Sch. Bus., Nat. Louis U., Nowy Sacz, Poland, 1992—. Chmn. Moderata Ungdomsforbundet, Luleå, 1971-73, Luleå Fria Studenter, 1972; v.p. Found. for Wysza Szkola Brnesu, Nat. Louis U., Novy Sacz, 1992—. Recipient Silver cross Polish Order of Merit by Pres. Watesa, 1991. Mem. Moderata Samlingspartiet. Lutheran. Avocation: history. Home: Berga-Odensala, S-19592 Marsta Uppland, Sweden Office: Scania Russia, Leninsky Prospekt 11311, 117198 Moscow Russia

NILSSON, RALPH INGEMAR, occupational and environmental health physician; b. Helsingborg, Sweden, Sept. 9, 1949. MD, Lund (Sweden) U., 1974; PhD, Göteborg (Sweden) U., 1998. Staff physician Ctrl. Hosp., Västerås, Sweden, 1974-77; staff physician Sahlgrenska U. Hosp., Göteborg, 1978-89, cons., 1989-99, 2000—; assoc. prof. dept. epidemiology Inst. Pub. Health, U. Copenhagen, 1999-2000; med. cons. Indsl. Safety Inspectorate, Borås, Sweden, 1985—. Contbr. articles to books and med. jours. Mem. Internat. Commn. on Occupl. Health. Home: Linnegatan 55, SE 41308 Göteborg Sweden Office: Sahlgrenska Univ Hosp, St Sigfridsgatan 85, SE 41266 Göteborg Sweden

NILSSON, SIGWARD, physics educator; b. Veta, Sweden, July 9, 1927; s. Oscar and Ragnhild (Karlsson) N.; m. Kerstin Blom, July 9, 1956; children: Katarina, Petra. Degree in engring., Katrineholm (Sweden) Tech.Sch., 1945; grad., Hermods, Malmo, Sweden, 1948; BSc, Uppsala (Sweden) U., 1953, PhD in Physics, 1958. Engr. Asea Brown Boveri, Vasteras, Sweden, 1946-50; rsch. asst. Uppsala U., 1953-56, asst. lectr., 1956-60; rsch. asst. CERN, Geneva, 1960-62; sr. univ. lectr. Stockholm U., 1962-92, dean dept. physics, 1977-82; bd. dirs. Vallentuna Energy Inc.; sci. assoc. CERN, 1973-74, 82-84; project leader Spiral Reader, Stockholm, 1974-76; lectr. in field. Author: The World of Quarks, 1985, (poetry) The System's Consequences, 1997; initiator use of computers in undergrad. univ. tchg., 1992, Cybernetic Pedagogics Web, 1997. Mcpl. councillor Vallentuna City Coun., 1970-76; mem. Energy Commn., Vallentuna, 1976-80; mem. steering group Swedish U. Computer Network, Stockholm, 1985-88. Radar engr. Swedish Royal Air Force, 1949-50. Recipient Wallmark prize Royal Swedish acad. Scis., 1983. Mem. Swedish Phys. Soc., Gesellschaft für Pedagogik und Info., Swedish Assn. for Distance Edn. Mem. Swedish Social Dem. Party. Home: Nyhagavagen 13, 18642 Vallentuna Sweden Office: Stockholm U, Fysikum Box 6730, 11385 Stockholm Sweden

NILVA, LEONID, scientist, researcher; b. Leningrad, USSR, Dec. 15, 1956; came to U.S., 1987; s. Alexander and Tamara (Ginzburg) N.; (div. May 1987); children: Maria, Tamara. BS in Applied Maths., Inst. Elec. Engring., Leningrad, 1977, MS in Computer Sci., 1979; postgrad., Inst. for Control Technique, Leningrad, 1979-81. Cert. handwriting analyst Inst. Integral Handwriting Studies. Programmer Inst. Elec. Equipment, Leningrad, 1981-83; sr. programmer Geol. Inst., Leningrad, 1983-86, Inst. of Hydrotechnology, Leningrad, 1986-87; sr. design engr. Answer Computer, Sunnyvale, Calif., 1987-88; staff scientist Ricoh Calif. Rsch. Ctr., Menlo Park, Calif., 1988-91; mgr. imaging group Harvest Software, Inc., Sunnyvale, Calif., 1991-93; rsch. asst. All-Union Astronomic Soc., Leningrad, 1981-87; cons. Informax Inc., Washington, 1990-91; staff scientist Inst. Integral Handwriting Studies, Palo Alto, Calif., 1993-94; mgr. Info. Net. Tech. Corp., San Jose, 1994-96; v.p. software development Simply Interactive Internet Tech., San Jose, 1996-98; founder, CTO Creative Sci. Sys., Inc., San Jose, Calif., 1998—. Patentor variable spectral analysis for OCR, binary tree recognition for OCR. Mem. IEEE, Assn. for Computing Machinery. E-mail: leonid@nilva.com. Office: Creative Sci Sys Inc 1475 S Bascom Ave Ste 108 Campbell CA 95008-0628

NIMCEVIC, DRAGAN IVAN, biochemical engineer; b. Subotica, Yugoslavia, Oct. 17, 1960; s. Simon and Antonija (Kvala) N.; m. Ivanka Kalaci, Oct. 21, 1981 (div. 1991); children: Ivana, Ivan. Diploma Engring., U. Novi Sad, 1986; Doctor Tech., Vienna U. Technology, Austria, 1996. Chartered engr., Europe. Asst. U. Novi Sad, 1986; technologist Veterinarski Zavod, Subotica, Yugoslavia, 1986-88, head of prodn., 1988-91; rschr. Inst. of Chem. Engring., Vienna, 1992—. Contbg. author: Umweltbiotechnologie in osterreich, 1997; contbr. articles to profl. jours. Mem. Austrian Chemist's Soc., N.Y. Acad. Scis. Avocations: music, sports. Office: Inst Chem Engring, Getreidemarkt 9/159, 1060 Vienna Austria

NINDL, INGO, molecular biologist; b. Ingolstadt, Bavaria, Germany, Sept. 16, 1964; s. Anton and Franziska (Dasch) N. Diploma in biology, U. Aachen, Germany, 1991; PhD, U. Heidelberg, Germany, 1994. Sci. vice dir. Friedrich-Schiller U., Jena, Germany, 1994-95, sci. group leader, 1997-99; postdoctoral Vrije U., Amsterdam, The Netherlands, 1996; sci. project leader MTM-Labs., Heidelberg, Germany, 1999—; student Max Planck Inst. Cologne, Germany, 1990-91. Author: (book) HPV Infection: a Clinical Atlas, 1997; also articles in profl. jours. Grantee: Max Planck Inst., Cologne, Germany, 1990, European Commn. Human Capital and Mobility, 1996, Deutsche Forschungs Gemeinschaft, Bonn, 1997, Deutsche Krebshilfe, Bonn, 1999. Mem. AAAS, Deutsche Hochschulverband, Gesellschaft fuer Virolgie, Cologne. Avocations: diving, travel, biking, guitar. Office: Im Neuenheimer Feld 519, 69120 Heidelberg Baden Germany

NINEHAM, DENNIS ERIC, retired theology educator; b. Southampton, Eng., Sept. 27, 1921; s. Stanley Martin and Bessie Edith (Gain) N.; m. Ruth Corfield Miller, Aug. 13, 1946; children: Elizabeth, Clare, Hugh, Christopher. BA, Oxford U., 1943, MA, 1947; BD, Cambridge U., 1964; DD (hon.), Yale U., BDS, 1965; DD (hon.), U. Birmingham, Eng., 1972; DD, Oxford U., 1978. Fellow, chaplain Queen's Coll., Oxford, Eng., 1946-54; prof. London U., 1954-64; regius prof. Cambridge U., 1964-69; fellow Emmanuel Coll., Cambridge, 1964-69; warden Keble Coll., Oxford, 1969-79; prof. Bristol U., Eng., 1980-86; vis. prof. Trinity Coll., Toronto, Ont., Can., 1992, Rikkyo U., Tokyo, 1994. Author: The Gospel of St. Mark, 1963, The Use and Abuse of the Bible, 1976, Explorations in Theology, 1977, Christianity Medieval and Modern, 1993; editor: Studies in the Gospels, 1955, 2d edit. 1957, The Church's Use of the Bible, 1963. Proctor Ch. of Eng. Assembly, 1955-70, Ch. of Eng. Gen. Synod, 1970-76. Fellow King's Coll., U. London, 1963, hon. fellow Keble Coll., Oxford U., 1980, fellow King Edward VI Sch. Southampton, 1986, hon. fellow Queen's Coll., Oxford U., 1991. Home: 9 Fitzherbert Close, Oxford OX4 4EN, England

NING, JOHN TSE-TSO, urologic surgeon; b. Tso-Ying, Taiwan, Aug. 25, 1951; came to U.S., 1963; s. Joseph Pei-Ying and Yuan-Chen (Chow) N.; m. Linda J. Ching, July 27, 1975; children: Lena, Jonathan. BS in Chemistry, MIT, 1978; MS in Pharmacology, Northeastern U., 1981, MS in Med. Lab. Sci., 1982; PhD Biochemistry & Molecular Biophysics, Med. Coll. of Va., 1988, MD, 1991. Diplomate Nat. Bd. Med. Examiners; lic. M.D., S.C.; cert. clin. chemist Nat. Registry Clin. Chemistry. Postdoctoral fellow dept. biochemistry/molecular biophysics Med. Coll. V., Va. Commonwealth U., Richmond, Va., 1988-91; postdoctoral fellow radiation biology br. Ctr. Devices and Radiol. Health FDA, Rockville, Md., 1991-92; affiliated rsch. assoc. Dept. of Biochemistry & Molecular BioPhysics Med. Coll. Va., Richmond, 1990-92; rsch. assoc. dept. of elect. engring. U. Md., College Park, 1991-92; vis. scholar Quindao (People's Rep. of China) Med. Coll. Affiliated Hosp., 1987-92; vis. scientist Peking (People's Rep. of China) Third Hosp., 1992; gen. surgery intern dept. surgery Med. U. of S.C., Charleston, 1992-93; gen. surgery resident dept. surgery Med. U. of S.C., 1993-94; urologic surgery resident dept. urology Brown U., Providence, R.I., 1994-98; chief urology, Alaska Native Med. Ctr. Alaska Area Native Health Svc., Indian Health Svc., USPHS, Anchorage, 1998—; co-chmn. com. prostate disorders and minorities NIH, 1997; mem. APOAC adv. com. to Surgeon Gen., pres. Alaska Br. Commn. Officer's Assn.; bd. dirs. Soc. Govt. Svc. Urologists. Contbr. to Annals of N.Y. Acad. Sci., 1992. Cultural chmn. MIT Chinese Student Club, Cambridge, Mass., 1974; bd. dirs. South CDVC Cmty. Health Ctr., Boston, Mass., 1979. Recipient Commemorative medal of honor Am. Biographical Inst., 1987. Fellow Am. Inst. Chemists; mem. Soc. Govt. Urologists (bd. dirs. 1999—), Bioelectromagnetics Soc., Biolect. Repair and Growth Soc., Soc. of Govt. Svc. Urologists (bd. dirs.), Am. Med. Assn., Sigma Xi, Rho Chi (life), Phi Lambda Upsilon (life). Republican. Roman Catholic. Achievements include contributions to knowledge of effects of extremely low frequency electromagnetic fields on gene expression; effects of extremely low frequency electromagnetic fields on genitourinary system in rabbits; health effects of electromagnetic fields and potential therapeutic applications in medicine and surgery; rsch. in prostate cancer. Avocations: swimming, tennis, playing trumpet and saxophones,

bowling. Office: PHS Alaska Native Med Ctr ANC-SUR 4315 Diplomacy Dr Anchorage AK 99508-5926

NING, KE, neurosurgeon; b. Zhangjiang, China, Apr. 26, 1963; s. Hangzhong and Suying (Huang) N.; m. Yongrong Chen, Aug. 1, 1988; 1 child, Xiaoqi. BS, First Mil. Med. Univ., Guangzhou, China, 1985; MD, Sun Yatsen U. Med. Sci., Guangzhou, China, 1991; PhD, Third Mil. Med Univ., Chongqing, China, 1996. Resident doctor of surgery Zhujiang Hosp., Guangzhou, 1985-88; lectr. and doctor-in-charge/neurosurgery Zhujiang Hosp. tal, Guangzhou, China, 1988-97; assoc. prof. neurosurgery Zhujiang Hosp. tal, Guangzhou, 1997—; postdoctoral rsch. assoc. U. Notre Dame, Ind., 1999-2001; grad. student advisor First Mil. Med. U., Guangzhou, Chian; vice-dir. Neurosci. Ctr. of Zhujiang Hosp., Guangzhou. Grantee NSF of China., 1997-99; recipient award Assn. of Sci. and Technology of Guangdong Province, China, 1991. Mem. Assn. Chinese Traumotology (editor Jour. of Traumotlogy 1998—). E-mail: Ke.Ning.1@nd.edu. Office: Dept Neurosurgery/Zhujiang, Hosp/235 Gongye Rd, Guangdong 510282, China

NING, PINGZHI, physics educator; b. Peijing, May 12, 1938; s. Ju and Ruiyun (Sun) N.; m. Defen Min, July 24, 1965; children: Ke Ning, Yu Ning. BS, Nankai U., Tianjin, China, 1961; MS, Nankai U., 1964. Diplomate in Theoretical Physics. Lectr. Nankai U., 1965-82, assoc. prof., 1986-87, prof., 1988—, PhD supr., 1992—, vice chmn., dept. Physics, 1987-97; vis. scholar Western Mich. U., Kalamazoo, 1983-85; guest rschr. Inst. Theoretical Physics, Acad. Sinica, Peijing, 1990—; mem. editl. bd. Physics Bulletin (China), 1994—, Nuclear Physics Rev. (China), 1989—. Author: Vibrations and Waves, 1981, Transmission Technology of Microwave Information, 1985, Integral Transformations for Electronic Engineering, 1999; editor: C.N. Yang's Lectures, 1989 (highly rated books prize, 1991). Recipient Sci. and Tech. Progress prize State Edn. Commn., 1988, 1992, 1996. Mem. China Ctr. Advanced Sci. and Tech. (assoc.), Chinese Nuclear Physics Soc. (coun. mem. 1990—). Avocations: swimming, calligraphy, playing chess, collecting stamps. Office: Dept Physics Nankai U, 94 Weijin Rd, 300071 Tianjin China

NING, SHOUCHENG, cancer biologist, head and neck surgeon; b. Gao-Qing, Shandong, China, Aug. 1, 1951; came to U.S., 1988; s. Yun-You and Shu-Zheng (Gao) N.; m. Ling-Yi Zhang, Sept. 10, 1979; 1 child, Kevin X.B. MD, Shanghai 2d Med. U., 1978, MS, 1982, PhD, 1986. Asst. prof. Shanghai 2d Med. U., 1978-81, attending surgeon, 1982-88, assoc. prof., vice chief surgeon, 1988—; rsch. fellow Stanford (Calif.) U. Med. Sch., 1988-93, rsch. scientist, 1993—. Author: Modern Treatment in Internal Medicine, 1987, China Yearbook of Stomatology, 1988;; contbr. articles to Internat. Jour. Radiation Oncology and Biol. Physics, Jour. Cellular Physiology. Recipient award for outstanding young scientists Shanghai Assn. Sci. and Tech., 1985, nat. award in cancer rsch. China Ministry Pub. Health, 1986, nat. award for advancement of sci. and tech. China. Nat. Coun. for Edn., 1994. Mem. Am. Assn. for Cancer Rsch., N.Am. Hyperthermia Soc., Chinese Med. Assn. Office: Stanford U Med Ctr A010 300 Pasteur Dr Palo Alto CA 94304-2203

NING, XUE-HAN (HSUEH-HAN NING), physiologist, researcher; b. Peng-Lai, Shandong, People's Republic of China, Apr. 15, 1936; came to U.S., 1984; s. Yi-Xing and Liu Ning; m. Jian-Xin Fan, May 28, 1967; 1 child, Di Fan. MD, Shanghai 1st Med. Coll., People's Republic of China, 1960. Rsch. fellow Shanghai Inst. Physiology, 1960-72, leader cardiovasc. rsch. group, 1973-83, head, assoc. prof. cardiovasc. rsch. unit, 1984-87, prof. and chair hypoxia dept., 1988-90, vice chairperson academic com., 1988-90; NIH internat. rsch. fellow U. Mich., Ann Arbor, 1984-87, vis. prof., hon. prof., rsch. investigator, 1990-95; prof. and dir. Hypoxia Physiology Lab. Academia Sinica, Shanghai, 1989-90; acting leader, High Altitude Physiology Group, Chinese mountaineering and sci. expdn. team to Mt. Everest, 1975; leader High Altitude Physiology Group, Dept. Metall. Industry of China and Ry. Engring. Corps, 1979; vis. prof. dept. physiology Mich. State U., East Lansing, 1989-90; vis. prof. dept. pediat. U. Wash., Seattle, 1994-97; affiliate prof., U. Wash., 1997—; rsch. scientist Children's Hosp. and Regional Med. Ctr., Seattle, 1997—. Author: High Altitude Physiology and Medicine, 1981, Reports on Scientific Expedition to Mt. Qomolungma, High Altitude Physiology, 1980, Environment and Ecology of Qinghai-Xizang (Tibet) Plateau, 1982; mem. editl. bd. Chinese Jour. Applied Physiology, 1984—, Acta Physiologica, 1988-90; contbr. articles to profl. jours. Recipient Merit award Shanghai Sci. Congress, 1977, All-China Sci. Congress, Beijing, 1978, Super Class award Academia Sinica, Beijing, 1986, 1st Class award Nat. Natural Scis., Beijing, 1987, # 1 Best Article award Tzu-Chi Med. Jour., Taiwan, 1995. Mem. Am. Physiol. Soc., Am. Heart Assn., Internat. Soc. Heart Rsch., Royal Soc. Medicine, Shanghai Assn. Physiol. (bd. dirs. 1988-91), Chinese Assn. Physiol. (com. applied physiology 1984-93, com. blood, cardiovascular, respiratory and renal physiology 1988-93), Chinese Soc. Medicine, Chinese Soc. Biomed. Engring. Achievements include research in predictive evaluation of mountaineering performance, paradox phenomenon of cardiac pump function injury after climbing or giving oxygen, blood flow-metabolism-function relationship of heart during hypoxia and ischemia, effect of medicinal herbs on cardiac performance, cardiovascular adaptation and resistance to hypoxia and ischemia, Hypothermic adaptation protects heart from subsequent ischemia and hypoxia; the critical temperature 30 degrees celsius "temperature threshold" for modulating myocardial metabolism and gene expression to resist ischemia and hypoxia, first electrocardiograph recording at summit of Mt. Everest. Home: 7033 43rd Ave NE Seattle WA 98115-6015 Office: U Wash Dept Pediatrics Box 356320 1959 NE Pacific St Seattle WA 98195-0001

NINKE, ARTHUR ALBERT, accountant, management consultant; b. Aug. 20, 1909; s. Paul F. and Theresa Grace (Warskow) N.; m. Claudia Wagner, Sept. 13, 1930; children: Doris Ninke Hart, Donald, Marion, George, Arthur Jr., Thomas, Mark, Albert. Student acctg., Internat. Bus. Coll., 1928; diploma commerce, Northwestern U., 1932. Auditor Arthur Andersen & Co., CPAs, Chgo., 1929-36, Midwest Stock Exch., St. Louis, 1936-41, SEC, St. Louis, 1942-45; expense controller Butler Bros., Chgo., 1946-49; auditor Arthur Andersen & Co., CPAs, St. Louis, 1950-55; bus. mgr. Barrett Weber Ford, St. Louis, 1955-56; office mgr. Hargis Electronics, St. Louis, 1956-59; auditor HUD, Detroit, 1960-64; owner, cons. urban renewal projects and housing devel. Urban Tech. Staff Assoc., Detroit, 1965-81; pres. Simplified Systems & Computer Sales, Detroit, 1978—, More Benefits Acctg. Svcs., Phoenix, 1991-97; exec. dir. Urban Mgmt. Svcs., 1984—, Urban Computerized Svcs., Inc., 1984-88, Computer Mgmt. Svcs., 1985—, Complete Bus. Svc., Dallas, 1979-82; pres. Loving Shepherd Nursing Home, Warren, Mich., 1975-83; sec. Gideons Detroit North Woodward, 1981-83, treas., 1986-87. Author: Family Bible Studies; Computer Networking; developer simulated machine bookkeeping sys.; trademark holder Record-Checks-Systems, 1981—. Sec. Gideons Detroit North Woodward, 1981-83, treas., 1986-87; sec. Casa Campana Homeowners Assn., Glendale, Ariz., 1993-96; dir. Family Bible Hour Club, 1986—; controller Lake Superior R & D Inst., Munsing, Mich., 1973-76; lay min. Redford Luth. Ch., 1988-91; pres. Luth. Friendship Homes, Inc., 1975-85; lay evangelist Outer Drive Faith Luth. Ch., 1975-88, Faith Luth. Ch., 1986-88, treas., 1985-86; mng. dir. Family Evangelism Found., 1977—; controller S.E. Mich. Billy Graham Crusade, 1976-77; pres. Project Compassion Met. Detroit, Inc., 1982-91; cons. Highland Park, Mich., Housing Project, 1991—; bd. dirs. Luth. Credit Union Greater Detroit, 1982-88; mem. Nat. Coun. on Aging. Recipient tribute Mich. State Legis., 1982, 91, City of Warren, 1982, City of Detroit, 1991, Project Compassion of Mich., 1991, Detroit City Coun., 1991. Mem. Am. Mgmt. Assn., Nat. Soc. Pub. Accts., Nat. Assn. Housing and Redevel. Ofcls. (treas. 1975-81, dir. 1975-81), Internat. Luth. Laymen's League (treas. S.E. Mich. 1971-75, dir. 1976-81), Highland Park Lions Club (treas. 1999—), Fairlane Club of Dearborn, Gideon Internat. Home: PO Box 3471 Highland Park MI 48203-0471

NINNEKAR, HARICHANDRA ZARINATH, biochemist; b. Bidar, India, Feb. 10, 1955; s. Zarinath Lingappa and Ratnabai Zarinath (Udkar) N.; m. Pushpa Harichandra Kittur, Feb. 6, 1980; children: Shilpa, Vishal. BSc, Karnatak U., Dharwad, India, 1974, MSc, 1976, PhD, 1987. Rsch. fellow Indian Inst. Sci., Bangalore, India, 1976-77; from lectr. to reader Karnatak U., Dharwad, 1977-94, prof., 1994—; program dir. Civil Svcs. Coaching Ctr., India, 1986-89; guest lectr. dept. sericulture Karnatak U., Dharwad, 1992-94, 97, dir. students welfare K.U. Dharwad, prof., chmn. dept. biochemistry, 1999; acad. coun. faculty sci. and tech., 1994—. Contbr. articles to profl. jours. Fellow Indian Coun. Chemists; mem. Soc. Biol. Chemists. Avocations: reading, travel, TV, badminton. Home: Ashirwad CITB Plot No 68, Srinagar 3rd Main Rd, Dharwad 580 003, India Office: Karnatak Univ, Karnatak Univ, Dept Biochemistry, Dharwad 580 003, India

NINNI, VASSILIA, chemist; b. Athens, Greece, May 18, 1946; d. Lysimachus and Maria N.; m. Athanassios Spanos, Sept. 16, 1976; 1 child, Dimitrios-Emmanuel. Degree in chemistry, U. Athens, 1969; PhD in Bus. Adminstrn., Athens U. of Econs. and Bus., 1988. Asst. prof. dept. tech. of Goods Athens U. Sch. Econ. and Bus., 1969-92, sr. lectr., 1992—; presenter in field. Author: Technological Topics of Industry vol. I and II, 1990. Grantee State Scholarship Found., 1964-69. Mem. Greek Chemists Union, Greek Inst. Food Scientists, Greek Female Scientists Group. Greek Orthodox. Avocations: classical piano, foreign languages, travel.

NIR, ISAAC, medical educator; b. Radom, Poland, June 16, 1916; Immigrated to Israel, 1936; s. Mendel and Gela (Zylberberg) Grosfeld; m. Barbara Jean Morrison, Nov. 21, 1959. MSc in Biology, Hebrew U. Jerusalem, 1942, PhD in Biochemistry, 1945, MD, 1957. Dir. Inst. for Standardization Pharm. Products, Jerusalem, 1949-62; head of unit of chemicals in human use WHO, Geneva, 1957-60; vis. assoc. prof. Chgo. Med. Sch., 1963-65; head clin. pharm. Min. Health, Jerusalem, 1965-84; prof. pharmacology H.U. Med. Faculty, Jerusalem, 1965-85, prof. emeritus, 1985—; perm. panel mem. Expert Adv. Com. on Drugs & Chemicals WHO, Geneva, 1965-85; invited sci. expert on thalidomide German Ct., 1969; chair Israeli Compendium of Essential Drugs in Hosps., 1970-95; invited mem. Ciba Found. Mtg., London, 1970; assoc. participant Boston Collaborative Drug Surveillance Program, 1984-89; hon. vis. prof. Hong Kong U. Contbr. articles to sci. jours., chpts. to books. Mem. Sci. Corps. Israeli Army, 1947-49. Recipient prize Israel Chemical Soc., 1948. Mem. N.Y. Acad. Scis., Internat. Soc. Neuroendocrinology, Israeli Med. Assn. (prize 1977). Home: Gelber 1, 96755 Jerusalem Israel Office: Hebrew U, Hadassah Med Sch, 91120 Jerusalem Israel

NIR, RAPHAEL, communication educator; b. Hamburg, Germany, Sept. 9, 1930; s. Max and Irma (Orchudesch) Strauss; m. Miriam Maoz, Oct. 13, 1953; children: Ori, Eynat. BA summa cum laude, The Hebrew U., Jerusalem, 1955, MA summa cum laude, 1959, PhD, 1967. Cert. h.s. tchr. Dir. dept. tchrs.' tng. Hebrew U., 1964-67, prof., 1980—; head of Sch. of Edn. Ben-Gurion U., Beersheva, Israel, 1968-73; dir. Ctr. for Applied Linguistics, Hu J-M, Israel, 1970-75; vis. prof. U. Wis., Madison, 1972-73, U. Heidelberg, Germany, 1986-87, 91; project dir. and course writer, The Open Univ., Tel Aviv, 1981—; chmn. com. for tchg., Ministry of Edn., 1993—; vis. scholar MCA-Berkeley, 1996. Author: Language, Medium and Message, 1984, Word Formation in Modern Hebrew, 1993; contbr. articles to profl. publs. Maj. Israel Def. Force, 1949-52. Mem. AILA, Israel Assn. of Applied Linguistics (pres. 1983-86), Coun. on the Tchg. of Hebrew. Jewish. Office: Dept Comms/Journalism, Hebrew Univ, 91905 Jerusalem Israel

NIREGI, MITSUKI, counseling psychology educator; b. Utsunomiya, Tochigi, Japan, July 23, 1938; s. Kaisei Uchiyama and Sakae Niregi; m. Keiko Sakai, Feb. 11, 1940; children: Emiko Suzuki, Mamiko Yoshikawa. BSc, Tokyo Ednl. U., 1961; MA, Mich. State U., 1981; PhD, Jichi Med. Sch., Tochigi, 1992. Cert. clin. psychologist, counselor. Ednl. supr. Tochigi Ednl. Com., 1974-76; asst. prof. Jichi Med. Sch., Tochigi, 1976-86, assoc. prof., 1986-94, prof., 1995-97; prof. Ochanomizu U., Tokyo, 1997—. Author, editor: Medical Counseling, 1991; translator: How to Cope with Life Transition, 1993, Employee Assistance Program, 1997; author: Introduction to Industrial Counseling, 1995. Mem. Japanese Assn. Counseling Sci. (bd. dirs.), Japanese Assn. Indsl. Counseling (sec.). Home: 4-18 Misao-cho, Utsunomiya Tochigi 320-0863, Japan Office: Ochanomizu Univ, 2-11 Otsuka, Bunkyo-ku Tokyo 112-0012, Japan

NIRENBERG, MARSHALL WARREN, biochemist; b. N.Y.C., N.Y., Apr. 10, 1927; s. Harry Edward and Minerva (Bykowsky) N.; m. Perola Zaltzman, July 14, 1961. B.S. in Zoology, U. Fla., 1948, M.S., 1952; Ph.D. in Biochemistry, U. Mich., 1957. Postdoctoral fellow Am. Cancer Soc. at NIH, 1957-59; postdoctoral fellow USPHS at NIH, 1959-60; mem. staff NIH, 1960—; research biochemist, chief lab. biochem. genetics Nat. Heart, Lung and Blood Inst., 1962—; researcher mechanism protein synthesis, genetic code, nucleic acids, regulatory mechanisms in synthesis macromolecules, and neurobiology. Recipient Molecular Biology award Nat. Acad. Scis., 1962, award in biol. scis. Washington Acad. Scis., 1962, medal HEW, 1964, Modern Medicine award, 1963, Harrison Howe award Am. Chem. Soc., 1964, Nat. Medal Sci. Pres. Johnson, 1965, Hildebrand award Am. Chem. Soc., 1966, Research Corp. award, 1966, A.C.P. award, 1967, Gairdner Found. award merit Can., 1967, Prix Charles Leopold Meyer French Acad. Scis., 1967, Franklin medal Franklin Inst., 1968, Albert Lasker Med. Research award, 1968, Priestly award, 1968; co-recipient Louisa Gross Horowitz prize Columbia, 1968, Nobel prize in medicine and physiology, 1968. Fellow AAAS, N.Y. Acad. Scis.; mem. Am. Soc. Biol. Chemists, Am. Chem. Soc. (Paul Lewis award enzyme chemistry 1964), Am. Acad. Arts and Scis., Biophys. Soc., Nat. Acad. Scis., Washington Acad. Scis., Soc. for Study Devel. and Growth, Soc. Devel. Biology, Harvey Soc. (hon.), Leopoldina Deutsche Akademie der Naturforscher, Pontificial Acad. Scis.

NIROMA, TIMO I., systems analyst; b. Helsinki, Finland, Aug. 3, 1945; s. Olli I. and Gunvor E. (Palmen) N.; m. Paivi I. Koillinen, Dec. 19, 1969; children: Oskari, Raisa. M of Statis., U. Helsinki, 1980. Systems analyst Social Ins. Inst., Helsinki, 1969—. Contbr. articles to profl. jours. Mem. AAAS, N.Y. Acad. Scis. Avocations: science, movies, music. Office: Social Ins Inst, Hoylaamotie 1 a B, FIN00380 Helsinki Finland

NIRSCHL, ROBERT PHILLIP, orthopedic surgeon; b. South Milwaukee, Wis., Aug. 28, 1933; s. Boyd A. and Helen (Wozny) N.; m. Mary Ann Oleniczak, June 21, 1958; children: Suzanne, Robert C., Julie. Student, Coll. Holy Cross, 1951-53, Marquette U., 1953-54; MD, Marquette U., 1958; MS, U. Minn., 1965. Diplomate Am. Bd. Orthop. Surgery. Intern St. Mary's Hosp., Duluth, Minn., 1958-59; resident in orthop. Mayo Clinic, Rochester, Minn., 1959-63; lt. comdr. USN, Washington, 1963-65; pvt. practice Arlington, Va., 1965—; attending orthop. surgeon Arlington (Va.) Hosp., v.p. med. staff, 1980-83, dir. Hand Surgery Svc., 1975-85; chief orthop. surgery No. Va. Cmty. Hosp., 1971-82; founding dir. Nirschl Orthop. Sports Medicine Clinic, Va. Sports Medicine Inst., 1974—, Nirschl Orthop. Sports Med. Clinic Orthop. Sports Medicine Fellowship Program Arlington Hosp., 1987—; mem. clin. faculty Georgetown U. Med. Ctr., 1965—; orthop. cons. Pres.'s Coun. Phys. Fitness, Washington, 1981-87; mem. sports sci. com. USTA, N.Y.C., 1987-94; course dir. numerous symposia in field. Author: Arm Care, 1981, rev. edit., 1996, Isoflex Exercise System, 1983; chief med. editor Orthop. Today, 1983-93; mem. editl. bd. The Physician and Sportsmedicine, 1992—, The Med. Sentinel, 1996—; creator 6 video programs; contbr. chpts. to books and over 100 articles to profl. publs.; patentee in field. Chmn. Jeffersonian Health Policy Found., Williamsburg, Va., 1994-97. Grantee Pfizer Inc., 1992-93, Sano Corp, 1993-94, Iomed Corp. Mem. AMA, ACS, Am. Acad. Orthop. Surgery (health fin. com. 1994-2000, bd. counselors 2000—, comm. and state soc. coms. bd. of counselors 2000—), Am. Orthop. Sports Medicine Soc. (ethics com. 1992-97), Soc. Tennis Medicine and Sci. (exec. com.), Ea. Orthop. Assn., Washington Orthop. Soc., Va. Orthop. Soc. (pres. 1998-99), Med. Soc. Va. (chmn. sports medicine com. 1973-84, trustee polit. action com. 1990—, legis. com. 1995—), Arlington County Med. Soc. (pres. 1977, chmn. legis. com. 1987—, Welburn award 1995), Washington Golf and Country Club. Republican. Roman Catholic. Avocations: fitness activities. Office: Nirschl Orthop Sports Medicine Clinic 1715 N George Mason Dr Ste 504 Arlington VA 22205-3670

NIRSIMLOO, JAY, financial company executive; m. Josica Avena, Nov. 19, 1980; children: Lorjanie, Marjorie, Isalyne. BSc in Econs. with honors, London Sch. Econs., 1979. Expert comptable; commissaire aux comptes. Sr. mgr. KPMG, Paris, 1987-90, exec. ptnr., 1990—. Fellow Inst. of Chartered Accts. of Eng. and Wales. Avocation: golf. Office: KPMG, 1 Cours Valmy, 92923 Paris France

NISCE, LOURDES, radiologist; b. Manila, Apr. 13, 1923; m. Francisa N. and Elena (Zandueta) N. MD, U. Santo Tomas, Manila, 1946. Diplomate Am. Bd. Radiology. Intern Holy Name Hosp., Teaneck, N.J., 1952-53; resident N.Y. Hosp.-Cornell Med. Coll., N.Y.C., 1957-61; fellow Meml. Hosp. Sloan-Kettering Ctr., N.Y.C., 1961-62, attending radiation oncologist, 1965-86; prof. radiology N.Y. Hosp., 1965—, Cornell Med. Coll., 1965—. Contbr. articles to med. jours. Fellow Am Coll. Radiology; mem. Am. Coll. Radiologists, Radiol. Soc. N.Am., RADIUM, Am. Soc. Therapeutic Radiology and Oncology. Address: 525 E 68th St New York NY 10021-4870

NISCHIK, REINGARD MONICA, literature educator; b. Herford, Germany, Nov. 3, 1952. BA, MA, U. Cologne, Germany, 1977; PhD, U. Cologne, 1980, habilitation, 1990. Asst. prof. U. Cologne, 1980-86; prof. comparative lit. U. Mainz, Germany, 1988-92; prof. N.Am. lit. U. Freiburg, Germany, 1992-94; prof. Am. lit. U. Konstanz, Germany, 1994—. Author: Einsträngigkeit und Mehrsträngigkeit der Handlungsführung, 1981, Mentalstilistik: Stiltheorie und Narrativik, 1991; editor: Literary Criticism in Perspective, 1991-94, Short Short Stories Universal, 1993, American and Canadian Short Short Stories, 1994, American Film Stories, 1996, European Studies in American Literature and Culture, 1996—, Leidenschaften literarisch, 1998, Uni literarisch, 2000, New York Fiction, 2000, Margaret Atwood: Works and Impact, 2000; co-editor: (with others) Zeitschrift für Kanada-Studien, 1989—, (with Robert Kroetsch) Gaining Ground: European Critics on Canadian Literature, 1985, (with Barbara Korte) Modes of Narrative, 1990. Mem. selection com. German Acad. Exch. Svc., 1994—; chairperson English-Can. Lit. Gesellschaft für Kanada-Studien, 1989-94. Avocation: music, nature. Office: U Konstanz Dept Literature, HD 166, 78457 Konstanz Germany

NISENOFF, MARTIN, physicist; b. N.Y.C.; s. Louis and Ruth Nisenoff; m. Phyllis B. Simon, 1994; three children. BS, Worcester Poly. Inst., 1950; MS, Purdue U., 1952, PhD, 1960. Rsch. assoc. Purdue U., West Lafayette, Ind., 1960-61; physicist Ford Sci. Lab., Dearborn, Mich., 1961-70; low temperature physicist Stanford Rsch. Inst., Menlo Park, Calif., 1970-72; rsch. physicist U.S. Naval Rsch. Lab., Washington, 1972-99; physicist M. Nisenoff Assocs., North Bethesda, Md., 1999—. Mem. IEEE (sr.), Am. Phys. Soc., Applied Superconductivity Conf. Inc. (bd. dirs. 1982-88, 90-96, 98—). E-mail: m.nisenoff@ieee.org.

NISH, IAN HILL, political science educator; b. Edinburgh, Scotland, June 3, 1926; m. Rona Margaret Speirs, Dec. 29, 1965; 2 children. MA, Edinburgh U., 1951, London U., 1956; PhD, London U., 1961. Lectr. U. Sydney, Australia, 1957-62; from lectr. to prof. London Sch. Econs., 1962-91, prof. emeritus, 1991—. Author: Anglo-Japanese Alliance, 1966, Alliance in Decline, 1972, Japan's Foreign Policy, 1978, Origins of the Russo-Japanese War, 1986, Japan's Struggle with Internationalism, 1931-33, 1993. Served to capt. Brit. Army, 1944-48, PTO.

NISHI, HITOSHI, corporate communications consultant, critic; b. Kumamoto, Japan, Jan. 31, 1948; s. Hachiro and Mutsu (Ohmura) N.; m. Taeko Wakabayashi, March 25, 1971. BA, Meiji U., Tokyo, 1971. Mem. staff Hakuhodo Inc., Tokyo, 1971-90; v.p. Aoki Concept Designing Co., Ltd., Tokyo, 1990-95; CEO The Agency Review Ltd., Kanagawa, Japan, 1995—. Avocations: ocean sailing, target shooting, cooking. Home and Office: The Agency Review Ltd, 102 9-5-23 Sakurayama, Zushi City Kanagawa 249-0005, Japan

NISHI, OKIHIRO, ophthalmologist, surgeon; b. Osaka, Japan, Nov. 20, 1940; s. Taseki and Sono (Shiraishi) N.; m. Kayo Nakagawa, Nov. 22, 1975; children: Jinyu, Yutaro, Hiroyuki. B Culture, U. Tokyo, 1961; MD, U. Freiburg, Germany, 1967. Asst. physician in ophthalmology U. Tokyo, 1968-70; vice dir. Nishi Eye Hosp., Osaka, 1970-86, dir., 1986—; surgeon faculty eye camp Indo-Japan Ophthalmol. Found., Madras, India, 1987, bd. dirs., 1987—; tchr. in tng. of many Indian physicians for cataract surgery, 1986—; mem. faculty Congress of European Soc. of Cataract and Refractive Surgeons, Dublin, 1987—; lectr. 8th Ann. Meeting German Ophthalmic Surgeons, Nürnberg, 1995; dir. and sci. advisor Highlights of Ophthalmology, Panama, 1996—. Author: (with others) Techniques of Phacoemulsification & IOL Implantation, 1992; translator: Pathologie des Auges (Naumann & Apple) 1987; inventor surgical instrument for cataract surgery and restoration of accommodation by lens refilling using inflatable endocap balloon; editor Japanese Jour. Cataract and Refractive Surgery, 1986—, Japanese Jour. Ophthalmic Surgery, 1988; editl. bd. Jour. Am. Soc. of Cataract Refractive Surgery, 1998—; contbr. more than 120 articles to profl. jours. including Cataract Surgery. Mem. Japan Soc. Cataract and Refractive Surgery (bd. dirs. 1986—), Internat. Intraocular Implant Club, Internat. Ophthalmic Microsurg. Study Group. Avocations: yachting, scuba diving, skiing, golf, flamenco guitar. Office: Nishi Eye Hosp, Nakamachi 4-14-26, Higashinari-ku Osaka 537, Japan

NISHI, TOSHIO, political scientist, educator; b. Osaka, Japan, Dec. 13, 1941; s. Masashi and Chieko (Fujimura) N.; m. Maria Gotschall, Aug. 18, 1994; children: Leilan, Takeru. BA, Kwansei Gakuin U., Nishinomiya, Japan, 1964; MA, U. Wash., 1968, PhD, 1976. Account rep. J. Walter Thompson Co., N.Y.C., Tokyo, 1968-70; rsch. scientist Battelle Meml. Inst., Seattle, 1975-77; corr. NHK Jour., Seattle, 1985-91; postdoctoral fellow Hoover Instn., Stanford, Calif., 1977-91, rsch. fellow, 1996—; prof. Reitaku U., Chiba, Japan, 1991—; TV commentator TV Tokyo, 1998-99; guest commentator ABC News "45/85", 3 hr. program on Am. fgn. policies, 1985, "American Caesar", 5 hr. TV documentary based on William Manchester, 1985; lectr. in field. Author: Unconditional Democracy: Politics and Education in Occupied Japan, 1982, MacArthur no Hanzai (The Crime of MacArthur), 1983, Fukoku Jakumin: Nippon (Wealthy Nation, Weak People: Japan), 1996, Kuniyaburete MacArthur (The Invasion of MacArthur), 1998. Japan Soc. Rsch. grantee, 1973; Harry S. Truman Libr. Inst. scholar, 1977. Avocations: fencing, photography, survival hiking, weightlifting. Office: Reitaku Univ, 2-1-1 Hikarigaoka, Kashiwa Chiba 277, Japan

NISHIDA, ATSUHIRO, aerospace scientist. Dir. gen. Japanese Inst. Space Astron. Sci., Sagamihari Kanagawa. Office: Inst Space & Astro Sci, 3-1 Yoshinodai, Sagamihari Kanagawa 299, Japan

NISHIDA, HIROMI, biologist, researcher, educator; b. Osaka, Japan, Feb. 9, 1966; s. Koukichi and Hiroko Nishida. BS, U. Tokyo, 1990, M in Agr., 1992, PhD, 1995. Rsch. fellow Japan Soc. Promotion of Sci., Tokyo, 1994-96; postdoctoral rsch. fellow RIKEN Inst., Wako, Japan, 1996-97; asst. prof. U. Tokyo, 1997—. Mem. AAAS, Japan Soc. Biosci., Biotech., and Agrochemistry, Molecular Biology Soc. Japan, Soc. Evolutionary Studies Japan, Nat. Geog. Soc.

NISHIDA, KEIU, bank company executive. CEO Mitsui Trust & Banking, Tokyo, 1996—. Office: Mitsui Trust & Banking, 2-1-1 Nihonbashi-Muromachi, 103 Tokyo Japan

NISHIDA, MAMORU, Japanese government official. Min. home affairs Govt. of Japan, Tokyo, 1998—. Mem. Liberal Democratic Party. Address: Ministry Home Affairs, JT Honsha Bldg 2-2-1 Toranomon, Minato-ku Tokyo 105, Japan*

NISHIGAKI, KOJI, electronics executive. CEO NEC Corp., Tokyo. Office: NEC Corp, 5-7-1 Shiba, Minato-ku Tokyo 108-8001, Japan*

NISHIGAKI, SATORU, bank company executive. CEO Tokai Bank, Nagoya, Japan, 1996—. Office: Tokai Bank, 3-21-24 Nishiki Naka-ku, 460 Nagoya Japan

NISHIGAKI, TORU, information scientist, educator, science writer; b. Tokyo, Dec. 12, 1948; s. Osamu and Shigeko (Aoki) N.; m. Sachiko Koizumi, May 19, 1974; children: Taro, Junta. BS in Engring., U. Tokyo, 1972, PhD in Info. Engring., 1982. Rschr. Hitachi, Ltd., Japan, 1972-80; vis. scholar Stanford (Calif.) U., 1980-81; sr. rschr. Hitachi Ltd., Japan, 1981-86; assoc. prof. info. engring. Meiji U., Tokyo, 1986-91, prof. info. engring., 1991-96; vis. prof. info. engring. U. Reims, France, 1994-95; prof. info. engring. U. Tokyo, 1996—. Author: Digital Narcissus, 1991 (Suntory prize for social scis. and humanities 1991), Multi-media, 1994 (Telecom Social Sci. prize 1995), Pessimistic Cyborg, 1994, Sacred Virtual Reality, 1995. Recipient Best Paper prize Info. Processing Soc. Japan, 1979. Mem. Assn.

Computing Machinery, Japan PEN. Office: U Tokyo Interfac Init Info Studies, 7-3-1 Hongo Bunkyo, Tokyo 113-0033, Japan

NISHIKAWA, TOSHIFUMI, bank executive. Pres., CEO The Sumitomo Bank Ltd., Osaka, Japan. Office: Sumitomo Bank Ltd, 6-5 Kitahama 4-chome Chuoku, Osaka 541-0041, Japan*

NISHIKAWA, TOSHIO, electronics executive; b. Ishikawa, Japan, July 10, 1935; m. Atsuko Tokuda, Mar. 2, 1962; children: Satomi, Wataru. BEE, Kanazawa (Japan) U., 1958, DEng, 1990. Dir. Murata Mfg. Co., Ltd., Kyoto, Japan, 1989-97, gen. mgr. Yokohama R & D Ctr., 1996-97, gen. mgr. Microwave Product divsn., 1994-97, standing corp. advisor, 1997—; temporary lectr. Tohoku U., 1990-91, Saitama U., 1992-93, Ritsumeikan U., 1998—; guest prof. Utsunomiya U., 1994-95, Yamaguchi U., 1996-97, Saitoma U., 2000—. Fellow IEEE; mem. Inst. Electronics, Info. and Comm. Engrs., Inst. Elec. Engrs. Japan, Info. Processing Soc. Japan, N.Y. Acad. Sci. Home: 1-15-4 Takadai, Nagaoka kyo 617, Japan Office: Murata Mfg Co Ltd, 2-26-10 Tenjin, Nagaoka kyo 617, Japan

NISHIKAWA, YASUO, psychologist, educator; b. Chiba-shi Chiba-ken, Japan, July 30, 1939; s. Kenro and Fujiko (Oguchi) N.; m. Nobuko Nagatsuka, Dec. 11, 1970; 1 child, Yuichi. BA, Keio U., 1964, M, 1966, PhD, 1978. Asst. Sophia U., Tokyo, 1969-70, asst. prof., 1970-74, assoc. prof., 1974-81, prof., 1981-98, prof. emeritus, 1998—; prof. Hokkaido U., Sapporo, 1998—; vis. prof. Pa. State U., State College, 1974, 1990-91; specialist mem. Ctrl. Coun. for Edn., 1989-91. Author: What is Mind, 1975, Behavior Analysis, 1978, Human Being Viewed as a Black Box, 1979, Behavior Medicine, 1981, Pattern of Cognition, 1988, Experimental Science of Behavior, 1988, Frontiers of Mental Science, 1994; author, editor: Invitation to Modern Psychology, 1989, Cognitive Science, 1997, Life Style Related Diseases, 1998, Introduction to Cognitive Science, 2000; co-author: An Introduction to Linguistic Research, 1999, Engineering of Impression, 2000, Cognitive Science, 2000. Mem. Am. Psychol. Soc., Am. Psychol. Assn., N.Y. Acad. Scis., Planetary Soc., Cognitive Sci. Soc., Japanese Psychol. Assn., Japanese Cognitive Sci. Soc. (editor in chief 1987-90), Japanese Psychonomic Soc., Japanese Assn. for Philosophy of Sci. (editl. bd.). Avocation: classical music. Home: 13-2 Inage 3-chome Inage-ku, Chiba-Shi, Chiba 263-0034, Japan

NISHIMOTO, MARC MAKOTO, research chemist; b. Wailuku, Hawaii, Apr. 2, 1959; s. Sadao and Asaye (Flores) N.; m. Dina Sachie Shinozuka, Feb. 19, 1988; children: Eric Keith, Gregory Jordan. BS in Chemistry, Seattle U., 1981; MS in Chemistry, U. Wash., 1983, PhD in Chemistry, 1986. Teaching asst. U. Wash., Seattle, 1981-83; postdoctoral fellow Oreg. State U., Corvallis, 1987-88; chemist Nat. Marine Fisheries Svc., Seattle, 1983-87, rsch. chemist, 1988-94; chemist Maui Pineapple Co., Kahului, Hawaii, 1994-95, product safety officer, 1995-96, R&D coord., 1996-97, dept. head, 1997-99, dir. rsch. and product devel., 1999—; reviewer fellowship com. Soc. Environ. Toxicology and Chemistry, 1991. Contbr. articles to sci. publs.; reviewer Ctr. Indoor Air Rsch.; patentee in field. Recipient Outstanding Performance award Nat. Marine Fisheries Svc., 1984, Superior Performance award, 1985, Cert. of Merit, 1990, New Investigator award Air Force Office Sci. Rsch. and Soc. Environ. Toxicology and Chemistry, 1990. Mem. Am. Chem. Soc., Inst. Food Tech., Alpha Sigma Nu. Achievements include research in metabolism of xenobiotics in marine organisms, structure of major DNA adduct formed by fish liver enzymes using chromatography and low temperature fluorescence spectroscopy, level of oxidative DNA damage in marine organisms undergoing oxidative stress, changes in glutathione homeostasis in liver of fish exposed to pro-oxidant chemicals, exposure of fish to xenobiotics. Office: Maui Pineapple Co 120 Kane St Kahului HI 96732

NISHIMURA, AKITOSHI, electronics engineer; b. Ise, Mie, Japan, Apr. 14, 1950; s. Katsuhiko and Toshiko N.; m. Nori Noto, Oct. 9, 1983; 1 child, Kumi. BS, Kyoto U., Japan, 1972; MS, Tokyo U., Japan, 1974, DSc, 1977. Rsch. fellow Glasgow U., Scotland, 1977-79; rschr. High Energy Physics Lab., Tsukuba, Ibaraki, Japan, 1980-83; tech. staff Tex. Instruments Japan, Tokyo, 1983—; sr. mem. tech. staff Tex. Instruments Japan, Miho, 1992—. Patentee in field; contbr. articles to profl. publs. Mem. IEEE. Avocations: gardening, swimming. Office: 6-24-1 Nishi-Shinjuku, Shinjuki, Tokyo 160-8366, Japan

NISHIMURA, MASAO, banker. CEO, Indsl. Bank Japan, Tokyo. Office: Indsl Bank Japan, 1-3-3 Marunouchi Chiyoda-ku, Tokyo 100-8210, Japan*

NISHIMURA, TATSUYA, materials engineer, investigator; b. Kagoshima, Japan, Jan. 30, 1946; s. Keiji and Tsuyako (Tsuru) Sakoda; m. Toshi Nishimura, Mar. 20, 1970; children: Tamaki, Masanobu, Mitsumasa. BS in Metallurgy, Kyushu (Japan) Inst. Tech., 1969. First class radioisotope tech.; authorized inspector "B" endorse, lead auditor. Inspector engr. Sasebo (Japan) Heavy Industries, 1969-80, asst. mgr. bus. sec., 1980-82, asst. mgr. pressure vessel fab. shop, 1982-85; authorized inspector, ASME code inspector B.E.I., Inc., Tokyo, 1985-87; authorized inspector, ASME code inspector, shop auditor The Hartford Steam Boiler Inspection & Ins., 1987—; auditor ISP 9001, Japan, 1994—. Mem. ASME (N.Y.). Avocation: fishing. Home: 1309-8 Kashimae-Cho, 858 Sasebo Nagasaki, Japan Office: Hartford Steam & Boiler Ins, 7-9-201 Mitaki-Honmachi, Nishi-ku Hiroshima 733, Japan

NISHIMURA, TOSHIKAZU, anatomy educator; b. Higashiosaka, Osaka, Japan, Dec. 20, 1949; s. Hiromu and Chiyoko (Nanno) N.; m. Mitsuko Kawai, Aug. 13, 1983; children: Jitsumi, Ariko. MSc, Osaka (Japan) City U., 1975; D of Med. Sci., Aichi Med. U., Nagakute, Japan, 1987. Rsch. asst. Aichi Med. U., 1975-95, lectr., 1996—; vis. prof. Bern U. Inst. Med. Microbiology, Switzerland, 1991-92. Author: Methods in Cell Biology 14, 1976; contbr. articles to profl. publs. Mem. Friendly Found., Aichi, 1997—. Mem. Japanese Assn. of Anatomists, Japanese Soc. of Developmental Biologists, Japan Soc. for Cell Biology. Avocation: plant cultivation. Office: Aichi Med U Sch Medicine, Karimata Yazako, Nagakute 480-1195, Japan

NISHIMURA, TOSHIRO, lawyer; b. Mukden, China, Apr. 10, 1933; s. Katsuro and Fumiko N.; m. Keiko Saito, 1966; children: Naohiro, Hiroaki. LLB, U Tokyo, 1959. Rep. ptnr. Nishimura & Ptnrs., Tokyo, 1966—; vis. prof. Chuo U. Law Sch., Tokyo, 1997—. Mem. Internat. Bar Assn., Japan Fedn. Bar Assns., Rotary. Avocations: classical music, golf. Home: 5-16-35-409 Roppongi, 106-0032 Minato-ku Tokyo, Japan Office: Nishimura & Ptnrs, ARK Mori Bldg 29F 1-12-32, 107-6029 Akasaka Minato-ku Tokyo, Japan

NISHIMURO, TAIZO, electronics executive. CEO Toshiba Corp., Tokyo; chmn. Toshiba Corp. Office: Toshiba Corp, 1-1-1 Shibaura Minato-ku, Tokyo 105-8001, Japan*

NISHINARI, KATSUHIRO, physicist, educator; b. Tokyo, Jan. 8, 1967; s. Hiroshi and Akie (Makimura) N.; m. Yumiko Nojima, Sept. 13, 1995. B, Tokyo Univ., 1990, M, 1992, PhD, 1995. Assoc. Yamagata Univ., Yonezawa, Japan, 1995-97, assoc. prof., 1997-99; assoc. prof. Ryukoku U., Shiga, 1999—; cons. Tokyo Bobslei Assn., 1996—. Contbr. articles to profl. jours. Recipient grant Ministry of Edn., Sci. and Culture, 1995, 97. Mem. Physical Soc. Japan, Japan Soc. Mechanical Engring., Japan Soc. Industrial and Applied Math. Avocations: opera, driving. Office: Ryukoku Univ, Seta, Ohtsu Shiga 520-2194, Japan

NISHIOKA, SHUZO, environmental systems analyst; b. Tokyo, Dec. 8, 1939; s. Usaburo and Sueko (Kino) N.; m. Reiko Sato; children: Tomoyuki, Yousuke. BS in Engring., U. Tokyo, 1962, MS in Engring., 1964, PhD in Engring., 1967. Plant engr. Asahi Chem. Co., Tokyo, 1967-75; system analyst Asahi Rsch. Ctr., Tokyo, 1976-79; chief researcher Nat. Inst. for Environ. Studies, Tsukuba, Japan, 1979-90, dir., 1990-99; prof. Tokyo Inst. of Tech., 1996-99, Grad. Sch. of Media and Governance, Keio U., 1999—; vice-chmn. WGII IPCC, Geneva, 1991-92; mem. sci. com. START, Washington, 1998—; counselor Environ. Info. Ctr., Tokyo, 1992—; mem. GEF/UNEP/STAD, 1998—. author: Economics of Global Environment, Key concept of Global Environment, 1992; editor: Climate Change Impact on Japan, 1997; contbr. articles to profl. jours. Recipient Global Environ. Tech. prize Nikkei Shimbun, Tokyo, 1997. Mem. Climate Inst. (bd. dirs. 1990—), Japanese Assn. for Environ. and Symbionisis (vice chmn.). Avocation: rugby. Home: 4-10-16 Shimoochiai, Shinjuku Tokyo 161-0033, Japan Office: Keio Univ, 5322 Endo, Fujisawa 252-8520, Japan

NISHITA, EIJI, management consultant, planning executive; b. Toshimaku, Tokyo, Japan, Jan. 24, 1936; s. Toshinaga and Sei Nishita. BA in Law, Waseda U., Tokyo, 1959. Mem. div. staff Yutaka & Co., Tokyo, 1959-64, Topy Industries Ltd., Tokyo, 1965-66; sr. researcher JEEC Cons., Tokyo, 1967-69; mgr., planner Devel. Systems Inc., Tokyo, 1969-75; mng. dir. Regional Planning Union, Inc., Tokyo, 1975-79, pres., 1979—; v.p. Regional Planning Internat., Tokyo, 1975-79, pres., 1979—. Bd. dirs. City Planning Cons. Assn. Japan. Mem. Nat. Assn. Indsl. and Office Properties (U.S.) Assn. of Promotion of Internat. Cooperation (Japan), City Planning Cons. Assn. Japan (bd. dirs.). Home: 1207 Roi Ichibankan 6-1, Sakae Kanagawa-Ku, Yokohama 221-0052, Japan Office: Regional Planning Internat, Otsuka Gen Bldg 1-19-17, Kita Otsuka Toshimaku Tokyo 170, Japan

NISHIURA, HIROYUKI, physicist, educator; b. Itami, Japan, Feb. 15, 1953. BS, U. Osaka, 1976, MS, 1978, DSc, 1981. Postdoctoral fellow Soryushi Shogakukai Found., Kyoto, Japan, 1981-82, Japan Soc. Promotion Sci., Kyoto, 1982-83, Johns Hopkins U., Balt., 1983-85; lectr. U. Osaka, Japan, 1986—; assoc. prof. Jr. Coll. Osaka Inst. Technology, 1991-2000, prof., 2000—. Mem. Phys. Soc. Japan. Office: Osaka Inst Tech Jr Coll, 5-16-1 Omiya Asahi-ku, 535-8585 Osaka Japan

NISHIYAMA, HITOSHI, environmental engineer, consultant, researcher; b. Komae-shi, Tokyo, Japan, Jan. 12, 1962; s. Masao and Setsuko (Saito) N.; m. Toyoko Kikuchi, Nov. 19, 1995; children: Yuna, Keito. B in Engring., Musashi Inst. Tech., Tokyo, 1984, D in Engring., 1996. Registered profl. engr., Japan. Tech. expert Nippon Electric Corp., Tokyo, 1984-88; tech. expert Fuji Tech. Rsch. Ctr., Inc., Tokyo, 1988-92, asst. chief engr., 1992-96, chief engr., 1996—; cons. Akita (Japan) Prefecture, 1990—, Ministry Constrn., Tokyo, 1992—, City of Tokyo, 1995—, Japan Hwy. Pub. Corp., Tokyo, 1997—. Contbr. articles to profl. jours. Mem. Inst. Electronics, Info. and Comm. Engrs. of Japan, Japan Soc. for Simulation Tech., Japan Soc. Civil Engrs. Liberal Democrat. Buddhist. Avocations: music appreciation, listening to jazz, astronomical observation, motoring, swimming. Home: 3-1-6 Iwado Minami, Komae 201-0005, Japan Office: Fuji Tech Rsch Ctr Inc, 1-22-11 Higashi, Shibuya 150-0011, Japan

NISHIYAMA, TOSHIMASA, parasitologist; b. Osaka, Japan, Oct. 4, 1956; s. Toshio and Masami (Shimizu) N.; m. Yoshie Matsuoka, Apr. 21, 1984; children: Nobumasa, Masayuki, Mari. MD, Kansai Med. U., Osaka, 1982; DMS, Nara Med. U., Kashihara, Japan, 1987. Asst. Nara Med. U., Kashihara, 1986-91, lectr., 1991-2000; prof. dept. pub. health Kansai Med. U., 2000—; sec. gen. health advice for those who travel or stay overseas, Nara, Japan, 1995—; mgr. orphan drugs of the rsch. group for devel. of therapeutic drugs against tropical diseases, Ministry Health and Welfare, Japan, 1995-99; dir. health edn. for overseas passengers, Osaka, 1995-2000; core group Malaria Network Japan Internet, Himeji, Japan, 1995—; dir. Nara Prefectural Inst. Pub. Health, 1999-2000. Editor: Clinical Application of Praziquantel, 1993; co-editor: The Traveler's Medical Services, Japanese Homepage of Internet, 1995; contbr: Integrate Pharmacology, 1997. Fellow Royal Soc. Tropical Medicine and Hygine; mem. Japanese Soc. Parasitology, Am. Soc. Parasitologists, Japanese Soc. Internal Medicine, Japan Endocrine Soc. Office: Kansai Med U Dept Pub Health, 10-15 Humizono-cho, Moriguchi-shi Osaka 570-8506, Japan

NISHIYAMA, YAYOI, mycologist, educator; b. Japan, Apr. 22, 1945; d. Hidemitsu and Mutsuko (Yoshioka) Kanda; m. Fumiaki Nishiyama, June 19, 1983. B of Domestic Sci., Japan Womens U., 1968; PhD, Tokyo U., 1980. Asst. prof. medicine Teikyo U., Tokyo, 1973-80, assoc. prof. medicine, 1981-90, assoc. prof. med. mycology, 1991—; councilor The Japanese Soc. Electron Microscopy, 1989—, The Japanese Soc. Med. Mycology, 1991—, Japanese Soc. Bacteriology, 1997-99; trustee The Japanese Soc. Electron Microscopy. Author: Dimorphic Fungi in Biology and Medicine, 1993, Archaea, 1995; contbr. articles to profl. jours. Mem. Internat. Soc. Human and Animal Mycology. Office: Teikyo U Inst Med Mycology, 359 Otsuka Hachioji, Tokyo 192-0395, Japan

NISKANEN, RAIMO OLAVI, orthopedic surgeon; b. Pieksämäki, Finland, Jan. 6, 1954; s. Martti Mikael and Sirkka Marjatta (Rissanen) N.; m. Riitta Aulikki Virta, Oct. 1, 1983; children: Juho, Silja, Kalle. MD, 1st I.P. Pavlov Med. Inst., Leningrad, 1980. Cert. specialist in orthopedics and traumatology, Nat. Bd. Social Welfare and Health Svc. Asst. surgeon Ctrl. Hosp., Lahti, 1985-89, Rheumatism Found. Hosp., Heinola, Finland, 1989-90; sr. registrar Univ. Hosp., Helsinki, Finland, 1990-91, 94; asst. surgeon City Hosp., Lahti, Finland, 1981-85; specialist in orthopedics and traumatology City Hosp., Lahti, 1995-96; asst. chief, specialist in orthopedics and traumatology Päijät-Häme Ctrl. Hosp., Oikokadun, Yksikkö, 1997—; mem. investigative com. of traffic accidents of ins. cos. Contbr. articles on orthopedics and traumatology to profl. publs. Med. lt. Finnish mil., 1992-93. Mem. Finnish Med. Assn., Finnish Orthop. Soc. Lutheran. Avocations: exercise, boating, forestry.

NISLI, GÜNGÖR, pediatric hematologist, pediatrics educator; b. Ankara, Turkey, May 25, 1931; s. Mahmut Cavit and Makbule Muhlise (Denker) N.; m. Necla Sagiroglu, July 6, 1963; children: Tigin, Yulug. Grad., Ankara U., 1955, Ege U., Izmir, Turkey, 1962. Resident in pediat. Ege U., Izmir, 1957-62, chief resident pediat., 1962-67, assoc. prof. pediat., 1967-72, pediat. hematologist, 1970-98, prof. pediat., 1972-98, vice dean med. faculty, 1980-82, head dept. pediat., 1989-92, head sect. internal med. scis., 1995-98, ret. with high honor cert., 1998; mem. exec. com. faculty medicine Ege U., Izmir, 1972-75; mem. ethics com. Ege U. Hosp., 1990-98, cons. in pediatric hematology, 1998—. Contbr. articles to profl. jours. Pres. Izmir Thalassemia Assn., 1989—, Ege Hemophilia Assn., 1994—. Lt. Nebihan Hosp. Erzurum, Turkey, 1955-57. Lepetit scholarship grantee Perugia, Italy, 1960-61, Tubitak Scientist grantee U. Man., Can., 1990-92, Cilag Internat. grantee, Geneva, 1997. Mem. Internat. Soc. Pediat. Oncology, Internat. Soc. Hematology, Turkish Hematology Assn. (exec. com. 1996—). Avocations: traveling, camping, swimming. Home: 1441 Sok No 2/10, TR-35220 Izmir Turkey Office: Dept Pediat & Pediat Hemat, Ege Univ Hosp, TR-35100 Izmir Turkey

NISSAN, EPHRAIM, computer scientist; b. Tel-Aviv, May 9, 1955; s. Hayim and Albertina Yamin-Joseph Nissan. Laurea in Engring., Milan Inst. Technology, 1982; PhD in Computer Sci., Ben-Gurion U., Beer-Sheva, Israel, 1989. Cert. engr., Milan, Israel. Doctoral and postdoctoral fellow Ben-Gurion U., 1983-90; rschr. three Faculties of Bar-Ilan U., Israel, 1991-94; vis. prof. Istituto Metodologico Economico Statistico/U. Urbino, Italy, 1993, hon. overseas assoc., 1994—; rsch. fellow computing and math. scis. U. Greenwich, London, 1994—; invited speaker in field; adviser World Orgn. Law and Computer Sci., 1999—. Founder Internat. Jour. Expert Systems, 1985-87, assoc. editor, 1986-91; mem. editl. bd. numerous internat. rsch. publs.; editor: (with K.M. Schmidt) From Information to Knowledge, 1995; guest editor: Computers and Artificial Intelligence, 1998, Jour. Ednl. Computing Rsch., 1997, New Rev. Applied Expert Systems, 1998, 99, Artificial Intelligence and Law, 2001, Artificial Intelligence Engring. Design Analysis Mfg., 1999, Internat. Jour. Info. and Telecomms. Law, 1998, 2001; co-editor e-journal humanities, Melilah, 2000—, Tsur, 1999—; contbr. over 130 articles to profl. jours. and confs. Recipient IPA award in Computer Sci., Info. Processing Assn., Israel, 1988; hon. rsch. fellow Ctr. of Jewish Studies, U. Manchester, 1999—; award Burroughs Italiana thesis contest, 1982. Achievements include research in artificial intelligence, power plant engring., linguistics, literature and cultural studies, computing for law and humanities fields; authoring computational models of cognition, e.g. word-formation, deontic intentionality, humor or creativity. E-mail: e.nissan@gre.ac.uk. Office: CMS/Univ Greenwich, Wellington St Woolwich, London SE18 6PF, England

NISSAN, MOSHE, biomedical engineer and researcher; b. Haifa, Israel, May 8, 1946; s. Menachem and Rivka Nissalevitch; m. Ziva Wodislawsky, Apr. 4, 1971; children: Yael Kadit, Kfir Yoav, Assaf Ben-Zion. BSc in Physics, Technion-Israel Inst. Tech., Haifa, 1968, MSc in Bioengring., 1974; PhD in Bioengring., U. Strathclyde, Glasgow, U.K., 1978. Bioengr. Rambam Med. Ctr., Haifa, 1978-80; rschr. bioengring. Technion-Israel Inst. Tech., Haifa, 1980-82; lectr. Holon (Israel) Technol. Ctr., 1982-88; vis. rschr. Oxford (U.K.) Ortho. Engring. Ctr., 1987-88; rschr. Rappaport Inst. for Rsch., Haifa, 1988-93; bioengr., R&D officer Tel-Aviv Med. Ctr., 1993—. Contbr. articles to profl. jours., books. Lt. Israeli Def. Forces, 1968-71. E-mail: nissan@tasmc.health.gov.il. Office: Tel-Aviv Med Ctr, Orthop B' Dept, 6 Weizman St, 64239 Tel-Aviv Israel

NISSEL, MARTIN, radiologist, consultant; b. N.Y.C., July 29, 1921; s. Samuel David and Etta Rebecca (Ostrie) N.; m. Beatrice Goldberg, Dec. 26, 1943; children: Philippa Lyn, Jeremy Michael. BA, NYU, 1941; MD, N.Y. Med. Coll., 1944. Diplomate Am. Bd. Radiology. Intern Met. Hosp., N.Y.C., 1944-45, Lincoln Hosp., N.Y.C., 1947-48; resident in radiology Bronx Hosp., 1948-50, attending radiologist, 1952-54; resident in radiotherapy Montefiore Hosp., Bronx, 1950-51, attending radiotherapist, 1954-65; attending radiologist Buffalo (N.Y.) VA Hosp., 1951-52; attending radiotherapist Univ. Hosp. Boston City Hosp., 1965-69; asst. prof. radiology Boston U. Sch. of Medicine, 1965-69; chief radiotherapist,dir. radiation ctr. Brookside Hosp., San Pablo, Calif., 1969-77; group leader, radiopharm. drugs FDA, Rockville, Md., 1977-86; pvt. cons. radiopharm. drug devel., 1986—. Contbr. articles to profl. jours. Lectr. Am. Cancer Soc., Contra Costa County, Calif., 1973-76. Capt. MC AUS, 1945-47, Korea. Recipient Contra Costa County Speakers Bur. award Am. Cancer Soc., 1973, 76, Responsible Person for Radiol. Health Program for Radiopharm. Drugs award FDA, 1980-86. Mem. Am. Coll. Radiology, Radiol. Soc. N.Am. Avocations: photography, model train building, travel. Office: PO Box 5537 Eugene OR 97405-0537

NISSEN, BRUCE ALLEN, labor studies educator; b. Ames, Iowa, Jan. 20, 1948; s. Raymond A. and Irene A. Nissen; m. Karen L. Lieberman, Apr. 26, 1978; children: Jared A., Leif A. BA, Grinnell Coll., 1970; PhD, Columbia U., 1975. Prof. labor studies Ind. U. N.W., Gary, 1985-97, Fla. Internat. U., Miami, 1997—. Editor: Theories of the Labor Movement, 1987, Unions and Workplace Reorganization, 1997, Which Direction for Organized Labor?, 1999; author: Fighting for Jobs, 1995. Office: Ctr Labor Rsch and Studies Fla Internat U University Park Miami FL 33199-0001

NISSEN, HANS JÖRG, archaeology educator; b. Heidelberg, Germany, June 22, 1935; s. Stig Høffding and Huberta (Radloff) N.; m. Margarete Speer, Apr. 14, 1962; children: Annegret, Berta, Karen, Nils Frederik. Dr.phil., U. Heidelberg, 1963. Rsch. asst. German Archaeol. Inst., Baghdad, Iraq, 1963-67; asst. prof. Oriental Inst., U. Chgo., 1968-71; prof. archaeology Free U. Berlin, 1971—, v.p., 1977-81; excavating and archaeol. fieldwork, Iraq, Iran, Pakistan, Jordan, 1964—. Author: Datierung des Königsfriedhofes von Ur, 1966, The Early History of the Ancient Near East, 1988, Geschichte Alt-Vorderasieus, 1999, (with R.M. Adams) The Uruk Countryside, 1972, (with P. Damerow and R.K. Englund) Archaic Bookkeeping, 1993. Mem. German Archaeol. Inst., Am Oriental Soc., German Oriental Soc. Home: Nollendorfstr 28, D-10777 Berlin Germany Office: Free U Berlin, Huettenweg 7, D-14195 Berlin Germany

NISSEN, LOWELL ALLEN, education educator; b. Jan. 10, 1932; s. Nanning Henry and Marie Caroline (Chell) N.; m. Beverly Ann Chloupek, July 31, 1960; 1 child, Lois Ann Nissen Ganous. BA magna cum laude, U. Minn., 1954, MA, 1958; PhD, U. Nebr., 1962. Asst. prof., instr. U. Ark., Fayetteville, 1963-70, assoc. prof., 1970-79, prof., 1979—. Author: Teleological Language in the Life Sciences, 1997; co-author: Reflective Thinking: The Fundamentals of Logic, 1968, rev. edit., 76, John Dewey's Theory of Inquiry and Truth, 1966. Mem. Am. Philos. Assn. Philosophy Sci. Assn., British Soc. Philosophy Sci., Phi Beta Kappa. Home: 2163 S Smokehouse Trl Fayetteville AR 72701-7724

NISSENBAUM, GERALD, physician, educator, inventor; b. Jersey City, Feb. 5, 1932; m. Sylvia Sinakin, Sept. 4, 1957; children: Gary David, Eliot Mark, Robert Samuel. BA, Yeshiva U., 1954; MD, SUNY, 1958. Intern Brookdale Hosp., Bklyn., 1958-59, resident, 1959-60; sr. resident Jersey City Med. Ctr., 1960-61; NIH research fellow in gastroenterology Nat. Cancer Inst., 1962-63; asst. med. dir. Hebrew Hosp., Jersey City, 1962-73; clin. instr. medicine U. Medicine and Dentistry N.J., 1963-72; asst. attending dept. medicine Jersey City Med. Ctr., 1963-68, assoc. attending, 1968-69, attending, 1970—, dir. gastroenterology, 1973-76; clin. asst. prof. medicine U. Medicine and Dentistry N.J., 1972—; pvt. practice internal medicine and gastroenterology Jersey City; adminstrv. dir. gastroenterology Jersey City Med. Ctr., 1996—. Contbr. articles to profl. jours.; developed classic cytol. reagt. used worldwide in medicine and microbiology, "Nissenbaum's Fixative", 1953; patentee device for localizing gastrointestinal bleeding; inventor various med. devices. Capt. M.C., U.S. Army. Recipient Bernard Revel Meml. award Yeshiva U., 1972. Mem. AMA, Soc. Protozoologists, N.J. Med. Soc., NRA, Phi Lambda Kappa. Office: 126 Gifford Ave Jersey City NJ 07304-1704

NISSEN-MEYER, JON, biochemist, educator; b. Luster, Norway, June 6, 1948; s. Sven and Elna (Biong) Nissen-M.; m. Helene-Margrethe Svalland, June 12, 1947; children: Jostein, Sigurd-Erik, Margrete. Master, U. Bergen, Norway, 1975, PhD, 1982. Fellow Norwegian Cancer Soc., U. Bergen, 1976-80; rsch. scientist Norwegian Cancer Soc. Inst. for Cancer Rsch., Trondheim, 1981-88, Lab. Microbial Gene Tech., Ås, Norway, 1988-92; prof. dept. biochemistry U. Oslo, 1992—. Contbr. over 70 articles to profl. jours. Recipient Oncology Rsch. award Onkologist Forum, Norway, 1987. Avocation: cross country skiing. Home: Feltspatveien 16, 1430 Ås Norway Office: U Oslo, Dept Biochemistry 1041, 0316 Oslo Norway

NISSENSON, ALLEN RICHARD, physician, educator; b. Chgo., Dec. 10, 1946; s. Harry and Sylvia Lillian (Chapnitsky) N.; m. Charna H. Karp, May 28, 1978; 1 child, Ariel Rose. BS in Medicine, Northwestern U., 1967, MD, 1971. Diplomate Am. Bd. Internal Medicine, bd. cert. internal medicine and nephrology. Intern in medicine Michael Reese Hosp. and Med. Ctr., Chgo., 1971-72, resident in internal medicine, 1972-74; fellowship in nephrology Northwestern U., Chgo., 1974-76; assoc. medicine Northwestern U. Med. Sch., Chgo., 1976-77; asst. prof. medicine UCLA Sch. Medicine, 1977-82, assoc. prof. medicine, 1982-88, prof. medicine, 1988—; dir. dialysis program UCLA Ctr. for the Health Scis., 1977—, med. dir. renal mgmt. strategies; adj. attending physician Northwestern Meml. Hosp., Chgo., 1976-77; asst. attending physician UCLA Ctr. for Health Scis., 1977-82, assoc. attending physician, 1988—; attending physician nephrology Wadsworth VA Hosp., 1978—; cons. on peritoneal dialysis Baxter-Travenol Labs., 1981—; mem. nephrology adv. com. Nephrology Nursing Edn. Grant, Calif. State U., 1983-90; vice chmn. Forum of End Stage Renal Disease Networks, 1988-91; mem. sci. adv. bd. Nat. Kidney Found., 1989-91, chmn. coun. on clin. nephrology, dialysis and transplantation, 1989-91; cons. on End Stage Renal Disease reimbursement Rand Corp., 1990—, others. Editor-in-chief Advances in Renal Replacement Therapy, 1993—; mem. editl. bd. Dialysis and Transplantation, 1978—, UCLA Health Insights, 1981-89, Perspectives in Peritoneal Dialysis, 1983—, Internat. Jour. Artificial Organs, 1984—, Seminars in Dialysis, 1987—, Am. Jour. Nephrology, 1989—, Am. Jour. Kidney Diseases, 1989—, Geriat. Nephrology and Urology Jour., 1989—; mem. editl. adv. bd. Contemporary Dialysis, 1983—, Nephrology Practice Today, 1989—, Hematopoietic Therapy Index and Revs., 1993—, Primary Care Reports, 1994—; editl. cons. Am. Jour. Nephrology, 1981-88; contbr. chpts. to books, abstracts and articles to profl. publs. Recipient Nat. Kidney Found. So. Calif. Cmty. Svc. award, 1981; Robert Wood Johnson policy fellow Office of Sen. Paul Wellstone, 1994-95. Fellow ACP; mem. Am. Soc. for Artifical Internal Organs, Am. Fedn. for Clin. Rsch., Am. Soc. Nephrology, Internat. Soc. Nephrology, Internat. Soc. Artificial Organs, Western Soc. for Clin. Investigation, European Dialysis and Transplant Assn., N.Am. Soc. for Dialysis and Transplantation, Renal Physicians' Assn. (bd. dirs. 1993—, sec. bd. dirs. 1994—, pres.), Calif. Renal Physicians (bd. dirs. 1987—). Office: UCLA Med Ctr Dialysis Ctr Ste 565-59 200 Medical Plaza Los Angeles CA 90024-6945

NISSER, CARL GUSTAV, lawyer; b. Stockholm, Mar. 25, 1940; s. William Percy and Ulla (Tegnér) N.; m. Marie-Louise Carolson, June 29, 1963 (div. May 1984); children: Henry, Daniel; m. Gunilla Lofgren, Aug. 23, 1984 (div. May 1997). LLM, Uppsala (Sweden) U., 1966; Diplôme d'Etudes Supérieurs, Strasbourg (France) U., 1967; postgrad., Harvard Bus. Sch., 1981. Jr. judge Ct. of Appeals, Stockholm, 1967-71; dir. Gränges Metallverken, Paris and Brussels, 1971-73, Volvo, Brussels, 1973-74; dir.

corp. affairs Goodyear Internat., Brussels, Akron, Ohio and Jakarta, Indonesia, 1974-81; chmn. Am. Transocean, Westport, Conn., 1987—; v.p. Inter Matrix, Westport, Conn., 1981-89; resident counsel Landahl, Brussels, 1989-93; resident ptnr. Lindahl, Brussels, 1993-97; mng. ptnr. Advokatfirman Nisser, 1997—; founder European Govt. Bus. Rels. Coun., Heat Transfer Techs., 1982, Swedeponic Internat. NV, 1996; bd. dirs. UTEK Corp., Plant City, Fla., e-tel corp., Providence, R.I.; founder, chmn., CEO eCom Enterprises, Inc. Author: (books) How to Sell in France, 1972, How to Form a Company in the Common Market, 1974, The Entrepreneur and Europe, 1994, Practical Guide to European Union, 1994, EC Competition Law-Leading Cases, 1995. Cpl. Signal, 1960-61, Uppsala. Mem. ABA, Internat. Bar Assn., European Assn. Securities Dealers (mem. legal and tax coms.), Order of Lazarus (comdr.). Republican. Lutheran. Home: 12 Treadwell Ave Westport CT 06880-4727 also: 27 Beresford Rd, London N5 2HS, England Office: Sweden House, 3 rue du Luxembourg, 1000 Brussels Belgium

NISTICÓ, GIUSEPPE, pharmacology educator; b. Cardinale, Calabria, Italy, Mar. 16, 1941; m. Maria Louise Hipwood; children: Steven, Robert. MD, Univ. Degli Studi, Naples, Italy, 1965. Asst. prof. Univ. Degli Studi, Naples, 1966-72; specialist in neurology and psychiatry Univ. Degli Studi, Modena, Italy, 1968; assoc. prof. Univ. Degli Studi, Messina, Italy, 1973-75, dir. Inst. Pharmacology, 1976-82, prof., 1980; dir. Inst. Pharmacology Univ. Degli Studi, Catanzaro, Italy, 1983; mem. European Parliament, Brussels, Belgium. Author: Neurotransmitters and Anterior Pituitary Function, 1978, Farmacologia Comunicazione Sinaptica, 1986, Brain Messengers and the Pituitary Gland, 1988; co-editor: Progr. in Nonmammalian Brain Research, 1983, Neurotransmitters, Seizures and Epilepsy III, 1986, VII International Conference Tetanus, 1985; contbr. articles to profl. jours. Christian Democrat. Roman Catholic. Home: Vitale Giulio Cesare 61, I-00100 Roma Italy*

NITSCH, CAROLINA, art dealer, publisher; b. Düsseldorf, Germany, Nov. 18, 1963; came to U.S., 1990; d. Walter Carl and Marion Ingeborg (Forst) N.; m. Ronald W. Jones (div.); m. Dieter Von Graffenried; 1 child, Alma Cosima Nitsch-Von Graffenried. Degree, U. Vienna, Austria, 1989. bd. dirs. Printed Matter, Inc., N.Y.C. Mem. Art Table, Inc. Roman Catholic. Home: 101 Wooster St Apt 6F New York NY 10012-3895 Office: Brooke Alexander Inc 59 Wooster St New York NY 10012-4349

NITSCHKE, PETER, political scientist, historian, educator; b. Hilden, Germany, Oct. 11, 1961; s. Günter and Maria-Louise (Moll) N.; m. Annette Beate Sperling, Oct. 20, 1989; children: Christine Sophia, Maximilian. Dissertation, U. Münster, Germany, 1989, habilitation, 1994. Lehrbeauftragter U. Münster, 1990-94, vertreter hochschuldozentur, 1994, vertreter prof., 1995; fellow Kulturwiss. Inst., Essen, Germany, 1995-96; prof. U. Vechta, Germany, 1997—; dir. Inst. for Social Scis., 2000—; stipendiat Fritz-Thyssen Stiftung, Köln, Germany, 1990-93. Author: Verbrechensbekämpfung, 1990, Staatsräson kontra Utopie?, 1995, Einführung in die Politische Theorie der Prämoderne, 2000; editor: Deutsche Polizeigeschichte, 1996, Revision des Grundgesetzes?, 1997, Die Europäische Union der Regionen, 1998, Klassische Politik, 2000, Metamorphosen des Leviathan?, 2001. Mem. German Soc. for Police History (redakteur 1991—, vorstandsmitglied 1992—). Roman Catholic. Avocations: sports, painting. Office: Hochschule Vechta, Pstf 15 53, 49364 Vechta Germany

NITTA, DOUGLAS, family practice physician; b. Seattle, Mar. 30, 1954; s. Susumu and Donna (Tokuda) N. BA in Chemistry magna cum laude, U. Wash., 1976, MD, 1980. Diplomate Am. Bd. Family Practice. Internship, resident Irvine Med. Ctr. U. Calif., 1980-83; mem. active staff St. Jude Med. Ctr., Fullerton, Calif., 1982—; chmn. dept. family practice St. Jude Med. Ctr., Fullerton, 1989—; v.p., bd. dirs. St. Jude Med. Group, Inc., Fullerton, Calif., 1996—; mem. adv. bd. St. Jude Heritage Health Found., 1997-99; chmn. primary care dept. St. Jude Med. Ctr., 1999. Fellow Am. Acad. Family Physicians; mem. Calif. Med. Assn., Phi Beta Kappa. Office: 301 W Bastanchury Rd Ste 155 Fullerton CA 92835-3477

NITTA, HIDEO, physicist, educator; b. Tokyo, Japan, Nov. 4, 1957; s. Izuwo and Izumi (Takako) N. m. Tamiko Sakamoto, Mar. 22, 1988; children: Ryuma, Yushi. BS, Waseda U., Tokyo, 1982, MS, 1984, PhD, 1987. Physics rsch. assoc. Waseda U., Tokyo, 1987-88; physics rsch. assoc. Tokyo Gakugei U., 1988-95, assoc. prof., 1995—; lectr. U. Tokyo, 1997—, Rsch. Inst. for Sci. Measurement, Tohoku U., Sendai, 1998—; rschr. Nat. Exch. Program, Internat. Solvay Inst. Physics and Chemistry, Brussels, 1994-95, Nuclear Fusion Inst., Japan, 1998—. Author: Special Functions in Physics, 1997; co-author: New Perspectives on Problems in Classical and Quantum Physics, 1998; contbr. articles to profl. jours. Grantee Japan Soc. for Promotion of Sci., 1994, Ministry of Edn., Sci. and Culture of Japan, 1997, 98. Mem. Phys. Soc. Japan, Japanese Soc. Physics Edn. (bd. dirs. 2000—). Avocation: painting. Office: Tokyo Gakugei U, Dept Physics, Tokyo 184-8501, Japan

NITTA, KOH-HEI, physicist; b. Kanazawa, Ishikawa, Japan, June 23, 1959; s. Satoshi and Reiko (Kida) N.; m. Yuka Fujimoto; children: Ryosuke, Hiroyuki. BS in Polymer Chemistry, Kyoto (Japan) U., 1983, MS in Polymer Chemistry, 1985, PhD in Polymer Chemistry, 1991. Rschr. Rsch. Ctr. Mitsubishi Chem. Corp., Yokohama, Japan, 1988-90; rschr. Devel. Ctr. Mitsubishi Chem. Corp., Mizushima, Japan, 1990-93; assoc. prof. Ctr. for New Materials Japan Advanced Inst. Sci. and Tech., Tatsunokuchi, 1993-99, assoc. prof. Sch. Materials Sci., 1999—. Recipent SRJ Rsch. award, 1999. Mem. Soc. Polymer Sci., Soc. Rheology. E-mail: nitta@jaist.ac.jp. Home: C-34 1-50 Asahidai, 923-1211 Tatsunokuchi Ishikawa, Japan Office: Japan Adv Inst Sci & Tech, 1-1 Asahidai, 923-1292 Tatsunokuchi Ishikawa, Japan

NITZAN, ABRAHAM, chemistry educator, university dean; b. Tel Aviv, Israel, May 3, 1944; s. Baruch and Nehama (Bocian) N.; m. Raya Tatsa Silbert; children: Sigal-Shahaf, Sharon. BSc, Hebrew U., Israel, 1964, MSc, 1966, PhD, 1972. Rsch. assoc. MIT, Cambridge, Mass., 1972-74; asst. prof. Northwestern U., Evanston, Ill., 1974-75; assoc. prof. chemistry Tel Aviv U., Israel, 1975-81, prof., 1981—, chmn. Sch. Chemistry, 1984-87, dean Faculty of Sci., 1995-98; cons. AT&T Bell Labs., 1975-81; vis. prof. Northwestern U. Contbr. articles to profl. jours.; patentee in field. Recipient Kolthoff prize Technion, Israel, 1996; Fulbright grantee, 1972, Humboldt awardee, 1995. Fellow Am. Phys. Soc.; mem. Materials Rsch. Soc., Israel Chem. Soc. Office: Tel Aviv U, Sch Chemistry, 69978 Tel Aviv Israel

NIVEAU, GERARD, psychiatrist, researcher; b. Forbach, Moselle, France, May 12, 1958; s. Jean and Marie (Carl) N.; m. Jocelyne Bastien, Sept. 14, 1989; children: Nathan, Noemie. MD, U. Lyon, France, 1988; Cert. d'Etudes Superieures in Psychiatry, U. Lyon, 1988, Attestation d'Etudes in Criminology, 1989. Psychiatry asst. Pub. Hosp., Lyon, 1984-89; head clinic Inst. Forensic Medicine, Geneva, Switzerland, 1989-97; head unit forensic psychiatry Inst. Forensic Medicine, Geneva, 1997—; univ. lectr. U. Geneva, 1997—. Contbr. articles to profl. jours. Capt. Health Care Svc., 1986. Mem. Internat. Acad. Law and Mental Health, Assn. European Psychiatrists. Avocations: water skiing, skiing, hiking. Office: Inst U Medicine Legal, 9 Av de Champel, 1211 Geneva 4, Switzerland

NIVEN, ALASTAIR NEIL ROBERTSON, literature director; b. Edinburgh, Scotland, Feb. 25, 1944; s. Harold Robertson and Elizabeth Isobel Robertson (Mair) N.; m. Helen Margaret Trow; children: Isabella, Alexander. MA, U. Cambridge, Eng., 1966, U. Ghana, 1968; PhD, U. Leeds, Eng., 1972. Lectr. U. Ghana, 1968-69, U. Leeds, Eng., 1969-70, U. Stirling, 1970-78; dir. gen. Africa Centre, London, 1978-84; Chapman fellow Inst. Commonwealth Studies, London, 1984-85; spl. asst. sec. gen. Assn. Commonwealth U., London, 1985-87; dir. lit. Arts Coun. Eng., London, 1987-94, Arts County England, 1994-97, Brit. Coun., 1997—. Author: D.H. Lawrence: The Novels, 1978, The Yoke of Pity: The Fiction of Mulk Raj Anand, 1978, Truth Into Fiction: Raja Rao, 1988; co-author: The Commonwealth of Universities, 1987; editor: The Commonwealth Writer Overseas, 1976. Chmn. U.K. Coun. Overseas Student Affairs, 1987-92; mem. Booker Prize Judges, U.K., 1994. Avocations: theater, traveling, cats. Office: Arts Coun Eng, 14 Great Peter St, London SW1P 3NQ, England

NIWA, KIYOSHI, engineering educator; b. Hatano, Kanagawa, Japan, Oct. 25, 1946; s. Sueo and Mano (Takahashi) N.; m. Naoko Takahashi, Mar. 27, 1977; 1 child, Mari. B in Engring., Waseda U., Tokyo, 1970, M in Engring., 1972; DEng, Tokyo Inst. Tech., 1986. Rsch. scientist sys. lab. Hitachi, Ltd., Kanagawa, 1972-85; sr. rsch. scientist sys. lab. advanced rsch. lab. Hitachi, Ltd., Saitama, Japan, 1985-94; sr. rsch. fellow IC2 Inst., U. Tex., Austin, 1988—; assoc. prof. U. Tokyo, 1994-97, prof., 1997—; vis. prof. Portland (Oreg.) State U., 1989-91. Author: Knowledge-Based Risk Management in Engineering, 1989, Technology Management Strategy, 1999; co-editor: Innovation in Technology Management, 1997, Technology and Innovation Management, 1999; contbr. articles to sci. publs. Mem. IEEE, Japan Info. Soc., INFORMS. Avocation: fly fishing. Office: Univ Tokyo Dept Sys Sci, 3-8-1 Komaba, Meguro-ku, Tokyo 153-8902, Japan

NIWA, UICHIRO, financial company executive. CEO Itochu Corp., Osaka, Japan. Office: Itochu Corp, 5-1 Kita-Aoyama 2-chome, Minatoku Tokyo 107-8077, Japan*

NIWANO, SINICHI, physician, researcher; b. Johetsu, Niigata, Japan, Aug. 6, 1959; s. Noboru and Yuki (Takeuchi) N.; m. Hiroe Araki, Feb. 28, 1988. MD, Niigata U., 1984, PhD, 1991. Internship Niigata Univ. Hosp., 1982-84, resident, 1984-87; clin. fellow Niigata U. Hosp., 1984-87, 91-92, rsch. fellow, 1987-91, asst. prof., 1994-98; rsch. fellow Case Western Res. U., Cleve., 1992-94; lectr. Kitasato U., Sagamihara, Japan, 1998—. Contbr. articles to profl. jours. Medtronic fellowship, 1991, AHA, 1993; rsch. grant Kanagawa Acad., 1999. Mem. N.Am. Soc. of Pacing and Electrophysiology. Home: Minamidai 2-2-16, Clea House 1-302, Sagamihara 228-0814, Japan Office: Kitasato Univ Hosp, Kitasato 1-15-1, Sagamihara 228-8555, Japan

NIX, JOHN SYDNEY, retired business management educator; b. London, July 27, 1927; s. John William and Eleanor Elizabeth (Stears) N.; m. Mavis Marian Cooper, Oct. 7, 1950; children: Alison, Robert, Jennifer. BSc in Economics, U. London, 1948; MA, U. Cambridge, Eng., 1958. Agrl. economist U. Cambridge, Eng., 1951-61; farm mgmt. liaison officer, lectr. U. London, 1961-70, sr. tutor, 1970-72, sr. lectr., 1972-75, reader, head farm bus. unit, 1975-82, prof., head farm bus. unit, 1982-89. Author: Farm Management Pocketbook (31 edits.), 1966-2000; co-author (with others) Farm Planning and Control (2d edit.) 1979, Farm Mechanisation for Profit, 1983, Land and Estate Management (3rd edit.), 1998. Chmn. jour. editl. com. Ctr. Mgmt. in Agr., Eng., 1971-95; chmn. Bd. Farm Mgmt., Eng., 1979-81; pres. Agrl. Econs. Soc., Eng., 1990-91, Kingshay Farming Trust, Eng., 1991-96, Assn. Ind. Crop Cons., 1993-97, Guild Agrl. Journalists, 2000—. With British Navy, 1948-51. Recipient 1st nat. award for Outstanding and Continuing Contbn. to Advancement of Mgmt. in Agrl. Industry, Ctr. for Mgmt. in Agr., 1982. Fellow Royal Soc. Arts, Royal Agrl. Socs., Inst. Agrl. Mgmt.; mem. Brit. Inst. Mgmt. (companion). Avocations: theatre, cinema, travel, rugby, cricket. Office: U London, Farm Bus Unit Imperial Coll Wye, Ashford TN25 5AH, England

NIXDORFF, UWE, cardiologist, researcher, consultant; b. Hofheim/Ts., Hessen, Germany, June 12, 1958; s. Hans Jochen and Anita (Buch) N.; m. Sigrid Brigitte Maletzki, June 5, 1992; children: Caroline Sophie, Constantin Friedrich. MD, U. Frankfurt, Germany, 1986. Cert. cardiologist. Stabsarzt Bundeswehr, Giessen, Germany, 1985-86; postdoctoral fellow German Heart Ctr, Munich, Germany, 1986-88; guest investigator U. N.C., Charlottesville, 1988; resident U. Mainz, Germany, 1988-93, internist, 1993-95, cardiologist, 1995-98; asst. prof., cons. U. Erlangen, Germany, 1998—; diplomate visitor guiding German fgn. office Frankfurt, Germany, 1982-86. Author: (book) Cardiac Ultrasound, 1993; contbr. over 100 publs. to profl. jours. and books. Recipient Young Investigators award Internat. Coun. on ECG, 1988, Best Abstract award honorable mention Internat. Soc. Cardiovascular Ultrasound, 1996. Mem. Am. Heart Assn., European Heart Soc., German Soc. Cardiology, N.Y. Acad. Sci., Am. Soc. Echocardiography, Deutsche Gesellschaft für Innere Medizin. Avocations: tennis, jogging, climbing, paragliding, philosophy, arts. Fax: 0049 9131 85-33838. E-mail: uwe.nixdorff@rzmail.uni-erlangen.de. Home: Turmhugelweg 22, D-91058 Erlangen Germany Office: Friedrich-Alexander-U Med, Ostliche Stadtmauerstrasse, 91054 Erlangen Germany

NIXON, MARGARET SUE, telephone business executive, researcher; b. Hattiesburg, Miss., Jan. 10, 1948; d. Rufus Baxter and Martha Lee (Marshall) N.; children: Melinda Gayle Young, David Lamar Moore, Timmy Dewayne White. Student, So. Bus. Coll., Vicksburg, Miss., 1970, Hinds Jr. Coll., Vicksburg, Miss., 1979. Telephone op. Nixon's Mktg., Memphis, 1981—; op./mgr. Anserphone By Graves, Memphis, 1983-86; telemarketer McSwain-Mortgage, Germantown, Tenn.; mgr. Bus. Connection, Memphis, 1991—. Mem. NAFE (assoc.), U.S. Golf Assn. Avocations: collector of plates, reading, golf, walking. Home: 6724 Quail Hollow Ct Apt 3 Memphis TN 38120-4511 Office: Bus Connections PO Box 241312 Memphis TN 38124-1312

NIXON, ROBERT OBEY, SR., business educator; b. Pitts., Feb. 14, 1922; s. Frank Obey and Margurite (Van Buren) N.; m. Marilyn Cavanagh, Oct. 25, 1944 (dec. 1990); children: Nan Nixon Friend, Robert Obey, Jr., Dwight Cavanagh. BS in bus. adminstrn., U. Pitts., 1948; MS, Ohio State U., 1964; MBA, U. Phoenix, 1984. Commd. 2d lt. USAF, 1943, advanced through grades to col., 1970, master navigator WWII, Korea, Vietnam; sales, adminstrn. U.S. Rubber Corp., Pitts., 1940-41; asst. engr. Am. Bridge Corp., Pitts., 1941-42; underwriter, sales Penn Mutual Life Ins. Corp., Pitts., 1945-50; capt., nav. instr. USAF Reserves, 1945-50; ret. USAF Col., divsn. chief Joint Chiefs of Staff, 1973; educator, cons. U. Ariz., 1973-79; bus. dept. chmn., coord., founder weekend coll. Pima C.C., Tucson, 1979-90, prof. mgmt., 1991-98, coord. weekend coll. program, 1991—; adj. faculty Pima C.C., 1998—; founder, pres. Multiple Adv. Group ednl. cons., Tucson, 1978—. Author: Source Document: On Accelerated Courses and Programs at Accredited Two- and Four-Year Colleges and Universities, 1996; contbr. articles to profl. jours. Mem. Soc. Logistics Engrs. (sr., charter mem.), Phi Delta Theta. Presbyterian. Avocations: tennis, hiking, swimming. E-mail: eb58271@goodnet.com; bnixon@pimacc.pima.edu. Fax: 520-885-2378. Home: 1824 S Regina Cleri Dr Tucson AZ 85710-8664

NIXON, SCOTT SHERMAN, lawyer; b. Grosse Pointe, Mich., Feb. 7, 1959; s. Floyd Sherman and Marjorie Jane (Quermann) N.; m. Cathryn Lynn Starnes, Aug. 27, 1983; children: Jeffry Sherman, Kelsy Jane, James Robert. BABA, Mich. State U., 1981; JD, U. Denver, 1984. Bar: Colo. 1984, U.S. Dist. Ct. Colo. 1984, U.S. Ct. Appeals (10th cir.) 1984. Assoc. Pryor, Carney & Johnson, P.C., Englewood, Colo., 1984-89, shareholder, 1990-95; pres., shareholder Pryor, Johnson, Montoya, Carney & Karr, P.C., Englewood, 1995—. Officer, bd. dirs. Luth. Brotherhood Br. 8856, Denver, 1993-99, Mark K. Ulmer Meml. Native Am. Scholarship Found., Denver, 1994—; officer, mem. coun. Bethan Luth Ch., Englewood, 1993-95. Mem. ABA, Colo. Bar Assn., Denver Bar Assn., Colo. Def. Lawyers Assn. Avocations: music performance, physical fitness, carpentry/construction. Home: 6984 S Pontiac Ct Englewood CO 80112-1127 Office: Pryor Johnson Montoya Carney & Karr PC Ste 1313 6400 S Fiddlers Green Cir Englewood CO 80111-4939

NIXON, SIR EDWIN, company executive; b. June 21, 1925; s. William Archdale and Ethel (Corrigan) N.; m. Joan Lilian Hill, 1952 (dec. 1995); 2 children; m. Bridget Diana Rogers, 1997. MA with honors, Cambridge U., 1983; DSc (hon.), Aston U., 1985, U. Stirling, 1985; DTech (hon.), U. Brunel, 1986; LLD (hon.), U. Manchester, 1987, U. Leicester, 1990; DTech (hon.), CNAA, 1991. Mng. acct. Dexion Ltd., 1950-55; with IBM U.K. Ltd., 1955-90; mng. dir. IBM UK Holdings Ltd., 1965-79, chmn., CEO, 1979-86, chmn. bd., 1986-90; dir. Royal Ins. PLC, 1980-88, Internat. Westminster Bank PLC, 1987-95, Lloyd Instruments, 1987-91, Partnership Sourcing, 1990-96; chmn. Amersham Internat. Plc, 1988-96, dir., 1987-96; dir. Nat. Westminster Bank Plc, 1975-96, dep. chmn., 1987-96; dir. U.K.-Japan 2000 Group Ltd., 1987-96; alt. dir. bCH Property Ltd., 1988-96; chmn. Natwest Pension Trustees Ltd., 1992-98, Leicester BioScis. Ltd., 1996-99. Mem. coun. Found. for Automation and Employment, 1967-77; mem. CBI, 1971-96, chmn. standing com. on mktg. and consumer affairs, 1971-78; mem. Com. on Indsl. Policy, 1978-85, pres.'s com., 1986-88; mem. Found. for Mgmt. Edn., 1973-84, Brit. Com. of Awards for Harness Fellowships, 1976-82; adv. coun. Bus. Grads. Assn., 1976-87; bd. govs. United World Coll. of Atlantic, 1977—; bd. trustees Internat. Inst. for Mgmt. Devel., 1990-96; chmn. coun. Leicester U., 1992-98; mem. coun. Manchester Bus. Sch., 1974-86, chmn., 1979-86; mem. Bus. in the Cmty., 1981-88, companion, 1992; vice chmn. Westfield Coll., London, 1980-82; mem. coun. William Temple Coll., Manchester, 1972-80, Oxford Ctr. for Mgmt. Studies, 1973-83, Open U., 1986-92; mem. The Civil Svc. Coll., 1979-91; adv. coun. New Oxford English Dictionary, 1985-89, Coun. for Industry and Higher Edn., 1986-98; trustee Inst. Econ. Affairs, 1986-92, hon. trustee, 1992; mem. Chichester Cathedral Devel. Trust, 1986—, The Prince's Youth Bus. Trust, 1987—, Lloyd's of London Tercentary Found., 1987—; pres. Nat. Assn. for Gifted Children, 1980-91, hon. mem., 1991; v.p. Opportunities for People with Disabilities, 1980—; chmn. Joint Bd. for Pre-Vocat. Edn., 1983-87; mem. Study Commn. on the Family, 1979-83; chmn. bd. trustees, dir. Royal Opera House, Covent Garden, 1984-87, trustee, 1980-87; chmn. bd. trustees Monteverdi Choir and Orch., 1988—, trustee, 1980—; v.p. London Internat. String Quartet Competition Patron Assn. Internat. des Etudiantes en Sciences Economiques et Commerciales, 1980—. Fellow Inst. Mktg. (hon., hon. v.p. 1980-97). Avocations: music, tennis, golf, sailing. Office: Starkes Heath, Rogate Petersfield, Hants GU31 5EJ, England

NIYAZOV, SAPARMURAD ATAYEVICH, president of Turkmenistan; b. Ashgabat, Turkmenistan, Feb. 19, 1940; married, 2 children. Grad., Leningrad (USSR) Poly. Inst., 1967. Cert. power engring. Instr. Trade-Union Orgn. of mineral prospecting works, Turkmenistan, 1959-67; dep. dir., dir. Cen. Com. of Turkmen Communist Party, 1970-80; chmn. Coun. of Mins. of TSSR, Ashgabat, 1985; 1st sec. Cen. Com. of Turkmen Communist Party, 1985-90, Ashkhabad City Com. of Turkmen Communist Party, 1980-84; party workman Cen. Com. of Communist Party of Soviet Union, Moscow, 1984-85; chmn. Supreme Soviet of Turkmenistan, Ashgabat, 1990; now pres. Turkmenistan, Turkmenistan, 1990—; academician Acad. Scis. of Turkmenistan, dr. economy and policy; prof. Turkmen State U., Mahtumkuli and Istanbul U., Turkey. Chmn. Dem. Party. Recipient Internat. Prize after Mahtumkuli, 1992, Turkmen State prize after Al-Horezmi, 1994. Mem. Humanitarian Assn.of the Turkmens of the World (pres. 1885—). Avocations: philosophy, history, music, poetry. Address: Presidential Palace, 24 Karl Marx St, Ashgabat 744014, Turkmenistan*

NIYOGI, PARTHA, computer scientist, educator; b. Calcutta, July 31, 1967; s. Ranjit Kumar and Prabhati Niyogi; m. Parvati Krishnamurty, Nov. 24, 1995. B of Tech., Indian Inst. of Tech., New Delhi, 1989; MS, MIT, 1992, PhD, 1995. Rsch. assoc. MIT, Cambridge, 1995-96; mem. tech. staff Bell Labs., Murray Hill, N.J., 1996—; asst. prof. U. Chgo., 2000—; panelist Nat. Acad. Sci., 1997; speaker in field; cons. Inst. for Advanced Study, Princeton, 1999—. Author: Informational Complexity of Learning, 1997; contbr. articles to sci. and profl. jours. Fellow NSF, 1995; Beckman fellow U. Ill., 1995. Office: U Chgo Ryerson Hall 1100 E 58th St Chicago IL 60637-1588

NIZAMI, WAJIH AHMAD, parasitologist; b. Meerut, India, Aug. 22, 1950; s. Khaliq and Razia N.; m. Rahat Faridi, Jan. 18, 1981; children: Moin, Amin. BSc, Aligarh Muslim U., 1970, MSc, 1972, MPhil, 1974, PhD, 1976. From lectr. to prof. Aligarh Muslim U., India, 1979—; Royal Soc. fellow Br. Univs., England, 1984; Br. Coun. fellow Queens U., Belfast, Ireland, 1990-91; mgr. Ahmadi Sch. for Blind, Aligarh, 1991-94. Fellow Helminthological Soc. India, Soc. Bioscis. of India, Zool. Soc. India. Avocations: reading autobiographies, mysticism, machine repair, gardening. Home: Nizami Villa Sir Syed Rd, 202002 Aligarh India Office: Aligarh Muslim U, Dept Zoology, 202 002 Aligarh India

NIZAMOV, IL'YAS SAIDOVICH, chemist, researcher; b. Kazan, Russia, Jan. 3, 1958; s. Said Kamalovich and Madina Khusainovna (Bakhtiyarova) N.; m. Luiza Magdanovna Ikhsanova, Aug. 17, 1990; 1 child, Aliya. BS, U. Kazan, 1981, PhD, 1986. Probationer Arbuzov Inst., Kazan, 1981-82, jr. rschr., 1985-86, rschr., 1986-92, sr. rschr., 1992—. Contbr. articles to profl. jours.; inventor in field. Canvasser Election Campaign, Kazan, 1983-84. Grantee Russian Found. Basic Rschrs., Moscow, 1995-96. Mem. Internat. Coun. on Main Group Chemistry. Avocations: nature, cycle racing, skiing. Home: Arbuzov St 48-52, 420088 Kazan Russia Office: Arbuzov Inst Organic Chem, Arbuzov St 8, 420088 Kazan Russia

NIZAMSKA, MARINA VLADOVA, nuclear engineer, consultant; b. Sofia, Bulgaria, Apr. 19, 1966; d. Vlado Manolov and Elena Eftimova (Gerginova) N. MSc, Sofia U., 1989. Diploma-engr., physicist and specialization, nuclear technics and nuclear energetics. Radiation protection inspector Bulgarian Atomic Com., Sofia, 1990-92, head gammaspectrometric lab., 1992-95; radiation protection expert Civil Protection, Sofia, 1996-98; head divsn. emergency planning and responce Bulgarian Atomic Com., Sofia, 1999—; cons. Ministry of Environment, Sofia, 1993-94, Ministry of Energy, Sofia, 1994-95, Riskengineering Ltd., Sofia, 1996—. Author: Radiation Protection, 1991; contbr. articles to profl. jours. Mem. Bulgarian Nuclear Soc., Metrology Soc., Permanent Govt. Protection Commn. (sec. 1992—). Democrat. Avocations: photography, swimming, music, literature. Home: 12 Parchevich St, 1000 Sofia Bulgaria Office: Com Use Atomic Energy, 69 Shipchensky Prokhod Blvd, 1574 Sofia Bulgaria

NIZINSKI, JERZY JAN, hydrologist, researcher; b. Wrocław, Poland, June 1, 1951; arrived in France, 1980; s. Jozef and Janina (Murias) N.; m. Dominique Pascale Morand, 1971; children: Louis, Pierre. Degree in engring., U. Agriculture, Wrocław, Poland, 1977; diplome d'Etudes Approfondies, U. Paris XI, 1981, PhD, 1986. Hydrologist engr. Inst. Hydrology, Wrocław, Poland, 1977-80; rschr. Orstom, Cayenne, Guyana, 1986, Dakar, Senegal, 1989-93; rschr. Inra, Bordeaux, France, 1994-95, Orstom, Pointe Noire, Congo, 1996-99, U. Paris XI, France, 2000—, Inra, Bordeaux, France, 1994-95, U. Paris XI, 2000—. Contbr. articles to profl. jours. Under lt. Polish Army Res., 1978, Wrocław, Poland. Mem. Soc. Am. Foresters, Brit. Ecol. Soc. Mem. Catholic Ch. of Rome. Avocations: history, policy, economy, golf. Fax: 33-2-54-78-19-19. Home: 8 Rue du Commerce, 41000 Blois Loir et Cher France Office: Orstom, 213 Rue la Fayette, 75480 Paris France

NIZNIK, CAROL ANN, electrical engineer, educator, consultant; b. Saratoga Springs, N.Y., Nov. 10, 1942; d. John Arthur Niznik and Rosalia Sopko; m. Donald H. Walter, Jan. 11, 1964. AAS in Engring. Sci., Alfred (N.Y.) State Coll., 1962; BSEE, U. Rochester, N.Y., 1969, MSEE, 1972; PhD in Elec. Engring., SUNY, Buffalo, 1978. Technician Taylor Instrument Corp., Rochester, 1962-64; sr. technician IBM Corp., Poughkeepsie, N.Y., 1964-68; rsch. scientist Eastman Kodak Corp., Rochester, 1969-70; sr. engr. Xerox Corp., Webster, N.Y., 1971-74; rsch. asst. prof. SUNY, buffalo, 1979-80; assoc. prof. elec. engring. U. Pitts., 1980-83; pres., cons. NW Systems, Rochester, 1975—; adj. prof. math. Rochester Inst. Tech., 1993-94; vis. assoc. prof. Ctr. for Brain Rsch., Sch. Medicine, U. Rochester, 1983-84. Author tech. monograph on cerebellum prosthesis component; contbr. some 70 articles to profl. jours.; patentee in field. Recipient fellowships, grants and U.S. govt. contracts. Mem. IEEE (sr.), Sigma Xi, Eta Kappa Nu, Tau Beta Pi. Roman Catholic. Avocations: doll collecting, care of pets, gardening. Office: NW Sys PO Box 18133 Rochester NY 14618-0133

NIZON, PAUL, writer; b. Bern, Switzerland, Dec. 19, 1929; arrived in France, 1976; s. Max and Flora (Liechti) N.; m. Odile Roquet, Mar. 20, 1980; 1 child, Igor Odilon Maximilien. DPhil, U. Berne, 1957. Art critic Swiss and German media, 1957-72. Author: (novels) Canto, 1963, Stolz, 1975, Das Jahr der Liebe, 1981, Im Bauch des Wals, 1989, Hund, 1998, others. Recipient Bremer Lit. prize, 1975, Grosser Lit. prize der Stadt Zürich, 1992, Maria Luise Kaschnitz prize Acad. Tutzing, 1990, Prix Lit. de Radio France Culture, 1988. Mem. Internat. PEN Club. Avocations: dogs, classic cars, walking, night bars. Home: 262 Rue Saint Honoré, F75001 Paris France Office: Editions Actes Sud, Rue Séguier, 75007 Paris France

NIZZE, HORST KARL GERHARD, pathologist, educator; b. Schwerin, Germany, Apr. 14, 1942; s. Franz Ludwig Martin and Elisabeth Johanna Christa Nizze; m. Bärbel Renate Lange, Jan. 18, 1963; 1 child, Susanne. MD, U. Rostock, 1967, Habilitation, 1976. Postgrad. asst. Inst. Pathology Dist. Hosp., Schwerin, 1967-72; pathologist U. Rostock, 1973-78, reader in pathology, 1979-88, extraordinary prof. pathology, 1989-91, prof. pathology, 1992, head Inst. Pathology, 1993—, ednl. dean med. faculty, 1990-98. Mem. editl. bd. Der Pathologe, 1993—; contbg. author numerous pathology textbooks; contbr. more than 200 articles to profl. jours. Mem.

Deutsche Gesellschaft für Pathologie (vice sec. 1993-99, pres. 2000—), Gesellschaft Deutscher Naturforscher und Ärzte, Gesellschaft für Nephrologie Goethe-Gesellschaft, Internat. Acad. Pathology. Evang. Lutheran. Avocation: literature. Office: U Rostock Inst Path, Strempelstrasse 14 POB 100888, D-18055 Rostock Germany

NJINU, PETER KIMANI, controller; b. Kiamisu, Ctrl., Kenya, Oct. 31, 1960; s. Naftaly Njimu Mutungi and Mary Wamjiku (Kimani) Njimu; m. Josephine Kiangari Chege, Apr. 29, 1998; children: Wamjiku, Njimu, Wambui. B. Comm., U. Nairobi (Kenya), 1985. CPA. Audit sr. Deloitte & Touche, Nairobi, 1985-90; chief acct. Chloride Group, Nairobi, 1990-94; fin., adminstrv. mgr. S.I.T.A., Nairobi, 1994-99; fin. controller S.I.T.A., Johannesburg, South Africa, 1999—. Mem. I.C.P.A.K. (assoc., mem. convenor-peer review com. 1995-99), Thika Sports Club. Avocation: golf. Office: Barprop House, 36 Homestead Rd, Rivonia Sandton, South Africa also: Postnet ste No 89, Pvt Bag X51, 2128 Rivonia South Africa

NJOKAH, JOSEPH MUNENE MBUI, surgeon, educator, educator; b. Central Province, Kenya, Feb. 24, 1946; s. Paul Mbui and Penninah (Wanjira) N. MB, ChB, U. Makerere, Uganda, 1972; M Med, U. Nairobi, Uganda, 1985. Med. officer Ministry Health, Kenya, 1972-73; resident in surgery Aghakhan Hosp., Kenya, 1985; lectr. surgery U. Nairobi, Kenya, 1985—, chmn. dept. med. physiology, 1988—; cons. and relief surgeon Internat. M.C., Rwanda, Burundi, Sudan, 1995-96; medico-legal cons. to ins. cos. and lawyers, Kenya, 1985—; marine and hyperbaric medicine specialist; cons. neurosurg. and gen. surgeon. Mem. bd. govs. Karumandi Secondary Sch., 1996—. Maj. Kenya Navy, 1973-85. Kennedy scholar Kangaru Sch., 1965-66. Mem. Kenya Physiol. Soc. (sec. 1986-99), Kenya Resuscitation Coun. (instr. 1999—), Internat. Brain Orgn. Avocations: photography, farming, car mechanic, woodworking. Home: Market St, PO Box 40633, Nairobi Kenya Office: U Nairobi Chiromo Campus, PO Box 30197, Nairobi Kenya

NJOKU, ATHAN O., economist, educator. PhD, U. Ill., 1969. Prof. Benedict Coll., Columbia, S.C., 1970—. Home: 627 Glenthorne Rd Columbia SC 29203-3630

NJOKU, DAVIDSON, social scientist, educator; b. Anara Isiala Mbano, Imo state, Nigeria, Dec. 20, 1960; s. Reuben Oguguo and Betsy (Uwalaka) N.; m. Maria Chinenye Atuegbu, Dec. 27, 1997. BA in Pub. Adminstrn. with honors, Panjab U., Chandigarh, India, 1984, MA in Pub. Adminstrn., 1986. Sr. lectr. social sci. Abia State U., Uturu, 1990—; part-time lectr. Imo State U., 1996-98. Author: Government Administration and Citizens Welfare, 1987, Introduction to Local Government Administration, 1994; dep. editor New Pilot Comm., 1989; cons. editor Creative Ednl. Mgmt. Cons., 1998, Nigerian Acad. Jour., 1994-98; co-editor: Readings in Social Sciences: ABSU Freshman's Course in Citizenship Education, 1997. Hostel warden Abia State U., Uturu, 1997, mem. senate 1998-99; ctr. supr. Inst. for Distance Edn., 1998; pub. rels. officer Umuduru Emeghara, Anara, Nigeria, 1988-98; resource fellow Nat. Orientation Agy., Owerri, 1997. Avocations: reading, researching and playing football. Home: Umuduruemeghara, PO Box 157, Anara Isiala Mbano, Nigeria Office: Abia State Univ, PMB 2000, Uturu Abia State Nigeria

NJOROGE, ERNEST MWANGI, veterinarian; b. Muranga, Kenya, June 17, 1966; s. Geoffrey Njoroge and Jane Njoki Njuguna N.; m. Alice Watiri Wachira, Apr. 13, 1996. BVM, U. Nairobi, 1991; MS, U. Natrobi, 1993. Vet. Ilkerin-Loita, Nairobi, 1994-95; lectr. U. Nairobi, 1995-98; vet. AMREF, Nairobi, 1999—; cons. Animal Industry Consultancy Unit, U. Nairobi, 1997—. Inventor in field. Mem. Kenya Vet. Assn. Office: AMREE, PO Box 30125, Nairobi Kenya

NKUEBE, JOSHUA SEMPE, education testing officer, evaluator; b. Quthing, Lesotho, Dec. 15, 1947; s. Kenneth Makhaola and Elizabeth Maliako (Mebe) N.; m. Florence Nkomile Tsufu, June 1, 1973 (div. Nov. 1982); 1 child, Makhaola; m. Gertrude Mamojela Makatise, Dec. 4, 1980; children: Mojela, Maliako, Methalali. BSc, Nat. U. Lesotho, 1980; MEd, U. Ibadan, Nigeria, 1983. Tchr. Masitise H.S., Lesotho, 1966; statis. officer Bur. of Stats., Lesotho, 1970-71; tech. officer Land Survey Dept., Lesotho, 1972-74; tchr. Peka H.S., Lesotho, 1974-82; edn. testing officer Nat. Curriculum Devel. Ctr., Maseru, Lesotho, 1984—; advisor Primary Sch. Leaving Examination, Lesotho, 1985—. Mem. Lesotho Ednl. Rsch. Assn., African Curriculum Orgn. Mem. Lesotho Evang. Ch. Avocations: music, soccer, movies, gardening, travel. Home: PO Box 72, 700 Quthing Lesotho Office: Nat Curriculum Devel Ctr, Po Box 1126, 100 Maseru Lesotho

NNAJI, ESTHER NKECHI, meteorologist; b. Enugu, Nigeria, Oct. 11, 1972; d. Godswill Okafor and Grace Onyenweaku (Iwu) N. BS, Enugu State U., Nigeria, 1998. Meterologist Airport Authority, Portharcourt, Nigeria, 1996; conservationist Najek Park, Portharcourt, 1997; sec. Shape-Up, Lagos, 1998; mgr. Eshiwe Holdings, Aba, 1999. Mem. Internat. Soc. Tropical Foresters, Rotary Club Nigeria. Avocations: sewing, badminton, reading, travel. Home: 240 Ehi Rd PO Box 1233, Abia State Nigeria Office: Enugu State U Dept Meteorol, 224 Cameron Rd, 1233 Aba Abia State Nigeria

NNODIM, JOSEPH OGBONNA, biomedical researcher, educator; b. Owerri, Imo, Nigeria, Jan. 4, 1953; s. Maxwell Ogbonna and Joy Emelda (nee Okoro) N.; m. Gloria Ngozi Okeke, Feb. 28, 1981; children: Ljeoma, Kelechi, Ahamefula, Ebubechukwu. MBBS, U. Lagos, Nigeria, 1978; PhD, U. Wales, Cardiff, Eng., 1985. Cert. in reproductive medicine. Intern Lagos (Nigeria) U. Tchg. Hosp., 1978-79; med. officer Nat. Youth Svc. Corps Ife (Nigeria) U. Tchg. Hosps. Complex, 1979-80; lectr. Sch. Med. U. Benin, Benin City, Nigeria, 1980-82, 85-87; sr. lectr. Sch. Med. U. Benin, Benin City, 1987-91, ag. head dept. Sch. Med., 1989-91, 93-95, assoc. prof, cons. Sch. Med., 1991-95; doctoral scholar U. Wales, Cardiff, 1982-85; term lectr., rsch. investigator Sch. Med. U. Mich., Ann Arbor, 1996—. Contbr. articles to profl. jours. Ad-hoc chaperone Angell Elem. Sch., Ann Arbor, 1999—; vol. Hunger Coalition, Ann Arbor. Roman Catholic. Avocations: music (flautist), photography, leisure running, tennis. Fax: 734-763-1166. E-mail: Jnnodim@umich.edu. Office: U Mich Sch Med 1150 W Medical Center Dr Ann Arbor MI 48109-0726

NNOLIM, DOROTHY ADAKU E., management consultant, educator; b. Enusu, Nigeria, Feb. 27, 1941; arrived in U.S., 1973.; d. Edmund Emekaezuru and Mercillina Onyeuchealu (Igbogionu) E.; m. Benedict Nwankwo Nnolim, Feb. 12, 1970; children: Neme, Chukwuma, Chiemedinam, Uche. BBA, U. Mich., 1967, MBA, 1969. Rsch. asst. Bureau of Bus. Rsch., Ann Arbor, 1968-69, Am. Enterprise Inst., Washington, 1969; mgr. in tng. Sybron Corp., Rochester, 1969-70; analyst, production planner Eastman Kodak, Rochester, N.Y., 1970-73; lectr. U. Nigeria, Enucu, 1973—; dir. U. Nigeria Gen. Enterprises, Ltd., 1993—, assoc. dean. faculty bus. admin., U. Nigeria, 1989-90. Author: (books) International Marketing, 1994, Principles and Practice of Marketing, 1996; co-author: Marketing in Nigeria, 1998; contbr. articles to profl. jours. Pres. Catholic Women Orgn., 1995-99, Ladies of St. Mulumba, 1998—, sec. 1994-98; chair-person bldg. com. U. Nigeria, 1999—. Mem. Nigerian Economic Soc., N.Y. Acad. Sci., Am. Mktg. Assn. Roman Catholic. Office: Dept Mktg, U Nigeria Enugu, Enugu Nigeria

NOACH, ARTHUR BERNARD JOSEPH, pharmacologist, pharmacist; b. Leiden, The Netherlands, Mar. 1, 1962; s. Erik L. and Mathilde L. J. (De Clerck) N. BS, U. Leiden, 1983, MS, 1987, PhD, 1994. Lic. pharmacist. Rsch. scientist Organon Pharm. Co., Oss, The Netherlands, 1994-98; dir. preclin. rsch. Kinesis Holding BV, Breda, The Netherlands, 1999—. Contbr. articles to sci. jours. Mem. AAAS, Am. Assn. Pharm. Scientists, Dutch Assn. Pharm. Sci., Dutch Pharmacol. Soc., Royal Dutch Assn. Advancement Pharmacy, Am. Soc. Microbiology, N.Y. Acad. Scis. E-mail: a.noach@wxs.nl. Avocation: violinist in amateur symphony orchestras. Home: Meijer Van Leeuwenstraat 32, NL-5348 JW Oss The Netherlands Office: Smederijstraat 2, 4814 DB Breda The Netherlands

NOAKES, MICHAEL, portrait and landscape painter; b. Brighton, Sussex, Eng., Oct. 28, 1933; s. Basil Henry and Mary Josephine (Gerard) N.; m. Vivien Langley, July 9, 1960; children: Anya, Jonathan, Benedict. Nat. diploma in Design, Reigate Sch. Art, Surrey, Eng., 1954; cert., Royal Acad. Schs., London, 1960. TV art corr. Town and Around BBC-TV, London, 1964-68; a gov. Fedn. Brit. Artists, 1972-81, bd. dirs., 1981-83; judge Australian Bicentennial Portrait Competition, 1988; broadcast and televised widely on art subjects. Exhibits include Royal Acad., Royal Inst. Oil Painters, Royal Soc. Brit. Artists, Royal Soc. Marine Artists, Royal Soc. Portrait Painters, Royal Glasgow Inst. Fine Arts, Contemporary Portrait Soc., Grafton Galleries, Grosvenor Galleries, Nat. Soc., New Grafton Galleries, Upper Grafton Galleries, Upper Grosvenor Galleries, Woodstock Galleries, Young Contemporaries; permanent collections include for The Queen for Royal Collection, Windsor, The Prince of Wales, Nat. Portrait Gallery, London, The Brit. Mus., London, Guildhall, London, others; portrait sitters include The Queen, The Duke of Edinburgh, Queen Elizabeth The Queen Mother, The Prince of Wales, The Princess Royal as Princess Anne, Princess Margaret, The Earl of Snowdon, President Clinton, Lord Boothby, Princess Ashraf of Iran, Sir Alec Guinness, John J. Louis, Jr., Robert Morley, J. B. Priestley, Charles Price, Sir Ralph Richardson, Edmund de Rothschild, Dame Margaret Rutherford, Archbishop Runcie of Canterbury, Margaret Thatcher, Sir Donald Wolfit, Sir Frank Whittle, Sir Martin Roth, and many others; designed coin for 50th birthday of Prince of Wales; author: A Professional Approach to Oil Painting, 1968; contbr. to various art jours. Freeman City of London; liveryman Co. of Woolmen. Recipient Platinum Disc award for record-sleeve of Portrait of Sinatra, 1977. Mem. Royal Inst. Oil Painters (v.p. 1968-72, pres. 1972-78, hon. coun. mem. 1978—), Royal Soc. Portrait Painters (mem. coun. 1969-71, 72-74, 78-80, 93-95), Garrick Club. Address: c/o New Grafton Gallery, 49 Church Rd, London 3W139HH, England Home and Studio: 146 Hamilton Terr, St John's Wood, London NW8 9UX, England*

NOAMESI, SEEWU KOMLA, food scientist; b. Amedzofe, Ghana, July 26, 1949; s. Gottlieb Kofi and Mary Alice (Kakraba) N.; m. Comfort Adjo Amoah, Jan. 7, 1983; children: Vera Ama, Eunice Abra, David Yao, Daniel Kodjo. BS in Agr. with honors, U. Ghana, 1975, MS in Food Sci., 1979. Cert. food scientist, agriculturist. Farmer Akpafu, Ghana, 1976-90; subject matter specialist (agronomy) Volta Region Agrl. Devel. Project, Ho, Ghana, 1982; sr. tng. officer Volta Region Agrl. Devel. Project, Ho, 1984-87, head, tng. and communication, 1988-90; agriculturist State Com. for Econ. Cooperation, Accra, Ghana, 1987-88; scientific sec. Food Rsch. Inst., Accra, 1990—; pres. Food Rsch. Inst. Rsch. Staff Assn., Accra, 1993-95; sec. Agrl. Mgmt. Tng. for Africa Assocs. Internat., Accra, 1988—. Editor Volta Region Agrl. Programme, 1984-86, 1984 (newspaper commendation for excellence 1984); compiler, rschr. agrl. projects. Mem. Student Rep. Coun., U. Ghana, 1973-74. Mem. Bible Soc. of Ghana (life), Scripture Union of Ghana (life), Ghana Fellowship of Evangel. Students (ptnr., life). Avocations: music, art and craft, horticulture, Bible study. Home: PO Box 277, Hohoe Ghana Office: Food Rsch Inst, PO Box M20, Accra Ghana

NOBEL, JORIS ROELOF, civil servant, statistician, researcher; b. Utrecht, The Netherlands, Nov. 25, 1954; s. V.J. and M. (Zilver) N.; m. Anke Suzanne Dronkert; children: Jeroen, Sander. D of Polit. Sci., Free U., Amsterdam, 1984. Rschr., lectr. Free U., Amsterdam, 1980-85; rschr. Statistics Netherlands, Voorburg, 1985-87, staff officer, 1987—. Mem. Internat. Stats. Inst., Network Social Network Analysis, Internat. Assn. Official Statisticians. Office: Stats Netherlands, PO Box 4000, 2270 JM Voorburg The Netherlands

NOBEL, PETER, lawyer, researcher; b. Stockholm, Dec. 8, 1931; s. Leif Jurij Nobel and Anna Elisabeth (Mellen) Molander; m. Agnes Waldenstrom, Oct. 7, 1961 (div. Dec. 1993); m. Weini Kahsai, Mar. 18, 1994; children: Leif Jakob, Andreas, Jonas. Juris kandidat, U. Uppsala, Sweden, 1963, JD (hon.), 1985. Bar: Sweden 1968-86. Assoc. Advokatfirman, Chrysander, Uppsala, 1963-68, ptnr., 1968-86; assigned expert Swedish Govt. Com. for Reform of Law on Arrest and Custody in Criminal Procs.,, 1974-80, 83-85, on Law of Asylum, 1985, on Internat. law and disarmement, 1991-95, on Spl. Crisis Support, 1997-98; del. Swedish Govt. on Children and Youth, 1991-95; lectr. Law Sch., Uppsala, 1964-69; apptd. ombudsman against ethnic discrimination Govt. of Sweden, 1986-91; sec. gen. Swedish Red Cross, 1991-94; commr. for counseling relatives of victims after the shipwreck of Estonia, 1994-96; mem. coun. fgn. affairs peace and security promoting, 1995-97; cons. inf field; mem. com. Ethics of the Press, 1996. Author: (with G. Melander) Invandrarrätt, 1984, Refugee Law in the Sudan, 1982, The Alien Under Swedish Law, 1989, Tankar i Tigertid, 1992, Lag och Ratt och nya religioner, 1999; editor: Refugees and Development in Africa, 1987; (with G. Melander) African Refugees and the Law, 1971, International Legal Instruments on Refugees in Africa, 1979, After Estonia, 1997, Lag Och ratt ock rya religioner, 1999; editor: Advokaten, Tidskrift for Sveriges Advokatsamfund, 1973-86. Bd. dirs. Uppsala-Gavle Mpcl. Theatre, 1986-80; mem. Social Welfare Com., 1976; hon. treas., trustee European Human Rights Found., Amsterdam/London, 1981—; vice chmn. Swedish NGO Fund for Human Rights, 1991-93; trustee Internat. Alert, London, 1998; pres. Transnational Found. for Peace and Future Rsch., 1994-97; mem. com. elimination racial discrimination UN, 1998. Mem. Swedish Bar Assn. (dep. bd. dirs. 1970-78), Internat. Inst. Humanitarian Law (coun. mem. San Remo chpt. 1988-97). Home: Vasagatan 1A 3d Fl, S-75313 Uppsala Sweden

NOBLE, ADRIAN, artistic director; b. Eng., July 19, 1950; s. William John and Violet Ena (Wells) N. BA, Bristol U., 1972; student dir. program, Drama Ctr. London, 1972-74. IBA dirs. traineeship Bristol's Old Vic theatre, 1976-79; resident dir. Royal Shakespeare Co., 1980; guest dir. Royal Exchange Theater, 1980-81; assoc. artistic dir. Royal Shakespeare Co., London, 1982-90, artistic dir., 1990—. Office: care Barbican Theater, London EC2Y 8BQ, England

NOBLE, JOHN JOSEPH, diplomat; b. Newton, Mass., Apr. 4, 1945; s. Ronald Harding and Marion Cope (Smith) N.; m. Linda June Styan, Aug. 20, 1966; children: Christine Noble-Seller, Michael, Sarah. BA, Acadia U., Wolfville, N.S., Can., 1965, BA (hons.), 1966. Joined Can. Fgn. Svc., 1966—; served with Can. Embassy, Dakar, 1968-70, Ankara, Turkey, 1973, London, 1973-77; mem. Can. Mission to UN and GATT, Geneva, 1980-83; spokesman, dir. press office External Affairs, Ottawa, Ont., 1983-84, dir. gen. U.S. rels., 1984-88, dir. gen. internat. security, 1988-90, dir. gen. internat. orgns., 1991-93; amb. of Can. to Hellenic Republic Athens, Greece, 1993-94; minister plenipotentiary Can. Embassy, Paris, 1994-98; amb. of Can. to Switzerland and Liechtenstein, 1998—; permanent observer Coun. of Europe in Strasbourg, 1998—. Contbr. articles to profl. jours., chpts. to books. Bd. govs. Acadia U., Wolfville, 1991-93. Lt. COTC, 1962-66. Fellow Ctr. for Internat. Affairs, Harvard U., Cambridge, Mass., 1990-91. Mem. East India and Devonshire Club (life). Baptist. Office: Canadian Embassy, Kirchenfeldstrasse 88, 30056 Bern Switzerland

NOBLE, LAWRENCE ALAN, artist; b. Tampa, Fla., Nov. 11, 1948; s. Clymer Marlay and Mary Alice (Cortes) N.; m. Elizabeth Wearden, May 22, 1982; children: Casey Josephine, John Marlay. Student, Tex. Acad. Art, 1969, Houston Mus. Fine Art Sch., 1974-75. Illustrator U.S. Army, Ft. Sheridan, Ill., 1970, San Francisco, 1971; staff artist, promotion dept. The Houston Chronicle, Houston, 1972; art dir., designer, illustrator Middaugh Assocs., Houston, 1973; freelance illustrator Noble Studio, Houston, 1973-88; designer, sculptor Noble Studio, Crestline, Calif., 1988—; sculptor, com. mem. San Bernardino County Peace Officers Meml. Com., San Bernardino, 1995—, designer sculptor Victor Salmones galleries, 1995—, sculptor, com. mem. Jack Benny Meml. Com., 1992-93, Ft. Sheridan Centennial Com., 1989-90. Sculptor, designer various art galleries. Hon. firefighter City of Redlands Fire Dept., 1997; marshall 4th July Parade Crestline Resorts C. of C., 1996, vol. McGovern for Pres., Dem. party, 1972. With U.S. Army, 1969-71. Recipient 4th U.S. Army Leadership and Integrity medal, 1986. Mem. Nat. Sculptors Soc., Internat. Sculpture Ctr., Calif. Profl. Firefighters, Star Wars Fan Club, Star Trek Fan Club. Republican. Roman Catholic. Avocations: surfing, reading, history. Office: Noble Studio PO Box 2229 Crestline CA 92325-2229

NOBLE, PETER SCOTT, language educator; b. Aberdeen, Grampian, Scotland, May 20, 1941; s. Peter Scott and Mary (Stephen) N.; m. Margaret Emma Leask, Mar. 30, 1968; children: Alexander, Stephen, Alasdair. BA, Cambridge U., 1963; PGCE, Kings Coll., 1964; PhD, Birkbeck Coll., 1973; dipl., Inst. Francais, London, 1986. Tchr. Surrey County Coun., Reigate, Eng., 1964-67; lectr., reader U. Reading, Eng., 1967-97, head dept., 1991-99, prof. medieval and Que. lit., 1997—; examiner UCLES, Cambridge, 1993—; chief examiner SUJB, Bristol, 1983-93. Author: Le Voyatge D'Oultremer, 1975, Love and Marriage in Chretien de Troyes, 1982, Beroul and La Folie Tristan de Berne, 1982, Hebert les Fous de Bassan, 1995; editor Reading Medieval Studies, 1975-92; contbr. articles to profl. jours. Recipient Can. Govt. Faculty Enrichment award, 1982, 92. Office: Dept French Studies, Univ Reading, Reading Berks RG6 6AA, England

NOBLE, SUNNY A., business owner; b. Moorhead, Minn., May 22, 1940; m. Eric Scott Noble, Apr. 11, 1980. MBA, U. Calif., Berkeley, 1960; qualified parapsychologist, U. Minn., 1979. Mgr. Spear & Hill Attys., N.Y.C., 1969-70; mgr. exec. property mgmt. May Co. Dept. Stores, La Jolla, Calif., 1981-82; owner, pres. The Computer Tutor, L.A., 1984—. Author: (newspaper column) That Computes, 1984-88, The Storyteller, 1987-91; humor columnist Chit-Chat, The Westside Examiner, 1996—; author stage plays: The Garlic Eater (Writer's Digest Mag. nat. writing competition award 1998), Mother's Day (Writer's Digest Mag. nat. writing competition award 1998), (screen play) The Black Mirror. Mem. Internat. Platform Assn., Toastmasters Internat. (ednl. v.p. 1988), Mensa, Beta Sigma Phi. Home and Office: 4152 W Avenue L2 Quartz Hill CA 93536-4216

NOBLITT, NANCY ANNE, aerospace engineer; b. Roanoke, Va., Aug. 14, 1959; d. Jerry Spencer and Mary Louise (Jerrell) N. BA, Mills Coll., Oakland, Calif., 1982; MS in Indsl. Engring., Northeastern U., 1990. Data red specialist Universal Energy Sys., Beaver Creek, Ohio, 1981; aerospace engr. turbine engine divsn. components br. turbine group aero-propulsion lab. Wright-Patterson AFB, Ohio, 1982-84; engine assessment br. spl. engines group Wright-Patterson AFB, 1984-87; lead analyst cycle methods computer aided engr. GE, Lynn, Mass., 1987-90; Lynn PACES project coord. GE, Lynn, 1990-91; software sys. analyst Sci. Applications Internat. Corp.; with artificial intelligence Sci. Applications Internat. Corp., McLean, Va., 1991-92; software engring. mgr., intelligence applications integration Sci. Applications Internat. Corp., Hampton, Va., 1992-93; mgr. test engring. and sys. support Sci. Applications Internat. Corp., Hampton, 1993-94, mgr. configuration mgmt., 1994, mgmt. asst. to TBMCS program mgr., 1994-95; sr. simulation engr. Chem Demil, 1995-98; supervisory engr. Analytical Mechanics Assocs., Hampton, 1998-99; sr. project engr. Newport News (Va.) Shipbuilding Inc., 1999-00, Coll. William an dMary Law Sch., Williamsburg, Va., 2000—; math and sci. tutor Centerville Sch. Bd., Ohio, 1982-86, math. and physics tutor Marblehead Sch. Bd., Mass., 1988-90; tutor math, chemistry & physics Poquoson Sch. Bd., Va., 1994—; rep. alumnae admissions Mills Coll., Boston area, 1987-91; mem. bd. trustees/bd. govs. Mills Coll., 1995-98; mem. Citizens for Hilton Area Revitalization, 1994—. Math. and sci. tutor Centerville Sch. Bd., Ohio, 1982-86, math. and physics tutor Marblehead (Mass.) Sch. Bd., 1988-90; tutor math., chemistry and physics Poquoson Sch. Bd., Va., 1994—; rep. alumnae admissions Mills Coll., Boston area, 1987-91, trustee/bd. govs., 1995-98; mem. Citizens for Hilton Area Revitalization, 1994—. Recipient Notable Achievement award USAF, 1984, Spl. award Fed. Lab. Consortium, 1987. Mem. Soc. Mfg. Engrs. Avocation: book collecting. Home: 58 Hopkins St Newport News VA 23601-4034 Office: Newport News Shipbuilding Newport News VA 23607

NOBUKI, SABURO, publisher; b. Tokyo, May 5, 1923; s. Mokusaburo and Kiyono (Akiyama) N.; m. Tsugiko Suwa, Oct. 7, 1955; children: Soichiro, Haruo. BA in Sociology, Tokyo U., 1946. Editor, writer, high sch. tchr., translator, 1946-53; sales mgr. C.E. Tuttle, 1953-61; Japan rep. Feffer & Simons, 1961-62; mng. dir. Kodansha Internat., 1962-87; spl. adviser, 1967-84; v.p. Kodansha Internat./U.S.A., 1986-87; mng. dir. Kodansha Famous Sch.; pres. NST Internat. Co., Quadriga NST Internat. Pubs. Ltd., London, 1982—, Internat. Pub. Inst., 1987—, Japan Ave., Inc., 1995—; spl. adviser baseball mag. Ko Bunsha Pub., 1994—, Koshiwisha Pub., 1999—. Bd. dirs. newsletter Asian Culture Ctr. for UNESCO, 1994-98; mem. Japan Film Censorship, 1995-99. Mem. Japanese Animal Welfare Soc., Japan. Sociol. Assn., Internat. Soc. Ednl. Info., Inc. (exec. dir. 1988-93), Gakushikai, PEN Club, Editorogical Soc. Japan (mem. masters exec.), Tokyo Ginza Rotary, Keiza, Doyukai. Home and office: 3-17-14 Akatsutsumi Setagaya-ku, Tokyo 156-0044, Japan Office: 2-12-21 Otowa, Bunkyo-ku, Tokyo 112, Japan

NOBUYUKI, ONIMURA, transportation executive; b. Hagi, Yamaguchi, Japan, Mar. 15, 1938; s. Shigeharu and Shizuko (Yokoyama) O.; m. Kimiko Tanaka, Apr. 10, 1965; children: Shigehito, Kazunori. Navigator, Marine Tech. Coll., 1958-59, master class, 1961-63. Marine navigator First Shipping Co. Ltd., 1959-61; with marine dept. Nickel & Lyons Co., Kobe, Japan, 1963-70, Everett Steamship Corp. S.A., Tokyo, 1970-87; with traffic dept. Showa Enterprise, Kobe, 1987-88; with transport dept. Mitsuboshi Kaiun Co. Ltd., Osaka, 1988-95; agy. broker, cons. Hayakoma Shoji Co. Ltd., Himeji, Japan, 1995—; gen. gmr. Agy. Brokering Dept., Himeji, 1995—; port capt. Transport Dept., Osaka, 1988-95; gen. mgr. Traffic Dept., Kobe, 1987-88; gen. mgr. Marine Dept. Maintenance Brokering and Agy., Tokyo-Kobe, 1982-87. Mem. Japan Overseas Parent Assn. Home: 3-9-23-502 Hiyodoridai, Kita-ku, Kobe 651-1123, Japan Office: Agy Dept. 301 Suka Shikama-ku, Himeji 672-8063, Japan

NOCERA, LUIGI, research physicist; b. Gallipoli, Lecce, Italy, Jan. 13, 1957; s. Giovanni and Angela (Barra) N.; m. Laura Josefina Palumbo, Feb. 12, 1994; 1 child, Guglielmo-Giovanni. Laurea in physics, U. Pisa, Italy, 1980. Rsch. fellow U. Florence, Italy, 1981-82; vis. rschr. Acad. Scis., Moscow, 1982-83; rsch. fellow U. St. Andrews, Scotland, 1983-86; rschr. 3rd level NRC, Pisa, 1986—; contract lectr. U. Pisa, 1991-92; sci. counsellor NRC, 1993-96, project rep., 1992-94; referee Jour. Plasma Physics, INTAS Programs; guest lectr. NASA/WIND Space Program; guest investigator NASA/WIND Project; mem. organizing com. World Inst. Space Sci. Rsch. Contbr. articles to sci. publs. Fund raiser Scientists for Global Responsibility, 1992-93. Rsch. grantee Czech Acad. Scis., Prague, Czech Republic, 1989-91. Mem. Internat. Astron. Union, European Astron. Soc., N.Y. Acad. Scis. Avocations: woodwork, bicycling, painting. Home: Via Calcesana 171, 56010 Ghezzano Italy Office: Ist Fisica Atom e Molecolar, Via Alfieri 1, 56010 Ghezzano-Pisa Italy

NOCHMAN, LOIS WOOD KIVI (MRS. MARVIN NOCHMAN), retired educator; b. Detroit, Nov. 5, 1924; d. Peter K. and Annetta Lois (Wood) Kivi; m. Harold I. Pitchford, Sept. 6, 1944 (div. May 1949); children: Jean Wood Pitchford Scott, Joyce Lynn Pitchford Undiano; m. Marvin A. Nochman, Aug. 15, 1953; 1 child, Joseph Asa. AB, U. Mich., 1946, AM, 1949. Tchr. adult edn. Honolulu, 1947, Ypsilanti (Mich.) H.S., 1951-52; spl. instr. English Wayne State U., Detroit, 1953, 54; tchr. Highland Park (Mich.) Coll., 1950-51, instr. English, 1954-83; ret., 1983; mem. exec. bd. Highland Park Fedn. Tchrs., 1963-66, 73, del. to Nat. Conv., 1964, 71-74, rep. higher edn. to Mich. Fedn. Tchrs. Exec. Com., 1972-76; mem. faculty adv. com. Gov.'s Commn. on Higher Edn., 1973—. Contbr. poems to mags. Tchr. Baha'i Schs., Davison, Mich., 1954-55, 58-59, 63-66, Beaulac, Que., Can., 1960, Greenacre, Maine, 1965; sec. local spiritual assembly Baha'is, Ann Arbor, 1953, sec., Detroit, 1954, chmn., 1955; mem. nat. com. Baha'is U.S., 1955-68; sec. Davison Bahai Sch. Com. and Coun., 1956, 58, 63-68; Baha'i lectr. Subject of local TV show Senior Focus, 1992. Recipient Women's Movement plaque Women Lawyers Assn. Mich., 1975, Lawrence award Mich. Masters Swimming, 1991, 6 World Master Records in Age Group short course meters, 1994-95, 5 records in Long Course Meters, 1995, 23 Nat. Masters Records, 1994-96, 6 Nat. YMCA records, 1995, 2 U.S. Nat. Sr. Sports Classic Records, 1995, 2 World Sr. Games Records, 1993, All-Am. award, 1990-99, U.S. Long Distance All Star, 1995, 96, 97, 98, 99, U.S. MS Finals All Star, 1995, 8 Huntsman World Sr. Games Records, 1996, 9 Huntsman World Sr. Games Records, 1998, 5 Huntsman Masters World Records short course meters, 1999, 5 Masters World Records long course meters, 1999, 9 Huntsman World Games Records in age group 75-79, 1999; named one of 10 Best of 1995 Swim Mag., one of 12 Best Swimmers of 1999, Swim Mag., 2000. Mem. NOW, MLA, Nat. Coun. Tchrs. English, Mich. Coll. English Assn., Am. Fedn. Tchrs., Nat. Soc. Lit. and Arts, Women's Equity and Action League (sec. Mich. chpt. 1975-79), Alpha Lambda Delta, Alpha Gamma Delta. Avocations: U.S. Swimming Master Champion.

NOCKER, MARGIT, chemist, webmaster; b. Brunico, BZ, Italy, Jan. 13, 1961; d. Amedeo and Erta (Gargitter) N. BS, U. Innsbruck, 1989; D in Chemistry, U. Bologna, Italy, 1990. Cert. chemist. Chemist Chem. Lab. Province Bolzano, Bolzano, Italy, 1991-93; dir. sterilization plant Hosp. S. Candido, Brunico, Italy, 1996; internet webmaster Brunico, 1998, with com-

panies, Obiettivo Lavoro, Adecco and Manpower at Bolzano, 1999—; security expert, 1999. Fellow Highlander Club; mem. Chamber of Chemists, Assn. Webmasters Italy, Club of Rome. Avocations: sports.

NODA, MAMI, pharmacology educator; b. Tokyo, Mar. 9, 1957; d. Kanemaru and Sumiko (Miyahara) Urata; m. Terumi Noda, Nov. 22, 1981; children: Yuki, Yumi. BD, Kyushu U., Fukuoka, Japan, 1979; PhD, Kyoto (Japan) U., 1986. Asst. prof. Kyushu U., Fukuoka, 1979-81, 96-99, assoc. prof., 1999—; fellow Rockefeller U., N.Y.C., 1986-90; rschr. Kanazawa (Japan) U., 1990-96. Active Met. Mus. Art, 1997—. Mem. N.Y. Acad. Sci. Home: 1-21-2 Ikimatsu-dai, Fukuoka 819-0044, Japan Office: Kyushu U Grad Sch Pharmacy, 3-1-1 Maidashi Higashi-ku, Fukuoka 812-8582, Japan

NODA, NAO-AKI, mechanical engineering educator, researcher; b. Bisai-city, Japan, Dec. 25, 1956; s. Akikatsu and Kayoko (Asai) N.; m. Kaoru Miyoshi Noda, Dec. 23, 1990; children: Kanako, Yoshihisa. B in Engring., Kyushu Inst. Tech., Kitakyushu, Japan, 1979; M in Engring., 1981; PhD in Engring., Kyushu U., Fukuoka, Japan, 1984. Asst. prof. Kyushu Inst. Tech., Kitakyushu, Japan, 1984-87; vis. prof. Lehigh (Pa.) U., 1985-86; assoc. prof. Kyushu Inst. Tech., Kitakyushu, Japan, 1987—; vis. lectr. Nishi-Nippon Inst. Tech., Kitakyushu, Japan, 1989-90, Oita (Japan) U., 1990-91, Kyushu Sangyo U., Fukuoka, Japan, 1994-96. Contbr. technical papers to profl. jours. Fellow Japanese Min. Edn. and Sci., 1985-86; named hon. prof. Shandong (China) U. Tech., 1996. Mem. Japan Soc. Mech. Engrs., Japan Soc. Material Sci. Achievements include contributions to stress analysis for notched and stepped bars, cracked bodies, and various shaped inclusions by the application of body-force method coupled with a singular integral equation formulation. Home: 1-2-37 Kawanaka-yutakamachi, Shimonoseki 751-0853, Japan Office: Kyushu Inst Tech, 1-1 Sensui-cho Tobata, Kitakyushu 804-8550, Japan

NODA, YUTAKA, physician, otolaryngologist; b. Toyonaka, Osaka, Japan, Sept. 22, 1937; s. Masayuki and Yukiko (Yuasa) N.; m. Hiroko Tamura, Nov. 19, 1963; children: Maki, Miki. BA, Med. Faculty Keio U., Tokyo, 1962; MD, Nihon U., Tokyo, 1972. Intern Keio U. Hosp., Tokyo, 1962-63; resident Nihon U. Hosp., Tokyo, 1963-65, asst., 1965-68, asst. lectr., 1972-73; asst. Hamburg (Fed. Republic of Germany) U. Hosp., 1968-72; assoc. prof. Ryukyu U. Hosp., Naha-Shi, Okinawa, Japan, 1973-81, prof., 1981-83; prof. medicine Ryukyu U., Nishihara, Okinawa, 1983—. Contbr. articles to profl. jours. Mem. Japanese Soc. Stomatopharyngology (bd. dirs. 1988—), Otorhinolaryngology Soc. Japan (councilor 1978—), German Soc. Throat, Nose and Ear Medicine, Soc. Head and Neck Surgery (corr.), Soc. for Promotion Rsch. in Otorhinolaryngology in Ryukyus (chief dir. 1983—). Avocations: Japanese archery, travel. Office: U Ryukyus, Aza-Uehara 207, Nishihara-Cho Okinawa 903-01, Japan

NODDINGS, SARAH ELLEN, lawyer; b. Matawan, N.J.; d. William Clayton and Sarah Stephenson (Cox) Noddings; children: Christopher, Aaron. BA in Math., Rutgers U., New Brunswick, N.J., 1965, MSW, 1968; JD cum laude, Seton Hall U., Newark, 1975; postgrad., UCLA, 1979. Bar: Calif. 1976, Nev. 1976, N.J. 1975, U.S. Dist. Ct. (ctrl. dist.) Calif. 1976, U.S. Dist. Ct. N.J. 1975. Social worker Carteret (N.J.) Bd. Edn., 1970-75; law clk. Hon. Howard W. Babcock, 8th Jud. Dist. Ct., Las Vegas, Nev., 1975-76; assoc. O'Melveny & Myers, L.A., 1976-78; atty. Internat. Creative Mgmt., Beverly Hills, Calif., 1978-81, Russell & Glickman, Century City, Calif., 1981-83; atty. Lorimar Prodns., Culver City and Burbank, Calif., 1983-87, v.p., 1987-93; atty. Warner Bros. TV, Burbank, Calif., 1993—, v.p., 1993—, sr. atty., 1999—. Dir. county youth program, rsch. analyst Sonoma County People for Econ. Opportunity, Santa Rosa, Calif., 1968-69; VISTA vol. Kings County Cmty. Action Orgn., Hanford, Calif., 1965-66; officer, PTA bd. Casimir Mid. Sch. and Arlington Elem. Sch. Mem. Acad. TV Arts and Scis. (nat. awards com. 1994—), L.A. Copyright Soc. (trustee 1990-91), Women in Film, L.A. County Bar Assn. (intellectual property sect.), Women Entertainment Lawyers, Media Dist. Intellectual Propr. Bar Assn. (bd. dirs. 1999—). Avocations: travel, tennis, skiing, bicycling, swimming. Office: Warner Bros TV 300 Television Plz Burbank CA 91505-1372

NODES, JAMES THOMAS, biochemist; b. London, Mar. 7, 1932; s. Percy Clarence and Florrie Clara (Thomas) N.; m. Kathleen Elizabeth Blackie, Mar. 3, 1962; children: Michael James, Andrew John. BSc in Zoology, Kings Coll., London, 1955, MSc in Biochemistry, 1959, PhD in Biochemistry, 1964. Chartered biologist. Rsch. asst. Chester Beatty Rsch. Inst., London, 1955-62; lectr. Brunel U., London, 1963-73, sr. lectr., 1973-92, acting head of dept., 1992-93, ret., 1993; nat. assessor in biology ONC/OND Sci. Courses, Great Britain, 1967-85; mem. scientific adv. com. Marie Curie Rsch. Found., Great Britain, 1968-73; mem. examination and validation com. Inst. of Biology, Great Britain, 1981-84; mem. scientific adv. com. Assn. for Internat. Cancer Rsch., Great Britain, 1981-82. Fellowship Inst. of Biology, 1986. Mem. Biochem. Soc. Home: 83 North View, Eastcote HA5 1PX, England

NODLAND, BORGE HEMING, physicist; b. Oslo, Norway, Apr. 7, 1964; came to U.S., 1989; s. Ingebjorg (Loken) N.; m. Angela Christine Spendal, Sept. 9, 1994; children: Sean, Eric. BS, U. Trondheim (Norway), 1989; MS, U. South Fla., 1991; PhD, U. Kans., 1995. Tech. support engr. Wolfram Rsch. Inc., Champaign, Ill., 1995-96; rsch. fellow U. Rochester (N.Y.), 1996-98; scientist advanced programs divsn. Silicon Valley Group Lithography Sys., Inc., 1998—. NSF grad. trainee, 1994. Mem. Am. Phys. Soc. Achievements include experimental findings with a developed theory indicating that the universe is anisotropic with respect to electromagnetic interactions. Avocation: swimming. Office: Quaker chem Corp 24 Drayton St Ste 800 Savannah GA 31401-2733

NOE, VIRGILIO CARDINAL, archbishop; b. Zelata di Bereguardo, Italy, Mar. 30, 1922. With titular ch. St. John Bosco; vicar gen. Vatican City State; archpriest St. Peter Basilica; with titular Ch. Voncaria; elevated to Sacred Coll. Cardinals, 1991. Office: 00120 Vatican City State Vatican City State*

NOEL, TREY LEONARD, III, strategic planning executive; b. New Orleans, Nov. 4, 1967; s. Leonard Leon Jr. and Jennifer Lynn (Tujague) N.; m. Samantha Shea Cronley, June 13, 1998. BS, So. Meth. U., 1990, MBA, 1994. Assoc. Willis Corroon, Seattle, 1990-92; bus. devel. exec. Orthofix, Dallas, 1993-95; fin. planning exec. Dr. Pepper/Seven Up, Dallas, 1995-99; strategic planning exec. Cadbury Schweppes, London, 1999—. Mem. Kappa Alpha (pres. 1985-86). Avocations: golf, skiing, reading. Home: 32 Milliners Ct, Saint Albans Herts AL1 3XT, England

NOETHLING, VICTORIA ANN, delivery service executive; b. Pitts., Jan. 8, 1958; d. James Ralph and Elizabeth Mary Sage; m. Robert August Noethling, June 23, 1979; children: Samantha, Rebecca. Bus. cert., Bradford Bus. Sch., Pitts. Adminstrv. asst. Grant Thornton, Pitts., 1977-86, Margolis Wine & Spirits, Pitts., 1986-87; supr., adminstr. Arby's, Inc., Atlanta, 1987-91; supr., adminstr. UPS Hdqs., Atlanta, 1991-93, supr. customer info. mgmt., 1993—. Mentor Girl Scouts Am., 2000, assoc. Boys & Girls Club Met. Atlanta, 1993—, torchbearer 1996 Olympics, Atlanta. Recipient Ember award Camp Fire Girls, Atlanta, 1998. Mem. NAFE, Toastmasters Internat. (pres., v.p. edn., sec. 1998-2000, Competent Toastmaster award 1998). Roman Catholic. Avocations: reading, water skiing, crafts, cooking. E-mail: vnoethling@ups.com. Office: UPS 55 Glenlake Pkwy NE Atlanta GA 30328-3474

NOFFKE, JANE BUNGE, sculptor; b. Madison, Wis., Oct. 28, 1957; d. William Wheeler and Elizabeth Ann (Carpenter) Bunge; m. Stephen Henry Noffke, Apr. 25, 1991; children: Payvand, Aaron, Anne Rose. BS with honors, U. Wis., 1987; student, Ea. Mich. U., Ypsilanti, 1989-91. Artist, 1980—; pvt. sculpture tchr. Ann Arbor, 1996—; author/lectr., 1995—; tchr./sculpture juror U. Mich., Ann Arbor, 1994-98; mentor/tchr. U. Mich./Eaton Acad., Detroit, 1998; art tchr. Crane Correctional Instn. for Women Women Caucus for the Arts, 1997-98. Exhbns. include photographs at UN, 1996-2000, bronze sculpture at Smithsonian Art Inst., 1994—, commd. bronze at the White House, photographs at Nat. Mus. of Women, 1995—, gallery bronzes at Toledo Mus. Art, 1992—, gallery bronzes at Galerie Alain Daune, Paris, 1995-98, Swords Into Plowshares UN Global Focus, 1997; contbr. articles to profl. jours. Recipient Dick Blick award for Artistic Excellence, 1992, Transforming Visions award Swords Into Plowshares Gallery, Detroit, 1993, 1997, Outstanding Achievement award Washtenaw Coun. for the Artists, 1997, 1998, Ethel Odegard scholarship for Artistic Excellence U. Wis., 1987, Outstanding Artistic Citation U. Wis., 1986, Gov.'s award for Outstanding Citizenship & Achievement, 1985, Outstanding Artistic Excellence award Internat. Exhbn., Russia, 1985, Nat. Endowment for the Arts grant Milw. Found., 1982; work selected to go on world tour UN Beijing Women's Conf., 1995-96. Mem. Nat. Sculpture Soc., Nat. Women's Caucus for the Arts, Chgo. Coalition of Artists, Detroit Artists Mkt., Ann Arbor Art Ctr. Avocations: photography, painting, running. E-mail: steven@rust.net. Studio: Technology Ctr Noffke Studio 410 W Washington St # 20 Ann Arbor MI 48103-4230

NOFUENTES, GUSTAVO, science educator; b. Jaen, Spain, Dec. 8, 1967; s. Eduardo and Asuncion N. Diploma in telecomm. engring., U. Poly. Madrid, 1993, MS, 1998. Rschr. U. Jaen, 1993, lectr., 1993—; project rschr. European Commn., Jaen, 1993-95, 96-98. Contbr. articles to profl. jours. Avocations: travel, music, collecting Roman coins. Fax: 34.953.212400. E-mail: gnofuen@ujaen.es. Home: Paseo de la Estacion 9, 23007 Jaen Spain Office: U Jaen, Ave de Madrid 35, 23071 Jaen Spain

NOGAMI, GYOICHI, physical chemist; b. Tobata-city, Fukuoka, Japan; s. Yasuko Nogami, June 1, 1975; children: Keitaro, Natsu, Shaw. BSc, Waseda U., 1966, MSc, 1968, PhD, 1974. Rsch. asst. Kyushu Inst. of Tech., 1969-75; assoc. prof. Kyushu Inst. of Tech., Kitakyushu, Japan, 1975-82, prof., 1982—. Author: The History of Meiji College of Technology, 1994. Avocations: mountain climbing, yachting, wild flowers, essay. Home: 1-4-13 Wakagidai Fukuma, Fukuoka 811-3221, Japan Office: Kyushu Inst of Tech, 1-1 Sensuicho Tobata, Kitakyushu 804-8550, Japan

NOGAMI, YOSHIKO, mathematics and statistics educator; b. Tennoji, Osaka, Japan, Dec. 10, 1942; d. Takumi and Chizue Nogami. BS in Math., Tsuda Coll., Tokyo, 1966; PhD in Stats. and Probability, Mich. State U., 1975. Rsch. asst. Inst. Statis. Math., Tokyo, 1966-69; asst. prof. Daito Bunka U., Tokyo, 1977-79; asst. prof. U. Tsukuba, Ibaraki, Japan, 1979-85, assoc. prof., 1985—.

NOGATA, FUMIO, engineering educator; b. Saga City, Japan, Feb. 5, 1947; parents Juzou and Nui N.; m. Tsuneko Koga, Mar. 23, 1980; children: Fumiyasu, Kanako, Kumiko. M in Engring., Kanto Gakuin U., 1973; D in Engring., Tohoku U., 1986. Lectr., assoc. prof. Himeji Inst. Technology, Japan, 1974-98; prof. Gifu U., Japan, 1998—. Office: Gifu U, 1-1 Yanagido, Gifu 501-1193, Japan

NOGI, TIAKI, textile designer; b. Kyoto, Japan, Dec. 17, 1937; s. Shogo and Namie (Kumon) N.; m. Yoshie Seto, May 10, 1964; children—Yuko, Akiko. BA, Kansai U. (Japan), 1961. Studio mgr. Shogo Nogi Studio, Kyoto, 1969-75; owner, mng. dir. Nogi Tiaki Designs, London and Kyoto, 1975—; designer wallcoverings, upholsteries, bedlinen. Roman Catholic. Avocations: coin collecting, Sunday carpentry, operas, classical music. Home: 23 Okamachi Misasagi Yamasina, 607 Kyoto Japan Office: Nogi Tiaki Designs, 23 Okamachi Misasagi, 607-8431 Kyoto Japan

NÓGRÁDI, ANTAL, ophthalmology educator, researcher; b. Békés, Hungary, Apr. 23, 1961; s. Antal and Éva (Forray) N.; m. Stefánia Borda, Oct. 30, 1993; children: Eszter, Bernat. MD, Albert Szent-Györgyi Med. U., Szeged, Hungary, 1986, PhD, 1995. Med. diplomate. Intern P. Réthy Hosp., Békéscsaba, Hungary, 1985-86; asst. prof. Albert Szent Györgyi Med. U., Szeged, 1986-90, 94—; rsch. fellow U. Coll., London, 1991-94, assoc. prof., 1997—. Author: Transplantation of Neural Tissue Into the Spinal Cord, 1994; contbr. articles to profl. jours. Recipient Lenhossék award Soc. Hungarian Anatomists, 1995; named prof. Ministry Higher Edn., 1999. Mem. Internat. Brain Rsch. Orgn., Hungarian Neurosci. Soc., Brit. Brain Rsch. Soc. Office: Dept Opht Albert Szent-Györgyi, Korányi fasor 1o-11, H-6720 Szeged Hungary

NOGUCHI, HIROSHI, structural engineering educator; b. Tokyo, Aug. 9, 1946; s. Kou and Kimie (Ohtake) N.; m. Yoriko Ito, Jan. 8, 1982; children: Mariko, Eriko. B in Engring., U. Tokyo, 1970, M in Engring., 1972, DEng, 1976. Registered architect 1st class. Rsch. assoc. U. Tokyo, 1976-77; asst. prof. Chiba (Japan) U., 1977-79, assoc. prof., 1979-90; prof. Chiba U., 1991, chmn. dvsn. environ. sci. Grad. Sch. Sci. and Tech., 1995; vis. researcher U. Toronto, 1984-85, U. Tex., 1997-98. Author: (with others) Shear Analysis of Reinforced Concrete Structures, 1983, Finite Element Analysis of Reinforced Concrete Structures, 1986, Shear Resistance Mechanisms of Beam-Column Joints Under Reversed Cyclic Loading, 1987, Guidelines for Application of FEM to RC Design, 1989, Development of Mixed Structures in Japan, 1990, Experimental Studies on Shear Performances of RC Interior Column-Beam Joints with High-Strength Materials, 1992, Finite Element Analysis of Reinforced Concrete Structures II, 1993, Analytical Study on the Shear Performance of Beam-Column Connections in Hybrid Structures with RC Column and S Beams, 1995, Nonlinear Finite Element Analysis on Shear and Bond of RC Interior Beam-Column Joints with Ultra High-Strength Materials, 1995, Analytical Study on the Shear Performance of Steel Beam-R/C Column Connections in Hybrid Structures, 1996, Analysis of Beam-Column Joints in Hybrid Structures, 1997, Shear Strength of Beam-Column Joints with High-Strength Concrete, 1998, FEM Analysis for Structural Performance Design of Concrete Structures, 1999, Research on RC/SRC Column Systems, 2000, FEM Analysis of Hybrid Structural Frames with R/C Columns and Steel Beams, 2000; author: State-of-the-Art of Theoretical Studies in Membrane Shear Behavior in Japan, 1991, Recent Developments of Researches and Applications of RCFEM in Japan, 1991, Finite Element Analysis of Shear Behavior of RC Members with High Strength Materials, 1993, Shear Resisting Mechanisms of Reinforced Concrete Members Based on FEM Analysis, 1994, Concrete Model Code for Asia, 1996. Mem. ASCE, Archtl. Inst. Japan (Meritorious Paper award 1997), Japan Concrete Inst. (Meritorious Paper award 1985), Tokyo Soc. Architects, Am. Concrete Inst., Internat. Assn. Bridges and Structural Engring. Avocations: swimming, skiing, classical music. Home: 5-9-2 Arima, Miyamae-ku, Kawasaki-City, Kanagawa 216-0003, Japan Office: Chiba U Dept Design & Arch, 1-33 Yayoi-cho, Inage-ku Chiba 263-8522, Japan

NOGUCHI, THOMAS TSUNETOMI, author, forensic pathologist; b. Fukuoka, Japan, Jan. 4, 1927; came to U.S., 1952; s. Wataru and Tomika Narahashi N. D of Medicine, Nippon Med. Sch., Tokyo, 1951; prof. honoris causa, U. Braz Cubas Fedn. Faculties Mogi Das Cruzes, Sao Paolo, Brazil, 1980; DSc (hon.), Worcester State Coll., 1985. Dep. med. examiner Los Angeles County Dept. Chief Med. Examiner, L.A., 1961-67, coroner, 1967-82; prof. forensic pathology U. So. Calif. Med. Sch., L.A., 1982-99, prof. emeritus forensic pathology, 1999—. Author: Coroner, 1983 (N.Y. Times Bestseller 1984), Coroner At Large, 1985; (fiction) Unnatural Causes, 1988, Physical Evidence, 1990. Recipient Imperial medal Order of Sacred Treasure, His Majesty the Emperor of Japan, 1999. Fellow Am. Acad. Forensic Sci. (chmn. sect. 1966); mem. AMA, Internat. Acad. Legal and Social Medicine, Nat. Assn. Med. Examiners (pres. 1983), Calif. State Coroners Assn. (pres. 1974), World Assn. Med. Law (v.p.). Republican. Avocations: fine arts, gourmet Oriental cooking, painting stills and abstracts. Fax: 323-733-9860. Office: U So Calif Med Ctr 1200 N State St Rm 2520 Los Angeles CA 90033-1029

NOGUEIRA, CARLOS MAIA, computer company executive; b. Lisbon, Portugal, Jan. 24, 1943; s. António and Maria (Maia) N.; m. Clemencia F. Maia Nogueira, Feb. 12, 1972 (dec.); children: Vasco Diogo, Ana Luisa; m. Lucia F. Maia Nogueira; 1 child, Joana. Degree in electrotech. and mechs., Lisbon Indsl. Inst., 1969. Office mgr. Mensor, Lisbon, 1962-65; bus. ptnr. Ciope Sarl, Lisbon, 1966-68; ptnr., gen. mgr. Soternica, Lisbon, 1969-72; indsl. pool and water treatment co. mgr. Sebes, Lisbon, 1972-77; indsl. equipment co. mgr. Diamante Internat., Lisbon, 1978-80; computer co. gen. mgr. Landry, Lisbon, 1980-83, Solbi, Lisbon, 1983—. Editor: Basic, 1980; editor (first Portuguese computer mag.) Cérebro, 1982; inventor, patentee in field. Sgt., Portuguese Army, 1965-69, Paço d'Arcos. Mem. Clube Empresários. Roman Catholic. Avocations: hand works, collecting gold, bronze, and watches. Office: Solbi Lda Edificio Solbi, R Casal Do Canas 14, 2795 Carnaxide Portugal

NOGUEIRA, DIOGO PUPO, occupational health educator; b. São Paulo, Brazil, May 14, 1919; s. Octavio Pupo and Judith Pupo Nogueira; m. Lucia Gomes Pinto, Sept. 14, 1944; children: Diogo Jr., Maria Judith, Marcelo. MD, U. São Paulo, 1943, D in Occupational Hygiene, 1968. Med. dir. Linhas Corrente, São Paulo, 1944-84; prof. occupational health U. São Paulo, 1968-90, prof. emeritus, 1990—; bd. dirs. Internat. Commn. on Occulpational Health. Contbr. chpts. to books, articles to profl. jours. With Brazilian Army, 1937-38. Recipient Moinho Santista prize, 1988. Mem. Nat. Assn. on Occupational Health (bd. dirs.). Avocations: amateur radio, photography. Home: 67 Apt 61, Rua Cássio Costa Vidigal, 01456 São Paulo SP, Brazil Office: Av Dr Arnaldo 715, 01255000 São Paulo SP, Brazil

NOGUEIRA, GUILHERME DE PAULA, veterinary educator, researcher; b. Mirandópolis, Sao Paulo, Brazil, Dec. 20, 1965; s. Marcos da Costa and Myriam Azevedo (de Paula) N.; m. Maria Beatriz de Azevedo Passos, Nov. 25, 1995. B in Veterinary Medicine, U. Fed. Rural do Rio de Janeiro, 1988; MS, Faculdade de Medicina Veterinaria e Zootecnia da Universidade de Sao Paulo, 1994; PhD in Animal Reproduction, FMVZ U. Sã Paulo, 1997. Cow keeper Kibutz Brorchall, Askelon, Israel, 1988; horse keeper Yarkon Stable, Petartivka, Israel, 1989; stud farm inspector Assn. Brasileira dos Criadores de Cavalo de Corrida, qão Paulo, Brazil, 1989-90; asst. prof. animal physiology U. Estadual Paulista Julio de Mesquita Filho, Arçatuba, Brazil, 1991—; postdoctoral study U. Wis., Madison, 1998-99; Zool. cons., Araçatuba, 1991—. Contbr. book chpt. to Applied Pharmacology to Veterinary Medicine, 1996, 99. Recipient Young Rschr. award Brazilian Coll. Animal Reproduction, 1995. Mem. Brazilian Zool. Soc. Home: Apt 121 Vila São Paulo, Rua Euclides da Cuhna # 11, 16015220 Araçatuba S Paulo, Brazil Office: UNESP Araçatuba, Rua Clóvis Pestana 793, Araçatuba S Paulo, Brazil

NOGUEIRA E SILVA, JOSE AFONSO, engineering executive; b. Lisbon, June 30, 1946; s. Afonso Lourenco Dias Da and Maria Jose Barata (Nogueira) Silva; m. Isabel Rivera, Sept. 17, 1990. Diploma, Inst. Superior Technico, Lisbon, 1972. Student travel guide Student Travel Svc., Europe, 1966-69; nat. travel guide Portuguese Travel Agys., Europe, 1970-72; engr. Prof. Costa Lobo/Prof. Johnson Marshall, Regional Porto Plan, 1973-74; minister cons. Internal Affairs Minister, Lisbon, 1976; engr. cons. Portuguese Town Halls, Portugal, 1977-78; travel engr. cons. Nat. Travel Assn., Lisbon, 1978-79; CEO Nogueira e Silva Group of Co., Portugal, 1978—; dir. APIL Portugese Indsl. Assn., Luxembourg, 1994-95; founder, pres. Zona do Pinhal Rural Bank, Serta, 1982-84; pres. Agr. Coop., 1984-91. Avocation: stamp collection. Home: Rua Artilharia Um 46-2 DT, PT-1070 Lisbon Portugal Office: Rua Prof R Santos 50-B, PT-1500 Lisbon Portugal

NOHL, WERNER, landscape architect, researcher; b. Gummersbach, Rheinland, Germany, July 18, 1938; s. Otto and Emmy (Lang) N.; m. Ursula Friederike Bindl, Apr. 2, 1979; children: Friederike, Johannes, Cornelius. Student, Tech. Univ. Berlin, Germany, 1967, U. Calif., Berkeley, 1968; Dr, Tech. Univ. Hannover, Germany, 1979. Diplomate landscape architecture. Planner Priv. Planning Office, San Francisco, 1968-69; rsch. fellow Tech. Univ. Hannover, 1970-75; asst. prof. Tech. Univ. Munich, Germany, 1976-83; pvt. practice/rsch. Kirchheim, Germany, 1984—; lectr. Weihenstephan Coll., Germany, 1977-87, Univ. Kassel, Germany, 1981-84, Tech. Univ. Munich, 1983-93; hon. prof. Tech. U. Munich, 1994—; cons. Upper Bavarian County, Germany, 1996—. Author: Experiencing Abandoned Sites, 1976, Landscape Architecture and Emancipation, 1980, Reproduction of Men in Open Spaces, 1983, Open Spaces and the Ecological City, 1993. Japan Sci. and Tech. Corp. fellow, 1999—. Mem. Chamber of Architects, Inst. of Urbanistics (bd. mem.), Soc. of Rural Lanscape Germany. Avocations: piano, hiking. Home: Stockäckerring 17, D-85551 Kirchheim Germany

NOHRDEN, PATRICK THOMAS, lawyer; b. Santa Cruz, Calif., Mar. 7, 1956; s. Thomas Allen and Roberta Eugenia (Brydon) N.; m. Debora Ann Heintz, Sept. 19, 1981; children: Steven, Laura, Maranda, Patricia. AS, SUNY, Albany, 1980; BA in English with great distinction, San Jose State U., 1984; JD, U. Akron, 1992. Bar: Nev. 1993, U.S. Dist. Ct. Nev. 1993. Regional dir. CareerPro, Inc., Roseville, Calif., 1984-91; cons. Patrick T. Nohrden & Assocs., Youngstown, Ohio, 1991-93; pvt. practice, Las Vegas, Nev., 1993—; exec. dir. Geisa Project; bd. dirs. Profl. Resume Svc., Inc., Las Vegas, Las Vegas Diamondbacks, Inc., Clark County Pro Bono Project, Maui Land Devel. Co., Inc., World Internat. Intelligence Bur., Inc.; adj. prof. C.C. So. Nev. Sgt. U.S. Army, 1975-81. Recipient 2 Spirit of Pro Bono awards, Meritorious Svc. award. Mem. ATLA, ABA (family law sect.), Fed. Bar Assn., Nev. Trial Lawyers Assn., State Bar Nev. (family law and bankruptcy sects.), Clark County Bar Assn., Phi Kappa Phi. Republican. Roman Catholic. Office: 608 S 8th St Las Vegas NV 89101-7005

NOIN, DANIEL JEAN, geographer, educator, researcher; b. Ecouen, Val D'oise, France, Mar. 2, 1930; s. Pierre A. and Jeanne H. (Bélard) N.; m. Maddy M. Ledanois, Dec. 26, 1953; children: Katia, Sylvia. M in Geography, U. Paris, 1953, agregation geography, 1955, D in Geography, 1970; Doctorate (hon.), U. Zaragoza, Spain, 1991. Asst. U. Rabat, Morocco, 1962-69; lectr. U. Poitiers, France, 1969-70; sr. lectr. U. Rouen, France, 1970-73; prof. U. Paris (Sorbonne), 1973—, v.p., 1981-82; pres. Commn. on Population Geography, Internat. Geography Union, Paris, 1988-96; cons. UNESCO, 1996—. Author: La Population du Maroc, 1965 (Silver medal 1966), L'espace français (9 edits.), 1976, La Population de la France (4 edits.), 1986, Atlas de la Population Mondiale, 1993, Paris, 1997, People on Earth, 1997, The Population of Sub-Saharan Africa, 2000; also others; editor: The Changing Population of Europe, 1993. Recipient Palmes Academiques, Ministry of Edn., Paris, 1975, 88. Avocation: fruit tree cultivation. Home: 27 rue Marcille, F-41100 Vendome France Office: Univ Paris, 191 rue Saint-Jacques, F-75005 Paris France

NOIREAUD, JACQUES MICHEL RENE, physiologist; b. Bressuire, France, May 18, 1952; s. Rene and Suzanne (Raymond) N.; m. Dominique Bodin Louisot, June 21, 1973 (div. 1979); 1 child, Nadege; m. Christine Malburet, June 20, 1986; children: Sandy, Yann. BS, U. Poitiers, 1974, MD, 1977; DSc, U. Nantes, 1985. 010. Asst. prof. U. Calgary, Canada, 1978-79; rsch. asst. U. Homburg, Germany, 1980-81; med. attache U. Nantes, 1982-84; fellow U. Edinburgh, Scotland, 1985-86; rsch. asst. INSERM, Nantes, France, 1987-91, dir. rsch., 1992—. Mem. Fedn. Cardiology, Rsch. Def. Soc., Physiol. Soc. Fax: 33 02 40 08 75 23. E-mail: jacques.noireaud@nantes.inserm.fr. Home: 6 rue de la Cedraie, F-44240 La Chapelle Erdre France Office: INSERM U533, Hotel Dieu, F-44093 Nantes France

NOITSAKIS, BASILE, agronomy educator; b. Edessa, Greece, Mar. 15, 1947; s. John and Athanasia (Fragaki) N.; m. Helene Doumani; children: Athanasia, John, Leo. BS in Forestry, U. Thessaloniki, Greece, 1969, BS in Biology, 1976; MS in Ecology, U. Sci. and Technique, Montpellier, France, 1979, PhD in Ecophysiology, 1981. Diplomate in forestry and biology. Grad. rsch. asst. U. Thessaloniki, 1974-83, asst. prof., 1983-92, assoc. prof., 1992-97; prof. Aristotle U. Thessaloniki, 1997—. Author: Rangeland Ecology, 1993; also many scientific articles. Mem. Am. Soc. Agronomy, Assn. Francaise de Pastoralisme. Christian Orthodox. Avocations: music, philosophy. Home: 15 P Mela St, 54622 Thessaloniki Greece Office: U Thessaloniki, 236 Thessaloniki 54006, Greece

NOJAROV-ISSELHARD, ROLAND MICHAILOV, management consultant; b. Sofia, Bulgaria, Nov. 29, 1950; arrived in Germany, 1984; s. Michail Krustev and Gina Zaharieva (Krusteva) Nojarov. MSc, Sofia U., 1974, PhD, 1982; Habilitation, U. Tübingen, Germany, 1989. Physicist faculty of physics Sofia U., 1975-77; rsch. assoc. Inst. Nuclear Rsch. and Nuclear Energy Bulgarian Acad. Scis., Sofia, 1978-84; rsch. assoc. Inst. Theoretical Physics U. Tübingen, 1985-95, privatdozent Inst. Theoretical Physics, 1996-98; mgmt. cons. Computer Scis. Corp., Stuttgart, Germany, 1998-99, Origin Corp., 1999—. Referee internat. physics jours.; contbr. sci. articles to profl. jours. Fellow Alexander von Humboldt Found., 1985-86, 88. Mem. AAAS, N.Y. Acad. Scis. Avocations: philosophy, history, politics, economics, psychology. E-mail: roland.isselhard@uni-tuebingen.de.

NOJIMA, YOSHIKO, nursing educator; b. Ibara, Okayama, Japan, Feb. 10, 1939; d. Matsuichi and Hideko (Sano) N. BA, Ritsumeikan U., Japan,

1974. Reg. nurse. Assoc. prof. Fukui Prefectural Coll., Japan, 1975-77; lectr. Faculty Edn., U. Tokushima, Japan, 1977-82, assoc. prof., 1982-86; assoc. prof. Inst. Univ. Extension, U. Tokushima, 1986-91, prof., 1991-93; prof. Hiroshima U. Sch. Medicine, Japan, 1993—. Author: (book) Introduction to Humanistic Nursing, 1976, Techne of Nursing, 1977, A Theory of Nursing, 1984, Nursing Theory and Structural Formula For Nursing, 1988, Nursing Diagnosis and Independent Nursing Intervention, 1996. Recipient Nursing prize Med. Pub. Co., 1972, 73, Rsch. award Four Univ. Soc. Nursing Rsch. Mem. Japanese Soc. Nursing Rsch. Dir., Japanese Soc. Nursing Diagnosis, Sigma Theta Tau Insternat. Avocations: swimming, gardening, theater-going, reading books. Office: Hiroshima U Sch Medicine, Seta Tsukinowa Ohtsu-shi, Shiga 520-2192, Japan

NOLAN, BENJAMIN BURKE, retired civil engineer; b. Detroit, Oct. 6, 1931; s. Benjamin Augustus and Helen Louise (Boughey) N.; m. Katherine Mary Zeman, may 14, 1961. BSCE, U. Calif., Berkeley, 1958. Registered civil engr., Calif. City engr. City of Newport Beach, Calif., 1965-78, pub. works dir., 1978-94; mem. Orange County Transp. Authority, Calif., 1978-94, Transp. Corridor Agys., Orange County, 1984-94; active City Engrs. Assn., Orange County, 1965-94. With USAF, 1951-53, France. Mem. ASCE (life), Am. Pub. Works Assn. Achievements include participation in creation of Orange County Transp. Corridor Agys.; beach erosion solutions; hwy. and bridge constrn. and widening; coastal estuary restoration; harbor facilities and ocean pier improvements; water supply, sanitary sewerage, and storm drainage improvements; and publ. parks and bldgs. constrn. Home: 614 Hassett St Brookings OR 97415-8206

NOLAN, GARRY FRANCIS, company director and secretary; b. Sydney, Australia, Sept. 6, 1947; s. Geoffery and Rita Nolan; m. Joanne Elizabeth Andries; children: Samantha, Stuart, Briony. MBus, U. Tech., Sydney, 1993. Sec. Nat. Australia Bank Ltd. Authro: Structured Financing, 1973. Served with Australian mil. Fellow Australian Inst. Co. Dirs., Chartered Inst. Co. Secs., Australian Inst. Banking and Fin.; mem. Fin. and Treasury Assn., Securities Inst. Australia (assoc.). E-mail: garry.nolan@nag.national.com.au. Office: Nat Australian Bank Ltd, 500 Bourke St, 3000 Melbourne 3000, Australia

NOLAN, PETER JOHN, physics educator; b. N.Y.C., Mar. 25, 1934; s. Peter John and Nora (Gleeson) N.; divorced 1978; children: Thomas, James, John, Kevin. BS in Physics, Manhattan Coll., 1956; cert. in meteorology, UCLA, 1958; MS in Physics, Adelphi U., 1966, PhD in Physics, 1974. Engr. various corps., N.J., N.Y., 1956-63; systems analysis engr. on lunar module Gruman Aircraft Engring. Corp., Bethpage, N.Y., 1963-66; asst. prof. Physics SUNY, Farmingdale, 1966-68, assoc. prof. Physics, 1968-71, prof. Physics, 1971—; chmn. Physics dept. SUNY, Farmingdale, 1970-77. Author: Experiments in Physics, 1982, 2d edit. 1995, Fundamentals of College Physics, 1993, 2d. edit. 1995, Electromagnetic Theory for Electrical Technology Students, 1995. Mem. Am. Assn. Physics Tchrs. Home: 47 Fairdale Dr Brentwood NY 11717-1337 Office: SUNY Dept Physics Farmingdale NY 11735

NOLAN, RICHARD THOMAS, clergyman, educator; b. Waltham, Mass., May 30, 1937; s. Thomas Michael and Elizabeth Louise (Leishman) N.; life ptnr. Robert C. Pingpank, Sept. 14, 1955. BA, Trinity Coll., 1960; cert. in clin. pastoral edn., Conn. Valley Hosp., 1962; diploma, Berkeley Divinity Sch., 1962; MDiv., Hartford Sem. Found., 1963; postgrad., Union Theol. Sem., N.Y.C., 1963; MA in Religion, Yale U., 1967; PhD, NYU, 1973; postgrad., Ctr. Career Devel. and Ministry, Newton Center, Mass., 1987, Harvard U., 1991, U. Wales at Lampeter, 1998-99. Ordained deacon Episcopal Ch., 1963, priest, 1965; cert. in death, dying and bereavement Waterbury Hosp. Health Ctr., Conn., 1977; notary pub., Fla. Instr. Latin and English Watkinson (Conn.) Sch., 1961-62; instr. math. Choir Sch. of Cathedral of St. John the Divine, N.Y.C., 1962-64; instr. math. and religion, assoc. chaplain Cheshire (Conn.) Acad., 1965-67; instr. Hartford (Conn.) Sem. Found., 1967-68, asst. acad. dean, lectr. philosophy and edn., 1968-70; instr. Mattatuck C.C., Waterbury, Conn., 1969-70, asst. prof. philosophy and history, 1970-74, assoc. prof., 1974-78, prof. philosophy and social sci., 1978-92, prof. emeritus, 1992—; vicar St. Paul's Parish, Bantam, Conn., 1974-88; pastor emeritus St. Paul's Parish, Bantam, 1988—; pres. Litchfield Inst., Conn. and Fla., 1984-96; adj. lectr. in philosophy Palm Beach C. C., Fla., 2000—; ethics com. Waterbury Hosp. Health Ctr., 1984-88; vis. and adj. prof. philosophy, theology and religious studies Trinity Coll., Conn., L.I. U., U. Miami, St. Joseph Coll., Conn., Pace U., Teikyo Post U., U. Conn., Hartford Grad. Ctr., Ctrl. Conn. State U., Broward C.C., Fla., 1964-95; lectr. philosophy and theology Barry U., Fla., 1973, 89-92, 97-98; adj. assoc. in continuing edn. Berkeley Div. Sch. Yale U., 1987-89; Rabbi Harry Halpern Meml. lectr., Southbury, Conn., 1987; adj. prof. philosophy Fla. Atlantic U., 1998-99; adj. prof., The Union Inst., Fla., 1999; guest spkr. various chs. and orgns. including Cathedral of St. John the Divine, N.Y. and Trinity Cathedral, Miami; mem. faculty of consulting examiners Charter Oak State Coll., Conn., 1990-93; assoc. for edn. Christ Ch. Cathedral, Hartford, Conn., 1988-94, hon. canon, 1991—; cons. Dept. Def. Activity Non-Traditional Ednl. Support, Ednl. Testing Svcs., Princeton, 1990; vis. scholar Coll. Preachers Washington Nat. Cathedral, 1994; retired assisting priest Episcopal Ch. of Bethesda-by-the-Sea, Palm Beach, Fla., 1994-98; supply priest Episcopal Diocese of S.E. Fla., 1997—. Author: (with H. Titus and M. Smith) Living Issues in Philosophy, 7th edit., 1979, Indonesian edit., 1984, 8th edit., 1986, 9th edit., 1995, (with F. Kirkpatrick) Living Issues in Ethics, 1982, 2d edit., 2000 (Honored Author for Books Exceeding 100,000 Copies award 1986); editor, contbr. Diaconate Now, 1968; host Conversations with ..., 1987-89; editor philosophy-religion.org. Founding mem. The Heritage Soc. of The Episcopal Ch. of Bethesda-by-the Sea, Palm Beach. Rsch. fellow Yale U., 1978, 87; recipient Founder's Day award NYU, 1973. Mem. Am. Acad. Religion, Am. Philos. Assn., Authors Guild, Hemlock Soc. Fla. (adv. bd. 1998—), Interfaith Alliance, Integrity, Boston Latin Sch. Alumni Assn., Tabor Acad. Alumni Assn., McCook Fellows Soc. Trinity Coll., Cavalier King Charles Spaniel Club, Am. Friends of Anglican Centre in Rome, Anglican Assn. Bibl. Scholars, PFlag, Phi Delta Kappa. Avocation: Cavalier King Charles Spaniels. E-mail: canonn@adelphia.net. Home: 2527 Egret Lake Dr West Palm Beach FL 33413-2161

NOLAND, MARCUS, economist, educator; b. Greensboro, N.C., Mar. 29, 1959. BA, Swarthmore Coll., 1981; PhD, Johns Hopkins U., 1985. Sr. fellow Inst. for Internat. Econs., Washington, 1985—; asst. prof. U. So. Calif., L.A., 1990-91; sr. economist Coun. Econ. Advisers, Washington, 1993-94; vis. prof. Saitama U., Urawa, Japan, 1988-89; vis. scholar Korea Devel. Inst., Seoul, 1991; vis. assoc. prof. Johns Hopkins U., Balt., 1991-98; vis. prof. Tokyo U., 1996, U. Ghana, 1997; cons. Internat. Food Policy Rsch. Inst., 1999—. Author: Pacific Basin Developing Countries, 1991, Avoiding the Apocalypse: The Future of the Two Koreas, 2000; editor: Economic Integration on the Korean Penninsula, 1998; co-author: Japan in the World Economy, 1988, Reconcilable Differences?, 1993, Global Effects of the Asian Currency Devaluations, 1998; co-editor: Pacific Economic Dynamism, 1993. Japan Soc. for Promotion of Sci. fellow, 1988, Internat. Affairs fellow Coun. on Fgn. Rels., 1993, Coun. for Internat. Exch. of Scholars fellow, 1997. Mem. Coun. on Fgn. Rels. E-mail: mnoland@iie.com. Office: Inst for Internat Econs 11 Dupont Cir NW Washington DC 20036-1207

NOLD, AURORA REYES, business and economics educator; b. Honolulu, Apr. 21, 1958; m. Allan Jeffrey Nold, Aug. 1, 1995. BSBA cum laude, St. Louis U., 1979, MS in Bus. Adminstrn. magna cum laude, 1982, PhD, 1986. Exch. prof., dept. chairperson mgmt. St. Louis U., Baguio City, Philippines, 1980-86; rsch. asst. East/West Ctr. for Am. Studies, Honolulu, 1986-87; dir. Am. studies United State Info. Svcs., Washington, 1987-89; fin. cons. Shadow Hill Samaritan, Long Beach, Calif., 1989-93; dir. A&A Edu Care Consultancy Programs, Inc., Las Vegas, Nev., 1993—; bd. advisors Am. Biog. Inst., Raleigh, N.C., 1995—, Internat. Biog. Ctr., Cambridge, Eng., 1995—; rschr. S.H.S. Inc., Las Vegas, 1995—; prof. econs., bus and mgmt. C.C. So. Nev.; prof. stats. U. Nev., Las Vegas; tutor C.C. So. Nev. Author: Business Education in the Philippines, 1986; contbr. articles to profl. jours. Pres. Rep. Presdl. Task Force, Las Vegas, 1995—. Cultural Exch. grant Fulbright Am. Studies, 1987, scholarship grant St. Louis U., 1979-86; recipient Appreciation award Nat. Humane Edn. Soc., 1996, Nat. Park Trust, 1996, Nat. Law Enforcement Officers Meml. Fund, 1997, Oustanding Cmty. and Profl. Achievement Commemorative medal Am. Biog. Inst., 1997, internat. cultural diploma of honor, 2000. Mem. AAUW, NAFE, Asian Am. Studies Assn., U.S. Profl. Bookkeepers Assn., Nev. Faculty Alliance. Republican. Mem. LDS Ch. Avocations: collecting rare coins, writing, reading, music and art collecting. Office: A&A Edu Care Consultancy Programs Unit 657-10 7812 Clarkdale Dr Las Vegas NV 89128-3866

NOLDIN, JOSÉ ALBERTO, agricultural researcher; b. Brusque, Brazil, Nov. 3, 1953; s. Ernesto Armelino and Adélia (Pretti) N.; m. Pedra Claumann, Dec. 29, 1979; children: Candi, Calu, Dante. BSc, U. Fed. Santa Catarina, Florianópolis, Brazil, 1979; Msc, U. Fed. do Rio Grande do Sul, Porto Alegre, Brazil, 1985; PhD, Tex. A&M U., 1995. Cert. agronomist. Rschr. Itajai (Brazil) Experiment Sta./Epagri, 1980—. Mem. Weed Sci. Soc. Am., Sociedade Brasileira da Ciência das Plantas Daninhas, Sociedade Sul Brasileira de Arroz Irrigado (pres. 1998-99), Rotary Internat. Roman Catholic. Avocations: reading, soccer. Office: Epagri-Itajai Expert Sta, PO Box 277, 88301970 Itajai Brazil

NOLEN, ROY LEMUEL, lawyer; b. Montgomery, Ala., Nov. 29, 1937; s. Roy Lemuel Jr. and Elizabeth (Larkin) N.; m. Evelyn McNeill Thomas, Aug. 28, 1965; 1 child, Rives Rutledge. BArch, Rice U., 1961; LLB, Harvard U., 1967. Bar: Tex. 1968, U.S. Ct. Appeals (5th cir.) 1969. Law clk. to sr. judge U.S. Ct. Appeals (5th cir.), 1967-68; assoc. Baker Botts LLP, Houston, 1968-75, ptnr., 1976—; co-head Corp. Dept., 1985-90, mem. exec. com., 1988-91, adminstrv. ptnr., 1997—. bd. dirs. Houston Ballet Found., 1980-92, Rice Design Alliance, 1995-96; exec. com. Contemporary Arts Mus., 1990-96, 97—; exec. com. Houston Symphony Soc., 1994-99, gen. counsel, 1994-98; bd. dirs., exec. com. Menil Found. (Menil Collection), 1999—, sr. warden Christ Ch. Cathedral, 1991-92; chmn. Houston area devel. initiative Episcopal Diocese of Tex., 1997. 1st lt. USMC, 1961-64. Mem. ABA, State Bar of Tex., Houston Bar Assn., Coronado Club, Allegro, Paul Jones Dancing Club. Episcopalian. Office: Baker Botts LLP 3000 One Shell Plz 910 Louisiana St Ste 3000 Houston TX 77002-4991

NOLL, ARMIN JOHANNES, editor; b. Dautphetal, Germany, Aug. 4, 1954; s. Heinrich and Elfriede (Reuter) N.; m. Heide Haffer, May 18, 1993; 1 child, Pauline. Staatsexamen, Fachhochschule, Fulda, Germany, 1976. Tchr. Gesamtschule, Wächtersbach, Germany, 1977-81; editor Vox-Culture Mag., Kassel, Germany, 1983-86, Pflasterstrand-City Mag., Kassel, Frankfurt, 1986-87; press chief Team 3, Kassel, 1987-89; editor Weber & Weidemeyer Verlag, Kassel, 1990-94, Publikom Z Verlagsgesellschaft, Kassel, 1995—. Avocations: travel, art, music. Office: Publikom Z Verlagsges, Frankfurter Strasse 168, 34121 Kassel Germany

NOLL, BERNHARD FRIEDRICH, food engineer, researcher; b. Ulm, Germany, Jan. 25, 1963; s. Klaus Reinhold and Susanne Annelise (Lenzinger) N.; m. Cornelia Michael, Feb. 27, 1987; children: Annika, Evelyn, Katja. Dr. rer.nat. in Engr. Food Tech; diplomate, U. Hohenheim, Germany, 1990. Rsch. asst. U. Hohenheim, 1991-97; product mgr. Rettenmaier, Ellwangen, Germany, 1997—. Author: Image Analysis, 1995 (Rsch. award 1996). Baptist. Avocations: song writing, hiking, skiing, computing, family. E-mail: bernhardnoll@online.de. Home: Buttlar Str 30, D-74541 Vellberg-Talheim Germany

NOLL, RICHARD DEAN, JR., psychologist, educator and historian; b. Detroit, Oct. 27, 1959; s. Richard Dean and Betty Ann (Adamczak) N.; children: Dylan James Patterson, Wolfgang Naylor Noll; m. Mary Beth McAndrews, Apr. 27, 1986 (div. 1993); m. Susan J. Naylor, May 13, 1994; 1 child, Wolfgang Naylor Noll. BA, U. Ariz., 1979; MA, New Sch. for Social Rsch., 1982; PhD, New Sch. for Rsch., 1992. Lic. clin. psychologist, Pa. Staff clin. psychologist Ancora Psychiat. Hosp., Hammonton, N.J., 1985-88; clin. psychologist in pvt. practice Phila., 1988-92; instr. dept. psychology West Chester (Pa.) U., 1992-94; postdoctoral fellow Harvard U., Cambridge, Mass., 1994-96, Lectr. in History of Sci., 1997-98; resident fellow Dibner Inst. History of Sci. and Tech. MIT, Cambridge, Mass., 1995-96; asst. prof. psychology De Sales Univ., Center Valley, Pa., 2000—; invited lectr. Acad. Scis., Budapest, Hungary, 1991, Warsaw U., 1991, Chinese Acad. Scis., Beijing, 1994; vis. scholar MIT, 1995-96. Author: The Encyclopedia of Schizophrenia and the Psychotic Disorders, 1992, 2d rev. edit., 2000, Vampires, Werewolves and Demons: Twentieth Century Case Reports in the Psychiatric Literature, 1992, The Jung Cult, 1994 (named best book in psychology Assn. Am. Publishers 1994), The Aryan Christ, 1997, Encyclopedia of Schizophrenia and Other Psychotic Disorders, rev. 2d edit., 2000; contbr. articles to profl. jours. Wenner-Gren Found. for Anthropol. Rsch. grantee, 1993. Mem. History of Sci. Soc.

NOLL, RONALD LEROY, psychologist, organization development consultant; b. Waukegan, Ill., Mar. 15, 1936; s.Reihardt and Amanda (Van der Mark) N.; m. Barbara Marie Rohnert, July 3, 1993; 1 child, Aron Leonard. BS, Western Ill. U., 1960; MA, U. Nebr., Lincoln, 1965; PhD, U. Oreg., 1970. Lic. clin. psychologist, U.S. Founder, counselor United Cmty. Counseling Orgn., Eugene, Oreg., 1966-70; GS 12-4 psychologist U.S. Army Mil. VA Hosp., Ft. Sheridan, Ill., and Rota, Spain, 1971-76; founder ACT Seminars, Chgo., , 1976-86; psychologist to missionaries East and Ctrl. Asia, 1988—; co-founder Comty, Recovery Network, Singapore, 1995—. Bd. mem. Luth. Family Svc. Mem. Internat. Assn. Cross-Cultural Pscyhology, Nat. Christian Counselors Assn., Singapore Assn. for Counseling (bd. mem.), Member-Care Assocs. Asia (founder). Avocation: biking, rebuilding used computers for donation to 3d world pastors. E-mail: 73422.3170@compuserve.com. Home and Office: MemberCare Network Internat, CFC Postfach 100262, 35332 Giessen 0821, Germany

NOLLER, PATRICIA, psychologist, educator; b. Sydney, Australia, Mar. 13, 1938; d. James and Beryl Jean (Black) Tate; m. Charles Geoffrey Noller, May 14, 1960; children: Deborah Lynne, Geoffrey Stuart, Caroline Louise, Alison Ruth. BA, U. Queensland, 1976, PhD, 1981. From tutor to prof. U. Queensland, Brisbane, Australia, 1980—; dir. U. Queensland Fam. Ctr., 1996—; vis. prof. UCLA, 1990, Fuller Theol. Sem., Pasadena, Calif., 1993, vis. scholar, U Wis., Madison, 1986. Author: Nonverbal Communication and Marital Interaction, 1984; co-author: Adolescents in the Family, 1991, Communication in Family Relationships, 1993; editor: Perspectives on Marital Interaction, 1988; founding editor Personal Relationships, 1994-98; contbr. articles to profl. jours. Fellow Acad. Social Scis. in Australia, Nat. Coun. Family Rels.; mem. Australian Psychol. Soc., Internat. Soc. Study of Personal Rels.(pres 1998-2000). Avocations: reading, walking, church activities. Home: 34 Middle St, 4101 West End QLD, Australia Office: U Queensland, Sch Psychology, 4072 Brisbane QLD, Australia

NOLLET, FRANCISCUS, physiatrist; b. Amsterdam, Netherlands, Jan. 13, 1958; s. Elbert Ludovicus and Afra Anna (Dam) N.; m. Engelina Jansje Romeijn, Nov. 21, 1986 (div. Aug. 1988); 1 child, Nina Robin; m. Maria Sophia Hendriks, May 2, 1990; children: Jef Marx Xavier, Edgar Elbert. MD, U. Amsterdam, 1985; postgrad., Acad. Med. Ctr. U. Amsterdam, 1994. Cert. physician in rehab. medicine, Netherlands. Resident in internal medicine Slotervaart Hosp., Amsterdam, 1985; resident in orthopedic surgery Med. Ctr. Alkmaar, Netherlands, 1985-87; resident in orthopedic surgery Acad. Med. Ctr. U. Amsterdam, 1987-88, resident in rehab. medicine, 1988-90, 1992-94; physiatrist West Fries Gasthuis, Hoorn, Netherlands, 1994-96, Acad. Hosp. Vrije Universiteit, Amsterdam, 1996—; sci. advisor Hogeschool van Amsterdam, 1987—; physician Dutch Nat. Speed Skating Team, Amersfoort, 1987-96. Co-author: Polio and its consequences, 1996, also articles. Physician, mem. Dutch delegation Winter Olympics, Lillehammer, Norway, 1988; bd. dirs. Turning Spirit Gymnastics, Amsterdam, 1999; mem. nat. steering com. Polio de wereld uit, Baarn, Netherlands, 1997—. Recipient grants in field. Mem. Dutch Association Rehab. Medicine, Dutch Assn. Sports Medicine, INternat. Soc. Prosthetiocs and Orthotics. Avocations: speed skaing, cycling. E-mail: f.nollet@azvu.nl. Office: Acad Hosp Vrije U, Dept Rehab Med PO Box 7057, 1007 MB Amsterdam Netherlands

NOLTE, JOHN MICHAEL, lawyer, consultant; b. England, Mar. 20, 1941; s. Ernest H. Nolte and Katheryn A. (Reinhart) Robertson; m. S.K. Marren (div. 1979); children: Stephanie Ann, Jennifer Lee, Sarah Sookwang; m. Diane L. Staufenbeil, Apr. 1982. BS, Ariz. State U., Tempe, 1963; MBA in Fin., U. Calif., Berkeley, JD, 1966. Bar: Oreg. 1966, Calif. 1973. Assoc. Keane, Haessler, Bauman & Harper, Portland, Oreg., 1966-71; assoc. gen. counsel Boise Cascade Corp., Palo Alto, Calif., 1972-73, Larwin Group, L.A., 1973-74; mng. ptnr. Leahy, O'Dea & Givens, San Francisco, 1974-81; pvt. practice law and cons. Canterbury and Tunbridge Wells, Eng., 1981-88, Montecito, Calif., 1988-99, Dorset, England, 1999—; officer Larwin Co., Encino, Calif. Hon. mem. East Sussex Conservative Party, Buxted, Eng., 1986—; pres. Glen Oaks Comty. Assn., Montecito, 1990-92; bd. trustees Castaic Union Edn. Found. With USMC, 1960-66; lt. comdr. USNR, 1966-70. Mem. ABA, Calif. Bar Assn., Oreg. Bar Assn., L.A. Bar Assn., Am. Judicature Soc., Order of Coif, Phi Kappa Phi. Republican. Avocations: skiing, historic automobile racing, cricket, mountaineering, antiques. Home and Office: Pamphill Manor, Pamphill Wimborne, Dorset BH21 4EE, England

NOLTE, WILHELM, physician; b. Minden, Westfalia, Germany, Nov. 5, 1960; s. Heinrich and Elisabeth (Döpke) N.; m. Christiane Bartel; children: Christoph-Heinrich, Cornelia-Helene, Carolin-Elisabeth. MD, U. Münster, Germany; habil., 1999. Physician U.Göttingen, 1987—. Contbr. articles to profl. jours. Mem. German Soc. Endocrinology. Office: Med Dept, Robert-Koch-Strasse 40, 37075 Göttingen Germany

NOMA, SOWAKO, publishing executive; widowed; 4 children. Pres., CEO Kodansha Ltd., Tokyo, 1987—. Named One of World's 50 Most Prominent Businesswomen, World Bus. mag., 1996. Office: Kodansha Ltd 12-21 Otowa, 2 chome Bunkyo-ku, Tokyo 112, Japan*

NOMER, ERGIN NAMI, law educator, university administrator; b. Istanbul, Turkey, Jan. 7, 1935; s. Mustafa Resit and Sefika (Gozubuyuk) N.; m. Esin Ayas, Aug. 13, 1962; children: Haluk Nami, Nedret Fusun. Lawyer, Istanbul U., 1957, LLD, 1961. Lectr. Faculty of Law-Istanbul U., 1966-73, prof., 1973—, dean, 1980-82; v.p. Istanbul U., 1974-80, 94-97, pres. civil law, 1998—. Author: International Private Law, 10th edit., 2000, Law of Nationality, 12th edit., 1999, Foreign Law in Civil Proceedings, 1972, Maintenance in International Private Law, 1967. Pres. discipline com. The Green Crescent, 1964—. Lt. Land Force, Turkish Army, 1967-69. Mem. Turkish Bar Assn. Avocations: bridge, chess, walking. Home: Erenkoy Etemefendi Cad 9, Gokova Apt D5, TR 81060 Istanbul Turkey Office: Istanbul U, Faculty of Law Bayazit, TR 34452 Istanbul Turkey

NOMICOS, NICHOLAS EUGENE, emergency medicine physician; b. Memphis, May 22, 1962; s. Eugene Nicolas and Melva Ann (Adams) N. BS, Coll. of Idaho, 1983; MD, Am. U. of the Caribbean, 1987. Rsch. assoc. Harbor UCLA Med. Ctr., Torrance, Calif., 1987-89; cert. family life educator Harbor Free Clinic, San Pedro, Calif., 1987-89; intern/resident St. Joseph Mercy Hosp., Pontiac, Mich., 1989-91; ind. emergency physician Coldwater, Mich., 1991—; med. dir. Br. County Med. Control Authority, Coldwater, Mich., 1994—; resident educator, instr. Cmty. Health Ctr. of Br. County, 1994—; ATLS instr. Ind. U./Wishard Meml. Hosp., Indpls., 1995—; bd. county rep. S.W. Mich. Trauma Coalition, Kalamazoo, 1994—; emergency dir. Cmty. Hosp., Watervliet, Mich., 1992; presenter in field. Author, photographer: Expedition: Bikini Atoll Diving Ground Zero of Operation Crossroads, 1997; contbr. articles to profl. jours. Mem. AMA (Physicians Recognition award 1994, 97), Assn. of Emergency Physicians, Am. Assn. of Physician Specialists, Am. Coll. of Physician Execs., Masons. Republican. Greek Orthodox. Avocations: concert violinist, master scuba diver/underwater photographer, travel, sports, fine arts. Office: CHC of Branch County 274 E Chicago St Coldwater MI 49036-2041

NOMIKOS, IAKOVOS NICOLAS, general surgeon; b. Syros Island, Cyclades, Greece, Oct. 1, 1951; s. Nicolas and Sofia (Baïla) N.; m. Anastasia Koutsouveli, Sept. 30, 1978; children: Nicolas, George, Thalassini. MD, Athens (Greece) U., 1975. Cert. in gen. surgery Greek Bd. Certification. Submarine base surgeon Greek Navy, Salamis Island, 1980-81; attending surgeon Larissa (Greece) Gen. Hosp., 1981-83; pvt. practice Ygeia Hosp. Athens, 1983-84; attending surgeon Evangelismos Med. Ctr., Athens, 1984-85; fellow Barbara Davis Diabetes Ctr., U. Colo., 1985-86; fellow dept. surgery N.Y. Med. Coll., Valhalla, 1986-87; sr. registrar liver unit Queen Elizabeth Hosp., Birmingham, Eng., 1991; attending surgeon Tzanion Gen. Hosp., Piraeus, Greece, 1987—; lectr. surgery Athens U., 1990-94, asst. prof., 1994—. Author: Diagnostic and Therapeutic Approach to the Critically Ill Surgical Patient, 1993; contbr. articles to profl. jours. Fellow ACS; mem. Am. Assn. Clin. Anatomists, N.Y. Acad. Scis. Avocations: aviation, running marathons. Office: 55 Psarron Str, 18120 Koridallos Piraeus, Greece

NOMMELA, MARI, art history educator; b. Rakvere, Estonia, Sept. 21, 1950; d. Valdu and Selma-Leontine (Värv) Männilo; m. Kalev Tähepöld (div. May 1977); 1 child, Piret; m. Kalev Nõmmela (div. Oct. 1985); children: Kadi, Krõõt. Grad., Tartu (Estonia) Art Coll., 1969, Tartu U., 1977; MA in Philosophy, Tartu U., 1993. Sr. rschr. Tartu (Estonia) Art Mus., 1977-83, dir., 1983-96; founder Kivisilla Art Gallery, 1988; lectr. art dept. landscape arch. Estonian Agrl. U., 1996—, prof. Estonian Agr. U., 1999—; lectr. Tartu U., 1996—. Contbr. articles to profl. jours. Mem. Internat. Coun. Mus., Estonian Artist' Union. Avocation: painting.

NOMO, HIDEO, professional baseball player; b. Osaka, Japan, Aug. 31, 1968. Pitcher Kintetsu, Japan, 1990-94, L.A. Dodgers, 1995-97; traded to N.Y. Mets, 1997-99, Milw. Brewers AAA baseball, 1999—; mem. Japanese Olympic Baseball team, 1988. Named Nat. League Rookie Pitcher of Yr. The Sporting News, 1995, Nat. League Rookie of Yr. Baseball Writers Assn., 1995; strikeout leader Japanese Pacific League, 1990-93, Nat. League, 1995. Office: care Milw Brewers County Stadium PO Box 3099 Milwaukee WI 53201-3099

NOMOTO, SHINICHI, telecommunications engineer; b. Tokyo, July 12, 1957; s. Noboru and Yoshiko (Mori) N.; m. Yukiko Nomoto, Dec. 7, 1985; children: Yutaro, Mana. BSEE, Waseda U., Tokyo, 1980, MSEE, 1982, PhD, 1993. Rsch. engr. KDD R&D Lab., Tokyo, 1982-92; prof. assignee INMARSAT, London, 1992-95; sr. rsch. engr. KDD R&D Lab., Kamifukuoka, Japan, 1995—. Inventor: Reflector antennas; contbr. articles to profl. jours. Recipient Young Engr. award IEICE, Tokyo, 1988, Piero Fanti Internat. prize INTELSAT/Telespazio, Italy, 1988, Radio Disting. award ARIB/Min. of Post & Telecom., Tokyo, 1991. Mem. IEEE, IEICE, AIAA. Avocations: skiing, mountaineering, football. Office: KDD R&D Labs, 2-1-15 Ohara, Kamifukuoka 356, Japan

NOMURA, KANEO, architect; b. Ohta, Tokyo, Japan, June 9, 1935; s. Tsurunosuke and Senko (Tsukagoshi) N.; m. Yuko Sugawara, Oct. 16, 1965; children: Gaku, Cho. BArch, Tokyo Nat. U. Fine Arts/Music, 1958. 1st class architect, Japan. Assoc. Isoya Yoshida Architect & Assocs., Tokyo, 1958-60, prin. assoc., 1963-73, prin., 1974-77; architect Kaneo Nomura Architect & Assocs., Tokyo, 1978—; diplomatic architect Japan Ministry Fgn. Affairs, Rome, 1960-63; lectr. Yamaha Archtl. Seminar, 1983, Japanese Architecture Seminar, 1987; guest prof. Tokyo Nat. U. Fine Arts and Music, 1997—. Archtl. designer Shigeru Yoshida Meml. Hall, 1987, Mitsukoshi Mus., 1991, Japanese amb.s residence, Columbia, 1996, pub. residence Imperial Highnesses Prince and Princess Akishinomiya, 1998. Recipient Gold Medal, Kanagawa Archtl. Contest, Japan, 1980, 82, 84, Gold medal Italian Marble Archtl. Awards, 1992. Mem. Japanese Inst. Architects (corp.), Archtl. Inst. Japan (corp.), the Japan-Italy Assn., Kyoto Traditional Assn. Architecture. Buddhist. Avocations: travel, skiing, driving, photography. Home: 15-13 Nishimagome 1 Chome, Ohta-ku Tokyo 143-0026, Japan

NOMURA, KICHISABURO, air transporation company executive. Grad. in law, Waseda U., Tokyo. With All Nippon Airways Co., Ltd., 1959—, bd., sr. dir. personnel issues, sr. mng. dir., gen. mgr. Ea. Japan, pres., CEO; safety promotion chmn., corp. restructuring com., corp. strategy com., All Nippon Airways, 2000. Office: All Nippon Airways, 3-5-10 Haneda Airport, Ota-ku Tokyo 144-0041, Japan*

NOMURA, RYÔKI, chemistry educator; b. Kobe, Japan, Sept. 3, 1954. B Engring., Osaka (Japan) U., 1977, M Engring., 1979, D Engring., 1982. Lectr. Osaka U., 1982-93, asst. prof., 1993-94; assoc. prof. Osaka Inst. Tech., 1994-98, prof. inorganic chemistry, 1998—. Co-author: (with Matsuda, Nomura, Ikeda and Baba) (in Japanese) Industrial Organic Chemistry, 1999. Mem. Chem. Soc. Japan, Japan Petroleum Inst. Avocations: walking, con-

tract bridge, go. Office: Osaka Inst Tech, Ō-Miya 5-16-1, Osaka 535-8858, Japan

NOMURA, SETSUZO, microbiologist, researcher; b. Sannan-cho, Hyogo, Japan, Feb. 11, 1934; s. Uichi and Fuyuko (Fujimoto) N.; m. Miho Haruna, Apr. 20, 1965; children: Yasushi, Tadashi. BS, Tokyo Coll. Sci., 1957; DSc, Nagoya (Japan) U., 1972. Mem. staff Kitasato Inst., Tokyo, 1957-76; lectr. Sch. Hygiene Kitasato U., Tokyo, 1966-70, lectr. Sch. Pharm. Sci., 1970-74; rsch. fellow dept. chemistry Harvard U., Cambridge, Mass., 1974-75; asst. prof. Sch. Fisheries Scis. Kitasato U., Sanriku, Japan, 1976-80, prof., 1980-99, chief Lab. Aquatic Microbiology, 1980-99, curatory Libr. Fisheries Sci., 1990-92, head prof. dept. marine biochemistry, 1994-96, prof. emeritus, 1999—; councilor Kitasato Ednl. Instn., Tokyo, 1994-97; internat. tech. cons. UN, 1999—. Author: Ozone Annual, 1992, New techniques of ozone utilization, 1993, others; contbr. articles to profl. jours. Mem. Japanese Soc. Bacteriology, Japanese Soc. Fisheries Sci., Japanese Soc. Fish Pathology, Intelligent Cosmos Rsch. Inst., Japanese Soc. Symposium on Toxins, Asian Fisheries Soc., N.Y. Acad. Scis. Avocations: angling, photography, mineral collection. Home: 67-5 Sugishita, Okirai, Sanriku-cho Iwate 022-0101, Japan Office: Kitasato U Sch Fisheries Sc, 160-4 Uto, Okirai, Sanriku-cho, Iwate 022-0101, Japan

NONAKA, TAIJIRO, structural engineering educator; b. Osaka, Japan, May 16, 1936; s. Kyotaro and Shizu N.; m. Mihoko Takata, Nov. 5, 1966; 1 child, Shin. BSc, Kyoto U., Japan, 1959, MSc, 1961, DEng, 1976; PhD, Brown U., 1965. Asst. prof. Disaster Prevention Rsch. Inst., Kyoto U., 1965-79, prof., 1979-2000; prof. structural engring. Grad. Sch. Engring., Chubu U., Kasugai City, Japan, 2000—, dir. Inst. Sci. and Tech. Contbr. articles to profl. jours. Fulbright grantee, 1961, Sakkokai Found. grantee, 1967, Matsunaga Sci. Found. grantee, 1967, 70. Mem. Archtl. Inst. Japan (medal 1979), Japan Soc. Materials Sci., Sigma Xi. Home: 8-4 Daigo Furumichicho, Fushimiku, Kyoto 601-1316, Japan Office: Chubu U Inst Sci and Tech, 1200 Matsumoto-cho, Kasugai 487-8501, Japan

NONDI, RICHARD OWINO, management educator; b. Siaya, Nyanza, Kenya, Dec. 30, 1950; s. Daniel Nondi and Norah Kinani; m. Joyce Achieng, Oct. 20, 1976; 4 children. MSc in Purchasing and Supply, U. Ulster, No Ireland, 1994. Supply officer Govt. Press, Nairobi, Kenya, 1973-79; supply trainer Office of Pres., Nairobi, 1980-81; lectr. Kenya Poly., Nairobi, 1984-87; lectr. mgmt. dept. Govt. Tng. Inst., Mombasa, Kenya, 1982-84, sr. lectr., 1987-95, prin. lectr., 1995-99, sr. prin. lectr., 1999—, head dept., 1997—. Contbr. articles to profl. jours., including Purchasing and Supply Mgmt., Acct. Jour., European Jour. Purchasing and Supply, Mgmt. Jour. Mem. Chartered Inst. Purchasing and Supply (U.K.), Nat. Assn. Purchasing Mgmt. (U.S.), Kenya Inst. Mgmt., Inst. Cert. Pub. Secs. (Kenya), Internat. Purchasing and Supply Edn. Rsch. Assn. (U.K.). Anglican. Avocations: football, reading. Office: Govt Tng Inst, PO Box 84027, Mombasa Kenya

NONG DUC MANH, Vietnamese government official; b. Cuong Loi, Sept. 11, 1940. Grad., Leningrad Forestry Inst. Sec. Provincial Party Com., Bac Thai, 1976-80; alternate mem. Communist Party CC, 1986-89, mem., 1989—; mem. nat. assembly Govt. of Vietnam, Lang-Son, 1989—; chmn. nat. assembly Govt. of Vietnam, Hanoi, 1992—; vice-chmn. CC Coun. of Nationalities, 1989—; 10th ranked mem. Communist Party Politburo, 1991—. Communist Party. Office: Quoc Hoi, Office of the Chairman, Hanoi Vietnam*

NONNEMAN, GERD, international politics researcher, educator; b. Temse, Flanders, Belgium, May 16, 1959; arrived in Eng., 1984; s. Ward and Aldegonde (Meersman) N. Lic. in Oriental Philology, Ghent (Belgium) U., 1980, Lic. in Devel. Studies, 1981; MA in Politics, Exeter (Eng.) U., 1985, PhD in Politics, 1993. Lectr. in govt. Manchester (Eng.) U., 1987-88; country author Economist Intelligence Unit, London, 1987-91; rsch. assoc. Exeter U., 1991-92; vis. prof. Internat. U. Japan, Urasa, 1992; rsch. fellow Middle East politics Exeter U., 1992-93; sr. lectr. in internat. rels. Lancaster (Eng.) U., 1993-98, reader internat. rels. & mid. east politics, 1999—; Mid. East cons., Exeter and Lancaster, 1987—. Author: Development, Administration and Aid in the Middle East, 1988, War and Peace in the Gulf, 1991; editor, chief contbr.: The Middle East and Europe, 1993, Muslim Communities in the New Europe, 1996, Political and Economic Liberalization, 1996. Recipient Rsch. and Publ. grant European Comty. Commn., Brussels and London, 1990. Fellow Brit. Soc. for Mid. Ea. Studies (exec. dir.); mem. Polit. Studies Assn. Avocations: music (renaissance to early classical), dining, travel, nature walking, reading. Office: Lancaster Univ, Lancaster LA1 4YL, England

NOOL, ERKI, Olympic athlete; b. Voru, Estonia, June 25, 1970. Winner Silver Medal decathlon European Championships, 1998; winner Gold Medal decathlon Sydney, 2000. Broke 8,600 pt. barrier 3 times, 1998. Office: Estonian Olympic Assn, Regati pst 1, Tallinn EE0019, Estonia*

NOONAN, ROBERT HARRY, art and music educator; b. Mpls., Sept. 18, 1924; s. William Earl and Nellie Morene Noonan; m. Azalie Cecile Pulling, Feb. 14, 1983 (div. July 1999). BS in Chemistry, Northwestern State Coll., 1948; MusB in Music Edn., Centenary Coll., 1963. Cert. tchr. music, chemistry, sci., math., visually talented and musically talented, La. Sr. chemist Ark. Fuel Oil Co., Shreveport, La., 1948-53; grad. asst. U. Wyo., Laramie, 1953-54; asst. chief chemist Atlas Processing Co., Shreveport, 1955-58; Frenh horn player Shreveport Symphony Orch., 1948-72; sch. sys. employee East Baton Rouge Sch. Sys., Baton Rouge, La., 1972-81; pub. sch. tchr. Ascension Parish Schs., Donaldsonville, La., 1981-95; tchr. visually talented St. James Parish Schs., Lutcher, La., 1997-99. Composer, arranger: (music) One Step from the Edge, 1999-00; one-person shows include Jones Creek Libr., Baton Rouge, 1993, Donaldsonville (La.) H.S., 1994, Galvez (La.) Libr., 1994, Westbank Libr., Harvey, La., 1995, Bruno Gallery, New Orleans, 1997; exhibited in group shows New Orleans, Baton Rouge, Jackson, Plaquemine, Morgan City, numerous others; represented in pvt. collections in La., Tex., Miss., Ala., Okla., others. Chmn. La. Sch. Employees Coun., 1977-81. With Army Air Corps, 1943-46. Goals 2000 grantee State of La., 1995-96, Spl. Arts grantee, 1997-99. Mem. Am. Chem. Soc. (sr. grade chemist 1948-58), New Orleans Art Assn. (v.p. 1998-00), St. Bernard Art Guild (pres. 1999-00), Jefferson Art Guild, La. Partnership for the Arts, others. Avocations: outdoor painting, writing articles for newspapers. Home: 11254 E Lanoux PO Box 713 Gonzales LA 70707-0713

NOONAN, WILLIAM DONALD, lawyer, physician; b. Kansas City, Mo., Oct. 18, 1955; s. Robert Owen and Patricia Ruth Noonan. AB, Princeton (N.J.) U., 1977; JD, U. Mo., Kansas City, 1980; postgrad., Tulane U., 1981-83; MD magna cum laude, Oreg. Health Scis. U., 1991. Bar: Mo. 1980, U.S. Ct. Appeals (5th cir.) 1982, U.S. Patent & Trademark Office 1982, U.S. Ct. Appeals (D.C. cir.) 1984, Oreg. 1985, U.S. Ct. Appeals (9th Cir.) 1985. Assoc. Shurgue, Mion, Zinn, Washington, 1983-84, Keaty & Keaty, New Orleans, 1984-85; ptnr. Klarquist, Sparkman, Portland, Oreg., 1985—; intern in internal medicine Portland Providence Med. Ctr., 1993-94; resident in ophthalomology Casey Eye Inst., Portland, 1994-95; adj. prof. patent law Tulane U., New Orleans, 1984-85, U. Oreg., 1992-93. Casenotes editor U. Mo. Law Rev., 1979. Nat. Merit scholar. Mem. ABA, AMA (Leadership award 1994), Alpha Omega Alpha (pres. Oreg. chpt. 1990-91). Republican. Avocation: raising horses, mountain climbing, hiking. Office: Klarquist Sparkman 121 SW Salmon 1600 World Trade Ctr Portland OR 97201

NOONE, KATHLEEN MARY, art educator; b. Wynnewood, Pa., Mar. 16, 1971; d. John Francis and Mary Louise (McCahon) N. BS, Kutztown U., 1993. Art educator Villa Maria Acad., Malvern, Pa., 1994—, cons. fine arts ctr., 1995-97, dept. chair visual arts, 1996-97; art tchr. summer enrichment program Archbishop John Carroll H.S., Radnor, Pa., summers 1996, 97. Bd. dirs. Archdiocesan Curriculum Com. for Fine Arts, Phila., 1996—; vol. tchr. aide GED course Ardmore Libr., 1995. Recipient Connelly Art Connection award Connelly Found., Mus. Am. Art, 1997. Mem. NEA, Nat. Art Edn. Assn., Pa. Art Edn. Assn., Am. Crafts Coun., Phila. Mus. Art, Main Line Art Ctr. Roman Catholic. Avocations: coaching field hockey. Home: 316 E Athens Ave Ardmore PA 19003-3108

NOOR, MOHAMED AHMED, biology educator, researcher; b. Sydney, Australia, Jan. 1, 1971; came to U.S., 1971; s. Ahmed Khairy and Zakia Mahmoud N.; m. Juliet Kathleen Noor, Sept. 3, 1995; 1 child: Megan Zakaya. BS, Coll. William and Mary, 1992; PhD, U. Chgo., 1996. Rsch. assoc. Cornell U., Ithaca, N.Y., 1996-98; asst. prof. La. State U., Baton Rouge, 1998—. Recipient Young Investigator prize Am. Soc. Naturalists, Vancouver, B.C., Can., 1998, Regional Young Investigator prize Sigma Xi, 1998.

NOORLANDER, PETER JAN LEENDERT, lawyer, human rights advocate; b. Soest, Utrecht, The Netherlands, July 30, 1971; m. Thao Phuong Lee. Grad., U. Maastricht, The Netherlands; LLM, U. Nottingham, Eng. Legal policy officer JUSTICE, London, 1996—; lectr. human rights and policing Nat. Police Staff Coll., Bramshill, Eng.; mem. adv. bd. Found. Info. Policy Rsch., London; spkr. confs. Author: Covert Surveillance and Human Rights Standards, 1999. Mem. Am. Soc. Internat. Law, Netherlands Commn. Jurists for Human Rights. E-mail: humanrights@petern.dircom.co.uk. Office: Ind Human Rights Consultant, 12 Cintra Ct Patterson Rd, London SE19 2LB, England

NORCROSS, JOHN C(ONNER), psychologist, educator; b. Camden, N.J., Aug. 13, 1957; s. George E. and Carol C.; m. Nancy A. Caldwell, June 25, 1981; children: Rebecca, Jonathan. BA, Rutgers U., 1980; MA, U. R.I., 1981, PhD, 1984. Lic. psychologist, Pa. Psychology intern Brown U. Sch. Medicine, 1984-85; rsch. fellow self-change lab. U. R.I., 1982-86; pvt. practice, 1986—; prof. psychology U. Scranton, Pa., 1985—; chmn. dept. U. Scranton, 1987-93; vis. prof. U. Guadalajara, 1990; vis. fellow U. London, 1990. Author: Toward Integration: John Norcross in a Dialogue with Windy Dryden, 1991, Changing for Good, 1994, Authoritative Guide to Self-Help Resources in Mental Health, 2000; co-author: Insider's Guide to Graduate Programs in Clinical and Counseling Psychology, 2000, Systems of Psychotherapy - A Transtheoretical Analysis, 1998; editor: Therapy Wars, 1990; editor Jour. Clin. Psychology, 2000—; co-editor: Handbook of Psychotherapy Integration, 1992, APA Psychotherapy Videotape Series, 1994—, Psychologists Desk Reference, 1998; assoc. editor Jour. Psychotherapy Integration, 1990-2000; mem. editl. bd. 12 jours.; contbr. articles to profl. jours. Recipient Pa. Prof. Yr. award, 1992; named Disting. Practitioner in Psychology, 1999. Fellow APA (Jack Krasner award 1992), Internat. Acad. Eclectic Psychotherapists, Pa. Psychol. Assn.; mem. Assn. for Advancement of Psychology, Ea. Psychol. Assn., Soc. for Psychotherapy Rsch., Soc. for Applied and Preventive Psychology, Soc. for Exploration of Psychotherapy Integration. Home: 300 Lake Spangenberg Rd Lake Ariel PA 18436 Office: U Scranton Dept Psychology Scranton PA 18510-4596

NORCROSS, KEITH, surgeon; b. Oldham, Lancashire, Eng., May 29, 1929; s. Frank and Elizabeth (Parker) N.; m. Kathleen Ellis, Oct. 26, 1954; 1 child, Catharine Hilary. B.A., Oxford U., Eng., 1951, M.A., 1954, B.M., 1954, B.Ch., 1954. Resident posts in surgery Nat. Health Service, Manchester, Eng., 1954-55, 58-66; fellow in orthopedics Hosp. for Spl. Surgery, N.Y.C., 1964; cons., surgeon in orthopoedics, Nat. Health Service, Birmingham, Eng., 1966—; tutor in orthopoedics, Med. Sch., Birmingham, 1975—; lectr. in surgery for podiatrists, Matthew Boulton Tech. Coll., Birmingham, 1966-86; environ. control assessor, Nat. Health Service, Birmingham, 1976—. Author: (with others) Visual Dictionary of Sex, 1978. Contbr. articles to profl. jours. Editorial adviser, British Jour. of Sex Medicine, London, 1973—. Mem., sec. Oxford U. Socrates Club, 1950—; mem. Howard League for Penal Reform, U.K., 1960—, Albany Trust, U.K., 1960—, Nat. Assn. Mental Health, U.K., 1970—, "Sequal", U.K., 1979, Vol. Euthanasia Soc., U.K., 1975. Served to capt. Eng. Army, 1955-58. Theodore Williams scholar in pathology, Med. Sch. Oxford U., 1950, Bradley scholar in surgery, Med. Sch., Manchester, 1953. Fellow, Brit. Orthopedic Assn., Royal Coll. Surgeons, Royal Soc. Medicine; mem. Med. Soc. for Disabled, Brit. Med. Assn., Naughton Dunn Club (sec. 1970-77), Savage Club, Soc. of Recorder Players, Polmetsch Found. Avocations: music; reading; diving; camping; ethical controversy; marine biology; human biology; decorative glass.

NORCROSS-MEHLMAN, KARYL, neurologist, educator; b. Joliet, Ill.; d. Anthony S. Music and Mary Anne Music-Ressler; m. Dan Nechay, Aug. 8, 1988 (dec. Dec. 1990); m. Myron A. Mehlman, Apr. 14, 1999. BA, Northwestern U., 1973, MD, PhD, 1978. Intern in general medicine Northwestern Meml. Hosps., Chgo., 1978-79, resident in neurology, 1979-82; asst. prof. neurology U. Tex. Med. Br., Galveston, 1982-87, assoc. prof neurology, 1987-2000, clin. prof. neurology, 2000—, dir. electroencephalography-evoked potential dept., 1982-2000, dir. EEG-evoked potential and intracoop. monitoring dept., 1982-2000, adj. prof. pediat., 1985-2000, assoc. prof. pharmacology, 1991-2000, assoc. prof. anesthesiology, 1996-2000; pres. Med. Neuro. Tox., RLLP, Princeton, N.J., 2000—; cons., advisor, reviewer BlueCross BlueShield of Tex., Richardson. Contbr. articles to profl. jours. Panel mem. diving adv. bd. Tex. A&M U., Galveston, 1984—. Mem. AMA, Tex. Neurol. Soc. (v.p. 1989), N. Am. Spine Soc., 1998—. Avocations: open water diving (cert.), computer graphics. Fax: (609) 683-0838. E-mail: mehlman@rcn.com. Home: 7 Bouvant Dr Princeton NJ 08540-1208 Office: U Tex Med Br EEG/EP Dept 300 University Blvd Galveston TX 77555-5301 also: Med Neuro Tox RLLP 7 Bonvant Dr Princeton NJ 08540

NORDAL, JOHANNES, banker; b. Reykjavik, Iceland, May 11, 1924; s. Sigurdur and Olof (Jonsdottir) N.; m. Dora Guojonsdottir, Dec. 19, 1953; children: Bera, Sigurdur, Gudrun, Salvor, Olof, Marta. BSc in Econs., London Sch. Econs., 1950; PhD, U. London, 1953. Econ. adviser Nat. Bank of Iceland, Reykjavik, 1954-59, gen. mgr., 1959-61; gov. Ctrl. Bank of Iceland, Reykjavik, from 1961-93, chmn. bd. govs.; gov. for Iceland Internat. Monetary Fund, Washington, 1965-93; chmn. Nat. Power Co., 1965-96. Editor Fjarmalatioindi Fin., 1954-94, Helgafell literary, 1955-59. Fellow Icelandic Sci. Soc.; mem. Sci. Fund Iceland (chmn. humanities div. 1965-87, chmn. sci. coun. 1987—, nat. libr. bd. 1994—). Home: Laugarasvegur 11, 104 Reykjavik Iceland Office: Central Bank of Iceland, Kalkofnsvegur 1, 150 Reykjavik Iceland

NORDBERG, ERIK MAGNUS, physician, researcher; b. Harnosand, Sweden, Feb. 2, 1935; arrived in Kenya, 1996; s. John and Gunnel Maria (Huss) N. MD, U. Gothenburg, 1965, BA in Sociology, 1971; MPH, Nordic Sch. Pub. Health, Gothenburg, 1987; PhD in health care rsch., Karolinska Inst., Stockholm, 1995. Provincial med. officer Ministry of Health, Nakamte, Ethiopia, 1971-74; dep. head med. svcs. Min. Health, Addis Ababa, Ethiopia, 1974-75; dep. provincial med. officer Harnosand, Stockholm, 1975-78; med. dir. African Med. and Rsch. Found., Nairobi, Kenya, 1978-82, 96-99; dep. provincial med. officer Stockholm, 1982-85; rschr. dept. internat. health care rsch. Karolinska Inst., 1985-96; cons. in internat. health Swedish Internat. Devel. Agy., 1983-95. Author: Environmental Hygiene in Developing Countries, 1979; editor: Society, Environment and Health in Low Income Countries, 1990; contbr. articles to profl. jours. Avocations: sports, science fiction. Home: Jungfrugatan 15, SE11444 Stockholm Sweden Office: IHCAR, Karolinska Inst, SE17176 Stockholm Sweden

NORDBERG, M. MONICA, science educator; b. Karlskrona, Sweden, Aug. 14, 1944; d. P. Arne and Maud I.S. (Langton) Akesson; m. Gunnar F. Nordberg, Oct. 30, 1970; children: Petra, Johan. BSc in Biochem., Microbiol. and Genetics, U. Stockholm, 1968; PhD in Environ. Hygiene, Karolinska Inst., Stockholm, 1977. Head dept. environ. hygiene Karolinska Inst., 1969-81, assoc. prof., dir. ednl. program dept. environ. hygiene, 1983—, temp. prof. dept. environ. hygiene, 1985, prof. in environ. medicine, 1990—; temp. tchg. prof. dept. environ. studies Umeå U., Sweden, 1980, temp. rsch. asst., asst. prof., 1980-83, temp. prof. dept. environ. medicine, 1982-85; mem. edn. policy com. for toxicology and pub. health Karolinska Inst., 1984-93; dep. mem. work employment sect. Bd. Health Care for State Employees, 1985-92; mem. editl. bd., referee various jours. in field; presenter, spkr. in field; mem. Internat. Commn. on Occupl. Health IUPAC, COST. Contbr. over 120 articles to profl. jours.; author/co-author books in field. Mem. Swedish Soc. Toxicology (bd. dirs. 1985-92, treas. 1988-92). Avocations: gardening, reading, golf, swimming. Office: Karolinska Inst, Inst Environ Medicine, S-17177 Stockholm Sweden

NORDEIDE, JARLE TRYTI, biologist, educator; b. Voss, Hordaland, Norway, Dec. 20, 1959; p. Magne and Helga Tryti Nordeide; 1 child, Anna Baustad Nordeide. DSc, U. Bergen, Norway, 1993. Scientist III Inst. Marine Rsch., Bergen, 1987-92, scientist II, 1992-93; assoc. prof. Bodx (Norway) Regional U., 1993—, vice dean faculty fisheries and natural scis., 1997—. Contbr. articles to profl. jours. Mem. Internat. Soc. Behavioral Ecology, Assn. for the Study of Animal Behaviour, Human Behavior and Evolution Soc. E-mail: Jarle.Nordeide@hibo.no. Fax: 47 7551 7349. Office: Bodx Regional Univ, Mxrkved, N-8049 Nordland Norway

NORDEN, KARL ELIS, management consultant; b. Stockholm, Feb. 27, 1921; s. Daniel Henrik and Ella Amanda (Larsson) N.; m. Beatrice Buff; children: Jan-Henrik, Gunilla, Carl-Magnus. BEE, Royal Inst. Tech., Stockholm, 1954. Devel. engr. Swedish Radio AB, 1940-44; chief radar devel dept. Royal Swedish Air Bd., 1944-54; founder, pres. Elenik Automation AB, Stockholm, 1955-64, Norden Automation Systems AG, Zurich, Switzerland, 1964-79, NAS Austria, Vienna, 1966-79, NAS Holland, Woudenberg, 1968-79; mgmt. cons. to airlines, and specialized on yield improvement in iron, steel and chem. industry, specialist in motion weighing, computer controlled material handling; pres. Norden Consulting Internat. Ltd., Sargans, Switzerland, 1987—, Inst. Yield Tech., Ltd., Sargans, Switzerland, 1999—; course dir. modern electronic weighing Ctr. Profl. Advancement, East Brunswick, N.J.; tchr. Royal Swedish Air Force High Sch., 1955-64; chmn. bd. dirs. Inst. Yield Tech. Ltd., Sargans, Switzerland, 1999—. Author: The Inventors Book, 1963, Pulp and Paper, 1968, Aufbereitungstechn, 1972, Electronic Weighing in Industrial Processes, 1984, Electronic Weighing, 1992, Handbook of Electronic Weighing, 1998; patentee in field. Mem. Swedish Inst. Tech., Swedish Assn. Elec. Engrs., Assn. Instrument Tech., Verein Deutscher Eisen-Hüttenleute, Inst. Materials London (affiliate). Home and Office: Grossfeldstrasse 76, CH-7320 Sargans Switzerland

NORDENBERG, MARK ALAN, law educator, university official; b. Duluth, Minn., July 12, 1948; s. John Clemens and Shirley Mae (Tappen) N.; m. Nikki Patricia Pirillo, Dec. 26, 1970; children: Erin, Carl, Michael. BA, Thiel Coll., 1970; JD, U. Wis., 1973. Bar: Wis. 1973, Minn. 1974, U.S. Supreme Ct. 1976, Pa. 1985. Atty. Gray, Plant, Mooty & Anderson, Mpls., 1973-75; prof. law Capital U. Law Ctr., Columbus, Ohio, 1975-77; prof. law U. Pitts., 1977—, acting dean Sch. Law, 1985-87, dean Sch. Law, 1987-93, interim univ. sr. vice chancellor and provost, 1993-94, Univ. Disting. Svc. prof., 1994—, interim univ. chancellor, 1995-96, univ. chancellor, 1996—; mem. U.S. Supreme Ct. Adv. Com. on Civil Rules, Washington, 1988-93, Pa. Supreme Ct. Civil Procedure Rules Com., Phila., 1986-92; mem. large and complex case panel Am. Arbitration Assn.; reporter civil justice adv. group U.S. Dist. Ct., Pitts., 1991-96; bd. dirs. Mellon Financial Corp. Author: Modern Pennsylvania Civil Practice, 1985, 2d edit., 1995. Trustee Thiel Coll., Greenville, Pa., 1987-97; bd. dirs. Inst. for Shipboard Edn. Found., Pitts. Tech. Coun., Pitts. Regional Alliance, Pitts. Digital Greenhouse, Boy Scouts of Allegheny County, Urban League of Pitts., United Way of Allegheny County, World Affairs Coun. of Pitts., The Carnegie Mus., Pitts., Allegheny Conf. on Cmty. Devel., Pitts.; chair Pitts. Coun. on Higher Edn. Named Vectors Pitts. Person of Yr. in Edn., 1996, Person of Yr., 1997. Fellow Am. Bar Found.; mem. ABA, Pa. Bar Assn., Pa. Assn. Colls. and Univs. (bd. dirs.), Allegheny County Bar Assn., Acad. Trial Lawyers Allegheny County, Pa. Assn. Colls. & Univs., Pitts. Athletic Assn., Law Club Pitts., Univ. Club, Duquesne Club, Wildwood Golf Club. Office: U Pitts Cathedral of Learning Pittsburgh PA 15221-3662

NORDENFELT, JOHAN, foreign service official. B in Law, Stockholm U., 1963; LHD (hon.), Jurmiata Coll., 2000. Mem. UN divsn. Ministry for Fgn. Affairs Swedish Embassy, Rio de Janeiro, Tel Aviv and Brussels, 1965-77; counsellor permanent mission of Sweden UN, N.Y.C., 1977-83, del. gen. assembly coms. human rights and legal affairs, 1977-83, chmn. working groups on code of conduct for law enforcement, 1977-83, com. vice chmn. econ. and social coun., 1977-83; counsellor Embassy of Sweden, Mexico City, 1983-84; depl. asst.-under sec., divsn. security policy Ministry Fgn. Affairs, Stockholm, 1984-85, asst.-under sec. for human rights and pub. law, 1985-87; dir. dept. disarmament affairs UN, N.Y.C., 1987-91, lead chem. weapons investigation team to Mozambique, 1992, dir. Centre against Apartheid, 1992, dir. gen. assembly, 1994, dir. Ams. divsn., 1995—; amb. for disarmament Ministry of Fgn. Affairs, Sweden, 1997; amb. of Sweden to India, 2000; lectr. U. Toronto, U. Wis., Pace U., Upsala U., Nordic Forum for Security Policy, Baker Inst. for Peace and Conflict Studies; amb. Seden to Sri Lanka, India, Blutan, Nepal and the Maldives, 2000—. Translator anthologies short stories from Portuguese to Swedish; contbr. articles to profl. jours. including Nordic Jour. Internat. Law, Human Rights Internat. Reporter, Strategic Studies, Environment and Internat. Security, among others. Decorated Knight of the Order of So. Cross (Brazil), Comdr. of the Order of Leopold II (Belgium). Mem. Internat. Assn. Univ. Pres.'s Disarmament Edn. Commn. Office: Embassy of Sweden, Ministry for Fgn Affairs, S-10323 New Delhi India

NORDENFELT, LENNART, philosophy educator; b. Jönköping, Sweden, Apr. 8, 1945; s. Olof and Runa (Granér) N.; m. Kerstin Maria Höök, Oct. 20, 1973; children: Ulrika, Anders. BA, U. Uppsala, Sweden, 1965, MA, 1968, PhD in Theoretical Philosophy, 1974. Assoc. prof. dept. philosophy U. Stockholm, 1975-82, acting prof., 1975, 80, 81; assoc. prof. dept. health and society U. Linköping, Sweden, 1982-87, prof., 1987—, dean Faculty of Tema, 1990-93; rsch. fellow U. Western Ont., London, Can., 1976, Swedish Rsch. Coun. for Humanities and Social Scis., Stockholm, 1981-84; vis. prof. Inst. for Advanced Studies in Humanities, Edinburgh, 1989, U. Warwick, Eng., 1998. Author: On the Nature of Health, 1987, On Crime, Punishment and Psychiatric Care, 1992, Quality of Life, Health and Happiness, 1993, Talking about Health, 1997, Action, Ability and Health, 2000; editor: Concepts and Measurements of Quality of Life in Health Care, 1994. Bd. dirs. U. Linköping, 1994—.

NORDENFORS, HELENA ERICA, biologist, researcher; b. Västervik, Sweden, Apr. 24, 1967; d. Nils-Erik Johansson and Karin Nordenfors; m. Jonas Fredric Öhr, Aug. 12, 2000; children: Harry, Hanna. MSc, Uppsala (Sweden) U., 1994. Rsch. scientist Nat. Vet. Inst., Uppsala, 1994—. Contbr. articles to profl. jours. Bd. dirs. Örsundsbro Montessori Presch., 1999—. Mem. Scandinavian Soc. for Parasitology. Avocations: painting, photography, riding. E-mail: helena.nordenfors@sva.se. Office: Nat Vet Inst, 751 89 Uppsala Sweden

NORDENSTAM, (RUNE) BERTIL, botanist, educator; b. Nykoping, Sweden, Feb. 20, 1936; s. Bengt Torgny and Greta Hulda Sofia (Lundh) N.; m. Gunilla Madeleine Lindberg, Apr. 5, 1966; 1 child, Felicia. PhD candidate, U. Lund, 1958, Fil. Mag., 1958, Fil. Lic., 1966, PhD, 1968, docent, 1969. Asst. U. Lund, Sweden, 1956-58, 61, 67, lectr., 1964-66, rsch. asst., 1968-69; curator Swedish Mus. Natural History, Stockholm, 1969-74, 1st curator, 1974-80, prof., 1980—, dir. rsch. divsn., 1982-84, dep. mus. dir., 1989-95; hon. adv. bd. Queen Sirikit Botanic Garden, Thailand; mem. internat. prize com. Cosmos, Japan; v.p. bd. dirs. Natur och Kultur Pub. House, 1995—. Author: Carl Peter Thunberg, 1993; editor: Plant Systematics for the 21st Century, 2000, Botaniska Notiser, 1965-66, sci. serial Opera Botanica, 1965-66, Compositae Newsletter, 1990—; contbr. over 150 articles to bot. books and jours. Bd. dirs. Swedish Natural Sci. Rsch. Coun., 1983-86, dir. biology com., 1980-86; mem. Univ. Libr. Bd., Stockholm, 1981-87; mem. bd. Hedin Found., Stockholm, Swedish Linn Soc., Bergius Botanic Garden. Recipient Linnaeus prize in Botany, Royal Physiographic Soc., 1980; Smuts Meml. fellow Nat. Botanic Gardens, Kirstenbosch, South Africa, 1962-63. Mem. SW African Sci. Soc. (corr.), Bayerische Botanische Gesellschaft (corr.), World Wildlife Fund (past v.p. Swedish chpt), Royal Swedish Acad. Scis. (coun. 1988—, v.p. 1992-95), Royal Patriotic Soc., Swedish Nat. Com. Biology, Abisko Sci. Sta. (mem. bd.), Royal Physiographic Soc. Lund, Societas Ad Sciendum (Primus praeses, 1995—), Travellers Club (pres. 1997—), Idun Soc., The Explorers Club. Fax: 46-8-51954221.. Home: Krutvagen 4 Sollentuna, SE-19255 Stockholm Sweden Office: Swedish Mus Natural History, Sec of Botany PO Box 50007, SE-10405 Stockholm Sweden

NORDHEIM, ECKHARD VON, clergyman; b. Wittenberg, Germany, May 20, 1942; s. Erich and Hiltrud (Zaenglein) von N.; m. Ingrid Groneberg, Sept. 15, 1967; children: Micha, Miriam. ThD, U. Munich, 1973; D Habilitation, U. Frankfurt, Germany, 1990; Hon. Degree, U. Giessen, 1983. Asst. U. Munich, 1969-74; asst. prof. U. Giessen, 1974-79, prof., 1979-80; oberkirchenrat evangelical Ch. of Germany, 1980-82; oberkirchenrat

evangelical Ch. of Hassia, 1982-90, pastor, 1991—; evangel. pres. of German Coord. Coun. of assn. for Christian-Jewish Cooperation, Bad Nauheim, 1984-98; pres. Buber-Rosenzweig-Found., Frankfurt, 1989-98; scientific cons. European Ctr. for Jewish Music, 1992—, Ashkenas: Jour. for History and Culture of the Jews, 1991—; bd. dirs. Assn. Study in Israel: A Yr. of Studies at Jerusalem, Frankfurt. Author: Jesus von Nazareth, 1974, Die Lehre der Alten I: Das Testament als Literaturgattung im Judentum der hell. roem. Zeit, 1980, Die Lehre der Alten II: Das Testament als Literaturgattung im Alten Testament und im Alten Vorderen Orient, 1985, Die Selbstbehauptung Israels in der Welt des Alten Orients, 1992; contbr. articles to profl. jours. Lt. German Air Force, 1961-63. Recipient Hedwig-Burgheim medal City of Giessen, Germany, 1988. Lutheran. Avocations: archaeology, Egyptology, interreligious dialogue. Home: Justus-Liebig-St 3, 64839 Münster Hassia, Germany

NORDIN, BENGT ÅKE, literary agent; b. Mjölby, Sweden, Mar. 5, 1947; s. Oscar Bernhard and Maibritt Ebba (Carlsson) N.; m. Inger Agneta Marie Erikson, Nov. 30, 1968; children: Camilla, Mikael, Jenny. Sales mgr. Bonniers Förlag, Stockholm, 1975-80, mktg. mgr., 1983-86, book club mgr., 1986-87; mng. dir. B. Wahlströms Bokförlag, Stockholm, 1987-90; pres., founder B. Nordin Agy., Värmdo, Sweden, 1991—. Office: Bengt Nordin Agy AB, Roddvägen 14, S-13955 Värmdö Sweden

NORDIN, HOLGER ZACHARIAS, naval architect; b. Gavle, Sweden, Dec. 10, 1936; s. Per Zacharias and Ida Kristina (Sundin) N.; m. Maud Florence Jacobsen Nordin, May 23, 1963; children: Marika Kristina, Henrik Zacharias. MS, Kungl Technic Hogskolan, Stockholm, 1964. Technician Finnboda Varf AB, Stockholm, Sweden, 1964-65; head of class dept. Kockums AB, Malmo, Sweden, 1965-70; rschr. Lloyd's Register of Shipping, London, 1970-71; head of hull design dept. Kockums AB, Malmo, Sweden, 1971-76, project leader, 1976-87; v.p. Kockums Engring. AB, Malmo, Sweden, 1987—. Contbr.: Ship of the Future, 1990; inventor: Turret, 1996. Home: Ornvagen 31, S-23932 Skanor Sweden Office: Kockums Engring AB, Varvsgatan 1, S-20555 Malmö Sweden

NORDLING, BERNARD ERICK, lawyer; b. Nekoma, Kans., June 14, 1921; s. Carl Ruben Ebben and Edith Elveda (Freeburg) N.; m. Barbara Ann Burkholder, Mar. 26, 1949. Student, George Washington U., 1941-43; AB, McPherson Coll., 1947; JD, U. Kans., 1949. Bar: Kans. 1949, U.S. Dist. Ct. Kans. 1949, U.S. Ct. Appeals (10th cir.) 1970. Pvt. practice Hugoton, Kans., 1949—; ptnr. Kramer, Nordling & Nordling, Hugoton, Kans., 1950-99; mem. Kramer, Nordling & Nordling, LLC, Hugoton, Kans., 1999—; city atty. City of Hugoton, 1951-87; county atty. Stevens County, Kans., 1957-63; Kans. mem. legal com. Interstate Oil Compact Commn., 1969-93; mem. supply tech. adv. com. nat. gas survey FPC, 1975-77. Editor U. Kans. Law Rev., 1949. Mem. Hugoton Sch. Bds., 1954-68, pres. grade sch. bd., 1957-63; trustee McPherson Coll., 1971-81, mem. exec. com., 1975-81; mem. Kans. Energy Adv. Coun., 1975-78, mem. exec. com., 1976-78. With AUS, 1944-46. Recipient Citation of Merit, McPherson Coll., 1987, Disting. Alumnus award Kans. U. Law Sch., 1993, Lifetime Achievement award Hugoton Kans. Area C. of C., 1994. Fellow Am. Bar Found. (Kans.); mem. ABA, Kans. Bar Assn., S.W. Kans. Bar Assn., Am. Judicature Soc., City Attys. Assn. Kans. (exec. com. 1975-83, pres. 1982-83), Nat. Assn. Royalty Owners (bd. govs. 1980-99), S.W. Kans. Royalty Owners Assn. (exec. sec. 1968-94, asst. exec. sec. 1994—), U. Kans. Law Soc. (bd. govs. 1984-87), Kans. U. Endowment Assn. (trustee 1989—), Kans. U. Alumni Assn. (bd. dirs. 1992-97, Fred Ellsworth medallion 1997), Order of Coif, Phi Alpha Delta. Address: 4404 Nicklaus Dr Lawrence KS 66047

NORDLING, CARL OLOF, architect, urban planner, retired, researcher; b. Helsinki, Finland, Dec. 16, 1919; arrived in Sweden, 1940; s. Ole and Karin Maria (Schauman) N.; m. Margit Ester Karlsson, Mar. 4, 1944 (dec. Sept. 1995); children: Danne, Nikus. Architect's diploma, Finland Inst. Tech., Helsinki, 1939. Rsch. asst. Royal Inst. Tech., Stockholm, 1944-47, prof. pro tem, 1946; cons. in pvt. practice Stockholm, 1948-53; architect Vattenbyggnadsbyran, Stockholm, 1953-74; tchr. The Bd. of Edn., Stockholm, 1968; rschr. Faktainformation A-Z, Lidingo, Sweden, 1974—; expert valuer various expropriation cts., Sweden, 1960-70. Author: Defence or Imperialism? An Aspect of Stalin's Military and Foreign Policy 1933-1944, 1984, The Creation of Finnish and the Finns, 1995; contbr. articles to profl. jours. Chmn. Swedish Freedom Coun., 1974-75. Corp. Finnish Army, 1941-42, 44. Mem. Econs. Union. Home: Sporrvagen 16, S-181 41 Lidingo Sweden

NORDLINGER, GERSON, investor; b. Washington, Feb. 2, 1916; s. Gerson and Camille (Bensinger) N. BA, George Washington U., 1935; BCS, Benjamin Franklin U., 1939. Head Navy Dept. Bur. Aeros. Budget, 1946-50; pres. Nordlinger Investment Corp., Washington, 1955—; trustee Washington Real Estate Investment Trust, 1961-98. Chmn. D.C. Arts Commn., 1965-67; v.p. Nat. Symphony Assn., 1953-59, Nat. Ballet, 1966-70, Alliance Francaise, 1980-97; pres. Prevention of Blindness Soc., 1960-67; treas. Friendship House, 1951-69; vice chmn. D.C. Recreation Bd., 1960-67; trustee Washington Performing Arts Soc., Mt. Vernon Coll., Washington Opera, Phillips Collection; mem. state com. Republican Party, 1952-64. Lt. comdr. Supply Corps, USNR, 1941-46, PTO. Mem. D.C. Inst. CPAs, Cosmos Club, Met. Club. Home: 2700 Calvert St NW # 515 Washington DC 20008-2621 also: 3900 Galt Ocean Dr Fort Lauderdale FL 33308-6631

NORDMARK, DAG K., comparative literature researcher, educator; b. Lindesberg, Sweden, Feb. 18, 1945; s. Erik A. and Elsa T. (Skog) N.; m. Karin Arvidsson; children: Viktor, Aron. BA, Uppsala (Sweden) U., 1968; PhD, Umeå (Sweden) U., 1978. Lectr. Umeå U., 1972-73, asst. prof., 1973-84, assoc. prof., 1984—, prof., 1995—; prof. Tromsø (Norway) U., 1991-96, Karlstad U., 1998—. Author: Bildspråkets betydelser, 1976, Samhället på scenen, 1978, Det förenande samtalet, 1986, Tiljorna vid vägen, 1996. With Finrummet och lekstugan, 1999. Avocation: gardening. Home: Skolgaten 10, 666 06 Molkom Sweden Office: Karlsta U, S-651-88 Karlstad Sweden

NORDSHUS, TORE, pediatric radiologist; b. Oslo, June 12, 1944. MD, U. Oslo, 1971. Intern med. dept. Trondheim, Norway, 1969; intern surg. dept. Trondheim, 1970; resident dept. radiology Ulleval, Oslo, 1972-77; fellow dept. pediat. radiology Nat. Hosp., Oslo, 1977-82; cons. dept. pediat. radiology Ulleval Univ. Hosp., Oslo, 1982—. Capt. Royal Norwegian Air Force, 1971. Mem. Norwegian Ultrasound Assn. (pres. 1983-86), European Fedn. Ultrasound (sec. 1981-85), European Soc. for Pediat. Radiology (pres.-elect), Scandinavian Assn. Pediatric Radiology (leader 1991-96).

NORDSIECK, KAREN ANN, custom apparel company executive; b. Ft. Campbell, Ky., Nov. 2, 1955; d. Reuben James and Shirley Jean (Walters) Simpson; m. Kenneth M. Farber, Mar. 5, 1977 (div. July 1982); children: Carissa Ann, Laurie Jean; m. Derrell E. Hiett, May 10, 1985 (div. May 1989); m. Michael Louis Nordsieck, June 2, 1989. Student, El Paso Community Coll., 1976, 84. Sales clk. Busy B Gift Shop, El Paso, Tex., 1973; svc. rep. Bell System, El Paso and Seattle, 1974-85; substitute tchr. Cleburne County Elem. Sch., Heflin, Ala., 1986; credit clk. Wakefields, Anniston, Ala., 1986-87; svc. rep. Ala. Power, Anniston, 1986-88; beauty cons. May Kay Cosmetics, El Paso and Heflin, Ala., 1983-88; mgr. Rock's T-Shirts & Screen Printing, El Paso, 1988-92; owner Custom Designs and Promotions, Richmond, Mo., 1992-96; svc. rep. Southwestern Bell Telephone Co., Kansas City, Mo., 1993—; owner Kreations by Karen, Richmond, 1996—; liaison for ptnrs. in edn. El Paso Ind. Sch. Dist., Rock's T-Shirts and Screen Print, El Paso, 1990—; co-chairperson quality of work life com. Southwestern Bell, El Paso, 1984; union steward Communication Workers Am., El Paso, 1974-75. Troop leaders Brownies, Girl Scouts U.S.A., troop # 126, Heflin, 1985-88, mag. chairperson, 1986; v.p. Clendenin Elem. PTA, El Paso, 1989-90, pres., 1990-92; family support leader Ft. Bliss Family Support, El Paso, 1990-91; mem. El Paso Ind. Sch. Dist. Strategic Planning Com., 1990-91; mem. campus improvement com. Clendenin Elem., 1991-92, vol. pub. schs., 1989-92; mem. parent adv. com. ctrl. area El Paso Ind. Sch. Dist., 1989-92; mem. Richmond PTA, 1992—; mem. com. Richmond A-Plus Sch. Planning, 1994-95; co-chairperson Jr. Class Parents After Prom/Project Graduation, 1995-96; mem. Battlefield Piece Makers Quilt Guild, 1995—; chmn., editor CWA Local 6327 newsletter, The Localizer, 1997-98, union steward, 1996-98; mem. Southwestern Bell/CWA United Way com., 1997-98; chair office improvement com. Southwestern Bell Kansas City Soc., 1997-98. Recipient Outstanding Troop Leader award Girl Scouts U.S.A., Anniston, 1987, cert. outstanding svc. Clendenin PTA, El Paso, 1990, 91, 92; cert. of honor Clendenin Elem. Sch., 1990, 91, 92, Cert. of Appreciation, 1991, 92; Cert. of Appreciation, Ft. Bliss Army Family Support, 1991, plaque Vols. in Pub. Sch., El Paso, 1991, 92, Ptnrs. in Edn., El Paso Ind. Sch. Dist., 1991, 92, Desert Storm vol. pin Ptnrs. in Edn., 1991, Pres. Appreciation award S.W. Bell, 1997. Mem. Battlefield Piecemakers Quilt Guild (sec., chair newsletter 2000—), Order Ea. Star, Telephone Pioneers. Mem. Assembly of God. Avocations: sewing, painting, quilting, reading, sailing. Office: Kreations by Karen 15601 E 3rd Street Ct S Independence MO 64050-1970

NORDSTRÖM, OLLE, mechanical engineer; b. Uppsala, Sweden, July 29, 1935; s. Nils Johan and Estrid (Hansen) N.; m. Anna Birgitta Kristina Wirdefeldt, Oct. 7, 1967; children: Lena, Anders, Kristina. MME, Royal Inst. Tech., Stockholm, 1960. Asst. Royal Inst. Tech., Stockholm, 1960-61; rsch. engr. Nat. Swedish Road Rsch. Inst., Stockholm, 1961-69, head mech. dept., 1969-71; chief engr. Swedish Road and Traffic Rsch. Inst. (VTI), Stockholm, 1971-75, Linköping, Sweden, 1975—; chief engr. Swedish Road and Transp. Rsch. Inst. (VTI), Linköping, 1993—. Author tech. reports. Recipient award U.S. DOT, 1991. Mem. Soc. Automotive Engrs., ASTM (mem. E17 1983—), Svenska Mekanisters Riksförening, Swedish Vehicular Engring. Assn., Internat. Assn. for Vehicle System Dynamics (hon.). Avocations: photography, video, windsurfing. Home: Vitsippevägen 14, 58935 Linköping Sweden Office: VTI, Swedish Road & Transp Rsch Inst, 58195 Linköping Sweden

NORDYKE, ELEANOR COLE, population researcher, public health nurse; b. Los Angeles, June 15, 1927; d. Ralph G. and Louise Noble (Carter) Cole; m. Robert Allan Nordyke, June 18, 1950; children: Mary Ellen Nordyke-Grace, Carolyn Nordyke-Cozzette, Thomas A., Susan E., Gretchen Nordyke Worthington. BS, Stanford U., 1950; P.H.N. accreditation, U. Calif.-Berkeley, 1952; MPH, U. Hawaii, 1969. RN. Pub. health nurse San Francisco Dept. Health, 1950-52; nurse-tchr. Punahou Sch., Honolulu, 1966-67; clinic coordinator East-West Population Inst., East-West Ctr., Honolulu, 1969-75, population rschr., 1975-82, rsch. fellow, 1982-92; cons. Hawaii Commn. on Population, Honolulu, 1970-83; mem. Hawaii Policy Action Group for Family Planning, Honolulu, 1971-89, chmn., 1976-77. Author: The Peopling of Hawaii, 1977, 2d rev. edit., 1989, A Profile of Hawaii's Elderly Population, 1984, (with Robert Gardner) The Demographic Situation in Hawaii, 1974, Pacific Images from Cook's Third Voyage, 1999; mem. editorial bd. Hawaiian Jour. History, 1980—; contbr. articles to profl. jours. Bd. dirs. YMCA, Honolulu, 1970-85, YMCA Camp Erdman Br., 1985—, vice-chmn. 1978-79, chmn. YMCA Camp Erdman, 1989-92; bd. dirs. Hawaii Planned Parenthood, 1974-78, Friends of Libr. of Hawaii, 1985-87; trustee Hawaiian Hist. Soc., 1978-82, Arcadia Retirement Residence, Honolulu, 1978-87; mem. liberal arts coun. Hawaii Pacific U., 1988—. Mem. Population Reference Bur., Am. Statis. Assn., Hawaii Econ. Assn., Hawaiian Hist. Soc., Friends of East-West Ctr., Friends of Univ. Hawaii Sch. Medicine, Stanford Nurses Alumni Assn., Stanford Alumni Assn. (bd. dirs. Hawaii chpt.), U. Hawaii Sch. Pub. Health Alumni Assn. (life), Gen. Fed. Women's History Club, Adventurers' Club of Honolulu, Book Reading Club, Outrigger Canoe Club, Morning Music Club, Caledonian Soc., NAIC Wiki Kala Investment Club, Phi Beta Kappa. Democrat. Congregationalist. Avocations: music, art, swimming, birds, travel. Home: 2013 Kakela Dr Honolulu HI 96822-2158

NORENKOV, IGOR PETROVICH, computer educator, researcher; b. Penza, USSR, Aug. 19, 1933; s. Petr Vasilevich and Larisa Alexandrovna (Savvina) N. DSc, Bauman Moscow High Tech. Sch., 1973. Engr. Bauman Moscow High Tech. Sch., 1960-65, asst. prof., 1965-82; head of chair Bauman Moscow State Tech. U., 1982—; dean of Robotics faculty Bauman Moscow High Tech. Sch., 1987-89; sci. rschr. Bauman Moscow State Tech. U., 1965—. Author: Introduction of CAD, 1980, CAD System Engineering, 1990; author, editor: CAD Systems, 1986; chief editor: Information Technologies, 1995—. Recipient State Award of USSR, 1975. Mem. IEEE, Internat. Info. Acad., Russian Nature Sci. Acad. E-mail: norenkov@wwwcdl.bmstu.ru. Home: Bldg 66 Apt 30, Leningrdsky Prospect, 125315 Moscow Russia Office: Bauman Moscow State Tech U, 2nd Baumaskaya St Bldg 5, 107005 Moscow Russia

NORES, CARLOS, biologist, researcher, educator; b. La Corunna, Spain, Jan. 3, 1953; s. Antonio Nores and Maria Luisa Quesada; m. Dolores Moro, Aug. 14, 1984; 1 child, Marta. Diploma in biology, U. Oviedo, Asturias, Spain, 1978, PhD in Biology, 1989. Asst. lectr. U. Oviedo, Asturias, 1980-89, assoc. prof., 1989-91; prof. U. Oviedo, Spain, 1991—; vis. lectr. Nat. U. Cordoba, Argentina; sub.-dir. INDUROT, U. Oviedo, 1993-97; v.p. Brown Bear Found., 1992—. Co-author: Bears, Status Survey and Action Plan, 1999. 2d lt. Spanish Army, 1976-78. Mem. Mammal Soc., Marine Mammal Soc., European Cetacean Soc. Avocation: music. Fax: 34985104868. Office: U Oviedo, Independencia 13, 33071 Oviedo Spain

NORES, JEAN-MARC, rheumatologist; b. Alger, Algerie, Apr. 27, 1953; s. Paul and Arlette (Jarry) N.; m. Beatrice Cuisenier, June 11, 1982; four children. MD, U. Paris, 1981, PhD, 1997. Intern Hosp. Paris, 1979-84, resident, 1984-87; chief of clinic Faculty of Medicine U. Paris, 1984-87; physician U. Paris V, 1988—. Mem. European Assn. Internal Medicine, French Soc. Rheumatology, French Soc. Philosophy, N.Y. Acad. Scis. Home: 40 rue du Mont-Valerien, 92210 Saint-Cloud France

NORFOLK, DAVID HUGH, business executive, consultant; b. London, July 9, 1945; s. Alfred Thomas and Pamela Mary (Spurling) N. BS with honors, U. East Anglia, 1967. Market rsch. officer B.I.S., Birmingham, U.K., 1968-72; market rsch. mgr. Stephens & Carter, London, 1972-77, Stone-Platt Elec., Crawley, U.K., 1977-81; investment analyst Spencer-Thornton, London, 1981-82; bus. planning mgr. Weidmüller Ltd., Sheerness, U.K., 1982-99; cons., 2000—. Mem. Inst. Mgmt. Mem. Ch. England. Avocations: golf, sailing, ornithology. Address: 48 The Metropole, The Leas, Folkestone Kent CT20 2LU, England

NORGAARD, CARL AAGE, law educator; b. Svenstrup, Denmark, Sept. 15, 1924; m. Hedvig Hauberg, Mar. 17, 1951; 1 child, Helene Hauberg Lehrmann. CandJur, U. Aarhus, Denmark, 1954, DrJur, 1962; postgrad., U. Cambridge, Eng., 1954-55, Inst. Internat. Studies, Geneva, 1959-60; DrJur (hon.), U. Lund, Sweden, 1994. Asst. U. Aarhus, 1955-58, lectr., 1958-64, prof. law, 1964-91; mem. European Commn. of Human Rights, Strasbourg, France, 1973-95, v.p., 1976-81, pres., 1981-95; mem., chmn. various Danish law preparing coms.; ind. jurist with regard to release of polit. prisoners in Namibia, UN, 1989-90; cons. South African Ministry of Justice, 1994-96. Author: The Position of the Individual in International Law, 1962; Administrative Law Procedure, 1972, 4th edit., 1995; co-author: Administration and Citizens, 1973, 2d edit., 1984; contbr. articles to profl. jours. Served to lt. Danish Army, 1945-47. Decorated Danish Grand Cross; German Grand Order of Merit with star and sash; recipient French Prix de la Tolerance, 1998. Home: Skjoldsbergvej 2A, Skjorring, 8464 Galten Denmark Office: U Århus, Inst Pub Law, 8000 Århus Denmark

NORIN, TORJBÖRN, chemistry educator; b. Örnsköldsvik, Sweden, Sept. 16, 1933; s. Carl Einar and Elisabeth (Wik) N.; m. Ingergerd Andersson, July 18, 1959; children: Martin, Elisabeth, Magdalena. M Engring., Royal Inst. Tech., Stockholm, 1957, Tech. Lic., 1962, Tech.D., 1964. Tchr. and rsch. asst. Royal Inst. Tech., Stockholm, 1956-61, 62-64, asst. prof. organic chemistry, 1964-65, prof. organic chemistry, 1969—; postdoctoral rschr. Dyson Derrins Lab., Oxford (Eng.) U., 1961-62; dir. rsch., head chemistry dept. Swedish Forest Products Lab., Stockholm, 1966-72, chmn., 1966-68. Contbr. over 200 articles to profl. pubis. Recipient medal U. Helsinki, 1980, U. Kyoto, 1991. Fellow Royal Acad. Engring. Scis. Sweden, Royal Acad. Scis. Sweden, Academia Europaea, Royal Norwegian Soc. Scis. and Letters, Swedish Chem. Soc. (pres. 1989-99, Norblad-Eustrand award 1966, Oscar Carlson medal 1999); mem. Internat. Union of Pure and Applied Chemistry (pres. organic chemistry divsn. 2000—), Swedish Inst. Surface Chemistry (chmn. bd. dirs. 1989—). Office: Royal Inst Tech, Organic Chemistry, S-10044 Stockholm Sweden

NORKUS, EUGENIJUS, chemist; b. Vilnius, Lithuania, Jan. 21, 1955; s. Povilas and Danute (Kairyte) N.; m. Ruta Rasikaitė, Nov. 19, 1977; children: Ausra, Saule. MSc, U. Vilnius, 1978; PhD, Inst. of Chemistry, 1988. Rsch. scientist Inst. of Chemistry, Vilnius, 1978-92, sr. rsch. scientist, 1992-96, head of dept. of catalysis, 1996—, asst. prof., 1992-95, assoc. prof., 1995-99, prof., 2000—; Contbr. numerous articles to profl. jours. Recipient J. Matulis award in chemistry Lithuanian Acad. Scis., 1997. Roman Catholic. Avocations: numismatics, underwater sports, swimming, fishing. Home: Zirgo 1-29, Vilnius 2040, Lithuania Office: Inst of Chemistry, A Gostauto 9, Vilnius 2600, Lithuania

NORLANDER, JONAS ROLF, treasury executive; b. Jukkasjärvi, Sweden, June 17, 1958; s. Paul Rune Rolf and Anne-Marie Mathilda (Lindmarker) N.; m. Kerstin Gunvor Brynander, July 7, 1990; children: Erik, Axel. MBA, Stockholm Sch. of Econs., 1984. Asst. salesman Johnson Matthey AB, Stockholm, 1984-86; dealer money markets Nordbanken, Stockholm, 1986-89; asst. fin. mgr. Hexagon AB, Stockholm, 1989-91; corp. dealer AlfaLaual AB, Brussels, 1991-93, treasury mgr., 1997—; sr. corp. dealer Tetra Laual S.A., Lausanne, Switzerland, 1993-97. Soccer coach Skanör-Falsterbo If, Skanör, Sweden, 1998—; treas. Pvt. Rd. Maintenance, Skanör, 1999—. Mem. Fin. Mgrs. of So. Sweden. Avocations: squash, skiing. Home: Väktarevägen 5A, S-23933 Skanör Sweden Office: Alfa Laual Treasury International AB, PO Box 73, S-22100 Lund Sweden

NORLANDER, TORSTEN GEORG, psychology educator, researcher; b. Gothenburg, Sweden, Aug. 8, 1950; s. Kurt Karl and Anna Britta (Olsson) N.; m. Anne Sofie Inez Strandh, ept. 6, 1985; 1 child, Arvid. Tchr.'s cert., Linköping (Sweden) U., 1986; PhD, Gothenburg U., 1997. Tchr. various high schs., Örebro, Sweden, 1986-95; instr. dept. psychology Karlstad (Sweden) U., 1995-97, lectr., 1997—, dir. dept. psychology, 1997—, dir. dept. rsch. on sport and exercise, 1997-2000. Contbr. articles to profl. jours., including Jour. Creative Behavior, Creative Rsch. Jour. Grantee Adlerberth Rsch. Found., 1995, Högskolan Rsch. Found., 1998, Swedish Nat. Ctr. for Rsch. in Sports, 1999, 2000. Office: Karlstad U, Dept Psychology, S-651 88 Karlstad Sweden

NORLIN, MALCOLM CARL, leasing company executive; b. Stockholm, Apr. 29, 1947; s. Per Adolf Norlin; m. Madeleine Brita Mörner, Sept. 22, 1979; children: Carl, Henrik, Louise. Degree in econs., Stockholm Sch. Econs., 1971; MBA, Stanford U., 1973. Project team mgr. U.S. Bank of Am., 1973-75; dep. head group Ship Financing Bank of Am., London, 1975-78; head Swedish Regional Office Bank of Am., Copenhagen, 1978-81; dep. head treas., liability mgmt. Emea Region Bank of Am., London, 1981-84; mng. dir., founder Comml. Aircraft Leasing and Trading Blenheim Group, London and Rotterdam, 1984—; chmn. bd., prin. Domsjö Fabriker AB. Mem. Nya Sallskapet, Sallskapet. Lutheran. Avocations: tennis, wine, boating, shooting. Home: Johannesgatan 20 III, S-11138 Stockholm Sweden Office: Blenheim Aviation Svcs AB, 20 Johannesgatan III, S-11138 Stockholm Sweden

NORLING, BERNARD, retired history educator; b. Hunters, Wash., Feb. 23, 1924; s. Thomas Frederick and Catherine (Lucey) N.; m. Mary Theresa Norling, Jan. 30, 1948. BA, Gonzaga U., Spokane, Wash., 1948; MA, U. Notre Dame, 1949, PhD, 1955. Lectr. history U. Notre Dame, Ind., 1950-52; asst. prof. history U. Notre Dame, 1952-60, assoc. prof., 1960-70, prof. history, 1970-85, prof. emeritus history, 1985—. Author: Towards a Better Understanding of History, 1964, Timeless Problems in History, 1970, Understanding History Through American Experience, 1976, Return to Freedom, 1983, Behind Japanese Lines, 1986, Nazi Impact on a German Village, 1993, Lapham's Raiders, 1996, Intrepid Guerrillas of North Luzon, 1999. Sgt. U.S. Army, 1943-46. Avocations: reading, golf, travel, softball, volleyball. Home: 504 E Pokagon St South Bend IN 46617-1326

NORMAN, ALBERT GEORGE, JR., lawyer; b. Birmingham, Ala., May 29, 1929; s. Albert G. and Ila Mae (Carroll) N.; m. Catherine Marshall DeShazo, Sept. 3, 1955; children: Catherine Marshall, Albert George III. BA, Auburn U., 1953; LLB, Emory U., 1958; MA, U. N.C., 1960. Bar: Ga. 1957. Assoc. Moise, Post & Gardner, Atlanta, 1958-60, ptnr., 1960-62; ptnr. Hansell & Post, Atlanta, 1962-86, Long, Aldridge & Norman, Atlanta, 1986-2000. Served with USAF, 1946-49. Mem. ABA, Ga. Bar Assn., Atlanta Bar Assn., Lawyers Club Atlanta (pres. 1973-74), Am. Law Inst., Am. Judicature Soc. (dir. 1975-78), Old War Horse Lawyers Club, (pres. 1991-92), Cherokee Town and Country Club. Episcopalian.

NORMAN, GREGORY JOHN, professional golfer; b. Mt. Isa, Australia, Feb. 10, 1955; m. Laura Norman; children: Morgan-Leigh, Gregory. Profl. golfer, 1976—; chmn., CEO Gt. White Shark Enterprises Inc., Hobe Sound, Fla. Winner Brit. Open Championship, 1986, 93, 18 PGA Tour titles, 68 additional internat. titles; winner Vardon trophy, 1989, 90, 94; recipient Arnold Palmer award for leading money winner, 1995, Byron Nelson trophy for the lowest scoring average, 1995; ranked #1 by Sony; named PGA Player of Yr., 1995, PGA Tour Player of Yr., 1995. Achievements include being the leading Money Winner PGA Tour 1986, 90.

NORMAN, HERBERT JOHN LA FRENCH, writer, organ consultant; b. London, Jan. 15, 1932; s. Herbert La French and Hilda Caroline (West) N.; m. Jill Frances Sharp, Aug. 11, 1956; children: Elizabeth Mary, Sarah Jane, Bernard John. BS, London U., 1953; A, Royal Coll. of Sci., London, 1953. Organ builder Wm. Hill & Son and Norman & Beard Ltd., London, 1953-70, mng. dir., 1970-74; computer mktg. exec. IBM, UK, Ltd., London, 1974-90; organ cons. Lancing Coll., Sussex, Eng., 1983-87, Mill Hill Sch., London, 1984-87, Sherborne Abbey, Dorset, Eng., 1984-88, English & Am. Ch., The Hague, Holland, 1985-88, Pershore Abbey, Worcestershire, Eng., 1988—, St. Lawrence Whitchurch (The Handel organ), London, 1993-95, St. Mary's Pro-cathedral, Dublin, Ireland, 1994-95, St. Helen's, Bishopsgate, London, 1994-96, Oakham Parish Ch., Rutland, Eng., 1994-96, St. Mary's, Twickenham, London, 1995-96, Mullingar Cathedral, Ireland, 1996-97, Palace of Westminster (Houses of Parliament), London, 1995-2000; mem. organs com. Coun. for the Care of Chs. Author: The Organ Today, 1966, The Organs of Britain, 1984; editor: Jour. The Organbuilder, 1983—, Musical Instrument Technology, 1965—; contbr. articles to profl. jour. Organist's Review, 1980—. Mem. St. Albans Diocesan Synod, 1980-86; ch. warden Holy Trinity Ch., Lyonsdown, New Barnet, 1986-88. Fellow Inst. Musical Instrument Tech., Inc. Soc. Organ Builders; mem. Cahtedrals Fabric Commn. for Eng., Freeman (City of London), Liveryman (Musician's Co.). Mem. Church of England. Club: 41 (Hornsey). Home and Office: 15 Baxendale, London N20 OEG, England

NORMAN, JESSYE, soprano; b. Augusta, Ga., Sept. 15, 1945; d. Silas Sr. and Janie (King) N. B.M. cum laude, Howard U., 1967; postgrad., Peabody Conservatory, 1967; M.Mus., U. Mich., 1968; MusD (hon.), U. South, 1984, Boston Conservatory, 1984, U. Mich., 1987, U. Edinburgh, 1989, Cambridge U., 1989. Debut, Deutsche Oper, Berlin, 1969, Italy, 1970; appeared: in operas Die Walküre, Idomeneo, L'Africaine, Marriage of Figaro, Aida, Don Giovanni, Tannhauser, Gotterdammerung, Ariadne auf Naxos, Les Troyens, Dido and Aeneas, Oedipus Rex, Hérodiade, Les Contes d'Hoffmann; debut in operas, La Scala, Milan, Italy, 1972, Salzburg Festival, 1977, U.S. debut, Hollywood Bowl, 1972, appeared with, Tanglewood Festival, Mass., also Edinburgh (Scotland) Festival, debut, Covent Garden, 1972; appeared in 1st Great Performers recital, Lincoln Center, N.Y.C., 1973—; other guest performances include, L.A. Philharm. Orch., Boston Symphony Orch., Am. Symphony Orch., Chgo. Symphony Orch., San Francisco Symphony Orch., Cleve. Orch., Detroit Symphony, N.Y. Philharm. Orch., London Symphony Orch., London Philharm. Orch., BBC Orch., Israel Philharm. Orch., Orchestre de Paris, Nat. Symphony Orch., English Chamber Orch., Royal Philharm., London Phila. Orch., Milw. Symphony Orch., Stockholm Philharm. Orch., Vienna Philharm. Orch., Berlin Philharm. Orch.; tours, Europe, S. Am., Australia, numerous recs., Columbia, EMI, Philips Records; PBS TV spcls. include Kathleen Battle and Jessye Norman Sing Spirituals, 1991, Concert at Avery Fisher Hall, 1994; recordings include Amazing Grace, Brava, Jessye!, Jessye Norman at Notre Dame, Lucky to Be Me, Sacred Songs, With a Song in My Heart, In The Spirit. Recipient 1st prize Bavarian Radio Corp. Internat. Music Competition, 1968, Grand Prix du Disque, Acad. du Disque Francais, 1973, 76, 77, 82, 84, Deutsche Schallplatten, Preis, 1975, 81, Alumni award U. Mich., 1982, Outstanding Musician of Yr. award Musical Am., 1982, Grand Prix du Disque Academie Charles Cros, 1983, Commandeur de l'Ordre des Arts et des Lettres, France, 1984, Grammy awards, 1980, 82, 85, numerous other awards; named hon. life mem. Girl Scouts U.S., 1987. Mem. Royal Acad. Music (hon.), Alpha Kappa Alpha, Gamma Sigma Sigma, Sigma Alpha Iota, Pi Kappa Lambda.

Club: Friday Morning Music (Washington). Office: L'Orchidee PO Box S Crugers NY 10521-0710*

NORMAN, MAGNUS, pro tennis player; b. Filipstad, Sweden, May 30, 1976. Mem. ATP, 1995—; winner Auckland Open, 2000, Italian Open Tennis Master's Series, Rome, 2000, Swedish Open, Bastad, Sweden, 2000, The Hamlet Cup, Commack, N.Y., 2000. Office: ATP Tour 201 ATP Tour Blvd Ponte Vedra Beach FL 32082*

NORMAN, MARY MARSHALL, educator, counselor, therapist; b. Auburn, N.Y., Jan. 10, 1937; d. Anthony John and Zita Norman. BS cum laude, LeMoyne Coll., 1958; MA, Marquette U., 1960; EdD, Pa. State U., 1971. Cert. alcoholism counselor. Tchr. St. Cecilia's Elem. Sch., Theinsville, Wis., 1959-60; vocat. counselor Marquette U., Milw., 1959-60; dir. testing and counseling U. Rochester (N.Y.), N.Y., 1960-62; dir. testing and counseling, dean women, assoc. dean coll. Corning (N.Y.) C.C., Corning (N.Y.) C.C., 1962-68; asst. dean students, dir. student activities, asst. prof. ps Corning (N.Y.) C.C., University Park, 1962-68; rsch. asst. Ctr. for Study Higher Edn. Pa. State U., University Park, Pa., 1969-71; dean faculty South Campus C.C. Allegheny County, West Mifflin, Pa., 1971-72, campus pres., coll. v.p., 1972-82; pres. Orange County C.C., 1982-86; alcohol counselor Sullivan County Alcohol Drug Abuse Svc., 1985-90; sr. counselor Horton Family Program, 1990-96, ednl. cons., writer, 1996—; cons. Boricua Coll., N.Y.C., 1976-77; reader NSF, 1977-78; mem. govtl. commn. com. Am. Assn. Cmty. and Jr. Colls., 1976-79, bd. dirs., 1982—; mem. and chmn. various middle state accreditation teams. Contbr. articles to profl. jours. Bd. dirs. Orange County United Way, Orange County Alcoholism and Drug Abuse Coun., 1993-96, Seneca County Hist. Soc., 1997—, Guild and Altar Soc., 1999—, Seneca Falls Kiwanis; active St. Patrick's Ch. Mem. Nat. Women's Hall of Fame. Mem. Am. Assn. Higher Edn., Nat. Assn. Women Deans Counselors, Am. Assn. Women in Cmty. and Jr. Colls. (charter, Woman of Yr. 1981), Pa. Assn. Two-Yr. Colls., Pa. Assn. Acad. Deans, Pitts. Coun. Women Execs. (charter), Nat. Am. Coun. on Edn. (Pa. rep. identification women for adminstrn. 1978-82, bd. dirs., pres. 1980-96), Pa. Coun. on Higher Edn., Concerned Citizens for Good Govt. (charter), Amnest Internat. (charter mem. women's coun. 2000—), Orange County C. of C. (bd. dirs.), Kiwanis, Gamma Pi Epsilon. Home: 9 S Park St Seneca Falls NY 13148-1423

NORMAN, NEVILLE ROBERT, economist; b. Melbourne, Australia, Mar. 18, 1946; s. Alfred Stanley and Florence Elsie (Arnott) N.; m. Margaret Anne Goodfellow, Jan. 8, 1969; children: David R.J., Geoffrey W.B., Jennifer M.C., Katherine R.M. B of Commerce with honors, U. Melbourne, 1968, MA with honors, 1970; PhD, U. Cambridge, Eng., 1974. Sr. tutor in econs. U. Melbourne, 1968-70; tchr. econ. stats. U. Cambridge, Eng., 1971-73; from lectr. to sr. lectr. U. Melbourne, 1973-84, reader in econs., 1984-91, assoc. prof., 1992—; project leader Econs. of Immigration Project, Melbourne, 1982-86; ratings dir. Australian Ratings, Melbourne, 1982-92; investment advisor Transport Accident Commn. Victoria, Melbourne, 1987-96; pres. Cambridge Australia Trust, 1998—. Author: (book) Economics of Personal Tax Escalation, 1986. Dir. Firbank Anglican Sch., Melbourne, 1978-98; pres. Brighton Grammar Boys' Sch., Melbourne, 1986-89; dir. Brighton Grammar Sch. Found., 1990—. Recipient U.K. award Govt. of Gt. Britain, 1970-73. Mem. Econs. Soc., Athenaeum Club Melbourne. Anglican. Avocations: classical music, genealogy. Home: 97 Dendy St, Brighton Vic 3186, Australia Office: U Melbourne, Dept Econs, 3052 Parkville Vic 3010, Australia

NORMAN, WYATT THOMAS, III, landman, consultant; b. Austin, Tex., Dec. 30, 1952; s. Wyatt Thomas Jr. and Frances Claire (Bliss) N. BS in Agronomy, Tex. A&M U., 1975. Cert. profl. landman, environ. site assessor. Mgr. farm and ranch Bennett Bros., Inc., Pearsall, Tex., 1975-78; landman Corpus Christi, Tex., 1978—. Mem. Flour Bluff (Tex.) Vol. Fire Dept., 1984-90. Mem. Am. Assn. Profl. Landmen, Soc. for Creative Anachronism, Corpus Christi Assn. Profl. Landmen, Assn. Former Students, Century Club, Padre Isles Property Owners Assn., Internat. Game Fish Assn., Corpus Christi Town Club, Single Action Shooting Soc., Coastal Conservation Assn., Tex. Riviera Pistoleros. Republican. Presbyterian. Avocations: hunting, fishing, skiing. Home: 13946 Man O'War Ct Corpus Christi TX 78418-6340 Office: 615 Leopard St Ste 434 Corpus Christi TX 78476-2225

NORMIE, LAWRENCE ROBERT, technologist; b. Manchester, Eng., Dec. 31, 1957; arrived in Israel, December, 1988; s. Gerald and Shirley Riva (Zatman) N.; m. Claudia Miriam Citronenbaum, May 28, 1996; 1 child, Raphael. BSc in Physics, U. Manchester Inst. Sci./Tech., Eng., 1981; MSc in Elec. Engring., Univ. Coll. London, 1985. Chartered physicist. Systems engr. Marconi Def. Sys., London, 1981-85; sr. cons. Sema, London, 1985-88; devel. enr. Elta, Ashdod, Israel, 1989-92; tech. dir. Plexus Cons., Jerusalem, 1992-98; profl. examiner grants Office Chief Scientist, Ministry Industry and Trade, Jerusalem, 1995-98; part-time faculty mem., lectr. dept. indsl. engring. mgmt. Jerusalem Coll. Tech., 1998—. Contbg. editor Photonics Spectra, 1995-99, Biophotonics Internat., 1995-99, Asia-Pacific Telecomm., 1996-99, Asia-Pacific Broadcasting, 1997-99; project evaluator European Commn., 1998—, dir. GeronTech Israel Ctr. Assistive Tech. Aging, 1998—. Recipient gold award Duke of Edinburgh, 1976. Mem. Inst. Physics Eng., Assn. Engrs. Israel, Assn. for Advancement of Assistive Tech. in Europe, Coun. of Internat. Soc. for Gerontechnology, North Amer. Soc. for Rehab. Engrg. Avocations: scuba, watercolors, photography, fencing.

NORO, YOSHIO HAYASHI, theological educator, writer; b. Tokyo, Aug. 2, 1925; s. Kametaro and Hide (Yoshino) H.; m. Ruth Komatsu, June 3, 1951; children: Naomi, Yoshiaki Edwin, Yoshinobu Carl, Mizuki Ann, Michiru Michelle. Student, Keio U. Law Sch., 1942-45, Tokyo Union Theol. Sem., 1945-48; BD, Drew Theol. Sem., 1952; ThD, Union Theol. Sem., N.Y., 1955; PhD in Lit., Kyoto (Japan) U., 1970. Lectr. Aoyama Gakuin U., Tokyo, 1956-57, asst. prof., 1957-62, prof., 1962-72; dean Sch. Lit., Aoyama Gakuin U., 1969-71; prof. Rikkyo U., Tokyo, 1972-91, chmn. dept. theology grad. sch., 1984-91; lectr. Asahi Newspaper Culture Ctr., 1997—. Author: John Wesley, 1963, An Existentialist Theology, 1964, Life and Theology of John Wesley, 1975, God and Hope, 1980, Christianity and Japanese Popular Religions, 1991; contbg. author Reimei (Dawn) mag., 1995—. Min. United Ch. of Christ. Mem. Soc. Christian Studies Japan (trustee 1980-82), Soc. for Japanese Systematic Theologians (pres. 1980-82). Home: 3-21-13 Midoricho, Akishima-shi, Tokyo 196-0004, Japan

NORRBACK, JOHAN OLE, Finnish government official; b. Övermark, Finland, Mar. 18, 1941; m. Vivi-Ann Lindqvist, 1959. Tchr., 1966-67; dist. sec. Swedish People's Party, Ostrobothnia, Finland, 1967-71; exec. mgr. Provincial Union Swedish Ostrobothnia, 1971-89; polit. sec. to min. comm. Finland, Helsinki, 1976-77, M.P., 1979-87, 91-99, min. def., 1987-90, min. Agrl. & Forestry Fisheries & Game Dept., Helsinki, 1987-91; first min. edn. and sci. Finland, Helsinki, 1990-91, min. transp. and comms., 1991-95, min. Nordic coop., 1991-99, min. European affairs and fgn. trade, 1995-99; chmn. parliamentary group Swedish People's Party, 1983-87; amb. of Finland in Norway, Oslo, 1999—. Mem. Vaasa City Coun., Finland, 1981-92; chmn. Swedish People's Party, 1990—. Office: Min Fgn Affairs Embassy Finland, Thomas Heftyes g 1, 0244 Oslo Norway

NORRBY, ERLING CARL JACOB, virology educator; b. Stockholm, Sweden, Aug. 28, 1937; s. Carl Tore Nikolaus and Anna Gertrud (Lofgren) N.; m. Margareta Norrby; children: Jacob, Lars, Christina. MD, Karolinska Inst., Stockholm, 1963, PhD, 1964. Prof. Karolinska Inst., 1972-90, prof., dean, 1990-96; sec. gen. Royal Swedish Acad. Scis., Stockholm, 1997—. Author: Allmanna Forlaget, 1987; editor: (textbook) Almqvist & Wiksell, 2d edit. 1981; contbr. numerous articles to profl. jours. Home: Tykovagen 21, Lidingo S-181 61, Sweden Office: Royal Swedish Acad Scis, PO Box 50005, S-10405 Stockholm Sweden*

NORRBY, KLAS CARL VILHELM, pathology educator; b. Shanghai, China, Jan. 8, 1937; s. Åke Vilhelm and Ingrid Maria (Wedblad) N.; m. Ulla Margareta Hjort, June 17, 1961; children: Katarina, Cecilia, Jacob. BSc, Uppsala (Sweden) U., 1957; MB, Göteborg (Sweden) U., 1959, MD, 1964, PhD, 1970. Asst. prof. pathology Göteborg U., 1967-71; sr. lectr. in pathology Linköping U., 1972-84, chmn. Inst. Med. Microbiology and Pathology, 1980-84; prof. pathology, regal chair Göteborg U., 1985—; vis. prof. in cell biology Harvard Med. Sch., Boston, 1989-90; chmn. Inst. Labor Medicine Sahlgrenska U. Hosp., Göteborg, 1997—. Author over 200 articles to profl. jours. Sub.-lt. Royal Swedish Navy Med. Corps, 1972-86. Fellow European Study Group for Cell Proliferation, European Histamine Rsch. Soc., N.Y. Acad. Sci. Office: Sahlgrenska U Hosp, Dept Pathology, SE-41345 Göteborg Sweden

NORRGREN, HANS RIKARD, physician; b. Stockholm, July 5, 1960; s. Ulf and Britt (Hansson) N.; m. Ingrid Rydholm, June 13, 1987; children: Axel, Lisa, Anna. Med. Degree, Uppsala (Sweden) U., 1988, PhD, 1998. Med. legitimization, 1990; splst. in infectious diseases. Physician dept. infectious diseases U. Hosp. Lund (Sweden), 1990-92, 95-97, 1999—; physician Regional Ctr. Infectious Disease Control, Malmö, Sweden, 1998; clin. researcher Swedish Inst. Infectious Disease Control and Microbiology, Tumor Biology Ctr. Karolinska Inst., Stockholm, stationed in Guinea-Bissau, 1992-95. Contbr. articles to profl. jours. Home: Vallkärratorns Bygata 14, S-22650 Lund Sweden Office: U Hosp Lund, Dept Infectious Diseases, S-22185 Lund Sweden

NORRID, HENRY GAIL, osteopathic physician and surgeon, biologist, researcher, human anatomy and physiology educator; b. Amarillo, Tex., June 4, 1940; s. Henry Horatio and Johnnie Belle (Combs, Cummins) N.; m. Andreia Maybeth Hudson, Jan. 29, 1966 (dec. 1988); children: Joshua Andrew, Noah Adam; m. Cheryll Diane Payne, Mar. 19, 1989; stepchildren: Kim Sheri Payne, Matthew Dominic Payne. AA, Amarillo Coll., 1963; BA, U. Tex., 1966; MS, W. Tex. State U., 1967; DO, Kirksville Coll., 1973. Diplomate Bd. Osteo. Physicians and Surgeons, Nat. Bd. Examiners Osteo. Physicians and Surgeons; cert. basic sci. tchr. Iowa, Tex., Colo. Intern Interboro Gen. Hosp., Bklyn., 1973-74; attending physician dept. gen. practice Osteo. Hosp. and Clinic N.Y., N.Y.C., 1974-77; gen. practice medicine specializing in osteo. Amarillo, Tex., 1978—; emergency care physician Amarillo Emergency Receiving Ctr. Amarillo Hosp. Dist., 1978-79, Ready Care Emergency Ctr., Arlington and Bedford, Tex., 1990-92, St. Anthony Hosp., Amarillo, 1992; emeritus mem. consulting staff physician dept. family practice Northwest Tex. Hosp., Amarillo, 1995; emergency/trauma physician Tex. EM Care, 1995—; mem. mass casualty nat. disaster response team ARC, 1995; contract staff physician Tex. Tech. Univ. Sch. Medicine and Health Scis. Ctr., med. dept. and infirmary Tex. Dept. Corrections, Tex. Dept. Criminal Justice, 1992-94; med. cons. rehab. medicine vocat rehab. divsn. Tex. Rehab. Commn., Plano, 1992-94; cattleman, ranch owner, Van Zandt County, Tex.; lectr. osteo. prins. and practice, The Osteo. Hosp. and Clinic N.Y., 1974-77, mem. credentials com., 1975-76; mem. exec. com. Southwest Osteo. Hosp., Amarillo, 1983-84, chief of staff, 1984-85; sec. dept. family practice Northwest Tex. Hosp., Amarillo, 1981-82, mem. credentials com., 1984-85, joint practice com. dept. family practice, 1986-87; mem. orgnl. com. for devel. of dept. osteo. prins. and practices, chmn. N.Y.C. group N.Y. Coll. Osteo. Med., 1977; mem. founding com. N.Y. Coll. Osteo. Medicine, N.Y. Inst. Tech., Old Westbury L.I., 1976-77; mem. North Tex. Support Group, Dallas; instr. human anatomy and physiology dept. biol. scis. Amarillo Coll., 1998—. Contbr. articles to Tex. Jour. Sci., other publs. Scout physician Llano Estecato council Boy Scouts Am., Tex., 1978-85. Served to E-4 U.S. Army, 1956-63. Recipient William M. Giltner Meml. Fund award 1972, Humanitarian award Am. Cath. Conf., 1979, Century award Boy Scouts Am., 1982, Pfizer Sr. Med. Student award, 1973; Maxwell D. Warmer Meml. scholar 1973; scholar Kirksville Coll. Osteo. Medicine, 1970; Tex. Legislature scholar, 1969-73; named to Eminent Soc. Border Legionaires, 11th Armored Cavalry Regiment, Germany, 1958. Mem. Am. Coll. Gen. Practitioners, Tex. Osteo. Med. Assn. (pres. dist. I, mem. ho. of dels. 1981-82, 95), Tex. C.C. Tchrs. Assn., SAR, The Sons of Republic of Tex., Am. Congress Rehab. Medicine, Am. Osteo. Assn., World Future Soc. (profl.), Gen. Soc. War of 1812, Tex. & Southwest Cattle Raisers Assn., N.Y. Acad. Scis., Ex-Student's Assn. of The Univ. Tex. (life), 11th Armored Cavalry Regiment Assn., 36th (Tex.) Inf. Divsn. Assn. (life), Baron of the Magna Charta (Somerset chpt. Magna Charta Barrons 1994—), Masons, Am. Legion, Beta Beta Beta, Sigma Sigma Phi (pres. 1972), Alpha Phi Omega, Psi Sigma Alpha, Theta Psi, Theta Psi Clowns (1969-73). Avocations: astronomy, short wave listening, camping, fishing, anthropology. Office: 1422 S Tyler St Ste 102 Amarillo TX 79101-4238

NORRIE, PHILIP ANTHONY, family physician, historian; b. Sydney, Feb. 5, 1953; s. Ernest Walter and Agnes Johnstone (Fleming) N.; m. Belinda Jill Vivian, June 6, 1974; children: Andrew Charles, Alexander Edward. B Medicine, B Surgery, Univ. New South Wales, Sydney, 1977; MS, Univ. Sydney, Sydney, 1993; M Social Sci. with honors, Charles Sturt Univ., Wagga, Australia, 1998; postgrad., U. Western Sydney, 1998—. Intern St. Vincent's Hosp., Sydney, 1977; sr. resident Ryde Hosp., Sydney, 1978-79; family physician Sydney, 1980—; owner Pendarves Estate Vineyard, Belford, Australia, 1986—; wine & medical historian Sydney, 1990—; mem. adv. bd. Assocs. into Rsch. for Sci. of Enjoyment, 1996. Author: Vineyards of Sydney, 1990, Lindeman, 1993, Australia's Wine Doctors, 1994, Penfold, 1994, Leo Buring, 1996, Wine and Health Diary, 1998—, Wine and Health-A New Look at an Old Medicine, 2000, Dr. Norrie's Advice on Wine and Health-Thinking and Drinking Health, 2000; mem. editorial bd. Alcohol in Moderation, 1994, Robert Mondavi Mission, 1994. Mem. Australian Medical Friends of Wine Soc. (founder), Australian Soc. History of Medicine, New South Wales Soc. of the History of Medicine, Royal Australian Historical Soc. Avocations: reading history, writing history, wine, travel, watching movies. Home: 22 Ralston Rd, Palm Beach 2108, Australia Office: 2/50 Kalang Rd, Elanora 2101, Australia

NORRILD, BODIL, molecular biologist, educator; b. Copenhagen, Denmark, Nov. 5, 1943; d. Viggo Peter-August and Betty Bodil Mathilde (Hjorth) Hougs; m. Peter Norrild, Mar. 5, 1966 (div.); children: Jens Christian, Kathrine. PhD, U. Copenhagen, 1968, DS, 1980. Rsch. fellow, lectr., asst. prof. U. Copenhagen, Denmark, 1968-80; assoc. prof. U. Copenhagen, 1980—. Contbr. articles to 101 sci. pubs. Grantee Kaj Hansen Found., 1979; recipient Poul Astrup award, 1981, L.F. Foght award, 1988. Mem. EEC (com. regulatory nature), Am. Soc. Microbiology, Danish Soc. Cancer Rsch., Danish Cancer Rsch. Found. (profl. chmn.). Avocations: Italian languages, classical music, golf. Office: Panum Inst Inst Mol Pathol, 3C Blegdamsvej Bld 6 2, DK-2200 Copenhagen N, Denmark

NORRIS, CHARLES HEAD, JR., lawyer, manufacturing executive; b. Boston, Sept. 14, 1940; s. Charles Head and Martha Marie N.; m. Diana D. Strawbridge, July 27, 1974 (div 1994); 1 child, Margaret Dorrance. BA, U. Pa., 1963; JD, 1968; MA, U. Wash., 1965. Mem. Morgan, Lewis & Bockius, Phila., 1968-77; pres., chief exec. Artemis Corp., 1978-79; chmn. bd., chief exec., 1979-91; chmn. exec. com., vice-chmn. bd. Remington Rand Corp., 1979-81; ptnr. Artemis Energy Co., 1980-92; chmn., CEO Norris Investment Co., 1992—; chmn. Norris Mfg. Co., 1994—, Garret Precision Products, 1996—; chmn., CEO Precision Technologies, 1996—; trustee maj. stockholders' voting trust Campbell Soup Co., 1987-90; bd. dirs. SBSF Funds, Inc., 1988-91, Del. trust, 1987-91. Mem. Harvard U. Overseas Com. to Visit Libr., 1989—; mem. Pa. Commn. to Crime and Delinquency, 1980-84; mem. Thouron Award Selection Com., 1985-90; mem. Pa. Electoral Coll., 1980; mem. West Pikeland Twp. Suprs., 1969-72; mem. bd. visitors Carnegie Mellon U. Sch. Urban and Pub. Affairs, 1988-90; corp. mem. Belmont Hill Sch., 1990—. Served with USAF, 1960. Mem. ABA, Pa. Bar Assn., Am. Econ. Assn., Phila., Knickerbocker, Union League, Vicmead Hunt, Everglades (bd. dirs. 1986-91, Bath and Tennis Club (treas., bd. dirs. 1985-91), Sunningdale Golf (Eng.), The Country (Brookline). Office: PO Box 112 Boston MA 02117-0112

NORRIS, GLENN L., lawyer; b. Clarinda, Iowa, Sept. 25, 1946; s. Harold E. and Darlene Louise (Crane) N.; m. Dale Bailey, Jan. 28, 1967 (div. June 1990); m. Tiffinny C. Sparks, Nov. 14, 1998; children: Christopher, Catherine. BA, Simpson Coll., 1968; JD, U. Iowa, 1971. Bar: Iowa 1971, So. Dist. Iowa 1971, U.S. Dist. Ct., no. dist., Iowa, 8th circuit, 1972, U.S. Supreme Ct., 1976. Law clerk U.S. Dist. Judge Hanson, Ft. Dodge, Iowa, 1971-73; assoc. Hawkins, Hedberg & Ward, Des Moines, Iowa, 1973-78; ptnr. Hawkins & Norris, P.C., Des Moines, Iowa, 1978—. Editor: Iowa Academy of Trial Lawyers Handbook, 3d edit., 1999. Mem. tech. com. Iowa Supreme Ct. Commn. for Planning for 21st Century, 1996-98, Iowa Supreme Ct. Budget Adv. Com., 1997—; dir. men's chorus Sacred Heart Knights of Columbus. Fellow Iowa Acad. Trial Lawyers; master C. Edwin Moore Am. Inn of Ct. (pres. 1998-2000); mem. Am. Bd. Trial Advs. (cert. civil trial advocate 2000—), Iowa State Bar Assn. (mem. fed. practice com. 1999—). Roman Catholic. Home: 6205 Oakwood Hills Dr Johnston IA 50131-1962 Office: Hawkins & Norris PC 2501 Grand Ave Ste C Des Moines IA 50312-5311

NORRIS, JOHN STEVEN, healthcare company executive; b. Chgo., Apr. 25, 1943; s. Norris Dale and Olive (Grissinger) N.; m. Susan Jean Armstrong, May 3, 1975; children: Lindsey Jean, Whitney Ann, John Scott. BA, U. Ariz., 1967; B in Fgn. Trade, Am. Grad Sch. Internat. Mgmt., 1968; MPH, U. Ariz., 1995. Diplomate Am. Coll. Healthcare Execs.; lic. nursing home adminstr., gen. contractor, real estate broker. Inspection officer Citicorp, Brazil, Columbia, Mex., Venezuela, Peru, Ecuador, 1968-72; asst. cashier Citicorp, N.Y.C., 1972-74; pres., gen. mgr. Phoenix Athletic Club, 1974-76; bus. mgr. Phoenix Pub. Inc., 1976-77; project mgr. Environ. Constn. Co., Phoenix, 1977-79; pres. AGN Devel. Corp., Phoenix, 1979—, Valley View Realty, Inc., Phoenix, 1981-87; exec. v.p., sec., pres. RGW Constrn. Co., Inc.; pres. Norris/Roberts Group, Inc., Phoenix, 1987-90; CEO Christian Care Cos., Inc., Phoenix, 1990—; bd. dirs. Covenant Health Network. Ex officio bd. dirs. Christian Care Inc.; elder 1st Christian Ch., bd. dirs. Promise Endowment; bd. dirs. region 1 Area Agy. Aging. Recipient award of honor Ariz. Assn. Homes and Svcs. for Aging, 1999. Fellow Am. Assn. Home Svcs. Aging, Am. Coll. Healthcare Adminstrs.; mem. Rotary Internat. (past pres. Phoenix club, Paul Harris fellow), Moon Valley Country Club, Phi Delta Theta. Republican. Avocations: golf, skiing, racquetball. E-mail: jnorris@christiancare.org. Home: 111 W Tam O'Shanter Dr Phoenix AZ 85023-6241 Office: Christian Care Cos 2002 W Sunnyside Dr Phoenix AZ 85029-3534

NORRIS, LONNIE HAROLD, dean; b. Houston, Nov. 22, 1942; s. Mary Ethel (Jacobs) King; m. Donna M. Farmer, June 18, 1966; children: Marlaina M., Michael A. BA in Chemistry, Fisk U., 1964; DMD, Harvard U., 1976, MPH, 1977. Asst. prof. oral & maxillofacial surgery Tufts U. Sch. Dental Medicine, Boston, 1981-88, assoc. prof., 1988-95, prof., 1995—, interim dean, 1995-96, dean, 1996—; mem. com. on dental accreditation. Mem. Gov.'s Commn. to Study the Oral Health Status and Accessibility of Dental Care Svcs. for Residents of the Commonwealth of Mass. Named Disting. Practitioner Nat. Acads. of Practice, Dentist of Yr., New England chpt. Pierre Fauchard Acad. Fellow Am. Acad. Dental Sci., Am. Coll. Dentists, Am. Assn. Oral/Maxillofacial Surgeons, Am. Bd. Oral/Maxillofacial Surgery, Mass. Dental Soc. Anesthesiology, Internat. Coll. Dentists, Phi Beta Kappa, Omicron Kappa Upsilon. Avocations: travel, family. Office: Tufts U Sch Dental Medicine 1 Kneeland St Boston MA 02111-1527

NORRIS, THOMAS FRIEDRICH, marine biologist; b. Eng., June 8, 1965; came to U.S., 1966; s. Patrick Joseph and Maria Luise Norris. BA in Zoology, U. Calif., Santa Barbara, 1987; MS in Marine Sci., San Jose State U., 1995. Sr. scientist Sci. Application Internat. Corp., San Diego, 1998—. Recipient rsch. grant Am. Mus. Natural History, rsch. grant Sigma Xi Sci. Rsch. Soc., award The Packard Found., award The Animal Behavior Soc. Mem. Soc. Marine Mammalogy, Acoustical Soc. Am. E-mail: Thomas.f.norris@saic.com. Office: Sci Application Internat Corp 3990 Old Town Ave Ste 105A San Diego CA 92110-2974

NORRIS, TODD D., speech and theatre educator, actor; b. Columbus, Ohio, July 13, 1969; s. Clifford Max and Donna Lee (Bland) N. BA, U. Findlay, Ohio, 1991; MFA, U. Louisville, 1996. Asst. mgr. Costume Holiday House, Columbus, 1991-92; grad. tchg. asst. U. Louisville, 1993-96; performer nat. tour Mr. Wizard Sci. Assembly Programs, 1996-97; adj. asst. prof. theatre Wright State U., Dayton, Ohio, 1997-98; adult programmer Washington-Centerville (Ohio) Pub. Libr., 1998-99; instr. New Horizons Computer Learning Ctr., Columbus, 1999; instr. speech and theatre, dir. coll. theatre Alice Lloyd Coll, Pippa Passes, Ky., 2000—; cons. Mayhem & Mystery Dinner Theatre, Dayton, 1999-00. Dir. and actor in plays Love's Labour's Lost, 1998, Antigone, 1994-96, Pterodactyls, 1996. Democrat. Fax: 606-368-6212. E-mail: toddnorris@alc.edu. Home: PO Box 37 Pippa Passes KY 41844-0037 Office: Alice Lloyd Coll 100 Purpose Rd # 55 Pippa Passes KY 41844-9005

NORRIS, TRACY HOPKINS, retired public relations executive; b. Ainsworth, Iowa, Nov. 1, 1927; s. Lee E. and Ruth C. (Simpson) N.; m. Emilie Lathrop, Nov. 11, 1956; 1 child, Shawn Tracy. BA, Cornell Coll., Mt. Vernon, Iowa, 1952; MA, U. Iowa, 1957. Admissions counselor Cornell Coll., Mt. Vernon, 1952-54; dir. news bur. Wittenberg U., Springfield, Ohio, 1956-70; exec. dir. univ. relations and communications Ball State U., Muncie, Ind., 1970-88. Active United Way Springfield, Ohio, Muncie, 1965—. Served with USN, 1945-48. Recipient Silver Anvil award Pub. Relations Soc. Am., 1967. Mem. Council for Advancement and Support Edn., Exchange Club. Lutheran. Avocations: golf, travel, lawn and garden activities. Home: 3810 S Burlington Dr Muncie IN 47302-8498

NORRIS, WILLIAM VERNON WENTWORTH, lawyer; b. Bedford, Eng., May 11, 1937; s. William Henry and Eileen Louise (Willmott) N.; m. Penelope Anne Dimmock (div. 1982); children: Sally, Richard; m. Catherine Jean Knowles, June 6, 1982; 1 child, Katie. Barrister (Lincoln's Inn), formerly solicitor Supreme Ct. Eng. Law lectr. Coll. of Law, London, 1959-61; assoc. Allen & Overy, London, 1961-64, ptnr., 1964-97; barrister London, 1997—; dir. Interights, London, 1995—; adv. bd. Jubilee Ctr., Cambridge, Eng., 1996. Contbr. Brit. Tax Rev., 1974-96. Chmn. tax com. Law Soc., 1987-90. Fellow Chartered Inst. of Taxation, 1994. Avocations: poetry, theatre, Tuscan landscape. Home: 21A Ovington Sq, SW3 London England Office: 9 Old Square, Lincoln Inn, London WC2A 3SR, England

NORSTRAND, IRIS FLETCHER, psychiatrist, neurologist, educator; b. Bklyn., Nov. 21, 1915; d. Matthew Emerson and Violet Marie (Anderson) Fletcher; m. Severin Anton Norstrand, May 20, 1941; children: Virginia Helene Norstrand Villano, Thomas Fletcher, Lucille Joyce. BA, Bklyn. Coll., 1937, MA in Biochemistry, 1965, PhD in Biochemistry, 1972; MD, L.I. Coll. Medicine, 1941. Diplomate Am. Bd. Psychiatry and Neurology, cert. geriat. psychiatry. Intern Montefiore Hosp., Bronx, N.Y., 1941-42; asst. resident in neurology N.Y. Neurol. Inst.-Columbia-Presbyn. Med. Ctr., N.Y.C., 1944-45; pvt. practice Bklyn., 1947-52; resident in psychiatry Bklyn. VA Med. Ctr., 1952-54, resident in neurology, 1954-55, staff neurologist, 1955-81, asst. chief neurol. svc., 1981-91, staff psychiatrist, 1991-95; neurol. cons. Indsl. Home for Blind, Bklyn., 1948-51; clin. prof. neurology SUNY Health Sci. Ctr., Bklyn., 1981—; attending neurologist Kings County Hosp., Bklyn., State U. Hosp., Bklyn.; cons. in field. Contbr. articles to profl. jours. Mem. Nat. Rep. Congl. Com., Rep. Senatorial Inner Circle. Recipient Spl. plaque Mil. Order Purple Heart, 1986, Spl. Achievement award PhD Alumni Assn. of CUNY, 1993, Lifetime Achievement award Bklyn. Coll., 1995, others. Fellow Am. Psychiat. Assn., Am. Acad. Neurology, Internat. Soc. Neurochemistry, Am. Assn. U. Profs. Neurology, Am. Med. EEG Soc. (pres. 1987-88), Nat. Assn. VA Physicians (pres. 1989-91, James O'Connor award 1987), N.Y. Acad. Scis., Sigma Xi. Republican. Presbyterian. Avocations: writing, piano, travel, reading. Home: 7624 10th Ave Brooklyn NY 11228-2309

NORSWORTHY, JOHN RANDOLPH, economist, educator; b. Norfolk, Va., Aug. 26, 1939; s. John Tignor and Annie Vivian (Smith) N.; m. Elizabeth Krassovsky, June 24, 1961 (div. 1962); 1 child, Leonid Alexander; m. Susan Foster, Aug. 15, 1964 (div. 1971); 1 child, Ann Randolph; m. Irene Jacobsohn, June 19, 1991. BA with distinction, U. Va., 1961, PhD in Econs., 1966. Asst. prof. econs. U. Ill., Chgo., 1966-68; asst., then assoc. prof. Temple U., Phila., 1968-71; chief applied econs. divsn. Office of Emergency Preparedness, Exec. Office Pres., Washington, 1971-73; chief productivity rsch. divsn. Bur. Labor Stats., Washington, 1973-82; chief ctr. for econ. studies Bur. Census, U.S. Dept. Commerce, Washington, 1982-85; cons. economist, 1985-86; prof. econ. and mgmt. Rensselaer Poly. Inst., 1986—; mem. Brookings Panel on Econ. Activity, 1979; dir. Ctr. Sci. and Tech. Policy, 1990-92; cons. in telecom. and productivity AT&T, 1995-97. Author: (with S.L. Jang) Pub. Analysis of Technological Change and Productivity: Applications in High Technology and Service Industries, 1992, (with D.H. Tsai) The Macroeconomic Environment as Implicit Industrial Policy, 1997, (with Nan L. Pitt) Technological Change and Productivity in U.S. Commercial Airlines, 1999; contbr. articles to profl. jours. Recipient Disting. Achievement award for Rsch., U.S. Dept. Labor, 1980, Lawrence R. Gordon award for Grad. Tchg. and Rsch. in Econs., Rensselaer Poly. Inst., 1988; NDEA fellow, U. Va., 1961-65, postdoctoral fellow econs. U. Chgo.,

1965-66, NSF/Am. Statis. Assn. fellow U.S. Bur. Census, 1990-91. Mem. Am. Econ. Assn., Am. Statis. Assn., Econometric Soc., Am. Fin. Assn., Fin. Mgmt. Assn. Internat., Conf. on Rsch. in Income and Wealth (exec. com. 1981-85), Phi Beta Kappa, Phi Eta Sigma, Tau Kappa Epsilon.

NORTH, ALASTAIR MACARTHUR, retired academic administrator; b. Aberdeen, Scotland, Apr. 2, 1932; s. Norman Richard and Anne (Macarthur) N.; m. Charlotte Muriel Darroch, Mar. 28, 1934; children: David Macarthur, Alison Mary Ross, Corinne Elizabeth Wilson, Andrew Russell. BSc with first class hons., Aberdeen U., 1954, PhD, 1957; DSc, Aberdeen U., Scotland, 1965; ScD honoris causa, Tech. U. Łodz, Poland, 1978; PhD honoris causa, Ramkhamhaeng U., Thailand, 1991; D of Univ. honoris causa, Strathclyde U., Scotland, 1993; PhD honoris causa, Inst. Nat. Poly. Toulouse, France, 1995; DTech honoris causa, AIT, Thailand, 1997. Asst. lectr. Aberdeen U., 1956-57; rsch. fellow U. So. Calif., 1957-58; ICI fellow U. Liverpool, Eng., 1958-59; lectr. in inorganic, phys. and indsl. chemistry U. Liverpool, 1959-67; Burmah prof. phys. chemistry U. Strathclyde, 1967-83, dean Sch. Chem. and Materials Scis., 1972-75, vice prin., 1976-80, dep. prin., 1980-81; pres., prof. applied sci. Asian Inst. Tech., Bangkok, Thailand, 1983-96; vis. prof. Chiang Mai U., 1984—, Mahidol U., 1987—; cons. in field; mem. chemistry panel Scottish Cert. of Edn. Examining Bd., 1971-78, convener, 1971-76; chmn. Scottish Cen. Com. on Sci., 1971-72, 79-83, Scottish Cen. Subcom. on Chemistry, 1971-72, 78-81, CNAA Chemistry Bd., 1978-81, Coun. for Scotland, 1979-83; lectr. in field. Editorial bd. Jour. Macromolecular Sci., Macromolecular Rev., 1966-79, Advances in Molecular Relaxation Processes, 1970-83, Polymer, 1970-83, Russian Jour. Phys. Chemistry, 1970-83, Rev. Reactive Intermediates, 1978-83, Polymer Photochemistry, 1980-83; author 2 books; editor various books; contbr. articles to profl. jours. Mem. ILL European Neutron Beam Facility Polymer Sci. Subcom., 1980-83. Decorated Order of the Brit. Empire; named Comdr. dans l'Ordre des Palmes Academiques, France, Comdr. in the Order of King Leopold II, Belgium, Prasidda Prabala Gorkha Dakshim Bahu, Nepal; recipient Marlow medal Faraday Soc., 1965. Fellow Royal Inst. Chemistry, Royal Soc. Edinburgh; mem. Assn. Univ. Tchrs. Scotland (exec. com. 1978-81). Avocations: golf, sub-aqua diving.

NORTH, ANITA, secondary education educator; b. Chgo., Apr. 21, 1963; d. William Denson and Carol (Linden) N. BA, Ind. U., 1985; MS in Edn., Northwestern U., 1987. Cert. tchr., Ill. High sch. social studies and English tchr. Lake Park High Sch., Roselle, Ill., 1987-89; high sch. social studies tchr. West Leyden High Sch., Northlake, Ill., 1989—; exch. program coord. West Leyden High Sch., 1989—, head coach boys' tennis team, 1989—, asst. coach girls' tennis team, 1994—, asst. speech coach, 1992-93. Humanities fellow Nat. Coun. Humanities, 1995; recipient Fern Fine Tchg. award West Leyden H.S., 1992. Mem. AAUW, Nat. Coun. for Social Studies, Ill. Coun. for Social Studies, Orgn. Am. Historians, Ill. Tennis Coaches Assn., Phi Delta Kappa. Christian. Avocations: wilderness backpacking, tennis, orienteering, gardening, antique books and maps.

NORTH, DOUGLASS CECIL, economist, educator; b. Cambridge, Mass., Nov. 5, 1920; s. Henry Emerson and Edith (Saitta) N.; m. Elisabeth Willard Case, Sept. 28, 1972; children by previous marriage: Douglass Alan, Christopher, Malcolm Peter. BA, U. Calif., Berkeley, 1942, PhD, 1952; D in Natural Scis. (hon.), U. of Cologne, Federal Republic of Germany, 1988, U. Zurich, Switzerland, 1993, Stockholm Sch. of Econs., Sweden, 1994, Prague Sch. Econs., 1995. Asst. prof. econs. U. Wash., 1950-56, assoc. prof., 1957-60, prof., 1960-83, prof. emeritus, 1983—, chmn. dept., 1967-79; dir. Inst. Econ. Research, 1960-66, Nat. Bur. Econ. Research, 1967-87; Spencer T. Olin prof. in arts and scis. Washington U., St. Louis, 1983—; Pitt prof. Am. history and instns. Cambridge U., 1981-82; fellow Ctr. for Advanced Study on Behavioral Scis., 1987-88. Author: The Economic Growth of the U.S. 1790-1860, 1961, Growth and Welfare in the American Past, 1966, (with L. Davis) Institutional Change and American Economic Growth, 1971, (with R. Miller) The Economics of Public Issues, 1971, 74, 76, 78, 80, (with R. Thomas) The Rise of the Western World, 1973, Structure and Change in Economic History, 1981, Institutions, Institutional Change and Economic Performance, 1990. Guggenheim fellow, 1972-73; grantee Social Sci. Rsch. Coun., 1962, Rockefeller Found., 1960-63, Ford Found., 1961, 66, NSF, 1967-73, Bradley Found., 1986—. Recipient Nobel Prize in Economic Science, Nobel Foundation, 1993. Fellow Am. Acad. Arts and Scis.; mem. Am. Econ. Assn., Econ. History Assn., The British Acad. (corr. mem.). Office: Washington U Dept Econs PO Box 1208 Saint Louis MO 63188-1208

NORTH, GERALD DAVID WILLIAM, lawyer; b. N.Y.C., Feb. 15, 1951; s. David North and Isabella (Leonard) Cadgene; m. Jeanne Curtis, Nov. 1970 (div. 1977); m. Carmela Benvenuto, Feb. 21, 1980; 1 child, David II. BA (hon.) with distinction, U. Iowa, 1972, JD with high distinction, 1975; postgrad., Oxford (Eng.) U., 1975-76. Bar: Iowa 1975, Ill. 1977, U.S. Dist. Ct. (no. dist.) Ill. 1977, U.S. Supreme Ct. 1982, U.S. Dist. Ct. (no. dist. trial bar) Ill. 1983, U.S. Ct. Appeals (fed. cir.) 1984, Ariz. 1985, U.S. Dist. Ct. Ariz. 1985, U.S. Ct. Appeals (9th cir.) 1985. Assoc. Sidley & Austin, Chgo., 1976-81; ptnr. Brace & North, Chgo., 1981-82; v.p., gen. counsel Trans-Global Group, Chgo., 1983-84; of counsel McCabe, Polese, Pietzsch, Phoenix, 1984-87; founder, shareholder North & Barron, Phoenix, 1987-92; sr. shareholder North & Vaira, Phila., Phoenix, 1992-93; prin. counsel IMPRA, Inc., Phoenix, 1984-93; chmn. bd. Fibrin Techs., Inc., Wilmington, Del., 1993-97; prin. counsel MinTec, Inc., Freeport, Bahamas, 1995-96; bd. dirs. Fenders Auto Leasing Inc., Vancouver, Can., 1996-97; asst. sec. Summit Spirits, Ltd., Grand Cayman, Cayman Islands, 1998—. Contbg. author: European Investment in U.S. and Canadian Real Estate, 1990, Directory of Asian High Tech Companies in the U.S., 1991. Fellow Ariz. Bar Found.; past mem. ABA (antitrust sec. 1975-93) Am. Intellectual Property Law Assn., Assn. Trial Lawyers Am., Fed. Cir. Bar Assn., Univ. Club (Chgo.), United Oxford and Cambridge Club (London), Legal Club (Chgo.); mem. National Club (Moscow), Order of Coif, Monte Carlo Country Club, Phi Beta Kappa, Omicron Delta Kappa. Home: 3977 E Paradise View Dr Paradise Valley AZ 85253-3808

NORTH, PETER MACHIN, academic administrator, lawyer; b. Nottingham, Eng., Aug. 30, 1936; s. Geoffrey Machin and Freda Brunt (Smith) N.; m. Stephanie Mary Chadwick, Aug. 13, 1960; children: Jane, Nicholas, James. BA, Oxford (Eng.) U., 1959, BCL, 1960, MA, 1963, DCL, 1976; LLD, Reading (Eng.) U., 1992; Nottingham U., 1996, Aberdeen U., 1997. Teaching assoc. Northwestern U., Chgo., 1960-61; lectr. U. Wales, Aberystwyth, 1960-63, U. Nottingham, Eng., 1964-65; fellow Keble Coll./Oxford U., 1965-76; law commr. Law Commn., London, 1976-84; prin. Jesus Coll./Oxford U., 1984—; vice-chancellor Oxford U., 1993-97. Author: Occupiers' Liability, 1971, Modern Law of Animals, 1972, Private International Law, 1999, Essays in Private International Law, 1993. Chmn. Rd. Traffic Law Rev., London, 1985-88; chmn. Rev. of Parades and Marches in No. Ireland, 1996-97, chmn., Independent Com. for the Supervision of Standards of Telephone Information Svcs., 1999—. Lt. English Army, 1954-56. Decorated Knight Bachelor, Comdr. Order Brit. Empire, Queens Counsel. Fellow British Acad.; mem. Inst. Internat. Law, Internat. Acad. Comparative Law. Mem. Ch. of Eng. Home and Office: University of Oxford Jesus Coll, Principals Lodgings, Oxford OX1 3DW, England

NORTH, ROBERT (ROBERT NORTH DODSON), dancer, choreographer, artistic director; b. Charleston, N.C., June 1, 1945; came to Eng.; s. Charles Edward and Elizabeth Almerine (Thomson) Dodson; m. Janet Smith, Aug. 18, 1978. Ed. Central Sch. Art, London, Royal Ballet Sch. Mem. London Contemporary Dance Co., 1967-81, Ballet Rambert, London, 1981—; guest artist Royal Ballet, London, 1976, Martha Graham Co., N.Y.C., 1968-69, dir.,Corpo di Ballo dell'Arena di Verona, coreographer ballets including: Conversation Piece, Troy Game, The Annunciation, Death and the Maiden, Pribaoutki, Colour Moves, Still Life, Peflections, Running Figures. Mem. Equity Brit. Actors, AGMA. Office: Corpo di Ballo dell'Arena di Verona, Piazza Bra 28, I-37121 Verona Italy

NORTH, SAM, writer, literary agent; b. Bury St Edmunds, Suffolk, U.K., Aug. 30, 1960; s. Jeremy North and Annabelle Alexander Reynolds; m. Abigail Chaytor Philbrow; children: Esme, Diggory, Louie. Head of devel. WW Internat., London, 1995-97; dir. A.P. Watt, London, 1998—. Author: The Automatic Man, 1990 (Somerset Maugham award 1990), Chapel Street, 1991, The Gifine Programme, 1994, By Desire, 1996, The Lie of the Land, 1998. Mem. Soho House. Home: Batnorthy Rvin, Chagford TQ13 8EO, England Office: AP Watt Ltd, 20 John St, London WC1N 2DR, England

NORTHCUTT, WAYNE, history educator; b. New Orleans, July 5, 1944; s. Bernard Duke and Clara Lenore N. BA in History, Calif. State U., Long Beach, 1966, MA in History, 1968; PhD in European History, U. Calif., Irvine, 1974; postgrad., Ecole Partique des Hautes, Etudes, Paris, 1978. Asst. prof. of history and head western European area study Monterey (Calif.) Inst. of Internat. Studies, 1975-78; lectr. in history and internat. rels. Schiller Coll., Paris, 1978; tchg. assoc. U. Calif., Irvine, 1979-80; fgn. expert Chinese People's U., Beijing, 1983; coord. internat. studies program Niagara (N.Y.) Univ., 1985—, prof. of history, 1980—. Author: The Regions of France, 1996, Mitterrand: A Political Biography, 1992, Historical Dictionary of the French Fourth and Fifth Republic, 1946-1991, 1992, The French Socialist and Communist Party Under the Fifth Republic, 1958-1981, 1985.

NORTHOVER, BASIL JOHN, pharmacologist, educator; b. Northampton, Eng., July 7, 1936; s. Eric and Winifred (Mead) N.; m. Ann Howden, aug. 30, 1958; 3 children. B in Pharmacology, London U., 1958, M in Pharmacology, 1959, PhD, 1965; DSc, Coun. Acad. Awards, 1988. Lectr. pharmacology Christian Med. Coll., Vellore, South India, 1959-64; sr. lectr. pharmacology De Montfort U., Leicester, Eng., 1965-88; prof. pharmacology De Montfort U., Leicester, 1989—; cons., external examiner, Eng. Author: The Electrical Activity of Mammalian Tissues, 1992; mem. editl. bd. rsch. jours.; contbr. articles to profl. publs. Mem. British Pharmacol. Soc., British Microcirculation Soc. Home: 12 Newport Terr, Barnstaple Devon EX32 9BB, England

NORTHRUP, STEPHEN JAMES, professional association executive; b. Schenectady, N.Y.; s. James Reed and AnnMary Northrup. BA, Hamilton Coll., 1989; MPA, George Mason U., 1996. Legal asst. Steptoe & Johnson, Washington, 1989-90; legis. analyst Williams & Jensen, P.C., Washington, 1990-91, Assn. Am. Med. Colls., Washington, 1991-96; dir. govt. and cmty. rels. Loyola U. Med. Ctr., Maywood, Ill., 1996-98; exec. dir. Med. Device Mfrs. Assn., Maywood, 1998—. Mem. Am. Soc. Assn. Execs., St. Andrews Golf Club. Fax: (559) 663-7777. E-mail: snorthrup@medicaldevices.org. Home: 3410 Broad Branch Ter NW Washington DC 20008-2019 Office: Med Device Mfrs Assn 1900 K St NW Ste 100 Washington DC 20006-1102

NORTON, CHRISTOPHER DAVID, legal assistant; b. Sydney, Australia, June 12, 1970; s. William Edwin and Kay Ellen (Patterson) N. BA with honors, U. Sydney, 1993, LLB with honors, 1995. Rschr. Ctr. for Plain Legal Lang., Sydney, 1993-95; tipstaff to chief judge Land and Environment Ct NSW, Sydney, 1995-96; solicitor Doyles Solicitor, Sydney, 1997-98; sr. solicitor Environ. Defender's Office NSW, Sydney, 1998—; state rep. Outdoor Recreation Coun. Australia, Sydney, 1993—. Editor SUSS Bull., 1995-97. Mem. Sydney U. Speleological Soc. (pres. 1991-92), NSW Speleological Coun. (exec. mem. 7-2000, pres. 2000—), Australian Speleological Fedn. Avocation: speleology. Home: 32 Crows Nest Rd, Wollstonecraft NSW 2065, Australia Office: Environ Defender's Office, L9, 89 York St, Sydney NSW 2000, Australia

NORTON, EUNICE, pianist; b. Mpls., June 30, 1908; d. Willis I. and Charlotte (O'Brien) N.; m. Bernard Lewis, May 4, 1934; 1 child, Norton Lewis. Student, U. Minn., 1922-24, Tobias Matthay Pianoforte Sch., London, 1924-31, Artur Schabel Master Piano Classes, Ger., 1931-33, Arthur Schabel Master Piano Classes, Italy, 1933; MusD (hon.), Wooster Coll., 1977. vis. prof. piano Carnegie Mellon U.; lectr. U. Pitts., Cath. U. Am.; lectr., condr. master piano classes univs.; condr. pvt. master classes, Pitts., N.Y.C., Vt.; dir. Peacham (Vt.) Piano Festivals; founder, musical dir. Pitts. New Friends of Music, Pitts. Concert Artists; pres. Norvard, Inc. Classic CD's. Concert pianist in U.S. and Europe, 1927—; soloist with numerous symphony orchs., including N.Y. Philharm., Boston, Phila., Pitts., Mpls., London, Berlin symphony orchs., also orchs. in Leipzig, Germany, Vienna, Austria, Birmingham, Eng., Manchester, Eng.; chamber musician with Budapest, Juilliard and Griller string quartets, Am. Chember Orch.; recorded Well Tempered Clarier (J.S. Bach); performed Beethoven's entire piano sonatas, Carlow Coll., Pitts., 1983, U. Pitts., 1988, recorded ltd. edit., 1988; recorded 4 one-hour illustrated lectrs. on video Teaching of Arthur Schnabel, U. Pitts., 1987, video The Teaching of Tobias Matthay, 1995. Recipient Bach prize, 1927; recipient Chappell Gold medal Chappell Piano Co., London, 1928. Mem. Am. Matthay Piano Assn. (founder mem.), Sigma Alpha Iota (hon.). Club: Tuesday Musical (hon.) (Pitts.). Home: 5863 Marlborough Ave Pittsburgh PA 15217-1415

NORTON, JAY LEWIS, lawyer, recording company executive; b. Olathe, Kans., Nov. 26, 1968; s. Joseph Lewis and Jane Marie (Bushfield) N.; m. Katherine Lucy Rampton, Dec. 30, 1993. BA, U. Kans., 1991, JD, 1994. Assoc. Moriarty, Erker & Moore, Overland Park, Kans., 1994-96; ptnr. Erker & Moore, Olathe, 1996-98; pres. Iconoclastic Pop Records, Lawrence, Kans., 1993—; pntr. Erker, Norton & Hare, Olathe, 1999—. Author: Art of War for Criminal Defense Attorneys, 1997. Coach Nat. Mock Jury competition, Shawnee Mission, Kans., 1997. Named one of Kansas City's 29 most influential people under age 30, Kansas City mag., 1996. Mem. Nat. Coll. of DUI Def., Kans. Assn. Criminal Def. Lawyers, Kans. Bar Assn. Libertarian. Avocations: guitar playing, painting, writing. Home: 4221 Oak St Kansas City MO 64111-1616 Office: Erker Norton & Hare 130 N Cherry St Ste 203 Olathe KS 66061-3460

NORTON, JERRY WILLIAM, journalist, news executive; b. North Bend, Oreg., May 16, 1946; s. William Wellington and Lydia Hillis (McCall) N.; m. Kim Thoa Nguyen, Nov. 18, 1982; 1 child, Michael Hoai Vu. BA, U. Oreg. Honors Coll., 1968; postgrad., Georgetown U., 1970-71; MS, Columbia U., 1974. Exec. editor Unicom News, London, 1982-83; bus. editor S. China Morning Post, Hong Kong, 1983-86; sub-editor Reuters, Hong Kong, 1986-87; chief sub-editor Reuters, Tokyo, 1987-89, news editor Japan, 1989-93; bur. chief Reuters, Singapore, 1993-99, dep. editor Asia Desk, 1999—. With U.S. Army, 1968-70, Vietnam. Decorated Purple Heart U.S. Army, Vietnam, 1969. Mem. DAV, Fgn. Corrs. Assn. Singapore (sec. 1994-95, pres. 1995-97), Fgn. Corrs. Club Hong Kong, Nat. Press Club, Soc. Profl. Journalists, Hong Kong Journalists Assn. (exec. com. 1981-82), Mensa, Custer Battlefield Hist. and Mus. Assn., Phi Beta Kappa, Kappa Tau Alpha. Home: 09 02 Orchard Bel Air, 245 Orchard Blvd, Singapore 248648, Singapore Office: Reuters, 18 Science Park Dr, Singapore 118229, Singapore

NORTON, LINDA LEE, pharmacist, educator; b. Vallejo, Calif., Aug. 12, 1953; d. Don Leroy and Pearl Etta (Cain) Hartzell; m. Lawrence Henry Norton, Aug. 19, 1972; children: Joshua David, Gabriel Aaron. PharmD, U. Pacific, 1991. Lic. pharmacist, Calif., Nev. Pharmacy resident St. Joseph's Med. Ctr., Stockton, Calif., 1991-92, U. Ariz., Tucson, 1992-93; fellow in pain rsch. and drug info. U. of Pacific and Am. Acad. Pain Mgmt., Stockton, 1993-95; asst. prof. pharmacy practice U. of Pacific, Stockton, 1995-99, assoc. coord. postgrad. profl. edn., 1995-99, assoc. prof., dir. postgrad. profl. edn., 1999—; mng. editor Enjoying Good Health, 1997-99; contbr. articles to profl. jours. Bd. dirs. SMART Coalition, Sacramento, 1998—. Mem. shared governance com. Liberty Union H.S., Brentwood, Calif., 1995-97, health careers acad. com., 1995-97. Recipient Award for outstanding article in pain mgmt. Am. Jour. Pain Mgmt., 1997; grantee Valley Mountain Reg. Ctr., 1998—, Diagnostek, 1994; Thomas J. Long Faculty fellow, 1997, 98. Mem. Am. Assn. Colls. Pharmacy, Am. Soc. Health-Sys. Pharmacists, Calif. Soc. Health-Sys. Pharmacists (co-chair C.E. Focus '98), Rho Chi. Avocations: small-scale farming and ranching, horse shoe pitching, fishing. Office: Univ of the Pacific Sch of Pharmacy 751 Brookside Rd Stockton CA 95211-0001

NORTON, WILLIAM ALAN, lawyer; b. Garretsville, Ohio, Apr. 26, 1951; s. Hugh Delbert and Tommie (Leet) N.; m. Denise Ann, May 2, 1991; children: Rachel, Sarah Megan, William Tucker. AA, U. Fla., 1972, BS, 1973, JD, 1976. Bar: Fla. 1977, U.S. Dist. Ct. (so. and mid. dist.) Fla. 1995. Assoc. Law Office of David Paul Horan, Key West, Fla., 1978-79; asst. pub. defender 16th Jud. Cir., Monroe County, Fla., 1979-81, 1st Jud. Cir., Ft. Walton Beach, Fla., 1981-85; assoc. Jones & Foster, P.A., West Palm Beach, Fla., 1985-88, Montgomery Searcy & Denney, West Palm Beach, 1988-89, Searcy Denney Scarola Barnhart & Shipley, P.A., 1989-93; atty./shareholder Searcy Denney Scarola Barnhart & Shipley, P.A., West Palm Beach, 1989—, shareholder; lectr. in civil trial and securities litigation. Bd. dirs. Ctr. for Children in Crisis, West Palm Beach, 1994—. Mem. Fla. Bar Assn. (cert. civil trial litigation), Pub. Investors Arbitration Bar Assn., Palm Beach County Bar Assn., Acad. Fla. Trial Lawyers. Home: 8152 Needles Dr Palm Bch Gdns FL 33418-6074 Office: Searcy Denney Scarola et al 2139 Palm Beach Lakes Blvd West Palm Beach FL 33409-6601

NORTON-LARSON, MARY JEAN, lawyer, planned giving officer; b. Adrian, Minn., Feb. 18, 1955; d. Robert Eugene and Natalie Norma (Nelson) Norton; m. Richard Allan Larson, Apr. 2, 1977; children: Kathryn, Bennett, Jackson. BA, Bethel Coll., St. Paul, 1977; JD, Hamline U., St. Paul, 1981. Bar: Minn. 1981. Assoc., ptnr. Eastlund, Solstad & Hutchinson, Ltd., Mpls., 1982-95; sole practitioner Cambridge, Minn., 1995-97; planned giving officer Bethel Coll. and Sem., St. Paul, 1997—. Editor notes and comments Hamline Law Rev., 1980-81. Mem. Minn. Women Lawyers. Methodist. Avocations: travel, golf, reading, volleyball. Home: 32299 Jackson Rd NE Cambridge MN 55008-6879 Office: Bethel Coll and Sem 3900 Bethel Dr Saint Paul MN 55112-6902

NORWOOD, SAMUEL WILKINS, III, financial consultant; b. Chgo., Apr. 6, 1941; s. Samuel Wilkins and Miriam Lois (Cary) N.; m. Julianne Parker Jones, Jun. 15, 1962 (div. Sept. 1981); children: Samuel Parker, Elizabeth Cary; m. Alice Ann Lynch, Jan. 13, 2000. Student, Vanderbilt U., 1959-61; BA, Tulane U., 1964; MBA, U. Chgo., 1965. Supr. spl. studies Allied Corp., N.Y.C., 1965-67; mgr. analysis and planning ITT Semiconductors Corp., West Palm Beach, Fla., 1967-69; dir. fin. planning Fuqua Industries, Atlanta, 1969-73, v.p. planning, 1976-81, v.p. corp devel., exec. asst. to chmn., 1981-89; pres., CEO, dir. Vista Resources, Inc., Atlanta, 1991-95; ptnr. Tatum CFO Ptnrs., LLP, Atlanta, 1997—; cons., Atlanta, 1973-76. Founder N. Atlanta Mediation Ctr., 1972. Mem. Planning Execs. Inst. (bd. dirs. 1979-85, chmn. 1984-85, pres. Atlanta chpt. 1976-77), The Planning Forum (bd. dirs. 1985-87), Atlanta Yacht Club (bd. govs. 1984-87, commodore 1989), Allatoona Canoe and Sailing Club (commodore 1988-89), Assn. for Corp. Growth, Soc. Internat. Bus. Fellows (bd. dirs. 1996-99, exec. com. bd. 1998-99). Avocations: competitive sailing, skiing, mountain climbing/hiking. Home: 42 Camden Rd NE Atlanta GA 30309-1508

NOSAKA, TETSUYA, molecular biologist; b. Toyonaka City, Osaka, Japan, Mar. 8, 1961; s. Masao and Eiko (Shimada) N.; m. Terumi Uchiyama, May 4, 1990; 1 child, Yoshiaki. MD, Mie U., Tsu, Japan, 1985; PhD, Kyoto (Japan) U., 1989. Asst. prof. Kyoto U., 1989-96; postdoctoral rsch. assoc. St. Jude Children's Rsch. Hosp., Memphis, 1994-96; asst. prof. U. Tokyo, 1996-99, assoc. prof. molecular biology, 1999—. Contbr. articles to profl. jours. Recipient Merit award Am. Soc. Hematology, 1995. Mem. Japanese Soc. Hematology, Japanese Molecular Biol. Soc., Japanese Cancer Assn. Avocation: taking photographs. Office: Inst Med Sci U Tokyo 4-6-1, Shirokanedai Minato-ku, Tokyo 108-8639, Japan

NOSKE, RAINER, writer, translator; b. Euskirchen, Germany, Oct. 29, 1965; s. Horst and Irmgard (Rieger) N. MA, Bonn U., 1992, PhD, 1996. Freelance writer, 1990—. Author: Philosophy of Language, 1996; contbr. articles to profl. jours. Mem. MENSA. Home: Kirchstrasse 8, 53879 Euskirchen Germany

NOSKO, MICHAEL GERRIK, neurosurgeon; b. Montreal, Feb. 24, 1957; came to U.S., 1991; s. Joseph John and June Elizabeth (Salter) N.; m. Deborah Anne Branciere, May 23, 1981; children: Douglas Joseph, Denise Elizabeth, Keith Michael. BS, McMaster U., 1978; MD, U. Toronto, 1982; PhD, U. Alberta, 1986. Intern U. Toronto (Ont., Can.) Gen. Hosp., 1982-83; resident U. Alberta Hosps., Edmonton, Can., 1986-91; assoc. prof. neurosurgery Robert Wood Johnson Med. Sch., New Brunswick, N.J., 1991—, chief, divsn. neurosurgery, 1991—; cons. and presenter in field. Contbr. articles to profl. jours., chpts. to books. Rsch. fellow Alberta Heritage Found., 1983-86; Chancellor' scholar McMaster U., 1975, Univ. scholar, 1976, Edwin Marwin Dalley Meml. scholar, 1977; recipient Acad. award Am. Acad. Neurol. Surgery, 1986. Fellow Am. Coll. Surgeons (Resident Rsch. award 1986), Royal Coll. Surgeons Can., Acad. Medicine N.J.; mem. AMA, Am. Assn. Neurol. Surgeons, Can. Neurosurg. Soc., N.J. Neurosurg. Soc., N.Y. Acad. Scis., Middlesex County Med. Soc., Soc. Critical Care Medicine, Congress Neurol. Surgeons, Alpha Omega Alpha. Anglican. Avocations: aircraft/helicopter pilot/instructor, fishing. Office: Divsn Neurosurgery 125 Paterson St Ste 2100 New Brunswick NJ 08901-1962

NOSRATIAN, FARSHAD JOSEPH, internist, cardiologist; b. Tehran, Iran, Sept. 1, 1956; came to U.S., 1979; s. Yahoude Nosratian and Violet (Pousadeh) N.; m. Faranak Daravi, June 24, 1990; children: Michelle, Blake, Brooke. Student, U. Tehran, 1974-78; MD, Albert Einstein Coll. Medicine, Bronx, N.Y., 1983. Diplomate Am. Bd. Internal Medicine, Am. Bd. Cardiovascular Diseases. Resident in internal medicine Harbor-UCLA Med. Ctr., Torrance, 1983-86; fellow in cardiology U. Calif., Irvine, 1986-89, asst. clin. prof., 1989—; clin. staff cardiologist UCLA, 1990—, Centinela Hosp. Med. Ctr., Inglewood, Calif., 1989—, Daniel Freeman Meml. Hosp., Inglewood, 1989—, Little Company of Mary Hosp., Torrance, 1990—, Santa Monica (Calif.) Med. Ctr., 1990—; clin. staff cardiologist Kennedy Med. Ctr., Hawthorne, Calif., 1989—, chmn. critical care com., 1992—. Contbr. chpt. to book, articles to profl. jours. Fellow Am. Coll. Cardiology; mem. Los Angeles County Med. Assn., Alpha Omega Alpha. Avocations: stamp collecting, coin collecting, skiing, tennis, soccer. Office: 4477 W 118th St Ste 301 Hawthorne CA 90250-2258

NOSS, ANDREW JAY, conservationist; b. Stoughton, Wis., Dec. 24, 1964; s. Philip Andrew and Cecilia Audelle (Arnold) N.; m. Lauren Inga Samuels, July 15, 1989; children: Wesley James, Jesse Philip. BA, Carleton Coll., 1986; MA, Johns Hopkins U., 1989; PhD, U. Fla., 1995. Rschr. World Bank, Washington, 1989-91; assoc. conservation scientist Wildlife Conservation Soc., Santa Cruz, Bolivia, 1996—. Contbr. articles to profl. jours. Democrat. Lutheran. Avocations: soccer, Lepidoptera. Home: 8540 S Wabash Ave Chicago IL 60619-5618 Office: WCS Internat Programs 185th St & Southern Blvd Bronx NY 10460

NOSSAL, GUSTAV JOSEPH VICTOR, medical research institute administrator, biologist, educator; b. Bad Ischl, Austria, June 4, 1931; m. Lyn B. Dunnicliff, Nov. 18, 1955; children: Katrina, Michael, Brigid, Stephen. BSc, U. Sydney, 1952, MBBS, 1954; PhD, U. Melbourne, 1960. Jr. and sr. resident officer Royal Prince Alfred Hosp., Sydney, 1955-56; rsch. fellow Walter and Eliza Hall Inst. Med. Rsch., Melbourne, 1957-59, dep. dir., 1961-65, dir., 1965-96; ptnr. Foursight Assoc. Pty., 1996—; asst. prof. dept. genetics Stanford U., 1959-61; prof. med. biology U. Melbourne, 1965—, prof. emeritus dept. pathology, 1996-99; chair WHO Global Programme for Vaccines and Immunization, 1992—; vis. scientist Pasteur Inst., 1968-69; vis. prof. U. Oreg., 1970, U. Calif., Berkeley, 1978; mem. adv. com. med. rsch. WHO, 1973-80, spl. cons., 1976; chmn. Western Pacific Regional Adv. Com. on Med. Rsch., 1976-80; mem. Australian Indsl. R&D Incentives Bd. Author: Antibodies and Immunity (Phi Beta Kappa award), 1968, rev. edit., 1978, Antigens, Lymphoid Cells and the Immune Response, 1971, Medical Science and Human Goals, 1975, Nature's Defences (1978 Boyer Lectures); contbr. numerous articles to profl. jours. Created knight, 1977; recipient Emil von Behring prize Phillipps U. Marburg, 1971, Rabbi Shai Shacknai Meml. prize U. Jerusalem, 1973; named Australian of Yr., 2000. Fellow Australian Acad. Sci. (treas. 1973-76), Royal Soc. (London), Nat. Acad. Scis. (fgn. assoc.); mem. Australian Sci. and Tech. Coun., Am. Assn. Immunologists, Transplantation Soc. (v.p. 1971-73), Am. Acad. Arts and Scis. (fgn.), Melbourne Club, Rosebud Country Club. Office: Royal Melbourne Hosp, W and E Hall Inst Med Rsch, Parkville Vic 3050, Australia*

NOSU, KIYOSHI, communication science researcher; b. Gifu, Japan, June 19, 1949; s. Shoichi and Tamae Nosu; m. Yuki Maruyama, Apr. 12, 1981. B Engring., Keio U., Tokyo, 1972; PhD, Tokyo U., 1977; MBA, Tsukuba U., Tokyo, 1993. Rsch. engr. NTT, Yososuko, Japan, 1977-95, mgr., 1995-97; mgr. NTT, Tokyo, 1997—. Guest editor IEEE Jour. Selected Areas Comm., 1990, IEEE Jour. Lightwave Tech., 1993, IEEE Comm. mag., 1994. Recipient Young Engr.'s award IEICE, 1980, Achievement award, 1991. Mem. Inst. Electronics, Info. and Comm. Engrs. Fax: 81-422-59-6364. E-mail: nosu.kiyosz@lab.ntt.co.jp. Home: 4-35-20-1-804 Sekimachikita, Tokyo

177-0051, Japan Office: NTT, 3-9-11 Midori-cho Musashino, Tokyo 180-8585, Japan

NOTARBARTOLO DI SCIARA, GIUSEPPE, marine biologist; b. Venice, Italy, Nov. 27, 1948; s. Marco and Emma (Vanzetti) Notarbartolo di Sciara; m. Flavia Pizzi, June 18, 1988; children: Marco, Bianca. Degree in Biol. Scis., U. Parma, Italy, 1974, Degree in Natural Scis. cum laude, 1976; PhD in Marine Biology, U. Calif., San Diego, 1985. Rsch. assoc. Hubbs Sea World Rsch. Inst., San Diego, 1977-80; coord. Centro Studi Cetacei, Italy, 1985-90; pres., dir. Tethys Rsch. Inst., Italy, 1986-97; pres. Inst. Centrale Ricerca Applicata al Mare, Rome, 1996—; cons. UN Environ. Program, Mediterranean Action Plan, 1996—; dir. marine mammal working group C.I.E.S.M., Monaco, 1992-95; mem. species survival commn. IUCN, 1991—; dep. chair Cetacean Spec. Group, IUCN, 1997—. Author: L'Orca, 1981 (1st prize Glaxo 1982), Guida dei Mammiferi Marini del Mediterraneo, 1994 (Premio Gambrinus 1994). Recipient Tridente d'oro Accademia Internat. Sci. Tech. Subacquee, Ustica, Italy, 1993. Fellow Linnean Soc. London; mem. European Cetacean Soc. (pres. 1993-97), Soc. for Marine Mammalogy (life). E-mail: disciara@tin.it. Office: ICRAM, Via Casalotti 300, I-00166 Rome Italy

NOTARIS, SOTIRIOS E., mathematics educator; b. Athens, Greece, July 3, 1960; s. Eftychios S. and Anastasia I. (Amarantidi) N.; m. Maria I. Arzimanoglou, Sept. 25, 1993; children: Anastasia, Ioannis. BSc in Math., U. Athens, 1983; MSc in Math., Purdue U., 1985, PhD, 1988. Tchg. asst. math. Purdue U., West Lafayette, Ind., 1983-85, rsch. asst. math., 1985-88; vis. asst. prof. math. Ind. U./Purdue U. at Indpls., 1988-90; asst. prof. math. U. Mo., Columbia, 1990-94, U. Athens, 1995—. Contbr. articles to profl. jours. Mem. Am. Math. Soc., Swiss Soc. Chronometry. Christian Orthodox. Avocations: watchmaking, travel, reading. Home: 103 Deinokratous St, 11521 Athens Greece Office: U Athens, 5 Stadiou St, 10562 Athens Greece

NOTARTE, ROMMEL DE GUZMAN, accountant; b. Baguio City, Benguet, Philippines, Oct. 17, 1969; s. Dominador Necesito and Lydia (de Guzman) N. Student, Nagasaki Wesleyan Jr. Coll., Japan, 1988; acctg., U. Baguio, 1991; MBA, Baguio Coll. Found., 1997. Savings acct. bookkeeper Allied Banking Corp., Baguio City, 1992-93, current acct. bookkeeper, 1993, distributing clk., 1993-94; gen. acctg. bookkeeper Allied Banking Corp., La Trinidad, Philippines, 1994-98; OOP trainee Allied Banking Corp., Makati City, Philippines, 1998-99; acct. Allied Banking Corp., Pasay City, 1999—. Mem. Bankers' Assn. Philippines. Roman Catholic. Avocations: writing poetry, singing, movies, dining out, cooking for special occasions. Home: Navy Base Compound, 2600 Baguio City Benguet, Philippines Office: Allied Banking Corp, 6754 Ayala Ave Cor Legaspi St, 1224 Makati City Philippines

NOTEBAERT, RICHARD C., telecommunications industry executive; b. 1947; married. With Wisconsin Bell, 1969-83; v.p. marketing and operations Ameritech, Chicago, 1983-86; pres. Ameritech Mobile Comm., 1986-89, Indiana Bell Telephone Co., 1989-92; pres. Ameritech Services, 1992-93, pres., COO, 1993-94; chmn., pres., CEO Ameritech Corp., Chicago, 1994-2000; ret., 2000. Office: Aon Corp 4951 Indiana Ave Lisle IL 60532-3818

NOTGHI, ALP, physician; b. Abadan, Iran, Sept. 19, 1950; s. Hamid and Ayten (Bayraksan) N.; m. LesleyMurray Henderson, 1986; children: Anne Ayten, Alp Aslan, Alp Aydin. MD, Shiraz U., Iran, 1975; MS in Nuclear Medicine, London U., 1992. House officer, sr. house officer, registrar Western Gen. Hosp., Edinburgh, Scotland, 1980-94; sr. registrar nuclear medicine City Hosp. NHS Trust, Birmingham, England, 1990-94, cons., 1994—. Fellow Royal Coll. Physicians Edinburgh, Royal Coll. Physicians London; mem. British Nuclear Medicine Soc. (coun. mem. 1999—). Avocations: photography, computers, music, motorcycle, sailing. Office: City Hosp Dept Nuclear Med, Dudley Rd, Birmingham B18 7QH, England

NÖTH, WINFRIED MAXIMILIAN, semiotics and linguistics educator, researcher; b. Gerolzhofen, Bavaria, Germany, Sept. 12, 1944; s. Ernst and Frida (Feldt) N.; children: Dorothea, Annette, Frithjof. PhD, Ruhr U., Bochum, Germany, 1971, Habilitation, 1976. Rsch. asst. Ruhr U., 1969-76, lectr., 1976-77; acting prof. Technische Hochschule, Aachen, Fed. Republic Germany, 1977-78; prof. semiotics and linguistics U. Kassel, Fed. Republic Germany, 1978—, dean Faculty Modern Langs., 1981-82, 95-96; dir. Rsch. Ctr. for Cultural Studies, 1999—; vis. prof. U. Wis., Green Bay, 1985-86, Cath. U., São Paulo, 1994—. Author: Strukuren des Happenings, 1972, Dynamik semiotischer Systeme, 1978, Literatursemiotische Analysen, 1980, Handbuch der Semiotik, 1985, 2000, Handbook of Semiotics, 1990, Origins of Semiosis, 1994, Semiotics of the Media, 1997, Imagem: Cognicao semiotica, midia, 1998, Medientheorie und die digitalalen Medien, 1998. Mem. Hochschulverband, Anglistentag, German Soc. for Semiotics (pres. 1999—), Internat. Semiotic Assn., Internat. Assn. Visual Semiotics (hon.). Lutheran. Home: Auf der Bünte 1, D-34130 Kassel Germany Office: U Kassel, Georg-Forster-Strasse 3, D 34109 Kassel Germany

NOTHOMB, SIMON-PIERRE, government official; b. Habay La Neuve, Luxembourg, Belgium, July 4, 1933; s. Pierre and Chislaine (Montens D'Oosterwyck) N.; m. Dominique D'Aspremont-Lynden, May 31, 1960; children: Philippe, Pierre, Eva. Diploma, Ecole Des Scis. Politique, Paris, 1960; BA, U. Louvain, France, 1963; Master degree, Paris VIII U., 1992. UN observer in Palestine UNTSO, 1955-57; advisor Belgian Ministry of Fgn. Trade and Tech. Assistance, 1962-65; dep. dir. UN Inst. for Rsch. and Tng., Geneva, 1972-75; dep. sec.-gen., dir.-gen. for culture Agy. for Cultural and Tech. Coop., Paris, 1976-82; from dir. to dir.-gen. Cath. U. Louvain, Belgium, 1965-72, 83-92; sec.-gen. Econ. and Social Com. of the European Cmtys., Brussels, 1992—; pres. Cercle Richelieu Senghor, Paris, 1979—; vice-chmn. Union of Belgians Living Abroad, sec.-gen. Europeans in the World, 1996—; founder, sec.-gen. First European Network of Thirty Univs., 1985—. Lt. col. Para-Commando, 1952-57, Korea and Palestine. Office: Europeans Through the World, 11 Rue d Egmont, B1000 Brussels Belgium

NOTO, HIROSHI, internist; b. Yokosuka, Japan, July 29, 1968; s. Yasushi and Keiko (Maruta) N.; m. Kaori Ueno, June 11, 1994; children: Kenji J., Mikio. MD, U. Tokyo, 1993. Diplomate Am. Bd. Internal Medicine. Med. res. Tokyo U. Hosp., 1993-94, Beth Israel Med. Ctr., N.Y.C., 1994-97; med. fellow Tokyo Kosei-Nenkin Hosp., 1997-98; med. fellow Tokyo U. Hosp., 1998-99, attending physician, 1999—. Contbr. articles to profl. jours. Mem. Am. Assn. Clin. Endocrinologists, Japanese Soc. Internal Medicine, Japanese Soc. Endocrinology. Avocation: alternative medicine. Home: 2-42-2-401 Futamatagawa, Asahi, Yokohama 241-0821, Japan Office: Tokyo U Hosp Dept Diabetes, 7-3-1 Hongo, Tokyo 113-0033, Japan

NOTO, LUCIO A., gas and oil industry executive; b. Apr. 24, 1939. BS in Physics, U. Notre Dame; MBA, Cornell U.; Woodrow Wilson Fell., U. Notre Dame; Bache Fell., Cornell U. With Mobil Corp., 1962—; pres. Mobil Saudi Arabia, 1981-85, chmn., 1985-86; v.p. planning and econs. Mobil Corp./Mobil Oil Corp. (now Exxon Mobil Corp.), 1986-88, CFO, 1989-93, pres., 1993—, chmn. bd., CEO, COO, 1994-99, vice chmn., 1999—. Internat. Business Machines Corp. (dir.), Amer. petroleum Inst. Public Policy Committee, The Business Council, The Council on Foreign Relations & Business Roundtable. Office: Exxon Mobil Corp 5959 Las Colinas Blvd Irving TX 75039-2298

NOTOWIDIGDO, PRI, executive search consultant; b. Klaten, Cen. Java, Indonesia, May 14, 1947; s. Moekarto and Martaniah (Brodjokumoro) N.; m. Rigianti Gandarum; 1 child, Nikita Karti. BA in Polit. Sci. with honors, Carleton U., Ottawa, Can., 1974, MA in Internat. Devel. Edn. programme officer Canadian U. Svc. overseas, Ottawa, 1975-77; planner/project mgr. Indonesia programme Can. Internat. Devel. Agy., Hull, Que., 1977-84; mgr. of human resources cons. group Price Waterhouse Mgmt. Cons., Jakarta, Indonesia, 1984-87; ptnr. in charge, human resources cons. KPMG Peat Marwick Mgmt. Cons., Jakarta, 1987-94; mng. ptnr. TASA Internat., Jakarta, 1994-96, AMROP Internat., Jakarta, 1996—; cross-cultural comm. cons. various orgns. in pub. and pvt. sectors in N. Am. and Asia Pacific, 1974—; session lectr. Indonesian Inst. for Mgmt. Devel., Jakarta, 1988—; commr. Gandarum Ganda Architects, Jakarta, 1990—. Contbr. articles to profl. jours. Mem. Am. Mgmt. Assn., Assn. Exec. Search Cons., Soc. for Intercultural Edn., Tng. and Rsch. Avocations: reading, music, tennis, swimming. Office: AMROP Internat, Bapindo Plz, Jl Jend Sudirman 54-55, Jakarta 12190, Indonesia

NOTT, DAVID OWEN, French educator; b. London, June 17, 1939; s. John Charles and Gladys Evelyn (Owen) N.; m. Elizabeth Jane Owen, Aug. 10, 1963 (divv. Apr. 1981); children: Susan Ella, Jonathan Owen; m. Françoise Jeanne Stephens, Nov. 5, 1981; children: Nicole Anne Stephens, Mark Ian Stephens. BA, Cambridge (Eng.) U., 1961, postgrad. cert. edn., 1962, MA, 1969. English asst. Lycée Champollion, Grenoble, France, 1962-63; tchr. French, Manchester (Eng.) Grammar Sch., 1963-72, head French dept., 1972-80; lectr. U. Wales Sch. Edn., Bangor, 1981-85; lectr. dept. French studies Lancaster (Eng.) U., 1985-93, sr. lectr., 1993—; mem. subject com. for modern fgn. langs. No. Exams. and Assessment Bd., Manchester, 1974-87, 90-96. Co-author: Actualités Françaises, Parts 1 and 2, 1971; author: Points de Départ, 1993, French Grammar Explained, 1998; editor: Language Teaching 16-19: A Handbook, 1977; co-editor: French 16-19, A New Perspective, 1981. Decorated Palmes Académiques, France, 1984. Mem. Assn. for Lang. Learning, Assn. for French Lang. Studies, Assn. Friends Roger Vailland, Soc. French Studies. Mem. Labour Party. Avocations: fellwalking, opera and theatre going, classical music, gardening, literature. Office: Lancaster U, Dept European Langs/Culture, Lancaster LA1 4YN, England

NOTT, JONATHAN FREEMAN, science educator, researcher; b. Sydney, Australia, June 19, 1959; s. John Freeman Nott and Lorna Aileen (Bourke) Congdon; m. Jeana Krista Harper, Dec. 9, 1989; children: Jemma Elizabeth, Benjamin Patrick, Samuel Joseph. BSc with Honors, U. Wollongong, Australia, 1980, MSc, 1984, Diploma Edn., 1982, PhD, 1991. Lectr. U. Wollongong, 1984-90, No. Territory U., Darwin, Australia, 1991-93, Australian Nat. U., Canberra, Australia, 1993-95; sr. lectr. James Cook U. North Queensland, Cairns, Australia, 1995—; scientific cons. No. Terr. U., 1991-93, Australian Nat. U., 1993-95, James Cook U., 1995—. Contbr. chpt. to book and articles to sci. jours. Advisor Old Emergency Svcs., 1996, Cairns City Coun., 1997—. Recipient Rsch. grant Australian Rsch. Coun., 1991—, James Cook U., 1996. Mem. Geol. Soc. Australia, N.S.W. Geographical Soc. Avocations: swimming, surfing, golf, tennis. Office: James Cook U, PO Box 6811, 4870 Cairns Australia

NÖTZEL, RICHARD, physicist, researcher; b. Munich, May 18, 1963; s. Wolfgang and Irene (Sichelschmidt) N. Diploma, Tech. U., Munich, 1989; D in Natural Scis., U. Stuttgart, 1992. Rschr. Max-Planck-Inst. fü Festkörperforschung, Stuttgart, 1990-92; postdoctoral fellow NTT Opto-Electronics Labs., Atsugi, Japan, 1993; assoc. prof. Rsch. Ctrl. for Interface Quantum Electronics Hokkaido U., Sapporo, Japan, 1994; rschr. Paul-Drude-Inst. fü Festkörperelektronik, Berlin, 1995-99; assoc. prof. COBRA Inter-Univ. Rsch. Inst. Eindhoven (Netherlands) U. Tech., 2000—. Contbr. articles, revs. to profl. jours.; patentee in field. With German Army, 1989. Recipient Otto Hahn medal Max Planck Soc., 1992, Rsch. award NTT Opto-Elec. Labs., 1993, Acad. award Berlin-Brandenburg Acad. Sci., 1996. Office: COBA Inter-Univ Rsch Inst, Eindhoven Tech Postbus 513, 5600 MB Eindhoven Netherlands

NOUGARET, ROGER, archivist; b. Thiers, France, Aug. 14, 1957; m. Christine Chapalain; children: Pierre, Guillaume, Philippe. Lic. ih History, U. Toulouse, France, 1978; degree in archive-paleography, Nat. Sch. Chartes, Paris, 1982. Cert. curator of nat. heritage. Dep. archivist Archives de Loire-Atlantique, Nantes, France, 1982-91; head archivist Crédit Lyonnais, Paris, 1991—. Author: Hôpitaux, le'Proseries et Bodomies de Rodez, 1340-1676, 1986 (1st prize French Soc. Hospital History), Kléber: Mémoires Politiques et Militaires, 1793-1794, 1989; editor (collection) Archives Économiques du Crédit Lyonnais, 1996-99. Mem. French Assn. Archivists, European Assn. Banking History (mem. acad. adv. coun. 1997—), Internat. Coun. Archives (mem. steering com. sect. bus. and labour archives). E-mail: roger.nougaret@creditlyonnais.fr. Home: 36 Blvd Voltaire, 75011 Paris France Office: Archives Hist Credit Lyon, 6 Rue de Hanovre, 75002 Paris France

NOUR, BAKR M., surgeon, health facility administrator; s. Mohamed Mahmoud Nour and Fatheya A. Hussein; m. Sohair A. Kheir, Dec. 23, 1976; children: May, Mohamed. MD, U. Alexandria, 1974, M in Surgery, 1978, D in Surgery, 1986. Diplomate Bd. Gen. Surgery, Egypt. Intern U. Alexandria, Egypt, 1975-76, resident in gen. & pediatric surgery, 1976-79, instr. surgery, 1979, asst. lectr. pediatric surgery, 1979-82, sr. asst. lectr. pediatric surgery, 1984-86, asst. prof. pediatric surgery, 1987-89; clin./rsch. fellow, vis. asst. prof. surgery dept. pediatric surgery U. Pitts. Med. Ctr., Children's Hosp. Pitts., 1982-84, 90; clin. fellow U. Pitts. Med. Ctr., Transplantation Inst., 1990-92, asst. prof. surgery, 1992-94; chief pediatric liver transplantation, adult liver transplant surgeon Okla. Transplantation Inst., Bapt. Med. Ctr., Oklahoma City, 1994-97; chief abdominal transplantation Oklahoma Transplantation Inst., Integris Bapt. Med. Ctr., Oklahoma City, 1997-98, dir. abdominal organ transplant divsn., 1998-99, interim dir., 1999—; past mem. staff Presbyn. U. Hosp. Pitts., Montefiore Hosp., Pitts.; mem. human rights com. Children's Hosp. Pitts., 1993-94; mem. libr. com. Bapt. Med. Ctr. Okla. Contbr. articles to profl. jours. Founding mem. Innocent Childhood Benevolent Charity Assn., Alexandria; mem Islamic Charity Assn. Recipient World Cmty. award Results, 1998. Mem. AMA, ACS, Arab Am. Med. Assn., Am. Coll. Physician Execs., Am. Assn. Study of Liver Disease, Am. Soc. Transplant Surgeons, Egyptian Physician's Syndicate, Egyptian Med. Assn., Egyptian Soc. Surgeons, Egyptian Assn. Pediatric Surgeons, Alexandria Med. Assn., Brit. Assn. Pediatric Surgeons, Okla. State Med. Assn., Okla. County Med. Soc., Internat. Coll. Surgeons, Internat. Gastro-Surg. Club, Internat. Liver Transplantation Soc., Tex. Transplant Soc., Soc. Surgery Alimentary Tract, Alexandria Sporting Club, Oklahoma City Golf and Country Club. Moslem. Achievements include research in cell model to study bacterial translocation in transplanted small bowel, FK506 as immunosuppressive agent, small bowel transplantation, causes of anemia in transplant patients, Alpha interferon therapy, for viral hepatitis. E-mail: NourBM@Integris-Health.com. Home: 11511 Red Rock Rd Oklahoma City OK 73120-5318 Office: Okla Transplantation Inst Nazih Zuhdi 3300 NW Expressway Oklahoma City OK 73112-4418

NOUSIA-ARVANITAKIS, SANDA, pediatrician; b. Thessaloniki, Greece, Jan. 27, 1939; d. Thomas and Efterpi (Giannouta) Nousia; m. Constantine Arvanitakis, June 3, 1967; 1 child, Marianna. Diploma, Anatolia Coll., 1958; MD, U. Thessaloniki, Greece, 1964; diploma in child health. Resident NHS, England, 1967-70, U. Wis., 1970-73; asst. prof. pediatrics U. Kans., 1973-77, assoc. prof. pediatrics, 1977-78; asst. prof. pediatrics U. Thessaloniki, Greece, 1986-91, assoc. prof., 1991—; dir. dept. pediatrics Kentrikon Hosp., Thessaloniki, 1986-91. Contbr. articles on pediatric gastroenterology, nutrition, and cystic fibrosis to profl. jours., chpts. to books; mem. editl. bd. Annals of Gastroenterology. Cons. Assn. Parents with Children with Cystic Fibrosis, 1980—. U. Wis. fellow, 1970-73. Fellow Am. Acad. Pediatrics, European Bd. Gastroenterology; mem. Am. Gastroenterological Assn., Hellenic Soc. Gastroenterology, Hellenic Soc. Pediatrics, Soc. Pediatric Rsch., European Soc. Pediatric Gastroenterology Nutrition (pres. 30th meeting 1997), N.Am. Soc. Pediatric Gastroenterology Nutrition, European Soc. Cystic Fibrosis (coun. mem.). Avocations: gardening, swimming, music, literature. Home: PO Box 322, 57001 Thermi Greece Office: U Thessaloniki AHEPA Gen Hosp, 4th Dept Pediatrics, 54006 Thessaloniki Greece

NOUTSOS, PANAGIOTIS CHRISTOS, philosophy educator; b. Ioannina, Epirus, Greece, Aug. 8, 1948; s. Christos Charalampus and Phedra Christos (Grestas) N.; m. Maria Emmanuel Hatzigiakoumi, Mar. 26, 1950. Grad., Philos. Faculty, U. Ioannina, Greece, Philosophische Fakultät, FU, Berlin. Lectr. U. Ioannina, Greece, 1980-83, assoc. prof., 1983-88, prof., 1988—; vice chancellor U. Ioannina, 1991-94. Author: Utopia and History, 1979, Le Marxisme Européen, 1989, The Socialist Thought in Greece 1990-94, Sozialpolitische Theorie, 1994, Greek-Australia, 1996, Language and Power, 1998, A Guide for Research Methodology, 1998, Database, 2000. Home: N Zerva 11, Ioannina 45332, Greece Office: U Ioannina, 45110 Ioannina Greece

NOVAES, LUIZA HELENA VINHOLES SIQUEIRA, pediatrician, educator; b. Pelotas, Brazil, Aug. 5, 1957; d. Sergio Vieira and Zaira Lessa (Vinholes) Siqueira; m. Luis Eduardo Silveira da Mota Novaes, Jan. 16, 1982. MD, Cath U Pelotas, Brazil, 1981, MS, 1996; postgrad., U. Aveiro, Portugal. Pediatrician Hosp. Univ. Pelotas, 1985—; tchr. medicine Cath. U. Pelotas, 1988—; pediatrician U. Fed. de Pelotas, 1997—; pvt. clinic pediatrician, Pelotas, 1985—; mental health rschr. Cath. U. Pelotas, 1994—; tech. mgr. therapeutic recreation rm. Hosp. Univ. Pelotas, 1995—. Author: Neonatologia-notinas hospitalares, 1993, Brincar é Saúde-O alívio do estresse na crianca hospitalizada, 1998; contbr. articles to profl. jours. Mem. Soc. Brasileira Pediatria, Soc. Medicina Pelotas, Conselho Regional Medicina Rio Grande Sul. Roman Catholic. Avocations: movies, music, books, photography, travel. Home: Apt 203, Gonçalves Chaves 3657, 96015560 Pelotas Brazil Office: Univ Aveiro Dept Edn Scis, Bamfars de Santiago, 3810-193 Aveiro Brazil

NOVAK, ALEXEJ, speech pathologist; b. Dritec, Czech Republic, Dec. 1, 1930; m. Eva Horova, May 10, 1955; 1 child, Martin. MD, Charles U., Prague, 1956. Asst. ENT dept. Usti n Orlici, 1956-60, asst. phoniatr., 1960-83; asst. prof. phoniatric dept. Charles U., 1983-87, prof., dir. phoniatric dept., 1987-97. Contbr. numerous articles to profl. jours. and publs. in field of phoniatry. Pres. Union of European Phoniatricians, 1991-93, Congress of IALP, 1989. Recipient Hermann Gutzmann medal, 1985. Mem. German Assn. for Phoniatrics and Pedaudiology, Austrian Assn. for Phoniatrics, Logopedics and Pedaudiology. Avocations: music, painting. E-mail: vydfon@mbox.vol.cz. Home: Bouckova 1746, 162 00 Praha 6 Czech Republic

NOVAK, ANDREAS ROBERT, acoustic consultant, educator; b. Stockholm, Nov. 25, 1965. MSc, Royal Inst. Tech., Stockholm, 1989, Lic. of Engring., 1992, PhD, 1995. Rschr., tchr. Royal Inst. Tech., 1989-95; acoustic cons. Ingemasson Tech. AB, Stockholm, 1996—. Contbr. articles to profl. jours. Recipient grant Swedish Coun. Bldg. Rsch., 1989, 92, Devel. Fund of Swedish Constrn. Industry, 1989. Mem. Civil Engring. Soc., Swedish Acoustical Soc., Swedish Bldg. Soc. Avocations: pilot, racing driver, scuba diving. Office: Ingemansson Tech AB, Instrumentvagen 31 Bx 47321, S-10074 Stockholm Sweden

NOVAK, DARWIN ALBERT, JR., chemical engineer, consultant; b. Quincy, Ill., Nov. 25, 1935; s. Darwin Albert and Mildred Luisa (Schuermann) N.; m. Carol Joan Stephany, Apr. 22, 1961; children: Robert Brian, Linda Susan. B Chem. Engring., Cornell U., 1958; MS, Washington U., St. Louis, 1966, DSc, 1973. Registered profl. engr., Mo. Pilot plant engr. Mallinckrodt, St. Louis, 1958-60; rsch. engr. Monsanto Co., St. Louis, 1960-64; with tech. svc. dept. Monsanto Co., Brussels, 1964-66; engring. specialist Monsanto Co., St. Louis, 1966-81, mgr. engring., 1981-87; dir. engring. Henkel, Ambler, Pa., 1987-92; consulting engr. BE&K DE, Newark, Del., 1992-95; mgr. engring. Cabot Performance Materials, Boyertown, Pa., 1995-96, sr. technologist, 1997-99; cons. Horsham, Pa., 1999—; affiliate prof. Washington U., 1984-87; mem. assessment bd. NAE, Gaithersburg, Md., 1981-86. Patentee for detergent process, oil recovery. Fellow AIChE (dir., chmn. mgmt. div. 1986-89); mem. NSPE, Am. Chem. Soc. Republican. Avocations: photography, personal computing. Home and Office: 27 Timber Rd Horsham PA 19044-3810

NOVAK, ERICH, mathematician, educator; b. Nürnberg, Fed. Republic Germany, Jan. 9, 1953; s. Heinrich and Esther (Braun) N. Diploma in math., U. Erlangen, Fed. Republic Germany, 1979, D of Math., 1983, habilitation, 1987. Asst. prof. math. U. Erlangen, 1983-92; vos. Columbia U., N.Y.C., 1985, 88, 89, 92, U. Calif., Berkeley, 1993, Internat. Computer Sci. Inst., 1993; lectr. Beijing Normal U., 1990. Author: Deterministic and Stochastic Error Bounds in Numerical Analysis, 1988; contbr. articles to profl. jours. Recipient Emmy Noether prize 1991, First prize for achievement in info.-based complexity Jour. of Complexity, 1999; Heisenberg Rsch. scholar 1991. Mem. Am. Math. Soc., Deutsche Mathematiker-Vereinigung, Soc. Ind. Applied Math. Home: Am Messehaus 14, 90489 Nürmberg Germany Office: U Erlangen Dept Math, Bismarck Str 1 1/2, 91054 Erlangen Germany

NOVAK, GREGORY, marketing professional; b. Johnstown, Pa., Oct. 19, 1949; s. Eugene F. and Joan (Tross) N.; m. Naomi Sosia Wall; children: Rebecca, Jeffrey, Jacqueline. BA, U. Vt., 1971. Project dir. Dun & Bradstreet, N.Y.C., 1973-74; sr. analyst Colgate Palmolive, N.Y.C., 1974-76; mgr. brand research R.J. Reynolds, Winston-Salem, N.C., 1976-77, mgr. group new brand rsch., 1977-80, dir. new bus., 1980-81, dir. group mktg., 1981-84; nat. dir. mktg. Deloitte Haskins & Sells, N.Y.C., 1984-90; pres. Novak Mktg. Inc., 1990—. Mem. Princeton Club N.Y. Office: Novak Mktg Inc 237 Park Ave Fl 21 New York NY 10017-3140

NOVAK, HELMUT FRANZ, neurologist; b. Vienna, Austria, May 16, 1961; s. Franz and Elisabeth Anna (Schmid) N. MD, U. Vienna, 1986; diploma, Austrian Soc. for Acupuncture, 1987. Vol. Health Care Project City of Vienna, 1986-89; guest doctor 2 Surg. DTP U. Hosp., Vienna, 1986; nursing doctor Rudolph's Hosp., Vienna, 1987; mil. asst. doctor Vienna Mil. Hosp., 1987-88; intern Lorenz-Böhler Trauma Ctr., Vienna, 1988-89; resident Psychiat. Hosp., Vienna, 1989-90; intern Glanzing Children's Hosp., Vienna, 1990; intern med. dept. Elisabeth's Hosp., Vienna, 1990-91; intern Semmelweis Women's Hosp., Vienna, 1991; resident neurol. dept. Salzburg County Neuro Hosp., 1991-98; attending physician neuro ICU dept. neurology Salzburg Christian Doppler Hosp., 1998—; trainer Vienna Sports H.S., 1988. Mem. Austrian Doctor's Assn., Diving and Hyperbaric Medicine Austrian Soc., Undersea and Hyperbaric Medicine Soc., Neurology and Psychiatry Austrian Soc., Acupuncture and Auriculotherapy Austrian Soc., Manual Medicine Austrian Doctor's Soc. Avocations: diving, underwater rugby, traveling. Office: Neuro Intensive Care, Ignaz Harrer Str 79, A-5020 Salzburg Austria

NOVAK, IVAN, pediatrician, consultant; b. Prague, Czech Republic, Jan. 9, 1944; s. Josef and Eva (Roubickova) N.; m. Jitka Lehovcova Panznerova, Oct. 25, 1968 (div. Dec. 1973); 1 child, Ondrej; m. Marie Vinklarkova, Jan. 24, 1974. Degree in pediatrics, Charles U., Prague, 1967, candidate of scis., 1984. Cert. 2d degree of postgrad. diploma in pediats. Bd. Exam. House officer Dist. Hosp., Slany, Czech Republic, 1967-68; sr. house officer Pediat. Dept., Prague, 1969-74; sr. lectr. Charles U., Prague, 1974-76, Postgrad. Med. Sch., Prague, 1977-84; head of dept. Thomayer Hosp., Prague, 1985-95, Postgrad. Med. Sch., Prague, 1996—; cons. pediatrician Ministry of Health, Prague, 1995; chmn. pediat. com. Czech Med. Chamber, Prague, 1995. Author: Handbook of Emergency Pediatrics, 2d edit., 1996; contbr. articles to profl. jours. Capt. Czech Army Med. Svc., 1967-68. Rsch. grantee Leverhulme Trust, London, 1988, Ministry Health, Prague, 1993. Mem. Czech Pediat. Soc. (com. mem.). Avocations: soccer, cocker spaniel. Home: Kostelec u Krizku 160, 251 68 Prague Czech Republic Office: Thomayer Tchg Hosp, Videnska 800, 140 59 Prague 4, Czech Republic

NOVAK, JOSEPH ANTHONY, lawyer; b. Detroit; s. Thomas Paul and Mary Cecilia N. AA, Macomb C.C., Warren, Mich., 1984; BA, Oakland U., 1986; JD, Mich. State U., 1991; M Libr. and Info. Sci., Wayne State U., 1998. Intern Wayne County Pub. Defender's Office, Detroit, 1986; intern Office of Jud. Assistance 3d Jud. Ct. Mich., Detroit, 1993, law clk. to Hon. Diane M. Hathaway, intern, 1996; law libr. St. Louis Correctional Facility, 2000—. Vol., Vol. Income Tax Assistance Program, Detroit, 1995—. Recipient Outstanding Vol. Volunteer Income Tax Assistance Program, 1995, 96, 98, 99, 2000, The Spirit of Am. Is In the Heart of Its Volunteers IRS, 1995, 96, 97, 99. Mem. Am. Assn. Law Librs., Spl. Librs. Assn., Acctg. Aid Soc. Democrat. Roman Catholic. Avocations: coin and stamp collecting, water skiing, walking. Home: 1820 S Crawford St Apt C3 Mount Pleasant MI 48858-6150

NOVAK, KAREL, entomologist; b. Roudnice, Czech Republic, Dec. 8, 1925; s. Karel and Marie (Petrackova) N.; m. Vera Brukova, Aug. 5, 1953. RNDr, Charles U., 1950, PhD, 1956. Scientific asst. Charles U., Prague, Czech Republic, 1950-54; researcher Inst. Entomology Czech Acad. Sci., Prague, 1954-90; scientific sec. Inst. Entomology Czech. Acad. Sci., 1954-81, deputy dir., 1981-90. Author: Cockchafers and their Control, 1953, Method of Collecting and Mounting Insects, 1968; contbr. articles to profl. jours. Recipient Silver medal of Gregor Mendel Czech Acad. Sci., 1985. Mem. Czech Entomological Soc., Czech Zool. Soc. (scientific sec. 1955-80). Home: Smeralova 15/390, 170 00 Prague Czech Republic Office: Inst Entomology, Branisovska 31, 370 05 Ceske Budejovice Czech Republic

NOVAK, LESLIE HOWARD, lawyer; b. Chgo., May 10, 1944; s. Sidney and Sadie (Jensky) N.; m. Nancy Ruth Sherman, July 2, 1967; children: Heidi Ellen, Shani Beth. BS in Bus. with high distinction, U. Minn., 1966, JD cum laude, 1969. Bar: Minn. 1970, U.S. Dist. Ct. Minn. 1970, U.S. Ct. Appeals (8th cir.) 1974, U.S. Supreme Ct. 1995. Assoc. Robins, Kaplan, Miller & Ciresi, Mpls., 1969-77, ptnr., 1977-92; ptnr. Mackall, Crounse & Moore, PLC., Mpls., 1992—, mng. ptnr., 1997-99. Bd. dirs. Am. Israel C. of C. and Industry of Minn., Mpls., 1981—, founding pres., 1981-91; founding sec., founding bd. dirs. Assn. N.Am.-Israel Chambers Commerce, Inc., 1993—; bd. dirs. United Jewish Fund and Coun., St. Paul, 1986—; founding dir. Illusion Theater and Sch.; past bd. dirs., past pres. Jewish Family Svc. of St. Paul; past bd. dirs. Mt. Zion Temple. Mem. Hillcrest Country Club, Phi Delta Phi, Beta Gamma Sigma. Avocations: biking, golf, tennis, skiing. Office: Mackall Crounse & Moore PLC 1400 AT&T Tower 901 Marquette Ave Minneapolis MN 55402-3205

NOVAK, MARK, lawyer; b. Buffalo, N.Y., Jan. 28, 1952; s. Eugene Francis and Joan (Tross) N.; m. Charlene Mary Ingoglia, Sept. 2, 1972; children: Jason Charles, Jennifer Rose. BA, U. Rochester, 1974; JD, Loyola U., Chgo., 1977. Bar: Ill. 1977, U.S. Dist. Ct. (no. dist.) Ill. 1977, U.S. Ct. Appeals (7th cir.) 1978. Assoc. Anesi, Ozmon & Lewin, Ltd., Chgo., 1977-83; ptnr. Anesi, Ozmon, Rodin, Novak & Kohen, Ltd., Chgo., 1983—. Fundraiser Christmas is for Kids Charity, Chgo., 1992—. Mem. ATLA (product liability sect. 1985—), ABA, Ill. Trial Lawyers Assn., Trial Lawyers for Pub. Justice, Chgo. Bar Assn. (jud. evaluation com. 1995—). Avocations: painting, gardening, traveling. Home: 1212 N Lake Shore Dr Chicago IL 60610-2371 Office: Anesi Ozmon Rodin Novak & Kohen Ltd 161 N Clark St Fl 21 Chicago IL 60601-3206

NOVAK, MICHAEL (JOHN), religion educator, author, editor; b. Johnstown, Pa., Sept. 9, 1933; s. Michael John and Irene (Sakmar) N.; m. Karen Ruth Laub, June 29, 1963; children: Richard, Tanya, Jana. AB summa cum laude, Stonehill Coll., North Easton, Mass., 1956; BT cum laude, Gregorian U., Rome, 1958; MA, Harvard U., 1966; LLD, Keuka (N.Y.) Coll., 1970, Stonehill Coll., Mass., 1977, Thomas More Coll., 1992; LHD, Davis and Elkins (W.Va.) Coll., 1971, LeMoyne (N.Y.) Coll., 1976, Sacred Heart U., 1977, Muhlenberg Coll., 1979, D'Youville Coll., 1981, Boston U., 1981, New Eng. Coll., 1983, Rivier Coll., 1984, Marquette U., 1987; D en Ciencias Sociales, U. Francisco Marroquin, Guatemala, 1993; Jacksonville U., 1994; HHD, Saint Xavier U., 1995. Teaching fellow Harvard U., 1961-63; asst. prof. Stanford U., 1965-68; assoc. prof. philosophy and religious studies State U. N.Y., Old Westbury, 1968-71; assoc. dir. humanities Rockefeller Found., N.Y.C., 1973-75; provost Disciplines Coll., SUNY, Old Westbury, 1969-71; vis. prof. Jan. session Carleton Coll., Northfield, Minn., 1970, Immaculate Heart Coll., Hollywood, Calif., 1971; vis. prof. U. Calif., Santa Barbara, 1972, Riverside, 1975; Ledden-Watson disting. prof. religion Syracuse U., 1977-79; journalist nat. elections Newsday, 1972; writer in residence The Washington Star, 1976, syndicated columnist, 1976-80, 84-89; columnist Forbes Mag., 1989—; George Frederick Jewett chair pub. policy research Am. Enterprise Inst., Washington, 1983—, dir. social and polit. studies, 1987—; chmn. working seminar on family and Am. welfare policy Ind., 1986; faculty U. Notre Dame, Ind., 1986-87, vis. W. Harold and Martha Welch Prof. Am. Studies, 1987, 88; judge Nat. Book awards, 1971, DuPont Broadcast Journalism awards, 1971-80; speechwriter nat. polit. campaigns, 1970, 72; mem. Bd. Internat. Broadcasting, 1983—; mem. Presdl. Task Force Project Econ. Justice, 1985-87, Council Scholars Library of Congress, 1986—; mem. monitoring panel UNESCO, 1984; vice chmn. Lay Commn. Cath. Social Teaching and U.S. Economy, 1984-86; U.S. Ambassador to Experts Meeting on Human Contacts of the Conf. On Security and Cooperation in Europe, Bern, Switzerland, 1986; U.S. rep. to human rights commn. UN, 1981-83; hon. prof. U. Cuyo, Argentina, 1992. Author: novel The Tiber was Silver, 1961, A New Generation, 1964, The Experience of Marriage, 1964, The Open Church, 1964, Belief and Unbelief, 1965, 3d edit., 1994, A Time to Build, 1967, A Theology for Radical Politics, 1969, American Philosophy and the Future, 1968, Story in Politics, 1970, (with Brown and Herschel) Vietnam: Crisis of Conscience, 1967, Naked I Leave, 1970; Politics: Realism & Imagination, 1971, Ascent of the Mountain, Flight of the Dove, 1971, A Book of Elements, 1972, All the Catholic People, 1971, novel Naked I Leave, 1970, The Experience of Nothingness, 1970, The Rise of the Unmeltable Ethnics, 1972, Choosing Our King, 1974, The Joy of Sports, 1976, The Guns of Lattimer, 1978, The American Vision, 1978, Rethinking Human Rights I and II, 1981, 82, The Spirit of Democratic Capitalism, 1982, Confession of a Catholic, 1983, Moral Clarity in the Nuclear Age, 1983, Freedom with Justice, 1984, Human Rights and the New Realism, 1986, Will It Liberate? Questions About Liberation Theology, 1986, Character and Crime, 1986, The New Consensus on Family and Welfare, 1987, Taking Glasnost Seriously: Toward an Open Soviet Union, 1988, Free Persons and the Common Good, 1989, This Hemisphere of Liberty, 1990, The Spirit of Democratic Capitalism, 1991 (Anthony Fisher award 1992), Choosing Presidents, 1992, The Catholic Ethic and the Spirit of Capitalism, 1993, Awakening from Nihilism, Joy of Sports, rev. 1995; Belief and Unbelief, rev, 1995; Business as a Calling, 1996, The Fire of Invention, 1997, with daughter Jana Novak, Tell Me Why: A Father Answers His Daughter's Questions About God, 1998, On Cultivating Liberty, 1999, To Empower People, anniv. ed, 1995, The Free Society Render ed, 2000; numerous other articles and books transl. into all maj. langs.; assoc. editor Commonweal mag., 1966-69; contbg. editor Christian Century, 1967-80, Christianity and Crisis, 1968-76, Jour. Ecumenical Studies, 1967—, This World, 1982-89, First Things, 1990—; religion editor Nat. Rev., 1979-86; founder, pub. Crisis, 1982—, editor-in-chief, 1993-95. Decorated K.M.G., Soverign Mil. Order of Malta, 1987, Order of the Byzantine Cross Republic of Slovakia, 1996; Kent fellow, 1961—; fellow Hastings Inst., 1970-76; named Most Influential Prof. Sr. Class Stanford U., 1967, 68; Man of Yr. Johnstown, Pa., 1978; recipient Faith and Freedom award Religious Heritage Am., 1978, HIAS Liberty award, 1981, Friend of Freedom award, 1981; Newman Alumni award CCNY, 1984; George Washington Honor medal, 1984; award of Excellence, Religion in Media, 8th annual Angel Awards, 1985, Ellis Island Honor medal, 1986, Anthony Fisher award, 1992, Wilhelm Weber Prize, 1993, One Million Dollar Templeton prize for progress in religion, 1994, Internat. prize Inst. World Capitalism, 1994, Award for the Arts City of Bratislava, 1998, Gold Medal Slovak Acad. Scis., 2000; diploma as vis. prof. U. Francisco Marroquin, 1985; named acad. corr. mem. from U.S., Argentina Nat. Acad. Scis., Morals & Politics, 1985, others. Mem. Soc. Religion in Higher Edn. (ctrl. com. 1970-73), Am. Acad. Religion (prog. dir. 1968-72), Coun. Fgn. Rels., Cath. Theol. Soc., Soc. Christian Ethics, Inst. Religion and Democracy (dir. 1981—), Nat. Ctr. Urban and Ethnic Affairs (dir. 1982-86). Office: Am Enterprise Inst 1150 17th St NW Washington DC 20036-4603

NOVÁK, MILAN, mineralologist, educator; b. Vyskov, Czechoslovakia, Oct. 19, 1952; s. František and Zdenka (Čížková) N.; m. Drahomíra Janečková, May 26, 1979; children: Jirí, Jana. BS, U. J.E. Purkyně, Brno, Czechoslovakia, 1977, M of Natural Scis., 1979; PhD, Charles U., Prague, Czechoslovakia, 1988. Rsch. assoc. dept. mineralogy Moravian Mus., Brno, 1977-93, head. dept. mineralogy, 1994-99, dir. Inst. Earth Scis., 1997-99; head dept. mineralogy, petrology and geochemistry Masaryk U., Brno, 1999—; sr. lectr. Masaryk U., Brno, 1996-99. Contbr. articles to profl. jours. Postdoctoral fellow U. Man., Winnipeg, Can., 1991-93. Mem. Soc. Mineral Mus. Profls. E-mail: mnovak@sci.muni.cz. Home: Dukelská 9, 682 01 Vyskov Moravia, Czech Republic Office: Masaryk U/Dept Mineralogy, Kotlarska 2, 611 37 Brno Czech Republic

NOVÁK, RUDOLF, physics educator, consultant; b. Prague, Czech Republic, Apr. 11, 1942; s. Rudolf B. and Miluše (Rozsypalová) N.; m. Jindřiška Šípová, Nov. 14, 1964 (div. 1976); m. Danuše Trková, May 19, 1977; 1 child, Ludmila. MS, Czech Tech. U., Prague, 1966, Charles U., Prague, 1972; PhD, Charles U., Prague, 1975, Czech Tech. U., Prague, 1981. Asst. prof. applied physics Czech Tech. U., 1966-87, assoc. prof. applied physics, 1987—; cons. Surtec Ltd., Prague, 1993—; dir. Pragomef Ltd., Prague, 1992-94. Co-author: Physical Measurements, 1984 (Czech Tech. U. Rector's award 1985). Sgt. Czechoslovak Army, 1967-68, Milovice. Mem. Wolfson Coll., Oxford. Avocation: collecting and restoring ancient clocks. Office: Czech Tech U Dept Physics, K202 Technicka 4, 16607 Prague Czech Republic

NOVÁK, VILÉM, mathematician, educator; b. Bruntál, Czechoslovakia, June 21, 1951; s. Vilém and Nina (Krasilová) N.; m. Irina Perfilieva; children: David, Martin. MSc, Mining U., Ostrava, Czechoslovakia, 1975, Charles U., Prague, Czechoslovakia, 1982; PhD, Charles U., Prague, Czechoslovakia, 1988; DSc, Polish Acad. Scis., Warsaw, 1995. Advance designer Automation of Mgmt., Ostrava, 1975-84; researcher Mining Inst., Czechoslovak Acad. Scis., Ostrava, 1984-95; prof., sr. scientist, dir. inst. U. Ostrava, Olomouc, Czech Republic, 1995—; prof. Masaryk U., Brno, Czech Republic, 2000; educator Mining U., 1978-80. Author: Fuzzy Sets and Their Applications, 1986, rev. edit., 1989 (Czechoslovakian Literal Fund award 1987), The Alternative Mathematical Model of Linguistic Semantics and Pragmatics, 1992, (with I. Perfilieva, J. Močkoř) Mathematical Principles of Fuzzy Logic, 1999; contbr. over 100 articles to profl. jours. Mem. Soc. Czechoslovak Mathematicians and Physicists, Internat. Fuzzy Systems Assn. Avocation: music. Office: U Ostrava Inst Rsch Fuz Mdl, 30 dubna 22, Ostrava 1, Czech Republic

NOVAK-LYSSAND, RANDI RUTH, engineer, computer scientist; b. Chgo., July 10, 1954; d. Bernard Richard and Shirley Ann (Fiedorczyk) Novak; children: Rona Rachel, Bonnie Shaina. BS in Math., U. Calif., Santa Cruz, 1976, BA in Econs. with honors, 1976; postgrad., U. Rochester, 1976-78. Rsch. asst. U. Calif., Santa Cruz, 1974-76; Russian translator U. Chgo., 1977-78; intern economist Congl. Budget Office, Washington, 1977; engr. Lockheed MSC, Sunnyvale, Calif., 1978-82; software engr. contractor Silicon Valley Systems, Belmont, Calif., 1982, 83-84, Data Encore (subs. of Verbatim), Sunnyvale, 1982-83; systems programmer CompuPro/Viasyn Corp., Hayward, Calif., 1984-87; mem. tech. staff Network Equipment Techs., Redwood City, Calif., 1987-89; v.p. engring., founder Segue Setups, Burlingame, Calif., 1989-92, ptnr., 1992—; sr. mem. tech. staff NEC Am., San Jose, Calif., 1992-94; sr. systems engr. Hitachi Computer Products, Santa Clara, Calif., 1994-96; prin. engr. Rapid-City Comms./Bay Networks/Nortel Networks, Santa Clara, Calif., 1996—. Fellow Dept. Treasury, 1974-76, NSF, 1977-78, U. Rochester, Rush Rhees fellow. Mem. IEEE Computer Soc., Am. Math. Assn., Computer Profls. for Social Responsibility, Soc. for Computing and Info. Processing, Internat. Platform Assn., Calif. Scholarship Fedn. (life). Avocations: piano, oboe, music, photography, mathematics. Home: 4166 School St Pleasanton CA 94566-6218

NOVA'KOVA', OLGA, chemist, researcher; b. Brno, Czech Republic, Sept. 25, 1960; d. Karel and Jiřina Očkova'. PhD, Inst. Chem. Tech., Prague, Czech Republic, 1984. Rschr. LACHEMA, Brno, 1984-86; rsch. scientist State Phytosanitary Adminstrn., Brno, 1986—. Contbr. articles to profl. jours. Office: State Phytosanitary Adminst, Zemedelska 1A Dept Chem, 613 00 Brno Czech Republic

NOVAKY, ERZSEBET, economics educator; b. Keszthely, Zala, Hungary, Oct. 20, 1945; d. Jeno and Erzsebet (Cserpes) N. M Econs., U. Econ. Sci., Budapest, 1970; PhD Econs., Hungarian Acad. Scis., Budapest, 1980; DSc Econs., Hungarian Acad. Scis., 1991. Instr. U. Econs. Scis., Budapest, 1970-76, asst. prof., 1976-80, assoc. prof., 1981-91, prof. econs., 1991—, head dept. futures rsch., 1989—; vice-pres. futures rsch. com. Hungarian Acad. Sci., 1990—, habilitation Com., U. Econ. Sci., 1994—. Co-author: (books) Practice of Future Research and Forecasting, 1977 (pub. award 1978), Technological Development in Education, 1986 (rsch. award 1986), Vocational Training and Future, 1998; co-author/editor: (books) Developing Environmental Strategies Through Futures Research, 1991, Futures Research, 1992, 97, Chaos and Futures Research, 1995; mem. editl. bd. Jour. of Futures Studies. Named Outstanding Mem. Area of Edn., Min. for Edn. Budapest, 1979, Master Tchr., 1999. Mem. World Futures Studies Fedn. (exec. bd.), World Future Soc., N.Y. Acad. Sci. Avocation: classical music. Office: Budapest U Econ Scis, Fovam ter 8 PO Box 489, 1828 Bp5 Budapest Hungary

NOVELO-GUTIÉRREZ, RODOLFO, biologist, researcher; b. Mexico City, Nov. 27, 1955; s. Rodolfo Novelo-Silva and María Teresa Gutiérrez-Serrano; m. Marcela Galicia-Alcántara, July 3, 1982; children: Daniel Novelo-Galicia, Eric Novelo-Galicia. MS, Nat. Autonomous U. Mex., Mexico City, 1983, DSc, 1996. Tchg. asst. Nat. Autonomous U. Mex.-X, 1978-84, assoc. prof., 1983-86, titular prof., 1987-89; assoc. rsch. Inst. Ecology A.C., Xalapa, Mex., 1989-92, sr. rschr., 1993—; cons. Fed. Electricity Commn. (CFE), Zimapan, Mex., 1993-96. Editor Folia Entomologica Mexicana, 1993. Grantee NSF, 1989, Osaka Prefecture, Japan, 1993. Mem. Mex. Entomology Soc. (SME), Internat. Odontological Soc. (SIO), N.Am. Benthological Soc. (NABS), Washington Entomol. Soc., Mex. Acad. Scis. Avocations: football, soccer, swimming, guitar. Home: Bourbon No 36 La Mata, 91583 Coatepec Veracruz, Mexico Office: Inst Ecology AC, Km 25 Carretera Antigua Cpc, 91000 Xalapa Veracruz, Mexico

NOVETZKE, SALLY JOHNSON, former ambassador; b. Stillwater, Minn., Jan. 12, 1932; married; 4 children. Student, Carlton Coll., 1950-52; PhD (hon.), Mt. Mercy Coll., 1991. Amb. to Malta, Am. Embassy, Valletta, 1989-93. Past mem., legis. rep. Nat. Coun. on Vocat. Edn.; past mem. adv. coun. for career edn., past mem. planning coun. Kirkwood C.C.; bd. dirs., life trustee Cedar Rapids (Iowa) Cmty. Theater; past bd. dirs. James Baker III Pub. Policy Inst., Rice U.; past trustee, v.p. bd. dirs. Shattuck-St. Mary's Sch., Faribault, Minn., Mt. Mercy Coll., Cedar Rapids; vice chmn., life trustee, mem. exec. com. Hoover Presdl. Libr., 1982—, v.p. Hoover trustees; state chmn. Iowa Rep. Ctrl. Com., 1984-86; co-chair rep. Ctrl. Com.; chmn. Linn County Rep. Com., 1980-83; mem. adv. bd. Iowa Fedn. Rep. Women, 1987-89; vice chmn. campaign adv. bd. Nat. Fedn. Rep. Women, 1987-89; co-chmn. V.P. Bush Inauguration, 1980; Iowa co-chmn. George Bush for Pres.; mem. Coun. Am. Ambs.; bd. dirs. Ambs. Forum; trustee 4-Oaks Juvenile Facility; chmn. Nat. Coun. Youth Leadership. Decorated dame Order of Knights of Malta; recipient Disting. Alumnus award Stillwater High Sch., 1991; Disting. Alumni award for outstanding achievement Carleton Coll., 1994. Home: 4747 Mount Vernon Rd SE Cedar Rapids IA 52403-3941

NOVIKOV, ILYA, engineering educator; b. Moscow, July 21, 1926; s. Izrail and Senya (Rafalovskaya) N.; m. Nadejda Serdeckkina, June 22, 1946; 1 child, Alexander. Degree in engring., Moscow Inst. Non-Ferrous Metal, 1948, PhD, 1951; DSc, Moscow Inst. Steel and Alloys, 1964. Asst. Kazakstan Poly. Inst., Alma-Ata, USSR, 1951-54, asst. prof., 1954-55; asst. prof. Moscow Inst. Non-Ferrous Metals and Gold, 1955-61; asst. prof. Moscow Inst. Steel and Aoolys, 1962-64, prof., head dept. phys. metallurgy of non-ferrous metals, 1965-90, prof., 1991—; head dept. metal/physics Inst. Solid State Physics, Acad. Sci. of Kazakstan, Alma-Ata, 1953-55; editor Jour. Nonferrous Metallurty, 1995—, mem. editl. bd., 1965-95; vice chmn. Russian com. Superplastic Materials, Moscow, 1985-90. Author: Hot-Cracking of Non-Ferrous Metals and Alloys, 1966, Superplasticity of Alloys with Ultra-Fine Grain (in Russian), 1981, (in German) 1984, (prize of 2d degree Russian Sci.-Tech. Soc. 1982), Theory of Heat-Treatment of Metals, 1962, 4th edit., 1986 (English, Arabic, Portuguese and Chinese translations); developer of platinum alloys for highest work temperatures (State prize of USSR Laureate 1982). Recipient Meritorious Sci. and Engring. Worker of Russia award Parliament of Russia, 1991. Mem. Internat. Info. Acad. Avocations: badminton, kayaking. Office: Moscow Steel & Alloys Inst, Leninski Prospect 4, 117936 Moscow Russia

NOVIKOV, NIKOLAJ NIKOLAEVITCH, physics educator, researcher; b. Chernihiv, Ukraine, USSR, June 22, 1933; s. Nikolaj Ananievich and Anastasija Ivanovna (Djachenko) N.; m. Agnesa Nikolaevna Zubkovskaja, Feb. 7, 1957; children: Vladimir, Irina. Grad. in Physics, U. Kiev, Ukraine, 1956, PhD in Physics and Math., 1960, DSc, 1975. Asst. Physics Faculty U. Kiev, 1957-62, asst. prof., 1962-75, prof. physics, 1975—, dean Faculty for Higher Edn. Tchrs., 1985-93. Author: The structure and structure-sensitive properties of real crystals, 1983, How and why metals are hardened, 1998, others; contbr. numerous articles to profl. jours.; 35 patents in field. Mem. sci. coun. Taras Shevchenko U., 1985-94; mem. Znannaja Soc., 1971-85. Recipient Gold and Silver medals VDNH, 1986, 89, State award of the Ukraine, 1987; Soros Sci. Edn. Program grantee, 1997. Mem. Acad. of Higher Sch. of Ukraine, Ecology Acad. Ukraine. Avocations: gardening, swimming. Home: Vasilkovskaja str 40a f52, Kiev 03022, Ukraine Office: Kiev Taras Shevchenko U, Vladimirskaja str 64, Kiev 03033, Ukraine

NOVIKOV, ROMAN GENNADIEVICH, mathematician, researcher; b. Moscow, Mar. 27, 1965; s. Gennadi Henkin and Natalia Novikova. PhD, Moscow U., 1989; Habilitation Diriger des Recherches, Nantes (France) U., 1996; DSc, St. Petersburg, 1998. Rschr. Acad. Sci. Russia, Moscow, 1989—, CNRS, Nantes, France, 1992—. Contbr. articles to profl. jours. Office: CNRS UMR 6629 Dept Math, BP 92208, F-44322 Nantes Cedex 03, France

NOVOKSHCHENOV, VLADIMIR ILICH, civil engineer; b. Tkvarchels, Georgia, USSR, Aug. 11, 1941; came to U.S. 1979.; s. Ilia Elimovitch and Anna Danilovna N.; m. Kristine (Uhlman), (div. 1995); 1 child, Vladimir Vladimirovich. MS, U. Civil Engring., Odessa, Russia, 1965; PhD, U. Civil Engring., 1972. Cert. Profl. Engr., Ontario, Canada. Asst. prof., assoc. prof. U. Civil Engring., Odessa, Russia, 1967-75; concrete rsch. engr. Portland Cement Assoc., Skokie, Ill., 1979-89; cons. Concrete Clinic Internat., Gibsonia, Pa., 1989—. Contbr. articles to profl. jours. Mem. Assoc. Profl. Engring., Am. Concrete Inst., Nat. Assoc. Corrosion Engrs. Avocations: tennis, traveling, fishing. Office: Concrete Clinic Internat 5600 William Flynn Hwy Gibsonia PA 15044-9585

NOVOSAD, JAN, chemical engineer; b. Zlin, Czech Republic, June 12, 1930; s. Jan and Libuse (Popelkova) N.; m. Alena Seifertova, July 20, 1993; children: Tomas, Jana. Degree in engring., Prague Tech. U., 1951; PhD, Czech Acad. Scis., 1962. Rsch. fellow Czech Acad. Scis., Prague, 1954-62, head rsch. group, 1962-91; exec. sec. Czech Soc. Chem. Engring., Prague, 1991—. Author: Mechanics of Particulate Solids, 1983; contbr. articles to profl. jours.; mem. editl. bd. Powder Tech. Internat. Jour., 1971—; patentee in field. Mem. Czech Chem. Soc. (exec. bd. 1975-88, exec. bd. chem. engring. sect. 1958-90), European Fedn. Chem. Engring. (chmn. working party on mechanics of particulate solids 1971—, exec. bd. 1996—, Behrens Medal award 1999), Czech Assn. Sci. and Tech. Socs. (exec. bd. 1998—). Avocations: gardening, travel. Home: Krohova 2212, 160 00 Prague 6, Czech Republic Office: Czech Soc Chem Engring, Novotneho lavka 5, 116 68 Prague 1, Czech Republic

NOVOSAD, TOMA'Š, armed forces officer; b. Brno, Czech Republic, Oct. 7, 1959; s. Karel and Jarmila (Hlava'čova') N.; m. Eva Putzova', Oct. 15, 1983; children: Veronika, Toma'š. Student, Mil. Sch., Martin, Czech Republic, 1978. Sgt. Czech Rep. Armed Forces, Holy'šov, 1978-80; commd. officer Czech Rep. Armed Forces, 1980, advanced through grades to capt.; officer Czech Rep. Armed Forces, Kramolin, 1980-90, Brno, 1990-98, 99—; officer SFOR Czech Rep. Armed Forces, Ljubija, Bosnia, 1998. Home: 5 Rybizova, 62100 Brno Czech Republic Office: Tř Gen Píky, 61300 Brno Czech Republic

NOVOTNA, JANA, tennis player; b. Brno, Czech Republic, Oct. 2, 1968. Profl. tennis player, 1993—; winner four Grand Slam doubles titles Australian Open and Wimbledon, 1995; winner Grand Slam singles title Wimbledon, 1998. Office: c/o WTA Tour 1266 E Main St 4th Fl Stamford CT 06902-3546*

NOVOTNY, DEBORAH A., management consultant; b. Oak Lawn, Ill., Sept. 23, 1964; d. Russell Anthony and Barbara J. (Doran) N. BA in Econs., Northwestern U., 1986; postgrad., U. Minn., 1988-91. Lic. mutual fund mktg. analyst; cert. PowerBuilder developer-profl., instr., PowerSoft divsn. Sybase, Inc., 1993—; cert. project mgr.; cert. QMS coord. Mgr. lab., cons. Northwestern U., Evanston, Ill., 1983-86; asst. mgr. microcomputer services Sara Lee Corp., Chgo., 1986; sr. cons. Lante Corp., Chgo., 1987-88; fin. exec. IDS Fin. Svcs., Inc., Mpls., 1988-91; fin. system coord. Met. Water Reclamation Dist. of Greater Chgo., Chgo., 1991-92; mgmt. systems cons., pres., CEO Deborah A. Novotny, Inc., Chgo., 1992—; various mgmt. positions Sybase, Inc., 1993—, area project mgmt. office mgr., 1999—; invited spkr., instr. ann. Powersoft User Conf., Comdex Trade Show, homeless children Christmas gift program, 1994—. Active teen retreat team St. Michael's Ch., Orland Park, Ill., 1978-84; vol. Greater Chgo. Food Repository, 1997—; vice chmn., chair fin. com. Mount Assisi Acad. Bd. of Dirs., 1997-99. Ill. State scholar. Mem. MacIntosh Users Group, Chi Omega Rho (charter, chmn. housing assn. 1986-91). Avocations: piloting aircraft, photography, travel, reading, writing.

NOVOTNY, JAROMIR, federal agency administrator; b. Ostrava, Czech Republic, Aug. 24, 1947; s. Jaromir and Vlasta (Kovalova) N.; m. Katrina Smrkovska, Jan. 15, 1970 (div. Nov. 1996); children: Ondrej, Katerina; m. Dana Matejkova, Oct. 24, 1997. M, Prague Sch. Econs., Czech Republic, 1970. Deputy chief gov. com. internat. rels. Czech Govt., 1991-92; dir. dept. TV Cable Plus, Prague, Czech Republic, 1992; chief fgn. rels. dept. Czech Govt., 1993-91, gen. dir. fgn. rels. sect., 1993-97, deputy min. def., 1997, first deputy min. def., 1997—. Contbr. articles to profl. jours. Mem. Rotary. Avocations: skiing, history. Office: Czech Min Def, Tychonova 1, 160 00 Prague 6, Czech Republic

NOVOTNY, JIRI, biophysicist; b. Kladno, Czech Republic, Dec. 15, 1943; came to U.S., 1979; s. Jaroslav and Eva (Foustkova) N.; m. Jarmila Novotny, Feb. 26, 1967; 1 child, Paula. RNDr, Charles U., Prague, Czechoslovakia, 1970, PhD, 1970. Scientist Inst. Organic Chemistry & Biochemistry, Prague, 1970-77; sr. scientist Inst. Molecular Genetics, Czech Acad. Sci., Prague, 1971-79; from asst. to assoc. prof. Harvard Med. Sch., Boston, 1980-88; dir. dept. Bristol-Myers Squibb Rsch. Inst., Princeton, N.J., 1988-98; vis. scientist Oxford U., Eng., 1979; vis. scholar dept. molecular biology Princeton U., 1993—; dir. rsch. Pasteur Inst., Paris, 1987; adj. prof. U. Pa., Phila., 1989-95; cons. Creative Biomolecules Inc., Hopkinton, Mass., 1987-88, Roussel UCLAF, Romainville, France, 1987, Howard Hughes Med. Inst., Boston, 1986-87; mem. sci. adv. bd. Procept, Inc., Cambridge, 1989-92, Ctr. Biomolecular Simulation Columbia U., N.Y.C., 1994-98, Novalon Inc., Durham, N.C., 1999—. Contbr. articles to jours., including procs. NAS, Nature, Biochemistry; contbg. author: Advances in Protein Chemistry, 1996, Ency. Molecular Biology, 1995, Ency. Immunology, 1993, Current Opinions in Structural Biology, 1997. Recipient prize of the Czechoslovak Acad. of Scis., 1979, Bristol-Myers Squibb Presdl. award, 1998. Mem. Am. Phys. Soc., Am. Soc. Biol. Chemists, Am. Biophys. Soc., Am. Chem. Soc., Princeton Chess Club, Belle Meade Friends of Music. Achievements include patent for single-chain T cell receptor fragments; for alpha-helical heterotetramers; for peptides derived from the obese gene; for mutant penicillin G acylases; development of empirical free energy potential, of molecular theory of protein antigenicity; identification of C1q binding site on antibody molecules; research on secondary structure prediction algorithm. Home: 101 Red Hill Rd Princeton NJ 08540-1307 Office: Dept Molecular Biology Princeton U Princeton NJ 08544-0001

NOVOTNY, LADISLAV, experimental oncologist, educator; b. Svitavy, Czechoslovakia, Oct. 5, 1955; s. Ladislav and Zdenka (Ruzickova) N.; m. Jozefina Valova, Aug. 6, 1983; children: Robert, Barbora, Martina. B Pharm., Kharkov Pharm. Inst., Ukraine, 1980; D Pharm., Charles U., 1981; PhD, Czechoslovak Acad. Sci., Prague, 1984; DSc, Slovak Acad. Sci., Bratislava, 1997. Chemist Czechoslovak Acad. Scis., Prague, 1986-87, 92-93; vis. scientist med. oncology U. Tex., Houston, 1986-87; asst. prof. pharm. chemistry Comenius U., Bratislava, Slovak Republic, 1985-88; from scientist to leading scientist Cancer Rsch. Inst. Slovak Acad. Scis., Bratislava, 1988-98; assoc. prof. pharm. chemistry, acting chair dept. Kuwait U., 1998—. Mem. Kuwait Pharm. Assn., European Assn. Cancer Rsch., Am. Assn. Cancer Rsch., Slovak Pharmacol. Soc., Slovak Pharm. Soc. E-mail: novotny@hsc.kuniv.edu.kw. Office: Kuwait U Faculty Pharmacy, PO Box 24923 Safat, 113110 Kuwait Kuwait

NOVOTNY, MIROSLAV, mathematics educator; b. Tovačov, Czech Republic, May 11, 1922; s. František and Ružena (Kapounková) N.; m. Věra Zábojníková, Apr. 24, 1948; children: Zdeňka, Dagmar. D of Natural Scis., Masaryk U., Brno, Czech Republic, 1948, diploma in phys. and math. sci., 1956; D of Phys. and Math. Sci., U. Prague, 1962. Reader Tech. U., Brno, 1947-51, Mil. Acad., Brno, 1951-53; assoc. prof. math. Masaryk U., Brno, 1953-63, vice-dean faculty of sci., 1954-56, dir. dept. math. analysis, 1963-70, prof. math., 1963-71; leading rschr. Math. Inst. Czechoslovak Acad., Brno, 1971-90; prof. math. Masaryk U., 1990—. Author: With Algebra From Language to Grammar and Back, 1988; contbr. articles to profl. jours. Recipient Gold medal B. Bolzano Czechoslovak Acad. Sci., 1992. Mem. Union Czechoslovak Mathematicians and Physicists. Avocation: Moravian folklore music. Home: Chlupova 3, 602 00 Brno Czech Republic Office: Masaryk U Faculty Computer Sci, Botanická 68a, 602 00 Brno Czech Republic

NOVOTNY, VLADIMIR, educator, consultant; b. Olomouc, Czech Rep., Aug. 30, 1938; came to U.S., 1969, naturalized, 1983; s. Vladimir and Frantiska (Havrankova) N.; m. Lynn Emily Braasch, June 14, 1975; children: Paul Martin, Eric Vladimir. Diploma in Engring., Tech. U., Brno, Czech Rep., 1963, degree in Sci., 1968; PhD, Vanderbilt U., 1971. Rsch. engr. Water Mgmt. Inst., Brno, Czech Rep., 1962-69; rsch. assoc. Vanderbilt U., Nashville, 1969-71; project engr. Aware, Inc., Nashville, 1970-73; pres. Aquanova Internat., Ltd., Mequon, Wis., 1989—; prof. Marquette U., Milw., 1973—; dir. Inst. Urban Environ. Risk Mgmt. Marquette U., Milw., 1998—; dir. workshop NATO, Viena, 1994; expert pollution abatement Venezia Nuova, Venice, 1989-98. Author: Handbook of Nonpoint Pollution, 1981, Water Quality, 1994; editor: Management of Degraded River Basins, 1995. Rsch. grantee Water Environ. Rsch. Found., Alexandria, Va., 1992, 95, U.S. EPA, Washington, 1993, 97. Mem. Internat. Water Assn. (chmn. com. 1993-98, chair internat. conf., Chgo., 1993, Edinburgh, 1998), Internat. Water Resource Assn., Am. Water Resources Assn. (dir. 1985-89), Water Environ. Fedn. E-mail: v.novotny@marquette.edu. Home: 10122 Lake Shore Dr Mequon WI 53092-6110 Office: Marquette Univ 1515 W Wisconsin Ave Milwaukee WI 53233-2222

NOVOZHILOV, VASILY BORISOVICH, mathematician, researcher; b. Moscow, Russia, Nov. 24, 1963; s. Boris Vasilievich and Ludmila Mikhailovna N.; m. Natalia, Oct. 5, 1997. MS, Moscow Inst. Oil & Gas, Russia, 1986; PhD, Moscow Aviation Inst., Russia, 1993. Engr. Inst. of Physics of the Earth, Moscow, Russia, 1986-87; jr. rschr. Inst. for Problems in Mechanics, Moscow, 1987-93; rsch. asst. U. Sydney, Australia, 1994-97; computational fluid dynamics engr. Orbital Engine Co., Perth, 1997-99; rsch. assoc. U. Sydney, 1999—; cons. All-Russian Rsch. Inst. for Fire Protection, Balashikha, Russia, 1997—, Orbital Engine Co., Perth, Australia, 1997—, Orbital Engine Co., Perth, Western Australia. Contbr. over 40 articles to profl. jours. and chpt. to book. Fellow Japan Soc. Promotion of Sci., 1997. Mem. The Combustion Inst. (Travel Grant 1997), The Internat. Assn. for Fire Safety Sci., Asia-Oceania Assn. for Fire Sci. and Tech. (com. 2000—). Avocation: classical music listening. Office: Nanyang Tech U Sch Mech and Prodn Engring Nanyang Ave Singapore 639798 Singapore

NOWACKI, WOJCIECH KRZYSZTOF, solid mechanics educator; b. Mielec, Poland, Feb. 22, 1938; s. Witold Jozef and Janina Kazimiera (Sztaba) N.; m. Alicja Maria Kurowska, Feb. 8, 1977; 1 child, Deelman Ewa. MS, Warsaw Tech. U., 1961; PhD, Polish Acad. Scis., Warsaw, 1965, DS, 1975. Teaching asst. Warsaw Tech. Acad., 1961-65; asst. prof. Polish Acad. Scis., Warsaw, 1965-75, assoc. prof., 1975-82, prof., 1982—; dir. Lab. Applied Plasticity, Warsaw, 1978, Ctr. Mechanics and Info. Tech., Warsaw, 1995. Author: Stress Waves in Non-Elastic Solids, 1978; editor-in-chief Jour. theoretical and Applied Mechanics, 1992—; contbr. articles to profl. jours. Mem. Soc. Theoretical and Applied Mechanics (v.p. 1992). Home: Grzybowska 5m902, 00-132 Warsaw Poland Office: Inst Fundamental Tech Rsch Swietokrzyska 21, 00-049 Warsaw Poland

NOWACZEK, FRANK HUXLEY, venture capital executive; b. Bklyn., July 6, 1930; s. Frank Huxley and Louise (Blake) N.; m. Alice Elaine Novak, May 21, 1955; children: Richard Alan, Elaine. Student, St. Lawrence U., 1948-50; BS in Hotel Adminstrn., Cornell U., 1952; postgrad. in polit. sci. and pub. rels., George Washington U., 1954-58, Am. U., 1954-57. Spl. agt. spl. ops. br. security divsn. Def. Dept., Nat. Security Agy., 1954-59; asst. to pres., dir. Nat. Cable TV Assn., Washington, 1959-64; asst. to pres. TeleSystems Corp., Glenside, Pa., 1964-66; v.p., part-owner Newport Cablevision, Vt., 1966-68; v.p. Blackburn & Co., Inc., Washington, 1968-76; v.p. Mid Atlantic region Warner Amex Cable Comms., N.Y.C., 1976-80; sr. v.p. eastern divsn. Ft. Washington, Pa., 1980-82; sr. v.p. nat. divsn. Columbus, Ohio, 1982-83; owner Cable Media Co., Washington, Ohio, 1983-86; pres. Newcable TV Corp., 1985-86; COO Bachow & Elkin, Inc., Phila., 1986-92; ops. dir. Communications Industries Bachow & Assocs., Bala Cynwyd, Pa.; sr. advisor Bachow Investment Ptnrs., 1992-95; mng. dir. Bachow and Assocs., Inc., 1995—; v.p. Digital Access, Inc., 1999—; bd. advisors Columbus Investment Interest Group; spkr. various orgns. Served with CIC, U.S. Army, 1952-54. Mem. IEEE, Pub. Rels. Soc. Am., Soc. Relay Engrs. (Gt. Britain), Cable TV Adminstrn. and Mktg. Assn., Nat. Cable TV Pioneers Assn., Nat. Acad. Cable Programmers, Soc. Cable Telecom. Engrs., Pa. Cable TV Assn. (pres., dir.), Pa. Calbe TV Pioneers Assn. (Founders award), Phila. Cable TV Club (founder), Cornell Soc. Hotelman (life), Am. Mgmt. Assn., Nat. Cable TV Assn. (sec. tech. stds. com. 1961 chmn. membership com. 1965-66), World Futurist Soc., Soc. Telecomm. Engrs., Ohio Hist. Soc., Cornell U. Alumni Club, Phi Delta Theta. Republican. Roman Catholic.

NOWAK, GRZEGORZ, conductor, music and artistic director; b. 1951. M Music Conducting, Poznan Acad. Music; postgrad., Eastman Sch. Music, Rochester, N.Y.; studied with, Leonard Bernstein, Seiji Ozawa, Eric Leinsdorf, Maurice Abravanel. Mus. dir. Slupsk Symphony Orch., 1976-80, Biel Symphony and Opera, Switzerland, 1985-91, Teatr Narodowy, Warsaw; music dir. Edmonton Symphony Orch., 1995—, New Warsaw Philharm., Sinfonia Helvetica, Swiss Festival Musique & Amitié, Calgary Millennium Music Found., Vancouver Chopin Soc.; assoc. prof. Bowling Green (Ohio) U., 1982-90; asst. condr. Kurt Masur & N.Y. Philharmonic, 1992; hon. prof. U. Alta, 1996; music and artistic dir. Jeunesses Musicales Chamber Orch., Poznan, 1971-76, engagements include London Symphony, Montreal Symphony, Orchestra Nat. de France, orchestras in Rome, Oslo, Stockholm, Copenhagen, Helsinki, Monte Carlo, Jerusalem, Madrid, Lisbon, Balt., Cin., San Diego, Vancouver, Ottowa, Tokyo, Hong Kong, Geneva, Zurich, Baden-Baden, Saarbrucken, Rotterdam, Milan, Florence, Goteborg, Malmo, Birmingham, Bournemouth, Liverpool, Manchester, Belfast, and Glasgow. Recs. include London Symphony, Martha Argerich and Sinfonia Varsovia, (CDs) Edmonton Symphony (Juno award 1998), Polish Symphonic Music of the 19th Century (CD of Yr. 1996, Bronze Bell prize), Chopin Piano Concerti with Janusz Olejiniczak and Sinfonia Varsovia (CD of Yr. 1995, Fryderyk 1996 Grammy award). Recipient 1st prize Ernest Ansermet Conducting Competition, Geneva, 1984, Grand Prix Patek Philippe, Swiss prize, Rolex prize, and Am. Patronage prize, Europäische Förderpreis für Musik as European Musician of Yr.; Tanglewood fellow, 1981-82. Fax: 1 604 266-1794. E-mail: maestro@nowak.net. Mailing: 3715 W 51 Ave, Vancouver, BC Canada V6N 3V9 Office: care Mujsicians Corp Mgmt Ltd PO Box 589 Millbrook NY 12545-0589 also: Teatr Narodowy, Plac Teatralny 1, 00-950 Warsaw Poland also: Edmonton Symphony Orch, 9720 102 Ave NW, Edmonton, AB Canada T5J 4B2

NOWAK, JOHN E., law educator; b. Chgo., Jan. 2, 1947; s. George Edward and Evelyn (Bucci) N.; m. Judith Johnson, June 1, 1968; children: John Edwin, Jeffrey Edward. AB, Marquette U., 1968; JD, U. Ill., 1971. Law clk. Supreme Ct. of Ill., Chgo., 1971-72; asst. prof. U. Ill., Urbana, 1972-75, assoc. prof., 1975-87, law prof., 1978—, grad. coll. faculty, 1982—, Baum Prof. Law, 1993—; chmn. Constl. Law Sch. Sect.; faculty rep. Big Ten Intercollegiate Conf., Schaumburg, Ill., 1981-91; vis. prof. law U. Mich., Ann Arbor, 1985; Lee Disting. vis. prof. Coll. William and Mary, 1993. Co-author: Constitutional Law, 6th edit. 2000, Treatise on Constitutional Law, 1986, 3d edit., 1999, Story's Commentaries on the Constitution, 1987. Scholar-in-Residence, U. of Ariz., Tucson, 1985, 87. Mem. Assn. of Am. Law Schs. (chm. constl. law sect., accreditation com. 1980-88), Nat. Collegiate Athletic Assn. (mem. infractions com. 1987—), Am. Law Inst., Am. Bar Assn., Ill. Bar Assn., Order of the Coif (Triennial Book award com.). Roman Catholic. Home: 1701 Mayfair Rd Champaign IL 61821-5522 Office: U Ill Coll Law 504 E Pennsylvania Ave Champaign IL 61820-6909

NOWAKOWSKI, ANDRZEJ MARIA, mathematician; b. Gniewkowo, Poland, May 11, 1949; s. Jozef and Agnieszka (Kulczyk) N.; m. Iwona Danuta Sedziak, Apr. 29, 1993; 1 child, Lilianna. MS, U. M. Kopernikus, Poland, 1970; PhD, U. Lodz, Poland, 1978; habilitation, Tech. U. Warsaw, 1989. Asst. prof. U. Lodz, 1978-89, assoc. prof., 1989-90, prof., 1990—; dir. inst. math. U. Lodz, 1993-96, dean faculty math., 1996—. Contbr. articles to profl. jours. Home: Malachitowa 14, 91360 Lodz Poland Office: Faculty Math U Lodz, Banacha 22, 90238 Lodz Poland

NOWAKOWSKI, TOMASZ TADEUSZ, technology educator; b. Wrocław, Poland, July 28, 1953; s. Tadeusz and Barbara (Jakimowicz) N.; m. Mariola Sedzimirska. MS, U. Tech., Wroclaw, 1976, PhD, 1980, DSc, 1999. Cert. in mech. engring. Univ. tchr. Inst. Machine Design and Operation, U. Tech., Wroclaw, 1980-86, rschr., 1986—, adj. prof., 1993-96, dep. dir., 1996—. Co-author: (books) Bus Reliability, 1993, Information Systems and Technologies in Research and Practice, 1996, Zuverlassigkeit Technischer Systeme, 1988. V.p. Estate Coun., Wroclaw, 1992-94. Mem. Polish Sys. Soc. Office: Wrocław U of Tech, Lukasiewicza 7/9, 50-371 Wrocław Poland

NOWE, DENNIS ANTHONY, chef; b. Pitts., Apr. 19, 1956; s. Richard Edward and Conchita Nena Nowe; m. Stella Maris, Apr. 1, 1989. Exec. chef Loew's Lenfant Plz., Washington, 1980-84, Hotel Bristol, Washington, 1984-85, Watergate Hotel, Washington, 1985-86, Inter Am. Bank, Washington, 1986-90; exec. chef, owner What Nowe, Alexandria, Va., 1990-92; exec. chef Mohonk Mountain Ho., New Paltz, N.Y., 1992-95, Albert Uster Imports, Gaithersburg, Md., 1995—; mem. adv. bd. Pvt. Industry Coun., Washington, 1984-86. Food stylist Road to Wellville, 1994; columnist Capital Chefs, 1998-99 (Best Newsletter 1999). Culinary organizer Diabetes Found., Washington, 1997-99. Mem. Am. Culinary Fedn. (cert. exec. chef, Gold medal 1999), Worlds Assn. Cooks Socs., Nations Capital Chefs Assn. (bd. dirs. 1984—, v.p. 1996—, Chef of the Yr. 1987, 99), Washington Sculpture Group. Office: Albert Uster Imports Inc 9211 Gaither Rd Gaithersburg MD 20877-1419

NOWELL, LINDA GAIL, organization executive; b. Ft. Worth, Apr. 24, 1949; d. Jesse Wayne and Bennie Dale (Flint) Stallings. BA in English, North Tex. State U., 1970. Cert. secondary edn. tchr., Tex. Ind. sales rep. Jostens Printing & Pub. Div., Owatona, Minn., 1980-84; v.p. Nowell Equipment Co., Cranfils Gap, Tex., 1984-89; edn. coord. Tex. Farm Bur., Waco, Tex., 1987-90; account exec. MAC Printing, Las Vegas, 1991-94; mgr. frontier health outreach program Nev. Rural Health Ctrs., Inc., 1994-97; state coord. Nev. 5-A-Day Coalition, 1995-96; exec. dir. No To Abuse, Pahrump, Nev., 1999—. Grant writer, editor (health newsletter) Ridin' the Circuit. Participant Landmark Edn., Inc. Recipient South Cen. Regional Pacer Sales award, 1982, Sales Commitment Achiever award, 1982, 83, 84. Mem. NAFE. Avocation: oil painting. Office: PO Box 2869 Pahrump NV 89041-2869

NOWELL-SMITH, PATRICK HORACE, philosophy educator; b. Polzeath, Eng., Aug. 17, 1914; s. Charles Nowell and Cecil Violet (Vernon-Harcourt) Smith; m. Perilla Thyme Southwell, 1945 (div. 1967); children: Richard Wingate, Viola Margaret, Robert Vernon, Timothy David; m. Felicity Margret Ward, 1968 (div. 1985); children: Harriet Flora, Kate Prudence. BA, New Coll., Oxford, Eng., 1937; AM, Harvard U., 1939. Fellow Trinity Coll., Oxford, 1945-56; prof. Leicester U., Eng., 1956-64, U. Kent, Canterbury, Eng., 1964-69; prof. York U., North York, Can., 1969-85, prof. emeritus, 1985—. Author: Ethics, 1954; contbr. numerous articles to profl. jours. Com. mem. Vol. Euthanasia Soc., London, 1985-89; pres. Dying with Dignity, Can., 1972-85, World Fedn. Right to Die Socs., 1986-88. Maj. Royal Army Svc. Corps, 1940-42, Royal Indian Army Svc. Corps, 1942-45. Liberal/Liberal Democrat. Avocations: music, reading. Home: 7 Wyndham House, Plantation Rd, Oxford OX2 6JJ, England

NOWICK, ARTHUR STANLEY, metallurgy and materials science educator; b. N.Y.C., Aug. 29, 1923; s. Hyman and Clara (Sperling) N.; m. Joan Franzblau, Oct. 30, 1949; children: Jonathan, Steven, Alan, James. A.B., Bklyn. Coll., 1943; A.M., Columbia U., 1948, Ph.D., 1950. Physicist NACA, Cleve., 1944-46; instr. U. Chgo., 1949-51; asst. prof., then assoc. prof. metallurgy Yale U., 1951-57; mgr. metallurgy research IBM Corp Research Center, Yorktown Heights, N.Y., 1957-66; prof. metallurgy Columbia U., 1966-90, Henry Marion Howe prof. metallurgy and materials sci., 1990-95, prof. emeritus, 1996—; A. Frank Golick lectr. U. Mo., 1970; vis. prof. Technion, Haifa, Israel, 1973; co-chmn. Internat. Conf. Internal Friction, 1961, 69 (medal 1989); cons. in field. Author: Crystal Properties Via Group Theory, 1995; co-author: Anelastic Relaxation in Crystalline Solids, 1972; co-editor: Diffusion in Solids, 1975, Diffusion in Crystalline Solids, 1984; contbr. articles to profl. jours. Named David Turnbull lecturer Materials Rsch. Soc., 1994. Fellow AIME, Am. Phys. Soc.; mem. Materials Rsch. Soc. (Turnbull lectr. 1994), Sigma Xi (pres. Kappa chpt. 1983-85). Office: 1144 Mudd Bldg Columbia U New York NY 10027

NOWICKA-JEŻOWA, ALINA MARIA, philology educator; b. Zakopane, Poland, May 24, 1946; d. Kazimierz and Katarzyna (Witowska) Nowicki; m. Marian Jeż, Sept. 15, 1968; children: Łukasz, Tomasz, Justyna, Anna. MA, Jagiellonian U., Cracow, Poland, 1968, PhD, 1974; DA, U. Warsaw, Poland, 1989. Asst. Jagiellonian U., Cracow, 1968-69; asst. U. Warsaw, 1969-74, asst. prof., 1974-92, adj. prof., 1992-98, prof., 1998—; prof. Cath. U. Lubelski, Lublin, Poland, 1991-94; dir. Polish Lit. Inst., U. Warsaw, 1993-96; chmn. sci. com., Warsaw, 1996-99. Author: Madrygały staropolskie, 1978 (award Ministry Edn. 1979), Presni crasu inierci, 1992 (award Ministry Edn. 1993), Sarmaci i inierc, 1992; editor: Kasper Miaskowski, Zbror rytniow, 1995. Mem. Solidarity, 1981. Grantee Polish Com. Sci. Rsch., 1997-99. Mem. Warsaw Sci. Soc. Roman Catholic. Avocation: music.

NOWICKI, MAREK, physicist; b. Drezdenko, Poland, Aug. 16, 1968; s. Mirosław Kazimierz and Jadwiga Kazimiera (Kwiatkowska) N.; m. Maria Opacka, Oct. 2, 1993. MS in Physics, U. Wrocław, Poland, 1992, PhD in Physics, 1996. From technician to asst. prof. Inst. Exptl. Physics-U. Wrocław, 1992-97, assoc. prof., 1997—. Contbr. articles to profl. jours. U. Zurich scholar, 1995; Alexander von Humboldt fellow, 1998. Avocations: sailing, sightseeing, music, guitar, percussion. Fax: (48) 71-328-7365; e-mail: nowicki@max.ifd.uni.wroc.pl. Office: Inst Exptl Phys U Wroclaw, Pl Maxa Borna 9, 50-204 Wrocław Poland

NOWIK, HENRY IAN, marketing executive, consultant; b. Posen, Poland, Feb. 3, 1917; came to U.S., 1979; s. Alexander Joseph and Elizabeth Augusta (von Kuhn) N.; m. Evelyn Phyllis Barnard, Sept. 17, 1949 (dec. 1992); m. Kathleen Yvonne Jones, May 12, 1995. BS in Econs., London U., 1949; PhD, U. Lyon, 1948. Student advisor U. London, 1948-52; export mktg. exec. Parke Davis Ltd., Eng., 1952-54; mgr. market rsch. Mather & Crowther, Eng., 1954-56; mgr. new products Hoover Ltd., Eng., 1956-58; mgr. market rsch. Petfoods Ltd. div. Mars, Inc., Eng., 1958-64; v.p. mktg., sales Uncle Ben's, Australia, 1964-68, gen. mgr., mng. dir., 1968-78; v.p. mktg. Mars, Inc., U.S., 1979-80, group pres., 1980-84; cons. mktg., 1984—; sr. cons. Food System Assocs., Washington, 1985—; prof., lectr. Georgetown U., Washington, 1984—. Author: Disciplined Entrepreneur, 1976, Research in Marketing, 1964, (with others) Product and Process Development in the Food Industry, 1985; contbr. articles to profl. jours. Justice of Peace, Sydney, Australia, 1973; bd. dirs. Australian Ballet Found., Melbourne, 1975; trustee World Wildlife Fund, Australia, 1976; chmn. Decentralization Adv. Bd., Canberra, Australia, 1977-78. Served with RAF, 1939-45. Decorated Officer of Most Excellent Order Brit. Empire, Officer of Order of Australia, Comdr. with Star of Polonia Restituta, Polish Gold Cross of Merit, Knight Supreme Mil. Order Temple Jerusalem. Fellow Royal Statis. Soc., Brit. Inst. Mgmt., Australian Inst. Mgmt., Advt. Inst. Australia, Inst. Dirs. Australia; mem. Internat. Law Assn., Acad. Polit. Sci. (life), Lloyds of London (underwriting), Market Rsch. Soc., Chartered Inst. of Mktg., Am. Mgmt. Assn., N.Y. Acad. Sci., London Reform Club, Georgetown Club (Washington), Royal Yacht Squadron Club (Sydney, Australia). Roman Catholic. Avocations: collecting coins, stamps and first edition books.

NOWINSKI, WIESLAW LUCJAN, medical researcher; b. Tomaszow-Maz, Poland, July 24, 1953; arrived in Singapore, 1991; s. Ludwik and Janina (Hejdus) N.; m. Anna Szydlowska, 1980; children: Marta, Natalia. MSc, Warsaw (Poland) Tech. U., 1977; PhD with honors, Lodz (Poland) Tech. U., 1985; DSc, Polish Acad. Scis., Warsaw, 1994. Cert. engr. Assoc. prof. Polish Acad. Scis., Warsaw, 1985—; vis. staff Inst. Systems Sci., 1991-92, rsch. staff, 1992—; vice chief Internat. Lab. Computer Systems Architecture, Polish Acad. Scis., Warsaw, 1986-88; prin. investigator brain imaging Inst. Systems Sci., Singapore, 1993-97; program dir. Med. Imaging Inst. Sys. Sci., Singapore, 1997-98; dir. bio-med. lab., dep. dir. Kent Ridge Digital Labs., Singapore, 1998—. Author: Introduction to Parallel Image Reconstruction, 1992; co-author: Brain Atlas for Functional Imaging, 2000; prin. editor: (CD-ROM) The Electronic Clinical Brain Atlas, 1997; 1st co-inventor Curved surg. instruments and method of mapping of a curved path for stereotactic surgery; contbr. over 100 articles to profl. jours. and internat. confs. Recipient East European scholarship Commn. of European Cmty., 1993, Bronze Cross of Merit, Summa Cum Laude citation Am. Soc. Neuroradiology, 1997, Outstanding Univ. Rschr. award Nat. U. Singapore, 1998. Mem. Internat. Soc. Computer Aided Surgery, European Congress Radiology. Avocation: playing music. Office: Kent Ridge Digital Labs, 21 Heng Mui Keng Ter, 119613 Singapore Singapore

NOWOTNY, HELGA, social sciences educator, researcher; b. Vienna, Austria, Aug. 9, 1937. JD, U. Vienna, 1959; PhD, Columbia U., 1969. Head dept. sociology Inst. for Advanced Studies, Vienna, 1970-72; vis. rschr. Kings's Coll., Cambridge (Eng.) U., 1972-73; founding dir. European Ctr., Vienna, 1974-87; prof. social scis. U. Vienna, 1987—; dir. Collegium Helveticum, ETH, Zurich, Switzerland, prof. social studies of sci.; vis. prof. U. Bielefeld (Fed. Republic Germany), 1978-79; fellow Wissenschaftskolleg, Berlin, 1981-82; dir. studies Maison Scis. l'Homme, Paris, 1987, 90; resident fellow Rockefeller Study Ctr., Bellagio, Italy, 1988; guest prof. Sci. Ctr., Berlin, 1988—; chmn. standing com. social scis. European Sci. Found., Strasbourg, France, 1985-91. Author 12 books; contbr. more than 100 articles on social studies of sci. and tech., social policy, time studies, and sociology to profl. jours. Mem. Academia Europea (exec. coun.), Internat. Soc. for the Study of Time. Home: Haldeneggsteig 5, CH-8006 Zurich Switzerland Office: Collegium Helveticum ETH, Schmelzbergstr 25, CH-8092 Zurich Switzerland

NOXON, MARGARET WALTERS, community volunteer; b. Detroit, Dec. 16, 1903; d. George Alexander and Ethelwyn (Taylor) Walters; grad., Liggett Sch. for Girls, Det., 1922; life teaching certificate Wayne State U., 1925; student Columbia Tchrs. Coll., 1939-40; m. Herbert Richards Noxon, July 15, 1926 (dec. Aug. 4, 1971). Bd. dirs. Coll. Club, Detroit, 1925-30; mem. Salvation Army Aux., Detroit, 1926—; mem. Coll. Club, Summit N.J., 1941—; historian D.A.R., N.Y.C., 1943-46, vice regent, 1946-49; dir. New Eng. Women, 1961-64; dir. Woodycrest-Five Points Child Care, 1961-77; bd. dirs. ARC, Summit, N.J., service com. chmn. uniforms and insignias, 1943-45; v.p. N.Y. Infirmary Aux., N.Y.C., 1948-58, bd. dirs., 1959-80. Recipient award for meritorious personal service ARC, 1945. Mem. Nat. Inst. Social Scis., Grand Jury Assn. N.Y. County, D.A.R. (dir. 1950-70), St. David's Soc. State N.Y., English-Speaking Union, Daus. Am. Colonists, AAUW, Southampton Colonial Soc., Nat. Woman's Farm and Garden Assn. (dir. met. br. 1975—, dir. N.Y. State div. 1978-80, mem. nat. council 1978-80), Ch. Women's League for Patriotic Service, Women's Bible Soc. N.Y., Alpha Sigma Tau. Republican. Presbyterian. Clubs: Southampton (N.Y.) Bath and Tennis, City Gardens (dir. 1963-68, mem. adv. com. 1968-74, dir. 1974-80, adv. bd. 1980-83), York (bd. govs. 1965-66, 73-77), Barnard (trustee 1979-81), Sorosis (v.p. 1979-81), Regency (N.Y.C.). Home: care Virginia W Rider 634 Silvermine Rd New Canaan CT 06840-4324

NOYER, CHRISTIAN, central banker; b. Soisy, France, Oct. 6, 1950. Lic., U. Rennes, France, 1971; diploma higher studies, U. Paris, 1972, degree in polit. sci., 1972; student, Nat. Sch. Adminstrn., France, 1974-76. Fin. attache Permanent Rep. to EEC, Brussels, 1980-82; various positions French Treasury, 1976-86, dep. asst. sec., asst. sec., 1988-93, under sec., 1993-95; advisor Ministry of Economy and Fin., Paris, France, 1986-88; chief of staff Min. of Economy and Fin., Paris, 1995-97; v.p. European Ctrl. Bank, Frankfurt, Germany, 1998—; chmn. Paris Club of Creditor Countries, 1993-97; alt. gov. IMF World Bank, 1993-95. Author: Banks: The Rules of the Game, 1990. Decorated Ordre Nat. du Merite, 1994, Commdr. Ordre Nat. du Lion, 1995, Chevalier Ordre Nat. Legion d' Honneur, 1998. Office: Kaiserstrasse 29, D-60311 Frankfurt am Main Germany

NOYER, JACQUES, bishop; b. Le Touquet, France, Apr. 17, 1927. Tchr. Inst. Haffreingue, Boulogne sur Mer, France; headmaster Grand Séminaire, Arras, France; vicar Le Touquet, France; bishop Amiens, France. Legion d'Honneur, Chevalier, 1992. Home: 21 Rue Saint Leu, 80090 Amiens France Office: Centre diocesain, Parc de Beauville Bat G1, 80044 Amiens Cedex, France

NOZAKI, HISAYOSHI, biologist, educator; b. Meguro-ku, Japan, Aug. 28, 1955; s. Yoshihei and Fukiko (Iida) N.; m. Tomoko Tsuchiya, Oct. 8, 1995. BS, Tokyo Met. U., 1978; DSc, U. Tsukuba, Japan, 1988. Tchr. high sch. Keio Sr. H.S., Yokohama, Japan, 1978-92; sr. sientist Nat. Inst. for Environ. Studies, Tsukuba, 1992-95; assoc. prof. U. Tokyo, Bunkyo-ku, Tokyo, Japan, 1995—; guest researcher U. Tokyo, 1990-91, Inst. für Gewaesseroekologie und Binnenfischerei im forschungsverbund Berlin e.V, Germany, 1997. Mem. editorial bd. Jour. Phycologia, 1989-92, European Jour. Phycology, 1993—, Jour. Phycology, 1995-97; assoc. editor Phycological Rsch., 2000—. Recipient Young Scientist award Botanical Soc. Japan, 1994, Young Scientist award Japan Soc. Culture Collections, 1998. Mem. Japanese Soc. Phycology (exec. coun. 1997-98). Avocations: boxing, Origami, Sumou wrestling, sightseeing. Home: 4-15-2 Shimohoya Hoya-shi, Tokyo 202 0004, Japan Office: U Tokyo Dept Biol Scis, Grad Sch Sci 7-3-1, Hongo 113, Japan

NOZAKI, RYOICHI, gastroenterologist; b. Kumamoto, Japan, Oct. 31, 1958; s. Akira and Tomeyo (Fujimoto) N.; m. Chiyoko Kurokawa, May 3, 1984; children: Ryotaro, Mari. B Medicine, Jichi (Japan) Med. Sch., 1983, MD, 1998. Resident Kumamoto (Japan) Red Cross Hosp., 1983-85; staff Kawaura Mcpl. Hosp., Kumamoto, 1983-88, Taragi Mcpl. Hosp., Kumamoto, 1988-90, Tamana Chuo Hosp., Kumamoto, 1990-93; head Takano Hosp., Kumamoto, 1993-95, vice dir. Coloproctology Ctr., 1995—; Cert. in gastroenterol. endoscopy. Contbr. chpt. to book, articles to profl. jours. Recipient award Japan Soc. Multiphasic Health Testing and Svcs., 1996. Fellow Japan Gastroenterol. Endscopy Soc. (bd. cert.), Japanese Soc. Gastroenterol. Mass Survey (bd. cert.). Avocations: baseball, walking, computer games. Office: Takano Hosp Coloproc Ctr, Obiyama 4-2-88, Kumamoto City 862-0924, Japan

NOZAWA, KAZUNORI, technological studies educator; b. Utsunomiya, Japan, June 30, 1951; s. Tomonori and Aiko N.; m. Fujiko Katayama, Nov. 4, 1981; 1 child, Satoshi. BEdn, Utsunomiya U., 1974; MA, Kans. U., 1978. Instr. Nagoya Internat. Coll., Japan, 1978-81; from asst. to assoc. prof. Toyohashi U. Technology, Japan, 1981-98; prof. Ritsumeikan U., 1998—. Co-editor: TEFL-10th Anniversary Collected Papers, 1985, Computers and Foreign Language Education, 1993; translator: (books) the Pickled Plum and the Japanese Sword, 1992, Soichiro Honda: The Endless Racer, 1993. Grantee Br. Coun., Min. Edn., 1983, 1994-95, NTT Found., 1997. Mem. Japan Assn. Lang. Tchrs. (program chair 1981-82, pub. rels. chair 1987-91, Call elec. jour. editor 1995-99, co-editor Call-EJ Online 1999—). Avocations: telecommunications, golf, tennis, travel. Office: Ritsumeikan U Coll Econs, Nojihigashi Kusatsu, Shiga 525-8577, Japan

NQWABABA, BONGANI, petroleum company executive; b. Harare, Zimbabwe, Mar. 5, 1966; arrived in South Africa, 1993; s. Victor Vushumuzi and Rosemary Ntombiyethemba (Mohlaohla) N.; m. Lungile Zittah Ngcobo, March 29, 1996; 1 child, Alwande. B in Accountancy (hons), U. Zimbabwe, 1989; MBA, U. Wales and Manchester, 1999. Articled clk. Price Waterhouse, Bulawayo, Zimbabwe, 1988-91, asst. audit mgr., 1992-93; audit mgr. Price Waterhouse, Durban, South Africa, 1993-94; corp. accountant Columbus Stainless, Middleburg, South Africa, 1995, treas. adminstrn. mgr., 1996-97; head. fgn. exch. FBC Fidelity Bank, Johannesburg, South Africa, 1997-99; treas. Shell SA PTY Ltd., Cape Town, South Africa, 1999—. Fin. advisor Highlanders Football Club, Bulawayo, 1989-93; audit com. mem. Greater Johannesburg Met. Coun., 1999. Mem. Zimbabwe Inst. Chartered Accountants. Avocations: travelling, reading, e-commerce. E-mail: bonganibnqwababa@shell.co.za. Fax: 27-21-408-4313. Office: Shell SA PTY Ltd, Shell House Riebler St, Cape Town 8000, South Africa

NTLOLA, PETER MAKHWENKWE, retired translator; b. Phillipstown, Cape, South Africa, July 7, 1908; s. Fanteni and Sarah Notsitsa (Bonani) N.; m. Constance Nomalanga Siningwa, July 7, 1949 (dec. Mar. 1976). Pub. serials on Man's Footprints on the Moon in state-sponsored monthly, 1963-76; columnist to 3 African monthly periodicals. Journalist, editor, reporter, proofreader, photographer, layout artist 5 books translated from English, 1966-86. Served as sgt. in World War II. Home: PO Box 77396, Mamelodi West, 0101 Gauteng Province South Africa

NUCCIOTTI, ANGELO ENRICO LODOVICO, physicist, educator; b. Catania, Sicilia, Italy, Oct. 21, 1967; s. Alessandro and Marina (Sebastiani) N.; m. Monica Sisti, June 27, 1999. Laurea in Physics, U. Milan, Italy, 1992, PhD in Physics, 1996. Guest scientist M.P.I. für Physik, Munich,

Germany, 1992-93; technol. rschr. I.N.F.N., Milan, 1996—. Contbr. articles to profl. jours. Avocations: windsurfing, theatre, music, literature, travel. Office: Nat Inst Nuclear Physics, Via Celoria 16, 20133 Milan Italy

NUCIFORO, ANDREA FRANCESCO, JR., state legislator, lawyer; b. Pittsfield, Mass., Feb. 26, 1964; s. Andrea Francesco Sr. and Irene G. (Wojtkowski) N. BA, U. Mass., 1986; JD, Boston U., 1989. Mem. Mass. Senate, Boston, 1997—, chmn. joint com. banks and banking, 1999—; law clk. to Hon. Frank H. Freedman U. S. Dist. Ct. Mass., 1989-92; assoc. Posternak, Blankstein & Lund, 1992-95; pvt. practice Pittsfield, 1995—. Roman Catholic. Office: Mass State Legis Rm 213B State House Boston MA 02133

NUCKOLLS, JOHN HOPKINS, physicist, researcher; b. Chgo., Nov. 17, 1930; s. Asa Hopkins and Helen (Gates) N.; m. Ruth Munsterman, Apr. 21, 1952 (div. 1983); children—Helen Marie, Robert David; m. Amelia Aphrodite Liaskas, July 29, 1983. B.S., Wheaton Coll., 1953; M.A., Columbia U., 1955; D.Sc. (hon), Fla. Inst. Tech., 1977. Physicist U. Calif., Lawrence Livermore Nat. Lab., 1955—, assoc. leader thermonuclear design div., 1965-80, assoc. leader laser fusion program, 1975-83, div. leader, 1980-83, assoc. dir. physics, 1983-88, dir., 1988-94, assoc. dir. at large, 1994-97, dir. emeritus, 1997—; mem. U.S. Strategic Command Strategic adv. group; cons. def. sci. bd. Dept. Def. Recipient E.O. Lawrence award Pres. and AEC, 1969, Fusion Leadership award, 1983, Edward Teller medal Internat. Workshop Laser Interaction and Related Plasma Phenomena, 1991, Resolution of Appreciation, U. Calif. Regents, 1994, Sec. of Def. Outstanding Pub. Svc. medal, 1996, Disting. Assoc. award U.S. Dept. Energy, 1996, Career Achievement award Fusion Power Assocs., 1996. Fellow AAAS, Am. Phys. Soc. (J.C. Maxwell prize 1981); mem. NAE. Office: Lawrence Livermore Nat Lab PO Box 808 Livermore CA 94551-0808

NUCKOLS, WILLIAM MARSHALL, electrical goods manufacturing executive; b. Washington, Nov. 1, 1939; s. Edgar Marshall Jr. and Helen Abigail (Potter) N.; m. Margaret Louise Beebe, July 9, 1963 (div. 1980); children: Teryl K., Kerena A.; m. Maureen Joy Ryan, July 18, 1981 (div. 1990); children: Lauren E., Lindsay A.; m. Tuula Elina Renko, June 8, 1991; children: Wilson M., Julia A. BEE, Cornell U., 1962; MS in Indsl. Mgmt., MIT, 1965. Ops. and fin. analyst Ebasco Industries, N.Y.C., 1965-69; mktg. mgr. Gen. Cable Corp., N.Y.C., 1970-73; dir. corp. planning Gen. Cable Corp., Greenwich, Conn., 1974, group v.p., 1975-81; v.p. ops. devel. Penn Ctrl. Corp., Greenwich, 1982-83; group v.p. electronics Burndy Corp., Norwalk, Conn., 1984-89; dir. bus. devel. Uponor Group, Helsinki, 1990-91; chmn., pres., CEO, Pass & Seymour/Legrand, Syracuse, N.Y., 1991-98, chmn., 1999, cons., 1999—; bd. dirs. Ortronics, Inc., Pass & Seymour Can., Inc., The Watt Stopper, Inc.; v.p. Legrand Holding, Inc., 1991-99. Dir. Hiawatha coun. Boy Scouts Am., Syracuse, 1992-99. Mem. IEEE, Elec. Mfrs. Club, Am. Electronics Assn. (dir. 1985-88), Mfrs. Assn. Ctrl. N.Y. (dir. 1993-99). Avocations: sailing, skiing, genealogy, shop, computers.

NUDELHOLE, SUSA, journalist; b. Liège, Belgium, May 11, 1927; s. Simon and Haïa (Schnaider) N.; m. Eliane Françoise Nicolas, Mar. 15, 1952; 1 child, Simone. Internat. chronicler Le Drapeau Rouge, Brussels, 1954-73, chief editor, 1974-77, internat. editorialist, 1978-91; internat. editorialist Libertes, Brussels, 1991, Cittadini Europei, Brussels, 1991-92; free-lance journalist Brussels, 1992—. Mem. Inst. Royal Relations Internat. Home: Rue J-B Labarre 34, B 1180 Brussels Belgium

NUDELMAN, NORMA SBARBATI, chemist, educator; b. Pigue, Argentina, June 2, 1937; d. Humberto and Juana Dorotea (Alonso) Sbarbati; m. Osmar Nudelman, Aug. 14, 1965; children: Alejandra, Guillermo, Luis. BSc, U. Buenos Aires, 1961, MSc, 1962, PhD, 1965. Postdoctoral fellow MIT, Cambridge, 1965-66; rsch. asst. U. Calif. Santa Cruz, 1967; prof. U. Buenos Aires, 1980—; vis. prof. U. Porto Alegre, Brazil, 1992, U. Valence, Spain, 1991, U. E. Anglia, Eng., 1978; prin. rschr. CONICET, Argentina, 1976—; nat. rep. IUPAC, Oxford, Eng., 1995-97. Author: Stability of Drugs, 1975, Carbonylation of Main Group Organometalic Compounds, 1989, The SnAr by Amines in Aprotic Solvents, 1996. Mem. Argentine Chem. Soc., Argentine Organic Chem. Rsch. Soc. (founder). Home: Sucre 2950 5 13, 1428 Buenos Aires Argentina Office: Facultad de Ciencias Exactas, Univ de Buenos Aires, 1428 Buenos Aires Argentina

NUDURUPATI, KISHORE KRISHNA, engineering educator; b. Hyderabad, India, Nov. 16, 1960; s. Prakasarao Nudurupati Venkata Satya Subramanya Surya Parvati N.; m. Hemalatha Balakrishnan, Nov. 8, 1990; 1 child, Uma. B, Osmania U., Hyderabad, 1983; M, Indian Inst. Sci., Bangalore, India, 1985, PhD, 1991. Sci. officer Indian Inst. Sci., 1987-91; lectr. Indian Inst. Tech., Kharagpur, 1991-93, asst. prof., 1993-99, assoc. prof., 1999—. Mem. IEEE (sr. mem.). Office: Indian Inst Tech, Elec Engring Dept, Kharagpur 721302, India

NUE, STEEN, management educator, consultant; b. Aarhus, Denmark, Aug. 26, 1946; s. Alfred and Agnes Nue (Møller) Nielsen; m. Inge Hein-Sørensen, July 20, 1974; children: Anita, Ditte, Vicki. Grad., U. Aarhus, 1974. Mgmt. cons. LEC, Aarhus, 1971-74; chief mgmt. cons. Regnecentralan, Aalborg, Denmark, 1974-76; fin. dir. Chloride Scandanavia, Aalborg, 1976-78; prof. U. Aalborg, 1977—; prof. Aalborg Bus. Coll., 1981—, chief mgmt. cons., 1981—; fin. mgr. Aalborg Portland, 1978-79, Autocentralan, Aalborg, 1979-81. Author: Operations Research, 1982. Mgr. Skovbakken, Aarhus, 1971-74, Danish Basketball Fedn., Copenhagen, 1972-74. Recipient Mgr.'s award Danish Basketball Fedn., 1972. Home: Jens Stoffersens Vej 36, DK-9000 Ålborg Denmark Office: Aalborg Bus Sch, Porthusgade 1, DK-9000 Ålborg Denmark

NUEBLER-MORITZ, MICHAEL, oralmaxillofacial surgeon; b. Oberhausen, Rheinland, Germany, Oct. 2, 1962; s. Heinz Joachim and Ursula Maria (Sippli) M.; m. Gundula Nuebler, Oct. 1, 1994; 1 child, Sarah Ann-Kathrin. DMD, U. Mainz, Germany, 1988, MD, 1991. Oral and maxillofacial surgeon U. Regensburg (Germany), 1991-96; cranio-maxillofacial surgeon U. Zurich, Switzerland, 1996-98; vis. prof. Inst. for Laser Medicine, U. Duesseldorf, 1996-98; mem. staff OMF Clinic Applied Laser Dentistry, Tafers, Switzerland, 1998-2000, OMF Clinic Applied Dentistry and Medicine, Amberg, Germany, 2000—. Mem. editl. bd. Internat. Jour. Oral and Maxillofacial Surgery, 1998-99; contbr. articles to profl. jours. Mem. Internat. Soc. Lasers in Dentistry (country rep. Switzerland 1997-2000), Deutsche Gesellschaft für Laser-Zahnheilkunde, Deutsche Gesellschaft für Mund-Kiefer-Gesichts-Chirurgie, Swiss Study Group for Laser Surgery, Schweizerische Gesellschaft für Oro-Faziale Lasermedizin (sec. 1998-2000). Roman Catholic. Achievements include research in applications of fibers and lasers in the field of cranio-maxillofacial surgery. Office: OMF Clinic Applied Laser Dentistry and Medicine, Obere Nabburger Str 1, D-92224 Amberg Germany

NUGAPITIYA, MANOSHANTHA BANDARA, civil and mining engineer, management consultant; b. Colombo, Sri Lanka, Apr. 6, 1961; came to Australia, 1991; s. Bernard and Marie (Gunasekera) N.; m. Chandini Antoinette Kapuwatte, Aug. 8, 1991. BSc in Engring., Moratuwa U., Colombo, 1985; M in Civil and Mining Engring., U. Sydney, Australia, 1993; PhD student in project mgmt., U. Tech. Sydney, 1996—. Chartered profl. engr. Asst. project mgr. Sydney Internat. Airport Refurbishment, 1993-95; project cons. Airport Link Rlwy. Project, NSW, Australia, 1996, Homebush Bay (Olympic 2000) Infrastructure Devel., NSW, Australia, 1996-98, Thredbo Landslide Repairs and Alpine Way Reconstrn., Australia, 1998-99, Sydney Internat. Airport SA 2000 Project, Australia, 1999—. Served as flight lt. Sri Lanka Air Force Directorate of Civil Engring., 1985-91, commdg. officer civil engring. ea. zone, 1988-91. Recipient Partnering Excellence commendation Master Builders Australia, 1994, Engring. Excellence award, 1998. Mem. ASCE, Inst. Engrs. (Australia). Roman Catholic. Achievements include notable findings in ignition temperatures of pyrites, comparisons between thermal tests and explosion tests on pyrites, influence of particle sizes on explosion data on pyrites; microscopic analysis of products from thermal and explosion tests; current research in project interface management through use of symbolism, culture and behavioral science. Home: 22/76 Lenthall St, Kensington 2033, Australia Office: APP Infrastructure & Mgmt Cons, L4 53 Berry St, North Sydney 2060, Australia

NUGAYEV, RINAT MAGDIEVICH, physicist, philosopher of science, researcher; b. Kazan, Tatarstan, Russia, May 30, 1953; s. Magdi Alimjanovich and Nafisa Khasanovna (Masoutova) N.; m. Gulnur Schamilevna Galieva, Aug. 19, 1984; children: Schamil, Nafisa. Student, Kazan U., 1970-75, Inst. Space Rsch., Moscow, 1975-76; MS, Moscow U., 1979; PhD, Russian Acad. Sci., Moscow, 1991. With Kazan Inst. Tech., 1979-82; docent, prof. Kazan U., 1982-93; head dept. Kazan Med. U., 1994, Tatarstan Acad. Sci., Kazan, 1995—; mem. organizing com. Internat. Seminar on Geometrization of Physics, Kazan, U. Author: Reconstruction of Scientific Theory Change, 1989, Reconstruction of Mature Theory Change: A Theory Change Model, 1999; contbr. articles to profl. jours. Named Outstanding Scientist of Russia, Pres. Yeltzin, 1994-97, 2000—; Soros Found. grantee, 1989, 91, 93, 95, 99, Russian Found. Basic Rsch. grantee, 1998, 2000. Mem. Am. Phys. Soc., Brit. Soc. for Philosophy of Sci. (acad. com. of phys. interpretations of relativity). Avocation: numismatics. Home: Chekhov St 4v-2, 420012 Kazan Tatarstan Russia Office: Acad of Sci, Volgogradskaya 49, 420044 Kazan Russia

NUGEE, EDWARD GEORGE, Queen's counsel; b. Godalming, Surrey, U.K., Aug. 9, 1928; s. George Travers Nugee and Violet Mary Richards; m. Rachel Elizabeth Makower, Dec. 1, 1955; children: John Francis, Christopher George, Andrew James, Richard Edward. BA with 1st class honors jurisprudence, Oxford U., 1952, MA, 1956. Barrister-at-law, 1955. Pvt. practice London, 1955—, Queen's counsel, 1977—; dep. high ct. judge Supreme Ct. Eng. and Wales, London, 1982-97; mem., vice chmn. and chmn. bd. studies Coun. Legal Edn. Eng., 1967-90; mem. Lord Chancellor's Law Reform Com., Eng., 1973—; mem., chmn. Common Professional Edn. Bd., Eng., 1976-90. Author: Nathan on Charities Act 1960, 1962; editor: Halsbury's Laws of England, Landlord and Tenant, 3d edit., 1958, Real Property, 3d edit., 1960, 4th edit., 1982, reissue, 1998, others. Chmn. Govt. Com. on Mgmt. of Blocks of Flats, Eng. and Wales, 1984-85; chmn. bd. govs. Brambletye Sch., East Grinstead, 1972-77; mem. coun. Radley Coll., 1975-95; ch. commr. Ch. of Eng., 1989—; trustee Lambeth Palace Libr., 1999—. Decorated Territorial Decoration, Her Majesty the Queen, 1964; Eldon Law scholar Oxford U., 1953. Mem. Bar of Eng. and Wales (gen. coun. 1962-66), The Inst. (pres. 1986-87), Inner Temple (treas. 1996). Home: 10 Heath Hurst Rd, London NW3 2RX, England Office: Wilberforce Chambers, 8 New Square, Lincoln's Inn, London WC2A 3QP, England

NUGÉE, JOHN FRANCIS, bank executive; b. London, Nov. 9, 1956; s. Edward George and Rachel Elizabeth (Makower) N.; m. Victoria Mary Elinor Simpson, Feb. 11, 1989; children: Jennifer Kate, Emma Charlotte, Samuel John. BA with honors, Cambridge U., England, 1977, MA, 1980. Various positions fgn. exch. divsn. Bank of England, London, 1986-91, tech. advisor fgn. exch. divsn., 1991-92; exec. dir. Hong Kong Monetary Authority, 1992-96; dir. Hong Kong Note Printing Ltd., 1996; chief mgr. fgn. exch. divsn. Bank of England, 1996—. Fellow Royal Geographical Soc.; mem. Worshipful Co. Weavers (warden 1997-98). Avocations: field hockey, wine connoisseur. Office: Bank of England, Threadneedle St, London EC2R 8AH, England

NUGENT, HELEN MARION, bank executive; b. Brisbane, Queensland, Australia, Feb. 13, 1949; d. Murray Robert and Elfa Barbara (Napier) Illingworth; m. Michael Nugent, Jan. 30, 1971; children: Elizabeth Marion, James Michael. BA with honors, U. Queensland, Brisbane, 1971, PhD, 1978; MBA, Harvard U., 1982. Sr. tutor history dept. U. Queensland, Brisbane, 1971-80; assoc. McKinsey & Co., Melbourne, 1982-87; ptnr. McKinsey & Co., Melbourne and Sydney, Australia, 1987-92; prof. in mgmt., dir. MBA program Australian Grad. Sch. Mgmt., Sydney, 1992-94; dir. strategy Westpac Banking Corp., Sydney, 1994-99; non-exec. dir. TAB Queensland, Brisbane, 1999—, United Energy, Melbourne, 1999—, Macquarie Bank, Sydney, 1999—. Chmn. Ministerial Inquiry into Major Performing Arts, Sydney, 1999; dep. chmn. Australia Coun., Sydney, 1997—, chmn. major orgn. fund, 1997—; dep. chmn. Opera Australia, Sydney, 1994-98. Mem. Australian Inst. Co. Dirs. (bd. dirs. 1999), Harvard Club of Australia. Avocations: opera, tennis, reading. Office: Macquarie Bank Level 11, 1 Martin Pl, Sydney 200 NSW, Australia

NUGENT, LORI S., lawyer; b. Peoria, Ill., Apr. 24, 1962; d. Walter Leonard and Margery (Frost) Meyer; m. Shane Vincent Nugent, June 14, 1986; 1 child, Justine Nicole. BA in Polit. Sci. cum laude, Knox Coll., 1984; JD, Northwestern U., Chgo., 1987. Bar: Ill. 1987, U.S. Dist. Ct. (no. dist.) Ill. 1988, U.S. Ct. Appeals (7th cir.) 1995. Assoc. Peterson & Ross, Chgo., 1987-94; assoc. Blatt, Hammesfahr & Eaton, Chgo., 1994, ptnr., 1994—. Co-author: Punitive Damages: A Guide to the Insurability of Punitive Damages in the United States and Its Territories, 1988, Punitive Damages: A State-by-State Guide to Law and Practice, 1991, Japanese edit., 1995, Pocket Part, 1999; contbr. articles to law jours. E-mail: lnugent@bhelaw.com. Office: Blatt Hammesfahr & Eaton 222 S Riverside Plz Ste 1500 Chicago IL 60606-6000

NUGENT, NELLE, theater, film and television producer; b. Jersey City, May 24, 1939; d. John Patrick and Evelyn Adelaide (Stern) N.; m. Donald G. Baker, June 6, 1960 (div. 1962); m. Benjamin Janney, June 22, 1969 (div. Apr., 1980); m. Jolyon Fox Stern, Apr. 7, 1982; 1 child, Alexandra Fox Stern. BS, Skidmore Coll., 1960, DHL (hon.), 1981. Chmn. bd. McCann & Nugent, Prodns. Inc., N.Y.C., 1976-86; pres. Foxboro Prodns., Inc., N.Y.C., 1985-94; pres., CEO Foxboro Entertainment, 1990-94; pres. The Foxboro Co., Inc.; co-prin. Golden Fox Films, Inc. Stage mgr. various off-Broadway shows, 1960-64; prodn. asst.: Broadways plays Any Wednesday, 1963-64, Dylan, 1964, Ben Franklin in Paris, 1964-65; stage mgr. Broadway shows, 1964-68; prodn. supr., then gen. mgr., 1969-76, assoc. mng. dir. Nederlander Corp., operating theaters and producing plays in N.Y.C. and on tour, 1970-76; prodr.: Dracula, 1977 (Tony award), The Gin Game (Tony nom.), The Elephant Man, 1978 (Tony award, Drama Critics award), Morning's at Seven, 1980 (Tony award), Home, 1980 (Tony nomination), Amadeus, 1981 (Tony award); also produced: Rose and Piaf, 1980, Otherwise Engaged, The Life and Adventures of Nicholas Nickleby, 1981 (Tony award, Drama Critics award), The Dresser (Tony award nominee), 1981, Mass Appeal, 1981; The Lady & The Clarinet, 1982; The Glass Menagerie (revival), 1983; Painting Churches (Obie award), 1983; Total Abandon, 1983; All's Well That End's Well, 1983 (Tony nominee); Pilobolus Dance Company, 1983; Pacific Overtures (revival), 1984; Much Ado about Nothing/Cyrano de Bergerac (repertory) (Tony award nominees), 1984; Leader of the Pack (Tony award nominee), 1985, The Life and Adventures of Nicholas Nickleby (revival) (Tony award nominee), 1986; prodr.: TV spls.; Morning's At Seven, Piaf; Pilobolus; prodr. A Fighting Choice, 1986-88, A Conspiracy of Love, 1987, The Final Verdict, 1990 (Cable Ace award nominee Best Picture); exec. prodr. (TV pilot) Morning Maggie, 1987, Dick Clark Prodns., 1988-90, (feature films) Student Body, 1993, Getting In, 1994, Jane Doe, 1996; (TV films) In the Presence of Mine Enemies, 1995-96 (Houston Festival Silver Star award), A Town Has Turned to Dust, 1997 (World Festival Silver medal 1998), After the Storm, 2000. Mem. Am. Women's Econ. Devel. Corp. (bd. dirs.). Office: Foxboro Co Inc 133 E 58th St Ste 301 New York NY 10022-1236

NUGENT, WALTER TERRY KING, historian; b. Watertown, N.Y., Jan. 11, 1935; s. Clarence A. and Florence (King) N.; children from previous marriage: Katherine, Rachel, David, Douglas, Terry, Mary; m. Suellen Hoy, 1986. AB, St. Benedict's Coll., 1954, DLitt, 1968; MA, Georgetown U., 1956; PhD, U. Chgo., 1961. Instr. history Washburn U., 1957-58; asst. prof. Kans. State U., 1961-63; asst. prof. history Ind. U., 1963-64, assoc. prof., 1964-68, prof., 1968-84, assoc. dean Coll. Arts and Scis., 1967-71, dir. overseas study, 1967-76, chmn. history dept., 1974-77; Andrew V. Tackes prof. history U. Notre Dame, 1984-00, Andrew V. Tackes prof. emeritus, 2000—; Paley lectr., Fulbright vis. prof. Hebrew U., Jerusalem, 1978-79; vis. prof. U. Hamburg, 1980, U. Warsaw, 1982; Mary Ball Washington Fulbright prof. U. Coll., Dublin, 1991-92; summer seminar dir. NEH, 1979, 84, 86; bd. mem. U.S.- Israel Ednl. Found., 1985-89; USIA acad. specialist, lectr., Brazil, 1996. Author: The Tolerant Populists, 1963, Creative History, 1967, The Money Question During Reconstruction, 1967, Money and American Society 1865-1880, 1968, Modern America, 1973, From Centennial to World War: American Society 1876-1917, 1977, Structures of American Social History, 1981, Crossings: The Great Transatlantic Migrations 1870-1914, 1992, (with Martin Ridge) The American West: The Reader, 1999, Into the West: The Story of Its People, 1999. Newberry Libr. fellow, 1962, Guggenheim fellow, 1964-65, Huntington Libr. fellow, 1979, 85, Beinecke fellow Yale U., 1990. Mem. Western Hist. Assn., Soc. Am. Historians, Soc. of Historians of the Gilded Age and Progressive Era (pres. 2000—). Democrat. Roman Catholic.

NUIJTEN, WIM, computer scientist; b. Gilze, The Netherlands, Aug. 27, 1966; m. Annemieke van Gorkom, Aug. 30, 1996. Degree in computer sci. cum laude, U. Eindhoven, The Netherlands, 1990, DSc, 1994. Rschr. U. Eindhoven, The Netherlands, 1990-94; project mgr. ILOG Scheduler, Paris, 1995-99; dir. optimization tech. ILOG, 1999—; cons. RIKS, Maastricht, The Netherlands, 1992-94; vis. rschr. Netherlands Orgn. for Sci. Rsch., Pitts. and Waterloo, Can., 1992, Boulder, Colo., 1994. Contbr. articles to profl. jours. Recipient ITEA prize European Cmty. for ILOG Scheduler, Brussels, 1995. Mem. Soc. for Computing Engrs. Office: ILOG SA, 9 rue de Verdun, F-94253 Gentilly France

NUISSL VON REIN, EKKEHARD, adult education educator; b. Kiel, Germany, June 15, 1946; children: Henning, Alexander, Benjamin. PhD, U. Bremen, 1974; Habilitation, U. Hannover, 1987; Dr. h.C., U. Temesvas, 2000. Editor, scientist newspaper, Heilbronn, Germany, 1966-67; pub. rels. officer U. Heidelberg, 1970-73; chmn. AFEB Rsch. Inst., Heidelberg, 1974-88; dir. Adult Continuing Edn. Ctr., Hamburg, Germany, 1989-91; prof. U. Marburg, Germany, 1991—. Author: Adult Education in Germany, 1995, Adult Education in the European Community, 1988; contbr. articles to profl. jours. Mem. German Inst. for Adult Edn. (chmn. 1992—). Office: DIE, Hansaallee 50, D-60320 Frankfurt Germany

NUJOMA, SAM DANIEL, president of Namibia; b. Ongandjera, Namibia, May 12, 1929; s. Utoni Daniel and Mpingana (Kondombolo) N.; married; 4 children. LLD, Ahmadu Bello U., Zaria, Nigeria, 1982, Roma U., Maseru, Lesotho, 1983. Pres. South West Africa People's Orgn. of Namibia (SWAPO), Windhoek, 1960—; pres. of Namibia, Windhoek, 1990—. Recipient Ho Chi Minh award World Peace Council, 1986, Masters Degree Order of Brasilia Fed. Dist. Gov. Brasilia, 1987; named citizen of Silvester mayor, Calif., 1965. Avocations: reading, swimming, fishing, gardening. Office: Office of Pres, State House Mugabe Ave Pvt Bag 13339, Windhoek 9000, Namibia

NULL, ELISABETH HIGGINS, librarian; b. Worcester, Mass., Dec. 1, 1942; d. Carter Chapin Higgins and Katharine Huntington (Bigelow) Doman; m. Henry Harrison Null IV, July 13, 1963 (div. 1970); children: John Higgins, Jacob Van Uechten. BA, Sarah Lawrence Coll., Bronxville, N.Y., 1983; MA, Yale U., 1985, MPhil in Am. History, 1989; MA in Folklore, U. Pa., 1987; M Libr. and Info. Sci., Cath. U. Am., 1995. V.p. Abington Pub. Co., Clark's Summit, Pa., 1966-70; CEO Green Linnet Records, Danbury, Conn., 1971-81; vis. lectr. Am. Musical Life, Georgetown U., 1991-98; libr. and conversion specialist nat. digital libr. program Libr. of Congress, Washington, 1996-98, expert cons., 1995; ind. writer, coord. editor, cybrarian on edn issues Rural Sch. and Cmty. Trust, 1999—; bd. dirs. Horizon Comm., New Haven, 1978—; program chair Folklore Soc. Greater Washington, 1993-94; humanities scholar-in-residence Conn. Coun. for Humanities and Conn. Dept. for the Arts, Waterbury, Conn., 1986-87; program co-chair Washington Folk Festival, 1999—; fieldworker in folklore Waterbury Ethnic Music Project, 1986-87. Singer 2 recordings: The Feathered Malden, 1977, American Primitike, 1981; performance career with guitarist Bill Shute included 6 appearances with Garrison Keillor's A Prairie Home Companion; major venues include Phila. Folk Festival, Bklyn. Mus., Mus. Natural History. Incorporator John Woodman Higgins Armory, Worcester, Mass., 1966—; sec. Stanton Park Neighborhood Assn., Washington, 1990; bd. dirs. Johna and Clara Higgins Found., 1999—. Folger Shakespeare Libr. Seminar fellow, 1989-91. Mem. ALA, Am. Folklore Soc., Soc. for History of Early Am. Rep., Folklore Soc. Greater Washington (bd. dirs., program dir., festival com.). Democrat. Episcopalian. Avocations: folk music performer, song writer. E-mail: elisabeth.null@tcs.wap.org. Home and Office: 706 Bonifant St Silver Spring MD 20910-5534

NULTSCH, WILHELM, botany educator, plant physiologist; b. Magdeburg, Germany, Mar. 20, 1927; s. Wilhelm and Elfriede (Lehmann) N.; m. Dorothea Simon, Apr. 1, 1950; children: Wolf-Rüdiger, Sibylle. D Natural Scis., U. Halle, Germany, 1953, Habilitation, 1959. Asst. prof. U. Halle, 1953-54; microbiologist various chem. cos., Magdeburg, 1954-59; lectr. U. Tübingen, Germany, 1959-65, assoc. prof., 1965-66; prof. botany U. Marburg, Germany, 1966-95, dir. Bot. Inst., 1966-71, dir. Bot. Garden, 1966-75; dir. Biol. Inst. Helgoland, Hamburg, 1994-98. Author: Allgemeine Botanik, 1996, Mikroskopisch Botanisches Praktikum, 1995. Recipient Order of Merit, Germany, 1996. Mem. German Bot. Soc. (pres. 1985-94), Am. Soc. for Photobiology (assoc. editor 1981-88), European Soc. for Photobiology (pres. 1991-93), Internat. Phcological Soc., Union German Biol. Socs. (pres. 1994-95), Fed. Republic Germany (order of merit 1996). Avocation: chess. Home: Hasenmoor 6, D-25462 Rellingen Germany

NUMANO, ALLEN STANISLAUS MOTOYUKI, musician, writer; came to U.S., 1974; Grad., St. Joseph's Coll., Colombo, Ceylon, 1929; postgrad., Worcester Coll., Oxford, Eng., 1940, Royal Coll. Music, London, 1940. Sr. examiner, translator Gen. Hdqs. Supreme Comdr. for Allied Powers, Tokyo, 1945-47; cons., chief tech. translator U.S.-Japanese joint venture Pfizer Taito Co. Ltd., Tokyo, 1954-68; lectr. English composition Sophia U., Tokyo, 1967-68; founder Safilta Tech. Translation Svc., 1969—. Author: (as A.L.A. Corenanda) Music and Reminiscences, 1982-83; translator: All About Christmas (Maymie R. Krythe), 1962; pioneering originator in new field of study Mentalogy; contbr. concert revs., recital critiques and mus. news briefs Nippon Times (now Japan Times), also articles to Times of Ceylon, Organic Forum, Indian Labour Rev.; pencil sketches exhibited at 55th Ann. Exhbn. of Ceylon Soc. of Arts, Colombo, 1952; performed as violinist at Royal Coll. Hall, Colombo, 1940; inventor tech. innovations. Del. Sr. Citizens of Honolulu to Gov.'s State Conf. on Aging. Recipient Gov.'s Cert. of Appreciation, 1980, certs. of appreciation Pres. Ronald Reagan and Pres. George Bush; named Citizen of Yr. 1994 Principality of Hutt River Province Australia. Fellow Inst. Linguists; mem. Soc. Authors, London (assoc.), Translator's Assn., London, Smithsonian Instn. (nat. mem.), George Bush Presdl. Libr. Mus.

NUMBERE, DAOPU THOMPSON, petroleum engineer, educator; b. Buguma, Nigeria, Mar. 30, 1951; came to the U.S., 1975; s. Thompson and Norah (West) N.; m. Tonye Eugenia Higgwe, Dec. 29, 1987. BS in Mech. Engring., U. Coll. Swansea, 1975; MS in Petroleum Engring., Stanford U., 1977; PhD, U. Okla., 1982. Asst. prof. U. Mo., Rolla, 1982-88, assoc. prof., 1988-96, prof., 1996—, head dept. petroleum engring., 1996—; cons. Sigma Cons., Mattoon, Ill., 1987-93, Marathon Oil Co., 1998; chmn. Mo. Oil and Gas Coun., 1996—. Author: Petroleum Reservoir Class Manual, 1991, Principles of Waterflooding, 1998. Recipient Shell-BP award, 1971-75, Selwyn Caswell prize U. Coll. Seansea, 1975, Okla. Rsch. award Okla Rsch. Coun., 1981. Mem. ASME, Internat. Soc. for Computer Methods and Adv. in Geomechanics, Soc. Petroleum Engrs., Sigma Xi. Achievements include development of an innovative method for streamline generation for oil recovery prediction, simultaneous prediction of oil recovery and water influx for oil and gas reservoirs. Office: U Mo Rolla 119 Mcnutt Hall Rolla MO 65401

NUNES, RAUL, civil engineer; b. São Paulo, Brazil, Oct. 9, 1943; s. Antônio and Filomena (da Conceição) N. m. Margarida Maria Nunes; children: Newton, Adriana. Student, Claretian Sem., Rio Claro, 1960; Civil Engr., São Paulo U., 1968, postgrad., 1969-71. Tchr. physics St. Augustin Coll., 1966; sci. programming coord. Cyberplan S/A, São Paulo, 1969-70; mgr. tech. applications Proconsult, São Paulo, 1971-72; systems analyst, database supr., cons. geog. info. systems Prodam S/A, São Paulo, 1971-74; prof. physics St. Augustin Coll., São Paulo, 1964; prof. informatics St. Cross Coll., São Paulo, 1985-86; dir. VV Ltd., São Paulo, 1980-98; cons., analyst, programmer Datamec, Perwa, Eletropaulo, Votorantin, Prodam, others, 1974-88. Author: Rule and Compass Problems, 1963, Introduction to Fortran II, 1964, Oscillations, 1966, Data Bank Management System, 1974; translator: Problems of Descriptive Geometry, 1963, Simulation with GASP II, 1971; contbr. articles to profl. jours.; inventor Little Strings Method; developer softwares for civil engring., system for mktg. rsch. analysis using techniques of automatic programming, 1969-72; creator Universal Syntax Analyzer and the Standard Logic for Sequential Files Processing, 1969-85.

Recipient Premio Marina Cintra, 1962. Office: Caixa Postal 45350, 04010970 São Paulo Brazil

NUNEZ DE ARCO, JORGE ALBERT, psychiatrist; b. La Paz, Bolivia, Apr. 23, 1950; arrived in Spain, 1975; s. Ernesto Manuel and Sara Vitaliana (Mendoza) N. de A.; m. Maria Dolores Valenzuela; children: Georgina, Laura. MS in Biology, U. San Andres, La Paz, 1973; MD, U. Seville, Spain, 1979, degree in psychology, 1988, PhD, 1991. Asst. prof. biology and genetics U. San Andres, 1973-75; resident in psychiatry Psychiat. Hosp. U. Macarena, Seville, Spain, 1979-81, Psychiat. Hosp. Almeria, Spain, 1981-84; psychiatrist Hosp. Valme de Seville, 1985-91; tchr. psychobiology U. Seville, 1985, assoc. prof. psychobiology, 1986-88; official psychiatrist Penitentiary Psychiat. of Min. Justice, Seville, 1991-94; chief psychiatry Santa Isabel Clinic, Seville, 1993—; dir. mental health area, Hosp. de Valme, Seville, 1990-91, didr. acute patients, Unity Hosp., Penitentiary Psychiat. Min. Justice, Seville, 1992-94; organizer com. Congress of Psychobiology, Seville, 1985, 86. Author: Evaluacion y percepcion de paisajes naturales en niños en situacion quirurgica, 1993; contbr. articles to profl. jours. Hon. Consul of Bolivia, Seville, 1995-98. Mem. APA (fgn. affiliate), L.Am. Neurol. Sci. Soc., L.Am. Assn. Study of Mental Retardation, Royal Med. Coll. Seville. Roman Catholic. Avocations: computer science, photography, Aimara books. Office: ADIMSA, Av Republica Argentina 22-A 3, E-41011 Seville Spain

NUNEZ-ESCOBAR, ROBERTO, soil science educator; b. Autlan, Jalisco, Mex., Apr. 28, 1934; ss. Francisco Nunez-Garcia and Maria Guadalupe Escobar-Curiel; m. Maria Carmen Elisea-Cuevas, May 26, 1956; children: Roberto, Ana Gloria, Maria Carmen. Degre in agronomy engring., Nat. Sch. Agr., Chapingo, Mex., 1958; MSc, U. Calif., Davis, 1961; PhD in Soil Sci., N.C. State U., 1967. Rsch. asst. Rockefeller Found., La Piedad, Mex., 1956-59; rschr. Inst. Agrl. Rsch., Ciudad Obregon, Mex., 1961-62; rsch. prof. Postgrad. Coll., Chapingo, 1962-64, chmn. soils dept., 1967-74, rsch. dir., 1983-94; subdir. Inst. Natural Resources Postgrad. Coll., Montecillo, Mex., 1997-99; nat. investigator Sistema Nal. de Investigadores, Mex., 1984—. Editor: Agrociencia, 1997. Mem. Mexican Soc. Soil Sci. (pres. 1968-70), Internat. Soc. Soil Sci. (v.p. Mex. 1990-94), Am. Soc. Agronomy, Mexican Acad. Engrs. Office: Postgrad Coll, Edafologia, 56230 Montecillo Mexico

NUNEZ-LAWTON, MIGUEL G., international finance specialist; b. Havana, Cuba, Feb. 8, 1949; came to U.S., 1964; s. Miguel Nunez-Portuondo and Silvia Lawton-Alfonso. BSBA, Georgetown U., 1971, postgrad. in Econs., 1973. Asst. treas. Deltec Securities Corp., N.Y.C., 1971; debt specialist internat. econs. dept. World Bank, Washington, 1973-95; internat. cons. Miami, Fla., 1995—; UNCTAD chief tech. adviser Bureau of the Treasury, Manila, Philippines, 1989-90. Bd. dirs., treas. Friends of Art Mus. of the Americas, OAS, Washington, 1988-90; bd. dirs. Friends of Peru, 1991—; panel mem. The Lawrenceville Sch., 1992; mem. Presdl. Inaugural Com., Washington, 1997. Roman Catholic. Avocations: art collecting, genealogy. Home: 8860 SW 123rd Ct # K106 Miami FL 33186-4152

NUNEZ-MORA FERNANDEZ, MARIBEL, lawyer; b. Mexico City, Feb. 12, 1973; d. Fernando Nuñez-Mora Escobedo and Maria Isabel Fernandez Gallegos. Student in law, Inst. Tecnologico Autonomo Mex, Mexico City, 1992-97. Civil law litigator Hegewisch Abogados S.C., Mexico City, 1995-96, Consultores Exprofesso S.C., Mexico City, 1997; cons. mcpl. and constl. law Centro Nacional Desarrollo Mcpl. Govt., 1997—; civil litagator, 1998—. Recipient Latino Scholar award, State of Ind., 1992. Mem. Phi Delta Phi Internat. (pres. 1996—, treas. 1995-96, legal cons. 1994—). Avocations: equitation, aerobics, social service, paramedics. Home: Puebla #49 Col Contreras, 10700 Mexico City DF, Mexico Office: Arroyo, Galindo y Lara, Insurgentes Sur # 1377 12, 03920 Mexico City Mexico

NUNLEY, JULIA RILEY, physician, educator; b. Cleve., Aug. 22, 1957; d. Cyril Penn and Lauer Ann Agnes (Riley) N. BS, Purdue U., 1979; MD, CWRU, 1983. Diplomate Am. Bd. Internal Medicine, Nephrology and Dermatology. Intern, resident Med. Coll. Va., Richmond, 1983-86, fellow nephrology, 1986-89, clin. instr., asst. prof., 1989-93; chief dialysis dept. McGuire VA Med. Ctr., Richmond, 1990-93; resident dermatology Med. Coll. Va., Richmond, 1993-96, asst. prof. dermatology, 1996—. Contbr. chpt. in book, articles to profl. jours. Recipient Women's Inner Circle Achievement award, 1991, 92. Mem. Am. Soc. Nephrology, Internat. Soc. Nephrology, Am. Acad. Dermatology, Phi Beta Kappa. Roman Catholic. Office: Med Coll Va PO Box 980164 Richmond VA 23298-0164

NUNN, TREVOR ROBERT, theater director; b. Ipswich, Eng., Jan. 14, 1940; s. Robert Alexander and Dorothy May (Piper) N.; m. Janet Suzman, 1969 (div. 1985); 1 child; m. Sharon Lee Hill, 1986 (div. 1991); 2 children; m. Imogen Stubbs, 1994; 2 children. Student, Ipswich Coll., Downing Coll., Cambridge, Eng.; LLD, U. Warwick, 1982; MA (hon.), U. Newcastle-upon-Tyne, 1982. Trainee dir. Belgrade Theatre, Coventry; assoc. dir. Royal Shakespeare Co., Warwickshire, Eng., 1964-68, artistic dir., 1968-78, joint artistic dir., 1978-86, chief exec., 1968-86, dir. emeritus, 1986—; artistic dir. Royal Nat. Theatre, London, 1997—. Dir. plays including Tango, 1965, The Revenger's Tragedy, 1965, 69, The Taming of the Shrew, The Relapse, The Winter's Tale, 1969, Hamlet, 1970, Henry VIII, 1970, Roman Season: Antony and Cleopatra, Coriolanus, Julius Caesar, Titus Andronicus, 1970, Macbeth, 1974, 76, Hedda Gabler (own version) 1975, Romeo and Juliet, 1976, Comedy of Errors, 1976, The Alchemist, 1977, As You Like It, 1977, Every Good Boy Deserves Favour, 1977, Three Sisters, 1978, The Merry Wives of Windsor, 1979, Once in a Lifetime, 1979 (Evening Standard Best Dir. award), Juno and the Paycock, 1980, The Life and Adventures of Nicholas Nickleby (with John Caird), 1980 (Tony Best Dir. award 1981, Evening Standard Best Dir. award), touring revival, 1985, Cats, 1981 (Best Dir. Tony award 1982), All's Well That Ends Well, 1981, Henry IV (parts I and II), 1981, 82, Peter Pan (with John Caird), 1982, Starlight Express, 1984, Les Miserables (with John Caird), 1985 (Tony award for best dir. 1987), Fair Maid of the West, 1986, Chess, 1986, Aspects of Love, 1989, Othello, 1989, The Baker's Wife, 1989, Timon of Athens, 1991 (Evening Standard Best Dir. award, Best Dir. Critics' Cir. award), The Blue Angel, 1991, Measure for Measure, 1991, Heartbreak House, 1992, Arcadia, 1993, Sunset Boulevard, 1993 (Tony nominee - Direction of a Musical, 1995), Enemy of The People, 1997, Mutabilite, 1997, Not About Nightingales, 1998, Oklahoma, 1998, Betrayal, 1998, Troilus and Cressida, 1999, The Merchant of Venice, 1999, Summerfolk, 1999, Albert Speer, 2000; (opera) Idomeneo, 1982, Porgy and Bess, 1986, revived 1987,92, Cosi Fan Tutte, 1991, Peter Grimes, 1992, Katya Kabanova, 1994; TV shows Include: Anthony and Cleopatra, 1975, Comedy of Errors, 1976, Every Good Boy Deserves Favour, 1978, Three Sisters, 1978, Macbeth, 1978, Great Hamlets, 1983, Othello, 1990, Porgy and Bess, 1993, Oklahoma!, 1999, Merchant of Venice, 2000; writer, dir. Shakespeare Workshops Word of Mouth, 1979, films Hedda, Lady Jane, 1985, Twelfth Night, 1996; author: British Theatre Design, 1989. Recipient London Theatre Critics Best Dir. award, 1969; Soc. Film and TV Arts award, 1975, Ivor Novello award for best Brit. Musical, 1976; numerous others.

NUNZ, GREGORY JOSEPH, aerospace engineer, program manager, educator, entrepreneur; b. Batavia, N.Y., May 28, 1934; s. Sylvester Joseph and Elizabeth Marie (Loesell) N.; m. Georgia Monyea Costas, Mar. 30, 1958; children: Karen, John, Rebecca, Deirdre, Jaimie, Marta. BSChemE, Cooper Union, 1955; postgrad., U. So. Calif., Calif. State U.; MS in Applied Math., Columbia Pacific U., 1991, PhD in Mgmt. Sci., 1993. Adv. design staff, propulsion mgr. U.K. project Rocketdyne div. Rockwell, Canoga Park, Calif., 1955-65; mem. tech. staff Aerospace Corp., El Segundo, Calif., 1965-70; mem. tech. staff propulsion div. Jet Propulsion Lab., Pasadena, Calif., 1970-72; chief. monoprop. engring. Bell Aerospace Corp., Buffalo, N.Y., 1972-74; group supr. comb. devices Jet Propulsion Lab., Pasadena, 1974-76; dep. group leader, asst. div. leader, program mgr. internat. HDR geothermal energy program, program mgr. space-related projects Los Alamos (N.Mex.) Nat. Lab., 1977—; assoc. prof. electronics L.A. Pierce Coll., Woodland Hills, Calif., 1961-72; instr. No. N.Mex. C. C., Los Alamos, 1978-80, div. head scis., 1980-92; adj. prof. math. U. N.Mex., Los Alamos, 1980—; sr. mgmt. rep. Excel Telecommunications, Inc., 1995-98. Author: Electronics Lab Manual I, 1964, Electronics in Our World, 1972; co-author: Electronics Mathematics, vol. I, II, 1967; contbg. author Prentice-Hall Textbook of Cosmetology, 1975, Alternative Energy Sources VII, 1987, The Xerolithic Geothermal ("Hot Dry Rock") Energy Resource of the United States: An Update, 1993; contbr. articles to profl. jours.; inventor smallest catalytic liquid N2H4 rocket thrustor, co-inventor first monoprop/biprop bimodal rocket engine, tech. advisor internat. multi-prize winning documentary film One With the Earth. Mem. Aerial Phenomena Research Orgn., L.A., 1975. Fellow AIAA (assoc., liquid propellants com. on stds.); mem. Tech. Mktg. Soc. Am., Math. Assn. Am., ARISTA, Shrine Club, Masons, Ballut Abyad Temple. Avocations: travel, archaeology, fgn. langs., golf. Office: Los Alamos Nat Lab PO Box 1663 Los Alamos NM 87545-0001

NURBAKHSH, MOHSEN, bank executive; b. Tehran, 1948. Mem. Majlis; dep. min. of fin. and econ. affairs Govt. of Iran; gov. Ctrl. Bank; min. of econ. affairs and fin. Govt. of Iran, v.p.; gov. Bank-e Markazi Jomhouri-ye Islami ye Iran, Tehran. Office: Bank Markazi Jomhouri Islami Iran, 213 Ferdowsi Ave, 11365 8551 Tehran Iran*

NURGALIEV, TIMERFAIAZ CHAMATSHINOVICH, physicist, researcher; b. Bashkiria, Russia, Jan. 3, 1952; s. Chamatsha and Galima Nurgaliev; m. Snejanka Ivanova Miteva, Aug. 12, 1977; children: Emil, Ruslan. Grad. in Radio-Physics, St. Petersburg (Russia) State U., 1975, PhD, 1985. Engr., physicist Bashkirian State U., Ufa, Russia, 1981-87; rschr./fellow 2nd degree Inst. Electronics BAS, Sofia, Bulgaria, 1988-93, rschr./fellow 1st degree, 1993-96, sr. rschr., 1996—. Contbr. articles to profl. jours. Office: Inst Electronics, 72 Tzarigradsko Chaussee, 1784 Sofia Bulgaria

NURHALIM, PURNOMO SANTOSO, banking executive; b. Rembang, Indonesia, Dec. 11, 1951; s. Slamet N.; m. Linawati Sutedja, May 29, 1977; children: Laurensia, Diana. BS, Inst. Tech. Bandung, 1974. From sys. engr. to gen. mgr. IBM, Jakarta, Indonesia, 1973-93. Office: Bank Ctrl Asia, Jl S Parman Kav 79, Barat Jakarta 11420, Indonesia

NURHUSSEIN, MOHAMMED ALAMIN, internist, geriatrician, educator; b. Adwa, Ethiopia, Apr. 4, 1942; came to U.S., 1972; s. Hagos and Teberih (Yusuf) N.; m. Zahra Said, June 10, 1972; children: Nadia, Siham, Safy. BS, Haile Selasie Mil. Acad., Harar, Ethiopia, 1961; MD, Zagreb (Yugoslavia) U., 1968. Intern, resident, then fellow Bklyn.-Cumberland Med. ctr., 1972-77; emergency rm. physician Cumberland Hosp., Bklyn., 1977-79; attending physician in medicine Kings County Hosp. Ctr., Bklyn., 1979—; faculty practice medicine, geriatrics SUNY Univ. Hosp., Bklyn., 1983—; instr., then asst. prof. SUNY Health Sci. Ctr., bklyn., 1979—; med. cons., dir. drug abuse treatment Coney Island Hosp., Bklyn., 1982-84; adv. bd. Bklyn. Alzheimer's Disease Assistance Ctr., 1992—. Fellow ACP; mem. Am. Geriatric Soc., Am. Lung Assn., N.Y. Acad. Scis., Amnesty Internat., Physicians for Human Rights. Democrat. Moslem. Office: SUNY Health Sci Ctr 450 Clarkson Ave Brooklyn NY 11203-2056

NURIDSANY, CLAUDE, filmmaker; b. Paris, Apr. 11, 1946; m. Marie Pérennou. Filmmaker: The Looking-Glass Inhabitants, 1984, Microcosmos, 1996 (5 awards); author (with Marie Perennou) Éloge de L'Herbe, 1988, Microcosmos. Recipient Grand prize Cannes Film Festival, 1996. Office: Editions de la Martinière, 2 rue Christine, 75006 Paris France*

NURMI, HANNU JUHANI, political science educator; b. Turku, Finland, Aug. 24, 1944; s. Leo Emil and Laina Lemmitty (Hakanpaa) N.; m. Maire Irmeli Jaska, 1969; children: Lasse Juhani, Hanna Liina Maria. MA, Univ. Turku, 1969; PhD, U. Turku, 1974. Assoc. prof. U. Turku, 1975-95, prof. polit. sci., 1995—, dean faculty social scis., 1991-96; vis. prof. Finnish studies U. Minn., Mpls., 1998. Author: Comparing Voting Systems, 1987, Rational Behaviour and the Design of Institutions, 1998, Voting Paradoxes and How to Deal with Them, 1999. Fulbright-Hays scholar The Johns Hopkins U., Balt., 1972-73; Wolfson fellow Brit. Acad., Colchester, Essex, Eng., 1978. E-mail: hnurmi@utu.fi. Fax: 358-2-3335090. Home: Varusmestarink 6 C 17, 20360 Turku Finland Office: U Turku Dept Polit Sci, Arwidssonink 2, 20014 Turku Finland

NÜRNBERG, BERND E.R., molecular pharmacology educator; b. Kassel, Hessen, Germany, Mar. 17, 1958; s. Eberhard K.U. and Käte (Kalkofen) N.; m. Angelika H.E. Wiesener, Dec. 10, 1957; children: Daniela, Christina. Degree in Pharmacy, U. Würzburg, Germany, 1982; Dr.rer.nat., U. Erlangen, Germany, 1986, Degree in Medicine, 1989, MD, 1990; pvt. dozent, U. Berlin, 1997. Cert. specialist pharmacology and toxicolgy; cert. pharmacist. Postdoctoral staff U. Erlangen, 1986-88, Royal North Shore Hosp., Sydney, Australia, 1988-89, Free U., Berlin, 1989-96; group leader Free U., 1996-2000; prof. U. Ulm, Germany, 2000—; cons. U. Iowa, 1987, German Drug Adminstrn., Berlin, 1990—. Author: Handbook of Experimental Pharmacology, 1997, 2000. Cpl. German Army Air Force, 1977-78. Home: Colmarer Weg 19, D-14169 Berlin Germany Office: Dept Pharmacology & Toxicol, Univ Ulm, D-89069 Ulm Germany

NÜRNBERGER, GÜNTHER, mathematician; b. Marktredwitz, Bavaria, Germany, Jan. 13, 1948; s. Rudolf and Lotte (Schodner) N.; m. Gudrun Tiller, Apr. 7, 1982; 1 child, Sandra. Mathematician, Erlangen U., Nuremberg, Germany, 1974, D of natural scis., 1975, D of natural scis. habilitation, 1979. Asst. prof., assoc. prof. Erlangen U., Nuremberg, 1974-83, 85-89; assoc. prof Mannheim U., Germany, 1983-85; prof. Mannheim U., 1989—, dean, 1993-94; cons. Siemens Inc., Nuremberg, 1985-88; organizer internat. sci. confs. Author: Approximation by Spline Functions, 1989; editor: Delay Equations, Approximation and Application, 1985, Numerical Methods of Approximation Theory, 1987, Multivariate Approximation and Splines, 1997; editor Jour. of Approximation Theory, 1988, Comms. Applied Analysis, 1996; contbr. over 70 articles to profl. jours. Fiebiger prof. Munich 1985. Avocations: music, sports. Office: U Mannheim, Faculty Math & Computers, 68131 Mannheim Germany

NURSER, JOHN SHELLEY, retired religious organization administrator; b. Northampton, Eng., May 26, 1929; s. Arthur and Florence (Shelley) N.; m. Elizabeth Kimber, Aug. 30, 1956; children: George, Isabelle, Henry, Louise. PhD, Cambridge (Eng.) U., 1958. Ordained priest Episcopal Ch., 1958. Curate Tankersley Parish, Yorkshire, Eng., 1958-61; dean Trinity Hall, Cambridge, 1961-68; warden St. Mark's Inst. of Theology, Canberra, Australia, 1968-74; rector Freckenham Parish, Suffolk, Eng., 1974-76; chancellor Lincoln Cathedral, Eng., 1976-92; dir. Christianity and the Future of Europe, Cambridge, 1992-97; sr. rsch. assoc. Von Hugel Inst., Cambridge, 1996-99; ret., 1999; spl. prof. theology U. Nottingham, Eng., 1989-92; vice chmn. coun. Lincoln Theol. Coll., 1976-92; sec. Com. for Christian Work in Delhi, 1962-68; mem. steering com. Liberty Under the Law, Magna Carta Tour for U.S. Constitutional Bicentennial, 1985-87; fellow human rights ctr. U. Essex, 1998—; Cecil Woods fellow Va. Theol. Sem., 1999. Author: The Reign of Conscience (Lord Acton), 1987; co-author: Non-Stipendiary Ministry, 1988; contbr. to books: Churches on the Wrong Road, 1986, A History of Lincoln Minster, 1994. Trustee Sudbury Common Lands, 1995—; chmn. Lincoln Archeol. Support Group, 1985-88; canon emeritus Lincoln Cathedral, 1999—. Lt. Royal Navy, U.K., 1950-53. Recipient Templeton prize, 1994; Commonwealth fellow Harvard Div. Sch., 1956-57. Mem. Ecclesiastical History Soc. (mem. com. 1984-87), Cambridge Theol. Fedn. (sr. assoc.). Avocations: sculpture, gardens, archeology. Home: 68 Friars St, Sudbury Suffolk CO10 2AG, England

NUSBAUM, GEOFFREY DEAN, psychotherapist; b. Berkeley, Calif., Apr. 1, 1946; s. Wayne Dale and Jeanne (Hankins) N.; m. Barbara Ann Pierfy, June 1, 1986; 1 child, Michael Wayne. BA, Washington U., St. Louis, 1967; MA, Hartford Sem. Fdn. Consortium, 1971, PhD, 1978. Diplomate Am. Bd. Med. Psychotherapy; cert. therapist Am. Assn. for Marriage and Family Therapy; lic. therapist, N.J. Pvt. practice Marlton, N.J. and Phila., 1972—; cons. N.Y. Fertility Rsch. Found., N.Y.C., 1978-83, Bancroft Sch., Haddonfield, N.J., 1983-87; fellow Internat. Coun. Sex. Edn. and Parenthood Am. U. Author: Community, Self Identity, 1978; peer manuscript reviewer to sci. jours. Bd. dirs. Calcutta House AIDS Hospice. Mem. Am. Soc. for Reproductive Medicine, Am. Soc. for Psychosomatic Ob-Gyn., N.Y. Acad. Scis.

NUSCHELER, FRANZ, political science educator; b. Bad Wörishofen, Bavaria, Germany, Apr. 11, 1938; s. Konrad and Maria (Hierl) N.; m. Karin Beiermeister, Jan. 13, 1967; children: Ulrike, Max. PhD, U. Heidelberg, Germany, 1967. Asst. prof. U. Hamburg, 1969-74; prof. U. Duisburg, Germany, 1974—; vis. prof. Dokkyo U., Japan, 1987-88; dir. Inst. for Devel. and Peace, U. Duisburg, Germany, 1990—; cons. Found. for Devel. and Peace, Bonn, Germany, 1990—, Goethe Inst., Munich, 1995—, NGOs; mem. adv. bd. German Overseas Inst., Hamburg, 1995—. Author: (books) Walter Bagehot, 1968, Nowhere at Home, 1985 (Peace award 1985), Development Policy, 1995; editor (Handbook) Handbook of Third World (8 vols.), 1992-94, (Political Book of 1995, Friedrich Ebert Found., Bonn, 1995). Recipient Gustav-Heinemann- Peace award Jury of State Govt., North-Rhine-Westfalia, 1985. Office: U Duisburg, Lotharstrasse 68, 47048 Duisburg Germany

NUSINOVICH, GREGORY SEMEON, physicist, researcher; b. Berdichev, Russia, July 18, 1946; came to U.S., 1991; s. Semeon and Esther (Burdo) N.; m. Yelena Naydich, July 2, 1968; children: Maria, Liza, Paulina. MSc, Gorky (Russia) State U., 1968, PhD, 1975. Rsch. scientist Radiophys. Rsch. Inst., Gorky, 1968-77; sr. rsch. scientist, group leader Inst. Applied Physics, Acad. Scis. of Russia, Gorky, 1977-90; sr. rsch. scientist Inst. for Plasma Rsch., U. Md., College Park, 1991—; mem. sci. coun. on phys. electronics Acad. Scis. Russia, 1981-90; cons. Phys. Scis., Inc., Alexandria, Va., 1991—, Sci. Applications Internat. Corp., McLean, Va., 1991-93, Omega-P, New Haven, Conn., 1995—. Co-editor: Gyrotron, 1981, Gyrotrons, 1989; guest editor spl. issues IEEE-PS on high-power microwaves, 1996, cyclotron resonance masers and gyrotrons, 1999; assoc. editor IEEE-PS; contbr. chpts. to books. Fellow IEEE, Am. Phys. Soc. Achievements include development of the theory of multimode gyrotrons, the nonlinear theory of relativistic gyrodevices, theory of gyroamplifiers and the gyrotron producing 100 KW power at the frequency of 500 GHZ. Office: University of Maryland Inst For Plasma Rsch College Park MD 20742-0001

NUSS, JOANNE RUTH, sculptor, artist; b. Gt. Bend, Kans., May 2, 1951; d. Melvin Oliver and Ruth Helen (Brauer) N. Student, Valparaiso U., 1969-71, U. Kans., 1972-73, U. Copenhagen, 1974; BA, Ft. Hays State U., 1975; MFA, Santa Fe Inst. Fine Arts, 1991. lectr. Noon Edition Sta. KCMO-TV, Kansas City, 1981, Menoriah Hosp., Brookridge Elem. Sch., The Jill Shurin Show Telecable 10, Kansas City, 1982, Barton County C.C., Gt. Bend, Nelson-Atkins Mus., Kansas City, Mo., 1984; artist-in-residence Helen Wurlitzer Found., Taos, N.Mex., 1984, 90. One-woman shows include Bette Moses Gall., Gt. Bend, 1980, Art Expo Ctr., San Francisco, 1981, Univ. Gall., Ft. Hays State U., 1985, Am. Legation Mus., Tangiers, Morocco, 1986, Inma Gall., Dhahran, Saudi Arabia, 1994, 96, Bab Rouah Gallery, Rabat, Morocco, 1996, others; group exhbns. include Second Internat. Sculpture Fair, Boston, 1980, Joan Cooke Gall., Kansas City, Mo., 1983, The Batz Lawrence Gall., Kansas City, 1984, Galerie de Rond Point des Champs Elysees, Paris, 1989, Tetouan & La Kabila Gallery, Tetouan, Morocco, 1991, N.Mex. Sculptors Guild, Fuller Lodge Art Gall., Los Alamos, 1992, Hermosa Fine Arts Gall., Durango, Colo., 1995, Tanjah Flandria Art Gall., Marrakech, Morocco, 1997, others; represented in permanent collections including King Hassan II of Morocco, Am. Legation Mus., Prince Mohammed Bolkiah of Bandar Seri Begawan, Brunei, others. Recipient 1st Kans. Artist Purchase award Ft. Hays State U., 1985, Best 3-D Works award Wichita Art Assn., 1983; 1st female fgn. artist commd. for archtl. major project, Tangiers, 1988-90. Mem. Nat. Assn. Women Artists, Nat. Sculpture Soc., Nat. Mus. of Women in the Arts, Internat. Sculpture Ctr., Kans. Sculptor's Assn., Internat. Platform Assn. Avocations: travel, working with other artists, gardening; listed in Dictionary of American Sculptors, 1984. Studio: PO Box 2080 Great Bend KS 67530-2080

NUSSBAUM, HOWARD JAY, lawyer; b. N.Y.C., Dec. 17, 1951; s. Norman and Ruth (Rand) N.; children: Martin Garrett, Daniel Todd. BA, SUNY, Binghamton, 1972; JD, Boston Coll., 1976. Bar: Fla. 1977, U.S. Dist. Ct. (so. dist. trial and bankruptcy bar) Fla. 1977, U.S. Ct. Appeals (5th and 11th cirs.) 1981. Mng. atty. Legal Aid. Svc., Ft. Lauderdale, Fla., 1976-88; ptnr. Weinstein, Zimmerman & Nussbaum, P.A., Tamarac, Fla., 1988-92; pres. Howard J. Nussbaum, P.A., 1993—; chmn. Legal Aid com. North Broward Bar Assn., Pompano Beach, Fla., 1986-87; cons. Police Acad. of Broward County, Ft. Lauderdale, 1985-87.; gen. counsel Gene Glick Mgmt. Corp. Author: Florida Landlord/Tenant Law and the Fair Housing Act, 1989. Gen. counsel Registered Apt. Mgrs. Assn. South Fla., 1993—, Wynmoor Cmty. Coun., 1993—, The Accutrack Safety Systems Corp., 1997—, Dominium Mgmt. Svcs, Inc., J&B N. Am. Movers, Inc. Regents scholar N.Y. State, 1968-72, Presdl. scholar Boston Coll. Law Sch., 1973-76. Mem. ABA (litigation sect.), ATLA, Acad. Fla. Trial Lawyers, Broward Bar Assn., Justice Lodge J.C.C. Avocations: softball, tennis, swimming. Office: 3029 NW 28th Ave Boca Raton FL 33434-6023

NUSSBAUM, JEFFREY JOSEPH, musician; b. N.Y.C., July 7, 1952; s. Eli and Dorothy (Wolkowitz) N.; m. Alison Knopf (div. 1984); m. Joan Feigenbaum, April 5, 1990; 1 child, Samuel Leonard Baum. BA in Music, Hunter Coll., N.Y., 1977; MA in Edn., Bklyn. Coll., 1987; MFA in Early Music, Sarah Lawrence Coll., Bronxville, Tex., 1989. Cert. N.Y.S., N.Y.C. Freelance musician (trumpet, cornetto, natural trumpet), 1979—; tchr. music Park West H.S., N.Y., 1984—; pres., founder Historic Brass Soc., N.Y., 1989—; dir. Manhattan Early Wind Ensemble, N.Y., 1992—, Pan Brass Quintet, N.Y., 1978-84; organized Internat. Hist. Brass Symposium, Amherst, Mass., 1995; organizer Early Brass Colloquium, Royal Acad. Music, London, 1997, Internat. Hist. Brass Symposium, co-sponsored by Cité de la Musique, Paris, 1999, Internat. Symposium co-sponsored with Stimu, Utrecht, Germany, 2000, HBS Cornetto Symposium, Bate Coll., Oxford U. Author: Brass Teaching and Learning: History, Development and Technology of Brass Instruments, 1998; contbr. articles to jours. in field. Mem. Am. Fedn. Musicians, Am. Musicological Soc., Internat. Trumpet Guild, Galpin Soc. Jewish. Home: 148 W 23rd St Apt 2A New York NY 10011-2447

NUSSBAUM, LAUREEN, retired foreign language educator; b. Frankfurt, Germany, Aug. 3, 1927; came to the U.S., 1957; d. Edmund Joseph and Marianne Felicitas (Blumenthal) Klein; m. Rudi H. Nussbaum, Oct. 15, 1947; children: Ralph E., Fred D., Elka N. BA, Portland State U., 1962; MA, U. Wash., 1966, PhD, 1977. Instr. Portland (Oreg.) State U., 1962-77, asst. prof., 1978-81, assoc. prof., 1981-86, full prof., 1987-88, prof. emerita, 1989—. Author: (yearbook) Exilforschung 5 & 11, 1987, 93, (anthologies) Women Writing in Dutch, 1994, Children in the Holocaust—Children in Exile, Children Under Fascism, 1998, Anne Frank: Reflections on Her Life and Legacy, 2000, (handbook) Yale Companion to Jewish Writing and Thought in German Culture, 1997, (reference companion) Bertolt Brecht, 1997; editor: Unvorhanden und Stumm, 1991. Recipient Mosser award Oreg. State Bd. Higher Edn., 1967; Rsch. and Pub. grantee Portland State U., 1983; Visitor's fellow Netherlands Orgn. for Pure Rsch., Leiden, 1985. Mem. Am. Assn. Netherlandic Studies, Am. Assn. Tchrs. German, Internat. Brecht Soc. (exec. com. 1980-82), Soc. for Exile Studies, Assn. for German Studies, Women in German, Am. Friends Svc. Com., Women's Internat. League for Peace and Freedom. Avocations: hiking, swimming, sailing, grandparenting, supporting husband's research. Office: Portland State Univ Dept FLL Box 751 Portland OR 97207

NUSSBAUM, NORBERT, architectural historian, researcher; b. Cologne, Germany, June 24, 1953. PhD, U. Cologne, 1982. Lectr. history of art U. Cologne, 1984-96; prof. archtl. history U. Dortmund, Germany, 1996—. Author: Deutsche Kirchenbaukunst der Gotik, 1985, Bauforschung, Dokumentation and Auswertung, 1992, Spätgotische Dreistützenbauten, 1982, Das gotische Gewölbe, 1999; editor: Der Mittelalterliche Baubetrieb, 1978. Mem. Koldewey Assn. Office: Univ Dortmund, August-Schmidt-Strasse 6, 44221 Dortmund Germany

NÜSSLEIN-VOLHARD, CHRISTIANE, medical researcher; b. Magdeburg, Germany, Oct. 20, 1942; d. Rolf Volhard and Brigitte (Haas) Volhard. Diploma in Biochemistry, U. Tübingen, 1968, PhD, 1973; ScD (hon.), Yale U. Rsch. assoc. lab. of Dr. Schaller Max-Planck Inst. for Devel. Biology, Tübingen, 1972-74; postdoctoral fellow lab. of Dr. W. Gehring, Biozentrum, Basel, Switzerland, 1975-76; postdoctoral fellow lab of Dr. K. Sander U. Freiburg, 1977; head rsch. group European Molecular Biology Lab., Heidelberg, 1978-80; rsch. group leader Friedrich-Miescher Lab. Max-Planck-Gesellschaft, Tübingen, 1981-85; sci. mem. Max-Planck Assn., dir. Max-Planck Inst. for Devel. Biology, Tübingen, 1985-90, dir. genetics dept., 1990—; hon. prof. U. Tübingen. Contbr. numerous articles to profl. jours. Recipient Albert Lasker Basic Med. Rsch. award Albert and Mary Lasker

Found., 1991, Louisa Gross Horowitz prize Columbia U., 1992, Forderpreis award Deutschen Forschungsgemeinschaft, 1986, Franz Vogt prize U. Giessen, 1986, Carus medal German Acad. Leopoldine, 1989, Rosenstiel medal Brandeis U., Nobel Prize in Medicine, 1995; Schering prize, Berlin, 1993. Mem. European Molecular Biology Orgn., Berlin Brandenburgische Acad., Am. Philosophical Soc. Achievements include rsch. in using embryos, created a series of genetic screens that led to the identification of most of the genes responsible for the organism's body segment development, establishing that genes encode signaling molecules that tell cells where they are in the organism's overall structure and what their function is to be. Office: Max Planck Inst Entwicklung, Sbiologie Spemannstr 35, D-72076 Tübingen Germany

NUTTER, DAVID GEORGE, urban planner; b. Manchester, Conn., Nov. 25, 1939; s. George Huitt and Catherine Lavina (Casey) N.; m. Ellen Marie Manfredonia, Sept. 7, 1968; children: Susan Katharine, Anne Amelia. BA in English cum laude, Tufts U., 1961; MS in Urban Planning, Columbia U., 1967. City planner Balt. City Planning Commn., 1967-69; dir. planning Charles Ctr.- Inner Harbor Mgmt., Inc., Balt., 1969-72, v.p., 1972-76; pvt. cons. Balt., 1976-83; dir. downtown mall mgmt. dist. Denver Partnership, Inc., 1983-85; exec. dir. Rochester (N.Y.) Downtown Devel. Corp., 1985-87; prin. Nutter Assocs., Rochester, 1987-2000; dir. Salisbury-Wiconico Planning and Zoning Commn., 2000—. Author: Selecting a Developer, 1983. Bd. dirs. Soc. Preservation of Fed. Hill, Balt., 1969-73, Arts for Greater Rochester, 1986-90, Rsch. Ctr. for Delmarva, History and Culture, Salisbury (Md.) State U., 1998—; chmn. Town of Brighton (N.Y.) Conservation Bd., 1992-95. Sgt. U.S. Army, 1962-65. William F. Kinne Travelling fellow Columbia U., 1967. Mem. Am. Inst. Cert. Planners, Am. Planning Assn., Urban Land Inst. (assoc.), Canal Soc. of N.Y. State, N.Y. Planning Fedn. Avocations: historical map and atlas collecting, American and English history, computer mapping, hiking, history of urbanism. Home: 240 Allens Creek Rd Rochester NY 14618-4136

NUTTON, VIVIAN, history of medicine educator; b. Halifax, Eng., Dec. 21, 1943; s. Eli and Constance (Mortimer) N.; m. Christine Clements, July 7, 1973; children: Alice A., Christopher W., Rosemary G. BA, Cambridge (Eng.) U., 1965, MA, 1969, PhD, 1970. Fellow Selwyn Coll., Cambridge U., 1967-77; lectr. Univ. Coll., London, 1977-93, prof. history of medicine, 1994—; head acad. unit Wellcome Inst. History of Medicine, London, 1996-2000. Author: From Democedes to Harvey, 1988, The Western Medical Tradition, 1995; Editor: (Galen) On Prognosis, 1979, (Galen) On My Own Opinions, 1999. Fellow Internat. Acad. History of Medicine, Internat. Acad. History of Sci., Royal Coll. Physicians of London (hon.), Academia Europaea. Avocations: campanology, singing.

NUTZINGER, HANS GOTTFRIED, economics professor; b. Hauingen, Fed. Republic Germany, May 25, 1945; s. Richard and Luise K. (Keller) N.; m. Christel L. Bretzer, 1970; children: Verena, Heidi. Diploma in Econs., U. Heidelberg, Fed. Republic Germany, 1968; D in Polit. economy, U. Heidelberg, 1973, Habilitatio, 1976. Asst. U. Heidelberg, 1968-73, U. Dortmund, Dortmund, Fed. Republic Germany, 1973-74; rsch. fellow Deutsche Forschungsgemeinschaft, Bonn, Fed. Republic Germany, 1974-76; provisionary U. Bielefeld, U. Heidelberg, 1977-78; prof. econs. U. Kassel, Kassel, Fed. Republic Germany, 1978—; dean Dept. of Econs., U. Kassel, 1988-89. Author: (with others) Arbeit ohne Umweltzerstorung, 1983, 2d edit., 1988, Mitbestimmung in der Krise, 1987, Mitbestimmung: Norm und Wirklichkeit, 1984, Unternehmenskultur und innerbetriebliche Kooperation, 1995, Zwischen Nationalökonomie und Universalgeschichte, 1995, Naturschutz-Ethik-Ökonomie, 1996, Die Enstehung des Arbeitsrechts in Deutschland, 1997, Perspektiven der Mitbestimmung, 1999, Eigentumsrechte verpflichten, 1998, Instutionen pragen Menschen, 1999; editor: (with others) Codetermination, 1989, Erwerbsarbeit und Dienstgemeinschaft, 1991. Cons. Bund für Umwelt und Naturschutz Deutschland, Bonn, 1981—. Fellow Inst. Advances Studies, Berlin, 1992-93. Mem. Am. Econ. Assn., Royal Econ. Soc., Verein fur Socialpolitik. Home: Poststr 4, 69151 Neckargemund Germany Office: U Kassel FB7, Nora Platiel Str 6, 34109 Kassel Germany

NUWER, HENRY JOSEPH (HANK NUWER), journalist, educator; b. Buffalo, N.Y., Aug. 19, 1946; s. Henry Robert and Teresa (Lysiak) N.; m. Alice May Cerniglia, Dec. 28, 1968 (div. Mar. 1980); 1 child, Henry Christian; m. Jenine Howard, Apr. 9, 1982; 1 child, Adam. BS in English, SUCNY, Buffalo, 1968; MA in English, N.Mex. Highlands U., 1971; PhD equivalency, Ball State U., 1987. Freelance author, journalist, 1969—; asst. prof. Clemson (S.C.) U., 1982-83; assoc. prof. Ball State U., Muncie, Ind., 1985-89; sr. editor Rodale Press, Emmaus, Pa., 1990-91; editor in chief Arts Ind. Mag., Indpls., 1993-95; assoc. prof. journalism U. Richmond, Va., 1995-97; Hazing expert-lectr., 1990—; Hazing cons. NBC Movie-of-the-Week Moment of Truth: Broken Pledges, Indpls., 1994; adj. prof. journalism Ind. U. Sch. Journalism, Indpls., 1995—, Anderson U., 1998—; nat. advisor/NCAA study and survey on hazing in coll. athletic groups Alfred U., 1999. Author: Steroids, 1990, Broken Pledges: The Deadly Rite of Hazing, 1990, How to Write Like an Expert, 1995, The Legend of Jesse Owens, 1998, Wrongs of Passage, 1999, High School Hazing, 2000; mem. editl. staff Chic Mag., 1976-77; corr. Onhealth.com. Network On-Line mag., 1998-99; contbr. articles to profl. jours. Grantee Nat. Endowment for the Arts, 1976, Idaho Humanities Coun., 1985, Gannett Found., 1988; named Mag. Adviser of Yr., Coll. Media Advisers, 1988, Disting. Alumnus, Buffalo State Coll., 1999. Mem. Soc. Profl. Journalists, Investigative Reporters and Editors. Democrat. Roman Catholic. E-mail: hnuwer@iupui.edu.

NUYTTEN, HERMAN H.J., chemist, laboratory director; b. Roeselare, Belgium, June 25, 1952; s. Gerard H.P. Nuytten and Anna M.F. Courtens; m. Martine L.F.M. Claeys, Sept. 8, 1975; children: Christophe, Philippe, Olivier. Degree in Chemistry, U. Ghent, Belgium, 1973, licentiaat in Chemistry, 1975, PhD in Chemistry, 1980, specialist in Clin. Chemistry, 1982. Dir. AZM, Menen, Belgium, 1982—. Contbr. articles to profl. jours. Mem. BVKC (bd. dirs.), ACCC, ASM, WKBWV (bd. dirs.). Avocations: reading, hiking, music. Home: Vinderhoutsedam, Mariakerke 9030, Belgium Office: AZM Lab, Rijselstraat 71, Menen 8930, Belgium

NUZHDINA, MAJA ANATOLIVNA, astronomer, astrophysicist, researcher; b. Omsk, Siberia, Russia, Apr. 19, 1940; d. Anatoliy and Anna (Demidova) N. MS, State U., Kiev, Ukraine, 1963; PhD in Physics and Math., State U., St. Petersburg, Russia, 1995, Acad. Scis., Kiev, 1966. Cert. in physics and math., solar-terrestrial physics. Lectr. Kiev Planetarium, 1963-68; tchr. boarding sch. Yamal, Russia, 1968-70; from jr. rschr. to sr. rschr. Astron. Obs. of U. Kiev, 1970-85, leading rschr., 1995—. Contbr. sci. papers to profl. jours. Avocations: trips, reading, walking. E-mail: mn@aoku.freenet.kiev.ua. Home: Geroey Dnepra 30 39, 04214 Kiev 214, Ukraine Office: Astron Obs, Observatorna 3, Kiev 53 04053, Ukraine

NUZZO, ANNE L., artist; b. St. Clairsville, Ohio, July 24, 1924; d. Louis and Edna Duchoslav; m. John A. Nuzzo, Sept. 16, 1944; children: Frances, James, Thomas, Robert, Frances, MaryAnn. Student, Cleve. Art Inst., 1950, Tri-C Coll., Parma Heights, Ohio, 1975-78, Cleve. State Coll., 1995. Artist dept. art Boise Casacade, Brooklyn, Ohio, 1975-88; artist Brenda Kloos Gallery, Cleve., Marco Art Gallery, Marco Island, Fla. Chmn. art shows Green Briar Art League, Parma Heights, 1975-99, Metro Parks Fall fest, 1987—. With WAC, 1944-46. Mem. Marco Art League, Greenbriar Art League, Metro Parks of Cuyahoga County. Republican. Roman Catholic. Avocations: stone sculpture, woodcut printing. Home: 5837 Flower Dr Parma Heights OH 44130-1501

NUZZO, ANTHONY GERALD, banking executive; b. New Haven, Aug. 9, 1951; s. Michael Anthony and Theresa Mary (Aitro) N.; m. Julie Nuzzo, Mar. 22, 1975; children: Beth, Michael, Cortney. BA, Boston Coll., 1973; MBA, Columbia U., 1975. CLU. Brand asst. Procter & Gamble, Cin., 1975-76, sales rep., 1976, asst. brand mgr., 1976-77; asst. product dir. Johnson & Johnson, New Brunswick, N.J., 1977-78, spl. project dir., 1978-79; product dir. Johnson & Johnson, Milltown, N.J., 1979-82, group product dir., 1982-84; v.p. Am. Express Travel Related Services, New York, 1984-87; v.p., exec. com. Am. Express Can., Inc., Markham, Ont., 1987-88; v.p. internat. mktg. Am. Express, N.Y., 1988; v.p. Chemical Bank, N.Y.C., 1988-90, sr. v.p., 1990-91; pres., CEO Chemical Bank Del., Wilmington, 1991-92; pres., founder Advanced Mktg. Assocs., Inc., East Brunswick, N.J., 1992-93; pres., CEO Fidelity Trust Co., Salt Lake City, 1993-98, chmn., 1998-99; pres., CEO Fidelity TempWorks/TempSource, Boston, 1998-99; chmn., pres., CEO @Bank, Framingham, Mass., 1999—; mem. Visa Mktg. Advisors, 1989-92, 93-98. Editor: Physiology, 1984. Dir., co-chair, co-founder Citizens Against UnSafe Environments, East Brunswick, N.J., 1981-93; bd. dirs. Utah Bd. Fin. Instns., 1995-98. Named to PS&D Merchandising Hall of Fame Procter & Gamble, Cin., 1977, named Scholar of the Coll., Boston Coll., 1973; recipient Bus. Sch. Service award Columbia U., 1975, Excellence award Package Designer Coun., N.Y.C., 1980, Clio Creative Excellence award Clio Adv. Body, N.Y.C., 1981, Effie award, N.Y.C., 1989. Mem. Boston Coll. Alumni Assn., Columbia Bus. Sch. Alumni Assn. (dir. N.Y. club 1975), Utah Bankers Assn. (bd. dirs. 1996-98), Utah Assn. Fin. Svcs. (bd. dirs. 1993-98, treas. 1995-96). Avocations: golf, skiing, baseball coaching, hockey managing, reading. Fax: (508) 661-2402. Office: @Bank 111 Speen St Ste 410 Framingham MA 01701-2090

NVODARU, ION, zoologist; b. Slobozia Conache, Romania, Mar. 7, 1955; s. Constantin and Zurnia N.; m. Adriana Popa, Nov. 22, 1980; children: Cristian, Irina. Diploma in engring., Dunarea de Jos U., 1981, PhD, 1997. From rsch. asst. to sr. scientist Danube Delta Rsch. & Design Inst., Tulcea, Romania, 1981-99; sr. scientist Danube Delta Nat. Inst. Rsch. & Devel., Tulcea, 1999—. Mem. Romanian Fishers Assn., The Shad Found. Office: Danube Delta Nat Inst, Babadag, Tulcea 8800, Tulcea

NWADIANI, MON, educational planner, education educator; b. Agbor Town, Delta, Nigeria, Dec. 24, 1958; s. Nwadiani Emefiele and Ororonwa Enyihon Nwadiani; m. Comfort Onaigho Irabor, Apr. 8, 1990; children: Ekaose, Oseoma, Kpamiose, Ogenose. BE in Geography with honors, U. Benin, Bening City, Nigeria, 1980; MEd in Ednl. Planning, U. Ibadan, Nigeria, 1982; PhD in Ednl. Planning, U. Ibadan, 1985. Lectr. II U. Benin, 1988-90, lectr. I, 1990-93, sr. lectr., 1993-96, assoc. prof., 1996—; sr. master Bapt. Girls H.S., Agbor Town, 19985-88; coord. part-time postgrad. program dept. ednl. adminstrn. and founds. U. Benin, 1990-96, coord. dept. doctoral programs Faculty of Edn., 1996—, asst. dean Postgrad. Sch., 1997-99; cons., mayor Monose Amalgamates, Benin City, 1993—; chmn. univ. staff sch. mgmt. bd., 1998-99. Author: Demand for Tertiary Education in Nigeria, 1994, Financing Education: Strategies and Matters Arising, 1997. Chmn. bd. govs. Justice Internat. Sch., Benin City, 1992—; bd. govs. Iyoba Girls Secondary Sch., Benin City, 1996—; edn. resource person Politico Bur., Boji-Boji, Nigeria, 1986; mem. Delta State Boundary com., 1999—, Delta State Scholarship com., 1999—. Secondary Sch. Merit scholar Midwest State of Nigeria, 1973-75, scholar Fed. Republic of Nigeria, Lagos, 1983-85, U. Ibadan, 1981-85. Mem. Nigerian Assn. Edn. Adminstrn. and Planning (sec. Edo-Delta State chpt. 1990—), Nigerian Soc. Ednl. Planning (asst. editor 1989—), Nigerian Ednl. Rsch. Assn. Avocations: gardening, domestication of animals, motorcycling, music, football. Home: PO Box 1957, 20 Iwaseh St, Agbor Town Delta, Nigeria Office: Faculty Edn U Benin, Ugbowo Campus, PMB 1154 Benin City Nigeria

NWANA, HYACINTH SAMA, computer scientist; b. Bamenda, Cameroon, Sept. 11, 1964; arrived in Eng., 1982; s. Elias Muthas and Odilia Mantan (Domatob) N.; m. Bertha Andin Gwanyama, Aug. 8, 1992; children: Gima, Gana, Lena. BSc with honours, U. Birmingham, Eng., 1985; MSc, Aston U., Eng., 1986, PhD, 1989; MEd, Cambridge (Eng.) U., 1997; MBA, London Bus. Sch., 1999. Chartered engr. Asst. prof. U. Liverpool, Eng., 1989-91, U. Keele, Eng., 1991-94; sr. rsch. scientist BT Labs., Ipswich, Eng., 1995-97, prin. rsch. scientist, 1998, tech. group leader, 1998-99; chief tech. ofcr./dir. Antfactory, 1999—; edn. cons. U. Buea, Cameroon, 1992-95. Editor: Software Agents and Soft Computing, 1997, Mathematical Intelligent Learning Environments, 1997. Recipient DEC European Artificial Intelligence award, 1991, Folon award, 1991. Mem. Brit. Computer Soc. Roman Catholic. Avocations: football, jogging, running, playing with kids, tennis. Office: antfactory Ltd Prospect Ho. 80-110 New Oxford St, London WC1A 1MB, England

NWEEIA, MARTIN THOMAS, dentist, musician, composer, anthropologist; b. New Britain, Conn., Apr. 15, 1954; s. Alexander and Nellie (Lazar) N. BA in English and Biology, Trinity Coll., Hartford, Conn., 1977; DDS, Case Western Res. U., 1984; cert., Brånemark Clinic, Göteborg, Sweden, 1989. Pvt. practice, Honolulu, 1984-95, Sharon, Conn., 1995—; dental corr. Sta. KGMB-TV, CBS, 1988-92; dental columnist Honolulu Star-Bull., Gannett-USA Today, 1988-95; attending cons. Sharon Hosp., 1995—; dental dir. World Health Network, Phila., 1997-98; leader exptn. to study adult tooth morphology of living Ticuna Indians of Colombian Amazon, 1978; leader expdn. to study childhood dental diseases of Micronesia Ulithi Atoll, Yap State, 1983; expert witness for dental malpractice MedQuest, 1998—. Author: (pamphlet) Baby-Bottle Tooth Decay, 1989, The Whole Tooth, Answers to Questions You Always Wanted to Ask Your Dentist, 1999; editor Hawaii Dental Jour., 19990-94 (Golden Pen award 1994); contbr. articles to profl. jours., including Am. Jour. Dental Rsch., Internat. Jour. Dental Rsch., Am. Jour. Phys. Anthropology; music dir. As One Hawaii, 1992, Do It Together, Honolulu, 1993, Cool Notes, Hawaii Dept. Edn., 1994; PBS documentaries including; Light in Art, 1988, Facets, 1989 (Kona Gold, Blue Ribbon Am. Film and Video Assn.), Dark After Daylight, Taiwan, 1990, Dialog, 1994, to debut video for Waikiki Aquarium Jellyfish (Bronze award N.Y. Internat. Film Festival, Cine Golden Eagle 1994). Constrn. worker rep. United Ch. Fedn., Tarsus, Turkey, 1972. Rsch. grantee in anthropology Explorers Club N.Y., Colombian Amazon, 1978; Joseph Silber fellow Am. Cancer Soc., 1982-83, grad. student rsch. fellow Smithsonian Instn., 1981. Fellow Amer. Col. of Dentists, Acad. Gen. Dentistry (Editl. award of excellence 1999), Acad. Dentistry Internat. (hon.), Internat. Coll. Dentists (hon.), Pierre Fauchard Acad. (hon.), Explorers Club (nat.); mem. Hawaii Dental Assn. (trustee 1993-95), Hawaii Acad. Gen. Dentistry (pub. info. award 1990-93, pres. 1993-95, nat. award for cmty. involvement 1990, nat. award for media rels. 1992, nat. award for editorials, 1999). Republican. Mem. United Ch. of Christ. Avocations: documentary composer and arranger, anthropologist, windsurfing, skiing, tennis and squash. E-mail: boo@snet.net. Home: 16 Grandview Ln Sharon CT 06069-2040 also: 358 Kupaua Pl Honolulu HI 96821-2152 Office: 6 New St Sharon CT 06069-2077

NWOGU, KEVIN NGOZI, linguist, educator; b. Umuohie-Ukwu, Nigeria, Sept. 19, 1953; s. Anthony Ejike and Fidelia Ngbeke (Chigbu) N.; m. Emilia Eleje Isu, Oct. 30, 1981; children: Chigozie, Ogechi, Iauoma, Ndidiamaka, Onyekachi. BA in English, U. Ife, Nigeria, 1978; M in English, U. Jos, Nigeria, 1982; PhD in Linguistics, Aston U., Birmingham, Eng., 1989. Lectr. Fed. Coll. Edn., Kontagora, Nigeria, 1979-80, Yola, Nigeria, 1981-82; from asst. lectr. to lectr. II Fed. U. Tech., Yola, Nigeria, 1983-89, from lectr. I to assoc. prof., 1990-97, prof., 1997—. Author: Technical Report Writing, 1998; editor Systemic Functional Linguistics Forum, 1992—, Yolde, 1998; mem. editl. bd. Dougirei Jour. Edn., 1992—. Spl. marshal Fed. Rd. Safety Corps., Yola, 1995-98. Sgt. Biafran Army, 1967-70. Recipient Commonwealth Acad. Staff award Commonwealth Secretariat, U.K. Mem. Linguistics Assn. Nigeria, Nigeria Assn. Lectrs. English. Roman Catholic. Avocations: table-tennis, basketball. Home: Fed Univ Tech Girei Campus, PO Box 2076, Yola Nigeria Office: Fed Univ Tech, PO Box 2076 Dept Mgmt Gen S, Yola Nigeria

NWOYE, MAY IFEOMA, accountant, business educator, consultant; b. Onitisha, Anambra, Nigeria, Feb. 16, 1956; d. Fidelis Oraekwu and Virginia Achua (Okonkwo) Agulue; m. Gregory Onuigbo Nwoye, Aug. 27, 1977; children: Nneka, Osita. BBA, George Washington U., 1980; MBPA, Southeastern U., 1981; PhD, U. Benin, Nigeria, 1997. Cert. in acctg., Nigeria. Acct. Nutrition Inc., U.S., 1980-81, U.B.T.H., Nigeria, 1981-82; bus. analyst Isomex Nigeria Ltd., 1983-84; sr. acct. U. Benin, 1986-89, prin. acct., lectr., 1990-94, chief acct., assoc. lectr., 1995—; cons. in small bus. mgmt.; assoc. lectr. U. Benin Faculty of Bus.; exec. dir. Highcliff Comms., 1995—. Author: Endless Search, 1984, Small Business Enterprise, 1991, Tides of Life, 1995, othersBlind Expectation, 1997, (with others) Mobilization and Management of Financial Resources in Nigerian Universities, 1995, Death By Installments, 1999; author articles. Mem. Nigerian Inst. Mgmt. (assoc.), Assn. Nat. Accts. of Nigeria, MBA Exec. Inc. Roman Catholic. Avocations: reading, writing, cooking, music, sports, interacting with youth. Office: U Benin, PMB 1154, Benin City Nigeria

NYAGURA, LEVI MARTIN, mathematics and education educator, administrator; b. Rusape, Zimbabwe, Aug. 26, 1946; s. Martin Chizanga and Emeriah (Chidongo) N.; m. Stella Flora Sanyangore, Aug. 27, 1971; children: Nhena, Tatenda, Kudzai, Shingirai. BSc, U. London, 1970; BSc with honors, U. Zimbabwe, Harare, 1975; MSc, U. South Africa, Pretoria, 1980; PhD, So. Ill. U., 1986. Grad. cert. in edn., 1972. Chmn., dep. dean U. Zimbabwe, 1982-83, chmn., 1986-89, dir., 1990-95, pro vice chancellor, 1995—; cons. USAID, Zimbabwe, 1987, 90, World Bank, Zimbabwe, 1990, 91, UNESCO, Zimbabwe, 1991, 93, 95, U. Fort Hare, Alice, South Africa, 1994, 95, U. Botswana, 1993. Author: Strategies to Improve Motivation in Education, 1996; contbr. articles to profl. jours.; editor-in-chief Zimbabwe Jour. Ednl. Rsch., 1990-95. Vice chmn. Nat. Yr. 2K Compliance com., Harare, 1998, Zimbabwe Sch. Exams. Coun., Harare, 1996—; nat. coord. rsch. awards Internat. Devel. Rsch. Ctr., Zimbabwe, 1995. Fulbright scholar 1983-86. Mem. Southern African Math. Scis. Assn., Zimbabwe Ednl. Rsch. Assn. Seventh-Day Adventist. Avocations: golf, soccer, music, information technology, reading management books. Home: 7 Maidenhead Lane, Borrowdale, Harare Zimbabwe Office: U Zimbabwe Box MP 167, Mt Pleasant, Harare Zimbabwe

NYALALI, FRANCIS LUCAS, chief justice; b. Mwanza, Tanzania, Feb. 3, 1935; s. Lucas Makali and Salome (Sato) Madiya; m. Loyce Phares, Dec. 28, 1968; children—Emmanueli, Karoli, Victor, Lulu. B.A. with honors (London), Univ. Coll. of East Africa, Makerere, 1961. Mem. Lincoln's Inn, London, 1965. Bar: Tanzania. Resident magistrate Judiciary Dept., Tanzania, 1966-71, judge High Ct., 1974-77, chief justice, 1977—; chmn. labor tribunal, Labor Dept., Tanzania, 1971-74. Author: Aspect of Industrial Conflicts in Tanzania, 1978. Chmn. presdl. commns. on polit. pluralsim in Tanzania, 1991-92; patron Tanzania Youth Assn., 1993—; appointer Tanzania Social Action Trust Fund, 1994—. Decorated Order of United Republic (Tanzania). Mem. Tanzania Judges and Magistrates Assn. (patron), Soc. For Reform in Internat. Criminal Law, Indian Soc. Internat. Law (hon.) Lincolns Inn Ct. (hon. bencher). Avocations: reading; nature watching. Office: Ct of Appeal, High Court Bldg, Dar es Salaam Tanzania*

NYAM, DENIS CHRISTOPHER, colorectal surgeon; b. Seremban, N Sembilan, Malaysia, Aug. 31, 1962; s. Andrew Thian-Swee and Brenda Liew-Kam N.; m. Adeline Ming-Lee Mow, Apr. 14, 1988; children: Alyssa En Mei, Abigail En Hui. MB, BS, Nat. U., Singapore, 1986, M in Medicine, Surgery, 1991. Intern Nat. U. Hosp., Singapore, 1986-87, resident in surgery, 1988-90, sr. resident in surgery, 1990-91; med. officer dept. colorectal surgery Singapore Gen. Hosp., 1991-92, surg. registrar dept. colorectal surgery, 1992-95; surg. registrar dept. surgery Tan Tock Seng Hosp., Singapore, 1992-93; acting sr. registrar Royal Infirmary of Edinburgh, Scotland, 1993-94; fellow in colon and rectal surgery Mayo Clinic and Mayo Grad. Sch. Medicine, 1995—; sr. surg. registrar dept. colorectal surgery Singapore Gen. Hosp., 1995—, cons. surgeon dept. colorectal surgery, 1997—, dir. lab. surgery, 1998—; clin. coord. Master Medicine course in Surgery, 1992; clin. tchr. Nat. U. Singapore, 1992—; mem. Ministry of Health Sports Coun. (volleyball convenor), 1992-96; social chmn. organizing com. 25th Internat. Soc. Univ. Colorectal Surgeons, Singapore, 1994, course coord. for laparoscopic colorectal surgery workshop pre-congress; instr. Trauma Advanced Life Support Course for Physicians, Singapore, 1995, course dir., 1999—; fellowship divsn. colon and rectal surgery Mayo Clinic, Rochester, Minn., 1995-96; vis. colorectal surgeon Jichi Med. Sch., Tochighi, Japan, 1996; sec., treas. organizing com. on rectal surgery workshop Internat. Coll. Surgeons Overseas meeting and New Changi Hosp. Sci. Meeting, 1997; mem. Singapore Gen. Hosp. perioperative charts computerization com. and social and recreation com.; chmn. Family Day, 1997; mem. standing adv. com. SGH Postgrad. Med. Inst., 1998—. Contbr. over 30 articles to profl. jours. and chpts. to books; presenter at more than 60 sci. confs.; mem. editl. bd. Singapore Med. Jour., 1998. Surgeon officer Singapore St. John's Ambulance Brigade, 1993—, judge First Aid and Home Nursing Competition, 1993, 94; vol. doctor Singapore Cancer Soc.; leader med. team to Cambodia in conjunction with Meth. Ch. Mission to Cambodia, 1997—. Recipient Nat. U. Singapore scholarship 1987, 91, Ministry of Health Singapore scholarship award for colorectal surgery fellowship at Mayo Clinic, 1995, Best Sci. Presentation award VI Congress Nat. Soc. Italiana di Coloproctologia, 1996. Fellow Acad. Medicine Singapore (com. mem. surgeons' chpt.), Royal Coll. Surgeons Singapore, Royal Coll. Surgeons and Physicians Glasgow, Internat. Coll. Surgeons (U.S.); mem. AAAS, Biomed. Rsch. and Exptl. Therapeutics Soc. Singapore, Am. Soc. Colon and Rectal Surgeons, Singapore Med. Assn., Priestley Soc. (Mayo Clinic), Mayo Clinic Alumni Assn., N.Y. Acad. Scis., Soc. for Surgery of Alimentary Tract (U.S.), Singapore Hospice Assn. Office: Singapore Gen Hosp, Colorectal Surg/Outram Rd, Singapore 169608, Singapore

NYBERG, RIITTA HELINÄ, communications and advertising manager; b. Saarijärvi, Finland, July 4, 1947; d. Otto V. and L. Maria Mesiäinen; m. Tapio Nyberg, May 16, 1970; 1 child, Mikko. BSc in Econs., Helsinki Sch. Econs./Bus. Adm., Finland, 1969. With Algol Oy, Espoo, Finland, 1969—, mgr. advt. and comms., 1977—; lectr. in field. Mem. Finnish Assn. Grads. in Econs. and Bus. Adminstrn., Finnish Mktg. Fedn. (chmn. pub. rels. divsn. 1982-83). Avocations: writing, reading, discussing, music. Office: Algol Oy, PO Box 13 Karapellontie 6, 02611 Espoo Finland

NYBORG, HELMUTH, psychoneuroendocrinologist; b. Losning, Denmark, Jan. 5, 1937; s. Kaj and Gerda Sørensen; m. Merete Østrup, June 23, 1961 (div. 1994); children: Casper, Catrine; m. Charlotte Bondesen, Feb. 1, 1994 (div. 1999). BA, U. Copenhagen, 1968; PhD, U. Aarhus, Denmark, 1971, U. Aarhus, 1977. Asst. prof. Inst. Psychology U. Aarhus, 1968-74, assoc. prof. Inst. Psychology, 1974-94, prof. devel. and child psychology, 1994—; dir., founder Internat. Rsch. for Psychoneuroendocrinology Inst. Psychology U. Aarhus, 1986—. Author: Hormones, Sex, and Society: The Science of Physicology, 1994, 4 others; editor: The Scientific Study of Human Nature: Tribute to Hans J. Eysenck of Eighty, 1997; contbr. articles to profl. jours., chpts. to books. Recipient Lehman prize Lehman Found. Copenhagen Royal Acad. Sci., 1996. Office: PNE-Ctr Inst Psychol, Asylvej 4, DK-8240 Risskov Denmark

NYBORG, ROLF, physicist; b. Oslo, Norway, Jan. 5, 1960; s. Per Nyborg and Anne Alvik; m. Ellen Elisabeth Hemstad, Sept. 24, 1982; three children. MSc, Norwegian Inst. Technology, Trondheim, 1983. From rsch. engr. to prin. rsch. scientist Inst. Energy Technology, Kjeller, Norway, 1983—. Mem. Norwegian Soc. Chartered Engrs., Nace Internat. Office: Inst Energy Technology, PO Box 40, N-2007 Kjeller Norway

NYCANDER, SVANTE OSCAR ELIS, editor; b. Stockholm, Sweden, Jan. 2, 1933; s. Gunnar and Aina (Bratt) N.; m. Viola Jönsson, July 3, 1956; children: Jonas, Maud, Gunnel. MA, Uppsala (Sweden) U., 1964, Dr (hon.), 1996. Editorial writer Dagens Nyheter, Stockholm, 1960-69, 74-79, reporter, 1969-74, chief editor, 1979-94. Author: Swedes and Alcohol, 1967, updated 1996, Abolish Forensic Psychiatry, 1970, The Damned Scientologists, 1977, Freedom of Speech, 1995, The War against the Unions, A Study of the American Model, 1998. Recipient prize Journalism Ragnar and Torsten Söderbergs Foundations, 1992.

NYE, EDWIN RICHARD, physician, writer; b. Liege, Belgium, June 22, 1926; arrived in New Zealand, 1960; s. Edwin Herbert and Hortensia (Stephens) N.; m. Pauline Mahalski, Sept. 1967 (div. 1982); 1 child, Bruce; m. Brenda Jeanette Leigh Borrie, Aug. 28, 1982. BSc, London U., 1952, MB BS, 1956; PhD, London Sch. Hygiene & Trop Med, 1960. House physician, house surgeon Kingston Hosp., Surrey, Eng., 1956-57; jr. lectr. London Sch. Hygiene & Tropical Medicine, 1957-60; med. rsch. officer U. Otago Med. Sch., New Zealand, 1960-64; from lectr. to assoc. prof. Otago Med. Sch., 1966-90, ret., 1990—, hon. sr. fellow; physician in cardiology Dunedin Hosp. Author: Exercise and the Coronary Patient, 1971, Medicinsk Ordbok Tekniskaord, 1990, Ronald Ross, Malariologist and Polymath, 1997; editor: Med. Rsch. in Otago, 1922-97. Mem. New Zealand Internat. Physicians for the Prevention of Nuclear War, 1992-97; chmn. Otago Br. Heart Found. New Zealand. Recipient Knight of the Pole Star Govt. Sweden, 1990. Fellow Royal Entomological Soc. London; mem. Cardiac Soc. Australia and New Zealand, Linnaean Soc. London. Avocations: tchr. Swedish lang., entomology and gen. natural history, fencing coach. Home: The Cove, 51 Irvine Rd, Dunedin New Zealand Office: Sch Medicine, Box 913, Dunedin New Zealand

NYE, JOHN ROBERT, furniture company executive, transportation consultant; b. Phila., Apr. 18, 1947; s. William E. and Mary B. (Brick) N.; m. Judy Burris, May 31, 1969 (div. Dec. 1977); children: Keith, Lanny, John; m. Grace M. Adams, Feb. 28, 1981 (div. Aug. 1993); children: Annette, Mark. BA, N.C. State U., Raleigh, 1969. Prodn. mgr. Highland House, Hickory, N.C., 1969-79; distbn. mgr. Hickory Chair Co., 1979-97; mgr. Tydings House, Hickory, 1983—; distbn. mgr. Baker Furniture, 1998—; owner J.R. Investments, 1989. Mem. Catawba Valley Traffic Club; vice-chmn. Catawba County Mayors Com. for Handicapped, 1987-89. Mem. Met. Planning Assn. Republican. Lutheran. Home: PO Box 3136 Hickory NC 28603-3136

NYE, PETER HAGUE, soil scientist, researcher; b. Hove, Sussex, Eng., Sept. 16, 1921; s. Haydn Percival and Jessie Mary (Hague) N.; m. Margaret Sophia Aron, Dec. 4, 1950 (div. 1953); m. Phyllis Mary Quenault, Dec. 21, 1953; children: Isobel Jessie, Philip David, Vivien Alice (dec.). BA, Oxford (Eng.) U., 1943, BSc, 1944. Agrl. chemist Colonial Svc., 1946-50; lectr. in soil sci. U. Ibadan, Nigeria, 1950-52; sr. lectr. in soil sci. U. Ghana, 1952-60; rsch. officer rsch. and isotopes dept. Internat. Atomic Energy Agy., Vienna, 1960-61; reader in soil sci. Oxford (Eng.) U., 1961-88, reader emeritus, 1988-2000, fellow St. Cross Coll., 1966-88, emeritus fellow, 1988—; hon. rsch. prof. Scottish Crops Rsch. Inst., Invergowrie, 1996-2000. Author: (with D.J. Greenland) The Soil Under Shifting Cultivation, 1960, (with P.B. Tinker) Solute Movement in the Root-Soil System, 1976, (with P.B. Tinker) Solute Movement in the Rhizosphere, 2000; contbr. articles to profl. jours. Fellow Royal Soc. London., Inst. Brit. Soil Scientists; mem. Brit. Soc. Soil Sci. (pres. 1966-68). Avocations: Scrabble, computing, watching cricket. Home: Hewel Barn Common Rd, Beckley Oxford OX3 9UR, England

NYEANCHI, EMMANUEL BONGKIYUNG, physicist; b. Jakiri, Cameroon, Nov. 26, 1968; s. Nsaichia and Angelicah (Yekwah) N. BS in Physics with honors, Hull U., U.K., 1989; MS in Physics, Sussex U., U.K., 1990; PhD in Physics, Sussex U., 1995. Chartered Physicist. Postdoctoral rsch. fellow Nat. Accelerator Ctr., S. Africa, 1995-96, rsch. scientist, 1996-98; rsch. scientist in exptl. physics Umea U., Sweden, 1998—.

NYENHUIS, HORST FRIEDRICH, geographer; b. Furstenau, Germany, Aug. 6, 1939; s. Heinrich Dietrich and Ella Margarete (Kogelberg) N. Apprentice Deutscher Konditoren Bund, Osnabruck, Germany, 1956-58; scientist Osnabruck, Germany, 1982—. Contbr. articles to profl. jours.; inventor in field. Fellow Club Nat. de Becassiets, Internat. Union Game Biologists; mem. Deutscher Jagdschutz Verband, Nat. Geog. Soc., Gesellschaft fur Wildtier und Jagdforschung. Avocations: wildlife ecology, painting. Home: Deichstrasse 13, 49584 Furstenau Germany Office: Bergstrasse 1, 49076 Osnabruck Germany

NYER, RAYMOND JEAN PIERRE, quality and environment executive; b. La Mure, France, Apr. 1, 1938; s. Auguste Louis and Raymonde Marie (Dauphiné) N.; m. Christiane Marie Schmutz; children: Marie Nöelle, Alain, Laurence. Degree in engring., Ecole Centrale de Paris, 1962, Inst. Nat. Sci. & Nuclear Tech, Grenoble, France, 1963; MS, U. Calif., Berkeley, 1966. Cert. sr. assessor European Found. for Quality Mgmt. Semi-condr. process engr. IBM France, Corbeil Essonnes, 1966-69, mgr. product engring., 1969-72, mgr. very large-scale integration prodn. unit, 1975-82; logic tech. mgr. IBM World Trade, White Plains, N.Y., 1972-75; mgr., sr. advisor sys. and tech. IBM Europe, Paris, 1982-89; quality and environ. dir. IBM Europe Mid. East Africa, Paris, 1990—; bd. dirs. Global Quality Svcs., Paris, 1995-96; pres. Ctrl. Quality, Paris, 1994-96; v.p. Ctrl. Informatique, Paris. Lt. French Navy, 1963-65. Mem. IEEE, Am. C. of C., Am. Electronics Assn. (mem. environ. com.), Conf. Bd. Europe (mem. Coun. on Environ. Coun. on Quality). Roman Catholic. Avocations: skiing, cycling, golf. Home: 56 Rue Charles Laffitte, 92200 Neuilly-sur-Seine France Office: IBM EMEA, Tour Descartes, 92066 Paris La Defense, France

NYERS, REZSO, Hungarian politician; b. Budapest, Hungary, Mar. 21, 1923. Printer, until 1945; mem. Social-Dem. Party,, 1940, dep. sec. Kispest dist., 1945; dep. mem., ofcl. Hungarian Worker's Party Cen. Com.,, 1948-53, mem. Cen. Com., 1954; min. food industry, 1956-57, min. fin.,, 1960-62; sec. Hungarian Socialist Workers' Party Cen. Com.,, 1962-74, mem. Politburo and sec., 1988-89; chmn. Hungarian Socialist Party, Budapest, 1989-90; dep. chmn. Nat. Assn. Coops., 1954-56, chmn., 1957-60; dep. from Bacs-Kiskun Megye dist. Nat. Assembly, 1958-90, from Budapest, 1990—, chmn. commerce com., 1980; chmn. Econ. Commn., Hungarian Social Workers' Party, 1962-64, candidate mem. Politburo, 1962-66, mem., 1966-74, dir. Inst. of Econs., 1974-81, mem. econ. working group, 1980. Chmn. Hungarian Socialist Party, 1989-90. Mem. Polit. Economy Soc. (dep. chmn. 1981—). Office: Kopint-Datorg Ec Rsch Co Lt, Csokonai u3 H, Budapest 1389, Hungary

NYFORS, EBBE GUSTAF, radio engineer, researcher; b. Esbo, Finland, Mar. 13, 1956; s. Börje Gustav and Marita Ingeborg (Jansson) N; m. Brit Luktvasslimo; children: Malin, Emil. Diploma in Engring., Helsinki (Finland) U. Tech., 1980, lic. in Tech., 1990, DSc in Tech., 2000. Rsch. asst. Helsinki U. Tech., 1979-80, rsch. engr., 1980-82, acting lab. mgr., 1983-85, lab. mgr., 1985-95; radio operator Marine Rsch. Inst., Helsinki, 1991-92, radio operator, base comdr., 1993-94, radio operator, cook, 1997-98; sr. engr. Multi-Fluid ASA, Forus, Norway, 1995-97; head R&D Roxar ASA, Forus, 1997—; participant in Finnish Expdn. to Antarctica, 1992, 94, 97; tchr. Helsinki Inst. Tech., Finland, 1985-95; supt. Faculty of Elec. Engring. of Hut, Finland, 1990-96. Author: Industrial Microwave Sensors, 1989; contbr. over 50 articles to profl. jours. Mem. IEEE, Tekniska Föreningen i Finland, Norske Sivilingenjørers Forening. Evangelical Lutheran. Achievements include patents in field of microwave sensors. Avocations: nature photography, sports diving, sports shooting, hiking. Home: Einartangen 26A, N-4309 Sandnes Norway Office: Roxar ASA, Gamle Forusvei 17 Box 112, N-4065 Stavanger Norway

NYGAARD, JENS, conductor, music educator; b. Longview, Tex., Oct. 26, 1931; s. Marius Jensen Nygaard and Lois McClurkin. BS, Juilliard Sch. Music, 1957, MS, 1958. Founder, condr. Westchester Chamber Chorus and Orch., White Plains, N.Y., 1967-76, Jupiter Symphony, N.Y.C., 1979—; condr. Naumburg Orch., N.Y.C., 1979-93, Rutgers U. Orch., New Brunswick, N.J., 1983-93; tchr. conducting Columbia U., N.Y.C., 1981-83; organist, harpsichordist Mostly Mozart, N.Y.C. Composer Stephen Foster Medley, cadenzas for various Mozart concertos, various marches and waltzes. Organizer musical activities Washington Heights YMHA, N.Y.C., 1970-93, Jewish Guild for the Blind, N.Y.C., 1985-88; presenter numerous concerts for underprivileged and handicapped, 1960's—. Avocation: reading. Home and Office: 155 W 68th St New York NY 10023-5808

NYGAARD, LANCE COREY, nurse, data processing consultant; b. Casper, Wyo., June 21, 1952; s. Miles Adolph and Jenile Hansine (Mosman) N.; m. Susan Leigh Wilson, May 8, 1995; 1 child from previous marriage, Kari Melissa. AA in Nursing, U. S.D., 1980; BS in Chemistry, 1974; MLS, U. Ill., 1975. Libr. asst. Brookings Pub. Libr., S.D., 1971-75, asst. dir., 1975-77; emergency med. technician Brookings Hosp., 1976-78; sr. emergency med. technician Vermillion Ambulance, S.D., 1978-80; nurse McKennan Hosp., Sioux Falls, S.D., 1980-91, VA Hosp., 1991-96, Sioux Valley Hosp., 1996—, cardiovasc. data sys. coord., 1997—; owner operator Data Processing Svcs., Sioux Falls, 1983—; applications cons. Computer Dimensions, Sioux Falls, 1984-85. Fin. sec., mem. ch. coun. Holy Cross Luth. Ch., Sioux Falls, S.D., 1986-91, info. resources coord., 1991-92; troop leader Minn-Ia-Kota coun. Girl Scouts U.S., 1989—, region troop supr., 1991-95. Mem. Vermillion Chemistry Club (pres. 1973-74), Sioux Valley Rose Soc. (v.p. 1988-89, pres. 1989-90), Sons of Norway (guard 1976-77). Republican. Lutheran. Avocations: World War II military history, photography, amateur radio. Home: 3500 S Grace Cir Sioux Falls SD 57103-7226 Office: Sioux Valley Hosp 1100 S Euclid Ave Sioux Falls SD 57105-0496

NYGREN, LARS JOHAN, transportation executive; b. Kyrkslätt, Finland, May 9, 1940; s. Lars and Eva (Andersin) N.; m. Silvia Kristina; children: Björn, Diana, Johan, Filip, Madelene. PhD, Century U., L.A., 1986. Mng. dir. Investor Ab, Helsingfors, Finland, 1966-81; pres. Fr. Krupp gmbh, Essen, 1980—, Olympic Airways, Amsterdam, 1981—; shipowner Onassis Line, 1981—; bd. dirs. Exxon Corp., N.Y.C., Fiat, Turin, Italy, Citibank, Munich, Can. Int., UPM Kymmene, Mitsubishi, Tokyo, Smith, London, Repson, Barcelona, Citibank Brisbane, Citibank, Vancouver; gen. dir. Tapiola Yhtymä Helsinki, Helsinki Bank Ltd. Espoo Kartano Yhtymä, Leningrad factories; chief dir. East Indian Co.; mng. dir. Kungahuset. Mem. Dir.'s Lodge Club, Svenska Club. Mem. Lut Ev.

NYIDE, THABISILE GRACIOUS, communications company executive; b. Johannesburg, South Africa, Jan. 31, 1958; d. Petrus Gcinabakubo and Fakazile Loveline (Mlaba) N.; m. Samson Makhudu Gulube, Nov. 27, 1982; children: Sukumani Gulube, Mbeko Gulube, Hlobisile. AA, Acad. New Church, 1978; BS, Westchester Coll., 1981; MS, Atlanta U., 1987. Tchg. asst. dept. anthropology Westchester (Pa.) State Coll., 1980-81; refugee counselor Internat. Svc. Ctr., Phila., 1980-81; internat. student advisor AAI, N.Y.C., 1985; counselor Midtown Hosp., Atlanta, 1986-87; social svcs. coord. Grady Meml. Hosp., Atlanta, 1987-90; sr. clin. social worker U. South Fla., Tampa, 1991-93, sr. human svcs. specialist, 1993-96; cons. program officer IFESH, Johannesburg, South Africa, 1996; dir. pub. affairs Bristol-Myers Squibb, South Africa, 1996-99; dir. corp. affairs Pfizer, Johannesburg, 2000—; presenter in field; social svcs. coord. Counseling and Svc. Mgmt., 1988. Bd. dirs. Bridgland Found., 1999—; project leader South Africa Secure the Future, 1998-99; mem. coun. IDASA, South Africa, 1997—. Mem. Black Mgmt. Forum, Soroptimist. Mem. African Nat. Congress. Mem. Gen. Ch. of New Jerusalem. Avocations: volleyball, reading, writing poetry and fiction. Home: 497 Cliff Ave, 0181 Waterkloof Ridge Gauteng, South Africa Office: Pfizer So Life Bldg, 201 Rivonia Rd, 2146 Sandton Gauteng, South Africa

NYIRI, JOSEPH ANTON, sculptor, art educator; b. Racine, Wis., May 24, 1937; s. Joseph Anton Nyiri and Dorothy Marion (Larson) Zink; m. Laura Lee Primeau, Aug. 29, 1959 (dec. Mar. 1982); children: Krista, Nicole, Page; m. Melissa Trent, July 28, 1985. BA, U. Wis., 1959, MS, 1961. Tchr. art Madison (Wis.) Sch. Dist., 1959-62; art cons. San Diego Unified Schs., 1962-65, dist. resource tchr., 1965-73, regional tchr. occupational art, 1973-76, mentor tchr., 1985-95; sculptor San Diego, 1962—, fine arts cons., 1966—; head dept. art edn. Serra H.S., San Diego, 1976-95; tchr. art Zool. Soc. San Diego, 1991-2000; cons. gifted and talented edn. program San Diego City Schs., 1995—, gifted programs Escondido, Calif. and Poway, Calif. Schs., 1995—, Boston Schs., 1996-98, Romona, Calif. Pub. Schs., 1996—; instr. art U. Calif. at San Diego, La Jolla, 1967-80, San Diego State U. Extension, 1969—; fine art restorer, 1963—, lectr. art and art edn., 1963—; pvt. art tchr. San Diego City Zoo. Exhibited sculpture in numerous one-man, two-person, juried and invitational shows, 1960—, U. Mex.-Baja Calif., 1983; rev. Calif. Art Rev., 1989. Active Art Guild San Diego Mus. Art; bd. dirs. San Diego Art Inst. Sgt. Wis. N.G., 1955-61. Named One of 3 Tchrs. of Yr., San Diego County, 1983, One of Outstanding Art Tchrs. in U.S., RISD, 1984, Secondary Tchr. of Yr., San Diego City Schs., 1982; recipient creativity award Pacific Inst., 1969. Mem. Arts/Worth: Nat. Coun. Art (charter), Allied Craftsmen San Diego, Internat. Platform Assn., San Diego Art Inst. (bd. dirs.), San Diego Mus. Art (mem. Art Guild), Zool. Soc. San Diego. Democrat. Mem. Christian Ch. Avocations: running, hiking, travel, reading, writing poetry. Office: 3525 Albatross St San Diego CA 92103-4807 Also: Zool Soc San Diego Edn Dept PO Box 551 San Diego CA 92112-0551

NYKÄNEN, TIMO JUHANI, engineering educator, researcher; b. Kotka, Kymi, Finland, May 9, 1953; s. Eino Olavi and Helvi Kaarina (Ylönen) N.; m. Sirpa Ilona Käkelä. MSc, Lappeenranta (Finland) U. Tech., 1979, Licentiate in Tech., 1987, D in Tech., 1993. Asst. strength materials dynamics Lappeenranta U. Tech., 1979-86, sr. asst. strength materials, 1987—; Contbr. articles to profl. jours. Mem. Finnish Assn. Structural Mech. (bd. dirs. 1997—). Avocations: nature, fishing, boating, forestry, amateur radio. Office: PO Box 20, Skinnarilankatu 34, 53851 Lappeenranta Finland

NYKLES, OLDRICH, retired engineering company administrator; b. Klatovy, Czech Republic, Aug. 12, 1936; s. Vojtech and Filomena (Stuchlova) N.; m. Marie Maresova, Feb. 18, 1961; children; Oldrich, Marek. MSc in Mech. Engring., Western Bohemia U., Plzen, Czech Republic, 1960. Nuclear reactor commissioning project mgr. Skoda, Concern Nuclear Machinery Ltd., Plzen, 1965-69; nuclear reactor commissioning site mgr. Skoda, Concern Nuclear Machinery Ltd., Jaslovske Bohunice, Slovak Republic, 1970-73; nuclear power plant decommissioning project mgr. Skoda, Concern Nuclear Machinery Ltd., Plzen, 1978-90, nulcear spent fuel storage facilities project mgr., 1991-94; desalination plant constrn. mgr. Brown & Root Skoda, Ltd. Co., Plzen, 1994-95, project mgr., asst., cons., 1995-98; cons. Ministry Industry and Trade, Praha, Czech Republic, 1995—. Patentee conditioning of spent nuclear fuel for transport and storage. Fellow Czech Nuclear Forum, Brit. Coun. Roman Catholic. Avocations: English language, tourism, hiking. Home: Mandlova 21, 320 03 Plzen Czech Republic

NYLIN, BRITTA, veterinarian; b. Copenhagen, Aug. 28, 1953; d. Jorgen and Ann-Lise Nylin; m. Bjarne Nikolajsen; 1 child, Tine. DVM, Royal Vet. and Agrl. Sch., Copenhagen, 1979, PhD, 1999. Vet. practitioner Olgod, Denmark, 1979-84; rschr. Danish Dairy Bd., Aarhus, 1984-99, Danish Vet. Lab., 1999—. Mem. Danish Vet. Assn. (bd. dirs. 1996-99), Danish Vet. Orgn. Social Democrat. Lutheran. Avocations: epidemiology, dressage riding. Home: Foldingbrovej 54, 6650 Broerup Denmark Office: Danish Vet Lab, Hangovej 2, 8200 Århus N, Denmark

NYMAN, GUNNAR BO LABBE, chemistry educator; b. Uppsala, Sweden, Apr. 4, 1957; s. Bo Karl Labbe and Gun Ingegärd (Nilsson) N.; m. Gunilla Anne Wallin, July 26, 1986; children: Matilda, Anna, Sara. BS, Göteborg (Sweden) U., 1981, PhD, 1987, docent, 1992; MS, U. Calif., San Diego, 1982. Vis. scholar U. New South Wales, Canberra, Australia, 1987-88, U. Sydney, Australia, 1987-88; rsch. assoc. Chalmers U. of Tech., Göteborg, 1988; rsch. assoc. Göteborg U., 1989-92, sr. lectr., 1994—; rsch. assoc. Cambridge (Eng.) U., 1992-94; expert Chemistry Rchrs. Resource Ctr.; sec. Ctr. for Kinetics, Göteborg, 1989-92, chmn., 1995-2000; Sweden's rep. IXth Internat. Chemistry Olympics, 1977, head phys. chemistry, 1999—. Mem. Sch. Adv. Bd. Knappekullaskolan, Lerum, 1996-99, chmn. parents assn., 1996-99. Sgt. Swedish Army, 1977-78. Rotary Found. internat. scholar, 1981-82. Mem. Swedish Chem. Soc. (bd. dirs. 1987-91), Molecular Beams and Dynamics Group. Avocations: swimming, jogging, diving. Home: Kring-Alles v 12, 44334 Lerum Sweden Office: Göteborg Univ, Dept Chem/Phys Chem, 41296 Göteborg Sweden

NYMAN, SVEN ÅKE BÖRJE, legal administrator, judge; b. Kristianstad, Sweden, Aug. 15, 1925; m. Gunnel Nilsson; children: Ulf, Louise, Maud. LLB, U. Lund, Sweden, 1952. Dep. atty. gen. Sweden, 1971-75; judge Appellate Ct., 1972-75; judge Supreme Ct., 1975-92, div. head, 1988, chmn., pres., 1990; ret., 1992. Recipient King's Own Medal 12th degree with collar, 1993. Mem. Ogn. Swedish Justices.

NYREN, NEIL SEBASTIAN, publisher, editor; b. Boston, June 13, 1948; s. Karl Edwin and Dorothy Elizabeth (Smith) N.; m. Lois Miriam Sharfman, Oct. 11, 1970; 1 child, Alexander. B.A., Brandeis U. V.p. G.P. Putnam's Sons Pub., N.Y.C., 1997—; editor Random House Pubs., N.Y.C., 1974-77, Arbor House Pubs., N.Y.C., 1977-78; exec. editor Atheneum Pubs., N.Y.C., 1978-84; sr. editor G.P. Putnam's Sons Pub., N.Y.C., 1984-86, editor-in-chief, 1986—, pub., 1989—, sr. v.p., 1997—. Democrat. Jewish. Office: GP Putnam's Sons 375 Hudson St New York NY 10014-3658

NYRKE, TIMO JUKKA, neurophysiologist; b. Vehmaa, Vakka-Suomi, Finland, Oct. 27, 1955; s. Tauno Ilmari and Liisa Inkeri (Vuori) N.; m. Eija Helena Vierola, Sept. 27, 1980; children: Vesa, Joanna. MD, Turku (Finland) U., 1980, PhD, 1991. Physician dept. neurophysiology U. Turku, 1979-86; rschr. Acad. Finland, Turku, 1986-89; pvt. practice Hemo Med. Ctr., Finland, 1982—; chief physician, head dept. Päijät-Häme Ctrl. Hosp., Lahti, Finland, 1989—; cons. neurophysiologist Mcpl. Health Care, Päijät-Häme, 1989—; mem. lab. quality assurance bd. Min. Health, Helsinki, 1992-95; mem. quality assurance bd. Soc. of Clin. Neurophysiology, 1995—. Rsch. grantee Farmos Co., 1987, Emil Aaltonen Found., 1988, Med. Co. Orion, 1989. Avocations: gardening, competitive dance sport. Office: Paijat-Hame Ctrl Hosp, Keskussair K 7, 15850 Lahti Finland

NYS, PAULINE S., health facility adminstrator, educator; b. Zhitomir, Ukraine, Russia, Oct. 4, 1937; d. Simon P. and Genia I. (Fuks) Chuck; m. David A. Nys, July 16, 1959; 1 child, Igor D. M, U. Kazan, Russia, 1960; PhD, Physical Chem. Inst., Moscow, 1968; D in Chem. Scis., Inst. Antibiotics, Moscow, 1984. Postgrad. fellow Inst. Antibiotics, Moscow, 1962-67, jr. rschr., 1968-71, sr. rschr., 1971-84, chief rschr., 1985-92; chief lab. Ctr. for Antibiotics, Moscow, 1993—; full prof. Inst. Antibiotics, Moscow. Contbr. articles to profl. jours. Recipient State prize of Russia, 1984. Mem. N.Y. Acad. Scis. Avocations: literature, painting, architecture, journey. E-mail: davidnys@writeme.com. Home: Rechnikov st 26-2-66, 115407 Moscow Russia Office: Nat Rsch Ctr Antibiotics, Nagatinskaya St 3A, 113105 Moscow Russia

NYSTROM, FREDRIK HANS, endocrinologist, researcher; b. Gothenburg, Sweden, Sept. 3, 1963; s. Hans Gunnar and Marianne Gisela (Frey) N.; m. Eva-Lotta Östlund, July 13, 1992; children: Viktor, Max. BS, Uppsala U., Sweden, 1985; MD, Uppsala U., 1988; PhD, Linkoping U., Sweden, 1997. Intern Finspang (Sweden) Hosp., Finspang, Sweden, 1988-90; resident, fellow Linkoping (Sweden) Hosp., 1990-95, registrar, 1995-97; vis. assoc. NIH, Bethesda, Md., 1997-99; rschr. Swedish Soc. Med. Rsch., Sweden, 1999—; tchr. Linkoping U., 1999—. Mem. Swedish Soc. for Physicians, Swedish Soc. for Endocrinologists, Swedish Soc. for Hypertension. Avocation: welding furniture. Office: Linkoping U Hosp, Fac Health Sci, 58185 Linkoping Sweden

NYVLT, JAROSLAV, chemist, researcher; b. Bratislava, Czechoslovakia, Mar. 20, 1932; s. Antonin and Anna (Rihova) N.; m. Eva Muchova, Dec. 28, 1957; 1 child, Alice. Ing., Tech. U., Praha, 1956, PhD, 1960, DSc, 1967. Registered profl. engr., Czechoslovakia. Researcher Inst. Inorganic Chems. Ústi n.L., 1959-62; dept. head Inst. Inorganic Chems., 1963-68, head lab., 1969-78; vis. prof. Univ. Coll., London, 1968-69; head lab. Inst. Inorganic Chems. of Czechoslovakia Acad. Sci., Praha, 1978-93; mem. redaction bd. Chemicky Prumysl, Praha, 1965-90, Crystal Rsch. Tech., Leipzig, 1991—; lectr. chemistry and postgrad. courses Tech. U., Praha, 1963-98. Author: Industrial Crystallization From Solns, 1977, Solid-Liquid Phase Equil., 1977, Industrial Crystallization, 1978, 82, (with others) Kinetics of Industrial Crystallization, 1985, Design of Crystallizers, 1992, Admixtures in Crystallization, 1995, (Brazil version) Cristallizaçao. Mem. European Fedn. Chem. Engring., Working Party of Crystallization.

NZIRAMASANGA, CHENJERAI SAMBOKU, marketing professional; b. Hacare, Zimbabwe, Jan. 2, 1949; s. Charles Samboku and Enia (Matiiria) N.; m. Violet Mukwata, Dec. 22, 1973; 1 child, Kudakwashe. BBA, Wash. State U., Pullman, 1984; postgrad., North Tex State U., Denton, 1985. Cert. mktg. Sales exec. Minerals Mktg. Corp., Zimbabwe, 1987-96; chief mktg. mgr. Nat. Rwy. Zimbabwe, Bullawayo, 1996—. Mem. AMA. Christian Apostolic. Avocations: reading, golf, church, game viewing. Home: 50 Townsend Rd, Suburbs, Bullawayo Zimbabwe Office: Nat Rwys Zimbabwe, Box 596, Bullawayo Zimbabwe

NZOIKA, PETER NDALU, medical technologist; b. Machakos, Eastern, Kenya, Oct. 28, 1968; s. Ngolwa and Dorcas Kalondu (Mutisya) N.; m. Catherine Minoo Mutuku, Jan. 23, 1999; 1 child, Steven. Student, Tenwek Hosp., Nairobi, Kenya, 1991-93. Cert. med. lab. tech., supervisory skills Nairobi, 2000. Lab. asst. Mbitini Health Ctr., Emali, Kenya, 1989-90, technologist, 1993-96; technologist P.C.E.A. Chogoria Hosp., Nairobi, 1996-97, technologist in charge, 1997—; cons. Kikoko Mission Hosp., Nairobi, 1995, Nyina Wa Mumbi Maternity, Nairobi, 1995-99, Matiliku Mission Health Ctr., Nairobi, 1998, St. Anns Maternity, Nairobi, 1999. Mem. Assn. Kenya Med. Lab. Sci. Officers, Map Internat. (HIV/AIDs counselor 1995). Mem. Social Dems. Avocations: volleyball, reading, traveling, singing, gospel music. Home: Sultan Hamud, 49 Nairobi Kenya Office: Plea Chogoria Hosp, Chogoria, 35 Nairobi Kenya

NZOMO, NZELE DAVID, accounting educator; m. Nwanzia Juliana Wavinya; children: Brian Muusi, Joy Mutheu, Paul Tele. BA, Fish U., 1965; MBA, NYU, 1967; MA, Columbia U., 1969, EdD, 1972. CPA, Kenya. Instr. Peace Corp, 1967; acct. UN, 1967-70; rsch. fellow U. Nairobi, Kenya, 1971; lctr. Taylor Bus. Inst., New York, 1972; asst. prof. Castleton State Coll., VT, 1972-75, Stockton State Coll., NJ, 1975-76, U. Nairobi, 1976—; mem. Task Force Kenya Govt., Nairobi, 1983-85, Parastatals Adv. Com., Kenya, 1979-87; team leader Coffee Com., Kenya, 1986; fin. cons. UNCTC study on joint ventures, 1987. Author: (books) Advanced Financial Accounting, 1992, Education for Executive Jobs, 1978, Manual for Research and Writing, 1980, Socio-Economic Consequences, 1985. Chmn. Sengani Secondary Sch., Machakos, 1979-83, Indusl. Devel. Bank, Nairobi, 1983-85, KIRDI, Nairobi, 1985-92; dir. Savings and Loan, Nairobi, 1992—. Fellow ICPA; mem. United Kenya Club (life); AIC Plainsview (treas./elder). Avocations: music, composing. Office: U of Nairobi, Box 50117, Nairobi Kenya

OAK, H(ELEN) LORRAINE, academic administrator, geography educator; b. Toronto, July 19, 1951; d. James Wilfred George and Helen Mary (Towers) O.; m. Athol Denis Abrahams, Jan. 3, 1976; 1 child, Geoffrey James Oak Abrahams. BA Honours, U. Alta., 1973; PhD in Geomorphology, Macquarie U., Sydney, 1982. Mng. editor Assn. Am. Geographers, Washington, 1981-85; rsch. adminstr. SUNY, Buffalo, 1987-92, asst. vice provost rsch., 1992-93, dep. provost, 1993-96, assoc. dean for interdisc. affairs Sch. Med. & Biomed. Scis., 1996—, assoc. vice provost rsch., 2000—; mem. steering com. Environ. Inst., SUNY, Buffalo, 1994-2000, Inst. Rsch. and Edn. on Women and Gender, 1997—, exec. com., 1999-2000. Freelance tech. editor, 1985-86; contbr. articles to profl. jours. and reviews. Mem. Assn. Am. Geographers (nat. acad. leadership round table 1995—), N.Y. Sea Grant Inst. (bd. govs. 1993—, exec. com. 1999—), Sigma Xi (exec. com., pres. SUNY Buffalo chpt. 1993-94). Avocations: travel, reading. E-mail: loak@buffalo.edu. Office: SUNY 128 Biomed Edn Bldg Sch Med and Biomed Scis Buffalo NY 14214 also: U at Buffalo 562 Capen Hall Buffalo NY 14260-1600

OAK, JEFFREY CHARLES, ethicist; b. Weymouth, Mass., July 1, 1959; s. Wayne LeRoy and Myrna Eloise (Noble) O.; m. Carol Pinkham, Oct. 11, 1986; children: Nathaniel Charles, Julia Elizabeth. BA, Gettysburg (Pa.) Coll., 1981; MDiv, Yale U., 1985, STM, 1986, PhD, 1996. Ordained Methodist Church. Clergyman United Meth. Conf. Ea. Pa., Valley Forge, 1986-87, United Meth. Conf. N.Y., White Plains, 1987-91; lectr., tchg. asst. Yale U., New Haven, 1991-96; healthcare ethicist Arden Hill Health Care, Goshen, N.Y., 1996-98; v.p. corp. integrity and ethics Arden Hill Sr. Health System, Goshen, 1998-99; sr. v.p. Coun. of Ethical Orgns., Alexandria, Va., 1999—; chmn. U.S. code of ethics Health Care Compliance, Phila., 1998-99, chmn. nat. edn. com., 1998-99. Editor Pastin Report on Healthcare Compliance, 2000; assoc. editor Report on Healthcare Compliance, 1999—; contbr. articles to profl. jours. Trustee, vice chair Arden Hill Health System, Goshen, 1993-96; chmn. ethics com. Arden Hill Hosp., Goshen, 1990-99, Hospice of Orange County, Middletown, N.Y., 1996-99; mem. steering com. Hudson Valley Healthcare Ethics Network, Bronx, 1993-97. Recipient Keith Pappas award Gettysburg Coll., 1981, Disting. Alumni award Manheim Twp. H.S., 1998; John Wesley fellow Found. for Theol. Edn., 1992-95, Yale U. fellow, 1994. Mem. Southold Yacht Club of N.Y. Avocations: sailing, woodworking, jogging, kayaking, Nordic skiing. Office: Council of Ethical Orgns Health Ethics Trust 214 S Payne St Alexandria VA 22314-3530

OAKES, ELLEN RUTH, psychotherapist, health institute administrator; b. Bartlesville, Okla., Aug. 19, 1919; d. John Isaac and Eva Ruth (Engle) Harboldt; m. Paul Otis Oakes Sr., June 12, 1937 (div. April 1974); children: Paul Otis Jr., Deborah Ellen, Nancy Elaine Masters; m. Siegmar Johann Knopp, Nov. 24, 1975 (div. Feb. 1998). BA in Sociology, Psychology summa cum laude, Oklahoma City U., 1961; MS in Clin. Psychology, U. Okla., 1963, PhD, 1967. Lic. clin. psychologist, Okla. Chief psychometrist Okla. U. Guidance Ctr., Norman, 1962; psychology trainee VA Hosp., Oklahoma City, 1962-64, Cerebral Palsy Ctr., Norman, Okla., 1964-65; psychology intern Guidance Service, Norman, 1965-66, staff psychologist, 1966-67; asst. prof. psychology Okla. U. Med. Sch., Oklahoma City, 1967-70; supr. psychology interns Okla. Univ. Health Scis. Ctr., 1967-80; founder, dir. Timberridge Inst., Oklahoma City, 1970-90, pres., 1980-90; pvt. practice clin. psychologist Oklahoma City, 1970-92; instr. Okla. U. extension course, Tinker AFB, Oklahoma City, 1963, U. Okla., 1965-66; discussion leader Inst. for Tchrs. of Disadvantaged Child Oklahoma City Sch. System, 1966; leader

group therapy sessions Asbury Meth. and Westminster Presbyn. Chs., Oklahoma City, 1966; mem. psychology team confs. for hearing disorders, Okla. U. Med. Sch., 1967-70; cons. Oklahoma City Pub. Schs., 1970-72; cons., group leader halfway house, 1972; lectr. chs., PTAs, hosps.; reviewer Am. Psychol. Assn. Civilian Health and Med. Program of the Uniformed Svcs., 1978-89. Workshop conductor on Shame & Sexuality, Zurick Jungian Inst. winter seminar, 1992; attended Européen Congrès de Gestalt Thérapie in Paris, 1992; contbr. articles to profl. jours. Speaker Okla. County Mental Health Assn. Annual Worry Clinic, St. Luke's Ch., Oklahoma City, 1968-92, psychology dept. Sorosis Club, St. Luke's Ch.; charter mem. English spkg. Christian Congregation mission outreach Pauluskirche, Bochum, Germany, 1993-97, exec. coun., 1996-97. Mem. Am. Psychol. Assn. (peer rev. project with CHAMPUS, 1978-89), Okla. Psychol. Assn. (pres. 1975-76). Avocations: art, travel, poetry, photography, walking.

OAKES, MARIA SPACHNER, nurse; b. Cinn., Mar. 27, 1947; d. A. William and Roberta Mae (Linville) Stephens; m. John Cullwell Oakes, Nov. 27, 1976; children: John Cullwell II, Laura Suzann. Diploma Sch. Nursing, King's Daughters' Hosp., 1968. Cert. med./surg. nurse. Staff nurse Ohio State U. Hosp., Columbus, Lawrence County, Ironton; head nurse, neonatal intensive care King's Daughters' Med. Ctr., Ashland, Ky., staff nurse; staff nurse neonatal IC, Huntington Hosp. Behavioral Medicine. Bd. dirs. Am. Cancer Soc.; deacon bd. sessions, pres. Women's Assn. First Presbyn. Ch.; v.p. West Ironton Parent-Tchr. Group; pres. Kingsbury Parents for Better Schs.; past pres. Kings Daus. Hosp. Sch. Nursing Alumni Assn.; mem. strategic planning com. Ironton City Sch. Dist., Acad. Boosers Assn., H.S. Band Boosters mem., band nurse. Mem. ANA, Ky. Nurses Assn. (state offices nursing practice comm., legis. com., state nominating com., nurse practice commn., past pres., v.p., treas. Dist. 4, former v.p., program chmn., seminar planner, continuing edn. coord., current v.p. Dist. 4, mem. ad hoc com. health care reform), Ironton Cooperative Club. (pres.-elect.). Home: 2210 N 3rd Ave Ironton OH 45638-1068

OAKES, TIM SIMON NEVILLE, manufacturing company executive; b. Leighon Sea, Essex, Eng., Jan. 3, 1953; s. Denis Frederick and Priscilla Elizabeth (Neville) O.; m. Barbara Ann Johnston, May 8, 1982; children: Simon, Charlotte, William. Student, Oxford U., 1975. Field engr. Schlumberger, Iran and Egypt, 1975-76; trainee acct. Lever Bros., Kingston, Eng., 1977-79, cons., 1979-82; cons. Unilever Australia, Sydney, 1982-84, sys. acct., 1984-85; fin. acct. Streets Ice Cream, Sydney, 1985-86, frozen foods marketeer, 1987; mgmt. acct. Unifoods, Sydney, 1988-92; global sourcing comml. exec. Unilever Rsch., Port Sunlight, Eng., 1992-96; leader Internat. Mfg. Investment, 1996-2000; supply chain strategy for Asia/Mid. East Unilever Rsch., Port Sunlight, 2000—. Recipient Scholarship Oxford U., 1972-75. Mem. Chartered Inst. Mgmt. Accts. Avocations: sports, music, reading, walking, family fun. Office: Unilever Rsch, Quarry Rd E, Bebington L63 3JW, England

OAKLEY, JOHN BILYEU, law educator, lawyer, judicial consultant; b. San Francisco, June 18, 1947; s. Samuel Heywood and Elsie-Maye (Bilyeu) O.; m. Fredericka Barvitz, May 25, 1969; children: Adélie, Antonia. BA, U. Calif., Berkeley, 1969; JD, Yale U., 1972. Bar: Calif. 1972, U.S. Dist. Ct. (no. dist.) Calif. 1974, U.S. Dist. Ct. (ctrl. and ea. dists.) Calif. 1975, U.S. Supreme Ct. 1977, U.S. Ct. Appeals (5th cir.) 1979, U.S. Ct. Appeals (9th cir.) 1992. Rsch. atty. chief justice Donald R. Wright Supreme Ct. of Calif., 1972-73, sr. rsch. atty. chief justice Donald R. Wright, 1974-75; sr. law clk. chief judge M. Joseph Blumenfeld U.S. Dist. Ct. Conn., Hartford, 1973-74; acting prof. law U. Calif., Davis, 1975-79, prof. law, 1979—; reporter Speedy Trial Planning Group, U.S. Dist. Ct., Sacramento, 1977-82, Civil Justice Reform Act Adv. Group, 1991-94, U.S. Jud. Conf. Com. on Fed.-State Jurisdiction, 1991-96, Western Regional Conf. on State-Fed. Jud. Relationships, 1992-93, 2000; scholar-in-residence, sr. trial atty. Civil Rights Divsn., U.S. Dept. Justice, Washington, 1979-80; vis. scholar U. Coll., Oxford (Eng.) U., 1982-83; apptd. counsel death penalty appeal Supreme Ct. Calif., 1984-96; cons. Calif. Jud. Coun. Commn. on the Future of the Cts., 1992-93; mem. Calif. Appellate Process task force, 1997—. Co-author: Law Clerks and the Judicial Process, 1980, An Introduction to the Anglo-American Legal System, 1980, 2d edit., 1988, Civil Procedure, 1991, 2d edit., 1996, Federal Courts, 10th edit., 1999; contbr.: Restructuring Justice, 1990. Pub. mem. New Motor Vehicle Bd. Calif., Sacramento, 1976-82, Calif. Jud. Coun. Appellate Process Task Force, 1997—; bd. dirs. Fallen Leaf Lake (Calif.) Mutual Water Co., 1980-82, 94—; western regional assoc., field assoc. Duke U. Primate Ctr., 1986-91, bd. visitors, 1997-2000. With U.S. Merchant Marine, 1969, Vietnam. Nat. Merit scholar, 1964. Mem. Am. Law Inst. (reporter Fed. Jud. Code Revision Project 1995—), Assn. Am. Law Schs. (chair sect. on civil procedure 1979-80, 96-97), Am. Judicature Soc. (bd. dirs. 1996-98), Am. Inns of Ct., Phi Beta Kappa. Avocations: aviation, photography, railroads, rugby, running. Office: Univ Calif Sch Law Davis CA 95616

OAKLEY, WANDA FAYE, management consultant, educator; b. Durham, N.C., June 27, 1950; d. Joseph Napolian and Doris Gray (Thomas) O. BSBA, U. N.C., 1971, postgrad., 1972-73. CPA, N.C.; cert. fraud examiner. Acct. Oakley Motors, Durham, 1965-73; controller Airheart Ins. Agy., Inc., Durham, 1973-75; controller, owner Quality Car Wash, Durham, 1974-83; acct. computer svcs. dept. William H. Mitchell, P.A. and CPAs, Durham, 1983-84; mgr. John Anderson & Assocs., Inc., Durham, 1984-85; v.p. CMS Svcs., Inc., York, S.C., 1985-86; adminstr. N.C. State U., Raleigh, 1986-89; pvt. practice bus. cons. Raleigh, 1989—; instr. Wake Tech. Community Coll., Raleigh, 1985—, Small Bus. Ctr., Johnston Community Coll, Smithfield, N.C., 1990—; proctor N.C. State Bd. CPA Examiners, Raleigh, 1986—; bus. cons. in field. Fellow N.C. Assn. CPAs, AICPA; mem. NAFE, Assn. Cert. Fraud Examiners, Exersafety Internat. (master's cert. 1984), U. N.C. Alumni Assn. (life). Home: PO Box 3257 Durham NC 27715-3257 Office: 4404 Ryan St Durham NC 27704-1808

OATES, GEOFFREY DONALD, surgeon, consultant; b. Wolsingham, Durham, England, May 16, 1929; s. Thomas and Dorothy Verne (Jones) O.; m. Mollie Parfitt Edwards, June, 1954 (dec. Dec. 1972); children: John, Susan; m. Elizabeth Anne Wife, Mar. 31st, 1973. BSc with honors, U. Birmingham, England, 1950, MB Ch.B, 1953; MS in Surgery, U. Ill., 1964. Lectr. in anatomy U. Birmingham, England, 1954-55; with surg. tng. program U. Birmingham Hosps., West Midlands Health Authority, England, 1957-66; cons. surgeon U. Birmingham Hosps., 1966-94, emeritus, 1994—; instr. surgery, rsch. fellow U. Ill., Chgo., 1963-64, vis. prof., Thomas Bombek lectr., 1994; vis. rsch. fellow U. Wis., Madison, 1966; Frickman lectr. U. Minn., Mpls., 1989; mem. working party colorectal cancer Med. Rsch. Coun., colorectal subcom. U.K. Coord. Com. Cancer Rsch. Author: (with others) The Pathological Basis of Medicine, 1972, Clinical Trials, 1977; editor Updates in Colo-Proctology, 1992; contbr. articles to profl. jours. Capt. Royal Army MC, 1955-57. Exch. Travel Fulbright fellow, 1963-64. Fellow Royal Coll. Surgeons, Royal Soc. Medicine (pres. oncology sect. 1980-81, pres. coloproctology sect. 1989-90); mem. Assn. Coloproctology Great Britain and Ireland (pres. 1990-91), Internat. Soc. Surgery, Internat. Assn. Endocrine Surgeons. Avocations: skiing, golf, fishing. Home: 14 Hintlesham Ave, Birmingham West Midlands, England B15 2PH Office: 81 Harborne Rd, Birmingham West Midlands, England B15 3HG

OATES, JEREMY JOHN, management consultant; b. London, Aug. 20, 1963; s. John and Sylvia Mary (Harris) O.; m. Laura Chapman Jury, July 11, 1987; children: James, Barnaby. Degree in Econs., Trinity Coll., Cambridge, Eng., 1985. Sys. engr. IBM UK Ltd., London, 1985-88, sr. sys. engr., 1989; tech. svcs. mgr. ASTEC Ltd., London, 1989-90; mgr. Andersen Cons., London, 1990-96, assoc. ptnr., 1996-99, ptnr., 1999—. Jr. treas. Cambridge U. Conservative Assn., 1985; del. Nat. Union of Students, Cambridge, 1983-84. Mem. Athenaeum. Mem. Conservative Party. Ch. of England. Home: 55 Southlands Dr, London SW19 5QL, England Office: Andersen Consulting, 2 Arundel St, London WC2R 3LT, England

OATES, JOYCE CAROL, author; b. Lockport, N.Y., June 16, 1938; d. Frederic James and Caroline (Bush) O.; m. Raymond Joseph Smith, Jan. 23, 1961. BA, Syracuse U., 1960; MA, U. Wis., 1961. Instr. English U. Detroit, 1961-65, asst. prof., 1965-67; prof. English U. Windsor, Ont., Can., 1967-87; writer-in-residence Princeton (N.J.) U., 1978-81, prof., 1987—. Author: (short story collections) By the North Gate, 1963, Upon the Sweeping Flood, 1966, The Wheel of Love, 1970, Marriages and Infidelities, 1972, The Hungry Ghosts, 1974, The Goddess and Other Women, 1974, Where Are You Going, Where Have You Been?: Stories of Young America, 1974, The Poisoned Kiss and Other Stories From the Portuguese, 1975, The Seduction and Other Stories, 1975, Crossing the Border, 1976, Night-Side, 1977, All the Good People I've Left Behind, 1978, The Lamb of Abyssalia, 1980, A Sentimental Education: Stories, 1981, Last Days: Stories, 1984, Wild Nights, 1985, Raven's Wing: Stories, 1986, The Assignation, 1988, Heat: And Other Stories, 1991, Where is Here?, 1992, Haunted: Tales of the Grotesque, 1994, Will You Always Love Me? and Other Stories, 1995; (novels) With Shuddering Fall, 1964, A Garden of Earthly Delights, 1967 (Nat. Book award nomination 1968), Expensive People, 1967 (Nat. Book award nomination 1969), them, 1969 (Nat. Book award for fiction 1970), Wonderland, 1971, Do With Me What You Will, 1973, The Assassins, 1975, Childwold, 1976, The Triumph of the Spider Monkey, 1976, Son of the Morning, 1978, Unholy Loves, 1979, Cybele, 1979, Bellefleur, 1980 (L.A. Times Book award nomination 1980), A Sentimental Education, 1981, Angel of Light, 1981, A Bloodsmoor Romance, 1982, Mysteries of Winterthorn, 1984, Solstice, 1985, Marya, 1986, You Must Remember This, 1987, (as Rosamond Smith) The Lives of the Twins, 1987, American Appetites, 1989, (as Rosamond Smith) Soul-Mate, 1989, Because It Is Bitter, and Because It Is My Heart, 1990, (as Rosamond Smith) Nemesis, 1990, I Lock My Door Upon Myself, 1990, The Rise of Life on Earth, 1991, Black Water, 1992, (as Rosamond Smith) Snake Eyes, 1992, Foxfire: Confessions of a Girl Gang, 1993, What I Lived For, 1994 (PEN/Faulkner award nomination 1995); (poetry collections) Women in Love, 1968, Expensive People, 1968, Anonymous Sins, 1969, Love and Its Derangements, 1970, Angel Fire, 1973, Dreaming America, 1973, The Fabulous Beasts, 1975, Season of Peril, 1977, Women Whose Lives are Food, Men Whose Lives are Money: Poems, 1978, The Stepfather, 1978, Celestial Timepiece, 1981, Invisible Women: New and Selected Poems, 1970-1972, 1982, Luxury of Sin, 1983, The Time Traveller, 1987; (plays) The Sweet Enemy, 1965, Sunday Dinner, 1970, Ontological Proof of My Existence, 1970, Miracle Play, 1974, Three Plays, 1980, Daisy, 1980, Presque Isle, 1984, Triumph of the Spider Monkey, 1985, In Darkest America, 1990, I Stand Before You Naked, 1990, The Perfectionist and Other Plays, 1995; (essays) The Edge of Impossibility, 1972, The Hostile Sun: The Poetry of D.H. Lawrence, 1973, New Heaven, New Earth, 1974, Contraries: Essays, 1981, The Profane Art, 1984, On Boxing, 1987, (Woman) Writer: Occasions and Opportunities, 1988; editor, compiler: Scenes from American Life: Contemporary Short Fiction, 1973, (with Shannon Ravenel) Best American Short Stories of 1979, 1979, Night Walks, 1982, First Person Singular: Writer's on Their Craft, 1983, (with Boyd Litzinger) Story: Fictions Past and Present, 1985, (with Daniel Halpern) Reading and Fights, 1988, The Oxford Book of American Short Stories, 1992, The Sophisticated Cat: An Anthology, 1992; editor (with Raymond Smith) Ontario Rev.; contbr. to nat. mags. including N.Y. Times Book Rev., Mich. Quarterly Rev., Mademoiselle, Vogue, North Am. Rev., Hudson Rev., Paris Rev., Grand Street, Atlantic, Poetry, Esquire. Recipient O. Henry award, 1967, 73, Rosenthal award Nat. Inst. Arts and Letters, 1968, O. Henry Spl. award continuing achievement, 1970, 86, Award of Merit Lotos Club, 1975, St. Louis Lit. award, 1988, Rea award for the Short Story, 1990, Alan Swallow award for fiction, 1990, Nobel Prize in Lit. nomination, 1993; Guggenheim fellow, 1967-68, Nat. Endowment for the Arts grantee, 1966, 68. Mem. Am. Acad. and Inst. Arts and Letters. Office: care John Hawkins 71 W 23rd St Ste 1600 New York NY 10010-4102 also: Princeton U Dept Creative Writing 117 185 Nassau St Princeton NJ 08544-0001

OBAGAH, MAMUDU OMOSAH NASIRU, educational evaluator; b. Iyakpi, Nigeria, Oct. 15, 1952; s. Nasiru Imiegbala and Rametu (Nasiru) O.; m. Hazara Momoh, June 2, 1977, children: Lukman, Fatimah, Yanetu, Aloaye. BEd with honors, U. Ilorin, 1982; MEd, U. Ibadan, 1985, PhD, 1990. Adminstrv. officer Inst. of Edn., U. Ibadan, 1983-86; bus. mgr. Inst. Ibadan (Nigeria), 1986-91; lectr. Inst. of Edn., U. Sci. and Tech., Port Harcourt, 1991—; asst. coord. Project Time Lagos, 1985-91; supr. of tchg. practice Faculty of Tech. Sci., 1991-98; coord. postgrad. porgrams Inst. of Edn. RSUST, 1993—. Author: Joint, Matriculations Exams, 1987; co-author: Nigerian Education Research Association, 1986, Perspective in Teaching, 1994; contbr. articles to profl. jours. Contra-examiner Coll. of Edn. Rivers State, Rumuolumeni, 1992—; active peace conf. Nat. Orientations Agy., 1994. Recipient Outstanding Contbns. award Muslims Students Soc., 1981. Mem. Assn. for Quality Edn. in Nigeria, Edn. Devel. in Nigeria, Edn. Rsch. and Mgmt. in Africa. Avocations: reading, jogging, TV reviewing, photography, gardening. Home: No 4 Mannion, Campus Guest House RSUST, Port Harcourt Nigeria Office: Inst Edn FTSE, PMB 5080 Nkpolu, Port Harcourt Nigeria

OBAIDAT, MOHAMMED TALEB, civil engineering educator; b. Kufrsaum, Irbid, Jordan, Oct. 25, 1961; s. Taleb Mefleh and Amneh (Khasim) O.; m. Hekmat Hamzeh Obaidat, July 23, 1988; children: Bahá, Deyá, Ahmed. BSc, Yarmouk U., Irbid, 1983; MSc, Jordan U. Sci. and Tech., Irbid, 1988, U. Ill., 1994; PhD, U. Ill., 1994. Registered profl. engr. Dist. projects mgr. Ministry of Edn., Irbid, 1985-89; from rsch.-tchg. asst. to asst. prof. civil engring. Jordan U. Sci. and Tech., Irbid, 1989-99, assoc. prof, civil engring., 1999—; dean student affairs Jordan U. Sci. and Tech., 2000; bd. dirs. Jordanian U. Sports Fedn., 2000; cons. Ministry of Edn., Jordan, 1985-88; mem. evaluation and planning com. Royal Jordanian Geog. Ctr., 1995; cons. for authoring computer books for high schs., Jordan, 1995. Contbr. articles to profl. jours.; patentee in field. Active Jordanian Olympic Com., 2000. With Jordanian Army, 1983-85. U. Ill. Advanced Constrn. Tech. Ctr. fellow, 1990-93, Leica Inc. Photogrammetric fellow, 1992. Mem. ASCE, Indian Rd. Congress, Am. Soc. Photogrammetry and Remote Sensing, Jordanian Profl. Engring. Soc., Soc. for Prevention of Rd. Accidents Jordan. Avocations: football game, chess, swimming, computers, racing cars. Home: Al-Amari Apt Complex, Cairo St, Irbid Jordan Office: Jordan U Sci Tech, Civil Engring Dept Box 3030, Irbid Jordan

OBAIDULLAH, KHURSHID AHMED, geophysicist; b. Ahmedabad, India, Apr. 28, 1940; s. Mohammed Tajuddin and Iqbal Begum (Abdullah) O.; m. Hendrika Tahira Brouwer, Feb. 9, 1973; children: Shireen Tahira, Farah Yasmin. BSC in Math. with honors, Panjab U., Lahore, Pakistan, 1959, MSc in Geology, 1961; MSc, Imperial Coll., London, 1965, PhD in Geophysics, 1969. Lectr. Panjab U., Lahore, 1961-62; rsch. scientist U. Miami, 1970-71; rsch. geophysicist Deutsche Texaco, Wietze, Germany, 1973-74; ops. geophysicist Nederlandse Aardolie My., Assen, Netherlands, 1974-79; rsch. geophysicist Shell Rsch., Ryswyk, Netherlands, 1980-84; chief geophysicist Shell Gabon, Port Gentil, 1984-86; sr. processor Shell U.K. E&P, London, 1986-88; sr. geophysicist Shell Internat. Petroleum My., The Hague, Netherlands, 1988-93; cons., 1993—. Served to comdr. Pakistani Air Force, 1971-73. Mem. European Assn. Exploration Geophysicists, Soc. Exploration Geophysicists of Am., Planetary Soc. Am., Am. Assn. Petroleum Geophysicists, Am. Assn. Petroleum Geologists. Muslim. Home: Rederserf 27, 2586 M The Hague The Netherlands

OBAL, FERENC FRANCIS, science educator; b. Budapest, Hungary, Sept. 28, 1916; s. Ferenc and Anna (Barczy) O.; m. Magdolna Nagy, Jan. 31, 1941; children: Ferenc, Gyorgyi. MD, Pazmany Peter U., 1940, PhD, 1939; DS, Acad. Sci., 1967; MD honoris causa, Tg-M., 1996. Asst. prof. physiology U. Kolozsvar (Hungary), 1940-45; prof. physiology U. Bolyai, Tirgu-Mures, Romania, 1945-53, Inst. Neurosurgery, Budapest, Hungary, 1954-58, U. Szent-Györgyi, Szeged, Hungary, 1958-86; prof. emeritus U. Szent-Györgyi, Szged, Hungary, 1986—; head U. Bolyai dept. physiology and pharmacology, 1947-48, 48-53; dir. Inst. Conservation and Transfusion Blood, Tirgu-Mures, 1947-48, Ctr. Welfare of Students, Tirgu-Mures, 1945-47. Author/editor: The Human Body, vols. I-II, 1957-86; editor: Environmental Physiology, 1987; contbr. articles to profl. jours. Fellow Dept. Pathophysiology, Budapest, 1939-40. Mem. European Sleep Rsch. Soc. (hon. mem., v.p. 1986-88), Hungarian Neurophysiol. Soc. (pres. 1971-79). Pavloviai Soc. N.Am., Med. Acad. Bucharest (hon.). Lutheran. Avocations: drawing, painting, fine art. Home: Batthyany St 6/a, H-6722 Szeged Hungary Office: Szent-Gyorgyi Med U, Dom Squer 10, H-3720 Szeged Hungary

OBAME, PAULIN, Gabonese government official. Sec. gen. Govt. of Gabon, Libreville, prime min. and head of govt., 1994—, min. pub. health and population. Office: Min Pub Health-Population, BP 50, Libreville Gabon*

OBAMOGIE, MERCY A., physician; b. Lagos, Nigeria, Jan. 18, 1954; d. Godwin I and Janet E. (Amiolemen) O.; m. Abiodun O. Odunmbaku, June 20, 1980 (div. 1995); children: Abisola, Adenike, Abiodun. BS, Columbia U., 1980; MD, U. Medicine and Dentistry N.J., Piscataway, 1984; MPH, Johns Hopkins U., 1987. Diplomate Am. Bd. Family Practice, Nat. Bd. Med. Examiners. Intern in internal medicine Muhlenberg Hosp., Plainfield, N.J., 1984-85; resident in gen. preventive medicine Johns Hopkins U., Balt., 1985-86; resident in family practice Georgetown U./Providence Hosp., Washington, 1986-89; pvt. practice Washington, Greenbelt, Md., 1989—; med. dir. Doctors Slim and Fitness Ctr., Greenbelt, 1996-98; med. adv. bd. Metra Health Ins. Co., 1992-94; utilization com. Aetna Ins. Co., 1993-95, credentialing com., 1996; med. adv. com. United HealthCare, 1997; mem. planning com. Providence Hosp., Washington, 1996-98; with Prince George's Hosp. Ctr., Cheverly, Md., Howard U. Hosp., Washington, Doctors Cmty. Hosp., Lanham, Md., Providence Hosp., Washington; pres., med. dir. Mercy Med. Ctr., Benin City, Nigeria, 1996—; pres., CEO ASAKI Corp., Greenbelt, Md., 2000—. Contbr. articles to profl. jours. Home: 25 Atwood Ct Silver Spring MD 20906-2089 Office: 7323 Hanover Pkwy Ste A Greenbelt MD 20770-3617

OBANDO BRAVO, MIGUEL CARDINAL, archbishop; b. La Libertad, Nicaragua, Feb. 2, 1926. Ordained priest Roman Cath. Ch., 1958. Titular bishop of Puzia di Bizavena and aux. bishop of Matagalpa, 1968—, archbishop of Managua, 1970—, elevated to Sacred Coll. of Cardinals, 1985. Address: Arzobispado, Apto 3058, Managua Nicaragua*

O'BANION, MICHAEL KERRY, molecular neurobiologist; b. Ft. Myers, Fla., June 10, 1958; s. Terry U. and Mary L. (Coyner) Rogers; 1 child, Colin P.; m. Dorothy Petrie. BS in Biology, U. Ill., 1980, PhD in Microbiology, 1987, MD, 1987. Instr. medicine U. Rochester (N.Y.), 1990-91, asst. prof. dept. neurology, 1991-97, assoc. prof. dept. neurology and neurobiology and anatomy, 1997—. Contbr. articles to profl. jours. Wilmot Found. Cancer Rsch. fellow, 1988-91. Mem. AAAS, Soc. Neurosci., Alpha Omega Alpha. Achievements include discovery of glucocorticoid and cytokine regulated cyclooxygenase-2. Office: U Rochester Med Ctr 601 Elmwood Ave # 603 Rochester NY 14642-0001

OBARA, MARIAN ZYGMUNT, gynecologist, consultant; b. Wola Cieklińska, Poland, Aug. 5, 1933; s. Józef and Aniela (Olszewska) O.; m. Urszula Jadwiga Ducka, Nov. 30, 1963; 1 child, Monika. Degree in engring., U. Poznań, Poland, 1953; MD, Med. Acad., Poznań, 1960. Surveyor Ministry of Home Trade, Warsaw, Poland, 1953-55; asst. City Hosp., Poznań, 1963-66; asst. lectr. Clinic Ob-Gyn., Poznań, 1966-70; lectr. Inst. Ob-Gyn., Poznań, 1970-78; sr. lectr. Inst. Ob-Gyn., 1978-88; prof., chief Dept. Med. Pedagogy, Poznań, 1989—; cons. Med. U. Poznań, 1972—. Co-author: Organization of the Evaluation System in Medical Education, 1978 (award Polish Ministry of Health 1979), Psychological and Educational Problems in Medical Education, 1978 (award Polish Ministry of Health 1983), Foundations of Medical Education (award Polish Ministry of Health 1984). Mem. provincial office Soc. for Popularization of Culture and Sci., Poznań, 1962-89, Birth Control Soc., Poznań, 1962-89, Assn. of Lovers of City of Poznań, 1953-89, Anti-Cigarettes Leauge, Poznań, 1962-90. Decorated Silver Cross of Merit, People's State Coun., Poland, 1970; named Meritorious Tchr., People's State Coun., 1986. Mem. Polish Med. Soc., Polish Gynecology Soc. (didactic sect.), Polish Acad. Medicine. Roman Catholic. Avocations: tourism, cultivating flowers, raising birds, antique collecting. Home: Marcelińska 4 B m 6, 60-801 Poznań Poland Office: Dept Med Edn, Jackowskiego 41, 60-513 Poznań Poland

OBARA, TOSHIYUKI, chemistry educator; b. Hokkaido, Japan, May 31, 1956; s. Azusa and Kimiko (Sasaki) O.; m. Ritsuko Seki, Oct. 9, 1988; children: Kazuya, Kengo. DEng, Hokkaido U., Sapporo, 1985. Asst. Tohoku U., Sendai, Japan, 1985-88; lectr. chemistry Hakodate (Japan) Nat. Coll. Tech., 1988-92, assoc. prof., 1992—. Contbr. articles to sci. jours., including Carbon, Fuel, Chemistry Letters, Biosci., Biotech. and Biochemistry. Recipient adv. sci. award Japan Inst. Energy, 1993. Avocations: movies, reading. Office: Hakodate Nat Coll Tech, Tokura-cho 14-1, Hokkaido Hakodate 042-0953, Japan

OBASANJO, OLUSEGUN (MATTHEW OLUSEGUN FAJINMI AREMU OBASANJO), president of Nigeria; b. Nigeria, Mar. 5, 1937; s. Obasanjo Bankole and Bernice Ashabi; m. Oluremi Akinlawon, June 22, 1963 (div.); 6 children; m. Stella Abebe; 1 child. Cert., London Gen. Cert. Edn. Clerical worker United African Co.; tchr. African Ch. Modern Sch., Ibadan; cadet Regular Officer's Spl. Tng. Sch. Nigerian Army, Teshie, Ghana, 1958; advanced through grades to gen. Nigerian Army, 1979, various positions, 1958-63; comdr. field engring. squadron Nigerian Army, Kaduna, 1963; head 3rd marine commando Nigerian Army, 1969, comdr. engring. corps, 1970-75, commr. works and housing, 1975, chief of staff armed forces, 1975; head of state Nigeria, 1976, pres., 1999—; founder, chair African Leadership Forum, 1987—; dir. Better World Soc., Washington, 1987-93; with Carter's Internat. Negotiations Network, 1991—; involved in various mediation efforts in Namibia, Angola, Sudan, South Africa, Mozambique, Burundi; bd. dirs. Ford Found. Author: My Command, 1980, Africa in Perspective: Myths and Realities, 1987, Nzeogwu, 1987, Africa Embattled, 1988, Constitution for National Integration and Development, 1989, Not My Will, 1990, Elements of Development, 1992, Elements of Democracy, 1993, Africa: Rise to Challenge, 1993, Hope for Africa, 1993. Address: PO Box 2286, Abeokuta Ogun, Nigeria Address: Presdl Villa, Oslo Rock, Abuja Federal Capital Territory*

OBASI, GODWIN OLU PATRICK, United Nations agency administrator, scientific organization administrator, meteorologist; b. Ogori, Kwara, Nigeria, Dec. 24, 1933; s. A.B. and R. (Akande) Patrick; 6 children. BSc in Math. and Physics with honors, McGill U., Montreal, Can., 1959; MSc in Meteorology with distinction, MIT, 1960, DSc in Meteorology, 1963; grad., Inst. Statisticians, Eng., 1971; D of Physics (honoris causa), U. Bucharest, Romania, 1991; LLD (honoris causa), U. Philippines, 1992; DSc (honoris causa), Fed. U. Tech., Akure, Nigeria, 1992; DSc (hon.), Alpine Geophys. Rsch. Inst., Nal-Chik, Russian Fedn., 1993, U. Nairobi, Kenya, 1998. Demonstrator dept. physics McGill U., 1958-59; rsch. asst. dept. meteorology MIT, Cambridge, 1959-63; sr. meteorologist in-charge rsch. and tng. Nigerian Meteorol. Dept., 1963-67; sr. meteorologist in-charge tech. adminstrn. Nigerian Meteorological Dept. Hdqrs., Lagos, 1966-67; sr. meteorologist in-charge meteorol. svcs. Lagos Airport, Ikeja, 1964-65; chmn. working group tropical meteorology World Meteorol. Orgn., 1965-67; World Meteorol. Orgn./UN Devel. Programme expert, sr. lectr. U. Nairobi, Kenya, 1967-74, acting head dept. meteorology, 1972-73, prof., chmn. dept. meteorology, 1974-76, dean faculty sci., World Meteorol. Orgn. expert; adviser in meteorology, asst. dir. Nigerian Govt., 1976-78; dir. edn. and tng. dept. secretariat World Meteorol. Orgn., Geneva, 1978-83; sec.-gen. World Meteorol. Orgn., 1984—; vis. rsch. fellow Fla. State U., 1973; v.p., mem. adv. group commn. atmospheric scis. World Meteorol. Orgn., 1978; mem. bd. advisors The Bower Award and Prize for Achievement in Sci., Benjamin Franklin Meml. Cons. editor Weatherwise, 1964—; contbr. over 133 articles and papers to profl. jours. Chmn. New Sun Found. Decorated Officer Order of Fed. Republic of Nigeria, 1983, comdr. Nat. Order of Côte d'Ivoire, 1992, comdr. Nat. Order of Niger, 1994, Gold medal Govt. of Paraguay, 1988, Cross medal Venezuelan Air Force, 1989, comdr. Nat. Order of Lion Republic of Senegal, 1995, comdr. Nat. Order of Benin, Republic of Benin, 1997, Comdr. of the Nat. Order of Burkina Faso, 1997, Order of the Grand Duke of Lithuania Gediminas and the medal of the Order of Gediminas, Republic of Lithuania, 1998; recipient Gold Plaque Merit award Czechoslovakian Acad. Scis., 1986, Appreciation cert. and medal Inst. Meteorology and Water Mgmt., Poland, 1989, Washington Climate Inst. award, 1990, Medal of Freedom of Ho Chin Minh City, Vietnam, 1990, Ogori Merit award, Nigeria, 1991, DINAC Honour of Merit award, Paraguay, 1992, Recognition of Merit, Nat. U. Asuncion, 1993, medal of Merit for the Devel. Hydrology and Meteorology Slovak Hydormeteorological Inst., 1994, medal of honor and cert. of merit Front for Ebira Solidarity, Okene, Kogi State, Nigeria, 1995, Balkan Phys. Union Golden medal, Greece, 1997, award for promotion of hydrometeorology Socialist Republic of Viet Nam, 1998, Presdl. award of medal of friendship Socialist Republic of Viet Nam, 1998, plaque of appreciation Islamic Republic of Iran, 1999, Head of State Commendation award, Kenya, 1999, Carl Rossby award in meteorology for best doctoral thesis; named to Nat. Roll of Honour for Environ. Achievement,

Nigeria, 1999. Fellow Nigerian Meteorol. Soc., Colombian Meteorol. Soc., Dominican Republic Meteorol. Soc., Ecuadorian Meteorol. Soc., Royal Meteorol. Soc., African Meteorol. Soc. (Gold Medal award 1993), Royal Statis. Soc., African Acad. Scis., Third World Acad. Scis. (v.p. 1999), Internat. Energy Found.; mem. Academician of the Internat. Acad. Scis. Nature and Soc. (Armenian br.), Indian Meteorol. Soc., Kenya Meteorol. Soc. (hon.), Hellenic Meteorol. Soc. (hon.), Brit. Inst. Statisticians, Am. Meteorol. Soc., Cuban Meteorol. Soc. (fgn.), Kenya Meteorol. Soc. (hon.), Burkina Faso Meteorol. Soc., Chinese Meteorol. Soc. (hon.), Acad. Agrl. and Forestry Scis. Romania (hon.), Sigma Xi. Office: World Meteorol Orgn, 7 bis ave de la Paix, 1211 Geneva 2, Switzerland

OBAYA, MARIA CRISTINA, chemical engineer, researcher; b. Havana, Cuba, Dec. 5, 1949; d. Manuel and Merice (Abreu) O.; m. Alberto Roca, Dec. 16, 1973 (div. 1978); children: Adrian, Alberto. BS, Havana U., 1972, MS, 1984. Jr. rschr. Cuban Rsch. Inst. of Sugar Cane Byproducts, Havana, 1973-84, sr. rschr., 1985—; cons. Sugar Ministry, Havana, 1976—. Author: Handbook of Sugar Cane Derivatives, 1988, 90, Subproductos y derivados de la agro industria azucarera, 1988. Mem. N.Y. Acad. Scis., Latin Am. Network Anaerobic Digestors, Cuban Assn. San. Engring. Avocations: music, reading, ornamental plant culture, movies, dancing. Home: Milagros No 259, Armas y Lawton 10 de Octubre, Havana Cuba Office: Cuban Rsch Inst Sugar Cane Byproducts, Via Blanca 804 PO Box 4026, 11000 Havana Cuba

OBE, ERIC MOONMAN, radio educator; b. Liverpool, Eng., Apr. 29, 1929; s. Borach and Leah (Bernstein) M.; divorced; children: Daniel, Natasha, Josh. MSc, U. Manchester, Eng., 1966; diploma in social scis., Royal Soc. Arts, 1956. Adviser Brit. Inst. Mgmt., London, 1956-62; sr. rsch. fellow U. Manchester, 1964-66; M.P., Ho. of Commons, London, 1966-70, 74-79; prof. City U., London, 1990—; chmn. Essex (Eng.) Radio PLC, 1990—; gov. Brit. Film Inst., 1979-85; v.p. Bd. of Deps., 1985-91, 94-2000; cons. Internat. Red Cross, South Africa, 1992-94; mem. Internat. Rsch. Coun., Potomac Inst., Washington. Author: The Manager and The Organization, 1965, Communications in an Expanding Organization, 1970, The Violent Society, 1987, also others. Mem. London Coun., 1960-64. With Inf. King's Regt., 1951-53. Jewish. Avocations: theatre, football, cinema. Home: 1 Beacon Hill, London N7 9LY, England Office: Essex Radio PLC, Clifftown Rd Southend, Essex England

OBEID, LINA M., medical educator; b. N.Y.C., July 22, 1955; p. Sami J. and Rosette S. Obeid; m. Yusuf A. Hannun, June 9, 1983; children: Reem, Awni, Marya. BS, Rutgers U., Piscataway, N.J., 1978; MD with distinction, Am. U. Beirut, 1983. Diplomate Am. Bd. Internal Medicine. Resident medicine dept. internal medicine Duke U. Med. Ctr., 1983-86; endocrinology fellow Duke U., 1986-90; assoc. Duke Med. U., Durham, 1990-92, asst. prof., 1992-96, assoc. prof., 1996-98; prof. Med. U. S.C., Charleston, 1998—, Boyle endowed chair prof. medicine, 1998—; rsch. fellow Duke U. Med. Ctr., 1986-87, rsch. assoc., 1988-92; mem. search com. dept. microbiology/immunology Med. U. S.C., Charleston, 1999—, chair internal rsch. and sponsored programs, 1999—. Grantee NIH, Bethesda, Md., 1995-2000, 98—; Paul Beeson Physician faculty scholar in aging Am. Fedn. Aging Rsch., 1995-2000. Fellow Ctr. for Study Aging and Human Devel. (sr.); mem. Am. Fedn. Clin. Rsch., Am. Soc. Biochemistry and Molecular Biology. E-mail: obeidl@musc.edu. Fax: 843-876-5172. Office: Med Univ SC 114 Doughty St Rm 604 Charleston SC 29403-5729

O'BEIL, HEDY, artist; b. Bronx, N.Y.; d. Leo Gersten and Viola Cymberg; m. Jerome Liebowitz (div. Sept. 1981); children: S. Jay Liebowitz, Josh E. Liebowitz. Student, Traphagen Sch. Art, 1949, Art Students League, 1953-55, Skowhegan Sch. Art, 1958, Bklkyn Mus. Arts, 1961-64; BS, CUNY, 1974; MFA, Goddard Coll., 1976. Art lectr. Art Ctr. of No. N.J., New Milford, 1976—; curator Chuck Levitan Gallery, N.Y.C., 1998, Broom St. Gallery, N.Y.C., 1999. Exhbns. include Hofstra U., Hempstead, N.Y., 1965, Heckscher Mus., Huntington, N.Y., 1970, Phila. Mus. Art, 1986, Arlene Bujese Gallery, East Hampton, N.Y., 1993, Katherina Perlowe Gallery, N.Y.C., 1998, Savannah (Ga.) Coll. Art and Design, 1999, La Mama La Galleria, N.Y.C., 2000; art critic Arts Mag., N.Y.C., 1976-85. Recipient 1st pl. award L.I. Artists, Guild Hall, East Hampton, N.Y., 1971, Pen & Brush-Sussman/Stevenson award, 1997, 99; fellow Yaddo, 1985; scholar Bob Blackburn Printmaking Workshop, 1991; grantee Richard Florsheim Art Fund, 1999. Mem. AICA, ASCA, CAG, N.Y. Artists Equity, Pen & Brush. Avocations: voice, guitar, piano. Home: 463 West St Apt A1103 New York NY 10014-2040

OBEL, NILS JOHAN, veterinary surgeon, educator; b. Höör, Skåne, Sweden, Mar. 28, 1914; s. Frans and Ebba (Sjöström) Andersson; m. Anna Elisabeth Tägtström (dec. 1975); children: Henning, Johan, Gunilla, Martin; ptnr. Berit Dagny Elisabeth Funkquist; children: Pia-Maria Funkquist, Eva-Lotta Funkquist. DVM, Royal Vet. Coll., Stockholm, 1941, PhD, 1948; Jubilee D of Vet. Medicine (hon.), Swedish U. Agrl. Scis., 1998. Clin. tchr. depts. surgery and medicine Royal Vet. Coll., Stockholm, 1936-37, assoc. prof. dept. surgery, 1949-51, prof. surgery, 1952-76; prof. surgery Swedish U. Agrl. Scis., Uppsala, 1976-80, prof. emeritus, 1980—; dist. vet. officer, clin. tchr., Sweden, 1941-47; head dept. surgery Royal Vet. Coll., Stockholm, 1952-76, Swedish U. Agrl. Scis., Uppsala, 1976-80; fellow sci. bd. vet. svc. Swedish Army, 1957-59; fellow sci. bd. vet. govt. office, Sweden, 1960-68. Contbr. numerous sci. articles to profl. jours.; inventor in field. Vet. surgeon Swedish Army, 1947-53. Decorated Officer 1st class Royal Order of Polar Star, 1957, Knight 1st class Order of White Rose Finland, 1969; recipient Silver medal Swedish Vet. Assn., 1948, hon. plaque Coll. Vet. Medicine, Helsinki, Finland, 1995. Mem. Swedish Pointer Club (hon.), Cen. Swedish Club Bird Dogs (hon.). Lutheran. Avocations: electronics, hunting, bird dog-breeding, etology. Home: Bonadsvägen 34, 757 57 Uppsala Sweden Office: Swedish U Agrl Scis, Box 7037, 750 07 Uppsala Sweden

OBERDANK, LAWRENCE MARK, lawyer, arbitrator; b. Cleve., Nov. 1, 1935; s. Leonard John and Mary (Pavelich) O.; m. Arlene C. Baldini, Aug. 25, 1962; 1 child, Karen A. BA, Western Res. U., 1958, JD, 1965. Bar: Ohio 1965, U.S. Dist. Ct. (no. dist.) Ohio 1966, U.S. Ct. Appeals (6th cir.) 1968, U.S. Supreme Ct. 1970. Assoc. Law Offices Mortimer Riemer, Cleve., 1965-69; ptnr. Riemer and Oberdank, Cleve., 1969-76; prin. Lawrence M. Oberdank Co., L.P.A., Cleve., 1976—; arbitrator Ohio Employment Rels. Bd., 1985-89, Cleve. Civil Svc. Commn., 1983—, FMHA, 1989—; chmn. mandatory arbitration panel Ct. Common Pleas; mem. Nat. Mediation Bd., 1986—; instr. indsl. rels. law Cleve. State U., 1982-85; instr. labor rels. Cuyahoga C.C., 1983; arbitrator/mediator U.S. Dist. Ct. (no. dist.) Ohio, ea. divsn. fee dispute panel Cleve. Bar Assn.; mem. securities arbitration panel Am. Stock Exch., N.Y. Stock Exch., 1995—. Bd. mediators U.S. EEOC. Mem. ABA (labor and employment sect., labor arbitration, law collective bargaining agreements, alternate dispute resolution sect., fed. ct. annexed/connected programs com., sr. lawyers sect.), Am. Arbitration Assn. (securities arbitrator, nat. labor panel 1973—, comml. arbitration panel, nat. panel of employment arbitrators), Nat. Assn. Securities Dealers, Inc. (bd. mediators), Bar Assn. Greater Cleve. (labor law com.), Cuyahoga County Bar Assn., Am. Judicature Soc., Internat. Soc. Labor Law and Social Legislation, Ohio State Bar Assn. (chmn. labor law sect. 1970-73), Indsl. Rels. Rsch. Assn., Pub. Sector Labor Rels. Assn., Soc. Profls. in Dispute Resolution (bd. dirs. Southwest Ohio chpt.), Nat. Inst. Dispute Resolution (assoc.), Masons, Phi Gamma Delta. Roman Catholic. Avocations: golf, Civil War history. Home: 8051 Lakeview Ct N Royalton OH 44133-1214 Office: 6450 Rockside Woods Blvd S Cleveland OH 44131-2230

OBEREDER, ERICH ANTON, financial analyst; b. Linz, Austria, Aug. 5, 1948; s. Eduard and Theresia (Kunzfeld) O.; m. Helene Geier, Aug. 25, 1978; children: Eva, Lisa. Grad. high sch., Linz, 1966. Acct. Chemie Linz, 1966-76, asst. balance dept., 1976-83, head balance dept., 1991-93; CFO Agrolinz, Linz, 1983-91; CFO proxy Agrolinz Melamin, Linz, 1994—. Avocations: tennis, skiing. Office: Agrolinz Melamin GmbH, Saint Peter Str 25, A-4020 Linz Austria

ÖBERG, TOMMY ROLAND, biomechanic and orthopaedic educator; b. Borås, Sweden, Oct. 17, 1943; s. Roland Alexander and Hanna Linnéa (Dinér); m. Ulrika Ebba Ragnarsdotter Smeds, Nov. 2, 1972; children: Gabriella, Magdalena, Johannes. MB, U. Gothenburg, Sweden, 1964, MD, 1970; MSc in Ergonomy, U. Linköping, Sweden, 1992, PhD, 1992. Med. diplomate; specialist diploma in gen. practice, diploma occpl. medicine, occpl. health specialist diploma; cert. profl. ergonomist, Europe. Intern different clinics, Sweden, 1970-73; dep. chief physician Med. Clinic, Skene, Sweden, 1973-74; pvt. practice Sweden, 1974-76, 77-78; chief med. officer Nat. Bd. Health and Safety, Sweden, 1976-77, Occupational Health Unit, Jönköping, Sweden, 1978-89; dep. dir. dept. biomechancis U. Coll. Health Scis., Jönköping, Sweden, 1989-91, dir., asst. prof. biomechanics, 1991—, also bd. dirs.; bd. drs. WHO Collaborating Ctr., Jönköping, 1991—; assoc. prof. orthopaedics U. Linköping, Sweden, 1992—; acting prof. sports biomechanics U. Poznan, Poland, 1995; prof. biomechanics U. Coll. Health Scis., Jönköping, 1996. Mem. editl. bd. Jour. Rehab. R&D; contbr. numerous articles to books and profl. jours.; patentee in field. Dep. dir. County Coun., Jönköping, 1984-89; mem., chmn. numerous coms. and bds., 1970—; v.p. Com. for Competence Evaluation, Sci. Coun. Mem. AAAS, N.Y. Acad. Scis., Swedish Med. Assn., Swedish Soc. Medicine, Internat. Soc. Electromyography and Kinesiology. Mem. Liberal Party. Home: Överåsgatan 7, S 575 35 Eksjö Sweden

OBERGUGGENBERGER, MICHAEL BERND, mathematician, educator; b. Innsbruck, Austria, Sept. 10, 1953; s. Herbert and Sophie (Böhler) O.; m. Elisabeth Marx, July 16, 1982; 1 child, Anne Sophie. M in Natural Scis., U. Innsbruck, 1979; PhD, Duke U., 1981. Habil., 1987. Teaching asst. Duke U., Durham, N.C., 1979-81; teaching asst. U. Innsbruck, Austria, 1975-79, head dept. constrn. mgmt., 1995-96, asst. prof. math., 1981-86, assoc. prof., 1987—, head dept. tech. math., 1999—. Author: Multiplication of Distributions, 1992; co-author: Solution of Nonlinear PDEs Through Order Completion, 1994; editor Pubs. Math. Belgrade, 1995—. Recipient Prize of the City of Innsbruck, 1983. Mem. Am. Math. Soc., Austrian Math. Soc. (prize 1993), S.African Math. Soc. Avocation: music. Office: U Innsbruck Inst Tech Math, Technikerstr 13, A 6020 Innsbruck Austria

OBERIN, COLIN J., patent lawyer; b. Melbourne, Australia, Oct. 2, 1946; m. Anne C. Oberin, Dec. 18, 1970; children: Rebekah, Hayden, Ptolemy, Dante. Diploma in applied chemistry, Swinburne U., Melbourne, 1971. Registered patent atty., 1974. Ptnr. Phillips Ormonde & Fitzpatrick, Melbourne, 1977-87, Oberins Arthur Robinson & Hedderwicks, Melbourne, 1987-99, McMaster Oberin Arthur Robinson & Hedderwicks, 1999—. Co. mem. Melbourne Rudolf Steiner Sch., Melbourne, 1985—; founder Sophia Mundi Rudolf Steiner Sch., Melbourne, 1986. Fellow Inst. Patent and Trade Mark Attys. Australia; mem. AIPPI (Australian group), Internat. Fedn. Indsl. Property Attys., Internat. Trademark Assn., Royal Australian Chem. Inst., Intellectual Property Soc. Australia and New Zealand, Inst. Patent and Trade Mark Attys. Australia (trade marks com. 1986—), Asian Patent Attys. Assn. (trade marks com. 1994—). Office: McMaster Oberin Arthur, GPO Box 1776Q, Melbourne VIC 3001, Australia

OBERMAN, STEVEN, lawyer; b. St. Louis, Sept. 21, 1955; s. Albert and Marian (Kleg) O.; m. Evelyn Ann Simpson, Aug. 27, 1977; children: Rachael Diane, Benjamin Scott. BA in Psychology, Auburn U., 1977; JD, U. Tenn., 1980. Bar: Tenn. 1980, Tenn. Supreme Ct. 1980, Tenn. Criminal Ct. Appeals 1980, U.S. Dist. Ct. (ea. dist.) Tenn. 1980, U.S. Ct. Appeals (4th cir.) 1981, U.S. Ct. Appeals (6th cir.) 1983, U.S. Supreme Ct. 1985. Law clk. Daniel, Duncan & Claiborne, Knoxville, Tenn., 1978-80; assoc. Daniel, Claiborne & Lewallen, Knoxville, Tenn., 1980-82; ptnr. Daniel, Claiborne, Oberman & Buuck, Knoxville, 1983-85, Daniel & Oberman, Knoxville, 1986—; pres., Project First Offender, Knoxville, 1983-86; bd. dirs. Fed. Defender Svcs. Eastern Tenn., Inc., v.p. 1994-97, pres. 1998—; guest instr. U. Tenn. 1988-90; guest lectr. U. Tenn. Law Sch., 1982-88; guest instr. U. Tenn. Grad. Sch. Criminal Justice Program, 1983, 84; guest speaker Ct. Clk's Meeting, Cambridge, Eng., 1984; guest instr. legal clinic , trial advocacy program U. Tenn., 1984—; adj. prof. U. Tenn. Law Sch., 1993— (Forrest W. Lacey award for outstanding faculty contbn. to U. Tenn. Coll. Law Moot Ct. Program, 1993-94; coach U. Tenn. Law Sch. Nat. Trial Team, 1991-96; spl. judge Criminal Divsn. Knox County Gen. Sessions Court; founding mem. Nat. Coll. for DUI Def.; speaker in field. Author: D.U.I.: The Crime and Consequences in Tennessee, 1991, 2d edit., 1997, supplemented annually; co-author: D.W.I. Means Defend With Ingenuity, 1987; contbr. legal articles on drunk driving to profl. jours. Bd. dirs. Knoxville Legal Aid Soc., Inc., 1986-88 (pres. 1990), Arnstein Jewish Community Ctr., 1987-91, pres. 1990; bd. dirs. Knoxville Racquet Club, 1991-93, pres. 1992-93. Col. Aide de Camp Tenn. Gov.'s Staff, 1983, Moot Ct. Bd. Spl. Svc. award, 1995-96. Mem. ATLA, Nat. Assn. Criminal Def. Lawyers (co-chair DUI advocacy com. 1995—), Nat. Coll. DUI Def. (founding, bd. regents 1999), Tenn. Assn. Criminal Def. Lawyers (bd. dirs. 1983-89), Knoxville Bar Assn. Jewish. Office: Daniel & Oberman 550 W Main St Ste 950 Knoxville TN 37902-2536

OBERMANN, RICHARD MICHAEL, governmental technology and policy analyst; b. May 21, 1949; s. Baird J. and Phyllis L. (Weber) O. BS of Engring. in Aerospace and Mech. Scis. cum laude, Princeton U., 1971, PhD in Engring., Aerospace and Mech. Scis., 1977; MS of Engring. in Astronautics and Aeros., Stanford U., 1972; postgrad., Va. Poly. Inst. and State U., Am. U. With MITRE Corp., McLean, Va., 1977-88, engr. transp. systems analysis, transp. energy analysis, telecommunications, project leader, mem. tech. staff in communications and system design; sr. staff officer aeros. and space engring. bd. NRC, Washington, 1988-90, study dir. and analyst technol. and policy issues; mem. profl. staff for space subcom. U.S. Ho. of Reps. Com. on Sci., Space and Tech., Washington, 1990-95; minority staff dir., space subcom. U.S. House of Reps. Com. on Sci., Washington, 1995—. Author tech. papers and presentations. Fellow AIAA (assoc.), Brit. Interplanetary Soc.; mem. IEEE, AAAS, N.Y. Acad. Scis., Japan-Am. Soc., Asia Soc., Am. Astronaut. Soc. (bd. dirs., exec. com.), Nat. Space Club, Pacific Telecomms. Coun., Women in Aerospace (bd. dirs.), Internat. Acad. Astronautics (corr.), World Affairs Coun. Avocations: Japanese, Chinese and Spanish langs., sports, trumpet.

OBERMAYER, HERMAN JOSEPH, newspaper publisher; b. Phila., Sept. 19, 1924; s. Leon J. and Julia (Sinsheimer) O.; m. Betty Nan Levy, June 28, 1955; children: Helen O. Levy-Myers, Veronica O. Atnipp, Adele O. Malpass, Elizabeth Rose. Student, U. Geneva, Switzerland, 1946; AB cum laude, Dartmouth U., 1948. Reporter L.I. Daily Press, Jamaica, N.Y., 1950-53; classified advt. mgr. New Orleans Item, 1953-55; asst. to pub. Standard-Times, New Bedford, Mass., 1955-57; editor, pub. Long Branch (N.J.) Daily Record, 1957-71, No. Va. Sun, Arlington, 1963-89; adj. prof. journalism U. Md., 1989-93; vis. lectr. U. West Indies, Jamaica, 1994-95; publ. com. Commentary Mag., 1989—; Pulitizer Prize juror, 1983, 84; chmn. fin. com. Washington Journalism Rev., 1990-91; lectr. publs. mgmt. seminars, Hungary, Poland, Lithuania, Latvia, Estonia, Ukraine, Moldova, Slovenia, Macedonia, Russia, 1990-2000, Internat. Ctr. Journalists, 1992—. Contbr. articles to numerous mags. and newspapers. Bd. dirs. Monmouth Med. Ctr., 1958-71; mem. exec. coun. Monmouth Boy Scouts Am., 1958-71, mem. exec. com. Nat. Capital coun., 1971-79, v.p., 1974-77; mem. Va. Legis. Alcohol Beverage Control Study Commn., 1972-74; trustee Arlington (Va.) Bicentennial Commn., Am. Jewish Com. Cmty. Svc. award, 1986, nat. bd. govs., 1989-96, nat. coun., 1996—; trustee Jewish Inst. for Nat. Security Affairs, 1996—. With AUS, 1943-46, ETO. Rhineland Campaign Star; Recipient Silver Beaver award Boy Scouts Am., 1977, Knight Internat. Press fellow, 1994-95. Mem. Am. Soc. Newspaper Editors, So. Newspaper Pubs. Assn. (dir. 1981-84), Soc. Profl. Journalists, Nat. Press Club (Washington), Cosmos Club (Washington), Washington Golf and Country Club (Arlington, Va.), Dartmouth Club (N.Y.C.), Econ. Club (Washington), Sigma Chi. Jewish. Rotarian. Home: 4114 N Ridgeview Rd Arlington VA 22207-4711

OBERMAYER, MICHAEL ERIK MAX, management consultant; b. Stockholm, May 8, 1948; s. Adolf Max and Gerd Sigrid Ulrica (Malm) O.; m. Marianne Linnander, May 2, 1991; children: Anna Catharina, Johan Georg, Marie Louise, Erik Richard. MSChemE, Royal Inst. Tech., Stockholm, 1973; DSc in Biochemistry with honors, Ludwig Maximilians U., Munich, 1976; MBA with honors, European Inst. Adminstrn. Affairs, Fontainebleau, France, 1977. Fellow Max Planck Inst. Biochemistry, Munich, 1974-76; assoc. McKinsey & Co., Copenhagen, 1977-83; prin. McKinsey & Co., Stockholm, 1983-86; prin., head of office McKinsey & Co., Oslo, 1986-90; dir., head of office McKinsey & Co., Stockholm, 1990-93; dir., chmn. Ea. Europe McKinsey & Co., St. Petersburg, Russia, 1993-94; chmn. Ea. Europe McKinsey & Co., Prague, Czech Republic, 1994-96, Moscow, 1996-2000, London, 2000—; vis. prof. bus. strategy Faculty Econs. Moscow State U., 1996—. Mem. adv. bd. State Hermitage Mus., St. Petersburg, 1994; mem. Mir Iskusstvo/World of Art Found., Moscow, 1997. Lt. C.E., German Army, 1967-68.

OBERNDORFER, WOLFGANG JOHANNES, engineering educator; b. Steyr, Austria, Feb. 28, 1941; s. Karl and Annelise (Mayr) O.; m. Christine Mittendorfer, Mar. 22, 1969; children: Birgit, Christian, Georg. Diploma in engring., Tech. U. Vienna, Austria, 1964; MS, U. Calif., Berkeley, 1965; PhD, Tech. U. Vienna, 1966. Rsch. asst. U.Calif., Berkeley, 1964-65; design engr. Voest-Alpine, Linz, Austria, 1965-66; constrn. engr. Mayreder, Linz, 1966-76; exec. Stuag, Vienna, 1976-81; prof. engring. Tech. U. Vienna, 1981—. Author: Baustellen U Betriebsanalyse, 1981, Kalkulation von Baupreisen, 1988, Handwoerterbuch der Bauwirtschaft, 1987, Preisumrechnung von Bauleistungen, 1992, Kommentar zu den Oenormen betreffend das Verdingungswesen, 1992. Mem. Internat. Assn. Bridge and Structural Engring., Verein der Gerichtssachverstandigen, Oeïav, Austrian Soc. Contractural Law in Constrn. Roman Catholic. Avocations: sports, cycling, jogging, mountain climbing. Home: Ludwig Kaiser Strasse 34, 3021 Pressbaum Austria Office: Tech U Vienna, Karlsplatz 13, 1040 Vienna Austria

OBERNEIER, KLAUS HENNER, health care executive; b. Prussia Holland, Germany, Apr. 11, 1943; arrived in Namibia, 1989; s. Wilhelm and Elfriede (Linnenkamper) O.; m. Annemarie Bezuidenhoud, May 7, 1993; children: Regina, Elfriede. PhD in Engring., U. Wupputal, Germany, 1968; PhD in Sci., U. Krefeld, Germany, 1970; MS in Canonica, U. Köln, Germany, 1984, cert. secondary education tchr., 1975; MD, U. Bonn, Germany, 1980. Cert. engr., airline transport pilot, air traffic controller, aircraft dispatcher, flight instr. Prof. U. Köln, 1984-85, U. Wupputal, 1985-90, Raum Quanten Forshung, Switzerland, 1990-92; educator Namibia Prisons Sys., Windhoek, 1992-93; pres. Quadrapilegic Trust Namibia, 1993—; also bd. dirs. Author, editor: Education Central Prison I, 1993, II, 1994, The Quadripelgic Patient, 1994, A Future for Education. Walker, peace pilgrim on behalf of para and quadriplegic patients. Recipient award Amb. of U.S., 1996, 2000, Fed. Rep. Germany, 1995, Ministry of Health and Social Svcs., Windhoek, 1996. Mem. Physicians Assn. Antrhoposophical Medicine, Schweizer Paraplgiker Stiftung, N.Y. Acad. Scis. Roman Catholic. Office: QTN, Privat Bag 12032, Windhoek 9000, Namibia

OBERRAUCH, KARL, investment banker; b. Bolzano, Italy, Aug. 18, 1957; s. Hermann and Laura (Bensi) O.; m. Daniela Salerno, Oct. 26, 1991; children: Caroline, Claudia, Cinzia. Maturita sci., Liceo Scientifico, Bolzano, 1976; D Econs. summa cum laude, U. Padua, 1980; MBA, Columbia U., 1986. CPA, Italy. Ptnr. Karl Oberrauch & Ptnrs., Bolzano, 1982-84; mgr. Nomura Internat. Plc, London, 1986-89, exec. dir., 1990-93; mng. dir. Babcock & Brown SpA, Milan, 1993—; dep. chmn. SEIM SpA, Milan, 1990-93. Mem. Beta Gamma Sigma. Avocations: golf, skiing, piano. Home: Via Cornaiano 30, 39057 Appiano Bolzano Italy Office: Babcock & Brown SpA, Via Serbelloni 4, 20122 Milan Italy

OBERST, ULRICH HERBERT GÜNTER, mathematics educator; b. Berlin, Oct. 4, 1940; arrived in Austria, 1972; s. Hermann and Ruth (Winchenbach) O.; m. Karla K. Thöle, Apr. 3, 1965; children: Corinna Sonderegger, Hilmar. Bachelor, U. Heidelberg, Germany, 1961, M in Math., 1963; PhD, U. Munich, 1965. Asst. U. Munich, 1963-65, assoc. prof., 1969-72; asst. prof. U. Calif., San Diego, 1965-67; instr. U. Chgo., 1967-69; prof. U. Innsbruck, Austria, 1972-99; vis. prof. U. Fla., Gainesville, 1988; head of dept. U. Innsbruck, 1972—. Contbr. articles to profl. jours. Mem. Austrian Math Soc., MPG (chmn.). Avocations: piano playing, chamber music, mountaineering. Home: Franz-Gastl-Weg 11, A-6170 Zirl Austria Office: Dept Math U Innsbruck, Technikerstrasse 25, A-6070 Innsbruck Austria

OBERSTEIN, MARYDALE, geriatric specialist; b. Red Wing, Minn., Dec. 30; d. Dale Robert and Jean Ebba-Marie (Holmquist) Johnson; children: Kirk Robert, Mark Paul, MaryJean. Student, U. Oreg., 1961-62, Portland State U., 1962-64, Long Beach State U., 1974-76. Cert. geriatric specialist, Calif. Florist, owner Sunshine Flowers, Santa Ana, Calif., 1982—; pvt. duty nurse Aides in Action, Costa Mesa, Calif., 1985-87; owner, activity dir., adminstr. Lovelight Christian Home for the Elderly, Santa Ana, 1987—; activity dir. Bristol Care Nursing Home, Santa Ana, 1985-88; evangelist, speaker radio show Sta. KPRZ-FM, Anaheim, Calif., 1985-88; adminstr. Leisure Lodge Resort Care for Elderly in Lake Forest, Lake Forest, Calif., 1996—; nursing home activist in reforming laws to eliminate bad homes, 1984-90; founder, tchr. hugging classes/laughter therapy terminally ill patients, 1987—; founder healing and touch therapy laughter therapy Merry Sunshine, 1991-93; bd. dirs. Performing Arts Ctr.; speaker for enlightenment and healing. Author (rewrite) Title 22 Nursing Home Reform Law, Little Hoover Commn.; model, actress and voiceovers. Bd. dirs. Orange County Coun. on Aging, 1984—; chairperson Helping Hands, 1985—, Pat Robertson Com., 1988, George Bush Presdl. Campaign, Orange County, 1988; bd. dirs., v.p. Women Aglow Orange County, 1985—; evangelist, pub. spkr., v.p. Women Aglow Huntington Beach; active with laughter therapy and hugging classes for terminally ill; helped write AB 180 Nursing Home Reform Bill and revised title 22. Recipient Carnation Silver Bowl, Carnation Svc. Co., 1984-85, Gold medal Pres. Clinton, 1994; named Woman of Yr., Kiwanis, 1985, ABI, 1990, Woman of Decade, Am. Biog. Soc., 1995, Little Hoover Commn., 1995; honored AM L.A. TV Show, Lt. Gov. McCarthy, 1984. Mem. Calif. Assn. Residential Care Homes, Orange County Epilepsy Soc. (bd. dirs. 1986—), Calif. Assn. Long Term Facilities. Home: 2050 Oak St Santa Ana CA 92707-2921

OBIALA, RAPHAEL UZODINMA, pediatrician, family medicine physician; b. Bukuru, Nigeria, June 18, 1951; arrived in Mex., 1981.; s. Peter and Felicia (Otuechere) O.; children: Elizabeth, Victoria, Victor, Raphael. BS, U. Wis., 1980; MD, U. Xochicalco, Mex., 1991. Cert. pediatrician El Consejo Mex. Cert. Pediatria. Resident in pediatrics Gen. Hosp. Ensenada, Mex., 1992-95; pvt. practice Ensenada, 1995—; on-call staff Clin. Hosp. Issste, Ensenada. Vol. Mex. Red Cross, Ensenada. Mem. AAAS, N.Y. Acad. Scis. Roman Catholic. Home: PO Box 2548, Ensenada Mexico Office: Colonia Ampliacion Reforma, Calle 11 674 y Colon, 22835 Ensenada Mexico

OBIANG NGUEMA MBASOGO, TEODORO, president of Equatorial Guinea; b. June 5, 1942. Ed. in Spain. Army officer; now pres. Govt. of Equatorial Guinea, Malabo; minister of def., 1986-1989; overthrew former pres. in coup; pres., 1979—; head Supreme Mil. Council, 1979—. Office: Office of President, PO Box 597, Malabo Equatorial Guinea*

OBINAJU, JOSEPH NWABUEZE, foreign language educator; b. Onitsha, Anambra, Nigeria, Apr. 1, 1952; s. Jonas Chinwuba and Virginia Matagu (Okafor) O.; m. Queendoleen Idongesit Udom, Feb. 26, 1983; children: Lawrence, Blessing, Queenette, Raymond, Precious. BA in French with honors, U. Nigeria, Nsukka, 1976, MA in French, 1982; PhD in Lit. in French, U. Port Harcourt, Nigeria, 1988; exec. diploma in computer sci., Delta State U., Abraka, Nigeria, 1997. Asst. lectr. Coll. Edn., Uyo, Nigeria, 1977-83; lectr. II/I Unicross, Uyo, 1983-91; sr. lectr. U. Uyo, 1991-97, assoc. prof., 1997—, acting head dept. fgn. langs., 1992-97, 2000—, vice dean faculty arts, 1995-97, chmn. faculty arts exam com., 1995-96; external examiner U. Port Harcourt, 1995, 96, 99; vis. scholar Delta State U., Abraka, 1997-98. Author: Ferdinand Oyono: L'Itinéraire d'un Romancier, 1999; co-author: African Literature Series, 1998; editor-in-chief Agora, 1997—; mem. editl. adv. bd. Ago Go, 1991; contbr. articles to profl. jours. Patron Anambra Students Assn., U. Uyo, 1995-96; mem. Nat. Commn. for Colls. Edn. Accreditation Team, Kaduna, Nigeria, 2000. Mem. Nat. Assn. for Francophone Studies (coord. 1988-92), Assn. for Promoting Quality Edn. in Nigeria, Nigeria Univ. French Tchrs. Assn. (editl. cons. 1999—), Cath. Men Orgn. Roman Catholic. Avocations: reading, writing, music, traveling, meeting people. Home: 2 Udosen Uboh St, Uyo Nigeria Office: Univ Uyo, PMB 1017, Uyo Nigeria

OBIORA, CHRIS SUNNY, architect; b. Lagos, Nigeria, Sept. 2, 1954; came to U.S., 1978; s. Patrick M. and Virginia E. Obiora. Diploma in Physics, Chemistry, and Biology, Christ the King Coll., Onitsha, Anambra, 1974; A in Econs. and Current Affairs, Christ the King Coll., 1976; postgrad., Tex. A&M U., 1986, Coll. Profl. Mgmt., Lintas, Lagos, 1992. CFP; cert. tng. adminstr. Accounts clk. Lintas, Ltd., Lagos, 1976-78, media accounts clk., 1977-78; with San Jacinto Jr. Coll., Houston, Tex., 1980-81;

The Wacherhit Corp., Coral Gables, Fla., 1980-84; gen. merchant Joncod Overseas Ltd., Lagos, 1974—; world trade strategist Joncod Overseas Ltd., Houston, 1987—; retail trader Star Liquor Store, Hempstead, Tex., 1987—; owner, prin. Chris & Chris Assocs., 1989; coord. Jancod/Bexpharm, Houston, 1987-88; cost acct. Jancod Overseas Ltd., Houston, 1980—; founder, pres. Joncod Internat., Inc., 1987—; founder, com. group head Star Liquor Store, Hempstead, 1987—. Active ARC, 1967-70, PTO, also numerous charitable activities, Lagos, 1970-74. Recipient Professionalism Cert. AMA, 1994, Meritorious Svc. award AIA Students, 1985, Recognition award Nat. Fire Protection Assn., 1986. Fellow The Highlanders Club (svcs. prof. 1993—), Nat. Shrine, Oxford Club, Oblates Mission Mary Immaculate; mem. ACLU, NAFE, ATLA, AIChE, N.Y. Acad. Sci., Am. Chem. Soc., Am. Fin. Assn., Nat. Audubon Soc., Internat. Assn. Fin. Planners, Soc. Applied Learning Tech., Assn. Corp. Tech. Computer Profls., Instr. of Profl. Mgmt. and Adminstrn., Internat. Assn. of Account Practitioners, Constrn. Specs. Inst., Nat. Hist. Soc., Nat. Soc. Accts., Sherrifs Assn. Tex., Soc. Human Rels. Mgmt. Avocations: table and lawn tennis, photography, swimming. Office: Joncod Overseas Ltd PO Box 87549 Houston TX 77287-7549

OBLOY, LEONARD GERARD, priest; b. Cleve., Sept. 1, 1951; s. Henry Joseph and Ruth Elsie (Walter) O. AB, Borromeo Coll. of Ohio, 1973; MDiv, St. Mary's Seminary, 1977; SSL, Pontifical Biblical Inst., Rome, 1983, postgrad., 1984. Ordained priest Roman Cath. Ch., 1977. Assoc. pastor St. Helen Parish, Newbury, Ohio, 1977-80, St. Rose of Lima Parish, Cleve., 1984-88; vice-rector St. Mary's Sem., Emmitsburg, Md., 1988-97; asst. prof. sacred scripture and computer sci. Mt. St. Mary's Sem., Emmitsburg, Md., 1988-99; dir. aux. svcs. Mt. St. Mary's Sem., Emmitsburg, 1997-99; assoc. pastor St. Francis of Assisi Parish, Gates Mills, Ohio, 1999—; adj. prof. St. Mary's Sem., Cleve., 1984-88, 1999—; tech. com. Cath. Distance U., Hamilton, Va., 1986—, dean grad. divsn., 1995—, also bd. dirs.; guest lectr. Our Lady of Holy Cross Coll., New Orleans, 1988—; lectr. in field. Author, narrator pub. TV series And God Said, Witness; author various pamphlets/audio casettes for Cath. Distance U. Mem. IEEE Computer Soc., Assn. for Computing Machinery, N.Y. Acad. Scis., Cath. Bibl. Fedn., Cath. Distance U., Corp. for Pub. Broadcasting, Nat. Cath. Edn. Assn., Sacred Congregation for Doctrine of Faith, Vatican Radio, Eternal Word TV Network. Avocations: computers, audio engineering, audio recording, auto mechanics. Home and Office: St Francis of Assisi Parish 6850 Mayfield Rd Gates Mills OH 44040-9635

OBOH-IKUENOBE, FRANCISCA EMIEDE, geologist, educator, researcher; b. Lagos, Nigeria, Aug. 23, 1962; came to U.S., 1990; d. Joseph and Christiana (Atiomo) O.; m. Thomas Ikuenobe, Nov. 4, 1995; children: Ordia, Aita. BSc, U. Ife, Nigeria, 1983, MSc, 1986; PhD, U. Cambridge, Eng., 1990. Reg. geologist, Mo. Prodn. geologist Shell Petroleum Co., Lagos, 1983-84; palynologist Shell Petroleum Co., War, Nigeria, 1984; geologist, palynologist GEOTREX Sys. Ltd., Lagos, 1987; asst. prof. U. Mo., Rolla, 1991-97, assoc. prof., 1997—; grad. asst. U. Ife, 1985-87, asst. lectr., 1987; demonstrator, supr. U. Cambridge, 1988-90; cons. Mobil Exploration Producing, Dallas, 1991-95, Shell Petroleum Co., Warri, 1992-94; shipboard sedimentologist Ocean Drilling Program, College Sta., Tex., 1995. Contbr. articles to Palaeogeography, Palaeoclimatology, Palaeoecology, Palynology, Jour. Petroleum Geology Palaios, Geol. Soc. Am. Bulletin. Commonwealth scholar, 1987; grantee Am. Chem. Soc., 1992, NSF, 1994. Mem. Am. Assn. Stratigraphic Palynologists (Best Poster award 1994), Am. Assn. Petroleum Geologists, Soc. Sedimentary Geology, Mo. Acad. Sci. (sect. chair 1994-98), Optimist Club (bd. dirs. 1995-98), Sigma Xi. Office: U Mo 125 Mcnutt Hl Rolla MO 65409-0001

OBOT, PATRICK ENEFIOK, workshop manager; b. Uyo, Nigeria, May 5, 1962; s. Thomas Dickson and Theresa Mercy (Inyans) O.; m. Maria Augustine Inyang, Feb. 2, 1992; three children. Postgrad. cert., Brunel U., U.K., 1996; M in Advanced Mfg., Brunel U., 1999. Process engr. St. Microelectronics, Kirkop, Malta, 1990-93; workshop mgr. Trismegitus Co. Ltd., Luqa, Malta, 1993—. Mem. ASME (assoc.). Avocations: table tennis, football, lawn tennis, golf, basketball. Home: 4 Seychell Bldg Wilya Str, Luqa LQA 02, Malta

O'BOYLE, PATRICK JOHN, urologist, consultant; b. Glasgow, Scotland, Apr. 12, 1941; s. James and Elizabeth (Dunlop) O'B.; m. Emilia Maria Galli, Sept. 4, 1968; children: Marie-Claire Elizabeth, Stephen James. MBChB, Glasgow U., 1965. Clin. rsch. fellow U. Leeds, Eng., 1971-73; sr. registrar U. Liverpool, Eng., 1974-78; cons. urologist Taunton (Eng.) and Somerset Hosp., 1979—. Author: Top Tips in Urology, 1995; contbr. articles to med. jours., chpts. to books. Mem. Royal Soc. Medicine, Brit. Assn. Urol. Surgeons, Brit. Laser Urol. Evaluation Soc. Avocations: golf, sailing, running, skiing, music. Home: Wild Oak Cottage, Wild Oak Ln, Trull, Taunton TA3 7JS, England Office: Taunton and Somerset Hosp, Musgrove Park, Taunton TA1 5DA, England

OBREBSKI, JAN BOGDAN, civil engineer, educator; b. Miedzyrzec Podlaski, Poland, Jan. 27, 1943; s. Czeslaw and Wiktoria (Sierpinska) O.; m. Maria Krystyna Świrkowska, Dec. 31, 1971; children: Konrad Bartlomiej, Michal Ziemowit. MSc, Warsaw U. Tech., 1966, habilitation, 1980; PhD, Polish Acad. Scis., Warsaw, 1972. Engr., constrn. works mgr. Chemobudowa-Pulawy, Pulawy, Poland, 1966-69; asst. Warsaw U. Tech., 1972-73, asst. prof., 1973-81, assoc. prof., 1982-96, prof., 1996—, vice dir. for didactic affairs Inst. Structural Mechanics, 1987-88, vice dir. for sci. affairs Inst. Structural Mechanics, 1988-91, dir. Inst. Structural Mechanics, 1991-96; from assoc. prof. to prof. Agr.-Tech. Acad., Olsztyn, Poland, 1990—; cons. prof. Inst. Civil Engrng. Tech., Warsaw, 1991-95; lectr. in field; mem. scientific or adv. coms. numerous internat. scientific confs., 1994—; organizer confs. on lightweight structures in civil engrng., 1995—. Co-author: Statistical Computations of Structural Roofs, 1980, Statische Berechnung der Raumstabiwerke, 1985; author: Thin-Walled Elastic Bars, 1991, 99, Strength of Materials, 1997; contbr. numerous articles and papers to profl. jours. and internat. confs. procs.; mem. editl. bd. Internat. Jour. Space Structures, Internat. Jour. Structural Stability and Dynamics. Cpl., inf. Polish Army Res. Decorated Silver Cross of Merit (Poland); recipient Individual Sci. award Minister Nat. Edn., 1981, 90. Mem. Polish Assn. Civil Engrs., Internat. Assn. for Shell and Spatial Structures (exec. coun. 1996—), Internat. Assn. for Bridge and Structural Engrng. (founder Polish chpt. 1996—), Polish Assn. for Tourism. Roman Catholic. Avocations: sailing ocean-going yachts and ocean-going motorboats, chess, stamps. Office: Warsaw U Tech Struct Mechs, Armii Ludowej 16, 00-637 Warsaw Poland

O'BRIEN, BRIAN JOHN, environmental and strategic consultant; b. Sydney, Australia, Feb. 27, 1934; s. Richard Ignatius and Thelma (Hoban) O'B.; m. Aril Searle, Apr. 10, 1959; children: Richard, John (dec.), Rosalind, Caroline. BSc with honors, U. Sydney, 1954, PhD in Physics, 1957. Dep. chief physicist Antarctic Div., Melbourne, Australia, 1958-59; asst. prof., then assoc. prof. Iowa State U., Iowa City, 1959-63; prof. space sci. Rice U., Houston, 1963-68; vis. prof., scientist Sydney U., 1964, 69-70; dir. environ. protection, chmn. EPA, Perth, Australia, 1971-77; mng. dir. Brian J. O'Brien & Assocs. P/L, Perth, 1977—; cons. Communication Adv. Com., Perth, 1978—. Inventor thermomagnetic refrigerator, thermoelectric refrigerator, radiation instruments, charged particle lunar environment expt., lunar dust detector, other devices; author: Postponing Greenhouse, 1990, Nationalising the Australian Environment, 1993, Statewide Waterways Management, 1996, Fatal Flaws in Life Cycle Assessment Methodologies, 1998, Communications Impact Assessments, 1998, Australian Greenhouse Governance: The Twilight Zone, 1999; editor: Science and Environment, 1979; contbr. numerous articles, sci. papers to profl. publs. Recipient medal for exceptional sci. achievement, NASA, 1973, Paul Harris medal, Perth Rotary, 1988. Fellow Australian Acad. Technol. Scis. and Engrng.; mem. AAAS, Australian and New Zealand Assn. Advancement Sci., Inst. Urban Studies, Rotary (coord. East Java Hearing Ctr. 1997—). Avocations: reading, writing, music, photography, grandchildren. Home and Office: 12 Caithness Rd, Floreat Park WA 6014, Australia

O'BRIEN, CATHERINE LOUISE, museum administrator; b. N.Y.C., July 21, 1930; d. Edward Denmark and Cathrine Louise (Browne) O'B.; m. Philip R. James (div.); m. Sterling Noel (div.). BA, Finch Coll., 1952; postgrad, Williams Coll., 1954, Marymount Coll., 1954. Reprodn. mgr. Met. Mus. Art, N.Y.C., 1975—; dir. sales Simon Pearce Gallery, N.Y.C. Exhibited in group shows at Parrish Art Mus., Southampton, N.Y., 1965-70, Met. Mus. Art, N.Y.C., 1975-85, Guild Hall Exhibit, East Hampton, N.Y., 1965-85; founding mem. Parrish Art Mus. Players, Southampton, 1958, Williamstown (Mass.) Theater, 1955; mem. John Drew Theater Co., Guild Hall, 1956-59. Mem. aux. Southampton Hosp., 1970-85; founder East Hampton Horse Show, Ladies Village Improvement Soc., East Hampton, 1970—; mem. fair coms. St. James Ch., N.Y.C., St. Luke's Ch., East Hampton, 1970-85; mem. alumnae adv. bd. Marymount Coll., N.Y.C., 1984-86, chmn. alumnae event, 1994; mem. Women's Nat. Rep. Club, N.Y.C.; chmn. Landmark and Tree Planting Com. for Madison Ave. Assn., N.Y.C., 1994—; mem. founding com. Internat. Debutante Ball, Waldorf Astoria, N.Y.C., 1955; founding mem. Williamstown (Mass.) Theater, 1955; founder Parrish Art Mus. Players, Southampton, N.Y., 1955. Mem. DAR (founding; vice regent East Hampton chpt. 1974-85), Colonial Dames Am. (archives com. 1980-85), Daus. Brit. Empire (historian 1978-85), United Daus. Confederacy (state historian 1970-85), Daus. Colonial Wars (corr. sec. 1983-85), Sons and Daus. of Pilgrims (corr. sec. 1983-85), Victorian Soc., Soc. Mayflower Descs. (life), English Speaking Union, New Eng. Soc. (mem. ball com. 1983-86), Daus. of Cin. (historian 1979-85), Squadron "A", Devon Yacht, Maidstone, Southampton Yacht, Metropolitan Club (women's com., chmn. debutante ball 1980-84), Reciprocal/India House, St. Anthony Union League. Republican. Episopalian. Avocations: show horses, dogs. Home: 605 Park Ave New York NY 10021-7016 also: Seacote PO Box 1488 East Hampton NY 11937-0711 Office: Met Mus of Art 5th Ave New York NY 10028 also: Simon Pierce Gallery 500 Park Ave New York NY 10022-1606

O'BRIEN, DANIEL DION, track and field athlete, Olympic athlete; b. Portland, Oreg., July 18, 1966. Student, U. Idaho, 1989. Track and field athlete Reebock Racing Club; pub. personality; broadcaster NBC, CBS, ESPN, TBS. Vol. asst. coach Wash. State U. Winner Decathlon World Championship, 1991, 93; ranked No.1 in Decathlon Track & Field News, 1991; recipient Gold medal Atlanta Olympics, 1996; Footlocker A.C. World Record holder. Office: USA Track and Field 1 Rca Dome Ste 140 Indianapolis IN 46225-1023 Agent: Gold Medal Management Attn Janey Miller 1750 14th St Ste 200 Boulder CO 80302-6322*

O'BRIEN, DANIEL ROBERT, lawyer; b. Peoria, Ill., May 7, 1951; s. William Patrick and Irene Cornelia O'Brien; m. Eileen Mary Kahn, Aug. 17, 1974; children: Colleen, Patrick, Bridget. BS, No. Ill. U., 1973; JD, Wash. U., St. Louis, 1976. Bar: U.S. Dist. Ct. (so. dist.) Ill. 1977. Ptnr. Smith Moos Schmitt & O'Brien, Peoria, 1976-82, Moos, Schmitt & O'Brien, Peoria, 1982—; lectr. Peoria County Bar Assn., Ill. Continuing Legal Edn., Springfield. Dem. precinct committeeman Dem. Party, 1986. Named to Greater Peoria Sports Hall of Fame, 1967. Fellow Ill. Bar Found. (charter mem., Leading Ill. Atty. award), Beta Gamma Sigma. Avocations: coaching children's basketball. Office: Moos Schmitt & O'Brien 331 Fulton St Ste 740 Peoria IL 61602-1499

O'BRIEN, DAVID A., lawyer; b. Sioux City, Iowa, Aug. 30, 1958; s. John T. and Doris K. (Reisch) O'B. BA, George Washington U., 1981; JD with distinction, U. Iowa, 1984. Bar: Iowa 1985, U.S. Dist. Ct. (no. dist.) Iowa 1985, Nebr. 1990, U.S. Dist. Ct. Nebr. 1990. Legis. asst. Nat. Transp. Safety Bd., Washington, 1978-81; assoc. O'Brien, Galvin & Kuehl, Sioux City, 1985-88; ptnr. O'Brien, Galvin Moeller & Neary, Sioux City, 1989-94; chair Wage Appeals Bd. & Bd. of Svc. Contract Appeals U.S. Dept. Labor, Washington, 1994-96, acting dir. Office Adminstrv. Appeals, 1995-96, chair adminstrv. review bd., 1996-98; ptnr. O'Brien & Beyer, Cedar Rapids, Iowa, 2000—. Dem. candidate for Congress, 6th dist. of Iowa, Sioux City, 1988; chmn. Woodbury County Dem. Party, Sioux City, 1992-94, chair Iowa campaign Clinton for Pres., Des Moines, 1992; bd. dirs. Mid-Step Svcs. Inc., Sioux City, 1986-91, Mo. River Hist. Devel., Sioux City, 1989-94. Mem. Nat. Assn. Trial Lawyers, Iowa Trial Lawyers Assn. (bd. govs. 1991-94). Roman Catholic. Avocations: sports, politics. Office: O'Brien & Beyer PO Box 1231 Cedar Rapids IA 52404-1231

O'BRIEN, DAVID MICHAEL, law educator; b. Rock Springs, Wyo., Aug. 30, 1951; s. Ralph Rockwell and Lucile O'Brien; m. Claudine M. Mendelovitz, Dec. 17, 1982; children: Benjamin, Sara, Talia. BA, U. Calif., Santa Barbara, 1973, MA, 1974, PhD, 1977. Fulbright lectr. Oxford (Eng.) U., 1987-88; lectr. U. Calif., Santa Barbara, 1976-77; asst. prof. U. Puget Sound, Tacoma, Wash., 1977-79; Spicer prof. U. Va., Charlottesville, 1979—; Fulbright rschr., Tokyo, Kyoto, Japan, 1993-94, Fulbright chair, Bologna, Italy, 1999; jud. fellow U.S. Supreme Ct., Washington, 1982-83; vis. postdoctoral fellow Russell Sage Found., N.Y.C., 1981-82; lectr. USIA, Burma, Japan, France, 1994-95. Author: Supreme Court Watch, 1991—, Constitutional Law and Politics, 2 vols., 3d edit., 1997, Storm Center: The Supreme Court in American Politics, 4th edit., 1996, To Dream of Dreams: Constitutional Politics in Postwar Japan, 1996, To Dream of Dreams: Religious Freedom in Postwar Japan, 1996; editor: Views from the Bench, 1985, Judges on Judging, 1997. Rappatour, jud. selection 20th Century Fund Task Force, N.Y., 1986-87. Tom C. Clark Jud. Fellow, Jud. Fellows Commn., Washington, 1983. Mem. ABA (Silver Gavel award 1987), Am. Judicature Soc., Am. Polit. Sci. Assn., Supreme Ct. Hist. Soc. (editl. bd. 1982—), Internat. Polit. Sci. Assn. Democrat. Avocations: painting, travel. Home: 916 Tilman Rd Charlottesville VA 22901-6338 Office: U Va 232 Cabell Hall Charlottesville VA 22901

O'BRIEN, DAVID PETER, business executive; b. Montreal, Que., Can., Sept. 9, 1941; s. John Lewis and Ethel (Cox) O'B.; m. Gail Baxter Corneil, June 1, 1968; children: Tara, Matthew, Shaun. B.A. with honors in Econs., Loyola Coll., Montreal, 1962; B.C.L., McGill U., Montreal, 1965. Assoc. and ptnr. Ogilvy, Renault, Montreal, 1967-77; v.p., gen. counsel Petro-Can., Calgary, Alta., 1977-81; sr. v.p. Petro-Can., Calgary, 1982-85, sr. v.p. fin. and planning, 1982-85, exec. v.p., 1985-89; pres., chief exec. officer Noverco Inc., Montreal, 1989; chmn. bd., pres., chief exec. officer PanCan. Petroleum Ltd., Calgary, Alta., Can., 1990-94; pres., COO Can. Pacific Ltd., Montreal, 1995-96; chmn., pres., CEO Can. Pacific Ltd., Calgary, 1996—; bd. dirs. Air Can., Westburne Inc., Fording Coal Ltd., Inco Ltd., Royal Bank Can., Conf. Bd. Can., C.D. Howe Inst., Can. Pacific Ltd.; chmn. bd. dirs. PanCan. Petroleum Ltd., Bus. Coun. Nat. Issues; mem. exec. com. Bus. Coun. on Nat. Issues. Bd. govs. U. Calgary. Mem. Quebec Bar Assn., Glencoe Club, Calgary Petroleum Club, Calgary Golf and Country Club. Office: 1800 Bankers Hall East, 855 2nd St SW, Calgary, AB Canada T2P 4Z5

O'BRIEN, DENIS PATRICK, economics educator; b. Knebworth, Herts, Eng., May 24, 1939; s. Patrick Kevin and Dorothy Elizabeth (Crisp) O'B.; m. Eileen Patricia O'Brien, Aug. 5, 1961 (dec. 1985); children: Ann Elizabeth, Alison Mary, Martin Michael; m. Julia Stapleton, Sept. 11, 1993; 1 child, Juliet Florence. BSc in Econs., U. Coll., London, 1960; PhD, Queen's U., Belfast, 1969. Asst. lectr. Queen's U., 1963-65, lectr., 1965-70, reader, 1970-72; prof. Durham (Eng.) U., 1972-97, prof. emeritus, 1998—. Author: J.R. McCulloch, 1970, The Classical Economists, 1975, Lionel Robbins, 1988, Thomas Joplin and Classical Macroeconomics, 1993; editor: Correspondence of Lord Overstone, 1971. Fellow Brit. Acad. Roman Catholic. Avocation: violin. Office: U Durham, 23-26 Old Elvet, Durham DH1 3HY, England

O'BRIEN, DENNIS JAY, economics educator; b. Omaha, Mar. 5, 1936; s. Cornelius James and Blanche Lenore (Gardipee) O'B.; children: Pamela Anne, Kevin Gardipee. BA, U. Nebr., 1961, MA, 1963; PhD, U. Mo., 1974. Instr., asst. prof. Mo. State U., Kirksville, 1962-68; instr. U. Mo., Columbia, 1965-68; asst. to assoc. prof. Calif. State U., Sacramento, 1969-80; project leader fgn. policy and nat. security rev. John F. Kennedy Libr., Boston, 1968-70; asst. dir. internat. energy and faculty fellow U.S. Gen. Acctg. Office, Washington, 1975-77; dep. asst. sec. for internat. oil and gas U.S. Dept. Energy, Washington, 1981-83, sr. petroleum officer, 1978-80; faculty petroleum mgmt. program Institut Francais du Petrole, Paris, 1994—; chief economist, mgr. econs. dept. Caltex Petroleum Corp., Dallas, 1983-95, advisor to the chmn., 1995-98; exec. dir. Pacific Econ. Cooperation Coun. Energy Forum, Washington, 1996—; dir. Inst. for Energy Econs. and Policy, U. Okla., Norman, 1998—, John A. & Donnie Brock chair prof. energy econs., bus., 1998—; adj. prof. Econs. Dept. Colo. Sch. of Mines, 1990-91, Internat. Mgmt. Program, U. Tex., Dallas, 1986—, Sch. of Engrng., U. Regina, 1998—; assoc. bd. dirs. Cox Sch. of Bus., So. Meth. U., 1985—, sr. fellow inst. for the study of earth and man, 1985—; global adv. bd. Thunderbird Mgmt. Sch., Glendale, Ariz., 1988—; v.p., program dir. Com. on Fgn. Rels., Dallas, 1984—; mem. internat. adv. com. Internat. Energy Found., Regina, 1985—; mem. Pacific Coun. on Internat. Policy, L.A., 1994—, Coun. on Fgn. Rels., N.Y., 1986—; dir., mem. exec. com. U.S. Nat. Com. for Pacific Econ. Cooperation, 1985—; mem. internat. adv. bd. East-West Ctr., Honolulu, 1996-99; adv. bd. U. of Houston Sch. of Bus. Energy Ctr., 1997-99. Editor: OPEC and Future World Oil Supply, 1988; author: Oil and Foreign Policy of Wilson Administration, 1974; contbr. articles to profl. jours. Bd. dirs. Ctr. for Energy Studies, U. Houston Sch. of Bus., 1997—. With USMC, 1956-58. Named Ky. Col., Frankfort, 1982; sr. fell., Inst. for the Study of Earth and Man, 1987, Tex. Higher Edn. Coord. Bd., Austin, 1990. Sr. Fellow U.S. Assn. for Energy Econs. (sr.); mem. Internat. Assn. for Energy Econs. (pres. 1993-95, 97), U.S. Assn. for Energy Econs. Fax: 405-325-3180. E-mail: dobrien@ou.edu. Office: Univ of Okla 100 E Boyd St Rm 540 Norman OK 73019-1028

O'BRIEN, ELMER JOHN, librarian, educator; b. Kemmerer, Wyo., Apr. 8, 1932; s. Ernest and Emily Catherine (Reinhart) O'B.; m. Betty Alice Peterson, July 2, 1966. A.B., Birmingham So. Coll., 1954; Th.M., Iliff Sch. Theology, 1957; M.A., U. Denver, 1961. Ordained to ministry Methodist Ch., 1957; pastor Meth. Ch., Pagosa Springs, Colo., 1957-60; circulation-reference librarian Boston U. Sch. Theology, 1961-65; asst. librarian Garrett-Evang. Theol. Sem., Evanston, Ill., 1965-69; librarian, prof. United Theol. Sem., Dayton, Ohio, 1969-96, prof. emeritus, 1996—; abstractor Am. Bibliog. Center, 1969-73; dir. Ctr. for Evang. United Brethren Heritage, 1979-96; acting libr. Iliff Sch. Theology, 2000—; chmn. div. exec. com. Dayton-Miami Valley Libr. Consortium, 1983-84; rsch. assoc. Am. Antiquarian Soc., 1990. Author: Bibliography of Festschriften in Religion Published Since 1960, 1972, Religion Index Two: Festschriften, 1960-69; contbg. author: Communication and Change in American Religious History, 1993, Essays in Celebration of the First Fifty Years, 1996; pub. Meth. Revs. Index, 1818-1985, 1989-91; contbr. essay to profl. jour. Recipient theol. and scholarship award Assn. Theol. Schs. in U.S. and Can., 1990-91; Assn. Theol. Schs. in U.S. and Can. library staff devel. grantee, 1976-77, United Meth. Ch. Bd. Higher Edn. and Ministry research grantee, 1984-85. Mem. ALA, Acad. Libr. Assn. Ohio, Am. Theol. Libr. Assn. (head bur. personnel and placement 1969-73, dir. 1973-76, v.p. 1977-78, pres. 1978-79), Am. Antiquarian Soc. (rsch. assoc. 1990), Delta Sigma Phi, Omicron Delta Kappa, Eta Sigma Phi, Kappa Phi Kappa. Club: Torch Internat. (v.p. Dayton club 1981-82, pres. 1982-83). Home: 4840 Thunderbird Dr Apt 281 Boulder CO 80303-3829

O'BRIEN, EUGENE PATRICK, humanities educator; b. Thurles, Tipperary, Ireland, Oct. 20, 1958; s. William and Alice (Carroll) O'B.; m. Aine Noreen McElhinney, July 7, 1991; children: Eoin, Dara. EdB, Mary Immaculate Coll., Limerick, Ireland, 1981; MA, Univ. Coll., County Cork, Ireland, 1988; PhD, U. Limerick, 1995. Tchr. St. Brigid's Sch., Limerick, 1981-86; prin. Bruce Coll., Limerick, 1987-92; lectr. Dublin (Ireland) City U., 1992—, U. Limerick, 1993—, Mary Immaculate Coll., 1994—. Author: The Question of Irish Identity in the Writings of W.B. Yeats and James Joyce, 1997, The Epistemology of Nationalism, 2000; editor Ireland in Theory; contbr. articles to profl. jours. Mem. MLA, Brit. Assn. Irish Studies, Internat. Assn. for Study of Irish Lit. Avocations: reading, films, fitness, music. E-mail: Eugene.obrien@oceanfree.net. Home: 58 Lansdowne Park, Ennis Rd, Limerick Ireland Office: Univ Limerick, Dept Langs, Cultural Study, Limerick Ireland

O'BRIEN, GEORGE DENNIS, retired university president; b. Chicago, Ill., Feb. 21, 1931; s. George Francis and Helen (Fehlandt) O'B.; m. Judith Alyce Johnson, June 21, 1958; children: Elizabeth Belle, Juliana Helen, Victoria Alyce. AB in English, Yale, 1952; PhD in Philosophy, U. Chgo., 1961. Tchr. humanities, Carnegie rsch. fellow U. Chgo., 1956-57; from instr. to asst. prof., asst. dean Princeton (N.J.) U., 1958-65; on leave in Athens, Greece, 1963-64; spl. honors seminars LaSalle Coll., spring 1963, fall 1964, spring 1965; assoc. prof. philosophy Middlebury (Vt.) Coll., 1965-71, prof., 1971-76, dean of men, 1965-67, dean of coll., 1967-74, dean faculty, 1975-76; pres. Bucknell U., 1976-84, U. Rochester, N.Y., 1984-94; ret., 1994; dir. Salzburg Seminar in Am. Studies. Author: Hegel on Reason in History, 1975, God and the New Haven Railway, 1986, What to Expect from College, 1991, All the Essential Half-Truths About Higher Education, 1997; contbr. articles to profl. jours. Trustee LaSalle Coll., Phila., 1965—; bd. dirs. Union Theol. Sem., 1985-90, Rsch. Librs. Group, 1994-96; v.p. Commonweal Found., 1994—. Fellow Am. Coun. Learned Socs., London, 1971-72; Nat. Phi Beta Kappa scholar, 1996-97. Mem. Am. Philos. Assn., Phi Beta Kappa. Home: 153 Wildflower Ln Middlebury VT 05753-9172

O'BRIEN, GREGORY FRANCIS, book publisher, writer, producer; b. New Rochelle, N.Y., Mar. 22, 1950; s. Francis Xavier and Virginia (Brown) O'B.; m. Mary Catherine McGeorge, Apr. 19, 1977; children: Brendan, Colleen, Conor. BA, U. Ariz., 1972. Reporter The Ariz. Republic, Phoenix, 1976-79; staff writer Boston Herald Am., 1979-82; sr. writer Boston Mag., 1982-84; reporter The Cape Codder, Inc., Orleans, Mass., 1973-76, editor, pres., 1985-93, also bd. dirs.; editor The Cape Codder Press, Orleans, 1988-93; pres. The Cape Codder Printery, Inc., Orleans, 1989-93, also bd. dirs.; pres., pub. Stony Brook Pub. and Prodns., Inc., Brewster, Mass., 1993—; editor-in-chief Cape Cod Bus. Jour., Orleans, 1988-89; editor, pres. The Register, Yarmouth Port, Mass., 1990-93; pres., pub. Cape Cod Pub. Co., Orleans, 1990-93; bd. dirs. Community Newspaper, Inc., North Shore Weeklies, Inc., Community Pub. Co.; editor, pub. Cape Cod Newspapers, Osterville, Mass., 1992-93. Author, editor: An Insider's Guide to Cape Cod and the Islands, 1988, The Sea, The Land, The Life, 1988, A Guide to Nature on Cape Cod and the Islands, 1990, O'Brien's Original Guide to Cape Cod and the Islands, 1996, Secrets In The Sand-the Archaeology of Cape Cod, 1997; contbr. numerous articles to newspapers and mags. Trustee Cape Cod Mus. Natural History, Brewster, Mass.; past bd. trustees Trinity Sch. of Cape Cod, Yarmouth, Mass.; vice chmn. Nauset Regional Sch. Bd. Award recipient The Ariz. Press Club, Hearst Newspapers, New England Newspaper Assn. Mem. New Eng. Newspaper Assn., New Eng. Press Assn. Roman Catholic. Avocations: writing, sports, gardening, family activities. Home: 25 Stony Hill Rd Brewster MA 02631-1612 Office: Stony Brook Pub and Prodns Inc Stony Hill Rd Brewster MA 02631

O'BRIEN, JAMES EDMOND, journalist, editor, educator; b. Schenectady, N.Y., June 30, 1952; cre; s. James Joseph and Marie Crooks (Wilkie) O'B.; m. Ronni Michele Rosenberg, Dec. 1, 1996; children: Ariel Melissa, Alex Michael. BA, SUNY, Potsdam, 1974; MA, Binghamton (N.Y.) U., 1976; MBA, N.Y. Inst. Tech., 1999. Freelance journalist Boston Phoenix, The Real Paper, Boston, 1977-81; reporter Globe Comm. Corp., Boca Raton, Fla., 1981-88; staff writer Your Health mag., Boca Raton, 1988-97; exec. dir. Unicorn Children's Found., 1998-99; assoc. editor Nat. Enquirer, Lantana, Fla., 1999—; instr. French, ESL The Lang. Exch., Delray Beach, 1988—; pres. Moondance Enterprises, Inc., Delray Beach, Fla., 1989—; tchr. French Palm Beach County Schs./Boca Raton Cmty. H.S., 1992—. Author: Garlic and Vinegar, 1989, Lower Cholesterol 30 Points in 30 Days, 1992, Fat Burning Foods, 1994, Herbal Cures for Common Ailments, 1997. Scholar Bryn Mawr Coll., 1976; recipient Excellence in Journalism award Am. Acad. Allergy and Asthma, N.Y.C., 1986. Avocations: fitness activities, computer programming, dog training, yoga, meditation. Home: 6508 Stonehurst Cir Lake Worth FL 33467-7374

O'BRIEN, JOAN SUSAN, lawyer, educator; b. New York, Apr. 14, 1946; d. Edward Vincent O'Brien and Joan Therese (Kramer) Quinn; m. Michael P. Wilpan, May 27, 1979; children: Edward B. Wilpan, Anabel T. Wilpan. BA, NYU, 1967; JD, Georgetown U., 1970. Bar: N.Y. 1971, Mass. 1971, U.S. Dist. Ct. (so. and ea. dist.) N.Y. 1972, U.S. Ct. Appeals (2d cir.) 1971. Law clk. to Hon. Frank J. Murray U.S. Dist. Ct. Mass., Boston, 1970-71; asst. U.S. atty. Office of U.S. Atty. U.S. Dist. Ct. (ea. dist.) N.Y., Bklyn., 1972-76; pvt. practice N.Y.C., 1976-79; trial atty. Mendes & Mount, N.Y.C., 1979-84; asst. prof. St. Johns U., Jamaica, N.Y., 1984-90; adminstrv. law judge N.Y. State Workers Compensation Bd., Hempstead, N.Y., 1990-93; appellate atty. Scheine, Fusco, Brandenstein & Rada, Woodbury, N.Y., 1993-97; trial atty. Grey & Grey, L.L.P., Farmingdale, N.Y., 1997—. Editor: Georgetown Law Jour., 1968-70. Pres. Nassau County Dem. Com. Women's Caucus, Westbury, N.Y., 1988-90; leader Girl Scouts Nassau County, 1990-93. Unitarian-Universalist. Office: Grey & Grey LLP 360 Main St Farmingdale NY 11735-3592

O'BRIEN, KATHLEEN ANN, economist; b. Augusta, Ga., Apr. 25, 1959; d. John Anthony O'Brien and Rita Jennie Dell Veneri. BA in Econs., U. Colo., 1981. Rschr. Internat. Rsch. Ctr. for Energy and Econ. Devel., Boulder, Colo., 1979-87, Bus. Rsch. Divsn., Boulder, 1987-88; com. mem. Bus.-Econ. Outlook Forum, Denver, 1987-99; pub. info. staff Colo. State Registration Nursing, Denver, 2000—. Chair justice com. LWV, Boulder; bd. U.S.-Internat. Ctr. for People with Disabilites, Boulder. Mem. 501 Club World Trade Orgn. Roman Catholic. Avocations: flying, swimming, knitting, chess, prayer. Home: 8989 W 14th Ave Apt 207 Lakewood CO 80215-4838

O'BRIEN, KEITH MICHAEL PATRICK, archbishop; b. Ballycastle, Antrim, Mar. 17, 1938; s. Mark Joseph and Alice Mary (Moriarty) O'B. BSc, Edinburgh U., 1959, DipEd, 1966; student, St. Andrew's Coll., Drygrange, Moray Ho. Coll. Edn., Edinburgh. Ordained priest Roman Cath. Ch., 1965. Priest Holy Cross, Edinburgh, 1965-66, St. Bride's, Cowdenbeath, 1966-71; chaplain, tchr. maths and sci. St. Columba's High Sch., Cowdenbeath and Dunfermline, 1966-71; priest St. Patrick's, Kilsyth, 1972-75, St. Mary's, Bathgate, 1975-78; spiritual dir. St. Andrew's Coll., 1978-80; rector St. Mary's Coll., Blair, Aberdeen, 1980-85; archbishop of St. Andrews and Edinburgh, 1985—. Office: St Bennet's, 42 Greenhill Gardens, Edinburgh EH10 4BJ, Scotland

O'BRIEN, KEVIN, college dean, consultant; b. Bayonne, N.J., Jan. 10, 1948; s. Vincent and Anne (Sullivan) O'B. BA, U. Dayton, 1969; MA, Calif. State U., San Diego, 1977; MS, Ind. U., 1991. Cert. in social sci. Tchr. Inst. Mont., Zug, Switzerland, 1978-90, dean, 1990—; coll. counselor, Zug, 1990—; IB coord., Zug, 1990—. Author: American Press Attitudes Toward Egypt, 1952-56. Mem. NACAC, Swiss Am. C. of C. Roman Catholic. Office: Inst Mont, Zugerberg, CH-6300 Zug Switzerland

O'BRIEN, KEVIN JAMES, investment banking executive; b. Tucson, July 19, 1956; s. Murray Andre and Sigrid (Kostoff) O'B. BSBA in Fin., No. Ariz. U., 1983. V.p. spl. situations Drexel Burnham Lambert, Inc., L.A., 1983-91; spl. projects mgr. Gtr. Flagstaff (Ariz.) Econ. Coun., Inc., 1992-95; pres. Sovereign Capital, Inc., Flagstaff, 1995—; advisor World Bank, Washington, 1995—. Contbr. articles to profl. jours. Bd. dirs. No. Ariz. Econ. Devel. Dist., Flagstaff, 1992-95, No. Ariz. U. Students in Free Enterprise, Flagstaff, 1998. Mem. Nat. Tax Lien Assn. (charter). Avocations: flying, skiing, writing, travel, hiking. Office: Sovereign Capital Inc 2387 Augusta Dr Flagstaff AZ 86004-7537

O'BRIEN, KEVIN PATRICK, business and management educator; b. Kapunda, Australia, Feb. 23, 1942; s. William John and Eileen (Kevin) O'B.; m. Anne Eileen Penman, Dec. 3, 1966; children: Mark Damian, Suzanne Louise. B Econs. with honors, U. Adelaide, South Australia, 1968; MSc in Econs., U. Stirling, Scotland, 1977. With rsch. dept. Res. Bank Australia, Sydney, 1968-70; lectr., sr. lectr. South Australian Inst. Tech., Adelaide, 1970-85, assoc. prof., head Sch. Accountancy, 1986-92; dean faculty bus. and mgmt. U. South Australia, Adelaide, 1992-98, pro vice chancellor, divsn. bus. and enterprise, 1998—; vis. lectr. MBA Program U. Adelaide and Flinders U., 1988; expert commentator profl. devel. program South Australian Health Commn., Hosps. Assn. Australia Conf., 1989; researcher geriatric assessment rsch. project Flinders Med. Ctr., 1984-90; econ. evaluator of limiting rotavirus cross infection in hosps.; mem. selection and placement team Vietnam Joint Fellowship, Australian Internat. Devel. Assistance Bur., Hanoi, 1992; mem. acads. liaison tour and Univ. Mobility in Asia and Pacific Forum, Japan, 1993. Author: The Australian Business Framework, 1986; (with others) Macroeconomics: The Australian Context, 1987, The Australian Financial System, 1993, Nosocomial Rota Virus Infection: The Economics of Prevention, 1993, The Australian Financial System: Evolution, Policy and Practice, 1997; contbr. articles to profl. jours. Fellow Australian Soc. CPAs.; mem. Econs. Soc. Australia, Grange Golf Club. Office: U South Australia, North Terrace, Adelaide SA 5000, Australia

O'BRIEN, MARK STEPHEN, pediatric neurosurgeon; b. West New York, N.J., Jan. 2, 1933; s. Mark Peter and Hannah (Dempsey) O'B.; m. Mary Morris Johnson, June 3, 1961 (div.); children: David, Derek, Marcia; m. Karen-Marie Sampson, June 1, 1984; children: Blythe, Blake, Lauren-Blair, Connor. A.B. cum laude, Seton Hall U., 1955; M.D., St. Louis U., 1959. Diplomate Am. Bd. Neurol. Surgery, Am. Bd. Pediat. Neurol. Surgery. Intern St. John's Hosp., St. Louis, 1959-60; resident in surgery St. John's Hosp., 1960; resident in neurology Charity Hosp., New Orleans, 1962-63; resident in neurosurgery St. Vincent's Hosp., N.Y.C., 1963-64; resident in surgery St. Vincent's Hosp., 1965; sr. resident, chief resident Cin. Children's Hosp., U. Cin., 1965-68, research fellow in neurosurgery, 1966-67, 67-68; NIH spl. fellow in neuroradiology Albert Einstein Coll. Medicine, N.Y.C., 1968-69; mem. faculty dept. surgery Emory U. Sch. Medicine, Atlanta, 1969—; prof. surgery, assoc. prof. pediatrics Emory U. Sch. Medicine, 1979—; chief neurosurgery Henrietta Egleston Hosp. for Children, Atlanta, 1971—; trustee Elaine Clark Center for Exceptional Children; mem. med. adv. bd. Nat. Found., March of Dimes; trustee Henrietta Egleston Hosp. for Children; mem. profl. adv. panel Spina Bifida Assn. Am. Editorial bd. Pediatric Neurosurgery; contbr. chpts. to books, articles to med. jours. Served with USNR, 1960-62. Mem. Am. Assn. Neurol. Surgeons, Soc. Neurol. Surgeons, Congress Neurol. Surgeons, Internat. Soc. Pediatric Neurosurgery, Greater Atlanta Pediatric Soc., Med. Soc. Atlanta, AMA, ACS, Ga. Neurosurg. Soc., Am. Acad. Pediatrics, Am. Soc. Pediatric Neurosurgery, Pediatric Oncology Group, Am. Bd. Pediatric Neurol. Surgery (sec.), Acad. Pediatric Neurosurgeons. Home: 889 W Wesley Rd NW Atlanta GA 30327-1306 Office: 1900 Century Blvd NE Ste 4 Atlanta GA 30345-3307

O'BRIEN, MARLYS CAROL HOWE, retired library director; b. St. Paul, Dec. 10, 1937; d. James Melvin and Emma Linda (Luthi) Howe; m. Gerald Thomas O'Brien, Mar. 29, 1970 (dec. Aug. 1993); stepchildren: Michael, David, Joseph, Kristine, Patrick, Colleen. Cert., U. Oslo, Norway, 1958; BA, U. Minn., 1960, MA, 1963. Libr. asst. St. Paul Pub. Libr., 1954-63; pub. libr. cons. Minn. Office of Libr. Devel. and Svc., St. Paul, 1963-65; librarian Cass County Libr., Pine River, Minn., 1965-69; dir. Kitchigami Regional Libr., Pine River, Minn., 1969-99; ret., 1999; bd. dirs. Minn. Libr. Found., St. Paul, 1983-86. Mem. ALA (pub. libr. assn. cmty. info. sect., pres. 1994), Minn. Libr. Assn. (councilor Minn. chpt. 1974-78, pres. 1982-83, Cert. of Merit award 1967, 91). Lutheran. Avocations: reading, fishing, baking, church bell choir, sign language. Home: Norway Lake 2338 19th St SW Pine River MN 56474-7909

O'BRIEN, MARY DEVON, communications executive, consultant; b. Buenos Aires, Argentina, Feb. 13, 1944; came to U.S., 1949, naturalized, 1962; d. George Earle and Margaret Frances (Richards) Owen; m. Gordon Covert O'Brien, Feb. 16, 1962 (div. Aug. 1982); children: Christopher Covert, Devon Elizabeth; m. Christopher Gerard Smith, May 28, 1983. BA, Rutgers U., 1975, MBA, 1976. Project mgmt. cert., 1989. Contr. manpower Def. Comm. divsn. ITT, Nutley, N.J., 1977-80, adminstr. program, 1977-78, mgr. cost, schedule control, 1978-79, voice processing project, 1979-80; mgr. project Avionics divsn. ITT, Nutley, 1980-81, sr. mgr. projects, 1981-93, cons. strategic planning, 1983-95; pres. Anamex, Inc., 1995—; bd. trustees South Mountain Counseling Ctr., 1987-98, chmn. bd. trustees, 1994—; bd. dirs. N.J. Eye Inst.; session leader Internet Conf., Florence, Italy, 1992; session moderator, panel mem. MES Conf., Cairo, Egypt, 1993, spkr., session leader Vancouver, 1994, keynote spkr. New Zealand, 1995; lectr. in field;. Author: Pace: System Manual, 1979, Voices, 1982; contbr. articles to profl. jours. and Maplewood Community calendar. Chmn. Citizens Budget Adv. Com., Maplewood, N.J., 1984-87, chmn. recreation, libr., pub. svcs., 1982-83, 94-96, chmn. pub. safety, emergency svcs., 1983-84, chmn. schs. and edn., 1984-85, chmn. gen. gov. and fin., 1998-2000; first v.p. Maplewood Civic Assn., 1987-89, pres., 1989-91, 2000—, sec. 1993-94, bd. dirs., officer, 1984—; chmn. Maple Leaf Svc. award Com., 1987-89, 94—, Community Svc. Coun. of Oranges and Maplewood Homelessness, Affordable Housing, Shelter Com., 1988—; chmn. speaker's bur. United Way, 1989-93; bd. trustees United Way Essex and West Hudson Cmty. Svc. Coun., 1988—; v.p. mktg. United Way Community Svc. Coun. of Oranges and Maplewood, 1990-93, v.p. 1994; mem. Maplewood Zoning Bd. of Adjustment, 1983-95; officer, mem. exec. bd. N.J. Project Mgmt. Inst., 1985—, pres., 1987-88, 95-2000, v.p. adminstrn., 1994-95; bd. dirs. Performance Mgmt. Assn.; chmn. Charter Com.; chmn. Internat. Project Mgmt. Inst. Jour. and Membership survey, 1986-87, mktg. com., 1986-89, long range planning and steering com., 1987—; bd. dirs., vice chmn. Coun. Chpt. Pres. Interaction Com., 1986-90, chmn., 1991—, pres. Internat. Project Mgmt. Inst., 1991, chmn., 1992, v.p. Region II, 1989-90; adv. bd. Project Mgmt. Jour., 1987-90, N.J. PMI Ednl., 1987—; liaison officer, PMI internat. liaison to Australian Inst. of Project Mgmt. and Western Australia Project Mgmt. Assn.; apptd. fellow Leadership N.J., 1993—, Internat. Project Mgmt. Inst. and Performance Mgmt. Assocs.; mem. MCA/N.J. Blood Bank Drive; chmn. Maplewood Community Calendar, 1990-98; trustee community svc. coun. and edn. program United Way Essex and West Hudson, 1988—, also, chmn. leadership div., chmn. speakers bur., 1991— and mem. communications com.; pres. N.J. Project Mgmt. Inst., 1995—; chmn. Maplewood Rep. County Com., 1996—; chair, sec. Essex County Rep. County Com. Recipient Spl. commendation for Community Svc. Twp. Maplewood, 1987; First Place award Anti-Shoplifting Program for Distributive Edn. Club Am., 1981, N.J. Fedn. of Women's Clubs, 1981, 82, Retail Mchts. Assn., 1981, 82; Commendation and Merit awards Air Force Inst. Tech., 1981; Pres.'s Safety award ITT, 1983; State award 1st Pl. N.J. Fedn. of Women's Clubs Garden Show, 1982, Outstanding Pres. award Internat. Project Mgmt. Inst., 1988, Outstanding Svc. and Contbrn. award 1986-87; Cert. Spl. Merit award N.J. Fedn. of Women's Clubs, 1982, Disting. Contbn. award United Way, 1990, Pursuit of Exellence Cost Savings Achievement award ITT Avionics, 1990, Meritorious Svc. Recognition award Internat. Project Mgmt. Inst., 1989-90, Maple Leaf award for outstanding community svc., 1992, Phoebe and Benjamin Shackelford award United Way, 1992, U.S. Ho. Reps. citation, 1992, N.H. Gen. Assembly Senate resolution for Community Leadership and Svc., 1992, resolution of Appreciation Township of Maplewood; N.J. Leadership fellow, 1993, awarded fellow of Internat. Project Mgmt. Inst., 1995. Mem. Internat. Platform Speakers Assn., Grand Jury Assn., Telecommunications Group and Aerospace Industries Assn., Women's Career Network Assn., Nat. Security Indsl. Assn., Assn. for Info. and Image Mgmt., Internat. Project Mgmt. Inst. (liaison officer pres. 1991—), Performance Mgmt. Assn, Indsl. Rels. Rsch. Assn., ITT Mgmt. Assn., NAFE, Rutger's Grad. Sch. Bus. Mgmt. Alumni Assn., Maplewood LWV (chair women and family issues com., voter registration bd. dirs.), Maplewood Women's Evening Membership Div. (pres. 1980-82), Lions (Maplewood dir. 1992-95, program chmn. 1991-92, treas. 1994-95, N.J. dist. 16E zone gov., chmn. 1992-93, 95-96, cabinet sec. internat. dist., region chmn. 1993-94, 96—, trustee Eye Bank N.J., internat. dist. 16-E cabinet sec. 1994-95, dist. 16-E chmn. peace poster contest 1995-99, pres. Newark 1995-97, sec. 1997—, N.J. State chmn. youth outreach and quest 1995-98, internat. dist. 16-E gov., 1999—, dist. MD16 treas., 1999—). Home: 594 Valley St Maplewood NJ 07040-2616 Office: 21 Madison Plz Ste 152 Madison NJ 07940-2354

O'BRIEN, MICHAEL DERMOD, physician, consultant neurologist; b. Sleima, Malta, Apr. 4, 1938; s. Dermod Donatus and Helen Doreen (O'Connor) O'B. MBBS, U. London, 1962, MD, 1973. Intern, resident Guy's Hosp., London, 1962-67; resident Nat. Hosp. for Neurology, London, 1967-68; sr. resident Neurol. Ctr., Newcastle, Eng., 1968-71; NIH-MRC fellow U. Minn., Mpls., 1971-72; chief asst. in neurology Guy's Hosp., London, 1972-78, cons. neurologist, 1978—, clin. dir. neuroscis., 1990—; group clin. dir. Guy's and St. Thomas' Hosp., London, 1993-95, exec., 1993-95. Contbr. chpts. to books, numerous articles to profl. jours.; lectr. on cerebral hemodynamics. Fellow Royal Coll. Physicians (London), Royal Geog. Soc., Med. Artists' Assn.; mem. Med. Soc. London, Am. Heart Assn. (fellow stroke coun.), Royal Archaeol. Inst. Conservative. Roman Catholic. Avocations: ancient civilizations, travel, general aviation. Office: Guy's Hosp, Dept Neurology, London SE1 9RT, England

O'BRIEN, NORA MARY, nutrition educator; b. Cork, Ireland, Jan. 26, 1960; d. Michael and Mary (Cashman) O'B.; m. Thomas O'Connor, Jan. 26, 1985; children: Stephen, Aideen. BSc, U. Coll. Cork, Ireland, 1981; MS, U. Minn., St. Paul, 1983; PhD, Cornell U., 1987. Postdoctoral fellow U. Louvain, Belgium, 1988; lectr. U. Coll. Cork, 1989-98, sr. lectr., 1999—; cons. Food Safety Authority, Ireland, 1995—; mem. Royal Irish Acad., Ireland, 1995—. Contbr. articles to profl. jours. Recipient fellowship Nat. U. Ireland, 1982, Internat. Inst. Cellular and Molecular Pathology, Belgium, 1998, rsch. grants Irish, indsl. and European sources. Mem. Brit. Nutrition Soc., Biochem. Soc., Irish Soc. Toxicology. Avocations: hill walking, reading, swimming, cooking. Office: U Coll Cork Western Rd, Nutritional Scis, Cork Ireland

O'BRIEN, PAMELA C., communications educator; b. Wilmington, Del., Sept. 27, 1969; d. Bruce Redfearn and Lestina Larsen Colby; m. Sean D. O'Brien, July 9, 1994; 1 child, Eilean Donan. BA with honors, So. Meth. U., 1991; MA in Mass Comm., Ind. U., 1994, PhD candidate in telecomm., 1994-96. Assoc. instr. Ind. U., Bloomington, 1991-96; vis. prof. comm. George Washington U., Washington, 1996-98, asst. prof. comm., 1998—. Co-writer (TV show) A Tribute to Arthur Miller, 1990. Sec. Greenbrook Estates, Greenbelt, Md., 1998-99. Ednl. fellow Nat. Assn. TV Program Execs., 1998. Mem. Broadcast Ednl. Assn., Internat. Comm. Assn., Popular Culture Assn., Soc. Animation Studies. Avocations: animation studies, commercialization of media. E-mail: pcobrien@gwu.edu. Office: George Washington U 812 20th St NW Washington DC 20052-0001

O'BRIEN, PATRICK KARL, economic history educator; b. London, Aug. 12, 1932; s. William Patrick and Elizabeth (Stockhausen) O'B.; m. Cassy Cobham, Apr. 15, 1959; children: Karen, Helen, Stephen. BSc in Econs., London Sch. Econs., 1958; DPhil, Oxford (Eng.) U., 1966, MA, 1970; PhD (hon.), U. Carlos III, Madrid, 1966; Doctorate honoris causa, Uppsala (Sweden) U., 2000. Rsch. fellow Sch. Oriental and African Studies, London, 1960-63, lectr., 1964-66, reader, 1966-70; reader, profl. fellow St. Anthony's Coll., Oxford, Eng., 1983-90, lectr., fellow, 1970-83; prof., dir. Inst. Hist. Rsch. London U., 1990-98; Centennial prof. London Sch. Econs., 1999—; vis. prof. Yale U., European U., Florence, Princeton U., Columbia U., U. Calif., San Diego, Va. U., Carlos III U., Madrid. Author: The Revolution in Egypt's Economic System, 1966, The New Economic History of Railways, 1977, Economic Growth in Britain and France, 1780-1914, 1978, The Industrial Revolution and British Society, 1992. Fellow Royal Hist. Soc., Brit. Acad., Royal Soc. Arts. Home: 66 St Bernards Rd, Oxford OX2 6EJ, England Office: London U Inst Hist Rsch, Senate House, London England

O'BRIEN, (MICHAEL) VINCENT, horse trainer, owner, breeder; b. Apr. 9, 1917; s. Daniel P. and Kathleen (Toomey) O'B.; m. Jacqueline Wittenoom, 1951; 5 children. Grad., Mungret Coll., Ireland; LLD (hon.), Nat. U. Ireland, 1983; DSc (hon.), U. Ulster, 1995. Champion trainer Nat. Hunt Gt. Britain, 1952-53, champion trainer Flat, 1966, 67; winner of all major English and Irish hurdle & steeplechases; winner 3 consecutive Grand Nats., 4 Gold Cups and 3 Champion Hurdles; trained flat racing winners of 44 Classics including 6 Epsom Derbys, 6 Irish Derbys and 1 French Derby; also 3 Prix de l'Arc de Triomphe, Breeders Cup Mile and Washington Internat.; trainer of Nijinsky. Named trainer of century both for flat and nat. hunt racing in Gt. Britain and Ireland, 1999. Avocation: golfing. Fax: (62) 61677. Address: Ballydoyle House, Cashel, County Tipperary Ireland

OBRUBOV, YURI VICTOR, mathematics educator; b. Dushanbe, Tajikistan, USSR, Feb. 2, 1950; s. Victor Sergey Obrubov and Anna Davydova; m. Galina Polyakova, Oct. 15, 1973; children: Vitaliy, Olga. Math. Educator, State Univ., Dushanbe, Tajikistan, 1972; PhD, State Univ., Moscow, 1982, DSc, 1994; Hon. Sr. Scientific Worker, Highest Attestation Com., Moscow, 1991; Assoc. Prof. (hon.), Internat. Soros Sci. Edn., Program, USA, 1997, 98; prof. (hon.), Internat. Soros Sci. Edn., 2000. Engr. Astrophys. Inst., Dushanbe, Tajikistan, 1974-76, jr. sci. worker, 1976-83, sr. sci. worker, 1983-92, head of lab., 1992-94; assoc. prof. Moscow Agrl. Acad., Kaluga, Russia, 1995—, prof., 1995-98; head math. dept., dean faculty Moscow Agrl. Acad., Kaluga, 1998—; assoc. prof. Moscow Tech. U., Kaluga, 1995-96, prof., 1996—; cons. Internat. Astron. Union, Paris, 1982—. Juror People Ct., Dushanbe, 1979-85. Sr. lt. Soviet Army, 1972-74, Russia. Grantee Am. Astron. Soc., 1992, 94, Internat. Sci. Found., 1994, Internat. Edn. Program, 1997. Mem. N.Y. Acad. Scis., European Astron. Soc. (founding mem.), Internat. Meteor Orgn. Avocations: tourism, fishery, computers. Office: Math Dept/Moscow Acad, Vishnevskiy str 27, 248007 Kaluga Russia

O'BRYON, DAVID SCOTT, association executive; b. Washington, Nov. 14, 1949; s. Tom Watson and Mary O'Bryon; m. Margaret Elisabeth Keller, Sept. 13, 1975; children: Elisabeth Cady, David Bahr. BA, Gettysburg Coll., 1972; JD, Potomac Sch. of Law, 1980. Staff U.S. Congress, 1972-79; dir. ACA, Arlington, Va., 1980-85; v.p. Assn. & Soc. Mgmt. Internat., Falls Church, Va., 1985-88; exec. v.p. Real Estate Securities & Syndication Inst., Washington and Chgo., 1988-90; pres. O'Bryon & Co., Bethesda, Md., 1990—; sr. cons. Assn. Soc. Mgmt. Internat., 1990—; exec. dir. Assn. Chiropractic Colls., Bethesda, 1996—, Retirement Industry Trust Assn., Bethesda, 1995—. Past co-pres. Rock Creek Forest PTA, Chevy Chase; treas. Disabled Sports USA, 1992—. Mem. Am. Soc. Assn. Execs. (cert.). Republican. Lutheran. Office: O'Bryon & Co 4424 Montgomery Ave Ste 102 Bethesda MD 20814-4409

OBUDHO, ROBERT ABACKUCK, communications company executive; b. Nyanza, Kenya, Nov. 28, 1942; m. Peninah Akeyo Obudho; children: Justus, Grace, Gerald, Christine. AAS, SUNY, Cobleskill, 1964; BSc, SUNY, Albany, 1966; postgrad. diploma edn., U. Nairobi, Kenya, 1966-67; MA, Rutgers U., 1970, PhD, 1974. Asst. to the contr. Met. Hosp., Phila., 1968-69; planning analyst Johnson & Johnson, N.J., 1976-79; asst. prof. Rutgers U., N.Y., 1979-82; vis. asst. prof. Vassar Coll., N.Y., 1982-83; assoc. prof. SUNY, 1984-89; assoc. prof. U. Nairobi, 1994—, chmn. dept. geography, 1995-96, internal examiner, 1999, bd. mem., 1999; editor faculty arts U. Nairobi, 1992-97. Co-compiler Kenya Coast Handbook: Problems and Perspectives; co-editor: Municipality of Mombasa & IB Environs: A Study in Urban and Regional Planning, National Heritage, Resource Management and Development; editor African Urban Quarterly. Chmn., mem. Kenya Nat. Preparatory Com., Nairobi, 1994; rep. of Nairobi, Worldwide Megacities Project, 1999; advisor local and nat. govt., 1999; cons. UNICEF, UNCHS, UNESCO, Nairobi, 2000. Mem. Internat. Geog. Union (v.p. 1989-2000), Geog. Assn. Kenya (sec. 1989-2000), Union for African Popk. Office: African Urban Quarterly Ltd, Pvt Bag 51336, Nairobi Kenya

OBUKHOVSKY, IGOR TIMOPHEEVITCH, nuclear physics theorist, educator; b. Moscow, Dec. 12, 1936; s. Timophei Kalennikovitch and Antonina Nikolaevna (Dremakina) O.; m. Ludmila Anatol'evna Golikova, July 4, 1967; children: Alexander, Vadim. Engr., Moscow Energy Inst., 1960; postgrad., 1960; physicist, M.V. Lomonosov State U., Moscow, 1965; postgrad., Moscow State U., 1965-67, PhD, 1970. Jr. scientific worker Inst. Nuc. Physics, Moscow State U., 1968-73, sr. scientific worker, 1973—. Contbr. articles to profl. jours. Grantee Russian Found. Basic Rsch., Moscow, 1994-95, 96-98, Deutsche Forschungsgemeinschaft, 1997-98, 99-01, St Petersburg (Russia) U., 1993-94. Home: 15-2-45 Acad Volgin St, 117485 Moscow Russia Office: Moscow State U Inst Nuc Phy, Vorobjovy gory, 119899 Moscow Russia

OBUSHENKO, IVAN MAKAROVICH, chemist; b. Kiev, Ukraine, Jan. 19, 1952; arrived in U.S., 1994; s. Makar P. and Nadia P. (Danilenko) O.; m. Olena M. Andriash, Jan. 15, 1994; 1 child, Oles. MS in Chemistry, Kiev State U., 1974; PhD in Chemistry, Material Sci. Inst. Acad. Sci., Kiev, 1981. Rsch. assoc. Material Sci. Inst., Kiev, 1974-85; sr. rsch. scientist Colloidal & Water Chemistry Inst., Kiev, 1985-93, Sorption & Endoecology Problem Inst., Kiev, 1993-94, Photran Corp., Lakeville, Minn., 1994-98; cons. Rescue Technologies, St. Paul, 1999—. Co-author: Physical Chemistry in Inorganic Matter, 1988; contbr. inventions and articles to profl. jours. Mem. Am. Chem. Soc. Achievements include work with nuclear waste treatment and disposal, metals recovering processes, thin films and displays technologies.

O'BYRNE, ELIZABETH MILIKIN, pharmacologist, researcher, endocrinologist; b. Miami, Fla., May 19, 1944; d. Richard Mershon and Anne (Smith) Milikin; m. Brian Kenneth O'Byrne, July 1, 1972; children: Lucy Milikin, Kenneth Daniel. AB in Chemistry, Emory U., 1965, MS in Biochemistry, 1968; PhD in Biochemistry, N.Y. Med. Coll., 1985. Assoc. scientist Eli Lilly Rsch. Labs., Indpls., 1968-70; sr. rsch. scientist CIBA-GEIGY Pharms., Summit, N.J., 1970-96; rsch. fellow Novartis Pharms., Summit, N.J., 1997—. Contbr. articles to profl. jours. Mem. AAAS, N.Y. Acad. Sci., Inflammation Rsch. Assn., Osteoarthritis Rsch. Soc. Achievements include isolation, characterization and development of radioimmunoassay for hormone relaxin to monitor production and secretion, of assays of cytokine and enzyme degradation of cartilage in vitro and in vivo, of proton and sodium magnetic resonance properties of cartilage; demonstration of therapeutic efficacy of matrix metalloprotease inhibitors to retard tissue damage in animal models of diseases; investigation of autologous bone marrow-derived mesechymal stem cells to repair osteoarthritic lesions in cartilage and bone, co-founder of CIBA-GEIGY Partnership in Sci. in which scientists work with teachers to bring hands-on experiences in laboratory investigation to high school students. Home: 234 Sagamore Rd Millburn NJ 07041-2136 Office: Novartis Morris Ave Summit NJ 07901

OCAL, AKAR, academic administrator. Rector U. Anatolia, Turkey. Office: Yunus Emre Kampusii, 26470 Eskisehir Turkey*

O'CALLAGHAN, BRYAN IRVINE, physician, radiologist, neuroradiologist; b. Geneva, May 18, 1962; s. Michael and Fiona (O'Doherty) O'C.; m. Frederique Zihlmann, July 2, 1994; 1 child, Marc. BEE, Ecole Technique Superieure, Geneva, 1982; MD, U. Geneva, 1990; D in Medicine, U. Berne, 1994. trained Cantonal Hosp., Fribourg, Hosp. Gruyere, U. Hosp. Bern; team medic Brit . Joint Svcs. Expdn., Smith Island, Antarctica, 1990-91. Contbr. articles to profl. jours. including Rev. Med. de la Suisse Romande, Radiology, Spine, Am. Jour. Sports Medicine, Mosby Yr. Book of Ultrasound Radiol. Documents, Ann. Hand Surgery, Schweiz Med. Wochemschr Neuropediatrics, 1 Belge Rad, European Soc. Neuroradiol. and Radiol. Soc. N.Am. Served with Swiss Army, 1982—. Avocations: family, music. Office: Caantonal Hosp, Fribourg Switzerland

O'CALLAGHAN, DONAL JOSEPH, engineering researcher; b. Cork, Ireland, Apr. 24, 1952; s. Timothy and Mary (Browne) O'C.; m. Evelyne Burkhard, Aug. 12, 1999. B of Elec. Engring., UCC, Cork, Ireland, 1975, MS, 1995; PhD, UC Dublin, 2000. Design engr. Telectron, Dublin, 1975-78; lectr. Cork Inst. Tech., Cork, Ireland, 1978-80; rsch. officer Teagasc, Fermoy, Ireland, 1980—; spkr. in field. Mem. Soc. Dairy Tech., Toastmasters Internat., Brit. Soc. Rheology. Avocation: Irish dancing, psychology. Office: Teagasc, Moorepark, Fermoy Ireland

OCANSEY, AARON AKROFI, game designer; b. Ada, Ghana, Africa, Sept. 16, 1949; came to U.S., 1969; s. Alfred Natea Ocansey and Grace Tay; m. Shirley Donaldson, Nov. 23, 1974 (div. Aug. 1990); children: Denis, Aba, Daniela; m. Gloria Jean Penrice, Aug. 25, 1992; 1 child, Layo Penrice. Stage III Level Acctg., Royal Inst. Tech., Accra, New Town, 1969. Cert. of Appreciation, Pres. Ronald Reagan, 1988. Acct. London Agy., Westwood, Calif., 1974-76, Kindle Inc., Inglewood, Calif., 1984-90, Rotex Exch., Gardena, Calif., 1990-92, Trak Auto Corp., Ontario, Calif., 1992; officer Advance Tech., Hollywood, Calif., 1992—; game designer Ocansey Ocean Inc., Accra, 1989—. Designer: (bd. games) Elmina Game, 1996, Ghana Empire Game, 1998. Avocation: game designing. Home: 16240 Vaquero Ct Riverside CA 92504-5856 Office: Ocansey Ocean, PO Box 6559, Accra Ghana

O'CARROLL, MARTIN JOSEPH, wholesale executive; b. Brisbane, Australia, Feb. 7, 1963; s. Martin Joseph and Valmai Joyce (Robinson) O'C. Automatic transmission tech. Graham's A1 Autmoatics, Redcliffe, Australia, 1981-87; carpet cleaner Myer Cleaning Svcs., Brisbane, Australia, 1987; steward Conrad Hotel Jupiters Casino, Gold Coast, Australia, 1987-89, Ana Hotel, Gold Coast, Australia, 1989-91; steward Hayman Island, Australia, 1991-93, store supr., 1993-99. Mem. Royal Automobile Club Queensland. Ofcl. Elvis Fan Club Australia. Avocations: travel, photography, motor sports, reading, model building. Home: 108 Fountain Rd, Burpengary Qsld 4505, Australia Address: PO Box 536, Morayfield QLD 4506, Australia

OCCHIONERO, FRANCO, astronomer, educator; b. Bologna, Italy, July 8, 1939; s. Giulio Occhionero and Olga Vittozzi; m. Marisa Ferrara, Mar. 18, 1967 (div. 1997); 1 child, Francesca. Diploma in physics, U. Rome, 1961, diploma, 1968. Rsch. fellow Nat. Rsch. Coun., Rome, 1963-83; assoc. prof. U. Rome, 1983-86, prof., 1972-83, 90—; chair astronomy Astronomy Ob-

servatory, Rome, 1986—. Editor: Birth of the Universe & Fundamental Physics, 1995; contbr. articles to profl. jours. Mem. Am. Astron. Soc., Am. Phys. Soc., Internat. Astron. Union, Internat. Soc. Gen. Relativity & Gravitation. Avocations: windsurfing, skiing, symphonic music. Fax: 39-06-35347802. Office: Osservatorio Astronomico, V.le Parco Mellini 84, 00136 Rome Italy

OCH, MOHAMAD RACHID, psychiatrist, consultant; b. Damascus, Syria, Apr. 1, 1956; came to U.S., 1981; s. Seifeddine and Souad (Oubari) O.; m. Marianne Noonan, July 24, 1960; children: Seifeddine, Adam. MD, Aleppo (Syria) U., 1980. Psychiat. cons. Human Resource Inst., Brookline, Mass., 1985; med. dir. Spectrum House, Westboro, Mass., 1986-87; assoc. med. dir. Boston Rd. Clinic, Shrewsbury, Mass., 1985-97, v.p., 1989—; med. dir. mental health unit Holden (Mass.) Hosp., 1988-90; med. dir. Basic Health Mgmt., Worcester, Mass., 1988-90; dir. clin. ops. Capstan, LLC, Worcester, 1997—, CEO, med. dir., 1999-2000; nat. med. dir. Civigenics, Marlboro, Mass., 1997-2000; gen. mng. ptnr. Prescott Healthcare, Worcester, Mass., 2000—; asst. med. dir. Boston Rd. Clinic, Shrewsbury, 1986-97, Holden Hosp., 1988—, Basic Health Mgmt., Worcester, 1988—; attending psychiatrist, asst. prof. U. Mass. Med. Ctr., Worcester; dir. mental health unit Milford Whitinsville Hosp., 1990-93, chmn. dept. psychiatry, 1991-92; med. dir. Seven Hills Intensive Residential Treatment Program, 1990-93; asst. chief psychiatry St. Vincent's Hosp., 1996-99; mem. adv. bd. Pfeizer, 1996—; med. dir. HMA behavioral health, 1995-99. Mem. Am. Psychiat. Assn., AMA. Moslem. Office: Prescott Health Care LLP 108 Grove St Worcester MA 01605-2651

OCHI, KOZO, microbiologist; b. Kamiura-cho, Ehime-ken, Japan, Jan. 1, 1949; s. Morio and Tatsuko (Soga) O.; m. Etsuko Yamanouchi, Jan. 3, 1977; children: Kensuke, Eriko. BSc, Hokkaido U., Sapporo, Japan, 1971, MSc, 1973, PhD, 1976. Postdoctoral fellow Georgetown U., Washington, 1977-78; vis. scientist NIH, Bethesda, Md., 1979-82; sr. scientist Fujisawa Pharm., Tsukuba, Japan, 1982-91; head of lab. Nat. Food Rsch. Inst., Tsukuba, 1991—. Recipient award for contbn. to edn. NIH, 1981. Mem. Soc. for Actinomycetes (sec. gen.), Japan Soc. for Biosci., Biotech. and Agrochemistry. Avocations: fishing, gardening. Home: Ninomiya 4-5-73, Tsukuba 305-0051, Japan Office: Nat Food Rsch Inst, 2-1-2 Kannondai, Tsukuba 305-8642, Japan

OCHIAI, MASAHIKO, cardiologist, educator; b. Hiratsuka, Kanagawa, Japan, Mar. 24, 1959; s. Kazumasa and Tomoko (Tokiwa) O.; m. Tomoko Yoshida, Oct. 3, 1985. MD, Tokyo U., 1984, PhD, 1992. Med. diplomate. Jr. resident Tokyo U. Hosp., 1984-85; jr. resident Mitsui Meml. Hosp., Tokyo, 1985-86, sr. resident, 1986-88; staff cardiologist Tokyo U. Sch. Medicine, 1988-92; staff cardiologist Teikyo U. Sch. Medicine, Tokyo, 1992-94, asst. prof., 1994—; co-dir. catheterization lab. Teikyo U. Hosp., Tokyo, 1994—, dir. outpatient clinic cardiology, 1998—. Contbr. articles to profl. jours. Fellow Am. Coll. Cardiology, Japanese Soc. Internal Medicine; mem. Japanese Circulation Soc. (bd. cert.). Avocations: wine, traveling. Home: 2-21-24 Yushima, Bunkyo-ku 113-0034, Japan Office: Teikyo U Dept Medicine, 2-11-1 Kaga, Itabashi-ku 173-8605, Japan

OCHOA, MANUEL, JR., oncologist; b. N.Y.C., Apr. 22, 1930; s. Manuel and Maria (Diaz) O.; m. Suzanne Ellen Recca, Sept. 1, 1956; children: Elizabeth, Suzanne Elise. AB, Columbia Coll., 1951; MD, Columbia U., 1955. Diplomate Am. Bd. Internal Medicine; lic. physician, N.Y., Mass. Asst. in medicine U. Rochester (N.Y.) Med. Sch., 1958-61; instr. medicine, assoc., asst. prof. Columbia U., N.Y.C., 1964-68; attending physician Meml. Sloan-Kettering Cancer Ctr., N.Y.C., 1973—; investigator Marine Biol. Lab., Woods Hole, Mass., 1965; assoc. prof. clin. medicine Cornell U., N.Y.C., 1982-96, prof., 1996—; cons. Harlem Hosp. Ctr., N.Y.C., 1966-68, Kingston (N.Y.) Hosp., 1970-85; vis. prof. U. Hawaii, Honolulu, 1971, U. Mex., Mexico City, 1979. Contbr. articles to profl. jours. Capt. USAF, 1956-58, ETO. Fellow Lalor Found., 1965. Fellow ACP, ACS. Republican. Roman Catholic. Achievements include discovering genetic code and protein synthesis in cancer cells, cancer chemotherapy. Home: 82 E Middle Patent Rd Bedford NY 10506-2106 Office: Meml Sloan-Kettering Cancer Ctr 1271 York Ave New York NY 10021-6007

OCHS, RICHARD WAYNE, artist, gallery owner; b. Newburgh, N.Y., Dec. 26, 1938; s. Harold John Ochs and Gertrude Adelaid Goetchius; m. Cindy Ochs, Apr. 14, 1968. AB in Econs. and Math., Hamilton Coll., 1960; postgrad., SUNY, New Paltz, 1961-70. Cert. secondary tchr., N.Y. Math. tchr. Newburgh Sch. Dist., 1960-92; artist, owner Richard Ochs Gallery, Newburgh, 1993—; represented by Art Nook Gallery, Newburgh, 1979-93, Irvington (N.Y.) Gallery, 1996-2000, Jordane Artworks, Fort Myers Beach, Fla., 1998-2000, Cerulean Gallery, Morristown, N.J., 2000—; mem. Coast Guard Artists' Program. Treas. Newburgh Tchrs.' Assn., 1965; pres. Dutchess County Art Assn., Poughkeepsie, N.Y., 1979, trustee, 1975-76. Staff sgt. N.Y. ARNG, 1963-69. Recipient Grumbacher Gold medal Mt. St. Mary Coll., 1997, 98, George Gray award USCG. Mem. Artist's Fellowship, Hudson Valley Art Assn., Kent Art Assn. (exec. bd. 1996—, 2nd v.p. 1999-2000), Am. Artist's Profl. League, North East Watercolor Soc. (treas. 1984-94, 1st v.p. 1995-97, pres. 1997—), Cmty. Arts Assn. (exec. bd. 1996—), Soc. Creative Artists of Newtown, Middletown, N.Y. Artist's Group, Watercolor Soc. Ala., Soc. Marine Artists, Artist's Fellowship, Ctrl. N.Y. Watercolor Soc., Salmagundi Club. Home and Office: 62 Dalfonso Rd Newburgh NY 12550-7203

OCHS, ROBERT DAVID, history educator; b. Bloomington, Ill., Mar. 27, 1915; s. Herman Solomon and Fannie Leah (Livingston) O. A.B., Ill. Wesleyan U., 1936; M.A., U. Ill., 1937, Ph.D., 1939; M.A., Oxford U., Eng., 1964. Research dir. Anti-Defamation League, 1939-41; mem. faculty U. S.C., 1946—, prof. history, 1957-76, disting. prof. emeritus, 1976—, chmn. dept., 1960-74; acting dean U. S.C. (Coll. Arts and Sci.), 1970-71; asso. editor U. S.C. Press, 1950-53; vis. prof. Merton Coll., Oxford U., 1964; Mem. S.C. Archives Commn., 1960-74. U.S. cons.: History of The 20th Century, 1967. Bd. dirs. Columbia Music Festival Assn., 1957-64, 77-85, v.p., 1961-62, pres., 1962-63; dir. Columbia Lyric Opera, Columbia Mus. Art, 1966-69, 74-77, McKissick Mus., 1991-96. Maj. AUS, 1941-46; lt. col. Mem. Am. Hist. Assn., So. Hist. Assn. (exec. council 1973-76), S.C. Hist. Assn. (editor 1947-55, pres. 1956-57), Am. Studies Assn., Orgn. Am. Historians, Southeastern Am. Studies Assn. (pres. 1960-61), Omicron Delta Kappa. Home: 100 Sunset Blvd Apt 401 West Columbia SC 29169-7565

OCHS, ROBERT HANSON, marketing professional; b. Quincy, Mass., Aug. 31, 1926; s. Harold Frederick and Mary Brown (Hanson) O.; m. Karen Astrid Scruton, Feb. 1, 1985; 1 child from previous marriage, Priscilla Jeanne Murphy. BSEE, Lehigh U., 1947; postgrad., Columbia U., 1958, 60; grad. dipl. in indsl. engring., U. Witwatersrand, Johannesburg, South Africa, 1986. Design and test engr. GE, 1947-51; engring. mgr. Manufacturera Gesa, Mexico City, 1951-54; sr. product engr. Internat. GE, N.Y.C., 1954-61; product mgr. GE, Phila., 1967-72; asst. dir. overseas mfg. Ingersoll-Rand, N.Y.C., 1961-67; mgmt. cons. Wendell Walker Assocs., N.Y.C., 1972-80, Whitehead Morris Ltd. Cons., Randburg, South Africa, 1980-86, Bus. Cons. Ltd., Valley Stream, N.Y., 1987; market analyst Automatic Switch Co. subs. Emerson Electric, Florham Park, N.J., 1987-92; computer engring. cons., 1992-93; sr. cons. Advanced Knowledge Sys. Consultancy, Randburg, South Africa, 1994-98; website market devel. Hillcrest, South Africa, 2000—. Contbr. articles to profl. jours. and papers to tech. socs. Active St. Dominic's, Hillcrest, South Africa. Mem. IEEE (sr.), Engring. Mgmt. Soc. (sr.), Toastmasters Internat., Assagay Valley Small Holders Assn. Roman Catholic. Avocations: computers, golf, walking, reading, backgammon. E-mail: ochs@cdrive.co.za. Home: PO Box 1775, 3650 Hillcrest South Africa

OCHSENBEIN, PETER ENGELBERT, library administrator, educator; b. Solothurn, Switzerland, July 15, 1940; s. Engelbert Paul and Agnes (Schwaller) O.; m. Rosmarie Rehmann, Mar. 8, 1968. PhD, U. Basel, Switzerland, 1969, PD PhD, 1987, prof. PhD, 1990. Asst. U. Basel, 1968-74; rsch. asst. Schweiz. Nationalfonds, Bern, 1975-81; dir. Abbey Libr., St. Gallen, Switzerland, 1981-2000. Author: Studies About Anticlaudian of Alanus ab Insulis, 1974, The Great Prayer of Swiss Citizen, 1989, Pray with Picture and Word, 1996. Avocation: music. Home: Girtannerstrasse 16, CH-9010 Saint Gallen Switzerland

OCHSNER, SEYMOUR FISKE, radiologist, editor; b. Chgo., Nov. 29, 1915; s. Albert Henry Ochsner and Fleda Fiske; m. Helen Keith, Sept. 8, 1945 (dec. Jan. 1976); children: Anne, Diana, Lida; m. Bobbie Sue Mercer, Dec. 31, 1981 (dec. Jan. 1997). AB, Dartmouth Coll., 1937; MD, U. Pa., Phila., 1947. Diplomate Am. Bd. Radiology, 1953. Intern Johnston-Willis Hosp., Richmond, Va., 1949-50; staff radiologist Ochsner Clinic, New Orleans, 1953-89, also chmn. dept., 1969-77; clin. prof. radiology Tulane Med. Sch., New Orleans, 1955-75; editor Orleans Parish Med. Bulletin, New Orleans, 1985-91. Contbr. articles to profl. jours. Pres. PTA, Metairie, La., 1964. Recipient Disting. Svc. medal So. Med. Assn., 1972, Disting. Svc. award AMA, 1993, fellow, Alton Ochsner Med. FOund., New Orleans, 1950-53. Fellow Alton Ochsner Med. Found.; mem. Radiol. Soc. La. (pres. 1965), So. Radiol. Conf. (pres. 1968), Am. Coll. Radiology (pres. 1972, Gold medal 1982), Am. Roentgen Ray Soc. (pres. 1975, Gold medal 1986), Rex Orgn., So. Yacht Club, Candlewood Club. Republican. Episcopalian. Avocations: reading, gardening, travel, sailing. Home: 107 Holly Dr Metairie LA 70005-3915

Ó CONGHAILE, MICHEÁL, writer, publishing executive; b. Galway, Ireland, Mar. 14, 1962; s. Colm Ó C. and Bríd Hernon. BA, U. Coll. Galway, Ireland, 1983, Higher Diploma in Edn., 1984, MA in History, 1986. Founder Cló Iar-Chonnachta, Galway, Ireland, 1985; mng. dir. Cló Iar-Chonnachta, 1985-95, dir., 1997—. Author: (short stories) Mac an tSagairt, 1986, (poetry) Comhrá Cailí, 1987, Conamara agus Árainn 1880-1980 (Irish Books award 1988), 1988, Gnéithe d'Amhráin Chonamara ár Linne, 1993, (short stories) An Fear a Phléasc, 1997 (nominated for Irish Times Literary Prizes 1997), (novel) Sna Fir, 1999; editor: Gaeltacht Ráth Cairn: Léachtaí Comórtha, 1986, (songs) Croch Suas É!, 1990, Sláinte: Deich mBliana de Chló Iar-Chonnachta, 1995. Recipient Hennesy Literary award 1997, Butler Literary award, 1997. Avocations: sports, reading, travel, walking. Home: Teach Mór Thoir, Indreabhán Galway, Ireland Office: Cló Iar-Chonnachta, Indreabhán Galway, Ireland

O'CONNELL, ANTHONY J., bishop; b. Lisheen, County Clare, Ireland, May 10, 1938. Ed., Mt. St. Joseph Coll., Cork, Ireland; Mungret Coll., Mangret Coll., Limerick, Ireland; ed., Kenrick Sem., St. Louis. Ordained priest Roman Cath. Ch., 1963. 1st bishop Diocese of Knoxville, 1988-99; 3d bishop Diocese of Palm Beach, Fla., 1999—. Office: Bishop of Palm Beach PO Box 109650 Palm Beach Gardens FL 33410-9650

O'CONNELL, BRIAN MICHAEL, lawyer; b. Hartford, Conn., Nov. 2, 1960. BA, Trinity Coll., Hartford, 1983; JD, U. Conn., 1987. Bar: Conn. 1988, U.S. Dist. Ct. Conn. 1988, U.S. Supreme Ct. 1992. Pvt. practice Farmington, Conn., 1988—; prof. law, ethics and computing Ctrl. Conn. State U., New Britain, 1997—. Office: Ctrl Conn State Univ New Britain CT 06050

O'CONNELL, DANIEL JAMES, lawyer; b. Evergreen Park, Ill., Aug. 14, 1954; s. Edmund J. and Kathryn J. (Hanna) O'C.; m. Nancy L. Eichler, March 21, 1992; children: Kelly Jacklyn, Kirby Kathryn. BS, Millikin U., 1976; JD, IIT, 1980; postgrad., DePaul U., 1981, U. Mich., 1997, U. Ill., 1999—. Bar: Ill. 1980, U.S. Dist. Ct. (no. dist.) Ill. 1980, U.S. Dist. Ct. Ariz. 1989. Ins. regulatory counsel Kemper Group, Long Grove, Ill., 1980-81, environ. claims counsel, 1981-82; sr. home office claim counsel Zurich Ins. Cos., Schaumburg, Ill., 1982-83; assoc. Clausen, Miller, Gorman et al, Chgo., 1983-86; ptnr. environ. toxic tort litigation O'Connell & Moroney, P.C., Chgo., 1986-90; ptnr. toxic tort litigation Burditt, Bowles & Radzius, Chgo., 1990-91; ptnr. Daniel J. O'Connell & Assocs., P.C., Elgin, 1991—. James S. Kemper Found. scholar, 1972-76. Mem. ABA, APHA, Ill. Bar Assn., Kane County Bar Assn., Def. Rsch. Inst., N.Y. Acad. Scis.,. Home: 177 Macintosh Ct Glen Ellyn IL 60137-6478

O'CONNELL, DAVID FRANCIS, psychologist; b. York, Pa., Aug. 21, 1953; s. John Vincent and Anne Marie (Pollard) O'C. BA, U. Pa., 1975; MS, Loyola Coll., 1978; PhD, Temple U., 1986. Diplomate Am. Acad. Psychologists Treating Addiction; lic. psychologist, Pa. Clin. supr. Berks Youth Counseling Ctr., Reading, Pa., 1981-84; staff psychologist ARC/The Terraces, Ephrata, Pa., 1984-87; pvt. practice Reading, Pa., 1989—; instr. in addictions studies Alvernia Coll., Reading, 1981—; adj. instr. Pat. State U., Berks, 1984—; attending psychologist St. Joseph's Hosp., Reading, 1989—; cons. New Beginnings At Hidden Brook, Bel Air, Md., 1987; sr. cons. Family Life Svcs., 1989-97; psychol. examiner Bur. Disability Determination, 1989—; cons. Caron Found., Wernersville, Pa., 1989-97, corp. clin. dir., 1997—, chmn. profl. staff orgn.; cons. Reading Police Svc. Bd.; lectr. in field; cons. dept. psychiat. Reading Hosp. and Med. Ctr.; mem. adv. bd. Inst. Sci. Tech. and Pub. Policy. Author: Treating the High Risk Adolescent: A Survey of Effective Programs and Interventions, 1989, Treating The Dually Diagnosed Patient in Addictions Setting, 1991, Counseling the Dually Diagnosed Patient, 1988, Relapse Prevention with Chemically Dependent Adolescents: Cogitive Therapy Approaches, 1994; editor: Managing the Dually Diagnosed Patient, 1990, 2d edit., 1999, Self Recovery, 1994, Dual Disorders: Essentials for Assessment and Treatment, 1998; contbr. articles to Jour. Coll. Student Pers., Alcoholism Quarterly, Jour. Chem. Dependence Treatment, and others; mem. editorial bd. Jour. of Adolescent Chem. Dependency, 1989—. Mem. APA, Pa. Psychol. Assn., N.Y. Acad. Scis., Berks Area Psychol. Soc. (pres.). Roman Catholic. Achievements include research on practical approaches in treating adolescent chemical dependency, managing the borderline alcoholic in addictions treatment settings, prevention of alcohol problems in colleges and universities, relapse prevention, treating impaired health professionals, inovative approaches to addictions therapy. Home: 26 Witman Rd Womelsdorf PA 19567-9425 Office: 25 Stevens Ave West Lawn PA 19609-1424

O'CONNELL, FRANCIS JOSEPH, retired lawyer, arbitrator; b. Ft. Edward, N.Y., Mar. 19, 1913; s. Daniel Patrick and Mary (Bowe) O'C.; m. Adelaide M. Nagro, Sept. 27, 1937; children: Chris, Mary Gaynor Lavonas. AB, Columbia U., 1934; JD, Fordham U., 1938; SJD summa cum laude, Bklyn. Law Sch., 1945. Bar: N.Y. 1938, U.S. Dist. Ct. (so. dist.) N.Y. 1942, U.S. Tax Ct. 1941. Counsel and asst. to chmn. exec. com. for labor law and litigation Allied Chem. Corp., N.Y.C., 1942-70; ptnr. Bill & O'Connell and predecessor, Garden City, N.Y., 1970-76; pvt. practice Garden City, N.Y., 1976-85, Cutchogue, N.Y., 1985—; now ret.; arbitrator, fact-finder, mediator Fed. Mediation and Conciliation Svc., 1970—, N.Y. State Mediation Bd., Am. Arbitration Assn., N.Y. State, Nassau and Suffolk County pub. employment rels. bds., 1970—; adminstrv. law judge N.Y. State Dept. Health, 1979—; instr. labor law and labor rels. Cornell U.; U.S. del. ILO, Geneva, 1948, 59, 69, 72. Author: Labor Law and the First Line Supervisor, 1945, Restrictive Work Practices, 1967, National Emergency Strikes, 1968. Trustee Village of Garden City, 1948-50; mem. bd. edn. Diocese of Rockville Centre (N.Y.), 1972-80; pres. various civic orgns., 1942—. Mem. ABA (labor and internat. law sects.), N.Y. State Bar Assn. (labor com.), Bar Assn. Nassau County (labor and arbitration coms., former chmn. arbitration andlabor law coms.), Mfg. Chemists Assn. (chmn. indsl. rels. com.), U.S. C. of C. (indsl. rels. com.), Southold Indian Mus. (bd. dirs.). Republican. Roman Catholic. Office: PO Box 819 Cutchogue NY 11935-0819

O'CONNELL, MARGARET SULLIVAN, lawyer; b. N.Y.C., Feb. 16, 1942; d. Thomas J. and Nora (Ryan) Sullivan; m. Anthony F. O'Connell, May 11, 1968 (dec. Mar. 1975); children: Noreen Anne, Joan Margaret, Alison Marie. Nursing diploma, St. Clare's Hosp. Sch. Nursing, N.Y.C., 1962; BA, Jersey City State Coll., 1973; JD, St. John's U., 1983. Bar: N.Y. 1984, U.S. Dist. Ct. (so. and ea. dists.) 1996; RN, N.Y. Staff nurse St. Clare's Hosp., N.Y.C., 1962-64, head nurse, 1964-67; clin. instr. medicine and surgery St. Clare's Sch. Nursing, N.Y.C., 1967-70; nursing supr. Menorah Home and Hosp., Bklyn., 1974-75; assoc. Costello, Shea & Gaffney, N.Y.C., 1987-95, ptnr., 1995—. Mem. ABA, N.Y. State Bar Assn., Assn. Bar City N.Y. (com. on med. malpractice 1996—), Am. Assn. Nurse Attys., Brehon Law Soc. Office: Costello Shea & Gaffney 44 Wall St New York NY 10005-2401

O'CONNELL, MAURICE, banker. Gov. Ctrl. Bank Ireland. Office: Ctrl Bank Ireland, PO Box 559 Dame St, Dublin 2, Ireland

O'CONNELL, MICHAEL, quaternary palaeoecologist, botanist, educator; b. Ireland, Apr. 20, 1946; s. Martin and Rita (Nugent) O'C.; m. Máire OBroin, Aug. 22, 1975. BSc with honors, U. Coll. Dublin, 1971, PhD, 1977. Jr. lectr. Nat. U. Ireland, Galway, 1974-86, statutory lectr., 1987-97, assoc. prof., 1997—; vis. prof. Shaanxi Normal U., Xi'an, China, 1997-99, Inst. Geobotanik U. Hanover, Germany, 1999-2000. Copy editor Vegetation History and Archaeobotany, 1990—; contbr. articles to profl. jours. A. von Humboldt fellowship A. von Humboldt Found., 1982, 83. Mem. Royal Irish Acad., Irish Assn. for Quarternary Studies, British Ecol. Soc., British Quaternary Rsch. Assn. Avocations: archaeology, hill-walking, photography. Office: Nat U Ireland Galway, Galway Ireland

O'CONNELL, MICHAEL ALEXANDER, social worker; b. Dayton, Ohio, May 28, 1948; s. William J. and Aida May (Duncan) O'Co. BS in econ., U. Pa., 1970; MSW, U. Wash., 1977, PhD in Counseling Psychology, 1997. Cert. social worker, Wash. Dir. Second Chance Youth Alcoholism Program, Seattle, 1977-78; social worker Riverton Hosp., Burien, Wash., 1979-80; therapist Robinson William & Assocs., Seattle, 1981-82; therapist & cons. Althean Assocs., Seattle, 1982-83, Everett/Mill Creek, 1983—. Author: Working With Sex Offenders, 1990. Pres. Wash. State Chpt., Assn. for the Treatment of Sexual Abusers, 1997—. Mem. Acad. Cert. Social Workers, Assn. Treatment of Sexual Abusers, Am. Profl. Soc. on the Abuse of Children. Office: Michael A O'Connell & Assocs 16300 Mill Creek Blvd Ste 202 Mill Creek WA 98012-1286

O'CONNELL, RICHARD (JAMES), English literature educator, poet; b. N.Y.C., Oct. 25, 1928; s. Richard James and Mary Ellen (Fallon) O'C.; BS, Temple U., 1956; MA, Johns Hopkins, 1957. Instr. English Temple U., Phila., 1957-61, asst. prof., 1961-69, asso. prof., 1969-86; sr. assoc. prof., 1986-93, assoc. prof. emeritus, 1993; guest lectr. poetry dept. writing seminars Johns Hopkins U., 1961-74; participant Poetry in Schs. Program, Pa. Council Arts, 1971-73; Fulbright lectr. Am. lit. U. Brazil, Rio de Janeiro, 1960, U. Navarre, Pamplona, Spain, 1962-63. Served with USN, 1948-52. Recipient prize Contemporary Poetry Press, 1972. Mem. PEN, MLA, Asso. Writing Programs, Walt Whitman Poetry Center (dir. 1975-84), Lit. Fellowship Phila. Author: From an Interior Silence, 1961, Cries of Flesh and Stone, 1962, New Poems and Translations, 1963; Brazilian Happenings, 1966, Terrane, 1967, Thirty Epigrams, 1971, Irish Monastic Poems (transl.), 1975, The Word in Time (selected transl. of Antonio Machado), 1975, Sappho (selected transl.), 1975, Lorca (selected transl.), 1976, Middle English Poems (transl.), 1976, More Irish Poems (transl.), 1976, Epigrams from Martial (transl.), 1976, One Hundred Epigrams from the Greek Anthology (trans.), 1977, Hudson's Fourth Voyage, 1978, The Epigrams of Luxorius (transl.), 1984, Temple Poems, 1985, Hanging Tough, 1986, Battle Poems, 1987, Selected Epigrams, 1990, Lives of The Poets, 1990, New Epigrams From Martial (transl.), 1991, The Caliban Poems, 1992, RetroWorlds, 1993 (translation) Simulations, 1993, Voyages, 1995, The Bright Tower, 1997; editor: Apollo's Day, 17th Century Songs, 1969; Atlantis Edits., 1962—, Poetry Newsletter, 1971-86. Home: 1147 Hillsboro Mile Apt 907 Hillsboro Beach FL 33062

O'CONNELL, TAAFFE CANNON, actress, publishing executive; b. Providence; d. Joseph Ceril and Edith Ethelyn (Dent) O'C. BA, U. Miss., MFA. Regional supr. Gloria Marshall Figure Salons, S.C.; v.p., co-founder Doc Sox Inc., Pacific Palisades, Calif., 1988-90; pres., founder Canoco Pub., L.A., 1991—, 1-800-266-DYNE, L.A., 1992-93; founder Rising Star Distbn., Canoco Prodn. Appeared in films, including Men Without Dates, Dangerous, Hot Chili, Cheech & Chong Nice Dreams, Rocky II, Galaxy of Terror, New Years Evil, Rich Man Poor Man Book I, Caged Fury; TV appearances include Malubu Branch, General Hospital, Dangerous Women, Dallas, Knight and Daye, The New Gidget, Knight Rider, Three's Company, Dr. Joyce Brothers Show, Blansky's Beauties, Peter Lupus Show, Fix-It City, Happy Days, Laverne & Shirley, Wonder Woman, The Incredible Hulk; theater appearances include Too True to be Good, Damn Yankees, Anastasia, Star Spangled Girl, The Beaux Stratagem, The Canterbury Tales; founder, pub. Astrocaster, 1991, Power Agent, 1993; Jan. founder Rising Star Distbn. and Canoco Prodns., 1999—; exec prodr.: Beanie & Twigg, Paranormal Private Eyes, Inside the industry, 2000. Mem. Screen Actors' Guild, Am. Fedn. TV Radio Artists, Actor's Equity, Actor's Forum (bd. dirs. 1985-94). Avocations: singing, spinning, sailing, travel. E-mail: industryedge@earthlink.net. Office: Canoco Pub 11611 Chenault St Ste 118 Los Angeles CA 90049-4574

O'CONNOR, BERNARD F., academic administrator; b. June 14, 1944. BA in Philosophy, Cath. U., 1969, MA in Philosophy, 1971, PhD in Philosophy, 1986; MA in Theology, DeSales Sch. Theology, 1974. Instr. philosophy Allentown Coll. St. Francis De Sales, Center Valley, Pa., 1974-76; asst. prof. philosophy Allentown Coll. St. Francis De Sales, Center Valley, 1980-87, assoc. prof. philosophy, chair philosophy and theology dept., 1987-93, assoc. v.p. for acad. affairs, 1993-94, acad. dean, 1994-97, exec. v.p., 1997-99, pres., 1999—; mem. com. on ecumenism Diocese of Allentown, 1991, mem. bd. edn., 1996; mem. exec. bd. Ctr. for Agile Pa. Edn., Bethlehem, 1999, Pa. Ednl. Telecom. Exch., Bethlehem, 1999. Author: A Dialogue Between Philosophy and Religion: The Perspective of Karl Jaspers, 1988. Recipietn Sears Roebuck Found. Tchg. Excellence and Campus Leadership award, 1990. Mem. Am. Philos. Assn., Am. Cath. Philos. Assn., Fellowship Cath. Schs. Roman Catholic. Office: Allentown Coll St Francis 2755 Station Ave Center Valley PA 18034-9565

O'CONNOR, BETTY LOU, service executive; b. Phoenix, Oct. 29, 1927; d. Georg Eliot and Tillie Edith Miller; m. William Spoeri O'Connor, Oct. 10, 1948 (dec. Feb. 1994); children: Thomas W., William K., Kelli Anne. Student, U. So. Calif., 1946-48, Calif. State U., Los Angeles, 1949-50. V.p. O'Connor Food Svcs., Inc., Jack in the Box Restaurants, Granada Hills, Calif., 1983-93; pres. O'Connor Food Svcs., Inc., Granada Hills, Calif., 1994—, Western Restaurant Mgmt. Co., Granada Hills, 1986—; sec. C.E.O. Foods, Inc., Victorville, Calif.; pres. City Snippers, Inc., Santa Clarita, Calif.; mem. adv. bd. Bank of Granada Hills; bd. dirs. Nat. Franchise Purchasing Coop., nc. Recipient Frannie award Foodmaker, Inc., Northridge, Calif., 1984, First Rate award, 1992. Mem. Jack in the Box Franchisee Assn., Spurs Hon. (sec. U. So. Calif. 1947-48), Associated Women Students (sec. U. So. Calif. 1946-47), Gamma Alpha Chi (v.p. 1947-48), Chi Omega. Republican. Roman Catholic. Avocation: sewing. Office: O'Connor Foord Svcs Inc 17545 Chatsworth St Granada Hills CA 91344-5720

O'CONNOR, BRIAN JOSEPH, physician, consultant; b. Dublin, Leinster, Ireland, Sept. 14, 1956; s. Timothy Christopher and Margaret Mary (Hanly) O'C.; m. Helena Diana Kingston, Aug. 1997; 1 child, Christopher. MD, U. Coll. Dublin, 1980; diploma in Child Health, Nat. U. Ireland, 1987. Intern Cavan Gen. Hosp. and St. Vincent's Hosp., Elm Park, Ireland, 1980-81; sr. house officer in gen. medicine Letterkenny Gen. Hosp., Donegal, Ireland, 1981-82; sr. house officer in hematology/oncology St. Laurence's and Mater Misericordiae Hosps., Dublin, 1982-83; registrar in respiratory medicine Mater Misericordiae Hosp., Dublin, 1983-85, clin. rsch. registrar in gastroenterology, 1985-86; clin. lectr. in medicine and cardiology dept. medicine Mater Misericordiae Hosp. and U. Coll. Dublin, 1986-87; sr. house officer/registrar in pediat. cardiology and med. Our Lady's Hosp. for Sick Children Crumlin & U. Coll. Dublin, 1987; clin. rsch. fellow dept. thoracic medicine Nat. Heart and Lung Inst., U. London, 1988-91; hon. registrar respiratory medicine Royal Brompton and Westminster Hosps., London, 1988-91; overseas sr. registrar in respiratory medicine Royal Brompton Hosp., London, 1992; sr. lectr. thoracic medicine Imperial Coll. Sch. Medicine, Nat. Heart and Lung Inst., London, 1992-97; hon. cons. respiratory medicine Royal Brompton Hosp., London, 1992-97; cons. respiratory medicine Kings Coll. Hosp., London, 1997—; locum cons. physician/med. registrar Louth County Hosp., Dundalk County, 1988; cons. gen. physician ABN Al Bitar Hosp., Baghdad, 1988. Editor: Key Advances in the Effective Management of Asthma, 1999; mem. editl. bd. Pulmonary Pharmacology and Therapeutics, European Jour. Clin. Pharmacology; reviewer Lancet, Am. Jour. Respiratory and Critical Care Medicine, European Respiratory Jour., Thorax, Jour. Allergy and Clin. Immunology, Respiratory Medicine, Respiration; contbr. articles to profl. jours., chpts. to books. Fellow Royal Coll. Physicians Ireland, Royal Coll. Physicians London; mem. Royal Soc. Medicine London (pres. respiratory medicine sect. 1997-99, Am. Thoracic Soc., British Thoracic Soc., European Respiratory Soc. Home: 31 Orlando Rd, London SW4 OLD, England

O'CONNOR, BRIAN KEVIN, pediatric cardiac electrophysiologist, researcher; b. Woodbury, N.J., Dec. 27, 1960; s. Frederick V. and Patricia

Mary O'Connor. BS magna cum laude, U. Notre Dame, 1981; MD, Georgetown U., 1985. Pediat. resident Boston, 1985-88; pediat. cardiology fellow U. Mich., Ann Arbor, 1988-91; pediat. electrophysiology fellow S.C. Children's Heart Ctr., Charleston, 1993-95; asst. prof. pediats. Sch. Medicine NYU Med. Ctr., N.Y.C., 1995—, dir. divsn. pediat. electrophysiology, 1995—. Author: (with others) Perspectives in Pediatric Cardiology, Vol. 2, 1990, Practical Pediatric Cardiac Pacing, 1995, Clinical Pediatric Cardiac Arrhythmias, 1998; contbr. articles to profl. jours. including Pacing and Clin. Electrophysiology, Pediat. Annals, Circulation, and Jour. Am. Coll. Cardiology. Fellow Am. Coll. Cardiology-Bristol-Meyers Squibb, 1994. Mem. Am. Coll. Cardiology, N.Am. Soc. Pacing and Electrophysiology, Phi Beta Kappa. Office: Children's Hosp NJ 201 Lyons Ave Newark NJ 07112-2027

O'CONNOR, CLINT HAYNIE, electrical engineer; b. Corpus Christi, Tex., June 23, 1955; s. Robert Barnard Jr. and Edith H. (Haynie) O'C.; m. Christine Ann Schroeder, Mar. 30, 1985. BA, Wabash Coll., Crawfordsville, Ind., 1978. Pres., dir. R&D Analytical Engines, Austin, Tex., 1982-86; sr. project engr. Gould Indsl. Automation, Andover, Mass., 1986-88; mgr. elect. engring. Webtron Corp., Fort Lauderdale, Fla., 1988-93; devel. mgr. Dell Computer Corp., Austin, 1993—; chmn. bd. Analytical Engines, 1982-86; cons. Marine Sci. Inst., Galveston, Tex., 1980. Vol. Dolphin Rsch. Ctr., Grassy Key, Fla., 1989-90. Mem. Sigma Xi. Achievements include development of first 68000 co-processor for Apple II, 68010 co-processor for IBM PC; author 68000 Applesoft BASIC compatible interpreter; software development of Gould C986 co-processor, printing press control systems, development of Dell battery gauge, Dell control, Dell PC-card central and utilities for Dell Latitude portables; 9 patents in field. Office: Dell Computer One Dell Way Round Rock TX 78682

O'CONNOR, EDWARD CORNELIUS, army officer; b. Middlesex County, Mass., June 22, 1931; s. Edward Denis and Gladys Marie (Devine) O'C.; m. Charlotte Hubble, June 1, 1958. A.B., Boston Coll., 1952; M.S., U. N.C., 1966; M.S. George Washington U., 1979. Commd. 2d lt. U.S. Army, 1952, advanced through grades to maj. gen., 1981; asst. for NATO Affairs, Office of Sec. Def., 1970-72; sec. Joint Staff, Vietnam, 1972; chief staff Joint Mil. Commn., Vietnam, 1973; arty. comdr. 1st Armored Div., Europe, 1973-74; Fed. Exec. fellow Brookings Inst., Washington, 1975-76; chief Army Initiatives Group, Army Staff, Pentagon, 1976-77; dep. dir. ops. Nat. Mil. Command Center, Joint Chiefs of Staff, Washington, 1977-78; asst. div. comdr. (maneuver) 1st Armored Div., Europe, 1978-79; chief nuclear activities SHAPE, Belgium, 1979-82; dir. ops., readiness and mobilization ODCSOPS, Dept. Army, 1982-83; comdg. gen. Security Affairs Command Army Material Command, 1983-86; chief exec. officer, pres. Global Mktg. Corp. (doing bus. as GMA Internat., Inc.), 1986—; chmn. Contraves, Inc., Pitts., 1992-97; mem. policy working group U.S. State Dept. Def. Trade Adv. Group, Washington, 1994—; bd. dirs. Gas Equipment Engring. Corp., Milford, Conn., 1997—; internat. lectr. in field. Author: Performance Appraisal, 1966. Chmn. Harvard U. Grad. Sch. rels. com. Decorated D.S.M., Legion of Merit with 3 oak leaf clusters, Bronze Star, Air medal with 6 oak leaf clusters, Army Commendation medal with V device and 7 oak leaf clusters, Def. Meritorious Service medal, Def. Superior Service medal, Joint Service Commendation with oak leaf cluster, Identification Badges of Sec. Def. Office, Joint Chiefs of Staff and Army Gen. Staff. Mem. Harvard U. Alumni Assn. (bd. dirs. 1989-93). Address: 10202 Eagle Landing Ct Burke VA 22015-2524

O'CONNOR, FRANCIS DAVID, automotive company executive; b. Perth, Australia, Jan. 6, 1937; s. Francis Patrick and Sybil Helen (Webster) O'Connor; m. Maria Ann Ellery, June 25, 1966; children: Anne Marie, Francis William (dec.), Damian Victor. Diploma in Acctg., Perth Tech. Coll., 1966. With Western Australian Trustee Executors & Adminstrs., Perth, 1953-64; sales rep. Shell Oil, Perth, 1964-68; proprietor various small bus. including svc. sta. Esso Svc. Sta., Gillford Tyres, Cygus Marine, Perth, 1968-81; CEO Capricorn Soc. Ltd., Perth, 1981—; dir./councillor Coop. Fedn. Western Australia, 1989—; chmn. Nat. Coop. Coun. Sydney, 1994-98. Capt. Australian Army, 1956-84. Recipient Efficiency Decoration ED, Australian Govt., Res. Forces Decoration. Fellow Australian Cert. Practicing Accts., Corp. Mgrs. and Adminstrs., Chartered Secs., Taxation Inst.; mem. Australian Auto Aftermarket Assn. (dir., chmn., councillor 1990—, area chair 1998—), Motor Trades Assn. Western Australian (divsn. chmn. 1974—), Credit Mgmt. Assn. (assoc.), Rotary, West Australian Cricket Assn., West Australian Turf Club, Royal Perth Yacht Club. Office: Capricorn Society Ltd, 172 Burswood Rd, Victoria WA 6100, Australia

O'CONNOR, GAYLE MCCORMICK, law librarian; b. Rome, N.Y., July 8, 1956; d. John Joseph and Barbara Jane (Molyneaux) McC. Head libr. Bolling, Walter & Gawthrop, Sacramento, 1987-88, Weintraub, Genshlea & Sproul, Sacramento, 1988-93, Brobeck, Phleger & Harrison, San Diego, 1993-96; legal cons., author, 1996—; owner Automated legal Solutions, Ft. Lauderdale, Fla., 1997—; legal industry mktg. specialist CourtLink, Seattle, 1998—; mktg. mgr. Pro2Net, Legal, 2000—; instr. law Lincoln U., Sacramento. Assoc. editor, rsch. advisor Alert Publs., Chgo.; contbr. articles to profl. jours. Mem. ABA (tech. show bd.), No. Calif. Assn. Law Librs., So. Calif. Assn. Law Librs., Am. Assn. Law Librs., Spl. Librs. Assn. (chair legal divsn. 1997-98). Avocations: bodybuilding, skiing. Office: 400 112th Ave NE Ste 250 Bellevue WA 98004-5550

O'CONNOR, JAMES JOHN, retired utility company executive; b. Chgo., Mar. 15, 1937; s. Fred James and Helen Elizabeth O'Connor; m. Ellen Louise Lawlor, Nov. 24, 1960; children: Fred, John (dec.), James, Helen Elizabeth. BS, Holy Cross Coll., 1958; MBA, Harvard U., 1960; JD, Georgetown U., 1963. Bar: Ill. 1963. With Commonwealth Edison Co., Chgo., 1963-98, asst. to chmn. exec. com., 1964-65, comml. mgr., 1966, asst. v.p., 1967-70, v.p., 1970-73, exec. v.p., 1973-77, pres., 1977-87, chmn., 1980-98, CEO, also bd. dirs., 1998; chmn., CEO Unicom Corp., Chgo., 1994-98, ret., 1998; bd. dirs. Corning, Inc., Tribune Co., United Air Lines, Am. Nat. Can., Smurfit-Stone Container Corp. Mem. The Bus. Coun.; bd. dirs. Lyric Opera, Joffrey Ballet, Helen Brach Found.; bd. dirs., trustee Mus. Sci. and Industry, Chgo. Symphony; past chmn. Met. Savs. Bond Campaign; trustee Northwestern U.; bd. dirs., past chmn. Chgo. Urban League, Chicagoland C. of C.; past chmn. bd. trustees Field Mus. Natural History; life trustee Adler Planetarium, Mus. Sci. and Industry; mem. exec. bd. Chgo. Area coun. Boy Scouts Am.; chmn. Cardinal Bernardin's Big Shoulders Fund; exec. v.p. The Hundred Club Cook County; dir., past pres. Cath. Charities; past chmn., hon. dir. Am. Cancer Soc., Chgo. Conv. and Tourism Bur. With USAF, 1960-63. Mem. ABA, Ill. Bar Assn., Chgo. Bar Assn.

O'CONNOR, JAMES PATRICK MEL, advertising agency director; b. Devizes, Wilts, Eng., Mar. 11, 1918; 3 children. Dir. Advt. Agy., London, 1946-52, Inst. Practitioners in Advt., London, 1953-77; cons. Ind. TV Cos. Assn., London, 1978-87. Editor: (textbook) The Practice of Advertising. 1978 other editions; contbr. articles to profl. jours. Flight lt. RAF, 1940-46, ETO. Decorated officer Order Brit. Empire, Silver Jubilee medal (Eng.), knight comdr. Order St. Gregory (Pope John Paul); recipient Mackintosh medal, Publicity Club London Cup, award Internat. Advt. Assn., 1971, numerous others worldwide. Fellow Chartered Inst. Secs., Inst. Practitioners in Advt.; mem. CAM Found., Inst. Advt. Practitioners in Ireland, Inst. for Markedsföring (Norway). Roman Catholic. Avocations: music, walking, birdsong. Home: Hoyland Down, Woodland Way, Kingswood, Surrey KT20 6NW, England

O'CONNOR, JOHN, hotel management educator, consultant; b. Bolton, Lancs., Eng., Mar. 31, 1934; s. Francis and Catherine (McGuinness) O'C.; m. Maureen Patricia Jones, Mar. 22, 1963; children: Michael Sean, James Anthony. BSc in Pure Sci., U. Birmingham, U.K., 1961. Trainee mgr. Warburtons Ltd., Bolton, 1956-57; asst. exptl. officer Baking Industries Rsch. Assn., Chorleywood, Herts., 1957; sect. officer Ranks-Hovis-McDougall Labs., London, 1961-64; lectr. in food sci. South Devon Tech. Coll., Torquay, Devon, 1964-66, U. Surrey, Guildford, 1966-73; cons. BLA Mgmt. Svcs. Group, London, 1973-76; prin. lectr. Oxford Polytechnic, Oxford, Oxon, 1976-78; head of sch. Oxford Brookes U., 1978-96, prof. hotel mgmt., 1988-96, prof. emeritus, 1996—; bd. dirs. U.K. Hotel and Catering Tng. Bd., London, 1982-90; chair U.K. Coun. on Hospitality Mgmt. Edn., 1982-85, Oxford Ctr. for Tourism and Leisure Studies, 1992-96; vice chair exec. com. World Travel and Tourism Environ. Rsch. Ctr., Oxford, 1992-96; vis. prof. Scottish Hotel Sch., U. Strathclyde, Glasgow, 1996—; mem. ct. U. Surrey, Guildford, Eng., 1997—. Founding editor-in-chief Internat. Jour. of Hospitality Mgmt., 1982—; editor (book series) Professional Hospitality Guides, 1989—, Internat. Series in Hospitality Mgmt., 1978-85; editor: Selections From the John Fuller Collection, 1985. With U.K. Army Catering Corps, 1952-54. Recipient Outstanding Svc. award Coun. on Hospitality Mgmt. Edn., 1996; Baking Industry Edn. Bd. scholar, 1954-56, Ministry of Edn. Tech. State scholar, 1957-61. Fellow Royal Statis. Soc., Hotel and Catering Internat. Mgmt. Assn.; mem. Reform Club (Pall Mall, London). Home and Office: 4 Feilden Grove, Oxford OX3 0DU, England

O'CONNOR, JOSEPH BENEDICT, surgeon; b. Dublin, Ireland, Aug. 12, 1945; s. Malachy Michael and Mary Josephine (O'Connor) O'C.; m. Bridget Ann Mullen, June 28, 1969; children: Roderick, Angus, Ashling, Avice. MB BChir, U. Coll., Dublin, 1969. Lectr. U. Glasgow, 1970-71; rsch. fellow U. Coll., Dublin, 1971-72; sr. surg. registrar Dublin, 1974-76; fellow Providence Med. Ctr., Seattle, 1976-77; sr. surg. registrar U. Coll. Hosp., Galway, Ireland, 1977-78; cons. surgeon Waterford (Ireland) Regional Hosp., 1981—. Fellow Royal Coll. Surgeons Glasgow, Royal Coll. Surgeons Edinburgh, Royal Coll. Surgeons Ireland, Royal Coll. Surgeons Eng. (cert. higher surg. training), British Horse Soc. Home: Chehalis Ballyglan, Woodstown Ireland Office: Waterford Regional Hosp, Waterford Ireland

O'CONNOR, KAREN LENDE, Olympic athlete; b. Feb. 17, 1958; m. David O'Connor, 1993. Mem. US Equestrian Olympic Team, Seoul, Korea, 1988, Atlanta, 1996; mem. U.S. Equestrian Team, 2000. Winner CCI, Boekelo (Holland), 1984, CCI, Chesterland (Pa.), 1985, placed 1st Role/Kentucky Internat. CCI Three Day Event, 1991, 1st Tetbury (Eng.) Horse Trials, 1991, 1st Fair Hill (Md.) Horse Trials, 1991, 3rd Burghley Three Day Event CCI (Eng.), 1991, 6th World Three Day Event Rider Rankings L'Annee Hippique, 1991, 3rd CCI, Loughanmore (Ireland), 1992, 6th Blenheim Audi Internat. Horse Trials (Eng.), 1993, 1st CCI, Punchestown (Ireland), 1993, 10th CCI Internat. de Saumur, 1994; recipient Silver medal, Olympic Games, Atlanta, 1996; named U.S. Combined Tng. Assn. Lady Rider of the Year, 1989, 90, 91, 95, 96, 97, 98, Female Equestrian Athlete of the Year Olympic Com., 1993, USET spring champion, winning Kentucky CCI, USET FAll Reserve champion, 2nd Fair Hill, 1999, World Equestrian Games Bronze Medal Team, 1998, USET spring champion, winner Kentucky CCI, 1997; grantee USET, 1991. Office: care US Equestrian Team Inc PO Box 355 Gladstone NJ 07934-0355*

O'CONNOR, KATHLEEN MARY, lawyer; b. Camden, Jan. 14, 1949; d. John A. and Marie V. (Flynn) O'C. BA, U. Fla., 1971, JD, 1981. Bar: Fla. 1981, U.S. Ct. Appeals (11th cir.) 1982, U.S. Supreme Ct. 1987. Atty. Walton, Lantaff, Schroeder & Carson, Miami, 1981-84, Thornton, Davis & Murray PA, Miami, 1984-98. Exec. editor U. Fla. Law Rev., 1981; contbr. articles to profl. jours. Legal advocate Miami Project to Cure Paralysis, 1992-97. Mem. ABA, Dade County Bar Assn. (vice-chair appellate cts. com. 1981), Def. Rsch. Inst., Fla. Def. Lawyers Assn.

O'CONNOR, KEVIN THOMAS, religious organization administrator; b. Dubuque, Iowa, Oct. 9, 1950; s. Francis John and Marion Helen (Rhomberg) O'C.; m. Abbie J. O'Connor, July 17, 1993; 1 child, Sean Francis. BS, Regis Coll., Denver, 1973. Spl. agt. Northwestern Mut. Life, Denver, 1973-78; account exec. Blue Cross/Blue Shield of Colo., Denver, 1978-82; pres., owner O'Connor Ins. Cons., Denver, 1982-92; dir. devel. Archdiocese of Denver, 1992-95, mgr. Cath. appeal, 1995-96; dir. devel. Archdiocese L.A., 1996—. Chmn. Regis Coll. Telefund, Denver, 1987-88, 90-91; treas., 1st vice chmn. Serra Trust Fund for Vocations, 1988-93, chmn., 1993-96; mem. fin. coun. St. James Parish, 1988-95, chmn. autumn bazaar, 1985, 87, mem. choir, 1993-95; sec. Mother Teresa Com., 1989; co-founder Pueblo Serra Club, 1992, Colorado Springs Serra Club, 1995, Greeley Serra Club, 1996; pres. Denver Serra Club, 1991-92; dist. 6 gov. Serra Internat., 1995-96. Recipient Share Serra Comm. award Serra Internat., 1989, Spl. Project award Dist. 6, 1986, 88, Spl. Recognition award, 1989, Outstanding Serran award, 1995, Jan Berbers award, 1996, Alumni Svc. award Regis Coll., 1990, Disting. Alumnus award Wahlert H.S., 1994. Mem. Serra Club L.A., Serra Internat. (bd. trustees 1997—, sec. bd. 1998—, chmn. internat. vocation com. 2000—). Roman Catholic. Avocations: golf, tennis, mountain climbing, handball, running. Home: 3510 Fallenleaf Pl Glendale CA 91206-4803 Office: Archdiocese LA 3424 Wilshire Blvd Los Angeles CA 90010-2241

O'CONNOR, KIM CLAIRE, chemical engineering and biotechnology educator. BS magna cum laude, Rice U., Houston, 1982; PhD, Calif. Inst. Tech., Pasadena, 1987. Postdoctoral rsch. fellow chemistry dept. Calif. Inst. Tech., Pasadena, 1987-88; postdoctoral rsch. fellow chem. engring., biochemistry, molecular biology, and cell biology depts. Northwestern U., Evanston, Ill., 1988-90; asst. prof. chem. engring. Tulane U., New Orleans, 1990-96, assoc. prof. chem. engring., 1996—, faculty molecular and cellular biology grad. program, Newcomb fellow, 1991—, co-dir. molecular and cellular biology grad. program, 1996-99, interim dir. molecular and cellular biology grad. program, 1997; mem. Tulane Cancer Ctr., 1994—; adj. assoc. prof. dept. surgery Tulane U. Sch. Medicine, 1999—; cons. in field. Contbr. articles and revs. to profl. jours.; patentee in field. Recipient NASA Space Act award, 1996, Outstanding Engring. Student award Tex. Soc. Profl. Engrs., 1982, Tulane award for excellence in undergrad. tchg., 1999; Robert A. Welch Merit scholar, 1978-82, Brown Engring. Merit scholar, 1980-82, Roy Merit scholar, 1981-82; Weyeryhaeuser Co. Found. fellow, 1982-83. Mem. Am. Assn. for Cancer Rsch., Am. Chem. Soc., Am. Inst. Chem. Engrs., Am. Soc. Engring. Edn., European Soc. Animal Cell Tech., Soc. In Vitro Biology, Tissue Engring. Soc., Sigma Xi, Tau Beta Pi, Phi Lambda Upsilon. Achievements include interdisciplinary research in engineering and the biological sciences. Office: Tulane U Dept Chem Engring Lindy Boggs Ctr Rm 300 New Orleans LA 70118

O'CONNOR, PATRICK DIGBY TAAFFE, engineer, consultant; b. London, Mar. 7, 1937; s. Philip Emmett Taaffe and Thora (Brand) O'C.; m. Ina Dziock, Oct. 15, 1963; children: Niall, Sean, Myles, Liam, Kieran. HND in Mech. Engring., RAF Tech. Coll., Henlow, Eng., 1959. Chartered engr., Eng. Engring. officer RAF, 1959-73; reliability mgr. British Aerospace Dynamics, Stevenage, Eng., 1975-93, British Rail Rsch., Derby, Eng., 1993-95; cons. engr. and mgmt. quality and reliability, Stevenage, 1995—. Author: Practical Reliability Engineering, 1981, The Practice of Engineering Management, 1994; contbr. articles to profl. jours. Mem. Royal Aero. Soc., Inst. Mech. Engrs., IEEE. Avocations: walking, music, squash, tennis. Home and Office: 62 Whitney Dr, Stevenage SG1 4BJ, England

O'CONNOR, SHEILA ANNE, freelance writer; b. Paisley, Scotland, Jan. 20, 1960; came to the U.S., 1988; d. Brian Aubrey Witham and Margaret Kirk (Reid) Davies; m. Frank Donal O'Connor, Aug. 9, 1986; children: David Michael, Andrew James, Christine Charlotte. BA in French and German, Strathclyde U., 1980, postgrad. diploma in office studies, 1981, MBA, 1992. Office asst. BBC, London, 1982-83; asst. to mng. dir. Unimatic Engrs. Ltd., London, 1983-84; freelance word processing operator London, 1984-88; staff asst. Internat. Monetary Fund, Washington, 1988-94; prin. Internat. Media Assn., Washington, 1988—. Contbr. articles to profl. jours. Mem. Am. Mktg. Assn., Bay Area Travel Writers Assn., Calif. Writers Club. Avocations: animals, travel. Home and Office: 1974 46th Ave San Francisco CA 94116-1005

O'CONNOR, SYLVIA CANNON, association legislative liaison, analyst, retired; b. Chgo., Sept. 9, 1934; d. LeGrand and Helen (West) Cannon; m. William Searls Van Bergen, Aug. 25, 1956 (div. 1983); children: Louise Van Bergen Holzhauer, Carolyn Van Bergen-Rylander, Amy E. Van Bergen; m. Raymond James O'Connor, Nov. 28, 1987. BA, Sangamon State U., 1984, MA with honors, 1986. Legis. liaison Chgo. Bar Assn., Springfield, Ill., 1983-84; asst. to bur. chief Ill. Dept. Aeronautics, Springfield, 1984-86; dir. Springfield Right to Life, 1986-89; Ill. capitol city task force coord. Am. Assn. Retired Persons, Washington, 1988-92; ret., 1992. Mem. policy com. Ill. Dept. Aging, Springfield, 1989—; chmn. fundraiser Christ Episc. Ch., Springfield, 1990, vestry mem., 1987-90; mem. Symphony Guild. Mem. PEO (v.p. 1981-82, 91—), Questers (pres.), Kappa Alpha Theta (alumnae rush chmn. 1980, pres. Alumnae Club of Sarasota 1997, 98). Republican. Episcopalian. Avocations: reading, symphony, theater, classic films, art. summer address: 4460 Deer Trail Blvd Sarasota FL 34238-5606

ODA, CHIKASHI, consultant; b. Reihoku, Kumamoto, Japan, Apr. 22, 1921; s. Oda and Oda (Tsugi) Naohiko; children: Masahiko, Mariko, Toshio. Degree, Coll. Paul Bert, Hanoi, Vietnam, 1939. Prof. Sakasegawa Jr. High Sch., Kumamoto, 1947-52; dir. Dainan Trading Co. Ltd., Tokyo, 1952-62; dep. dir. Nippon Koei Co. Ltd., Tokyo, 1962-71, dir., 1971-83, spl. advisor, 1983-94; gen. mgr. Uzo Uwani State Farm, Anambra, Nigeria, 1975-79, Nippon Koei Office, Saigon, Vietnam, 1971-75; chief mission for tech. investigation Japan Internat. Cooperative Agy., 1962-92; chmn. Vietconsult Internat. Inc., 1991-93. Recipient Chevalier de l'Ordre du Merite Agricole Royal Cambodian Govt., 1956, Chevalier de l'Ordre de Million D'Elephants et du Parasol Blanc Royal Laotian Govt., 1972, Chevalier de l'Ordre du Merite Nat. Republic of Mali, 1989. Mem. N.Y. Acad. Scis. Avocations: driving, cooking, gardening, carpentry, fishing. Home: 253-477 Fukawa, Tonemachi Kitasoma Gun, Ibaraki 300-1622, Japan Office: Nippon Koei Co Ltd, 4 Kojimachi 5-chome, Tokyo Chiyoda 102, Japan

ODA, JUN, hotel company executive; b. Kobe, Japan, Aug. 9, 1938; s. Hidesaburoh and Teruno (Miaki) O.; m. Yoshiko Isaji, Feb. 6, 1966; children: Megumi, Hiroshi. LLB, Kwansei Gakuin U., Kobe, 1961. Dir. planning and devel. Miyako Hotel, Tokyo, 1979-83, dir. sales, 1983-90, exec. mgr., food & beverage dept., 1990-94, exec. mng. dir. sales and mktg., 1994-98; exec. gen. mgr. Hotel Maiko Villa, Kobe, 1999—. Mem. Skål Internat. Avocations: tennis, golf, reading. Home: 20-9 Umegaoka Kukizakimachi, Inashiki-gun, Ibaraki-ken 300-1275, Japan Office: Hotel Maiko Villa, 18-11 Higashi Maiko-cho, Tarumi-ku Kobe 655-0047, Japan

ODA, MINORU, English literature educator; b. Kagoshima, Kyushu, Japan, Jan. 23, 1931; s. Tatsumi and Chieko (Fukushima) O.; m. Eiko Akiyoshi, Apr. 29, 1961; 1 child, Kuniko Oda Funaki. BA, Kagoshima (Japan) U., 1956; MA, Kyushu U., Fukuoka, Japan, 1959. Instr. in English Meijigakuen H.S., Kitakyushu, Japan, 1959-62; asst. in English Fukuoka U. Edn., Kurume, Japan, 1962-64; lectr. in English Fukuoka U. Edn., Kurume, 1964-66; asst. prof. English lit. Fukuoka U. Edn., Munakata, Japan, 1966-73; prof. English lit. Fukuoka U. Edn., Munakata, 1973-94, prof. English lit. Grad. Sch., 1990-94; dean faculty of edn., 1985-87; prof. emeritus Fukuoka U. Edn., Munakata, 1994—; prof. English lit. Fukuoka Jogakuin Coll., Ogori, Japan, 1994—, chmn. English cultures dept., 1996—; overseas rsch. worker Japanese Govt., U.K., 1968-69; domestic rsch. worker Kyushu U., 1984-85. Author: Characterization and Formation of Fate in the Novels of Thomas Hardy, 1974, Thomas Hardy: A Bird Deprived of Wings, 1990; contbr.: Thomas Hardy: The Harbinger of Twentieth-Century Literature, 1975, Thomas Hardy: An Annotated Bibliography of Writings About Him Volume II and Supplement for 1871-1969, 1983; fgn. corr. English Lit. in Transition: 1880-1920, 1983-90. Grantee for encouragement of sci. rsch. Ministry of Edn., Sci., and Culture, Japanese Govt., 1959, grant-in-aid for publ. sic. rsch. result Ministry of Edn., Sci. and Culture, Japanese Govt., 1989. Mem. The English Literary Soc. Japan (edtl. staff mem. Kyushu br. 1992—), The Thomas Hardy Soc. Japan (coun. mem. 1970—), All Japan Kyudo Fedn. (life hon. mem.), Fukuoka Kyudo Fedn. (coun. mem. Higashi br. 1987-94). Avocations: Kyudo (Renshi), classical music. Home: 6-7-7 Nozomigaoka, Ogori 838-0107, Japan Office: Fukuoka Jogakuin Univ, 2409-1 Ogori, Fukuoka 838-0141, Japan

ODA, SHIGERU, judge; b. Japan, Oct. 22, 1924; s. Toshio and Mioko (Horiuchi) O.; m. Noriko Sugimura, Mar. 3, 1950; children—Hiroshi, Yasuko. LLB, Imperial U., Tokyo, 1947; LLM, Yale U., 1952, JSD, 1953; LLD, Tohoku U., 1962, Bopal (India) U., 1980, N.Y. Law Sch., 1981. Assoc. prof. law Tohoku U., Sendai, Japan, 1953-59, prof., 1959-76, prof. emeritus, 1985—; spl. asst. to min. fgn. affairs, 1973-76; judge Internat. Ct. Justice, The Hague, 1976—, re-elected, 1985, 94, v.p., 1991-94; mem. Japan Acad., 1994—; bd. dirs. Internat. Devel. Law Inst. Author books, articles internat. law, law of sea. Mem. curatorium Hague Acad. Internat. Law, 1987—. Mem. Am. Soc. Internat. Law (hon.), Inst. de Droit Internat. (assoc. 1969-79, titulaire 1979—), Internat. Law Assn., Internat. Coun. Arbitration for Sport, Japanese Soc. Internat. Law. Clubs: Tokyo, Yale, Society, Koninklijke, Haagsche Country. Office: Internat Ct Justice, Peace Palace Carnegieplein 2, 2517KJ The Hague The Netherlands*

ODAGA, ASENATH BOLE (KITUOMBA), writer, poet, playwright; b. Rarieda, Kenya, July 5, 1937; d. Blasto Akumu Aum and Patricia Abuya Abok; m. James Charles Odaga, Jan. 27, 1957; children: Odhiambo, Odongo, Akelo, Adhiambo, Awuor. Attended, Kikuyu Tchr. Tng. Coll., 1955-56; BA with honors, U. Nairobi, Kenya, 1974, diploma in edn., 1974, MA, 1981. Tchr. Ch. Missionary Soc. Tchr. Tng. Coll., Ngiya, Kenya, 1957-58, Kambare Sch., 1957-58, Butere Girls Sch., Kakamega, Kenya, 1959-60; headmistress Nyakach Girls Sch., Kisumu dist., Kenya, 1961-63; asst. sec. Kenya Railways, Nairobi, 1964, Kenya Dairy Bd., Nairobi, 1965-68; sec. Kenya Libr. Svcs., Nairobi, 1968; advt. asst. East African Std., Nairobi, 1969-70; advt. and office mgr. Kerr Downey and Selby Safaris, Nairobi, 1969-70; asst. dir. curriculum and devel. program Christian Chs. Ednl. Assn., Nairobi, 1974-75; rsch. fellow Inst. African Studies, U. Nairobi, 1976-81; mgr. Thu Tinda Bookshop, 1982—, Lake Pubs. and Enterprises, 1982—; with Odaga & Assocs., 1984—. Writings include: (children's lit.) The Secret of Monkey Rock, 1966, Jande's Ambition, 1966, The Diamond Ring, 1967, The Hare's Blanket and Other Tales, 1967, The Angry Flames, 1968, Sweets and Sugar Cane, 1969, The Villager's Son, 1971, Kip on the Farm, 1972, Kip at the Coast, 1977, Kip Goes to the City, 1977, Poko Nyar Mugumba, 1978, Thu Tinda: Stories from Kenya, 1980, The Two Friends, 1981, Kenyan Folk Tales, 1981, (with Kenneth Cripwell) Look and Write Book One, 1982, (with Cripwell) Look and Write Book Two, 1982, My Home Book One, 1983, Ogilo Nungo Piny Kirom, 1983, Nyamgondho Wuod Ombare, 1986, Munde and His Friends, 1987, The Rag Ball, 1987, Munde Goes to the Market, 1987, Weche, Sigendi gi Timbe Luo Moko, 1987, Story Time, 1987, A Night on a Tree, 1992; (plays) The Bride, 1981, Simbi Nyaima (The Sunken Village), 1982, Nyamgondho, 1983; (fiction) The Shade Changes, 1984, The Storm, 1985, Between the Years, 1987, A Bridge in Time, 1987, The Silver Cup, 1987, Riana, 1987, A Taste of Life, 1988, Love Ash, Rosa and Other Stories, 1992, Luo-English Phrases, 1993, Endless Road, 1995, The Cloud Boy, 1996, Honey River, 1997, Secrets, 1999, Kisera, 1999, Jood Ogango, 1999; (other writings) Nyathini Koa e Nyuolne Nyaka Higni Adek, 1976, (with S. Kichamu Akivaga) Oral Literature: A School Certificate Course, 1982, Yesterday's Today: The Study of Oral Literature, 1984, Literature for Children and Young People in Kenya, 1985, Luo Sayings, 1991, Luo-English Dictionary, 1991; editor: The Mother of Girls and Other Stories, 1990, Why The Hyena Has a Crooked Neck, 1992, English-Luo Dictionary, 1997, Holding The Center, 1998, The Survivor, Moving to The Center, 1999; mem. editl. com. Wildlife Soc.; contbr. stories to numerous periodicals and jours. Chair bd. govs. Nyakach Girls H.S.; mem. mus. mgmt. com. Kisumu, 1984—, vice chair, 1984—; dir. Gender & Devel. Ctr., Kisumu. Recipient Best Story award Voice of Women mag., 1967, Best Play award Radio Play. Mem. Writers' Assn. Kenya (founding mem., sec. 1978-87), Kenya Assn. Univ. Women (chair Kisumu chpt. 1983-87), Kenya Bus. and Profl. Women's Club (past chair), Rarieda Women's Group, Akala Women's Group (patron), Kenya Women Writers Found. (chairperson), Internat. Bd. Books for Young People (Kenyan sect.). Avocations: reading, photography, music, cooking, walking. Office: PO Box 1743, Kisumu Kenya

ODAGAKI, TAKASHI, physics educator; b. Ochi-gun, Ehime, Japan, Oct. 7, 1945; s. Shigeo and Sue (Kashio) O.; m. Nobuko Kitayama, Aug. 18, 1976; children: Natsuki A., Marica M. BS, Kyoto U., 1968, MS, 1970, DS, 1975. Rsch. assoc. CCNY, N.Y.C., 1979-82; asst. prof. Brandeis U., Waltham, Mass., 1982-89; prof. Kyoto Inst. Tech., 1989-93, Kyushu U., Fukuoka, Japan, 1993—. Author: Introduction to Percolation Science, 1993, Science of Connectivity, 2000, Mathematical Methods in the Physical Sciences, 2000. Rsch. grantee Ministry of Edn., Tokyo, 1990—, Rsch. Corp., N.Y., 1985, Corning Japan, 1995, The Found. of Sanyo Broadcasting, 1997. Avocations: gardening, tennis, Go. Office: Kyushu U Dept Physics, 6-10-1 Hakozaki Higashi-ku, Fukuoka 812-8581, Japan

ODAMTTEN, GEORGE TAWIA, mycologist; b. Koforidua, Ghana, July 7, 1948; s. Theophilus Ayitey and Comfort Dewi (Quarcoo) O.; m. Catherine Neeney Wayoe, Apr. 18, 1974; 3 children. BSc, U. Ghana, Legon, 1973, MSc in Botany, 1977; PhD, Agrl. U., Wageningen, The Netherlands, 1986. Tchg. asst. U. Ghana, 1974-76, lectr., 1982-86, sr. lectr., 1987-91, assoc. prof., 1991-96, prof., 1996—, head dept. botany, 1988-92, dean grad. studies, 1996-97, head dept. botany, 1997—, assessor appointment and promotion

bd., 1998—, chmn. Volta Basin rsch. project, 1999—; sci. officer Ghana Atomic Energy Commn., Legon, 1977-82; vis. scholar, prof. Agrl. U., Wageningen, 1992-93; agrl. head dept. biology, food and agrl. Ghana Atomic Energy Commn., 1981-82; mem. UNU/INRA Coll. Rsch. Assocs., Tokyo, 1999—. Author: Fungi, Man's Allies or Enemies?, 1988; co-author, contbr.: Food Irradiation Processing, 1985, Medical Resources of the Tropical Forest, Biodiversity and Its Importance to Human Health, 1996, Mitigation of Stackburn in Woven Polypropylene Bagstack Maize Granis for Improved Food Security in Sub-Saharan Africa, 1996; contbr. articles to profl. jours. Rsch. fellow internat. Atomic Energy Agy., The Netherlands, 1979-81; scholar for secondary edn. Ghana Cocoa Mktg. Bd., 1962-67. Fellow African Mycological Assn. (v.p. 1995—); mem. Soc. for Econ. Botany, African Bioscis. Network (hon. sec. 1988—), N.Y. Acad. Scis. Avocations: sports, music, reading, counseling. Office: U Ghana Dept Botany, PO Box 55, Legon Accra Ghana

ODAMTTEN, HELEN MARY, English language educator; d. Solomon Edmund and Marion Adeline (Dove) O. BA in History and English, U. Southampton, Eng., 1959; Diploma in Edn., U. London, 1960; MA in Applied Linguistics, U. Essex, Colchester, Eng., 1971. Cert. in English phonetics Univ. Coll., London, 1981. Tchr. english and history, asst. housemistress Achimota Secondary Sch., 1960-62; producer, programme organizer in schs. broadcasting Ghana Broadcasting Co., 1963-66, head programme tng. sch., 1967-74; rsch. fellow Lang. Centre, U. Ghana, Legon, 1974-84, sr. rsch. fellow, 1984-98, retired, 1998; lectr. Sch. of Performing Arts, Legon, 1999—. Life mem. Ghana Soc. for Blind; mem. Internat. Phonetic Assn., Linguistics Assn. Ghana, West African Linguistic Soc., Hist. Assn. Ghana, Ghana U. Tchrs. Assn., Legon Women's Soc., Internat. Assn. Women in Radio and TV. Achievements include rsch. on TESL particularly in Ghana and other African nations. Home: D375 3 Cromer Rd, PO Box 438, Accra Ghana Office: Language Centre U Ghana, PO Box 119, Legon Ghana

ODAR-CEDERLÖF, INGEGERD ELISABET, internist, nephrologist, researcher, educator; b. Stockholm, Aug. 18, 1936; d. Bertil S. and Märta Elisabet (Thörngren) Odar; m. Sven E. Cederlöf, 1962 (dec. 1983); 1 child, Caroline. MD, Karolinska Inst., Stockholm, 1963, PhD, 1975. Lic. physician, Sweden. Asst. rsch. physician Karolinska Inst., Stockholm, 1963-65, asst. physician, 1965-77, sr. physician, 1977—, assoc. prof., 1977—. Contbr. articles to profl. jours. Mem. Swedish Med. Assn., European Dialysis and Transplant Assn., Am. Soc. Nephrology, European Asn. for Clin. Pharmacology and Therapeutics, N.Y. Acad. Scis., Internat. Soc. Nephrology. Lutheran. Avocations: music, literature, art. Home: Brahegatan 51, 11437 Stockholm Sweden Office: Njurmedicinska Kliniken, Karolinska Hosp, 17176 Stockholm Sweden

ODAWARA, KEN'ICHI, economist, educator; b. Tokyo, Mar. 8, 1933; s. Tsuneo and Kimie (Nagazumi) O.; m. Tsuneko Kurosawa, Sept. 25, 1965; children: Jun'ichi, Nobuo. BA, Jochi Sophia U., 1955, MA, 1957; postgrad., Columbia U., 1957-58; MA, Boston Coll., 1958. From rsch. asst. to assoc. prof. Jochi Sophia U., Tokyo, 1956-70, prof., 1970-97; prof. econs. and internat. rels. Nihon U., Tokyo, 1997—; lectr. Komaba Campus, U. Tokyo, 1973-84, 90-93, also others; ; cons. UN, Bankok, Thailand, 1965-68, 69-70, 74; vis. prof. and scholar Yale U., 1972, MIT, 1975, U. Pitts., 1977, Harvard U., 1994, Wharton Sch., U. Pa., 1995, Nat. Taiwan U., 1997, others; advisor on energy tax Ministry Fin., 1978, Sci. Coun. Ministry Edn., 1980-82; cons. U.S.-Japan Atomic Power Ageement, 1985; interviewer, examiner Econs. com. Fulbright Program, 1985, 91, 96; citizen-to citizen del. to Russia, 1992, 93, China, 1993, Czech., Poland, Hungary, 1996. Author: The Great American Disease, 1980, The Economic Friction Between The U.S., Europe and Japan, 1981, An Overview on International Economics, 1995, 2d edit. 1999, International Comparison of Companies and Labor Unions, 1997; author, co-editor: The Textbook of World Economy, 1981, International Political Economy, 1988; editor procs. Japan Soc. Internat. Econs. 1974-76; contbr. articles to profl. jours. Japan Found. grantee, 1978, 92, Union Nat. Econ. Assns. Japan grantee, 1983. Mem. Am. Econ. Assn., Japan Econ. Assn. Home: 1-3-4 Fujigaya, Kugenuma Fujisawa-shi 251-0031, Japan Office: 3-34-1 Shimouma, Setagaya-ku Tokyo 154-8513, Japan

ODAWARA, MASATO, physician, researcher; b. Kagoshima, Kyushu, Japan, Mar. 24, 1955; d. Tokuji and Akiko O.; Chikako Ozawa, Sept. 23, 1982; children: Sarah, Luli, Ellie. MA, Tokyo U., Tokyo, Japan, 1980, PhD, 2000. Resident Tokyo U. Hosp., Tokyo, Japan, 1980-82; staff physician Tokyo U., Tokyo, Japan, 1982-90, tchg. and rsch. assoc., 1990-92; asst. prof. U. Tsukuba, Tsukuba, Japan, 1992-2000; dir. Toranomon Hosp., Tokyo, Japan, 2000—; lectr. Oxford U., 1996-98. Contbr. articles to profl. jours. Grantee Ciba-Geigy Found. Promotion Sci., 1993, Japan Soc. Promotion Sci., 1995; recipient Ibaraki Med. Assn. Rsch. award, 1999. Mem. Am. Diabetes Assn., Japan Diabetes Soc., Japanese Soc. Molecular Medicine, N.Y. Acad. Sci., Japanese Soc. Internal Medicine (bd. qualification exam.), European Assn. Study Diabetes. Avocations: skiing, classical music, ballet, opera. Office: Toranomon Hosp, 2-2-2 Toranomon, Minato-ku Tokyo 105-8470, Japan

ODDI, SILVIO CARDINAL, archbishop; b. Morfasso, Piacenza, Italy, Nov. 14, 1910; s. Agostino and Esther (Oddi) O.; Doctorate in Canon Law, Rome, 1936; Dr. honoris causa, U. Buenos Aires, 1944, St. John's U., N.Y.C., 1981, St. Charles Sem., Phila. Ordained priest Roman Cath. Ch., 1933; named archbishop titular of Mesembria, 1953, cardinal, 1969. Mem. Vatican Diplomatic Service, Iran, Lebanon, Syria, Palestine, Egypt, France, Yugoslavia, Belgium and Luxembourg, 1936-69; spl. missions to Central Africa, Latin Am., Philippines, Cuba and Dominican Rep., 1961-74; mem. Congregations for Causes of Saints, Bishops, Oriental Chs. of Pub. Affairs of the Ch., Supreme Tribunal of Apostolic Segnatura, Amministrazionedel Patrimonio della Sede Apostolica, Congregation per l'Evangelizzazione dei Popoli, Sanctuaries of Loreto and Pompei; pontifical legate to Basilica and Convent of St. Francis (Assisi). Home: Via delle Grazie 3, 00193 Rome Italy*

ODDOYE, DAVID EMMANUEL MICHAEL, library and archival studies educator; b. Kibi, Ghana, June 4, 1930; s. Emmanuel Nicholas Victor and Lucy Matilda (Tawia) O.; m. Eleanor Asante, Aug. 18, 1960; 1 child, Emmanuel Okpoti Kofi. ALA, Leeds Coll. Commerce, Eng., 1954; FLA, Manchester (Eng.) Coll. Tech., 1962. Mem. Ghana Libr. Bd., 1950-82; dep. dir. Ghana Libr. Bd., Accra, 1966-82; part-time lectr. DLAS Dept. Libr. and Archival Studies, U. Ghana, Legon, 1982-83; sr. lectr. U. Ghana, Legon, 1983—, ag. head dept., 1987-90, sr. lectr., 1990—. Fellow Carnegie Corp., 1953, Brit. Coun., 1975-77, UNESCO, 1979. Anglican. Avocations: reading, bird watching, gardening. Home: PO Box 815, Accra Ghana Office: U Ghana, PO Box 60, PO Box 25, Legon Ghana

ODDSSON, DAVID, prime minister of Iceland; b. Reykjavik, Iceland, Jan. 17, 1948; s. Oddur Olafsson and Ingibjörg Kristin (Ludviksdottir) O.; m. Astridur Thorarensen, 1970. Grad., Reykjavik Sec. Grammar Sch., 1970; grad. lawyer, U. Iceland, 1976. Chief clk. Reykjavik Theatre, 1970-72; parliamentary reporter Morgunbladid newspaper, 1973-74; with Almenna Bokafelagid Pubs., 1975-76; office mgr. Reykjavik Health Ins. Fund, 1976-78, mng. dir., 1978-82; mayor City of Reykjavik, from 1982; elected vice-chmn. Independence Party, 1989, elected chmn., 1991; M.P. Althing, 1991; prime min. Govt. of Iceland, Reykjavik, 1991—; prodr. numerous radio programs Iceland State Broadcasting Svc., 1968-75; bd. dirs. Almenna Bokafelagid Pubs. Author: Sjalfstaedisstefnan (The Independence Movement), 1981, (plays) (with T. Eldjarn and H. Gunnlaugsson) Eg Vil Audga Mitt Land (For My Country's Benefit), 1974, (with H. Gunnlaugsson) Islendingaspjoll (Icelandic Confabulations), 1975, (TV dramas) Robert Eliasson Kemur Heim fra Utlondum (Robert Eliasson Returns from Abroad), 1977, Kusk a Hvitflibbanum (Stains on the White Collar), 1981; translator: Eistland-Smathjod undir Oki Erlends Valds (Estonia, a Small Nation under the Yoke of a Foreign Power, by Anders Küng), 1973, A Couple of Days Without Gudny, 1997. Bd. dirs. Independence Party Youth Fedn., 1973-75, Vardberg (Assn. for Western Cooperation), 1973-77, Reykjavik Mcpl. Youth Summer Sch., 1974-82; mem. Reykjavik City Coun., from 1974, mem. exec. com., from 1980, chmn., from 1982, mem. supervisory com., 1978-80; mem. negotiating com. State Social Security Inst., others, 1976-81; mem. exec. com. Independence Party, 1979—; mem. Reykjavik Traffic Com., 1974-78, Reykjavik Mcpl. Bd. Edn., 1974-82; bd. dirs. Kjarvalsstadir Art Mus., Reykjavik, 1974-82, vice-chmn., 1974-78; mem. Reykjavik Youth Coun., 1974-82, chmn., 1974-78; mem. Reykjavik Bd. Freshwater Fisheries & Pisciculture, 1974-82, vice chmn., 1974-78; chmn. exec. com. Reykjavik Arts Festival, 1976-78; mem. negotiating com. for merger of Landsvirkjun (Nat. Power Co.) and Laxarvirkjun Power Co., 1980-81; mem. bldg. com. Reykjavik Mcpl. Theatre, 1975-79, also from 1982, vice chmn., 1975-79, chmn., from 1982; chmn. bd. dirs. Shop and Office Workers' Pension Fund, from 1982; mem. editorial com. History of Reykjavik, from 1981, chmn., from 1982. Office: Prime Minister's Office, Stjórnarrádshusid v/Laekjartorg, 150 Reykjavik Iceland*

ODDY, WILLIAM ANDREW, museum official, author, editor; b. Bradford, Yorkshire, Eng., Jan. 6, 1942; s. William Tingle and Hilda Florence (Dalby) O.; m. Patricia Anne Whitaker, Aug. 4, 1965; children: William Guy, Frances Sarah. BA, Oxford (Eng.) U., 1964, BSc, 1965, MA, 1969, DSc, 1994. Sci. officer Brit. Mus., London, 1966-69, sr. sci. officer, 1969-75, prin. sci. officer, 1975-81, head conservation, 1981-85, keeper of conservation, 1985—; mem. numerous coms. relating to conservation of antiquities; adv. editor Butterworth/Heinemann, Oxford, 1990—; Chester Beatty lectr. Royal Soc. Arts, London, 1982; hon. rsch. fellow Univ. Coll., London, 1992; M. Victor Leventritt lectr. Harvard U. Art Mus., 1996; Forbes Prize lectr. to Internat. Inst. for Conservation, 1996. Author, editor: The Art of the Conservator, 1992; editor or joint editor 8 conf. procs.; contbr. over 200 articles, notes and revs. to scholarly jours. Fellow Soc. Antiquaries London, Internat. Inst. for Conservation, Worshipful Co. Goldsmiths (freeman), also other archaeology and mus. conservation orgns. Avocations: travel, church architecture. Office: The British Museum, Dept Conservation, London WC1B 3DG, England

O'DEA, SANDRA RENEE, sales professional; b. Oakland, Calif., Aug. 11, 1964; d. Jack Peter and Mary Elizabeth (Azevedo) Freethy; m. Timothy Desmond O'Dea, June 17, 1989; children: Kelsey Mary and Dakota Jack (twins). BA, Calif. State U., Chico, 1987. Adminstrv. asst. Fred Hutchinson Cancer Rsch. Ctr., Seattle, 1992, Toko's Med. Co., Seattle, 1992-93; sales supr., account exec. Trader Pub., Burlingame, Calif., 1993—. Mem. AAUW. Avocations: motocross, exercising, reading, family. Home: 137 Capstone Ct Napa CA 94559-4277

ODEGARD, MARK ERIE, geophysicist, consultant; b. Plentywood, Mont., Nov. 1, 1940; s. Harold Theodore and Edna Marcella (Jacobsen) O.; m. Elisabeth Snow, June 17, 1967; 1 child, Liv. AA, Dawson Coll., Glendive, Mont., 1960; BA, U. Mont., 1962; MS, Oreg. State U., 1965; PhD, U. Hawaii, 1975. Asst. prof. Hawaii Inst. Geophysics, Honolulu, 1974-78; dir. geology and geophysics program Office Naval Rsch., Arlington, Va., 1978-81; assoc. prof. N.Mex. State U., Las Cruces, 1981-83; staff rsch. geophysicist Sohio Petroleum Co., Dallas, 1983-86; prin. scientist Basalt Waste Isolation Program, Richland, Wash., 1986-88; rsch. assoc. Unocol Sci. & Tech., Brea, Calif., 1988-93; mgr. Potential Fields Group, Unocal, Sugar Land, Tex., 1993-98; bd. dirs., v.p. U.S. ops. Geophys. Exploration Tech., Sugar Land, 1998—. Contbr. over 50 articles to sci. jours. Chmn. San Bernardino County (Calif.) Svc. Area 48 Adv. Com., 1989-91; vice chmn. Chino Hills Planning Commn., 1992-93; mem. Chino Hills (Calif.) Mcpl. Adv. Coun., 1990-91. Recipient Antarctica Svc. medal U.S. Congress, 1966. Mem. Soc. Exploration Geophysicists, Am. Geophys. Union, Sigma Xi, Am. Planning Assn. Avocations: skiing, golf, hunting, fishing, marathon running. Home: 3418 El Dorado Blvd Missouri City TX 77459-2414 Office: Geophys Exploration Tech 12946 Dairy Ashford Rd Ste 250 Sugar Land TX 77478-3160

O'DELL, JOAN ELIZABETH, lawyer, mediator, business executive, educator; b. East Dubuque, Ill., May 3, 1932; d. Peter Emerson and Olive (Bonnet) O'D.; children: Dominique R., Nicole L. BA cum laude, U. Miami, 1956, JD, 111958. Bar: Fla. 1958, U.S. Supreme Ct. 1972, D.C. 1974, Ill. 1978, Va. 1987; cert. mediator; lic. real estate broker, Ill., Va. Trial atty. SEC, Washington, 1959-60; asst. state atty. Office State Atty., Miami, Fla., 1960-64; asst. county atty. Dade County Atty.'s Office, Miami, 1964-70; county atty. Palm Beach County Atty.'s Office, West Palm Beach, Fla., 1970-71; regional gen. counsel Region IV EPA, Atlanta, 1971-73; assoc. gen. counsel EPA, Washington, 1973-77; sr. counsel Nalco Chem. Co., Oakbrook, Ill., 1977-78; v.p., gen. counsel Angel Mining, Washington and Tenn., 1979-96; pres. S.W. Land Investments, Miami, 1979-88; v.p.m geb, ciybsek Events U.S.A., Washington, 1990—. Bd. dirs. Tucson Women's Found., 1982-84, U. Ariz. Bus. and Profl. Women's Club, Tucson, 1981-85; bd. dirs. LWV, Tucson, 1981-85, pres., 1984-85; bd. dirs. LWV Ariz., 1984-85, chmn. nat. security study; bd. dirs. LWV, Palm Beach County, Fla., 1990-92; mem. Exec. Women's Coun., Tucson, 1982-85. Mem. Fla. Bar Assn., D.C. Bar Assn., Va. State Bar Assn., Ill. Bar Assn. Avocations: camping, hiking, skiing.

O'DELL, WILLIAM FRANCIS, retired business executive, writer; b. Detroit, Jan. 24, 1909; s. Frank Trevor and Garnett (Aikman) O'C.; m. Bess Baer, June 10, 1933 (dec. July 1986); m. Helen M. Porter, May 16, 1987 (dec. 1997); children: Peggy, David. B.S., U. Ill., 1930. With Penton Pub. Co., 1933-37; v.p. Ross Fed. Research Corp., 1937-44; mng. dir. Statis Research Co., 1944-45; pres. Market Facts, Inc., 1946-64, chmn., 1964-74; pres. ROC Internat., 1961-64; mem. census adv. bd. Dept. Commerce, 1963-73; prof. mktg. McIntire Sch. Commerce U. Va., 1965-78; vis. prof. Chinese U. of Hong Kong, 1969. Author: Marketing Decision, 1968, Marketing Decision Making, 1976, 4th edit., 1988, How to Make Lifetime Friends—With Peers and Parents, 1978, Twelve Families—An American Experience, 1981, Effective Business Decision Making and the Educated Guess, 1991; mem. editorial rev. bd. Jour. Mktg., 1964-73. Recipient Leader in Mktg. award, 1970, Jour. Mktg. Research editorial award, 1979; William F. O'Dell professorship in commerce named in his honor U. Va., 1983. Mem. Am. Mktg. Assn. (pres. 1960-61), Colonnade Club (Charlottesville), Rotary, Delta Upsilon, Beta Gamma Sigma. Home: 5707 Junonia Ct Fort Myers FL 33908-1667

ODEN, FAY GILES, writer, educator; b. Nashville, Nov. 17, 1929; d. Charley Jr. and Phenizie (Hodge) Giles; m. Edward A. Oden, Apr. 16, 1961. BA, Tenn. A&I State U., Nashville, 1951. Cert. in cosmetology. Elem. tchr. Cin. Pub. Schs., 1954-84, substitute tchr., 1985-94; author, pub. Tennedo Pubs., Cin., 1992—; supervising tchr. Ctrl. State Coll./U. Cin., 1968-75; vol. tutor; storyteller at various schs. and day care ctrs., Cin., 1993—. Author: Calvin and His Video Camera, 1993, (inspirational poetry) Believe, 1995, Discover, 1998; author, illustrator: Where Is Calvin?, 1993, I Dream A Journey, 1997, Calvin's Curtain Call, 1999; author, editor: (pamphlet) The Flying School, 1995, (coloring book, poetry illustrated) The Good Ol' Days, 1999. Fin. sec. New Hope Bapt. Ch. Credit Union, Cin., 1982; vol. Pres.'s Coun. for a Drug Free Am., Cin., 1986; pub. speaker and mistress of ceremonies; piano tchr. to talented children, 1994—. Recipient award for Dedicated Vol. Svc., Cin. Charter of Ohio Credit Union League, 1983, other awards. Mem. Silverton Neighborhood Club (sec. 1987), Urban League of Greater Cin., Zeta Soc. Pub. Authors, Zeta Phi Beta. Avocations: music, cooking. Home: 6315 Elwynne Dr Cincinnati OH 45236-4013

ODENING, KLAUS, zoologist, parasitologist, researcher; b. Leipzig, Saxony, Germany, Dec. 29, 1932; s. Will and Hanna (Ulbricht) O.; m. Waltraud Wiegand, Aug. 18, 1956; children: Karen, Sven, Frank. Diploma in Biology, U. Halle, Saale, Germany, 1954, D in Natural Sci., 1958; Habil. in Natural Sci., U. Berlin, 1965. Sci. worker U., Jena, Germany, 1954-59; sr. sci. worker Acad. Scis., Berlin, 1959-72, head dept. ecology, 1973-86, head dept. parasitology, 1986-91; head dept. parasitology Inst. Zoo Biol. & Wildlife Rsch., Berlin, 1992—; prof. Acad. Scis., Berlin, 1976—, ret. Contbr. articles to profl jours. including Parasitology, Vet. Parasitology, Advances in Parasitology, and Zool. Jahrb. Syst., 1965—; editor-in-chief (German jour.) Applied Parasitology, 1980-96; mem. editl. bd. Folia Parasitologica, 1995—. Office: Inst Zoo Biol/Wildlife Rsch, PF 601103, D-10252 Berlin Germany

ODESCALCHI, EDMOND PÉRY, international financial consultant, author; b. Budapest, Hungary, Oct. 11, 1928; came to U.S., 1950; s. Prince Bela and Princess Charlotte (de Bay) O.; m. Esther de Kando, Sept. 30, 1961; children: Daniel, Dominic. Student, Cornell U., 1951, U. Pa., 1956-57; MS in Econs., St. Andrews U., Scotland, 1959. Adminstrv. asst. French Govt., Baden, Fed. Republic Germany, 1948-50; world trade specialist IBM Corp., Poughkeepsie, N.Y., 1952-60, project mgr., 1960-74; devel. mgr. IBM Corp., East Fishkill, N.Y., 1974; pres. Global Tech., Inc., N.Y.C., 1975-91; Internat. fin. cons., 1975-93. Author: The Global Arena, 1973, Faces of Reality, 1975, The Third Crown, 1997; contbr. articles to profl. jours. Mem. Rep. Nat. Com., 1984—. Mem. Bus. Cons. Assn., Am. Mus. Natural History (assoc.), Internat. Platform Assn., Acad. Polit. Sci. Home and Office: 1020 Freedom Rd Pleasant Valley NY 12569-7636

ODGERS, PETA MICHELLE, fire and emergency services administrator; b. Perth, Australia, Jan. 31, 1967; d. Dennis Samuel and Pamela Isabelle (Matthews) O. BS in Psychology with honors, U. Western Australia, Perth, 1990, diploma in edn., 1992, PhD, 1996. Registered psychologist. Rsch. asst. psychology dept. U. Western Australia, Perth, 1988-96, tutor Grad. Sch. Edn., 1992-96, lectr. Grad. Sch. Edn., 1994-96, rsch. asst. Grad. Sch. Edn., 1995-96; sr. rschr. Turning Point Alcohol and Drug Ctr., Melbourne, Australia, 1996-97; sr. rsch. officer Fire and Emergency Svc. of Western Australia, Perth, 1997—; hon. rsch. fellow U. Melbourne, 1996-97; cons. Western Australia Premier's Drug Task Force, Perth, 1995-97, Victorian Premier's Task Force on Drug Abuse, Melbourne, 1996-97; rsch. fellow U. Western Australia, 1997-99. Author: (book chpt.) Drug Use in Australia, 1998; contbr. articles to profl. jours. Vol. cons. on drug edn. Edn. Dept. Western Australia, 1995—; vol. cons. Princess Margaret Hosp. for Children, Australia, 1997—, Moreland Hall Drug Ctr., Melbourne, 1996, Life Edn. Ctr., Wesley Mission, Sydney, Australia, 1993—. Recipient Cameron prize in edn. Western Australian Inst. for Ednl. Rsch., 1996-97; postgrad. scholar Nat. Drug Strategy, 1993-96. Mem. Psychology Assn. Western Australia. Office: Fire and Emergency Svc WA, 480 Hay St, 6000 Perth Australia

ODIER, PIERRE ANDRE, educator, writer, photographer, artist; b. Lausanne, Switzerland, May 24, 1940; came to U.S., 1959; s. Leon Odier and Gretha (Vesper) Hough; m. Mary Ellen Patton, Apr. 2, 1967 (div. Apr. 1984); children: Yvette, Debbi. BA, U. Puget Sound, 1967; MFA, Calif. State U., L.A., 1974; postgrad., UCLA, 1976-83. Cert. tchr. Calif. Owner restaurant The End, Tacoma, Wash., 1961-64; owner gallery Place des Arts, Tacoma, 1964-65; interpreter Weyerhauser Corp., Tacoma, 1964; chairperson dept. fine arts Hoover H.S., Glendale, Calif., 1967—. Author: The Rock, A History of Alcatraz, 1983, Lummis Inside his Habitat, 1977 (State Hist. Soc. award 1981), A Discovery of Age, Students Look at Aging Process, 1992, A Discovery of Destitution, Students Look at Extreme Poverty; editor: Nat. Photographers Assn. quar., 1980-84. Served with U.S. Army, 1959-62. Recipient Tchr. of Yr. award Parent Tchrs. Student Assn., Glendale, Calif., 1979, Tchr. of Yr. award Glendale c. of C., 1983, Hon. Tchr. award Puiching Sch. China, 1994. Mem. Glendale Tchrs. Assn. (contract negotiator 1977), Nat. Photography Instrs. Assn. (chmn. election com., pres. 1980-85, chairperson conv. 1982), China Exploration and Rsch. Soc. (v.p., editor newsletter, expdn. leader China, Mongolia, Siberia, Russia, U.S.A. 1994), NEA, Adventurers Club (pres. 1999-2000), Explorers Club. Democrat. Lutheran. Home: 1255 Hill Dr Los Angeles CA 90041-1610 Office: Hoover High Sch 651 Glenwood Rd Glendale CA 91202-1597

ODIJK, THEO, physical chemist, educator; b. Rotterdam, The Netherlands, Sept. 30, 1952; s. Cornelus Theodorus Odijk and Johanna Maria Christina Kloos. Masters, State U. at Leiden, The Netherlands, 1978, Doctorate, 1983. Sci. asst. U. Leiden, 1978-82, postdoctoral grad., 1983-84, lectr., 1985-87; prof. Tech. U., Delft, The Netherlands, 1987—; adj. prof. Leiden U., The Netherlands, 1999—. Contbr. articles to profl. jours. Recipient Gold medal Royal Dutch Soc. Chemistry, 1986. Avocations: philosophy, lit., sports. Office: Theory of Complex Fluids, PO Box 11036, 2301 EA Leiden The Netherlands

ODINAK, MIROSLAV MIKHAILOVICH, physician, researcher; b. Borovtsi, Ukraine, Russia, Jan. 19, 1946; s. Michael Vasiljevich and Elena Ivanovna (Shevchik) O.; m. Klaudia Alexandrovna Zelejnaj, Feb. 3, 1968; children: Oleg Miroslavovich, Olga Miroslavovna. MD, Saratov, Russia, 1969. Sr. physician Regiment of Air Force, Sethcha, 1969-73; physician in nervous diseases Mil. Med. Acad., St. Petersburg, 1973-75, sr. ordinator, 1975-79, tchr., 1979-89, sr. tchr., 1989-94, chief tchr., 1994—; neurologist Ministry Defence, 1994—. Editor: Topical Diagnostics of Diseases and Traumas of Nervous System, 1996, Differential Diagnostics of Nervous System, 1999; author: Epilepsy, 1997, Vessels Pathology of Brain, 1997. Col. Ministry Defence, 1994—. Recipient numerous mil. medals Pres. Russia, Competition prize Internat. Acad. Nature and Soc., 1999. Mem. Assn. Neurologists (pres. 1997—), Nat. Assn. Neurologists (gov. mem. 1994—), Acad. Natural Scis. (corr. mem. 1999—). Democrat. Avocations: numismatics, woodcutting. Home: Kompositorov 29-1-415, 194355 Saint Petersburg Russia Office: Mil Med Acad, Desnoj 2, 194044 Saint Petersburg Russia

ODINTSOVA, NELLY ADOLPHOVNA, marine biologist, researcher; b. Novosibirsk, Russia, Dec. 23, 1954; d. Adolph Iosiphovich and Asia Abdurachmanovna (Mychametzaynova) L.; m. Viacheslav Sergeevich Odintsov; children: Alekzandra, Antonina. Grad. in biology, Far East State U., Vladivistok, Russia, 1977; PhD, Inst. Cytology, St. Petersburg, Russia, 1984; Doct. d., Medicine U., Vladivostok, 1999. Asst. Inst. Marine Biology, Vladivostok, 1977-79, jr. rschr., 1979-84, rschr., 1984-89, sr. rschr., 1989—, chief group, 1993—. Contbr. articles to sci. jours., including FEBS Letters, In Vitro, Biochim, Biophys. Acta. Grantee Internat. Soros Found., 1994-96, Russian Found. Fundamental Rsch., 1996-98. Mem. Russian Acad. Scis. (acad. sec. Far East br. 1994—), European Soc. Tissue and Cell Cultures. Achievements include part patent for cell culture of marine mollusks. E-mail: anodin@mail.ru. Office: RAS Inst Marine Biology, Palchevsky St 17, 690 041 Vladivostok Russia

ODLAND, BARBARA, medical association administrator; b. Bucyrus, Ohio, Mar. 25, 1923; d. E. Blair and Gladys Morgan (MacNaily) Ruhl; m. Paul Kenneth Odland, Sept. 16, 1945; children: Judy, Blair, Bruce. BS, Coll. William and Mary, 1944. Tour translator Colombia, 1960; tchr. Spanish Beloit (Wis.) Cath. H.S., 1967-86; dir. children's choir 1st Luth. Ch., Janesville, 1967-86; TV coord. 1st Luth. Ch., Janesville, Wis., 1984—; program coord. Pan Am. Drs. Assn., U.S.-Mex., 1972—, Mex.-Wis. orthop. meeting, Mexico City, 1976; translator Mercy Hosp., Janesville, City Health, Janesville, Riverview Clinic, Janesville. Guide Rotary Gardens, Janesville, 1994—. Named Tchr. of Yr., Cath. Diocese, Madison. Mem. AAUW, Women of Note, Janesville Art League. Home: 2255 N Parker Dr Janesville WI 53545-0715

ODLIND, BO GUNNAR, physician, educator; b. Östersund, Sweden, Jan. 13, 1946; s. Anders Wilhelm and Barbro Rut (Röste) O.; m. Viveca Lena Odeen, Sept. 25, 1970; children: Clara Cecilia, Jenny Katarina. MD, Uppsala (Sweden) U., 1972, PhD in Pharmacology, 1978. Rschr., tchr. pharmacology Uppsala U., 1972-78; physician internal medicine and nephrology U. Hosp. Uppsala, 1978-83; med. dir. Pharmacia Uppsala Sweden, 1983-88; sr. dir. Astra Arcus, Södertälje, Sweden, 1988-96; prof., head pharmacotherapeutic divsn. Med. Product Agy., Uppsala, 1996-2000; ptnr. European Regulatory and Drug Devel. Svcs., Uppsala, 2000—. Fellow Royal Soc. Medicine, Faculty Pharm. Medicine; mem. Internat. Soc. Nephrology, Swedish Med. Assn. Avocations: hunting, skiing, badminton, music. Home: Nordfeldts Vag 13, 64551 Strängnäs Sweden Office: EUREDA AB, Uppsala Sci Park, Dag Hammarskjoldsvag 10C, 75183 Uppsala Sweden

ODLUM, GEORGE WILLIAM, government official; b. Castries, Saint Lucia, June 24, 1934. Attended, St. Mary's Coll. St. Lucia, North Western Polytechnic, London; BA in English with honors, U. Bristol, England; MA in Politics Philosophy and Econs., Magdalen Coll. Oxford U. Pres. of the union Bristol U., England, 1959; perm. sec. min. of trade St. Lucia, 1961-64; economist commonwealth secretariat Marlborough House, London, 1964-67; exec. sec. coun. mins. West Indies Associated States, 1967-71; pres. Farmers and Workers Union, 1971-79; dep. prime min. and min. of trade, industry, tourism and fgn. affairs, 1979-82; publisher Crusader Newspaper, 1982-93; perm. rep. of St. Lucia U.N., 1994-96; fgn. min. St. Lucia, 1998—. Actor in numerous radio and stage plays; producer St. Lucia's Prodn. at Carifta Arts Festival, 1969. Rep. St. Lucia at Commonwealth Heads of Govt. in Zambia, 1979, Non-Alignment Movement Conf. in New Delhi, 1980, on admission to Orgn. of Am. States, 1979. Mem. Commonwealth Parliamentary Assn. Office: Min Fgn Affairs & Internat Trade, Block B Waterfront, Castries Saint Lucia*

ÖDMAN, CLAES STURE BERTIL, communications company executive; b. Malmo, Sweden, Apr. 19, 1965; s. Jan Sture Bertil and AnneMargret Bertilsdotter (Eriksson) V.; m. Lisa Frederika Fagberg, June 19, 1999. MBA, U. Tech., Gothenburg, Sweden, 1990; MSc in Engring. Physics, Chalmers U. Tech., Gothenburg, 1990. Trainee Saab Scania Combitech, Gothenburg, 1990-91; area mgr. Saab Marine Electronics, Gothenburg, 1991-94, Ericsson Radio Sys., Stockholm, 1994-98; v.p. Ericsson Taiwan Ltd., Taipei, 1998—. Fax: 886 2 2747 7412. E-mail: claes.odman@ert.ericsson.se. Office: Ericsson Taiwan Ltd, 4 Fl # 33 Ln 11 Kuang Fu N, Taipei Taiwan

ÖDMANN, JAN-CHRISTER, novelist, publicist; b. Stockholm, Apr. 10, 1920; arrived in France, 1971; s. John Gustaf and Rut Inga (Hagström) Ö.; m. Ella Fischbach-Engelberg, 1943 (div. 1957); children: Maria, Viveca, Sam; m. Anna Christina Norin, 1959 (div. 1961); 1 child, Christopher; m. Birgitta Margareta Lönnegardh, Oct. 21, 1962. ML, U. Stockholm, 1945. Assessor Dist. Judge, Kristinehamn, Sweden, 1946-48; mem. Magistrates' Ct., Kristinehamm, Sweden, 1948; officer Royal Bd. Civil Aviation, Stockholm, 1949-56; 1st asst. sec. Swedish Ministry Home Affairs, Stockholm, 1956-62; prin. asst. sec. Swedish Ministry Social Affairs, Stockholm, 1962-71; resigned, 1971. Author: (novels) Munk i Neutralien, 1968, Den missÿckade presentatören, 1971, Mission en Neutralie, 1983, Adieu à un été suédois, 1984, Kämpa för livet, 1985, Nya testamentet, 1986, Den inbillade rike, 1987, Munk i Neutralien-20 ar efterat, 1988, Doktorns pojke, 1992, (short stories, poems) Brackefejden, 1972; contbr. articles, short stories and poems to newspapers and mags. Mem. Sällskapet (Stockholm), New Sporting Club (Geneva). Roman Catholic. Avocations: painting, tennis. Home: 1068 Les Vertes Campagnes, F-01170 Gex France

ODNOPOSOFF, RICARDO, violinist, educator; b. Buenos Aires, Feb. 24, 1914; s. Mauricio and Juana Tauba (Wainstein) O.; naturalized U.S. citizen, 1953; m. Irmtraut Baum, Mar. 20, 1965. M.Mus., High Sch. Music, Berlin, 1932. Violinist, playing in concerts throughout the world, 1932—; tchr. U. Caracas, Venezuela, 1943-47; taught summer courses Mozarteum, Salzburg, 1956-60, Internat. Summer Acad., Nice, France, 1959-73; prof. High Sch. for Music, Vienna, 1956—, prof. emeritus, 1975—; tchr. High Sch. for Music, Stuttgart, Germany, 1964-94, Music High Sch., Zurich, 1975-84. Decorated chevalier des Arts et Lettres, France, chevalier de l'Ordre Rose Blanche, Finland, comdr. Order of Leopold II, Belgium, Grosses Verdienstkreuz des Verdienstordens, Federal Republic of Germany, Mun Hwa Po Chang, Republic of South Korea, medal for Merit, Argentina, medal of Honor in Silver, City of Vienna, 1979, Ehrenkreuz fü r Wissenschaft und Kunst I. Klasse, Austria, Medal of Merit in gold Govt. Baden-Wü rttemberg, W.Ger., others. Lodge: Masons. Home: 27 Singerstrasse, Vienna 1010, Austria

ODOM, PATRICIAN ANN (PATT ODOM), artist, educator; b. Hattiesburg, Miss., Nov. 21, 1942; d. Charles Casey and Katie Clara (Stringer) O.; m. Robert Frank Drake, Aug. 25, 1964 (div. Jan. 1970); children: Robert Charles, Thomas Casey. BS in Drawing and Painting, U. So. Miss., 1964, M in Art Edn., 1975; studied with Hon Chee Hee, U. Hawaii, 1968; studied with Douglas Walton, La. Tech. U., 1982; student, Ringling Sch. Art & Design, 1994; postgrad., U. Tenn., Arrowmont, 1994-96; numerous art workshops, 1987-98. Tchr. art E. Elem. Sch., Ocean Springs, Miss., 1966-67, Pecan Park, Ocean Springs, Miss., 1971-75, Ocean Springs H.S., 1975-79; art instr., gallery dir. Gulf Coast C.C., Gautier, Miss., 1980-99; guest lectr. Hinds C.C., 1997; guest spkr. Miss. Art Mus., Pascagoula Garden Club; panelist spkr. Miss. Assn. Colls. Conf., 1997; motorator Cmty. Bridges Project, Biloxi, Miss., 1997; guest spkr. Ocean Springs Art Assn, 1998. Designed logo for Gulf Coast YMCA, Hattiesburg Racquetball and Fitness Ctr.; executed mural at Keesler Air Force Base, 1992; represented in permanent collections 1st Magnolia Bank, Biloxi, Miss.; prin. works include sculpture Sen. John Stennis, Seabees Base, Gulfport, Miss., 1988; works appear in numerous calendars, (book) In Harmony with Nature, 1989. Recipient Nat. Tchrs Award of Excellence, 1989, Purchase award Cottonlandia Mus. Art, Greenville, Miss., 1998, Mobile Mus. Art, Ala., 1996, 1st place Miss. Art Colony Traveling Show, Hattiesburg, 1997. Mem. South Miss. Art Assn., Art Wave (show chair 1980-99), Jackson County Arts Coun., Singing River Art Assn. (show chair 1988), Ocean Springs Art Assn. (bd. dirs. 1986-87, 95-96, 99, pres. 1994, receiving chair 1988, receiving chair for annual show 1984-86, past v.p. 1980-81), Biloxi Art Assn., La. Mus. Art, Mobile Art Assn., Gulf Coast Art Assn., Fairhope Art Assn., Slidell Art League, Nart Art Edn. Assn., Miss. C.C. Art Instructors, Kappa Kappa Iota, Delta Psi Omega. A. Avocations: painting, gardening, commercial art. E-mail: patto@ametro.net. Home: 306 Porter St Ocean Springs MS 39564-3714

O'DONNELL, EDWARD EARL, physicist; b. Hobbs, N.Mex., Sept. 16, 1937; s. Thomas E. and Bessie L. (Rhodes) O'D.; m. H. Kathryn Jones; children: Damon L., Dari L., Doran L., Devon L. BS, N.Mex. State U., 1961, MS, 1963, PhD, 1965. Rsch. scientist Kaman Scis. Corp., Colorado Springs, Colo., 1965-74, Sci. Applications Internat. Corp., Colorado Springs, 1974-81; v.p. Sci. Applications Internat. Corp., Albuquerque, N.Mex., 1981—; mentor, program mgr. Sci. Applications Internat. Corp., Albuquerque, 1994—. Contbr. articles to profl. jours. Recipient Citation, U.S. Navy, 1996. Mem. AIAA. Avocations: fishing, reading. Home: 981-3 Highway 98E # 141 Destin FL 32541-2561 Office: Sci Applications Internat Corp 2109 Airpark Rd SE Albuquerque NM 87106-3258

O'DONNELL, EDWARD JOSEPH, bishop, former editor; b. St. Louis, July 4, 1931; s. Edward Joseph and Ruth Mary (Carr) O'D. Student, Cardinal Glennon Coll., 1949-53; postgrad., Kenrick Sem., 1953-57. Ordained priest Roman Cath. Ch., 1957, consecrated bishop, 1984; assoc. pastor in 5 St. Louis parishes, 1957-77; pastor St. Peter's Ch., Kirkwood, Mo., 1977-81; assoc. dir. Archdiocesan Commn. on Human Rights, 1962-70; dir. Archdiocesan Radio-TV Office, 1966-68, Archdiocesan Vocation Council, 1965; editor St. Louis Rev., 1968-81; vicar-gen. Archdiocese of St. Louis, 1981-84, aux. bishop, 1984-94; bishop Diocese of Lafayette, Lafayette, LA, 1994—; bd. dirs. Nat. Cath. Conf. for Interracial Justice, 1980-85, NAACP, 1964-66, Urban League St. Louis, 1962-68; chmn. Interfaith Clergy Coun. Greater St. Louis, 1963-67. Named to Golden Dozen Internat. Soc. Weekly Newspaper Editors, 1970, 77. Mem. Cath. Press Assn., Nat. Assn. TV Arts and Scis. Office: PO Box 3387 Lafayette LA 70502-3387

O'DONNELL, JOHN JOSEPH, JR., optometrist; b. Phila., Oct. 26, 1956; s. John Joseph and Mary Agnes (Hungrige) O'D.; m. Jane Susan Betz, June 28, 1980; children: Kathryn Marie, John Joseph III, Michael Charles. BS in Biology, St. Joseph U., 1978; BS in Ocular Sci., Pa. Coll. Optometry, 1981, OD with honors, 1983. Cardio-pulmonary perfusionist Hosp. U. Pa., Phila., 1978-80; staff optometrist Pa. Eye Assocs., Harrisburg, 1983-85; chief optometric svcs. Meml. Eye Inst., Harrisburg, 1986-93; optometrist, ptnr. Premier Eye Care Group, Harrisburg, 1994—; trustee Optometric Svc. Corp. Pa., Harrisburg, 1989. Contbr. articles to profl. jours. Fellow Am. Acad. Optometry; mem. Am. Optometric Assn., Pa. Optometric Assn. (trustee 1987-94, pres. 1994), Ctrl. Pa. Optometric Soc. (pres. 1985-86). Republican. Roman Catholic. Avocations: computers, writing, photography, digital imaging processing. Office: Premier Eye Care Group Inc 92 Tuscarora St Harrisburg PA 17104-1691

O'DONNELL, KATHLEEN MARY, social services administrator; b. Bklyn., Dec. 29, 1965; d. Ronald Joseph and Maureen Grace (Nutting) O'D. BA in Psychology, Tchr. of Handicapped, Kean Coll. N.J., 1990; MS in Psychiat. Rehab., U. Medicine and Dentistry N.J., 2000. Cert. social worker. Nursing asst. Carrier Found., Belle Mead, N.J., 1988; tutor Kean Coll. N.J., Union, 1989; case mgr. Project Live, Inc., Newark, N.J., 1990-92, U. Medicine & Dentistry N.J., New Brunswick, 1992—. Mem. NASW, Internat. Assn. Psychiat. Rehab. Svcs. Avocations: bowling, dancing, music, travel.

O'DONNELL, STELLA RAYNER, pharmacology educator; b. Harrogate, Yorkshire, Eng., July 6, 1938; d. James Booth and Irene (Rayner) Gregory; m. James Hamilton O'Donnell, Dec. 14, 1963 (dec. Apr. 1995); children: Anne Rayner, Susan Margaret Anderson. BS in Pharmacy, Leeds U., Eng., 1959, BS in Pharmacology, 1960, PhD, 1963, DSc, 1985. Asst. lectr. in pharmacology Leeds U., 1962; sr. demonstrator in pharmacology U. Queensland, Australia, 1964, lectr., 1965-68, sr. lectr., 1969-73, reader, 1974-89, prof., 1990—. Editor 2 books on asthma; contbr. over 100 rsch. articles to profl. jours. Officer Order of Australia. Fellow Royal Pharm. Soc. Gt. Britain, Pharm. Soc. Australia (pres. Queensland br. 1995-96); mem. Brit. Pharmacological Soc., Am. Soc. Pharmacology and Experimental Therapeutics, Australian Soc. Clin. and Experimental Pharmacologists and Toxicologists. Anglican. Avocations: piano, bushwalking, embroidery, travel. Office: U Queensland Dept Physiol and Pharm, St Lucia Campus, QLD Brisbane 4072, Australia

O'DONNELL, TERESA HOHOL, software development engineer, antennas engineer; b. Springfield, Mass., Nov. 25, 1963; d. Marion and Lena Hohol; m. Patrick Alan O'Donnell; children: Kelly Marie, Tracy Alana. BS in Computer Engring., MIT, 1985, BSEE, 1985, MSEE, MS in Computer Sci., 1986. Rsch. asst. MIT Rsch. Lab for Electronics, Cambridge, 1985-86; lead VHSIC insertion engr. USAF Electronic Systems Divsn., Hanscom AFB, Mass., 1986-88; intelligent antennas engr. USAF Rome Lab., Hanscom AFB, Mass., 1988-91; sr. scientist Arcon Corp., Waltham, Mass., 1991—. Composer: (choral mass setting) Mass of Rejoicing, 1989; inventor: patentee cab to cap gap filler, weather seal strip, infant stimulus toy. Performer Zbeide's Harem, Tewksbury, Mass., 1986-93; organist/composer St. Theresa's Choir, Billerica, Mass., 1987-95. Maj. USAF and USAFR. Decorated Commendation medal (2), Joint Svc. Achievement medal. Mem. IEEE, Nat. Assn. Pastoral Musicians, Am. Guild Organists, Assn. for Computing Machinery, Res. Officers Assn., Sigma Xi, Eta Kappa Nu (v.p. 1985-86). Roman Catholic. Avocations: music, dancing, theater, composing, roller skating. Office: Arcon Corp 260 Bear Hill Rd Ste 5 Waltham MA 02451-1000

O'DONNELL, WILLIAM DAVID, retired construction firm executive; b. Brockton, Mass., Aug. 21, 1926; s. John Frank and Agnes Teresa (Flanagan) O'D.; m. Dixie Lou Anderson, Jan. 31, 1951; children—Craig Patrick, Ginger Lynn. BS, U. N.Mex., 1953. Registered profl. engr., Ill., 1958. Engr. State of Ill., 1953-59; with Gregory-Anderson Co., Rockford, Ill., 1959—, gen. mgr., 1960-61, sec., 1961-81, pres., 1981-94; ret.; bd. dirs. Growth Enterprise, Davis Meml. Park, BankOne, Rockford. Dir. St. Anthony Med. Ctr., Youth Svcs. Network, Cath. Conf. of Ill.; bd. dirs. Rockford YMCA, pres., 1984. Served with USN, 1943-47. Decorated papal knight Order of St. Gregory; recipient Friend of the Boy award Optimist Club, 1966, Excalibur award for cmty. svc. Rockford Register Star, 1971; named Titan of Yr., Boylan H.S., 1974, Papal Knight Order of St. Gregory the Great; fellow Wisdom Hall of Fame. Fellow ASCE, NSPE, Soc. Am. Mil. Engrs.; mem. No. Ill. Bldg. Contractors, Aircraft Owners and Pilots Assn., Balloon Fedn. Am., World Future Soc., Am. Polar Soc., Nat. Sporting Clays Assn., Amateur Trapshooting Assn., Am. Legion (life), VFW (life), Sigma Tau, Chi Epsilon, Tau Beta Pi. Clubs: Forest Hills Country (Rockford), Metropolitan Club (Chgo.); Adventurers (Chgo.). Lodges: Rotary (Service Above Self award 1972; v.p. Rockford chpt. 1983, pres. 1984). Home: 2004 Bradley Rd Rockford IL 61107-1258 Office: PO Box 900 Rockford IL 61105-0900

O'DONOGHUE, DANIEL FRANCIS, advertising agency executive; b. Manchester, Eng., Mar. 27, 1947; s. Daniel and Sabina (Carey) O'D.; m. Suzanne Lynne Holman, Apr. 1, 1972; children: Timothy, James, ALexander, Johanna. BEng, Sheffield U., 1969. Trainee GUS, Manchester, 1968-69; rsch. mgr. Rowntree, York, England, 1969-76; mktg. officer Shepherd Bldg., York, 1976-77; account planner Ogilvy & Mather, London, 1977-79; planning dir. CDP Aspect, London, 1979-82; joint CEO Publicis, London, 1982-98; worldwide dir. strategic planning Publicis Worldwide, Paris, 1999—. Fellow Inst. Practitioners in Advt. (chmn. bibliography com. 1989-90, mem. coun. 1989-92); mem. Mktg. Soc., Designers and Art Dirs. Assn. (assoc., edn. com. mem.). Roman Catholic. Avocations: fine art, football, archaeology. Home: Woodcroft Castle Marholm, Peterborough PE6 7HW, England Office: Publicis, 82 Baker St, London W1M 2AE, England also: Publicis Worldwide, 1333 Champs Elysées, 75380 Paris Cedex 08, France

O'DONOGHUE, HEATHER, university educator; b. Stockton-on-Tees, England, July 12, 1953; d. Roderick and Sheila (Mason) Mackinnon; m. James Bernard O'Donoghue, July 23, 1977; children: Ellen, Tom, Josie. BA, U. London, 1974; MPhil, U. Oxford, 1976, DPhil, 1987. Fellow, tutor Somerville Coll., Oxford, England, 1978-91; reader in Old Norse Linacre Coll., Oxford, England, 1991—. Author: The Genesis of a Saga Narrative, 1991, Beowulf, 1999. Avocations: archaeology, Irish traditional music, crime novels. Office: Linacre Coll, Oxford OX1 3JA, England

O'DONOGHUE, JOHN, government official, solicitor; b. Caherciveen, Ireland, May 28, 1956; m. Kate Ann Murphy; 3 children. BCL, U. Coll. Cork; LLB, Inc. Law Soc. Ireland. Spokesman on justice Fianna Fail Front Bench; mem. Kerry County Coun., chmn., 1990-91; mem. Brit.-Irish Parliamentary Body; min. of state Dept. Fin., 1991-92; min. of justice, equality and law reform Ireland. Mem. Caherciveen Social Svcs. Com.; mem. Kerry County Libr. Com., Kerry Fisheries and Coastal Mgmt. Com., So. Health Bd., So. Health Bd. Psychiat. Svcs. Com., Dail Com. on Legislation and Security. Mem. St. Mary's GAA Club. Office: Dept Justice, 72-76 St Stephen's Green, Dublin 2, Ireland*

O'DONOGHUE, MICHAEL JOHN, gemological association executive, educator; b. Leicester, U.K., Nov. 30, 1934; s. Desmond and Sarah Ann (Ward) O'D.; m. Elizabeth Anne Borley, Feb. 26, 1968; children: Lucy, Clare, Peter. MA, Cambridge (Eng.) U., 1962. Curator Nat. Libr. Scotland, Edinburgh, 1960-62, The Brit. Mus., London, 1962-91; lectr., head gemmology London Guildhall U., London, 1991—; bd. dirs. Gemological Assn. and Gem Testing Lab. of Gt. Britain, 1998—. Author: Encyclopedia of Minerals and Gemstones, 1975, Synthetic Gem Materials, 1976, Synthetic Gems: The Case for Caution, 1976, Beginner's Guide to Mineralogy, 1983, Quartz, 1983, Identifying Man-made Gemstones, 1983, Gemstones, 1988, Pocket Guide to Rocks and Minerals, 1990, Illustrated Guide to Rocks and Minerals, 1991, Gemstones of Pakistan, 1991, Synthetic Imitation and Treated Gemstones, 1997; abstractor Mineral. Abstracts, 1976—; editor Gems and Mineral Realm, 1979-86, Gemmological and Synthetic Crystals Newsletters, 1970—, Information Sources in the Earth Sciences, 1986. Leader The Samaritans, London, 1967-91; pastoral asst. St. John's Ch., Sevenoaks, U.K., 1989—; chair Sevenoaks Early Years Forum, 1993—; exec. coun. mem. Age Concern, Sevenoaks, 1997—. Rsch. scholar Worshipful Co. Goldsmiths, London, 1976. Fellow Gemmological Assn. Great Britain (coun. mem. 1971-85), Geol. Soc. London (libr. com.), Mineral. Soc., Deutsche Gemmologische Gesellschaft (coun. mem.). Anglican. Avocations: playing the organ.

O'DONOGHUE, PHILIP NICHOLAS, zoologist; b. London, Oct. 9, 1929; s. Terence Frederick and Ellen Mary (Haynes) O.; m. Veronica Florence Campbell, 1955; children: Elizabeth Clare, Christine Jane. BSc, U. Nottingham, 1952, MSc, 1959. Exptl. officer Agrl. Research Council, 1952-61; sci. officer Nat. Inst. Research in Dairying, Reading, 1962-66; sr. lectr. U. London, 1966-82; gen. sec. Inst. Biology, London, 1982-89. Editor Jour. Laboratory Animals, 1967-82. Fellow Inst. Biology; mem. Royal Soc. Medicine (sect. pres. 1985-86). Club: Athenaeum (London). Avocations: music, family history. Office: Inst Biology, 20 Queensberry Pl, London SW7 2DZ, England

O'DONOVAN, YVONNE M., recording industry executive; b. Limerick, Munster, Ireland, Apr. 30, 1956; d. Donal and Katherine (Harrington) O'Donovan; m. Adam Paul Morris, Apr. 28, 1993 (div. 1996); children: Aine Sophie, Sean Peter, Niamh Catriona. Cert. Dipl.A.F., City of London Poly., 1981; MBA, Sheffield U., 1993; MA, Sheffield Hallam U., 2000. Acct. Ocean Inchcape Ltd., London, 1979-81; mgmt. acct. Salen Shipping Ltd., London, 1981-83; dir. The Photographers Gallery, Ltd., London, 1983-89, Modo Records and Tapes, Ltd., Sheffield, U.K., 1989-95; chief exec. Action for Bus. & Culture, 1999—; cons. Miners Arena Benefit trust, Sheffield, 1989-93, Amber Initiatives, 1993-99, Orb USA Inc., N.Y.C., 1992-94. Treas. Nat. Centre for Popular Music, Sheffield, 1994—. Fellow Royal Soc. for Arts, Inst. of Dirs., Inst. for Mgmt. of Info. Sys., Assn. of MBAs. Roman Catholic. Home: 47 Woodholm Rd, Sheffield S11 1HJ, United Kingdom Office: Action for Bus & Culture, 15 Paternoster Row, Sheffield S11 8TW, England

ODOR, RICHARD LANE, mental health administrator, psychologist; b. Oberlin, Ohio, Aug. 11, 1954; s. Frank and Marjorie Ann (Carpenter) O. Student, Moody Bible Inst., 1972-74; BA, Ohio State U., 1977, MA, 1978, PhD, 1986. Counselor children's groups Gladden Community House, Columbus, Ohio, 1978-79; partial hospitalization counselor Columbus Area Community Mental Health Ctr., 1979-81, residential counselor, 1978-82; grad. rsch. assoc. dept. family rels. and human devel. Ohio State U., 1983-85; emergency svcs. counselor S.E. Community Mental Health Ctr., Columbus, 1983-86, dir. emergency svcs., 1986-87; program dir., psychologist Southeast Counseling Svcs., Columbus, 1987-92; psychologist Psychol. and Counseling Svcs., Reynoldsburg, Ohio, 1989-98, Richard L. Odor, PhD, Inc., Reynoldsburg, Ohio, 1998—; psychologist, clin. supr. New Source Counseling Ctrs., Twinsburg, Ohio, 1990-97; psychologist, owner Psychol. and Recovery Svcs., Columbus, 1991-94; employee assistance program affiliate McDonnell Douglas Corp., Columbus, 1992-95; staff Grant Med. Ctr., Columbus, 1995—; mem. profl. adv. com. Mt. Carmel Behavioral Healthcare, 1998—. Profl. adv. bd. Ctrl. Ohio Chpt. Nat. Multiple Sclerosis Soc., 1995-97. Recipient Silver medal Pan Am. Master's Weightlifting Championships, 1999, Bronze medal Pan Am. Master's Weightlifting Championships, 2000. Mem. APA, Interact Behavioral Healthcare (credentialling com. 1996-98), Ohio Psychol. Assn., Ctrl. Ohio Psychol. Assn., U.S. Weightlifting Fedn., Ohio State U. Weightlifting Club (coach 1982-85, faculty advisor 1984-85), Rotary (bd. dirs. Reynoldsburg-Pickerington chpt. 1992-94), Phi Kappa Phi, Omicron Nu, Phi Upsilon Omicron. Republican. Avocations: skiing, water skiing, competitive weightlifting, sailing. Office: 7664 Slate Ridge Blvd Reynoldsburg OH 43068-8158

O'DRISCOLL, JOHN KEVIN, psychologist, retired educator; b. Sydney, Australia, June 3, 1924; s. Cornelius Joseph and Ellen Mary (Noonan) O'D. BA, U. Sydney, 1948, diploma in edn., 1949. Cert. tchr. Dept. Edn., Sydney, 1950. Sch. tchr. Sch. Edn., Moss Vale, Australia, 1950-51, Wollongong, Australia, 1960-75; novice monk Abbey of Mt. Melleray, Waterford, Ireland, 1953-55; counsellor, psychologist Sch. Edn., Sydney, 1976-94; Fedn. rep. Tchr.'s Fedn. New South Wales, 1961-74. Editor The A.E.F. (Assn. Ednl. Freedom), 1963-75. Sec. Dem. Labour Party NSW, Wollongong, 1965-75; found. mem. Right to Life Assn., Wollongong, 1968; pres. Wollongong Curia of Legion of Mary, 1970-75; mem. Gregorian choir Priestly Soc. St. Pius X, Sydney, 1975-85. Leading air craftsman Royal Australian Air Force, 1943-45. Recipient Pacific Star award Commonwealth Australia, 1949, Def. medal, 1949, War medal, 1949, Bronze medal Royal Life-Saving Soc., New SOuth Wales, 1951. Roman Catholic. Home: 46 Bryant St, Sydney 2216, Australia

ODULIO, SHERIDONI TORRES, illustrator; b. Apr. 4, 1973. Illustrator Omega IT Inc., Columbus, Ohio, 1997—; author 1st Books, Indpls., 1998—. Patentee in field.

O'DWYER, TONY, corporate secretary, accountant; b. Dublin, Leinster, Ireland, July 24, 1963; s. Michael and Catherine O'Dwyer; m. Terry Sargent, Aug. 24, 1991. Assoc., Accountancy and Bus. Coll., 1986, 96. Trainee PWC, Dublin, 1981-88; supr. Ernst and Young, Dublin, 1988-89; mgr. KPMG, Dublin, 1989—. Mem. Inst. Chartered Secs. and Adminstrs. (pres. Irish region 1999-00, chmn. Irish region 1995-99). Avocations: walking, listening to music, sword fencing, reading. Fax: 353 01 4121149. E-mail: tony.odwyer@kpmg.ie. Office: KPMG, 1 Stokes Pl St Stephens Grn, Dublin 2, Ireland

ODZA, RANDALL M., lawyer; b. Schnectady, May 6, 1942; s. Mitchell and Grace (Mannes) O.; m. Rita Ginness, June 19, 1966; children—Kenneth, Keith. B.S. in Indsl. and Labor Relations, Cornell U., 1964, LL.B., 1967. Bar: N.Y. 1967, U.S. Ct. Appeals (2d cir.) 1970, U.S. Dist. Ct. (so. and ea. dists.) N.Y. 1969, U.S. Dist. Ct. (we. dist.) N.Y. 1970, Fed. Dist. Ct. (we. dist.) N.Y. Assoc. Proskauer, Rose, Goetz & Mandelsohn, N.Y.C., 1967-69; assoc. Jaeckle, Fleischmann & Mugel, Buffalo, 1969-72, ptnr., 1972—. Past trustee, legal counsel, past treas. Temple Beth Am. Recipient Honor award Western N.Y. Retail Mchts. Assn., 1980. Mem. Indsl. Relations Rsch. Assn. Western N.Y., ABA, Erie County Bar Assn., N.Y. State Bar Assn. Office: Jaeckle Fleischmann & Mugel 12 Fountain Plz Rm 700 Buffalo NY 14202-2292

ŌE, KENZABURŌ, writer; b. Ehime, Shikoku, Japan, Jan. 31, 1935; m. Itami Yukari, 1960; three children. BA, Tokyo U., 1959. mem. Japan-China Literary Delegation, 1960; vis. prof. Collegio de México, 1976. Author: Shisha no ogori, 1958, Shiiku, 1958 (Akutagawa prize Japanese Soc. for Promotion of Literature 1958), Miru mae ni tobe, 1958, Memushiri kouchi, 1958, Warera no jidai, 1959, Seinen no omei, 1959, Kodoku na seinen no kyuka, 1960, Sevuntiin, 1961, Seiji shōnen shisu, 1961, Okurete kita seinen, 1962, Sakebigoe, 1962, Sekai no wakamonotachi, 1962, Seiteki ningen, 1963, Nichijō seikatsu no bōken, 1963, Kojinteki na taiken, 1964 (pub. as A Personal Matter, 1968), Sora no kaibutsu Aguii, 1964 (pub. as Aghwee the Sky Monster, 1977), Hiroshima nōto, 1965, Genshuku na tsunawatari, 1965, Man'en gannen no futtobōru, 1967 (pub. as The Silent Cry, 1974), Jizokusuru kokorozashi, 1968, Warera no kyoki o iki nobiru michi o oshieyo, 1969 (pub. as Teach Us to Outgrow Our Madness, 1977), Kowaremono to shite no ningen, 1970, Okinawa nōto, 1970, Kakujidai no sōzōryoku, 1970, Genbakugo no ningen, 1971, Kujira no shimetsusuru hi, 1972, Waga namida o nuguitamu hi, 1972 (pub. as The Day He Himself Shall Wipe My Tears Away, 1977), Dōjidai to shite no sengo, 1973, Kōzui wa waga tamashii ni oyobi, 1973, Jōkyō e, 1974, Bungaku nōto, 1974, Pinchiranna chōsho, 1976, Kotoba ni yotte: Jōkyō/Bungaku, 1976, Shōsetsu no hōhō, 1978, Dōjidai gemu, 1979, Gendai denkishu, 1980, Ō Kenzaburō dōjidaironshu (10 vols.), 1981, Shomotsu-sekai no in'yu, 1981, Chushin to shuen, 1981, Bunka no kasseika, 1982, "Ame no ki" o kiku onnatachi, 1982, Hiroshima kara Oiroshima e: '82 Yōroppa no hankaku heiwa undō o miru, 1982, Kaku no taika to "ningen" no koe, 1982, Atarashi hito yo mezameyo, 1983, Ika ni ki o korosu ka, 1984, Nihon gendai no yumanisuto Watanabe Kazuo o yomu, 1984, Ikikata no teigi: futatabi jokyo e, 1985, Shōsetsu no takurami chi no tanoshimi, 1985, Kaba ni kamareru, 1985, Natsukashii toshi e no tegami, 1986, M/T to mori no fushigi no monogatari, 1986, Atarashii bungaku no tame no, 1988, Kirupu no gundan, 1988, Saigo no shōsetsu, 1988, Chiryō no tō, 1991; editor: Itami Mansaku essei shu, 1971, Atomic Aftermath: Short Stories About Hiroshima-Nagasaki, 1984. Recipient May Festival prize, 1954, Shinchōsha prize, 1964, Tanizaki prize, 1967, Noma prize, 1973, Osaragi Jirō award, Nobel Prize in literature, 1994. Address: 585 Seiji-machi, Setagaya-ku Tokyo Japan*

OECHEL, WALTER CLARENCE, ecologist; b. San Diego, Jan. 15, 1945; s. Walter C. Oechel and Gloria Dawn Gordon; m. Judith Lynne Oechel, 1967. BA, San Diego State U., 1966; PhD, U. Calif., Riverside, 1970. Asst. to assoc. prof. McGill U., Montreal, Que., Can., 1970-78; rsch. prof. San Diego State U., 1978-83, prof., 1983—; dir. systems ecology rsch. group San Diego State U., 1982-87, Global Change Rsch. Group, 1992—; cons. in field, 1970—; polar rsch. bd. Nat. Acad. Sci., 1995—, mem. ecosystems panel for global change, 1996—; expert witness U.S. Govt., Bonn govt., UNESCO. Editor: Dynamics and Management of Mediterranean Type Ecosystems, 1981, Being Alive on Land, 1984, Plant Response to Stress, 1985, The Role of Fire in Mediterranean Type Ecosystems, 1994, Effects of Global Change on Arctic Ecosystems, 1994, Global Change and Mediterranean Type Ecosystems, 1995; contbr. 160 articles to profl. jours.; mem. many editorial bds. Grantee NSF, 1972-85, 92—, Dept. of Energy, 1978—, Nat. Park Svc., 1990-94. Mem. AAAS, Ecol. Soc. Am. (chmn. physiol. ecology sect. 1978-79), Nat. Acad. Scis. (ecosys. panel 1997—, polar rsch. bd. 1998—). Achievements include determination of response of arctic tundra to global change including elevated atmospheric CO_2 and temperature, current flux of CO_2 from arctic tundra in response to recent climate change; determination of the effects of global change on Mediterranean-type ecosystems, including Chaparral, Oak Woodlands and related vegetation. Office: San Diego State U Dept Biology San Diego CA 92182

OEFFNER, BARBARA DUNNING, biographer, educator, screenwriter; b. Southampton, N.Y., Aug. 25, 1944; d. Walter Arnold and Grace Dominy (Werner) Renkens; m. Michael Arthur Dunning, Oct. 1, 1966 (div. June 1984); children: Brendan, Ania, Amie, Heidi, Matt; m. F. Thomas Oeffner, Oct. 2, 1991. BS in Journalism, Northwestern U., 1966; postgrad., Fla. State U. Film copywriter Ency. Britannica, Chgo., 1966-69; pub. rels. dir. Eldred Auctions, East Dennis, Mass., 1982-85; editor Sandscript, Cummaquid, Mass., 1975-95; ins. agt. State Farm Ins., Delray Beach, Fla., 1992-95; biographer Cape Cod Writers, Inc., Cummaquid, 1995—; v.p. Caribbean

Coatings Corp., Moore Haven, Fla., 1996—, Native Am. Prodns., Palm Beach, Fla., 1994—; lectr. Glades County Hist. Soc. Author: (screenplay) The Cuban Accident, 1996; co-author: (screenplay) Chief, 1994; author: (book) Chief: Champion of the Everglades, 1995. Tchr. Meth. Bible Sch., Moore Haven, 1997; activities dir. Campers Club Am., Moore Haven, 1996-97. Grantee Mary Roberts Rinehart Found., 1975, Commonwealth of Mass.-Dept. of Arts and Humanities, 1984, Coord. Coun. Lit. Mags., 1976. Mem. DAR. Democrat. Avocations: water aerobics, line dancing, hiking, traveling, gardening. Fax: (561) 924-2271. Home: Box 1236 306 Yacht Club Way Moore Haven FL 33471-2809 Office: Clarence E Anthony Libr 375 SW 2d Ave South Bay FL 33493-2225

OEHLER, RICHARD DALE, lawyer; b. Iowa City, Dec. 9, 1925; s. Harold Lawrence Oehler and Bernito Babb; m. Rosemary Heineman, July 11, 1952, (div.); m. Maria Luisa Holguin-Zea, June 11, 1962; children: Harold D., Richard L. BA in Med. Scis., U. Calif., Berkeley, 1951; JD, Loyola U., L.A., 1961. Bar: Calif. 1962, Fla. 1968. Sales rep. Abbott Labs., Pasadena, Calif., 1951-63; with claims dept. Allstate Ins., Tampa, 1963-70; pvt. practice Tampa, 1970—; instr. Dale Carnegie Courses West Fla. Inst., Tampa, Scott Hitchcock & Assocs., Tampa, 1969—. Pres. U. South Fla. Parents Assn., Tampa, 1986-87. Mem. Fla. Bar Assn., Hillsborough County Bar Assn., Acad. of Fla. Trial Lawyers, Assn. of Trial Lawyers of Am., Masons (32d degree), Shriners, Phi Beta Kappa. Republican. Presbyterian. Avocations: jogging, road races, target shooting, fishing. Office: 200 N Pierce St Tampa FL 33602-5020

OEI, HOK LIANG, immunobiologist, researcher; b. Bandung, Indonesia, Mar. 31, 1943; s. Sioe Lam and Sik Nio (Tjoa) O.; m. Lian Eng Lie, Aug. 25, 1972; 1 child, Edwin Hong Gwan. DVM, Justus-Liebig U., Giessen, Germany, 1972, PhD, 1974. Scientist faculty vet. medicine Justus-Liebig U., 1972-74; sr. rsch. scientist Wageningen U. and Rsch. Ctr. Inst. Animal Sci. and Health, Lelystad, The Netherlands, 1974—; tech. contact person Ofcl. Medicines Control Labs. European Union, Strasbourg, 1993—; expert vet. immunobiology European Agy. for Evaluation of Medicinal Products, London, 1994—. Mem. European Soc. Vet. Virology, The Netherlands Soc. Microbiology. Home: Karveel 40-03, 8231DK Lelystad The Netherlands Office: Inst Animal Sci and Health, Edelhertweg 15, 8200 AB Lelystad The Netherlands

OEI, S. GUID, gynecologist; b. Leiden, The Netherlands, May 30, 1961; s. Tjien Tek and Bea (Gouw) O.; m. Nanette Laetitia Jacqueline van der Hagen, Apr. 6, 1990. MD, Leiden U., The Netherlands, 1986, PhD, 1996. Resident Rynstate Hosp., Arnhem, The Netherlands, 1987-88, Acad. Hosp., Rotterdam, The Netherlands, 1988-89, Leyenburg Hosp., The Hague, The Netherlands, 1989-90, Leiden U. Med. Ctr., The Netherlands, 1990-94, Groene Hart Hosp., Gouda, The Netherlands, 1994-95; gynecologist, cons. St. Joseph Hosp., Veldhoven, The Netherlands, 1996—, head of dept. obstetrics. Author: Past and Present of the Postcoital Test, 1996; contbr. articles to profl. jours. Mem. Dutch Assn. Ob-gyn. (author obstetric guidelines), Dutch Soc. Perinatal Medicine, Otterlo Working Party Perinatology. Avocation: juggling. Home: Vloeteind 33, 5502 PT Veldhoven The Netherlands Office: St Josephs Hosp, de Run 4600, 5500 MB Veldhoven The Netherlands

OEIRIA, DAVID SUDARTO, dermatologist, plastic and reconstructive surgeon, educator; b. Medan, N Sumatera, Indonesia, May 15, 1956; s. Darmawan Oei Lian Goan and Sulasmi Geok Sie O.; m. Ratna Maitri Dewi Gondowardojo, Sept. 25, 1983; children: Christopher Toshihiro, Stephen Akihiro, Andrew Yoshihiro. MD, Airlangga U., 1979, Airlangga U., 1982; dermatologist, dermatologic surgeon, Kanazawa Med. U., 1990. Bd. cert. dermatologist and venereologist. Dermatologist U. Indonesia, Jakarta, 1991; dir. Dermatology and Skin Laser Ctr., Surabaya, 1991—; plastic and reconstructive surgeon Kanazawa Med. U. Sch. Medicine, 1997; dir. Klinik Dr. Ratna, Surabaya, Indonesia; lectr. U. Wijaya Kusuma Sch. Medicine, Surabaya; dir. Indonesian-Internat. Med. Coop., Surabaya, 1996—, Indonesian-Japan Med. Assn., Surabaya, 1996—; chmn. Surabaya br. program Cutaneous Surgery Edn. Contbr. articles to profl. jours. Clin. rsch. fellow in plastic surgery Kanazawa (Japan) Med. U., 1995—. Mem. Am. Acad. Dermatology, European Acad. Dermato-Venereology, Indonesian Soc. Dermato-Venereology (regional chmn. dermatologic surgery study group 1999—), Japan Soc. Plastic and Reconstructive Surgery, Internat. Soc. for Dermatologic Surgery. Avocations: reading, art, music, sports, swimming. Office: Klinik Dr Ratna, Jl Raya Kertajaya Indah 121, Surabaya 60116, Indonesia

OELBERG, ROBERT NATHAN, landscape architect; b. Washington, May 7, 1956; s. George Robert and Elizabeth Abigail (Kepler) O. BA in Art magna cum laude, Maharishi Internat. U., Fairfield, Iowa, 1981; M.Landscape Arch., U. Va., 1985. Registered landscape architect, N.C. Landscape architect, sr. project mgr. Land Design Inc., Alexandria, Va., 1985-93; owner Robert N. Oelberg ASLA, Boone, N.C., 1994-97; dir. HMR Land Planning and Landscape Arch., Boone, 1997—; project landscape architect Heavenly Mountain Resort, Boone, 1994—, mem. archtl. rev. bd. and exec. bd., 1997—. Bd. dirs. Mcoi Devel. Corp., Washington, 1989-91. With USMC, 1974-76. DuPont fellow, 1984. Mem. Am. Soc. Landscape Architects. Democrat. Methodist. Avocations: designing and building a house, contra dancing. Home: 155 Briar Rose Trl Boone NC 28607-9422 Office: 639 Whispering Hills Rd Boone NC 28607-5599

OELLERICH, MICHAEL, chemistry educator, chemical pathologist; b. Heidelberg, Germany, July 15, 1944; s. Friedrich W. and Roswitha (Kamner) O.; m. Pushpa Singh, Mar. 12, 1976; children: Mark, Thomas, Diana. MD, U. Heidelberg, 1970; Habilitation, Med. U. Hannover, 1978; DHc, BNAM, Sofia, 1998. Intern U. Heidelberg, 1971-72; resident dept. internal medicine U. Düsseldorf, Fed. Republic of Germany, 1973-75; resident Inst. for Clin. Chemistry, Med. U. Hannover, Fed. Republic of Germany, 1972-73, 75-79, head physician, 1979-82, dep. chmn., 1982-91; prof. clin. chemistry U. Hannover/Göttingen, Fed. Republic of Germany, 1982—; dir. dept. clin. chemistry, ctrl. lab. Ctr. Internal Medicine U. Göttingen, 1991—, dean faculty medicine, 1996-98, vice dean faculty medicine, 1998-99; dep. chief exec. for rsch. and tchg. Georg-August U., Göttingen, 1999—; mem. DFG Commn. for Clin. Toxicol. Analysis, 1984-89; mem. coun. faculty of medicine, U. Göttingen, 1993—, mem. habilitation com., 1993-98; chmn. 4th Internat. Congress of Therapeutic Drug Monitoring and Clin. Toxicology, Vienna, 1995. Contbr. over 230 articles on hypoglycemia inducing substances, metabolic monitoring in clin. transplantation, therapeutic drug monitoring, including immunosuppressants, oxidant stress and liver injury, non isotopic immunoassay techniques to sci. jours., chpts to books; mem. editl. bd. Jour. Clin. Chemistry and Clin. Biochemistry, 1985-88, Clin. Biochemistry, 1995-96, Therapeutic Drug Monitoring, 1987—; assoc. editor Clin. Biochemistry, 1996—. Recipient Ludolf-Krehl prize S.W. German Soc. for Internal Medicine, 1971, Internat. Assn. Therapeutic Drug Monitoring and Clin. Toxicology award for exceptional contbns. to implementation of goals of society, 1999. Mem. German Assn. Lab. Medicine (pres.-elect 1999—), German Soc. for Clin. Chemistry (bd. dirs. 1984-86), Am. Assn. for Clin. Chemistry, Internat. Assn. of Therapeutic Drug Monitoring and Clin. Toxicology (pres.-elect 1995-97, pres. 1997-99, past pres. 1999—), Bulgarian Nat. Acad. Medicine. Lutheran. Achievements include invention of hypoglycemic hydrazonopropionic acid and of the MEGX liver function test. Office: Georg-August U Dept Clin Chemistry, Robert-Koch-Str 40, D-37070 Göttingen Germany

OELLERS-FRAHM, KARIN, law educator; b. Köslin, Pommern, Germany, July 7, 1942; d. Friedrich Wilhelm and Anneliese Franziska (Schumann) F.; m. Burkhard Ernst Wilhelm Oellers, June 26, 1970; children: Kathrin, Karsten. Diplom, U. Mainz, Germany, 1966; D in Legal Studies, U. Heidelberg, Germany, 1970. Interpreter European Cmtys., Brussels, 1966-67; rschr. Max Planck Inst., Heidelberg, 1970—; asst. prof. U. Heidelberg, 1982—, lectr. internat. jurisdiction, 1991; registrar Arbitral Tribunal, Heidelberg, 1989-90. Author: Interim Measures of Protection Before International Tribunals, 1975, Dispute Settlement in Public International Law, 1984, Fontes Iuris Gentium, World Court Digest, 1978, 4th edit., 1996; contbr. articles to profl. jours. Mem. CSCE (expert), Internat. Law Assn. (mem. com. 1992), German Assn. Internat. Law, Ctr. for Human Rights. Office: Max Planck Inst Pub Law, Im Neuerheimer Feld 535, 69120 Heidelberg Germany

OELMÜLLER, RALF, plant physiologist, researcher; b. Münster, Westfalia, Germany, Sept. 26, 1957; s. Wilhelm and Hannelore (Langenberg) O. Diploma, U. Freiburg, Germany, 1982, PhD, 1986; habilitation, U. Munich, 1996. Cert. in biology and plant physiology. Postdoctoral fellow U. Freiburg, 1986-87, Stanford U., Palo Alto, Calif., 1987-89; asst. prof. U. Munich, 1989-97; prof. U. Jena, Germany, 1997—. Contbr. numerous articles to internat. jours. Office: Inst Gen Botany, Dornburger Str 159, 07743 Jena Germany

OELOFSE, JAN HARM, game rancher, wildlife management consultant; b. Burgersdorp, Cape Province, South Africa, July 12, 1934; s. Andries and Johanna (Vorster) O. Diploma in agriculture, Agrl. Coll., Cradock Cape, South Africa, 1952. Animal and trapping staff Tanganykia Game Ltd., Arusha Tanganykia, 1954-63; sr. game warden game translocation Natal Parks Bd., Hluhluwe Gamereserve, Natal, South Africa, 1964-72; game rancher Farm Okonjati, Kalkfeld, Namibia, South Africa, 1974—; mem. Wilderness Leadership Sch., Durban, Natal, 1967—; mem. tourist bd. Namibia Adminstrn., Windhoek, 1984—. Discoverer technique to capture wild animals with plastic material. Named Most Outstanding Hunter of Yr., 1982; recipient Internat. Order of Merit, 1990. Mem. Safari Club Internat., Internat. Profl. Hunters Assn. Lodge: Etosha Otjiwarongo. Avocations: sculpture; wildlife photography. Home and Office: Mount Etjo Safari Lodge, PO Box 81, Kalkfeld 9000, Namibia

OERTEL, WOLFGANG HERMANN, physician, neurologist; b. Helmstedt, Germany, Feb. 15, 1951; s. Hermann August and Annelies (Lucke) O.; m. Heide-Lotte Hohage, Dec. 12, 1977. MD, Free U. Berlin, 1976, D of Medicine, 1978. Intern Free U. Berlin, Berlin, 1976-77; rsch. fellow NIH, NIMH, Bethesda, Md., 1978-81; resident dept. Neurology T.U., Munich, 1981-86; rsch. fellow Inst. of Neurology, London, 1987; cons., neurologist Klinikum Grosshadern, Munich, 1988-90, prof. neurology, 1990-96; chmn. dept. neurology Philipps U., Marburg, Germany, 1996—; coord. German med. network Parkinsonian Syndromes, 1999—. Contbr. articles to profl. jours. Heisenberg fellow German Rsch. Found., 1987-90; recipient Parkinson-Frosst-Price award German Soc. for Neurology, 1986. Mem. Soc. of Neurosci., N.Y. Acad. Sci., Am. Acad. Neurology, Movement Disorder Soc., European Neurosci. Assn., European Neurol. Soc. Avocations: piano, hiking. Office: Philipps U Zentrum Nervenheilkunde, Philips U Marburg Dept Neur, D-35033 Marburg Germany

OESTER, PAUL THOMAS, forestry educator; b. Corvallis, Oreg., Mar. 2, 1949; s. Louis Milton and Claire (Watson) O.; m. Margo Diane Wheeler, Jan. 26, 1968 (div. Oct. 1993); children: Mark, Ana, Heidi, Joel. BS, Oreg. State U., 1972, MS, 1977. Forester Oreg. Dept. Forestry, La Grande, 1977-79; ext. forester Oreg. State U., Coguille and La Grande, 1980—. Contbr. articles to profl. jours. including Can. Entomologist, New Forests. Mem. Gov.'s Eastside Forest Adv. Panel, Oreg., 1996—; mem., bd. dirs. Blue Mountain Forum, La Grande, 1998—. Cpl. USNG, 1969-75. Recipient Achievement award Nat. Assn. County Agrl. Agts., 1989. Mem. Soc. Am. Foresters (chmn. Blue Mountain chpt. 1980—). Office: Oreg State U Ext Svc 10507 N Mcalister Rd La Grande OR 97850-8716

OESTERGAARD, LEON FRODE, sociologist; b. Kildebrönde, Denmark, July 31, 1943; s. Frode Verner Hansen and Lily (Jensen) H.; m. Annelise Oestergaard, 1965 (div. 1984); children: Peter, Mette, Helle; m. Kirsten Oestergaard, 1995. MSc in Sociology, U. Copenhagen, 1972. Prin. Fedn. Danish Motorists, Denmark, 1972-76; campaign mgr. Danish Road Safety Coun., Denmark, 1976-87, acting dir., 1987-88; dir. info. Nat. Consumer Agy., Denmark, 1988-94; gen. mgr., CEO Danish State Info. Svc., Denmark, 1994-98; dir. info. Danish Contractors Assn., Copenhagen, 1998, Stats. Denmark, Copenhagen, 1999—; external examiner U. Roskilde, U. Odense, Denmark; mem. Govt. Com. on Pub. Info. Policy, Denmark, 1996-97. Initiator, councillor: Master of Public Relations, 1985; initiator, panel mem. for Consumer Radio Broadcast "Good Advice Is For Free", 1991-95 (Veuve-Cliquot prize 1993). Coun. mem. Mcpl. Coun., Karlebo, 1985-90. Knight of the Dannebrog, Her Royal Highness The Queen of Denmark, 1993. Mem. Danish Pub. Rels. Assn. (bd. mem. 1982-86, 92-93), Internat. Pub. Rels. Assn. (coun. mem. 1996-97)/. Avocations: opera, theatre, golf. Fax: 45 3975 1714. E-mail: LoE@DST.DK.

OESTERLING, JOSEPH EDWIN, urologic surgeon; b. Greensburg, Ind., May 28, 1956; s. Walter Bernard and Leona Martha (Muckerheide) O.; m. Carmen Teresa Noguera, June 9, 1984; children: Christopher Charles, Jennifer Marie. BA, Columbia Coll., 1978; MD, Columbia U., 1982. Diplomate Nat. Bd. Med. Examiners, Am. Bd. Urology; lic. in Md., Fla., Ariz., Minn., Mich. Intern, dept. gen. surgery Johns Hopkins U. Sch. of Med., Balt., 1982-83, resident, dept. gen. surgery, 1983-84, resident, dept. urology, 1984-87, chief resident, dept. urology, 1988, instr., dept. urology, 1988-89; cons. dept. urology Mayo Clinic, Rochester, Minn., 1989-94; asst. prof. urology Mayo Med. Sch., Rochester, 1989-93; assoc. prof. urology Mayo Clinic, Rochester, 1993-94; prof., urologist-in-chief, dir. Mich. Prostate Inst., U. Mich., Ann Arbor, 1994-97; dir. The Midwest Prostate Inst., Saginew, Mich., 1997—; cons./researcher in field; mem. Comprehensive Cancer Ctr. U. Mich.; physician cons. Ann Arbor Vet. Adminstrn. Hosp.; mem. prostate cancer adv. com. Mich. Cancer Consortium, 1988. Author: The ABCs of Prostate Cancer: The Book That Could Save Your Life, 1997; cons. The Jour. of Urology, The Prostate, 1990, Cancer, 1990, Cancer Rsch., 1990, New Eng. Jour. Medicine, Jour. Am. Med. Assn., 1991, Jour. Andrology, 1992, So. Med. Jour., 1992, The Clin. Jour. of Pain, 1992; editor-in-chief Urology; book editor: Urologic Oncology, Prostate-specific antigen: The Best Tumor Marker for Prostate Cancer; mem. editl. bd. Annals of Surg. Oncology, 1993, Urology Times, 1994, Men's Confidential, 1994, Jour. Urologic Pathology, 1995, Jour. Clin. Outcomes Mgmt., 1996, Infections in Urology, 1996, Prostate Diseases, 1996, Urology Bulletin, 1996. Recipient Emil T. Hofman Chemistry award Univ. Notre Dame, 1975, Albert B. Schweitzer award for Acad. Excellence, Columbia Coll., 1978, Salutatorian, Columbia Coll., 1978, Samuel W. Rover and Lewis C. Rover Biochemistry award Coll. of Physicians and Surgeons of Columbia U., 1982, Valedictorian, 1982, Am. Soc. Clin. Oncology Rsch. award 1987, Devel. award Am. Cancer Soc., 1988, others in field. Fellow ACS; mem. AMA, Am. Urol. Assn. (voting mem., Grand Champion prize 1991 Western sect., Prostate Educator of Yr. 1995, mem. BPH guidelines com., prostate cancer guidelines com.), N.Y. Acad. Sci., Sci. Rsch. Soc., Nat. Assn. Residents and Interns, Minn. State Med. Assn., Minn. Urol. Soc., Zumbro Valley Med. Soc., So. Minn. Med. Assn., Mich. Urol. Soc., Am. Soc. Andrology, Am. Assn. Clin. Urologists, Am. Geriatrics Soc., Am. Soc. Clin. Oncology, Can. Urol. Assn., European Assn. Urology, Endourol. Soc., Pan-Pacific Surg. Assn., Soc. for Basic Urologic Rsch., Soc. Internat. Urology, Johns Hopkins Med. and Surg. Assn., Soc. Univ. Urologists, North Cen. Sect. Am. Urologic Assn. (1st prize Clin. Rsch. 1986, 87, 1st prize Lab. Rsch. 1987), Mayo Alumni Assn., Sigma Xi. Avocations: landscape photography, cross country skiing, downhill skiing, sailing, gardening. Home: 5410 Meadowcrest Dr Ann Arbor MI 48105-9343 Office: The Midwest Prostate Inst 3406 Davenport Ave Saginaw MI 48602-3374

OESTERREICHER, JAMES E., department stores executive; b. 1941. B.S., Mich. State U., 1964. With J. C. Penney Co. Inc., 1964—; pres. Western Region J. C. Penney Co. Inc., 1987-88, exec. v.p., 1988-94; chmn., CEO J.C. Penney Co. Inc., 1994—. Office: J C Penney Co Inc 6501 Legacy Dr Plano TX 75024-3698

OESTMANN, MARY JANE, retired senior radiation specialist; b. Chgo., May 22, 1924; d. Charles Edward and Harriet Evelyn (Stoltenberg) O. BA in Math, Chemistry with honors, Denison U., 1946; MS, U. Wis., 1948, PhD, 1954; DSc., Denison U., 1975. Research chemist Inst. for Atom Energy, Oslo, 1954-55; vis. scientist AB Atom Energy, Stockholm, 1955-56; vis. prof. chem. dept. U. Iowa, Iowa City, 1957; sr. scientist Battelle Meml. Inst., Columbus, Ohio, 1957-61; assoc. chemist Argonne (Ill.) Nat. Lab, 1961-71; environ. project mgr. U.S. AEC, Washington, 1971-75; sr. radiation specialist U.S. Nuclear Regulatory Commn., Glen Ellyn, Ill., 1975-87; bd. dirs. U. Wis.-Madison Alumni Assn. of the So. Lakes, 1992—. Contbr. numerous articles to scientific jours. Mem. planning and zoning commn. Town of Burlington; bd. trustees Plymouth Congl. UCC Ch. Burlington, 1993-96. Recipient Internat. Women's Yr. award Nuclear Regulatory Commn., 1972, Dist. Alumni citation Denison U., 1971. Fellow Am. Inst. Chemists, Am. Nuclear Soc. (bd. dirs. 1983-86); mem. Am. Chem. Soc., Inst. Environ. Scis. (sr. mem.), Health Physics Soc. (sec.-treas. Midwest chpt. 1978, exec. com. 1983-86), N.Y. Acad. Scis., Wis. Acad. Scis., Arts and Letters, Wis. Fedn. Rep. Women (program dir. exec. com.), Burlington Woman's Club (treas., scholarship com. 1993—), Browns Lake Yacht Club (Burlington), Rep. Women Racine County-West Club (v.p. 1992-93, sec. 1994, pres. 1994-98, Anita Hunt award), Sigma Xi, Phi Beta Kappa, Sigma Delta Epsilon, Iota Sigma Pi. Home: 2520 Cedar Dr Burlington WI 53105-9174

OETTING, MILDRED KATHERINE See SQUAZZO, MILDRED KATHERINE

OETTMEIER, WALTER PAUL, chemist, educator; b. Schwandorf, Bavaria, Germany, Sept. 26, 1941; s. Fritz and Ferda (Bauriedl) O.; m. Ursula Hilgenstock, Feb. 12, 1981; children: Christina, Friedrich-Martin. Diploma in chemistry, Tech. U., Munich, 1965, PhD in Natural Scis., 1968; pvt. dozent, Ruhr-U., Bochum, Germany, 1982, prof., 1988. Rsch. assoc. Tech. U., 1968-70, Argonne Nat. Lab., Ill., 1974-76; rsch. assoc. Ruhr-U. Bochum, 1970-74, 76-87, prof., 1988—. Contbr. over 90 articles to sci. jours. Mem. Gesellschaft Deutscher Chemiker, Gesellschaft Biochemie und Molekularbiologie. Home: Wuppertaler Str 25, 45549 Sprockhövel NRhnWstf, Germany Office: Ruhr U, Biochemie der Pflanzen, 44780 Bochum NRhnWstf, Germany

OFFENBACKER, STEPHEN PHILLIP, translator; b. Seattle, Mar. 4, 1955; s. Phillip and Anne Marie (Rutledge) O. BA, Western Wash. U., 1980, U. Wash., 1983; MA, U. Wash., 1984. German tchr. U. Wash., Seattle, 1983-84; translator Munich, 1986-90; English instr. Euro Sprachschule, Munich, 1988-90; tech. translator Dr. Johannes Heidenhain GmbH, Traunreut, Germany, 1990-94; information developer SAP AG, Walldorf, Germany, 1995—. Translator (jour.) Restauro, 1988. Avocations: running, hiking, bicycling. E-mail: soffen@dusnet.de. Home: Rennbahnstrasse 55, D-69190 Walldorf Germany

OFFERSGAARD, JESPER FALDEN, physicist, researcher; b. Aarhus, Denmark, Feb. 24, 1967; s. Richardt Simoni and Anni (Nielsen) Falden; m. Lene Offersgaard, Aug. 5, 1989; children: Anna, Stine. MS, Aalborg U., Denmark, 1990; PhD, Tech. U. Denmark, 1994. Rschr. Tech. U. Denmark, 1994-95, Risoe Nat. Lab., Roskilde, Denmark, 1995-98, Delta Light & Optics, Lyngby, Denmark, 1998—. Mem. Optical Soc. Am. Mem. Kristeligt Folkeparti. Avocation: bicycle racing. Office: Delta Light & Optics, Hjortekaersvej 99, DK-2800 Lyngby Denmark

OFNER, GÜNTER ALOIS, journalist; b. Vienna, Austria, Nov. 13, 1958; s. Alois and Margaretha (Urban) O. Grad., Bundesreal Gymnasium, Vienna, 1977. Mem. Students Coun. Austria, 1991-95. Editor (monthly newspaper) Umfeld. Sec. gen. United Greens Austria, Vienna, 1990-93, Civic Greens Austria, Vienna, 1994-98; councilor Coun. Währing, Dist. of Vienna, 1991-96. Mem. Austrian-Israelic Soc., Amnesty Internat., Austrian Soc. Fgn. Policy. Roman Catholic. Avocations: books, newspapers, classical music. Home: Schulgasse 46, A-1180 Vienna Austria

OFNER, WILLIAM BERNARD, investor; b. L.A., Aug. 24, 1929; s. Harry D. and Gertrude (Skoss) Offner; m. Florence Ila Maxwell, Apr. 13, 1953 (div. 1956). AA, L.A. City Coll., 1949; BA, Calif. State U., L.A., 1953; LLB, Loyola U., L.A., 1965; postgrad., Sorbonne, 1951; cert. de Langue Francaise, 1987; postgrad., U. So. Calif., 1966, Glendale Community Coll., 1986-92. Bar: Calif. 1966, U.S. Dist. Ct. Calif. 1966, U.S. Supreme Ct. 1972. Assoc. Thomas Moore and Assocs., L.A., 1967-69; pvt. practice L.A., 1969-70, 74—; assoc. Peter Lam, L.A., 1981-94, mng. atty., 1993—; assoc. C.M. Coronel, 1986-87, Jack D. Janofsky, 1987-89, Mario P. Gonzalez, 1990-92, Genaro Legorreta, Jr., 1997-98; lectr. Van Norman U., 1975; property mgr., 1982—; investor 1984—. With USNR, 1947-54. Mem. Inst. Gen. Semantics, Toastmasters, Soc. des Amis De l'Universite de Paris, Safari Athletic Club, Sierra Club. Democrat. Avocations: painting, photography, linguistics, French tutoring, travel. Home: 13229 Setting Sun Ct Chino Hills CA 91709-1151

OFOEFULE, SABINUS IFEANYI, pharmaceutical technology educator; b. Orlu, Imo, Nigeria, Sept. 22, 1960; s. Cornelius Okonnia and Bridget (Ukazu) O.; m. Akuzuo Uwaoma Nwaozuzu, Aug. 10, 1988; children: Chidera Amarachukwu, Chiazam Chimdiebube. B Pharm, U. Nigeria, Nsukka, 1988, M Pharm, 1991, PhD, 1997. Intern pharmacist U. Nigeria, Nsukka, 1988-89, lectr., 1993-97, sr. lectr., 1997—, acting head dept., 1998, head dept. pharm. tech. and indsl. pharmacy, 2000—; supervising pharmacist Hosp., Ilesa, Nigeria, 1989-90, Cmty. Pharmacy, Maiduguri, Nigeria, 1990-93; cons. Biopharm.-Pharmacokinetics Rsch. Unit, Nsukka and Nnewi, Nigeria, 1993—; postgrad. external examiner Nnamdi Azikiwe U., Awka, Nigeria, Birla Inst. Tech., India. Contbr. articles to profl. jours. Recipient rsch. award Bashir-Thomas Rsch. Found., 1996. Mem. N.Y. Acad. Scis., Bioencapsulation Rsch. Group (assoc.), Pharm. Soc. Nigeria. Avocations: reading, football, travel, writing. Office: Dept Pharm Tech & Indsl, Univ Nigeria, Nsukka Nigeria

OFOMATA, GODFREY EZEDIASO KINGSLEY, geographer; b. Nnewi, Anambra, Nigeria, Aug. 28, 1936; s. Ezeatuma Ezebube and Juliana Ndayagwa (Nzuko) O.; m. Hope Obiageli Ejimbe, Aug. 2, 1969; children: Obianuju, Kenechukwu, Chijioke, Ogochukwu, Chinenye, Ijeoma. BA with honors, U. Coll., Ibadan, Nigeria, 1961; PhD, Troisieme Cycle, Strasbourg, France, 1963. From lectr. to reader geography U. Nigeria, Nsukka, 1963-76, prof. geography, 1976—. Editor: Nigeria in Maps: Eastern States, 1975, The Nsukka Environment, 1978; co-editor: (with C.C. Ukaegbu) Nigeria in Search of a Future, 1986. Chmn. Nat. Com. on Soil Conservation, 1978-90. Lt. col. Biafran Army, 1968-70. Commonwealth fellow Sheffield U., 1974-75. Fellow Nigerian Geog. Assn.; mem. Internat. Geog. Union (commn. on hist. monitoring environ. changes). Anglican. Avocations: walking, photography. Home: 17 Sir Louis Mbanefo St, Nsukka Nigeria Office: Univ Nigeria, Dept Geography, Nsukka Nigeria

OF SOUTHWOLD IN COUNTY OF SUFFOLK, BARONESS JAMES OF HOLLAND PARK See JAMES, P(HYLLIS) D(OROTHY)

ÖFVERHOLM, STEFAN, electrical engineer; b. Ludvika, Sweden, Nov. 21, 1936; s. Håkan and Ragnhild Gudrun (Andersson) Ö.; m. Eva Guy Tiselius, Sept. 9, 1966 (div. 1971); m. Ulrika Mathilda Marie Skaar, Oct. 10, 1975 (div. 1994); children: Harald, Ingegerd. MSEE, Chalmers U. Tech., Gothenburg, Sweden, 1963. Engr. microwave systems devel. Ericsson AB, Mölndal, Sweden, 1963-66; mgr. microwave lab. Trelleborgplast AB, Ljungby, Sweden, 1966-67; mgr. process and prodn. control projects Ericsson AB, Stockholm, Sweden, 1967-71; head computer devel. dept. Ericsson AB, Mölndal, Sweden, 1974-77; head testing methods and tech. Ericsson AB, Stockholm, Sweden, 1977-81; mgr. design and devel. Asea Lme Automation AB, Västerås, Sweden, 1971-74; v.p., gen. mgr. hybrid divsn. Rifa AB, Stockholm, Sweden, 1981-85; gen. mgr. controls divsn. Tour & Andersson AB, Västerhaninge, Sweden, 1985-89; dir. ops. mobile telephone systems divsn. Ericsson Radio Systems AB, Stockholm, 1989-90, v.p., gen. mgr. ops. divsn., 1990-92, v.p. bus. unit mobile tel. systems GSM, NMT and TACS, 1992-98; exec. v.p. Ericsson Turkey, 1998—. Avocations: classical music, linguistics, modern art. Home: Köybasi Caddesi 257, 80870 Istanbul Turkey

OGA, SEIZI, toxicology educator; b. Okayama, Japan, Sept. 4, 1937; arrived in Brazil, 1938, naturalized, 1963; s. Kizyuro and Sayono Oga; m. Sadako Ono, Apr. 30, 1941; children: Rosely Miyazaki, Silvio, Noemi. Degree in Pharmacy, U. São Paulo, 1965, PhD, 1969. Pharm. diplomate. Asst. prof. U. São Paulo, 1966-74, assoc. prof., 1974-93, full prof., 1993—, head dept., 1994-96, dean faculty pharm. scis., 1996—. Authro: Farmacologia Aplicada, 1979, Farmacologia Integrada, 1988, Medicamentos e suas interações, 1994, Fundamentos de Toxicologia, 1996. Mem. Soc. Pharmacy and Chemistry of San Paulo (pres. 1976-78), Rotary Club São Paulo-Aclimação (pres. 1987-88), Brazilian Soc. Pharmacology and Exptl. Therapy, Brazilian Soc. Toxicology. Avocations: tennis, painting. Home: Apt 83, Rua Calógero Calia 501, 04152101 São Paulo Brazil Office: U São Paulo Pharm Scis, Av Prof Lineu Prestes 580, 05508900 São Paulo Brazil

OGANYAN, VICTOR K., mathematics educator; b. Tbilisi, Georgia, USSR, Dec. 12, 1948; came to Armenia, 1966; s. Karo M. and Lilit N. (Nazaryan) O.; m. Narina S. Danielyan, June 28, 1975; 1 child, Lilit. Diploma, U. Yerevan, Yerevan, 1971; Candidate Scis. Physics and Math., Inst. Math., Leningrad, 1979; ScD in Physics and Math., St. Petersburg U., 1998. Tutor dept. math. U. Yerevan, Yerevan, Armenia, 1975-83, docent, 1983—; prof. probability theory and math. stats. dept. math. U. Yerevan, Armenia, 2000—; vis. lectr. Am. U. of Armenia, 1995—. Author: Probability Theory, 1986; contbr. to 33 papers. Internat. Sci. Found. (SOROS) grantee, 1994-95. Mem. Am. Math. Soc., Armenian Math. Soc. (treas. 1990-92, sci. sec. 1998—). Home: Khanjian 33 flat 18, 375010 Yerevan 375010, Armenia Office: Erevan State U, Yerevan State Univ, St A Manoukian 1, Yerevan 375025, Armenia

OGASAWARA, HIDEO, bank executive. Pres. Tokai Bank Ltd., Nagoya, Japan. Office: The Tokai Bank Ltd, 21-24 Nishiki 3-chome Naka, Nagoya 460-8660, Japan*

OGATA, KATSUHIKO, engineering educator; b. Tokyo, Jan. 6, 1925; came to U.S., 1952; s. Fukuhei and Teruko (Yasaki) O.; m. Asako Nakamura, Sept. 6, 1961; 1 son, Takahiko. B.S., U. Tokyo, 1947; M.S., U. Ill., 1953; Ph.D., U. Calif., Berkeley, 1956. Research asst. Sci. Research Inst., Tokyo, 1948-51; fuel engr. Nippon Steel Tube Co., Tokyo, 1951-52; mem. faculty U. Minn., 1956—, prof. mech. engring., 1961—; prof. elec. engring. Yokohama Nat. U., 1960-61, 64-65, 68-69. Author: State Space Analysis of Control Systems, 1967, Modern Control Engineering, 1970, 2d edit., 1990, 3d edit., 1996, Dynamic Programming, 1973, Ingenieria de Control Moderna, 1974, 3d edit., 1998, Metody Przestrzeni Stanow w Teorii Sterowania, 1974, System Dynamics, 1978, 3d edit., 1998, Engenharia de Controle Moderno, 1982, 2d edit., 1993, Teknik Kontrol Automatik, 1985, Discrete-Time Control Systems, 1986, 2d edit., 1995, Gendai Seigyo Riron, 1986, Dinamica de Sistemas, 1987, Solving Control Engineering Problems with MATLAB, 1994, Gendai Seigyo Kogaku, 1994, Designing Linear Control Systems with MATLAB, 1994, Kejuruteraan Kawalan Moden, 1996, Sistemas de Control en Tiempo Discreto, 1996, Projeto de Sistemas Lineares de Controle com MATLAB, 1996, Solucao de Problemas de Engenharia de Controle com MATLAB, 1997. Recipient Outstanding Adv. award Inst. of Tech., U. Minn., 1981, John R. Ragazzini Edn. award Am. Automatic Control Coun., 1999. Fellow ASME; mem. Sigma Xi, Pi Tau Sigma. Office: U Minn Dept Mech Engring Minneapolis MN 55455

OGATA, SADAKO, United Nations official; b. 1927. Min. Japan's Mission to UN, N.Y.C., 1978-79; spl. emissary UN; Japanese rep. Comm. on Human Rights, UN, 1982-85; former chair, exec. bd. UNICEF; former dir. Inst. Fgn. Rels. Sophia U., Tokyo, dean faculty of fgn. studies; high commr. UN High Commn. for Refugees, Geneva, 1991—. Office: UNHCR, Case postale 2500, 1211 Geneva 2 depot, Switzerland

OGATA, SHIJURO, banker; b. Tokyo, Nov. 16, 1927; s. Taketora and Koto (Hara) O.; m. Sadako Nakamura, Jan. 21, 1961; children: Atshushi, Akiko. BA, U. Tokyo, 1950; MA, Fletcher Sch. of Law/Diplomacy, 1955. Dep. gov. internat. rels. Bank of Japan, Tokyo, 1984-86; dep. gov. Japan Devel. Bank, Tokyo, 1986-91; dir. Barclays PLC & Barclays Bank PLC, London, 1991-95, Horiba, Kyoto, Japan, 1995—; advisor in Japan Swire Group, London, 1991-98; mem. internat. adv. coun. Chase Manhattan Bank, N.Y.C., 1991—; dir. Fuji Xerox, Tokyo, 1991—; chmn. Barclays Trust & Banking Co. (Japan) Ltd., 1993-97; advisor Imperial Hotel, Tokyo, 1991—; mem. Asia Pacific adv. com. N.Y. Stock Exch., 1991—; dep. chmn. Trilateral Commn. Contbr. numerous articles to profl. jours. Mem. Group of Thirty. Home: 3-29-18 Denenchofu, Ota-ku Tokyo 145-0071, Japan

OGATA, TOMOYUKI, chemist, researcher; b. Sakai, Osaka, Japan, Aug. 1, 1967; s. Ritsuo and Akiko (Yao) O.; m. Miho Takahashi, Apr. 23, 1995; children: Takamitsu, Hayato. PhD, Osaka U., Suita, Japan, 1995. Vis. scientist Brookhaven Nat. Lab., Upton, N.Y., 1995-96; researcher Mitsubishi Chem. Corp., Yokohama, Japan, 1996—. Mem. Japan Soc. Applied Physics. Avocation: volleyball. Office: Mitsubishi Chem Corp, 1000 Kamoshida Aoba-ku, 227-8502 Yokohama Kanagawa, Japan

OGAWA, HIDEMITSU, computer science educator; b. Kamo-gun, Hiroshima, Japan, Jan. 17, 1942; s. Mitsuyoshi and Utako (Kazuta) O.; m. Kyoko Tanaka, May 18, 1969; 1 child, Mitsunori. B in Engring., Tokyo Inst. Tech., 1965, DEng, 1977; hon. doctor, Lappeenranta U. Tech., Finland, 1994. Mem. rsch. staff Electrotech. Lab., Ministry Internat. Trade and Industry, Tokyo, 1965-72; rsch. asst. Tokyo Inst. Tech., 1972-78, assoc. prof., 1978-87, prof., 1987—; temp. lectr. Gunma U., Kiryu, Japan, 1978-95, Niigata (Japan) U., 1979-99, Kuopio (Finland) U., 1984-85, Tsukuba (Japan) U., Hitotsubashi U., Tokyo, 1990, Meiji U., Tokyo, 1991, Nagoya (Japan) U., 1991-92; vis. prof. Helsinki U. Tech., Otaniemi, Finland, 1984-85; cons. mem. evaluation com. on Inst. for Posts and Telecom. character recognition competition Inst. for Posts and Telecom. Policy, Ministry Posts and Telecom., Tokyo, 1992-94; cons., spkr. in field. Editor, co-author: New Horizons in Pattern Recognition and Understanding-Problems to be Challenged, 1994; contbr. articles to profl. jours. Active Nordic Cultural Soc. Japan. Grantee-in-aid for sci. rsch. The Ministry of Edn., Tokyo, 1978-83, 86-97, 99—; grantee for sci. rsch. Secom Sci. and Tech. Found., Tokyo, 1986-88, The Okawa Inst. Info. and Telecom., Tokyo, 1988. Mem. IEEE, Am. Math. Soc., Inst. Electronics, Info. and Comm. Engrs. (mem. various coms., bd. dirs. 1994-96, others), Info. Processing Soc. Japan (editor 1981-86), Audio Visual Info. Rsch. Group (many offices including auditor 1987-89), Pattern Recognition Soc. (assoc. editor 1992-98), Internat. Assn. for Pattern Recognition (tech. com. mem. 1994—), Japanese Soc. for Artificial Intelligence, Japanese Neural Network Soc., Internat. Neural Network Soc., others. Avocations: poetry, literature, music, painting, architecture. Office: Toyko Inst Tech Computer Sc, 2-12-1 Ookayama Meguro-ku, Tokyo 152-8552, Japan

OGAWA, MAKOTO, environmentalist, mycologist; b. Kyoto, Japan, Oct. 30, 1937; s. Chuji and Kimiko (Fukawa) O.; m. Yoko Katayama, July 22, 1969; children: Jun, Ryo. B in Agr., Kyoto U., 1961, MS in Agr., 1963, D in Agr., 1966. Sr. rschr. Forestry and Forest Products Rsch. Inst. Ministry Agr., Forests and Fishery, Tokyo, 1967-72, chief rschr. of soil microbiology, 1973-86; section leader planning Ministry Agr., Forests and Fishery, Japan, 1986-87, sect. leader mushroom scis., 1987-91; dir. biol. environ. inst., mgr. Kansai Environment Engring. Co. Ltd, Uji, Japan, 1991—, cons. Author: (books in Japanese) The Biology of Matsutake, 1978, Forest and Fungi, 1980, Natural History of Mushroom, 1983, Symbiotic Microorganisms Joining Root and Soil, 1985. Recipient Sci. Achievement award Internat. Union of Forestry Rsch. Orgns., Austria, 1981, recipient Japan Forestry Awd., Japan Forestry Assn., 1980, NIKKEI Global Environment Tech. Awd., 1998. Mem. Japan Mycological Soc. (award 2000), Japan Forestry Soc. (Japan Forestry award 1980), Japan Mycorrhiza Rsch. Soc. Avocations: reading, writing, painting, walking. Home: 4-1-33 Nanryo cho, Kyoto Uji 611-0028, Japan Office: KEEC Biol Environ Inst, 8-4 Ujimatabuti, Kyoto Uji 611-0011, Japan

OGAWA, TOHRU, electrical engineer, researcher; b. Kawasaki, Japan, Aug. 14, 1959; s. Tadashi and Shima (Hakari) O.; m. Kyoko Taira, May 30, 1992; 1 child, Mayu. B in Physics, Rikkyo U., Tokyo, 1984; D of Electronics, Tokyo Inst. of Tech., 1997. Engr. Canon Inc., Japan, 1985-90; sr. rsch. scientist SONY corp., Japan, 1990-96, mgr., 1999—; team leader Selete, Japan, 1997-99. Contbr. articles to profl. jours.; patentee in field. Mem. SPIE (program com. optical micro-lithography sect. 1994—). Achievements include patents for SiON inorganic anti-reflective layer; weak off-axis illuminaion in microlithography. Avocation: skiing. Office: SONY Corp Semiconductor Div, 4-14-1 Asahi-Cho, 243-0014 Atsugi-shi Japan

OGAWA, TORU, science laboratory administrator, educator; b. Naruto, Tokushima, Japan, Mar. 9, 1924; s. Masuji Saito and Machie Ogawa; m. Toshiko Suzue, Apr. 1, 1954; children: Mikiko, Atsushi, Keiko. BS, Kyoto U., 1949, DSc, 1961. Cert. in physics. Prof. Doshisha U., Kyoto, 1961-67; prof. Kyoto U., 1967-87, prof. emeritus, 1987—; prof. Osaka Electro-Comm. U., 1987-94; dir. HFD Lab., Kyoto, 1994—; vis. prof. Darian (China) Maritime U., 1994—; profl. mem. radio-wave tech. com. Ministry of Post, Japan, 1960-82; mem. com. of sci. satellite Inst. of Space and Astronautical Sci., Tokyo, 1968-81. Contbr. articles to profl. jours. Recipient Kokusai Denshin Denwa award, 1984. Avocations: classical music, traveling. Office: HFD Lab, Nagareda Kamitakano, 606 Kyoto Japan

OGAWA, TOSHIO, materials engineering educator; b. Ichikawa, Chiba-ken, Japan, Apr. 8, 1940; s. Susumu and Toku Ogawa; m. Akiko Wakabayashi, Oct. 10, 1969; children: Toshikazu, Miwako. BA, Yokohama (Japan) Nat. U., 1965, MS, 1967; D. of Engring., Kyoto (Japan) U., 1976. Sr. researcher Ube Industries, Osaka, Japan, 1976-85; prof. of materials engring. Kanazawa (Japan) Inst. Tech., 1985—, assoc. dean of career placement, 1994—; assoc. prof. Mich. Molecular Inst., 1978-80; rschr. in conservation sci., biodegradable polymers, surface treatment and characterization of polymer films. Author: Polyimides, 1989, Introduction to Polymeric Materials, 1993; editor: Jour. Adhesion Soc. Japan, 1997—. Avocations: tennis, fishing, private vegetable garden. Office: Kanazawa Inst Tech, 7-1 Ohgigaoka Nonoichi, Ishikawa 921, Japan

OGAWA, YASUO, pharmacology educator, researcher; b. Minato-ku, Tokyo, June 30, 1939; m. Toshiko Nobuoka, May 11, 1968; children: Megumi, Kaoru. MD, U. Tokyo, 1964, PhD, 1969. Rsch. assoc. U. Tokyo, 1969-76, Rockefeller U., N.Y.C., 1972-75; prof. Juntendo U., Tokyo, 1976—. Reviewer handbooks Exptl. Pharmacology, 1988, Critical Rev. Biochem. Molecular Biology, 1994; contbr. articles to profl. jours. E-mail: ysogawa@med.juntendo.ac.jp. Office: Juntendo U Sch Medicine, 2-1-1 Hongo, Bunkyo Tokyo 113-8421, Japan

OGAWA, YOSHIHIDE, urologist; b. Utsunomiya, Tochigi, Japan, Sept. 18, 1942; s. Hajime and Toyo (Komatsu) Gomi; m. Yumiko Sano, May 28, 1972; children: Yuho, Tomohide, Miho. MD, Keio U., Tokyo, Japan, 1970, PhD, 1982; MD, Med. Coll. Va., 1978. Clk. Neurol. Clinic, Tübingen U., Germany, 1968; asst. Sch. Medicine Keio U., Tokyo, 1971-76; clin. fellow Med. Coll. Va., Richmond, 1976-78; asst. prof. Sch. Medicine U. Tsukuba, Ibaragi, Japan, 1978-82, Juntendo U., Tokyo, Japan, 1982-94; assoc. prof. Faculty Medicine U. Ryukyus, Nishihara, Japan, 1994-95, prof. Faculty of Medicine, 1995—; vis. prof. U. Iowa, Mayo Clinic, 1998. Author: Studies on Oxalate In Urolithiasis, 1982 (Japan Urol. Assn. award 1982), Studies of Urolithiasis, 1993 (Spl. award Keio U. 1993); contbr. papers to profl. jours. Mem. Japan Urol. Assn. (con. 1979—, pres. Okinawa chpt. 1995), Japanese Soc. Nephrology (Cons. 1984—), The Japan Soc. for Transplantation (con. 1984—). Avocations: golf, jogging, baseball. Home: 2-96-1 # 3-103 Ryudai, Igakubu Shokuin Shukusha, Ishimine-cho Shuri 903-0804, Japan Office: Faculty of Med U Ryukyus, Dept Urology 207 Uehara, Nishihara, Okinawa 903-0215, Japan

OGAWARA, HIROSHI, biochemistry educator; b. Tokyo, Sept. 11, 1935; m. Hiroko Ogawara, Feb. 27, 1961; children: Yuki, Reiko. BS, U. Tokyo, 1958, MS, 1960, Dr.Pharm.Sci., 1968. Researcher Nat. Inst. Health of Japan, Tokyo, 1960-75; prof. biochemistry Meiji Pharm U, Tokyo, 1975—. Mem. Biochem. Soc. Japan (councilor), Pharm. Soc. Japan (councilor), Antibiotic Soc. Japan (councilor), Soc. Actinomycetes Japan (bd. dirs.), N.Y. Acad. Sci. Office: Meiji Pharm U, Noshio 2 Kiyose, Tokyo 204-8588, Japan

OGBAA, KALU, English literature educator; b. Umuchiakuma, Abia, Nigeria, Aug. 21, 1945; came to U.S., 1977; s. Stephen and Ogonna (Uche) O.; m. Clara Nwankwo, Apr. 5, 1975 (div. Mar. 1994); children: Ikenna, Ndubuisi, Emeka, Nneka, Enyinna, Kelechi; m. Glory Eke Uche, Dec. 27, 1996; children: Uchenna, Adanne. BA in English with honors, U. Nigeria, Nsukka, 1973; MA in Black Studies, Ohio State U., 1977; PhD in English, U. Tex., 1981. Asst. lectr. Alvan Ikoku Coll. Edn., Owerri, Nigeria, 1974-76; teaching assoc. Ohio State U., Columbus, 1977; asst. instr. U. Tex., Austin, 1978-81, lectr. English, 1981; asst. prof. Imo State U., Okigwe, Nigeria, 1982-85; assoc. prof. Imo State U., Okigwe, 1985-89, Oral Roberts U., Tulsa, Okla., 1989-90, Clark Atlanta U., 1990-92; assoc. prof. So. Conn. State U., New Haven, 1992-95, prof. English, 1995—; acting dir. gen. studies program Imo State U., Okigwe, 1987-89. Author: Gods, Oracles and Divination: Folkways in Chinua Achebe's Novels, 1992, Igbo, 1995, Understanding Things Fall Apart, 1999; editor: The Gong and the Flute: African Literary Development and Celebration, 1994. Grantee Fed. Nigeria scholarship Fed. Ministry Edn., 1971-73, Imo State Postgrad. scholarship Imo State Ministry Edn., 1980, Fed. Nigeria Postgrad. scholarship Fed. Ministry Edn., 1980-81; So. Conn. State U. scholar, 2000. Mem. MLA, CLA, African Lit. Assn., African Studies Assn., Commonwealth Lit. Assn., Assn. Grad. Students English (exec.), Imo State U. Faculty Asembly (sec. 1982-89), Phi Kappa Phi. Presbyterian. Avocations: choirmaster, laypreacher. Fax: 203-392-6731. Office: So Conn State U Dept English New Haven CT 06515

OGBAR, JEFFREY OGBONNA GREEN, history educator; b. June 10, 1969. BA, Morehouse Coll., 1991; MA, Ind. U., 1993, PhD, 1997. Jeffrey Campbell fellow St. Lawrence U., Canton, N.Y., 1996-97; asst. prof. U. Conn., Storrs, 1997—.

OGBECHIE, CHRIS IKE, marketing consulting executive; b. Zaria, Nigeria, Apr. 8, 1950; s. Christopher Onweazu and Felicia (Okonkuo) O.; m. Rose Kambili Chiedu, June 30, 1975; children: Ijeoma, Eneka, Ekene, Ikenna, Namdi, Onyeka. BSc with first class honors, Manchester (Eng.) U., 1974, MBA, 1976; mktg. diploma. Product mgr. Xerox Nigeria, Lagos, 1977-79; sr. product mgr. Nestle Nigeria, Lagos, 1979-81, Nestle Malaysia, Kuala Lumpur, 1981-83; head mktg. sales Nestle Nigeria, Lagos, 1983-90; mktg. dir., CEO Contact Mktg. Svcs., Lagos, 1991—; chmn., CEO Mktg. & Audit Rsch. Svcs., Lagos, 1994—; chmn. Project Mktg. Inst., Lagos, 1996—; resource person Lagos Bus. Sch., 1994—; cons. Ecobank, Lome/Toga, 1998—. Patron Madanna Sch. for Handicapped, Oupanam-Delta, Nigeria, 1995—; chmn. Oganihu Anioma, Lagos, 1996—. Home: 2 Ibimemi St Off Osoloway, Ajao Estate Lagos, Nigeria Office: Contact Mktg. Svcs., 149 Eleven Davys Babaniji, Ajao Estate Lagos, Nigeria

OGBEIBU, ANTHONY EKATA, zoologist, researcher; b. Emu, Edo, Nigeria, Oct. 19, 1959; s. Ogbeibu Imhanbe and Onore Alice (Osuenmhen) Ogbeibu; m. Beatrice Ekemheiyeva Aghenta, Aug. 23, 1987; children: Jim, Jerry. BSc, U. Benin, Nigeria, 1984, MSc, 1987, PhD, 1991. Cert. Environ. Edn., Glasgow. Master II Post Primary Edn. Bd., Benin City, Nigeria, 1987-90; conservation officer Nigerian Conservation Found., Benin City, 1989-90; asst. lectr. to sr. lectr. U. Benin, Benin City, 1990-1997, sr. lectr., 1997—; cons. Edo State Environ. Protection Agy., Nigeria, 1996—, Shell Petroleum Devel. Co., Nigeria, 1996—; bd. dirs. Bendel Pharms. Ltd., Nigeria, 1992-93. Author: Guide to Conservation Clubs, 1997; editor Tropical Freshwater Biology, 1993, 95, 96. Commr. (hon.) Edo (Bendel) State, Nigeria, 1993; pres. Men's Ministries Assemblies of God Ch., Nigeria, 1996, Full Gospel Bus. Men's Fellowship, Ugbowo, 2000. Rsch. grantee U. Benin, Nigeria, 1992. Fellow Nigerian Conservation Found.; mem. Nigerian Assn. Aquatic Scis., Nigerian Assn. Environ. Edn., U. Benin Alumni Assn. (pres. 1995, cert. honour 1995), N.Y. Acad. Scis. Avocations: jogging, swimming, karate, table tennis, photography. Office: Dept Zoology, U Benin, PMB 1154 Benin City Edo, Nigeria

OGBONNA, JOSEPH UZOECHINA, nutritional biochemist; b. Imo, Nigaria, Jan. 15, 1946; s. Nwaulu and Egbedie Ndie Ogbonna; m. Charity Chioma Nwokena, Sept. 28, 1969; children: Chinedu, Chinonye, Emeka, Chidi. BSc, U. Ibadan, Nigeria, 1979, MSc, 1982, PhD in Animal Sci., 1991. Asst. tutor Inst. Agrl. Rsch. and Tng., Ibadan, 1979-84, tutor II, 1984-87, tutor I, 1987-91, lectr. I, 1991-93, sr. lectr., 1993-96, prin. lectr., 1996—; resource person Osun State Agrl. Devel. Program, Nigeria, 1996—. Sec. Umuozu Devel. Union, Ibadan, 1982-92, chmn., 1996—. Rsch. grant Fed. Ministry of Sci. and Tech., Nigeria, 1998. Mem. Nigeria Soc. Animal Protection, Animal Sci. Assn. Nigeria, World Poultry Sci. Assn. Mem. Redeemed Christian Ch. of God. Avocations: reading, drama, singing, music, football. Office: Inst Agrl Rsch & Tng, PMB 5029 Moor Plantation, Ibadan Nigeria

OGBONNA, JOSHUA UZOMA, environmental and geographic science educator; b. Port-Harcourt, Nigeria, Dec. 25, 1962; s. Aaron Wogwugwu and Esther (Abel) O.; m. Florence Ugochi Madugba, May 7, 1994. ABA, Fed. Sch. Arts and Sci., Nigeria, 1980; BSc with honors, U. Ibadan, Nigeria, 1983, MSc, 1985, MSc in Geographic Info. Sys., 1998. Accounts clk. Nat. Elec. Power Plc., Lagos, Nigeria, 1977-78; youth corps person Nat. Youth Svc. Corps, Uyo, Nigeria, 1984; lectr., then sr. lectr. Abia State U., Uturu, Nigeria; cons. Spatial Comm., Okigwe, Nigeria, 1995—, Nigerian Nat. Commn. for UNESCO, 1996—, Abia State Environ. Protection Agy., 1998; bd. dirs. AMOJI Cmty. Bank. Author: Nigeria: Giant in the Tropics, 1993, Marine Pollution in Nigeria, Issues, Problems and Prospects, 1998; editor Jour. of Environ. Mgmt. and Tech., 1998; contbr. articles to sci. and profl. jours. Dir. Global Youth Radical Justice for Balance Environ., Nigeria, 1996—. Mem. N.Y. Acad. Scis., Nat. Geographic Soc., Nigerian Geographic Assn., Global Environ. Peace Initiative. Seventh Day Adventist. Avocations: reading, driving, board games, music. Home: 140 Owerri Rd, Okigwe Nigeria Office: Abia State U Sch Environ, Studies PMB 2000, Uturu Nigeria

OGBUEFI, JOSEPH UGOCHUKWU, real estate educator; b. Nsukka, Nigeria, Dec. 28, 1954; s. Simon Ezenyinwa and Lucy Oyiliona (Umeh) O.; m. Joy Obianuju Okafor, May 23, 1992; children: Nnubia, Sonoi, Ejielo, Enuma. BSc, U. Nigeria, Nsukka, 1978, MSc, 1983, PhD, 1988. Land officer Ministry Housing & Environment, Sokoto, Nigeria, 1978-79; lectr. Coll. Tech., Owerri, Nigeria, 1979-80, U. Nigeria, Nsukka, 1980-95; head dept. estate mgmt. U. Nigeria, Enugu, Nigeria, 1995-99; mem. Property Rating Tribunal, Nnewi, Nigeria, 1982-84; chmn. Anambra (Nigeria) State Indsl. Estate Devel. Bd., Enugu, 1989-92; mem. sch. bd. postgrad. studies U. Nigeria, Nsukka, 1992-96. Author: The Time Between, 1985; contbr. articles to profl. jours. Mem. Nnobi (Nigeria) Market Mgmt. Com., 1984-86; pres. Ifite-Nnobi Youth Assn., Anambra, 1998—. Fellow Nigerian Instn. Estate Surveyors and Valuers (sec. 1984-86); mem. Nigerian Environ. Soc. Avocations: reading, writing, swimming. Home: PO Box 9202, 31 Amokwe St, Uwani Nigeria Office: U Nigeria, Dept Estate Mgmt, Enugu Nigeria

OGDEN, DAVID WILLIAM, lawyer; b. Washington, Nov. 12, 1953; s. Horace Greeley and Elaine Celia (Condrell) O.; m. Wannett Smith, 1988; children: Jonathan Smith, Elaine Smith. BA summa cum laude, U. Pa., 1976; JD magna cum laude, Harvard U., 1981. Bar: D.C. 1983, Va. 1986, U.S. Dist. Ct. D.C. 1984, U.S. Dist. Ct. (ea. dist.) Va. 1988, U.S. Ct. Appeals (D.C. cir.) 1984, U.S. Ct. Appeals (4th cir.) 1986, U.S. Ct. Appeals (1st cir. 1989), U.S. Ct. Appeals (10th cir.) 1991, U.S. Supreme Ct. 1987, U.S. Ct. Appeals (5th cir.) 2000. Law clk. to presiding judge U.S. Dist. Ct. (so. dist.) N.Y., N.Y.C., 1981-82; law clk. to assoc. justice Harry A. Blackmun U.S. Supreme Ct., Washington, 1982-83; assoc. atty. Ennis, Friedman, Bersoff & Ewing, Washington, 1983-85; atty., ptnr. Ennis, Friedman & Bersoff, Washington, 1986-88, Jenner & Block, Washington, 1988-94; legal counsel, dep. gen. counsel U.S. DOD, Washington, 1994-95; assoc. dep. atty. gen. U.S. Dept. Justice, Washington, 1995-97, counselor to the atty. gen., 1997-98, chief of staff to atty. gen., 1998-99, acting asst. atty. gen. for Civil Divsn., 1999-2000, asst. atty. gen. for Civil Divsn., 2000—; adj. prof. law Georgetown U. Law Ctr., 1992-95. Author: (with Jerald A. Jacobs) Legal Risk Management for Associations, 1995. Recipient Disting. Pub. Svc. medal Dept. Def., 1995, Atty. Gen.'s medallion, 1999. Mem. ABA, D.C. Bar Assn., Phi Beta Kappa. Democrat.

OGDEN, GRAHAM RICHARD, oral and maxillofacial surgery educator; b. London, May 9, 1958; s. Dennis Richard and Margot Hope (Blenkinsop) O.; m. Anne Marie Dooley, May 4, 1985; children: Hannah, Thomas, Rosie. BDS, U. Sheffield, Eng., 1980; MDSc, U. Dundee, Scotland, 1988, PhD, 1992. Cert. in oral and maxillofacial surgery Royal Coll. of Physicians and Surgeons, Glasgow, 1993. Assoc. gen. practitioner dentistry Mansfield, Eng., 1980-81; sr. house officer Dudley Rd. Hosp., Birmingham, Eng., 1982, Bristol (Eng.) Dental Hosp., 1983; registrar Guy's Hosp., London, 1983-84; lectr. U. Dundee, Scotland, 1985-93, sr. lectr., 1993-99, hon. cons., surgeon, 1994—, prof. oral and maxillofacial surgery, 1999—; organizer, chair Ann. Meeting Lecturers in Oral Surgery, Dundee, 1990; session chair 8th Internat. Symposium on Prevention and Detection of Cancer, Nice, France, 1993; mem. editl. bd. European Jour. Cancer-Oral Oncology, London, 1995—, Brit. Jour. Oral and Maxillofacial Surgery, 1999—; external examiner PhD, U. London, 1996, 98, U. Wales, 1998, MDSc program U. Leeds, 1997—, BDS Glasgow, 1998, BDS U. Birmingham, 1999—, PhD U. Amsterdam, 1999, BDS Queens U., Belfast, No. Ireland, 2000—; sec. European Sci. Found. Network; specialist in oral surgery, surg. dentistry and oral medicine Gen. Dental Coun. U.K. Specialist Register. Contbr. numerous articles to profl. jours. including Lancet, Brit Med. Jour., Jour. of Nat. Cancer Inst., 1991—; interviewee on BBC World Svc. Broadcast, 1991. Recipient T.C. White prize lectureship, Royal Coll. Physicians and Surgeons, Glasgow, 1990, Brit. Soc. for Oral Medicine prize Brit. Soc. for Oral Medicine, 1990, Colgate prize Brit. Soc. for Dental Rsch., 1992, Howard Elder prize and medal for cancer rsch. U. Dundee, 1990; grantee Med. Rsch. Coun., Scottish Office. Fellow in dental surgery Royal Coll. Physicians and Surgeons (Glasgow), Brit. Assn. Oral and Maxillofacial Surgery, Internat. Assn. Oral and Maxillofacial Surgeons; mem. Nat. Dental Adv. Com. Scotland, Internat. Assn. for Dental Rsch., The Johnson Soc., Assn. Clin. Pathologists, Internat. Assn. Oral and Maxillofacial Surgery. Avocations: swimming, reading, tennis. Office: U Dundee Dundee Dental Hosp, Park Pl, Tayside Dundee DD1 4MN, Scotland

O'GEARY, DENNIS TRAYLOR, retired contracting/engineering company executive; b. Waverly, Va., Feb. 20, 1925; s. King William and Mary Virginia (Traylor) O'G.; m. Alice Stuart Baum, Aug. 3, 1947; children: Dennis Patrick, Mary Alice O'Geary Eisenbarth, Elizabeth Christina O'Geary Bernstorf. Surveying degree, Tri-State U., 1943; BS in Civil Engring., Ill. Inst. of Tech., 1947. Resident engring trainee Va. Hwy. Dept., Richmond, 1947-50; civil engring. supt. Wiley Jackson Co., Roanoke, Va., 1950-57; engr., asst. estimator, project mgr., v.p. and asst. to area mgr. S.J. Groves & Sons Co., Mpls. and Springfield, Ill., 1957-77, v.p., area mgr., 1978-82; v.p., asst. divsn. mgr., divsn. estimator S.J. Groves & Sons Co., Atlanta, 1982-84; pres. Peabody S.W., Inc., Houston, 1984-85; v.p. Houston ops. J.D. Abrams, Inc., Austin, Tex., 1985-99; ret., 1999; cons. J.D. Abrams, Inc. Served with USNR, 1943-46. Mem. ASCE (life), Am. Concrete Inst., Soc. Am. Mil. Engrs. (50 yr. mem.), Nat. Maritime Hist. Soc. Methodist. Home: 15402 Cresent Oaks Ct Houston TX 77068-2079 Office: 111 Congress Ave Austin TX 78701-4050

OGEDE, ODE, literature educator; b. Uchenyim Igede, Benue, Nigeria, Sept. 16, 1956; came to the U.S., 1994; s. Ogede and Margaret (Ogwuna) Ode; m. Shianyisimi Asabe, Apr. 5, 1986; children: Ochuole, Ogede, Shekwaga. BA in English Lit. with honors, Ahmadu Bello U., Zaria, Nigeria, 1979, MA in African Lit., 1982, PhD in English, 1987. Sr. lectr. in English Ahmadu Bello U., Zaria, 1988-94; Andrew Mellon faculty fellow U. Pa., Phila., 1994-95; vis. prof. Lincoln U., Pa., 1995-96; English prof. N.C. Ctrl. U., Durham, 1996—. Author: Art, Society and Performance, 1997, Ayi Kwei Armah: Radical Iconoclast, Pitting Imaginary Worlds Against the Actual, 1998, Achebe and the Politics of Representation, 2000; editor SAIWA (Roots), 1989-94; mem. editl. bd. Studies of Nigerian Cultures and Society, 1990-94; contbr. articles to profl. jours. Mem. MLA, MLA of Nigeria (v.p. 1989-91), African Lit. Assn. Am. Home: 129 Celeste Cir Chapel Hill NC 27514-8916 Office: NC Central U Comms Bldg Rm 327 Durham NC 27707

OGÉE, FRÉDÉRIC, English literature and art educator; b. Boulogne Billancourt, France, July 26, 1957; s. Alain and Genevieve (Rialan) O.; m. Marie Launay, July 23, 1997; children: Jacob, Raphaëlle. Grad., Ecole Normale Supérieure, Saint Cloud, France, 1982; Doctorat, U. Paris X, Nanterre, France, 1984, habilitation a diriger rech., 1994. Maitre de conf. U. Paris X, 1988-96; prof. U. Paris 7-, Denis Diderot, France, 1996—; pres. sci. coun. U. Paris 7, Denis Diderot, France, 1997—. Editor: The Dumb Show: Image and Society in the Works of William Hogarth, 1997; co-author: (with M.C. Rouyer) R.B. Sheridan: The Critic, 1995, (with P. Boucher) Grammaire Appliquee de L'Anglais, 1997. Vis. fellow Gonville and Caius Coll., Cambridge, Eng., 1994; rsch. fellow William Andrews Clark Meml. Libr., UCLA, 1997. Home: 13 Blvd Arago, 75013 Paris France Office: U F R d'Etudes Anglophones, U Paris 7 Denis Diderot, 75004 Paris France

OGG, ROBERT DANFORTH, corporate executive; b. Gardiner, Maine, June 10, 1918; s. James and Eleanor B. (Danforth) O.; m. Nancy Foote, Oct. 21, 1978; children by previous marriage: Richard Aasgaard, Robert Danforth, James Erling. Student U. Calif., Berkeley, Stanford U. Utilities engr. State of Calif., 1946-48; gen. mgr. Danforth Anchors, Berkeley, 1948-51, pres., chief exec. officer, 1951-59; mng. dir. Danforth div. The Eastern Co., 1959-79, dir., 1972-80; dir. Hodgdon Bros., East Boothbay, Maine, 1961-65; pres. Brewers Boatyard, West Southport, Maine, 1963-65; v.p.

Henry R. Hinckley Co., Manset, Maine, 1974-79; pres. Ogg Oceans Systems, 1980—; chmn. Alpha Ocean Systems, 1983—. Author: Anchors & Anchorin (8 editions); contbr. chpts. to books, articles to profl. jours.; patentee in field; inventor The Danforth Anchor, Inertial Altimeter, Digital Depth Sounder, others. Mem. adv. com. U. Calif. Rsch. Expeditions Program, 1979, co-chmn., 1983—; trustee U. Calif.-Berkeley Found., 1981, exec. com., 1983—, chmn. audit com., 1984-89, fellow, 1990, lifetime emeritus trustee; advisor Lawrence Hall Sci.; founder, sr. warden St. Ann's Episcopal Ch., Windham, Maine, 1976-79; life fellow U. Calif., Berkeley; contbr. to ABC and BBC documentaries on Pearl Harbor. With USN Intelligence, 1941-46. Recipient Wheeler Oak meritorious award U. Calif., 1987. Fellow Explorers Club (life), Calif. Acad. Scis. (life); mem. Navy League (founder Marin coun.), Soc. Naval Architects & Marine Engrs., Am. Soc. Naval Engrs., Am. Boat & Yacht Coun., Boating Writers Internat., Am. Geophys. Union, IEEE, Chancellors Cir. U. Calif., Sports Adv. Coun. U. Calif., Bodega Marine Lab., U.S. Naval Inst., R.G. Sproul Assocs., Tail Hook Assocs., Woodshole Assocs., Buncke Microsurgical Found. (bd. dirs. 1994—), Sierra Club, U. Calif.-Berkeley Alumni Assn., Engring. Alumni Assn., N.Y. Yacht Club, Pacific Union Club, Elks Club, Bear Backers Club, U. Calif. Berkeley Chancellor's Circle Club, U. Calif. San Francisco Heritage Club. Address: 11490 Franz Valley Rd Calistoga CA 94515-9549

OGG, WILSON REID, lawyer, poet, retired judge, lyricist, curator, publisher, educator, philosopher, social scientist, parapsychologist; b. Alhambra, Calif., Feb. 26, 1928; s. James Brooks and Mary (Wilson) O. Student, Pasadena Jr. Coll., 1946; AB, U. Calif., Berkeley, 1949; JD, U. Calif., 1952; Cultural D in Philosophy of Law, World U. Roundtable, 1983. Bar: Calif. 1955. Assoc. trust dept. Wells Fargo Bank, San Francisco, 1954-55; pvt. practice Berkeley, 1955—; adminstrv. law judge, 1974-93; real estate broker, cons., 1974—; curator-in-residence, Pinebrook, 1964—; owner Pinebrook Press, Berkeley, 1988—; rsch. atty., legal editor Dept. of Continuing Edn. of Bar U. Calif., 1958-63;instr. 25th Sta. Hosp., Taegu, Korea, 1954, Taegu English Lang. Inst., 1954; trustee World U., 1976-80; dir. admissions Internat. Soc. for Phil. Enquiry, 1981-84; dep. dir. gen. Internat. Biographical Ctr., England, 1986—; dep. gov. Am. Biographical Inst. Rsch. Assn., 1986—. Contbr. articles to profl. jours.; contbr. poems to mags. With AUS, 1952-54. Elected to Internat. Poetry Hall of Fame Nat. Libr. Poetry, 1997. Mem. VFW, AAAS, ABA, ASCAP, ACLU, Internat. Platform Assn., Internat. Soc. Unified Sci., Internat. Soc. Poets (life), Amnesty Internat., Internat. Soc. Individual Liberty, State Bar Calif., San Francisco Bar Assn., Am. Arbitration Assnl. (nat. panel arbitrators), Calif. Soc. Psychical Study (pres., chmn. bd. 1963-65), Intertel, Triple Nine Soc., Wisdom Soc., Inst. Noetic Scis., Men's Inner Circle of Achievement, Truman Libr. Inst. (hon.), Am. Legion, City Commons Club (Berkeley), commonwealth Club of Calif., Town Hall Club Calif., Marines Meml. Club, Masons, Shriners, Elks. Unitarian. Fax: 510-540-6052. Home: Pinebrook 8 Bret Harte Way Berkeley CA 94708-1611 Office: 1104 Keith Ave Berkeley CA 94708-1607 also: 39231 Liberty St Fremont CA 94538-1501

OGI, ADOLF, government official; b. Kandersteg, Switzerland, July 18, 1942. Diploma, Comml. Coll., La Neuveville, Switzerland; postgrad., Swiss Mercantile Sch., London. Mgr. Soc. Devel. and Improvement Meiringen and Hasli Valley, Canton Berne, 1963-63; tech. dir. Swiss Ski Assn., 1964-74, dir., 1975-81; vice chmn. World and European Com. of Internat. Ski Fedn., 1971-83; chmn. Swiss People's Party, 1984-87; mem. fed. legislature Nat. Coun., Berne, 1979, chmn. mil. com., 1986-87, chief fed. dept. transport, comm. and energy, 1988-95; v.p. Fed. Coun., Berne, 1992, 99; pres. Switzerland, 1993; chief Fed. Dept. Def., Civil Protection & Sports, Switzerland, 1996—. Office: Fed Dept Def Civil Protection & Sports, Bundeshaus-West, 3003 Bern Switzerland*

OGIELA, MAREK ROMUALD, computer science educator; b. Cracow, Poland, July 19, 1968; s. Julian and Izydora (Znamirowska) O. MS in Computer Sci., Jagiellonian U., Cracow, 1992; PhD in Automatics and Robotics, AGH Tech. U., Cracow, 1996. Assoc. prof. AGH Tech. U., Cracow, 1996—. Contbr. articles to profl. jours. Mem. SPIE, Soc. for Imaging Sci. and Tech., Soc. for Computer Applications in Radiology. Home: os Jagiellonskie 35/6, PL31-837 Cracow Poland Office: AGH Tech U Inst Automatics, 30 Mickiewicza Ave, PL30-059 Cracow Poland

OGIHARA, TOSHIO, medical educator; b. Ohta City, Gunma, Japan, Jan. 16, 1944; s. Kiyotoshi and Kino Ogihara; m. Mutsuko Shiraishi, Apr. 13, 1943; 1 child, Shunji. MD, Osaka U., 1968, PhD, 1977. Medical diplomate, 1968. Rsch. fellow U. Ariz., Tucson, 1974-75; instr. Osaka U., Japan, 1976-81, assoc. prof., 1981-88, prof., 1988—; dir. geriatric medicine, Osaka U., 1988—. Editor: Molecular Hypertensinolog, 1993. Fellow Am. Heart Assn.; mem. Endocrine soc., Coun. on Geriatric Cardiology, Interant. Soc. Hypertension (coun.). Office: Osaka U Dept Geriatric Medicine, Yamadaoka 2-2, Suita 565-0871, Japan

OGILVIE, DONALD GORDON, bankers association executive; b. N.Y.C., Apr. 7, 1943; s. John B. and Ann (Stephens) O.; m. Fan Staunton, Apr. 18, 1966; children: Jennifer B., Adam C. B.A., Yale U., 1965; M.B.A., Stanford U., 1967. Systems analyst Dept. of Def., Washington, 1967-68; pres., dir. ICF Inc., Washington, 1969-73; dep. assoc. dir. Office of Mgmt. and Budget, Washington, 1973-74, assoc. dir., 1974-76; assoc. dean Yale U., New Haven, 1977-80; v.p. Celanese Corp., N.Y.C., 1980-85; exec. v.p. Am. Bankers Assn., Washington, 1985—; dir. Colonial Bancorp, 1979-85, MacDermid Corp., 1986—, Marine Spill Response Corp., 1991—. Bd. dirs. N.Y.C. Ballet, 1981-88, Hospiec Edn. and Rsch., New Haven, 1978-81; mem. adv. bd. Yale Sch. Orgn. and Mgmt., 1992-94. Home: 3133 Connecticut Ave NW Apt 923 Washington DC 20008-5111 Office: Am Bankers Assn 1120 Connecticut Ave NW Washington DC 20036-3902*

OGISO, KEN, engineering educator, researcher; b. Tokyo, Sept. 9, 1931; s. Kin and Hana (Machida) O.; m. Kazuko Tazaki, May 17, 1964. B Engring., U. Tokyo, 1957, M Engring., 1959, D Engring., 1978. Sr. rschr. Nippon Telegraph & Telephone Co. Ltd., Tokyo, 1961-73; staff engr. Nippon Telegraph & Telephone Co. Ltd., 1973-86; prof. Tokyo U. Tech., 1986—; staff engr. Nippon Telegraph & Telephone Co., Tokyo, 1973-86; chairperson conf. Internat. Soc. Hybrid Microelectronics, Tokyo, 1990. Author: Entropy Generation Rate in Counter-Flow Heat Exchanger, 2000. Mem. Japan Soc. Mech. Engrs., Inst. Elec. Engrs. Japan (chairperson com. 1986-89), Inst. Electronics, Info. and Comm. Engrs. (chairperson conf. 1985), Soc. Univ. Grads. Avocations: music, reading, driving, travel. Home: 2-9-12 Kinuta Setagaya-ku, Tokyo-to 157-0073, Japan Office: Tokyo U Tech, 1404-1 Katakura Hachiouji, Tokyo 192-8580, Japan

OGITA, SHUHEI, surgeon, educator; b. Itami, Japan, June 20, 1947; s. Yoshitaka and Takae (Takahashi) O.; m. Tokuko Tanaka, Sept. 24, 1978; children: Keiji, Yasuo. MD, Kyoto Prefectural U. Medicine, Japan, 1972, PhD, 1980. Fellow Matsushita Hosp. and Maizuru Nat. Hosp., 1974-76; jr. resident Kyoto Prefectural U. Medicine, 1972-74, sr. resident, 1976-78, asst., 1979-84, assoc. prof., 1985—. Author: Neonatal Screening, 1994, New Encyclopedia of Surgical Science, 1997. Bd. dirs. Fund Carlos-Chan, 1992. Japanese Ministry Edn., Sci., Sports and Culture grantee, 1982, 89. Mem. Japan Surg. Soc., Japanese Soc. Pediatric Surgeons, Japanese Cancer Assn. Avocations: travel, skiing, driving, movies. Home: 2-9-19 Utsukushi-ga-Oka, Takasuki, 569-1111 Osaka Japan Office: Children's Rsch Hosp Kyoto, Kawaramachi Kamigyo-ku, 602-8566 Kyoto 602-8566, Japan

OGIWARA, HIROYASU, electrical engineering educator; b. Hakodate, Hokkaido, Japan, Sept. 10, 1934; s. Shinzo and Matsuko (Kameoka) O.; m. Teruko Miyamae, Apr. 1962; 1 child, Hideo. BSc, U. Tokyo, 1958, DEng, 1970. Scientist Toshiba Co., Yokohama, Japan, 1958-73; chief rschr. Toshiba Co., Kawasaki, Japan, 1973-78, dir. Energy Sci. and Tech. Lab., 1978-85, fellow scientist, 1985-91, chief fellow scientist, 1991-94; prof. elec. engring. Shonan Inst. Tech., Fujisawa, Japan, 1994—; tech. cons. Author, editor: Applied Superconductivity, 1986; author: Super Train, 1990, Presentology of Superconductivity, 1993, Introduction to Cryogenics, 1994. Author, editor: Applied Superconductivity, 1986; author: Super Train, 1990, Presentology of Superconductivity, 1993, Introduction to Cryogenics, 1994. Recipient sci. and tech. award Office of Prime Min., 1990. mem. Japanese Inst. Elec. Engring. (best publ. award 1975, contbn. to progress of tech. award 1980), Cyrogenic Soc. Japan (trustee 1982-94, exec. dir. 1994—), Internat. Inst. Refrigeration (internat. com. 1988—), Untraditional Tech. Assn. (bd. mem. com. new superconduting material forum 1987—). Avocations: woodblock printing, painting, collecting Kokeshi, cooking. Home: 1-5-47-809 Honkugenuma, Fujisawa Kanagawa 251-8511, Japan Office: Shonan Inst Tech, 1-1-25 Tsujido-Nishikaigan, Fujisawa 251 0046, Japan

OGLE, ROY CLINTON, molecular biologist; b. Clark AFB, Philippines, Nov. 28, 1950; s. Roy R. and Helen Ruth (Schultz) O.; m. Rebecca Elizabeth Adams, Apr. 6, 1978; children: Molly Elizabeth, Katharine Adams. BA in Biology, U. Va., 1972, PHD, 1985. Rsch. specialist dept. orthopaedics U. Va., Charlottesville, 1973, rsch. asst. dept. biology, 1976-80, grad. rsch. fellow dept. cell biology and anatomy, 1982-85; biologist, then guest rschr. lab. devel. biology NIH, Bethesda, Md., 1985-87; asst. prof. anatomy & cell biology Med. U. S.C., Charleston, 1987-92; asst. prof. plastic surgery & cell biology U. Va., 1990-96, assoc. prof. neurol. surgery, plastic surgery, cell biology, 1996—. Editor: Craniofacial Surgery: A Multi-Disciplinary Approach to Craniofacial Anomalies, 2000; contbr. articles to profl. jours., chpts. to books. Basil O'Connor fellow March of Dimes, 1988-91; grantee NIH, Am. Cancer Soc. Mem. Am. Soc. Cell Biology, Plastic Surger Rsch. Coun., AAAS, Friends of Nat. Inst. Dental Rsch. Avocations: fly fishing, gardening, bird watching. Home: 415 Hickory Dr Earlysville VA 22936-9630 Office: U Va HSC Charlottesville VA 22908

OGO, YOSHIAKI, chemist; b. Tokushima, Japan, Dec. 6, 1930; s. Satoru and Ichino (Furukawa) O.; m. Mariko Tauchi, Apr. 10, 1960. BS, Tokushima U., 1953; DEng, Osaka (Japan) City U., 1964. Rsch. fellow Resources Rsch. Inst., Kawaguchi, Japan, 1957-64; asst. prof. Osaka City U., 1964-67, from assoc. prof. to prof., 1969-95; rsch. assoc. N.Y. State U., 1967-69; dir. gen. Rsch. Inst. for Solvothermal Tech., Takamatus, Japan, 1997—; vis. prof. Strausbourg (France) U., 1973. Author: Prosesu-Kaiseki-Keisanho, 1971, High Pressure Chemistry, 1972, Polymer Handbook, 1989. Office: Rsch Inst Solvothermal Tech, 2217-43 Hayashi, 761-0301 Takamatsu Japan

O'GORMAN, JAMES VIVIAN, health executive; b. Cork, Munster, Ireland, July 1, 1938; s. John Patrick (dec.) and Maura Ellen (Hobart) O'G.; m. Mary Josephine Gilmartin, Sept. 8, 1964; 1 child, Deirdre Mary. BSc, U. Coll. Cork, Ireland, 1959; PhD, Pa. State U., 1971. Postdoctoral fellow U. London, 1971-72; sr. rsch. fellow Confedn. Brit. Industry, Stevenage, U.K., 1972-74; registrar Nat. Coun. for Ednl. Awards, Dublin, Ireland, 1974-79; head rsch. divsn. Nat. Bd. for Sci. and Tech., Dublin, 1979-87; mgr. Irish Sci. and Tech. Agy., Dublin, 1987-88; chief exec. Health Rsch. Bd., Dublin, 1988-98; dir. Office Rsch. and Tech. Transfer Royal Coll. Surgeons, Ireland, 1998—; chmn. Inst. Water Pollution Control, Ireland, 1980-83; nat. rep. European Union Biomed. and Health Rsch. Com., Brussels, 1990-98, European Union Healthcare Telematics, Brussels, 1992-98. Chmn. editl. bd. (internat. newsletter) European Union Biomed. and Health Rsch., 1994. Recipient Silver medal Soc. Chem. Industry, U.K., 1975; named Centennial fellow Pa. State U., 1996. Fellow Royal Soc. Chemistry; mem. Inst. Chemistry Ireland (coun. mem. 1984-87). Avocations: reading, gardening, music, sports. Office: Health Rsch Bd, Royal Coll Surgeons, 123 St Stephen's Green, Dublin 2, Ireland

OGORODNIKOVA, NATALIA ALEKSEEVNA, chemist, researcher; b. Dzerjinsk, Gorjkovskaya, Russia, Oct. 10, 1938; d. Aleksei Feodorovich and Marianna Iakovlevna (Kutcherenko) Volkov; 1 child, Uliana Bashtanova. Grad., Mendeleev Moscow Chem. Tech. Inst., 1960; PhD in Chemistry, A.N. Nesmeyanov Inst., Moscow, 1985. Rschr. Nesmeyanov Inst. Organo-Element Compounds, Moscow, 1964—. Contbr. articles to profl. jours. Avocations: writing poetry, painting. Home: Apt 30, Profsoyusnaya St 142/4, 117321 Moscow Russia Office: A N Nesmeyanov Inst Organo-Elem, Vavilov St 28, 117813 Moscow Russia

O'GRADY, BEVERLY TROXLER, investment executive, counselor; d. Robert Andrew and Beverly Beam (Barrier) Troxler; m. Robert Edward O'Grady, Aug. 6, 1966. BA, St. Mary's Coll., 1963; MA, Columbia U., 1965. Exec. v.p. Wilkinson & Hottinger Inc., N.Y.C., 1973-94, Helvetia Capital Corp., N.Y.C., 1987-94; pres. Wilkinson O'Grady & Co., Inc., N.Y.C., 1994—; mem. adv. bd. Charles Schwab Fin., San Francisco, 1991-93. Active Women's Nat. Rep. Club, N.Y.C., 1991-94. Mem. Assn. Investment Mgrs., N.Y. Soc. Security Analysts, Women's Bond Club (pres. 1992-94), Univ. Club. Roman Catholic. Office: Wilkinson O'Grady & Co Inc 520 Madison Ave New York NY 10022-4213

O'GRADY, JOHN CHARLES, forensic psychiatrist, consultant; b. Mallow, Ireland, Sept. 15, 1952; arrived in U.K., 1976; s. Henry A. and Veva (Thomasson) O'Grady; m. Alison Child Hooper; children: Tom, Robert. MD, U. Ireland, Cork, Eire, 1975; MBA, U. Durham, Ireland, 1995. Sr. house officer, registrar U. Oxford, 1976-81; sr. registrar Newcastle Upon Tyne U., 1981-83; cons. with specialization in intensive care Leeds West Health Authority, 1983-89; cons. gen. psychiatrist Newcastle Mental Health NHS Trust, 1989-96; cons. forensic psychiatrist Southampton Cmty. Mental Health Inst., 1996—; divisional mgr. mental health svcs. Newcastle City Health NHS Trust, 1994-95; mem. steering com. Rev. of Svcs. Mentally Abnormal Offenders, 1990-92; mem., chair mental health subcom. Health Adv. Com. to Prison Svc., 1992-99. Occasional referee Brit. Jour. Psychiatry. Mem. joint home office/Dept. Health Rev. of Prison Healthcare, 1998-99, fellow Royal Coll. Psychiatrists. Avocations: outdoor pursuits, tennis, cinema, music. Office: Ravenswood Home, Knowle, Fareham Hampshire PO17 5NA, England

O'GRADY, MARY JOSEPHINE, editor, foundation consultant; b. Chgo., Sept. 25, 1951; d. Valentine Michael and Lillian Mary (Quinlan) O'G. Student, St. Mary's Coll., Rome, Italy, 1970-71; BFA, Manhattanville Coll., 1973; MA, Georgetown U., 1996. Assoc. editor Magnum Photos, N.Y.C., 1973-76; asst. picture editor Modern Photography Mag., N.Y.C., 1976-78; freelance photographer, N.Y.C., 1978-80; sr. producer Trans-Atlantic Enterprises, N.Y.C., L.A., 1981-82; dir. pub. info. World Wildlife Fund, Washington, 1983-84; sr. analyst Mead Data Cen., Washington, 1985-87; editor photos U.S. News and World Report, Washington, 1987-90; program dir. Sacharuna Found., 1990-92; adminstr. Roland Films, 1991-92; assoc. dir. AIDS Control and Prevention Project Family Health Internat., Washington, 1994-97, assoc. dir. Implementing AIDS Prevention and Care Project, 1998—; cons. Time, Inc., N.Y.C., 1981, Exxon Corp., N.Y.C., 1981-82, U.S. News and World Report, Washington, 1987, The German Marshall Fund of U.S., Conservation Internat., Washington, 1992, W. Alton Jones Found., 1993-94. Asst. editor: The Family of Woman, 1978; producer (TV shows) A Conversation With..., 1982, The Helen Gurley Brown Show, 1982, Outrageous Opinions, 1982; photo editor America's Best Colleges, 1989, 90, Great Vacation Drives, 1989. Recipient Editorial Excellence award Natural Resources Coun. Am., 1984. Mem. Soc. Environ. Journalists, Worldwide Women in Environment and Devel., Monitoring the AIDS Pandemic Network, Nat. Orgns. Responding to AIDS Internat. Issues Working Group, Internat. Bioethics Orgn. (trustee).

OGUNC, KURTAY, investment advisor, manager; b. Istanbul, Jan. 30, 1967; s. Kurtul and Aysel Ogunc; m. Asli Ogunc, Aug. 20, 1990; 1 child, Patara. BBA, Marmara U., Istanbul, 1990; MBA, Western Mich. U., 1992; M of Applied Stats., La. State U., 1997. Fin. cons. Interdata, Istanbul, 1992-93; securities analyst Global Securities, Istanbul, 1993-94; rsch. asst. La. State U., Baton Rouge, 1994-97, Western Mich. U., Kalamazoo, 1990-92; instr. La. State U., Baton Rouge, 1996-99, quantitative analyst, 1997-98, investment mgr., 1998—. Mem. Am. Statis. Assn., Am. Finance Assn., Decision Scis. Inst., Phi Kappa Phi, Beta Gamma Sigma. Avocations: reading, travel, writing, soccer, football. Home: 2542 Chain Bridge Rd Apt 102 Vienna VA 22181-5549

OGUNJOBI, KAYODE ADE, chemistry educator, researcher; b. Ijebu, Nigeria, Nov. 12, 1964; s. Moses Ade and Mope Abeni (Sanni) O.; m. Adeola Bukanla Bakare, Mar. 30, 1996. BS in Chemistry, U. Ibadan, Nigeria, 1987, MS, 1990, postgrad., 1994—. Chartered chemist. Fin. min. Tedder Hall, U. Ibadan, 1984-85; vice chmn. chemistry week com. U. Ibadan, 1986-87; artist Nat. Youth Svc. Corps Drama Troupe, Enugu, Nigeria, 1987-88; adminstr., tutor Ultimate Continuing Edn. Ctr., Ago Iwoye, Nigeria, 1993-97; chmn. Citywide Garments, 1997—; deptl. rep. faculty of sci. exam com. Ogun State U., Ago Iwoye, 1993-94, deptl. project coord., 1994-97, 200 level chemistry student course advisor, 1994-96, final yr. chemistry student oral exam com., 1994-96. Contbr. articles to profl. jours. Band leader Ch. Choiristers, Ijebu, Nigeria, 1972—; capt. Boys Brigade, Ijebu, 1980-88; electoral officer World U. Svc., U. Ibadan, 1984-85; orderly Ebumawe Coronation Com., Ago Iwoye, 1994; mem. election monitoring team Ijebu-North local Govt., Nigeria, 1998-99, mem. zoning com., 2000—, apptd. del. political group, 2000. Attachee Mil. Hosp. Lab. 82 Mechanised Divsn., Nigeria, 1987-88. Mem. Nigeria Inst. Mgmt., Sci. Assn. Nigeria, Chem. Soc. Nigeria, Children-in-Agr. Programme, Nat. Geog. Soc. Methodist. Avocations: table tennis, Scrabble, chess, musicals, writing, entertainment.

OGUNMOKUN, GABRIEL OLAYINKA, academic administrator, marketing educator; b. Ikeji-Ile, Nigeria, Feb. 23, 1952; s. James Kolawole and Felicia Olaitan Ogunmokun; m. Ruth Lilian Pengelley, Sept. 20, 1980; children: Sandra Adodele, Peter Oluseyi, Joshua Olusegun. BBA, Churchlands Coll. Advanced Edn, Perth, Australia, 1979; grad. diploma in bus. adminstrn., Western Australian Inst. Tech., Perth, 1980, MBA with distinction, 1981; PhD, Monash U., Melbourne, Victoria, Australia, 1992. Primary sch. tcir. Ife-Ijesha Local Sch. Bd., Ilesha, Nigeria, 1971-72; internal auditor Brit-Am. Ins. Co., Auchi Dist. and Lagos, Nigeria, 1973-77; assoc. lectr. mktg. and adminstrn. U. of the Pacific, Suva, Fiji, 1982-84; lectr. in mktg. U. So. Queensland, Toowoomba, Australia, 1985-86; sr. lectr. mktg., mgmt. and adminstrn., head mktg. Monash U., 1986-90; sr. lectr. mktg. City U. Hong Kong, 1990-93; dir. Australian Nat. Inst. Higher Edn., Melton, Victoria, 1993; sr. lectr. info. mgmt. and mktg. U. Western Australia, Perth, 1993—, dir. Rsch. Ctr. for Internat. Mktg. and Exporting, 1994—; lectr. Edith Cowan U., Perth, 1980-82, Queensland U. Tech., 1984, Griffith U., Brisbane, Australia, 1984; bus. mgmt., mktg. and export mgmt. cons., Brisbane, 1985-86; co-editor Pacific Jour. Mgmt., 1982-84; chair course adv. coun. Australian Nat. Inst. Higher Edn., Perth;. Editor Jour. Internat. Mktg. and Exporting, 1995—; author: (with John Hailey) Organization and Management: South Pacific Cases, 1984, (with Rony Gabbay) Contemporary Issues in International Business and Marketing, 1998; contbr. numerous articles to profl. jours., chpts. to books. Sec., newsletter editor Churchlands Coll. Christian Fellowship, Perth, 1978-79; leader teenage sect. Children's Spl. Svc. Mission, 1978-81; mem. coun. Christ Ch., Hong Kong, 1991-93; advisor Latrobe Valley Tourism Com., Morwell, Victoria, 1987-90; mem. com. mgmt. Churchill Cmty. Health Ctr., 1987-90; chmn. ch. growth com. Hamersley Anglican Ch., Perth, 1994—; group leader home fellowship Holy Cross Anglican Ch., Balcatta-Hamersley, 1994—. Recipient John Storey Meml. prize Australian Inst. Mgmt., 1979, 80. Mem. Am. Mktg. Assn., Am. Assn. Consumer Rsch., Acad. Mktg. Sci., Acad. Internat. Bus., Asian Acad. Mgmt., Internat. Students Support Assn. (pres. 1994—). Avocations: soccer, leading Bible studies, speaking. Fax: 61 08 9380 1004. E-mail: gogunmok@ecel.uwa.edu.au. Address: PO Box K789, Perth WA 6001, Australia Office: U Western Australia, Dept Info Mgmt and Mktg, Nedlands Perth WA Australia

OGUNNIYI, ADESOLA, neurologist, consultant, educator; b. Lagos, Nigeria, Dec. 9, 1953; s. Oyedele Samuel and Oyedoyin Margaret (Ogunrinka) O.; m. Jaiyeola Olayemi Thomas, Aug. 11, 1984; children: Adedamola, Adebola. BSc, U. Ife, Ile Ife, Nigeria, 1975, MBBS, 1978. Med. diplomate. Intern Univ. Coll. Hosp., Ibadan, Nigeria, 1978-79, registrar, 1980-85, cons., lectr., 1987-90, cons., sr. lectr., 1990-97, prof., 1997—; med. officer N.Y.S.C., Saminaka, Nigeria, 1979-80; vis. fellow NIH, Bethesda, 1986-87; mem. sci. adv. panel Alzheimer Disease Inst., U.K., 1998. Contbr. over 100 articles to sci. jours. Mem. Landlord's Assn., Akobo, Ibadan, 1993. Recipient Nat. Acad. award Fed. Govt. Nigeria, 1972-8, Bruce Schoenberg award Am. Acad. Neurology, 1991. Baptist. Avocations: music, reading, movies, tennis, travel. Home: Pdcos Estate Block 18, Orita Bashorun Plot 7, Ibadan Oyo, Nigeria Office: PMB 5116, Univ Coll Hosp, Ibadan Oyo, Nigeria

OGUNSOLA-BANDELE, MERCY FUNICE, science educator; b. Minna, Niger, Nigeria, Mar. 25, 1957; d. Albert Folorunsho and Victoria Ayo (Omotosho) Ogunsola; m. Victor Iunde Bandele, Aug. 29, 1981; children: Seyi, Femi, Iope. EdB in Sci. Edn., Ahmedy Bello U., Zaria, Nigeria, 1980, MEd in Sci. Edn., 1981, PhD in Sci. Edn., 1987; postdoctoral study, Ind. State U., 1992. Curriculum coord. Coll. Agr. Ahmedy Bello U., 1982-83, head basic scis., 1984-90, sr. lectr., 1994—, head sci. edn., 1995-99; vis. prof. Ind. State U., Terre Haute, 1991-92; resource person UNESCO, Abuja, Nigeria, 1998-99; local expert cons. World Bank, Washington, 1999-2000, COL/BR D, Can. and Washington, 1999-2000; mem. panel for visitation to colls. of edn. Fed. Govt. of Nigeria, 1999. Editor publ. on state of edn. in Nigeria, UNESCO, 1998, resource person book on tchg. and learning in higher edn., 1999; contbr. 4 chpts. to books, articles to profl. publs. African ednl. rsch. scholar Ohio U., 1991. Mem. Nat. Sci. Tchrs. Assn., Nat. Assn. Rsch. in Sci. Tchg. (mem. grad. and new rschrs. com. 1999), Sci. Tchrs. Assn. Nigeria, Mich. Coun. Tchrs. of Math. and Sci., Hoosier Sci. Tchrs. Assn., Assn. Sci. Edn. Mem. All Peoples Party Nigeria. Baptist. Avocations: listening to music, singing, baking. Home: PO Box 900, 7 Adeleye Rd, GRA, Ilorin Kwara, Nigeria Office: Ahmady Bello U Dept Edn, Zaria Nigeria

OGURA, CHIKARA, neuropsychiatry educator; b. Osaka, Japan, May 1, 1937; s. Iwao and Sukako (Hirata) O.; m. Fumiko Kimura; children: Satoru, Yoshiko. MD, Tottori U., Yonago, Japan, 1962, PhD, 1968. Instr. Tottori U., 1969, asst. prof., 1969-81, assoc. prof., 1981-84; prof. neuropsychiatry U. Ryukus, Okinawa, Japan, 1984—; dir. Univ. Hosp., 1998—; chmn. XIth Internat. Conf. on Event-Related Potentials of the Brain, 1995. Chief editor: Recent Advances in Event-Related Potential Brain Research, 1996. Avocation: tennis. Home: 4-58 Ishimine, Naha Okinawa 903-0804, Japan Office: U Ryukus Faculty Medicine, 208 Uehara, Uehara Okinawa 903-0215, Japan

ÖĞÜTÇÜ, MEHMET, organization administrator; b. Ankara, Turkey, Mar. 15, 1962; s. Erol and Sadakat (Aricioglu) O.; m. Seylan Goral, Feb. 5, 1986; children: Halil Can, Melis. BS in Internat. Rels., U. Ankara, 1983; hon. degree in pub. info. techniques, Brit. Cen. Office of Info., London, 1984; MS in Internat. Econs., U. London, 1985; MA in European Studies, Coll. D'Europe, Bruges, Belgium, 1992. Cert. in internat. banking. Sr. analyst Office of Prime Min., Ankara, 1979-83; sr. rsch. fellow NATO Secretariat, Brussels, 1985-86; diplomatic corr. Turkish Daily News and Milliyet, London, 1984-86; diplomat Turkish Ministry of Fgn. Affairs, Ankara, Beijing, Brussels, Paris, 1987-94; prin. adminstr. Orgn. for Econ. Coop. and Devel., Paris, 1994—; writer Milliyet Newspaper, Istanbul, 1994—, investor 1999—; sr. advisor Turkish Assn. of Industrialists and Businessmen, Istanbul, 1994—. Author: (books) The New Economic Superpower: China, 1995, 2010 Turkey Vision, 1998, Rising Asia, 1998, Is Our Future With Asia?, 1999, Changing World, Unchanging Turkey: 2023 Vision, 2000; contbr. articles and reports to profl. jours. Res. officer Turkish mil., 1986-87. Jean Monnet fellow EC, 1991, sr. fellow 21st Century Trust, London, 1996, hon. sr. fellow U. Dundee, 1998—. Mem. World Future Soc., Internat. Assn. Energy Econs., Trans-European Policy Studies Assn., AFEMOTI, Mulkiyeliler Birligi. Avocations: writing, bird-watching, sailing, cycling. Fax: 33-1-45249395. E-mail: mehmet.ogutcu@oecd.org. Office: OECD/DAF DIR, 2 rue Andre Pascal, 75016 Paris France

OGUTU, JOSEPH OCHIENG, ecologist, educator, researcher; b. Kisumu, Nyanza, Kenya, Jan. 15, 1967; s. Richard and Teresa Aoko Ogutu; m. Phoebe Obura, June 1, 1991; 1 child, Laureen Laura. BSc in Wildlife Mgmt., Moi U., Eldoret, Kenya, 1990, MPhil in Wildlife Mgmt., 1994; Dr.rer.agr., Humboldt U., Berlin, 1999. Rsch. ecologist World Wide Fund for Nature, Nairobi, Kenya, 1990-92; grad. asst. Moi U., Eldoret, Kenya, 1990-94; tutorial fellow Moi U., Eldoret, 1994—. Rsch. grantee World Wide Fund for Nature, Gland, Switzerland, 1990-92; undergrad. and masters scholar Govt. Kenya, Nairobi, 1990-94, scholar, rsch. grantee German Acad. Exch. Svc., Bonn, 1994-99. Avocations: swimming, body building, sailing, fishing. E-mail: joseph.ochieng.ogutu@rz.hu-berlin.de. Fax: 0049-30-71426. Home: Triftstr 67, 13353 Berlin Germany Office: Humboldt U Berlin, Lentzeealle 75, 14195 Berlin Germany

OGUZ, YASEMIN NEYYIRE, physician, medical educator; b. Ankara, Turkey, July 27, 1963; d. Erdem Cetin and Hatice Guler (Goktan) Yalim; m. Sahin Oguz, Feb. 24, 1990; 1 child, Elif Deniz. MD, Ankara U., 1987, PhD, 1994. Lectr. faculty medicine Ankara U., 1995-98, assoc. prof. faculty medicine, 1998—; chairperson ethics unit Ankara Chamber Physicians, 1994-98; mem. ethics com. Ankara U. Faculty Dentistry, 1999. Author, editor:

Deontology, 1995, 99, Where is Ethics in This, 1997. Mem. Internat. Assn. Bioethics (assoc.), Royal Coll. Psychiatry Philosophy Group (assoc.), Turkish Philos. Assn. (chairperson bioethics unit 1998—), Hastings Ctr. (assoc.), Bioethics Assn. (founder, treas. 1993—). Avocations: computers, books, birdwatching, tracking, tennis. Home: Turangunes Bulvari 260/105, 06450 Ankara Oran, Turkey Office: Ankara Univ Faculty Med, Unit Med Ethics, 06100 Ankara Sihhiye, Turkey

OGUZER, TANER ABDULLAH, electrical and electronics engineer; b. Trabzon, Turkey, Sept. 26, 1967; s. Turgut and Sabiha (Temir) O. BS, Mid. East Tech. U., Ankara, Turkey, 1989; MS, Bilkent U., Ankara, 1991, PhD, 1996. Cert. in engring. Rsch. asst. Bilkent U., Ankara, 1989-96; asst. prof. Dokuz Eylül U., Izmir, Turkey, 1997—. Mem. IEEE. Office: Dokuz Eylül U, Tinaztepe Kampus Buca, 35160 Izmir Turkey

OH, CHOO-HIAP, physics educator; b. Kota Kinabalu, Sabah, Malaysia, Jan. 4, 1944; s. Soon-Tien and Soh (Ng) O. BSc with honors, U. Otago, New Zealand, 1969, PhD, 1972. Lectr. Sci. U. Malaysia, 1972-80, assoc. prof., 1980-83; sr. lectr. physics Nat. U. Singapore, 1983-88, assoc. prof., 1989-98, prof., 1998—. Editor: Conformal Field Theory, Anomalies and Superstrings, 1988, High Temperature Superconductivity and Other Related Topics, 1989; contbr. articles to profl. jours. Assoc. mem. Internat. Ctr. Theoretical Physics, Italy, 1981. Mem. Am. Phys. Soc. E-mail: phyohch@nus.edu.sg. Office: Nat U Singapore, Physics Dept Kent Ridge, Singapore 119260, Singapore

OH, DEOK KUN, microbiologist; b. Seoul, Korea, Sept. 18, 1961; s. Jae Hun Oh and Han Hee Cho; m. Young Sook Jung, May 2, 1992; children: Jong Moon, Jong Hoon. BS, Seoul Nat. U., 1984; MS, Korean Adv. Inst. Sci. & Tech., 1986, PhD, 1992. Visiting rschr. Osaka (Japan) U., 1991; rschr. Cheiljedang Co., Icheon, Korea, 1986=95; asst. prof. Woosuk U., Cheonju, Korea, 1995-2000, Sejong U., Seoul, Korea, 2000—. Contbr. articles to profl. jours. Mem. Korean Soc. Food Sci. and Tech., Korean Soc. Applied Microbilogy. Home: Jugong Apt 301-103, Byulyang Dong Kwacheon, Kyungki Do 427-040, Korea Office: Sejong U Dept Bioscience and Biotechnology, 98 Kunja-dong, Kwangjin-ku 143-747 Seoul Korea

OH, JONGTAEK, telecommunications engineering researcher; b. Seoul, Republic of Korea, Nov. 4, 1963; s. Heungseok Oh and Soonsik Lee; m. Bonjoo Koo, Dec. 20, 1994; 1 child, Youngsik Oh. BS, Han Yang U., Seoul, 1986; MS, KAIST, Seoul, 1989; PhD, Korea Adv. Inst. Sci. & Tech., Seoul, 1993. Dir. Korea Telecom, Seoul, 1993-2000; prof. Hansung U., Seoul, 2000—. Contbr. articles to profl. jours. Recipient citation Ministry Info. & Comm., Seoul, 1998. Mem. IEEE, Telecomm. Tech. Assn., Intelligent Transport Sys. Study Group (chmn. 1998—). Avocations: reading, mountain climbing, fixing home equipment. Office: Hansung U Info Divsn, 389 Samsun Sungbuk, Seoul 136-792, Republic of Korea

OH, JU-HWAN, history educator; b. Sanchung, Kyung-Nam, Korea, June 9, 1931; s. Jueng-Shik and Do-Ho (Bai) Oh; m. Kap-Suk Yoo, Jan. 15, 1957; children: Jun-Ki, Jun-Kyu, Bong-Kyung, Hen-Kyung. BA, Kyungpook Nat. U., Taegu, Korea, 1956, MA, 1958; postgrad., SUNY, Buffalo, 1978-79; PhD, Keimyung U., Taegu, 1983. Asst. prof. Taegu (Korea) Tchrs. Coll., 1964-68; assoc. prof. Kyungpook Nat. U., Taegu, 1968-80, chmn. dept. history, 1975-78, prof., 1980-96; ret., 1996; dean Coll. of Humanities Kyungpook Nat. U., Taegu, 1985-87; vis. prof. SUNY, Buffalo, 1978-79; rsch. fellow Modern History Faculty, U. Oxford, Eng., 1979-80; dir. Kyunpook U. Press, Taegu, 1983-85, Kyungpook U. Libr., Taegu, 1990-92; pres. Taegu Hist. Assn., 1986-88, Kyungpook Grad. Sch. Alumni Assn., Taegu, 1990-93; prof. history Coll. Social and Cultural Edn., Taegu, 1996. Author: History of World Civilization, 1972, Revolution, Thought and Social Change, 1992, Early Modern Society of England, 1992, Middle Class and Bourgeois Society, 1993, Local History of Province Sanchung, 1994-95; editor: Current Theory of History, 1988, Genealogy of "Oh" Family in Korea, 4 vols., 1997-98. Recipient award for spl. contbn. to edn. Korea Tchrs. Assn., 1986, Cultural award for outstanding acad. achievement citizen, City of Taegu, 1995; Order of Nat. Svc. Merit, Pres. Republic of Korea, 1996. Home and Office: 1071 Bongduck-dong NAM-KU, 705-751 Taegu HyoSung Town 107-1105, Republic of Korea

OH, KYUNGHWAN, educator, consultant; b. Seoul, Korea, Sept. 9, 1963; s. Kook Keun and In Ja (Kim) O.; m. Hyeyon Yoon, Aug. 9, 1989; children: Seiyon, Seijong. BS in Physics, Seoul Nat. U., 1986, MS in Physics, 1988; MS in Engring., Brown U., 1991, PhD in Physics, 1994. Tchg. asst. Seoul Nat. U., 1986-88; tchg. asst. Brown U., Providence, 1989-90, rsch. asst., 1990-94; postdoctoral rsch. asst. Lab for Lightwave Tech., Providence, 1995-96; sr. rschr. Lab. for Fiber Optics and Comm., Anyang, Korea, 1995-96; asst. prof. Kwangju (Korea) Inst. Sci. and Tech., 1996—; vis. asst. prof. rsch. divsn. engring. Brown U., 1998; cons. Samsung Electronics, Kumi, Korea, 1996—; vis. scientist Bell Labs., Lucent Techs., 2000—. Editor Jour. for Physics Dept. Undergrad. Seoul, 1984; contbr. articles to profl. jours. V.p. student union Osan H.S., Seoul, 1982, rep. for dept. physics Seoul Nat. U., 1982-83. Served with Inf., 1988-89. Recipient The Korea Nat. Scholarship Min. of Edn., 1989, The Korean Honor scholarship Korean Embassy U.S., 1992, The Excellence award in LG Skill Olympiad LG Group, 1996. Mem. IEEE (treas.), Optical Soc. Am., Am. Ceramic Soc., Korean Optical Soc. Avocations: golf, guitar, choir. Fax: 82 62 970 2204. E-mail: koh@eunhasu, kjist.ac.kr. Office: Kwangju Inst of Sci & Tech, 1 Oryong-dong Puk-ku, Kwangju 500-712, Korea

OH, SEI-CHULL, economics educator, political activist; b. Seoul, Rep. of Korea, Nov. 10, 1943; m. Jin-Hyang Choi, Aug. 5, 1985; children: Seung-Yun, Ja-Kyung, Jung-Lim, Yun-Sun. BA, Yonsei U., Seoul, 1965, MA, 1967; PhD, Northwestern U., 1975. Instr. Yonsei U., Seoul, 1970-72, asst. prof., 1975-77, assoc. prof., 1977-79, prof., 1980—, dir. Mgmt. Ctr., 1978-80, chmn. dept. mgmt., 1980-82, dean Coll. Bus. and Econs., 1994-96. Author: Culture and Social Psychological Theory, 1981 (Yonsei Academic award 1982), Organization and Change of Korean Society, 1986, Culture and Society of East European Countries, 1987, Marxism, Political Economy and Social Transformation of Korea, 1993. Pres. People's Coun., Seoul, 1991-93, People's Polit. Fedn., Seoul, 1993-94; co-rep. Power of the Working Class, 1999—. Mem. Korean Acad. Mgmt. (pres. 1999—). Office: Yonsei U Coll Bus and Econs, 134 Shin-chon-dong, 120-749 Seoul Republic of Korea

OH, SE-JUNG, physics educator; b. Seoul, Korea, Feb. 17, 1953; came to U.S., 1976; s. Chang-hwan and Kie-on (Yoon) O.; m. Nansil Hong, Jan. 3, 1990. BS in Physics, Seoul Nat. U., 1975; PhD in Physics, Stanford U., 1982. Vis. scientist Xerox Pal Alto Rsch. Ctr., Calif., 1981-84; asst. prof. physics Seoul Nat. U., 1984-88, assoc. prof. physics, 1988-94, prof. physics, 1994—, dir. Ctr. for Strongly Correlated Materials Rsch., 1999—; mem. Presdl. Commn. for 21st Century, Korea, 1989-94, Presdl. Coun. for Sci. and Tech., Korea, 1999—; internat. adv. bd. Internat. Conf. Vacuum Ultraviolet Radiation Physics, 1998—; assoc. mem. Internat. Ctr. Theoretical Physics, Trieste, Italy, 1987-94. Contbr. articles to profl. jours. Served with Korean Army, 1975-76. Recipient Korean Sci. award Pres. Korea, 1998. Fellow Korean Phys. Soc., Korean Vacuum Soc.; mem. Am. Phys. Soc. Office: Seoul Nat Univ, Dept Physics, Seoul 151-742, Republic of Korea

OH, TAI KEUN, business educator; b. Seoul, Korea, Mar. 25, 1934; s. Chin Young and Eui Kyung (Yun) O.; came to U.S., 1958, naturalized, 1969; B.A., Seijo U., 1957; M.A., No. Ill. U., 1961; M.L.S., U. Wis., 1965, Ph.D., 1970; m. Gretchen Brenneke, Dec. 26, 1964; children: Erica, Elizabeth, Emily. Asst. prof. mgmt. Roosevelt U., Chgo., 1969-73; assoc. prof. Calif. State U., Fullerton, 1973-76, prof. mgmt., 1976—; vis. prof. U. Hawaii, 1983-84, 86; advisor Pacific Asian Mgmt. Inst., U. Hawaii; internat. referee Asia-Pacific Jour. of Mgmt., 1990—; cons. Calty Design Research, Inc. subs. Toyota Motor Corp. The Employers Group; seminar leader and speaker. Named Outstanding Prof., Sch. Bus. Adminstrn. and Econs., Calif. State U., Fullerton, 1976, 78. NSF grantee, 1968-69, recipient Exceptional Merit Service award Calif. State U., 1984, Meritorious Performance and Profl. Promise award Calif. State U., 1987. Mem. Acad. Mgmt., Indsl. Relations Research Assn., Acad. Internat. Bus. Editorial bd. Acad. Mgmt. Rev., 1978-81; contbg. author: Ency. Profl. Mgmt., 1978, Handbook of Management 1985; contbr. articles to profl. jours. Home: 2044 E Eucalyptus Ln Brea CA 92821-5911 Office: Calif State U Dept Mgmt Fullerton CA 92634

OH, Y. JUNE CHOI, pianist, music educator; b. Seoul, Republic Korea, 1965; came to U.S., 1981; m. D.H. Oh; 1 child, S. MusB, Juilliard Sch., 1987, MusM, 1989; postgrad., Manhattan Sch. Music, 1995. Faculty Manhattan Sch. Music, N.Y.C., 1992-97, Johannesen Internat. Sch. of the Arts, Victoria, 1993; dir., founder Pacific Music Festival Calif., Stanford, 1995—; faculty San Francisco Conservatory Music, 1996—. Soloist Aspen (Colo.) Concert Orch., 1986, New Haven Symphony Orch., 1991, Filarmonica de Jalisco, Guadalajara, Mexico, 1991, 92; pianist San Francisco Symphony Chamber Music Series, 1998. Nat. Endowments for the Arts scholar The Juilliard Sch., N.Y.C., 1986, William Petschek scholar The Juilliard Sch., N.Y.C., 1988; recipient concerto competition award Aspen Music Festival, 1986, 1st prize Marcia Polayes Nat. Competition, New Haven Symphony Orch., 1990. Home: PO Box 18050 Stanford CA 94309-8050 Office: San Francisco Conserv Music Prep Dept 1201 Ortega St San Francisco CA 94122-4498

OH, YOUNG-TAEK, radiologist, oncologist, researcher; b. Seoul, Korea, May 30, 1963; s. Joosuk and Wookyung (Shim) O.; m. Kyung-Hee Kwak, Feb. 22, 1992; 1 child, Jiwon. MA, Yansei U., Seoul, Korea, 1995. Korean Bd. Therapeutic Radiology. Instr. Ajou U., Suwon, Korea, 1996-98; asst. prof. Ajou U., Suwon, 1999—. Mem. Korean Soc. Therapeutic Radiology/Oncology, Korean Cancer Assn. Office: Ajou U Hosp Dept Rad Onc, San5 Wonchon-Dong Paldal-Ku, 442-749 Suwon Korea

OH, YUNG-HWAN, science educator; b. Nonsan, Chungnam, Rep. of Korea, May 25, 1947; s. Kyung Jin Oh and Soon Chun Jun; m. Young Ock Lee, Feb. 7, 1974; children: Jeong soo, Yang Soo. BS, Seoul Nat. U., 1972, MS, 1974; PhD, Tokyo Inst. Tech., 1980. Mem. rsch. staff Tokyo Inst. Tech., 1975-77; asst. prof. Chungbuk Nat. U., Chungju, Rep. of Korea, 1981-85; prof. Korea Advanced Inst. Sci. and Tech., Taejon, Rep. of Korea, 1985—; instr. part-time Seoul Nat. U., 1981-83; vis. scholar U. Calif., Davis, 1984-85, Carnegie-Mellon U., Pitts., 1995-96. Author: Pattern Recognition Theory, 1991,, Spoken Language Processing, 1998; contbr. articles to profl. jours. Mem. Korea Info. Sci. Soc. (v.p. 1997-98). Avocations: mountain hiking, golf. Office: KAIST, 373-1 Kusong-dong Yusong-gu, Taejon 305-701, Republic of Korea

OHAMA, YOSHIHIKO, architectural engineer, educator; b. Shimonoseki, Japan, Mar. 29, 1937; s. Yoshihiro and Ritsuko O.; m. Ikuko Ohama, Mar. 24, 1966; children: Akiko, Noriko, Hiroshi. BE, Yamaguchi U., Japan, 1959; PhD, Tokyo Inst. Tech., 1974. Rsch. engr. ctrl. rsch. lab. Onoda Cement Co., Ltd., Koto-ku, Tokyo, 1959-66; rsch. engr. and dept. head Bldg. Rsch. Inst. Japanese Govt., Tokyo, 1966-76; from assoc. prof. to prof. Nihon U., Koriyama, Fukushima-ken, Japan, 1976—; rsch. engr. Inst. Indsl. Sci., U. Tokyo, 1972-81; adv. prof. Tongji U., Shanghai, 1990—; guest prof. Shandong Inst. Bldg. Materials, Jinan, China, 1991—; vis. prof. Katholieke Universiteit, Leuven, Belgium, 1990; dir. v.p., pres. Internat. Congress on Polymers in Concrete (ICPIC), Denver, 1981—; v.p. Internat. Ferrocement Soc., Bangkok, 1998—; dir. Japan Concrete Inst., 1995-97; trustee Inorganic Materials Soc., 1993—, Life Materials Soc., 1989—; chmn. Polymers in Concrete Com., Japan chpt. ICPIC, Tokyo, 1987—; v.p. Internat. Ferrocement Soc., Bangkok, 1998—. Author: Polymeric Waterproofing Work, 1972, Handbook of Polymer-Modified Concrete and Mortars, 1995; co-author: Plastics Concrete, 1965, Building Materials, 1981, Concrete Admixtures Handbook, 1984, Modern Construction Materials, 1990, Polymers in Concrete, 1994. Mem. ASTM, Am. Concrete Inst., Materials Rsch. Soc., Internat. Union Testing and Rsch. Labs. for Materials and Structures (chmn. tech. com. 151-APC), Soc. for Advancement of Material and Process Engring., Soc. Materials Sci. Japan, Archtl. Inst. Japan, Japan Concrete Inst. Avocations: travel, mountaineering, ham. Home: 14-10-402, Hiyoshi 2-chome, Kohoku-ku, Yokohama 223-0061, Japan Office: Nihon U, Coll Engring, Koriyama 963-8642, Japan

O'HANDLEY, DOUGLAS ALEXANDER, astronomer; b. Detroit, May 7, 1937; s. Malcolm Joseph and Georgie Roberta (MacPherson) O'H.; m. Christine Jeannette Stube, July 20, 1991; 1 child, Douglas Alexander, Jr. AB, U. Mich., 1960; MS, Yale U., 1964, PhD, 1967. Astronomer U.S. Naval Obs., Washington, 1960—; scientist Jet Propulsion Lab., Pasadena, Calif., 1985-86; dir. space station Ames Rsch. Ctr., Moffett Field, Calif., 1985-86; mgr. TRW Space Tech. Group, Redondo Beach, Calif., 1986-88; dep. asst. adminstr. office exploration NASA, Washington, 1988-92; dir. astrobiology acad. Ames Rsch. Ctr., Moffett Field, 1992—, ret., 1999; chmn. com. for protection of human subjects in med. rsch., 1982-85; lectr. grad. sch. Georgetown U., Washington, 1964-67; adj. prof. physics Santa Clara (Calif.) U., 1997—; spkr. in field. Contbr. articles to profl. jours. Bd. dirs. Big Bros.; extraordinary min. St. Bede's Roman Cath. Ch. Fellow AIAA (assoc.), ASMA, AAS, Royal Soc. Medicine; mem. Internat. Astron. Union, Internat. Acad. Astronautics. Home: 1580 Grackle Way Sunnyvale CA 94087-4715

O'HANLON, MARY TERESA, consultant psychiatrist; b. Ballinasloe, Ireland, Oct. 16, 1959; arrived in England, 1990; d. Ciaran Francis and Marie Teresa (Doyle) O'H.; m. John Gerard Boyan, May 24, 1991. Diploma, London Coll. of Music, 1977; MB, BCh, BAO, Univ. Coll. Dublin, Ireland, 1983; diploma in child health, Univ. Coll. Dublin, 1987. Intern Mater Hosp., Dublin, 1983-84; sr. house officer Mater Hosp., St. Michael's Hosp., Dublin, 1984-86; sr. house officer, registrar Dublin Tng. Sch., 1986-89; rsch. sr. registrar St. James/Trinity Coll., Dublin, 1989-90; psychiatry sr. registrar West Midlands Tng. Scheme, Eng., 1990-93; cons. psychiatrist Priority Health Dudley, Eng., 1993-98, Port Laoise, Ireland, 1998—; assoc. prof. Granada U., 1994—; tutor Royal Coll. Psychiatrists, England, 1994—; sr. clin. lectr. Birmingham U., England, 1994-98; examiner, Royal Coll. Psychiatrists, 1998—. Contbg. author: Approaches in Alcohol Dependence, 1993; contbr. articles to profl. jours. Rsch. fellow U. Warwick, England, 1992-95; recipient Prof. Norman Moore Rsch. prize, Dublin, 1989, Royal Acad. Medicine Ireland Pres. prize, Dublin, 1990. Fellow Royal Soc. Medicine; mem. Royal Coll. Physicians Ireland (diploma), Royal Coll. Psychiatrists (diploma), Brit. Assn. Psychopharmacology, Birmingham Med. Inst. Roman Catholic. Avocations: walking, cycling, swimming, skiing, boating. Office: St Fintans Hosp, Portlaoise, County Ladis Ireland

O'HANLON, REDMOND DOUGLAS, writer; b. Langton Matravers, Dorset, Eng., June 5, 1947. BA, Merton Coll., Oxford, Eng., 1969, MPh with distinction, 1971; MA, St. Anthony's Coll., Oxford, Eng., 1974, PhD, 1977. Sr. scholar St. Antony's Coll., 1971-74, research fellow, 1974; editor lit. supplement Times Newspaper Ltd., London, 1981—; mem. literary panel The Arts Council of Great Britain, London, 1971-74; sr. visitor St. Antony's Coll, 1985—. Author: Joseph Conrad and Charles Darwin, 1984, Into the Heart of Borneo, 1984, In Trouble Again, A Journey Between the Orinoco and the Amazon, 1988, Congo Journey, 1996 (best non-fiction title Am. Libr. Assn. 1997); contbr. to profl. jours. Fellow Royal Geog. Soc., Royal Soc. Lit.; mem. Soc. for History of Natural History, British Ornithological Union. Home: Pelican House, Ch Hanborough Witney, Oxford OX8 8AE, England Office: The Times Lit Supplement, 66-68 East Smithfield, London E1 9XY, England

O'HARA, DELIA IGLAUER, family nurse practitioner; b. Cin., Feb. 5, 1942; d. Arnold and Virginia (Dunn) Iglauer; children: Robert, Matthew, William. BS, Simmons Coll., 1965; Cert. Nurse Practitioner, George Washington U., 1975; JD, Howard U., 1987. Bar: D.C.; cert. family nurse practitioner. Dir. home care program for cancer patients George Washington U. Med. Ctr., 1975-79; occupational health nurse practitioner Libr. of Congress, Washington, 1979-84; lawyer FTC, Washington, 1987-89; dir. student health svcs. Presdl. Classroom for Young Ams., 1987-98; health svcs. mgr. Time-Life Books, Inc., Alexandria, Va., 1990-92; pvt. practice law Washington, 1990-99; occupational health nurse practitioner Washington Hosp. Ctr., 1993-96, nurse practitioner Admissions Testing Ctr., 1996-98; nurse practitioner dept. pre-surgery Kaiser Permanente Med. Ctr., Oakland, Calif., 1998—. Chmn. D.C. Home Care Task Force; vol. Winterhaven Shelter for Homeless Women; mem. Bd. Nursing, Washington; vestry mem. St. John's Episcopal. Ch., Montclair, 1999—. Recipient Trustee's scholarship Howard U. Fellow Am. Acad. Nurse Practitioners (bd. dirs. region 3 rep. 1991-94, rec. sec. 1994-96, treas. 1996-97, founder Found., bd. dirs. 1996—), Nurse Practitioner Assn. of D.C. (pres. 1992-95), Capitol Area Network of Nurse Attys. (v.p. 1992-93), Simmons Coll. Alumnae Assn. (class sec. Class of 1964, 1989-94). Home: 2525 Alida St Oakland CA 94602-2503 Office: Kaiser Permanente Med Ctr 280 W Macarthur Blvd Oakland CA 94611-5642

O'HARA, HIROSHI, internist; b. Kita, Tokyo, Japan, Sept. 9, 1952; s. Jun and Taki (Tsukada) O.; m. Narumi Ishikawa, Aug. 26, 1994. B of Medicine, Hirosaki U., 1978; PhD, MD, U. Tokyo, 1982. Cert. of med. practitioner conducting advanced clin. tng. Lectr. Toho U., Tokyo, 1985-88; assoc. prof. Saitama Med. Sch., Moroyama, Japan, 1989-92; chief med. advisor Japan Overseas Cooperation Vols., Tokyo, 1993-94; team leader Japan Internat. Cooperation Agy., Kathmandu, Nepal, 1995-96; sr. med. expert Internat. Med. Ctr. of Japan, Tokyo, 1996—; med. advisor Japan Overseas Cooperation Vols., Tokyo, 1979-94; team leader of med. edn. project Japan Internat. Cooperation Agy., 1995-96; team leader Bach Mai Hosp. Project, Hanoi, Vietnam, 2000—. Contbr. articles to profl. jours. Fellow Japanese Soc. of Internal Medicine, Japanese Soc. of Infectious Diseases, Am. Soc. of Tropical Medicine and Hygiene, Internat. Soc. Travel Medicine. Avocations: swimming, baseball. Home: 1-41-11 Ishiharamachi, Kawagoe 350, Japan Office: Internat Med Ctr of Japan, 1-21-1 Toyama, Shinjuku 162, Japan

OHARA, IKUO, nutrition educator; b. Higashiizumo, Shimane, Japan, Sept. 28, 1943; s. Masao and Atsuko Ohara; m. Etsuko Kotani, May 30, 1970; children: Masako, Akio. B in Agr., Chiba (Japan) U., 1967; M in Agr., Nagoya (Japan) U., 1969, D in Agr., 1980; D in Med. Sci., Kyoto (Japan) U., 1991. Rsch. scientist Amino Feed Co., Ltd., Yokohama, Japan, 1969-70, Ajinomoto Co., Inc., Yokohama, 1970-83; assoc. prof. nutrition Kobe (Japan) Women's U.-Faculty Home Econs., 1983-88, prof. nutrition, 1988—; head food and nutrition sect. Kobe Women's U., 1997-99. Mem. Am. Coll. Nutrition, Japanese Soc. for Hygiene, Japanese Soc. Nutrition and Food Sci. Home: 1165 Higashiizumo, Yatsuka Shimane 699-0102, Japan Office: Kobe Womens U Home Econs, 2-1 Aoyama Higashisuma Suma, Kobe 654-8585, Japan

O'HARA, PAUL ANTHONY, JR., retired art educator, artist; b. Indiana, Pa., Sept. 16, 1938; s. Paul Anthony and Hilda M. (Henderson) O;H.; m. Barbara Ann Zolock, May 24, 1965; children: Paul Anthony III, Polly Ann, Rebecca, Mark. BS in Art Edn., Edinboro (Pa.) U., 1961; MA in Painting/Sculpture, Pa. State U., 1965; postgrad., U. Pitts., Calif. U. Pa., 1963-64. Cert. tchr. K-12, supr., Pa. Tchr. jr. h.s. art Chartiers Valley Schs., Pitts., 1961-95; photographer Pa. State U., University Park, 1977-78; instr. ceramics Allegheny C.C., Pitts.; instr. art Everyday Poeple, Monessen and Donora, Pa. Sculptor, printmaker, painter; one-man shows include Calif. U. Pa., 1962-64, Lutheran Assn. State Coll, Pa., 1964, Pitts. Ctr. for Arts, 1964, 68, St. Francis Coll., Ft. Wayne, Ind., 1968, U. Iowa, Iowa City, 1968, U. Pitts., 1969, Pa. State U., University Park, 1972, Pitts. History and Landmarks Mus., Pitts., 1974, Adam's Art, Bellefonte, Pa., 1994, Pitts. History and Landmarks Mus., 1973; exhibited in group shows at Erie Mus. Spring Art Show, 1959-60, 89, 93, 95-96, 2000, Soc. Sculptors, Pitts., 1963-66, 68-84, Associated Artists, Pitts., 1962-63, 66-67, 68, 70, 72-73, 75-79, 81, 84, 86, Mini Print Internat., Cadaques, Spain, 1989-2000, Mini Print Internat. travelling show Mex., 1989, Spain, 1989-88, Italy, 1989, Colombia, 1989, Cadaques, 1990, 92, Japan, 1991-92, Eng., 1992-99, France, 1995-99, Korea, 1994, Finland, Pa. State U., University Park, Boston Printmakers, Boston, 1969, Vendome Gallery, Pitts., Pratt Internat., 1971, Pratt Internat. Travelling Show, 1971-74, William Penn Mus., Harrisburg, Pa., Pa. State Traveling Show, 1972-74, Ball State U., Muncie, Ind., 1973-74, Delmar Coll., Corpus Christie, Tex., 1973, Three Rivers Art Festival, Pitts., 1961-67, 71, 73-74, 76-78, 80, Pitts. Connection, Dunfermline, Scotland, 1985, Butler Inst. Am. Art, Youngstown, Ohio, 1987, Seton Hill Coll., Greensburg, Pa., 1989, Greensburg Mus. Art, 1989, Pitts. Ctr. Arts, 1962-68, Ann. Holiday Ornaments Exhbn. Palmer Mus. Art, Pa. State U., University Park, 1997-99, Soc. Am. Graphic Artists 67th Nat. Members Exhbn. Prince St. Gallery, N.Y.C., 1999, 2000. Recipient Frick award Frick Found., 1964. Mem. ADOGI Print Group, Internat. Sculpture Ctr., Soc. Am. Graphic Artists. Democrat. Roman Catholic. Avocations: landscaping, renovation, genealogy. Home: PO Box 132 Roscoe PA 15477-0132

O'HARE, DANIEL JOHN, electrical engineer; b. Bay City, Mich., Dec. 17, 1955; s. John William and Vida Flo (Roberts) O'H.; m. Betty Joanne Luczak, May 23, 1979; children: Jennifer Louise, Meghan Elizabeth, Amanda Jayne. BSEE, Mich. Technol. U., 1978; postgrad., U. Minn., 1979-84, SUNY, Binghamton, 1985. Jr. engr. IBM, Rochester, Minn., 1978-79; assoc. engr. hard file integration IBM, Rochester, 1979-82, sr. assoc. engr. hardfile integration, 1982-85, project engr., mgr. subsystem serviceability, 1985-88, devel. engr., mgr. hardware devel., 1988-91, adv. engr. interdivsnl. project leader, 1991-95; program mgr. storage adapter all IBM server syss., 1995-97; sr. program mgr. AS/400 Asia Pacific Mktg., 1997—. Referee Rochester Youth Baseball Assn., 1988, 89, coach, 1992, 93; line judge Rochester Youth Soccer, 1989; vol. tchr. for gifted and talented edn. at local pub. elem. sch., 1989-94; asst. youth competitive cheerleading squad, Rochester Youth Cheerleading Assn., 1995-98, h.s. cheerleading asst. coach, 1999—. Roman Catholic. Avocations: model building, computers, photography. Home: 2607 Westview Ln NW Rochester MN 55901-2362 Office: IBM Hwy 52 at 37th St NW Rochester MN 55901

OHASHI, HIROSHI, reinsurance company executive; b. Gifu City, Japan, Dec. 1, 1932; s. Eikichi and Wakako (Kojima) O.; m. Yoshiko Matsco, Apr. 25, 1960; children: Hidehiko, Kazuhiko, Makiko Colsey. BA, Hitotsubashi U., Tokyo, 1955. Exec. v.p. Tokio Marine Fire Ins. Co., Ltd., 1992-94; pres., CEO Toa Reinsurance Co., Ltd., Tokyo, 1994-2000; dir., sr. adviser, 2000—. Mem. Japanese Soc. Ins. Sci., Japanese Environ. Edn. Forum, Japan Assn. Corp. Execs., Internat. House Japan, Club Corp. Asia Internat. Club, Kawana Hotel Golf Course. Avocations: golfing, reading, music. Home: Shibuya-ku, 9-14 Tomigaya 2-chome, Tokyo 151 0063, Japan Office: Toa Reins Co, 6 Kanda Surugadai 3 chome, Chiyoda-ku Tokyo 101 8703, Tokyo

OHASHI, MITSUO, chemical company executive; b. Tokyo, Japan, Jan. 18, 1936; s. Takeo and Fujiko (Hamaguchi) O.; m. Kiyoko Iwasa, Mar. 27, 1962; children: Yoshihiro, Hiromasa. BA in Econs., Keio U., Tokyo, 1959. With Mitsui Bank Ltd., Tokyo, 1959-61; with Showa Denko K.K., Tokyo, 1961—, elected dir., 1989, elected sr. mng. dir., 1995, elected rep. dir., pres., CEO, 1997. Mem. Abrasive Industry Assn. (chmn. 1997—), Japan Carbon Assn. (chmn. 1999—), Japan Petrochem. Industry Assn. (chmn. 2000—). Avocations: opera, classical music, art appreciation, golf. Office: Showa Denko K K, 13-9 Shiba Daimon 1-chome, Minato-ku, Tokyo 105-8518, Japan

OHASHI, TETSUYA, materials scientist, researcher; b. Sapporo, Hokkaido, Japan, Aug. 21, 1951; s. Akira and Kikuko (Tadokoro) O.; m. Yoshie Yokouchi. BS, Hokkaido U., Sapporo, 1974, MS, 1976, PhD, 1981. Rschr. Hitachi Rsch. Lab., Hitachi Ltd., Japan, 1981-88, sr. rschr., 1988-98; rsch. fellow Nat. Rsch. Inst. for Metals, Tsukuba, Japan, 1997—; prof. Kitami Inst. of Tech., 1999—. Mem. steering com. Hitachi Chamber Music Festival, 1991—. Mem. AAAS, Materials Rsch. Soc., Japanese Soc. Mech. Engrs. (com. mem. 1993—, paper rev. mem. 1992-95, 98—), Japan Inst. Metals (com. mem. 1996-98). Avocations: playing stringed instruments, violin and viola. Home: Tanno 3-367-1 Tokoro, Hokkaido 099 2103, Japan Office: Kitami Inst Tech, Koencho 165, 090-8507 Kitami Hokkaido, Japan

OHASHI, YOICHI, surgeon, immunologist; b. Kokura, Fukuoka, Japan, Apr. 23, 1957; s. Kenpachiro and Saeko (Kimura) O. ; m. Yukiko Kamata, June 3, 1989; children:Ruriko, Rikako. MD, Tohoku U., Sendai, Japan, 1984, PhD, 1991. Resident in surgery Tohoku Rhosai Hosp., Sendai, 1984-85, Sendai Shakaihoken Hosp., Sendai, 1985-87; resident in surgery Tohoku U. Sch. Medicine, Sendai, 1991-93, asst. prof., 1996-97; surgeon Sendai Shakaihoken Hosp., 1997—. Contbr. articles to profl. jours. Postdoctoral fellow U. South Calif., 1994-95. Mem. Japanese Surg. Soc., Japanese Soc. Immunology, Japanese Cancer Assn. Office: Sendai Shakaihoken Hospital, 3-16-1 Tsutsumi-Machi Aobaku, Sendai 981-8501, Japan

OHAYON, MAURICE M., research center administrator, psychiatrist; b. Casablanca, Morocco, June 22, 1948; arrived in Can., 1990; MD, U. Aix Marseille II, France, 1979, Cert. d'Etudes Spéciales Psychiatry, 1980, D in Computer Scis., 1992; PhD in Human Biology, U. Calude Bernard, Lyon, France, 1997. Resident in psychiatry and neurology C.H.U. Marseille, 1975-77; hosp. psychiatrist France, 1980-90; sci. dir. Rsch. Ctr. Fernand Seguin, Montreal, Que., Can., 1990-92; dir. rsch. ctr. Inst. Philippe Pinel, Montreal,

1992—; rsch. coord. U. Montreal, 1992-96; pres. Ctr. Evaluation and Statistics, Montreal, 1998—; project dir. Ctr. for Human Sleep Rsch. Stanford (Calif.) U. Med. Ctr.; assoc. prof. U. Que. Trois-Rivières, 1993—; sci. conseiller Ctr. Hos. Vinatier, France, 1994—; vis. clin. scientist St. Mary's Hosp., London, 1995—; cons. prof. psychiatry Stanford U., 1995—; adj. prof. psychiatry NYU, 1998—. Author: Intelligence Artificielle et Psychiatrie, 1989, Apprentissage, Adaptation et Réadaptation: Etat de la Recherche, 1995; Dis-moi comment tu dors, 1997. Mem. APHA, Can. Psychol. Assn., N.Y. Acad. Scis. Office: Ctr Rsch Philippe Pinel, 10905 Henri Bourassa E, Montreal, PQ Canada H1C 1H1 Office: Ctr for Human Sleep Rsch Stanford Univ Med Ctr 401 Quarry Rd Ste 3301 Stanford CA 94305*

OHAYON, ROGER JEAN, aerospace engineering educator, scientific deputy; b. Meknes, Morocco, Jan. 3, 1942; s. David and Lily (Sassoon) O.; m. Ingrid Schmischke, Oct. 5, 1968; children: Carine, Philippe. D in Engring., U. Orsay, Paris, 1971; Habilitation Diriger Recherches, U. Paris 6, Marie Curie, 1990. Registered profl. engr., Chatillon. With Office Nat. d'Etudes et de Recherches Aerospatiales, Chatillon, France, 1970—, sci. dep., 1991—; prof., chair mechanic Conservatoire National des Arts et Metiers, Paris, 1992—; prof. Ecole Cen. Arts and Mfrs., Chatenay, France, 1978-86, Ecole Nat. Tech. Avancées, Paris, 1986—; external prof. U. Paris 6, 1986—; mem. sci. coun. Lab. Cen. des Ponts et Chaussées, Paris, 1987—. Co-author: Fluid-Structure Interaction, 1992, English edit., 1995, Structural Acoustics and Vibration, 1998; co-editor 5 books; mem. editl. bd. 9 jours.; contbr. numerous articles to profl. jours. Mem. and organizer of several Internat. Congresses. Recipient Acad. Sci. Price du Gen. Muteau award, 1989; named Chevalier Ordre des Palmes Académiques. Fellow Internat. Assn. Computational Mechs. (corr. of exec. com. 1994); mem. ASME, French Computational Structural Mechanics Assn. (pres. 1991), Spanish Soc. Computational Mechanics, Groupe pour Avancement Methodes Numeriques Ingenieur, Group for Aeronautical Rsch. and Tech. in Europe, Nat. Acad. Engring. Brazil (fgn.). Home: 22 Kellermann Blvd, 75013 Paris France

OHBA, HIROSHI, manufacturing executive. CEO, chmn. Kawasaki Heavy Industries, Kobe, Japan, 1996—. Office: Kawasaki Heavy Industries Kobe Crystal Tower, 1-1-3 Higashi Kawasakicho, 650-91 Kobe Japan*

OHBA, RYOJI, physics educator and researcher; b. Imaichi, Tochigi, Japan, Mar. 8, 1942; s. Ryojiro and Shina (Kamiyama) O.; m. Junko Kuge, Mar. 23, 1973; children: Yoriko, Ryohei, Hisanaga. BE, U. Tokyo, 1965, ME, 1967, D of Engring., 1970. Chartered physicist. Lectr. Hokkaido U., Sapporo, Japan, 1970-71, assoc. prof., 1971-88, prof. physics, 1988—, dir. Simulation Ctr., 1994-99; vis. rschr. Tech. U. Berlin, 1985, U. Manchester (Eng.) Inst. Sci. and Tech., 1985-86; bd. dirs. SICE, Tokyo, 1992-94. Author, editor: Intelligent Sensor Technology, 1992; contbr. article to profl. jours.; patentee in field. Recipient Ichimura prize New Tech. Devel. Found., Tokyo, 1988, Sound Tech. award Sound Tech. Found., Tokyo, 1987, Suhara Meml. Found. award, Saporro, 1988, Remarkable Invention award Min. of Sci. and Tech. Japan, Tokyo, 1999. Fellow Inst. of Physics, Soc. Instrument Control Engrs., Inst. Electronics Info. and Comm. Engrs., Japan Soc. Applied Physics. Avocation: gardening. Office: N-13 W-8 Kitaku, Hokkaido U, 060-8628 Sapporo Hokkaido, Japan

OHGA, NORIO, electronics and entertainment executive; b. Numazu, Shizuoka, Japan, Jan. 29, 1930; m. Midori Ohga. Grad., Tokyo Nat. U. Fine Arts and Music, 1953, Kunst U., Berlin, 1957. Cons., advisor Tokyo Tsushin Kogyo (later Sony Corp.), 1953-59; gen. mgr. tape recorder divsn., product planning divsn., indsl. design divsn. Sony Corp., Tokyo, 1959, bd. dirs., 1964-72, mng. dir., 1972-74, sr. mng. dir., 1974-76, dep. pres., 1976-82, pres., chief oper. officer, 1982-89, pres. and CEO, 1989-95, chmn. and CEO, 1995-99, chmn., rep. dir., 1999-2000, chmn. bd., 2000—; CEO Nobuyuki Idei; sr. mng. dir. CBS/Sony Group, Inc., 1968-70, pres., 1970-80, chmn., 1980-91; chmn. Sony Corp. Am., 1988-98; vice chmn. Keidanren, 1998. Decorated Cmdr. Cross First Class of the Order of Merit of the Rep. of Austria, 1987, Medal of Honor with Blue Ribbon by J.M. the Emperor of Japan, 1988, Officier de l'Ordre Nat. de la Legion d'Honneur France, 1996, Grande Ufficiale dell'Ordine Al Merito della Repubblica Italiana award Pres. Italian Republic, 1998. Mem. Japan Fedn. Econ. Orgn. (vice-chmn. 1998), Tokyo C. of C. and Industry (vice chmn.). Office: Sony Corp, 7-35 Kitashinagawa 6-chome, Shinagawa-ku Tokyo 141, Japan Office: Sony Corp Am 550 Madison Ave New York NY 10022-3211

OHHASHI, TOSHIO, physiology educator, researcher; b. Mito, Japan, Mar. 27, 1949; s. Takeo and Masa (Ono) O.; m. Yumiko Ichimura, Sept. 15, 1974; children: Tsukasa, Aya. MD, Shinshu U., Matsumoto, Japan, 1974; PhD, Shinshu U., 1979. Temp. lectr. physiology Queen's U. Belfast, No. Ireland, 1979-81; instr. physiology Shinshu U. Sch. Medicine, 1974-76, asst. prof., 1976-79, assoc. prof., 1981-84, prof., chmn. dept., 1985—, dir. Inst. Animal Rsch., 1987-89, 91-93, 1995-97, 99—, prof. Inst. Organ Transp. Reconstruct. Med. Tissue Engring., 2000—; honors guest rschr. in clin. scis. NIMH, Bethesda, Md., 1983, 85, 87; dir. Skinos Co. Ltd., 2000—. Author: Handbook of Physiological Sciences, Vol. 16 Cardiovascular Physiology, 1991, Textbook of Human Physiology by Studying Experiments and Experiences in Daily Life, 1996; author, editor: Emotional Perspiration and Its Clinical Application, 1993; mem. editl. bd. Microvascular Rsch., 1985-88, Internat. Jour. Angiology, 1992—, Am. Jour. Physiology (Heart and Circulatory Physiology), 1994-98; patentee device for continuously measuring local sweating rate in human beings (Japan, Am. Europe), device for self-evaluating character and condition of ego in human beings by means of measuring emotional perspiration (Japan). Dir. Nagano Prefecture Com. for Health Sci. in Human Beings and Its Bus. Application, 1993—. Recipient Disting. Rschr. award Japanese Heart Assn., 1983, Young Investigator award European Soc. Microcirculation, 1984; rsch. grantee Japanese Ministry Edn., Sci. and Culture, 1975, 77, 78, 84, 85, 86-88, 92-98, 98-99, 99-2000. Mem. Japanese Coll. Angiology (councillor 1994—), Japanese Soc. Microcirculation (councillor 1985—), Japanese Soc. Lymphology (councillor 1985—), Japanese Soc. Perspiration Rsch. (bd. dirs. 1992—). Avocations: golf, baseball. Office: Shinshu U 1st Dept Physiol, 3-1-1 Asahi, Nagano Matsumoto 390-8621, Japan

OHHIRA, IICHIROH, microbiologist, educator; b. Osaka, Japan, Feb. 6, 1936; s. Yutaka and Akiko (Tsubaki) Fujita. BS, Okayama U., 1960, MS, 1973, PhD, 1990; postgrad., Kagawa Med. Sch., 1992. With Wako Securities, 1960-71; rep. Ohhira Planning Office on Park and Garden, Okayama, Japan, 1973, Ohhira Rsch. Inst. on Tree Disease, Okayama, 1973; chmn. Bio Activity R&D Inst., 1977—; prof. Pusan (Korea) Fisheries Coll., Kangnung (Korea) Nat. U. Recipient Okayama Daily Newspaper award, 1980, Malaysia Sandakan Honor award, 1979, Malaysia Kota Kinabalu Honor award, 1980, Malaysia Sabah ADK award, 1981, Japan Dairy Sci. Soc. award, 1991. Avocations: Kendo (Japanese swordsmanship), reading, travel.

OHI, YOSHIHARU, consulting company executive; b. Kurashiki, Okayama, Japan, Oct. 6, 1947; s. Kazuo and Kaname (Ikawa) O.; m. Tomoko Miyamoto, Mar. 11, 1980; children: Mayumi, Kenji. Degree in Internat. Econs., Wakayama (Japan) U., 1970. Head investment banking divsn. Daiwa Europe Ltd., London, 1982-88; gen. mgr. Sydney (Australia) Br. Daiwa Securities Co. Ltd., 1988-90, Daiwa Securities Co. Ltd., Tokyo, 1990-96, Nippon Investment and Fin., Tokyo, 1996-97; chmn., CEO Global Bus. Consulting Corp. Ltd., Hong Kong, Japan, 1998—. Author: Commercial Law Review, 1978, International Financing Review, 1984, Cofri Journal, 1995. Mem. Chiba Lawn Tennis Club. Avocations: tennis, gardening, golf. E-mail: yohi@gbcc-jp.com. Fax: 81-43-226-5537. Office: Global Bus Cons Corp Ltd, Warblehills 7-53-3, Asumigaoka Midori-ku Chiba 267-0066, Japan

O'HIGGINS, NIALL JOHN, surgeon, educator; b. Dublin, Ireland, Jan. 28, 1942; s. Niall Bartholomew and Joan (O'Shea) O'H.; m. Rosaleen Elizabeth Healy; children: Amy, Eoin, Lisa, Conor. MB BChir BAO with honors, Nat. U. Ireland, Dublin, 1965, BS with honors, 1967. House surgeon, sr. house officer various hosps, Ireland and U.K.; rsch. registrar surgery Luton and Dunstable Hosp., England, 1970; sr. registrar, tutor surgery Royal Postgrad. Med. Sch., London, 1971-74; tutor surgery U. Coll. Dublin, Ireland, 1974-76; sr. lectr., cons. surgeon U. Coll. Hosp. Med. Sch., London, 1976-78; prof. surgery, dept. head U. Coll., Dublin, 1978—; cons. in field. Co-editor: Surgical Management; contbr. over 300 articles to profl. jours. Mem. Royal Coll. Surgeons Ireland, Fedn. European Cancer Socs. (past pres.), European Soc. Surg. Oncology (past pres.), World Fedn. Surg. Oncology Soc. (pres.), European Inst. Oncology, James IV Assn. Surgeons, Inc. Avocations: reading, cycling. Fax: 353-1-2839326. E-mail: niall.ohiggins@ucd.ie. Home: The Turret, 18 Park Dr, Dublin Ranelagh 6, Ireland Office: St Vincents U Hosp, Elm Park, Dublin 4, Ireland

O'HIGGINS, PAUL, law educator; b. Dublin, Irish Republic, Oct. 5, 1927; s. Richard Leo and Elizabeth O'H.; m. Rachel Elizabeth Bush, May 20, 1952; children: Maeve, Siobhan, Niall, Niav. MA, Trinity Coll., Dublin, Ireland, 1960; PhD, Cambridge (Eng.) U., 1962; LLD, Trinity Coll., Dublin, 1987, Cambridge (Eng.) U., 1989. Barrister King's Inn, Dublin, 1957, Lincoln's Inn, 1959. Vis. prof. Kent U., Canterbury, Eng., 1972-73; univ. lectr. in law Cambridge (Eng.) U., 1965-79, univ. reader in labour law, 1979-84; Regius prof. of laws Trinity Coll., Dublin, Ireland, 1984-87; prof. law King's Coll., London, 1987-92; fellow Christ's Coll., Cambridge, 1959—, vice master, 1992-95; mem. staff-side panel Civil Svcs. Arbitration Tribunal, 1972-86, Bur. of European Inst. of Social Security, 1990-95; hon. fellow Trinity Coll., Dublin, 1996; vis. prof. City U. London, 1992-96. Author: Bibliography of Periodical Literature on Irish Law, 1966, 75, 83, Censorship in Britain, 1972, Workers' Rights, 1976, Bibliography Brit. & Irish Social Security Law, 1986, Bibliography Irish Trials, 1986, Discrimination in Employment in Northern Ireland, 1984; editor: The Common Law Tradition-Essays in Irish Legal History, 1990, Lessons from Northern Ireland, 1991. Mem. Office of Manpower Econs. Com. on Equal Pay, 1970-72; chmn. Nat. Coun. Civil Liberties, Cambridge, 1970-78; patron Cambridge U. Grad. Soc., 1972-84; trustee Cambridge Union Soc., 1973-84; hon. treas. Alan Bush Music Trust, 1997—. Recipient Joseph L. Andrews Bibliographical award Am. Assn. Law Librs., 1987; emeritus fellow Leverhume Fund, London, 1992-93, hon. fellow Trinity Coll., Dublin, 1996. Mem. Royal Irish Acad., Brit. Inst. Human Rights (gov. 1988-98), Inst. Employment Rights (v.p. 1989—), Irish Soc. Labour Law (hon.), Acad. European Pvt. Lawyers, Cambridge Soc. (pres. Irish br.). Avocations: talk, travel in France and Italy, wine. Office: Christ's Coll, Cambridge CB2 3BU, England

OHIRA, KAZUTO, theatre company executive, writer; b. Hiroshima, Japan, Jan. 5, 1933; s. Kitaro and Ryo (Sugimoto) O.; m. Evelyn Lanham, Sept. 3, 1964. BA, Waseda U., Tokyo, 1956. Theatre mgr. Toho's La Brea Theatre, L.A., 1961-63; gen. mgr. Toho Cinema, N.Y.C., 1963-64; publicity mgr. Towa Co., Ltd., Tokyo, 1965-69; rep., dir., mgr. Toho Internat. Inc., N.Y.C., 1969, chief exec. officer, 1988-97; pres. Internat. Cultural Prodn. Inc., N.Y.C. Producer (dance performance and drama) Yasuko Nagamine's Musume Dojoji, 1982, Mandara, 1985, (drama) Yukio Ninagawa's Media, 1987, Takarazuka Show at Radio City Music Hall, N.Y., 1989, KanashibetsU: Furano Group at La Mama, Takarazuka Dance Concert at Joyce Theater, 1992, Sotoba Komachi, Yasuko Nagamine and Co., Beauty of Tokyo, Met. Tokyo, City Ctr., N.Y., 1993, Virtue Senpo Sugihara, Danny Kay Theater, N.Y.C., 1997, Gen: Hiroshima Atom Bomb's Kid, Danny Kay Theater, N.Y.C., 1998, The Winds of God, Am. Pl. Theater, N.Y.C., 1999, Rent, Japan, 2000, Boonah, Come Down, N.Y.C., 2000; author: Broadway parts I and II, 1982, 2d edit., 1987, Broadway, Broadway, 1987, Performing Arts of New York, 1989, Haiku Collection: Though The Travel is Short, The Charms of Broadway, 1994, Broadway Criticism, 1995, Japanese translation of Show Business Is No Business by Al Hirshfeld, 1997, Haiko Collection Flower Garden, 2000. Bd. dirs. Japan Musical Award Com. in U.S., 1994—; chair bd. dirs. Saeko Ichinohe Dance Co. Recipient 2d Fumiko Yamaji Cultural award, 1985, 1st Cultural Bridge award, 1998. Mem. UNESCO, Internat. Theatre Critics Assn., Internat. Theatre Inst. Japan, N.Y. Waseda Univ. Alumni Assn. (hon. dir.), Players Club. Avocation: golf. Home: 560 W 43d St Apt 3D New York NY 10036 Office: ICP Inc 235 W 48th St Apt 33B New York NY 10036-1431

OHIRA, TATSUYA, research industrial engineer; b. Kagoshima, Japan, Apr. 13, 1964; s. Masato and Kumiko (Otani) O.; m. Emi Itagaki, Mar. 15, 1992; 1 child. B in Engring., U. Tokyo, 1987, M in Engring., 1989, D in Engring., 1992. Rsch. engr. Mitsubishi Heavy Industries Co., Ltd., Yokohama, Japan, 1992-2000. Contbr. articles to scientific jours. Avocations: soccer, singing, books. Home: Narusedai 1-10-15, Machida Tokyo 194, Japan Office: Mitsu Heavy Ind Adv Tech Ct, 8-1 Sachiura 1 chome, Kanazawa-ku Yokohama 236, Japan

OHKADO, MASAYUKI, linguistics educator; b. Ise, Japan, Sept. 12, 1963; s. Masashi and Junko (Suzuki) O.; m. Kikuyo Suzuki, Nov. 3, 1990; children: Yuka and Yui. BA, Osaka U. Fgn. Studies, 1986; MA, Nagoya U., 1988. Lectr. Osaka-Kyoiku U., 1989-96; assoc. prof. Chubu U., Kasugai, Japan, 1996—; vis. scholar MIT, 1991-92, U. Amsterdam, 1994. Contbr. articles to profl. jours. Mem. English Literary Soc. of Japan (Chubu chpt., editl. bd. 1997—), Soc. of English Lit. and Linguistics (editl. bd.), English Linguistic Soc. of Japan (nat. conf. planning com. 1995-97), Japan Soc. for Medieval English Studies (organizing com. 1998—). Avocation: singing. Home: 470-0201 Aichi-ken Nishikamo-gun, Miyoshi-cho Kurozasa, Ibomichi 1033, Japan Office: Chubu U 487-8501 Aichi-ken, Kasugai-shi, Matsumoto-cho 1200, Japan

OHKOSHI, MASAAKI, medical company executive; b. Tokyo, Sept. 23, 1912; s. Tamotsu and Suzu (Hiramatsu) O.; m. Mitsuyo Toyama; chidlren: Yasumasa, Shinji, Kazuko. MD, Tokyo Imperial U., 1936. Asst. prof. Tokyo Imperial U., 1945-51; prof. Keio U., 1965-74, Tokai U., Kanagawa, 1974-84; prof. emeritus Tokai U., 1992—; chmn. Med. Corp. Showakai; emeritus pres. Internat. Symposium on Urinary Tract Infection, 1990. Author: Clinical Evaluation of Drug Efficacy in Urinary Tract Infection (K. Shiga and S. Hata Meml. award 1990). 1st lt. surgeon Japanese Army, 1937-42. Mem. Japan Urol. Assn., Japanese Soc. Chemotherapy (dir. 1969-75), Japanese Soc. Nephrology (dir. 1970-78), Japanese Soc. Infectious Disease (councilor 1977—). Anglican. Avocation: golf. Home: Minamiyukigaya 4-22-17, Ohta-ku Tokyo 145-0066, Japan Office: Med Corp Showakai, Shinyokohama 3-20-12, Yokohama Kanagawa 222-0033, Japan

OHKOSHI, NORIO, neurologist; b. Tone, Japan, Nov. 18, 1954; s. Cyuu and Aya O.; m. Mihoki, June 11, 1983; children: Yuki, Takaki, Hiroki. MD, U. Tsukuba, Japan, 1980, PhD, 1987. Resident U. Hosp. Tsukuba, Japan, 1980-88, asst. prof. neurology, 1988-90, 92—; chief neurologist Hitachi Hosp., Japan, 1990-92. Contbr. articles to profl. jours. Mem. Japanese Soc. Internal Medicine, Soc. Neurology Japan. Officee: U Tsukuba Inst Dept Neurol, 1-1-1 Tennodai, Tsukuba 305-8575, Japan

OHKURO, SHIGERU, mathematics educator; b. Sendai, Japan, Nov. 29, 1940; s. Ryoutarou and Masae (Kumagai) O.; m. Noriko Ohkuro, June 26, 1965; children: Naoko, Youko. MS, Tohoku U., Sendai City, Japan, 1965. Rsch. asst. Tohoku U., Sendai, Japan, 1965-84; lectr., 1984; asst. prof. Hachinohe (Japan) Inst. Tech., 1984—; expert C. of C. and Industry of Hachinohe, 1984; time limit mem. of rsch. spl. com. of relativity theory and gravitational wave The Inst. Electronics Info., and comm. Engrs., Tokyo, 1986-88. Contbr. articles to profl. jours.; inventor in field. Mem. IEEE Computer Soc., N.Y. Acad. Scis., AAAS, Assn. for Computing Machinery, Math. Soc. Japan, Internat. Assn. Math. Physics, Phys. Soc. Japan, Internat. Fedn. Nonlinear Analysts, Info. Processing Soc. of Japan. Avocations: tennis, skiing, music. Office: Hachinohe Inst Tech Myo, Hachinohe 031-8501, Japan

OHLENDORF, THOMAS CHARLES, systems analyst; b. Balt., Apr. 7, 1959; s. Bernard Joseph and Mary Dolores Ohlendorf; m. Andrea Marie Ohlendorf, Oct. 15, 1994. BS in Physics, Morgan State U., Balt., 1982, BS in Computer Sci., 1984. Programmer Sygnetron Protection Sys., Timonium, Md., 1984-87, Md. Dept. Econ. and Employment Devel., Balt., 1987-88; programmer, analyst Towson (Md.) U., 1988-98; sys. analyst Sea Internat., Inc., Balt., 1998—. Bd. dirs. 2d Dist. Rep. Club, Harford County, Md., 1998-99; Web master Harford County Rep. Women, 1998—, Upper Chesapeake Young Reps., Harford and Cecil Counties, 1998—. Mem. KC. Republican. Roman Catholic. Avocations: camping, fishing, computer tinkering, computer game development. E-mail: thomasohlendorf@home.com. Home: 3316 Trellis Ln Abingdon MD 21009-2878 Office: SRA Internat Inc 7102 Ambassador Rd Baltimore MD 21244-2707

OHLMAN, DOUGLAS RONALD, commodities and securities trader, investment consultant, lawyer; b. Rockville Centre, N.Y., Mar. 25, 1949; s. Maxwell and Miriam (Frucht) O.; m. Elat Menashe, Dec. 4, 1983 (div. Nov. 1996). B.A., Columbia Coll., 1971; J.D., Hofstra U., 1974. Bar: N.Y. 1975, U.S. Dist. Ct. (so. and ea. dists.) N.Y. 1976, (no. and we. dists.) N.Y. 1978, U.S. Tax Ct. 1978, U.S. Supreme Ct. 1978, U.S. Ct. Claims 1978, U.S. Customs Ct. 1978. V.p. Info. & Research Services, Inc., Roslyn, N.Y., 1975-81; assoc. Baer & Marks, N.Y.C., 1974-75, Rains, Pogrebin & Scher, Mineola, N.Y., 1975-76, Weisman, Celler, Spett, Modlin & Wertheimer, N.Y.C., 1976-79, Hoffberg, Gordon, Rabin & Engler, N.Y.C., 1979-80, Bergner & Bergner, Blum & Ruditz, N.Y.C., 1980-81; gen. counsel Greenfield Ptnrs., N.Y.C., 1981-86, gen. ptnr., 1982-86, dep. mng. ptnr., 1984-86, chief operating officer, sr. v.p., sec., dir. V.W. Investors, Inc., J.L. Investors, Inc., N.Y.C., 1985-88; commodities and securities trader for proprietary accts. Highland Beach, Fla., 1988—; dir. Track Data Corp., N.Y.C., 1983-87; allied mem. N.Y. Stock Exchange, Inc., 1982-88, options prin., 1985, 87. Mem. radio news team WKCR-FM, N.Y.C. (Writers Guild award, Peabody nomination 1968); notes and comments editor Hofstra Law Rev., 1973-74. Communications dir., dep. radiol. officer Nassau County Civil Def., Town of Roslyn, N.Y., 1964-74; mem. com. Nassau County Liberal Party, 1982. Mem. ABA, N.Y. State Bar Assn., N.Y. County Lawyers Assn., Assn. of Bar of City of N.Y. Home: 401 NE Mizner Blvd Apt T502 Boca Raton FL 33432-4024

OHLSSON, BERTIL GULLITH, molecular biologist; b. Malmo, Sweden, July 24, 1954; s. Nils Axel and Erna Henny (Albrechtsen) O. BS, U. Lund, Sweden, 1979, PhD, 1987. Asst. prof. U. Goteborg, Sweden, 1991—. Postdoctoral fellow Rockefeller U., N.Y.C., 1987-90. Mem. Swedish Soc. Medicine. Avocation: hiking. Home: Allmanna vagen 40C, S-41460 Göteborg Sweden Office: U Göteborg, sahlgrenska U Hosp Wallenberg Lab, S-41345 Göteborg Sweden

OHLSSON, NICLAS, technical director; b. Orebro, Sweden, Apr. 5, 1967; s. Goran and Barbro (Roman) O.; m. Maria Ivers, Sept. 20, 1997; children: Phillip, Naima. MSc, Linkoping U., 1993, PhD, 1998. Engr. Ericsson Telecom AB, Stockholm, Sweden, 1993; cons. Fides Ingenii, Linkoping, Sweden, 1994-98; tech. dir. Gratistel Internat. AB, Stockholm, 1998; v.p. tech. Iquity Syss. AB (formerly Gratistel Internat. AB), Stockholm, 1998-2000; v.p. engring. Odin AB, Stockholm, 2000—. Mem. IEEE. Avocations: brass music, sailing, football, cycling.

OHMORI, HIROMITSU, electrical engineering educator; b. Kita-ku, Tokyo, Aug. 14, 1960; s. Kazuo and Yukiko (Hirayama) O.; m. Hisako Nagase, Feb. 23, 1992. BE, Keio U., Tokyo, 1983, ME, 1985, PhD, 1988. Isntr. Keio U., 1988-91, asst. prof., 1991-96, assoc. prof., 1996—. Recipient Ando Incentive prize for study of electronics The found. of Ando Lab., 1993. Office: Keio U Dept Sys Design Engring, 3-14-1 Hiyoshi, Kohoku-ku, Yokohama 223-8522, Japan

OHNAMI, MASATERU, mechanical engineering educator; b. Kyoto, Japan, Apr. 6, 1931; s. Eijiro and Hisae O.; m. Hiroko Ohnami, Oct. 10, 1959; 1 child, Masahiro. B in Engring., Ritsumeikan U., Kyoto, Japan, 1954; D in Engring., Kyoto U., 1960; D Internat. Rels. (honoris causa), Am. U., Washington, 1995; LLD (honoris causa), U. B.C., Can., 1997; DSc honoris causa, Macquarie U., Australia, 1999. Asst. prof. Kyoto U., 1955-61; assoc. prof. Ritsumeikan U., Kyoto, 1961-67, prof., 1967—, dean acad. affairs, 1978-80, dean faculty sci. & engring., 1988-90, pres., 1991-98; pres. Kyoto Tachibana Women's U., 2000—; vis. rsch. prof. Columbia U., N.Y.C., 1963-64; mng. dir. Japan Assn. Pvt. Colls. and Univs., Tokyo, 1991-99; v.p. Japanese Univ. Accreditation Assn., Tokyo, 1997—; mem. Sci. Coun., Ministry Edn., 1984-86, 88-91; regular mem. Univ. Formation Coun., 1993—, Coun. Colls. and Univs., Ministry Edn., Tokyo, 1995-97; mem. steering com. Ctr. Entrance Exam. (DNC), 1996—; hon. consul Republic Philippines, Kyoto, 1997—. Author: Plasticity and High Temperature Strength of Materials, 1988, Fracture and Society, 1992. Mem. Deutscher Verband für Materialforschung und prüfung e.V. (hon.), Soc. of Materials Sci. Japan (bd. dirs. 1971-74, 81-84, 85-88, prize 1971), Japanese Soc. of Strength and Fracture of Materials (bd. dirs. 1984-99, hon. 1999), Sci. Coun. Japan (material rsch. liaison com. 1988-94, 95—), Engring. Acad. Japan. Avocations: oil painting, reading. Home and Office: 8-10 Hyugacho, Osaka Takatsuki 569-0024, Japan

OHNISHI, MINORU, film company executive; b. Mihara-cho, Japan, Oct. 28, 1925; s. Sokichi and Mitsu Ohnishi; m. Yaeko Yui, Nov. 13, 1951; children: Mitsuru, Masahiko. BS in Econs., Tokyo U., 1948. With Fuji Photo Film Co., Ltd., Tokyo, 1948—; mgr. N.Y. office Fuji Photo Film Co., Ltd., 1964-72; dir. overseas divsn. Fuju Photo Film Co., Ltd., Tokyo, 1972-76, mng. dir. overseas divsn., 1976-79, sr. mng. dir. domestic sales divsn., 1979-80, pres., 1980-96; chmn., CEO Fuji Photo Film Co., Ltd., Tokyo, 1996—. Decorated comdr. Order of Orange-Nassau, The Netherlands, 1986, Cruzeiro Do Sul, Brazilian Govt., 1990, Medal with Blue Ribbon, Emperor of Japan, 1990, Comdr. Crown of Belgium, King of Belgium, 1991, Order of Merit, Northrhine-Westphalia, Germany, 1992, Second Class of Order of the Rising Sun, Emperor of Japan, 1995; recipient Leadership award Nat. Assn. Photographic Mfrs. (U.S.), 1992. Mem. Photo-sensitized Materials Mfrs. Assn. Japan (pres. Tokyo chpt. 1980-96), Japan Rec.-Media Industries Assn. (chmn. 1994-96), Japan Chem. Industry Assn. (v.p. 1993-96), Photograph Soc. Japan (chmn. 1997—). Avocations: reading, golf. Office: Fuji Photo Film Co Ltd, 26-30 Nishi-Azabu 2-chome, Minato-ku Tokyo 106, Japan*

OHNO, EIICHI, electronics company executive; b. Gifu, Japan, Apr. 1, 1933. B in Engring., U. Tokyo, 1955, D of Engring., 1968. Rschr. rsch. lab. Mitsubishi Electric Corp., Amagasaki, Japan, 1955-82, gen. mgr. product devel. lab., 1982-86, gen. mgr. info. sys. lab., 1986-89, dir., gen. mgr. ctrl. rsch. lab., 1989-91; mng. dir. corp. rsch. and devel. Mitsubishi Electric Corp., Tokyo, 1991-95, advisor, 1995—; chmn. steering com. Internat. Robotics and Factory Automation Ctr., 1985-92. Author, editor: Introduction to Power Electronics, 1983, English edit., 1987; spkr. in field. Recipient Award for Persons of Sci. and Technol. Merits Japanese Govt., 1980, Mainichi Indsl. award, 1983. Fellow IEEE (vice chmn. Tokyo sect. 1997-98, Japan coun. 1999-2000), The Soc. of Instrument and Control Engrs. (chmn. 1996-97); mem. IEE Japan (auditor 1990-91), Japan Machinery Fedn. (chmn. indsl. tech. com. 1993—), Japan Soc. for Indsl. and Applied Math. (chmn. 1995-96). Avocations: playing flute, T'ai Chi Ch'uan. Office: Mitsubishi Electric Corp, 3-1-1 Maruno-chi Ciyoda-ku, Tokyo 100-0005, Japan

OHNO, KEIICHI, academic administrator, engineering educator; b. Numata, Gunma, Japan, Aug. 16, 1938; s. Shuji and Aki (Nishimura) O.; m. Akiko Kusano, Apr. 29, 1968; children: Shuichi, Ayako. B, U. Electrocomm., Tokyo, 1962; M, Tokyo Inst. Tech., 1964, D, 1967. From asst. to assoc. prof. faculty engring. Hokkaido U., Sapporo, Japan, 1967-90; prof. dept. info. engr. Polytech. U., Sagamihara, Japan, 1990-2000; pres. Hokkaido Polytechnic Coll., Otaru, Japan, 2000—. Author, editor: ESR Imaging: ESR Zeumatography and Its Applications, 1990, EPR Imaging and In Vivo EPR, 1991. Mem. Internat. Soc. Magnetic Resonance, Internat. EPR(ESR) Soc., Japan Soc. Applied Physics (dir. Hokkaido br. 1983-84), Chem. Soc. of Japan. Achievements include development of EPR imaging. Avocations: skiing, mountain climbing. Home: 3-3-102 Maeda Teine-ku, Sapporo 006-0813, Japan Office: Hokkaido Polytechnic Coll 3-190, Otaru 047-0282, Japan

OHNO, KIMIO, chemist; b. Tokyo, June 4, 1926; s. Ryuta and Akiko (Hara) O.; m. Akiko Toki, may 13, 1951; children: Hideo, Nobuko, Michio. BS, U. Tokyo, 1951, DS, 1957. Rsch. asst. U. Tokyo, 1952-61; prof. Uppsala U., Sweden, 1961-63, U. Fla., Gainesville, 1963-64, Hokkaido U., Sapporo, Japan, 1964-90, Nat. Ctr. for Sci. Info. Systems, Tokyo, 1990-92, Hokkaido Info. U., Ebetsu, Japan, 1992—; dir. Computer Ctr., Hokkaido U., 1976-82; dep. dir. gen. NACSIS, Tokyo, 1990-92; head satellite edn. dept., HIU, Ebetsu, 1994-97, pres., 1999—. Co-author: Quantum Mechanics of Electronic Structure of Simple Molecules, 1961, Quantum Chemistry Literature Data Base, 1976; editl. bd. Internat. Jour. Quant. Chemistry, 1985—. Office: Hokkaido Info Univ, 59-2 Nishi-Nopporo, 069-8585 Ebetsu-shi/Hokkaido Japan

OHNO, KOICHI, physical chemist; b. Asahikawa, Hokkaido, Japan, Sept. 19, 1945; s. Kimiyoshi and Shigeko (Mori) L.; m. Yaeko Himeno, Sept. 19, 1970; children: Shinya, Yumiko. BSc, U. Tokyo, 1968, MSc, 1970, DSc, 1973. Rsch. assoc. U. Tokyo, 1972-80, assoc. prof., 1980-89, prof., 1989-94; prof. phys. chemistry Tohoku U., Japan, 1994—. Recipient Ramsay Meml.

fellow, 1975-77. Mem. Chem. Soc. Japan (bd. dirs. 1997-99, acad. rsch. prize 1999). Avocation: skiing. Home: Kunimigaoka 1-16-6, Aobaku, 989-3201 Sendai Japan Office: Tohoku U Grad Sch Sci, Aramaki, Aobaku, Sendai 980-8578, Japan

OHNO, MOTONORI, biochemist; b. Chikushino City, Japan, Feb. 18, 1933; s. Toraji Umeda and Kimiyo O.; m. Yoshiko Takeshita, Apr. 27, 1963; children: Yuju, Keiju. BS, Kyushu U., 1956, MS, 1958, DSc, 1963. Asst. prof. Kyushu U., Fukuoka, 1963-68, assoc. prof., 1969-87, prof., 1988-96; prof. emeritus Kyushu U., 1996—; prof. Osaka U., Japan, 1993, Kumamoto Inst. Technology, Japan, 1997—; councilor Biodynamics Found., Kumamoto, 1997—; vis. assoc. NIH, Bethesda, 1966-68, vis. scientist NIH, Bethesda, 1980-82. Contbr. articles to profl. jours. Recipient award Mitsubishi Found., Tokyo, 1994. Mem. Chem. Soc. Japan (chmn. Kyushu br. 1994-95), Japanese Biochem. Soc. (councilor 1989—), Japanese Peptide Soc. (dir. Osaka 1990—), Am. Chem. Soc. Avocations: golf, rugby football. Home: 3-1-16-203 Kami-Kumamoto, 860 0079 Kumamoto Japan Office: Sojo U, 4-22-1 Ikeda, 860-0082 Kumamoto Japan

OHNO, TADAO, health science association; b. Akita, Japan, Nov. 21, 1942; s. Tadatoshi and Ai Ohno; m. Mitsuko Murata, June 30, 1985; children: Atsuko, Tadatsune. BSc, U. Tokyo, 1966, MSc, 1968, PhD, 1971. Rschr. U. Pa., Phila., 1971-73; engr. Kitasato Inst., Tokyo, 1973-75; rschr. Nat. Inst. of Radiol. Scis., Chiba, 1975-85; sr. rschr. Inst. of Phys. and Chem. Rsch., Wako and Tsukuba, 1985-93; dir. gene bank Inst. of Phys. and Chem. Rsch., Tsukuba, 1993—; pres. 3rd Internet World Congress on Biomed. Scis., Tsukuba, 1996. Contbr. articles to profl. jours.; patentee in field. Mem. Japanese Soc. of Alternatives to Animal Experiments (pres. 1999—). Office: Inst Phys and Chem Rsch, RIKEN Gene Bank, Tsukuba 305-0074, Japan

OHNO, YUTAKA, information sciences educator; b. Tokyo, Aug. 24, 1924; s. Teikichi Asai and Kin O.; m. Kyoko Okuno; children: Takashi, Junko. B of Engring., Tokyo U., 1946, DEng, 1962. Rschr. Railway Tech. Rsch. Inst., Japanese Nat. Railway, Tokyo, 1946-72; prof. Kyoto (Japan) U., 1972-88, dir. Ednl. Ctr. Info. Processing, 1978-88, prof. emeritus, 1988—; prof. Koshien U., Takarazuka, Japan, 1988-90; prof. Ritsumeikan U., Kyoto, 1990-95, dean dept. sci. and engring., 1992-94, dir. Integrated Info. Ctr., 1994-95; dir. rsch. ctr. Biwako Kusatsu campus Ritsumeikan U., Kusatsu, 1995—; pres. Kansai Tech. Licensing Orgn. Co., Ltd., 1998—; mem. Coun. Info. Processing Promotion, Ministry of Internat. Trade and Industry, Tokyo, 1985-96. Contbr. numerous rsch. articles to sci. publs. Recipient Gen. Dir. award Sci. and Tech. Agy., Japanese Govt., 1961, Purple Ribbon medal Japanese Govt., 1971, 2d Order of Sacred Treasure, 1996. Mem. Engring. Acad. Japan, Person Computer User's Applications Tech. Assn. (pres. 1991—), Info. Processing Soc. Japan (hon. life, pres. 1987-89), Assn. Computing Machinery (dir. Japan chpt. 1997-2000), Orgn. for Engring. Adventure Groups Linkage Prog. (pres. linkage program 1991-98). Buddhist. Avocations: game of Go, golfing, reading, calligraphy. Home: 1-14-4 Takadai, Kyoto Nagaokakyo 617 0847, Japan Office: Ritsumeikan U BKC, 1-1-1 Nojihigashi, Shiga Kusatsu 525 8577, Japan

OHNUMA, KATSUHIKO, prehistoric archaeologist; b. Itabashi, Tokyo, Japan, June 2, 1944; s. Yasoji and Kazuko Ohnuma; m. Junko Satoh, July 20, 1978; children: Sachi, Hiroshi, Michi. BA, Nanzan U., Nagoya, Japan, 1973, MA, 1976; PhD, London U., 1986. Lectr. Inst. Cultural Studies Ancient Iraq, Kokushikan U., Tokyo, 1982-87, assoc. prof., 1987-94, prof., 1994—, dir., 1997—; Field dir. Archaeol. Expdn. to Iraq, Kokushikan U., Tokyo, 1986-88, dir., 1997—, archaeol. expdn. to Syria, Kokushikan U., Tokyo. Editor Al Rafidan, Vol. 18, 1997, Archaeol. Expedition to Syria; author: British Archaeological Reports, 1988, The Emergence of Modern Humans, 1990, The Definition and Interpretation of Levallois Technology, 1995. Mem. Japanese Archaeol. Assn., Japanese Soc. West Asian Archaeology, Japanese Soc. Lithic Tech. (pres. 1994—). Avocations: reading, country music, fishing. Home: 6-8-15-501 Tsurukawa, Machida, Tokyo 195-0061, Japan Office: Kokushikan U, 1-1-1 Hirohakama, Machida 195-8550, Japan

OHRI, SANGEETA JEAN MARY, social educator; b. Mumbai, India, Sept. 12, 1943; d. Joseph Marshall and Hilda Mary (Varel) D'Aguiar; m. N. Ohri, Nov. 20, 1961 (div. May 1999); children: Sanjay, Sandeep. BA part I, Shrimati Nathibai Damodar Thackersey, Mumbai, 1980. Organiser day sch. Soc. for Edn. of Crippled, Mumbai, 1978-82, acting prin., 1979-81; resource person Indian Assn. Presch. Edn., Mumbai, 1979—, Indian Nat. chpt. Org. Mondiale Edn. Prescolaire (World Body Presch.), Mumbai, 1987-95; hon. treas. Indian Assn. Presch. Edn., Mumbai, 1979-81, hon. sec., 1981-86; adminstr. Soc. for Edn. Crippled, Mumbai, 1979-93; chairperson Rural Project, Pune, India, 1993-96. Joint hon. sec. Local Gen. Hosp., Santa Cruz, Mumbai, 1987-89; mem. State Commn. for Handicapped, Pune, India, 1996; v.p. All India Balkan-ji-Bari (Pioneer Child Welfare Assn.), Mumbai, 1996—; exec. v.p. Indian Assn. Presch. Edn., Mumbai, 1997; exec. Bombay Vigilance Assn., 1990—; cons. Save the Children, India; active PTO. Recipient Sahyog award for women's welfare and social work, 1999. Mem. Pers. Mgmt. and Tng. Assn. of Indian Women (v.p.). Avocations: creative dramatics, writing, travel, organising welfare activities. Home: A-14 Hill View Residency, Baner Rd, Baner Pune 411045, India

OHRI, SUNIL KUMAR, surgeon; b. Karpurthala, Punjab, India, Dec. 25, 1961; arrived in England, 1967; s. Manohar Lal and Anita (Puri) O.; m. Sonia Kumar, Oct. 14, 1990; children: Sereena India, Rikhil Arun, Nikhil Sunil, Raja Sahil. MB, Middlesex Hosp. Med. Sch., London, 1985; MB BS, Middlesex Hosp. Med. Sch., 1985; MD, U. London, 1994. Registrar cardiothoracic surgery Hammersmith Hosp., London, 1994-95; sr. registrar Hammersmith Hosp., 1995-97, Middlesex Hosp., London, 1995-96; sr. registrar in cardiac & thoracic surgery Harefield Hosp., England, 1996-97; cons. cardiac surgery Southampton Gen. Hosp., 1998—. Contbr. articles to profl. jours. Fellow Royal Coll. Surgeons; mem. Soc. Thoracic Surgeons, Assn. Cardiothoracic Surgeon Gt. Britian, British Med. Assn. Hindu. Avocations: writing, gardening. Home: Hamtun House, 9A Westrow Rd, Southampton S015 2NA, United Kingdom Office: Southampton Gen Hosp Cardiac Surg Unit, Tremona Rd, Southampton SO16 6YD, England

OHRT, KARSTEN, company executive; b. Copenhagen, Nov. 8, 1952; s. Hans Henrik and Helle (Olivarius) O.; m. Jane Havshøj; children: Eva, Christine. Magister Konferens, Århus U., 1979. Curator Nordjyllands Kunstmuseum, Ålborg, 1979-88; dir. Kunsthallen Brandts Klaedefabrik, Odense, 1988—; bd. dirs. Frederiksborgmuseet, New Carlsberg Found. Chmn. Govtl. Com. for Visual Arts, 1996-98; bd. mem. Nat. Com. for Expo 2000, Hannover, 1998—. Decorated Knight of the Order of Danebrog, 1997; recipient The Høyen award, 1998. Office: Brandts Klaedefabrik, Brandts Passage 37-43, 5000 Odense Denmark

OHSAKI, AYUMI, chemist; b. Kochi-City, Japan, Oct. 29, 1958; d. Azusa and Tokumi (Masaoka) Kawamura; m. Hisashi Ohsaki, Oct. 30, 1983; children: Mizu, Noboru. PhD, Osaka City U., 1987. Asst. prof. Kinki U., Osaka, Japan, 1983-91, Tokyo Med. & Dental U., 1992—. Mem. Am. Chem. Soc., Chem. Soc. Japan, Pharm. Soc. Japan. Phone: 81-55-3-5280-8153. Office: Med/Dental U Inst Biomed/Biomat Engring, 2-3-10 Surugadai Kanda, Chiyoda-ku Tokyo 101-0062, Japan

OHSAKI, KATSUICHIRO, otolaryngologist researcher, and educator; b. Kyoto, Kyoto-fu, Japan, Feb. 13, 1935; s. Kazuo and Tsuya Ohsaki; m. Reiko Miyoshi, Sept. 20, 1964; children: Yohichiro, Mari, Keijiro. MD, Okayama U., Okayama City, Japan, 1959, PhD, 1965; postgrad., NYU, 1962. Intern 6022 USAF Hosp., Japan, 1959-60; resident N.Y. Eye and Ear Infirmary, N.Y.C., 1961-62; otolaryngologist Hiroshima Citizens' Hosp., Japan, 1965-69; from vic chief otolaryngologist to chief otolaryngologist Kobe Nishishimin Hosp., Hyogo, Japan, 1970-75; otolaryngologist-in-chief Okayama Red Cross Gen. Hosp., Japan, 1975-76; prof. otolaryngology sch. medicine U. Tokushima, Japan, 1976-81, prof. divsn. clin. otology univ. hosp. Sch. Medicine, 1981-2000, prof. emeritus, 2000—; mem. Sudden Deafness Rsch. Com. Japan organized by Ministry of Health and Welfare of Japanese Govt., 1973-76; hon. chmn. Beijing Internat. Symposium Otolaryngology, 1988; guest prof. Beijing Med. U., 1992—, 4th Mil. Med. U., Xian, China, 1994—; mem. adv. com. 6th Internat. Conf. on Cholesteatoma and Ear Surgery, 2000—; session chmn. XVI World Congress Otorhinolaryngology-Head and Neck Surgery, 1997. Author: Sudden Deafness (Japanese edit.), 1985; co-author, co-editor Tinnitus (Chinese edit.), 1994; patentee remedy for sudden deafness and fluctuating sensorineural hearing loss, 1982, test equipment for tinnitus, 1992. Named Most Admired Man in the Decade, Am. Biog. Inst., 1995, 20th Century Award for Achievement, IBC, 1997, Internat. Man of the Year, 1996-97. Mem. N.Y. Acad. Scis., Otological Soc. Japan (councillor 1991-2000), Japan Soc. Infectious Diseases in Otolaryngology (adminstrn. com. 1991—), Internat. Soc. of Audiology, Tokushima-ken Med. Soc. (rep. 1994-2000), Am. Acad. Otolaryngology-Head and Neck Surgery (corr.), European Acad. Otology and Neuro-otology (assoc.), Oto-Rhino-Laryngological Soc. Japan (specialist 1984—). Buddhist. Avocations: calligraphy, golf, shogi. Home and Office: 5-25 Nanokaichi-Nishi-Machi, Okayama 700-0851, Japan Office: U Tokushima U Hosp Sch Medicine, 2-50-1 Kuramoto-cho, Tokushima 770-8503, Japan

OHSAKI, MAKOTO, architecture educator; b. Osaka, Japan, June 12, 1960; s. Haruo and Michiko O.; m. Noriko Shimada, June 16, 1985; children: Takeshi, Satsuki. BS, Kyoto (Japan) U., 1983, MS, 1985, DEng, 1993. Instr. Kyoto U., 1985-95, assoc. prof., 1995—; Mem. adv. bd. Showa Ednl. Found., Osaka, 1999—; bd. dirs. Archtl. Inst. Japan, Tokyo, 1998—. Recipient Promotive prize Archtl. Inst. Japan, 1996, Best Dissertation of Yr. award Maeda Found., Tokyo, 1994. Avocations: music, auto racing. Office: Dept Architecture Kyoto U, Sakyo, Kyoto 606-8501, Japan

OHSATO, HITOSHI, ceramic science educator; b. Mizushima, Okayama, Japan, July 7, 1944; s. Tuneo and Yuri (Mase) O.; m. Keiko Karasawa, Apr. 2, 1971; children: Motoko, Hajime. B in Engring., Nagoya (Japan) Inst. Tech., 1968, M in Engring., 1970; DSc, Tokyo U., 1984. Cert. sci. and engring. tchg. Asst. prof. Nagoya Inst. Tech., 1970-86, lectr., 1986-93, assoc. prof., 1993-99, prof., 1999—; lectr. Aichi Prefectural Seto (Japan) Ceramics H.S., 1989-92. Contbr. articles to profl. jours.; patentee in field. V.p. Park Protection Soc. Shimada Green, 1989—. grantee Ohkura Kazuchika Meml. Found., Tokyo, 1987, Ministry of Edn., Tokyo, 1985, 91, 98, Murata Sci. Found., Kyoto, Japan, 1992, Japan Sheet Glass Found., Tokyo, 1997; rsch. scholar Japanes Govt., Tokyo U., 1983-84, Northwestern U., 1993-94. Mem. Mineralogical Soc. Japan (jour. editor 1984-88), Crystallographic Soc. Japan (jour. editor 1996—), Am. Ceramic Soc., Ceramic Soc. Japan., Creative Sci. Soc. Japan (v.p. 1995-2000, pres. 2000—), Japan Soc. Applied Phys. Avocations: nature watching, mountain climbing, skiing, gardening. Home: 13-28 Hirabari-jutaku, Tempaku-cho Tempaku-ku, Aichi Nagoya 468-0021, Japan Office: Nagoya Inst Tech, Gokiso-cho Showa-ku, Aichi Nagoya 466-8555, Japan

OHSAWA, HIDEJIRO, oil industry executive. Ceo Nippon Oil, Tokyo. Office: Nippon Mitsubishi Oil Corp, 3-12 Nishi-Shimbashi 1chome, Minato-ku Tokyo 105-8412, Japan*

OHSAWA, YASUHARU, engineering educator; b. Osaka, Japan, Nov. 25, 1946; s. Mitsusaburo and Sue (Tsujimoto) O.; m. Chizuko Matsui, Mar. 24, 1975; children: Yasuyuki, Mariko. BS, Kyoto (Japan) U., 1969, MS, 1971, D of Engring., 1982. Rsch. assoc. Kyoto U., 1972-85; from asst. prof. to assoc. prof. Tsukuba (Japan) U., 1985-90; assoc. prof. Kobe (Japan) U., 1990-94, prof., 1994—. Author: (book) Electric Power Generation, 1985. Mem. IEEE, Inst. Elec. Engrs. Japan. Avocations: golf, driving cars, gardening. Home: 2-1-4 Taishibashi Asahi-ku, Osaka 535-0001, Japan Office: Kobe U, 1-1 Rokkodai Nada-ku, 657-8501 Kobe Hyogo, Japan

OHSHIMA, TOHRU, legal medicine educator; b. Asahi-machi, Toyama, Japan, June 10, 1956; Alexander von Humboldt Found. rsch. fellow Inst. Legal Medicine, U. Cologne, Germany, 1988-89.; s. Kanji and Fumiko (Uda) O.; m. Kaoru Ito-Uji, Oct. 18, 1986; 1 child, Yu. MD, Kanazawa (Japan) U., 1981, PhD, 1986. Instr. dept. legal medicine Kanazawa U. Sch. Medicine, 1986-87, asst. prof., 1987-90, assoc. prof., 1990-93, prof., dir. dept., 1993—; vis. prof. Dalian (China) U., 1998. Author: Burned Bodies (in English), 1991, The Essentials of Legal Medicine, 1993, Modern Textbook of Legal Medicine, 1995, A Manual of Death Certificate, 1997. Mem. Japan Com. for UNICEF, Tokyo, 1998. Recipient encouragement award Japanese Assn. Criminology, 1995; grantee Japan Med. Assn., 1999. Mem. Japanese Assn. Forensic Toxicology (bd. dirs. 1997—), Medico-Legal Soc. Japan (councilor 1992—, encouragement award 1992), Japanese Soc. Clin. Toxicology (councilor 1995—), Baltic Medico-Legal Assn. (hon.). Avocations: reading, travel, hot springs, classical music, opera. Office: Kanazawa U Dept Legal Med, 13-1 Takara-machi, Ishikawa Kanazawa 920-8640, Japan

OHTA, AKIHIDE, physician, researcher, educator; b. Fukae Town, Japan, Mar. 22, 1951; s. Tomoshi and Eiko (Shimoda) O.; m. Masumi Kurauchi, Mar. 21, 1982; children: Akiko, Chiaki, Kensuke. MD, Kagoshima U., Japan, 1976. Physician-in-tng. Saga (Japan) Prefectural Hosp., 1976-77, Kyushu U. Hosp., Fukuoka, Japan, 1977-78; rsch. fellow Kyushu U., Fukuoka, 1978-79; rsch. assoc. Harbor-UCLA Med. Ctr., Torrance, Calif., 1984-86; asst. prof. Saga Med. Sch., 1979-84, 86-90, asst. prof., instr., 1990-95, instr., dir. divsn. rheumatology and allergy, 1994, prof. dept. clin. nursing, 1995—. Contbr. articles to profl. jours. Mem. Japanese Soc. Internal Medicine, Japanese Rheumatism Assn., Am. Fedn. for Med. Rsch., Soc. for Investigative Dermatology, Am. Coll. Rheumatology, N.Y. Acad. Scis. Avocation: watching movies. Office: Saga Med Sch Dept Clin Nrsg, 5-1-1 Nabeshima, Saga 849-8501, Japan

OHTA, HITOYA, radiologist; b. Kobe City, Hyogo, Japan, Jan. 1, 1953; s. Takeshi and Chie (Inoue) O.; m. Nakamura Atsuko; children: Kaori, Yuko, Rie, Mio, Masahiro. BS, Kyoto (Japan) U., 1980, MD, PhD, 1998. Vice-dir. Wakayama (Japan) Red Cross Hosp., 1989-92, Osaka (Japan) Red Cross Hosp., 1992—. Contbr. articles to profl. jours. Mem. Japanese Radiol. Soc. Kodokan. Buddist. Avocations: noh-play, judo. Home: 1-23-21 Ishimaru, Mino-o City 562, Japan Office: Osaka Red Cross Hosp, 5-53 Fudegasakicho Tennohji, Osaka City 543, Japan

OHTA, ISAMU, mechanical engineer; b. Hitachi, Ibaraki, Japan, July 3, 1967; s. Hiroshi and Yuko (Narita) O.; m. Mizue Sawaike, Mar. 12, 1994. MME, Aoyama-Gakuin U., Tokyo, 1992. Rschr. Misawa Homes Inst. R & D Co. Ltd., Tokyo, 1995—; engr. Misawa Homes Co. Ltd., Tokyo, 1995—. Contbr. articles to profl. jours., including Trans. Japan Soc. Mech. Engrs. Grantee Aoyama Gakuin U., 1990. Avocations: tennis, cooking, raising tropical fish. Home: 4-19-10 Kugayama Suginami, Tokyo 168, Japan Office: Misawa Homes Co Ltd, 2-4-5 Takaido-higashi, Tokyo 168-0071, Japan

OHTA, NOBUO, psychology educator; b. Nishiharu, Aichi, Japan, Nov. 6, 1941; s. Haruzoh and Fuh Ohta; m. Hiroko Tsuchida; 2 children. BA, Aichi U. of Arts and Scis., 1965; MA, Nagoya U., 1968, PhD in Psychology, 1976. Asst. prof. Nagoya (Japan) Arts Univ., 1971-73; asst. prof. Tottori (Japan) Univ., 1973-75, assoc. prof., 1975-76; assoc. prof. U. Tsukuba, Japan, 1976-92, prof., 1992—, dir. grad. sch. Psychology, 1996-98; dean Coll. Human. Scis. U. Tsukuba, 1998—. Author, editor: Episodic Memory, 1988, Cognitive Psychology; Theory and Data, 1991, The Fronitesr of Memory Research, 2000; contbr. articles to profl. jours. Avocations: travel, movies. Home: 702-21 Shimohirooka, Tsukuba 305, Japan Office: U Tsukuba, Inst of Psychology, Tsukuba 305, Japan

OHTA, SHOZABURO, engineering educator; b. Mito-shi, Ibaraki, Japan, May 15, 1925; s. Keizaburo and Kana (Kani) O.; m. Mitsuko Ishizaki, Feb. 9, 1955; 1 child, Nobuyuki. B in Engring., Tokyo U., 1949, D in Engring., 1961. Tech. officer Japanese Nat. Rlwys., Tokyo, 1949-50; engr. Rlwy. Tech. Rsch. Inst., Tokyo, 1950-56, chief engr., 1956-71, head welding lab., 1971-77; prof. Musashi Inst. Tech., Tokyo, 1977-96, chief mfg. engring. Grad. Sch., 1988-92, prof. emeritus, 1996—; advisor tng. sch. for cons. engrs., Tokyo, 1988—. Author: Fastening and Joining Method, 1966, Strength of Welded Joints, 1972, Design and Standard of Welded Structures, 1978, Welding Encyclopedia, 1985. Avocations: music, travel, movies. Home: 27-2 Kakinokidai, Aoba-ku, Yokohama Kanagawa 227-0048, Japan Office: Musashi Inst Tech, 1-28-1 Tamazutsumi Setagaya, Tokyo 158-8557, Japan

OHTA, TETSUO, chemistry educator; b. Kanzaki-gun, Hyogo, Japan, Jan. 1, 1958; s. Katsumi and Sachiko (Tanaka) O.; m. Taeko Maeda, Mar. 26, 1989; 1 child, Tadahiro. Diploma in engring., Kyoto (Japan) U., 1980, M in Engring., 1982, DEng, 1988. Tech. assoc. Inst. for Molecular Sci., Okazaki, Japan, 1984-89, rsch. assoc., 1989; rsch. assoc. Kyoto U., 1989-95; assoc. prof. chemistry Doshisha U., Kyoto, 1995—; vis. prof. ENSC of Lille, France, 1991; vis. scholar Northwestern U., Evanston, Ill., 1993-94. Author: Future Opportunities in Catalytic and Separation Technology, 1990, Comprehensive Organic Synthesis, 1991, Homogeneous Transition Metal Catalyzed Reactions, 1992, Catalytic Asymmetric Synthesis, 1993. Office: Doshisha U Faculty Engring, Dept Molecular Sci and Tech, Kyoto 613-0394, Japan

OHTA, TOKIO, engineering educator, researcher; b. Kanazawa, Japan, Nov. 3, 1925; s. Sentario and Haru (Higashi) O.; m. Kimiko Nakagawa, Apr. 10, 1950 (dec. Dec. 1963); 1 child, Takeyo; m. Yohko Ishikawa, Sept. 27, 1964; children: Takaya, Yasuto. BA, Kyoto U., 1948, DrSc, 1962. Prof. Tchr.'s Coll., Kanazawa, Japan, 1950-54, Def. Acad., Yokosuka, Japan, 1954-68; prof. Yokohama (Japan) Nat. U., 1968-85, dean faculty of engring., 1985-88, pres., 1988-94, prof. emeritus, 1994-99; chmn. Frontier Info. and Learning Orgn., Kamakura, Japan, 1995—; supt. Internat. Network, U. Gifu, 1998—; chancellor Internat. Network U., 1998—; mem. sci. and tech. coun. Govt. Tokyo, 1974-94, mem. indsl. tech. coun., 1974-99. Author: Solar-Hydrogen Energy Systems, 1979, Energy Technology Sources, Systems and Frontier Conversions, 1994, Energy Viewed from the Numerical Data (in Japanese), 1991, Semiconductor Thermoelectricity (in Japanese), 1964. Advisor in sci. and tech. Gifu-Ken, 1992—, Kanagawa-Ken, Yokohama, 1988-94. Recipient Disting. Performance award U. Hawaii, 1984, Meritorious award Sao Paulo U., 1993, Jules Verne award Internat. Assoc. Hydrogen Energy, 2000. Avocations: haiku-poem, gardening. Office: Frontier Info & Learning, 4-8-15 Inamuragasaki, Kamakura Japan

OHTAHARA, SHUNSUKE, medical educator; b. Okayama, Japan, Feb. 11, 1930; s. Kazuyoshi and Shizue (Itano) O.; m. Sachiko Takahara, May 28, 1961. MD, Okayama U., 1956; PhD, Okayama U. Med. Sch., 1961. Intern Okayama Univ. Hosp., 1956-57, resident dept. pediat., 1957-61; asst. prof. Okayama U. Med. Sch., 1970-78, assoc. prof., 1978-79, prof., chmn. dept. child neurology, 1979-95, prof. emeritus, 1979—, dir. Inst. Neurobiology,, 1981-83, 87-89; prof. pediat., child neurology Kibi Internat. U. Health Sci. Sch., Takahashi, Japan, 1995—. Editor: New Trends in Pediatric Epileptology, 1991; contbr. articles to med. pubs. Pres. Rotary of Okayama Chuo, 1986-88. Mem. Japanese Soc. Child Neurology (pres. 1975-76), Japan Epilepsy Soc. (pres. 1979-80), Japanese Soc. EEG and EMG (pres. 1988-89), Internat. Child Neurology Assn. (exec. bd. dirs.). Avocations: collecting classic cameras, photography, travel. E-mail: ohtahara@med.okayama-u.ac.jp. Office: Okayama U Med Sch Child Neu, 2-5-1 Shikatacho, Okayama 700-8558, Japan

OHTAKA, HIROSHI, medicinal chemist; b. Tokyo, Feb. 27, 1949; s. Kiyoshi Masaki and Emiko O.; m. Midori Kobayashi, Jan. 10, 1973; children: Hiromi, Atsushi. PhD, Kyoto U., 1987. From rsch. scientist to dir. pharm. tech. rsch. Kanebo Ltd., Osaka, Japan, 1973-99; mgr. mfg. and tech. planning Nippon Organon K.K., Osaka, 1999—; lectr. Osaka Mcpl. U., Japan, 1991-95. Author: Progress in Drug Research, vol. 41, 1993, QSAR and Drug Design: New Developments and Applications, 1995, The Creation of New Drugs, 1995, Development and Application of Fluorinated Bioactive Compounds, 1999, Drug Design and Computer Science, 2000; contbr. articles to profl. jours. Mem. Chem. Soc. Japan, Pharm. Soc. Japan, The QSAR and Modelling Soc. Home: 2-12-24 Shiginonishi Jotoku, 536-0014 Osaka Japan Office: Nippon Organon KK 1-5-90, Tomobuchicho Miyakojimaku, 534-0016 Osaka Japan

OHTAKE, EIJI, radiologist; b. Tokyo, July 22, 1948; s. Kenji and Michiko (Takai) O.; m. Sumiko Sano, Apr. 29, 1979; children: Makoto, Shinji. MD, Gunma U., 1974; PhD in Med. Sci., Yokohama City U., 1982. Resident Yokohama City Univ. Hosp., 1974-76; radiologist Met. Geriatric Hosp., Tokyo, 1979-81; lectr. and radiologist Yokohama (Japan) City U., 1982-83, asst. prof., 1983-85; chief divsn. radiology Tokyo Senbai Hosp., 1985-88; chief divsn. radiotherapy Toranomon Hosp., Tokyo, 1988-94; chief dept. radiology Fujisawa (Japan) City Hosp., 1994—; assoc. prof. attendant Yokohama City U., 1985—. Contbr. articles to profl. jours. Mem. Japan Radiol. Soc., Japanese Soc. Nuclear Medicine, Soc. Nuclear Medicine, Radiol. Soc. N.Am. Home: 1-608 1510 Shinyoshida-cho, Kohoku-ku Yokohama 223-0056, Japan Office: Fujisawa City Hosp Radiolog, 6-1 Fujisawa 2-chome, Fujisawa 251-8550, Japan

OHTAKE, MASAKAZU, seismologist, educator; b. Tokyo, Nov. 26, 1939; s. Yozo and Nobuko (Okubo) O.; m. Nobuko Sasaki, Dec. 18, 1965; 1 child, Kazuo. BS, U. Tokyo, 1963, MS, 1965, PhD, 1979. Asst. prof. Earthquake Rsch. Inst., U. Tokyo, 1966-73; rschr. Bldg. Rsch. Inst., Tokyo, 1973-74, sr. rschr., 1975-77; rsch. assoc. Marine Biomed. Inst., U. Tex., Galveston, 1974-75; lab. head Nat. Rsch. Ctr. for Disaster Prevention, Tsukuba, Japan, 1977-88; prof. seismology Tohoku U., Sendai, Japan, 1988—, councilor, 1999—; v.p. Coordinating Com. for Earthquake Prediction, Tsukuba, 1998—; mem. Nuclear Plant Safety Judgement Com., Tokyo, 1985—; expert mem. Atomic Energy Safety Commn., Tokyo, 1995-98. Mem. Seimsological Soc. Japan, Volcanological Soc. Japan, Am. Geophys. Union, Assn. for Devel. of Earthquake Prediction Rsch. (coun. 1995—). Avocations: hiking, classical music, Go-game. Office: Tohoku U Dept Geophysics, Aoba-ku, Sendai 980-8578, Japan

OHTAKI, TETSUYA, biochemist, researcher; b. Nishinomiya, Japan, Jan. 16, 1959; s. Tetsuzo and Chikako (Takitani) O.; m. Naoko Shimauchi, March 14, 1986; children: Hiroya, Takaya, Kaya. BS, U. Tsukuba, 1981; MS, Osaka U., 1983; DSc, Hokkaido U., 1986. Rsch. fellow Takeda Chem. Industries, Ltd., Osaka, 1986-88; rsch. fellow Takeda Chem. Industries, Ltd., Tsukuba, 1988-92, assoc. rsch. head, 1992-97; rsch. head Takeda Chem. Industries, Ltd., 1997—. Author: BioMethods (Vol. 7): A Laboratory Guide to Biotin-Labeling in Biomoleculte Analysis, 1996; contbr. articles to profl. jours. Avocations: fishing, camping, mountaineering, gardening. Office: Takeda Chem Industries Ltd, 10 Wadai, Tsukuba, Ibaraki 300-4293, Japan

OHTANI, HARUO, pathologist, educator; b. Shibukawa, Japan, Oct. 2, 1951; s. Fumio and Yoshie (Iizuka) O.; m. Noriko Horibe, Apr. 20, 1980; 1 child, Kaoru. MD, Tohoku U., Sendai, Japan, 1976. Trainee Tohoku U. Sch. Medicine, 1976-80; rsch. assoc. dept. pathology Tohoku U. Hosp., 1980-85; rsch. assoc. dept. pathology Tohoku U. Sch. Med., 1985-97, assoc. prof., 1997—. Contbr. articles to sci. jours. Avocation: mountain hiking. Home: 427-903 Aramaki Aoba-ward, Miyagi Sendai 980-0845, Japan Office: Tokoku U Sch Med Dept Patho, 2-1 Seiryo-machi Aoba-ward, Miyagi Sendai 980-8575, Japan

OHTO, CHIKARA, molecular biologist, biochemist; b. Hita, Ohita, Japan, Apr. 18, 1963; s. Wataru and Toshiko (Isamoto) O. BS, Nagoya (Japan) U., 1986, MS, 1988; PhD, Tohoku U., 1999. Rschr. Toyota Motor Corp., 1988-94, asst. mgr., 1995—; violinist Toho Orch. Acad., 1996. Mem. Internat. Soc. Plant Molecular Biology, N.Y. Acad. Scis., Molecular Biology Soc. Japan, Japan Soc. Biosci. Biotech. and Agrochemistry. Avocations: violinist, conductor. Fax: 0565-23-5825. E-mail: ohto@square.mk.toyota.co.jp. Home: # 501 3-21-1 Kanaya-cho, Toyota 471-0876, Japan Office: Bio Rsch Lab Toyota Motor, 1 Toyota-cho, Toyota 471-8572, Japan

OHTSUBO, HISAO, physics educator; b. Hiroshima, Japan, Jan. 10, 1940; s. Ohtsubo Yoshihisa and Harumi (Oda) O.; m. Junko Shimizu, Feb. 14, 1967. DSc, Tokyo Inst. Tech., 1967. Rsch. assoc. Osaka (Japan) U., 1967-74, lectr., 1974-78, assoc. prof., 1978-89, prof. physics, 1989—. Mem. Phys. Soc. Japan, Am. Phys. Soc. Office: Osaka U Dept Physics, 1-1 Machikaneyama, Toyonaka Osaka 560-0043, Japan

OHTSUKA, KAZUMASA, chemist; b. Yokohama, Japan, May 6, 1924; s. Yakichi and Kyuno (Sugano) O.; m. Takako Ono, May 4, 1952; children: Masako, Naoko, Sachie. M, Tokyo U., 1946. Chem. rschr. Hodogaya Chem. Ind. Co., Yokohama, 1947-56, Japan Leather Co., Tokyo, 1956-62; vis. rsch. scientist Stanford Rsch. Inst., Menlo Park, Calif., 1962-64; chem. rschr. Japan Leather Co., Tokyo, 1964-86; ind. rsch. chemist Yokohama, Japan, 1994—. Inventor in field; contbr. articles to profl. jours. Achievements include research on chemical behavior between tri- and hexavalent

chromium ions, on redox potentials between Cr(VI) and Cr(III) in an alkaline medium, the oxidation from Cr(III) to Cr(VI) and the reverse reaction. Avocations: playing piano, playing "Go". Home: 87 Kamaya-cho, Hodogaya-ku Yokohama 240-0063, Japan

OHTSUKA, TOSHIYUKI, engineering educator; b. Tokyo, Sept. 28, 1967; s. Yuzo and Junko (Shinoda) O.; m. Yuumi Uemura, Mar. 14, 1999. B of Engring., Tokyo Met. Inst. Tech., Hino, 1990, M of Engring., 1992, D of Engring., 1995. Asst. prof. U. Tsukuba, Japan, 1995-99, Osaka (Japan) U., 1999—; vis. assoc. Calif. Inst. Tech., Pasadena, 1996-97. Contbr. articles to profl. jours. Mem. AIAA, IEEE, Japan Soc. Aeronautical and Space Scis., Japan Soc. Mech. Engrs., N.Y. Acad. Scis., Soc. Instrument and Control Engrs. Office: Osaka U Dept Mech Sys, 2-1 Yamadaoka Suita, Osaka 565-0871, Japan

O'HUIGINN, SEAN, diplomat. With Anglo-Irish Secretariat, Belfast, 1987-90; head Anglo-Irish Divsn., Dublin, 1991-97; amb. to U.S. Govt. of Ireland, Washington, 1997—. Office: Embassy of Ireland 2234 Massachusetts Ave NW Washington DC 20008-2870

OHYAMA, YOSHISHIGE, mechanical engineer; b. Iwaki, Fukushima, Japan, Mar. 7, 1938; s. Katsumi and Taka (Kusano) O.; m. Teruko, Feb. 1, 1964; children: Yumiko, Akiko. BS, Tohoku U., Sendai, Japan, 1960, DS, 1968. Rschr. Hitachi (Japan) Rsch. Lab., Hitachi Ltd., 1960-71, sr. rschr., 1971-84, chief rschr., 1984-90, sr. chief rschr., dir., sr. chief engr., 1990-97; chief engr., dir. Hitachi Car Engring. Co., Ltd., 1997-2000, cons., 2000—. Recipient award R & D Inc., 1984, Oliver Lucas Automotive Electronic award IEEE, 1991, Japan Sci. Tech. award, 1998. Fellow Soc. Automotive Engrs.; mem. Japan Soc. Automotive Engrs. (24th sci. award 1974), Japan Soc. Mech. Engrs. Achievements include patent for air flow meter for engine control system (Ichimura Indsl. award 1993). Home: 3-24-18 Higashi Ohshima, Hitachinaka Ibaraki 312-0042, Japan Office: Hitachi Car Engring Co Ltd, 2520 Takaba, Hitachinaka Ibaraki 312-8503, Japan

OHYANAGI, MITSUMASA, physician, medical educator; b. Himeji, Hyogo, Japan, Feb. 8, 1949; s. Genji and Aiko Ohyanagi; m. Sumiko Yahata, May 28, 1977; children: Shinya, Tatsuya, Noriko. MD, Kobe (Japan) U., 1975; PhD, Hyogo Coll. Medicine, Nishinomiya, Japan, 1988. Clin. fellow Hyogo Coll. Medicine, Nishinomiya, 1975-77, 78-79, asst. prof., 1979-88, 90-97, assoc. prof., 1997—; clin. fellow Kanebo Meml. Hosp., Kobe, 1977-78; postdoctoral fellow U. N.C., Chapel Hill, 1988-90. Fellow Japanese Circulation Soc., Japan Soc. Ultrasonics in Medicine; mem. Am. Heart Assn., N.Y. Acad. Scis. Office: Hyogo Coll Medicine, 1-1 Mukogawa-cho, Nishinomiya 663, Japan

OHZEKI, TOSHIAKI, English studies educator, prison chaplain; b. Fukuoka, Japan, Apr. 3, 1938; m. Harumi Ohzeki, Aug. 25, 1973; 1 child, Mari. BA, Kita-Kyushu U., Fukuoka, 1965; BTh, Seinan Gakuin U., Fukuoka, 1969; MTh, Southeastern Bapt. Theol. Sem., 1971. Asst. pastor Bapt. Ch., Fukuoka, 1971-72; min. New Southriver Bapt. Assn., 1972-74; asst. prof. Nakamura Gakuen U., Fukuoka, 1974-77, assoc. prof., 1977-85, prof., 1985—; part-time lectr. Saga Nat. U., 1975-77, Fukuoka U., 1977—; vis. prof. Waikato U., Hamilton, New Zealand, 1993; prison chaplain Nat. Prison, Fukuoka, 1973—. Author: Martin Heidegger, 1988; editor: Literature and Religion, 1988; contbr. articles to profl. jours. Named Hon. Citizen Henderson City, 1976. Mem. Japan Dem. Party. Baptist. Avocations: golf, classical music, driving, touring, walking. Home: 5-18-40 Nanakuma Jhonan-ku, Fukuoka 814, Japan Office: Nakamura Gakuen U, 50701 Befu Jhonan-ku, Fukuoka 814, Japan

OHZUKU, TSUTOMU, chemistry educator; b. Gose, Nara, Japan, June 16, 1949; s. Takeyoshi and Asako (Nishikawa) O.; m. Chizuko Nakatani, Feb. 17, 1980; children: Aya, Rina. BS in Chemistry, Doshisha U., 1973; MS in Electrochemistry, Kyoto (Japan) U., 1975, PhD in Electrochemistry, 1978. Rsch. assoc. dept. synthetic chemistry Okayama U. Faculty Engring., 1978-84, lectr., 1984-87; lectr. dept. applied chemistry Osaka City (Japan) U. Faculty Engring., 1987-89, assoc. prof., 1989-92, prof. electrochemistry and Inorganic Chemistry Lab., 1992—; spkr. over 30 internat. meetings; mem. tech. com. rsch. project on advanced lithium batteries for energy storage in large scale NEDO, Japan, 1992-97, chmn., 1997-99. Co-editor: Handbook of Batteries; contbr. over 90 articles on lithium batteries, electrochemistry of manganese dioxide, solid state electrochemistry of insertion materials for advanced lithium-ion batteries to sci. jours., chpts. to books. Recipient rsch. award for work on electrochemistry of manganese dioxide Internat. Battery Assn., 1991. Mem. Electrochem. Soc., Am. Chem. Soc., Internat. Soc. Electrochemistry, Chem. Soc. Japan, Ceramic Soc. Japan, Electrochem. Soc. Japan (Sano Meml. prize 1981). Avocations: fishing, watching green trees. Fax: 06-605-2693. Home: Nagao 221-12 Taima-cho, Kitakatsuragi-gun, Nara 639-2164, Japan Office: Osaka City U Fac Engring, Sugimoto 3-3-138 Sumiyoshi, Osaka 558-8585, Japan

OI, TAKAO, chemist, educator; b. Miyota, Japan, Jan. 17, 1952; s. Makio and Kaoru (Arai) O.; m. Kyoko Mizuno, Mar. 28, 1976; children: Naoki, Masaya. BS, Tokyo Inst. Tech., 1974; M. in Engring., 1976, DEng, 1979. Postdoctorate SUNY, 1979-84; asst. Sophia U., Tokyo, 1984-87, lectr., 1987-91, assoc. prof., 1991-96, prof., 1996—, chmn. grad. divsn. chemistry of sci. and tech., 1999—; vis. researcher Shikoku Nat. Indsl. Rsch. Inst., Takamatsu, Japan, 1993; mem. hon. editorial adv. bd. EOLSS, 1995—; mem. organizing com. Internat. Symposium on Isotope Separation and Chem. Exchange Uranium Enrichment, Tokyo, 1989-90; trustee Soc. of Sea Water Sci., Tokyo, 1996—; prin. investigator joint rsch. project Japan-China Sci. Coop. Program, 1998-2000; trustee Japan Assn. of Ion Exchange, 1997—. Author: New Development in Ion Exchange, 1991, Handbook of Separation Science, 1993; contbr. articles to profl. jours. Grantee Tokyo Club, 1992, 93, Salt Sci. Rsch. Found., Tokyo, 1991, 93, 94, 95, River Environ. Mgmt. Found., Tokyo, 1992, 93, 97, Sci. award Soc. of Seawater, 2000. Avocation: reading. Office: Sophia U, Kioicho 7-1, Chiyoda ku Tokyo 102-8554, Japan

OIARBIDE, MIKEL, chemist, educator; b. Altzaga, Spain, Dec. 28, 1963; s. Juan Jose Oiarbide and Antonia Garmendia; m. Ana Vicente, Mar. 7, 1998. PhD, U. Basque Country, San Sebastian, Spain, 1991. Postdoctoral rschr. U. Calif., Berkeley, 1991-93; asst. prof. U. Basque Country, 1994—. Contbr. numerous articles to profl. jours. Fulbright fellow, 1991-93. Mem. Am. Chem. Soc. Office: U Basque Country, Dept Quimica Org Apto 1072, 20080 San Sebastian Spain

OIDA, AKIRA, engineering educator; b. Fukui city, Japan, Dec. 21, 1942; s. Motoharu and Mitsui (Nobata) O.; m. Naoko Kaseda, Aug. 25, 1975; 2 children. B of Agriculture, Kyoto U., 1965, M of Agriculture, 1967, D of Agriculture, 1976. Asst. prof. Kyoto U., 1967-84, assoc. prof., 1989-99, prof., 1999—; lectr. Niigata (Japan) U., 1984-85, assoc. prof., 1985-89; guest prof. Jilin U. of Tech., Changchun, People's Republic of China, 1979, Munich U. Tech., Germany, 1976-78, 95-96; dispatched expert JICA, Bogor, Indonesia, 1992, Amman, Jordan, 1996; guest scholar Wageningen Agrl. U., 1996. Author 6 books including Dynamics Between Vehicle/Machine and Soil, 1993; contbr. numerous articles to profl. jours. Mem. Internat. Soc. for Terrain-Vehicle Systems (assoc. editor 1992, nat. sec. Japan 1999—, dir. 1999), JSAM (councillor), Asian Assn. for Agrl. Engring. (editl. bd. 1992), Japanese Soc. for Terramechanics (pres. 1999). Avocations: Shado, 9 dan.

OIKAWA, HIROSHI, college president, materials science educator; b. Sakhalin, Japan, Oct. 15, 1933; s. Torao and Tomi (Kumagai) O.; m. Ayako Otomo, May 4, 1963; children: Makoto, Junko. BE, Tohoku U., Sendai, Japan, 1956, ME, 1958, D in Engring., 1961. Instr. Tohoku U., 1961-63, lectr., 1963-64, assoc. prof., 1964-82; rsch. fellow U. Fla., Gainesville, 1966-68; prof. Tohoku U., 1982-97, councilor, 1993-97, dean faculty engring., 1995-97; prof. emeritus Tohoku U., 1997—; prof. Nat. Instn. Acad. Degrees, Yokohama, Japan, 1997-98; pres. Coll. Indsl. Tech., Amagasaki, Japan, 1998—. Co-editor: Metals Handbooks, 1990, Metals Databook, 1993. Mem. Engring. Acad. Japan (bd. dirs. 2000—), Japan Inst. Metals (bd. dirs. 1992-94, 96-97, chief dir. Tohoku chpt. 1991-93, pres. 1996-97), Iron and Steel Inst. Japan (bd. dirs. 1990-92), Japan Inst. Light Metals (bd. dirs. 1989-95), Minerals, Metals and Materials Soc., ASM Internat., Inst. Materials. Office: Coll Indsl Tech, Nishikoya 1, Amagasaki 661-0047, Japan

OIKAWA, HIROSHI, parasitologist, researcher; b. Sendai, Miyagi, Japan, June 25, 1932; s. Koushiro and Tomoyo (Isawa) O.; m. Junko Takagi, Mar. 8, 1963; children: Yoko, Wataru. M of Agr., Tohoku U., Sendai, 1958; PhD, Osaka (Japan) U., 1975. Rsch. staff Shionogi Pharm. Co. Ltd., Osaka, 1958-70; assoc. dir. Shionogi Aburahi Labs., Shiga, Japan, 1970-92; lectr. Setsunan U. Sch. Pharmacology, Hirakata, Japan, 1985-89; lectr. microbial diseases Osaka U., Suita, 1988-90, lectr. Sch. Medicine, 1993—; cons. Makki Internat. Acad., Kyoto, Japan, 1994-97. Author: (books) Biology of Dogs, 1969, Parasitology of Dogs and Cats, 1992; editor: (book) Biological Data Book on Experimental Animals, 1989; patentee in field. Mem. Japanese Soc. Toxicol. Sci. (bd. dirs. 1985—), Japanese Soc. Animal Models for Human Diseases (bd. dirs. 1984—), Kansai Lab. Animal Rsch. Assn. (bd. dirs. 1984—), Japan Malaysia Assn., N.Y. Acad. Scis. Avocations: flute, sightseeing in Malaysia. Home: 1-8-1 Kamigasa 2-chome, Shigaken Kusatsu 525-0028, Japan

OIM, PILL SOO, electrical and automotive engineering educator; b. Seoul, May 5, 1961; s. Yong Duck and Sook Won Kim; m. Soon Ok Song, Oct. 19, 1990; children: Byung Hyun, Hae Ram. BSEE, Dongguk U., 1984, MSEE, 1986, PhDEE, 1994. Lectr. Dongguk U., Seoul, 1994-97; prof. Chungcheong Coll., Cheongju, Korea, 1992-96, Daelim Coll., Anyang, Korea, 1996—; cons. Jungil Engring Co., 1996—, Jungil Co., 1996—, XIT Korea Co., Seoul, 1998—; dir. BoongBoong.com Co., 2000—, Mochan Precision & Ind. Co., 2000—. Author: Automotive Electricity, 1998, Electromagnetics, 1998, Automotive Electricity Experiment, 1999, Automotive Laws and Regulations of Korea, 1999, Automotive Electronic Control, 1999, Automotive Inspection, 2000, Fundamentals of Automotive Electricity and Electronics, 2000. 2d class Air Base, 1987-88. Mem. IEEE, AAAS, Korean Inst Elec. Engrs., Inst. Automotive Engring. of Korea, Soc. Automotive Engrs. Japan, N.Y. Acad. Sci., Nat. Geographic Soc., Inst. of Elect. Engring. of Japan, Internat. Assn. of Sci. and Tech. for Devel., European Power Electronics, London Diplomatic Acad. Avocations: travel, showing movies, music. Home: Dong-Go Apt 104-904, Umyon-dong Seocho-ku, Seoul 137-140, Korea Office: Daelim Coll 526-7, Bisan-dong Dongan-ku, Anyang-si Kyunggi-do 431-715, Korea

OJA, EVE, mathematician, educator; b. Tallinn, Estonia, Oct. 10, 1948; d. Feliks and Ilme (Kukk) Martin; m. Peeter Oja, Aug. 10, 1973; 1 child, Martin. MSc in Math., Tartu (Estonia) State U., 1972, PhD, 1975; student French Lang., Leningrad State U., 1976-77; postdoctoral, Aix-Marseille U., 1980-81. From asst. to prof. Tartu State U., 1975-92, prof., chair functional analysis, 1992—, dir. inst. pure math., 1994, 98; prof. math. Nat. Engring. Sch., Bamako, Mali, 1977-78. Author: Extensions of Functionals and the Structure of the Space of Continuous Linear Operators, 1991; co-author: (with P. Oja) Functional Analysis, 1991; mem. editl. bd. Acta Commentationes Univ. Tartuensis Math., 1990—, editor in chief, 1998—; contbr. over 45 articles to profl. jours. Grantee Internat. Sci. Found., 1993, Tempus, 1993, 95; Nordic Coun. Mins. scholar, 1995, German Acad. Exch. Svc. scholar, 1997. Mem. Am. Math. Soc., Estonian Math. Soc., N.Y. Acad. Scis., Tartu Acad. Tennis Club. Avocations: tennis foreign languages. Office: Faculty Math Tartu U, Vanemuise 46, EE51014 Tartu Estonia

OJANEN, EETU SAMULI, computer scientist; b. Helsinki, Finland, Sept. 10, 1976; s. Olli J. and Paula Irmeli (Ala-Lehtimäki) O. MSc in Info. Sys., U. Jyväskylä, 2000. Children's ednl. programmer, designer Kidsoft Oy, Jyväskylä, 1997; sys. designer Republica Oy, Jyväskylä, 1998-99, v.p. tech., 1999—; part-time tchr. U. Jyväskylä, 1997-98. Avocations: composing music, aikido. E-mail: eetu@ojanen.net. Office: Republica Ltd, Vaasankatu 2, 40101 Jyväskylä Finland

OJEBODE, JACOB OLUSOJI, radiation therapist; b. Gbongan, Osun State, Nigeria, Apr. 20, 1945; s. Gabriel Adedeji and Rebecca Subuola Ojebode; m. Rachael Olakusibe Anibaba, May 14, 1998; 4 children. DCR, Fed. Sch. Radiography, Lagos, Nigeria, 1971, Hammersmith Hosp., London, 1978. Diagnostic basic radiographer Ministry of Health Western Region, Ibadan, Nigeria, 1971-75; prin. II, radiographer to chief radiographer Lagos U. Tchg. Hosp., 1975-95; vis. radiotherapy, asst. chief technologist U. Coll. Hosp., Ibadan, Nigeria, 1990-91; external examiner Radiographer Regration Bd. of Nigeria, Lagos, 1991-95; lectr. Fed. Sch. of Radiography, Lagos, 1994-97; IAEA expert Ghana Atomic Energy Commn., Accra, 1997—; mng. dir. Olucob X-Ray Svc., Lagos, 1995-99; med. specialist, asst. chief radiographer on contact therapy Family Burport Trust Fund Hosp. for Women and Children, Abuja, Nigeria, 1999—. Inventor in field. Spl. marshal Fed. Rd. Safety Commn., Abuja, Nigeria, 2000; hon. sr. evengelst Celestial Ch. of Christ, Nigeria, Worldwide, 1997. Mem. Assn. of Radiographers of Nigeria, Soc. of Radiographers (life), N.Y. Acad. Scis. Avocations: Evangelism, fishing, swimming, computer operation, reading psychology and philosophy. Home: X-Ray House Celestial St, Iyana Iyesi Village, Sango-Otta Nigeria Office: Lagos U Tchg Hosp, PMB 12003 Surulere, Lagos Nigeria

OJEDA-CASTAÑEDA, JORGE, academic administrator, researcher; b. Oaxaca, Mex., Apr. 23, 1949; s. Adelaido and Emma De O.; m. Cristina Margarita Gomez, June 27, 1981. BS, Nat. U. Mex., Mexico City, 1972; PhD, U. Reading, Berkshire, Eng., 1976. With INAOE, 1972, 76-82; chmn. optical dept. INAOE, Puebla, Mex., 1978-82, gen. dir., 1984-92; prof. physics U. Las Americas, Mex., 1993-95, dean Sch. Sci., 1996—; vis. prof. Instituto De Optica, Madrid, 1980, 87, Centro De Investigaciones Opticas, La Plata, Argentina, 1986; vis. scientist Universitat Erlangen, West Germany, 1982-84, U. Valencia, Spain, 1992, U. Barcelona, 1993; v.p. Internat. Commn. for Optics, 1996—. mem. selecting bd. for nat. fellows Sec. of Pub. Edn., 1988-92; mem. selecting bd. ctr. for rsch. optics CONACyT-CIO, 1987—; mem. selecting bd. postgrad. programs Nat. Coun. of Sci. and Tech., CONACyT, 1989—; mem. editl. bd. Microwave and Optical Tech. Letters, Optical Memory & Neural Networks. Mem. jury Nat. Award Sci. and Art, Mex., 1988. Recipient Sci. Rsch. award Mexican Phys. Soc., 1996; Alexander von Humboldt fellow Fed. Republic of Germany, 1982-84. Fellow Soc. Photo Instrumentation Engrs., Mex. Acad. Optics (pres. 1996-98), Optical Soc. Am., Acad. of Sci., Internat. Soc. Optics Within Life Sci. (treas. 1992-95), Internat. Commn. for Optics (v.p. 1996—). Home: Zona Resicendial UDLA, Casa 6 Sta Catarina Martir, 7280 Cholula San Andres, Cholulu Mexico 72729 Office: U Las Americas, Apdo Postal 100, 72820 Cholula Puebla Mexico*

OJEDA EISELEY, JAIME DE, former Spanish ambassador, educator; b. Aug. 5, 1933. BL maxima cum laude in Law, U. Madrid, Spain, 1957; grad., Internat. Acad. of The Hague, The Netherlands; student, Naval War Coll. and Sr. Ctr. for Nat. Def. Studies, Madrid, Spain. Prof. polit. law Complutense U. Madrid, Spain, 1958; joined diplomatic svcs., 1958; served Washington, 1962-69; min.-counsellor Beijing, 1973-76; consul-gen. of Spain Hong Kong and Macao, 1976-79; fellow Ctr. Internat. Rels., Harvard U., Cambridge, Mass., 1979-80; dep. permanent rep. NATO, 1982-83, permanent rep., 1983-90; amb. to U.S.A., Spanish Embassy, Washington, 1990-97; pres. high level coun. fgn. affairs Min. F.A. Madrid, 1997; amb.-in-residence Shenandoah U., Winchester, Va., 1997—; vis. scholar Johns Hopking U., Washington, 1997; disting. adj. fellow CSIS, Washington, 1997. Lt. Reserve Marine Corps. Spanish Navy, 1957. Home: PO Box 57 3770 Leeds Manor Rd Markham VA 22643-1817 Office: Shenandoah U 1460 University Dr Winchester VA 22601-5195

OJEDA-RAMIREZ, MARIO MIGUEL, statistician, researcher; b. Miahuatlan, Mexico, Aug. 22, 1959; s. Martin Ojeda-Salinas and Sofia (Moreno) Ramirez de Ojeda; m. Antonia Olivia Jarvio-Fernandez, July 19, 1986. BS, Veracruzana U., Xalapa, Mex., 1982; MS, Postgrad. Coll. Mex., 1988; PhD, Havana (Cuba) U., 1988. Asst. prof. stats. Veracruzana U., 1981-91, prof. stats., 1991—, dir. postgrad. studies, 1997-98, dir. gen. acad. devel., 1998—; stats. cons. Veracruzana U., 1992—; dir. Calidad y Opinion, A.C., Mex., 1989-92. Author: Fundamental Aspects of Statistical Experimental Design, 1998; co-author (with A. Castillo): Principles of Nonparametric Statistics, 1994, (with Dellllleon) Basic Statistical methodology, 1997, (with Sahai H.) A Comparison of Approximations to the Percentiles of Noncentral Chi-Square, 1999, (with C. Sahai, H. and Macedo J.M.) A Handbook of Chi-Square, 2000; contbr. articles to profl. jours. Mem. Am. Statis. Assn., Internat. Biometric Soc., Internat. Statis. Inst. Avocations: reading, jazz, writing. Home: Mariano Escobedo 4, Zoncuantla, 91500 Coatepec Mexico Office: U Veracruzana, Juarez 55, 91000 Xalapa Mexico

OJENIYI, STEPHEN OLUSOLA, soil scientist, researcher, educator; b. Ikire, Osun, Nigeria, Feb. 16, 1951; s. Timothy Adedeji and Janet Abike (Adedeji) O.; m. Modupe Enitan Adetiba, July 27, 1978; children: Atinuke, Bukola, Ayokunnu. BSc, U. Ife, Nigeria, 1973; MSc, U. Ibadan, Nigeria, 1976; PhD, U. Adelaide, Australia, 1979. Rsch. officer Cocoa Inst., Ibadan, 1978-82; prin. lectr. Coll. Edn., Ila, Nigeria, 1982-83; sr. lectr. U. of Tech., Bauchi, Nigeria, 1983-84; sr. lectr., reader U. of Tech., Akure, Nigeria, 1984-92; prof. U. of Tech., Akure, 1987—; assoc. prof. Agr. U., Makurdi, Nigeria, 1992-93; prof., head soil sci. Agr. U., Makurdi, 1999-2000; dean of agr. Coll. of Edn., Ila, 1983; coord. of agr. U. of Tech., Bauchi, 1984; head of crop prodn. U. of Tech., Akure, 1994-95, dean of agr., 1995-97. Found. mng. editor Applied Tropical Agr. jour., 1996. Scholar Fed. Govt. of Nigeria, 1971, Rockefeller Found., 1974, Commonwealth of Australia, 1976. Mem. AAAS, Soil Sci. Soc. of Nigeria (sec., editor 1992-97), Internat. Soil Tillage Rsch. Orgn. (editor 1990-94), N.Y. Acad. Scis. Baptist. Avocations: music, dancing, socials, gardening, travel. Office: Fed U of Tech, PMB 704 Akure Nigeria

OJEWOLE, JOHN AKANNI OLUWOLE, pharmacology educator, pharmacist; b. Gbongan, Osun State, Nigeria, Nov. 25, 1948; arrived in S.Africa, 1997; s. Abraham Ojebode and Abigael Arinola Awero Ojewole; m. Elizabeth Bolanle Abiodun, Dec. 30, 1989; children: Abiola, Adegoke, Adedeji, Adebimpe, Adebayo. B in Pharmacy, U. Ife, Ile-Ife, Nigeria, 1972; PhD in Pharmacology, U. Strathclyde, Glasgow, Scotland, 1977; MS in Clin. Pharmacy, U. London, 1992. Grad. asst. Obafemi Awolowo U., Ile-Ife, Nigeria, 1973-76, lectr. pharmacology, 1977-80, sr. lectr., 1981-83, prof. pharmacology, 1984-97, vice dean Faculty Pharmacy, 1983-87, dean Faculty Pharmacy, 1988-91, head, chmn. Pharmacology Dept., 1983-87; prof. pharmacology U. Zimbabwe, Harare, 1996-97; head dept. pharmacology faculty health scis. U. Durban-Westville, Durban, S.Africa, 1998-99. Fellow Internat. Union Pharmacologists, 1984, Assn. Commonwealth Univs., 1988, 90, WHO, 1996. Mem. Am. Coll. Clin. Pharmacy, European Soc. Clin. Pharmacists, Pharm. Soc. Nigeria, Am. Coll. Clin. Pharmacology. Anglican. Avocations: music, photography, football, gardening, reading. Office: U Durban-Wdestville Dept Pharm, Private Bagf X54001, Durban 4000, South Africa

OJHA, CHANDRA SHEKHAR, environmental engineer; b. Ballia, India, Jan. 11, 1962; s. Uma and Kamala (Mishra) O.; m. Indumati Tiwari, July 7, 1983; children: Richa, Pragya. B in Engring., Gorakhpur U., 1982; M, Indian Inst. Sci., Bangalore, 1984; DIC, Imperial Coll. Sci. & Tech., London, 1993; PhD, U. London, 1993. Lectr. Inst. Technology, Bhu, India, 1984-86; lectr. U. Roorkee, India, 1986-96, asst. prof, 1996—. Mem. Am. Soc. Civl Engrs., Indian Soc. Tech. Edn. Office: Civil Engring Dept, U Roorkee, Roorkee Haridwar 247 667, India

OJIMA, TOSHIO, engineering educator; b. Toyama, Japan, Sept. 2, 1937; s. Haruo and Hisako Ojima; m. Reiko Matsui, Oct. 4, 1966; children: Ito, Kunikazu. Grad., Waseda U., Tokyo, 1960; M in Engring., Waseda U., 1962, D of Engring., 1965. Asst. prof., assoc. prof. Waseda Univ., Tokyo, 1965-73, prof., 1974—; lectr. Tokyo U. of Art, 1973—; vis. prof. Kogakuin U., Tokyo, 1992—, U. Tokyo, 1988-92; advisor prof. Zhejiang (China) U., 1980—; rschr. Acad. of China, Beijing, 1979-80; infrastructures planner Expo 70, Osaka, Japan (Spl. prize 1970), Expo 75, Okinawa, Japan, 1985, Expo 85, Tsukuba, Japan, 1978; environ. planner Barcelona (Spain) Olympic Indoor Stadium, 1992. Author: To Construct a Picturesque City, 1984, The Reconstruction of Tokyo, 1986, Housing in Future, 1988, Imageble Tokyo, 1991. Mem. Archtl. Inst. Japan (pres.), City Planning Inst. Japan (pres.), Soc. Heating, Japan Dist. Heating and Cooling (pres.), Nat. Land Agy. Office: Waseda U Sci & Engring Fac, Waseda U Sci & Engring Fac, 3-4-1 Okubo Shinjuku-ku, Tokyo 169-8555, Japan

OJOVAN, MICHAEL IVANOVICH, physicist, researcher; b. Dynjeni, Ocnitsa, Moldova, Mar. 6, 1955; arrived in Russia, 1972; s. Ion Matveevich and Maria Ivanovna (Scutelnic) O.; m. Natalia Vladimirovna Vlad, Mar. 5, 1977; children: Irina, Silvia. MSc, Engring. Phys. Inst., Moscow, 1979, PhD, 1982; DrSc, 1994. Sr. rsch. worker SIA Radon, Moscow, 1982-85; head lab. SIA (Scientific Indsl. Assn.) Radon, Moscow, 1985-91, head dept., 1991-95; dep. dir. Applied Rsch. Ctr., Moscow, 1995—; mem. Waste Mgmt. Internat. Conf., program advisory com. Internat. Conf. on Icineration and Thermal Treatment Technologies, IT3 1997—. Contbr. articles to profl. jours.; inventor in field. Recipient Silver medal All Union Exhbn., Moscow, 1987. Mem. Internat. Atomic Energy Agy., Russia Acad. Natural Scis., Material Rsch. Soc., 1999—, Am. Chem. Soc. Home: Yaroslovskoe Rd, 141300 Sergiev Posad Moscow, Russia Office: Scientific Indsl Assn Radon, 7th Rostovsky Ln 2/14, 119121 Moscow Russia

OK, ÜLGEN ZEKI, microbiologist, parasitologist; b. Ayvalik, Balikesir, Turkey, Apr. 15, 1963; s. Süleyman and Özlem (ülgen) O.; m. Gülsüm Eser Gürbüz, Oct. 11, 1986. MD, Ege U. Faculty Medicine, 1986, PhD, 1995; docent, Celal Bayar U. Faculty Medicine, 1996. Physician Tosya (Turkey) State Hosp., 1986-87, Govt., Izmir, Turkey, 1988-90, Ege U. Med. Faculty, Izmir, 1990-95; asst. prof. Celal Bayar U. Faculty Medicine, Manisa, 1995-96, assoc. prof., 1996—; assoc. dean, 1998—; asst. chief physician Celal Bayar U. Hosp., Manisa, 1996-98, head divsn. basic medicine, 1998, chief physician medico-social unit, 1998—; asst. chief doctor Celal Bayar U. Hosp., Manisa, 1996—. Sgt. Navy Air Force, 1987-88. Home: Venedik Sitesi Efes 4, 103/14 Bostanli Izmir Turkey Office: Celal Bayar U Fac Med, Dept of Parasitology, Manisa 45100, Turkey

OKA, KUNIO, chemistry educator; b. Shimoaso, Gifu, Japan, May 28, 1945; s. Akitaro and Kanayo (Kanai) O.; m. Sachiko Kawata, May 2, 1971; children: Tetsunori, Michiko. BS, Toyama U., 1968; M in Engring., U. Osaka Prefecture, 1970, D in Engring., 1990. Researcher Osaka Prefectural Radiation Rsch. Inst., Sakai, Osaka, 1975-85, sr. researcher, 1986-90; assoc. prof. U. Osaka Prefecture, Sakai, 1990—; mem. drafting com. Tech. Innovation Assn., Osaka, 1984-86. Co-author: Chitin, Chitosan and Related Enzymes, 1984, Fullerenes: Recent Advances in the Chemistry and Physics of Fullerenes and Related Materials, 1994, Inorganic and Organometallic Polymers II. Advanced Materials and Intermediates, 1994; contbr. articles to profl. jours. Recipient Osaka Nuclear Sci. Assn. award, 1996. Mem. Am. Chem. Soc., Chem. Soc. Japan, Kinki Chem. Soc., Silicon Chemistry Assn., Japan Assn. Synthetic Organic Chemistry, Nakamozu Lawn Tennis Club, Sakai Country Golf Club. Avocations: tennis, golf, gardening. Home: 4-34-3 Niwashirodai, Sakai Osaka 590-0133, Japan Office: Osaka Prefecture U, 1-2 Gakuencho, Sakai Osaka 599-8570, Japan

OKA, MILIND MADHUKAR, information systems specialist; b. Pune, India, Apr. 16, 1952; s. Madhukar Shankar and Shalini (Madhukar) O.; m. Nayana Milind; 2 children. BSc 1st class with distinction, U. Pune, India, 1971, MBA 1st class with distinction, 1973, PhD, 1977; diploma in Computer Mgmt., Datapro, Pune, 1985. Cert. assessor of quality systems. Exec. Pratibha Advt., Pune, 1973, Comml. Paper & Pulp Conversions Ltd., 1973-81; cons. market rsch. and econ. studies Kirloskar Cons., Ltd., 1981; mktg. mgr. Sudarshan Chem. Industries Ltd., Pune, 1981-91, sr. mgr. MIS, 1991-95, gen. mgr. MIS, 1995-98; ind. mgmt. cons., 1999—. Author: Management Information Systems, 1994, Computer Fundamentals, 1995, Business Applications of Computers, 1996, Systems Analysis and Design, 1997, Enterprise Resource Planning, 1999; contbr. articles to profl. jours. Home and Office: Crystal Nest 108/25, Bharati Niwas, Prabhat Rd, Pune 411004, India

OKADA, AKISHIGE, bank executive. Pres. The Sakura Bank, Ltd., Tokyo. Office: The Sakura Bank Ltd, 3-1 Kudan Minami 1-chome, Tokyo 100-8611, Japan*

OKADA, HAKUYU, science educator; b. Oita, Japan, Sept. 21, 1933; s. Magojuro and Matsuko Okada; m. Yoko Hikata, Mar. 15, 1962; 1 child, Aya. BS, Kyushu U., Fukuoka, Japan, 1956, MS, 1958, DSc, 1961. Asst. Kyushu U., 1961-70; assoc. prof. Kagoshima (Japan) U., 1970-72, prof., 1972-76; prof. Shizuoka (Japan) U., 1976-88, dean students, 1982-84; prof. Kyushu U., 1988-97; tech. advisor Oyo Corp., Minami Fukuoka, Japan, 1997—. Author: The Encyclopedia of Sedimentology, 1978, Environments of Earth Surface, 1979, Ocean Floor, 1979; author, editor: Eruption of Unzen Volcano, 1992, Cretaceous Environments of Asia, 2000. Mem. Geol. Soc. Japan (v.p. 1991-93, pres. 1994-96, prize 1993). Home: 4-8-36-601

Yoshizuka, Hakatu-ku, Fukuoka 812-0041, Japan Office: Oyo Corp Kyushu Office, 2-21-36 Ijiri, Minami-ku Fukuoka 811-1302, Japan

OKADA, HARUO, lawyer; b. Toyama, Japan, Mar. 2, 1954; s. Shinji and Mitsuko O.; m. Hisako Kitamura, Oct. 9, 1982; children: Yuki, Kosuke. B in Law, Tokyo U., 1977; LLM, U. Mich., 1986. Pub. ofcl. Ministry of Fin., Tokyo, 1978-79; legal apprentice Legal Tng. Inst., Tokyo, 1980-82; atty. Anderson, Mori & Rabinowitz, Tokyo, 1982-85; pvt. practice internat. law Osaka, Japan, 1987—. Recipient sports award Chichibunomiya Found., 1977. Mem. Osaka Bar Assn. (fgn. lawyers com. 1987—), Japan Fedn. Bar Assns. (fgn. lawyers com. 1993—). Home: 8-13 Hikarigaoka 1-chome, Takarazuka, Hyogo 665-0015, Japan Office: Yodogawa 5 bankan, 2-1 Toyosaki 3-chome, Kita-ku Osaka 531-0072, Japan

OKADA, HIDEAKI, information technology company executive; b. Tokyo, Oct. 27, 1935; s. Toyoji and Matsu Okada; m. Tomoko Takahashi, Sept. 5, 1964; children: Yujin, Fumiko. BS in Chemistry, Tokyo Inst. Tech., 1959. Cert. sys. engr. R & D Kyowa Hakko Kogyo Inc., Osaka, 1959-60; control sys. engr. Kyowa Hakko Kogyo Inc., Yamagiti, Mie, Japan, 1961-66; mgr. info. sys. engr. Kyowa Hakko Kogyo Inc., Tokyo, 1967-74; mgr. product mgmt. Kyowa Hakko Kogyo Inc., Shizuoka, Japan, 1975-79; dir. info. sys. divsn. Kyowa Hakko Kogyo Inc., Tokyo, 1980-87; consulting ptnr. NIX Rsch. Inst. Inc., Tokyo, 1988-89; dir. Puraido Inc., Tokyo, 1993-94; consulting ptnr. Lifepreneur Group Japan, Tokyo, 1995—; sr. cons. Lifepreneur Group Japan, Tokyo, 1995-99; advisor Bus. Rsch. Inst., Tokyo, 1987-99. Author: (book) Methodologies for Constructing the Strategic Information Systems, 1990; editor: (book) Handbook for the Intelligent Factories, 1990. Mem. IEEE. Avocations: playing Noh, Shodo (Knaji calligraphy), painting, swimming. Fax: 81 45 978 1378. E-mail: okadalp@iea.att.ne.jp. Office: Lifepreneur Group Japan, 1-18-16 Fujigaoka Aobaku, Yokohama Kanagawa 227-0043, Japan

OKADA, HIROAKI, pharmaceutical scientist, pharmacist; b. Fukuoka, Japan, Apr. 1, 1946; s. Hiroshi Abe and Kikuno Okada; m. Mineko Kunimatsu, June 6, 1976; children: Yuka, Hidekuni. BS, Kyushu U., Fukuoka, 1968, MS, 1970, PhD, 1982; postgrad., U. Kans., Lawrence, 1973-74. Lic. pharmacist. Rsch. asst. U. Kans., Lawrence, 1973-74; rsch. scientist Pharm. Rsch. Labs. Takeda Chem. Industries, Ltd., Osaka, 1970-87, rsch. head, 1987-93, sr. rsch. head DDS Rsch. Labs., 1993-97, dir. pharm. bus. devel., 1997—; vis. instr. Kyushu U., 1990-94, Okayama (Japan) U., 1998—; vis. prof. Kyushu U., 1999—. Co-author: Peptide and Protein Drug Delivery, 1991, others; contbr. more than 41 articles to profl. jours.; holder 25 U.S. patents. Recipient Kinki Invention award, 1994, Imperial Invention award Japan Inst. Invention and Innovation, 1995, Outstanding Rsch. award Soc. Powder Tech., 1997. Mem. Pharm. Soc. Japan (PSJ. award for Drug R&D 1991), Controlled Release Soc. (CRS/Nagai Found. Innovation award 2000), Am. Assn. Pharm. Scientists, Osaka Pharm. Mfg. Assn. (chmn. pharm. rsch. com. 1996), Kansai Econ. Fedn. (sci. and technol. com. 1998-99), Japan Soc. Drug Delivery Sys., Acad. Pharm. Sci. and Tech. (symposium com. 1995—). Avocations: golf, tennis, mountain climbing, reading. Home: 44-11-704 Yamada-minami, Suita, Osaka 565-0823, Japan Office: Takeda Chem Industries Ltd, 2-17-85 Juso-honmachi, Yodogawa, Osaka 532-8686, Japan

OKADA, JUNYA, home economics educator; b. Urawa, Saitama, Japan, Dec. 12, 1939; s. Kazuyoshi and Tiyoko (Inagaki) O.; m. Kiyoe Rikuta, Jan. 10, 1966; children: Shizuka, Soya. BA, Rikkyo U., Tokyo, MA in Lit.; PhD in Lit., Pacific Western U., L.A., 1996. Assoc. prof. Kyoto (Japan) Women's U., 1967-90, prof. home econs., 1990—, dean dept. home econs., 1994-96, dir. libr., 1996-98, prof. Postgrad. Sch., 1994—, headmaster elem. sch., 1998—. Author: Poetry of Haruo Sato, 1965, Fantasy of Kenji Miyazawa, 1966, Child Books and Child REader, 1974, History of Child Books in Japan, 1992, Fascinating Children's Literature, 1992, Picture Books and Child Play, 1992, History of Juvenile Literature in Japan, 1992. Bd. dirs. Japan Assn. for Child Culture, Tokyo, 1980—; active UNICEF, Tokyo, 1990—. Fellow Children's Lit. Assn. Japan; mem. Japan Child Book Assn. (bd. dirs.). Avocations: ceramic art, travel. Home: 2-18-6 Shiga, Otsu 520-2133, Japan Office: Kyoto Women Univ, 35 Kitahiyoshi Imakumano, Kyoto 605, Japan

OKADA, KENKICHI, retired physics educator; b. Chiba, Japan, Jan. 1, 1926; s. Kiyoshi and Hideko (Torikai) O.; m. Aiko Toyoda, Nov. 28, 1956; children: Ritsuko, Yoo. BA, Kyoto (Japan) U., 1951, PhD, 1961. Asst. Aichi Gakugei U., Nagoya, Japan, 1951-61; lectr. Nagoya Inst. Tech., 1961-62, asst. prof., 1962-68, prof., 1968-89; prof. computer sci. Nagoya Bunri Coll., 1989-96; ret., 1996; assoc. scientist I, P.R. Nuclear Ctr., 1963-65; guest prof. Autonomous U. Madrid, 1987-88. Author: (in Japanese) Introduction to Quantum Mechanics and Applications, 1982, (in English) Catastrophe Theory and Phase Transitions, 1994.

OKADA, RYOZO, educator, clinician and researcher; b. Kiryu, Gummaken, Japan, July 20, 1931; s. Kenji and Sachi (Ishihara) O.; m. Shigeko Shindo, May 25, 1958; children: Kyoko, Taro. MD, Tokyo U., 1956, PhD, 1961. Intern then resident; asst. Tokyo U. Sch. Medicine, 1962-63; rsch. fellow Hektoen Inst. Cook County Hosp., Chgo., 1963-66; attending physician Yoikuin Hosp., Tokyo, 1966-68; assoc. prof. Sch. Med. Juntendo U., Tokyo, 1968-83, prof., 1983-97, dir. cardiovascular lab., 1985-97, prof. emeritus, 1997—; rector Gumma Paz Sch. of Nursing, Japan, 1998—; councilor Cardiovascular Inst. Roppongi, Tokyo, 1990—, Indsl. Medicine Found., 1995—; mem. occupational diseases com. Ministry of Labor, Japan, 1987—. Contbr. chpts. to books, articles to profl. jours. Bd. dirs. Shirane Kaizen Sch.; Hotaka juridical person, Gumma, Japan. Fellow Am. Geriatrics Soc., Cardiovasc. Pathology, Internat. Electrocardiology, Internat. Union Angiology, Coun. Prevention Heart Disease, Japanese Circulation Soc., Japanese Angiology Soc., Japanese Geriatrics Soc.; mem. Japanese Soc. Medicine. Avocation: travel. E-mail: paz.offi@po.wind.ne.jp. Home: 6859-186 Nakayama, Takayamamura Agatsumagun, Gummaken 377-0702, Japan Office: Gumma Paz Coll, 6859-251 Nakayama Takayamamura, Gummaken 377-0702, Japan

OKADA, SHIGERU, pathology educator; b. Okayama, Japan, Feb. 15, 1940; s. Keizo and Moyoko (Nishigaki) O.; m. Naoko Kobashi, Nov. 7, 1965; children: Satoru, Rie, Mari. MD, Okayama U., Japan, 1964, PhD, 1969. Chief pathologist Kyoto (Japan) City Hosp., 1977-80; lectr. Sch. Medicine Kyoto U., 1980-90; asst. Med. Sch. Okayama U., 1969-71, lectr., 1971-77; prof. Okayama U. Med. Sch., Japan, 1990; dir. Isotope Ctr. Okayama U., Japan, 1995—; advisor to the pres. Okayama U., 1999; head radiation protection com. Okayama U., 1991. Contbr. articles to profl. jours. Mem. Japan Pathol. Soc. Tokyo, Japan Haematological Soc. Kyoto, Internat. Soc. Hematology, Japanese Cancer Assn. Tokyo, N.Y. Acad. Sci. Office: Okayama U Med Sch, 2-5-1 Shikata, Okayama 700-8558, Japan

OKADA, SHUICHI, physician, researcher; b. Yokosuka, Kanagawa, Japan, Aug. 26, 1957; s. Masao and Katako Okada; m. Mariko Kato, Jan. 24, 1988; 1 child, Akihiro. MD, Chiba (Japan) U., 1982, PhD, 1991. Resident Chiba U., 1982-83; head Chiba Cancer Ctr., 1988-90, Nat. Cancer Ctr. Hosp., Tokyo, 1990—. Author: Liver Cancer, 1998, Viral Hepatitis, 1998. Office: Nat Cancer Ctr Hosp, 5-1-1 Tsukiji, Chuo-ku, Tokyo 104-0045, Japan

OKADA, SUMIE MARY, educator, author; b. Nishinomiya, Japan, Oct. 14, 1940; permanent resident U.K.; d. Tokumi and Masae (Masaki) O. BA, U. Sacred Heart, Tokyo, 1963, MA, 1966; postgrad., Aoyma Gakuin U., Tokyo; student, Oxford U., 1973-74, 76-78; MLitt, Cambridge U., 1985. Lectr. in English Toyo (Japan) Women's Coll., 1970-72, asst. prof., 1972-79; Arthur Prowse fellow Durham (Eng.) U., 1991; assoc. prof. Immaculate Heart U., Kagoshima, Japan, 1996—; Author: Edmund Blunden and Japan: The History of a Relationship, 1988, Blunden no Ai no Tegami, 1995, Western Writers in Japan, 1999; contbr. articles to profl. jours. Grantee Gt. Britain-Sasakawa Found., London, 1986, 88, 97, Emmanuel Coll., Cambridge, Eng., 1988. Mem. Soc. Authors U.K., Internat. PEN. Office: Immaculate Heart U, 2365 Amatatsu, Sendai, Kagoshima 895, Japan

OKADA, TAKESHI, professional soccer coach, former player. Player Furukawa Electric Co., 1980, Furukawa FC, Japan Nat. Team; coach Furukawa FC, Japan Nat. Team, 1997—, World Cup, France, 1998. Recipient Japan Soccer League Championship medal, Japan Soccer League Cup Winners medals, Asian Club Championship Winners medal. Office: Japan Nat Team Fl 3 Nomura Bldg, 1-10-8 Dogenzaka Shibuya-ku, Tokyo 150-0043, Japan*

OKADA, TAKUYA, retail executive; b. Sept. 19, 1925; m. Yasuko Okada; children: Motoya, Katsuya, Masaya. BA, Waseda U., Japan, 1948. Pres. Jusco (USA), Inc.; founder, chmn., CEO JUSCO Co. Ltd., Tokyo; chmn. Talbots. Chmn. AEON Group Environs. Found., Okada Found. for Promotion of Hometown, Culture Found. Okada. Recipient Blue ribbon decoration 1985, Japanese Prime Minister commendation 1986, Internat. medal Nat. Retail Fedn., 1985; named Hon. Comdr. Order Brit. Empire, 1989. Mem. Japan Shopping Ctrs. Assn. (chmn. 1995—), Japan Retailers Assn. (chmn. 1995—), Tokyo C. of C. and Industry (vice chmn. 1987—), Japanese C. of C. (spl. adv. 1986—), Fedn. of Ecol. Orgn. (Keidanren) (exec. dir. 1979). *

OKADA, YOSHITAKA, radiologist; b. Hashima, Japan, Jan. 4, 1959; s. Shoji and Sekiko O.; m. Hitomi, Aug. 16, 1988; children: Naomichi, Eika. MD, U. Tokyo, 1983. Rsch. fellow U. Calif., San Francisco, 1987-88; asst. prof. radiology Kitasato U., Sagamihara, Japan, 1990-92, U. Tokyo, 1996-2000; assoc. prof. radiology Internat. U. Health and Welfare, Otawara, Japan, 2000—. Mem. Radiol. Soc. N.Am., Japan Radiol. Soc. Office: Sanno Hosp, 8-5-35 Akasaka, Tokyo 107-0052, Japan

OKAFOR, OKECHUKWU MICHAEL CHUKWU, forwarding agency executive; b. Enugu, Nigeria, Aug. 7, 1963; arrived in Germany, 1991; s. Emmanuel Ekegbo and Grace Chidi (Echedom) O.; m. Petra Rosa Pastari, Feb. 12, 1991; children: Fabienne, Ricardo, Rapheala. BSc, U. Nigeria, Nnuskka, 1988. Cert. in estate mgmt. and surveying. Pub., pres. Jinks Pub. Co., Enugu, 1984-86; CEO, pres. Cap Import and Export GdbR, Mannheim, Germany, 1993-94; CEO, co-pres. DLM Shipping Agy. GdbR, Schifferstadt, Germany, 1994—. Soccer trainer U. Nigeria, Nnuskka, 1987, 88. Avocations: reading, history, sports, current affairs. Fax: 06235 98804. Office: DLM Shipping Agy GdbR, Dannstadterstr 7-9, Schifferstadt 67105, Germany

OKAI, OSAMU, physician, educator; b. Kasagi, Taki-cho, Taki-gun, Japan, Nov. 21, 1933; s. Jiro and Etsu (Nakanisi) Okai; m. Itsuko Hosaka, Dec. 20, 1968. D Med. Sci., U. Tokyo, 1969; MD, Mie Prefecture U., Japan, 1964. Med. diplomate. Intern Mie Prefectual U. Hosp., Tsu, Japan, 1965; rsch. assoc. Tokyo Women's Med. Coll., 1970-82; assoc. prof. Kyorin U. Sch. Medicine, Mitaka, Japan, 1982-85; prof. Kyorin U. Sch. Health Sci., Hachioji, Japan, 1985-99; physician Musashi Inst. Tech., Tokyo, 1999—. Contbr. articles to profl. jours. Avocation: travel. Home: 1-20-8 Yamatocho, Nakano-ku, Tokyo 165-0034, Japan Office: Musashi Inst Tech, 1-28-1 Tamazutumi, Setagaya, Tokyo 158-8557, Japan

OKAJIMA, YASUTOMO, physiatrist; b. Tokyo, May 15, 1955; s. Jiro and Michiko (Murayama) O.; m. Midori Osa, June 11, 1985; children: Reina, Kohsuke. MD, Keio Univ. Sch. Medicine, Tokyo, 1980, D of Med. Sci., 1990. Cert. physiatrist, sports doctor, Japan. Fellow U. Ark. for Med. Scis., 1985-86; instr. Keio U. Sch. Medicine, 1986-88; chief dept. rehab. medicine Senbai Hosp., Tokyo, 1988-91; asst. prof. Tsukigase Rehab. Ctr. Keio U., Amagi-yugashima, 1991-97, assoc. prof., 1997—, v.p., 1998—. Contbr. articles to profl. jours. France-bed Co. grantee, Tokyo, 1994, Japan Ministry of Health rsch. grantee for aging, 1995, rsch. grantee Japan Ministry of Edn. and Sci., 1998. Mem. Japanese Assn. Rehab. Medicine (councilor 1994—, mem. editl. bd. 1997—, chmn. internat. com. 1999—). Avocations: tennis, skiing, golf. Office: Keio U Tsukigase Rehab Ctr, Keio U Tsukigase Rehab Ctr, Tsukigase 380-2, Amagi-yugashima 410-3293, Japan

OKAMOTO, JIRO, information scientist, educator; b. Kyoto, Japan, Dec. 25, 1938; s. Masao and Itsu Okamoto; m. Akiko Yabu, Mar. 28, 1965; children: Tetsuro, Yoko. B of Engring., Kyoto Tech. U., 1962; M of Engring., Osaka (Japan) City U., 1964, D of Engring., 1982. Asst. Osaka City U., 1964-70, lectr., 1970-88, assoc. prof., 1988-99, prof., 1999—. Contbr. sci. papers to profl. jours. Mem. Inst. Elec. Engrs. Japan (steering com. 1981-82), Inst. TV Engrs. (steering com. 1982-83), Inst. Electronics, Info. and Comm. Engrs. (steering com. 1988-89), Soc. Instrument and Control Engrs. (Kansai chpt. steering com. 1997-98, councilor 2000—). Avocations: gardening, Igo game. Home: 13 Fukakusa-Bocho, Fushimi Kyoto, Japan Office: Osaka City U, 3-3-138 Sugimoto, Sumiyoshi Osaka, Japan

OKAMOTO, KOICHI EUGENE, psychology educator; b. Takatsuki, Osaka, Japan, June 17, 1955; s. Nozomu and Yoshi (Wakino) O.; m. Yoshiko Yasuguchi, Apr. 5, 1981; children: Aya, Akane. BA, U. Tokyo, 1980, MA in Social Psychology, 1982, PhD in Social Psychology, 1990. Tchg. asst. Sophia U., Tokyo, 1983-85; instr. faculty of letters U. Tokyo, 1985-88; asst. prof. Toyo Eiwa Women's Jr. Coll., Yokohama, Japan, 1988-89; assoc. prof. Toyo Eiwa Women's U., Yokohama, 1989-97, prof. psycology, 1997—; rsch. supr. Ministry of Environment, Govt. of Japan, 1994—; mem. Nuclear Power Safety com., Sci. and Technol. Advancement Agy., Govt. of Japan, 1999—. Am. Field Svc. fellow, 1973, Fulbright fellow, 1993. Mem. Internat. Soc. Polit. Psychology (governing coun. 1998-2000), Japanese Psychol. Assn., Urasenke Internat. Assn. Buddhist. Avocations: tea ceremony of Urasenke tradition, Japanese chess. Home: 3-14-34-414 Higashi-Shinagawa, Shinagawa-ku, Tokyo 140-0002, Japan Office: Toyo Eiwa Women's U, 32 Miho-cho Midori-ku, Yokohama 226-0015, Japan

OKAMOTO, SACHIKO, biochemistry researcher; b. Kyoto, Japan, Mar. 30, 1973; d. Kunio and Junko (Nagata) O. B in Pharmacy, Kyoto U., 1996, M in Pharmacy, 1998. Rschr. Takara Shuzo Co. Ltd., Kyoto, 1998—. Contbr. articles to profl. jours. Avocations: scuba diving, tennis, playing contrabass. Office: Takara Shuzo Co Ltd, 2257 Sunaike Noji-cho, Kyusata City 525-0055, Japan

OKAMURA, HIDEKI, research scientist, physicist; b. Machida, Tokyo, Japan, Oct. 16, 1964; s. Muneki and Yoko (Kitada) O. BS, U. Tokyo, 1988, MS, 1990, PhD, 1994. Lectr. Japan Optometry and Hygienic Sch., Tokyo, 1988-93; rsch. scientist Inst. Phys. and Chem. Rsch., Saitama, Japan, 1994—; lectr. in physics Sophia U., Tokyo, 1998-2000; vis. scientist Nat. Rsch. Coun. Can., Ottawa, Ont., 2000—. Contbr. articles to profl. sci. jours. Mem. Atomic Energy Soc. Japan (isotope separation rsch. com. 1996-99), Japan Soc. Applied Physics, Optical Soc. Japan, Optical Soc. Am. Avocations: tennis, flying, swimming, horseback riding. Office: Steacie Inst Molcular Gen, 100 Sussex Dr Rm 2083, Ottawa, ON Canada K1A 0R6

OKAMURA, TADASHI, business executive; b. 1938. Grad., Tokyo U., 1962, U. Wis., Madison, 1973. Gen. mgr., Mktg. planning divsn., corp. mktg. group, 1989-93, group exec., info. processing and control systems group, 1993-94, v.p., dir., 1994-96; v.p., dir. Toshiba Corp., Tokyo, 1996, sr. v.p., dir., 1996, sr. v.p., dir. info. and comm. systems, dep. group exec., 1996-98, corp. sr. v.p., dir., 1998-99, corp. sr. v.p., dir. pres., CEO, 1999—. Office: Toshiba Corp, 1-1-1 Shibaura Minato-ku, Tokyo 105-8001, Japan*

O'KANE, ROSEMARY HEATHER TERESA, political scientist, educator; b. Enfield, Middlesex, Eng., Nov. 18, 1947; d. William Charles and Eileen Margaret Henrietta (Lovelock) O'K.; m. Leslie Rosenthal; 1 child, Harriet. BA with hons., U. Essex, Eng., 1970; MA, U. Essex, 1972; PhD, U. Lancaster, Eng., 1978. Lectr., sr. lectr. to prof. dept. politics U. Keele, Eng., 1973—. Author: The Likelihood of Coups, 1987, The Revolutionary Reign of Terror, 1991 (Outstanding Acad. Book, 1993), Terror, Force and States: The Path from Modernity, 1996, Revolution: Critical Concepts in Political Science (4 vols.), 2000. Mem. Polit. Studies Assn., Internat. Polit. Sci. Assn. Mem. Labour Party. Avocations: house decor, antiques. Office: Dept Politics, U Keele, Keele ST5 5BG, England

OKANO, KAORI HORNE, Asian studies educator; b. Innoshima, Japan, Aug. 3, 1959; d. Mamoru and Yukiko (Yatani) O.; m. David Matthew Horne, July 3, 1993; two children: Yukiko, Tom. BEd, Hiroshima U., 1983; MA with honors, Sydney U., 1987; PhD, Massey U., 1991. Cert. secondary tchr. Tchr. Mater Maria Coll., Sydeny, 1985, St. Matthews Coll., Rathkeale Coll., Masterton, New Zealand, 1986-87; lectr. LaTrobe U., Melbourne, 1991-94, sr. lectr., 1995—. Author: Education in Contemporary Japan: Inequality and Diversity, 1999, School to Work Transition in Japan: An Ethnographic Study, 1993; contbr. articles to acad. jours. Mem. The Asian Studies Assn. of Australia, Japanese Studies Assn. of Australia, Japan Soc. of Ednl. Sociology. Avocations: swimming, gardening. Office: Dpt Asian Studies LaTrobe U, Bundoora, Melbourne VIC 3083, Australia

OKANO, MASAYUKI, soccer player; b. July 25, 1972. Forward Urawa Red Diamonds, Japan; ctr.-forward Japan Nat. Team. Address: Japan Football Assn, 1-10-8 Dogenzaka Shibuya-Ku Fl 3, Tokyo 150-0043, Japan*

OKARMA, HENRYK, zoologist, researcher; b. Nysa, Poland, Nov. 12, 1959; s. Wladyslaw and Bronislawa Okarma; m. Elzbieta Serek, Sept. 19, 1987; children: Tomasz, Gabriela. MSc, Jagiellonian U., Cracow, Poland, 1983, PhD, 1989; assoc. prof., Warsaw (Poland) Agrl. Acad., 1996. Rsch. fellow Mammal Rsch. Inst., Bialowieza, Poland, 1989-96; assoc. prof. Inst. Nature Conservation, Cracow, 1997—; advisor World Wildlife Found., Gland, Switzerland, 1999, State Com. for Nature Protection, Warsaw, 1998. Author: (books) Wilk, 1992, Der Wolf, 1997. Mem. European Soc. Mammalogy, Cat Specialist Group Species Survival Commn. World Conservation Union (SSC-IUCN). Roman Catholic. Avocation: sports. Fax: 48 12 4210348. E-mail: okarma@ib-pan.krakow.pl. Office: Inst Nature Conservation, Lubicz 46, Cracow 31-512, Poland

OKASHA, SARWAT, art historian, educator, writer; b. Cairo, Feb. 18, 1921; s. Mahmoud Okasha and Sania Talaat; m. Islah Lofty, 1942; children: Mahmoud, Nora el-Labban. Student, Mil. Coll., Cairo, Staff Coll., Cairo; MA Lit., U. Cairo, 1951; D Lettres, U. Paris, 1960; HHD (hon.), Am. U., Cairo, 1995, Festschrift (hon.), 2000. Cavalry officer; mil. attaché Bern and Paris, 1953-56; amb. to Rome, 1957-58, Min. of Culture, 1958-62, 66-70; vis. prof. Coll. de France, 1973. Author: History of Arts, 22 vols.; transl. numerous works including Ovid's Metamorphoses, Ars Amatoria, Gibran Khalil Gibran's (in English) The Muslim Painter and the Divine, others. Mem. exec. bd. UNESCO, 1962-70. Recipient Légion d'Honneur, Arts et Lettres, Silver medal UNESCO, 1968, Golden medal UNESCO, 1970, Médaille d'argent de la Campagne de Nubie, 1999; corr. fellow Brit. Acad., 1975. Avocation: classical music. Address: Villa 34 Rd 14, Maadi, Cairo Egypt

OKAWARA, YOSHIO, former ambassador; b. Gunma Prefecture, Japan, Feb. 5, 1919; m. Mitsuko Terajima, Apr. 13, 1948; children: Akio, Nobuo, Tamio. LLB, Tokyo U., 1942. 2d and 1st sec. Japanese Embassy, London, 1954-56; 1st sec. Manila, 1956-58; fellow Ctr. for Internat. Affairs, Harvrd U., 1962; 1st sec. Japanese Embassy, Washington, 1962-63, counsellor, 1963-65; dir. pers. divsn. Ministry Fgn. Affairs, Tokyo, 1965-67, dep. dir. gen. Am. affairs bur., 1967-71, dir. gen., 1972-74, dep. vice minister for adminstrn., 1974-76; envoy extraordinary and min. plenipotentiary Japanese Embassy, Washington, 1971-72; amb. extraordinary and plenipotentiary of Japan to Australia, 1976-80; amb. of Japan to Fiji and Repiblic of Nauru, 1976-78; amb. to U.S., 1980-85; advisor Ministry Fgn. Affairs, 1985-2000; pres. Inst. Internat. Policy Studies. Mem. Tokyo Club, Chevy Chase Golf Club (Washington). Address: 1-22-20 Seijo Setagaya-ku, Tokyo 157 0066, Japan

OKAYAMA, HIDEAKI, opto-electronic engineer, researcher; b. Kamakura, Kanagawa, Japan, Jan. 13, 1958. BE in Applied Physics, Waseda U., Tokyo, 1981, MS in Physics, 1983, PhD in Applied Physics, 1993. Opto-electronic engr. R&D components Oki Electric Industry, Tokyo, 1983—; numerous conf. presentations in field. Contbr. numerou articles to sci. jours. Mem. IEEE, Optical Soc. Am., Japan Soc. Applied Physics, Inst. Electronics, Info. and Comm. Engrs. Office: Oki Electric Industry R & D, 550-1 Higashiasakawa, Hachioji Tokyo 193-8550, Japan

OKAYAMA, HIROSHI, physicist,; b. Zushi City, Japan, Mar. 29, 1943; s. Haruna and Toyo (Tahara) O.; m. Yumiko Kajino, Nov. 4, 1972; children: Akiko, Yuko, Sakiko. BS, Sci. Univ. Tokyo, 1965, MS, 1967, DSc, 1996. Asst. Chiba (Japan) U., 1972-77, lectr., 1977—. Author: Dictionary of Technical Terms on Remote Sensing, 1991; contbr. articles to profl. jours. Mem. Japan Resources Observation Sys. Orgn. (reviewer Applied Optics). Avocations: landscape gardening, ping pong, tennis, swimming. Home: 2-7-15 Kurosuna Inage-ku, Chiba 263-0042, Japan Office: Chiba U Env Remote Sensing, 1-33 Yayoi cho Inage-ku, Chiba 263-8522, Japan

OKAZAKI, MASAMI, manufacturing company executive; b. Tokyo, Japan, Oct. 12, 1929; s. Masatoshi and Tomoe (Kukizu) O.; m. Keiko Kawarasaki, May 7, 1961. BS, Meiji Pharm. Coll., Tokyo, 1951; BA, Waseda U., Tokyo, 1954. Import pharmacist for medicine and cosmetics Nippon Roche K.K., Tokyo, 1954-58; tech. dir. Tokyo Hoechst Japan, 1958-90; exec. cons. B.F. Goodrich Co., Cleve., 1991—. Mem. Am.-Japan Soc., Am. C. of C. in Japan, Chem. Soc. Japan. Methodist. Home: 2-27-8 Maruyama, Nakano-ku, Tokyo 165-0021, Japan

OKAZAKI, TSUNEKO, molecular biology educator; b. Nagoya, Japan, June 7, 1933; parents Takima and Hama (Kato) Hara; m. Reiji Okazaki, May 23, 1956 (dec. 1975); children: Ichiro, Junko. BS, Nagoya U., 1956, MS, 1958, DSc, 1963. Rsch. asst. dept. pharmacology Washington U., St. Louis, 1960-61; rsch. asst. dept. biochemistry Stanford U., Palo Alto, Calif., 1961-63; rsch. assoc. inst. molecular biology Nagoya U., 1965-76, assoc. prof. inst. molecular biology, 1976-83, prof. dept. molecular biology, 1983-97; prof. Inst. for Comprehensive Med. Sci. Fujita Health U., 1997—. Mem. Japanese Cell Biology Assn., Japanese Molecular Biology Assn.

OKE, FESTUS E., minister, religious organization administrator; b. Ofoni, Nigeria, Dec. 23, 1938; came to U.S., 1965; d. Ighojigbere Tom and Oghifo Okwede O.; m. Margret A. Ogwilaya, Nov. 7, 1960 (div. 1965); 1 child, Richard; m. Connie J., March 12, 1972; children: Richard, Okwede, Ejenobo, Ojeta, Aweshare. BS, Ind. U., 1969, MS, EdS, 1971, EdD, 1972; MDiv, Bethany Theol. Sem., 1994. Tchg. asst. Ind. U., Bloomington, 1969-72; dept. chair Fla. A&M U., Tallahassee, 1972-74, dir., 1974-76; dir. Ahmadu Bello U., Zaria, Nigeria, 1976-87; pastor Turkey Creek Ch. of the Brethren, Nappanee, Ind., 1993-94; factory worker Wells Aluminum Corp., Liberty, Ind., 1994-95; dir., chaplain Hope Rescue Mission, South Bend, Ind., 1995—. Avocations: photography, woodwork. E-mail: festus@michiana.org. Home: 28680 SR 4E North Liberty IN Office: Hope Rescue Mission 532 S Michigan St South Bend IN 46601-2499

O'KEEFE, FREDRICK REA, bishop, consultant, educator, writer; b. Washington, Mar. 26, 1944; s. Roy Fox and Kathryn Isabelle (Rea) O'Keefe; stepson of James Michael O'Keefe. Student, Fordham U., 1970-72; STD (hon.), StarReach Inst., Putnam Valley, N.Y., 1973; student, St. Augustines Sch. Theology, Fla., 1984; HHD (hon.), Trinity Hall Coll. & Sem., Santa Monica, 1987. Mgmt. trainer Sears Roebuck, Peekskill, N.Y., 1971-76, div. mgr., 1970-76; pres. Dreadnought Corp., Peekskill, 1974-76; gen. mgr. R. Shaw Co., Laguna Beach, Calif., 1977, N.D. Burger Co., L.A., 1980-84; mgmt., sales and mktg. trainer, v.p. mktg. Grand Am. Computers and Software Only, Irvine, Calif., 1984-86; tchr. Confraternity Christian Doctrine, Myrtle Beach, S.C., 1967-68; deacon to priest Old Cath. Ch. in N.Am., Peekskill, 1975-82; consecrated bishop Old Episcopal Ch., Scotland, 1982; vicar gen. Lomita, Calif., 1982-83; presiding bishop Redondo Beach, Calif., 1983—; archibishop-abbot Incarnation Abbey Found., Order of St. Benedict, 1987—; dir. customer svc. divsn., mgr. MIS networks Peter Lowe Internat. Inc., Tampa, Fla., 1992-94; mgmt. cons. Power Support Engring., Inc., Tampa, 1997-2000; dir. Conlegium Spiriti Refulgentis, Redondo Beach, 1975—; exec. dir. Am. Bd. Examiners in Pastoral Counseling, Washington, 1986—, sec., treas., 1982—; exec. dir. Am. Coun. on Schs. and Colls., Washington, 1982—; chmn. Grad. Coll. Theology, L.A., 1983-87; chaplain L.A. Sheriff's Dept., 1983-86; cons. CSR Cons., Clearwater, Fla., 1975-98, CEO, 1984-98, also dir.; dir. customer svc. Peter Lowe Internat., Inc., 1992-94; bd. dirs. Corp. Mgmt. Trust, Advanced Indsl. Techs. Contbr. articles to mags., poetry to collections; assoc. editor, journalist, mng. editor ANCHOR Mag., 1984—. Trustee St. Petersburg (Fla.) Theol. Sem., 1993-95; chmn. Trinity Hall Coll. and Sem., 1998—; bd. dirs. Carrollwood Civic Assn., Fla., 1995-97, Camp Endeavor, 1996—. With USAF, 1964-70. Recipient John Philip Sousa award, 1963. Mem. ASCAP, Am. Ministerial Assn. (sec. 1982-86, bd. dirs. 1985—, internat. pres. 1998—), Nat. Writers Union, Westchase Cmty. Assn. (dir. 1999—), Anglican Soc. N.Am., The Confraternity of the Blessed Sacrament, Silicon Valley Computer Soc., Pinellas IBM-PC Users

Group, Inc., Internat. Order of St. Luke the Physician, Soc. of Christian Letters, Soc. Mfg. Engrs., Small Press, Writers and Artists Orgn., Planetary Group Writers Club, Order of the Holy Redeemer, Ecumenical Ch. Fedn., Anglican Inst. Ecumenical Coun. of Cath. and Orthodox Bishops, Tampa Bay Skeptics Soc., Patrons of Husbandry, Carrollwood Sertoma Club. Avocations: composing, carpentry, screenwriting, liturgics. Office: Advanced Indsl Techs #363 N Dale Mabry Hwy Carrollwood FL 33618-2814

O'KEEFE, KATHLEEN MARY, state government official; b. Butte, Mont., Mar. 25, 1933; d. Hugh I. and Kathleen Mary (Harris) O'Keefe; BA in Comm., St. Mary Coll., Xavier, Kans., 1954; m. Nick B. Baker, Sept. 18, 1954 (div. 1970); children—Patrick, Susan, Michael, Cynthia, Hugh, Mardeen. Profl. singer, mem. Kathie Baker Quartet, 1962-72; research cons. Wash. Ho. of Reps., Olympia, 1972-73; info. officer Wash. Employment Security Commn., Seattle, 1973-81, dir. public affairs, 1981-90, video dir., 1990-95, ret., 1995; freelance writer, composer, producer, 1973—. Founder, pres. bd. Eden, Inc., visual and performing arts, 1975—; public relations chmn. Nat. Women's Democratic Conv., Seattle, 1979, Wash. Dem. Women, 1976-85; bd. dirs., composer, prodr., dir. N.Y. Film Festival, 1979; Dem. candidate Wash. State Senate, 1968. Recipient Silver medal Seattle Creative Awards Show for composing, directing and producing Rent A Kid, TV pub. svc. spot, 1979. Mem. Wash. Press Women. Democrat. Roman Catholic. Author: Job Finding In the Nineties, The Third Alternative, handbook on TV prodn., (children) So You Want to be President, 1995; composer numerous songs, also writer, dir., producer Job Service spots, Immigration & Naturalization Svc. spots, U.S. Dept. Labor spots, Dept. VA spots. Home: 4426 147th Pl NE # 12 Bellevue WA 98007-7191

OKEH, SAMSON EWRUJE, psychiatric nurse; b. Abraka, Nigeria, Nov. 5, 1943; s. Ovaguono Okeh; m. Pauline Okeh, Dec., 1969; children: Helen, Sunday, Debra, Abraka, John, Amber. Diploma, Bapt. Sch. Nursing, Eku Sapele, Nigeria, 1967; BA, U. Ill., Chgo., 1979; MA in Pub. Admistrn., Northeastern Ill. U., 1981. RN, Ill., Md., Calif. Asst. head nurse Loretto Hosp., Chgo.; nursing supr. Greater Laurel (Md.) and Beltsville Hosp.; charge nurse, part time supr. South Wood Hosp., Chula Vista, Calif.; asst. nurse mgr. Cedars Sinai Med. Ctr., L.A., 1991—. Mem. United Nurses Assn. Calif., Nigerian Assn. San Diego (pres. 1990-91), URHOBO Assn. So. Calif. (pres. 1992-93), Acad. Polit. Sci., L.A. World Affairs Coun. Home: 6639 Bellingham Ave North Hollywood CA 91606-1405 Office: Cedars Sinai Med Ctr 8700 Beverly Blvd Los Angeles CA 90048-1865

O'KELLY, MICHAEL E., engineering educator; b. Cork, Ireland, Apr. 10, 1937; s. Michael John and Margaret (Casey) O'K.; m. Jane Ann Walsh, July 4, 1968; children: Michael John, Eamon Eugene, Ita Margaret, Paul James, David Donogh, Jane Eugenie. B of Elec. Engring., U. Coll., Cork, Ireland, 1958; MSME, Calif. Inst. Tech., 1960, M of Mech. Engring., 1961; MS in Indsl. Engring. & Info. Systems, Columbia U., 1962; PhD in Applied Mechanics, Econs., Calif. Inst. Tech., 1964. Prodn. mgr. Ulmic S.A., Paris, 1964-65; mng. dir. Elec. Components, Ltd., Cork, Ireland, 1965-67; head manpower forecasting unit Dept. Labor, Dublin, Ireland, 1967-70; mng. engring. cons. Cork, 1970-71; prof. indsl. engring. U. Coll., Galway, Ireland, 1971—; deputy chmn. Electricity Supply Bd., Dublin, 1990-95; chmn. Nat. Manpower Adv. com., 1979-82, FAS Retail Sector Adv. Com., 1996-98; mem. governing body U. Coll., 1996-98; chmn. EirGrid, 2000—. Mem. editl. bd. Internat. Jour. Computer Integrated Mfg. Systems; contbr. articles to profl. jours. Fellow Instn. Elec. Engrs., British Inst. Mgmt. Avocations: gardening, cycling. Office: U Coll, Galway Ireland

OKEMWA, OBIRI LUKE, purchasing agent, consultant; b. Kisii, Nyanza, Kenya, July 12, 1953; s. Bernard and Sabina (Kemuma) O.; m. Theresa Nyaoso Nyarangi; children: Maureen, Robin, Emelliah, Ronnie, Lynah, Brian, Joy. B in Comms. with honors, U. Nairobi, Kenya, 1977; MSc in Purchasing and Supply, Ulster U., No. Ireland, 1992. Pers. officer Mumias Sugar Co., Kenya, 1977-79; supplies officer Ministry Fin., Kenya, 1980-87; sr. stock contr. Kenya Railways, Kenya, 1987-88, prin. stock contr., 1988-92, dep. head supplies, 1993-94; head purchasing Kenya Airways, Kenya, 1994-98; purchasing and supply mgr. Magadi Soda Co., Kenya, 1998—; cons. various firms in Kenya, 1983-96, BAT (Kenya), 1996. Author: Appraising of Purchasing Systems Within Central Medical Stores, 1984, KGG CU: Merchandise Distribution Systems, 1994; co-author: Quality Management Systems for Kenya Airways, 1995. Mem. Chartered Inst. Purchasing and Supply, Kenya Inst. Supplies Mgmt., Inst. MAterials Mgmt., Inst. Tng. and Devel., Muthaiga Golf Club, Kenya Railways Club, Magadi Soda Golf Club. Avocations: golf, snooker, squash, tennis, swimming. Office: Magadi Soda Co, PO Box 1 Magadi, Rift Valley Kenya

OKEN, ROBERT, neuroscientist, researcher, consultant; b. N.Y.C., Oct. 15, 1929; s. Milton and Etta (Weiner) O. BA, NYU, 1949, PhD, 1958. V.p., dir. Oken Fabrics Inc., N.Y.C., 1959-68, 71-73; rschr., cons. U.S. Army, USN, Washington, and Frederick, Md., 1955-56, Teller Environ. Systems, N.Y.C., 1969-70; businessman R.A. Siegel Galleries, N.Y.C., 1978-87; cons. to dir. N.Y. State Inst. for Basic Rsch., Staten Island, 1991-93; cons. Gerex Biotech. P.L. McGeer, Vancouver, B.C., Can., 1994-98. Contbr. papers and articles to various profl. jours., including Schizophrenia Bull., Am. Jour. Psychiatry, Annals of Pharmacotherapy, Jour. Dental Rsch., Alzheimer's Disease and Associated Disorders, Medical Hypotheses, Parkinson/Alzheimer Digest, Focus on Parkinson's Disease, Psychiatry Rev. Series. Scientific advisor Lifer Environ. Group, Roxbury, N.J., 1984-87; vol. Dover (N.J.) Gen. Hosp., 1989-90. With U.S. Army. 1955-56. Recipient medal of achievement Dover Gen. Hosp., 1990. Mem. AAAS, Am. Chem. Soc., Am. Philatelic Soc., N.Y. Acad. Scis., N.Y. Neuropsychology Group, Mensa Internat., Intertel, Phi Beta Kappa. Home and Office: PO Box 412 Hopatcong NJ 07843-0412

OKENFUSS, RONALD JOSEPH, brand manager; b. Cin.; m. Jenneke Oosterhoff. BA, Washington U., 1989, MA, 1993; M in Internat. Mgmt., Am. Grad. Sch. Internat. Mgmt., Glendale, Ariz., 1996. Interim merchandising mgr. Cin. Art Mus., 1990-91; compensation analyst WF Corroon, St. Louis, 1994-95; bus. analyst SmithKline Beecham, Buehl, Germany, 1996—. Office: SmithKline Beecham, Herrmannstr 7, Buehl Germany 77815

OKERE, CHIGOZIE, microbiologist; b. Owerri, Imo, Nigeria, Apr. 18, 1969; came to U.S., 1997; s. Geoffrey Owuamanna and Priscilla Agbachi O. B in Technology, Abubakar Tafawa Belewa U., Bauchi, 1991. Sci. rep. Ray Import Export Corp., Chgo., 1992-94; asst. rsch. scientist Abubakar Tafawa Belewa U., 1994-95; asst. quality control microbiologist Parkland Lab. Svcs., Owerri, 1996-97; biochem. oxygen demand personnel Gabriel Labs., Chgo., 1998—. Sec. youth wing Grassroots Dem. Movement, Owerri, 1998. Mem. Am. Soc. Microbiology, AAAS. Avocations: soccer, table tennis, swimming, volleyball, tennis.

OKERE, CHUMA ONYEAGHALA, neuroscientist; b. Enugu, Nigeria, Mar. 20, 1964; s. Geoffrey Chukwuma and Marian Nnenna (Ike) O.; m. Maria Anayo Iwuoha, Jan. 17, 1993; children: Chukwumerije Uzoma, Tochukwu Eziihe, Enyichukwu Nneoma. BSc, U. Ibadan, Nigeria, 1987, MSc, 1990; PhD, Kochi (Japan) Med. Sch., 1997. Lectr. U. Maiduguri, Nigeria, 1990-93; rsch. assoc. Kochi Med. Sch., 1999-2000, postdoctoral rsch. fellow, 1997-99; rsch. fellow Med. Coll. Pa. Hahnemann U., Phila., 2000—. Fgn. Rsch. fellow Ministry Sci. Culture and Sports, Japan, 1993. Mem. AAAS, Internat. Behavioral Neurosci. Soc., Japan Neuroendocrine Soc. Avocations: reading, nature viewing. Home: 7708 Lucretia Mott Way # 8 Elkins Park PA 19027-1007 Office: Hahnemann U Med Coll Pa 2900 Queen Dr Philadelphia PA 19129

OKEYA, EPHRAIM NKEM, biomedical engineer; b. Ndoni Rivers, Onelga, Nigeria, Oct. 5, 1956; s. Ambrose B.C. and Theresa (Nwachi) O.; m. Laura Naglaa Said, 1990. BA, UNESCO, 1975, PhD, 1976, DSc, 1990. Audtior Tourism Industry, Ndoni, Nigeria, 1970-71; editor, pub. Tourist Mag., Ndoni, Nigeria, 1972-75; engr. Nipsset/Unesco, Ndoni, Nigeria, 1975-77; med. dr. Magdalene Hosp., Ndoni, Nigeria, 1978-83; rsch. dir. Space U.-Ndoni-Unesco, Ndoni, Nigeria, 1986—; Nipsset sec. gen. Unesco Biotech/Engring., France, 1976—; mem. remote sensing program Nat. Space U. Editor: Toursit Mag.-Nigeria, 1974-79; contbr. articles to profl. jours. Presdl. aspirant Nat. Rep. Conv., Nigeria, 1992. UN Family scholar, 1992—; Unesco fellow, 1976-77, 92-93. Mem. World Parliament (knight comdr. 1991), Internat. Parliament (knight templar 1992), Maison Internat. Conferation of Chivalry. Roman Catholic. Achievements include research in space signals, biotherapy thermo therapy, brightness of source, power sources, immunoglobulins, gamma globins interaction in complex medium, earthquare decay. Office: Space U Ndoni Unesco, 149 Hospital Rd, Aba Nigeria

OKIGBO, PIUS NWABUFO, economist; b. Ojoto, Nigeria, Feb. 6, 1924; s. James Okoye and Anna (Onu) O.; divorced; m. Florence Nnakwe; children: Pius Nebolisah, Anne, Linda, Chantal, Victor, Obiajulu. BA with honors, London U., 1946, BScEcons, 1949, LLB, 1952, DSc in Econs., 1982; MA, Northwestern U., 1954, PhD, 1956; postgrad., Nuffield Coll., Oxford, 1954; LLD (hon.), U. Nigeria, 1966; DLitt. (hon.), Ahmadu Bello Univ.; DSc, Fed. U. Tech., Owerri; DSc Econ. (hon.), Univ. Lagos; DSc in Econs., London U., 1982; DSc in Econs. (hon.), London U., Abubako, Tafawa Balewa U., Nnamdi Azikiwi U. Chukwuma Devel. officer, 1948-52; economist Survey Nat. Income, 1958-60; econ. adv. Govt. of Eastern Nigeria, 1960-61, Fed. Govt. of Nigeria, 1962-67; ambassador of EEC, 1963-67, mem. constn. drafting com., 1975; chmn. Com. on Fin. System, 1976; mem. Constituent Assembly, 1977; chmn. Presdl. Commn. Revenue Allocation, 1979-80; mng. dir. Skoup & Co., Ltd., Enugu, Nigeria, 1971—; lectr. Northwestern U., 1955-57; studentship Nuffield Coll., 1954, 57; cons. to UNCTAD, ECA; dir. corps. Author: Nigerian National Accounts 1950-57, 1962; Nigerian Public Finance, 1965; Africa and the Common Market, 1967; Nigeria's Financial System: Structure and Growth, 1981, Nigerian National Development Planning 1900-1992, 1989, Essays in the Public Philosophy of Development, Vol. 1, 1987, Vols. 2-5, 1994. Decorated Comdr. Order of the Niger, 1977; recipient Nat. Merit award, 1983, Internat. Order Merit. Fellow Royal Econ. Soc., Nigerian Inst. Mgmt., Nigerian Econ. Soc. (past pres.); mem. Eonometric Soc., Am. Econ. Assn. Home: Plot 750 NZA St PO Box 39, Enugu Nigeria

OKIJI, AYAO, theoretical physicist, educator, administrator; b. Nishinomiya, Hyogo, Japan, Aug. 28, 1934; s. Masami and Chizu (Oishi) O.; m. Setsuko Kotake, Oct. 16, 1966; children: Miwa Takamoto, Masahiro. BS, Osaka (Japan) U., 1960, MS, 1962; DSc, U. Tokyo, 1967. Rsch. assoc. U. Tokyo, 1963-68; assoc. prof. Osaka U., 1968-84, prof., 1984-97, prof. emeritus, 1997—; pres. Wakayama Nat. Coll. Tech., Gobo, Japan, 1997—. Editor: Correlation Effects in Low-Dimensional Electron Systems, 1994, Elementary Processes in Exitations and Reactions on Solid Surfaces, 1996, Solid State Communications, 1990-97; editl. adv. bd. Surface Sci., 1996—. Mem. Phys. Soc. Japan (v.p. 1997-98, pres. 1998-99). Home: 1-9-10-205 Nigawa-cho, 662-0811 Nishinomiya Hyogo, Japan Office: Wakayama Nat Coll Tech, 77 Noshima Nada, 644-0023 Gobo Wakayama, Japan

OKIKIOLU, GEORGE OLATOKUNBO, scientific and industrial company executive, mathematician; b. Nigeria, July 18, 1941; arrived in U.K., 1959; s. James Adekunle and Anwan (Obong) O.; m. Patricia Natasha Edwards, Sept. 19, 1962 (div. 1980); children: Jeannie Adetokunbo, Katherine Adebola. B.Sc. (1st class), Sir John Cass Coll., U. London, 1963, M.Sc., 1964; D.Sc., U. London, 1971. Asst. lectr. Battersea Coll., London, 1964, U. Sussex, Brighton, Eng., 1965; lectr. U. East Anglia, Norwich, Eng., 1966-74; pres., propr. Okikiolu Sci. and Indsl. Co., London, 1972—. Author: Aspects of the Theory of Bounded Integral Operators in LP-Spaces, 1971; author, pub. Completion of the Magic Square of Even Order, 1976, Special Integral Operators, vol. I, 1980, vol. II, 1981, Divisibility and Numbers, 1989; (jours.) Bull. of Math., 1981—, Bull. of Inventions and Summary of Patent Specifications, 1981—. Patentee sci. processes and devices. Mem. N.Y. Acad. Scis. Achievements include inventions of photoconverter technology, magnetic propulsion systems, multiple station communication and broadcasting channel systms, applications of electro-optical signal distributor assemblies and remote effect devices and sub-micro-acoustic waves. Office: Okikiolu Sci & Idsl Co, 377 Edgware Rd, London W2 1BT, England Also: 8 Bradfield Ct Hawley Rd, London NW1 8RN, England

OKINAGA, LAWRENCE SHOJI, lawyer; b. Honolulu, July 7, 1941; s. Shohei and Hatsu (Kakimoto) O.; m. Carolyn Hisako Uesugi, Nov. 26, 1966; children: Carrie, Caryn, Laurie. BA, U. Hawaii, 1963; JD, Georgetown U., 1972. Bar: Hawaii 1972, U.S. Dist. Ct. Hawaii 1972, U.S. Ct. Appeals (9th cir.) 1976. Adminstrv. asst. to Congressman Spark Matsunaga Honolulu, 1964, 65-69; law clk. to chief judge U.S. Dist. Ct. Hawaii, Honolulu, 1972-73; assoc. Carlsmith Ball, Honolulu, 1973-76, ptnr., 1976—; mem. Gov.'s Citizens Adv. Com. Coastal Zone Mgmt., 1974-79; sec. Hawaii Bicentennial Corp., 1975-77, chmn., 1985-87, vice chmn., 1983-85; mem. Jud. Selection Commn., State of Hawaii, 1979-87, vice chmn., 1986; mem. consumer adv. coun. Fed. Res. Bd., 1984-86; chmn. State of Hawaii Jud. Conduct Commn., 1991-94; apptd. mem. Fed. Savings and Loan Adv. Council, Washington, 1988-89; mem. nat. adv. coun. U.S. Small Bus. Adminstrn., 1994-2000; mem. adv. coun. Fed. Res. Bank of San Francisco, 1995—. Bd. dirs. Moiliili Cmty. Ctr., Honolulu, 1965-68, 73-86, trustee 1993—; bd. visitors Georgetown U. Law Ctr., 1993—; trustee Kuakini Med. Ctr., 1984-88, 89-96. Capt. USAFR, 1964-72, 74-76. Mem. ABA (ho. of dels. 1991-94, standing com. on jud. selection tenure and compensation 1993-96, standing com. on jud. independence 1999—), Hawaii Bar Assn. (sec., bd. dirs. 1981), Am. Judicature Soc. (bd. dirs. 1986—, treas. 1995-97, pres. 1997-99), Georgetown U. Law Alumni Assn. (bd. dirs. 1986-91), Omicron Delta Kappa. Office: Carlsmith Ball PO Box 656 Honolulu HI 96809-0656

OKINO, YOSHIHIRO, science educator; b. Kyoto, Japan, June 8, 1939; s. Takatoshi and Toyo (Nojima) O.; m. Sumiko Okino, May 28, 1969; children: Toshihiko, Keiko. Rsch. engr. Matsushita Elec. Ind. Co. Ltd., Kadoma, Japan, 1963-99; guest rschr. Kansai U., Suita, Japan, 1999—; cons. to media, optical, mfg. cos., Tokyo, 1999—. Recipient Prize of Meml. of Dr. K. Sakurai, 1996. Mem. Internat. Symposium on Optical Memory (chair steering com. 1999—). Avocation: mountain climbing. Home: 1-1-131 Nagi Iseda-cho, Uji Kyoto 611-0044, Japan Office: Kansai U, 3-3-35 Yamate-cho, Suita Osaka 564-8680, Japan

OKOCHA, AUGUSTINE (JAY JAY OKOCHA), professional soccer player; b. Enugu, Nigeria, Aug. 14, 1973. Midfielder Rangers Internat. Football Club, Nigeria, Eintracht Frankfurt Football Club, Germany, 1994-95, Fenerbahce Football Club, Turkey, 1996-97, Nigeria Nat. Team, Paris St. Germain, 1998—. Recipient Olympic Gold medal Nigeria Team, 1996, Africa Cup 2000 with Nigeria and Nat. Team. Office: 24 Rue du Commandant, 30 Ave du Parc des Princes, 75016 Paris France*

OKOGUN, JOSEPH IBOMEIN, chemist, educator; b. Agbor, Nigeria, Oct. 23, 1939; s. Okogun John and Enimaluole Yawo Okdgun; m. Justina Isimankhomen Odigie, July 20, 1968; children: Margaret, Isi, Osahon, Erabor, Enomen, Aigue. BS, Univ. Coll., Ibadan, Nigeria, 1963; PhD, U. Ibadan, 1967; DIC, Imperial Coll., London, 1971. Chartered chemist, U.K. Lectr. U. Ibadan, 1966-77, dean of sci., 1980-82, head of chemistry, 1984-87, prof., 1977-95; prof., dir. Nat. Inst. for Pharm. Rsch. and Devel., Abuja, Nigeria, 1994—; vis. prof. U. Hannover, 1993, 97; chmn. Indsl. Tng. Fund, Nigeria, 1985-89; pres. Bevekt Gedu Chem. Co., Nigeria, 1995—. Patentee in field; contbr. articles to profl. jours. Mem. Cmty. Devel., Ewohimi, Nigeria, 1963—, St. Vincent de Paul Charity, Abuja, 1996—. Fellow Nigerian Acad. of Sci., 1979, Alexander von Humboldt Found., Germany, 1979, 87, 93, 97; named Best Chemistry Grad., U. Ibadan, 1963. Fellow Royal Soc. Chemistry, African Acad. of Scis.; mem. N.Y. Acad. Scis. Roman Catholic. Avocations: reading, music, walking. Office: Nat Inst Pharm R&D, PMB 21, Abuja/FCT Nigeria.

OKOH, ANTHONY JOSEPH, veterinarian, educator; b. Okpoga, Benue, Nigeria, Aug. 25, 1945; s. Okoh Abarike and Enega Ekle; m. Mary Lovina Ogbole; children: Simon, Christiana, Moses, Theresa, Emmanuel, Godwin, Maria. D of Vet. Medicine, Ahmadu Bello U., Zaria, Nigeria, 1971; M of Preventive Vet. Medicine, U. Calif., Davis, 1977; PhD, Ahmadu Bello U., Zaria, 1986. Vet. rsch. officer Nat. Vet. Rsch. Inst., Vom, Nigeria, 1971-74, prin. vet. rsch. officer, 1975-77, chief vet. rsch. officer, 1980-85; sr. lectr. U. Jos, Makurdi, Nigeria, 1985-88; assoc. prof. U. Agr., Makurdi, 1989-91; prof. vet. medicine Usmanu Danfodiyo U., Sokoto, Nigeria, 1992-99; dean Coll. Vet. Medicine, U. Agr., Makurdi, Nigeria, 1999—; cons. in diagnostics Nat. Vet. Rsch. Inst., Vom, 1980-85; cons. in rabies Fed. Livestock & Pest Control Svcs., Abuja, Nigeria, 1992—; dir. Vet. Tchg. Hosp., Usmanu Danfodiyo U., Sokoto, 1992-96; rsch. assoc. Wistar Inst. Anatomy and Biology, Phila. Co-author: (book) Rabies and Rabies-related Viruses, 1988, Viral Diseases of Animals in Africa, 1988, Education of Nomadic Families: Animal Health and Husbandry; contbr. numerous articles to sci. jours. Grantee Wistar Inst. of Anatomy and Biology, 1982-83. Mem. Nigerian Vet. Med. Assn., Nigerian Soc. for Animal Prodn. Roman Catholic. Avocations: reading, traveling, cooking, farming, cricket. Home: PO Box 579, Makurdi Benue, Nigeria Office: U Agr, PMB 2373, Makurdi Benue, Nigeria

OKOLO, JULIUS EMEKA, political science educator, researcher; b. Abatete, Nigeria, Feb. 18, 1944; s. Peter Iloka and Nwude Dinemeluaku (Onuorah) O. BA, Howard U., 1966, MA, 1968, PhD, 1970. Asst. prof. polit. sci. Howard U., Washington, 1970-74, assoc. prof. polit. sci., 1974-79; reader in polit. sci. Usmanu Danfodiyo U., Sokoto, Nigeria, 1979-91, prof. polit. sci., 1991—, head polit. sci. dept., 1997—; dir. grad. rsch. program in polit. sci., Howard U., 1972-74; head polit. sci. dept. Usmanu Danfodiyo U., 1979-85, dean social scis., 1982-83, dean postgrad. sch., 1983-88, 92-97. Editor: West African Regional Cooperation and Development, 1990, Political Economy of Foreign Policy in Ecowas, 1994; contbr. articles to profl. jours. Mem. Internat. Studies Assn., Nigerian Soc. Internat. Affairs (1st v.p. 1986—), Nigerian Polit. Sci. Assn. (exec. mem. 1979—), Igbo Cmty. Assn. Rockefeller Found. fellow, N.Y., 1987. Avocations: gardening, lawn tennis, music, rope making, reading. Home: 2 Benjamin Ln PO Box 1230, Onitsha Anambra, Nigeria Office: Usmanu Danfodiyo U, PMB 2346, Sokoto Nigeria

OKOLODKOV, YURI BORISOVICH, marine botanist researcher; b. Karabas, USSR, Oct. 27, 1956; s. Boris Ivanovich Okolodkov and Lidia Aleksandrovna (Rusakova) Okolodkova; m. Natalia Aleksandrovna Pekarskaya, Jan. 23, 1981; children: Boris Y., Aleksandr Y., Anna Y. MSc, Leningrad (USSR) State U., 1982; PhD, Komarov Bot. Inst., Leningrad, 1987; DSc, Komarov Bot. Inst., St. Petersburg, 2000. Lab. asst. Zool. Inst. Russian Acad. Sci., Leningrad, 1973-74, 76-82; jr. rsch. scientist Komarov Bot. Inst. Russian Acad. Sci., St. Petersburg, Russia, 1988-92, rsch. scientist, 1992-99, sr. rsch. scientist, 1999—. Author: (with J. Wiktor, K. L. Vinogradova) Atlas of the Marine Flora of Southern Spitsberger, 1995; contbr. articles to profl. jours. Recipient Antarctic Svc. medal U.S., 2000; Rsch. Coun. Norway scholar, 1996. Fellow Royal Soc. Eng.; mem. Peter Great Acad. Sci. & Arts, U.K. Systematics Assn. & Sys. Forum, Russian Bot. Soc. Avocations: foreign languages, swimming, playing guitar, table tennis, tourism. Office: Komarov Bot Inst, Prof Popov St. 2, 197376 Saint Petersburg Russia

OKONKWO, JOHN EMEWULU NICHOLAS, obstetrician-gynecologist, educator; b. Nnewi, Anambra, Nigeria, June 20, 1942; s. Akabogu Ezenyinna and Obomkaewe (Edoka) O.; m. Chinwe Christiana Okeke, Jan. 31, 1970; children: Chika, Nkechi, Ifeyinwa, Ijeoma, Nnenna, Onyinye, Obiajulu, Chisom. MB, BChir, U. Ibadan, Nigeria, 1971; ECFMG, U. Ibadan, 1972; LMCC, U. Sask., Can., 1977; ABOG, U. Sask., 1980. Ob-gyn., med. dir. Nigercem Hosp., Ikalagu, Nigeria, 1978-81; med. dir. Jeno Hosp., Enugu, Nigeria, 1981-92; lectr. Nnamdi Azikiwe U., Awka, Nigeria, 1992-95; sr. lectr. Nnamdi Azikiwe U., Awka, 1996—; ob-gyn. North Battleford Health Dist., Can., 1996; cons. Nnandi Azikiwe U. T. Hosp., Nnewi, 1992-99; dir. Chi Orgn., Awkunanaw, Enugu, 1999. Contbr. articles to profl. jours. Coun. mem. Soc. Ob-gyn. Nigeria, 1990-93, treas. Ea. sector, 1994-96. Fellow ACOG, Internat. Coll. Surgeons, West African Coll. Surgeons. Jehovah's Witness. Avocations: farming, car repairing, soccer, table tennis. Office: Box 8282, Enugu Nigeria

OKOSUN, IKE S., epidemiologist, educator; b. Ishan, Nigeria, May 20, 1954; came to U.S., 1975, naturalized, 1975; s. Stephen and Comfort Okosun; m. Martha Okosun, July 1, 1970; children: Vanessa, Bryan. BS in Bacteriology, N.D. State U., 1978; MS in Microbiology, Ala. A&M U., 1984; MPH in Epidemiology, U. Okla., 1987; PhD in Epidemiology, U. Pitts., 1996. Microbiologist Oklahoma City Health Dept., 1985-88; epidemiologist Devre Inc., Washington, 1991-92, Med. Care Devel., Washington, 1992-94; rsch. scientist Loyola U., Maywood, Ill., 1997-99; asst. prof. Mercer U., Macon, Ga., 1999—; vis. epidemiologist Edo State U., Ekpoma, Nigeria, 1994—; cons. in health WHO, N.Y., 1994; cons. in epidemiology Pan Am. Health Orgn., Washington, 1994—, African Devel. Bank, Cote d'Ivoire, 1994—. Author: (book) Stroke in Blacks, 1999; contbr. articles to profl. jours. Minority postdoctoral fellow NIH, 1998-99. Fellow Inst. Food Technologists, Royal Inst. Pub. Health and Hygiene; mem. APHA, N.Am. Soc. for Study of Obesity, Soc. for Epidemiologic Rsch. Roman Catholic. Avocations: traveling, soccer, music, writing. E-mail: okosun 1@mercer.edu. Office: Mercer U Coll Medicine 1550 College St Macon GA 31207-1500

OKREPILOV, VLADIMIR VALENTINOVICH, business executive, quality management specialist; b. Leningrad, Russia, Feb. 23, 1944; s. Valentin Ivanovich Okrepilov and Valentina Mihailovna Kirillova-Aristova; m. Gennadievna Irina Efremenko, July 6, 1987; children: Mihail, Vladimir. Engr. Mech., Baltic State Tech. U., St. Petersburg, Russia, 1970; Candidate degree in Econs., State U. of Econs. and Fin., St. Petersburg, 1986, D Econs., 1992, Prof., 1993. Engr. Plant of Radio-Tech. Equipment, St. Petersburg, 1965-70; chief engr. D.I. Mendeleyev Rsch. Inst. metrology, St. Petersburg, 1979-86; dir. Leningrad Ctr. of Standardization and Metrology, St. Petersburg, 1986-90; dir. gen. Ctr. for Testing and Certification, St. Petersburg, 1990—; asst. prof. State U. of Econs. and Fin., St. Petersburg, 1991-93, prof., 1993—; head of sub-faculty Acad. of Standardization, metrology and Cert., 1995—; chmn. Northwestern sect. for encouraging devel. of econ. sci. divsn. econs. Russian Acad. Scis., 1998—. Author: (books) Total Quality Management, 1996, Quality and Competitiveness, 1997, Quality Management, 1998. Recipient Disting. Figure in Sci. and Tech. Russian Fedn., Pres. Russia, 1994, also Russian Fedn. State award in Sci. and Engring. Mem. Russian Acad. for Quality Problems (pres. St. Petersburg Br. 1993—), Internat. Sci. Acad. for Ecology, Human and Nature Safety, St. Petersburg Union of Sci. and Engring. Socs. (mem. presdl. coun.), Order for Svc. to Fatherland. Avocations: sports, music, reading. Office: Ctr for Testing/Cert, 1 Kurlandskaya St, 198103 Saint Petersburg Russia

OKSA, JUHA AH, scientist; b. Kuopio, Finland, Dec. 30, 1958; s. Juho Olavi and Tuula Armi Oksa; m. Taina Tarja Utriainen, June 20, 1986; children: Tuuli Maria, Kaisli Katariina. MSc, U. Jyväskylä, Finland, 1987, PhD, 1998. Cert. exercise physiologist. Tchr. H.S., Konnevesi, Finland, 1986-87; scientist Oulu Regional Inst. Occupl. Health, 1987—; lectr. Health Care Inst., Oulu, 1989-92; vis. scientist Def. and Civil Inst. Environ. Medicine, Toronto, Can., 1998-99. Contbr. articles to profl. jours. Mem. Am. Coll. Sports Medicine, Internat. Commn. on Occupl. Health. Avocations: hiking, skiing, canoeing, photography. Home: Yli-Iintie 60, 80900 Kiiminki Finland Office: Oulu Regional Inst Occupl, Aapistie 1, 90220 Oulu Finland

OKU, SHOICHIRO, sales and marketing executive; b. Kitakyushu, Fukuoka, Japan, Dec. 18, 1944; s. Tadashi and Chiyose Oku; m. Fumiko Inoue, Oct. 10, 1973; children: Noburo, Mayuko. BS in Econs. and Fgn. Trade, Kanagawa U., Yokohama, Japan, 1969. Sales mgr. Comm. Sci. Corp., Tokyo, 1969-80; regional mgr. Asia region Onan Corp., Tokyo, 1980-90; gen. mgr. Pacific north region GNB Techs., Inc., Lombard, Ill., 1990—; v.p. GNB Battery Techs. Japan Inc., Tokyo, 1990—. Mem. World Wide Fund for Nature. Avocation: antique chinaware collecting. Home: 3-7-4-304 Hikarigaoka, Nerima-ku Tokyo 179-0072, Japan Office: GNB Bat Techs Japan Inc, 1-26-2 NishiShinjuku Nomura Bldg, Shinjuku-ku Tokyo 163-0528, Japan

OKUBOTE, AMOS OLAKUNLE, computer company executive, consultant; b. Sagamu, Remo, Nigeria, Dec. 17, 1956; s. James Olaitan and Sophian Adefunke (Ajayi) O.; m. Bolaji Omolara Alese, Apr. 3, 1981; children: Adewale, Adejoke, Oluwaseun, Olaitan. BSc in Computer Scis. with honors, U. Nigeria, Nsukka, 1982; MEd in Info. Scis., U. Ibadan, Nigeria, 1998. Programmer, analyst Fed. Dept. Agr., Benin City, Nigeria, 1982-83; edn. officer VI Ministry of Edn., Abeokuta, Nigeria, 1983-90; head dept. maths. and computers Fed. Coll. Edn., Abeokuta, 1990-96; head computer tech. dept. Lagos City Poly., Ikeja, Nigeria, 1996-97; sr. mgr. Electronics Data Processing Bemil Nigeria Ltd., Lagos, 1997; software mgr. Complete Tech. Ltd., Lagos, 1997-98; lectr., project coord. computer tech. Yaba Coll. Tech., Lagos, 1998—; vis. lectr. Ogun-State Poly., Abeokuta, 1990-96, Safe Assocs. Ltd., Lagos, 1996-97; cons. Emmersons Nigeria, Ltd., Lagos, 1997-98; bd. dirs. Obam Computers Ltd., Lagos, Complete Tech., Ikeja, Lagos. Author: Computer Studies: An Introductory Text, 1994, A First Course in

Computer Studies, 1995 (Pubs. Best award 1995). Assessor, examiner Inst. Chartered Accts. Nigeria, Lagos, 1993—; mem. Cmty. Devel. Assn., Lagos, 1996. Recipient Profl. Excellence award Nat. Assn. Computer Sci. Students, Abeokuta, 1995, Merita award Rotaract Club Osiele, Abeokuta, 1996. Mem. Computer Profl. Nigeria, Computer Assn. Nigeria (chpt. sec. 1993-96), Rotary Internat. (chpt. vocat. dir. 1994-95, LG coord. Polio Plus com. 1995). Avocations: reading, writing, traveling, games, music. Home: 25 Adeyemi St, Agege Laos, Nigeria Office: Yaba Coll Tech, Dept Computer Tech, Yaba Lagos Nigeria

OKUDA, HIROSHI, automotive executive; b. Mie Prefecture, Dec. 29, 1932; m. Kyoko Okuda; 1 son, 1 dau. Degree in bus., Hitotsubashi U., Tokyo. Mem. acctg. divsn. Toyota Motor Corp., 1955-72, overseer Philippine ops., 1972-79, gen. mgr. Asia and Oceania divsn., 1979-82, dir., 1982-87, mng. dir., 1987-88, sr. mng. dir., 1988-92, exec. v.p., 1992-95, pres., 1995-99, chmn., 1999—; mem. Econ. Strategy Coun. Japan, 1998—; chmn. Japan Fedn. Employers' Assns., 1999—; chmn. Japan Automobile Mfrs. Assn., 2000—, Japan Motor Indsl. Fedn., 2000—. Recipient Blue Ribbon medal for contbns. to Japanese Soc., 1996; named Grande Oficial Rio Branco, Govt. Brazil, 1997; recipient Grand Decoration of Honor in Silver with Star, Govt. Austria, 1999, Ordre National de La Legion d'Honneur Officer, Govt. France. Avocations: books, movies, judo (black belt). Office: Toyota Motor, 1 Toyota-cho, Toyota Aichi Pref 471-8571, Japan

OKUDA, YUKICHI, medical educator, endocrinologist; b. Maebashi, Japan, May 25, 1954; s. Kunio and Miyoko (Kousaka) O.; m. Harumi Nohara, Mar. 31, 1984; children: Itoko, Lisa. MD cum laude, Tsukuba U., 1980, PhD, 1987. Resident in internal medicine Tsukuba U. Hosp., Japan, 1980-83; rsch. asoc. endocrinology Baylor Coll. Medicine, Houston, 1987-88, rsch. instr. endocrinology, 1988; from asst. prof. to assoc. prof. Inst. Clin. Medicine U. Tsukuba, 1988—; dir. nutritional svc. U. Tsukuba Hosp., 1995—. Reviewer Endocrine Jour., 1995—, Jour. Clin. Metabolism, 1998—; contbr. articles to profl. jours. Mem. Am. Diabetes Assn., Japanese Soc. Internal Medicine, Endocrine Soc. Avocations: swimming, music, tennis, fishing. Office: U Tsukuba Inst Clin Med, Tennodai 1-1-1, 305-8575 Tsukuba shi, Japan

OKUDAIRA, MASAHIKO, pathologist, researcher; b. Hiroshima, Japan, Aug. 28, 1927; s. Minoru and Toshiko (Ohnogi) O.; m. Hiroko Naitou, Apr. 28, 1955; children: Takehito, Tsuneko Okudaira Kumagai. MD, Tokyo U., 1950, PhD, 1958. Rsch. assoc. dept. pathology Tokyo U., 1951-63, lectr. Sch. Medicine, 1963-74; med. examiner Tokyo Met. Govt., 1955-72; rsch. assoc. Jewish Hosp., Cin., 1960-61; prof. pathology Sch. Medicine Kitasato U., Sagamihara, Kanagawa, Japan, 1972-93; dir. hosp. pathology Kitasato U. Hosp., Sagamihara, 1984-93; adrritus prof. Kitasato U., Sagamihara, 1993—; head divsn. pathology Japan Bioassay Rsch. Ctr., Hadano, Kanagawa, 1993-2000; commr. Ministry of Labor, 1996—; vis. prof. Sch. Medicine Showa U., Tokyo, 1982-95. Contbr. articles to med. jours. Mem. Japanese Path. Soc. (registered, trustee 1962—), Japanese Soc. Med. Mycology (hon., pres. 1984-85, bd. dirs. 1974-94, acad. award 1987), Japan Soc. Hepatology (hon. award 1998), Japanese Med. Soc. Alcohol and Drug Studies (hon., pres. 1993-94), Internat. Soc. Human and Animal Mycology (hon., v.p. 1991-94), Liver Cancer Study Group Japan (hon., pres. 1989-90), Japan Soc. Portal Hypertension (hon.). Home: 3-23-19 Nakano, Nakano-ku, Tokyo 164-0001, Japan Office: Ministry of Labor, 1-2-2 Kasumigaseki, Chiyoda-ku Tokyo 100-8988, Japan

OKUDE, SHINGICHIRO, physicist, researcher; b. Kameyama, Japan, Dec. 9, 1960; s. Takuo and Kazuko (Sunami) O.; married 1991 (div. 1992). PhD, U. Tokyo, 1988. Rsch. fellow Japan Soc. Promotion Sci., Tokyo, 1988-89; with Toshiba Co., Kawasaki, Japan, 1989—. Contbr. articles to profl. jours. Avocations: artificial intelligence, personal computer, C language programming, data base theory, playing piano. Home: Ooaza Nihongi 1001-375, Ichishi-gun, Hakusan-cho 515-2605, Japan Office: R&D Ctr Toshiba Co, 1 Komukai Toshiba-cho, Kawasaki 210-8582, Japan

OKUMA, SATOSHI, physicist, educator; b. Hakodate, Hokkaido, Japan, May 1, 1959; s. Noboru and Teruko (Saikachi) O.; m. Akiko Osanai, Oct. 10, 1989; children: Gaku, Hikaru. BSc, U. Tokyo, 1982, MSc, 1984, DSc, 1987. Rsch. assoc. Tokyo Inst. Tech., 1987-91, assoc. prof., 1992—. Co-author: (book) Basic Physical Experiments (in Japanese), 1989; co-translator: Science Dictionary of Physics, 1994; contbr. articles to profl. jours. Grantee: Ministry of Edn., Sci., Sports and Culture, 1994-97, 99-2000, The Sumitomo Found, 1995, The Kawasaki Steel Found., 1996-97. Office: Tokyo Inst Tech, 2-12-1 Ohokayama Meguro-ku, Tokyo 152-8551, Japan

OKUMURA, FUKUICHIRO, anesthesiology educator; b. Osaka, Japan, Aug. 15, 1938; s. Takatsugu and Toshiko (Tabuchi) O.; m. Mutsuko Yoshikawa, Nov. 23, 1968; children: Ayako, Asako. MD, Osaka U., 1963, PhD, 1969. Intern Osaka Univ. Hosp., 1963-64, resident in surgery and anesthesiology, 1964-68; instr. Osaka U., 1968-71, lectr., 1973-76; fellow in cardiothoracic anesthesia Green Lane Hosp., Auckland, New Zealand, 1971-73; postdoctoral fellow Australian Nat. U., Canberra, 1976-78; chief anesthesiology Nat. Cardiovasc. Ctr., Osaka, 1979-89; prof. anesthesiology, chmn. dept. Yokohama (Japan) City U., 1989—. Editor-in-chief Jour. Anesthesia, 1995-98; contbr. articles to med. jours. including Anesthesia and Analgesia, Brit. Jour. Anaesthesia, Brain Rsch., Anesthesiology. Rsch. grantee Japan Ministry Edn., Sci., Sports and Culture, 1990-95. Mem. Japan Soc. Anesthesiology (diplomate, elder 1985—, bd. dirs. 1996-99), Japan Soc. Cardiovasc. Anesthesia (bd. dirs. 1996—, pres. 1997-98). Avocations: fishing, swimming, stamp collecting. Home: 365-7-201 Shiba-cho, Kanazawa-ward, Yokohama 236-0012, Japan Office: Yokohama City U Dept Anes, 3-9 Fukuura Kanazawa-ward, Yokohama 236-0004, Japan

OKUNGU, JERRY, broadcast company executive, media consultant; b. Kisumu, Nyanza, Kenya, May 19, 1952; s. Nelson Akumu and Rosa Oigo (Asande) O.; m. Lillian Akinyi Odoyo, July 10, 1993; children: Rima, Arnold, Norah, Sonya Awour, Xernona Oigo. EdB, U. Nairobi, 1976; diploma, Inst. Social Studies, The Netherlands, 1985. Tchr. Tchrs. Svc. Commn., Nairobi, 1979-84; mktg. mgr. Alliance Fin., Nairobi, 1985-86; sales and mktg. mgr. Kicomi Textiles, Kicomi (1983) Ltd., Kisumu, Kenya, 1986-89; mktg. mgr. Eveready Batteries, Eveready PLC, Nairobi, 1989-90; group mktg. mgr. Nation Media Group, Nairobi, 1991-98; dir. advt. sales Worldspace, Nairobi, 1998—; chmn. Stella Moka Found., Nairobi, 1982-84; coun. mem. World Coun. Internat. Advt., Nairobi, 1996-99; bd. dirs. Dynamic Comm., Nat. Media Trust, Kenya; exec. dir., Pan African Broadcasting Heritage and Achievement awards, Abjuta, 2000, Exact Powerhouse, Nairobi. Chmn. Awasi Sch. Bd., Kisumu, 1992-97. Recipient Ford Found. Ednl. award, Guelph U., 1983, UNESCO Ednl. award, The Netherlands, 1985. Mem. Internat. Advt. Assn. (chmn. 1995-99, convenor Africa conf. 1997, Pro-Democracy conf. 1998), Internat. Pub. Relations Assn., Am. Mgmt. Assn. Democrat. Avocations: travel, theatre, concerts, photography, dancing. E-mail: jerryokungu@hotmail.com, okora19@yahoo.com. Home: Outer Ring Fedha Estate, PO Box 59272, Nairobi Kenya Office: Exact Powerhouse, PO Box 79559 Chaica Rd, Nairobi Kenya

OKUNO, TSUTOMU, medical researcher; b. Sendai, Japan, Sept. 30, 1955; s. Noboru and Akiko (Hasegawa) O.; m. Yasuko Kitaura Okuno, Apr. 29, 1983; 2 children. MS, Tohoku U., Sendai, Japan, 1980, DEng, 1993. Rschr. Nat. Inst. Indsl. Health, Kawasaki, Japan, 1980-89, sr. rschr., 1989—; committeeman for safety and health Japan Welding Engring. Soc., Tokyo, 1994-97. Contb. articles to profl. jours. Mem. Japan Occupational Hygiene Assn., Japan Soc. for Occupational Health, Phys. Soc. Japan. Home: 6-39-18 Kanai, Tokyo 195-0072, Japan Office: Nat Inst Indsl Health, 6-21-1 Nagao Tama Ku, Kawasaki 214-8585, Japan

OKUYAMA, AKIRA, trading company executive; b. Tokyo, Dec. 8, 1947; s. Takatoshi and Fukika (Asanuma) O.; m. Satomi Sakamoto, May 1, 1982. B. Law, Keio-Gijyuku U., Tokyo, 1972. Asst. mgr. Kanematsu-Gosho Ltd., Tokyo, 1982-90; pres. New Materials & Components Co., Ltd., Tokyo, 1990—; v.p. H.A. Internat. Inc., Tokyo, 1998—. Buddhist. Avocations: music, travel, driving. Home: 1-22-7 Jiyugaoka Meguro-Ku, Tokyo 152-0035, Japan Office: New Materials & Components, 1-22-7 Jiyugaoka Meguro-Ku, Tokyo 152-0035, Japan

OLAFSSON, JON HJALTALIN, dermatology educator; b. Reykjavik, Iceland, July 12, 1949; s. Olafur and Arntrud (Jonsdottir) O.; m. Thorunn Thorhallsdottir, Jul. 15, 1972; children: Arntrud, Solveig. MD, U. Iceland, 1976; special degree dermatology, U. Gothenburg, Sweden, 1982, PhD, 1985. Specialist in dermatology Sahlgrens Hosp., Gothenburg, Sweden, 1982-85; chief outpatient clinic tchr. Schlgrens Hosp., Gothenburg, Sweden, 1982-85; chief outpatient clinic Heilsuvernrarstod, Reykjavik, 1986-88; chief outpatient clinic Nat. Univ. Hosp., Reykjavik, 1989—, chief outpatient and inpatient dept., 1997—; pvt. practice, Reykjavik, 1986—; assoc. prof. dermatology U. Iceland, Reykjavik, 1988—. Contbr. numerous articles to profl. jours. Fellow Am. Acad. Dermatology, Swedish Dermatology Soc., Finnish Dermatologic Soc., Icelandic Dermatology Soc.; mem. European Acad. Dermatology and Venerelogy (bd. dirs.). Home: Hraunton, 210 Gardabaer Iceland Office: Landspital Univ Hosp, Tverholt 18, 105 Reykjavik Iceland

OLAFSSON, OLAFUR, public health official, consultant; b. Reykjavik, Iceland, Nov. 11, 1928; s. Bjarnason and Asta (Olafsdottir) O.; m. Inga Olafsson, Feb. 19, 1959; 7 children. MD, U. Iceland; JPHD, London Sch. Hygiene, 1966. Cert. specialist in cardiology and internal medicine, Iceland. Chief physician Heart Prevention Clinic, Reykjavik, 1967-72; dir. gen. Pub. Health in Iceland, Reykjavik, 1972-98; assoc. prof. social medicine U. Iceland, Reykjavik, 1977-82; chmn. Icelandic Med. Coun., Reykjavik, 1972; mem. Icelandic CD, 1972. Editor Scandinavian Social Medicine; contbr. numerous articles to profl. jours. Decorated knight and grand falcon Icelandic Falcon Order; recipient Gold award Internat. Traffic Soc., Stockholm, 1980, gold award Iceland Traffic Medicine, 1998. em. Norse Traffic Medicine (hon.), Iceland Med. Assn. (hon.). Home: Grenimel 38, Reykjavik Iceland Office: Divsn Gen Pub Health, Laugavegur Iceland

OLAH, GEORGE ANDREW, chemist, educator; b. Budapest, Hungary, May 22, 1927; came to U.S., 1964, naturalized, 1970; . Julius and Magda (Krasznai) O.; m. Judith Agnes Lengyel, July 9, 1949; children: George John, Ronald Peter. PhD, Tech. U. Budapest, 1949, D (hon.), 1989; DSc (hon.), U. Durham, 1988, U. Munich, 1990, U. Crete, Greece, 1994, U. Szeged, Hungary, 1995, U. Veszprem, Hungary, 1995, Case Western Res. U., 1995, U. So. Calif., 1995, U. Montpellier, 1996, SUNY, 1998. Mem. faculty Tech. U. Budapest, 1949-54; assoc. dir. Ctrl. Chem. Rsch. Inst., Hungarian Acad. Scis., 1954-56; rsch. scientist Dow Chem. Can. Ltd., 1957-64, Dow Chem. Co., Framingham, Mass., 1964-65; prof. chemistry Case Western Res. U., Cleve., 1965-69, C.F. Mabery prof. rsch., 1969-77; Donald P. and Katherine B. Loker disting. prof. chemistry, dir. Hydrocarbon Rsch. Inst., U. So. Calif., L.A., 1977—; vis. prof. chemistry Ohio State U., 1963, U. Heidelberg, Germany, 1965, U. Colo., 1969, Swiss Fed. Inst. Tech., 1972, U. Munich, 1973, U. London, 1973-79, L. Pasteur U., Strasbourg, 1974, U. Paris, 1981; hon. vis. lectr. U. London, 1981-95; cons. to industry. Author: Friedel-Crafts Reactions, Vols. I-IV, 1963-64; (with P. Schleyer) Carbonium Ions, Vols. I-V, 1969-76, Friedel-Crafts Chemistry, 1973, Carbocations and Electrophilic Reactions, 1973, Halonium Ions, 1975; (with G.K.S. Prakash and J. Somer) Superacids, 1984; (with Prakash, R.E. Williams, L.D. Field and K. Wade) Hypercarbon Chemistry, 1987; (with R. Malthotra and S.C. Narang) Nitration, 1989, Cage Hydrocarbons, 1990; (with Wade and Williams) Electron Deficient Boron and Carbon Clusters, 1991; (with Chambers and Prakash) Synthetic Fluorine Chemistry, 1992; (with Molnar) Hydrocarbon Chemistry, 1995 (with Laali, Wang, Prakash) Onium Ions, 1998; also chpts. in books, numerous papers in field; patentee in field. Recipient Alexander von Humboldt Sr. U.S. Scientist award, 1979, Calif. Scientist of Yr. award, 1989, Pioneer of Chemistry award Am. Inst. Chemists, 1993; Mendeleev medal Russian Acad. Scis., 1992, Kapitsa medal Russian Acad. Natural Scis., 1995; Nobel prize in Chemistry, 1994; Guggenheim fellow 1972, 88. Fellow AAAS, Chem. Inst. Can., Brit. Chem. Soc. (hon., Centenary lectr. 1978); ; mem. NAS, Italian NAS Lincei, Royal Soc. London (fgn.), Royal Soc. Can., European Acad. Arts, Scis. and Humanities, Royal Chem. Soc. (hon.), Italy Chem. Soc. (hon.), Hungarian Acad. Sci. (hon.), Am. Chem. Soc. (award petroleum chemistry 1964, Leo Hendrik Baekeland award N.J. sect. 1966, Morley medal Cleve. sect. 1970, award Synthetic organic chemistry 1979, Roger Adams award in organic chemistry 1989, L. Arthur C. Cope award 2001). Home: 2252 Gloaming Way Beverly Hills CA 90210-1717 Office: U So Calif Labor Hydrocarbon Rsch Inst Los Angeles CA 90007

OLAITAN, ADEMOLA ABAYOMI, oral and maxillofacial surgeon; b. Ile-Ife, Nigeria, Aug. 22, 1957; s. Magbagbeola Adedayo Olaitan and Morenike Omilewo Elufisan; m. Taibat Iyabode Bello, Aug. 11, 1984; children: Akeem, Olamide (dec.), Ademola Jr., Olanrewaju, Oluwabukola. B Dental Surgery, U. Ibadan, Nigeria, 1980; diploma in dental surgery, Nat. Postgrad. Med. Coll., Nigeria, West African Coll. Surgeons. House surgeon Oyo State Health Coun., Ibadan, 1980-81; with nat. youth svc. Govt. Dental Clinic Dental Hdqrs., Ilorin, Nigeria, 1981-82; dental surgeon II Oyo State Health Coun., Ibadan, 1982-84; sr. house officer, registrar Univ. Coll. Hosp., Ibadan, 1984-86; sr. registrar Ahmadu Bello U. Tchg. Hosp., Kaduna, Nigeria, 1987-89; lectr. 1, cons. Ahmadu Bello U., Zaria, Nigeria, 1990-96, sr. lectr., 1996-99; chief cons. oral and maxillofacial surgeon Nat. Hosp. for Women and Children, Abuja, Nigeria, 1999—; mem. faculty bd. dental surgery Nat. Postgrad. Med. Coll. Nigeria, Lagos, 1993—; hon. cons. Ahmadu Bello U. Tchg. Hosp., 1990—. Contbr. articles to profl. jours. Sec. Chess Barons, Kaduna, 1987-92; asst. sec. Chapel of Goodnews, Kaduna, 1990-91. Mem. Med. and Dental Cons. Assn. Nigeria (sec. 1993-99), Nigerian Med. Assn. (asst. sec. gen. 1993), N.Y. Acad. Scis., Nigerian Med. Assn. (sec. 1990-92, sub-editor newsletter 1991), Kaduna State Chess Assn. (acting chmn. 1994-96, chmn. 1997-99). Avocations: chess, table tennis, lawn tennis, reading. Fax: 234 62 240 465. E-mail: olaitana@skannet.com. Home: Nabil Court Yedseram St, Maitama Abuja Nigeria Office: Nat Hosp, Plot 132 Ctrl Dist, Abuja PMB 425, Nigeria

OLAJUWON, HAKEEM ABDUL, professional basketball player; b. Lagos, Nigeria, Jan. 21, 1963; s. Salaam and Abike O. Student, U. Houston, 1980-84. With Houston Rockets, 1984—. Named to Sporting News All-Am. First Team, 1984, NBA All-Rookie Team, 1985, All-Star team, 1985-90, 92-94, All-NBA First Team, 1987-89, 93-94, NBA All-Defensive First Team, 1987-88, 90, 93-94; named MVP 1993-94, NBA Defensive Player of Yr., 1993-94, mem. NBA championship team, 1994-95; named MVP NBA finals, 1994-95; recipient award IBM, 1993. Office: Houston Rockets The Summit Two Greenway Plz Ste 400 Houston TX 77046-3865

OLAÑO, SERVILLANO SAN BUENAVENTURA, JR., chemical engineer, educator; b. Botolan, Zambales, The Philippines, Jan. 19, 1944; s. Servillano Gonzales Sr. and Consuelo Gonzaga San Buenaventura O.; m. Carmerina Daco, Dec. 23, 1978; children: Ma Carmina Aileen, Jerome Tristan. BS in Chem. Engring., U. St. Tomas, Manila, The Philippines, 1965; MEng. in Chem. Engring., U. of the Philippines, Manila, 1981; DEng. in Chem. Engring., Tokyo Inst. Tech., 1996. Lab. supr. Chem. Engring. Labs U. St. Tomas, Manila, The Philippines, 1969-74, prof., 1976-78; exec. dir. Indsl. Rsch. Devel. Ctr. De La Salle U., Manila, 1974-76; chmn. chem. engring. dept. De La Salle U., Manila, 1978-82, assoc. dean Coll. of Engring., 1982-89, dean Coll. of Engring., 1989-92, dir. Grad. Sch. of Engring., 1996-97, vice-dean Coll. Engring., 1997-98; rsch. Internat. Chem. Industries, Manila, 1970; cons. Edwardson Mfg. Co., Manila, 1976-78; accreditor Philippine Accrediting Assn. of Schs., Colls. and Univs., 1984—. Author: (book) Experiments in Unit Operations, 1992; co-author: Theory and Problems of Mass Transfer, 1983. Treas. Philippine Assn. Tech. Edn., Manila, 1988; bd. dirs. Philippine Productivity Movement, Manila, 1992. Named exchange scientist Japan Soc. for Promotion of Sci., 1986, 98, Univ. fellow, De La Salle U., 1988, Vis. Embassy of France in the Philippines, 1989. Mem. Japan Soc. of Chem. Engrs., Philippine Inst. of Chem. Engrs. Roman Catholic. Avocations: table tennis, badminton, chess. E-mail: coesbo@mail.dlsu.edu.ph. Home: 14 Dahlia St Pacita Complex, Laguna San Pedro 4023, The Philippines Office: De La Salle U, 2401 Taft Ave, Manila 1004, The Philippines

OLAOSEBIKAN, EBIKABOERE BOLANLE, law educator; b. Lagos, Nigeria, Mar. 4, 1959; d. Harrowell and Bolajoko (Sawyer) D.; m. Adebayo Olaosebikan, Aug. 28, 1993. BA, U. Lagos, 1983, LLB, 1987, LLM, 1992. Lectr. law Rivers State U. Sci. & Technology, Port Harcourt, Nigeria, 1989—. Mem. editl. bd. Health and Rights of Women, 1998—. Marriage counseling com. Four Square Gospel Ch., Port Harcourt, 1989. Mem. Fedn. Internat. Women Lawyers. Mem. Pentecostal Ch. Avocations: cooking, dancing, singing, acting. Office: Portharcourt Rivers State, PO Box 9727, Port Harcourt Nigeria

OLARIU, IOAN VASILE, civil engineer, educator; b. Deva, Romania, Feb. 16, 1943; Andrei and Elena (Nemes) O.; m. Felicia Claudia Moldovan; children: Mihaela Elena, Andrei Iulian. MS, Tech. U., Cluj-Napoca, Romania, 1966, PhD, 1980. From jr. asst. to prof. Tech. U., Cluj-Napoca, 1966-91, prof., 1991—; dir. Contur SRL, Cluj-Napoca, 1990—. Author: Structural Analysis, 1981, Génie Parasismique, 1983, Design of Concrete Structures, 1986, Earthquake Engineering, Vol. I, 1985, Vol. II, 1988, Vol. III, 1990 (prize Romanian Acad. Sci.). Recipient Prize Romanian Acad. Sci. Mem. ASCE (stds. com. on seismic isolation sys.), Internat. Ctr. for Disaster-Mitigation Engring., Computer-Aided Design Assn., Assn. Francaise du génie parasismique, European Assn. of Earthquake Engring. (task group seismic structural control). Avocations: amateur radio, internet. Home: Bolintineanu 24, 3400 Cluj Napoca Romania Office: Tech U, Daicoviciu 15, 3400 Cluj-Napoca Romania

OLARU, MARIA, olympic athlete; b. Suceava, Romania, June 4, 1982. Mem. gymnastics team Romania; co-winner second pl. in vault European Championship, 1998; winner gold all-around World Championship, Tianjin, China, 1999, winner team gold, 1999, winner bronze in vault, 1999; winner gold team all-around Olympics, Sydney, Australia, 2000. Office: Romanian Gymnastics Ctr Romanian Studies, Ofcl Postal I Casuta Postala 108, 6600 Iasi Romania*

OLARU, RADU, electrical engineering educator; b. Botosani, Romania, Feb. 12, 1949; s. Petru and Maria (Abalasei) O.; m. Mariana Popescu, Mar. 23, 1956; children: Cristian, Vlad. Univ. degree, Tech. U., Iasi, 1972, PhD, 1994. Engr. Mill of Footwear, Suceava, Romania, 1972-74; sci. rschr. Inst. R&D for Tech. Physics, Iasi, 1974-79; asst. prof. Tech. U., Iasi, 1979-87, lectr., 1987-95, assoc. prof., 1995-99, prof. elec. engring., 1999—. Author: Magnetic Fluid Transducers and Devices for Measuring and Control, 1997; contbr. articles to profl. jours.; inventor in field. Tech. U. Faculty Coun. fellow, 1996-2000. Orthodox. Achievements include contributions to investigation and development of magnetic fluid based sensors and transducers. Avocation: recreational activities. Home: Sf Lazar 49 Bl A3, 6600 Iasi Romania Office: Tech Univ Fac Elec Engring, 53 Mangeron Blvd, 6600 Iasi Romania

OLASZ, LAJOS, dental surgeon, oncology researcher; b. Szegvár, Hungary, June 21, 1948; s. Lajos and Lajosné (Juhász) Szatmári; m. Aranka Fejes, Mar. 23, 1974; children: Lajos, Katinka. MD cum laude, Szent-Gyorgyi Albert Med. UJ., Szeged, Hungary, 1973; DMD, Med. U. Pécs, Hungary, 1976; PhD, Hungarian Acad. Scis., Budapest, 1994. Clin. physician Med. U., Pécs, Hungary, 1973-76, asst. lectr., 1976-87, lectr., 1987-97, assoc. prof., 1997—; cons. Orvosi Hetilap, Budapest, 1992. Contbr. articles to profl. jours. Mem. Hungarian Dental Soc. (dir. 1978—), Hungarian Oral and Maxillofacial Surgery Soc. (sec. 1990-96, dir. 1996—), Hungarian Scientific Acad. (corp.). Avocations: fishing, swimming. Office: Dischka 5, 7621 Pécs Hungary

OLAYAN, SULIMAN SALEH, finance company executive; b. Onaiza, Saudi Arabia, Nov. 5, 1918; s. Saleh and Heya (Al Ghanem) O.; m. Mary Perdikis, Feb. 22, 1974; children: Khaled, Hayat, Hutham, Lubna. Student, Pub. Schs., Bahrain Islands. Rsch. specialist Arabian Am. Oil Co., Saudi Arabia, 1937-47; founder, chmn. The Olayan Group, Saudi Arabia, 1947—; included in Olayan Group: Olayan Investments Co. Establishment, Olayan Europe Ltd., Olayan Devel. Corp., Ltd., Olayan Am. Corp., Crescent Holding GmbH, Olayan Financing Co., Olayan Saudi Holding Co.; mem. supreme coun. Saudi Arabian Oil Co., 1989—; founding chmn., 1977-89, bd. dirs. The Saudi Brit Bank, Riyadh, Saudi Arabia, 1977-89, internat. adv. bd. Am. Internat. Group, 1982-99; mem. internat. coun. J.P. Morgan & Co., Inc., N.Y., 1979-90; internat. councillor, mem. adv. bd. Ctr. for Strategic and Internat. Studies, Washington, 1977-95; bd. dirs. CS First Boston, Inc., 1988-95. Mem. internat. adv. coun. SRI Internat., Menlo Park, Calif., 1965—; alumnus mem. The Rockefeller U. Coun., N.Y.C., 1978—; trustee Am. U. of Beirut, 1979-84; co-chmn. U.S.-Saudi Arabian Businessmen's Dialogue under the U.S.-Saudi Arabian Joint Commn. on Econ. Cooperation, 1980-92. Decorated Knight Comdr. Brit. Empire, 1987, comdr. 1st class Royal Order of the Polar Star (Sweden), 1988; recipient Great Cross of the Order of Merit (Spain), 1984, medal of honor Madrid C. of C., 1985. Mem. Internat. Indsl. Conf., San Francisco (internat. chmn. 1985), Inst. for Internat. Econs., Washington (bd. dirs.), The Conf. Bd. of N.Y. (internat. counselor emeritus), Riyadh Handicapped Children Assn. (vice chmn. 1983-88), Equestrian Club (Riyadh), Knickerbocker Club (N.Y.C.), N.Y. Athletic Club (N.Y.C.), Pacific Union and Bohemian Clubs (San Francisco), Royal Automobile Club (London). Fax: 212-486-4001. Office: The Olayan Group, PO Box 8772, Riyadh 11492, Saudi Arabia also: Olayan Am Corp 505 Park Ave Fl 11 New York NY 10022-1106

OLAYIWOLA-OLOSUM, BOLA ADIGUN, priest; b. Osogbo, Nigeria, Oct. 13, 1963; arrived in Germany, 1994; s. Iyanda and Anike (Orisawayi) Olayiwola-O.; m. Birgit Kolling, June 29, 1993; children: Sangolana, Ogunsakin; m. Annelie Pungs, Mar. 1, 1996; m. Monika Passon, Sept. 4, 1997. BA, Obafemi Awolowd U., Ife, Nigeria, 1990; Diploma, Nigerian Inst. of Journalism, Lagos, 1993; MA, U. Lagos, Nigeria, 1995; BA, Wilhelms U., Munster, Germany, 1997. Pres. Yoruba Heritage Club, Osogibo, Nigeria, 1983-90; high priest Ibile Faith Soc., Osogibo, 1984—; parliament mem. Ace Student Union, Omdo, Nigeria, 1987-88; pres. Osun State Student U., Omdo, 1989-90; sec. Yoruba Students Assn. of Nigeria, Omdo, 1988-89; pub. Akede Asa Mag., Osogbo, 1987; tchr. Lagos State Govt., Nigeria, 1990-94; chmn. Asala Comm. Bank, Osogbo, Nigeria, 1997—, Adigun Olesun Troupe, Munster, 1995—; patron IFA Art Trust, London, 1997—. Pub. V. Ase Mag. founder, dir. Iyadudu Ctrr. Yoruba Culture, Ibile Faith Soc. Mem. World Trade Ctr., Nigerian Union of Tchrs., Ibile Faith Soc. Yoruba. Avocations: travel, reading, writing, people, pub. speaking. Fax: 490 251 1366883. Office: Ibile Faith Soc, Dechanaistr 24, 48145 Münster Germany

OLAZABAL, JOSE MARIA, professional golfer; b. Fuenterrabla, Spain, Feb. 5, 1966. Profl. golfer PGA European Tour, 1985—; mem. European Ryder Cup Team, 1987, 89, 91, 93, 97, Kirin Cup Team, 1987, Four Tours World Championship Team, 1989, 90, World Cup Team, 1989, Dunhill Cup Team, 1986, 87, 88, 89, 92. Winner Italian Amateur award, 1983, Spanish Amateur award, 1983, European Masters-Swiss Open, 1986, Sanyo Open, 1986, Belgian Open, 1988, German Masters, 1988, Tenerlfe Open, 1989, Dutch Open, 1989, Benson & Hedges Internat., 1990, Irish Open, 1990, Lancome Trophy, 1990, Visa Talhoyo Club Masters, 1989, 90, Catalonia Open, 1991, Turespana Open de Tenerlfe, 1992, Open Mediterrania, 1992, British Boys Champion, 1993, British Amateur Champion, 1994, Masters, 1994, Mediterrania pen, 1994, Volvo PGA, 1994, British Youth Champion, 1995, Open Ferrier de Paris, 1995, Turespana Masters, 1997; tour victories include NEC World Series of Golf, 1990, The Internat., 1991, Dubai Desert Classic, 1998, Masters, 1999, Benson & Hedges Internat. Open, 2000. Avocations: music, cinema. Office: PGA European Tour, Wentworth Dr Virginia Water, Surrey GU25 4LX, England

OLBRICK, VALERIE LYN, management consultant, information technologist; b. Pitts., Feb. 9, 1959; d. Kenneth Donald and LaVerne Estelle (Aiken) O. BS, Grove City Coll., 1981. Sr. telecomm. analyst Timken Co., Canton, Ohio, 1981-85; network planning mgr. Leaseway Transp. Inc., Cleve., 1985-87; group mgr. Network Strategies, Fairfax, Va., 1987-88; sr. mgr. Ernst & Young, L.A., 1988-95; prin. Ernst & Young, N.Y.C., 1995, dir. tech. planning and deployment Internat. divsn., 1995—. Avocations: sailing, skiing, bicycling, gardening, reading. Office: Ernst & Young Internat 787 7th Ave Fl 14 New York NY 10019-6085

OLCZAK, PAUL VINCENT, psychology educator; b. Buffalo, N.Y., May 25, 1943; s. Vincent Henry and Helen (Babula) O.; m. Marie Rose Oliveri, Oct. 20, 1973; children: Paul V. II, Patrick J., Drew M. MA, No. Ill. U., 1969, PhD, 1972. Clin. psychologist Family Ct. Psychiat. Clinic, Buffalo, 1975-77, cons. supervisory psychologist, 1977—; supr. psychol. svcs. Hopevale, Inc., Hamburg, N.Y., 1977-89; clin. psychologist Amherst (N.Y.) Police Dept., 1989—; asst. prof. psychology SUNY, Geneseo, 1977-83, assoc. prof. psychology, 1983-90, prof. psychology, 1990—, chairperson, 1999—; clin. psychologist child and adolescent psychiatry Niagara Falls Meml. Hosp., 1996—. Co-editor: Community Mediation, 1991; contbg. author: The POI in Clinical Situations: A Review, 1991, Self-actualization-Polemics Sur-

rounding Its Use, 1991; contbr. articles to profl. jours./publs. Mem. APA, Ea. Psychol. Assn., Midwestern Psychol. Assn., Psychonomic Soc., Soc. Exptl. Social Psychology, Internat. Assn. for Conflict Mgmt., Psi Chi, Sigma Xi. Home: 150 Briarhill Rd Buffalo NY 14221-1811 Office: SUNY Dept Psychology Geneseo NY 14454

OLD, JOHN MICHAEL, molecular geneticist; b. London, Apr. 15, 1949; s. John William and Florence Mary (Straw) O.; m. Ruth Jean Barwell, July 7, 1974; 1 child, Gillian Sarah. BSc, Liverpool (Eng.) U., 1971, PhD, 1974. State registered clin. scientist in molecular genetics. Med. Rsch. Coun. rsch. fellow Nuffield dept. clin. medicine Oxford (Eng.) U., 1974-79; reader in hematology; Med. Rsch. Coun. staff scientist, unit molecular haematology John Radcliffe Hosp., Oxford, 1979-81, clin. scientist Nat. Haemoglobinopathy Reference Svc., 1981—; mem. Birthright Rsch. Adv. Com., 1990-91. Mem. editorial bd. Jour. Prenatal Diagnosis, Molecular and Cellular Probes; author 10 chpts. in books; contbr. numerous articles to profl. jours. Asst. county commr. The Scout Assn., Oxford, 1991-97. Fellow Royal Coll. Pathologists (chmn. panel of examiners in genetics 1999—); mem. Biochem. Soc., Cin. Molecular Genetics Soc. (sec. 1988-91). Avocations: mountaineering, science fiction. Office: Inst Molecular Medicine, John Radcliffe Hosp, Oxford OX3 9DS, England

OLDENBURG, CLAES THURE, artist; b. Stockholm, Sweden, Jan. 28, 1929; s. Gosta and Sigrid Elisabeth (Lindforss) O.; m. Patricia Joan Muschinski, Apr. 13, 1960 (div. Apr. 1970); m. Coosje van Bruggen, July 22, 1977. B.A., Yale, 1951; student, Art Inst., Chgo., 1952-54. One-man shows include Reuben Gallery, N.Y.C., 1960, Green Gallery, N.Y.C., 1962, Sidney Janis Gallery, N.Y.C., 1964-70, Galerie Ileana Sonnabend, Paris, 1964, Robert Fraser Gallery, London, 1966, Moderna Museet, Stockholm, 1966, 77, Mus. Contemporary Art, Chgo., 1967, 77, Irving Blum Gallery, Los Angeles, 1968, Mus. Modern Art, N.Y.C., 1969, U. Calif. at Los Angeles Art Gallery, 1970, Stedelijk Mus., Amsterdam, 1970, 77, Tate Gallery, London, 1970, Nelson-Atkins Mus., Kansas City, 1972, Art Inst. Chgo., 1973, Leo Castelli Gallery, N.Y.C., 1974, 76, 80, 90, Kunstmus., Basel, 1992, Margo Leavin Gallery, Los Angeles, 1975, 76, 78, 88, Art Gallery of Toronto, Ont., 1976, Centre Georges Pompidou Musée National d'Art Moderne, Paris, 1977, Kröller-Muller Mus., 1979, Mus. Ludwig, Cologne, 1979, Wave Hill, Bronx, N.Y., 1984, Pace Gallery, 1992, 94, Nat. Gallery of Art, Washington, 1995, Mus. Contemporary Art, L.A., 1995, Solomon R. Guggenheim Mus., N.Y.C., 1995, Kunst und Ausstellungshalle der Bundersrepublik Deutschland, Bonn, 1996, Hayward Gallery, London, 1996; group shows include Martha Jackson Gallery, N.Y.C., 1960, 61, Dallas Mus. Contemporary Art, 1961, 62, Sidney Janis Gallery, 1962, 64, Inst. Contemporary Arts, London, 1963, Art Inst. Chgo., 1962, 63, Allen Art Mus. Oberlin (Ohio) Coll., 1963, Mus. Modern Art, N.Y.C., 1963, 88, 90, 91, Washington Gallery Modern Art, 1963, Am. Pavilion, Venice, 1964, Moderna Museet, Stockholm, 1964, Gulbenkian Found. Tate Gallery, London, 1964, Rochester (N.Y.) Meml. Mus., 1964-65, Worcester (Mass.) Mus., 1965, Met. Mus. Art, N.Y.C., 1969, Walker Art Center, 1975, others, numerous commd. works, rep. permanent collections at, Guggenheim Mus., N.Y.C., Mus. Modern Art, Albright-Knox Art Gallery, Buffalo, Centre Georges Pompidou, Stedelijk Mus., Tate Gallery, Mus. Ludwig, Moderna Museet, Rose Art Mus. Brandeis U., Waltham, Mass., Oberlin Coll., Nat. Gallery Art, Canberra, Art Gallery Ont., Toronto, Art Inst. Chgo., Hirshorn Gallery and Sculpture Garden, Whitney Mus. Modern Art, N.Y.C., Mus. Contemporary Art, L.A., many others; Numerous outdoor works in corporate and private collections. (Recipient Sculpture award Am. Ann., Chgo. Art Inst. 1976, medal AIA 1977); author: Store Days, 1967, Proposals for Monuments and Buildings, 1969, Notes in Hand, 1971, Raw Notes, 1973, Multiples in Retrospect, 1991, Claes Oldenburg Coosje van Bruggen: Large Scale Projects, 1994, Claes Oldenburg Coosje van Bruggen, 1999. Recipient Sculpture award Brandeis U., 1971, Skowhegan Sculpture medal, 1972, Wolf Prize in Arts, 1989, Jack I. and Lillian Poses medal Brandeis U., 1993, Lifetime Achievement award Contemporary Sculpture Internat. Sculpture Ctr., 1994. Mem. Am. Acad. & Inst. Arts & Letters. Office: care Pace Gallery 32 E 57th St 4th Fl New York NY 10022-2513

OLDENBURG, RICHARD ERIK, auction house executive; b. Stockholm, Sept. 21, 1933; came to U.S., 1936, naturalized, 1959; s. Gösta and Sigrid Elisabeth (Lindforss) O.; m. Harriet Lisa Turnure, Dec. 17, 1960 (dec. Apr. 1998). A.B., Harvard U., 1954. Mgr. design dept. Doubleday & Co., Inc., N.Y.C., 1958-61; mng. editor trade div. Macmillan Co., Inc., N.Y.C., 1961-69; dir. publs. Mus. Modern Art, N.Y.C., 1969-72, dir., 1972-94, dir. emeritus, hon. trustee, 1995—; chmn. Sotheby's North and South America, N.Y.C., 1995-2000, hon. chmn., 2000—. Served with AUS, 1956-58. Home: 447 E 57th St New York NY 10022-3064 Office: Sotheby's Inc 1134 York Ave New York NY 10021-8300

OLDENBURG, RONALD TROY, lawyer; b. Eldora, Iowa, June 2, 1935; s. Lorenz Frank and Bess Louise (Lewis) O.; m. Vickie Yu; children: John, Keith, Mark. BA, U. N.C., 1957; postgrad., Brunnsvik Folkhogskola, Sorvik, Sweden, 1957-58; JD, U. Miss., 1961. Bar: Miss. 1961, Hawaii 1975. Mgr. Continental Travel Svc., Chapel Hill, N.C., 1956-57, Meridian Travel Svc., Raleigh, N.C., 1961, Linmark Internat. Devel., Seoul, 1972-74; fgn. atty. Li Chun Law Office, Taipei, Taiwan, 1965-67; pvt. practice, Taipei, 1967-72, Honolulu, 1975—. Compiler: International Directory of Birth, Death, Marriage and Divorce Records, 1985; contbr. articles on immigration law to legal jours. Capt. JAGC, USAF, 1962-65. Mem. Am. Immigration Lawyers Assn. Office: 737 Bishop St Ste 2400 Honolulu HI 96813-3215 also: 17800 Castleton St Ste 588 City Industry CA 91748-5758

OLDENZIEL, RUTH, history educator, researcher; b. Amsterdam, The Netherlands, May 13, 1958; d. Jan-Germ and Rosa Rachel (Knorringa) O.; 1 child, Alexander. BA, MA in History, U. Amsterdam, The Netherlands, 1985; Ma in Am. Studies, Smith Coll., Northampton, 1982; MA in Am. History, U. Mass., Amherst, 1983; PhD in Am. History, Yale U., 1992. Postdoc. U. Twente, The Netherlands, 1991-92; assoc. prof. U. Amsterdam, The Netherlands, 1992—; founder, pres. Soc. Gender and Tech., The Netherlands, 1993-99. Author: Making Technology Masculine, 1999; editor: Schoon Genoeg, 1998, Crossing Boundaries, Building Bridges, 2000. TV commentator Am. Polit. Affairs, The Netherlands. Mem. Soc. of History and Tech. Home: Weesperzyde 105, 1091EM Amsterdam The Netherlands Office: University of Amsterdam, Rokin 84, 1012KX Amsterdam The Netherlands

OLDER, JAY JUSTIN, ophthalmic plastic surgeon; b. Jersey City, N.J., Feb. 7, 1940; m. Lois Rosner; children: Benjamin, Jessica. AB, Rutgers U., 1961; MD, Stanford U., 1966. Diplomate Am. Bd. Ophthalmology. Intern, resident in internal medicine Cornell U./Bellevue Hosp. Ctr., N.Y.C., 1968; resident in ophthalmology Stanford (Calif.) U., 1973; fellow in ophthalmic plastic and reconstructive surgery Stanford U., San Francisco, 1974; pvt. practice Tampa, Fla., 1974—; clin. prof. ophthalmology U. South Fla. Coll. Medicine, Tampa, 1975—, dir. oculoplastic svc., 1974-89, 90—. Author: Eyelid Tumors: Clinical Diagnosis and Surgical Treatment, 1987. Fellow Am. Acad. Ophthalmology (Sr. Honor award 1995), Am. Soc. Ophthalmic Plastic and Reconstructive Surgery (pres. 1987, sec. 1983-84), ACS; mem. Phi Beta Kappa (v.p. Greater Tampa Bay Assn. 1995-96). Office fax: 813 977-2611. Office: Ophthalmic Plastic Surgery Assocs 4444 E Fletcher Ave Ste D Tampa FL 33613-4937

OLDERMAN, MURRAY, columnist, cartoonist; b. N.Y.C., Mar. 27, 1922; s. Max and Jennie (Steinberg) O.; m. Nancy J. Calhoun, Feb. 28, 1945; children: Lorraine Imlay, Marcia Lynn, Mark. BJ, U. Mo., 1943; BS in Humanities, Stanford U., 1944; MJ, Northwestern U., Evanston, Ill., 1947. Sports editor Rockland Leader, Spring Valley, N.Y., 1938-40; cartoonist, writer McClatchy Newspapers, Sacramento, 1947-51, Mpls. Star-Tribune, 1951-52; cartoonist, writer, exec. editor Newspaper Enterprise Assn., N.Y.C., 1952-87; asst. prof. San Francisco State U., 1974-80, U. Redlands, Calif., 1987, U. Oreg., Eugene, 1991-97; sr. editor Palm Springs (Calif.) Life, 1995—; project dir. Hall of Fame, Oakland (Calif.) Raiders, 1995-99. Author: (books) The Pro Quarterback, 1966, The Running Back, 1969, The Defenders, 1972, Tennis Clinic, 1979, Super: "Just Win, Baby", 1984, Starr, 1987; (book series) My Best Year, 1969-71. Pres. Calif. Alliance for Mentally Ill, Sacramento, 1994-95. Lt. M.I., U.S. Army, 1944-45, ETO. Recipient Bert McGrane award Football Writers Assn. Am., 1991; named to Nat. Sportswriters and Sportscasters Hall of Fame, Salisbury, N.C., 1993, Internat. Jewish Sports Hall of Fame, Netanya, Israel, 1997. Mem. Nat. Cartoonists Soc. (Best Sports Cartoonist 1973, 78), Golf Writers Assn. Am. (Best Feature 1982), Pro Football Writers Assn. (Dick McCann award 1979, Best Feature 1983), Baseball Writers of Am., Basketball Writers of Am. (Best Feature 1959), Football Writers Assn. Am. (pres. 1960-61), Phi Beta Kappa. Democrat. Avocations: tennis, photography. Home: 832 Inverness Dr Rancho Mirage CA 92270-1451

OLDFIELD, FRANK EUGENE, retired aerospace engineering executive; b. Ft. Morgan, Colo., Apr. 20, 1931; s. Henry Johnstone and Florence Ona (King) O.; m. Mary Rose Barrett, Sept. 20, 1975; children: Vanessa L. Lawson, Perry D. BS in Electronics, San Diego State U., 1958. Aerospace engr. Teledyne Ryan Aero., San Diego, 1958-63, computer sys. mgr., 1963-68, advanced projects dir., 1968-88, v.p., chief engr., 1988-93, ret., 1993—; aerospace cons. AAI Corp., Hunt Valley, Md., 1988-94. Author: (book) Mankind Metamorphosis, 1997. Mem., v.p., treas., pres. Smoketree Condo. Assn., 1988-98. Sgt. U.S. Army, 1955-58. Recipient Pioneer award Assn. for Unmanned Vehicle Sys., 1987; tribute to Frank Oldfield recorded in Congl. Records, Ho. of Reps., 1987. Mem. Early Am. Coppers. Republican. Home: 6050 Henderson Dr Unit 14 La Mesa CA 91942-4012

OLDHAM, CHRISTOPHER RUSSELL, communications executive; b. Basingstoke, U.K., Sept. 18, 1946; came to U.S., 1986; s. Henry Russell Oldham and Esme Grace (Craufurd) Anderson; m. Elizabeth Jacoba Graham, Jan. 9, 1971 (div. 1978); children: Justin, Mark; m. Janet Patricia Gough, Dec. 9, 1978; children: Carro, Nicholas. Student, Rugby Sch., U.K., 1965, Madrid U., 1967, London Bus. Sch., 1972. Mgmt. exec. Guthrie & Co. (U.K.) Ltd., London and Singapore, 1973-74; mktg. dir. Guthrie & Co. (U.K.) Ltd., London, 1974-75; mng. dir. William Armes & Son, Sudbury, U.K., 1975-76; chmn. Transmarine Air Holdings Ltd., Luton, U.K., 1976-80; pres., owner S.C.E.A. Du Chateau De Lacaze, Gabarret, France, 1980-87; corp. devel. dir. Chateaux Shippers Ltd., London, 1984-95; pres. Wine Link Inc., San Diego, 1987-95; pres., CEO Global Link Corp., 1999—; cons. Transmarine Holdings Ltd., London, 1980-97; chmn. Internat. Wine Consortium, 1995-99. Author: Armagnac and Eaux-De-Vie, 1986; author, editor (bi-monthly pub.) Wine Line, 1990-98; contbr. articles to profl. jours. Hist. rsch. Societe Borda, Pau, France, 1981-87; mem. Worshipful Co. of Glaziers, City of London, Liveryman; bd. trustees New Hampton Sch., N.H., 1994-97. Capt. U.K. Cavalry, 1967-71. Recipient Freedom of City of London by Lord Mayor of London, 1975. Mem. British Inst. of Mgmt., Confrerie Cadets de Gascogne, Cavalry Club London, Southwestern Yacht Club (San Diego). Avocations: ocean sailing, wine collecting, golf, computing, literature. Office: Global Link Corp PO Box 2275 South Hamilton MA 01982-0275

OLDHAM, GAVIN DAVID REDVERS, brokerage house executive; b. London, May 5, 1949; s. David George Redvers and Penelope Barbara O.; m. Virginia Russell, May 17, 1975; children: 4 daughters. MA in Mgmt. Studies, Cambridge U., Eng., 1971. Systems analyst CSE (aircraft svcs.) Ltd., Oxford, Eng., 1971-76; office mgr. Wedd, Durlacher, Mordaunt, London, 1976-86, ptnr., 1984-86; secretariat Barclays, De Zoete, Wedd, London, Eng., 1984-86; CEO Barclayshare, Ltd., Watford, Eng., 1985-89, chmn., 1989-90; CEO, chmn. The Share Ctr. Ltd., Tring, Eng., 1990—; chmn. Share plc, 2000—. Elected mem. Gen. synod Anglican Ch., 1995—, ch. commr., 1999—. Mem. Inst. Dirs London, Leander Club. Avocations: rowing, hill walking, sailing. Office: The Share Ctr Ltd, St Peter's House Mkt Pl, Herfdshr Tring HP23 5XD, England

OLDHAM, JOHN, family physician; b. Manchester, Eng., Aug. 17, 1953; s. Kenneth and Marion (Booth) O.; m. Julia Robinson, Oct. 17, 1987. MB, BChir, Manchester (Eng.) U., 1978; MBA with distinction, Manchester Bus. Sch., 1992; diploma in child health, London U., 1980. Ho. physician Manchester Royal Infirmary, 1978-79; ho. surgeon Stepping Hill Hosp., Stockport, U.K., 1979; sr. ho. officer Royal Manchester Children's Hosp., 1979-80; gen. practice registrar Darbishore House, Manchester, 1980-81; sr. ho. officer St. Marys Hosp. for Women, Manchester, 1982-83; prin. gen. practitioner Dr. Rowley & Ptnrs., Glossop, U.K., 1984-89; sr. ptnr. Manor House Surgery, Glossop, 1989—, head natural primary care devel. team, 1999—; founder, chair N.W. GP Tng. Orgn., Eng., 1979-81; advisor Mersey Regional Health Authority, Liverpool, Eng., 1989-91; med. advisor Derbyshire Family Health Svcs., Derby, Eng., 1990-95; primary care advisor NHS Hdqrs., London, 1996-99. Civil chair SDP Health and Social Svcs. Group, London, 1982-87. Mem. Royal Coll. Gen. Practitioners. Avocations: cooking, hiking, sailing, Blues music. Office: Manor House Surgery, Manor St, Glossop SK13 8PS, England

OLDMAN, GARY, actor; b. London, Mar. 21, 1958; m. Lesley Manville (div.); 1 child, Alfred; m. Uma Thurman (div.); m. Donga Fiorentino; children: Guliver, Charlie. BA, Rose Buford Coll. Speech and Drama, 1979. Appearances include (TV movies) Remembrance, 1982, Meantime, 1984, Honest, Decent and True, 1985, Fallen Angels: Dead End for Delia, 1993 (Cable Ace award, Actor in a Dramatic Series); (video) Since I Don't Have You by Guns n' Roses, 1994; (film) Sid and Nancy, 1986, Prick Up Your Ears, 1987 (Brit. Acad. Film and TV Arts nomination 1988), Track 29, 1988, We Think the World of You, 1988, Criminal Law, 1988, Paris by Night, 1989, Chattahoochee, 1990, State of Grace, 1990, Rosencrantz and Guildenstern Are Dead, 1991, JFK, 1991, Bram Stoker's Dracula, 1992, True Romance, 1993, Romeo is Bleeding, 1994, The Professional, 1994, Immortal Beloved, 1994, Murder in the First, 1995, The Scarlet Letter, 1995, Basquiat, 1996, The Fifth Element, 1997, Air Force One, 1997, Lost in Space, 1998, Nil By Mouth, 1998 (also dir., author), The Contender (also exec. prodr.), Anasazie Moon, 1999 (also prodr.); (theatre) Massacre at Paris, 1980, Chinchilla, 1980, Desperado Corner, 1980, A Waste of Time, 1980, Summit Conference, 1982, Rat in the Skull, 1984, The Pope's Wedding, 1984 (Drama Mag. Best Actor award 1985, Fringe Best Newcomer award 1985-86), The War Plays, 1985, The Desert Air, 1985, Women Beware Women, 1986, Real Dreams, 1986, Serious Money, 1987. Recipient Outstanding Brit. Film award Brit. Acad., Best Screenplay award Brit. Acad., Dirs. prize Edinburgh Festival Channel Four, Best Dir. prize Cannes Film Festival, Best Actor and Best Newcomer, Brit. Ind. Film Awards Best Actors. Office: c/o Douglas J Urbanski Douglas Mgmt Inc 515 N Robertson Blvd Los Angeles CA 90048-1730

OLDROYD, DAVID ROGER, historian of science; b. Luton, Eng., Jan. 20, 1936; arrived in Australia, 1969; s. Kenneth Ainsley and Gladys (Buckley) O.; m. Elizabeth Jane Dawes, Sept. 5, 1958; children: Benjamin Paul, Nicholas. BA, Cambridge (Eng.) U., 1958, MA, 1962; MSc, London U., 1967; PhD, U. NSW, 1974, DLitt, 1993. Sci. master John Lyon Sch., Harrow, Eng., 1958-62, Hastings (New Zealand) Boys H.S., 1962-65, Christ's Coll., Christchurch, New Zealand, 1966-69; lectr. Sch. Sci. and Tech. Studies U. NSW, 1969-76, sr. lectr., 1976-85, assoc. prof., 1986-94, prof., 1995-96, hon. vis. prof., 1996—. Author: Darwinian Impacts, 1980, The Arch of Knowledge, 1986, The Highlands Controversy, 1990, Thinking About the Earth, 1996, Sciences of the Earth, 1998; contbr. articles to profl. jours. Recipient Sue Tyler Friedman medal Geol. Soc., 1994, History of Geology award Geol. Soc. Am., 1999; fellow Geol. Soc., Australian Acad. Humanities. Mem. Australasian Assn. for History, Philosophy and Social Studies of Sci. (pres. 1993-95), Internat. Commn. on History of Geol. Scis. (sec.-gen. 1996—), History of Earth Scis. Soc. (councilor 1993-96). Avocation: playing cello. Home: 28 Cassandra Ave, Saint Ives NSW 2075, Australia Office: Univ NSW, Sydney NSW 2052, Australia

OLDSHUE, JAMES Y., chemical engineering consultant; b. Chgo., Apr. 18, 1925; s. James and Louise (Young) O.; m. Betty Ann Wiersema, June 14, 1947; children: Paul, Richard, Robert. B.S. in Chem. Engring., Ill. Inst. Tech., 1947, M.S., 1949, Ph.D. in Chem. Engring., 1951. Registered engr., N.Y. With Mixing Equipment Co., Rochester, N.Y., 1950-92, dir. research, 1960-63, tech. dir., 1963-70, v.p. mixing tech., 1970-92; pres. Oldshue Techs. Internat., Inc., Rochester, N.Y., 1992—; adj. prof. chem. engring. Beijing Inst. Chem. U., 1992—. Author: Fluid Mixing Technology, 1983; contbr. chpts. and articles to books and jours. Chmn. budget com. Internat. div. YMCA; bd. dirs. Rochester YMCA. Served with AUS, 1945-47. Recipient 1st Disting. Svc. award N.E. YMCA Internat. Com., 1979, J.E. Purkynse medal Czech Republic Acad. Sci.; named Rochester Engr. of Yr., 1980. Fellow AIChE (pres. 1979, treas. 1983-89, chmn. internat. activities com. 1989-92, Founders award 1981, Eminent Chem. Engr. award 1983, Svc. to Soc. award 1989, F.J. and Dorothy van Antwerpen award for Svc. to the Inst. 1999); mem. NAE, Am. Assn. Engring. Socs. (chmn. 1985, K.A. Roe award 1987), Am. Chem. Soc., Internat. Platform Assn., World Congress Chem. Engrs. (v.p. 1986, pres. 1992-96), N.Am. Mixing Forum (chmn. 1990-93, Mixing Achievement rsch. award 1992), Interam. Confedn. Chem. Engrs. (sec. gen. 1991-93, v.p. 1993-95, pres. 1995-96), Victor Marquez award 1983), Rochester Engring. Soc. (pres. 1992-93, Rochester Engr. of Yr. 1980). Mem. Reformed Ch. in Am. (gen. program coun.). Achievements include design and scale-up procedures in field of fluid mixing. Home and Office: 141 Tyringham Rd Rochester NY 14617-2522

OLDSTEIN, CHARLES RODNEY, small business owner; b. Apr. 12, 1960. AS, Guam C.C., 1988; student, U. North Tex., 1989-90. Owner, prodr. Oldsein Prodn. Studios, Jefferson, La., 1997—. Office: Oldstein Prodn Studios 839 S Clearview Pkwy # 305 Jefferson LA 70121-3119

O'LEARY, (DENIS) BRENDAN, political science educator, journalist; b. Cork, Ireland, Mar. 19, 1958; s. Donal Joseph and Margery (O'Mahony) O'L. BA in Philosophy, Politics and Econs., Oxford (Eng.) U., 1981; PhD, LSE, London, 1988. Lectr. LSE, 1983-90, sr. lectr., 1990-92, reader, 1992-96, prof. polit. sci., 1996—; vis. prof. U. Notre Dame, 1991—, U. Western Ont., Can., 1995-96; cons. to project on Somalia, UN/EU, 1995-96. Author: The Asiatic Mode of Production, 1989; co-author: The Politics of Antagonism, 1993, Explaining Northern Ireland, 1995; co-editor, contbr. The Politics of Conflict Regulation, 1993. Constnl. advisor to Kevin McNamara MP, 1988-94, Marjorie Mowlam MP, 1994—; broadcaster Nationalism, numerous networks. Fellow Ctr. for Study of Nationalism. Avocations: cinema, travel, visiting hot-spots. Office: London Sch Econs, Houghton St, London WC2A 2AE, England

O'LEARY, PAUL ALISTAIR, civil engineer; b. Chester, Eng., Dec. 5, 1942; s. Daniel and Gwendoline (Dickie) O'L.; m. Vivien Emery, Sept. 19, 1968; children: Mark, Robert. B.A., Cambridge U., Eng., 1964, M.A., 1968; Sc.M., Brown U., 1966. Registered profl. engr., Singapore; chartered engr., Gt. Britain. Asst. engr. Kirk & Kirk, Ltd., London, Eng., 1965-69; engr. Harris & Sutherland, London, 1969-72, sr. engr., 1972-75, assoc. ptnr., 1975-80; dir. Harris & Sutherland Pte., Ltd., 1980-96, Harriland Perunding Teknologi Pembinaan Sdn. Bhd., 1987-96; dir. Computer Consortium, Ltd., London, 1976-80, Charles Haswell Cons. Pte., Ltd., Singapore, 1986-92, Harris & Sutherland Ltd., London. 1992-97 ; regional dir. Harris & Sutherland Holdings Ltd., 1989-94; cons. Harris & Sutherland (Asia), 1996—, Harris & Sutherland, London, 1998—. Vice chmn. Round Table Great Britain, Epping, Eng., 1979-80. Univ. scholar Inst. Civil Engrs., Cambridge/Brown Univs., 1961-65; fellow Brown U., R.I., 1964-65. Fellow Inst. Civil Engrs., Inst. Strl. Engrs., Inst. Hwys. and Transp.; mem. Singapore Concrete Inst. (bd. dirs. 1983-86), Inst. Engrs. Singapore, Assn. Cons. Engrs. Singapore (council 1983-92). Club: Tanglin (Singapore). Avocations: Tennis; badminton; swimming. Home: The Barn House, Fair Green, Sawbridgeworth CM21 9AG, England Office: Harris and Sutherland, 82/83 Blackfiars Rd, London SE1 8HA, England

O'LEARY, ROBERT THOMAS, physiatrist; b. Scranton, Pa., Aug. 29, 1964. BS, U. Scranton, 1986; DO, Phila. Coll. Osteo. Medicine, 1990. Diplomate Am. Acad. of Phys. Medicine and Rehabil. Cons. BOSS, Scranton, Pa., 1995; dir. N.E. Rehab. Assocs., Scranton, 1995; co-med. dir. N.E. Occupl. and Rehab. Medicine, Dunmore, Pa., 1995; chmn. ethics com. Allied Svcs. Found., Scranton, 1997—; med. dir. Back and Neck Ctr., Scranton, 1996—. Contbr. articles to profl. jours. Biomechanics fellow NIH, 1994; recipient Physicians Recognition award Am. Med. Soc., 1996. Fellow Am. Acad. of Pain Mgmt., Am. Acad. Disability Evaluating Physicians, Am. Bd. Ind. Med. Examiners; mem. AMA, Am. Med. Acupuncture Assn., Sigma Xi, Alpha Epsilon Delta. Avocations: scuba diving, skiing, bicycling. Office: NE Rehab 475 Morgan Hwy Scranton PA 18508-2605

O'LEARY, TERESA, controller; b. N.Y.C., Jan. 21, 1960; d. Donald James and Frances W. (McGowan) O'L. BS, N.Y. Inst. Tech., 1981; JD, N.Y. Law Sch., 1994. Lic. fin. and ops. prin. Sr. compliance examiner Nat. Assn. Securities Dealers, N.Y.C., 1982-85; asst. v.p., sr. compliance officer Ryan, Beck & Co., West Orange, N.J., 1985-89; v.p., contr. Chapdelaine & Co., N.Y.C., 1989—. Avocations: boating, travel. Office: Chapdelaine & Co 199 Water St Fl 17 New York NY 10038-3529

OLECHOWSKI, ANDRZEJ, government official, economist; b. Cracow, Poland, Sept. 9, 1947; married; 2 children. MA in Econs., Ctrl. Sch. Planning and Stats., Warsaw, Poland, 1973, PhD in Econs., 1979. Assoc. econ. affairs officer Multilateral Trade Negotiations Project, Geneva, 1974-75; head dept. analysis and projections Fgn. Trade Rsch. Inst., Warsaw, 1978-82; econ. affairs officer UN Conf. Trade and Devel., Geneva, 1982-84; economist internat. econ. rsch. divsn.-devel. rsch. dept. The World Bank, Washington, 1985-87; advisor to pres. Nat. Bank Poland, 1987, dep. gov., 1989-91, dir. World Bank Corp. Bur., 1988; dir. dept. Ministry Fgn. Econ. Coop., 1988-89; sec. of state Ministry Fgn. Econ. Rels., 1991-92; min. fin. Warsaw, 1993-95, min. fgn. affairs, 1995; chmn. Bank Handlowy w Warszawie S.A. Ctrl. Europe Trust Poland Ltd., Warsaw, 1995—. Office: 1 Parkingowa Str, 00-517 Warsaw Poland

OLEGO, OSCAR, psychiatrist; b. Cordoba, Argentina, Mar. 20, 1946; s. Arturo and Elena (Acevedo) O.; m. Susana Traba, May 10, 1973 (div. 1984); 1 child, Nicolas Martin. MD summa cum laude, Buenos Aires U., 1970. Staff mem. med. dept. Clinicas Hosp., Buenos Aires, 1970-74; dir. adolescent psychiat. dept. Jewish League Hosp., Buenos Aires, 1974-82, gen. dir. psychiat. dept., 1982—; prof. Mental Health Cathedra, Med. Sch., U. Buenos Aires, 1988—. Mem. Am. Psychiatric Assn., Argentine Psychoanalytic Assn. (assoc.). Home: Las Heras 3767 10o D, 1425 Buenos Aires Argentina

OLEISKY, ROBERT EDWARD, lawyer; b. Mpls., Nov. 23, 1966; s. Allen L. and Marcia E. O. BA, U. Minn., 1989; JD, Hamline U., 1992. Bar: Minn. 1992. Atty. Oleisky & Oleisky P.A., Mpls., 1993—. Bd. dirs. Jewish Family & Children's Svcs., Mpls., 1998-99, vol., 1995-98. Mem. Minn. Assn. Criminal Defense Lawyersm Douglas Andahl Inn of Ct. Democrat. Avocations: basketball, softball, rollerblading, movies, volunteer work. Office: Oleisky & Oleisky PA 250 2d Ave S #225 Minneapolis MN 55401

OLEJNICEK, JIRI, entomologist, researcher; b. Brno, Czechoslovakia, Aug. 5, 1946; s. Vilem and Libuse (Mahelkova) O.; m. Anna Ondrejkova; children: Jiri, Jana, Lukas. MSc, J.E. Purkyne U., Brno, Czech Republic, 1969, RNDr, 1975; PhD, Czech Acad. Scis., Prague, 1980. Rschr. Inst. of Parasitology, Acad. Sci. Czech Republic, Prague, 1970-80; sr. scientist Inst. of Parasitology, Ceske Budejovice, Czech Republic, 1980—; thesis supr. South Bohemian U. Ceske Budejovice, 1982—; cons. Pharmallerga C. Budejovice, 1992—. Co-author: Key to identification of Czechoslovak Fauna, 1977, Check-list of Czechoslovak Insects Dolichopodidae, 1987; editor procs.; author some 100 sci. papers. Recipient prize for best sci. paper Czech Lit. Found. Prague, 1987. Mem. Soc. for Vector Ecology, Czech Soc. Entomology, Czech Soc. Zoology, Czech Soc. Parasitology, Am. Mosquito Control Assn. Christian. Home: U Tri dubu 25, CZ 37010 České Budějovice Czech Republic Office: Czech Acad Scis Inst Parasitology, Branisovska 31, CZ 37005 České Budějovice Czech Republic

OLEKSY, JOZEF, former prime minister of Poland; b. Nowy Sacz, Poland, June 22, 1946; married; 2 children. Sci. worker Main Sch. of Commerce, Warsaw, Poland, 1969-78; worker Ctrl. Com. PZPR, Warsaw, 1978-81; min., mem. Coun. Mins., Warsaw, 1989; dep. to Sejm, 1989—; prim. min. Govt. of Poland, Warsaw, 1995-96; chmn. Social-Democratic Party, Warsaw, 1996—; spkr. Parliament, 1993-95. Contbr. articles to profl. jours. Avocations: walking, history, futurology, parapsychology. Office: ul Rozbrat 44 A, 00-419 Warsaw Poland also: ul Wiktorii Wiedenskiej 5, m4, 02-951 Warsaw Poland*

OLENIC, LILIANA, chemist, researcher; b. Cluj-Napoca, Romania, Sept. 3, 1955; d. Nicolae and Ana (Crisan) Bogdan; m. Liviu Olenic, July 7, 1977; 1 child, Lucian. Diploma of Licentiate, Babes-Bolyai U., Cluj, 1978; Grad. Diploma, Faculty of Chem. Tech., Cluj, 1984; PhD in Chemistry, Faculty of Chem. Tech., 1998. Chemist Oficiu Pt. Nutreturi Combinate, Bucharest,

1978-79, ICME, Bucharest, 1979-82, Carbochim, Cluj, 1982-83; chemist/rschr. Inst. Chemistry, Cluj, 1983—. Contbr. articles to profl. jours.; patentee in field. Mem. Analytical Chem. Soc. Romania. Mem. Ch. of Jesus Christ of Latter-Day Saints. Avocations: reading, hymns, travel, swimming, sports. Home: Fantanele Str #7 Ap 42, 3400 Cluj-Napoca Romania Office: Inst Chemistry Raluca Ripan, Fantanele Str #30, 3400 Cluj-Napoca Romania

OLER, WESLEY MARION, IV, executive; b. Washington, Apr. 13, 1955; s. Wesley Marion III and Virginia (Craemer) O.; m. Debra Brown, Apr. 16, 1993; children: Wesley V, Phoebe. BA, Yale U., 1978. CFA. Deputy mgr. instl. sales Brown Bros. Harriman & Co., Zurich, 1982-88; mgr. internat. bankers Brown Bros. Harriman & Co., N.Y.C., 1988-95, sr. mgr. equity trading, 1995—; mem. ITS/CAES subcom. Nasdaq Stock Market, N.Y.C., 1996—; mem. N.Y. Stock Exch., N.Y.C., 1998. Mem. SAR (treas. 1995-96), Soc. Colonial Wars (coun. mem. 1993-94), Soc. Mayflower Descs., Securities Industry Assn. (mem. instnl. brokerage com. 1997—). E-mail: wesley.oler@bbh.com.

OLES, STUART GREGORY, lawyer; b. Seattle, Dec. 15, 1924; s. Floyd and Helen Louise (La Violette) O.; m. Ilse Hanewald, Feb. 12, 1954; children: Douglas, Karl, Stephen. BS magna cum laude, U. Wash., 1947, JD, 1948. Bar: Wash., 1949, U.S. Supreme Ct. 1960. Dep. pros. atty. King County, Wash., 1949; chief civil dept. King County, 1949-50; gen. practice law Seattle, 1950-95; sr. ptnr. firm Oles, Morrison & Rinker and predecessor, 1955-90, of counsel, 1991-95. Author: A View From the Rock, 1994, On Behalf of My Clients -- A Lawyer's Life, 1998. Chmn. Seattle Cmty. Concert Assn., 1955; pres. Friends Seattle Pub. Libr., 1956; mem. Wash. pub. Disclosure Commn., 1973-075; trustee Ch. Divinity Sch. of Pacific, Berkeley, Calif., 1974-75; mem. bd. curators Wash. State Hist. Soc., 1983; former mem. Seattle Symphony Bd.; pres. King County Ct. House Rep. Club, 1950, U. Wash. Young Rep. Club, 1947; Wash. conv. floor leader Taft, 1952, Goldwater, 1964; Wash. chmn. Citizens for Goldwater, 1964; chmn. King County Rep. convs., 1966, 68, 76, 84, 88, 90, 92, 96, Wash. State Rep. Conv., 1980. Served with USMCR, 1943-45. Mem. ABA (past regional vice-chmn. pub. contract law sect.), Wash. Bar Assn., Order of Coif, Scabbard and Blade, Am. Legion, Kapoho Bay Club (pres.), Am. Highland Cattle Assn. (v.p. and dir.), Phi Beta Kappa, Phi Alpha Delta. Home: 22715 SE 43rd Ct Issaquah WA 98029-5200 Office: Oles Morrison & Rinker 701 5th Ave Ste 3300 Seattle WA 98104-7082 also: RR 2 Pahoa HI 96778-9802

OLESEN, DORTE MARIANNE, mathematician, educator; b. Hillerød, Denmark, Jan. 8, 1948; d. Knud Henning and Irene Mariane (Pedersen) O.; m. Gert K. Pedersen, Feb. 26, 1971; children: Just, Oluf, Marianne. MS, U. Copenhagen, 1973; PhD, U. Odense, Denmark, 1975; DSc, U. Copenhagen, 1981. Rsch. assoc. U. Odense, Denmark, 1973-74; acad. sec. Ministry of Edn., Copenhagen, 1974-76; postdoctoral fellow U. Copenhagen, 1976-79, lectr., 1980-88; prof. U. Roskilde, Denmark, 1988-89; mem. Math. Scis. Rsch. Inc. Berkeley, 1984-85; dean Faculty of Natural Scis., Copenhagen, 1986-88; mng. dir. Danish Computing Ctr. for Rsch. and Edn., 1989—. Contbr. articles to profl. jours. Mem. Danish Coun. for Rsch. Policy and Planning, 1987-93, Danish Def. Rsch. Coun., 1998—. Recipient Gold medal U. Copenhagen, 1973; travel grantee Tagea Brandt Com., 1987, Marie Loenggaard Com., 1988. Mem. Danish Math. Soc., Am. Math. Soc., Danish Assn. for Advancement of Sci. (pres. 1988—), Danish Acad. Natural Scis. Office: UNI-C, Vermundsgade 5, 2100 Copenhagen Denmark

OLESEN, MARIE, fashion designer; b. Klokkerholm, Denmark, Jan. 13, 1952; d. Ole Christian and Cecily Lauretta (Axelsen) O. Diploma, Gullaksen, Aalborg, Denmark, 1970. Owner Olesen Design Svcs., Cumbria, Eng., 1985-90, Renaissance Bridal Gowns, Whitehaven, Eng., 1990—; designer and mfr. freelance, 1992—; cons. in field. Patentee in field. Recipient Small Bus. Competition award, 1989. Avocations: bottani, dancing, country walks, photography. Office: Renaissance Bridal Gowns, 133 Queen St, CA28 7QF Whitehaven CA28 79F Cumbria, England

OLESEN, OLE FRILEV, neurobiologist, researcher; b. Harboore, Denmark, June 30, 1965; s. Kristian and Norma (Nielsen) O.; m. Elisabetta Vaudano; children: Camilla, Andreas. BSc, Arhus U., Arhus, Denmark, 1989, MSc, 1991; PhD, Cambridge U., 1994; MBA, Copenhagen Bus. Sch., 1996. Asst. prof. Arhus U., 1993-94; rsch. mgr. H. Lundbeck, Copenhagen, 1994-98; internatl. proj. mgr. Ferring Pharmaceuticals, Copenhagen, 1998—; writer Bergen Pub. Co., 1991—; asst. lectr. Arhus U., 1994-97; sci. adv. Bonniers Pub. Co., 1995-98. Author: (book) Mr. Dupond, 1991. Recipient Hoejgaard award Knud Hoejgaard Found., 1990, Rsch. grantee Arhus U. Rsch. Found., 1991, Rsch. award Danish Rsch. Acad., 1992. Mem. Am. Soc. Cell Biology, Soc. Neuroscience, Internat. Project Mgmt. Assn. Avocations: poetry, cross-country skiing, crocodiles, finnish films. Home: Strindbergsvej 50, 2500 Copenhagen-Valby Denmark Office: Ferring A/S, Borups Alle 177, Copenhagen Denmark

OLESZEK, WIESLAW ALEKSANDER, chemist; b. Belzyce, Lublin, Poland, Feb. 27, 1948; s. Kazimierz and Janina (Kozinska) O.; m. Ewa Gozdzicka, Sept. 15, 1973; children: Malgorzata, Magdalena. MS, Maria Sklodowska-Curie U., Lublin, 1975; PhD, Inst. Soil Sci./Plant, Cultivation, Pulawy, 1985, Docent, 1991. Rsch. asst. Inst. of Soil Sci. and Plant Cultivation, Pulawy, 1980-85, prof., 1992—, head biochemistry dept., 1992—, v.p. scientific coun., 1992-98; vis. fellow Cornell U., Geneva, N.Y., 1979-80; adj. asst. prof. Inst. Soil Sci. and Plant Cultivation, Pulawy, 1985-91; vis. prof. Cornell U., 1987, Inst. of Food Rsch., Norwich, U.K., 1989, INRA, Avignon, France, 1993. Translator: Introduction to Ecological Biochemistry (by G. Harborne), 1997; contbr. articles to profl. jours.; contbg. author: (books) Allelopathy, Basic and Applied Aspects, 1995, Allelopathy in Pests Management for Sustainable Agriculture, 1996, Current Trends in Fruit and Vegetables Phytochemistry, 1996, Saponins Used in Food and Agriculture, 1996, Principles and Practices in Plant Ecology, 1999, Recent Advances in Allelopathy, 1999, Natural Food Antimicrobial Systems, 2000, Phytochemicals as Bioactive Agents, 2000; editor: Saponins in Food, Feedstuffs and Medicinal Plants, 2000. Mem. com. Misericordes, Pulway, 1987-93. Recipient award Polish Acad. of Scis., Warsaw, 1992. Mem. N.Y. Acad. Scis., Phytochem. Soc. of Europe, Polish Phytochem. Soc. (sec. 1996—), Polish Biochem. Soc., Internat. Allelopathy Soc. (founding mem.). Roman Catholic. Avocations: beekeeping, bicycling, gardening. Office: Inst Soil Sci/Plant Cultiv, Czartoryskich 8, Pulawy 24-100, Poland

OLFF, MIRANDA, psychologist, researcher; b. Kortenhoef, The Netherlands, June 19, 1962; d. Tertius and Gerarda Johanna (Van Oyen) O.; m. Antoon Opperhuizen; children: Martijn, Roman, Onno, Anneloes, Alette. M in Psychology, Utrecht (The Netherlands) U., 1987, PhD in Social Scis., 1991. Rschr., European astronaut selection European Space Agy., Noordwyk, The Netherlands, 1990-91; assoc. clin. rsch. dir. Solvay, Weesp, The Netherlands, 1991-96; postdoctoral rschr. Groningen (The Netherlands) U., 1996-97; sr. scientist Trimbos Inst. (Netherlands Inst. Mental Health & Addiction), Utrecht, 1998—; vis. prof., Lund (Sweden) U., 1997-99; cons. Norwegian Med. Assn., Oslo, 1993-98; dir. stress rsch., Hilversum, The Netherlands, 1995-99. Author: Stress, the impact of stress on body and mind, 1995; author, editor: Quantification of human defense mechanism, 1991; editor (jour.) Preventie Periodiek. 1999. Office: Neth Inst Mental Health, Dept Prevent POB 725, NL3500AS Utrecht The Netherlands

OLGAARD, ANDERS, economics educator; b. Aabenraa, Denmark, Sept. 5, 1926; s. Axel O. and Anna Lebeck; m. Alice Christiansen, 1951; three children. Dr. Polit., Univ. Copenhagen, 1966. Civil servant Econ. Sec., 1953-60; prof. econs., Univ. Copenhagen, 1962-96 ; adviser in Malaysia, Harvard U. Devel. Adv. Service, 1968-69; mem. Econ. Council, 1966-68, chmn., 1970-76. Author: Growth, Productivity and Relative Prices, 1966; The Danish Economy, EEC Economic and Financial Series, 1980. Mem. Danish Econ. Assn. (pres. 1983-88). Home: 12 Lerbaekvej, DK-2830 Virum Denmark Office: U Copenhagen Inst Econs, Studiestraede 6, DK-1455 Copenhagen Denmark

OLIET, SEYMOUR, endodontics educator, dean, dentist; b. Perth Amboy, N.J., July 12, 1927; s. Asher Jacob and Sarah Oliet; m. Sherry Roseff, July 2, 1949; children: Eric Jay, Amy Ellen Oliet Heller. Student, Rutgers U., 1945-46, 47-49; DDS with distinction, U. Pa., 1953. Diplomate Am. Bd. Endodontics. Instr. oral medicine Sch. Dental Medicine U. Pa., 1953-56, assoc. oral medicine, 1956-61, asst. prof. oral medicine, 1961-65, assoc. prof. oral medicine, 1965-71, prof. oral medicine, dir. undergrad. endodontics, 1971-72, founding chmn. dept. endodontics, 1972-80, prof. endodontics, interim chmn. endodontics, 1990-91, prof. emeritus, 1994—; attending dentist Albert Einstein Med. Ctr., Phila., 1953-60; sr. attending, chmn. endodontics Albert Einstein Med. Ctr., 1960-84; prof. endodontics Coll. Dental Medicine Nova Southeastern U., Ft. Lauderdale, Fla., 1996—, chmn. task force to estab. Dental Sch., 1995-96, dean Coll. Dental Medicine, 1996—; cons. endodontics U.S. Army, Ft. Dix, N.J., and Walter Reed Army Hosp., Washington, 1955-80, VA Hosp., Phila., 1965-80; chmn. internat. to estab. I.B. Bender Endowment Fund, Israeli Endodontic Soc., Hebrew U., 1990-91; reviewer Jour. Am. Dental Assn., 1970—. Author: (with others) Endodontics Practice, 11th edit., 1988, Diagnosis and Treatment of Endodontic Emergences, 1981, Current Therapy in Dentistry, 1977, Diagnosis and Treatment Planning in Management of Diseases of the Pulp, 1963, Programmed Text Endodontics; editor Alpha Omega, 1956, (newsletter) Am. Assn. Endodontics, 1966-69; contbr. articles to profl. jours. Named Hon. Citizen of New Orleans; inducted Perth Amboy H.S. Hall of Fame, 1998; recipient Mayor's Citation, Perth Amboy, 1998. Fellow AAAS, Royal Soc. Health (Brit.), Internat. Assn. Dental Rsch., Am. Assn. Endodontists, Am. Coll. Dentists (sec.-treas. Phila. chpt. 1965-76, pres.-elect 1976-77, pres. 1976-77), Internat. Coll. Dentists, Phila. Coll. Surgeons; mem. ADA (life), Pa. Acad. Endodontics (founder, pres. 1977-79, adv. to pres. 1979), Phila. County Dental Soc. (membership com. 1954, indsl. dentistry com. 1954, chmn. sci. program com. 1963, chmn. essay and clins. com. 1964-65, chmn. mediation com. 1965-66, bd. govs. 1985-87, chmn. ad hoc com. ins. 1985-96, com. peer rev. 1985-96, com. on continuing edn. 1989-96, dir. liberty dental conf. 1987-91, gen. chmn. 1991-92, chmn. awards and banquets 1988-89, dir. sci. exhibits and programs 1989-90, del. Pa. Dental Assn. 1985-96, long-range planning com. 1993-96, historian, bd. govs. 1994-96), Brazilian Dental Soc. (hon.), N.Y. Acad. Sci., Am. Assn. Endodontists (arrangements com. 1958-60, libr. com. 1960-61, membership com. 1961-67, publ. chmn., editor newsletter, sci. 1966-69, sci. prof. chmn. 1970-71, bd. govs., exec. com. 1972-78, awards and hons. com. 1992-95), Eastern Dental Soc. (chmn. membership 1956-57, program com. 1957-59, chmn. publicity, editor 1957-59, sec. 1960-62, bd. dirs. 1958 , pres.-elect chmn. bd. govs. 1968-69, pres. 1969-70), Acad. Stomatology, Am. Assn. Dental Editors, Alpha Omega (Phila. alumni chpt., editor 1956, treas. 1956-60, adv. to alumni chpt., regent 1960-61, nat. dept. marshall 1961-62, pres.-elect 1961-63, pres. 1963-64). Avocations: tennis, golf, horseback trail riding, fishing. Office: Nova Southeastern U Coll Dental Medicine 3200 S University Dr Fort Lauderdale FL 33328-2018

OLIGER, TATIANA IVANOVNA, research scientist; b. Russia, June 8, 1941; d. Ivan Mikhailovich and Ksenia Vladimirovna (Fedyai) O.; m. Shaldybin Sergei Lvovich; children: Nadezhda, Nastasia. Dr., U. Gorky, 1963; PhD in biology, U. Kazan, 1972. Prof. U. Cheboksary, Russia, 1969-74; sr. rsch. scientist Lazovskii State Nature Reserve, Primorie, Russia, 1975-82; engr. Mariculture Base, Valentin, Russia, 1983-84; leading rsch. scientist Nizhnesvirskii State Nature Reserve, Leningrad, Russia, 1985—. Author: Spiders of Nizhnesvirskii Reserve, 1996; contbr. articles to profl. jours. Mem. Internat. Soc. Arachnology. Avocations: study of spiders, fishing, travel. Office: Lodeinoye Polye, zapovednik, 187710 Saint Petersburg Russia

OLINGER, CHAUNCEY GREENE, JR., investment executive, editorial consultant; b. Long Beach, Calif., Jan. 16, 1933; s. Chauncey Greene and Cora Blount (Urquhart) O.; m. Carla R. Dragan, May 30, 1981. BA in Philosophy with honors, U. Va., Charlottesville, 1955; MA, Columbia U., N.Y., 1971. CFP. Coadjutant in philosophy Rutgers U., New Brunswick, N.J., 1968-72; rep. N.Y. World Federalists, USA, N.Y.C., 1970; dir. subcom. U.S. sec. of state adv. com. Dept. of State, Washington, 1972; editl. cons. Columbia U., N.Y.C., 1973-82; editor, pres. Metropolitan Rsch. Co., N.Y.C., 1982-91; investment exec. First Albany, N.Y.C., 1991-92, Janney Montgomery Scott, N.Y.C., 1992—; sec. sem. on human nature Columbia U., N.Y.C., 1968-72, mem. sem. on orgnl. mgmt., 1972-84, mem. com. to increase corp. philanthropic giving, 1980-83, founder, co-chmn. U. seminar Hist. of Columbia U., 1998. Editor: World Enough, (Margaret Mead and Ken Heyman), 1975, A Celebration of Thanksgiving For the Life of I.I. Rabi, 1991, Columbia and the City: The University's Commitment to New York City, 1993, Courtney C. Brown: In Memory, 1995; author: New York City: An Economic Resource Profile, 1989, The I.I. Rabi Memorial Room, 1996. Pres. Fellowship of Young Churchmen, Episcopal Diocese of So. Va., 1950-52; nat. chmn. Coalition to Stop SST Environmental Damage, N.Y., 1975-78; pub. mem. human rights in rsch. com. N.Y. Hosp.-Cornell Med. Ctr., 1975-80; pres. grad. faculty alumni Columbia U., N.Y., 1977-81. Recipient Conspicuous Alumni Svc. medal Columbia U., 1980, Svc., Loyalty and Dedication award Grad. Faculty Alumni of Columbia U., 1988. Mem. Am. Philos. Assn., Nat. Inst. Social Science (dir. 1988-92), Pilgrims of the U.S., Am. Soc. Most Venerable Order of Hosp. of St. John of Jerusalem, St. Andrew's Soc. of the State of N.Y. (sec. 1991-95), St. George's Soc. N.Y., 1977—, Century Assn., The Ch. Club of N.Y. (v.p. 1985-86, 88-89, 96-97, pres. 1997-2000), Laymen's Club of the Cathedral of St. John the Divine (pres. 1988). Episcopalian. Avocations: reading, writing, walking, theatre, ballet. Office: Janney Montgomery Scott 575 Lexington Ave New York NY 10022-6102

OLIPHANT, CHARLES ROMIG, retired physician; b. Waukegan, Ill., Sept. 10, 1917; s. Charles L. and Mary (Goss) R.; m. Claire E. Canavan, Nov. 7, 1942; children: James R., Cathy Rose, Mary G., William D. Student, St. Louis U., 1936-40, MD, 1943; postgrad., Naval Med. Sch., 1946. Intern Nat. Naval Med. Ctr., Bethesda, Md., 1943; pvt. practice medicine and surgery San Diego, 1947-99; ret., 1999; bd. dirs. Midway Med. Enterprises; former chief staff Balboa Hosp., Doctors Hosp., Cabrillo Med. Ctr.; chief staff emeritus Sharp Cabrillo Hosp.; mem. staff Mercy Hosp., Children's Hosp., Paradise Valley Hosp., Sharp Meml. Hosp.; sec. Sharp Sr. Health Care, S.D., 1985-98; mem. exec. bd., program chmn. San Diego Power Squadron, 1985-93, 95; charter mem. Am. Bd. Family Practice. Served with M.C., USN, 1943-47. Recipient Golden Staff award Sharp Cabrillo Hosp. Med. Staff, 1990. Fellow Am. Geriatric Soc. (emeritus), Am. Acad. Family Practice, Am. Assn. Abdominal Surgeons; mem. AMA, Calif. Med. Assn., Am. Acad. Family Physicians (past pres. San Diego chpt., del. Calif. chpt.), San Diego Med. Soc., Pub. Health League, Navy League, San Diego Power Squadron (past comdr.), SAR, San Diego Yacht Club, Cameron Highlanders. Home: Riverview Terr Unit # 109 1970 W Harvard Ave Roseburg OR 97470-2746

OLISA, KEN APHUNEZI, venture marketing company executive; b. Nottingham, Eng., Oct. 13, 1951; s. Charles H. and Barbara E. (Laskey) O.; m. Julia B. Sherwood, July 26, 1976; children: Elinor, Auriol. BA in Natural, Polit., Managerial Scis., Fitwilliam Coll., Cambridge, Eng., 1974, MA, 1978. Salesman IBM, London, 1974-80; U.K. mktg. dir. Wang, London, 1981-87; v.p. mktg. Wang Labs. Inc., Boston, 1987-90; sr. v.p. Wang Labs. Inc., Brussels, 1990-92; CEO Interregnum Venture Mktg., London, 1992—; chmn. DMATEK, Tel Aviv, 1996-98; chmn., CEO Interregnum plc, 2000—; chmn. Voss Net, London, 1994-97, Open Text Inc., 1998—. Dir. Lambeth NHS Trust, 1995-98; chmn. Thames Reach Homeless Charity, 1994—; trustee Fitzwilliam Soc. Trust, 1995—, gov. Peabody Trust; commr. Postal Svc., 2000—. Fellow Royal Soc. Arts; mem. Worshipful Co. Info. Tech. (liveryman). Office: Interregnum Venture Mktg, 22-23 Old Burlington St, London W1X 1RL, England

OLISEH, SUNDAY, soccer player; b. Abavo, Belgium, Sept. 14, 1974. Midfielder Reggiana, 1994-95, 1 FC Koeln, 1994-97, Ajax Amsterdam Football Club, 1998-99, Juventus, 1999-2000, Borussia Dortmund, Germany, 2000—. Address: Borussia Dortmund, Strobelallee 50, 44139 Dortmund Germany*

OLIVA, AURELIO ANDRÉS, physics researcher; b. Havana, Cuba, Oct. 17, 1949; s. Pío Genaro and Benita (Viera) O. Lic. en Física, U. Havana, 1972. Cert. physicisit, sr. rschr. Young rschr. Inst. Fundamental Tech. Rsch., Havana, 1974-85; rschr. Inst. Cybernetics, Maths. and Physics, Havana, 1985-90; sr. rschr. Ctr. Devel. Sci. Equipments & Instruments, Havana, 1990—; cons. Laser Nat. Commn., Havana, 1986—, Group of Laser Experts, Havana, 1988-91, Group of Instrumentation Experts, Havana, 1991—. Patentee in field. Mem. Internat. Com. Optics (pres. Cuban territorial com. 1993—), Cuban Soc. Physics (head optics sect.). Avocations: chess, classical music. Home: Lawton, Calle 9 No 65 e/C y D, 10700 Havana Cuba Office: Ctr Devel Sci Equip & Instr, Luz # 375 Picota y Compostela, 10100 Havana Cuba

OLIVA, DOMINADOR PAGKALINAWAN, engineering and technical educator; b. Pateros, Metro Manila, The Philippines, Aug. 7, 1920; s. Arcadio L. and Olimpia P. (Pagkalinawan) O.; m. Clemencia Borja Mendiola, Dec. 23, 1945; children: Antonio, Wilfredo, Renato, Danilo, Cynthia, Monina. BS in Radio and Electronics Engring., Featì U., Manila, 1966, MPA, 1968; BSEE, Mapua Inst. Tech., Manila, 1957. Amateur radio operator Radio Sta. KAITS Philippine Sch. Arts and Trades, Manila, 1938-39; ship radio officer Luzon Stevedoring Co./Visayan Stevedoring Co., Manila/Iloilo, 1939-40; chief radio officer Madrigal & Co., Manila, 1940-41; pvt. practice radio technician Pateros/Manila, 1941-45; radio engr./announcer/newscaster Radio Sta. KMPI, U.S. Army, Ft. William McKinley, The Philippines, 1945-46; chief radio officer U.S. War Shipping Adminstrn., Manila, 1946, Am. Pres. Lines, Manila, 1946; aero. radio officer, flight radio officer Far Eastern Airline Transport, Inc., Manila, 1946; aero. radio operator/technician Pan Am. World Airways, Manila, 1946-47; aero. radio operator, flight radio officer China Airlines, Inc., Manila, 1946; with Civil Aeronautics Adminstrn., Manila, 1948-80; prof. electronics and comms. engring. dept. FEATI U., Manila, 1960—, head radio-TV and electronics dept., 1960—; spl. lectr./resource spkr. Nat. Def. Coll. Philippines and Naval Air Group, Philippine Navy, Nat. Def. Forces, Manila, 1978-79; project co-mgr. UN Devel. Programme, 1977-81, Country Programme Project, 1977-81; reviewer Electronics and Comms. Engrs. Licensure Examination, and Bd. Examinations for Comml. Radio-Telegraph and Radiotelephone Examinations, Manila Rev. Inst./United Profl. Rev. Ctr./Dynamic Rev. Ctr./Reviewmasters, Manila, 1977—; cons. Antonio S. Dimalanta Assocs., Manila, 1985-88, Angel Lazaro Assocs., Inc., Manila, 1989-90; cons. on tech. and vocat. edn. Tech.-Vocat. Edn. Accrediting Assn. Philippines, Manila, 1989—; cons., project mgr. Teleconsultant, Inc., Manila, 1989—; cons. tech. adv. bd. Technol. U. Philippines, Manila, 1993—; cons. Ednl. Devel. Program Implementing Task Force, Manila, 1994—; mem. Tech. Panel for Engring. Edn., Manila, 1980-85; mem. tech. Panel for Tech. and Vocat. Edn., Manila, 1990—, bd. judges Metrobank Found., Inc. 1997 Search for Outstanding Tech.-Vocat. Tchr. of the Philippines; cons. Metrobank Found., Inc. 1998 Search for Outstanding Tech.-Vocat. Tchr. of the Philippines; cons. ELECTROCOM Mgmt. & Manpower Svcs., Inc.; pres. emeritus Philippine Aviation Tng. Program Alumni Assn., 1999. Contbr. numerous articles to profl. jours. Co-founder, former chmn. bd. and pres. So. Rizal Inst., Inc., Pateros, Metro Manila, 1955-68; instr. first aid course Philippine Nat. Red Cross and Civil Aeronautics Adminstrn., 1956-58; co-founder (now adviser) Pateros Cmty. Welfare Orgn., 1953—, Pateros Puericulture Ctr., Inc., 1954—; founding mem. Pateros Credit Coop., Inc., 1990—, Pateros People's Econ. Coun. Found., 1991—; former chmn. (now advisor) Pateros Mcpl. Scouting Com., 1993—; adviser Boy Scouts of Philippines, South Coun., Pateros, 1993—; mem. Sr. Citizens Affairs, Pateros, 1993—; mem. Fedn. Sr. Citizens Assns. of Philippines, Inc., 1993—; adviser FEATI U. Red Cross Youth Coun., Manila, 1993—. Recipient Award as Most Outstanding for Leadership of Philippine Pensionados in Aviation, Oklahoma City, 1948, Cert. of Appreciation, BOAC, 1955, Cert. of Appreciation for Valuable Assistance to Philippine Amateur Radio Assn., 1959, Boy Scouts of Philippines, 1957-68, Silver Pin and Cert. of recognition, Inst. Electronics and Comms. Engrs. of Philippines, 1970, Most Outstanding Instr. of Radio, TV and Electronics Dept., FEATI U. by Sigma Beta Epsilon, 1972, Cert. of Merit as Ofcl. of Dept. Pub. Wks., Transp. and Comms., 1974, Cert. of Merit, So. Rizal Inst., Pateros, 1978, 1987 Most Outstanding in Industry award PSAT/PCAT/Technol. U. Philippines Alumni Assn., 1987, Leadership award, 1991, Meritorious Svc. award, 1991, Outstanding Alumnus Rizal H.S., 1992, Plaque of Achievement as 1992 Most Outstanding Tech. Tchr. of the Philippines, Ayala Found. Inc. and DECS Bur. of Tech. and Vocat. Edn., 1992, Plaque of Merit as Favorite Son of Pateros, Mayor Jose T. Capco, Jr. and Mcpl. Coun. Pateros, 1993, Outstanding Electronics and Comm. Engr. in Edn., award, Insts. of Electronics/Engr., Philippines, 1992, Outstanding Electronics and Comms. Engr. of Philippines, Profl. Regulation Commn., Manila, 1993, Lifetime Achievement award, PSAT/PCAT/Technol. U. Philippines Alumni Assn., 1994, others. Mem. Inst. Electronics and Comms. Engrs. of Philippines (life, dir. 1956—, chmn. pub. com. 1966, chmn. internat. rels. com. 1967, chmn. R&D com. 1979), PSAT/PCAT/Technol. U. Philippines Alumni Assn. (life, dir. 1967—, Most Outstanding Alumnus 1987, Leadership award 1991, Meritorious Svc. award 1991), Philippine Assn. Pvt. Tech. Instns. Inc. (dir. 1968—), Techn.-Vocat. Edn. Accrediting Assn. of Philippines, Fedn. of Accrediting Assns. of Philippines, Philippine Assn. Vocat. Edn., Pvt. Edn. Retirement Annuity Assn., Pateros Tennis Club (pres. 1985-88). Roman Catholic. Home: 520 M Almeda St, Pateros Metro Manila 1621, The Philippines Office: FEATI Univ, Helios St Sta Cruz, Manila 1003, The Philippines

OLIVA-LOPEZ, EDUARDO, information scientist, educator, consultant; b. Acambaro, Guanajuato, Mex., Feb. 16, 1941; s. Jesus Oliva-Davis and Luz Lopez-Delgado. BSc, ESIME-IPN, Mex., 1967, MSc, 1975; MSc, Birmingham U., Eng., 1976; PhD, Cranfield U., Eng., 1980. Elec. maintenance mgr. CHESA, Mex., 1963-69; acad. vice dir. UPIICSA, Mex., 1972-74; tech. devel. coord. IPN, Mex., 1980-83; planning mgr. ININ, Mex., 1984-85, tech. svcs. dir., 1986-90; prof. UPIICSA-IPN, Mex., 1991—; cons. Trasnvac, Mex., 1970-71. Founding dir. Ergonomics Rsch. Inst., Mexico City, 1996. Conacyt-Mex. scholar, 1975-79; Fulbright grantee, 1995. Mem. Human Factors and Ergonomics Soc., Internat. Soc. Sys. Sci. E-mail: ediva@redipn.ipn.mx. Home: Playa Mirador 430, 08830 Mexico City Mexico

OLIVEIRA, ALEXANDRE BORGES, international relations consultant; b. Luziânia, Go, Brazil, Nov. 29, 1975; s. Joaõ Batista and Nilva Borges (Jesus) O. BSc, U. Brasilia, Brazil, 1997. Advisor Embrapa, Brasilia, 1996—; assoc. editor Brasilia Newspaper, 1997—; adminstrv. asst. SBF, Brasilia, 1996—; cons. Interam. Inst. for Agrl. Cooperation, 1997—; advisor Embrapa, Brasilia, 1996-99; procurement specialist Fundo de Fortalecimento da Escola-Ministry Edn./World Bank, 1999-2000; procurement asst. World Bank, 2000—. Author various websites. Rsch. grantee Nat. Counc. for Rsch. and Technol. Devel., Brasilia, 1996. Home: HIGS, 703 Bloco N Casa 16, 70331714 Brasilia Brazil Office: SCN Qua 02 Lote A Ed Cor Fin Ctr, Salas 303/304/603, 70712900 Brasilia Brazil

OLIVEIRA, HAROLDO DE CASTRO, aviation company executive, consultant; b. Rio de Janeiro, Brazil, Feb. 15, 1940; s. Salvino De Castro and Antônia Oliveira; m. Raquel Cardoso Oliveira, Dec. 15, 1966; children: Christian de Castro Oliveira, Erik Luís de Castro Oliveira. Superior, Aman, Resende, Brazil, 1963. Capt. Brazilian Army, 1963-77; adviser Pres. of Republic, Brasilia, Brazil, 1971-79; turism dir. State Govt., Brasilia, 1979-81; dir. Digibras, Brasilia, 1981-82; state sec. State Govt., Brasilia, 1982-85; v.p. mgmt. coun. VASP, Brasilia, 1994—; pres. FSS/GDF, Brasilia, 1982-85, SHIS/GDF, Brasilia, 1982-85; advisor GDF, Brasilia, 1982-85; v.p. adv. coun. VASP, Brasilia, 1996—. Author: The Economic Factor of Tourism, 1979, Brasilia and Its Touristic Potencialities, 1979, Tourism and the Economic Factor, 1980, Habitation in the Federal District, 1983. Active Dem. Social Party/PDS, Brasilia, 1980, Rondon Project Coun., Brasilia, 1983, C. of C. Brazil/Ukraine, Curitiba, Brazil, 1997, C. of C. Brazil/Paraguai, Brasilia. Recipient medals Order of Merit Brasilia/GDF, 1979, Order of Merit Armed Forces, Brasilia, 1995, Order of Merit Mil./Army, Brasilia, 1996. Mem. Soc. of Friends of the Navy (pres. 1981-98), Brasilia Pioneers Club, Lions Club. Democrat. Roman Catholic. Avocations: soccer, reading, hat collecting, music, movies. Home: Shis QI 27, Conjunto 13 Casa 16, 71675130 Brasilia DF, Brazil Office: VASP Brazilian Airlines, Hangares Lt 23 A 26, Brasilia DF, Brazil

OLIVEIRA, MANUEL DE, film director; b. Oporto, Portugal, 1908. Film director Douro, Faina Fluvial, 1931, Aniki-Bóbó, 1942, O Pinto e a Cidade, 1956, O Pão, 1959, O Acto da Primavera, 1963, A Caça, 1964, O Passado e Presente, 1972, Benilde ou A Virgem Mãe, 1975, Amor de Perdição, 1979, Francisca, 1981. Office: Mandragoa Films, Ave D Manuel I No 3, 2890 014 Alcochete Portugal

OLIVEIRA, MARIO MARTINS, physician; b. Lisbon, Portugal, Apr. 23, 1963; s. Joao Santos Oliveira and Adelaide Martins Zeferino; m. Isabel Jorge Pinto, Aug. 19, 1989; children: Marta, Mariana, Pedro. MD, Med. U., 1988;

M Sports Medicine, Med. U., Lisbon, 1992. Medical diplomate. Rsch. asst. Med. U., London and Lisbon, 1986-88; faculty asst. Med. U., Lisbon, 1988-90, gen. intern, 1990-91; cardiology fellow Hosp. St. Marta, Lisbon, 1992-96; rsch. fellow St. George Hosp., London, 1995; clin. tng. Ann Arbor Med. Ctr., Mich., 1996; cardiology asst. Hosp. Santa Marta, Lisbon, 1997-99; cardiology cons. Hosp. St. Louis, Lisbon, 1997-99. Contbr. articles to profl. jours. Affil. Sch. of Music and Arts, Lisbon, 1979, 97. Sub-lt. Portuguese Army, 1991-92. Mem. NASPE, European Soc. Cardiology, European Working Arrhythims and Echocardiography, N.Y. Acad. Scis., Internat. Soc. of Holter and Noninvasive Electrocardiology. Roman Catholic. Avocations: music, sports, travel. Office: Hosp Santa Marta, RNA de Santa Marta, 1150 Lisbon Portugal

OLIVEIRA, ROSE MARIE, elementary educator; b. N.Y.C., June 26, 1950; d. Manuel and Carmen A. Matos; m. Jose Oliveira, Nov. 28, 1969; children: Francisco José, Lori Anne Jose Jr. BS in Edn., Old Westbury (N.Y.) U., 1984; MS in TESOL, Hofstra (N.Y.) U., 1989; sch. cert. in staff devel., Coll. New Rochelle, N.Y., 1999, sch. dist. adminstrn., 2000. Sci. mentor Westbury (N.Y.) Pub. Schs., 1992-98, educator, 1984—; adminstrv. intern Coll. New Rochelle, 1999; adj. prof. ESL Suffolk C.C., Brentwood, N.Y., 1990—. Co-developer: (handbook) Cultural Teacher Training Resource Guide, 1989. Vol. Brentwood/Bay Shore Breast Cancer Coalition, 1995—. Roman Catholic. Avocations: flamenco dancing, painting, meditation, reading, listening to New Age Music. Home: 120 Deer Park St Bay Shore NY 11706-1322

OLIVEIRA, TANIA CRISTINA, epidemiologist; b. Rio de Janeiro, Dec. 29, 1957; d. Hildeberto Camargo Oliveira and Maria De Fátima Teixeira; m. Roberto Antonio Facio; children: Julio C. Azevedo, Vitor O. Facio. MPH, State U. Campinas, Brazil, 1992, PhD, 1997; degree in quality of healthcare, Med. Coll. Va., 1996. Epidemiology fellow Fiocruz, Rio de Janeiro, 1984; rschr. Pub. Health Dept., Rio de Janeiro, 1984—; chief Infection Control Svc., Araras, Mogi-Mirim, Campinas, Brazil, 1991—, Infectology Dept., Araras, Mogi-Mirim, Campinas, Brazil, 1990—. Contbr. articles to profl. jours. Mem. Societá, Mogi-Mirim, 1999. Recipient Brazilian award of medicine Abramge, 1997; Fulbright fellow, 1995-96. Mem. Soc. for Healthcare Epidemiology Am., Associaçaó Paulista de Controle de Infecção, Soc. Brasileira de Infectologia. E-mail: taniao@ft.com.br. Home: Rua Alcides Hortencio 71, 13800000 Mogi-Mirim Brazil Office: Rua Olavo Bilac 283, Cambuí Campinas SP, Brazil

OLIVEIRA LIMA, RONALDO MATTOS, maritime official; b. Rio de Janeiro, Brasil, May 6, 1957; s. Waldemiro Oliveira Lima dn Maria Dulce Mattos Oliveira Lima; m. Mabel Hubbard Graham-Bell, Oct. 2, 1993; m. Gisela Mac Larem, June 21, 1984 (div.); m. Joao Pedro Graham Bell de o Lima, Fernanda Graham Bell de O Lima. Diploma, Sta. Ursula U., Rio de Janeiro, 1981; MBA, Nova U., Fla., 1986. Registered civil engr. Comml. mgr. Sul Am. Ins., Brasil, 1979-84; fin. dir. Mac Laren Shipyard, Brasil, 1984-90; CEO Astromaritima Navegacao S.A, Brasil, 1990—. With Brazilian Assn. Ship Owners, 1994-97. Office: Astromaritima Navegacao SA, Rua Lauro Muller 116-GR1703, 22290160 Rio de Janeiro Brazil

OLIVEIRA MACIEL, MARCO, Brazilian government official; b. 1940; married; 3 children. BA in Juridical and Social Scis., Cath. U. of Pernambuco, Brazil. Fed. dep. Pernambuco Govt., 1966, pres. Chamber of Deps., 1977-79, gov., 1979-82; senator Govt. of Brazil, 1982-94, min. edn., 1990, leader of senate, v.p., 1994—. Office: Praça dos Tres Poderes, Anexo II do Palacio Planato, 70150900 Brasilia DF, Brazil*

OLIVELLA, CARME, chemist, researcher; b. Barcelona, Spain, July 12, 1956; d. Joan Olivella and Carme Pedregal. MSc in Chemistry, U. Barcelona, 1982, PhD in Chemistry cum laude, 1996. Rschr. Inst. Rsch. i Tecnologia Agroalimentaries, Cabrils, Spain, 1982-96, Lab. Agroalimentary, Cabrils, 1996—. Contbr. articles to profl. jours. Pres. Amnesty Internat., Catalunya, 1985-87; councillor Dist. Coun., Barcelona, 1999—. Mem. Societat Catalana de Quimica Barcelona, Tennis Club Fontmartina-Palautordera (sec. 1999—). Office: Lab Agroalimentari, Carr de Cabrils s/n, 08348 Cabrils Spain

OLIVER, ANN BREEDING, secondary education educator; b. Hollywood, Fla., Sept. 21, 1946; d. Harvey James and Ruth (Lige) Breeding; m. John Russell Kelso, July 22, 1972 (div. Feb. 1984); 1 child, Anna Liege; m. Ted J. Oliver, June 29, 1996. BA in Fgn. Lang., U. Ky., 1967; MA in History of Art, Ohio State U., 1971. Curatorial intern Lowe Art Mus., Coral Gables, Fla., 1972; adj. faculty Fla. Atlantic U., Boca Raton, Fla., 1972-73, 78; lectr. Miami (Fla.) Dade C.C., 1974, with art-music workshop, 1980-81, lectr.-cons., 1972—, adj. faculty music dept., 1991; curator of edn. Ctr. for the Fine Arts, Miami, 1987-92, High Mus. of Art, Atlanta, Ga., 1992-96; Spanish tchr. Sprayberry H.S., Cobb County Bd. Edn., Marietta, Ga., 1997—; mem. Artists in Edn. Panel, Ga. Coun. for Arts, 1994; field reviewer Inst. Mus. Svcs., 1994; adj. faculty in art history Kennesaw State U., Marietta, Ga., 1996—; Spanish tchr. Cobb County Bd. Edn., Atlanta, Spray H.S., Marietta, Ga. Contbg. editor African Art: An Essay for Teachers, 1993; project mgr. and contbg. author: Rings: Five Passions in World Art: Multicultural Curriculum Handbook, 1996. Mem. Cobb County Com. for Fgn. Lang. Curriculum Alignment. Recipient Nat. award for graphics Mead Paper Co., 1989, Gold Medal of Honor publication design S.E. Mus. Educators Publ. Design, 1994. Mem. Am. Assn. of Mus., Inst. Mus. Svcs., Nat. Art Edn. Assn., Am. Coun. Tchrs. Fgn. Langs., Fla. Art Edn. Assn. (dir. mus. divsn.), Ga. Art Edn. Assn. (dir. mus. divsn., Mus. Educator of Yr. 1993), Fgn. Lang. Assn. of Ga. Home: 2420 Mitchell Rd NE Marietta GA 30062-5321

OLIVER, BRUCE LAWRENCE, information systems specialist, educator; b. Westfield, Mass., Nov. 20, 1951; s. Ernest Lawrence and Elizabeth (Welchek) O. AS, Greater Hartford C.C., 1972; BS, U. Mass., 1974; MBA, U. Hartford, 1989. Cert. tchr. sec. and vocat. edn., Mass., Conn. Comml. sales Gordon Realty, Enfield, Conn., 1972-75; forestry tech. rsch. Dept. Environ. Protection, State of Conn., Hartford, 1973, 1974; res. sales Forsman Realty, Enfield, 1975-77; substitute sec. tchr. Enfield Sch. Systems, 1975-78; collections mgr. New Eng. Bank & Trust, Enfield, 1978-79; ops. CCEC/McCullahg Leasing, Inc., S. Windsor, Conn., 1979-81; pres. Ollie & Ike's, Inc., Enfield, 1985-86; MBA Adj. U. Hartford, West Hartford, Conn., 1988-89; workstation engr. Travelers, Hartford, 1982-89; v.p. 1st Class Expert Sys., Inc., Wayland, Mass., 1989-90, Microsoft Corp., Boston, 1991-94; cons., pres. Profl. Office Solutions, Enfield, 1981—; pres. New Venture Inc., Enfield, 1994—; owner, nvi: Ednl. Multimedia Group, nvi: Webmaster Internet Devel.; del. leader Comparative Studies Assn.; Internat. Cultural Exch. with China, Washington; pub. spkr. Spkrs. Bur., U. Hartford; vis. mem. faculty mgmt. info. sci. U. Hartford, 1989-91. Author: A Novice's Guide to Personal Computer Buying, New Ventures to Egypt, New Ventures to China. Gubernatorial appointee Conn. bd. trustees Reg. C.C.s, 1985-89; vice chmn. Student Affairs and Acad. Policies Com. Hartford, 1987; chmn., trustee Conn. Data Processing Curriculum Com., Hartford, 1989; elected com. mem. Enfield Dem. Com., 1975; chmn. regional adv. coun. Asnuntuck C.C.; notary pub. Conn., 1972—; gubernatorial appointee Conn. bd. trustees Community Tech. Colls., 1990-93. Recipient CTM degree Toastmaster Internat., Hartford, 1987, State Farmer degree Conn. Future Farmers Am., DeKalb Agrl. Accomplishment award, cert. of recognition Bicentennial (USA) Commn., Enfield, 1976, Vigil Hon. BSA Order of the Arrow, Hartford, 1972, Merit award State of Conn. Community-Tech. Colls. Bd. of Trustees, 1994. Mem. World Affairs Coun. of Hartford, Computer Soc. of IEEE, Am. Assn. for Artificial Intelligence, Assn. C.C. Trustees, Am. Assn. Cmty. and Tech. Colls., Microsoft AlumNet Assn., Internat. Platform Assn., Oldefield Farms Homeowners' Assn. (residence com. sec. 1990-91), Hartford County Soil and Water Conservation Dist., Nat. Press Club Found., Robert Schueller's Eagles Club, Masons. Democrat. Roman Catholic. Avocations: travel, refinishing antiques, tennis, hiking, real estate investment, photography. Home: 71 Oldefield Farms Enfield CT 06082-4565

OLIVER, DAVID JOHN, physician, consultant; b. Oxford, Eng., Feb. 17, 1954; s. Ray and Lucy Leslie (Williams) O.; children: Ben, Tom. BSc, Univ. Coll., London, 1975; MBBS, U. Coll. Hosp., London, 1978. House physician St. Pancras Hosp., London, 1978-79; house surgeon Stoke Mandeville Hosp., Aylesbury, Eng., 1979; gen. practice trainee Swindon, Wiltshire, Eng., 1979-82; registrar St. Christopher's Hospice, London, 1982-83, sr. registrar, 1983-84; cons. physician palliative medicine, med. dir. Wisdom Hospice, Rochester, Kent, Eng., 1984—; med. dir. North Kent Healthcare NHS Trust, 1996-98, Thames Gateway NHS Trust, 1998-99; Mem. Ken Hopkins Tribute Working Party, Motor Neurone Disease Assn., Eng., 1991-93; chmn. Palliative Medicine Specialty Subcom., S.E. Thames Region, 1994-96; adviser on palliative care Brit. Nat. Formulary, London, 1984—. Author: Motor Neurone Disease, 1986, 2nd edit., 1994, Motor Neurone Disease-A Family Affair, 1995. Recipient Thumbs Up award Motor Neurone Disease Assn. Eng., 1993. Fellow Royal Soc. Medicine (London), Royal Coll. Gen. Practitioners; mem. Brit. Med Assn., Brit. Med. Assn. (hon. treas. local divsn. 1989-95, chmn. local divsn. 1997-99), Royal Coll. Obstetricians and Gynecologists (diploma). Avocation: photography, walking. Office: Wisdom Hospice, St Williams Way, Rochester ME12NU, England

OLIVER, DIANE FRANCES, publisher, writer; b. N.Y.C., Feb. 7, 1935; m. Ben Martin Oliver, Sept. 3, 1960 (div. 1973). BA, Syracuse U., 1955. Reporter Millinery Rsch. mag., N.Y.C., 1956-58; with N.Y.C. Bur., London Daily Mail and London Daily Sketch, 1964-69; editor The Celebrity Bull., Celebrity Svc. Inc., N.Y.C., 1971-78; pub. The Celebrity Bull., pres., owner Celebrity Svc. Ltd., London, 1978—; former publicist Lake Lucerne (N.Y.) Playhouse, Bklyn. Acad. Music, Statler Hilton Hotel, N.Y.C. Author: Older Woman/Younger Man, 1975; columnist Palm Beach Social Pictorial mag., 1981-85. Avocations: music, ballet, films, theater, travel. Home: 44 Lennox Gardens, London SW1X 0DJ, England Office: Celebrity Svc Ltd, 93/97 Regent St, London W1B 4ES, England

OLIVER, DOMINICK MICHAEL, business educator; b. Niagara Falls, N.Y., Apr. 12, 1962; s. Dominick Jr. and Priscilla (Prenatt) O.; m. Vicki Anne Sellig, May 18, 1991. AAS, Niagara County C.C., Sanborn, N.Y., 1982; BS in Bus., Niagara U., N.Y., 1984, MS in Edn., 1986. Lic. tchr. bus. and distributive edn., N.Y.; bus. sch. lic. bus., mgmt., acctg., gen. academics, N.Y. Temporary instr. Niagara County C.C., Sanborn, 1986-87; tchr. on spl. assignment LaSalle Sr. H.S., Niagara Falls, N.Y., 1986-87; instr. St. Joseph Parochial Elem. Sch., Niagara Falls, 1987-88; instr., acad. dean Kelley Bus. Inst., Niagara Falls, 1988-91; instr. Cheryl Fell's Sch. Bus., Niagara Falls, 1991-92; instr., advisor Bryant and Stratton Bus. Inst., Buffalo, 1992—, sr. mentor, portfolio textbook curriculum com., 1996—; bus. mgr. Dove Artworks, Buffalo, 1996—; instr. Adopt-A-H.S., Seneca Vocat. H.S., Kensington H.S., Lafayette H.S., Riverside H.S., Buffalo, 1996—. Life mem. Buffalo and Erie County Naval and Servicemen's Park, Buffalo, 1991—. Mem. Nat. Bus. Edn. Assn., Nat. Coun. Tchrs. English, Assembly for Tchg. English Grammar, Nat. Soc. Pub. Accts., Collegiate Press, N.Y. State Assn. Two Yr. Colls., N.Y. State Ind. Accts., Phi Delta Kappa. Republican. Roman Catholic. Avocations: sports (baseball, football, hockey), political history of United States, reading classical literature. Home: 119 Wendover Ave Buffalo NY 14223-2731 Office: The Huntington Learning Ctr 3086 Delaware Ave Kenmore NY 14217-2056

OLIVER, ELIZABETH KIMBALL, writer, historian; b. Saginaw, Mich., May 21, 1918; d. Chester Benjamin and Margaret Eva (Allison) Kimball; m. James Arthur Oliver, May 3, 1941 (div. July 1967); children: Patricia Allison (dec.), Dexter Kimball. BA, U. Mich., 1940. Tchr. Dexter (Mich.) High Sch., 1940-41; libr. Sherman (Conn.) Libr. Assn., 1966-75; pres. Sherman (Conn.) Libr. Assn., 1983-84; writer, historian, 1976—; reporter Sherman Sentinel, 1965-70; editor newsletter Sherman Hist. Soc., 1977-78; columnist Citizen News, Fairfield County, Conn., 1981-83. Author: History of Staff Wives-AMNH, 1961, Background and History of the Palisades Nature Association, 1964, History and Architecture of Grace United Methodist Church, 1990, Legacy to St. Augustine, 1993, Franklin W. Smith and His Casa Monica Hotel, 2000; guest columnist Mandarin News, 1995-97; columnist St. Augustine Record, 1998—. Vol. N.Y. Hist. Soc., N.Y.C., 1961-65; treas. Coburn Cemetery Assn., Sherman, 1976-82; historian Greenbrook-Palisades Nature Assn., Tenafly, N.J., 1962-64; mem. St. Augustine Hist. Soc., Naromi Land Trust (life), Cedar Key Hist. Soc.; adv. bd. IBC (Eng.). Mem. AAUW, Friends of Libr. (life), Inst. Am. Indian Studies, Marjorie Kinnan Rawlings Soc. (charter), St. Augustine Woman's Club (archivist, cert. of appreciation 1990), Sherman Hist. Soc., Mandarin Hist. Soc. Republican. Congregationalist. Avocations: sacred choral music, research, reading, piano and dulcimer playing, botany. Home: 2292 Commodores Club Blvd Saint Augustine FL 32080-9161

OLIVER, G(EORGE) BENJAMIN, educational administrator, philosophy educator; b. Mpls., Sept. 17, 1938; s. Clarence P. and Cecile (Worley) O.; m. Paula Rae Foust, Sept. 15, 1963; children: Paul Benjamin, Rebecca Lee. BA with honors, U. Tex., 1960; MDiv, Union Theol. Sem., N.Y.C., 1963; MA, Northwestern U., 1966, PhD, 1967. Lectr. Northwestern U., Evanston, Ill., 1966-67; asst. prof. Hobart & William Smith Coll., Geneva, N.Y., 1967-71, chmn. dept. philosophy, 1969-77, assoc. prof., 1971-77, prof., 1977; dean Southwestern U., Georgetown, Tex., 1977-89, provost, 1986-89; pres. Hiram (Ohio) Coll., 1989-2000, pres. emeritus, 2000—; chmn. Coun. Acad. Deans and V.P.s of Tex., 1987-88. Contbr. articles to profl. jours. Trustee John Cabot U., Rome, 1989—, Grand River Acad., Austinburg, Ohio, 1991—, N.E. Ohio Coun. Higher Edn., 1991-2000, Ohio Found. Ind. Coll., 1989—, vice-chair, 1999-2000, exec. com., 1994-2000, co-chair strategic planning com., 1997-98; trustee Assn. Ind. Colls. and Univs. Ohio, 1993—, Nat. Assn. Ind. Colls. and Univs. Pol. Com. on Student Aid, 1999-2000, Am. Coun. Edn. Commn. Govtl. Rels., 1994-97, Cleve. Coun. on World Affairs, 1996-2000; chmn. bd. trustees East Ctrl. Coll. Consortium, 1993-95. Rockefeller Found. fellow, 1960-61, Internat. fellow Columbia U., 1962-63; rsch. grantee NEH, 1973-74. Mem. AAUP, Am. Coun. Edn. (commn. on govtl. rels.), Soc. for Values in Higher Edn., Assn. Ind. Coll. and Univs. Ohio (treas. 1993-94), East Ctrl. Colls. Consortium (chair, bd. trustees 1993-95), Ohio Found. Ind. Colls. (exec. com. 1994-2000, vice chair elect 1999-2000), Am. Assn. Higher Edn., Cleve. Coun. on Fgn. Rels. Episcopalian. Office: Hiram Coll Office of Pres Hiram OH 44234

OLIVER, GILDA MARIA, sculptor, artist; b. Manhattan, N.Y., Nov. 16, 1961; d. Thomas Tobin and Francoise Marie (Bonamy) Krampf; m. Shawn James Francis McLean, Aug. 1, 1983 (div. Dec. 1986); 1 child, Cory Shawn McLean; m. Marc Scott Oliver (div. 1998); m. Anthony Lamont Dowdell, 2000. BFA cum laude, Wells Coll., Aurora, N.Y., 1984; BFA, N.Y.S. Coll. of Ceramics at Alfred U., 1994; MFA, Cranbrook Art Acad., 1997. Artist-in-residence Powasi Pottery, Detroit, 1997-98; dir. corp. sales and rentals Cambridge (Mass.) Art Assn., 1988-92; tchrs. asst. art dept. Wells Coll., Aurora, 1980-84; prof. Ctr. for Creative Studies, Detroit, 1999—. Commissioned sculptures include Heather, 1984, Mark Phillips, 1987, Dr. Cutler-West, 1987, George Orwell, 1988, B.F. Skinner, 1988, Margaret Gibson, 1993 (nom. Pulitzer Prize award 1995), David McKain, 1992 (nom. Pulitzer Prize award 1995); shows include U. Pitts., Bradford, Hanley Gallery, 1995; represented in collections Wells Coll., Aurora, 1984, Lillian Hellman, N.Y.C., 1984, Victoria and Richard MacKenzie-Childs, Ltd., Aurora, 1988, B.F. Skinner, Cambridge, 1989, Robert and Jane Saltonstall, Jr., Concord, Mass., 1989, David McKain and Margaret Gibson, Providence, R.I., 1995; represented in galleries including Copley Soc., Boston, 1985-89, Cambridge Art Assn., 1988-90, Bella Luna Gallery, Boston, 1992-93, Brickbottom Gallery, Somerville, Mass., 1989-95, Loveed Gallery, 1995—; featured (cover) Am. Ceramics mag., Art in Am. Nominated Tiffany Comfort award, 1999.

OLIVER, JAMES ANTHONY, writer, editor, consultant; b. Plymouth, Devon, Eng., Jan. 17, 1956; s. Thomas Gabriel and Mary Anne (McKearney) O. Student, Exeter Coll., Eng., 1973-76; student mech. engring, City U., London, 1976-77; BSc, Plymouth Polytech., Eng., 1982; Read MSc in Applied Energy, Cranfield Inst. Tech., Eng., 1985. Intern British Gas, London, 1980-81; cons. Energy Conscious Design Partnership, London, 1985-86; dir. A Company of Writers, Ltd., London, 1988-90; prin. James A. Oliver, Cons., London, 1991—; freelance writer, 1978—; mem. conf. adv. com. World Devel. Coun., Honolulu, 1992, Singapore, 1993, Barcelona, 1994; spl. cons. to Chmn. Interhemispheric Bering Strait Tunnel and R.R. Group, Washington, 1994; founder intercontinental conv. to create a world railway system (four links: Bering Strait, Strait of Gibraltar, Bosporos Strait, Ctr. Am. Land-Bridge), 1996; dir. World Editl. Network, 1997—. Editor, author: (jour.) The Seychelles Islands Jour., 1990-92; editor-in-chief Te Global Railway.com., 1999—; author Proceedings of First Super Projects Conf. in Honolulu, Conway Data, U.S., 1992. Mem. The Soc. of Authors, Writers' Guild of Great Britain, Wig and Pen Club, London. Avocations: writing, reading, travel, sailing, deep-sea fishing. E-mail: baneau@worldeditorialnetwork.com.

OLIVER, MARLYS MAE, retired editor, writer; b. St. Paul, Mar. 23, 1930; d. Earle R. and Margaret A. (Parrott) Benner; m. Alfred Leo Oliver, Apr. 28, 1951; children—Stephanie Margaret, David Earle. AA, Lakewood C.C., 1970; student Metro State U., 1976-77. Graphic artist Lakewood C.C., White Bear Lake, Minn., 1968-70; corr. Women Sports mag., N.Y.C., 1973-77; editor Press Publs., White Bear Lake, 1972-76; mng. editor Frogtown Forum, St. Paul, 1976-77; mayor City of Birchwood, Minn., 1977-83; exec. editor Press Publs., White Bear Lake, 1982-92; owner Dolls by Marlys, 1992—; host weekly cable tel. talk show Come for Coffee, 1988-90; pres., dir. Cable Access Corp., 1985-87. Mem. White Bear Lake Arts Council, dir., 1975; bd. dirs. Lakeshore Players, 1984-85, White Bear Lake Area Hist. Soc.; chmn Ramsey Washington Counties Cable TV Commn. Recipient numerous awards in journalism. Mem. Minn. Press Women (past treas.), Midwest Writers Conf (com.) Mem. Democratic Farm Labor Party. Lodge: Job's Daus. (Queen 1949). Contbr. numerous articles and poems to popular mags. Home and Studio: 139 Birchwood Ave Saint Paul MN 55110-1611

OLIVER, MICHAEL FRANCIS, physician, consultant cardiologist, educator; b. Wales, July 3, 1925; s. Wilfrid F.L. and Cecilia B. (Daniel) O.; m. Margaret Y. Abbey, Oct. 12, 1948 (div. 1979); children: John (dec.), Sarah, Mark, Paul; m. Helen Louise Daniel, June 28, 1985. MB, U. Edinburgh, Scotland, 1947, MD, 1957; MD (hon.), Karolinska Inst., Stockholm, 1980, Bologna (Italy) U., 1986. Personal prof. cardiology U. Edinburgh, 1974-78; prof. medicine and cardiology, chmn. dept. U. Edinburg, 1978-89; dir. Wynn Inst. for Metabolic Rsch., London, 1989-93; hon. prof. Nat. Heart and Lung Inst. U. London, 1993-99; com. mem. Med. Rsch. Coun., London, 1982-86; chmn. panel on cardiac fitness Dept. Transport, 1989-90; cons. Dept. Health, U.K., 1980-99, WHO, Geneva, 1975—. Editor 5 books on sci. aspects of heart disease; contbr. over 300 articles on heart disease, biochemistry and epidemiology to med. jours. Decorated comdr. Order Brit. Empire. Fellow Royal Soc. Edinburgh, Royal Coll. Physicians (London), Royal Coll. Physicians (Edinburgh) (pres. 1986-89), Brit. Cardiac Soc. (pres. 1980-84), Athenaeum (London), New (Edinburgh). Avocation: Italy and Italians. Office: Keepier Wharf 12 Narrow St, London E14 8DH, England

OLIVER, RODNEY JOHN, solicitor; b. Southampton, Hants, Eng., June 1, 1937; s. Frank Austin and Ruby Moya (Davidson) O.; m. Judith Sydney, Aug. 19, 1966; children: Justin, Barnaby, Lucy. Degree, Law Soc. Sch. Law, 1960. Ptnr. Huggins Oliver & Taylor, Reading, Eng., 1964-89; cons. Thompson Leatherdale, Reading, 1989—; chmn. social security appeal Tribunal, Reading, 1984—; spl. immigration adjudicator Taylor House, London, 1990—. Chmn. Reading Civic Soc., 1977-80. Fellow Chartered Inst. of Arbitrators, Arbitrators Co. (liveryman), Freeman of the City of London. Avocations: marathon running, English church architecture. Home: 1 Highmoor Rd, Caversham Reading RG47BN, England Office: Thompson Leatherdale, 23 Russell St, Reading RG1 7XD, England

OLIVER, WILLIAM DONALD, orthodontist; b. Montreal, Dec. 14, 1945; s. Austen William and Margaret Kay (Donald) O. BS in Physics, Mt. Allison U., 1964; DDS, McGill U., 1968; MSD in Orthodontics, U. Pa., 1970. Pres. Orthodontic Enterprises Internat., Geneva, Switzerland, 1973-78; practice dentistry specializing in orthodontics Barrington, R.I., 1979-84; instr. Frankfurt Carolinium, 1972-74; witness Senate Armed Services Com., 1975. Inventor Piezo Electric Bone Healing; contbr. articles to profl. jours. Mem. Olympic Ski Team, Squaw Valley, 1960. Served with USAF, 1970-73. Recipient Carter Meml. award, 1964, M.T. Dohan prize, 1966. Mem. ADA, Can. Assn. Orthodontists, Am. Assn. Orthodontists, European Orthodontic Soc., Can. Dental Assn., Fedn. Internat. d'Automobile (qualified and registered mem.), Royal Ocean Racing Club. Republican. Office: 10812 19th Ave SE Everett WA 98208-5153

OLIVER, WILLIAM EDWARD, JR., mental health nurse; b. Providence, Apr. 22, 1945; s. William E. and Lillian E. (Keeling) O.; m. Jane S. Oliver, May 23, 1970; children: Lydia J., Lynnette K. BS in Psychology, Howard U., 1973; AAS in Nursing, U. D.C. cert. substance abuse nurse, behavior modification. Psychiat. technician Sibley Meml. Hosp., Washington, 1965-68; dir. resident svcs. Overbrook Children's Ctr., Falls Church, Va., 1967-68; nursing asst. Psychiat. Inst. Washington, D.C., 1968-72; team leader, counselor Dominion Psychiat. Treatment Ctr., Falls Church, 1974-77; ins. agt. Mut. Life Ins. Co., Washington, 1977-81, United Ins. Co. Am., Washington, 1981-83; RN Leland Meml. Hosp., Washington, 1988-89, Approtech Agy., Washington, 1989, J and E Agy., Washington, 1989—; counselor Comprehensive Alcohol and Drug Abuse Ctr., Washington, 1986-90; psychiat. nurse, team leader St. Elizabeth Hosp., Washington, 1991—; mem. libr. staff, student asst. U. D.C., Washington, 1984-87. With U.S. Army, 1964-67. Mem. D.C. Nurses' Assn., Psy-Chi.

OLIVERE, RAYMOND LOUIS, illustrator, artist, portrait painter; b. Wilmington, Del., Aug. 31, 1924; s. Louis Ronald and Natalie Adele (Caldara) O.; m. Kathryn Howett, May 9, 1949 (dec. July 1964); children: Marc, Laura Sopp, Gina Burcham; m. Betty Field, Mar. 22, 1968 (dec. Sept. 1973); m. Kathryn Marks Wakefield, June 9, 1984. Student, Art Students League, N.Y.C., 1948-49. Studio illustrator Kent Studio, N.Y.C., 1951-59, Graphic Directions, N.Y.C., 1961-67; freelance illustrator N.Y.C., portrait painter. Painter of more then 300 book covers; exhibited at Nat. Acad. Design, Allied Artist and Audubon shows. Staff sgt. U.S. Army, 1943-46. Howard Pyle scholar, 1934-40. Mem. Am. Soc. Portrait Artists, Portrait Inst. N.Y.C., Allied Artists Am., Soc. Illustrators. Home: 1435 Lexington Ave New York NY 10128-1625

OLIVER-SIMON, GLORIA CRAIG, human resources advisor, consultant, lawyer; b. Chester, Pa., Sept. 19, 1947; d. Jesse Harper and Lavinia Craig Cuff; m. James Russell Norwood, Sept. 1970 (div.); 1 child, James Russell Jr.; m. Joseph M. Simon, Jan. 1993. BS, U. Md., 1987; JD, Am. U., 1990, MS, 1992. Bar: Pa. 1991, U.S. Ct. Appeals (fed. cir.) 1994, D.C. 1997. Pers. specialist VA Med. Ctr., Phila., 1974-80; pers./human resources specialist VA Ctrl. Office, Washington, 1980-90, human resources mgr., 1990-97; atty./adviser human resource mgmt./sr. human resources cons. VACO; mem. VA Work Group on Minority Initiatives, 1990, 93—; VA coord., rep. Coun. for Excellence in Govts. Spkrs. Bur. Project, 1991-92, Pub. Employees Roundtable for Pub. Svc. Recognition Week, 1991-92; subcom. chair Student Employee Programs, Office of Pers. Mgmt. Work Group, 1993; coord. VA Caring and Courtesy Campaign Focus Group, 1993; mem. VA Veterans Health Adminstrn. Nursing Shortage Task Group, 1987, 93, VA Work Group on the Nat. and Cmty. Svc. Program, 1993-94, 95-96, Veterans Health Adminstrn. Healthcare Reform Work Group on Customer Svc., 1993-94; VA's Nat. Com. on Employment of Disabled Vets. and People with Disabilities, 1992-93; VA Office Human Resources Mgmt. coord. Pres.'s Com. on Employment of Persons with Disabilities/Dept. of Def. Student Employment Initiative, 1994-95; VA Office of Human Resources Mgmt. steering com. 1994-96; mem. Dept. of Energy Student Employment Task Group, 1994-96; VACO coord. Welfare to Work Initiative, 1997—; VACO coun. mem. VA Early Mediation Program, 1999—; mem. VACO Workgroup on Position Sensitivity and Suitability Adjudication, 1999—; mentor VA VACO Fed. Women's Program, 1999—. Bd. dirs. So. PG County Cmty. Charities, Inc., 1999—, pres., CEO, 2000. Mem. ABA, Fed. Bar Assn., Nat. Bar Assn., Fed. Cir. Bar Assn., D.C. Bar Assn., Bar Assn. of D.C., Phi Delta Phi, U. Md. Alumni Assn. (mentor program), Am. U. Alumni Assn. (admissions com., mentor program for grad. and law students), Leadership VA Alumni Assn. (chair promotions com. 1997-2000), AKA Sorority Inc., DAV Aux. (fed. unit 1), Zonta Internat., Am. Legion Aux. Avocations: reading, traveling. Home: 809 Braeburn Dr Fort Washington MD 20744-6022 Office: Dept Vets Affairs 810 Vermont Ave NW Washington DC 20420-0001

OLIVER-WARREN, MARY ELIZABETH, retired library science educator; b. Hamlet, N.C., Feb. 23, 1924; d. Washington and Carolyn Belle (Middlebrooks) Terry; m. David Oliver, 1947 (div. 1971); children: Donald D., Carolyn L.; m. Arthur Warren, Sept. 14, 1990 (dec. Feb. 1995). BS, Bluefield State U., 1948; MS, South Conn. State U., 1958; student, U. Conn., 1977. Cert. tchr., adminstr. and supr., Conn.; cert. pub. sch. substitute tchr., K-12, N.J. Media specialist Hartford (Conn.) Pub. Schs., 1952-86; with So. Conn. State U., New Haven, 1972—, asst. prof. Sch. Libr. Sci. and Instruc-

tional Tech., 1987-95, ret., 1995; mem. dept. curriculum com. So. Conn. State U., 1987-95, adj. prof., 1995—; cert. substitute tchr. Somerset County Pub. Schs., 1997—. Author: My Golden Moments, 1988, The Elementary School Media Center, 1990, Text Book Elementary School Media Center, 1991, I Must Fight Alone, 1991, (textbook) I Must Fight Alone, 1994. Mem. ALA, Conn. Ednl. Media Assn., Black Librs. Network N.J. Inc., Assn. Ret. Tchrs. Conn., Black and Hispanic Consortium, So. Conn. State U. Women's Assn., Cicuso Club (v.p.), Friends Club (v.p.), Delta Kappa Gamma, Alpha Kappa Alpha. Avocations: reading, music, piano, walking. Home: 224 High Path Rd Windsor CT 06095-4103 Office: So Conn State U 501 Crescent St New Haven CT 06515-1330

OLIVIERI, DARIO, university administrator, educator; b. Brindisi, Italy, Sept. 26, 1940; s. Francesco and Ada (De Luca) O.; m. Silvana Mazza, Aug. 31, 1968; children: Francesco, Stefano, Matteo. Grad., U. Parma, Italy, 1964, postgrad. in Respiratory Disease, 1966, postgrad. in Internal Medicine, 1969; postgrad. in Immunology, U. Firenze, Italy, 1975. Fellowship in pulmonary medicine U. Parma, 1964-68; rsch. asst. U. Napoli, Italy, 1969-83, assoc. prof., 1983-86; prof. U. Parma, 1986—; dir. dept. respiratory diseases U. Parma, 1986—, Postgrad. Sch. Respiratory Medicine, 1986—. Editor: Airway Obstruction and Inflammation, 1990, Asthma Treatment-A Multidisciplinary Approach, 1992. Mem. European Respiratory Soc. (pres. 1994), Am. Coll. Chest Physicians (regent 1992—), Am. Thoracic Soc. (bd. dirs. 1994). Home: Via Palestro 2, 43100 Parma Italy Office: Univ Parma Respiratory Dis, Via Rasori 10, 43100 Parma Italy

OLLER, JOSE ANTONIO, physicist, researcher; b. Onil, Alicante, Spain, Jan. 17, 1972; s. José Antonio Oller and María Dolores Berbel; m. Maria José Clemente, Sept. 21, 1997; 1 child, Maria José. Diploma in physics, U. Valencia, Spain, 1995, D in Physics, 1999. Rschr. Inst. Kernphysic Forschungszentrum, Jülich, Germany, 1999—. Contbr. articles to profl. jours. Recipient 3d award Spanish Ministry Culture and Sci., 1996; scholar Colegio Mayor San Juan de Ribera, 1989-95. Roman Catholic. Office: Inst Kernphysic, Forschungszentrum, D-52425 Jülich Germany

OLLIER, WILLIAM ERNEST ROYCE, immunogeneticist; b. Crewe, Eng., Jan. 22, 1952; s. Dennis Royce and Hilda Mary (Bordell) O.; m. Janet Hilda Christison, Sept. 14, 1974; children: Bryony, Christian. BSc with honors, Aberystwyth, Wales, 1973; PhD, London U., 1980. Rsch. asst. Charing Cross Hosp., London, 1974-80; lectr. Royal London Hosp., 1980-88; from sr. scientist to reader Manchester U., Eng., 1988-96, prof., 1996—. Fellow Inst. Biomed. Scientists, Royal Coll. Pathologists; mem. British Soc. for Histocompatibility and Immunogenetics (chmn. 1995—), British Soc. for Rheumatology, British Soc. for Immunology, British Transplant Soc. Office: Manchester U Med Sch, Oxford Rd, M139PT Manchester England

OLLILA, JORMA JAAKKO, chief executive officer; b. Seinäjoki, Finland, Aug. 15, 1950; m. Liisa Annikki Metsola; children: Jaakko, Anna, Matti. MSc in Polit. Sci., U. Helsinki, 1976; MSc in Econs., London Sch. Econs., 1978; MSc in Engring., Helsinki U. Tech., 1981; PhD (hon.), U. Helsinki, 1995; DSC (hon.), Helsinki U. Tech., 1998. Account mgr. Citibank N.A., London, 1978-80; from account officer to mem. bd. mgmt. Citibank Oy, Helsinki, Finland, 1980-85; from v.p. internat. ops. to sr. v.p. fin. Nokia Group, Helsinki, 1985-89, mem. group exec. bd., 1986—, dep. mem. bd. dirs., 1989-90, 1989-90; pres. Nokia Mobile Phones, Salo, Finland, 1990-92; pres., CEO Nokia Group, Helsinki, 1992-99, chmn. bd. dirs., CEO, chmn. group exec. bd., 1999—; bd. dirs. UPM-Kymmere, Otava Pub. Co., Ford Motor Co.; mem. European Round Table of Industrialists, 1997—, internat. bd. United World Colls., 1995—, numerous other couns. and coms. Mem. dean's coun. John F. Kennedy Sch. Govt. Harvard U. Decorated Commdr.'s Cross of the Order of Merit, Fed. Republic of Germany, 1997, Commdr., 1st Class of Order of the White Rose of Finland, 1996, Order of Merit of the Hungarian Republic, Officer's Cross, 1996, Order of White Star, Estonia, 1995, Commdr. of Order of Orange-Nassau, 1995. Mem. Confedn. Finnish Industries and Employers (dep. chmn.), Finnish-Swedish C. of C., Assn. Finnish Cultural Found, State Tech. Rsch. Ctr., Econ. Info. Bur., Ctr. for Finnish Bus. and Policy Studies EVA, Sci. and Tech. Policy Coun., Min. Trade and Industry (tech. del.), Savonlinna Opera Festival Promotional Assn., Am.-Scand Found. (overseas adv. trustee), others. Avocations: langs. include Finnish, Swedish and English. Office: Nokia Oy, PO Box 226, FIN-00045 Nokia Group Finland

OLLJUM, ALAR J. RUDOLF, ambassador; b. Vancouver, B.C., Can., Oct. 30, 1959; arrived in Estonia, 1991; s. Rudolf and Irene Gunhild (Dyrberg) O.; m. Lia Silvia Peet, Dec. 31, 1994; children: Liv Malena, Laura Sofia, Linda Irene. BA, U. B.C., Vancouver, 1988; postgrad., Stockholm U., 1989-91, Göteborg (Sweden) U., 1995-96. Freelance journalist Can., 1984-89; spl. advisor MFA, Estonia, 1990-91, head divsn., 1991-92, permanent under-sec., 1992-94, amb.-at-large, 1994-96; Estonian amb. to Lithuania Vilnius, 1996—; nat. coord. Baltic Coun. of Min., 1994-95; chmn. com. sr. ofcls. Coun. Baltic Sea States, 1993-94; guest scholar Swedish Inst., 1990. Active Baltic Christian Student Union, 1978—. Rsch. grantee Swedish Fgn. Ministry, 1996. Mem. Rotalia Acad. Corp. Lutheran. Avocations: skiing, bicycling, tennis. Office: Ministry Fgn Affairs, Islandi Valjak 1, 15049 Tallinn Estonia

OLMAN, MARYELLEN, human resources administrator; b. Grand Rapids, Mich., Dec. 24, 1946; d. Norman Adolph and Mary Irene (McCarthy) O.; m. Richard Isaac Fine, Nov. 25, 1982; 1 child, Victoria Elizabeth. BA in Cmty. Svc., Mich. State U., 1968. Legis. rschr. to Hon. Gerald R. Ford, U.S. Ho. of Reps., 1969-71, spl. asst. to Hon. Jack F. Kemp, 1971-74; personnel analyst L.A. City Housing Authority, 1975-78; profl. placement rep. Gen. Telephone of Calif., Santa Monica, 1978-81, mgmt. staffing adminstr., 1981-84; human resource adminstr. Law Offices Richard I. Fine & Assocs., 1985—. Mem. Founders Cir., L.A. Music Ctr., L.A. World Affairs Coun., Chmn.'s Cir., L.A. Art Mus., Mus. Contemporary Art. Republican. Home: 12097 Summit Cir Beverly Hills CA 90210-1376

OLMSTEAD, MARJORIE ANN, physics educator; b. Glen Ridge, N.J., Aug. 18, 1958; d. Blair E. and Elizabeth (Dempwolf) O. BA in Physics, Swarthmore Coll., 1979; MA in Physics, U. Calif., Berkeley, 1982, PhD, 1985. Rsch. staff Palo Alto (Calif.) Rsch. Ctr. Xerox Corp., 1985-86; asst. prof. physics U. Calif., Berkeley, 1986-90; asst. prof. physics U. Wash., Seattle, 1991-93, assoc. prof., 1993-97, prof., 1997—; prin. investigator materials sci. divsn. Lawrence Berkeley Lab., 1988-93. Contbr. articles to profl. jours. Named Presdl. Young Investigator, Nat. Sci. Found., 1987; recipient Devel. awards IBM, 1986, 87. Fellow Am. Vacuum Soc. (Peter Mark Meml. award 1994); mem. Am. Assn. Physics Tchrs., Am. Phys. Soc. (chair com. on status of women in physics 1999, Maria Goeppart-Mayer award 1996), Materials Rsch. Soc., Assn. Women in Sci., Phi Beta Kappa, Sigma Xi. Office: U Washington Dept Physics PO Box 351560 Seattle WA 98195-1560*

OLMSTED, CRAIG WILLIAM, mortgage banker; b. Glendale, Calif., Dec. 8, 1964; s. Ronald David Olmsted and Susan Mary Lancaster; m. Suzanne Lara Wasylenko, Dec. 7, 1993; children: Joseph David, Jessica Marie. BBA, Western Mich. U., 1986. Commodities asst. Chgo. Bd. of Trade Drexel, Burnham and Lambert, Chgo., 1986; processing mgr. First Savs. Assn. of Ypsilanti, Mich., 1986-89; sales mgr. Mortgage Connection, Farmington Hills, Mich., 1989-92; v.p., gen. mgr. Mutual Fin. Svcs., Farmington, Mich., 1992-97; pres., owner Home Loan Securities, Inc., Livonia, Mich., 1997—. Mem. Mortgage Bankers Assn. of Mich. Republican. Orthodox. Avocations: ice hockey, softball, fishing, travel. Home: 47645 Wellesley Ct Novi MI 48374-2870 Office: Home Loan Specialists 13961 Farmington Rd Livonia MI 48154-5403

OLNAS, FELIX J., retired Slavic language educator; b. Tartu, Estonia, Mar. 6, 1911; m. Lisbet Kõve, July 12, 1937; children: Helina (Mrs. Charles Piano), Valdar. Student in Finno-Ugric and Slavic langs., Budapest (Hungary) U., 1935-36; MA in Finno-Ugric Lang., Tartu U., 1938; student in Slavic and English langs., Heidelberg (Germany) U., 1946-48; PhD in Linguistics and Slavic Lang., Ind. U., 1952; hon. doc., Tartu U., 1999. Lectr. various univs., 1938-50; lectr. Russian studies Ind. U., Bloomington, 1950-52, instr. Slavic studies, 1952-55, asst. prof., 1955-61; assoc. prof. Slavic langs. and lits., 1961-65, prof., 1965-81, prof. Uralic and Altaic studies, 1965-81, fellow Folklore Inst., 1965-81, prof. emeritus, 1981—; vis. prof. Slavic and Finnic folklore, U. Calif., Berkeley, spring 1976; lectr. and presenter in field. Author: Truth and Justice of Vargamäe: Essays, 1984, Studies in Finnic Folklore: Homage to the Kalevala, 1985, Essays on Russian Folkore and Mythology, 1985, Immortal Kalevipoeg, 1994, others; editor: How Writers Write Lund, 1978, European Folklore: Readings from the Journal of the Folklore Institute, 1981, others; mem. adv. bd. Russian Lang. Jour., 1976-77; cons. Ency. Am. Popular Beliefs and Superstitions, 1984; mem. editl. com. The Slavic and East European Jour., 1966—; assoc. editor Uralic and Altaic Series, 1960—; contbr. over 350 articles to profl. publs. Recipient Cultural award Found. Estonian Arts and Letters, 1978, Kalevala medal Finnish Govt., 1985, Lauri prize Found. Estonian Culture in U.S., 1985, medal of Kreutzwald's Mus., Võru, 1991, awarded Presdl. Order of the Estonian State Coat of Arms, II Class, 1997; Finno-Ugric, Slavic and Folklore fellow Tartu U., 1942-44; Fulbright grantee for Finland, 1961-62, Guggenheim grantee, 1961-62, 66-67, Fulbright-Hays grantee for Yugoslavia, 1964-65, grantee Am. Philos. Soc., 1966, Ford Found., summer 1967, travel grantee ACLS, 1973, Rsch. grantee NEH, 1974-75. Fax:(812) 855-2107. E-mail: iuslavic@indiana.edu. Office: Ind U Dept Slavic Langs and Lit 502 Ballantine Rd Bloomington IN 47401-5018

OLNEY, PETER JAMES STEPHEN, zoologist; b. Bournemouth, Eng., July 2, 1931; s. James and Margaret (Stephen) O. BSc, U. Durham, 1958, diploma in Edn., 1959. Research biologist Wildfowl Trust, 1959-64; head of research Royal Soc. Protection of Birds, 1964-69; curator of birds Zool. Soc. London, 1969-81, curator of birds & reptiles, 1981-91; mem. emeritus Survival Service Commn., Glans, Switzerland, 1974—. Editor: International Zoo Yearbook, 1975—; author/editor: Birds of the Western Palearctic, 1977, 80, 83, 85; author: Paintings of Henry James, 1987, children's books; contbr. Encylopedia Britannica, 1980-94. Coord. Internat. Studbook, 1975—; trustee Herpetol. Conservation Trust, 1990—; dir. Fedn. Zoos, 1991-96. Fellow Inst. Biology, London, Linnean Soc.; mem. Internat. Council Bird Preservation (chmn. Brit. sect. 1982-88), Brit. Ornithologist's Union (v.p. 1985-88. Social Democrat. Avocations: reading, bird watching, theatre, music. Home: 3 Dukes Ave, London N3 2DE, England Office: Zool Soc London, Regent's Park, London NW1 4RY, England

OLOFSSON, JAN GUNNAR VILHELM, otolaryngologist, educator; b. Malmoe, Sweden, Mar. 28, 1940; s. Gunnar Valdemar and Siri Elisabeth (Persson) O.; m. Margareta Ingegerd, 1973 (div. 1989); children: Charlotta, Matilda, Lovisa; m. Anne Berit Guttormsen; 1 child, Jan Stefan. MD, Lund U., Sweden, 1967; PhD, Linköping U., Sweden, 1973. Specialist in otorhinolaryngology/head and neck surgery. Asst. prof. Dept. Otolaryngology Linköping (Sweden), 1973-75, assoc. prof., 1975-87, head Dept. Otolaryngology, 1986-87; prof., chmn. Dept. Otolaryngology/Head and Neck Surgery Univ. Hosp., Bergen, Norway, 1987—; dir. head and neck divsn. Univ. Hosp., 1995-99; dep. CEO Haukeland U. Hosp., Bergen, 1999—. Sem. editl. bd. Acta Otolaryngologica, 1988-2000, Clin. Otolaryngology, 1980—, Jour. Otolaryngology, 1972-95; editl. bd. European Archives Otorhinolaryngology, 1998-99, mng. editor, 2000—; contbr. over 200 articles to internat. jours., chpts. to textbooks. Mem. Collegium Oto-Rhino-Laryngologicum Amicitae Sacrum, Swedish Med. Assn., Swedish Soc. of Medicine, Swedish Otolaryn. Soc., Norwegian Otolaryn. Soc., Soc. Surgical Oncology, Norwegian Med. Assn., Danish Soc. Otolaryngology/Head and Neck Surgery, Danish Soc. Head and Neck Oncology, Can. Soc. Otolaryngology/Head and Neck Surgery, Scandinavian Soc. for Head and Neck Oncology (pres.), Assn. of Head and Neck Oncologists of Gt. Britain, Internat. Fedn. Head and Neck Oncolog. Socs., Soc. Surg. Oncology, The European Soc. for Surg. Oncology, Am. Head Neck Soc., The Laryngeal Cancer Assn., The Scandinavian Soc. for Laser Therapy, The European Soc. for Laser Therapy, The European Laryngological Assn. (pres.-elect), La Societa de Scienze Mediche di Conegliano Vittorio Veneto, The Royal Soc. Medicine (Gt. Britain), German Otorhinolaryngol. Head & Neck Soc., Rotary Internat., Bergenhus Rotary Club (past pres.). Fax: 47-55974956. E-mail: jan.olofsson@.haukeland.no. Office: Haukeland U Hosp, Dept Otolaryngol/Head Neck Surgery, N-5021 Bergen Norway

OLOFSSON, KURT STEFAN, development engineer; b. Pitea, Norrbotten, Sweden, Aug. 23, 1957; s. Sven Olof and Ragnhild Anna (Bergstrom) O.; m. Kerstin Elisabet Bergman, July 15, 1989; children: Anna-Lotta, Nils. MSc, Lulea U. Tech., Sweden, 1981, Tech. Lic., 1995. Devel. engr. ABB STAL, Finspong, Sweden, 1981-85; project leader devel. ABB PLAST, Pitea, 1985-89; project leader rsch. Swedish Inst. Composites, Pitea, 1989—. Contbr. articles to profl. jours.; patentee in field. With Swedish Army, 1976-77. Mem. SAMPE, ICCM-10 (vice chmn. 1995), ICCM-11 (exec. coun. 1997), ICCM-12 (exec. coun. 1999). Avocations: tennis, squash, golf, sailing. Office: Swedish Inst Composites, Fibervagen 2 Box 271, 94126 Pitea Sweden

OLOPADE, OLUFUNMILAYO FALUSI, oncologist, geneticist, educator. MBBS with distinction, U. Ibadan, Nigeria, 1980. Diplomate Am. Bd. Internal Medicine, Am. Bd. Med. Oncology, Am. Bd. Hematology; lic. MD Ill., Ind. Intern in medicine, surgery, pediatrics, ob-gyn. Univ. Coll. Hosp., Ibadan, 1980-81; intern in internal medicine Cook County Hosp., Chgo., 1983-84, resident in internal medicine, 1984-86, chief resident in medicine, 1986; postdoctoral fellow jt. sect. hematology/oncology U. Chgo., 1987-91; clin. instr. U. Ill. Abraham Lincoln Sch. Medicine, Chgo., 1986-87; asst. prof. hematologyo/oncology, Pritzker Sch. Medicine U. Chgo., 1991—, mem. Cancer Rsch. Ctr., 1991—, mem. Cancer Biology com., 1994—, mem. Genetics com., 1996—; attending physician Cook County Hosp., Chgo., 1987; dir. Cancer Risk Clinic, U. Chgo., 1992—, dir. fellowship program hematology and oncology sect., 1993—. Ad hoc reviewer Jour. AMA, Genes, Chromosomes and Cancer, Genomics, Human Molecular Genetics, Cancer Rsch., Blood, Molecular Carcinogenesis, New Eng. Jour. Medicine; contbr. articles to profl. jours. Mem. AAAS, Am. Assn. Cancer Rsch. (membership credentialing com. 1994-95, program com. carcinogenesis subcom. 1993), Am. Soc. Clin. Oncology (mem. program com. subcom. tumor biology and genetics 1997), Am. Assn. Preventive Oncology , Women in Cancer Rsch., Am. Soc. Hematology, Am. Cancer Soc. (adv. com. cancer control investigations, epidemiology, diagnosis, therapy 1994-97). Office: U Chgo Med Ctr 5841 S Maryland Ave # Mc2115 Chicago IL 60637-1463

OLORUNFEMI, BABATUNDE OLATUNDE, dental surgeon; b. Ibadan, Nigeria, June 3, 1958; s. Josiah Oladiji and Christianah Alake (Odetola) O.; m. Olanike Mosunmola Falola, May 1990. B Dental Surgery, U. Ibadan, 1983; M of Med. Sci., U. Sheffield, Eng., 1992. Houseman State Hosps. Mgmt. Bd., Ibadan, 1983-84, dental surgeon, 1985-87; registrar Lagos (Nigeria) U. Tchg. Hosp., 1987-90, sr registrar, 1990-93; specialist, cons. Ministry of Health, Abha, Saudi Arabia, 199499; trustee Edn. and Health Resources, Lagos, 1999—; coord. Nigerian Osseointerelation and Dental Implant Soc., 1999—; examiner Ministry of Health, Abha, 1994—; cons. Julianah Meml. Dental Clinic, Lagos, 1992—. Contbr. articles to profl. jours.; inventor in field. Treas., U. Ibadan Med. Students Assn., 1980-81; pres. Nigerian Assn. Dental Students, 1981-82. Recipient 3d prize Mediterranean Congress Prosthetic Dentistry, 1996. Mem. Internat. Assn. for Dental Rsch., World Dental Fedn., Am. Acad. Implant Dentistry. Avocations: walking, Scrabble, Monopoly, novels. Office: Assir Dental Ctr, Box 1393, Abha Saudi Arabia

O'LOUGHLIN, JOHN KIRBY, retired insurance executive; b. Bklyn., Mar. 31, 1929; s. John Francis and Anne (Kirby) O'L.; m. Janet R. Tag, July 5, 1952; children: Robert K., Steven M., Patricia A., John A. BA in Econs., St. Lawrence U., Canton, N.Y., 1951. State agt. Royal Globe Ins. Group, 1953-58; with Allstate Ins. Co., 1958—, mktg. v.p., group v.p., then exec. v.p., 1972—; pres. Allstate Life Ins. Co., 1977—; chmn. bd. Allstate Ins. Co. and Life Co. Can., 1976—, sr. exec. v.p., chief planning officer, 1980-90; ret.; bd. dirs. all cos. in Allstate Ins. Group and Allstate Enterprises, Inc.; former pres. Allstate Enterprises, Inc.; pres., CEO Royal Link Ventures, Ltd., Pinehurst, N.C. Trustee St. Lawrence U.; bd. trustees, pres. U.S. Marine Corps U. Found., Inc.; bd. dirs. Marine Corps Assn., Am. Ireland Fund, USMC Scholarship Found. Inc., Coun. on Ind. Colls.; past chmn. No. Suburban Chgo. United Way; elder 1st United Presbyn. Ch. Capt. USMCR, 1951-53. Mem. Sales and Mktg. Execs. Internat. (bd. dirs., past chmn., pres.), Whispering Woods Golf Club, Pinehurst Country Club, Lahinch Club, Country Club of N.C., Army-Navy Club, Washington. Office: Royal Links Ventures Ltd PO Box 3579 Pinehurst NC 28374-3579

OLOV, HALLENBERG NILS, mycology educator, researcher; b. Kil, Närke, Sweden, Aug. 3, 1947; s. Eyvind Torbjörn and Svea Kristina (Löthstam) H.; m. Laia Hovedskou, June 19, 1976; 1 child, Karl. PhD., U. Göteborg, Sweden, 1981. Asst. prof. mycology U. Göteborg, 1981-87, as-soc.prof., 1987—, head dept. systematic botany, 1996—. Author: Lachnocladiaceae of North Europe, 1985; sect. editor Nordic Jour. Botany, 1994—. Mem. Mycol. Soc. Am., Brit. Mycol. Soc., Göteborg Mycol. Club (chmn. 1986—). Avocation: gardening. Office: U Göteborg Dept Sys Bot, Carl Skottsbergs Gata 22, S-41319 Göteborg Sweden

OLSCHWANG, ALAN PAUL, lawyer; b. Chgo., Jan. 30, 1942; s. Morton James and Ida (Ginsberg) O.; m. Barbara Claire Miller, Aug. 22, 1965; children: Elliot, Deborah, Jeffrey. BS, U. Ill., 1963, JD, 1966. Bar: Ill. 1966, N.Y. 1984, Calif. 1992. Law clk. Ill. Supreme Ct., Bloomington, 1966-67; assoc. Sidley & Austin and predecessor firms, Chgo., 1967-73; with Montgomery Ward & Co. Inc., Chgo., 1973-81, assoc. gen. counsel, asst. sec., 1979-81; ptnr. Seki, Jarvis & Lynch, Chgo., 1981-84, dir., mem. exec. com.; exec. v.p., gen. counsel, sec. Mitsubishi Electronics Am. Inc., N.Y.C., 1983-91, Cypress, Calif., 1991—; dir. Mitsubishi Electrics and Electronics USA, Inc. Mem. ABA, Am. Corp. Counsel Assn., Calif. Bar Assn., Ill. Bar Assn., Chgo. Bar Assn., N.Y. State Bar Assn., Bar Assn. of City of N.Y., Am. Arbitration Assn. (panel arbitrators). Office: Mitsubishi Elec & Electronics USA Inc 5665 Plaza Dr Cypress CA 90630-5023

OLSEN, CLIFFORD WAYNE, retired physical chemist, consultant; b. Placerville, Calif., Jan. 15, 1936; s. Christian William and Elsie May (Bishop) O.; m. Margaret Clara Gobel, June 16, 1962 (div. 1986), remarried, Mar. 4, 2000; children: Anne K. Olsen Cordes Bothe, Charlotte Marie; m. Nancy Mayhew Kruger, July 21, 1990 (div. 1993). AA, Grant Tech. Coll., Sacramento, 1955; BA, U. Calif.-Davis, 1957, PhD, 1962. Physicist, project leader, program leader, task leader Lawrence Livermore Nat. Lab., Calif., 1962-93; ret., 1993, lab. assoc., 1993-95, 96—; cons. Holmes & Narver, 1995, Keystone Internat., 1996—, Am. Techs. Inc., 1997, Profl. Analysis, Inc., 1997-99; mem. Containment Evaluation Panel, U.S. Dept. Energy, 1984—, mem. Cadre for Joint Nuclear Verification Tests, 1988; organizer, editor procs. for 2nd through 7th Symposiums on Containment of Underground Nuclear Detonations, 1983-93. Contbr. articles to profl. jours. Mem. bd. convocators Calif. Luth. U., 1976-78. Recipient Chevalier Degree, Order of DeMolay, 1953, Eagle Scout, 1952. Mem. AAAS, Am. Radio Relay League, Seismol. Soc. Am., Livermore Amateur Radio Klub (pres. 1994-96), Sigma Xi, Alpha Gamma Sigma (life), Gamma Alpha (U. Calif.-Davis chpt. pres. 1960-61). Democrat. Lutheran. Avocations: photography, amateur radio, music, cooking.

OLSEN, DAVID MAGNOR, chemistry and astronomy educator; b. Deadwood, S.D., July 23, 1941; s. Russell Alvin and Dorothy M. Olsen; m. Muriel Jean Bigler, Aug. 24, 1963; children: Merritt, Chad. BS, Luther Coll., 1963; MS in Nat. Sci., U. S.D., 1967. Instr. sci., math. Augustana Acad., Canton, S.D., 1963-66; instr. chemistry Iowa Lakes Community Coll., Estherville, Iowa, 1967-69; instr. chemistry Merced (Calif.) Coll., 1969—, instr. astronomy, 1975—, div. chmn., 1978-88, coord. environ. hazardous materials tech., 1989—. Trustee Merced Union High Sch. Dist., 1983—, pres., 1986-87, 97. Mem. NEA, Am. Chem. Soc., Astron. Soc. of the Pacific, Calif. Tchrs. Assn., Planetary Soc., Calif. State Mining and Mineral Mus. Assn. (bd. dirs., sec. 1990-93), Nat. Space Soc., Merced Coll. Faculty Assn. (pres. 1975, 93, 94, treas. 1980-90, 96, 97, bd. dirs., sec. 1990-91), Castle Challenger Learning Ctr. Found. (bd. dirs.), Merced Track Club (exec. bd. 1981), M Star Lodge, Sons of Norway (v.p. 1983), Rotary Internat. (pres. Merced Sunrise 2000-01). Democrat. Lutheran. Home: 973 Idaho Dr Merced CA 95340-2513 Office: Merced Coll 3600 M St Merced CA 95348-2806

OLSEN, DONALD EMMANUEL, architect, educator; b. Mpls., July 23, 1919; s. Clarence Edward and Thea (Scharnell) O.; m. Helen Karen Ohlson, Apr. 2, 1944; 1 child, Alan Edward. B.Arch., U. Minn., 1942; M. Arch., Harvard U., 1946; postgrad. in civic design, U. Liverpool, Eng., 1953; postgrad. in philosophy of sci., London Sch. Econs., 1962-63, 68. Registered architect, Calif. Archtl. designer Saarinen, Swanson & Saarinen, Bloomfield Hills, Mich., 1946; project mgr. Skidmore, Owings & Merrill, San Francisco, 1948; designer, draughtsman Wurster, Bernardi & Emmons, San Francisco, 1949-51; pvt. practice architecture Berkeley, Calif., 1954—; prof. architecture U. Calif.-Berkeley, 1954-90, prof. emeritus, 1990—; guest prof. various univs., lectr. in field, U.S., Eng., Germany, Denmark; lectr., tchr. Ecoles D'Art Améicaines de Fontainebleau, France; nominator Carnegie Grant Personality Assessment and Research Creativity Study Architects, 1959; profl. adviser City of San Francisco, 1961-62; juror, critic, evaluator, various programs, projects. Contbr. articles, chpts. to profl. publs.; subject of numerous profl. publs. Numerous exhibits throughout U.S., Europe; prin. works include numerous design commns. Recipient awards, including nat. awards of Excellence Archtl. Record, Houses of 1966; scholar Harvard U., Cambridge, Mass., 1945-46; A. W. Wheelwright fellow Harvard U., 1953. Fellow AIA (2 nat. honor awards 1970, 8 various regional, local Honor, Excellence and Merit awards 1967-89); mem. Brit. Soc. for Philosophy of Sci., Soc. for Philosophy and Tech., Open Soc. and Its Friends. Avocations: study of philosophy; travel and travel photography; opera. Office: Donald E Olsen & Assocs Architects 771 San Diego Rd Berkeley CA 94707-2025

OLSEN, EGIL, former soccer coach. Head coach nat. soccer team Norway, World Cup Championships, 1994; head coach Norwegian Nat. Team; ret., 2000; head coach nat. soccer team Norway, 1990-98. Address: Storkenebbveien 15, 0860 Oslo Norway*

OLSEN, ERLING HEYMANN, Danish government official; b. Copenhagen, Apr. 18, 1927; s. Albert Georg and Agnete (Bing) O.; m. Annette Unmack Larsen, 1969; children: Tore, Ida. Degree in econs., U. Copenhagen, 1953, Dr. of Econs., 1971. Mem. Folketing for Copenhagen, 1964-98; min. housing Govt. Denmark, 1978-82, min. justice, 1993-94; spkr. Danish Parliament, 1994-98; chmn. Kredit Danmark SA, Paris, 1989. Author 12 books; contbr. articles to profl. jours. Mem. Danish Fgn. Policy Soc. (chmn. 1988). Mem. Social Dem. Party. Avocations: skiing, DIY. Home: Søbredden 14, DK-2820 Gentofte K, Denmark

OLSEN, FLEMMING OVE, mechanical engineer, educator; b. Sorø, Denmark, Jan. 24, 1948; s. Ove K. G.a nd Sofie K. (Jacobsen) O.; m. Grethe Elholm, Apr. 17, 1976; children: Louise, Ingrid. MSc, Tech. U. Denmark, Lyngby, 1977, postgrad., 1982; PhD in Mech. Engring., Tech. U. Denmark, 1982. Sr. engr. IPU, Lyngby, Denmark, 1980-82; postdoctoral rschr. Tech. U. Denmark, Lyngby, 1982-85, asst. prof., 1985-89, assoc. prof., 1989—, divsn. mgr. Thermal Processing Matls., 1995—; nat. coord. EUREKA projects in indsl. laser tech., 1989—. Patentee in field. County counsellor Vestsjaellands Amt, 1994—; bd. dirs. Vestsjaelland Transport Authority, 1994—. Mem. Laser Inst. Am., Int. Inst. Welding (chmn. laser cutting work group 1986—), Schwerpunktprogramm (steering com. 1995—). Avocations: rowing, cross country skiing. Home: Egevangs Alle 23, 4180 Sorø Denmark Office: Tech U Denmark, Bldg 425, 2800 Lyngby Denmark

OLSEN, HAAKON ANDREAS, educator; b. Tromsø, Norway, Sept. 18, 1923; s. Johan and Gurine (Østrem) O.; m. Betty Ugedahl, May 20, 1952; children: Hanne, Guri. Degree physics engring., Norges Tekniske Høgskole, Trondheim, Norway, 1950, Dr. techn., 1953; postdoctoral, Cornell U., 1954-55, Calif. Inst. of Tech., 1955-56. Asst. prof. Norges Tekniske Høgskole, 1956-62, prof., 1962-64; chief Radiation Sec., Nat. Bur. of Stds., Washington, 1964-65; prof. U. Trondheim, 1965-99, prof. emeritus, 1999—; pres. Coll. Arts & Scis. U. Trondheim, 1969-75; chmn. Norway CERN com., Oslo, 1980—; bd. dirs. NORDITA, Copenhagen, 1970-89, chmn. bd., 1977-81. Author: Springer Tracts in Modern Physics, Vol. 44, 1968; contbr. numerous articles to profl. jours. Mem. Royal Norwegian Soc. of Sci. and Letters (pres. 1990—), Norwegian Phys. Soc., Am. Phys. Soc., European Phys. Soc., Norwegian Acad. of Scis., Norwegian Acad. of Tech. Scis.

OLSEN, JAN TERJE, corporate treasurer; b. Skien, Telemark, Norway, Sept. 26, 1958; s. Ole Andreas and Konstanse (Grinilia) O.; m. Margrethe Oldrup, Aug. 16, 1986; children: Trond Olaf, Inger Helene. Siviløkonom/MBA, Norw. Sch. Econs. & Bus. Adm., Bergen, Norway, 1983. Acct. mgr. Norsk Finans A/S, Tromsø, Norway, 1984-87; v.p. Fabin Nord A/S, Tromsø, Norway, 1987-90; corp. treas. A/S Union, Skien, Norway, 1990—; chmn. bd. SKK Nett AS, Prosgrunn, Norway, 1998—; mem. Corp. Assembly of Skiensfjordens Energy Co., 1995-99; dir. Skien Mcpl. Pension

Fund, Skien, 1995—; A/S Kontorbygg, Skien, 1996—; dir. Grenland Investment Fund, Skien, 1997—; fin. dir. Worske Skog Union, Skien, 1999—. Mem. town coun., Skien, 1995—, exec. coun., 1995—. Chief petty officer Royal Norwegian Navy, Tromsø, 1983-84. Norwegian Conservative Party. Avocations: scouting, outdoor activities. Home: Falkaasen 91, B-3727 Skien Norway Office: A/S Union, PO Box 66 Sentrum, N-3701 Skien Norway

OLSEN, M. KENT, lawyer, educator; b. Denver, Mar. 10, 1948; s. Marvin and F. Winona (Wilker) O.; m. Shauna L. Casement; children: Kristofor Anders, Alexander Lee, Nikolaus Alrik, Amanda Elizabeth. BS, Colo. State U., 1970; JD, U. Denver, 1975. Bar: Colo., U.S. Dist. Ct. Colo. 1982, U.S. Tax Ct. Law clk. Denver Probate Ct., 1973-75; assoc. ptnr. Johnson & McLachlan, Lamar, Colo., 1975-80; assoc. Buchanan, Thomas and Johnson, Lakewood, Colo., 1981-82, William E. Myrick, P.C., Denver, 1982-83; referee Denver Probate Ct., Denver, 1983-89; ptnr. Haines & Olsen, P.C., Denver, 1989-95; pvt. practice Denver, 1995—; adv. bd. Denver Paralegal Inst., 1993—, Elder Law Inst., 1994—. Mem. Gov.'s Commn. on Life and the Law, Denver, 1991-2000; bd. dirs. Adult Care Mgmt., Inc., Denver, 1985-95; bd. dirs. Arc of Denver, Inc., 1990—, pres., 1995-97; bd. dirs. Colo. Guardianship Alliance, Denver, 1990-91; bd. dirs., pres. Colo. Fund for People with Disabilities, 1994—. Recipient Outstanding Vol. Svc. award Adult Care Mgmt., 1990, Outstanding Svc. award The Arc of Denver, 1991, Vol. Svc. award Colo. Gerontol. Soc., 1997, Pres.'s award Arc of Denver, 1998. Mem. ABA, Colo. Bar Assn. (chair probate sect.), Am. Assn. Home for Aging, Nat. Acad. Elder Law Attys., Denver Bar Assn. Episcopalian. Avocations: running, skiing, racquetball, art, hiking. Home: 3030 S Roslyn St Denver CO 80231-4153 Office: 650 S Cherry St Ste 1250 Denver CO 80246-3805

OLSEN, MORTEN HARRY, writer, editor, consultant; b. Narvik, Nordland, Norway, Aug. 15, 1960; s. Harry Georg and Inger Karen (Ytterstad) O.; m. Anne Gro Dyvik, Feb. 26, 1988 (div. July 1995); 1 child, Torkild Dyvik. Cons. Norwegian Writers' Ctr., Oslo, 1986-88; editor Forlaget Oktober, Oslo, 1991-92; editor-in-chief De norske Bokklubbene, Oslo, 1992-96; editor Aschehoug, 1997-98; cons. Gyldendal Norsk Forlag, 1998—; chmn. Norwegian Writers' Ctr., 1989-91, The Brage Com., Oslo, 1991-95; vice chmn. Norwegian Writers' Union, 1997-99. Author: For alt hva vi er verdt, 1985 (Best Debut Fiction 1985), Tråder, 1988, Begjaerets pris, 1993 (Best Crime Novel 1993), Tilfeldig utvalg, 1996, Naken for leseren, naken for Gud, 1998, Mord og galskdap, 2000. Sgt. Norwegian Field Artillery, 1979-80. Mem. Norwegian Writers' Union, Crime Writers' Assn., Mystery Writers Am. Avocation: music, Pauline and NT studies.

OLSEN, OLAF, archaeologist, former museum director; b. Copenhagen, June 7, 1928; s. Albert and Agnete (Bing) O.; m. Jean Catherine Dennistoun Sword; 1 child, Morten; m. Rikke Agnete Clausen, May 21, 1971. Cand. mag., Copenhagen U., 1953, PhD, 1966; Dr. (hon.), St. Petersburg. Asst. Nat. Mus. Copenhagen, 1950, asst. keeper, 1958-71, dir. mus., keeper nat. antiquities, 1981-95; prof. medieval archaeology Aarhus U., Denmark, 1971-81; dir. Hielmstierne-Rosencrone Found., 1980—; v.p. Det Kongelige Nordiske Oldskriftselskab, 1981-95. Author: Horgr, hof and church, 1966, Five Viking Ships, 1969, Fyrkat, 1977; contbr. articles to profl. jours. Recipient awards various Danish and Swedish Founds., The Rosenkjaer prize, The Hartmann prize. Fellow Soc. Antiquaries London (hon.); mem. Royal Danish Acad. Sci. and Letters, Vetenskapssoc. i Lund (Sweden), Deutsche Archaeologische Institut, Royal Norwegian Acad., Gustav Adolf Acad. Uppsala (Sweden), Academia Europaea. Home: 2 Strevelshovedvej Alro, DK-8300 Odder Denmark

OLSEN, RICHARD JAMES, artist, art educator; b. Milw., Nov. 15, 1935; s. Edward Marinus and Ann Frances (Keymar) O.; m. Nina Marsh Civilette-Olsen, July 25, 1969; children: Dayna Kim, Dawn Beth, Josh Keymar. BS, U. Wis., 1958, MFA in Painting and Printmaking, 1966. Tchg. asst. U. Wis., 1965-66; art tchr. grade 8 Winnequah Grade Sch., Monona, Wis., 1966-67; instr. printmaking Oper. Area Arts, Green Bay, Wis., 1967-69; instr. painting and drawing U. Ga., Athens, 1969-73, asst. prof., 1974-78, assoc. prof., 1978-94, prof., 1994-2000, Sandy Beaver prof., 1998-2000, emeritus prof., 2000—; represented by Berman Gallery, Atlanta, 1986-97, Novus Inc., Atlanta, 1990-98, Maurine Littleton Gallery, Washington, 1990, Miriam Perlman Gallery, Chgo., 1991, EDL & Assocs., Atlanta, 1994, Elements of Art, Columbus, 1995, Ellen Wallace-Paushter, Art Cons., Chgo., 1999; wrestling coach Monona Grove (Wis.) H.S., 1966-67; panelist Steinham Arts Festival St. Lawrence U., N.Y., 1987, Crossroads in Cultural Studies, Tampere, Finland, 1996; head preparator Reflexes and Reflections Russell Rotunda Capitol Hill, Washington, 1983, Lincoln Ctr., N.Y.C., 1984. One person exhibns. include Claywork Gallery, Atlanta, 1986, H. Smith Gallery U. S.C., Spartanburg, 1991, Nat. Vietnam Vets. Art Mus., Chgo., 1999; group exhibns. include Third Brit. Internat. Print Biennale, Bradford, Yorkshire, Eng., 1971, U. Wis., Madison, 1975, SECAC, Winston-Salem, N.C., 1981, Chattahoochee Valley Arts Assn., LaGrange, Ga., 1982, N.A.M.E. Gallery, Chgo., 1982, Washington Project for the Arts, 1983, Cannon Rotunda, 1983, Russell Rotunda, 1983, Lincoln Ctr., N.Y.C., 1984, LBJ Libr., 1984, Savannah Coll. Art and Design, 1989, R.H. Love, Contemporary, Chgo., 1992, Mus. Fine Arts, Ho Chi Ming City, Vietnam, 1994, Nat. Mus. Fine Arts, Hanoi, Vietnam, 1994, Berman Gallery, Atlanta, 1994; featured Vietnam Reflexes and Reflections, N.Y. Times, New Art Examiner, Chgo. Tribune, "Q" A Jour. of Art, Panorama, AP, Vets. of Fgn. Wars mag., Stars and Stripes, Gravitas mag., War Lit. in the Arts, Bloomsbury Rev., Ninety Six Inc., (documentary) Reflexes/Reflections PBS, 1984; permanent collections Nat. Vietnam Vets. Art Mus., Chgo., Nat. Mus. Fine Art, Hanoi, Vietnam. With U.S. Army, 1959-63, Vietnam. Decorated Purple heart, 1963; Visual Arts fellow So. Arts Fdn./NEA, 1988; Sr. Faculty grantee U. Ga. Rsch. Found., Inc., 1991-93, 96-98, Individual Artist grantee Ga. Coun. Arts, 1993-94; recipient Purchase award 8th Annual Maine/Maritime Internat. Flatworks Exhibn., 1990. Mem. VFW, Mil. Order of the Purple Heart (comdr. 1999-2000). Home: 165 Springdale St Athens GA 30605-1237

OLSEN, STEIN HAUGOM, humanities educator; b. Oslo, Dec. 22, 1946; s. Odd Werner and Aase Karine (Haugom) O.; m. Agnete Birkrem, Dec. 21, 1991; m. Gyrd Anne Larsen (div. 1988). B Lit., Oxford U., Eng., 1974; PhD, U. Bergen, Norway, 1978. Rsch. fellow Norwegian Rsch. Coun., Oslo, 1978-81; sr. lectr. U. Oslo, 1981-85, prof., 1985-97; chair prof. Lingnan U., Hong Kong, 1997—; adj. prof. Oslo Coll. Architecture, 1994-97. Author: The Structure of Literary Understanding, 1978, The End of Literary Theory, 1987; (with Peter Lamarque) Truth, Fiction and Literature A Philosophical Perspective, 1994. Fellow Norwegian Acad. Sci. and Letters. Office: Lingnan U, Tuen Mun NT, Hong Kong China

OLSEN, STEVEN KENT, dentist; b. Spanish Fork, Utah, Nov. 20, 1944; s. Earl Clarence and Adela (Faux) O. BS, Brigham Young U., 1969; DDS, U. Pacific, 1974. Ptrn. practice dentistry in surg. and endodontics Brooks & Olsen, Salt Lake City, 1974—; gen. practice dentistry Steven K. Olsen, D.D.S., San Francisco, 1974-75; pres. S.K. Olsen, P.C., San Francisco, 1975—; ptnr. Olsen, H. & P., San Francisco, 1977-83; instr. U. Pacific, San Francisco, 1978—; chmn. bd. Am. Dentists Ins. Corp., Grand Cayman, W.I., 1978-81; instr. Stanford (Calif.) Inst., 1979-82; med. staff Latter-day Saints Hosp.; cons. Calif. Inst., San Francisco, 1981—; ptnr. John Berghoff Devel. Co.; ptnr. Russell Harris Restorations, Dale Westington Mgmt. Co., Dave Olsen & Co.; bd. dirs. Wilks & Topper, Inc., San Francisco, Curt Facchino Ltd., Woodside. Author: Accolade, 1963, (play) Lancer Ballade, 1963, (acad. course) World Religions, 1979; editor corr. course Calif. Inst., 1981. Recipient Good Citizenship medal SAR, 1963. Mem. Assn. Coll. of Physicians and Surgeons, ADA, Calif. Dental Assn., Utah Dental Assn., Physicians and Surgeons Club (San Francisco), Alpha Epsilon Delta. Home: 385 Old La Honda Rd Woodside CA 94062-2617

OLSEN, TILLIE, author; b. Omaha, Nebr., Jan. 14, 1912; d. Samuel and Ida (Beber) Lerner; m. Jack Olsen; children: Karla, Julie, Kathie, Laurie. LittD (hon.), U. Nebr., 1979, Knox Coll., 1982, Hobart and William Smith Coll., 1984, Clark U., 1985, Albright Coll., 1986, Wooster Coll., 1991, Mills Coll., 1995, Amherst Coll., 1998. Writer-in-residence Amherst Coll., 1969-70; vis. faculty Stanford U., 1972; Writer-in-residence, vis. faculty English M.I.T., 1973-74, U. Mass., Boston, 1974; internat. vis. scholar Norway, 1980; Hill prof. U. Minn., spring 1986; writer-in-residence Kenyon Coll., 1987—; Regents lectr. U. Calif. at San Diego, 1977—, UCLA, 1987; commencement spkr. English dept. U. Calif., Berkeley, 1983, Hobart and William Smith Coll., 1984 Bennington Coll., 1986. Author: Tell Me A Riddle, 1961 (title story received First prize O'Henry award 1961), Rebecca Harding Davis: Life in the Iron Mills, 1972, Yonnondio: From the Thirties, 1974, Silences, 1978, The Word Made Flesh, 1984; editor: Mother to Daughter, Daughter to Mother, 1984; Preface Mothers and Daughters, That Special Quality: A Exploration in Photographs, 1987, 95, Essay Afterword: Saxton's Bright Web in the Darkness, 1998; short fiction published in over 200 anthologies; books translated in 11 langs. pres. women's aux. Calif. CIO, 1941-43, dir. war relief, 1944-45. Recipient Am. Acad. and Nat. Inst. of Arts and Letters award, 1975, Ministry to Women award Unitarian Universalist Fedn., 1980, Brit. Post Office and B.P.W. award, 1980, Mari Sandoz award Nebr. Libr. Assn., 1991, REA award Dungannon Found., 1994, Disting. Achievement award Western Lit. Assn., 1996; Grantee Ford Found., 1959, NEA, 1968; Stanford Univ. Creative Writing fellow, 1962-64, Guggenheim fellow, 1975-76, Bunting Inst. Radcliffe Coll. fellow, 1985; Tillie Olsen Day designated in San Francisco, 1981. Mem. Authors Guild, PEN, Writers Union. Address: c/o Elaine Markson Agency 44 Greenwich Ave New York NY 10011-8347

OLSHAKER, MARK BRUCE, author, film maker; b. Washington, Feb. 28, 1951; s. Bennett and Thelma A. (Abramson) O.; m. Carolyn M. Clemente, Aug. 28, 1977. BA, George Washington U., Washington, 1972. Spl. correspondent St. Louis Post Dispatch, Washington Bur., 1974-75; writer, author, film maker Washington Area, 1972—; v.p. Unicorn Projects, Inc., Washington, 1983—, Mindhunters, Inc. Vienna, Va., 1995—; bd. dirs. Shakespeare Guild, Washington. Author: (novels) Einstein's Brain, 1981, Unnatural Causes, 1986, Blood Race, 1989, The Edge, 1994, The Mindhunters: Broken Wings, 1999; (anthology) Unusual Suspects, 1996; (non-fiction) The Instant Image, 1978; co-author (with John Douglas), Mindhunter, 1995 (Anthony award nomination, Brit. Gold Dagger nomination, Edgar nomination, Mystery Writers of Am.), Unabomber: On the Trail of America's Most-Wanted Serial Killer, 1996, Journey into Darkness, 1997, Obsession, 1998, The Anatomy of Motive, 1999, The Cases That Haunt Us, 2000; (with C.J. Peters) Virus Hunter, 1997; (screen writing) Stormchasers, 1995, (CINE Golden Eagle), The Edge, 1996 (TV Writing and Prodn.) We All Came to America, 1974, A Moment in Time, 1975, Patent Pending, 1975 (silver medal Internat. Film & TV Festival N.Y.), Lewis Mumford: Toward Human Architecture, 1979, Castle, 1983 (Am. Film Festival Red Ribbon), Cathedral, 1985 (Am. Film Festival Blue Ribbon, Cine Golden Eagle) Pyramid, 1988 (CINE Golden Eagle, Nat. Ednl. Film and Video Festival Gold Apple), What's Killing the Children?, 1990, Discovering Hamlet, 1990 (Am. Film Festival Red Ribbon, Bronze medal Inst. Film & TV Festival N.Y.), Mind of a Serial Killer, 1992 (Emmy nomination news and documentary 1993), Roman City, 1994 (Emmy award), Bridge, 1998; contbr. articles to newspapers, mags., wrote exhibition films for Nat. Park Svc., and Nat. Bicentennial Grand Parade, 1976. Media advisor, NEH, Corp. Pub. Broadcasting, Washington, 1984, 89, 91, 98, D.C. Comm. Arts and Humanities; hearing com. D.C. Ct. of Appeal Bd. on Profl. Responsibility, 1988-91. Mem. Writers Guild of Am. East, The Authors Guild, The Cosmos Club, Nat. Press Club. Office: PO Box 1957 Vienna VA 22183-1957

OLSHEN, ABRAHAM CHARLES, actuarial consultant; b. Portland, Oreg., Apr. 20, 1913; m. Dorothy Olds, June 21, 1934; children: Richard Allen, Beverly Ann Jacobs. AB, Reed Coll., 1933; MS, U. Iowa, 1935, PhD, 1937. Chief statistician City Planning Commn., Portland, Oreg., 1933-34; rsch. asst. math. dept. U. Iowa, 1934-37; biometrics asst. Med. Ctr., 1936-37; actuary, chief examiner Oreg. Ins. Dept., 1937-42, 45-46; actuary West Coast Life Ins. Co., San Francisco, 1946—, chief actuary, 1953-63, v.p., 1947—, 1st v.p., 1963-67, senior v.p., 1967-68, bd. dirs., 1955-68; cons. actuarial and ins. mgmt., pres. Olshen & Assocs., San Francisco, 1979—; bd. dirs. Home Federal Savs. & Loan Assn., San Francisco, 1972-85, vice-chmn. bd. 1979-85, bd. chmn. 1985-86; guest lectr. various univs. Contbg. writer Ency. Britannica, Underwriters' Report, The Nat. Underwriter, Life Underwriters Mag., Annals of Math. Stats., other publs. Mem. Calif. com. Health Ins. Coun., U. Calif. Med. Care Adminstrn. com., San Mateo County Retirement Bd. (1975-77). Rsch. assoc. Div. of War Rsch., 1942-44, Ops. Rsch. Gp., H/Q Comdr.-in-Chief, U.S. Fleet, 1944-45. Recipient U.S. Navy Ordnance Devel. award, 1945, Disting. Service award U.S. Office of Sci. Rsch. & Devel., 1945, Presdl. Cert. Merit, 1947. Fellow AAAS, Sigma Xi; mem. Health Ins. Assn. Am. (mem., past chmn. Blanks Com., actuarial & stat. com.), Actuarial Club of Pacific States (past pres.), Actuarial Club of San Francisco (past pres.), Am. Acad. of Actuaries (charter), Am. Math. Soc., Am. Risk and Ins. Assn., Calif. Math. Coun., Commonwealth Club (life), Fellow Conf. of Actuaries in Public Practice, Inst. Mgmt. Scis., Inst. Math. Stats., Internat. Actuarial Assn., Internat. Assn. Consulting Actuaries, Internat. Cong. Actuaries, Ops. Rsch. Soc. (charter), San Francisco Press Club (life). Office: Olshen & Assocs 760 Market St Ste 739 San Francisco CA 94102-2302

OLSNES, SJUR, biochemistry educator; b. Bergen, Norway, Aug. 23, 1939; s. Sigvald and Maria (Berge) O.; m. Barbara Tubylewicz Kwiatkowska, Jan. 5, 1971; 1 child, Astrid Marta. MD, U. Bonn, Germany, 1964; PhD, U. Oslo, 1972; Dr. honoris causa, Engelhardt Inst. Molec. Biol., Moscow, 1997. Intern Hammerfest/Vadsø/Sjøholt, Norway, 1965-66; rsch. fellow Bergen U., Norway, 1966-68; vis. scientist Acad. Scis., Moscow, 1968; rsch. fellow Norwegian Radium Hosp., Oslo, 1969-73, sr. scientist, 1974-89, prof., 1989—; dir. U. Oslo Centre Med. Studies, Moscow, 1993-97. Contbr. articles to profl. jours. Recipient Anders Jahres Med. prize for younger scientist U. Oslo, 1979, Shipley award Harvard U., Boston, 1986, Schunk award Giessen U., 1988, Stiansen Med. award Norwegian Acad. Scis., 1995. Mem. European Molecular Biology Orgn. (life), Academia Europaea (life), Det Norske Videnskaps-Akademi (life), Russian Acad. Scis. (fgn. and life mem.). Home: Vestveien 8, 0284 Oslo Norway Office: Inst Cancer Rsch, Norwegian Radium Hosp Montebello, 0310 Oslo Norway

OLSON, DANIEL JAY, surgeon, researcher, educator; b. Racine, Wis., June 17, 1944; s. Roy Oscar Olson and Laura Lillian (Chaussee) Black; m. Kathryn Mary Mahkovtz, Dec. 27, 1985; children: Lisa R., Loren D.; children: Marisa L., Meredith L., Matthew D., Ryan D., Ivy Agnes Rose. BA, UCLA, 1967, DDS, 1972; PhD, U. Wash., 1992. Diplomate Am. Bd. Oral & Maxillofacial Surgery. Resident oral surgery Mass. Gen. Hosp., Boston, 1972-75; clin. fellow Haravard Med. Sch., Boston, 1974-75; pvt. practice Santa Cruz, Calif., 1975-85; postdoctoral fellow Syntex, Palo Alto, Calif., 1991-92; asst. prof. biochemistry, molecular biology, surgery Pa. State U., Hershey, 1993-96, asst. prof. surgery, 1993-96; asst. prof. oral molecular biology Oreg. Health Scis. U., Portland, 1996-98, asst. prof. oral pathology, 1998—. Contbr. articles to profl. jours. Grantee U.S. Army Breast Cancer, 1993-97, Pa. State U., 1994-96, Oreg. Health Scis. Found., 1999. Fellow Am. Assn. Oral & Maxillofacial Surgeons; mem. ADA, AAAS, Oreg. Dental Soc., Oreg. Assn. Oral & Maxillofacial Surgeons, Umpqua Dental Soc. (pres.). Avocations: golf, surfing. Office: 1813 W Harvard Ave Ste 207 Roseburg OR 97470-2791

OLSON, DENNIS OLIVER, lawyer; b. Seminole, Tex., Oct. 19, 1947; s. Edwin and Beulah Matilda (Strang) O.; m. Leonee Lynn Claud, Jan. 30, 1971; children: James Edwin, Stacy Rae. BA in English, U. Tex., 1969; JD, Tex. Tech U., 1974. Bar: Tex. 1974, U.S. Ct. Mil. Appeals 1974, U.S. Dist. Ct. (no. dist.) Tex. 1978, U.S. Dist. Ct. (we. dist.) Tex. 1978, U.S. Ct. Appeals (5th cir.) 1984, U.S. Supreme Ct. 1985. Commd. USMC, 1969, advanced through grades to capt., 1973, infantry officer various locations including Vietnam, 1969-74; judge advocate USMC, various locations, 1974-78; resigned USMC, 1978; assoc. Carr, Evans, Fouts & Hunt, and predecessor, Lubbock, Tex., 1978-81, ptnr., 1981-85; sole practice Dallas, 1985-88; shareholder, co-chmn. bankruptcy sect. Godwin & Carlton, P.C., Dallas, 1989-94; ptnr. Olson Gibbons Wilbur Nicoud Birne & Gueck, LLP & predecessor, Dallas, 1994—. Bd. dirs. Presbyn. Ctr. Doctor's Clinic, Lubbock, 1983-85, United Campus Ministry, Tex. Tech U., Lubbock, 1984-85; elder Canyon Creek Presbyn. Ch., Richardson, Tex.; treas. bd. dirs. Lubbock chpt. ARC, 1975-77; vol. Lubbock United Way, 1978-80. Decorated Bronze Star; named Outstanding Young Man of Am., 1983. Fellow Tex. Bar Found. (sustaining life); mem. Dallas Bar Assn., Lubbock County Bar Assn. (bd. dirs. 1983-85), Tex. Young Lawyers Assn. (bd. dirs. 1981-83), Judge Advocates Assn. (bd. dirs. 1976-78), Lubbock C. of C. (grad. Leadership Lubbock program 1981), Phi Delta Phi. Home: 313 Forest Grove Dr Richardson TX 75080-1937

OLSON, DONALD GEORGE, computer services administrator; b. Minot, N.D., May 16, 1941; s. George James and Ellen (Ranta) O.; m. LuAnn Hiniker; 1 child, Tod B. BME, U. N.D., 1963; MMS, N.D. State U., 1968. Registered profl. engr., cert. data processor. Analyst, programmer Bur. Reclamation, Denver, 1963-66; asst. dir. computer ctr. N.D. State U., Fargo, 1966-69; data processing mgr. U. Calif. Sci. Lab., Los Alamos, 1969-74; dir. data processing nat. assessment ednl. progress Edn. Commn. States, Denver, 1974-77; staff mgr. Mountain Bell, Denver, 1977-80; dir. computer svcs. Mankato (Minn.) State U., 1980-86, assoc. v.p. computer and info. svcs., 1986-96, interim dir. MSUS/PALS automated libr. system, 1993-96; chief info. officer Murray (Ky.) State U., 1996-2000; dir. info. tech. So. Ill. U., Carbondale, 2000—; bd. dirs. Minn. Regional Network; cons. in field. mem. Assn. Computing Machinery, Rotary, Elks, Phi Delta Theta. Republican. Roman Catholic. Home: 539 White Tail Rd Murphysboro IL 62966-6415 Office: So Ill U Info Tech Carbondale IL 62901

OLSON, EDWARD CHARLES, entrepreneur, conservationist, writer, business consultant, foundation administrator; b. Jacksonville, Fla., July 6, 1956; s. Edward Charles and Marcine Era (Hall) O.; m. Krista Lynn Neuberger, Aug. 5, 1978; children: Laura Ellen, Edward Charles, Natalie Rose. BS, Miami U., Oxford, Ohio, 1978; MS, Wash. State U., 1980; PhD, Ohio State U., 1983. State dir. Nature Conservancy, Columbus, Ohio, 1983-86; pres., CEO Florida Keys Land & Sea Trust, 1986-93, Catalina Island Conservancy, Avalon, Calif., 1993-96; chmn., CEO E.C. Olson & Assocs., 1996—; ptnr. Oceanwatch Prodn. Group, 1996—; cons. non-profit orgns., 1987—; chmn., CEO Man-O-War Clothing, Co., 1996—; pres., CEO St. Lucie Wetland Solutions, Inc., 1997—, Fla. Wetlands Stewardship Group, Inc., 1998—; dir. Reef Relief, 1997—; chmn., CEO Fregata Publ. Co., 1998—; pres. MitBank-USA, 1999—. Editor: Guide to the Florida Keys, 1989; author: Winds of the Marquesas, 1996, Hardball, 1998, After Matthias, 1999. Bd. dirs. Catalina Cmty. Pub. Radio, 1993-96, Fla. Nat. Parks and Monuments Assn., Homestead, 1988-93, Fla. Keys Meml. Hosp., Key West, 1989-91, Fla. Keys Guidance Clinic, Marathon, 1990-92. Recipient Leadership Fla. Grad. award Fla. C. of C., 1990, Outstanding Young Floridian, Fla. Jaycees, 1991; named Man of Yr., Marathon Jaycees, 1990. Avocations: fishing, travel, reading, writing, Civil War study. E-mail: ecolson@inetw.net. Office: 205 Olive Ave Port Saint Lucie FL 34952-1347

OLSON, HARRIETT JANE, corporate lawyer; b. Phila., May 5, 1958; d. Charles L. and G. Elizabeth O. BA, Houghton Coll., 1980; JD, Harvard Law Sch., 1983. Bar: N.J., Tenn. Ptnr. Pitney, Hardin, Kipp & Szuch, Morristown, N.J., 1990-96; sr. v.p. publ. United Meth. Publ. House, Nashville, 1996—. Methodist.

OLSON, JEANNE INNIS, technology and technical management executive; b. South Bend, Ind., May 10, 1960; d. Francis Bedford and Mary Ann (Szachnia) Innis; m. Thomas Hilton Olson, Apr. 12, 1992; 1 child, Walter Samuel. Student, Purdue U., 1978-80; BS in Tech. & Mgmt. summa cum laude, U. Md., 1986; MS in Sys. Mgmt. with honors, U. So. Calif., 1991. Analyst Potomac Rsch., Inc., Alexandria, Va., 1980-82; staff specialist SWL, Inc., McLean, Va., 1982-87; sr. staff Advanced Tech., Inc., El Segundo, Calif., 1987-89; prin. staff/section mgr. PRC, Inc., El Segundo, Calif., 1989-95, dep. dir. space sys. acquisition support, 1995-96, dir. space sys. acquisition support and LA operations, 1997-98; v.p. Litton PRC, 1998—. Mem. South Bay Friends Planned Parenthood, Calif., 1992—, v.p. fund raising, 1994. Recipient Vol. Recognition award Planned Parenthood L.A., 1994, 96. Mem. Innes Clan Soc. (v.p. 1984-91, pres. 1991-92), Innes Clan Ctr. Assn. (bd. dirs. 1993—), Nat. Def. Indsl. Assn. (bd. dirs. Greater L.A. chpt.), Phi Kappa Phi. Avocations: skiing, music, travel, Scottish heritage, family planning edn. Office: Litton PRC Ste 1310 222 N Sepulveda Blvd El Segundo CA 90245-5648

OLSON, LEE CHARLES, biochemistry educator; b. Austin, Minn., June 2, 1936; s. Lee Kaius and Hazel Elizabeth (Miller) O.; children: Charles, Ingrid, Robert, Michelle. BS, S.D. State U., 1958; MS, U. Wis., 1962, PhD, 1965. Asst. prof. U. Minn., St. Paul, 1964-70; prof. Christopher Newport U., Newport News, Va., 1970—. Mem. AAUP, Am. Chem. Soc., Am. Soc. Plant Physiologists, Soc. for In Vitro Biology, N.Y. Acad. Sci., Sigma Xi. Avocations: farming, bicycling, canoeing. E-mail: lolson@worldnet.att.net. Home: 723 Plymouth Cir Newport News VA 23602-7016 Office: Biol Dept Christopher Newport Coll Newport News VA 23606

OLSON, LESLIE, music educator; b. Scottsbluff, Nebr., Apr. 20, 1950; d. Kenneth Merle Peck and Audrey Doris Laessle; m. Paul A. Olson, May 25, 1974; 1 child, Krista. BA in Music Edn., San Diego State U., 1988. Music tchr. Christ Luth. Sch., La Mesa, Calif., 1984—; pvt. music tchr., La Mesa, 1988—; music dir. Atonement Luth. Ch., Spring Valley, Calif., 1989—. Treas San Diego Concert Band, La Mesa, 1997—; sec.-treas. H.B. Goodlin Scholarship Bd., San Diego, 1999—. Recipient awards for compositions, 1998, 99. Mem. Music Tchrs. Assn. (adjudicator, treas. 1998-99). Avocations: old car restoration, boating, gardening. Home: 4220 Lovett Ln La Mesa CA 91941-6919

OLSON, LYNDON LOWELL, JR., ambassador; b. Waco, Tex., Mar. 7, 1947; s. Lyndon Lowell and Frances (McLaughlin) O.; m. Nancy Swenson, Mar. 6, 1970 (div. Dec. 1980); m. Kathleen Woodward, Nov. 22, 1982. BA in Polit. Sci. and Religion, Baylor U., 1969, postgrad. Mem. Tex. Legislature, 1973-78; apptd. chmn. Tex. State Bd. Ins., Austin, 1979-81, 83-87, apptd. mem., 1981-83; pres. and chief exec. officer Nat. Group Ins. Cos., Waco, Tex., 1987—; amb. to Sweden Stockholm, 1997; lectr. UN Conf. on Trade and Devel., Phillipines, 1985; mem. Expert Com. on Reinsurance for UN, Geneva, 1986-87; negotiator U.S.-Israeli Free Trade Agreement, 1986-87. leader trade delegation People to People for Russia and People's Republic of China, 1985; chmn., bd. dirs. Tex. Arts Alliance, Austin, 1984, chmn. and pres. Tex. Opera Theater, Houston, 1980-82; mem. exec. com. Houston Grand Opera, 1985—; pres. Tex. Lyceum, The Woodlands, 1987; chmn. Baylor U. Honors Council, 1969; bd. dirs. Am. Income Life Ins., Behrens Drug Inc., Gulf Life Ins. Co., United Bank of Waco, Tex. Mcpl. League Ins. Trust, Paul Quinn Coll., 1987. Recipient Disting. Alumni award Baylor U., 1985, Distinguished Pub. Servant award Tex. Med. Assn., 1986, Gates of Jerusalem award State of Israel, 1986; named Outstanding Pub. Ofcl. Tex. Mcpl. League, 1986. Mem. Nat. Assn. Ins. Commrs., Profl. Liability Ins. com. of the State Bar of Tex., Omicron Delta Kappa. Democrat. Presbyterian. Lodge: Masons. Office: Am Embassy Stockholm Sweden Dept State Washington DC 20521-0001

OLSON, LYNN, sculptor, painter, writer; b. Chgo., Mar. 23, 1952; s. Ellen (Nelson) Olson. instr. direct cement sculpture workshops Montoya Art Studios, West Palm Beach, Fla., 1988-89, Alta. Sculptors Assn., Edmonton, Can., 1990, Mendocino (Calif.) Art Ctr., 1992-93, Sierra Nev. Coll. at Lake Tahoe, Incline Village, 1993, Lighthouse Art Ctr., Crescent City, Calif., 1990-96, Elisabet Ney Sculpture Conservatory, Austin, Tex., 1995, Tarrant County Jr. Coll., Ft. Worth, 1995, Arts Students League of Denver, 2000. Prin. works include Good Shepherd, Ch. Good Shepherd, Albion, Ind., Kneeling Figure, Manta Ray. World of Concrete, Addison, Ill., Rose, Carter Meml., Chesterton, Ind., Redwood Tree, Lighthouse Art Ctr., Crescent City, Calif., George Bartholomew Meml., Bellefontaine, Ohio, Color Concerto, Purdue U., Hammond, Ind., Continuity III, Tower East, Shaker Heights, Ohio, Aluma Beam, Aluma Corp., Toronto; one-person show No. Ind. Arts Assn., Munster, CCT Gallery, Evanston Hall, Northwestern U. Settlement, Chgo., 2000—; exhibited in group show at Danada Sculpture Show, Cantigny Park, Wheaton, Ill., 1999, Prairie Arts Coun., Rensselaer, Ind., 2000; author, pub.: Sculpting with Cement, 1981-99; contbr. over 50 articles to mags. Mem. Am. Concrete Inst. (com. 124 concrete aesthetics). Home and Office: Steelstone 4607 Claussen Ln Valparaiso IN 46383-1526

OLSON, ROGER NORMAN, health service administrator; b. Spokane, July 3, 1936; s. Harry Leonard and Evelyn Helen (Pearson) O.; m. Joyce Marlene Markert, June 28, 1959; children: Leonard Mark, Brent Norman. BA, Pacific Luth. U., 1958; MDiv, Augustana Theol. Sem., 1962; MSW, U. Wash., 1970. Pastor Christ Luth. Ch., Des Moines, 1962-64; asst. pastor First Immanuel Luth. Ch., Portland, Oreg., 1964-68; planner Tri-County Community Coun., Portland, 1970-71; project coord. City-County Commn. on Aging, Portland, 1971-73; evaluation coord. Portland Bur. of Human Resources, 1973-74; asst. dir. Multnomah County Project Health Div., 1974-83; interim pastor Augustana Luth. Ch., 1984-85; dir. family

support svcs. Met. Family Svc., 1985-91; dir. planning and rsch. Met. Family Svcs., 1992-94; dir. info. exch. Luth. Family Svc., 1994-98; performance imrpovement mgr. Kerr Youth and Family Ctr., Portland, 1998—. Rockefeller Bros. fellowship Rockefeller Fund for Theol. Edn., 1958-59, fellowship NIMH, 1968-69, Adminstn. on Aging, 1969-70. Democrat. Lutheran. Avocations: music, reading, theatre. Home: 3939 NE 21st Ave Portland OR 97212-1432 Office: Kerr Youth and Family Ctr 722 NE 162nd Ave Portland OR 97230-5760

OLSON, ROY ARTHUR, government official; b. Dec. 8, 1938; s. Elof Herman and Beatrice Lorraine (Dolezal) O.; m. Elisabeth Rigge Behrens, June 24, 1967; children: Heather Elisabeth, Peter Roy. BS, Northwestern U., 1960. Lic. real estate salesman, Ill. Writer, editor Chgo. Am., 1956-68; pres. Roy Olson Pub. Rels. Co., Oak Park, Ill., 1968-70; asst. regional adminstr. SBA, Chgo., 1970-95; Chgo. spokesman Ill. Dept. Transp., 1995—; dir. Am. Food Industries, Chgo., Covenant Village Retirement Ctr., Northbrook, Ill., 1975-81, Brandel Care Ctr., Northbrook, 1975-81, Swedish Covenant Hosp., Chgo., 1995—. Chmn. Northbrook Covenant Ch., 1980-81, 97-2000. Mem. Soc. Profl. Journalists, Art Inst. Chgo., City Club (media com.), Execs. Club, Chgo. Press Club, Chgo. Headline Club (past dir. 1964-66), Northwestern Club. Home: 2015 Prairie St Glenview IL 60025-2824 Office: 310 S Michigan Ave Chicago IL 60604-4207

OLSON, WILLIAM JEFFREY, lawyer; b. Paterson, N.J., Oct. 23, 1949; s. Walter Justus and Viola Patricia (Trautvetter) O.; m. Janet Elaine Bollen, May 22, 1976; children: Robert J., Joanne C. AB, Brown U., 1971; JD, U. Richmond, 1976. Bar: Va. 1976, D.C. 1976, U.S. Ct. Claims 1976, U.S. Ct. Appeals (4th, 9th and D.C. cirs.) 1976, U.S. Supreme Ct. 1982. Assoc. Jackson & Campbell, Washington, 1976-79; ptnr. Gilman, Olson & Pangia, Washington, 1980-92; prin. William J. Olson PC, McLean, Va. and Washington, 1992—; sec., treas. bd. dirs. Victims Assistance Legal Orgn., Virginia Beach, Va., 1979—; presdl. transition team leader Legal Svcs. Corp., Washington, 1980; chmn. and bd. dirs. nat. Legal Svcs. Corp., 1981-82; mem. Pres.'s Export Coun. Subcom. on Export Adminstrn., Washington, 1982-84; spl. counsel bd. govs. U.S. Postal Svc., Washington, 1984-86. Author: Tuition Tax Credits and Alternatives, 1978; co-author: Debating National Health Policy, 1977, Executive Orders and National Emergencies, 1999. Trustee Davis Meml. Goodwill Industries, Washington, 1980-86, 88-93; chmn. Fairfax County Rep. Com., Fairfax, Va., 1980-82; mem. Rep. State Ctrl. Com., Richmond, Va., 1982-86. Mem. Va. Bar Assn., Assn. Trial Lawyers Am., Va. Trial Lawyers Assn., Christian Legal Soc. Republican. Baptist. Avocation: gardening. Office: 8180 Greensboro Dr Ste 1070 Mc Lean VA 22102-3860

OLSON-HELLERUD, LINDA KATHRYN, elementary education educator; b. Wisconsin Rapids, Wis., Aug. 26, 1947; d. Samuel Ellsworth and Lillian (Dvorak) Olson; m. H.A. Hellerud, 1979; 1 child, Sarah Kathryn. BS, U. Wis.-Stevens Point, 1969, tchg. cert., 1970, MST, 1972; postgrad., U. Wis., Whitewater, 1975; EdS, U. Wis.-Stout, 1978. Cert. K-12 reading tchr. and specialist. Clk. U. Counseling Ctr. U Wis., Stevens Point, 1965-69; elem. sch. tchr. Wisconsin Rapids, Wis., 1970-76, sch. counselor, 1976-79, dist. elem. guidance dir., 1979-82, elem. and reading tchr., K-1 early intervention team, 1982—, also cons. Advocate Moravian Ch. Sunday Sch. Mem. NEA, Wisconsin Rapids Edn. Assn., Internat. Reading Assn., Wis. Reading Assn. (spl. emergent reader com.), Ctrl. Wis. Reading Assn. (family lit. com.), Wis. State Hist. Soc., Wood County Hist. Soc., Wood County Lit. Coun. (cons.). Mem. United Ch. of Christ. Avocations: gardening, piano, Spanish, French, cross-country skiing. Home: 1011 16th St S Wisconsin Rapids WI 54494-5371 Office: Howe Elem Sch Wisconsin Rapids WI 54494

OLSSON, ANN-MARGRET See ANN-MARGRET

OLSSON, BIRGITTA E., economics educator, researcher; b. Hudiksvall, Sweden, Aug. 31, 1948; d. Arne Olsson; m. Evald John Pettersson; children: Camilla, Theresia. PhD in Bus., Stockholm U., 1994. Lectr. Sch. Bus. Stockholm U., 1970-75, asst. prof., 1990-95, assoc. prof., head Pers. Econs. Inst. Sch. Bus., 1995—, dir. doctoral studies, 1997-2000; rschr. Metal Workers Union, Stockholm, Sweden, 1976-83; head dept. Ministry of Industry, Stockholm, Sweden, 1983-86; polit. advisor to min. Ministry of Environment, Stockholm, Sweden, 1986-90; cons. Bonlaboris, Täby, Sweden, 1996—. Author: Kortare Arbetsdag-en väg till ett mer ekologiskt arbetsliv?, 1994. Avocations: painting, gardening, skiing. Office: Stockholm U, Sch Bus, 10691 Stockholm Sweden

OLSSON, CURT GUNNAR, banker; b. Mjällby, Sweden, Aug. 20, 1927; s. N.E. and Anna (Nilsson) O.; m. Asta Engblom, 1954; two daughters. BS in Econs., Stockholm Sch. Econs., 1950, D in Econ. honoris causa, 1992. Mng. dir. Skandinaviska Enskilda Banken, Stockholm, 1972-76, mng. dir., chief exec. officer, head office, 1976-82, first dep. chmn. bd., group dir., 1982-84, chmn. bd., 1984-96; bd. dirs. Hufvudstaden AB; consul gen. h.c. for Finland, 1989-99. Knight of Order of Vasa, 1976; King Carl XVI Gustaf's Gold medal 1982; comdr. Royal Norwegian Order of Merit, 1985; comdr. 1st class, Order Lion of Finland, 1987. Mem. Royal Swedish Acad. Engring. Sci. Office: Skandinaviska Enskilda Banken, Kungsträdgårdsgatan 8, S-106 40 Stockholm Sweden

OLSSON, ELISABETH E.C., physical therapist, educator; b. Stockholm, Sweden, Feb. 26, 1942; d. Carl E.K. and Ebba C. (Thott) Lewenhaupt; m. Kjell T.G. Olsson, June 12, 1970; children: Caroline, Greger. Diploma in Phys. Therapy, Stockholm, 1965; PhD, Karolinska Inst., Stockholm, 1986. 1st phys. therapist, orthopedic dept. Karolinska Hosp., Stockholm, 1970-86, rsch. phys. therapist, 1986-92; assoc. prof., sr. lectr. dept. phys. therapy Karolinska Inst., 1992-99, head dept. phys. therapy, 1993—, prof. in phys. therapy, 2000—; mem. various bds. of healthcare and rehab. in Sweden. Contbr. some 40 articles to profl. jours. Lady-in-waiting H.M. Queen Silvia, Royal Court, 1978-86. Decorated orders from Eng., France, Spain, Germany, Mex., Austria and Yugoslavia. Home: Östermalmsgatan 97, S-11459 Stockholm Sweden Office: Karolinska Inst, Dept Phys Therapy, S-14157 Huddinge Sweden

OLSSON, KARL ANDERS, American literature educator, researcher; b. Söderhamn, Sweden, July 16, 1949; s. Allan Karl and Gudrun Alina (Boström) O.; m. Lillemor Ingrid Eliasson, June 27, 1971 (div. 1988); children: Patrik, Per, Hans; m. Karin Elisabeth Johansson, July 25, 1990. MA, Uppsala (Sweden) U., 1973; Tchr.'s diploma, Uppsala Tchr. Tng. Coll., 1974. Tchr., head tchr. Härnösand (Sweden) Gymnasium, 1974-87; sch. insp. Vasternorrland County Sch. Bd., Härnösand, 1988; rsch. asst. Inst. for Pedagogic Texts, Härnösand, 1988-89; lectr. Mid Sweden U., Härnösand, 1989—, dir. English studies, 1990-97, internat. coord., 1992-97, mem. rsch. bd., 1993-97, mentor tchr. trainees dept. humanities, 1999—; mem. divsn. rsch. bd. comm. arts and humanities Mid Sweden U., 1992—, mentor newly appointed tchrs., 1993-95, mem. departmental bd. dept. arts and humanities, 1994—; instr. tchr. tng. project European Union Project, Härnösand, 1995. Author: Studies in U.S. Literature, 1996, Managing Diversity: The Anthologization of American Literature, 1999; co-author: The Art of Persuasion, 1993; author (project) Arts and Humanities in a European Context, 1996. Recipient Rsch. grant Bank of Sweden Tercentenary Found., 1997-99; vis. scholar Austin Peay State U., Clarksville, Tenn., 2000. Mem. Härnösand Theater Soc. (chmn. 1985-89), Härnösand Music Soc. (bd. dirs. 1999—). Avocations: choir singer, pianist, traveller. E-mail: anders.olssen@hum.mh.se. Home: Torngatan 3, S-87162 Härnösand Sweden Office: Mid Sweden Univ, Dept Humanities, S-87188 Härnösand Sweden

OLSSON-LILJEQUIST, BARBRO ELISABET, microbiologist, researcher; b. Stockholm, Sept. 25, 1949; d. Bo Christer and Margareta (Rahmberg) Olsson; m. Klas Goran, Jan. 7, 1978; children: Magnus, Henrik. PharmM, Pharm. Inst., Stockholm, 1972; DMS, Karolinska Inst., Stockholm, 1980. Assoc. prof., 1993. Chemist Sabbatsberg Hosp., Stockholm, 1972, Karolinska Hosp., Stockholm, 1973; microbiologist Nat. Bacteriological Lab., Stockholm, 1973-85, chief microbiologist, 1986-93; chief microbiologist Swedish Inst. for Infectious Disease Control, Stockholm, 1993—; sec. Swedish Reference Group for Antibiotics, Stockholm, 1980—. Contbr. articles to Jour. of Antimicrobial Chemotherapy, Jour. Infectious Diseases and others. Mem. Swedish Med. Soc., Swedish Pharm. Soc. Office: Swedish Inst for, Infectious Disease Control, SE-17182 Solna Sweden

OLSTEAD, CHRISTOPHER ERIC, consulting executive, talent manager; b. Gainesville, Fla., Feb. 10, 1956; s. George Elias Olstead and Myra (Mahlow) Hinman; m. Rebecca Lynn Jeffries, Feb. 14, 1978; 1 child, Reneé. BS, SUNY, Albany, 1991; MBA in Internat. Bus., U. St. Thomas, 1994. Control sys. specialist Soltex Polymer, Etc., Houston, 1975-82; sr. instrument inspector Sohio Constrn. Co., Prudhoe Bay, Alaska, 1983-84; instrument engr. Arco Alaska, Kuparuk, 1984-85, Standard Alaska Prodn. Co., Prudhoe Bay, 1985-87; control sys. supr. S & B Engring., Houston, 1987-88; sr. control sys. engr. Bechtel Corp., Houston, 1988-90, microcomputer ops. mgr., 1990-92, project quality mgr., 1992-95, supply chain mgr., 1995-97; sr. exec. Arthur Andersen Bus. Cons., Houston, 1997-99; COO U.S. Space & Rocket Ctr., Huntsville, Ala., 1999-2000; sr. exec. Arthur Andersen Bus. Cons., Houston, 2000—; spkr. ASME-IEEE Internat. Conf., Boston, 1990; panelist Constrn. Industry Inst., San Antonio, Tex., 1993, Constrn. Productivity Inst., Austin, Tex., 1993. Lead author: Advances in Applied Business Strategies, 1995; contbr. articles to profl. jours. Mem. Project Mgmt. Inst., Instrument Soc. Am. (bd. dirs. 1989-92). Avocations: entertainment and management collectibles. Office: Arthur Andersen Bus Cons 711 Louisiana St Ste 1300 Houston TX 77002-2716

OLSZAK, NORBERT, lawyer, educator; b. Freyming, Moselle, France, June 7, 1950; s. Wladislas and Irene (Lorych) O.; m. Adrienne Baston, Mar. 19, 1975; children: Nicolas, Ivan, Sarah. Diploma, Inst. d'Etudes Politiques, Strasbourg, France, 1971; LLD, U. Robert Schuman, Strasbourg, France, 1987. Asst. U. Robert Schuman, Strasbourg, 1981-87, sr. lectr., 1987-90, prof. law, 1990—, dir. Rsch. Ctr. for Labor Law, 1991-98, dean faculty of law, 1995-2000. Author: History of Monetary Unions, 1996, History of Central Banks, 1998, History of French Labor Law, 1999; contbr. articles to profl. jours. Adminstr. Social Security (URSSAF), Strasbourg, 1996; mem. Nat. Com. for History of Social Security, 1997. Mem. Legal History Soc. (bd. dirs. 1996), Ind. Law and Econs. Profs. Union. Home: 6 rue de la Garenne, F-67700 Saverne France Office: Univ Robert Schuman, BP 66 1 place d'Athenes, F-67045 Strasbourg France

OLSZEWSKA, MARIA JOANNA, biologist, researcher; b. Dabrówka P-Sanok, Poland, Apr. 21, 1929; d. Tadeusz and Stefania (Strzelbicka) Skwarczynski. MSc, U. Łodź, Poland, 1950, PhD, 1956, habil., 1960. Asst. H.S. Agronomy, Łodź, Poland, 1949-50, Pedagogical Coll., Łodź, Poland, 1950-53, U. Łodź, Poland, 1953-61; asst. prof. U. Łodz, 1961-69, assoc. prof., 1969-76, prof., 1976-99; head dept. plant anatomy and cytology M. Curie Skłodowska U., Lublin, 1961-65; head lab. cytochemistry U. Łódź, 1961-70, head dept. plant cytology and cytochemistry, 1971-99; vice dean Faculty Biology and Earth Scis., U. Łodź, Poland, 1966-69, dean, 1969-72. Author: (book) Plant Cytology, 1971 (Ministry of Edn. award 1972); contbr. articles on rsch. studies (Polish Acad. Scis. awards 1957, 65, 66). Recipient Polonia Restituta Cross III Class, Pres. Poland, 1972, Polonia Restituta Cross II Class, Pres. Poland, 1990, Cross I Class, Pres., 1999. Mem. Polish Acad. Scis. (pres. Łodź br. 1992-98), Polish Histo and Cytochem. Soc. (pres. Łodź br. 1964-67), Soc. Scientiarum Lodzense (sec. III Dept. 1963-72, pres. 1972-75, Sci. award 1982). Home: Platynowa 38/43, 90-245 Łódź Poland Office: U Lódź Dpt Plant Cyto, Banacha 12/16, 90-237 Lódź Poland

OLSZEWSKI, STANISŁAW MARIAN, physical chemist; b. Warsaw, Poland, Dec. 8, 1932; s. Paweł and Teodora Marianna (Żuchniewska) O.; m. Anna Halina Kalinowska, Sept. 7, 1980 (dec. Mar. 1996); 1 child from previous mariage, Mateusz. Degree in chem. engring., Poly. Inst., Warsaw, 1954; MSc in Theoretical Physics, U. Warsaw, 1954; D of Solid State Physics, U. Paris, 1962; Habilitation, Polish Acad. Scis., Warsaw, 1964. Rsch. worker Inst. Phys. Chemistry, Polish Acad. Scis., Warsaw, 1955—, prof., 1971—, head of divsn., 1985—; lectr. gen. physics and quantum theory Acad. Cath. Theology, Warsaw, 1964-70; vis. prof. U. Paris-Sud, 1988, U. J. Fourier, Grenoble, 1982, 89. Contbr. articles to profl. jours. Mem. European Acad. Scis. and Arts. Home: Platynowa 8/97, 00-808 Warsaw Poland Office: Inst Phys Chem Polish Acad Scis, Kasprzaka 44/52, 01-224 Warsaw Poland

OLTEAN, STEFAN, English educator; b. Cluj, Romania, July 28, 1950; s. Stefan and Gizella (Fogarasi) O.; m. Iuliana Florea, Oct. 5, 1950; children: Ion-Stefan, Alexandru. BA in English, Babes-Bolyai U., Cluj, Romania, 1973; PhD in Philology, U. Cluj, 1984. Instr. English U. Cluj, 1973-90, asst. prof. English, 1990-94, assoc. prof. English, 1994-98, prof., 1998—; vis. prof. Kent (Ohio) State U., 1984-86, Cornell U., Ithaca, N.Y., 1990-92; chmn. professorial coun. faculty letters U. Babes-Bolyai, 1996-2000, dean, 2000—; bd. e xperts Nat. Ctr. U. Rsch., Romania, 1997—. Author: Teoria textului narativ si discursul indirect liber, 1994, Fictiunea, lumile posibile si discursul indirect liber, 1996; contbr. articles to profl. publs. Mem. Romanian Group Applied Linguistics, Romanian Soc. Philol. Studies, European Soc. for Study of English, Romanian Soc. for Anglo-Am. Studies. Avocations: photography, hiking. Office: Faculty Letters, Horea St 31, 3400 Cluj-Napoca Romania

OLUFOLAJI, DAVID BABATUNDE, pathologist, microbiologist; b. Ado-Ekiti, Ekiti, Nigeria, July 20, 1951; s. Daniel Olatunji and Elizabeth Adebire (Ajibola) O.; m. Olusolape Adenike Osoba, May 21, 1978; children: Oluwaseun, Oluwasegun, Oluwayemisi, Korede. BSc in Agribiology, U. Ibadan, Nigeria, 1975, MPhil in Plant Pathology, 1985; PhD in Plant Pathology and Microbiology, U. Ilorin, Nigeria, 1989. Jr. rsch. fellow U. Ilorin, Nigeria, 1980-85, rsch. fellow II, 1986-87, rsch. fellow I, 1988-90; lectr. I Fed. Univ. Tech., Akure, Nigeria, 1990-92, sr. lectr., 1993-95, assoc. prof., 1996—; dept. exam. officer Fed. Univ. Tech., Akure, 1992-94, coord. postgrad. studies, 1996—, head dept., 1997-99. Contbr. articles to profl. publs. Mem. N.Y. Acad. Scis., Nigerian Soc. Plant Pathology, Internat. Soc. Sugarcane Tech., Internat. Congress Plant Pathology. Mem. Christian Apostolic Church. Avocations: photography, travel, lawn tennis, reading, computers. Home: Christ Apostolic Ch Ijigbo, Ado-Ekiti Nigeria Office: Fed Univ Tech, PMB 704, Akure Nigeria

OLUFSEN, METTE SOFIE, mathematician; b. Roskilde, Denmark, Mar. 31, 1966; d. Peter Las and Inger (Michelsen) O. MS in Math. and Computer Sci., Roskilde U., 1993, PhD in Applied Math., 1998. Lectr. dept. math. Roskilde U., 1994-98; indsl. rschr. Math-Tech, Copenhagen, 1994-98; rsch. assoc. dept. math. Boston U., 1998—; programmer UN Environment Programme, Riso Nat. Lab., Roskilde, 1992-93. Mem. Soc. Indsl. and Applied Math. Avocations: biking, scuba diving. Office: Boston U Dept Math 111 Cummington St Boston MA 02215-2411

OLUJOBI, TOLA ABIMBOLA, advertising and marketing executive; b. Abeokuta, Ogun State, Nigeria, Apr. 25, 1941; d. Solomon Adebayo and Eudora Ebun (Ajibode) O.; m. Bola Januario Marquis, July 1, 1965 (div. 1976); 1 child, Tola Jr. Higher diploma, Inst. Dirs., London, 1984; profl. diploma in Bus. Adminstrn., 1992. With Ogilvy Benson & Mather Nigeria Ltd., Lagos, Nigeria, 1970—, exec. sec., personal asst., 1970-75, rsch. coord., 1975-98, exec. dir., co. sec., 1976-98, head adminstrn. dept., 1976-98, head creative dept., 1985-90; mng. dir. Tango Oscar Ltd. Nigeria, Kresta Laurel Complex Maryland, Lagos, 1998—; dir. Kresta Laurel Ltd. Maryland, Nigeria. Chmn. Police Cmty. Rels. Com., Sabo Yaba Lagos, 1996—; vice-chmn. Nigeria Amateur Cycling Assn., Nigerian Sports Commn., Lagos, 1978-85. Recipient Nigeria women award for excellence Internat. Women Found., 1998, Chieftaincy award EGBA Christians Coun., Abeokuta, Nigeria, 1988, IFE Coun. Chiefs Nigeria, 1991. Fellow Inst. Dirs. London; mem. Assn. Advt. Pracitioners Nigeria (vice-chmn. 1985), Internat. Advt. Assn. (dir. pub. affairs Nigeria chpt. 1993—), Nigerian Inst. Mgmt., Advt. Practitioners Coun. Nigeria, Enabling Environ. Forum Nigeria. Anglican. Home: Akoka Yaba, 18 Afolabi Brown St, Lagos Nigeria Office: Kresta Laurel Complex, 376 Ikorodu Rd Maryland, Lagos Nigeria

OLUMIDE, YETUNDE MERCY, dermatologist, educator, researcher; b. Jos, Nigeria, Sept. 21, 1943; d. George Idowu and Eunice Adebambi (Ogunle) Okege; m. Adekunle Aina Olumide, Oct. 22, 1967; children: Oyindamola, Adekunle Jr., Babatunde, Oloyede. B Medicine B Surgery, U. Ibadan, Nigeria, 1968, MD, 1990; diploma in dermatology, U. London, 1974; postgrad., Nat. Postgrad. Med. Coll., Nigeria, 1979. House officer Gen. Hosp. Lagos, Nigeria, 1968-69; med. officer Apapa Health Ctr., Lagos, 1970-71; lectr., cons. Coll. Medicine U. Lagos, 1980-82, sr. lectr., cons., 1982-90, assoc. prof., cons., 1990-91, prof., cons., 1991—, head dept. medicine, 1992-95, dean Coll. Medicine, 1995—; registrar Lagos U. Tchg. Hosp., 1974-79, sr. registrar, 1979-80, cons., 1980—. Author: A Pictorial Self-Instructional Manual on Common Skin Diseases, 1989, Global Dermatology, 1994. Mem. coun. Food and Drugs Adminstrn., Fed. Ministry Health, Lagos. Scholar Fed. Govt. Nigeria, 1964, Brit. Commonwealth, 1973-74. Fellow West African Coll. Physicians, Nigerian Acad. Sci.; Am. Acad. Dermatology; mem. Brit. Assn. Dermatologists, African Assn. Dermatology (sci. sec.), N.Y. Acad. Scis. Mem. Anglican Ch. Avocation: singing. E-mail: adeolu89@alpha.linkserve.com. Office: U Lagos Coll Medicine, Idiaraba Surulere PMB 12003, Lagos Nigeria

OLVER, IAN NORMAN, medical oncologist; b. Melbourne, Victoria, Australia, May 10, 1953; s. Norman Henry and Rebie Alison (Reid) O.; m. Jennifer Robyn Turner, Jan. 14, 1978; children: Scott, Christopher, Robert. MBBS, U. Melbourne, 1976, MD, 1991; PhD, Monash U., 1997. Fellow in med. oncology Cancer Ctr. U. Md., Balt., 1983-85; clin. asst. dept. cancer medicine Peter McCallum Cancer Inst., Melbourne, 1985-93, head med. oncology, 1990-91; dir. med. oncology Royal Adelaide Hosp., 1991—, clin. dir., 1993—; clin. prof. U. Adelaide, 1999—; mem. Australian Drug Evaluation Com., 1995-99. Author book and chpts. to books; contbr. more than 90 articles to profl. jours. Fellow Royal Australasian Coll. Physicians; mem. Clin. Oncol. Soc. Australia, Am. Soc. Clin. Oncology, European Soc. Med. Oncology. Avocations: traveling, photography, science fiction. Home: 1 Mountainview Pl, Mount Osmond SA 5064, Australia Office: Royal Adelaide Hosp, North Terrace, Adelaide SA 5000, Australia

OM, HARI, agronomist, researcher; b. Sonipat, India, Jan. 10, 1959; s. Shiv Narain and Sruti; m. Bimlesh Kumari, June 25, 1984; children: Chetna, Vijay. BSc in Agr. with honors, Haryana Agrl. U., Hisar, India, 1980, MSc in Agronomy, 1982, PhD in Agronomy, 1995. Asst. scientist H.A.U., 1982-95, agronomist, 1995—. Contbr. articles to profl. jours. Mem. Indian Soc. Agronomy (life). Radha Swami Satsang. Avocations: meditation, reading religious and scientific books, playing volleyball and chess. Office: CCS HAU, Rice Rsch Station, Kaul, 136021 Kaithal India

OMABU, PATRICK CHIZOBA, publishing executive; b. Nimo, Anambra, Nigeria, Mar. 27, 1939; s. Okonkwo Omabu and Agnes Mgbafor Anatuanya; m. Rosemary Nkeiruka Ndubisi; 5 children. BSc in Bus. Mgmt., Pacific Western U., 1995. Mgr. Ness (Nig.) Bookshop, 1962-73; founder, mng. dir. Africana Pub. Ltd., Nigeria, 1974-81; mng. dir. Africana-FEP Pub., Onitsha, Nigeria, 1982-96, exec. chmn., 1997-99; founder, exec. chmn. Rex Chaires & Patrick Ltd., 1997-99; bd. dirs. Dolbic Fin. Ltd., Nigeria, Omagba Comty. Bank Ltd., Nigeria. Vice chmn. Parish Coun., 1994-99. Knighted Order of St. Mulumba, 1984. Mem. Nigeria Pubs. Assn. (v.p. 1982-85). Office: Africana-FEB Pubs Ltd, #1 Africana-FEP Dr PMB 1639, Onitsha Nigeria

OMAGARI, KATSUHISA, internist, educator; b. Sasebo, Nagasaki, Japan, Dec. 10, 1959; s. Takanobu and Tsuyako O.; m. Masako Urata. MD, Nagasaki (Japan) U., 1994. Resident Nagasaki U., 1984-86, med. staff, 1988-92, instr., 1992—; med. staff Sasebo (Japan) Hosp., 1986-88; vis. scientist Monash U., Australia, 1993-94. Office: Nagasaki U Sch Med 2d Dept, Internal Med 1-7-1 Sakamoto, Nagasaki 852-8501, Japan

O'MAHONY, GEORGE BARRY, hospitality educator, researcher; b. Dublin, Jan. 22, 1961; arrived in Australia, 1986; s. Michael Joseph and Diana Mary (Cubitt) O'M.; m. Noirin Martina O'Connor, Jan. 18, 1985; children: Ciaran, Eoin, Grace. BBus, Victoria U., Melbourne, Australia, 1994, MEd, 1997; grad. adminstrn., U. Melbourne, 1996. Cert. chef, master craftsman Catering Inst. Australia. Chef tournant Chef Ctr., London, 1985-86; sous chef Sheraton Hotel, Darwin, Australia, 1986-87; exec. sous chef Sheraton Mirage Hotel, Gold Coast, Australia, 1987-88; lectr. profl. cookery New South Wales Dept. Tech. Edn., Sydney, 1988-92; lectr. food studies No. Met. Inst., Melbourne, 1992-94, Victoria U., 1994—; bd. dirs. Robin Foods Catering Cons., Cork, Ireland, 1983-85. Contbr. articles to profl. jours. Mem. Hotel, Catering and Internat. Managers Assn., Assn. Culinaire Francaise. Home: 3 Charlotte St, Melbourne VIC 3013, Australia Office: Victoria U, Ballarat Rd, Footscray VIC 3012, Australia

O'MALLEY, CARLON MARTIN, judge; b. Phila., Sept. 7, 1929; s. Carlon Martin and Lucy (Bol) O'M.; m. Mary Catherine Lyons, Aug. 17, 1957; children: Carlon Martin III, Kathleen B. O'Malley Aikman, Harry Tighe, John Todd, Cara M. BA, Pa. State U., 1951; LLB, Temple U., 1954. Bar: Pa. 1955, Fla. 1973, U.S. Supreme Ct. 1973. Practiced law, 1957-61; asst. U.S. atty. for Middle Dist. Pa., Dept. Justice, 1961-69, U.S. atty., 1979-82; ptnr. O'Malley & Teets, 1970-72, O'Malley, Jordan & Mullaney (and predecessor firms), 1976-79; pvt. practice Pa. and Fla., 1972-79, 82-87; judge Ct. Common Pleas of Lackawanna County (45th Judicial Dist.), 1987-97, sr. judge, 1998—; dir. pub. safety City of Scranton, 1983-86; lectr. Lackawanna Jr. Coll., 1982-86. Editorial bd.: Temple Law Rev, 1952-53. Pres. Lackawanna County (Pa.) unit Am. Cancer Soc., 1966-67; bd. dirs. Pa. Cancer Soc., 1967-68, Lackawanna county chpt. ARC, 1967-69; mem. solicitation team, govtl. divsn. Lackawanna United Fund, 1963-68; chmn. profl. divsn. Greater Scranton (Pa.) YMCA Membership Drives; trustee Everhart Mus., Scranton, 1987—. Pilot USAF, 1955-57, Pa. N.G., 1957-59. Mem. Am. Judges Assn., Nat. Assn. Former U.S. Attys., Pa. Bar Assn., Lackawanna County Bar Assn., Fla. Bar Assn., Country Club of Scranton, Elks (pres. Pa. chpt. 1978-79, judiciary com. 1985-89, justice Grand Forum 1991, 1995-97, chief justice 1992-93, nat. pres. 1997-98), K.C., Phi Kappa (pres.), Delta Theta Phi (pres.). Democrat. Office: Judges Chambers Lackawanna County Courthouse Scranton PA 18503

O'MALLEY, E. MICHAEL, international trade consultant; b. Chgo., Sept. 27, 1971; s. Edward Michael and Carole Jean O'M.; m. Carolyn Joy O'Malley, Sept. 1, 1996. BS, U. Ill., 1993; MS, London Sch. Econs., 1995. Assoc. bus. devel. officer Canadian Consulate Gen., Chgo., 1996-98; legis. asst. State of Ill., Washington, 1998-99; sr. assoc. Internat. Trade Svcs. Corp., Washington, 1999—. James H. Dunn Meml. fellow Office of Gov., State of Ill., 1993-94. Mem. Washington Internat. Trade Assn., Am. Friends of London Sch. Econs. (co-chair 1999—). E-mail: emomalley@earthlink.net. Home: 5229 Tancreti Ln Alexandria VA 22304-8648 Office: Internat Trade Svcs Corp 1150 17th St NW Ste 402 Washington DC 20036-4622

O'MALLEY, JOHN PATRICK, dean; b. Hoosick Falls, N.Y., Nov. 27, 1928; s. Thomas Joseph and Mary Alice (Mulvihill) O'M.; m. Margaret Parlin, June 24, 1989. BA, Villanova U., 1950; MA, PhD, Cath. U., 1969. Tchr. Archbishop Carroll High Sch., Washington, 1954-68, prin., 1987-89; asst. prof. Cath. U., Washington, 1968-69; asst. prof. Merrimack Coll., North Andover, Mass., 1969-74, dean humanities, 1976-78; chair edn. dept. Emmanuel Coll., Boston, 1974-76; dean coll. arts and scis. Villanova (Pa.) U., 1978-84; provost St. Thomas U., Miami, Fla., 1985-86; assoc. prof. Widener U., Chester, Pa., 1990-99, ret., 1999. Editor: Non-Fiction, Books I and II, 1968. Home: PO Box 586 Norfolk CT 06058-0586

O'MALLEY, PATRICK PEARSE, neurologist, psychiatrist; b. Newtown Hamilton, Ireland, Apr. 22, 1918; s. Patrick and Susan (McKee) O'M.; m. Mary Hickey, Sept. 16, 1947; children: Kieran Darragh, Donal Lysaght, Conor Plunket. MB, BChir, BAO, Queen's U., Belfast, No. Ireland, 1941; Diploma in Psychol. Medicine, Royal Coll. Physicians, Dublin, Ireland, 1942; Diploma in Pub. Health, Univ. Coll., Dublin, 1943, MRCP, 1945. Med. officer St. Patrick's Hosp., Dublin, 1941-44; clin. asst. Bristol (Eng.) Mental Hosp., 1944-45; clin. clk. Nat. Hosp. for Nervous Diseases, London, 1945-46; rsch. asst. in neuropathology Maudsley Hosp., London, 1945-46; dir. setting up Neuro-Psychiat. Clinic, Mater Hosp., Belfast, 1946-81; clin. tchr. Queen's U., Belfast, 1946-81; cons. neurologist and psychiatrist Ulster Ind. Clinic, 1981-92, ret., 1992; mem. Mental Health Appeals Tribunal, Northern Ireland, 1960-71. Author: Clinical Neuro-Pschiatry, 2000; contbr. articles to med. jours., 1944—; co-founder Threshold Literary mag., 1957. Co-founder lyric Players Theatre, Belfast, 1951; found. trustee Lyric Cultural Charitable Trust, 1960; founder Granuaile Trust of O'Malley Clan, Dublin, 1986. Fellow Royal Coll. Physicians (Ireland), Royal Coll. Psychiatrists (London); mem. Brit. Med. Assn., Irish Med. Assn. Home: St Helens Wood, Booterstown, 73 Hampton Park, Dublin Ireland

O'MALLEY, SEAN, bishop; b. Lakewood, Ohio, June 29, 1944. Ed., St. Fidelis Sem., Herman, Pa., Capuchin Coll. and Cath. U., Washington. Ordained priest Roman Cath. Ch., 1970. Espiscopal vicar of priests serving

Spanish speakin Washington archdiocese, 1978-84; exec. dir. Spanish Cath. Ctr., Washington, from 1973; bishop Roman Cath. Ch., St. Thomas, V.I., 1985-92, Fall River, Mass., 1992—. Office: Bishop of Fall River PO Box 2577 47 Underwood St Fall River MA 02722-2577

OMAN, HENRY, retired electrical engineer, engineering executive; b. Portland, Oreg., Aug. 29, 1918; s. Paul L. and Mary (Levonen) O.; m. Winifred Eleanor Potter, June 17, 1944 (dec. Nov. 1950); m. Earlene Mary Boot, Sept. 11, 1954; children: Mary Janet, Eleanor Eva, Eric Paul. BSEE, Oreg. State U., 1940, MSEE, 1951. Registered profl. engr., Wash. Application engr. Allis Chalmers Mfg. Co., Milw., 1940-48; rsch. engr. Boeing Co., Seattle, 1948-63, engring. mgr., 1963-91. Author: Energy Systems Engineering Handbook, 1986; contbr. numerous articles to profl. jours. Mem. team that restarted amateur radio communication to the outside world from the People's Republic of China, 1981. Recipient prize paper award Am. Inst. Elec. Engrs., 1964. Fellow IEEE (founder power electronics systems confs., 1970—, v.p. Aerospace and Electronics Systems Soc. 1984-88, Harry Mimno award 1989, Third Millenium medal 2000, editor-in-chief IEEE Aerospace and Electronic Sys. mag. 1995-99/rated in top two by Inst. for Scientific Info.), AIAA (assoc.); mem. AAAS (bd. dir. Pacific divsn. 1992—). Republican. Methodist. Achievements include development of concepts for solar power satellite which generates power in geo-synchronous orbit 24 hours per day and beams it to the Earth surface with a microwave beam; research in simple battery-powered electric bicycles for low-cost, pollution-free transportation in developing nations. Home: 19221 Normandy Park Dr SW Seattle WA 98166-4129

OMAN, JULIA TREVELYAN, theatrical designer; b. London, July 11, 1930; d. Charles Chichele and Joan (Trevelyan) O.; m. Roy Strong, 1971. Ed., Royal Coll. Art; DLitt (hon.), Bristol U., 1987. Designer BBC-TV, 1955-67; designer for theater, opera and ballet, London, N.Y.C., Boston, Toronto, Vienna, Stockholm and, West Germany, Japan, The Netherlands and Italy, 1967—. Designer Mme. Tussaud's Hall of Historical Tableaux, 1979; art dir. various films including The Charge of the Light Brigade, 1967, Laughter in the Dark, 1968; prodn. designer film Julius Caesar, 1969; design cons. film Straw Dogs, 1971; dir. Oman Prodns. Ltd.; author: (with B.S. Johnson) Street Children, 1964; (with R. Strong) Elizabeth R., 1971, Mary Queen of Scots, 1972, The English Year, 1982, A Celebration of Gardens, 1991, (with R. Strong) A Country Life, 1994, Vanitas Designs, Gianni Versace, 1994, (with R. Strong) Happiness, 1997, (with R. Strong) Garden Party, 2000. Mem. vis. com. dept. edn. and sci. Royal Coll. of Art, 1980. Decorated Comdr. of the Order of the Brit. Empire; recipient Silver medal Royal Coll. of Art, Designer of Yr. award, 1967, ACE award for best art direction NCTA, 1983; named Royal scholar; elected Royal Designer for Industry, 1977. Address: Oman Prodns Ltd, The Laskett-Much Birch, Hertfordshire HR2 8HZ, England

ÖMAN, PERTTI JUHANI, auditor; b. Muurame, Finland, Aug. 23, 1953; s. Erik Wilhelm and Airi Dagmar (Mäkinen) Ö.; m. Ulla Johanna Paunonen, Aug. 6, 1977; children: Olli Erik, Isa Johanna. MS in Econs., Helsinki Sch. Econs. Bus. Sci., 1978. Cert. auditor. Inspector Finnish State Economy Comptroller's Office, Helsinki, 1979-80, sr. inspector, 1980-82; internal auditor Kansallis-Osake-Pankki, Helsinki, 1983-86, 89-91, dir. auditing, sr. v.p., 1992-95; internal auditor Kansallis Fin. Ltd., Helsinki, 1986-89, audit mgr., 1995-96; dir. auditing (sr. v.p.) Postipankki Ltd./Leonia plc, Helsinki, 1996—. Avocation: literature. Office: Leonia plc, Unionink 22, FIN00007 Helsinki Finland

OMARA-OTUNNU, AMII, history and human rights law educator; b. Kitgum, Acholi, Uganda, Aug. 15, 1952; came to U.S., 1977; s. Yusto Abwola and Josephine Amato Otunnu; m. Elizabeth Jane Omara-Otunnu, Aug. 15, 1985; children: Larib Lapyem, Tekowa Lakica. BA in Social Studies, Harvard U., 1980; MSc in Polit. Sci., London Sch. Econs., 1981; BA in Jurisprudence, U. Oxford, Eng., 1995, DPhil in History, 1985. Asst. prof. U. Mass., Boston, 1987-88; asst. prof. U. Conn., Storrs, 1988-92, dir. Ctr. for African Studies, 1990-94, prof. history, 1992—; dir. Comparative Human Rights, Storrs, 1998—; exec. dir. U. Conn.-African Nat. Congress of South Africa Partnership, Storrs, 1998—; project mgr. U. Conn.-U. Ft. Hare (South Africa) Internat. Linkage, 2000—; vis. scholar Ctr. for Internat. Affairs, Harvard, Mass., 1986-88. Author: (book) Politics and Military, 1895-1995, 1987, (poetry book) Dispossessed Lyrics, 1983. Mem. African Studies Assn., Conn. Acad. Sci., Ugandans for Peace and Dem. Pluralism (sec. gen. 1989—), U. Conn. Pres. Adv. Bd., Coun. for Devel. of Econ. Social Rsch. Avocations: soccer, debating, traveling, community service, canoeing, jogging. Home: 29 Ellise Rd Storrs Mansfield CT 06268 Office: U Conn U-103 241 Glenbrook Rd Storrs Mansfield CT 06269

OMATA, KEN, physician; b. Nishigo, Fukushima, Japan, Apr. 4, 1950; s. Nagao and Kane (Takahashi) O.; m. Reiko Nakayama, May 3, 1984; children: Kei, So, Ei, Mei. MD, Tohoku U., Sendai, Japan, 1976, PhD, 1983. Physician Sendai (Japan) City Hosp., 1976-78; physician Tohoku U. Hosp., Sendai, 1978-80, 82-87, asst. instr., 1991-94, sr. instr., 1994-99, asst. prof. internal medicine, 1999-2000; prof. Health Adminstrn. Ctr., Miyagi U. Edn., Sendai, 2000—; vis. fellow Henry Ford Hosp. Detroit, 1980-82; chief physician JR Sendai Hosp., 1987-89; vis. scientist N.Y. Med. Coll., Valhalla, 1989-91; sr. instr. China Med. U., Shenyang, 1994. Recipient Young Investigator award Internat. Kinin Symposium, 1984. Home: 1-3-11 Kaigamori Aobaku, Sendai Miyagi 981-0942, Japan Office: Health Adminstrn Ctr Miyagi U Edn, Aobaku Aramaki Aoba, Sendai 980-0845, Japan

OMATA, YOSHIAKI, research educator; b. Tokyo, June 20, 1954; s. Nobuo and Masako (Momiyama) O. BS, Sci. U. of Tokyo, 1977, MS, 1979, PhD, 1987. Vis. fellow NIH, Bethesda, Md., 1988-91, vis. assoc., 1991-94; asst. Kurume Univ. Sch. Medicine, Japan, 1994-95, lectr., 1995-99; assoc. prof. Kurume Univ. Sch. Medicine, 1999—. Office: Kurume U Sch Medicine, 67 Asahi-machi, Fukuoka Kurume 830 0011, Japan

OMBAKA, CHRISTINE ODUOR, humanities educator, researcher; b. Kisumu, Nyanza, Kenya, Nov. 23, 1956; d. Jacob and Elizabeth (Owaga) Ochola; m. Wycliff Oduor Ombaka. BEd with honors, Nairobi U., Kenya, 1977; MA, Lancaster U., U.K., 1990. Tchr. Tchrs. Svc. Commn., Kenya, 1977-89; prin. Sinyolo Girls H.S., Kenya, 1984-89; lectr. Moi University, Kenya, 1990-92, Maseno U., Kenya, 1992—; head dept. Maseno U., Kenya, 1994-97; rsch. coord. Population Coun., Kenya, 1997; rsch.-dir. Ctr. Study of Adolescence, Kenya, 1997—. Author: (poetry) An African Lullaby, 1995, The Coming of Dawn, The Space Between, Holding the Centre, 1999. exec. mem. Aaword, Nairobi, 1996—; gov. Ulumbi Secondary Sch., Nyanza, 1996—, Nyakach Girls High Sch., Nyanza, 1997—; sec. Formart, Kisumu, 1998—. Grantee Brit. Coun., 1989-90. Mem. Internat. Soc. Poets (life, Internat. Poet of Merit 1994). Avocations: writing poetry, swimming, counseling young people. Office: Maseno U, 333 Maseno Kenya

O'MEARA, JOHN FRANCIS, lawyer; b. Chgo., Apr. 14, 1936; s. John J. and Mary (Joyce) O'M.; children: Marcia A. Hiehle, John A., Timothy D. BS, Loyola U., 1959; JD, Northwestern U., 1960. Bar: Ill. 1961, U.S. Dist. Ct. (no. dist.) Ill. 1964, U.S. Ct. Appeals (7th cir.) 1992. Assoc., ptnr. Lord, Bissell & Brook, Chgo., 1961-74; atty. pvt. practice, Chgo. and Park Ridge, Ill, 1975—; instr. John Marshall Sch. Law, Chgo., 1966-71. Author: Tort Liability of Illinois Land Occupiers, 1968. Bd. dirs. St. Mary of Angels, 1987—; founder, officer Ind. Precinct Orgn., Chgo., 1969-71. With U.S. Army Res., 1960-66. Mem. Holy Name Soc. Roman Catholic. Office: 1737 N Wolcott Ave Chicago IL 60622-1350

O'MEARA, MARK, professional golfer; b. Goldsboro, N.C., Jan. 13, 1957; m. Alicia; children: Michelle, Shaun. BS in Mktg., Long Beach State U., 1980. Profl. golfer PGA, 1980—; mem. nat. team Ryder Cup, 1985, 89, 91, 97, Nissan Cup 1985, Dunhill Corp. 1985, 86, 87, 96, 97, Pres. Cup 1996. Named All-Am., Long Beach State U., Rookie of Yr., 1981; mem. Ryder Cup team, 1985, 89, 91; won U.S. Amateur, 1979, Greater Milw. Open, 1984, Bing Crosby Pro-Am., 1985, Hawaiian Open, 1985, Fuji Sankei Classic, 1985, Australian Masters, 1986, Lawrence Batley Internat., 1987, AT&T Pebble Beach Nat. Pro-Am., 1989, 90, 92, H-E-B Tex. Open, 1990, Walt Disney World/Oldsmobile Classic, 1991, Tokia Classic, 1992, Argentine Open, 1994, Honda Classic, 1995, Bell Can. Open, 1995, Mercedes Championships, 1996, Greater Greensboro Open, 1996; tied (with Corey Pavin) Bob Hope Chrysler Classic, 1990; AT&T Pebble Beach National Pro-Am, 1997; Buick Invitational, 1997; Masters Tournament, 1998; British Open Championship, 1998. Office: c/o PGA Box 109601 Ave of Champions Palm Beach Gardens FL 33410

OMELCHUK, ANATOLII AFANASIEVICH, electrochemist; b. Lopatin, Ukraine, Apr. 14, 1950; s. Afanasii and Mariya (Vinnik) O.; m. Galina Illinichna Borovskaya, Feb. 15, 1985; 1 child. BS, U. Kiev, 1972; PhD, Inst. Gen. & Inorganic Chem., Kiev, Ukraine, 1977, DSc, 1991. From engr. to dept. head Inst. Gen. & Inorganic Chemistry, Kiev, 1972—; mem. coun. for def. of thesis, Inst. Gen. & Inorganic Chemistry. Mem. editl. bd. Ukrainian Chem. Jour. Mem. Ukrainian Electrochem. Soc., Scientific Coun. Inst. Kiev. E-mail: zakharchenko n@ionc.kar.net. Office: Inst Gen Inorganic Chem, Palladina 32-34, 03142 Kiev Ukraine

OMER, MOHAMED IBRAHIM ALI, pediatrician, educator; b. Kassala, Sudan, Jan. 1, 1940; arrived in Trinidad and Tobago, 1999.; s. Ali Omer and Fatma Osman Sheikh; m. Zeinab Mohamadain Mahmoud, July 2, 1969; children: Rahab, Hesham, Rasha, Mayada, Salma. Cambridge Sch. cert., Hantoub, Medani, Sudan, 1959; MB BChir, U. Khartoum, Sudan, 1965; diploma in child health, Royal Coll. Physicians & Surgeons Eng., London, 1968. Prof., dir. postgrad. med. edn. U. Khartoum, 1980-86, prof. pediat. and child health, 1980-90; prof. pediats. Sana'a (Yemen) U., 1990-93; chief pediats. King Fahad Specialist Hosp., Al-Qassim, Saudi Arabia, 1993-95, med. dir., 1995-99; prof. child health U. W.I., Champs Fleurs, Trinidad and Tobago, 1999—; short-term cons. WHO, Sana'a, 1990, Alexandria, Egypt, 1990, Amman, Jordan, 1992, UNICEF, Sana'a, 1991, 92; convenor Postgrad. Program in Pediats., 1977-80. Editor: Sudanese Jour. Pediats., 1985-89, Procs. of 1st Nat. Symposium on Continued Med. Edn., 1996. Fellow Royal Coll. Physicians Edinburgh, Royal Coll. Physicians Glasgow, Royal Coll. Physicians London, Royal Coll. Pediats. and Child Health (U.K.); mem. Sudan Pediat. Assn., Sudan Med. Soc., Brit. Med. Assn. Muslim. Avocations: reading, listening to classical music. Office: Faculty Med Scis, Uriah Butler Hwy, Champs Fleurs Trinidad and Tobago

OMHOLT, BRUCE DONALD, product designer, mechanical engineer, consultant; b. Salem, Oreg., Mar. 27, 1943; s. Donald Carl and Violet Mae (Buck) O.; m. Mavis Aronow, Aug. 18, 1963 (div. July 1972); children: Madison, Natalie; m. Darla Kay Faber, Oct. 27, 1972; 1 child, Cassidy. BSME, Heald Coll. Engring., San Francisco, 1964. Real estate salesman R. Lea Ward and Assocs., San Francisco, 1962-64; sales engr. Repco Engring., Montebello, Calif., 1964; various mfg., engring. and mgmt. positions Ford Motor Co., Rawsonville, Saline, Owosso and Ypsilanti, Mich., 1964-75; chief engr. E.F. Hauserman Co., Cleve., 1975-77; dir. design and engring. Am. Seating Co., Grand Rapids, Mich., 1977-80; pres. Trinity Engring., Grand Rapids, Mich., 1980-81, Rohnert Park, Calif., 1981—; cons. in mfg., carrier rack apparatus, motorcycle improvements. Patentee in vertical mitre machine, merchandise display unit.

OMI, MAKOTO, speech communication educator; b. Shizuoka, Japan, Mar. 18, 1941; s. Akira and Kiyoko (Koitabashi) O.; m. Sachiko Omi, May 1998; children: Nao, Sadami. BA, Nanzan U., Nagoya, Japan, 1963; M of Applied Tchg. in Speech Comm., Ind. U., 1970; postgrad., Columbia U., 1988. Instr. Aichi Prefectural Jishukan Sr. H.S., Toyohashi, Japan, 1963-69; lectr. Nanzan Jr. Coll., Nagoya, 1974-76, assoc. prof., 1976-83, prof., 1984—; part-time lectr. Nanzan Jr. Coll., Nagoya, 1971-73. Author: (books: Introduction to Oral Interpretation, 1984, How to Learn English through Mind, Heart and Body, 1988, The Theory and Practice of English Communication—from the Standpoint of Speech, 1996 (Japan Assn. Coll. English Tchrs. award 1997). Fulbright grantee Japan U.S. Ednl. Commn., 1967. Mem. Comm. Assn. Japan (pres. 1990-93), Japanese Assn. Coll. English Tchrs. (award 1997). Avocation: music. Home: A-908 26-1 Takiawa-cho, Showa-ku Nagoya 466-0826, Japan Office: Nanzan Jr Coll, 19 Hayato-cho Showa-ku, Aichi Nagoya 466-0826, Japan

OMICHI, HIDEKI, chemist; b. Amagasaki, Hyogo, Japan, Apr. 21, 1942; s. Hiroshi and Aiko (Endo) O.; m. Harue Nakamura, Nov. 24, 1970; 2 children. M.Engring., U. Tokyo, 1967, Dr.Engring., 1979. Scientist Advanced Radiation Tech. Ctr., Atomic Energy Rsch. Inst., Takasaki, Japan, 1967-85, prin. scientist, 1985-88, sr. staff, 1988-91, head, 1991-96, dep. dir., 1996—. Co-author: Degradation and Stabilisation of Polyolefins, 1983, Processing of Polymers by Means of Beams, 1986, CRC Handbook of Radiation Chemistry, 1991, Handbook of Polymer Degradation, 1992. Mukaibo Fund grantee Nuclear Sys. Assn., 1996. Mem. The Chem. Soc. Japan, Japanese Soc. Radiation Chemistry, Japan Radioisotope Assn. Avocations: swimming, driving. Home: 908-18 Itai, Tamamura Sawa-gun 370-11, Japan Office: Japan Atomic Energy Rsch Inst, 1233 Watanuki, Takasaki 370-12, Japan

OMIDVAR, BIJAN, structural engineer, researcher; b. Tehran, Iran, Sept. 3, 1959; came to U.S., 1991; s. Reza and Parvin (Fekrazad) O.; m. Nahid Razmara, June 8, 1994. BS, U. Tehran, 1984, MS, 1986; PhD, U. Wis., Milw., 1995. Registered prof. engr., Iran. Structural engr. Sano Consulting Co., Tehran, 1984-86; project mgr. Djahad Assocs., Hamadan, Iran, 1986-90; mem. faculty Bu-Ali-Sina U., Hamadan, 1986-91; lectr. U. Wis., 1991-95, rsch. assoc., 1996—; engr. lead combustion design GE Power Sys., Schenectady, N.Y., 2000—; adj. asst. prof. U. Wis. Ctr. Continuing Edn., 1994—, adj. asst. prof., 1996—. Contbr. articles to profl. jours. Scholar Asian Inst. Tech., 1986; grad. sch. fellow U. Wis., 1993; recipient 3d pl. award Student Rsch. Contest Soc. Exptl. Mechanics, Milw., 1995, Winner Best Rsch. Paper award, 1998. Mem. ASCE (assoc.). Achievements include development of new approach in defining "shear coefficient" in beams under bending. Home: 1200 Hillside Ave Apt 408 Niskayuna NY 12309-3580

OMLAND, TOV, physician, medical microbiologist; b. Kviteseid, Telemark, Norway, May 15, 1923; s. Hans Omland and Torbjorg Lid; m. Ellen-Margrethe Soderstrom, Aug. 13, 1949 (dec. Mar. 1981); children: Anne Katerine, Hans Harald. MD, Oslo U., 1949, specialist med. microbiology, 1959. Med. officer Internat. Tb Campaign, Greece, 1950-51; gen. practice medicine Norway, 1951-52; med. office WHO, Egypt and Turkey, 1952-53; trainee internal medicine and surgery Oslo City Hosp., 1954-55, trainee, asst. prof., 1955-63; dir. State Microbiology Lab., Lillehammer, Norway, 1963-68, Norwegian Def. Microbiology Lab., Oslo, 1968-88; bd. dirs. Ellen-Margrethe and Tov Omland's Lab. for Med. Microbiology, Ski, Norway, 1973—; adv. on disarmament biol. weapons Ministry of Fgn. Affairs, Norway; mem. various nat. and internat. expert panels. Contbr. chpts. books and articles to profl. jours. Served to 2nd lt. Norwegian Mil., 1944-45, col. Norwegian Med. Corps, 1978. Recipient prize Schering Corp. U.S.A., 1986. Mem. Norwegian Soc. Microbiology (pres. 1973-75), Norwegian Soc. Pathology, Norwegian Soc. Infectious Diseases, Soc. Gen. Microbiology (U.K.), Am. Soc. Microbiology, Norwegian Res. Officers' Fedn. (pres. regional divsn. 1992-94), Oslo Militaere Samfund. Conservative. Lutheran. Home: Gamlevegen 55, 1400 Ski Norway Office: EM & T, Omland's Lab Med Microbiology, 1400 Ski Norway

OMNES, FRANCK, electrical engineering researcher; b. Paris, Mar. 12, 1960; s. Roland and Liliane (Dieny) Omnes; m. Guylaine Sabardak, Mar. 3, 1990; children: Etienne, Claire-Elisabeth, Eve-Marie. Diploma in engring., Ecole Supérieuse Physique Chimie Industrielles Ville Paris, 1984; PhD in Physics, U. Paris VI, 1993. Rsch. engr. Thomson-CSF/Ctrl. Rsch. Lab., Orsay, France, 1985-91; product mgr. EFEREL, Neauphle le Chateau, France, 1991-94; rschr. Nat. Ctr. Scientific Rsch. (CNRS)/CRHEA, Valbonne, France. Contbr. over 70 articles to profl. jours.; extensive patentee in field of semiconductor physics. Office: CNRS-CRHEA, rue Bernard Gregory Sophia-Antipolis, F-06560 Valbonne France

OMOLE, DAVIDSON ADEGOKE, economist; b. Ilesa, Osun, Nigeria, Feb. 22, 1956; s. David Adedoyin and Dorcas Olateju O.; m. Adebimpe Olubunmi Fenuga, Nov. 12, 1988; children: Adewumi, Adedayo. NCE, Coll. Edn., Ilesa, 1983; BSc with hons., Econs. U. Ibadan, Nigeria, 1987; MSc in Econs., Econs. U. Ibadan, 1988, PhD in Econs., 1997. Rsch. asst. Nigerian Inst. Social Econ. Rsch., Ibadan, 1988-90, jr. rsch. fellow, 1990-92, rsch. fellow II, 1993-95, rsch. fellow I, 1996-98, sr. rsch. fellow, 1999—; cons. Lagos (Nigeria) State Govt., 1990-91; cons., lectr. Nat. Ctr. for Econ. Mgmt. and Adminstrn., Ibadan, 1996—; rsch. assoc. African Econ. Rsch. Consortium, Nairobi, Kenya, 1989—, Ctrl. Bank Nigeria, 1996—. Contbr. chpts. to books. Recipient Sir James Robertson prize, 1987; grantee African Econ. Rsch. Consortium, 1994, Codesria, 1994. Mem. African Econ. Rsch. Consortium, Nigerian Inst. Mgmt., Nigerian Econ. Soc., Ibadan Socio-Econ. Group, Rockefeller Foudn. Leadership Environ. Devel. Programme. Jehovah's Witness. Avocations: reading, travelling, music. Office: Nigerian Inst Social Econ, PMB 5, Ibadan Nigeria

OMOLE, GABRIEL GBOLABO, international venture capitalist; b. Akungba-Akoko, Nigeria, Mar. 15, 1940; came to U.S., 1975; s. Amos Akindele and Victoria Ola (Olutu) O.; children: Juliana Olufunke, Esther Oluremi, Christiana Oluseun, George Abayomi. PhD, D MSc. Chmn. Gay Omole & Co., Ltd., Lagos, Nigeria, 1968—, Akoko Indsl. Devel. Ltd., 1973—, Akoko Mktg. & Investment Ltd., 1973—, Johngay Enterprises, Ltd., Accra, Ghana, 1977—, Gayom Travel & Tours, Ltd., 1977—, Unifood Industries Nigeria Ltd., 1979—, Unity Village Complex, 1979—, 1st Akoko Internat. Corp., N.Y.C., 1978—, UCM Services Corp., N.Y.C., 1979—, The Akoko Group, Ltd., London, 1983—, Gay Omole Internat. Ltd., London, 1983—, Gay Omole Investment Ltd., Brunei Internat. Investors (West Africa) Ltd.; pres., CEO Mastercard Internat. Svcs. Ltd., 1996—; mng. dir. Galleria Tourist Devel. Property Co. Ltd., Lagos, 1993—, Galleria Transp. Systems Ltd., Lagos, 1993, Combined Billionaires Network Svcs. Ltd., 1996—, Direct Resources Internat. Ltd., 1996—, Galleria City Devel. Ltd., 1996—; Co-founder Brunei Resources (West Africa) Ltd., 1990—; pres., co-founder African Continental Corp., Miami, Fla.; dir.-gen. IBB World Leaders Gallery, Gay Omole Petroleum. Chmn. bd. dirs. Akoko Specialist Hosp., N.Y.C.; trustee, chmn., Gay Omole Found., Lagos, 1979—; founder Unity Ch. Mission, 1976, chmn. devel. fund, 1979—. Mem. Am. Mgmt. Assn., Akungba Devel. Union, Am. Mgmt. Internat., Assn. Venture Founders, Akure C. of C., N.Y.C. C. of C., Nigerian-Am. C. of C., Nigerian-ASEAN C. of C., Nigerian-South Africa C. of C., N.Y. Acad. Scis., Nat. Geo. Soc., London Inst. Dirs., U.S. C. of C. Home: PO Box 74147 Victoria Island, Lagos Nigeria also: PO Box 4447, Garki Abuja Nigeria

OMORI, KOICHI, otolaryngologist, educator; b. Kobe, Japan, July 8, 1959; s. Takashi and Shukuko (Okajima) O.; m. Fujiko Shino, Nov. 7, 1987; 2 children. MD, Kyoto (Japan) U., 1985, PhD, 1992. Resident Kyoto U. Hosp., 1985; med. staff Kurashiki (Japan) Ctrl. Hosp., 1985-87; instr. Kyoto U. Hosp., 1991-93; rsch. assoc. Lenox Hill Hosp., N.Y.C., 1993-95; instr. Kyoto U., 1995-96; dir. dept. otolaryngology Nishi-Kobe Med. Ctr., 1996—. Contbr. articles to profl. jours. Recipient Young Faculty award Am. Laryngol. Assn., 1995; grantee Ministry Edn., Japan, 1990-91, 92-93, 96-97. Mem. AAAS, Am. Laryngol. Assn., Acoustical Soc. Am., Triological Soc., Oto-rhino-laryngological Soc. Japan. Avocations: golf, reading. Fax: 81-78-993-3728. E-mail: koichi.omori@nifty.ne.jp. Office: Nishi Kobe Med Ctr 5-7-1, Kouji-dai Nishi-ku, Kobe 651-2273, Japan

O'MULLAIN, CIARAN, accountant; b. Ireland, Mar. 31, 1949; s. Sean and Maria (Casey) O'M.; m. Claire Casey, Mar. 25, 1974; children: Fiona, Eanna. Audit clk. Pelman Plunkett, Waterford, Ireland, 1969-74; asst. acct. C.A.H. Ltd., Carlow, Ireland, 1974-75; ptnr. Plunkett Cook & Co., Waterford, Ireland, 1975-77; proprieter O'Mullain & Co., Waterford, Ireland, 1978—; ptnr. O'Mullain News Agts., 1997—; proprieter T.C. Marine Svcs., 1998—; dir. Internat. Fin. Svcs., 1990—. Crew mem. Dunmore East Lifeboat, 1984—, coxwain, 1996—; driver, firefighter Waterford County Fire Svc., 1985—. Mem. Inst. Fin. Accts., Internat. Assn. Bookkeepers. Roman Catholic. Avocations: sailing, gardening, films, books, music. Home and Office: Leckawn Dunmore E, Waterford Ireland

OMURA, EMILY FOWLER, dermatologist, educator; b. Oklahoma City, Okla., Oct. 19, 1938; d. Richard William and Emma (Fraiser) Fowler; m. George A. Omura, Dec. 27, 1962; children: June, Susan, Ann, George F. BA cum laude, Barnard Coll., 1960; MD, Cornell U., 1964. Cert. Am. Bd. Dermatology, Am. Bd. Dermatopathology. Intern in mixed-medicine Roosevelt Hosp., N.Y.C., 1965-66; resident in dermatology Cornell/N.Y. Hosp., N.Y.C., 1966-69, clin. instr. dermatology, 1969-70; asst. prof. dermatology U. Ala., Birmingham, 1970-75; assoc. prof. U. Ala. Med. Ctr., Birmingham, 1975-83, prof. dermatology, dir. dermatopathology, 1983-99, emeritus prof. dermatology, 1999—; with dermatopathology Skin Path P.C., Birmingham, 1999—; dir. dermatopathology fellowship training program U. Ala., Birmingham, 1983-99. Med Stud. Awd. for Outstanding Performance in Dermatology established by U. Ala. Birmingham, named for Emily F. Omura, 1999—. Fellow Am. Acad. Dermatology, Am. Soc. Dermatopathology (pres.-elect 1999-00). Methodist. Avocations: dance, reading, mus. docent. Office: Skin Path PC 3550 Independence Dr Birmingham AL 35209-5710

OMURA, GEORGE ADOLF, medical oncologist; b. N.Y.C., Apr. 30, 1938; s. Bunji K. and Martha (Pilger) O.; m. Emily Fowler, Dec. 27, 1962; children: June Ellen, Susan, Ann, George Fowler. B.A. magna cum laude, Columbia U., 1958; M.D., Cornell U., 1962. Intern Bellevue Hosp., N.Y.C., resident, 1965-67; fellow Meml. Sloan Kettering Cancer Ctr., N.Y.C., 1967-70; asst. prof. medicine U. Ala., Birmingham, 1970-73, assoc. prof. medicine, 1973-78, prof. medicine, 1978-95, prof. emeritus, medicine, 1995—, prof. ob-gyn., 1991-95; v.p. clin. devel. BioCryst Pharms., Inc., Birmingham, 1995-99, med. dir., 1996-99; prof. emeritus, ob-gyn U. Ala., Birmingham, 1996—; cons. Nat. Cancer Inst., 1975-97; chmn. Southeastern Cancer Study Group, 1983-87; cons. to FDA, 1994-95; prin. investigator cancer and leukemia Group B for Ala., 1986-95. Contbr. articles to profl. jours. Served with USNR, 1963-65. Am. Cancer Soc. jr. faculty clin. fellow, 1971-74. Fellow A.C.P.; mem. Gynecol. Oncology Group (co-prin. investigator for Ala. 1988—), Am. Soc. Clin. Oncology, Am. Soc. Hematology, Am. Assn. Cancer Research, Phi Beta Kappa, Alpha Omega Alpha. Home: 3621 Crestside Rd Birmingham AL 35223-1514 Office: University Sta Birmingham AL 35294-0001

OMURA, MINORU, toxicologist; b. Shizuoka-City, Japan, June 27, 1962; s. Tsuneo and Yone (Tominaga) O. PhD, Kyushu U., Fukuoka, Japan, 1992. Instr. Kyushu U., 1992—. Home: Nishizin 1-7-25-303, Sawara-ku, Fukuoka 814-0002, Japan Office: Dept Hygiene Kyushu U, Maidashi 3-1-1 Higashi-ku, Fukuoka 812-8582, Japan

ONADEKO, BABATUNDE OWOLABI, medical educator, consultant; b. Ishara, Ogun, Nigeria, Nov. 14, 1938; s. Adeniyi Gabriel and Edith Modupe (Martins) O.; m. Modupe Onayinka Onabamiro, Dec. 24, 1968; children: Sola, Jade, Wole, Kemi. BA, U. Dublin, Ireland, 1964, MB BChir, 1966, MA, 1973, MD, 1977. Intern Birkenhead (Eng.) Gen. Hosp., 1966-67; sr. house officer U. Coll. Hosp., Ibadan, Nigeria, 1967-68; registrar Univ. Coll. Hosp., Ibadan, 1968-70; clin. asst. City Hosp., Edinburgh, Scotland, 1970-72, Western Gen. Hosp., Edinburgh, 1970-71; sr. registrar U. Coll. Hosp., Ibadan, 1972-74; lectr. U. Ibadan, 1974-76, sr. lectr., 1979-87; prof. medicine King Faisal U., Dammam, Saudi Arabia, 1987-90, U. Ibadan, 1990-2000; dir. clin. svcs. and tng. Univ. Coll. Hosp., Ibadan, 1996—. Editor: African Jour. Medicine and Med. Scis., 1991-96. Med. advisor Nigerian Soc. for Asthmatics, Ibadan, 1995—. Commonwealth scholar Brit. Govt., 1970; Nuffield West African Trust fellow, 1977. Fellow ACP (Blaine Bower scholar 1993), Royal Coll. Physicians London, Royal Coll. Physicians Edinburgh, Coll. Chest Physicians; mem. Am. Thoracic Soc., Brit. Thoracic Soc., Internat. Union Against Tuberculosis and Lung Disease. Anglican. Avocations: reading novels, singing, table tennis, lawn tennis, music. Office: Univ Coll Hosp Dept Medicine, Queen Elisabeth Rd, Ibadan Oyo, Nigeria

ONAT, TEOMAN, pediatric cardiologist; b. Istanbul, Turkey, Nov. 8, 1931; s. Ahmet Rasim and Neyire Onat; children: Suzan, Erol Rasim. BSc in Natural Sci., Robert Coll., Istanbul, 1951; MD, U. Zurich, Switzerland, 1957; PhD, U. Istanbul, 1966. Resident pediat. clinic U. Zurich, 1957-61; pediatrician-in-chief newborn dept. Am., Admiral Bristol Hosp., Istanbul, 1964-74, chief resident, head dept. pediat. cardiology, 1964-66; asst. prof. pediat. U. Istanbul, 1966-67, assoc. prof., 1967-72, prof., 1972—, head pediat. cardiology Cerrahpasa med. faculty, 1966-98. Co-author: Differential Diagnosis of Congenital Heart Disease, 1963; author: Growth and Development (sexual and skeletal) of Girls During Puberty, 1976; editor: Textbook of Pediatrics, 2 vols., 1996; others; contbr. articles to profl. jours. Lt. Turkish mil., 1962-64. Recipient Internat. Schleussner prize for radiology, 1962, Eczacibasi sci. award, Istanbul, 1976, Myrtle Watt journalist award med. subjects unit Am. Topical Assn., 1990, Haktan award pediat. rsch. Am. Jour. Human Biology, 1997. Mem. Assn. European Pediat. Cardiologists (chmn. 1976), Turkish Pediat. Assn. (pres. 1975), Turkish Soc.

Cardiology (directorial bd. 1978-84), Am. Soc. Human Biology, Soc. Med. History. Avocations: medical philately, jazz and classical music, playing keyboard and piano, bridge, sports. Home: Nisbetiye Cad 17/6A, 80630 Istanbul Akatlar, Turkey

ONDA, KAZUO, engineering educator; b. Tokyo, Japan, June 20, 1941; s. Sanjiroh and Kama (Yamada) O.; m. Chieko Shohji, Apr. 22, 1972; children: Naoko, Takuroh. BS, Tokyo Inst. Tech., 1964, MS, 1966, PhD, 1993. Sr. rschr. Electrotech. Lab., Tanashi, Japan, 1974-83; chief officer Electrotech. Lab., Tsukuba, Japan, 1983-84, mgr., 1984-95; prof. engring. Toyohashi (Japan) U. Tech., 1995—; vis. scientist Stanford (Calif.) U., 1976-77. Author: The Carbon Monoxide Laser, 1976, Spectral Emission from Combustion Gas Containing Scattering Media, 1993, Thermal Engineering for Global Environmental Protection, 1996; editor: Global Warming Gas and Fossil Fuel Power Generation System, 1992. Recipient Naoji Iwatani meml. award, Tokyo, 1973. Mem. Inst. Elec. Engrs. Japan, Japanese Soc. Mech. Engrs., Japan Soc. Energy and Resources. Avocations: golf, hiking, classical music, reading. Office: Toyohashi U Tech, 1-1 Hibarigaoka Tenpaku-cho, Toyohashi 441-8580, Japan

ONDA, MORIO, sociology educator; b. Akita, Japan, Jan. 30, 1955; s. Hiroshi and Ryoko (Watanabe) O.; m. Fusae Takeda Onda, Sept. 23, 1991; children: Takahiro, Masanori. BA, Keio U., Tokyo, 1978; B in Econ., Kobe U., 1983; PhD, U. Tokyo, 1996. With Japan Travel Bur., Inc., Tokyo, 1978-92; assoc. prof. Ryutsu Keizai U., Ibaraki-ken, Japan, 1993-99, prof., 1999—; rschr. Japan Travel Bur. Found., Tokyo, 1984-91. Author: Management Diagnosis of Leisure Business, 1992, Economic Sociology of Development, 1997. Mem. Internat. Sociol. Assn., The Soc. for Internat. Devel., The Soc. for the Advancement of Socio-Economics. Avocations: car driving, music. Fax: 81-48-688-2675. E-mail: morio.onda@nifty.ne.jp. Home: 556-505 Horisaki-cho, Omiya-shi 330-0022, Japan

ONDO BILE, PASTOR MICHA, ambassador; b. Equatorial Guinea, Dec. 2, 1952; married; 6 children. MS in Engring., Univ. Inst. Mines, Krivoirog, 1982. Engr. Dept. Mines and Hydrocarbons of Malabo, Equatorial Guinea, 1982, chief mines and quarries sect., 1983-84, gen. dir., 1984-85; sec. gen. Min. of Mines and Energy, Equatorial Guinea, 1994-95; amb. E. and P. Republic of Equatorial Guinea, Washington, 1995—; permanent rep. UN, N.Y.C., 1995—. Decorated Knight of 2d class Order of Independence of Republic of equatorial Guinea. Office: Embassy of Republic of Equatorial Guinea 1712 I St NW Ste 410 Washington DC 20006-3702

ONDOH, TADANORI, space scientist; b. Ochiai, Okayama, Japan, Jan. 3, 1935; s. Hajime and Shizue (Yoshioka) O.; m. Takako Seki, Jan. 7, 1968. BS, Kyoto (Japan) U., 1958, MS, 1960, DS, 1965. Rsch. scientist Radio Rsch. Lab. Ministry of Posts and Telecomms., Tokyo, 1963-75, chief space physics sect., 1975-84, dir. Lab. for Space Science, 1984-89, dir. Comms. Rsch. Lab., 1990-95; NAS-NASA rsch. assoc. Goddard Space Flight Ctr., Greenbelt, Md., 1968-70; dir. Space Earth Environ. Lab., Tokorozawa, Japan, 1995—; mem. nat. com. on space rsch. Sci. Coun., Japan, 1983-94, mem. nat. com. on radio sci., 1973—; prin. investigator Dynamics Explorer Guest Investigator program NASA, Washington, 1985—; assoc. Com. on Space Rsch., 1994—. Editor: Radio and Space Data, 16 vols., 1970-85, Geospace Environmental Science, 2000; contbr. articles to profl. jours. Dep. dir. gen. for Asia, Internat. Biographical Ctr., Cambridge, Eng., 1995—, LFIBA, 1998—. Recipient Tanakadate Gold medal Soc. Terrestrial Magnetism and Electricity, 1973, Gold medal for Disting. Scientist, Minister Sci. and Tech., Japan, 1993. Mem. Am. Geophys. Union, Soc. Geomagnetism and Earth, Planetary and Space Scis. (mem. adv. com. 1989-94). Achievements include investigations on characteristics and generation mechanism on auroral and magnetospheric radio emissions observed by ISIS and DE-1 satellites; first geomagnetic field observation by ETS-VI near the geostationary orbit. Home: 5186 Kitano, Tokorozawa 359-1152, Japan Office: Space Earth Environ Lab, Tokorozawa Saitama 359-1152, Japan

O'NEAL, CLARENCE ROYAL, economist; b. L.A., Oct. 1, 1928; s. Clarence Burt and Geraldine Beatrice (Whiteside) O'N.; m. Tamara Maria Eisenhut, May 16, 1959; children: Kevin Roderick, Danika Verena. BA, Stanford U., 1951, MA, 1955; B Fgn. Trade., Am. Grad. Sch. Internat. Mgmt., 1952; postgrad., Johns Hopkins U., 1955-56. Cons. Econometric Specialists Inc., N.Y.C., 1956-57, Ebasco Svcs., N.Y.C., 1957-58; ofcl. IAEA, Vienna, Austria, 1958-78, adviser to dir. gen., 1978-83, coord. regional coop. arrangements for promotion nuclear sci, 1983-87; adviser to dir. Internat. Ctr. for Theoretical Physics, Trieste, Italy, 1976-88; adviser to pres. Third World Acad. Scis., Trieste, 1988; cons. Fox, Marinelli, O'Neal, Vienna, 1988-94; lectr. in field. Co-author (computer manual) N/Joy-World of Objects, 1990; contbr. articles to profl. publs. Served in USMC, 1946-48. Fellowship Johns Hopkins U., 1955-56. Mem. UN Assn. of Austria.

O'NEAL, SHAQUILLE RASHAUN, professional basketball player; b. Newark, Mar. 6, 1972; s. Philip A. Harrison and Lucille O'Neal. Student, La. State U. Center Orlando Magic, 1992-96, L.A. Lakers, 1996—. Appeared in movie Blue Chips, 1994, Kazaam, 1996. Named to Sporting News All-American first team, 1990-91; recipient Rookie of the Yr. award NBA, 1993; mem. NBA All-Star team, 1993, 94, Dream Team II, 1994; first pick overall, 1992 draft. Office: LA Lakers 3900 W Manchester Blvd Inglewood CA 90305-2200

O'NEAL, STEVEN G., chemist, educator; b. Peru, Ind., Oct. 28, 1947; s. George Buckley and Myra Joan (Alger) O.; m. Cheryl Anne Poore, Jan. 24, 1970; 1 child, Kristina Marie. BA in Chemistry, Wabash Coll., Crawfordsville, Ind., 1970; PhD in Chemistry, U. S.C., 1977. Cert. tchr. secondary sci., Ariz., Okla. Instr. biology Wabash Coll., Crawfordsville, 1970-72; asst. prof. chemistry Okla. U., Norman, 1980-85; tchr. chemistry Norman (Okla.) H.S., 1989-97, Chandler (Ariz.) H.S., 1997-98, Hamilton H.S., Chandler, 1998-99; adj. prof. chemistry Chandler Gilbert C.C., 1999—; tchr. honors chemistry Desert Vista H.S., Tempe, 1999—; advanced placement chemistry reader Coll. Bd., Princeton, N.J., 1999, 2000, chemistry cons., 2000—. Fellow AAAS; mem. Am. Chem. Soc., Nat. Sci. Tchrs. Assn., Sigma Xi (Okla. chpt. v.p., sec. 1995-97). Avocations: science fiction, walking, basketball, classical music. Home: 1435 W Remington Dr Chandler AZ 85248-1396 Office: Desert Vista High Sch 16440 S 32d St Phoenix AZ 85044

ONEGLIA, CARLO, cardiologist; b. Savona, Italy, Mar. 30, 1948; s. Angelo and Marcella (Pasqualini) O.; m. Carla Ricco, May 10, 1980; children: Andrea, Emanuele. MD, U. Padua, Italy, 1973. Intern Padua U., 1973-75; asst. Gen. Hosp., Brescia, Italy, 1977-83; dep. dir. divsn. medicine Iseo (Italy) Hosp., 1983-88; dep. dir. divsn. cardiology S. Orsola Hosp., Brescia, 1988—. Contbr. articles to profl. jours. Capt. police Italian mil., 1975-76. Office: S Orsola Hosp, V Emanuele II 27, 25122 Brescia Italy

O'NEIL, ROBERT MARCHANT, university administrator, law educator; b. Boston, Oct. 16, 1934; s. Walter George and Isabel Sophia (Marchant) O'N.; m. Karen Elizabeth Elson, June 18, 1967; children—Elizabeth, Peter, David, Benjamin. AB, Harvard U., 1956, AM, 1957, LLB, 1961; LLD, Beloit Coll., 1985, Ind. U., 1987. Bar: Mass. 1962. Law clk. to Justice William J. Brennan Jr. U.S. Supreme Ct., 1962-63; acting assoc. prof. law U. Calif.-Berkeley, 1963-66, prof., 1966-67, 69-72; exec. asst. to pres., prof. law SUNY-Buffalo, 1967-69; provost, prof. law U. Cin., 1972-73, exec. v.p., prof. law, 1973-75; v.p., prof. law Ind. U., Bloomington, 1975-80; pres. U. Wis. System, 1980-85; prof. law U. Wis.-Madison, 1980-85; prof. law U. Va., Charlottesville, 1985—, pres., 1985-90; gen. counsel AAUP, 1970-72, 91-92. Author: Civil Liberties: Case Studies and the Law, 1965, Free Speech: Responsible Communication Under Law, 2d edit., 1972, The Price of Dependency: Civil Liberties in the Welfare State, 1970, No Heroes, No Villians, 1972, The Courts, Government and Higher Education, 1972, Discriminating Against Discrimination, 1976, Handbook of the Law of Public Employment, 1978, 2d rev. edit., 1993, Classrooms in the Crossfire, 1981, Free Speech in the College Community, 1997; co-author: A Guide to Debate, 1964, The Judiciary and Vietnam, 1972, Civil Liberties Today, 1974. Trustee Tchrs. Ins. and Annuity Assn.; bd. dirs. Commonwealth Fund, Fort James Corp., Sta. WVPT Pub. TV, Am. Law Inst. Home: 1839 Westview Rd Charlottesville VA 22903-1632 Office: Thomas Jefferson Ctr Protection Free Expression 400 Peter Jefferson Pl Charlottesville VA 22911-8691

O'NEILL, BRADFORD KNIGHT, lawyer, legal translator; b. Abington, Pa., May 12, 1942; arrived in Honduras, 1964; s. Louis Andrew and Katharine Matilda (Cross) O'N.; m. Helga Idalia Martínez, Apr. 27, 1964; children: Francesca Melissa, Michelle Katarina, Helga Consuelo, Natalie Anne. BS in Langs., Georgetown U., 1969; postgrad. in law, U. Madrid, 1970-71; lic. in juristic and social scis., Nat. Autonomous U. Honduras, Tegucigalpa, 1990. Assoc. Bufete Ortez Colindres, Tegucigalpa, 1976; co-founder, ptnr. Bufete Tugliani, González and O'Neill, Tegucigalpa, 1976-77; ptnr. Bufete Gutiérrez Falla, Tegucigalpa, 1977—. Bd. dirs. Am. Sch. of Tegucigalpa, 1981; co-founder, treas. Honduran Am. C. of C., Tegucigalpa, 1983. Mem. Honduran Bar Assn. Roman Catholic. Office: Bufete Gutiérrez Falla, Ave La Paz No 2702, Tegucigalpa 11101, Honduras

O'NEILL, CASTEEN, artist; b. Orange, Calif., Aug. 17, 1976; d. William Allen Casteen and Micheleen O'Neill. BA in Fine Arts and Cultural Studies, Evergreen State Coll., Olympia, Wash., 1994. Designer fantasy ballgown Red Queen, 1999; exhbns. include GeoCon Art Show, Evergreen State Coll., Olympia, Wash., 1997, 98; mem. local comedy troupe Out on a Limb, 2000—. Avocations: role playing, painting, writing, dancing, reading. E-mail: dracora@hotmail.com.

O'NEILL, ELIZABETH STERLING, trade association administrator; b. N.Y.C., May 30, 1938; d. Theodore and Pauline (Green) Sterling: m. W.B. Smith, June 18, 1968 (div. Aug., 1978); 1 child, Elizabeth S. Kroese; m. Francis James O'Neill, May 19, 1984. BA, Cornell U., 1958; postgrad. studies, Northwestern U., 1959-60. Social sec. Perle Mesta Ambassador Luxembourg, N.Y.C.; spl. asst. Vivian Beaumont Allen, philanthropist, N.Y.C.; rep. Prentice-Hall Pub. Co., Eastern Europe; exec. dir. New Caanan (Conn.) C. of C., 1985-97; speaker various orgns. including Lions Club, Exchange Club, Kiwanis, Rotary, Poinsettia Club; apptd. Commn. Small Bus. State of Conn., 1996. Pres. Newcomers, New Caanan, Conn.; pub. rels. rep. Girl Scouts of U.S., Fairfield County; bd. dirs. Young Women's Rep. Club; mem. Gov. Weicker's Com. for Curriculum Reform; mem. community bd. Waveny Care Ctr., New Caanan; apptd. mem. Gov. John Roland's Commn. on Small Bus., Conn., 1996—; bd. dirs., trustee Clinton (N.J.) Mus. Art, Hunterdon Mus. Art, 2000. Recipient Service awards New Caanan YMCA, N.Y. ASPCA, certs. of appreciation New Caanan Lions Club, President Bush. Mem. AAUW (bd. dirs. New Caanan chpt.), Kiwanis. Christian Scientist. Avocations: tennis, horses, travel. Home: 17 Lance Rd Lebanon NJ 08833-5007

O'NEILL, JAMES ARTHUR, physicist, software developer; b. Hinckley, Eng., Jan. 7, 1953; came to Can., 1977, Australia, 1994; s. John Arthur and Edith Mary (Jacques) O'N.; m. Julie Elisabeth Tinson, May 28, 1988; 1 child, Charlotte. BA, Oxford U., Eng., 1973, MA, DPhil in Physics, 1977. Postdoctoral fellow U. Alberta, Edmonton, Can., 1977-79; engring. physicist Ont. Hydro, Toronto, Ont., Can., 1979-85; dir. sci. and tech. Ctr. for Indsl. Laser Applications, Sydney, Australia, 1986-87; sr. physicist Ont. Hydro, Toronto, 1987-93; prin. scientist BHP Rsch., Australia, 1994-96, mgr. rsch., steel coatings, 1996-99; dir. advanced processes JDS Uniphase, Ottawa, 1999—; mem. gen. physics grant selection com. Nat. Sci. and Engring. Coun., Can., 1989-92; adj. prof. York U., Toronto, 1988-93. Contbr. articles to profl. jours. including Jour. of Optical Soc. of Am., Phys. Review, Astronomy and Astrophysics, Jour. of Physics B, Jour. of Physics D, Review of Sci. Instruments, Physica Scripta. Mem. Can. Indsl. Laser Assn. (pres. 1988-93). Achievements include patents in laser isotope separation; development of commercial technology for isotope detection by IR spectroscopy; development of equipment for laser vibration measurements in nuclear reactors; developed and marketed "Quick Returns" software program (3d on Can. best seller list 1993). Avocations: snow skiing, windsurfing.

O'NEILL, KEVIN, plastic engineer, consultant; b. Jersey City, Feb. 7, 1933; s. John Joseph and Camille Lois O'Neill; m. Jacqueline Reilly, Sept. 12, 1953 (div. Oct. 1, 1965); children: Patricia, Sean, Moira, Kevin, Deirdre; m. Theresa Ann, Dec. 20, 1997. BS, Seton Hall U., 1955; AA, Newark Coll., 1958; MBA, C.W. Post Coll., 1964. Plastic engring., sales Celanese Corp. Am., N.Y.C., 1955-59; product mgr. cellulose acetate Columbian Carbon Co., N.Y.C., 1959-67; mkt. devel. mgr. Polymer Materials Inc., Farmingdale, N.Y., 1968-79; sales and mktg. mgr. Georgia Pacific Corp., Oak Brook, Ill., 1979-84; cons. Synergistics Chemicals Ltd., Toronto, Can., 1984-87, Hoechst A.G., Lonstein, Germany, 1989, Erkwepa A.G., Erkrath, Germany, 1990, 9A7 Specialty Chemicals, Wayne, N.J., 1991. Mem. Soc. Plastic Engrs. Assn., Plastic Pioneers Assn., Am. Mgmt. Assn. Avocation: tennis. Home: 13380 Polo Rd W Apt A202 West Palm Beach FL 33414-7277

O'NEILL, PAUL HENRY, aluminum company executive; b. St. Louis, Dec. 4, 1935; s. John Paul and Gaynald Elsie (Irvin) O'N.; m. Nancy Jo Wolfe, Sept. 4, 1955; children: Patricia, Margaret, Julie, Paul Henry. BA, Fresno State Coll., 1960; Haynes Found. fellow, Claremont Grad. Sch., 1960-61; postgrad., George Washington U., 1962-65; MPA, Ind. U., 1966; hon. degree, Clarkson U., 1993, Edinboro U., 1997, California U. Pa., 1998, Duquesne U., 1999, Calif. State U., Fresno, 1999. Site engr. Morrison-Knudsen, Inc., Anchorage, 1955-57; systems analyst VA, Washington, 1961-66; budget examiner Bur. of Budget, Washington, 1967-69; chief human resources program div. U.S. Govt. Office of Mgmt. and Budget, Washington, 1969-70; asst. dir. U.S. Govt. Office of Mgmt. and Budget, 1971-72, assoc. dir., 1973-74, dep. dir., 1974-77; v.p. Internat. Paper Co., N.Y.C., 1977-81, sr. v.p., 1981-85, pres., dir., 1985-87; CEO Alcoa Inc., Pitts., 1987-99, chmn., 1987—, also bd. dirs.; bd. dirs. Rand Corp, chmn.; bd. dirs. Lucent Techs., Eastman Kodak Co.; chmn. Pres.'s Edn. Policy Adv. Com., 1989-92; bd. govs. Nat. Assn. Securities Dealers, Inc. Bd. dirs. Gerald R. Ford Found., 1981—, Pub. Oversight Bd.; chmn. Manpower Demonstration Rsch. Corp., 1981—, Coun. for Excellence; trustee Am. Enterprise Inst., H. John Heinz III Ctr. for Sci., Econs. and the Environment. Recipient Nat. Inst. Pub. Affairs Career Edn. award, 1965, William A. Jump Meritorious award, 1971; Fellow Nat. Inst. Pub. Affairs, 1966. Mem. Bus. Coun., Nat. Acad. Social Ins. (founding mem.), Inst. Internat. Econs. (bd. dirs.), Internat. Primary Aluminum Inst. (former chmn.), Mgmt. Exec. Soc. Methodist. Office: Alcoa 201 Isabella St Pittsburgh PA 15212-5859

O'NEILL, ROBERT JOHN, historian; b. Melbourne, Victoria, Australia, Nov. 5, 1936; arrived in Eng. 1982; BE with honors, U. Melbourne, 1960; BA in Philosophy, Politics, Econs., Oxford (Eng.) U., 1963, MA, 1965, D of Philosophy in Modern History, 1965. Student with regular army Royal Mil. Coll. of Australia, Duntroon, 1955-58; commd. lt. Australian Regular Army, 1958, advanced through grades to capt., 1962; war svc. Australian Regular Army, Vietnam, 1966-67; promoted to maj. Australian Regular Army, 1967; instr. mil. history Royal Mil. Coll., Duntroon, 1967-68; res. Australian Regular Army, 1968; sr. lectr. history U. New South Wales, Australia, 1968-69; sr. fellow Rsch. Sch. Pacific Studies Australian Nat. U., 1969-77, prof. fellow in internat. rels., 1977-82; head Strategic and Def. Studies Ctr. Australian Nat. U., 1971-82; dir. Internat. Inst. for Strategic Studies, London, 1982-87; Chichele prof. history of war, fellow All Souls Coll., Oxford, 1987—, co-dir. Fgn. Policy Studies programme, 1990—; Australian ofcl. historian Korean War, 1970-82; chmn. bd. dirs. Ctr. Def. Studies U. London, Sir Robert Menzies Ctr. Australian Studies U. London, mem. Commonwealth Sec. Gen.'s Consultative Group on Small States, 1984-85; chmn. Brit. Working Group Internat. Nuclear History Programme, 1987-95, Internat. Studies Task Force Campaign for Oxford, Delegacy for Mil. Instrn. U. Oxford, 1991-2000; bd. dirs. Shell Trading and Transport Co. Plc (U.K.), Capital Income Builder, World Growth and Income Fund, L.A.; mem. adv. bd. Investment Co. Am., L.A., 1987—. Author: The German Army and the Nazi Party 1933-39, 1966, Vietnam Task, 1968, General Giap--Politician and Strategist, 1969, Australia in the Korean War 1950-53, 2 vols., 1979, 85; editor: (books) Insecurity: The Spread of Weapons in the Indian and Pacific Oceans, 1978, Security in East Asia, 1984, The Conduct of East-West Relations in the 1980's, 1985, New Technology and Western Security Policy, 1985, Doctrine, The Alliance and Arms Control, 1986, East Asia, the West and International Security, 1987, Prospects for Security in the Mediterranean, 1988; co-editor: New Directions in Strategic Thinking, 1981, Australian Defence Policy for the 1980s, 1982, Hedley Bull on Arms Control, 1987, The West and the Third WOrld, 1990, Securing Peace in Europe, 1945-61, 1992, War, Strategy and International Politics, 1992, Alternative Nuclear Futures, 1999; armed svcs. editor Australian Dictionary of Biography, 1970—. Trustee Imperial War Mus., 1990—, chmn., 1998—; mem. Commonwealth War Graves Commn., 1991—; gov. Internat. Peace Acad., N.Y., 1990—, Ditchley Found., 1990—. Decorated officer Order of Australia; named Hon. Col. 5th Vol. Royal Green Jackets, 1993; Rhodes scholar for Victoria, Oxford U., 1961; hon. fellow Brasenose Coll., Oxford, 1990. Fellow Australian Acad. Social Scis., Australian Inst. Engrs., Royal Hist. Soc.; mem. Internat. Inst. Strategic Studies (vice chmn. coun., chmn. exec. com. 1994-96, chmn. 1996—), Brit. Internat. Studies Assn. (exec. com. 1983-88), Royal Inst. Internat. Affairs, Australian Inst. Internat. Affairs (v.p. Canberra Br. 1971-72, rsch. com. 1970-79), Royal United Svcs. Inst., Royal United Svcs. Inst. of Australia (coun. mem. ACT 1971-79, pres. ACT 1976-77), The Fifth Royal Green Jackets (hon. colonel 1993-99). Avocations: walking, local history. Office: All Souls Coll, Oxford OX1 4AL, England

O'NEILL, SUSIE, Olympic athlete; b. Mackay, Queensland, Australia, Aug. 2, 1973; d. John and Trish O'Neill; m. Cliff Fairley, Mar. 1999. Recipient Gold medal 200 fly Atlanta Olympics, 1996, Silver medal 400 x 100m medley relay, Bronze medal 4 x 200m freestyle relay, Silver medal 100 butterfly Pan Pacific Championships, 1999, Gold medal 200 free and 200 butterfly, Gold medal 200m freestyle Sydney Olympics, 2000; 200 butterfly world titleist, 1998; named most successful Commonwealth Games athlete in history; set new world record for 200 fly Olympic Trials, Australia, 2000. Office: Australian Swimming Inc, PO Box 940, Dickson ACT 2602, Australia*

ONET, TRAIAN I., civil engineering educator, researcher; b. Dealul Negru, Cluj, Romania, May 29, 1937; s. Ioan I and Rafila G. (Trif) O.; m. Hortenzia Viorica Pop, July 24, 1960; children: Mircea Calin, Horia Aurelian. Degree in civil engring., Polytechnic Inst., Cluj, 1959, PhD, 1972. Design engr. Prefab Concrete Factory, Turda, 1959-61; chief engr. Bldg. Site, Turda, 1961-63; asst. Tech. U., Cluj-Napoca, 1963-70; asst. prof. Tech. U., Turda, 1970-74, assoc. prof., 1974-78, prof., 1978—, dep. dean civil engring. faculty, 1977-81, dean civil engring. faculty, 1984-89, head reinforced concrete lab., 1992—. Author: Reinforced Concrete, 1982, Structural Concrete Design, 1975, Partially Prestressed Concrete, 1993 (Romanian Aacd. Anghel Saligny prize 1993), Durability of Reinforced Concrete, 1994. Mem. Parochial Coun., Club, 1990—. Recipient Hon. Prof. award Romanian Edn. Ministry, 1984. Mem. Romanian Assn. Structural Design Engrs., Romanian Concrete Soc., Internat. Fedn. Structural Concrete. Orthodox. Avocation: gardening. Office: Tech U, Str C Daicoviciu 15, 3400 Cluj-Napoca Romania

ONG, EDMUND LIANG CHAI, infectious diseases physician, consultant; b. Kuching, Sarawak, Malaysia, Jan. 2, 1956; arrived in Eng., 1976; s. Keebian and Lee Kheng (Tan) O.; m. Sally Patricia Nield, Aug. 15, 1987; children: Stephanie Elizabeth Hui Ling, Emily Sarah Mei Ling. MB, BChir, U. Newcastle-upon-Tyne, Eng., 1983; MSc, U. London, 1987. Cert. in gen. medicine; cert. in infection and tropical medicine. House officer South Cleveland Hosp., Middlesbrough, Eng., 1983-84; house officer in surgery Freeman Hosp., Newcastle-upon-Tyne, 1984; sr. house officer South Cleveland Hosp./Middlesbrough Hosp., 1984-86, Whittington Hosp., London, 1986; rsch. fellow Hosp. Tropical Diseases London Sch. Tropical Medicine and Hygiene, U. London, 1986-87; registrar Monsall Hosp., Manchester, Eng., 1988-89; sr. registrar in infectious diseases and gen. medicine Monsall and North Manchester Gen. Hosp., 1989-91; cons. physician, sr. lectr. Newcastle Gen. Hosp., Newcastle-upon-Tyne, 1991—. Contbr. articles to nat. and internat. sci. jours. Grantee, Med. Rsch. Coun. Fellow Royal Coll. Physicians London, Ireland, Royal Soc. Tropical Medicine and Hygiene; mem. Brit. Soc. for Study of Infection, Brit. Thoracic Soc., Internat. AIDS Soc., Royal Coll. Physicians (London, diplomat in tropicalmedicine hygiene 1987). Avocations: badminton, walking, reading. Office: Newcastle Gen Hosp, Westgate Rd, Newcastle-upon-Tyne NE4 6BE, England

ONG, GIOK LIM, real estate executive; b. Semarang, Indonesia, Mar. 16, 1949; arrived in France, 1982; s. Bing Tjin and Hiang Bwee (Liem) O.; m. Sian Hoa Lauw, Nov. 20, 1976; children: Wan, Ing, Kim, Yen. BA, U. Antwerp (Belgium), 1970; MBA, Webster U., Geneva, 1980. Chief exec. Bunge, Antwerp, Belgium, 1971-75; mktg. mgr. Cast Europe, Rotterdam, The Netherlands, 1976-80; trades banking Dierickx & Co., Marseille, France, 1982-86; fin. dir. California Internat., Puget-Sur-Argens, France, 1987-92; comml. v.p. real estate Fria Internat., Le Muy, France, 1993—. Liberal. Roman Catholic. Avocations: skiing, golf, swimming, diving. Home: Villa Paradiso St Cassier, F-83490 Le Muy France Office: Fria Internat, 36 Allee des Lilas, F-83490 Le Muy France

ONG, KAH LAM, polymer technologist; b. Taiping, Malaysia, Aug. 14, 1936; arrived in Australia, 1992; s. Chen Huah Ong and Swee Luan Lim; m. Dorcas Leow (div. 1982); children: Marlene, Stephen, Henry; m. Edwina C. Goh, 1984; children: Mevelyn, Melarie. Grad. diploma in rubber tech., London Sch. Polymer Tech., 1960; MS, U. Akron, 1964; PhD, Case Western Res. U., 1968. Chemist Durable Rubber Mfg. Co., Middlesex, Eng., 1960-62; devel. chemist Gen. Tire and Rubber Co., Akron, Ohio, 1963-65; head chem. process tech. dept. Singapore Polytech., 1968-74; mng. dir. Allied Chem. Products Co., Malaysia, 1974-84; mng. ptnr. Goodrich Enterprise, Malaysia, 1984-92; ptnr. Blendrich Consulting, Melbourne, Australia, 1992—; cons., dir. Seal Polymer Industries, Malaysia, 1984-92; dir. mfg. Superior Healthcare Products Inc. (USA), Malaysia, 1988-89; cons. Ctr. for Advanced Material Tech., Monash U., Australia, 1992, RMIT U. Polymer Tech. Ctr., Australia, 1993-94. Environ. Studies grantee Esso Singapore Pte. Ltd., 1970, U.S. Tertiary Instns. Studies co-grantee Asia Found. Inc., 1973. Fellow Plastic & Rubber Inst. U.K., Inst. Materials U.K., Australasian Plastics and Rubber Inst. Avocations: reading, swimming. Office: Blendrich Consulting, Blendrich Consulting, 9 Lovell Close, 3178 Rowville Victoria, Australia

ONG, KIAN CHYE, psychologist; b. Singapore, Feb. 21, 1949; s. T.K. Ong and S.E. Kuah; m. Jean Koh; 1 child, Jacquelyn Wang. B in Psychology, U. Western Australia, 1973; MSc with distinction, U. Hull, Eng., 1986; M in Tech., Nat. U., Singapore, 1999. Chartered psychologist, U.K. Psychologist Ministry of Health, Singapore, 1975-81; head psychol. svcs., psychologist pers. rsch. dept. Ministry of Def., Singapore, 1981-83, head pers. rsch. dept., 1986-89, head applied behavioural scis. dept., 1989—, chief psychologist, 1999—; head aviation psychology Rep. of Singapore Air Force, 1983-86; part-time lectr. Nat. U. Singapore, 1987-95; cons. police psychology unit Republic of Singapore Police, 1992—; cons. pers. guidance unit pub. svc. divsn. Prime Mins. Office, 1995—. Maj. Singapore Mil. Res., 1975-95. Recipient Presdl. Commendation, Pres. of the Republic of Singapore, 1991, Pub. Adminstrn. medal Singapore Govt., 1995; Colombo Plan scholar Australian Govt., 1969, Commonwealth scholar Commonwealth Scholarship Commn. in the U.K., Eng., 1986; Mindef scholar, 1995-99. Mem. Brit. Psychol. Soc. (assoc. fellow), Ergonomics Soc. in U.K. (Ulf Aberg award 1986). Methodist. Office: Appl Beh Sci Dept (MINDEF), Defence Tech Tower B Depot Rd, Singapore 109681, Singapore

ONG, SIOW-HENG, communications consultant, educator, education consultant; b. Singapore, July 24, 1960; s. Sing-Say and Sow-Kun (NG) O.; m. Nirmala Govindasamy, Dec. 28, 1985; children: Benjamin, Deborah. BS, U. Oreg., 1985; MDiv, Fuller Theol. Sem., Pasadena, Calif., 1988; PhD, Northwestern U., 1994. Prof. Sch. of Comm. Studies Nanyang Tech. U., Singapore, 1994—; ednl. cons. TIME Asia Inc., others. Author: (book) A Strategy For a Metaphorical Reading of the Epistle of James, 1996; co-author: (book) Metaphor and Public Communication: Selected Speeches of Lee Kuan Yew & Goh Chok Tong, 1996. Recipient Norman Vincent Peale Preaching award Fuller Theol. Sem., 1987. Avocations: cinema, music, books, swimming. Home: 25 Colchester Grove, Singapore 558364, Singapore Office: Nanyang Tech U, Sch Comm Studies, Singapore 639798, Singapore

ONGHENA, PATRICK, psychologist, statistician, educator; b. Deurne, Antwerpen, Belgium, Feb. 3, 1965; s. Ludo and Frieda (Kerckhofs) O.; m. Adelheid Kennes, Oct. 1, 1988; children: Bieke, An. Lic., K. U. Leuven, 1988, D, 1994. Civil svc. U.C. Kortenberg, Belgium, 1988-90; rsch. asst. N.F.W.O., Leuven, Belgium, 1990-95; hoofddocent K.U. Leuven, 1995—. Contbr. articles to profl. jours. Mem. APA, Am. Ednl. Rsch. Assn., Belgische Vereniging voor Statistiek. Roman Catholic. Home: Hondseinde, B-2260 Westerlo Belgium Office: K U Leuven, Vesaliusstraat, B-3000 Leuven Belgium

ONI, OLUSOLA OLUMIDE AKINDELE, orthopaedic surgeon, consultant; b. Ibadan, Nigeria, Apr. 5, 1949; arrived in England, 1974; s. David

Babajide and Mary Monilola (Ogunsola) Oni; m. Merle Molly Campbell; children: Olutolani, Georgette, Babajide, Julia. MB BS, U. Ibadan, Nigeria, 1973; MD, U. Leicester, Leicester, Eng., 1987, MSc, 1994. House officer U. Coll. Hosp., Ibadan, 1973-74; sr. house officer New Castle (Eng.) Hosp., 1974-78; registrar Medway Hosp., Gillingham, Eng., 1980-81; cons. U. Teaching Hosp., Benin, Nigeria, 1981-82; sr. registrar Gen. Hosp., Watford, Eng., 1983-85; lectr., sr. lectr. U. Leicester, Leicester, Eng., 1985-93; examiner Royal Coll. Surgeons of Edinburgh, 1994. Inventor in field. Fellow Postgrad. Med. Coll. Nigeria. Fellow British Orthopaedic Assn., Royal Coll. Surgeons (Edinburgh), West African Coll. Surgeons; mem. British Orthopaedic Rsch. Soc. Office: The Glenfield Hosp, Groby Rd, Leicester LE3 9OP, England

ONIANG'O, RUTH KHASAYA, food scientist, educator; b. Kakamega, Kenya, Sept. 9, 1946; d. Benjamin Barwa and Philista (Ndakala) Shiare; m. Clement Meshack Oniang'o, Aug. 7, 1971; children: (twins) Masuka and Makeba, Tete, Joseph, Lulu. BSc with distinction, Wash. State U., 1971, MSc, 1973; PhD, U. Nairobi, Kenya, 1983. Asst. lectr. Kenyatta U., Nairobi, 1978-81, lectr., 1981-84, sr. lectr., 1984-88, assoc. prof., 1988-96; full prof. Jomo Kenyatta U. Agr. and Tech., Nairobi, 1996—; bd. mem. Kenya Gatsby Charitable Trust, Nairobi, 1995—; mem. UN Com., Geneva, 1996-99, Kenya Govt. Poverty Eradication Commn., 1999—. Author, editor: Feeding the Children, 1989, Not by Bread Alone: Food Security and Governance in Africa, 1999; co-author: Complete Kenya Cookery, 1990. Exec. dir. Non-Govtl. Orgn.-Rural Outreach Program, Kenya, 1993—; bd. mem. secondary schs., Kenya. Recipient Outstanding award People's Ednl. Program, Jackson, Miss., 1974, Silver Star, Pres. of Kenya, 1996, Disting. Svc. medal Pres. of Kenya, 1998. Mem. Nutrition Assn. Kenya (chair 1992-96), Kenya Profl. Assn. Women in Agr. Avocations: cooking, writing, family activities.

ONIFADE, ADEBIMPE ABRAHAMS, biochemist; b. Saki, Nigeria, Sept. 20, 1965; s. Adedokun Abraham and Olanihun Marian O.; m. Olajumoke Iyabo Adekola, Sept. 18, 1993; children: Folakemi Esther, Damilola Deborah, Olufemi Abraham. PhD, U. Ibadan, Nigeria, 1993; MS with distinction, U. Ibadan, 1990, BS with 1st class, 1987. Tech. officer Nigerian Pres. Task Force, Lagos, 1990-92; lectr. and rschr./rsch. supr. animal sci. U. Ibadan, 1994-97; rsch. assoc. Dept. Biological Scis., Kuwait U., 1997—; cons. Michael Stevens Assocs., Lagos, 1996-97. Contbr. to articles in profl. jours in field of animal sci. including Brit. Poultry Sci., Animal Feed Sci. and Tech., Jour. of Applied Animal Scis., Archives of Animal Nutrition, Archivos de Zootechnia. Exec. dir. Network for Eradication of Drug Abuse and Traffiking, Ibadan, Nigeria, 1995-97, dir. gen. Club Accord, Saki, Nigeria, 1994-97, asst. sec. Saki Consultative Forum, Nigeria, 1994-97, exec.-coord. Change 93, local govt. Ifedapo, Nigeria, 1993. Recipient scholarships U. Ibadan, 1988, Nigerian govt., 1988, others, Senate prize in agr. and forestry U. Ibadan, 1987. Mem. Am. Soc. Animal Sci., Poultry Sci. Assn., Nigerian Soc. Animal Prodn. Baptist. Avocations: conselling, reading, singing. Office: Dept Biological Scis, Kuwait U PO Box 5969, Safat 13060, Kuwait

ONIPCHENKO, VLADIMIR GERTRUDOVICH, biologist, educator; b. Moscow, Sept. 19, 1957; s. Gertrud Fedorovich and Valentina Stepanovna (Tyulpakova) O.; m. Olga Vital'evna Yurtseva, Jan. 19, 1980; 1 child, Elena. MS, Moscow State U., 1980, PhD, 1984, D in Biol. Sci., 1996. Biologist diplomate. Sci. rschr. Moscow State U., 1984-90, assoc. prof., 1991-96, prof., 1997—. Editor, co-author: Experimental Investigation, 1994; contbr. articles to profl. jours. Grantee Russian Found. Fundamental Rsch., Moscow, 1993—, Sweden Acad. Sci., 1994-96, J. and K. MacArthur Found., Moscow, 1995. Mem. Internat. Assn. for Vegetation Sci., Brit. Ecol. Soc., Moscow Soc. Naturalist. Office: Dept Geobotany Biol Fac, Moscow State Univ, 119899 Moscow Russia

ONISCHENKO, EVGENI FEDOROVISH, physician, researcher; b. Tsheliabinsk, Ural, Russia, Jan. 24, 1961; s. Ivan Fedorovish and Maria Fedorovna Onischenko; m. Svetlana Michailovna Poyasik; 1 child, Fedor Evgenievish. MD, Med. Inst., Tsheliabinsk, 1984; PhD, Med. Inst. Postgrad. Studies, Leningrad, Russia, 1991. Physician Hosp. Railway South-Ural, Tsheliabinsk, 1984-87; aspirant Med. Inst. Postgrad. Studies, 1987-90; asst. prof., lectr. Med. Acad. Postgrad. Studies, St. Petersburg, Russia, 1991—; physician cons. Consulat Gen. French in St. Petersburg, 1992-98. Contbr. articles to profl. jours.; inventor in field. Fellow Gen. Practice Assn. St. Petersburg; mem. Nat. Geog. Soc., N.Y. Acad. Scis., Planetary Soc. Home: Telejnaya str 9 6, 193024 St Petersburg Russia Office: St Petersburg Med Acad Postgrad Studies, 41 Kiroshnaya str, 193015 St Petersburg Russia

ONISHCHUKOV, GEORGE, physicist, researcher; b. Vladimir, Russia, June 13, 1957. MS, Moscow Inst. Physics & Tech., 1980, PhD, 1984. Rsch. asst. Moscow Inst. Physics and Tech., 1984-87, sr. rsch. asst., 1987-93; rsch. asst. Inst. Applied Physics U. Berne, Switzerland, 1991-94; vis. prof. Inst. Applied Physics, Friedrich-Schiller U. Jena, Germany, 1995—. Office: Inst Applied Physics, Max-Wien-Platz 1, D-07743 Jena Germany

ONISHI, AKIRA, executive, economics and global modeling educator; b. Tokyo, Jan. 5, 1929; s. Tatunosuke and Tomi (Fusegawa) O.; m. Noriko Shimizu, Sept. 27, 1963; children: Kimihiro, Masahiro. BA in Econs., Keio U., Tokyo, 1954, MA in Econs., 1958, PhD in Econs., 1963; PhD in Sys. Engring., Tokyo Inst. Tech., 1994. Rsch. officer Inst. Devel. Econs., Tokyo, 1963-65; assoc. prof. Chuo U., Tokyo, 1965-67; econ. affairs officer UN Econ. Commn. for Asia and Far East, Bangkok, Thailand, 1967-68, ILO, Geneva, 1968-70; chief economist Japan Econ. Rsch. Ctr., Tokyo, 1970-71; from prof. to v.p. Soka U., Tokyo, 1971-91, v.p., 1991—; bd. dirs. Inst. Systems Sci. Author: Japanese Economy in Global Age, 1974; contbr. articles to profl. jours. Grantee Japan Found., 1958-60, Japan Econ. Rsch. Found., 1974-75, Australia-Japan Found., 1981-82; recipient SGI Culture award 1985, Supreme Article award Japan Assn. Planning Adminstrn., 1991, 20th Century award Internat. Bibliog. Ctr., Eng., 1993, Excellent Article award ECAAR, 1997. Fellow Japan Soc. Internat. Econs., Japan Assn. Planning Adminstrn., Japan Assn. Simulation and Gaming (v.p. 1989-92, pres. 1993-97, award 1998), First Five Hundred, Internat. Bibliog. Ctr. (Eng.). Buddhist. Achievements include development of futures of global interdependence global model used by UN, 1982—. E-mail: onishi@t.soka.ac.jp. Home: 4-9-4 Seijyo Setagaya-Ku, Tokyo 157-0066, Japan Office: Soka U, 1-236 Tangi-cho Hachiji-shi, Tokyo 192-8577, Japan

ONISHI, TAKEHITO, economics educator; b. Nara, Japan, July 1, 1948; s. Shigeru and Eiko (Hirata) O.; m. Mayumi Okita, Mar. 23, 1977; children: Takahito, Anna, Atsuto. BS, Kyoto (Japan) U., 1973, B of Econs., 1976; M of Econs., Osaka City U., Japan, 1978, D of Econs, 1984. Univ. lectr. Osaka U. Econs., 1985, Osaka U. Econs. and Law, 1986-88; univ. lectr. Kinki U., Osaka, 1988-91, univ. assoc. prof., 1991—. Co-author: World Capitalism and Non-White Labour, 1983, Labour Migration in the Modern World, 1992; co-editor: Problems of Social Science, 1995, Reconstruction of Modernity, 1998. Mem. Internat. Soc. for the Study European Ideas (chair), Soc. for Advancement of Socio-Econs., Assn. Social Thought. Avocations: music, gardening, travel, mountaineering. Home: 4-12 Kumoi-cho, Nishinomiya 662-0064, Japan Office: Kinki U, 3-4-1 Kowakae, Higashi, Osaka 577, Japan

ONISHI, TETSURO, urology educator; b. Okayama, Japan, Feb. 24, 1951; s. Hiroyuki and Fumiko Onishi; m. Kimiko Komoto, Apr. 15, 1979; 3 children. MD, Jikei U., Tokyo, 1971, BM, 1985. Cert. Japanese Bd. Urology. Intern Jikei U. Sch. Medicine, Tokyo, 1978-80, med. asst., 1980-86, resident in urology, 1983-84; assoc. prof. urology Jikeo U. Sch. Medicine, Tokyo, 1986—. Author: Year Book of Urology, 1992, Essentials of Urology, 1995; contbr. articles to med. jours., including Japan Jour. Urology, Internat. Jour. Urology. Grantee Aid for Encouragement Young Scientists, 1989, Aid for Sci. Rsch., 1992-93, 95-97. Mem. Japan Urol. Assn. (instr. 1990—), Am. Urol. Assn. (corr.). Avocations: cooking Italian food, driving, reading. Office: Jikei U Sch Med Dept Urol, 25-8 3-chome Nishi-shinbash, Tokyo 105-8461, Japan

ONITSUKA, HIDEO, radiologist, health facility administrator; b. Fukuoka, Japan, July 7, 1947; s. Toshio and Teru (Hida) O.; m. Kumiko Sato, Sept. 15, 1973; children: June, Ryo, Ken. MD, Kyushu U., Fukuoka, Japan, 1972, D of Med. Sci., 1989. Diplomate Am. Bd. Radiology. Resident U. Mich., Ann Arbor, 1975-79; instr. Kyushu U., 1979-84, lectr., 1984-90, assoc. prof. radiology, 1990-92; dir. dept. radiology Iizuka (Japan) Hosp., 1992-98, v.p., 1997-98; v.p. Tanushimaru Ctrl. Hosp., Japan, 1998-2000, pres., 2000—; cons. Radiation Effects Rsch. Found., Hiroshima, Japan, 1979-89; vis. lectr. Kyushu U., 1992—. Mem. Japan Radiol. Soc., Radiol. Soc. N.Am., Am. Coll. Radiology, Am. Roentgen Ray Soc. Avocations: computer, camera, travel. E-mail: onitsuka@intermix.ne.jp. Home: Gojo 2-23-5, Dazaifu 818-0125, Japan Office: Tanushimaru Ctrl Hosp, 892 Masuoda, Tanushimaru Uhika Fukuoka 839-1213, Japan

ÖNKAL-ATAY, DILEK, management educator; b. Istanbul, Turkey, Mar. 31, 1961; d. Yasar and Ilhan (Yenilmez) Ö; 1 child, Cagil. BA, Bogazici U., Istanbul, 1982; PhD, U. Minn., 1988. From asst. to assoc. prof. Bilkent U., Ankara, 1988—; vis. instr. U. Minn., 1987-88. Contbr. articles to profl. jours. including Internat. Jour. Forecasting, Jour. Forecasting, Jour. Behavioral Decision Making, and European Jour. Operational Rsch. V.p. Minn. Turkish-Am. Assn., 1983-84. Recipient Rsch. award Turkish Acad. Scis., 1995, 96, 97, 98, 99. Mem. Informs, Internat. Inst. Forecasters, Turkish Statis. Assn., Internat. Soc. on MCDM, Ops. Rsch. Soc. Turkey, N.Y. Acad. Scis. Office: Bilkent U, Faculty Bus Adminstrn, 06533 Ankara Turkey

ONNIS, LUIGI, psychotherapist, educator; b. Iglesias, Cagliari, Italy, Feb. 28, 1944; s. Corrado and Palmira (Giacobbe) O.; m. Caterina Selvaggi, Dec. 22, 1984. MD, Med. Sch., Cagliari, 1969; degree, Psychiatry Sch., Parma, Italy, 1972; family psychotherapy cert., Family Therapy Sch., Rome, 1974. Clin. assoc. U. Padova, Italy, 1970-73; asst. prof. U. Rome, 1973-80, rsch. prof., 1980-90, prof. psychiatry, 1990—; family therapy supr. Family Therapy U. Sch., Barcelona (Spain), 1988—; family therapy tchr. Family Therapy Ctr., Paris, 1987—; cons. Family Therapy U. Ctr., Lausanne, Switzerland, 1988—; founder, dir., tng. dir. Inst. Europeo Formazione Consulenza Sistemica, Rome, 1992—. Editor: (jour.) Psicobiettivo, 1981—; mem. editl. bd. Jour. Systemic Therapies, 1988—, Cahiers Critiques de Therapie Familiale, 1980—, Reviste de Psicoterapia, 1985—; author: Corpo e Contesto, 1985, Famiglia e Malattia Psicosomatica, 1988, La Terapia Relazionale e i suoi contesti, 1993, Les langages du corps, 1996, La palabra del ceurpo, 1997. Active Nat. Com. for Psychotherapy Regulation, 1990—. Hon. mem. Assn. des Therapeutes Systemiques Françaises, Paris, 1989; approved supr. Am. Assn. Marriage Family Therapy, 1993. Mem. Soc. Italiana Psicoterapia Relazionale (bd. dirs.), European Family Therapy Assn. (founder, bd. dirs.), Soc. Italiana di Psichiatria, Am. Family Therapy Acad. Roman Catholic. Home: Viale Eritrea 136, 00199 Rome Italy Office: U Dept Psychiatry, Via Panama 68/70, 00198 Rome Italy

ONO, ELIZABETH ORIKA, science educator; b. Embu, Brazil, Nov. 21, 1963; d. Yoshio and Masami Kogima Ono. B in Biology, UNESP, Botucatu, Brazil, 1986, MS, 1991, D, 1994. Prof. UNITAU, Taubate, Brazil, 1988-97, UNESP, Botucatu, 1997—. Author: Rooting of Stem Cuttings: Geral Aspects, 1996. Mem. Brazilian Plant Physiology Soc., Brazilian Bot. Soc., Sao Paulo Bot. Soc. Roman Catholic. Avocations: cinema, music, tourism. Fax: 55148213744. Home: 439 Ap 14, Rua Cel Manoel Luiz dos Santos, 18603310 Botucatu Brazil Office: UNESP, Dept Botonica-IB, 18618000 Botucatu Brazil

ONO, HIROSHI, health facility administrator; b. Sendai, Miyagi, Japan, May 30, 1937; s. Sosaburo and Tomi (Hirama) O.; m. Shizue Orii, Aug. 27, 1965; children: Naoko, Wahei. MD, Tohoku U., Sendai, 1962, PhD, 1967. Instr. Tohoku U. Sch. Medicine, Sendai, 1967-69, asst. prof., 1973-75; chief physician Wakayanagi Pub. Hosp., Miyagi, 1970-73; chief rschr. Hatano Rsch. Inst., Hadano, Japan, 1975—, dir. gen., 1989—; vis. lectr. Yamanashi Med. Coll., Kofu, Japan, 1982—, Tohoku U. Sch. Medicine, 1989—; mem. Ctrl. Coun. Pharmaceutical Affairs, 1981-97. Author: Functional Toxicology, 1990, The Dictionary of Food Safety, 1998. Recipient Mochizuki Kitaji Meml. prize Biosafety Rsch. Found., 1993. Mem. Japan Soc. Alternatives Animal Experiments (pres. 1995-96). Home: 793-12 Shibusawa, Hadano 259-1322, Japan Office: Hatano Rsch Inst, 729-5 Ochiai, Hadano 257-8523, Japan

ONO, JUNJI, acupuncturist; b. Yokohama, Kanagawa, Japan, Oct. 4, 1948. Diploma, Dr. Liu's Acupuncture Clinic, Taipei, Taiwan, 1972, Meishinkai Acupuncture Acad., Tokyo, 1972, Toyo Acupuncture and Moxibustion Coll., Tokyo, 1973, Dr. Wu Wei Ping's Chinese Acupuncture Hosp., Taipei, 1974. Lic. acupuncturist, Calif., Japan. Dir., owner Chinese Acupuncture Hosp., Tokyo, 1974-79, Chinese Acupuncture Clinic, Tokyo, 1979—; master trainer acupuncture schs., U.S.A., Japan, 1978—. Mem. Internat. Friendship Ctr., Tokyo. Recipient Chinese Acupuncture Assn., 1976. Mem. Internat. Acupuncture Assn. Japan (pres. 1994—). Avocations: karate, weight lifting, swimming. Office: Chinese Acupuncture Clinic, 2-15-1-613 Dogenzaka Shibuya-ku, Tokyo 150-0043, Japan

ONO, KOTARO, materials scientist, educator; b. Abu-Gan, Yamaguchi, Japan, Jan. 7, 1946; s. Ryoji and Misao Ono; m. Chitose Suyama; children: Shintaro, Yoshiko. BS, Hiroshima (Japan) U., 1968, MS, 1970, ScD, 1975. Rsch. assoc. Hiroshima U., 1973-87; postdoctoral fellow, lectr. Northwestern U., Evanston, Ill., 1985-87; assoc. prof. Shimane U., Shimane-Mastue, 1987-94; prof. materials sci. Shimane U., Mastue, 1994—, dept. chmn., 1994-95, faculty chmn. student com., 1999—; vis. rschr. Argonne (Ill.) Nat. Lab., 1998. Contbr. articles to profl. jours. Chmn. local Citizen Com., Matsue, 1997. Mem. Phys. Soc. Japan, Japan Inst. of Metals, Japan Soc. Electron Microscopy. Avocations: fishing, tennis, music, chorus. Office: Shimane Univ, 1060 Nishikawatsu, Mastue 690-8504, Japan

ONO, SHUN, journalist; b. Tokushima, Japan, Sept. 17, 1953; parents Akitoshi and Kazuyo (Amo) O.; m. Chieko Obara, Nov. 15, 1984; children: Yu, Aya. BA, Kyushu U., Fukuoka, Japan, 1978; MA, U. of The Philippines, Quezon City, 1992. Staff writer Mainichi Shimbun, Nagano, Japan, 1978-82, Osaka, Japan, 1982-89, Tokyo, 1989-90; corr. Mainichi Shimbun, Manila, 1990-95; sr. writer Mainichi Shimbun, Osaka, 1995-97, asst. editor, 1997—; lectr. Internat. Buddhist U., Habikino, Japan, 1998—. Author: (books) The Present Situation of Wild Animals, 1984, Red River, 1985, Hapon: Long Agony of Japanese-Filipinos After the Pacific War, 1992, Non-Tourism Courses in the Philippines, 1997. Mem. Assn. of The Philippines (fgn. corr., pres. 1994-95). Avocations: swimming, scubadiving. E-mail: oono@sakuranet.or.jp. Home: 1-17-9 Niwashirodai, Sakai-shi Osaka 590-0133, Japan

ONODERA, SUKEO, chemistry educator; b. Shizukawa, Japan, May 29, 1944; s. Choji Watabe and Tamiko Onodera; m. Kyoko Satoh, Oct. 10, 1978; children: Shin-ichiro, Keisuke, Yuko. BSc, Sci. U. of Tokyo, 1967, MSc, 1969, PhD, 1972. Rschr. Sci. U. Tokyo, 1973-84, asst. prof., 1985—; expert The Office Nat. Environment Bd., Bangkok, 1984-85. Author: Current Public Health, 1998, A Technical Manuals for Surface Treatment, 1997, A View for PCDD Pollution, 1993, Water Pollution and Quality Control, 1985; editor: The Pharm. Soc. Japan, 1995—; dir. Japan Soc. Environ. Chem. (dir. 1991—), Japan Toxicol. Sci. (trustees 1990—). Mem. N.Y. Acad. Scis., Pharm. Soc. of Japan, Chem. Soc. Japan. Office: Sci U Tokyo Faculty Pharm Scis, 12 Ichiga ya-funagawara, Shinjuku-ku Tokyo 162-0826, Japan

ONOÉ, KAZUNORI, immunologist, educator, pathologist; b. Sapporo, Hokkaido, Japan, Aug. 28, 1945; s. Tamenori and Yoshiko (Ohno) O.; m. Yaeko Terada, Jan. 23, 1971; children: Kazuyuki, Megumi. MD, Hokkaido U., Sapporo, 1970, PhD, 1976. Instr. Hokkaido U., Sapporo, 1970-81, assoc. prof., 1981-85, prof., chmn., 1985—, dir. Animal Facility Inst. Immunol. Sci., 1991-96, dir. Inst. Immunol. Sci., 1996—, dir. Inst. Gene. Med., 2000—; vis. investigator Sloan-Kettering Cancer Ctr., N.Y.C., 1977-79. Contbr. articles to profl. jours. including Jour. Exptl. Medicine and Proceedings Nat. Acad. Scis., USA. Grantee Health Sci. Found., Akiyama Found., 1987, Suhara Meml. Found., 1990, Uehara Bio Sci. Found., 1991, Sagawa Cancer Found., 1994. Achievements include research in NK-T-cell selection and differentiation in the thymus, immunobiology of bone marrow chimera, and peptide-based vaccine. Fax: 011-707-6838. Home: Minami-7 Nishi-26 Chuo-ku, Sapporo 064-0807, Japan Office: Hokkaido U Inst Gene Med, N-15 W-7 Kita-ku, Sapporo 060-0815, Japan

ONORATO, GIOVANNI, company executive; b. Torte del Greco, Nov. 19, 1960; s. Mario and Yolanda (Matesca) O.; m Daniela Aletti, Sept. 30, 1989; 1 child, Lorenzo. Grad., Inst. Orientale, Naples, Italy, 1984. Asst. dir. F&B Ops., Zerbowe Cat, Italy, 1985-92, dir. catering ops., 1992-98; v.p. ops. Costa Crociere, Genova, Italy, 1998—. Office: Costa Crociere Spa, Via de Marini 60, 16149 Genova Italy

ONOUE, YOSHIO, marine biology educator; b. Hirao-cho, Yamaguchi, Japan, Sept. 5, 1937; s. Susumu and Chieko (Higaki) O.; m. Chifumi Onoue, Mar. 19, 1966; children: Takuya, Kazuya. BS, Hiroshima U., 1961; MS, U. Tokyo, 1963; PhD, U. Wash., 1977. Sect. head Zenyaku Kohgyo Co., Ltd., Tokyo, 1963-66; rsch. assoc. U. Tokyo, 1966-70; tchg. and rsch. asst. U. Wash., Seattle, 1971-76; rsch. assoc. U. Tokyo, 1977-82; assoc. prof. Kagoshima U., Japan, 1983-88, prof., 1989—; dir. Fisheries Libr., Kagoshima U., 1995—; councillor Kagoshima U., 1998-99. Author: (book) Marine Toxins, 1979; contbr. articles to profl. jours. Mem. N.Y. Acad. Scis., AAAS, World Aquaculture Soc. Office: Faculty of Fisheries/Kagoshima U, 4-50-20 Shimoarata, Kagoshima 890-0056, Japan

ONSAGER, DAVID RALPH, cardiothoracic surgeon, educator; b. Phoenix, Feb. 15, 1962; s. Ralph William and Margaret Carol (Engel) O. BA in Biochem., History & Sociology Sci., U. Pa., 1984; MD, Rush Med. Coll., 1988. Diplomate Nat. Bd. Med. Examiners, Am. Bd. Surgery, Am. Bd. Thoracic Surgery. Resident in gen. surgery Med. Coll. Wis. affiliated hosps., Milw., 1988-94; fellow in cardiopulmonary transplantation U. Wis. Hosp. and Clinics, Madison, 1994-95, fellow in cardiothoracic surgery, 1995-97, lectr. in cardiothoracic surgery, 1997-2000; attending surgeon Meth. Hosp., Omaha, 2000—. Contbr. articles to profl. jours. Recipient House Staff Excellence in Tchg. award Med. Coll. Wis., 1991, Cmty. Health Svc. award Rush Med. Coll., Chgo., 1988; Cancer Ctr. grantee Med. Coll. Wis., 1991. Fellow ACS (assoc.); mem. AMA, State Med. Soc. Nebr., Internat. Soc. Heart and Lung Transplantation, Soc. Thoracic Surgeons (candidate). Dem. Avocations: tennis, basketball, skiing, sailing, flying. Home: 1337 S 101st St Apt 314 Omaha NE 68124-1098 Office: Cardiothoracic and Vascular Surgery 8111 Dodge St Ste 220 Omaha NE 68114-4117

ONTON, ANN LOUISE REUTHER, chemist; b. Bridgeport, Conn., Sept. 29, 1943; m. Aare Onton, 1965; children: Alan David, Daryl John, Julie Ann. BS in Chemistry, Purdue U., 1965. Lab. chemist Great Lakes Chem. Corp., 1965-67; rsch. asst. Geigy Chem. Corp., 1967-70; abstractor Chem. Abstracts Svc., 1970-72; rschr. Cancer Prevention II Study, 1980-90; chemist Prototek, Inc., 1992-93; rsch. assoc. Applied Biotech Concepts, Inc., 1995-98, Genaissance Pharms., 1999-2000; mgr. rsch. devel. and prodn. AllExcel.com, Inc., 2000—. NIH grantee, 1996, 97. Mem. Am. Chem. Soc., Assn. for Women in Sci. Achievements include development of novel materials and methods for improved electrophoresis and DNA sequencing technologies, development of methodologies for purification and testing of enzymes, U.S.A., Nat. and world medalist in Masters and Senior Olympic Swimming. Avocations: running, cycling, triathlon, competitive swimming. Office: AllExcel.com Inc Ste 200 135 Wood St West Haven CT 06516-3700

ONUKWULI, OKECHUKWU DOMINIC, mechanical engineering educator, researcher; b. Umuoji, Idemili, Nigeria, Aug. 5, 1955; s. Matthias Okafor and Mercilina (Okonkwo) O.; m Vivian Ozoemena Umerah, Apr. 13, 1998. BSc, U. Veszprem, Hungary, 1979, MSc, 1981; PhD, U. Lagos, Nigeria, 1998. Cert. chem. engr. Lectr. II, Enugu (Nigeria) State U. Tech., 1982-88, lectr. I, dept. coord. postgrad. program, 1988-91; sr. lectr. mech. engring. Nnamdi Azikiwe U., Awka, Nigeria, 1991-96, assoc. prof., 1996—, dept. seminar coord., 1996-98. Editor: Jour. Engring. and Applied Scis., 1998—; contbr. articles to profl. jours., including Chem. and Engring. Tech., Petroleum Sci. and Tech. Scholar Hungarian Govt., 1975, Nigerian Govt., 1984. Mem. Nigerian Soc. Chem. Engrs., Nigerian Soc. Engrs. Roman Catholic. Avocations: football, table tennis, travel. Home: Umuoli-Umuoji, Idemili Local Govt Anambra, Nigeria Office: Nnamdi Azikiwe U Dept Mech, Engring, PMB 5025, Awka Anambra, Nigeria

ONUMA, NAOKI, audiologist, educator for hearing impaired; b. Miyagi, Japan, Jan. 12, 1942; m. Reiko Onuma, May 6, 1966; children: Fuyuko, Hitomi. BA, Tohoku U., Sendai, Japan, 1965; Diploma of Audiology, Ctrl. Inst. for the Deaf, St. Louis, 1981; MD, Showa U., Tokyo, 1994. Sr. rschr. Nat. Inst. Spl. Edn., 1984-88; prof. Tsukuba Coll. Tech., 1988-98, dean, 1998—; cons. Comm. Rsch. Lab., Ministry of Posts and Telecomms., 1996—; pres. Internat. Symposium on Childhood Deafness, Tokyo, 1997—. Author: Educational Audiology Handbook, 1997, Assistive Listening Guidebook for Hearing Impaired People, 1997. Mem. Japan Audiol. Soc. (councilor 1993—), Japan Soc. Edn. Audiology (prs. 1994—). E-mail: ohnuma@tsukuba-tech.ac.jp. Office: Tsukuba Coll Tech, 4-3 Amakubo, Tsukuba, Ibaraki 305-0005, Japan

ONWU, EMMANUEL NLENANYA, religious studies educator; b. Ututu, Abia, Nigeria, Mar. 22, 1948; s. Nlenanya and Mgbeke O.; m. Alu Nlenanya Eke Alu Ugwo, Dec. 21, 1972; children: onwu, Eberechukwu, Inya, Chioma, Ogonna, Amarachi. BA with honors, U. Nigeria, Nsukka, 1977; ThM, Princeton (N.J.) Theol. Sem., 1979; PhD, U. Nigeria, U. Durham, 1983. From asst. lectr. to sr. lectr. U. Nigeria, 1980-86, prof. New Testament, 1988—, acting head dept. religion, 1994—; vis. prof. U. Zimbabwe, 1993, U. Cambridge, 1995, U. Edinburgh, 1995. Author: A Critical Introduction to the Traditions of Jesus, 1991; editor African Jour. Biblical Studies, 1985-90, Nsukka Jour. Religious Studies, 1995—. Recipient Theol. Edn. Fund award World Coun. Chs., 1974-77; scholar Princeton Theol. Sem., 1978-79, Commonwealth of Eng. Staff scholar, 1983. Mem. Nigerian Assn. Biblical Studies, Internat. Assn. Promotion of Christian Higher Edn., Soc. Study of New Testament. Avocations: jogging, gardening. Home: Ututu Postal Agy, Arochukwu Local Govt Area, Ututu Abia Sta, Nigeria Office: U Nigeria, Dept Religion, Nsukka Nigeria

ONWUEMESI, AJANA GODWIN, geophysics educator, researcher; b. Inyi, Enugu, Nigeria, Nov. 22, 1957; s. Onwuemesi Matthew and Nebe Matina (Nwokedi) O.; m. Ekwutosi Faustina Okpara, Jan. 16, 1997; 1 child, Bonaventure. BS in Geology, UNN, Nigeria, 1982, MS in Geophysics, 1986; PhD in Geophysics, Nnamdi Azikime U., Awka, Nigeria, 1995. Mem. faculty Nnamdi Azikiwe U., 1987—, head dept. geophysics, 1997-99; mem. NMGS, Nigeria, 1990—; coord. dept. postgras. program Nnamdi Azikiwe U., 1990—, univ. senate, 1997-99; cons. geophysicist Environ. Co., Nigeria, 1988-94, Water Drilling Co., Nigeria, 1987—, Mineral Exploration Co., Nigeria, 1988—. Mem. editl. bd. Jour. Scis., 1996—; contbr. articles to profl. jours. Sec. Town Union, Nigeria, 1987-90, chmn., 1990-93, peace com., 1999—. Mem. NAH, Exploration Geophysicists. Avocations: footballing, swimming, music, writing, travelling. Home: 12 Igwebuike St, Awka Nigeria Office: Nnamdi Azikime Univ, Geol Scis Dept PMB 5025, Awka Nigeria

ONYEMELUKWE, GEOFFREY CHUKWUBUIKE, physician, consultant; b. Nanka, Anambra, Nigeria, Apr. 7, 1944; s. Samuel Okeke and Grace (Ezeonodu) O.; m. Ifeoma Mabel Nwakalor, Mar. 14, 1977; children: Onyekachi, Obiageli, Mmaegbunam, Ogochuwu, Ikechukwu. BSc in Med. Scis., U. Ibadan, Nigeria, 1967, MB BS with honors, 1973. House officer U. Ibadan, 1972-74; physician Ahmadu Bello U. Hosp., 1974-75, rsch. fellow, 1978-79, dep. dean, 1987-89, prof., head dept., 1992—; rsch. fellow U. Liverpool, 1980. Co-author: Renal Disease in Nigeria, 1984; contbr. articles to profl. jour. Immunology and Internal Medicine. Robert White fellow Brit. Soc. for Immunology. Fellow Internat. Coll. Angiology, Inst. Adminstrv. Mgmt., Med. Coll. Physicians of Nigeria, West African Coll. of Physicians; mem. Diabetes Assn. Nigeria (pres. 1992—), Pan African Diabetes Study Group, Pan African Environ. and Mutagenicity Soc., Internat. League Against Rheumatism, Internat. Toxicol. Soc., Tennis Club, Zaria Club. Anglican. Avocations: football, cricket, tennis, literature. Office: Ahmadu Bello U Tchg Hosp, Dept Medicine, Zaria Kaduna, Nigeria

ONYENEKE, EUSEBIUS CHUKWU, biochemist, researcher; b. Ishiagu, Nigeria, Sept. 1, 1958; s. Damian and Mary Theresa (Ngwoke) Chukwu; m. Chika Catherine Ezekwesili, June 19, 1990; children: Somto, Obumkelu, Chikaodili. BSc, U. Nigeria, Nsukka, Nigeria, 1978, MSc, 1982, PhD, 1989. Med. lab. scientist NAF, Kano, Nigeria, 1978-79; asst. lectr. U. Nigeria, Nsukka, Nigeria, 1983-84, lectr. II, 1985-87, lectr. I, 1988-91; sr. lectr. U. Benin, Nigeria, 1991—; sec. African Conf. on the Biochemistry of Lipids. Co-editor: African Conf. on the Biochemistry of Lipids Series, 1988—; editor: (newsletter) African Conf. on the Biochemistry of Lipids, 1988—.

Mem. Inst. of Biology, Assn. Clin. Biochemistry, The Biochem. Soc. Nigeria. Roman Catholic. Avocations: reading, soccer, badminton, table tennis, athletics. Home: Chukwu Ori Compound, Amata Ishiagu Nigeria Office: Dept Biochemistry, U Benin, Benin City PMB 1154, Nigeria

ONYSZKIEWICZ, JANUSZ, mathematics educator, former federal official; b. Lwow, Dec. 18, 1937; m. Joanna Jaraczewska-Pilsudska, May, 1983; 5 children. D of Math., Warsaw U., PhD in Math., 1967, MSc in Math.; DSc (hon.), U. Leeds, England. Rsch. asst. Inst. Math Machines Polish Acad. Scis., 1959-61; mem. faculty dept. math. Warsaw U., 1961—; min. nat. def. Warsaw, Poland, 1992-93, 98—; vis. prof. Oxford U., London U., Leeds U., Manchester U. Paris U., Aarhus U. Islamabad U., Kabul U., 1976-79; co-founder, vice-chmn. Warsaw U. Ind. Sci., Tech. and Edn. Workers Trade Union, 1980; mem. Bd. Internat. Union History and Philosophy Sci., 1984-88. Co-worker Robotnik newspaper, 1979—. Active nat. exec. com. "Solidarity", nat. spokesman, 1981-89; dep. to Parliament, 1989—; mem. exec. com. Inter-Parliamentary Union, vice chmn. Polish group, 1989-91; vice minister Nat. Def., 1990-92; bd. dirs. Inst. East-West Security Studies, N.Y., 1991-94; commr. Ctr. Strategic and Internat. Studies, Washington, 1991; mem. Coun. Found. Edn. for Democracy, Warsaw, 1991; pres. Polish Parliament Delegation to North Atlantic Assembly, 1991-93; mem. Union for Freedom and Union for Freedom Nat. Coun., 1996—; v.p. Asia and Pacific Coun., 1996—; mem. Fgn. Policy Coun., 1996—; mem. Euro-Atlantic Assn., 1994—, pres., 1994-98; min. Nat. Def., 1997—; chmn. def. affairs com. Coun. of Mins., 1997—. Mem. Solidarity (nat. spokesman, mem. nat. exec. com. 1981-89). Home: Narbutta 17, Warsaw 02 536, Poland Office: Ministry Nat Defense, ul Klonowa 1, 00-909 Warsaw Poland

OOI, HONG-KEAN, veterinary parasitologist; b. Sungai Petani, Malaysia, Jan. 17, 1956; s. Yeok Ba Ooi and Guat See Tan. B in Vet. Sci., Hokkaido U., 1980, M in Vet. Sci., 1982, PhD, 1987. Sr. rschr. Hokkaido Vet. Ctr., Sapporo, Japan, 1985-88; instr., adj. lectr. Hokkaido U., 1990-94; assoc. prof. Nat Chung Hsing U., Taichung, Taiwan, 1995-99, prof., 1999—. Office: Nat Chung Hsing U Dept Vet, 250 Kuo Kuang Rd, 40227 Taichung 40227, Taiwan

OOMMEN, GEORGE, architect, painter; b. Munnar, India, Feb. 27, 1942; came to U.S., 1968; s. George and Achy (Abraham) O.; children: Mia, Christie, Sarah. BArch, Delhi U., 1964; MArch in Urban Design, Harvard U., 1970. Registered arch., planner. Prin. Khanna, Oommen, Jain, New Delhi, 1964-65, George Oommen & Assocs., Mepral, Kerala, India, 1964-67; archtl. designer Ewing Miller Assocs., Terre Haute, Ind., 1967-68; project planner Harvard U., Cambridge, Mass., 1970-72; planning officer Harvard U., Cambridge, 1972-79, spl. asst. to v.p. adminstrn., 1979-84, critic Grad. Sch. Design, 1973-74, faculty Grad. Sch. Design and Continuing Edn., 1983—, sr. property devel. officer Planning Group, 1984-95, sr. project mgr. Harvard Planning & Real Estate, 1995—; faculty Boston Archtl. Ctr., 1970-73, Babson Exec. Edn. Program, 1985-86; cons. in field. Author: Program for Athletic Facilities, 1975; urban designer various jours., Eng., Greece, Italy, India, Japan, U.S.A.; creator first outdoor fine tuned track McCurdy Track, Harvard U., 1984; exhbns. include Wellbridge Ctr., Boston, 1994, Harvard Club Boston, 1994, Dru Arstark, N.Y.C., 1994, Kresge Gallery, Boston, 1994, Rocco's Charles St. South, Boston, 1994; guest artist Ellison Ctr. Arts, Duxbury, Mass. Art Heritage, New Delhi, Mingo Gallery, Beverly, Mass., Open Studio at 8 Elm St., Woodstock, Vt., Holyoke Ctr., Cambridge. Exec. coun. Harvard/Radcliffe Child Care Coun., Cambridge, 1974; mem. Gov.'s Task Force Commonwealth of Mass., 1975; athletic cons. L.I. U., Franklin & Marshall Coll., Drew U., Babson Coll., Western Mont. Sports Medicine & Fitness Ctr., DePaul U., Assumption Coll., St. Marks Sch., McDonough (Md.) Sch., Mansfield U., The Nutrasweet Co., Hamline U., Adelphi U., St. Xavier U., SUNY New Paltz, Brooks Sch., North Andover, Mass., Brewster Acad., Wolfboro, N.H., Blair Acad., Blairstown, N.J. Recipient award of distinction for exhibit Internat. Conf. Archs., India, 1964, Cert. of Merit, Winthrop Housing Design Competition, Boston, 1975, Athletic Bus. Facility of Merit award, 1987, 88, 89, 90, Preservation Honor award Nat. Trust Hist. Preservation, 1987; John D. Rockefeller III Found. grantee, 1969. Mem. AIA (assoc.), Am. Inst. Cert. Planners, Am. Planning Assn., Am. Inst. Planners, Boston Soc. Archs., Mass. State Assn. Archs., Indian Inst. Archs. (assoc.), Harvard Club (Boston), Harvard Varsity Club (hon.). Office: Harvard Planning Group 912 Holyoke Ctr 1350 Massachusetts Ave Cambridge MA 02138-3846

OONISHI, HIRONOBU, orthopedic surgeon; b. Osaka, Japan, July 13, 1935; s. Ichiro and Fukue (Kosumi) O.; m. Yasuko Hirata, Nov. 1, 1969; children: Hiroyuki, Takako. MD, Osaka City U. Med. Sch., 1962, PhD, 1975. Lectr. Osaka City U. Med. Sch., 1978—; chief dept. orthopedic surgery Osaka Minami Nat. Hosp., 1978—, vice dir., 1993—; lectr. Osaka U. Med. Sch., 1980—; guest prof. Nat. Biomechanics Rsch. Ctr., Montpelier, France, 1975-76, Kyoto U., 1993—; pres. 1st through 6th Internat. Symposium on Ceramics in Medicine, 1989-92. Contbr. articles to profl. jours. Mem. Internat. Hip Soc., European Soc. for Biomaterials, Am. Soc. Biomaterials, Orthop. Rsch. Soc. in USA, Japanese Assn. of Orthopedic Surgery, Japanese Soc. for Orthop. Ceramic Implants (nat. chmn., editor proceedings), Japanese Soc. for Orthop. Biomechanics, Ctrl. Japanese Orthop. Surgery Soc., Japanese Soc. for Joint Surgery, Japanese Soc. for Artificial Joints, Future Scis. in Japanese Min. of Sci., Japanese Soc. for Biomaterials, Japanese Soc. for Artificial Organs, others. Home: 6-23 2-chome Fuminosato, Abeno-ku, Osaka 545-0004, Japan Office: Osaka-Minami Nat Hosp, 2-1 Kidohigashi-Machi, Kawachinagano-Shi Osaka 586-8521, Japan

OOSTERLINCK, WILLEM, urologist, educator; b. Aalst, Belgium, Sept. 10, 1944; s. Maurits and Elsa Helena (Van Durme) O.; m. Margarete Nelly Mortier, May 2, 1969; children: Dirk, Henk, Mark. MD, U. Ghent, 1968, PhD, 1992. Resident urology dept. Univ. Hosp., Ghent, 1973-79, docent, 1979-91, prof., 1991—, head of dept., 1993—, pres. dept. surgery, 1995—. Mem. Belgian Urol. Assn. (sec. 1984-92, v.p. 1992-94, pres. 1994-95), European Urol. Assn., Soc. Internat. Urology, Am. Urol. Assn. E-mail: willem.oosterlinck@rug.ac.be. Home: Leiepark 4, 9051 St Denijs Westrem Belgium Office: Univ Hosp, De Pintelaan 185, 9000 Ghent Belgium

OOSTHUIZEN, BERENDIEN LAURIKA, information scientist, educator; b. Rustenburg, South Africa, Aug. 11, 1936; d. Pieter Frederik and Hester Johanna (Groenewald) Kruger; m. Johannes Joachim Oosthuizen, Feb. 2, 1963; 5 children. BA, Potchefstroom (South Africa) U, 1958; B in Libr. Sci. with honors, Rand Afrikaans U., Johannesburg, South Africa, 1976, M in Libr. Sci., 1981, D Lit. and Philosophy, 1992. Br. libr. Johannesburg Pub. Libr., 1959-61; head of divsn. CSIR, Pretoria, South Africa, 1961-64; cataloguer University Libr., Johannesburg, 1970-73; part-time lectr. Rand Afrikaans Univ., Johannesburg, 1974-85, sr. lectr., 1986-98; ret., 1998; researcher South African Broadcasting Corp., Johannesburg, 1985. Co-author Die Nuwe Bibliotekaris, 1987; contbr. articles to profl. jours. Mem. South African Inst. Libr. and Info. Sic. (sec. 1985-86), South African Online User Group (profl.). Avocations: birding, indigenous fauna and flora, reading, the arts.

OPACICH, MILAN, protective services official, musician; b. Gary, Ind., Apr. 12, 1928; s. Mile and Roza (Perpic) O.; m. Rosalyn Helen Nicolich, Oct. 20, 1951; 1 child, Karin Joann. Grad. high sch., Gary, Ind. Tool and die maker Gary Screw and Bolt Co., 1947-58; lt. Gary Fire Dept., 1958-78; instr. Purdue U. NW, Hammond, Ind., 1978-80; luthier Schererville, Ind., 1950—; lectr. in field; guest on numerous radio and TV shows. Writer Serb World, USA, 1984—; exhbns. include Mall, Washington, 1976, Remwick Gallery, Washington, 1978, 79-80, Smithsonian Inst., Washington, 1981, Bailey Ctr., 1982, Balzekas Lithuanian Culture Mus., Chgo., 1988, Arie Crown Theater, Chgo., 1990, Old Town Sch. Music, 1998; represented in permanent collection Roy Acuff Mus., Nashville; recordings include Bleda Djeva, Kreni Kreni, Jamin with Julius, Drina and Mel Dokich, Vintage 59 and Patriotic Songs of the Serbs; featured in numerous books, magazines and newspaper articles. Founder, co-dir. Tamburitza Orch. St. Sava Orthodox Ch., 1964-70; founder First Tamburitza Extravanganza, 1971—. Recipient Pres.'s award for 50 Yrs. of Beautiful Tamburitza Music, 1999; Am. Slavic Assn. honoree, 2000; Ind. Arts Commn. grantee, 2000. Mem. Assn. Stringed Instrument Artisans. Ea. Orthodox. Avocations: collecting 78-RPM records, rare vintage instruments, documenting historical data, photographs, memorabilia tamburitza orchs., photography, historian family archives. Home and Office: 2255 Robinhood Blvd Schererville IN 46375-1847

OPARA, UKACHUKWU EUGENE, university administrator, researcher; b. Irete Owerri, Imo, Nigeria, Sept. 23, 1957; s. Cleophas Onuegbu and Eunice Nwakaego (Ugorji) O.; m. Ronke Saratu Musa, Apr, 1991; children: Ogechi, Uchenna, Chinenye, Ugoeze, Nkechinyere. BSc, U. Nigeria, Nsukka, 1982; MSc, Heriot-Watt U., Edinburgh, Scotland, 1985. Registered estate surveyor and valuer. Mem. editl. bd. Nigerian Instn. Estate Surveyors and Valuers, 1995-96, mem. edn. com., 1996-97; dir. oil and gas Imo State Govt., 1999—, mem. petroleum intelligence com., 2000—; panel mem. NUC Accreditation Panel, 1990, 98; head estate mgmt. dept. U. Lagos, Nigeria, 1990-92, 93-94, 94-95, 95-96. Contbr. articles to profl. jours. Dir. socials EMSA, U. Nigeria, Enugu campus, 1981-82; gen. sec. Holy Ghost Coll. Old Boys Assn., Lagos br., 1995-99; mem. strategy com. Redemption '99 Campaign, People's Dem. Party, Owerri, Imo, 1998-99. Postgrad. scholar Fed. Govt. Nigeria, U.K., 1983. Mem. Nigerian Instn. Estate Surveyors and Valuers, U. Lagos Sr. Staff Club. Mem. People's Dem. Party of Nigeria. Roman Catholic. Home: Umunbe-Umuoma Irete, PO Box 14, Owerri Imo, Nigeria Office: U Lagos, Akoka-Yaba, Lagos Nigeria

OPAT, JAROSLAV, historian, carpenter; b. Vojnuv Městec, Czech Republic, Apr. 11, 1924; s. Antonín and Anastázie (Nováková); m. Vlastimila Minarikova, Apr. 4, 1953 (div. 1976); children: Jaroslava, Miloslav. Grad. in carpentry, Secondary Tech. Sch., Prague, Czech Republic, 1947; PhD, U. Polit. and Social Scis., Prague, Czech Republic, 1953. Tchr. U. Prague, 1953-61; miner Uranian Mines (polit. persecution), Pribram, 1961-63; rschr. Inst. History, Acad. Scis., Prague, 1964-70; carpenter, heater, bldg. worker various orgns. (polit. persecution), 1970-89; rschr. Inst. History, Acad. Scis., 1990-91; dir. Masaryk Inst., Prague, 1991-97. Author: For New Democracy, 1966, Philosophy of Politician T.G. Masaryk, 1882-1893, 1985, Masarykiana and Other Studies, 1994; co-author, editor World War I, Modern Democracy and T.G. Masaryk, 1995, T.G. Masaryk: Citizen of Europe and of the World, 1999. Signatory Charter-77 Human Rights Movement, 1976—. Mem. Masaryk Soc. (founding mem. 1988, bd. dirs.).

OPATRNY, JOSEF, historian, educator; b. Skryje, Czechoslovakia, Nov. 19, 1945; s. Václav and Libuše (Krausová) O.; m. Olga Titerova, Feb. 20, 1970; children: Olga, Eva, Jan. MA, Charles U., Prague, Czechoslovakia, 1968, PhD, 1969, prof. in History, 1995. Rschr. Ctr. for Latin Am. Studies, Charles U., Prague, 1969; head Ctr. for Latin Am. Studies, Charles U., 1990—; dir. Yearbook Ibero-Americana Pragensia, Prague, 1987—. Author: U.S. Expansionism and Cuban Annexationism in the 1850's, 1993, Historical Pre-Conditions of the Origin of the Cuban Nation, 1994; editor: (book) Cuba. Algunos Problemas de su Historia; contbr. articles to profl. jours. Mem. N.Y. Acad. Scis., European Latinoamericanists Assn. (exec. com. 1990-93, head working group 1993—, v.p. 1996-99). Avocations: family, literature, sport. Office: Ctr Latin Am Studies, n j Palach 2, 116 38 Prague Czech Republic

OPHOF, HENRI P. J., lawyer, law educator; b. Gouda, The Netherlands, July 5, 1939. Degree in Bus. Econs., Erasmus U., Rotterdam, Holland, 1968, Degree in Civil Law, 1971. Tchr. Municipality of Rotterdam, 1963-69; lectr. Erasmus U., Rotterdam, 1969-71, prof. law, 1991-94, part-time prof. law, 1994—; lawyer Nauta Dutilh, Rotterdam, 1971-91, 94—, chmn., 1997—; bd. supervisory dirs. Robein Bank NV, The Hague, The Netherlands, 1993—; pres. Herbel Beleggingen NV, Rotterdam, 1991—. Contbr. numerous articles to profl. jours. Fax: 31-10-2240169. E-mail: ophofh@nautadulh.com. Office: Nauta Dutilh, Weena 750 PO Box 1110, 3000 BC Rotterdam The Netherlands

OPIE, SIMON ANDREW ROBERT, lighting designer, mathematician, project manager; b. Chatham, Kent, Eng., Apr. 8, 1957; s. Michael Wallace and Susan Jane (Robinson) Garland; m. Jacqueline Susan Grove, June 15, 1985; children: Gregory Jonathan, Laurence Gabriel. BS with honors, Open U., U.K., 1994. Prodn. mgr. Kent Opera, U.K., 1978-80, Royal Shakespeare Co., London, 1980-87; dir. P.M.A. Ltd., London, 1987-95; project mgr. Tussauds Group Studios, London, 1995-98, gen. mgr., 1998—; lighting designer, 1977—; rsch. mathematician Open U., 1995—. Lighting designer (plays) Dead Funny, 1994-95, The Clandestine Marriage, 1994, Nuremberg, 1996, Jeffrey Bernard is Unwell, 1999, Versekkel Kartyazo, 2000; (operas) Masque in Dioclesian, 1995, The Prodigal Son, 1994, El Cimarron, 1999, Eight Songs For a Mad King, 1999. Mem. Brit. Soc. for History of Math., London Math. Soc. Avocations: soccer, mountain biking, chess. Office: Tussauds Studios, 43-55 the Vale, London W3 7RR, England

ÖPIK, ILMAR, power engineering educator, thermal physicist; b. Tallinn, Estonia, June 17, 1917; s. Paul and Ella (Pani) Ö.; m. Elsa Aarma, June 4, 1946 (div. 1978); 1 child, Andres; m. Lia Raud, May 6, 1978. DiplEngr, Tech. U., Tallinn, 1940, PhD, 1953; DSc, Power Engring. Inst., Moscow, 1963. Constructor Franz Krull Ltd., Tallinn, 1937-41; engr. Teploelektroproekt, Sverdlovsk, Russia, 1942-44, oil shale industry, Tallinn, 1944-48; tchr., lab. head Tech. U., Tallinn, 1944-68; divsn. head Estonian Acad. Sci., Tallinn, 1968-77, v.p., 1977-87, emeritus, 1987—; prof. Tech. U., Tallinn, 1968-77; advisor Ministry Econ. Affairs, Tallinn, 1990—; bd. dirs. RAS Kiviter, Kohtla-Jarve, 1992-97. Decorated The Arms of Estonian Order; recipient medal of Merit, Tech. U., 1967, Paul Kogerman medal, Acad. Sci. and Tech. U., 1991. Mem. Estonian Naturalists Soc. (K.E. v. Baer medal 1984), Estonian Acad. Sci. (v.p., medal, 1987), Finnish Acad. Tech. (fgn. mem., medal of Merit 1992). Lutheran. Avocation: bridge. Home: Raja 7a-28, 12616 Tallinn Estonia Office: Estonian Acad Sci, Kohtu 6, 10130 Tallinn Estonia

OPINYA, GLADYS NABUBWAYA, dental educator, consultant; b. Kenya, Kenya, Nov. 25, 1952; d. Tom Wanjusi and Fridah Nang'Oni (Wamukota) Wanjala; m. Harun Walumbe Opinya, Dec. 3, 1977; children: Jonathan Wamukota, Joel Quentin Wanjala, Noel Caleb Manyasi, Rachael Jael Namwaya. BDS, U. Nairobi (Kenya) Dental, 1978; CAGS, MSD, Golman Sch. Grad. Dentistry, Boston, 1984; PhD, U. Nairobi Dental, 1993. Diplomate Kenya Med. Practitioners and Dentist Bd. Tutorial fellow Dept. Dental Surgery, Nairobi, 1980-84; lectr. and divsn. head Paediatric Dentistry Orthodontics, Nairobi, 1984-87, sr. lectr. and divsn. head, 1987-91, assoc. prof. and divsn. head, 1991-95, assoc. prof. and chmn., 1995-96, prof. and chmn., 1996—; coord. internat. elective students Dental Sch., Nairobi, 1984-87, chmn. syllabi devel. postgrad. & undergrad., 1988-93; cons. Paediatric Dentistry Kenyatta Nat. Hosp., Nairobi, 1984—; dir. Imani Dental Ctr. Ltd., Nairobi, 1990—. Contbr. articles to profl. jours. Recipient award Fulbright Hayes U.S. Cultural Exchg., 1981, Internat. Scholars award Boston U., 1983. Mem. Kenya Dental Assn. (treas. 1985-87, sec. 1990-91), Kenya Med. Women's Orgn. (vice chmn. 1987-90), Third World Orgn. Mem. Pentecostal Ch. Avocations: studying bible, charity athletics, cooking, watching nature. Home: Kabarnet Ct, 56605 East Africa Nairobi Kenya

OPITZ, HANS-PETER MANFRED, electrical engineer; b. Heidelberg, Germany, June 30, 1957; s. Manfred E. and Ingeborg (Lanz) O.; m. Claudia Krotz, Dec. 12, 1980; children: Patrick C., Saskia A. Dipl. engr., U. Karlsruhe, 1980; D of Engring., U. German Armed Forces, 1984. Sci. asst. Degussa AG, Hanau-Wolfgang, Germany, 1984-86; head R&D dept. Rheinmetall GmbH, Dusseldorf, Germany, 1986-91; corp. officer Gebr. Roechling, Mannheim, Germany, 1991-97; pres., CEO FHF Funke & Huster, Velbert, Germany, 1998—. Mem. IEEE (sr.). Home: Nelkenweg 5, D-40882 Ratingen Germany Office: FHF Funke & Huster, Eintrachtstr 95, D-42551 Velbert Germany

OPITZ, NORBERT, physicist, researcher; b. Herdecke, Germany, May 6, 1947; s. Heinrich and Hildegard (Nettmann) O.; m. Nina Bulgaru, Dec. 29, 1973; children: Stephanie, Martin. Diplom-Physiker, Aachen, Germany, 1973; PhD, U. Marburg/Lahn, Germany, 1976. Scientist sys. physiology Max-Planck-Inst., Dortmund, Germany, 1973-87; sr. scientist molecular physiology Max-Planck-Inst., Dortmund, 1989—; mgr. AVL-Prof. List Gmbh, Graz, Austria, 1987-89; cons. AVL-Prof. List Gmbh, Graz, 1980-85. Contbr. articles to profl. jours.; inventor in field. Avocations: chess, swimming, volleyball.

OPITZ-VON-BOBERFELD, WILHELM, agriculturist, researcher; b. Poznan, Poland, Mar. 7, 1941; arrived in Germany, 1945; s. Konstantin and Gerda (von-Born-Fallois) O.; m. Ursula Buchta, Aug. 16, 1985; 1 child, Carola. Dipl.Ing.agr., U. Bonn, Germany, 1968, Dr.agr., 1971, Dr.agr.habil., 1978; Dr.h.c., U. Brno, Czechoslovakia, 1995. Asst. U. Bonn, 1968-84; prof. agr. U. Goettingen, Germany, 1984-85; prof. agr. U. Giessen, Germany, 1985—, dean faculty of agr., 1988-89. Author: Gruenlandlehre, 1994; co-author: Grundfutterproduktion, 1986, Graeser-/Kraeuterschluessel, 1988, 95, Taschenbuch der Graeser, 1990. Mem. German Agronomy Soc. (pres. 1997-99), German Grassland Soc. (pres. 1990-96). Fax: 49-641-9937519. Office: University of Giessen, Ludwigstr 23, D-35390 Giessen Hessen, Germany

OPOCENSKY, MILAN, church alliance official; b. Hradec Kralové, Czech Republic, July 5, 1931; m. Jana Juránková; 3 children. MDiv, Comenius Evang. Fac. Theology, 1954, DTh, 1965; DTh (hon.), U. Faculty of Theology, Brussels, 1984; DD (hon.), Coll. of Wooster, 1986; ThD (hon.), Protestant Faculty Debrecen, 1995. Ordained to ministry Evang. Ch. of Czech Brethren, 1955. Lectr. Comenius Faculty of Protestant Theology, Prague, 1954-67, prof. theology, 1973-90; European sec. World Student Christian Found., 1967-73; sec.-gen. World Alliance of Reformed Chs., 1989-00; mem. Bd. of Bossey, 1976-91. Author: Christians and Revolutions, 1977, Widerstand und Revolution, 1982; editor: Sprung über die Mauer, 1990, The Field is the World, 1990, Towards a Renewed Dialogue, 1996, The Message for the Last of Days, 1998, Justification and Sanctification, 1999, From the Reformation to Tomorrow, 2000. mem. Ctr. for Theol. Inquiry, Princeton, N.J., 1985—. Office: PO Box 2100, 150 route de Ferney, CH-1211 Geneva 2, Switzerland

OPOKU, WISDOM KOMLA, academic administrative assistant; b. Amedzofe, Volta, Ghana, Nov. 6, 1951; s. Otto Kwaku and Hilda Ama (Dzradosi) O.; m. Elizabeth Yawa Anumah; children: Otto Komla, Allysha Yawa. Diploma in pub. adminstrn., U. Ghana, Legon, 1987, postgrad., 1999—. Clk. grade I Ghana Edn. Svc., Accra, 1978-82; sr. clk. Ho (Ghana) Poly., Ghana Edn. Svc., 1982-88, adminstrv. asst., 1988-92, sr. adminstrv. asst., 1992-97, sr. adminstrv. officer, 1997—; staff rep. to bd. govs. Ho. Poly., 1988-90, mem. poly. coun., 1994-95. Chmn. choir New Apostolic Ch., Ho, 1982-91, reverend. min., 1987—, sec. coun., 1989-91. Mem. Tchrs. and Ednl. Workers Union of Trades Union Congress (chmn. Ho Poly. local 1990-91). Democrat. Avocations: reading, correspondence, singing. Home: Volta, PO Box 756, Ho Ghana

OPOKU-MENSAH, EDWARD, construction company administrator, real estate developer, contractor; b. D/nkwanta, Ghana, Dec. 18, 1952; s. Sampson Kwaku and Elizabeth Abena (Adoma) Opoku; m. Comfort Mavis Arthur, Apr. 28, 1979; children: Emmanuel, Josiah, Esther, Edward Jr., Ewuradwoa. BS in Civil Engring., U. Sci. and Tech., Kumasi, Ghana, 1977; Cert., Ghana Inst. Mgmt. and Pub. Adminstrn., Accra, Ghana, 1983, Internat. Labour Orgn., Roads Sch., Sefwi Wiawso, Ghana, 1988. Project engr. Ghana Water and Sewerage Corp., Kumasi, 1978-79; civil works mgr., civil engr. Glksten Ltd., Sefwi Wiawso, 1979-83, acting mng. dir., 1983, forest mgr., 1983-85; gen. mgr. Akaasu Constrn. Works Ltd., S/Bekwai, Ghana, 1985-87; mng. dir. Opm Constrn. Works Ltd., Accra, 1987—; chmn. bd. dirs. Maranatha Nursery and Kindergarten Sch., Dansoman, Accra; lectr. Labour Intensive Rd. Sch., Koforidua, Ghana, 1993; chief exec., cons. African Coll. Mgmt. and Computer Sci., Ghana. Cons. tech. svcs. Sefwi Wiawso Community and Dist., 1979—. Mem. Ghana Instn. Engrs., Labour Intensive Rd. Contractors Assn. (nat. sec. 1989-94, nat. chmn. 1994—), Full Gospel Bus. Men's Fellowship Internat. (life, pres. 1989-91, area field rep. 1991—). Roman Catholic. Avocations: football, chess, scrabble, photography, preaching the gospel. E-mail: e opm@usa.net. Home: Hse No A 832/15, Dansoman Accra Ghana Office: Opm Constrn Works Ltd, Box 4856, Accra Ghana

OPPEDAHL, PHILLIP EDWARD, computer company executive; b. Renwick, Iowa, Sept. 17, 1935; s. Edward and Isadore Hannah (Gangstead) O.; m. Sharon Elaine Ree, Aug. 3, 1957 (dec. Aug. 1989); children: Gary Lynn, Tamra Sue, Sue Ann, Lisa Kay. BS in Naval Sci., Navy Postgrad. Sch., 1963, MS in Nuclear Physics, 1971; MS in Sys. Mgmt., U. S.C., 1978. Commd. ensign U.S. Navy, 1956, advanced through grades to capt., 1977; with Airborne Early Warning Squadron, 1957-59, Anti-Submarine Squadron, 1959-65; asst. navigator USS Coral Sea, 1965-67; basig jet flight instr., 1967-69; test group dir. Def. Nuclear Agy., 1972-74; weapons officer USS Oriskany, 1974-76; program mgt. for armament Naval Air Sys. Command, Washington, 1977-79; test dir. Def. Nuclear Agy., Kirtland AFB, N.Mex., 1979-82; dep. comdr. Def. Nuclear Agy., 1982-83; pres., CEO Am. Systems, Albuquerque, 1983—; bd. dirs. BASIS Internat., 1991—. Author: Energy Loss of High Energy Electrons in Beryllium, 1971, Understanding Contractor Motivation and Incentive Contracts. Decorated DSM. Mem. Nava. Inst., Am. Nuclear Soc., Aircraft Owners and Pilots Assn., Assn. Naval Aviation, Navy League. Lutheran. Home and Office: 5850 Eubank Blvd NE Ste B 49 Albuquerque NM 87111-6111

OPPELT, WOLFGANG DIETRICH HERMANN, culture scientist, researcher; b. Ansbach, Bavaria, Germany, Jan. 11, 1945; s. Paul and Elisabeth (Dorn) O.; m. Fatoumata Kanouté, Jan. 21, 1996. PhD, U. Würzburg, Germany, 1974. Cert. in ethnology, history, German philology. Sci. vol. Stuttgart (Germany) Mus., 1974-76; sci. collaborator U. Tübingen, Germany, 1976, Germanic Nat. Mus., Nürnberg, 1978-85, 90, Frankonian Open Air Mus., Bad Windsheim, Germany, 1986-87, Jewish Mus. Frankonia, Fürth, Germany, 1991-93, Jewish Cmty., Nürnberg, 1994-95, savs. bank, Höchstadt/Aisch, 1996-98; appointed prof. U. Erlangen, Nürnberg, 1989-93. Contbr. articles and revs. on social and cultural history, history of crime and punishment, folk jewellery, Jewish history, history of travelling, history of savs. banks to profl. publs. Active mem. com. Art Club, Nürnberg, 1980-98. Mem. Deutsche Gesellschaft für Volkskunde, Tübinger Vereinigung für Volkskunde, Gesellschaft für Goldschmiedekunst, Deutscher Verein für Kunstwissenschaft, Kestnergesellschaft Hannover. Avocations: jazz, literature, psychology, philosophy, African history. Home: Frauentormauer 18, D-90402 Nürnberg Bavaria, Germany

OPPENHEIM, FRANK MATHIAS S.J., philosophy educator; b. Coldwater, Ohio, May 18, 1925; s. Theodore Henry Oppenheim and Anna Elizabeth Mathias. AB, MA, Loyola U., Chgo., 1947, PhL, 1949, STL, 1956; PhD in Philosophy, St. Louis U., 1962. Assoc. prof. history philosophy St. Paul's Maj. Sem, Wau, Sudan, 1976-77; asst. prof. Xavier U., Cin., 1961-68, assoc. prof., 1968-78, prof., 1978—. Author: Royce's Mature Philosophy of Religion, 1987, Royce's Mature Ethics, 1993, Behind the Bits, 1998, others; also articles. Mem. Am. Philos. Assn., Soc. for Advancement of Am. Philosophy (mem. exec. com., Herbert W. Schneider citation 1999), Jesuit Philos. Assn. (pres. 1971-72). Roman Catholic. Avocations: walking, bicycling, swimming. E-mail: oppenhei@xu.edu. Home: 5367 S Milford Rd Milford OH 45150-9744 Office: 3800 Victory Pkwy Unit 1 Cincinnati OH 45207-1035

OPPENHEIM, ROBERT, beauty industry executive; b. N.Y.C., May 21, 1925; s. Hyman and Hannah (Lieberman) O.; m. Ruth Wigler, Feb. 7, 1954; children: Nancy Ellen, David Paul, Howard P. BS cum laude, Syracuse U., 1950. Product sales specialist McKesson & Robbins, Yonkers, N.Y., 1950-55; asst. sales mgr. Clairol, Inc., N.Y.C., 1955-60, pres. Salon div., 1976-83, chmn. Profl. Products div., 1983-87; dir. mktg. Haircolor div. Revlon, Inc., N.Y.C., 1960-68, dir. mktg. and sales Salon div., 1968-70; exec. v.p. Milton R. Barrie Co., Inc., 1970-71; pres. Oppenheim Communications, N.Y.C., 1987—; pub. Beauty Salon Newsletter, N.Y.C., 1971-83, Salon Update, 1988-95, The Oppenheim Letter, 1988-95; mgmt. cons., 1988—; contbg. commentator Beauty Store Bus., 1998—, Profl. Beauty Mfr., 1998-99; bd. dirs. Cosmetology Advancement Found., 1995-98, Internat. Haircolog Exch., 1995-96. Author: 101 Salon Promotions, 1999. With AUS, 1942-44, ETO. Decorated Purple Heart; recipient Spirit of Life award City of Hope, 1989, Showman Wall of Fame award Internat. Beauty Show, 1994; inducted into Nat. Cosmetology Assn. Hall of Fame, 1994, Barber & Beauty Supply Inst. Hall of Leaders, 1998. Mem. Nat. Beauty and Barber Mfrs. Assn. (pres. 1984-85), Am. Beauty Assn. (pres. 1985-86), Masons. Home: 241 Sickletown Rd West Nyack NY 10994-2905 Office: Oppenheim Communications PO Box 700 West Nyack NY 10994-0700

OPPENHEIMER, TAMAR MARIAMNE, international government specialist; b. London, Nov. 20, 1925; arrived in Can., 1931; d. Lionel Joshua and Lea (Young) Shine; m. Hans Herman Oppenheimer, Oct. 22, 1949. BA in Econs. and Polit. Sci. with honors, McGill U., 1946; MA in Internat. Law, Columbia U., 1953; LLD (hon.), McGill U., 1994. With UN, N.Y.C., 1946-82; chief, adminstrv. unit, div. human rights UN, 1968-74, exec. officer Habitat-UN Conf. Human Settlements, 1974-77, chief recruitment programs, office personnel svcs., 1977-79, chief tng. and examinations svc., 1979-82; dep. to dir. gen. UN Office at Vienna, Austria, 1982-86; dir. div. narcotic drugs UN Office at Vienna, 1982-86, asst. sec. gen. U.N. Secretariat, officer in charge Ctr. Social Devel., Humanitarian Affairs, 1986-87, sec.-gen Internat. Conf. on Drug Abuse & Illicit Trafficking, 1985-87; cons. Govt. of Can., Dept. External Fgn. Affairs, Royal Can. Mounted Police, Ottawa, 1988-89; cons., lectr. Coun. Drug Awareness, Carleton U., Ottawa, 1988; lectr. Diplomatische Akademie Ministry for Affairs, Austria, 1990-91. Contbr. articles to various publs. Bd. dirs., sr. adviser Alliance for Drug-Free Can., Ottawa, 1988-94; adviser Can. del. UN Commn. on Narcotic Drugs, 1991-94, UN Drug Control Programme, 1993-96; bd. dirs., chmn. Found. for Responsible Computing, 1989-99; sr. advisor HOPE 87, Austria, Tafelmusik, Can.; bd. govs. Portage Program for Drug Dependencies, Inc., Canada; mem. internat. adv. com. Inst. for Leadership Devel. Can. Named officer Order of Can., 1987; recipient Knight Comdr.'s Cross Order of Merit of Austria with Star, 1991. Mem. Can. Inst. Internat. Affairs, Internat. Assn. Penal Law, Assn. Former Internat. Civil Servants. Home: Engelsberggasse 5/11, A 1030 Vienna M5S 2X3, Austria also: Ste 1105, 62 Wellesley St W, Toronto, ON Canada

OPPERMAN, DWIGHT DARWIN, publishing company executive; b. Perry, Iowa, June 26, 1923; s. John H. and Zoa L. Opperman; m. Jeanice Wifvat, Apr. 22, 1942 (dec.); children: Vance K., Fane W. JD, Drake U., 1951, LLD (hon.), 1998. Bar: Iowa 1951, U.S. Supreme Ct. 1976, U.S Ct. Internat. Trade, 1988. Editor, asst. editorial counsel West Pub. Co., St. Paul, Minn., 1951-64, mgr. reporters and digest depts., 1964-65; v.p. West Pub. Co., 1965-68, pres., 1968-93, CEO, 1978-96, chmn., 1993-96; chmn. emeritus West Group, Eagan, 1996; chmn. Key Investment, Mpls., 1996—; dir. Inst. Judicial Adminstrn. Chmn. Supreme Ct. Hist. Soc.; dir. Inst. Jud. Adminstrn.; bd. govs. Drake U., Des Moines; dir. Minn. D.A.R.E. Inc.; dir. Brennan Ctr. for Justice; trustee NYU Law Sch.; dir., Nat. Legal Ctr. for Pub. Interest, Nat. Ctr. for State Cts. Recipient Herbert Harley award Am. Judicature Soc., 1984, Justice award, 1992, 1st George Wickersham Founder's award Friends of Law Libr. of Congress, 1993, Lifetime Achievement award Minn. State Bar Assn., 1997. Fellow Am. Bar Found.; mem. ABA, Fed. Bar Assn., Am. Judicature Soc., Am. Law Inst., Drake U. Nat. Alumni Assn. (disting. svc. award 1974, Centennial award 1981, Outstanding Alumni award 1988), Minn. Club (pres. 1975-76), Mpls. Club. Office: Key Investment 601 2nd Ave S Ste 5200 Minneapolis MN 55402-4317

OPPEY, MARK OFOSY, military employee; b. Takoradi, Ghana, May 27, 1965; s. James and Juliana (Ogyerewaa) O.; m. Barbara Asamoah, July 11, 1992; 1 child, Dorcas Darkoah. Lines and exch. operator, radio operator 1st Signal Regiment Burma Camp, Accra, Ghana, 1989—. Presbyterian. Avocations: football, hockey, sports, films, international news. Office: 1st Signal Regiment, Burma Camp, Accra Ghana

OPRISAN, IONEL, literary historian, folklorist; b. Cavadinesti, Romania, Apr. 17, 1940; s. Ioan and Smaranda (Dabija) O.; m. Ecaterina Popescu; 3 children. BA, U. Bucharest, 1963, PhD, 1980. Rschr. Inst. Literary Theory and History-G. Calinescu, Bucharest, Romania, 1963—; sci. sec. Inst. Literary Theory & History G. Călinescu, 1980-90; sci. sec. dept. philology, lit. and arts Acad. Romania, Bucharest, 1985-90; sec. Folklore Commn. Acad. Romania, 1986—. Author: Mihail Sadoveanu's Work, 1986, Critical Edition: I.M. Sadoveanu Writings I-VIII, 1969-1985, 1986, The Story of B. P. Hasdeu' Life, 1989, Critical Edition: B.P. Hasdeu Works, I-III, and The Man of Flowers, 1997, G. Calinescu. The Performance of the Personality, 1999. Mem. Romanian Writers Assn. Home: 5 Ciucea St Bl L19 Top 216, 74696 3 Bucharest J-72, Romania

OPTALE, GABRIELE, psychotherapist, physician; b. Venice, Italy, Nov. 25, 1949; d. Guerrino and Maria Luisa (Rubini) Optale. MD, U. Padua, Italy, 1975, specialization in gynecology, 1980; specialization in sex psychotherapy, Rsch. and Tng. Inst., Genoa, Italy, 1994. Med. intern Pub. Hosp., Venice, Italy, 1976-77; med. resident dept. gynecology Verona (Italy) U. Hosp., 1978-80; rsch. gynecologist U. Padua, 1976-80; pvt. practice gynecology Venice, 1980-91; physician Pub. Health Svc., Venice, 1980—; sex psychotherapist Assn. for Rsch. in Sexology, 1991—; rsch. cons. Pub. Hosp., Venice, 1995-99; presenter Nat. Sex Therapist Conf., 1993. Contbr. articles to profl. publs. Recipient Most Original Work award Nat. Sex Therapist Conf., 1993. Mem. Assn. Med. Psychotherapists (gen. sec. 1997—), Lions (pres. club 1997-98). Roman Catholic. Avocations: tennis, windsurfing, skiing, golf. E-mail: optale@tin.it.

OQBAL, SYED MOHAMMED, otolaryngologist; b. Kurnool, India, Mar. 16, 1946; s. Syed Abdul and Bijan Gaffoor; m. Iqbal Padmini Parveen; children: Javed, Rahila. BSc, S.V. Univ., Tirupati, India, 1966, MBBS, 1971; MS, Postgrad. Inst., Chandigarh, India, 1977. Sr. resident otorhinolaryngology Post Grad. Inst., 1977-79; from sr. specialist to head dept. otorhinolaryngology JLN Hosp. & Rsch. Ctr., Bhilai, India, 1979—. Avocations: reading, sports. Home: D-15 Hospital Sector, 490 006 Bhilai India Office: JLN Hosp & Rsch Ctr, Sector 9, 490 006 Bhilai MP, India

OQUENDO, SERGIO, lawyer; b. Lima, Peru, Dec. 16, 1964; s. Abelardo C. and Carmen E. (Heraud) O. BA in Law, Cath. U., Lima, 1990, JD summa cum laude, 1992; LLM, Columbia U., 1994. Bar: Lima's Bar Assn. 1992. With Instituto Libertad & Democracia, Lima, 1986-88, Garcia-Calderon, Ghersi & Cateriano Abogados, Lima, 1988-89, Centro de Investigacion y Estudios Legales, Lima, 1991-92; outside legal adviser Spl. Com. Privatization-Telecom, Lima, 1993; with Milbank, Tweed, Hadley & McCloy, N.Y.C., 1994-95; ptnr. Muniz Forsyth Ramirez Perez-Taiman & Luna-Victoria Abogados, Lima, 1995—; asst. prof. Cath. U., Lima, 1989-92, San Marcos Nat. U., Lima, 1992, U. Lima, 1992. Editor Colombia Jour. Transnat. Law, 1993-94; columnist Gestion Daily, Lima. Fulbright Commn. scholar, Lima, 1993, Friedmann fellow Columbia U., N.Y.C., 1993. Mem. Am. Mus. Natural History (assoc.), Lima Bar Assn. (assoc.), Columbia Law Sch. Assn. Avocations: red wines, travel, conservationism and ecology, Internet. Home: Apt 301, Madrid # 269, Lima 18, Peru Office: Muniz Forsyth Ramirez etal, Las Begonias 475, San Isidro Piso 6 Lima 27, Peru

O'QUINN, NANCY DIANE, nurse, educator, consultant; b. Walton County, Ga., Nov. 22, 1944; d. L.C. Jr. and Eula Sandra (Hegwood) Kennedy; m. Charles Frank O'Quinn, Sept. 12, 1965; children: Robert, Spencer, Alan. Diploma, Ga. Bapt. Hosp., 1965; BSN, Valdosta State Coll., 1979, MEd, 1983; MSN, Valdosta State U., 1986; PhD in Social Work Adminstrn. & Policy, Fla. State U., 1999. Sr. nurse Tift County Health Dept., Tifton, Ga., 1979-80; instr. Abraham Baldwin Coll., Tifton, 1980-85, assoc. prof., 1992-94; asst. prof. Valdosta (Ga.) State Coll., 1985-94; asst. prof. nursing Albany (Ga.) State U., 1990-92, 94-97; rsch. assoc. Fla. State U., 1998-99, Health Occupations Cook County, Ga., 1999; asst. dir. econ. devel. U. Ga., 2000—. Lt. USNR, 1989—. Mem. Sigma Theta Tau, Alpha Chi.

ORAEFO, JOHNNY NDUBUISI, geologist, corporation executive, consultant; b. Jos, Plateau, Nigeria, June 26, 1945; s. George Madubike and Comfort O. (Onwuamaegbu) O.; m. Comfort Chinwe Onyekaba, July 9, 1976; children: Adaora, Ebeleann, Oge, Obi, Amy. AB, U. N.C., 1982; Diploma, Computer Electronics, 1993. Cert. profl. geologist, N.C. Dir. Flamingo Imports Exports, Inc., Raleigh, N.C., 1984—; pres., co-owner African Supermarkets and Gift Shop, Raleigh, 1987—; pres. B.J. Internat., 1994—; dir. African Safari Stores, 1995—; cons. Internat. Trades, Raleigh, 1984—. Pres. Nigerian Student Assn. of U.S.A., Raleigh, 1981; dir. World Missions Living Faith Apostolic Ministries, U.S.A., 1995—. Recipient cert. Merit Internat. Traders Assn., 1982. Mem. Am. Assn. Petroleum Geologists, Soc. Econ. Paleontologists Mineralogists, Dip. Computer Electronics Tech., Travel Internat. Club. Mem. Christian Ch. Avocations: tennis; travel; singing; ping-pong; reading. Home: 1716 River Knoll Dr Raleigh NC 27610-4582

ORAEVSKY, ANATOLY NIKOLAYEVICH, physicist, educator; b. Ivanovo, Russia, Jan. 26, 1934; s. Nikolay Alekseevich and Alexandra Evgraphovna (Grafova) O.; m. Iraida Sergeevna Timantseva, Dec. 30, 1955; children: Alexander, Alexey, Anna. PhD, Inst. Radioengring. & Elec., Moscow, 1960; DSc, P.N. Lebedev Phys. Inst., Moscow, 1965. Jr. fellow P.N. Lebedev Phys. Inst., Moscow, 1957-60, sr. fellow, 1960-65, lab. dir., 1965-90, head rschr., lab. dir., 1990—; prof. physics Moscow Engring.-Physics Inst., Moscow, 1962—; head Soviet Union Acad. Sci. Coun. on Laser Chemistry, Moscow, 1972-91, Soviet Union Sci. Coun. on Coherent and Nonlinear Optics, Moscow, 1965-92, Russian Acad. Sci. Coun. on Laser Physics and Optics, 1998—; mem. adv. com. Internat. Symposium on Gas-Flow and Chem. Lasers, 1978—. Mem. editl. bd. Jour. High Energy Chemistry, 1971-93, Jour. Quantum Electronics, 1998—; several inventions. Recipient Lenin prize Soviet Union Govt., Moscow, 1984; named hon. scientist Russian Fedn., 1999. Mem. Acad. Natural Scis. Russia, Optical Soc. Russia, Moscow Phys. Soc., Optical Soc. Am. Avocation: chess. Office: PN Lebedev Phys Inst, 53 Lenin Prospect, 117924 Moscow Russia

O'RAHILLY, STEPHEN PATRICK, clinical endocrinologist, researcher, educator; b. Dublin, Ireland, Apr. 1, 1958; s. Patrick Francis and Teresa Emer (Hyland) O'R.; m. Suzy Oakes, Sept. 9, 1990. MBBCh, B Obstetrics, Nat. U. Ireland, Dublin, 1981, MD, 1987. Fellow Royal Coll. Physicians (U.K.), Fellow Royal Coll. Physicians of Ireland. Rsch. fellow in endocrinology Oxford (Eng.) U., 1984-87; clin. registrar John Radcliffe Hosp., Oxford, 1987-88, Radcliffe Infirmary, Oxford, 1988-89; med. rsch. coun. traveling fellow Harvard U. Med. Sch., Cambridge, Mass., 1989-91; Wellcome Trust sr. rsch. fellow in clin. sci. Cambridge (Eng.) U., 1991-95, prof. metabolic medicine, 1996—; panel mem. Wellcome Trust Clin. Interest Group, London, 1996—, chmn. 1999; lectr. Clin. Endocrinology Trust, 1999, Soc. Enocrinology, 2000; Kroc lectr. U. Seattle, 1999; Macallum lectr. U. Toronto, Can., 2000; Rufus Cole lectr. Rockefeller U., N.Y.C., 2000. Contbr. over 100 articles to internat. med. jours. Redcliffe-Maud fellow, Brit. Diabetic Assn., 1986, R.D. Lawrence lectr., 1996; recipient Medal Soc. for Endocrinology, Graham Bull prize Royal Coll. Physicians Eng., 2000. Fellow U. Cambridge Churchill Coll. (professorial), Acad. of Medicine. Avocations: literature, music, good food, wine, tennis, Manchester United. Office: U Cambridge Sch Medicine, Addenbrooke's Hosp Level 5, Cambridge CB2 2QR, England

ORAL, SÜMER, Turkish government official; b. Izmir, Turkey, 1938; married; two children. Student, Istanbul U. Sch. Econs. True Path Party dep. from Manisa; former dir. Gen. Budget and Fin. Control Min. of Labour and Social Security, Ankara, Turkey; min. fin. and customs Min. of Labour and Social Security, Ankara, 1991-93; now min. fin. Ministry Fin and Customs, Ankara. Office: Ministry Fin and Customs, Ilkadim Cad Dikmen, Ankara 6, Turkey*

ORALLO, FRANCISCO, pharmacologist, researcher, educator; b. Lugo, Spain, Feb. 17, 1958; s. Manuel and Gemma (Cambeiro) O. BS in Pharmacy with spl. distinction, U. Santiago de Compostela, Spain, 1980, PhD in Pharmacy with spl. distinction, 1984. Predoctoral fellow Sch. Pharmacy U. Santiago de Compostela, 1981-84, asst. prof. Sch. Pharmacy, 1984-86, prof. Sch. Pharmacy, 1987—, head cardiovascular rsch. Sch. Pharmacy, 1987—; postdoctoral fellow U. Autónoma, Madrid, 1987-88, U. Louis Pasteur, Strasbourg, France, 1991-92. Contbr. articles to profl. jours. (Dolores Trigo award, Brit. Jour. Pharmacology 1993, Eloy Diez award Pharm. Coll., Pontevedra, 1984). Recipient SEQT award Spanish Soc. Therapeutic Chemistry, Madrid, 1987, Dr. Esteve Hon. Mention award Dr. Esteve Found., Barcelona, 1992, Xunta de Galicia research award, 1996. Mem. Am. Assn. for the Advancement of Sci., N.Y. Acad. Scis., Spanish Soc. Pharmacology, Pharm. Soc. Latin Mediterranean, Spanish Soc. Therapeutic Chemistry. Avocations: research, classical music. Home: Dr Maceira 5-2 A, de Compostela Santiago 15706, Spain Office: U Santiago Compostela, Dept Pharmacology Fac Pharmacy, Santiago La Coruña 15706, Spain

ORATI, VITTORANGELO, economist, educator; b. Rome, Jan. 8, 1943; s. Gino Orati and Olga Recchi Murso;; m. Maria Rosaria Petrellese, Nov. 18, 1972. D of Econs., U. Navale Napoli, Italy, 1969, postdoctoral, 1971; postdoctoral, Nat. Ctr. Rsch., Rome, 1969-71. Rschr. Formez, Rome, 1971-72; vis. prof., asst. lectr. 1st U. Navale Napoli, 1974; lectr. SDA Boconi U., Milan, 1978; prof. U. Reggio Calabria, Italy, 1982-91; lectr. Politecnico, Milan, 1987-93; mgr. Ambrosetti Consulenza, Milan, 1991-92; prof. econs. U. La Tuscia, Viterbo, Italy, 1991—, dir. Econ. Inst., 1995—; cons. IDIMER, Napoli, 1980—; econ. commentator Il Diario, Napoli, 1980; rschr. Isveimer, Napoli, 1980; vis. prof. Roskilde (Denmark) U., 1993-94, U. Capetown, Johannesburg, South Africa, 1994; mem. editl. bds. Il Ponte, Firenze, Italy, 1998—, Internat. Jour. Devel. Planning, Rohtak, India, 1998—; mem. internat. adv. com. Jan Timbergen Inst. Devel. Planning, Rohtak, 1998—. Contbr. numerous articles to profl. jours. Mem. Am. Econ. Assn., Italian Soc. Economists. Home: via PO n2, 01100 Viterbo Italy Office: U Tuscia Econ Inst, Via del Paradiso n47, 01100 Viterbo Italy

ORAZI, ATTILIO, anatomic pathologist, researcher, educator; b. Milan, Aug. 2, 1954; came to U.S., 1992; s. Luigi Mario and Giulia (Formiga) O.; m. Maria Lupieri; children: Giulia, Rita. MD cum laude, U. Milan, 1979; specialist in anatomic pathology, U. Pavia, Italy, 1987; specialist in hematology, U. Milan, 1991. Diplomate Am. Bd. Pathology. Intern U. Milan, 1979-80; resident physician Ballochmyle Hosp., Mauchline, Scotland, 1980-81; sr. house officer Leicester (Eng.) Royal Inf., 1981-82; registrar in pathology Northampton (Eng.) Gen. Hosp., 1982-83; postdoctoral fellow Nat. Cancer Inst., Milan, 1983-85, staff pathologist, 1985-92; assoc. prof. pathology, dir. immunohistochemistry Ind. U. Sch. Medicine, Indpls., 1992-97, prof. pathology, 1997-98; prof. pathology Coll. Physicians and Surgeons, Columbia U., 1998—; dir. divsn. hematopathology Columbia U., The Presbyn. Hosp., N.Y.C., 1998—. Contbr. numerous sci. reports, book chpts., editls. to profl. jours. including Nature Genetics, Lab. Invest., Procs. NAS USA, Am. Jour. Physiology, Blood, Am. Jour. Surg. Pathology, Am. Jour. Clin. Pathology, Cancer Rsch., Jour. Clin. Oncology, Exptl. Hematology, Brit. Jour. Haematology. Mem. Internat. Acad. Pathology, Royal Coll. Pathology, European Assn. for Haematopathology, Am. Soc. Hematopathology. Republican. Roman Catholic. Achievements include research on clinical and experimental hematology; on diagnostic hematopathology; spleen pathology. Avocations: mountaineering, skiing, sailing, literature, arts. Office: Coll of Physicians and Surgeons Columbia Univ Dept Pathol 630 W 168th St New York NY 10032-3702

ORBAN, GUY ANGÈLE, neurophysiology educator; b. St. Niklaas, Belgium, Nov. 4, 1945; s. Louis Charles and Christiaene Eugenie (Boelens) O.; m. Chantal Marie Gaudissart, Dec. 12, 1987; children: Pauline, Rodolphe, Nicolas. MD, Cath. U. Leuven, Belgium, 1969, PhD in Neurophysiology, 1975; degree in engring., Cath. U., Louvain-la-Neuve, Belgium, 1974. From rsch. asst. to sr. rsch. asst. Nat. Fund Sci. Rsch., Leuven, 1970-79; assoc. lectr. Cath. U. Leuven Med. Sch., 1976-82; prof. Cath. U. Leuven Med. Sch., Leuven, 1982—, U. Limburg Med. Sch., Diepenbeek, Belgium, 1987-99. Author: Neuronal Operations in the Visual Cortex, 1984; editor: Cognitive Neuroscience, 1991, Articial and Biological Vision Systems, 1992. Recipient Ophthalmology prize Faes Found., 1994. Mem. Royal Golf Club Belgium. Avocations: golf, roses, skiing. Office: Lab voor Neuro Psychofysiol, Herestraat 49, B-3000 Leuven Belgium

ORBAN, LASZLO, biologist; b. Varpalota, Hungary, July 25, 1957; s. Laszlo, Sr. and Julianna (Albert) O.; m. Ildiko Zsuzsanna Szeverenyi, Aug. 8, 1981; children: Andras, Csaba. MS in Biology, Jozsef Attila U., 1981, D in Biochemistry, 1983; Candidacy degree in Biochemistry, Hungarian Acad. of Scis., Budapest, 1997. Postgrad. Jozsef Attila U., Szeged, 1981-83, postdoctoral fellow, 1983-86; Fogarty fellow NICHD, NIH, Bethesda, Md., 1986-89; staff scientist, project leader Agrl. Biotechnology Ctr., Godollo, Hungary, 1989-98; sr. scientist, prin. investigator Inst. Molecular Agrobiology, Singapore, 1998—; mem. editl. adv. bd. Aquaculture, Elsevier, Amsterdam, 1994—; mem. Fisheries Rsch. Coun., Szarvas, Hungary, 1996—; referee Found. for Rsch., Sci. and Tech., 1994—, Jour. Biotech., 1997—, Jour. Fish Biology, 1998—, others. Recipient fellowship Hungarian People's Republic, 1979-80. Avocations: basketball, fishing, music. Office: Inst Molecular Agrobiology, 1 Research Link NUS Campus, Singapore 117604, Singapore

ORBÁN, VIKTOR, prime minister of Hungary; b. Székesfehérvár, Hungary, May 31, 1963; s. Győző Orbán; married; 3 children. Grad. Faculty of Law, Eötvös Loránd U. Arts & Scis., 1987; trainee sociologist, Man. Sch. Ministry Agr. and Food Industry. Rschr. Middle Europe Rsch. Group, 1989-91; founding mem. Spl. Juristic Sociol. Coll. (now István Bibó Spl. Coll.); cofounder Fedn. Young Dems. (Fidesz), 1988, chmn., 1993—; chmn. parliament com. European integration affairs, Budapest, 1994-98, prime min., 1998—. Avocation: soccer. Office: Office of Prime Minister, Kossuth Lajos ter 1-3, 1055 Budapest Hungary

ORBERSON, WILLIAM BAXTER, lawyer, educator; b. Jeffersonville, Ind., Aug. 24, 1962; s. William B. and Nancy Lee Orberson; m. Lea Lynn Mater, May 18, 1984; children: Katherine, Madeline, Allyson. BA in Bus. Adminstrn. magna cum laude, Bellarmine Coll., 1983; JD cum laude, U. Louisville, 1986. Bar: Ky. 1986, U.S. Dist. Ct. (ea. dist.) Ky. 1987, U.S. Dist. Ct. (we. dist.) Ky. 1990. Ptnr. Phillips, Parker, Orberson and Moore P.L.C., Louisville, 1986—; adj. prof. U. Louisville Sch. Law, 1994—. Bd. dirs. Chapel Creek Neighborhood Assn., New Albany, Ind., 1997, v.p., 1998. Mem. ABA, Am. Judicature Soc., Def. Rsch. Inst., Ky. Bar Assn., Louisville Bar Assn. (exec. com. litigation sect. 1994), St. Xavier Legal Soc., Ky. Def. Counsel, U. Louisville Sch. Law Alumni Assn. (class dir. 1994—). Republican. Roman Catholic. Avocations: golf, fishing. Fax: 502-587-1927. Office: Phillips Parker Orbersond Moore PLC Aegon Ctr 716 W Main St Ste 300 Louisville KY 40202-2634

ORCHARD, JOHN WILLIAM, sports physician, researcher; b. Melbourne, Australia, Jan. 22, 1967; s. William Henry and Elspeth Alice (Bott) O. BA, MB, BS, Melbourne U., 1989; PhD, U. NSW, Sydney, 1999. Med. intern Box Hill Hosp., Melbourne, 1990-91; sr. tutor Melbourne U., 1991-92; sports physician Australian Coll. Sports Physicians, Melbourne, 1992-93; fellow Australian Inst. Sport, Canberra, 1993-94; med. dir. Sydney (Australia) Swans Football Club, 1994-97; sports physician Ea. Suburbs Sports Med. Ctr., Sydney, 1994-97; med. dir. Sydney City Roosters Rubgy League Club, 1997—. Author: Life, The Universe and Football, 1989; contbr. articles to Am. Jour. Sports Medicine, Med. Jour. Australia, Clin. Jour. Sport Medicine, Brit. Jour. Sports Medicine. Fellow Australian Coll. Sports Physicians, Am. Coll. Sports Medicine; mem. Australian Sports Medicine Fedn. (life, commendation for rsch. paper 1995, Syntex rsch. grantee 1995). Office: South Sydney Sports Med, 111 Anzac Pde, Kensington, NSW 2033, Australia

ORD, LINDA BANKS, artist; b. Provo, Utah, May 24, 1947; d. Willis Merrill and Phyllis (Clark) Banks; m. Kenneth Stephen Ord, Sept. 3, 1971; children: Jason, Justin, Kristin. BS, Brigham Young U., 1970; BFA, U. Mich., 1987; MA, Wayne State U., 1990. Asst. prof. Sch. Art U. Mich., Ann Arbor, 1994—; juror Southeastern Mich. Scholastic Art Award Competition, Pontiac, 1992, Scarab Club Watercolor Exhbn., Detroit, 1991, Women in Art Nat. Exhbn., Farmington Hills, Mich., 1991, U. Mich. Alumni Exhbn., 1989-90. One-woman shows Atrium Gallery, Mich., 1990, 91; group shows include Am. Coll., Bryn Mawr, Pa., Riverside (Calif.) Art Mus., Kirkpatrick Mus., Oklahoma City, Montgomery (Ala.) Mus. Fine Arts, Columbus (Ga.) Mus., Brigham Young U., Provo, Utah, Kresge Art Mus., Lansing, Mich., U. Mich., Ann Arbor, Detroit Inst. Arts, Kirkpatrick Ctr. Mus. Complex, Oklahoma City, 1994, Riverside (Calif.) Art Mus., 1995, San Bernadino County Mus., Redlands, Calif., 1996, Neville Mus., Green Bya, Wis., 1996, Downey Mus. Art, Calif., 1996, Detroit Inst. Arts, 1996, Gallery Contemporary Art, U. Colo., Colorado Springs, 1996, Saginaw (Mich.) Art Mus., 1998, Springfield (Mo.) Art Mus., 1998, Art Inst. So. Calif., Laguna Beach, 1998, San Diego Art Inst., 1998, U. Mich., Dearborn, 1998. Hillsdale (Mich.) Coll., 1998, Ferris State U., Big Rapids, Mich., 1998, Sangre de Cristo Arts Ctr., Pueblo, Colo., 1999; works in many pvt. and pub. collections including Kelly Svcs., Troy, Mich., FHP Internat., Fountain Valley, Calif., Swords Into Plowshares Gallery, Detroit; work included in: (books) The Artistic Touch, 1995, Artistic Touch 2, 1996, Best of Watercolor-Painting Color, 1997, Best of Watercolor-Painting Light; Shadow, 1997, Artistic Touch 3, 1999; (mag.) Watercolor, An Am. Artist, 1996; subject of articles. Chairperson nat. giving fund Sch. Art, U. Mich., 1993; Sch. Art rep. Coun. Alumni Socs., U. Mich., 1992—. Recipient 1st Pl. award Swords Into Plowshares Internat. Exhbn., Detroit, 1989, Silver award Ga. Watercolor Soc. Internat. Exhbn., 1991, Pres.'s award Watercolor Okla. Nat. Exhbn., Oklahoma City, 1992, Flint Jour. award Buckham Gallery Nat. Exhbn., 1993, Ochs Meml. award N.E. Watercolor Soc. Nat. Exhbn., Goshen, N.Y., 1993, Color Q award Ga. Watercolor Soc., 1994, St. Cuthberts award Tex. Watercolor Soc., 1996, Daler-Rowney award San Diego Watercolor Soc. Internat. Exhbn., 1998, Hon. Mention award Nat. Watercolor Okla. Exhbn., 1998, Winsor:Newton award N.e. Watercolor Soc., 22d Annual Nat. Exhbn., 1998; many state and nat. painting awards. Mem. U. Mich. Alumni Assn. (bd. dirs. 1992—, Sch. Art rep.), U. Mich. Sch. Art Alumni Soc. (bd. dirs. 1989-91, pres.), Mich. Watercolor Soc. (chairperson 1992-93, bd. dirs. adv. 1993-94). Avocations: music, theatre, tennis, golf, reading.

ORDA, RUBEN, surgeon; b. Dec. 22, 1935; s. Moshe and Esther (Oiberman) O.; m. Sara Grossberg, Mar. 12, 1960; children: Ariel, Ruth Miriam. MD with honors, Buenos Aires U., 1959; M Surgery, Tel Aviv U., 1975. Resident Fiorito Hosp., Buenos Aires, 1959-64; sr. surgeon Rawson Hosp., Buenos Aires, 1964-67, Tel Aviv Med. Ctr., 1968-83; head surgery Assaf Harofe Hosp., Zerifin, Israel, 1983—; chmn. divsn. surgery Tel Aviv U., 1991-95; clin. and rsch. fellow Westminstern Hosp., London, 1976-77; lectr. surgery Buenos Aires U., 1964-67; lectr. anatomy Tel Aviv U., 1967-73; assoc. prof. surgery Tel Aviv U., 1983-92, prof. surgery, 1992—; examiner gen. surgery Israel Bd. Examinations, 1983—; mem. adv. com. for surgery Ministry of Health, Israel, 1986-93; sec.-gen. 9th World Congress of Collegium Internat. Chirurgiae Digestivae, Jerusalem, 1986, nat. del., chmn. Israeli chpt., 1988-98. Chmn. coun. Israel Surg. Soc., 1990-94, chmn., 1994-97. Grantee Gordon Rsch. Found., 1978, Tel Aviv U., 1978, 80-82, 85. Fellow ACS (pres. Israeli chpt. 1997—, gov. 1995—), Royal Soc. Medicine (Eng.); mem. Societe Internationale de Chirurgie, Collegium Internationale Chirurgiae Digestivae, European Soc. Surg. Rsch., N.Y. Acad. Scis., Israel Surg. Soc. (chmn. 1994-97), World Assn. Hepato-Pancreato-Biliary Surgery, Asian Surg. Assn., Senologic Internat. Soc. (pres. elect 2000—), Nat. Acad. Surgery France. Home: Keren Hayesod 3/27, Ramat Ilan Givat Shmuel 54051, Israel Office: Assaf Harofe Hosp Surgery A, Tel Aviv U, Zerifin 70300, Israel

ÖRDÖG, ADAM, mechanical engineer; b. Kecskemét, Hungary, Oct. 13, 1934; s. István and Iren (Moricz) Ö.; m. Eva Monory, Aug. 25, 1962; 1 child, Adam. Diploma in engring., Müszakiegyetem, Budapest, Hungary, 1962. Design engr. Power Plants Maintenance Enterprises, Budapest, 1960-63; dir. Danubian Petroleum Refinery, Százhalombatta, Hungary, 1963-84; project mgr. Hungarian Acad. Sci./Cen. Rsch. Inst. Physics, Budapest, 1984-85; main adviser Vegyepszer, Budapest, 1985-89; dir. Techno-Team Ltd., Budapest, 1989-92; main adviser Hungarian Oil and Gas Co., Budapest, 1992-99; leading instr. engr. Honeywell, Hungary, 1999—; cons., Rsch. Inst. Measuring, Budapest, 1968-73. Editor profl. periodical, 1973-84. Mem. Sci. Assn. for Orgn., Sci. Assn. for Automatization. Lutheran Evangelic. Avocation: wind surfing. Home: Radnoti M u 14/A, H 1137 Budapest Hungary Office: Honeywell Engring Sol Ltd, Barbtok B u 152/c, H 1113 Budapest Hungary

ORDONEZ, NELSON GONZALO, pathologist; b. Bucaramanga, Santander, Colombia, July 20, 1944; came to U.S., 1972; s. Gonzalo and Itsmenia Ordonez; m. Miranda Lee Ferrell, Dec. 18, 1976 (div. June 1983); 1 child, Nelson Adrian; m. Catherine Marie Newton, Nov. 6, 1987; 1 child, Sara Catherine Itsmenia. BA and Sci., Instituto Daza Dangond, Bogota, Colombia, 1962; MD, Nat. U. Colombia, Bogota, 1970. Resident pathology U. N.C., Chapel Hill, 1972-73; resident pathology U. Chgo., 1974-76, asst. prof. pathology, 1977-78; asst. prof. pathology U. Tex. M.D. Anderson Cancer Ctr., Houston, 1978-82, assoc. prof., 1983-85, prof., 1985—, dir. immunocytochemistry sect., 1981—, dir. electron microscopy sect., 1996—. Author: (with others) Renal Biopsy Pathology and Diagnostic and Therapeutic Implications, 1980, Tumors of the Lung, 1991; contbr. chpts. to books, numerous articles to med. jours. Nat. Kidney Found. fellow, 1977-78. Mem. AMA, Am. Assn. Pathologists, Internat. Acad. Pathology, Am. Soc. Clin. Pathologists, Am. Soc. Cytology, Am. Soc. Investigative Pathology, Internat. Acad. Cytology, Arthur Purdy Stout Soc. Surg.

Pathologists, Latin-Am. Soc. Pathology. Office: U Tex MD Anderson Cancer Ctr 1515 Holcombe Blvd Houston TX 77030-4009

ORDONEZ, ULISES SCHMILL, Mexican supreme court justice. Judge, pres. Supreme Ct. of Mexico, Mexico City. Office: Supreme Ct of Mexico, Pino Suarez Num 2, 06065 Mexico City Mexico*

ORDOÑEZ-JONAMA, RAMIRO, lawyer; b. Guatemala, Dec. 27, 1945; s. Ramiro Ordoñez-Paniagua and Graciela Jonama-Gonzalez. Licenciado, Universidad Rafael Landivar, Guatemala, 1970. Roman Catholic. Home: 12 calle 11-51 zona 1, 01001 Guatemala Guatemala

ORDOÑO, ADELINO VALDEZ, retired goverment official, farmer; b. Balaoan La Union, The Philippines, Apr. 15, 1927; s. Prospero Lopez Ordoño and Arsenia Manzano Valdez; m. Rebecca Rilloraza; children: Cynthia, Aureo, Sixto, Nilda. BS in Agr., U. of The Philippines, 1952; MA, U. of the East, The Philippines, 1968; cert. in regional planning, Settlement Study Ctr., Rehovot, Israel, 1972; PhD, U.S.T. Grad. Sch., The Philippines, 1983. Vocat. agr. tchr. Philippine Dept. Edn., 1952-64; edn. and info. officer Agrl. Credit and Coop. Office, The Philippines, 1965-74, coop. officer, 1975-80, agrl. coop. specialist, 1978-80; chief resource allocation divsn. bur. cooperatives Dept. Agrl., The Philippines, 1981-90, acting dir., 1990-91; from assoc. lectr. to prof. Poly. U. of The Philippines, 1972-91; prof. Grad. Schs. Pamantasan Ng Kungsad, The Philippines, 1985-91; economist, cons. ASEAN, Thailand, 1986-97. 1st v.p. Pastoral Parish Coun., 1997-99; mem. Food Security Coun.; pres. Environ. Ret. Assn., San Fernando, 1993-95; chmn. Provincial Coop. Union, San Fernanco, 1997-99; dir. Regional Coop. Union, Tuboa, The Philippines, 1998—; chmn., pres. Sr. Citizen's Assn., Carlatan, The Philippines, 1994—. Travel grantee USDA, 1979; recipient Outstanding Area Chmn. in Econ. award La Consolacion Coll., 1984, award of appreciation Ministry of Agr. and Food, 1986, Outstanding Elderly for Leadership award Provincial Govt. of La Union, 1990, Leadership award Pastoral Parish Coun., 1999. Roman Catholic. Avocations: farming, chess. Home: 261 Carlatan, San Fernando 2500, The Philippines Office: KS St William Parish, City of San Fernando, La Union 2500, The Philippines

OREFICE, UMBERTO, clinical researcher; b. Ragusa, Sicilia, Italy, Sept. 15, 1952; s. Ernesto and Giulia O.; m. Paola di Luccio, July 26, 1980; 1 child, Filippo. Licenza liceale, Liceo Scientifico Galileo, Naples, Italy; MD, U. Naples. Specialist Pneumologic Sch., Naples; specialist allergy and immunology Padua, Italy; diplomate public hygiene Florence, Italy; chief dept. phisiopatology respiratory Civil Hosp., Udine, Italy; cons. U. Padua. Fellow Am. Coll. Chest Physicians; mem. AAAS, Am. Thoracic Soc., Internat. Assn. Allergology and Clin. Immunology (mem. Acad. Scis.), European Respiratory Soc., Assn. for Study of Asthmatic and Allergic Diseases (pres.), N.Y. Acad. Scis., World Assn. Sarcoidosis & Other Granulomatosis. Home: Via Pordenone 50, 33100 Udine Italy

O'REILLY, FRANCIS JOSEPH, academic administrator; b. Dublin, Ireland, Nov. 15, 1922; s. Charles Joseph and Dorothy Mary (Martin) O'R.; m. Teresa Mary Williams, May 9, 1950; children: Mary, Charles, Jane, Olivia, Margaret, Rose, Louise, Peter, Paul, Julie. BA, U. Dublin, Ireland, 1943, LLD (hon.), 1978; LLD (hon.), Nat. U. Ireland, 1987. Cert. civil engr. Chmn. John Power & Son Ltd., Dublin, 1946-66, Player & Wills Ltd., Dublin, 1964-81, Irish Distillers Ltd., Dublin, 1966-83, Ulster Bank Ltd., Belfast, Ireland, 1982-89; dir. Nat. Westminster Bank Plc, London, 1982-89; chancellor Trinity Coll. U. Dublin, 1985-98, ret., 1998; pres. Mktg. Inst. Ireland, Dublin, 1983-85, Inst. Bankers of Ireland, Dublin, 1985-86. Pres. Equestrian Fedn. Ireland, Dublin, 1963-79, Royal Dublin Soc., 1986-89; chmn. Coll. des Irlandais, Paris, 1987—; mem. Royal Irish Acad., Dublin, 1987—. Lt. Royal Engrs., 1943-46. Named Hon. Life. Del., Fedn. Equestrian Internat., Berne, Switzerland, 1979; recipient Grand Cross of St. Lazarus of Jerusalem, Mil. and Hospitaller Order, 1992. Fellow Inst. Engrs. in Ireland, Inst. Mgmt. in Ireland, Trinity Coll. Dublin (hon.); mem. Kildare Street and Univ. Club, Irish Turf club, Kildare Hunt Club, Fairyhouse Race Club. Roman Catholic. Avocations: horse racing, gardening. Home: The Glebe House, Rathmore Naas, Ireland Office: The Univ Dublin, College Green, Dublin Ireland

O'REILLY, JOHN JAMES, electronic engineer, educator; b. Bromsgrove, Eng., Dec. 1, 1946; s. William Patrick and Dorothy Ann (Lewis) O'R.; m. Margaret Brooke, July 18, 1968; children: Jenny Ann, Edward James. B-Tech with 1st class honors, Brunel U., Eng., 1969; PhD, Essex U., Eng., 1982; DSc, Brunel U., 1993. Chartered engr. Engr./apprentice Royal Radar Establishment, Malvern, Eng., 1962-69; rschr. Ultra Electronics Ltd., London, 1969-72; lectr. U. Essex, Colchester, 1972-78, sr. lectr., 1979-85; vis. rschr. Post Office Rsch. Centre, Ipswich, Eng., 1978-79; head Sch. Elec. Engring. U. Wales, Bangor, 1985-93; dir., chief exec. Indsl. Devel. Bangor Ltd., Bangor, 1985-93; bd. dirs. Videoconferencing Wales, IDB Ltd., Bangor; prin. rsch. fellow BT Labs., Ipswich, Eng., 1993-94; chair telecomms. Univ. Coll., London, 1994—, head dept. electronic & elec. engring., 1997—. Author: Telecommunication Principles, 1984; editor: Mathematical Topics in Telecommunications, Vols. 1 and 2, 1984. Chmn. SERC-DTI Comms. and Distributed Systems Com., Eng., 1990-94; mem. Info. Tech. Adv. Bd., Eng., 1990-94; mem. English Adv. Com. on Telecomms.; chair UK Network Interoperability Com., 1996—. Fellow Royal Acad. Engring., Inst. Elec. Engrs. (Paper Premium award 1972); mem. The Athenaeum. Office: Univ Coll London Electronic, Elec Engring Torrington Pl, London WC2E 7JE, England

O'REILLY, KENNETH WILLIAM, military officer; b. N.Y.C., July 17, 1953; s. Thomas Michael and Dorothy Marie (Garvin) O'R.; m. Ginger Lee Jacobs, Apr. 22, 1978; children: Ryan, Erin. AAS, SUNY, Farmingdale, 1973; BS, Dowling Coll., 1975; MA, Webster U., 1982. Sales rep. N.W. Airlines, N.Y.C., 1976-78; commd. 2d lt. USAF, 1978—, advanced through grades to lt. col.; student navigator 452 Flight Tng. Squadron, Mather AFB, Calif., 1979-80; KC135 unit navigator 11th Air Refueling Squadron, Altus AFB, Okla., 1980-83; instr. navigator 11th Air Refueling Squadron, Altus AFB, 1984-85; wing exec. officer 340 Air Refueling Wing, Altus AFB, 1984-85; chief of navigation 34 Strategic Squadron, Zaragoza AB, Spain, 1985-88; strategic plans advisor 2 Airborne Command and Control Squadron, Offutt AFB, Nebr., 1988-91; action officer Hdqrs. SAC/Directorate of Strategic Plans, Offutt AFB, 1991-92; chief of tanker plans Hdqrs. Air Mobility Command/Dir. Ops. and Transp., 1992-93, chief personnel mgmt. br., 1993-96; chief opers. watch divsn., headqrs., dir. ops. and plans The Pentagon, Washington, 1996-97, chief command control and comms. divsn., dir. ops. and tng., 1997-2000, chief global command and ctrl. sys. br., dep. dir. cur. ops., 2000—. Committeeman Levittown South-North Wantagh, Rep. Club, N.Y.C., 1971-78. Decorated 3 Meritorious Svc. medal, 2 Commendation medals, others. Mem. Air Force Assn., Inst. of Navigation, Airlift Tanker Assn. Roman Catholic. Home: 6361 Regal Oak Dr Springfield VA 22152-2861 Office: The Joint Staff 20318-3000 Pentagon Washington DC 20330-0001

O'REILLY, MYRA FAITH, artist; b. Boston, Aug. 6, 1938; arrived in Great Britain, 1946; d. James George Sheehey and Eileen Theresa (O'Reilly) Gibbon. Nat. diploma, Royal Berkshire Coll., 1959; diploma, Royal Acad., 1964; teaching diploma, Hornsey Coll., 1972. Head art dept. Sherwood Hall Sch., Nottinghamshire, Eng.; lectr. I Found. Arts, Essex, Eng.; lectr. II Thomas Huxley Coll., London, Goldsmith's Coll., London; sr. lectr. Brighton Polytechnic, Sussex, Eng., 1976—. Home: 13 Walpole Terr, BN22EB Brighton England Studio: Le Vernet, 34240 Lamalous-Les-Bains France Studio: Garnet House, Brighton BN2 1EU, England

OREKHOV, ALEXANDER NIKOLAEVICH, biochemist, researcher; b. Putivl, Russia, June 30, 1949; s. Nikolay Semenovich and Nina Vladimirovna (Kamenskaya) O.; m. Natalie Mikhailovna D'yachkova, June 25, 1976; children: Alexandra, Veronica, Gregory, Barbara, Elisabeth, Nina. PhD, Moscow U., 1978. Jr. rschr. Moscow U., 1972-77; jr. rschr. Cardiology Ctr., Moscow, 1977-80, sr. rschr., 1980-84, leading rschr., 1984-98; leading rschr. Moscow U., 1998—. Contbr. articles to profl. jours. Recipient Forschungspreis, Martin Luther U., Halle, Germany, 1987, Young Investigator award XI World Congress of Cardiology, Manila, 1990; Outstanding Scientist grantee Govt. Russia, Moscow, 1993. Mem. Am. Heart Assn., Russian Sci. Soc. of Cardiologists, Internat. Arteriosclerosis Soc. Russian Orthodox. Home: Osennyaya 4-1-207, 121609 Moscow Russia

OREL, VALERI EMMANUILOVICH, medical physicist; b. Tehran, Iran, Aug. 11, 1945; s. Emmanuil Michelevich and Polina Grigorievna (Zlotnik) O.; m. Rozalia Konstantinovna Vesnovskay, July 30, 1985; 1 child, Irina Valerievna. B, Tech. Coll. Kiev, 1964; M, Kiev Polytechnick Inst., 1974; PhD, Kiev Inst. Problems Oncology, 1978, Dr. Hab. Biology Sci., 1987. Chief phys.-tech. lab. Ukrainian Rsch. Inst. Oncology and Radiology, Kiev, 1973—; prof. Internat. U. Solomon, Kiev, 1993—; cons. Comeetet New Med. Tech., Kiev, 1993—. Author: Peroxide Oxidation and Radiation, 1991, Chemiluminescence in Oncology, 1984; patentee in field. Mem. Internat. Orgn. Med. Physicists, Assn. Med. Physicists Ukraine (v.p. 1993-97), Literat Club Eng. Avocation: sports. Home: 28 Gorcogo str fl 4, 252005 Kiev Ukraine Office: Ukraine Rsch Inst Oncology, 33/43 Lomonosov str, 252022 Kiev Ukraine

OREL, VLADIMIR, linguist, educator; b. Moscow, Feb. 9, 1952; arrived in Israel, 1990; s. Emmanuil and Leah (Potiagailo) O.; m. Maria Osipov, July 1, 1981 (div. 1986); 1 child, Artiom; m. Natalia Zakharov, Mar. 25, 1989; children: Miriam, Elizabeth. BA, Moscow U., 1970, MA, 1973; PhD, Russian Acad. Scis., 1981. Rschr. Russian Acad. Scis., Moscow, 1981-87, sr. rschr., 1988-90; sr. lectr. Hebrew U., Jerusalem, 1991, Tel Aviv U., 1991-97; lectr., acad. dir. Coll. Pluralistic Judaism, Jerusalem, 1996—; sr. lectr. Bar-Ilan U., Ramat Gan, Israel, 1997-98, assoc. prof., 1998-2000; dir. linguistics ZI Corp., Calgary, Alta., Can., 2000—; vis. scholar Wolfson Coll., Oxford, Eng., 1995-96. Author: Hamito-Semitic Etymological Dictionary, 1995, The Language of Phrygians, 1997, Albanian Etymological Dictionary, 1998, A Historical Grammar of Albanian, 2000; translator: Alice in Wonderland, Through the Looking Glass, 1980-85; contbr. articles to profl. jours. Guastalla Found. prize, 1991. Mem. Philol. Soc., Writers' Union Russia, World Union Jewish Studies. Jewish. Home: 155 Stradwick Rise SW, Calgary, AB Canada T3M 1G7 Office: 500 4th Ave SW Ste 300, Calgary, AB Canada T2P 2V6

ORELLANA, EDMUNDO, Honduran government official. Atty. gen. Govt. Honduras, Tegucigalpa; permanent rep. to UN N.Y.C. Office: Perm Mission of Honduras UN 866 U N Plz Rm 417 New York NY 10017-1822*

OREM, HENRY PHILIP, retired chemist, chemical engineer, consultant; b. Campbellsburg, Ky., Feb. 28, 1910; s. Mal Lee and Alice (Green) O.; m. Lydia C. Orem (dec. Feb. 1988). BS in Indsl. Chemistry, U. Ky., 1932, MS, 1934; postgrad., Pa. State U., 1934-36. Grad. asst. phys. chemistry U. Ky., 1933; grad. rsch. scholar Pa. State Coll., 1934-37; with rsch. dept. Calco Chem. Co. subs. Am. Cyanamid Co., Bound Brook, N.J., 1937-39; plant rschr./process developer Am. Cyanamid Co., Bound Brook, 1939-42; asst. chief chemist Azo Dye and Intermediate divsn. Am. Cyanamid Co., Bound Brook, N.J., 1942-46; departmental chemist Azo Dye and Intermediate divsn. Am. Cyanamid Co., Bound Brook, 1947, tech. supt., 1947-50; rsch. chemist Sloss Sheffield Steel and Iron Co. (now U.S. Pipe and Foundry Co. subs. Jim Walter Co.), Birmingham, Ala., 1950-52, rsch. ehcm. engr., 1952-65, group leader, 1965-75, ret., 1975; cons. Jim Walter Resources, Inc., Arichem, Inc. (now subs. Jim Walter Resources, Inc.). Contbr. articles to on black powder and ballistics to publs. Fellow Am. Inst. Chemists (profl. accredited chemist); mem. AIChE (life, 1st sect. N.J. sect. 1949-50, chmn. 1963, treas. Ala. sect. 1971, 72), Am. Chem. Soc. (emeritus life, sec.-treas. Raritan Valley group N.J. sect. 1948, chmn. 1950, sec. Ala. sect. 1956-57), NRA (life), Nat. Muzzle Loading Rifle Assn. (life, contbr. and reviewer articles Muzzle Blasts, technical advisor muzzle blasts, powder and ballistics), U.S. Revolver Assn. (life), Ala. Gun Collectors Assn. (life), Magic City Gun Club (life), Va. Gun Collectors Assn. (life), Kate Carpenter Muzzleloaders Inc., Stonewall Rifle and Pistol Club (Churchville, Va.), Shenandale Gun Club (Buffalo Gap, Va.), Homestead Shooting Club (Hot Springs, Va.), Va. Muzzle Loading Rifle Assn., Va. State Rifle and Revolver Assn., Ft. Lewis Hunting Club (life), Am. Def. Preparedness Assn., Sigma Xi. Achievements include 22 patents in field (U.S. and Can.), numerous publs. in chemistry and ballistics. Home: HC 2 Box 259 Warm Springs VA 24484-9508

ÖREN, ERSIN EMRE, materials engineer, physicist, researcher; b. Antalya, Turkey, Feb. 13, 1975; s. Muharrem and Münevver (Hacibekiroglu) Ö. Grad. solid state physics, Middle East Tech. U., Ankara, Turkey, 1997, grad. metall. and materials engring., 1997, MS in metall. and materials engring., 2000. Cert. metall. and materials engring.; cert. solid state physics. Student asst. Middle East Tech. U., Ankara, 1996-97, rsch. asst., 1997—. Contbr. articles to profl. jours. Mem. Turkish Amatuer Astronomers Soc., Amateur Astronomy Soc., Chamber Metall. Engrs. Avocations: amateur astronomy, swimming, diving, parachuting, riding. Home: No 8, Kiziltoprak Ave 939 St, 07300 Antalya Turkey Office: Mid East Tech U Metall and, Materials Engring, Inonu St, 06531 Ankara Turkey

OREN, JOHN BIRDSELL, retired coast guard officer; b. Madison, Wis., Dec. 27, 1909; s. Arthur Baker and Lucile Grace (Comfort) O.; m. Harriet Virginia Prentis, Feb. 9, 1934; children—Virginia Joan (Mrs. Luther Warren Strickler II), John Edward. B.S., USCG Acad., 1933; M.S. in Marine Engring, MIT, 1942. Commd. ensign USCG, 1933, advanced through grades to rear adm., 1964; chief engring. div. (11th Coast Guard Dist.), 1957-59, (12th Coast Guard Dist.), 1960-61; dep. chief (Office Engring.), Washington, 1962-63; chief Office of Engring. (Office Engring.), 1964-68; now ret.; Mem. Mcht. Marine Council, 1964—; chmn. ship structures com. Transp. Dept., 1964—; exec. dir. Maritime Transp. Research Bd., Nat. Acad. Scis., 1968—; mem. nat. adv. bd. Am. Security Council. Recipient Legion of Merit. Mem. Soc. Am. Mil. Engrs. (pres. 1966, Acad. of Fellows), Am. Soc. Naval Engrs. (pres. 1965), Internat. Inst. Welding (vice chmn. Am. coun. 1964), Ret. Officers Assn. (bd. dirs. 1978), Pan Am. Inst. Naval Engring., Vinson Hall Residents Assn. (v.p. 1998), Mason. Republican. Episcopalian. Home: Apt 221 6251 Old Dominion Dr Mc Lean VA 22101-4806

ORGLER, YAIR E., engineer; b. Tel Aviv, Oct. 10, 1939; married; two children. BS, Technion Israel Inst. Tech., Haifa, 1963; MS, U. So. Calif., L.A., 1965, Carnegie-Mellon U., 1967; PhD, Carnegie-Mellon U., 1967. Rsch. dir. Israel Inst. Bus. Rsch./Tel Aviv U., 1969-73, 75-80; chmn. com. of bus. adminstrn. colls. Coun. for Higher Edn., Israel, 1979-80; dean faculty of mgmt. The Leon Recanati Grad. Sch. Bus./Tel Aviv U., 1981-85; vice-rector Tel Aviv U., 1985-90, sr. lectr., 1969-72, assoc. prof., 1972-77, prof., 1977—, incumbent of The Goldreich Chair in Internat. Banking, 1982—; fin. economist FDIC, Washington, 1967-69; asso. prof. bus. adminstrn. The George Washington U., Washington, 1968-69; vis. fin. economist FDIC, 1973-74, vis. economist/bd. govs. Fed. Res. System, Washington, 1974-75; dir. Israel Devel. and Mortgage Bank, Ltd., 1983-86, Israel Bank of Agr., 1977-80; cons. Bank Leumi le Israel, Ltd., 1976-80, Israel Examiner of Banks, Bank of Israel, 1969-73; mem. fin. mgmt. com. Israel Mgmt. Ctr., 1970-82; chmn. Tel Aviv Stock Exch. Mem. editl. bd. Jour. of Fin. Svcs. Rsch., Advances in Working Capital Mgmt., Issues in Banking/Hebrew, Quarterly Banking Rev.; assoc. editor: Multinational Fin. Jour.; scientific editor article series, 1996-98; author several books, including: Multinational Banking: The Israeli Experience, Jerusalem: The Bank of Israel, 1979, Analytical Methods in Finance and Banking: A Book of Readings in the Memory of Benjamin Cohen, 1977, Bank Capital, 1976, others; contbr. numerous articles to profl. jours. Bd. dirs. U.S. Israel Ednl. Found., 1999—. Mem. Am. Fin. Assn., European Fin. Assn., Fin. Mgmt. Assn., Multinational Fin. Soc. (bd. dirs. 1998—), Assn. of Univ. Heads of Israel (chmn. wage com. 1992-96).

ORHON, MINE, civil engineer, educator, dams specialist; b. Zonguldak, Turkey, Dec. 4, 1952; d. Mehmet and Nezihe Türkyilmaz; m. Gafur Mete Orhon, Nov. 26, 1976; 1 child, Yosun. BSCE, Middle East Tech. U., Turkey, 1974, MSCE, 1977, PhDCE, 1989. Cert. dam specialist. Rsch. asst. Middle East Tech. U., Ankara, Turkey, 1974-76, part-time instr., 1983-85; rch. engr. State Hydraulic Works, Ankara, 1976-84, design engr., 1984-94, sect. mgr., 1994-97, dep. dept. head, 1997—; exec. sec. Turkish Nat. Com. on Large Dams, 1994-98; mem. ICOLD Com. on Reservoir Sedimentation, 1995—; mem. Turkish nat. com. World Energy Coun.; instr. (part-time) Middle East Tech. U., 1983-85. Mem. Internat. Hydropower Assn. Avocations: tennis, skiing, reading. Home: 5 Cadde Zirvekent B, Blok 52/48, Ankara 06550, Turkey Office: DSI Genel Mudurlugu, Inönü Bulvari, Ankara 06100, Turkey

ORIANA, FEDERICO FILIPPO, lawyer, educator; b. Genoa, Italy, Aug. 4, 1952; s. Giuseppe and Wilma (Risso) O.; m. Franca Piccini, July 25, 1987; children: Fiorenza, Francesca. Diploma in English Lang., Internat. Lang. Ctr., London, 1973; diploma in French Lang., U. Rennes, France, 1974; diploma in comparative law, Georgetown U., 1975; JD, U. Genoa, 1975; LLM, U. Chgo., 1976. CPA; Bar: Rome. Asst. to pres. Confindustria, Genoa, 1974-77; sec. gen. Confindustria Liguria, Genoa, 1977-83; pres. Regional Agy. for Devel., Genoa, 1983-87; CEO Bosco Spa, Terni, Italy, 1988-90; internat. affairs v.p. Ente Finanziamento Industria Manifatturiera, Rome, 1990-93; adminstr. Fin. Invest (now FederCasa), Genoa, 1993—; chmn. CIFIN, Genoa, 1984-90, MEDIOFIDI, Genoa, 1985-88; vice chmn. ASSOFIR, Ro, 1986-88. Translator: Taking Rights Seriously of R. Dworkin, 1982; contbr. articles to profl. jours. City mgr., commr. City of Terni, 1995-97. Fulbright fellow U.S. Govt., 1975; recipient Economia Ligure prize City of Genoa Com., 1985. Mem. Interant. Soc. Legal Philosophy, Nat. Soc. Real Estate Promoters (vice-chmn. Aspesi 2000—), Rotary Club Genoa. Office: FederCasa, Via XII Ottobre 2/181, 16121 Genoa Italy

ORIHUELA NICOLAU, RAFAEL, urology educator; b. La Paz, Murillo, Bolivia, Oct. 20, 1946; s. Nestor Zenon and Amparo (Nicolau) O.; m. Wilma Graciela Salinas, May 17, 1980; children: Rodrigo Rafael, Alvaro Sergio. Surgeon, U. San Andres, La Paz, 1974; urologist, St. Joseph Hosp., Paris, 1978; urologist surgeon, Med. Sch. Bolivia, La Paz, 1994; honors diploma, Tech. U. Beni, Trinidad and Bolivia, 1994. Lic. urologist surgeon. Prof. physiology and biophysics U. San Andres, La Paz, 1976—, prof. urology, 1978—; postgrad. prof. Nat. Sec. of Health, La Paz, 1988—. Author: (books) Outline of Practical Works of Biophysics and Nuclear Medicine, 1980, Diagnostic and Treatment of the Sexually Transmitted Disease, 1987, Applied Biophysics, 1995, (mag.) Argentine Magazine of Dermatology, 1990. Recipient Gold medal IX Nat. Congress of Urology, 1986. Mem. Urol. Am. Assn., Am. Confedn. Urology, French Speaking Soc. Uridinamics (founder mem. 1978), Bolivian Union Against Sexually Transmitted Diseases (pres. 1986-90), Bolivian Soc. Urology (v.p. 1987-91, pres. 1991-93), Bolivian Soc. Sexology and Sexual Edn. (founder 1996), Bolivian Soc. Transplantation of Organs and Tissue (founder 1988), N.Y. Acad. Scis. Avocations: photography, cinematography, astrophysics, relativity, reading. Home: Calle 14 de Septembre 555, La Paz Bolivia Office: Av Arce 2082 Esquina, Montevideo La Paz, Bolivia

ORIO, OSCAR ANGEL, chemistry educator; b. Buenos Aires, June 1, 1927; s. Angel and Maria Angèlica (Mangiante) O.; m. Elena Haavardsholm, June 4, 1993; children: Maria Julia, Maximiliano Oscar. Lic. in chemistry, U. La Plata, Argentina, 1952, D of Chemistry, 1955. Asst. U. La Plata, 1954-55; rsch. chief, govt. oil fields Florencio Varela, Argentina, 1955-58; prof. Nat. U. Córdoba, Argentina, 1958-80, dean chemistry faculty, 1971-73; prof. organic chemistry Nat. U. Tech., Córdoba, 1980—, head fuels rsch. group, 1980-95; nat. com. for catalysis Sci. and Tech. Rsch. Coun. of Province of Córdoba, 1987—, U. Rschrs. Help System Nat. Sci. and Tech. Coun. Argentina, 1989—. Recipient Biennial award for outstanding tech. contbn. Union Carbide Argentina, 1982. Mem. Assn. Quimica Argentina, Assn. Investigadores in Ingenieri a Quimica y Quimica Aplicada, Assn. Argentina Investigadores in Quimica Orgánica, Soc. Argentina Enseñanza de la Ingeniera, Internat. Union for Pure and Applied Chemistry. Roman Catholic. Office: Universidad Tecnológica Nacional, Casilla de Correos 36, 5016 Córdoba Argentina

ORIORDAN, TIMOTHY, environmental sciences educator, consultant; b. Edinburgh, Scotland, Feb. 21, 1942; s. Kevin Denis and Norah Joyce (Lucas) O.; m. Ann Morison Philip, May 18, 1968; children: Katharine Louise, Alice Janet. MA in Geography, U. Edinburgh, 1963; MS in Water Resources, Cornell, Ithaca, 1965; PhD in Geography, U. Cambridge, 1987. Asst. prof. Simon Fraser U., Burnaby, 1967-71; assoc. prof. Simon Praser U., Burnaby, 1971-74; reader U. Ea. Anglia, Norwich, 1971-80, prof., 1980—. Author: Environmentalism, 1981; co-author: Sizewell B, 1987, Controlling Pollution, 1991, Environmental Science for Environmental Management, 1994, 99, The Transition to Sustainability, 1998, Globalism, Localism and Identity, 2000, Re-interpreting the Precautionary Principle, 2000. Chair environment com. Broads Authority, Norwich, 1981-98; chair environment sci and society program European Sci. Found., 1989-92; dep. lt. County of Norfolk, 1998. Recipient Gill Meml. award, Royal Geographical Soc., London, 1983. Fellow Brit. Acad. Avocations: classical double bass playing. Home: Wheatlands Hethersett Ln, Coloney, NR4 7TT Norwich England Office: Sch Environmental Sciences, U East Anglia, NR4 7TJ Norwich England

ÖRKÉNY, ANTAL, sociology educator; b. Budapest, Hungary, Jan. 6, 1954; s. István Örkény and Angéla Nagy. MA, Eötvös Loránd U., Budapest, 1978, PhD, 1986. Diplomate in sociology and history. Assoc. prof. Eötvös Loránd, Budapest, 1987—; vis. prof. Columbia U., N.Y.C., 1984; lectr. U. Calif. Edn. Abroad Program, Budapest, 1988-89, 90-91, 92—, acad. dir., 1992—; lectr. Am. U. Edn. Abroad Program, Budapest, 1991-94; asst. prof. Inter-Univ. Gasorgium Postical & Social Rsch., Ann Arbor, Mich., 1992, 93; vis. prof. polit. sci. dept. Oreg. State U., Corvallis, 1994; dir. ELTE UNESCO Ethnic and Minority Studies Program, Budapest, 1992—, Minority Rsch. Inst., Budapest, 1995—. Author: (with G. Csepeli) Ideology and Political Beliefs in Hungary. The Twilight of State Socialism, 1992; contbr. articles to profl. jours. Office: Eötvös Loránd Univ, Pollack M tes 10, 1088 Budapest Hungary

ORLEDGE, ROBERT NICHOLAS, music educator, researcher, musicologist; b. Bath, Avon, Eng., Jan. 5, 1948; s. Rex Edward Mark and Maisie Irene (Clark) O. BA in Music with honors, Clare Coll., Cambridge, Eng., 1968, MA, 1972, PhD, 1973. Lectr. U. Liverpool, Eng., 1971-80, sr. lectr., 1980-86, reader, 1986-91, prof., personal chair, 1991—; head music dept. U. Liverpool, 1990-93. Author: Gabriel Fauré, 1979, Debussy and the Theatre, 1982, Charles Koechlin: His Life and Works, 1989, Satie the Composer, 1990, Satie Remembered, 1995; contbr. numerous articles to profl. jours. Mem. Assn. Univ. Tchrs., Assn. Des Amis De L'Oeuvre Koechlin, Fond. Satie, Centre De Documentation Claude Debussy. Avocations: gardening, music manuscripts collector, jazz piano. Home: Windermere House, Windermere Terr, Liverpool L8 3SB, England Office: U Liverpool, 80 Bedford St South, Liverpool L69 3BX, England

ORLIAGUET, GILLES ANDRÉ, anesthesiologist, researcher; b. Paris, Nov. 6, 1961; s. Jean-Claude Germain and Claude Georgette (Joubert) O.; m. Jocelyne Durin; children: Antoine, Adrien. MD, U. Paris, 1991. Licensed anesthesiologist. Resident in anesthesiology U. Paris, 1989-93, asst. prof., 1993—; med. dir. pediat. anesthesiology Necker-Enfants Malades Hosp., Paris, 1998-99. Contbr. articles to profl. jours. Mem. Assn. Anesthesiologists Reanimateurs Pediat. Expression Francaise (treas. 1998-99), Soc. Francaise Anesthesie Reanimation, Am. Soc. Anesthesiologists. Avocations: computer, books, movies, music. Home: 8 rue du 18 Juin 1940, 94700 Maisons-Alfort France Office: Necker-Enfants Hosp, 149 rue de Sevres, 75743 Paris France

ORLIC, MIRKO, oceanographer; b. Zagreb, Croatia, May 26, 1955; s. Ignac and Gabrijela (Batic) O.; m. Alemka Penzar, June 14, 1980; children: Niksa, Ivana. BS, U. Zagreb, 1978, MS, 1981, PhD, 1988. Asst. Ruder Boskovic Inst., Croatia, 1979-83; asst. U. Zagreb, 1983-89, asst. prof., 1989-95, assoc. prof., 1995—; vis. scholar Scripps Instn. Oceanography, 1993; head Andrija Mohorovicic Geophys. Inst., Croatia, 1996—. Contbr. articles to profl. jours.; editor: Geofizika, 1990-92. Recipient Fulbright award USIA, 1993. Mem. Commn. Internat. pour L'Exploration Scientifique de la Mer Mediterranee, Am. Geophys. Union. Avocations: swimming, bicycling. Home: Grskoviceva 9, 10000 Zagreb Croatia

ORLIKOV, GREGORY ALEXANDER, medical educator; b. Kijev, USSR, Aug. 24, 1940; arrived in Latvia, 1947; s. Alexander Efrem and Sara Girsch (Roitman) O.; m. Rimma Paul Negodjajeva, Aug. 31, 1967; 1 child, Alexei. Diploma, Medicine Inst., Riga, Latvia, 1963, MD, 1969, Habil. MD, 1986. Physician Dist. Hosp., Uraljsk, Kazakhia, 1963-66; aspirant Medicine Inst., Riga, 1966-69, asst., 1969-79, docent, 1979-87; prof. internal medicine Latvian Acad. Medicine, Riga, 1987—; chief Internal Diseases Clinics, Latvian State Hosp., 1995—; chief propedeutic course Latvian Acad. Medicine, Riga, 1995—. Author: Visible Symptoms in Internal Clinics, 1983, (student manual) Historia Morbi, 1993, Internal Diseases Propedeutic Course, 1998, Propedeitike Praktiskais Kurss, 2000; contbr. numerous articles to internat. jours. Mem. Latvian Soc. Physicians, Soviet Soc. Gastroenterology, N.Y. Acad. Scis. Social Democrat. Avocations: literature, fishing. Home: 6-6

Šarlotes str, LV 1001 Riga Latvia Office: Latvian Acad Medicine, 16 Dzirciema str, LV 1007 Riga Latvia

ORLOVA, LUDMILA VLADIMIROVNA, agricultural management company executive; b. Pokhvistnevo, Russia, Apr. 12, 1956; d. Vladimir Nickolaevich Orlov and Iraida Petrovna Vashurina; m. Alexander Jurjevich Tsybrov, Nov. 21, 1976 (div. May 1985). Gen. practice medicine Mcpl. Hosp., Samara, 1979-84, dir. dept. rehab., 1984-85; instr. socio-econs. Samara Mcpl. Party Com., 1985-89; mng. dir. Interindsl. State-Coop. Sotrudnichestvo, Samara, 1989-92, MPS Mgmt. and Prodn. Systems ZAO, Samara, 1992—, AHT Systems GmbH, Essen, Germany, 1996—, Eurotechnika AO, Samara, 1998—; bd. dirs. AgroLeasing, Samara, AHT Group GmbH, Germany, Samara Grain Co., Samara Solana. Co-founder Acad. Humanitarian Scis., Agrl. Tng. Found.; asst. to chmn. Com. for Budget of Russian Fedn., Fed. House of Russia, Moscow, 1994—. Avocations: reading, music, art, fashion, design. Office: MPS Mgmt and Prodn Sys ZAO, Kuibysheva 88, 443099 Samara Russia

ORLOVA-BIENKOWSKAYA, MARINA YAKOVLEVNA, zoologist; b. Moscow, Russia, Aug. 19, 1969; d. Yakov Gershovich Dorfman and Galina Ilyinichna Orlova, m. Andrei Olegovich Bienkowski, June 14, 1991; children: Andrei Andreevich Bienkowski, Vladislav Andreevich Bienkowski. Magister, Moscow State U., 1991; D of Zoology, Russian Acad. Scis., Moscow, 1995. Rsch. scientist Russian Acad. Scis., Moscow, 1993—. Contbr. articles to profl. jours. Home: Zelenograd 1130 Apt 101, 103460 Moscow Russia Office: Russian Acad Sc Leninsky 33, Inst Ecology and Evolution, 117071 Moscow Russia

ORLOVSKY, DONALD ALBERT, lawyer; b. East Orange, N.J., May 15, 1951; s. Manuel Martin and Eleanor Marie (Karr) O.; m. Nancy Ann Richmond, Nov. 21, 1987; children: Kyle Lee, Donald Albert Jr. AB, Cornell U., 1973; JD, Rutgers U., 1976. Bar: Fla. 1976, U.S. Ct. Appeals (5th cir.) 1976, N.J. 1977, U.S. Dist. Ct. (so. dist.) Fla. 1977, U.S. Dist. Ct. N.J. 1977, U.S. Supreme Ct. 1980, U.S. Ct. Appeals (11th cir.) 1981. Assoc. Smathers & Thompson, Miami, 1976-77; ptnr. McCune, Hiaasen, Crum, Ferris & Gardner, P.A., Ft. Lauderdale, Fla., 1978-86, Kamen & Orlovsky PA, West Palm Beach, 1988—; bd. dirs. Comprehensive Alcoholism Treatment Program, Inc., Fla. Lawyers Assistance, Inc., supervising monitor and counselor, 1991—. Author: Nova U. Law Review, 1977, U. Miami Law Review, 1978. Alumni bd. St. Andrew's Sch., Boca Raton, Fla., 1996—. Recipient All-Am. recognition in springboard diving, 1966-69; inducted Hall of Fame Newark Acad., Livingston, N.J., 1997. Mem. ABA, Fla. Bar (civil procedure rules com. 1981), Acad. Fla. Trial Lawyers, Assn. Trial Lawyers Am. Episcopalian. Office: 1601 Belvedere Rd Ste 402 West Palm Beach FL 33406-1541

ORLOWSKA-WARREN, LENORE ALEXANDRIA, art educator, fiber artist; b. Detroit, May 22, 1951; d. William Leonard and Aloisa Clara (Hrapkiewicz) Orlowski; m. Donald Edward Warren, May 11, 1990. AA, Henry Ford C.C., 1972; BS in Art Edn., Wayne State U., 1974, M in Spl. Edn., 1978; BFA, Ctr. for Creative Studies, 2000. Tchr. arts and crafts Detroit Pub. Schs., 1974—; fiber artist Detroit Inst. Arts; cons. Arts Detroit Cmty. Plan, TRIACO Arts & Crafts, 1996—; instr., demonstrator weaving Detroit Inst. Arts. One-woman show at Dearborn C. of C., Ctr. for Creative Studies, 2000; exhibited in group shows, including alumni exhibit Henry Ford C.C., 1989, Detroit Artist Market, 1995—, Scarab Club, 1996, Lansing Art Gallery, 1997, Ctr. for Creative Studies, 1997, Yr. of the Woman Exhibit, 1998, Tom Thompson Meml. Art Gallery Juried Ontario Artists Exhibit, 1998, One Focus, Two Worlds Exhibit, 1999, Fashion Exhibit and Felt the Feeling of Fiber, U.245 Gallery, 1999, Tom Thompson Meml. Act Gallery Juried Ont. Artist Exhibit, 1998, Fiber U. 245 Gallery, 1999, Ctr. Creative Studies, 2000; contbr. to Sch. Arts Mag. Mem. exec. bd. Springwells Pk. Assn., 1989-99, pres., 1994-96, chairperson youth act workshops; com. mem. Dearborn cmty. art coun. Art on the Ave., 1993-99, Gallery Crawl chairperson, 1998; chair Nat. Woman's History Month workshop, 1995; mem. LWV, Cranbrook Acad. Art, Art Inst. Chgo., Met. Mus. Art, Cleve. Mus. Art, Nat. Mus. of Women in the Arts, Art Gallery of Ontario, Colonial Williamsburg Burgesses, Textile Mus., Surface Design Assn. Mem. Nat. Art Edn. Assn. (electronic gallery coord. 1992-99), Mich. Art Edn. Assn. (presenter art advocacy workshop), Card Weaving Workshop presenter, 1999, Am. Craft Coun., Detroit Artist Market, Detroit Inst. Arts-Founders Soc., Birmingham Bloomfield Art Assn., Met. Mus. of Art, The Cleve. Mus. of Art, The Nat. Mus. of Women in the Arts, Art Gallery of Ont., Colonial Williamsburg Burgessess, The Textile Mus., Surface Design Assn. Avocations: fiber art, travel, colonial gardening, reading colonial history and biographies. Home: 10 Berwick Ln Dearborn MI 48120-1102

ORLOWSKI, ANDRZEJ JERZY, acoustician, educator; b. Sopot, Gdansk, Poland, June 10, 1947; s. Zygmunt Roman and Donata Barbara (Szymanska) O.; m. Nora Cristina Scerpella, Aug. 12, 1975; children: Andrzej Pawel, Mariola Nora. MSc, Tech. U. Gdańsk, Poland, 1970, PhD, 1977; DSc, Acad. Agrl., Szczecin, 1988. Cert. acoustical engr. Engr. Sea Fisheries Inst., Gdynia, Poland, 1970-76, prof. asst., 1976-90, asst. prof. dept. biology and conservation of resources, 1991—; prof. Sea Fisheries Inst., 1998—; fisheries biologist UN Devel. Program/UNESCO/FAO Project, Aden, Yemen, 1990-91; lectr. Gdańsk U., Gdynia, Poland, 1989-90; acoustic team leader research vessel Profesor Siedlecki cruises at Atlantic, Pacific, Indian Ocean and Baltic Sea, 1973-89; cons. Northeast N. Fishery Ctr., Woods Hole, Mass., 1985; mem. fish tech. group Internat. Coun. for Exploration of the Sea, 1989—; lectr. ichthyology dept. Sea Fisheries Inst., Gdynia, 1974-89. Co-author: Commercial and Scientific Correspondence in Spanish, 1996. Recipient grant Polish Com. Sci., Warszawa, 1996-97. Mem. Polish Acoustic Soc. (sec. 1994), Polish Com. Ocean Rsch. (sect. physics), Polish Acad. Scis. (mem. com. acoustic sect. 1993—), Polish Soc. Spanishists, Sopot Lovers Assn. Avocations: music, painting, tourism, cross-country skiing, kayaking. Office: Sea Fisheries Inst, Kollataja 1, 81-332 Gdynia Poland

ORŁOWSKI, TADEUSZ, medical educator; b. Kazan, Russia, Sept. 13, 1917; arrived in Poland, 1919; s. Witold Eugeniusz and Alina Maria (Trzeciakowska) O. Physician, U. Warsaw, Poland, 1943; MD, U. odź, Poland, 1948; PhD, Warsaw Med. Sch., 1952, prof. medicine, 1962; Dr. honoris causa, Jagellonian U., Cracow, Poland, 1990, Warsaw Med. Sch., 1999. Sr. asst. dept. medicine 2d U., Warsaw, 1945-48; sr. asst., assoc. prof., head 1st dept. medicine Warsaw Med. Sch., 1945-52, 63-75; head Transplant Inst., Warsaw, 1975-87; prof. Inst. Biocybernetic and Biomed. Engring., Warsaw, 1987—; dir. Polish Red Cross Tchg. Hosp., Ham-Hyn, Korea, 1958; dep. sr. sec. dept. medicine Polish Acad. Scis., Warsaw, 1963-68, sci. sec. dept. medicine, 1968-71, 1st dep. sci. sec., 1971-79. Editor, author: (chpts.) Textbook of Internal Medicine, I-IV, 1979, I-IX, 1988-92, Kidney Transplantation, 1995; editor: Nephrology, 1976, 83, 92, 97; contbr. numerous papers in field to profl. jours. and books. Officer Polish Underground Army, 1939-44. Recipient 2d Polish State award Govt. Com., 1968, Big Cross of Polonia Restituta Medal, 1997; Rockefeller Found. fellow, 1959-60. Mem. Polish Nephrol. Soc. (pres.), European Dialysis and Transplant Assn. (coun. mem. 1966-68), Kidney Internat. (mem. mgmt. com. 1974-76), Internat. Soc. Nephrology (coun. mem. 1974-76), Hungarian Acad. Scis. (hon.), Polish Acad. Scis., Internat. Acad. Scis. (fgn. mem.), German Soc. for Nephrology, Polish Alpine Club (hon. mem.). Avocations: Alpinism, traveling. E-mail: torlows@ikp.atm.com.pl. Home: Al Roz 6 m 13, 00556 Warsaw Poland Office: Transplantation Inst, Nowogrodzka 59, 02 006 Warsaw Poland

ORLU, LEVENT ÖZCAN, business executive, management consultant; b. Istanbul, Turkey, Oct. 21, 1959; s. Erdógan and Gönül (Celikkol) O.; divorced; 1 child, Candogan. Doctoral degree, U. Istanbul, 1984, cert. in econs., 1991; cert., Cambridge (Eng.) Acad. Transp., 1994. Physician Ministry of Health, Gümüshane, Turkey, 1984, Municipality of Besiktas, Istanbul, 1986; project mgr. Les Labs. Servier, Paris, 1987, Servier ILAC, Istanbul, 1988-91; CEO Orlu Ltd., Istanbul, 1991—, Sigor Ltd., Istanbul, 1995—, Galev A.S., 1999—, Ordent A.S., 1999—; gen. coord. rsch. studies in field, 1989; cons. SSM&A, Istanbul, 1993-98. With Turkish Air Force, 1985-86. Mem. Am. Mgmt. Assn. (Belgium), Alexander Hamilton Inst., C. of C. Istanbul, Cir. d'Orient, Lions (founder, pres. club Leo 1980, gen. sec. com. 1982, Loyalty plaque 1981, Gratitude plaque 1982-83), Rotary, Turkish Footballmen Assn. Liberal. Moslem. Avocations: tennis, skiing, graphology, astronomy, social politics. E-mail: orlu@turk.net. Office: Soyak Sitesi 1 Blok D007, 81190 Istanbul Turkey

ORMAN, GABRIEL V., mathematician, educator; b. Balti, Romania, Nov. 15, 1933; s. Virgiliu Gh. and Varvara Gh. (Tanasescu) O.; m. Olivia I. Dumitrache, Aug. 22, 1954. MS, Univ., Cluj, Romania, 1957; Prof., Transylvania U., Brasov, Romania, 1974; Dr in Scis., Univ., Bucharest, Romania, 1973. Lectr. U. Brasov, 1962-74; prof. Transylvania U., 1974—, head dept. math., 1985—, head lab. of math., 1990—, pres. Univ. House, 1985-93. Author: Formal Languages, 1982; editor procs. Mem. Sindical, Brasov, 1985-98. Recipient grants in field. Mem. European Math. Soc., N.Y. Acad. Sci. Christian Orthodox. Avocation: travel. E-mail: ogabriel@unitbv.ro. Office: Transylvania U, Iuliu Maniu 50, 2200 Brasov Romania

ORMAN, NANETTE HECTOR, psychiatrist; b. Highland Park, Ill., Feb. 1, 1943; d. William Joseph and Agnes (Daly) Hector; m. John Christopher Orman, July 2, 1964; children: Laurel Anne, Nathaniel William. BA in Journalism, U. Calif., Berkeley, 1964; postgrad., Stanford U., 1978-81; MPH in Epidemiology, U. Calif., Berkeley, 1984, MS in Health and Med. Scis., 1985; MD, U. Calif., San Francisco, 1987. Diplomate Am. Bd. Psychiatry and Neurology; lic. physician, Calif. Psychiatrist San Jose (Calif.) State U., 1989-93; pvt. practice Los Altos, Calif., 1991—; staff El Camino Hosp., 1991-94, assoc. staff, 1994—; staff Stanford (Calif.) U. Hosp. and Med. Ctr., 1998—; asst. clin. prof. Stanford (Calif.) U. Sch. Medicine, 1995—; oral bd. examiner Am. Bd. Psychiatry & Neurology, Deerfield, Ill., 1995—, chief resident in psychiatry, 1991; spkr. and cons. in field. Editor San Mateo County Planned Parenthood Assn. Newsletter, 1968-69. Bd. dirs. Mid-Peninsula Task Force for Integrated Edn., 1972-82; consumer mem. San Mateo County Mental Health Adv. Bd., 1987. Mem. Am. Psychiat. Assn. (pub. info. com. 1989—), No. Calif. Psychiat. Soc. (chair membership com. 1996-98, pub. info. com., media spokesperson, moderator ann. meetings 1993-94), Nat. Alliance for the Mentally Ill, San Francisco Depressive and Manic Depressive Assn. Office: 851 Fremont Ave Ste 98 Los Altos CA 94024-5602

ORME, MICHAEL L'ESTRANGE, pharmacologist, educator; b. Derby, Eng., June 13, 1940; s. Christopher L'Estrange and Muriel Janet (Thomson) O.; m. Joan Patricia Abbott, Apr. 15, 1967; 1 child, Robert L'Estrange. MA, Cambridge U., 1965, MB BCh, 1965, MD, 1975. Lectr. clin. pharmacology Royal Postgrad. Med. Sch., London, 1969-75; sr. lectr. pharmacology and therapeutics U. Liverpool, Eng., 1975-84; prof. pharmacology and therapeutics U. Liverpool, 1984—, dean Faculty of Medicine, 1991-96; dir. edn. and tng. N.W. Regional Office Nat. Health Svc., Eng., 1996—; cons. Royal Liverpool U. Hosps. NHS Trust, 1975—. Author: Medicine-The Self Help Guide, 1987; editor: Therapeutic Drugs, 1989. Gov. Birkenhead Sch., Eng., 1989—. Fellow Royal Coll. Physicians London, Faculty of Pharm. Medicine; mem. Brit. Pharmacol. Soc. (sec. clin. sect. 1981-86), Brit. Med. Assn., Gen. Med. Coun. Avocations: sailing, astronomy, gardening. Home: 80 Brimstage Rd, Merseyside CH60 1XG, England Office: NW Regional Office NHS Exec, 930-932 Birchwood Blvd, Millenium Park WA3 7QN, England

ORMENYI, IMRE, environmental scientist; b. Budapest, Hungary, Sept. 15, 1932; s. Zoltan Ormenyi and Blanka Kastner; m. Klara Komary, June 26, 1974 (div. 1982). Meteorologist, U. Budapest, 1956; PhD, Hungarian Acad. Sci., 1986. Rschr. Nat. Inst. Rheumatology and Physiotherapy, Budapest, 1956-93; v.p. Internat. Com. Study Environ. Factors, Brussels, 1984—. Editor: Weather Sensitivity, 1988; contbr. several articles to profl. jours. Mem. Internat. Soc. Biometeorology (chair), Hungarian Biometeorology Soc. (pres. 1996). Home: Kiraly-v 52, 1061 Budapest Hungary

ORMEROD, LAWRENCE PETER, thoracic physician, consultant; b. Rossendale, Lancashire, Eng., Aug. 28, 1950; s. Milton Blackburn and Dorothy (Sellers) O.; m. Pauline Morris; children: Adam James, Heather Jane. BSc in Pharmacology with hons., U. Manchester, Eng., 1971, MB ChB with hons., 1974, MD, 1986, D of Med. Scis., 2000. House surgeon Manchester (Eng.) Hosp., 1974-75, house physician, 1975, sr. house officer, 1975-77, registrar, 1977-78, sr. registrar, 1978-80; cons. thoracic physician Blackburn, Eng., 1981—; prof. medicine Postgrad. Sch. of Medicine and Health U. Cen. Lancashire, Preston, Eng., 2000—. Author: (with others) Thorax, 1990. Fellow Royal Coll. Physicians; mem. Brit. Thoracic Soc. (chmn. joint TB com. 1995—). Office: Blackburn Acute Nat Health Trust, Chest Clin Royal Infirmary, Lancs Blackburn BB2 3LR, England

ORMEZZANO, UGO, mechanical engineering company executive; b. Andorno, Italy, July 29, 1948; s. Primino and Ellia (Brusotti) O.; m. Magda Ramilli, Jan. 12, 1973; children: Greta, Giulia. BSME, Q. Sella U., Biella, Italy, 1967. Sales engr. Biffi, Milan, Italy, 1970-76; gen. mgr. Polimat, Bologna, Italy, 1976-78; sales mgr. Grove, Rome, 1978-81; gen. mgr. Ledeen, Voghera, Italy, 1981-86, pres., 1986—; pres. Ledeen Flow Control Sys., Ponca City, Oklahoma, 1985-88. Mem. Golf Castell 'Arquato, Golf Club Chamonix. Avocations: skiing, golf. Office: Ledeen, Via Gandini 4, 270058 Voghera Italy

ORMOND, LEONEE, English literature educator; b. Kingston-on-Thames, England, Aug. 27, 1940; m. Richard Louis Ormond, May 11, 1963; children: Augustus Jasper, Marcus Conrad. BA, Oxford U., 1962; MA, Birmingham U., 1965. Asst. lectr. in English City of Birmingham (Eng.) Coll. Edn., 1963-65; lectr. in English King's Coll., London, 1965-85, sr. lectr., 1985-89; reader King's Coll., 1989-96, prof. Victorian studies, 1996—. Author: (biographies) George Du Maurier, 1969, Lord Leighton (with Richard Ormond), 1974, J.M. Barrie, 1987, Alfred Tennyson, 1993. Fellow English Assn. Mem. Ch. of Eng. Club: Women's U. (London). Avocations: mountain hiking, hill walking. Office: U London Kings Coll, Strand, London WC2, England

ORMOS, JENŐ, pathologist; b. Hódmezövasarhely, Csongrad, Hungary, Dec. 21, 1922; s. Pál and Ilona (Fülöp) O.; m. Katalin Koller, Sept. 3, 1949 (div. 1959); children: István, Pál; m. Judit Lantos, Dec. 27, 1960. MD, Pázmány Péter U., Halle, Germany, 1945, U. Szeged, Hungary, 1946; PhD, Hungarian Acad. Scis., Budapest, 1963, DSc, 1980. Resident pathology U. Szeged, 1946-47, asst. dept. pathology, 1947-54, assoc. prof., 1955-62, prof. and chmn. dept. pathology, 1963-92, com. chmn. dept. pathology, 1992-93, prof. emeritus, 1993—; cons. pathologist Szeged, 1954-55; rsch. fellow dept. pathology U. Düsseldorf, Germany, 1961-62; dep. rector U. Medicine, Szeged, 1967-73. Pres. Trade Union of U. Medicine, Szeged, 1984-90. Recipient Purkyne award Czechoslovak Med. Soc., 1987, Thomasius, Martin Luth U., 1987, Jancsó Miklós, U. of Medicine, Szeged, 1989. Mem. Hungarian Soc. Pathology (pres. 1964-66), Polish Pathol. Soc. (hon.), Cuban Pathol. Soc. (hon.). Unitarian. Avocations: rowing, touring. Home: Tömörkény u 2/c, H-6720 Szeged Hungary

ORMOS, PAL, biophysicist, researcher; b. Szeged, Hungary, Oct. 14, 1951; s. Jenö and Katalin (Koller) O.; m. Zsuzsa Boros, Mar. 13, 1976 (div. July 1996); 1 child, Peter; m. Judit Gerhardt, Oct. 12, 1996. MS, Jozsef U., Szeged, 1970-75, PhD, 1982; ScD, Hungarian Acad. Sci., 1992. Jr. scientist Inst. Biophysics, Biol. Rsch. Ctr., Szeged, 1975-82, sr. scientist, 1982-85, sci. advisor, 1991-93, dir., 1994—; vis. prof. U. Ill., Urbana, 1985-91. Mem. Hungarian Biophys. Soc. Avocation: soccer. Home: Zarda u 16/A, 6721 Szeged Hungary Office: Biological Rsch Ctr, Temesuári Krt 62, 6701 Szeged Hungary

ORMS, R. NORRIS, healthcare society administrator; b. St. Louis. BA, McKendree Coll.; MBA, Keller Grad. Sch. Mgmt., Chgo. Cert. assn. exec. Exec. dir. Nat. Safety Coun. Found., Itasca, Ill., 1985-97, dir. cause related mktg., dir. coun. rels.; acting exec. dir. Healthcare Info. and Mgmt. Systems Soc., Chgo., 1997—. Office: HIMSS 230 E Ohio St Ste 500 Chicago IL 60611-3270

ORMSBY, ERIC LINN, educator, researcher, writer; b. Atlanta, Oct. 16, 1941; s. Robert and Virginia (Haire) O.; m. Dorothy Louise Hoffmann, July 22, 1967; children: Daniel Paul, Charles Martin. BA summa cum laude, U. Pa., 1971; MA, Princeton U., 1973, PhD, 1981; MLS, Rutgers U., 1978. Near East bibliographer libr. Princeton U., N.J., 1975-77; Near East curator libr. Princeton U., 1977-83; libr. dir. Cath. U. Am., Washington, 1983-86; libr. dir. McGill U., Montreal, Can., 1986-96, assoc. prof. Inst. Islamic Studies, 1986-96, prof., 1996—; cons. NYU, 1981-82; mem. libr. com. Mid. East Inst., Washington, 1985-87, Al Akhawayn U., Morocco, 1994-95, Saudi Arabian Monetary Agy., Riyadh, 1995-96; chmn. continuing edn. com. Washington Consortium, 1983-86; mem. bd. Ctr. Rsch. Librs., 1989-95. Author: Theodicy in Islamic Thought, 1984 (Choice Mag. award 1984), Bavarian Shrine and Other Poems, 1990 (QSPELL award for poetry 1991), (poems) Coastlines, 1992, (with others) Handlist of Arabic Manuscripts, 1986, For a Modest God: New and Selected Poems, 1997; editor: Moses Maimonides and His Time, 1989; contbr. articles and book revs. to profl. jours., poetry and essays to various mags., including New Republic, New Yorker, Grand St., Shenandoah, The New Criterion, The Yale Rev., So. Rev. and Chelsea. Instr. Princeton Adult Sch., 1978-80. DAAD fellow German Acad. Exch., 1973-74; recipient Ingram Merrill award, 1993. Mem. Middle East Librs. Assn. (v.p. 1981-82, pres. 1982-83), Hoelderlin Gesellschaft, Societe des Amis de Jean de la Fontaine, Can. Assn. Rsch. Libs. (v.p. 1988-89), Can. Libr. Assn., Assn. pour l'Avancement des Scis. et des Techniques de la Documentation, Conseil des recteurs et des principaux des univs. du Québec, Sous-Comité des Bibliotheques (pres. 1989-91). Roman Catholic. Avocations: natural history, writing, cooking, photography. Office: McGill U Inst Islamic Studies, 3458 McTavish St, Montreal, PQ Canada H3A 1Y1

ORNELLAAS, WALDECK VIEIRA, Brazilian government official. Minister social security Govt. of Brazil, Brasilia, 1998—. Office: Ministry Social Security, Espl Ministerios Bloco f, 8 andar Brazilia 70059900, Brazil*

ORNER, LINDA PRICE, family therapist; b. Gettysburg, Pa., June 27, 1943; d. John Robert and Ruby Pearl (Vines) Price; m. Ted Arnold Orner, Mar. 29, 1963; children: Penni Ann, Jennifer Lynne. AA, North Harris Coll., 1991; BA summa cum laude, U. St. Thomas, 1994; MEd in Counseling Psychology, U. Houston, 1997, postgrad.; MA in Family Therapy, U. Houston-Clear Lake, 1998. Therapist Houston VA Hosp./Trauma Recovery Program, 1996, U. Houston Counseling and Testing Svcs., 1997, U. Houston-Clear Lake Psychol. Svcs., 1998-99; intern/assoc., family therapist Houston Galveston Inst., 1998—. Vol. Women's Ctr.; vol. seminar instr., counselor Tex. Prison; keynote spkr. Christian Women's Clubs Internat., Cmty. Bible Study Internat. Mem. ACA, Am. Assn. for Marriage and Family Therapy, Tex. Assn. for Marriage and Family Therapy, Houston Assn. for Marriage and Family Therapy, Am. Psychol. Assn. of Grad. Students, Tex. Counseling Assn., Am. Psychotherapy Assn., Am. Assn. of Christian Counselors, Houston Psychol. Assn. Presbyterian. Avocations: travel, scuba diving, hiking, antiques, art. Home: 4684 Stone Manor Hts Colorado Springs CO 80906-8605

ORNISH, DEAN, medical educator, administrator. MD, Baylor Coll. Medicine. Resident in internal medicine Mass. Gen. Hosp., Boston, 1981-84; clin. fellow in medicine Harvard Med. Sch., 1981-84; clin. prof. medicine U. Calif., San Francisco, 1984—, co-founder Osher Ctr. Integrative Medicine, 1998; founder, pres. Preventive Medicine Rsch. Inst., Sausalito, Calif., 1984—; also bd. dirs.; physician cons. to Pres. Bill Clinton, U.S. Congress, others; U.S. bd. dirs. UN High Commn. on Refugees. Author: 5 books including Dr. Dean Ornish's Program for Reversing Heart Disease, 1990, Eat More, Weigh Less, 1993, Love & Survival: The Scientific Basis for the Healing Power of Intimacy, 1998; contbr. numerous articles to profl. jours. Recipient Outstanding Young Alumnus award U. Tex., 1994, U.S. Army Surgeon Gen. medal, Beckmann medal German Soc. Prevention and Rehab. Cardiovascular Diseases, 1996. Mem. Calif. Acad. Medicine. Fax: 415-332-5730. E-mail: deanornish@aol.com. Office: Preventive Med Rsch Inst 900 Bridgeway Ste 1 Sausalito CA 94965-2100

ORNOY, ASHER, pediatrician, researcher; b. Daraban, Romania, June 19, 1941; arrived in Israel, 1950; s. Shalom and Eti Ornstein; m. Amira Ben-Arzi, July 7, 1963; 4 children. MD, Hebrew U., Jerusalem, 1968. Intern Hadassah Hosp., Jerusalem, 1966-67, resident in pediat., 1970-72, 79-81; instr. in anatomy Hebrew U., Jerusalem, 1968, sr. lectr. Hadassah Med. Sch., 1972-76, assoc. prof. anatomy Hadassah Med. Sch., 1976-79, prof. anatomy, embryology, & teratology, 1979, chmn. dept. anatomy & embryology, 1975-80, 87-90, dir. lab. teratology dept. anatomy & embryology, 1980—, vice dean Hadassah Med. Sch., 1990-92, asst. to dean Hadassah Med. Sch., 1992-96, chmn Diabetes Rsch. Ctr./Hadassah Med. Sch., 1993-99; head child devel. and rehab. Israeli Ministry Health, 1996—; dir. Jerusalem Child and Family Devel. Ctr., 1980-97; cons. UNICEF, 1984-87; vis. prof. UCLA, 1982, Jefferson Med. Coll., Phila., 1987, U. Calif., San Francisco, 1992. Contbr. 175 articles to profl. jours. Major Israeli Med. Corps, 1968-70. Mem. European Network Teratogen Info. (pres. 1999—), Teratology Soc., European Teratology Soc. (mem. coun. 1998-00). Avocations: music, sports. E-mail: ornoy@cc.huji.ac.il. Home: 9 Burla St, 93714 Jerusalem Israel Office: Hebre U, Hadassah Med Sch, 91120 Jerusalem Israel

ORNSTEIN, SHEILA WALBE, architect, educator; b. Sao Paulo, Brazil, Dec. 31, 1954; d. Jonel and Bella (Walbe) O. Degree in architecture/urban planning, U. Sao Paulo, 1978, PhD, 1988. Prof., vice dean Sch. Architecture and Urban Planning U. Sao Paulo, 1998—. Mem. Environ. Design Rsch. Assn., Nat. Assn. Built Environment. Office: Rua do Lago 876, Cidade Universitaria, 05508900 São Paulo Brazil

ORO, FELISA PANAL, education supervisor; b. Maasin, The Philippines, Apr. 23, 1918; d. Alberto L. and Restituta Saludo P.; m. Braulio Kangleon (dec.). BEd, ETC, Cebu Normal Sch., 1940; BSSE, U. Visayas, Cebu City, The Philippines, 1949; MA, U. Visayas, 1985, LLB magna cum laude, 1960. Emergency tchr., 1938-39, critic tchr., 1941, supr. instrn. elem. and high sch., 1949-51, supr. instrn. coll., 1960, supr. interns, 1965-72, 96—, dean coll. commerce, 1972-76; v.p. adminstrn. U. Visayas, 1994-96, adminstrv. officer Grad. Sch.,, 1996-98, acad. cons., 1998—. Home: Bacayo Guadalupe, M Veloso St, Cebu City 6000, The Philippines

ORO, ROBERT JOHN, dentist, consultant, writer; b. Bklyn., Apr. 22, 1952; s. Philip Edward and Marie Catherine (Bruno) O.; m. Debra Ann Haas, June 17, 1979; children: Philip, Anna. BS in Econs. with honors, SUNY, Queens, 1974; DMD, U. Pa., 1979; Fellow, Acad. Gen. Dentistry, 1985, Master, 1988. Lic. dentist, N.Y., Ariz. Founder, dentist Free Dental Clinic, Guadalajara, Mex., 1976; jr. resident Brookdale Hosp. and Med. Ctr., Bklyn., 1979-80, sr. resident, 1980-81; pres., CEO Hudson Valley Dental Medicine, Cortlandt Manor, N.Y., 1981-96, Penn Dental Consultanta, Cortlandt Manor, N.Y., 1996; v.p. Oro-Dontics, Inc., Oro Valley, Ariz., 1996—; CEO On Valley Denta Medicine, Ariz., 1998—; clin. instr. Brookdale Hosp. Med. Ctr., 1981-84; attending Hudson Valley Hosp. Ctr., 1981-96; officer Peekskill (N.Y.)-Yorktown Dental Soc., 1984-87, pres., 1988; co-founder, v.p. Dentistry as Children's Advocates. Author: How to Choose Your Dentist: Confessions of an Adrenaline Addict, 1997. Active health fairs/fundraisers Hudson Valley Hosp., 1981-96; fundraiser Casa del los Ninos, Tucson, 1996, 97, St. Elizabeth's of Hungary, Tucson, 1996, 97; active health fairs Tucson Pks. and Recreation, 1997. Named Mr. Congeniality, Mrs. Ariz./USA Pagent, 1997; cited as one of four top clinicians Acad. Gen. Dentistry Ann. Meeting, 1997. Mem. ADA, Ariz. Dental Assn., N.Y. State Dental Soc., Pima County Dental Study Club, Peekskill Yorktown Dental Soc. (pres. 1981-96), Delta Omicron. Avocations: writing, sports, hiking, playing with my children. Office: Oro-Dontics Inc 991 W Wheatgrass Pl Tucson AZ 85737-8654

ORON, MOSHE B., physicist; b. Pamagusta, Cyprus, June 21, 1948; arrived in Israel, 1949; s. Haim and Gittel (Beck) Orlinski; m. Esther Brener, Aug. 8, 1972; children: Efrat, Yoav, Shaul. BS, Tel Aviv U., 1972, MS, 1974, PhD, 1981. Tech. staff mem. AT&T Bell Labs., Holmdel, N.J., 1981-83; rschr. Soreq Nuclear Rsch. Ctr., Yavne, Israel, 1983-89, project mgr., 1990-93, dept. head solid state phys., 1994-99; vis. scientist AT&T Labs., Holmdel, 1989-90; vis. prof. engring. Tel Aviv U., 1990-94. Contbr. articles to profl. jours. Mem. Israel Phys. Soc. (exec. coun. 1985-89), Israel Crystal Growth Soc. (exec. coun. 1990-94, treas., organizing com. 12th Internat. Conf.), Optical Soc. Am. Office: Soreq NRC, SSP Dept, 81800 Yavne Israel

ORONA, ERNEST JOSEPH, real estate and construction company executive; b. Belen, N.Mex., Oct. 5, 1942; s. Joseph B. and Melinda (Sanchez) O.; m. Margaret M. Guinan, Aug. 22, 1964; children: Mary Melinda, Marie-Jeanne. BA in Latin Am. Affairs and Spanish, U. N.Mex., 1968. Vol. cmty.

devel. Peace Corps, Colombia, S.Am., 1962-64; instr. Peace Corps tng. U. Mo., Kansas City, summer 1964, Baylor U., Waco, Tex., summer 1965, also U. Ariz., N.Mex. State U., Las Cruces, 1966, U. N.Mex., Albuquerque, 1966; exec. dir. Mid-Rio Grande Cmty. Action Project, Los Lunas, N.Mex., 1965-66; cmty. devel. cons. Ctr. for Cmty. Action Svcs., Albuquerque, 1967-68; project dir. Peace Corps Tng. Ctr., San Diego State U., Escondido, Calif., 1968-70; propr., developer GO Realty and Constrn. Co., Albuquerque, 1970—; pres. La Zarzuela de Albuquerque, Benchmark Real Estate Investment Inc. Mem. Albuquerque Sister Cities; trustee N.Mex. Performing Arts Ctr. Mem. Nat. Bd. Realtors, Albuquerque Bd. Realtors, Albuquerque C. of C., Albuquerque Com. on Fgn. Rels. Roman Catholic. Home: 733 Valverde Dr SE Albuquerque NM 87108-3467 Office: GO Realty & Constrn Co 2034 2nd St NW Albuquerque NM 87102-1043 also: Benchmark Real Estate Inv Albuquerque Profl Bldg 909 Virginia St NE Ste 103 Albuquerque NM 87108-2578

O'RORKE, JAMES FRANCIS, JR., lawyer; b. N.Y.C., Dec. 4, 1936; s. James Francis and Helen (Weber) O'R.; m. Carla Phelps, Aug. 6, 1964. A.B., Princeton U., 1958; J.D., Yale U., 1961. Bar: N.Y. 1962. Assoc. Davies, Hardy & Schenck, 1962-69; ptnr. Davies, Hardy, Ives & Lawther, 1969-72, Skadden, Arps, Slate, Meagher & Flom, N.Y.C., 1972—; dir. Clinipad Corp.; mem. adv. bd. Chgo. Title Ins. Co. N.Y. Trustee Mus. Am. Indian-Heye Found., 1977-80; dir. James Lenox House Assn., Inc. Mem. ABA, N.Y. State Bar Assn., Assn. Bar City N.Y., Am. Coll. Real Estate Lawyers, Princeton Club N.Y.C. Office: Skadden Arps Slate Meagher & Flom 4 Times Sq Fl 24 New York NY 10036-6595 Address: C/O Skadden Apts 4 Times Sq Rm 44200 New York NY 10036-6522

OROS, GYULA, biologist, researcher; b. Csorna, Hungary, Aug. 17, 1946; s. László and Valéria (Makkos) O. BS, Gorky U., Charkow, Ukraine, 1969; MS in Plant Physiology, Eötvös U., Budapest, Hungary, 1973; PhD in Phytopharmacology, Hungarian Acad. Sci., Budapest, 1991. Assoc. rsch. biologist dept. plant pathophysiology Plant Protection Inst., Budapest, 1969-71, rsch. biologist biochemistry, 1972-77; vis. rsch. fellow dept. pesticide and plant chemistry Plant Protection Inst., Havana, Cuba, 1977-78; rsch. biologist dept. biochemistry Plant Protection Inst., Budapest, 1979-88, sr. rsch. biologist dept. herbology and toxicology, 1988—; assoc. prof. dept. microbiology Atrl. U., Gödöllő, Hungary, 1991. Contbr. numerous articles to profl. jours.; patentee in field. Recipient Emininent Worker of Plant Protection award Ministry of Agr., Cuba, 1977, Eminent Inventor award Hungarian Patent Office, 1987. Mem. Internat. Biometric Soc., N.Y. Acad. Scis. Office: Plant Protection Inst, Herman Ottó ut 15, 1022 Budapest Hungary

OROSA, MARILY YSIP, book publisher, graphic designer; b. Manila, The Philippines, May 26; d. Bonifacio Ortiz Luis Jr. and Maria Luisa V. (Villanueva) Ysip; m. Jesus Hemedes Hernandez, Sept. 2, 1967 (dec. Nov. 1987); children: Jerome, Justin, Bonifacio, Christopher, Maria Carmela; m. Jose De Santos Orosa, Dec. 21, 1993. AB, Maryknoll Coll., The Philippines, 1968. Pub. Studio 5 Pubs., Manila. Books pub. include: Philippines 2000: A Vision for the Nation, 1994, In Excelsis (The Mission of Dr. Jose R. Rizal), 1996, The Tragedy of the Revolution, 1997, Visions of the Possible, 1998, Dynamic Partnership, 1998, The Millennium President, 1999. Bd. dirs. Maryknoll Found., 1992—; v.p. Women for Bus., 1996—; dir. Med. Ambassadors, 1992—; mem. Women for Women, Women's Bus. Coun. Recipient Gold award for hotel collateral design Philippine Ad Congress, 1985, Excellence award for calendar design, 1987, 89, Nat. Book award of excellence, 1996, 97, 98, Anvil award of excellence, 1999. Mem. Zonta Internat. (Dist. 17 pres. 1992-94, chmn. 1994-96, area coord. 1994-96, dir. 1996—). Avocations: writing, gardening, reading. Fax: (632) 890-9345. E-mail: studio5@info.com.ph. Office: Studio 5 Publishing Inc, 28 Paseo de Roxas, Makati Manila, The Philippines

OROSEL, GERHARD OSKAR, economics educator; b. Vienna, Austria, July 31, 1946; s. Egon Walter and Auguste (Studnicka) O.; m. Renate Taubenbeck, July 30, 1971 (div. 1979); children: Christian, Stefan. JD, U. Vienna, 1970, Habilitation in Econ. Theory, 1974. Asst. Inst. Advanced Studies, Vienna, 1971; asst. dept. econs. U. Vienna, 1971-74, prof. econs., 1977—; wissenschaftlicher rat and prof. econs. U. Bonn, Fed. Republic Germany, 1974-77; vis. scholar NYU, 1984, U. Calif., San Diego, 1987-88, dean of the sch. of social and econ. scis., 1989-91; acad. vis. London Sch. Econs., 1993; vis. scholar U. Boston, 1996-97, Harvard U., 1999-2000; vis. prof. Ctr. Econ. Studies, Munich, 1995. Mem. Amnesty Internat., 1975—. Mem. Am. Econs. Assn., Theoretischer Ausschuss des Vereins für Socialpolitik, Nationalökonomische Gesellschaft, European Econ. Assn., Econ. Soc. E-mail: gerhard.orosel@univie.ac.at. Home: Neubauguertel 4/17, A-1070 Vienna Austria Office: U Vienna Dept Econs, Hohenstaufeng 9, A-1010 Vienna Austria

OROSZ, FERENC, biochemist; b. Hatvan, Hungary, Jan. 1, 1958; s. Ferenc Tibor and Ida (Dobrossy) O.; m. Valeria Julianna Lenkei, Aug. 31, 1991; children: Áron, Ferenc. MS, Eötvös Lorand U., 1982, PhD, 1990; PhD, Inst. of Enzymology, 1989. Rsch. scientist Inst. Enzymology, Budapest, Hungary, 1982-91, sr. scientist, 1993—; rsch. scientist U. La Sapienza, Rome, 1988-89, U. Calif., Riverside, 1992-93; vis. prof. U. Barcelona, 1999; mem. Coun. of Rsch. Insts., Budapest, 1990-94. Co-author: From Metabolite, to Metabolism, to Metabolon, 1992, Channelling in Intermediary Metabolism, 1996; contbr. articles to profl. jours.; patentee in field. Mem. regional presidium FIDESz-Hungarian Civic Party, Budapest, 1991-92, Dunakeszi, 1996—. Recipient Jr. prize Hungarian Acad. of Scis., 1987, prize Qualitas Biologica, 1997. Mem. Raoul Wallenberg Assn. (mem. presidium 1989-90, 95-2000), Internat. Raoul Wallenberg Found., Hungarian Chem. Soc., Hungarian Biochem. Soc., N.Y. Acad. of Scis, Hungarian Biol. Soc. Avocations: sports, music, politics. Home: Stromfeld Aurel 14, H-2120 Dunakeszi Hungary Office: Inst of Enzymology, Hungarian Acad Scis Karolina 29, H-1113 Budapest Hungary

OROSZ, GYÖRGY, chemist; b. Békéscsaba, Hungary, Aug. 26, 1958; s. György and Maria (Balaj) O.; m. Valéria Oroszné Gombos; children: Gergely, Balint. MSc, Eötvös U., 1982, PhD, 1989. Rsch. chemist Crop Protection Ctr., Budapest, Hungary, 1982-90; postdoctoral rsch. assoc. U. Kans. Dept. of Chemistry, Lawrence, 1990-92; rsch. fellow Eötuös Univ., Budapest, 1992-93, sr. rsch. fellow, 1994—. Editor, author: Organic Laboratory Textbook, 1998; contbr. articles to profl. jours.; patentee in field. Home: 5 Mogyorodi ut, H-1143 Budapest Hungary Office: Dept Organic Chemistry, Eotvos U PO Box 32, H-1518 Budapest Hungary

O'ROURKE, JAMES LOUIS, lawyer; b. Bridgeport, Conn., July 5, 1958; s. James G. and Margaret Elizabeth (Fesco) O'R.; m. Margaret C. DiCicco, Sept. 18, 1994. BS, U. Bridgeport, 1984, JD, 1987. Bar: Conn. 1988, U.S. Dist. Ct. Conn. 1989, Mashantucket Pequot Tribal Bar 1995, Supreme Ct. of U.S., 1998. Pvt. practice Stratford, Conn., 1987—. With USN, 1976-79. Mem. ABA, Assn. Am. Trial Lawyers Assn., Conn. Trial Lawyers Assn., Conn. Bar Assn., Greater Bridgeport Bar Assn. Roman Catholic. Avocations: boating, cycling, swimming, golf. Office: The Barnum Profl Bldg 1825 Barnum Ave Stratford CT 06614-5333

O'ROURKE, JOAN B. DOTY WERTHMAN, educational administrator; b. N.Y.C., June 7, 1933; d. George E. Doty and Lillian G. Bergen; 10 children, 8 stepchildren. BA summa cum laude, Marymount Manhattan Coll., 1953; MA, Columbia U., 1958; PhD, St. John's U., 1971. Tchr. History Marymount High Sch., N.Y.C., 1953-55; hist. instr. Marymount Manhattan Coll., 1957-59; acting chmn. hist. dept. Nassau Community Coll., Mineola, N.Y., 1959-60; prof. history Westchester Community Coll., Valhalla, N.Y., 1963-74; prin. Pius X Sch., Scarsdale, N.Y., 1974-77; assoc. dir. alumni relations Fordham U., N.Y.C., 1980-84; co-founder, dir. Assn. for Profl. Psychol. and Ednl. Counseling, Wilmette, Ill., 1987-91; ptnr., pres. O'Rourke and Assocs., 1993-97; ret., 1997; dir., writer Sta. WFAS Radio, White Plains, 1963-64; adj. prof. social sci. Fordham U., 1974-76. Teaching fellow St. John's U., Jamaica, N.Y., 1968; recipient Alumni award Marymount Coll., 1987-88. Mem. Soc. Mayflowers Descs. Ill., Michigan Shores Club. Democrat. Roman Catholic.

O'ROURKE, MARY, public representative; b. Athlone, Ireland, 1937. Student, U. Coll., Dublin, Maynooth Coll. Sen. Dublin, 1981-82; front bench spokesperson Dept. Edn., 1982-87, min. for edn., 1987-91; min. for Health, 1991-92; min. Trade & Mktg., 1992-93, Labor Affairs, 1993-94; front bench spokesperson Dept. Enterprise & Employment, 1995-97; min. Pub. Enterprise, Dublin, 1997—. Office: Dept Pub Enterprise, 44 Kildare St, Dublin 2, Ireland

O'ROURKE, VINCENT JOHN, management consultant; b. Longreach, Queensland, Australia, Dec. 26, 1940; s. Patrick Frederick and Ellen Veronica (Doherty) O'R.; m. Margaret Mary Clarke, Dec. 6, 1966; children: Maree Therese, Megan Anne, Anne Louise. BA, U. Queensland, 1968, B in Econs., 1973, BA with honors, 1976, MLit Studies, 1981; BA, U. Villanova, 1962; MA, St. Mary's U., San Antonio, Tex., 1991. Secondary sch. tchr., 1966-72; rsch. officer Dept. Edn., 1973-76; planning officer Brisbane Cath. Edn. Office, Queensland, 1977-83, dir., 1983-98; mng. dir. V.J. O'Rourke Consulting Svcs. Pty. Ltd., Queensland, 1998—; cons. Cath. Inst. Edn., South Africa, 1994, 97, Cath. Edn., Zimbabwe, 1997; advisor Min. Edn., Rep. of Ireland, 1997, Sarasas Sch. Bangkok, Commn. for Sch. Accommodation, Rep. of Ireland, 1997; presenter at numerous internat. confs. Melbourne and South Africa. Bd. govs. So. Cross Cath. Coll. Fellow Australian Inst. Mgmt.; Australian Coll. Edn., Queensland Inst. for Ednl. Adminstrn., Australian Coun. for Ednl. Adminstrn., Commonwealth Coun. for Ednl. Adminstrn. Home: 33 Devon St, Annerley QLD 4103, Australia Office: VJ O'Rourke Consulting, PO Box 1, Annerley QLD 4103, Australia

ORPEN, ANTHONY GUY, chemistry educator; b. Pointe-a-Pierre, Trinidad and Tobago, Oct. 5, 1955; arrived in Eng., 1960; s. Christopher Martin Willson and Shirley (Esselen) O.; m. Carolyn Louise Pooler, July 14, 1984. BSc, U. Cape Town, South Africa, 1975; PhD, U. Cambridge, Eng., 1979. Univ. lectr. U. Bristol, Eng., 1979-90, univ. reader, 1990-94, prof., 1994—. Contbr. articles to profl. jours. Mem. Royal Soc. Chemistry (Meldola medal and prize 1983, Corday Morgan medal and prize 1989, Tilden lectr. 1999-2000), Am. Chem. Soc., British Cystallographic Assn. Avocations: sports, Italian, football. Office: Univ of Bristol, Sch Chemistry, Bristol BS8 ITS, England

ORPEN, CHRISTOPHER EDWARD, management educator; b. Cape Town, South Africa, Sept. 14, 1942; s. Terence and Mary (Cronin) O.; m. Anna Judith Coles, June 28, 1975; children: Katherine, James, Timothy. BA, Rhodes U., Cape Town, 1963; BA with honors, Natal (South Africa) U., 1964; MA, U. Cape Town, 1986, PhD, 1990. Mktg. analyst South African Mutual Life, Cape Town, 1965-70; lectr. U. Cape Town, 1970-75; prof., head dept. U. Witwatersrand, South Africa, 1975-80; prof., dep. dean Deakin U., Australia, 1980-90; reader in mgmt. Bournemouth U., Eng., 1990—; vis. prof. U. Tenn., Knoxville, 1987; dir. Deakin U. Cons. Author: Productivity and Black Workers in South Africa, 1976, Principles of Personnel Psychology, 1978, Behavior in Work Organizations, 1980; editor Internat. Jour. Mgmt.; editl. bd. Psychology, Jour. of Human behavior, South african Jour. Bus. Mgmt.; contbr. numerous articles to profl. jours. Chrysler Corp. Internat. scholar, 1968, Johnson's Wax scholar, 1968, Rhodes U. scholar, 1961, others. Roman Catholic. Avocations: swimming, walking, golf, reading. Home: 141 Middelhill Rd, Wimbourne BH21 2HJ, England Office: Bournemouth Univ, Dept Mgmt, Bournemouth BH1 3LG, England

ORPEN, MICHAEL GERALD, farmer; b. Capetown, South Africa, Dec. 2, 1939; s. Neil Newton Darcy and Margaret Dorothy (Josephs) O.; m. Judy Bain Orpen, July 15, 1946; children: Rosemary, Neil Michael, Iain Michael. B in Comm., UCT, South Africa, 1960; P.R.E.P., U. South Africa, 1970. Commd. South Africa Active Citizens Army, 1962, advanced through grades to maj., 1967; sales mgr. WG Thompson Pry Ltd, Capetown, South Africa, 1970-72; mgr. Schus & Co., Capetown, South Africa, 1973-75; branch mgr. Murray & Stewart Homes, Belleville, South Africa, 1975-77; mgr. Syfrets Trust Real Estate, Belleville, South Africa, 1977-78; mng. dir. Hudlor Housing Ltd., Belleville, South Africa, 1979-82; exec. chmn. Sunter Solar Sys., Somerset West, South Africa, 1983-95; fruit and wine farmer, 1996—; exec. mem. Bldg. Industry Fedn. South Africa, 1975-80; found. exec. mem. Nat. Assn. Homebuilders South Africa, 1978-80; assoc. South Africa Inst. Bldg., 1980-95; trustee, executor several estate trusts. Patentee: Harmony Solar Water Heaters. Com. Roundtable, South Africa, 1976. Mem. C. of C., Master Builders Assn., Teerwaters Kloof Club, W.P. Sports Club. Mem. Anglican Ch. Avocations: fishing, hunting, genealogy. Office: Dawn Mountains Farm, PO Box 172, Simondium Capetown 7670, South Africa

ORPHANIDES, GUS GEORGE, research chemist; b. N.Y.C., Jan. 27, 1947; s. Gus G. and Savesta (Agapetus) O.; m. Jeanne Wood, Feb. 3, 1968; children: Alyson, Paul, Lindsay. BS with honors, Hobart Coll., 1967; PhD, Ohio State U., 1972. Chemist E.I. Du Pont de Nemours & Co., Wilmington, Del., 1974-79, Beaumont, Tex., 1979-81; chemist Air Products, Allentown, Pa., 1981-84, applications mgr., 1984-85, comml. mgr., 1985-88, rsch. mgr., 1988-91, sr. comml. devel. mgr., 1991-94, comml. devel. mgr., 1995-96, R&D mgr., 1996-98, global tech. svc. mgr., 1998—. Contbr. articles to profl. publs.; patentee in field; developed new polymers for adhesives, non-wovens, paper coatings, polyurethane elastomers, rubber cross-linking. Phys. rehab. hosp. vol. in occupl. therapy. 1st lt. U.S. Army, 1972-74. Decorated Army Commendation medal; recipient Army Cert. of Achievment, Raker Meml. award Good Shepherd Hosp.; N.Y. State Regents scholar, 1963-67. Mem. Am. Chem. Soc. Republican. Presbyterian. Achievements include development of novel emulsion polymers and polymer intermediates, international technology transfer, technology licensing, lab-to-plant technology transfer, plant start-up, commercialized new products. Avocations: traveling, classical music, crossword puzzles, reading. Home: 4046 Providence Ct Schnecksville PA 18078-3524 Office: Air Products 7201 Hamilton Blvd Allentown PA 18195-1526

ORPHANIDES, NORA CHARLOTTE, ballet educator; b. N.Y.C., June 4, 1951; d. M.T. and Mary Elsie (Tilly) Feffer; m. James Mark Orphanides, July 1, 1972; children: Mark, Elaine, Jennine. BA, CUNY, 1973; student, Joffrey Ballet Sch., N.Y.C., 1970-75; postgrad., Princeton Ballet Sch., 1976-86. Cert. speech and hearing handicapped tchr. With membership dept. M.M.A., N.Y.C., 1987—; mem. faculty Princeton (N.J.) Ballet Sch., 1983—, trustee emeritus, 1992—. Mem. cast Princeton Ballet ann. Nutcracker, 1985-90, now Am. Repertory Ballet Co., 1993—; appeared in Romeo & Juliet, 1995-96, 2000. Fundraising gala chmn. Princeton Ballet, 1985, 86, 91-92, chmn. spl. events, 1987—, trustee, 1986—, chmn. Nutcracker benefit, 1990—, Dracula benefit, 1991, honoree, 1999; dept. chmn. June Fete to benefit Princeton Hosp., 1988, 90-91, 92, 96, 2000; vol. Nat. Hdqrs. Recording for the Blind, 1991-93; dinner chmn. Nassau Ch. Music Festival, 1992, Handel Festival, Nassau Ch., 1993, Princeton Chamber Symphony, 1993; hon. chmn. Princeton Ballet Gala, 1993; chmn. Christmas Boutique, Princeton Med. Ctr., 1993; trustee, Princeton Med. Ctr. Aux. Bd., 1992—, trustee 1995—, pres., 1997-99, past pres., 2000—; choreographer Stuart Country Day Sch., Princeton, 1996-99; chmn. benefit dinner Eden Inst., 2000. Named honoree Princeton Ballet, 1999. Democrat. Avocations: piano, skiing, tennis. Office: 301 N Harrison St Princeton NJ 08540-3512

ORR, CAROLE, artist; b. Alexandria, Ind., June 10, 1933; d. Carl Victor and Marian Martha (Long) Coonse; m. Larry D. Ribble (dec. July 1953); m. Thomas LeRoy Orr, Nov. 10, 1950 (div. Oct. 1979); children: Karen Sue, Terri Ribble, David Thomas; m. Lev C. Hamblet Jr., Feb. 5, 1982 (div. Oct. 1998); stepchildren: James, Jean, Laura, Anne. Cert., Famous Artist Sch., Westport, Conn., 1956, Art Instrn. Schs., Mpls., 1962. Asst. art dir. La Gallerie du Mall, Houston, 1975-78; freelance fine artist Lantern Ln. Gallery, Houston, 1968-81, asst. mgr., design cons., 1979-81; artist Artist Showroom, Houston, 1982—; participating artist Assistance Guild, Houston, 1968, Beaux Arts, Houston, 1968-70, Houston Gamma Phi Gallery, 1971-72, Houston Delta Gamma Found., 1978-81, Glassell Sch. of Art Houston, 1983; art instr. children's art Houston Park and Recreational Programs, 1964-68. One-woman shows include Nobler Gallery, Houston, 1967, Art Gallery, Pasadena, Tex., 1968, Gallarie La Rue, Austin, Tex., 1971, Gallery 12, Houston, 1972, Main St., Houston, 1974, La Galerie de Mall, Houston, 1976-78, Triumvirate Gallery, Santa Fe, N.Mex., 1980, Houshang's Gallery, Dallas, 1980-82, Battle Horn Galleries Ltd., Santa Fe, 1984, New Trends Inc., Santa Fe, 1985-88, Horizons Galleries, Houston, 1990-93, Houston C.C., 1992, Heinen Theatre, 1992, Windsor Gallery, Ft. Lauderdale, Fla., 1994; exhibited in group shows at Motorola Invitational, Houston, 1964, Assistance Guild Houston, 1968, Am. Gen. Bldg., Houston, 1968, Beaux Arts, Houston, 1968-70, Gamma Phi Gallery, Houston, 1971-72, Lantern Ln. Gallery, Houston, 1971-72, Delta Gamma Found., Houston, 1978-81, Glassell Sch. Art, Houston, 1983, New Trends Gallery Inc., Santa Fe, N.mex., 1985-88, Pasadena (Tex.) Art Invitational, 1988, Double Tree Hotel, Houston, 1990, Horizons Gallery, Houston, 1990-93, Windsors Gallery, Dania, fla., 1993. Art instr. adults Ch. of the Advent, Houston, 1968-70; adult edn. instr. arts Ch. Sch. Conf., Dept. Christian Edn., Trinity Ch., Diocese of Tex., Houston, 1969. Recipient Profl. Best Ann. Competition Art Instrn. Schs., Mpls., 1965. Avocations: self-study in psychology, music, dance. Home and Studio: Artist Showroom DBA 880 Tully Rd Apt 29 Houston TX 77079-5418

ORR, JOSEPH ALEXANDER, educational administrator; b. West Palm Beach, Fla., Nov. 20, 1929; s. Joseph Alexander and Eula (Terry) O.; m. Ardis W. Orr (div.); children: Eric, Pamela, Tracey; m. Linda F. Orr. BS, Fla. A&M U., 1951; MS, Mich. State U., 1953; MEd, Fla. Atlantic U., 1965; PhD, Fla. State U., 1972. Sci. tchr. Roosevelt Sr. H.S., West Palm Beach, Fla., 1953-68; counselor, coord. Adult Edn. Dept. Sch. Sys., Palm Beach County, Fla., 1960-72; dean of students Palm Beach H.S., West Palm Beach, 1968-70; asst. dean Fla. A&M U., Tallahassee, 1970-72; adj. prof. Ind. U., Bloomington, 1972-73; prin. Ctrl. Sr. H.S., Louisville, 1972-74, Jupiter (Fla.) H.S., 1974-78; adj. prof. Fla. Atlantic U., Boca Raton, 1978—; asst. supt. Palm Beach County (Fla.) Sch. Bd., 1978-84, assoc. supt., 1984-92; exec. dir. Palm Beach County Sch. Adminstrs. Assn., 1992—; chair State Adv. Bd. for Severely Emotionally Disturbed. Contbr. articles to profl. jours. Bd. dirs. Children's Home Soc. of Fla., Palm Beach County Coun. of Arts; past chair Health and Human Svcs. Bd., Palm Beach County, Fla., Inst. of New Dimensions, Palm Beach C.C., Assn. for Retarded Citizens, Inc., West Palm Beach; past pres. Scholastic Achievement Found. Palm Beach County. Recipient Disting. Svc. award NEA, Pioneer award for excellence in pub. svc. Nat. Forum of Pub. Adminstrn., Outstanding Achievement award Fla. Assn. Cmty. Educators, Four Seasons award Nat. Assn. for Year Round Edn. Mem. ASCD, Fla. Assn. Sch. Adminstrs., Am. Assn. Sch. Adminstrs., Nat. Assn. Secondary Sch. Prins., Nat. Cmty. Edn. Assn. (Sch. Leadership award), Kiwanis Internat. Democrat. Episcopalian. Avocation: boating. Office: Palm Beach County Sch Adminstrs Assn PO Box 31511 Palm Bch Gdns FL 33420-1511

ORR, KEVIN BRIDSON, surgeon, educator; b. Balmain, Sydney, Australia, July 17, 1927; s. Clarence Montague and Vera Ruth (Bridson) O.; m. Shirley Hope Frost, Dec. 16, 1950; children: Sandra Carol, Karen Elizabeth, Diane Margaret, Stuart Kelvin Ross, Iain Phillip Angus. MB, BS, U. Sydney, 1950. Registered med. practitioner, U.K. and NSW. Resident med. officer Grafton Base Hosp., NSW, 1950-51; surg. registrar Red Hill County Hosp., Surrey, Eng., 1954-56, Essex County Hosp., Colchester, Eng., 1956-58; surg. tutor U. Sydney, NSW, 1963-69, U. NSW, Sydney, 1969—; vis. med. officer St. George Hosp., Sydney, 1963—, sec. planning com. med. staff coun., 1965-70, sec. dept. surgery, 1965-75, chmn. med. staff coun., 1983-85, chmn. dept. gastrointestinal surgery, 1992-96. Contbr. numerous articles to med. jours. Fellow ACS, Royal Coll. Surgeons Eng., Royal Australasian Coll. Surgeons; mem. Australian Med. Assn. Presbyterian. Avocations: music, bushwalking, photography, golf, theological science. Home: 42 Castle St, Blakehurst NSW 2221, Australia Office: 22 Belgrave St, Kogarah 2217 NSW, Australia

ORR, ROBIN KEMSLEY, composer, emeritus educator; b. Brechin, Scotland, June 2, 1909; s. Robert Workman and Florence Mary (Kemsley) O.; m. Margaret Ellen Mace, Dec. 29, 1937 (div. 1979); children: Alison, David, Jean (dec.); m. Doris Ruth Winny-Meyer, July 14, 1979. Student, Royal Coll. Music, London, 1926-29; MusB, BA, Cambridge U., 1932; studied with Casella, Italy, 1934; MA, Cambridge U., 1938; studies with Boulanger, France, 1938; MusD, Cambridge U., 1949; DMus (hon.), U. Glasgow, Scotland, 1972; LLD (hon.), U. Dundee, Scotland, 1976. Asst. lectr. U. Leeds, Eng., 1936-38; organist, dir. music St. John's Coll., Cambridge U., 1938-51; prof. Royal Coll. Music, London, 1950-56; lectr. U. Cambridge, 1947-56; The prof. of music U. Glasgow, 1956-65; The prof. of music U. Cambridge, 1965-76, emeritus, 1976—; chmn. Scottish Opera, Glasgow, 1962-76; bd. dirs./trustee Arts Theatre, Cambridge, 1965-76; bd. dirs. Welsh Nat. Opera, Cardiff, 1977-83. Composer: (operas) Full circle, 1967, Hermiston, 1975, On the Razzle, 1987; composer 3 symphonies, also chamber music, ch. music, lyric pieces, others. Decorated Comdr. Brit. Empire; liveryman Musicians' Co., London; fellow St. John's Coll., Cambridge, 1948-56, 65-76, hon. fellow, 1987—, hon. fellow Pembroke Coll., Cambridge, 1988—. Fellow Royal Coll. Music, Royal Scottish Acad. of Music and Drama. Avocations: gardening, mountain walks. Home: 16 Cranmer Rd, Cambridge CB3 9BL, England

ORR, WENDY ANN, occupational therapist, writer; b. Edmonton, Alta., Can., Nov. 19, 1953; d. Anthony Malcolm and Elizabeth Ann (Jenkins) Burridge; m. Thomas Hugh Orr, Nov. 8, 1951; children: James Anthony, Susan Elizabeth. Diploma in Occupl. Therapy, London Sch. Occupl. Therapy, Melbourne, Australia, 1976. Occupational therapist Murray Regional Health Ctr., Albury, Australia, 1976-80, Lang. and Devel. Clinic, Shepparton, Australia, 1982-92; free-lance writer Cobram, Australia, 1978—. Author: Amanda's Dinosaur, 1988, Ark in the Park, 1994 (Book of Yr. Jr. Readers Children's Book Coun. of Australia 1995), A Light in Space, 1994, Peeling the Onion, 1996 (Honour book for Older Readers Children's Book Coun. of Australia 1997, ALA Best Books award 1998, N.Y. Pub. Libr. Book for Teenager award 1998), Arabella, 1998, Nim's Island, 1999. Mem. Australian Soc. Authors, Children's Book Coun. of Australia. Avocations: reading, travel, walking, pets. Home: 401 Arthur's Seat Rd, Red Hill VIC 3937, Australia

ORROM, WILLIAM JOHN, surgeon; b. London, Jan. 19, 1955; s. Vernon John and Moan May (Thompson) O.; m. Irene Roseychuk, Dec. 8, 1984. MD, Queens U., Kingston, Ont., Can., 1981; MSc, U. Alta., Edmonton, Can., 1987. Diplomate Am. Bd. Surger, Am. Bd. Colon and Rectal Surgeyr. Asst. prof. surgery U. Alta., 1990-98; cons. Oxford Clinic, Christchurch, New Zealand, 1998-99, Surg. Cons., Victoria, B.C., Can., 1999—. Contbr. articles to profl. jours., chpt. to book. Fellow ACS, Royal Coll. Physicians and Surgeons Can. (Detweiler scholar 1988); mem. Am. Soc. Colon and Rectal Surgeons. Office: 203-2020 Richmond Rd, Victoria, BC Canada V8R 6R5

ORSKOV, EGIL ROBERT, agriculturalist; b. Herning, Denmark, May 24, 1934; s. Anders and Maren (Poulsen) O.; m. Joan Pamela Scott, Sept. 30, 1967; three children. BSc, KLV Univ., Copenhagen, 1961; PhD, Reading U., U.K., 1965, DSc, 1975. Fgn. rsch. assoc. USDA, 1965-66; from head sheep sect. to dir. internat. feed resource Rowett Inst., Scotland, 1967—. Officer of Order of Brit. Empire. Fellow Royal Soc. of Edinburgh, Polish Acad. of Sci.; mem. Br. Soc. Animal Sci., Br. Nutritional Soc. Home: Craigie Park, Whitecairns AB23 8UN, Scotland

ORSZÁG-LAND, THOMAS ERVIN, poet; b. Budapest, Hungary, Jan. 12, 1938; arrived in Eng., 1962; s. Jenö Ország and Iren Hamburger; children: David James, Benjamin Peter. Student, Acadia U, Wolfville, Can. Self-employed writer. Fellow Internat. PEN; mem. Royal Inst. Internat. Affairs (London), Fgn. Press Assn. (London), Soc. Authors (London). Home: PO Box 1213, London N6 5HZ, England

ORTEGA Y ALAMINO, JAIME LUCAS CARDINAL, archbishop. Archbishop of San Cristóbal de Habana, Roman Cath. Ch., Cuba; elevated to cardinal Roman Cath. Ch., 1994—. Office: Calle Habana 152 esq a, Chacón, Apdo 594, Havana 10100, Cuba*

ORTEL, THOMAS LEE, oncologist, hematologist, educator; b. Greenfield, Ind., Aug. 27, 1957; s. Donald William and Shirley Radine (Abbott) O. BS with high distinction, Ind. U., 1979, PhD in Chemistry, 1983, MD, 1985. Diplomate Am. Bd. Internal Medicine, Hematology Subspeciality. Intern Duke U. Med. Ctr., Durham, N.C., 1985-86, resident, 1986-88, fellow in hematology and oncology, 1988-91, assoc. in medicine, 1991-93, asst. prof. medicine, 1993-98, med. dir. Clin. Coagulation Lab., 1994—, assoc. prof. medicine, 1999—, asst. prof. pathology, 1994—; med. dir. Platelet Antibody Lab., 1999—. Recipient Am. Heart Assn. Clinician Scientist award, 1991-96, Pew Scholar award, 1995-2000.

ORTH, PAUL WILLIAM, lawyer; b. Balt., May 7, 1930; s. Paul W. and Naomi (Howard Bevard) O.; m. Isle Haertle, June 15, 1956; children: Ingrid,

Ilse Christine. AB, Dartmouth Coll., 1951; JD, Harvard U., 1954. Bar: Mass. 1954, Conn. 1957, U.S. Dist. Ct. Conn. 1958, U.S. Ct. Appeals (2d cir.) 1960, U.S. Ct. Appeals (1st cir.) 1983, U.S. Supreme Ct. 1960. Assoc. Hoppin, Carey & Powell, Hartford, Conn., 1957-62, ptnr., 1962-86; ptnr. Shipman & Goodwin, Hartford, 1987—; instr. Sch. Law U. Conn., 1959-81. Editor: Every Employee's Guide to the Law, 1993, 96. Chmn. Farmington Conservation Commn., 1982-83; mem. town com. Town of Farmington, 1973-81; dir. Conn. Opera Assn., 2000—. With AUS, 1954-56. Fellow Am. Bar Found., Conn. Bar Found.; mem. ABA, Hartford County Bar Assn. (pres. 1983-84), Conn. Bar Assn. (chmn. coms.). Democrat. Office: Shipman & Goodwin LLP One American Row Hartford CT 06103

ORTHWEIN, WILLIAM COE, mechanical engineer; b. Toledo, Jan. 27, 1924; s. William Edward and Millie Minerva (Coe) O.; m. Helen Virginia Poindexter, Feb. 1, 1948; children—Karla Frances, Adele Diana, Maria Theresa. B.S., M.I.T., 1946; M.S., U. Mich., 1951, Ph.D., 1959. Registered profl. engr., Ill., Ind., Ky. Aerophysicist Gen. Dynamics Co., Ft. Worth, 1951-52; research asso. U. Mich., 1952-59; adv. engr. IBM Corp., Owego, N.Y., 1959-61; dir. computer centers U. Okla., Norman, 1961-63; research scientist Ames Lab., NASA, Moffett Field, Calif., 1963-65; mem. faculty So. Ill. U., Carbondale, 1965—; prof. engring. So. Ill. U., 1967—; cons. in field. Author: Clutches and Brakes, 1986, Machine Component Design, 1990; papers, revs., books in field. Pres. Jackson County (Ill.) Taxpayers Assn., 1976. Served with AUS, 1943-46. Mem. ASME (Outstanding Svc. award 1972), Am. Gear Mfrs. Assn., Am. Acad. Mechanis, Soc. Automotive Engrs., Ill. Acad. Sci., Ill. Soc. Profl. Engrs. (chmn. salary and employment com. 1974, chmn. ad hoc com. continuing edn. 1975), NRA, Aircraft Owners and Pilots Assn., Sigma Xi. Mem. LDS Ch. Home: 15091 Ford Rd Apt 602 Dearborn MI 48126-4648

ORTINAU, DAVID JOSEPH, marketing specialist, educator; b. Harvey, Ill., Dec. 14, 1948; s. Harold Raymond and Lois Agnice (Reich) O.; m. Shirley Keating, Aug. 15, 1975 (div. Nov. 1979); m. Renee Susan Hess, Apr. 30, 1983 (div. Aug. 1993). BS in Mgmt., So. Ill. U., 1970; MS in Bus. Adminstrn., Ill. State U., 1971; PhD in Mktg., La. State U., 1979. Sr. research analyst, dir. projects Rabin Research Co., Chgo., 1971-73; adminstrv. asst., instr. mktg. Coll. Bus., Ill. State U., Normal, 1973-76; grad. teaching assoc., instr. mktg. Coll. Bus., La. State U., Baton Rouge, 1976-79; from asst. prof. mktg. to assoc. prof. Coll. Bus., U. South Fla., Tampa, 1979-84, assoc. prof., 1984-95, prof., 1995—, coord. PhD program dept. mktg., 1989-91; dir. mktg. and rsch. Market Research Group, Tampa, 1980-83; v.p. mktg. Neaves, Neaves and Ortinau, Normal, 1974-77. Co-author: Marketing Research: A Practical Approach in the New Millennium, 2000; mem. editl. rev. bd. Jour. Acad. Mktg. Sci., 1989— (Disting. Merit award for Outstanding Reviewer 1992-93, 97-2000, Outstanding Jams Rev. 1997-2000), Jour. Bus. Rsch., 2000—; contbr. articles to Jour. Health Care Mktg., Jour. Mktg. Edn., Jour. Bus. Rsch., Jour. Svcs. Mktg., Jour. Acctg. Horizons, Jour. Retailing, others. Recipient Disting. Merit award Advt. Fedn. S.W. Fla., 1983, Coba Outstanding Rsch. award U. South Fla., 1987, Outstanding Tchg. award, 1980, 81, 82, 86, 90, 95. Mem. Am. Mktg. Assn. (doctoral consortium fellow 1978, reviewer 1982—), Assn. Consumer Rsch., So. Mktg. Assn. (reviewer 1975—, chmn. 1976—, sec. 1990-91, treas. 1992-95, pres. elect 1995-96, pres. 1996-97, chmn. Svcs. Mktg. Customer Satisfaction Track Program 1990-92, co-chair doctoral consortium 1998, 99, Outstanding Articles award 1981, 86, 87, 90, 92), Acad. Mktg. Sci. (reviewer 1988—, chmn. 1989, 92, Reviewer of Yr. 1992, session chair new tech. and retail store images at 1999 conf.), Acad. Bus. Adminstrn. (track program chmn. 1993), Soc. for Mktg. Advances (bd. dirs. 1998—, co-chair doctoral consortium 1998-99), Beta Gamma Sigma (pres. Fla. chpt. 1990-91). Avocations: all sports, reading, gardening, the arts. Research and consulting specializations focus on attitudinal, motivational, multivariate measurement and data analysis methods in areas of services marketing and quality, customer satisfaction and evaluation models, advertising, marketing education topics/issues, diffusion and diagnostic performance processes of product innovations, consumer services and interactive marketing techniques. Home: 2305 Windsor Oaks Ave Lutz FL 33549-5880 Office: U South Fla Mktg Dept Tampa FL 33620

ORTIZ, EDUARDO LEOPOLDO, mathematician, historian; b. Buenos Aires, Mar. 28, 1931; s. Ricardo M. and Leopoldina (Crespo) O.; m. Susana Ortiz; 1 child, Miguel Eduardo. Student, Coll. Nat. Belgrano, Buenos Aires, 1945-49, U. Nacional Buenos Aires, 1950-55. Sci. officer Commn. Atomic Energy, Buenos Aires, 1956-58; asst. prof. U. Buenos Aires, 1958-61; scholar Inst. for Advanced Studies, Dublin, Ireland, 1961-63; lectr. Imperial Coll., London, 1963-64; prof. U. Buenos Aires, 1964-66; prof., dept. head Univ. Nacional, Lima, Peru, 1966-68; head numerical analysis sect., co-dir. postgrad studies Imperial Coll., London, 1968—, full prof., 1986—, sr. rsch. fellow, 1997—; prof. emeritus U. London, 1997. Contbr. over 180 rsch. articles to profl. jours.; author, editor 12 books; editor Internat. Jour. Computers and Math., Applied Math. Letters, Mathesis, Bull. Hellenic Math. Soc., Abacus, Jour. Spanish Soc. History of Sci., The Humboldt Libr. (London). Fgn. fellow Nat. Acad. Sci., Argentina, 1988, Royal Acad. Sci., Spain, 1991, Nat. Acad. Sci., cordoba, Argentina, 2000, fellow Inst. Math. Gt. Britain, 1978; recipient J. Babini Nat. prize, Argentina, 1990, prof. de la lere class U. Orleans, 1992, Rouan, 1998, Guggenheim Rsch. fellow Harvard U., 1996-98, rsch. fellow MIT, 1998, Vietor Rsch. fellow Brown U., 1999, A. Mellon Rsch. fellow Am. Philosophical Soc., 2000. E-mail: e.ortiz@ic.ac.uk. Home: 115 Studdridge St, London SW6 3TD, England Office: Imperial Coll, 180 Queens Gate, London SW7 2BZ, England

ORTIZ, FERNANDO, JR., municipal budget official; b. Havana, Cuba, Dec. 2, 1951; came to the U.S., 1961; m. Frances K. Ortiz; children: William, Fernando III. Attended, Miami-Dade C.C., 1972-74, U. Miami, Coral Gables, Fla., 1974-75, Fla. Internat. U., Miami, 1975-76; MD, U. Centro Estudios Technicos, Santo Domingo, Dominican Republic, 1981; postgrad, Syracuse U., postgrad., 1998—. Mgr. Ortiz Transp., Miami, 1981-84; ptnr. Astrum, Syracuse, N.Y., 1984-91; bus. developer Rebuild Syracuse, Inc., 1991-92; coord. Urban Bus. Opportunity Ctr. City of Syracuse, 1992-96, sr. econ. devel. officer, 1996-2000, budget dir., 2000—; mem. adv. bd. Greater Syracuse Small Bus. Loan Program, 1993—; bd. dirs. Consol. Industries, Inc., Child Care coun. of Onondago County; mem. educare com. Success By Six, 2000. Sec. bd. dirs. Onondaga Spanish Action League, Syracuse, 1994-95, pres., 1996—; Cultural Resources Coun., 1997—; active Onondaga Citizens League, Syracuse, 1995, bd. dirs. Syracuse Neighborhood Housing Svcs.; corp. mem. United Way Ctrl. N.Y.; mem. Ctrl. N.Y. Childcare Coun., 2000—; mem. bus. and industry adv. bd. Onondaga C.C.; mem. Leadership Greater Syracuse Class of '93; bd. dirs. Metro. Water Bd., 1998—; active F.O.C.U.S. Greater Syracuse, 1997—. Named Min. Small Bus. Adv. of Yr., U.S. SBA, Syracuse, 1995. Mem. U.S. Assn. Small Bus. and Entrepreneurship. Avocations: reading, gardening, music. Home: 1412 Lemoyne Ave Syracuse NY 13208-1339 Office: City of Syracuse Office Econ Devel 221 City Hall Syracuse NY 13202

ORTIZ, FERNANDO, JR., film researcher, stage manager; b. N.Y.C., Mar. 28, 1965; s. Fernando and Helen Ortiz. BA in Comm., St. Francis Coll., Bklyn., 1988; MA in Liberal Studies, NYU, 1996. Asst. photo rschr./filer The Bettmann Archive, N.Y.C., 1985-88; rsch. asst. Fleishman-Hillard, Inc., N.Y.C., 1988-90; rsch. coord. NYU, 1990-95; patron rschr. Carnegie Hall, N.Y.C., 1996-98; asst. bldg. mgr. Columbia U., N.Y.C., 1998-99; stage mgr. various prodns., N.Y.C., 1998—; film rschr. Archive Films, N.Y.C., 1999—; casting asst. Casting Solutions, 2000—. Asst. stage mgr. Mutt Repp Prodns., N.Y.C., 1998, property master, mem. crew, 1998; asst. stage mgr. Infinite Prodns., N.Y.C., 1999; stage mgr. The Shakespeare Project, N.Y.C., 1999. Vol. Lower East Side Tenement Mus., N.Y.C., 1998—, Hartley Ho., N.Y.C., 1983-85. Mem. Actor's Equity Assn., Film Soc. of Lincoln Ctr., Ford Falcon Club of Am. Democrat. Roman Catholic. Avocations: writing, running, music, dance, photography.

ORTIZ, JOSÉ ARTURO, psychologist, researcher, educator; b. Mexico City, Mex., Nov. 17, 1954; s. Jose and Maria (Castro) O.; m. Susana Ortiz; children: Isabel, Marco. BD in Psychology, U. Iberoamericana, Mex., 1979; MD in Clin. Psychology, U. Nat. Autonoma de Mex., 1981; PhD in Psychoanalytical Psychology, U. Intercontinental Mex., 1986. Head Info. Ctr. on Drugs Mex. Inst. Psychiatry, 1986-96, head spl. rsch. dept., 1996—; titular rschr. B Ministry of Health, Mex., 1996—, titular rschr. A., 1989-96; mem. Nat. Sys. Rschrs., 1990—; supr., tng. analyst Inst. Clin. and Social Psychol. Rsch., Mex., 1987—; prof. U. Nuevo Mundo, 1996—; cons. Bicigato, Mexico City, 1996—; tutor mastery in pub. mental health Nat. Autonomous U. Mexico, 1999—. Author: Information Reporting System on Drugs, 1986—; editor: Aletheia (Jour. Psychology), 1987—; contbr. more than 100 articles to profl. jours. Advisor Renascence Found., Mexico City, 1998. Mem. Social and Clin. Rsch. Inst. (pres. 1997—, mem. acad. bd. 1987—, sec. 1985-87, founding mem. 1979). Avocation: road cycling. Office: Inst Mex de Psiquiatria, Calz Mexico-Xochimilco 101, 14370 Mexico City Mexico

ORTIZ, JUAREZ, medical diagnostic center director; b. Sao Paulo, Jan. 1, 1948; s. Julio and Lucrecia (Bagarelli) O.; divorced; children: Marcos, Sergio, Mariana. MD, Santos Faculty of Medicine, 1972; DSc, U. Sao Paulo, 1981. Chief echo lab Heart Inst., Sao Paulo, 1976-82; dir. Non Invasive Cardiology Ctr., Sao Paulo, 1976—; gen. dir. Omni Diagnostic Ctr., Sao Paulo, 1993—; chmn. sci. com. III World Congress Echocardiography and Vascular Ultrasound, 1998; pres. Brazilian Soc. Cardiology, 1999—. Author, editor: Semiologia Cardiologica Nao Invasiva, 1980; author: O Ecocardiograma, 1993, 2d edit., 1997; (with others) Comparative Approaches to Medical Reasoning, 1995; contbr. articles to profl. jours. Recipient Award of Honor Sao Paulo Police Dept., 1983, Award of Honor, Soc. Braz. Est. Mun., 2000. Mem. Brazilian Soc. Cardiology (pres. echo dept. 1987-91, dir. pubs. 1995), Internat. Soc. Cardiovascular Ultrasound (sci. com. 1993—, exec. bd. 1993—), N.Y. Acad. Scis., Brazilian Soc. Cardiology, Brazilian Med. Assn. Avocations: ocean fishing, scuba diving. Fax: 55(011)570-7851. Home: Apto 142, Alameda Dos Aicás 956, 04086002 São Paulo Brazil Office: Omni Servicos Diagnosticos, Rua Cubatao 726, 04013002 São Paulo Brazil

ORTIZ-CONDE, ADELMO ANTONIO, electrical engineering educator, researcher; b. Caracas, Venezuela, Nov. 28, 1956; s. Adelmo Antonio Ortiz and Alicia Cristina Conde. BS, U. Simon Bolivar, Caracas, 1979; M Engring., U. Fla., 1982, PhD, 1985. Mem. tech. staff AT&T Bell Labs., Reading, Pa., 1985-87; prof. elec. engring. U. Simon Bolivar, 1987—. Editor IEEE Internat. Caracas Conf. on Devices, mem. editl. adv. bd. Microelectronics and Reliability, 1995; contbr. articles to sci. jours., including IEEE Trans. on Electron Devices, IEEE Electron Devel. Letters, Solid State Electronics, IEE Circuit Devices and Sys., Jour. Applied Physics, Japanese Jour. Applied Physics, Electronics Letters, and Microelectronics and Reliability. Mem. IEEE (sr.), Internat. Caracas Conf. on Circuit Devices & Systems (gen. chmn. 1995—). Office: U Simon Bolivar, Dept Electronics Apdo 89000, Caracas 1080-A, Venezuela

ORTIZ DE ZARATE, JULIO CESAR, physician; b. Buenos Aires, Mar. 2, 1919; s. Raymundo Diego and Maria Dolores (Maraver) O.; m. Aurora Marta Rizzi, June 9, 1954; children: Maria Julieta, Cesar Octavio, Juan Raymundo Martin, Pedro Facundo. MD, U. Buenos Aires, 1943. Chief neurology svc. Hosp. Castex, Buenos Aires, 1956-78; chief neurol. sect. Policlinica Bancaria, Buenos Aires, 1978-82; chief neurol. svc. Hosp. Clinicas, Buenos Aires, 1980-82; prof. U. Salvador, Buenos Aires, 1957-85, U. Buenos Aires; dir. Hosp. M.R. Castex, San Martin, Buenos Aires, 1956-58; cons. prof. U. Buenos Aires, 1985—, U. Buenos Aires, 1985—. Contbr. chpts. to books and contbr. articles to profl. jours. Grantee Nat. Coun. of Investigations, 1965. Mem. Royal Soc. of Medicine, Deutsche Gessellschaft fur Neurologie, Am. Soc. of Human Genetics, Am. Acad. of Neurology, N.Y. Acad. Scis., Sociedad Neurologica Argentina. Avocations: history of medicine, artistic handycrafts. Home: Llerena 2558, 1427 Buenos Aires Argentina

ORTIZ-PULIDO, RAUL, ornithologist, researcher, educator; b. Xalapa, Mex., Jan. 22, 1969; s. Rodolfo Ortiz Santos and Guadalupe Pulido Sarmiento; m. Martha Elvira Carvallo Campos, Jan. 1995. BS, U. Veracruzana, Mex., 1994; DSc, Inst. of Ecology, Xalapa, 2000. With Instituto Nacional de Geografia e Informatica, Xalapa, 1990; prof. U. Veracruzana, Xalapa, 1999—. Contbr. articles to profl. jours. Recipient various student travel awards. Mem. Ecol. Soc. Am., Am. Ornthologists Union, Assn. Field Ornithologists, Sigma Xi. Avocations: science fiction lectures, playing guitar, sports. E-mail: ortizrau@ecologia.edu.mx. Office: Instituto de Ecologia AC, Apartado 63, Xalapa Veracruz, Mexico 91000

ORTIZ RUIZ, AIDA M., university administrator, educator; b. Barranquitas, P.R., Oct. 3, 1940; d. Higinio and Joaquina (Ortiz) O.; m. William Ruiz; 1 child, Philip. BA, U. P.R., 1971; MA, NYU, 1973; MEd, Columbia U., 1988. Tchr. N.Y.C. Bd. Edn., 1972-74; instr. English Queens Coll., N.Y.C., 1974-78; lectr. English Hostos Community Coll., Bronx, N.Y., 1978-83; asst. dean of faculty Hostos Community Coll., Bronx, 1984-86, assoc. dean of academic affairs, 1988-91; coord. freshman yr. programs CUNY, 1991-93, assoc. dean academic affairs, 1998—; mem. test of std. written English com. Coll. Bd., 1985-90; reader SAT Composition, GMAT, TOEFL-Test of Written English, 1990—; mem. coun. internat. edn. CUNY, 1989—, United Way campaign fund drive, 1990—, mem. chancellors task force on writing, 1984-88, chair univ. adv. com. on transfer and articulation; grants adminstr. Title III, Vocat. Edn. Act, Ford Univ. C.C. Transfer Opportunity Program, Diamond Found. grant Minority Project for Tchg. Professions, 1993—, Gear Up/BEA steering com., 1999—; CUNY coord. univ. skills immersion program, 1991-93; coord. Hostos Coordinated Freshmen Yr. Program, 1996—; bd. dirs. China Exchange Program; mem. Writing Across the Curriculum com., CUNY, 1998—. Contbr. articles to profl. jours. Mem. Inst. for P.R. Policy, N.Y.C., 1986—, CUNY Women's Coalition, 1984—. Fellow Ford Found., 1971-73. Fellow ASCD, Acad. Affairs Adminstrs., Coll. Compositions and Comm., TESOL, Assn. Tchrs. English, Acad. for Humanities and Scis., Internat. Platform Assn. Avocations: multiethnic literature, gender studies, new media tech., Latino/U.S. literature. Office: Hostos Community Coll 500 Grand Concourse Bronx NY 10451-5323

ORTIZ SANTOSCOY, RAUL, human resources consultant; b. Mexico City, Mexico, May 17, 1945; s. Eduardo and Magdalena Ortiz; m. Reyna Zapata Valdez (div. March 1993); children: Sandra, Raul, Daniel; m. Lourdes Vargas Snyder, April 7, 1995. Degree, U. Nat. Autonoma de Mexico, 1970, Inst. Tech. Estudios Superiores De Monterrey, 1972; MA in Labor Rels., U. Am., Puebla, Mexico, 1979. Human resources mgr. Ortiz Weiss Co., Mexico City, 1967-72; chmn. Asesores Grupo Omicron, S.A., Mexico City, 1972-99; tchr. Inst. PanAm. de Alta Dirección, Mexico City, 1983-86; cons. Confed. Patronal de la Rep. Mexicana, Mexico City, 1982-99; speaker in field. Author: Mi Legado, Lo Saben en Casa, 1996. Mem. Mexico Unido, Programa Lazos, Mexico City, 1992-99, Ctr. Empresarial de la Ciudad de Mexico, Mexico City, 1982-99, Alianza Para La Edn. Superior, Mexico City, 1996-99; chmn., founder Centro ITARI Hosp., A.C. Mem. Am. Soc. Indsl. Security. Mem. Accion Nat. Party. Avocations: toy car collector, antiques. E-mail: omicros@infosel.net.mx. Office: Asesores Grupo Omicron, Luz Savinon 305 Col del Valle, 03100 Mexico City Mexico

ORTIZ VERA, LUIS TOMAS, biologist, educator; b. Madrid, July 22, 1957; s. Luis Ortiz and Julia Vera; m. Lydia Peña, Feb. 5, 1987; children: Julia, Lucia, Mar. PhD in Biology, U. Complutense, Madrid, 1991. Rschr. Nat. Inst. Agrl. Investigation, Madrid, 1981-87, NRC, Madrid, 1991-92; rschr. U. Complutense, 1987-91, assoc. prof., 1993—. Contbr. articles to sci. publs. Mem. Spanish Red Cross, Madrid, 1978-84. Mem. Am. Poultry Sci. Assn., Fedn. Animal Sci. Socs., European Soc. Biologists. Avocations: tennis, soccer. Office: U Complutense Faculty Veter, Avda Puerta de Hierro S/N, 28040 Madrid Spain

ORTLIP, MARY KRUEGER, artist; b. Scranton, Pa.; d. John A. and Ida Mae (Phillips) Smale; m. Emmanuel Krueger, June, 1940 (dec. Nov. 1979); children: Diane, Keith; m. Paul D. Ortlip, June 26, 1981. Student, New Sch. Social Rsch., N.Y.C., 1957-59, Margarita Madrigal Langs., N.Y.C., Montclair (N.J.) Art Mus. Sch., 1978-79; Nomina Accademico Conferita, Accademia Italia, Italy, 1986; DFA (hon.), Houghton Coll., 1988. Dancer, dance instr. Fleischer Dance Studio, Scranton, Pa., 1934-38. One-woman shows include Curzon Gallery of Boca Raton, Fla. and London, 1986-93, Galerie Les Amis des Arts, Aix-en-Provence, France, 1987; group exhbns.: Salmagundi Club, N.Y.C., 1980, James Hunt Barker Galleries, Nantucket, Mass. and N.Y.C., 1983, Salon Internationale Musée Parc Rochteau à Revin, France, 1985, 90, Accademia Italia, Milan, 1986, many others in Europe and Am.; permanent collections Musée de parc Rocheteau, Revin, France, Pinacothèque Arduinna, Charleville-Meziéres, France. Named Invité d'Honneur, Le Salon des Nations a Retenu L'oeuvre, Paris, 1983, Artist of the Year, La Cote des Arts, France, 1986; recipient La Medaille d'Or, Du 13ème Salon Internationale al du Parc Rocheau au Revin, France, 1985, Medaille d' Honneur Ville de Marseille, France, 1987, Targo D'Oro, Accademia Italia Premio D'Italia, 1986; Trophy Arts Internationale Exposition de Peinture Marseille, Plaquette d' Honneur, Palais des Arts, 1987, Grand Prix Salon de Automne Club Internationale, 1987, Connaissance de Notre Europa Ardennes Eifel, Revin, France, 1990. Mem. Nat. Mus. Women in Arts, Accademia Italia (charter), Instituo D'Art Contemporanea Di Milano, Nat. Soc. Arts and Letters, Gov.'s Club, Salmagundi Club. Home (summer): 2917 S Ocean Blvd Apt 703 Highland Bch FL 33487-1836 Office: The Curzon Gallery 501 E Camino Real Boca Raton FL 33432-6127

ORTLIP, PAUL DANIEL, artist; b. Englewood, N.J., May 21, 1926; s. Henry Willard and Aimee (Eschner) O.; m. Mary Louise Krueger, June 1981; children from previous marriage: Carol, Kathleen, Sharon (dec.), Danielle (dec.), Michelle. Diploma, Houghton Acad., 1944; student, Art Students League, 1947-49; diploma, Acad. la Grande Chaumiere, Paris, 1950; DFA (hon.), Houghton Coll., 1988. Tchr. Fairleigh Dickinson U., Teaneck, N.J., 1956-68; artist in residence, curator Fairleigh Dickinson U., Rutherford, N.J., 1968-72; official USN artist on assignment, Cuban missile crisis, Fla., 1963, Gemini 5 Recovery, Atlantic Ocean, 1965, Vietnam, 1967, Apollo 12 recovery, Pacific Ocean, 1969, Apollo 17 recovery, Pacific Ocean, 1972, Internat. Naval Rev., N.Y. harbor, 1976, USCG Sta., Key West, Fla., 1985; mem. USN Art Coop. and Liason Com. Exhbns. include Salonde L'Art Libre, Paris, 1950, Nat. Acad. Design, 1952, Allied Artists of Am., N.Y.C., Acad. Sci., Rundell Gallery, Rochester, N.Y., Monclair Art Mus., Hist. Mus, Lima, Ohio, Butler Art Inst., Youngstown, Ohio, Fine Arts Gallery, San Diego, State Capitol Bldg., Sacramento, Calif., Capitol Mus., Olympia, Wash., Mus. Gt. Plains, Lawton, Okla., Witte Meml. Mus., San Antonio, Nimitz Meml. Mus., Fredericksberg, Tex., Pentagon Collection of Fine Arts, James Hunt Barker Galleries, Palm Beach, Fla., Nantucket, Mass, N.Y.C., Smithsonian Inst., Gallerie Vollem Breuse, Biarritz, France, Galerie Mouffe, Paris, Guggenheim Gallery, London, Wickersham Gallery, N.Y.C., Soc. Illustrators, N.Y.C.; retrospective exhbn. Bergen Community Mus., Paramus, N.J. 1970, The Curzon Gallery, 1987, 88, 89, 93, Ardennes et de l'Eifel, Charleville Mézières, France, June-Sept. 1990; represented permanent collections including Salmagundi Club N.Y.C., Houghton (N.Y.) Coll., Portrait Meml. J.F. Kennedy Library, Fairleigh-Dickinson U., Nat. Air and Space Mus., Smithsonian Inst., Intrepid Sea-Air Space Mus., N.Y.C., Hist. Mural Visitors Ctr., Palisades Interstate Pk., Ft. Lee, N.J., Vets. Med. Ctr., East Orange, N.J., USN Exhbn. Ctr., Washington Navy Yard, Am. Coll. Clin. Pharmacology, N.Y.C., N.J. U. Dentistry & Medicine, Newark, Bergen County Ct. House, Hackensack, N.J., Dickinson Coll., Carlisle, Pa., George Washingtogn Meml Pk., Paramus, N.J., Marietta (Ohio) Coll., Mcpl. Bldg., Ft. Lee, N.J., Navy League U.S., Arlington, Va., Nat. Archives and Records Adminstrn., Washington, (mural) Pub. Libr., Fort Lee, N.J., Bush Presdl. Libr., College Station, Tex., UDT Seal Mus., Fort Pierce, Fla. Served to sgt. U.S. Army, 1944-47, ETO, PTO, 1946-47. Recipient 1st prize Am. Artists Profl. League State Exhibit N.J. chpt., Paramus, 1960, 1st prize U.S. Armed Forces Exhibit Far East, Seoul, Korea, Tokyo, 1946, Franklin Williams award, Salmagundi Club, N.Y., 1967, Outstanding Achievement award for oil painting, USN, 1968, Artist of Yr. award, Hudson Artists, Jersey City (N.J.) Mus., 1970, Statue of Victory World Culture prize, Accademia Italia, Parma, 1982, Men of Achievement medal Cambridge, Eng., 1990, Connaissance de Notre Europe Gold medal Charleville-Mézières, France, 1990. Mem. Allied Artists Am. (art coop. and liaison com. with USN), Nat. Soc. Mural Painters, Nat. Soc. Arts and Letters, Bergen County Artists Guild (pres. 1960-62), Portrait Soc. Am., Inc., Artists Fellowship, Inc., U.S. Coast Guard Art Program, Art Students League N.Y. (life), Navy League U.S., VFW (life), Am. Legion. Clubs: Salmagundi (N.Y.C.) (art chmn. 1979-81); Gov.'s of the Palm Beaches (Fla.). Home: 2917 S Ocean Blvd Apt 703 Highland Bch FL 33487-1836 Office: care The Curzon Gallery 501 E Camino Real Boca Raton FL 33432-6127

ORTLIP, STEPHEN JUDE, musician; b. Englewood, N.J., Aug. 13, 1920; s. Henry Willard Ortlip and Aimee Eschner; m. Doris Ruth Armstrong, Jan. 22, 1946; children: Stephanie, Pamela, Benjamin. BS, Houghton Coll., 1942; MA, Cath. U., 1944; M in Sacred Music, Union Theol. Sem., 1951. Organist, choirmaster Westside Presbyn. Ch., Englewood, N.J., 1948-51, First Congl. Ch., Wakefield, Mass., 1951-55, Lookout Mountain (Tenn.) Presbyn. Ch., 1955-70; dir. Chattanooga Boys Choir, 1957-75; choir dir. Baylor Sch. Glee Club, Chattanooga, 1958-60; condr. Chattanooga Concert Choir, 1964-70; founder, dir. Atlanta Young Singers Callanwolde, 1975-97; organist, choirmaster Decatur (Ga.) Presbyn. Ch., 1970-88; ret.; guest dir. Atlanta Symphony & Robert Shaw, Atlanta, 1978-93. Condr. Festival of Trees, Egleston Children's Hosp., Atlanta. Mem. Am. Guild Organists (dean Chattanooga chpt. 1964-66), Rotary Internat. (Paul Harris fellow), Am. Choral Dir. Assn. (childrens choir chair so. divsn. 1991-93). Presbyterian. Avocations: walking, trail hiking, woodworking, brickworking, household handiwork. Home: 26 Dartmouth Ave Avondale Estates GA 30002-1410 Office: Atlanta Young Singers Callanwolde 980 Briarcliff Rd NE Atlanta GA 30306-2618

ORTMEYER, CARL EDWARD, retired demographer; b. Charles City, Iowa, Mar. 12, 1915; s. Arthur Herman and Sarah Emilie (Stoeber) O.; m. Anne Babuska O'Brien, Aug. 3, 1947 (dec. Dec. 15, 1995); 1 child, Kerry Michael; m. Ruth Forberg, Oct. 5, 1996. BA, U. Iowa, 1939; MS, Iowa State U., 1948, PhD in Rural Sociology, Demography, 1954. Rsch. assoc. bur. pub. health econs. Sch. Pub. Health U. Mich., Ann Arbor, 1954-56; demographer social security adminstrn. Libr. Congress, Washington, 1956-57; rsch. assoc. Sch. Medicine Howard U., 1958-59; demographer Nat. Ctr. Health Statistics Pub. Health Svc. U.S. Dept. HEW, 1959-68, demographer Nat. Inst. Occpl. Safety and Health CDC, 1968-80. Vol. caregiver Benedictine Nursing Ctr., Mt. Angel, Oreg., 1990-96, Wesley Homes Health Ctr., Des Moines, Wash., 1996—; mem. Wesley Found., Ams. for Democratic Action. Sgt. U.S. Army, 1941-45. Travel grantee London Sch. Econs. Rockefeller Found., 1969. Fellow APHA AAAS; mem. N.Y. Acad. Sci. Democrat. Mem. United Meth. Ch. Avocations: dancing. Home: 815 S 216th St Apt 200 Des Moines WA 98198-6332

ORTNER, EVELYN MAVIS JACOBS, organization executive; d. Samuel Jacobs and Bronislawa Wilson; m. Robert Ortner, May 21, 1947; children: Peter Colby, Nicole Jane. BA, Montclair State U., 1972; MA, Drew U., 1973. Lectr. contemporary lit. Brandeis U. Studies Group, N.J., 1970's; sr. advisor, speechwriter Sec. Health and Human Svcs., U.S. Govt., Washington, 1980's; founder, exec. dir. The Unity Group, Inc., Millburn, N.J., 1990—; bd. dirs. Drew U., Madison, N.J.; spkr. in field; appeared on numerous TV and radio programs. Author: By Nature a Sociable Fellow; contbr. chpt. to book, articles to profl. publs., mags., newspapers. Founder Inter-Group Com., Essex County, N.J., 1950's; officer LWV, Short Hills, N.J., 1960's; commr. Essex County (N.J.) Commn. on Status of Women, 1990's. Recipient Cert. of Appreciation, U.S. Dept. Justice, Washington, 1998, Commending Resolution, N.J. Senate and Gen. Assembly, Trenton, 1999, Annual Vol. award Gov. N.J., 1999. Avocations: theater, writing, reading, dancing. Office: The Unity Group Inc PO Box 333 Millburn NJ 07041-0333

ORTNER, GUSTAV, Austraian diplomat; b. Vienna, Austria, Feb. 17, 1935; s. Gustav and Felicitas (Weiss Von Tessbach) O. D Econs., U. Vienna, 1958; postgrad. in piano, Conservatory of City of Vienna, 1962. Attache Fgn. Office, Vienna, 1960-62; sec. Austrian Embassy to Holy Sea, Rome, 1962-67, Fed. Chancellor, Vienna, 1967-70; 2d counsellor Austrian Embassy, Paris, 1970-73; 1st counsellor Austrian Embassy, Tel Aviv, 1973-75; with Fgn. Office, Vienna, 1975-77; dep. permanent rep. UN, N.Y.C., 1977-79; dir. security coun. UN, 1979-88; chief of protocol Austrian Ambassador, Vienna, 1988-96; Austrian amb. to the Holy See Vatican, Rome, 1997—. Recipient Magistral Knight-Grand Cross, Souvereign Order of Malta; named Familiare, Teutonic Order, Rome. Mem. N.Y.C. Century Club, Vienna Club, St. Johanns Club, Jockey Club Austria, Circolo della Caccia. Home and Office: Via Reno 9, 00198 Rome Italy also: Nibelungengasse 3, A-1010 Vienna Austria

ORTNER, JOHANNES, former Austrian space agency administrator; b. Vienna, Austria, May 31, 1933; s. Gustav and Felicitas (Weiss-Tessbach) O.; m. Katharina Hackenschmidt, Aug. 21, 1961 (div. 1976); children: Nikolaus, Marie-Therese; m. Martina Haffner, Nov. 9, 1979. PhD in geophysics and

meteorology, U. Vienna, 1960. Rsch. physicist Geophys. Observatory, Kiruna, Sweden, 1957-62; sr. scientist European Preparatory Commn. for Space Orgn., Paris, 1962-65; asst. dir. for sci. projects European Space Rsch. Orgn., Noordwijk, The Netherlands, 1965-68; asst. dir. for program planning European Space Rsch. Orgn., Paris, 1968-74; mng. dir. Austrian Space Agy., Vienna, 1974-98; ret., 1998; pres. Internat. Astronautical Fedn., Paris, 1986-88; vice chmn. trustees Internat. Space U., Strasbourg, 1989-98, chmn. bd. trustees, 1998—; v.p. European Assn. for the Internat. Space Yr., Paris, 1993—; trustee Internat. Space Sci. Inst., Berne, 1998—; bd. dirs. European Forum Alpbach, Tyrol, Austria. Editor: Introduction to Solar Terrestrial Relations, 1961 (European Space Agy.-Team Achievement award 1983). Named Professor, Pres. of Austria, 1981. Mem. Internat. Acad. Astronautics, Techniker Cercle, Rotary Club. Roman Catholic. Avocations: bridge, skiing, photography. Home: 3 Nibelungengasse, A-1010 Vienna Austria

ORTON, GEORGE FREDERICK, aerospace engineer; b. Flushing, N.Y., Aug. 8, 1941; s. Harry and Evelyn (Brostrom) O.; m. Susan K., Dec. 21, 1962; children: Karen, Kevin, Kristen. BS in Aeron. Engring., U. Md., 1964; MS in Engring. Mechanics, St. Louis U., 1971. Engr. propulsion McDonnell Douglas Co. (now The Boeing Co.), St. Louis, 1964-73, sr. engr. propulsion, 1973-77, unit chief propulsion, 1977-81, sect. chief propulsion, 1981-86, br. chief nat. aerospace plane, 1986-90, staff dir. nat. aerospace plane, 1990-92, dir. space programs, 1992-93, program mgr. Hypersonics Ctr. Excellence, 1993—, mem. air force sci. adv. bd., 2000—; mem. adv. bd. Ga. Inst. Tech., 1998—. Contbr. articles to profl. jours. Advisor Explorer Post 9005, St. Louis, 1980-87; sci. advisor University City (Mo.) Schs. Fellow AIAA (assoc., mem. liquid propulsion tech. com. 1980-84, 91-96, mem. hypersonics program com. 1994—, Best Paper award 1986), St. Louis Head Injury Assn. Methodist. Achievements include patent for propellant acquisition device for zero-g engine starts, patent for propellant resupply system, NASA technology cash award for work on shuttle auxiliary propulsion. Office: The Boeing Co PO Box 516 Mailcode S1067250 Saint Louis MO 63166-0516

ORTON, LESLIE WILLIAM, economics educator; b. Sevenoaks, England, May 12, 1942; s. William George and Myrtle Mary Madeline (Haine) O.; m. Moraig Anne Webster, July 2, 1969; children: Keith Malcolm, Gail Lesley. MA in Social Sci., U. St. Andrews, Scotland, 1967; MEd, U. Dundee, Scotland, 1970. Rsch. and tutorial asst. U. Dundee, 1967-69; tchr. econs. High Sch. Dumfermline, 1970-72, prin. tchr. econs., 1972-77; tchr. econs. European Sch., Brussels, 1977—; coord. secondary years 1 and 2 Brussels, 1988—, setter in O grade econs., 1975-77. Mem. Scottish Br. Econs. Assn. (sec. 1974-77), Brussels St. Andrews & Dundee Alumnus Assn. (co-sec. 1990—), Scottish European Assn. Avocations: golf, skiing, trumpet, water color, dogs. Office: European Sch, 46 Ave Du Vert Chasseur, 1180 Brussels Belgium

ORUÇ, SELÇUK, dentist; b. Kastamonu, Turkey, Apr. 23, 1949; s. Hayri and Meliha (Caglar) O.; m. Nilgun Göze, Mar. 7, 1977; children: Onur, Elif. Degree in dentistry, Istanbul (Turkey) U., 1973. Chief apprentice Guilhane Mil. Med. Acad., Ankara, Turkey, 1974-75; chief Mil. Hosp., Agri, Turkey, 1975-80, Derince, Turkey, 1980-85; asst. prof. Guilhane Mil. Med. Acad., 1986-90, assoc. prof., 1991—; asst. prof. Mil. Hosp., Camlica, Turkey, 1990-91; cons. Guilhane Dept. Prosthodontics, 1991—. Inventor in field. Col. Turkish armed forces, 1993—. Mem. Internat. Prosthodontics and Implantology Assn., Ilgaz Group, Kascetvak. Avocations: tennis, gardening, fishing, travel, billiards. Home: Büyuksehir Sit, 645 Sek No 16, Konutkent Turkey Office: Guilhand Mil Med Acad, Dental Sci Ctr, 06010 Ankara Turkey

ORVANANOS, MARCELA DE ROVZAR, philanthropist; b. Mexico City, Oct. 20, 1950; d. Eduardo Zuniga and Teresa (Hernández) O.; m. Alexis E. Rovzar, Dec. 1, 1972; 4 children. Degree in architecture, Iberoamericana U., Mex., 1972; cert. in mgmt. non-profit/fundraising, Indiana Ctr. Philanthropy, 1993. Vol. Mex. Found. Rural Devel., Mex., 1989-90, dir. of devel., 1990-92, v.p., 1992-94; founder Procura A.C., Mex., 1994-2000, mem. hon. bd., 2000—. Mem. cmty. bd. Jr. League, Mex., 1997—; bd. dirs. UNICEF, Save the Children, 1999—; trustee CEMEFI, Mex., 2000—. Roman Catholic. Avocations: painting, sculpture, ceramics. Home: Au Desierto de Los Leones, 6153-2 Mexico City Mexico

ÖRVELL, CLAES GUNNAR, virologist, researcher, physician, educator; b. Stockholm, Apr. 22, 1945; s. Gunnar Emanuel and Margit (Borg) Ö; m. Eva Reimert, May 5, 1987; 3 children. MD, Karolinska Inst., Stockholm, 1973, PhD, 1977. Lic. med. doctor, virologist. Rschr. dept. virology Karolinska Inst., Stockholm, 1978-79; rschr. in virology Nat. Bacteriological Lab., Stockholm, 1980-92; sr. physician Stockholm City Coun., 1992—; assoc. prof. virology Karolinska Inst., Stockholm, 1988—. Contbr. articles on virological rsch. to profl. jours. Mem. AAAS, N.Y. Acad. Scis. Avocations: golf, literature. Office: Huddinge Univ Hosp, Dept Clin Virology, S-14186 Huddinge Sweden

ORY, STEVEN JAY, physician, educator; b. Houston, Aug. 4, 1950; s. Edwin Marvin and Norma Gertrude O.; m. Kathleen Higgins, Jan. 10, 1981; children: Eleanor Claire, Edward Michael. BA, Washington and Lee U., 1972; MD, Baylor Coll., 1976. Diplomate Am. Bd. Obstetrics and Gynecology, subsplty. cert. in Reproductive Endocrinology and Infertility. Asst. prof. Duke U., Durham, N.C., 1981-82, Northwestern U., Chgo., 1982-85; assoc. prof., cons. Mayo Clinic, Rochester, Minn., 1985-95, chmn. sect. reproductive endocrinology and infertility, 1985-95; pvt. practice reproductive endocrinology and infertility; mem. ob-gyn. staff N.W. Ctr. for Infertility and Reproductive Endocrinology, Margate, Fla., 1995—; assoc. clin. prof. obstets. and gyn. U. Miami, Fla., 1999—; assoc. dir. Am. Fertility Soc., Birmingham, Ala., 1986-87. Asst. editor: Fertility and Sterility, 1988-96; contbr. articles to profl. jours. Mem. Internat. Soc. for Advancement of Humanistic Studies in Medicine (bd. dirs. 1999—), Am. Soc. Reproductive Medicine (chmn. practice com. 1998—, bd. dirs., 1999—), Soc. Reproductive Endocrinologists (sec.-treas., pres. elect), Ft. Lauderdale Ob-Gyn. Soc. (pres. 1998-2000). Address: 2825 N State Road 7 Ste 302 Margate FL 33063-5737

ORZA, JOSÉ M., chemist, researcher; b. Vedra, La Coruña, Spain, Apr. 1, 1931; s. José Orza and Dolores Segade; m. Joaquina Negro, June 24, 1958 (div. May 1978); m. Josefina Marco, Sept. 28, 1989. Grad. in Chemistry, Madrid U., 1954, D in Chemistry, 1959. Asst. prof. chem. physics U. Complutense, Madrid, 1954-61; lectr. quantum mechanics, quantum chemistry, 1970-76; scientific collaborator, scientific researcher Coun. Scientific Rsch., Spain, 1967-71; rsch. prof., 1971-96, researcher (ad honorem), 1997—; dir. Inst. Estructura de la Materia, Madrid, 1979-87; lectr. laser spectroscopy U. Autónoma, Madrid, 1988-91; vis. prof. Unicamp U., Campinas, São Paulo, 1978, Asociación Física Argentina, Buenos Aires, 1992. Author: Espectroscopia I, 1972, Láseres: Nuevas Tendencias, 1986; editor: Gas Flow and Chemical Lasers, 1987-91; contbr. numerous articles to profl. jours. Scientific dir. Fundación Madrid-Láser, 1989-92; dir. Researchers Residence, Madrid, 1975-78. Postdoct. grant Fundación Juan March, 1958. Fellow Real Soc. Española Física; mem. Grupo Español Espectroscopia (pres. 1986-90, Silver medal 1993). Mem. Partido Socialista Obrero Espanol. Roman Catholic. Avocations: photography, travel, chess. Home: Numancia 24, 28039 Madrid Spain Office: Inst Estructura Materia, Serrano 123, 28006 Madrid Spain

OSA, TETSUO, pharmaceutical science educator; b. Tokyo, Aug. 6, 1932; s. Jiro and Mine (Irie) O.; m. Reiko Uemura, Oct. 26, 1960; children: Minako, Yumiko. B Engring., U. Tokyo, 1955, M Engring., 1957, D Engring., 1964. Sr. researcher Coal Chem. Lab., Hokkaido Colliery and Steamship Co., Toda-shi, Japan, 1957-62; assoc. prof. faculty engring. U. Tokyo, 1962-74; prof. Pharm. Inst. Tohoku U., Sendai, Japan, 1974-96; rsch. & devel. advisor ctrl. lab. Asahi Glass Co., Yokohama-shi, Japan, 1996—. Recipient Purple ribbon Japanese Govt., 1997. Mem. Pharm. Soc. Japan (v.p. 1994), The Japan Petroleum Inst. (bd. dirs. 1989-96, soc. award 1989), Chem. Soc. Japan (Soc. award 1994), Soc. Cyclodexcrins Japan (pres. 1996-98, society award 1999). Avocation: travel. Office: 1150 Hazawa-cho Kanagawa-ku, Yokohama 221, Japan

OSAKA, NAOYUKI, psychology educator; b. Kyoto, Japan, Dec. 16, 1946; s. Ryoji and Ritsuko Osaka; m. Mariko Yamamoto. BA, Kyoto U. Edn., 1971; MA, Kyoto U., 1973, PhD, 1979. Asst. prof. Otemon-Gakuin U., Osaka, Japan, 1977-81, assoc. prof., 1981-87; assoc. prof. Kyoto U., 1987-94, prof., 1994—, chmn. psychology dept., 1994—. Editor Japanese Psychol. Rev., 1994—. Mem. Japan Color Sci. Assn. (pres. 1998—). Avocations: tennis, skiing, travel. Home: 3-28-1 Minegado-cho Goryo, Nishikyo-ku Kyoto 610-1103, Japan Office: Kyoto U Dept Psychology, Grad Sch Letters, Kyoto 606-8501, Japan

OSAKWE, CHRISTOPHER, lawyer, educator; b. Lagos, Nigeria, May 8, 1942; came to U.S. 1970, naturalized 1979; s. Simon and Hannah (Morgan) O.; m. Maria Elena Amador, Aug. 19, 1982; 1 child, Rebecca E. LLB, Moscow State U., 1967, PhD, 1970; JSD, U. Ill., 1974. Bar: Moscow, 1967, Kazakhstan, 1997. Prof. sch. law Tulane U., New Orleans, 1972-81, 86-88; ptnr. firm Riddle and Brown, New Orleans, 1989—; Eason-Weinmann prof. comparative law, dir. Eason-Weinmann Ctr. for Comparative Law Tulane U., New Orleans, 1981-86; ptnr. Riddle and Brown, 1988—; vis. prof. U. Pa., 1978, U. Mich., 1981, Washington and Lee U., 1986; vis. fellow St. Anthony's Coll., Oxford U., Eng., 1980, Christ Ch. Coll., Oxford U., 1988-89, Lomonosov Moscow State U., 1999-2000; cons. U.S. Dept. Commerce, 1980-85. Author: The Participation of the Soviet Union in Universal International Organizations, 1972, The Foundations of Soviet Law, 1981, Joint Ventures with the Soviet Union: Law and Practice, 1990, Soviet Business Law, 2 vols., 1991, (with others) Comparative Legal Traditions in a Nutshell, 1982, Comparative Legal Traditions--Text, Materials and Cases, 1985, The Russian Civil Code Annotated: Translation and Commentary, 2000; editor Am. Jour. Comparative Law, 1978-85. Carnegie doctoral fellow Hague Acad. Internat. Law, 1969; Russian rsch. fellow Harvard U., 1972; USSR sr. rsch. exch. fellow, 1982, rsch. fellow Kennan Inst. for Advanced Russian Studies, 1988. Mem. ABA, Am. Law Inst., Am. Soc. Internat. Law, Supreme Ct. Hist. Soc., Soc. de Legislation Comparée, Order of Coif. Republican. Roman Catholic. Home: 339 Audubon Blvd New Orleans LA 70125-4124 Office: 201 S Charles Ave Ste 3100 New Orleans LA 70170

OSAWA, AKIRA, ecologist; b. Kawagoe, Japan, Apr. 19, 1954; s. Isao and Yuki O.; m. Nahoko Kurachi, Aug. 25, 1991; 1 child, Hatena. BS, Nagoya U., 1978; MS, Cornell U., 1983; PhD, Yale U., 1986. Rschr. Forestry and Forest Products Rsch. Inst., Sapporo, Japan, 1988-96; assoc. prof. Ryukoku U., Ohtsu, Shiga, Japan, 1996—. Contbr. sci. articles to profl. jours. Postdoctoral fellow U. Wash., Seattle, 1986-87. Mem. Ecological Soc. Am., Forestry Soc. Japan, Ecological Soc. Japan. Home: 1-13-10 Aoyama, Otsu Shiga 520-21, Japan Office: Ryukoku U, 1-5 Yokoya Seta-Ohe, Otsu Shiga 520-21, Japan

OSAWA, PAULA MARIANI, trading company executive; b. St. Petersburg, Fla., Jan. 31, 1951; d. Alfred and Velma Mariani; m. Yuichi Osawa, 1999. BS, U. Fla., 1972, MS, 1973. Pres. Orientations Japan, Hawaii and Tokyo, 1979-87; protocol advisor Mitsui & Co., Ltd., Tokyo, 1987—, Japan External Trade Orgn., Tokyo, 1992—; TV commentator Japan Ednl. TV, 1991—; radio commentator Japan Ednl. Radio, 1985-90. Contbr. articles to profl. jours.; profiled on CNN TV as successful Am. woman working in Japan, on CBS TV as success in Japan market. Mem. Am. C. of C. in Japan. Avocations: Kung Fu (Black Belt), marathon running. Office: Mitsui & Co Ltd, 1-2-1 Otemachi, Chiyoda-ku, Tokyo 100-0004, Japan

OSAWA, SATOSHI, chemistry educator; b. Tokyo, June 5, 1961; s. Masaru and Keiko Osawa; m. Etsuko Osawa; children: Yuri, Yukari. BS, Sci. U. Tokyo, 1986, PhD, 1991. Departmental asst. U. Mass., 1991-93; rsch. assoc. Sci. U. Tokyo, 1993-96; asst. prof. Kanazawa Inst. Tech., 1996-98, assoc. prof. chemistry, 1998—; organizer Indsl. Materials Workshop, Kanazawa, 1996—, Polymer Workshop, Kanazawa, 1997—. Author: Recent Research Developments in Macromolecules Research, 1998; contbr. articles to profl. jours. NSF grantee U. Mass., 1991-93; recipient Grant-ini-Aid Ministry of Edn. Sci. and Culture, 1998. Mem. Am. Chem. Soc., Chem. Soc. Japan, The Soc. Polymer Sci. Avocations: golfing, painting, motorcycling. Home: Wakunami 1-7-16, Kanazawa, Ishikawa 920, Japan Office: Kanazawa Inst Tech, Kanazawa 921-8501, Japan

OSAZUWA, ISAAC BABATUNDE, physics educator, researcher; b. Ijagba, Nigeria, Mar. 20, 1947; s. Francis Osazuwa Arikalu and Elizabeth Igbekele (Obadan) Arikalu; m. Catherine Ayoka Osayameh, Jan. 22, 1987; children: Stephen, Christopher, Joy. BSc, U. Ibadan, Nigeria, 1973; MSc, Ahmadu Bello U., 1978, PhD, 1985. Lectr. CMS Grammar Sch., Lagos, Nigeria, 1973-74, Fed. Govt. Coll., Sokoto, Nigeria, 1974-76; lectr. Ahmadu Bello U., Zaria, Nigeria, 1978-86, sr. lectr., 1986-91, reader, 1991-94, prof., 1994—; coord. Geophysics Rsch. Ahmadu Bello U., 1992—; chmn. U. Bd. Rsch., 1997-2000; head dept. physics Ahmadu Bello U., 1997-2001; dep. dean Faculty of Sci. Ahmadu Bello U., 1999-2001; team leader W. African Examination Coun., 1975—; mem. coun. Nat. Math. Ctr., Abuja, Nigeria, 1990-94. Mem. editl. bd. Nigerian Jour. Physics, 1992-97; contbr. articles to profl. pubs. Fellow Internat. Programs in the Physical Scis., Uppsala, Sweden, 1983-84, 91-92. Mem. N.Y. Acad. Scis., Nigerian Inst. Physics (fin. sect. 1988-92). Avocations: traveling, computer programming, reading, politics, visiting. Home: No 19 Sarkin Musulmi St Area A, Zaria Kaduna State Nigeria Office: Ahmadu Bello U, Dept Physics, Zaria Kaduna State Nigeria

OSBERG, TIMOTHY MICHAEL, psychologist, educator, researcher; b. Buffalo, Aug. 11, 1955; s. John Carlton and Adeline Rose (Weichsel) O.; m. Debra A. Morreale, July 14, 1990; children: John Peter, Erika Evelyn. BA, SUNY, Buffalo, 1977, MA, 1980, PhD, 1982. Lic. psychologist, N.Y. Intern VA Med. Ctr., Buffalo, 1981-82; asst. prof. Niagara U., N.Y., 1982-86; assoc. prof., 1986-90, prof., 1990—; pvt. practice Niagara U., Niagara Falls, N.Y., 1985—, Niagara Falls, N.Y., 1985—; psychologist Optifast Weight Loss Program, Niagara Falls, 1989-92; editorial bd. Jour. Personality and Social Psychology, 1988-92, Teaching of Psychology, 1991-99, Jour. Correctional Edn., 1993-97, Jour. Clin. Psychology, 1999—; instr. Attica Correctional Facility, 1980-93; presenter in field. Contbr. articles to profl. jours. Vol. group leader pre-release program Attica (N.Y.) Correctional Facility, 1984-90, exec. com. Psychol. Assn. Western N.Y., Buffalo, 1982-87. Recipient Feldman-Cohen Meml. award SUNY, Buffalo, 1977, Disting. Faculty award Consortium of Niagra Frontier, 1993. Fellow APA; mem. Am. Psychol. Soc., Eastern Psychol. Assn., Soc. for Personality Assessment, Assn. Advancement Behavior Therapy, Phi Beta Kappa. Democrat. Roman Catholic. Avocations: spectator sports, running, golf, tennis, hockey. Home: 2652 David Dr Niagara Falls NY 14304-4619 Office: Niagara U Dept Psychology Niagara University NY 14109

OSBORN, FREDERICK HENRY, III, foundation executive; b. Phila., Dec. 31, 1946; s. Frederick Henry Osborn Jr. and Anne de Witt (Pell) O.; m. Anne Hampton de Peyster Todd, July 10, 1971; children: Frederick Henry IV, Elisabeth Van Cortlandt, Graham Livingston. Student in Econs., Princeton U., 1964-66; BA in Bus. Adminstrn., Colby Coll., 1971; postgrad., Nat. Planned Giving Inst., 1987, Philanthropy Tax Inst., 1988. Registered investment advisor. Pres. Call-Us, Inc., Edgartown, Mass., 1969-72; exec. v.p. Hall Labs., Boston, 1972-74; fin. officer Episcopal Diocese Mass., Boston, 1972-76; diocesan adminstr. Episcopal Diocese Maine, Portland, 1976-80; dir. adminstrn. Episcopal Diocese Conn., Hartford, 1980-86; dir. of devel. and planned giving Nat. Episcopal Ch., N.Y.C., 1987-94; dir. of devel. programs Episcopal Ch. Found., N.Y.C., 1995-97; dir. devel. The Nature Conservancy of N.Y., N.Y.C., 1997-99; dir. philanthropic svcs. Episcopal Ch. Found., 1999—; bd. dirs. Living Music, Inc., Ulysses Co., William O. Benson Co., FAN Trusts, Oslands, Inc., Boscobel Restoration, Inc., Garrison Sta. Plz., Inc., Garrison Landing Assn., Covenant Svcs., Inc.; prin. Cat Rock Counsel, Garrison, N.Y., 1990—. Co-author: Planned Giving for the Episcopal Parish, 1989. Bd. dirs. The Giraffe Project, chmn. 1989-93, Alice Desmond & Hamilton Fish Libr.; chmn. bd. dirs. Hudson Highlands Land Trust; v.-chair., bd. dirs. Scenic Hudson, Berkeley Divinity Sch. Yale U., Nature Conservancy (lower Hudson chpt. chair 1994-97); trustee Tabor Acad., 1993-99, Cathedral Ch. St. John the Divine, chair Hudson Highlands Music Festival, 1994-96, 99—, St. Francis Found., The Constn. Island Assn. With U.S. Army, 1966-68, Vietnam. Mem. Nat. Soc. Fund Raising Execs., Nat. Planned Giving Assn., Nat. Environ. Le adership Coun., Planned Giving Group Greater N.Y., Social Investment Forum, Coun. Econ. Priorities, Social Venture Network, Century Assn., St. Andrews Soc. of N.Y., Highlands Country Club, N.Y. Yacht Club, Portland Yacht Club, Dauntless Club, Garrison Yacht Club, Princeton Club (N.Y.), Internat. Platform Assn. Avocations: sailing, music, photography. Home: PO Box 347 Garrison NY 10524-0347 Office: The Episcopal Ch Found 815 2nd Ave New York NY 10017-4503

OSBORN, JOHN EDWARD, lawyer, pharmaceutical and biotechnology industry executive, former government official, writer; b. Davenport, Iowa, Sept. 4, 1957; s. Edward Richard and Patricia Anne (O'Donovan) O.; m. Deborah Lynn Powell, Aug. 11, 1984; children: Delaney Powell, Keeley Rush. Student, Coll. William and Mary, 1975-76; BA, U. Iowa, 1979; cert., Georgetown U., 1980; JD, U. Va., 1983; cert., Wadham Coll., Oxford U., 1987; M Internat. Pub. Policy, Johns Hopkins U., 1992; cert., Wharton Sch., U. Pa., 1994-95; postgrad., Princeton U., 1997-99. Bar: Mass. 1985. Law clk. to Hon. Albert V. Bryan U.S. Ct. Appeals (4th cir.), Alexandria, Va., 1983-84; assoc. Hale and Dorr, Boston, 1984-88, Dechert Price & Rhoads, Phila., 1988-89; spl. asst. to legal adviser U.S. Dept. State, Washington, 1989-92; sr. counsel DuPont Merck Pharm. Co., Wilmington, Del., 1992-94, assoc. gen. counsel, 1994-96, v.p., assoc. gen. counsel, asst. sec., 1996-97; v.p. legal affairs Cephalon, Inc., West Chester, Pa., 1997-98, sr. v.p., gen. counsel, sec., 1998—; legal cons. Amnesty Internat. USA, 1987-88; vis. scholar East European studies, Woodrow Wilson Internat. Ctr. for Scholars, Washington, 1991; assoc. scholar Fgn. Policy Rsch. Inst., Phila., 1992—; vis. lectr. U. Mich. Bus. Sch., Ann Arbor 1997—; vis. fellows seminar Ctr. Internat. Studies, Princeton U., 1998; bd. advisors U. Pa. Inst. Law and Econs., Phila., 1999—. Contbr. articles to profl. jours., newspapers and periodicals including N.Y. Times, Wall St. Jour., Wash. Post, Christian Sci. Monitor, Am. Jour. Internat. Law; articles editor: Va. Jour. Internat. Law, 1982-83. Mem. Friends of Child Devel. Ctr., Georgetown U. Med. Ctr., Washington, 1999—, Johns Hopkins U. Alumni Coun., Balt., 1997—, U. Va. Law Sch. Bus. Advisory Coun., Charlottesville, 1996—, U. Iowa Liberal Arts Dean's Adv. Bd., Iowa City, 1999—; rsch. aide, speechwriter George Bush for Pres. Com., 1979-80, 87-88, mem. Del. Rep. State Com., 1995-99, del. to Rep. Nat. Conv., 1996, mem., bd. dirs. Del. Ctr. for the Contemporary Arts, 1994—, v.p. 1997-99, Am. Civil Liberties Found. Del., 1995-98, adv. bd. 1998—; trustee Tower Hill Sch., Wilmington, Del., 1997—, Del. Art Mus., 1999—. Eisenhower fellow, Ireland, 1998; postdoctoral grantee Andrew W. Mellon Found., 1999. Mem. Am. Corp. Counsel Assn., Am. Soc. Corp. Secs., Atlantic Coun. of the U.S., Coun. Fgn. Rels., Mortar Board, Greenville Country Club, Capitol Hill Club, Princeton Club N.Y., Phi Beta Kappa, Phi Delta Phi, Omicron Delta Kappa. Republican. Roman Catholic. Home: 5 Doe's Lane Greenville DE 19807-1548 Office: 145 Brandywine Pkwy West Chester PA 19380-4245

OSBORN, JOHN ROBERT, retired mechanical engineer; b. Kansas City, Mo., Aug. 11, 1924; married, 1945; 3 children. BS, Purdue U., 1950, MS, 1953, PhD in Mechanical Engring., 1957. Jr. engr. Thiokol Chem. Corp., 1950-51; asst. Purdue U., West Lafayette, Ind., 1951-57, from asst. prof. to assoc. prof. mechanical engring., 1957-61, prof., 1961-70, 71-79, prof. aeronautical and astronautical, 1980-89, ret., 1990; br. chief Ballistics Rsch. Lab. Aberdeen Proving Ground, 1970-71. Mem. AIAA (Wyld propulsion award 1995), Soc. Automotive Engrs. Achievements include research in combustion instability in rockets; high frequency response instrumentation; combustion in solid rockets and interior ballistics. Address: 40 Stayman Ct Lafayette IN 47905-4446

OSBORN, KENNETH LOUIS, financial executive; b. Belleville, Ill., Jan. 9, 1946; s. William Arthur and Louise Mary (Brueggemann) O.; BBA, U. N.Mex., 1968; m. Roberta Marie Vodicka, Oct. 23, 1971; 1 son, David Anthony. Auditor, Ernst & Ernst, Albuquerque, 1968; budge mgr. Rockwell Internat., Chgo., 1970-74; mgr. internat. acctg. Allied Van Lines, Chgo., 1974-76; fin. mgr. Sealy, Inc., Chgo., 1976-79; sr. fin. analyst Newark Electronics, Chgo., 1979-80, internat. dir. credit, 1980-82; bus. mgr. Prime Computer, 1982-90; acctg. mgr., CFO Flexonics, Inc., Chgo., 1990-96; contr. and chief fin. ofcr. Jackson Industries, Chgo., 1996—; fin. cons. Am. European Expres. Mem. Rep. Nat. Com., presdl. task force. With AUS, 1968-70. Decorated Air medal. Mem. Mensa, Soc. Am. Baseball Rsch., Inst. Mgmt. Accts.

OSBORN, LA DONNA CAROL, clergywoman; b. Portland, Oreg., Mar. 13, 1947; d. T.L. and Daisy (Washburn) O.; m. Cory A. Nickerson, Dec. 11, 1981; children: Tommy O'Dell, LaVona Thomas, Daneesa Dolan, Donald O'Dell. Student, Assemblies of God Coll., 1963; BA, Okla. City U., 1994; DD, Bethel Coll., 1995; Doctor of Humane Letters (hon.), Wesley Synod, 1998; MA, Oral Roberts U., 2000. Fgn. mission corr., purchaser, personnel agt. Osborn Found., Tulsa, 1969-75, exec. asst., 1975-76, internat. gen. mgr., 1976-81, internat. editor-in-chief, 1981-86, corp. pres., 1986-93; assoc. pastor Internat. Gospel Ctr., Tulsa, 1986-89, sr. pastor, 1989-94, sr. pastor, overseer, 1994-97; bishop Internat. Gospel Ctr. (IGC) Chs., Tulsa, Okla., 1997—; mem. Coll. of Bishops Internat. Communion of Charismatic Chs., 1998—; v.p., CEO OSFO Internat., 1998—; internat. minister, religious tchr., and motivational spkr. Nigeria, Kenya, Uganda, Colombia, Papua New Guinea, France, Russia, Belarus, Kazakhstan, Kyrgyzstan, Ukraine, Russia, Sweden, Eng., Holland, Can., India, Zambia, China, U.S.; internat. spiritual advisor Christian Women's Fellowship Internat. Nigeria; founder Internat. Gospel Ctr. Ch. and Ministries, Believers' Network Internat., Internat. Gospel Ctr. Fellowship of Chs. and Ministries. Author, editor Bible tng. courses. Republican. Avocations: Jewish Biblical history, interracial issues, Biblical equality, women's issues. Office: Internat Gospel Ctr 3111 E 89th St Tulsa OK 74137-3362

OSBORN, MALCOLM EVERETT, lawyer; b. Bangor, Maine, Apr. 29, 1928; s. Lester Everett and Helen (Clark) O.; m. Claire Anne Franks, Aug. 30, 1953; children: Beverly, Lester, Malcolm, Ernest. BA, U. Maine, 1952; postgrad., Harvard U., 1952-54; JD, Boston U., 1956, LLM, 1961. Bar: Maine 1956, Mass. 1956, U.S. Dist. Ct. Mass. 1961, U.S. Tax Ct. 1961, U.S. Claims Ct. 1961, N.C. 1965, U.S. Supreme Ct. 1979, U.S. Ct. Appeals (4th cir.) 1980, Va. 1991. Tax counsel State Mut. Life Assurance Co., Worcester, Mass., 1956-64; v.p., gen. tax counsel Integon Corp. and other group cos., Winston-Salem, N.C., 1964-81; ptnr. House, Blanco & Osborn, P.A., Winston-Salem, N.C., 1981-88; v.p., gen. counsel, dir. Settlers Life Ins. Co., Bristol, Va., 1984-89; prin. Malcolm E. Osborn, P.A., Winston-Salem, 1988—; lectr. The Booke Seminars, Life Ins. Co., 1985-87; adj. prof. Wake Forest U. Sch. Law, Winston-Salem, 1974-82; Disting. guest lectr. Ga. State U., 1965; guest lectr. NYU Ann. Inst. Fed. Taxation, 1966, 68, 75, 80. Com. editor The Tax Lawyer, ABA, 1974-76; author numerous articles in field. Trustee N.C. Coun. Econ. Edn., 1968-76; bd. dirs. Christian Fellowship Home, 1972-80; co-founder Bereaved Parents Gropu Winston-Salem, 1978—. Mem. ABA (chmn. com. ins. cos. of taxation sect. 1980-82, chmn. subcom. on continuing legal edn. and publs. 1982-88), Am. Bus. Law Assn. (mem. com. fed. taxation 1968—, chmn. 1972-75), Assn. Life Ins. Counsel (com. on co. tax, tax sect. 1965—), N.C. Bar Assn. (com. taxation 1973—), Fed. Bar Assn. (taxation com. 1973—), Maine State Bar Assn., Va. State Bar Assn., Internat. Bar Assn. (com. on taxes of bus. law sect. 1973—), AAUP, Southeastern Acad. Legal Studies in Bus., Masons (Lincoln, Maine). Office: PO Box 5192 Winston Salem NC 27113-5192

OSBORN, MARK ELIOT, dentist; b. Buffalo, Apr. 22, 1950; s. Thomas Earl and Ruth Frances (Martin) O. BA, U. Mo., Columbia, 1972; DDS, U. Mo., Kansas City, 1977. Dir. Westport Free Health Clinic, Kansas City, Mo., 1974-76; clinician St. Louis Dept. Health, 1977-82; gen. practice dentistry Troy, Mo., 1978-92; pvt. practice St. Louis, 1993-94; mem. gen. practice staff Gravois-Gustine Dental Group, St. Louis, 1994-96; pvt. practice gen. dentistry St. Louis, 1996-97, pvt. practice, 1997—. Mem. ADA, Greater St. Louis Dental Soc. (bd. dirs. 1999—), Am. Soc. Dentistry for Children, St. Louis Dental Rsch. Group, Delta Sigma Delta, Troy C. of C., Rotary (Troy chpt., dir. dental program 1985—, sec. 1988, pres. 1989, bd. dirs. 1989-91). Home: 360 W Point Ct Saint Louis MO 63130-4028 Office: Chestnut Park Dental 4583 Chestnut Park Plz Ste 201 Saint Louis MO 63129-3163

OSBORN, RALPH J., retired electrical engineer; b. Pawhuska, Okla., Oct. 26, 1923; s. Ray J. and Lena (Tebo) O.; m. Ruth Rains, Nov. 6, 1943; children: Marsha Hayes, Ronald J. BSEE, Kans. State U., 1948. Registered profl. engr., Kans. Engr. Arco Pipeline, Independence, Kans., 1948-53, supervisor elec. engring. divsn., 1953-74; project mgr. Bayport/Olefins Arco Pipeline, Houston, 1974-76; mid-continent regional mgr. Arco Pipeline, Independence, 1976-85; ret. Bd. dirs. Independence Pub. Schs., 1956-60, 62-

64, Independence C.C., 1972-74, 94-98, Independence Pub. Libr., 1988-98. Ensign USN, 1943-46. Mem. IEEE (pipeline subcom. 1954-75), Am. Petroleum Inst. (pipeline automation com. 1960-76). Disciples of christ. Avocations: photography, computers, travel. Home: 419 S 4th St Independence KS 67301-3938

OSBORN, SUSAN CHANEY, educator, writer; b. Ft. Campbell, Ky., Jan. 7, 1953; d. Lawrence Elvie and Wilma Barbara (Powell) Howard; m. Nicholas Lourick, Aug. 1, 1976 (div. Oct. 1981); m. Steve Osborn, Mar. 20, 1993; 1 child. BS, Ga. State U., 1989; MS, U. Colo., 1997. Lic. tchr., Colo, pvt. occupational tchr., Colo. Owner, photographer Creative Assistance, Atlanta, 1979-89; educator St. Mary's Acad., Cherry Hills Village, Colo., 1989-90, Denver Pub. Schs., 1990-92; internet resource coord. Nat. Renewable Energy Lab., Golden, Colo., 1993-95; writer Diners Club Internat., Englewood, Colo., 1995-96; owner, writer, coord. Publs. Resolution, Denver, 1996—; website advisor Colo. Dept. Pub. Health and Environment, Denver, 1998-99; advisor Houghton-Miffilin Co., Boston, 1992; mem. math. text seclection com. Denver Pub. Schs., 1991; cons. Hauser Chem. Co., Boulder, Colo., 1994. Author: Public Service Company Classroom Connection, 1992, photography manual. Art/photography dir. Boy's Club, Marietta, GA., 1987; art show sect. organizer Girl's Club, Atlanta, 1988; implementor Bear Creek Blvd. Civic Assn., Lakewood, Colo., 1995; pub. rels. coord. Resolve Rocky Mountain Assn., Denver, 1996. Fellow Colo. Writing Project; mem. NEA, Golden Key. Avocations: creative writing, creative photography, theatre, hiking, mountain biking. Office: Publs Resolution PO Box 37263 Denver CO 80237

OSBORNE, CHARLES THOMAS, writer, musicologist; b. Brisbane, Queensland, Australia, Nov. 24, 1927; s. Vincent Lloyd and Elsa Louise (Raumer) O. D (hon.), Griffith U., Australia, 1994. Asst. editor The London Mag., 1958-66; asst. lit. dir. Arts Coun. Gt. Britain, London, 1966-71, lit. dir., 1971-86; chief theatre critic Daily Telegraph, London, 1987-92. Author: The Complete Operas of Verdi, 1969 (Italian Critics award 1969), The Complete Operas of Puccini, 1981 (Yorkshire Post Music award 1981), W.H. Auden: The Life of a Poet, 1979, The Bel Canto Operas, 1994, Oxford Opera Guide, 1996, others. Recipient Gold medal Amici di Verdi, 1993. Fellow Royal Soc. Lit., Royal Philharm. Soc.; mem. Critics Circle (chmn. 1993—). Avocations: reading, traveling.

OSBORNE, DUNCAN ELLIOTT, lawyer; b. Orange, N.J., May 24, 1944; s. Walter Dodd Osborne and Anne (Boaz) Treanor; m. Elizabeth May Bachman, Dec. 29, 1965; children: Ellen Osborne Ray, Mark Elliott, Michael Cleveland. BA, Stanford U., 1966; MA, U. Tex., 1968, JD with honors, 1971. Bar: Tex. (cert. estate planning and probate law) 1971, U.S. Supreme Ct. 1975, U.S. Tax Ct. 1975, U.S. Fed. Ct. Claims 1997. Atty. Graves Dougherty, Austin, Tex., 1971-93, Osborne, Lowe, Helman & Smith L.L.P., Austin, 1993—; bd. dirs. Boatmen's Nat. Bank Austin, 1995-97, Hill Country Bank, Austin, 1998. Author, editor: Asset Protection: Domestic and International Law and Tactics; contbr. articles to profl. jours.; mem. adv. bd. Jour. Asset Protection; mem. Tex. Law Rev. Trustee Susan Vaughan Found., Houston, Still Water Found., Austin; chair bd. trustees St. Stephens Episcopal Sch., Austin, 1985-91, St. Andrews Episcopal Sch., Austin, 1978. Fellow Am. Coll. Trust and Estate Counsel, Coll. of State Bar of Tex.; mem. Internat. Tax Planning Assn., Offshore Inst., Internat. Acad. Estate and Trust Law (exec. com.), Asset Protection Planning Commn. (chair 1996-98)), Order of Coif. Avocation: scuba diving. Office: Osborne Lowe Helman & Smith LLP 301 Congress Ave Ste 1900 Austin TX 78701-2959

OSBORNE, EVAN W., economics educator; b. Berkeley, Calif., May 17, 1964; s. Weymar Zack and Estelle Barbara (Chodor) O.; m. Toyoko Miwa, July 29, 1995; 1 child, Weymar Chiune Miwa Osborne. BA, U. Tex., 1985; MA, UCLA, 1989, PhD, 1993. Asst. prof. Wright State U., Dayton, Ohio, 1994—. Contbr. articles to profl. jours. Mem. Am. Econ. Assn., Am. Law and Econs. Assn., Western Econ. Assn., Pub. Choice Soc. E-mail: evan.osborne@wright.edu. Office: Wright State Univ Dept Econs 3640 Col Glenn Hwy Dayton OH 45435

OSBORNE, FRANK R., lawyer, educator, lecturer; b. Cleve., Dec. 7, 1946; s. Thomas L. and Doris E. O.; m. Charlotte A. Caston, July 8, 1972; children: James, Thomas, Patricia, Janet, Karen, Kathleen, Linda, Jennifer. AB in Polit. Sci., John Carroll U., 1969; JD, Cleve. State U., 1973. Bar: Ohio 1973, U.S. Dist. Ct. (no. dist.) 1975, U.S. Supreme Ct. 1979, U.S. Ct. Appeals (6th cir.) 1979, U.S. Tax Ct. 1980, U.S. Ct. Appeals (7th cir.) 1982. Law clk. to Hon. John V. Corrigan Ohio Ct. Appeals (8th appellate dist.), Cleve., 1973-76; atty. Roudebush, Brown & Ulrich, LPA, Cleve., 1976-86, Arter & Hadden, LPA, Cleve., 1986—; adj. prof. law Ohio civil procedure Cleve. Marshall Coll. Law, Cleve. State U., 1994—; alternative dispute resolution neutral U.S. Dist. Ct. (no. dist.), Cleve., 1990—. Co-author: Civil Discovery Practice in Ohio, 1995. Mem. Ohio State Bar Assn., Cleve. Bar Assn. Fax: 216-696-2645. E-mail: fosborne@arterhadden.com. Home: 1278 Croyden Rd Lyndhurst OH 44124-1413 Office: Arter & Hadden LPA 1100 Huntington Bldg Cleveland OH 44115

OSBORNE, HARRY ALAN, orthodontist; b. Youngstown, Ohio, Mar. 9, 1934; s. Kenneth L. and Marguerite (Filmer) O.; m. Carol June Williams, June 30, 1956 (dec. 1989); children: Elizabeth Ann, J. Scott, Linda J., Robert K.; m. Linda Sue Leister Simmons, May 9, 1993; stepchildren: William A. Simmons, John S. Simmons, Susan Jane Simmons. Student, Westminster Coll., New Wilmington, Pa., 1952-55; DDS, U. Pitts., 1959; MS, Northwestern U., 1962. Diplomate Am. Bd. Orthodontics. Intern Youngstown Hosp. Assn., 1959; practice dentistry specializing in orthodontics Canton, Ohio, 1964—. Supt. adv. com. North Canton Sch. Dist., 1960-87; mem. adv. com. Soc. Bank, Canton, 1962-89; chmn. bldg. com. Faith United Meth. Ch., 1975-80; chmn. cmty bd. YMCA, North Canton, 1986-96, charter mem. Heritage Club (Canton YMCA); v.p. Hills and Dales Homeowners Assn., 1993-96; trustee Christ Presbyn. Ch., Canton, Ohio, elder. Recipient Disting. Service award, Jaycees, 1968. Mem. ADA, Pierre Fauchard Acad., Am. Assn. Orthodontists, Coll. of Diplomates of Am. Bd. Orthodontists (charter), Gt. Lakes Orthodontic Assn., Ohio Dental Assn., Cleve. Orthodontic Soc. (pres. 1983), Stark County Dental Soc. (pres. 1975-76), World Fedn. Orthodontists, Internat. Coll. Dentists, Shady Hollow Country Club (Massillion, Ohio) (bd. dirs. 1984-85, 87—), Brookside Country Club. Republican. Avocation: golf. Home: 2410 Strathmore Dr NW Canton OH 44708-1364 Office: 1021 Schneider St SE Canton OH 44720-3857

OSBORNE, JERRY RAMON, lawyer; b. New Orleans, Dec. 22, 1938; s. Gerald Woodrow and Mildred Irene (Durkee) O.; m. Marianne Muse, June 1965 (div.); children: Carol Osborne Carriere, David Gerald; m. Linda Margaret Le Blanc, Aug. 26, 1987. BBA, Tulane U., 1961, JD, 1962. Bar: La. 1962, U.S. Dist. Ct. (ea. dist.) La. 1962, U.S. Ct. Appeals (5th cir.) 1973. Assoc. then ptnr. Cox, Huppenbauer & Osborne and predecessor firms, New Orleans, 1965-84; ptnr. Foley & Judell L.L.P., New Orleans, 1985—. Bd. dirs. Alliance for Good Govt., 1977-85, Common Cause, Baton Rouge, La., 1990, Planned Parenthood, 1990; mem. Met. Area Com., New Orleans, 1986—. 1st lt. U.S. Army, 1962-65. Mem. New Orleans Tennis Club, Audubon Tennis Club. Democrat. Methodist. Avocations: tennis, cycling. Home: 5518 Prytania St New Orleans LA 70115-4237 Office: 2600 One Canal Pl 365 Canal St New Orleans LA 70130-1112

OSBORNE, JOHN, German language educator; b. Lincoln, Eng., Dec. 31, 1938; s. Leonard and Gladys Ellen (Ward) O.; m. Janet Elizabeth Hart, Sept. 7, 1962; children: Helen, Josephine, Mary, Luke. BA, U. Wales, Swansea, 1962, DLitt, 1995; PhD, Cambridge (Eng.) U., 1966. Lectr. German, U. Southampton, Eng., 1965-68; lectr., reader U. Sussex, Eng., 1968-79; prof. U. Warwick, Coventry, Eng., 1979—; dean Faculty of Arts U. Warwick, Coventry, 1998—. Author: J.M.R. Lenz, 1975, The Meiningen Court Theatre, 1988, C.F. Meyer; Vom Nutzen der Geschichte, 1994, T. Fontane: Vor den Romanen, 1999. Rsch. fellow Alexander von Humboldt Found., Germany, 1972-73, 76-77. Mem. English Goethe Soc. (coun. 1970—, Goethe essay prize 1968), Translators Assn., Fontane Gesellschaft. Avocations: foreign travel, swimming, music. Home: 30 Waverley Rd, Kenilworth CV8 1JN, United Kingdom Office: U Warwick, Dept German, Coventry CV4 1AL, United Kingdom

OSBORNE, KEITH LANGFORD, retired oil industry executive; b. Woodford, Eng., Dec. 10, 1921; s. Frederick Langford and Ruby May (Woods) O.; m. Mary Grey West, Sept. 23, 1950. Officer cadet, Royal Mil. Acad. Sandhurst, Camberley, Eng., 1942. Supply exec. Shell Internat. Petroleum, London, 1947-67; tng. mgr. Shell UK, Chester, Eng., 1967-73, UKF Fertiliser Ltd., Chester, Eng., 1973-80; ret., 1980; prin. assessor, inst. supervisory mgmt. Carlett Park Coll., Eastham, Eng., 1975-89. Editor British Rowing Almanack, 1956—; author: Boat Racing in Britain 1815-1975, One Man Went to Row, 1998, Berlin or Bust, 2000; contbr. articles to profl. jours. Vol. Tonbridge Sch. Clubs, London, 1940—, hon. sec., 1954-59, hon. treas., 1960-95, bd. dirs., 1947—. Lt. Brit. Army, 1942-46, Territorial Army, 1947-50. Inst. Supervisory Mgmt. fellow, 1987; recipient Silver Jubilee medal Her Majesty the Queen, 1977, Gold award Nat. Assn. Boys Clubs, 1982, Torch Trophy Trust award, 1995, Lord Mayor of Chester's Star Citizen Millenium award, 2000. Mem. Kings Sch. Rowing Club (pres. 1989—), Royal Chester Rowing Club (v.p. 1975—, hon. treas. 1978-96), Leander Club. Avocations: rowing, motoring, gardening, music, theatre. Home: Fir Tree Cottage, 30 Eggbridge Ln, Waverton Chester CH3 7PE, England

OSBORNE, MARTIN ROY, research chemist; b. Chelmsford, England, Nov. 9, 1946; m. Ursi Fenner, July 26, 1980; 1 child, David. MA & PhD, Cambridge U., 1971. Rsch. asst. Imperial Coll., London, 1970-72; scientist Inst. Cancer Rsch., London, 1973—. Author: Benzopyrenes, 1987; contbr. scientific papers to profl. publs. Reader Ch. of England, 1991—. Home: 67 Broadlands Ave, Chesham HP5 1AL, England Office: Inst Cancer Rsch, 15 Cotswold Rd, Sutton SM2 5NG, England

OSBORNE-GOLLOP, MARGARET BEVERLEY, administrator; b. Bridgetown, Barbados, Dec. 20, 1948; d. Selwyn Archibald and Germain Camilla (Niles) Osborne; divorced, May 1992. Consular U.S. Embassy, Barbados, 1969-70; clk. typist BWIA, Barbados, 1970-83, sales rep., 1977-81, customer svc. rep., 1981-83; sales rep. B T I C, Barbados, 1995-96; mgr. Club Caribbean, Barbados, 1996—; clk. typist Cable & Wireless, Barbados, 1966-67. Avocations: meeting people, entertaining, dancing. Office: Caribbean Airways, Grantley Adams Airport, Christ Church Barbados

OSBURN, HUGH JACK, business valuation consultant, accountant; b. Gwanda, South Rhodesia, Sept. 7, 1945; arrived in Eng., 1964; s. Henry Stuart and Gladys Evelyn Marion (Bacon) O.; m. Margaret Fowler, Sept. 19, 1970. BA, Cambridge (Eng.) U., 1967, MA, 1971; MSc, U. Newcastle-upon-Tyne, Eng., 1968; MBA, Manchester (Eng.) Bus. Sch., 1972. Chartered engr., Eng. Tech. asst. ironworks Brit. Steel, Scunthorpe, Eng., 1968-70; fin. analyst Brit. Steel, London, 1973-75; works acct. cold rolled products Brit. Steel, Port Talbot, Wales, 1975-78; engring. cons. Knight Wegenstein, Manchester, 1972-73; operational auditor Esso Europe Inc., Hamburg, Germany, 1978-80; sr. auditor Lear Siegler Inc., Germany, 1980-81; fin. dir. Precision Gear Machines & Tools, Coventry, Eng., 1982-83; mgr. mgmt. acctg. Royal Ordnance PLC, Chorley, Eng., 1984-88; v.p. internat. fin. appraisal Am. Appraisal (UK) Ltd., Manchester, 1989—; mem. Ct. of U. of Lancaster, Eng. Fellow Chartered Inst. Mgmt. Accts. (pres. Lancashire and Cumbria br. 1989-90, mem. nat. coun. U.K. 1994-97, mem. internat. com., mem. disciplinary com. 1995-98, investment subcom. 1997-2000), Inst. Materials (profl.), Am. Soc. Appraisers (accredited sr. appraiser), Inst. Investment Mgmt. and Rsch. (assoc.), Hawks (Cambridge U.). Anglican. Avocations: swimming, flying, languages. Home: 1 The Croft Euxton, Chorley PR7 6LH, England Office: Am Appraisal (UK) Ltd, 127-129 Portland St, Manchester M1 4PZ, England

OSCARSON, MATS ÅKE, foreign language educator, researcher; b. Storfors, Sweden, June 9, 1939; s. Klas Henning and Astrid Emy (Emilsson) Oskarsson; m. Lisa Ingeborg Örtengren, Dec. 2, 1978; children: Jacob, Sofia. MA, Gothenburg U., Sweden, 1964, PhD, 1972. Tchr. h.s., 1964-67; ednl. rsch. fellow U. Gothenburg, 1972—, asst. prof., 1973—; lang. testing cons. Coun. of Europe, Strasbourg, France, 1973—; internat. tchg. and rsch. assignments Swedish Internat. Devel. Authority, Latvia and Mozambique, 1994-95. Author: Approaches to Self-Assessment in Foreign Language Learning, 1980, One Two Three-English Grammar, 1976, Catch on 1-4, 1990-91; mem. editl. bd. System, Internat. Jour. Ednl. Tech., 1978—, Language Testing, 1998—; contbr. articles to profl jours. including Lang. Testing, System, Moderna Sprak. Mellon rsch. fellow Nat. Fgn. Lang. Ctr., Johns Hopkins U., 1996. Mem. Internat. Lang. Testing Assn. Home: Snackeskarsg 10, S-42157 V Frolunda Sweden Office: Göteborg U Dept of Edn, PO Box 300, SE 40530 Göteborg Sweden

OSEI-OFEI, EMMANUEL, auditor, accountant; b. Mampong Akwapim, Ghana, Oct. 5, 1942; s. Ebenezer Bernard Ofei and Emilyl Kare Asamoah-Bekoe; m. Vida Abbeyguaye, July 9, 1977; children: Ebenezer, Abena Kare, Yaa Adwo, Gottfried Kwame Ampofo. BA with honors, U. Ghana, 1969. Tchr. Wesley Grammar Sch., Accra, Ghana, 1965-66; team leader 1970 Population Census, Ghana, 1969; tchr. Okuapemman Secondary Sch., Akropong, Ghana, 1969-71; auditor Ghana Audit Svc., Accra, 1972-79; internal auditor Dept. Social Welfare & Cmty. Devel., Accra, 1975-78; prin. internal auditor Accra City Coun., 1979; tech. asst. Audit Office, Maseru, Lesotho, 1979-81; controller of audits Auditor Gen., Gaborone, Botswana, 1981-95; sr. prin. acct. Acct. Gen.on Coun. Botswana Inst. Accts., Botswana, 1996—; auditor African devel. bank projects, jr. secondary schs., 1985-95. Mem. Inst. Internal Auditors. Methodist. Avocations: gardening, classical music, social work. Office: Acct Gen, Pvt Mail Bag 0030, Gaborone Botswana

OSELEDCHIK, YURIY SEMENOVICH, physicist, educator; b. Urupinsk, Russia, Mar. 11, 1942; s. Semen Mironovich Oseledchik and Olga Sergeevna Alekseeva; m. Ludmila Alekseevna Petrova, Dec. 15, 1960; children: Sergey, Katrine. MD, U. Novosibirsk, Russia, 1966, Phd (hon.), 1969; DSc, Acad. Sci. Novosibirsk, 1986. Lectr. Indsl. Ins., Zaporozhye, Ukraine, 1969-76, head dept. physics, 1976-95; head dept. physics Engring. Acad., Zaporozhye. Contbr. articles to profl. jours. Mem. N.Y. Acad. Scis. Home: Budenov Ave 18-16, 330097 Zaporozhye Ukraine Office: Engring Acad, Lenine Ave 226, 330006 Zaporozhye Ukraine

OSEN, KIRSTEN KJELSBERG, anatomy educator, researcher; b. Alta, Finnmark, Norway, July 20, 1928; d. Paul Amandus and Helga (Brun) K.; m. Knut Bjørnør Osen, Jan. 1, 1955; children: Per, Karl. MD, U. Oslo, 1954, PhD, 1970, cert. pathology, 1963; D (hon.), U. Salamanca, Spain, 1997. Intern, 1954-55; sr. registrar in pathology Norwegian Radium Hosp., 1958-62; asst. prof. Anatomical Inst. U. Oslo, 1962-71, prof., 1976—; prof. morphology U. Tromsoe, 1971-76. Contbr. more than 40 articles to profl. jours. including Brain Rsch., Am. Jour. Anatomy, Neurosci., European Jour. Neurosci., among others. Vice chair Norwegian Physicians Against Nuclear Weapons, 1993—. Mem. Am. Assn. Rsch. Otolaryngology (Merit award 1995), Norwegian Acad. Sci. Avocation: peace activism. Office: U Oslo Inst Basic Med Scis, PB 1105 Blindern, 0317 Oslo Norway

OSEN, LYNN M., women's studies educator, writer; b. Roanoke, Ala., Nov. 13, 1920; d. William Benjamin and Portia Bailey Moses; m. Donald Shotwell Osen, May 20, 1950; 1 child, Frank Sanford. BS, U. Calif., Irvine; MS, Calif. State U., Fullerton, 1968. Statistician USN, Alameda, Calif., 1940-45; v.p. Osen-Ojeda Devel. Corp., Santa Ana, Calif., 1961-63; math. tchr. Eldorado Sch. for Gifted, Orange, Calif., 1964-67; prof., lectr. women's studies U. Calif., Irvine, 1969-73; assoc. rschr., mem. adv. bd. U. Calif., Irvine; cons. U. Calif. Santa Ana Women's Opportunity Ctr., 1972. Author: Women in Mathematics, 1974, Women in Science, 1976, In the Wake of Women Pirates, 1976; contbr. articles to profl. jours. and mags. Recipient Outstanding Alumni award U. Calif., Irvine, 1972. Mem. Assn. Women in Math., U. Calif. Irvine Found., U. Calif. Irvine Alumni Assn. (Outstanding Alumna commendation 1972), Newport Beach (Calif.) Libr. Assn., U. Calif. Irvine Chancellor's Club. Avocations: sailing, computers, support group volunteering. E-mail: osen@aol.com. Home: 515 Dunnegan Dr Laguna Beach CA 92651-1432

OSETROV, ALEXANDER VLADIMIROVICH, physics educator, researcher; b. Saint Petersburg, Russia, Nov. 3, 1962; s. Vladimir Sergeevich Osetrov and Nina Anatolievna Smurova. MS in Electrophysics with honors, State Electrotech. U., St. Petersburg, 1985, PhD, 1988, DSc, 1999. Sci. rschr. St. Petersburg State Electrotech. U., 1988-91, asst. prof., 1991-97, assoc. prof., 1997—; head temp. sci. group Ctrl. Rsch. Inst. Materials, St. Petersburg, 1995-99; cons., rschr. in field. Contbr. articles to profl. publs. Grantee Internat. Sci. Found., 1993, Russian Pres., 1994-96, Russian Found. Fundamental Investigation, 1996, 98-2000. Avocations: gardening, outdoors. Home: Apt 9, Bolshaya Konushennaya St 5, 191186 Saint Petersburg Russia Office: State Electrotech U, Prof Popova St 5, 197376 Saint Petersburg Russia

OSETSKY, YURI NICOLAI, physicist, researcher; b. Lvov, Ukraine, May 3, 1959; s. Nicolai Boleslav and Alla Nicolai Osetsky; m. Alla Vladimir Souvorova; children: Nicolai, Tatiana. BSc, MSc with honors, Moscow Engring. Physics Inst., 1982; PhD in Physics and Math., I. V. Kurchatov Atomic Energy Inst., Moscow, 1991. Rsch. scientist Atomic Energy Inst., Moscow, 1982-90; sr. rsch. scientist Russian Rsch. Ctr. "Kurchatov Inst.", Moscow, 1991-93; expert investigator CIEMAT Nuc. Tech. Inst., Madrid, 1993-94; vis. rschr. Poly. U. Catalunya, Barcelona, 1994-95, vis. prof., 1995-97; univ. rsch. fellow U. Liverpool, Eng., 1997—. Contbr. articles to profl. jours. Recipient II Kurchatov prize, 1986, awards Atomic Energy Ministry of Russia, 1989, 94, III Kurchatov prize, 1991. Avocations: informatics, alpine skiing. E-mail: osetsky@liv.ac.uk. Office: U Liverpool, Dept Materials Sci-Engring, Liverpool L69 3GH, England

OSGOOD, CHRISTOPHER MYKEL, radio sales executive; b. Northampton, Mass., Nov. 8, 1963; s. Robert Mansfield and Susanne (Mykel) O.; m. Angela Baxter. BS, Cornell U., 1989. Media rsch. mktg. analyst Vitt Media Internat., N.Y.C., 1988-89; acct. exec. KAOI AM/FM Radio, Maui, Hawaii, 1989-91, KTXH-TV, Houston, 1991-92; dir. advt. Oilers News, Browns News Illustrated, 49ers Report, Cleve., 1992-93; acct. exec. KRBE-FM, Houston, 1993-96, KLOL-FM, Houston, 1996-99; local sales mgr. KUCD-FM, Honolulu, 1999—. Coach Bear Creek Basketball League, Houston, 1993-94. Mem. Cornell Alumni Assn. of Greater Houston, Cornell Soc. Hotelmen. Office: Star 101.9/KUCD-FM 650 Iwilei Rd Ste 400 Honolulu HI 96817-5319

OSGOOD, FRANK WILLIAM, urban and economic planner, writer; b. Williamston, Mich., Sept. 3, 1931; s. Earle Victor and Blanche Mae (Eberley) O.; children: Ann Marie, Frank William Jr. BS, Mich. State U., 1953; M in City Planning, Ga. Inst. Tech., 1960. Prin. planner Tulsa Met. Area Plnning Commn., 1958-60; sr. assoc. Hammer & Co. Assocs., Washington, 1960-64; econ. cons. Marvin Springer & Assocs., Dallas, 1964-65; sr. assoc. Gladstone Assocs., Washington, 1965-67; prof. urban planning Iowa State U., Ames, 1967-73; pres. Frank Osgood Assoc./Osgood Urban Rsch., Dallas, 1973-84; dir. mktg. studies MPSI Americas Inc., Tulsa, 1984-85, Comarc Systems/Roulac & Co., San Francisco, 1985-86; pres. Osgood Urban Rsch., Millbrae, Calif., 1986-95; freelance writer Millbrae and L.A., Calif., 1994—; VISTA vol. coord. Chrysalis, Santa Monica, Calif., 1995-96; pres. Osgood Urban Rsch., L.A., 1996—; adj. prof. U. Tulsa, 1974-76; lectr. U. Tex., Dallas, 1979, U. Tex., Arlington, 1983. Author: Control Land Uses Near Airports, 1960, Planning Small Business, 1967, Continuous Renewal Cities, 1970; contbr. articles to profl. jours. Chmn. awards Cub Scouts Am., Ames, 1971-73; deacon Calvary Presbyn. Ch., San Francisco, 1987-90. 1st lt. USAF, 1954-56. Recipient Community Leaders and Noteworthy Americans award 1976. Mem. Am. Inst. Cert. Planners (peninsula liaison 1987-89, dir. protem 1990 No. Calif. sect., edn. coord. 1991-92, Calif., dir. N. Cen. Tex. sect., Tex. chpt. 1983), Am. Planning Assn., Am. Inst. Planners (v.p. Okla. chpt. 1975-77), Okla. Soc. Planning Cons. (sec., treas. 1976-79), Urban Land Inst., Nat. Assn. Regional Couns., So. Calif. Assn. Govts. (regional adv. coun. 1998—, vice-chmn. 1999-2000, chair 2000—), Writer's Bloc & Novel Group, Cypress. Home: 5605 Nelson St Cypress CA 90630-3148

OSHAROVA, IRINA A., lawyer; b. Nejin, Ukraine, June 7, 1946; d. Alexandr E. and Bella J. Osharova; m. Ely B. Doubinskiy, Aug. 6, 1988. Engr., Poly. Inst., Kiev, Ukraine, 1970; Patent Agt., Pub. Patent Inst., Kiev, 1973; Patent Atty., State Patent Tng. Inst., Moscow, 1975. Patent agent Ukrainian Inst. of Local Industry, Kiev, 1973-80; head patent, trademark and licensing dept. Inst. Biochemistry, Kiev, 1980-93; sr. ptnr., patent and trademark atty. Intels Agy., Kiev, 1993—; atty. Interregional Acad. Personnel Mgmt., 1998; patent cons., advisor Inst. Biochemistry, Kiev, 1997—. Recipient award lettern medal Ukrainian State Patent Office, Kiev, 1997. Mem. Ukrainian Assn. Patent Attys. (mem. audit com. 1997), Internat. Assn. for Protection of Indsl. Property, Internat. Trademark Assn., Internat. Bar Assn. Avocations: travel, theater, literature, art. Office: Intels Agy, Ste 41, 14-A Borschagovskaya Str, 03055 Kiev Ukraine

O'SHEA, LYNNE, management consultant, educator. BA in Polit. Sci., U. Mo., BJ, MA in Info. Theory; PhD, Northwestern U., 1977; postgrad., U. Calif., 1988. Corp. officer, v.p. Internat. Harvester, Chgo., 1979-83; divsn. head, dir. mktg. and comms. Arthur Andersen, Chgo. and Geneva, 1983-85; v.p. bus. devel. mktg. and sales Gannett Co., Arlington, Va., 1986-94; cons. ptnr. Innova, London, 1994-97, A.T. Kearney, Chgo., 1998—; adj. prof. Northwestern U., The J.L. Kellogg Grad. Sch. Mgmt., Evanston, 1982-83, 93-94, 2000—; disting. vis. prof. Syracuse U., 1983-84; lectr. in mktg. U. Chgo., 1982-83. Contbr. articles to profl. jours. Bd. dirs. Nat. Ctr. for Children's Illustrated Lit., Abilene, Tex., Off-the-Street Club, Chgo.; bd. dirs. inner city com. Chgo. Crime Commn.; bd. govs. Mid-Am. Club; chair Circle of Friends, YWCA; co-chair New Trier Parents; bd. dirs. Internat. Women's Forum, membership co-chair, comm. co-chair. Mem. Woman's Athletic Club Chgo., Cleve. Yachting Club, Exec. Club Chgo. Office: A T Kearney Inc 1200 Bank One Ctr 222 W Adams St Fl 23 Chicago IL 60606-5227

OSHEROFF, DOUGLAS DEAN, physicist, researcher; b. Aberdeen, Wash., Aug. 1, 1945; s. William and Bessie Anne (Ondov) O.; m. Phyllis S.K. Liu, Aug. 14, 1970. B.S. in Physics, Calif. Inst. Tech., 1967; M.S., Cornell U., 1969, Ph.D. in Physics, 1973. Mem. tech. staff Bell Labs., Murray Hill, N.Y., 1972-82, head solid state and low temperature physics research dept., 1982-87; prof. Stanford (Calif.) U., 1987—, J.G. Jackson and C.J. Wood prof. physics, 1992—; chair physics, 1993-96. Researcher on properties of matter near absolute zero of temperature; co-discoverer of superfluidity in liquid 3He, 1971, nuclear antiferromagnetic resonance in solid 3He, 1980. Co-recipient Simon Meml. prize Brit. Inst. Physics, 1976, Oliver E. Buckley Solid State Physics prize, 1981, Nobel prize in physics, 1996; John D. and Catherine T. MacArthur prize fellow, 1981. Fellow Am. Phys. Soc., Am. Acad. Arts and Scis., Nat. Acad. Scis. Office: Stanford U Dept Physics 4060 Stanford CA 94305-4060

O'SHIELDS, JUNE CRUCE, lawyer; b. Atlanta, June 27, 1928; d. Marshel Ember and Anne Beatrice (Cruce) O'S.; m. Joseph Candler Hutchinson, Aug. 12, 1950 (div.); children: June O'Shields, Joseph Candler Jr. BA, Vanderbilt U., 1948; MS, Georgetown U., 1970; JD, Monterey (Calif.) Sch. Law, 1977. Bar: Calif. 1983. Sole practice Salinas, Calif., 1983—. Contbr. article to profl. jours. Past election judge State of Va., Fairfax; mem. Dem. Cen. Com., Monterey, 1973-75. Mem. Calif. Bar Assn., Assn. Trial Lawyers Am., Calif. Trial Lawyers Assn., Monterey County Trial Lawyers Assn., Calif. Women Lawyer's Assn., LWV (v.p. Fairfax chpt., chmn. ad hoc com. Monterey chpt.). Democrat. Roman Catholic. Home: 13918 Monte Del Oro Castroville CA 95012-2912

OSHIMA, MASAHARU, chemistry educator; b. Izushi, Hyogo, Japan, Mar. 17, 1949; s. Toshio and Hisako (Nanjo) O.; m. Satoko Terabayashi, Mar. 12, 1977; children: Kumiko, Chihiro. BS, U. Tokyo, 1972, MS, 1974, D in Engring., 1984. Rschr. Nippon Telegraph and Tel., Tokyo, 1974-85, sr. rschr., 1985-87, group leader, 1987-95; prof. U. Tokyo, 1995—. Author, editor: Materials Characterization for Nanoelectronics, 1996, Applications of Synchrotin Radiation, 1998. Mem. Am. Vacuum Soc., Electrochem. Soc., Japan Soc. Synchrotron Radiation Rsch. Avocations: tennis, baseball, golf, music. Office: U Tokyo Dept Appl Chem, 7-3-1 Hongo, Bunkyo-ku Tokyo 113-8656, Japan

OSHIMA, MASUMI, nuclear physicist, educator; b. Toyota, Japan, Jan. 31, 1950; s. Fumio and Kimiko (Sarai) O.; m. Hiromi Ozutsumi, Feb. 6, 1983; children: Maki, Mitsuhiro. Bachelor's, Nagoya (Japan) U., 1972; MS, Tohoku U., Sendai, Japan, 1974, PhD in Nuclear Physics, 1977. Fellow of advanced sci. Japan Atomic Energy Rsch. Inst., Tokai, Japan, 1977-78; rsch. scientist Japan Atomic Energy Rsch. Inst., Tokai, 1978-87, sr. scientist, 1987-92, prin. scientist, 1992—; guest prof. Tohoku U., 1996—. Avocations:

gardening, camping, tennis, walking, reading. Home: Nakane 3337-66, Hitachinaka-shi 312-0011, Japan Office: Japan Atomic Energy, Rsch Inst Shirakata, Tokai-mura 319-1195, Japan

OSHIMA, MICHAEL W., lawyer; b. Big Rapids, Mich., Apr. 4, 1957; s. Walter W. and Mitsue (Marutani) O. AB, Brown U., 1979; MA, Harvard U., 1984; JD, NYU, 1987. Bar: N.Y. 1988, D.C. 1989. Sr. rsch. asst. Harvard U. John F. Kennedy Sch. Govt., Cambridge, Mass., 1981-84; assoc. Davis Polk & Wardwell, N.Y.C., 1987-90; assoc. Arnold & Porter, N.Y.C., 1990-96, ptnr., 1997—. Contbr. articles, reports to profl. publs. Mem. Am. Sociol. Assn., Law and Soc. Assn., N.Y. State Bar Assn., Assn. Bar City N.Y. Office: Arnold & Porter 399 Park Ave Fl 35 New York NY 10022-4690

OSHIMA, TOSHIYUKI, science educator; b. Muroran, Japan, July 29, 1946; s. Kazue and Fumiko Oshima; m. Saori Tadano; children: Koyuki, Yuji. BS, Hokkaido U., Sapporo, Japan, 1969; MS, Muroran (Japan) Inst. Japan, 1972; PhD, Hokkaidoo U., 1983. Assoc. prof. Kitami (Japan) Inst. Tech., 1975-91, prof. bridge engring. & earthquake engring., 1991—; vis. prof. Va. Inst. Tech. and State U., Blacksburg, 1990-91. Avocations: tennis, golf. E-mail: oshima@stce2.civil.kitami-it.ac.jp. Home: Toryocho 171-8, Kitami 090, Japan Office: Kitami Inst Tech, Koencho 165, Kitami 090, Japan

OSHINUSI, OLADAPO NURUDEEN, oil company executive; b. Lagos, Nigeria, Feb. 28, 1956; s. Olaonipekun and Atinuke (Bakare) O.; m. Helen Bassey Henshaw, Oct. 10, 1990; children: Bolanue, Adebayo, Eniola. BSc with honors, U. Ibadan, Nigeria, 1979. Field svc. mbr. Schumberger Dowell, Walm, Nigeria, 1987-88; ops. mgr. Schumberger Dowell, Port Harcourt, Nigeria, 1988-90; tng. mgr. Schlumberger, Eng., 1990-94; tech. mgr. Europe and Africa region Schlumberger, 1994-95; ops. mgr. Schlumberger, Nigeria, 1995-99; quality health, security & environ. mgr. West/South Africa Schlumberger, 1999—. Avocations: golf, reading, travel. Office: Dowell Schulmber, 50 Ave Jean Jauves, BP 360 Montrouse France

OSHIYAMA, ATSHUSHI, physical scientist; b. Kofu, Yamanashi, Japan, Nov. 9, 1952. BS in Physics, U. Tokyo, 1976, MS in Physics, 1978, PhD in Physics, 1981. Rsch. assoc. U. Tokyo, 1981-84; vis. scientist IBM Watson Rsch. Ctr., Yorktown Heights, N.Y., 1983-84; rsch. mgr. NEC Fundamental Rsch. Labs., Tsukuba, Japan, 1984-95; prof. U. Tsukuba, 1995—; vis. prof. U. Hiroshima, Japan, 1991, U. Hokkaido, Sapporo, Japan, 1992, U. Tohoku, Sendai, Japan, 1997—. Contbr. articles to profl. jours. Mem. Am. Phys. Soc., Phys. Soc. Japan. Office: Inst Physics, U Tsukuba, Tsukuba 305, Japan

OSHTRAKH, MICHAEL IOSIFOVICH, physicist, biophysicist; b. Sverdlovsk, USSR, Sept. 18, 1956; s. Iosif Z. and Maya Z. (Yantovsky) O. MS engring. physics, Ural Poly. Inst., Sverdlovsk, 1979, PhD molecular physics and biophysics, 1990, DSc molecular physics and biophysics, 2000. Engr. Div. Applied Biophysics, Physico Tech. Dept. Ural Poly. Inst., Sverdlovsk, 1979-87; jr. rsch. worker divsn. applied biophysics Physico-Tech. Dept., Ural Poly. Inst., Sverdlovsk, 1987-91; sr. rsch. worker div. applied biophysics, physico-tech dept Ural State Tech. U., Sverdlovsk, 1991—; leader rsch. projects, 1991—; sci. cons. Sci.-Prodn. Bus. Uralcomplex, Sverdlovsk, 1990. Contbr. numerous articles to profl. jours. Organizer Sverdlovsk Soc. Jewish Culture, 1988-89, bd. dirs., 1989-90, v.p., 1990-94, pres., 1994—; mem. organizing com. and del. I, II and III Congresses of Jewish Orgns. and Communities, Moscow, 1989, 91, Odessa, 1992, I, II and III Congresses of Fedn. Jewish Orgns. and Communities of Russia, N. Novgorod, 1992, St. Petersburg, 1995, Moscow, 1999; organizer Sverdlovsk Assn. for Jewish Studies, 1991, pres., 1991—; pres. Jewish Nat. Cultural Autonomy of Sverdlovsk Region, 1997—. Mem. United Phys. a Soc. Russian Fedn., Regional Coun. Jewish Orgns. and Communities Ural Region, Assn. Med. Physicists of Russia, Presidium of Fedn. Jewish Orgs. and Cmtys. of Russia, City Ctr. Nat. Cultures, Pub. Chamber of Sverdlovsk Region (coord. coun. 1999—). Achievements include research in biophysical and biomedical applications of Mössbauer spectroscopy, the Mössbauer study of normal hemoglobins with different molecular structure and hemoglobins from patients with leukaemias and erythremia, the Mössbauer and positron annihilation studies of hemoglobin radiolysis and iron-containing pharmaceutical compounds. E-mail: oshtrakh@mail.utnet.ru. Home: Zavodskaya str 32/3 Apt 45, Ekaterinburg Russia 620131 Office: Ural State Tech U-UPI, Div Applied Biophysics, Ekaterinburg Russia 620002

OSIANDER, ANDREAS, political science educator; b. Bonn, Germany, Feb. 19, 1962. Diploma, Inst. Polit. Studies, Paris, 1985; PhD, Oxford (Eng.) U., 1991. Hedley Bull jr. rsch. fellow Balliol Coll., Oxford, 1989-92; Wissenschaftlicher asst. Humboldt U., Berlin, 1992—. Author: The States System of Europe 1640-1990, 1994. Home: Fürbringerstr 4, 10961 Berlin Germany Office: Humboldt U, Unter Den Linden 6, 10099 Berlin Germany

OSIAS, RICHARD ALLEN, international financier, investor, real estate investment executive, corporate investor; b. N.Y.C., Nov. 13, 1940; s. Harry L. and Leah (Schenk) O.; children: A. Kimberly, Alexandra Elizabeth. Grad., Columbia U., 1963; postgrad., David Lipscomb U., 1988-92. Ptnr. Osias Enterprises, Inc., numerous locations, 1953-98; mem. bus. cabinet David Lipscomb U.; bd. dirs. Am. 21. Prin. works include city devel., residential and apt. units, founder City North Lauderdale, Fla., co-founder City of Lauderhill, Fla., complete residential housing communities, shopping centers, country clubs, golf courses, hotel chains, comprehensive housing communities; contributed Greystone Raquet and Tennis Club to Nolensville, Tenn.; owner, operator Coolsprings Exec. Plz., landmark office bldg., Internat. Common Market Shopping Complex and other office bldgs., shopping ctrs. in mid-southern region; co-author: South Florida Uniform Building Code. Mem. North Lauderdale City Coun., 1967—, mayor, 1968, police and fire commr., 1967—; mem. Gold Cir., Atlanta Ballet; benefactor Atlanta Symphony Soc.; founder Boys Clubs Broward County, Tower coun. Pine Crest Prep. Sch. (founder), v.p., bd. dirs. LaCiel Park Tower Condominium Assn.; bd. dirs. Tenn. Children's Home, MASS, Tenn. chpt. MADD, MADD Tenn. Children's Home. Recipient Best Am. House award Am. Home mag., 1962, Westinghouse award, 1968, Cert. of Merit for outstanding achievement and contbn. to City of Atlanta by Mayor Andrew Young, 1982; named Builder of Yr., Sunshine State Info. Bur., Fla. and Sunshine State Sr. Citizen, Fla., 1967-73, Builder of Month, Builder/Arch. Mag., 1992, Hon. Police Chief, Nashville, Tenn., 1995, N.Y.C.; profiles on nat. and internat. media, including Dateline/CBS TV, NBC TV, CBS TV and Fuji Network (Japan). Mem. Ft. Lauderdale BBB, N.Y. BBB, Nashville BBB, Offshore Power Boat Racing Assn., Fraternal Order Police Assn. (pres.), U.S. C. of C., Fla. C. of C., Margate C. of C., Ft. Lauderdale C. of C., Smithsonian Instn., Soc. Founders U. Miami, Tower Coun., Columns Soc., Pinecrest Prep. Sch. (founder), Nat. Assn. Home Builders, Bankers Club (Miami, Fla.), Bankers Top of First Club, Quarter Deck Club (Galveston, Tex.), Boca Raton (Fla.) Yacht and Country Club, Maunalua Bay Club (Honolulu), Tryall Golf and Country Club (Jamaica), Top of the Home Club, Svc. Plus Club (France), Ensworth Red Gables Soc., Hawaii Loa Ridge Assn., Cannes Island Yacht Club, Canary Islands Yacht Club, Collier's Reserve Country Club (Naples, Fla.), Grey Oaks Country Club (Naples), Le Ciel Club (Naples; v.p. bd. dirs.). E-mail: osias1@aol.com Fax: 808-373-9980. Home: 482 Maono Loop Honolulu HI 96821

OSICEANU, PETRE CONSTANTIN, physicist, researcher; b. Bals, Olt, Romania, Jan. 11, 1949; s. Constanin Petre and Victoria Constantin (Teodorescu) O.; m. Magdalena Petre Barbu, Apr. 30, 1974; children: Ana Maria, Elena Victoria. M in Physics, U. Bucharest, Romania, 1973, PhD, 1988. Rschr. Inst. Physics U. Bucharest, 1973-77, rschr. Inst. Phys. Chem., 1978—; rschr. Inst. Nuclear Energy, Pitest, 1977-78; vis. rschr. Internat. Ctr. Theoretical Physics, Trieste, Italy, 1991; invited prof. Internat. Microelectronics Ctr., Leuven, Belgium, 1993; assoc. prof. Polytech. U. Bucharest, 1994-96; cons. Ministry of Tech. Rsch., Bucharest, 1995-99; nat. rep. Coun. European Synch. Soc., France, 1990-92, Internat. Union of Vacuum, Sci. Technique and Applications-Applied Surface Sci. Divsn., U.S., 1992-98. Author: Surface Analysis Methods, 1998; contbr. articles to profl. jours. Recipient Nicolae Teclu award Romanian Acad., 1996. Mem. N.Y. Acad. Scis. Romanian Orthodox. Avocations: sports, music, pure biological agriculture. Office: U Bucharest Inst Phys Chem, Spl Indep 202, 77208 Bucharest Romania

OSIEGBU, PATRICK IFE, finance educator, consultant, researcher; b. Issele-Uku, Delta, Nigeria, Sept. 13, 1944; s. Iyiegbu and Osodi (Diei) O.; m. Florence Kosekwu Nwomeneh, Dec. 23, 1973; 5 children. BBA, Kent (Ohio) State U., 1974; MBA, Atlanta U., 1977; PhD, Fed. U. Tech., Owerri, Nigeria, 1996. Charge hand Alumna Co., Lagos, Nigeria, 1962-67; bookkeeper Nigerian Motion Pictures, Lagos, 1967-70; machine operator Parker-Hanifin Corp., Ravenna, Ohio, 1973-74; lectr. Voorhees, Denmark, S.C., 1977-91; sr. lectr. fin. and banking U. Port Harcourt, Nigeria, 1981—; head fin. and adminstrn. Honda Plaza, Isolo Lagos, 1994-96. Author: Introduction to Cost and Management Accounting, 1997, Money, Banking and Economy in Nigeria, 1998. Chmn. Otu Nmuta, Port Harcourt, 1996—. Grantee Coun. for Social Sci. Rsch. in Africa, Dakar, Senegal, 1994, U. Port Harcourt, 1998. Mem. Chartered Inst. Bankers Nigeria, Nigerian Acctg. Tchrs. Assn. (v.p. 1990-93), Rotary (dir. vocat. svc., editor 1985-90). Avocations: tennis, music. Homee: 3 Ali-Cape Verde, PO Box 256, Choba Port Harcourt Rivers, Nigeria Office: U Port Harcourt Fac Mgmt Sc, Dept Fin-Banking PO Box 256, Choba Port Harcourt Rivers, Nigeria

OSINSKY, SERGEY, oncologist, researcher; b. Mytischy, Russia, Nov. 5, 1945; s. Peter Aleksandrovich and Maria Yakovlevna (Britvina) O.; m. Larissa Nikitichna Bubnovskaya, June 23, 1970; 1 child, Dmitriy. MD, Med. U., Kiev, Ukraine, 1969; PhD, Inst. Oncol. Problems, Kiev, 1973, DrSci (med), 1987. Postgrad. student Inst. Oncology Problems, Kiev, 1969-72, minor rsch. fellow, 1972-76, sr. rsch. fellow, 1976-84, sci. sec., 1977-84; leading rsch. fellow Inst. Exp. Pathol. Oncol. Radiobiology, Kiev, 1984-90, head of dept., 1990—; prof. Inst. Exp. Pathology Oncology Radiobiology, Kiev, Ukraine, 1993; cons., adv. Ctr. of Intravascular Neuroradiosurgery, Kiev, 1990—; mem. editl. bd. Exptl. Oncology, Sensitization Newsletter, Kiev, 1997—, Kyoto, Japan, 1994—. Author: Hyperthermia and Hyperglycemia in Oncology, 1987; editor: Experimental Oncology, 1995; patentee: Eight patents in oncology, 1992-99; contbr. articles to profl. jours. Recipient INTAS, Belgium, 1993, Cancer Rsch. Inst., N.Y.C., 1995, CRDF, Arlington, Va., 1996. Mem. Internat. Clin. Hyperthermia Soc., Ukrainian Oncol. Soc. Avocations: color photography, geography, soccer. E-mail address: osion@onconet.kiev.ua. Fax: 380-44-267-16-56. Home: 9 Ozernaya Str flat 18, Kiev 03110, Ukraine Office: Inst Experimental Pathology, 45 Vasilkovskaya Str, Kiev 03022, Ukraine

OSIPENKO, KONSTANTIN YUR'EVICH, mathematician, educator; b. Moscow, Feb. 23, 1950; s. Yurii Konstantinovich and Cicely Danielovna (Plotkina) O.; m. Natalia Valentinovna Novojilova, Feb. 15, 1975; children: Xenia, Kirill. MS, Moscow State U., 1972, PhD, 1976; Dr in Physics and Math., Steklov Math. Inst., Moscow, 1994. Asst. prof. Russian State Tech. U., Moscow, 1975-79, assoc. prof., 1979-94, prof. math., 1994—, head math. dept., 1995—. Contbr. articles to profl. jours. Grantee Internat. Sci. Found., 1993, 94, 95, Russian Found. for Basic Rsch., 1995-96, 96-98, 97-99, 98-2000, 99-01, 2000-02. Mem. Moscow Math. Soc., Am. Math. Soc. Home: pr Vernadskogo 113-245, 117571 Moscow Russia Office: Russian State Tech U MATI, Orshanskay Str 3, 121552 Moscow Russia

OSIPOV, YURII SERGEYEVICH, mathematician, mechanical scientist, educator; b. Tobolsk, Russia, July 7, 1936; s. Sergey F. and Natalia S. (Kevlich) O.; m. Nadezhda B. Lipovetskaya, Mar. 1, 1960 (div. Aug. 1990); 1 child, Natalia Yu.; m. Marina V. Dortzeva, Mar. 28, 1992. PhD in Physics and Maths., Ural State U., Sverdlovsk, Russia, 1971; Doctor (hon.), Bar-Ilan U., Ramat-Gun, Israel, 1992, U. Santiago, Chile, 1993. Head chair of optimal control Moscow State U.; rschr. Inst. Maths. and Mechanics, Sverdlovsk, 1970-86, head sect. differential equations, 1972—, dir., 1987-93; dir. V. A. Steklov Inst. Maths., Moscow, 1993—; pres. Russian Acad. of Scis., Moscow, 1991—. Mem. editorial bd. Jour. Doklady Acad. Scis., Izvegtiya Acad. Sci., Jour. Computational Maths. and Math. Physics, Automation and Telemechanics; contbr. articles to profl. jours. Recipient Lenin prize Govt. of U.S.S.R., 1976, State prize, Govt. of Russia, 1993. Mem. Am. Math. Soc., Acad. of Scis. of U.S.S.R. (corr. 1984—, academician 1987—), World Acad. Arts and Scis., Washington Acad. Scis. Home: Leninskie Gory, MGU korp L kv 3, 117234 Moscow Russia also: ul Marshala Zhukova 11 62, 620077 Sverdlovsk Russia Office: Russian Acad Scis, Leninski Prospect 14, 117901 Moscow Russia also: Inst Math and Mechanics, ul Kovalevskoi 16, 620066 Sverdlovsk Russia*

OSKARSON, PETER O.H., theatre director; b. Stockholm, June 13, 1951; s. Per Otto S. Oskarson and Margareta G. DuRietz; m. Kajsa Reingardt (div. June 1979); m. Gunilla E. Kindstrand, Apr. 20, 1983; children: Love, Gro, Mikaela, Li, Saga. Student in actor edn., State Sch., Stockholm, 1973. Artistic dir. Skanska Theatre, Landskrona, Sweden, 1973-82, Folk Theatre Gavleborg, Gavle, Sweden, 1982-90, 97—, Helsingegarden, Jarvso, Sweden, 1990—, Orion Theatre, Stockholm, 1993-2000, World Theatre Project, Stockholm, 1999—; mem. Swedish Theater Acad., Swedish World Culture Forum. Recipient Alf Sjöberg prize Royal Dramatic Theatre, Stockholm, 1979, Theatre prize Swedish Acad., Stockholm, 1983, Expressen, Stockholm, 1989, Thalia prize Svenska Dagbladet, Stockholm, 1990, Malmoe, 1994, Wilhelm Moberg prize, 2000. E-mail: peter@oskarson.com. Home: Helsingegarden, S 820 40 Jarvso Sweden Office: Folkteatern Box 146, Gävle 80103, Sweden

OSKOUIE, ALI KIANI, chemical and environmental engineer; b. Tabriz, Iran, Aug. 9, 1960; came to U.S., 1988; s. Mohammad Kiani Oskouie and Azam Heidari; m. Mojgan Rassouli, June 14, 1989; children: Suzanne, Melissa. BS, U. Tabriz, 1986; MS of Engring., U. Mich., 1990; PhD, Ill. Inst. Tech., 1996. Tchg. asst. Ill. Inst. Tech., Chgo., 1990-95, rsch. asst., 1996, postdoctoral faculty rsch. assoc., 1996-97, faculty dept. of chem. and envrion. engring., 1997—, faculty Stuart Sch. of Bus., Environtl. Mgmt. Program, coord. water program jt. project with City of Chgo.; cons. Amherst (Mass.) Process Instruments, 1992—; supr. grad. students, particle lab. establishment Ill. Inst. Tech., Chgo., 1996—; coord. pharmaceutical rsch. with Gen. Hosp. and U. of Ottawa, Can. Mem. grad. and undergrad. housing focus group Ill. Inst. Tech., Chgo., 1996. Rsch. grantee Am. Air Liquide, 1996. Mem. ASCE, Am. Assn. Aerosol Rsch., Am. Water Works Assn. Achievements include devel. of new technique to determine particle size, density and shape factor using time-of-flight sizers in supersonic flow field; invented a multi-beam system in time-of-flight sizers; patented an apparatus for generating aroma upon electronic signal, developed a new technique for surfactant characterization. Office: Ill Inst Tech 10 W 33rd St Chicago IL 60616-3730

OSMAK, MAJA, biologist, researcher, educator; b. Zagreb, Croatia, Oct. 13, 1950; m. Veljko and Sonja (Marcelja) Mandić; m. Zeljko Osmak, Nov. 10, 1973 (dec. 1989); 1 child, Zoran. BSc, Faculty Natural Sci., Zagreb, 1974; MSc, U. Zagreb, 1978, PhD, 1982. Rsch. asst. Rudjer Bošković Inst., Zagreb, 1975-84, rsch. assoc., 1984-90, sr. rsch. assoc., 1990-93, rsch. advisor, 1993—, head lab., 1995—; prof. postgrad. studies U. Zagreb, 1986—; pres. sci. bd. Rugjer Bošković Inst., 1995-97. Co-author: Clinical Oncology, 1996. Mem. Croatian Radiation Protection Assn. (pres. 1995-97), Croatian Genetic Soc., European Soc. Radiation Biology, N.Y. Acad. Scis. Roman Catholic. Avocations: reading, swimming, climbing. Office: Rudjer Bošković Inst, Bijenička Cesta 54, HR-10000 Zagreb Croatia

OSMAN, ALI, medical educator, researcher; b. Kluang, Malaysia, Oct. 23, 1955; s. Buntar and Mohd-Amin (Sabidah) O.; m. Abd Manaf Rabitah; children: Marina, Mohd Helmi, Mohd Hamidi, Juliana, Suriana, Mohd Hazimi. MD, Univ. Kebangsaan, Malaysia, 1981; MPH, Tulane Univ., 1984; PhD, Univ. Kebangsaan, 1994. Medical officer Min. of Health, Malaysia, 1981-84; lectr. Univ. Kebangsaan, Malaysia, 1984-94, head of dept. assoc. prof., 1992-94, head of dept., prof., 1994—. Recipient Annual Rsch. award Royal Coll. Physicians, 1994. Fellow Acad. of Medicine; mem. Pub. Health Soc. Malaysia (pres.), Asia Pacific Clin. Nutrition Soc. (treas.). Avocations: reading cartoons, writing.

OSMAN, FREDERICK, mathematics educator, researcher; b. Fairfield, Australia, Sept. 23, 1971; s. Edward Yoad and Norma (Polus) O. BS, U. We. Sydney MacArthur, Campbelltown, Australia, 1994, BS with honors, 1995, PhD, 1998. Grad. Cert. in Tchg. Lab. attendant U. We. Sydney MacArthur, Campbelltown, 1992-93, peer tutor, 1992-99, assoc. lectr., 1993-99; lectr. U. We. Sydney Nepean, Kingswood, Australia, 1999—. Mem. Australian Inst. Physics (mem. com. 1994-99), Statis. Soc. (mem. com. 199—), Atomic Agy. Fusion Rsch. (mem. com. 1996-99), Australian Inst. Nuclear Sci. and Engring., Australian Nuclear Sci. Tech. Orgn. Avocations: reading, tennis, touch football. Home: 31 McCarthy St, 2165 Fairfield West Australia Office: UWS Nepean, PO Box 10, 2747 Kingswood Australia

OSMAN, MOHAMED SAYED, dean, mathematics educator; b. Cairo, Egypt, Oct. 11, 1941; s. Sayed Aly and Fatma (Hasan) O.; m. Sekina Hanafy Mohamed; children: Nagla, Lamia, Amr. BSc in Elec. Engring., Cairo U., 1963; PhD in Math. and Physics, Charles U., Prague, 1975. Prof. math. Mil. Tech. Coll., Cairo, 1986—, chmn. computers and ops. rsch. dept., 1986-87, chmn. basic sci. br., 1989-90, dep. dir. for grad. studies and rsch., 1990-91, vice dean mil. tech. coll., 1991-92; assoc. dean in charge engring. depts. Higher Tech. Inst., Cairo, 1994—; mem. grad. studies com. Cairo U., 1987-91. Editor confs.; contbr. more than 100 articles to profl. jours. Maj. gen. MTC, 1963-92. Recipient Nat. award for Math., Egypt, 1974, medal of long period svc. in Army, 1981, Highest Egyptian medal of 2d class, 1992. Mem. Internat. Soc. Math., Egyptian Soc. Ops. Rsch., Egyptian Soc. Appled Ops. Rsch., Mil. Sprots Clubs, El-Shams Sports Clubs. Avocations: reading, sports, walking, community service. Office: Higher Tech Inst, Ahmed Hamdi St, First Zone, Tenth of Ramadan City Egypt

OSMAN, TAREF BAHIJ, publisher; b. Beirut, Lebanon, Jan. 14, 1956; s. Bahij Salim and Sadouf Ibrahim (Kamal) Osman; m. Hala Zuheir Barakat; 3 children. B in Mech. Engring., Kans. State U., 1979. Prodn. mgr. DAR Shehrazad, Beirut, 1980-81; site engr. A.T.C.O. Engring., Qatar, 1981-82; prodn. mgr. Dar el Ilm Lilmalayin, Beirut, 1982-86, v.p. printing, 1986-89, CEO, 1989—; v.p., cons. Ednl. Pubs., beirut, 1986-97; cons. eirut Fatwa Pub. Libr., 1993—. Mem. Lebanese Pubs. Assn. (pres. 1993—). Mem. Nadwai Alamal Alwatani Party. Avocations: swimming, reading, golf. Office: Dar El Ilm Lilmalayin, Mar Elias St, 1085 Beirut Lebanon

OSMANOV, SALADIN KAMILOVITCH, microbiologist; b. Buinaksk, Russia, Mar. 24, 1951; s. Kamil Osmanov and Ayshat Daibova; m. Marifat Gafurova, Nov. 6, 1977; children: Sabira, Farida, Kamil. Degree in medicine, 2d Med. Inst., Moscow, 1976; postgrad., Med. inst., Moscow, 1977, Inst. Fng. Lang., Tula, Russia, 1978; PhD in Microbiology, Metchnikov Rsch. Inst., Moscow, 1983. Sr. rschr. Meichikov Inst. Vaccines and Sera, Moscow, 1983-85, chief lab. immunodiagnostics, 1985-87; sr. rschr. Inst. Epidemiology, Moscow, 1987-88; scientist Global Program on AIDS, WHO, Geneva, 1988-96; virologist, vaccine specialist Joint UN Program on HIV/AIDS, Geneva, 1996—. Contbr. over 70 articles to profl. jours., chpts. to books. Avocations: classical music, tennis, travel.

OSNOS, PETER LIONEL WINSTON, publishing executive; b. Bombay, India, Oct. 13, 1943; s. Joseph Lionel and Marta (Bychowski) O.; m. Susan R. Sherer, Aug. 18, 1973; children: Katherine Mason, Evan L.R. BA, Brandeis U., Waltham, Mass., 1964; MS in Journalism with honors, Columbia U., 1965. Editorial asst. I.F. Stone's Weekly, Washington, 1964-65; corr., editor Washington Post, 1966-84; v.p. assoc. pub. Random House Trade Books and pub. Times Books, Random House, Inc., N.Y.C., 1984-96; cons. 20th Century Fund, 1996-97; pub., chief exec. Public Affairs, 1997—. Contbr. articles to profl. publs. Bd. dirs. Human Rights Watch, chmn. Europe and Ctrl. Asia divns.; bd. dirs. Baltic-Am. Partnership, U. Mich. Fellowship Jounralists, 2000. Fellow NEH, 1973-74. Mem. Assn. Am. Pubs. (vice chmn. gen. pub. divsn. 1993-96), Coun. on Fgn. Rels., Century Club. Office: Pub Affairs 250 W 57th St New York NY 10107

OSOFF, JEFFREY ARLIN, media executive; b. Everett, Mass., June 5, 1936; s. Meyer and Minerva (Cogan) O. (dec.); m. Arlene Shuman, Sept. 23, 1962 (div. Jan. 1988); children: Judith Robin (dec.), David Eric. BA, Bowling Green State U., 1958; MS, Columbia U., 1959. Reporter Boston Post, 1954-55; reporter Boston Globe, 1955-64, rewriteman, 1962-63, acting asst. city editor, 1963-64; dir. News Bur. Brandeis U., Waltham, Mass., 1964-67; asst. dir. pub. affairs Brandeis U., 1967-69, dir. pub. affairs, 1969-76; chmn. bd. Jansson, Inc., Waltham, 1976-87; pres., chief exec. officer JAO Enterprises, Ltd., Lexington, Mass., 1987—; chmn. Dorian Enterprises, Ltd., 1992—, D & J Enterprises, Ltd., Lexington, Mass., 1995—; lectr. in journalism and pub. rels. cons. First v.p. Dysuatonomia Found., 1965-66, bd. dirs., 1965-76, pres., 1973-74; bd. dirs. New Eng. region Anti-Defamation League. Served with USAF, 1961-62. Recipient citation for outstanding journalistic reporting Mass. N.G., 1961; several awards for high achievement in graphics. Mem. New Eng. Press Assn., Internat. Thermographic Assn., Printing Industries Am., Printing Industries New Eng., Am. Coll. Pub. Rels. Assn., Jewish Pub. Relations Soc. Am., Pub. Rels. Soc. Am., Publicity Club Boston, Sigma Delta Chi, Zeta Beta Tau. Jewish. Home and Office: 136 Stow Rd Marlborough MA 01752-6510

OSOLSOBĚ, IVO, performing arts educator; b. Brno, Moravia, Czech Republic, Mar. 26, 1928; s. Jan and Zofie (Lefnerová) O.; m. Libuše Imrichová, Dec. 22, 1957; children: Jan. Petr. PhD, Masaryk U., 1953; postgrad., Netherlands Inst., 1980-81, CUNY, 1992-93. Dramaturgist State Theatre in Brno, Czech Republic, 1953-89; assoc. prof. Janáček Acad. of Performing Arts, 1994; lectr. Masaryk U., Brno, 1965, Summer Sch. of Semiotics, 1981, 83, U. Urbino, Italy, U. Leuven, 1987; internat. visitor USIA, 1990. Author: Musical Is..., 1967, Theatre That Sings, Speaks, and Dances, 1974 (Suphraphon award 1975), Much Ado About Semiotics, 1992, Marsyas, Apollo & Dionysos, 1996; editor: (by Otakar Zich) Esthetics of Dramatic Art, 1987, (by Siri Veltrusky) Drama as Literature, 1999. Pvt. Czechoslovakia Army, 1953-55. Mem. Semiotic Soc. of Am. (hon.), Internat. Assn. of Visual Semiotics (hon. com.). Roman Catholic. Home: Vackova 57, 61200 Brno Czech Republic Office: Janacek Acad Performing Art, Mozartova 1, 60200 Brno Czech Republic

OSPEL, MARCEL, bank executive. Grad., Higher Sch. Econs., Basel, Switzerland. With dept. olanning & mktg. Swiss Bank Corp., 1977-80; with capital markets Swiss Bank Corp., London, N.Y.C., 1980-87, dir., 1987-90, mem. enlargement group, 1990-92, CEO capital markets & treasury, 1992-95; with Swiss Bank Corp., Warburg, 1995-96, group pres., 1996—; CEO Union Bank Switzerland, Zurich, 1998—. Office: UBS AG, Bohnhofstrasse 45, CH-8098 Zurich Switzerland*

OSPELT, ALOIS, archivist, state librarian; b. Vaduz, Liechtenstein, Jan. 31, 1946. PhD, Fribourg (Switzerland) U., 1972. Gymnasium tchr. Liechtenstein Gymnasium, Vaduz, 1972-74; dir. Liechtenstein State Archives and Library, Vaduz, 1974—. Author: Liechtenstein 1938-1978: Bilder und Dokumente, 1978, Das Liechtensteinische Landesarchiv: eine Einführung, 1978, Das Wappen der Gemeinde Vaduz, 1978, Ein Lebenswerk: zum 65. Geburtstag ihrem Seniorchef Toni Hilti als Festgabe im Namen der Geschäftsleitung und der Mitarbeiter überreicht, 1979, Bericht über Wappen, Farben, Siegel und Embleme des Fürstentums Liechtenstein, 1981, Die Alpwirtschaft im Fürstentum Liechtenstein/Hippolyt Ludwig von Klenze, 1985, Besuchsdiplomatie zwischen Vaduz und Bern, Besuche schweizerischer Bundesräte im Fürstentum Liechtenstein, 1988; editor: 100 Jahre Pfarrkirche Vaduz: 1873-1973/Hundert Jahre Pfarrei und Pfarrkirche Vaduz, 1973, 100 Jahre Pfarrei Ruggell: 1874-1974: ein Beitrag zur Pfarreigeschichte Festschrift Pfarrei Ruggell, 1974, Landeskunde des Füstentums Liechtenstein, 1979, Der Vaduzer Wald, 1981, Das Vaduzer Rathaus: Festschrift zur Eröffnung des renovierten Rathauses am 10 Oktober 1984, 1984, Wappen, Farben, Siegel und Embleme des Fürstentums Liechtenstein, 1985; co-editor: 25 Jahre Liechtensteinische Landesbibliothek, Festschrift, 1986; contbr. numerous articles to profl. jours. and newspapers. Rep. Liechtenstein Parliament, 1989-92. Office: Liechtensteinisches, Landesarchiv/bibliothek, 9490 Vaduz Liechtenstein

OSPINA, JULIO ENRIQUE, pathologist, medical education expert; b. Ibagué, Tolima, Colombia, Jan. 12, 1936; s. Julio and Teodolinda (Lugo) O.; m. Clara Téllez, Nov. 21, 1964; children: Mónica, Tatiana. BS, Colegio Mayor del Rosario, Bogotá, 1953; MD, U. Brasil, Rio de Janeiro, 1961; Diploma, Ednl. Coun. Fgn. Med. Grads., Evanston, Ill., 1965. Intern in pathology Hosp. Santa Clara de Misericordia, Rio de Janeiro, 1960; resident in pathology U. Nacional de Colombia, 1961-63, instr. pathology/faculty medicine/prof./faculty odontology, 1963-64, asst. prof., 1969-91; postdoctoral fellow in cancer rsch. Roswell Park Meml. Inst., Buffalo, 1968; chief of pathology Clinica Palermo, Bogotá, Colombia, 1972—; exec. dir. Colombian Assn. Med. Schs., Bogotá, 1992—; dir. Inst. Nat. de Cancerologia, Bogotá, 1974-86; sci. dir. Hosp. San Juan de Dios, Bogotá, 1987-88; dir. Ctr. of Rsch., Escuela Coll. Medicina, Bogotá, 1988-89; coord. projects U. Nat. de Colombia, 1988-92; dir. projects faculty medicine U. de la

Sabana, Bogotá, 1992; cons. expert in cancer O.M.S. (WHO), Ginebra, Switzerland, 1992—; pres. CICA-UICC, Ginebra, 1992—; prof. ultraestructura celular dept. biology U. Los Andes, Bogotá, 1972-75; pres. congress Latinoamericanos e Iberoamericanos de Microscopá Electrónica y Biología Celular, 1981; exec. dir. Nacional de Hospitales e Instituciones de Salud Pública, 1980; founding mem. Coop. Trabajo Médico Asociado, Bogotá, 1993; mem. Com. Yr. 2000 Plan, U. Nacional de Colombia, 1989; sci. evaluator Proy. Investigac. Colciencias, Bogotá, 1986; sci. assessor Biolog Exptl. Inst. Nal. de Cancerologia, Bogotá, 1986. Author: Conferencia Andina de Educación Médica, 1993, Atlas Ultraestructural Celular-Publicaciones Experimentales, Aspectos Básicos del Cáncer, Proyecto Centro Hospitalario Nacional II, III, Proyecto Centro Médico Nacional, 1988, Plan Nacional de Cáncer de Colombia, 1975, II, 1985; co-author: Bocio y Cáncer del Tiroides, 1976; editl. com. L.Am. Electronic Microscopy Rev., 1978, Oncology, 1980-82, Jour. Exptl. and Clin. Cancer Rsch., 1983-92; med. adv. bd. Cancer Mag.; contbr. over 130 articles to profl. jours. Mem. Internat. Assn. Breast Cancer Rsch. (bd. govs. 1985), Fed. L.Am. Soc. Cancerologia (v.p. 1981), Soc. Iberoam. Biology Celular (adv. bd. 1981—), L.Am. Soc. Electronic Microscopics (pres. 1978-85, del. for Colombia 1972-78), L.Am. Asssn. for Insts. of Cancer (v.p. 1981), Soc. Col. Medic Fisica y Rehabilit., Soc. Col. del Cancerologia, Pathology Soc. of Bogotá, Internat. Union contra el Cáncer, Columbian Soc. pediatrics, AAAS, Internat. Acad. Pathology, Sociedad Mexicana de Estudios Oncológicos, Assn. de exalumnos Univ. de Yale (founding mem.), Assn. de Exalumnos del Inst. Nacional de Cancerologia (founding mem.), Cofundador Centro Internat. de Fisica, Assn. Colombiana para el Avance de la Ciencia (sci. assessor 1986). Avocations: sports, reading, classical music, Colombian music. Home: Calle 119 #12-68 Apto 101, Santafé Bogotá Colombia Office: Colombian Assn of Med Schs ASCOFAME, Calle 39A No 28-63 AA53751, Santafé Bogotá Colombia

OSPINA-LONDOÑO, OSCAR FRANCISCO, educator; b. Medellín, Antioquia, Colombia, July 3, 1930; s. Luis María and Sofía (Londoño) Ospina; m. Gladys María Parra, Aug. 6, 1960; children: Oscar Fernando, Jorge Mario, Marcela. MS, Mich. State U., 1957; Ingeniero Agronomo, U. Nat. Colombia, Agosto, 1960; PhD, U. Calif., Riverside, 1967. Prof., investigator soil sci. Nat. U. Colombia, Medellin, 1957-89, prof. emeritus, 1989—, pres. comision decanos, 1969-72; cons. Estudios De Suelos, Medellin, 1989—; gerente Agroestudios, Medellin, 1989—. Participant NGO, Medellin, 1992. Mem. Latin Am. Soc. Ciencia del Suelo (v.p. 1974-76), Colombian Soc. de la Ciencia del Suelo (honorable mention 1986). Liberal. Roman Catholic. Avocation: filatelia. Home: Carrer 85C No 34-81, Medellin Colombia Office: Agroestudios, Consultant, Cales Rio Claro Circ 4a, 69-42 Medellin Colombia

OSSEI-ANTO, THEOPHILUS AQUINAS, science educator; b. Bechem, Brong-Ahafo, Ghana, Feb. 4, 1948; s. Albert Cletus and Mary Akua (Pokuaah) A.; m. Esther Agyeiwaa Basoah, Feb. 4, 1978; children: Martina, Mary, Esther, Theophilus, Josephine. BS in Gen. Edn., U. Cape Coast (Ghana), 1972, BS in Physics with honors, 1973; MEd in Gen. Edn., SUNY, Buffalo, 1981, PhD in Sci. Edn., 1996. Demonstrator dept. physics U. Cape Coast (Ghana), 1972-73, lectr., 1986-92, sr. lectr., 1998—; asst. registrar West African Examinations Coun., Accra, Ghana, 1976-78; asst. sec. Ghana Atomic Energy Commn., Kwabenya, Ghana, 1977-78; lectr. Coll. Edn., Owerri, Nigeria, 1978-82; sr. lectr. Coll. Tech., Owerri, 1982-85; edn. officer Mbale (Uganda) Sr. Secondary Sch., 1973-75; physics tutor Opoku Ware Assisted Secondary Sch., Kumasi, Ghana, 1975-76. Co-author: (govt. SSS textbook) Physics for Sr. Secondary Schools, 1991; advisor: GAST: Physics for Senior Secondary Schools, 1990, GAST: Core Science for Senior Secondary Schools, 1990; mem. editl. bd.: GAST: Ghanaian Science Teacher's Sorucebook, 1991. Mem. nat. svc. team Cath. Charismatic Renewal Movement, Kumasi, Ghana, 1986-91. Sci. Performance Assessment Rsch. grantee Nat. Sci. Tchrs. Assn., 1994-95; recipient Undergrad. Studies Full Tuition award Govt. of Ghana, 1968-73, Grad. Studies Full Tuition award, 1992-95. Mem. Ghana Assn. Sci. Tchrs. (life, nat. exec., nat. pres. (1989-91)), Ghana Sci. Assn. (exec.), Phi Delta Kappa. Roman Catholic. Avocations: scripture writing, music, ice hockey, American football, sleeping. Home: PO Box AH 8930, Ahensan Kumasi, Ghana Office: U Cape Coast, Dept Sci Edn, Cape Coast Ghana

OSSIKOVSKI, RAZVIGOR BOJIDAROV, research and development engineer, physicist; b. Russe, Bulgaria, June 8, 1967; arrived in France, 1991; s. Bojidar Tzvetanov and Vania Danova (Mileva) O.; m. Marie Madeleine Gallardo, Dec. 23, 1995; 1 child, Anne. BSc, High Tech. Sch., Russe, Bulgaria; MSc, Ecole Poly., Palaiseau, France, 1992, PhD, 1995. R & D engr. Instruments SA, Longjumeau, France, 1996-99; with Corning SA, Fontainebleau, France, 1999—. Contbr. articles to profl. jours.; inventor in field. Mem. French Physics Soc. European Commn. Scientific Expert, Bulgarian Amateur Radio Assn. Avocations: amateur radio, rowing, bridge. Home: 13 Ave du Gen de Gaulle, 91140 Villebon sur Yvette France Office: Corning SA, 7 Av De Valvins, 77210 Avon France

OSTACHOWICZ, WIESŁAW MIECZYSŁAW, mechanical engineer, educator; b. Zabrze, Poland, Feb. 12, 1947; s. Mieczysław Zbigniew and Krystyna Franciszka (Unterszic) O.; m. Maria Jolanta Kłodnicka, Apr. 25, 1970; 1 child, Małgorzata. MS, Tech. U., Gdansk, Poland, 1970, PhD, 1975, DSc, 1980. Cert. prof., Pres. Poland. Rsch. asst. Polish Acad. Scis., Gdansk, 1970-72; sr. designer Navy Shipbuilding Yard, Gdynia, Poland, 1972-73; sr. rsch. asst., adj. prof. Tech. U., Gdansk, 1973-81, assoc. prof. mech. engring., 1981-87; assoc. prof. mech. engring. Polish Acad. Scis., Gdansk, 1986-92, prof. mech. engring., 1992—; chmn. dept. mechs. Tech. U. Gdansk, 1982-87; dep. dir. Polish Acad. Scis., 1986-92; vis. prof. mech. engring. Syracuse (N.Y.) U., 1980-81, Intst. Investigaciones Electricas, Cuernavaca, Mex., 1987, 90, head dept. statics and dynamics in fluid flow machinery, 1992—, head Ctr. for Mechanics and Machines, 1998—; presenter in field. Co-author: Finite element Method in Dynamic of Structures, 1984, Theoretical Mechanics, 1981, Theoretical Mechanics—Collection of Problems: Kinematics and Dynamics, 1985; contbr. articles to profl. jours.; contbr. chpts. to books; referee Jour. Sound and Vibration, ASME Jour. Vibration and Acoustic, ASME Jour. Dynamic Systems, Measurement and Control, ASCE Jour. Engring. Mechanics, An Internat. Jour. Structural Engring. and Mechanics, Internat. Jour. Solids and Structures, An Internat. Jour. Composites Engring., Finite Elements in Analysis and Design, Internat. Jour. Solids and Structures, Theoretical and Applied Mechs., and Mechs. and Computer; mem. editl. bd. Composites Engring. Jour. Scholar IREX, U.S., 1980-81, Brit. Coun., 1992-93, 95-96, U.S. Army and USAF, 1992, 95-98, KOSEF, South Korea, 1996, Royal Soc. (U.K.), 1994-98, DFG, Germany, 1993, Royal Irish Acad., 1998-99, FRD, South Africa, 1998, others; recipient awards Minister Sci. and Higher Edn. for scientific achievements, 1976, 80, 82, 84; grantee State Com. for Scientific Rsch., 1992—, Brit. Coun., 1993-96, U.S. Army, 1994-96. Mem. ASME, Internat. Fedn. Theory of Machines and Mechanisms (tech. com. ROTORDYNAMICS), Internat. Cmty. Composites Engring., Internat. Assn. Boundary Element Methods, Polish Nat. Com. Theory of Machines and Mechanisms, Polish Soc. Theoretical and Applied Mechs. Home: Hoene Wronskiego 7/2, 80-210 Gdańsk Poland Office: Inst Fluid Flow Machinery, 14 Gen J Fiszera St, 80-952 Gdańsk Poland

OSTADAL, IVAN, physicist, researcher; b. Sumperk, Czech Republic, Feb. 2, 1956; s. Jaromir and Bozena (Durcova) O.; m. Sylvie Kudrnova, Aug. 16, 1980; 1 child, Adam. MSc, Charles U., 1980, PhD, 1987. Rschr. Charles U., Prague, Czech Republic, 1983-86, sr. lectr., 1986-95, sr. sci. worker, 1996-98, assoc. prof., 1998—; postdoctoral student Kings Coll., London, 1989-90; leader Scanning Tunneling Microscopy Group, Charles U., 1989—. Brit. Coun. fellow, 1989; Tempus grantee European Commn., 1993, grantee Charles U., 1993-95, 97-99, 99—, Govt. of Czech Republic, 1997-99. Mem. Union of Czech Mathematicians and Physicists, N.Y. Acad. Scis. Avocations: art (drawing), philosophy, nature, sports. Home: Kubelikova 60, 130 00 Prague 3, Czech Republic Office: Charles U, Electronics/Vac Physics, V Holesovickach 2, 180 00 Prague 8, Czech Republic

OŠŤÁDAL, OLDŘICH, internist, educator; b. Olomouc, Czech Republic, May 16, 1935; s. Oldřich and Božena (Talášková) O.; m. Irena Skupniková, July 3, 1959; 1 child, Libor. MD, Palacky U., Olomouc, 1959, PhD, 1987. Physician Hosp. Karviná, Czech Republic, 1959-64; physician Univ. Clinic, Olomouc, 1964-67, head physician dept. pneumology, 1967-83; head Pneumological Clinic U. Hosp./Palacky U., Olomouc, 1983—; coord. WHO for Czech Republic for Drug Resistens on Treatment of Tuberculosis, 1995—; lectr. in field. Mem. editl. bd. Remedia Praha, 1991—, Klinická Mikrobiologie a Infekční Lékařství, 1995—, Remedia Klinická Mikrobiologie, 1996—; mem. internat. hon. bd. Czech med. jour. Studia Pneumol.phtiseol., 1992—; contbr. articles to profl. jours. Leader Civic Forum in Velveti Revolution, U. Hosp. Olomouc, Czech Republic, 1989. Recipient award for young rschrs. Czech Med. Soc., 1967; named to internat. hon. bd. Czech Med. Jour., 1992—. Mem. Internat. Union Against Tuberculosis and Lund Disease, European Respiratory Soc., European Soc. for Oxygenoterapie, German Pneumological Soc., Austrian Pneumological Soc., Czech Assn. Physicians (hon.), Czech Pneumological Soc. (ctrl. com. 1986—, pres. 1991-95). Roman Catholic. Avocations: music, playing piano, painting, sports, traveling. Home: Wellnerova 21, 779 00 Olomouc Czech Republic Office: Univ Hosp, IP Pavlova 6, 775 20 Olomouc Czech Republic

OSTAPENKO, GEORGY TIKHONOVICH, mineralogy, crystal growth researcher; b. Kharkov, Ukraine, Jan. 20, 1935; s. Tikhon Terentyevich and Ulyana Petrovna (Abramenko) O.; m. Rosa Yakovlevna Semikina, Jul. 21, 1960 (dec. Nov. 1970); children: Vladislav, Yelena; m. Marina Vladimirova, Sept. 9, 1990. Specialist, State Univ., Kharkov, 1958; PhD in geology, Inst. of Geochemistry, Moscow, 1967; D in scis., Inst. Geochemistry & Mineral Physics, Kiev, Ukraine, 1980. Sr. geologist Geological Expedition, Ust'-Kamenogorsk, 1958-62; sr. scientist Inst. of Mineral Synthesis, Aleksandrov, 1965-71; head of lab. Inst. of Mineralogy & Ore Formation, Kiev, 1971-95; head dept. Inst. of Magnetism, Kiev, 1995—; prof. Nat. Univ., Kiev, 1987—; sub-faculty mineralogy, petrology and geochemistry. Author: Thermodynamics of Non-Hydrostatic Systems, 1977, Physical and Chemical Conditions of Metamorphism, 1984; inventor in field of crystal growth; contbr. articles to profl. jours. Juryman People's Ct. of Leningrad Dist., Kiev, 1981-84. Recipient Kiev 1500 Year Anniversary medal, Kiev Mcpl., 1982. Mem. Ukrainian Mineralogical Soc., Commn. on Experimental Mineralogy. Avocation: jogging. Home: Tupolev St 17a Apt 26, 252128 Kiev Ukraine Office: Inst of Magnetism, Vernadsky Ave 36 B, 252142 Kiev Ukraine

OSTASIEWICZ, WALENTY, statistics educator; b. Krasnowies, Bielsk, Poland, Mar. 4, 1942; s. Jan and Olga (Babulewicz) O.; m. Stanislawa Nitek, July 21, 1970; children: Agata, Katarzyna, Pawel. Magister, Stats. Econs., Moscow, 1967; D, Acad. Econs., Wroclaw, Poland, 1974, Habilitation, 1986. Asst. Acad. Econs., Wroclaw, 1967-73, adj., 1973-88, asst. prof., 1988-91, prof., 1991—, head dept. stats., 1995—; prof. math. U. Trento, Italy, 1983-86. Author: Automated Data Processing, 1970 (Ministry Edn. award 1970, 73), Applications of Fuzzy Sets, 1987, Line Fitting Problems, 1995; editor, mem. editl. bd. Badania Operacyjne i Decyzje, Fuzzy Econ. Rev. Recipient scholarship Swiss Govt., Zurich, 1976-77, Golden Cross of Merit, State Coun. Poland, Warsaw, 1988, diploma AMSE Tassin-la-Lune, France, 1991. Mem. Polish Statis. Soc., Polish Math. Soc., Internat. Soc. Fuzzy Econs., Internat. Soc. Modeling and Simulation, Assn. for Advancement of Modelling and Simulation Techniques in Enterprises. Home: Szarych Szeregow 45, 52-245 Wroclaw Poland Office: Acad Econs, Komandorska 118/120, 53-345 Wroclaw Poland

OSTASZEWSKA-PUCHALSKI, IWONA, dermatologist; b. Bialystok, Poland, May 8, 1965; d. Aleksander and Olga (Kubajewska) O.; m. Andrzej Puchalski. MD, Bialystok Med. Acad., 1990. Med. diplomate. Resident Oncological Hosp., Bialystok, 1990-91; asst. Ctr. STD Rsch. and Diagnostics, Bialystok, 1992-94, specialist in dermatology and venerology, 1995-97, asst. for doctoral dissertations, 1998—. Contbr. articles to sci. jours. Mem. Polish Soc. Dermatology, Soc. Young Dermatologists. Avocations: interior design, music. Home: Konstytucji 3 Maja 30/5, 15 776 Bialystok Poland Office: Ctr STD Rsch Diagnostics, Ul SW Rocha 3, 15 879 Bialystok Poland

ÖSTBERG, GUSTAF, metallurgical engineer, educator; b. Sollentuna, Sweden, Apr. 11, 1926; s. Clas and Elsa (Steffenburg) Ö; m. Harriet Öfwerberg, Aug. 11, 1956. Metall. engr., Royal Inst. Tech., Stockholm, Sweden, 1950, Tekn. Lic., 1961, Docent, 1965. Rsch. asst. Royal Inst. Tech., 1950-52; rsch. metallurgist Ford Motor Co., Dearborn, Mich., 1952-53, Sveriges Mekanförbund, Stockholm, 1953-56, Falu Kopparverk, Falun, Sweden, 1956-58, Swedish Atomic Energy Co., Stockholm and Studsvik, Sweden, 1959-75; prof. engring. materials U. Lund, Sweden, 1975-91; adv. bd. Jour. Nuclear Materials, 1961-91, Scandinavian Jour. Metallurgy, 1972-86. Mem. editl. bd. Atomic Energy Review, 1977-83. Mem. Royal Physiographical Soc., Royal Swedish Acad. Engring. Scis., Royal Soc. Letters Lund, Swedish Soc. Phys. Metallurgy (pres. 1980-86), Societé Française de Métallurgie (hon.). Home: Linnégatan 8D, S 224 60 Lund Sweden Office: Univ Lund, PO Box 118, S-221 00 Lund Sweden

OSTENDORF, JOAN DONAHUE, fund raiser, volunteer; b. Boston, Dec. 9, 1933; d. John Stanley and Genevieve Catherine (Morrissey) Donahue; m. Edgar Louis Ostendorf, Feb. 10, 1962; 1 child, Mary Elizabeth. BA, Marymount Coll., Tarrytown, N.Y., 1956; postgrad., Boston U., 1956. Tchr. Boston pub. schs., 1956-57, Waltham (Mass.) pub. schs., 1957-62. Trustee Cleve. Inst. Music, 1984—, mem. trustees coordianting coun., 1989; mem. Jr. League Cleve., 1964, 1st v.p. 1972-73; founder adv. coun. pub. rels. com. Cleve. Orch., 1974, 1st v.p., 1975-76; mem. del. assembly United Way, 1977-87; chmn. benefits Vis. Nurse Assn., 1987-88, March Dimes, 1982; trustee women's com. U. Hosps. Case Western Res. U. Med. Sch., 1974—; mem. nominating com. Inst. Music, 1990-91; 2d v.p. Music and Drama Club, 1991-93, corresponding sec., 1993-95; chair Lyric Opera, 1992, Platform Assn., 1992—; pres. bd. trustees Cleve. Inst. Music, 1980-82, pres. women's com., 1980-82; mem. adv. bd. Women's Community Found., 1991—; v.p. Cleve. Internat. Piano Competition, 1994—; women's coun. Cleve. Mus., 1996. Mem. Internat. Platform Assn., Longwood Cricket Club, Intown Club, Chagrin Valley Hunt Club. Republican. Roman Catholic. Address: 3425 Roundwood Rd Chagrin Falls OH 44022-6634

OSTENDORF, LANCE STEPHEN, lawyer, investor, financial consultant and planner; b. New Orleans, Aug. 16, 1958; 1 child, Christine Marie Ostendorf. BBA summa cum laude, Loyola U., 1976, JD, 1980. Bar: La. 1980, U.S. Dist. Ct. (ea. dist.) La. 1981, U.S. Dist. Ct. La., U.S. Supreme Ct. 1980, U.S. Dist. Ct. (we. and mid. dists.) La. 1983. Ptnr. McGlinchey Stafford Lang, New Orleans, 1980-92, Campbell McCranie Sistrunk, Anzelmo & Hardy, New Orleans, 1992—; treas., CFO Campbell McCranie, New Orleans; owner RCO Internat. Inc.; treas., CFO La. State U. Med. Ctr. Found., New Orleans, 1992—; lectr. Lorman Ednl. Seminars; bd. dirs. La. State U. Med. Ctr. Found., New Orleans, tech. transfer com.; speaker and tchr. Lorman Ednl. Svcs., Inc. Author: Insurance Law; contbr. articles to profl. jours. Mem. ABA, Fed. Bar Assn., Internat. Bar Assn., Metairie Bar Assn., Maritime Law Assn., Comite Maritime Internat., Assn. for Transp. Law, Logistics and Policy, Assn. Average Adjusters of U.S., Jefferson Bar Assn., New Orleans Bar Assn., La. Restaurant Assn., Am. Trial Lawyers Assn., La. Bar Assn., Jefferson Bar Assn., Fifth Cir. Bar Assn., Def. Rsch. Inst., La. Trial Lawyers Assn., Law Def. Lawyers Assn., Houston Mariners Club, Southeastern Adm. Law Inst., St. Thomas Moore Club, La. Notary Soc., Blue Key Honor Soc. Home: 838 Gravier St New Orleans LA 70112-1408 Office: 3445 N Causeway Blvd Ste 800 Metairie LA 70002-3728

OSTER, LEONID, physicist, researcher; b. Tashkent, Uzbekistan, Soviet Union, Feb. 15, 1956; arrived in Israel, 1990; s. Naum and Evgenya (Lutskaya) O.; m. Natalya Polyakova, Sept. 11, 1976; children: Olga, Inna, Revital. MSc, Tashkent U., 1978, PhD, 1986. Cert. physicist-tchr. Rschr. Inst. Nuclear Physics, Tashkent, 1978-80; sr. rschr. Tashkent U., 1986-90; rschr. Tel Aviv U., 1991; sr. lectr. Negev U., Beer-Sheva, Israel, 1991-97, Negev Acad. Coll. Engring., Beer-Sheva, 1997—; cons. Negev U., Beer-Sheva, 1997—. Contbr. articles to sci. jours. Grantee Faculty Natural Scis. Seed Funding, 1994, U.S.-Israel Binat. Sci. Found., 1999; Guastalla fellow Raschi Found., 1997. Mem. AAAS, Internat. Solid State Dosimetry Orgn., N.Y. Acad. Sci. Office: Negev Acad Coll Engring, 71 Bazel St, 84100 Beer-Sheva Israel

ØSTERGÅRD, PATRIC RALF JOHAN, educator; b. Vasa, Finland, Jan. 29, 1965; s. Ralf Ingmar and Gretel Maj-Len (Bjørkqvist) Ø. MSc in Engring., Helsinki U. Tech., Esbo, Finland, 1990, licentiate in tech., 1992, DTech, 1993. Computer sci. rschr. Helsinki U. Tech., 1989-94; jr. fellow Acad. Finland, 1994-96, sr. fellow, 1996-2000; prof. Helsinki U. Tech., 2000—. Contbr. articles on coding theory to profl. jours.; leading constructor of gambling systems for football pools, lotteries and similar games. Fellow Inst. Combinatorics and Its Applications (assoc.); mem. IEEE. Lutheran. Avocation: sports. Home: Malmgatan 38B27, FIN-00100 Helsinki Finland Office: Helsinki U Tech, PO Box 5400, FIN-02015 HUT Finland

OSTERGREN, JAN B., physician, researcher; b. Stockholm, Sweden, June 7, 1950; s. Bertil and Birgitta (Andersson) O.; m. Elisabeth Svensson, May 9, 1973; children: Fredrik, Henrik, Anna. MD, Karolinska Inst., Stockholm, 1976, PhD, 1984. Cert. specialist in internal medicine and cardiology. Intern Stockholm, 1976-78, specialist tng., 1978-87; cons., asst. prof. Soderhosp., Stockholm, 1988-93; dir. studies, head cardiovascular medicine Karolinska Hosp., Stockholm, 1994-97, sr. lectr. and cons. dept. medicine, 1997—. Med. editor Lakartidningen, Jour. Swedish Med. Assn., 1997—; contbr. more than 80 sci. articles to profl. jours. Mem. Swedish Soc. for Med. Angiology (chmn. 1995-99), Swedish Soc. for Hypertension. Home: Vidargatan 3, 113 27 Stockholm Sweden Office: Karolinska Hosp, Dept Medicine, 17176 Stockholm Sweden

OSTERGREN BAITS, MARCIA, elementary education educator; b. Sao Paulo, Brazil, Oct. 24, 1944; came to U.S., 1965; d. Eduardo and Oraide G. Ostergren; m. David F. Baits, July 31, 1971; children: Mark David, Anelise Christine. MusB, Birmingham So. Coll., 1969; M of Music Edn., Wright State U., 1997. Cert. elem. tchr., Ohio. Music tchr. Sao Paulo Grad Sch., 1970-73, St. John Internat. Sch., Waterloo, Belgium, 1977-81; kindergarten tchr. ECLC, Columbus, Ohio, 1986-87; French immersion tchr. Columbus Pub. Sch., 1987-88, elem. tchr., 1988-89; music tchr. Wilmington (Ohio) City Sch., 1997-98, Dayton (Ohio) Pub. Schs., 1998—; asst. Montessori Acad., Dallas, 1969. Playwright: O Cedarville; co-founder Cedarville News, 1995; contbr. National Anthology, Poetic Voices of America, 1994. Founder Cedarville Opera House soc., 1994, Cedarville News, 1995; active Food for the Hungry, Crisis Pregnancy Ctr., Foster Care. Invited to Presdl. Prayer Breakfast The White House, Washington, 1969. Mem. Cedarville Opera House Soc. (co-founder 1994), Mortar Bd., Kappa Delta Pi, Phi Theta Kappa. Avocations: volleyball, tennis, guitar, piano, translator. Home: 179 Detroit Blvd Xenia OH 45385-2241 Office: Dayton City Schs Whittier Elem Sch 721 Miami Dayton OH 45408-2650

OSTERHAUS, GREG S., artist, graphic designer; b. Hinsdale, Ill., Apr. 28, 1963; s. Gordon Frederick and Leona Osterhaus; m. Janie D. Osterhaus, May 9, 1987; children: Taylor W., Madeline Q., Kyle J. BFA, Va. Poly. Inst. and State U., 1985. Artist oil paintings, also acrylics, watercolors, pastels. One-mans shows include Roanoke County Pub. Libr., 1987, Studios on the Square, Roanoke, 1994, 96, 99, YMCA Rotating Gallery, Roanoke, 1996, The Little Gallery, Smith Mt. Lake, Va., 1996, 99, Shenandoah Club, Roanoke, 1997, Frame Scapes, Roanoke, 1998, Allehany Highlands Ctr., Clifton Forge, Va., 1998, Artworks Gallery, Norfolk, Va., 1999; exhibited in group shows Depot Gallery, Roanoke, Studios on the Square, 1994, Gallery at Shanaz!, Lynchburg, Va., 1995, The Little Gallery, 1996, 97, Gallery at Szent Györgyi, Falmouth, Mass., 1998. Avocations: music, reading, guitar. Home and Studio: 2351 Denniston Ave SW Roanoke VA 24015-1904

OSTERHUS, ELIZABETH, pediatric academy administrator; b. Portland, Oreg., May 30, 1966; d. Robert Joel and Martha Meredith O. BA, Trinity Coll., 1989; MA, Northwestern U., 1993. Lic. profl. counselor. Rsch. asst. ICF Inc., Fairfax, Va., 1989-91; SASS counselor Mental Health Ctrs. Ctrl. Ill., Springfield, 1993-94; child and adolescent counselor Met. Family Svcs., Chgo., 1994-96; dir. Divsn. Children with Spl. Needs Am. Acad. Pediat., Elk Grove Village, Ill., 1996—; advisor numerous federally-funded child adv. programs, 1996—; exec. officer jount com. on infant hearing, Elk Grove Village, 1999—. Editor: Report of the Task Force on Newborn Screening, 1998—, Pediatrics, 1999, Every Child Deserves a Medical Home, 1999. Mem. Interagy. Coord. Coun., Evanston, Ill., 1996—; Big Sister, Chgo., 1997—. Grantee Shriners Hosps. for Children, Tampa, Fla., 1998—. Avocations: tennis, rollerblading, golf, running, skiing. E-mail: losterhus@aap.org. Fax #: (847) 228-6432. Office: Am Acad Pediatrics 141 NW Point Blvd Elk Grove Village IL 60007-1019

OSTERKAMP, DALENE MAY, psychology educator, artist; b. Davenport, Iowa, Dec. 1, 1932; d. James Hiram and Bernice Grace (La Grange) Simmons; m. Donald Edwin Osterkamp, Feb. 11, 1951 (dec. Sept. 1951). BA, San Jose State U., 1959, MA, 1962; PhD, Saybrook Inst., 1989. Lectr. San Jose (Calif.) State U., 1960-61, U. Santa Barbara (Calif.) Ext., 1970-76; prof. Bakersfield (Calif.) Coll., 1961-87, prof. emerita, 1987—; adj. faculty, counselor Calif. State U., Bakersfield, 1990—; gallery dir. Bakersfield Coll., 1964-72. Juried group shows include Berkeley (Calif.) Art, Ctr., 1975, Libr. of Congress, 1961, Seattle Art Mus., 1962. Founder Kern Art Edn. Assn., Bakersfield, 1962, Bakersfield Printmakers, 1976. Staff sgt. USAF, 1952-55. Recipient 1st Ann. Svc. to Women award Am. Assn. Women in C.C., 1989. Mem. APA, Assn. for Women in Psychology, Assn. for Humanistic Psychology, Calif. Soc. Printmakers. Home: PO Box 387 Glennville CA 93226-0387 Office: Calif State Univ Stockdale Ave Bakersfield CA 93309

ÖSTERLUND, ERIK DAVID, editor; b. Knista, Sweden, May 7, 1950; s. Erik David Harald and Stina (Laurell) Ö.; m. Karin Gunvi Birgitta Eriksson, June 1, 1974; children: Elin, Sofi, Nanny. Cert., U. Tchg., Linköping, Sweden, 1974. Editor Libris, Örebro, Sweden, 1975-84; editor layout Swedish Beekeeping Assn., Mantorp, Sweden, 1984—; editor layout Assn. for Biblical Creationism, Umeå, Sweden, 1989—; honeybee product prodr., Hallsberg, Sweden, 1984—. Contbr. articles to profl. jours.; patentee in field. Chmn. bd. Dksn-RIA, Hallsberg, 1982-93, bd. dirs., 1994-98; bd. dirs. Bapt. Ch., Hallsberg, 1994—; promotor youth music and drama. Mem. AAAS, Bee Breeding Assn. (rsch. organizer, chmn. 1989—).

OSTERRIETH, BERNARD FRÉDÉRIC, import-export company executive; b. Berchem, Antwerp, Belgium, Nov. 4, 1931; s. Frédéric Walter and Rosita Cécile (Grutering) O.; m. Marie-Hélène Castelein, Jan. 17, 1956; children: Marie-Hélène, Jean, Annick. Student, Nat. Leather-Sellers Coll., London, 1950-52. Technician Teneria Ancla Ltda., Medellin, Colombia, 1955-60; mgr. Inversiones Comerciales Antioquenas Ltda., Medellin, 1960-63; dir. Max Osterrieth & Co., Antwerp, Belgium, 1975. With Belgian mil., 1953-54. Office: Max Osterrieth & Co, Frankrijklei 104, 2000 Antwerp Belgium

OSTERTUN, BURKHARD, radiologist; b. Bonn, Germany, Jan. 3, 1960; s. Dettmar and Elfriede (Rothe) O.; m. Monika Nolden, Aug. 22, 1996; children; Jan-Philipp and Felix. MD, U. Bonn, 1984. Lic. physician, Germany; cert. in radiology and neuroradiology. Resident in radiology Städt. Kliniken, Cologne, 1985-86; resident in radiology Univ. Hosp., Bonn, 1986-91, resident dept. epileptology, 1992-93, resident dept. neuroradiology, 1993-95, attending radiologist, 1995—, chief cons. neuroradiology, 1996—, lectr., 1997. Contbr. articles to profl. jours. Flute player Acad. Symphony Orch., U. Bonn. Office: Klinik Osnabrueck/MRT, Am Finkenhuegel 1, D-49076 Osnabrueck Germany

ÖSTLING, MIKAEL LARS, microelectronics researcher; b. Sundsvall, Sweden, Aug. 26, 1955; s. Lars Olov and Inger Elisabeth (Mården) Ö; m. Carina Irene Zaring, Aug. 8, 1992. MSc in Engring. Physics, Uppsala (Sweden) U., 1980, D in Electronics Tech., 1983; docent, Royal Inst. Tech., Stockholm, 1987. Rsch. asst. Uppsala (Sweden) U., 1980-83; asst. prof. Royal Inst. Tech., Stockholm, 1983-90, assoc. prof., 1990-96, prof., 1996—; dir. studies Royal Inst. Tech., Stockholm, 1987-93, acting prof., 1991, dir. grad. studies microelectronics, 1995—, head dept., 2000—; consortium coord. Swedish Nat. Bd. Tech. Devel., Stockholm, 1994—. Editor: Refractory Metals and Silicides, 1991; contbr. articles to profl. jours. ALM scholar Royal Inst. Tech., 1992; Sr. vis. scholar Fulbright Commn. Stanford U., 1993-94. Mem. IEEE (sr.), Am. Vacuum Soc., Electro Chem. Soc. Avocations: running, swimming, alpine and cross country skiing, biking, hiking. Home: Holmvägen 25C, S-75651 Uppsala Sweden Office: Royal Inst Tech, Electrum 229, S-16440 Kista Stockholm, Sweden

OSTOJA-STARZEWSKI, MARTIN, engineering educator; b. Cracow, Poland, Apr. 22, 1954; s. Witold and Anna Wierzbianska; m. Iwona Jasiuk, Dec. 1991; 1 child, Pauline. Engr., Cracow Technol. U., 1977; M in Engring., McGill U., Montreal, Que., Can., 1980, PhD, 1983. Pres. Quadra Dynamics Inc., Montreal, 1984-85; asst. prof. aeronautics and astronautics Purdue U., West Lafayette, Ind., 1985-90; asst. prof. materials sci. and

mechanics Mich. State U., East Lansing, 1990-95; prof. engring. Inst. Paper Sci. and Tech., Atlanta, 1995—. Roman Catholic. Avocations: classical music, literature, skiing. E-mail: martin.ostoja@ipst.edu. Fax: 404-894-4778. Office: Inst Paper Sci & Tech 500 10th St NW Atlanta GA 30318-5794

OSTRIKER, JEREMIAH PAUL, astrophysicist, educator; b. N.Y.C., Apr. 13, 1937; s. Martin and Jeanne (Sumpf) O.; m. Alicia Suskin, Dec. 1, 1958; children—Rebecca, Eve, Gabriel. A.B., Harvard, 1959; Ph.D. (NSF fellow), U. Chgo., 1964; postgrad., U. Cambridge, Eng., 1964-65; hon. degree, U. Chgo., 1992. Rsch. assoc., lectr. astrophysics Princeton (N.J.) U., 1965-66, asst. prof., 1966-68, assoc. prof., 1968-71, prof., 1971—, chmn. dept. astronomy, dir. obs., 1979-95, Charles A. Young prof. astronomy, 1982—, provost, 1995—. Author: Development of Large-Scale Structure in the Universe, 1991; mem. editl. bd., trustee Princeton U. Press; contbr. articles to profl. jours. Recipient Vainu Bappu Meml. award Indian Nat. Sci. Acad., 1993, Karl Schwarzschild medal Astronomische Gesellschaft, 1999; Alfred P. Sloan Found. fellow, 1970-72. Fellow AAAS; mem. NAS (bd. govs. 1993-95, counselor 1992-95), Am. Astron. Soc. (councilor 1978-80, Warner prize 1972, Russel prize 1980), Internat. Astron. Union, Am. Philos. Soc., Am. Acad. Arts and Scis., Royal Astron. Soc. (assoc.), Am. Mus. of Natural History (trustee 1997—). Home: 33 Philip Dr Princeton NJ 08540-5409 Office: Princeton Univ Office of the Provost 3 Nassau Hl Princeton NJ 08544-0001

OSTROM, KATHERINE ELMA, retired educator; b. L.A., Dec. 30, 1928; d. Charles W. and Mabel M. (Christensen) Shults; m. Carl R. Ostrom, Jan. 29, 1949 (dec.); children: Margaret K. Larson, Carl R. Jr. BA cum laude, U. Wash., 1966, MA in Tchg. English, 1973, EdD, 1994. Std. tchg. cert. grades K-12, Wash.; continuing prins. cert.-secondary, Wash. Substitute tchr. Renton, Kent & South Ctrl. Sch. Dists., 1966; tchr. Foster H.S., Tukwila, Wash., 1966-67, 75-76; tchr. Showalter Middle Sch., Tukwila, 1967-79, dept. chair, 1968-87, vice prin., 1979-87; tchr., supr. student tchrs. U. Wash., Seattle, 1989-91; subs. tchr. Tukwila Sch. Dist., 1999—; tchr. Western Wash. State Coll., Bellingham, 1967-68; liaison, supr. Jr. Achievement, Seattle, 1988-89; cons., trainer Nat. Assn. Elem. Sch. Prins., 1992—; vol. tchr. Immigrant & Refugee Resources Ctr., Seattle, 1996—; dir. Forum on Edn., PDK, Seattle, 1997. Host, del. Tukwila-Ikawa (Japan) Sister Cities, 1980—, chair, 1999—; block watch organizer King County (Wash.) Sherrif's, 1994—; key communicator Renton (Wash.) Sch. Dist., 1996—; tutor Skyway Meth. Ch., Seattle, 1997—. Named Vol. of Yr., BPW, Tukwila, Wash., 1990; Coll. scholar U. Puget Sound, Tacoma, Wash., 1946. Mem. Assn. Wash. Sch. Prins. (chair state vice prins.' conf. 1986, regional dir. 1986-88), Wash. Physicians for Social Responsibility (del. to Mid. East 1994), Phi Delta Kappa (pres. chpt. 1991-95, newsletter editor 1988-90, 95—, area coord. 1995—), Phi Beta Kappa (Pathfinder award 1997). Democrat. Home: 12817 80th Ave S Seattle WA 98178-4911

ÖSTROS, THOMAS, federal official; b. Gällivare, Sweden, Jan. 26, 1965; married. BSc in Pub. Adminstrn., U. Uppsula, 1990, postgrad., 1992-94, licentiate degree in Econs., 1994. Rsch. officer Trade Union; organizing sec. Social Dem. Party Youth, 1988-89; spl. advisor Ministry of Fin., 1990; mcpl. councilor Uppsala, Sweden, 1991-96; rsch. asst. Trade Union Inst. Econ. Rsch., 1990-93; min. taxation, min. fiscal affairs Ministry of Fin., 1996-98; min. Ministry of Edn. and Sci., Stockholm, 1998—; bd. mem. Uppsala Homes Corp., 1992-96. Dep. mem. Swedish Parliamentary Standing Com. Fin., Standing Com. Civil Law Legis., 1994-96; bd. mem. Uppsala County Tax Authority. Office: Ministry Edn and Sci, S10333 Stockholm Sweden

OSTROV, BENJAMIN CHARLES, political science educator; b. Bklyn., July 21, 1953; arrived in Hong Kong, 1979; s. Bernard and Mary Ann (Fidlow) O.; m. Genevieve Suk-han Tsang, Aug. 22, 1976. BA in Asian Studies & Relig. with honors, Hamilton Coll., Clinton, N.Y., 1975; MA in Internat. Rels., U. Chgo., 1977, PhD in Polit. Sci., 1987. Tutor Chinese U. Hong Kong, Shatin, New Terrs., 1979-81, asst. lectr., 1981-87, lectr., 1987—; coach English debate team Chinese U., Hong Kong, 1992-94; vis. assoc. prof. dept. polit. sci. U. Oreg., 1996. Author: Conquering Resources: The Growth and Decline of the PLA's Science and Technology Commission for National Defense, 1991; contbr. articles to profl. jours., books. LaVerne Noyes Found. scholar U. Chgo., 1976; C.Y. Kwan Endowment Fund staff devel. grantee Chinese U. of Hong Kong, 1991. Mem. Israeli C. of C. Hong Kong, Hong Kong Fgn. Corrs. Club. Jewish. Avocations: bicycling, photography, short-wave radio, hiking, computer internetting, reading. Office: Chinese U Hong Kong, GPA Dept United Coll, Shatin New Territories Hong Kong

OSTROVOY, DMYTRIY YURIYEVICH, research scientist; b. Kyiv, Ukraine, Dec. 4, 1958; s. Yuriy Dmytriyevich and Gulzifa Ramazanovna (Bedretdinova) O. Diploma Mech. Engring., Kiev Poly. Inst., 1982; Candidate Sci., Inst. Problems of Strength, Nat. Acad. Scis. Ukraine, Kiev, 1993; postgrad., Nat. Acad. Scis. Ukraine, Kiev, 1992-93; hon. degree, Inst. Problems of Strength, Ukraine, 2000. Engr. Design Bur., Inst. Problems of Srength Nat. Acad. Scis. Ukraine, Kyiv, 1984-87, jr. rsch. fellow Inst. Problems of Strength, 1987-92, rsch. fellow, sr. rsch. fellow Inst. Problems of Strength, 1993—; sr. rschr. Korean Inst. Sci. and Tech., Seoul, 1995-96; sec. tech. com. for standardization State Com. for Standardization Ukraine, Kyiv, 1997—. Contbr. articles to profl. jours. Grantee Internat. Sci. Found, 1994. Avocations: philately, literature. Home: 2/6 Boychenko St Apt 76, 02206 Kyiv Ukraine Office: Inst Problems of Strength, 2 Timiryazevskaya St, 01014 Kyiv Ukraine

OSTROVSKAYA, LARISA ANATOLIEVNA, biologist, researcher; b. Moscow, Apr. 16, 1941; d. Anatoly Pavlovich Ostrovsky and Henrietta Vladimirovna Speranskaya; m. Alexander Stepanovich Pouzirevsky, Feb. 26, 1983; 1 child, Antony. MSc in Organic Chemistry, Inst. Petrochem. & GasIndustry, Moscow, 1963; PhD in Biology, Inst. Biophysics Acad. Scis., Moscow, 1968; DSc in Biology, Acad. Scis., Moscow, 1978. Jr. rschr. Inst. Chem. Physics Acad. Scis., Moscow, 1963-68, head rsch. group, 1968-79, sr. rschr., 1979-85, prin. rsch., 1985-96; prin. rsch. Emanuel Inst. Biochem. Physics Acad. Scis., Moscow, 1996—; head project in program Nat. Priorities Medicine, Moscow, 1990-91; head of project in program Remote Affects of Irradiation, Moscow, 1989-93; head of 2 projects in program Sci. and Tech. Devel., Moscow, 1997-98; head of 2 projects partnership ASGL Study of New Antitumor Drugs, Saint Petersburg, Russia, 1999—. Author: Alkylnitrosoureas-The Novel Class of Antitumor Drugs, 1978; contbr. articles to profl. jours., chpts. to books. Recipient Silver medal Exhibition Nat. Economy Advances, 1981; State Sci. scholarship Edict of Pres. Russian Fedn., 1994—. Mem. Soc. Oncologists, N.Y. Acad. Scis., Russian Acad. Med. Scis. (mem. expert coun. antitumor drugs therapy 1989—). Office: Emanuel Inst Biochem Physic, ul Kosygina 4, 117334 Moscow Russia

OSTROVSKY, GEORGE MAXIMOVITCH, engineering educator; b. Leningrad, Russia, Feb. 11, 1944; s. Maxim Filippovitch and Alexandra Vladimirovna (Prokochina) O.; m. Larisa Dmitrievna Rybina, Dec. 11, 1967 (div. Aug. 1982); 1 child, Maxim Georgievitch; m. Margarita Nikolayevna Simakova, Oct. 26, 1985. Degree in Engring., Leningrad Inst. Tech., 1967, D in Tech. Scis., 1972, M in Tech. Scis., 1987. Modelist of wooden models Transport Machine Bldg. Plant, Leningrad, 1961-62; engr. Leningrad Inst. Tech., 1967-71, asst. tchr., 1971-75, sr. tchr., 1975-82, asst. prof., 1982-91, prof., 1991—. Author: Pneumatic Transport of Free Flowing Materials in Chemical Industry, 1984, Machines and Apparatus of Chemical Industry, 1992. Recipient Hon. Sign, The Ministry of Higher Edn., Moscow, 1979, Silver medal of the State Exhbn. of Economy Achievements, Chief Com. Exhbn., Moscow, 1988. Mem. Russian Chem. Soc. (dep. chief of seminar mass and energy transfer in technol. processes 1986-97, chief of seminar 1997—). Avocation: visiting country house on the beach. Home: Bldg 1 Flat 188, April St 6, 195176 St Petersburg Russia Office: St Petersburg State Inst, Moskovsky Ave 26, 198013 St Petersburg Russia

OSTROVSKY, ILIA SEMENOVICH, limnologist, educator; b. Kiev, Ukraine, Dec. 14, 1954; arrived in Israel, 1990; s. Semen Ostrovsky and Isa Poliakina; m. Alexandra Ostrovskaya (div. 1987); children: Victoria, Natalia; m. Valentina Kurdumova, Sept. 14, 1988; children: Elena, Elizabeth. MSc, Kaliningrad (Russia) U., 1977; PhD, Zool. Inst., Leningrad, Russia, 1983. Chief rsch. assoc. Hydrobiol. Sta., Sevan, Armenia, 1977-88; head of lab. Inst. Water & Environ. Problems, Barnaul, Russia, 1988-90; assoc. prof. Altai U., Barnaul, 1988-90; sr. scientist Israel Oceanographic Limnol. Rsch. Kinneret Limnol. Lab., Tiberias, Israel, 1991—. Grantee USSR Acad. Sci., 1988-90, Ministry Sci. and Tech., Lake Kinneret, Israel, 1991-94, German-Israel Found., Lake Kinneret, 1997-99. Mem. Internat. Soc. Limnology, Israel Soc. Limnology & Oceanography. Avocations: N.Am. Benthol. Soc., Am. Soc. Limnology & Oceanography. Avocations: fishing, hunting, scuba diving. Home: PO Box 4258, 10300 Hazor Haglilit, Israel Office: Israel Oceanog Limnol Rsch, Kinneret Limnol Lab Box 345, 14102 Tiberias Israel

OSTROVSKY, LEV ARONOVICH, physicist, oceanographer, educator; b. Vologda, USSR, Dec. 10, 1934; s. Ahron L. Ostrovsky and Lidiya A. (Warshawskaya) Khvilivitskaya; children: Svetlana, Alexander. Cert. rsch. physicist in radiophysics, U. Gorky, USSR, 1957; PhD, U. Gorky, 1964; Dr Sci, Acoust. Inst., Moscow, 1973. Lead engr. Design Bureau, Gorky, 1957-59; asst. prof., then assoc. prof. physics Poly. Inst., Gorky, 1962-65; sr. researcher Radiophys. Rsch. Inst., Gorky, 1965-77; chief scientist and head lab. Inst. Applied Physics Russian Acad. Sci., Nizhni Novgorod (formerly Gorky), 1977—; assoc. prof to prof. U. Nizhni Novgorod, 1966-94; prof. sr. rsch. scientist U. Colo./NOAA Environ. Tech. Lab., Boulder, 1994—; Orson Andersen fellow Inst. Geophys. and Planet. Physics Los Alamos Nat. Lab., 1998-99. Co-author: Nonlinear Wave Processes in Acoustics, 1990, English edit., 1998, Modulated Waves, 1999; author or co-author 3 lectr. notes, numerous articles in profl. jours., patented various inventions; editor 3 book translations from English to Russian, 3 paper collection books, a topical dictionary; mem. editorial and adv. bds. Chaos, Ultrasonics, various Russian sci. jours. Recipient State Prize of USSR, 1985, USSR State Discovery Cert., 1982. Fellow Acoustical Soc. Am.; mem. Acoustical Soc. Russia, European Geophys. Soc., Am. Geophys. Union. Office: NOAA ETL R/E/ET1 Boulder CO 80303

OSTROW, RONA LYNN, librarian; b. N.Y.C., Oct. 21, 1948; d. Morty and Jeane Goldberg; m. Steven A. Ostrow, June 25, 1972; 1 child, Ciné Justine. BA, CCNY, 1969; MS in LS, Columbia U., 1970; MA, Hunter Coll., 1975; PhD., Rutgers U., 1998. Cert. libr., N.Y. Br. adult and reference libr. N.Y. Pub. Libr., N.Y.C., 1970-73, rsch. libr., 1973-78; asst. libr. Fashion Inst. Tech., N.Y.C., 1978-80; assoc. dir. Grad. Bus. Resource Ctr., Baruch Coll., CUNY, 1980-90, assoc. prof., 1980-90; assoc. dean of librs. for pub. svcs. Adelphi U., Garden City, N.Y., 1990-94; chief libr. Marymount Manhattan Coll., N.Y.C., 1994-98; asst. provost Teaneck (N.J.) Campus, Fairleigh Dickinson U., Teaneck, N.J., 1998-2000; chief libr. Lehman Coll. CUNY, Bronx, 2000—. Author: Dictionary of Retailing, 1984, Dictionary of Marketing, 1987; co-author: Cross Reference Index, 1989. Mem. ALA, AAUW, Assn. Coll. and Rsch. Librs. Office: CUNY Lehman Coll Libr 250 Bedford Park Blvd W Bronx NY 10468-1527

OSTROWSKA, TERESA HALINA, medical historian, researcher; b. Warsaw, Poland, Oct. 3, 1928; d. Władysław and Stephania (Kuzłejko) O. Diploma, Med. Acad., Warsaw, 1952; ArtsD, U. Lódź, Poland, 1971; MD habilitatus, Med. Acad., Szczecin, Poland, 1982; prof. arts, 1996. Rschr. State Inst. Hygiene, Warsaw, 1952-60; sr. libr. Ctrl. Med. Libr., Warsaw, 1960-66; rschr. Polish Acad. Scis., Warsaw, 1966-78. Author: Polish Medical Periodicals in the 19th Century, 1973, Physicians in Warsaw Society of Friends of Sciences, 1982; co-author: History of Medicine, 1988 (award 1988), History of Surgery in Poland, 1989 (award 1991), History of teaching medicine and pharmacy in Warsaw, 1990. Recipient medal, diploma Social Antialcoholic Com., Poland, 1987, Polish Soc. History of Medicine and Pharmacy, 1994. Mem. Polish Soc. History of Medicine and Pharmacy (hon.), Warsaw Med. Soc. (recipient medal). Roman Catholic. Avocations: reading, thinking. Home: Szczęśliwicka 21 m 10, 02-353 Warsaw Poland

OSTROWSKI-MEISSNER, HENRY, nutritional biochemist, educator, researcher, administrator; b. Grochowce, Poland, Apr. 18, 1940; arrived in Australia, 1977; s. Tadeusz-Alfred and Janina (Sliwiak) O.; m. Teresa Krystman, Aug. 15, 1973; children: Misia, Henia, Rysia, Witold; m. Dorothy Renata Szyszka, June 21, 2000; 1 child, Kasia. BS, Agrl. Coll. Cracow U., 1961, MS in Environ. Physiology, 1963, PhD in Nutritional Biochemistry, 1968. Rsch. asst. Nat. Inst. Animal Production, Cracow, Poland, 1963-70; head feed divsn. Nutritional Biochemistry Lab., Balice-Cracow, Poland, 1966-70; dept. head Quality Ctrl. Lab. Feed Industry, Lublin, Poland, 1970-72, 76; project leader protein extraction and herbal biomass fractionation Ruakura Rsch. Ctr., Hamilton, New Zealand, 1973-76; sr. lectr. dept. biochemistry Bendigo (Australia) Coll. Advanced Edn., 1977-78; lectr. U. Sydney (Australia), 1978-79; program leader Ctr. Animal Rsch. and Devel., Bogor, Indonesia, 1979-82; sr. rsch. scientist CSIRO, Blacktown-Sydney, Australia, 1979-92; dir. AFIC Nat. Facilities, Sydney, 1984—; exec. dir. rsch. & devel. TTD Internat., Sydney, 1986—; sr. tech. advisor China Internat. Ctr. for Econ. Tech Exch., UN Devel. Program, Beijing, China, 1995—; vis. prof. U. Nagoya (Japan), 1992-96; guest prof. Hubei Agrl. Coll., China, 1993-98; chief rsch. scientist joint rsch. project Chinese Acad. Scis., Beijing, 1995—; exec. dir. R&D Ecotech Labs., Melbourne, Australia, 1995-96; dir. R & D Nutriceutical Devel., Melbourne, 1997-98, Wild Herbs Australia Pty. Ltd., Sydney, 1998—; mem. exec. com., regional coord. Asia-Pacific INFIC, Sydney, 1984—; sr. internat. cons. UN Indsl. Devel. Orgn. Investment Promotion Svc., Beijing, 1996—; rsch. coord. joint aquaculture project Oceanic Inst., Hawaii, 1992-96; project coord. Joint Australian-Polish rehab. and recreation project Copper Mining Region, Legnica, Poland, 1995-98; sr. R&D cons. in functional foods Freedom Foods, Melbourne, 1995—, herbal therapeutics Regional Pharms., Sydney, 1995—; internat. exec. project coord. Joint China-Australian Environ. Project on Ecol. Rehab. and Regeneration, 1996—; prof., hon. rschr. Inst. Animal Sci., Chinese Acad. Agrl. Sci., Beijing, 1996—; dir. rsch. and devel. Wild Herbs Australia Pty. Ltd., Sydney, 1998—; chmn. Therapeutics Rsch., Charles Sturt U. Found., Bathurst, Australia, 1999—; assoc. prof. therapeutic rsch. Charles Sturt U., Bathurst, 1999—; internat. coord. distant edn. program, govt. accredited courses in herbal therapeutics and alternative medicine Rsch. Inst. for Medicinal Plants, Poznan, Poland. Author 18 books; contbr. 277 articles to profl. jours. Pres. Soc. for Green Vegetation Rsch., Calcuta, India, 1991-96. Rsch. fellow Rowett Rsch. Inst., Bucksburn, Aberdeen, 1968, Rsch. Adv. Coun. fellow Ruakura Rsch. Inst., Hamilton, New Zealand, 1972-76. Roman Catholic. Achievements include design of functional dietary preparations, health and herbal therapeutic products and establishment of comml.-scale extraction and fractionation techs. for processing green medicinal herbs and biomass from wide range of cultivated plant and native wild-growing species; establishment of installations to recover functional dietary supplements and refined biologically-active pharmaceutical compounds for dietary therapeutic, and medicinal use; design, establishment and coordination of multi-disciplinary internat. environ. projects for ecological rehabilitation and sustainable agro-indsl. devel. in semi-arid mountainous region surrounding Beijing, China; design and implementation of computerized sys. for use in quality control and standardisation of traded agri-commodities worldwide; establishment of a Therapeutic Rsch. in Australia, operating from mid 1999 as an extension of the Charles Stuart Univ. Found. located in the Fac. of Health Studies, simultaneously accepting position of the chmn. of the fund and professorship in natural and non-invasive therapeutic studies focusing on rsch. and devel. of appropriate therapeutic programs for preventive and cure of adverse med. conditions affecting modern soc. worldwide; establishment of commercial-scale production of preventive therapeutics, functional foods and refined pharmaceuticals based on herbal extracts distributed under the registered Trade Marks: Quintessence, Bio-essence and Bio-Life, Herbatonin, etc. helping to deal with such disorders as insulin non-dependent diabetes, obesity, hyper-cholesterolemia, vitamin A deficiency, osteoarthritis, various dermatological conditions, coeliac disease and other food intolerances; also design lines of health products customized for various disciplines of sport and performance including therapeutics based on herbal extracts and functional foods with therapeutic properties derived from natural sources; design and coordination of distant edn. courses in herbal therapeutics and complementary medicine as an extention of govt.-accredited studies, initially in Poland (with their dissemination to other countries in Ctrl. Europe) delivered for GPs and pharmacists through collaboration with local rsch. and edn. instns. Home: 17/1 Waruda St, Kirribilli Sydney 2061, Australia Office: TTD Internat, GPO Box 4792, Sydney 2001, Australia

OSUCHOWSKI, JACEK KAROL, neurosurgeon, consultant; b. Lublin, Poland, Dec. 8, 1963; s. Stanisław and Urszula Osuchowski; m. Dorota Bartoszek; children: Olga, Ida. MD, U. Med. Sch. Lublin, 1988, specialist in neurosurgery I, 1992, specialist in neurosurgery II, 1995. Med. diplomate Polish Bd. Neurosurgeons; cert. microneurosurgery European Assn. Neurosurg. Soc. Courses. Asst. dept. neurosurgery U. Lublin, 1990-95, cons. dept. neurosurgery, 1995—; ct. expert in neurosurgery The Province Ct., Lublin, 1997—; presenter in field. Co-author: A Manual for European Trainees in Neurosurgery, 1993, An European Manual of Neurosurgery, 1995; contbr. articles to profl. jours. Mem. Polish Soc. Neurosurgeons, Ctrl. European Neurosurg. Soc. Avocations: yachting, computers, guitar, country house, traveling. Home: Orla 5M2, 20-022 Lublin Poland Office: Dept Neurosurgery SPSK 4, Jaczewskiego 8, 20-954 Lublin Poland

O'SULLIVAN, BREDA, psychologist; b. Limerick, Ardpatrick, Ireland, July 2, 1940; d. Timothy O'Sullivan and Kathleen Fitzgibbon. BS with honors, U. Coll., Cork, Ireland, 1963; HDpEd, U. Coll., Dublin, 1966; MA, Anna Maria Coll., 1981; PhD, Boston U., 1985. Sci. dept. staff Cardinal Wiseman, Coventry, Eng., 1963-65; head sci., religion St. Paul's, Dublin, 1965-72, mgr. of sch., 1972-77; staff psychotherapist HOA, Boston, 1980-85; dir. Heronbrook House, Knowle, Eng., 1986-96; cons. Heronbrook House, Knowle, 1996—; lectr. in field; cons. psychologist, 2000—. Contbr. articles to profl. jours. Leadership team St. Paul the Apostle, Birmingham, 1986-92, Sister of Charity of St. Paul the Apostle, 1958—, on-going formation working party, 1992-98; dir. Heronbrook House, 1998-2000. Danielsen fellow Boston U., 1981-85, internat. scholar, 1985. Mem. APA, World Mental Health Fedn., Brit. Psychology Soc. (assoc. fellow). Roman Catholic. Avocations: golf, reading, writing, travel, music.

O'SULLIVAN, JOHN CONOR, gynecological surgeon, educator, consultant; b. London, Sept. 25, 1932; s. James Vincent and Maura (O'Connor) O'S.; m. Maureen Mitchell, Apr. 26, 1958; children: Marika, Claire, Catherine, Hugh. B.M., B.Ch., MA, Oxford (Eng.) U., 1959. Examiner ob-gyn. Gen. Med. Coun., U. London and U. Cambridge, Eng.; cons. ob-gyn. Cen. Middlesex Hosp., London, 1974-87; sr. lectr. Royal Postgrad. Med. Sch., London, 1976—; cons. gynecol. oncology Hammersmith Hosp., London, 1976—. Contbr. articles to profl. jours. Maj. Royal Army Med. Corps, 1960-62. Fellow Royal Coll. Surgeons (diplomate), Royal Coll. Obstetricians and Gynecologists (diplomate), Royal Soc. Medicine; mem. Gynaecological Cancer Soc., Worshipful Soc. Apothecaries (liveryman), Royal Wimbledon Golf Club (past capt.). Avocations: golf, skiing, fishing. Office: 8 Pennant Mews, London W85 1JN, England

OSUNTOGUN, CALEB ADENIYI, agricultural economist; b. Ibadan, Oyo, Nigeria, Apr. 14, 1943; s. Joseph Adesokan and Yinyinola Felicia Osuntogun; m. Bolanle Abeni Shonubi, Sept. 14, 1968; 4 children. BSc in Econs., U. Ibadan, 1967; PhD in Agrl. Econs., U. Leeds, Eng., 1971. Banker Ctrl. Bank of Nigeria and United Bank for Africa Plc, Lagos, 1967-68; lectr. U. Ife, Ile-Ife, Nigeria, 1972-78; lectr., sr. lectr. Obafemi Awolowo U., Ile-Ife, Nigeria, 1978-80; prof. agrl. econs. Obafemi Awolowo U., Ile-Ife, 1980-89, vice-chancellor, 1990-91; nat. program dir. Feden/Lead Nigeria, Lagos, 1992—; dir. Agrl. and Coop. Bank, Kaduna, Nigeria, 1977-80; cons. FAO, Rome, 1980, World Bank, Lagos, 1983, 85, 88; team leader, cons. agrl. economist on the project Involvement of Women in Cooperatives in Nigeria and Population Edn., 1980; chmn. Nat. Adv. Coun. for Coop. Devel., Lagos, 1985-87; trustee Nigerian Internet Group, Lagos, 1993—; cons. environtl. economist on biodiversity country study UN Environ. Program/Nigeria's Fed. EPA, 1992. Editor: Rural Banking in Nigeria, 1983, Cooperatives and Nigeria and Agricultural Development, 1984, Development of Nigerian Agriculture-Suggestions for the Future, 1985, Population and the Nigerian Environment, 1994, Poverty, Health and the Nigerian Environment, 1998. Mem. Oyo State Postgrad. Scholarship Bd., Ibadan, 1976-79; advisor Fed. Ministry of Coops. and Supply, Lagos, 1979-81; cons. UNEP/FFPA, Nigeria Biodiversity Study, Lagos, 1992. Recipient Brit. Soc. of Agr. Econs. prize, U.K., 1973; Western Nigeria Postgrad. scholar, Ibadan, 1968-77. Mem. YMCA, Oluyole Club, Fountain Hope Internations, Network of Environmental Econ. of West Africa (pres. 1998—). Anglican. Avocations: jogging, footballing. Home: 12A Enugu Close Amuwo Odofin, PO Box 74277 Victoria Isle, Lagos Nigeria Office: 8 Thorburn Ave, PO Box 664 Yaba, Lagos Nigeria

OSVAY, KÁROLY, physicist, reader; b. Miskolc, Hungary, July 29, 1964; s. Károly Sebő O. and Erzsébet Jáky; m. Zsuzsanna Gaál, June 23, 1989 (div.). MS, U. Szeged, Hungary, 1990, PhD, 1995. Vis. scientist Rutherford Applied Lab., Chilton, Eng., 1992, 94, 96; asst. lectr. U. Szeged, 1995, reader, 1996—. Szechenyu prof. Hungarian Ministry Edn., 1996; recipient Physics award Hungarian Acad. Scis., 1997. Mem. Soc. Photo-Optical Instrumentation Engrs., Roland Eötvös Phys. Soc., Soc. Pro-Scientia Medalists (pres. 1994—), Optical Soc. Am. Avocations: music, sports, philosophy. Office: Dept Optics U Szeged, Dóm tér 9, H-6720 Szeged Hungary

OSWALD, WINFRIED, veterinarian; b. Freiburg, Germany, Aug. 11, 1966; s. Dietrich and Gisela (Doelle) O. Diploma in vet., Justus Liebig U., Geissen, Germany, 1991, Dr.med.nat., 1994. Lab. tech. Inst. Vet. Hygiene & Infectious Disease, Giessen, Germany, 1992-94; vet. surgeon Humboldt, Germany, 1994-95; asst. scientist Inst. Med. Microbiol. & Infectious Disease, Munich, Germany, 1995-96; rschr. Inst. Med. Microbiol. & Infectious Disease, Hannover, Germany, 1996-99. Contbr. articles to profl. jours. With German Army, 1985-86. Mem. ASM, Deutsche Vet. Assn. Roman Catholic. Avocation: mountain climbing.

OSYKA, VICTOR F., chemist, ecologist; b. Belogorsk, Russia, Nov. 7, 1950. Student, Kharkov State U., 1973; postgrad., Inst. Basic Chemistry, Kharkov, 1979-81; PhD, Kharkov Poly. U., 1981. Rschr., sr. sci. rschr. Kharkov Sci. Rsch. and Design Inst. Basic Chemistry, 1975-85; chief lab. for monitoring water condition, head Analytical Ctr. of the USSR Environ. Ministry, 1985-93; cons. environ. rsch. projects Analytical Ctr. of tehe Ukrainian Environ. Ministry, 1993-95; advisor, cons., project mgr. Environ. Rsch. Projects, Kiev-Kharkov, 1995—; mem. coordinating group on unification of methods for environ. objects analysis Coun. of Mutual Econ. Assistance, 1986-91; co-founder Union of Scientists of Kharkov Region, 1990; initiator of establishment Profl. Union of Leading Analytical and Environ. Scientists of the Former USSR Ecoanalytika, Moscow, 1990. Author, editor: Protection of Waters Against Contamination, 1990, Control of Structure and Properties of Waste Waters, 1995, Quality of Measurements of Composition and Properties of the Objects of the Environment and Sources of Their Pollution, 1997. Sr. lt. Ukrainian Infantry, 1973-75. Grantee Ukraine for the Environ. Policy Devel. and Regulatory Capacity Bldg., World Bank, 1996. Mem. Sci. Couns. on the Analytical Chemistry of the Acads. of Scis. Ukraine and Former USSR Countries, N.Y. Acad. Scis. Avocations: recreational activities, tourism, literature. Office: Ukrainian Sci Ctr Water, 6 Bakulin St, 310888 Kharkov Ukraine

OTA, HIROJI, electric company executive. B in Elec. Engring., Tokyo U., 1955; doctoral degree, Nagoya (Japan) U., 1995. Dir., gen. mgr. Tokyo office Chubu Electric Power Co., Nagoya, Japan, 1985-89, mng. dir., 1989-91, exec. v.p., dir., 1991-95, pres., 1995—; chmn. Fedn. Elec. Power Cos. Japan, 1999—. Office: Chuba Electric Power Co, 1 Toshin-cho Higashi-ku, Nagoya 461-8680, Japan*

OTA, HIROTAKA, gynecologist; b. Sendai, Miyagi, Japan, Nov. 17, 1950; s. Naoyuki and Asa (Sasaoka) O.; m. Hiroko Sato, Apr. 24, 1977; children: Tatako, Norio. MD, Akita (Japan) U., 1976, PhD, 1983. Instr. ob-gyn. Akita U., 1981-86, asst. prof., 1986-88; dir. dept. ob-gyn. Akita Kumiai Gen. Hosp., 1988-97; asst. prof. dept. ob-gyn. Akita U., 1995-98, assoc. prof., 1998—. Mem. Am. Fertility Soc., Japanese Soc. Ob/Gyn. (counselor), Japanese Soc. Oriental Medicine, Japanese Soc. Immunology of Reproduction, Japanese Soc. Fertility and Sterility (counselor), Japanese Soc. Fertilization and Implantation (counselor), Japanese Soc. Ob/Gyn. Endoscopy (counselor), Japanese Soc. Gynecol. and Obstet. Microsurgery (counselor). Avocations: golf, fishing, jogging. Home: 3-5-8 Sakuraga Oka, Akita 010-0043, Japan Office: Dept Ob-Gyn, Akita U Hosp 1-1-1 Hondo, Akita 010-8543, Japan

OTA, TAKAO, American literature and studies educator; b. Minakuchi, Shiga, Japan, Mar. 25, 1942; s. Toshio and Chieko Ota; m. Reiko Arai, Feb. 26, 1946; children: Michiko, Takuo. BA in Math. and English, North Ctrl. Coll., Naperville, Ill., 1966; MA in Religion, Garrett-Evang. Theol. Sem., Evanston, Ill., 1975. Instr. English U. Hirosaki, Japan, 1975-78, assoc. prof., 1978-83; prof. English Niijima Gakuen Women's Jr. Coll., Takasaki, Japan,

1983-2000, dean of acad. affairs, 1983-86, 93-97, dean of admissions, 1997-2000; pres. Internat. Multi-Cultural Studies, 2000—. Chief editor: Marty, 1986, Printer's Measure, 1980, Crime in the Streets, 1993, Introduction to Area Studies, 1997; editor periodicals Studies in Broadcasting Arts, Studies in Comparative Culture. Fulbright sr. rsch. fellow, 1981-82. Mem. United Ch. of Christ in Japan. E-mail: tota@mail.wind.ne.jp. Office: 3413-3 Saginomiya, Annaka 379-0124, Japan

OTA, YORITO, electronics engineer, researcher; b. Kobe, Japan, Feb. 23, 1960; s. Junzo and Shizuko (Kato) O.; m. Keiko Harada, Feb. 16, 1986; children: Hiroto, Eri, Yuto. BS, Kobe U., 1982, MS, 1984, PhD, 1996. Engr. wireless rsch. lab Matsushita, Osaka, 1984-89; sr. engr. semiconductor rsch. ctr. Matsushita, 1989-95, prin. engr. elec. rsch. lab, 1995-97, mgr., 1997—; mem. com. Semi-Standard, Tokyo, 1990-94, Hard-Elec., Tokyo, 1995-97. Co-author: Design of Intelligent power IC/Intelligent power module, 1996. Mem. IEEE, Japan Soc. Applied Physics, Inst. Elec., Info. Comm. Engrs. Japan. Avocations: tennis, railroad models. Office: Matsushita Elec Rsch Lab, 3-1-1 Yagumo-nakamachi, Osaka Moriguchi 570-8501, Japan

OTAKE, YOSHIÉ, physicist, researcher; b. Shibuya, Japan, Oct. 8, 1960; d. Noboru and Kyoko O. BS, Waseda U., Tokyo, 1984, MS, 1986, DSc, 1989. Rsch. assoc. Nat. Coll. Tech., Ibaraki, Japan, 1989-90, asst. prof. physics, 1990-96; rsch. fellow Kyoto (Japan) U., 1993-94; vis. scientist Inst. Laue-Langevin, Grenoble, France, 1995; rsch. scientist Riken Inst. Phys. and Chem. Rsch., Hyogo, Japan, 1996-98, sr. rsch. scientist, 1998—. Author: Problems in Quantum Physics II, 1989, Quantum Aspects of Optical Communications, 1990; co-author: Quantum Coherence and Decoherence, 1999; contbr. articles to profl. jours. Alexander von Humboldt Found. rsch. fellow, 1996; recipient grant-in-aid for scientific rsch. Ministrn Edn., Sci. and Culture, Japan, 1992-97, 98-2000. Avocations: classical music (playing and listening), hiking. Office: RIKEN Coherent Optics Lab, 1-1-1 Kohto Mikazuki, Sayo-gun Hyogoken 679-5148, Japan

OTAL, JAVIER, secondary education educator; b. Zaragoza, Aragón, Spain, May 14, 1951; s. Francisco Otal and Consuelo Cinca; m. María Sol, July 14, 1979; children: Marta, Jorge, Laura. Student, San Agustín, Zaragoza, 1968; degree in math, U. Zaragoza, 1972, PhD in math, 1975. Asst. prof. U. Zaragoza, 1972-77, lectr., 1977-78, prof., 1978—. Author: Characters, 1994; contbr. articles to profl. jours. Mem. Am. Math. Soc., Assn. Am. Math, London Math Soc. Office: Fac Ciencias, U Zaragoza Dept Math, Zaragoza 50009 1, Spain

OTANI, YASUTERU, linguist, educator; b. Maizuru, Kyoto, Japan, Mar. 13, 1933; s. Shiro and Itsue (Kuroda) O.; m. Katsuko Mikawa, Dec. 8, 1963; children: Mami, Kumi. Student, Osaka (Japan) City U., 1952-60, Internat. Christian U., Tokyo, 1960-61, UCLA, 1974-75. Memm asst. prof. to assoc. prof. Momoyama Gakuin U., Osaka, 1963-76, prof., 1976-78; prof. Kansai U., Osaka, 1978-90, Osaka U., 1990-96, U. Shiga Prefecture, Japan, 1996—; prof. emeritus Osaka U., 1996—; lang. edn. adviser Ministry of Edn., Tokyo, 1991-93. Author: Omoigakenai Namida, 1988 (Japan Writer's award 1989), Meiji No Besuboru, 1992 (Japan Writer's award 1993). Grantee Rockefeller Found., 1960-61, Japan Soc. for Promotion of Sci., 1974-75, Brit. Coun., 1992. Mem. Japan Assn. Coll. English Tchrs. (pres. 1990-92, dir. 1990—), Inst. for Rsch. in Lang. Tchg. councilor 1984—). Home: 2-6-3 Higashi Tomigaoka, Nara 631-0002, Japan Office: U Shiga Prefecture, 2500 Hassaka, Hikone Shiga 522-8533, Japan

OTAZÚ, IVONE BEATRIZ, geneticist, researcher; b. Puerto Rico, Misiones, Argentina, Jan. 16, 1965; arrived in Brazil, 1995; d. Juan José Raul and Beatriz (Brandt) O.; m. Marcelo Castier, Dec. 8, 1998. BSc, Nat. U. Misiones, Posadas, Argentina, 1993; MSc, Fed. U. Rio de Janeiro, 1997, postgrad., 1997—. Rschr. Nat. U. Misiones, Posadas, 1988-90, Nat. Hosp. Pediatry, Buenos Aires, 1991-95, Nat. Inst. Cancer, Rio De Janeiro, 1995—; cons. Fertilab, Buenos Aires, 1994, Progenética Lab., Rio de Janeiro, 1999—; vis. rschr. U. Vigo, Spain, 1999. Avocation: fishing. Office: Inst Nacional do Cancer, Praca Cruz Vermelha 23, 20230130 Rio de Janeiro Brazil

OTČENÁŠEK, KAREL, archbishop of Roman Catholic church; b. Ceske Mezirici, Czechoslovakia, Apr. 13, 1920; s. František and Žofie O. Degree in theology, Lateran U., 1945; Doctorate (hon.), Pedagogical U., 1995. Ordained priest, 1945, bishop, 1950. Bishop Internation Communist Prison, 1951-62; dairy laborer, 1962-65, priest Czech borderland, 1965-90, archbishop, 1998, diocesan bishop, 1990-98, now bishop emeritus. Recipient Golden Medallion of Merit of City of Hradec Králové, 1994, Golden Medallion of Honors, Charles U. 1995, Order of T.G. Masaryk, 1995. Office: Biskupství královéhradecké, Velké náměstí 35, 500 01 Hradec Králové Czech Republic

OTERO, KEVIN A., consumer products executive; b. Albuquerque, Sept. 9, 1964; s. Gerge G. Otero and Jacque K. Hillman; m. Gina Kay Harrison, June 11, 1988; 1 child, Grant. B in Arts and Sci., U. N.Mex., 1987. Unit mgr. paper products Procter and Gamble, L.A., 1993-95; assoc. dir. sales tech. Procter and Gamble, Cin., 1995-96, assoc. dir. consumer dir. N.Am., 1996-98; assoc. dir. consumer direct Europe, Middle East and Africa Procter and Gamble, Brussels, 1998—; cons. Grocery E-Commerce. Avocations: golf, running. E-mail: otero.ka@pg.com.

OTERO, MIGUEL ANGEL, biochemist, researcher; b. Havana, Cuba, Oct. 18, 1947; s. Jose and Maria Elena (Rambla) O.; m. Gilda Iglesias, Dec. 15, 1968 (div. Aug. 1969); m. Alba Marina Fumero, Feb. 27, 1974; children: Miguel A., Alba M. BS in Chemistry, Havana U., 1972; postgrad. Rschr. ICIDCA, Havana, 1973-80, head dept., 1980-92, project mgr. dept. biochemistry, 1995—; cons. Barcelone U., Barcelona, Spain, 1985, Arinor Ltd., London, 1995; mem. expert com. Sugar Ministry, Havana, 1987-90; vis. prof. UAM, Mex., 1991, U. Nat. De La Plata, Argentina, 1996; spl. cons. Termotecnica Ltd., Brazil, 1996. Author: By-Product of Sugar Cane, 1990. Mem. N.Y. Acad. Scis. Avocations: reading, movies, sports. Home: 1A25 162d St, Alamar Havana Cuba Office: ICIDCA, 804 Via Blanca, 11000 Havana Cuba

OTERO GONZÁLEZ, ANSELMO JESUS, microbiologist; b. Havana, Cuba, Oct. 15, 1953; s. Anselmo and Guadalupe Herminia (González) O.; m. Tania Bilbao, July 22, 1977; children: Anabel, Juan Carlos. Grad., Faculty of Biology, 1978. Rschr. Nat. Ctrl. Sci. Rsch., Havana, 1978-85, attached rschr., 1985-89; aux. rschr. Inst. Tropical Medicine, Havana, 1989-95, sr. rschr., 1995—; head immunology lab./faculty biology Havana U., 1998—; head cell culture dept. Nat. Ctrl. Sci. Rsch., 1984-89; head hybridoma unit Inst. Tropical Medicine, 1989-95; attached sr. prof. Faculty Biology, Havana, 1995; vis. prof. Harvard U., 2000. Author: (with others) Monoclonal Antibodies, 1984; contbr. articles to profl. jours. Fellowship Swedish Inst., 1991. Mem. Internat. Mycoplasmology Assn., Planetary Soc. Avocations: baseball, classic guitar, book collecting, reading. E-mail: aoterog@infomed.sld.cu. Home: Calle Luz Caballero No 464, Municipio 10 de Octubre, Havana Cuba Office: Havana U Fac Biology, Calle 25 XJ Vedado CP10 400, Habana Cuba

OTEY, RHEBA L., librarian; b. Xenia, Ohio; d. E. Byron and Lottie (Myers-Jenkins) Washington; m. Robert C. Otey (dec.); 1 child, James Edward. AB cum laude, Wilberforce U., 1942; Libr. Cert., Ohio Dominican Coll., 1964; MA in English, Ohio State U., 1969, PhD in English Edn., 1978. Cert. tchr. English, libr. sci., earth sci., Ohio. Lectr., coord. job devel. Ohio Bur. Employment, Columbus, 1956-62; columnist Ohio Sentinel, Columbus, 1960-64; head libr. Columbus Pub. Schs., 1964—, mem. prin.'s adv. coun., 1965-71, chmn., 1972, 77-80, coord. gifted and talented program, 1980-96, advisor libr. stds., 1998—; pub. rels. cons., 1960—; former ptnr. Assocs. Resource Inst., Inc., cons. in human devel. svcs.; columnist Columbus Post; dir. Black Studies program Monroe Jr. H.S., Columbus, 1969-73, Medina Mid., 1974—; moderator Edn. Devel. Model Cities Workshops, 1970-73; presenter Phi Delta Kappa Workshop; del. Ohio White House Conf. on Libr. and Info. Svc.; chair tech. plan Medina Mid., 1997; mem. Medina Mid. Sch. Continuous Improvement Plan, 1998—. Author: Mercury Identifies: A Study of The Nature of Man, (collection short stories) That's the Way Life Is; contbr. articles, papers to profl. jours.; author poems. Vol. United Negro Coll. Fund, Columbus Cmty. House, numerous others; nat. pub. rels. officer Continental Socs., Inc.; founder Columbus chpt. Chums, Inc., past local pres., nat. officer; pub. spkr. Holistic Approach to Successful Goal Setting. Recipient Ohio gov.'s proclamation for outstanding cmty. svc., award for outstanding cmty svc. Columbus sect. Nat. Coun. Negro Women, also numerous certs. of merit from Ohio and U.S. govt. agys.; named Famous Poet, Famous Poet Soc., 1996. Mem. NEA, Ohio Edn. Assn., Columbus Edn. Assn., Phi Delta Kappa, Zeta Sigma Pi, Sen Mer Rekh. Roman Catholic.

OTHERSEN-KHALIFA, CHERYL LEE, insurance broker, realtor; b. Bay City, Mich., Aug. 17, 1948; d. Andrew Julius and Ruth Emma (Jacoby) Houthoofd; m. Wayne Korte Othersen, Sept. 5, 1964 (div.); 1 child, Angela; m. Imed M. B. Salah Khalifa, Sept. 27, 1997. Lic. ins., Mich. State U., 1980, lic. realtor, 1981. Owner, operator Glad Rags Boutique, Unionville, Mich., 1976-79; dept. mgr. Gantos, Saginaw, Mich., 1979-80; agt., bookkeeper Othersen Ins. Agy., Inc., Unionville, 1979-81, v.p., 1981—; realtor Osentoski Realty Corp., Unionville, 1981—; benefits specialist AFLAC Ins. Co., 1995—. Active Mich chpt. Nat. Head Injury Found., Mich. chpt. Crohn's and Colitis Found. Am., Inc., Nat. Mus. In the Arts, Nat. Trust for Hist. Preservation; vol. local Rep. campaigns, 1982, 84, 86; assoc. mem. Am. Mus. Natural History; charter supporter U.S. Holocaust Meml. Mus. Fellow (hon.) John F. Kennedy Libr. Found.; mem. Profl. Ins. Agts., Unionville Bus. Assn., Nat. Mus. Women in the Arts (charter), Saginaw Twp. Bus. Assn., Saginaw County C. of C, Saginaw County Homebuilders Assn., Saginaw Christian Women's Assn. Mem. Moravian Ch. Club: Sherwood-on-the-Hill Country (Gagetown, Mich.). Avocations: sports, painting, travel, gardening, reading. Home: 2575 Ranier St Saginaw MI 48603-3325 Office: Othersen Ins Agy Inc 6639 Center St Unionville MI 48767-9482

OTHMAN, TALAT MOHAMAD, financial consultant, investment banker; b. Betunia, Palestine, Apr. 27, 1936; came to U.S., 1947, naturalized, 1954; s. Mohamad Racheed and Damelize (Ahmed) O.; widowed; children—Joseph, Suad, Jamil, Rashid; m. Isabelle Othman. Student Northwestern U. With Harris Bank, Chgo., 1956-78, v.p., div. head, 1974-78; gen. mgr., chief exec. officer Saudi Arab Fin. Corp., S.A., Paris, 1978-83; pres. Dearborn Financial, Inc., Arlington Hts., Ill., 1983-95; chmn. Grove Fin. Inc., 1995—; bd. dirs. Bank One Wis. Corp., Milw., Harken Oil and Gas Co., Dallas, Pathogenesis Corp., Seattle; chmn. Dansk Internat. Designs, Inc., Mt. Kisko, N.Y., 1985-91, Goodson Polymer, Inc., Troy, Ohio, 1987-88. Contbr. chpts. to Technique of Foreign Exchange Trading, 1975; also articles and booklets. Bd. dirs. Inst. World Affairs, Milw., 1986-89, Khail Gibran Meml. com., Washington, D.C., 1987-89; pres. Islamic Cultural Ctr.; mem. adv. bd. Kennedy Sch. Govt., Harvard U.; mem. hon. bd. Mid. East Studies Ctr., U. Chgo. Recipient Outstanding Pres. award proclaiming Talat M. Othman Day, Islamic Cultural Ctr., 1997. Mem. Arab Bankers Assn. (pres. 1985-87, bd. dirs. 1984-89, recipient plaque of Appreciation), Forex Assn. of N.Am. (chmn., founding pres. Chgo. chpt. 1976, recipient plaque of Appreciation), Mid Am. Arab C. of C. (bd. dirs. 1974-78, 84-91, founding pres. 1977, recipient plaque of Appreciation), Chgo. Club. Moslem. Avocations: tennis, racquetball, reading.

OTIS, JOHN JAMES, civil engineer; b. Syracuse, N.Y., Aug. 5, 1922; s. John Joseph and Anna (Dey) O.; m. Dorothy Fuller Otis, June 21, 1958; children: Mary Eileen Dawn, John Leon. BChemE, Syracuse U., 1943, MBA, 1950, postgrad., 1951-55. Registered profl. engr., Ala., Tex. Jr. process engr. GM, Syracuse, 1951-53, prodn. engr., 1954-58, process control engr., 1958-59, process engr., 1960-61; engr., writer GE, Syracuse, 1961-63; configuration control engr. GE, Phila., 1969; assoc. rsch. engr. Boeing Co., Huntsville, Ala., 1963-65; assoc. Planning Rsch. Corp., Huntsville, 1965-67; prin. engr. Brown Engring. Co. subs. Teledyne Co., Huntsville, 1967-69; mech. designer Drever Co., Beth Ayres, Pa., 1970-71; civil engr. U.S. Army Corps Engrs., Mobile, Ala., 1971-74, Galveston, Tex., 1974—. Lector, lay minister Roman Cath. Ch. Served with USNR, 1944-50. Mem. Am. Inst. Indsl. Engrs. (past v.p. Syracuse and Huntsville chpts.), Tex. Soc. Profl. Engrs. (dir. Galveston County chpt. 1976-79, sec.-treas. 1979-80, v.p. 1980-81, pres. 1982-83), Am. Legion, Tau Beta Pi, Phi Kappa Tau, Alpha Chi Sigma, Chi Eta Sigma. Home: 2114 Yorktown Ct N League City TX 77573-5056 Office: US Army Corps Engrs Jadwin Bldg 2000 Fort Point Rd Galveston TX 77550-3038

OTIS, ROY JAMES, lawyer; b. San Rafael, Calif., 1946; m. Susan Leslie Wish, 1975; children: Lindsay Elizabeth, Ryan James. BA, Stanford (Calif.) U., 1968; JD, Golden Gate U., 1980. Bar: Calif. 1980, U.S. Dist. Ct. (no. dist.) Calif. 1980; cert. specialist in workman's compensation. Tchr. Albany Children's Ctr., Albany, 1972-77; assoc. atty. Beauzay, Bledsoe, Hammer, et al, San Jose, Calif., 1981-83, Boxer, Elkind & Gerson, Oakland, Calif., 1983-85; assoc. Airola, Williams, Otis et al, San Francisco, 1985-87; ptnr., 1988-92; pvt. practice Walnut Creek, Calif., 1992-93; assoc. Law Offices of Mark Gearheart, Pleasant Hill, Calif., 1993-95; ptnr. Gearheart & Otis, Pleasant Hill, 1996—. Mem. Calif. Applications Atty. Assn. (pres. no. Calif. chpt., 1994-96, bd. govs. 1997—), Assn. of Trial Lawyers of Am. (workplace injury litigation group sect. 1996—). Democrat. Avocations: skiing, tennis, bicycle riding, fiction. Office: Gearheart & Otis 367 Civic Dr Ste 17 Pleasant Hill CA 94523-1935

OTON, CLAUDIO ANTONIO, radiology educator, oncologist; b. Cartagena, Murcia, Spain, Apr. 3, 1947; s. Claudio Oton and Elena Sanchez; m. María Elena Nieto, Nov. 1, 1973; children: Elena, Claudio José, Laura. MD, U. Granada, Spain, 1970; PhD, U. Madrid, 1975. Resident in radiology and oncology Univ. Hosp. San Carlos, Madrid, 1970-73; asst. prof. U. Madrid Faculty Medicine, 1973-77; prof. radiology, chmn. Faculty Medicine, U. Córdova, Spain, 1977-78; prof. radiology, chmn. Faculty Medicine, U. La Laguna, Canary Is., Spain, 1978—, dean, 1995-97, dir. radiobiology sect., 1982—, coord. Physiotherapy Sch., 1984-94, head studies, 1997; head dept. Univ. Hosp. Canary Islands, 1978—; mem. nat. com. radiation oncology Spanish Ministry Health, 1990-95. Author: Questions and Answers in Physical Therapy, 1976; co-editor: Manual of Clinical Radiology, 1995, 97. Recipient plaque Bishopric of Tenerife, Spain, 1980, honor prize Spanish Assn. Physiotherapy, 1994. Mem. Royal Acad. Medicine (acad. corr.), Spanish Soc. for Med. Informatics (vice chmn. 1972-75), European Soc. Therapeutic Radiology and Oncology. Avocations: informatics, mythology, astronomy. E-mail: coton@ull.es. Office: Univ Hosp Canary Islands, Ofra La Cuesta, 38320 La Laguna Canary I, Spain

O'TOOLE, DESMOND KEITH, microbiologist, food scientist; b. Brisbane, Qld., Australia, July 22, 1941; s. Vincent and Thelma (Buckmaster) O'T.; m. Elizabeth Margaret Symington, Oct. 31, 1970; 1 child, John Vincent. BSc, U. Queensland, Australia, 1968, MSc, 1983. Bacteriologist N.S.W. Dept. Agr., 1968-74; dairy rsch. officer N.S.W. Dept. Agr. and Fisheries, 1974-80, sr. livestock rsch. officer, 1980-89; assoc. prof. microbiology and food sci. City U. of Hong Kong, 1989—. Contbr. articles to profl. jours. Chmn. Staff Assn. of City Poly. of Hong Kong, 1991-93. Office: City U Hong Kong Dept Biology/Chemistry, 83 Tat Chee Ave, Kowloon Hong Kong

O'TOOLE, SHANE, architect, critic; b. Dublin, Ireland, July 5, 1955; s. James Patrick and Caroline Louise (Hannan) O'T.; m. Maeve O'Neill, May 28, 1984; children: Alice, Tadg. BArch, Univ. Coll. Dublin, 1979. Arch. Lynch O'Toole Walsh, Dublin, 1979-82, assoc., 1982-86; project mgr. energy rsch. group Univ. Coll. Dublin, 1986-91; dir. Group 91 Archs., Dublin, 1991-98; prin. Shane O'Toole Arch., Dublin, 1992-98; co. arch. Tegral Bldg. Products, Dublin, 1994—; chmn. Irish Standards Com. Slating and Tiling, 1998—; convenor The Pillar Project, 1988, Tales Two Cities: Emerging Architects in Dublin & Edinburgh, 1994; architectural critic The Sunday Times, U.K., 1999—; architectural advisor Nation Bldg., 2000; advisor Mies van der Rohe award for European Architecture, 1992—, 6th Veronica Rudge Green prize in Urban Design, Harvard U. Grad. Sch. of Design, 2000. Co-editor, designer Kevin Roche Architect, 1983 (book design commendation 1984); designer The Ark: A Cultural Centre for Children, 1992-95 (Bldg. of Yr. award 1996, Downes medal Archtl. Assn. Ireland 1996), Pedestrian Archway Meetinghouse Sq. Temple Bar, 1992-97); mem. editl bd. A & D Architecture and Design, Stuttgart, Germany, 1995—, Tracings, Dublin, 1999—, internet-based Planning Architecture Design Database Ireland, Belfast, 2000—. Recipient Silver medal Sofia Biennale, 1987, Grand Prix, Cracow Biennale for the Pillar Project, 1989, Sunday Tribune award, 1989. Mem. Royal Inst. Archs. Ireland (v.p. 1988, 97, regional award 1996, elected fell., 1998), Royal Inst. Brit. Archs. (award 1997), Archtl. Assn. Ireland (hon. mem., pres. 1982-83, editor Green Book yearbook 1975-96), DoCoMoMo Ireland (founder). Office: Tegral Bldg Products, Athy, County Kildare Ireland

O'TOOLE, TARA JEANNE, federal official; b. Newton, Mass., May 3, 1951; d. Harold J. and Jeanne (Whalen) O'T. BA, Vassar Coll., 1974; MD, George Washington U., 1981; MPH, Johns Hopkins U., 1988. Diplomate Am. Bd. Internal Medicine, Am. Bd. Preventive/Occupational Medicine. Rsch. asst. Sloan-Kettering Cancer Inst., N.Y.C., 1974-77; resident in internal medicine Yale New Haven (Conn.) Hosp., 1981-84; physician Balt. Cmty. Health Ctrs., 1984-87; fellow in occupational medicine Johns Hopkins U., Balt., 1987-89; sr. analyst Office Tech. Assessment, Washington, 1989-93; asst. sec. energy for environ., safety and health Dept. Energy, Washington, 1993-97; dep. dir. Johns Hopkins U. Ctr. Civilian Biodefense Studies, 1998—. Democrat.

O'TOOLE, WILLIAM GEORGE, lawyer; b. Chgo., Oct. 25, 1934; s. George P. and Margaret (Battenhouse) O'T.; m. Gail M. McGregor, Aug. 13, 1960; children: Joyce M. Masterton, Paul G., Katherine A. Gorski. BS, U. Detroit, 1956; JD, DePaul U., 1961. Bar: Ill. 1961, U.S. Dist. Ct. (no. dist.) Ill. 1962. Assoc. Jaros, Tittle & O'Toole (and predecessor firm), Chgo., 1961-74, ptnr., 1974-90, pres., 1990—. Mem. ABA, Ill. Bar Assn., Ill. Mortgage Bankers Assn. (bd. dirs.), Chgo. Bar Assn., Southwest Bar Assn. (past pres.), Chgo. Athletic Assn., Abbey Springs Country Club, Ridge Country Club, Elks, K.C., Beta Alpha Psi. Roman Catholic. Home: 10736 S Kolmar Ave Oak Lawn IL 60453-5349 Office: Jaros Tittle & O'Toole 20 N Clark St Ste 510 Chicago IL 60602-4188

OTOROWSKI, CHRISTOPHER LEE, lawyer; b. Teaneck, N.J., Nov. 20, 1953; s. Wladyslaw Jerzy and Betty Lee (Robbins) O.; m. Shawn Elizabeth McGovern, Aug. 4, 1978; children: Kirsten, Hilary. BSBA cum laude, U. Denver, 1974, MBA, 1977, JD, 1977. Bar: Wash. 1977, Colo. 1977, U.S. Dist Ct. (we. dist.) D.C. 1977, U.S. Dist. Ct. (we. dist.) Wash. 1978. Asst. atty. gen. Wash. State Atty. Gen., Spokane, 1978-79; atty. Bassett, Gemson & Morrison, Seattle, 1979-81; pvt. practice Seattle, 1981-88; atty. Sullivan, Golden & Otorowski, Seattle, 1988-91, Morrow & Otorowski, Bainbridge Island, 1996—; pvt. practice Morrow and Otorowski, Bainbridge Island, Wash., 1991-96. Contbr. articles to profl. jours. Bd. dirs. Bainbridge Edn. Support Team, Bainbridge Island, 1991-97. Mem. Fed. Bar Assn. We. Dist. Wash. (sec. 1979-82, trustee 1990-93), Wash. State Trial Lawyers Assn. (bd. govs. 1991-93), Assn. Trial Lawyers Am., Seattle Tennis Club, Seattle Yacht Club. Avocations: photography, sailing. Office: 298 Winslow Way W Bainbridge Is WA 98110-2510

OTRZAN, DURDA, author, composer; b. Bjelovar, Yugoslavia, May 1, 1953; d. Nikola and Lucija (Bojanic) O.; m. Vladan Svacov, July 3, 1976 (div. 1980); 1 child, Thomas. BA in Musicology, Comparative Lit., Faculty Philosophy/Music Acad., Zagreb, Yugoslavia, 1975. Editor Radio Zagreb, 1979—; head music Croatian Radio, Zagreb, 1994—; leader Croatian Euroclassic team European Broadcasting Union, 1999—. Author: Scene with Spear/Angel of the Fatherland, 1988; contbr. essays on arts to various publs.; composer scores for theatrical presentations; writer screen plays including Volunteer, 1984, Parthian Shot, 1990, Silicon Horizon, 1990; chief music editor Channel III, 1992—. Mem. Croatian Soc. Composers. Avocation: athletics. Home: Veslacka 14, 10000 Zagreb Croatia Office: Croatian Radio and TV, Prisavlje 3, 10000 Zagreb Croatia

OTSTERWALD-LENUM, CARSTEN, engineer; b. Copenhagen, Aug. 19, 1958; s. Kurt and Jytte (Laustrup) Osterwald-Lenum. MSc in Engring., Tech. U. Denmark, Copenhagen, 1984. Field engr. Schlumberger, S.Am., 1985-86; engr. Royal Danish Air Force, 1986-88; cons. Simcorp A/S, Copenhagen, 1988-93; data mgr. Riva Hugin-Sweda, Copenhagen, 1993-94; ctr. mgr. Euromath Ctr., Copenhagen, 1994-98, Bone Marrow Transfer, 1998-99; project mgr. Bus. IT, 1999-2000, ECSoft Danmark A/S, Copenhagen, 2000—; sec. EMNET/NIS, Copenhagen, 1994-98. Mem. Soc. Danish Engrs., Danish Math. Soc., European Math. Soc.

OTSUBO, MAYUMI, management educator, writer, commentator; b. Kyoto, Japan, Apr. 13, 1929; s. Kunimasu and Toshi (Icho) O.; m. Atsuko Sakamoto, Mar. 23, 1958; children: Motoki, Saiko. BA in Econs., U. Tokyo, 1953; MBA, UCLA, 1957. Gen. mgr. corp. planning Bridgestone Corp., Japan, 1969-72, gen. mgr. advt., 1976-82; mng. dir. Bridgestone Tire Am., Japan, 1972-76; prof. U. Shizuoka, Japan, 1987-98, asst. to pres., dean Sch. Informatics and Adminstrn.,, 1996-98; prof. Shizuoka Sangyo U., 1998—, pres., 2000—; radio commentator SBS Radio, Shizuoka, 1990—; chair TV program review com. Daiich-TV, Shizuoka, 1993—; assoc. N.C. Japan Ctr. N.C. State U., 1993—. Author: Marketing for Engineers and Scientists, 1988, Corporate Communications, 1992, How to Develop Strategic Mind, 1994; author, editor: Information Society and Management, 1998. Vice-chair Prefectural Long Range Planning Coun., Shizuoka, 1988—; chair Employment Stabilization Coun., Shizuoka, 1988—, EEO Act Mediation Bd., Shizuoka, 1994—; councilor Shizuoka Sci. and Edn. Promotion Found. Inc., 1996—. Mem. Japan Mktg. Assn. (vice-chair internat. divsn. 1988—), Acad. Soc. Orgn. (auditor 1996-99), Acad. Soc. Advt. (direction councilor 1995-98), Acad. Soc. Corp. Comm. (dir. 1995-98). Avocations: gardening, music, travel, collection of prints. Home: 2174 Isshiki Hayama, Kanagawa 240 0111, Japan Office: Shizuoka Sangyo Univ, 4-1-1 Surugadai, Fujieda Shizuoka 426 8668, Japan

OTSUKA, AKIO, lawyer, consultant; b. Utsunomiya, Tochigi, Japan, Jan. 28, 1959; s. Yoshijiro and Yoshi (Suzuki) O. BA in Law, Hitotsubashi U., Tokyo, 1984; LLM, So. Meth. U., 1990, MBA, 1991; postgrad., Tsukuba U., Tokyo, 1998—. Bar: Japan. Legal trainee Legal Study & Rsch. Inst. Supreme Ct., Tokyo, 1984-86; assoc. Shinmyo & Osanai, Tokyo, 1986-89, Hamayotsu & Hamayotsu, Tokyo, 1991-96; ptnr. Hamayotsu & Hamayhotsu, Tokyo, 1996-99, Aoyama Century Internat. Law Office, Tokyo, 1999—; advisor Tokyo Consulting Internat. Inc., Dallas, 1994-97, Japan Consulting Internat., Inc., Tokyo, 1997—; vis. scholar So. Meth. U. Sch. of Law, 1998; statutory auditor T.G.I. Friday's Japan, Inc., Tokyo, 1998—. Mem. Japan Fedn. Bar Assns., Daiichi-Tokyo Bar Assn. Buddhist. Avocations: music, driving. Home: 27-4 Yoyogi 4-chome # 105, Shibuya-ku, Tokyo 151, Japan

OTSUKA, KAZUHIRO, engineering educator; b. Hamamatsu, Shizuoka, Japan, Mar. 8, 1937; s. Kichihei and Yayoi (Tanaka) O.; m. Motoko Iwashita, Oct. 22, 1967; children: Kay, Ryo, Jun. BS, U. Tokyo, 1961, D Engring., 1972; MS, U. Ill., 1966. Rschr. Furukawa Electric Co. Ltd., Nikko, Japan, 1961-64; rsch. assoc. Osaka U., Japan, 1966-73, assoc. prof., 1973-79; prof. U. Tsukuba, Japan, 1979-2000; sr. scientist Nat. Inst. for Advanced Interdisciplinary Rsch., MITI, Tsukuba, Japan, 2000—; dir. Cryogenic Rsch. Ctr. U. Tsukuba, 1980-81; vis. assoc. prof. U. Ill., Urbana, 1974-76; vis. prof. Katholieke Univ. Leuven, Belgium, 1989; mem. Internat. Adv. Com. Martensitic Transformations, 1989—. Author: Metallic Funtional Materials, 1985; author, editor: Shape Memory Materials, 1997; contbr. articles to profl. jours. Recipient Fulbright Travel grant, 1964. Fellow Am. Soc. Metals Internat.; mem. Japan Inst. Metals (meritorious award 1982, Tanigawa Harris award 1997), Materials Rsch. Soc. Avocations: music, travel, reading. Home: 31-20 2-chome Umezono, Tsukuba 305-0045, Japan Office: Nat Inst Adv Rsch MITI, 1-1-4 Higashi, Tsukuba 305-8562, Japan

OTT, GILBERT RUSSELL, JR., lawyer; b. Bklyn., Apr. 15, 1943; s. Gilbert Russell Sr. and Bettina Rose (Ferrel) O.; m. Lisa S. Weatherford, Apr. 12, 1986; children: Gilbert R. III, Laura Elisabeth. BA, Yale U., 1965; JD, Columbia U., 1969, MBA, 1969. Bar: N.Y. 1970. Assoc. Chadbourne, Parke, Whiteside & Wolff, N.Y.C., 1969-72, LeBoeuf, Lamb, Leiby & MacRae, N.Y.C., 1972-78; assoc. gen. counsel Kidder, Peabody & Co., Inc., N.Y.C., 1978-96, asst. sec., 1978-91, asst. v.p., 1978-79, v.p., 1979-86, mng. dir., 1986-91, sr. v.p., sec., 1992-96; v.p. Kidder, Peabody Group Inc., N.Y.C., 1989-96, asst. sec., 1986-96; exec. v.p., gen. counsel, sec. Rodman & Renshaw Capital Group, Inc., Chgo. and N.Y.C., 1996-98; counsel Cadwalader, Wickersham & Taft, N.Y.C., 1998-99; dep. gen. counsel Datek Online Holdings Corp., Edison, N.J., 1999—, N.Y.C. Mem. Assn. of Bar of City of N.Y., Piping Rock Club, Univ. Club. Home: 260 Highwood Cir Oyster Bay NY 11771-3205

OTT, JAMES DANIEL, journalist, educator; b. Dayton, Ky., Mar. 24, 1938; s. Arthur Daniel and Grace Mary (Bennett) O.; m. Charlotte Elizabeth Freihofer, Aug. 1, 1964; children: Alec, Stephen, Anthony, James, Michael. AB in English Lit., Thomas More Coll., 1961; MEd in Comms. Arts, Xavier U., 1973. Reporter Cin. Enquirer, 1959-65, Ky. editor, 1965-69; pub. rels. dir. Thomas More Coll., Crestview Hills, Ky., 1969-74, Cath. U. Am., Washington, 1974-78; transport editor Aviation Week and Space Tech., Washington, 1978-84, sr. transport editor, 1984-94; contbg. editor Aviation Week and Space Tech., Ft. Mitchell, Ky., 1994—; freelance writer, McGraw-Hill, Inc., Ft. Mitchell; online editor Aviation Week Group, Ft. Mitchell. Author: Jets, Airliners of the Golden Age, 1993, Airline Odyssey, 1995. Mem. adv. bd. The Messenger, 1999—. With USAR, 1956-63. Mem. Soc. Aerospace Communicators, Cathedral Found. (bd. dirs. 1997—). Republican. Roman Catholic. Avocations: swimming, hiking, reading. E-mail: jim ott@aviationnow.com. Office: Aviation Week and Space Tech 825 Rosewood Dr Crescent Spgs KY 41017-1383

OTT, ULRICH, physicist, researcher; b. Kettenbach, Hesse, Germany, Dec. 9, 1947; s. August and Amalie E.C. (Hofmann) O.; m. Brigitte J. Görisch; 1 child, Joachim P. Physics Diploma, U. Mainz, Germany, 1974, PhD, 1977, habilitation nuc. chemistry, 1997. Postdoctoral fellow Max Planck Inst. for Chemistry, Mainz, 1977-78, rsch. scientist, 1980—; postdoctoral fellow U. Calif., Berkeley, 1978-80; vis. rsch. assoc. prof. Washington U., St. Louis, 1993. Assoc. editor Geochimica et Cosmochimica Acta, 1995—, Geochem. Jour., 1998—. Fellow Meteoritical Soc.; mem. German Phys. Soc., Indian Soc. Mass Spectrometry (life). Home: Königsberger Str 60a, D55268 Nieder-Olm Germany Office: Max Planck Inst for Chem, Becherweg 27, D-55128 Mainz Germany

OTTAVIANI, MARIA GIOIA, performing arts educator; b. Perugia, Umbria, Italy, Sept. 1, 1948; d. Gino and Elvira (Locascio) O.; m. Marcello Aldega, Apr. 12, 1975; 1 child, Federico Giovanni Aldega. Letters, U. Rome, 1973. Fellow U. Rome, 1974-75, Nat. Coun. Rsch., Italy, 1976-80; asst. prof. Inst. Performing Arts U. Rome, 1981-83, asst. prof. Dept. Oriental Studies, 1984-98; tchr. dept. Italian studies and performing arts U. Rome, La Sapienca, 1998—. Author: Introduction to the Study of Japanese Theatre, 1994, 2nd edit., 2000, The Actor and the Shaman, 1984, rsch. on theatre anthropology and drama therapy; contbr. articles to profl. jours. Achievements include research ont heatre anthropology and drama therapy. Avocation: embroidering. Home: Via G. Pier Luigi, da Palestrina 63, 00193 Rome Italy Office: U Rome La Sapienza Dept Oriental Studies, Piazzale Aldo Moro, 00185 Rome Italy

OTTAWAY, DAVID BLACKBURNE, journalist; b. Endicott, N.Y., Oct. 27, 1939; s. James Haller Sr. and Ruth Blackburne (Hart) O.; m. Marina Seassaro, July 18, 1963; children: Eric, Robin. BA, Harvard U., 1962; MA, Columbia U., 1964, PhD, 1972. Dep. fgn. editor Washington Post, 1971-73, Africa correspondent, 1974-79, Mid. East correspondent, 1981-85, nat. security correspondent, 1985-90, South Africa corr., 1990-92, Ea., So. and Ctrl. South Europe correspondent, 1992-94, investigative reporter, 1994—; chmn., pres. Buck Hill Falls Co., Buck Hills, Pa., 1995-98, bd. dir. Co-author: (with Marina Ottaway) Algeria - The Politics of a Socialist Revolution, 1965, Ethiopia - Empire in Revolution, 1978, Arfocommunism, 1983; author: Chained Together - Mandela, De Klerk and the Struggle to Remake South Africa, 1993. Pres. NBO Found., 1995-98, trustee, 1998—; trustee Lawrenceville Sch., 1998—. Mem. Harvard Club of Washington. Avocations: skiing, hiking, jogging, tennis. Office: Washington Post 1150 15th St NW Washington DC 20071-0002

OTTE, KJELD ERIK, medical consultant; b. Skodborg, Denmark, May 24, 1954; s. Peter Petersen and Ingeborg Marie (Hansen) O.; m. Doris Roed Jakobsen, Jan. 22, 1977; children: Camilla, Andreas, Helena, Kjeld Erik. MD, U. Arhus, Denmark, 1982. Resident Med. Dept., Vejle, Denmark, 1982-84, sr. resident, 1984-88; resident Dept. Nephrology, Odense, Denmark, 1988-89, sr. resident, 1990-94; sr. resident Dept. Nephrology, Arhus, Denmark, 1995-98; cons. Dept. Medicine, Fredericia, Denmark, 1998—; assoc. prof. internal medicine I. Arhus, 1995-98. Author: International Asbestos Medical Research, 1991, Xenotransplantation, 1991. Fellow Danish Soc. Nephrology; mem. Danish Soc. Internal Medicine, European Renal Assn. Avocations: history, politics, hunting, fishing. Home: Mosebakken 1, 7120 Vejle Denmark Office: Fredericia Hosp, Dronningens Gade 97, 7000 Fredericia Denmark

OTTER, MANFRED WERNER, space scientist; b. Graz, Styria, Austria, Nov. 6, 1954; s. Josef and Gertrude (Heinrich) O. MS, Tech. U., Graz, Austria, 1980; PhD, U. Graz, 1982. Rsch. fellow U. Graz, 1980-81, asst. prof., 1981-82; space scientist European Space Agy., Noordwijk, The Netherlands, 1982-85; space sys. engr. European Space Agy., Darmstadt, Germany, 1985-94; mng. dir. Anetel, Stockport, U.K., 1995—; cons. World Meteorol. Orgn., Geneva, Switzerland, 1995—; mem. Space Frequency Coord. Group, Paris, 1986—. Patentee in field; contbr. articles to profl. publs. Avocations: tennis, skiing, water sports, traveling. Home: Steinberg 76, A-8151 Hitzendorf Styria, Austria

OTTESON, HOLLY CAROL HARVICK-WARD, poet; b. Bismarck, N.D., Dec. 20, 1941; d. Bennie Arthur and Mary Laura (Bawden) Harvick; m. Denis Martin Ward, June 7, 1963 (dec. Dec. 1986); children: Scott John Ward Harvick, Lauren Heather Ward; m. Lyle William Otteson, Feb. 3, 1996. BS, U. N.D., 1963; MA, U. Mo., Kansas City, 1982. Life cert. tchr., Mo.; cert. counselor. pvt. art tutor, Bismarck, N.D., 1962-69, Oswego, N.Y., 1974. Author: (poetry) The Desert Sun, Anthology of N.Am. Poetry, A View from the Edge, New American Poetry Anthology, Great Poems of Our Time, Selected Works of Our World's Best Poets, Our Worlds Favorite Poems, Whspers in the Wind; poetry pub. various jours. Active Jr. Women's Symphony Alliance, Symphony Women's League. With USMC, 1980-88, U.S. Army, 1963. Recipient Silver and Bronze medals for working with disabled vets. Mem. AAUW, Internat. Soc. Poets, Nat. Geog. Soc., Nat. Hist. Trust, Smithsonian Instn., Comdrs. Club of DAV, Kappa Alpha Theta. Republican. Lutheran. Avocations: swimming, skiing, skating, bike riding, walking. Home and Office: 441 W Oakdale Ave Apt 13C Chicago IL 60657-5968

OTTEWILL, GERALDINE ASTRID, chemistry educator; b. Cambridge, Eng., Sept. 17, 1956; d. Ronald Harry and Ingrid Geraldine (Roe) O.; m. Donald Robert Bootle, Aug. 19, 1978; 1 child, Rosalind Gillian. BSc in Chemistry with honors, U. Nottingham, Eng., 1978, PhD in Phys. Chemistry, 1982; MA, U. Portsmouth, U.K., 1996. Univ. demonstrator U. Nottingham, 1981-82; extra mural rsch. worker UKAEA Harnell, Didcot, U.K., 1984-87; rsch. chemist U. Southampton, U.K., 1988-91; sr. lectr. chemistry U. Portsmouth, 1992—; lectr. in phys. chemistry U. Bournemouth, Poole, U.K., 1989-90; lectr. in math. Fareham Tertiary Coll., Fareham, 1990-91; external examiner, moderator Hampshire Access Validation Agy., Portsmouth, 1992—. Contbr. articles to profl. jours. Avocation: playing piano and clarinet. Office: U Portsmouth Chemistry Dept, White Swan Rd, Portsmouth PO1 2DT, England

OTTINO, JULIO MARIO, chemical engineering educator, scientist; b. La Plata, Buenos Aires, Argentina, May 22, 1951; came to U.S., 1976; naturalized, 1990; s. Julio Francisco and Nydia Judit (Zufriategui) O.; m. Alicia I. Löffler, Aug. 20, 1976; children: Jules Alessandro, Bertrand Julien. Diploma in Chem. Engring., U. La Plata, 1974; PhD in Chem. Engring., U. Minn., 1979; exec. program Kellogg Sch. Mgmt., Northwestern U., 1995. Instr. in chem. engring. U. Minn., Mpls., 1978-79; asst. prof. U. Mass., Amherst, 1979-83, adj. prof. polymer sci., 1979-91, assoc. prof. chem. engring., 1983-86, prof., 1986-91; Chevron vis. prof. chem. engring. Calif. Inst. Tech., Pasadena, 1985-86; sr. rsch. fellow Ctr. for Turbulence Rsch. Stanford (Calif.) U., 1989-90; Walter P.Murphy prof. chem. engring. Northwestern U., Evanston, Ill., 1991-2000, chmn. dept. chem. engring., 1992—; McCormick Inst. prof., 2000—; George T. Piercy Disting. prof. U. Minn., 1998; cons. to U.S. and European corps.; Allan P. Colburn Meml. lectr. U. Del., 1987; Merck Sharp & Dohme lectr. U. P.R., 1989, Stanley Corrsin lectr. Johns Hopkins U., 1991; Centennial lectr. U. Md., 1994, William N. Lacey lectr. Calif. Inst. Tech., 1994, P. V. Danckwerts Meml. lectr. Inst. Chem. Engring., Eng., 1999; mem. tech. adv. bd. Dow Chem.; mem. bd. dirs. Coun. Chem. Rsch. Author: The Kinematics of Mixing: Stretching, Chaos and Transport, 1989; contbr. articles to profl. jours.; assoc. editor Physics Fluids A, 1991—; mem. editl. bd. Internat. Jour. Bifurc. Chaos, 1991—; assoc. editor Am. Inst. Chem. Engring. Jour., 1991-95, assoc. editor., 1995—; one man art exhibit, La Plata, 1974. Recipient Presdl. Young Investigator award NSF, 1984; Univ. fellow U. Mass., 1988, Alpha Chi Sigma award AIChE, 1994; Lacey lectureship, Calif. Inst. Tech., 1994, Danckwerts lectureship Royal Instn., 1999. Fellow Am. Phys. Soc., AAAS; mem. Am. Chem. Soc., Am. Phys. Soc., Soc. Rheology, Am. Soc. Engring. Edn., Nat. Acad. Engring., Sigma Xi (disting. lectr. 1997-99), Pau Beta Pi (gov. bd. coun. for chem. rsch.). Achievements include research in fluid dynamics, chaos, complex systems, mixing and granular flows. Avocations: visual arts, painting. Home: 1092 Crescent Ln Winnetka IL 60093-1501 Office: Northwestern U Dept Chem Engring 2145 Sheridan Rd Evanston IL 60208-0834

OTTLEY, JEROLD DON, retired choral conductor, educator; b. Salt Lake City, Apr. 7, 1934; s. Sidney James and Alice (Warren) O.; m. JoAnn South, June 22, 1956; children: Brent Kay, Allison. B.A., Brigham Young U., Provo, Utah, 1961; M.Mus., U. Utah, 1967; Fulbright study grantee, Fed. Republic Germany, 1968-69; D.M.A. (grad. teaching fellow), U. Oreg., 1972. Tchr. public schs. Salt Lake City area, 1961-65; mem. faculty U. Utah, Salt Lake City, 1967-99, asst. prof. music, 1971-78, adj. assoc. prof. music, 1978-81, adj. prof. music, 1981-99; assoc. conductor Salt Lake Mormon Tabernacle Choir, 1974-75, conductor, 1975—; also guest conductor throughout U.S. Conducted Mormon Tabernacle Choir in 13 concert tours U.S., 25 fgn. countries, Utah Phila. and Milw. Orchestra in performance; rec. artist CBS Masterworks, London/Decca Records, Bonneville Records and Laserlight; prepared choirs for Eugene Ormandy, Maurice Avravanel, Stanislaw Skrowaczewski, Michael Tilson Thomas, Robert Shaw, Julius Rudel, Sir David Willcocks, Ling Tung. Past mem. gen. music coms. Mormon Ch., cultural arts com. Salt Lake City C. of C. (Honors in the Arts award), past bd. advs. Barlow Endowment Music Composition; v.p., past bd. dirs., com. chair Chorus Am. Served with U.S. Army, 1957-59. Faculty Study grantee U. Utah, 1971-72; recipient Brigham Young U. Alumnus Achievement award, 1990, Disting. Alumnus award U. Oreg. Sch. of Music, 1996. Mem. Am. Choral Dirs. Assn., Am. Choral Found., Master Tchr. Inst. Arts (past trustee). Office: Mormon Tabernacle Choir 50 E North Temple 20th Fl Salt Lake City UT 84150-0002*

OTTLINGER, CLAUDIA, English educator; b. Witten, Germany, Feb. 25, 1962; d. Hellmut Georg and Gertrud (Blum) O. Cert. tchr., Ruhr U., Bochum, Germany, 1987, PhD, 1995. Instr., adminstrv. asst. Inst. Theatre, Film and TV Studies, Bochum, 1988-94; instr. English dept. Ruhr U., 1994—. Mem. German Shakespeare Soc., Assn. German Anglicists. Office: Ruhr U English Dept, Universitätsstrasse 150, 44801 Bochum Germany

OTTNAD, ADRIAN BERNHARD HUBERT, economist; b. Freiburg, Breisgau, Germany, Apr. 7, 1956; s. Bernd J. and Margarethe C. (Roesch) O.; m. Maria-Arabella Fach, Apr. 11, 1980; children: Konstantin, Camilla, Jonathan, Samuel. Rsch. asst. U. Freiburg, 1984-90; sr. econ. IWG Bonn, Germany, 1991—. Author: Wohlstand Auf Pump, 1996; co-author: Grundzuge der Mikrookonomik, 1993, Risse im Fundament, 1995, Foederalen Wettbewerb statt Verteilungsstreit, 1997, Zwischen Markt und Mildtaetigkeit, 2000. With German Army, 1975-76. Mem. Am. Econ. Assn., Verein F. Social Pol. Fax: 49-228-375-869. E-mail: ottnad-iwg.bonn@t-online.de.

OTTO, CARL, statistical sciences educator, researcher; b. Kalisz, Posen, Poland, Apr. 28, 1928; s. Emil Karl and Emma Frieda (Sauer) O.; m. Karin Eva Schneiderheinze, July 24, 1967 (div. Jan. 1977); m. Edeltraut Irene Schulze, Dec. 29, 1978. Abitur, Humboldt U., Berlin, 1949, MS, 1952, PhD, 1959, DSc, 1962. Tchr. Potsdam (Germany) h.s., 1945-46; dep. dir. CMEA, Moscow, 1962-65; vice dean Faculty of Arts and Social Scis., Berlin, 1970-76; asst. dir. UN Statis. Office, N.Y.C., 1976-80; dean, dep. dean Humboldt U., Berlin, 1968-89, prof., dir., 1954-89, dir., 1968-69; cons. Ministry of Higher Edn., Berlin, 1969-76, Statis. Office, Berlin, 1965-89, Statis. Bundesamt, Weisbaden, 1996—. Co-author, editor: Mathematical Manual, 1972, 74; co-author: Encyclopedia for Accounting and Statistics, 1974; editor: Mathematik und Wirtschaft, 1977, 8th edit., 8 vols., 1977; editor World Stats. in Brief, 4th edit., 1979. Mem. Statis. OFfice, Berlin, 1965-89; cons. Bd. Cultural Performance, Berlin, 1970-89; mem. Intergovtl. Commn., Berlin, 1965-89; adviser Commn. Univ. Degrees, Berlin, 1980-89. Recipient Vaterlandvecher Kerchienstorden, 1978. Mem. N.Y. Acad. Scis., Forschungs-Inst. Avocations: photography, travel, statistics, history, psychology. Home: Lichtenberger Str 27, 10179 Berlin Germany

OTTO, HARRY CLAUDE, manufacturing executive; b. Chgo., Feb. 7, 1957; s. Edward and Carol (Greengard) Urbanski; m. Linda Jean Schneller, Sept. 13, 1980. Diagnostic ctr. mgr. Panafax Corp., Chgo., 1979-83; spl. project mgr. Panafax Corp., Melville, N.Y., 1983-86; product mgr. Brother Internat. Corp., Piscataway, N.J., 1986—; dir. mktg. Toshiba Am. Info. Systems, Irvine, Calif., 1990-92; exec. v.p. Danka Omnifax, L.A., 1992—; gen. mgr. Samsung Electronics Am., 1997—. Contbr. articles to profl. jours. Mem. Facsimile Systems Equipment Engring., Electronic Industries Assn., Telecommunications Industry Assn., Am. Mgmt. Assn. Republican. Methodist. Avocations: skiing, weightlifting, bridge. Office: Samsung Electronics Am 18600 S Broadwick St Rncho Domingz CA 90220-6434

OTTO, JOHAN LODEWIKUS, financial executive; b. Johannesburg, South Africa, Jan. 29, 1942; s. Johannes Lodewikus and Susanna Magdalena Elzabeth (Pretorius) L.; m. Drinai Patricia Esterhuyse Otto, June 14, 1980; children: Teresa, Tanja, Leslie, Wikus. Student, Chartered Inst. Secs. and Adminstrs., South Africa, 1972, Inst. Credit Mgmt., South Africa, 1974. Trainee merchant banker Cen. Merchant Bank, South Africa, 1968-73; sr. gen. mgr. Capital Market Mgmt. Volkskas Merchant Bank/ABSA, South Africa, 1973-83; mng. dir. CM Interbank, South Africa, 1987-94; exec. and mng. dir. Sechold Group, South Africa, 1991-93; chmn. MCI Ltd., South Africa, 1993, Harpers Motoring Group, South Africa, 1995—. Bd. dirs. Beafort Inst., 1998. Recipient Comrades Marathon bronze medal Comrades Com., 1979, 80, 2 Oceans Marathon, Two Oceans Com., 1979, 80. Mem. CIS, CICM. Avocations: reading, collecting art, science, sports, music. Home: A11 World's View, Northcliff Ridge, 2095 Johannesburg South Africa Office: Cascade House 1st Fl, Constantia Office Park South Africa

OTTO, MICHAEL, sales executive; b. Kulm/Bromberg, Germany, Apr. 12, 1943; m. Christi von Klier. Mem. exec. bd. Otto Versand, Hamburg, Germany, 1971-81, chmn. bd., pres., 1981—, chmn. bd.; chmn. bd. dirs. Otto AG fur Beteiligungen, Hamburg, Spiegel Inc., Chgo.; chmn. supervisory bd. Schwab AG, Hanau; mem. adminstrv. bd. Deutsche Einkaufs-Ctr.-Gesellschaften, Hamburg, 3 Suisse Internat. S.A., Croix, France; mem. supervisory bds. Axel Springer Verlag AG, Berlin, Deutsche Bank AG, Frankfurt am Main, Gerling-Konzern Versicherungs-Beteiligungs-AG, Cologne; chmn. adv. bds. Versandhaus Heinrich Heine, Karlsruhe, Alba Moda Europa, Bad Salzuflen. V.p. Hamburg Chamber of Trade; mem. presidium Aubenhandelsvereinigung des Deutschen Einzelhandels e.V., Cologne; chmn. Messe Ptnr. des Fortschritts, Berlin; chmn. bd. govs. Gesellschaft fur Politik und Wirtschaft e.V., Hamburg; bd. govs. Otto Found., Hamburg, Found. Promotion of Hamburg Art Collections, Hamburg; founder, chmn. Freundeskreis der Hochschule fur Bildende Kunste, Cultural Circle Fedn. German Industry, Cologne. Recipient Fed. Cross of Merit First Class, Govt. of Germany, 1989. Avocations: tennis, volleyball, modern arts. Office: Otto Versand, Wandsbeker Str 3-7, Hamburg 22172, Germany also: Via Triste #24, 20068 San Bovio Milan Italy*

OTTO BUCZKOWSKA, EWA, pediatrician, researcher; b. D—browa Górnicza, Silesia, Poland, July 29, 1935; d. Stefan and Janina (Bem) Otto; m. Mieczysław Buczkowski, Mar. 19, 1960. MD, Med. Acad., Katowice, Poland, 1963, specialist in pediatrics, 1967, Habilitation, 1974; specialist in diabetes, Ctr. Med. Postgrad. Edn., Warsaw, Poland, 1994. Asst. prof. dept. anatomy Med. Acad., Zabrze, Poland, 1958-64; dir. Regional Diabetes Ctr. for Children and Adolescents, Gliwice, Poland, 1964-74; cons. Regional Diabetes Ctr. for Children and Adolscents, Gliwice, Poland, 1974-94; head dept. pediat. City Hosp., Gliwice, 1974-94; assoc. prof., cons. diabetologist Outpatient Clinic Diabetology for Children and Adolescents, Gliwice, 1995—. Author: Compendium of Diabetes, 1995, Diabetes in Young People, 1999; editor: Diabetes in the Young, 1998; contbr. articles to med. jours., including Z. Kinderheilkunde, Mschr. Kinderheilkunde, Archives Exptl. Immunology and Therapy. Mem. Internat. Soc. for Pediatric and Adolescent Diabetes, European Assn. for Study Diabetes, Polish Diabetes Assn. (v.p. pediatric divsn., dir. supervisory com. of exec. coun.). E-mail: em.buczkowski@pro.onet.pl. Home: Jasnogórska 16 m 21, PL-44100 Gliwice Silesia, Poland

OTTOLENGHI, MARINELLA, architectural educator; b. Turin, Italy, Mar. 15, 1926; d. Enrico and Silvia (Mortara) O. DArch, U. Sapienza, Rome, 1950; MArch, U. Pa., 1951. Prof.-in-charge U. Sapienza, Rome, 1969-80, prof., planning chmn., 1981—; guest prof. N.H. Bouwkunst En Stedebow, Antwerp, Belgium, 1975; vis. prof. U. S.C., Clemson, 1978; dir. planning dept. U. Roma Tre, 1992. Author: Conoscere L'Urbanistica, 1976, Viaggio South Carolina: trarinnovo urbano e Territorio, 1979, Roma: Three Univerisities in Search of Actors, 1998; contbr. articles in field. Mem. Inst. Nat. Urbanistica, Internat. Soc. City and Regional Planners, Internat. Coun. Monuments and Sites, Internat. Assn. for Environ. Design. Home: Via dei Villini 26, 00161 Rome Italy

OTTONE, JORGE ANTONIO, marketing management executive, consultant; b. Genova, Ikliz, Apr. 30, 1931; arrived in Argentina, 1935; s. Estoban Jose Lando Ottone and Lijdio Kenatz Risso Narice. Degree, U. Buenos Aires, PhD in Economy. Sr. auditor Price Waterhouse, Peat & Co., 1956-61; cons. Estudio del Doctor Luis S. Mey, Buenos Aires, 1961-63; adminstr. Siam Di Tella S.A., Buenos Aires, 1963-65; finance dir. Planeamiento Comercial en Bodegas y Vinedos Narice S.A., Buenos Aires, 1965-67; sr. auditor Delcitte, Plender, Haskins & Sells, Buenos Aires, 1968-70; adminstrv. dir. Empresa Soc. Cementos Armados Centrifugados, Buenos Aires, 1970-73; financial mgr. OMS, Buenos Aires, 1975-80; cons. Jorge Hones PA, Buenos Aires, 1980—; ptnr. OHome o Assn., Buenos Aires, 1980—. Mem. Conseja Profl. Economists. Roman Cath. Avocations: music, film, tennis, swimming, literature. Home: Av Los Heros 2928-7, 1920 Buenos Aires Argentina Office: Juncal 1695, 3 Piso C, 1062 Buenos Aires Argentina

OTTONELLO, CARLO MAURIZIO, radiologist; b. Savona, Liguria, Italy, July 7, 1965; s. Giacomo and Rosa (Arecco) O. MD cum laude, Genova (Italy) U., 1991, B in Radiology/Imaging Scis. cum laude, 1996. Resident rschr. radiology dept. Genova U., 1992-97; rschr. Italian Army Gen. Hosp., Rome, 1996—; Imaging Scis. chair Italian Army Sch. for Health Svc. Warrant Officers, Rome, 1998—; emergency diagnostic imaging chair Radiology Sch. Genova U., 2000—. Contbr. articles to profl. jours. Capt. M.C., Italian Army, 1996. Mem. Italian Assn. Radiology, Italian Mil. Med. Assn., European Congress of Radiology, European Soc. Cardiovascular Imaging. Office: Italian Army Gen Hosp, Piazza Celimontana 50, 00184 Rome Italy

OTTORO, ZELEKE WOLDE TENSSAY, microbiology educator; b. Wacca, Keffa, Ethiopia, Jan. 1, 1957; s. Wolde Tenssay Ottoro Erybaye and Abaware Ayelech; m. Zenash Kebede; children: Bemnet Zeleke, Beza Zeleke. BSc, Addis Ababa U., Ethiopia, 1981, MSc, 1990. Cert. microbiologist. Secondary sch. biology tchr. Gofa, Ethiopia, 1981-85; dir. Pub. Health Lab., Regional Health Dept., Jimma, Ethiopia, 1985-86; lectr. microbiology Jimma Inst. Health Scis., Ethiopia, 1991—, chmn. dept. microbiology, 1995—; asst. prof. Jimma U. Contbr. articles, papers to profl. jours. Mem. Biol. Soc. Addis Ababa, Tchr. Assn. Jimma. Avocation: table tennis. Home: PO Box 596, Jimma Ethiopia Office: Jimma Inst Health Scis, Jimma 378, Ethiopia

OTUBUSIN, SAMUEL OLU, aquaculturist educator, consultant; b. Ijebu-Ode, Ogun, Nigeria, May 4, 1948; s. Issac Otuyelu and Lydia Oladunni (Ogunyoye) O.; m. Ajibola Olu Smith, Dec. 10, 1977; children: Shalom, Tomi. BSc in Zoology with honors, U. Ife, Ile-Ife, Nigeria, 1975; MSF in Aquaculture, U. The Philippines, Iloilo, 1981; PhD in Fisheries, Ahmadu Bello U., Zaria, Nigeria, 1992. Cert. aquaculture, fisheries mgmt. Statis. asst. Fed. Office Stats., Lagos, Nigeria, 1967-69; accts. clk. Mobil Oil Nigeria Ltd., Lagos, 1969-71; vacation trainee Ibru Seafoods Ltd., Lagos, Nigeria, 1974; rsch. officer Kainji Lake Rsch. Inst., New Bussa, Nigeria, 1976-91; asst. chief rsch. officer Nat. Inst. for Freshwater Fisheries Reserve, New Bussa, Nigeria, 1992-94; sr. lectr. U. Agr., Abeokuta, Nigeria, 1994—; cons., dir. food roads & rural infrastructure, Lagos, Nigeria, 1987-90; prog. head Aquaculture-NIFFR, New Bussa, Nigeria, 1988-94; dept. head Aquaculture and Fisheries Mgmt. UNAAB, Abeokuta, Nigeria, 1996—; consulting dir. Otiacs Nigeria Ltd., Lagos, 1993—. Author, co-editor: Fish Cage Culture Technology, 1989; contbr. articles to profl. jour. Leader Nigerian cmty., Panay, The Philippines, 1981-82; chmn. Senate Staff Assn. NIFFR, New Bussa, Nigeria, 1987-90; membership dir. Full Gospel Bus. Fellowship Internat., Abeokuta Ctrl., Nigeria, 1996-97. Recipient fed. govt. inservice award Kainji Lake Rsch. Inst., U. Philippines, 1979-81; Lagos State Govt. scholar Univ. Ife, 1971-75; travel fellow Pfizer Nigeria Ltd., Lagos, 1987. Mem. Fisheries Soc. Nigeria, Nigerian Assn. Aquatic Scis., Ecol. Soc. Nigeria. Mem. Deeper Christian Life Ministry. Avocations: photography, cycling, traveling, reading, aquariums. Office: Univ Agr Box 2033 Sapon, Dept Aquaculture Fisheries, Abeokuta Ogun, Nigeria

OTUNGA, MAURICE MICHAEL CARDINAL, archbishop; b. Chebukwa, Kenya, Jan. 1923; Ordained priest Roman Catholic Ch., 1950; Formerly tchr. Kisumu Maj. Sem.; attaché apostolic del. Mombasa, 1953-56; titular bishop of Tacape; also aux. Kisumu, 1957; bishop of Kisii, 1961, titular archbishop of Bomarzo, 1969, coadjutor of Nairobi, 1969-71; archbishop of Baitobi Nairobi, 1971-98; archbishop emeritus of Nairobi, 1998—; elevated to Sacred Coll. of Cardinals, 1973; titular ch. St. Gregory Barbarigo; mil. vicar of Kenya, 1981; primate of Kenya, 1983—; dir. Castrense for Kenya. Mem. Congregation of Sacraments and Divine Worship, Congregation of Religious and Secular Insts., Commn. Revision Code of Canon Law. Address: Archbishop's House, PO Box 14231, Nairobi Kenya*

OU, JONATHAN TSIEN-HSIONG, microbiology educator; b. Taiwan, July 31, 1934; U.S. citizen; s. Chin-Shi and Chhyu-Kyok (Chen) O.; m. Chhu-Swei Chang, Mar. 17, 1962; children: Steven S., June S. BS, Nat. Taiwan U., Taipei, 1957; PhD, U. Pa., 1967. Rsch. assoc. U. Pa., Phila., 1967-68; rsch. assoc. Inst. for Cancer Rsch., Phila., 1968-74, asst. mem., 1974-78, assoc. mem., 1978-82; sr. microbiologist Walter Reed Army Inst. Rsch., Washington, 1984-89; mem. genetic faculty U. Pa., Phila., 1978-84; prof., vice chancellor for student affairs Chang Gung U. Med. Coll., Kweishan, Taoyuan, Taiwan, 1989-92. Editor: (book) Pili, 1978; contbr. articles to profl. jours. Grantee NSF, 1975-78, Nat. Sci. Coun., Taipei, 1989—, Nat. Health Rsch. Inst., Taipei, 1996—; Japan Soc. for Promotion of Sci. fellow, 1981, NRC fellow, 1984. Mem. Am. Soc. for Microbiology, Genetic Soc. Am. Democrat. Avocations: tennis, swimming, bridge, mahjong, chess. Office: Chang Gung U Coll Medicine, 259 Wenhwa 1 Rd, Kweishan Taoyuan 33332, Taiwan

OU, SHAN-HWEI, dean, engineering educator. BS, Nat. Cheng Kung U., Tainan, Taiwan, 1968, MS, 1971, PhD, 1977. Asst. rschr. dept. hydraulics and ocean engring. Nat. Cheng Kung U., Tainan City, Taiwan, 1974-75, lectr. dept. hydraulics and ocean engring., 1975-78, assoc. prof. dept. hydraulics and ocean engring., 1978-82, prof. dept. hydraulics and ocean engring., 1982—, dean coll. engring.; chmn. dept. hydraulics and ocean engring. Nat. Cheng Kung U., Tainan, 1986-92; vis. rschr. U. Hawaii, U. Del., 1978-79. Fax: 886-6-2741463. Office: Nat Cheng Kung U, 1 Ta-Hsueh Rd, Tainan Taiwan

OUANE, M. MOCTAR, diplomat. Perm. rep. of Mali to UN N.Y.C., 1995—. Office: Perm Mission of Mali to UN 111 E 69th St New York NY 10021-5004*

OUCHI, ISUKE, engineering educator; b. Kyoto, Kyoto, Japan, Nov. 24, 1931; m. Masako Yamamoto; 2 children. BS, Kyoto U., 1954, MS, 1956, DEng, 1983. Mgr. 2d Films Lab., dept. plastics rsch. Teijin Ltd., Sagamihara, Japan, 1970-80; mgr. Advanced Film Products Lab. dept. ctrl. rsch. Teijin Ltd., Hino, Japan, 1981-85; asst. to gen. mgr. rsch. and prodn. divsn. Teijin Ltd., Tokyo, 1980-81, sr. staff mem. rsch. planning dept., 1985-89; prof. Tottori (Japan) U., 1989-97, Tokushima Bunri U., Shido, Japan, 1997—. Contbr. papers to sci. jours. including Japanese Jour. Applied Physics, Polymers for Advanced Tech., others. Mem. Japanese Phys. Soc. (life), Polymer Soc. Japan, Applied Physics Soc. Japan. Avocation: tennis. Office: Faculty Engring, Tokushima Bunri U, Kagawa Shido 769-2193, Japan

OUCHI, SEIJI, plant pathology educator; b. Hiroshima, Japan, Jan. 9, 1933; s. Fumio and Koen (Fujiwara) O.; m. Naoko Kitamura, Mar. 17, 1962; children: Takashi, Yuko, Junko. BSc, Kagawa (Japan) U., 1955; MSc, Kyoto (Japan) U., 1957, PhD, 1971; postgrad., So. Ill. U., 1961-63. Rsch. asst. microbiology So. Ill. U., Carbondale, 1961-63; asst. prof. Kyoto U., 1963-70; assoc. prof. Okayama (Japan) U., 1970-85; prof. Kinki U., Nara, Japan, 1985—, chmn. agronomy dept., 1994-96, dir. grad. program, 1996—, dir. Inst. for Comprehensive Agrl. Scis., 1991—; asst. dean student affairs Kinki U., Osaka, 1991-94. Author: Annual Review of Phytopathology, 1983; author, editor: Plant Infection, 1982, (in Japanese) Physiological Plant Pathology, 1990, Molecular Strategies of Pathogens and Host Plants, 1991. Fellow Phytopathol. Soc. Japan (pres. 1996-97), Am. Phytopathol. Soc.; mem. Am. Soc. Microbiology. Achievements include research in molecular strategies of pathogens to induce accessibility in host plant cells by means of production of suppressor moleculas. Home: 6-7-21 Suzaku, Nara Nara-ken 631-0806, Japan Office: Kinki U Faculty Agr, 3327-204 Naka-machi, Nara Nara-ken 631-8505, Japan

OUCHTERLONY, ÖRJAN THOMAS, physician, educator; b. Stockholm, Jan. 14, 1914; s. Gunnar Fabian and Lisa Ludovica (Pripp) O.; m. Marianne Selma Schröder, 1942 (dec. 1985); children: Finn, John, Mats, Frank, Björn, Tim. Med. Lic., Karolinska Inst., Stockholm, 1942; MD, Karolinska Inst., 1949; MD (hon.), Helsingfors U., Finland, 1990. Vol. asst. State Bacteriology Lab., Stockholm, 1935-38, asst., 1938-49, head diagnostic dept., 1949-52; prof. med. bacteriology U. Gothenburg, Sweden, 1952-80; prof. emeritus U. Gothenburg, 1980—; vis. scientist Pasteur Inst., Paris, Algiers, Tunis, 1950, 52, 53, WHO, India, Bangladesh, 1953, 54, Harvard Med. Sch., Boston, 1954-55, U. Mont., 1971-72. Chmn. Town Planning, Kunjah, Sweden, 1970-80. Recipient Paul Ehrlich prize BRD Germany, 1961, Pasteur Gold medal Swedish Assn. Physicians, 1970, Fernström prize Lund (Sweden) U. Mem. Royal Acad. Scis. Lutheran. Avocations: hiking, gardening. Home: Fontinvägen 24, 44231 Vumgelu Sweden Office: Inst Med Microbiology, Guldhedsgatan 10, 41346 Göteborg Sweden

OUDENDIJK, ALEX P., communications executive; b. Jakarta, Indonesia, May 22, 1953; s. Maria-Louisa Oudendijk; m. Anne-Marie Beckers; children: Lotte, Jesse, Joris, Sander, Joshua. MSc, U. Tech., Delft, The Netherlands, 1980. Bus. devel. dir. Spar Comstream, Can., 1992-95; sales and mktg. dir. Hughes Olivetti Telecom, Milton Keynes, U.K., 1995-96; v.p., mng. dir. Hot Telecomms., Griesheim, Germany, 1996—. Mem. Am. C. of C. Avocations: walking, reading, writing. Office: Hot Telecomms GmbH, Ottostr 9, D-64347 Griesheim Germany

OUEDRAOGO, BOUKARY, banker. Gov. Ctrl. Bank Burkina Faso. Office: Ministry of Economy and Finance, 01 BP 6444, Ougadougou 01, Burkina Faso*

OUÉDRAOGO, ELIE JUSTIN, government official; b. Boromo, Burkina Faso, Aug. 8, 1952; married; children. PhD in Econs. Attaché Soc. for Rsch. and Exploitation of Mines of Burkina, 1983-88, mng. dir., 1988-90, dir. gen., 1990-92, provisional adminstr., 1992-95; minister of energy and mines Govt. Burkina Faso, 1995—. Mem. Orgn. for Popular Democracy/Labor Movement. Office: Ministry of Energy & Mines, 01 BP 3922, Ouagadougou Burkina Faso*

OUEDRAOGO, IDRISSA, film director; b. Burkina Faso, 1954. Studied at film sch., Burkina Faso. Director: Yam Daabo, 1987, Yaaba, 1989, Tilaï, 1990 (Cannes Grand prize 1990, Grand Prize Pan-African Film Festival 1991), A Karim Na Sala, 1991, Samba Traore, 1992, The Three Friends, 1993, Lumiè et Compagnie, 1995, Kini and Adams, 1997; co-dir. Gorki, 1994, The Heart's Cry, 1994, Afrique mon Afrique, 1994; prodr., writer Guimba, A Tyrant and His Era, Kini and Adams, 1997. Office: FEPACI, 01 BP 2524, Ouagadougou 01, Burkina Faso*

OUEDRAOGO, KADRE DESIRE, foreign government official; b. Sanmatenga, 1953; married; 4 children. BAC, 1972; HEC, Sch. Commerce, France, 1977; M in Econ. Scis., Sorbonne U., Paris. Past tchr. U. Quagadougou; mem. staff divsn. fin. Solidarity Funds and Cmty. Devel., 1980; fin. counselor Econ. Cmty. W. African States, 1983; vice gov. Ctrl. Bank W. African States, 1993; econ. affairs counselor Ministry Commerce and Indsl. Devel., 1977-80; prime min. Burkina Fasco Govt. of Burkina Faso, Quagodougou, 1996—; exec. sec. Econ. Cmty. W. African States, 1983. Office: Office of the Prime Minister, BP 7027, Ougadougou Burkina Faso*

OUEIJAN, NAJI BOULOS, English literature educator, researcher; b. Beirut, Lebanon, Nov. 1, 1951; s. Boulos Nicolas and Alice Semaan (Deeb) O.; m. Nawal Rizkallah Askar, Nov. 18, 1978; children: Harvey, Roy, Sami-Joe. BA, Lebanese U., Beirut, 1977, MA, 1979; PhD, Baylor U., 1985. Cert. tchr. Instr. English St. Joseph U., Beirut, 1977-80; Writing Ctr. aide Baylor U., Waco, Tex., 1983-85; asst. prof. English Lebanese U., 1985-89; prof. English Notre Dame U., Beirut, 1990—; chmn. dept. English Lebanese U., 1989-92; ednl. cons. Rosarey Insts. Edn., Beirut, 1985-90. Author: The Progress of an Image: The East in English Literature, 1996; A Compendium of Eastern Elements in Byron's Oriental Tales, 1999, The Progress of an Image: The East in English Literature, 1995; contbr. articles and revs. to profl. jours. Lebanese U. Faculty Devel. scholarship, 1979-85; McCall grantee, Waco, 1982-85; Notre Dame U. rsch. fellow, 1992; Hellenic Byron Soc. fellow, Athens, 1994. Mem. MLA, Internat. Byron Soc. (bd. dirs. 1995—), Lebanese Byron Soc. (pres. 1993—), Am. Conf. on Romanticism, Baylor Alumni, Lions Clubs Internat. (dist. pres. 1994-95, pres. 1991). Greek Orthodox. Avocations: playing guitar, painting, reading, travel, jogging and walking. Home: Ndu St, Zook Mosbeh Lebanon Office: Notre Dame U, PO Box 72 Zouk Mikael, Zouk Mosbeh Lebanon

OUELLET, ANDRÉ, business executive; b. St. Pascal, Que., Can., Apr. 6, 1939; s. Albert and Rita (Turgeon) O.; m. Edith Pagé, July 17, 1965; children: Sonia, Jean, Olga, Pierre. BA, U. Ottawa, Ont., Can., 1960, D (hon.), 1995; LLL, U. Sherbrooke, Can., 1963. Mem. Can. Parliament, Ottawa, 1967-93, min. consumer and corp. affairs, 1974-76, 80-83, min. state urban affairs, 1976-78, min. public works, 1978-79, min. labor, 1983-84; postmaster gen. Can., Ottawa, 1972-74, 80-81; min. fgn. affairs Can. Parliament, Ottawa, 1993-96; chmn. bd. Can. Post Corp., Ottawa, 1996-99; pres., CEO Can. Post Corp., 1999—. Office: Canada Post Corp, 2701 Riverside Dr Ste N1250, Ottawa, ON Canada K1A 0B1

OUGH, RICHARD NORMAN, lawyer, physician; b. Loscoe, Derbyshire, Eng., Jan. 25, 1946; arrived in Can., 1973; s. Conrad Jocelyn and Alice Louisa Ough; m. Shelley Jean Henshaw (div. 1985); children: Geoffrey, Eliza; m. Mary Jane Alison Payne, 1991; children: Thomas, James. MB, BS, London U., 1973; MA in Law, City U. London, 1986; MSc in Mgmt., London Bus. Sch., 1995. Lic. physician, Can.; barrister, 1985; chartered arbitrator, 1999. Intern, house physician King Edward Meml. Hosp. & Whittington Hosp., London, 1972-73; resident in ob-gyn. Vancouver, B.C., Can., 1973-74; pvt. practice in medicine Stratford, Ont., Can., 1977-84; pvt. practice in law London, 1986—. Sloan fellow, London Bus. Sch., 1995; recipient Cert. of Merit in psychiatry St. Mary's Hosp., 1970. Fellow Royal Soc. Medicine, Chartered Inst. Arbitrators; mem. AMA, Brit. Med. Assn. Anglican. Avocations: family life, music, walking. Office: Lamb Chambers Temple, London EC4Y 7AS, England

OULD DEDDACH, MAHFOUDH, diplomat. Mauritania rep. UN, N.Y.C. Office: Ste 200 211 E 43d St New York NY 10017

OULTON, RICHARD JAMES, lawyer, entrepreneur; b. Peekskill, N.Y., Jan. 8, 1945; s. John and Martha (Smith) Outhouse; m. Ava Liu, July 4, 1986; children: John Lawrence, Alexis Xaioying Oulton, Jamie Richard. BA, SUNY, Buffalo, 1970, JD, 1973; MBA, CUNY, N.Y.C., 1976. Bar: N.Y. 1974, Va. 1989, D.C. 1990; U.S. Ct. Appeals (4th cir.) 1989. Asst. adminstr., atty. Roosevelt Hosp., N.Y.C., 1973-77, N.Y. Med. Coll., N.Y.C., 1977-78; 2d v.p. Va. Ins. Reciprocal, Richmond, 1978-87, v.p., 1987-88; pres. Oulton Assocs. Inc., Glen Allen, Va., 1988—, Affiliated Attys., Inc., Richmond, 1989—, Attys. Ins. Agy., Inc., Richmond, 1989—, Affiliated Accts., Inc., Richmond, 2000—; mem. Adv. Bd. on Edn. and Pubs., 1984-88, Adv. Bd. Joint Commn. on Accreditation of Hosps., Chgo.; asst. prof. dept. health care adminstrn. Va. Commonwealth U., Richmond, 1982-87, assoc. prof., 1987—; liaison, legis. officer Order of Purple Heart VA, 1991-92; speaker numerous seminars; founding dir. 1st Battalion, 9th Marines Network Inc., The Walking Dead, 1997—. Editor: quality assurance risk mgmt. newsletter; mem. editorial adv. com. Quality Rev. Bull., 1984-89; contbr. articles to profl. jours. With USN/USMC, 1964-67, Vietnam. Decorated Purple Heart, USMC Combat Action Ribbon, Vietnam Cross of Gallantry. Mem. ABA, Va. Bar Assn., Am. Coll. Health Care Execs., Am. Acad. Hosp. Attys., Nat. Health Lawyers Assn., Outhouse Family Hist. Soc., Inc. Home: 11900 Alor Ct Glen Allen VA 23059-7068 Office: Affiliated Attys Inc 8515 Mayland Dr Richmond VA 23294-4701

OURA, TOSHIAKI, pediatrician, health facility administrator; b. Kohno Village, Fukui, Japan, Mar. 8, 1921; s. Teiichi and Takano K. Oura; m. Hiroko Kashima; children: Toshihiro, Hiroaki. MD, Osaka (Japan) City Med. Coll., 1949, PhD, 1959. Intern Osaka City Transp. bur. Hosp., 1949; resident Luth. Med. Ctr., N.Y.C., 1957-59; lectr. pediatrician Osaka City U., 1961-63; pediatrician-in-chief Children's Med. Ctr. Osaka City, 1965-79, dir., 1979-81; dir. Osaka City Rehab. Tng. Ctr., 1984-99; chief dir. Inclusion, Osaka City, 1995-99. Author, co-editor: Phenylketonuria, 1971, Handbook of Inborn Errors of Metabolism and Immune Diseases, 1982; editor: Inborn Errors of Metabolism in Children, 1980. Recipient Med. award Mayor of Osaka, 1954, 66, 68, award for Disting. Achievement in Svcs., Internat. Assn. for Sci. Study of Mental Retardation, 1991. Home: Kasugaoka 2-136-3, A-101, Itami City 664-0893, Japan

OUSSANI, JAMES JOHN, stapling company executive; b. Bklyn., Jan. 3, 1920; s. John Thomas and Clara (Tager) O.; m. Lorraine G. Tutundgy, Apr. 25, 1954; children: James J., Gregory P., Rita C. B.M.E., Pratt Inst., 1938-42; J.D. (hon.), Coll. Boca Raton, Lynn U.; LLD. Dir. research, mfg. Supertronic Co., N.Y.C., 1943-46; sr. partner Perl-Oussani Machine Mfg. Co., N.Y.C., 1946-49; founder The Staplex Co., Bklyn., 1949, pres., 1949—; exec. dir. Lourdes Realty Corp.; dir. Junios Corp.; producer air sampling equipment for radioactive fallout AEC, 1951—. Mem. Bur. Research Air Pollution Control, Pres.'s Council on Youth Opportunity, Cardinal's Com. for Edn.; trustee Ch. of Virgin Mary; bd. dirs. St. Joan Arc Found., Boca Raton; founding mem. Lumen Christi-Palm Beach Diocese; founder, bd. dirs. Oussani Found.; founder James J. & Lorraine G. Oussani Scholarship Fund, Coll. Boca Raton; mem. cardinal's com. of laity, bishop's com. of laity; mem. Lumen Christi Found.; bd. overseers Lynn U., Boca Raton. Recipient Blue Ribbon Mining award, Sch. Mgmt. award, Aerospace Pride Achievement award; installed Knight of Jerusalem. Mem. Adminstrv. Mgmt. Soc., Office Adminstrn. Assn., Nat. Stationery and Office Equipment AssOffice Equipment Assn., Office Execs. Assn., Nat. Office Machine Mfg. Assn., Nat. Office Machine Dealers Assn., Nat. Office Products Assn., Bus. Equipment Mfrs. Assn., Our Lady Perpetual Help Holy Name Soc., Knights of Holy Sepulchre, Knights of St. Gregory, Knights of Malta, Rotary, Salaam Club, Mahopac Golf Club (Lake Mahopac, N.Y.), Internat. Club of Boca Raton, Boca Raton Hotel and Resort Club. Inventor automatic electric stapling machine. Patentee in field. Office: 777 5th Ave Brooklyn NY 11232-1626

OUSSET, JEAN CLAUDE, physics educator, researcher; b. Saint Lary, Ariege, France, Jan. 24, 1949; s. Clement and Helene (Tougne) O.; m. Catherine Estaque, Sept. 30, 1995; 1 child, Adrian. Master, P. Sabatier U., Toulouse, France, 1972, PhD, 1975, DSc, 1980. Cert. professor, researcher. Rschr. CNRS, Toulouse, 1975-85, sci. responsible High Magnetic Field Facility, 1993—; rschr. CNRS-St. Gobain, Nancy, France, 1986-90; prof. Nat. Edn., Toulouse, 1991—; sci. sec. Nat. Com. Sci. Rsch. (Solid State Physics), 1982-86. Contbr. articles to profl. jours. including Physics Rev. B, Jour. Magnetism and Magnetic Materials, others; contbr. procs. to internat. confs. Avocations: rugby, hunting, ramble, jogging, gardening. Home: 27 rue de l'Autan, 31320 Pechabou France Office: CEMES-CNRS, 29 rue Jeanne Marvig BP 4347, 31055 Toulouse Cedex 4, France

OUT, HENK JAN, clinical scientist; b. Velsen, The Netherlands, Jan. 5, 1961; s. Hartman and Neeltje (Piet) O.; m. Jetty Van Der Graaf; children: Mischa, David. MD, Free U., Amsterdam, The Netherlands, 1987; PhD, State U., Utrecht, The Netherlands, 1991. Med. advisor Organon, Oss, The Netherlands, 1992-99; med. dir. Organon Labs., Cambridge, Eng., 1999—. Editor: Recombinant Fsh, 1996; coord. Human Reprodn. Excerpts, 1996. Home: Middle House, Carmel St, Great Chesterford Essex, England Office: Organon Labs, Sci Park, Cambridge England

OUT, THEO ANTHONIUS, immunologist; b. Edam, The Netherlands, Oct. 1, 1946; s. T.A. and A.G. (Hoogland) O.; m. G.M. Boon, Dec. 19, 1969; children: Gaia, Welmoed. B in Chemistry, U. Amsterdam, 1967, MS in biochemistry, 1971, PhD of Biochemistry, 1977. Rsch. fellow U. Amsterdam, 1971-76; rsch. fellow CLB Sanguin Blood Supply Found., Amsterdam, 1976-84, dept. head, 1984—; dept. head Acad. Med. Ctr., Amsterdam, 1984—. Mem. editl. bd. Jour. Immunol. Methods. Mem. European Respiratory Soc., Dutch Soc. Immunology, Brit. Soc. Immunology. Office: Acad Med Ctr, B1-236 Meibergdreef 9, 1105 AZ Amsterdam The Netherlands

OUTMAN, WILLIAM DELL, II, lawyer; b. St. Petersburg, Fla., Nov. 10, 1940; s. Boyd Johnson and Marion Lucetta (Banks) O.; m. Sally Rockwell June 29, 1963 (dec. Sept. 1998); children: William Dell III, Stephanie O. Kiker, Sarah O. Brophy. BS in Bus. Adminstrn., Wash. & Lee U., 1962; JD, Georgetown U., 1965, LLM in Taxation, 1968. Bar: D.C. 1966, N.Y. 1999. Assoc. atty. Baker & McKEnzie, Wash., 1965-70, ptnr., 1970-97; mng. ptnr. Baker & McKEnzie, N.Y.C., 1997-2000; ptnr. Baker & McKEnzie, Washington, 2000—. Staff sgt., U.S. Army, 1965-71. Mem. Customs and Internat. Trade Bar Assn. (v.p., bd. dirs. 1992—), Ct. Internat. Trade Adv. Com. (current chmn. 1990—), Congl. Country Club, Met. Club, Omicron Delta Kappa. Office: Baker & McKenzie 815 Connecticut Ave NW Ste 900 Washington DC 20006-4004

OUTRATA, EDVARD, public information administrator, statistician; b. Brno, Czech Republic, Aug. 9, 1936; s. Edvard and Emma (Cepková) O.; m. Jana Maria Veselá, Sept. 3, 1958. MSc, Prague Sch. of Econs., 1959. Chief informatics Statistics Can., Ottawa, 1972-73, dir. gen. survey systems, 1973-74, dir. systems devel., 1974-82, dir. informatics svcs., 1982-84, dir. gen. informatics, 1984-93; pres. Czech Statistical Office, Prague, Czech Republic, 1993-99, Can.-Czech Rep. C. of C., 1999—. Jr. lt. Czech Army, 1959-61. Mem. Internat. Statis. Inst. Home: U Písecké brány 18, 16000 Prague 6, Czech Republic Office: Can.-Czech Rep C of C, Celetná 19, 116 22 Prague 1, Czech Republic

OUTTEN, KRISTINA MARIE, secondary education educator; b. Ogden, Utah, Dec. 6, 1973; d. Burrett William and June J. Clay; m. Todd Edgar Outten, Nov. 16, 1996. BA in English Edn., U. Ariz., 1996, MA in Ednl. Psychology, 2000. Lead trainer Macayo's Mexican Food, Tucson, 1991-95; bar mgr. Bushwacker, Tucson, 1995-96; student tchr. Tucson H.S. Tucson Unified Sch. Dist., 1996, tchr. Alice Vail Mid. Sch., 1996—; bartender Applebee's Thomas & King, Tucson, 1996—; com. mem. 504 rev. team, awards and site-based decision making team Vail Mid. Sch., 1998—. Author: And So It Begins..., 1999; contbr. poetry to Nat. Libr. of Poetry-Libr. of Congress, A View from Afar, The Peace We Knew, A Muse to Follow, Blossom in the Dawning, The Colors of Thought, Serenity at Daybreak; author poems (Editor's Choice awards 1996, 97, 98). Regents scholar U. Ariz., 1991; Vocal Talent scholar Am. Legend, 1991. Mem. Tucson Edn. Assn., Internat. Soc. Poets. Avocation: writing, singing, reading, travel. Home: 6001 E Pima St Apt 61 Tucson AZ 85712-4360

OUZTS, EUGENE THOMAS, minister, secondary education educator; b. Thomasville, Ga., June 7, 1930; s. John Travis and Livie Mae (Strickland) O.; m. Mary Olive Vineyard, May 31, 1956. BA, Harding U., Searcy, AR, 1956, MA, 1957; postgrad., Murray State U., KY, U. Ark., U. Ariz., Ariz. State U., No. Ariz. U. Cert. secondary tchr., Ark., Mo., Ariz.; cert. c.c. tchr., Ariz.; ordained minister Church of Christ, 1956. Min. various chs., Ark., Mo., Tex., 1957-65; tchr. various pub. schs., Ark., Mo., Ariz., 1959-92; min. Ch. of Christ, Clifton and Morenci, Ariz., 1965—; 1st lt. CAP/USAF, 1980, advanced through grades to lt. col., 1989; chaplain CAP/USAF, Ariz., 1982—; asst. wing chaplain CAP/USAF, 1985—; adviser student activities Clifton (Ariz.) Pub. Schs., 1965-92; bd. dirs. Ariz. Ch. of Christ Bible Camp, Tucson, 1966—. Mem. airport adv. bd. Greenlee County, Clifton, Ariz., 1992—. Recipient Meritorious Svc. award, 1994, Exceptional Svc. award, 1997, Civil Air Patrol; named Ariz. Wing Chaplain of Yr, 1984, Thomas C. Casaday Unit Chaplain of Yr., 1985, Ariz. Wing Safety Officer of Yr., 1989, Ariz. Wing Sr. Mem. of Yr., 1994, Southwest Region Sr. Mem. of Yr., 1995, Civil Air Patrol. Mem. Mil. Chaplains Assn., Disabled Am. Vets., Am. Legion, Elks. Democrat. Avocations: flying, building and flying model aircraft, reading. Home and Office: HC 1 Box 557 Duncan AZ 85534-9720

OVADIA, MICHAEL, toxicology and anatomy educator; b. Aden, Yemen, Israel, Oct. 23, 1941; s. Shua and Bracha (Nagar) O.; m. Ruth Liberty, Nov. 4, 1971; children: Yaron, Yael, Yuval, Yehonathan. BSc, Tel-Aviv U., 1967, MSc, 1969, PhD, 1976. Instr. Tel-Aviv U., 1967-77, lectr., 1979-83, sr. lectr., 1983-91, assoc. prof. toxicology and anatomy, 1991-98, prof., 1998—; vis. asst. prof. U. Pa., Phila., 1977-79; vis. scholar Vanderbilt U., Nashville, 1986-87. Contbr. articles to profl. jours., including Biochemistry, Arch. Biochem., Biophys, Biochim, Biophys. Acta, Cell Differentiation, Toxicon, Med. Biology, Am. Zoologist, Anticancer Rsch., Jour. Applied Physiology, Biochemistry Internat., Life Scis., Histochem. Jour., Biol. Bull., Comp. Biochem. Physiol, Jour. Exptl. Zoology, Antiviral Rsch., Procs. NAS USA. Maj. Israel Def. Forces, 1961-64, Res., 1964—. Grantee, Muscular Dystrophy Assn., 1979, Israel Acad. Scis., 1980-82, U.S. Agy. for Internat. Devel., 1991-95. Mem. Internat. Soc. Toxinology, Internat. Soc. Antivinal Rsch., European Soc. Clin. Virology, Israel Biochem. Soc., Israel Soc. Microbiology, N.Y. Acad. Scis. Jewish. Avocation: folk dancing. Home: 25 Hagalil St, 44233 Kfar-Saba Israel Office: Tel-Aviv Univ, Dept Zoology, 69978 Ramat-Aviv Israel

OVCHINNIKOV, BORIS MIKHAILOVICH, physicist, researcher; b. Krasnogvardeisk, Russia, July 5, 1933; s. Mikhail Mikhailovich and Evdokia Georgievna Ovchinnikov; m. m. Raisa Dmitrievna Krasovskaja, Aug. 15, 1957 (div. Sept. 1962); 1 child, Dmitry Borisovich; Valeria Nicolaevna Solyankina, Apr. 8, 1963; 1 child, Yuri Borisovich. Degree in physics and math., Leningrad Inst. Physics & Tech, 1971; D of Physics and Math., Russian Acad. Scis., Moscow, 1988. Engr. Sci. Inst. Rlwy. Connections, Kolomna, 1957-60; jr. sci. rschr. Inst. of Physics and Tech., Acad. Scis. of USSR, Leningrad, 1961-71, Inst. Nuclear Physics, Acad. Scis. of USSR, Leningrad, 1971-73; sr. sci. rschr. Inst. Nuclear Rsch., Acad. Scis. USSR, Moscow, 1973-89; lead sci. rschr. Inst. Nuclear Physics, Acad. Scis. of USSR, Moscow, 1989—; dir. sci. rsch. coop., ISTOK, Troitsk, Russia, 1988-96. Contbr. articles to profl. jours. Recipient medal Govt. of Soviet Union, 1975, 86, Russian Govt., 1989, 97. Avocations: skiing, bicycling. Home: Solnechnaja St 12 Apt 40, 142092 Troitsk Russia Office: Rus Acad Sci Inst Nucl Rsch, 60-October Ann Prospect 7a, 117312 Moscow Russia

OVCHINNIKOV, LEV PAVLOVICH, molecular biology educator; b. Ruza, Moscow, Jan. 21, 1943; s. Pavel Dmitrievich Ovchinnikov and Elena Maximovna Novozhilova; m. Albina Borisovna Zubareva, July 14, 1967; children: Ilya, Natalia. MS, Lomonosov State U., Moscow, 1965; DSc, Lomonosov State U., 1982; PhD in Biochemistry, USSR Acad. Scis., 1970. Jr. rschr. Inst. Protein Rsch., Russian Acad. Scis., Pushchino, 1968-72, sr. rschr., 1972-81, head Lab. Protein Synthesis Regulation, 1981—, dep. dir. Inst., 1988—, prof., head advanced course molecular biology, 1993—; prof. molecular biology Lomonosov State U., Moscow, 1970—; prof., head dept. Lomonosov State U., Pushchino, 1998—. Contbr. over 100 articles on translational regulation of protein biosynthesis and on Y-box binding cold-shock domain containing proteins to sci. jours. Recipient Lenin prize for rsch., 1976; grantee NSF/U.S. Civilian R&D Found., 1996-98, Russian Found. for Basic Rsch./Internat. Assn. for the Promotion of Cooperation with Scientists from the Ind. States of the Former Soviet Union 1996-99, Internat. Assn. for the Promotion of Cooperation with Scientists from the Ind. States of the Former Soviet Union, 1998-00. Mem. Russian Acad. Scis., Russian Biochem. Soc. (presidium 1994—). Achievements include study on messenger ribonucleoprotein particles informosomes; discovery and study of RNA-binding proteins. Avocations: canoeing, fishing. Office: Russian Acad Scis, Inst Protein Rsch, 142290 Pushchino Moscow, Russia

OVCHINNIKOV, VITALY VITAL'EVICH, chemistry educator, researcher; b. Kazan, Russia, Nov. 29, 1947; s. Vitaly Ivanovich Ovchinnikov and Sofia Nikolaevna Mikhailova; m. Nataly Domracheva, July 19, 1971 (div.); children: Kate, Olga; m. Ludmila Omel'chenko Lapteva, Dec. 16, 1988. Candidate of chem. scis., Kazan State U., 1974, D of Chem. Scis., 1989. Sci. worker Kazan State U., 1972-92; prof. dept. chemistry Kazan State Acad. of Constrn. and Arch., 1992—; chief thermochem. lab. Inst. Organic and Phys. Chemistry, Kazan Br. Acad. of Scis. of Russia, 1997—. Contbr. articles to profl. jours. Named Honored Worker of Scis., Tatarstan Republic, Russia, 1996. Avocations: table tennis, volleyball. Office: Kazan State Acad Constn & Arch, Zelionaya St 1, 420043 Kazan Russia

OVERBEEK, JAN THEODOOR GERARD, retired chemistry educator, consultant; b. Groningen, The Netherlands, Jan. 5, 1911; s. Adam Adolf and Johanna Cornelia (Van Rijssel) O.; m. Johanna Clasina Edie, Aug. 18, 1936; children: Reina Elisabeth, Antoinetta Wilhelmina, Marijke, Titia Edie. D in Math. and Scis., U. Utrecht, The Netherlands, 1941; DSc (hon.), Clarkson U., 1967, Bristol (Eng.) U., 1984. From pvt. to ensign Dutch Mil., 1933-34; rsch. worker Free U., Brussels, 1934-35; asst. U. Ghent, Belgium, 1935-36; asst. in phys. chemistry U. Utrecht, 1936-41, prof. phys. chemistry, 1946-81; rsch. worker N.V. Philips, Eindhoven, The Netherlands, 1941-46; cons. I.C.I., Manchester, Eng., 1965-83, others; vis. prof. chem. engring. MIT, Cambridge, Mass., 1952-53, 66-67, 68-81, U. So. Calif., 1959-60; lectr. in field. Co-author: (with E.J.W. Verwey and J. Th. G. Overbeek) Theory of the Stability of Lyophobic Colloids, 1948; editor: Chemistry, Physics and Applications of Surface Active Substances, Vol. II, 1964; contbr. over 200 articles to profl. jours., chpts. to books; author, performer 2 video series and study guides. Named Knight Royal Order of the Netherlands Lion, 1971. Fellow Royal Soc. Chemistry (hon.); mem. Royal Netherlands Acad. Scis., Royal Netherlands Chem. Soc. (hon.), Royal Belgian Acad. Scis., Letters and Fine Arts (fgn.), Am. Acad. Arts and Scis. (fgn. hon.), Kolloidgesellschaft (hon., Wolfgang Ostwald prize 1989), Sigma Xi. Home: Zweerslaan 35, 3723 HN Bilthoven The Netherlands Office: Van't Hoff Lab Utrecht U, Padualaan 8, 3584 CH Utrecht The Netherlands

OVERCASH, SHELIA ANN, nurse; b. Columbia, Mo., Dec. 17, 1962; d. William Edgar and Lea Rosalee (Pilotte) Bacon; m. Stephen Harry Overcash, July 20, 1990; children: Kari Heller, Julie Keehnast. Diploma, Spoon River Coll., 1992. Cert. in intravenous therapy. Charge nurse Lindenwood Health Ctr., Peoria, Ill., 1992-93, Havana (Ill.) Health Care, 1993-94; staff nurse Graham Hosp, Canton, Ill., 1994-95, Pekin (Ill.) Hosp., 1995-97. Mem. AACN, CCNA, Phi Theta Kappa. Avocations: gardening, continuing education.

OVERGAAUW, EEF, paleographer, researcher, educator; b. Leidschendam, The Netherlands, Aug. 29, 1957; arrived in Germany, 1990; s. Henk and Gré (Van Winden) O. DPhil, U. Leiden, The Netherlands, 1990. Rschr. U. Leiden, 1986-88, Univ. Libr., Münster, Germany, 1990-94, Landeshauptarchiv, Koblenz, Germany, 1994-98, U. Libr., Dusseldorf, 1998-2000; head manuscript dept. Staatsbibliothek zu Berlin, 2000—; lectr. paleography Humboldt U., Berlin, 1995—. Author: Martyrologes Manuscrits des Anciens Diocèses d'Utrecht et de Liège, 1993, Die mittelalterlichen Handschriften der Universitäts- und Landesbibliothek Münster, 1996. Roman Catholic. Office: Staatsbibliothek zu Berlin, Abteilung III A, 10772 Berlin Germany

OVERGARD, ROBERT SHAWN, database marketing professional; b. Cheyenne, Wyo., May 3, 1970; s. Mary Irene Overgard; m. Christine Ann Soika, May 16, 1998. BS, U. Wyo., 1992, 93; MBA, Vanderbilt U., 1996. Econ. rsch. asst. Ctr. for Econ. and Bus. Data, Cheyenne, 1993-94; grad. rsch. asst. Vanderbilt U., Nashville, 1994-96; mktg. intern AT&T, Bridgewater, N.J., 1995; mktg. analyst Fed. Express, Memphis, 1996-97; mktg. mgr. Sprint, Overland Park, Kans., 1997—. Mem. Kansas City Direct Mktg. Assn., Kansas City Wine Enthusiasts, Mensa. Democrat. Avocations: wine tasting, traveling, gardening. E-mail: rovergard@yahoo.com and robert.overgard@mail.sprint.com. Fax: 913-762-0511. Home: 12708 W 125th St Overland Park KS 66213-5037 Office: Sprint Mail Stop KSOPHE0406-4B524 6360 Sprint Pkwy Shawnee Mission KS 66251-6100

OVERILL, RICHARD EDWARD, computer scientist, researcher; b. Halstead, Essex, Eng., Jan. 29, 1950; s. Charles Harold and Evelyn Agnes (Doe)

O.; m. Geraldine Crossley, July 3, 1976; children: Ralph Edmund Charles, Keith Aidan Francis. BSc, U. Leicester, Eng., 1971, PhD, 1977. Program advisor King's Coll. London, 1975-77, sr. analyst/advisor, 1977-85, asst. dir. sci. engring. support, 1985-87, lectr. computer sci., 1987-94, sr. lectr. computer sci., 1994—. Contbr. over 50 articles to profl. jours. Fellow Brit. Computer Soc. (chartered engr., European engr., info. security specialist group), Inst. Math. and its Applications (chartered mathematician); mem. Inst. Elec. Engrs., Royal Soc. Chemistry (chartered chemist), Chelmsford and Dist. Organists Assn. (com. 1996-98). Anglican/Quaker. Avocations: early keyboard music, Shotokan karate, steam engines, mills, lepidoptery. Office: Kings Coll London, Comp Sci Dept The Strand, London WC2R 2LS, England

OVERLAND, JANE ELIZABETH, nurse consultant; b. Murray Bridge, Australia, Nov. 27, 1963; d. Malcolm James and Pauline Temple (Shunke) O.; m. Peter Scott Hopkins, Feb. 5, 1994; 1 child, Sophie. Degree in nursing, Royal North Shore, Sydney, Australia, 1985; MPH, U. Sydney, 1996. Cert. in nursing diabetes edn. Nurse Woden Valley Hosp., Australia, 1985-88; sr. staff nurse King Edward Hosp., London, 1988-90; rsch. cons. U. Sydney, 1998—; clin. nurse cons. Royal Prince Alfred Hosp., Australia, 1990—; mem. econ. task force Internat. Diabetes Fedn., Brussels, 1994—; cons. Project Hope, U.S., 1995-96; chairperson diabetes task force Cen. Sydney Area Health Svc., Australia, 1997—; moderator profl. session Australian Diabetes Edn. Assn., coord. low literacy workshop, coord. rsch. workshop NSW br.; hon. rsch. assoc. faculty nursing U. Sydney. Author: (books) What Is Diabetes?, 1995, The Food You Eat, 1995, The Complications of Diabetes, 1995, Diabetes: Looking After Your Feet, 1995, Diabetes: Looking After Your Blood Vessels, 1994, Living with Diabetes, 1995; contbr. articles to profl. jours. and chpts. and reports to books. Recipient Hoechst award, 1992, Ames Scholarship award, 1992; ADEA travel grantee, 1994, D.K. Baird Bicentennial Traveling Fellowship grantee, 1997, rsch. grantee Eli Lilly Fund, 1992, Diabetes Australia Rsch. Trust, 1995. Avocation: cooking.

OVERSKEID, GEIR, psychologist; b. Levanger, Nord-Trond, Norway, July 19, 1963; s. Kare Harald and Unni (Westermark) O.; 1 child, Knut Hakedal Overskeid. Cand. Psychol., U. Oslo, 1989, D Psychol., 1995. Lic. clin. psychologist. Freelance journalist, 1980-88; rsch. psychologist Inst. Transport Econs., Oslo, 1989-91; rsch. fellow U. Oslo, 1991-96; assoc. prof. Norwegian Sch Mgmt., Sandvika, Norway, 1997—. Editor: (book) The Unconscious and Modern Science, 1997; dir., author, composer and actor: (play) The Russian Review, 1981; actor: Til Lykke Med Dagen, 1982. With Norwegian Army, 1986, 90-91. Scholar The Norwegian Work Life Ctr., Oslo, 1991, The Rsch. Coun. of Norway, Oslo, 1992, U. Oslo, 1995, Norwegian Non-Fiction Writers Assn., 1998, The Rsch. Coun. Norway, 1999. Mem. Elgens Venner Soc. (hon.). Avocations: family life, friends, reading, running, cinema. Office: Norwegian Sch Mgmt, PO Box 580, 1301 Sandvika Norway

OVERTON, CAROLINE ELIZABETH, obstetrician, gynecologist; b. Oxford, England, Dec. 4, 1962; d. Jeremy Richard and Gillian Mary (Trace) Naish; m. Timothy Graeme Overton, Febr. 6, 1993. MBBS, U London, Royal Free Hosp., 1987; MD, U. London, 1996. Sr. house officer Royal Free Hosp. London, 1988-89, John Radcliffe Hosp., Oxford, 1989-90; clin. rsch. fellow Nuffield Dept. Obstetrics & Gynecology, John Radcliffe Hosp., 1990-93; sr. house officer Addenbrooks Hosp., Cambridge, 1993; registrar Addenbrookes & Peterborough Hosps., 1993-95; sr. registrar Addenbrookes & Norfolk & Norwich Hosps., 1995-97; subspecialist trainee in reproductive medicine U. Coll. Hosp., London, 1997-2000; cons. ob-gyn Norfolk and Norwich Hosp., Norwich, Eng., 2000—; U.K. trainees rep. European Assn. Obstetricians & Gynecologists, 1994-95; mem East Anglian Trainees Com., 1995-97; asst. editor European Assn. Obstetricians & Gynecologists, 1996-97. Contbr. articles to profl. jours. Avocation: sailing.

OVERTON, EDWIN DEAN, campus minister, educator; b. Dec. 2, 1939; s. William Edward and Georgia Beryl (Fronk) O. BTh, Midwest Christian Coll., 1963; MA in Religion, Ea. N.Mex. U., 1969, EdS, 1978; postgrad., Fuller Theol. Sem., 1980. Ordained to ministry Christian Ch., 1978. Min. Christian Ch., Englewood, Kans., 1962-63; youth min. 1st Christian Ch., Beaver, Okla., 1963-67; campus min. Cen. Christian Ch., Portales, N.Mex., 1967-68, Christian Campus House, Portales, 1968-70; tchr. religion, philosophy, counseling Ea. N.Mex. U., Portales, 1970—, acting chmn. religion dept., 2000—; dir. Campus Christian House, 1980—; farm and ranch partner, Beaver, Okla., 1963—. State dir. Beaver Jr. C. of C., 1964-65; pres. Beaver H.S. Alumni Assn., 1964-65; elder Cen. Christian Ch., Portales, 1985-88, 90-93; chmn. Beaver County March of Dimes, 1966; neighborhood chmn. Portales March of Dimes, 1997; pres. Portales Tennis Assn., 1977-78. Mem. U.S. Tennis Assn., Am. Assn. Christian Counselors, Ea. N.Mex. U. Faith in Life Com., Lions Club. Republican. Home: 1129 Libra Dr Portales NM 88130-6123 Office: 223 S Avenue K Portales NM 88130-6643

OVIASU, EFOSA, medical educator, consultant physician; b. Benin City, Edo, Nigeria, Jan. 5, 1953; s. Humphrey Ehiobo and Rebecca Nobiomano (Bazuaye) O.; m. Stella Amechi Osunkwo, Apr. 25, 1981; children: Osaretin, Osarugue, Itohan. B of Medicine and Surgery, U. Lagos, Nigeria, 1976; postgrad., Med. Coll. Nigeria, 1987. Diplomate in internal medicine. Clin. and rsch. fellow Guy's Hosp., London, 1987-89; lectr. in medicine U. Benin, Benin City, 1989-93, sr. lectr., 1993-96, assoc. prof., 1996—, acting head dept. medicine, 1994-96, 98—; house officer, sr. house officer U. Benin Teaching Hosp., 1976-79, registrar, sr. registrar, 1979-87, cons. physician, 1989—. Contbr. articles to profl. jours. U. Benin rsch. grantee, 1990. Fellow Med. Coll. Physicians; mem. Internat. Soc. Nephrology, Nigerian Assn. Nephrology (sec. 1994-96), Nigerian Med. Assn. (treas. 1993-97). Avocations: chess, lawn tennis, current affairs. Home: PO Box 6684, 7 Medical Stores Rd, Benin City Nigeria Office: U Benin, Dept Medicine, Benin City Nigeria

OVISSI, NASSER, artist; b. Tehran, Iran, Aug. 13, 1934; s. Shaban and Batool O.; m. Ruby; 1 child, maryam. LLB, Tehran U., 1959; BA, U. Rome, 1965. Diplomat fgn. ministry, 1960-79; art cons., 1979-85. Artworks exhibited in Italy, France, Eng., Greece, Germany, Switzerland, Sweden, Spain, India, Can., U.S., Turkey, Brazil, Yugoslavia, Monaco, China, and Iran; permanent collections in mus. in Athens, Barcelona, Belgrade, Brussels, Campione, Italy, N.C., Kerman, Iran, Madrid, N.Y., Ottawa, Paris, Pasadena, Calif., Rome, Tehran, Washington, in palaces in His Royal Majesty Juan Carlos of Spain and Her Imperial Majesty Farah Pahlevi of Iran. Recipient numerous awards including gold medal Internat. Salon of Campione (Italy), 1968, grand prize Internat. Art Exhbn. in Monaco, 1974, gold medal, Madrid, 1979. Home: 1381 Park Lake Dr Reston VA 20190-3936

OVITZ, MICHAEL S., communications executive; b. 1946; m. Judy Reich, 1969; 3 children. Grad., UCLA, 1968. With William Morris Agy., 1968-75; co-founder, chmn. Creative Artists Agy., L.A., 1975-95; pres. Walt Disney Co., Burbank, Calif., 1995-97; owner CKE Cos., Beverly Hills, Calif., 1998—; chmn. exec. bd. dirs. UCLA Hosp. and Med. Ctr.; bd. advisors Sch. Theater, Film and TV UCLA; bd. dirs. Livent, Inc., Gulfstream Aero. Corp., J. Crew Group, Inc. Trustee St. John's Hosp. and Health Ctr., Santa Monica, Calif., Mus. Modern Art, N.Y.C.; bd. govs. Cedars-Sinai Hosp., L.A.; mem. exec. adv. bd. Pediatric AIDS Found.; bd. dirs. Calif. Inst. Arts, Sundance Inst. Mem. Coun. Fgn. Rels., Zeta Beta Tau. Avocations: contemporary art, African antiques, Chinese furniture. Office: Artists Management Group 9465 Wilshire Blvd Ste 212 Beverly Hills CA 90212-2610

OVODOV, YURY SEMYONOVICH, chemist, researcher, educator; b. Khar'kov, Ukraine, USSR, Aug. 28, 1937; s. Semyon Ivanovich and Mariya Feodorovna (Lavrukhina) O.; m. Raisa Grigorievna Lipeyko, Apr. 29, 1961; 1 child, Sergey Urievich. Degree chemistry, U. Moscow, 1959; Candidate of Chem. Sci., 1963. Sr. lab. asst. Inst. of Organic Chemistry, Novosibirsk, USSR, 1959-60; postgrad. fellow Inst. of Chemistry of Natural Compounds, Moscow, USSR, 1960-62; jr. rsch. worker Lab of Chemistry of Natural Compounds, Vladivostok, USSR, 1962-64; head of lab. carbohydrate chemistry Pacific Inst. Bioorganic Chemistry, Vladivostok, USSR, 1964-75, 89-94, dep. dir., 1967-87, dr. chem. sci., 1972—, prof., 1973—, head of dept. molecular immunology, 1975-94; univ. prof., Vladivostok, 1974-81, Syktyvkar, Republic of Komi, Russia, 1995—; head of dept. molecular immunology and biotech. Inst. Physiology, Komi Sci. Ctr., Syktyvkar, 1994—; corr. mem. USSR Acad. Sci., 1990-92; academician Russian Acad. Sci., 1992—. Author: Introduction to Immunochemistry, 1983, Chemistry of Immunity, 1997, The Selected Chapters of Bioorganic Chemistry, 1998; contbr. articles to profl. publs. Grantee Russian Ministry of Sci., 1999. Mem. N.Y. Acad. Sci., Scientific Couns., Presidium of Komi Sci. Ctr. Avocations: opera music, Russian songs, numismatics, philately, sports. Office: Inst Physiology, 50 Pervomayskaya str, 167982 Syktyvkar Russia

OVSEPIAN, ZHANNA IOSIFOVNA, law educator; b. Rostov-on-Don, Russia, July 6, 1956; d. Iosif Asaturovich and Elizabeta Alekseevna (Tarasova) O. Diploma, Rostov State U., Rostov-on-Don, 1978; degree in law, Saratov (Russia) Law Sch., 1985; DSc in Law, Acad. Sci. Russian Fedn., Moscow, 1994. Sr. lab. asst. Rostov State U., 1978-81, tchr., 1981-87, asst. prof. law, 1987-89, assoc. prof. law, 1989-95, prof. law, 1995—; expert Govtl. Fund of Fundamental Rsch., Moscow, 1997—; head law procedure dept. Acad. State Svc. Sch. Law, Rostov-on-Don, 1997-98, head adminstrv. and mcpl. dept., 1998—. Author: Law Defence of the Constitution, 1992; editor, preface author: Collection of Legislations on the Constitutional Law of Russian Federation, 1997; co-editor, preface author: Constitutions, Regulations and Agreements of the Subjects of the Russian Federation in the North Caucasus, 1998; contbr. articles to profl. jours. Avocations: traveling, gardening, theater, museums. Home: Geltsa 60, 344048 Rostov-on-Don Russia Office: Rostov State U Law Faculty, M Gorky Str 88, 344007 Rostov-on-Don Russia

OWADA, HISASHI, government official; b. Shibata, Nigata, Japan, Sept. 18, 1932; s. Takeo and Shizuka (Tamura) O.; m. Yumiko Egashira, Oct. 7, 1962; children: Masako, Reiko, Setsuko. BA, U. Tokyo, 1955; LLB, Cambridge U., Eng., 1956. Dir. legal affairs Ministry Fgn. Affairs, New York, 1959; pvt. sec. to min. Ministry Fgn. Affairs, Tokyo, 1971, dir. UN polit. affairs div., 1972-74, dir. treaties div., 1974-76; pvt. sec. to prime min. Govt. of Japan, Tokyo, 1976-78; min. Japanese Embassy, Washington, 1979-81, Moscow, 1981-84; dir. gen. treaties bur. and for law of sea Ministry Fgn. Affairs, 1984-87, dep. vice minister, 1987-88; amb. extraordinary and plenipotentiary Permanent Mission of Japan to OECD, Paris, 1988-89; dep. min. fgn. affairs Min. Fgn. Affairs, Tokyo, 1989-91, vice min., 1991-93, advisor to mins. fgn. affairs, 1993-94; perm. rep. of Japan UN, N.Y.C., 1994-98; assoc. Inst. Internat. Law; adj. lectr. U. Tokyo, 1963-88; vis. prof. Harvard U., Cambridge, Mass., 1979-81, 87, 89; adj. prof. Internat. Law Columbia U., 1994-2000; Inge Rennert disting. vis. prof. N.Y.U., 1994—; sr. advisor to Pres. of World Bank, advisor to Min. Fgn. Affairs of Japan, Pres. Japan Inst. Internat. Affairs, 1999—. Author: Practice of Japan in International Law, 1984, From Involvement to Engagement, 1994, Diplomacy, 1996. Bd. dirs. Aspen Inst., Ditchley Found., Salzburg Sem. Mem. Japanese Assn. Internat. Law (exec. coun.). Avocations: skiing, mountain walking, music. Fax: 03-3503-7292. Office: Japan Inst Internat Affairs, 3-2-5 Kasumigaseki Chiyoda-ku, Tokyo 100-6011, Japan

OWADOWSKA, EDYTA MARIA, forester, researcher; b. Toninek, Poland, Sept. 28, 1968; d. Zbigniew and Helena (Pyrc) O. BSc, Agrl. U., Warsaw, Poland, 1993, D, 1998. Asst. Agrl. U., Warsaw, 1992-93; asst. Kampinos Nat. Pk., Izabelin, Poland, 1993-98, sr. asst., 1998—. Avocations: travel, cycling, sailing, wild nature. Office: Kampinos Nat Pk, Tetmajera 38, 05080 Izabelin Warszawa, Poland

OWAKI, KENICHI, computer scientist, inventor; b. Kochi, Japan, Aug. 25, 1910; s. Yasu and Ikushi (Kawaguchi) O.; m. Shizuko Saito, Apr. 4, 1939; children: Yasuko, Tsutomu, Masako, Osamu. PhD, Osaka U., 1948. Bd. dirs. Kobe Kogyo Ltd., 1962-68, Fujitsu Co. Ltd., Kawasaki, Japan, 1968-73; prof. Hiroshima Inst. of Tech., 1975-86; pres. Hiroshima (Japan) Coll. of Computer Sci., 1983-88. Inventor in field. Recipient Hyogo Prefecture Culture award Hyogo Prefecture Govt., 1949, Nat. Award medal with blue ribbon Prime Min. Office Nat. Govt., 1950, Recognition award Soc. Info. Soc. Am., 1974. Avocations: computer graphics, cruising, gardening. Home: Herios, Yokohama 20-1 Kochi 781-02, Japan

OWCZAREK, ROBERT MICHAL, physicist; b. Szczecin, Poland, Apr. 20, 1963; s. Stanislaw and Miroslawa (Galaj) O.; m. Hanna Ewa Makaruk. MS, Warsaw (Poland) U., 1988; PhD summa cum laude, Polish Acad. Scis., Warsaw, 1993. Rsch. assoc. Inst. Fundamental Tech. Rsch., 1988-93; assoc. prof. Polish Acad. Scis., Warsaw, 1993—; postdoctoral assoc. theoret. disvn. Los Alamos (N.Mex.) Nat. Lab., 1997—. Referee 4 jours.; contbr. articles to profl. jours., chpts. to books in field. Fellow for outstanding rschrs., Warsaw, 1994, Internat. fellow Found. for Polish Sci., 1996, Sr. Fulbright fellow, 1997. Mem. Internat. Soc. for Interaction Between Mechanics and Math., Polish Soc. for Applied Electromagnetism, Am. Mathematical Soc. Roman Catholic. Achievements inlcude explaining role of topologically mon-trivial vortices in phase transition in He4, finding string-like solution with non-zero helicity. Avocations: classical music, basketball, hiking. Office: Los Alamos Nat Lab T13 B213 Los Alamos NM 87595

OWCZAREK, STEFAN, engineering educator; b. Kludno, Poland, Mar. 16, 1936; s. Wincenty and Malgorzata (Lerka) O.; m. Maria Miroslawa Balcerzak, Oct. 28, 1972; 1 child, Mariusz. MSc, Warsaw Tech. U., 1962; PhD, Inst. Fundamental Tech. Rsch., 1970, postdoctoral, 1992. Asst. Warsaw Tech. U., 1963-64; asst. Inst. Fundamental Technol. Rsch., 1965-70, adj. prof., 1970-93, assoc. prof., 1993-98; chmn. process engring, orgn. and bldg. econs. Bialystok (Poland) U. Tech., 1999—. Co-author: Foundations of Optimum Design in Civil Engineering, 1980. Criteria and methods of Structural Optimization, 1980; contbr articles to profl. jours. Mem. Sci. Coun. Inst. Fundamental Technol. Rsch., internat. Solar Energy Soc., N.Y. Acad. Scis. Roman Catholic. Avocations: music, dancing, walking. Home: Malborska 8/54, 03-286 Warsaw Poland Office: Biatystok U Tech, Wiejska, 13-351 Biatystok Poland

OWEN, ARTHUR S., Barbados government official; b. Barbados, Oct. 17, 1949; married. BA in Econs. and History, MSc in Econs. From asst. econ. planner to chief econ. planner Nat. Planning Agy., Jamaica, 1974-81; econs. dir. Jamaica Bauxite Inst., 1979-81; chief project analyst Min. Fin. and Planning, Barbados, 1981; parliamentary sec., 1985, leader of the opp., 1993-94; prime min., min. fins. and econ. affairs, min. civil svc., min. def. and security govt. Barbados, St. Michael, 1994—. Contbr. article to profl. jours. Recipient the Josè Marti award, Cuba, 1999. Office: Office Prime Min, Govt Hdqs Bay St, Saint Michael Barbados

OWEN, CHARLES THEODORE, journalist, publisher; b. Beech Grove, Ind., June 14, 1941; s. James Robert and Helen Maurine (Sayre) O.; m. Kathleen Rose Dellaria, Apr. 29, 1967. AS in Journalism, Vincennes U., 1972; BA in Social Sci., Chapman U., 1976; MBA, Nat. U. San Diego, 1984. Enlisted U.S. Marine Corps, 1959-72, commd. 2d lt., 1973, advanced through grades to capt., 1979; combat journalist/photographer, Vietnam, 1967-68; dep. dir. Joint Pub. Affairs Office, Camp Pendleton, 1976-79; dir. Pub. Affairs Office, Marine Corps Recruit Depot, San Diego, 1980-81; dir. comm. and mil. affairs div. Greater San Diego C. of C., 1981-82, v.p. 1987—, bd. dirs., 1982-87; now pres., pub. San Diego Bus. Jour., 1987—; host TV program Focus on San Diego Bus. Bd. dirs. San Diego Conv. and Visitors Bur., San Diego Econ. Devel. Corp.; econ. devel. advisor to Mayor of San Diego; presenter in field. Decorated Cross of Gallantry, Joint Svc. Commendation medal with Combat V (3 awards), medal of Honor 2d class (Vietnam); recipient Thomas Jefferson award, 1981. Republican. Pub. Newswriting Program Instruction, 1972. Office: 4909 Murphy Canyon Rd Ste 200 San Diego CA 92123-5381

OWEN, DANIEL PAUL MICHAEL, anthropologist; b. London, Jan. 12, 1966; s. Paul Robert and Margaret Anne (Baron) O. BA, Cambridge U., 1988, MA, 1992; MPA, Harvard U., 1991; postgrad., London Sch. of Econs. Anthropologist The World Bank, Washington, 1991-95, Maputo, Mozambique, 1995-96; tech. advisor Ministry of Planning, Govt. of Mozambique, 1996-97; rsch. advisor Eduardo Mondlane U., Maputo, 1996-98; cons. U.K. Dept. Internat. Devel., London, 1998-99; social devel. specialist World Bank/Internat. Fin. Corp., Washington, 1999—; cons. in field. Kennedy Meml. scholarship, 1989. Avocations: rowing, theatre, football, music. Office: 1818 H St NW Washington DC 20433-0001

OWEN, LORD DAVID ANTHONY LLEWELLYN, former British government minister, physician; b. July 2, 1938; s. John William Morris and Mary (Llewellyn) Owen; m. Deborah Schabert, 1968; three children. Student, Bradfield Coll., Sidney Sussex, Coll., Cambridge U., St. Thomas' Hosp. Mem. med. staff St. Thomas' Hosp., 1962-64, neurol. and psychiat. registrar, 1964-66, rsch. fellow med. unit, 1966-68; M.P. Sutton div. of Plymouth, 1966-74, Devonport div., 1974-92; under-sec. of state for def. Royal Navy, 1968-70; min. of state Dept. Health and Social Security, 1974-76; privy councillor, 1976; min. of state Fgn. Office, 1976-77; sec. of state Fgn. and Commonwealth Affairs, 1977-79; opposition spokesman for energy, 1979-80; chmn. Middlesex Holdings, 1995—; bd. dirs. Coats Viyella plc, Abbott Labs., Europe-Steel.com; chancellor Liverpool U., 1996—, chmn. New Europe, 1999—; dep. chmn. Europe-Steel.com, 2000—; mem. Ind. Commn. on Disarmament and Security Issues, Ind. Commn. on Internat. Humanitarian Issues, Carnegie Commn. Preventing Deadly Conflict, Eminent Persons Group on Curbing Illicit Trafficking in Small Arms and Light Weapons; dir. New Crane Pub. Author: The Politics of Defense, 1972; In Sickness and in Health: the Politics of Medicine, 1976; Human Rights, 1978; Face the Future, 1981; A Future That Will Work, 1984; A United Kingdom, 1986, Our NHS, 1988, Time to Declare, 1991, Seven Ages, 1992, Balkan Odyssey, 1995. Co-founder Social Dem. Party, 1981, leader, 1983-87, 88-90; European Union co-chmn. Internat. Conf. on the Former Yugoslavia, 1992-95. E-mail: lordowen@nildram.co.uk. Home: 78 Narrow St Limehouse, London E14 8BP, England Office: House of Lords Westminster, London SW1A 0PW, England

OWEN, GORDON PETER, fundraising professional; b. Lonond, June 28, 1953; s. William and Lucy Theodosia (Adams) O.; m. Janice Joel, Sept. 12, 1981; children: Matthew David Peter, Andrew William Richard. Fundraising and devel. officer London Borough of Newham Swimming Club, 1995—; part-time prin. Messrs. G. Owen & Co., 1972—; part-time proprietor Messrs. Rent-A-Bar Svc., 1981—. Fete chairperson, coord. Friends of Barking Ch. of Eng. Sch. PTA, 1993-94; vice chmn. Newham Youth Leader's Assn., 1978-79, chmn., 1979-85, exec. officer, 1985-87; chmn. Newham Youth Trust Ltd., 1983-85, founder, mem., dir., trustee, co. sec.; chmn. youth and cmty. worker St. Barhtolomew's Social Club, 1984-85; mem. London Borough of Newham Edn. Com., youth panel 1983-84, 85-88; mem. Newham Vol. Agys. Coun., children and young people steering com., 1981-83; founder, developer Newham Youth Lodge Hostel Project, 1979-94; youth worker St. Barbabas Youth Club; past mem. Nat. Youth Bur., Nat. Assn. of Youth Clubs, and London Union of Youth Clubs; chmn., co-coord. NYLA-All Our Own, 1980-85; regional health authority appointee Newham Cmty Health Coun., 1982-85; mem. St. Bartholomew's Devel. com., 1977-84; mem. Parochial Ch. Coun.-Parish of East Ham, London, 1977-87, 2000—, parish warden; sec., mem. St. Bartholomew's Dist. Ch. Coun., 1977-87, 98—; mem. Newham Deanery Synod, London, 1980-81, 82-84, Stop Seward, 1982-84, 86-93; worker, coord. Turn-Around Newham Night Shelter, 1998—; former mem. Nat. Union Licenses Victuallers Assn., The Carnival Guild, Nat. Camping & Caravanning Club, Conway Owners Club. Mem. Inst. Charity Fundraising Mgrs., Brit. Apple Sys. Users' Group (Apple 2000), London Macintosh Users' Group, NYT Never-Land, NYT Met. Police Newham Vol. Cadet Corps., Royal Hort. Soc., Brit. Mountain Bike Fedn., Cyclists' Touring Club. Home: Owen House, Twenty Three Beverly Rd, East Ham London E6 3LH, England Office: PO Box 45, London E6 3LR, England

OWEN, JUNE LOIS, artist; b. Berlin, N.H., June 10, 1930; d. Raymond and Maude (O'Bryan) Legru; m. Frank Swain Owen, June 21, 1952; children: Jody Ann, Polly Swain. BFA, R.I. Sch. Design, 1952. Solo exhbns. include New Britain (Conn.) Mus. Am. Art, 1973, Munson Gallery, New Haven, Chatham, Mass., 1979, Pindar Gallery, N.Y.C., 1986-88, Slater Meml. Mus., Norwich, Conn., 1994, Main St. Gallery, Nantucket, Mass., 1975-97, Kerygma Gallery, Ridgewood, N.J., 2000; group exhbns. include Mattatuck Mus., Waterbury, Conn., 1977, DeCordova Mus., Lincoln, Mass., 1972. Avocation: cooking.

OWEN, LYNETTE ISABEL, book publisher; b. Bangor, Wales, June 29, 1947; d. Warwick Jack Burgoyne and Betty Isabel (Drummond) O. BA in English with honors, U. London, 1968. Rights asst. Cambridge U. Press, London, 1968-73; rights mgr. Pitman Pub., London, 1973-75; N.Am. sales mgr. Marshall Cavendish, London, 1975-76; rights and contracts dir. Pearson Edn. Ltd., Harlow, Eng., 1976—. Author: Selling Rights, 1st edit., 1991, 2d edit., 1994, 3d edit., 1997; gen. editor, contbr.: Publishing Agreements, 1997; contbr. numerous articles to internat. profl. jours. Office: Pearson Edn Ltd, Edinburgh Gate, Harlow Essex CM20 2JE, England

OWEN, MICHAEL, ballet dancer; b. Carlisle, Pa.. Studied with Marcia Weary; student, Pa. Ballet Sch., Sch. Am. Ballet, Am. Ballet Theatre Sch. Mem. Ballet Reportory Co.; with Am. Ballet Theatre, 1974-97, soloist, 1977-87, prin. dancer, 1987-97; head dance dept. Walnut Hill Sch., Natick, Mass., 1998—. Appeared in ballets including La Bayadere, Coppelia, Fall River Legend, Giselle, Jardin aux Lilas, The Leaves are Fading, Manon, Pillar of Fire, Romeo and Juliet, The Sleeping Beauty, Swan Lake, Undertow; created leading role in Americans We. *

OWEN, MICHAEL JAMES, professional soccer player; b. Chester, Eng., Dec. 14, 1979. Forward Liverpool Football Club, Eng., 1996—; with English Nat. Team, 1998. Office: SFX Sports Group (Europe), 35-36 Grosvenor St, London W1X 9FG, England

OWEN, MICHAEL JOHN, psychiatrist, geneticist; b. Birmingham, Eng., Nov. 24, 1955; s. John Robson and Mary Gillian (Dowsett) O.; m. Deborah Anne Cohen, Sept. 27, 1985. PhD, Birmingham U., 1982, MB ChB, 1983, BSc, 1987. Lectr. Inst. Psychiatry, London, 1987-90; rsch. fellow St. Mary's Med. Sch., London, 1987-90; sr. lectr. U. Wales Coll. Medicine, Cardiff, 1990-95, prof. dept. psychiatry and med. genetics, 1995—; head dept. psychol. medicine U. Wales Coll. Medicine, 1998—. Contbr. articles to profl. publs. Fellow Royal Coll. Psychiatry, Acad. Med. Sci. Office: U Wales Coll Medicine, Health Park, Cardiff CF4 4XN, Wales

OWEN, PETER LOTHAR, publisher; s. Arthur and Winifred (Friedman) O.; m. Wendy De Moulins (div.); children: Antonia, Georgina, Benedict; m. Jan Kenny, 1995. Pub. Peter Owen Ltd., London. Editor: Peter Owen Anthology, 1992, Publishing the Future, 1989, Publishing Now, 1993, rev. edit., 1996, Peter Owen 50th Anniversary Anthology, The Delicate Prey and Other Fiction, An Anthology. Office: Peter Owen Pubs, 73 Kenway Rd, London SW5 0RE, England

OWEN, ROBERT DEWIT, lawyer; b. St. Louis, Nov. 15, 1948; s. Kenneth Campbell Owen and Mary Elenor (Fish) Luebbers; m. Rebecca Roberts Baxter, June 4, 1977; children: Abigail Mary, James Roy, Charlotte Grace. BA, Northwestern U., 1970; JD cum laude, U. Pa., 1973. Assoc. Sullivan & Cromwell, N.Y.C., 1973-81; ptnr. Towne, Dolgin, Furlaud, Sawyier & Owen, N.Y.C., 1981-83, Owen & Fennell, N.Y.C., 1983-87, Owen & Davis, N.Y.C., 1987—; instr. Nat. Inst. Trial Advocacy, Boulder, Colo., 1988—; faculty mem. ABA Nat. Inst. 1992, 93. Bd. dirs. St. Christopher's-Jennie Clarkson Child Care Svcs., Dobbs Ferry, N.Y., 1991-97. Mem. Assn. Bar City N.Y., Fed. Bar Coun., Nat. Assn. Securities Dealers (bd. arbitrators 1985—), Nat. Futures Assn. (bd. arbitrators 1999—), Colonial Springs Club (pres. 1986-94), India House. Episcopalian. Avocations: boating, running. Office: Owen & Davis 805 3rd Ave New York NY 10022-7513

OWEN, ROBERT FREDERICK, internist, rheumatologist; b. Poplar Bluff, Mo., Oct. 19, 1927; s. John Clarence and Lydia Anna (Laverty) O.; m. Edith Suzanna Trugly, June 11, 1960; 1 child, Suzanne Marie. AB summa cum laude, Princeton U., 1948; MD, Yale U., 1952. Diplomate Am. Bd. Internal Medicine, Nat. Bd. Med. Examiners. Med. intern Barnes Hosp. (Washington U.), St. Louis, 1952-53; asst. resident in internal medicine St. Louis City Hosp. (Washington U. Med. Svc.), 1953-54, 56-57, med. resident, 1957-58; pvt. practice in internal medicine and rheumatology St. Louis, 1958—; instr. clin. medicine Washington U. Sch. Medicine, St. Louis, 1958—; cons. Arthritis Clinic Washington U. Clinics, St. Louis, 1958-78; attending physician inpatient and outpatient tchg. svcs. at Washington U. and Mo. Baptist, St. Luke's, and Deaconness Hosps., St. Louis, 1958-79. Chmn. Instnl. Rev. Bd. Mo. Baptist Hosp. (monitoring biomed. and behavioral rsch.), 1977-96; mem. St. Louis Cmty. Clin. Oncology Program Human

Subjects Rsch. Instnl. Rev. Bd., 1983-96. Capt. U.S. Army Med. Corps, 1954-56, Korea. Commendation by surgeon, Eighth U.S. Army, Far East, 1955. Fellow ACP; mem. AMA (Physician's Recognition award annually 1977—), Sigma Xi, Phi Beta Kappa. Avocations: piano, organ, photography. Office: St Francois Med Ctr 1224 Graham Rd Ste 3008 Florissant MO 63031-8028

OWEN, ROY, editor; b. Grantham, Lincs, U.K., Dec. 6, 1935; m. Virginia Marquez Amparo, Aug. 3, 1988. BS, Columbia Pacific U., 1983, PhD, 1986. Higher clerical officer Hosp. Svc., St. Albans, U.K., 1962-64; editor Hosp. Equipment and Supplies, Hosp. Devel., 1965-85, Biomedical Scientist, Inst. Biomed. Sci., 1985-2000; adj. asst. prof. Am. Univ. London, Eng., 1987. Candidate spl. duties officer Royal Navy, 1952-62. Fellow Royal Soc. Health, Royal Soc. Arts. Avocations: church history, homeopathic medicine. Office: Inst Biomedical Sci, 12 Coldbath Sq, London EC1R 5HL, England

OWEN, THOMAS JAMES, artist, educator; b. Coca-Rockledge, Fla., Aug. 20, 1945; s. Irwin Arthur and Esther Ethel (Sensinig) O.; m. Judith Lea Pasternak, June 21, 1969 (div. Feb. 1983); m. Koreen Clay, June 26, 1986; 1 child, Gillian Clay. BS in Edn., N.W. Mo. State U., 1968. Cert. tchr., Mo., Nebr. Secondary educator Avon-Grove Sch. Dist., West Grove, Pa., 1968-69, Dist. # 60 Schs., Pueblo, Colo., 1969-72, Wymore (Nebr.) Unified Dist., 1972-73; art educator Sangre De Cristo F.A.C., Pueblo, 1981-86, Colorado Springs (Colo.) F.A.C. Bemis Art Sch., 1982-96, Cottonwood Art Acad., Colo. Springs, 1997—; pvt. practice Black Forest, Colo., 1996—; art dir. Columbine Cellers, Denver and Palisade, Colo., 1989-96; guest instr. Adams State Coll., Alamosa, Colo., 1990-95. Exhibited Kans. Watercolor Soc. (Purchase selection), Wichita Ctr. for Arts. Recipient Juror's Choice award San Diego Nat. Watermedia, 1981, Adirondack's Wilderness award, The Rouse Gold medallion, Adirondack's Nat. Exhbn. Am. Watercolors, 1995, Florene and H. Samuel Slater meml. award, 1999, Gold Medal New World Internat. Wine Label Competition, 1994, Dr. Martin's award Soc. Watercolor Artists, 1997, Silver Brush award 1999, New West award Watermedia IX, 1998, Meyer award Rocky Mt. Nat. Water Media Exhbn. Signature, 1998, 2000, Best Transparent Watercolor Watermedia X, 1999, Omni Trax award, 1999, Mid Continent Engring. award Kans. 7 state exhbn., 1999, 2000, Atlantic Papers award Western Colo. Nat. Watercolor Exhbn., 1999, Best of Show award Soc. Watercolor Artists, 2000, Carillion Gallery award, Best of Show award, 2000, Honorarium award Kans. Watercolor Soc., 2000, Connoisseur Art award, 2000, 4th Pl. medallion Pa. Watercolor Soc., 2000. Mem. Nat. Watercolor Soc. (signature mem., Rocky Mtn. br. bd. dirs., Hariett Wexler Bartsch Meml. award 1994), Colo. Artists Assn. (v.p. 1982-86), Nickerbocker Artists (assoc.), Pikes Peak Watercolor Soc. (v.p. 1990—), Watercolor West (juried mem. 1999), Acad. Sertoma Club. Avocations: trout fishing, skiing, model railroading. E-mail: tomowen@hotbot.com. Home and Office: 11935 Vollmer Rd Colorado Springs CO 80908-4086

OWEN, THOMAS LLEWELLYN, investment executive; b. Patchogue, N.Y., June 24, 1928; s. Griffith Robert and Jeanette Roberts (Hatfield) O. AB in Econs., Coll. William and Mary, 1951; postgrad., Columbia U., 1952, N.Y. Inst. Fin., 1960-62; MBA, NYU, 1966. Exec. trainee Shell Oil Co., N.Y.C. and Indpls., 1951-59, supr., 1958-59; petroleum and chem. investment analyst Paine, Webber, Jackson & Curtis, N.Y.C., 1959-62; sr. oil investment analyst DuPont Investment Interests, Wilmington, Del., N.Y.C., 1962-66; dir. rsch. DuPont Investment Interests, Wilmington, N.Y., N.Y.C., 1964-66; v.p., sr. investment officer, mem. policy, investment coms. Nat. Securities and Rsch. Corp., N.Y.C., 1966-75; sr. investment exec., v.p., portfolio mgr. F. Eberstadt & Co. and Eberstadt Asset Mgmt., Inc., N.Y.C., 1975-85, mem. policy com., 1979-85, also dir. portfolio rev. com.; sr. investment exec., portfolio mgr. Brown Brothers Harriman, N.Y.C., 1985-89; pres., CEO Owen Capital Mgmt., N.Y.C., 1989—. Contbr. chpt. "Oil and Gas Industries" to Financial Analysts Handbook, 1975. Chmn. bd. trustees Congl. Ch. Patchogue, N.Y. Mem. N.Y. Soc. Security Analysts, Assn. of Investment Mgmt. and Rsch., Oil Analysts Group N.Y., Am. Econ. Assn., Investment Assn. N.Y., Am. Petroleum Inst., Nat. Assn. Petroleum Investment Analysts, Internat. Assn. Energy Economists. Home and Office: 251 E 32nd St New York NY 10016-6304

OWEN-JONES, LINDSAY, cosmetics executive; b. Mar. 17, 1946; s. Hugh A. and Esmee (Lindsay) O.- J.; m. Cristina Furno, 1994; 1 child. BA, Oxford U.; postgrad., European Inst. Bus. Adminstrn., 1969. Product mgr. L'Oreal, Clicy, France, 1969, head pub. products divsn., 1971-74; mgr. SCAD (L'Oreal subs.) L'Oreal, Paris, 1974-76, mktg. mgr. pub. products divsn., 1976-78; gen. mgr. SAIPO (L'Oreal subs.) L'Oreal, Italy, 1978-81; pres. L'Oreal, Clichy, 1981-83, v.p. mgmt. com., bd. dirs., 1984, pres., COO, 1984-88; CEO, chmn. bd. dirs. L'Oreal, Clichy, France, 1988—; chmn. COSMAIR (L'Oreal agt.) L'Oreal, USA, 1991—; bd. dirs. Banque Nat. de Paris, LAFARGE, Air Liquide. Avocation: private helicopter pilot. Office: L'Oreal SSA, 41 rue Martre, 92117 Clichy France*

OWENS, BETTY RUTH, lawyer; b. Texas City, Tex., Dec. 21, 1951; d. Marvin Lee Jr. and Ellen Frances (Nunnally) O.; m. Robert Foster Geary, Oct. 1, 1994. BS, La. State U., 1973, MA, 1975; JD, U. Tex., 1988. Bar: Tex., U.S. Dist. Ct. (so. dist.) Tex. 1989, U.S. Ct. Appeals (5th cir.) 1989, U.S. Dist. Ct. (we. dist.) Tex. 1999. Ptnr. Vinson & Elkins LLP, Houston, 1988—. Author: (with others) ABA Antitrust Law Developments, 4th edit., ABA Annual Review of Antitrust Law Developments, 1992-95; editor ABA Antitrust Summary Judgment Newsletter, 1996-98. Trustee St. Luke's United Meth. Ch., Houston, 1998, mem. adv. com. Senior's Place, 1994-98, personnel com. 1999—. Mem. ABA (vice chair civil practice and procedure com., antitrust sect. 1993-98, v. chair books and treatises com. 2000—), Am. Law Inst., Tex. Bar Found., Houston Bar Found. Avocations: reading, cooking, travel. Office: Vinson & Elkins LLP 1001 Fannin St Ste 2300 Houston TX 77002-6760

OWENS, JOHN ROBIN, finance company executive; b. Shillong, India, May 26, 1939; s. Theobold David Cogswell and Irene Hamilton (Franklyn) O.; m. Margaret Ann Overton, Dec. 21, 1963 (dec. Feb. 1998); children: Nicholas, Philippa. Degree in mech. scis., Emmanuel Coll., Cambridge, Eng., 1963. Auditor Price Waterhouse, London, 1968-72; mgr. Midland Bank, London, 1972-78; dir. Midland Montagu Leasing, London, 1978-80, Forward Trust Group, London, 1980-84, GATX Leasing, London, 1984-85; mng. dir. Park pl. Fin., Epsom, England, 1985-86, Medens Trust, Crawley, England, 1986-89; dir. Brown Shipley, London, 1989-95; chmn. Will Hire, Newmarket, England, 1991-95; chief exec. Bldg. Ctr. Group, 1996—. Patentee in field. Capt. Brit. Army, 1958-68. Mem. Oxford and Cambridge Univ. Club, Royal Engrs. Yacht Club, Medway Yacht Club. Mem. Ch. of England. Avocations: sailing, tennis, opera. Office: 26 Store St, London WC1E 7BT, England

OWENS, LUVIE MOORE, association consultant; b. Cleve., July 26, 1933; d. Dan Tyler and Elizabeth (Oakes) Moore; m. Lloyd Owens, Jan. 1, 1955; children: Luvie Owens Myers, Elizabeth, Lloyd H. Student, Smith Coll., Northampton, Mass., 1956. Tchr. Howard Jr. High Sch., Wilmette, Ill., 1971-75; U.S. ops. mgr. Frank T. Ross & Co., Evanston, Ill., 1976-86; dir. Internat. Platform Assn., Winnetka, Ill., 1972—, chief exec. officer, 1986-98. Mem. jr. league Cleve. Mus. Art, 1954-98, treas., mem. jr. coun., 1964-65; commr. Police and Fire Commn., Winnetka, 1980-86; chmn. bd. Lake Shore Unitarian Ch., Winnetka, 1986-87; mem. alumnae bd. Madeira Sch., Greenway, Va., 1984-88. Mem. Rotary. Office: Internat Platform Assn PO Box 250 Winnetka IL 60093-0250

OWENS, MARSHA, library director; b. Birmingham, Ala., Apr. 5, 1956; d. Clarence Austin and Virginia (Hamilton) O.; m. James Alfred Smith, May 19, 1984 (div. Dec. 1990); m. William Kelly Key, Jan. 7, 1995. BS in Journalism, U. Ala., 1982, MLS, 1992. Staff photographer, reporter Daily Mountain Eagle, Jasper, Ala., 1983-84; paraprofl. librarian Birmingham Pub. Libr., 1988-90; dir. Orange Beach Pub. Libr., 1992—. Bd. dirs. South Baldwin Literacy Coun., Foley, Ala., 1993-97; mem. Ala. Electronic Access Com., 1997-98. Mem. ALA, Ala. Libr. Assn. (convention com. 1994-97, 98), Beta Phi Mu. Avocations: hiking, camping, reading, sports cars, gardening. E-mail: owensmar@hotmail.com. Home: 26759 Magnolia Ave Orange Beach AL 36561-4915 Office: Orange Beach Pub Libr 4101 Orange Beach Blvd PO Box 1649 Orange Beach AL 36561-1649

OWENS, ROBERT GEORGE, psychologist, researcher; b. Devils Lake, N.D., Oct. 10, 1932; s. Clarence George and Anne Marie (Ebner) O.; m. Ruth Ann Johnson, Aug. 21, 1955 (dec. Sept. 1993); children: Scott George, Bruce Robert, Laura Marie. PhB, U. N.D., 1954, MA, 1955. Lic. psychologist, Wis. Lectr. U. Wis., Madison, 1964-66; cons. psychologist various mental health facilities and cts., Wis., 1966-86; profl. spkr. in field of psychology Wis., N.Y., 1962—. Founder, pub., editor The Internat. Jour. of Clin. Neuropsychology, 1979-84; contbr. articles to profl. publs. Mem. APA, Am. Psychol. Soc., Nat. Register Health Svc. Providers in Psychology, Nat. Acad. Neuropsychologists (life). Republican. Episcopalian. Avocation: book collecting. Home and Office: 6666 Odana Rd Madison WI 53719-1012

OWENS, VIVIAN ANN, plant science educator, researcher; b. Conway, S.C., Sept. 2, 1948; d. Zack Jr. and Frances (Mishoe) O. BS, Howard U., 1971, MS, 1974; PhD, Cornell U., 1984; MLS, U. Md., 1998. Assoc. prof. plant sci. Hampton (Va.) U., 1988-95; faculty fellow EPA, Washington, summer 1990. Contbr. articles to profl. jours. Vol. Friends of Kennedy Ctr., 1996.

OWOLABI, E. AMOLE, computer scientist; b. Eruwa, Nigeria, May 22, 1935; s. Moses Alamu and Awopeju Agbeke Owolabi; m. Victoria Bolape Ogunwole; children: Babatunde, Adetokunbo; m. Theresa Charity Ogette; children: Olukemi, Adepeju, Modupeola. BEd, U. Ibadan, Nigeria, 1967, postgrad. diploma in stats., 1969; MS in Computing Sci., U. Alta., Edmonton, Can., 1973. Tchr. Bapt. Day Sch., Igboora, Nigeria, 1954; tchr. Bapt. H.S., Iree, Nigeria, 1959-60, 63-64, Ejigbo, Nigeria, 1967-68; rsch. asst. Nigerian Inst. Social and Econ. Rsch. U. of Ibadan, 1969-70; jr. rsch. fellow NISER, U. of Ibadan, 1973-74; asst. mgr. data processing Nat. Elec. Power Authority, Lagos, Nigeria, 1974-75; prin. sys. analyst computer Ctr. U. Lagos, 1975-78; programme specialist UNESCO, Paris, 1978-92; regional informatics adviser for Africa UNESCO, Nairobi, Kenya, 1992-95; mem. exec. com. UNESCO Staff Assn., Paris, 1980-85; mem. mgmt. bd. UNESCO Savs. and Loans Svc., Paris, 1985-86; mem. sr. pers. adv. bd. UNESCO, 1984-86, mem. appeal bd., 1990-92; bd. dirs. Caretaker Cmty. Bank, Ogbomoso, Nigeria. Mem. editl. bd. Info. Tech. for Devel., 1986-90; contbr. to book: Informatics and Industrial Development, 1982; author reports in field. Study fellow Can. Internat. Devel. Agy., 1970-73. Mem. IEEE, Am. Mgmt. Assn., Computer Assn. Nigeria. Baptist. Home: PO Box 471, Ogbomoso Nigeria

OWOR, RAPHAEL, histopathologist, educator; b. Tororo, Uganda, July 7, 1934; s. Tadeo and Magadalena (Athieno) Omiel; m. Mary Francis Nyakecho, Jan. 2, 1965; children: Maureen, Geraldine, Stella, Ancila, Andrew. MB BS, U. Makerere, Uganda, 1962, MD, 1970. Intern Ministry of Health, Uganda, 1962-63; registrar Glasgow Royal Infirmary, 1965-69; demonstrator Makerere U., 1963-64, lectr., 1964-65, reader, 1969-72, prof. histopathology, 1972—, head dept. pathology, 1972-81, dean med. sch., 1981-89; coord. health rsch. UNDP, Geneva, 1991-92; vice chair Coun. on Health Rsch. for Devel., Geneva, 1996—. Editor: The Child in the African Environment, 1975; contbr. more than 100 sci. articles to East African Med. Jour., Brit. Med. Jour. Internat. Jour. Cancer, Cancer, Tropical Geog. Medicine, others. Chmn. Health Policy Rev. Commn., Uganda, 1987. Recipient Benemerenti award Vatican City, 1961, cert. of merit for Honourable Contrn. to the Med. Profession Uganda Med. Assn., 1999; Carnegie Corp. N.Y. rsch. grantee, 1995-97. Fellow Royal Coll. Pathologists; mem. Uganda Joint Med. Store (chair 1995—), Uganda Nat. Med. Equipment, African Health Rsch. Network (chair 1995—). Roman Catholic. Avocation: gardening. Office: Makerere U Dept Pathology, Box 7072, Kampala Uganda

OWSLEY, MARK D., lawyer; b. Talladega, Ala., Dec. 10, 1959; s. Buford H. and Betty J. Owsley; m. Carol Ann Summers, June 17, 1989; children: Tammy, Michael, Shannon. BA in Polit. Sci. with spl. honors, Jacksonville State U., 1980; JD, U. Ala., 1984. Bar: Ala. Assoc. atty. Law Firm Ray F. Robbins, II, Talladega, 1984-86, atty., ptnr., 1986-97; atty., sr. ptnr. Law Offices Mark D. Owsley, Talladega, 1997—. Webmaster, tech. cons. alabamalawyers.com, author, editor, 1998-2000; webmaster, editor, author Kurios, 1999-2000. Spl. asst. atty. gen. State of Ala., Talladega; adminstr., moderator Polit. Issues Network Mailing List, 1997-2000. Hugo L. Black scholar U. Ala., 1981-84. Mem. Ala. State Bar Assn., Talledega County Bar Assn. Avocations: numismatics, politics, theology, internet web development. Home: 736 Jackson Trace Rd Talladega AL 35160-6128 Office: Law Offices Mark D Owsley 211 North St E Talladega AL 35160-2109

OWUAMA, CHUKWUNONYE OZIOMA, civil engineering educator, consultant; b. Umunkwo, Nigeria, Sept. 29, 1955; s. Igboejesi and Mabel Nwaorji (Okoronta) O.; m. Eunice Chinagorom Chibundu, Dec. 20, 1986; children: Henry Chukwunonye, Kingsley Chukwuemeka, Charles Chukwudi. BS in Geology, U. Ibadan, Nigeria, 1978; MS, U. London, 1981; PhD in Engring., U. Benin, Nigeria, 1994. Geotech. engr. Shawmont Engrs., Ltd., Lagos, Nigeria, 1982-83; materials engr. Samek, Ltd., Aba, Nigeria, 1983-84; rsch. fellow R/S Unitech, Portharcourt, Nigeria, 1985-92; sr. lectr. Fed. U. of Technology, Owerri, Nigeria, 1992—; prin. cons. Hybrid Tech., Owerri, 1991—, nat. cons. UNDP, Lagos, 1995-96; vis. cons. Niger Trigon, Ltd., PH, Nigeria, 1995-97, Delta Works, Warri, 1995-97, Geoscan Ltd., Port Harcourt, 1998—. Contbr. articles to profl. jours. Mem. 1.5 Percent Mineral Derivation Fund Com., Port Harcourt, 1985, 1-Percent Ecol. Fund Com., Port Harcourt, 1986, Environ. Protection Com., Owerri, 1995, UNDP Projects Profile Com., Owerri Imostate, 1996; mem. stakeholders bd. UNDP/FGN Projects, Owerri, 1999—. Mem. AAAS, Nigerian Soc. Engrs., N.Y. Acad. Scis. Mem. Anglican Ch. Avocations: reading, sightseeing, table tennis, war games, card playing. Office: Fed Univ of Tech, PMB 1526, Owerri Nigeria

OXENSTIERNA, MARIA TERESA DORADO ORTIZ (COUNTESS MARIA TERESA DORADO OXENSTIERNA), political-military advisor; b. Quezon City, Philippines, July 10, 1964; came to Guam, 1966.; d. Eduardo Agustin Ortiz and Inday Dorado; m. Count David Gabriel Christerson Oxenstierna, May 31, 1996. BA in Polit. Sci., UCLA, 1986; MA in Law and Diplomacy, Tufts U., Harvard U., 1989; diploma, U. Cambridge, 1997; PhD in War Studies, King's Coll., U. London, 1999. Staff asst. The White House, Washington, 1986-87, presidential historian, 1989; political-military analyst U.S. Dept State, 1989-92; foreign affairs specialist U.S. Dept Energy, 1992-95; rsch. assoc. Los Alamos Nat. Lab., 1995-99; dir. european strategy Raytheon Sys. Ltd., London, 1999; asst. lectr. King's Coll., U. London, 1996-97; vis. scholar U. Guam, 1995. Contbr. articles to profl. jours. Mem. Republicans Abroad. Lt. U.S. Navy Res., 1993. MacArthur fellow. Mem. Fed. Am. Scientists, Internat. Inst. Strategic Studies, Royal United Svcs. Inst., Women in Internat. Security, Harvard Club of London, Am. Women's Club, Am. Soc. London, Rotary Club of London. Republican. Roman Catholic. Avocations: history, antiques, scuba-diving, sailing.

OXHØJ, HENRIK, pediatric cardiologist, consultant; b. Copenhagen, Denmark, Mar. 17, 1941; s. Paul and Else Birgitte (Johannsen) O.; m. Ingrid Køng Hansen, May 3, 1970. MD, Aarhus U., Denmark, 1967; MS, Gothenburg U., Sweden, 1977. Cert. pediat. cardiologist. Various positions various hosps., Sweden, Denmark, 1967-86; cons. clin. physiology Odense (Denmark) U. Hosp., 1986-95, cons. Pediat. Cardiology Unit, 1995—; reader Odense U., 1978—, Gothenburg U., 1977—. Author, editor: Practical Use of Lung Function Tests, 1990; contbr. numerous rsch. articles to profl. pubs. Recipient Honor medal Swedish Red Cross, 1968. Mem. European Assn. Pediat. Cardiologists. Home: Kaersangervaenget 2, DK 5210 Odense NV, Denmark Office: Odense U Hosp, Pediat Cardiology Unit, DK 5000 Odense C, Denmark

OXLADE, ZENA ELSIE, retired nursing officer; b. London, Apr. 26, 1929; d. James and Beatrice May (Oliver) O. Sister Tutor diploma, U. London, 1956; Doctor (hon.), U. Surrey, Eng., 1993. RN. Sister tutor Nat. Health Svc., Ipswich, Suffolk, 1963-66; prin. tutor Nat. Health Svc., Bury St Edmunds, Suffolk, 1966-71; chief nursing officer Nat. Health Svc., West Suffolk, 1971-78; area nursing officer Nat. Health Svc., Suffolk, 1978-81; regional nursing officer Nat. Health Svc., East Anglia, 1981-87; ret., 1987; mem. Gen. Nursing Coun., Eng. and Wales, 1975-77, chmn., 1977-83; mem. U.K. Ctrl. Coun. for Nursing and Midwifery, 1983-89; chmn. Gen. Nursing Coun. Trus, Eng. and Wales, 1983—. Author: Ear, Nose and Throat Nursing, 1968. Decorted comdr. Brit. Empire. Mem. Ch. of Eng. Avocations: motoring, reading, handicrafts, travel. Home: 5 Morgan Ct, Claydon Ipswich, Suffolk IP6 0AN, England

OXLEY, JAMES GRIEVE, mathematics educator; b. Sale, Victoria, Australia, Feb. 4, 1953; s. William A. and Dilys C. (Grieve) O.; m. Judith Danute Surkevicius; children: Margaret Catherine, David Grieve (dec.). BSc, U. Tasmania, 1974; MSc, Australian Nat. U., 1975; PhD, U. Oxford, 1978. Lectr., rsch. fellow Australian Nat. U., 1978-82; asst. prof. La. State U., Baton Rouge, 1982-85, assoc. prof., 1985-90, prof., 1990-99, alumni prof., 1999—; vis. instr. U. N.C., Chapel Hill, 1978. Author: Matroid Theory, 1992.; mem. editorial bd. Combinatorics, Probability and Computing; reviewer Mathematical Reviews, Zentralblatt for Mathematik; contbr. chpts. to books, articles to profl. jours. Grantee NSF, 1985-87, 89-91, La. Edn. Quality Support Fund, 1987-94, Nat. Security Agy., 1994—, others; Fulbright postdoctoral fellow U. N.C., 1980; named Disting. Rsch. Master of Engring, Sci. and Tech., La. State U., 1999. Mem. Am. Math. Soc., London Math. Soc. Office: La State U Math Dept Baton Rouge LA 70803-0001

OXLEY, MARGARET CAROLYN STEWART, elementary education educator; b. Petaluma, Calif., Apr. 1, 1930; d. James Calhoun Stewart and Clara Thornton (Whiting) Bomboy; m. Joseph Hubbard Oxley, Aug. 25, 1951; children: Linda Margaret, Carolyn Blair Oxley Greiner, Joan Claire Oxley Willis, Joseph Stewart, James Harmon, Laura Marie Oxley Brechbill. Student, U. Calif., Berkeley, 1949-51; BS summa cum laude, Ohio State U., 1973, MA, 1984, postgrad., 1985, 88, 92. Cert. tchr., Ohio. 2d grade tchr. St. Paul Sch., Westerville, Ohio, 1973—; presenter in field. Mem. editl. bd. Reading Tchr., vol. 47-48, 1993-94, Jour. Children's Lit., 1996—; co-author: Reading and Writing, Where it All Begins, 1991, Teaching with Children's Books: Path to Literature-Based Instruction, 1995, Adventuring With Books, 2000. Active Akita Child Conservation League, Columbus, Ohio, 1968-70. Named Columbus Diocesan Tchr. of Yr., 1988; Phoebe A. Hearst scholar, 1951, Rose Sterheim Meml. scholar, 1951; recipient Mary Karrer award Ohio State U., 1994. Mem. Nat. Coun. Tchrs. English (Notable Children's Books in the Lang. Arts com. 1993-94, chair 1995-96, treas. Children's Literature Assembly bd. dirs. 1996-99, co-chair fall 2000 breakfast children's lit. assembly), Internat. Reading Assn. (Exemplary Svc. in Promotion of Literacy award 1991), Literacy Connection (pres.), Children's Lit. Assembly, Ohio Coun. Tchrs. English Lang. Arts (Outstanding Educator 1990), Phi Kappa Phi, Pi Lambda Theta (hon.). Democrat. Roman Catholic. Avocations: reading, writing, travel, gardening, working with children. Home: 298 Brevoort Rd Columbus OH 43214-3826

OXLEY, ROLAND ROSS, construction executive, food service executive; b. Tomahawk, Wis., May 9, 1939; s. Ross Phillip Oxley and Margrett Ledyard; m. Sarah Ann Grant, June 15, 1960 (div. Jan. 1966); children: Gordon, Kathy, Anna Marie; m. Anna Marie Lutt, July 3, 1985; 1 child, Brent. Owner mill Oxley Shake Co., Humptulips, Wash., 1970-74; baker, mgr. Albertson's Grocery, Boise, Idaho, 1975-85; owner Oxley Constrn., Mackay, Idaho, 1985—; pres. High Country Baking, Mackay, 1997—. Avocation: bowling. E-mail: HCBC@ATCNET.NET. Home: PO Box 266 Mackay ID 83251-0266

OXTOBY, RICHARD MARKHAM, psychology educator, consultant; b. Durban, Natal, South Africa, Mar. 18, 1939; s. Charles Francis and Kathleen (Lister) O.; m. Colleen Joy Nero, Apr. 17, 1976; children: Christopher Charles, Oliver Francis, Sven Richard. BS, U. Natal, Durban, South Africa, 1961; BS cum laude with honors, U. Natal, 1962; MS cum laude, U. Cape Town (South Africa), 1971, PhD, 1978. Dir. Internat. Arts League of Youth, Durban, South Africa, 1963-65, Musica Antiqua, Cape Town, South Africa, 1966—; lectr. dept. psychology U. Cape Town (South Africa), 1975-78, sr. lectr. dept. psychology, 1978-99; chmn. Cape Psycho-Social Oncology Trust, Cape Town, South Africa, 1989-96; cons. Richard Oxtoby Assocs., Cape Town, 1991—, sr. neuropsychologist Radcliffe Infirmary, Oxford, Eng., 1990-91; psychotherapist (hon.) Pollsmoor Prison, Cape Town, 1994-98. Author: Consumer marketing, 1973, Industrial Marketing, 1974, DCF for Capital Investment Analysis, 1975, Computers for Management, 1976, Parenting Without Pain, 1987, Loving: A Guide to Better Relationships Between Men and Women, 1989. Vice-chmn. bd. govs. Bergvliet Primary Sch., Cape Town, South Africa, 1996-97. Fellow Trinity Coll.; mem. Brain and Behavior Soc. (mem. com.), Soc. Abolition of Phys. Punishment in Schs. (mem. com.), Soc. for Promotion of Early Music (founder, dir. 1999—). Anglican. Mem. Soc. of Friends. Avocations: music, gardening, reading. Home: 17 Roderick Way, 7806 Constantia Cape, South Africa Office: U Cape Town, Rondesbosch, 7701 Cape Town South Africa

OYA, TAKIO, engineering educator; b. Musashino-shi, Japan, Aug. 5, 1924; s. Takijiro and Chiyo (Nishigai) O.; m. Eiko Nagoya, Apr. 8, 1956; children: Nobuyuki, Toshio. BE, Tokyo U., 1949, DE, 1971. Rschr. Printing Bur. of Fin. Office, Tokyo, 1949-56; chief Tokyo - Hatzudoki Inc., 1958-64; from instr. to dean engring. Meiji Univ., Kawasaki-shi, Japan, 1964-89; dean Sch. Sci. and Tech. Meiji Univ., Kawasaki-shi, 1989-90, prof. Sch. Sci. and Tech., 1990-95, prof. emeritus, 1995—. Editl. com. chief Bicycle Handbook, 1991. Chmn. com. Japan Bicycle Mfrs. Assn., Tokyo, 1993—; chmn. com. MITI of Japan, Tokyo, 1991—. Mem. Soc. Automobile Engrs. Internat., Soc. Automobile Engrs. Japan, Japan Soc. Mech. Engring. Home: 2-27-2 Kyonan-cho, Musashino Tokyo 180-0023, Japan

OYABU, TAKASHI, information science educator; b. Unazuki, Japan, Jan. 11, 1949; s. Ryozo and Jitsuko (Watanuki) O.; m. Masako Shimabukuro, Sept. 1, 1981; children: Hiroshi, Taijirou. B of Engring., Kogakuin U., 1971, M of Engring., 1973; B of Lit., Waseda U., 1975; D of Engring., Kogakuin U., 1984. Researcher Denki Onkyo Co., Tokyo, 1975-80; lectr. Kanazawa (Japan) Women's Coll., 1980-84, assoc. prof., 1984-88, prof., 1988-91; prof. Toyama (Japan) U. Internat. Studies, 1991-98, Kanazawa (Japan) U. Econs., 1998—. Contbr. articles to profl. jours. Avocations: tennis, skiing, stamp collecting. Home: 5-11-12 Suzumidai, Kanazawa 920-1161, Japan Office: Kanazawa U Econs, Gosho-machi, Kanazawa 920-8620, Japan

OYAMA, TSUTOMU, anesthesiologist; b. Kushiro, Japan, June 9, 1923; s. Masanobu Oyama and Yone Kohno; m. Kei Oyama, Nov. 5, 1959; children: Takayo, Hiroko. MD, Hokkaido U. Med. Sch., Sapporo, Japan, 1949; PhD, Hokkaido U. Med. Sch., 1957. Resident U. Oregon, Portland, 1955-57; rsch. fellow Harvard Med. Sch., Boston, 1958-59; assoc. prof. Anesthesiology Hokkaido U. Med. Sch., Sapporo, Japan, 1961-65; prof., chmn. dept. Kirosaki U. Med. Sch., Japan, 1965-89; visiting prof. U. Miami Med. Sch., 1973-74; prof. Dept. Anesthesiology Med. Coll. Wisc., 1974-75; adj. prof. U. Tex. Health Sci. Ctr., San Antonio, 1995—. Contbr. articles to profl. jours., presenter in field. Mem. Japanese Anesthesia Soc., Japanese Pain Clinic Soc., Japanese Pain Soc.

OYANAGI, MITSUMASA, medical educator; b. Himeji, Hyogo, Japan, Feb. 8, 1949; s. Genji and Aiko (Takayama) O; m. Sumiko Yahata, May 28, 1977; children: Shinya, Tatsuya, Noriko. MD, Kobe (Japan) U., 1975; PhD, Hyogo Coll. Medicine, Nishinomiya, Japan, 1988. Clin. fellow Hyogo Coll. Medicine, Nishinomiya, 1975-77, 1978-79, asst. prof., 1979-88, 1990—; clin. fellow Kanebo Hosp., Kobe, 1977-78; postdoctoral fellow U. N.C., Chapel Hill, 1988-90. Fellow Japanese Circulation Soc., Japan Soc. Ultrasonics in Medicine; mem. Am. Heart Assn., N.Y. Acad. Scis. Office: Hyogo Coll Medicine, Hyogo Coll Medicine, 1-1 Mukogawa-cho, Nishinomiya 663-8501, Japan

OYARZABAL, ANTONIO, diplomat; b. Stockholm, Oct. 12, 1935; m. Beatriz Lodge; children: Matilde, Marta, Juan, Gloria, Iñigo, Borja. Grad., Complutense U., Madrid, 1957; postgrad., Spanish Diplomatic Sch., 1959-61. Staff mem. Exec. Office Ministry Fgn. Affairs, 1967-70, Embassy of Spain, U.K., 1970-74; counselor Exec. Office Prime Min., Madrid, 1974-76; gov. Santa Cruz de Tenerife, 1976-77, Guipúzcoa, 1977-79; asst. sec. State for Pub. Info., 1979-81; amb. to Ecuador, 1981-83; sec. Joint Spanish-Am. Com. for Sci. and Technol. Cooperation, Madrid, 1983-86; dir. bilateral sci. cooperation Min. Fgn. Affairs, Madrid, 1983-86; asst. sec. State for Internat. Cooperation, 1986-90; amb. to Japan, 1990-94, amb. to Denmark, 1994-95, amb. to Rep. Lithuania, 1995-96; amb. to U.S. Washington, 1996—. Recipient numerous Spanish and fgn. honors and awards. Fax: 202-833-5670. Office: Embassy of Spain 2375 Pennsylvania Ave NW Washington DC 20037-1736

OYEH, HENRY KWASHIE, bank officer; b. Lolobi-Kumasi, Volta, Ghana, Mar. 16, 1951; s. Casmiel Komla and Paulina Afua (Addae) O.; m. Vicentia Adzo Oware, 1976 (div. 1983); children: Bernice Adzovi, Edwin Yaw; m. Ellen Honoria Onai, Mar. 30, 1986; children: Felix Kwaku, Florence Portia Afi. BA in Econs. with Stats., U. Ghana, Accra, 1984, postgrad., 1989; postgrad., Inst. Manpower Planning, Sussex, Eng., 1992. Head tchr. Ghana Edn. Svc., Madina, 1978-79; asst. mgmt. analyst mgmt. svcs. div. Ghana Civil Svc., Accra, 1984-85; rsch. officer rsch. div. Ghana Comml. Bank, Accra, 1985-87; supervisory officer br. banking Ghana Comml. Bank, Wa, 1987-89; schedule officer for manpower planning and tng. Ghana Comml. Bank, Accra, 1989-99, corp. rels. officer Accra Area Office, 1999—. Sec. edn. com. Roman Cath. Ch., Madina, 1977-79; organizer, adviser Coop. Farmers Assn., Lolobi, Ghana, 1983-86; chmn. Lolobo-Kumasi Devel. Assn., Accra, 1991-98. Mem. Nat. Patriotic Party. Avocations: small scale farming, lawn tennis, classical music, chess, reading. Home: SSNIT Flats, Block 9, B2, Adenta, Accra Ghana Office: Ghana Comml Bank, Ghana Comml Bank, Area Office PO Box K 96, Accra, New Town Ghana

OYEKANMI, RAFFIU ADEKUNLE, maintenance engineer, consultant; b. Iressi, Osun, Nigeria, Feb. 17, 1966; s. Lasisi Olabode Oyekanmi and Safurat Arinpe Gbolade; m. Medinat Bolanle Alako, Oct. 2, 1999. B in Engring., U. Ilorin, Nigeria, 1992. Cert. engr. Site asst. Gan-Rovet, Ilorin, 1984-87; trainee engr. Accolade Engr., Port Harcourt, Nigeria, 1993-94; field engr. Adeyanju and Stadus, Nigeria, 1994; maintenance engr. Isrma Ltd., Port Harcourt, 1995, Topsam Ltd., Port Harcourt, 1995—; cons. Well Engring., Port Harcourt, 1996—; exec. dir. Develop. Alternative Incorporations, Port Harcourt, 1996—. Inventor in electronics infrared ray security system, design and constrn. of phase failure relay. Mem. IEEE, Nat. Geog. Soc. Islamic. Avocations: reading, traveling, music, photography, swimming. Home: 278 Aba Rd, Port Harcourt Rivers, Nigeria Office: Adeyanju & Stadius Ltd, L/96 Ilepa St PO Box 451, Ikare Ondo, Nigeria

OYÉ-MBA, CASIMIR, Gabonese government official, banker; b. Libreville, Gabon, Apr. 20, 1942; s. Ange Mba and Marie-Jeanne Nse; married; 6 children. Ed., College Bessieux, Libreville, 1954-61; student, Faculté de Droit etdes Sciences Economiques, Rennes, France, 1961-65, Faculté de Droit etdes Sciences Economiques, Paris, 1965-67, Centre D'Etudes Financieres et Bancaires, Paris, 1967-68. Dep. dir. Banque des Etats de Afrique Centrale, Libreville, 1969-70, dir., 1970-76; dep. mng. dir. Banque des Etats de Afrique Centrale, Yaounde, Cameroon, 1977-78, gov., 1978-90; prime min., head of govt. Govt. of Gabon, Libreville, 1990-94, min. fgn. affairs, 1994, now min. planning and devel. Mem. Lions. Roman Catholic. Office: Min Planning Environ and, Tourism, BP 165, Libreville Gabon*

OYENUGA, VICTOR ADENUGA, agricultural scientist, educator; b. Isonyin, Nigeria, Apr. 9, 1917; s. Thomas and Matilda Afikorisa O.; m. Sabinah Babafunmike Onabajo, Apr. 11, 1950 (dec. Nov. 1996); children: Victor Adetokunbo, Victoria Olusimbo Abubakar, Olusomidotun Adetilewa, Adeyinka Badejoko, Olabisi Adebimpe Shi-Shi Gyer. BSc, Durham U. King's Coll., Eng., 1948, PhD, 1951; DSc, U. Newcastle Upon Tyne, Eng., 1978, U. Ife, Ile-Ife, Nigeria, 1977, Ogun State U., 1996; DAgr honoris causa, U. Agr., Abestruta, Nigera. Chartered chemist, London. Tchr. Anglican Ch. Mission, Ijebu, 1935-42; clerical work Nigerian Colonical Gov., Lagos, 1942-45; lectr. in animal nutrition U. Ibadan, Nigeria, 1951-58, sr. lectr. in animal nutrition, 1958-61, head sub dept. agrl. chemistry, 1960-61; prof. agr., head dept. U. Ife, 1961-64; prof., head dept. U. Ibadan, 1964-66, prof., head dept. animal sci., 1966-77, dean faculty agr., forestry and vet. sci., 1966-69, dep. vice chancellor, 1972-74, 74-76, prof. animal prodn. and nutrition biochemistry, 1977-79; chmn., mng. dir. Vabo Agrl. Industries Ltd.; master hall I U. Ife, 1962-64, chmn. com. of deans, 1962-64, master sultan bello hall U. Ibadan, 1966-71, chmn. com. deans, 1968-69; chmn. bd. nutrition U. Ibadan, 1970-76, chmn. senate com., 1971-72, chmn., bd. dirs. U. BKSHP Ltd., U. Ibadan, 1971-76, chmn. bd. post grad. studies, 1972-76, chmn. libr. com., 1972-76, chmn. bd. dels. Inst. of Edn., 1972-76, chmn. profl. com. Inst. of Edn., 1972-76, mem. gov. coun., U. Ibadan, 1969-76, mem. provisional coun., 1963-64, U. Ife. Author: Agriculture in Nigeria, 1967, Herbage, Flesh and the Quality of HUman Existence, 1976, Nigeria's Foods and Feeding Stuffs: Their Chemistry and Nutritional Value, 1966, 2nd edit., 1959, 3rd edit., 1968, Our Needs and Resources in Food and Agriculture, 1960, Choose You This Day Whom You Will Serve, 1995; editor: Animal Production in the Tropics, 1974; contbr. some 210 articles to profl. jours. Chmn. Nigerian Coun. for Sci. and Tech., 1970-74, Commn. of Enquiry into The Affairs of Western Nigeria Devel. Corp., 1967-68, Agricultural Schemes Com. Western Nigeria Devel. Com., 1955-57; dir. Nigeria Western Nigeria Devel. Corp., 1957-62; mem. Nat. Exec. Coun. Action Group Nigeria, 1954-66; mem. exec. coun. Internat. Grassland Congress, 1977-87; trustee CIAT, Cali, Colombia, 1974-77; exec. mem. Ibadan C. of C. and Industries, 1989-91, chmn. agrl. and allied trade group, 1989-92; mem. exec. coun. Internat. Union Nutritional Scis., 1966-72, exec. commn. World Assn. Animal Prodn., 1974-87. Recipient Gold Merit award Animal Sci. Assn., 1997, African Nutritive award, 1979, Disting. Pioneer award U. Ibadan Dept. Animal Sci., 1998. Fellow Nigerian Soc. Animal Prodn. (1st pres. 1974-75), Nigerian Acad. Sci. (1st pres. 1977-79), Royal Soc. Chemistry (London), Royal Inst. Chemistry (London); mem. Agrl. Soc. Nigeria (1st pres. 1963-64), Sci. Assn. Nigeria (trustee), Agrl. Soc. Nigeria (trustee), Assn. for Advancement of Agrl. Scis. in Africa (pres. 1968-75), West African Sci. Assn. (pres. 1968-71). Home: 34 Awolowo Ave Bodija, Ibadan Nigeria Office: Univ Ibadan, Dept Animal Sci, Ibadan Nigeria

OYLER, AMY ELIZABETH, medical/surgical nurse; b. Roanoke, Va., Aug. 20, 1971; d. James Thomas and Vivian Yvonne (Mills) O. AS, Va. Western C.C., 1991; BSNB, Radford U., 1993. RN, Va.; cert. med. surg. nurse. Nursing asst. Roanoke Meml. Hosp., 1989-93, med.-surg. nurse in diabetic care and renal transplants, 1993—. Avocations: reading, aerobics, family. Home: 950 John Arthur Rd Boones Mill VA 24065-4072

ÖYMEN, ONUR, diplomat from Turkey, NATO official; b. Istanbul, 1940; married; 2 children. Grad., Faculty of Polit. Scis., Ankara, 1963, PhD on Def. Policies, 1970. Joined Ministry of Fgn. Affairs, Turkey, 1964; 2d sec. NATO Dept., 1966-68; 1st sec. Permanent Delegation to Coun. of Europe, Strasbourg, 1968-72; chief of section, Policy Planning Dept. Ministry of Fgn. Affairs, 1972-74; counsellor Embassy of Turkey, Nicosia, 1974-78; spl. adviser to Ministry of Fgn. Affairs, 1978-80; counsellor Embassy of Turkey, Prague, 1980-82, Madrid, 1982-84; head of Policy Planning Dept. Ministry of Fgn. Affairs, 1984-88; amb. Embassy of Turkey, Copenhagen, 1988-90, Bonn, 1990-95; under-sec. Ministry of Fgn. Affairs, 1995-97; permanent rep. of Turkey NATO, Brussels, 1997—. With Turkish Armed Forces, 1964-66. Mem. Internat. Inst. for Strategic Studies. Office: NATO Hdqrs, Blvd Leopold III, 1110 Brussels Belgium*

OYONO, FERDINAND LÉOPOLD, Cameroonian government official; b. Sept. 14, 1929. Grad., Faculty of Law and Econ. Sci., Paris. Former amb. to Liberia Govt. of Cameroon, 1963-65, amb. to Belgium (also accredited to Luxembourg and The Netherlands), 1965-68, amb. to France (also accredited to Italy, Morocco, Algeria, Tunisia), 1969-74; permanent rep. to UN Govt. of Cameroon, N.Y.C., 1974-82; amb. to U.K. Govt. of Cameroon, London, 1984-85; sec. gen. at the Presidency Govt. of Cameroon, 1985-87, min. in charge of town planning and housing, 1987-90; min. external rels. Govt. of Cameroon, Yaoundé, Cameroon, 1992-97, sr. min. of culture, 1997—; chair UNICEF Ctrl. Com., 1977-78; vice chmn. conf. human rights Vienna, Austria, 1993; chmn. OAU Coun. Mins., 1996. Author: Une vie de boy, 1956, Le vieux nègre et la médaille, 1967, Le pandemonium, Chemin d'Europe. Decorated comdr. Legion of Honor, others. Office: Ministry of Culture, BP 1588, Yaoundé Cameroon*

OYONO NDONG, MIGUEL, Equatorial-Guinean government official. Min. of state for fgn. affairs and coop. Rep. Equatorial Guinea, 1994—, first dep. prime min. Office: Office of Prime Minister, Ministry Fgn Affairs and Cooperation, Malabo Equatorial Guinea*

OYOSHI, KEIJI, scientist; b. Tokyo, June 6, 1961; m. Shoko Kato, Sept. 13, 1992; 1 child, Ryo. Bachelor, Chiba Inst. Tech., Japan, 1983; Master, U. Tsukuba, Japan, 1985, PhD, 1992. Cert. material scientist. Rschr. Nippon Sheet Glass Co., Ltd., Tsukuba, 1985-93, NSG Techno-Rsch. Co., Ltd., Tsukuba, 1993-94; sr. rschr. Nat. Inst. for Rsch. in Inorganic Materials, Tsukuba, 1995—. Contbr. articles to profl. jours. Sec. Coun. of Mountain Garbage, Chiba Pref., Narashino, Japan, 1981-84. Mem. Japan Soc. Applied Physics. E-mail: oyoshi@nirim.go.jp. Fax: 81-298-52-7449. Home: Ninomiya 1-25-13, Tsukuba, Ibaraki Japan 3050051 Office: Nat Inst Rsch Inorganic Mat, Namiki 1-1 Tsukuba, Ibaraki Japan 3050044

OZ, AMOS, author; b. Jerusalem, 1939; m. Nily Zuckerman; children: Fania, Gallia, Daniel. BA, Hebrew U., Jerusalem; MA, Oxford U., 1970; D (hon.), Hebrew Union Coll., Western New Eng. Coll., Tel Aviv U. Mem. Kibbutz Hulda, Israel, 1957-86; full prof., Agnon chmn. Hebrew Lit. Ben-Gurion U. Negev, Beer-Sheva, Israel, 1986—; author-in-residence Hebrew U., Jerusalem, 1975, 90, Boston U., 1987, U. Calif., Berkeley, 1980, Colo. Springs Coll. Am., 1984-85; vis. fellow Oxford U., 1969-70; vis. writer N.Y. State Writers Inst., 1997. Author: (collection) Where the Jackals Howl, 1965, Elsewhere Perhaps, 1966, adapted for stage1982, My Michael, 1968, film version, 1975, Unto Death, 1971, Touch the Water, Touch the Wind, 1973, The Hill of Evil Counsel, 1976 (Brenner prize Lit. 1977), (children's book) Soumchi, 1978, (collection) Under This Blazing Light, 1979, The Slopes of Lebanon, 1981, A Perfect Peace, 1982, In the Land of Israel, 1983, Black Box, 1987 (Prix Femina Etranger 1988), To Know a Woman, 1989, The Third Condition (Fima), 1991, The Silence of Heaven, 1993, Don't Call It Night, 1994, Israel, Palestine & Peace, 1994, Panther in the Basement, 1995, The Story Begins, 1996, short stories; editor: The Seventh Day, (anthology) Stories from the Kibbutz; contbr. 450 articles and essays to profl. jours. and newspapers. Active various groups Israeli Peace Movement, 1967—, Peace Now, 1977—. Served with Israeli Army. Recipient Holon prize for Lit., 1966, B'nai Brith Ann. Lit. award, 1972, Bialik prize, 1986, Wingate prize, 1988, German Friedenspreis Internat. Peace prize, 1992, French Cross of Knight of Légion d'Honneur, Pres. Jacques Chirac, 1997; Am. Israel Cultural Found. fellow. Mem. I.T.I., Internat. PEN Assn., Acad. Hebrew Lang. Office: Ben Gurion U Negev, Beer Sheva Israel*

OZ, YILMAZ, lawyer; b. Ankara, Turkey, Apr. 10, 1930; s. Hilmi and Zuhtiye (Muslim) O.; m. Nihal Ipek, Nov. 29, 1951; children: F. Simin, Y. Sinan, Selmin. LLB, U. Ankara, 1951; LLM, Yale U., 1952. Bar: Turkey 1956. Atty.-at-law Ankara, 1956—; panelist Ctr. European Legal Studies, U. Cambridge, Eng., 1994. Co-editor: (chpt.) Comparative Report on Force Majeure in Western Europe (Turkey), 1982; translator: Quotations from Ataturk, 1981; reviser (law directory) Martindale-Hubbell Law Directory, 1986—; contbr. articles to profl. jours. Recipient Ataturk's Centennial award State Min., Ankara, 1982. Mem. Ankara Bar Assn., World Jurist Assn., Yale Law Sch. Alumni Assn., Turkish-Am. Assn. (pres. 1965-74), Rotary (Ankara club pres. 1966-67, internat. svc. consultative com. 1967). Avocations: historical research, tennis, skiing.

OZAIR, SYED MOHAMMAD, business educator; b. Darbhanga, Bihar, India, Aug. 25, 1950; s. Mir Mohammad Ayyub and Bibi Zeenat Kubra; m. Shaheda Khatoon, Dec. 31, 1970; children: Ghazala Roomi, Ahsan Jamal Ayyubi, Mohsin Jamal Ayyubi, Naushaba Nazneen. BA, Patna (India) U., 1968; MBA, Aligarh (India) Muslim U., 1974, PhD in Bus. Adminstrn., 1988; FDPM, IIMA, Ahmedabad, India, 1985. Lectr. Aligarh Muslim U., 1977-84, reader, 1984-88, prof., 1988—, chmn. dept. bus. adminstrn., 1988-91, 93-96, dean faculty commerce, 1993-95, dean students welfare, 1995-98, dean FMS&R), 1996-98. Patron Anjuman Farooqia Chandan Patti Darbhanga, 1964-71. Lance cpl. N.C.C., 1965-67. Merit scholar Bihar Madrasa Exams. Bd., Patna, 1961-67; jr. fellow U. Grant Commn., New Delhi, 1975-77. Mem. Aligarh Mgmt. Alumni Assn., Aligarh Muslim U. Staff Assn., Alumni Assn. I.I.M.A. Avocations: listening and singing Ghazals and Hamd and Naat. Office: Dept Bus Adminstrn, Aligarh Muslim Univ, Aligarh 202002, India

OZAKI, GEORGE TADASHI, patent agent; b. Seattle, July 4, 1928; s. Saiichi Frank and Komatsu (Shima) O.; m. Shizue Cee, March 26, 1955; children: Glenn Masao, Susan Mari. AA, Wright Jr. Coll., 1952; BS in Chemical Engring., Ill. Inst. Tech., 1963; LLB, U. Balt., 1967. Engr. in tng. State of Ill., Chgo., 1962-63; patent examiner U.S. Patents & Trademark Office, Washington, 1963-88; registered patent agent Litman Law Offices, Ltd., Arlington, Va., 1993—. Cpl. U.S. Army, 1952-53. Mem. Japanese Am. Citizens League. Republican. Presbyn. Avocation: photography. Fax: (703) 486-7000. E-mail: litman@4patent.com. Home: 4905 Bangor Dr Kensington MD 20895-1213

OZAKI, JUMBO, professional golfer; b. Tokushima, Japan, May 18, 1956. Profl. golfer, 1973—. Named Rookie of the Yr., 1973; winner 5 times PGA tour. Office: c/o PGA Tour PO Box 109601 100 Ave of the Champions Palm Beach Gardens FL 33410-9601

OZAKI, NANCY JUNKO, performance artist, educator; b. Denver, Feb. 14, 1951; d. Joe Motoichi and Tamiye (Saki) O.; m. Gary Steven Tsujimoto, Nov. 12, 1989. BS in Edn., U. Colo., 1973; postgrad., U. Colo., Denver, 1977, Metro State Coll., 1982, Red Rocks C.C., 1982-83, U. No. Colo., 1982, U. N.Mex., 1985, U. No. Colo., 1988. Elem. tchr. Bur. Indian Affairs, Bloomfield, N.Mex., 1973-75, Aurora (Colo.) Pub. Schs., 1977-83, Albuquerque Pub. Schs., 1983-84, Denver Pub. Schs., 1984-87, Oak Grove Sch. Dist., San Jose, Calif., 1988-89, San Mateo (Calif.) City Elem. Dist., 1990-92; performing artist Japanese drums Young Audiences, San Francisco, 1992-93, Denver, 1994-97; performing artist Japanese drums Walt Disney World, Epcot Ctr., Orlando, Fla., 1993-97; co-dir., mgr., performer One World Taiko, Japanese Drum Troupe, Denver, 1997—. Vol. worker with young Navajo children; co-sponsor girl's sewing and camping groups. Mem. Kappa Delta Pi (Theta chpt.). Avocations: reading, sewing, skiing, hiking, snorkeling. Home: 6713 W 53rd Ave Arvada CO 80002-3937 Office: One World Taiko PO Box 12252 Denver CO 80212-0252

OZAKI, TORU, physicist, educator; b. Fukuyama, Japan, Sept. 9, 1950; m. Naoko Kanako. BS, Hiroshima U., Higashi-Hiroshima, Japan, 1973, MS, 1975, DSc, 1980. Rsch. scientist Hiroshima U., 1980-85, rsch. assoc., 1985-99; assoc. prof. physicis Hiroshima Inst. of Tech., 1999—. Contbr. articles to profl. jours. Mem. Phys. Soc. of Japan, Crystallographic Soc. of Japan. Avocations: playing music, swimming. Office: Hiroshima Inst Tech, 2-1-1 Miyake Saeki-ku, Hiroshima 731-5193, Japan

OZAKI, YUKIO, artist, educator; b. Tokyo, Jan. 3, 1948; came to U.S., 1971; s. Shigeo and Shoko Ozaki; m. Elizabeth Davis Train, Oct. 4, 1986; children: Reef, Clay. BA, Gakushuin U., Tokyo, 1971; MFA, U. Hawaii, 1977. Asst. prof. art Chaminade U. Honolulu, 1986-91, assoc. prof., 1991-97, prof., 1997—. Murals executed in wood carvings and ceramics State of Hawaii, Honolulu, 1978-99. Recipient 13 purchase awards for state bldgs. Hawaii Found. on Culture and Arts, 1973-98, hon. mention Internat. Ceramics Festival, Mino, Japan, 1986, Living Treasure award Houpa Honganji Mission, HOnolulu, 1994; named Prof. of Yr., Carnegie Found., 1998. Avocation: free diving. E-mail: ozakitrain@compuserve.com. Home: 3720 Mariposa Dr Honolulu HI 96816-3914 Office: Chaninade U Honolulu 3140 Waialae Ave Honolulu HI 96816-1510

OZAWA, AKIRA, nuclear scientist, physicist; b. Shizuoka-shi, Japan, Oct. 22, 1963; s. Masaji and Kikue (Kuboyama) O.; m. Waki Chiba, June 19, 1993. Bachelor, Osaka (Japan) U., 1985, Master, 1987, PhD, 1992. Spl. posdoc. rschr. Inst. Physical Chem. Rsch., Wako, Japan, 1992-94; rschr. Inst. Physical Chem. Rsch., Wako, 1994—. Contbr. articles to profl. jours. Avocations: hiking, volleyball, reading. Home: Hirosawa 2 2 507, Wako Shi 351-0106, Japan Office: Inst Phys Chem Rsch RIKEN, Hirosawa 2 1, Saitama Wako Shi 351-0198, Japan

OZAWA, HIKARU, retired science educator, editor; b. Gifu, Japan, Oct. 10, 1914; s. Moriichi and Kishi (Kawamura) O.; m. Eiko Hashiguchi, Nov. 10, 1945; children: Kazufumi, Terutaka. B of Pharmacy, Tokyo U., 1939, PhD in Pharmacology, 1951; MD, Tokyo Med. Coll., 1957. Med. diplomate; lic. physician, pharmacist, pharmacologist. Rsch. scientist Tanabe Pharm. Co., Tokyo, 1948-53; prof. Nihon U., Tokyo, 1957-60; prof. Tohoku U., Sendai, Japan, 1960-78, hon. prof., 1978—; v.p. Toyama (Japan) Med. and Pharm. U., 1979-82. Chief editor Oyo Yakuri, 1942—. Mem. Japan Pharm. Soc. (pres. 1977-78, Acad. prize for pharm. sci.). Home: 4-15-406 Katahira-1-chome, Aoba-ku Sendai 980-0812, Japan Office: Oyo Yakuri Kenkyukai, 11-12-609 Ichibancho-2-chome, Aoba-ku Sendai 980-0811, Japan

OZAWA, KATSUMI, Japanese literature educator, researcher; b. Itabashi-ku, Tokyo, Japan, Aug. 23, 1933; s. Yoshikazu and Asao (Sasaguchi) O.; m. Sadako Ishikawa, Oct. 30, 1961; children: Chizuko, Misako. BEd, Tokyo Gakugei Univ., 1959. Tchr. Sr. H.S. Attached to Kogakuin Coll., Shinjuku-ku Tokyo, Japan, 1959-76; lectr. Wako Coll., Machida Tokyo, Japan, 1975-76; lectr. Hosei Univ., Chiyoda-ku, Japan, 1976-78, asst. prof., 1978-83, prof., 1983—. Author: Tokoku and Kunisaburo Akiyama, 1974, Literature-Esp. Tokoku and Soseki, 1979, Tokoku Kitamura-Original Figure and Stream, 1982, Tokoku and Soseki-Literature of Liberty and Civil Rights, 1991, Studies on "My Three-Day Paradise" by Tokoku Kitamura - Literary Visions of Hope for Kawaguchi Village in Hachioji and its People, 1997. Councilor Hachioji Kuruma Ningyo Supporters' Assn., Hachioji, 1985—. Mem. Japanese Lit. Assn. (com. 1968-91, 94-98, steering com. 1976-85, mgr. 1977-79, inspector 1989-90), Japanese Social Lit. (councilor 1985-91, steering com. 1989-90, com. 1998—), Soc. for Study of the History, Culture and Natural Environment in Tama Area (steering com. 1997), Soc. for Study of Tokoku Kitamura (com. 1999—). Home: 353-60 Kamiichibukata-machi, Hachioji Tokyo 1930811, Japan Office: Hosei Univ, 4342 Aihara, Machida 194, Japan

OZAWA, KYOSUKE SAMUEL, retired medical company executive; b. Yokohama, Kanagawa, Japan, Dec. 25, 1932; s. Tsuneo and Asa (Ueda) O.; m. Yoko T. Osako, June 1, 1963; 1 child, Hideo. BS, Osaka (Japan) Liberal Arts U., 1957; PhD, D in Med. Sci., Toho U., 1972. Rsch. scientist Meguro Inst., Ikeda, Japan, 1957-62, sr. rschr., 1962-72; rsch. fellow Inst. for Virus Rsch. Kyoto (Japan) U., 1965-72; rsch. dir. Meguro Inst., 1972-84, exec. dir., 1984-90, mng. dir., 1990-96, rsch. exec., 1996-98. Patentee in field. Mem. The Japanese Assn. for Infectious Diseases (Disting. Achievement award 1973), Japanese Soc. for Bacteriology. Mem. Orthodox Ch. of Osaka. Home: 5-3-25 Seiwadai-higashi, Kawanishi-shi Hyogo-ken 666-0142, Japan Office: Meguro Inst 5-3-25 Seiwadai-higashi, Kawanishi-shi, Hyogo-ken 666-0142, Japan

OZAWA, MASAKI, nuclear chemical engineering scientist; b. Kōfu, Japan, Sept. 1, 1950; s. Masao and Kazuko (Matsuo) O.; m. Yoshie Kaneko, Feb. 5, 1977. B of Engring., Yamanashi U., 1973, M of Engring., 1975; D of Engring., U. Tokyo, 1993. With Power Reactor and Nuc. Fuel Devel. Corp., Tokyo, 1975; engr. Tokai Reprocessing Plant, Power Reactor/Nuc. Fuel Devel. Corp. (P.N.C.), Tokai-mura, Japan, 76-84, mgr., 84, assoc. chief engr., 1984-91, sr. staff reprocessing tech. devel. divsn., 1991-96, sr. engr. reprocessing tech. devel. divsn., 1996-98; sr. scientist FBR cycle system planning sect. Japan Nuclear Cycle Devel. Inst., 1998—; rschr. Kernforschungszentrum, Karlsruhe, Germany, 1981-82; com. mem. Japanese Sci. and Tech. Agy., Tokyo, 1988-90, Japan Atomic Energy Rsch. Inst., Tokyo, 1989-95, Inst. Rsch. and Innovation, Tokyo, 1991—; reviewer Jour. Nuc. Sci. Tech., 1993—; mem., sr. session chair internat. tech. program com. Global '97, '99 (Internat. Conf. on Future Nuclear Systems). Contbr. articles to sci. jours.; inventor in field separation chemistry for nuc. fuel reprocessing. Mem. AAAS, Electrochem. Soc. Japan, Atomic Energy Soc. Japan, Japan Nuc. Fuel Ltd. (com. mem. 1995—), Planetary Soc. Avocations: outdoor sports. Fax: 81-29-267-7518. E-mail: ozawam@hq.jnc.go.jp. Home: E-101 Minowa-danchi, 1230-2 Terunuma, Ibaraki-ken Japan Office: Japan Nuc Cycle Devel Inst, Ooarai Marita-machi 4002, Ibaraki-ken Post 311-1393, Japan

OZAWA, TAKAYUKI, biomedical chemistry educator, physician; b. Shimada, Shizuoka, Japan, Dec. 21, 1932; s. Minoru and Kaoru (Kambara) O.; m. Izumi Norimatsu, June 8, 1980; children: Chizuko, Naoyuki. MD, U. Nagoya (Japan), 1957, DMS, 1962. Asst. prof. biomed. chemistry U. Nagoya, 1962-67, assoc. prof., 1767-76, prof., 1976-96, dir. dept., 1976-96, prof. emeritus, 1996—; rsch. assoc. Enzyme Inst., U. Wis., Madison, 1965-67. Co-author: Mitochondoria, 1971, Transport and Bioenergetics, 1982, Bioenergetics, 1990; editor: New Horizons in Biological Chemistry, 1980, Heart and Vessel, 1989, Biochemistry International, 1990; hon. editor Internat. Jour. Biochemistry, 1980. Japanese Ministry Edn., Sci. and Culture grantee, 1987—. Fellow Am. Coll. Angiology; mem. Japanese Biochem. Soc. (coun. 1978-80, 83-85, 88—), Japanese Sci. Coun. (com. 1984—), Am. Thoracic Soc., Internat. Heart Rsch. Assn. (pres. 1985—), N.Y. Acad. Scis. Avocation: art. Home: 2492, Shimada City 427-0044, Japan Office: U Nagoya, 65 Tsuruma-cho Showa-ku, Nagoya 466, Japan

OZBOLT, SIMONE TRACY, investment company executive; b. London, Aug. 1, 1962; d. Hans and Rosemary Josephine (Ozbolt) Berndt; m. Roger Edwin Careless (div. 1998); children: Iain Stewart, Jessica Josephine, Megan Rosmairi; m.Ian Fullerton Nicol, 1998. BBA, U. South Africa, Johannesburg, 1986. Cert. CMEA. Dir. Egrin Co., Johannesburg, 1986—, Egret Investments, Johannesburg, 1989—; mem. Megonic Trading, Johannesburg, 1993—; with Forin Investments, 1998—. Mem. Credit Mgmt. Edn. Assn. (cert.). Roman Catholic. Avocations: philately, numismatics, Internet, reading, writing, business. Office: Forin Global, POB 1343 Rosettenville, 2130 Johannesburg South Africa

OZBUN, MICHELLE ADAIR, science educator; b. Craig, Colo., Feb. 16, 1965; s. Jerald Allen and Janet Adair O.; m. Latisha Kay Frederick. AS, Mesa Coll., 1985; BS, Colo. State U., 1987; PhD, Baylor Coll. Medicine, 1994. Asst. prof. U. New Mexico Sch. Med., Albuquerque, 1988—. Democrat. Avocations: guitar, golf, running. Fax: 505-272-6029. E-mail: mozbun@salud.unm.edu. Office: U New Mexico 915 Camino De Salud NE Albuquerque NM 87131-0001

OZDAMAR, SUKRU, pathology educator; b. Istanbul, Turkey, Aug. 14, 1959; s. Mehmet Emin and Sermin (Ugur) O. MD, Anadolu U., Eskisehir, Turkey, 1984. Intern Hosp. of Anadolu U. Med. Sch., Eskisehir, Turkey, 1983-84; resident in pathology Ministry of Health Ankara Hosp., Turkey, 1986-90; specialist Military Service, Istanbul, 1990-92, Aksaray Hosp., Turkey, 1992-93; specialist dept. pathology Ondokuz Mayis U., Samsun, Turkey, 1993-94, asst. prof. dept. pathology, 1994-97; specialist dept. pathology Hacettepe U., Ankara, Turkey, 1997-98, assoc. prof., 1998. Recipient 1st place award (poster competition) Nat. Congress of Cancer (Turkey), 1995, 96. Mem. Soc. of Protection of Wild Life, Planetary Soc., European Soc. of Pathology, Turkish Soc. of Pathology, Ankara Soc. of Pathology. Avocations: archaeology, astronomy, photography, classical guitar, table tennis (nat. champion). E-mail: sozdamar@hacettepe.edu.tr. Home: 7 Sokak No 21-3, 06500 Ankara Turkey Office: Hacettepe Univ, Sch Medicine Dept Pathology, 06100 Ankara Turkey

ÖZDEMIR, ENVER, urologic surgeon, researcher; b. Palu, Turkey, Jan. 25, 1966; s. Resul and Hatun Özdemir; m. Dudu Erdem, 1989; 1 child, Muhammed Emin. MD, Ankara (Turkey) U., 1988; PhD, Kyoto U., 1997. Asst. prof. urology Dicle (Turkey) U., 1994—. Mem. Am. Urol. Assn. Islam. Home and Office: Dept Urology, Dicle U, Diyarbakr Turkey

OZDEMIR, YILDIZ EMINE, ophthalmologist; b. Elazig, Turkey, Feb. 7, 1957; d. Orman Selim and Zumal (Ersoy) O.; m. Ismet Inan, June 29, 1987 (div. Dec. 1995); 1 child, Beril Inan. MD, Ankara (Turkey) U., 1980. Ophthalmologist Ankara Hosp., 1985-90; ophthalmologist, asst. chief Eye Clinic I Ankara Numune Hosp., 1990—. Mem. Turkish Ophthalmology Assn. (del. 1991—). Muslim. Avocations: reading, swimming. Home: Sanoak Mah. 233. Sok. 6/12, 06550 Ankara Turkey Office: Ankara Numune Hosp, Eye Clinic I, 06550 Ankara Turkey

OZDILEK, H. GOKSEL, environmental engineer; b. Çankiri, Turkey, Jan. 2, 1972; came to U.S., 1996; s. Osman and Ayla Ozdilek. BS in Environ. Engring., Firat U., Elaziğ, Turkey, 1994; MS in Environ. Engring., N.Mex. State U., 1998; postgrad., Worster Poly. Inst., 1998—. Computer rsch. asst. N.Mex. State U., Las Cruces, 1997-98; rsch. engr. S.W. Tech. Devel. Inst., Las Cruces, 1997-98. Scholar Turkish Ministry State, 1989-94, Turkish Ministry Nat. Edn., 1995—. Mem. Am. Water Works Assn., New Eng. Water Works Assn. Fax: 508-831-5808. Office: Worcester Poly Inst Kaven Hall 100 Institute Rd Worcester MA 01609-2247

OZEKI, TOMOYASU, outsourcing company executive; b. Gifu, Japan, June 13, 1954; s. Hidetaro and Naoko (Takahashi) O.; m. Tomoyo Nonaka, Oct. 30, 1988; 1 child, Marina. BA in Econs., Keio U., Tokyo, 1978; MBA with honors, U. Notre Dame, 1981. CPA, N.Y. Auditor Price Waterhouse, N.Y.C., 1981-84, Touche Ross, N.Y.C., 1984-87; dep. contr. Morgan Stanley

Japan, Tokyo, 1987-90; contr. Lehman Bros. Japan, Tokyo, 1990-93, CS First Boston Asia, Tokyo, 1993-94; v.p. L&M Internat., Tokyo, 1994-97; pres. Nippon Outsourcing Corp., Tokyo, 1997-99, Pricewaterhouse Coopers BPO Japan, Tokyo, 1999—. Co-author: Outsourcing, 1997. Mem. AICPA, Japan Young Pres. Orgn., Am. C. of C. Japan, Tokyo Am. Club, Beta Gamma Sigma. Avocations: golf, tennis, skiing, pottery. Office: Pricewaterhouse Coopers, 402-03 Ebisu Shibuya-ku, Tokyo 150-6014, Japan

ÖZER, A. YEKTA, pharmacist, researcher; b. Ankara, Turkey, Jan. 9, 1953; d. M. Muammer and H. Sevim (Aktur) Uysal; m. M. Vasfi Özer, July 10, 1978; 1 child, Basak. Cert. of Basic Scis., U. Hacettepe, 1972, B.Pharm., 1975, PhD, 1981. Rsch. assoc. Hacettepe U., Ankara, 1976-88, assoc. prof. faculty pharmacy, 1988-95, prof., 1995—, head radiopharmacy dept., 1993—, mem. exec. com. faculty pharmacy, 1991—; sci. cons. Poison Control Ctr., U. Hacettepe, 1992—, coord. 2d apprenticeship program, 1989-98; vis. specialist dept. pharmaceutics U. Utrecht, The Netherlands, 1986-87; lectr. in field. Sci. referee Jour. Hacettepe U. Faculty Pharmacy, Jour. Pharm. Sci., Internat. Jour. Pharmacy; contbr. articles to profl. jours., chpts. in books; editor: Turkish Pharm. Scientists Assn. News, 1992—; sci. bd. Jour. FABAD Pharm. Sci., 1996—. Recipient Ihsan Dogramaci award Hacettepe U., 1975, Best Poster award Internat. Pharm. Tech. Symp-IPTS, 1994, 98, 4th Liposome Rsch. Days Conf., 1995. Mem. Assn. of Turkish Pharm. Tech. Scientists (gen. sec. 1995—), Assn. Hacettepe Pharms. (exec. com. 1996-99), Turkish Pharmacists Assn., Pharmacists Chamber of Ankara, Assn. Pharm. Scis. of Ankara, Internat. Microencapsulation Soc., World Scientists, Internat. Cosmetic Scientists Assn. Office: Hacettepe Univ, Fac Pharmacy Dept Radiophar, Ankara 06100, Turkey

OZER, MARTHA ROSS, school psychologist; b. Richmond, Ky., Sept. 4, 1932; d. Robert Lee and Virginia Eudelle (Hurst) Ross; m. John Dudley Redden, Dec. 27, 1953 (dec. June 1969); children: Mary, Patricia, Robert, Mark; m. Mark N. Ozer, Aug. 12, 1979. BA in Elem. Edn., Georgetown Coll., 1954; MA in Counseling, Murray State U., 1966, MS in Psychology, 1968; EdD in Edn. Adminstrn., U. Ky., 1976; LLD (hon.), Georgetown Coll., 1995; postdoctoral cert. in infant and young child mental health program, Wash. Sch. Psychiatry, 1995-96. Cert. sch. psychologist with autonomous functioning, Ky.; lic. sch. psychologist, Va., D.C., lic. profl. counselor; Sch. Psychologist, Washington, D.C. Elem. tchr. Jefferson County Pub. Schs., Louisville, 1954-58, Hickman County Pub. Schs., Campbellsburg, Ky., 1960-62; tchr. emotional disturbed, dir. psychol. svcs. Paducah (Ky.) Pub. Schs., 1965-70; psychologist, program dir. Louisville Pub. Schs., 1970-74; doctoral intern Bur. Edn. for Handicapped U.S. Dept. Edn., Washington, 1974-75; program dir. project sci. tech. and disability AAAS, Washington, 1975-86; postdoctoral intern NYU Brain Trauma Program NYU Med. Ctr., N.Y.C., 1986-87; program dir., adminstr., asst. prof. dept. rehab. medicine Med. Coll. Va., Richmond, 1987-89; psychologist MCV Pediatric Devel. Ctr., Richmond, 1989; sch. psychologist Fairfax (Va.) County Pub. Schs., 1989-98; pvt. practice, 1998—; cons. Am. Coun. on Edn., Washington, 1976-97; project coord. Higher Edn. and the Handicapped Am. Coun. on Edn., 1976-86; cons. rehab. and spl. edn., Brazil, Saudi Arabia, Qatar, Turkey; numerous other profl. and disability orgns. Authored more than 20 books and contbr. articles to profl. jours. on access for persons with disabilities to sci. edn. and careers, contbn. of sci./tech. to persons with disabilities. Advisor Disability Rights, 1975—. Recipient U.S. Presdl. Pvt. Sector award, award Am. Coalition Citizens with Disabilities, 1980, Alumni award Geotgetown Coll., 1985, Disting. Alumni award Murray St. U., 1996; grantee U.S. Dept. Edn., 1975-86, U.S. Dept. Civil Rights, 1975-90, Grant Found., 1975-77, Exxon Found., 1976, IBM, 1976, NSF, 1977-86, Nat. Inst. for Rehab. Rsch., 1978-84. Mem. NSTA (award), APA (bd. dirs. rehab. sect.), NASP (nat. cert.), Va. Psychol. Assn., Assn. Handicapped Student Svc. Programs in Post-Secondary Edn. (editor jour. 1988-91). Avocations: photography, pottery, travel. E-mail: mr2oz@aol.com. Home: 3420 38th St NW Apt A-415 Washington DC 20016-3032

OZER, MUAMMER, business educator; b. Erzurum, Turkey, May 21, 1963; s. Ismet and Hadice Ozer; m. Yasemin Gunderen, May 30, 1998; 1 child, O. Fatih. BS in Engring., Istanbul (Turkey) Tech. U., 1984, MS in Engring., 1987; MBA, St. Louis U., 1989; PhD, U. Pitts., 1996. Instr. U. Pitts., 1994-96; lectr. City U. Hong Kong, 1996—. Contbr. articles to profl. jours. Mem. Am. Mktg. Assn., Beta Gamma Sigma. Avocations: hiking, travel, swimming. Office: City U Hong Kong Dept Mgmt, 83 Tat Chee Ave, Kowloon Hong Kong

OZESMI, MUSTAFA, chest physician, consultant; b. Odemis, Turkey, Sept. 5, 1942; s. Mehmet and Emine (Bozdag) O.; m. Cigdem Cankaya, July 12, 1968; children: Uygar, Deniz. MD, U. Istanbul, 1966; PhD, U. Uppsala, Sweden, 1988. Specialist internal medicine, 1970, chest medicine, 1973. Lectr. U. Hacettepe, Ankara, Turkey, 1970-73, asst. prof., 1974-75; asst. prof. U. Erciyes, Kayseri, Turkey, 1978-79, assoc. prof., 1979-88, prof., 1988—, head chest dept., 1978-90, cons. chest dept., 1990—; vis. rschr. U. Uppsala, Sweden, 1984-85; fellow Klinik St. Blasien, Germany, 1975-78. Contbr. articles to profl. jours. Lt. Turkish Mil., 1973-74. Recipient Bedii Gorbon Cancer Rsch. prize, 1984. Mem. Swedish Nat. Assn. Against Chest and Heart Disease (award 1984), Uppsala Assn. Against Tuberulosis (Amanda Ahlströms award 1985), Soc. Thorax, Soc. Tb and Thorax, Assn. Pneumology Germany, European Respiratory Soc., Soc. for Protection Nature. Social Democrat. Islamic. Avocations: gardening, cross country skiing. Home: Univ Lojmanlari 1B/25, Kayseri 38039, Turkey Office: U Erciyes, Med Faculty, Kayseri 38039, Turkey

OZET, AHMET, medical educator; b. Eskisehir, Turkey, Mar. 10, 1960; s. Musa and Ayse Ozet; m. Gulaim Enlistan, Sept. 6, 1986; 1 child, Mehmet Erdem. MD, Haceteppe Med. Faculty, Ankara, Turkey, 1983. Intern Hacettepe Med. Faculty, Ankara, 1982-83; internal medicine fellow Gulhane Mil. Med. Acad., Ankara, 1986-90, med. oncology fellow, 1991-93, asst. prof. medicine, 1995-97, assoc. prof. medicine, 1997—; clin. rsch. fellow Boston U. Med. Sch., 1994-95; physician Meyki Mil. Hosp., Ankara, 1990-91; med. oncologist Gulhane Mil. Med. Acad., Ankara, 1993-95. Mem. ASCO, ESMO, IBMTR. Muslim. Avocations: table tennis, soccer, chess. Home: Uran St B-2 Block Daire 3, Ankara Turkey

ÖZGEN, MEHMET TANKUT, electrical engineer, researcher; b. Ankara, Turkey, Apr. 15, 1965; s. Ali Riza and Semra (Sevil) Ö. BSc in Elec. Engring., Mid. East Tech. U., Ankara, 1987; MSc in Elec. Engring., Bilkent U., Ankara, 1990; MS in Elec. Engring., Stanford U., 1992; PhD in Elec. Engring., Mid. East Tech. U., 1999. Rsch. and tchg. asst. Bilkent U., Ankara, 1987-90, Mid. East Tech. U., Ankara, 1993-98. Contbr. articles to profl. jours. Lt. Turkish Armed Forces, 1999—. Recipient univ. scholarship Turkish Sci. and Rsch. Coun., Ankara, 1983-87. Mem. IEEE. Avocations: journeys, book reading, mysticism and spirituality, movies, sports. Home: 16 Sokak 18B-4, Bahcelievler, 06490 Ankara Turkey

OZGORKEY, SELIM M., food processing company executive, auto dealer; b. Izmir, Turkey, Jan. 27, 1969; s. Erdogan and Ruchan (Kardicali) O. BS, cert. hotel mgmt., Northeastern U., Boston, 1993. Trainee Coca-Cola Co., Atlanta, 1993-94; human resources mgr. Ea. Cen. Europe divsn. Coca-Cola Co., Vienna, Austria, 1994-96; gen. mgr. Ozgorkey Group of Cos., Izmir, 1997—; with BMW dealership, svc. Recipient championship awards for horseback riding and car racing. Mem. Izmir Tennis Club Alliance, Horseback Riding Club, Izmir Motor Sports Club. Avocations: paint ball, fitness, offroading/ATVing, snowboarding, go-carting. Office: Ozgy Ozgorkey, Universite Cad # 66 Bornova, 35100 Izmir Turkey

OZGÜR, SERVET, public health educator, researcher; b. Mersin, Icel, Turkey, Nov. 25, 1948; s. Ali and Fatma (Benli) O.; m. Sumru Alpat, Jan. 27, 1975; children: Anil, Cagdas. MD, Hacettepe U., Ankara, Turkey, 1973. Asst. Haceteppe U., Ankara, 1973-77, specialist, 1977-80; asst. prof. Cumhuriyet U., Sivas, Turkey, 1980-83; assoc. prof. Cumhuriyet U., Sivas, 1983-88, prof., 1988-95; prof. pub. health Gaziantep (Turkey) U., 1995—; chief med. officer Sincan Health Ctr., Etimescut Dist., Ankara,1974-80; dir. Ulas Health Dist., Sivas, Turkey, 1981, dept. pub. health Faculty of Medicine Cumhuriyet U., Sivas, Turkey, 1980-95, Caziantep (Turkey) U., 1995—. Author: Örneklerle Sağlik Ocagr Hekiminin El Kitabi, 1985, Saglik Alanmda Arastwma Yontemlein Ders Notlari, 1999; translator: Saglik istatistigi Ögretimi-Vium Model Devs ue Seminer; contbr. articles to profl. jours. Recipient Zubitak award, 1996, award for First Nat. Family Planning Congress, Ankara, Turkey, 1999. Mem. Turkish Med. Soc., Soc. Pub. Health Specialists, Soc. Fighting Against AIDS, Soc. Ataturk's Philosophy. Avocations: swimming, walking. Office: Gaziantep U, Fac Med Dept Pub Health, 27310 Gaziantep Turkey

OZHIGOV, YURI IGOREVICH, mathematician, educator, researcher; b. Volgograd, Russia, Mar. 29, 1958. PhD in Math., Moscow State U., 1983, DSc in Physics and Math., 2000. Rschr. Inst. Automation in Bldg., Moscow, 1982-85; assoc. prof. Moscow Inst. Textiles, 1985-87; prof. Moscow Inst. Tech., 1987—. Editor Quantum Computations; contbr. articles to profl. jours. including Info. and Computation, Complex Sys., Chaos, Solitons and Fractals, and Proceedings of the Royal Soc. Grantee Integration of Sci. and Edn., 1999. Mem. Moscow Math. Soc. Office: Moscow State U Stankin, Vadkovsky per 3a, 101472 Moscow Russia

OZIMEK, EDWARD, acoustician, researcher; b. Koztów, Poland, Jan. 21, 1939; s. Feliks and Wiktoria (Falinska) O.; m. Ewa Sobczak, Mar. 28, 1978; children: Maciej, Anna, Joanna, Małgorzata. MS in Physics, A. Mickiewicz U., Poznań, Poland, 1961, DSc in Acoustics, 1969. Cert. in acoustics. Asst. Inst. Acoustics, Poznań, 1961-63, sr. asst., 1964-69, adj. prof., 1970-78, asst. prof., 1979-88, prof., 1989—; dir. Inst. Acoustics, Poznań, 1981-85; head Lab. Psychoacoustics and Rm. Acoustics, Poznań, 1985—; chmn. Internat. Subjective and Objective Evaluation of Sound, 1990. Author: Theoretical Foundations of the Spectral Analysis of Signals, 1985; editor: Subjective and Objective Evaluation of Sound, 1990; contbr. articles to profl. jours. Recipient Hon. Badge of Poznań, Pres. of Poznań, 1980, Golden Cross of Merit, Pres. of Poland, 1982, Knight's Cross of Order of Polonia Restituta, Pres. Poland, 1990. Mem. Polish Acoustical Soc. (Poznan br. sec. 1963-74, chmn. 1976-82), Polish Soc. of Learned Friends, Polish Acad. Sci. (acoustical com. 1972—), Acoustical Soc. Japan, Acoustical Soc. Am. Roman Catholic. Avocations: gardening, fishing. Home: Kozotwskiego 5, 61-606 Poznan Poland Office: Inst Acoustics Poznan ul, Umultowska 85, 61-614 Poznan Poland

ÖZKAN DE QUINONES, ALEV, economist, banker, consultant; b. Istanbul, Turkey, July 11, 1955; d. Dogan Özkan and Üner (Cagatay) Gözen; m. Quinones S. Manuel Ricardo, May 13, 1986; children: Richard James, Alev Melissa, Alessandra Dilara. BS in Econ., U. Istanbul, 1976; MS in Operational Rsch., LSE, U. London, 1981. Rsch. analyst Indsl. Devel. Bank, Istanbul, 1981-83; spl. projects mgr. Turkish Glass Works, Istanbul, 1983-85; treas. Chem. Mitsui Bank, Istanbul, 1988-98; mng. dir. A&A International. Inc., Istanbul, 1998-99; exec. v.p. Emlakbank, Istanbul, 1999—, Sumerbank, Istanbul, 2000—; bd. dirs. Romanian Internat. Bank, Bucharest, Nippon Ins. Co. Mem. European Soc. Opinion and Mktg. Rsch., Turkish Market Rshc. Soc., Fin. Club Turkey. Avocations: reading, skiing, horse riding, cultural activities. E-mail: alevozkan@yahoo.com. Fax: 90 212 279 19 78. Home: Akcam Sokak No 9/4 Levent, Istanbul Turkey Office: Sümerbank, Eski Buyukdere Caddesi 13, 80670 Maslak Istanbul Turkey

ÖZKAYA, ERDOGAN, engineer; b. Kirklareli, Turkey, Mar. 10, 1971; s. Fikret and Hatice (GÜn) O.; m. Sehnaz Isik, Aug. 17, 1994; 1 child, Hande Nur. BS, Dokuz Eylul U., Izmir, Turkey, 1992; MS, Celal Bayar U., Manisa, Turkey, 1995. Rsch. asst. Celal Bayar U., 1993—. Recipient award Turkish Sci. and Tech. Rsch. Assn., Ankara, 1997. Mem. Assn. for Scientific Rsch. Muslim. Avocations: soccer, tennis, swimming, basketball, volleyball. Office: Celal Bayar Univ, Engrng Dept/Muradiye Campus, 45140 Manisa Turkey

ÖZMEN, YASAR, construction executive; b. Ikizdere, Rize, Turkey, July 10, 1965; s. Ali Osman and Emriye (Kircal) Ö; m. Tugba Akyildiz, Apr. 11, 1993; 1 child, Ali Osman. BS in Econs., N.Y. Inst. Tech., N.Y.C., 1986; MA in Econs, Fordham U., N.Y.C., 1987. Mgr. Yapi Mktg. Ltd., Bursa, Turkey, 1988-90; dir. A.O. Özmen Constrn. Co., Ankara, Turkey, 1990—. Mem. Math. Soc. of Mid. East Tech. U., Omicron Delta Epsilon. Avocations: reading, jogging. Office: A O Özmen Constrn Corp, Nenehatun Caddesi #56, 06700 Ankara Turkey

OZOLINS, PETERIS, physiologist, researcher; b. Riga, Latvia, Mar. 5, 1923; s. Peteris and Olga (Green) O.; m. Gundega Liepina, May 8, 1954. Biologist-physiologist, Latvian U., Riga, 1951, cand. Biol. Scis., 1958, D in Biol. Scis., 1973. Libr. States' Hist. Libr., Riga, Latvia, 1944-46; investigator Latvian Inst. Exptl. and Clin. Medicine, Riga, 1958-62, leading investigator, 1962-92, prof., 1992-97, prof. emeritus, 1997—; assoc. prof. Latvian U., Biolog. faculty, Riga, 1970-90. Author: (book) Adaptation of Peripheral Circulation to Sports Training, 1976, 2d rev. edition, 1984 (both in Russian), The Fatigue, 1989 (in Latvian); also jour. articles. Mem. N.Y. Acad. Scis., Latvian Physiol. Soc. Mem. Social Dem. Workers' Party. Home: Blaumana Str 26-70, LV-1011 Riga Latvia Office: Latvian Inst Exptl Medicine, O Vacietis 4, LV-1004 Riga Latvia

OZOLS, ANDRIS, physics researcher and lecturer; b. Riga, Latvia, Dec. 6, 1944; s. Olgerts and Nina (Zvirgzde) O.; m. Vera Palazhenko, June 12, 1971; children: Kaspars, Anna. MSc, U. Gorky, USSR, 1968; PhD, Latvian Acad. Sci., Salaspils, USSR, 1980, Dr Phys.-Math. Sci., 1991; habilitation, U. Latvia, Riga, 1992. Jr. rschr. Inst. of Physics/Latvian Acad. Sci., Salaspils, 1975-84, sr. rschr., 1984-91; asst. prof. Tech. U. Riga, Latvia, 1991-94; vis. rschr. U. Joensuu, Finland, 1992-93; leading rschr. Inst. Solid State Physics/U. Latvia, Riga, 1993-94; prof. physics Riga Tech. U., 1994—. Contbr. articles to profl. jours. Dep. chmn. Latvian Social Dem. Party, 1994-99. Mem. SPIE, Latvian Acad. Scis. (corr.). Avocations: jogging, downhill skiing, philosophy. Office: Riga Tech U/Inst Tech Phys, Azenes iela 14/24, LV-1048 Riga Latvia

OZOLS, ANTONS EDMUNDS, animal physiologist, educator; b. Riga, Latvia, July 26, 1927; s. Jānis and Tekla (Šlakota) O.; m. Velta Raibe, Feb. 7, 1953; children: Mudīte, Anta. Degree in higher edn., Acad. Agr., Riga, 1954, D of Agrl. Sci., 1960; D of Biology, Acad. Sci. Inst. Physiology, St. Petersburg, Russia, 1983. Sr. rsch. assoc. Inst. Animal Sci., Riga, 1955-62; asst. prof. Latvia U., Riga, 1962-64; leading rsch. assoc. Inst. Biology Acad. Sci., Riga, 1964-89, head of lab., 1989-96, prof. animal physiology, 1993-96, prof. emeritus, 1997—. Author: Enteral Uptake of Carbohydrates, 1984. Mem. Latvia Acad. Agrl. and Forest Sci., Latvian Physiology Soc. Achievements include patents for methods of obtaining feed addition from remains of fish-factory and for system producing dry concentrate of fish protein. Home: Raunas Str 45/4 Apt 194, LV 1084 Riga Latvia Office: Latvian Acad Sci, Inst Biology Animal Lab, LV 2169 Riga Latvia

OZOLS-KALNINŠ, VALĒRIJS, physicist, researcher; b. Riga, Latvia, May 12, 1952; s. Garry and Nina (Ermush) Ozols-K. Grad. in Math., Latvian State U., 1979; Candidate of Phys. and Math. Scis., Moscow State U., 1990; D of Physics, Inst. Physics of Rigid Body, Latvia, 1995. Engr. Inst. Wood Chemistry, Latvian Acad. Scis., Riga, 1975-80, sr. engr., 1980-86, jr. sci. worker, 1986-91; sci. worker Latvian State Inst. Wood Chemistry, Riga, 1991-93, leading rschr., 1993—. Contbr. articles to profl. jours. Recipient 2d prize Presidium of Latvian Acad. Scis. Mem. N.Y. Acad. Scis. Avocations: music, airing in the forest and at the sea shore, gathering mushrooms, reading historical an philosophical literature. Home: Unijas 76a Apt 55, LV1084 Riga Latvia Office: Latvian State Inst Wood Chemistry, 27 Dzerbenes Str, LV 1006 Riga Latvia

OZORNEK, MURAT HAKAN, obstetrician-gynecologist; b. Istanbul, Turkey, Aug. 26, 1965; s. Yuksel Cetin and Inci (Senuzun) O.; m. Sema Otrakcier, Nov. 13, 1991. MD, Cerrahpasa Med. Faculty, Istanbul, 1991. Med. staff State Prison, Yozgat, Turkey, 1991-93; resident dept. ob-gyn. Heinrich-Heine U., Dusseldorf, Germany, 1993-99; med. dir. Pvt. Assisted Reproductive Techniques (ART) Ctr., Istanbul, 1999—; rschr. Immunology Lab., Heinrich Heine U., Dusseldorf, 1994-2000. Translator: Gynekologische Chirurgie des Beckenbodens, 1999; contbr. articles to profl. jours. Recipient Sci. Rsch. award Tukiye Bilimsel ve Teknik Arastirma Kurumu, 1993, Heinrich Hertz Found., Germany, 1994, Young Scientist award Rochester Traphoblast Group, Banff, Can., 1996. Mem. European Soc. Human Reproduction and Embryology, Internat. Fedn. Placental Assn., N.Y. Acad. Scis., Am. Soc. Reproductive Medicine. Avocations: music, computers. Home: Fahrettin Kerim Gokay Cad, Beyaz Kosk Sitesi B2 Blok, 81040 Kadikoy Istanbul Turkey Office: Eurofertil, Nuhkuyusu Cad No 90, Altunizade Istanbul 81190, Turkey

OZOROWSKI, EDWARD, theology educator; b. Wasilkow, Poland, May 1, 1941; s. Antony and Maria (Sosnowska) O. ThD, Cath. U., Lublin, Poland, 1970. Ordained priest Roman Cath. Ch., 1964, bishop, 1979. Adj. prof. Acad. Cath. Theology, Warsaw, Poland, 1970-78, docent, 1978-87, prof. theology, 1987—; rector Priest Sem., Bialystok, Poland, 1979-92; vicar gen. Archdiocese of Bialystok, 1979—; pres. Mixt Ecumenical Commn. Poland, 1980-96; bishops commn. Poland for Ecumenism, 1980-86, Poland for Liturgy and Sci., 1996—; sec. Studia Theol. Varsaviensia, 1970-79; redaktor Studia Theologica, 1980-92. Editor, author: Lexikon of Polish Catholique Theologiens; contbr. articles to profl. jours. Home: Warszawska 46, 15-077 Bialystok Poland

OZTUGRAN, ALI OKYAY, air express executive; b. Kirklareli, Turkey, Nov. 6, 1970; s. Ibrahim and Sevil Oztugran; m. Arzu Basaktar, July 21, 1994; 1 child, Sarp. BS in Indsl. Engring. with honors, Bogazici U., Istanbul, Turkey, 1992, MA in Managerial Fin., 1996. Cert. indsl. engr., Turkey. Ops. rsch. analyst Turkish Airlines, Inc., Istanbul, 1992-95; product responsible for TOFAS-FIAT Automative Industries A.S., Istanbul, 1995-96; team mgr. export and logistics Procter & Gamble A.S., Istanbul, 1996-97; project mgr. ops. DHL Worldwide Express, Istanbul, 1998—; area mgr., implementor of work processes transport harmonization project best DHL sta. in world, 1999. Outstanding Performance award for completing TROYA software Turkish Airlines, Inc, Istanbul, 1995. Avocations: sports, volleyball, trekking, being a social aide to homeless children, internet. Fax: 90-212-221 78 17. Home e-mail: okyayoztugran@hotmail.com. Office e-mail: ooztugra@tr.dhl.com. Home: Semsettin Gunaltay Cad Gunesli Sk, Group Apt 7 D 8, Kazasker Istanbul 81090, Turkey Office: DHL Worlwide Exp Tas Tic AS, Piyalepasa Bulvari Famas Plz Zemin Kat, 80270 Istanbul Okmeydani-Sisli, Turkey

OZTURK, CENGIZHAN, biomedical engineer; b. Turkey, 1966. MD, Marmara Med. Sch., Istanbul, Turkey, 1990; PhD, Drexel U., 1997. Postdoctoral rsch. fellow med. imaging lab. Johns Hopkins U., Balt., 1997—; rsch. fellow lab of cardiac energetics Nat. Heart Lung Blood Inst., Bethesda, Md., 1999—. Falk Found. fellow, 1998-2000. Mem. IEEE, Soc. Biomed. Engring., Internat. Soc. MRI in Medicine, Internat. Soc. Optical Engring. Office: Med Imagin Lab JHU 407 S Taylor Ave Bldg Rutland Baltimore MD 21221-6846

OZTURK, VELI, mechanical engineer; b. Istanbul, Turkey, Sept. 15, 1954; s. Sait and Kibriya (Elhan) O.; m. Nevin Semen, Oct. 9, 1989; 1 child. BSc, Instanbul Tech. U., 1977. Divsn. mgr. Alarko Almut, Istanbul, 1984-91; mgr. Argus Ltd., Istanbul, 1991—. Office: Argus Ltd, Macka Cad Narmanli Apt 32, Macka Istanbul 80200, Turkey

PAAJANEN, ERKKI MATTI, consultant company executive; b. Parikkala, Finland, Jan. 9, 1944; s. Lauri and Helli Katri (Heiskanen) P.; m. Riita Liisa Saari, Nov. 23, 1968; children: Sami, Satu. MS in Econs., Vaasa U., 1982; MBA, Henley Mgmt. Coll., 1994. Cert. mgmt. cons. Internat. Coun. Mgt. Cons. Insts. Area sales mgr. Rank Xerox, Vaasa, Finland, 1969-79; regional dir. Fennia Ins., Vaasa, Finland, 1979-82; cons. PA Cons. Group, Helsinki, Finland, 1982-86; mktg. dir. Oy Norcar AB, Vaasa, 1986-87; sr. cons. PA Cons. Group, 1987-89; mng. dir. Oy Erkki Paajanen AB, Vaasa, 1990—. Mem. Finnish Mgmt. Cons. Assn., Strategic Mgmt. Soc. Finland, Personnel Mgmt. Group Assn., Internat. Coun. Mgmt. Cons. Inst. (cert.), Rotary. Avocations: tennis, golf, fishing, literature. Home: Koulukatu 3-5 A 36, FIN65100 Vaasa Finland Office: Hovioikeudenpuistikko, 5 A 11, FIN65100 Vaasa Finland Office: Mariankatu 15 A 13, 00170 Helsinki Finland

PAÁL, ZOLTÁN, chemical engineer, researcher; b. Budapest, Hungary, Mar. 1, 1936; s. József and Etelka (Varga) P.; m. Julia Lukács, Mar. 5, 1983; children by previous marriage: György, Edina. MSc, Tech. U. Budapest, 1959, Dr.Tech., 1962; CScHung, Acad. Sci. Budapest, 1967, DScHung, 1978; Dr.Habilitation, Tech. U. Budapest, 1995. Rsch. assoc. Hungarian Oil and Gas Rsch. Inst., Budapest, 1959-63; rsch. fellow Inst. Isotopes, Budapest, 1966-78, sr. rsch. fellow, 1978-83, head dept. catalysis, 1983-92, dir., 1993-98, sci. advisor, 1998—; adj. prof. U. Szeged, Hungary, 1979—, U. Veszprém, 1993—. Co-editor: (with P.G. Menon) Hydrogen Effects in Catalysis, 1988; contbr. articles to profl. jours. Recipient Hungarian State prize Govt. of Hungary, 1983. Mem. Hungarian Engring. Acad. Office: Inst of Isotopes, Hungarian Acad Sci PO Box 77, H-1525 Budapest Hungary

PAALMAN, MARIA ELISABETH MONICA, public health executive; b. Zwolle, Overyssel, The Netherlands, Dec. 7, 1951; d. Herman J. and Wieb (Lievestro) P. MS in Clin. Psychology, U. Groningen, 1977; postgrad., Pesso Psychomotor, Boston, 1982; MSc in Health Policy, Planning & Financing, U. London, 1996. Staff mem. Hoog Hullen-Ther. Comm., Eelde, Netherlands, 1977-79; asst. dir. Krauweelhuis-Ther.Comm., Amsterdam, 1979-82; dir. STD Found., Utrecht, 1983-93; cons. WHO, Geneva, 1990; mem. Nat. Com. AIDS Control, The Netherlands, 1983-93; nat. coord. campaigns on STDs, AIDS, safer sex, 1985-93; tech. asst. STD/AIDS EC, Tanzania, 1993-95; adviser health planning MoH Vietnam, 1997, sr. health planner, MoH Palestine, 1999—. Editor: Dutch Std. Bull., 1983-93; editor Promoting Safer Sex, 1990; mem. editl. bd. Internat. Jour. on STD and AIDS, 1989-93, AIDS Health Promotion Exch., 1991-96, AIDS Edn. and Prevention, 1992-97; contbr. articles to profl. jours. Mem. Internat. Soc. for STD Rsch. (bd. dirs. 1989-95). Fax: 972-7-483-4255. Home: PO Box 4054 Abu Khadra, Gaza via Israel, Palestine

PAAR, VLADIMIR, physicist; b. Zagreb, Croatia, May 11, 1942; s. Vladimir and Elvira (Potočnjak) P.; m. Nada Pandur, Dec. 30, 1978; children: Dalibor, Nils, Petar, Elizabeta. BSc, U. Zagreb, 1965, MSc, 1969, PhD, 1971. Asst. Inst. R. Bošković, Zagreb, 1966-71; guest scientist Niels Bohr Inst., Copenhagen, 1971-72; guest prof. Natuurkundig Lab., Amsterdam, 1975; prof. U. Zagreb, Croatia, 1976—; guest scientist Lawrence Livermore Nat. Lab., Calif., 1985, 89, KFA Jülich, Germany, 1986, 88. Editor: Nuclear Structure, Reactions and Symmetries, 1986; contbr. articles to profl. jours. Recipient State award for Sci. Ministry of Sci. Mem. Am. Phys. Soc., European Phys. Soc., German Phys. Soc., Croatian Acad. of Scis. and Arts. Roman Catholic. Avocations: soccer, gardening, popularization of science.

PAASI, JAAKKO ANTTI JUHANI, physicist, educator; b. Ulvila, Finland, June 21, 1964; s. Antti and Aino (Arvela) P.; m. Paivi Jokinen, Aug. 13, 1994; children: Johanna, Antti. MSc, Tampere U. Tech., Finland, 1988, Lic. in Tech., 1992, D in Tech., 1995. Rschr. ABB, Sweden, 1988; rschr. Tampere U. Tech., 1989-95, sr. scientist, 1996-2000; scientist Acad. Finland, 1996-99; sr. scientist VTT Automation, Tampere, Finland, 2000—. Contbr. numerous articles on electromagnetism and superconductivity to sci. jours. Recipient Sci. award Town of Tampere, 1996, Sci. award IVO Found., 1997. Lutheran. Office: VTT Automation, PO Box 1306, 33101 Tampere Finland

PAASIO, PERTTI KULLERVO, Finnish government official; b. Helsinki, Apr. 2, 1939; s. Kustaa Rafael and Mary Regina (Wahlman) P.; m. Kirsti Kaarina Johansson, 1967; children: Ari, Paivi, Heli, Jouni. MSc in Polit. Sci., 1968. Mem. Turku (Finland) City Coun., 1965-90; dep. head Tourist Office City of Turku, 1968-73; head Regional Employment Svc., Turku, 1973-87; spl. asst. to min. fin. Helsinki, 1972; aide to prime min., Govt. of Finland, Helsinki, 1975; M.P. Helsinki, 1975-79, 82-96; mem. exec. com. Social Dem. Party Finland, Helsinki, 1978-87, chmn. parliamentary group, 1984-87, 96—, chmn., 1987-91; mem. Parliamentary Fgn. Affairs Com., 1975-79, 82-89, chmn., 1991-96, min. for fgn. affairs, 1989-91; mem. European Parliament, 1996-99; chmn. Finnish Nat. Com. for European Security, 1985-87. Vice pres. Internat. Social Dem. Youth League (Falcom Movement), 1975-81. *

PAASWELL, ROBERT EMIL, civil engineer, educator; b. Red Wing, Minn., Jan. 15, 1937; s. George and Evelyn (Cohen) P.; m. Rosalind Snyder, May 31, 1958; children: Judith Marjorie, George Harold. BA (Ford Found. fellow), Columbia U., 1956, BS, 1957, MS, 1961; PhD, Rutgers U., 1965. Field engring. asst. Spencer White & Prentis, Washington, 1954-56; engr. Spencer White & Prentis, N.Y.C., 1957-59; rsch. scientist Davidson Lab.,

N.J., 1964; rsch. fellow Greater London Council, 1971-72; rsch. and teaching asst. Columbia U., 1959-62; asst. prof. civil engring. SUNY, Buffalo, 1964-68; chmn. bd. govs. Urban Studies Coll., 1973-76, assoc. prof., 1968-76, prof. civil engring., 1976-82; dir. Center for Transp. Studies and Research, 1979-82, chmn. dept. environ. design and planning, 1980-82; prof. transp. engring. U. Ill., Chgo., 1982-86, 89-90, dir. Urban Transp. Ctr., 1982-86; exec. dir. Chgo. Transit Authority, 1986-89; dir. transp. rsch. consortium, prof. civil engring. CCNY, 1990—, disting. prof., 1991—; faculty-on-leave Dept. Transp., 1976-77, cons., 1981—; v.p. Faculty Tech. Cons., Inc., Midwest Sys. Scis., Inc., 1982-86; dir. Urban Mass Transp. Adminstrn. Summer Faculty Workshop, 1980, 81; cons. transp. planning, energy and soil mechanics; spl. cons. to Congressman T. Dulski, 1973; vis. expert lectr. Jilin U. Tech., Changchun, Peoples Republic of China, 1985, hon. prof. transp., 1986—; bd. dirs. E'Escuto Archs. and Engrs., Chig, Hickling Co., Ottawa, Can., Transic Devel. Corp.; chmn. transp. steering adv. bd. Office of Tech. Assessment for Infrastructure and the Urban Core Project, 1994—; faculty Lincoln Inst. of Land Policy, 1994-95; vis. scholar Tel Aviv U., Israel, 1995—; arbitrator in productivity Met. Transp. Authority, N.Y.C., 1996—; mem. exec. com. Coun. on Transp., 1996—, NSF Ctr. for Infrastructure Sys.; cons. Coun. of North East Govs., 1997—; faculty "Conflict Resolution," NYU, 1998—; mem. exec. com. Inst. for Civil Infrastructure Sys. (NSF), 1998—; chair panel new paradigms in transit Transp. Rsch. Bd.; bd. dirs. Transit Stds. Consortium, chmn., 2000—. Author: Problems of the Carless, 1977; contbg. author: Transport and Urban Development, 1995, Panels for Transportation Planning, 1997, Studies in Israel Planning, 1996, Dynamic Networks and Spatial Change; editor: Site Traffic Impact Assessment, 1992; contbg. author: Decisions for the Great Lakes, 1982, World Book Encyclopedia, 1992, 93, 94, Transport and Urban Development, 1995, Israel Planning Studies, 1996, 97, Panels for Transportation Planning, 1997, New Contributions to Transportation Analysis in Europe, 1999; mem. bd. editors Jour. Environ. Systems, 1974—, Transp., 1978—, Jour. Urban Tech., 1992—; contbr. articles to profl. jours. Mem. Buffalo Environ. Mgmt. Commn., 1972-74; mem. Area Com. for Transit, Mayor's Energy Adv. Bd., 1974, Block Grant Rev. Com., City of Buffalo; chmn. com. on transp., mem. rev. adv. bd. Rsch. and Planning Coun. Western N.Y.; mem. transp. com. Chgo. 1992 Worlds Fair; mem. citizens' adv. bd. Chgo. Transit Authority, 1985—; mem. strategic planning com. Regional Transp. Authority, 1985; mem. steering com. Nat. Transit Coop. Rsch. Program, 1991—, Borough pres. (Manhattan) Trans. Adv. Bd., Bronx Ctr. Devel. Project; bd. dirs. Transit Devel. Corp., 1992—; exec. bd. Transp. Council, 1996—; mem. exec. com. Colin Powell Ctr. Recipient Dept. Transp. award, 1977; SUNY faculty fellow, 1965-66. Fellow ASCE (past pres. Buffalo sect., chmn. steering com. 1992 specialty conf. traffic impact analysis); mem. AAAS, Transp. Rsch. Bd. (chmn. com. on transp. disadvantaged, mem. exec. com., peer rev. com. nat. transp. ctrs. 1988—), Inst. Transp. Engrs. (transit coun., exec. com., chmn. legis. policy com., rsch. com. surface transp. policy project 1995—), Coun. on Transp. (bd. dirs. 1996—), N.Y. Acad. Scis., Sigma Xi. Office: CCNY Inst Transp Systems Rm 220-Y 135th St and Convent Ave New York NY 10031

PABISCH, PETER KARL, German and European studies educator; b. Vienna, Austria, Apr. 17, 1938; came to U.S., 1969; s. Ernst and Gertrude (Engel) P.; m. Patricia Ann Trench, Nov. 25, 1959; 1 child, Angela. MA, U. Ill., 1971, PhD, 1974. Tchr. pub. schs. Vienna, 1959-69; dir. summer children's homes Vienna Social Welfare Sys., Italy, 1964-69; co-dir. German summer sch. U. N.Mex., Albuquerque, 1976—, from asst. prof. to assoc. prof., 1972-84, prof. German and European studies, 1984—. Author: (books) Austrian Poet H. C. Artmann, 1978, Modern German Lyrics, 1992, also 5 poetry books; editor 7 books on German, Swiss, and Austrian studies, 1977—. Pres. Atlantic Bridge on the Camino Real Orgn., 1997—, Austrian-Am. Coun. of N.Mex., Inc., 1999—. Decorated Order of Merit 1st Class, Fed. Republic of Germany, 1985, Gt. Order of Merit, Republic of Austria, 1986; recipient Award of Recognition, Goethe-Inst. Munich, 1995, poetry awards, 1992, arts award, 1993, Friedestrom prize, 2000; named Best German Tchr., Am. Assn. Tchrs. of German, 1982. Democrat. Avocations: skiing, scuba diving, playing music, traveling. Home: 417 Jefferson St NE Albuquerque NM 87108-1279 also: House Pabisch, Polidendri, Larisas 40003, Greece Office: U N Mex German Program Fls Albuquerque NM 87131-0001 also: Ariadne Inst Global Studies, Amaliaodos 4, Larissa 41336, Greece

PABITO, BEATRIZ VARGAS, foreign language educator; b. Iriga, Bicol, The Philippines, May 10, 1938; d. Francisco Ibarrientos Vargas Sr. and Bernarda Malaca Matalota; m. Diosdado Rufa Pabito Jr., (dec.); children: Bedi Raquel Pabito Casilihan, Edwin. BSc in Edn., Adamson U., Manila, 1967; MA in Spl. Edn., Nat. U., 1985. Chairperson Spanish dept. Adamson U.; liaison officer Nat. U., Manila; spl. edn. adviser Burgos Elem. Sch., Manila; cooperating tchr. St. Bridget's Coll., Batangas, The Philippines; adviser student orgn. Adamson U., Manila. Pres. PTA, Las Piñas, Homeowners Assn., Las Piñas, Iriga Varsitarians, Aquing Bicol; nat. pres. Ladies of Charity-Assn. Internat. Charity Philippines. Scholar Agencia Española de Cooperacion Internat., Inst. Coop. Iberoamericano, Internat. Mendendez Pelayo, Santander, Entro Cultural de España en Manila. Mem. Philippine Assn. Women, Cath. Womens League, Adamson Univ. Tchrs. Club, Adamson U. Alumni Assn. (dir.). Avocations: reading, writing, cross stitch designing, swimming. Home: Blk 21 Lot 14, Marcos Alvares Corner, Las Piñas Manila, The Philippines Office: Adamson Univ, 900 San Marcelino St, Ermita The Philippines

PÁCA, JAN VÁCLAV, bioengineering educator; b. Prague, Czech Republic, Aug. 20, 1945; s. Jan and Justina (Podana) P.; m. Jana Anna Novotná, Oct. 31, 1975; children: Jan, Hana. MSc, Tech. U., Prague, 1968; PhD, U. Chem. Tech., Prague, 1975, DSc, 1993. Cert. bioengring., microbiology, fermentation chemistry and tech. Designer Wiener Brückenbau, Vienna, Austria, 1969; rschr. Rsch. Inst. Ft Industry, Prague, 1969-70; asst. prof. U. Chem. Tech., Prague, 1973-90, assoc. prof., 1990-95, prof. bioengring., 1995—; sr. reader Tech. U., Prague, 1983-91; referee NSF, Washington, 1976-78; supr. Czech Acad. Sci., Prague, 1989-92; dir. Bioproc, Prague, 1991—; sr. reader Charles U., Prague, 1995-96, FH Magdeburg, 1997. Author: Bioengineering, 1986, Production of Alcohol, Fooder and Baker's Yeast, 1988; co-author, co-editor: Biotechnologie, 1987, 91; mem. editl. bd. ACTA BIOTECHNOLOGICA, Wiley-VCH Verlag, Berlin, 1998—. Grantee Czech Grant Agy., Prague, 1993, 96, 99, Tempus, Brussels, 1995, 96, European Tng. Found., Turin, 1996, Copernicus, Brussels, 1997. Mem. Sci. Coun. Czech Acad. Sci., Sci. Coun. U. Chem. Tech., Czech Microbiol. Soc. (head com. applied microbiology 1989-95), Czech Chem. Soc., Czech Biochem. Soc., Czech Soc. Chem. Engrs., Czech Biotech. Soc., Czech Nat. Com. of Feani (v.p.), Czech Grant Agy. (mem. exec. com. for tech. sci. 1999—, mem. com. for tech. chemistry 1999—), N.Y. Acad. Sci. Avocations: white water canoeing, classical music. Home: Podolska 21, 14700 Prague 4, Czech Republic Office: U Chem Tech, Technicka 5, 16628 Prague 6, Czech Republic

PACCALONI, GIOVANNI, chemist; b. Porto Potenza Picena, Italy, Mar. 29, 1945; s. Giuseppe and Germana (Venanzetti) P.; m. Angela de Angelis, Sept. 11, 1071; children: Daniele, Chiara, Francesca. MS in Indsl. Chemistry, U. Bologna, Italy, 1969. Cert. of profl. chemist. Drilling engr. AGIP, Milan, Italy, 1972-74, prodn. engr., 1975-77; mgr. stimulation tech. sect. AGIP Spa, Milan, Italy, 1978-83, mgr. prodn. optimization dept., mgr. prodn. labs, 1993-96; v.p. E&P lab. ENI-AGIP, Milan, Italy, 1997—. Author: Oil and Gas Journal, 1979, Journal of Petroleum Technology, 1993, SPE Production and Facilities, 1996. Lt. Italian Army Sch. of Artillery Missiles, 1970-71, Rome. Mem. SPE Italian Sect. (chmn. 1990-92), SPE Internat. (bd. dir. 1995-98). Avocations: chess, photography, music. Office phone: 0039-02-52036570. Home: via Agadir 10A, 20097 Milan Italy Office: ENI-AGIP Divsn, via Maritano 26, 20197 Milan Italy

PACE, GEORGE ERNEST, hospital engineer; b. Sliema, Malta, May 16, 1961; s. Joseph and Mary Carmela (Antignolo) P. Degree in elec. engring., U. Malta, 1992; MBA, Henley U., 1998. Engrs. warrant. Technician Telemalta Corp., Malta, 1986-87; trainee engr. Malta Devel. Corp., 1987-92, engr., 1992-93; hosp. engr. dept. health St. Luke's Hosp., G'Mangia, Malta, 1993—. Avocations: reading, music, gardening. Home: 15/3 Sappers St, Valletta VLT 11, Malta Office: Dept Health, St Lukes Hosp St Lukes Rd, G'Mangia MSD 07, Malta

PACE, STANLEY DAN, lawyer; b. Dayton, Ohio, Dec. 10, 1947; s. Stanley Carter and Elaine (Cutchall) P.; m. Judy Roehm, Sept. 8, 1973; children: Stanley Carter, Barbara Roehm. BA, Denison U., Granville, Ohio, 1970; JD, U. Toledo (Ohio), 1975. Bar: U.S. Dist. Ct. (so. dist.) Ohio 1975, U.S. Dist. Ct. (no. dist.) Ohio 1977, U.S. Ct. Appeals (6th cir.) 1975. Atty. ARMCO Steel Corp., Middletown, Ohio, 1975-77; assoc. Spieth, Bell, McCurdy & Newell, Cleve., 1977-82, dir., 1982—, co-mng. dir., 1987—; bd. mem. Indsl. Rels. Rsch. Assn., Cleve., 1985. Bd. pres. Judson Retirement Community, Cleve., 1985; bd. mem. Arthritis Found. N.E. Ohio, Cleve., 1984, Western Res. Hist. Soc., 1998. Mem. ABA, Ohio Bar Assn., Greater Cleve. Bar Assn., The Country Club, Pepper Pike Club, Tavern Club, Rolling Rock Club. Office: Spieth Bell McCurdy & Newell 2000 Huntington Bldg Cleveland OH 44115

PACH, JÁNOS, mathematician, computer scientist, researcher; b. Budapest, Hungary, May 3, 1954; s. Zsigmond Pal and Clara (Sos) P.; m. Anna Jemnitz, July 11, 1985; 2 children. MA in Math., Eötvos U., Budapest, 1977, PhD in Math., 1980. Research asst. Math. Inst. Hungarian Acad. Scis., Budapest, 1977-80, research assoc., 1980-85, sr. research fellow, 1986—; research fellow Univ. Coll. London, 1981-82; vis. scientist McGill U., Montreal, Can., 1984; vis. prof. NYU Courant Inst., N.Y.C., 1986—; vis. asst. prof. SUNY, Stony Brook, 1985-86; prof. CCNY. Author: (with W.O.J. Moser) Research Problems in Discrete Geometry, 1985, New Trends in Discrete and Computational Geometry, 1993, (with P. Agarwal) Combinatorial Geometry, 1995; editor Discrete and Computational Geometry, 1987—, Computational Geometry: Theory and Applications, 1991—, Combinatorica, 1991—, Geombinatorics, 1996—, Graphs and Combinatorics, 1999—; contbr. articles on graph theory, combinatorics, convexity, discrete and computational geometry to profl. jours. Recipient Order of Higher Edn. Council Ministers Hungary, 1978, Gold Ring Pres. of Hungary, 1983, Young Researcher's award Hungarian Acad Scis., 1984, Lester R. Ford award Math Assn. Am., Rényi prize Hungarian Acad. Scis., 1993, Acad. award, 1998. Mem. J. Bolyai Math. Soc. (editor Combinatorica 1981—, Grunwald medal 1982). Avocation: painting. Home: Nemetvolgyi ut 72/C, H-1124 Budapest Hungary Office: Hungarian Acad Scis Math Inst, Realtanoda utca 13-15, H-1053 Budapest Hungary

PACH, ZSIGMOND PAL, historian, educator; b. Oct. 4, 1919; s. Lipot and Rozsa (Weisz) P.; m. Klara Edit Sos, 1945; 2 children. Student, Budapest U. of Arts and Scis.; D. (hon.), Tartu U., 1982, Budapest U., 1989. Tchr. high sch., 1943-48; reader Budapest U. of Econs., 1948-52, prof. econ. history, 1952-93, prof. emeritus, 1995—, rector, 1963-67; dep. dir. Hungarian Acad. Sci. Inst. History, 1949-56, dir., 1967-85. Author: Gazdasagtortenet-a feudalizmus hanyatlasaig (Economic History up to the decline of Feudalism, 1947; Az eredeti tokefelhalmozas Magyarorszagon (Previous accumulation of capital in Hungary), 1952; A foldesuri gazdasag porosz-utas fejlodese Oroszorszagban a 19 sz masodik feleben (Development of the Prussian type manorial economy in Russia in the second part of the 19th century), 1958; Nyugateuropai es magyarorszagi agrarfejlodes a 15-17 sz-ban (West European and Hungarian Development of Agrarian Relations in the 15th to 17th centuries), 1963; Die ungarische Agrarentwicklung im 16-17 Jahrhundert, 1964; Problemi razvitiya vengerskoy marxistskoy istoricheskoy nauki, 1966; A nemzetkozi kereskedelmi utvonalak 15-17 sz-i athelyezodesenek kerdesehez (On the shifting of internat. trade routes in the 15th to 17th centuries), 1968; The Role of East Central Europe in International Trade: 16th and 17th Centuries, 1970; Le commerce du Levant et la Hongrie au Moyen Age, 1976; Tortenetszemlelet es tortenettudomany (History and Its View), 1978; The Transylvanian Route of Levant Trade at the Turn of the 15th and 16th Centuries, 1980; East Central Europe and World Trade at the Dawn of Modern Times, 1982; Business Mentality and Hungarian National Character, 1985; Történelem és nemzettudat (History and National Consciousness), 1987, Von der Schlacht bei Mohács bis zur Rückeroberung Budas, 1989, A harmincadvám eredete: The Origins of the Frontier Customs Duty in Hungary, 1990, The East-Central European Aspect of Overseas Discoveries and Colonization, 1991, The Turnabout in the Historiography of the Levant between 1879 and 1918, 1993, Hungary and the European Economy in Early Modern Times (Collected Studies), 1994, The Oldest Guild Privilege of Cloth Makers in Hungary, 1995, How the Frontier Customs Duty Changed from a Thirtieth into a Twentieth, 1996, Sorts of Cloth in Turkish Customs Journals, 1997, History of Hungarian Clothing Industry in the 16th Century, 1999; mem. editorial bd. Jahrbuch fur Wirtschaftsgeschichte, Berlin, 1960-91, The Economic History Rev., 1966-75. Mem. Hungarian Acad. Sci. (v.p. 1976-85, editor in chief Acta Historica 1972-92), Istituto Internat. di Storia Economica, Internat. Econ. History Assn. (pres. 1978-82, hon. pres. 1982—), Russian Acad. Scis. (fgn. mem.), Bulgarian Acad. Scis. (fgn. mem.), Laureate Hungarian Republic. Office: Nemetvolgyi ut 72/C, H-1124 Budapest Hungary

PACHECO, FERNANDO ANTONIO LEAL, aquatic engineer; b. Maputo, Mozambique, Feb. 18, 1967; s. Antonio and Julieta (Leal) P.; m. Paula Soares, Feb. 8, 1992; three children. Degree in engring. geology, U. Coimbra, 1991; degree in aquatic chemistry, U. Utrecht, 1991; MSc, U. Coimbra, 1996; PhD, Tras-Os-Montes U., 2000. Asst. Tras-os-Montes U., Vila Real, Portugal, 1993—, Alto Douro U., 2000—. Mem. Internat. Assn. Hydrogeologists. Office: Tras-Os-Montes e Alto Douro, Quinta de Prados, 5000 Vila Real Portugal

PACHECO, HUMBERTO, JR., lawyer; b. San José, Costa Rica, Jan. 10, 1940; s. Humberto and Julia (Alpizar) P.; m. Cynthia Ortiz, Mar. 7, 1975; children: Humberto III, Miguel. JD, U. Costa Rica, 1964; MCL, U. Miami, Fla., 1971; postgrad., Harvard U., 1972, 76. Costa Rican Bar: 1965. With Pacheoco Coto, San José, 1959-64, sr. ptnr., 1964—; legal adviser to pres. Costa Rica, sec. state fgn. affairs, 1970-78; scholar in residence Law Sch., U. San Diego, 1984; dir. Internat. Fin. Adv. Corp. Contbr. articles to profl. jours. Mem. Internat. Bar Assn., Inter-Am. Bar Assn., Costa Rican Bar Assn., Assn. of Bar of City of N.Y., Internat. Fiscal Assn., Am. C. of C. Costa Rica, Union Club, Costa Rica Country Club. Office: PO Box 6610, 1000 San José Costa Rica

PACHECO, MARCOS TADEU, engineering educator, researcher; b. Recife, Brazil, Oct. 31, 1951; s. Geraldo Castro and Carmencita Tavares Pacheco. Degree in Engring., Inst. Tech. Aeronautica, SJ Campos, São Paulo, 1976, MS, 1979; PhD, Southampton (Eng.) U., 1986. Cert. engring. CREA. Rschr. Centro Ticnico Aeroespacial, SJ Campos, 1976-89; full prof. U. do Vale do Paraiba, SJ Campos, 1990—; group leader Centro Ticnico Aeroespacial, SJ Campos; dir. U. do Vale do Paramba, SJ Campos. Author: Optics Design, 1998. Aspirante a Oficial, Aeronautica, 1982-83. Recipient Mattos Pimenta award Referees of the Brazilian Med. Laser Soc., Rio de Janeiro, 1987. Roman Catholic. Avocations: reading, movies, music, animals. E-mail: mtadeu@univap.br and fivek@directnet.com.br. Fax: 012 347 11 49. Office: UNIVAP, Shishima Nifumi 2911, 12244000 SJ Campos Brazil

PACHER, PA'L, physicist, educator; b. Györ, Hungary, Sept. 2, 1944; s. Aloysius and Ilona (Kerényi) P.; m. Irene Gisela Bolfert, July 30, 1968; children: Pal Joseph, Tünde Gabriella, László Zoltán. MSc in Elec. Engring., Tech. U. Budapest, Hungary, 1967; PhD in Physics, Eötvös U., Budapest, 1976. Mem. faculty, dept. atomic physics Tech. U. Budapest, 1967-78; sr. scientist, Lab. of Neutron Physics JINR, Dubna, Russia, 1978-86; lectr., assoc. prof. physics Tech. U. Budapest, 1986-90; vis. prof. physics Lake City (Fla.) C.C., 1991; assoc. prof. physics Tech. U. Budapest, 1991—. Author, editor: Measurements in Atomic Physics, 1976; author: Optics I-II, 1990. IAEA scholar, Trieste, Italy, 1973. Mem. Eötvös Phys. Soc., SEFI Working Group on Physics. Avocations: sailing, tennis, opera, concerts. Office: Tech U Budapest Dept Phys, Budafoki ut. 8, H-1111 Budapest Hungary

PACI, PIERELLA, economist; b. Rome, Italy, Aug. 18, 1957; d. Orazio and Rosa (Galassetti) P.; m. Adam Wagstaff, July 15, 1989; children: Benedict, Lilli Ruth. Grad., U. Rome, 1980; diploma, U. York, Eng., 1981; PhD, U. Manchester, Eng., 1986; diploma, Liceo Classico, Rieti, Italy, 1975. Lectr. U. Sussex, Brighton, Eng., 1985-89; from lectr. to sr. lectr. City U., London, 1989-99; hon. rsch. fellow Inst. Edn., London, 1994—; cons. World Bank, Washington, 1998—, Dept. Internat. Devel., London, 1999—. Author: Wage Differentials between Men and Women: Evidence from Cohort Studies, 1996, Unequal Pay for Women and Men, 1998 (Noteworthy Books in Indsl. Rels. and Labor Econs. award 1999); contbr. articles to profl. jours. including Jour. Health Econs., Social Sci. and Medicine, Jour. Human Resources, Cambridge Jour. Econs., others. Rsch. grantee Dept. for Edn. and Employment London, 1994, Econ. Social Rsch. Coun., 1997, European Union, 1998. Mem. Royal Econ. Soc., European Assn. Labour Economists. Office: The World Bank 1818 H St NW Washington DC 20433-0002

PACIFICI, GIAN MARIA, clinical pharmacology educator, researcher; b. Lucca, Tuscany, Italy, Apr. 7, 1944; s. Giuliano and Adriana (Pardini) P.; m. Elena Sorbi, Oct. 31, 1971; children: Stefano, Alessandro, Marco. Grad. in pharmacology, U. Pisa, Italy, 1971. Asst. prof. pharmacology U. Pisa, 1978-83, assoc. prof., 1983—. Fellow Brit. Coun., Rome, 1978, NATO, Rome, 1980, Nobel Com., Stockholm, 1982. Home: Via S Andrea 32, 56100 Pisa Italy Office: U Pisa Dept Biomedicine, Via Roma 55, 56126 Pisa Italy

PACINI, GLENN ALLEN, electrical engineer; b. Great Falls, Mont., Sept. 14, 1950; s. Nello John and Iva Lou (Griner) P.; m. Suzanne Dianne Olson, June 28, 1975; children: Shane Allen, Lindsey Jacquelyn. BSEE, Mont. State U., 1975; MBA, U. Mont., 1986. Registered elec. engr., Mont. Tng. engr. Mont. Power Co., Butte, 1975, relay engr., 1976-77; divsn. engr. Mont. Power Co., Great Falls, 1978-80, sr. divsn. engr., 1981-91, mgr. ops., 1991—. Served to e-5 USNG, 1970-76. Roman Catholic. Home: 1113 22nd Ave SW Great Falls MT 59404-3434

PACKA, DANIEL E., federal agency administrator; b. Canton, Ohio, July 12, 1952; s. Richard E. and Marie C. Packa; m. Janet Wolfe, Dec. 10; 1 child, Janet K. BS, Ohio State U., 1974, MS, 1974. Cert. real property adminstr. Bldg. mgmt. spcialist GSA, Chgo., 1978-82; bldg. mgr. GSA, Columbus, Ohio, 1982-85; facility mgr. Nat. Archives and Records Adminstrn., Washington, 1985-89; mgr. bldg. ops. br. U.S. GAO, Washington, 1989-94, facilities modernization analyst, 1994—. Avocations: computers, electronics, hiking. Home: 7672 Sheffield Village Ln Lorton VA 22079-1754 Office: US GAO 441 G St NW Rm 1800 Washington DC 20548-0001

PACKARD, PETER, medical educator, retired internist; b. Evanston, Ill., Mar. 14, 1927; s. George and Marianna (Dickinson) P.; m. Jenifer Carr, Aug. 28, 1951 (div. 1969); m. Mary Jane P., Nov. 8, 1969; children: Patricia Ann Langlais, Charles Barklay Langlais, Georgia Packard, Caroline L. Gregger, Louise Moskowitz-Packard, Victoria P. Aase, Adam L. Packard. BA, U. Calif., Berkeley, 1945; MD, U. Calif., San Francisco, 1948. Diplomate Am. Bd. Internal Medicine. Intern San Francisco Gen. Hosp., 1948-49; vol. arzt fellow infectious diseases Children's Hosp., Zurich, 1949-50; asst. res. in medicine Franklin Hosp., U. Calif., San Francisco, 1950-51; capt., med. corps USAF, Riverside, Calif., 1951-53; asst. res. medicine Ft. Miley VA Hosp., San Francisco, 1953-54, U. Calif. Hosp., San Francisco, 1954-55; pvt. practice Mills Hosp., Peninsula Med. Lab., San Mateo, Burlingame, Calif., 1955-91; med. dir., vice chmn. bd. dirs., Peninsula Med. Lab., Menlo Park, Calif., 1980-94; chief of medicine, chief of staff Mills Hosp., San Mateo, 1967-74; assoc. clin. prof. medicine, U. Calif. San Francisco, 1955—. Founding trustee, v.p. Mills-Peninsula Found., 1974-90, trustee emeritus, 1990—; pres., mem. bd. San Mateo County Heart Assn., 1964-74. Capt., USAFR Med. Corps, 1951-53, Korea. Mem. AMA, Calif. Med. Assn., San Mateo County Med. Assn. (various coms., bd. dirs., 1959-91), Am. Soc. Internal Medicine, Calif. Soc. Internal Medicine (del. off and on 1960-93), Calif. Soc. Medicine, U. Calif. San Francisco Assn. Clin. Faculty. Avocations: tennis, golf, teaching, history, politics. Home: 720 Seabury Rd Hillsborough CA 94010-6532

PACKENHAM, RICHARD DANIEL, lawyer; b. Newton, Pa., June 23, 1953; s. John Richard and Mary Margaret (Maroney) P.; m. Susan Patricia Smillie, Aug. 20, 1983. BA, Harvard U., 1975; JD, Boston Coll., 1978; LLM in Taxation, Boston U., 1985. Bar: Mass. 1978, Conn. 1979, U.S. Dist. Ct. Mass. 1979, U.S. Dist. Ct. Conn. 1979, U.S. Ct. Appeals (1st cir.) 1981, U.S. Supreme Ct. 1985. Staff atty. Conn. Superior Ct., 1978-79; ptnr. McGrath & Kane, Boston, 1979-94, Packenham, Schmidt & Federico, Boston, 1994—. Mem. ABA, Mass. Bar Assn., Conn. Bar Assn., Boston Bar Assn., Mass CLE (faculty). Democrat. Roman Catholic. Club: Harvard (Boston). Home: 1062 North St Walpole MA 02081-2307 Office: Packenham Schmidt & Federico 4 Longfellow Pl Boston MA 02114-2838

PACKER, CLAUDE MONTGOMERY, college president; b. Kingston, Jamaica, W.I., June 6, 1944; m. Lissa Joy Taylor, Dec. 19, 1973; children: Corrine Faith, Claudia Melissa. BA, U. W.I., 1972; MS, Cen. Conn. State U., 1975; MA, Cornell U., 1978, PhD, 1979. Lectr. Mico Coll., Kingston, 1979-86; head dept. math. Mico Coll., 1981-86; pres. Mico Coll., Kingston, 1995—; lectr. dept. econs. U. W.I., Kingston, 1986-90, head dept. econs., 1990-93, sr. lectr., 1992-95; sr. assoc. fellow U. W.I. Inst. of Bus., Kingston, 1995-97, dir. UNDP Math. Project, 1993-95; mem. U. W.I. Mona Campus Coun., 1999—; external examiner Caribbean Exam Coun., Barbados, 1995—, Tchr.'s Coll., Jamaica, Bahamas, Belize, 1992-95; mem. adj. faculty Nova Southeastern U., Miami, Fla., Ctrl. Conn. State U. Author: (books) Calculus for University Students, 1986, New Practice Papers in Math, 1993, Remedial Mathematics, 1995, Pre-Calculus Mathematics, 1995. Bd. dirs. Wolmer's Boy's Sch., Kingston, 1998—; chmn. Mico Practising Sch. Bd., Kingston, 1995—; bd. dirs. PALS, Kingston, 1997—; mktg. dir. Mico Found., 1995; Justice of the Peace, Kingston. Recipient Jamaica Silver Musgrave medal Inst. of Jamaica, 1997, Gold medal Mico Coll., Kingston, 1986, 25th Anniversary award Student Loan Bur., Jamaica, 1991. Mem. Joint Com. on Tertiary Edn. (chmn. 1997—), Jamaica Assn. of Tertiary Edn. (pres. 1997—), Jamaica Tchrs. Assn. (mem. exec. 1997—). Avocations: cricket, football, boxing. Office: Mico Coll, Kingston 5 Jamaica

PACKER, JAMES DOUGLAS, publishing and broadcasting executive; s. Kerry Francis and Roslyn Parker. Dir. Pub. and Broadcasting Ltd., 1991-92; gen. mgr. CPH Group, 1992-96; CEO Pub. and Broadcasting Ltd., 1996-98; now exec. chmn., CEO Pub. and Broadcasting Ltd., CPH Group, 1998; dir. Australian Consol. Press Group Ltd., 1991—, gen. mgr., 1993—; dir. Nine Newtwork Australia Ltd., 1992—, Huntsman Corp., Utah, 1994—, Optus Vision Pty. Ltd., 1995—, Valassas Inserts. Office: Pub & Broadcasting Ltd, 24 Artarmon Rd, Willoughby NSW 2068, Australia*

PACKER, KENNETH JOHN, spectroscopist; b. Kettering, Northants, Eng., May 18, 1938; s. Harry James and Alice Ethel (Purse) P.; m. Christine Frances Hart, Aug. 18, 1962; children: James Vernon, Alison Frances. BSc 1st class with honors, London U., 1959; PhD, Cambridge (Eng.) U., 1962. Chartered chemist. Postdoctoral researcher E.I. duPont de Nemours, Wilmington, Del., 1962-63; SERC rsch. fellow U. East Anglia, Norwich, Eng., 1963-64, lectr. chemistry, 1964-71, sr. lectr., 1971-78, reader in chemistry, 1978-82, prof. chemistry, 1982-84; chief rsch. assoc. BP Rsch., Sunbury-on-Thames, Eng., 1984-93; rsch. prof. in chem. U. Nottingham, 1993—; mem. sci. bd. UK Sci. and Engring. Rsch. Coun., London, Swindon, Eng., 1988-91. Co-author: Nuclear Magnetic Resonance in Solid Polymers; editor Molecular Physics jour., 1982-85; contbr. articles to profl. jours. Rsch. grantee UK Sci. and Engring. Rsch. Coun., 1964-84. Fellow Royal Soc. Chemistry London (coun. Faraday div. 1988-91), Royal Soc. London for the Improvement of Natural Knowledge. Avocations: fly-fishing, skiing, music, gardening, sailing. Home: The Coach House Bunny Hall Lane, Loughborough Rd Bunny, Notts NG11 6QT, England Office: Univ Nottingham Dept Chem, University Park, Nottingham NG7 2RD, England

PACKER, KERRY FRANCIS BULLMORE, media company executive; b. Sydney, Australia, Dec. 17, 1937; s. Frank and Lady P.; m. Roslyn Weedon, 1963; 2 children. Student, Cranbrook Sch., Geelong Ch. of Eng. Grammar Sch. Chmn. Consol. Press Holdings Ltd., 1974—. Decorated companion Order of Australia. Mem. Royal Sydney Golf Club, Australian Golf Club, Elanora Country Club, Tattersall's Athanaeum (Melbourne) Club. Avocations: polo, tennis, cricket, golf. Office: Consol Press Holdings Ltd, 54 Park St, Sydney NSW 2000, Australia*

PACKIRISAMY, SHANMUGAM, chemist; b. Pulivalam, India, Dec. 14, 1955; s. Shanmugam Ramasamy and Amsavalli S.; m. Veda Arumugam, June 3, 1984; 2 children. BSc, Puspam Coll., 1976; MSc, Indian Inst. Technology, Kharagpur, 1978, PhD, 1982. UNESCO fellow Tokyo Inst. Technology, 1982-83; rsch. officer Berger Paints India Ltd., Calcutta, India, 1984-86; scientist Vikram Sarabhai Space Ctr., Thriuvananthapuram, India, 1986-91, 94—; vis. scientist Mich. Molecular Inst., Midland, 1993-94; rsch.

assoc. Case Western Res. U., Cleve., 1992-93. Author: Key Polymers, 1985; contbr. articles to profl. jours.

PACNER, KAREL, journalist; b. Janovice, Klatovy, Czechoslovakia, Mar. 29, 1936; s. Karel and Bedřiška (Čeřovská) P.; divorced. MA, Inst. Economy, Prague, 1959. Sr. editor Mladá Fronta, Praha, Czech Republic, 1959-90, Mladá Fronta Dnes, Praha, 1990—; dep. editor-in-chief Daily Mladá Fronta, 1989; chief dept. Mladá Fronta Sunday Supplement, 1990-92; sci. editor MF Dnes, 1993—. Author: On the Both Sides of Space, 1968, ...and the Giant Leap for Mankind, 1971, 72, We are Searching Space Civilizations, 1976, 79, The Columbuses of Space, 1976, Soyuz Calling Apollo, 1976, The Constructor-in-Chief, 1977, The Nine Days in Space, 1978, Salyut-Soyuz, 1978, The Trip on the Mars, 1990-99, 1979, The Astro & Commonauts of the 20th Century, 1986, Towns in Space, 1986, 88, The Humanized Galaxy, 1987, The Message of Space Worlds, 1987, The Discovered Secrets of UFS's, 1991, The Atomic Spies, 1994, The Fatal Moments of Czechoslovakia, 1997, (TV series) From the Earth to Stars, 1971, 76. Chmn. Orgn. Employees of Mladá Fronta, 1989-90. Recipient prize Czechoslovak Acad. Scis., 1967, 84, 97. Mem. Czechoslovak Union of Journalists (mem. com. Prague chpt. 1968-69), Club of Sci. Journalists (v.p. 1966-69), Sceptic Club (mem. com. 1995—). Office: Mladá Fronta Dnes, Mladá Fronta Dnes, Na Prikope 31 POB 1080, 11121 Prague 1, Czech Republic

PACOSTE, COSTIN CALMANOVICI, civil engineer, educator; b. Bucharest, Romania, Aug. 24, 1960; arrived in Sweden, 1991; s. Cornel and Georgeta (Chitu) P.; m. Ina Pacoste Calmanovici, Apr. 4, 1991; children: Maria, Alexandra, Laura. MS in Civil Engring., Tech. U., Timisoara, Romania, 1985; PhD, Royal Inst. Tech., Stockholm, 1992. Civil engr. Indsl. Bldg. Co., Timisoara, 1985-87; rschr. Bldg. Rsch. Inst., Bucharest, 1987-91; assoc. prof. structural enging. Royal Inst. Tech., Stockholm, 1997—. Author: Advanced Methods in Structural Mechanics, 1988; contbr. articles to profl. jours. Fellow European Cmty. Computational Mechanics, Nordic Assn. Computational Mechanics. Avocations: tennis, bridge. Office: Dept Structural Enging, Royal Inst Tech, S-10044 Stockholm Sweden

PACURAR, VASILE, oncologist, educator; b. Subpiatra, Romania, Aug. 25, 1952; s. Aurel and Viorica (Urs) P.; m. Iuliana Ratiu, Aug. 16, 1975; 1 child, Mihaela Bianca. Doctor-medic, U. Medicine and Pharmacy, Cluj-Napoca, 1978, Internal Medicine Postgrad., 1981, Med. Oncology Postgrad.; Doctor in Med. Scis., U. Medicine and Pharmacy, 1997. Gen. practicioner Oradea Travel Hosp., Oradea, Romania, 1978-81; med. resident Co. Hosp., Oradea, 1981-85, med. specialist, 1985-91, cons. med. oncologist, 1991-93, head med. oncology dept., 1993-95; asst. prof. oncology U. Oradea, 1995—; cons. med. oncology Clin. Hosp., Oradea, 1991, dep. dir., 1997—; dir. Co. Oncology Network, Bihor-Oradea, Romania, 1999—. Author: (book) Elements, Practice of Oncology, 1997, Cancerul Colo-Rectal Pentru O Corecta Intelegere, 1999. V.p. Romanian Cancer Soc., 1993—. Fellow Romanian Soc. Oncological Therapy; mem. Balcan Union Oncology, European Associated Mastology, N.Y. Acad. Sci. Nat. Pesant Christian and Democratic Party. Christian-Orthodox. Avocation: mountain hiking. Office: Clinica De Oncologie, Republicii 37, 3700 Oradea Romania

PACYNA, ANDRZEJ WOJCIECH, physicist, researcher; b. Cracow, Poland, May 2, 1946; s. Tadeusz Antoni and Janina Władysława (Kwiecinska) P.; m. Irena Anna Lichtenberg, Apr. 5, 1975; children: Wojciech Paweł, Michał Mikołaj, Katarzyna Irena. M Physics, Jagellonian U., Cracow, 1971; postgrad., Acad. Mining and Metallurgy, Cracow, 1971-72; D Physics, Inst. Nuclear Physics, Cracow, 1986. Asst. Inst. Nuclear Physics, 1972-75, sr. asst., 1975-89, adj., 1989—. Contbr. articles to sci. jours., including Jour. Physics E: Sci. Instruments, Physica C., Jour. Magnetism and Magnetic Materials, Jour. Alloys and Compounds, Acta Physica Polonica A., Molecular Physics Reports. Recipient collective prize Office of Atomic Energy, 1973, Silver award of honor League for Preservation of Nature, 1978; Golden award Polish Tourist Country-Lover's Assn., 1978, Silver award of honor Polish Tourist Country-Lover's Assn., 1980. Roman Catholic. Avocations: family genealogy, bicycling, mountain climbing. Home: Sereno Fenna 10/5, 31-143 Cracow Poland Office: Henryk Niewodniczanski Inst Nuc Physics, Walerego Eljasza Radzikowskiego, 31-342 Cracow Poland

PADAKANDLA, JOHN SUNDER RAO, clergy member; b. Bangalore, India, June 21, 1949; s. Padakandla John Michael and Suvartha Sujanamma (Koylakuntla) P.; m. Mary Kasturi-Bai Manne, May 31, 1983; 1 child, Michael Sudarshan Rao. Pre-univ., Banglore U., 1968; intermediate, Bombay U., 1968; BD, Bishop's Coll., Calcutta, India, 1988; D in Min., Univ. South, Tenn., 1996. Ordained deacon Ch. of South India, 1989, presbyter Ch. of South India, 1990. Ship wright grade II Mazagon Docks Ltd., Bombay, 1973-83; priest in charge St. Mary's Ch., Vizianagram, India, 1988-89, 91-97, St. Thomas Ch., Kakinada, India, 1989-90, St. Gile's Ch., Rajahmundry, India, 1990-91, Hans Bapt. Ch., Vizianagram, 1997-98, London Mission Ch., Chittivalasa, 1998—; assoc. Bridge of Hope, Gotlam, India, 1997—. Avocations: reading, corrospondence, traveling, camping, social work. Office: London Mission Ch, PO Box # 2, Chittivalasa 531 162, India

PADBERG, HELEN SWAN, violinist; b. Shawnee, Okla.; d. Frank P. and Birdie B. (Rudell) Swan; m. Frank Padberg, Feb. 6, 1943; children: Frank, Kristen. AA, Stephens Coll., 1938; MusB, U. Okla., 1940; MusM, Northwestern U., 1941; student, Jacques Gordon. Solo performances and concerts, 1932—; mem. faculty string quartet and symphony soloist Stephens Coll., 1937-38; violinist Oklahoma City Symphony Summer Concerts, 1940; soloist Northwestern U. Symphony, 1941; violinist USO Tours World War II, 1941-43; mem. Nat. Orchestral Assn. and Am. Youth Orch., N.Y.C., 1944-46; tchr. strings Maywood (Ill.), 1946-47; asst. concertmaster West Suburban Symphony, Chgo., 1947-48; mem. Chgo. Women's Symphony, Chgo. Civic Orch. and chamber music groups, 1947-51; violinist Ark. String Trio, 1952-58; concertmaster Ark. Symphony and Little Rock Philharmonic, 1953-57, Marjorie Lawrence TV Series, Ark., 1953-54; pvt. tchr. violin Little Rock, 1953-66; accompanist and performer on piano, harp. Pres. Ark. Med. Soc. Aux., 1962-63, historian, 1963-94; co-founder Little Rock Chamber Music Soc., 1954; pres. bd. dirs. Vis. Nurse Assn. of Pulaski County, Ark., 1967-69; bd. dirs. Internat. Visitors Ctr., Chgo., 1988—, Stephens Coll. Alumna Assn. Bd.; elder, trustee Presbyn. ch. Mem. Am. Harp Soc., Chgo. Harp Soc. (sec. 1979-84), Am. Fedn. Musicians, Am. Opera Soc. (historian 1987—), Am. Opera Soc. of Chgo. (v.p. and program chmn. 1981-82, pres. 1984-87), Internat. Women Assocs. (pres. 1988-91), Pi Kappa Lambda, Mu Phi Epsilon, English Speaking Union (local chpt., bd. govs. 1997—), Pi Beta Phi (pres. Little Rock Alumnae Club), Aesthetic (pres. Little Rock) club, Women's Athletic of Chgo. Club, Musicians' Club of Women (Chgo.). Home: 175 E Delaware Pl Chicago IL 60611-1756

PADDEN, ANTHONY ALOYSIUS, JR., federal government official; b. Kearny, N.J., Apr. 3, 1949; s. Anthony Aloysius and Harriet Margaret (Dolan) P. B.A., Fairleigh Dickinson U., 1970; postgrad. U. Tenn. Sch. Law, 1970; M.A. in Pub. Adminstrn., Fairleigh Dickinson U., 1980. Employment interviewer N.J. Dept. Labor, Trenton, 1970-76, prin. procedure analyst, 1976-79; nat. procedure coordinator Interstate Compendium Employment Service Activities Project, Trenton, 1979-80; mgmt. analyst Dept. Justice, Washington, 1980-83, chief clerk of ct. U.S. Immigration Ct., Falls Church, Va., 1983—, adj. faculty mem. Nat. Judicial Coll., Reno, Nev., 1998-99; cons., Dumfries, Va., 1978—. Author Dept. Labor tech. report, 1980. Contbr. and editor for other profl. studies. Presdl. Mgmt. intern, 1980; Logan Chambers grantee Internat. Assn. Personnel in Employment Security, 1979. Mem. Pi Alpha Alpha (Adminstr. of Yr. 1991). Democrat. Roman Catholic. Home: 15272 Larkspur Ln Dumfries VA 22026-1076 Office: US Dept Justice Exec Office for Immigration Rev 5107 Leesburg Pike Ste 2545 Falls Church VA 22041-3234

PADDISON, DAVID ROBERT, lawyer; b. Savannah, Ga., May 15, 1949; s. Richard Milton and Josephine Butler (Bowles) P.; m. Frances M. Phares (div. Mar. 1995) children: Hunt, Brian, Margery; m. Jane Ingrid Caddell, Mar. 30, 1996; 1 child, Ethan David. BSBA, La. State U., 1971; JD, Tulane U., 1976. Bar: La. 1976; U.S. Dist. Ct. (ea. dist.) 1976; U.S. Ct. Appeals (5th cir.) 1976; bd. cert. specialist in family law La. State Bar Assn., 1995. Asst. dist. atty. Dist. Atty.'s Office, Covington, La., 1983-86, New Orleans, La., 1978-83; pvt. practice Covington, La., 1986—; advisor Contemporary Arts Ctr., New Orleans, 1978-79; clin. advisor Tulane U. Sch. Law, New Orleans, 1980-81; spl. cons. Dist. Atty.'s Office, New Orleans, 1981. Legal advisor Christ Episcopal Church (sch. planning com., lector, usher). Mem. Covington Bar Assn., La. Trial Lawyers Assn., ATLA. Republican. Episcopalian. Avocations: golf, sailing, snow skiing. Office: PO Box 1830 Covington LA 70434-1830

PADGET, JOHN E., management professional; b. L.A., Aug. 26, 1948; s. LeRoy and Gladys (Black) P. BA, U. Kans., 1969, postgrad., 1970. Instr. bridge Am. Contract Bridge League, 1971-77; owner Hectors, Kirkland, Wash., 1978-84; producer TV show Sta. 2, Oakland, 1985-88; regional mgr. Keithwood Agy.-Am. Health Care Adv., Pleasanton, Calif., 1991-92; exec. v.p. J. & J. Warren Co., Walnut Creek, Calif., 1991-97; pres. BBH Ltd., 1997—; pres. BBH Ltd. Author: Winning Style, 1977. Mem. AAAS, Mensa, Internat. Platfrom Soc. Jewish. Avocations: hiking, reading, travel, internet publishing. Office: BBH PO Box 792 Concord CA 94522-0792

PADHI, RABINDRA NATH, geologist; b. Ganjam, Orissa, India, May 3, 1939; s. Braja Mohan and Kamala (Das) P.; m. Sanjukta Panda, July 3, 1964 (wid. Aug. 1982); children: Madhabi, Madhumeeta, Mugdha. BS with hons., Indian Sch. of Mines, Dhanbad, India, 1959, MS, 1960, AISM, 1960; Diploma in Photogeology, ITC, Delft, Holland, 1966. Asst. geologist GSI, Simla, India, 1961-64; jr. geologist GSI, Lucknow, India, 1964-69; sr. geologist GSI, Hyderabad, India, 1969-81; dir. GSI, Bhubaneswar, India, 1981-86; dir. (s.g.) GSI, Bhubaneswar, 1986-92; dep. dir. gen. GSI, Nagpur, India, 1992-97; cons. Pasminco/India, New Delhi, 1997-99, Tarrara Pty. Ltd., Broken Hill, Australia; advisor MDA Pvt. Ltd., Nagpur, India, 1999—; dir. MP Mining Corp., Bhopal, India, 1992-97; mem. senate Nagpur U., 1995-2000. Editor: (book) Geothermal Energy In India, 1996; supr. (book) Deccan Basalts, 1996, (projects) Project Crumansonata, 1993, Exploration for Diamond, 1996 (Nat. Mineral award for Workers 1998). Mem. Indian Red Cross Soc., Bhubaneswar, 1981-92, Rover's Crew, Cuttack, 1953-57. Recipient Nat. Mineral award Govt. of India, New Delhi, 1972, Disting. Alumni award Indian Sch. Mines, Dhanbad, 1986, Univ. Gold medals Bihar U., Muzzafarpur, 1959, 60. Fellow S. Asian Soc. Econ. Geologists (vice-chmn. 1997-99), Maharashtra Acad. Sci., Orissa Acad. Sci.; mem. Mining Geologists Assn. (pres. 1995-99), Rotary (pres. Nagpur Club 1999-2000, Best Bulletin Editor 1988). Hindu. Avocations: gardening, photography. Home: c/25 Manavseva Nagar, Seminary Hills, Nagpur 440006, India

PADHILA, ELISEU, Brazilian government official. Min. of transport Govt. of Brazil, Brasilia, 1997—. Mem. Brazilian Dem. Movement Party. Office: Min Transport, Espl dos Mini Bloco E, 6 andar Brasilia DF 70044900, Brazil*

PADISAK, JUDIT, biologist, researcher; b. Budapest, Hungary, Oct. 1, 1955; d. Padisak Mihaly and Paal Roza; m. G.-Toth Laszlo, Nov. 16, 1978; children: Marcell, Kamilla, Franciska. Diploma in biology, U. Budapest, 1979, D Natural Sci., 1989; PhD, Hungarian Acad. Sci., Budapest. Asst. scientist U. Budapest, 1979-80; asst. lectr. Tchr.'s Tng. Sch., Budapest, 1981; curator Natural History Mus., Budapest, 1982-93; sr. scientist Hungarian Acad. Sci., Tihany, 1994-98, Inst. Biol. Univ. Veszprem, 1999—. Editor: Developments in Hydrobiology 81, 1993, Developments in Hydrobiology 100, 1993. Mem. Hungarian Algological Soc. (co-pres. 1990—), Internat. Soc. Limnology, Internat. Phycological Soc. Lutheran. Office: Hungarian Acad Scis, Balaton Limnological Inst, H-8237 Tihany Hungary

PADMACHANDRAN, KORAMBATH PAYYANADAN, surgeon, consultant; b. Cannanore, Kerala, India, Sept. 24, 1936; s. Kumaran Payyanadan and Devi Korambath Cherumanalil; m. Sambasalini Narikkuni Padmachandran, Jan. 12, 1969; children: Ivan, Surya. MB BChir, Stanley Med. Coll., Madras, India, 1958. Diplomate Am. Bd. Surgery. Pre-registration intern Govt. Stanley Hosp., Madras, 1959-60; rotating intern Deaconess Hosp., Buffalo, N.Y., 1960-61, resident in surgery, 1961-63, resident in anatomic pathology, 1963-64; chief resident in surgery Meml. Hosp., Albany, N.Y., 1964-65; surg. preceptee St. Clares Hosp., Schenectady, N.Y., 1965-67; asst. pres. anatomic pathology Queens U., Kingston, Can., 1967-68; surgeon SSN Mission Hosp., Vrkala, India, 1969-70, SN Trust Mission Hosp., Quilon, India, 1970-71; chief surgeon med. supt. Kunaran Meml. Hosp., Cannanore, India, 1976-99; cons. gen. surgeon Cannanore, 1999—. Fellow Royal Coll. Physicians and Surgeons Can.; mem. Indian Med. Assn., Assn. Surgeons India, Theosophical Soc., Lions Club Internat. Avocation: music. Home and Office: Shalin Talap, 670002 Cannanore Kerala, India

PADMANABHAN, KUPPUSWAMY ANANTHA, metallurgy and materials science educator; b. Thiruvananthapram, India, Apr. 5, 1945; s. Palamadai Subbier Kuppnswamy and Subbulakshmi (Ananthanarayanan) K.; m. Gita Ramamurthi, Feb. 8, 1973; children: Vivek, Anand, Amar. BS in Metall. Engring, Banaras Hindu U., Varanasi, India, 1968; PhD in Metallurgy and Materials Sci., Cambridge U., England, 1971. Lectr. dept. metall. engring Banaras Hindu U., 1972-74, reader, 1974-79; prof., head metal forming lab. Indian Inst. Tech., Madras, 1980-97, head dept. metallurgy, 1982-85, dean acad. rsch., 1996-97; dir. Indian Inst. Tech., Kanpur, 1997—; vis. scientist U Sheffield, England, 1976; vis. prof. Tech. U. Darmstadt, Germany, 1994-95; cons. in field; academician, Russia. Author: Superplasticity, 1980; editor: Energy Optimisation of Manufacturing and Materials Processing, 1989, Understanding Combustion, 1989, The Frontier Between Physics and Astronomy, 1989, Catalysis, 1991, Thermo Mechanical Aspects of Manufacturing and Materials Processing, 1992; contbr. over 170 articles to profl. jours.; inventor, patentee in field. Pupil leader Ramaseshier Higher Secondary Sch., 1960-61. Recipient rsch. prize Alexander von Humboldt Found., 1994-95; rsch. grantee German Sci. and Tech. Collaboration Agreement, 1986-95; Alexander von Humboldt fellow, Germany, 1985-86, 89, 90. Fellow Indian Nat. Acad. Engring., Indian Acad. Scis., Inst. Materials (London), Indian Inst. Metals, Instn. Engrs. (India). Avocations: reading, travel. Home: Director's Bungalow, Kanpur 208016, India Office: Indian Inst, Kanpur 208016, India

PADMANABHAN, MUKUND, researcher company executive; b. ysore, India, Aug. 31, 1965. B in Tech. (hons.), Indian Inst. Tech., Kharagpur, India, 1987; MEE, U. Calif., L.A., 1989, PhD in Integrated Cir., 1992. From rsch. staff to mgr. IBM T.J. Watson Rsch. Ctr., Yorktown Heights, N.Y., 1992-98, mgr. telephony speech algorithms, 1998—. Author: Feedback Based Orthogonal Digital Filters, 1995; patentee in field; contbr. articles to profl. jours. Mem. IEEE (sr.). E-mail: mukund@us.ibm.com. Office: IBM TJ Watson Rsch Ctr PO Box 218 Yorktown Heights NY 10598-0218

PADMANABHAN, TATTAMANGALAM RAMACHANDRAN, engineering executive; b. Tattamangalam, Palghat, India, Sept. 26, 1941; s. Tattamangalam Sivaramakrishnan and Ramachandran Iyer (Parvathi) P.; m. Uma Chidambaram, Aug. 19, 1972; 2 children. BSc in Engring., Kerala U., Trichur, 1964; M in Tech., Indian Inst. Tech., Kharagpur, 1968, PhD, 1974. Various positions Indian Inst. Tech., Kharagpur, 1964-75, asst. prof., 1975-79; asst. supt. electronics Tata Steel, Jamshedpur, 1979-82; mgr. R & D Crompton Greaves, Bombay, 1982-94, gen. mgr. R & D, 1994-95; gen. mgr. R & D Premier Polytronics, Coimbatore, 1995—. Author: Digital Systems & Microprocessors, 1982. Fellow Instn. Engrs.; mem. IEEE (sr.). Avocations: reading, classical literature, homeopathy, Indian classical music. Home: S-8 Mithila Sathyamurthy Rd, Ram Nagar Coimbatore 641 009, India Office: Premier Polytronics, 304 Trichy Rd, Singanallur Tamil Nadu 641005, India

PADMORE, ELAINE MARGUIRITE, artistic director; b. Haworth, Yorkshire, Eng., Feb. 3, 1947; d. Alfred and Florence (Stockman) P. BMus, Birmingham (U.K.) U., 1970, MA, 1971. Prodr. Radio 3 BBC, U.K., 1971-76, head of opera, 1976-83; artistic dir. Wexford (Ireland) Festival Opera, 1982-94, DGOS Opera Ireland, Dublin, 1989-93, Royal Danish Opera, Copenhagen, 1993-99, Royal Opera, Covent Garden, London, 2000—; artistic cons. Classical Prodns., London, 1990-92, London Opera Festival, 1992. Author: Wagner, 1971; producer (operas) Miss Julie, Die Liebe der Danae, The Tigers, Carmen, Don Giovanni, Tosca, Imeneo, many others. Office: Royal Opera House, Covent Garden, London WC2E 9DD, England

PADOVANO, ANTONIO, writer; b. Mola di Bari, Italy, Feb. 19, 1948; s. Giuseppe Padovano and Domenica Susca. Author: Processo Alla Malavita Barese, 1976, Racconti Allegri E Amari, 1994, L'Antiere, 1996, Il Sogno Della Ragione, 1998, Ditta Ottavio Cicoriella, 1999. Mem. N.Y. Acad. Scis. Roman Catholic. Avocations: reading, writing, travel. Home: Via Vittorio Emanuele 17, 70042 Mola di Bari Italy

PADRÓN, RUBÉN SALVADOR, endocrinologist, educator; b. Puerto Padre, Tunas, Cuba, Aug. 6, 1939; s. Rubén Juan and Maria Josefa (Durán) P.; children: Olga Maria, Rubén Luis; m. Mayda Guillén, July 1, 1972; 1 child, Dayma. MD, Havana (Cuba) U., 1965; Dr. Med. Scis., Acad. Scis., Havana, 1985. Dir. Rural Hosp./Regional Hosp., various locations, Cuba, 1965-68; resident Nat. Inst. Endocrinology, Havana, 1968-72, head endocrinology ward, 1974-78, head infertility group, 1975-82, head human reprodn. dept., 1982-98; head endocrinology dept. Camaguey (Cuba) Provincial Hosp., 1972-74; titular prof. Havana U., 1990—; cons. Nat. Group of Endocrinology, Ministry of Pub. Health, Havana, 1974—, Nat. Com. of Family Planning and Reproductive Health, Havana, 1990—; investigator human reprodn. programme WHO, 1977—; titular investigator Acad. Sci., Cuba, 1985—; reviewer L.Am. Programme of Capacitation and Investigation in Human Reprodn., 1993—;. Editor: Infertilidad Femenina, 1998 (Premio de la Critica 1999), Temas de Reproduccion Masculina y Diferenciación Sexual, 1991 (Premio de la Critica 1992), Temas de Reproducción Femenina, 1991, Manual de Diagnóstico y Tratamiento en Endocrinología, 1985; editl. bd. Revista Cubana de Endocrinologia, 1975. Pres. ethics com. Nat. Inst. Endocrinology, Havana, 1983-96, mem. sci. and ethics rev. com., 1996—. Recipient Manuel Fajardo medal Trade Union of Health Workers, Havana, 1990, 30th Anniversary Cuban Acad. Sci. medal, 1995, Distinción por la Edn. medal Ministry Higher Edn., 1998; named Disting. Guest, Oruro City, Bolivia, 1991; Human Reprodn. Program/WHO Rsch. grantee, 1978-79. Mem. Cuban Soc. Endocrinology (pres.), Internat. Soc. Andrology, L.Am. Assn. for Investigation in Human Reprodn., Cuban Soc. Reproductive Health and Reproductive Medicine (pres.), Cuban Multidisciplinary Soc. for Sexuality Studies. Avocations: chess, baseball. Home: Vedado, Calzada 115 Apto 5, Havana Cuba Office: Nat Inst Endocrinology, Zapata and C Vedado, Havana 10400, Cuba

PADUANI, CLEDERSON, physicist, researcher; b. Divinopolis, Brazil, Apr. 13, 1958; s. Cesar and Clelia (Araujo) P.; m. Ana Maria Daldegan, July 30, 1987; 1 child, Victor. BA, U. Fed. Minas Gerais, 1984, DSc in Physics, 1991. Prof. U. Fed. de Santa Catarina, Florianopolis, 1992—. Mem. SBF, Soc. Brasileira de Fisica. Avocations: guitar, swimming, chess. Office: UFSC, Campus, 88040900 Florianopolis Brazil

PADULA-PINTOS, VICTOR HORACIO, telecommunications engineer; b. Buenos Aires, Feb. 11, 1925; s. Victor Padula and María Lucinda Pintos; m. Graciela Belloni, July 5, 1948; children: Graciela Susana, Patricia Inés, Victor Horacio. Midshipman, Naval Acad., Argentina, 1945; Telecomm. Engr., La Plata U., Argentina, 1951. Dir. ARA Ionospheric Lab., Argentina, 1962-71; dir. electronics dept. Inst. Tech. Buenos Aires, Argentina, 1972-76; chmn. Nat. Com. Geo-Heliophys. Rsch., Argentina, 1976-77; dir. radiocomm. and electromagnetic Radiocomm. and Electromagnetic Compatibility Rsch. Ctr., Argentina, 1979-96; dir. sci. and technol. rsch. Inst. Tech. Buenos Aires, 1996—; prof. antenas and radiopropagation Inst. Tech. Buenos Aires, 1964-94. Contbr. articles to profl. jours. Lt. comdr. Argentine Navy, 1941-61. Fellow Argentine Assn. Geophysics and Geodesy (life); mem. IEEE (life sr.), Profl. Coun. Electronics and Telecomm. Engring. (life, chmn. 1959-63), Argentine Naval Ctr. (life), Argentine Yacht Club (life). Home: Peña 2446 7A, C1125ACD Buenos Aires Argentina Office: CAERCEM, Av Madero 399, 1106 Buenos Aires Argentina

PAEFGEN, FRANZ-JOSEF, automotive executive; b. Büttgen, Germany, May 10, 1946. Student, U. Kaslsruhe, Germany; D Mech. Engring. and Econs., U. Aachen, Germany. Trainee Ford, Germany, 1976-80; mgr. interior equipment and electronics Audi, Neckersulm, Germany, 1980-87; head body trim and equipment, climate control sys. Audi, Ingolstadt, Germany, 1987-91, head product planning and project mgmt., 1991-94, acting head R&D, 1994-95, mem. bd. mgmt., 1995-97, dep. chmn., 1997, spokesman mng. bd., 1997—. Office: Audi AG I/FF-12, Finanzanalytik und Publizitat, D-85045 Ingolstadt Germany*

PAGALA, MURALI KRISHNA, physiologist; b. Sri Kalahasti, Andhra, India, Oct. 2, 1942; came to U.S., 1970; s. Lakshmaiah and Radhamma (Bhimavaram) P.; m. Vijaya Bhimavaram, Dec. 12, 1969; children: Sobhan, Suresh. PhD in Zoology, S. V. Univ., Tirupati, A.P., India, 1969; MS in Computer Sci., Pratt Inst., N.Y., 1985. Postdoctoral fellow Inst. for Muscle Disease, N.Y.C., 1970-73, asst. mem., 1974; assoc. rsch. scientist NYU, N.Y.C., 1974-75; asst. to dir. Neuromus Disease Div. Maimonides Med. Ctr., Bklyn., 1975-89, dir. neuromuscular rsch., 1990—; vis. scientist II Physiol. Inst., U. Saarlandes, Hamburg, Germany, 1981, 82; sci. cons. UNDP/TOKTEN Program, Calcutta, India, 1990, NIGMS/FASEB MARC Program Grambling State U., La., 1992, 95; chair sci. confs., participated in Sci. Congress, Germany, 1990, Israel, 1992, Japan, 1994, 95, Australia, 1998. Reviewed and contbr. articles to profl. jours. Life mem. Telugu Assn. of North Am., 1989; sci. fair judge N.Y. Acad. Scis., N.Y.C., 1986—. Named Best speaker Zool. Soc. of S. V. Univ., 1964, Best Basic Rsch. paper Maimonides Med. Ctr., 1983, 88, 94, 95, 97; grantee Maimonides Rsch. Devel. Found., fatigue rsch., 1986—, drug abuse rsch., 1989-75, aging rsch., 1995—, urinary bladder rsch., 1997—, spinal cord protection, 1997—, anesthesiology rsch., 1997—. Mem. N.Y. Acad. Scis., Am. Physiol. Soc., Assn. Scientists of Indian Origin in Am. (pres. 1993-94). Democrat. Hindu. Achievements include devel. in vitro electromyographic, electrocardiographic and multi-muscle chambers to evaluate the function of skeletal muscle, heart and smooth muscle preparations from experimental animals and human subjects; and development of consumer products. E-mail: mvsspagala@msn.com. Home: 82 Pacific Ave Staten Island NY 10312-6212 Office: Maimonides Med Ctr 4802 10th Ave Brooklyn NY 11219-2844

PAGANI, OLIVIA, oncologist; b. Como, Italy, May 4, 1958; d. Gaetano and Mariola (Smiraldi) Santoro; m. Norberto, Nov. 14, 1986. MD, U. Milan, Italy, 1985. Sr. registrar Inst. Oncology So. Switzerland, 1992—. Mem. European Soc. Med. Oncology. Avocations: travel, cinema, reading. Office: Inst Oncology Switzerland, Ospedale Beata Vergine, 6850 Bellinzona Switzerland

PAGANO, FILIPPO FRANK, financial broker, commercial loan consultant; b. East Paterson, N.J., Feb. 4, 1939; s. Frank and Katherine (Tavano) P.; m. Rose Ann Melisi, June 10, 1960 (div. Dec. 1972); children: Paul, Cynthia Pagano Grube, Stefanie; m. Darlene Ann Coryea, Mar. 1987 (div. June, 1998). BS in Pharmacy, Rutgers U., 1960. Registered pharmacist, profl. ski instr.; lic. capt. master USCG. System analyst Parke-Davis & Co., Detroit, 1964-72; sr. mktg. analyst internat. Schering-Plough Pharm. Co., Kenilworth, N.J., 1972-73; v.p. Robert S. First, N.Y.C., 1973-74; pres. M-P Consultations Inc., N.Y.C., 1974-75; chief exec. officer Nordic Inn, Landgrove, Vt., 1975-83; sea capt. Bahamas, 1983-85; food and beverage dir. Meredith Guest House, Durham, 1985-86, gen. mgr., 1986-88; pres. Flagship Yachts, Durham, N.C., 1988—; gen. mgr. Inter-Global Capital, Raleigh, N.C., 1989—. Co-author: Nordic Inn Book of Soups, 1979; contbr. articles on skiing to newspapers and mags. Mem. Vt. Ski Touring Operators Assn. (pres. 1979-81), Beaufort Off-Shore Sailing Soc., Boss Club (Beaufort), Kappa Psi. Republican. Roman Catholic. Avocations: sailing, snow skiing, culinary interests. Home and Office: PO Box 145 Beaufort NC 28516-0145

PAGANO, NICHOLAS JOSEPH, materials engineer; b. Torrington, Conn., Jan. 11, 1933; s. Nicholas and Helen Lodzia Pagano; m. Marianne Waugh, Apr. 16, 1955; children: Nicholas, Theresa, Karen, Janet, Mark, Kathy, Christopher, Paul. BS in Civil Engring., Drexel U., 1955, MS in Civil Engring., 1961; PhD in Engring. Mechanics, Lehigh U., 1967. Instr. Drexel Inst. Tech., Phila., 1955-57, asst. prof., 1957-66; materials engr. Air Force Materials Lab., Dayton, Ohio, 1966-68; materials rsch. engr. Air Force Materials Lab., Dayton, 1968-90; sr. scientist Air Force Rsch. Lab., Dayton, 1990—; affiliate prof. Washington U., St. Louis, 1967-70; vis. prof. Drexel U., Phila., 1970; adj. prof. Ohio State U., Columbus, 1990-92; vis. scientist Air Force Office Sci. Rsch., Washington, 1985-86; mem. adv. bd. Ga. Inst. Tech., Atlanta, 1998-2000. Author: Elasticity: Tensor, Dyadic and Engineering Approaches, 1967; editor, author: Composite Materials Work-

shop, 1967, Interlaminar Response of Composite Materials, 1989; mem. editl. bd. four jours., 1985-2000; contbr. chpt. to book and articles to profl. jours. Bd. mem. PTA, 1970-72; spl. projects officer PTO, Centerville, Ohio, 1972-75; coach, organizer Soccer For Am. Youth, Centerville, Ohio, 1972-76; coach Washington Baseball League, Centerville, 1974-77, bd. treas., 1975-78; coach West Carrolton (Ohio) Adult Soccer League, 1983-84; booster club bd. mem. Centerville H.S., 1973-74; vol. for patient discharge Kettering (Ohio) Med. Hosp., 1980-85; vol. phys. therapist Montgomery County Devel. Ctr. for Handicapped Children, Kettering, 1982-84, chmn. fundraising, 1983-87; mem. Alliance for Edn., Dayton, Ohio, 1996. Recipient Air Force Basic Rsch. award USAF, Washington, 1984, award for outstandng tech. achievement The Affiliate Socs. Coun. of the Engring. and Sci. Found. Dayton, Ohio, 1991, Ohio Senate Spl. Recognition, Columbus, 1991; named Disting. lectr. NASA, Va. Poly. Inst. and State U., Blacksburg, 1987. Fellow Am. Soc. Composites (Disting. Rsch. award 1989); mem. Internat. Soc. Composite Engring. (Permanent Keynote Spkr. 1999). Avocations: bicycling, powerwalking, reading, sports. E-mail: nicholas.pagano@wpafb.af.mil. Home: 571 Brandywynne Ct Dayton OH 45459-3015 Office: Air Force Rsch Lab/MLBC 2941 P St Wright Pat OH 45433-7749

PAGANO, PATRICK JOSEPH, biomedical researcher; b. Bronx, July 26, 1963; s. Giuseppe and Catherine (La Valle) P.; m. Maria Eugenia Cifuentes, Feb. 12, 1994; children: Caterina, Daniella. BA in Chemistry, Binghamton U., 1985; MS in Pharmacology, N.Y. Med. Coll., 1987, PhD in Pharmacology, 1991. Asst. prof. Sch. Medicine Boston U., 1996-98; sr. staff investigator Henry Ford Hosp., Detroit, 1998—. Recipient FIRST award NIH. Fellow AHA (grantee-in-aid, fellow Coun. High Blood Pressure, Coun. Circulation, Coun. Basic Scis.); mem. Am. Physiol. Soc., Oxygen Soc. Office: Henry Ford Hosp Rm 7044 Hypertension/Vas Rsch Divsn Detroit MI 48202

PAGE, (JOHN) DAVID, newscaster; b. Winchester, Mass., Jan. 7, 1952; s. John William and Claire Alison (Mooers) P.; m. Danielle Roberte De Leurence; 1 child, Alexander Louis. BA, Williams Coll., 1974. News dir. WRQX Radio, Washington, 1985-87, WMC Radio, Memphis, 1987-91; news commentator RFI, Paris, 1991—; radio show host Europe 2, Paris, 1991; editor, anchor AITV, Paris, 1991-95; corr. NBC Radio News, Paris, 1992—; cons. Festival FM, Cannes, France, 1996, Club 9516 Music Awards, Paris, 1993—; anchor, host TV festival Cannes Film Festival, 1998—. Author: Washington 2057, 1997, Talked Out, 1993, (screenplay) Lafayette, 1987; actor Man in the Iron Mask, 1997, Le Nombril du Monde, 1993. Bd. dirs. Hist. Mus., Le Treport, France. Recipient UPI Newsleader award, 1984; named Club 9516 Favorite Radio Personality, 1996. Mem. Reporters Sans Frontieres Paris. Avocations: polo, tennis, parasailing, piano, speed skating. Office: 116 Ave du Pres Kennedy, 75016 Paris France

PAGE, GENEVIEVE, actress; b. Paris, Dec. 13, 1927; d. Jacques Bonjean and Germaine Lipmann; m. Jean-Claude Bujard, 1959; 2 children. Student Lycee Racine, Paris, Sorbonne, Paris, Conservatoire nat. d'art dramatique. Prin. actress in the Comedie Francaise and Jean-Louis Barrault Co., T.N.P. Jean Vilar; appeared in many famous classical and tragic stage roles; numerous film appearance include: Ce siecle a cinquante ans, Pas de pitie pour les femmes, Fanfan la tulipe, Lettre ouverte, Plaisirs de Paris, Nuits andalouses, L'etrange desir de M. Bard, Cherchez la femme, L'homme sans passe, Foreign Intrigue, The Silken Affair, Michael Strogoff, Un amour de poche, Song Without End, Le bal des adieux, El Cid, Le jour et l'heure, L'honorable correspondent, Youngblood Hawke, Le majordome, Les corsaires, l'or et le plomb, Trois chambres a Manhattan, Grand Prix, Belle de jour, Mayerling, A Talent for Loving, The Private Life of Sherlock Holmes, Les Gemeaux, Decembre, Buffet Froid, Les Larmes Ameres de Petra von Kant (prix de la critique meilleure actrice), , La Femme sur Le Lit, Les Bois Noirs, Mere Courage, Le Soulier de Satin, L'Echange. Le Balcon, Les Grandes Forets, Colombe, 1996 (prix plaisir du theatre meilleure actrice), Les Grandes Forets, 1998, Delicate Balance, 1998. Decorated Chevalier du Merite sportif; recipient Prix de la Critique, 1980, Memoreen Fuite, 2000.

PAGE, JEREMY NEIL, editor; b. Folkestone, England, Feb. 23, 1958; s. Harold and Doris (Hawker) P.; m. Maria Jane Maguire Judd, June 29, 1991; children: Harry Benjamin, Lily Alexandra, Dominic Louis, William Arthur. BA, U. Warwick, 1980; MA, U. Bristol, 1983. Tchr. Internat. House, Arezzo, Italy, London, Hastings, England, 1983-88; trainer Internat. House, Nice, France, London, 1989-95; dir. studies Internat. House, London, 1995—; mng. editor Frogmore Press, England, 1983—; mem. editl. bd. The IH Jour. of Edn. and Devel., 2000—. Author: (poetry) Bliss, 1989, Secret Dormitories, 1993; co-author: Think Ahead to First Certificate Workbook, 1993, The Alternative Version, 2000; editor: The Frogmore Poetry Prize Anthology, 1992, The Frogmore Papers Anthology, 1993, Poetry South East 2000, 2000; co-editor: Frogmore Poetry, 1989, Decade, 1996. Avocations: theatre, film, cricket, ornithology, languages.

PAGE, JOHN GRAHAM, emergency medicine educator, consultant; b. Liverpool, Eng., Feb. 16, 1943; s. George Ronald and Lilian Alice (Kay) P.; m. Jessie Sandra Hossack, Aug. 30, 1968; children: Andrew, Caroline, Alison. MB, ChB, Aberdeen (Scotland) U., 1968, ChM, 1977. Registered med. practitioner. Resident house officer in medicine Aberdeen (Scotland) Royal Infirmary, 1968-69, resident house officer in surgery, 1969, sr. house officer in surgery, 1970-71, registrar in surgery, 1971-79, registrar in accident and emergency medicine, 1979-81, cons. in accident and emergency medicine, 1981—; lectr. pathology Aberdeen U., 1969-70; rsch. fellow Harvard U., Boston, 1974-75; hon. prof. emergency medicine Robert Gordon U., Aberdeen, 1993—; hon. med. cons. Brit. Antarctic Survey, 1981-96; chief med. officer Brit. Assn. Ski. Patrollers, 1991. Author: (with K.L.G. Mills and R. Morton) A Colour Atlas of Plaster Techniques, 1986, (with Mills and R. Siweck) A Colour Atlas of Low Back Pain, 1990, (with Mills and Morton) A Colour Atlas and Text of Emergencies, 1995 (high commendation award Royal Soc. Medicine 1995); contbg. author: Infection in Surgical Practice, 1992. Fellow Royal Coll. Surgeons (Edinburgh) (examiner part 2 accident and emergency exams.), Faculty Accident and Emergency Medicine (regional advisor for N.E. Scotland, chmn. higher tng. com. 1996—), Faculty of Occupl. Medicine; mem. Brit. Assn. Accident and Emergency Medicine, Brit. Med. Assn., European Undersea Baromed. Soc., Aberdeen Medico-Chirurg. Soc. Home: 16 Kingswood Ave Kingswells, Aberdeen AB15 8AE, Scotland Office: Aberdeen Royal Infirmary, Accident and Emergency Dept, Aberdeen AB25 2ZN, Scotland

PAGE, LEWIS WENDELL, JR., lawyer; b. Scottsboro, Ala., Nov. 6, 1947; s. Lewis Wendell and Maymie Elizabeth (Parks) P.; m. Dollie Lucretia Roberts, Dec. 24, 1977; children—Margaret Amelia, Katherine Elizabeth. B.A., Auburn U., 1970; J.D., U. Ala., 1973; LL.M., George Washington U., 1975. Bar: Ala. 1973, U.S. Dist. Ct. (no. dist.) Ala. 1974, U.S. Ct. Appeals (5th cir.) 1973, U.S. Ct. Appeals (11th cir.) 1978, U.S. Supreme Ct. 1982. Assoc. firm Sadler, Sadler, Sullivan & Sharp, Birmingham, Ala., 1973-74; assoc. firm Lange, Simpson, Robinson & Somerville, Birmingham, 1975-80, ptnr. 1980-93, Page Law Firm, 1993—; pres., CEO Controllex, L.L.C., 1997—. Served to 2d lt. U.S. Army, 1973. Mem. Ala. State Bar Assn. (chmn. antitrust sect. 1983-84, co-chmn. permanent code commn. 1986-88), Birmingham Bar Assn. (panel chmn. grievance com. 1983-84, chmn. fee arbitration com. 1984-85, exec. com. 1998—), ABA (antitrust sect., litigation sect., patent, copyright and trademark sect.), Auburn U. Bar Assn. (pres. 1993-94).*

PAGE, LORNE ALBERT, physicist, educator; b. Buffalo, July 28, 1921; s. John Otway and Laura (Stewart) P.; m. Muriel Emily Jamieson, Sept. 7, 1946; children: J. Douglas, Kenneth L., James F., Donald S., David K. BSc, Queen's U., Can., 1944; PhD, Cornell U., 1950. Mem. faculty U. Pitts., 1950—, prof. physics, 1958-86, prof. emeritus, 1987—; vis. physicist Stanford U., Palo Alto, Calif., 1962, Lawrence Livermore Lab., Calif., 1970. Contbr. articles to Phys. Rev., Rev. Modern Physics, Ann. Rev. Nuc. and Particle Sci. Lt. Royal Can. Navy, 1944-45. Guggenheim fellow Upsala U., Sweden, 1957-58; Alfred P. Sloan research fellow, 1961-63. Fellow Am. Phys. Soc.; mem. Sigma Xi. Episcopalian. Achievements include definitive measurement of electron-electron (Moller) scattering, measurement of the positron's mass, identification of positronium in condensed matter; development of method for analyzing circular polarization of high energy x-rays, first measurement of inherent polarization of positive beta particles. Home: 157 Lloyd Ave Pittsburgh PA 15218-1645

PAGE, LOUIS RAJKUMAR, broadcasting company executive; b. Colombo, Sri Lanka, Sept. 18, 1949; s. Albert Athisayaratnam and Lucy (Aloysious) P.; m. Kahirabdhi Tanaya Padmanabht, Jan. 11, 1973; 3 children. FCA, Inst. Chartered Accts., Ceylon, Sri Lanka, 1971; FCMA, Inst. Cost & Mgmt. Accts., England, 1973. Chief acct. Cargills Ltd., Ceylon, Sri Lanka, 1973-74; chief acct. Shaw Group Cos., Hong Kong, 1974-79, group sec., fin. controller, 1979-82; sec. Television Broadcasts Ltd., Hong Kong, 1983-87, exec. dir., 1987-95; exec. dir. Shaw Group Cos., Hong Kong, 1983—; mng. dir. Television Broadcasts Ltd., Hong Kong, 1995—. Office: Television Broadcasts Ltd, TV City Clear Water Bay Rd, Kowloon Hong Kong

PAGE, SALLY JACQUELYN, university official; b. Saginaw, Mich., 1943; d. William Henry and Doris Effie (Knippel) P. BA, U. Iowa, 1965; MBA, So. Ill. U., 1973. Copy editor C.V. Mosby Co., St. Louis, 1965-69; editl. cons. Editl. Assocs., Edwardsville, Ill., 1969-70; rsch. adminstr. So. Ill. U., 1970-74, asst. to pres., affirmative action officer, 1974-77; office of instn. U. N.D., Grand Forks, 1977—, lectr. mgmt., 1978—; polit. comentator Sta. KFJM, Nat. Public Radio affiliate, 1981-90; mem. mayor's com. Employment of People With Disabilities, 1980-97. Contbr. articles to profl. jours. Chmn. N.D. Equal Opportunity Affirmative Action Officers, 1987-2000; pres. Pine to Prairie coun. Girl Scouts U.S., 1980-85; mem. employment com. Ill. Commn. on Status of Women, 1976-77; mem. Bicentennial Com., Edwardsville, 1976, Bikeway Task Force, Edwardsville, 1975-77, Bus. Leadership Network; bd. dirs. Grand Forks Homes, 1985—, pres., 1996—; mem. Civil Svc. Rev. Task Force, Grand Forks, 1982, civil svc. commr., 1983-98, chmn., 1984, 86, 88, 92, 96; ruling elder 1st Presbyn.; mem. Grand Forks Mayor's Adv. Cabinet, 1998-2000. Mem. AAUW (dir. Ill. 1975-77), PEO, Coll. and Univ. Pers. Assn. (rsch. and publs. bd. 1982-84), Soc. Human Resource Mgmt., Am. Assn. Affirmative Action. Democrat. Presbyterian. Home: 3121 Cherry St Grand Forks ND 58201-7461 Office: U ND Grand Forks ND 58202

PAGEL, THEO, curator; b. Duisburg, Germany, Jan. 14, 1961; s. Theo and Margaret (Wagner) P.; m. Iris Lunghard, 1984; children: Anne, Julia. Degree in Biology/Geography, U. Duesseldorf, Germany, 1990. Curator Zoo Cologne, Germany, 1991—; cons. in field. Author: (book) Loris, 1997. Avocations: traveling, birding, hunting. Office: Zoo Koln, Riehlerstr, 50735 Koln Germany

PAGELS, JÜRGEN HEINRICH, balletmaster, dance educator, dancer, choreographer, writer; b. Lübeck, Germany, Apr. 16, 1925; came to U.S., 1955; s. Heinrich and Margret (Haas) P. Artists diploma, Hamburg (Fed. Republic Germany) State Exam Bd., 1947; advanced soloist exam. with honors, Assn. Russian Ballet, London, 1952, advanced tchrs. exam. with honors, 1961, sr. tchrs. exam. with honors, 1969; DFA, Pacific Western U., 1988. Ballet soloist Atlantic Theater, Lübeck, 1945-46, Stadt-Theater, Lübeck, 1946-47; prin. dancer Dortmund, Fed. Republic Germany, 1947-48, Operette and Stattl. Schauspielhaus Theater, Hamburg, 1949-50; ballet soloist Ballet Theater Co., Hamburg, 1950-51; prin. dancer Ballet Legat, London, 1951-52, Ballet Legat and Yugoslav Nat. Ballet, touring throughout Europe, 1952-53; guest ballet soloist Ballet Etoile, Paris Opera, Paris, 1954; dir., owner Pagels Legat Sch. Ballet, Dallas, 1955-62; guest tchr. ballet numerous dance acads. and ballet cos., worldwide, 1962-70; prof. dance Ind. Univ., Bloomington, 1970-90; prof. emeritus Ind. U., Bloomington, 1990—; guest tchr. ballet numerous orgns. including Vaganova Choreography Inst., Leningrad, USSR, Ballet do Rio de Janeiro, Egypt Nat. Ballet of Cairo, Ballet Intezet, Hungary, Nat. Ballet, Istanbul, Turkey, Royal Danish Ballet, Tex. Christian Univ., Ft. Worth, Nat. Ballet, Nicaragua; condr. master classes for Ballet Guatemala, Escuela Nacional de Danza, San Salvador, Academia de Danza Classica, Costa Rica, Nat. Ballet Venezuela, T.W. Univ., Nat. U. Costa Rica, Bellas Artes, Honduras, Ballet Nacional Nicaragua; co-founder, dir. Dallas Civic Ballet; art dir. Ballet Guatemala, 1978-79, Nat. Ballet Salvador, Ulm Theatre, Germany, Ballet Co., 1995, Ballet Nat.-Mcpl., Lima, 1999, Artemis, Amsterdam, Holland; Internat. Ballet competition Managuq, Nicaragua, 1995. Author of character dance books and ballet dance books in English, German and Spanish, 1991; collaborator and coach to Dame Margot Fonteyn. U.S. judge Internat. Ballet Competition, Trujillo, Peru, 1989-91, 99, Internat. Competition, Camaguey, Cuba, 1999. Served as sgt. German Army, 1942-45. Research grantee Ind. Univ., 1977. Avocations: exhibited sculptor, tennis, deep-sea fishing. Home: 934A S Maxwell Ter Apt A Bloomington IN 47401-5264 Office: Ind U Sch Music Ballet Dept Bloomington IN 47405 also: Curtius Str 6, 23568 Luebeck Germany

PAGENDARM, HANS-GEORG, mechanical engineer; b. Hagen, Westphalia, Germany, Oct. 22, 1954; s. Johann Heinrich Josef and Marianne (Börstinghaus) P.; m. Nora Gattner, Oct. 10, 1981; children: Eva, Bastian. M in Engring., Ruhr U., Bochum, Germany, 1979; diploma in fluid dynamics, von Karman Inst., Rhode-St. Genese, Belgium, 1980; PhD in Engring., Ruhr U., 1985. Rsch. asst. Ruhr U., Bochum, 1980-85; scientist DLR German Aerospace Ctr., Göttingen, 1985-2000, head software tech. group for fluid mechanics, 1987-2000; head dept. info. tech. and measurement techs. German-Dutsch Windtunnerl DNW, 2000—; lectr. Georg August U., Göttingen, Germany. Author: Optimierung von Diffusoren bezüglich der Diffusorströmung und der Diffusorwände, 1987; contbr. articles to profl. jours. Mem. IEEE Visualization (conf. co-chair 1995-98, editl. bd. Trans. on Visualization and Computer Graphics), Eurographics (chmn. visualization working group 1997—), Sun User Group of Germany (co-chair 1988-90), Genealogic Heraldic Soc. Göttingen, Java User Group of Germany (chmn. 1999—). Roman Catholic. Office: DLR German Aerospace Ctr, Bunsenstrasse 10, 37073 Göttingen Germany

PAGES, MONTSERRAT, biologist; b. Torredembarra, Spain, Feb. 24, 1945; d. Vicens and Montserrat (Torrens) P.; m. Marti Borrell; children: Marti, Marie, Anna. Lic., U. Barcelona, 1971; PhD, U. Autonoma Madrid, 1976. Asst. Centro Investigación y Desarrollo, Madrid, 1975-78; rsch. scientist Consejo Superior Investigaciones Cientificas, Barcelona, 1978-82, investigator, 1982-92, head dept., 1993—. Contbr. articles to profl. jours. Mem. Soc. Catalana Biologia. Office: CSIC, Jorge Girona 18-26, 08034 Barcelona Spain

PAGLIARULO, MICHAEL ANTHONY, physical therapy educator; b. Amityville, N.Y., May 15, 1947; s. Anthony and Louise (Cipriani) P.; m. Patricia Marilyn Salm, Mar. 22, 1975; children: Michael, David, Elisa. BA in Biology, SUNY, Buffalo, 1969, BS in Phys. Therapy, 1970; MA in Phys. Therapy, U. So. Calif., 1974; EdD in Postsecondary Edn. Adminstrn., Syracuse U., 1988. Lic. phys. therapist, N.Y., Calif. Staff phys. therapist Brunswick Hosp. Ctr., Amityville, 1970; lectr. U. So. Calif., L.A., 1974-75, U. Calif., San Francisco, 1975-80; curriculum coord. Ithaca (N.Y.) Coll., 1980-82, asst. prof., 1982-84, acting dir., 1986-89, assoc. prof., dir., 1989-94, assoc. prof. phys. therapy, 1994-2000, chair, 1997-2000. Author: Introduction to Physical Therapy, 1996. Bd. dirs. Marin/Roundtree Homeowners Assn., San Rafael, Calif., 1978-80; cubmaster Boy Scouts Am., Ithaca, 1989-91. Capt. U.S. Army, 1970-72. Named to Copiague H.S. Hall of Achievement, 1998. Mem. Am. Phys. Therapy Assn. (bd. dirs. Calif. chpt. 1979-80, treas. N.Y. chpt. 1989-91, Merit award 1988, 95, 97, Norma Chadwick award 1993, Outstanding Svc. award 1997, Dr. Marilyn Moffat Disting. Svc. award 1998). Congregationalist. Avocations: scuba diving, water and snow skiing, model trains. Office: Ithaca Coll Dept Phys Therapy Danby Rd Ithaca NY 14850-1328

PAGLINI, SEVERO, educator; b. Gualeguaychu, Entre Rios, Argentina, Nov. 25, 1920; s. Adolfo Pedro and Carolina (Lencioni) P.; m. Ada Guillerma Solari, July 23, 1951; children: Patricia Adriana, Victoria Monica, Julieta Alejandra, Maria Gabriela. Bachelors degree, Luis Clavarino, Gualeguaychu, 1939; pharmacist, Farmacia Y Bioquimi, Cordoba, Argentina, 1945, D in Biochemistry, 1947; PhD, Instituto Ciencias Quimicas, Cordoba, Argentina, 1964. Minor practitioner Faculty of Med. Scis., Cordoba, 1945-46; sr. practitioner Faculty of Med. Schs., Cordoba, 1946-47, chief lab., 1947-48; second chief lab. Italian Hosp., Cordoba, 1949-60; rsch. chief Alergy Inst., Cordoba, 1955-60; full prof. Sch. Pharmacy and Biochemistry, Cordoba, 1955-64, Virology Inst., Cordoba, 1960-90; cons. prof. Nat. U. of Cordoba, 1993—; rsch. career mem. Nat. Rsch. Coun., Argentina, 1961—; dir. Virology Inst., Cordoba, 1978-85; chief of cellular receptors Inst. Virology, Cordoba U. Author: La Electromigracion Como Tecnica Analitica, 1964, Introduccion Al Estudio Biofisico de Las Macromoleculas, 1979, Los Virus: Capitulo En Microbiologia Clinica, 1984, Identification of a Second Cellular Receptor for a Coxackie Virus B-3 Variant CB3-RD, 1990, Virus Receptores y Correceptores Celulares, 1999; contbr. chpts. to books and over 70 articles to profl. publs. Recipient numerous grants Nat. Rsch. Coun., Sci. and Tech. Sec., Argentina, 1962—. Mem. Am. Soc. for Microbiology, Argentinian Biochemistry Rsch., N.Y. Acad. Sci., Cordoba Med. Circle (hon.), Argentinian Assn. for Microbiology (hon.). Mem. Radical Civic Union. Avocations: hunting, fishing, cooking. E-mail: spaglini@cmefcm.uncor.edu. Office: Inst de Virologia Ciudad U, Agencia 4, 5016 Cordoba Argentina

PAGNOTTA, MARIO-AUGUSTO, educator; b. Rome, Sept. 13, 1960; s. Emidio Pagnotta and Giovanna Castaldo; m. Stefania Turbessi, July 15, 1987; children: Mattia-Federico, Susanna-Maria. Grad. in agrl. sci., U. Perugia, Italy, 1984; PhD, Reading (Eng.) U., 1991. Cert. agronomist. Profl. expert U. Perugia, 1986; rsch. assoc. Internat. Ctr. for Agrl. Rsch. in the Dry Areas, Aleppo, Syria, 1986-91; asst. prof. U. Viterbo, Italy, 1992—; prof. conservation biodiversity U. Viterbo, 1998-99; prof. genetics U. Maputo, Mozambique, 1994; mem. organizing com. 1998 Eucarpias's Gen. Congress, Viterbo, 1995-98. Editor: Seed Science and Technology, 1993, Italian Contribution to Plant Genetics and Breeding, 1999, Genetics and Breeding for Crop Quality and Resistance, 1999. Sub-lt. Logistic Group, Rome, 1995-96. Mem. European Assn. Plant Breeding, Italian Soc. Agrl. Sci. Fax: 39-0761-357242. E-mail: pagnotta@unitus.it. Office: Tuscia Univ, Via S Camillo de Lellis, 01100 Viterbo Italy

PAGONE, GAETANO TONY, barrister; b. Melbourne, Victoria, Australia, July 31, 1955; s. Salvatore Eduardo and Maria Bianca (Consoli) P.; m. Margaret Lorraine Mioni, Jan. 6, 1977; children: Clara Francesca, Richard Salvatore. BA, Monash U., Australia, 1976, diploma in edn., 1977, LLB, 1979; LLM, Cambridge (Eng.) U., 1983. Queen's Counsel, Victoria, Australia. Tchr. Edn. Dept., Melbourne, 1976-78; articled clk. Frederick Owen and Assocs., Melbourne, 1979-80; tutor Melbourne State Coll., 1980-81; tutor law faculty Monash U., Melbourne, 1981-83, lectr. law faculty, 1984-87; barrister Victorian Bar, Melbourne, 1985—; chmn. edn. com. Taxation Inst. Australia, Melbourne, 1994-95, 97-98; treas. bus. law sect. Law Coun. Australia, Melbourne, 1997-99; chmn. bus. law sect., Law Coun. Australia, 1999. Author: Introducing the Law, 1984. Sec. Victorian Coun. for Civil Liberties, Melbourne, 1986-88; chmn. Internat. Commn. Jurists in Victoria, Melbourne, 1994-97. Mem. Australian Club, Melbourne Savage Club, Victorian Bar. Avocations: reading, films, food, Royal tennis. music.

PAGTALUNAN, FLORA ZENAIDA DIAZ, pediatrician; b. Zamboanga City, Philippines, Dec. 22, 1936; d. Lorenzo Sayson Diaz and Carmen Fuentebella Larracochea; m. Redentor J. Giongco Pagtalunan, Feb. 27, 1960; 1 child, Enrica. BA, U. Philippines, 1954, MD, 1959. Diplomate Am. Bd. Pediatrics, Philippine Pediat. Soc. Staff cons. pediatrics Med. Ctr. Manila, Philippines, 1978-80, 82-83, 1986-89; assoc. clin. prof. pediatrics Aguinaldo Coll. Medicine, Manila, 1988-90; staff cons. Manila Doctors Hosp.; chmn., bd. sec. Marianne Doctors Hosp., Manila.

PAGTALUNAN, REDENTOR JUAN GUILLERMO, general surgeon, consultant; b. Manila, Mar. 3, 1931; s. Angel Karangan and Merced Pugeda (Giongco) P.; m. Flora Zenaida Larracochea Diaz, Feb. 27, 1960; 1 child, Maria Enrica. AA, U. Philippines, Quezon City, 1949, MD, 1955; MS Colorectal Surgery, U. Minn., 1964. Diplomate Am. Bd. Surgery, Philippine Bd. Surgery, Pan Am. Med. Assn. Intern Philippine Gen. Hosp., Manila, 1954-55; resident in radiology UP-PGH Med. Ctr., 1955-58; resident in gen. surgery Lakewood Hosp., Cleve., 1958-61; resident in colorectal surgery Mayo Clinic, Rochester, Minn., 1961-64; resident in gen. surgery St. Luke's Hosp., St. Paul, 1964-65; assoc. clin. prof. surgery E. Aguinaldo Medicine, Manila, 1987-89; staff cons. gen. surgery Med. Ctr., Manila, 1972—, chmn., 1987-89; staff cons. gen. surgery Manila Doctors Hosp., 1984—, bd. dirs. med. staff, 1992-96; gov. Philippine Bd. Surgery, 1969-80, examiner, 1969-97; cons. gen. surgery/gastroenterology Philippine Cancer Soc., 1966-85. Recipient Cert. of Appreciation, Philippine Bd. Surgery, Manila, 1990, Rsch. award Cleve. Surg. Soc., 1960, plaque of appreciation Philippine Cancer Soc., 1986. Fellow ACS, Philippine Coll. Surgeons, Philippine Soc. Laparoscopic Surgeons, Surg. Oncology Soc. of Philippines; mem. Doctors Mayo Soc., U. Minn. Alumni Assn. Office: Med Ctr Manila, Gen Luna, 1122 Ermita Manila Philippines

PAGUIO-TORREYILLAS, DIMPNA DURAN, pediatrician, educator; b. Vigan, Ilocos Sur, The Philippines, May 15, 1938; d. Juan Santiago and Rosa (Duran) Paguio; m. Eusebio Godinez Torreyillas, Aug. 25, 1976; 1 child, Juan Alfonso. AB, U. of the Philippines, 1957, MD, 1967. Diplomate Am. Bd. Pediat., Philippine Pediat. Soc. Pediat. resident Mt. Sinai Hosp., Chgo., 1963-65; chief pediat. resident Babies Hosp., Newark, 1965-66; fellow clin. pediat. N.Y. Down State U., Bklyn., 1966-67; chair dept. pediat. Dr. Uy Hosp., The Philippines, 1974-92; clin. preceptor pediat. Mindanao State U. Coll. Medicine, The Philippines, 1992-94; pediat. dept. chair Mindanao Sanitarium & Hosp., The Philippines, 1992—; pediat. cons. Mercy Cmty. Hosp., The Philippines, 1992—. V.p. Birth Devel., The Philippines, 1996—; chmn. Punla PPS-Unilab for El Nino Cmtys., Rotabato, The Phillppines, 1998-99. Fellow Philippine Pediat. Soc. (pres. 1973-74, trustee 1996-98); mem. Iligan Med. Soc. (pres.-elect 2000—), U. Philippines Alumni Assn. (pres. 1993-94), Rotary-Down South Iligan (pres.). Roman Catholic. Avocations: crossword puzzles, cross-stitch, digong, reading, cooking. Home: 0033 D Tibanga, Iligan City M9200, The Philippines Office: Mindanao Sanitarium Hosp, Tibanga, Iligan M9200, The Philippines

PAHOR, AHMES LABIB, physician; b. Cairo, Egypt, Sept. 15, 1942; Brit. citizen; MB, BCh, Cairo U., 1964, DLO, 1966; DMSc in Pathology, Ain Shams U., Cairo, 1968; MA, Inst. Higher Coptic Studies, Cairo, 1986; Diploma in History of Medicine, Soc. Apothecaries, London, 1994. Cert. in otolaryngology Gen. Med. Coun., London, 1995. Intern Cairo U. Hosp., 1964-65; sr. house officer Ministry of Health, Cairo, 1965-66; asst. rschr. pathology and cytology dept. Nat. Rsch. Ctr., Ministry Sci. Rsch., Cairo, 1966-70; sr. house officer ENT dept. Waveney Hosp., Ballymena, No. Ireland, 1970-72, Birmingham (Eng.) and Midland Ear, Nose and Throat Hosp., 1972; registrar Eye and Ear Clinic Royal Victoria Hosp. and Belfast (No. Ireland) City Hosp., 1972-74; registrar, tchr. various hosps., Eng., 1974-78; cons. ENT surgeon Dudley Road Hosp./West Birmingham Health Authority, 1978—, Sandwell Dist. Gen. Hosp./Sandwell Dist. Health Authority, 1978—; hon. sr. clin. lectr. Med. Sch., Birmingham U.; examiner Royal Coll. Surgeons, Edinburgh. Referee Jour. Laryngology and Otology, 1992—; contbr. numerous articles to profl. jours.; rschr. in field. Fellow Royal Coll. Surgeons (Edinburgh) (adv. bd.), Internat. Coll. Surgeons; mem. Royal Coll. Physicians (London); mem. Brit. Med. Assn., Royal Soc. Medicine, Brit. Assn. Otolaryngologists, Brit. Assn. Pediatric Otorhinolaryngologists, Irish Soc. Otolaryngology, Midland Inst. Otology (hon. libr.), Brit. Assn. for Cancer Rsch., Brit. Soc. for History of ENT (founder mem., sec.), Internat. Soc. ENT, Birmingham Soc. History of Medicine, Brit. Soc. History of Medicine, Internat. Soc. History of Medicine, Internat. Hippocratic Found. of Kos, European Rhinologic Soc., N.Y. Acad. Scis., Freedom of the City of London. Office: City Hosp NHS Trust, Dudley Rd, Birmingham B18 7QH, England

PAHOR, DUŠICA, ophthalmologist, consultant; b. Murska Sobota, Slovenia, Oct. 29, 1957; d. Venčeslav and Irena (Rogl) Svatina; m. Artur Pahor, Dec. 19, 1981; 1 child, Jan. MD, Med. Faculty Ljubljana, Slovenija, 1981; MS, Med. Faculty Zagreb, Croatia, 1994, PhD in Medicine, 1997. Gen. practitioner Health Inst., Maribor, Slovenia, 1981-85, pediatric ophthalmologist, 1990-92; specialist in ophthalmology Eye Clinic, Ljubljana, 1986-90; cons. in ophthalmology Teaching Hosp. Maribor, 1992—; lectr. High Med. Sch., Maribor, 1995—. Contbr. articles to profl. jours. Grantee European Soc. Ophthalmology, Milan, Italy, 1995. Mem. Austrian Ophthalmological Assn., N.Y. Acad. Scis., European Soc. Cataract and Refractive Surgeons (award 1996), Austrian Ophthalmol. Assn. Avocation: classic guitar. Home: Presernova 11, 2000 Maribor Slovenia Office: Teaching Hosp Opthalmol Dpt, Ljubljanska 5, 2000 Maribor Slovenia

PAI, TONSE RAMESH UPENDRA, business executive; b. Udupi, Karnataka State, India, Oct. 22, 1924; s. Upendra Anantha and Parvathi Upendra Pai; m. Shanti Ramesh Parvathi Baliga, May 29, 1949; children: Shobha, Sudhakar, Sheela, Shantharam. Grad. (hon.), Acad. of Genl. Edu-

cation, Manipal, 1944. Mng. dir. G.I.C.C. Ltd., Udupi, 1943-55, Canara Land Investments Ltd., Udupi, Maha Rashtra Apex Corp. Ltd., Udupi/Manipal, 1956-84; chmn., mng. dir. Indsl. Credit & Devel. Syndicate Ltd., Manipal, 1984-95; chmn., mng. dir. Maha Rashtra Apex Corp. Ltd., Manipal, 1995-99, chmn., 1999—; emeritus chmn. Kurlon Ltd., Bangalore; bd. dirs. Reliance Industries Ltd., Bombay, Andhra Sugars Ltd., Tanuku, Lingapur Estates Ltd., Bangalore, Manipal Control Data Electronic Commerce Ltd., Dupont Kurlon Ltd.; chmn. Maipal Home Fin. Ltd. Past pres. The Kasturba Med. Coll. Trust, Manipal; past mem. Senate of Madras U., Senate of Mangalore U., Syndicate of Mysore U.; active Ct. of Goa U., 1990-96; former v.p. Family Planning Assn. of India (25 yrs.); dir. Rotary Intl., Evanston, Ill., 1992-94. Recipient Key to the City of Miami Beach, Vidyadhiraj award H.H. Gokarn Parthagali Jeevottam Mutt, GOA, citation Internat. Planned Parenthood Fedn., London, Karnataka Rajyotsava award, 1998. Mem. Rotary (pres., Golden Century citation 1995-96, mem. nomination com. for pres. of Rotary Internat. 2000-2001, 1998—), Udupi C. of C. Industry (pres.), All India Mfrs. Orgn. (chmn.), Karnataka State Bd., Rotary Club of Udupi-Manipal. Home: Chitrakala 5 Anant Nagar, Manipal Karnataka 576119, India Office: Maha Rashtra Apex Corp Ltd, Syndicate House, Manipal Karnataka 576119, India

PAIGE, ANITA PARKER, retired English language educator; b. Valparaiso, Ind., Feb. 5, 1908; d. Eugene Mark and Grace Agnes (Noon) Parker; m. Robert Myron Paige, Aug. 12, 1933 (dec. 1965); children: Susan Marlowe Paige Morrison, Amy Woods Paige Dunker, Caroline Parker Paige McClennan. AB, Vassar Coll., 1929; MA, U. Chgo., 1930, postgrad., 1931-32. Instr. English Hillsdale (Mich.) Coll., 1930-31, asst. prof., 1931-33; bd. edn. Anglo-Am. Schs., Athens, Greece, 1948-51; tchr. secondary sch. Am. Sch., Teheran, Iran, 1957-58; instr. English Republic of China Mil. Cartographic Sec. group, Taipei, Taiwan, 1960-61; instr. dept. English Nat. Taiwan U., Taipei, 1961-62; intermittent lectr., 1988—; bd. dirs. Ginling Girls Mid. Sch., Taipei, 1960-62. Bd. dirs. (Presbyn.) Cmty. Ch., Teheran, 1957-58. Mem. LWV (chmn. Cook County, Ill. child welfare dept. 1933-36, mem. bd. Overseas Edn. Fund 1966-68), Diplomatic and Consular Officers Ret., Assn. Am. Fgn. Svc. Women, Asian Am. Forum (founding mem.), Friends of Soochow U., Phi Beta Kappa. Democrat.

PAIGE, GLENN DURLAND, political scientist, educator; b. Brockton, Mass., June 28, 1929; s. Lester Norman and Rita Irene (Marshall) P.; m. Betty Gail Grenier, Jan. 2, 1949 (div.); children: Gail, Jan, Donn, Sean, Sharon, Van; m. Glenda Hatsuko Naito, Sept. 1, 1973. Grad., Phillips Exeter Acad., 1947; A.B., Princeton U., 1955; M.A., Harvard U., 1957; Ph. D., Northwestern U., 1959; PhD (hon.), Soka U., 1992. Asst. prof. pub. adminstrn. Seoul Nat. U., 1959-61; asst. to assoc. prof. politics Princeton U., 1961-67; prof. polit. sci. U. Hawaii, Honolulu, 1967-92, prof. emeritus, 1992—; cons. Fla. Martin Luther King, Jr., Inst. for Nonviolence, 1997. Author: The Korean Decision, 1968, The Scientific Study of Political Leadership, 1977, To Nonviolent Political Science, 1993; editor: Political Leadership, 1972, (with George Chaplin) Hawaii 2000, 1973, (with Sarah Gilliatt) Nonviolence in Hawaii's Spiritual Traditions, 1991, Buddhism and Nonviolent Global Problem-Solving, 1991, (of Petra K. Kelly) Nonviolence Speaks to Power, 1993, (with Chaiwat Satha-Anand) Islam and Nonviolence, 1993; social sci. editor: Biography, 1977-2000. Program chmn. Hawaii Gov.'s Conf. on Yr. 2000, 1970; faculty UN Univ. Internat. Leadership Acad., 1997; pres. Non-profit Ctr. for Global Nonviolence, 1994—. With U.S. Army, 1948-52. Decorated Commendation medal; recipient Seikyo Culture prize, 1982, Dr. G. Ramachandran award for internat. understanding, 1986, Anuvrat award for internat. peace, 1987, Jai Tulsi Anuvrat award, 1995; named Woodrow Wilson nat. fellow, 1955-56, Princeton U. Class of 1955 award, 1987, 3rd Gandhi Meml. lectr., New Delhi, 1990. Mem. Internat. Peace Rsch. Assn., Internat. Polit. Sci. Assn., World Future Studies Fedn., Am. Polit. Sci. Assn, Phi Beta Kappa. Home: 3653 Tantalus Dr Honolulu HI 96822-5033

PAIK, HYUN-DONG, microbiologist; b. Seoul, Mar. 19, 1961; parents Hyo-Saeng Paik and Young-Ja Jung; m. Eun-Mi Hong, Nov. 8, 1986; children: Ji-Yeon, Sarah. BS, Yonsei U., 1983; MS, Iowa State U., 1992, PhD, 1995. Rschr. Hyundai Heavy Industries, Co., Yongin, Korea, 1984-88, Korea Chem. Co., Yongin, 1988-90; postdoctoral rschr. Korea Rsch. Inst. Biosci. & Biotechnology, Taejeon, 1995; assoc. prof. Kyungnam U., Masan, Korea, 1995—; advisor Sunchundang Pharm. Co., Pusan, Korea, 1997—. Mem. Am. Soc. Microbiology, Inst. Food Technologists, Soc. Indsl. Microbiology, Korean Soc. Food & Technology. Presbyn. Avocation: movies. Home: 212-802 Dong A Apt, Wolyoung-Dong Habpo-Gu, Masan Kyungsangnam-Do Korea 631-701 Office: Kyungnam U, 449 Wolyoung-Dong Habpo-Gu, Masan Kyungsangnam-Do Korea 631-701

PAIK, JEOM KEE, marine architect; b. Sacheon, Korea, Jan. 7, 1957; s. Yon Do and Ya Moo (Chun) P.; m. Yun Hee Kim, Feb. 19, 1984; children: Myung Hoon, Yun Jung. BS, Pusan Nat. U., 1981; MS, Osaka U., 1984, PhD, 1987. Sr. rschr. Korea Inst. of Machinery and Metals, Taejon, Korea, 1987-89; prof. Pusan Nat. U., 1989—; adv. com. mem. Korean Register of Shipping, Taejon, 1993—; session organizer Internat. Soc. of Offshore and Polar Engrs., Colo., 1987—; vis. prof. Tech. U. Denmark, 1993-94, Va. Poly. Inst. and State U., 1999-2000, Am. Bur. Shipping, 1999-2000. Author: Energy Principles in Structural Mechanics, 1996, Theory of Reliability Engineering, 1996; contbr. articles to profl. jours.; chief editor Jour. Rsch. Inst. Indsl. Technology Pusan Nat. U., 1998—. Recipient Outstanding Paper award Royal Instn. of Naval Architects, 1995, Korean Fedn. of Sci. and Tech. Socs., 1996, Soc. of Naval Architects of Korea, 1996, Engrng. prize Faculty of Engrng. Pusan Nat. U., 1995. Mem. Internat. Ship and Offshore Structures Congress, Soc. of Naval Architects and Marine Engrs./N.J. (best paper award 2000), Royal Instn. of Naval Architects/London. E-mail: jeompaik@hyowon.pusan.ac.kr. Office: Pusan Nat U Dept of Naval Arch/Ocean Engrng, 30 Changjeon-Dong, Kumjeong-ku Pusan 609-735, Republic of Korea

PAIK, UNGYU, ceramic scientist, educator; b. Masan, South Korea, Mar. 2, 1964; s. Keum-Seog Paik and Jeong-Je Ok; m. Yeonsook Hwang, Sept. 28, 1991; 1 child, Juhee. BS, Hanyang U., 1986; MSc, Va. Poly. U., 1988; PhD, Clemson U., 1991. Rschr. Nat. Inst. Standards & Technology, Gaithersburg, Md., 1991-92; lectr., asst. prof. Changwon Nat. U., Korea, 1992-98; vis. scholar Nat. Inst. Standards and Technology, 1995-96; assoc. prof. Changwon Nat. U., 1997-99, Hanyang U., Seoul, 1999—. Mem. Korean Ceramic Soc. (publs. com. 1992—), Korean Assn. Crystal Growth (assoc. editor 1992—), Am. Ceramic Soc. Avocations: swimming, scuba diving, climbing. Office: Hangyang U Dept Ceramic Eng, Seongdong-Ku, 133-791 Seoul Korea

PAIKEDAY, THOMAS M., lexicographer and language consultant; b. Kerala, India, Oct. 11, 1926; came to U.S., 1962, Can. 1964; s. Manuel Thomas and Anna (Poovelickal) P.; m. Mary Kurien Kizhakethottam, Jan. 4, 1967; children: Anthony, Anne-Marie. L.Ph., Coll. of the Jesuits, Shembaganur, India, 1955; BA with 1st class honors, Madras Christian Coll., Tambaram, India, 1958; MA, U. Madras, India, 1960; postgrad, Boston Coll., 1962-63, U. Mich., 1963-64. Lectr. English St. Joseph's Coll., Tiruchy, Madras, 1958-59, Ramjas Coll., Delhi, India, 1960-61; copy editor The Statesman, New Delhi, India, 1961-62; asst. lexicographer W.J. Gage Ltd., Toronto, Ont., Can., 1964-66; editor Ont. Min. Edn., Toronto, 1966-67; head lexicography div. Holt, Rinehart & Winston, Toronto, 1967-73; chief lexicographer Lexicography, Inc., Mississauga, Ont., 1973—; cons. Collier-Macmillan Can., Toronto, 1980-81, Can. advisor Collins Publishers, Glasgow, Scotland, 1981-82, assoc. Applied Linguistics Rsch. Working Group, York U., Toronto, 1984—. Chief editor: Winston Interm. Dictionary, 1969, Compact Dictionary of Canadian English, 1970, Winston Canadian Dictionary, elem. edit., 1975, New York Times Everyday Dictionary, 1982, The Penguin Canadian Dictionary, 1990, The User's Webster, 1997; author: The Native Speaker is Dead!, 1985; contbr. articles to profl. jours. Mem. Authors Guild, European Assn. Lexicography, Dictionary Soc. N.Am., MLA, Tchrs. of English to Speakers of Other Langs., Can. Coun. Tchrs. of English, Am. Dialect Soc., Am. Name Soc., Assn. Computing and Humanities, Assn. Lit. and Linguistic Computing. Roman Catholic. Avocations: computer applications in lexicography, tennis, swimming. Office: Lexicography Inc, 7014 Royal Manor Dr Ste 208, Niagara Falls, ON Canada L2G 7L9

PAILLET, ALAIN, automotives executive; b. Saint Etienne, Loire, France, Mar. 17, 1947; arrived in Poland, 1997; s. Gaston and Marie-Louise (Blanc) P.; m. Bogumila Szubska, Aug. 17, 1974; 1 child, Philippe. Degree of engrng., Inst. Nat. Scis. Appliquées, Lyon, France, 1968; PhD in Physics, U. C. Bernard, Lyon, France, 1972. Sales engr. Valeo, Paris, 1973-82; divsn. mgr. Valeo, Stuttgard, Germany, 1982-93; East European divsn. mgr. Faurecia, Paris, 1994-97; mng. dir. Bertrand Faure Automobil/Faurecia, Warsaw, Poland, 1998—. Co-pres. Bus. Club, Stuttgart, 1988-93; bd. dirs. French C. of C., Germany, 1989-93; mem. Conseiller Commerce Ext., France, 1990-95. Mem. Bus. Ctr. Club, Bus. Club Grójec (pres. 1999). Roman Catholic. Home: Graniczna 15, PL 05501 Piaseczno Poland Office: Bertrand Faure Automobil, ul Spoldziecka, PL 05600 Grójec Poland

PAINE, ERIC, society executive; b. Chingford, Eng., June 9, 1927; s. Henry Nelson and Ethel Alice (Frost) P.; m. Joyce Koeke, Dec. 18, 1961 (dec. Dec. 1992); children: Terence, Theresa. Diploma in Higher Edn., Wolverhampton U., 1984. Accountancy asst. Oxon County Coun., Oxford, Eng., 1942-59; various adminstrv. posts Eng., 1960-65; sales adminstr. Telcon Metals, Crawley, Eng., 1965-73; tennis coach, TESL Sussex, Eng.; bookkeeper, salesman, other positions, 1973-90; hon. sec., treas. Thomas Paine Soc., U.K., 1989—. Editor T.P.S. newsletter. Mem. Selsey Town Coun., West Sussex, Eng.; Green Party candidate in gen. election, 1992, in European elections, 1994; active Amnesty Internat., Charter 88, UNO, Campaign Against the Arms Trade, Friends of Earth, Campaign for Nuclear Disarmament, Conscience. Mem. Chichester Tennis and Squash Club, Chichester Folk Club, Casuals Squash Club (hon. treas.). Green Party. Avocations: tennis, squash, history, folk music. Home: 43 Wellington Gardens, Selsey West Sussex P020 0RF, England

PAINE, GORDON ALLAN, barrister, educator; b. Dunedin, New Zealand, Jan. 4, 1955; s. Andrew Graham and Catherine Shirley Ellen (O'Brien) P.; m. Lynnette Rae Moses, Mar. 8, 1980 (dec. Dec. 1997); 1 child, Allan Brendon; m. Diane Mary Grant, Oct. 24, 1998. LLB, Otago U., Dunedin, 1979; LTCL, Trinity Coll. Music, London, 1979. Admitted to practice 1979. Prodn. mgr. Radio Otago Ltd., New Zealand, 1977-79; staff solicitor Sinclair, Horder, O'Malley, New Zealand, 1979-83, assoc. ptnr., 1983-84; staff solicitor Wheeler & Pahl, New Zealand, 1985, Rowe McBride, New Zealand, 1986-88; ptnr. Fitzherbert Rowe, Palmerston North, New Zealand, 1988-2000; barrister sole, 2000—; hon. solicitor Manawatu Theatre Soc., New Zealand, 1995-2000, Manawatu Justice of the Peace, 1993-2000, Manawatu Marching, 1995-2000. Author: (Study Guide) Legal Issues in Aviation, 1994—. Trustee Regent Theatre Trust Bd., New Zealand, 1993—; v.p. Birthright Inc., New Zealand, 1989—. Mem. Balloon Assn. of New Zealand. Avocations: hot air ballooning, sports watching, antiques. Office: 1st Fl AMF Bldg Broadway, Palmerston North New Zealand

PAINTAUD, GILLES, pharmacologist; b. Saint-Mandé, France, Sept. 10, 1959; s. Michel and Josyane (Flaud) P.; m. Sabine Merle, Jan. 18, 1986; children: Agathe, Anaïs. MD, U. Nancy and Besançon, France, 1989; Specialist in Gastroenterology, U. Besançon, 1991; Postgrad. Diploma in Pharmacology, U. Nancy, 1988; PhD, Karolinska Inst., Stockholm, 1993. Intern, house physician Univ. Hosp., Besançon, 1984-90; jr. lectr. U. Hosp., Besançon, 1992-95; sr. lectr., hosp. physician Univ. Hosp., Besançon, 1995-98, Tours, France, 1998-99; prof. Univ. Hosp., Tours, 2000—; adj. scientist, clin. pharmacology, Karolinska Inst. at Huddinge, Sweden, 1994—; mem. Med. Faculty Coun., Besançon, 1992-96; mem. Transparency Commn., French Agy. of Medicines, Paris, 1996-2000. Co-editor: (book) Cost B1 Conference on Variability and Specificity In Drug Metabolism, 1995; contbg. author: Organ Transplantation and Tissue Grafting, 1996; contbr. articles to profl. jours. Grantee Karolinska Inst., Stockholm, 1992; rsch. grantee Contrat Normalisé d'Etudes Pilotes en Recherche Clinique, Inst. Nat. de la Santé et de la Recherche Médicale France, 1993, mission grantee European Action cost B1, Brussels, 1996. Mem. French Soc. Pharmacology, Internat. Assn. Therapeutic Drug Monitoring & Clin. Toxicology. Office: Dept Pharmacology, CHU Bretonneau, F-37044 Tours Cedex, France

PAINTER, CHRISTOPHER, public management educator; b. Worcester, U.K., Aug. 7, 1948; s. Gwyn and Brenda (Davis) P.; m. Norah Catherine Mahon, Sept. 7, 1968; children: Anthony James, Claire Elizabeth, Jennifer Mary. BA with joint honors, U. Hull, U.K., 1969; PhD, U. Aston, U.K., 1973. Lectr. Birmingham (U.K.) Poly., 1972-88; part-time tutor Open U., 1973-88; vis. lectr. U. Aston, Birmingham, 1994; prin. lectr. U. Ctrl. Eng., Birmingham, 1988-96, prof., head dept. pub. policy, 1996—; contbr. to adminstrn. trainee courses Civil Svc. Coll., London, 1988-91; cons. West Midlands Local Authorities Joint Com., Birmingham, 1994-95, Local Govt. Assn., 1998-2000; polit. analyst Ctrl. Ind. TV, Birmingham, 1992-95, 2000, Birmingham Live, 1997-98; external examiner Southampton Inst., 1992-96, U. Aston, 1996-99. Joint editor: Management in the Public Sector, 1993, 2d edit., 1997; contbr.: Next Steps: Improving Management in Government?, 1995; chair editl. bd. The Stakeholder, 1996-99; contbr. articles to profl. jours. Rsch. grantee Local Govt. Mgmt. Bd., 1994-95, West Midlands Local Authorities Joint Com., 1993-94. Mem. Joint Univ. Coun. (pub. adminstrn. com. rsch. sec. 1991-94), Econ. and Social Rsch. Coun. (sem. recent developments in new pub. mgmt. 1999—). Roman Catholic. Avocations: reading, music, cricket. Office: Univ of Central England, Perry Barr, Birmingham B42 2SU, England

PAINTER, MARK PHILIP, judge; b. Cin., Apr. 6, 1947; s. John Philip and Marjorie (West) P.; m. Sue Ann Painter. BA, U. Cin., 1970, JD, 1973. Bar: Ohio 1973, U.S. Dist. Ct. (so. dist.) Ohio 1973, U.S. Supreme Ct. 1980. Assoc. Smith & Schnacke and predecessor firm (now part of Thompson, Hine & Flory), 1973-78; pvt. practice Cin., 1978-82; judge Hamilton County Mcpl. Ct., Cin., 1982-95, Ohio 1st Dist. Ct. Appeals, Cin., 1995—; adj. prof. law U. Cin., 1990—; lectr. in field. Co-author: Ohio DUI Law, 1988, 9th edit., 2000; mem. editl. bd. Criminal Law Jour. Ohio, 1989-92; contbr. articles to profl. jours. Bd. dirs. Citizens Sch. Com., Cin., 1974-76; trustee Freestore Foodbank, Cin., 1984-90, Mary Jo Brueggeman Meml. Found., Cin., 1981-92; bd. commrs. on grievances and discipline Ohio Supreme Ct., 1993-95; mem. Rep. Ctrl. Com., Cin., 1972-82. Recipient Superior Jud. Svc. award Ohio Supreme Ct., 1982, 84, 85. Mem. ABA, Ohio State Bar Assn., Cin. Bar Assn. (trustee 1988-90), Am. Judges Assn., Am. Judicature Soc., Am. Soc. Writers on Legal Subjects, Potter Stewart Inn of Ct. (master of bench emeritus), Bankers Club. Home: 2449 Fairview Ave Cincinnati OH 45219-1170 Office: Ct of Appeals William Howard Taft Law Ctr 230 E 9th St Cincinnati OH 45202-2174

PAINTSIL, ROBERT, marketing professional; b. Kumasi, Ashant, Ghana, June 15, 1965; s. Paintsil Braukmann Svans and Mary Ansah. BA, Ghana Polytechnic Tutorial, Sch. Mktg., 1986. Libr. asst. Nat. Svc., Kumasi, 1987-88; tchr. Nat. Svc., Ejisu, 1988-89; mktg. mgr. Joe Best Co., Kumasi, 1990-92; mng. dir. Nehppon Enterprise, Kumasi, 1992—. Editor publs. in field. Organizer Watch-Door Neighbor Com., Agafo Dist., 1990-92. Mem. U.K. Million Dollar Club, Knight of Marshall. Mem. Christian Ch. Avocations: football, travel, rsch. reading, music. Home: PO Box X50 FNT, Kumasi/Ashanti Ghana

PAISLEY, IAN RICHARD KYLE, clergyman, political activist; b. Apr. 6, 1926; s. J. Kyle and Isabella Paisley; m. Eileen E. Cassells, 1956; 5 children. Ed., South Wales Bible Coll., Ref. Presbyn. Theol. Coll., Belfast, No. Ireland; D.D. (hon.), Bob Jones U., Greenville, S.C., 1966. Ordained to ministry, 1946. Minister Martyrs Meml. Free Presbyn. Ch., Belfast, from 1946; moderator Free Presbyn. Ch. of Ulster, from 1951; pub. Protestant Telegraph, from 1966; M.P. for North Antrim, Westminster, from 1970; M.P. for Bannside, County Antrim, North Ireland Parliament, 1970-72, leader of opposition, 1972, chmn. public accounts com., 1972; mem. No. Ireland Assembly, 1973-74; mem. European Parliament, from 1979; mem. Constl. Conv., 1975-76; co-chmn. World Congress of Fundamentalists, 1978; leader Democratic Unionist Party, 1971—; pres. Whitfield Coll. of the Bible, 1979—. Author: History of the 1859 Revival, 1959, Christian Foundations, 1960, Ravenhill Pulpit, Vol. I, 1966, Vol. II, 1967, Exposition of the Epistle to the Romans, 1968, Billy Graham and the Church of Rome, 1970, The Massacre of Saint Bartholomew, 1972, Paisley, The Man and His Message, 1976, America's Debt to Ulster, 1976, The Life of Dr. James Kidd, 1982, Those Flaming Tenants, 1983, Be Sure, 1987, Jonathan Edwards: Theologian of Revival, 1987, What a Friend We Have in Jesus, 1994, Understanding Events in Northern Ireland: An Introduction for Americans, 1995; editor: The Revivalist, 1950, Protestant Blueprint, 1987—. Fellow Royal Geog. Soc.; mem. Internat. Cultural Soc. Korea. Office: Parsonage, 17 Cyprus Ave, Belfast BT5 5NT, Northern Ireland also: Dem Unionist Party, 296 Albertbridge Rd, Belfast BT5 4GX, Northern Ireland*

PAIVA, MANUEL, physicist, educator; b. Oporto, Portugal, Jan. 7, 1943; s. Manuel and Amália Elisa (Pinto) P.; m. Irina Veretennicoff, July 26, 1968; children: Isabelle, Nathalie. M in Physics, U. Brussels, 1968, PhD in Physics, 1973. Researcher U. Brussels, 1968-79, sr. rsch. scientist, 1979—, prof. sch. medicine, 1991—; chmn. life scis. working group European Space Agy., Paris, 1991-93. Author: Dialogos sobre Portugal, 1998; editor: Gas Mixing and Distribution in the Lung, 1984, Respiratory Physiology: An Analytical Approach, 1989; contbr. over 100 sci. articles to profl. jours. Home: 3 Italiëlaan, 3090 Overijse Belgium Office: Biomed Physics Lab, 808 Rte de Lennik, B1070 Brussels Belgium

PAIVA, MELQUÍADES PINTO, marine biologist, educator; b. Lavras da Mangabeira, Ceará, Brazil, Mar. 6, 1930; s. José Rodrigues Tavares and Creusa Pinto (Nogueira) P.; m. Maria Arair Bezerra, Jan. 4, 1961; children: Paloma, Gabriela, Rodolpho, Bernardo. Agronomy Engr., Sch. Agronomy, Fortaleza, Brazil, 1952; D Biology, U. São Paulo, Brazil, 1972. Prof. Fed. U. Ceará, Fortaleza, Brazil, 1954-87; dir. Marine Scis. Inst. Fed. U. Ceará, Fortaleza, 1961-76; adviser, engr. Brazilian Ctrl. Electric, Rio de Janeiro, 1976-91; prof. Fed. U. Rio de Janeiro, 1992-98; rschr. Brazilian Nat. Coun. Sci. and Tech. Devel., Brasília, Brazil, 1993—; mem. Interministerial Commn. for Marine Resources, Brasília, 1979-86, Nat. Commn. Antarctic Matters, Brasília, 1982-86. Contbr. chpts. to books, more than 240 articles to profl. jours. Brazilian rep. on 19 diplomatic missions principally concerned with conservation in western hemisphere. Recipient Amigo da Marinha medal, 1971, Pres. Castelo Branco medal State of Ceará, 1984, Sci. Merit medal Fed. U. Ceará, 1987, Francisco Gonçalves de Aguiar medal State of Ceará, 1999, hon. citation City of Fortaleza, 1982. Home: Baronesa de Pocone 71/701, 22471-270 Rio de Janeiro Brazil Office: Fed U Rio de Janeiro Marine Biol Dept, Ilha do Fundão, 21944-970 Rio de Janeiro Brazil

PAJAK, MARCIN IRENEUSZ, information scientist; b. Cracow, Poland, Aug. 7, 1968; s. Janusz Wiesław and Barbara Lidia (Norwecka) P. Grad., Informatics Coll., 1996. Info. scientist U. Mining and Metallurgy, Cracow, 1990-91; computer network supr. Dist. Post Office, Cracow, 1994; owner Marcin Pajak Oprogramowanie Komputerow, Cracow, 1991—; computer network supr. Elektromontaz, Cracow, 1995-98; field maintenance specialist Polska Telefonia Cyfrowa, Rzeszów, 1998; cash register servicer Consortia, Cracow, 2000—. Avocation: tourism. Home: ul Okolna 8/36, 30-684 Cracow Poland

PAJALIC, OLEG, chemical engineer, consultant, researcher; b. Krk, Croatia, Apr. 21, 1964; arrived in Sweden, 1992; s. Anton and Emilija (Vujicic) P.; m. Zada Catovic, Apr. 30, 1988; children: Katarina, Filip. BSc, U. Tuzla, Bosnia-Hercegovina, 1986, MSc, 1991. Cert. in energy mgmt. Asst. lectr. U. Tuzla, 1986-88; asst. rschr. Inst. Chem. Engrng., Tuzla, 1988-90, jr. rsch. fellow, 1990-91; asst. lectr. U. Tuzla, 1991; engr. for info. Soda Factory, Lukavac, Bosnia-Hercegovina, 1991-92; cons. Adviesbureau voor Energiestrategie, Teraar, Netherlands, 1994-95; R & D engr. Perstorp (Sweden) AB, 1995—; pro-rector U. Tuzla, 1985-86; mem. sci. bds. Assns. Univs. Bosnia-Hercegovina and Yugoslavia, 1986-87. Author procs. of sci. congresses; patentee in field. U. Tuzla scholar, 1985; Energy Mgmt. in Small Industries fellow U. Twente, Enschede, Netherlands, 1991. Mem. Swedish Assn. Grad. Engrs. Avocations: computers, fishing. Home: Sodra Langgatan 31, 29159 Kristianstad Sweden

PAJARES, GONZALO MARTINSANZ, physics educator; b. Trijueque, Spain, July 29, 1957; s. Perfecto Tavira Pajares and Carmen Pajares Martinsanz; m. Alicia Gomez Alvarez, Aug. 6, 1988; 1 child, Belen Alvarez. D in Physics. Assoc. prof. U. Complutense, Madrid, 1995—. Contbr. articles to profl. jours. E-mail: pajares@eucmax.sim.ucm.es. Office: U Complutense Fac Fisicas, Giudad Universitaria, 28040 Madrid Spain

PAJARES, RAMON, hotel company executive; b. Jaen, Andalucia, Spain, July 6, 1935; s. Juan Antonio and Rosario (Salazar) P.; m. Jean Kathleen Porter, July 13, 1963; children: Sofia, Maria, Roberto. Grad., Inst. Hotel & Tourism Studies, Madrid. Numerous seasonal positions learning langs., Spain, France, Switz., Germany; asst. mgr. Reina Isabel, Las Palmas, Spain, 1963-69; food and beverage dir. Inn-on-the-Park, London, 1969-72; gen. mgr. Hotel San Antonio, Lazarote, 1972-75; gen. mgr., v.p. Four Seasons, London, 1975-94; mng. dir. Savoy Group, London, 1994—. Served with Spanish Navy, 1955-57. Decorated ofcl. Order of Isabel the Cath., Merito Civil (Spain); named Hotelier of Yr., Brit. Hotel and Catering Industry, 1984, Personality of Yr. for Hotel Industry, London, 1986. Fellow Skål; mem. French Culinary Assn., Cookery and Food Assn., European Hotel Mgrs. Assn., Caballeros del Vino, Chevaliers du Tastevin, Ordre des Coteaux de Champagne, Confrerie de la Chaine des Rotisseurs, Confrerie des Chevaliers du Sacavin, Las Ambassadeurs, Annabels Club, others. Roman Catholic.

PAJASOVÁ, LIBUŠE, physicist, researcher; b. Proseč, Chrudim, Czechoslovakia, Apr. 24, 1937; d. Jan and Emilie (Sejnohová) Rejent; m. Petr Pajas, Feb. 10, 1960; children: Patrik, Petr. MSc, Lomonosov U., Moscow, 1962. Exptl. physicist. Rsch. asst. Inst. of Solid State Physics, Prague, Czech Republic, 1962-68, rsch. fellow, 1968-78; rschr. Inst. of Physics, Prague, Czech Republic, 1978-91; chief rschr. Inst. Physics, Prague, Czech Republic, 1991-95. Contbr. articles to profl. jours. Recipient award Czechoslovakian Acad. Sci., 1987. Mem. Union of Czechoslovakian Mathematicians and Physicists, Czechoslovak Spectroscopic Soc., European Synchrotron Radiation Soc. Avocations: mountain hiking, cooking. Office: Inst Physics Acad Sciences, Inst Physics Acad Sciences, Na Slovance 2, 18221 Prague Praha8, Czech Republic

PAJITNOV, ANDREI VLADIMIROVICH, mathematics educator; b. Moscow, Aug. 1, 1957; s. Vladimir Konstantinovich and Nadejda Vassilievna (Scherbakova) P. Grad., Moscow State U., 1979, PhD, 1984; DSc, Math. Inst. Steklov, 1990. Researcher Inst. Chem. Physics, Moscow, 1982-91, Inst. New Tech., Moscow, 1991-92; prof. dept. math. U. Nantes, France, 1992—. Contbr. articles to profl. publs. Office: U Nantes Dept Math, 2 Rue de la Houssiniere, 44072 Nantes France

PAJNO, GIOVANNI BATTISTA, allergist, pediatrician; b. Valdina, Italy, July 5, 1955; s. Felice Pajno and Maria Viglianti; m. Graziella Antonina Cucinotta, Dec. 17, 1963; children: Valentina, Cristina. MD, U. Messina, Italy, 1982. Resident in pediats. U. Messina, 1986, resident in respiratory medicine, 1990, asst. pediatrician, 1989-96, reader in pediats., 1992-99; cons. pediatrician Messina, 1996—; hon. cons. physician Royal Brampton Hosp., London, 1996-97; hon. rsch. fellow dept. allergy and respiratory medicine Guy's Hosp., London, 1997. Mem. Italian Soc. Pediats. (exec. com. respiratory diseases 1999), European Acad. Allergy and Clin. Immunology. Roman Catholic. Home: Via Marche 12/7, 98124 Messina Italy Office: Messina U Inst Pediats, Via Consolare Valeria, 98124 Messina Italy

PAK, BO HI, foundation administrator; b. Ah-San, Chung Nam, South Korea, Aug. 18, 1930; s. Dong Hyun and Pyung Chun (Han) P.; m. Ki Sook Yoon, Nov. 29, 1953; children: Na Kyung, Jun Sun, Jin Sung, Hoon Sook, Yun Sook, Jin Kyung. Student, Georgetown U., 1962-64; HHD, La Plata Cath. U. of Argentina, 1984. Pres. The Washington Times Corp., Washington, 1982-92, CAUSA Internat., N.Y.C., 1981—; chmn., pres. Korean Cultural Found., Seoul and Washington, 1969—; pres. Universal Ballet Found., Washington, 1986—; chmn. bd. Panda Motors Corp., Hong Kong, 1990—; chmn. Kumgangsan Internat. Group, Seoul, 1998—; pres. The Summit Coun. for World Peace, Washington, 1987-97; pres., pub. News World Comm., Inc., N.Y., 1976-90; asst. mil. attache Embassy of Korea, Washington, 1961-64; spl. asst. to vice min. of def. Govt. of Republic of Korea, 1958-68. Author: The Truth is My Sword, 1999, Messiah: My Testimony to Reverend Sun Myung Moon, 2000. Lt. col. Republic of Korean Army, 1950-64. Decorated Medal of Gold Star Hwa-Rang Republic of Korea Govt., 1953, Nat. medal Dong Baek, 1971; recipient Investiture of Acad. Mexican Acad. of Internat. Law, 1990, Order of Liberty and Unity

Assn. for the Unity of Latin Am., 1992. Office: Summit Coun for World Peace 3rd Fl 3600 New York Ave NE Fl 3 Washington DC 20002-1947

PAK, SE RI, professional golfer; b. Daejeon, Korea, Sept. 28, 1977. Professional golfer LPGA Tour, 1997—; mem. KLPGA, 1996, 97. Recipient Rolex Rookie of Yr. award. Winner Seoul Ladies Open, 1997, Jamie Farr Kroger Classic, 1998, 99; Giant Eagle LPGA Classic, 1998, McDonald's LPGA Championship, 1998, U.S. Women's Open, 1998, ShopRite LPGA Classic, 1999; qualified for 14 events, winning 6 times and placing 2d 7 times. Address: LPGA 100 International Golf Dr Daytona Beach FL 32124-1082*

PAK, SONG-CHO'OL, vice president of Democratic People's Republic of Korea; b. Kiongsan Province, Korea, Sept. 21, 1913. Student, Soviet Mil. Coll., 1948-50. In emigration in China, 1921-45; hon. v.p. SPA, North Korea; activist Anti-Japanese Movement, from 1931; mem. Kim Il Sen's partisan units, Manchuria; dep. comdr. marine forces Korean War; Korean ambassador to Bulgaria, 1945; dep. minister fgn. affairs, head fgn. dept. Korean Workers Party; minster fgn. affairs, 1959-70; dep. prime minister, 1966-70; dep. chmn. Council of Ministers, chmn. Com. of Service to the People, 1970-76; prime minister Dem. People's Republic of Korea, 1976-77, v.p., 1977—. Address: Office of Vice Pres, Pyongyang Dem Peoples Republic of Korea*

PAK, TAE-CHUN, former prime minister of South Korea; b. Seoul, South Korea, Sept. 29, 1927; m. Jang Ock Ja; 5 children. Student, Waseda U., 1946; grad., Korean Mil. Acad., 1948; Doctor degree (hon.), Carnegie Mellon U., 1988, U. Sheffield, U.K., 1988, U. Birmingham, U.K., 1989, U. Waterloo, Can., 1991, U. Moscow, 1991. Sec.-gen. to chmn. Supreme Coun. for Nat. Reconstruction, 1961, mem. coun. for commerce and industry, 1961; chmn. bd. dirs., pres. Korea Tungsten Mining Co., Ltd., 1964; pres. Pohang Iron and Steel Co., Ltd., 1968, chmn., 1981; mem. parliament South Korean Nat. Assembly, 1981-2000, chmn. fin. com., 1981; prime min. Republic of Korea, 2000; chmn. founding com. Pohang Inst. Sci. and Tech., 1985; dep. chmn. Fedn. Korean Industries, 1987; chmn. Dem. Justice Party, 1990; co-chmn. Dem. Liberal Party, 1990; pres. United Liberal Dems., 1997; hon. chmn. Pohang Iron and Steel Co., Ltd., 1992; pres. Korea-Japan Parliamentarian's Union, 1998. Chmn. Korea Iron and Steel Assn., 1975, Korea-Japan Econ. Assn., 1981; chmn. POSCO Ednl. Found., 1976. Maj. gen. Korean Army, 1963, ret. Recipient Order of Mil. Merit, Hwarang, 1954, Order of Indsl. Svc. Merit, 1971, Order of Civil Merit, Mugunghwa medal, 1974, Order of Grand Decoration in Honour in Gold for Svcs., Republic of Austria, 1979, Merit Order for Disting. Svcs. in deg. of Grand Officer, Republic of Peru, 1979, Order of Great Cross of Rio Brando, Republic of Brazil, 1981, Comdr.'s Cross of Order of Merit, Republic of Germany, 1983, Bessemer Gold medal Brit. Inst. Metals, 1987, Order of So. Cross, Republic of Brazil, 1987, Merit Order for Disting. Svcs. in Degree of the Great Cross, Republic of Peru, 1987, Grand Decoration of Honour in Silver with Star for Svcs., Republic of Austria, 1993, Woon-Kyung prize Woon-Kyung Found., 1996, Grand Cordon of Order of Rising Sun, Japan, 1999. Office: 183-8 Bukahyun-Dong, Seodaemun-Gu, Seoul Republic of Korea*

PAKARINEN, ARVO JUHANI, metals manufacturing company executive; b. Tampere, Hame, Finland, Apr. 6, 1944; arrived in Australia, 1966; s. Arvo Armas and Maire Margaretta (Kankaanpaa) P.; m. Eve Hillary Caris, Dec. 6, 1976, (separated); children: Adam Christopher, Sean Aaron. Degree in effective speaking, Australian Inst. Mgmt., Melbourne, 1976, degree in applied mgmt., 1976. Cert. pub. speaking Coun. Adult Edn., 1997. High frequency applicator Sandvik, Lidkoping, Sweden, 1963-66; overseer Ericsson Telecomms., Melbourne, 1966-67; salesperson McEwan City, Melbourne, 1967-69; sales mgr. Eutectic (Australia), Melbourne, 1972-76; pres. Ausweld, Melbourne, 1977—; guest spkr. Benchmark, Melbourne, 1996—; welding cons. Esso, BHP, 1977. Contbr. rsch. articles to profl. publs. With Mil. Police, Karelian Brigade, 1964-65. Mem. Am. Soc. for Metals (cert. in metallurgy and joining Metals Engring. Inst.), Am. Welding Soc. Lutheran. Avocations: chess, golf, traveling, gardening. Office: Ausweld, 4/46 Holloway Dr, 3153 Bayswater Victoria, Australia

PAKCHUNG, WARREN GREGORY, engineer consultant; b. Sydney, Australia, Dec. 10, 1948; s. Edward and Marjorie P.; m. Andrea MacKenzie, Nov. 8, 1980. B in Elec. Engring., U. Sydney, 1973; BS in Pure Math., U. New South Wales, Australia, 1979. Chartered profl. engr. Instn. Engrs., Australia. Lead engr. The Permutit Co. Australia Ltd., 1988-89; sr. projects engr. (elec./instrumentation) ICI Australia Opers. Pty. Ltd., 1989-90; project mgr. Sydney Water Bd., 1990-92; site comms. mgr. Caltex Refining Co. Pty. Ltd., 1993-95; sr. bldg. svcs. engr. Connell Wagner, 1996-99; sr. project engr. Alstom Australia Projects, 1999—. Recipient Award of Excellence Lighting award I.E.S., 1998, Internat. Lighting award, Illuminating Engring. Soc./Australia New Zealand, 1998, Edwin F. Guth Meml. award for interior lighting Illuminating Engring. Soc. N.Am., 1999. Mem. IEEE, Inst. Instrumentaion and Control, Instn. Engr. Australia (chartered profl. engr.), Instrument Soc. Am. Avocations: opera, skiing, swimming, reading. Address: PO Box 41, Enfield NSW 2136, Australia

PAKENHAM-WALSH, NEIL MARTIN, health information consultant; b. Crowborough, Sussex, Eng., Apr. 2, 1960; s. Samuel Neil Pakenham-Walsh and Lorna Brunskill. MBBS, St. George's U., London, 1983; diploma, Royal Coll. Ob-gyns., London, 1985, Child Health, London, 1988. Jr. hosp. dr. NHS, 1983-89; contbg. dep. editor Medicine Digest, Eng., 1991-96; program mgr. Internat. Network for Availability of Scientific Publs., Oxford, Eng., 1996—; Med. officer Rio Mazan Expedition, Ecuador, 1986, Cusichaca Project, Peru, 1987; project officer Tropical Medicine Resource, Wellcome Trust, Eng., 1994-98. Mem. UN Assn., Amnesty Internat. Avocations: photography, golf, guitar. Fax: 44-(0) 1608-811338. E-mail: 101374.3615@compuserve.com.

PAKESCH, GEORG, psychiatrist, educator; b. Graz, Austria, June 6, 1951; s. Erich and Gertrude (von Kaan) P.; m. Karin Podolak, Mar. 5, 1993; children: Isabella, Christoph. MD, U. Vienna, 1977; diploma, Diplomatic Acad., 1979. Lic. psychiatrist, neurologist, psychotherapist. Asst. prof. dept. psychiatry U. Vienna, Austria, 1980-92, assoc. prof. dept. psychiatry, 1992—; bd. dirs. Med. Coun., Vienna, dir. pub. rels. and press dept., 1985—, dir. dept. rsch., 1989—. Author 4 books; contbr. numerous articles to sci. jours.; editor: (jour.) Wiener Arzt. Recipient Billroth prize Med. Coun., 1992. Mem. Assn. European Psychiatry, European Coll. Neuropsychopharmacology, Assn. Austrian Psychiatry and Neurology, Assn. Psychiatry Vienna, Gesellschaft der Arzte Vienna, Assn. Neuropsychopharmacology Austria. Avocations: theater, music, skiing, tennis. Home: Neulinggasse 18, Vienna A-1030, Austria Office: U Vienna Dept Psychiatry, Waehringer Guertel 18-20, Vienna A-1090, Austria

PAKHALINA, YULIA, Olympic athlete; b. Penza, Russia, Sept. 12, 1977; d. Vladimir. Winner European Championships, 1997, 2nd place World Championships, 1998, winner springboard competition Goodwill Games, 1999; winner Gold medal synchronized diving 3 meter springboard Sydney, 2000. Office: All-Russia Athletic Fedn, Luzhnetskaya Nab 8, Moscow 119871, Russia*

PAKKALA, SEPPO TAPIO, hematologist, researcher; b. Helsinki, Finland, Jan. 18, 1951; s. Kalervo and Pirita I. (Järventaus) P.; m. Arja U. Kaltula, June 29, 1974; 1 child, Tuomas A. Licenciate of Medicine, U. Helsinki, 1977, Dr. Medicine and Surgery, 1991, Docent of Exptl. Hematology, 1995. Registered physician, Finland. Physician Hyvinkää Dist. Hosp., 1977-80; fellow in internal medicine U. Helsinki, 1980-84, fellow in clin. hematology, 1984-86, rschr. transplantation lab., 1986-91, sr. rschr., 1993-96; assoc. prof. medicine Cedars Sinai Med. Ctr., L.A., 1992-93; dir. Inst. Clin. Rsch. Helsinki U. Ctrl. Hosp., 1996—, CEO Clin. Rsch. Inst.; CEO NC-Treatment Ltd. Contbr. articles to profl. jours. Mem. Finnish Med. Assn., Internat. Soc. Hematology, European Haematology Assn. Avocation: sailing. Office: Clin Rsch Inst HUCH, PO Box 105, 00029 Hus Finland

PAKOU, ATHENA, physics educator; b. Parga, Epirus, Greece, May 27, 1953; d. Adreas and Penelope Pakou. Diploma in Physics, U. Ioannina, Greece, 1975; PhD, U. Oxford, Eng., 1982. Lectr. U. Ioannina, 1982-87, asst. prof., 1987-93; assoc. prof., 1993—; vis. rschr. Rutgers U., New Brunswick, N.J., 1984-88, U. Padova, Italy, 1988-90, U. Manchester, Eng., 1991-92, Saclay/Dapnia, France, 1994—. Contbr. more than 40 articles to profl. jours. Mem. Am. Phys. Soc. Office: Univ Ioannina, Dept Physics, Ioannina GR451 10, Greece

PAL, HARIDAS, scientist, researcher; b. Jateswar, India, Dec. 14, 1959; s. Purnachandra and Dulali P.; m. Tanusree Bhadra, Apr. 23, 1993; 1 child, Ananya. BSc in Chemistry with honors, North Bengal U., West Bengal, India, 1981, MSc in Chemistry, 1984; PhD, Bombay (India) U., 1992. Sci. officer Bhabha Atomic Rsch. Ctr., Mumbai, 1985—; postdoctoral fellow Inst. Molecular Sci., Okazaki, Japan, 1994-96. Contbr. numerous rsch. papers to profl. jours. Mem. Indian Soc. Radiation and Photochem. Scis. (life), Chem. Rsch. Soc. India (life). Hindu. Avocation: reading. Home: A-17 Sarang Pin-400094, Mumbai India Office: Bhabha Atomic Rsch Ctr, RC&CD Divsn PIN-400085, Mumbai India

PAL, LENARD, physicist; b. Gyoma, Hungary, Nov. 7, 1925; s. Imre and Erzsebet (Varga) P.; m. Angela Danoci, 1963; 1 child. Student, Budapest U., Moscow U. Dept. head Ctr. Rsch. Inst. for Physics, Budapest, Hungary, 1953-56, dep. dir., 1956-69, dir., 1970-71, 75, dir. gen., 1975-77; prof. nuc. physics Eotvos Lorand U., Budapest, Hungary, 1961-77, 89—; pres. State Office Tech. Devel., 1978-80, 84-85, Nat. Atomic Energy Commn., 1978-80, 84-85; mem. Sci. Policy com. Council of Ministers, 1978-85; sec. Central Com. of the Hungarian Socialist Worker's Party, 1985-88. Contbr. articles to profl. jours. Recipient Gold medal Order Labour, 1956, 68, Kossuth prize, 1962, Meml. medal 25th Anniversary of the Liberation, 1970, Kurcsatov Meomry medal, USSR, 1970, Gold medal Hungarian Acad. Scis., 1975, Red Banner Order of Labor, USSR, 1975, Medal Eotvos Lorand Phys. Soc., 1975, Red Banner Order of Work, 1985. Mem. Hungarian Acad. Sci. (gen. sec. 1980-84, pres. Intercosmos Coun. 1980-84), Acad. Scis. USSR, Acad. Sci. German Democratic Republic, Acad. Scis. Czechoslovakia, Leibniz-Sozietat e.V. Home: II Széheruu 21/a, H-1021 Budapest Hungary

PAL, MAHENDRA, veterinary public health educator, researcher; b. Delhi, India, Apr. 10, 1946; s. Piarey Lal and Kartari Devi Pal; m. Raj Rani Pal, Jan. 17, 1968; 2 children. B in Vet. Scis., Vet. Coll., Mathura, India, 1969; M in Vet. Pub. Health, All-India Inst. Hygiene and Pub. Health, Calcutta, 1975; PhD, Kumaun U., Nainital, India, 1981; DSc, Utkal U., Bhubaneshwar, India, 1988. Mem. Indian Vet. Pub. Health Assn. Vet. surgeon Animal Husbandry Dept., Delhi, India, 1970-77; asst. rsch. officer Dr. R.P. Ctr. Ophthalmic Scis., New Delhi, 1977-78; disease control officer Animal Husbandry Dept., Delhi, 1978-80; mycologist Nat. Dairy Devel. Bd., Anand, India, 1980-82; lectr., V.P. Chest Inst. U. Delhi, 1982-84; assoc. prof., head Coll. Vet. Sci., Anand, 1984—; vis. scientist Massey U., Palmerston North, New Zealand, 1984; rschr. Inst. Tropical Medicine, Antwerp, Belgium, 1985-86; Japanese Soc. Promotion Sci. rsch. scientist U. Tokyo, 1989-90. Author 3 books; contbr. over 115 articles to profl. jours.; inventor staining solution Narayan for study of morphology of fungi, Pal's sunflower seed medium for quick diagnosis of cryptococcosis; mem. editl. bd. Revista Ibero-Americana de Micologia, Spain, 1991—; founder, editor Delhi Vet. Jour., 1979; editor Vet. Pub. Health Jour. Founder Poor Children Edn. Soc., India, 1977. Recipient Jawaharlal Nehru award Indian Coun. Agrl. Rsch., New Delhi, 1982, Sandoz Med. Times prize for Spot the Diagnosis, Bombay, 1995. Fellow Nat. Acad. Vet. Scis. India, Korean Soc. Vet. Clin. Medicine; mem. N.Y. Acad. Scis., Animal Welfare Bd. India Ministry Environment and Forests (hon.), Vet. Pub. Health Assn. (life), Indian Soc. Cryptococcois (founder, pres.), Gujarat Vet. Assn. Avocations: scientific and religious literature, music, movies, TV. Home: Flat 4 Aangan No 1, Jagnath-Ganash Rd Anand, 388001 Gujarat India Office: Coll Vet Sci, Dept Vet Pub Health Anand, 388001 Gujarat 388001, India

PAL, RANENDRA NATH, engineering educator; b. Dighali, Dhaka, Bangladesh, 1945; s. Nani Gopal and Mrinalini Pal; m. Sikha Pal, Nov. 27, 1977; children: Rashmi, Shreya. B.Engring., Jadavpur U., Calcutta, India, 1966, M.Engring., 1969; PhD in Engring., Indian Inst. Tech., Bombay, 1975. Design engr. Electric Control devices Corp., Calcutta, 1966-67; mem. tech. staff Electronics & Radar Devel. Estab., Bangalore, India, 1969-70; lectr. Indian Inst. Tech., Kharagpur, 1975-80, asst. prof., 1980-89, prof., 1990—, coord. radar and comm. ctr., 1989-91, prof., acting head E&ECE Dept., 1990-95; vis. fac. Hiroshima U., Japan, 1995-96; mem. Tech. Internat. Conf. on Microwave and Com., Kharagpur, 1981, Internat. Symposium on Electronics Devices and Comm., Kharagpur, 1987. Patentee in field; contbr. articles to profl. jours., specialization in signal processing. Fellow Inst. Electronics and Telecom. Engrs.; mem. IEEE (sr.). Avocations: music, watching football. E-mail: ranen@ece.iitkgp.ernet.in. Home: Qrs #A-12, IIT Campus, Kharagpur 721 302, India Office: Indian Inst Tech, Dept E&ECE, Kharagpur 721 302, India

PAL, SURENDRA, communications engineer, electronics engineer, space technologist, educator, researcher; b. Khetri, Rajasthan, India, Mar. 10, 1948; s. Singh Mal and Keshar Devi Pareek; m. Ranjana Purohit, Dec. 11, 1974; 1 child, Ankit. BSc, Birla Inst. Tech. and Sci., Pilani, India, 1966, MSc in Physics, 1968, MSc in Tech. Electronics, 1970; PhD in Comms. Engring., Indian Inst. Sci., Bangalore, 1985. Scientist SC-2 Tata Inst. Fundamental Rsch., Bombay, 1970-71; scientist, engr. SC Indian Space Rsch. Orgn., Trivandrum, India, 1971-72; scientist, engr. SD2 Indian Space Rsch. Orgn., Bangalore, 1972-78, scientist, engr. SE, 1978-82, head comms. divsn. Satellite Ctr., 1982-92, group dir. comms. Satellite Ctr., 1992-96, dir. comms. Satellite Ctr., scientist engr. H, 1996—; cons. Internat. Telecom. Union, 1989-90, Regional African Satellite Comm. Definition, 1994-97. Editor: (book) Perspectives in Communications, 1987; guest editor: IETE Tech. Rev., 1993, 99; editor: Jour. Space Craft Tech., 1992-99; mem. editl. bd. Jour. of Scientific and Indsl. Rsch., 1994 . Recipient Vikaram Sarabhai Rsch. award phys. rsch. lab., Ahmedabad, India, 1989, Independence Day Rsch. award Nat. Rsch. Devel. Corp. India, 1994, 95, Republic Day award, 1997. Fellow IEEE (sr. mem.), Instn. Electronics and Telecom. Engrs. India (mem. coun. 1992 , guest editor spl. issue Jour.), Indian Nat. Acad. Engring., Nat. Acad. Scis., Astronaut. Soc. of India. Avocations: photography, painting, playing bridge, reading books. Office: ISRO Satellite Ctr, Airport Rd, 560017 Bangalore India

PAL, UMAPADA, physics professor; b. Midnapore, W Bengal, India, Jan. 23, 1960; s. Kishorimohan and Indu Bala (Masanta) P.; m. Mou Pramanik Pal, Nov. 19, 1992; children: Lisa, Shreya. B Sc with honours in Physics, Midnapore Coll., 1981; MSc in Physcis, U. Calcutta (India), 1984, B Ed, 1985; PhD, Indian Inst. Tech., 1991. Rsch. fellow Indian Inst. Tech., Kharagpur, India, 1985-90; scientific officer Indian Inst. Tech., 1991-92; postdoctoral fellow U. Complutense de Madrid, Madrid, Spain, 1993-94; prof. investigator U. Automona de Puebla, Puebla, Mexico, 1995—; guest tchr. Vidyasagar U., 1990-92. Contbr. articles to prof. jours. and books. Recipient STA fellow JRDC (Japan), 1996; AIST fellow, MITI (Japan), 1999. Mem. AAAS, Soc. Mexicana de Fisica, Soc. Mexicana de Cristalografia. Avocations: football, cricket, fishing. Office: Inst de Fisica, 18 SUR y Av San Claudio, 72570 Puebla Mexico

PALABAY, CARMILITA LLABRES, principal; b. Marikina City, The Philippines, Feb. 6, 1944; d. Agapito Santiago and Perfecta Santos (Angeles) Llabres; m. Jesus Cruz Palabay, Nov. 27, 1965 (dec. July 1993); children: Jemellie, Jessemel, Jescié, Jesci James. MA in Edn., Cebu Normal, 1985, EdD, 1987. Tchr. DECS, The Philippines, 1965-87, prin. I, 1987-89, prin. II, 1989-93, prin. III, 1994-96, prin. IV, 1996—. Mem. MAPESPA, IMESPA, PESPA, RECGAM (1st v.p. 1995). Mem. Iglesia ni Cristo. Avocations: book writing, bowling, table tennis. Home: Rancho Estate IV, 12 Lilac St, Marikina City 1800, The Philippines Office: 67 Gen Ondõng St, Marikina City 1800, The Philippines

PALACIO, FRANCISCO JOSE, chemical engineer, researcher; b. Bogota, Colombia, Oct. 15, 1956; s. Jose Miguel and Maria Gloria (Ramirez) P.; m. Adriana Maria Gonzalez, June 24, 1989. Grad. in chem. engring., U. Pontificia Bolivariana, Medellin, Colombia, 1977; postgrad., Sch. Adminstrn. and Fin., Medellin, 1992—. Process assessment engr. Cia. Colombiana de Tabaco, Medellin, 1977-81, dir. R & D, 1981—; dean faculty chem. engring. U. Pontificia Boliviana, 1995-2000; instr. chem. engring. U. Pontificia Bolivariana, 1980-82; mem. adv. bd. Polimeros y Adhesivos Especializados, Medellin, 1989-93, Tecnicas Adhesivas Colombianas S.A., Medellin, 1990-92. Mem. Am. Chem. Soc., Am. Mgmt. Assn., Am. Soc. for Quality Control, Inst. Food Technologists, Rotary. Roman Catholic. Home: Casa 113, Carrera 29A No 4Sur-87, Medellin Colombia Office: Coltabaco, Carrera 50 No 5-115 Apt 828, Medellin Colombia

PALACIOS, RONALD, immunologist; b. Camiri, Bolivia, Jan. 11, 1953; came to U.S., 1992; s. Enrique and Leddy (Castrillo) P.; m. Patricia Ibarra, June 4, 1977; children: Catherine, Patricia. B Humanities, Colegio Sagrado Corazon, Sucre, 1970; MD with distinction, U. Nat. Autonoma de Mex., Mexico City, 1976, degree in internal medicine splty., 1979; PhD, Karolinska Inst., Stockholm, 1982. Cert. Mexican Bd. Internal Medicine. Instr. histology U. Nat. Mexico, Mexico City, 1973, asst. prof. introduction to medicine; fellow immunology Inst. Nat. Nutrition, Mexico City, 1979-80; mem. Basel (Switzerland) Inst. Immunology, 1982-92; prof., dep. chmn. dept. immunology U. Tex. M.D. Anderson Cancer Ctr., Houston, 1992—. Contbr. articles to profl. jours., chpts. to books. Fellow Swedish Inst., Stockholm, 1980-82, WHO, 1980-81. Fellow Mexican Bd. Internal Medicine; mem. AAAS, Am. Assn. Hematology, Assn. Medicos Internistas Mexico, Assn. Medicos Instituto Nat. Nutrition, Am. Assn. Immunology, Am. Assn. Microbiology, Scandinavian Soc. Immunology, U. Tex. M.D. Anderson Assocs., N.Y. Acad. Scis. Home: PO Box 2795, Santa Cruz Bolivia

PALACIOS-PAWLOVSKY, ALBERTO, engineering educator; b. Lima, Peru, Nov. 1, 1955; arrived in Japan, 1985; s. Gilberto Palacios and Juana (Pawlovsky Delgado) Pawlovsky de Palacios; m. Erglantina Ramirez Andrade, Feb. 2, 1992; children: Rossana, Stephanie. BS, U. Nacional de Ingenieria, Lima, 1981, elec. engr., 1982; MS, Nagaoka (Japan) U. Tech., 1988, DEng, 1991. Registered profl. engr. Engr. Entel Peru S.A., Lima, 1981-85, planning engr., 1983-84, projects engr., 1984-85; vis. rschr. Hitachi Ltd. Cen. Rsch. Lab., Tokyo, 1991-94; lectr. electronics and info. engring. Toin U. Yokohama, Japan, 1994—. Patentee in field. Monbusho scholar Ministry of Edn. of Japan, 1985, 88. Mem. IEEE (sr.), Inst. Electronics, Info. and Comm. Engrs. (Japan), Assn. for Computing Machinery (voting mem.). Avocations: jogging, aikido, chess, soccer. Office: Toin U Yokohama, Kurogane-cho 1614, Yokohama 225-8502, Japan

PALACZ, OLGIERD JAN, ophthalmologist, educator; b. Toruń, Poland, Feb. 8, 1933; s. Józef and Władysława (Trzebska) P.; m. Janina Henryka Woźniak, Aug. 28, 1965; 1 child, Andrzej. MD, Pomeranian Med. Acad., Szczecin, Poland, 1957, PhD, 1966. Med. diplomate. Asst. Pomeranian Med. Acad.-Dept. Ophthalmology, Szczecin, 1957-65, asst. prof., 1965-76, assoc. prof., 1976-84, full prof., 1984—, dean, 1976-81, 85-86, prorector, 1988-91; regional cons. in ophthalmology Ministry of Pub. Health, Szczecin, 1994—. Author: Visual System - Anatomy and Physiology "Okulistyka Współczesna, 1986; co-author: Functional Human Diagnostics Applied Physiol, 1999; contbr. articles to profl. jours. Lt. med. br. Polish Army, 1966—. Recipient 2nd grade Rector's awards, Szczecin, 1966, 71, 76, 91, 1st grade award Ministry of Pub. Health, Warsaw, 1985. Mem. Polish Ophthalmol. Soc. (bd. mem.), German Ophthalmol. Soc., European Glaucoma Soc. (bd. mem. 1990—). Roman Catholic. Avocations: ancient history, classical music, traveling, bicycling. Home: Wszystkich Świetych 43/2, 71-457 Szczecin Poland Office: Katedra Klinika Okulistyki, Al Powstancow Wlkp 72, 70-111 Szczecin Poland

PALADE, DMITRIY MIKHAYLOVICH, chemistry educator; b. Slobodzia-Mare, Vulkanesht, Moldova, Jan. 13, 1932; s. Mikhayl Dmitrievich and Nadeja Vikentjevna (Strujik) P.; m. Olga Ivanovna Matushina, Aug. 23, 1958 (div. May 1971); children: Anatoly Dmitrievich, Vitaly Dmitrievich. Diplome in Chemistry, Kishinev (Moldova) State U., 1955; Diplome Candidate Chem. Scis., Aspirantura Sci., Kishinev, 1963; Diplome D chem. Scis., Moscow State U., 1986. Tchr. chemistry mid. sch. Chernovitskay, Ukraine, 1955-56; asst. Acad. Scis., Kishinev, 1956-59, sci. worker, 1959-62; scientist, sec. Inst. Mutual Chemistry, Kishinev, 1962-64; docent Ivano-Frankovsk (Ukraine) Oil Inst., 1964-66, Donetsk (Ukraine) Polytech. Inst., 1966-87; prof. chemistry Donetsk State Tech. U., 1987—; prof. State Com. USSR of People Edn., Moscow, 1988; mem. inorganic chemistry coordinative, Coun. Sci. Acad., Moscow, 1975-91, Coun. Ukraine Sci. Acad., Kiev, 1975. Contbr. articles to profl. jours. Recipient personal grant Internat. Soros Suppor Edn. Programm Ukraine State, 1993. Mem. Mendeleev Russian Chem. Soc., Acad. Scis. N.Y., Coun. Conf. Sci. Degre Donetsk State U. Achievements include research in coordination chemistry of cobalt, synthetic oxygen carriers, mathematical simulation of complicated chemical processes. Office: Donetsk State Tech U, Artemy 58, 340000 Donetsk Ukraine

PALADE, GEORGE EMIL, biologist, educator; b. Jassy, Romania, Nov. 19, 1912; came to U.S., 1946, naturalized, 1952; s. Emil and Constanta (Cantemir) P.; m. Irina Malaxa, June 12, 1941 (dec. 1969); children—Georgia Teodora, Philip Theodore; m. Marilyn G. Farquhar, 1970. Bachelor, Hasdeu Lyceum, Buzau, Romania; M.D., U. Bucharest, Romania. Instr., asst. prof., then assoc. prof. anatomy Sch. Medicine, U. Bucharest, 1935-45; vis. investigator, asst. assoc., prof. cell biology Rockefeller U., 1946-73; prof. cell biology Yale U., New Haven, 1973-83; sr. research scientist Yale U., 1983-89; prof.-in-residence, dean sci. affairs Med. Sch., U. Calif., San Diego, 1990—. Author sci. papers. Recipient Albert Lasker Basic Research award, 1966, Gairdner Spl. award, 1967, Horwitz prize, 1970, Nobel prize in Physiology or Medicine, 1974, Nat. Medal Sci., 1986. Fellow Am. Acad. Arts and Scis.; mem. Nat. Acad. Sci., Pontifical Acad. Sci., Royal Soc. (London), Leopoldina Acad. (Halle), Romanian Acad., Royal Belgian Acad. Medicine. Achievements include research in interests correlated biochem. and morphological analysis cell structures.

PALADINO, ALBERT EDWARD, venture capitalist; b. N.Y.C., Aug. 4, 1932; s. Albert E. and Jennie (Fiato) P.; m. Dorothy M. Hayes (div. June 1979); children: Thomas A., Robert E., Catherine J., Paul F.; m. Susan Flynn, June 11, 1983. BS in Ceramic Engring., Alfred U., 1954, MS in Ceramic Engring., 1956; ScD in Materials Sci., MIT, 1962. Registered profl. engr., Mass. Staff mem. Raytheon Co. Rsch. Div., Waltham, Mass., 1955-59; mgr. materials and crystal growth lab. Raytheon Co. Rsch. Div., Waltham, 1962-69; mgr. materials and techniques group Raytheon Co. Microwave & Power Tube Div., Waltham, 1969-72, mgr. electronics materials group, 1972-75; program mgr. materials Office of Tech. Assessment U.S. Congress, Washington, 1975-78; asst. dir. telephone ops. tech. ctr. GTE Labs., Waltham, 1978-79; dep. dir. Office Energy Programs U.S. Dept. Commerce, Nat. Inst. Standards and Tech., Washington, 1979-81; mng. ptnr. Advanced Tech. Ventures, Boston, 1981-98; chmn. Telaxis Comm. Corp., South Deerfield, Mass., 1988—, Electro-Scan Corp., Billerica, Mass., 1990-95, OMEX Comm. Corp., 1999—; bd. dirs. TranSwitch Corp., Shelton, Conn., 1988—, Microwave Networks, Houston, 1990-95, Micro Devices, Greensboro, N.C., 1992—, Thunderbird Techs., Morrisville, N.C., 1992-98; chmn. OMEX Comm., 1999—; telecomm. bd. advisors Prisom Ventures, 1997—, Early Stage Enterprises, 1997—. Contbr. articles profl. jours.; patentee in field. Pres. West Needham (Mass.) Civic Assn., 1967-69; bd. trustees Alfred U., 1991—; mem. Needham Town Meeting, 1973-74, Rep. Nat. Com., 1988—. Recipient Disting. Svc. resolution Office of Tech. Assessment U.S. Congress, 1978. Fellow Am. Ceramic Soc. (chmn. basic sci. div. 1968-69, chmn. New Eng. sect. 1969-70, Disting. New Eng. Ceramic award), Nat. Venture Capital Assn. Avocations: painting, music, physical fitness, hiking, tennis, reading. Office: Telaxis Comm 20 Industrial Dr E South Deerfield MA 01373-7301

PALADUGU, RAMAMOHANARAO, botany and biotechnology educator, researcher; b. Chinaogirala, India, Nov. 25, 1937; s. Ramayya and Nagaratnamma (Velagapudi) P.; m. Seetaramamma Nagabhiru, Oct. 13, 1967; children: Lakshmi Paladugu, Kalyanchakravarthy, Paladugu. BS with honors, Andhra U., Visakhapatnam, India, 1958, MS, 1960; cert. in German, Delhi (India) U., 1964, diploma in German, 1965, PhD, 1966; MA (hon.), Cambridge (Eng.) U., 1967, PhD, 1967. Asst. lect. dept. botany Delhi U., 1964-67; postdoctoral fellow Cambridge (Eng.) U., 1967-71; rsch. assoc. dept. botany Delhi U., 1971-75; asst. prof. dept. bioscis. Himachel Pradesh U., Shimla, India, 1976-78; lectr., reader dept. botany Nagarjuna (India) U., 1978-84, prof. dept. botany, 1984—; vis. prof. Ctrl. U. Venezuela, Caracas, 1980, Paris U., 1986-87; Swedish Inst. guest Uppsala U., 1982-83; head dept. botany and microbiology Nagarjuna U., 1990-92, dir. Ctr. for Biotechnology, 1992-97, chmn. bd. studies botany and microbiology, 1995-97, chmn. bd. studies biotechnology, 1992-97. Recipient Andhra Pradesh Govt. Best Univ.

Tchr. award, 1997-98; grantee U. Grants Commn., New Delhi, 1984-89, Coun. Sci. and Indsl. Rsch., New Delhi, 1984-89, Bot. Survey India, 1984-89; UGC fellow, 1999—. Mem. Orchid Soc. India (founding life mem., edit. adv. bd., joint sec., asst. editor 1984—), Internat. Soc. Plant Morphologists (life), Swamy Bot. Club (found. mem.), N.Y. Acad. Scis. Avocations: reading natural history books, nature photography, orchid hunting. Home: Krishnanagar 3-29-11/1, 522006 Guntur India Office: Nagarjuna Univ, Dept Botany, 522510 Nagarjunanagar India

PALAKKANDY, ARUN, computer program educator, researcher; b. Telecherry, India, Feb. 18, 1969; s. K.C. Raghavan and Vasantha P. BS, ARSD Coll., New Delhi, India, 1990; MS, Dept. Physics and Astrophysics, Delhi, India, 1992, PhD, 1998. Lectr. Hansraj Coll., Delhi, India, 1995-97, SGTB Khalsa Coll., Delhi, India, 1997—. Author in field. Mem. N.Y. Acad. Sci. Hindu. Avocations: photography, electronic circuit design. Home phone: 6468401. Office: SGTB Khalsa Coll, University of Delhi, Delhi 110007, India

PALANT, ALEXEI ALEXANDROVICH, hydrometallurgist, researcher; b. Charkov, Ukraine, Russia, Aug. 10, 1941; s Alexandr Isaakovich and Eugenia Alexandrovna ((Atlasner) P.; m. Inna Naumovna Lesnovskay, Aug. 10, 1963; children: Natali, Leonid. Degree in Engring., Moscow State Acad. Fine Chem., 1965; Cand. Tech. Scis., Inst. Metallurgy, Moscow, 1970, ScD, 1989. Jr. scientist Inst. Metallurgy/Russian Acad. Scis., Moscow, 1965-74, sr. scientist, 1975-88, head scientist, 1989—; cons. Inst. of sci. and Tech. Info., Moscow, 1976—. Contbr. articles to profl. jours. Recipient The Ministry Prize Laureate, USSR, 1984. Mem. Spl. Sci. Soviet Moscow Acad. Fine Chem. Avocations: chess, travel, books. Home: Sivachskay 6-1-77, 113149 Moscow Russia Office: IMET RAN, Leninsky Prospect 49, 117911 Moscow Russia

PALARCA, DOMINGO CRISTOBAL, lawyer; b. Manila, Mar. 14, 1947; s. Jose and Querubina (Cristobal) P.; m. Maria Teresa Del Castillo, Feb. 22, 1975; children: Jose Miguel, Jose Domingo, Maria Teresa Francesca. AB in Philosophy, U. of The Philippines, 1968, LLB, 1972, LLM, 1977. Ptnr. Jose F. Palarca Law Offices, The Philippines, 1973-86; founding ptnr. Domingo C. Palarca Law Offices, The Philippines, 1987—; exec. v.p. Ctrl. Inst. Tech., The Philippines, 1987-98; pres. Philippine Concorde Trading Co., 1988-92, Femex Inc., The Philippines, 1993-96, C.I.T. Colls., The Philippines, 1999; legal cons. Sensormatic, Malaysia, 1997—, Kalaw Estate, The Philippines, 1987—, P.C.I.B. Properties, The Philippines, 1997-98, Nishiura Kenethu, Ltd., Japan, 1999, Sunyou Giken Co. Ltd., Japan, 1999. Exec. v.p. Philippine Jaycees, 1986; senator Jaycees internat., 1990; pres. Rizal Lawyers Assn., The Philippines, 1988; legal counsel Liberal Party, The Philippines, 1987. Recipient Papal award Vatican, 1985. Fellow Upsilon Sigma Phi (citation 1973); mem. Integrated Bar of The Philippines. Roman Catholic. Avocations: golf, target shooting, fishing, raising tropical fish, basketball. Home: 10 Data St, 1100 Quezon City The Philippines Office: Domingo C Palarca Offices, Palarca Bldg Q Blvd, 1008 Manila The Philippines

PALAT, KAREL, pharmacy educator; b. Trebic, Czech Republic, Oct. 6, 1957; s. Karel and Sona Palat. PharmDr, Charles U., Hradec Kralove, Czech Republic, 1982, PhD, 1992. Lectr. faculty pharmacy Charles U., Hradec Kralove, 1985—. Mem. Czech Chem. Soc., Czech Pharm. Soc. (com. mem. sect. of the synthetic drugs). Achievements include patentee in field. Avocations: skiing, basketball, photography. E-mail: palat@faf.cuni.cz. Fax: 49-5512423. Home: Benesova 1550, 500 12 Hradec Kralove Czech Republic Office: Charles U Fac Pharmacy, Heyrovskeho 1203, 500 05 Hradec Kralove Czech Republic

PALATIANOS, GEORGE MICHAEL, surgeon; b. Athens, Oct. 26, 1946; came to U.S., 1976; s. Michael G. and Anastasia (Psaltis) P.; m. Elisabeth Grapsas, Apr. 28, 1985; children: Stacie Marie, Joanna Iole, Alexandra Sofia. MD, U. Athens, 1971. Diplomate Am. Bd. Surgery, Am. Bd. Thoracic Surgery. Clin. instr. surgery U. Miami Sch. Medicine, 1983-84, asst. prof. surgery, 1984-91, assoc. prof., 1991—; chief cardiothoracic surgery VA Med. Ctr., Miami, 1989-93; attending staff Jackson Meml. Hosp., Miami, 1983—; chief cardiac surgery Onassis Cardiac Surgery Ctr., Athens, 1993—; cons. physician children's med. svcs. Dept. Health and Rehab. Svcs., State of Fla., Miami, 1985-91; physician advisor VA, Medipro, Miami, 1988-92. Contbr. articles to profl. jours. 2d lt. M.C., 1972-74, Greece. Fellow ACS, Am. Coll. Cardiology, Am. Coll. Chest Physicians; mem. Soc. Thoracic Surgeons, Soc. Internat. de Chirurgie, Am. Soc. Artificial Internal Organs., Am. Assn. Thoracic Surgery. Office: Onassis Cardiac Surgery Ctr, 356 Sygrou Ave, Athens 176-74, Greece

PALAZZI, RUBEN OSCAR, career military officer; b. Cruz Alta, Cordoba, Republic of Argentina, Feb. 26, 1944; s. Ricardo Angel and Zulema Elsa (Monti) P.; m. Ana Maria Lenardon, Apr. 11, 1969; children: Pablo Andres, Gustavo Gabriel. 2nd lt., Air Force Sch., Cordoba, Argentina, 1960-63, mil. pilot, 1964; asst. staff officer, Air War Coll., Buenos Aires, 1997. Ops. chief Air Ops. Command, Buenos Aires, 1988-89; air atache Air Force, Santiago de Chile, 1989-90; dir. Air War Coll., Buenos Aires, 1992-93, Air Force Sch., Cordoba, 1993-94; dep. chief Air Force, Buenos Aires, 1996-97, Joint Staff, Buenos Aires, 1997—; prof. Air War Coll., Buenos Aires, 1982-88. Author: Antartida Y Archipielagos Subantarticos, 1987, Book II, 1989, Book II, 1993, Escuela de Aviacion Militar-Genesis FAA, 1995, Puente Aereo A Malvinas, 1997, Alas Sobre El Sexto Continente, 1999. Mem. CARI (Antarctic studies com. 1990—), CAEE. Roman Catholic. Avocations: aeronautic history, Antarctic, golf, cookings and wines. Office: Estado mayor Conjunto FFAA, Azopardo 250 Piso 13, 1328 Buenos Aires Argentina

PALCHAEV, DAIR KAIROVICH, physics educator, researcher; b. Akhty, Daghestan, Russia, Nov. 24, 1946; s. Kair Abdurakhimovich and Gulselem Abdulfatakhovna (Radzhabova) P.; m. Khanum Seyfedinovna Gashumova, July 22, 1972; 1 child, Farida Dairovna. Diploma, U. Makhachkala, Russia, 1972; diploma Candidate of Sci., U. Rostov, Russia, 1982; cert. Docent, U. Moscow, 1992. Lab. asst. U. Makhachkala, 1972-75, sr. rsch. asst., 1975-84, lectr., 1985-89, docent, 1990—, sci. leader Students Rsch. Bur., 1987-90; Soros assoc. prof. Internat. Soros Sci. Edn. Program, 1997; mem. dissertational coun. Inst. Acad. Sci., Makhachkala, 1994—; rationalizator, inventor, Russia, 1984. Author: Review Information N3(35), 1982. Recipient award cert. Vystavka Dostizhenly Narodnogo Khozyaystva, USSR, 1977. Home: Kazbekova 180 a-32, 367027 Makhachkala Russia Office: Daghestan State U, Gadjieva 43 a, 367025 Makhachkala Russia

PALEČEK, EMIL, biochemist, educator; b. Brno, Czechoslovakia, Oct. 3, 1930; s. Josefa Palečková; m. Eva Borovcová; children: Jan, Emil, Pavel. MSc, Masaryk U., Brno, Czechoslovakia, 1956, PhD, 1959; DSc, Czechoslovak Acad. Sci., Prague, 1976. Rsch. asst. Inst. Biophysics, Brno, 1959-62, rsch. assoc., 1964-66, head dept., 1967—; postdoctoral fellow dept. biochemistry Brandeis U., Waltham, Mass., 1962-63; assoc. prof. U. Brno, 1968-92; prof. Masaryk U., Brno, 1992—; chmn. Natural Scis. Commn. Grant Agy., Czech Republic, 1993-94, mem., 1994-97. Contbr. articles to profl. publs. Recipient State Prize for Sci., Govt. of Czechoslovakia, 1976, Silver medal of G. Mendel, Czechoslovak Acad. Sci., 1980, Gold medal of G. Mendel, 1990. Mem. Acad. Scis. of Czech Republic (acad. coun. 1993-97, prize 2000), Bioelectrochem. Soc. (founding mem.), Czech Learned Soc. (founding mem.). Office: Inst Biophysics Acad Sci, Královopolská 135, 61200 Brno Czech Republic

PALECEK, PETER VACLAV, management consultant; b. Prague, Bohemia, Czech Republic, Apr. 28, 1940; s. Vaclav and Anna (Zmekova) P.; m. Hana Kazdova, Nov. 15, 1968; children: David, Michael, Tom. MS, Czech Inst. Tech., 1965; MBA, Stanford U., 1971. Mktg. analyst Peterbilt Motors, Newark, Calif., 1976-77; sr. mgmt. cons. SRI Consulting, Menlo Park, Calif., 1977-87; sr. v.p. Landbank, Redwood City, Calif., 1987-90; v.p. corp. devel. Bata Shoe Co., Prague, 1990-92; advisor to chmn. Xenel Industries, Jeddah, Saudi Arabia, 1992-95; v.p., mng. dir. Arthur D. Little, Prague, 1995—; exec. dir. World Freedom Found., Redwood City, Calif., 1981-86; exec. bd. trustees Czech Mgmt. Ctr., Celakovice, Czech Republic, 1995-99; advisor to bd. dirs. Škoda, Pilsen, Czech Republic, 1997-99. Mem. Nat. Ski Patrol, Alpine Meadows, Calif. 1st lt. Czech Army, 1966. Republican. Avocations: scuba diving, mountain climbing. Office: Arthur D Little Internat, Konviktska 24, 11000 Praha 1, Czech Republic

PALECZ, BARTLOMIEJ, chemist, educator; b. Radomsko, Poland, Nov. 30, 1949; s. Jozef and Marianna (Bakiewicz) P.; m. Danuta Maria Swiatlowska, Oct. 6, 1973; 1 child, Radoslaw. MS in Chemistry, U. Lodz, 1973, PhD of Phys. Chemistry, 1982. Asst. U. Lodz, Poland, 1973-82; rsch. lectr. U. Lodz, 1982—. Contbr. articles to profl. jours. Mem. Solidaronsc, Lodz, 1980—. Avocations: belles-lettres, sightseeing, modern history, amino acids. E-mail: paleczb@krysia.uni.lodz.pl.que. Home: Julianowska 1, 91-473 Łódź Poland Office: Univ Łódź Dept Phys Chem, st Pomorska 165, 90-236 Łódź Poland

PALEN, JOE JOHN, sociology educator; b. Dubuque, Iowa, Feb. 24, 1939; s. Joseph John Palen and Mary (Rowan) Toner; m. Karen Ann Doody, June 9, 1962; children: Joseph John, Elizabeth Ann, Ellen Marye. BA, U. Notre Dame, 1961; MS, U. Wis.-Madison, 1963, PhD, 1967. Demographer, UN, Addis Ababa, Ethiopia, 1971-72; assoc. prof. U. Wis., Milw., 1972-77, prof., 1977-80; vis. prof. Nat. U. Singapore, 1983-84; prof. sociology, chmn. dept. Va. Commonwealth U., Richmond, 1980—; cons., writer UN, 1983—. Author: Gentrification, Displacement and Revitalization, 1984; Urban World, 5th edit. 1997; City Scenes, 2nd edit. 1981, The Suburbs, 1995; Social Problems for the Twenty-first Century, 2000. Leader Boy Scouts Am., Wis., 1973-80; active Big Bros. Capt. U.S. Army, 1967-69. Rockefeller Found. grantee, 1985; NIH grantee, 1980-82; Ford Found. grantee, 1979, NIMH grantee, 1976, NSF grantee, 1985, Sr. Fulbright Scholar, Taiwan, 1992, Fulbright Disting. Lecturer and Chair in North American Studies, Univ. Calgary, 1997, Disting. Scholar, Va. Commonwealth Univ., 1995. Fellow Am. Sociol. Assn., So. Sociol. Soc.; mem. Urban Affairs Assn. Avocations: hiking, canoeing, civil war. Home: 500 Gardiner Rd Richmond VA 23229-6919 Office: Va Commonwealth U Dept Sociology And Anthropo Richmond VA 23284

PALEN, PETER HASBROUCK, retired mechanical engineer, consultant; b. N.Y.C., Nov. 7, 1920; s. Lewis Stanton and Laura Humphreys (Cooke) P.; m. Janet Grace Tilton, Nov. 27, 1948; children: Laura G., Brouck H., Pamela A. BA in Elem. Math., U. D'aix Marseilles, Nice, France, 1940; student, Stevens Inst. Tech., 1941. Layout designer Wright Aeronautical Group, Paterson, N.J., 1941-45; instr. Stevens Inst. Tech., Hoboken, N.J., 1945-46; sr. design engr. Reaction Motors, Inc., Rockaway, N.J., 1946-50; chief engr. Marotta Valve Corp., Boonton, N.J., 1950-53; staff engr. Bergen Rsch. Engring., Teterboro, N.J., 1953-58; prin., owner Captive Seal Corp., Caldwell, N.J., 1958-64; asst. to pres. Valcor Engring., Kenilwort, N.J., 1964-65; prin., owner Sigma-Netics Inc., Fairfield, N.J., 1965-94, retired, 1994. Field worker Am. Red Cross, Cannes, France, 1940-41; air raid warden Civil Defense WWII, Paterson, N.J., 1941-42. Recipient Quality Excellence award Dept. Defense, 1982. Mem. Nat. Space Soc., Planetary Soc. Achievements include the design and making of fuel valve and press, switch for Bendk Jet Engine starter, solenoid valve (anhydrous NH_3) for Hound Dog Missile, press switch on Mercury Capsule Retro-Rocket, ball valves handling UDMH & N_2O_4 to Titan Launcher of Gemini, all press switches and the pneumatic solenoid valve controlling X-15 Rocket motor, MX-774 Rocket motor and control valving, pressure switches in F-14 Swing Wing actuator, F-14 and C-5A brakes, C-141 flight controls; design, build and fire large caliber SABOT amo. Inventions include 8 U.S. patents and 5 foreign patents as the basis for critical designs of Reaction Motors, Captive Seal and Sigma-Netics. Home: 1 Union St Wiscasset ME 04578-4000

PALEOLOGOS, EVANGELOS, hydrologist, educator; b. Athens, Greece, June 26, 1958; came to U.S., 1983; s. Constantine E. and Kathy A. (Michos) P.; m. Cleo L. Kalemkeris, Apr. 30, 1989; children: Katrina, Demi. BSCE, Poly. U., 1986, MSCE, 1986; PhD in Hydrology, U. Ariz., 1994. Tchg. asst. Poly. U., N.Y.C., 1984-85, adj. lectr., 1985-86; grad. rsch. asst. U. Ariz., Tucson, 1986-92; sr. staff cons. Intera Inc., Las Vegas, Nev., 1992-95; asst. prof. U. S.C., Columbia, 1995—. Editl. bd. Jour. Stochastic Hydrology and Hydraulics, Stochastic Environ. Rsch. and Risk Assessment, 1998—, over 20 publs; author 2 books on environmental risk analysis. Organizing com. Champman Conf., 1998; faculty senator U. S.C., 1997—. Dept. Energy Nat. Water Rsch. Ctr. and Environ. Mgmt. grantee, 1997; U. S.C. Rschr. scholar, 1995-96; recipient Initializers award S.C. Rsch. Inst., 1998. Mem. Am. Geophys. Union, European Geophys. Soc. Greek Orthodox. Avocations: art collecting, gardening. Office: Dept Geol Scis U Sc Columbia SC 29208-0001

PALERMO, ROBERT JAMES, architect, consultant, inventor; b. N.Y.C., Mar. 25, 1949; s. Vitorio and Simone (DiFlorio) P.; m. Lore Bernadette Bilbao, July 22, 1972 (dec. Feb. 1977); m. Patricia Dolores Ward, June 14, 1981; children: Jaime, Justin, Kristen Leigh. BS, CCNY, 1971, BArch, 1972; MBA, Baruch Grad. Ctr., 1974; postgrad., Nat. Asbestos Tng. Inst., 1987. Lic. asbestos investigator; registered architect, N.Y., N.J. Architect Rongved, Wilcox, Erickson, N.Y.C., 1972-73, Welton Becket Assocs., N.Y.C., 1973-75; architect, prin. Jaime Lore Design, Bklyn., 1976—; bd. dir. Nat. Meddlex Med. Constrn. Corp., Hicksville, N.Y., 1981-85; pres. Corp. Design of Am., P.C., 1989—. Mem. Am. Inst. Archs., Soc. Am. Registered Archs., Cert. Interior Decorators Assn., Phi Sigma Kappa. Republican. Roman Catholic. Avocations: rare coin collecting, philatelics, Beaux Art prints. Home: 160 Pelican Rd Middletown NJ 07748-3042 Office: Corp Design of Am PC 461 Park Ave S New York NY 10016-6822

PALERMOS, JOHN GEORGE, immunologist, military officer; b. Salamis, Greece, June 14, 1947; s. George John Palermos and Sophia E. Skouterakou; m. Bia D. Davou, 1980; children: George, Sophia. MD, Med. U., Thessaloniki, Greece, 1972; officer Air Force, Mil. Med. Acad., Thessaloniki, Greece, 1972; bacteriologist, U. Athens, Greece, 1981. Cert. rsch. assoc. in immunology. Commd. lt. Hellenic Air Force, 1972, advanced through grades to col., physician, officer, 1972-81; cons. Air Force Hosp. Hellenic Air Force, Athens, 1981-87, dir. dept. Air Force Hosp., 1989—; rsch. assoc. U. Ala., Birmingham, 1987-89; bd. dirs. Air Force Hosp., Athens. Contbr. articles to profl. jours. Mem. Am. Assn. Clin. Chemistry, Am. Soc. for Microbiology, Hellenic Armed Forces Med. Rev. (bd. editors). Home: Evagelistrias 8, 18901 Salamis Greece

PALESKY, CAROL EAST, tax accountant; b. Orange, N.J., May 13, 1940; d. Neil Norell and Marie R. Reiss; m. Jacob Palesky; children: Donna, Lewis. AB, Am. Inst., Pleasantville, N.J., 1973; postgrad., Am. Inst., Portland, Maine, 1980; student, Atlantic C.C., Mays Landing, N.J., 1971-73. With mgmt. First Nat. Bank of South Jersey (now First Fidelity), Pleasantville, N.J., 1967-74; loan officer Maine Savs. Bank, Portland, 1980-81; acct., owner East Acctg. Assocs., Topsham, Maine, 1985—; pres. Sensible Tax Limits Coalition, 1995—. Treas., bd. dirs. Congl. Term Limits Coalition, Topsham, 1993—; bd. dirs. Maine Citizens Rev. Bd., Portland, 1993—. Scholar Nat. Taxpayer Union, 1992, 94; recipient United to Serve Am. award, 1992. Mem. Nat. Assn. Small Business Owners, Maine Taxpayers Action Network (pres. 1990—), Topsham Taxpayer Assn. (pres. 1991—). Roman Catholic. E-mail: cep@mtan.org. Home and Office: 24 Sokokis Cir Topsham ME 04086-1615

PÁLFFY, GYÖRGY ANTAL, neurologist, educator; b. Budapest, Hungary, Mar. 24, 1920; s. Sándor Pálffy and Gabriella Dobsa; m. Györgyné Simon, Aug. 31, 1950; children: György József, László Zoltán. MD, Pázmány Péter Univ., Budapest, 1944; candidate med. scis., Hungarian Acad. Scis., Budapest, 1969, D in Med. Scis., 1987. Intern, resident dept. internal medicine Pázmény Péter U., Budapest; intern, resident Rokus Hosp., Budapest; chmn. dept. neurology and psychiatry County Hosp., Kaposvar, 1960-72; intern, resident dept. neurol. psychiatry U. Pecs; chmn., prof. Univ. of Pécs (Hungary) Med. Sch., 1972-88, prof. neurology dept. neurology, 1988-90, prof. emeritus, sci. cons. dept. neurology, 1990—; vis. prof. Nat. Inst. Neurology and Psychiatry, Tokyo-Kodaira, Japan,1 986, Nat. Inst. Neurol. and Comm. Disorders and Stroke, NIH, Bethesda, Md., 1986. Author: Epidemiology of Multiple Sclerosis Neurology, 1986; mem. editl. bd. Acta Medica Hubgarica Clin. Neurosci., 1966. Recipient Star Distinction, Hungarian Republic Budapest, 1990. Mem. Internat. Fedn. Multiple Sclerosis Socs. (internat. med. adv. bd. 1977—). Roman Catholic. Avocations: swimming, literature. Home: Semmelweis U 9, 7623 Pécs Hungary Office: Dept Neurology, Univ Pécs Med Sch, 7623 Pécs Hungary

PÁLFI, TAMÁS, mechanical engineer; b. Nagykanizsa, Zala, Hungary, Feb. 14, 1970; s. Tihamér and Tihaméné (Kőfalvi Mária) P. MS, Tech. U., 1993. Engr. BKM Inc., San Diego, 1993-94; tchr. Sch., Nagykanizsa, 1994-99; asst. to prof. Sch., 1999—; cons. High Sch., Nagykanizsa, 1996—, U. Miskolc, 1996—. E-mail: palfit@cserhati.sulinet.hu. Home: Herman Ou 1, 8800 Nagykanizsa Hungary Office: Cserháti SzKI, Ady E. u. 74/a., 8800 Nagykanizsa Hungary

PÁLFY, MIKLÓS, solar company executive; b. Budapest, Hungary, Dec. 19, 1941; s. Sandor and Edit (Kerekes) P.; m. Ildiko Erzsebet Gallo, Aug. 3, 1965; children: Gabor, Tamas. MS in Elec. Engring., Tech. U. Budapest, 1964. Researcher Rsch. Inst. Elec. Engring., Budapest, Hungary, 1964-89; asst. prof. Tech. U. Budapest, 1979-95; dir. Solar Lab., Budapest, 1989-92, Solart-System Ltd., Budapest, 1990—; researcher U. Denmark, 1974; cons. TET Co., Cegled, Hungary, 1985—. Contbr. articles to profl. jours; inventor in field. Mem. Internat. Solar Energy Soc. (Hungarian sect.), Hungarian Electrotech. Assn. Home: Gulyás u 20, 1112 Budapest Hungary Office: Solart-System Ltd, Gulyas U 20, 1112 Budapest Hungary

PALGRAVE, DEREK AUBREY, chemist; b. Norwich, England, Sept. 16, 1932; s. Aubrey William and Doris Mary (Richardson) P.; m. Pamela Pearl Spilling, Sept. 21, 1957; children: Catharine, Nicholas, Christopher. MA, Cambridge U., 1957. Chartered chemist. Rsch. chemist Albright & Wilson, Oldbury, England, 1957-64; chief chemist J.W. Chafer Ltd., Doncaster, England, 1964-74, tech. dir., 1974-88; divisional dir. Britag Industries, York, England, 1988-91; cons. Bury St. Edmunds, England, 1991—; cons. Fertilizer Manufacturers' Assn., London, 1971—, British Standards Instn., London, 1972—, Internat. Standards Orgn., Geneva, 1973—; lectr. Chem. Industries Assn., London, 1988—; extra-mural tutor U. East Anglia, 1992—, U. Cambridge, 1997—. Contbr.: Mellor Treatise: Phosphorus, 1971; editor, contbr.: Fluid Fertilizer Science and Technology, 1991; patentee in field; editor: Family History News and Digest, 1977-82, Family History Digest, 1989—. Pilot officer RAF, 1952-54. Fellow Soc. Genealogists, Royal Hist. Soc., Royal Soc. Chemistry; mem. Fedn. Family History Socs. (vice chmn. 1978-82, mem. editorial bd., chmn. 1977-2000), Guild One-Name Studies (chmn. 1981-87, pres. 1987—), Suffolk Family History Soc. (chmn. 1989-98), Doncaster and District Family History Soc. (pres. 1989—), Coll. of Tchrs. Mem. Ch. of England. Avocations: gardening, heraldry, calligraphy, conservation, photography. Home: Crossfield House Dale Rd, Stanton Bury Saint Edmunds Suffolk 1P31 2DY, England

PALHOTO, GLAUCO BIETREZATTO, electrical engineer; b. Sao Paulo, Brazil, Jan. 17, 1961; s. Nuno Domingos Carbo and Eunice Bietrezatto Palhoto; m. Vania Fuscella, Nov. 20, 1987 (div. 1995); 1 child: Guilherme Fuscella. Technician, ITO, Sao Paulo, 1979; engring., FEI, Sao Paulo, 1986. Project designer ABB, Sao Paulo, 1986-91, sales mgr., 1991-93, v.p., 1993-95; dir. ABB-The U.S., Sao Paulo, 1995—. Mem. Apine. Roman Catholic. Avocation: judo. Home: Av Martin Luther King 2386, Apt 75, Sao Paulo 05352010, Brazil Office: ABB, Av Dos Autonomistas, Sao Paulo 06020902, Brazil

PALICA, MICHAŁ PAWEŁ, environmental sciences educator, consultant, researcher; b. Katowice, Silesia, Poland, July 30, 1942; s. Ryszard and Hildegarda (Kłosok) P.; m. Jadwiga Maria Jarosz, June 30, 1973; children: Joanna, Zofia, Jan-Paweł, Adam. MSc, Silesian Tech. U., Gliwice, Poland, 1966, PhD, 1972, DSc, 1983. Asst. Silesian Tech. U., 1966-72, lectr., 1972-85, reader, 1985-92, prof., 1992—; prof. Rsch. Ctr. Barowent, Katowice, Poland, 1994—; cons. environ. protection Izopol, Trzemeszno, Poland, 1983-85; mem. sci. bd. chem. faculty Silesian Tech. U., 1983—. Co-author student texts; contbr. over 105 articles to profl. jours. Recipient Co-award Min. of Edn., Warsaw, Poland, 1978, award, 1985. Mem. Soc. Chem. Engrs. (hon.), Barowent (sci. bd. 1994—). Roman Catholic. Avocations: books, gardening, carpentry. Office: Silesian Tech Univ, Ul Strzody 7, 44-100 Gliwice Upper Silesia Poland

PALIN, MICHAEL EDWARD, actor, screenwriter, writer; b. May 5, 1943; s. Edward and Mary P.; m. Helen M. Gibbons, 1966; 3 children. BA, U. Oxford, Eng., 1965. Writer, performer BBC Corp., 1965-69; presenter in field. Actor, writer: (TV shows) Monty Python's Flying Circus, 1969-74, Ripping Yarns, 1976-80; (films) And Now for Something Completely Different, 1970, Monty Python and the Holy Grail, 1974, Monty Python's Life of Brian, 1978, Time Bandits, 1980, Monty Python's The Meaning of Life, 1982, American Friends, 1991; TV presenter, writer Great Railway Journeys of the World, 1980, Around the World in 80 Days, 1989, Pole to Pole, 1993, Palin's Column, 1994, Great Railway Journeys of the World, 1994, Full Circle, 1997, Michael Palin's Hemingway Adventure, 1999; actor: (TV shows) Three Men in a Boat, 1975, GBH, 1991, Ex-S, 1997; (films) Jabberwocky, 1976, A Private Function, 1984, Brazil, 1985, A Fish Called Wanda (Best Supporting Actor Brit. Acad. Film and TV Arts, 1989), Fierce Creatures, 1998; actor, writer and co-producer: The Missionary, 1982; writer (stage play) The Weekend, 1994; author: Monty Python's Brand New Book, 1973, Dr. Fegg's Encyclopaedia of All World Knowledge, 1984, Limericks, 1985, Around the World in 80 Days, 1989, Pole to Pole, 1993, Pole to Pole: The Photographs, 1994, Hemingway's Chair 1995, Full Circle, 1997, Full Circle: The Photographs, 1997, Michael Palin's Hemingway Adventure, 1999; (children's books) Small Harry and the Toothache Pills, 1981, The Mirrorstone, 1986, The Cyril Stories, 1986. Co-recipient (with Monty Python) Michael Balcon award for outstanding contribution to cinema British Academy of Film and TV Arts, 1987. Avocations: reading, running, railways. Office: 34 Tavistock St, London WC2E 7PB, England

PALIN, MICHAEL GURDON, portfolio manager; b. Cheltenham, Eng., Aug. 26, 1944; s. Anthony Gurdon and Gabrielle Everard (White) P.; m. Libby Ann Halliday Croom, Oct. 4, 1980; children: Olivia Francesca, Amanda Halliday. LLB, Bristol U., 1967; law exams, Guildford Law Sch., 1970. Solicitor of Supreme Ct. Solicitor Slaughter and May, London, 1967-71; mgr. Slater Walker WestLB, London, Hong Kong, 1972-77, Grindlays Asia, Hong Kong, 1978-81; regional mgr. Std. Chartered Bank, 1981-90; regional dir. Hill Samuel Bank, London, 1991-93; dir. Investec Pers. Portfolio Mgmt. Guernsey Ltd, Hong Kong, 1994—; hon. lectr. Hong Kong U., 1974-80, United U., 1984-86, Calif. State U., 1984-86. Contbr. articles to profl. jours. Trustee Brit. Sporting Arts Trust, U.K., 1997—. Bristol U. Flying scholar. Mem. Inst. Dirs., Hong Kong Club, Hong Kong Yacht Club, LR Club, Asia Soc., Penang Club, Singapore Polo Club. Avocations: magic, music, chess, sailing, investmenting. Office: Investec Asset Mgmt, 2108 Jardine House Central, Hong Kong Hong Kong

PALIS, JACOB, mathematics educator; b. Uberaba, Brazil, Mar. 15, 1940. B, Red. U. Rio de Janerio, 1962; M, U. Calif., Berkeley, 1966, PhD, 1967. Prof. Inst. Pure and Applied Math., Rio de Janeiro; postdoctoral fellow Guggenheim Found., 1993. Author: (with W. De Melo) Geometric Theory of Dynamical Systems, 1982; (with F. Takens) Hyperbolicity and Sensitive-Chaotic Dynamics and Homoclinic Bifurcations, Fractal Dimensions and Infinitely Many Attractors, 1993, 2d edit., 1994. Recipient prize Moinho Santista, 1976, Math. prize Third World Acad. Scis., 1988, Nat prize for sci. and tech., Brazil, 1990, Interamerican Sci. prize OAS, 1995. Mem. Brazilian Acad. Scis. (Brazilian Nat. Sci. prize 1976, 90), Inst. Pure Math. Applications, Internat. Math. Union (pres. 1999—), Internat. Coun. Sci. Unions (v.p. 1996—), Third World Acad. Office: Inst Pure and Applied Math, Estrada Dona Castorina 110, 22460-320 Rio de Janeiro RJ, Brazil*

PALIWAL, SHRIKRISHNA TARACHAND, retired civil engineer, researcher; b. Chopda, Maharashtra, India, July 22, 1932; s. Tarachand Abaji and Avantika Paliwal; m. Kamala Kanungo, Mar. 16, 1960 (dec. July 1962); 1 child, Sushama; m. Lata Deshpande, Oct. 10, 1970; 1 child, Bharat. B in Engring., Birla Viswakarma Mahavidyalaya, Vallabh Vidya Nagar, Anand, India, 1958. Rsch. asst. Ctrl. Water and Power Rsch. Sta., Pune, India, 1958-62; extra asst. dir., asst. engr. Ctrl. Water Commn., New Delhi, 1962-65; rsch. officer engring. Ctrl. Water and Power Rsch. Sta., Pune, 1965-70, sr. rsch. officer engring., 1970-78, chief rsch. officer engring., 1978-90; sr. level expert Water and Power Consultancy Svcs., New Delhi, 1978-79, 88-90, 91-92; ret., 1990; mem. nat. adv. com. for soils and materials Ctrl. Bd. Irrigation and Power, New Delhi, 1983-88. Contbr. more than 19 articles to profl. jours. and more than 50 technical notes. Recipient Gold medal in engring. technology Ctrl. Bd. Irrigation and Power, New Delhi, 1986. Fellow Indian Geotech. Soc. Avocations: reiki, yoga, light music, reading. Home: Trupti Apts, 109/3 Erandwana, Pune 411004, India Office: Ctrl Water & Power Rsch Sta, Khadakwasla S, Pune 411024, India

PALIWODA, STANLEY JOSEPH, marketing educator; b. Renfrew, Strathclyde, Scotland, June 2, 1948; came to Can., 1990; s. Stanislaw and Helen Buchanan (Rome) P.; m. Helen McIsaac, Mar. 1989; 2 children. BA with honors, Ulster U., Northern Ireland, 1974; MSc, Bradford U., Eng., 1975; PhD, Cranfield U., Eng., 1980. Sales/relief br. mgr. Glasgow, Scotland, 1966-70; mktg. rschr. London, England, 1975-76; lectr. mktg. U. Westminster, London, England, 1979-80; lectr. mktg. and internat. bus. U. Manchester (Eng.) Inst. Sci. and Tech., England, 1980-90; prof. mktg., chair U. Calgary, Alta., Can., 1990-99; prof. internat. mktg. U. Birmingham, Eng., 1999—; lectr. in field. Author: AMBA Guide to Business Schools, 8th edit., 1990, New Perspectives in International Marketing, 1992, International Marketing, 3d edit., 1998, Essence of International Marketing, 1994, Investing in Eastern Europe, 1995, International Marketing Reader, 1995; co-author: Research in International Marketing, 1986. Constituency chmn. Liberal Democrats, Manchester, Wythenshawe, 1988-90. Recipient Export Rsch. prize Cranfield (Eng.), 1980, Case Study of Yr. prize Unilever/Case Clearing House, Bedford, 1981, award Indsl. Mktg. Rsch. Assn., Lichfield, Eng., 1984; Econ. and Social Rsch. Coun. London doctoral scholar, 1976-77, 78-79, Polish State scholar, 1977-78. Fellow Chartered Inst. Mktg.; mem. Acad. Internat. Bus. (U.K. treas. 1980-90), Assn. MBAs London (dir. 1979-90), Inst. Export London (examiner mktg. 1987-88), Am. Mktg. Assn., Brit. Inst. Mgmt., Brit. Assn. Slavic and Eastern European Studies, European Mktg. Acad., European Internat. Bus. Acad., Adminstr. Scis. Assn. Canada, Internat. Mgnt. Devel. Assn. (v.p.). Presbyterian. Avocation: karate. Office: U Birmingham, Ashley Bldg, Edgbaston Birmingham B15 2TT, England

PALLASMAA, JUHANI UOLEVI, architect, educator; b. Hameenlinna, Finland, Sept. 14, 1936; s. Harry and Aili (Kannisto) P.; m. Ulla Maria Rejstrom, 1957 (div. 1976); children: Pirja, Nanneli; m. Hannele Kersti Jaameri, Oct. 1990; children: Aaro, Meri. MS in Arch., Helsinki U. Tech., 1966, D (hon.), 1998; D (hon.), U. Indsl. Arts, Helsinki, 1992. Dir. exhbn. dept. Mus. Finnish Arch., Helsinki, 1968-72, 74-83; asst. prof. Haile Sellassie I U., Addis Ababa, Ethiopia, 1972-74; rector Inst. Crafts and Design, Helsinki, 1970-72; dir. Mus. Finnish Arch., Helsinki, 1978-83; state artist prof. Ministry of Edn., Helsinki, 1983-88; prof. Helsinki U. Tech., 1991-97. Designer numerous city planning and archtl. comms. in Finland and abroad; writer, editor numerous books on arch. and art; editor more than 30 exhbn. catalogues; graphic designer numerous exhbns. Chmn. Finnish Art Acad., Helsinki, 1992-94, Beautiful Helsinki Com., 1996-98, Alvar Aalto Acad., Helsinki, 1999—; mem. bd. reps. Mus. Finnish Arch., Helsinki, 1983-94, Finnish Assn. for Crafts and Design, Helsinki, 1980-85. Decorated Order of the White Rose (Finland); recipient Fritz Schumacher Arch. prize Alfred Toepfer Found., 1997, Arch. award of the Russian Fedn. Pres. Yeltsin, 1996, Finland State Arch. award Ministry of Edn., 1992, Jean Tschumi prize Internat. Union Archs., 1999. Mem. AIA (hon.), Finnish Assn. Archs., Internat. Com. Archtl. Critics. Avocation: philosophy and psychology of art. Office: Juhani Pallasmaa Archs, Tehtaankatu 13B, FIN00140 Helsinki Finland

PALLEN, MAX MORATILLO, martial arts educator; b. Pasacao, Philippines, Jan. 31, 1941; s. Zacarias and Luz Moratillo P.; m. Purificacion de Jarme, May 29, 1964; children: Joseph, Max, Jr., Jordan. Diploma in Gen. Automotive Repair, Sequoia Inst., Fremont, Calif., 1987; 8th Degree Blackbelt, Kajnkenbo Assn. Am., Inc., Oakland, Calif., 1997; Grandmaster, Balintawak World Arnis Assn., Cebu City, Philippines, 1998. Founder, chmn. Pallens Martial Arts Assn., San Leandro, Calif., 1969—; pres. Affil. Martial Arts Promoters, San Leandro, 1995-98, World Escrima Kali Arnis Fedn., Cebu City, 1998—; dir. we. region World Escrima Kali Arnis Fedn., 1996-98; prodr., exec. Asian Martial Arts Exposition, Oakland, 1975. Author: (book) Palarong Arnis, 1995, (videotapes) Arnis Master, 1992-98, Arnis Master II, 1993-98. Pres. World Escrima Kali Arnis Fedn., Cebu City, The Philippines, 1998. Recipient Outstanding Svc. award Philippine-Am. Civic Club, Oakland, 1977, Apo award World Assn. Martial Artists, Milpitas, Calif., 1996. Mem. Jaycees (dir. memb. Bayanihan club, Oakland 1974-75, Presdl. award of leadership 1975), Freemasons, K.C. Democrat. Roman Catholic. Avocations: martial arts tng., jogging. Office: Pallens Martial Arts Assn 13730 Doolittle Dr San Leandro CA 94577-5532

PALLETT, RAY(MOND) DAVID, civil servant; b. Luton, Eng., May 22, 1947; s. Reginald Thomas and Tagalie May (Marriott) P.; m. Jeanette Welham, Oct. 25, 1975; children: Bryony Clare, Rosanna Fay. Student, Southend Coll. Tech., 1963-64. Telecom. exec. Brit. Post Office, London, 1966-74; tax exec. Her Majesty's Customs and Excise, Southend-on-Sea, Eng., 1974-81; sys. analyst Her Majesty's Customs and Excise, Southend-on-Sea, 1981-90; sys. test mgr. Her Majesty's Customs and Excise, Southend-on-Sea, 1990-92, computer svc. mgr., 1992-94, bus. analyst, 1994—; Author: Goodnight Sweetheart-The Life and Times of Al Bowlly, 1986; editor, journalist, rschr. Memory Lane, 1972—; broadcaster (radio) BBC, 1988-92. Anglican. Avocations: music appreciation, record collecting, chess, badminton. Home: PO Box 1939, Leigh-on-Sea SS9 3UH, England

PALLINI, ANDREA, statistician, educator; b. Rapolano Terme, Italy, Sept. 29, 1961; s. Teseo and Anna (Meoni) P.; 1 child, Eugenio. Grad. in Statis. and Econ. Scis., U. Siena, Italy, 1985. Rschr. U. Siena, 1985-88; rschr. U. Venice, Italy, 1990-92, assoc. prof., 1992-97; assoc. prof. U. Bologna, Italy, 1997—; dir.'s del. U. Venice, 1996-97. Contbr. articles to profl. jours. Fellow Italian Statis. Soc. Office: Dept Statis Sci, Via Delle Belle Arti 41, T-40126 Bologna Italy

PALLOT, JOSEPH WEDELES, lawyer; b. Coral Gables, Fla., Dec. 23, 1959; s. Richard Allen Pallot and Rosalind Brown (Wedeles) Spak; m. Linda Fried, Oct. 12, 1956; children: Richard Allen, Maxwell Ross. BS, Jacksonville U., 1981; JD cum laude, U. Miami, Coral Gables, Fla., 1986. Bar: Fla. 1986. Comml. lending officer S.E. Bank, N.A., Miami, 1981-83; ptnr. Steel Hector & Davis, Miami, 1986—. Bd. dirs. MOSAIC: Jewish Mus. Fla., Miami Beach, 1993—; dir. Fla. Grand Opera, 1996—; mem. exec. com. The Beacon Coun. Mem. Fla. C. of C. (dir. 2000—), Miami City Club. Avocations: golf, tennis.

PALL-PALLANT, TERI, paleontologist, inventor, behavioral scientist, design engineer, advertising agency executive; b. Somerville, N.J., Jan. 6, 1921; d. Stanley and Milicent P.-P. BA, Imperial Coll., London, 1948; MS, Imperial Coll., 1949; postgrad., Warren Sch. Aero., L.A., 1950, Calif. Inst. Tech., 1951; PhD, London U., 1954, 66; student, UCLA, 1955; PhD, Columbia U., 1963; ScD, London Inst. Applied Rsch., 1973; cert. rehab. counselor, U. So. Calif., 1975. Design engr. Simmonds Aerocessories Ltd., London, 1949, dir. vocat. rehab., 1950; founder, owner Teri Pall Advt. Agy., L.A., 1951—, Pall Indsl. Surveys, Pasadena, Calif., 1952—, Pall Tech. Industries, Tarzana, Calif., 1979—; chmn. bd. Pall Industries, Ltd., Taipei, Taiwan and Tarzana, Calif., 1980—; vertebrate paleontologist Am. Mus. Natural History, N.Y.C., 1965-69; leader Teri Pall Trio, L.A., 1951-69; exec. dir. Hoffman House, Long Beach, Calif., 1970-72; sr. adminstrv. analyst Econ. and Youth Opportunities, L.A. County, 1973-74; dep. dir. Head Start Program L.A. County, 1974-75; assoc. dir. Casa del las Amigas, Pasadena, dir. rsch. and evaluation projects Nat. Inst. Alcohol Abuse and Alcoholism, Washington, 1977; pvt. practice vocat. rehab. counseling, Beverly Hills, Calif., 1977; exec. dir. Little House L.A. County, 1978; robotics cons. Jet Propulsion Lab., Pasadena, 1974-95, NASA, 1990—. Author: (play) El Rancho Verde, 1951, (novel) With Banners Flying, 1953, Chinese and Western Worlds from 1800 B.C. to Modern Times, 1950, 4000 Years of Egyptian History, 1950, The Integrating Power Meter, 1956, About the Mammoth, 1962, Look, a Travelogue in Time, 1967, The History of Our Calendar, 1977; designer robotics exhibit Calif. Mus. of Sci. and Industry, L.A., 1990; inventor proximity warning device for aircraft. Fossil exhibit contbr. L.A. County Mus., 1968-77; chmn. Mayor's Commn. on Barrier-Free Arch., 1978—; vice chmn. rsch. and coordinating com. Gov.'s Commn. on Safe Energy Alternatives, 1979—; mem. Cancer Rsch. Coordinating Com., 1979—; lectr. Long Beach Hosp., 1978; office bd. Inventor's Workshop Internat. Edn. Found., 1980—, Am. Guild of Inventors, 1990—; bd. dirs. Commn. Conserve Chinese Culture. Recipient Spl. Contbns. award Engring. and Grading Constructors Assn., 1968, Interkamera Gold award Cannes Art Festival, 1969, Spkr. of Yr. award Toastmasters Calif., 1971, Woman of Yr. for Civil Leadership award Long Beach, 1971, Outstanding Achievement award Am. Cancer Soc., 1979, others. Mem. AAUW, Statis. Quality Control Engrs. (sec. 1951—), Assn. Bus. Publs., Nat. Rehab. Counseling Assn., Archs. and Engrs. Inst., Nat. Soc. Vertebrate Paleontologists, Phi Beta Kappa. Republican. Episcopalian. Achievements include developer 2-mile cordless telephone, 1978, wrist chronograph calculator, 1979, Etch-A-Sketch, 1962, AC-DC multimeters, 1954, Miniaturized transcutaneous nerve stimulator, 1969, Electronic remote control system, 1972, proximity warning device for aircraft 1986.

PALM, ENOK JOHANNES, mathematician; b. Kristiansand, Norway, Dec. 5, 1924; s. Hjalmar and Siss (Konsmo) P.; m. Ruth Solveig Aadne, Mar. 20, 1954; children: Oyvind, Sverre. BS, U. Oslo, 1948, MS, 1950, PhD, 1954. Rsch. assoc. Weather and Climate Inst./Norwegian Acad. Sci., 1950-60; prof. mechanics Norwegian Inst. Technology, 1960-63; prof. applied math. U. Oslo, 1960—. Contbr. articles to profl. jours. Apptd. Knight 1 Class of Royal Norwegian Order of St. Olav, 1993. Mem. Norwegian Acad. Sci. (bd. dirs. 1968-74, 85-90), Norwegian Tech. Acad. Sci. Office: U Oslo, PO Box 1053 Blindern, 0316 Oslo Norway

PALM, MAUD EVA, veterinarian; b. Hjulsjö, Sweden, Aug. 19, 1941; d. Folke Söderberg and Eva (Öhman) Söderberg; m. Claes Henry Palm, Oct. 13, 1961; children: Viveka, Tommy. Lab. Technician, Laborantskolan, Stockholm, 1963; DVM, Swedish U. Agrl. Scis., Uppsala, 1981, PhD, 1990. Lab. technician Royal Vet. Sch., Stockholm, 1963-76; veterinarian Bagarmossens Djursjuhkus, Stockholm, 1982-84; rschr. Kabi, Stockholm, 1984-90; assoc. dir. Astra, Södertälje, Sweden, 1990-95; dir. AstraZeneca, Södertälje, 1995—. Contbr. articles to profl. jours. Mem. N.Y. Acad. Scis., Internat. Soc. for Animal Clin. Biochemistry, European Soc. Vet. Clin. Pathology, Swedish Soc. for Toxicology. Avocations: skiing, skating, wind surfing. E-mail: maud.palm@astrazeneca.com. Office: AstraZeneca, Safety Assessment B681, 151 85 Södertälje Sweden

PALM, MICHAEL MARTIN, college administrator, artist; b. Oakland, Calif., Aug. 4, 1944; s. Douglas F. and Marianne T. Palm. BFA, Ea. Ill. U., 1972, MS in Edn., 1973. Asst. dean of students U. Ky., Lexington, 1973-89; dir. student svcs. Greenbrier C.C., Lewisburg, W.Va., 1990—. Dir. Beta Sigma Pi Nat. Ednl. Found., 1988-96. Sgt. U.S. Army, 1966-69. Named Nat. Outstanding Fraternity Advisor, 1988. Mem. Assn. Fraternity Advisors (v.p. 1976), W.Va. AACRO, Rotary (pres. White Sulphur Springs 1997-98). Democrat. Lutheran. Avocations: antiques, Napoleonic artifacts, gourmet cooking, weight lifting, art collecting. Home: 520 W Main St Ronceverte WV 24970-1751 Office: Greenbrier CC 101 Church St Lewisburg WV 24901-1303

PALMASON, PALMI RAGNAR, geotechnical engineer, consultant; b. Reykjavik, Iceland, Jan. 31, 1940; s. Palmi and Ragnhildur (Thoroddsen) Hannesson; m. Agusta Gudmundsdottir, July 6, 1963 (div. Aug. 1994); children: Ingibjorg Yr, Anna Theodora, Gudmundur. BS in Civil Engring., U. Iceland, 1963; MS in Soils and Structural Engring., Tech. U. Norway, 1965. Registered profl. engr., Va., 1986. Project engr. Norwegian Geotech. Inst., Oslo, 1965-67, VST Cons. Engrs. Ltd., Reykjavik, 1967-69, 71-76; staff engr. Golder & Assocs., Soil Cons., Toronto, Can., 1969-70, Mueser, Rutledge, Wentworth & Johnston, N.Y.C., 1970-71; head soil sect. VST Cons. Engrs. Ltd., Reykjavik, 1976-85, 86-87; sr. soils engr. Schnabel Engring. Assocs., Richmond, Va., 1985-86; mgr. hydro, soils and mech. sects. VST Cons. Engrs. Ltd., 1987-95; chief engr. Gaza Br. office E. Pihl & Son A.S. Engrs. and Contractor, Lyngby, Denmark, 1995-96; sr. soil specialist VST Consulting Engrs. Ltd., 1996—; adj. soil mechanics U. Iceland, 1976-85; gen. mgr. Tech. Rsch. Ltd., Reykjavik, 1973-80, Icelandic Submarine Cables Ltd., Reykjavik, 1991; mgr. GECA group, Reykjavik, 1993; bd. dirs. GECA Ltd., Icelandic State Hosps. Chmn. bd. dirs. Tech. Coll. Reykjavik, 1981-85. Mem. ASCE, Soc. Chartered Engrs. Iceland (bd. dirs. 1977-78), Norwegian Geotech. Soc. Home: Silungakvisl 29, 15-110 Reykjavik Iceland Office: Armuli 4, IS-108 Reykjavik Iceland

PALMATIER, MALCOLM ARTHUR, editor, consultant; b. Kalamazoo, Nov. 11, 1922; s. Karl Ernest and Cecile Caroline (Chase) P.; m. Mary Elizabeth Summerfield, June 16, 1948 (dec. Oct. 1982); children: Barnabus, Timothy K., Duncan M.; m. Marie-Anne Suzanne van Werveke, Jan. 12, 1985. BS in Math., Western Mich. U., 1945; MA in English, UCLA, 1947; MA in Econs., U. So. Calif., 1971. Instr. English Pomona Coll., Claremont, Calif., 1949-51; editor Naval Ordnance Test Sta., Pasadena, Calif., 1951-54; head editl. unit Rocketdyne, L.A., 1954-55; editor The RAND Corp., Santa Monica, Calif., 1955-87; cons. editor The RAND Corp., Santa Monica, 1987—; instr. English UCLA, L.A., summer 1950. Mng. editor, cons. editor Jour.: Studies in Comparative Communism, L.A., 1968-80; co-editor Perspectives in Economics, 1971; contbr. chpts. to book, book revs. and articles to profl. jours. Chmn. bd. New Start, West L.A., 1982-84. With USNR, 1943-45. Mem. Jonathan Club. Avocations: music, travel. Home: 516 Avondale Ave Los Angeles CA 90049-4804 Office: The RAND Corp 1700 Main St Santa Monica CA 90401-3297

PALMEDO, HOLGER, nuclear medicine physician; b. Mannheim, Germany, Apr. 7, 1966; s. Peter Claus and Charlotte (Fiebig) P.; m. Jeannette Gisela Ilona Maire, May 16, 1991; children: Viviane, Fabienne, Benedikt. Med. exams, U. Bonn/Rennes, Germany/France, 1987-92; MD, U. Bonn, Germany, 1994. Sci. asst. Inst. of Anatomy, Bonn, Germany, 1987; sci., clin. asst. Erasmus Program, Rennes, France, 1989-90; resident internal medicine U. Bonn, 1992, resident nuclear medicine, 1993-96, sr. resident, 1997-99, asst. prof., 1999—; rev. Jour. Nuclear Medicine, 1997—. Author: (book) The Role of Nuclear Medicine in the Diagnosis of Breast Cancer, 1997, Radionuclide Imaging of the Breast: Clinical Applications, 1997; editor (book): Atlas of Clinical PET in Oncology, 2000; contbr. articles to profl. jours. Recipient Grant for new techniques in nuclear breast imaging DFG, 1997, Grant for oncologic pain therapy with radionuclides Biomed./Euro Com., 1997. Mem. Soc. Nuclear Medicine, European Assn. Nuclear Medicine (sec. workgroup on nuclear imaging of breast cancer 1995-97, task group breast imaging 1997—). Avocations: tennis, music. Office: U Bonn Dept Nuclear Med, Sigmund-Freud Str 25, 53127 Bonn Germany

PALMER, ALAN MICHAEL, neuroscientist; b. Neath, Wales, U.K., Jan. 4, 1958; came to U.S., 1989; s. John Hugh and Joan Mary (Richards) P.; m. Susan Elizabeth Hawton, children: Dean Richard, Steven Russell, Gavin Hugh, Rosalie Joan. BS, Warwick U., Coventry, U.K., 1980; MS, London U., 1981, PhD, 1987. Asst. prof. psychiatry U. Pitts., 1989, asst. prof. pharmacology, 1990; neuroscientist Western Psychiatric Inst. and Clin., Pitts., 1989-94; head neurochemistry Wyeth Rsch., Taplow, U.K., 1994-95; dir. neurochemistry Cerebrus, Wokingham, U.K., 1995—. Office: Cerebrus, 613 Reading Rd, Winnersh Wokingham RG41 5UA, England

PALMER, ANDREW CLENNEL, petroleum engineering educator, consultant; b. Colchester, Essex, Eng., May 26, 1938; s. Gerald Basil and Muriel Gertrude (Howes) P.; m. Jane Rhiannon Evans, Aug. 10, 1963; 1 child, Emily. BA, Cambridge (Eng.) U., 1961; PhD, Brown U., 1965. Chartered engr. Lectr. U. Liverpool, Eng., 1965-67; lectr. U. Cambridge, 1967-75, rsch. prof., 1996—; chief engr. R.J. Brown and Assocs., Rijswijk, The Netherlands, 1975-79, v.p., 1982-95; mng. dir., tech. dir. Andrew Palmer & Assocs., London, 1985-96; mng. dir. Bold Island Engring., London, 1997—; fellow Churchill Coll., Cambridge, 1967-75, 96—. Author: Structural Mechanics, 1976; contbr. articles to profl. publs.; patentee in field. Fellow Royal Soc., Royal Acad. of Engring., Instn. of Civil Engrs., Pipeline Industries Guild (pres.). Avocations: travel, glass blowing. Home: 49 Ashley Gardens, Ambrosden Ave, London SW1P 1QF, England Office: U Cambridge Engring Dept, Trumpington St, Cambridge CB2 1PZ, England

PALMER, ANN PATRICIA, public health physician; b. Clevedon, Eng., Dec. 29, 1945; d. Ronald Arthur and Marion Agnes Kate (Tranmer) Shadwell; m. John Herbert Palmer, Dec. 2, 1967; children: Edward, Stephen, Henrietta. MSc, London U., 1983, MBA, 1996; MD, Edinburgh (Scotland) U., 1989. House officer Greenbank Hosp., Plymouth, Eng., 1969-70; gen. practitioner Torquay, Eng., 1978-80; gen. practitiner London, 1980-82; pub. health trainee, 1982-86, pub. health cons., 1986-89, pub. health dir., 1989-94; with West Kent Health Authority, Aylesford, Eng.; cons. in pub. health medicine West Kent Health Authority, 1994—; hon. sr. rsch. fellow Ctr. for Health Svcs. Studies, U. Kent, Canterbury, Eng., 1986—; cons. in pub. Fellow Royal Coll. Physicians (faculty pub. health medicine). Anglican. Avocations: French culture, gardening, jazz. Home: 1 King Edward Rd, Rochester ME1 1UA, England Office: West Kent Health Authority, West Kent Health Authority, Preston Hall, Aylesford ME20 7NJ, England

PALMER, ARNOLD DANIEL, professional golfer; b. Youngstown, Pa., Sept. 10, 1929; s. Milfred Jerome and Doris M. Palmer; m. Winnie Walzer, Dec. 20, 1954 (dec. Nov. 1999); children: Peggy Palmer Wears, Amy Palmer Saunders. Student, Wake Forest Coll., LLD, 1970. Profl. golfer, 1954—, businessman, entrepreneur, 1960—; nat. spokesman Pennzoil Petroleum Products, Sears Can., Rolex, Agrobiotech, Cadillac Motor Car, GTE, Golf mag., Rayovac, Textron, Lexington Furniture, Office Depot, Cooper Tires, Callaway Golf, PNC Bank Corp.; designer numerous golf courses. Author: Arnold Palmer's Golf Book, 1961, Portrait of a Professional Golfer, 1964, My Game and Yours, 1965, rev. edit., 1983, Situation Golf, 1970, Go for Broke, 1973, Arnold Palmer's Best 54 Holes of Golf, 1977, Arnold Palmer's Complete Book of Putting, 1986, Play Great Golf, 1987, (with Thomas Hauser) A Personal Journey, 1994, (with James Dodson) Arnold Palmer, A Golfer's Life, 1999. With USCG, 1951-54. Winner over 90 major golf tournaments, 1955—, including Masters Championship, 1958, 60, 62, 64, U.S. Open, 1960, U.S. Amateur, 1954, Brit. Open, 1961, 62; recipient numerous golf awards including Bob Jones award U.S. Golf Assn., William D. Richardson award Golf Writers Assn. Am., Herb Graffis award Nat. Golf Found.; named AP Athlete of Decade, 1969, Sportsman of Yr. Sports Illustrated mag., 1960, Player of Yr. Profl. Golfers Assn., 1960, 62; Profl. Golfers Assn. Tour Money Leader, 1958, 60, 62, 63; elected to World Golf Hall of Fame, Profl. Golfers Assn. Hall of Fame. Mem. Latrobe (Pa.) Country Club, Laurel Valley Golf Club, Rolling Rock Club (Ligonier, Pa.), Bay Hill Club, Duquesne Club (Pitts.). Avocation: aviation. Home and Office: PO Box 52 Youngstown PA 15696-0052

PALMER, CHARLES BRIAN, solicitor; b. London, Jan. 30, 1944; s. Everett Elmslie and Elsie Doris (Gibbs) P.; m. Hilary Ruth McCallum, June 21, 1975; children: Alexander Charles, Catharine Ruth. MA, Cambridge (Eng.) U., 1966. Articled clerk Durham & Co., Leatherhead, Surrey, Eng., 1966-69; solicitor Theodore Bell Cotton & Co., Epsom, Surrey, Eng., 1969-72; ptnr. Gumersalls, Epsom, Surrey, Eng., 1973—. Anglican. Office: Gumersalls, Gumersalls, White House 16 Waterloo Rd, Epsom KT19 8AZ, England

PALMER, CHRISTINE (CLELIA ROSE VENDITTI), operatic singer, performer, pianist, vocal instructor, lecturer, entertainer; b. Hartford, Conn., Apr. 2; d. John Marion and Immacolata (Morcaldo) Venditti; m. Raymond Smith, Oct. 5, 1949 (div. June 1950); m. Arthur James Whitlock, Feb. 25, 1953. Student, Mt. Holyoke Coll., 1937-38, New Eng. Conservatory of Music, 1941-42; pvt. studies, Boston, Hartford, N.Y.C., Florence and Naples, Italy; RN with honors, Hartford Hosp. Sch. Nursing, 1941. Artist-in-residence El Centro Coll., Dallas, 1966-71; pvt. vocal instr.-coach, specializing in vocal technique for opera, mus. comedy, supper club acts, auditions, Dallas, 1962-94; voice adjudicator San Francisco Opera Co., 1969-72, Tex. Music Tchrs. Assn., 1964-75, others; lectr. in field; appearances with S.M. Chartocks' Gilbert and Sullivan Co.; now performing lecture/entertainment circuit. Leading operatic soprano N.Y.C. Opera, Chgo., San Francisco, San Carlo, other cities, 1944-62; presented concert N.Y. Town Hall, 1951; soloist with symphony orchs. maj. U.S. Cities, 1948-62; soloist Marble Collegiate Ch., Holy Trinity Ch.; coast-to-coast concert tour, 1948; numerous appearances including St. Louis Mcpl. Opera, MUNY Opera, Indpls. Starlight Theatre, Lambertville Music Circus; soloist Holiday on Ice, 1949-50; rec. artist; TV performer, including Home Show on NBC, Telephone Hour on NBC, Holiday Hotel; performer various supper clubs, N.Y.C., Atlanta, Bermuda, Catskills, others, including Number One Fifth Avenue, The Embers, The Carriage Club, Viennese Lantern. Hon. mem. women's bd. Dallas Opera Assn.; mem. adv. bd. Tex. Opera News; mem. Tex. Music Tchrs. Cert. Bd., Collegiate Chorale, Don Craig Singers, The Vikings; mem. women's bd., Dallas Bapt. Univ. Oliver Ditson scholar, 1942; recipient Phi Xi Delta prize in Italian, 1937; named Victor Herbert Girl, ASCAP; Spl. Recognition Gold book of Dallas Soc. Mem. Nat. Assn. Tchrs. of Singing (pres. Dallas chpt. 1972-74), Nat. Fedn. Music Clubs, Tex. Fedn. Music Clubs, Dallas Fedn. Music Clubs (pres. 1972-74), Dallas Symphony League, Dallas Music Tchrs. Assn. (pres. 1971-72, Tchr. of Yr. 1974), Thesaurus Book Club (pres. 1990-91, 97-98), Friday Forum (Dallas, bd. dirs.), Dallas Women's C. of C., Eagle Forum, Pub. Affairs Luncheon Club, Dallas Fedn. Music Club, Pro Am., Wednesday Morning Choral Club, Dallas Knife and Fork Club, Prestoncrest Rep. Club. Presbyterian. Home: 6232 Pemberton Dr Dallas TX 75230-4036

PALMER, CHRISTOPHER RALPH, medical statistician; b. Maidstone, Kent, Eng., Aug. 11, 1961; s. Ralph George and Joyce (Herd) P.; m. Cathy-Joan MacDonald, Dec. 30, 1989; children: Laura, Carolyn. BA, U. Oxford, Eng., 1982; MA (hon.), U. Oxford, 1987; MS, U. N.C., 1986, PhD, 1988. Lectr. applied statistics U. Reading, Eng., 1989-91; sr. rsch. asst. U. Cambridge, Eng., 1991-97; dir. ctr. applied med. statistics U. Cambridge, 1996—, asst. dir. rsch., 1997—. Dep. editor Stats. Medicine, 1996—; European office acting editor Statistician Medicine, 1999-2000; statis. referee The Lancet, 1992—; contbr. articles to profl. jours. Harvard U. fellow, 1988-89, Hughes Hall fellow U. Cambridge, 1993—. Fellow Royal Stats. Soc.; mem. Soc. Clin. Trials, Internat. Soc. Clin. Biostats., World Assn. Med. Editors. Office: U Cambridge Inst Pub Health, Robinson Way, Cambridge CB2 2SR, England

PALMER, DANIEL LEE, data communication manufacturing company executive; b. Norman, Okla., July 6, 1958; s. James Daniel and Margret (Kupka) P.; m. Kathleen Marie Connolly, Aug. 31, 1985; children: Jonathan Daniel, Elizabeth Marie, Robert Edward. BSEE, U. Colo., 1980; MSEE, U. Santa Clara, 1985. Engr. GTE Lenkurt, San Carlos, Calif., 1980-82; div. mgr. Granger Assocs., Santa Clara, Calif., 1982-84; v.p. DSC Comm., Santa Clara, 1984-89; v.p. engring., corp. officer Digital Link, Sunnyvale, Calif., 1989-95, pres., COO, 1995; sr. v.p., corp. officer Allied Telesyn, Sunnyvale, 1996-97, pres., COO, 1997; pres., CEO Tiara Networks, Inc., Fremont, Calif., 1998—. Contbr. articles to profl. jours. Mem. IEEE, Eta Kappa Nu. Avocations: piano, exercise, windsurfing, skiing, kids. Home: 45961 Hidden Valley Ter Fremont CA 94539-6845 Office: Tiara Networks Inc 525 Race St Ste 100 San Jose CA 95126-3405

PALMER, DAVID SCOTT, political scientist, educator; b. Boston, July 16, 1937; s. Walter S. and Jean (Stuart) P.; m. Sarah Crawford, 1966 (dec. Nov. 1985); children: Walter Scott, Henry Crawford, Asa MacAdam; m. Diane Nagel, 1998. BA in Internat. Rels. cum laude, Dartmouth Coll., 1959; MA in Hispanic Am. Studies, Stanford U., 1962; PhD in Comparative Govt., Cornell U., 1973. Vol. leader Peace Corps, Peru, 1962-64; asst. dean freshmen, asst. to dir. admissions Dartmouth Coll., Hanover, N.H., 1964-68; from instr. to asst. prof. dept. govt. Bowdoin Coll., 1972-76; professorial lectr. Sch. Advanced Internat. Studies Johns Hopkins U., Washington, 1977-88; assoc. dean for programs Fgn. Svc. Inst., Dept. State, 1984-88, chair Latin Am. and Caribbean studies, 1976-88; prof. polit. sci. Boston U., 1988—, prof. internat. rels., 1990—, assoc. chair undergrad. studies internat. rels. dept., 1997-99, chair dept. polit. sci., 1998—; vis. lectr. Princeton U., 1978-79, Georgetown U., 1985. Author: Peru: The Authoritarian Tradition, 1980, (with Kevin Middlebrook) Military Government and Political Development: Lessons from Peru, 1975 (with Robert Wesson and others) The Latin American Military Institution, 1985; editor, contbr.: Shining Path of Peru, 1992, 2d edit., 1994; contbr. chpts. to books, articles and revs. to profl. jours. Recipient Meritorious Honor award U.S. Dept. of State, 1981; Daniel Webster nat. scholar, 1955-59; Edward John Noble Found. leadership grantee 1959-62. Mem. Latin Am. Studies Assn. (exec. com. 1983-86), New Eng. Coun. Latin Am. Studies (exec. com. 1989-98, pres. 1993-94), Interam. Coun. of Washington (pres. 1978-79), Phi Beta Delta, Phi Kappa Phi, Sigma Delta Pi. Home: 69 Waverley St Belmont MA 02478-1958 Office: Boston U 152 Bay State Rd Boston MA 02215-1501

PALMER, FELICITY JOAN, mezzo-soprano opera singer; b. Cheltenham, U.K.; d. Henry Marshall and Sylvia Constance Palmer. Student, Guildhall Sch. Music and Drama, London, MunichHochschulle Musik. Appeared in major opera houses throughout world, including La Scala, Chgo., San Francisco, Paris, London, Glyndebourne; recordings for maj. labels. Named Comdr. of Brit. Empire, 1993; recipient Kathleen Ferrier Meml. prize, 1970. Address: c/o AOR Mgmt Ltd, Westwood Lorraine Park, Harrow Weald HA3 6BX, England

PALMER, FRANK ROBERT, linguist, educator; b. Westleigh, Gloucestershire, Eng., Apr. 9, 1922; s. George Samuel and Gertrude Lilian (Newman) P.; m. Jean Elisabeth Moore, June 18, 1948; children: Peter Frank, Robert George, Jane Margaret, Andrew Mark, Ruth Elisabeth May. Student, U. Oxford, Eng., 1941-42, 45-48; MA, Merton Coll., Oxford, 1949. Lectr. linguistics Sch. Oriental and African Studies U. London, 1950-60; prof. linguistics U. Coll. North Wales, Bangor, 1960-65; prof. linguistic sci. U. Reading, Eng., 1965-87; dean Faculty Letters Social Scis. U. Reading, 1969-72. Author: The Morphology of the Tigre Noun, 1962, A Linguistic Study of the English Verb, 1965, Grammar, 1970, The English Verb, 1974, 2d edit., 1981, Modality and the English Modals, 1979, 2d edit., 1990, Mood and Modality, 1986, Grammatical Roles and Relations, 1994; editor: Selected Papers of J.R. Firth (1951-1958), 1968, Prosodic Analysis, 1970; editor Jour. Linguistics, 1969-79. Served to lt. Brit. Army, 1942-45, Africa. Fellow Brit. Acad. (mem. coun. 1980-83); mem. Academia Europaea, Philol. Soc. (v.p.), Linguistic Soc. Am. (profl. 1971), Linguistics Assn. Gt. Britain (chmn. 1965-68). Home: Whitethorns Roundabout Ln, Winnersh Wokingham, Berkshire RG41 5AD, England

PALMER, HUBERT BERNARD, dentist, retired military officer; b. San Antonio, Sept. 6, 1912; s. Hubert Victor and Rosemary (Garvey) P.; student St. Mary's U., 1931-34; D.D.S., Baylor U., 1938; postgrad. George Washington U., 1946-47, U. Md., 1950-53; m. Elizabeth Harriet McAlary, Aug. 16, 1945; children—Hubert Bernard II, Robert Leldon. Commd. 1st lt. USAAF, 1938, advanced through grades to col. USAF, 1971; chief dept. dental research U.S. Army, 1946-50; chief dept. exptl. dentistry, USAF, 1953-54, chief research dentistry div. 1954-56; command dental surgeon, 1958-59, 63-65, 65-68; dental staff officer, 1959-62, dir. dental services, 1968-71; dir. Eastside Dental Clinic San Antonio Met. Health Dist., 1972-81; dir. Mirasol Dental Clinic, 1982-83; clin. asst. prof. U. Tex. Dental Sch., San Antonio, 1973-76. Decorated Legion of Merit, Commendation medal First Oak Leaf Cluster, Meritorious Service medal. Fellow AAAS; mem. Am. Dental Assn., Internat. Assn. Dental Research, Soc. Gen. Microbiology, Am. Soc. Microbiology, Omicron Kappa Upsilon. Contbr. articles to profl. jours. Research reduction decalcification tooth enamel. Home: 6115 Forest Timber St San Antonio TX 78240-3357

PALMER, JOHN DAVID, property manager; b. Wailuku, Hawaii, Sept. 3, 1970; s. Edward Raymond Jr. and Marilouise (Volper) P. BA, St. Mary's Coll., Moraga, Calif., 1992; MA, Dominican Sch. Philosophy, 1999. Adminstrv. asst. St. Mary's Coll.; mgr. St. Stephen L.L.C., Calif.; tchg. asst. De LaSalle Inst., Napa, Calif.; comml. property mgr. St. Helena, Calif. Editor, author (website) The Aquinas Cafe. Mem. Our Lady of Perpetual Help Men's Club. Roman Catholic. Avocations: writing, reading, research, art, wine. E-mail: boethius@jps.net. Office: St Stephen LLC 1780 Dean York Ln Saint Helena CA 94574

PALMER, KENNETH NORMAN, research chemist; b. High Wycombe, U.K., June 28, 1928; s. Henry Norman and Alice (Wibberley) P.; m. Angela Mary Hoare, Aug. 28, 1962; children: Susan, Jill. MA, Cambridge (Eng.) U., 1952. Chartered chemist; chartered engr. Rsch. scientist Fire Rsch. Sta., Borehamwood, U.K., 1949-83, dir., 1983-88; cons. London, 1988—; vis. prof. U. Manchester (U.K.) Inst. of Sci. and Tech., 1986-92. Author: Dust Explosions and Fires, 1973; contbr. articles to profl. jours. Recipient Disting. Svc. Cert. British Stds. Instn., 1992, Franklin medal Inst. Chem. Engrs. (U.K.), 1994. Fellow Royal Soc. of Chemistry, Inst. of Energy, Inst. of Petroleum, Instn. of Fire Engrs.; mem. Combustion Inst. Avocations: horticulture, music, travel.

PALMER, LYNNE, writer, astrologer; b. El Centro, Calif., Dec. 14, 1932; d. Clarence Lee and Paquita Mae (Hartley) Hafer; m. Bruno Cazzaniga, Mar. 13, 1964 (div. 1965); m. Sidney Latter, Nov. 29, 1997. Student, Ch. of Light, 1957-62, Calif. Sch. Escrows, L.A., 1960; theatre mgmt. degree, Mus. Arenas Theatres Assn., N.Y.C., 1963. Asst. teller Western Mortgage, L.A., 1957-58; head teller Sutro Mortgage Svc., L.A., 1958-61; freelance astrologer N.Y.C., 1961-92, Las Vegas, Nev., 1962—; owner, operator, tchr. astrology sch. N.Y.C., 1970-72; owner Star Bright Pubs., Las Vegas, 1996—; spkr. women's clubs, indsl. shows, astrol. orgns.; interviewed in N.Y. Post and other major newspapers and mags. including Life and Oggi (Italy), Veja (Brazil), Wall St. Jour., People Mag., Globe, Die Welt am Sonntag (West Germany), New Woman Mag., Forbes. Author: Signs for Success, Prosperity Signs, Nixon's Horoscope, Astrological Almanac, Astrological Compatibility (Profl. Astrologers award for outstanding contbn. to art and sci. of astrology 1976), Horoscope of Billy Rose, ABC Basic Chart Reading, ABC Major Progjressions, ABC Chart Erection, Pluto Ephemeris (1900-2000), Daily Positions, Is Your Name Lucky For You?, Do-It-Yourself Publicity Directory, Your Lucky Days and Numbers, Money Magic, Astro-Guide to Nutrition and Vitamins, Gambling to Win, The Astrological Treasure Map, Dear Sun Signs, Are You Compatible With Your Boss, Partner, Coworkers, Employee, Client?; columnist mags. and newsletters including Self, House Beautiful, Gold; record album: Cast and Read Your Horoscope; TV appearances include The Johnny Carson Tonight Show, What's My Line, 60 Minutes, CBS News Night Watch, Cosmos (BBC), Sci. Series (Italian TV), Fantastico (Brazilian TV), Japan TV, News (Nippon), Do We Really Need It? (ASAHI), The World is Calling (Uranai); contbr. articles to mags. and newspapers. Mem. AFTRA, Am. Fedn. Astrologers (cert.). Avocation: travel. Home: 850 E Desert Inn Rd Apt 912 Las Vegas NV 89109-2100 Office: Star Bright Pubs 2235 E Flamingo Rd Las Vegas NV 89119-5129

PALMER, MONA GENE, humanities educator; b. Bristol, Va., Apr. 10, 1935; d. James Hal and R. Kathryn Hodgson; m. Donald S. Baird, Sept. 6, 1957 (div. Oct. 1968); 1 child, Dylan H.; m. Fred E. Palmer, June 28, 1970. BA, San Diego State U., 1958, MA, 1973; postgrad., UCLA, 1962-63. Instr. English Southwestern Coll., Chula Vista, Calif., 1975-85; instr. English San Diego State U., 1975-87, lectr. in Classics and Humanities, 1987—; instr. humanities Miramar Coll., San Diego, 1988—; instr. San Diego Mus. of Art, 1997-99; faculty advisor Umanisti, San Diego, 1995-98; v.p. docent coun. San Diego Mus. of Art, 1997-99. Contbr. articles to profl. jours. Bd. dirs. Coll. Area Cmty. Coun., San Diego, 1982-88; script evaluator Old Globe Theatre, 1985—. Named Citizen of Yr. C. of C., 1987. Mem. Friends of Classics (bd. dirs. 1986—), Hellenic Cultural Soc., San Diego Mus. of Art (docent), Timken Mus. (docent), Phi Kappa Phi, Eta Sigma Phi. Avocations: piano, theatre, gardening. Office: San Diego State U 5500 Campanile Dr San Diego CA 92182-0002

PALMER, PATRICK ASA, former banker, lecturer; b. Amherst, N.S., Can., Mar. 29, 1943; s. James Asa and Evelyn Elizabeth (Hatt) P.; m. Margaret Ann Teixeira, Feb. 8, 1964; children: Mark, Ingrid, Petrina, Kara-Lynn. B in Commerce with honors, U. Windsor, Ont., Can., 1970; FICB, U. Toronto, 1972. Mgr. mktg. program Royal Bank of Can., Toronto, Ont., 1976-78; mgr. nat. bus. met. Royal Bank of Can., Toronto, 1978-79, mgr. comml. markets, 1979-81; v.p. comml. mktg. and svcs. Royal Bank of Can., Ont., 1981-82; v.p. comml. mktg. Royal Bank of Can., Can., 1982-83; v.p. planning, comml. banking and nat. accounts Royal Bank of Can., 1983-86; v.p. sales and svcs. Royal Bank of Can., Can., 1986-88, v.p. corp. mktg. and sales, 1988-89, v.p. retail banking, 1989-94; sr. v.p. channel mgmt. RBFG, 1994-97; pres. Where Eagles Soar, Inc., 1997—; lectr. Sheridan Coll., Oakville, Ont., 1979-81, George Brown Coll., Toronto, 1979; adviser to superhost Ont.; bd. dirs. Janes Family Foods Ltd., Kinfolk Mgmt. Inc., Penetangore Ridge Inc.; mem. adv. bd. Mphasis. Author papers and essays in field. Mem. devel. bd. U. Windsor; founder Cappy Ride, Motorcycle Charity Ride; bd. dirs. spl. envoy Ont. province Ont. Export, Inc., past bd. dirs. Ont. C. of C., U. Windsor, CDN Tourism Assn., Econ. Devel. Assn. Can., CDN Tourism Mgmt. Ctr., other non-profit orgns. Mem. Alliance for Ont. Univs. (hon.). Home: 49 Wildwood Rd, Georgetown, ON Canada L7G 2W9 Office: Where Eagles Soar Inc, 5720 Timberlea Blvd Ste 201, Mississauga, ON Canada L4W 4W2

PALMER, PAUL RICHARD, librarian, archivist; b. Cin., Jan. 21, 1917; s. Gardiner O. and Sarah Ellen (Christy) P. BA, U. Cin., 1949; MS, Columbia U., 1950, MA, 1955. Asst. br. libr. Bklyn. Pub. Libr., 1950-51; libr. Columbia U., N.Y.C., 1951-67, libr. sch. libr. svc., 1968, libr. and curator Brander Matthews Dramatic Mus., 1969-73, bibliographer Avery Archtl. Libr., 1974, curator Columbiana Collection, 1974—; cons. Am. Libr. Assn., Chgo. and N.Y.C., 1954-59. Contbr. articles to profl. jurs. With U.S. Army, 1942-46, ETO and NATOUSA. Fellow The Pierpont Morgan Libr.; mem. Theatre Libr. Assn. (exec. coun. 1970-74), Mus. Modern Art, Metro. Mus. Art, Am. Film Inst., Am. Mus. Britain, French Inst., Soc. Hist. Preservation, Lincoln Ctr. Film Soc., Manuscript Soc., Grolier Club, Church Club N.Y., St. George Soc. N.Y., VFW, Order St. John of Jerusalem, Phi Beta Kappa. Episcopalian. Home: 560 Riverside Dr Apt 21-b New York NY 10027-3236

PALMER, PHILIP ISHAM, JR., lawyer; b. Dallas, June 25, 1929; s. Philip I. and Charlene (Bolen) P.; m. Eleanor Hutson, Mar. 7, 1951; children—Stephen Edward, Michael Bolen. B.B.A., So. Methodist U., 1952; LL.B., U. Tex., 1957. Bar: Tex. 1957, U.S. Dist. Ct. (no. dist.) Tex. 1957, U.S. Ct. Appeals (5th cir.) 1958, U.S. Supreme Ct. 1963, U.S. Dist. Ct. (we. dist.) Tex. 1968, U.S. Ct. Appeals (9th cir.) 1973, U.S. Ct. Appeals (10th cir.) 1974, U.S. Supreme Ct. 1974, U.S. Ct. Appeals (11th cir.) 1981, U.S. Dist. Ct. (ea. dist.) Tex. 1987. Since practiced in Dallas; ptnr. Palmer & Palmer P.C. (and predecessor firms), 1957—; chmn. bd. Carolina Mfg. Corp., 1973—, pres., 1969-73; chmn. bd. Commonwealth Nat. Bank, 1967-69; pres. Pennyrich Corp., 1969-72. Co-author: Texas Creditors Rights; Contbr. articles to profl. jours. Vice consul Republic Costa Rica, 1973—; bd. dirs. Shepherd's Care, 1987—. Fellow Am. Coll. Bankruptcy; mem. Am. Bar Assn., Am. Judicature Soc., 5th Cir. Bar Assn. (atty. mem. 5th cir. jud. conf.), Dallas Bankruptcy Bar (chmn. bd. 1986—). Club: City. Office: Palmer & Palmer PC 1201 Main St Ste 1510 Dallas TX 75202-3985

PALMER, RICHARD WARE, lawyer; b. Boston, Oct. 20, 1919; s. George Ware and Ruth French (Judkins) P.; m. Nancy Fernald Shaw, July 8, 1950; children: Richard Ware Jr., John Wentworth, Anne Fernald. AB, Harvard U., 1942, JD, 1948. Bar: N.Y. 1950, Pa. 1959. Sec., dir. N.Am. Mfg. Co., Natick, Mass., 1946-48; assoc. Burlingham, Veeder, Clark & Hupper, Burlingham, Hupper & Kennedy, N.Y.C., 1949-57; ptnr. Rawle & Henderson, Phila., 1958-79; ptnr. Palmer, Biezup & Henderson, Phila., 1979-95, of counsel, 1996—; sec. Underwater Technics, Inc., Camden, N.J., 1967-85; adv. on admiralty law to U.S. del. Inter-Govtl. Maritime Consultative Orgn., London, 1967; mem. U.S. Shipping Coordinating Com., mem. Washington legal sub com., 1967—; U.S. del. 30th-34th internat. confs. Titular mem. Comité Maritime Internat.; v.p., sec., bd. dirs. Phila. Belt Line R.R.; bd. dirs. Mather (Bermuda) Ltd. Editor: Maritime Law Reporter. Mem., permanent adv. bd. Tulane Admiralty Law Inst., Tulane U. Law Sch., New Orleans, 1975—; trustee Seamen's Ch. Inst., Phila., 1967—, pres., 1972-84; Harvard Law Sch. Assn., Phila., Pa. (exec. com. 1986—); bd. dirs. Havrford (Pa.) Civic Assn., 1972-85, pres., 1976-79; consul for Denmark in State of Pa., 1980-91, consul emeritus, 1992—. Lt. comdr. USNR. Fellow World Acad. Art and Sci. (treas. 1988—); mem. ABA (former chmn. stdg. com. on admiralty and maritime law 1978-79), N.Y.C. Bar Assn., Phila. Bar Assn., Am. Judicature Soc., Maritime Law Assn. (chmn. limitation liability com. 1977-83, 2d v.p. 1984-86, 1st v.p. 1986-88, pres. 1988-90, immediate past pres. 1990-92), Internat. Bar Assn., Assn. Average Adjusters USA and Gt. Britain, Port of Phila. Maritime Soc., Harvard Law Sch. Assn. of Phila. (exec. com. 1986—), Fgn. Consul assn. of Phila., Danish Order of Dannebrog, Merion Cricket Club, Phila. Club, Rittenhouse Club, India House, Geneal. Soc. Pa. (bd. dirs. 1997—), Harvard Club of N.Y.C. and Phila. (exec. com. 1983-86, 94-97). Republican. Episcopalian. Home: 432 Montgomery Ave Haverford PA 19041-1559 Office: Palmer Biezup & Henderson Pub Ledger Bldg 620 Chestnut St Philadelphia PA 19106-3413

PALMER, ROBERT MARSHALL, geriatrician; b. Detroit, Jan. 5, 1946; s. Harry and Henrietta (Greenberg) P.; m. Miriam Rachel Brooks, Dec. 31, 1972; children: Adam, Alex. BA, U. Mich., 1967, MD, 1971; MPH, UCLA, 1977. Unit chief physician Los Angeles County Dept. Health Svcs., Pico Rivera, Calif., 1975-78; asst. dir. med. edn. Providence Med. Ctr., Portland, Oreg., 1978-80; program dir. internal medicine Oreg. Health Scis. U., Portland, 1981-84; med. dir. Elder Health Ctr., Univ. Hosps. Cleve., 1985-94, head sect. geriatric medicine, 1994—. Author, editor: Clinics in Geriatric Medicine, 1998. Mem. ACP, Am. Geriatrics Soc. Avocations: classical music, sports, reading. E-mail: palmerr@ccf.org. Office: Cleve Clinic Found 9500 Euclid Ave Cleveland OH 44195-0001

PALMER, ROBERT TOWNE, lawyer, banker; b. Chgo., May 25, 1947; s. Adrian Bernhardt and Gladys (Towne) P.; m. Anne Therese Darin, Nov. 9, 1974; children: Justin Darin, Christian Darin. BA, Colgate U., 1969; JD, U. Notre Dame, 1974. Bar: Ill. 1974, D.C. 1978, U.S. Supreme Ct. 1978. Law clk. to Hon. Walter V. Schaefer Ill. Supreme Ct., 1974-75; assoc. McDermott, Will & Emery, Chgo., 1975-81, ptnr., 1982-86; ptnr. Chadwell & Kayser, Ltd., Chgo., 1987-88, Connelly, Mustes, Palmer & Schroeder, Chgo., 1988-89; of counsel Garfield & Merel Ltd., Chgo., 1990-2000; mem. adj. faculty Chgo. Kent Law Sch., 1975-77, Loyola U., 1976-78; mem. adv. com. Fed. Home Loan Mortgage Corp., 1988-89; dir. Ctrl. Fed. Savs. & Loan Assn. of Chgo., 1988—, chmn. 2000—; mem. Chgo. Ctr. Adv. Bd. Voyageur Outward Bound Sch., 1988-91. Contbr. articles to legal jours. and textbooks. Mem. ABA, Ill. State Bar Assn. (Lincoln award 1983), Chgo. Bar Assn., Internat. Assn. Def. Counsel, Chgo. Club, Dairymen's Country Club, Lambda Alpha. Office: Central Fed Savs 1601 W Belmont Ave Chicago IL 60657-3044

PALMER, STUART BEAUMONT, physicist, educator; b. Ilkeston, Derbyshire, Eng., May 6, 1943; s. Frank Beaumont and Florence Beryl (Wilkinson) P.; m. Susan Mary Clay, Aug. 10, 1966; children: Richard Stuart, Anthony John, Katherine Mary. BSc. with hons., U. Sheffield, Eng., 1964, PhD, 1968, DSc, 1986. Asst. lectr. U. Hull, Eng., 1967-70; from lectr. to sr. lectr. U. Hull, 1970-83, reader, 1983-87; prof. exptl. physics U. Warwick, Coventry, Eng., 1987—; chmn. physics dept. U. Warwick, 1989—, pro vice-chancellor, 1995—; chmn. Sci. and Engring. Rsch. Coun. Magnetism Initiative, 1989-93. Author: Advanced University Physics, 1995, Quantum Physics, 1999, Solid State Physics, 2000; editor Nondestructive Testing and Evaluation, 1988—, Jour. Physics D: Applied Physics, 1989-99; contbr. over 250 articles to Sci. Jours.; holder 5 patents (Gt. Britain). Fellow Inst. Elec. Engring (chartered engr.), Inst. Physics (chartered physicist), Inst. Nondestructive Testing, Royal Acad. Engring. Avocations: sailing, music, tennis. Office: U Warwick, Dept Physics, Coventry CV4 7AL, England

PALMER, SUSAN SMITH, dietitian; b. Columbia, S.C., Feb. 15, 1961; d. Zeb Vance, Jr. and Barbara Jean (La Casse) S.; m. Chester D. Palmer, III, Feb. 5, 1994. BS, Winthrop Coll., 1983; MS, S.C. State Coll., 1998. Dietitian Orangeburg (S.C.) Calhoun Regional Hosp., 1985-93; cmty. dietitian S.C. Dept. Health Environ. Control, West Columbia, 1993—; liaison Carolina Health Styles/Dept. Health Environ. Control, Columbia, 1993-96. Mem. Am. Dietetic Assn. (reg.), S.C. Dietetic Assn., Episcopal Ch. Women. Avocations: reading, needlework. Office: SC Dept Health Environ Control 112 Hospital Dr W West Columbia SC 29169-3406

PALMER, VENRICE ROMITO, lawyer, educator; b. Springfield, Mass., Jan. 11, 1952; s. Venrice Wellesley and Mildred Adlay (Foster) P. Higher diploma, U. Besançon, France, 1973; AB maxima cum laude, King's Coll., Wilkes-Barre, Pa., 1974; JD, Harvard U., 1977. Bar: N.Y. 1978, U.S. Dist. Ct. (so. and ea. dists.) N.Y. 1979, Ill. 1986, Calif. 1997. Spl. asst. atty. gen. Office N.Y. Atty. Gen., N.Y.C., 1977-79; staff atty. SEC, N.Y.C., 1979-82, br. chief, 1982-83, spl. trial counsel, 1983-85, acting asst. regional adminstr., 1984-85; sr. counsel Sears, Roebuck and Co., Hoffman Estates, Ill., 1985-97, Bank of Am., San Francisco, 1997-99; counsel McCutchen, Doyle, Brown & Enersen, LLP, San Francisco, 1999—; guest lectr. St. John's U. Bus. Sch., N.Y.C., 1984; lectr. Practicing Law Inst., N.Y.C., 1995—, Glasser LegalWorks, Little Falls, N.J., 1997—. Contbr. articles to various law publs. Recipient cert. of appreciation N.Y. State Bar Assn., 1978. Mem. ABA, Am. Soc. Corp. Secs. (lectr. N.Y.C. 1997—). Avocations: opera, ballet, reading. Home: 1200 Gough St Apt 7A San Francisco CA 94109-6616 Office: McCutchen Doyle Brown & Enersen LLP Three Embarcadero Ctr San Francisco CA 94111

PALMER, WILLARD ALDRICH, III, magician, writer, actor; b. Houston, July 25, 1942; s. Willard Aldrich and Ruby Lenoir (Touchstone) P.; m. Carol Ann Houston. BA in Germanics, Rice U., 1964. Instr. Charlie Cash Music Studios, Houston, 1962-70; performer various venues, Houston, Montreal, Can., 1965—; writer Alfred Music Co., Los Angeles, 1968-86; official magician Todd Mission, Tex., 1984—; owner, operator Bill Palmer Magic Shows, Bellaire, Tex., 1984—; dir. Tex. Renaissance Festival, Todd Mission, 1978-79; writer, dir. Ren Fair Prodns., Inc., Houston, 1979-81; writer, cons. Exclusive Magical Pubs., Houston, Mexico City, 1986— (mem. editoral bd. 1986). Author: (books) How To Play Folk and Bluegrass Banjo, 1965, A Guide For The Texas Renaissance Festival Performer, 1978, Early History of the Paddle Trick in Print, 1995, How to be a Professional Entertainer, 1996; translator: Magical Adventures and Fairy Tales (Punx) 1987, Punx's Fourth Dimensional Mysteries, 1990, Farewell Performance (Punx), 1990, Paramiracles, 1996. Dir., pres. Houston Soc. for Psychic Research, 1972—. Mem. Soc. Am. Magicians (pres. Houston chpt. 1985-86), Internat. Brotherhood Magicians (pres. Houston chpt. 1984-85), Tex. Assn. Magicians, Houston Assn. Magicians (pres. 1978-79), The Inner Magic Circle (assoc.), Phi Mu Alpha (warden 1966-67), Delta Phi Alpha. Lutheran. Avocation: psychic research. E-mail: bill@billpalmer.com. Home and Office: Bill Palmer Magic Shows 7902 Roos Rd Houston TX 77036-6440

PALMIERI, SAMUEL NICOLARI, artist, educator; b. Jersey City, May 25, 1932; s. Carmine and Anna Maria (Nicolari) P.; m. Catherine Palmieri (div. July 1971); children: Michael, Anne, Patricia, Gina; m. Susan Palmieri, Aug. 24, 1976. BA, U. Calif., Northridge, 1969; MFA, U. Guanjuato, San Miguel, Mex., 1971. Tchr. Manatee Pub. Sch., Bradenton, Fla., 1968-70. Exhibited in group shows at N.Y. Art Expo, Gallery A., Taos, N.Mex., Treasure Art Gallery, Sedona, Ariz., Elaine Horwitch Gallery, Sedona, Jim Clark & Assocs., Scottsdale, Ariz., Kessel-Long Gallery, Scottsdale, Nat. Heritage Gallery, Beverly Hills, Calif., Galleria San Miguel, Mex.; pub. and pvt. collections include Tropicana Corp., Titan Capital Corp., U.S. Senate Bldg., actress Ann Miller, Sen. Barry Goldwater. Sgt. U.S. Army, 1950-53; PTO; ETO.

PALMISANO, LEONARDO, chemistry educator, researcher; b. Termini Imerese, Palermo, Italy, Apr. 13, 1950; s. Giovanni and Vincenza (Sammartano) P.; m. Maria Carmela Cipolla; children: Giovanni, Claudia. Degree in Chemistry, U. Palermo, 1973. Rsch. asst. U. Palermo, 1976-91, prof. chemistry, 1992—; prof. chemistry U. Cosenza, Italy, 1992-93; prof. chemistry U. Palermo, Italy, 1993-99, full prof., 2000—. Contbr. articles to profl. jours. 2d lt. Italian Army, 1975-76. Avocation: philately. E-mail: palmisan@dicpm.unipa.it. Office: U Palermo Dept Chem Engring, Viale Delle Scienze, 90128 Palermo Sicily, Italy

PALMITER, P. RUSSEL, mechanical engineer; b. Chattanooga, Feb. 18, 1975; s. Charles William and Peggy Jean (Scruggs) P. BSME, U. Memphis, 1997. Product engr. Paker Hannifin Corp., Memphis, 1997—. Mastersinger Rhodes Mastersingers Chorale, 1998. Mem. Memphis Fencing Alliance; outreach vol. Germantown Bapt. Ch., Memphis, 1998. Early scholar Tenn. Bd. Regents, 1993-97. Mem. AIAA (br. chmn. 1996-97), ASME, Phi Kappa Phi. Avocations: sketching, painting, performing arts, web sites. Home: 5916 Birdie Cv Memphis TN 38115-2102 Office: Parker Hannifin Corp 5300 E Raines Rd Memphis TN 38118-7015

PALMSTIERNA, TOM KRISMAN KULE, psychiatrist, researcher; b. Solna, Stockholm, Sweden, Feb. 26, 1956; s. Hans Allan Kule and Lena (Jovinge) P.; m. Toril Dybvig, Oct. 20, 1979; children: Caroline, Hans, Christian, Anna, Magnus. MD, Karolinska Inst., Stockholm, 1983, degree in psychotherapy, 1988, Dr.Med.Sc., 1992. Authorized physician, 1985, psychiatrist, 1989. Resident in geriatrics Geriatric Clinic, Södertälje, Sweden, 1980-81; resident in psychiatry Psychiat. Clinic, Huddinge, Sweden, 1981-82; resident in gen. medicine Gen. Hosp., Västerås, Sweden, 1983-85; resident in psychiatry Psychiat. Clinic, Västerås, 1985-89; med. head of psychiat. dependency unit Västerås Gen. Hosp., 1989-91; sr. psychiatrist Arboga Outpatient Clinic, 1990-94; sr. psychiatrist and psychiat. rschr. Psychiat. Dependency Clinic, St. Goran's Hosp., Stockholm, 1993—; head of acute and cmty. based dependency treatment Ctr. for Dependency Disorders, Karolinska Inst., 1996—; cons. psychiatrist Treatment Facility Orgn. of Swedish Client Orgn. for Former Drug Addicts, 1989-91, Stockholm City Coun. Treatment Bur. for Drug Addicts, 1990-94, Swedish Bd. for Involuntary Treatment of Drug Addicts, 1994—; sci. sec. First European Congress on Aggression in Clin. Practice, 1992. Contbr. articles to profl. jours. Grantee Gadelius Fund for Psychiat. Rsch., 1985, Swedish Wk. Environment Fund for Psychiat. Rsch., 1986, Lundbeck Found. for Psychiat. Rsch., 1989. Home: Glimmervägen 11, S-18734 Täby Sweden Office: Karolinska Inst St Gorans Hosp, BCN/Plan 12, 11281 Stockholm Sweden

PALOCZI, KATALIN, haemoto immunologist, consultant; b. Pacin, Hungary, May 7, 1946; d. Janos and Ilona P.; m. Istvan Szent-Kiralyi, Apr. 11, 1970 (div. 1983); children: Katalin, Agnes. MD, U. Med. Sch., Debrecen, Hungary, 1970; PhD, Acad. Sci., Budapest, Hungary, 1986, DSc, 1992. Bd. cert. Diplomate Internal Medicine, Haematology and Clin. Immunology. Postdoc. fellow U. Med. Sch., Debrecen, Hungary, 1970-75, asst. prof., 1976-80; assoc. prof. Nat. Inst. Haematology & Immunology, Budapest, Hungary, 1985-97; prof., chair Nat. Inst. Haematology & Immunology, Budapest, Hungary, 1998—; cons., 1987-92, sr. cons., 1993-95, deputy dir., 1998—, Nat. Inst. Haemotology & Immunology, Budapest, Hungary; chair immunology U. Health Sci., Budapest, Hungary, 1998—. Author: Monography, 1994; contbr. articles to profl. jours. Pres. Hungarian Soc. for Immunology, Budapest, Hungary, 1998; mem. CLWP of EBMT, London, 1997, European and Internat. Cytokine Soc., Paris, 1996, IACRLRD, 1994. Recipient Excellent Work prize, Min. of Health, Debrecen, Hungary, 1985, Acad. Prize Hungaryan Acad. Sci., Budapest, 1995. Mem. Hungarian Acad. Sci., Ethical Scientific Com., Hungarian Acad. Sci. Immunology Subcom. Presbyterian. Avocations: jogging, aerobics, psychology, para-psychology. Office phone: (36-1) 209-2311. Office: Nat Inst Haemot & Immun, Daroci str 24, H-1113 Budapest Hungary

PALODA, MARTIN, aircraft company executive; b. Prague, Czechoslovakia, Nov. 25, 1951; s. Lubos and Miloslava (Bila) P.; m. Daniele Honcova, Jan. 5, 1978; children: Zuzana, Hana. MSc, Mil. Tech. Acad., Brno, Czechoslovakia, 1975; PhD, Czech Acad. Sci., Prague, 1987. From aircraft designer to mktg. dir. Aero Vodochody Ltd., Odolena Voda, Czech Republic, 1975—. Mem. Czech Aeronautical Soc., Czech Soc. Mechs., Club of Friends of Fine Arts. Avocations: fine arts, literature, yachting, flying, horseback riding. Home: Cs Armady 364, 250 70 Odolena Voda Czech Republic

PALOLA, HARRY JOEL, international affairs executive, consultant; b. Kaukola, Viipuri, Finland, May 13, 1943; came to U.S., 1961; s. Heikki and Mary Dagmar (Ahokas) P.; m. Rita Hannele Ahokas, Sept. 15, 1968 (div. July 1992); children: Christine, Kathy, Kimberly. AA, L.A. City Coll., 1966; BS in Mech. Engring., Calif. State U., Long Beach, 1971; MA in Internat. Affairs, Calif. State U., Sacramento, 1995. Registered engr.-in-tng., Calif. Design engr. Northrop Corp., Hawthorne, Calif., 1971-77, Ford Aerospace and Comm. Corp., Newport Beach, Calif., 1977-81, B&M Assocs., San Diego, 1982; mech. engr. Raytheon Corp., Goleta, Calif., 1982-84; electronic packaging engr. LPL Tech. Svc., Seattle, 1984-86; design/test engr. Boeing Co., Seattle and Vandenberg, Calif., 1986-92; CEO Internat. Consultancy Corp., Santa Ynez, Calif., 1993—; cons. in basic and applied rsch. in human comm., 1993—. Author: International Finnish Studies: Language, History and Culture, 1995, The Karjala Question-Thoughts on Religious Directions, 1997. Econ. devel. student intern City of Sacramento, 1992-93. Sgt. USNG, 1966-72. Republican. Lutheran. Avocations: ocean sailing, private flying, Finno-Urgic and Ural-Altaic languages. Office: Internat Consultancy Corp 1041 N Refugio Rd Santa Ynez CA 93460-9316

PALOMÄKI, JARI JUHANI, philosopher, librarian, educator; b. Turku, Finland, May 24, 1961; s. Tarmo Tapani and Anja Inkeri (Nieminen) P. MS, U. Turku, 1989; Lic. Philosophy, U. Tampere, Finland, 1994, PhD, 1994. Libr. asst. Turku City Libr., 1981—; docent theoretical philosophy U. Tampere, 1996—, libr., 1994—; asst. rsch. prof. Tech. U. Denmark, Lyngby, 1997; tchr. U. Tampere, Turku, Tech. U., Tampere, Denmark, Turku Sch. Econs., 1986—; rschr. U. Tampere, 1990—; vis. rschr. Tech. U. Denmark, Lyngby, 1994, Acad. Scis. Czech Republic, Prague, 1994—, CNR, Pisa, 1999. Author: From Concepts to Concept Theory, 1994; co-editor: On the Formal Representation of Knowledge (in Finnish), 1997. Grantee NorFA, 1993, Finnish Cultural Found., 1999, 2000. Mem. Philos. Soc. Finland, Finnish Artificial Intelligence Soc. Avocation: art. E-mail: fijapa@uta.fi. Home: Vuorikatu 7aA4, FIN20700 Turku Finland Office: U Tampere PO, Dept Math Stats and Philos, FIN33014 Tampere Finland

PALOMARES, ANTONIO EDUARDO, chemist, educator; b. Tavernes Valldigna, Valencia, Spain, Jan. 9, 1968; s. Antonio Palomares and Encarna Gimeno. BS in Chemistry, U. Valencia, 1990, PhD in Chemistry Sci., 1995. Postgrad. U. Twente, Enschede, Netherlands, 1995-96; assoc. prof. Polytechnic U., Valencia, 1996. Patentee in field; contbr. articles to profl. jours. Grantee Regional Govt., Valencia, 1990-94, U. Valencia, 1995. Office: Polytechnic U Valencia, eno Vera Sin, 46022 Valencia Spain

PALOMBI, GUIDO, publisher; b. Rome, Lazio, Italy, Feb. 17, 1923; s. Carlo and Angeli Antonietta (Bambini) P.; m. Maria Pumelli (dec. Aug. 1991); children: Carlo, cristina, Alessandro, Francesca. D Economy and Commerce, U. Rome, 1949. Adminstr. Unico Fratelli Palombi S.r.l., Rome; pres. Centro Studi ed Esperienze Scout Baden Powel, 1974—. Pub. books, mags., others. Mem. Rotary. Home: Via Achille Papa 17, 00195 Rome Italy Office: Fratelli Palombi, Via Dei Gracchi 181/185, 00192 Rome Italy

PALOM IZQUIERDO, FRANCISCO JAVIER, management consultant, educator; b. Barcelona, Catalunya, Spain, Feb. 8, 1935; s. Agustin Palom Paradeda and Eulalia (Izquierdo) Cervera P.; m. Carmen Rico Garcia, July 14, 1961; children—Francisco Javier, Jorge, Santiago, Jose Oriol, Carlos. Prof. Mercantil, High Sch. Commerce, Barcelona, 1955. Cert. mercantil. Orgn. mngr. Umlever Co. Barcelona, Madrid, 1959-65; sr. cons. Asfor J.A., Barcelona, 1965-70, gen. mgr., 1973-99; pres. Ode S.A., Barcelona, 1974-99, and GPI S.A., Barcelona, 1979—; prof. high sch. bus. adminstrn. ESADE, Barcelona, 1965-80; cons. Centro Comercio Internacional, UN, Geneva, 1974-75; cons. Assn. Pri. Schs., Rome, 1980; lectr. univs. Author: Presupuesto Base Cero, 1979, 81; (manual) Cuadro de Mando del Entorno, 1979; (manual) Time Management, 1982, contbr. 25 articles to books, manuals and videotapes; editor videos and seminars. Mem. Mgmt. Assn. Execs. Fin. Club. Assn. Progreso de la Dirección, Assn. Iberomericana Mgmt. (pres. founder Barcelona). Club: Hispano-Frances (Barcelona). Home: Escorial 50 7 8a, Barcelona 24, Spain Office: Escorial 50 1 2a, Caspe 33, Barcelona 08010, Spain

PALOMO, CLAUDIO NICOLAU, chemist, educator, researcher; b. Barcelona, Catalunya, Spain, Sept. 4, 1951; s. Antonio Luis Coll and francisca Aloy (Nicolau) P.; m. Adoracion Ostiza Irigoyen, Mar. 4, 1981; 1 child, Marta Palomo Irigoyen. Chem. Engr., Instituto quimico Sarria, Barcelona, 1975, M.Organic Chemistry, 1976; BA in Chemistry, U. Barcelona, 1981; PhD in Chemistry, U. Basque Country, 1983. Rsch. assoc. Gema S.A., Barcelona, 1976-79; assoc. prof. U. Basque Country, San Sebastian, 1979-89, prof. chemistry, 1989—; vis. prof. U. Calif.-Berkeley, 1993. Contbr. articles to profl. jours., chpts. to books. Mem. AAAS, Spanish Royal Soc. Chemistry, Am. Acad. Sci. Office: Univ del Pais Vasco, Facultad de Quimica #1072, 20080 San Sebastian Spain

PALOTASI, ANDRAS, electrical engineer, researcher; b. Budapest, Hungary, Nov. 30, 1941; s. Kornel Palotasi and Ilona Kovacs; m. Magdolna Bizinger, Dec. 8, 1966; 1 child, Andrea. Student, German Lang. Sch., Budapest, 1974, English Lang. Sch., Budapest, 1979. Registered profl. engr., Hungary. Technician Gamma Works, Budapest, 1965-70; engr. Computer and Automation Inst., Budapest, 1970-79; researcher Computer and Automation Inst. Hungarian Acad. Scis., Budapest, 1979-90; chief engr. Itex Laser & Computer Technics, Ltd., Budapest, 1990-92; head elec. lab. Computer and Automation Inst. Hungarian Acad. Scis., Budapest, 1992—. Patentee in field. Steward Trade Union, Budapest, 1970. Lt. Signal Corps, 1963-65. Roman Catholic. Avocations: tennis, skiing. Home: 111 Jablonka Koz 4/a, 1037 Budapest Hungary Office: Hungarian Acad Scis XI, Kende-u 13-17, 1111 Budapest Hungary

PALOUKIS, DIMITRIOS, chemical engineer; b. Maroussi, Athens, Greece, July 5, 1960; married, 1985. M degree, Tech. U., Athens, 1983. Project engr. Asprofos Engring. S.A., Athens, 1986-91, project mgr., 1991—. Active Greek Red Cross, Athens, 1991. With Greek Mil., 1983-85. Mem. Greek Chamber of Chem. Engrs. Avocations: Internet, writing, arts, gymnastics. Home: Marathonodromou 120, GR 15125 Maroussi, Athens Greece Office: Asprofos Engring SA, El Veniselou 284, GR 17675 Kallithea Greece

PALSER, BETH ANNE, painter; b. Chester, Pa., Nov. 26, 1964; d. John Frank Palser Jr. and Barbara Mower Urban; adopted d. John Frank and Anita (Dietrich) P.; m. William Joseph Quindlen III, Aug. 26, 1963. AD in Specialized Tech., Art Inst. Phila., 1984. Mech./paste-up artist, draftsman Southco, Inc., Concordville, Pa., 1985; artist, asst. David E. Gordon Studios, Phila., 1985-87; freelance artist Franklin Mint, Wawa, Pa., 1988; artist, owner Beth Palser Studios, Oxford, Pa., 1988—; bd. dirs. Rittenhouse Sq. Fine Arts Assn., Phila., 1991-94, 98—, treas., 1992-94; exhbn. chair Artist Guild of Delaware County, Springfield, Pa., 1996-98; bd. dirs. Rittenhouse Sq. Fine Arts Annual, 1998—. Exhibited in one-woman show at Darlington Fine Arts Ctr., Wawa, 1994, 95, 97; exhibited in group shows including Pavilion Galleries Nat. Art Exhbn., Mt. Holly, N.J., 1992, Camden County Cultural Heritage Regional Watercolor Exhbn., Camden, N.J., 1994 (2d place award 1994), Pearl S. Buck Found. Regional Show, Lehigh Valley, Pa., 1995, Lansdale (Pa.) Fine Art Show, 1994, 96 (Best of Show award 1994, Excellence in Watercolor award 1996), Cape May (N.J.) Promenade Art Show, 1996, Phila. Sketch Club Watercolor Exhbn., 1997, Bianco Gallery Ann. Regional Exhbn., Buckingham, Pa., 1997, Cape May (N.J.) Promenade Fine Art Show, 1997 (2d place award 1996, 1st pl. award 1997), Chestnut Hill Art Show, Pa., 1998 (hon. mention 1998), Spirit of Art, Wilmington, Del., 1998 (hon. mention 1998), Roxborough Fine Art Festival, Phila., 1999 (Award of Merit, watercolor 1999), Rittenhouse Sq. Fine Arts Festival (2d place award 2000), Cape May (NJ) Promenade Art Show (2d place award 2000); exhibited in charity art shows at Children's Hosp. Phila., 1994-95, South Jersey Arthritis Found., 1995-98, Brandwine Sch. Nursing, 1998-99, United Cerebral Palsy Del., 1998-99, Ronald McDonald House Art Fest, Del.; represented in Newman Galleries, Phila, Chadds Ford Art Gallery, Pa., Tyme Gallery, Haverton, Pa., Deck the Walls, Exton, Pa.; represented by The Total Picture Gallery, Hockessin, Del., Artworks Gallery, Kennett Square, Pa.; exhibited in two-person show Artworks Gallery, Kennett Square, Pa., 1999. Recipient numerous awards for art. Mem. Balt. Watercolor Soc. (signature mem.), Chester County Art Assn., Phila. Watercolor Club, Pa. Watercolor Soc. (signature mem.). Republican. Avocations: photography, travel, cooking, aerobics. Home: 107 Midland Dr Oxford PA 19363-1125

PALSSON, GUNNAR, diplomat. Permanent rep. to UN Govt. Iceland, N.Y.C., 1994-98; head Iceland mission to NATO & European Union, Brussels, Belgium, 1998-. Office: Iceland's Mission to NATO, NATO Hdqrs Blvd Leopold III, 1110 Brussels Belgium*

PALSSON, PALL ARNOR, lawyer; b. Reykjavik, Iceland, June 5, 1948; s. Pall S. and Gudrun (Stephensen) P.; m. Ragnheidur Valdimarsdottir; children: Thordis, Pall Sigthor, Haukur. Cand.Juris, U. Iceland, 1974. Bar: Iceland, 1975—. Advocate Logmannastofan, Reykjavik, 1975—, Supreme Ct. Iceland, 1981—; consul gen. in Iceland State of Israel, 1993—. Mem. ABA (hon.), Icelandic Bar Assn. (v.p. 1984-86), The Parlex Group of European Lawyers. Home: Háaleitisbraut 119, 108 Reykjavik Iceland Office: Lögmannastofan, Laugavegi 7, 101 Reykjavik Iceland

PALSSON, THORSTEINN, Icelandic diplomat; b. Oct. 29, 1947; m. Ingibjorg Rafnar; 3 children. Grad., Comml. Coll.; LLD, U. Iceland, 1974. Journalist Morgunbladid; editor Visir newspaper, 1975-79; dir. Confedn. Icelandic Employers, 1979; M.P. Iceland, 1983—; chmn. Independence Party, 1983-91; min. fin. Iceland, Reykjavik, 1985-87, prime min., 1987-88, min. of fisheries, 1991—, min. justice, from 1991, min. eccles. affairs, from 1991; amb.-designate to India Iceland Embassy, New Delhi. Office: Ministry Fisheries, Skúlagata 4, 150 Reykjavik Iceland*

PALTA, JAIRO ALBERTO, plant scientist; b. Cali, Colombia, Nov. 23, 1953; arrived in Australia, 1981; s. Jaime Palta and Tulia Paz. BSc, U. Del Valle, Cali, Colombia, 1976; MSc, CINVESTAV, Mex., 1977; PhD, LaTrobe U., Australia, 1985. Cert. agriculturist. Postdoctoral rsch. assoc. U. North Wales, Bangor, U.K., 1985-87; plant physiologist UCLA, 1987-89; rsch. scientist CSIRO Plant Industry, Perth, Australia, 1989-92, sr. rsch. scientist, 1993-97, subprogram leader, 1993-2000, prin. rsch. scientist, 2000—; vis. scientist Ctr. Internat. Agrl. Tropical, Cali, Colombia, 1979-81, IARC-Long Ashton, U.K., 1998; associated scientist Ctr. for Legumes in Mediterranean Agrl., Perth, 1993—. Author: Isla de Gorgona, 1986; editor: Market Value and Profitability of Lupins, 1994. Australian oilseeds rsch. fellow, 1981; scholar UNESCO-PNUD, Mex., 1975, rsch. scholar CIAT, Cali, Colombia, 1979; rsch. fellow Australian Oilseeds Rsch. Coun.; sr. rsch. fellow GRDC, 1998. Mem. Am. Soc. Agronomy, Am. Soc. Plant Physiologists, Australian Soc. Plant Physiologists. Avocations: traveling, tennis, mountaineering. Office: CSIRO Plant Industry, Private Bag #5, Wembley WA 6913, Australia

PALTA, PRABHAT, reproductive biologist, researcher; b. Hisar, India, Sept. 16, 1958; s. Randhir Singh and Krishna (Passi) P.; m. Harvinder Risma Palta, Aug. 12, 1987; 1 child, Aniruddha. MS, Nat. Dairy Rsch. Inst., Karnal, India, 1979, PhD, 1987. Scientist Indian Veterinary Rsch. Inst., Izatnagar, India, 1986-93; sr. scale scientist Nat. Dairy Rsch. Inst., Karnal, India, 1993—. Author: Radio and Enzymeimmunoassay, 1996, In Vitro Fertilization Embryo Transfer and Associated Techniques in Farm Animals, 1997; contbr. articles to profl. jours. Mem. N.Y. Acad. Scis., Soc. Biol. Chemists. Avocations: reading, writing, listening to music. Office: Embryo Biotech Ctr, Nat Dairy Rsch Inst, Karnal 132 001, India

PALTAUF, FRITZ, biochemist; b. Graz, Austria, Feb. 27, 1936; m. Henriette Bauer. PhD, U. Graz, 1963. Head dept. biochemistry Graz U. Tech., 1973—. Editor: (book) Ether Lipids, 1983, (jour.) Chemistry and Physics of Lipids, 1984—; contbr. articles to profl. jours. Mem. Austrian Biochemical. Office: Graz U Tech Dept Biochmstry, Petersgasse 12, A-8010 Graz Austria

PALTRIDGE, BRIAN RICHARD, applied linguistics educator; b. Auckland, New Zealand, May 28, 1947; arrived in Australia, 1981; s. Henry Alfred Cecil and Muriel Gertrude (Loring) P. BA, Victoria U., Wellington, New Zealand, 1981; assoc. diploma in cmty. langs., U. Western Sydney, Macarthur, Australia, 1984; grad. diploma in TESOL, U. Tech., Sydney, 1987; MA, U. Sydney, 1989; PhD, U. Waikato, New Zealand, 1994. RSA/Cambridge diploma in TEFLA; RSA/Cambridge cert. in TEFLA. ESL tchr. Australian Coll. English, 1984-88; lectr. in TESOL U. Sydney, 1989; sr. lectr. in TESOL Internat. Pacific Coll., New Zealand, 1990-91; sr. lectr. in applied linguistics U. Waikato, 1992-94, U. Melbourne, 1995-2000; prof. applied linguistics Auckland U. Tech., 2000—. Author: Genre, Frames and Writing in Research Settings Amsterdam: John Benjamins, 1997, Making Sense of Discourse Analysis, 2000; contbr. articles to profl. jours. MAK Halliday scholar Applied Linguistics Assn. Australia, 1990. Mem. TESOL, TESOL Assn. Aeotearoa New Zealand, Applied Linguistics Assn. Australia, Am. Assn. Applied Linguistics. Office: Auckland U Tech, Private Bag 92006, Auckland 1020, New Zealand

PALTRIDGE, ROSEMARY, social welfare administrator; b. Adelaide, Australia, Aug. 2, 1952; d. Ivan Josiah Castle and Betty May (Taylor) C.; m. Robert Wayne Paltridge, Dec. 19, 1970 (dec. Apr. 1995); children: Roslyn Jennifer Farley, Norman Wayne. Student, Tabor Coll. Australia Inc., 1988, 99, Adelaide Inst., 1996. Tchr. aid Trinity Christian Schs., Rosewater, South Australia, 1981-84; asst. adminstr. Hebron Christian Ctr., West Lakes, 1984-86; receptionist Coull and Prior Tax Cons., Port Adelaide, South Australia, 1986-87; missionary, acct. Christian Revival Crusade, Port Moresby, Papua New Guinea, 1989-91; coord. Crusade Mercy Ministries, Ethelton, South Australia, 1995—; advisor Australian Cambodia Overseas Support Inc., Taperoo, South Australia, 1997—; coord. humanitarian aid Overseas Pharm. Aid for Life, 1997-98; missions coord. Portside Cmty. Ch. Inc., 1998—; tchr.'s aid Trinity Christian Schs., Rosewater, South Australia, 1981-84. Com. mem. St. John's Ambulance, Port Adelaide Divsn., 1988. Mem. Asian Action Love Australia (life). Avocations: reading, relating to people, public speaking, arts and crafts, singing and music. E-mail: rosepal@senet.com.au. Office: Crusade Mercy Ministries, 1 Causeway Rd, Ethelton 5015, South Australia

PALTROW, GWYNETH, actress; b. Los Angeles, CA, Sept. 28, 1973. Appeared in films Shout, 1991, Hook, 1991, Malice, 1993, Flesh and Bone, 1993, Mrs. Parker and the Vicous Circle, 1994, Jefferson in Paris, 1995, Moonlight and Valentino, 1995, Seven, 1995, The Pallbearer, 1996, Emma, 1996, Hard Eight, 1996, Sliding Doors, 1998, (voice) Out of the Past, 1998, Duet, 1998, Great Expectations, 1998, Hush, 1998, A Perfect Murder, 1998, Shakespeare in Love, 1998, The Talented Mr. Ripley, 1999, Duets, 1999, The Intern, 2000, Bounce, 2000; TV films Cruel Doubt, 1992, Deadly Relations, 1993; theatre Picnic, The Adventures of Huck Finn, Sweet Bye and Bye, The Seagull. Won Golden Satellite Best Actress in a Motion Picture Emma, 1997, Best Actress Oscar, American Academy Awards, Shakespeare in Love, 1999; Golden Globe Awards, Best Actress, Shakespeare in Love, 1999, Best Actress FFCC, 1999. Mem. Screen Actors Guild (Outstanding Performance (with others)). Office: CAA c/o Rick Kurtzman 9830 Wilshire Blvd Beverly Hills CA 90212-1804 also: Screen Actors Guild 5757 Wilshire Blvd Los Angeles CA 90036-3635*

PALUMBO, MATTHEW ALOYSIUS, marketing executive; b. Queens, N.Y., Sept. 17, 1961; s. John Christopher and Seiko (Murakami) P. BS, Cornell U., 1986; MBA in Mktg. Mgmt., St. John's U., 1990. Mortgage clk. Salomon Bros., Inc., N.Y.C., 1986; mut. fund adminstr. Bank of N.Y. Co., Inc., N.Y.C., 1986-88; copywriter Pierce Assocs., N.Y.C., 1988-90; dir. mktg. cons. Palumbo Assocs., S.I., 1989-90; adj. prof. St. John's U., S.I., 1990; mktg. dir., copy dir. Flaghouse Inc., Mt. Vernon, N.Y., 1990-93; spl. projects mgr., group product mgr. Global Computer Supplies, Port Washington, N.Y., 1993-97; dir. product mktg. Cyberian Outpost, Kent, Conn., 1997—; guest lectr. Am. direct mktg. techniques Sheffield Halleron U. (Eng.), 1993; guest lectr. designed and acquired funding Cornell U., Ithaca, 1992—. N.Y. State Regents scholar, 1979, Annette Brodsky scholar, 1988. Mem. Am. Assn. MBA Execs., Cornell Asian Alumni Assn. (v.p. alumni affairs 1993-95), Cornell ILR Alumni, Direct Mktg. Club N.Y., Cornell Club N.Y., Cornell Club Fairfield County, Cornell U. Quadrangle Club, Beta Gamma Sigma. Avocations: reading, sports, music.

PALUMBO-FOSSATI CASA, ISABELLA, humanities educator, writer, researcher; b. Trieste, Italy, Aug. 8, 1951; arrived in France, 1977; d. Carlo Palumbo-Fossati and Sylvia Lekner; m. Jean Michel Casa, May 18, 1988; children: Mathilde, Sophie. Laurea in lettere, U. Venice, 1977; doctorate de 3rd cycle histoire, E.H. E. SS, Paris, 1982. Boursière Ecole des Hautes Etudes Scis. Sociales, Paris, 1977-78; lectr. U. Picardie, Amiens, 1978-79; asst. U. Picardie, 1982-86, maitre de confs. 2nd cloz, 1986-93, maitre de confs. 1st cloz, 1993—. Author: La casa dell'artigiano e dell'artista, 1984, Livres et lecteurs Venice, 1986, Venezia e Parigi, 1990, Istanbul et Les Langues Orientales, 1995, Gaspare Fossati, Architetto Italiano At Istanbul, 1995; contbr. articles to profl. jours. Mem. Ateneo Veneto, Deputazione Storia Patria, Fonti per La Storia Veneta, AFCA, AHAI, ARHES. Home: 28 rue Gay Lussac, 75005 Paris France Office: U Picardie, UFR de Langues, 80025 Amiens France Address: Et S Marco 2597, 30124 Venice Italy also: UFR CLERC U Picardie, Campus Univ., 80025 Amiens France

PALVA, ILMARI PELLERVO, haematologist; b. E. Pirkkala, Finland, May 5, 1932; s. Lauri Ilmari and Aili Elisabet (Tyni) P.; m. Seija Liisa Kaivola, June 9, 1956; children: Katri, Tiina, Hanna, Lauri. MD, U. Helsinki, Finland, 1956, PhD, 1962. Resident Dept. Medicine, U. Hosp., Helsinki, 1959-63, instr., 1963-64, cons., 1964-65; assoc. prof. internal medicine U. Oulu, Finland, 1965-74; prof. U. Kuopio, Finland, 1974; acting prof. med. edn. U. Tampere, Finland, 1975-76; cons. City Hosp. of Tampere, 1977-92. Author: Veritaudit, 1976, 3d edit. 1981, Guide for Evaluation in Medical Education, 1976; contbr. over 200 articles to profl. jours. Lt. Finnish Army, 1957. Decorated Knight of 1st Order of Finnish White Rose, 1986. Mem. Finnish Soc. Haematology (chmn. 1975-76, hon. mem. 1992), Internat. Soc. Haematology (coun. 1976-81), Am. Soc. Hematology, Finnish Med. Soc., Finnish Soc. Internal Medicine. Lutheran. Home: Oikotie 8A, FIN33950 Pirkkala Finland

PALYGA, STEPHEN MICHAEL, lawyer; b. Adelaide, Australia, May 8, 1954; s. Miecyslaw Boleslaw and Kathleen (Shields) P. LLB, U. Adelaide, 1975. Bar: Australia 1980. Articled clk. Gurry, Condon & Harding, Adelaide, Australia, 1979-80, solicitor, 1980-82; ptnr. Condon & Co., Adelaide, 1982-84; solicitor Lynch & Meyer, Adelaide, 1984, ptnr., 1985—; bd. dirs. Prin. Fin., Adelaide, Colleque Pty. Ltd., Adelaide, Strait Talking Pty. Ltd.; ex-officio councillor Housing Industry Assn., South Australia, 1989-95. Contbr. articles to legal publs. Mem. Law Soc. South Australia. Avocations: classic cars, motorcycles, squash, Australian rules football, rural life. Office: Lynch & Meyer, 190 Flinders St, Adelaide 5000, Australia

PÁLYI, ISTVÁN, biologist, researcher; b. Mezötur, Hungary, June 25, 1932; s. István and Jolán (Szücs) P.; m. Vilma Mária Szeidel, Sept. 29, 1962. Degree, U. Natural Scis., Szeged, Hungary, 1954; PhD, Hungarian Acad. Scis., Budapest, Hungary, 1964, DSc, 1985; univ. prof. (hon.), U. Natural Scis., Szeged, Hungary, 1988. Biological diplomate. Postdoctoral fellow Nat. Inst. Oncology, Budapest, Hungary, 1954-64, rsch. fellow, 1964-70, sr. scientist, 1970-79, dept. head, 1979—, vice dir. rsch., 1986-92, dir. rsch., 1992—; sec. sci. coun. Nat. Inst. Oncology, Budapest, 1984; prof. biology József Attila U., Szeged, 1988. Patentee in field. Nat. Ctr. Sci. Rsch. fellow, France, 1963, Internat. Union Against Cancer fellow, U.S., 1971; recipient award for sci. work Ministry of Health, Hungary, 1982. Avocations: swimming, classical music and jazz, yoga, travel. Home: Edömér u 4, 1113 Budapest Hungary Office: Nat Inst Oncology, Ráth György 7-9, 1122 Budapest Hungary

PAMAN, URBANA JOSE, linguistics educator, researcher, consultant; b. Pangasinan, The Philippines, June 1, 1939; d. Pascual Ebtil José and Cerila Sereño Apresto. BS in Edn., English and Guidance, U. of The Philippines, 1960; MA in English, TESL, Lit., U. Santo Tomas, Manila, 1971, PhD in English, 1979. Tchr. English St. Theresa's Coll., Baguio City, The Philippines, 1960-61; instr. English Siena Coll., Quezon City, The Philippines, 1961-67, La Salle Green Hills, Makati City, The Philippines, 1967-69, Far Ea. U. and U. of East, Manila, 1969-70, U. of The Philippines, Baguio City, 1970-71, Philippine Normal U., Manila, 1971-76; asst. prof. I U. of the Philippines Coll. Iloilo, 1976-79, asst. prof. IV, 1979-81, assoc. prof. I, 1981-92, assoc. prof. 2, 1992-96, assoc. prof. 3, 1996, assoc. prof. 5, 1997—; Diamond Jubilee prof. chair U. Philippines, 1984-85, Dionisia A. Rola prof. chair ni English, 1991-92, 96-98;; chmn. com. on info. and publ. UPV, reader and panel mem. Grad. Sch., 1986; chmn. UPCI-UPV Conf., 1976-78; prof. Women's Fedn. for World Peace, 1986—, chmn. com. on higher edn. U. of the Philippines Found. Inc., 1996—, rschr., project leader, 1996—. Editor 19 Manuals, 1985, 86, 87-88; co-editor CAS-ORC, 1977; contbr. articles to profl. jours. Mem. Assn. Am. Studies, Assn. Edn. in Journalism. Roman Catholic. Avocations: organ player, writing poetry, stories and technical books, interior decoration, swimming. Home: 66 Rimando Rd Baguio City, 102 Hyacinth St Gen Roxas, Quezon City The Philippines Office: Univ of The Philippines, Humanities Coll Arts Scis, 5023 Iloilo 5000, The Philippines

PAMBOU-KOMBILA, BENJAMIN, judge. Pres. Supreme Court of Gabon, Libreville. Office: Supreme Ct, BP 1043, Libreville Gabon*

PAMENSKY, JOSEPH LEON, financial executive; b. Port Elizabeth, South Africa, July 21, 1930; s. Samuel and Freda Judith (Brisk) P.; m. Pamela Hazel Goldberg, July 10, 1957; children: Martin, Beverly, Kevin. Diploma in acctg., U. Witwatersrand, Johannesburg, South Africa, 1954. Articled clk. Schwartz, Fine, Kane & Co., Johannesburg, 1949-56; exec., then mng. dir. Schlesinger Orgn., Johannesburg, 1956-76; mng. dir. Trump Orgn., Johannesburg, 1976-77; mng. dir., chmn. Internat. Fin. Svcs. (Pty) Ltd., Johannesburg, 1977—. Recipient Order of Meritorious Svc. Gold medal South African Govt., 1987. Mem. South African Inst. Chartered Accts. (Chartered Acct. of Yr. 1984), Marylebone Cricket Club (hon. life), United Cricket Bd. South Africa (hon. life), Gauteng Cricket Bd. (pres. 1996, hon. life). Jewish. Home: 27 Limpopo Rd Emmarentia, Johannesburg 2195, Republic of South Africa Office: Internat Fin Svcs Pty Ltd, 70 Fox St, Johannesburg 2001, Republic of South Africa

PAMIĆ, JAKOB JAKOB, geologist, researcher; b. Požega, Slavonija, Croatia, Sept. 10, 1928; s. Jakob Mato and Roza Mijo (Herner) P.; m. Marija Nikola Musladin, Oct. 6, 1954 (div. Dec. 1962); children: Danko, Vlatko; m. Olga Vasilij Sunarić, Feb. 12, 1965. B in Engring. Geology, Faculty of Scis., Zagreb, Croatia, 1951; PhD, U. Zagreb, 1960. Cert. engring. of geology. Tech. faculty asst. U. Sarajevo, Bosnia, 1951-60; faculty of forestry asst. prof. U. Sarajevo, 1961-78; geologist, reschr. Inst. Geology, Sarajevo, 1961-72, 72-80; sci. supr. Inst. Geology, Zagreb, 1981-95; chief geologist Inst. Geology, Sarajevo, 1971-72; vis. prof. Faculty of Sci., U. Shiraz, Iran, 1975-76; part-time prof. Faculty of Sci., U. Zagreb, 1983—. Author: Magmatic Formations of the Dinarides, 1996; contbr. articles to profl. jours. Sec. Geol. Soc. Bosnia, Sarajevo, 1954-80. Mem. Internat. Geol. Correlation Program (chmn.), Croatian Acad. Scis., Geophys. Soc. Am., Geol. Soc. Croatia. Roman Catholic. Avocations: classical music, belles letres, sport. Home: V Filakovca 1, HR-10000 Zagreb Croatia

PAMIN, DIANA DOLHANCYK (DIANA DOLHANCYK), poet; b. Cleve., Dec. 13; d. Peter and Diana (Dribes) Dolhancyk; m. Leonard Pamin, Aug. 28; children: Diana Anne, Louis Peter. Grad., Titus Coll. Cosmetology. Author: The Parting in Journey of the Mind, 1994 (Editor's Choice award), The Parting in East of the Sunrise, 1995 (Editor's Choice award), Stormy in Songs on the Wind, 1994 (Editor's Choice award), Stormy in Beyond the Stars, 1995 (Editor's Choice award), Shadow Side in At Water's Edge, 1995 (Editor's Choice award), Eclipse in A Delicate Balance, 1995 (Editor's Choice award), Burnt By Love in Windows of the Soul, 1995 (Editor's Choice award), Web of Guilt in Where Dawn Lingers, 1996 (Editor's Choice award), The View in A Muse to Follow, 1996 (Editor's Choice award), The View in Portraits of Life, 1996 (Editor's Choice award), Photographer in Fields of Gold, 1997 (Editor's Choice award), Photographer in Dappled Sunlight, 1997 (Editor's Choice award), Shadow Side II in Of Moonlight and Wishes, 1997 (Editor's Choice award), Love No More in Best Poems of 1996 (Editor's Choice award), The Happening in Best Poems of the '90s, 1997 (Editor's Choice award), Rain in Journey to Our Dreams, 1996 (Accomplishment of Merit award for Literary Achievement), CAT in Promises to Keep, 1996 (Editor's Preference award of Excellence for Lit. Achievement), CAT in Starburst Jour., Winter Wedding, in Of Sunlight and Shadows, 1997 (Editor's Preference award of Excellence for Lit. Achievement), Unrequited Love, Web of Guilt, Sighs of Love, Autumn Symphony, A Dream, Happiness, Swan Song, Lost Song, in Of Sunlight and Shadows, 1997, Red Satin Box, in The Golden Wings of Time, 1997 (Editor's Preference award of Excellence for Lit. Achievement), Snowscape, Rain, Letters, Love No More, Happiness, in Best New Poems, 1996, 10 Elite award winning poems for Lit. Excellence in The Fourth Dimension, 1998, The Swing, Seasons of Love, The Goodbye, Betrothal, Not Our Own, Association, Gypsy, Heady Lilacs, Our Enchantment, Love No More, Sea of Dreams, A Furtive Tear, The Treasure, When Lips Cared, others; Association (poem), artwork cover Starburst Jour., 1999, Sea of Dreams, Starburst Jour., 1999 (elite award lit. excellence), Winter Wedding, Winds of the Universe, You, Loves Deception, The Soothing, Caress, He in Starburst Jour., 1997, His Name is Peter, "But, Isn't The Flower Lovely?," PaPa, in the Sparrowgrass Family Poetry Album, 2000, others. Inducted Internat. Poetry Hall of Fame Mus. Mem. Internat. Soc. Poets (life), Poet's Guild, Internat. Soc. Authors and Artists, Nat. Authors Registry. Home: 6282 Akins Rd N Royalton OH 44133-4904

PAMPLIN, ROBERT BOISSEAU, JR., manufacturing company executive, minister, writer; b. Augusta, Ga., Aug. 3, 1941; s. Robert Boisseau and Mary Katherine (Reese) P.; m. Marilyn Joan Hooper; children: Amy Louise, Anne Boisseau. Student, Va. Poly. Inst., 1960-62, BS in Acctg., 1965, BS in Econs., 1966, LHD (hon.), 1995, DHL (hon.), 1995; MBA, U. Portland, 1968, LLD (hon.), 1972, MEd, 1975; MCL, Western Conservative Bapt. Sem. (name now Western Sem.), 1978, DMin, 1982, D of Sacred Letter (hon.), 1991, MA, 2000; PhD, Calif. Coast U.; DHL (hon.), Warner Pacific Coll., 1988; LLD (hon.), Western Baptist Coll., 1989; cert. in wholesale mgmt., Ohio State U., 1970; cert. labor mgmt., U. Portland, 1982; cert. in advanced mgmt., U. Hawaii, 1975; DD (hon.), Judson Baptist Coll., 1984; DBA (hon.), Marquis Giuseppe Scicluna Internat. U. Found., 1986; LittD (hon.), Va. Tech. Inst. and State U., 1987, LHD (hon.); LHD (hon.), Western Seminary, 1991; DD, Western Evang. Sem., 1994; DBA (hon.), U. S.C., 1996; D Pub. Svc. (hon.), U. Puget Sound, 1999. Pres., COO R.B. pamplin Corp., Portland, Oreg., 1964—; chmn. bd., CEO Columbia Empire Farms Inc., Lake Oswego, Oreg., 1976—, United Tile Co., Pamplin Comms., Oreg. Wilbert Vault; chmn. bd., CEO Mt. Vernon Mills Inc.,; pres., CEO Ross Island Sand & Gravel; lectr. bus. adminstrn. Lewis and Clark Coll., 1968-69; adj. asst. prof. bus. adminstrn., U. Portland, 1973-76; pastor Christ Cmty.

Ch., Lake Oswego; lectr. in bus. adminstrn. and econs. U. Costa Rica, 1968, Va. Tech. Found., 1986; chmn. bd. dirs. Christian Supplly Ctrs. Inc.; prof. with tenure U. Portland, 1999. Author: Everything is Just great, 1985, The Gift, 1986, Another Virginian: A Study of the Life and Beliefs of Robert Boisseau Pamplin, 1986, (with others) A Portrait of Colorado, 1976, Three in One, 1974, The Storybook Primer on Managing, 1974, One Who Believed, Vol. I 1988, vol. II, 1991, Climbing the Centuries, 1993, heritage the Making of an American Family, 1994, American Heroes, 1995, Prelude to Surrender, 1995; editor Oreg. Mus. Sci. and Industry Press, 1973, trustee, 1971, 74—; editor Portrait of Oregon, 1973, (with others) Oregon Underfoot, 1975. Trustee Lewis and Clark Coll., 1989—, chmn. bd. trustees, 1991; hon. life pres. Western Conservative Bapt. Sem.; chmn. regents Western Sem., 1994; mem. nat. adv. coun. on vocat. Edn., 1975—; mem. Western Interstate Com. on Higher Edn., 1981-84; co-chmn. Va. Tech. $50 Million Campaign for Excellence, 1984-87, Va. Tech. Found., 1986—, Va.-Oreg. State Scholarship Commn., 1974—, chmn. 1976-78; mem. Portland dist. adv. coun. SBA, 1973-77; mem. rewards rev. com., City of Portland, 1973-78, chmn., 1973-78; bd. regents U. Portland, 1971-79, chmn. bd., 1975-79, regent emeritus, 1979—; trustee Oreg. Episc. Schs., 1979, Linfield Coll., U. Puget Sound, 1989—; dr. pub. svc., U. Puget Sound, 1999. Recipient Disting. Alumnus award Lewis and Clark Coll., 1974, ROTC Disting. Svc. award USAF, 1974, Albert Einstein Acad. bronze medal, 1986, Disting. Leadership medal Freedoms Found., Disting. Bus. Alumnus award U. Portland, 1990, Nat. Caring award Caring Inst., 1991, Pride of Portland award Portland Lions Club, Hero Ath,E,lete award 1994, Herman Lay Entrepreneurship award, 1995, Thomas Jeffersonard Oreg. Hist. Soc. 1998, Aubrey R. Watzek award Lewis and Clark Coll., 1998, Leadership award Portland Living Mag., 1998 ; named Outstanding Philanthropist of Yr. award Nat. Soc. Fund Raising Execs., 1997, Textile World's Top 10, 1999, Portland First Citizen, Portland Met. Assn. Realtors, 1999; Va. Tech. Coll. Bus. Adminstrn. renamed R.B. Pamplin Coll. Bus. Adminstrn. in his honor; Western Conservative Bapt. Sem. Lay Inst. for Leadership, Edn. Devel. and Rsch. named for R.B. Pamplin Jr., 1988. Mem. Acad. Mgmt., Delta Epsilon Sigma, Beta Gamma Sigma, Sigma Phi Epsilon, Waverley Country Club, Arlington, Multnomah Athletic Club, Capitol Hill Club, Greenville Country Club, Poinsett Club, Eldorado Country Club, Thunderbird Country Club, Rotary. Republican. Episcopalian. Office: RB Pamplin Corp Inc 900 SW 5th Ave Ste 1800 Portland OR 97204-1259

PAN, CHENG-LIEH, management executive, educator; b. Changzhou, Jiangsu, China, June 30, 1928; s. Cun-Cui Pan and May-Yin Xue; m. Jia-Fang Fu, Apr. 26, 1961; children: Pan Qi, Pan Wei. BS, Tsing Hna U., Beijing, 1950. Indsl. engr. First Auto Works, Chang Chun, China, 1955-72; asst. to Prof. Hue Loo-Keng (v.p. Chinese Acad. Sci.) Chinese Acad. Sci., China, 1972-79; dep. dir. Inst. Econs. and Mgmt., State Econ. Commn., China, 1982-85; dep. dir.-gen. China Enterprise Mgmt. Cons. Co., Beijing, 1980—, pres., 1984-91; vis. prof. U. N.S.W., Australia, 1986. Author: Corporate Strategy & Entrepreneurship, 1986, spl. paper on XX World Mgmt. Congress (CIOS) congl. summit mtg., In Search of Chinese Style of Management, Kuala Lumpur, Malaysia, 1985; contbr. articles to profl. jours. Co-sponsor China Bus. Summit with world econ. forum, Beijing, 1981-96, China-Australia Sr. Exec. forum, China, Australia (altenately), 1983-95. Rsch. fellow (hon.) U. Birmingham, Eng., 1979. Avocations: classical chinese poetry, classical music, photography. Office: China Enterprise Mgmt Assn, 17 Zizhuyuan Nanlu, Beijing 100044, China

PAN, CYNTHIA X., geriatrician, educator, researcher; b. Taipei, Taiwan, Aug. 17, 1965; d. James T.M. pan and Hsiang Yu; m. Darrell C. Sandel. BA, Harvard/Radcliffe U., 1987; MD, SUNY, Stony Brook, 1992. Diplomate Am. Bd. Internal Medicine. Asst. prof. in geriatrics, dir. edn. palliative care program Mt. Sinai Sch. Medicine, N.Y.C., 1997—. Mem. AMA, ACP, Am. Geriatrics Soc. (com. mem.), Am. Acad. Hospice and Palliative Medicine. Avocations: swing dancing, movies, travel. E-mail: cynthia.pan@mssm.edu. Office: Mount Sinai Sch Medicine PO Box 1070 New York NY 10029-0310

PAN, DON XIAO DONG, engineering company executive, consultant; b. Shanghai, China, Sept. 11, 1955; arrived in Eng., 1985; s. Chen Liang Pan and Hui Zhen Zhang; m. Min Yu, Apr. 17, 1983; 1 child. BSc, Tongji U., Shanghai, 1982, MSc, 1985; PhD Royal Sch. Mines, Imperial Coll., London, 1988; sr. mgmt. program, Cranfield (Eng.) U., 1998. Cert. engr. Asst. lectr. Tongji U., 1982-85; rsch. fellow Brunel U., London, 1989-90; engr. Sir William Halcrow & Ptnrs. Ltd., London, 1990-92, sr. engr., 1993-95; prin. engr., dir. Halcrow Asia Partnership Ltd., Hong Kong, 1995-99; dir. Halcrow Group Ltd., London and Hong Kong, 1999—; bd. dirs. Halcrow China Ltd., Hong Kong; chief rep. Halcrow Shenzhen Office, China, 1997-99; mng. dir. Halcrow China Ltd., Hong Kong, 2000—. Mem. steering com. Hong Kong Jocky Club Landslip and Land Devel. Ctr., 1998-99. Steven and Anna Hui fellow Imperial Coll., 1985-88. Mem. Inst. Mining and Metallurgy, Hong Kong Instn. Engrs. (com. mem. geotech. divsn. 1997-99). Avocations: wine, hiking, swimming. Office: Halcrow China Ltd 23/F, Central Plz 18 Harbour Rd, Wan Chai Hong Kong

PAN, FEIXIA, aeronautical engineeer; b. Songmen, Zhejiang, China, Oct. 30, 1963; came to U.S., 1992; d. Juhan and Shaoxiu (Jiang) P.; m. Weiquan Zhao, Mar. 14, 1992; 1 child, Jalen Zhao. BS, Nanjing U., 1984, MS, 1987; PhD, U. Nebr., 1996. Aircraft design engr. Shanghai Aircraft Rsch. Inst., 1987-92; tchg. asst. U. Nebr., Lincoln, 1992-97; rsch. staff Xerox Wilson Rsch. Ctr., Webster, N.Y., 1997—. Contbr. articles to profl. jours. E-mail: fpan@wrc.xerox.com.

PAN, HENRY YUE-MING, clinical pharmacologist; b. Shanghai, Dec. 27, 1946; came to U.S. 1969; s. Chia-Liu and Siu-Ging (Sung) P.; m. Mary Agnes Tse; children: Lincoln Jonathan, Gregory Kingsley. BSc (hon.), McGill U., Montreal, 1969; MS in Toxicology, U. Hawaii, 1973, PhD in Pharmacology, 1974; MD, U. Hong Kong, 1979. Rsch. asst. U. Hawaii, Honolulu, 1969-74, tchg. asst., 1970-74; med. officer Queen Mary Hosp., Hong Kong, 1979-81; asst. prof. medicine U. Hong Kong, 1981-85; vis. asst. prof. Stanford (Calif.) U., 1983-85; from asst. clin. pharmacology dir. to exec. dir. clin. rsch. Squibb Inst. Med. Rsch., Princeton, N.J., 1985-91; v.p. clin. rsch. Bristol-Myers Squibb Pharm. Rsch. Inst., Princeton, 1991-92; v.p. clin. R & D DuPont Merck Pharm. Co., Wilmington, Del., 1992-93, sr. v.p. drug devel., 1993-96; exec. v.p. R & D DuPont Merck Pharm. Co., 1996-97; pres. MDS Pharm. Svcs., 1997-99; pres., CEO, mng. ptnr. Integrated Drug Devel. Svcs. and Pharmacologics, LLC, 1998-2000; mng. dir. incuVest, LLC, N.Y.C., 2000—; dir. BioDesign, Inc., Springface, LLC, Predict, Inc., PanLabs internat., Inc., MDS Capital Corp., MDS SCI, Pharm. Devel. Corp., Proband, Inc., PharmaVentures (USA), Inc.; chmn. EastWest Pharm. Internat. LLC. Contbr. articles to profl. jours. Stanford Asian Med. Fund grant, 1983-85. Fellow Am. Coll. Clin. Pharmacology, Am. Heart Assn. Coun., Am. Coll. Cardiology, Acad. Medicine N.J., Inst. Biol. and Clin. Investigation; mem. AAAS, AMA, Am. Assn. Pharm. Scientists, Am. Soc. Clin. Pharmacology and Therapeutics, Am. Soc. for Pharmacology and Exptl. Therapeutics, Am. Fedn. Med. Rsch., Drug Info. Assn., Am. Coll. Clin. Pharmacology, Am. Heart Assn., Am. Coll. Cardiology. Roman Catholic. Avocations: tennis, golf, distance running, cycling, baseball. Office: incuVest LLC 590 Madison Ave New York NY 10022

PAN, HUO-HSI, mechanical engineer, educator; b. Fuzhou, Peoples Republic of China, Nov. 11, 1918; came to the U.S., 1948; s. Bai-ming and Won-ching (Chen) P.; m. Chao Pan, June 4, 1960; children: Lillian, Nina. BS in Mech. Engring., Nat. S.W. Associated U., Kunming, Peoples Republic of China, 1943; MS in Mech. Engring., Tex. A&M U., 1949; MS in Applied Mechanics, Kans. State Coll., 1950; PhD, U. Calif., Berkeley, 1954. Asst. engr. Yunnan Smelting Plant, Peoples Republic of China, 1942-43; from mem. tech. staff to head inspection dept. 21st Arsenal, Peoples Republic of China, 1943-47; from teaching asst. to assoc. mech. engring. U. Calif., Berkeley, 1950-53; rsch. engr. Portland Cement Assn., 1954; asst. prof. U. Toledo, 1954-55, U. Ill., Champaign, 1955-57; asst. prof. engring. mechanics NYU, 1957-59, from asst. prof. to prof. applied mechanics, 1957-73; prof. applied mechanics, mech. engring. Poly. U., 1973-90, prof. emeritus, 1990—; cons. Frankford Arsenal, Picatinny Arsenal, Petro-Chem Devel. Co.; referee Jour. Applied Mechanics, AIAA Jour., Internat. Jour. Mech. Sci., Internat. Jour. Solid and Structures, NSF; reviewer Applied Mechanics Revs.; sect. chmn. Internat. Modal Analysis Confs.; lectr. Kunming Inst. Tech., Tsinghua U., Jilin U. Tech., Jilin U., 1984. Contbr. numerous articles to Jour. Applied Mechanics, AIAA Jour., Jour. Mecanique, Jour. Engring. Mechanics, Jour. Applied Math. and Physics, Quar. Jour. Mechanics and Applied Math., Quar. Applied Math., Internat. Jour. Mech. Sci., Bull. Acad. Polonaise des Scis., Jour. Sound and Vibration, many others. Grantee NSF, 1964-67, NASA, 1966-68. Mem. ASME, AIAA, Am. Acad. Mechanics, Soc. Engring. Sci., Soc. for Indsl. and Applied Math., U.S. Assn. for Computational Mechanics, Internat. Assn. for Computational Mechanics, Phi Kappa Phi, Sigma Xi, Tau Beta Pi, Pi Tau Sigma, Pi Mu Epsilon. Achievements include development of method for reduction of vibrational systems, general method of modal analysis, solution for ordinary differential equation containing symbolic functions, eigenfunction expansion method in vibration problems of viscoelestic bodies. Home: 76 Edgars Ln Hastings Hdsn NY 10706-1137 Office: Poly U Dept Mech Engring 6 Metrotech Ctr Brooklyn NY 11201-3840

PAN, I. HUNG, microbiologist, geneticist; b. Taipei, China, Sept. 24, 1922; s. Nai Teh and Tson (Chien) P.; m. Lu Chin Huang, Dec. 24, 1956; children: Fu-Shih, Fu-Tao, Yoko Homma, Fu-Dy. MD, Kyoto (Japan) U., 1947, DMS, 1956. Intern Tokyo City Okubo Hosp., 1947-48; pvt. practice Osaka, Japan, 1948-51; rsch. fellow Osaka City Med. Sch., 1951-56; from instr. to prof. Nat. Taiwan U., Taipei, 1956-88; pres. emeritus The Chinese Soc. of Genetics, 1988—; dept. chmn. Nat. Taiwan U., Taipei, 1975-76; vis. prof. Osaka City U. Med. Sch., 1979-80, 92-94; v.p. Internat. Conf. Genetics, Beijing, 1998; lectr. in field. Contbr. articles to profl. jours. Rsch. fellow Harvard U. Sch. Pub. Health, Boston, 1964-66. Mem. AAAS, Chinese Soc. Genetics (pres. 1987-93), Genetics Soc. Korea (hon.), Soc. for Exptl. Biology and Medicine, Chinese Soc. Microbiology, Transplantation Soc. the Republic of China, Formosan Med. Assn. Buddhist. Avocations: walking, watches, classical music, travel. Fax: 886-2-2521-6120. Office: Nat Taiwan U Coll Medicine, No 1 Jen AI Rd Sec 1, 10018 Taipei China

PAN, JIXING, science history educator; b. Beizhen City, Liaoning, China, July 27, 1931; s. Guocheng Pan and Yuxiu Li; m. Dayan Li, Mar. 21, 1997. Grad. in chem. tech., Dalian (China) U. Tech., 1954, grad. in fgn. langs., 1957. Vis. prof. U. Pa., Phila., 1981-82; Bye fellow Robinson Coll., U. Cambridge, Eng., 1982; prof. Inst. History of Sci. Chinese Acad. Sci., Beijing; vis. prof. Inst. for Humanistic Studies, Kyoto (Japan) U., 1986-87; part-time prof. Dalian (China) U. Tech., 1984-87. Author: History of Papermaking Technology in China, 1979 (1st class award 1989), Collation, Explanation and Research of the Tiangong Kaiwu (Exploitation of the Works of Nature), 1989 (1st class award), Critical Biography of Song Yingxing, A Thinker and Scientist of the 17th Century, 1991 (2d class award); editor-in-chief: Collected Papers of Joseph Needham, 1986 (1st class award 1989). Mem. Internat. Assn. Paper Historians, China Soc. History Sci. (mem. coun. 1980-89), Internat. Acad. History Sci. (corr.). Avocations: western classical music, Peking opera, collecting books, bookbinding. Home: 10-509 Yong-an nan-li, Jianwai Beijing 100022, China Office: Inst History of Sci, 137 Chao-nei St, Beijing 100010, China

PAN, JUNZHENG, agricultural engineering educator; b. Shanghai, China, Dec. 25, 1922; s. Shuxun and Muyin (Fan) P.; m. Ninmei Ke, Apr. 4, 1951; children: Yongkong, Yongxin. BSc, Jiaotong U., Shanghai, 1946. Engr. S.W. Metal Works, Shanghai, 1946-48; mem. China Merchants Navigation Corp., Shanghai, 1948-49; engr. N.E. China Electric Industry Adminstrn., Mukden, 1949-50; lectr., asst. prof. Nanking U./Nanjing (China) Agrl. Coll., 1950-70; asst. prof., prof. Zhenjiang (China) Inst. Agrl. Machinery, 1970-80, 85; prof. dean Nanjing Agrl. U., 1985-90. Author: (with Lee) Agricultural Rheology, 1990; contbr. articles to profl. jours.; inventor chain-paddle drive for wetland. Dep. Jiangsu Provincial Congress, 1964—, 78-87, Nat. Congress China, Beijing, 1988-92; counsellor Jiangsu Provincial Govt., Nanjing, 1991-96. Cpl. Chinese Army, 1945. Recipient govt. spl. grant State Coun., Beijing, 1991, Sci. and Tech. Process awards Nat. Edn. Com., Beijing, 1997. Mem. Internat. Soc. Terrain-Vehicle Systems, Internat. Commn. Agrl. Engring., Jiangsu Soc. Agrl. Engring. (v.p. 1986-93), Chinese Soc. Agrl. Engring. (dir. 1988-95). Mem. Democratic League China. Avocations: Chinese chess, contract bridge. Office: Agrl Engring Coll NAU, 40 Dian Jiang Tai Rd Puzhen, Nanjing 210032, China

PAN, LUNG KWANG, educator; b. Keelung, Taiwan, May 13, 1959; s. Zie Ren Pan and Mei Yui Tsai; m. Szu Ru Yu, Oct. 25, 1985; children: Ker-Wei, Ker-Arn. BS, Chung Cheng Inst. Tech., Tashi, Taiwan, 1981; MSc, Nat. Tsing Hua (Taiwan) U., 1985; PhD, Ga. Inst. Tech., 1997. Tchr. asst. Chung Cheng Inst. Tech., 1981-83, lectr., 1985-91, assoc. prof., 1991-2000, prof., 2000—; referee Nat. Bu. Stds., Taipei, 1997; cons. Navtek, Chung Her, 2000,. Col. Taiwanese Army, 1970. Recipient award for excellent rsch. Nat. Sci. Coun. Taiwan, 1992. Mem. People's First Party. Avocations: swimming, badminton. Fax: 886-3-389-1519. E-mail: lkpan@ccit.edu.tw. Home: 3d Fl, No 32, Ln 10, Yung Li Rd, Yung Her, Taipei 234, Taiwan Office: Chung Cheng Inst Tech, Yuan Chul Lin, Taoyuan Tashi 335, Taiwan

PAN, PING-QI, mathematician; b. PingLiang, Gansu, China, Aug. 28, 1942; s. Chao and Yi-Yun (Yan) P.; m. Ming-Hua Jiang, Oct. 12, 1972; 1 child, Yun-Peng. BSc, Lanzhou U., China, 1967; MSc, Nanjing U., 1982. Engr. Jinling Shipyard, Nanjing, 1967-78; tutor Nanjing Forestry U., 1981-82, lectr., 1982-86, assoc. prof., 1986-93, prof., 1993-94; prof. Southeast U., Nanjing, 1994—. Contbr. articles to profl. jours. Mem. Chinese Math Soc., Chinese Ops. Rsch. Soc., Chinese Soc. Math. Prog. (coun. mem. 1994—). Office: Southeast Univ, Dept Applied Math, Nanjing 210096, China

PAN, TZU-MING, biotechnologist; b. Ching-Shui, Taiwan, Republic of China, Jan. 9, 1947; s. Wan-Chih and Teng (Yang) P.; m. Mei-Lan Chang, Dec. 25, 1973; children: Chia-Ying, Chia-Yu, Chia-Yueh. BS, Nat. Taiwan U., 1969, MS, 1972, PhD, 1978. Assoc. prof. Chinese Culture U., Taipei, 1978-82, prof., 1982-93, chmn., dir., 1988-92; prof. Yang-Ming U., 1980-94, Nat. Taiwan U., 1995—; chief divsn. bacteriology Nat. Inst. Preventive Medicine, Taipei, 1993-98; com. of patent screening Ministry of Econ. Affairs, Taipei, Taiwan, 1987—, com. of waste reduction task force, 1991—; com. of standard method EPA, Republic of China, 1990—;. Author: Organic Chemistry, 1984, Experiment in cHemistry, 1984, 86, 94, 96, 98, Experiment in Organic Chemistry, 1990, 96, 99, Preventive Medicine, 1995-99. Recipient Award of Rsch. and Writings Ministry of Edn., 1977, 79, Outstanding Tchrs. award, 1989, Youth Medal award Ministry of Youth, 1978, Outstanding Teaching Material award Ministry of Edn., 1992. Mem. Chinese Biochem. Soc., Chinese Tchrs. Assn. (exec. dir.), Biotech. Indsl. Assn. (exec. dir.), Chinese Agrl. Chem. Assn. (exec. dir.), Am. Chem. Soc., Am. Soc. Microbiology. Achievements include research on new recovery method of glutamic acid using ion-exchange resin, new microorganism to produce dedecanedic acid from n-dodecane, new microorganism to produce vitamin B12 from methanol, method of immobilization of papain and bromelain for beer chill-proffing, Lyme and Legionnaires' diseases in Taiwan, bioreagent for wastewater of papermaking industry, treatment of wastewater of food factory with microorganisms; production of vitamin B2 by microorganism; food poisoning in Taiwan area; rapid identification method of Salmonella typhi; detection of Legionella in environment; characteristics of Bordetalla pertussis isolated in Taiwan; determination of methyl mercury in fish and shellfish; production of rosmarinic acid with cell culture; production of monacolin K and GABA from Monascus anka; determination of E. coli 0157:H7 with PCR. Office: Nat Taiwan U, 1 Roosevelt Rd Sec 4, Taipei Taiwan 106, Taiwan

PAN, WYNN HWAI-TZONG, neuropharmacology educator, neurochemist; b. Taipei, Taiwan, July 2, 1961; s. Li Ming and Shio Chin (Chuang) P.; m. Angel Chin-Lien Yu, June 18, 1988; children: Roman, Roy. BS in Chemistry, Soochow U., Taipei, 1983; PhD, Emory U., 1990. Rsch. asst. Ctrs. for Disease Control, Atlanta, 1986-90; sr. scientist Schering-Plough Corp., Kenilworth, N.J., 1990-91; assoc. prof. neuropharmacology Nat. Yang Ming U., Taipei, 1991-97, prof., 1997—, dir. Instrumentation Ctr., 1995-98; secretariat Yang-Ming Med. U., 1998-99; invited lectr., Taiwan, U.S.A., Shanghai; lectr. in field. Reviewer Jour. Pharm. Sci., Chinese Jour. Physics, Jour. Food and Drug Analysis, Am. Chem. Soc. Symposium Series, proposals for Nat. Sci. Coun. (Taiwan), Nat. Rsch. Inst. Chinese Medicine; author over 40 publs. and rsch. papers on neuropharmacology and neuroscience in sci. jours. world-wide. Mem. Am. Chem. Soc., Soc. for Neurosci., Soc. for Pharmacology, Soc. for Physics (Taiwan), N.Y. Acad. Scis., Toastmasters Internat., Motor Neuron Disease Assn. (sec. in gen. 1999—, nat. asseblyman 1996—). Home: Fu-Jir Rd, 2F 21, Alley 7, Ln 14, Shih-lin, Taipei Taiwan Office: Nat Yang Ming U, Inst Pharmacology, Taipei 11221, Taiwan

PANAGIOTOU, GEORGE NICOLAS, mining engineering educator; b. Piraeus, Greece, Apr. 12, 1955; s. Nicolas and Maria (Sdralia) P.; m. Olga Matsouki, Sept. 5, 1991; 1 child, Mariella. Diploma in engring., Nat. Tech. U. Athens, 1978; MS, U. Newcastle, Eng., 1979; PhD, Nat. Tech. U. Athens, 1989. Cert. engr. Sci. assoc. Nat. Tech. U. Athens, 1980-89, lectr., 1989-92, asst. prof., 1992-98, assoc. prof., 1998—; presenter in field. Editor: Mine Simulation, 1997, Information Technologies in the Minerals Industry, 1998, Mine Planning and Equipment Selection, 2000; contbr. articles to profl. jours. Mem. AIME, Soc. Mining Engring., Internat. Soc. for Rock Mechanics, Internat. Soc. Computer Simulation, Internat. Sailing Fedn. (constn. com. 1986—), N.Y. Acad. Scis. Avocation: yacht racing. Home: 10 Korai St N Smyrni, GR-17122 Athens Greece Office: Nat Tech U Athens Dept Min-, Engring/Zographou Campus, GR-15780 Athens Greece

PANAGOPOULOS, PANAGIOTIS, political scientist; b. Athens, Aug. 8, 1970; s. Vasilios and Maria (Nieder) P. BA, McGill U., Montreal, Can., 1994; M in Internat. Studies, U. Birmingham, 1995. Rschr. Inst. for German Studies, Birmingham, Eng., 1995-97; lectr., rschr. Aalborg (Denmark) U., 1997-2000; conf. prodr. defense SMi, London, 2000; conf. mgr. Euromoney Instnl. Investor, London, 2000; conf. prodr. IBC Global Confs., London, 2000—; spkr. in field. Mem. editl. bd. Rsch. Inst. Internat. and European Studies, 1995—; contbr. articles to profl. jours. Rsch. grantee Inst. for German Studies, 1995-97, Aalborg U., 1997-00. Mem. U. Birmingham Alumni Assn., McGill U. Alumni Assn. Avocations: organizing conferences, languages. Office: IBC Global Confs, 37-41 Mortimer St, London W1T 3JH, United Kingdom

PANANGATTU, VISWANATHAN HAREESH KUMAR, oceanographer; b. Ernakulam, India, Mar. 20, 1961; s. Viswanathan and Amma (Lakshmikutti) P.; m. Hareesh Beena, Aug. 17, 1988; two children. BSc, Kerala U., 1981; MSc, Cochin U., 1984, PhD, 1994. Scientist Naval Phys. & Oceanographic Lab., Cochin, India, 1985—. Home: Geetham Kothakulangara, Angamaly, 683572 Ernakulam India

PANAS, RAYMOND MICHAEL, pharmaceutical researcher; b. Titusville, Pa., Sept. 12, 1963; s. Michael William and Shirley Jean (Sorrell) P. BS, U. Pitts., 1986, MPH, 1991. Rsch. supr. Montefiore Hosp., Pitts., 1988-89; microbiologist Allegheny County Pub. Health Labs., Pitts., 1989-95; sr. clin. rsch. assoc. ClinTrials Rsch., Research Triangle Park, N.C., 1995-99, TAP Holdings, Inc., Deerfield, Ill., 1999—; adj. prof. C.C. Allegheny County, Pitts., 1993-95. Author: AIDS Counseling and Testing: The Concepts, 1991. Mem. Renaissance City Choir, v.p., 1992-95. Mem. APHA, Am. Soc. Clin. Pathologist (cert.), Assn. Clin. Rsch. Profls. (cert.). Republican. Catholic. Avocations: swimming, racquetball, singing, rollerblading. Home: 5320 N Kenmore Ave Unit D Chicago IL 60640-2487 Office: TAP Pharm Products Inc 675 N Field Dr Lake Forest IL 60045-4832

PANASOFF, JOSEF HUGO, allergist; b. Parana, Argentina, Nov. 14, 1955; arrived in Israel, 1979; s. Aron and Regina (Frenkel) P.; m. Elisabeth Stibbe, Oct. 23, 1980; children: Shai, Adi, Itai, Michal. MD, U. Buenos Aires, 1978; splst. in internal medicine, Rambam Med. Ctr., Haifa, Israel, 1988; specialist in allergy/clin. immunology, B'nai-Zion Med. Ctr., Haifa, Israel, 1993. Resident Rambam Med. Ctr., 1981-87; staff Lin Med. Ctr., Haifa, 1988—; resident B'nai-Zion Med. Ctr., 1991-93; staff Rakhati Med. Ctr., Allergy Dept., Tiberias, Israel, 1988—; staff Degani Med. Ctr., Hadera, Israel, 1994—. Contbr. numerous articles to med. jours. Fellow Israeli Soc. Allergy and Clin. Immunology, European Acad. Allergy and Clin. Immunology. Avocations: reading, electronic organ playing. Office: Lin Med Ctr Allergy Dept, 35 Rostchild Ave, 35152 Haifa Israel

PANAWIDAN, HADJI HASAN ADIONG, university chancellor, foundation administrator; b. Ditsaan-Ramain, The Philippines, June 12, 1942; s. Aguam Barodi and Naima (Adiong) P.; m. Faidah Adiong, Sept. 28, 1968; children: Casan A. Jr., Faizah A., Hamdanie A. BBA, U. of East, Manila, 1963; MBA, Internat. Acad. Econs. & Mgmt., Manila, 1989. CPA. Clk. Mindanao State U., Marawi City, Philippines, 1964-65, acct., 1965-67, chief acct., 1968-76; fin. dir. Mindanao State U., Marawi City, The Philippines, 1990-92, chancellor I, 1992—; chief acct. Mindanao State U.-Iligan (The Philippines) Inst. Tech., 1976-89; pres. Muslim Mindanao Agr. Indsl. Devel. Corp., Marawi City, 1970-80, Islamic Libr. Found., Marawi City, 1980-90, Kharonisha Devel. Found., Marawi City, 1990-92; chmn. Ditsaan-Livelihood Multi-Purpose Coop., Marawi City, 1992—. Dir. Ansarol Islam, Marawi City, 1965. Lt. col. The Philippines mil., 1992—. Recipient gold medals Jamiatul Philippines Al-Islamia, 1959, 64, cert. of appreciation Colombo Plan Staff Coll., Singapore, 1979, profl. achievement award Media for Devel. & Progress Inc., Quezon City, Philippines, 1992. Mem. Philippine Inst. CPAs (cert. 1964), Asian Inst. Mgmt. Alumni Assn. (cert. 1976), U. East Alumni Assn. (cert. 1963), Lions (dir. 1970, cert. of merit 1975), Rotary (dir. 1976, Presdl. Plaque of Merit 1980), Jammah Tableegh. Lakas. Islam. Avocations: swimming, jogging, reading, exercising, golf. Home: Raya Saduc, Marawi City 9700, Philippines Mailing Address: PO Box 5580, Iligan City 9200, Philippines Office: Mindanao State U, Campus, Marawi City Philippines

PANAYEAS, SOTIRIOS GEORGE, flying surgeon, pathologist; b. St. Nikon, Greece, Dec. 8, 1936; s. George Nick and Stavroula Petez (Moundreas) P.; m. Vasiliki Nick Grammi, Sept. 22, 1975; children: Vanessa, Nick. Pathologist Evangelismos Hosp., Athens, 1980-83; pathologist, dir. 251st Air Forces Hosp., Athens, 1973-75; rschr., pathologist histology dept. Greek Social Security Found., Athens, 1975—; founder, 1st dir. Pathology Dept. Air Forces Hosp., 1973-75. Contbr. articles to profl. jours. Founder Greek Polit. Party Justice, Right Here, Right Now, Athens, 1985. Maj. Greek Air Forces, 1962-79. U. Athens pathology scholar, 1964, 67-71. Mem. Hellenic Assn. Study Med. Edn., Internat. Acad. Pathology (Hellenic divsn.), World Assn. Sarcoidosis and Other Granulomatous Disorders. Greek Orthodox. Avocations: literature, photography, travel, mountain climbing, swimming. Office: Greek Social Security Found, 181 Pireos Str, 11853 Athens Greece

PANAYI, GABRIEL STAVROS, medical educator; b. Nov. 9, 1940. BA with honors, U. Cambridge, Eng., 1962, MB, 1965, MD, 1972. House physician Queen Elizabeth II Hosp., Welwyn Garden City, Eng., 1965-66; med. rsch. coun. jr. fellow Kennedy Inst. Rheumatology Cen. Middlesex Hosp., London, 1967-69; house surgeon St. Mary's Hosp., London, 1966; sr. house officer in pathology Cen. Hosp., Nottingham, Eng., 1966, Cen. Middlesex Hosp., London, 1967; clin. rsch. fellow arthritis and rheumatism coun. diseases Northern Gen. Hosp., Edinburgh, Eng., 1970-73; lectr. in rheumatology dept. of medicine Guy's Hosp., London, 1973-76, sr. lectr., cons. arthritis and rheumatism coun. dept., 1976-80, prof. arthritis and rheumatism coun., chair rheumatology, 1980—; lectr. in field. Mem. editorial bd. Brit. Jour. Rheumatology, Clin. and Exptl. Immunology, Scandinavian Jour. Rheumatology, Scandinavian Jour. Immunology, Clin. Rheumatology, Jour. of Rheumatology, Clin. and Exptl. Rheumatology.; referee The Lancet, The New Eng., Jour. of Medicine, Arthritis and Rheumatism, Annals of Rheumatic Diseases; contbr. numerous articles to profl. jours. Recipient Margaret Holroyde prize Heberden Soc., 1975, Allessandro Robecci prize European League Against Rheumatism, 1979, Ballabio prize Italian Soc. Rheumatology. Mem. Am. Coll. Rheumatology, Brit. Soc. Immunology, Biochem. Soc., Brit. Soc. Rheumatology (past mem. exec. com., Heberden Orator 1992), Royal Soc. Medicine (past hon. sec. sect. of medicine, exptl. medicine and therapeutics 1977-79, libr. rep. sect. allergy and clin. immunology 1988-90, pres. sect. allergy and clin. immunology 1993-95), Greek Rheumatology Soc. (hon.), Italian Rheumatology Soc. (hon.). Achievements include research in the diagnosis and management of inflammatory joint diseases. Office: Guys Hosp, Rheum Dept GKT Sch Medicine, 5th Fl Thomas Guy House, London SE1 9RT, England

PANAYIOTIS, CHINAS, school psychologist, consultant; b. Cyprus, July 19, 1948; arrived in Greece, 1982; BA in Psychology, U. Lyon, France, 1974; degree in psychology, U. Paris V, 1979, Diplome Etudes Approfondies, 1980; Diplome Etudes Superieures Specialisees, Inst. Psychology, France, 1981. Asst. child and family welfare Social Svcs., Cyprus, 1975-76; rsch. exec. Middle East Rsch. Bur., Cyprus, 1976-78; counsellor office for adult

edn. Ministry of Edn., Athens, 1983-84; dir. dept. spl. edn. svc. Mental Health Ctr., Athens, 1984-89; sch. psychologist Exptl. Spl. Sch. Maraslio Didaskalio Dimotikis Ekpedeusis-Tchrs. Coll., 1989—; tchr. psychology and spl. edn. Sch. Social Work, IAKE, Athens, 1982-85; tchr. psychology and group work Sch. of Nurses, PIKPA, 1983-85; dir. specialization courses, social educator and spl. needs Ministry of Youth, CEE, 1986-89; coord. seminars and workshops on spl. needs Dist. Pieria, Greece, 1985; spl. edn. coord. Best Buddies U. Athens, 1993-96; v.p. coun. Nat. Welfare Orgn. for the Child and Mother, Athens, 1993-96; mem. commn. for reform of spl. edn. Ministry of Edn., 1994; mem. commn. for tng. needs and the devel. of social svcs. Ministry of Health and Social Svcs., 1997-99. Editor, translator; contbr. articles to profl. jours. Mem. Assn. Greek Psychologists, Internat. Sch. Psychology Assn., Am. Soc. for Quality Control, Greek Assn. Sch. Psychologists (founding mem., pres. 2000—). E-mail: chinas@iname.com. Home: Antifanous 3, 15773 Athens Greece

PANAYIOTOU, BARNABAS NICOS, consultant physician, educator; b. Nicosia, Cyprus, June 17, 1959; arrived in Eng., 1974; s. Nicos and Machi (Constantinou) P.; m. Sandra Panayiotou. B Med. Sci. with honors, Nottingham (Eng.) U., 1981, BMBS, 1983; MD, Keele (Eng.) U., 1999. Registrar Gen. Hosp., Bolton, Eng., 1988-90; sr. registrar Gen. Hosp., Barnet, Eng., 1990-91; rsch. registrar Gen. Hosp., Leicester, Eng., 1991-93; sr. registrar Manor Hosp., Walsall, Eng., 1993-94, City Gen. Hosp., Stoke-on-Trent, Eng., 1994-96; cons. Manor Hosp., Walsall, 1996—; sr. clin. lectr. Geriatrics Dept. Keele U. Contbr. articles to profl. jours., chpt. to book. Master Royal Coll. Physicians; mem. Brit. Med. Assn., Med. Rsch. Soc., Brit. Geriatrics Soc., Royal Coll. Physicians Eng. Greek Orthodox. Office: Manor Hosp, Elderly Care Dept, South Wing, Walsall WS2 9PS, England

PANAYIOTOU, GEORGHIOS S., economist, researcher; b. Peyia, Paphos, Cyprus, Dec. 12, 1937; s. Sophoclis and Pelaghia (Agathangelou) P.; m. Nina Chr. Galanou, Sept. 27, 1966; children: Christos, Sophoclis. Diploma in teaching, Tchr.'s Coll., Nicosia, Cyprus, 1958; BS in Agr., A.U.B., Beirut, 1971; MS in Agrl. Econs., Md. U., 1977; BA in Econs., Grad. Sch. Econ. Scis. and Bus, Athens, Greece, 1981. Tchr. elem. Ministry of Edn., Paphos, 1958-67; tchr. Ministry of Edn., Limassol, Cyprus, 1971-74; agrl. rsch. officer Ministry of Agr. & Natural Resources, Nicosia, 1974-92; rschr. Agrl. Rsch. Inst., Nicosia, 1975-95, sr. agrl. rsch. officer, 1995; cons. FAO/ESCWA, Sanaa, 1983; counsellor permanent delegation Rep. Cyprus to European Cmtys., Brussels, 1993-98; counsellor European Union affairs Ministry Agr., Natural Resources and Environment, Nicosia, 1998-2000. Contbr. articles to profl. jours. Mem. exec. coun. Pancyprian Trade Union Civil Servants, Nicosia, 1980-86. Mem. Pancyprian Union Agriculturists, Pancyprian Union Economists. Avocations: beekeeping, gardening, stamp and coin collecting. Office: Agrl Rsch Inst, Nicosia Cyprus

PANCHA, KESORNTHONG, federal official; b. Aug. 25, 1931. Grad. H.S., Phetpitaya. Mem. Ho. of Reps., 1969, 75, 76, 79, 83, 92, 95, 96, spkr., 1988-91; dep. min. Ministry of Edn., 1975, min., 1998—; min. Prime Min. Office, 1994-95. Chart Thai Party. Office: Govt House, Thanon Nakhon Pathom, Bangkok 10300, Thailand*

PANCHAL, CHANDRAKANT B., chemical engineer, researcher; b. Naroli, India, June 14, 1948; came to U.S., 1977; s. Bhanabhai C. and Kamlaben (Mistry) P.; m. Padma C. Mistry, Feb. 10, 1978; children: Surbhi, Vishal. BS in Chem. Engring., U. Bombay, 1972, MS in Chem. Engring., 1974; PhD in Chem. Engring., U. Manchester (Eng.), 1977. Rsch. assoc. Okla. State U., Stillwater, 1977-79; asst. chem. engr. Argonne (Ill.) Nat. Lab., 1979-82, chem. engr., 1982—; cons. devel. program UN, New Delhi, 1985-86, NASA, Cleve., 1987-88. Editor: Fouling Mitigation, 1997; contbr. chpt. to book. Recipient FLC Award Tech. Transfer Fed. Lab. Consortium, 1995. Mem. AIChE (divsn. chair 1998). Achievements include revitalization of research on fouling mitigation. Avocations: travel, camping, cycling, reading. Office: Argonne Nat Lab 9700 Cass Ave Bldg 362 Argonne IL 60439-4815 also: Energy Concepts Co 627 Ridgeley Ave Annapolis MD 21401

PANCHENKO, YURII NIKOLAEVICH, chemistry researcher; b. Kharkov, USSR, Apr. 6, 1934; s. Nikolai Korneyevich and Lyudmila Fiodorovna (Sudakova) P.; m. Larisa Grigorievna Tashkinova, Sept. 22, 1972 (div. Oct. 1975); 1 child, Viktor. Diploma in chemistry rsch., Moscow State U., 1959, PhD in Phys. Chemistry, 1970. Jr. rschr. Karpov Phys. Chemistry Inst., Moscow, 1959-61; jr. rschr. Moscow State U., 1961-77, sr. rschr., 1977—. Contbr. articles to profl. jours. Fellow World Assn. Theoretically Oriented Chemists. Office: Moscow State U, Dept Chem Vorobiovy gory, Moscow 119899, Russia

PANCHIN, YURI, research scientist; b. Kiev, USSR, Nov. 27, 1954; s. Valentin Vasiljevich Panchin and Margarita Sergeevna Marova; m. Nadia Alexandrovna Krasnobaeva; 1 child, Alexander Yurjevich. B, Moscow State U., 1977, PhD in Biology, 1984, DSc in Biology, 1990. Jr. scientist Bogomolez's Inst. Physiology, Kiev, USSR, 1977-79; sr. sci. rschr. INst. Problems Info. Transmission Russian Acad. Sci., Moscow, 1990—; sci. rschr. Moscow State U., 1990—; vis. rsch. assoc. U. Bristol, Eng., 1990-91, U. Calif., San Diego, 1991-92, 93-95. Contbr. articles to profl. jours. Fellow Russian Asian Assn. Office: Russian Acad Sci, Bolshoi Karetny pereulok 19, 101447 Moscow Russia

PANCHOLI, HEMENDRA BHUPENDRABHAI, chemist; b. Rajpipla, Hindu, India, Apr. 19, 1967; s. Bhupendrabhai Chhitalal and Hiraben (Bhupendrabhai) P.; m. Sangitaben Hemendra, Mar. 8, 1994; 1 child, Vishwa. BSc in Chemistry, M.R. Arts & Sci., Rajpipla, India, 1986; MSc, B.K.M. Sci., Valsad, India, 1988; PhD in Chemistry, Sardar Patel U., V.V. Nagar, India, 1992. Sr. asst. R&D United Phosphorous, Ankleshwar, India, 1992-93; officer R&D Sun Pharma Advance Rsch. Ctr., Baroda, India, 1993-95; asst. mgr. R&D Gujarat Organics, Ankleshwar, India, 1995-99; mgr. tech. Gujarat Organics, Ankleshwar, 1999—. Contbr. articles to profl. jours. Avocations: chess, reading, computers. Home: B/169 Surbhi Park Society, Vishwamitri Rd, Baroda 390 011, India Office: Gujarat Organics Ltd, 127/1 GIDC, Ankleshwar 393 002, India

PANDA, RAJESH KUMAR, ceramics and materials engineer; b. Berhampur, India, 1972; s. Jagannath and Jyoshna Panda; m. Smruti Rekha Panda, 1999. B Tech. in Metall. Engring., Indian Inst. Tech., Bombay, 1994; MS in Ceramics and Materials Engring., Rutgers U., 1996, PhD in Ceramics and Materials Engring., 1998. Undergrad. rsch. asst. Indian Inst. Tech., 1993-94; grad. rsch. asst. Rutgers U., Piscataway, N.J., 1994-98, tchg. asst., 1997-98; R&D design engr. Hewlett Packard Co., Andover, Mass., 1998—; cons. Ethicon (a J&J Co.), Somerville, N.J., 1997-98, Exogen Inc., Piscataway, 1996-97; presenter, spkr. in field. Contbr. articles to profl. jours.; patentee in field. Tchr. Nat. Social Svc. Orgn., Bombay, 1990-92. Recipient Best Paper award SAMPE, 1996, Rsch. Excellence award N.J. Ctr. for Biomaterials and Med. Devices, 1996, award for excellence Literati Club, 1999. Mem. IEEE. Avocations: current affairs, hiking, travel. E-mail: rkpanda@yahoo.com. Office: Agilent Techs 3000 Minuteman Rd # Ms0095 Andover MA 01810-1032

PANDA, SARAT CHANDRA, chemical engineer; b. Jeypore, Orissa, India, June 16, 1943; s. Nityananda and Sakuntala (Mahapatra) P.; m. Kumudini Brahma, Nov. 24, 1968; 1 child, Siddhartha. BSChemE, UDCT, Mumbai, India, 1964; M in Tech., Indian Inst. Tech., Chennai, India, 1966. Assoc. lectr. Regional Engring. Coll., Warangal, India, 1967-71; scientist Regional Rsch. Lab., Bhubaneswar, India, 1971—. Assoc. editor 1 book; contbr. articles to profl. jours.; patentee in field. mem. editl bd. Jour. Indsl. Pollution Control, India, 2000. Mem. Orissa Environ. Soc. (life), Soc. Geoscientists Allied Technologists (life). Hindu. Avocations: reading, news, science, economics. Home: 517 RRL Colony, Bhubaneswar 751 013, India Office: Regional Rsch Lab, Sachivalaya Marg, Bhubaneswar 751 013, India

PANDA, SHYAMAL KANTI, chemistry educator; b. Mugberia, W. Bengal, India, Jan. 31, 1949; s. Sudhangsu Sekhar and Chameli (Misra) P.; m. Chhanda Bhattacharya, Dec. 4, 1973; 1 child, Suparba. BS in Chemistry, Calcutta U., 1967, MS in Chemistry, 1969, PhD in Chemistry, 1976. Chartered chemist Instn. of Chemist, India. Lectr. in chemistry Diamond Harbour Coll., India, 1970-72, S.D.B. Coll., Howrah, India, 1972-73; sr. lectr. in chemistry MMC Coll., Calcutta, 1973-79; sr. rsch. assoc. Boston U. Sch. of Medicine, 1978-81; sr. lectr., mem. governing body Maharaja Manindra Chandra Coll., Calcutta, 1982-86; reader in chemistry Manaraja Mamindra Chandra Coll., Calcutta, 1986—. Author of books on phys. sci. and practical chemistry (textbooks chosen by Bd. of Sec. Edn./India and H.S. Coun., India); contbr. numerous articles to profl. jours. and publs. Prof.-in-charge Nat. Svc. Scheme, Calcutta U., 1972-73. Grantee Univ. Grants Commn., New Delhi, 1978, 84. Fellow Instn. of Chemists/India, Indian Chem. Soc., Internat. Congress of Chemistry and Environment. Avocations: rsch., librs., photography, travel. Office: Maharaja Manindra Chandra, Coll/20 RK Bose Str, 700003 Calcutta/W Bengal India

PANDAY, BASDEO, prime minister; b. Prince's Town, Trinidad and Tobago, May 25, 1933; s. Sookchand and Kissoondaye (Ajodha) P.; m. Norma Mohammed (div. 1981); 1 child, Niala; m. Oma Ramkissoon; children: Niala, Mickela, Nicola, Vastala. Barrister-at-Law degree, Lincoln's Inn, London, 1962; BS in Econs., U. London, 1965. Leader opposition Ho. Reps., Port of Spain, Trinidad and Tobago, 1976-86; minister external affairs Govt. Trinidad and Tobago, Port of Spain, Trinidad and Tobago, 1986-88, 87. Polit. leader United Labour Front, Trinidad and Tobago, 1976-85; dep. now prime min.; sole practice, San Fernando, Trinidad and Tobago, 1965-86; pres.-gen. All Trinidad Sugar and Gen. Workers Trade Union, Couva, 1973-polit. leader Nat. Alliance for Reconstrn., 1985—. Mem. Commonwealth Parliamentary Assn. (exec. mem. Trinidad and Tobago br.). Hindu. Avocations: chess, Indian music. Home: 1A Bryansgate Phillipine, San Fernando Trinidad and Tobago Office: Office of Prime Minister, Ctrl Bank Tower Eric Williams Plz, Independence Sq Port of Spain Trinidad and Tobago*

PANDE, BRIJ MOHAN, retired archaeologist; b. New Delhi, India, Oct. 2, 1938; s. Mathura Dutt and Bhagwati (Pant) P.; m. Munni Pant, Feb. 17, 1966; children: Mahima, Siddhartha. MA, Delhi U., India, 1959. Tech. asst. Archeol. Survey of India, Delhi, 1961-71, dep. supr. archeologist, 1971-76, supr. archeologist, 1976-88; dir. Inst. Archaeology, Delhi, 1988-91, Archaeol. Survey of India, Delhi, 1991-96. Author: (books) Symbols and Graphic Representations in Indian Inscriptions, 1999, Puratattva Prasanga, 1992; co-editor: Ecology and Archaeology of Western India, 1976, Archaeology and History: Essays in Memory of Shri A. Ghosh, 1987, Corpus of Indus Seals and Inscriptions, 2000. Assoc. mem. India Internat. Ctr., New Delhi. Recipient Shankar Puraskar award, K.K. Birla Found., New Delhi, 1996. Fellow Royal Asiatic Soc.; life mem. Indian Archaeol. Soc., Indian Soc. Prehistory and Quarternary Studies, Indian Place Names Soc., Indian History Congres, Indian Nat. Trust for Art and Cultural Heritage, Peoples Assn. for Himalayan Area Rsch., Rock Art Soc. India. Hindu. Home: Y-81 Hauz Khas, 110016 New Delhi India

PANDE, HARI KRISHNA, agronomist, educator; b. Pandepur, India, Nov. 30, 1926; s. Sadanand and Basanti (Mishra) P.; m. Shakuntla Pathak, June 8, 1938; children: Madhuri, Gopal, Girish. BSc, R.B.S. Coll., Agra, India, 1947, MSc in Crop Husbandry, 1949; PhD in Agronomy, Agra U., 1956. Asst. prof. agrl. sci. R.B.S. Coll., 1949-55; from asst. prof. agrl. engring. to head rice process engring Indian Inst. Technology, Kharagpur, 1956-77; dir. Ctrl. Rice Rsch. Inst., Cuttack, India, 1977-86; sr. cons. irrigation mgmt. tng. program LBII and WAPCOS, 1987-92; cons. in field; sr. rice agronomist FAO Mission in Sierra Leone, West Africa, 1989. Author: Upland Rice, 1990, Deficit Irrigation, 1991. Hindu. Avocations: gardening, reading, religious pilgrimage. Home: 33/33-88 Rohit Nagar, PO BHU-221005, Varanasi UP, India Office: Ctrl Rice Rsch Inst, 753 006 Cuttack Orissa, India

PANDE, HEM CHANDRA, Russian language educator; b. New Delhi, Sept. 24, 1943; s. Mathura Datt and Bhagwati (Pant) P.; m. Amita Joshi, Feb. 3, 1972; children: Shailaja, Juhi. MA, U. Delhi, India, 1965. Instr.. Russian Hindustan Aeronautics Ltd., Nashik, India, 1964-66; prof. Jawaharlal Nehru U., New Delhi, 1987—. Author: Language, Brain and Consciousness (Hindi), 1990, Patte ki Kahaanii tathaa, 2000; translator: Apni Zabaan Men Kuchh Kaho, 1983 (Soviet Land Nehru award 1984), Antim Gharii, 1985, Tiin Rusi Upanyaas, 1996. Mem. Indian Sci. Translators Assn. (editor Jista 1979-91), All India Inst. Russian Lang. (gen. sec. 1993—). Hindu. Avocations: travel, trekking. Home: Y-81 Hauz Khas, New Delhi 110016, India Office: Ctr Russian Studies, Jawaharlal Nehru U, New Delhi 110067, India

PANDEY, DHIRENDRA KUMAR, palaeontologist; b. Varanasi, India, Jan. 2, 1957; s. Shrikant and Parvati (Upadhayay) P.; m. Aruna Dubey, Feb. 21, 1979; children: Arudheer, Arunima. BS with honors, Banaras Hindu U., 1975; MS in Geology, Banaras Hindu U., Varanasi, India, 1977; PhD, Banaras Hindu U., 1984. Asst. prof. U. Rajasthan, India, 1982-95; assoc. prof. U. Rajasthan, Jaipur, India, 1995—. Contbr. articles to profl. jours. Recipient Alexander Von Humboldt fellowship, Bonn, 1991. Fellow Coun. of Geological Soc. India; mem. Indo-German Soc., Rollo Club. Avocations: driving, tennis. E-Mail: dhirendrap@hotmail.com and dhirendrap@satyam.net.in. Home: 4/284 SFS Agrawal Farm, 302020 Jaipur India Office: Dept Geology, U Rajasthan, 302004 Jaipur India

PANDEY, GIRISH CHANDRA, petrochemical company executive; b. Faizabad, India, June 30, 1946; s. H.D. and Annapurna D. (Shukla) P.; m. Chitralekha Misra, May 11, 1971; children: Sonal, Anurag, Abhishek. BS, Lucknow (India) U., 1965, MS, 1967, PhD, Indian Inst. Tech., Kanpur, 1970. Rsch. fellow Indian Inst. Tech., Kanpur, 1967-69, sr. rsch. fellow, 1969-71; lectr. in chemistry Bhagalpur (India) U., 1971-76; rsch. assoc., asst. prof. Sch. Environ. Scis. J. Nehru U., New Delhi, 1976-84; sr. mgr. R&D Indian Petrochems. Corp. Ltd., Baroda, India, 1984—; cons. thermal energy project Ctr. for Energy Studies, Indian Inst. Tech., New Delhi, 1979-82; mem. rsch. adv. com. Regional Sophisticated Instrumentation Ctr., Indian Inst. Tech., Bombay, 1984-88; mem. rsch. adv. bd. Sch. Environ. Scis., J. Nehru U., New Delhi, 1980-82; organizer confs. and symposia including Symposium on Indsl. Applications of NIR Spectroscopy (SIANIRS), 2000; Mem. Recognition Com. Universities. Contbr. numerous articles to profl. jours. Co-recipient Hari Om Ashram Prerit S.S. Bhatnagar award, 1980. Mem. Solar Energy Soc. India, Indian Soc. for Analytical Scientists (nat. exec. com. 1996—, chmn. Baroda chpt.); exec. mem. Assn. Chemical Technologists India. Avocations: cultural studies, travel. Home: D-24 Petrochems Twp, Baroda 391345, India Office: Indian Petrochems Corp Ltd, Rsch Ctr, Baroda 391346, India

PANDEY, GIRJA SHANKER, researcher, veterinary pathologist, educator; b. Pratapgarh, India, Jan. 8, 1945; s. Ram Bodh and Dhanraji Pandey; m. Savitri Pandey, May 30, 1965; children: Rajeev, Reenu, Meenu, Beenu, Anuradha. BSc in Agr., U. Allahabad, India, 1964; B Vet. Sci., Vet. Coll. MHOW, Jabalpur, India, 1968; MVSc, IVRI, Izatnagar, India, 1976; PhD, Azabu U., Tokyo, 1988. Cert. in vet. pathology, wildlife diseases, tropical vet. medicine. Vet. surgeon Dept. Animal Husbandry, Lucknow, India, 1968-73; jr. rsch. fellow IVRI, Izatnagar, India, 1974-75; livestock devel. officer Dept. Animal Husbandry, Sultanpur, U.P., India, 1976-79; vet. rsch. officer CVRI, Lusaka, Zambia, 1980-85; sr. lectr. U. Zambia, Lusaka, 1986-90, assoc. prof., 1991-95, prof., 1996—; vis. lectr. U. Glasgow, Scotland, 1991, NIES, Tsukuba, Japan, 1991; vis. prof. Azabu U., Tokyo, 1997, vis. rschr., 1998. Editor Wildlife Diseases and their conservation; author: Diseases of Lechwe, 1998; contbr. articles to profl. publs.; discovered many diseases of Lechwe. Jr. rsch. fellow ICAR, 1974, Brit. coun. fellow, 1991; grantee Japan Pvt. Sch. Fund, 1998. Mem. IAVP (life), VAZ (treas. 1992-96), Commonwealth Vet. Assn. (councillor). Home: Anapur Patti, Pratapgarh UP, India Office: U Zambia, Sch Vet Medicine Box 32379, Lusaka Zambia

PANDEY, LAKSHMAN, physics, materials science educator, researcher; b. Village Baburi, India, Jan. 30, 1953; s. Murari Ram and Dhanvanti (Tiwari) P.; m. Ujjwala Sakalkar, Apr. 27, 1984; 1 child, Shukdev. BSc, Banaras Hindu U., Varanasi, India, 1970, MSc, 1972; PhD, Indian Inst. Tech., Kanpur, India, 1980. Fellow U. Alberta, Edmonton, Can., 1980-83; rsch. scientist Sch. Materials Sci. Banaras Hindu U., 1984-89; reader Rani Durgavati U., Jabalpur, India, 1989-98, mem. bd. studies in physics, 1990-93, prof. physics dept., 1998—; vis. scientist U. Alberta, 1984, vis. prof., 1986, vis. asst. prof., 1990. Contbr. over 40 articles to profl. jours. Mem. Interreligious Forum, Jabalpur, 1992—. Mem. Materials Rsch. Soc. (life), Indian Inst. Metals (life), Nat. Magnetic Resonance Soc. (life), Indian Physics Assn. (life), Indian Assn. Physics Tchrs. (life), Sangeet Samaj, Third World Acad. Sci. (assoc.). Achievements include research in areas of NMR in solids and gases, electronic ceramics, glass, impedance spectroscopy, solidification, modelling, scientific concepts in Vedas and ancient Sanskrit texts. Avocations: playing flute, classical music, yoga, meditation, vedic literature. Office: Rani Durgavati U, Dept Physics, Jabalpur 482001, India

PANDEY, MANOJ, oncologist; b. Saharanpur, India, May 1, 1966; s. Pratap Narain and Pushpa (Chaudhary) P.; m. Mridula Shukla. DSSCE, Gov. Boys Sr. Sec. Sch., Lajpat Nagar, New Delhi, India, 1981; DSSCE, Gov. Boys Sr. Sec. Sch., Lajpat Nagar, India, 1983; MBBS, Inst. of Med. Sci., BHU Varanasi, India, 1989, MS, 1993. Jr. resident Inst. of Med. Sci., Varanasi, 1991-93, sr. resident, 1994-96; fellowship Gujarat Cancer Rsch. Inst., Ahmedabad, India, 1996; lectr. Regional Cancer Ctr., Trivandrum, India, 1996-98, asst. prof., 1998—; cons. Regional Cancer Ctr., 1996—. Contbr. numerous articles to profl. jours. Recipient Millineum medal of honour 2000. Mem. Indian Assn. Surgical Oncology, Assn. Surgeons India, Assn. Surgeons India, Indian Soc. Wound Mgmt., Trivandrum Surgical Club, Shushuruta Club. Avocations: photography, cricket, football, literature, music. E-mail: manojpandey@eth.net. Office: Regional Cancer Ctr, Medical Coll PO, 695011 Trivandrum India

PANDEY, SANJEEV ULRICH, physicist; b. Calcutta, India, Jan. 2, 1965; s. Ram and Ursula (Söhle) P. BA, Grinnel (Iowa) Coll., 1987; MS, U. Pitts., 1988, PhD, 1993. Rsch. asst. U. Pitts., 1988-92; vis. scientist Ohio State U., Columbus, 1992-93, postdoctoral rschr., 1993-96; asst. prof. physics Wayne State U., Detroit, 1996—; vis. fellow Ctr. of European Nuclear Rsch., Geneva, Switzerland, 1989-96, contact rep. for data acquisition, 1989-93; head silicon detector lab. Ohio State U., 1993-96; local coord. SVT Collaboration Brookhaven Nat. Lab., Upton, N.Y., 1996—. Contbr. articles to profl. jours. Treas. Forest Conservation Soc., Crozet, France, 1991-92. Mem. IEEE, AAAS, Am. Phys. Soc. Office: Brookhaven Nat Lab Bldg 510A-Star Upton NY 11973-5000

PANDEY, VIVEK K., finance educator, researcher; b. Chapra, Bihar, India, Feb. 4, 1965; came to U.S., 1987; s. Gopal K. and Shobha (Tiwary) P. BCom, Andhra U., India, 1986; MBA, Western Carolina U., Cullowhee, N.C., 1988; DBA, Miss. State U., 1994. Grad. rsch. asst. Western Carolina U., 1987-88, Miss. State U., 1988-93; instr. Miss. U. for Women, Columbus, 1993, asst. prof., 1994-98; asst. prof. dept. econs. and fin. Murray (Ky.) State U., 1998—; asst. prof. U. Tex., Tyler, 1999—. Contbr. articles to profl. jours. Recipient Outstanding Paper award Southwestern Fin. Assn., 1991, Anbar Highest Quality rsch. award, 1998, Distig. Rsch. award Allied Acads., 1999; named Faculty Mem. of Yr., Divsn. of Bus., Miss. U. for Women, 1995. Mem. Am. Fin. Assn., Fin. Mgmt. Assn., Eastern Fin. Assn., So. Fin. Assn. Avocations: philately, camping, biking, reading. Office: U Tex at Tyler 3900 University Blvd Tyler TX 75701-6622

PANDHI, VIJAY KUMAR, journalist, petroleum chemist; b. Dehradun, India, Feb. 5, 1946; s. Satyapal and Bimla (Behal) P.; m. Margaret edith Danler, Sept. 23, 1972. MS in Organic Chemistry, Agra (India) U., 1968; postgrad., Indian Inst. Petroleum, 1968-70. Rsch. chemist Lab. for Therapeutic Rsch., L.I. U., N.Y., 1970-76; UN corr. The Himachal Times Group, Allied Press Internat., N.Y.C., 1976-81; chmn., mng. dir. Petroleum & Energy Pub. Pvt. Ltd., Dehra Dun, India, 1981—. editor, pub. Karma Mag., 1974; chief editor: Petroleum Asia Jour. and Energy India. Mem. Govt. Advt. Approval Com., 1989-91, Govt. Press Accreditation Com., 1992-95, telephone Adv. Com., 1993—; sec.-gen. World Fellowship of Religions, N.Y.C., 1976-83, Gita Temple Ashram, N.Y., 1973. NIH grantee, 1973. Mem. Indian Newspaper Soc., All India Newspaper Editors Conf., Indian Lang. Newspaper Assn., Indo-French Tech. Assn., Dehra Dun Club, Press Club of India, Aero Club of India, No. India C. of C. and Industry. Avocations: swimming, golf, palmistry. Office: The Himachal Times, 57-B Rajpur Rd, Dehradun India

PANDIA, RAJEEV MAHENDRA, petrochemical company executive, chemical engineer; b. Nadiad, Gujarat, India, Dec. 17, 1949; s. Mahendra N. and Mahashweta M. (Yajnik) P.; m. Smita S. Jhala, Feb. 20, 1976; children: Keya R., Shaili R. B of Tech., Indian Inst. Tech., Mumbai, India, 1971; MS, Stanford U., 1972. Project officer Indsl. Credit and Investment Corp. India Ltd., Mumbai, 1973-76; sr. project officer Gujarat Carbon Ltd., Vadodara, 1976-79; engring. officer Nat. Organic Chem. Industries Ltd., Mumbai, 1979-81; project devel. mgr. Herdillia Chems., Ltd., Mumbai, 1981-84, project planning mgr., 1984-86, gen. mgr. projects, 1986-89, sr. v.p., 1990-92, mng. dir. (CEO), 1992—; bd. dirs. Herdillia Unimers Ltd., Mumbai, Herdillia Oxides & Electronics Ltd., Mumbai; chmn., bd. dirs. Herdillia Investments Ltd., Mumbai, 1993—; G.P. Kane vis. prof. dept. chem. tech. U. Bombay, 1993; spkr. in field. Author: (handbook) International Projects, 1992; mem. editl. adv. bd. Chem. Industry News, 1986—. Recipient Disting. Alumnus award Indian Inst. Tech., Mumbai, 1997, Group Study Exch. Program award Rotary Internat., 1981, tchg. assistantship Stanford U., 1971-72; Merit scholar Indian Inst. Tech., 1970. Mem. Indian Chem. Mfrs. Assn. (v.p. 1998-2000, pres. 2000—), Associated Chambers of Commerce and Industry (chmn. expert com. on environment 1995-96), Confedn. of Indian Industry (nat. com. on chems. and petrochems. 1995—), Am. Chem. Soc. Avocations: reading, writing, traveling, chess, swimming. Home: 701 Benson Saibaba Rd, Santa Cruz (West) Mumbai 400 054, India Office: Herdillia Chems Ltd, Air India Bldg Nariman Pt, Mumbai 400 021, India

PANDIMAN, DIEN, chemist; b. Balai, Indonesia, Apr. 7, 1966; m. Hariana Pandiman, Oct. 1, 1999. BSc, U. Huddersfield, Eng., 1989, MSc, 1994, PhD, 1997. Lectr. Unsyiah Poly. U., Aceh, Indonesia, 1990-93; sr. chemist Setsco Svcs. Pte. Ltd., Singapore, 1997—. Contbr. articles to sci. jours., including Jour. Polymer Engring. and Sci., TECHNIP. Scholar World Bank, Indonesia, 1987; rsch. grantee U. Huddersfield, 01994. Mem. Royal Soc. Chemistry (chartered), N.Y. Acad. Scis. Avocations: travel, sports, cooking, reading. Home: HJ Hts, No 3 Merbok Crescent 02-01, Singapore 597665, Singapore Office: Setsco Svcs Pte Ltd, 18 Teban Gardens Crescent, Singapore 608925, Singapore

PANDIT, ANIRUDDHA BHALCHANDRA, chemical engineering educator, consultant, researcher; b. Mumbai, India, Dec. 7, 1957; s. Bhalchandra Ramachandra and Sumati Bhalchandra Pandit; m. Anala Aniruddha Kulkarni, Aug. 11, 1990; 1 child, Sphoorti. B of Tech., Inst. Tech./Benaras Hindu U., Banaras, India, 1980; PhD, Univ. Dept. Chem. Tech., Mumbai, India, 1984. Asst. lectr. Mumbai U., 1982-84; rsch. assoc. U. Cambridge, U.K., 1984-90; reader U. Mumbai, 1991-95, prof., 1996—; tech. dir. Sarang Chem., Mumbai, 1991—; cons. Asian Paints, Mumbai, 1992—, Marico, Mumbai, 1995—, Electric Power Rsch. Inst., Pitts., 1996-97. Contbr. over 100 articles to profl. jours.; inventor in field. Mem. Indian Inst. Chem. Engrs. (life, coun. 1993-94, MRC hon. sec. 1991—). Avocations: music, hiking, trekking. Home: Prashant SB Marg, Mumbai 400016, India Office: Univ Mumbai, Chem Tech, Mumbai 400016, India

PANDOLFI, FRANCES, health facility administrator; b. N.Y.C., Sept. 7, 1944; d. Frank Pandolfi and Rose McGinn; m. Edmund Lewiska Menelik Bobbitt, May 19, 1973. BA, Vassar Coll., 1965; MPA, NYU, 1990. Health planner N.Y.C. Dept. City Planning, 1965-74; planner West Midlands County Coun., Birmingham, Eng., 1974-81, dir. recreation and tourism planning, 1981-85; dir. strategic planning West Midlands County Coun., Birmingham, 1985-86; dep. dir. housing coord. N.Y.C. Mayor's Office, 1987-89; dir. nurses housing N.Y.C. Health & Hosps. Corp., 1989-92, exec. asst. to v.p., 1992-94, asst. v.p., 1994-97; chief of staff N.Y.C. Health and Hosps. Corp., 1998—. Dir. Women in Housing and Fin., N.Y.C., 1990-96. Mem. Am. Soc. Pub. Adminstrn., Royal Town Planning Inst. Office: NYC Health & Hosps Corp 125 Worth St New York NY 10013-4006

PANDYA, DINESH KANT, physicist, educator; b. Mathura, India, Nov. 20, 1948; s. Ganpat R. and Sitara P.; m. Shashi Nagar, Mar. 8, 1981; children: Rohit, Dhruv, Dhaval. BSc in Physics with hons., U. Delhi, 1968, MSc in Physics, 1970; PhD, Indian Inst. Tech., Delhi, 1975. Lectr. Indian Inst. Tech., Delhi, 1977-81, asst. prof., 1981-90, prof., 1990—. Author: (chpt.) Physics of Thin Films Vol. 12, 1982. Mem. Materials Rsch. Soc. India, Solar Energy Soc. India., Indian Vacuum Soc. Avocations: music,

drama, reading. Home: 6 St M-2 IIT Campus, New Delhi 110016, India Office: Indian Inst Tech, Hauz Khas Physics Dept, New Delhi 110016, India

PANE, ANTONIO NICOLA, lawyer; b. Melbourne, Victoria, Australia, July 18, 1960; s. Natale and Virginia (Cacace) P.; m. Elizabeth Anastasia Grzesiak, Nov. 24, 1984; children: Bryce Natale, Thomas Stanislaw. BA, Monash U., Melbourne, 1982, LLB, 1984, LLM, 1995. Barrister, solicitor Victorian Supreme Ct. Articled clerk, solicitor Herbert Geer & Rundle, Melbourne, 1984-85; tax. cons. KMG Hungerfords/KPMG Peat Marwich Hungerfords, 1985-88; sr. assoc. Clayton Utz, Melbourne, 1988-90, ptnr., 1990-99; chief tax counsel Village Roadshow Ltd., Melbourne, 2000—. Fellow Tax. Inst. Australia; mem. Law Coun. Tax. Com. Roman Catholic. Avocations: family activities. Office: Village Roadshow Ltd, 206 Bourke St, Melbourne 3000, Australia

PANE, GERALD LOUIS, banker; b. N.Y.C., July 21, 1945; m. Ewa J. Pane; children: Marc, Kate, Adrianna. BA, Queens Coll., 1967; MBA, NYU, 1968. Sr. analyst Fed. Res. Bank N.Y., N.Y.C., 1970-78; v.p., regional head ctrl. bank rels. J.P. Morgan, London, 1970—. E-mail: pane gerald@jpmorgan.com. Home: 72 Minster Rd, London England, NW231E Office: JP Morgan, 60 Victorian Embankment, London EC4 Y0JP, England

PANE, LUIGI, biologist, researcher; b. Oristano, Italy, May 21, 1951; s. Giovanni and Maddalena (Sanna) P.; m. Graziella Merega, Apr. 21, 1951; children: Gianluca, Stefano. Degree in biology, U. Genoa, Italy, 1975; degree prize, U. Genoa, 1976. Tchr. pub. h.s. Genoa, 1975-80; sci. rschr. U. Genoa, 1986-92, rschr., prof. ecology, 1992-93, rschr., prof. planktology, 1993—; cons. hospital Santa Corona, Savona, Italy, 1980-83; mem. expedition Program Nat. Rsch. Antartide, Baia Terra Nova, Antarctica, 1995. Author: Elementi di Ecologia Applicata-Atmosfera, (ECIG award 1998), Elementi di Ecologia Applicata-Acque, (ECIG award 1998), Elementi Ecologia Applicata-Ecotossicologia (ECIG award 1998). Soldier, 1976-77, Verona, Genoa, Italy. Mem. Internat. Soc. Ecology, Internat. Soc. Indsl. Hygienists, Internat. Marine Biology, Internat. Soc. Limnology, Oceanology, N.Y. Acad. Scis., Commn. Internat. Exploration Scientifique Mer Mediterranee. Avocations: fishing, music. Office: DI BI SAA Univ, V Le Benedetto XV 5, 16132 Genoa Italy

PANEK, JAROSLAV, historian; b. Prague, Czech Republic, Jan. 23, 1947; s. Antonín and Antonie (Dostalova) P.; m. Markéta Vrbová, Nov. 18, 1994. PhD, Charles U., 1971, Czech Acad. Scis., Prague, 1980; DSc, Czech Acad. Scis., Prague, 1991. Archivist County Archive, Benešov, Czech Republic, 1970-75, Provincial Archive, Prague, 1975-76; rsch. fellow Inst. History Czech Acad. Scis., Prague, 1976-90, head Early Modern history, prof., 1990—, dir. Inst. History, 1998—; prorector Charles U., Prague, 1997-2000. Author: The Estate Opposition and Its Struggle Against the Habsburgs (1547-1577), 1982, Last Lords of Rožmberk—The Magnates of Czech Renaissance, 1989, The Death of Emperor Rudolf II, 1997, The Slovenian Culture in the Czech Republic, 1997, Vilém of Rožmberk, Politician of Conciliation, 1998, Jan Hus in Vatican, (with M. Polivka) The International Discourse on a Czech Reformer of the 15th Century and His Reception on the Eve of the Third Millennium, 2000, (with E. Procházková) Archive and Region, 2000; editor: The Lexicon of Contemporary Czech Historians, 1999, Select Bibliography on Czech History 1990-99, 2000. Mem. Assn. Czech Historians (pres. 1996—), Collegium Carolinum, Czech and Slovak History Conf.

PANEK, MAREK, wildlife biologist, researcher; b. Kostrzyn, Poland, Sept. 10, 1959. PhD, Wrocław (Poland) U., 1991. Rschr. Polish Hunting Assn., Czempiń, 1984—. Contbr. articles to profl. jours. Office: Polish Hunting Assn Rsch Sta, Sokolnicza 12, 64-020 Czempiń Poland

PANETH, DONALD JOSEPH, editor, writer; b. N.Y.C., Feb. 28, 1927; s. Irving and Maud (Kramer) P.; m. Elma Olans, Apr. 10, 1949 (dec. 1987); children: Thea, Ira. BBA, CCNY, 1948; postgrad., Columbia U., 1949-50. Reporter N.Y. Times, 1947-49; free-lance journalist N.Y.C., 1950-56, 73-75, 77-83, 94—; rewriteman Daily Mirror, N.Y.C., 1956-63; copy editor The Morning Telegraph, N.Y.C., 1964-65; staff writer Med. Tribune, N.Y.C., 1966-72; copy editor L.I. Press, Queens, N.Y., 1975-77; editor-in-chief News Dictionary: People, Places and Events, 1977-80; editor, writer Yearbook of the UN, N.Y.C., 1986-93; documents editor UN Office Conf. Svcs., N.Y.C., 1993-94; adj. lectr. English York Coll., CUNY, 1983-86; cons. study of lit. of far right extremist groups in U.S. Anti-Defamation League, N.Y., 1995-96. Author: William Baziotes: A Literary Portrait, 1961, Current Affairs Atlas, 1979, The Ency. of American Journalism, 1983; contbr. articles to Commentary mag., The Nation, Village Voice, Current Biography, Peacework, WorldPaper, others; work included in anthologies Commentary on the American Scene, 1953, New York City Folklore, 1956. Mem. The Authors Guild, Willa Cather Pioneer Meml., Am.-Scandinavian Found. Avocation: reading. Home and Office: 240 Cabrini Blvd Apt 1E New York NY 10033-1113

PANG, DAI-WEN, chemist, educator; b. Songzi, Hubei, China, July 14, 1961; s. Wan-Ming Pang and Zu-Feng Wei; m. Min Zhang, Feb. 4, 1986; 1 child, Bo. BS, Wuhan (China) U., 1982, PhD, 1992. Lectr. dept. chemistry Wuhan U., 1982-87, post-doctoral rsch. assoc., 1992-94, assoc. prof., 1994-96, prof., 1996—; vis. scientist Cornell U., Ithaca, N.Y., 1997-98; cons. Wuhan Tobacco Corp., 1999—. Contbr. articles to sci. jours., including Jour. Electroanalytical Chemistry, Analytical Chemistry, others; mem. editl. com. Jour. Analytical Sci., 1999—; patentee in field. Recipient Young Scientist prize Hubei Province, China, 1995, Sci. Progress prize State Edn. Commn. China, 1995, State Spl. award State Coun. China, 1999. Fellow Chinese Chem. Soc.; mem. Instruments Soc. Hubei Province. Avocations: long-distance running, sightseeing. Office: Dept Chemistry, Wuhan U, Hubei Wuhan 430072, China

PANG, HERBERT GEORGE, ophthalmologist; b. Honolulu, Dec. 23, 1922; s. See Hung and Hong Jim (Chuu) P.; m. Dorothea Lopez, Dec. 27, 1953. Student, St. Louis Coll., 1941; BS, Northwestern U., 1944. Diplomate Am. Bd. Ophthalmology. Intern Queen's Hosp., Honolulu, 1947-48; postgrad. course ophthalmology N.Y.U. Med. Sch., 1948-49; resident ophthalmology Jersey City Med. Ctr., 1949-50, Manhattan Eye, Ear, & Throat Hosp., N.Y.C., 1950-52; practice medicine specializing in ophthalmology Honolulu, 1952-54, 56—; mem. staffs Kuakini Hosp., Children's Hosp., Castle Meml. Hosp., Queen's Hosp., St. Francis Hosp.; asst. clin. prof. ophthalmology U. Hawaii Sch. Medicine, 1966-73, now assoc. clin. prof. Cons. Bur. Crippled Children, 1952-73, Kapiolani Maternity Hosp., 1952-73, Leahi Tb. Hosp., 1952-62. Mem. AMA, Am. Acad. Ophthalmology and Otolaryngology, Assn. for Rsch. Ophthalmology, ACS, Hawaii Med. Soc. (gov. med. practice com. 1958-62, chmn. med. spkrs. com. 1957-58), Hawaii Eye, Ear, Nose and Throat Soc. (pres. 1960), Pacific Coast Oto-Ophthalmological Soc., Pan Am. Assn. Ophthalmology, Mason, Shriner, Eye Study Club (pres. 1972—). Home: 346 Lewers St Honolulu HI 96815-2345

PANG, SAMUEL CHOW-ERN, reproductive endocrinologist, gynecologist-obstetrician; b. Singapore, Oct. 28, 1959; came to U.S., 1988; s. Teck Soon and Wendy Chew-Eng (Poh) P. Student, Vancouver (B.C., Can.) C.C., 1976-77; BSc, U. B.C., 1982, MD, 1983. Diplomate Am. Bd. Ob.-Gyn., Am. Bd. Reproductive Endocrinology. Adj. asst. prof. UCLA Sch. Medicine, 1988-90; asst. prof. Loma Linda (Calif.) U. Sch. Medicine, 1990-93; assoc. med. dir. Reproductive Sci. Ctr., Boston, 1993—; chief ob-gyn. Deaconess Waltham (Mass.) Hosp., 1995-00. Fellow ACOG, Royal Coll. Surgeons (Can.); mem. Am. Soc. Reproductive Medicine, Mass. Med. Soc., Soc. Reproductive Endocrinologists, Boston Fertility Soc. (pres.-elect), Soc. Male Reproduction and Urology (charter). Avocations: masters swimming, tennis, piano, choral singing, stamp and coin collecting. Office: Deaconess Waltham Hosp Hope Ave Waltham MA 02453-2774

PANG, TING SUN, music educator. MusB, Ctrl. Conservatory of Music, Beijing, 1957. Prof. Ctrl. Conservatory of Music, Beijing, 1957-80, Hong Kong Bapt. U., 1980-91; 1st violinist Hong Kong Philharm. Orch., 1980-91; tchr. violin, piano, music Hong Kong, 1980-91; prof. Pang's Music Studio, Vancouver, Can., 1991—. Recipient 2d prize China's First Nat. Violin competition. Office: Can-Am Cons Inc, 1066 W Hastings St Ste 2000, Vancouver, BC Canada V6E 3X2

PANG, YUAN-PING, synthetic and computational chemist; b. Shanghai, China, Sept. 9, 1962; came to U.S., 1987, naturalized, 1999; s. Qi-Yang and Li-Kang (Wang) P.; m. Bee-Darn Chao, July 26, 1996. BS, Amoy U., Xiamen, China, 1984; PhD, U. Pitts., 1990. Rsch. assoc. Mayo Clinic, Jacksonville, Fla., 1991-92, assoc. cons., 1992-97, chief rational drug design lab., 1996-97, mem. rsch. exec. subcom., 1995-97; sr. assoc. cons. Mayo Clinic Cancer Ctr., Rochester, Minn., 1997—; inventor neuroprotectives, drugs for Alzheimer's, drugs for schizophrenia, and antidotes for organophosphate poisonings; lectr. Bristol-Myers Squibb Pharm. Rsch. Inst., Wallingford, Conn., 1990, U. degli Studi, Perugia, Italy, 1991, Salk Inst., San Diego, 1992, Nat. Cancer Inst., Frederick, Md., 1992, Louis Pasteur U., Strasbourg, France, 1992, Mayo Clinic Rochester, Minn., 1993, 96, Brookhaven Nat. Lab., Upton, N.Y., 1994, Inst. de Recherches Internat. Servier, Paris, 1996, Weizmann Inst. Sci., Rehovot, Israel, 1997, Sandia Nat. Labs., Livermore, Calif., 1997; asst. prof. dept. pharmacology Mayo Med. Sch., Rochester, 1997—. Author: (with others) Excitatory Amino Acids, 1991, Trends in QSAR and Molecular Modeling '92, 1993, QSAR and Molecular Modelling: Concepts, Computational Tools and Biological Applications, 1995; contbr. more than 50 articles to profl. jours. including Nature, Nature Struct. Biol., Procs. NAS USA, Jour. Phys. Chemistry, Jour. Medicinal Chemistry, Jour. Biol. Chemistry, Molecular Pharmacology, Jour. Organic Chemistry, Jour. Am. Chem. Soc., Protein Sci., others. Grantee NIH, NIMH. Achievements include inventions of the multiple template approach for developing nonpeptidic mimetics, the cationic dummy atom approach to molecular modeling of metalloproteins and the dimeric analog approach for prototype drug optimization; contbn. to conformational selection mechanism for bindings of biologically active proteins; and leadership in developing automated computer docking program, ligands of cholinesterase and neurotensin receptor, and model of ligand binding site of transmembrane receptor for neurotension. Avocations: playing the violin, computer programming. Office: Mayo Clinic Dept Pharmacology 200 1st St SW Rochester MN 55905-0002

PANG, ZHAN-JUN, medical researcher; b. Henan, China, Feb. 1, 1973; s. G.S. and N.H. (Lan) P.; m. Jun-Gui Zhou, July 13, 1998; 1 child, Bo. BA, 1st Mil. Med. U., Guangzhou, China, 1995, MD, 1997, postgrad. Rschr. in field. Recipient awards for Advancement in Sci. and Tech., 1998, 1999. Mem. N.Y. Acd. Sci. Avocations: music, computers. E-mail: pangzhan@163.net. Home: Tong He, Guangzhou China Office: Rsch Lab Free Radical Med, 1st Mil Med U Tong He, Guangzhou 510515, China

PANGANIBAN, TERESITA MACATANGAY, manufacturing executive; b. Nasugbu, Batangas, The Philippines, Jan. 27, 1957; d. Teodoro Macaraig and Eleuteria Macatangay Panganiban. BS in Applied Math., U. of the Philippines, Las Baños, Laguna, 1978; postgrad., Ateneo Grad. Sch. Bus., Makati City, The Philippines, 1989. Rsch. asst. Cotton Rsch. and Devel. Inst., 1978; rschr. in market rsch. Nat. Steel Corp., Makati City, 1980-87, sr. rsch. asst. for market rsch., 1987-90, sr. supr. for market rsch. domestic market sect., 1990-97, dept. head market rsch. and intelligence, 1996-97, mgr. for market intelligence rsch. and advocacy/bus. devel., corp. devel., 1997—; county rep. S.E. Asia Iron and Steel Inst. Statis. Com., Malaysia, 1996—; industry rep. Philippine Customs Valuation Com., 1998—. Mem. The Club Metal Bull. Office: Nat Steel Corp, 377 Sen Gil Puyat Ave, 1200 Makati City The Philippines

PANGAS, JULIO CESAR, physician, educator; b. Buenos Aires, Mar. 18, 1947; s. Julio Cesar Pangas and Susana Luisa Trojan; m. Carolina Mariana Monica Graciela Pettenazza, Jan. 18, 1974 (div. Aug. 1999). Bachelor's degree, Nat. Coll. Buenos Aires, 1965; physician, U. Buenos Aires, 1972; expert in Orientalism, U. of the Salvador, Buenos Aires, 1978; PhD, U. Buenos Aires, 1998. Coroner Poder Jud., Rio Negro, Argentina, 1987-94; physician Supt. Admin. de Fondos Jubilaciones y Pensiones, Buenos Aires, 1994—; tchr., chair history medicine U. Buenos Aires, 1996—; assoc. prof. history of medicine Inst. Univ. de Ciencias de la Salud Barcelo, Buenos Aires, 1997—. Contbr. sci. articles to profl. jours. Recipient Borsa per Stranieri del la Scuola Normale de Pisa Italy Scuola Normale di Pisa Sezione di Lettere Italy, 1982-83, Chercheur Associé, CNRS France, Coll. France Cabinet D'Assyriologie, 1983-84; Conicet-Sorbonne fellow, 1979-82, fellow Smithsonian Instn., Nat. Mus. Natural History, 1992. Avocations: ancient literature and languages, Oriental philosophy, sports. Home: Jose Evaristo Uriburu 1029, Buenos Aires 1114, Argentina

PANG-WHITE, ANN A., philosophy educator, researcher; b. Taichung, Taiwan, China, June 23, 1964; came to U.S., 1989; d. Jee-Zen and Ai-Chu (Huang) Pang; m. David Alan White, July 22, 1995. BA, Tung-Hai U., Taichung, 1986; MA, U. S.C., 1991; PhD, Marquette U., 1997. Asst. prof. philosophy U. Scranton, Pa., 1997—, mem. instn. rev. bd. for protection human subjects, 1998—, parliamentarian faculty senate, 1998-2000, mem. honors com., 1999—. Contbr. articles to profl. jours. Mem. adv. bd. St. Pius X Sem., Dalton, Pa., 1998—. Recipient James W. Oliver prize in logic U. S.C., 1991, Faculty Svc. and Tchg. award Dexter Hanley Coll. Student Govt., U. Scranton, 1999. Mem. Am. Philos. Assn., Soc. of Medieval and Renaissance Philosophy, N.Am. Patristic Soc., Am. Cath. Philos. Assn. Office: Univ of Scranton Dept Philosophy Scranton PA 18510

PANIAGUA, RICARDO, cell biologist, educator; b. Cordoba, Spain, Aug. 21, 1948; s. Jesus and Carmen (Gomez-Alvarez) P.; m. Pilar Bravo, July 17, 1978. B in Biology, U. Navarra, Pamplona, Spain, 1969, D Biology, 1976. Asst. prof. cytology and histology Autonomous U., Madrid, 1976-83; assoc. prof. cytology and histology U. Salamanca, Spain, 1983, prof. cell biology, 1984-88; prof. cell biology U. Alcala, Alcala de Henares, Spain, 1988—, head dept. of cell biology and genetics, 1990-94, 98—, head Ctr. Molecular Biology, 1994-98; mem. nat. com. for evaluation of sci. rsch. Ministry of Edn., Spain, 1995-96; referee Nat. Agy. for Sci. Rsch. Evaluation, Ministry of Edn., 1990—; referee, mem. editl. bd. several sci. jours. in field. Author: Testicular and Epididymal Pathology, 1994, Urologic Surgical Pathology, 1997, Molecular and Cellular Endocrine Pathology, 2000. Mem. govt. coun. U. Alcala, 1990-2000. Roman Catholic. Avocations: classical music, football, drawing, reading. Office: U Alcala, Dept Cell Biology/Genetics, E-28871 Alcala de Henares Spain

PANIC, MILAN, pharmaceutical and health products company executive; b. Belgrade, Yugoslavia, Dec. 20, 1929; came to U.S., 1956, naturalized, 1963; s. Spasóje and Zorka (Krunich) P.; children—Dawn, Milan (dec.), Vivian; stepchildren—Jane, Mark, Patricia. B.S., HU Belgrade, 1955; postgrad., U. Heidelberg, Germany, 1955-56, U. So. Calif., 1957-59. Metallurgist Kaiser Steel Corp., 1956-57; chemist Cyclo-Chem. Corp., Los Angeles, 1957-58; research asst. dept. chemistry U. So. Calif., 1958-59; research chemist Biochem. Research, Los Angeles, 1959-61; chmn. bd., chief exec. officer ICN Pharms., Inc., Costa Mesa, Calif., pres., chmn. bd., chief exec. officer, 1961—; prime min. Govt. of Yugoslavia, Belgrade, 1992-93; chmn. Ribapharm Inc.; assoc. Calif. Inst. Tech. Trustee Intra-Sci. Research Found.; sponsoring com. program health scis. and tech. Harvard-Mass. Inst. Tech.; bd. dirs. Freedom's Found., Valley Forge, Pa. Served with Yugoslavian Army in Partisan Resistance, WWII. Recipient Ellis Island Medal of Honor, 1986. Mem. Serbian Orthodox Ch. Office: ICN Pharms Inc 3300 Hyland Ave Costa Mesa CA 92626-1503*

PANICALI, JOHN ANTHONY, chiropractor; b. Bklyn., Mar. 20, 1961; s. Marco and Josephine (Fusco) P.; m. Lisa Ann DeMarco, Sept. 25, 1987; children: Samantha, Nicholas. AS, St. John's Coll., 1981; D Chiropractic, N.Y. Chiropractic Coll., 1985. Chiropractor Bay Ridge Chiropractic, Bklyn., 1985-86; owner Panicali Chiropractic, Bklyn., 1986—, Spinecare, Bklyn., 1994—; lectr. in field. Inventor new lower back support device. Mem. Am. Chiropractic Assn., Fla. Chiropractic Assn., N.Y. State Chiropractic Assn. (peer reviewer 1994). Republican. Roman Catholic. Avocations: weight training, golf, skiing, cars, boating. Home: 20 Country Club Ln Colts Neck NJ 07722-2222 Office: Colony Chiropractic 1694 Central Ave Albany NY 12205-4002

PANICH, ALEXANDER, physicist; b. Krivoi Rog, Ukraine, July 5, 1949; arrived in Israel, 1992; s. Moisei P. and Riva Kvetnaya; 1 child, Eugene. MS in Radiophysics and Electronics, Donetsk (Ukraine) U., 1971; PhD, Inst. Physics, Krasnoyarsk, Russia, 1981. Engr. Inst. Inorganic Chemistry, Novosibirsk, Russia, 1971-74, rsch. scientist, 1974-88, sr. rsch. scientist, 1988-92; rschr. Infodisk Ltd., Dimona, Israel, 1992-93; sr. rsch. scientist Ben-Gurion U., Beer Sheva, Israel, 1993—. Contbr. more than 50 articles to sci. jours. Recipient Gold medal in electronics for sch. children, Exhbn. Nat. Achievements USSR, Moscow, 1966; recipient rsch. grant Ministry Scis., Israel, 1994-96; Giladi, 1996, KAMEA fellow, 1999; scholar German Acad. Exch. Svc., 1997. Achievements include rsch. in solid state nuclear magnetic resonance spectroscopy. Avocations: travel, mountain hiking. Office: Ben-Gurion U Dept Physics, PO Box 653, 84105 Beer-Sheva Israel

PANICHAS, GEORGE ANDREW, English language educator, critic, editor; b. Springfield, Mass., May 21, 1930; s. Andrew and Fotini (Dracouli) P. BA, Am. Internat. Coll., 1951, LittD (hon.), 1984; AM, Trinity Coll., Conn., 1952; PhD, Nottingham (Eng.) U., 1962. Instr., English and comparative lit. U. Md., College Park, 1962-63; asst. prof. U. Md., 1963-66, assoc. prof., 1966-68, prof., 1968-92; mem. Richard M. Weaver fellowship awards com., 1984-88, Ingersoll Prizes Jury Panel, 1986; co-chmn. Conf. on Irving Babbitt: Fifty Years Later, 1983. Author: Adventure in Consciousness: The Meaning of D.H. Lawrence's Religious Quest, 1964, Epicurus, 1967, The Reverent Discipline: Essays in Literary Criticism and Culture, 1974, The Burden of Vision: Dostoevsky's Spiritual Art, 1977, The Courage of Judgment: Essays in Criticism, Culture and Society, 1982, The Critic as Conservator: Essays in Literature, Society, and Culture, 1992, The Critical Legacy of Irving Babbitt: An Appreciation, 1999, Growing Wings to Overcome Gravity: Criticism as the Pursuit of Virtue, 1999; Editor: (with G.R. Hibbard and A. Rodway) Renaissance and Modern Essays: Presented to Vivian de Sola Pinto in Celebration of His Seventieth Birthday, 1966, Mansions of the Spirit: Essays in Literature and Religion, 1967, Promise of Greatness: The War of 1914-1918, 1968, The Politics of Twentieth-Century Novelists, 1971, The Simone Weil Reader, 1977, Irving Babbitt: Representative Writings, 1981, (with C. G. Ryn) Irving Babbitt in our Time, 1986, Modern Age: The First Twenty-Five Years, A Selection, 1988, In Continuity: The Last Essays of Austin Warren, 1996; editorial advisor Modern Age: A Quar. Rev., 1971-77; assoc. editor, 1978-83, editor, 1984—; adv. bd. Continuity: A Jour. of History, 1984-88, Humanitas, 1993—; contbr. articles and revs. to profl. jours. Mem. Acad. Bd. Nat. Humanities Inst., 1985—; trustee Found. for Faith in Search of Understanding, 1987. Grantee Earhart Found., 1982. Fellow Royal Soc. Arts (U.K.). Eastern Orthodox. Home and Office: PO Box Ab College Park MD 20741-3025

PANICKER, GIRISH KUMAR, agricultural scientist, consultant; b. Paravur, Kerala, India, Jan. 11, 1949; s. Sukumar and Pankajam Panicker; m. Rani Girish Kumar, Apr. 27, 1988; 1 child, Aja Girish. BS in Agr., U. Kerala, 1972; MS in Agronomy, Alcorn State U., 1992; PhD in Hort., Miss. State U., 1999. Rsch. asst., tech. officer Dept. Agr., Kerala, 1972-78, asst. dir., 1978-80; prin. inspector agr. Dept. Sci. and Tech., Sokoto, Nigeria, 1980-89; grad. rsch. asst. agr. Alcorn State U., Lorman, Miss., 1990-92; rsch. assoc. soil conservation rsch. project USDA, Lorman, Miss., 1992-96; grad. rsch. asst. Miss. State U., Starkville, 1996-99; project coord. soil conservation rsch. project USDA, Lorman, 1999—; recruitment bd. cons. agr. Pub. Svc. Commn., Sokoto, Nigeria, 1986-89; cons. in agronomy for gen. pub., Miss., 1997—. Contbr. more than 25 articles to profl. jours. Coord. India Assn., Sokoto, 1986-89. Mem. Am. Soc. Agronomy, Soil Sci. Soc. Am., Crop Sci. Soc. Am., Soil and Water Conservation Soc. Am., World Assn. Soil and Water Conservation, Am. Soc. Hort. Sci. Avocations: ornamental and vegetable gardening, reading, writing scientific articles, watching the discovery channel. Office: Alcorn State U 1000 Asu Dr # 1434 Lorman MS 39096-7510

PANIGHI, MÓNICA PATRICIA, biological marketing professional; b. Rosario, Santa Fe, Argentina, June 3, 1964; d. Raul Reyes and Emilia Saida (Isa) P. Grad. high sch., Jujuy, Argentina, 1981. Biology diplomate. Rschr., prof. biology and agronomy U. Tucumán, Argentina, 1987-92; tech. sales rep. Network Internat. Technologies, Buenos Aires, 1993-94, sci. tech. asst., 1994-95, tech. mgr., 1995-96; product specialist Organon Teknika, Buenos Aires, 1996-97, product mgr., 1998-99, mktg. and svc. mgr., 1999—. Mem. Nat. U. Superior Coun., Tucumán, 1987-88. Scholar Ctr. Investigacion en Ciencias Vets.-Inst. Nacional de Tecnologia Agropecuaria, Buenos Aires, 1990. Mem. Am. Soc. Microbiology, Argentine Soc. Microbiology. Roman Catholic. Avocations: reading, ancient civilizations, swimming. E-mail: panighi@uol.com.ar, panighi@yahoo.com.

PANIGRAHI, BIBHU PRASAD, engineering educator, researcher; b. Kankalu, India, June 5, 1968; s. Bhaskar and Kamini Manjari (Dash) P.; m. Puspita Pani, Feb. 15, 1997. BSc in Engring., Sambalpur U., Orissa, India, 1989; M Tech., Indian Inst. Tech., Bombay, 1997. Asst. engr. F.C.I. Ltd., New Delhi, 1989-91; sr. lectr. Indira Gandhi Inst. Tech., Sarang, India, 1992—; cons. Nalco, Angul, India, 1993. Contbr. articles to profl. jours. Mem. Indian Soc. Tech. Edn. (life), Orissa Sci. Acad. (life). Avocations: reading, newspapers, magazines, research. Home: Kankalu Via Meramandali, Dist Dhenkanal, 759 121 Orissa India Office: Indira Gandhi Inst Tech, Dhenkanal, 759 146 Sarang India

PANIGRAHI, DEBADATTA, microbiology educator; b. Biswanathpur, Orissa, India, May 24, 1950; s. Bauribandhu and Laxmipriya (Dash) P.; m. Nirupama Hota, Feb. 21, 1976; children: Priyankar, Deepankar. MBBS, MKCG Med. Coll., Berhampur, India, 1973; MD, PGIMER, Chandigarh, India, 1976. Tutor med. microbiology, 1975-79; sr. microbiologist Steel Plant Main Hosp., Bhilai, India, 1979-81; asst. prof. microbiology Postgrad. Med. Inst., Chandigarh, India, 1981-85, assoc. prof. microbiology, 1986-87, 87-93; prof. microbiology PGIMER, Chandigarh, 1987-93, chmn. med. microbiology, 1991-93; assoc. prof. microbiology Kuwait U./Health Sci. Ctr., 1993-96, prof. microbiology, 1996—; adviser microbiology, Def. Rsch. Orgn., Govt. of India, 1991-93, bacterial and parasitic infections, Ind. Coun. of Med. Rsch., 1990-93, Regional Rsch. Ctr., Jabalpur, India, 1989-93; cons. Clin. Microbiologist, Ministry of Pub. Health, Kuwait, 1993—. Author: Hospital Administration and Management, 1989; contbr. articles to profl. jours. Gen. sec. Med. Coll. Studion Union, Berhampur, India, 1970-72; pres. Jr. Doctors Assn., Postgrad. Med. Inst., Chandigarh, 1978-79; gen. sec. Faculty Assn. PGIMER, Chandigarh, 1982-83, pres., 1987-88. Fellow WHO, Laussane, Switzerland, 1984; recipient Fogarty Internat. award NIH, 1985-87. Mem. Internat. Soc. Inf. Diseases, Internat. Assn. Advancement of Sci., Internat. Fedn. of Hosp. Inf. Control, others. Hindu. Avocations: tennis, badminton, photography, music.

PANIKKAR, RAIMON, priest; b. Barcelona, Spain, Nov. 2, 1918; came to U.S., 1967; s. Rammuni and Carmen (Alemany) P. Philosophy Licenciate, U. Barcelona, 1941, Chem. Sci. Licenciate, 1942; PhD, U. Madrid, 1946, D Chem. Scis., 1958. Ordained priest Roman Cath. Ch., 1946. Chaplain U. Madrid, 1946-50, U. Salamanca (Spain), 1950-53, U. Rome, 1950-63, Diocese Varanasi (India), 1964—; prof. U. Calif., Santa Barbara, 1971-87, prof. emeritus, 1987—. Author: The Unknown Christ of Hinduism, 1981, Blessed Simplicity, 1982, Vedic Experience, 1989, The Silence of God, 1989, A Dwelling Place for Wisdom, 1993, The Cosmotheandric Experience, 1993, Cultural Disarmament: A Way to Peace, 1995, Invisible Harmony, 1995, Intrareligious Dialogue, 1999. Mem. Teilhard de Chardin Centre (v.p.), Am. Acad. Religion, Internat. Inst. Philosophy. Office: U Calif Dept Religious Studies Santa Barbara CA 93106

PANIKOV, NICOLAI SERGEYEVICH, microbiologist, researcher; b. N-Udinsk, Russia, Mar. 1, 1950; s. Sergey Dmitriyevich and Alexandra Fedorovna (Tichomirova) P.; m. Elena Livovna (Stepanova), Feb. 20, 1974, (div. Feb. 1994); children: Anna, Sergey; m. Maria Vyacheslavovna Sizova, Mar. 24, 1994. BSc, Moscow Univ., Russia, 1972; PhD, Moscow Univ., 1976, DSci, 1989. Jr. researcher Moscow Univ., 1975-83; postdoctoral Queen Elizabeth Coll., London, 1976-77; sr. researcher Moscow Univ., 1983-89; head of lab. Inst. of Moscow, 1989—; vice dir. Microbiology Russian Acad. of Sci., Moscow, 1991-96; prof. dept. chemistry and chem. biology Stevens Inst. Tech., 1999—; vis. prof. Mich. State Univ., East Lansing, 1995-96, Univ. of Louisville, 1996-97. Author: Microbial Growth Kinetics, 1995, The Kinetics of Microbial Growth: General Principles and Ecological Applications, 1992, Individual Components of Soil Humus, 1984; contbr. articles to profl. jours. Recipient numerous rsch. grants, 1995, 1998—, 1992-94. Avocations: poetry, tourism, swimming. E-mail: npanikov@stevens-tech.edu. Fax: 201-216-8240. Home: Zagorodnoye Sh 15/1 App 46, 113152

Moscow Russia Office: Inst of Microbiology, Prospect 60 Let Octabrya 7, 117811 Moscow Russia Home: 2 Ninth St Hoboken NJ 07030 Office: Stevens Inst Tech Castle Point on Hudson Hoboken NJ 07030

PANIN, LEV EVGENYEVICH, biochemist, researcher; b. Tobolsk, Tyumen, Russia, Nov. 15, 1935; s. Evgenii Dmitrievich and Zoya Nikolaevna (Minervina) P.; m. Galina Ivanovna Schvets, July 31, 1980; 1 child, Vera L'vovna. Physician, Tomsk State Med. Inst., Russia, 1960; PhD, Leningrad State Inst. Hygiene, Russia, 1965; MD, Inst. Clin. & Exptl. Medicine, Novosibirsk, Russia, 1976. Asst. prof. Tomsk State Med. Inst., 1963-71; chief biochemistry lab. Inst. Clin. Exptl. Medicine, Novosibirsk, 1971-88, dep. dir., 1981-87; dir. Inst. Biochemistry, Novosibirsk, 1988—; prof. Inst. Clin. & Exptl. Medicine, Novosibirsk, 1984—. Author: (books) Psychosomatic Interrelations in Chronic Emotional Stress, 1981, Biochemical Mechanism of Stress, 1983, Lysosomes: Role in Adaptation and Restoration, 1987 (Pirogov's award 1994); contbr. numerous papers to profl. jours.; patentee in field. Recipient Hildes medal Internat. Union for Circumpolar Health, 1996. Mem. Russian Acad. Med. Scis. (corr., academician). Avocation: classical music. Home: Krylov St 41-187, 630005 Novosibirsk Russia Office: Inst Biochemistry, Acad Timakov St 2, 630117 Novosibirsk Russia

PANIS, OLIVIER, race car driver; b. Oullins, Lyon, France, Sept. 2, 1966; m. Anne Montanari; children: Aurelien, Caroline. Race car driver, 1988—. 2d pl. finisher French Formula Renault, 1988, 5-time winner, champion, 1989, 2d pl. French Formula 3, 1991, champion, 3-time winner Internat. Formula 3000, 1993. Office: Prost Grand Prix, 7 Ave Eugene Freyssenet, 78286 Guyancourt France*

PANITZ, LAWRENCE, physician; b. Apr. 30, 1928; s. Max and Gussie (Gorenstein) P.; m. Adrienne Ruth Luke, June 20, 1965; children: Jennifer, Michael. BA, NYU, 1962, MD, 1966. Diplomate Am. Bd. Family Practice. Intern St. Joseph's Hosp., Syracuse, N.Y., 1966-67; practice gen. medicine Elmsford, N.Y., 1967-90, Hawthorne, N.Y., 1968—; affiliated with Docs Physicians Beth Israel Med. Ctr., N.Y.C., Shrub Oak, N.Y., Hartsdale, N.Y., Larchmont, N.Y., Yonkers, N.Y., Thornwood, N.Y., Crestwood, N.Y., New City, N.Y., West Haverstraw, N.Y., and numerous other cities, 1992-97; mem. staff New Rochelle (N.Y.) Hosp., St. Agnes Hosp., White Plains, N.Y., Phelps Meml. Hosp., North Tarrytown, N.Y., Westchester County Med. Ctr., Valhalla, N.Y., Dobbs Ferry Hosp., Beth Israel Hosp. Med. Ctr., N.Y.C., New Rochelle Hosp. Med. Ctr., Sound Shore Med. Ctr.; dep. dir. dept. family practice Phelps Meml. Hosp.; dir. Elmsford Med. Ctr.; police surgeon Tarrytown and North Tarrytown, Sleepy Hollow, Elmsford, Town of Greenburgh; med. dir. Margaret Chapman Sch. for Exceptional Child, Hawthorne; med. dir., prin. rschr. Clin. Tech. Assoc., Elmsford, N.Y., CNS Biosvcs., Pleasantville, N.Y.; physician Westchester County Correctional Health Dept., Valhalla; sch. physician Elmsford, N.Y. With U.S. Army, 1946-48, 82-88; lt. col. M.C. USAR; ret. Fellow AMA, Am. Acad. Family Physicians, Med. Soc. State of N.Y., Westchester County Med. Soc., Westchester Acad. Medicine, Shriners, Masons. Jewish. Home and Office: Riveredge 3 David Ln Yonkers NY 10701-1117 Office: 5 Bradhurst Ave Hawthorne NY 10532-2154

PANKOV, ANDREY ANATOLEVICH, aerospace scientist, educator; b. Gubaha, Perm, Russia, Mar. 23, 1965; s. Anatoliy Andreevich and Ludmila Mihailovna (Kotyaeva) P. ScD, Inst. Continuous Media Mechanics, Perm, 1993. Asst. Perm Poly. Inst., 1991-94; docent Perm State Tech. U., 1994—; lectr. Perm State Tech. U., 1988-2000. Author: Lectures on a Mechanics of Composite Structures, 1999, Elastic Wave Difraction in Stochastic Composite, 2000; contbr. articles to profl. jours. Eastern Orthodox. Avocations: mountain and water tourism, skiing, photography. E-mail: mkmk@cpl.pstu.ac.ru. Office: Perm State Tech Univ, 29-a Komsomolskiy Ave, 614600 Perm Russia

PANKOV, GRADIMIR KRUNISLAV, ballet artistic director; b. Skopje, Macedonia, Yugoslavia, Oct. 25, 1938; s. Krunislav Ivan and Dragica Isak (Mihajlovska) P.; m. Margret Maria Kaufmann, Dec. 30, 1980. Baccalaureat, Josip Broz Tito Gymnasium, Skopje, 1956; diploma, State Conservatory of Dance & Music, Skopje, 1957. Dancer Nat. Theatre Macedonia, Skopje, 1956-63; guest artist Nat. Theatres, Belgrade, Zagreb, Sarajevo, 1963-67; soloist City Theatres, Nuremberg, Karlsruhe, Wuppertal, Fed. Republic Germany, Theater Am Gärtnerplatz, Munich, 1967-74, Nat. Theatre, Mannheim, Fed. Republic Germany, 1974-76; ballet master City Theatre, Dortmund, 1976-80; artistic dir., tchr. Netherlands Dance Theatre Jr. Co., The Hague, 1980-81; artistic dir. Nat. Ballet of Finland, Helsinki, 1981-84; artistic dir., tchr. Cullberg Ballet, Stockholm, 1984-88; artistic dir. Ballet du Grand Theatre, Geneva, 1988-96, Les Grands Ballets Canadiens de Montreal, 2000—. Ballet roles include Mercutio in Romeo and Juliet, 1963, title role in Petrushka, 1965, title role in Pulcinella, 1971, The Faun in Afternoon of a Faun, 1975; choreographer (operas) Eugene Onegin, 1977, Carmen, 1978, Don Giovanni, 1978. Office: Les Grands Ballets Canadiens de Montreal, 4816 Rivard, Montreal, PQ Canada

PANKOV, YURI ALEXANDROVICH, molecular biologist, biochemist; b. Leningrad, Russia, Feb. 10, 1930; s. Alexandr Alexeevich and Anna Kusminichna (Ershova) P.; m. Svetlana Sergeevna Chumachenko Pankova, June 9, 1964; children: Denis, Darya. Diploma in Biochemistry, State U., Leningrad, Russia, 1953, diploma in Biophysics, 1970; D in Biol. Scis., Sci. Coun. Acad. Med. Scis., Moscow, Russia, 1968. Jr. scientist Inst. Biol. and Med. Chemistry, Moscow, 1953-65; sr. scientist Inst. Experimental Endocrinology and Hormone Chemistry, Moscow, 1965-70, deputy dir., 1970-83, dir., 1983-90; head of lab. Endocrine Rsch. Ctr., Moscow, 1990—; dir. World Health Orgn. Collaborating Ctr. of Spl. Program of Rsch., Devel. and Rsch. Tng. in Human Reproduction, Moscow, 1984-97; mem. Scientific and Tech. Adv. Group of Spl. Program of Rsch. Devel., and Rsch. Tng. in Human Reproduction, Geneva, Suisse, 1985-90. Author: Biochemistry of Hormone and Hormonal Regulation, 1976; contbr. papers in field. Hon. mem. Cuba Endocrinology Soc., 1984; hon. citizen Lexington Urban Govt., 1987. Grantee: Internat. Sci. Found., 1994. Mem. The Endocrine Soc., European Assn. for Study of Diabetes, Moscow House of Scientists, Russian Acad. of Med. Scis. Avocations: boating, fishing, skiing, vegetable growing. E-mail: yuri-pankov@mtu-net.ru. Fax: (7095) 112-35-47. Office: Endocrine Rsch Ctr, Moscvorechye St 1, 115478 Moscow Russia

PANKOW, MARIA STEFANIA, astronomer; b. Lvov, Poland, Apr. 17, 1932; d. Stefan and Maria (Wanczura) P. MS, Jagiellonian U., Cracov, Poland, 1955; D of Astronomy, U. Silesia, Katowice, Poland, 1971. Sci. dir. Planetarium, Chorzow, Poland, 1955-76; lectr. in pedagogical sch. Katowice, Poland, 1957-68; dir. dept. observational astronomy U. Silesia, Katowice, Poland, 1973-80, lectr., 1974—. Editor: (handbook) Wydawnictwa Szkolne i Pedagogiczne, 1981, Wydawnictwo Uniwersytetu Slaskiego; contbr. numerous articles to profl. jours. Bd. dirs. Polish Dem. Party, Katowice, 1969-92; mem. Polish Cmty., Katowice. Mem. Planetary Soc., Polish Astron. Soc. (bd. dirs. 1960, pres. Silesian br. 1983). Polish Dem. Party. Roman Catholic. Avocations: books, listening to classical music, gardening. Home: Tysigclecia 80/29, 40-871 Katowice Poland Office: U Silesia, Uniwersytecka 4, 40-007 Katowice Poland

PANKRATOV, OLEG ALEXANDROVITSCH, physics educator; b. Naltschik, Russia, Sept. 15, 1949; s. Alexander Jakovlevitsch and Valentina Ivanovna (Loboda) P.; m. Lioudmila Pavlovna Polenova, May 19, 1977; 1 child, Evgueniia. Diploma engr.-physicist, Moscow Phys. Tech. Inst., 1973, PhD, 1977; DSc, Lebedev Phys. Inst., 1988. Rsch. staff Inst. for Semiconductor Materials, Moscow, 1977-78; sr. rsch. staff Inst. for Applied Physics, Moscow, 1978-84, Lebedev Phys. Inst. of Russian Acad. of Scis., Moscow, 1984-89; rsch. staff Fritz-Haber Inst. of Max Planck Soc., Berlin, 1990-95, Lawrence Livermore Nat. Lab., Calif., 1995-97; prof. physics U. Erlangen-Nürnberg, Germany, 1997—; guest prof. Johannes-Kepler U., Linz, Austria, 1989, guest prof., 1992; rsch. leader Inst. Ctr. for Theoretical Physics, Trieste, Italy, 1990. Contbr. articles to profl. jours. Humboldt Rsch. fellowship Humboldt Found., 1990. Mem. Am. Phys. Soc. Avocations: music, skiing, tennis. Office: U Erlangen-Nürnberg, Staudtstrasse 7-B2, D-91058 Erlangen Germany

PANNEBAKER, JAMES BOYD, lawyer; b. Middletown, Pa., Mar. 9, 1936; s. Boyd Alton and Kathryn Kennedy (Brindle) P.; divorced; children: Jeffery B., Renee E. Pannebaker Bench, Traci Lee Pannebaker. BS, Elizabethtown Coll., 1958; JD, U. Mich., 1961. Bar: Pa. 1962, U.S. Dist. Ct. (mid. dist.) Pa., U.S. Ct. Appeals (3d cir.), U.S. Supreme Ct. 1969. Pvt. practice, Harrisburg, 1965-86; pres. Pannebaker & Jones, P.C., Middletown, 1986—; mem. regional adv. bd. Mellon Bank, Harrisburg, 1980—. Bd. dirs. Cmty. Gen. Osteo. Hosp., harrisburg, 1970-98; trustee Elizabethtown (Pa.) Coll., 1972-78; mem. adv. bd. Villa Teresa Nursing Home, Harrisburg, 1985—; past chmn. Middletown chpt. ARC; pres. Keystone Area coun. Boy Scouts Am. Capt. U.S. Army, 1962-65. Mem. Am. Legion, Masons, Shriners, Elks. Republican. Methodist. Avocations: skiing, sailing, horseback riding, outdoor activities. Office: Pannebaker & Jones PC 4000 Vine St Middletown PA 17057-3565

PANNELL, CLIFTON WYNDHAM, geography educator, writer; b. Tuscaloosa, Ala., Mar. 24, 1939; s. Henry Clifton and Anne Thomas (Gary) P.; m. Laurie Preston deBuys, Feb. 14, 1964 (dec. Aug. 1992); children: Alexander, Richard, Charles, Thomas; m. Sylvia Hillyard, Dec. 9, 1994. AB, U. N.C., 1961; AM, U. Va., 1962; postgrad. Inter-Univ. Ctr., for Chinese Lang. Studies, Taipei, 1968-69; PhD, U. Chgo., 1971. Lectr. U. Md. Far East Divsn., Taiwan, 1970-71; asst. prof. geography U. Ga., Athens, 1971-75, assoc. prof., 1975-80, prof., 1980—, dir. Ctr. for Asian Studies, 1987-92; assoc. dean Franklin Coll. Arts and Scis. U. Ga., 1994—; vis. prof. U.S. Mil. Acad., 1984, U. Hong Kong, 1993; mem. adv. bd. Ga. Rev., 1982-86. Author: China: The Geography of Development and Modernizatin, 1983, East Asia: Geographical and Historical Approaches to Foreign Area Studies, 1983; contbr. articles and revs. to profl. jours. and mags., chpts. to textbooks. Served to lt. USNR, 1962-66. NSF rsch. grantee 1979-82; recipient medal for creative research U. Ga. Research Found., 1981. Mem. Nat. Coun. Geog. Edn., Assn. Am. Geographers, Am. Geog. Soc., Assn. Asian Studies, Can. Assn. Geographers.

PANNER, JEANNIE HARRIGAN, retired electrical engineer; b. Malone, N.Y., Jan. 4, 1948; d. Martin Thomas and Marjorie (Boyea) Harrigan; m. John Charles Panner, Aug. 17, 1974. BS summa cum laude, SUNY, Plattsburgh, 1970; MA in Math., U. Vt., 1974, MSEE, 1993. Programmer Microelectronics Divsn. IBM, Burlington, Vt., 1970-71, assoc. programmer, 1971-74, sr. assoc. programmer, 1974-79, staff engr., 1979-85, adv. engr., 1985-90, sr. engr., 1990-97, sr. tech. staff, 1997-2000. Contbr. articles to engrng. jours.; patentee in field. Mem. IEEE. Avocations: golf, travel, gardening. Home: 55 Maple Leaf Farm Rd Underhill VT 05489-9361

PANNETON, JACQUES, librarian; b. Trois-Rivières, Que., Can., May 7, 1943; s. Marcel and Bernadette (Page) P.; married; children—Anne-Marie, Luce. B.L.S., U. Montréal, 1964. Cataloguer Bibliothèque de Trois-Rivières, 1964-65; dep. librarian, then head librarian Bibliothèque Centrale de Pret de la Mauricie, Trois-Rivières, 1965-74; head librarian Bibliothèque de la Ville de Montréal, 1974—; prof. pub. libraries U. Montréal Library Sch., 1974-75; mem. Com. Cons. du Livre, Govt. Que., 1976; mem. adv. bd. Nat. Library Can., 1978—; mem. com. d'étude sur bibliothèques publiques Govt. Qué., 1987; invited guest German libraries, German Fed. Republic, summer 1976, Brit. libraries, spring 1978; mem. Planning Com. for a New Provincial Libr. in Que., 1997; bd. dirs. La Grande Bibliothiques du Que., 1998—. Contbr. articles to profl. jours. Mem. Canadian, Am., Que. library assns., Corp. Profl. Librarians Que. (past pres.), Assn. pour l'avancement des sci. et des techniques de la documentation, Council Adminstrs. Large Urban Pub. Libraries, Internat. Fedn. Library Assns., Internat. Assn. Met. City Libraries. Office: Bibliothèque de Montreal, 5650 d'Iberville St Ste 400, Montreal, PQ Canada H2G 3E4

PANNKE, PEGGY M., long term care insurance agency executive; b. Chgo., Oct. 26; d. Victor E. and Leona (O'Leary) Stich; m. Craig D. Smith, July 18, 1998; children from previous marriage: Thomas Scott, David Savonne, Heidi Mireille, Peter. V.p. long term care ins. Sales & Seminars, Des Plaines, 1986-90; pres., founder Nat. Consumer Oriented Agy., Des Plaines, 1990—; columnist Senior News, Senior Connection, Senior Marketplace News, Front Ranger News; cons. on long-term care ins. The Travelers, Tchrs. Ins. & Annuity Assocs., others; speaker Exec. Enterprises, N.Y.C., 1988-93. ontbr. articles to profl. jours. Sponsor Ill. Alliance for Aging, Chgo., 1990—, Ill. Assn. Homes for Aging, 1990-91; bd. govs. St. Matthew Luth. Home, Park Ridge, Ill., 1993-95. Recipient Speakers awards Health Ins. Assn. Am., Washington, 1990, Retired Officers Assn., Glenview, Ill., 1991, 93, Nat. Assn. Sr. Living Industries, Denver, 1992, Exec. Enterprises, N.Y.C., 1993, Gov.'s Conf. on Aging, Chgo., 1996. Mem. Nat. Assn. Sr. Living Industries, Nat. Assn. Long Term Care Profls. (charter), Ctr. for Applied Gerontology, Nat. Coun. on Aging, Mature Ams. (ad hoc com.), Am. Mensa (program dir. in Ill. 1983-85, Colo. chpt. 1999—), Kiwanis (bd. dirs. Park Ridge 1992-98, pres. 1996-97), Am. Soc. on Aging, Internat. Soc. for Retirement Planning, Park Ridge C. of C., Boulder C. of C., Colo. Mountain Club, Friends of the Colorado Trail. Avocations: showshoeing, travel, sketching wildflowers, hiking. Office: Nat Consumer Oriented Agy 2200 E Devon Ave Ste 359 Des Plaines IL 60018-4505 also: Cherry Creek 300 S Jackson St Denver CO 80209-3176 also: 4450 Arapahoe Ave Boulder CO 80303-9123

PANNURU, VENKA TESU, chemistry educator; b. Tirupati, Indai, June 14, 1966; s. Chetty and Alimelumma (Kalappa) P. BS, S.V. Arts Coll., Tirupati, India, 1987; MS, S.V. Arts Coll., 1989, PhD, 1994. Post-doctoral fellow Warsaw U. Tech., Warsaw, Poland, 1997-98. Contbr. articles to profl. jours. Recipient rsch. assoc., Coun. Scientific & Indsl. Rsch., New Delhi, 1995, fellowship, Warsaw U. Tech., 1997. Avocation: reading. Home: Mogarala Damal Cheruru, Chitton India Office: Dept Chemistry, SV Univ, Tirupata India

PANOPOULOS, GEORGE, internist; b. Athens, Greece, Oct. 26, 1957; s. Nicholas and Catherine Panopoulos; m. Gesthimani Pandazi, Nov. 20, 1983; children: Catherine, Nicholas. MD, U. Thessaloniki, Greece, 1975. Intern, resident in internal medicine, rsch. asst. Athens U. Hosp., 1986-91; pvt. practice, Athens, 1992—; participant, presenter internat. confs., including 5th Internat. Conf. on Thalassaemias and Haemoglobinopathiies, Cyprus, 1993. Mem. N.Y. Acad. Scis. Home: 98 Gortinias St, 16561 Ano Glyfada Attica, Greece Office: 97 Gennimata St, 165 61 Ano Glyfada Attica Greece

PANOTOPOULOS, GEORGE, internist, nutritionist; b. Athens, Greece, Aug. 18, 1959; s. Athanassios and Marina P.; m. Helen Papaskeva, June 23, 1989. MD in Internal Medicine, Athens U. Med. Faculty, 1983; Nutritionist, U. Paris, 1994. Sr. registrar Alexandra/U. Hosp., Athens, Greece, 1991-92; chef de clinique des universites Hotel Dieu, Paris, 1992-94; pres. Hellenic Soc. Obesity, Athens, 1994—. Contbr. articles to profl. publs. Mem. Athens Med. Orgn., European Assn. for Study of Obesity, Ordre Des Medecins. Office: 119 Vas Sofias Ave, 11521 Athens Greece

PANOV, BRANKO MITO, historian, educator; b. Strumica, Republic of Macedonia, Mar. 22, 1932; s. Mito and Kaliopa (Samardzitrajkova) P.; m. Zoja Mishaykova, Nov. 11, 1962; children: Tatyana, Mitko. BA in History, Faculty of Philosophy, U. Skopje, Macedonia, 1955, PhD, 1965; postdoctoral studies, Inst. Slavic Studies, Moscow, 1967. Asst. Inst. History Faculty of Philosophy, Skopje, Macedonia, 1956-65, asst. prof., 1966-71, assoc. prof., 1971-76, prof., 1976—; founder and head dept. of Byzantine Studies Faculty of Philosophy, U. Skopje, Macedonia, 1966—; head Inst. of History, Faculty of Philosophy, U. Skopje, 1979-83, head of postgrad. studies in history, 1986—; head of Internat. Sci. Project on Cyril and Methodius commd. by Univs. Warsaw and Skopje, 1986-91. Author: (books) Theophylactes of Ohrid as a Source for the Medieval History of the Macedonian People, 1971 (Sci. award Skopje, "13 Nov." 1972), Medieval Macedonia Vols II-III, 1985 (Sci. award Republic of Macedonia, 1986), Albania and the Albanians in the Middle Ages, 1998, Macedonia Throughout History, 1999, A History of the Macedonian People, vol. I, 2000; editor Vol. I. Documents on the Struggle of the Macedonian People for Independence and a Nation State, vols. I-II, 1985; pres. editorial bd. Annual of the Faculty of Philosophy, 1978; contbr. more than 100 articles to historical publs. and jours. Pres. Coun. Faculty of Philosophy, Skopje, 1978-80; mem. Yugoslav Byzantine Com., Belgrade, 1971-91, administrative coun. of Macedonian-Russian Soc., Skopje, 1993—; pres. Macedonian-Ukranian Soc., Skopje, 1994—. Recipient Labour medal with golden wreath Pres. S.F.R.Y., 1978, Decoration of Univ. Ss. Cyril and Methodius, Skopje, 1984, St. Clement of Ohrid award for edn. and cultural achievement Republic of Macedonia, 1992; and other medals and awards. Mem. Coun. of Balkanology, Macedonian Acad. Scis. and Arts, Sci. Forum, Soc. of Historians of Republic of Macedonia. Home: Kej 13 Noemvri 20/33, 91000 Skopje Macedonia Office: Faculty of Philosophy, Bul Krste Misirkov bb, 91000 Skopje Macedonia

PANOV, DMITRY ALEKSANDROVICH, physicist; b. Moscow, Nov. 21, 1929; s. Aleksandr and Yutta (Voizekhovskaja) P.; m. Valentina Petrovna Zaizeva, Dec. 21, 1952; two children. BS, Moscow U., 1952. From jr. scientific collaborator to lab. chief Kurchatov Inst., Moscow, 1952—.

PANOV, KIRIL PANTELEEV, astronomist; b. Belogradchick, Bulgaria, Sept. 1, 1943; s. Pantaleij Kirov and Nadezhda Vasileva Christova P.; m. Kostadinka Tzvetanova Bakalova, Aug. 14, 1972; children: Nadezhda Kirilova, Marianna Kirilova. Astronomer, U. Sofia, 1968; PhD, Astrophysikalisches Inst., Potsdam, Germany, 1974; Sr. Rschr., Bulgarian Acad. Scis., Sofia, 1985. Rschr. Bulgarian Acad. Scis., Sofia, 1975-85, sr. rschr., 1985—; dir. Inst. Astronomy, Sofia, 1995—. Co-author: Participation in Building the National Astronomy Observatory (cert. of honor 1981). Mem. Internat. Astron. Union, N.Y. Acad. Scis. Avocation: skiing. Home: Komplex Banishora Bl 24/A, 1233 Sofia Bulgaria Office: Inst Astronomy, 72 Zarigradsko Chosse, 1784 Sofia Bulgaria

PANSU, ROBERT BERNARD, physical chemist; b. Lyon, France, Mar. 9, 1958; s. Claude and Danielle (Esclangon) P.; m. Anne Astier; children: Vincent, Bruno, Camille. Agrégation, France, 1981; Doctorate, U. Paris XI, 1988. Chargé de rsch. Lab. Phys. Chem. Rayonnements, Orsay, France, 1983-89; postdoctoral staff Inst. for Molecular Scis., Okasaki, Japan, 1988-89; chargé de rsch. dept. chemistry Ecole Normale Supérieure de Cachan, France, 1989-2000. Contbr. articles to profl. jours. Sgt. Sci. Infantry, 1983. Mem. Soc. Française Chimie, Groupe Française Photochimie (pres. 2000). Office: UMR 8531 CNRS, 61 ave du Pres Wilson, 94235 Cachan Cedex, France

PANT, HEM CHANDRA, veterinarian; b. Pithoragarh, India, May 15, 1937; s. Chanchala Ballabh and Basanti (Pande) P.; m. Usha Joshi, May 17, 1969; children: Prarthana, Tripti, Ashish. B.Vet. Sci. and Animal Husbandry, Agra (India) U., 1957, MVSc, 1961, PhD, 1968; PhD, Liverpool (U.K.) U., 1974. Demonstrator Coll. Vet. Sci. and Animal Husbandry Chandra Shekhar Azad U., Mathura, India, 1957-61, lectr., 1961-63, rsch. officer, 1963-67, asst. prof., 1967-69, sr. rschr., 1969-74, officer/sr. scientist, 1974-75, prof., 1975-97; adv. Sabarmati Ashram Gaushala, Gujarat, 1998—; vis. prof. Coll. Vet. Medicine, Baghdad, Iraq, 1980-83, Uppsala, Sweden, 1981, 83, 87; expert IAEA, Vienna, Austria, 1997; lectr. in field. The Commonwealth Scholarship Commn. postdoctoral fellow, 1970, U. Liverpool fellow, 1971, Ford Found. fellow, 1972, Nat. Acad. Vet. Scis. fellow, 1996. Mem. Indian Assn. Fertility and Sterility (life), Indian Soc. for Study of Animal Reprodn. (life). Fax: (02694) 88562. Home: B-4 Veterinary College, Mathura 281001, India Office: Bidaj Farm PO Lali, Dist Kheda, Gujarat 387120, India

PANT, MUKTESH, marketing professional; b. Almora, India, Sept. 1, 1954; s. Shukdeo and Gaura (Pande) P.; m. Vinita Pant, Apr. 19, 1980; 1 child, Sara. B Tech. in Chem. Engrng., Indian Inst. Tech., Kanpur, 1976. Gen. mgr. mktg. Unilever India, Bombay, 1976-90; exec. dir. Pepsico India Holdings, New Delhi, 1990-94; mng. dir. Reebok India, New Delhi, 1994-97; regional dir. Africa/Middle East/India Reebok Internat. Ltd., 1998—; chmn. Dukes Beverages, Bombay, 1993-96, Panagarh Beverages, Calcutta, 1993-94; spkr. bus. seminars in U.S. and Australia; cons. Ministry Commerce, Govt. India, 1992. Editor: Pepsi Handbook of Indian Exports, 1991; contbr. articles to profl. jours. Recipient nat. merit scholarship Govt. India, 1971-76. Hindu. Avocations: astronomy, running, bridge. Home: D1/25 Vasant Vihar, New Delhi India Office: Reebok Internat Ltd 100 Technology Center Dr Stoughton MA 02072-4705

PANTALEO, JACK, writer, composer, social worker, harpist; b. Melrose Park, Ill., Nov. 30, 1954; s. Jack Sam Pantaleo and Sophia Mannozzi Pantaleo Cicero. Psychiat. Tech., C.C., San Francisco, 1981; BA in Humanities, New Coll. Calif., San Francisco, 1986; MA in Writing, U. San Francisco, 1988. Lic. psychiat. technician. Asst. to dean U. San Francisco Sch. Nursing, 1984-88; grammar sch. tchr. St. Michael's Cath. Sch., San Francisco, 1989-91; instr. English Vista C.C., Berkeley, Calif., 1990-93; social worker City and County of San Francisco, 1991—; founder, dir. Evangelicals Concerned, San Francisco, 1978-85; co-founder, co-dir. AIDS InterFaith Network, San Francisco, 1983-88. Author: (novel) Mother Julian and the Gentle Vampire, 2000; Playwright/composer musical The Gospel According to the Angel Julius translated into German and performed in Hamburg, Germany, 1999; (one-act play): Uncle Fred's Ex-Staight Ministry in Wilma Loves Betty, 1999; contbg. author: (collection of meditations) The Road to Emmaus, 1990; author booklet and articles. Caregiver for babies with AIDS, The Bridge, San Francisco, 1989-93. Work included in Silver Quill, The David Ross Meml. Competition, Wichita, 1996. Mem. Social Workers Union, Nat. Writers Union. Democrat. Episcopalian. Avocations: harp, lecturing. Office: Child Protection Ctr San Francisco Gen Hosp 995 Potrero Ave San Francisco CA 94110-2859

PANTELARAS, PANTELIS JOHN, chemical engineer; b. Chios, Greece, July 23, 1956; s. John and Angeliki (Sandonas) P.; m. Maria Moutafi, Nov. 5, 1983. BSChE, Aristotilian U., 1979; BSBA, Aegean U., 1992; deg. leather tech., Nene Coll., 1982. Tech. dir. N. Zafirakis & Sons S.A., Chios, 1981-89; tech. advisor George Vretos, Athens, Greece, 1990-91; tech. advisor, ptnr. Damivret George Vretos EPE, Athens, 1991-92; owner Damivret Agys. EPE, Athens, 1993—; external asst. El. Ke. De. SA, Athens, 1995—; gen. mgr. Hellenic Tanners Assn., Athens, 1996. Mem. Am. Leather Chemists Assn., Soc. Leather Technologists and Chemists Eng., Water Environment Fedn. Nat. Democrat. Christian Orthodox. Avocations: swimming, travel, selections. Office: Damivret Agys EPE, 180 Piraeus and Lamias St, GR 17778 Tavros Greece

PANTIĆ, VLADIMIR RADIVOJE, cytologist, neuroendocrinologist; b. Medjulužje, Serbia, Yugoslavia, Apr. 5, 1921; s. Radivoje Radovan and Stanica Radovan (Urošević) P.; m. Olivera Vido Jablan, July 11, 1949; children: Zoran, Sanja. DVM, U. Belgrade, Yugoslavia, 1950, DVM Sci., 1954. Asst. Inst. Histology and Embryology U. Belgrade Vet. Faculty, 1950-57, lectr., 1957-63, extraordinary prof., 1963-72, ordinary prof., head dept. histology and embryology, 1972-86, head dept. cytology and embryology Inst. Biol. Rsch., 1963-86; mem. Serbian Acad. Scis. and Arts, Belgrade, 1970—, sec. dept. natural scis. and math., 1981—, mem. presidium, 1981-94; chief Lab. for Electron Microscopy, Inst. Application Nuclear Energy, Zemun, 1964-75; mem. Matica Srpska, Novi Sad, 1990—. Author: Cell Biology, 1974, 97, Embryology, 6th edit., 1996, Histology, 4th edit., 1995, Morphology of Domestic Animals, 7th edit., 1997; contbr. articles to sci. jours., author monograph. Recipient Serbian Republic prize for sci., 1960, hon. diploma Serbian Soc. Biologists, 1972, Belgrade prize for biomed. scis., 1975, Yugoslavian prize for biomed. sci., 1984. Mem. Internat. Soc. Cell Biology, Internat. Soc. Electron Microscopy, Internat. Found. for Biochem. Endocrinology (v.p. 1989—), European Soc. Comparative Endocrinology (exec. coun. 1977-88, hon. v.p. 1986-87), Yugoslav Soc. for Electron Microscopy (pres. 1975-78), Yugoslav Soc. Veterinarians (pres. 1994-98), Yugoslav Acad. Scis. and Arts, Union Yugoslav Socs. Anatomists and Histologists, Soc. Anatomists and Histologists Bulgaria (hon.), Yugoslavian Soc. Orthodontists, Serbian Med. Soc. (hon.), Serbian Socs. for Electron Microscopy (hon. pres.), Soc. Italian Anatomists (hon.), Acad. Serbian Vet. Soc., Acad. Engrng. Yugoslav Soc. Orthodox. Home: Dobračina 12, 11000 Belgrade Yugoslavia Office: SANU, Knez Mihajlova 35, 11000 Belgrade Yugoslavia

PANTÓ, GYÖRGY, geochemist; b. Budapest, Hungary, July 29, 1936; s. Endre and Ilona (Botar) P.; m. Marta Juhasz, July 29, 1961; children: Tamás, Zsuzsanna. Diploma in Geology, Eötvös U., Budapest, 1959; Candidate Sci., Hungarian Acad. Scis., Budapest, 1966, DSc, 1980. Mine geologist Hungarian Mineral and Ore Mines, Budapest, 1959-62; rschr. Lab. Geochem. Rsch. Hungarian Acad. Scis., Budapest, 1965-76, sci. dir., 1976-2000, head dept. earth sci., 1999—, dir. gen. Rsch. Ctr. for Earth Scis., 2000—. Contbr. articles to profl. jours. Scholar Hungarian Acad. Scis., Budapest, 1962-65. Avocations: gardening, tourism. Home: Báthori u. 4, H-1054 Budapest Hungary

PANTZARIS, CHRISTOS STAVROU, bank executive; b. Nicosia, Cyprus, Feb. 23, 1934; s. Stavros and Eleni (Tsigarides) P.; B.Sc. in Tech. with honours in C.E., Manchester U., 1957; m. Annita George Colocassides, Nov. 9, 1958; children: Avgusta, Eleni, Stavros. Asst. dist. engr. P.W.D., Nicosia, 1958; exec. dir. S&G Colocassides, Ltd., Nicosia, 1959-93; exec. chmn. Dexel Battery Makers, Ltd., Nicosia, 1970—; chmn. Electricity Authority of Cyprus, 1974-79; dir. Bank Cyprus Group, Ltd., Nocosia, 1974—, group v.p., chmn., CEO; chmn. Kermia Ltd., Nicosia, 1975—. Mem. exec. coun. Cyprus Employers and Industrialists Fedn., 1968—, chmn. 1969-72; bd. dirs. Cyprus Productivity Centre, 1969-73. Mem. Cyprus Civil Engrs. and Archs., Cyprus Profl. Engrs. Assn. (founding mem., 1st vice chmn.). Home: 2, Sachtouris St, 1080 Ay. Omoloyites, Nicosia Cyprus Office: Airport Rd, Nicosia,, 51, Stassinos St, 1599 Nicosia Cyprus

PANUSZKA, RYSZARD, acoustic engineer, educator; b. Wieliczka, Pland, Apr. 1, 1946; s. Jozef and Stefania (Jaworska) P.; m. Maria Bobowiec, June 22, 1974; 1 child, Justyna. MSc, Tech. U. Mining Metallurgy, Krakow, Poland, 1969, PhD, 1976. From rsch. engr. to profl. Tech. U. Mining Metallurgy, 1970—, prof. vibroacoustics, 1994—. Author: Energy Methods in Vibroacoustics, 1994, Using of Intregral & Finite Element Methods in Acoustics, 1995; co-author: The Fundamentals of Acoustics, 1990; contbr. articles to profl. jours. Mem. Polish Acoustical Soc. (pres. Cracow chpt. 1986), Polish Acad. Sci. (com. on acoustics 1986). Office: Tech U Mining Metallurgy, Al Mickiewicza 30, 30-059 Cracow Poland

PANWAR, OMVIR SINGH, research physicist; b. Kakripur (Baghpat), India, Mar. 15, 1954; s. Vijay Singh and Vidya; m. Anjana Panwar, Feb. 23, 1980; children: Sharad Panwar, Sapna Panwar. BSc in Physics, Math., Stats. with honors, Meerut U., 1973, MSc in Physics, 1975; PhD, Panjab U., Chandigarh, India, 1980. Postdoctoral fellow physics dept. Panjab U., 1980-81; rsch. assoc. physics dept. Indian Inst. Tech. Delhi, New Delhi, 1981-82, sr. scientific officer, 1982-83; scientist B thin film divsn. Nat. Phys. Lab., New Delhi, 1983-88, scientist C, 1988-93; scientist E-I, 1993—; rsch. fellow in microelectronics and elec. engring. Trinity Coll., Dublin, Ireland, 1987-88; hon. rsch. fellow in elec. and electronic engring. dept. Queens U., Belfast, No. Ireland, 1988; participant nat. and internat. confs. and workshops. Contbr. over 80 papers to Indian Jour. Pure and Applied Physics, Phys. Stat. Sol. A, Nat. Acad. Sci. Letters, Jour. Non-Crystal Solids, Phil. Mag. B, Jour. Inst. Electronics and Telecom. Engrs., Appl. Phys. Lett., Thin Solid Films, Jour. Applied Physics, NPL Tech. Bull. and Rsch. Report, Applied Surface Sci., Solar Energy Materials and Solar Cells, Jour. Solar Energy Soc. India, Infrared Phys. Tech., Jour. Vacuum Sci. Tech. A, IETE Jour. Rsch., Surface and Coatings Tech., Vacuum, and others; also papers in edited books; patentee for improved process for prodn. high resistivity amorphous hydrogenated silicon films. Merit scholar, 1969-71, Bursary scholar, 1971-73, Nat. scholar, 1973-75; rsch. fellow Coun. of Scientific and Indsl. Rsch., 1976-80. Mem. Materials Rsch. Soc. of India (life). Avocation: yoga. Home: DGII/285D Vikaspuri, New Delhi 110018, India Office: Nat Phys Lab Thin Film Tech Group, Dr KS Krishnan Rd, New Delhi 110012, India

PANWAR, SURENDRA SINGH, military officer; b. Dehradun, India, Jan. 7, 1921; s. Thakur Kundan Singh and Jaya Devi; m. Lakshmi Singh, Nov. 18, 1948; children: Rajendra S., Rajul Singh, Manjul Rana, Madhvi Bajekal, Shivendra S. BA, Allahabad U., India, 1939; grad., Def. Svcs. Staff Coll., Wellington, Conoor, India, 1954. 2d lt. Indian Army, 1942-43, lt., 1943-45; capt., instr. Kitchner Coll., India, 1945-46; maj. long gunnery staff course Sch. Arty., U.K., 1949-51; lt. col., chief instr., comdg. officer, staff officer Indian Army, 1956-63; brigadier, chmn. Internat. Commn. for Supervision and Control, Indochina, 1969-70; brigadier, sub-area comdr. Indian Army, Lucknow, India, 1970-72, Ambala, India, 1971-73; brigadier brigade comdr. Indian Army, 1994-96, brigadier dep. dir. arty., 1996-98. Pres. All India Gorkha Ex-Servicemens Welfare Assn., New Delhi Ministry of Def., 1983—, Uttra Khand Ex-Servicemens Assn., Dehradun, 1995—, Gorkha Mil. Coll., Dehradun, 1985-95; bd. trustees Cambrian Hall Sch., Dehradun, 1976—; active welfare of ex-servicemen, war widows, and orphans, 1973—. Home: 184 Kalidas Rd, UP248001 Dehradun India Office: All-India Ex-Servicemen, Naya Gaon Po Anarwala, 248001 Dehradun India

PANYASORN, SAWAT, mechanical engineer; b. Chiangrai, Thailand, June 3, 1946; m. Sumalee Rithakorn, Nov. 11, 1977; children: Jessada, Jinhatha, Judhinant. B in Engring., Rangoon (Burma) Inst. Tech., 1969; BS in Physics, Mandalay Arts & Sci. U., Burma, 1966. Sales engr. Siemssen GmbH, Bangkok, Thailand, 1970-80, sales dir., 1980-84, mng. dir., 1984-87; mng. dir. Ferrostaal, Bangkok, Thailand, 1987-95, Texpro Engring. Co. Ltd., Bangkok, Thailand, 1995—; textile engring. trainer Monchenglabach, Germany, 1974, Uster, Switzerland, 1975. Named Best Machine Supplier, Gov. Bangkok, 1992. Fellow Thai Centenarian Club. Avocations: reading, traveling, meeting people. Office: Texpro Engring Co Ltd, 33/822 Tor Ruamchoke 18, 10230 Bangkok Thailand

PANZ, VANESSA ROSE, medical scientist, researcher; b. Johannesburg, South Africa, Apr. 10, 1948; d. Alan and Edith Mary (Moore) Cunliffe; m. Helmut Elmar Panz, Jan. 23, 1970; 1 child, Jeannette. MSc in Medicine, U. Witwatersrand, Johannesburg, 1992, PhD in Medicine, 1998. Med. technologist South African Inst. Med. Rsch., Johannesburg, 1965-70, City Health Dept., Johannesburg, 1971-77; sr. med. technologist Nat. Inst. Virology, Johannesburg, 1977-83; sr. rsch. officer U. Witwatersrand, 1984—; presenter at numerous congresses in field. Contbr. numerous articles to profl. jours. Recipient Prof. Bobby Grieve Rsch. award, 1989, Fleischmann award U. Witwatersrand, 1993. Fellow Soc. Med. Lab. Technologists of South Africa; mem. South African Med. and Dental Coun. (registered), South African Coun. for Sci. Professions (registered), Soc. for Endocrinology, Metabolism and Diabetes of South Africa. Office: U Witwatersrand Med Sch, 7 York Rd Parktown, Johannesburg 2193, South Africa

PAOLAGGI, JOSEPH ANTOINE, physician, medical educator; b. Santa Maria Sicche, Corse, France, Oct. 11, 1925; s. Dominique and Jeanne (Massimi) P. MD, Faculty of Medicine, Paris, 1955, Prof Agrege, 1966. Diplomate in medicine. Chief of clinic Faculty of Medicine, Paris, 1956-58; med. asst. Hosps. of Paris, 1961-66, physician, 1966-94; chief of svvc. Hosp. Beaujon, Paris, 1975-91; med. cons. Hosp. Bichat, Paris, 1991-94, med. conciliator, 1995-97. Contbr. more than 400 articles to profl. jours. Decorated officer Nat. Order Legion of Honor (France). Mem. Assn. Charles Debray (pres. 1990—), Club Francais d'Echoendoscopie (pres. 1988-95). Roman Catholic.

PAOLETTI, RODOLFO, pharmacology educator; b. Milan, Aug. 23, 1931. MD summa cum laude, U. Milan, 1955; MD (hon.), Karolinska Inst., Stockholm, 1983; PharmD (hon.), U. Urbino, 1985; MD (hon.), U. Montpellier, 1993, U. Gdansk, Poland, 1996; PhD (hon.), U. Buenos Aires, Buenos Aires, 1999. Asst. prof. pharmacology U. Milan, 1955-62, assoc. prof., 1962-67, prof., chmn. Inst. Pharmacol. Scis., 1970—, chmn. coun. postgrad. edn., 1986—, dean sch. pharmacy, 1982-2000; prof. pharmacology, chmn. dept. U. Cagliari, Sardinia, Italy, 1967-70; adj. prof. pathology U. Pitts., 1986-97, adj. prof. pharmacology, 1992; fgn. adj. prof. Karolinska Inst., Stockholm, 1992. Editor: (with others) Drugs affecting lipid metabolism, 1961, Recent advances in atherosclerosis, 1968, Pharmacology of hormonal polypeptides and proteins, 1968, Pharmacological control of lipid metabolism, 1972, Lipids, lipoproteins and drugs, 1975, Thrombosis and urokinase, 1977, Molecular biology and pharmacology of cyclic nucleotides, 1978, Chemical toxicology of food, 1978, Drugs affecting lipid metabolism, 1980, The Menopause and Postmenopause, 1980, New trends in nutrition, lipid research and cardiovascular diseases, 1981, Factors in formation and regression of atherosclerotic plaque, 1982, Arterial pollution: an integrated view on atherosclerosis, 1983, Diet, diabetes and atherosclerosis, 1984, Developmental neuroscience: physiological, pharmacological and clinical aspects, 1984, Peptides and ion transport, 1985, Biotechnology in clinical medicine, 1987, Serotonin: from cell biology to pharmacology and therapeutics, 1990, Growth factors of Vascular and Nervous Systems: Functional Characterization and Biotechnology, 1992, Brunched-Chain Amino Acids: biochemistry, physiopathology and clinical science, 1992, Drugs and the Liver: High Risk Patients and Transplantation, 1993, Low Blood Cholesterol; Health Implications, 1993, others; contbr., editorial bd. numerous profl. jours. Pres. Giovanni Lorenzini Med. Found., Milan and Houston, 1976—, Nutrition Found. Italy, 1976—; Italian pres. sci. coun. NATO, Brussels, 1981-92; mem. nat. univ. coun. Ministry Pub. Instrn., Rome, 1985-89; dir. Milan Molecular Pharmacology Lab, 1985—, sci. dir., 1992—; sci. com. Nat. Inst. Applied Sci. Lyon, France, 1991—; pres. Ctr. Study, Prevention, and Therapy Vascular Atherosclerosis, 1991—; pres. G. Ronzoni Inst. Chemistry and Biochemistry, 1992—; pres sci. com. Ctr. Biologia e Tossicologia Cosmetologia, Milan, 1992—; mem. Nat. Drug Com., Rome, 1994—. Recipient Medal Prukyne Med. Soc. Prague, 1962, Award for Atherosclerosis Rsch., Am. Acad. Arts and Scis., 1963, Pamiotkowy medal Polish Pharmacol. Soc., 1973, Kravkov medal Pharmacol. Soc. Soviet Union, 1977, Gold medal Pres. Rep. Italy, 1977, medal Hungarian Soc. Atherosclerosis, 1981, Internat. prize Madonnina, 1982, award U. Chieti Med. Sch., 1984, Kaufmann Meml. award Internat. Soc. Fat Rsch., 1986, Grande Ufficiale Rep. Italy, 1989, Leloir medal Republic Argentina, 1996. Fellow N.Y. Acad. Sci.; mem. AAAS (corr.), Italian Soc. Pharmacology, Italian Soc. Biochemistry, Italian Soc. Study Arteriosclerosis, Italian Soc. Toxicology, Italian Soc. Psychiat. Biology, Soc. Italiana Studio Sostanze Grasse, Italian Soc. Normal and Pathological Metabolism, Italian Soc. Human Nutrition, German Med. Soc., Neuroimmunomoduliation (hon.), Soc. Italiana Farmacologia Ospedaliera (hon.), Assn. Riva Rocci Study and Cure of Arterial Hypertension (hon.), Italian Soc. Pharmacognosy, Italian Pharmacol. Soc. (pres. 1986-90), Italian Soc. Pharm. Scis. (pres. 1990—), Acad. Europaea, Mediterranean Acad. Sci., Acad. Nat. dell'Olivo, Am. Heart Assn. (corr., coun. atherosclerosis), Am. Oil Chemists Soc., Am. Pharm. Assn., Fedn. Nutrition Founds. (pres.), Assn. Studio della Farmaci Antitromobici, Assn. Biologi Farmacia, Assn. Cardiol. Found. Princess Lilian de Rethy (councillor), Internat. Atherosclerosis Soc. (Disting. Svc. award 1982), Internat. Union Pharmacologists (councillor 1975-81), Assn. Amici di Emilio Trabucchi, Assn. Italiana Dermatologia e Cosmetologia, Biochem. Soc. (Eng.), Brit. Pharmacol. Soc., European Sci. Found., European Acad. Scis. (hon.), European Neuropeptide Club, European Soc. Clin. Investigation, European Soc. Neurochemistry, European Membrane Soc. (pres. 1984), European Soc. Toxicology, European Soc. Study Drug Toxicity, Acad. Santae Clarae (hon.), European Soc. Biochem. Pharmacology (hon.), Argentinian Soc. Pharmacology (hon.), European Atherosclerosis Group (pres. 1980-87), European Atherosclerosis Soc., Med. Soc. Hosps. France (corr., Medal 1980), French Soc. Atherosclerosis Rsch., European Fedn. Pharmacologists (pres. 1992—), European Union Soc. Exptl. Biology (sec. 1990—), European Fedn. Pharm. Socs. (pres. 1993—), Group European Nutritionists, Internat. Soc. Cardiovascular Pharmacotherapy, Internat. Soc. Neuroimmunomodulation, Internat. Soc. Devel. Neurosci., Internat. Atherosclerosis Soc. (pres. elect 1996), Internat. Soc. Neurochemistry, Internat. Soc. Psychoneuroendocrinology, Internat. Soc. Pathophysiology, Internat. Union Therapeutics, Internat. Union Angiology, Internat. Union Pharmacology (rep. nat. rsch. coun. 1991—), Inst. Lombardo Acad. Sci. and Letters, Mediterranean Acad. Scis., Soc. Biological Psychiatry, Internat. Soc. Fedn. Cardiology, Soc. Atherosclerosis Hungary (hon.), French Soc. Atherosclerosis Rsch. (hon.), Argentinian Acad. Pharmacy and Biochemistry (hon.). Royal Soc. Medicine, Royal Acad. Medicine, World Fedn. Neurology, World Fedn. Scientists, Calcium Club (pres. 1991.). Office: Dept Pharmacol Scis, via Balzaretti 9, Milan 20133, Italy

PAOLI, LAETITIA ALINE, mathematics educator, researcher; b. Marseille, France, Mar. 23, 1967; d. Charles and Ghislaine Aline (Bonnet) P. Degree in Civil Engring., Nat. Sch. Pub. Civil Works, Lyon, France, 1989; PhD, U. C. Bernard Lyon, 1993. Asst. prof. U. Jean Monnet of St. Etienne, France, 1993-99, assoc. prof., 1999—. Contbr. articles to profl. jours. Office: U Saint Etienne, 23 rue P Michelon, 42023 Saint Etienne Cedex 2, France

PAOLICCHI, FERNANDO ALBERTO, veterinary educator; b. Mar del Plata, Argentina, July 11, 1958; s. Miguel and Juana (Abad) P. Grad. in Vet. Med., UNCPBA, Argentina, 1984; Magister Biol. Sci., U. Chile, 1995. Asst. prof. vet. sci. Faculty Vet. Sci., Tandil, Argentina, 1982-86; fellow CONICET/CIC, Mar del Plata, 1986-92, PLACIRH, Santiago, Chile, 1992-93; assoc. prof. faculty agr. sci. Nat. U. Mar del Plata, Balcarce, Argentina, 1990-99; rschr. INTA, Balcarce, 1997—; assoc. rschr. FAO-OIEA, Chile, 1993-95; assoc. rschr. FAO-INTA, Argentina, 1995; responsible serodiagnos Lab. Bacteriology, INTA, 1998—. Contbr. articles to profl. jours. Mem. Internat. Assn. Agr. Avocations: running, rugby. Home: 36 Marmol, 7600 Mar del Plata Argentina Office: CC 276 INTA, 226 National Rt, 7620 Balcarce Argentina

PAOLINI, CLAIRE JACQUELINE, dean, educator; b. Newton, Mass., May 19, 1934; d. Frank and Angelina Landro; m. Gilberto Paolini, June 18, 1960; children: Angela J., John F. BA, Boston U., 1956; MA, Middlebury (Vt.) Coll., 1958; PhD, Tulane U., 1982. Instr. Spanish U. Mass., Amherst, 1956-60, U. New Orleans, 1970-75; from dir. internat. student affairs to assoc. dean Loyola U., New Orleans, 1975-83, assoc. dean arts and scis., 1983-97; dean coll. arts and scis., prof. spanish Sacred Heart U., Fairfield, Conn., 1997—. Author: The Narrative Art of Domingos Monteiro, 1979, Valle-Inclán's Modernism: Use and Abuse of Religious and Mystical Symbolism, 1986; editor: LA CHISPA '95: Selected Proceedings, 1995, LA CHISPA '97: Selected Proceedings, 1997; co-editor: La CHISPA '99: Selected Proceedings, 1999; assoc. editor: LA CHISPA '93: Selected Proceedings, 1993; mem. editl. bd. LA CHISPA, 1983, 85, 87, 89, NACADA Jour., 1995-97. v.p. Soc. Espanola, New Orleans, 1977-81, bd. mem. 1976-97. Mem. Nat. Assn. Academic Affairs Administrators (Administrator of Yr. award 1996-97), Modern Lang. Assn., Council Colls. Arts Scis., Am. Assn. Tchrs. Spanish and Portuguese, Coll. Consortium Internat. Studies (bd. mem. 1997—), Am. Assn. Higher Edn. E-mail: paolinic@sacredheart.edu. Home: 3 Gregory Farm Rd Easton CT 06612-2049 Office: Sacred Heart Univ 5151 Park Ave Fairfield CT 06432-1000

PAOLINO, RICHARD GERALD, physician, consultant; b. Phila., Mar. 25, 1943; s. Rocco Richard and Theresa Irene (Caraffa) P.; m. Elaine Marie Sodl, Aug. 29, 1970; children: Richard G. II, Robert Jon. BS in pharmacology, Temple U., 1969; DO, Phila. Coll. of Osteopathic Medicine, 1975; postgrad., John Hopkins Med. Inst., 1976, 94-96, Yale U., 1996-97. Diplomate Osteo. Physicians and Surgeons; registered pharmacist, 1970; bd. cert. forensic examiner, forensic medicine. Physician, med. dir. Brookhaven Family Med. Ctr., Phila., 1975-95; physician phys. med. Hotspur Med. Fitness Ctr., Bensalem, Pa., 1987—; physician occupational med. Phys. Performance Ctr., Bensalem, 1992—; physician family med. Health Ctr., Ltd., Bensalem, 1992—; founder, pres. World Health Ctr., Ltd., Newtown, Pa., 1996—; workers compensation panel physician Thunder Hollow, Bensalem, 1993—; workers compensation panel mem. First Am. Home Care, Horsham, Pa., 1995—; consulting occupl. physician Am. Belt Co., Bensalem, 1995—; leadership vol. mem. Phila. Coll. Osteo. Medicine construction campaign, 1995—; adj. facuolty Phila. Coll. Osteo Medicine, 1997. Mem. Father's Assn. (pres. 1993-94) Holy Ghost Prep H.S., Cornwell Heights, Pa., 1989-95; mem. Father's Assn. Pennington (N.J.) Prep H.S., 1993-95; cert. CPR tchr. Am. Red Cross, Pendall, Pa., 1991—. Recipient Pres. award Holy Ghost Prep H.S., 1994, Teaching award Students-Coll. Pre-Med, Bensalem, 1994. Fellow Am. Coll. Forensic Examiners, Am. Coll. World Health Physicians (Disting., founder pres. 1996); mem. ABA (assoc., mem. dispute resolution sect., mem. health law sect., mem. individual rights and responsibilities sect., mem. family law sect.), AMA, Am. Osteo. Assn., Am. Osteo. Sports Med., Am. Osteo. Coll. Family Med., Am. Osteo. Coll. Occupational and Preventative Med., Am. Coll. Med. Quality, Pa. Osteo. Med. Assn., Am. Osteo Coll. Rehab. Medicine, Am. Coll. Occup. and Environ. Medicine, Pa. Osteo. Family Physicians Soc., Phila. Occupational and Environ. Med. Soc. Avocations: music, numismatics, Philately, opera, gardening. Home: 507 Wheatfield Ln Newtown PA 18940-2800 Office: Health Ctr Ltd PO Box 965 3554 Hulmeville Rd Bensalem PA 19020-4366

PAOLINO, RONALD MARIO, clinical psychologist, consultant, psychopharmacologist, pharmacist; b. Providence, Mar. 15, 1938; s. Lawrence and Mary Corinne (Guglielmi) P.; m. Eileen Frances Quimby, June 18, 1960; children: Lisa Katherine, David Lawrence. Student, Providence Coll., 1955-56; BS in Pharmacy, U. R.I., 1959, MS, 1961; PhD in Pharmacology/Toxicology, Purdue U., 1963; postdoctoral studies Exptl. Psychology, Yale U., 1963-65; doctoral studies in clin. psychology, Purdue U., 1972-74; postdoctoral studies in existential analytic psychotherapy, Okla. Inst. Existential Analysis and Psychotherapy, 1974-75; Hostage Negotiation, FBI, 1991, Advanced Hostage Negotiation, 1995; Crisis Negotiation, FBI Acad., 1994; MA (hon.), Brown U., 1977. Lic. psychologist, R.I., pharmacist R.I.; nat. registered health svc. provider in psychology; cert. arbitrator; cert. nat. registered group psycho-therapists; cert. edn. provider N.Y.; diplomate Am. Bd. Forensic Examiners, Am. Bd. Forensic Medicine. Intern dept. psychiatry and behavioral scis. U. Okla. Health Scis. Ctr., 1974-75; David Ross predoctoral fellow dept. pharmacology/toxicology Purdue U., 1961-63; NIMH postdoctoral fellow in psychology dept. psychology Yale U., 1963-65; asst. prof. pharmacology U. Conn. Sch. Pharmacy, 1965-67; assoc. prof. psychopharmacology Purdue U., 1967-74; NIMH fellow in clin. psychology U. Okla. Health Scis. Ctr., 1974-75; coord. group psychotherapy tng. program Brown U. Program in Medicine, 1983-85, assoc. prof. psychiatry and human behavior, 1976-90; pvt. practice; chief drug dependency treatment program VA Med. Ctr., Providence, 1975-87, dir. biofeedback clinic, 1977-87, primary hostage negotiator, 1991—; psychiatric cons. VA Police, alternative Dispute Resolution Mediator, New Eng. Veterans Integrated Svc. Network, 1996—, pain mgmt. bd., 1999—; mem. Pharmacology and Therapeutic Agts. Com., 1979-87, VA Med. Ctr., coord. VA Contracted Half-Way Project for Substance Dependent Vets., 1981-85, chmn. Pain Mgmt. Task Force, 1984-85, mem. Supervisory Level Pharmacy Profl. Standards Bd., 1990—, mem. Mgmt. Suicidal and Violent Patient Task Force, 1990-91, chmn. Com. Prevention & Mgmt. of Disturbed Behaviors, 1991—, chief crisis mgmt. program, 1993-96, advisor FBI Hostage Negotiations, 1991—, Instr. R.I. State Police Acad., 1994, Instr., Drug Recognition Experts Recert PRGM, R.I. Dept Health, 1995, Faculty, Law Enforcement Mgmt. Command Sch. U.R.I., 1991—, Va. Nat. Law Enforcement Tng. Ctr., 1997; chmn. Outpatient Psychiatry Svcs. Reorganization Task Force, 1991, mem. VA DOD Desert Storm Emergency Plan Com., 1991; advisor OSHA Dept. Labor for Violence in the Work Place, 1994-95; mem. E. Prov. Clergy & Mental Health Providers Alliance, 1995—; mem. substance abuse and prevention grant application rev. com. R.I. Adv. Coun. on Substance Abuse, 1982-92, prevention, edn. and tng. com. on substance abuse, 1981—, chmn. 1981-82; adj. assoc. prof. psychology, U. R.I., 1982—, clin. assoc. prof. pharmacy U. R.I., 1998—; mem. planning com. State Conf. on Substance Abuse in the Hispanic Community, 1986; mem. alcohol awareness commn. Episc. Diocese of R.I., 1983-85; gubernatorial appointee Gov.'s Permanent Coun. on Drug Abuse Control, 1978-82; mem. rev. com. for funding of state drug abuse programs R.I. Single State Agy. on Drug Abuse, R.I. Dept. Mental Health Retardation and Hosps., 1978-82; cons. Nurses Renewal Com., 1980-81, substance abuse prevention edn. for elem. sch. children R.I. chpt. ARC, 1977, mem. suicide prevention steering com., 1977; mem.Interagy. Drug Abuse Steering Com., Lafayette, Ind. 1969-72; bd. dirs. Providence VA Med. Ctr. Credit Union; mem. bd. cert. for alcoholism counselors R.I. Assn. Alcohol Counselors, 1979-81; mem. Gov.'s Task Force on Substance Abuse at Adult Correctional Instn., 1977-78, Gov.'s Task Force on Mental Health Svcs. at Adult Correctional Instn., 1977-78, chmn. reclassification of inmates com., 1977-78; chmn. com. on edn. and cert. biofeedback practioners Conn. Biofeedback Soc., 1977-78; summer faculty fellow U. Conn., 1967; vis. scientist lectr. Assn. Am. Colls. Pharmacy, 1972-73; cons. to bus., unions, law enforcement. Author: (2 chpts.) Drug Testing: Issues and Options, 1991; contbr. 37 articles to profl. jours. Bd. dirs. R.I. chpt. Samaritans Internat. Suicide Prevention Orgn., 1978-84; v.p. Experience Jesus Inc.; mem. com. adv. bd. Cpina Bifida Assn. R.I., 1980-83; mem. R.I. East Bay Interfaith Mental Health Alliance; congressman appointee (Patrick J. Kennedy); mem. veterans adv. commn., 1995—. Recipient Citation award for svc. and contbns. to formulation of state policy for treatment and prevention of drug abuse Gov. R.I., 1983, Letter of Commendation, Gov.'s R.I. Adv. Coun. on Substance Abuse, 1986, vc. Recognition award DAV, 1990, Spl. Contbn. award Providence VA Med Ctr., 1990. Fellow Am. Coll. Forensic Examiners; mem. AMA, Am. Psychotherapy Assn., Am. Soc. Pharmacology Exptl. Therapeutics, Internat. Brain Rsch. Orgn., Internat. Narcotic Enforcement Officers Assn., R.I. Group Psychotherapy Soc. (pres. 1991-93, continuing edn. dir. psychologists 1990-95, exec. bd. 1986—, tng. faculty 1985—, co-dir. tng. 1986-87, tng. adv. bd. 1985-86), R.I. Psychol. Assn. (chmn. substance abuse ins. subcom. 1986-87, rep. Gov.'s Coun. on Mental Health State Plan Com. 1982-84), Hostage Negotiators Am. Office: PO Box 159 Barrington RI 02806-0159

PAONESSA, M. SUZANNE, financial aid administrator; b. Albany, N.Y., May 1, 1974; d. Thomas and Mary Laura (Maresca) P. BS in Fin., Siena Coll., 1996. Fin. mgmt. specialist U.S. Dept. Energy, Schenectady (N.Y.) Naval Reactors Office, 1996-99; assoc. dir. fin. aid Siena Coll., 1999—; treas. Schenectady Naval Reactors Office Employee Assn., 1997-98. Co-dir. Siena Coll. Friendly's Fanfest, 1997-98; mem. Siena Coll. Career Advisory Network. Mem. Fin. Mgmt. Assn., N.Y. State Fin. Aid Assn., 21st Century Leaders Soc., DOE Women's Golf League (treas. 1998—, named Most Improved Player 1998), Kensho-Do Karate Club (asst. instr.), Alpha Kappa Alpha, Delta Epsilon Sigma, Sigma Beta Delta. Roman Catholic. Avocations: karate (brownbelt), golf.

PAPA, MICHAEL JOSEPH, real estate broker; b. Bklyn., Sept. 29, 1948; s. Joseph and Lena Helen (Bellofatto) P.; m. Lana Susan Turner, Oct. 30, 1967 (div. Dec. 1969); 1 child, Dawn Michelle; m. Barbara Moehringer-Papa, May 17, 1992 (div. Dec. 1997). Lic. Real Estate Broker, Fla. Real Estate Careers, Orlando, 1992; Lic. Mortgage Broker, Kambuck Inst., Inc., Orlando, 1994. Pres. Universal Trading Co., Huntington, N.Y., 1969-70; v.p. Interspec Trading, Inc., Lake Grove, N.Y., 1970-72; pres. Quality World Ctrs., Inc., Deer Park, N.Y., 1973-83, Jewels By Shalet, Inc., Deer Park, 1983-87; v.p. Quality Treasures, Inc., Patchogue, N.Y., 1980-81; pres. Select Acquisitions, Inc., Denver, 1987-91, Watches "R" Us, Inc., Smithtown, N.Y., 1988-91, Time for You, Inc., Smithtown, 1989-91, Progressive Realty Am., Inc., Cocoa, Fla., 1993—; owner Success Foundation.com, 1998—, Realty Executives Specialists, Sacramento, 2000—; pres. Investors Home Realty, Inc., Cocoa, All Svc. Mortgage of Am., Universal Satellite, Success Found., 1998—; real estate and mortgage broker, owner realty-execs. specialists, Sacramento, 2000. Author: "Good Communication" A Lost Art, 1998. Cert. Housing and Urban Devel., Brevard County, Fla., 1994-95. Mem. Rosicrusian Order (guard 1980-89). Avocations: holography, lighting effects, weapons, coins and stamps, 1st Degree Black Belt/Moo Do Kwan Tang Soo Do-Tai Kwan Do. Fax: 916-966-1231. E-mail: michaelpapa@realtyexecutives.com. Home: 5740 Audrey Way Fair Oaks CA 95628-3004 Office: Realty Execs 165A Commerce Cir Sacramento CA 95815-4201

PAPACHATZIS, PETROS NIKOLAOS, finance, insurance executive; b. Athens, Greece, Oct. 7, 1968; s. Nikolaos Athanassios and Vassiliki Hr. Hatchadourian P.; m. Kyriaki Athanassios Limniou, Nov. 3, 1997. Diplôme d'études supérieures, Inst. Français d'Athènes, 1985; Diploma Electronics Engring., Tech. U. Piraeus, Greece, 1992. Bank assurance cons. I.N.G.-Nationale Nederlanden, Athens, 1991—. With Hellenic Navy, 1994-96. Christian Orthodox. Avocations: singing, guitar playing, personal computing. Office: ING Nationale Nederlanden, Lazaraki 43, 16674 Glyfada Greece

PAPACONSTANTINOU, ADONIS MILTIADES, computer company executive; b. Nicosia, Cyprus, Dec. 20, 1953; s. Miltiades and Maria (Kyriakou) P.; m. Eleni Ioannidou, Sept. 1, 1980. BS, London U., 1977. Systems analyst NCR (Cyprus) Ltd., Nicosia, 1977-78, sales acct. mgr., 1979-81, vocat. mgr., 1981-83; area vocat. mgr. NcR (N. Africa) Ltd., Nicosia, 1981-84; area vocat. dir. NCR (Gulf) Ltd., Nicosia, 1985-86; gen. mgr. NCR Near East, Nicosia, 1987-89; mktg. dir. Middle East and Africa AT&T GIS, Nicosia, 1990-93, gen. mgr. Near East and Subsahara, 1994-95; asst. v.p. sales adn mktg. NCR Middle East and Africa, Nicosia, 1996-97, v.p., bus. unit leder Fin. Solutions Group, 1998—. Served with Army of Cyprus, 1972-74. Mem. Brit. Computer Soc. Avocations: tennis, classical music. Home: 14 Athanasiou Diakdu, 164 Ayios Dhometios Nicosia Cyprus Office: NCR Corp, PO Box 1823, Nicosia Cyprus

PAPADAKI, MARIA, chemical engineer; b. Chania, Crete, Greece, Apr. 25, 1970; came to U.S., 1992; d. Georgios Papadakis and Niki Bobolaki; m. Stelios Kouvroukoglou, May 25, 1998. BS, Aristotle U., Thessaloniki, Greece, 1992; PhD, Rice U., 1997. Registered engr., Greece. Postdoctoral fellow MIT, Cambridge, Mass., 1997—. Contbr. articles to profl. jours.; patentee in field. Recipient Whitaker award Biomed. Engring. Soc., 1996; NATO fellow, 1998. Mem. ACS, AIChE, AAAS. Avocations: swimming, traveling, reading, hiking. Home: 75 Sciarappa St Cambridge MA 02141-1705 Office: PMB #168 1 Kendall Sq Ste 600 Cambridge MA 02139-1562

PAPADAKIS, CHARITON E., physician, consultant; b. Heraklion, Crete, Greece, Oct. 24, 1960; s. Emmanuel C. and Katherine L. (Skordalakis) P.; m. Sevasti G. Kamilakis, July 18, 1992; children: Irene, Katherine. MD, U.

Thessaloniki, Greece, 1984. Cert. ENT surgeon, Greece. Lect. Univ. Hosp. of Crete, Heraklion, 1993—. 2d lt. Greek Army, 1984-85. Mem. Am. Acad. Otolaryngology-Head and Neck Surgery (corr.), Am. Auditory Soc., Assn. for Rsch. in Otolaryngology. Greek Orthodox. Avocations: soccer, basketball. Home: Psaron 7 St, 71307 Heraklion Crete, Greece

PAPADAKIS, CONSTANTINE N., university executive; b. Athens, Greece, Feb. 2, 1946; came to U.S., 1969; s. Nicholas and Rita (Masciotti) P.; m. Eliana Apostolides, Aug. 28, 1971; 1 child, Maria. Diploma in Civil Engring., Nat. Tech. U. Athens, 1969; MS in Civil Engring., U. Cin., 1970; PhD in Civil Engring., U. Mich., 1973. Registered profl. engr., Ohio, Greece. Engring. specialist, geotechnical group Bechtel, Inc., Gaithersburg, Md., 1974-76; supr. and asst. chief engr. geotechnical group Bechtel, Inc., Ann Arbor, Mich., 1976-81; v.p., bd. dirs. water resources div. STS Cons. Ltd., Ann Arbor, 1981-84; v.p. water and environ. resources dept. Tetra Tech-Honeywell, Pasadena, Calif., 1984; head dept. civil engring. Colo. State U., Ft. Collins, 1984-86; dean Coll. Engring. U. Cin., 1986-95, dir. Groundwater Rsch. Ctr., 1986-95; dir. Ctr. Hill Solid and Hazardous Waste Rsch. Ctr. EPA, Cin., 1986-93; pres. Drexel U., Phila., 1995—; adj. prof. civil engring. U. Mich., 1976-83; cons. Gaines & Stern Co., Cleve., 1983-84, Honeywell Europe, Maintal, Fed. Republic of Germany, 1984-85, Arthur D. Little, Boston, 1984-85, Camargo Assocs., Ltd., Cin., 1986, King Fahd U. Rsch. Inst., Dhahran, Saudi Arabia, 1987, King Abdulaziz City for Sci. and Tech., Riyadh, Saudi Arabia, 1991, Henderson & Bodwell Cons. Engrs. Inc., 1991, Cin. Met. Sewer Dist., 1992, Ohio River Valley Water Sanitation Commn., 1994; acting pres. Ohio Aerospace Inst., 1988-90; interim pres. Inst. Advanced Mfg. Scis. Ohio Edison Tech. Ctr., 1989-90; bd. govs. Edison Materials Tech. Ctr., 1988-95; adv. bd., founding mem. Hamilton County Bus. Incubator, 1988-95; bd. dirs. Nat. Commn. for Coop. Edn., U. City Sci. Ctr., Ben Franklin Tech. Ctr., WHYY Inc., Fidelity Fed. Bank, Opera Co. of Phila., Corcell, Inc., Greater Phila. First, Hellenic Coll./Holy Cross Acad. Author: Problems on Strength of Materials, 1968, Sewer Systems Design, 1969; editor: Fluid Transients and Acoustics, 1978, Pump-Turbine Schemes, 1979, Small Hydro Power Fluid Machinery, 1982; Megatrends in Hydraulics, 1987; contbr. more than 65 articles to profl. jours. Mem. Greater Cin. C. of C. Blue Chip Campaign for Econ. Devel. Task Force, 1988-93, bd. dirs. Bus. Assistance Ctr., 1989-95; mem. Ohio Coun. on Rsch. and Econ. Devel., 1988, Ohio Sci. and Tech. Commn. Adv. Group, 1989-90, 92-95; coun. mem. St. Nicholas Ch. Parish, Ann Arbor, 1981-84; mem. City of Ft. Collins Drainage Bd., 1984-86; bd. dirs. Dan Beard coun. Boy Scouts Am., 1995, Intelligent Vehicle Hwy. Soc. Ohio, 1994-95; bd. dirs. Liberty Bell Coun. of the Boy Scouts of Am., 1996—. Recipient Horace W. King scholarship civil engring. dept. U. Mich., 1971-73, 6 Bechtel Merit awards, 1974-79, Young Engr. of Yr. award Mich. Soc. Profl. Engrs., Ann Arbor, Mich., 1982, Disting. Engr. award Engrs. and Scientists Cin. Tech. Socs. Coun., 1989, Acad. of Achievement in Edn. award Am. Hellenic Ednl. Progressive Assn., 1995, Hellenic Univ. Club of Phila. Achievement award, 1996, Krikos Disting. Hellene Leader award, 1996. Fellow ASCE (pres. Ann Arbor br. 1980-81, pres.-elect Mich. sect. 1983-84, hydraulics divsn. publ. com. 1980-83), ASME (chmn. fluid transients com. 1978-80, mem. fluids engring. divsn. awards com. 1981-84), Am. Soc. Engring. Edn.; mem. NSPE (legis. and govt. affairs com. 1994-95, chair profl. engrs. in edn. divsn. 1995), Order of the Engr., Internat. Assn. for Hydraulic Rsch., Ohio Engring. Dean's Coun. (chmn.-elect 1989-91), Rotary, Sigma Xi, Chi Epsilon, Tau Beta Pi. Greek Orthodox. Avocations: photography, classical music, travel, swimming, racquetball. Home: 75 Crestline Rd Wayne PA 19087-2611 Office: Drexel Univ 3141 Chestnut St Philadelphia PA 19104-2875

PAPADAKIS, PANAGIOTIS AGAMEMNON, financier, international business executive; b. Athens, Greece, Mar. 29, 1935; s. Agamemnon Ioannou and Anna Karyatis (Kyriakopoulou) P.; m. Alexandra Argyropoulou, July 12, 1959. Student, U. Athens, 1953-57. Registered rep., Del., Athens, Greece, Zurich, Switzerland, Washington, 50 other countries. Pub., owner newspaper Peristeri, Athens, 1953-64; owner, gen. dir. printing house, advt. office, ins. agy., Athens, 1953-64; leader Nat. Radical Party Youth, Athens, 1958-59; founder, gen. dir. Servis Advt., Athens, 1963-78, Book-Servis, Athens, 1974-78; pres. Investments Promotions and Assocs. of Chgo., Athens, 1979-85; chmn. Internat. Investments World Co. Inc., Athens and Zurich, 1985—, Internat. Bus. Co. Inc., Internat. Comml. Co. Inc., Athens and Zurich, 1985—, Papadakis Internat. Fin. Co. Inc., Guarantor Co. Inc., Athens and Zurich, 1992—, Internat. Banker Fin. Co. Inc., Athens and Zurich, 1992—; chmn. Internat. Pap Financing and Investment Group, Vaduz Liechtenstein, Konekt Financing Investment Group AG, Griscaviation AG, Graubunden, Switzerland. Author, editor: Historical Biography of President Karamanlis, 1974-77; author: Why the Revolution of 21 April 1967 Happened, 1968; author numerous articles in Recently Humanity '93, Human Rights. Mem. Internat. C. of C., Internat. Soc. Financiers, World Trade Ctr. of Basel, Acad. Scis. Zurich (hon.), Assn. de Soutier A L'Universite De Dalout (hon.). Mem. New Democracy Party. Christian Orthodox. Home and Office: Usteristrasse 23, 8001 Zurich Switzerland Home: Karlihof 8-11, Malans Graubunden Switzerland also: Charilaou Trikoupis 113, Kifissia Athens Greece Office: Internat Investment World Group Cos, Inter Invest World Grp Cos, PO Box 140 88, 115 10 Athens Greece also: Pontou 24, Ilissia Athens Greece also: 1329 Connecticut Ave NW Washington DC 20036-1846

PAPADAKIS, VAGELIS G., chemical engineer; b. Elika, Greece, Jan. 5, 1964; s. George D. and Garyfalia (Dermatis) G. Diploma, U. Patras, Greece, 1986, PhD, 1990. Tchg. staff U. Patras, Greece, 1994-96; rschr. Danish Technol. Inst., Copenhagen, Denmark, 1997-99; head lab. Titan SA, Elefsis, Greece, 1999—; cons. Indusl. Enterprises, Greece, 1994-96, Concrete Enterprises, Denmark, 1997-99. Contbr. articles to profl. jours. Hellenic Naval Acad., Pireaus, Greece, 1990-92. Recipient Wason medal, Am. Concrete Inst., 1993; grantee Marie Curie, European Commn., 1997. Mem. Am. Concrete Inst. (Wason medal 1993), Marie Curie Assn. (grantee 1997), Technol. Chamber of Greece. Avocations: music, history, literature, travel, swimming. Office: Titan Cement Co SA, PO Box 18, GR 19200 Elefsis Greece

PAPADEMOS, LOUKAS, bank executive. Gov. Bank of Greece, Athens. Office: Bank of Greece, 21 Eleftherion Venizelou St, 102 50 Athens Greece*

PAPADIAS, BASIL C., education educator; b. Volos, Thessaly, Greece, Sept. 18, 1932; s. Constantinos B. and Pelagia C. (Kalozakis) P.; m. Vassiliki B. Klotsas, July 10, 1965; children: Constantinos, Alexandros. Mech.-Elec. Engr., Nat. Tech. U., Athens, 1956, D Engring., 1969; MEE, Rensselaer Polytechnic Inst., 1972, D Engring., 1975. Elec. engr. Pub. Power Corp., Athens, 1959-68, head rsch. sect., 1968-71, tech. cons., 1976—; rschr. RPI, Troy, 1971-73; head of system studies RPI, Athens, 1973-76; prof. elec. engring. dep. Nat. Tech. U., Athens, 1976—. Author: (text books) Transmission Lines of Electric Energy, 1985, Analysis of Electric Energy Systems, Vol. I and II, 1985, Transient Phenomena in Electric Power Systems, 1997; author/co-author articles in profl. jours. and publs. Fellow IEEE; mem. Nat. Acad. Scis. of N.Y., Tech. Chamber of Greece. Avocations: country hiking, classical music, cinema. Home: 9 Meg Alexandrou St, Maroussi, 15122 Athens Greece Office: Nat Tech U, 9 Iroon Polytechniou Str, 15773 Zografou Greece

PAPADIMITRIOU, DIMITRI BASIL, economist, college administrator; b. Salonica, Greece, June 9, 1946; came to U.S., 1965, naturalized, 1974; s. Basil John and Ellen (Takas) P.; children: Jennifer E., Elizabeth R. BA, Columbia U., 1970; PhD, New Sch. U., 1986. V.p., asst. sec. ITT Life Ins. Co. N.Y., N.Y.C., 1970-73; exec. v.p., sec., treas. William Penn Life Ins. Co. N.Y., N.Y.C., 1973-78, also dir.; exec. v.p., provost Bard Coll., 1978—, Jerome Levy prof. econs., 1978—; exec. dir. Bard Ctr., 1980—; pres. Jerome Levy Econs. Inst., 1988—; adj. lectr. econs. New Sch. U., 1975-76; fellow Ctr. for Advanced Econ. Studies, 1983; Wye fellow Aspen Inst.; bd. dirs. William Penn Life Ins. Co. N.Y.; mem. adv. com. Hudsonia, Inc.; bd. govs. Jerome Levy Econs. Inst., 1986—; mem. subcoun. capital allocation Competitiveness Policy Coun.; mem., vice-chmn. Congrl. Commn. to Rev. the Trade Deficit; mem. adv. com. Women's World Banking; radio econs. commentator Sta. WAMC, Monitor Radio, NPR, Money Radio. Author: Employment Policy Community Development and the Underlcass, 1997, Employment Policy: Theory and Practice, 1998; co-author: Community Development Banking, 1993, A Path to Community Development, 1993, An Alternative in Small Business Finance, 1994, Monetary Policy Uncovered: The Federal Reserve's Experiment with Unobservables, 1994, Targeting Inflation: The Effects of Monetary Policy on the CPI and Its Housing Component, 1996, The Fed Should Lower Interest Rates More, 1998, What to Do With the Surplus, 1998, How Can We Provide for the Baby Boomers in their Old Age?, 1999, Can Social Security Be Saved, 1999; editor, contbr. Profits, Deficits and Instability, 1992, Aspects of Distribution of Wealth and Income, 1994, Stability in the Financial System, 1996, Modernizing Financial Systems, 1998, Employment Policies: Theories and Evidence, 1999; co-editor, contbr.: Poverty and Prosperity in the USA in the Late Twentieth Century, 1993, Financial Conditions and Macroeconomic Performance, 1992; bd. editors Ea. Econ.Jour., Rev. of Income and Wealth; book reviewer Econ. Jour., Ea. Econ. Jour. Bd. dirs. Catskill Ballet Theatre, William Penn Life Ins. Co.; trustee ACHAEA Found., Am. Symphony Orch. Mem. Am. Econ. Assn., Am.-Hellenic Banker Assn., Royal Econ. Soc., Am. Fin. Assn., Econ. Club N.Y., European Econ. Assn., Eastern Econ. Assn., Econ. Sci. Chamber of Greece, Assn. for Evolutionary Econs., Econ. Club N.Y. Home and Office: Bard Coll Annandale On Hudson NY 12504

PAPADOPOULOS, CONSTANTINE DENIS, cardiology educator; b. Pyrgos, Greece, Feb. 6, 1939; s. Leonidas and Anna (Diamantopoulou) P.; (div. 1985); children: Leonidas, Paul. MD, PhD, Aristotle U., Thessaloniki, Greece, 1963. Asst. resident, sr. resident 2nd dept. internal medicine Aristotle U., Thessaloniki, 1963-69, lectr. 2nd dept. internal medicine, 1970-75, sr. lectr., 1975-78, asst. prof., 1978-85, assoc. prof. of cardiology, 1985—; head sect. cardiology 2nd univ. dept. internal medicine Hippokration Gen. Hosp., Thessaloniki, 1969-80, dir. 2nd univ. dept. cardiology, 1985—; dir. dept. cardiology Gen. Pref. Hosp., Larissa, Greece, 1973-74; head sect. cardiology 1st univ. dept. cardiology Ahepa Gen. Hosp., Thessaloniki, 1980-85, dir., 2nd Univ., Dept. of Cardiology, Hippokration Gen Terrotorial Hosp., Thesaloniki, Greece, 1985—. Contbr. numerous articles to profl. jours. Fellow Internat. Coll. Angiology, Internat. Coll. Chest Physicians and Surgeons, European Hypertension Soc., European Soc. Cardiology (working group on nuc. cardiology and magnetic resonance imaging), Am. Coll. Angiology, Am. Coll. Chest Physicians, Am. Coll. Cardiology; mem. Internat. Soc. on Thrombosis and Haemostasis, Internat. Soc. on Mechanocardiology, European Soc. on Mechanocardiology, N.Am. Soc. Pacing and Electrophysiology, Am. Soc. Nuc. Cardiology, Mediterranean League on Thrombosis and Haemostasis, Union Med. Balcanique, Am. Heart Assn. (clin. cardiology coun.), Hellenic Soc. Cardiology (former v.p.), Hellenic Soc. Hypertension (former pres.), Cardiol. Soc. No. Greece (former pres.), Hellenic Soc. Pediat. Cardiology, Hellenic Soc. Nephrology, Hellenic League Thrombosis Hemost, Hellenic Soc. Respiration Physiopathology, Hellenic Soc. Biochemistry, Hellenic Soc. Study and Application Ultra-sounds in Medicine and Biology, Hellenic Soc. Pharmacology, Hellenic Soc. Atherosclerosis, Med. Soc. Thessaloniki (past gen. sec.), N.Y. Acad. Scis. Greek Orthodox. Avocations: astronomy, palaeontology, philosophy, painting. Home: 83 Vas Olgas Ave, 54642 Thessaloniki Greece Office: Hippokration Gen Terr Hosp, Constantinoupoleos 49, 54642 Thessaloniki Greece

PAPADOPOULOS, CONSTANTINOS VASSILIOS, systems analyst; b. Athens, Greece, Dec. 12, 1962; s. Vassilios C. and Paraskevi V. (Makri) P. BS, U. Athens, 1984; postgrad., U. Essex, Eng., 1986, U. Lancaster, Eng., 1996—. Sys. programmer INTRACOM S.A., Athens, 1990; prof. European U., Athens, 1990-91; cons. Control Data, Inc., Athens, 1990-92; sys. analyst Ministry Fin., Athens, 1992—; lectr. Am. Coll. Greece, Athens, 1991-97; mem. com. 1st Nat. Hungarian Conf. on Med. Computing, Budapest, 1994; rep. of Greece to E.D.I. Working Group of European Union, Brussels, 1996-98; project leader Computerization of the Anti-fraud Dept., Greek Ministry Fin., 2000—. Author: Advanced Unix and C, 1992; contbr. articles to profl. jours. Sgt. Greek Army, 1988-90. Recipient 2d prize for composition Greek Ministry of Edn., 1980. Mem. IEEE, Assn. for Computing Machinery. Orthodox Christian. Avocations: Byzantine hagiography, classical music, chess. E-mail: k.papadopoulos@gsis.gov.gr. Home: 77 Aristeidou St, GR-17671 Kallithea Athens Greece Office: Ministry of Finance, 1 Thessalonikis and Handri St, GR-18346 Moschato Greece

PAPADOPOULOS, DEMETRIOS PANAGIOTOU, engineering educator; b. Papari, Arkadias, Greece, May 18, 1942; s. Panagiotis Konstantinou and Eleni Demetriou (Katsoulou) P.; m. Evangelie A. Panagopoulos; 1 child, Eleni Demetriou. BSEE, Marquette U., 1965, MSEE, 1968, PhDEE, 1970. Registered profl. engr. Engr. R&D Allis-Chalmers Mfg. Co., Milw., 1965-67; lectr. Marquette U., Milw., 1967-70; asst. prof. engring. Gonzaga U., Spokane, Wash., 1970-72; engr. and spl. cons. Pub. Power Corp. of Greece, Athens and Xanthi, Greece, 1972-97; asst., assoc. prof. Democritos U. of Thrace, Xanthi, 1981-85; prof. Democritos U. of Thrace, Xanthi, Greece, 1985—; vice rector Democritos U. of Thrace, Komotini, Greece, 1987-88, dir. energy systems engring. sect. Democritos U. of Thrace, Xanthi, 1988-89, 94-99; chmn. rsch. com. Democritos U., Komotini, Greece, 1987-88. Mem. editl. bd. Slovak Jour. Elec. Engring., 1992—; author of 4 books in the field of theory and lab. exercises in elec. machines; contbr. articles to profl. jours. Gen. sec. Ea. Macedonia-Thrace Region, Komotini, Greece, 1989-91, mem. energy office sci. com., 1994—. Recipient Hellenic Club of Writers award, 1995, award of prefecture of Arkadia, Greece, 1998; scholar Marquette U., Milw., 1961-70; grantee EEC, Brussels, 1983-94. Mem. IEEE (sr., chmn. power engring. chpt. Greek sect.), HKN, Tech C. of Greece. Greek Orthodox. Avocations: sports, traveling, music. Fax: 30-541-27955. E-mail: papadop@xanthi.cc.duth.gr. Home: Praxitelous 64-66, 671 00 Xanthi Greece Office: Electrical Machine Lab, Sch Engring Democritos U, 671 00 Xanthi Greece

PAPADOPOULOS, EVANGELOS, engineering educator, consultant; b. Athens, Greece, Nov. 4, 1957; s. George and Vasiliki (Vasilogeorgopoulou) P.; m. Eugenia Efstathiou; children: Ellie, George. Diploma, Nat. Tech. U., Athens, 1981; MS, MIT, 1983, PhD, 1991. Registered profl. engr., Greece. Rsch. asst. MIT, Cambridge, Mass., 1982-84, 87-91, lectr., 1991; analyst Hellenic Navy, Athens, 1985-87; asst. prof. McGill U., Montreal, Que., Can., 1991-97, assoc. prof., 1997; adj. prof. McGill U., Montreal, Can., 1997—; asst. prof. Nat. Tech. U. Athens, 1997—; cons. FERIC, Montreal, 1992, Aqua Vision, Montreal, 1993-94, Med-Eng. Sys., Ottawa, Ont., 1995, CAE Electronics, Montreal, 1995—. Contbr. articles to profl. jours., chpts. to 2 books. Petty officer Hellenic Navy, 1995-97. Recipient Hon. Title of scholar, Hellenic Min. Edn., 1976-81; TEE Scholarship awardee Tech. Chamber Greece, 1978-81, Thomaidion Scholarship award Nat. Tech. U. Athens, 1981. Mem. IEEE (sr.), AIAA (sr.), ASME, N.Y. Acad. Scis., Sigma Xi. Avocations: model trains, computing, fishing, remote controlled vehicles, robotics. Home: 5 Armonias St, 16671 Vouliagmeni Athens, Greece Office: Nat Tech Univ, Heroon Polytechniou 9, 15780 Zografou Greece

PAPADOPOULOS, GEORGE ARISTIDES, mechanics educator; b. Messini, Greece, Oct. 20, 1945; s. Aristides Anastasios and Eleni (Roditi) P.; m. Ionna Gini, June 27, 1950; 1 child, Eleni. Degree in physics, Nat. U. Athens, 1970; PhD in Exptl. Mechs., Nat. Tech. U. Athens, 1983. Asst. applied mechs. Nat. Tech. U. Athens, 1973-83, lectr. applied and theoretical mechs., 1983-87, asst. prof., 1987-93, assoc. prof., 1993—. Author 7 books in field, including Fracture Mechanics, 1993; contbr. over 180 articles to profl. publs. Recipient Ebirikion award Greece, 1992. Mem. ASME, Soc. Exptl. Mechs., Greek Soc. Theoretical and Applied Mechs., Greek Soc. Polymeric. Fax: (301) 7721302. Office: Nat Tech U Athens Sect Mech, 5 Heroes of Polytech Ave, GR15773 Zografou Athens Greece

PAPADOPOULOS, THEOHARIS, chemical engineer, consultant; b. Xanthi, Greece, June 20, 1961; s. Fanoula Albanidou; m. Maria Goulimari, Feb. 1991. Bachelor's degree, W.Va. Inst. Tech., 1985, ME, 1987; PhD, Stevens Inst. Tech., 1992. Rschr. Polymer Processing Inst., Hoboken, N.J., 1992-93; dep. dir. Thrace Papermill S.A., Xanthi, 1995-97; analyst Gen. Chemistry State Lab., Xanthi, 1997—; cons. Aristotelio U. Thessaloniki, 1993—; adj. prof. Democritian U. Thrace, Xanthi, 1996—. Contbr.: (electronic database) How to Manage Plastic Waste—Technology and Market, 1994. Mem. N.Y. Acad. Sci. Avocations: music, traveling. E-mail: thpapad@otenet.gr. Office: Gen Chemistry State Lab, 39 Agiou Eleftheriou St, Xanthi 67100, Greece

PAPADOPOULOU, ALEXANDRA, pediatrician; b. Patra, Greece, Jan. 3, 1958; d. Konstantinos and Athina Papadopoulou; m. Mark Avrousin, Sept. 12, 1982; 1 child, Liliana. MD summa cum laude, Pediat. Med. Acad., St. Petersburg, Russia, 1983. Med. diplomate. Resident pediat. gastroenterol unit Children's Hosp. Vilnius, Lithuania, 1983-84; resident Gen. Hosp., Thesprotia, Greece, 1985-86, Peuteli's Children's Hosp., Athens, Greece, 1986-89; registrar in pediat. Children's Hosp. P & A Kyriakou, Athens, 1989-91; clin. rsch. fellow in pediat. gastroenterology and nutrition Inst. Child Health, Birmingham, Eng., 1991-94; head outpatient pediat. gastroenterology and nutrition clinic, Faculty of Nursing, Dept. Pediat., U. Athens, P & A Kyriakou Children's Hosp., 1994—; presenter in field. Contbr. articles to profl. jours., chpts. to books; inventor in field. Grantee Bone Marrow Transplantation Rsch. Fund, 1992-94. Mem. Greek Pediat. Soc., Greek Gastroenterology, European Soc. Pediat. Gastroenterology and Nutrition. Avocation: dancing. E-mail: papadop@flash.gr. Home: Ag Anargyron 32B Marousi, 151 24 Athens Greece Office: P & A Kyriakou Childrens Hosp, Thivon and Levadias, 115 27 Athens Greece

PAPAGEORGIOU, ATHANASIOS, thoracic surgeon, educator; b. Trikala, Thessaly, Greece, Nov. 7, 1956; s. Antipas and Efterpi (Zafraka) P.; m. Sabine Hildegard Hedwig Meyer, Dec. 15, 1990; children: Antipas Joern-Axel, Inge-Efferpi. Medical Diploma, Med. Sch. Thessaloniki, Greece; MD, U. Hamburg, Germany. Asst. prof. medicine Aristoteles U. of Thessaloniki; registrar of propedeutic surg. clinic Ahepa U. Hosp., Thessaloniki. Mem. editorial bd. Rettungsdienst (German), 1993. Mem. German Soc. for Thoracic and Cardiovascular Surgery. Avocations: photography, trumpet playing. Office: Ahepa Univ Hosp, St Kiriakidi 6, 54006 Thessaloniki Greece

PAPAGEORGIOU, MARKOS, engineering educator; b. Thessaloniki, Macedonia, Greece, Sept. 29, 1953; s. Vassilios and Irene (Tsakmaka) P. Diploma, Tech. U. Munich, 1976, D Engring., 1981. Rsch. assoc. Tech. U. Munich, 1976-82, prof., 1988-94; free assoc. Dorsch Consult, Munich, 1982-86; scientific cons. INRETS, Paris, 1986-97; prof. Tech. U. Crete, 1994—; vis. prof. Poly. Milan, 1982, Ecole Nat. Ponts Chaussees, Paris, 1985-91, U. Calif. Berkeley, 1993, 97, 2000, MIT, Cambridge, 1997, 2000. Author: (books) Applic.Autom.Control Concepts to Traffic Flow, 1983, Optimierung, 1991, 2nd edit. 1996; editor: (book) Concise Encyclopedia of Traffic and Transportation, 1991. DAAD scholar, Germany, 1971-76, Eugen Hartmann, VDI scholar, Germany, 1983; recipient Fulbright award, 1997. Fellow IEEE; mem. Daimler-Benz Circle. Office: Tech U Crete, Dynamic Sys/Simulation Lab, 73100 Chania Crete, Greece

PAPAGEORGIOU, VASSILIOS PETER, chemistry educator; b. Thiva, Greece, June 4, 1942; s. Peter Vassilios and Evangelia Kostas (Vrettopoulou) P.; m. Charicleia Jordan Stergiou, Apr. 9, 1967; children: Peter, Dan-Paris, Eudoxia. BS with honors, Univ., Thessaloniki, Greece, 1966, PhD, 1970, DS, 1976. Lectr. Sch. Medicine, Thessaloniki, Greece, 1974-75; rsch. assoc. Coll. Pharmacy, Ky., 1975-76; reader Sch. Chem. Engring., Thessaloniki, 1978-82, asst. prof., 1982-83, assoc. prof., 1983-87, prof. lab. organic chemistry, 1987—; dean Sch. Engring., Thessaloniki, 1997; head Faculty Chem. Engring., Thessaloniki, 1991-97; dir. chemistry dept. Faculty Chem. Engring., 1996—. Inventor in field. 2d lt. Greek Mil., 1971-73. E-mail: vaspap@vergina.eng.auth.gr. Home: Anixeos 32 Panorama, 55236 Thessaloniki Greece Office: Faculty Chem Engring, Thessaloniki Univ, 54006 Thessaloniki Greece

PAPAGIANNIS, JOHN, pediatrician; b. Thessaloniki, Greece, Aug. 19, 1959; s. Constantine Byron and Alice Paraskeriv (Scabardonis) P.; m. Constantina Giaprou, Oct. 30, 1983; children: Paraskevi, Catherina, Marina, Constantinos. MD, Aristotelian U., Thessaloniki, Greece, 1983. Diplomate Am. Bd. Pediatrics, Am. Bd. Pediat. Cardiology. Intern pediatrics St. Louis Children's Hosp., 1985-86; pediatric resident Washington U., St. Louis, 1985-88; fellow in pediat. cardiology Duke U., Durham, N.C., 1988-91, fellow pediat. electrophysiology, 1995-96; fellow in cardiatric pathology Harvard U., Boston, 1991-92; attending physician Onassis Cardiac Ctr., Athens, Greece, 1993-98, assoc. dir. pediat. cardiology, 1998—; cons. Riyadh (Saudi Arabia) Armed Forces Cardiac Ctr., 1993; dir. pediat. electrophysiology Lab., Onassis Cardiac Ctr., Athens, 1996—. Mem. Assn. European Pediat. Cardiologists, Hellenic Soc. Cardiology. Office: Onassis Cardiac Surgery Ctr, 356 Sygrou Ave, 17674 Athens Greece

PAPAKONSTANTINO, STACY, English language educator; b. San Francisco, Feb. 27, 1967; d. Demetrios and Eugenia (Yiallely) P. AA, City. Coll. of San Francisco, 1987; BA in English Lit., San Francisco State U., 1989, MA in English Lang. Studies, 1991. Cert. in tchg. composition and postsecondary reading. English, ESL tutor City Coll. of San Francisco, 1986-87, instr. of English, 1991—; Greek instr. Holy Trinity Sch., 1988-90; chair student grade and file rev. com., City Coll. of San Francisco, 1996—, resource mem. student success com., 1997—, mem. student complaint com., 1997—, mem. composition/lit./reading com., 1996—. Mem. Nat. Coun. Tchrs. of English. Democrat. Orthodox. Avocations: reading, movies and plays, helping needy people, spiritual worship, fitness. Home: 48 Westpark Dr Daly City CA 94015-1055 Office: City Coll San Francisco 50 Phelan Ave San Francisco CA 94112-1821

PAPAKONSTANTINOU, ZOE, marketing professional; b. Athens, Greece, Dec. 11, 1972; d. Meletis and Athina P. Sales BIC SA, Athens, Greece, 1993-94, Ford S.A., Athens, 1996-97; mktg. and comms. dept. Altec S.A., Athens, 1997—. Avocations: gymnastics, reading, theater.

PAPAKOSTAS, ACHILLEAS, telecommunications engineer, researcher; b. Larissa, Greece, Sept. 23, 1967; came to U.S., 1990; s. Ioannis and Dimitra Papakostas; m. Sheila Ann Papakostas, Apr. 27, 1996; children: Maria Margarita, Demitra Eleni. MS, U. Mass., 1993; PhD, U. Tex., Dalls, 1996. Cert. engr., Greece. Software engr. Tom Sawyer Software, Berkeley, Calif., 1995; telecom. engr. NEC Am., Irving, Tex., 1996—. Contbr. articles to profl. jours. Tchr. Greek Orthodox Ch., Dallas, 1994-97; pres. Hellenic Cultural Soc. Dalls, 1996-97. Mem. IEEE, Greek Tech. Chamber, Soc. Indsl. and Applied Math. Avocations: reading, teaching Greek, cycling. E-mail: papakos@asl.dl.nec.com. Office: NEC Am 1525 W Walnut Hill Ln Irving TX 75038-3797

PAPALEXANDROU, CHRISTOS ELIAS, retired Greek government official, economist; b. Petrina, Lakonia, Greece, Mar. 28, 1925; s. Elias George and Erasmia John (Poulimenakou) P.; m. Kostantina Philip Ragazou, Nov. 1, 1959; children: Elias, Athanasios. BA, Athens Sch. Econs., 1953. Dir. Nat. Statis. Dept., Athens, 1955-87, 1982-87, Ministry Nat. Economy, Athens; econ. cons. Ministry Coordination, Athens, 1978-82; ret., 1987. Author: Inflation and Unemployment; contbr. over 1000 articles to econ. publs. and mags. With Greek Army, 1947-50. Recipient award for nat. resistance, 1944. Mem. Social Democratic Party. Christian Orthodox. Home: Michael Boda 144, 10446 Athens Greece

PAPANDONIOU, IOANNIS, Greek government official; b. Paris, July 27, 1949. Student econs., U. Athens, U. Wis.; student history, U. Paris; PhD in Econs., U. Cambridge, Eng. Lectr. econs. U. Athens; researcher Ctr. Planning and Econ. Rsch., 1977-78; mem. staff econ. dept. OECD, Paris, 1978-81; adv. PASOK, 1980-81, mem. European parliament, 1981-84; adv. to Prime Min. on EC affairs Govt. of Greece, 1984-85, dep. min. nat. econ., 1985-89, min. trade, 1989; MP Athens, 1989, 1993—; alternate min. nat. econ., 1993-94, min. nat. econ., 1994—. Mem. Panhellenic Socialist Movement. Office: Ministry Nat Economy, 5 Nikis Plateia Syntagmatos, 101 80 Athens Greece*

PAPANDREOU, GEORGE ANDREAS, parliamentarian; b. St. Paul, June 16, 1952; s. Andreas George and Margaret (Chant) P.; divorced; 1 child, Andreas. Student, Stockholm U., 1972-73; BA in Sociology, Amherst Coll., 1975; MS in Sociology and Devel., London Sch. Econs., 1977. Parliamentarian Govt. of Greece, Athens, 1981—, minister edn. and religious affairs, 1988—; undersec. for cultural affairs Greek Parliament, Athens, 1985-87; chmn. parliamentary com. on edn.; vice chmn. multi-partisan parliamentary com. for free radio. Active cen. com. Panhellenic Socialist Movement, Greece, 1984—, mem. exec. com., 1987, sec. agrl. coops., mem. internat. relations com., dep. sec. orgnl. com.; govt. coordinator for the Athens candidacy for the 1996 Olympic Games, 1988. Recipient award for promotion of journalism for the establishment of Free Radio in Greece, Botsis Found. Mem. Found. Mediterranean Studies (mem. research teams), Found.

Research and Self-Edn. Mem. Panhellenic Socialist Movement. Office: 17 Aghias Phicotheis, 10556 Athens Greece

PAPANTONIOU, NICOLAS ELPIDOFOROS, obstetrician, gynecologist, researcher; b. Athens, Greece, June 5, 1951; s. Elpidoforos A. and Rosalind A. P.; m. Annika Nominos, June 18, 1981; children: Antony, Anastasios, Angel. MD, U. Athens, 1976, MD Thesis, 1986. Lectr. U. London/Hammersmith Hosp., 1985-86; registrar U. Athens, 1986-91, sr. registrar, 1991-97, asst. prof., 1997—. Contbr. articles to profl. jours. Lt. Greek Navy, 1977-78. Mem. Internat. Fetoscopy Working Group, Internat. Soc. Ultrasound in Ob/gyn., Soc. Perinatal Obstetricians. Home: 4 Benaki Str, 154 52 Athens Greece Office: Alexandra U Maternity Hosp, Lourou 1 Str, 115 28 Athens Greece

PAPANTONIS, ANTONY, wine company executive; b. Athens, Greece, June 17, 1950; s. Dimostenes Papantonis and Katerine Dousias. BBA, Hamilton Coll., Mason City, Iowa, 1974. Gen. mgr. Inachos S.A., Athens, Greece, 1975-2000; owner, mgr. Papantonis Winery, Argos, Greece, 2000—; dir. Edok-Eter-Mandilas, Nigeria, Thalis S.A., Saudi Arabia, Overseas Engr. and Gen. Contractor, Libya. Served in the Greek Army, 1970-72. Office: Papantonis Winery, 48 Kanari Str, GR-21200 Argos Greece

PAPASOLOMONTOS, CHRISTINA, elementary educator, researcher; b. Famagusta, Cyprus, Mar. 2, 1970; arrived in Eng., 1993; d. George and Vasiliki Papasolomontos. Diploma, Pedagogical Acad. Cyprus, 1990; MEd, U. Manchester, Eng., 1995, MSc, 1996, PhD, 1997. Primary sch. tchr. Ministry Edn., Cyprus, 1990-93; rschr. U. Manchester, 1998—. Author: Educational Research, 1998. Mem. APA, Brit. Psychol. Assn. Office: U Manchester, CFAS Sch Edn Oxford Rd, Manchester M13 9PL, England

PAPASOTIRIOU, ALEXIOS, journalist; b. Athens, Greece, Jan. 12, 1967; s. Sotirios and Heide (Fetkoter) P. BA in History, Bates Coll., Maine, 1992; certs. in French lang., Sorbonne, Nouvelle Sorbonne, France, 1986; cert. comparative lit., U. Tubingen, Germany, 1992, Diploma in Translation, 1995; postgrad., U. Plymouth, Exeter, Eng., 1995-96. Freelance translator London, 1993-94, Exeter, Eng., 1994-96, Athens, 1998—; tchr. English Link, Prague, Czech Republic, 1996-97, Air Nav. Svc. Czech Rep., 1997-98; corres. Radio Free Europe/Radio Liberty, Greece, 1999—; co-editor Hellenic Star Weekly Newspaper, Athens, 1999—. Author: The Island Within, 1990-93, Ypsilon, 1990, Brandau, 1995; translator Twelve and One Lies, 1993; contbr. articles to newspapers. Mem. Inst. of Linguists. Avocation: literature. Home: PO Box 57, 19003 Markopoulo Greece Office: S Sisni, St 6, 11528 Athens Greece

PAPASPYRIDES, CONSTANTINE DIMITRIOS, chemical engineering educator, consultant; b. Athens, May 20, 1952; s. Dimitrios Constantine and Lefki Issidoros (Lunji) P.; m. Constantina Dionysios Kartsona, Jan. 28, 1979; children: Lefki-Maria, Dimitra. Diploma, Nat. Tech. U. Athens, 1975, D of Engring., 1982, privatdozent, 1985; MS, U. Technology, Loughborough, U.K., 1977. Lectr. chem. engring. Nat. Tech. U. Athens, 1982-85, asst. prof., 1985-90, assoc. prof., 1990-94, prof., 1994—, vice chmn. dept., 2000—; vis. scientist MIT, Cambridge, Mass., 1986-88, Swiss Fed. Inst. Tech. (ETH), Zurich, 1988-90, E.I. DuPont Nemours and Co., Inc., Wilmington, Del., 1991-92, cons., 1992—; dir. Lab. Polymer Tech. Nat. Tech. U. Athens, 1994—, dir. dept. sect. IV: Synthesis and Devel. of Indsl. Processes, 1999-2000. Patentee in field; contbr. articles to profl. jours., books, and encys. With Greek Army, 1978-80. State scholar Inst. of Greece, 1970-74, rsch. scholar R&D divsn. Imperial Chem. Industries Ltd., 1976, Fulbright sr. rsch. scholar USA Ednl. Found., Greece, 1987-88. Mem. N.Y. Acad. Sci. Office: Nat Tech Univ Athens, Lab Polymer Tech Zographou Campus, 157 80 Athens Greece

PAPASTEFANOU, CONSTANTIN, physics educator; b. 1944. PhD in Physics, Aristotle U., Thessaloniki, Greece, 1976. Assoc. rschr. in health physics divsn. CERN, Geneva, 1977, assoc. rschr. in exptl. physics divsn., 1982-84; assoc. rschr. in environ. scis. divsn. Oak Ridge (Tenn.) Nat. Lab., 1984-85, 87; prof. physics, dir. Environ. Radioactivity Lab. Aristotle U., Thessaloniki, 1970—. Author: Radiation Physics and Applied Radiation and Isotopes, 1989, Chernobyl '86: The nuclear accident, 1990; contbr. articles and sci. paper to profl. jours. and procs. internat. confs. Office: Aristotle Univ, Aristotle U, Nuclear Physics Dept, Thessaloniki 540 06, Greece

PAPASTEPHANOU, MARIANNA KYRIAKI, educator; b. Rhodes, Greece, July 16, 1970; d. Ioannis Papastephanou and Sophia Paraskeya. BA in Philosophy, U. Crete, Greece, 1992; postgrad., Tech. U., Berlin, 1994; PhD in Philosophy, U. Wales, Cardiff, 1996. Lectr. U. Cardiff, 1994-96, 96-97; lectr. philosophy of edn. U. Cyprus, 1997—; cons. convener, Haifa, Israel, 1998. Editor: From a Transendental Point of View, 1998, Truth, Relativism and Philosophy of Science, 2000; conf. convener 7th Internat. Conf. Approaching the Millenium, Bergen, Norway, 2000; contbr. articles to profl. jours. Fax: 003572753702. Office: U Cyprus Dept Edn, Dramas 13, Nicosia Cyprus

PAPATHANASIOU, THANASIS D., chemical engineer; b. Larissa, Greece, Aug. 6, 1961; came to U.S., 1997; s. Dimitrios and Lina (Themeli) P. BSc in Engring., Nat. Tech. Athens, Greece, 1985; MSc, U. Calgary, Can., 1987; PhD, McGill U., Montreal, 1991. Postdoctoral fellow Los Alamos Nat. Lab., 1991-92; lectr. Imperial Coll., London, 1992-97; assoc. prof. U. S.C., Columbia, S.C., 1997—. Editor: Flow-Induced alignment in Composites, 1997. Grantee Dept. of Energy, 1998, Dept. of Def., 1999. Mem. ASME, AIChE, Soc. Rheology, Am. Soc. Chem. Engrs. Office: U SC Dept Chem Engring Columbia SC 29208-0001

PAPAVASSILIOU, ATHANASIOS GEORGE, molecular biologist, educator; b. Thessaloniki, Greece, Mar. 13, 1961; s. George A. and Ioanna T. (Gelitsali) P.; m. Effie K. Basdra, Feb. 18, 1984; children: George A., Konstantinos A. MD with 1st class honors, Aristotelian U. Thessaloniki, 1984; PhD in Cellular, Molecular, and Biophys. Studies, Columbia U., 1989. Grad. rsch. asst. dept. microbiology Columbia U. Coll. Physicians and Surgeons, N.Y.C., 1984-89, postdoctoral rsch. scientist, 1989-90; postdoctoral fellow differentiation program European Molecular Biology Lab., Heidelberg, Germany, 1990-91, staff scientist, 1991-96, organizer, instr., 1993-96; assoc. prof. dept. biochemistry Sch. Medicine, U. Patras, Greece, 1994-2000, prof., 2000—. Co-author: Methods Manuals, 1994, 2000, Pediatric Neurology, 1995, 99; co-author, invited editor: Transcription Factors in Eukaryotes, 1997; guest editor (jour.) Methods in Molecular and Cellular Biology, 1995; contbg. editor (jour.) Molecular Medicine; contbr. articles to profl. jours.; mem. editl. bd. Frontiers in Biosci., Molecular Medicine Today, Expert Opinion on Investigational Drugs, Electronic Jour. Oncology. Fellow Ministry Nat. Edn., 1978-84; recipient Acad. Scis. Greece award, 1999. Fellow European Molecular Biology Orgn., Molecular Medicine Soc.; mem. AAAS, Internat. Bone Mineral Soc., Am. Chem. Soc., Am. Soc. Microbiology (Young Investigator award 1990), Am. Soc. for Biochemistry and Molecular Biology, Am. Assn. Cancer Rsch., N.Y. Acad. Scis., Biochem. Soc., Soc. for Gen. Microbiology, Biophys. Soc., Am. Soc. Bone and Mineral Rsch., Signal Transduction Soc. Greek Orthodox. Avocations: poetry, quantum physics and chemistry, soccer. Office: U Patras Sch Medicine, Dept Biochemistry, 26110 Patras Greece

PAPAY, FRANCIS ANTHONY, plastic surgeon, researcher; b. Lorain, Ohio, Sept. 24, 1953; s. Frank Steven and Virginia Kay (Plato) P.; m. Patricia Lynn Lake, Dec. 27, 1991 (div. Aug. 1998). BA in Chemistry, Zoology cum laude, Ohio U., 1975; MS in Biomed. Engring., Case Western Res. U., 1984; MD, Northeastern Ohio U., Rootstown, 1984. Diplomate Am. Bd. Plastic Surgery, Am. Bd. Otolaryngology, Nat. Bd. Med. Examiners, Am. Bd. Clin. Engrs. Clin. engr. Lake County Meml. Hosp., Willoughby, Ohio, 1976-77; biomed. engr. NASA, Cleve., 1978-79; intern Riverside Meth. Hosp., Columbus, Ohio, 1983-84; intern in gen. surgery Cleve. Clinic Found., 1984-85, resident in otolaryngology, 1985-89, resident in plastic and reconstructive surgery, 1989-91, clin. staff, 1992—, co-dir. craniofacial-occuloplastic surgery, 1992—, head sect. pediat. plastic surgery, 1992—, head sect. craniofacial plastic surgery, 1995—, co-acad. chairperson dept. plastic surgery sch. medicine, 1995—, dir. cleft palate clinic; fellow craniofacial surgery Primary Childrens Med. Ctr., U. Utah, 1991-92; preceptor facial plastic surgery New Orleans Facial Plastic Surg. Ctr., 1988; co-founding dir. Northeast Ohio Tissue Engring., Cleve., 1998—; surg. staff Primary Children's Med. Ctr., Salt Lake City, 1991, Holy Cross Hosp., Salt Lake City, 1991; courtesy staff LDS Hosp., Salt Lake City, 1991; asst. prof. Ohio State U.; with dept. plastic reconstructive surgery Fairview Health Sys., Cleve.; dir. craniomaxillofacial clinic Elyria (Ohio) Health Dept., Lake and Ashtabula Counties, Painesville, Ohio; co-dir. Kaiser Permanente Craniomaxillofacial Clinic, Beachwood, Ohio; vis. prof. Hosp. Clinicas Jose San Martin, Buenos Aires, 1997, Hosp. Clincias Dept. Pediat. Surgery, Puerto Montt, Chile, 1997; mem. Children's Oncology Svcs. Northeastern Ohio, Inc.; presenter in field. Co-author: (chpt.) The Otolaryngologic Clinics of North America: Advance Techniques for Management of Head and Neck Neoplasms, Vol. 24, 1991, Instructional Courses-Otolaryngology-Head and Neck Surgery, Vol. 4, 1991, Complications of Head and Neck Surgery, 1993, Duane's Clinical Ophthalmology, Vol. 2, 1993; mem. editl. bd. Pediat. Perspectives, 1994—; sect. editor Cleft Palate-Craniofacial Jour., 1994, 98, Jour. Craniofacial Surgery, 1998; contbr. articles to Jour. Craniofacial Surgery, Laryngoscope Jour., Annals Plastic Surgery, Otolaryngolgoy, Head and Neck Surgery, Am. Jour. Ophthalmology, Plastic Reconstructive Surgery Jour., Internat. Jour. Aesthetic Restorative Surgery, Archives Pediat. Adolescent Medicine, Jour. Am. Acad. Dermatology, Cleft Palate Craniofacial Jour., Surg. Forum, Facial Plastic Surgery, Jour. Burn Rehab., Operative Techniques Otolaryngology, Head Neck Surgery, Ear Nose Throat Jour., Otolaryngol. Clinic N.Am., Laryngoscope, Am. Jour. Rhinology, Cleve. Clinic Jour. medicine, Archives Otolaryngology, Ear Nose Throat Jour., Ohio State Med. Jour. Prin. Ambulatory Care. Founding mem. Interplast Ohio, surg. vol. mission, Puerto Viejo, Ecuador, 1990, Santiago, Chile, 1991, Temuco, Chile, 1992, Orsono, Chile, 1992, 94, 95, 96, Puerto Montt, 1995, 96; Nat. judge BF Goodrich Collegiate Inventors Program, Cleve., 1997, 98; founding mem. Aboutface, Cleve.; trustee Ronald McDonald House, Cleve. Recipient Northeastern Ohio Otolaryngology and Maxillofacial Surgery Rsch. award, 1989, Outstanding Young Men In USA award Jaycees, 1992, Servico Salud Osorno, 1996; Melvin E. Jones Rsch. Found. Meml. scholar, 1981, axillofacial Internat. scholar A-O Synthes, 1990; George and Grace Crile Traveling Surg. fellow U. Basel Kantonspital, 1991, Craniomaxillofacial and Pediat. Plastic Surgery fellow Primary Children's Ctr., 1991-92; grantee Cleve. Clinic Found., 1987-88, 90-96, 98, U. Utah, 1992-93, Calif. Birth Defects Monitoring Program, 1995, NIH, Leibinger Surg., others. Fellow ACS, Am. Acad. Pediat., Am. Acad. Otolaryngology; mem. AAAS, Internat. Coll. Surgeons, Internat. Soc. Craniofacial Surgeons, Lipoplasty Soc. N.Am. (continguing med. edn. com.), Am. Cleft Palate-Craniofacial Assn. (internat. rels. com., publs. com.), Am. Soc. Plastic Reconstructive Surgeons (ednl. tech. com., internat. rels. com., managed care com., rep. young plastic surgeons com.), Am. Rhinologic Soc., Assn. Am. Med. Instrumentation, Am. Bd. Clin. Engrs., Am. Soc. Maxillofacial Surgeons., Utah State Med. Assn., Ohio State Med. Assn. (pres. med. student sect. 1983, coun. 1983, Student Leadership award 1983), Ohio Valley Soc. Plastic Reconstructive Surgeons (Resident Rsch. award 1990), Tissue Engring. Soc., Bur. Children Med. Handicaps, Plastic Surgery Rsch. Coun., No. Ohio Pediat. Soc. (assoc.), Cleve. Med. Soc., Robin Anderson Soc. (founding), A-O Maxillofacial Fellowship Alumni. Republican. Roman Catholic. Achievements include patents for Subcutaneous Mandibular Bone Distractor, Pneumatic Cranial Molding Helmet, Osseous Integrated Bone Anchor, Anti Sids Sleep Cradle. Home: 30548 Royal Woods Pl Westlake OH 44145-3771 Office: Cleve Clinic Found 9500 Euclid Ave Cleveland OH 44195-0001

PAPAZISSIS, MICHAEL GEORGE, lawyer; b Serres, Macedonia, Greece, Jan. 2, 1935; s. George and Zoe (Katsaridou) P.; m. Athena Vogassari, Oct. 25, 1959; children: Byron, Joan, Georgia, Natalie. LLB, U. Thessaloniki (Greece), 1961, Postgrad. Diploma Law, 1967; LLM, U. Montreal, 1968. Bar: Thessaloniki 1965, Athens 1980, Supreme Ct. Athens 1969. Pvt. practice, Athens, 1980—; legal advisor Citibank N.Y., 1969—, Credit Commercial de France, Athens, 1981-82, B.I.A.O. of Paris, Athens, 1982-85, Bank of Macedonia and Thrace, 1984—. Ford Found. scholar, U. Montreal, 1968-69, medal Youth for Understanding, Student Exchange Program, Ann Arbor, Mich., 1974. Mem. Youth for Understanding Student Exchange Program (nat. chmn. Hellenic com. 1970—). Greek Orthodox. Home: 41 Spefsippou St, 10676 Athens Greece Office: 5 Xanthou St, 10673 Athens Greece

PAPE, HELMUT WOLFGANG, philosopher; b. Hildesheim, Germany, July 30, 1950; s. Helmut and Anneliese (Papenburg) P.; m. Astrid Mattern, Mar. 7, 1984; children: Almut and Hermine (twins). MA, U. Hamburg, Germany, 1977, PhD, 1981; habilitation, U. Hannover, Germany, 1993. Lectr. U. Hamburg, 1978-82; asst. prof. U. Freiburg, Germany, 1985-91; scientific employee U. Hannover, 1991-95, assoc. prof., 1995—; rsch. assoc. U. Tours, France, 1995—,U. Paris XII, Val de Marne, 1996—, Rsch. Ctr. for Linguistic & Semiotic Studies, Bloomington, Ind., 1977-78; co-founder, acting dir., v.p. Acad. du Midi-Inst. for Philosophy, 1988—; vis. prof. Humboldt U., Berlin, 1995-96. Author: Erfahrung und Wirklichkeit als Zeichenprozess, 1989; mem. adv. bd. Peirce-Edition Project, 1995—; mem. editl. bd. Jour. Speculative Philosophy, 1993—. Ctr. for Philosophy Sci. fellow U. Pitts., 1987, 90. Mem. Charles S. Peirce Soc., Deutsche Assn. for Semiotik (chmn. philosophy divsn. 1987-90), Soc. for the Advancement Am. Philosophists (corres.). Office: Univ Hannover, Philosophisches Seminar, D-30167 Hannover Germany

PAPE, STUART M., lawyer; b. Paterson, N.J., Dec. 24, 1948. BA, U. Va., 1970, JD, 1973. Bar: Va. 1973, U.S. Ct. Appeals (6th cir.) 1975, U.S. Supreme Ct. 1976, D.C. 1980. Law clk. to Hon. Leonard Braman Superior Ct. D.C., 1973-74; exec. asst. to commr. FDA, 1979; mng. ptnr. Patton Boggs LLP and predecessors, Washington. Mem. ABA (com. food and drug law, sect. adminstrv. law 1973-92), Va. State Bar, D.C. Bar. Addresss: 2950 Chain Bridge Rd NW Washington DC 20016-3408

PAPERNIK, JOEL IRA, lawyer; b. N.Y.C., May 4, 1944; s. Herman and Ida (Titefsky) P.; m. Barbara Ann Barker, July 28, 1972; children: Deborah, Ilana. BA, Yale U., 1965; JD cum laude, Columbia U., 1968. Bar: N.Y. 1969. Assoc. Shea & Gould, N.Y.C., 1968-76, ptnr., 1976-91; ptnr., chmn. corp. and securities dept., mem. mgmt. com. Squadron, Ellenoff, Plesent & Sheinfeld, N.Y.C., 1991-2000; ptnr., mem. bus. fin. dept. Mintz, Levin, Cohn, Ferris, Glovsky and Popeo PC, 2000—; lectr. various panels. Author: Risks of Private Foreign Investments in the U.S. Served with 11th Spl. Forces, USAR, 1967-73. Mem. ABA (sect. on corp. law, mem. forum on sports and entertainment law), N.Y. State Bar Assn. (lectr. various panels, mem. securities law com.), Assn. of Bar of City of N.Y. (chmn., lectr., mem. corp. law com., mem. securities regulation com. 1992-95(, N.Y. Tri-Bar Opinion Com., Yale Club. Office: Mintz Levin Cohn Ferris Glovsky and Popeo PC 666 3rd Ave New York NY 10017-4011

PAPI, LIZA RENIA, artist, writer, educator; b. Malacacheta, Minas Gerais, Brazil, Jan. 19, 1949; came to U.S., 1978; d. Rivadavia and Lair Bronzon P.; 1 child, Mourrice O. BA, Inst. Fine Arts Rio de Janeiro, 1974; MFA, CUNY, 1992. Art instr. CUNY, Henry St. Settlement, N.Y.C., Third St. Music; illustrator Studio T. Graphics; artist in residence Mus. del Barrio, N.Y.C.; dir. publicity Art Sphere Cultural Ctr., N.Y.C., 1990-91; coord. Americanos, N.Y.C., 1990-94. Author: The Vanishing Beetles, 1991, Carnavalia, African Brazilian Folklore and Crafts, 1994. Residency planning grantee N.Y. Found. Arts, 1994, Anneberg Art-in-Edn. grantee, 1998—. Mem. Soka Gakkai Internat., Coll. Art Assn., The Fgn. Press. Buddhist. Avocations: contemprary dance, biking. Office: Papi Studio 231 W 25th St Apt 3D New York NY 10001-7113

PAPINI, ROBERTO AMERIGO, veterinary scientist, researcher; b. San Giulliano, Pisa, Italy, June 5, 1958; s. Sergio and Mirella (Madrigali) P. Degree in vet. sci., U. Pisa, 1986. Fellow CNR, Pisa, 1983-90; collaborator Faculty of Vet. Medicine, Pisa, 1990-96, sr. collaborator, 1996—; monitor Bayer, Milan, 1998. Trade union rep. U. Pisa, 1999. Mem. Italian Soc. Vet. Sci., Italian Fedn. Human and Animal Mycology. Avocations: cinema, languages, travel. Office: Dept Clin Vet, Viale Delle Piagge, 56124 Pisa Italy

PAPOUIN, GÉRARD, cardiologist; b. Le Pas, Mayenne, France, Feb. 19, 1947; arrived in French Polynesia, 1980; s. Theo and Simone (Tourrier) P.; m. Rauzy Micheline, Dec. 23, 1969; children: Vaea, Jean-Christophe, Maïre. MD, U. Angers, France, 1973, cert. in cardiology, 1978, cert. in sports medicine, 1979. Asst. of medicine Papeete Hosp., French Polynesia, 1980-83, chief div. cardiology, 1983—. Contbr. articles to profl. jours. Mem. French Soc. Cardiology, South Pacific Internat. Cardiology Cong. (pres. organizing com. 1987). Avocation: karate. Office: Ctr Hosp Territorial, Box 1640, Papeete, Tahiti French Polynesia

PAPOUTSAKIS, ELEFTHERIOS TERRY, chemical engineering educator, consultant; b. Alexandroupolis, Greece, May 29, 1951; came to U.S., 1975; s. Efstratios and Eleni Papoutsakis; m. Maria Papoutsakis; 1 child, Ellie. Diploma in Engring., Nat. Tech. U. Athens, Greece, 1974; MS, Purdue U., 1977, PhD, 1980. Asst. prof. Rice U., Houston, 1980-85, assoc. prof., 1985-87; assoc. prof. Northwestern U., Evanston, Ill., 1987-89, prof., 1989—; cons. to numerous cos. Mem. editl. bd. Jour. Biotech., Tissue Engring., Metabolic Engring.; editor 2 books; editor Biotech. and Engring. Jour., 1990-96, assoc. editor, 1996—; contbr. over 150 articles to profl. jours. Recipient FPBD award Am. Inst. Chem. Engrs., 1995, M.J. Johnson award Am. Chem. Soc., 1998. Fellow AAAS, Am. Inst. Med. and Biol. Engring. E-mail: E-Paps@northwestern.edu. Office: Northwestern Univ Dept Chem Engring Evanston IL 60208-0001

PAPP, ERHARDT SABIN, physics educator; b. Timisoara, Banat, Romania, Jan. 24, 1944; arrived in Germany, 1981; s. Ingrid Bastius; children: Erhardt, Eduard. Grad. in Physics, U. Bucharest, Romania, 1966; PhD, Babes-Bolyai U., Cluj, Romania, 1974; Habilitation, Tech. U., Clausthal, Germany, 1993. Diplomate physics. Prof. asst. Poly. Inst., Cluj, 1966-81; prof. physics U. Baia Mare, Romania, 1996—. Author: The Derivation of Analogs, 1997; referee The Phys. Rev., 1986—; contbr. articles to profl. jours., chpt. to book. Recipient 1st prize Student's Physics Olympiad, Ministry Higher Edn., Bucharest, 1967; postdoctoral grantee Deutsche Forschungsgemeinschaft, Munich, 1983-85, Deutsche Forschungsgemeinschaft, Clausthal, Germany, 1988-90. Avocations: classical music, rock and roll, Greek philosophy, history. Office: U Baia Mare Dept Physics, Str Victoriei nr 76, RO-4800 Baia Mare Maramures, Romania

PAPP, FERENC, scientific consultant, educator; b. Budapest, Hungary, Sept. 19, 1930; s. Ferenc and Ferencné (Dózsa) P.; m. Maria Pátkai, Jan. 26, 1952; children: Ferenc, Mária. PhD, Hungarian Acad. Scis., Budapest, 1956; Doctorate (hon.), U. Debrecen, Hungary, 1992. Prin. asst. U. Lajos Kossuth, Debrecen, Hungary, 1953—; asst. prof. U. Lajos Kossuth, Debrecen, 1955—, univ. prof., 1965—; univ. prof. U. Eötvös Loránd, Budapest, 1966—; chief Russian dept. U. L. Kossuth, Debrecen, 1955-85; sci. cons. Acad. Scis., 1985—. Author, editor: A Reverse Alphabetised Dictionary of the Hungarian Language, 1969; author: Könyv az orosz nyelvröl, 1979; co-author, editor: Kurs Sovremennogo Russkogo Jazika, 1968; co-author: Ady Endre összes költoi müveinek fonémastatisztikája, 1974. Mem. Hungarian Linguistic Soc., John Neumann Soc., Hungarian Acad. Scis. Home: Gogol utca 27, 1133 Budapest Hungary Office: Hungarian Acad Scis, 1102 Szinház u 5-9, Budapest Hungary

PAPP, THILO, molecular biologist; b. Selters, Rheinland, Germany, July 16, 1957; s. Hugo and Brigitte (Sayn) P.; m. Petra Schlechtendahl, Aug. 22, 1991; 1 child, Fabian. Diploma in biology, U. Marburg, Germany, 1984; D in Natural Scis., U. Hannover, Germany, 1988. Postdoctoral fellow U. Freiburg, Germany, 1988-90, U. Wuerzburg, Germany, 1990-95, U. Rostock, Germany, 1995—. Avocations: music, drawing, nature. Office: U Rostock Dep Animal Physio, Uniplatz 2, D-18051 Rostock Germany

PAPP, ZOLTAN, physicist, educator; b. Hajduszoboszlo, Hungary, May 15, 1959; s. Karoly and Ilona (Kiss) P.; m. Aniko Patai, Sept. 9, 1965; children: Zoltan, Teodora. Dr.Univ., U. Kossuth Lajos, Hungary, 1988, PhD, 1998. Rsch. scientist Kossuth Lajos U., 1983-89, asst. lectr., 1989—. Contbr. articles to profl. jours. Mem. Lorand Eotvos Phys. Soc., Hungarian Acad. Scis. Office: U Debrecen Isotope Lab, Egyetem Ter 1 PO Box 8, 4010 Debrecen Hungary

PAPPALARDO, SALVATORE CARDINAL, archbishop; b. Villafranca, Sicula, Sicily, Sept. 23, 1918. Ordained priest Roman Cath. Ch., 1941; entered diplomatic secretariat of state, 1947; titular archbishop of Miletus, 1966; pro-nuncio in Indonesia, 1966-69; pres. Pontifical Ecclesiastical Acad., 1969-70; archbishop of Palermo, 1970—; elevated to Sacred Coll. of Cardinals, 1973; titular ch. St. Mary Odigitria of the Sicilians; mem. Congregation of Oriental Chs., Congregation of Clergy. Office: Casa Diocesana, Piazza Baida 1, 90136 Palermo Italy*

PAPPAS, BARBARA ESTELLE, Biblical studies educator, author; b. Chgo., July 26, 1941; m. George G. Pappas, Sept. 20, 1964; children: Dheanna Pappas Fikaris, Michele Pappas Glavanovits, Laina Pappas Krabbe. Lay asst. Holy Apostles Ch., Westchester, Ill., 1976—; sec., lectr. Diocese of Chgo. Religious Edn. Commn., 1982—; founder, dir. Holy Apostles Resource Ctr., Westchester, 1984—. Author: Are You Saved?, The Orthodox Christian Process of Salvation, 4th edit., 1997, The Christian Life in the Early Church and Today, Commentaries on Paul's Epistles to the Corinthians, Vol. I, 1989, Vol. II, 1998, God's Bubbly, Gurgly, Overwhelming, Overflowing Love, 2000. Mem. ASCD. Greek Orthodox. Home: 379 Arboretum Cir Wheaton IL 60187

PAPPAS, CHRISTOPHOROS, agriculturist, researcher; b. Kosmira, Ioannina, Greece, Feb. 3, 1937; s. Petros and Heleni (Tsiangaveli) P.; m. Vassiliki Tektonos, Nov. 21, 1965; children: Konstantinos, Heleni, Athanasios. Diploma, Zosimaea Sch., Lyceum, Ioannina, 1955; BSc with distinction, Agrl. U., Athens, 1962; MSc in Dairy Sci., Reading (Eng.) U., 1969, PhD in Food Sci., 1979; postgrad., England, 1971. Rschr. Dairy Rsch. Inst., Nat. Agrl. Rsch. Found., Epirus, Greece; sub dir., tchr. Dairy Sch. Ioannina GS, 1971-78; creator Dairy Rsch. Inst., 1984, dir., 1984-99; ret., 1999; cons. Ministry Agr., Athens, Greece, 1979-99, Hellenic Productivity Ctr., Ioannina GS, 1982-97, planner, establisher of new, modern pilot tng. plant, 1980-83, different pvt. orgns., 1984-99, other food industries; mem. Sci. Coun. Nat. Agrl. Rsch. Found., Athens, 1996-97; pres. Adminstrn. Coun. Union Geotech. Scientists, Epirus, Greece, 1992-2000l; establisher of different depts., labs., new lab. equipment to bring inst. up to date, 1984-99. Contbr. articles to profl. jours. Lt. Mech. branch, Greek Army, 1962-64. Scholar Greek State Scholarship Found., Athens, 1956-62, Reading, England, 1968-71, 79; grantee British Coun., Reading, Norwich, England, 1990, 98. Mem. N.Y. Acad. Sci., Geotechnical Chamber Greece, Epirus Agrl. Assn. Mem. Panhellenic Socialistic Party. Greek Orthodox. Achievements include establishing a pilot ednl. plant. Avocations: classic literature, music, agricultural activities. Home: Chaonon St 11-A, 45221 Ioannina Epirus, Greece Office: Dairy Rsch Inst, Nat Agrl Rsch Found, 45216Katsikas Ioannina Epirus, Greece

PAPPAS, EDWARD HARVEY, lawyer; b. Midland, Mich., Nov. 24, 1947; s. Charles and Sydell (Sheinberg) P.; m. Laurie Weston, Aug. 6, 1972; children: Gregory Alan, Steven Michael. BBA, U. Mich., 1969, JD, 1973. Bar: Mich. 1973, U.S. Dist. Ct. (ea. dist.) Mich. 1973, U.S. Dist. Ct. (we. dist.) Mich. 1980, U.S. Ct. Appeals (6th cir.) 1983, U.S. Supreme Ct. 1983. Ptnr. firm Dickinson & Wright, P.L.L.C., Detroit and Bloomfield Hi, Mich., 1973—; mediator Oakland County Cir. Ct., Pontiac, Mich., 1983—; hearing panelist Mich. Atty. Discipline Bd., Detroit, 1983—, chmn., 1987—; mem. bus. tort subcom. Mich. Supreme Ct. Com. Standard Jury Instructions, 1992-94; bd. commrs. State Bar Mich., 1999—. Trustee Oakland Community Coll., Mich., 1982-90, Oakland-Livingston Legal Aid, 1982-90, v.p., 1982-85, pres., 1985-87; trustee, adv. bd. Mich. Regional Anti-Defamation League of B'nai B'rith, Detroit, 1983-90; planning commr. Village of Franklin, Mich., 1987-91, chmn. 1989-91, councilman, 1991-92, chmn. charter com., 1993-94; chmn. State Bar Mich. Long Range Planning com.; pres.-elect Oakland County Bar Assn., 1996-97, pres., 1997-98, chmn. Jud. Selection Task Force, 1997; bd. dirs. Franklin Found., 1989-92; trustee The Oakland Medication Ctr., 1992-96. Master Oakland County Bar Assn. Inn of Ct.; fellow Mich. State Bar Found., Oakland Bar-Adams Pratt Found., ABA Found.; mem. ABA, Fed. Bar Assn., State Bar Mich. (co-chmn. nat. moot ct. competition com. 1974, 76, com. on legal aid, chmn. standing com. on atty. grievances 1989-92, comml. litigation com., civil procedure com. 1992-94, bd. commrs. 1999—), Oakland County Bar Assn. (vice-chmn. continuing legal edn. com., chmn. continuing legal edn. com. 1985-86, mediation com. 1989-90, chmn. mediation com. 1990-91, bd. dirs. 1990-98, chmn. select

com. Oakland County cir. ct. settlement week 1991, chmn. strategic planning com. 1992-93, editor Laches monthly mag. 1986-88, co-chair task force to improve justice systems in Oakland County 1993—, pres.-elect, bd. dirs. 1996-97, pres. 1997-98), Am. Judicature Soc., Mich. Def. Trial Lawyers, Def. Rsch. and Trial Lawyers Assn. (com. practice and procedure), B'nai B'rith Barristers. Home: 32223 Scenic Ln Franklin MI 48025-1702 Office: Dickinson Wright Moon Van Dusen & Freeman 525 N Woodward Ave Bloomfield Hills MI 48304-2971

PAPPAS, JAMES PETE, university administrator; b. Price, Utah, June 30, 1939; s. Pete S. and Dia P. (Metrakis) P.; m. Peggy Ann Kunz, Aug. 30, 1964; children: C. Jennifer, Peter T. AS in Psychology, Coll. Eastern Utah, 1959; BA in Psychology, U. Utah, 1961; MS in Counseling Psychology, Ohio U., 1964; PhD in Clin. Psychology, Purdue U., 1968; cert. in Mgmt., Stanford U., 1979; cert. in adminstrn., Harvard U., 1985. Asst. dir. counseling ctr. U. Utah, Salt Lake City, 1969-72, dir. ctr. for acad. advising, assoc. dean liberal edn., 1975-78, assoc. dean divsn. of continuing edn., 1978-87; prof. ednl. psychology and liberal studies U. Okla., Norman, 1987—, v.p. for univ. outreach; dean Coll. of Continuing Edn., 1994-00, Coll. of Liberal Studies, 2000—. Author: (book) Windows of Opportunity: Preparing University Based Residential Continuing Education for the Twenty-First Century, 1992, The University's Role in Economic Development: From Research to Outreach, 1997; co-author: (workbook) Promotional Techniques, 1987. Mem. Norman Econ. Devel. Coalition, 1996—; state chmn. Utah Endowment for Humanities, 1985-88; pres. Norman Arts and Humanities Coun., 1994-95. Recipient St. Paul award Greek Orthodox Ch. of N. Am., Denver, 1990, Christopher Outstanding Leadership and Bittner Svc. awards U. Continuing Edn. Assn.; inductee Internat. Adult and Continuing Edn. Hall of Fame, 1997. Mem. Am. Assn. Counseling and Devel. (nat. senator 1975-77), Assn. Acad. Affairs Adminstr. (bd. dirs. 1977-78), Adult Edn. Assn. Utah (bd. dirs. 1979-82), Univ. Continuing Edn. Assn. (pres. 1996-97), Nat. Assn. State Univs. and Land Grant Colls. (bd. dirs. 1994-97). Avocations: reading, cmty. svc., writing, sports, travel. Office: Coll Continuing Edn 1700 Asp Ave Rm 111 Norman OK 73072-6407

PAPPAS, MICHAEL, financial services company executive; b. N.Y.C., Sept. 10, 1940; s. Michael Papadopoulos and Despina (Vrioni) Kokindo; m. Eileen McGovern, Jan. 25, 1969. BBA in Acctg. and Data Processing, Pace U., N.Y.C., 1973. Mgr. acctg. E.F. Hutton, N.Y.C., 1972-75, bus. unit mgr., 1976-77; mgr. payroll and commn. acctg. Drexel Burnham Lambert, N.Y.C., 1977-81, v.p., project mgr., 1981-83, v.p., mgr. gen. acctg., 1983-85, v.p., mgr. fin. info. systems, 1985-86, v.p., govt. reporting coord., 1986-89; dir. compensation Gruntal & Co., Inc., N.Y.C., 1989-2000; v.p. Donaldson, Lufkin, Jenrette, N.Y.C., 2000—. Sgt. U.S. Army, 1963-65. Mem. Am. Payroll Assn. (N.Y. Met. chpt. pres. 1998—), Securities Industry Assn. (tech. tax com. 1986-88), Hellenic Am. Bankers Assn. (bd. dirs. 1991-92, v.p. 1992-94, pres. 1995-98, treas. 1998—). Greek Orthodox. Avocations: golf, bowling, collecting award winning movies. Office: Gruntal & Co Inc 1 Liberty Plz Fl 18 New York NY 10006-1404

PAPPAS, THOMAS NICHOLAS, insurance brokerage executive, consultant; b. Phila., Dec. 14, 1942; s. Thomas and Marcedes Madden; m. Carol Ann Pappas, Nov. 13, 1965; children: Thomas Nicholas Jr., Karen, Suszanne, Debora Pappas Herman. BS in Mktg., La Salle U., Phila., 1970; Exec. MBA, U. Pa., 1994. Sales rep. comsu,er [a[er [rpdicts Kimberley Clark Corp., Phila., 1966-67; regional sales and mktg. mgr. Xerox Corp., White Plains, Greenwich, Conn., 1968-74; br. sales mgr. Xerox Corp., Mountainside, N.J., 1974-75, sales mgr., 1975-76; mem. hdqs. mktg. staff Xerox Corp., Rochester, N.Y., 1976-77; sales rep. Xerox Corp., Phila., 1977-79; exec. v.p. Users, Inc., Glen Hardie, Pa., 1979-80; ptnr. Winklevoss & Assocs., Phila., 1981-82; mng. prin., sr. v.p., mgr. global sales and mktg. Johnson & Higgins, N.Y.C. and Phila., 1982-98; mem. sr. exec. transition team for merger Johnson & Higgins and Marsh & McLennan, Inc., 1997-98; chmn., CEO TNP Holdings Inc., Radnor, Pa., 1998—; mem. adv. bd. dirs. Rittenhouse Trust Co. Mem. president's coun. LaSalle U.; trustee Acad. Notre Dame de Namur, Villanova, Pa., 1983-88, chmn. bd. trustees, 1987-88, chmn. endowment com., 1989. Named Man of Yr., Cath. Youth Orgn., 1994, Holy Family Coll., 1999. Mem. Union League Phila. (bd. dirs. 1991-96, v.p. 1994-96, pres. 1997-98, mem. Benson table, chmn. membership com., chmn. membership devel. com. 1991-95), Sunday Breakfast Club, Kindergarten Club, Cross Keys. Home: 105 Rock Rose Ln Radnor PA 19087-3736

PAPPS, BRUCE WILLIAM, investment company executive; b. Mt. Kisco, N.Y., Jan. 19, 1962; s. Ernest W. and Annette (Lazration) P. BS in Econs., Wharton Sch., 1985. Broker, trainee Shearson Lehman, N.Y.C., 1989-93; broker Oppenheimer Co., N.Y.C., 1993-94; asst. v.p. Merrill Lynch, N.Y.C., 1994-96; pres., CEO Papps Capital Group, Inc., N.Y.C., 1996—; adj. prof. SUNY, Valhalla, N.Y., 1995—. Mentor P.R.I.D.E., Harlem, N.Y., 1996—. Avocations: sky diving, scuba diving, boating, skiing. Office: Papps Capital Group Inc 67 Wall St Ste 2411 New York NY 10005-3101

PAPRIKA, ZITA ZOLTAY, economist; b. Szentes, Hungary, Sept. 10, 1957; d. Benö and Irén (Kovács) P.; m. Ákos Zoltay, Nov. 21, 1987; 1 child, Richard. Bachelor, Karl Marx U. of Econs., 1981, doctorate, 1983; PhD, Budapest U. Econ. Studies, 1999. Analyst State Com. for Tech. Devel., Budapest, 1981-87; asst. prof. Budapest U. of Econs., 1987-90, assoc. prof., 1991—; cons. Mgmt. Ltd., Budapest, 1989—. Author: (with others) Implementing Systems for Supporting Management Decisions, 1996, Decision Support in Organizational Transformation, 1997, Context Sensitive Decision Support Systems, 1998. Mem. Multi Criteria Decision Making, Internat. Fedn. Info Processing (sec. working group decision support sys. 1998—). Avocation: traveling. Home: Torma Károly 22, H-1031 Budapest Hungary Office: Budapest U of Econs, Veres Pálné 36, 1053 Budapest Hungary

PAPROCKI, THOMAS JOHN, lawyer, priest; b. Chgo., Aug. 5, 1952; s. John Henry and Veronica Mary (Bonat) P. BA, Loyola U., Chgo., 1974; student Spanish lang. study, Middlebury Coll., 1976, student Italian lang. study, 1987; M in Divinity, St. Mary of the Lake Sem., 1978; student Spanish lang. study, Instituto Cuannahuac, 1978; Licentiate in Sacred Theology, St. Mary of the Lake Sem., 1979; JD, DePaul U., 1981; JCD, Gregorian U., Rome, 1991. Bar: Ill. 1981, U.S. Dist. Ct. (no. dist.) Ill. 1981, U.S. Supreme Ct. 1994. Assoc. pastor St. Michael Ch., Chgo., 1978-83; pres. Chgo. Legal Clinic, 1981-87, 91—; exec. dir. South Chgo. Legal Clinic, 1981-85, bd. dirs., 1987—; adminstr. St. Joseph Ch., Chgo., 1983-86; vice-chancellor Archdiocese of Chgo., 1985-92, chancellor, 1992-99; adj. faculty Loyola U. of Law, 1999—; senator Presbyteral senate Archdiocese of Chgo., 1985-87, mem. Presbyteral coun., 1992—, mem. Cardinal's cabinet, 1992—, sec. coll. consultors, 1992—; chmn. incardination com., 1991—, chmn. policy devel. com., 1998—, chmn. Fgn. Priests Inititive, 1998—; asst. to the Gen. Sec., Vatican Synod of Bishops, Spl. Assembly for Am., Rome, 1997; bd. dirs. Cath. Conf. Ill., 1985-87; adj. faculty Loyola U. Sch. Law, 1999—. Editorial Adv. Bd. Chicago Catholic Newspaper, 1984-85; contbr. articles to profl. jours. Bd. dirs. United Neighborhood Orgn., Chgo., 1982-85, S.E. Community Youth Svc. Bd., Chgo., 1985, Ctr. for Neighborhood Tech., Chgo., 1986-87, Chgo. Area Found. for Legal Svcs., 1994—; active Chgo. Cmty. Trust Com. on Children, Youth and Families, 1991—, Ill. Family Violence Coordinating Coun., 1994—. Recipient Humanitarian award Polish Am. Congress, 1997; named Man of Yr., Nat. Advs., 1999. Fellow Leadership Greater Chgo.; mem. Ill. Bar Assn., Chgo. Bar Assn. (bd. mgrs. 1999—, Maurice Weigle award 1985), Advs. Soc. (award of merit 1996), Cath. Lawyers Guild, Polish Am. Assn. (bd. dirs. 1998—), The Chgo. Jr. Assn. Commerce and Industry (Ten Outstanding Young Citizens award 1986), Union League Club of Chgo., Pi Sigma Alpha, DePaul U. Alumni Assn. Avocations: hockey, running, reading. Home: 730 N Wabash Ave Chicago IL 60611-2514 Office: Archdiocese of Chgo PO Box 1979 155 E Superior St Chicago IL 60611-2911

PAPUNEN, HEIKKI TAPANI, geologist, educator; b. Ikaalinen, Finland, Dec. 28, 1936; s. Kalle V. and Ella (Isotalo) P.; m. Aila Irma Koivusaari, June 5, 1960; children: Paula, Marja, Pirjo. MSc, Helsinki U., 1960; lic., Turku U., 1968, PhD, 1971. Asst. tchr. Turku U., 1960-70, lectr. in geology, 1970-71, assoc. prof., 1971-81, prof., 1981—; assoc. cons. field geologist Outokumpu Oy exploration, Finland, 1960-74; cons. econs. geologist several cos. and surveys, Finland, 1975—. Author: Ni-Cu Deposits of the Baltic Shield, 1985, Economic Geology of Finland, 1986; editor, author: Economic Geology, 1979; contbr. more than 50 articles to profl. jours. 1st lt. Finland Mil. Engring., 1962-63. Decorated Honour Order of the White Rose Knighthood, 1994. Fellow Mineral. Soc. Am., Geol. Soc. Finland (chmn. 1975-76), Soc. Geology Applied to Mineral Deposits (pres. 1999—). Evangelic-Lutheran. Office: Turku U Dept Geology, FIN20014 Turku Finland

PAQUAY, RAYMOND, agronomist, educator; b. Faymonville, Liege, Belgium, Aug. 4, 1940; s. Ernest and Philomene (Hermann) P.; m. Liliane Noel, May 26, 1968; children: Michel, Noelle. Grad., Cath. U. Louvain, Belgium, 1963, PhD, 1968. Rschr. I.R.S.I.A., Brussels, 1963-73; prof. physiology U. Namur, Belgium, 1973—, dean faculty sci., 1981-84, 98—; dean faculty sci. U. Namur, 1981-84, 98—, gen. sec., 1986-95. Author: Alimentation du Mouton, 5 vols., 1989-91; contbr. over 200 articles to profl. jours. Recipient Gilbert Mullie prize Boerenbond, Louvain, 1973. Home: Rue des Pinsons NR 5, S100 Jambes, Namur Belgium Office: Facultes Universitaires, Rue de Bruxelles Nr 61, 5000 Namur, Namur Belgium

PAQUIN, THOMAS CHRISTOPHER, lawyer; b. Quincy, Mass., Feb. 12, 1947; s. Henry Frederick and Rita Marie (St. Louis) P.; m. Jean Jacqueline O'Neill, Aug. 5, 1972; children: Martha, Edward. BS in Acctg., Bentley Coll., 1969; JD, U. Notre Dame, 1974. Bar: Mass. 1974, U.S. Dist. Ct. Mass. 1976. Tax atty. Coopers and Lybrand, Boston, 1974-76; assoc. Cargill, Masterman & Cahill, Boston, 1976, Wilson, Curran & Malkasian, Wellesley, Mass., 1976-77; ptnr. Bianchi and Paquin, Hyannis, Mass., 1977-98; shareholder, dir. Quirk and Chamberlain, P.C., Yarmouthport, Mass., 1998—; bd. dirs., chmn. nominating com. Elder Svcs. Cape Cod and Islands, Inc., Dennis, Mass., 1986-91; bd. dirs., corporator Vis. Nurse Assn. Cape Cod Found., Inc., Dennis, 1988-97; pres. Life Svcs. Inc., 1991-95; bd. dirs. Woodside Cemetery Corp., 1998—, pres., 1999—. Mem. Bass River Golf Commn., Yarmouth, Mass., 1980-83, chmn., 1982-83; chmn. Yarmouth Golf Course Bldg. Com., 1985-89; mem. hearing com. bd. Bar Overseers of the Supreme Jud. Ct., 1989-95; bd. dirs. Project Coach, Inc., 1990-97; conciliator Barnstable Superior Ct., 1992—; trustee Cape Symphony Orch., 1999—. Fellow Mass. Bar Found.; mem. ABA, Mass. Bar Assn. (del. 1986-87, mem. com. on bicentennial U.S. Constn. 1986-88, fee arbitration bd. 1985-86, chmn. spkrs. and writers subcom. 1986-88), Barnstable County Bar Assn. (chmn. seminar com. 1979-83, mem. exec. com. 1981-84, v.p. 1984-86, pres. 1986-87), Estate Planning Coun. Cape Cod (exec. com. 1985-98, sec. 1991-93, pres.-elect 1993-95, pres. 1995-97), Mass. Conveyancers Assn., Mid-Cape Men's Club (v.p. 1992, pres. 1993), Cummaquid Golf Club. Office: Quirk and Chamberlain PC PO Box 40 Yarmouth Port MA 02675-0040

PĀQUIN, TRUDY, gerontological nurse; b. Wantagh, N.Y., May 23, 1954; d. William Carl and Gertrude Mary (Kryl) Bauer; m. Alfred Joseph Pāquin III, July 30, 1977. AAS, John Tyler C.C., Chester, Va., 1982; BA magna cum laude, So. Conn. State U., 1993; gerontol. nurse cert., U. Conn., 1994, nurse mgmt. cert., 1995. RN, Va.; cert. psychiat. and mental health nurse. Animal trainer, 1972—, pet therapist, 1974—; nurse, educator, therapy dog tng. C.O.C. at Elm City, New Haven, 1983—; Alzheimer's rschr., 1995; mem. Antarctic Expedition, 1996. Author: Pet Therapy Handbook, 1998, One Man's Journey to America, 1996, Trainer of Therapy Dogs, 1999; composer numerous musical works. Mem. Harness Goat Soc. Avocations: songwriting, fiddling, dog training, swimming, packing with llamas. Office: COC at Elm City 50 Mead St New Haven CT 06511-5106

PARA, GERARD ALBERT, lawyer, real estate broker, consultant; b. Oak Park, Ill., June 27, 1953; s. Bruno Joseph and Bernice Agnes Para; m. Gayle Louise Keegan, Sept. 15, 1979; children; Eric, Teresa. BA with honor, De Paul U., 1973, JD, 1976. Bar: Ill. 1977, U.S. Dist. Ct. (no. dist.) Ill. 1977, U.S. Ct. Appeals (7th cir.) 1977, Fed. Trial Bar. 1984; lic. real estate broker, Ill. Jud. law clk. Ill Appellate Ct. (1st dist.), Chgo., 1977-78; divsnl. counsel Household Internat. Franchisor Divsns., Prospect Heights, Ill., 1978-85; v.p. Bannockburn (Ill.) Pk. Concepts, Inc., 1986-93; dir. real estate ops., asst. gen. counsel Ben Franklin Stores, Carol Stream, Ill., 1994-96; v.p., gen. counsel DiMucci Devel. Corp., Palatine, Ill., 1996-97; gen. counsel Urban Investment Trust Inc., Chgo., 1998-99; prin. Franchise ESQ.sm, Lincolnshire, Ill., 1999—; arbitrator 19th Jud. Cir., Lake County, Ill., 1999—; real estate broker, Long Grove, Ill., 1987—; franchise cons. Elliotts' Off Broadway Deli, Oak Brook, Ill., 1993—. Editor: Medical Malpractice, 1975, Trial Technique, 1975. Asst. coach Little League Buffalo Grove (Ill.) Recreation Assn., 1988—; asst. scoutmaster Boy Scouts Am., Long Grove, 1995—. Mem. ABA, Internat. Coun. Shopping Ctrs., Internat. Corp. Real Estate Execs. (bd. dirs. Chgo. chpt.), Chgo. Bar Assn., Internat. Franchise Assn., Coun. Franchise Suppliers. Roman Catholic. Avocations: lap swimming, boating, scuba diving, weightlifting. Office: Franchise ESQ sm 125 Shelter Rd #450 Lincolnshire IL 60069

PARACHA, MUHAMMAD SALIM, mechanical engineer; b. Darya Khan, Punjab, Pakistan, Nov. 1, 1948; s. Abdur Rahim and Fatima Rahim Paracha; m. Fauzia Paracha, May 7, 1975; three children. B in Mech. Engring., Engring. Coll., Peshawar, Pakistan, 1970; student, Islamia Coll., Peshawar, Pakistan. Sr. engr. EM-Hidromontaza, Tarbela, 1971-76; prin. mech. engr. Acres Internat. Ltd./Pakistan Engring. Svcs. Ltd., Tarbela, Pakistan, 1976-83, chief tech. engr., 1983-86; prin. engr. Nat. Engring. Svcs. Pakistan, 1983-86; mech. discipline leader Gibbs & Hill, Inc. N.Y., Guddu, Sindh, Pakistan, 1986-92; resident engr. Muzaffargarh Thermal Power Cons., Pakistan, 1992-94; sr. project mgr. Pvt. Power & Infrastructure Bd., Islamabad, Pakistan, 1994—; discipline leader Mech. Power Plant, Pakistan, 1983-86; project engr., Pakistan, 1986-92, project cons., 1992-94; cons. Pvt. Power and Infrastructure Bd., Pakistan, 1994-98. Mem. Pakistan Engring. Coun., Inst. Engrs. Home: House No 4, Main Double Rd F10/2, Islamabad Pakistan Office: House No 1, St 42 F 7/1, Islamabad Pakistan

PARACHA, SAMYA KADRI, investment banker; b. Karachi, Sind, Pakistan, May 18, 1970; d. Iqbal Bakshsh and Mumtaz (Hadi) Kadri; m. Saleem Asmatullah Paracha, Oct. 6, 1995; 1 child, Mustafa Saleem. BA in Econs., Allegheny Coll., Meadville, Pa., 1992. Accounts exec. Bear Stearns Jahanger, Karachi, 1992-93; asst. v.p. Livon Group, Karachi, 1993-96; v.p. Bankers Equity Ltd., Karachi, 1996—. Muslim. Avocations: reading, fishing, yoga, swimming, travel.

PARADA, ARTURO, foreign language and literature educator; b. Ourense, Spain, June 24, 1960; s. Arturo Parada and Társila Dieguez; m. Barbara Kuegler, April 1992; children: Antonio, Adrian. MA in Spanish Lang. and Literature, U. Santiago Compostela, Spain, 1985; PhD in German Lang. and Literature, U. Complutense, Madrid, 1994. Assoc. prof. Georgia Agusta U., Göttingen, 1988-92; asst. prof. U. Complutense, Madrid, 1994-96, U. Europea, Madrid, 1997-98; prof. U. de Vigo, Spain, 1999—; translator, advisor editl. Cátedra, Alianza editl. Author: Offene literarische Welten, 1997, Aleman en Construction, 1996, Deutsch für Die Bank, 1997; translator: H.G. Gadamer El Giro Hermeneutico, 1998, Weiss La estética de la resistencia. Active Medicos sin Fronteras, 1995. Mem. Assn. Cervantistas, Soc. Literatura Gral Ycomparada, Hispanisten Verband Deutschland, European Soc. Translators. Avocations: painting, sports, hiking, music. E-mail: aparada@uvigo.es. Home: Fonte do Bispo 1 4oi, 32002 Ourense Spain Office: U de Vigo, Facultade de Humanidades, 36200 Vigo Spain

PARADI, ELEMER, geneticist, researcher; b. Budapest, Hungary, May 22, 1939; s. Elemer and Izabella (Nyerges) P.; m. Lidia Kardos, Aug. 3, 1967 (div. 1977). MSc, Eötvös U., Budapest, 1962; PhD, Hungarian Acad. Sci., Budapest, 1985. Cert. secondary sci. tchr., Hungary. Asst. Hungarian Acad. Sci., 1962-65; rschr. Eötvös L. U., Budapest, 1965-85, rsch. assoc., 1985—. Author: Genetics, 1976, Genetics Problem Solver, 1995. Mem. European Environ. Mutagen Soc., Hungarian Genetic Soc., Hungarian Biol. Soc. Avocation: terraristics. Home: Döbrentei u 8, 1013 Budapest Hungary

PARADIES, HASKO HENRICH, chemistry educator, executive, consultant; b. Bremen, Germany, Feb. 18, 1940; s. Henry J. and Erna (Poppinga)P.; m. Gundrun K. Patzelt, June 28, 1973; children: Gesa-Kundry, Jan-Henry, Felix-Benjamin. PhD in Biochemistry (hon.), Albert Einstein-Found., 1990; diploma chemistry, MD, U. Munster, 1966, PhD in Medicine, 1967, postgrad., 1970; PhD in Chemistry, U. Uppsaa, 1969; postgrad., King's Coll., 1969-71, MIT, 1970-71; D in Biochem. Sci. (hon.), Royal Crown Spain, 1986. Rsch. assoc. U. Munster, 1966; postdoctoral fellow King's Coll., 1969-71, Boston, 1971-72; rsch. assoc. Max Planck Inst., Berlin, 1971; prof. biochemistry Free U. Berlin, 1974-83, chmn. dept. chemistry and biochemistry, 1974-77, chmn. dept. plant physiology and cell biology, 1980-82; prof. biotech. and phys. chemistry U. Applied Scis., 1988—; faculty chemistry and chem. engring. U. Paderborn, 1997—; guest and vis. prof. chemistry Cornell U., Ithica, N.Y., 1977-79; dir. rsch. and devel. Medice-Corp., Ltd., 1984-86, dir. 1986—; sr. lectr. tech. chemistry dept. engring. U. Hagen, 1985-86; sci. cons., counsel Sherex, Inc., Dublin, Ohio, Witco, Inc., Greenwich, Conn., Medice, Inc., Fed. Republic Germany, Octapharma, Fed. Republic Germany, SKW AG, Symbiopharm; guest prof. Biotech. and Phys. Chem. Märkische Hochschule Iserlohn, 1987-88, chaired prof. biotech. and phys. chemistry U. Paderborn, 1997—; vis. prof. La. State U., 1991-93, Ohio State U. chemistry dept., 1992—; vis. scientist Joule Physics Lab., Salford U., Manchester, Eng., 2000—. Author 13 books; contbr. articles to profl. jours., chpts. to books. Recipient Albert Einstein Internat. Acad. Found. Bronze medal for Peace, III class; Deutsche Forschungsgem fellow, 1967-71, grantee, 1974-79; Umweltbundesant grantee, 1979, 82, colloid and surface sci., 1982—, Internat. Copper Rsch. Assn., 1987, European Cmty. Microbiology, 1991, Min. Rsch. and Tech., 1989-91, 95—, Brite-Euram, 1991-94, 95—, Advanced In-Tech., 1995, Biomaterials grantee, 1996—. Fellow Royal Soc. Chemistry (Eng.); mem. ACS, Am. Materials Rsch. Soc., Am. Neutron Scatter Soc., N.Y. Acad. Sci., Charles Darwin Assn., Gesellschaft Deutscher Chemiker, Gesellschaft Deutsche Naturforscher und Artze. Achievements include over 175 patents in field. Fax: (049) 2371-149-705. E-mail: HParadies@aol.com. Home: 38 Goerresstrasse, D-58636 Iserlohn Germany Office: U Applied Scis, Frauenstuhlweg 31, D 58644 Iserlohn Germany

PARADISE, PAUL RICHARD, writer, editor; b. N.Y.C., July 4, 1950; s. Paul L. and Ann (Ho) P. BA in Journalism, Wash. State U., 1975. Staff writer T.F.H. Publs., Neptune, N.J., 1977-79; legal indexer Matthew Bender, N.Y.C., 1980-86; free-lance writer, 1988—. Contbg. editor: Parent Guide Mag., N.Y.C., 1993—; author: Raccoons, 1976, Amazon Parrots, 1978, African Gray Parrots, 1979, Cockatiels, 1987, Trademark Counterfieting, Product Piracy and the Billion Dollar Threat to the U.S. Economy, 1999. Mem. Soc. Profl. Journalists. Home: 722 Willow Ave Hoboken NJ 07030-4034

PARAMESHVARA, VISHVANATHAPURA, internist, cardiologist; b. May 8, 1930; s. Narasimha Bhatta and Parvathi Hande; m. Nalini Rao, Mar. 8, 1962; children: Ashok, Aparna, Ashvin. M.B.B.S., Mysore Med. Coll., U. Mysore (India), 1957. Asst. surgeon Mysore Med. Coll, 1958-59; med. registrar Gen. Hosp., Birmingham, 1964-65; asst. prof. gen. medicine Bangalore Med. Coll., India, 1966-71; pvt. practice medicine as cons. physician and cardiologist, Bangalore, 1971—; med. referee Life Ins. Corp. India; ofcl. cons. physician and cardiologist for various Indian cos.; chmn. Sharada Dhanvantari Hosp., Sringeri, India, 1979—; dir. Nat. Inst. Primary Health Care; dir., advisor Kirloskar Investment & Fin. Ltd.; chmn. Sri Abhinava Vidyatheertha Swamigal Sci. Rsch. Acad., Sringeri, 1979—, World Acad. of Med. Scis.; trustee Med. Edn. and Rsch. Trust, Bangalore, 1980—, sec., 1980—; trustee Dr. V. Parameshvara Charitable Trust, Bangalore, 1980—; bd. dirs. Clin. Rsch. Lab., Bangalore; mem. adv. bd. Indian Drugs and Pharmaceuticals; organiser, condr. various mass med. and cardiac check-up camps, Bangalore and Karnataka State, 1965; speaker in field. Author: Medical Emergencies in General Practice, 1970; editor: Jour. Mysore Med. Assn., 1967-77; founder, editor: Indian Med. Assn. Bangalore br. News Bull., 1979-80, IMA Focus, 1982—; mem. editorial bd. Indian Hart Jour., 1976-77; chmn. Ency. Indian Medicine, 8 vols. Fellow Am. Coll. Cardiology, Am. Coll. Chest Physicians, Internat. Coll. Angiology, Indian Soc. Electrocardiology, All India Inst. Diabetes, Internat. Med. Scis. Acad., Royal Coll. Physicians London, Internat. Coll. Nutrition, Assn. Physicians of India (founder), Indian Med. Assn. (pres. 1985-86, chmn. standing com. med. edn., Mysore br. Dr. Govinda Setty Meml. orator 1981), Indian Med. Assn. of Med. Specialities (chmn. 1986—); mem. Brit. Med. Assn., Assn. Physicians India (mem. governing coun. 1981-83, v.p. 1986—), Indian Assn. Experimental Medicine (pres.), Fedn. Voluntary Agencies in India, Assn. History Medicine, Cardiological Soc. India, Soc. Nuclear Medicine, Indian Assn. Occupational Health (Silver Jubilee Commemoration award 1980), Asthma Rsch. Soc. (founder sec. Bangalore 1975). Clubs: Bangalore Turf, Century, Bangalore Golf (Bangalore). Lodge: Lions (founder pres.). Home: 54 Kumarakrupa Rd, Bangalore 560 001, India Office: Bharat Apts, 44 Race Course Rd, Bangalore 560 001, India

PARAMESWARAN, ANANTANARAYANAN, dental educator; b. Madras, Tamilnadu, India, Sept. 18, 1938; s. Anantanarayaman and Anantanarayanan Parvatry; m. Sita P., Jan. 24, 1969; children: Ratna, Anantanarayanan. BS in Botany, Loyola Coll., Madras, India, 1957; B in Dentistry, Govt. Dental Coll., Madras, India, 1961; M in Dental Surgery, Govt. Dental Coll., Bombay, 1973. Demonstrator Madras Med. Coll., 1962-63; asst. surgeon Govt. Hosp., Cudallore, India, 1963; asst. reader Madras Med. Coll., 1963-70, asst. prof., 1973-78; prof. in dentistry Stanley Med. Coll., 1978-79; faculty in dentistry Uni Garyounis, Bengaazi, Libya, 1979-82; prof. in conservative dentistry, Govt. Dental Coll., Madras, 1982—; sr. civil surgeon Tamilnadu Med. Svc., Madras, 1994—; prin. Tamilnadu Govt. Dental Coll., Madras, 1995-96; prof., dir. of postgrad. studies Meenashi Coll., Madras, 1997—. Author: (books) Recent Advances in Operative Dentistry, 1985, Anterior Restoratives, 1986, Current Trends in Endodontology, 1988, others; co-author: Practitioners Handbook on Endodontics and Conservative Dentistry, Compendium of Fodi, 1994, Advanced Dental Biomechanics, 1996, Postgraduate Lectures, 1997, Dental Caries: A Dynamic Phenomenon, 2000, others; mem. editl. bd. Asian Jour. of Aesthetic Dentistry, 1992—. Cons. Tamilnadu Electricity Bd., Madras, 1995; oration spkr. and vis. prof. A.B.Shetty Dental Coll., Mangalore, India, 1996-99;. Fellow Royal Soc. Health/U.K.; mem. Material Rsch. Soc./Bombay, Indian Acad. of Implantology (exec. com. 1991—), Fedn. of Operative Dentistry of India (pres. 1994-95), Indian Endontic Soc., Asian Soc. Endodontics. Avocations: music, reading. E-mail: anantparam@vsnl.com. Office: Meenakshi Coll, Maduraroyal, 602 102 Madras/Tamil Nadu India

PARAMESWARAN, SUBRAMANIAN, tour company executive, accountant; b. Rangoon, Myanmar, Feb. 17, 1938; parents Periyaannan and Visalatchi Subramanian; m. Chitralekha Srinivasan; children: P. Sheela, P. Suseendran. MA, Annamalai U. Chidambaram, 1958; fellow, Chartered Accts. Inst. India, New Delhi, 1963. CPA Singapore; chartered acct. Chennai. Chartered acct. S. Parameswaran & Co., Chennai, India, 1965—; CPA S. Parameswaran & Co., Singapore, 1974—; chmn. Assoc. Tours Madras (P) Ltd., Chennai, 1978—; fin. cons. ATA Fin. Svcs. Pvt. Ltd., Chennai, 1995—; dir. Madras Metro. Water Supply and Sewage Bd., Chennai, 1977-87, Harijon Housing and Devel. Corp., Chennai, 1980-85. Mem. com. Nehuru Meml. Coll., Trichy, India, 1980—, Dr. M.G.R. Janaki Coll. Arts and Sci. Women, Chennai, 1998—. Office: Assoc Tours Madras (P) Ltd, 89/1 Anna Salai, 600 002 Chennai India also: S Parameswaran & Co, 41 Thambusamy Rd, 600 010 Chennai India

PARAMGURU, RAJA KISHORE, metallurgist; b. Khurda, Orissa, India, Aug. 4, 1948; s. Chintamoni and Bimala (Dash) P.; m. Binapani Dash, June 29, 1974; children: Kakali, Kamrakali. BSc in Engring with honors, Sambalpur (India) U., 1970; M in Tech., Indian Inst. Tech., Kharagpur, India, 1972, PhD, 1979. Chartered engr., India. Scientist B Regional Rsch. Lab., Coun. Sci. & Indsl. Rsch., Bhubaneswar, India, 1973-78; scientist C Regional Rsch. Lab., Coun. Sci. & Indsl. Rsch., Bhubaneswar, 1978-84, scientist EI, 1984-89, scientist EII, 1989-94, scientist F, 1994—; cons. Rajasthan State Indsl. and Mineral Devel. Corp., Rajasthan, India, 1975-78, The Tata Iron & Steel Co. India Ltd., Jamshedpur, 1989—, Orissa Industries Ltd., Rourkela, India, 1990-93, Mideast Integrated Steel Ltd., New Delhi, 1993-94, Directorate of Geology and Mining, Govt. of Nagaland, Dimapur, India, 1993-94, Western Indian Mining Svcs. Pvt. Ltd., Calcutta, India, 1994; guest scientist Inst. für Metallurgie, Metallhüttenkunde Tech. U., Berlin, 1984-85, 92. Co-editor: Production of Liquid Iron Using Coal, 1994; contbr. articles to profl. jours.; patentee in field. Merit scholar Govt. Orissa, India, 1958-70; fellow Indian Inst. Tech., Kharagpur, 1970-73, fellow Alexander Von Humboldt Found., Bonn, Germany, 1984-85, 92. Fellow Instn. Engrs. India; mem. Indian Inst. Metals (life), Orissa Vigyan Acad. (life), Indian Inst. Chem. Engrs., Indian Inst. Mineral Engrs. (life), Internat. Soc. Tchrs. and Rschrs. in Chemistry (life). Avocations: literature, drama, bridge, astrology. E-mail: drrkparamguru@yahoo.com. Home: Jemadei, Khurda 752057, India Office: Regional Rsch Lab, 516 RRL Campus, Bhubaneswar 751013, India

PARANICH, ANATOLY VALENTINOVICH, biology and biophysics educator, researcher; b. Sakhnovshchina, Kharkiv, USSR, July 22, 1952; s. Valentin Ivanovich and Valentina Ivanovna (Ridaeva) P.; m. Lyudmila Ivanovna Penchenko, May 25, 1975; children: Valentina, Ivan. Biologist, Kharkov State U., Ukraine, USSR, 1976, D in Physiology, 1985; M in Biology, Kiev Inst. Physiology, Ukraine, 1996. Lab. asst. Scientific Rsch. Inst. Biology Kharkov (Ukraine) State U., USSR, 1969; sr. researcher, asst. lectr., docent, prof. Kharkov (Ukraine) Nat. U., 1986—; worker nursery garden, Kharkov, 1970-71; sr. lab. asst. Ukraine S.R.I. Poultry Keeping, Borky, Ukraine, 1976-79; sr. engr. Kharkov Inst. Pub. Nutrition, 1979-86; sr. researcher Inst. Ambulance Surgery, Kharkov, Ukraine, 1995-97. Contbr. over 140 articles to profl. jours. Mem. Physiology Soc. Ukraine, Biochemistry Soc. Ukraine, Biophys. Soc. Ukraine, Trade Union Orgn. Radiophys. Faculty (chmn. 1987—). Avocation: gardening. Home: Lenin str No 36 Flat 9, 313410 Borky Zmiiv District, Ukraine Office: Nat U, Svoboda sq 4, 610077 Kharkov Ukraine

PARANJPE, AKALPITA SHRINIWAS, research scientist; b. Indore, Madhya, India, Nov. 20, 1947; d. Balkrishna Ramachandr and Radhabai Balkrishna Abhyankar Vaze; m. Shriniwas Krishnarao Paranjpe, May 17, 1970; children: Jayashri, Asmita, Shriram. BS, Holkar Sci. Coll., Indore, 1967, MS, 1969; PhD, Bhabha Atomic Rsch. Ctr., Mumbai, 1981. Cert. physicist. Scientific officer Bhabha Atomic Rsch. Ctr., Mumbai, India, 1971—. Contbr. articles to profl. jours. Mem. Indian Physics Assn. (life), Indian Women Scientists Assn. (life), Uttan Herbal Medicinal Rsch. Orgn. Achievements include rsch. in homeopathy, Indian med. systems, herbal farming and preparing new herbal medicines. Office: SSOD Bhabha Atomic Rsch Ctr, Trombay, 400085 Mumbai/Maharashtra India

PARANQUE, BERNARD, economist; b. Marseille, France, June 15, 1958; s. Michel and Claude Paranque; m. Joelle Comte, Feb. 4, 1989; 1 child, Estelle. PhD, U. Lyon-Lumiere, Lyon, France, 1984. Economist Acctg., Lyon, 1984-89, Banque de France, Paris, 1990—. Mem. N.Y. Acad. Scis. Avocations: Tae Kwon Do, astronomy, walking. E-mail: bernard@bparanque.com. Home: 21 Allee clos gagneur, 93160 Noisy-le-Grand France Office: Banque de France, 39 rue croix petits champs, Paris France 75001

PARAPPULLY, JOSE OUSEPH, psychologist, consultant; b. Kaduppisserry, Kerala, India, Dec. 18, 1949; s. Ouseph Kunjeeyoo and Thressia Vareed (Punneliparambil) P. MEd, Annamalai (India) U., 1986, MA, 1988; MA, Loyola U., Chgo., 1992; PhD, Calif. Inst. Integral Studies, San Francisco, 1997. Ordained priest Roman Cath. Ch., 1978. Tchr. Don Bosco Sch., Calcutta, India, 1972-75, vice-prin., 1979-85; dir. Bandel Retreat, Calcutta, 1984-89, Bosco Psychol. Svcs., New Delhi, 1997—; cons. psychologist Sadhana Inst., Lonavla, India, 1997—, Antara Psychiat. Ctr., Calcutta, 1999—; vis. lectr. Montfort Coll., Bangalore, India, 1998—. Editor: (periodical) Our Lady of Bandel, 1985-89; contbr. articles to profl. jours. Active Salesians of Don Bosco, Calcutta, 1969-96, New Delhi, 1997—; regional coord. Leadership Tng. Svc., Calcutta, 1980-84. Mem. APA, Soc. for Personality Assessment, Indian Assn. Clin. Psychologists. Roman Catholic. Avocations: drama, music, sports, games. Office: Bosco Psychol Svcs, Okhla Rd, 110 025 New Delhi India

PARASCHIV, MARIUS CORNELIU, physicist; b. Ploiesti, Prahova, Romania, Aug. 27, 1953; s. Constantin and Elisabeta (Costache) P.; m. Adriana Stănculescu, Mar. 1, 1979; children: Ioana, Marius-Martin. Degree in Physics, U. Bucharest, Romania, 1982. Physicist engr. Inst. for Nuclear Rsch., Pitesti, Romania, 1982-88, sci. rschr., 1988-90, sr. sci. rschr., 1990—. Contbr. articles to profl. jours. Mem. Romanian Soc. Physics, N.Y. Acad. Scis. Avocations: swimming, mountain travel, children's education. Home: Petrochimistilor B5b/c/12, R-0300 Pitesti Arges, Romania Office: Inst for Nuclear Research, PO Box 78, R-0300 Pitesti Arges, Romania

PARASCHIVESCU, LUCIAN, physician; b. Alexandria, Romania, Mar. 10, 1939; s. Iacob and Florica (Sandulescu) P.; m. Valeria Videscu, Sept. 27, 1970; 1 child, Eduard. MD, Inst. of Medicine, Bucharest, Romania, 1962. Physician Village Surgery, Alexandria, 1962-66; resident physician Emergency Hosp., Bucharest, 1966-70; internal medicine specialist Alexandria, 1971-90; physician Physician first, Alexandria, 1991—. Author: The Medical Research in Teleorman, 1999; contbr. articles to profl. jours. Mem. Physician Collegium-Teleorman (pres.), N.Y. Acad. Sci. Liberal. Christian Orthodox. Avocations: painting, poetry. Home: Ion Creanga, 0700 Alexandria Romania Ofifce: Alexandria Hosp, Libertati 1, 0700 Alexandria Romania

PARASCOS, EDWARD THEMISTOCLES, engineering consultant; b. N.Y.C., Oct. 20, 1931; s. Christos and Nina (Demitrovich) P.; m. Jenny Morris, July 12, 1978; children: Jennifer Mellissa, Edward T., Jr. BSME, CCNY, 1956, MSME, 1958; postgrad. ops. rsch., NYU, 1964. Registered profl. engr., Calif. Design engr. Ford Instrument, 1957-61; reliability engring. supr. Kearfott divsn. Gen. Precision Inc., 1961-63; staff cons. Am. Power Jet, 1963-64; reliability mgr. Perkin Elmer Corp., 1964-66; dir. system effectiveness CBS Labs., Stamford, Conn., 1966-72; pres. Dipar Cons. Svcs. Ltd., East Elmhurst, N.Y., Lapa Trading Corp.; gen. mgr., prin. reliability engr. engring. Consol. Edison Co., N.Y.C., 1972-95, mgr. transp. and stores environ. affairs, 1995-98, ret., 1998; sr. reliability engring. cons. Morris Cons. Agy.; pres., chmn. bd. RAM Cons. Assocs.; pres., 1978-80; chmn. 1st Reliability Engring. Conf. Electric Power Industry, 1974, also 4th and 18th confs.; chmn. bd. Inter-Ram Q Conf. for electric power industry; gen. chmn. 18th Inter-Ramq Conf. for electric power industry; lectr. in field. Fellow Am. Soc. Quality Control (vice chmn. Reliability divsn. 1968-70, sr. mem.); mem. ASME, Soc. Reliability Engrs., Edison Engring. Soc. Home: 30-02 83rd St Jackson Heights NY 11370-1919

PARASHOS, PETER, endodontist; b. Grenfell, NSW, Australia, Aug. 28, 1957; s. Theo and Olga (Indou) P.; m. Mary Branka Tutnjevic, Jan. 21, 1989; 1 child, Ethan Peter. B in Dental Sci., U. Melbourne, Australia, 1980, Lic. Dental Surgery, 1980, M in Dental Sci., 1988. Pvt. practice Melbourne, 1980-86, 89—; house officer Royal Dental Hosp., Melbourne, 1987-88; clin. demonstrator U. Melbourne, 1991—, sr. fellow, 2000—. Editor (jour.) Australian Endodontic, 1996—. Fellow Royal Australasian College Dental Surgeons; mem. Australian Soc. Endodontology (fed. sec. 1991-93, pres. 1992), Internat. Assn. for Dental Rsch., Australian and New Zealand Soc. Pediatric Dentistry, Internat. Orgn. for Forensic Odontostomatology, Australian and New Zealand Acad. Endodontists, Am. Assn. Endodontists, Brit. Endodontic Soc., Internat. Assn. for Dental Traumatology. Avocations: reading, old movies, driving, motor sports. Office: 20 Collins St 11th Fl, 3000 Melbourne Australia

PARASKEVAS, SPYRIDON MICHAEL, chemical engineer; b. Athens, Hellas, Feb. 1, 1937; s. Michael Spyridon and Vassiliki Thomas (Taskaris) P.; m. Mary Vassilios Keskos, Dec. 26, 1974; children: Michael, Marianne Vassiliki. Chem. engr., U. Stuttgart, Stuttgart, Germany, 1965, PhD, 1968; habilitation, U. Athens, Greece, 1977; dipl. (hon.), Assn. Hellenic Writers. Lab. asst. Sch. of Tech., Stuttgart, 1966-68; from chief lab. attendant to assoc. prof. organic chemistry U. Athens, 1970-94, prof. organic chemistry, 1994—; dir. organic chemistry lab. U. Athens, 1992—, dir. sector II dept. chemistry, 1993-95. Author: ESR Studies on Hydroquinoues, 1977, Topics on Organic Chemistry, 1995; contbr. articles to profl. jours. Sgt. Greek Army, 1968-70. Recipient Medal of Honor First Gymnasium, 1985, Diploma of Honor, Greek Assn. Literateurs, 1995. Fellow Parnassos Lit. Assn.; mem. Hellenic Chemists Assn., Tech. Chamber of Greece, Allgemeine Chemische Gesellschaft für Apparatenwesen. Avocations: painting, philosophical studies, music. Fax: 7249101. Home: Odos Trivonianou 77, 116 36 Athens Greece Office: Univ Athens Lab Organic Chemistry, Panepistimiopolis, 15771 Athens Greece

PARDEE, JEFFREY CLARK, county government official; b. N.Y.C., May 14, 1944; s. Jack Howard II and Florence (Brennan) P.; m. Mary Anna Weil, Dec. 23, 1966; children: Brennan James, Kennedy Clark. BBA, Eastern Mich. U., 1968; MBA in Fin., U. Detroit, 1971; postgrad., Nova U., 1975-81. Fin. analyst Sterling Axle Plant div. Ford Motor Co., Sterling Heights, Mich., 1968-73; budget dir. Genesee County, Flint, Mich., 1973-76, Oakland County, Pontiac, Mich., 1976—; treas. Flint-Genesee Corp. for Econ. Growth, 1978-81; pres. Genesee County Econ. Devel. Corp., Flint, 1982-84; bd. dirs. Forward Devel. Corp; chmn. bd. dirs. Communications Services Network, Inc.; adj. prof. pub. budgeting U. Mich., Flint, 1984-85. Editor Statewide News-Mich. Rental Housing Assn. Newsletter, 1985—. Merit counselor Boy Scouts Am., Grand Blanc, Mich., 1982—, dist. com. chmn. Tall Pines Coun., 1998—; councilman City of Grand Blanc, 1985—; treas. Crime Watch Assn., Grand Blanc, 1985—, Genesee County Met. Alliance, Flint, 1986-91; bd. dirs. Flint-Genesee Revolving Loan Fund, 1980-90; treas. Partnership Saginaw Bay Watershed, 1987—, Grand Blanc Vision 2020, 1998—; pres. Mich. Mcpl. Fin. Officers Assn., 1995-96; mem. GFOA Mgmt. Budget Com., 1998—. Mem. Govt. Fin. Officers Assn. U.S. and Can. (review com. 1984—, Disting. Budget Presentation award, Excellence in Fin. Reporting award), Am. Soc. Pub. Adminstrs., G.M.I. Mgmt. and Engring. Inst. (adv. bd. 1984-87). Republican. Mormon. Avocations: racquetball, auto racing. Home: 11390 Grand Oak Dr Grand Blanc MI 48439-1219 Office: Oakland County Dept Mgmt & Budget 1200 N Telegraph Rd Pontiac MI 48341-1032

PARDEE, MARGARET ROSS, violinist, violist, educator; b. Valdosta, Ga., May 10, 1920; d. William Augustus and Frances Ross (Burton) P.; m. Daniel Rogers Butterly, July 4, 1944. Diploma, Juilliard Sch. Music, 1940, grad. diploma, 1942; diploma, Juilliard Grad. Sch., 1945. Instr. violin and viola Manhattanville Coll. Sacred Heart, N.Y.C., 1942-54, Juilliard Sch., N.Y.C., 1942, Meadowmount Sch. Music, Westport, N.Y., 1956-84, 88-92, Bowdoin Coll. Music Festival and Sch., Maine, summer 1987; mem. faculty Estherwood Sch. and Summr Festival, 1984-86, Killington (Vt.) Music Festival, 1993—, Mannes Sch. Music, 1996—; concert master Gt. Neck (L.I., N.Y.) Symphony, 1954-85; adj. assoc. prof. Aaron Copeland Sch. Music, Queens Coll., CUNY, Flushing, 1978—, Adelphi U., Garden City, N.Y., 1979-83; adj. prof. SUNY, Purchase, 1980-93; vis. prof. Simon Bolivar Youth Orch. and Conservatory, Caracas and Barquisimeto, Venezuela, 1988, 89, Conservatorio Orch. Nat. Juvenil, Caracas, 1988, 89; mem. jury for internat. competitions; guest artist profl. 1st Internat. Festival for Young Violinists, Caracas, 1988; guest vis. prof. Orch. Filarmonica Nat. y Mcpl. Sinfonica Caracas, 1992, 97. Debut N.Y. Town Hall, 1952; toured U.S. as soloist and in chamber music groups; soloed with symphony orchs., Miss., N.J., D.C., N.Y. Bd. dirs. Meadowmount Sch. Music. Recipient Andres Bello award Venezuela Min. Edn., 1993. Mem. Soc. for Strings (dir. 1965-92), Assoc. Music Tchrs. League N.Y. (cert.), N.Y. State Music Tchrs. Assn. (cert., citation 1989), Music Tchrs. Nat. Assn., Am. String Tchrs. Assn. (citation for exceptional leadership 1990), Am. Fedn. Musicians, Viola Rsch. Soc. Office: care Juilliard Sch Lincoln Ctr Plz New York NY 10023

PARDHAN, SHAHINA, optometrist, educator; b. Mwanza, Tanzania, Jan. 21, 1962; d. Rajabali and Khatijabai (Kurji) P. BSc in Optometry, U. Bradford, Eng., 1984, PhD in Optometry, 1989. Registered optician, U.K., optometrist, U.K. Rsch. fellow U. Bradford, 1989-91, part-time lectr., 1991-93, lectr., 1993—, module leader dept. optometry, 1993—, sr. lectr., 1999—. Contbr. articles to profl. jours. Recipient Award for Excellence, Ismaili Coun., London, 1992. Mem. Am. Acad. Optometrists, Assn. for Rsch. in Vision and Ophthalmology, The Gen. Optical Coun. Avocations: swimming, music, cooking, charity clinics in Tanzania. Home: 50 Frensham Dr, Bradford BD7 4AS, England Office: Dept Optometry, Richmond Rd, Bradford BD7 1DP, England

PAREJA-HEREDIA, DIEGO, mathematics educator, bookseller consultant; b. San Pablo, Colombia, Dec. 23, 1939; s. José Euclides and Rosa Victoria (Heredia) Pareja; m. Neira Cerón de Pareja, July 30, 1966; children: Sandra Natalia, Leslie Sofia, Mauricio. Licenciado, U. Libre, Bogotá, Colombia, 1966; MS, U. Colo., 1972. Prof. math. U. Quindio, Armenia, Colombia, 1967—; gen. mgr. Libreria Primavera, Armenia, 1993—; vis. prof. NYU, 1981-82; cons. Librería Primavera, Armenia, Colombia, 1990—. Author: El Análisis Matemático, 1973, Historia de las Matemáticas, 1979; editor: Jour. Memorias del Seminario Interno, 1986. Recipient ICETEX scholarship, 1970, NSF scholarship, 1973. Mem. Math. Assn. Am., Am. Math. Soc., Nat. Geog. Soc. Home: Cra 15 No 12N32, Armenia Quindio Colombia Office: Librería Primavera, PO Box 1004, Armenia Colombia

PAREKH, DEEPAK, housing development finance executive. With Ernst & Ernst Mgmt. Cons. Svcs., N.Y.; with merchant-banking divsn. Grindlays Bank, Bombay; asst. rep. for South Asia Chase Manhattan Bank, with East Asia divsn.; chmn. Housing Devel. Fin. Corp., Bombay; v.p. Internat. Union for Housing Fin.; bd. dirs. Glaxo India Ltd., Otis Elevators (Co.) India Ltd., Burroughs Wellcome (India) Ltd., ICI India Ltd., Hindustan Lever Ltd., Exide Industries, Mahindra & Mahindra, Castrol India, Ltd., Nat. Housing Bank, Nat. Stock Exch., Nat. Thermal Power Corp. Ltd., The Indian Hotels Co. Ltd. Named Businessman of Yr., Bus. India mag., 1996; recipient JRD Corp. Leadership award 1996, Qimpro Platinum award for quality, 1998. Fax: 91-22-285-2336. Office: 5th Floor Ramon House, 169 Backbay Reclamation, Bombay India

PAREKH, KIRAN LAXMIDAS, early childhood care and education educator; b. Baroda, Gujarat, India, Sept. 8, 1939; d. Laxmidas Vallabhdas and Maniben Laxmidas (Gandhi) P. BS in Chemistry, M.S. U. of Baroda, 1959, Postgrad. in Presch. Edn., 1960, MS with Child Devel., 1970. Demonstrator M.S. U. Baroda, 1960-63, asst. lectr., 1963-65, lectr., 1965-82, lectr., supt. of a lab. sch., 1975-92, reader, 1983—; lectr. and supr. of Lab. Nursery Sch., Faculty of Home Sci., M.S. U., Baroda, 1975-92; cons. in field. Mem. World Orgn. for Early Childhood Edn. (sec. Indian chpt.), Indian Assn. for Presch. Edn. (v.p. Baroda br. 1993-99). Avocations: music, reading, cooking, attending socials, knitting. Office: Faculty of Home Sci, MS Univ Baroda/Univ Road, 390 002 Baroda/Gujarat India

PARELLADA CUADRADO, CARLOS MARIA, surgeon, consultant, researcher; b. Guatemala City, Guatemala, Sept. 12, 1964; s. Ramon Parellada Balsells and Luisa Teresa (Cuadrado) P.; m. Marisol Gonzalez Freeman, Mar. 17, 1990; children: Andrea, Isabella, Ignacio. BS, BL, Liceo Javier, Guatemala City, 1986; MD, U. Francisco Marroquin, Guatemala City, 1990. Med., surg. diplomate; cert. colon and rectal surgeon. Intern Hosp. Gen. San Juan de Dios, Guatamala City, 1989-90; gen. surg. resident Gen. San Juan de Dios, Guatemala City, 1991-94, laparoscopic, colorectal surgeon, cons. gen., 1997—; sr. registrar, asst. prof. The Gen. Infirmary, Leeds, Eng., 1995-96; prof. gen. surgery for med. students Univ. Francisco Marroquin, Guatemala, 1999—. Author papers; contbr. articles to profl. jours. Treas. Med. Residents Assn., Gen. San Juan de Dios, Guatemala City, 1992-93, pres. Photography Club, 1994; mem. com. for employed doctor Guatemalan Med. Bd., 1983. With Guatemalan Army Res., 1983-84. Recipient 1st prize paper award Ctrl. Am. Neurol. Congress, 1992. Mem. Guatemalan Colorectal Surgeons Assn., Guatemalan Surg. Assn. (candidate mem.), Spanish Assn. of Beneficency (assoc.), Assn. of Coloproctology of Gt. Britain and Ireland, Assn. of Endoscopic Surgeons of Gt. Britain and Ireland, European Soc. of Endoscopic Surgeons, Am. Soc. Colorectal Surgeons. Roman Catholic. Avocations: music, piano, cinema, countryside, travel, photography. Office: Edificio Clinicas, 6a Ave 3-22 Zona 10 7 nivel, 01010 Guatemala City Guatemala

PARERA BIOSCA, ALBERTO, business executive; b. Barcelona, Spain, July 10, 1955; s. Alberto Parera and Angeles Biosca; m. Angeles Anglada, June 9, 1984; 1 child, Cristina Parera. Grad., U. Barcelona. Sec. gen. Perfumeria Parera S.A., Spain, 1980-85; coun. del. Grupo Parera, S.A., Spain, 1985—; pres. Circulo de Valores Mobiliarios, S.A., Spain, 1985—. Mem. Real Club Polo Barcelona, Real Club de Golf Del Prat, Circulo Ecuestre. Avocations: golf, skiing, sailing. Office: Grupo Parera, Po de Gracia no 11 Esc C, 08007 Barcelona Spain

PARESKY, LINDA K., travel company executive; b. Cambridge, Mass., Mar. 18, 1943; d. Gilbert Milton and Marcia (Brown) Kotzen; m. David S. Paresky, Aug. 18, 1963; children: Pamela, Laura, Mark. BA, Simmons Coll., 1964; MA, Harvard U., 1965; PhD, Boston Coll., 1988. Chmn., CEO Travel Edn. Ctr., Cambridge, 1975-98; pvt. investor; v.p. Crimson Travel, Cambridge, 1965-89; co-chmn. Thomas Cook Travel, Cambridge, 1989-94; chair bd. trustees Simmons Coll., Boston, 1994-98; chair bd. dirs. Com. 200 Found., Chgo., 1997-98; bd. dirs. Thryoid Found. Am., Boston, 1994-97. Adv. com. Investment Svcs. and Policy Adv. Com., U.S. Trade Dept., Washington, 1995—. Recipient Bus. Leadership award New England Coun., 1994; named Outstanding Woman Entrepreneur, Pres. Reagan, 1986, Top 50 Women Bus. Owners, Nat. Found. Woman Bus. Owners and Working Woman Mag., 1994. Mem. Internat. Women's Forum, (Mass. chpt., pres. 1994-96), Travel Bus. Roundtable (policy com.), Acad. Travel and Tourism (adv. bd.), Com. 200. Avocations: travel, sports. Home: 7212 Fisher Island Dr Miami FL 33109-0725 Office: Travel Edn Ctr 41212 Fisher Island Dr Miami Beach FL 33109-1253

PARHI, NARAHARI, mathematician educator; b. Balimed, India, Feb. 24, 1942; s. Krushna Chandra and Umadevi (Parhi) P.; m. Kalpana Parhi, June 4, 1970; children: Sanghamitra, Smita, Ashutos. BSc (hons.), Utkal Univ., Bhubaneswar, India, 1964, MSc, 1966; PhD, Indian Inst. Tech., Kanpur, India, 1972. Rsch. fellow I.I.T., Kanpur, 1967-72; lectr. Berhampur Univ., Berhampur, India, 1972-77, reader, 1977-89, prof., 1989—, head dept. of math., 1990-92; supr. Berhampur Univ., 1987-89; vis. mathematician Hungarian Acad. Scis., Budapest, 1983, Internat. Ctr. for Theoretical Physics, Trieste, Italy, 1986. Inventor in field. Recipient Rsch. scheme U.G.C., New Delhi, 1994—. Mem. Orissa Math. Soc., Indian Math. Soc., Am. Math. Soc., ICTP (assoc.). Avocations: chess playing, gardening, novel reading, travelling. Home: Balimed, 756131 Orissa India Office: Berhampur U, Dept Math, Berhampur 760007 Orissa, India

PARIDA, BASANT KUMAR, aerospace engineer, researcher; b. Agria, Orissa, India, Mar. 28, 1943; s. Paramananda and Hemamani (Mohanty) P.; m. Bijaya Mohanty, June 26, 1970; children: Vasavadatta Parida Balachandran, Aparajitta. BSc in Engring., Utkal U., India, 1967; M in Engring., Indian Inst. Sci., Bangalore, 1968; PhD, Indian Inst. Tech., Kharagpur, 1977. Lectr. Indian Inst. Tech., Kharagpur, 1968-78, asst. prof., 1978-87, prof., head dept. aerospace engring., 1987-90; sr. NRC rsch. assoc. Nat. Acad. Scis., U.S., 1990-92; fellow, dep. dir. Nat. Aerospace Labs., Bangalore, 1992—; vis. prof. Mil. Tech. Coll., Baghdad, Iraq, 1983-85; sr. quality control mgr. Nat. Aerospace Labs., Bangalore, 1994—; coord. Ctr. for Ednl. Tech., Indian Inst. Tech., Kharagpur, 1987-90, chief design engr. AR&DB Project, 1983. Author: Procs. of 14th World Conf. on Nondestructive Testing, Trends in Nondestructive Evaluation Sci. and Tech., 1996; editor Procs. 6th Nat. Seminar on Aerospace Structures, Fatigue and Fracture of Materials and Structures, 1996. Recipient Cert. Appreciation, Dept. Def., Wright-Patterson AFB, Ohio, 1992, Samanta Chandra Sekhar award Orissa Sci. Acad., 1997; named Sr. Resident Rsch. Assoc., NAS, Wright-Patterson AFB, 1990; postdoctoral fellow Govt. USSR, Kiev Inst. Civil Aviation, 1976. Fellow Instn. Engrs. (India), fellow Aero. Soc. India; mem. ASTM, AIAA (sr.), European Structural Integrity Soc, Indian Soc. Advancement of Materials and Process Engring. Achievements include mathematical modeling of interaction effects of creep-fatigue-environment in titanium alloys and intermetallics at elevated temperature; environmental degradation effects and airworthiness certification of composite primary structures. E-mail: basant p@usa.net. Office: Nat Aerospace Labs, PO Box 1779, Bangalore 560017, India

PARIENTI, RAOUL SAÜL, engineering consulting company executive; b. Sfax, Tunisia, Jan. 18, 1948; s. Benjamin and Ida (Nataf) P.; m. Rosette Marie Monti, Jan. 17, 1970 (div. Nov. 1981); children: Michaël, David; m. Véronique Esteve, July 24, 1982 (div. July 1991); 1 child, Jérôme. Degree in engring., Conservatoire Nat. Arts/Metier, 1973; degree in math., U. Nice, France, 1974, MS, 1975. H.S. tchr. Nice, France, 1974-86; chmn., pres. TICFIR, Nice, 1987-91; CEO Eurinov, Nice, 1988-92, Alpha Innovations, Paris, 1995—; chmn., pres. Optima Cons., Paris, 1999—; freelance cons., Nice, 1992—. Patentee augomatically recharged urbain, electronic lock, contactless electronic purse, system for inputting, processing and transmitting information and data, electronic tourist voice guide system, electronic communication notepad, reading device for the blind. Recipient 6 awards Internat. Inventors Exhibns., Brussels, Geneva and Marseille, France, 1988, 89, 90, 91, prize French Agy. for Intellectual Property, 1991. Pres., founding mem. L'Arche du Temple, Nice, 1991. Avocations: piano, philosophy, martial arts, history of religions. Home: 5 rue de Belgique, 06000 Nice France

PARIHAR, MORADHWAJ SINGH, biochemistry educator, researcher; b. Rewa, India, Oct. 26, 1954; s. Shiladhwaj Singh and Basanti Sing (Baghel) P.; m. Arti Singh, June 20, 1983; 1 child, Abhilash. BS, Awadhesh Pratrap Singh U., Rewa, India, 1973; MS, Vikram U., Ujjain, India, 1975, MPhil, 1976, PhD, 1981. Asst. prof. Madhav U. Coll., Ujjain, India, 1981-92; reader in biochem. Sch. Studies in Zoology Vikram U., Ujjain, India, 1992—; adv. Ctr. Environ. Mgmt. Govt. India, Ujjain, 1996—, additional dir. (hon.), 1997—; coord. molecular cellular developmental bilogy and biochemistry, 1997—. Inventor in field. Warden Univ Postgrad. Hostal, Ujjain, India, 1996—. Mem. Acad. Biosci. Avocations: sitar music, cricket, tennis. Home: M 1/2 Univ Campus Dewas Rd, 456010 Ujjain MP, India Office: Vikram U SS in Zoology, Dewas Rd, 456010 Ujjain MP, India

PARIJA, SUBASH CHANDRA, microbiologist, researcher, educator; b. Cuttack, Orissa, India, Mar. 24, 1953; s. Managovinda and Nishamani Parija; m. Jyotirmayee Das; children: Madhuri, Mayuri. MB BS, SCB Med. Coll., Cuttack, India, 1977; MD, Inst. Med. Sci., Varanasi, India, 1981; PhD, JIMPER, Pondicherry, India, 1987. Jr. resident Inst. Med. Scis., Varanasi, 1978, sr. resident, 1979-81; microbiology lectr. Jawaharlal Inst. Postgrad. Med. Edn. & Rsch., Pondicherry, 1982, asst. prof., 1983-86, assoc. prof., 1986-91, prof., 1991-95, prof., head microbiology, 1998—; prof., head dept. B. P. Koirala Inst. Health Scis., Dharan, Nepal, 1995-98; mem. rsch. coun. BPK Inst. Health Scis., Dharan, 1999—; mem. task force on intestinal parasitic infections Indian Coun. Med. Rsch., 1999—. Author: Textbook of Medical Parasitology, 1996, Stool Microscopy, 1998, Sputum Microscopy, 1998; editor: Review of Parasitic Zoonoses; mem. editl. bd. Parasitology, Internat. Jour. Vet. Parasitology, Health Renaissance, Jour. Microbiol. World, Biomed. Rsch., Indian Jour. Allergy and Immunology. Fellow Indian Assn. Pathologists and Microbiologists (Smt. Kuntidevi Melhotra award 1990), Indian Assn. Biomed. Scientists, Internat. Med. Scis. Acad., Indian Coll. Allergy and Applied Immunology; mem. Indian Assn. for Devel. Vet. Parasitology, Nat. Acad. Med. Scis., Indian Assn. Med. Microbiologists, Indian Soc. for Parasitology (Dr. B.P. Pandey Oration award 1998). Hindu. Avocations: painting, traveling, graphology. Home: HIG 251, Pondicherry 605 008, India Office: JIMPER, Dept Microbiology, Pondicherry 605 006, India

PARIKH, ASHOK, economics educator; b. Ahmedabad, India, Nov. 24, 1936; s. Kanchanial and Champaben (Mehta) P.; m. Daksha (Mehta) Feb. 3, 1963; 1 child, Ami. B Com, H.L. Commerce Coll., 1957; M Com, R.A. Podar Coll., 1959; MSc in Econs., London Sch. Econs., 1962. Lectr. commerce Sardar Patel U., Anand, India, 1959-60; rsch. assoc. Inst. Econ. Growth, Delhi, India, 1963-65; reader in econs. Gokhale Inst. Politics, Poona, Maharashtra, India, 1965-66; lectr. econs. U. Sussex, Brigton, Eng., 1966-68; vis. prof. Columbia U., N.Y.C., summers 1967-69; rsch. economist IMF, Washington, 1969-70; lectr. econs. U. East Anglia, Norwich, Eng., 1968-69, 70-71, reader, 1971-80, prof., 1980—. Contbr. articles to profl. jours. Fellow Royal Statis. Soc. Home: 3 Cringleford Chase, Norwich NR4 7RS, England Office: U East Anglia, Sch Econ and Social Studies, Norwich NR4 7TJ, England

PARIKH, SHERWIN KIRIT, dermatologist, educator; b. Bethesda, Md., Dec. 19, 1969; s. Kirit and Vibha Parikh. BA, Harvard U., 1990; MD, Columbia U., 1994. Resident in internal medicine Columbia Presbyn. Med. Ctr., N.Y.C., 1994-95, resident in dermatology, 1995-98; pvt. practice, N.Y.C., 1998—; asst. clin. prof. dermatology N.Y.-Columbia Presbyn. Hosp., N.Y.C., 1998—, St. Vincent's Hosp., N.Y.C., 1998—. Contbr. articles to Jour. Am. Acad. Dermatology; dir. (play) For Colored Girls, 1997. Adams House arts and sci. scholar, Harvard U., 1990. Fellow Am. Acad. Dermatology (travel grantee Sydney, Australia 1997); mem. Greater N.Y. Dermatol. Soc. Avocations: biking, rollerblading, working out. E-mail: sherwin@post.harvard.edu. Office: 10 Union Sq E #5mi New York NY 10003-3314

PARIKH, SHRIKANT NAVNITLAL, computer scientist; b. Bombay, India, Feb. 25, 1956; s. Navnitlal Purshottamdas and Mandakini Navnitlal (Shah) P.; m. Vandana Purshottam Gujar, Aug. 18, 1984; 1 child, Adhishri. B Engring with honors, Bombay U., 1978; MS in Computer Sci. and Engring., U. Tex., Arlington, 1981; PhD in Computer Sci., So. Meth. U., Dallas, 1988. Cert. project mgmt. profl., Project Mgmt. Inst. Customer engr. Hindustan Computers Ltd., New Delhi, 1978-79; S.W. design engr. Tex. Instruments, Dallas, 1982-83; project mgr., sr. engr. United

Technologies, Carrollton, Tex., 1980-82, 83-85; sr. engr. Wang Labs, Allen, Tex., 1985-88; computer scientist, project leader IBM, Dallas, 1988-95; dep. gen. mgr. IBM India, 1995-98; co-founder GlobeRanger Corp., 1998—; IT cons., 1999—; referee Internat. Conf. Computer Arithmetic, 1989, 91, Fall Joint Computer Conf., Dallas, 1987. Patentee in field; contbr. tech. invention disclosure, 1990-94. Mem. IEEE (sec. IEEE-CS Dallas chpt. 1991-95, referee 1989, 90, 91, 92, presenter at symposium on computer arithmetic). Hindu, Swadhyayi. Avocations: chess, philosophy, real estate. Home: 454 Pirbhoy Mansion, 2d Fl A Block SVP Rd, Bombay 400004, India

PARIKH, VINAY, pharmacology scientist; b. Lucknow, India, Feb. 10, 1971; s. Vijay and Usha Parikh. BPharm, Sagar U., India, 1992; MPharm, Gujarat U., India, 1994; PhD, Punjabi U., India, 1998. Rsch. scientist, pharmacologist Sun Pharms., India, 1998—. Contbr. articles to Jour. Cardiovasc. Pharmacology, Molecular and Cellular Biochemistry, others. Recipient G.P. Nair award Indian Drug Mfrs. Assn., 1994. Mem. Indian Pharmacol. Soc. (Achari award 1996), Indian Sci. Congress Assn. (Young Scientist's award 1997). Avocations: sports (cricket, table tennis), singing, cooking, reading, writing. Office: Sun Pharma Advanced Rch Crt, Akota Rd, Akota, 390020 Vadodara, Gujarat India

PARINEH, PARIMA, artist; b. Tehran, Iran, Aug. 17, 1953; came to U.S., 1977; d. Khodadad and Pooran Khodabakhishian; m. Poorshasb Parineh, Dec. 31, 1975; children: Austiaj, Hormoz, Khasha. BA, Tehran U., 1976; studied with Bob Gerbracht, San Francisco, 1983-88; studied with Dan Greene, Carmel, Calif., 1986-92. Portrait painter, San Jose, Calif., 1986—. Exhibited in group shows Kaiser Gallery, Oakland, Calif., 1989 (1st place award), Triton Mus. Arts, Santa Clara, Calif., 1996, Presidio, San Francisco, 1997, Tower Gallery, Sacramento, 1998; work represented in The Best of Pastel, 1996, Portrait Inspiration, 1997. Mem. Pastel Soc. Am., Pastel Soc. West Coast (signature mem.), Western Soc. Artists, Saratoga Contemporary Artists. Home: 20978 Saraview Ct Saratoga CA 95070-4820 Studio: 7287 Coronado Dr San Jose CA 95129-4580

PARINOV, IVAN ANATOL'EVICH, mathematician; b. Ulan-Bator, Mongolia, May 6, 1956; s. Anatoly and Lyubov (Nimtzovitch) P.; m. Lidiya Vasil'eva, Feb. 16, 1979; two children. MSc, Rostov State U., 1978, PhD, 1990. From engr. to head lab. Mechs. & Applied Math. Rsch. Inst. Rostov State U., Rostov-on-Don, Russia, 1978—. Mem. N.Y. Acad. Scis., Am. Math. Soc. Office: Rostov State U Mechs/Math, 200/1 Stachki Ave, 344090 Rostov-on-Don Russia

PARIS, HARRY STUART, plant geneticist, researcher; b. Bklyn., May 3, 1951; arrived in Israel, 1978; s. Jack and Thelma (Fischer) P.; m. Yafa Faruhi, July 28, 1980; children: Effi Philip, Ohad Jonathan, Dorone Rosemary, Shirelle Siggalit. BSc, SUNY, New Paltz, 1973; PhD, Rutgers U., 1978. Rschr. vegetable crops Agrl. Rsch. Orgn. Newe Ya'ar Rsch. Ctr., Ramat Yishay, Israel, 1978—, mem. rsch. & governing bd.; breeder new cultivars cucurbits; chief scientist agrl. R&D Ctrl. Coastal Plain, Israel, 2000—. Contbr. more than 100 articles to profl. jours. Rsch. grantee Binat. Agrl. Rsch. & Devel. Fund, 1980, 84. Mem. Am. Soc. Horticultural Sci., Internat. Soc. Horticultural Sci., N.Y. Acad. Scis. Home: 12 Rehov Deqel, 20-692 Yoqne'am 'Illit Israel Office: Agrl Rsch Orgn Newe Ya'ar, PO Box 1021, Ramat Yishay Israel

PARIS, STEVEN MARK, software engineer; b. Boston, May 26, 1956; s. Julius Louis and Frances (Keleishik) P. BS, Rensselaer Poly. Inst., 1978; MS, Boston U., 1980, postgrad., 1980-84. Sr. software engr. Prime Computer Inc., Framingham, Mass., 1978-82; sr. analyst Computervision Corp., Bedford, Mass., 1982-84; prin. engr. Lotus Devel., Inc., Cambridge, Mass., 1984-88; pres. Tri-Millennium Corp., 1988-91; sr. researcher Tech. Edn. Rsch. Ctr., Cambridge, Mass., 1990-93; prin. engr. Beyond, Inc., Burlington, Mass., 1993, Bus. Matters Inc., Waltham, Mass., 1994-96; v.p. engr. Ambit, Inc., Brighton, Mass., 1996—. Dep. chief Civil Def., Somerville, Mass. Recipient Boston Sci. Fair 1st prize, 1973, 74, State of Mass. Sci. Fair 3d prize, 1973, 2d prize, 1974. Mem. Assn. for Computing Machinery, IEEE, Boston Computer Soc., Planetary Soc. Jewish.

PARIS, WAYNE, social worker, researcher; b. Claremore, Okla., Nov. 8, 1949; s. Arch LaVerne and Aileen Rosella (McGraw) P.; m. Donna Marie Lindley, Mar. 20, 1982; 1 child, Joel Michael. BA, Northeastern State U., 1972; MSW, U. Okla., 1979; postgrad., U. Huddersfield, Eng., 2000. Lic. clin. social worker, Okla. Med. social worker Bapt. Med. Ctr., Oklahoma City, 1979-84; clin. transplant social worker Nazih Zuhdi Transplantation Inst., Oklahoma City, 1985—; pvt. practice, cons. Wayne Paris & Assocs., Edmond, Okla., 1993—; grant reviewer The Wellcome Trust, London, 1999. Contbg. author: Yearbook of Surgery, 1994; mem. editl. bd. Jour. Transplant Coordination, 1996—; assoc. editor Progress in Transplantation, 2000, guest editor., 2000; invited reviewer Jour. Heart and Lung Transplantation, 1995, 99, Rsch. on Social Work Practice, 1999; contbr. numerous articles to med. jours. Mem. NASW, Soc. for Transplant Social Work (charter, past bd. dirs., Judy Middelfort Meml. award 1996), Soc. for Social Work and Rsch. (charter), Internat. Soc. for Heart and Lung Transplantation. Avocations: coin collecting, sailing. Office: Nazih Zuhdi Transplantation Inst 3300 NW Expwy Oklahoma City OK 73112-4418

PARISH, ANTHONY ROYAL, medical researcher; b. Norwich, Eng., May 6, 1931; children: Juliet, Jennifer, Peter, Benjamin, Joseph. Doctorate, N.Y. Acad. Scis., 1998. Self-employed carpet and flooring industry, 1950-68; founder, chmn. Queensway Warehouses Ltd., Norwich, Eng., 1968-78; ind. med. rschr., 1986—. With Royal Army Med Corps, 1948-50. Address: 59 Dereham Rd, Norwich NR2 4HU, United Kingdom

PARISI, MARIO NESTOR, medical educator; b. Buenos Aires, Oct. 1, 1939; arrived in France, 1977; s. Jose and Angela Maria (Petrone) P.; m. Margarita Freedman, 1966; children: Eric, Muriel. MD, U. Buenos Aires, 1962, PhD in Medicine, 1971. Adj. prof. biophysics U. Buenos Aires, 1973-76; research dir. Ctr. Nat. Recherche Sci., Paris, 1977-86; career investigator Consejo Nacional de Investigaciones Cientificas y Tecnicas, Buenos Aires, 1986—; prof. Dept. Physiology, Faculty Medicine, 1986—; vis. prof. dept. physiology Faculty Medicine, Sao Paulo, Brazil, 1976; vis. assoc. prof. Mt. Sinai Sch. Medicine, N.Y.C., 1975, 78; gen. dir. Nat. Found. for Sci. and Tech., Argentina, 1999—. Fellow Guggenheim Found., 1976. Office: Dept Physiology Faculty Medicine, Buenos Aires Argentina

PARISIER, CARLOS, lawyer, economist; b. Buenos Aires, Oct. 21, 1930; m. Alicia Parisier, Nov. 25, 1965; children: Martin, Jacqueline, Dario Werthein. BA, Colegio Nacional de Buenos Aires, 1948; LLB cum laude, U. Buenos Aires, 1954. Bar: Argentina, 1954, Uruguay, 1955, Spain, 1985. Owner, sr. ptnr. Estudio Parisier, Buenos Aires, 1954—; pres. Hermitage Hotel S.A., Mar del Plata, Argentina, 1958-75; founder Fundacion Pro Justitia, Buenos Aires, 1980; film producer, 1963—. Author: La nueva ley argentina en materia de convenciones de trabajo, 1955; contbr. articles on corp. and bankruptcy law to legal publs. Recipient motion picture award, Acapulco, Mexico, 1963. Mem. ABA, Buenos Aires Bar Assn., Uruguay Bar Assn., Madrid Bar Assn., Argentine Inst. Comml. Law, Comml. Bank Lawyers Argentina. Office: Estudio Parisier, Callao 220 4th Fl, Buenos Aires Argentina

PARISOTTO, GLORIA, publishing executive, poet; b. São Paulo, Brazil, July 4, 1938; came to U.S., 1980; d. Luiz and Antonia (Guimarães) P.; m. Onofre Pereira Mendonca, Dec. 13, 1954 (div. 1980); children: Marco Antonio, Marco Tulio, Maria Emilia. Degree in tchg., Inst. Fernando Costa, Prudente, 1954; student, Brazilian Acad. Fine Arts, Rio de Janeiro, 1985. Cert. tchr., Brazil. Tchr. Sch.-Pres. Bernardes, São Paulo, Brazil, 1954-56, Maristas H.S., Parana, P.R., 1954-66; hosp. supr. Sanatory Maringa Ltd., Parana, P.R., 1955-90; pres. Sunrising Publ. Co., N.Y.C., 1991—. Author: Learning Portuguese Without a Teacher, 1991, The Extraterrestrial and the Blue Planet, 1992, My Poems (3 langs.), 1992; (poems) The Flower (Poet of Merit award Am. Poetry Assn. 1990), Mother (Poet of Merit award Internat. Poetry soc. 1991); contbr. poetry to numerous anthologies; one-woman art show at Cricket Club, Nfianii, U.S., 1981; exhibited art in group shows at Assn. de Criticos y Comentaristas de Arte, Miami, Fla., 1981, Hispanic Heritage Festival, Miami, 1981, Internat. Festival, Nhan-@, 1982, Nouvelle Gailerie, Geneva, Switzerland, 1983, UNESCO, Paris, 1984, Brazilian Artists Show, Rio de Janeiro, 1985, Internat. Expo, N.Y.C., 1986, Internat. Art Expo, Montreal, Que., Can., 1986, Pub. Libr., Gt. Neck, N.Y., 1987 (Excellence medal), Am. Embassy, Brasilia, Brazil, 1987, House of Spain, Rio de Janeiro, 1987, Lever House, N.Y.C., 1987, Mcpl. Gallery, São Paulo, 1989, Lincoln Ctr. Cork Gallery, N.Y.C., 1989, Icaro Gallery, N.Y.C., 1990, Epiphany Gallery, N.Y.C., 1990, Vanderbilt Mus., L.I., N.Y., 1992, Rio Design Ctr. Gallery, 1993 (hon. mention), Portal Gallery, São Paulo, 1993, Who's Who Artists, Edinburgh, Scotland, 1994, IPS's Conv. Art Show, Washington, 1995, Art Show, Capetown, South Africa, 1995, Am. & Internat. Bio Ctr., San Francisco, 1996, Oxford (Eng.) Gallery, 1997. Rep. abroad Brazilian Ecology Assn., Rio de Janeiro, 1988, Pan Am. Writers Assn., Brazilian Acad. Fine Arts, Rio de Janeiro, 1988. Recipient Bronze medal L'Amounier Gallery, Rio de Janeiro, 1981, Hebrew Cmty., Rio de Janeiro, 1981, Silver medal Brazilian Assn. Drawing and Visual Arts, Rio de Janeiro, 1982, Mil. Assn. Art Show, Rio de Janeiro, 1982, Gold medal Internat. Blenal, Rio de Janeiro, 1983, Ho. of Reps., Rio de Janeiro, 1983, Planetarium Gallery, Rio de Janeiro, 1984, Nat. Acad. Fine Arts, Rio de Janeiro, 1985, Palace "Espelho D'Agua", Belem, Portugal, 1986, Civil Police Acad., Rio de Janeiro, 1986, Gold Palette award Exhbn. Brazilian Artists, Salvador, Bahia, Brazil, 1987, Editor's award Nat. Libr. of Poetry, Washington, 1993, 94, Excellentia Order of Merit award, 1995, 1st prize award Famous Poetry Soc., Calif., 1996; semi-finalist nat. contest Internat. Poetry Soc.; named Poet of Merit, Internat. Poetry Assn., Washington, 1990, 91, 92. Mem. Nat. League Am. Pen Women, Inc., Internat. Platform Assn., Writers and Poets Soc., Acad. Am. Poets, Française-Italian Cultural Inst. Avocations: tennis, gym, traveling, reading, music. Home and Office: 150 W 56th St Apt 3407 New York NY 10019-3843

PAŘÍZEK, JOHN FRANCIS, pediatric neurosurgeon, consultant; b. Paředly, Czech Republic, Jan. 17, 1931; s. Francis and Janet (Fiala) P.; m. Blanche Kožíšek, June 4, 1960; children: John, Ivan. MD, Charles U., Prague, Czech Republic, 1956. Med. diplomate, surgery, 1960, neurosurgery, 1971. House officer surgery Dist. Hosp., Partizánske, Slovakia, 1956-59, Tchg. Hosp. Hradec Králové, Czech Republic, 1959-60; sr. registrar neurosurgery Med. Faculty Charles U. Hradec, Králové, 1960-80; cons. pediat. divsn. Dept. Neurosurgery Charles U. Hradec Králové, 1980—. Contbr. articles to profl. jours. Mem. Soc. Czech Neurosurgeons, Regional Soc. Physicians. Home: Severní 761, 50003 Hradec Králové Czech Republic Office: Charles U, Dept Neurosurgery, 50005 Hradec Králové Czech Republic

PARK, BAE-SIG, physics educator, researcher; b. Taegu, Korea, Feb. 5, 1953; s. Hee-Soo Park and Duck-Seon Song; m. Wee-Sook Kim, May 24, 1981; children: Jin-Hee, Jae-Young. BS, Seoul (Korea) Nat. U., 1980; MS, U. Mass., Amherst, 1983; PhD, U. Md., 1988. Computer programmer Korea Bank Assn., Seoul, 1980-81; teaching asst. U. Mass., Amherst, 1981-83; teaching asst. U. Md., College Park, 1983-84, rsch. asst., 1984-88; postdoctoral fellow N.Mex. State U., 1988-90; asst. prof. Physics U. Suwon, Kyonggi-do, Korea, 1990-93; assoc. prof. Physics U. Suwon, Kyung-Gi Do, Korea, 1993—, dir. Inst. Moisture Measuring Tech., 1993—; founder, CEO New Idia Tech. Corp., 1998. Translator (books) Chaos, 1993, Does God Play Dice?, 1993, The Discovery of Subatomic Particles, 1994, In The Wake of Chaos, 1995, The Last Three Minutes, 1995. Mem. Am. Phys. Soc., Korean Phys. Soc. Roman Catholic. Avocations: reading scientific articles, meditation. Home: Keunyoung Apt 425-1104, Kyonggi-do Paldal-Gu, Suwon City 442-470, Republic of Korea Office: Suwon Univ, Dept Physics, Kyonggi-do 445-743, Republic of Korea

PARK, BONG-WOO, science educator; b. Seoul, Korea, Aug. 10, 1952; s. Chang-Ho Park and Bok-Ye Lee; m. Kyung-Suk Lee, Apr. 23, 1983; children: Shin-Young Park, Sung-Jin Park. BA, Korea U., Seoul, 1974, PhD, 1985; MLA, Seoul Nat. U., 1979. Chief rschr. KTQTA, Seoul, 1979-83; asst. prof. Sangji U., Wonju, Korea, 1983-86; prof. Kangwon Nat. U., Chunchon, Korea, 1986—; vis. scientist Colo. State U., 1990-91. Author: Woodchips and Landscape Management, 1997; co-author: Visiting Guide for the Beautiful Forests, 1996, Forest, Man and Culture, 1995; editor Forests and Culture Soc., Seoul, 1994-95. Mem. park. com. Kangwon Province, 1993—, cultural property com., 1995—. Sgt. Korean Army, 1974-76. Mem. Korean Inst. Forest Recreation (chmn. 1996—), Korean Nat. Park Assn. (bd. dirs. 1997-99), Soc. Am. Foresters, Soc. Conservation Biology. Avocations: hiking, photography, seal engraving. Office: Kangwon Nat U, Chunchon 200 701, Korea

PARK, BYEONG-JEON, engineering educator; b. Chill-Jeon, Chindo, Korea, May 5, 1934; s. Ho-June and Joo-Hyon (Kim) P.; m. Sung-Tcho, Oct. 27, 1956; children: Kwang-Yeol, Kwang-Hee, Kyu-Yeol, Yoo-Hee. BE, Seoul Nat. U., 1956; ME, Chonbuk Nat. U., 1975; D Engring., Chosun U., 1978. Architect diplomate. Lectr. Mokpo (Chonnam) Tech. High Sch., 1957-58, Coll. Engring., Chosun U., Kwangju, Chonnam, 1958-61, Chonnam Nat. U., 1962-63; lectr. Coll. Engring., Chonbuk Nat. U., Chonju, 1963-64, asst. prof., 1965-68, assoc. prof., 1968-71; prof. Coll. Engring. Chonbuk Nat. U., Chonju, 1971-99, prof. emeritus, 1999—, dean grad. sch. environ. studies, 1991-93; architect Shin Shin Architects & Assocs., 1999—; guest prof. Tokyo U., 1981-82; dir. Archtl. Inst. Korea, Seoul, 1966-76, Korea Inst. Fire Sci. and Engring., Seoul, 1989-93; mem. Archtl. Inst. Japan, Tokyo, 1979—; head Inst. Urban and Environ. Studies, Chonbuk Nat. U., Chonju, 1990-92; spl. work prof. Ministry of Constrn., Republic of Korea, 1989-93, mem. adv. com. Structures of Sound Insulation, Korea Nat. Housing Corp., 1990—; mem. archtl. com. of Chonju, 1993—, Chonbuk Provincial Govt., 1994—. Author: Building Equipments, 1981, Environmental Science for Architect, 1985, Science of Dewelling, 1987, Building Acoustics, 1989, Architectural Environmental Science, 1997, Sanitary Electricity Facilities and System, 1998, Air Conditioning System. Mem. com. Chonju City Planning Com., 1983-96, Com. for Energy Conservation, Chonbuk Provincial Govt., 1987-92, Traffic Policy Com. of Chonju City, 1990-91, Chonbuk Provincial Govt. Adv. Com., 1990-93, 95—; mem. tech. devel. com. for energy substitute and mgmt. coop. Mem. Acoustical Soc. Korea (v.p., dir. 1985-94). Home: 167-186 2Ga Tokjindong, Tokjinku Chonju, Chonbuk Chonju 560-190, Republic of Korea Office: Chonbuk Nat U, 664-14 1 Ga Tokjindong, Tokjinku Chonju 560-756, Republic of Korea

PARK, BYUNG-OK, materials scientist, engineering educator; b. Kyung ju, Korea, Dec. 14, 1950; s. Kyung-Re and Pil-Nam (Seu) P.; m. Il-Suk Kim, Dec. 24, 1980; children: Hea-Min, Jee-Min. BS in Engring., Kyung Pook Nat. U., Taegu, Korea, 1974, MS in Engring., 1980, PhD, 1987. Asst. prof. Pohang Coll., 1976-79, Ulsan Coll., 1980-83; lectr. Kyung Pook Nat. U., Taegu, 1987-88, asst. prof., 1988-92, assoc. prof., 1993-96, prof., 1997—, dept. chair, 1993-94. Author: Composite Materials, 1998; contbr. articles to profl. jours. including Materials Letters, Ferroelectrics. Pvt. corp. Korean Army, 1974-76. Mem. Korean Ceramic Soc. (editor 1992-93), Korean Crystal Growth Soc. Avocations: go, trekking. Home: 104-1003 Hanyang Gongjak, Upre-dong Pook gu, Taegu 702-200, Korea Office: Kyungpook Nat U, 1370 Sankyuk-dong Pook Gu, Taegu 702-701, Korea

PARK, CHOONG SEOK, political science educator; b. Sariwon, Republic of Korea, Sept. 13, 1936; s. Tae Cheong Park and So Jongneon Lee; m. Hyung Ja Lim, Mar. 24, 1966; children: You Sung, You Jin. BA in Polit. Sci., Yonsei U., 1961; MA in Polit. Sci., U. Tokyo, 1966, PhD in Polit. Sci., 1972. Asst. prof. Dankook U., Seoul, 1977-79; asst. prof. Ewha Woman's U., Seoul, 1979-80, assoc. prof., 1980-83, prof., 1983—; vis. prof., U. Tokyo, 1986-87. Cpl. Korean Army, 1957-58. Mem. Korean Polit. Sci. Assn. (head editorial com. 1980, 84, v.p. 1993, Prize for Excellent Writing 1982), Assn. Japanese Studies (pres. 1989-90), Inst. for Northeast Asian Studies (mem. editorial staff 1995—), Com. for Rsch. on Pacific Asia (mem. editorial staff 1993—). Home: 5-802 Daerim Apt 2, Okeum-dong, Songpa-ku, 138-130 Seoul Republic of Korea Office: Ewha Woman's U, 11-1 Daehyun-dong, 120-750 Seoul Republic of Korea

PARK, CHOON-KEUN, biology educator; b. Chunchon, Kangwon, South Korea, Sept. 20, 1958; s. Yong-Duk Park and Young-Mok Yu; m. Young-Sun Jang, Nov. 6, 1983; children: Sung-Hyun, Hyun-Young. BSc, Kangwon Nat. U., Chunchon, South Korea, 1986, MSc, 1987; PhD, Okayama (Japan) Nat. U., 1991. lic. tchr., South Korea. Lectr. Kangwon Nat. U., 1991-93, asst. prof., 1993-97, assoc. prof., 1997—; exch. prof. Laval U., Que., Can., 1994-95, Okayama Nat. U., 1997-98. Author: Embryo Transfer in Cow, 1995; contbr. articles to profl. jours. Sgt. South Korean Army, 1979-82. Recipient Intenrat. award Ryobiteien Found., Japan, 1990. Mem. Inst. Embryo Transfer Soc., Korean Soc. Animal Reprodn., Korean Soc. Embryo Transfer. Buddhist. Avocations: fishing, mountain climbing. Home: 303-506 Kumho 3 Cha Apt, Oneui-Dong, Chunchon Kangwon-do 200-190, South Korea Office: Kangwon Nat U, Hyoja 2 dong, Chunchon Kangwon-do 200-701, South Korea

PARK, CHUL AM, finance educator; b. Jecheon, Korea, Aug. 1, 1918; s. Yin Hyun and Poh Ok (Choe) P.; m. Soon Ok Kang; children: Sang Hee, Tae Jun. BA, Kyung Hee U., 1953, MBA, 1969. From lectr. to prof. Kyung Hee U., Seoul, 1961-92, dir. for planning and mgmt., 1980-81, chmn. dept. Chinese, 1980-82, chmn. devel. com., 1987-92, emeritus prof., 1994—; expedition leader Himalaya Dhaulagiri, 1962, Himalaya Lhotes Shar, 1971, Chooyu in China, 1991, Party of 8,000km in Western China, 1993, Party of 10,000km in Kailas, China, 1994, Ancient Kohkyuk Kingdom in China, 1995, Lintz Area, Tibet, 1995-96, Tsangpei Plateau, Tibet, 1996, Qangtang Plateau, Tibet, 1997, Namtso Area, Tibet, 1998. Author: Report of Inquiries of Himalaya Dhaulagiri, 1963, Study of the Novel of Late Ch'ing, 1983, Mysterious Lands, 1993, The Roof of the World-Tibet: Flowers, People and Things, 1998. dir. Korea Alpine Fedn., Seoul, 1966—; adv. com. Korea Red Cross, Seoul, 1968—; chmn. Korea Himalaya League, Seoul, 1994—; adv. Exploration Assn. Korea, 1997—. Named King of Mountaineering 6th Mount Surak Festival, 1971; recipient award Nepal Mountaineering Assn., Nepal, 1998. Avocation: mountaineering. Home: Jungrang-Gu, Kuk Dong Apt 1012, Seoul 130-120, Republic of Korea Office: Kyung Hee U, Dongdaemoon-ku, 1 Hoiki-dong Seoul 130-701, Republic of Korea

PARK, CHUNG, painter, educator, computer software developer; b. Pusan, Korea, Oct. 27, 1941; s. Byung Ho Park and Jung Sun Im; m. Sue Bok Park, May 9, 1974; children: Paul, Janet Suejean Park. Diploma, Pusan Tchr.'s Coll., 1962; BFA, U. Mich., 1979; MFA, Pratt Inst., 1981. Cert. secondary edn. tchr., Korea. Art prof. Pusan Women's U., Korea, 1984-87, Pusan Nat. U., Korea, 1983-84; painting instr. Sch. of Visual Arts, N.Y.C., 1990-92, 94—; art lectr. Nyack (N.Y.) Coll., 1992-93; asst. adminstr. Upsala Coll., Orange, N.J., 1993-94; exec. dir. Uran Tech., Inc., Tenafly, N.J., 1994—. Trustee Bd. of Edn., Tenafly, 1997—; chmn. Korean-Am. Elected Sch. Bd. Mem. Assembly, 1997—; mem. adv. com. N.J. State Dept. Edn., Bilingual Edn., 1998—; founder Korean-Am. Youth Ctr. N.J., 1998—, Korean-Am. Parents Assn. N.J., 1998—; exec. dir. Asian Am. Youth & Cultural Ctr., 2000—. Mem. Coll. Art Assn., Korean-Am. Tchrs. Assn. N.J. (founder), Korean-Am. Contemporary Artists Assn. Greater N.Y. (founder). Fax: 201-944-1388. Home: 101 Prospect Ave Apt 8-D Hackensack NJ 07601-1995 Office: Uran Tech Inc # 200 410 Broad Ave Ste 200 Palisades Park NJ 07650-2615

PARK, DAEWON, chemical engineering educator; b. Koseung-up, Kyungnam, Korea, July 26, 1953; p. Youngjin Park and Ilsun Lee; m. Eulmi Jeung, Mar. 18, 1979; 1 child, Sangkyung. BS, Seoul (Korea) Nat. U., 1972; MS, Korea Advanced Inst. Sci., Seoul, 1976; DS, U. Aix-Marseille (France) III, 1984. Rschr. Inst. de Petroedchimie et de Synthese Organique Industrielle, Marseille, 1984-85; sr. rschr. Korea Rsch. Inst. Chem. Tech., Daejeon, 1985-87; asst. prof. Pusan (Korea) Nat. U., 1987-91, assoc. prof., 1991-96, prof. chem. reaction engring. and catalysis, 1996—; vis. prof. Seoul Broadcasting Sta., 1998. Contbr. articles to profl. jours. and newspapers; patentee in field. Advisor Ministry of Commerce and Industry, Seoul, 1991-92, Ministry of Small and Middle Industries, Pusan, 1992-97; exec. Pusan Asian Game Supporting Group, 1995-96. French Govt. fellow French Ministry Fgn. Affairs, Paris, 1979-84; Rsch. grantee Korea Rsch. Found., Seoul, 1992-98. Mem. Korean Inst. Chem. Engring. (editor), Korean Soc. Indsl. and Engring. Chemistry (v.p. Pusan-Kyungnam br. 1998—, editor), Polymer Soc. Korea. Avocations: golf, tennis, hiking, traveling. E-mail: dwpark2@hyowon.cc.pusan.ac.kr. Fax: 82-51-512-8563. Office: Pusan Nat U/Chem Engring, Kumjeong-gu, Pusan 609-735, Korea

PARK, DONG SOO, physician; b. Seoul, South Korea, Oct. 26, 1959; s. Chong Beom and Tae Kon (Ryu) P.; m. Ok Jin Kim; children: Saeeun, Taewon. MD, Yonsei U., Seoul, South Korea, 1985, PhD, 1994. Diplomate Korean Bd. Urology. Intern Severance Hosp.-Yonsei U., Seoul, 1985-86, resident, 1986-90, fellow, 1994-96; asst. prof. Poncha CHA U., Sungnam, 1998—; vis. scientist U. Tex. M.D. Anderson Cancer Ctr., Houston, 1997-98. Physician Korean Armed Forces, 1990-93. Mem. Korean Urol. Assn., Korean Urol. Oncology Assn. Office: Pundang CHA Hosp-Univ, Pundang-gu, Sungnam 463-712, South Korea

PARK, DUCK-GUN, nuclear physics researcher; b. Pusan, Korea, Jan. 19, 1957; s. Dong-Hak Park and Jong-Lim Kim; m. Yang-Soon Huh, July 17, 1987; 1 child, Chae-Yeun. BSc, Pusan Nat. U., 1977, MSc, 1981; PhD in Engring., Korea Adv. Inst. Sci.-Tech., Taejon, 1991. Sr. rschr. Korea Atomic Energy Rsch. Inst., Taejon, 1986—. Contbr. articles to sci. jours., including Jour. Applied Physics, Jour. Materials Sci., Jour. Physique, IEEE Trans. on Magnatism, Jour. Magnetism Magnetic Materials, Jour. Korea Phys. Soc. Mem. Korea Nuclear Soc., Korea Phys. Soc. Home: Apt 103-902, Yusong-ku Eu-en Dong Hanbit, Taejon 305-333, Republic of Korea Office: KAERI, Yusong, PO Box 105, Taejon 305-600, Republic of Korea

PARK, EDWARD CAHILL, JR., retired physicist; b. Wollaston, Mass., Nov. 26, 1923; s. Edward Cahill and Fentress (Kerlin) P.; m. Helen Therese O'Boyle, July 28, 1951. AB, Harvard U., 1947; postgrad., Amherst Coll., 1947-49; PhD, U. Birmingham, Eng., 1956. Instr. Amherst (Mass.) Coll., 1954-55; mem. staff Lincoln Lab., Lexington, Mass., 1955-57, Arthur D. Little, Inc., Cambridge, Mass., 1957-60; group leader electronic systems Arthur D. Little, Inc., Santa Monica, Calif., 1960-64; sr. staff engr., head laser system sect. Hughes Aircraft Co., Culver City, Calif., 1964-68; sr. scientist Hughes Aircraft Co., El Segundo, Calif., 1986-88; mgr. electro optical systems sect. Litton Guidance and Control Systems, Woodland Hills, Calif., 1968-70; sr. phys. scientist The Rand Corp., Santa Monica, 1970-72; sr. scientist R&D Assocs., Marina Del Rey, Calif., 1972-1986, cons., 1986-89; sr. tech. specialist Rockwell Internat., N.Am. Aircraft, Seal Beach, Calif., 1988-94. Contbr. articles to profl. jours.; patentee in field. Served to 1st lt. USAAF, 1943-46. Grantee Dept. Indsl. and Sci. Research, 1953. Fellow Explorers Club (sec. So. Calif. chpt. 1978-79); mem. IEEE, Optical Soc. Am., Soc. Archtl. Historians, N.Y. Acad. Scis., Sigma Xi. Democrat. Clubs: 20-Ghost (Eng.), Harvard (So. Calif.). Avocations: music, art, architecture, body surfing, gardening. Home: 932 Ocean Frnt Santa Monica CA 90403-2410

PARK, GILBERT RICHARD, physician; b. London, May 17, 1950. BS, Edinburgh (Scotland) U., 1971, MB BChir, 1974, MD, 1991; MA, Cambridge (Eng.) U., 1987; D in Med. Sci. honoris causa, U. Pleven, 1991. MBChB/Edinburgh, FRCA/London. Intern dept. surg. neurology Western Gen. Hosp., Edinburgh, 1974; resident dept. orthopaedics Royal Infirmary, Edinburgh, 1974-75; resident in gen. medicine Bangour Gen., 1975; house officer dept. anesthesia Royal Infirmary, Edinburgh, 1975-76, sr. house officer dept. anesthesia, 1976, rotating registrar dept. anesthesia, 1976-79, sr. registrar dept. anesthesia, 1979-80; lectr. anesthesia, hon. sr. registrar Lothian Health Bd. U. Edinburgh, 1980-83; dir. intensive care Addenbrooke's Hosp., Cambridge, 1990—; cons. in anesthesia and intensive care, 1983—; vis. fellow INSERM Unit 128, Montpellier, France, 1991; cons. anesthesia and resuscitation Royal Army Med. Corps, Territorial Army, 1985-92; assoc. lectr. U. Cambridge, 1984—; vis. prof. Duke U., 1995. Recipient Territorial Decoration, HM Govt., 1988. Fellow Royal Coll. Surgeons (Hunterian prof. 1986-87), Royal Coll. Anaesthetists; mem. Bulgarian Soc. Anesthesia (hon.), World Fedn. Socs. Intensive and Critical Care Medicine (mem. coun.). Avocations: hill walking, writing. Office: JVF ICU Box 17, Addenbrooks Hosp/Hills Rd, CB2 2QQ Cambridge England

PARK, HAE SIM, allergist; b. Taegue, Korea, June 13, 1958; s. Young-Tae Park and Hee-Sun Lee; m. Ki-Suck Jung, June 27, 1986; children: Jung, Woo-Sung. MD, Yonsei U., Seoul, Korea, 1983; PhD, Yonsei U., 1989. Bd. cert. Internal Med., Allergy & Clinical Immunology. Intern Yonsei Med. Ctr., Seoul, Korea, 1983-84; resident Yonsei Med. Ctr., 1984-86, fellow, 1987-89; faculty Nat. Med. Ctr., Seoul, 1990-92; post-doctoral rsch. fellow Southampton (England) Gen. Hosp., 1993-94; assoc. prof. Ajou U. Hosp., Suwon, Korea, 1995—. Editor in chief: Official J. of Korean Acad. Allergy and Asthma; contbr. articles to profl. jours. Mem. Am. Acad. Allergy, Asthma, and Immunology, British Soc. Allergy and Immunology. Office:

Dept Allergy Ajou U Hosp, San 5 Wonchon Dong Paldalgu, Suwon 442749, Korea

PARK, HEE CHAN, materials engineering educator; b. Kangwon, Korea, Dec. 29, 1940; s. Sung Won and Jung Soon Yoon P.; m. Ok Hee Shin, Jan. 15, 1969; children: Gil Jae, Hyun Jae, Min Jae. BS, Hanyang U., Seoul, 1964; MS, U. Ala., 1975; PhD, Pusan Nat. U., Korea, 1979. Rschr. Ceramic Ctr., Changwon, 1968; prof. Pusan Nat. U., 1970—, vice-dean, 1993-95; rsch. assoc. Ohio State U., Columbus, 1981-83; dir. Rsch. Inst. Indsl. Tech., Pusan; cons. LG Electronics, Ltd., Changwon, Korea, 1996-98. Contbr. articles to profl. jours. Mem. Korean Ceramic Soc., Am. Ceramic Soc., Australasian Ceramic Soc. Home: 308-1203 Sunkyung Apt, 609-312 Pusan Republic of Korea Office: Dept Inorganic Materials, Pusan Nat Univ, 609-735 Pusan Republic of Korea

PARK, HYOSOON, clinical pathologist, educator; b. Taegu, Korea, July 27, 1961; s. Jongdoo and Byunghyun (Yoo) P.; m. Eunjoo Lee, Dec. 13, 1987; children: Sangmin, Sanga. MB, Seoul (Korea) Nat. U., 1986, M in Medicine, 1989, PhD, 1995. Lab. dir. Sejong Hosp., Buchon, Korea, 1993; chmn. dept. clin. pathology Dankook U. Med. Coll/Med. Ctr., Cheonan, Korea, 1994-97; lab. dir., assoc. prof. Kangbuk Samsung Hosp./Sungkyunkwan U. Med. Sch., Seoul, 1997—. Editor: Organizational Aspect of Medical Informatics, 1996. Recipient Euidang award Korean Med. Assn., Korean Hematol. Assn., 1997. Office: Kangbuk Samsung Hosp, 108 Pyungdong Jongro-ku, Seoul 100-634, Republic of Korea

PARK, HYUNWOOK, electrical engineer, educator; b. Chindo, Korea, July 5, 1959; s. Kinam and InJa (Cho) P.; m. Jinsook Choi, Oct. 25, 1987; children: Joonwoo, Jungwon. BS, Seoul Nat. U., 1981; MS, Korean Advanced Inst. Sci., 1983, PhD, 1988. Rschr. GoldStar Telecom Rsch. Ctr., Anyang, Korea, 1983-86; postdoctoral rschr. Korean Advanced Inst. Sci. and Tech., Seoul, 1988-89, assoc. prof., 1993—; rsch. assoc. U. Wash., Seattle, 1989-92; prin. rschr. Samsung Electronics, Kiheung, Korea, 1992-93; vis. assoc. prof. U. Wash., Seattle, 1998-99. Contbr. articles to profl. jours. Recipient Min. Prize for Contbn. to Multimedia Ministry of Communication, 1993. Mem. IEEE, Korea Soc. Med. Informatics (bd. dirs. 1994—), Korean Soc. Picture Archiving and Comm. Sys. (bd. dirs. 1994—). Avocation: reading. Home: Hanbit Apt 130-1005, Eoun-dong, Yusong-gu, Taejon 305-701, Republic of Korea Office: KAIST Dept EE, 373-1 Kusung-dong, Yusong-gu, Taejon 130-012, Republic of Korea

PARK, IAN GRAHAME, newspaper executive; b. Merseyside, Eng., May 15, 1935; s. William and Christina (Scott) P.; m. Anne Turner, Aug. 26, 1965; 1 child, Adam Edward. MA, Cambridge (Eng.) U., 1959. Trainee journalist The Press & Jour., Aberdeen, Scotland, 1959; asst. lit. editor The Sunday Times, London, 1960-63; mem. mgmt. staff The Thomson Orgn., London, 1964-65; mng. dir., editor-in-chief Liverpool (Eng.) Daily Post and Echo Group, 1965-82; mng. dir. Northcliffe Newspapers Group, London, 1982-95, chmn., 1995—; mem. newspaper panel Monompolies and Mergers Commn., London, 1986-95. Magistrate City of Liverpool, 1972-76; dir. Liverpool Playhouse, 1973-80; trustee Bluecoat Soc. Arts, Liverpool, 1973-92. 2d lt. Manchester Regiment, 1954-56. Fellow Royal Soc. Arts; mem. Press Assn. (chmn. 1978-79, 79-80), Newspaper Soc. (pres. 1980-81), Reform Club (London). Anglican. Avocations: 20th century British art, 18th century British pottery. Office: Northcliffe Newspapers Group Ltd, 31 John St, London WC1N 2QB, England

PARK, IL SOO, obstetrician, gynecologist, educator; b. Taegu, Korea, Mar. 29, 1949; m. Pan Jun and Gab Seon Kim P.; m. Jung Ja Kim, Oct. 21, 1974; children: Dong Ho, So Yoon. BS, Kyungpook Nat. U., 1973, MA, 1976, PhD, 1985. From intern to prof. Kyungpook Nat. U. Hosp., Taegu, 1973—; vis. prof. Mt. Sinai Hosp., N.Y.C., 1985-86. Office: Kyungpook U Hosp, 50 Samduk Dong 2GA Jung Gu, Taegu 700-721, Republic of Korea

PARK, JON KEITH, dentist, educator; b. Wichita, Kans., May 26, 1938; s. William Ray and Eleanor Jeanette (Cunningham) P. DDS, U. Mo., 1964; BA, Wichita State U., 1969; MS in Dental Hygiene Edn., U. Mo., 1971; MS in Oral Pathology, U. Md., 1982; cert. in dental radiology, U. Pa. Sch. Dental Medicine, 1982. Diplomate Am. Bd. Oral and Mixillo-facial Radiology. Pvt. practice dentistry Wichita, 1964-67; chmn. dept. dental hygiene Wichita State U., 1967-72; assoc. prof. oral diagnosis, dir. oral radiology Balt. Coll. Dental Surgery, U. Md., 1972—; program dir. U. Md. dental externship, 1974-77; lectr. Essex C.C., Harford County C.C.; cons. in radiology VA Hosp., Medix Sch. Dental Assisting; mem. Md. StateRadiation Control Adv. Bd., 1981—; chmn. devel. com. Introduction to Basic Concepts in Dental Radiography, Dental Assisting Nat. Bd., Inc., Am. Dental Assts. Assn., 1991;. Editor Am. Acad. Oral and Maxillofacial Radiology Newsletter; patentee pivotal design dental chair. Mem. Ute Pass Hist. Soc. Recipient U. Md. Media Achievement award, 1977, 78. Fellow Am. Acad. Dental Radiology; mem. ADA, Md. State Dental Assn., Balt. City Dental Soc. (ad hoc com. radiation safety, exec. coun.), Am. Acad. Oral Pathology, Am. Acad. Oral and Maxillofacial Radiology (edn1. standards com., editor newsletter), Orgn. Tchrs. oral Diagnosis, Am. Theater Organ Soc., Kans. Dental Hygienists Assn. (hon.), Balt. Music Club, Am. Assn. Dental Schs., Internat. Assn. Dental and Maxillofacial Radiology, Balt. Opera Guild, Engring. Soc. Balt., Met. Opera Guild, Balt. Symphony Orch. Assn., Ute Pass Cmty. Assn., Univ. Club, Omicron Kappa Upsilon, Psi Omega. Episcopalian.

PARK, JONG CHUL, engineering educator; b. Dalsung-kun, Kyung San Buk Do, South Korea, Mar. 14, 1927; s. Suk Kyu and Hyun-Shik (Lee) P.; m. Jong-Soon Kim, Apr. 26, 1954; children: Miesoon, Carolyn Haesoon, Genesoon, Sunsoon. BS, Seoul Nat. U., 1950; PhD, N.C. State U., Purdue U., 1958. Lectr. Hanyang U., Seoul, Republic of Korea, 1950, War-Time Consol. U./Yong Nam U., Taegu, Republic of Korea, 1952-54; asst. prof. Yong Nam U., Taegu, 1954; rsch. engr. R.A. Taft Environ. Engring. Ctr., Dept. HEW, Cin., 1957-58; rsch. engr., project leader Mass Transfer Lab. R&D Allied Signal Corp., Buffalo, 1958-67; v.p. Korea Engring. Cons. Corp., Seoul, 1967-68; advisor to pres. Hanhwa Corp., Seoul, 1968-70, Korea Gen. Chem. Corp., Seoul, 1968-70; prof. Kyung Hee U., Seoul, dean Engring. Coll., 1971-92, prof. emeritus, 1992—; mem. Petrochem. Project Coun., Ministry of Commerce & Trade, South Korea, 1967-69. Author: Venture Analysis Based on Decision Theory, 1982, Comparative Study of Fitting on the Ternary and Quaternary Systems, 1985, Representation of Multicomponent Phase Response Surface by Computer Graphics, 1987, Prof. Park, Jong-Chul, PhD 60th Birthday Memorial Thesis Collection, 1988, Mandang Park, Jong-Chul PhD Honorable Retirement Commemorative Thesis Collection, 1992; co-author: Comparative Performance of Expanded-Metal Plate in a Pulse Column Extractor, 1958, Suspension of Small Solid Particle in Liguid in Mixing Vessles, 1958, Developments in the Use if the A.I.S.I. Automatic Smoke Sampler, 1958; translator: General Chemistry 1 & 2, 1953, 54; contbr. articles to profl. jours.; inventor in field. 1st Lt. Republic of Korea Army, 1950-52. Recipient Outstanding Records of Experience and Scholastic Standing award AIChE, N.Y.C., 1964, Disting. Scholastic and Tchg. Contbn. to U. Kyung Hee, 1989, Recognition of Excellent Dedication to the Korea's Higher Edn., Ministry of Edn., Republic of Korea, Seoul, 1992. Mem AAAS, AIChE, Korean Inst. Chem. Engrs., Korean Chem. Soc., Korean Inst. Indsl. Engrs., Korean Indsl. Tech. Assn., Korean Resident Assn. at the Western Dist. State N.Y. (pres. 1963-67), N.Y. Acad. Scis., Seoul Nat. U. Engring., 4 Club (pres.), Kyungbuk Middle and High Alumni 27 Club (pres. 1994-97), Park Soonchon's Club (dir. adv. mem. 1980—), Seoul Nat. U. Engring. Coll. Alumni Assn. (dir. 1978-82). Avocations: golf, swimming, mountain climbing. Home: 1223-1501 Hanyang Apt, Kunpo Kyung-Gi Do 435-140, Republic of Korea Office: Kyung Hee Univ Suwon Campus, Yongin-gun, Kyung-Gi Do 449-701, Republic of Korea

PARK, JONG KUN, molecular cell biologist, educator; b. Iksan, Chonbuk, South Korea, July 25, 1958; s. Yong Hyun Park and Soon Buhn Kim; m. Soo Kyung Lee, May 28, 1990; 2 children. BS, Seoul (Korea) Nat. U., 1982, MS, 1984, PhD, 1990. Rsch. asst. Seoul Nat. U., 1982-86; lectr. Wonkwang U., Iksan, South Korea, 1987-88, asst. prof., 1989-93, assoc. prof., 1993-97, prof., 1998—, chair, 1992-94; vis. prof. U. N.C., Chapel Hill, 1997; cons. Somang Cosmetics, Seoul, 1995—. 2d lt. Korean Army, 1984. Mem. AAAS, Acad. Soc. Molecular Biology. Avocations: classical guitar, go game, table tennis, climbing, badminton. Office: Wonkwang U, Dept Molecular Biology, Iksan Chonbuk 570-749, South Korea

PARK, JONG WOO, electronics executive; b. Milyang, Kyungnam, Republic of Korea, July 10, 1952; s. Yoon Kyu Park and Dong Lee; m. Sungae Sohn, Nov. 7, 1980; children: Erica J., Eileen. BSEE, Yonsei U., Seoul, 1977; MSEE, Yonsei U., 1979; PhDEE, Purdue U., 1988. Nat. cert. 1st degree elec. engring. constrn. Mem. tech. rsch. staff Korea Scientific and Technol. Info. Ctr., Seoul, 1977-79; prof. electronic engring. Yuhan Tech. Coll., Seoul, 1979-81; chair electronic engring. dept. Yuhan Tech. Coll., 1979-81; rsch. asst. Pa. State U., State Coll., 1981-83, Purdue U., West Lafayette, Ind., 1983-88; tech. staff engr. IBM, N.Y.C., 1988-92. Contbr. about 50 articles to profl. jours. Mem. IEEE (mem. tech. com. Internat. SOI (Silicon-On-Insulator) Conf. 1996-98, IEDM (Internat. Electron Devices Meeting 1998-99, Asia Coordinate exec. com.). Methodis. Achievements include 6 international patents. Avocations: golf, skiing, racquetball, computers. Fax: 82331-209-3274. E-mail: ssparkjw@samsung.co.kr. Home: Chungdam-Dong 113-6, A-402 Jindo-Villa, Seoul Kangnam-ku 135-101, Republic of Korea

PARK, JOON BU, biomedical engineer, researcher, educator; b. Pusan, Korea, June 20, 1944; came to U.S., 1964; s. Sung Sub and Jung Ju (Kim) P.; m. Hyonsook Yoo, Apr. 15, 2000; children: Misun, Yoon Hi, Yoon Il, Lajong. Student, Seoul Nat. U., Korea, 1962-64; BS, Boston U., 1967; MS, MIT, 1969; PhD, U. Utah, 1972. NIH postdoctoral fellow U. Wash., Seattle, 1972-73; vis. asst. prof. U. Ill., Urbana, 1973-76; asst./assoc. prof. Clemson (S.C.), 1976-81; prof. Tulane U., New Orleans, 1981-83; prof. biomed. engring. U. Iowa, Iowa City, 1983—; advisor/cons. FDA, Rockville, Md., 1980—. Author: Biomaterials: An Introduction, 1979, 2nd edit., 1992, Biomaterials Science and Engineering, 1984, also more than 100 jour. articles, more than 100 abstracts. Recipient McQueen Quattlebaum award Clemson U., 1980. Fellow Am. Inst. Med. and Biol. Engring.; mem. Soc. for Biomaterials (founding mem.), Biomed. Engring. Soc., Orthop. Rsch. Soc., N.Y. Acad. Scis. Achievements include 7 patents. Home: 1810 Country Club Dr Coralville IA 52241-1183 Office: Univ of Iowa Dept Biomedical Engring Iowa City IA 52242

PARK, JUNG HAG, chemistry educator; b. Taegu, Aug. 20, 1953. PhD, U. Minn., 1988. Prof. Yeungnam U., Kyongsan, Korea, 1992—. Mem. Am. Chem. Soc., Korean Chem. Soc. (Acad. Excellence award in Anal. Chem. 1998). E-mail: jhpark@yu.ac.kr. Office: Dept of Chemistry, Yeungnam Univ, Kyongsan 712-749, Korea

PARK, JUNG-HAN, medical educator; b. Kyungpook, Korea, Aug. 8, 1945; s. Joo-Whan Park and Sung-Eu Bae; m. Jeong-Ok Hah, Nov. 18, 1972; children: Eun-Young, Eun-Jin, Sun-Joo. MD, Kyungpook Nat. U., Taegu, Korea, 1970, MS, 1973; MPH, Johns Hopkins U., 1975, DrPH, 1979. Diplomate Am. Bd. Preventive Medicine, Korean Bd. Preventive Medicine. Chief dept. advanced preventive medicine studies Walter Reed Army Inst. Rsch., Washington, 1979-81; asst. prof. Sch. Medicine Uniformed Svcs. U. Health Scis., Bethesda, Md., 1979-81; prof. Sch. Medicine Kyungpook Nat. U., 1981-92, assoc. dean Sch. Pub. Health, 1984-88; prof. Cath. U. Taegu-Hyosung Sch. Medicine, Taegu, Korea, 1992—, dean, 1992-97; temp. advisor WHO-Western Pacific Regional Office, Manila, The Philippines, 1983, 85, 86, 89, cons., 1988; vis. prof. Johns Hopkins Sch. Pub. Health, 1990-91; Govt. of Republic of Korea rep. to policy and coordination com. for reproductive health WHO, Geneva, 1998—; chmn. subcom. environment and welfare Com. for 21st Century, Taegu, 1995-97; mem. Health Reform Com. for Prime Min., Seoul, Republic of Korea, 1996-97; policy advisor for minister of health and welfare Republic of Korea, 1998-99, ombudsman Ministry Health and Welfare, 1999—. Co-author: Preventive Medicine and Public Health, 1995, National Health Promotion Targets and Strategies, 1995; contbr. 105 articles to profl. jours. Maj. Walter Reed Army Inst. Rsch., 1979-81. Recipient Meritorious Svc. medal Dept. Army Dept. of Def., 1982, Outstanding Internat. Alumnus award pub. health pratice Soc. Alumni Johns Hopkins Sch. Hygiene and Pub. Health, 1997, Nat. Decoration Camellia medal Korean Govt., 1998; tng. grantee USPHS, 1974-79; Fulbright sr. rsch. grantee Korea-Am. Edn. Coun., 1990. Fellow Am. Coll. Preventive Medicine; mem. Korean Soc. for Preventive Medicine (trustee 1989—, sec. gen. 1987-89, chief editor 1994-96, chmn. bd. examiners 1997-2000), Korean Soc. Maternal and Child Health (trustee, pres. 1996-2000). Roman Catholic. Avocation: mountain climbing. Home: 100 Whang Gum Dong, Garden Heights Apt 202-102, 706-040 Taegu Republic of Korea Office: Cath U Taegu-Hyosung Sch Medicine, 3056-6 Daemyung 4 Dong, 705-034 Taegu Republic of Korea

PARK, KUK-TAE, science educator, researcher; b. Pusan, Korea, Feb. 17, 1947; s. Kwan-Soo Park and Yong-Soon Kim; m. Myung-Ja Hong, April 3, 1976; children: Nah-Lee, Mee-Lee. BSc, Yonsei U., Seoul, 1973, MSc, 1975, PhD, 1978. Lectr. dept. chemistry Yonsei U., Seoul, 1975-78; asst. prof. dept. chemistry Jeonbug Nat. U., Jeonju, Korea, 1978-81; postdoctoral fellow dept. chemistry Queen's U., Kingston, Canada, 1981-82, U. Mich., Ann Arbor, 1982-84; prof. dept. chem. edn. Korea Nat. U. Edn., Chongwon, 1985—; vis. scholar dept. chemistry Queen's U., Kingston, 1990-91; chmn. dept. chem. edn. Korea Nat. U. Edn., Chongwon, 1988-90; vice dean coll. natural scis., 1992-94, head faculty of natural scis., 1994-96, dean coll. natural scis., 1996-98. Contbr. articles to profl. jours. With Korean Army, 1968-71. Recipient Internat. Sci. Exch. award Natural Scis. and Engring. Rsch. Coun. Canada, 1990, Basic Rsch. grant Korea Sci. and Engring. Found., 1992, Specified Rsch. grant Korea Min. Edn., 1995. Mem. Am. Chem. Soc., Korean Chem. Soc., Korean Environ. Scis. Soc. Avocations: swimming, photography, hiking, tennis. Office: Korea Nat U Edn Dept Chem, Chongwon-gun, Chungbuk 363-791, Korea

PARK, KWANG-KYUN, biochemist, educator, dentist; b. Seoul, South Korea, Mar. 4, 1953; s. Yong-Euon and Soon-Yae (Kang) P.; m. Hae-Jung Cho, Oct. 18, 1980; children: Eun-Bin, Na-Bin. BS, Yonsei U., 1975, DSD, 1980, M in Med. Scis., 1985, PhD in Med. Scis., 1988. Asst. prof. Wonju Coll. Medicine Yonsei U., Seoul, 1987-90, assoc. prof. Coll. Medicine, 1990-96, assoc. prof. Coll. Dentistry, 1996—, assoc. dean for student affairs, 1996-98; vis. prof. U. Wis., Madison, 1990-93; com. 2d Sci. and Tech. Policy Inst., Seoul, 1998—. Contbr. articles to profl. jours. including Carcinogenesis and Cancer Letters. Home: 264-448 Imun-2-Dong, Samick Townhouse #10-102, Dongdaemun-Gu Seoul 130-082, Republic of Korea Office: Yonsei U Coll Dentistry, 124 Shinchon-Dong, Seodaemun-Gu Seoul 120-752, Republic of Korea

PARK, KYIHWAN, mechanical and electrical engineering educator; b. Mokdo, Republic of Korea, Jan. 14, 1961; s. Kwanyong Park and Eunhee Jung; m. Jaekyung Shon; children: Jae Young, JaeHong. BS, Seoul Nat. U., 1985, MS, 1987; PhD, U. Tex., 1993. Rsch. scientist Korea Inst. Sci. and Tech., Seoul, 1988-89; rsch. asst. U. Tex., Austin, 1989-93, postdoctoral fellow, 1993-94; postdoctoral fellow Korea Inst. Sci. and Tech., Taejon, 1994-95; assoc. prof. Kwangju (Republic of Koreak) Inst. Sci. and Tech., 1995—; cons. Samsung Co., 1996-97. Contbr. articles to profl. jours. Mem. IEEE, Korean Soc. Mech. Engring. Avocations: tennis, golf. Office: Kwangju Inst Sci and Tech, Kwanju 500-712, Korea

PARK, KYONG WHA, hospital administrator; b. Whang-Ju, North Korea, Nov. 25, 1926; s. Kee Whan Park and Kwang Shin Ahn; m. Hyun Joo Seo, Feb. 7, 1952; children: Cheul-Min, Hay-won, Chung-Min. MD, Seoul (Korea) Nat. U., 1949; postgrad., Air U., San Antonio, 1957, Aero-Med. Ctr., San Antonio, 1960-61, U. Wash., 1967-68. Commd. Republic of Korea Air Force, 1953, advanced through grades to brig. gen.; flight surgeon flight tng. wing Republic of Korea Air Force, Sachun, 1953-58; dir. med. svc. divsn. Surgeon Gen.'s Office Republic of Korea Air Force, Seoul, 1958-60, comdr. Aero-Med. Ctr., 1966-67, surgeon gen., 1974-76; chmn. med. rev. com. Med. Ins. Corp., Seoul, 1981-84; supt. Ilsin Christian Hosp., Pusan, South Korea, 1985—; attending prof. Seoul Nat. U., 1966-67, Cath. Med. Sch., Seoul, 1967-68; supt. Eulchi Gen. Hosp., 1976-79. Author: Living in Aerobic Age, 1983, God, O! My god, 1993. Pres. Korea Oversea Med. Mission, Seoul and Dahka, Bangladesh, 1996; dir. Ctr. for Homeless People/House of Hope, Pusan, 1998. Mem. Korea Med. Assn. (auditor 1950—, Meritorious Svc. award 1976), Korea Christian Hosp. Assn. (pres. 1986-91, 97—), Soc. Gen. Surgery, Soc. Preventive Medicine. Presbyterian. Avocations: jogging, golf, classical music, reading. Home: 201-301 DaeLim Town, Hwa Myung Dong, Pusan Book-Ku Republic of Korea Office: Ilsin Christian Hosp, 471 Chwa Chun Dong Tong-ku, Pusan 601-050, Republic of Korea

PARK, KYU TAE, engineering educator; b. Kochang, Republic of Korea, June 11, 1933; s. Yang Mook and Yon Wol (Kim) P.; m. Moon Ja Shon, Oct. 25, 1970; children: Sung Jin, Sung Ho. BSc, Yonsei U., Seoul, South Korea, 1957; MSc, U. London, 1964; PhD, U. Southampton, Eng., 1969. Chartered engr., Eng. Prof. computer engring. Yonsei U., 1970—, chmn. dept. electronic engring., 1973-77, chmn. dept. computer sci. grad. sch. engring., 1977-91, dir. gen. affairs, 1980-84, dean Coll. Engring., 1988-92; mem. Presdl. Coun. on Sci. and Tech., Korea, 1992-98; vice chmn. Korea Sci. and Engring. Found., 1992—; dir. Ctr. for Signal Processing, Seoul, 1994-98; mem. Acad. Sci. and Tech., Korea, 1995—; chmn. Korea Coun. of Indsl. Tech., 1999—; mem. Policy Evaluation Com., Seoul, 1973-83; mem. adv. bd. Electronic Industries Assn. Korea, Seoul, 1983-86. Author: Digital Logic, 1975, Digital Signal Processing, 1986; contbr. articles to profl. jours. Pres. Brit.-Korean Soc., London, 1964-66, Union of Deans of Engring. Colls. of Korea, Seoul, 1990-92; presbyter Somang Presbyn. Ch., Seoul, 1988—. Sgt. Korean Army, 1961. Recipient Tongbaek medal Korean Govt., 1988. Fellow IEEE, Inst. Elec. Engrs.; mem. Inst. Elec. Engrs. Korea (pres. 1985-86, Acad. Excellence award 1973, 74, Grand Electronics award 1999), Korea Info. Sci. Soc. (pres. 1978-80), Korea Engrs. Club. Home: 651-2 Shinsa-Dong, Kangnam-Gu, 135-120 Seoul Republic of Korea Office: Yonsei U Dept Elec Engring, 134 Shinchon-dong Seopaemun, 120-749 Seoul Republic of Korea

PARK, LEE (LEE PARKLEE), artist; b. Seoul, South Korea; s. Chung-Kun Park and Mil-Hwa Kim; m. Chai Kyung Lim, June 3, 1994. MA, Fla. State U., 1986. Group shows include Shinpara Gallery, L.A., Up-Stairs Gallery, L.A., Beverly Plz. Hotel, Pacific Mus., Pasadena, Calif., Barnsdall Art Gallery, Hollywood, Calif., Brand XXII The Assn. of Brand Art Ctr., Glendale, Calif., Asia Invitation Art Exhibn., Sejong Cultural Ctr., Seoul, la Peintre Moderne Coreend '93, Paris, Korea-Japan Interchange Exhbn., Tokyo, 1994, Downtown Lives '96 Art Exhbn., L.A., City Hall of Paris, 4, Biennale Internat. de Paris, 1994, Musee d'Art Moderne de la Commanderie d'Unet, Paris, 1994, Bridgeport U., N.Y., 1995, San Bernardino County Mus., 1995, Kong-Ja Culture Art Exhbn., China, 1995, His Majesty the King's 50th Anniversary Art Exhbn., Thailand, 1996, 1st Venice Annual Internat. Open Art Exhbn., Venice, 1998, 1st Internat. Biennial Contemporary Art, Perugia, Italy, 1998, Heukyong-gangsung Internat. Art Exhbn., China, 1998, Ting Shao-Kuang Fine Art Ctr., Beverly Hills, Articulture Gallery, Hermosa Beach, Calif., 1998, '99 World Peace Art Exhbn., Sejong Cultural Ctr., Seoul, 1999; 2 person shows include Cosmos Gallery, Honolulu, The City of L.A. Cultural Affairs Dept.; solo exhibits include Modern Art Gallery, L.A., Olympic Gallery, L.A., Sun Space Gallery, L.A., Gallery Nuevo, Pusan, Korea; publ. artwork in American References, Art of California mag., Artweek mag., The Biweekly Art Jour., Seoul, Artprint mag., Washington, Art Exposure mag., Calif., Encyclopedia of Living Artists mag., Calif., Art 2000, Seoul, Art Diary Internat. 98/99, Milan, Italy. Recipient Bronze award Art of Calif., 1993, Gold award Art Addiction, Stockholm, 1997. Avocations: collecting stamps and antiques, music, reading books, jogging, playing tennis. Home: 1935 S La Salle Ave Apt 31 Los Angeles CA 90018-1627

PARK, LEE CRANDALL, psychiatrist; b. Washington, July 15, 1926; s. Lee I. and Alice (Crandall) P.; m. Barbara Ann Merrick, July 1, 1953; children: Thomas Joseph, Jeffrey Rawson; m. Mary Woodfill Banerjee, Apr. 27, 1985; stepchildren: Stephen Kumar, Scott Kumar. Grad., Putney Prep. Sch., Vt.; BS in Zoology, Yale U., 1948; MD, Johns Hopkins U., 1952. Diplomate Nat. Bd. Med. Examiners, Am. Bd. Psychiatry and Neurology. Intern medicine Johns Hopkins Hosp., Osler Clinic, Balt., 1952-53; resident psychiatry USN Hosp., Oakland, Calif., 1954, Henry Phipps Psychiat. Clinic, Johns Hopkins Hosp., Balt., 1955-59; asst. psychiatrist Henry Phipps Psychiat. Clinic, Johns Hopkins Hosp., 1955-59, staff psychiatrist, 1959—, staff dept. medicine, 1970—, hon. staff dept. medicine, 1991—, dir. psychiat. outpatient svcs. and community psychiatry program, 1972-74, asst. dir. clin. svcs. dept. psychiatry, 1973-74, mem. departmental coun., 1974-76; fellow psychiatry Johns Hopkins U., 1955-59, faculty in psychiatry, 1959—, assoc. prof., 1971—, physician charge psychiat. svcs. student health svc., 1961-73; vis. psychiatrist Balt. City Hosp., 1960-61; co-prin., prin. investigator NIMH Psychopharmacology Rsch. Br. Outpatient Study of Drug-Set Interaction, 1960-68, co-dir. (with Eugene Meyer) Time-Limited Psychotherapy Rsch. Grant, 1969-73; pvt. practice psychiatry, 1964—; cons. Met. Balt. Assn. Mental Health, 1961-63, Bur. Disability Ins., Social Security Adminstrn., 1964-81; attending staff Seton Psychiat. Inst., 1966-73, exec. bd., 1970-73; staff Sheppard and Enoch Pratt Hosp., 1974—; rsch. includes borderline and narcissistic conditions, long-term effects of childhood emotional abuse, psychotherapy, interrelationships of psychotherapy and pharmacotherapy, ethical considerations in clin. rsch. Co-author: Primer on Mental Disorders: A Guide for Educators, Families and Students, 2000; contbr. articles and chpts. to profl. jours. and books. Served to lt. M.C., USNR, 1953-55, div. psychiatrist 1st Marine Div., Korea, staff psychiatrist USN Hosp., Camp Pendelton, Calif., 1954-55; mem. Md. Interdisciplinary Coun. for Children and Adolescents, 1978-98, treas., 1980-87. Fellow AAAS, Am. Psychiat. Assn. (life; mem. assembly 1983-93, Pscyhiatr. Rsch. Network 1994—); mem. AMA, AAUP, Nat. Assn. Scholars, Md. Found. for Psychiatry (bd. dirs. 1995—, pres. 2000—), Am. Psychosomatic Soc., Internat. Soc. Study of Personality Disorders, Am. Soc. Adolescent Psychiatry, Am. Coll. Neuropsychopharmacology, Am. Assn. Pvt. Practicing Psychiatrists, Md. Assn. Pvt. Practicing Psychiatrists, Md. Psychiat. Soc. (pres. 1978-79), Soc. Psychotherapy Rsch., N.Y. Acad. Scis., Group Therapy Network, Med. and Chirurg. Faculty Md., Balt. City Med. Soc., Balt. County Med. Assn., Johns Hopkins Med. and Surg. Assn., Avery Assn., Denison Soc., Crandall Assn., Van Kouwenhoven-Conover Assn., Van Voorhees Assn., Parke Soc., SAR, Nat. Soc. of the Sons and Daus. of the Pilgrims, Gen. Soc. of War of 1812 (bd. dirs. State of Md. 1997-99, officer, surgeon 2000—), Nat. Huguenot Soc., Descendants of Mexican War Vets., Sons of Union Vets. of Civil War, Johns Hopkins Club (Balt.), Met. Club (Washington), Farmington Country Club (Charlottesville, Va.), Chevy Chase (Md.) Country Club, Phi Beta Pi. Episcopalian. Home: 308 Tunbridge Rd Baltimore MD 21212-3803 Office: 1205 York Rd Ste 35 Lutherville Timonium MD 21093-6211

PARK, MIN-SOO, engineer; b. Seoul, Korea, Sept. 19, 1967; s. Ki-Chul P. and Mee-Ja Chun; m. Hae-Won Moon, Oct. 16, 1997; 1 child, Soo-Jin. BS, Seoul Nat. U., Korea, 1990; MS, Pohang U. Sci. & Tech., Korea, 1992, PhD, 1997. Rsch. engr. LG Info. & Comm., Seoul, Korea, 1997-99. Contbr. articles to profl. jours. Mem. IEEE. Office: LG Info & Comm, 60-39 Lasan-Dong, Seoul 153-023, Korea

PARK, MOON SUH, otolaryngologist; b. Seoul, Korea, Feb. 25, 1954; s. Geun Ju Park and So Yon Eum; m. Hye Ki Han, Dec. 17, 1979; children: Eun Jung, Jun Wo. BS, Kyung Hee U., 1978, MS, 1982, DSc, 1989. Resident Kyung Hee Univ. Hosp., Seoul, 1979-82; instr. Hallym U., Seoul, 1983-86, asst. prof., 1986-91; vis. prof. Bonn U., Germany, 1986-87; from assoc. prof. to prof. Hallym U., 1987—. Author: Principles and Practices of Hearing Aids, 1998. Mem. Korean Audiol. Soc. Avocations: golf, traveling, swimming. Home: 13-102 Hyundai Apt, Abgujung-dong GangNam Gu, Seoul Republic of Korea Office: Hallym U Hangang Sacred Heart Hosp, 94-200 Youngdung-po dong, Seoul 150-020, Republic of Korea

PARK, MOON-JIN, oceanography researcher; b. Inchon, Korea, July 24, 1953; s. Jae-Kyu and Bock-Kyoung (Kim) P.; m. Dong-Yeon Lee; children: Caroline (Jieun), Tae-Joong. BS, Seoul Nat. U., 1977; MS, SUNY, Stony Brook, 1985, PhD, 1990. Sea grant scholar N.Y. Sea Grant Inst., 1987-88; cons. Marine Scis. Rsch. Ctr., SUNY, Stony Brook, 1990-91; asst. prof. dept. oceanography Chungnam Nat. U., 1991-95, assoc. prof., 1995-99, prof., 2000—; vis. assoc. prof. Marine Scis. Rsch. Ctr., SUNY, 1997-98; chmn. dept. oceanography Chungnam Nat. U., 1995-97; mem. governing bd. Korea Inter Univ. Inst. of Ocean Sci., 1995-97; chief planning and mgmt. divsn. Basic Scis. Rsch. Inst. Chungnam Nat. U., 1999—. Contbr. articles to profl. jours. Faculty fellow for rsch. overseas Korea Rsch. Found., 1997. Mem. Am. Geophys. Union, N.Y. Acad. Sci., Sigma Xi. Office: Chungnam Nat Univ, Dept Oceanog 220 Goongdong, Taejon 305-764, Korea

PARK, ROY HAMPTON, JR., advertising executive; b. N.C., 1938; s. Roy Hampton and Dorothy Goodwin (Dent) P.; m. Elizabeth Tetlow Parham; children: Elizabeth P. Fowler, Roy H. III. BA in Journalism, U. N.C., 1961; MBA, Cornell U., 1963. Sr. acct. exec., rev. bd. exec., advt. planning dir., J. Walter Thompson Co., N.Y.C. and Miami, 1963-70; v.p. mktg. and account

mgmt. Kincaid Advt. Agency divsn. First Union Nat. Bank Corp., Charlotte, N.C., 1970-71; v.p. Park Outdoor Advt., Ithaca, N.Y., 1971-75; v.p. advt. and promotion Park Broadcasting Inc., Ithaca, 1976-81; dir., 1993-95; mng. editor Park Comm. Newsletter, Ithaca, 1976-81; mng. dir. Agrl. Rsch. Advt. Agy., Ithaca, 1976-81; v.p., gen. mgr. Park Outdoor Adv., 1981-84; pres., CEO, dir. Park Outdoor Advt. of N.Y. Inc., 1984—; pres. Outdoor Advt. Coun. N.Y. Inc., 1986-91, chmn., dir., 1992-95; dir., sr. v.p. RHP Inc., 1994-96, RHP Properties Inc., 1994-96; mem. region I planning bd. Inst. Outdoor Advt., 1984-86. Dir. Boyce Thompson Inst. for Plant Rsch. Inc., 1995—; trustee Park Found. Inc., 1995—, Cornell U., 1999—; mem. adv. coun. Cornell U. Johnson Grad. Sch. Mgmt., 1996—, founding mem. alumni exec. com., 1984-88; bd. vis. U. N.C. Sch. Journalism and Mass Comm., 1994—; chmn. Ithaca Assembly Cotillion, 1979-81; dir. pub. rels. Tompkins County Conf. and Tourist Coun., 1976; exec. com. Tompkins County Rep. Fin. Com., 1983-84; chmn. fin. com. MacNeil for Assembly, 1984-86, co-chmn. 1978-82; bd. dirs. Tompkins County Coun. Arts, 1976; chmn. pub. rels. com. United Way Tompkins County, 1973-74, loaned publicity exec., 1977; bd. chmn., publicity dr. Jr. Olympics, 1973-74; dir. pub. rels. United Fund Raleigh, N.C., 1971; fin. com. Spl. Childrn's Ctr., 1979. Mem. Tompkins County C. of C. (chmn. legis. action com. 1976, acting chmn. nominating com. 1976, chmn. sign ordinance com., 1975-76, pub. rels. coun. 1976, Project of Yr. award 1974, Recognition award 1975), Charlotte C. of C. (pub. rels. com. 1970-71), N.C. Soc. of N.Y., Beach Preservation Assn. Pine Knoll Shores (adv.), Ithaca Yacht Club, Ithaca Country Club, Boca Bay Pass Club. Office: Park Outdoor Advt PO Box 6477 Ithaca NY 14851-6477

PARK, SANG WOO, research chemist; b. Kyong-ki, Korea, July 30, 1937; s. Chan Jin Park and Kyu Im Hwang; m. Hi Sook Han, Oct. 8, 1967; 1 child, Chun Il. BSc, Seoul Nat. U., Republic of Korea, 1962; diploma, Frankfurt (Germany U., 1972, PhD, 1975. Rsch. scientist U. Frankfurt, 1972-76; prin. rsch. scientist KIST, Seoul, 1976—; invited rschr. Ciba-Geigy, Basel, Switzerland, 1978-79; vis. scholar U. Calif., Berkeley, 1986-87; prof. extraordinary KAIST, Seoul, 1984-90, edn. chair/rsch. scientist, 1992—. Inventor in field; contbr. articles to profl. jours. 1st lt., Army of Republic of Korea, 1962-66. Recipient Mok-Ryon medal, Govt. Republic of Korea, 1988. Fellow Korea Acad. Sci. and Tech., Korea Chem. Soc., Pharm. Soc. Korea. Avocation: hiking. Office: KIST, PO Box 131 Cheongryang, Seoul 136-791, Republic of Korea

PARK, SANG-DAI, molecular biologist, educator; b. Kimhae, Kyung-nam, Korea, Aug. 20, 1937; s. Dong-Cho and Nam-Gi (Kang) P.; m. Kyungza Ryu, Dec. 20, 1969; 1 child, Kyungryul. BS, Seoul Nat. U., 1960, MS, 1962; PhD, St. John's U., N.Y., 1974. Instr. Seoul Nat. U., 1967-72, asst. prof., 1972-77, assoc. prof., 1977-82, prof. molecular biology, 1982—, dir. Inst. for Molecular Biology and Genetics, 1985-89, dean rsch. affairs, 1991-95; vis. prof. U. Calif., San Francisco, 1977-78; adv. com. Prime Minister of Korea, 1981-83; mem. Presdl. Commn. for Sci. and Tech., Korea, 1989-90; hon. v.p. 17th and 18th Internat. Congress Genetics, Birmingham/Beijing, 1993-98. Contbr. articles to profl. jours.; adv. bd. Jour. Biochemistry, Tokyo, 1994-97, Cytotech., London, 1987—. With Korean Army, 1962-63. Recipient Korea Sci. award (presdl.) Korea Sci./Engring. Found., 1987, Korea Nat. Acad. Sci. award, 1998. Fellow Korean Acad. Sci. and Tech.; mem. Korean Soc. for Molecular Biology (pres. 1991-92), Asian Soc. Toxicology (v.p. 1994-97), Korean Soc. Zoology (pres. 1994-95), Internat. Vaccine Inst. (chmn. planning support com. 1995—), Korean Assn. Biol. Scis. (pres. 2000—). Avocation: hiking. Home: Banpo-dong Seocho-ku 45-13, Daelim Villa B-103, Seoul 131-040, Republic of Korea Office: Seoul Nat U Dept Molecular Biology, San 56-1 Shinlim-dong, Seoul 151-742, Republic of Korea

PARK, SEOK-KYUN, civil engineer, educator; b. Seoul, Oct. 10, 1961; s. Keum-Churl and Chae-Bong (Kim) P.; m. Hyun-Joo Na, May 10, 1985; 1 child, Jeong-Min. BE, U. Hanyang, Seoul, Korea, 1984, M in Engring., 1986; PhD, U. Tokyo, 1996. Asst., tchr. U. Hanyang, Seoul, 1984-86; rschr. Ssangyong Rsch. Ctr., Taejon, 1986-94, sr. rschr., project mgr., 1995-96; postdoctoral fellow U. Tokyo, 1996-97; lectr. Korea Infrastructure Safety and Tech. Corp., Anyang, 1998—; asst. prof. U. Taejon, 1998—; vis. prof. Ssangyang Rsch. Ctr., Taejon, 1998—; expert advisor Korea Inst. of Contrn. Tech., Seoul, 1998—; cons. prof. Korea Infrastructure Safety and Tech. Corp., Anyang, 1999—; design cons. Adv. Com. of Cheonju City Hall, 1999—; hon. supr. Subway Constrn. Hdqs. Taejon City, 2000—; mem. Asian Model Code Com. Author: Evaluation and Repair of Concrete Structures, 1998; mem. editl. bd. Korea Concrete Inst., 1999—; contbr. articles to profl. jours., including Jour. Japan Soc. Civil Engrs., INSIGHT (jour. Brit. Inst. Non-Destructive Testing), Concrete Libr. Internat. Design cons. Adv. Com. Cheonju City Hall, 1999—; hon. supr. Subway Constrn. Hdqrs. Taejon City, 2000—. Recipient Best Acad. prize U. Hanyang, 1981, grand prize Ssangyong Cement Ind. Co. Ltd., 1993. Mem. Japan Soc. Civil Engrs. (Best Presentation award 1995, 96), Japan Concrete Inst., Korean Soc. Civil Engrs., Korea Inst. for Structural Maintenance Inspection, Taeduk Sci. Forum. Achievements include patent for ultrasonic measurement system for concrete setting time. Avocations: tennis, mountaineering, listening to music, seeing movies, cycling. Home: 102-801 Mulgeun APT, Wolpyung-dong Seo-gu, Taejon 302-280, Republic of Korea Office: U Taejon Dept Civil Engring, 96-3 Yongwoon-dong Tong-gu, Taejon 300-716, Republic of Korea

PARK, SEUNGJOON, research scientist; b. Seoul, South Korea, Feb. 7, 1966. BSE, Seoul Nat. U., 1988, MSE, 1990; PhD, Stanford U., 1996. Vis. fellow SRI Internat., Menlo Park, Calif., 1994; rsch. staff mem. dept. computer sci. Stanford (Calif.) U., 1996-98; rsch. scientist Rsch. Inst. Advanced Computer Sci., NASA Ames Rsch. Ctr., Moffett Field, Calif., 1998—. Contbr. articles to profl. jours. Mem. IEEE, Assn. Computing Machinery. E-mail: spark@ptolemy.arc.nasa.gov. Office: NASA Ames Rsch Ctr M/S 269-3 Moffett Field CA 94035

PARK, SONG HUI, system engineer, senior researcher; b. Chinhae, Kyung Nam, Republic of Korea, Nov. 30, 1949; s. Su Jang Park and Im Bae; m. Soon Young Moon, Aug. 26, 1980; children: Sang Jun Park, Sang Ah Park. BS, Seoul Nat. U., Republic of Korea, 1973; MS, Stevens Inst. Tech., 1980, PhD, 1983. Sect. chief Agy. Def. Devel., Chinhae, Republic of Korea, 1984-87, dept. head of torpedo, 1988-98, dir. R&D program, 1999—; project mgr. Torpedo Modernization Program, Devel. Heavy Weight Torpedo, Devel. Light Weight Torpedo. Recipient Decoration of Nat. Security Korean govt., 1999. Avocations: table tennis, golf, playing guitar. E-mail: shpark9@hananet.net.

PARK, SOO-GIL, chemical engineer, educator; b. Seoul, Korea, Sept. 21, 1956; m. Paik Sum-Young; 1 child. BS, Hamyang U., Seoul, 1979, MS, 1981; MS, Tokyo Inst. Tech., 1985, PhD, 1988. Postdoctoral fellow SUNY, 1988-90; rschr. Korea Atomic Energy Rsch. Inst., Dajeon, 1990-91; assoc. prof. Chungbuk Nat. U., Cheongju, 1991—. Author: Conductive Organic Thin-Film, 1998; editor: Polymer Battery, 1998. Recipient Best Paper Presentation prize Korean Soc. Indsl. and Engring. Chemistry, 1998, meritorious prize, 1998, Best Sci. prize Chungbuk Nat. U. Mem. Korean Electrochem. Soc. (organizing com. 1997—), Am. Electrochem. Soc., Japan Electrochem. Soc., Korean Inst. Electric and Electronic Materials Engring. (program com. 1991—), Inst. Surface Engring. (editl. com. 1991—), Inst. Elec. Engring. Home: 101-1002 Byuksam Apt, Gakyung-dong, Cheongin Chungbuk 361-230, Korea Office: Chungbuk Nat U/Indsl Chem, Som # 48 Gaeshin-dong, Cheongin Chungbuk 361-763, Korea

PARK, SOON J., cardiovascular surgeon; b. Seoul, Korea, Dec. 29, 1959; m. Seun Park; children: Issac, Tina, Peter, Joseph. BA in Chemistry, MS in Biochemistry, U. Chgo., 1983; MD, Pritzker Sch. Medicine, 1987. Staff surgeon VA Med. Ctr., Mpls., 1996—, Regions Hosp., St. Paul, 1996—; asst. prof. surgery Fairview U. Med. Ctr., Mpls., 1996—; guest spkr. Lifesource, St. Paul, 1996, lung transplant support group U. Minn., Mpls., 1999; surg. dir. lung and heart-lung transplantation program Fairveiw U. Med. Ctr., Mpls., 1999—. Contbr. articles to profl. jours. Rsch. grantee Minn. Med. Found. U. Minn., 1998, Am. Heart Assn., 1999. Mem. Twin City Thoracic and Cardiovascular Surg. Soc. (bd. dirs. 1999), Am. Soc. Transplant Surgeons, Internat. Soc. Heart/Lung Transplantation, Am. Soc. Artificial Internal Organs, Soc. of Thoracic Surgeons. Office: Fairview-U Med Ctr 420 Delaward St SE Minneapolis MN 55455

PARK, SOYEON, library science educator; b. Seoul, Nov. 20, 1967; s. Woojeong and Bocksoon P.;. MA in English Lit., Yonsei U., Seoul, 1992; MLS, Rutgers U., 1994, PhD, 1999. Lectr. English Yonsei U., Seoul, 1992; lectr. libr. and info. scis. Rutgers U., New Brunswick, N.J., 1997-99; vis. asst. prof. Rutgers U., 1999—; cons. Rutgers Assn. of Am. Univ. Profs. Contbr. articles to profl. jours. Recipient Marion-Johnson fellowship Rutgers Grad. Sch., New Brunswick, 1998. Mem. Am. Soc. Info. Sci., Assn. for Libr. and Info. Sci. Edn., Korean Soc. for Info. Mgmt. Roman Catholic. Avocations: swimming, movies, Broadway musical. E-mail: sypark@scils.rutgers.edu. Office: Dept Libr/Info Sci Rutgers Univ/4 Huntington New Brunswick NJ 08901-1071

PARK, TAE JOO, engineering educator; b. Pohhang, Kyongbuk, Korea, Dec. 13, 1950; s. Young S. Park and Sun Nam Choi; m. Jae Sook Rho, Oct. 2, 1977; children: Jong Kook, Cho Rong. BS, Pusan (Korea) Nat. U., 1976, PhD, 1989; MS, Korea U., Seoul, Republic of Korea, 1985. Cert. prof. engr., water quality mgmt. Staff Korea Export Indsl. Complex, Seoul, 1977-80; sect. chief Hyosung Engring. Co., Ltd., Seoul, 1980-85; mgr. Hyundai Precision & Industry Co., Ltd., Seoul, 1985-88; asst. prof. Pusan Cath. U., 1988-90; from asst. prof. to prof. Pusan Nat. U., 1990—; dir. Inst. Environ. Studies Pusan Nat. U., 1997—. Author: Environment and Safety Control in Laboratory, 1999. Adv. mem. Pusan Met. City, 1995—, Ulsan (Republic of Korea) Met. City, 1998—. Sgt. Republic of Korea Army, 1971-74. Mem. Internat. Water Assn. (editor 1999—), Korean Soc. Environ. Engrs. (dir. 1985—, prize Rsch. Paper 2000), Inst. Chem. Engrs., Korean Assn. Profl. Engrs. Roman Catholic. Achievements include patents for HINT BNR process, auto-control system of AOPs for petrochemical wastewater. Avocations: mountain climbing, sea fishing, travel, baduk. Fax: 82-51-514-9574. Home: 908-102 Dong LG Bilat Apt, Bugok2-Dong, 609-322 Pusan Republic of Korea Office: Pusan Nat U, San-30 Jang Jeon-Dong, 609-735 Pusan Republic of Korea

PARK, TA-RYEONG, physicist, educator; b. Dongkwangyang, Jonnam, South Korea, Jan. 20, 1961; s. Soo-Mahn and Jung-Eun (Jung) P.; m. Hyung-Ji Kim, Apr. 12, 1986; children: Gun-Tae, Sung-June, Sae-Gyul. BS, Seoul Nat. U., 1983, MS, 1985; PhD, Mich. State U., 1991. Sr. lectr. Hoseo U., Asan, South Korea, 1991-93, asst. prof., 1993-97, assoc. prof., 1997—. Contbr. articles to profl. jours. 2d lt. Korean Army, 1985-86. Mem. Am. Phys. Soc., Korean Phys. Soc. Avocation: audiophile. Office: Hoseo Univ, Dept Physics, Asan Choongnam 336-795, South Korea

PARK, WARN-GYU, mechanical engineering educator; b. Changwon, Kyungnam, Republic of Korea, Sept. 24, 1958; s. Sang-Rho and Jung-Soon (Joo) P.; m. Sun-Young Lee, Dec. 16, 1989; children: Jungsoo, Minjee, Sungmoon. BS, Pusan (Korea) Nat. U., 1981; MS, Korea Advanced Inst. Sci. & Tech., Seoul, 1983; PhD, Ga. Inst. Tech., 1993. Rsch. scientist Korea Inst. Sci. Tech., Seoul, 1983-88; rsch. asst. Ga. Inst. Tech., Atlanta, 1989-93; asst. prof. mech. engring. Pusan Nat. U., 1993—, chmn. dept. mech. engring., 1997-99; mem. internat. adv. com. Internat. Symposium on Fluid Machinery and Fluid Engring., Beijing, 1995—, Internat. Conf. Pumps and Fans, Beijing, 1997—. Author: Advances in Computational Methods in Fluid Dynamics, 1994; editor Jour. of Fluid Machinery, 1998—; contbr. articles to profl. jours. Recipient Sys. Engring. Rsch. Inst. award Korean Soc. Computational Fluid Dynamics, 1997. Fellow Korean Soc. Computational Fluid Engring.; mem. ASME, AIAA, Korean Soc. Mech. Engring., Korean Fluid Machinery R&D Assn. Avocations: climbing, tennis, travel. Home: Daelim 3-cha Apt 301-303, Haeundae-Gu Joa-Dong Republic of Korea Office: Pusan Nat U Dept Mech Engr, Changjun-Dong Kumjung-ku, Pusan 609-735, Republic of Korea

PARK, WILLIAM WYNNEWOOD, law educator; b. Philadelphia, Pa., July 2, 1947; s. Oliver William and Christine (Lindes) P. BA, Yale U., 1969; JD, Columbia U., 1972; MA, Cambridge U., 1975. Bar: Mass. 1972, D.C. 1980. Law practice Paris, 1972-79; prof. law Boston U., 1979—; counsel Ropes & Gray, Boston; v.p. London Ct. Internat. Arbitration; dir. Boston U. Ctr. Banking Law Studies, 1990-93; vis. prof. U. Dijon, France, 1983-84, Inst. U. Hautes Etudes Internat., Geneva, 1983, U. Hong Kong, 1990; fellow Selwyn Coll., Cambridge, Eng., 1975-77; arbitrator Claims Resolution Tribunal for Dormant Accts., Switzerland. Author: International Chamber of Commerce Arbitration, 1984, 3d edit., 2000, International Forum Selection, 1995, International Commercial Arbitration, 1997, Annotated Guide to the 1998 ICC Arbitration Rules, 1998, Arbitration in Banking and Finance, 1998; contbr. articles and book revs. to profl. jours. Trustee Mass. Bible Soc.; mem. vestry King's Chapel, Boston. Fellow Chartered Inst. Arbitrators (chartered arbitrator U.K.). Home: 36 King St Cohasset MA 02025-1304 Office: Boston U Law Sch 765 Commonwealth Ave Boston MA 02215-1401 also: Ropes and Gray 1 International Pl Boston MA 02110-2602

PARK, WON KUK, foundation administrator; b. Bukchang Dong, Chung-Ku, Korea, Mar. 24, 1929; s. Jun Seop and Kum Sun (Song) P. BA in Economics, Sungkyunkwan U., Seoul, Korea, 1957; MA in Economics, Am. U., 1960; PhD in Economics, Kyunghee U., Seoul, Korea, 1975. Asst. prof. Duksung Women's Coll., Seoul, Korea, 1961-63, Kyunghee U., Seoul, Korea, 1963-65; assoc. prof. Duksung Women's Coll., Seoul, Korea, 1965-67, v.p., 1965-70, prof., 1967-77, pres., 1970-77; v.p. Korean Pvt. Ednl. Found., Seoul, Korea, 1987-90, Korean Assn. for Univ. Found., Seoul, Korea, 1987-92; chmn. bd. trustees Duksung Sch. Found., Seoul, Korea, 1977-97; dir. Korean Pvt. Ednl. Found., Seoul, 1978—, Korean Assn. for Univ. Found., 1987—. Mem. Assn. for Promotion of Arts (pres. 1987-88), Korean Sect. World Edn. Fellowship (v.p. 1987—), Seoul Met. Chpt. The Republic of Korea Nat. Red Cross, Cooperation-Svc. Club Internat. (v.p. 1987-89), The Seoul Ctrl. Club of Good Will. Office: D-201 The Sungbookville Ho, 330-21 Sungbuk 2-dong, Dobong Ku Sungbuk-ku Seoul 136-012, Korea

PARK, WONDONG, science company administrator; b. Seoul, South Korea, Mar. 27, 1947; s. Wookyun Park and S. Chung; m. Youngran Choo, Jan. 25, 1972; 1 child, Jeeyoung. BA, Sungkyunkwan U., Seoul, 1970, Seoul Nat. U., 1976; MA, Chungang U., Seoul, 1984. Asst. mgr. Chase Manhattan Bank, Seoul, 1970-77; mgr. Samsung Co., Ltd., Seoul, 1978-80, McGraw Hill Book Co., Seoul, 1981-88; gen. mgr. Elsevier Sci., Seoul, 1989—. Editor: Publishing Management in Korea. active Lions Internat., Seoul, 1978-88. Mem. Korea Pub. Sci. Soc. Avocations: travel, mountain climbing, swimming, reading. Office: Elsevier Science, Kpo Box 315, Seoul 110-603, South Korea

PARK, WON-HOON, chemical engineer; b. Seoul, Feb. 10, 1940; s. Hyo-Hum and Soon-Ok (Yoo) P.; m. Oksoo Han, Sept. 25, 1971; children: Suzanne, Thomas. BE, Seoul Nat. U., 1964; PhD, U. Minn., 1971. Fellow U. Houston, 1971-72; vis. fellow SUNY, Buffalo, 1974-75; head lab. Korea Inst. Sci. & Tech., Seoul, 1972-81; prof. Sung Kyun Kwan U., Seoul, 1981-83; v.p. Korea Inst. Energy and Resource, Taejon, 1983-86; dir. Korea Inst. Sci. and Tech., Seoul, 1986-93; pres. Sci. and Tech. Policy Inst., Seoul, 1993; prin. investigator Environ. Rsch. Ctr. Korea Inst. Sci. and Tech., Seoul, 1994-95, pres., 1996-1999, rsch. fellow, 1999—; sec. gen. World Acad. Conf. of Seoul Olympiad '88, Seoul, 1987-88; chmn. Korea Sci. and Engring. Found., 1984-88; advisor Presdl. Commn. on Sci. and Tech., Seoul, 1989-90; mem. Presdl. Coun. on Sci. and Tech., 1995-98. Author: Fluidization-Japan and Korea, 1987; contbr. articles to profl. jours. With Korean Army, 1961-63. Recipient Nat. Medal (Sokryu) Korean Govt., 1980, Acad. Grand Prize, Kyunghyang Daily News, 1986, Citation, Pres. of Korea, 1989. Mem. Internat. Union Air Pollution Prevention and Environ. Protection Assns. (pres. 1998—), Korean Inst. Chem. Engrs. (v.p. 1999-00, pres. 2000—), Korean Soc. Energy Engring. (pres. 1998-99), Korean Solar Energy Soc. (pres. 1990-91), Korean Soc. Clean Tech. (pres. 1998-99). Home: 17-29 Kuki-Dong Chongro-Ku, Seoul 110-011, Republic of Korea Office: Korea Inst Sci and Tech, Sungbuk-Ku 39-1 Hawolgog-Dong, Seoul 136-791, Republic of Korea

PARK, YEON-SOO, government official; b. Jung Eupsi, Cheon Buk, Republic of Korea, Dec. 8, 1953; s. Jong-Tae and Yeon-Im (Lee) P.; m. Ok-Ki Shim, Apr. 7, 1979; children: So-Jin, So-Hyun. Bachelor, Korea U., Seoul, 1979; MSc, Yonsei U., Seoul, 1988, PhD in Urban Planning, 1997. Chief of sect. KyungNam Provincial Govt., Korea, 1979-85; dir. Inchon Mcpl. Govt., Korea, 1985-86, dir. gen., 1986-89; chief Inchon Dong-gu Mcpl. Govt., Korea, 1989-91; dir. gen. Inchon Mcpl. Govt., Korea, 1991-94; dir. Ministry of Home Affairs, Korea, 1995-97; dir. gen. Ministry of Govt. Adminstrn. and Local Autonomy, Korea, 1998-99; dir. gen. coun. promotion 2002 FIFA World Cup Korea/Japan Ministry of Govt. Adminstrn. and Local Autonomy, 1999—; vis. scholar Georgetown U., Washington, 1996-97. Author: (poem) Beside the Flower Garden, 1974. Pres. Inchon (Korea) City Ofcl.'s Club, 1984. Recipient Medal of Merit, 1998, Minister's award Ministry of Contrn., 1982, Excellent Thesis award Yonsei U., 1988. Fellow Korea Planners Assn., Korea Transp. Rsch. Soc., Korean Assn. for Policy Studies. Avocations: Taekwondo, Korean sword martial art, poem writing, golf. Address: Seocho Gu, #962-2 Bang Bae Dong, Seoul Republic of Korea

PARK, YONG-IL, biochemist, microbiologist, researcher; b. Choon-chun, Kangwon-Do, Republic of Korea, Jan. 5, 1962; s. Ki-Jun Park and Ok-Soon Min; m. Young-Nan Kim, July 5, 1992; 1 child, Hye-Seun. B Engring., Kon-Kuk U., Seoul, 1987, MS, 1989; PhD, U. Fla., 1996. Rsch. asst. Kon-Kuk U., 1988-89; rsch. and tchg. asst. U. Fla., Gainesville, 1992-96, postdoctoral assoc., 1997; postdoctoral and assoc. rsch. scientist Johns Hopkins U., Balt., 1997-99; rsch. scientist Korea Rsch. Inst. Biosci. and Biotech., Tae-Jon, Republic of Korea, 1999—. Contbr. articles to sci. jours., including Jour. Bacteriology, Applied and Environ. Microbiology, Molecular and Biochem. Parasitology. Sgt. Republic of Korea Marine Corps, 1982-84. Mem. Am. Soc. for Microbiology, Korean-Am. Scientists and Engrs. Assn. Avocations: fishing, playing soccer. Fax: 011-82-42-860-4598. Office: KRIBB KIST Environ Biomat, Rsch Unit, PO Box 115, Yusong Tae-Jon 305-333, Republic of Korea

PARK, YONGSUB, law educator; b. Masan, Korea, May 8, 1940; s. Konju Park and Myoungnam Lee. BS, Korea Maritime U., Pusan, 1963; LLM, Dong-A Univ., Pusan, 1977, PhD, 1983. Deck officer, master Korea Shipping Corp., Seoul, 1963-75; lectr., prof. Korea Maritime U., Pusan, 1975—; chmn. safety com. Korean Register of Shipping, Dejeon, 1990—; arbitrator Korean Comml. Arbitration Ct., Seoul, 1993—; sr. advisor Prime Min. of Korea Govt., Seoul, 1995-96, Pusan-Vladivostok Assn., Pusan, 1996—; spl. cons. com. of ILO to Korea Govt., Min. of Maritime and Fishery Dept., Seoul, 1998—; dir. Grad. Sch., Korea Maritime U., pres. 1992-94; chmn. Korea Assn. of Maritime Law, Pusan, 1993-98; vice-chmn. Korea Maritime Ednl. Assn., Pusan, 1993—; pres. Korea Maritime U., 2000—. Author: (book) Law of the Collision at Sea, 1986, Maritime Law, 1991, Marine Insurance, 1995, Combined Bills of Lading, 1992. Lt. Korean Naval Res., 1959-63. Recipient Presdl. commendation Pres. of Korea, 1984. Mem. Maritime Policy and Mgmt./London (regional advisor 1990—), Korea Maritime U. and U.K. Univs. (coord. 1987). Avocations: classical music, touring. Office: Korea Maritime Univ, No 1 Dongsamdong Youngdoku, 600101 Pusan Korea

PARK, YOONDONG, research scientist; b. Seoul, Republic of Korea; s. Kwonsik Park and Bokie Eun; m. Heesook Yoon, Mar. 2, 1991; 1 child, Nicola. BS, Hanyang U., 1988; MS, U. So. Calif., 1997, PhD, 1999. With Nat. Indsl. Tech. Inst., Seoul, 1989-95, Small and Med. Bus. Adminstrn., Seoul, 1995-99; rsch. assoc. U. So. Calif., L.A., 1999-2000; rschr. scholar Carnegie Mellon U., Pitts., 1993. Short-Term fellow Korean Govt., 1993, Long-Term fellow, 1995-99. Mem. IEEE (sr., mem. editl. bd. 1998-99, assoc. editor 1999-2000), Soc. Neuroscience. Fax: 213-740-0343. Home: 1200 Dale Ave Apt 101 Mountain View CA 94040-3331 Office: U So Calif OHE 500, BME Los Angeles CA 90007

PARK, YOUNG TAEK, industrial engineering educator; b. Dae-gu, Korea, Mar. 7, 1956; s. Keun and Duree (Lim) P.; m. Haeja Kang, June 12, 1957; children: Moonjoo, Yejoo. BS in Indsl. Engring., Seoul Nat. U., 1979; MS in Indsl. Engring., Korea Advanced Inst. Sci./Tech, 1981, PhD in Indsl. Engring., 1986. Registered industrial engr.; profl. cons. Asst. prof. Sungkyun-kwan Univ., Seoul, 1985-89, assoc. prof., 1989-94, prof., 1994—; chair Seoul Q&I Forum, 1997—; dir. Ctr. for Quality and Innovation at Sung-Kyun-Kwan U., Seoul, 1998—, dean sch. syss. mgmt. engring., 1999—; chair The Rsch. Group for Quality in the Pub. Sector, Seoul, 1997—; mem. adv. com. Indsl. Advancement Adminstrn. of Korean Govt., Seoul, 1991-95, head of com. for Korea Nat. Quality award, 1995; advisory editor of Quality Circle, Korea Std. Assn., 1990-95; lectr. Korea Productivity Ctr., Seoul, 1995, Inst. Govt. Officer Edn., Seoul, 1995; hon. vis. prof. U. Manchester, Eng., 1996. Editor-in-chief: Jour. of Quality Mgmt./Korean Soc. for Quality Mgmt., 1993-95; contbr. articles to profl. jours. Rsch. grantee Daewoo Electronics, Ltd., Korea, 1988, Korea Xerox, Ltd., Korea, 1990. Fellow Korea Acad. of Quality; mem. Human Engring. Soc. of Korea, Korean Soc. Quality Mgmt., Korean Soc. for Prodn. Mgmt. Achievements include devel. of many theoretical frameworks bridging gaps between theory and practice such as integrated model of maintenance policy and inventory control, dimensions of product innovation, others. Office: Sung-kyun-kwan U/Dept Indsl Engring, 300 Cheon-cheon-dong, 440-746 Suwon Republic of Korea

PARK, YOUNG-KEY, social science educator; b. Seoul, Korea, Jan. 3, 1948; s. Chang-Soo Park and Hyun-Ok Park-Byun; m. Kye-Nam Choi, Feb. 22, 1980; children: Jun-Kwan, Won-Kwan. BA, Yonsei U., Seoul, 1974; PhD, Yonsei U., 1989; MS, East Carolina U., 1979. Prof. Han Nam U., Taejon, Korea, 1981—, chmn. dept. pub. adminstrn., 1986-88, dean Sch. Law and Politics, 1989-91; chair faculty coun. Han Nam U., Taejon, 1998-99; dir. Korean Studies Program, Han Nam U., 1994—, Inst. Social Sci., Taejon, 1991-92; rsch. fellow Taejon Devel. Corp., 1990—. Author: Administrative Ideology, 1990. Adv. mem. Chung-Nam Provincial Govt., Korea, 1992-93; mem. Nat. Unification Coun., Korea, 1991. Mem. Korean Assn. Pub. Adminstrn. (v.p. 2000), Y's Men Taejon Club. Avocation: tennis. Home: Apt 119-1301, Dunsandong Clover, Taejon 302-222, Republic of Korea Office: Han Nam U, Taejon 300-791, Republic of Korea

PARK, YOUNG-MOON, electrical engineering educator; b. Masan, Kyungsang, Korea, Jan. 10, 1933; s. Chung-Sun and Choong-Dong Park; m. Chung-Hee Cho, Feb. 28, 1959. BS, Seoul Nat. U., 1956, MS, 1959, PhD, 1971. V.p. Assn. Elec. Power Ind., Seoul, 1987-88; pres. Korean Inst. Elec. Engrs., Seoul, 1989-90, Korea Elec. Engring. & Sci. Rsch. Inst., Seoul, 1990-96; prof. elec. engring. Seoul Nat. U., 1978-98, prof. emeritus, 1998—; chmn. Elec. Power and Energy Award Com., Seoul, 1990—, Examination Bd. of Elec. Engrs. Lic., Seoul, 1991—; co-chmn. Internat. Symposium on Power Sys. of Internat. Fedn. Automatic Control, 1989, mem. power plants and sys. tech. com., 1995—; chmn. Internat. Conf. on Intelligent System to Application to Power Systems, 1997. Author: Optimal Operational Planning, 1991, Power System Generation Expansion Planning Using Maximum Principle and Analytical Production Cost Model, 1991, Modern Power System Engineering, 1982. Recipient Disting. Svc. medal Korea Assn. Elec. Ind., 1979, Presdl. Svc. medal for sci. promotion Republic of Korea, 1991, Disting. Prof. award Seoul Nat. U., 1993. Fellow IEEE (co-chmn. internat. conf. on power sys. tech. 1991), chmn. elec. power and energy award com. 1990); mem. Korea Acad. Sci. and Tech. Avocation: travel. Home: 104-1502 Dae-Rim Apt, Dae-Bang-dong Tong-Jak-ku, 156-020 Seoul Republic of Korea Office: Seoul Nat U Sch Elec Engr, San 56-1 Sinlim-dong, 151-742 Seoul Republic of Korea

PARK, YOUNG-SUK, hospital equipment company executive; b. Bucheon, Republic of Korea, Sept. 13, 1941; s. Yong-Jae Park and Sung-Hee Hong; m. Eun-Young Jang, June 2, 1973; children: bo-Kyung, Chang-Won. BS, Seoul Nat. U., 1964. Mng. dir. Sang Chung Comml. Co. Ltd., Seoul, 1967-75; pres. Cho Sun Instrument Co., Seoul, 1975—; comml attaché U.S. Embassy, Seoul, 1976. Supt. Wallace Meml. Presbyn. Hosp., Busan, 1993. Mem. Lions (bd. dirs. 1990-98). Avocations: walking, singing, conversation. Home: #61-704 Hyundai Apt, Apgujeong-dong Kangnam-Gu, 135-111 Seoul Republic of Korea Office: Cho Sun Instrument Co, 151-11 Ssang Lim-Dong Joong-Gu, 100-400 Seoul Republic of Korea

PÁRKÁNYI, LÁSZLÓ, crystallographer, researcher; b. Budapest, Hungary, July 5, 1940; s. László Sr. and Margit (Gesztesy) P.; m. Ágnes Ladár, June 25, 1970; children: Balázs, Péter. Diploma in Chem. Engring., U. Tech. Budapest (Hungary), 1969, PhD, 1975, Prof. Chemistry, 1987; DSc, Hungarian Academy Sci., 1992. Chem. engr. Lectr. U. Tech. Budapest (Hungary), 1969-74; rsch. fellow Ctrl. Inst. Chemistry Hungarian Acad. Scis., Budapest, 1974-75, head rsch. group, 1975—. Avocations: computers, programming, fine arts, music, literature. Home: Vas u 5, H-1088 Budapest Hungary Office: Chem Rsch Inst Chemistry, Pusztaszeri ut 59/67, 1025 Budapest Hungary

PARKASH, WADIA VIKRAM, hotel facility executive, consultant; b. Shilong, Assam, India, Feb. 7, 1950; s. Ved and Lily (Shunbo) P.; m. Gurpreet Gill, Mar. 9, 1980; children: Karan, Varun. BA, Nowrosjee Western Coll., Pune, India, 1972; diploma in hotel mgmt., Oberoi Sch. of Hotel Mgmt., Delhi, India. Cert. hotel mgmt. Res. mgr. Oberoi hotels, Dammam, Saudi Arabia, 1987-90; gen. mgr. Oberoi hotels, Kuwait City, Kuwait, 1990, Hyderabad, India, 1990-94; gen. mgr. Ascott Internat., Jakarta, Indonesia, 1994-95; dir. Dharmala, Jakarta, Indonesia, 1995-96, Surabaya, Indonesia, 1996-97; dir. Oberol Sch. of Hotel Mgmt., Delhi, India, 1983-87; cons. Assn. Profl. Caterers, Hyderabad, India, 1993-96. Mem. SKAL (bd. dirs. 1993-96), Hoteliers Assn. Andhra Pardesh (v.p. 1992-93, pres. 1993-94). Home: C-220 Defence Colony, New Delhi 110024, India

PARKE, JOHN SHEPARD, marketing consultant; b. N.Y.C., Nov. 11, 1933; s. John S. and Dorothy (Simpson) P.; m. Mary J. Lundy, Aug. 20, 1955; children: John Shepard III, Suzanne Lundy. AB, Dartmouth Coll., 1956; MBA, Amos Tuck Sch., 1957. Sales mgr. Procter & Gamble Co., Cin., 1960, advt. mgr., 1961-69; mktg. dir. Ralston Purina Co., St. Louis, 1969-74, v.p. mktg., 1974-79; v.p. mktg. and sales Bausch & Lomb, Rochester, N.Y., 1979-81; founder, pres. PPI Mktg. Group, Rochester, 1982—. Mem. trustees coun. Rochester Inst. Tech.; bd. dirs. Episcopal Ch. Home, Rochester, Meml. Arts Gallery of U. of Rochester. Capt. USAF, 1957-60. Mem. Genesse Valley Club (Rochester), U.S. Tennis Assn. (chair umpire). Republican. Epsicopalian. Avocations: tennis, squash. Home and Office: 215 Ambassador Dr Rochester NY 14610-3404

PARKE, PAULA MARIE, nurse; b. Dorchester, Mass., Sept. 21, 1959; d. Robert Daniel and Carol Ann (Young) McEachern; m. Carlton William Parke, Aug. 7, 1982; children: Stefanie J., Caitlin M. Diploma, N.E. Deaconess Hosp., 1980; postgrad., St. Joseph's Coll., 1995-97, Regents Coll., 1998—. RN, N.H.; cert. Profl. Utilization Rev., Med. Surg. Nurse. Staff nurse Hampstead (N.H.) Hosp., 1981-85, supr., 1985-87; staff nurse Exeter (N.H.) Hosp., 1987-92; nurse reviewer Alicare Med. Mgmt., Inc., Salem, N.H., 1992-94, team leader, 1994-96, mgr., 1996-98; account mgr., cons. Interqual Products Group, Marlborough, Mass., 1998-2000; case mgr. Parkland Med. Ctr., Derry, N.H., 2000—. Mem. ANA, NAFE, Am. Assn. Managed Care Nurses, N.H. Nurses Assn. Avocations: sewing, community involvement, hiking. Home: 15 Blueberry Cir Hampstead NH 03841-2064

PARKER, ALAN WILLIAM, film director, writer; b. London, Feb. 14, 1944; s. William Leslie and Elsie Ellen P.; m. Annie Inglis, July 30, 1966; children: Lucy Kate, Alexander James, Jake William, Nathan Charles. Student Brit. schs. Advt. copywriter, 1966-69, dir. TV commls. Author: screenplay Melody, 1968; novel Bugsy Malone, 1975, Puddles in the Lane, 1977; author, dir.: No Hard Feelings, 1972, Our Cissy, 1973, Footsteps, 1973, Bugsy Malone, 1975 (5 Brit. Acad. awards), Come See the Paradise, 1990; dir.: The Evacuees (Brit. Acad. award, Internat. Emmy award, Press Guild U.K. award), Midnight Express (6 Golden Globe awards, 3 Brit. Acad. awards, 2 Oscar awards), Fame, 1980 (Brit. Acad. award, Golden Globe award, 2 Oscar awards), Shoot the Moon, 1982, Pink Floyd-The Wall, 1982, Birdy, 1984 (Grand Prix Spl. du Jury, Cannes Film Festival), A Turnip Head's Guide to the British Cinema, 1986 (British Press Guild award), Angel Heart, 1987, Mississippi Burning, 1988 (Oscar award), The Commitments, 1991 (4 BAFTA awards), The Road to Wellville, 1994, Evita, 1996 (3 Golden Globe awards), Angela's Ashes, 1999. Recipient 4 Brit. Acad. awards. Mem. Brit. Acad. Film and TV Arts, Brit. Film Inst. (chmn. 1997-99, chmn. film coun. 1999—), Dirs. Guild Am., Writers Guild G.B., Writers Guild Am., Dirs. Guild G.B., Acad. Motion Pictures Arts and Scis. Office: care Michael Wimer Creative Artists Agy 9830 Wilshire Blvd Beverly Hills CA 90212-1804

PARKER, ANDREW JAMES, physiologist, researcher, writer; b. Sheffield, Yorkshire, Eng., Dec. 24, 1950; s. Thomas Andrew and Irene (Lister) P.; m. Hilary Mary Barker, July 16, 1977; children: Eleanor Mary, Katherine Anne. BSc, Huddersfield U., 1978; MPhil, Sheffield U., 1989. Dir. Seaquariums (North) Ltd., Sheffield, 1969-71; rsch. asst. in zoology Sheffield U., 1971-75, rsch. worker in physiology, 1975-93, rschr. in biomed. sci., 1993—; cons. editor Sheffield U. Biomed. Info. Svc., 1978-89, Sheffield Acad. Press, 1989-96. Contbr. articles to profl. jours. including Jour. Physiology, Jour. Physiology and Behavior, Gut, European Jour. Pharmacology, Neuropeptides, Med. Sci. Rsch., and Exptl. Physiology. Social sec. Inland Waterways Assn., Sheffield, 1978-83; steward Meth. Ch., Sheffield, 1990—. Mem. Inst. Biology. Mem. Liberal Dem. Party. Avocations: walking, painting, inland waterways, classic cars. Office: Sheffield U Dept Biomed Sci, Alfred Denny Bldg, Sheffield S10 2TN, England

PARKER, ANDREW RICHARD, biologist; b. Wolverhampton, W Midlands, Eng., Oct. 28, 1967; arrived in Australia, 1993; s. Leslie Roy and Irene May (Creed) P. BSc (hons), John Moore's U., Liverpool, Eng., 1990; PhD, MacQuarie U., Sydney, Australia, 1996. Postdoctoral fellow Australian Mus., Sydney, 1996-99; assoc. physics U. Sydney, 1998—; lectr. zoology U. Reading, Eng., 1999; Royal Soc. rsch. fellow U. Oxford, Eng., 1999—; fellow Somerville Coll., Oxford, 2000—; cons. in environ. sci., Solihull M.B. Coun., Birmingham, Eng., 1991-92; speaker Australian Inst. Physics, 1997, Sydney TV, 1997, 98, 99; invited chmn. Internat. Optics Conf., 1998, 2000; lectr. in field. Selected to present Royal Inst. Lectr., 2000, London; contbr. numerous articles to internat. sci. jours.; inventor in field. Recipient Mus. award Australian Mus. Trust, 1993, Smithsonian Instn. award, Washington, 1995, Rsch. fellowship, Australian Mus., 1996. Achievements include discovery of antireflector now used on solar panels; discovery of light switch theory of evolution. Avocations: art, scuba diving and other sports, music. Office: U Oxford Dept Zoology, South Parks Rd, Oxford OX1 3PS, England

PARKER, DALLAS ROBERT, lawyer; b. Houston, Oct. 16, 1947; s. Richard Henry and Rosemary (McMillan) P.; m. Ingrid Elayne Thompson, July 1, 1972; children: Dallas Robert Jr., Nicholas Mattsson. BA, Vanderbilt U., 1969; JD, U. Tex., 1972. Bar: Tex. 1972. Assoc. Fulbright & Jaworski, Houston, 1972-79, ptnr., 1979-82; ptnr. Brown Parker & Leahy, Houston, 1982-99, Thomson, Knight, Brown, Parker & Leahy, LLP, Houston, 1999—; dir. Amigos de las Americas. Editor U. Tex. Law Rev., 1971. Dir. Odyssey House, Tex., Amigos de las Americas; adv. dir., chair adv. bd. Houston Tech. Ctr. Named to Chancellors U. Tex. Fellow Houston Bar Found., Tex. Bar Found.; mem. ABA, Tex. Bar Assn., Houston Bar Assn. Office: Brown Parker & Leahy LLP 3600 Two Allen Ctr Houston TX 77002

PARKER, DAVID, chemistry educator; b. Consett, Durham, Eng., July 30, 1956; s. Joseph William and Mary (Hill) P.; m. Fiona Mary MacEwan, July 27, 1979; children: Eleanor, Julia Rose, Philip. BA, Oxford (Eng.) U., 1978, D. Philosophy, 1980. NATO fellow U. Louis Pasteur de Strasbourg (France), 1980-81; univ. lectr. U. Durham (Eng.), 1982-89, sr. lectr., 1989-92, prof., 1992—; cons. Celltech Chiroscience, Slouth, U.K., 1985—, Guerbet S.A., Paris, 1992—. Contbr. numerous articles to profl. jours.; patentee in field. Recipient Rsch. prize in organic chemistry Imperial Chem. Industries, 1991, Inaugural awad in supramolecular tech. IBC, 2000; sr. rsch. fellow Royal Soc. Leverhulme Trust, 1999. Fellow Royal Soc. Chemistry (Interdisciplinary award 1996, Corday-Morgan medal and prize 1987, Hickinbottom fellow 1988, 89); mem. Am. Chem. Soc. Avocations: cricket, soccer, golf. Office: U Durham Dept Chemistry, South Rd, Durham DH1 3LE, England

PARKER, DIANA LYNNE, restaurant manager, special events director; b. Eureka, Calif., June 21, 1957; d. Carol Dean and Lynne Diane (Havemann) P. BA in English, Humboldt U., 1981, postgrad., 1982-84. Lic. real estate agent, Calif. Retail clk. Safeway, Inc., Eureka, 1977-84; caterer, owner TD Catering, Eureka, 1982-84; asst. buyer Macy's Calif., San Francisco, 1984-85; realtor Mason-McDuffie, Alameda, Calif., 1985-87; host, rotunda Neiman Marcus, San Francisco, 1987-89, asst. mgr., rotunda, 1989—, dir. spl. events, 1989—. Mem. Mus. Modern Art, Calif. Restaurant Assn., San Francisco Visitor and Conv. Bur., Common Wealth Club Calif. Republican. Avocations: gourmet chef, artist, antique collecting. Office: Rotunda at Neiman Marcus 150 Stockton St San Francisco CA 94108-5807

PARKER, ELLIS JACKSON, III, lawyer, broadcaster; b. Haleyville, Ala., Oct. 2, 1932; s. Ellis J. and Elizabeth (Funderburg) P.; m. Nancy Elizabeth Bealer; children: Francis Hill, Ellis Stuart. Student, U.S. Mil. Acad., West Point, N.Y., 1953-57; AB, U. Ala., 1958, LLB, 1960, JD, 1961; diploma, Droit Compare, Luxembourg, 1959; cert., Acad. Internat. Law, Hague, The Netherlands, 1960. Bar: Ala. 1960, U.S. Tax Ct. 1960, D.C. Ct. Appeals 1972, U.S. Supreme Ct. 1966, U.S. Ct. Appeals D.C. 1972, Md. Ct. Appeals 1973, U.S. Ct. Claims, 1977. Legis. atty. IRS, Washington, 1961-62; chief of staff to U.S. Congressman Grant Ala., 1963-64; pvt. practice Birmingham, Ala., 1964-84; spl. advisor to Pres. Richard Nixon White House, Washington, 1968-69; v.p., counsel Birmingham Broadcasting Co., 1964-83; ptnr. Taylor, Smith & Parker Law Office, Upper Marlboro, Md., 1970-86; prin., owner Ellis J. Parker, Law Office, Washington, 1986—; v.p., sec. Construction Components Corp., Upper Marlboro, Md., 1968-72; pres. Washington-Ala. News Reports, Washington, 1980—; pres. Sta. WNPT-AM-FM, Tuscaloosa, Ala.; v.p. Sta. WLPH, Birmingham, Parker Real Estate, Birmingham, N.B. Devel. Co., Washington; chmn. bd. Blackbelt Broadcasting Co., Selma, Ala.; founding mem. Women's Nat. Bank, Washington; CEO Birmingham Broadcasting Co.; ptnr. Linden Radio Joint Venture, Faunsdale, Ala.; v.p., bd. dirs. Hartford E. Bealer Devel. Corp., H.E. Bealer Properties, Washington; bd. dirs. 17th St L.L.C., Bealer-Parker, LLC, Washington. Mem. Presdl. Inaugural Com., inaugural protocol officer V.p. Agnew, 1968; mem. steering com. Rep. Party, Balt., 1972; chmn. bd. trustees Prince George's Hist. and Cultural Trust, Upper Marlboro, 1974, Hartford E. Bealer Found., Hamshire County, W.Va., 2000—; chmn. bd. advisors Prince George's Equestrian Ctr., Upper Marlboro, 1980; founder, pres. bd. dirs. Hospice of Prince George's County, Upper Marlboro, 1982; mem. Upper Marlboro Devel. Com. Mem. IEEE, ABA, FCC Bar Assn., Fed. Bar Assn., Inter-Am. Bar Assn., Ala. Bar Assn., Md. Bar Assn., Nat. Assn. Broadcasters Ala. Broadcasters Assn., Balt. Coun. Fgn. Affairs, Assn. Grads. U.S. Mil. Acad., Chevy Chase Club, Md. Club, St. Andrews Soc., Met. Club, Ala. Alumni Assn., Scabbard and Blade (chmn. nat. alumni coun.), Pi Kappa Alpha, Sigma Delta Kappa. Home: 9220 Cranford Dr Potomac MD 20854-2229 also: 306 Edgewater House Bethany Beach DE 19930-8013 also: 15227 Old Marlboro Pike Upper Marlboro MD 20772

PARKER, HAROLD TALBOT, history educator; b. Cin., Dec. 26, 1907; s. Samuel Chester and Lucile (Jones) P.; m. Louise Salley, July 9, 1980. PhB, U. Chgo., 1928, PhD, 1934; postgrad., Cornell U., 1929-30. Mem. faculty Duke U., Durham, N.C., 1939—, assoc. prof., 1950-57, prof. history, 1957-77, emeritus, 1977—; adj. prof. U. Ala., Huntsville, 1978-81; faculty U. N.C., Chapel Hill, 1984. Author: The Cult of Antiquity and the French Revolutionaries, 1937, Three Napoleonic Battles, 1944, 83, (with Marvin Brown) Major Themes in Modern European History, 3 vols., 1974, Bureau of Commerce in 1781, 1979, An Administrative Bureau During the Old Regime, 1993, History of St. Philip's Episcopal Church (Durham, N.C.) 1978-1994, 1997, Sermons From St. Philips, 1912-1994, 2000; editor: (with Richard Herr) Ideas in History, 1965, Problems in European History, 1979, (with Georg Iggers) International Handbook of Historical Studies, 1979, Theory and Social History, 1980, (with L.S. Parker) Proc. Consortium of Revolutionary Europe, 1981, 84, 85, 86; assoc. editor Historical Dictionary of Napoleonic France, 1985; regional editor, contbg. author: Great Historians of the Modern Age, 1991; contbr. articles to profl. jours. With USAAF, 1942-45. Recipient Disting. Svc. award Consortium on Revolutionary Europe, 1993, Disting Svc. award So. Hist. Assn. European History Sect., 1993. Mem. Soc. for French Hist. Studies (pres. 1957, Disting. Svc. award 1989), AAUP (pres. Duke U. chpt. 1960), Phi Beta Kappa (pres. Duke chpt. 1961). Episcopalian. Home: 137 Still Hopes Dr West Columbia SC 29169-7151

PARKER, HENRY GRIFFITH, III, insurance executive; b. Plainfield, N.J., Oct. 27, 1926; s. Henry Griffith and Ruth Martin (Van Auken) P.; m. Audrey Lansing Turner, May 11, 1957; children: Henry Griffith, IV, Elizabeth Wright. AB, Princeton U., 1948; postgrad., U. Pa. Sch. Law. With Chubb & Son, Inc., 1949-97, v.p., 1968-70, sr. v.p., dir., 1971-92, mng. dir., 1986-92; cons. to chmn., 1992-97; v.p. Fed. Ins. Co., 1966-73, sr. v.p., 1973-91; v.p. Vigilant Ins. Co., 1966-91, mgr. internat. div., 1967-84; chmn. Parker Assocs., Madison, N.J., 1997—; adv. bd. Firemark Global Ins. Fund II, L.P., 1997—, bd. dirs. Alliance Assurance Co. Am., N.Y.C., Sun Ins. Office Am. Inc., N.Y.C.; mem. industry sector adv. com. on svcs. U.S. Dept. Commerce, Washington; bd. dirs. Nat. Fgn. Trade Coun., chmn. declarations com., 1974-81, chmn. ins. com., 1976-81; chmn. internat. policy com. U.S. C. of C., 1970-73; chmn. U.S. del. XII-XIII-XX-XXII-XXII Hemispheric Ins. Conf., Chile, 1969, Paraguay, 1987, Panama, 1985, Buenos Aires, 1989; chmn. Internat. Ins. Adv. Coun., Washington, 1970-73, 85-90, chmn. Internat. Com. Am. Ins. Assn., 1991-93; mem. N.J. Commn. on Internat. Trade, 1986—; chmn. bus. adv. com. bus. coun. UN, 1988—; mem. adv. bd. Liaison Office Peoples Ins. Co. China, 1986-94. Appeared on numerous TV and radio programs; contbr. articles to profl. jours. Chmn. bd. Overlook Hosp., Summit, N.J., 1973-80; trustee Drew U., Madison, 1974—. Lt. (j.g.) USNR, 1944-46. Recipient Internat. Ins. award U.S. C. of C., 1981, Disting. Service award Internat. Ins. Council, 1988. Mem. Nat. Assn. Ins. Commrs. (chmn. internat. adv. com.), Am. Ins. Assn. (chmn. internat. com.), Psi Upsilon. Republican. Episcopalian. Clubs: Downtown Assn. (N.Y.C.), Princeton (N.Y.C.), River (N.Y.C.); Devon Yacht, Morris County (N.J.) Golf. Office: Parker Assocs 38 East Ln Madison NJ 07940-2652

PARKER, JAMES ROGER, chemist; b. L.A., July 19, 1936. BS, Pomona Coll., 1958; PhD, Iowa State U., 1964. Lab. asst. Ames (Iowa) Lab Atomic Energy Commn., 1958-64; analytical supr. PPG Industries, Natrium, W.Va., 1964-73, Corpus Christi, Tex., 1973-82; agrl. chemist PPG Industries, Barberton, Ohio, 1982-89; infrared spectroscopist PPG Industries, Monroeville, Pa., 1989-96, scientist, 1996—. Contbr. articles to profl. jours. Mem. Am. Chem. Soc., Soc. for Applied Spectroscopy, Spectroscopy Soc. Pitts., Soc. for Analytical Chemists Pitts., Phi Lambda Upsilon. Achievements include research in analytical chemistry of metal halides, iodine compounds, alkali metal oxides, coordination chemistry of phosphine oxides, qualitative identifications with proton magnetic resonance spectroscopy and polymer analyses with photoacoustic infrared spectroscopy. Office: PPG Industries 440 College Park Dr Monroeville PA 15146-1553

PARKER, JEFFREY SCOTT, law educator, university official; b. Alexandria, Va., Sept. 6, 1952; s. Clarence Franklin and Mary Florence (Partlow) P. B in Indsl. Engring., Ga. Inst. Tech., 1975; JD, U. Va., 1978. Bar: N.Y. 1979, U.S. Dist. Ct. (ea. and so. dists.) N.Y. 1979, U.S. Ct. Appeals (3d cir.) 1981, U.S. Ct. Appeals (2d cir.) 1984, U.S. Supreme Ct. 1984, U.S. Ct. Appeals (fed. cir.) 1985, U.S. Ct. Appeals (4th cir.) 1992, U.S. Ct. Appeals (D.C. cir.) 1997. Assoc. Sullivan & Cromwell, N.Y.C., 1978-86, Sacks Montgomery, N.Y.C., 1986-87; dep. chief counsel U.S. Sentencing Commn., Washington, 1987-88; of counsel Sacks Montgomery, N.Y.C., 1988-90; assoc. prof. of law George Mason U., Arlington, Va., 1990-94; prof. law, assoc. dean acad. affairs George Mason U. Sch. Law, 1994-96, prof. law, 1996—; cons. counsel U.S. Sentencing Commn., Washington, 1988-89. Contbr. articles to law revs.; mem. editorial bd. Va. Law Rev., 1976-78. Mem. ABA, Assn. of Bar of City of N.Y., N.Y. State Bar Assn., Am. Law and Econs. Assn., Am. Econs. Assn., Am. Judicature Soc. Office: George Mason U Sch of Law 3401 Fairfax Dr Arlington VA 22201-4411

PARKER, JIM (JAMES MAVIN PARKER), composer; b. Hartlepool, Eng., Dec. 18, 1934; s. James Robertson and Margaret (Mavin) P.; m. Pauline Ann George, Aug. 2, 1969; children: Claire, Amy; 1 child from previous marriage, Louise. Assoc., Guildhall Sch. of Music, London, 1959; lic., Royal Acad. Music, London, 1959. Oboist City of Birmingham (U.K.) Symphony Orch., 1960-61; oboe tutor Middlesex (U.K.) U., 1963-83; oboist, composer The Barrow Poets, London, 1963-93; freelance composer, condr. London, 1974—; bd. dirs. Rothko Ltd., London. Composer musicals (books and lyrics with Wally K. Daly) Follow the Star, 1975, Make Me a World, 1976 (with Jeremy Lloyd) The Woodland Gospels, 1984; composer chamber music for brass ensemble, wind quintet, brass quintet Clarinet Concerto TV series House of Cards, 1990 (Brit. Acad. Film and TV Arts nomination), House of Eliott, 1990-93, Soldier Soldier, 1990-94, Body and Soul, 1993, Goggle Eyes, 1993, To Play the King, 1994 (best original TV music award Brit. Acad. Film and TV Arts), The Final Cut, 1995, Moll Flanders, 1996 (Best Original TV Music award 1996), Tom Jones, 1997 (Best Original TV Music Brit Acad. award 1997), A Rather English Marriage, 1998 (Best Original TV Music Brit Acad. award 1998), also others. Avocations: art, literature. Home: 19 Laurel Rd, London SW13 0EE, England

PARKER, JOHN HENRY, building society executive; b. Cheltenham, Eng., May 10, 1949; s. Stephen John and Olive Maureen (Wiltshire) P.; m. Rosemary Parker; children: Emily Louise, Jessica Lucy, Natalie Catherine. MA, Cambridge (Eng.) U., 1971. Chief internal auditor Chelsea (Eng.) Bldg. Soc., 1975-78; fgn. exch. mgr. Burmah Oil, Swindon, Eng., 1979-81; chief acct. Burmah Oil Exploration, Swindon, Eng., 1982-84; chief acct. Stroud and Swindon Bldg. Soc., Stroud, Eng., 1984-89, mng. dir., 1989-94, CEO, 1994-99; dir. Pemberstone PLC, Worcester, Eng., 1995. Chmn. Stroud (Eng.) H.S., 1990-95. Fellow Inst. Chartered Accts. (panel on bldg. socs.); mem. Inst. Bankers (assoc.), Bldg. Socs. Assn. (new legis. working group). Avocations: skiing, cricket, golf, gardening, reading. Office: Stroud and Swindon Bldg Soc, Rowcroft, Stroud GL5 3BG, England

PARKER, JOHN MELVYN, materials engineering educator; b. Louth, Eng., Aug. 23, 1946; s. Robert and Eva (Blackbourn) P.; m. Mary Elizabeth Hopkins, Jan. 4, 1975; children: Claire, Rachel. MA, Cambridge U., 1967, PhD, 1970. Chartered engr. Postdoctoral fellow Cambridge U., England, 1970-72; from lectr. to sr. lectr. to reader dept. engring. materials Sheffield U., England, 1972—; vis. scientist Physik Inst. U. Zurich, 1971. Author: Stones and Cord in Glass, 1980; co-author: Flouride Glass Optical Fibres, 1990; co-author, editor: High Performance Glasses, 1991; co-editor: The Structure of Non-Crystalline Materials, 1983. Fellow Soc. Glass Technology, Inst. Materials. Office: U Sheffield Dept Engring Materials, Mappin St, Sheffield SI 3JD, England

PARKER, JOSEPH MAYON, printing and publishing executive; b. Washington, N.C., Oct. 11, 1931; s. James Mayon and Mildred (Poe) P.; m. Lauretta Owen Dyer, Mar. 23, 1957; children: Katherine Suzanne, Joseph Wilbur. Student, Davidson Coll., 1949-51; BA, U. N.C., 1953, MPA, 1992; postgrad., Carnegie Inst. Tech., 1955-56. Mgr. print div. Parker Bros., Inc., Ahoskie, N.C., 1956-71, chief editorialist, 1961-77, gen. mgr., 1971-77, pres., chief exec. officer, 1977—; dir. Governor's Hwy. Safety Program, 1993—; treas. Chowan Graphic Arts Found., Murfreesboro, N.C., 1971-90, pres. 1990-92. Editor, columnist five community newspapers, N.C.; panelist: (TV talk show) North Carolina This Week, 1986-89. Mem. Ind. Devel. Commn., 1974-86; vice chmn. N.C. Goals and Policy Bd., Raleigh, 1977-84; trustee Pitt County Meml. Hosp., 1980-88; pres. Com. of 100, Winton, N.C., 1984-87; chmn. Northeastern N.C. Tomorrow, Elizabeth City, 1981-84, sec., 1984-90; del. Dem. Nat. Conv., N.Y.C., 1980, platform com., 1988; dist. chmn. N.C. Dem. Ctrl. Com., 1980-82. With U.S. Army, 1953-54, col. USAR, 1954-88. Mem. Soc. Profl. Journalists, East N.C. Press Assn. (past pres.), N.C. Press Assn., Nat. Newspaper Assn. (state chmn. 1976-83), Roanoke Island Hist. Assn. (vice-chmn. 1987-89), Ea. C. of C. (past chmn.), Rotary, Raleigh Exec. Club. Democrat. Methodist. Avocations: golf, reading. Home: 4500 Connell Dr Raleigh NC 27612-5600 Office: 215 E Lane St Raleigh NC 27601-1035

PARKER, LEE DAVID, accounting and management educator, researcher, consultant; b. Berri, Australia, Mar. 18; s. Edward Jarvis James and Mavis Beatrice (Twining) P.; m. Susanne Dorothy Townley, Jan. 8, 1972 (dec. May 1991); children: Karen Claire, Jay Justin, Rhys Barclay; m. Gloria June Bonnett, May 18, 1992. B of Econ., U. Adelaide, Australia, 1970; MPhil, Dundee (Scotland) U., 1976; PhD, Monash U., Melbourne, Australia, 1983. Lectr. in acctg. Glasgow (Scotland) U., 1973-74, Dundee U., 1974-76; sr. lectr. in acctg. Monash U., 1976-85; prof. acctg. Griffith U., Brisbane, Australia, 1985-88; prof. acctg., fin. and mgmt. Flinders U., Adelaide, 1988-96; prof. commerce U. Adelaide, 1997—; vis. prof. Case Western Res. U., Cleve., 1984, U. Calif., Berkeley, 1984, U. Ala., Tuscaloosa, 1993, Manchester (U.K.) Bus. Sch., 1996. Author: Developing Control Concepts in the 20th Century, 1986; co-author: Accounting for the Human Factor, 1989; editor: Financial Reporting to Employees: From Past to Present, 1989; co-editor: The Public Sector: Contemporary Readings in Accounting and Auditing, 1990; contbr. numerous articles to rsch. and profl. jours. Recipient Walter Taplin prize Brit. Acctg. Assn., 1979, Rsch. grant Australian Rsch. Coun., 1990, Editor of Yr. award MCB Univ. Press, U.K., 1995, Ctr. of Excellence Rsch. grant Australian soc. CPAs, 1995. Fellow Inst. Chartered Accts. Australia, CPA Australia (divsn. councillor 1997—), Australian Inst. Mgmt. (divsn. bd. mem. 1996—), Ctr. for Social and Environ. Acctg. Rsch.; mem. Am. Acctg. Assn. (pres. pub. interest sect. 1998-2000), Acad. Acctg. Historians (trustee, pres. 1991), Australia Singapore Bus. Coun. (exe. com. 1995-97). Avocations: tennis, archery, tapestry, singing, antiquarian book collecting. Home: 651 Greenhill Rd Burnside, 5066 Adelaide Australia Office: Univ Adelaide, Sch of Commerce, 5005 Adelaide Australia

PARKER, M. IQBAL, biochemistry educator, health facility administrator; b. Cape Town, S. Africa, Oct. 20, 1952; s. Kamaludien and Halima Parker; m. Amina Mowzer, Aug. 8, 1976; children: Imran, Tasneem. BSc, U. Cape Town, 1974, BSc with honors, 1975, PhD, 1979. Assoc. prof. U. Cape Town, 1989-96, dir. Med. Rsch. Ctr., 1997—, chair, prof., 1998—. Chmn. St. Luke's Hospice, Cape Town, 1998. Mem. Acad. Sci. S. Africa, S. African Biochem. Soc. (pres. 1997—). Office: U Cape Town, Dept Med Biochemistry, Observatory 7925, South Africa

PARKER, MICHAEL SETH, energy engineer; b. Norwich, Conn., Jan. 30, 1964; s. Truman Kelly and Loretta (Hebert) P.; m. Cynthia Lynn Beck, May 23, 1998. BS in Mech. Engring., U. Hartford, 1986; MBA in Mgmt., U. N.Mex., 1999. Profl. engr., Ariz., Conn., N.Mex., Nev. Metal fabricator Crown Mfg. Corp., Waterford, Conn., 1980-86; project engr. Savage Engring., Inc., Bloomfield, Conn., 1986-94, Fletcher Thompson, Inc., Bridgeport, Conn., 1994-95; lead energy engr. Johnson Controls, Inc., Albuquerque, 1995—. Mem. ASHRAE, Assn. Energy Engrs. (sr.; cert. energy mgr., cert. demand side mgmt. profl., regional v.p. 2000—, cert. lighting profl., Internat. Energy Engr. of Yr. 1998, Western Regional Energy Engr. of Yr. 1997), Beta Gamma Sigma. Republican. Avocations: downhill skiing, Harley Davidsons, travel, guitar. Fax: 505-248-1929. E-mail: michael.s.parker@jci.com. Office: Johnson Controls Inc 3840 Commons Ave NE Albuquerque NM 87109-5831

PARKER, PETER JOSEPH JACQUES, medical researcher; b. London, Sept. 30, 1954; s. Philip Joseph Jacques and Phyllis Joyce Eileen (Aarons) P.; m. Jennifer Jean Jacques Cave, Dec. 31, 1976; 1 child, Joseph Philip Jacques. BSc in Biochemistry, Oxford (Eng.) U., 1976, PhD in Clin. Biochemistry, 1979. Postgrad. rschr. Med. Rsch. Coun., Dundee, Scotland, 1979-81; postgrad. rschr. Imperial Cancer Rsch. Fund, London, 1981-83, lab. head, 1983-85, prin. scientist, 1990—; lab. head Ludwig Inst. for Cancer Rsch., London, 1985-90; hon. prof. UCL, London, 1997—. Author: Molecular Biology of Oncogenes, 1990; chmn. editl. bd. The Biochem. Jour.; contbr. over 200 articles and reviews to profl. publs.; patentee delivery of radioisotopes, 1988. Mem. Biochem. Soc., Brit. Soc. Cell Biology, Am. Soc. for Biochemistry and Molecular Biology. Office: Imperial Cancer Rsch Fund, Woodlands Abinger Bottom, Abinger Common Dorking, England RHS 6JN

PARKER, RICHARD WILSON, lawyer, rail transporation executive; b. Cleve., June 14, 1943; s. Edgar Gael and Pauline (Wilson) P.; m. Helen Margaret Shober, Jan. 3, 1998; children from previous marriage: Brian Jeffrey, Lauren Michelle, Lisa Christine. BA in Econs. cum laude, U. Redlands, 1965; JD cum laude, Northwestern U., 1968. Bar: Ohio 1968, Va. 1974. Assoc. Arter & Hadden, Cleve., 1968-71; asst. gen. atty. Norfolk & Western Ry. Co., Cleve. and Roanoke, Va., 1971-74; asst. gen. solicitor Norfolk & Western Ry. Co., Roanoke, 1974-78, gen. atty., 1978-84; gen. atty. Norfolk So. Corp., 1985-88, sr. gen. atty., 1988-93, asst. v.p. real estate, 1993-99, v.p. properties, 1999-2000, v.p. real estate, 2000—. Mem. ABA, Va. State Bar, Va. Bar Assn., Norfolk-Portsmouth Bar Assn. Presbyterian. Office: 3 Commercial Pl Norfolk VA 23510-2108

PARKER, ROBERT, hospital administrator; b. Guildford, Surrey, Eng., Feb. 7, 1950; s. James Robert and Winifred (McLeish) P.; m. Janis Irene Linford, Feb. 11, 1989; 1 child, Lucy Mirtha. BSc, Univ. Coll. London, 1971; MSc, Brunel U., Uxbridge, Eng., 1974. Rsch. cell biologist Nat. Heart Hosp., London, 1971-76, head homograft dept., 1981-90; rsch. oncologist MRC Cyclotron Unit, London, 1976-81; heart valve bank mgr. Royal Brompton and Marefield NHS Trust, London, 1991—; chmn. Brit. Heart Valve Banks, London, 1993-95. Author: Cardiac Valve Allograft Update, 1996, Medico-Legal Perspectives in Health Care, 1996. Chmn. So. Region Youth Hostels, Salisbury, 1984-89. Mem. Brit. Assn. Tissue Banks (gen. sec.

1995-97, v.p. 1999—), European Assn. Tissue Banks (2nd gen. sec. 1999—). Ch. of Eng. Avocations: walking, swimming, sub-aqua. Office: Royal Brompton Hosp, Sydney St, London SW3 6NP, England

PARKER, ROBERT CHAUNCEY HUMPHREY, clergyman, publishing executive, psychic; b. N.Y.C., Apr. 6, 1941; s. Robert Humphrey and Edith Louise (Corya) P. Student, U. Va., 1960-61, 62-63; diploma, Inst. Psychorientology, Laredo, Tex., 1973. Ordained to ministry Ch. of Antioch-Malabar Rite, 1975. Law clk. Shearman & Sterling, N.Y.C., 1961-62; owner Parker's Pronto-Pups Inc., N.Y.C., 1962-64; asst. to pres. U.S. Packaging, N.Y.C., 1964-66; asst. nat. sales mgr. Elliott Svc. Co. Inc., Mt. Vernon, N.Y., 1966-67; pres., cons. Lenfield Assocs. & Cons., N.Y.C. and Washington, 1967-71; founder, pres. Occult Comm. Corp., N.Y.C., Washington, and Danbury, Conn., 1971-76, New Awareness Corp., London and Mpls., 1973-81; dir., resident minister The Healing Ctr. at St. Patricia's, Inver Grove Heights, Minn., 1975; lectr., minister Ch. of Antioch-Malabar Rite, 1975—; editor New Awareness News, 1975—; founder, pres. Parker/Tofte Comm., Robert Parker Assocs., Minnetonka, Minn., 1977—; pres., CEO Am. Energy & Alcohol Corp., Mpls., 1981-84; cons. Boat Owners Assn. U.S., Washington, 1967-70, Durance Co., 1994-95; rschr., cons. Am. Marine Corp., Marblehead, Mass.; new product devel., venture capital and cons. investment, banking houses, N.Y.C. and Washington, 1967-71; dir., cons. to regional and nat. healing orgns. and publs., 1973-81; pres. Field Harmonics Rsch. Group Inc., 1993-97, New Awareness Spkrs. and Pub. Group, Inc., 1997—; spkr., tchr. numerous orgns. Author: Watergate Flight 553, 1974, Reabsorption Energy, 1975, Finding Your Own Four-Leaf Clover, 1993; author Telsa Newsletter, 1979; editor New Awareness Mag., 1973-75, (newsletter) Sunbeams; editor, pub. New Awareness News and Book News, 1977—, New Awareness Computer News, 1995—, psychic/parapsychology internat. trade jours., 1971-75; designer, pub.: Henry's Hilarious One Liners, 1991, Henry's Just a Chuckle, 1992, Henry's Just a Laugh, 1992, Henry's Just a Witticism, 1992; contbr. articles to profl. jours.; guest spkr. various radio, TV and Internet programs, including Dimension, Sta. WCCO-AM-FM; featured on Dimension WCCO-TV (CBS), 1991, 93, Forbes Mag., 1996; host cable TV program Astrology and Mind, Etc., 1994-96; syndicated columnist. Bd. dirs. Toutorsky Ednl. Found., Washington, 1988-91. Mem. Nat. Press Club (Washington), Internat. Telsa Soc. Inc., Knickerbocker Greys Vet. Corps (N.Y.C.), Browning Sch. Alumni Assn. (N.Y.C.), Lenox (Mass.) Sch. Alumni Assn. Avocations: sailing, reading, gardening, traveling, golf. Home and Office: 5208 Woodhill Rd Minnetonka MN 55345-4751

PARKER, ROSS GAIL, lawyer; b. Council Bluffs, Iowa, July 13, 1948; s. Gail Francis and Mildred Julia P.; m. Deborah Jo LeVan, May 5, 1984; children: Sarah LeVan, Alexander LeVan. BS, Iowa State U., 1970; JD, U. Pitts., 1974. Bar: U.S. Dist. Ct. (ea. dist.) Mich. 1975, U.S. Ct. Appeals (6th cir.) 1975. Law clk. to Hon. Michael Cavanagh Mich. Ct. Appeals, Lansing, 1974-75; atty. Fink and LaRene, Detroit, 1975-78; asst. U.S. atty. U.S. Attys. Office, U.S. Dist. Ct. (ea. dist.) Mich., Detroit, 1978—, chief criminal divsn., 1981-89; chief asst. U.S. atty. U.S. Attys. Office, U.S. Dist. Ct. (ea. dist.) Mich., 1989-94; adj. prof. Detroit Coll. Law, 1980-82. Editor-in-chief U. Pitts. Law Rev., 1973-74. Coach Neighborhood Club, Grosse Pointe, Mich., 1998; mgr. SCH Hockey Assn., St. Clair Shores, Mich., 1998—. Recipient Dirs. award U.S. Dept. Justice, 1990. Mem. FBA (Leonard R. Gilman award 1997). Presbyterian. Avocations: reading, coaching, volunteering in church activities. Office: US Attys Office 211 W Fort St Detroit MI 48226-3202

PARKER, SIMON, software design consultant; b. Leeds, Eng., Apr. 19, 1954; s. Harry and Ivy Mary (Wilkes) P.; m. Sue Barrett, Mar. 19, 1981; children: David, Ian. Programmer Post Office, London, 1972-77; analyst, programmer Post Office, Cardiff, Wales, 1977-79; lectr. Altergo, Dublin, Ireland, 1979-84; cons. Eiffel Ireland, Dublin, 1984—; programmer Xiam Ltd., Dublin, 2000—. Active Non-profit Internat. Consortium for Eiffel (NICE), sec., 1994-97, chmn., 1996, 97. Mem. Irish Computer Soc. Home and office: 45 Hazelwood, Shankill Dublin, Ireland

PARKER, T. JOHN, shipping and shipbuilding company executive; b. Apr. 8, 1942; s. Robert and Margaret Elizabeth (Bell) P.; m. Emma Elizabeth Blair, 1967; two children. DSc, Queen's U. Belfast, 1985; DSc (hon.), Trinity Coll., Dublin, Ireland, 1986, U. Ulster, 1992, U. Abertay, Dundee, 1997. From student naval arch. to gen. mgr. sales and projects Nat. Physical Lab. (Ship Hydrodynamics), 1958-74; mng. dir. Austin-Pickersgill Ltd., Sunderland, 1974-78; from dir. mktg. to dep. CEO Brit. Shipbuilders, 1978-83; chmn., CEO Harland & Wolff, 1983-93; chmn. Babcock Internat. Group, 1993—; bd. dirs. GKN, B.G. Plc; gen. com. Lloyds Register Shipping, 1983—. Fellow Royal Acad. Engring., Royal Instn. Naval Architects (pres. 1996-99). Office: Babcock Internat Group plc, Badminton Ct Church St, Amersham Buckingham HP7 0DD, England

PARKER, THERESA ANN BOGGS, special education educator, music educator; b. Spencer, W.Va., Jan. 16, 1947; d. Harry Clay and Betty Jean (Richards) Boggs; m. Larry Glen Parker, Apr. 29, 1967; children: Carey Ann, Jill Renee, Timothy Preston, Jeremy David, Leanna Michelle. AA in Secretarial Studies, Glenville (W.Va.) State Coll., 1967, BA in Music Edn., 1970; MA in Spl. Edn., Coll. of Grad. Studies, 1991; EdS in Ednl. Leadership, W.Va. Grad. Coll., 1996. Cert. tchr. Pvt. practice piano teacher Spencer, 1967—; sub. tchr. Roane County Schs., Spencer, 1970-71; tchr. spl. edn. Roane County Schs., 1987—, educator team mem.-parent/educator resource ctr., 1989—; sub. tchr. Marietta (Ohio) City Schs., 1986; administrator Sand Hill Day Care Ctr., Reno, Ohio, 1986-87; spl. edn. rep. W.Va. Dept. Edn., Charleston, 1995—; dir. Safetytown Roane County, Spencer, 1989-93. Author: (with others) Selected Teaching Models Integrated with West Virginia's Academic Model for Gifted Education, 1991; poet with works appearing in Echoes of Yesteryear, America at the Millennium, 2000, Internat. Libr. Poetry. Chmn. Cub Scout Pack Boy Scouts Am., Reno, 1983-87, dist. trainer, Parkersburg, W.Va., 1986-87, chmn. Boy Scout Troop, Spencer, 1987-91; organizer First Bapt. Ch. Diabetes Sup. Group, 1995—. Safetytown grantee W.Va. Dept. Edn., Roane County, 1989, W.Va. Edn. Fund, Roane County, 1992; Dental Health grantee W.Va. Edn. Fund, Clover Sch., 1992; Diabetes Support Group grantee Benedium Found., Roane and Calhoun/Jackson Counties, 1995, youth and edn. grantee for Spencer Mid. Sch., Tri-County Partnership, Inc., 1998; named Tchr. of Yr. Spencer Middle Sch., 1999-2000. Mem. ASCD, W.Va. Profl. Educators, Blue Grass Riding Club, Lions (program chmn., pres. 1997-98, dist. Leo chmn. 1998—), Roane Arts and Humanities Coun. (charter mem., pres. 2000—). Democrat. Baptist. Avocations: reading, sewing, playing piano, attending children's activities, grandchildren. Home: PO Box 478 Spencer WV 25276-0478 Office: Roane County Schs 102 Chapman Ave Spencer WV 25276-1310

PARKER, VIVIENNE MARGARET, editor; b. Heswall, Eng., Nov. 7, 1943; d. John Jeffrey and Dorothy Blanche (Graham) Hancock; m. Hedley Parker, June 25, 1966 (div. 1992); children: Adam Scott, Austin Leigh; m. Keith Robert Vautier, July 13, 1996. Radiographer United Liverpool Hosps., England, 1963-70; handcraft tchr. Civilian Maimed Assn., Auckland, New Zealand, 1978-85; display cons. pvt. practice, Auckland, New Zealand, 1985-90; editl. advisor Inkster Pub. Rels., Auckland, New Zealand, 1991; editor New Zealand Soc. Genealogists, 1991-97, Genealogical Rsch. Inst. New Zealand, 1996-98; profl. rschr. Viva Rsch. and tchr. family history and genealogy. Mem. New Zealand Soc. Genealogists, Cheshire FHS, Derbyshire FHS, East Riding Yorkshire FHS. Home: 38 College Rd, Auckland 1005, New Zealand Office: Viva Research, PO Box 87-220, Meadowbank Auckland 1130, New Zealand

PARKER, W. BRADLEY, lawyer; b. El Paso, Tex., Dec. 15, 1959; s. William Ray Parker and Nancy Jo Thompson; children: Hayley Anne, Calyn Rae. BA in Govt., U. Tex., 1982; JD, Tex. Tech U., 1985. Bar: Tex. 1985, U.S. Dist. Ct. (no. dist.) Tex. 1985, U.S. Dist. Ct. (we. dist.) Tex. 1992, U.S. Ct. Appeals (5th cir.) 1985. Atty. Law, Snakard & Gambill, Ft. Worth, 1985-90; atty., shareholder Boswell & Kober, Ft. Worth, 1990-93, Kerr, Parker & Kerr, Ft. Worth, 1993-96, Watson & Parker, Ft. Worth, 1996—. Mem. Tex. Trial Lawyers Assn. (chmn. advocates 1998, bd. dirs. 1996—), Tarrant County Trial Lawyers Assn. (pres. 1998-99). Avocations: sailing, camping, outdoor activities. Home: 3505 Brookside Ct Bedford TX 76021-3537 Office: Watson & Parker 500 Throckmorton St Ste 1206 Fort Worth TX 76102-3710

PARKER, WALLACE O'NEIL, JR., research scientist; b. Raleigh, N.C., Apr. 12, 1958; arrived in Italy, 1988; s. Wallace O'Neil and Annie Faye (Morton) P. BA in Chemistry with emphasis of Physics, U. North Fla., 1982; PhD in Chemistry, Emory U., 1986; postdoctoral position, U. Calif., Davis, 1987. Vis. scientist U. Lund, Sweden, 1988; rsch. scientist Eni Tecnologie, Milan, Italy, 1988—. Contbr. articles to profl. jours. Home: Via Liberazione 39/3, 20068 Peschiera Borromeo Italy Office: Dept Phys Chemistry, Eni Tecnologie, 20097 San Donato Italy

PARKER, WARREN ANDREW, public health dentist, consultant; b. Swedesboro, N.J., May 31, 1932; s. Warren Henry and Mary Jane (Morrison) P.; m. Eileen Frances Grabosky, Oct. 12, 1957; children: Denise, Warren A., Gail Lamb, Stephen. DDS, U. Md., Balt., 1958; MPH, U. Calif., Berkeley, 1966. Diplomate Am. Bd. Dental Pub. Health. Pvt. practice dentistry, Swedesboro, 1958-60; resident in dental pub. health USPHS, San Francisco, 1967; asst. chief div. preventive dentistry Inst. Dental Rsch., Walter Reed Army Med. Ctr., Washington, 1967-74; chief health care studies divsn. Acad. Health Scis./U.S. Army, San Antonio, 1974-78, chief dental studies office, 1978-81; assoc. prof. grad. sch. Baylor U., Waco, Tex., 1978-92; prof. dept. cmty. health Baylor Coll. Dentistry, Dallas, 1981-88, prof., chmn. dept. cmty. health, 1988-92; dental pub. health cons. in pvt. practice, San Antonio, 1992—; cons. Agy. for Children and Families, Dept. HHS, Dallas, 1984—; cons. divsn. dental health Tex. Dept. Health, Austin, 1987-92; cons. Inst. for Family Studies, Tex. Tech. U., Lubbock, 1992—; mem. adv. com. Dental Health Programs, Inc., Dallas, 1989-92. Contbr. articles to profl. jours. Mem. exec. com. St. Vincent DePaul Soc., Lancaster, Tex., 1990-95; mem. com. Vis. Nurses Assn., Dallas, 1988-95; rep. Tex. Cancer Coun., Austin, 1989-90; vol. Habitat for Humanity. Col. U.S. Army, 1959-81. Decorated Legion of Merit; recipient Cert., Tex. Agy. on Aging, 1987. Fellow APHA, Am. Coll. Dentists, Tex. Pub. Health Assn. (chair oral health 1990-91, exec. dir. 1992—); mem. ADA, Am. Assn. Pub. Health Dentistry, Delta Omega. Avocations: fishing, gardening. Home: 2506 Shadowcliff San Antonio TX 78232-4012

PARKERSON, HARDY MARTELL, lawyer; b. Longview, Tex., Aug. 22, 1942; s. James Dee and Winifred Lenore (Robertson) P.; m. Janice Carol Johnson, Aug. 3, 1968; children: James Blaine, Stanley Andrew, Paul Hardy. BA, McNeese State U., Lake Charles, La.; JD, Tulane U., 1966. Bar: La. 1966, U.S. Supreme Ct. 1971. Assoc. Rogers, McHale & St. Romain, Lake Charles, 1967-69; pvt. practice Lake Charles, 1969—; chmn. 7th Congl. Dist. Crime and Justice Task Force, La. Priorities for the Future, 1980; asst. prof. criminal justice La. State U., 1986. Bd. dirs. 1st Assembly of God Ch., Lake Charles, 1980—; bd. regents So. Christian U., Lake Charles, 1993—; mem. La. Dem. State Ctrl. Com., 1992-96, Calcasieu Parish Dem. Com., 1988—, past sec.-treas., exec. com.; former mem. Gulf Assistance Program, Lake Charles; 7th Congl. Dist. La. mem. Imports and Exports Trust Authority, Baton Rouge, 1984-88. Mem. Federal Bar Assn. (chmn. federal courts com., sr. lawyer's divsn.), Pi Kappa Phi Housing Corp. of Lake Charles (bd. dirs., sec.-treas. 1985—), Optimists, Pi Kappa Phi (Beta Mu chpt.). Democrat. Mem. Assembly of God Ch. Avocations: political activist, television talk show host. Home: 127 Greenway St Lake Charles LA 70605-6821 Office: The Parkerson Law Firm 807 Alamo St Lake Charles LA 70601-8665

PARKES, COLIN MURRAY, psychiatrist, educator; b. London, Mar. 26, 1928; s. Gwyneth Ann Parkes; m. Patricia Ainworth, June 22, 1957; children: Elizabeth, Jennifer, Caroline. MB BS, Westminster Hosp. Med. Sch., London, 1951, DPM, 1959, MD, 1962. Lic. psychiatrist, Eng. Rsch. staff Med. Rsch Coun., London, 1960-62; social psychiat. unit staff Maudsley Hosp., London, 1960-62; project dir. Lab. of Cmty. Psychology, Harvard Med. Sch., Boston, 1965-69; rsch. staff Tavistock Inst., London, 1969-75; sr. lectr. London Hosp. Med. Coll., 1975-93; cons. psychiatrist St. Christopher's Hospice, London; pres. Cruse Bereavement Care. Author: Bereavement: Studies of Grief in Adult Life, 1972, 3d edit., 1998, Counseling in Terminal Care and Bereavement; co-author: The First Year of Bereavement, 1983; prodr. film The Life That's Left and Stillbirth, 1977 (Silver awards 1979). Served to 1st lt. RAF, 1954-56. Decorated Order Brit. Empire. Fellow Royal Coll. Psychiatry. Avocations: choral singing, antique blue-printed pottery. Home: High Marl South Rd., Chorleywood,, Hertfordshire WD3 5AS, England

PARKES, DIANNE LAURA, publisher, editor; b. Princes Risborough, Buckingham, Eng., Mar. 20, 1965; d. James Fredrick and Dorothy Mary (Perks) Bickmore; m. Nigel Parkes, Sept. 12, 1987. Student, Dubarry Coll., London. Freelance health and beauty cons. London, 1984-86; sales exec. Westminster Press, London, 1986; sales/mktg. exec. The Guardian Newspaper, London, 1986-89; pers. mgr. Jaeger, London, 1989-91; co. dir. Eversmile Ltd., London, 1990—; pub. Plus Partnership Ltd., Buckinghamshire, 1992—; design dir. The Design Wks., Buckinghamshire, 1995—. Writer/editor Health & Sport Plus mag., 1992—; contbr. articles to profl. jours. Avocations: business studies, environmental issues, art and design, sports, family. Office: The Old Raven, Great Gap Ivinghoe, Buckinghamshire LU7 9DZ, England also: Plus Partnership Ltd, 21 Bedford Square, London WC1B 3HH, England

PARKEY, ROBERT WAYNE, radiology and nuclear medicine educator, research radiologist; b. Dallas, July 17, 1938; s. Jack and Gloria Alfreda (Perry) P.; m. Nancy June Knox, Aug. 9, 1958; children: Wendell Wade, Robert Todd, Amy Elizabeth. BS in Physics, U. Tex., 1960; MD, S.W. Med. Sch., U. Tex., Dallas, 1965. Diplomate Am. Bd. Radiology, Am. Bd. Nuclear Medicine. Intern St. Paul Hosp., Dallas, 1965-66; resident in radiology U. Tex. Health Sci. Ctr., Dallas, 1966-69, asst. prof. radiology, 1970-74, assoc. prof., 1974-77, prof., chmn. dept. radiology, 1977—, Effie and Wofford Cain Disting. chair in diagnostic imaging, 1994—; chief nuc. medicine Parkland Meml. Hosp., Dallas, 1974-79, chief dept. radiology, 1977—. Contbr. numerous chpts., articles and abstracts to profl. publs. Served as catp. M.C., Army N.G., 1965-72. NIH fellow Nat. Inst. Gen. Med. Sci., U. Mo., Columbia, 1969-70; Nat. Acad. Scis.-NRC scholar in radiol. rsch. James Picker Found., 1971-74. Fellow Am. Coll. Cardiology, Am. Coll. Radiology; mem. Am. Coll. Nuclear Physicians (charter, ho. of dels. 1974—), Coun. on Cardiovascular Radiology of Am. Heart Assn., AMA, Assn. Univ. Radiologists, Dallas County Med. Assn., Dallas Ft. Wroth Radiol. Soc., Radiol. Soc. N.Am., Soc. Chmn. of Acad. Radiology Depts., Soc. Nuclear Medicine (acad. coun.), Tex. Med. Assn., Tex. Radiol. Soc., Sigma Xi, Alpha Omega Alpha. Avocations: gardening, golf, tennis. Achievements include academic research on nuclear cardiology, development of new imaging technologies, medical education. Office: U Tex Southwestern Med Ctr Dept Radiology 5323 Harry Hines Blvd Dallas TX 75390-7208

PARKHE, A., educator, researcher; b. Bombay, Aug. 8, 1948; s. Ramchandra D. and Sulabha R. P.; m. Kavita A., Sept. 15, 1996; children: Kiran, Roopali. MS, Ga. Inst. Tech., 1971; MBA, Ga. State U., 1979; PhD, Temple U., 1989. Computer ops. supr. Nat. Data Corp., Atlanta, 1972-79; mgr. purchasing and adminstrn. Gruner & Jahr, Hamburg, Germany, 1979-85; prof. internat. bus. Ind. U., Bloomington, 1989—. Mem. editl. review bd. Jour. Internat. Bus. Studies, 1992—, Acad. Mgmt. Jour., 1994-96. Mem. Acad. Mgmt. (editl. review bd. 1996—), Acad. Internat. Bus. Avocations: ping pong, indian music, travel. E-mail: aparkehe@indiana.edu. Home: 2728 Brigs Bnd Bloomington IN 47401-4402 Office: Indiana Univ Kelley Sch Business Bloomington IN 47405

PARKHURST, BEVERLY SUSLER, lawyer, former judge; b. Decatur, Ill.; d. Sewell and Marion (Appelbaum) Susler; m. Todd S. Parkhurst, Aug. 15, 1976. BA with honors, U. Ill., 1966, JD, 1969. Bar: Ill. 1969, U.S. Dist. Ct. (no. dist.) Ill. 1969, U.S. Ct. Appeals (7th cir.) 1975, U.S. Supreme Ct. 1980. Assoc. Pope, Ballard, Shepard & Fowle, Chgo., 1969-74; asst. U.S. atty. U.S. Atty.'s Office U.S. Dist. Ct. (no. dist.) Ill., Chgo., 1974-78, exec. asst. U.S. atty., 1978-81; pvt. practice law Offices of Beverly Susler Parkhurst, Chgo., 1982-86; trial judge Cir. Ct. Cook County, 1996-98; of counsel Witwer, Poltrock & Giampietro, Chgo., 1998—; mem. faculty trial advocacy programs Nat. Emory U., Hofstra U.; bd. dirs. Internat. Forum Travel and Tourism Advs., vice chmn. 2d Internat. Conf., Jerusalem, 1986, regional chmn. 3d Internat. Conf., San Francisco, 1987; chmn. inquiry bd. Ill. Atty. Registration and Disciplinary Commn., 1985-87; guest lectr. legal ethics Washington U., St. Louis, 1986; lectr. on travel law, fed. civic procedures and med. malpractice; adj. prof. John Marshall Law Sch., 1999—; mediator Jud. Disput Resolution. Contbr. articles to profl. jours.; spkr. in field. Mem. Ill. Toll Hwy. Adv. Com., 1985-90; bd. dirs. Ill. Soc. for Prevention of Blindness, Cook County Ct. Watchers, Chgo. State U. Found., 1997—. James scholar U. Ill., 1962-66; recipient Spl. Achievement award U.S. Dept. Justice, 1978, Dir.'s award, 1981, Cert. of Profl. Achievement in Mediation, DePaul U. Dispute Resolution Ctr.; U.S. Utility Patent grantee 1984. Mem. ABA (chmn. subcom. alternatives to discovery litigation sect. 1985-87), Ill. Bar Assn. (com. profl. responsibility), Women's Bar Assn., Fed. Bar Assn., Chgo. Bar Assn. (chmn. judiciary commn. 1988-90, bench bar symposium 1988-91, exec. com. Alliance for Women), Nat. Inst. Trial Advocacy (faculty N.E. region), Lincoln Inn of Ct. (v.p.), Legal Club of Chgo. Avocations: scuba diving, swimming, cooking. Office: Witwer Poltrock & Giampietro 125 S Wacker Dr Ste 2700 Chicago IL 60606-4401

PARKHURST, CHARLES LLOYD, electronics company executive; b. Nashville, Aug. 13, 1943; s. Charles Albert Parkhurst and Dorothy Elizabeth (Ballou) Parkhurst Crutchfield; m. Dolores Ann Oakley, June 6, 1970; children: Charles Thomas, Deborah Lynn, Jere Loy. Student, Hume-Fogg Tech. Coll., 1959-61; AA, Mesa Community Coll., 1973; student, Ariz. State U., 1973-76. Mem. design staff Tex. Instruments, Dallas, 1967-68; mgr. design Motorola, Inc., Phoenix, 1968-76; pres. LSI Cons., Inc., Tempe, Ariz., 1976-85, LSI Photomasks, Inc., Tempe, 1985-94, Charles Parkhurst Books, Inc., Prescott, Ariz., 1994—. Designer 1st digital watch chip, 1973. Mem. Rep. Congl. Leadership Coun., Washington, 1988; life mem. Rep. Presdl. Task Force, 1990. Served as cpl. USMC, 1961-64. Mem. Ariz. State U. Alumni Assn. (life), Antiquarian Booksellers Assn. of Am. Baptist. Achievements include design of the world's first digital watch chip. Avocations: genealogy, coin collecting, scuba diving, book collecting. Office: Charles Parkhurst Books Inc PO Box 10850 Prescott AZ 86304-0850

PARKHURST, EDWIN WALLACE, JR., healthcare management consultant; b. Waukegan, Ill., June 17, 1943; s. Edwin W. Sr. and Marie Violet (Wolf) P.; m. Grace Ann Dovemuehle, July 6, 1963; children: John Edward, Janet Lynn, Jeanine Marie, Julie Ann. BA, Carthage Coll., 1965; MBA, U. Chgo., 1968. Adminstrv. asst. West Allis (Wis.) Meml. Hosp., 1965-66; asst. dir., asst. prof. U. Mo. Med. Ctr., Columbia, 1968-71; from assoc., prin., to ptnr. Herman Smith Assoc., Hinsdale, Ill., 1971-88; ptnr. Herman Smith Assoc. divsn. Coopers & Lybrand, Chgo., 1988-93; ptnr. Herman Smith Assoc. Internat., Glen Ellyn, Ill., 1976—; mng. prin. MEDCO, Inc., Hatboro, Pa., 1997—, PRISM Healthcare Cons., Glen Ellyn, 1993—; spkr. in field; bd. dirs. Clin. Benchmaking. Contbr. articles to profl. jours. Bd. dirs., past pres. Lisle (Ill.) Cmty. Dist. 202 Bd. Edn., 1985—; scout leader Boy Scouts Am., Lisle, 1974-93. Named Disting. Alumni, U. Chgo., 1997; recipient Alumni Svc. citation U. Chgo., 1999. Fellow Am. Assn. Healthcare Cons. (bd. dirs., past pres., Chester A. Minkalis Svc. award 1999); mem. Health Issues Study Soc. (sec.-treas. 1972—), Am. Hosp. Assn., Am. Coll. Healthcare Execs. (cert. healthcare exec.), Soc. Healthcare Planning and Mgmt., Chgo. Health Exec. Forum. Avocations: fishing, hunting, hiking, camping, photography. E-mail: eparkhurst@prismcons.com. Home: 4239 White Birch Dr Lisle IL 60532-1252 Office: PRISM Healthcare Cons 799 Roosevelt Rd # B4s317 Glen Ellyn IL 60137-5908

PARKIN, ANDREW WARREN, political science educator, broadcaster, writer, editor, researcher; b. Adelaide, Australia, Nov. 2, 1952; m. Leonie Hardcastle. BA with honours, U. Adelaide, 1974, MA, 1976; MA, Harvard U., 1976, PhD, 1978. Tchg. fellow Harvard U., Cambridge, Mass., 1976-78; lectr. polit. sci. Flinders U., Adelaide, 1978-81, sr. lectr., 1982-92, reader, 1993-96, head Sch. Polit. and Internat. Studies, 1993-98, prof., 1997—; mem. corp. planning com. South Australian Housing Trust, 1985-88; cons. Rev. Com. on Local Govt. Boundaries, Adelaide, 1989-90. Editor, author: Government, Politics, Power and Policy in Australia, 1979, 6th edit., 1997, Machine Politics in the Australian Labor Party, 1982, The Bannon Decade: The Politics of Restraint in South Australia, 1992, South Australia, Federalism and Public Policy, 1996, The Machine: Labor Confronts the Future, 2000; contbr. over 70 articles to profl. jours.; editor Australian Jour. Polit. Sci., 2000—. Chmn. South Australian Housing Adv. Coun., Adelaide, 1985-89, South Australian Social Justice Com., Adelaide, 1986-87. Fulbright fellow, 1974-77, Frank Knox Meml. fellow Harvard U., 1974-77. Mem. Australasian Polit. Studies Assn. (pres. 1996-97), Am. Polit. Sci. Assn., Inst. Pub. Adminstrn. Australia. Office: Flinders U, GPO Box 2100, Adelaide SA 5001, Australia

PARKIN, DONALD PYSDEN, clinical pharmacologist, medical researcher; b. Krugersdorp, Transvaal, South Africa, May 23, 1940; s. Henry Norman and Hester Catherine (Pysden) P.; m. Ignatia Jean Bothma, July 8, 1961; children: Henry Norman, Ingrid, Andrew Le Roux, Sonya, Donald Edward. BSc, U. Stellenbosch, South Africa, 1967, BSc with honours, 1970; MB, ChB, U. Stellenbosch, Tygerberg, South Africa, 1975, PhD, 1996. Head toxicology unit Tygerberg Hosp., 1977—; specialist, lectr. pharmacology and toxicology U. Stellenbosch and Tygerberg Hosp., 1982-86, sr. specialist, sr. lectr., 1987—; mem. expert com. Med. Control Coun. South Africa, 1980-82. Guest editor Med. Intern/ South Africn Med. Jour.; contbr. articles to med. jours. including Jour. Chromatography, Jour. Antimicrobial Chemotherapy, Annals Tropical Paediatrics, Geneeskunde, Intensive Care Medicine, CNS Drugs, Am. Jour. Respiratory, Critical Care Medicine, Jour. Paediatrics, Ob. and Gyn., South African Jour. Sci. Anglican. Avocations: boat building, music, reading, mathematics, hiking. Home: 1 Riesling St, Paarl CP 7646, South Africa Office: Tygerberg Hosp, Tygerberg CP 7505, South Africa

PARKIN, GERARD FRANCIS RALPH, chemistry educator, researcher; b. Middlesbrough, Cleveland, Eng., Feb. 15, 1959; s. Ralph and Clementine (Gill) P.; m. Rita K. Upmacis. BA with honors, Oxford (Eng.) U., 1981, MA, 1984, PhD, 1985. NATO/SERC (U.K.) postdoctoral rsch. fellow Calif. Inst. Tech., 1985-88; asst. prof. Columbia U., N.Y.C., 1988-91, assoc. prof., 1991-94; prof., chmn. chemistry dept., 1994—, chmn. dept. chemistry. Contbr. numerous articles to profl. jours. Recipient Camille and Henry Dreyfus Tchr.-Scholar award, 1991, award in pure chemistry Am. Chem. Soc., 1994, Corday Morgan medal Royal Soc. Chemistry, 1995; A.P. Sloan rsch. fellow; NSF Presdl. faculty fellow, 1992—. Roman Catholic. Achievements include discovery that bond stretch isomerism in an artifact. Office: Columbia U 116th St And Broadway New York NY 10027

PARKIN, MALCOLM HIRST, chemical company executive; b. Delph, Yorkshire, Eng., July 11, 1939; s. Norman and Florence (Mellor) P.; m. Margaret Elizabeth Jefferson, Feb. 22, 1964; children: Helen Elizabeth, Andrew John. MRIC, Salford, 1962; MIWM, Manchester, Eng., 1967. Chemist Hardman & Holden, Manchester, 1955-67; sales exec. Manchem, Manchester, 1967-73, sales mgr., 1973-77; mktg. mgr. Manox Ltd., Manchester, 1977-84, comml. dir., 1984—; mnging. dir. RV Chem. Ltd., Widnes, 1989-98, Rika Internat. Ltd., Manchester, 1998—; pres. Rikamerica Inc., Princeton, N.J., 1998—. Home: 2 Rose Hill, Delph Oldham Manchester OL 3 5ED, England Office: Manox Ltd, Rika Internat Ltd, Greengate Middleton, Manchester M24 1GS, England

PARKINSON, CLAIRE L., climatologist; b. Bay Shore, N.Y., Mar. 21, 1948; d. C. V. and Virginia (Hafner) P. BA, Wellesley Coll., 1970; MA, Ohio State U., 1974, PhD, 1977. Rsch. asst. Inst. Polar Studies, Columbus, 1972-74; tchg. asst. Ohio State U., Columbus, 1973-76; rsch. asst. Nat. Ctr. Atmospheric Rsch., Boulder, Colo., 1976-78; rsch. scientist Goddard Space Flight Ctr., NASA, Greenbelt, Md., 1978-87, sr. rsch. scientist, 1987—; sci. colloquium com. mem. Goddard Space Flight Ctr., 1986-99; project scientist Earth Observing System Aqua Mission, NASA, 1993—; mem. sci. exec. com. Earth Observing Sys., 1996—; adv. panel climate and global change NOAA, 1990-95; climate rsch. com. Nat. Acad. Scis., 1994-96, sci. advisor earth & sky radio series, 1998—, sci. radio series Soundprint Media Ctr., 1998—; lead scientist NASA expedition to Resolute Bay and the North Pole, 1999. Author: Breakthroughs, 1985, Gospel Cryptograms, 1994, Earth from Above, 1997 (Spl. Act award 1997); co-author: Antarctic Sea Ice, 1983 (Group award 1982), Three-Dimensional Climate Modeling, 1986; lead author: Arctic Sea Ice, 1987 (Peer award 1988); co-editor: Atlas of Satellite Observations Related to Global Change, 1993 (Group award 1993); assoc. editor Internat. Glaciological Soc., Cambridge, Eng., 1989-92; mem. editl. bd. Earth Obs. Website, 1999—; contbr. articles to profl. jours. Vol. Spl. Olympics, Annapolis, Md., 1989, College Park, Md., 1998—; tutor Greenbelt Cares, 1989-94; sci. speaker, sci. fair judge local schs., 1989—. Mem. Am.

Polar Soc., Am. Meteorol. Soc. (history com. chmn. 1990), Assn. for Philosophy of Math., Oceanography Soc., Phi Beta Kappa, Phi Beta Kappa Fellows. Achievements include research in global change, satellite remote sensing, sea ice/climate connections, climate modeling, history of science. Home: 8345 Canning Ter Greenbelt MD 20770-2701 Office: Code 971 NASA Goddard Space Flight Ctr Greenbelt MD 20771-0001

PARKINSON, MURRAY LINTON, physicist, researcher; b. Sydney, NSW, Australia, Sept. 30, 1963; s. Linton Russell and Gloria Jean (Chaplin) P.; m. Maria Dolores Pifarre, Apr. 11, 1993. BS, U. Queensland, Brisbane, Australia, 1984, MS, 1988, PhD, 1993. Cert. physics. Physics tutor U. Queensland, Brisbane, 1986-93; rsch. assoc. La Trobe U., Melbourne, Australia, 1993-97; sr. rsch. assoc. La Trobe U., Melbourne, 1997—; summer physicist Australian Nat. Antarctic Rsch. Expeditions, Casey, Antarctica, 1996. Contbr. articles to profl. jours. Mem. Australian Inst. Physics. Avocations: scuba diving, bushwalking, tennis, oil painting, photography. Office: Dept Physics Bundoora Campu, La Trobe Univ, Melbourne 3083 VIC, Australia

PARKLEE, LEE See PARK, LEE

PARKS, CORRINE FRANCES, insurance agency owner; b. Pulaski, Ill., May 23, 1934; d. Elizabeth (Stanfield) Daniels; m. Charles Robert Parks, July 6, 1957; children: Reginald, Pierre. BA, Chgo. State U., 1976; student, Columbia Coll., 1986-87; MA, Gov.'s State U., 1981; postgrad., Chgo. U. Sem., 1990-94, Luth. Seminary of Theology. Exec. rep. Marsh & McLennon, Inc., Chgo., 1970-74; account exec. Internat. Ins. Cons., Chgo., 1974-77; mktg. rep. Alexander & Alexander, Chgo., 1977-79; mem. Nat. Coun. S.S. Reps., Chgo., 1981; pres. AA& A Ins. Agy., Chgo., 1981—; radio show host Sta. WBEE-1570 AM, Chgo., 1985—, WYAA Radio; bd. dirs. Unity Chgo., Chgo. Urban Day Unity COGIC C4. Talk show host Sta. WYBA-FM Radio. Sec. Englewood Redevel. Group, Chgo., 1987; rep. State Sun. Sch., N.I. Juris. Mem. Ind. Ins. Agts. Ill., Women in Radio and TV, Chgo. Bd. Underwriters, Nat. Assn. Black Journalists, Chgo. Mus. Sci. and Industry, Chgo. Assn. Black Journalists, Group V Video Club (dir. 1986), Order of Eastern Star (treas. 1983). Democrat. Avocations: theatre, singing, golf, reading. Fax: (773) 298-1562. Home: 100 Park Ave Calumet City IL 60409-5065 Office: AA & A Ins Agy 10016 S Western Ave # 2 Chicago IL 60643-1926

PARKS, DEBORA ANN, private school director; b. Homestead, Fla., July 23, 1954; d. Jack Wesley and Blanche Margaret (Shawver) Hardin; m. Lewis O'Dell Parks, Apr. 12, 1970 (div. May 1980); 1 child, Kerri Shane Parks. BS in Early Childhood Edn., U. Ala., Tuscaloosa, 1983, MA in Spl. Edn., 1984, MA in Early Childhood Edn., 1987, PhD in Elem. Edn., 1991. Kindergarten tchr. Martin Luther King Jr. Elem. Sch., Tuscaloosa, 1983-85; tchr. gifted grades 2-5 Martin Luther King Jr. Elem. Sch. and Univ. Place Elem. Sch., Tuscaloosa, 1985-86; early childhood edn. instr. Shelton State C.C., Tuscaloosa, 1985-88; instr. U. Ala., Tuscaloosa, 1987; elem. tchr. 1st grade Martin Luther King Jr. Elem. Sch., Tuscaloosa, 1988-89; tchr. gifted grades 3-6 Carthay Elem. Sch., L.A. Unified Sch. Dist., 1991; faculty-in-residence Sunset Village Residence Halls and Hitch Stes. UCLA, 1991-95; tchr. gifted grades K-8 Maimonides Acad., L.A., 1992-94; asst. rschr. So. Calif. Injury Prevention Rsch. Ctr. Sch. Pub. Health, UCLA, 1993-95; faculty liaison on campus housing com.'s darkroom UCLA, 1993-95, instr. dept. edn., 1994, 95, instr., rschr., 1989-95; tchr. gifted grades 2-8 Maimonides Acad., L.A., 1995, gen. studies prin., 1995—; grad. tchg. asst. elem. edn. U. Ala., Tuscaloosa, 1986-87; field coord., instr. Tchr. Edn. Lab., Grad. Sch. Edn., UCLA, 1989-93; enrichment tchr. grades 3-5 The Buckley Sch., Sherman Oaks, Calif., summer, 1991, 92, 93; evaluation coach/cons. Stanford Rsch. Inst., SB 620 Statewide Healthy Start Initiative Program, L.A., 1993-95; spl. faculty advisor UCLA Photographic Soc., 1993-95; evaluator lang. arts program, curriculum and tchrs. Maimonides Acad., L.A., 1994; enrichment tchr. grades 4-5 Buckley Sch., Sherman Oaks, Calif., summer 1994, enrichment tchr., summer 1995; evaluation coach, cons. Stanford Rsch. Inst., L.A., 1993-95; mem. governing bd. Nat. Assn. Creative Children and Adults, Ohio, 1992-94; rsch. adviser Phi Delta Kappa, UCLA chpt., 1992-94; mem. Adopt-A-Sch. Coun., L.A. Unified Sch. Dist., 1990-95; chairperson Tuscaloosa City Sch.'s Kindergarten Math. Com., 1984; presenter confs. and workshops. Author: The Newspaper Workbook, 1983, Pedestrian and Bicyclist Safety Curriculum for Grades K-5, 1994, Adopt-A-School Programs: A Guide for Pre-Service Teachers, 1995, Exercises and Tests in English Grammar, 2000; manuscript asst. editor Am. Mid. Sch. Edn., 1986-87; asst. editor Adopt-A-School Newsletter, 1993; contbr. articles to profl. jours. Vol. Rebuild L.A., 1992-93. Recipient award NEA and Kodak, N.Y. and Ala., 1985, scholarships Am. Bus. Women's Assn., Ala., 1988, Beta Chi of Delta Kappa Gamma, 1983, Epsilon chpt. Alpha Delta Kappa, 1984, Yewell R. Thompson Endowed scholarship, 1988; designee Ala. Tchr. of Yr. Program, 1984-85, 85-86. Mem. Phi Delta Kappa. Democrat. Avocations: photography, calligraphy, graphic arts, genealogy. Home: 311 Westbourne Dr West Hollywood CA 90048-1909 Office: Maimonides Acad 310 N Huntley Dr Los Angeles CA 90048-1919

PARKS, GERALD BARTLETT, educator; b. Bremerton, Wash., July 27, 1945; arrived in Italy, 1970; s. Bartlett Gilford and Margaret C. (Moulden) P.; m. Silvana Rancan; children: Elinor, Sylvia. BA in Latin, U. Wash., 1966; MA in Classical Studies, U. Mich., 1968. Cert. secondary tchr., Wash. Tchr. U. Trieste, Italy, 1970—. Author: (poetry) Lumen, 1992, (monograph) The Transilluminating Word: A Study of Robert Hayden's Poetry, 1983, (essay collection) Essays in the Methodology of Language Teaching, 1990; translator/editor: William Blake, Canti dell'innocenza e dell'esperienza, 1985-95. Recipient scholarship Stanford U., 1966, Salzburg seminar in Am. studies, Austria, 1973-81. Avocations: classical music, theatre, poetry. Home: Via Crispi 18, 34125 Trieste Italy Office: Scuola Superiore di Lingue, U Trieste/Via Filzi 14, 34100 Trieste Italy

PARKS, GRACE SUSAN, bank official; b. N.Y.C., Oct. 14, 1948; d. Marco A. and Gloria (Alvino) Vale; m. Louis Parks, Feb. 14, 1988. BS, Pa. State U., 1970; MA, New Sch. for Social Rsch., 1974; cert. in mgmt., Adelphi U., 1979, MBA, 1980; cert. in entrepreneurship, Hofstra U., 1996. Bus. office rep. N.Y. Tel. Co., Rockville Centre, 1971-74; social worker Children's Aid Soc., N.Y.C., 1974-75; EEO officer Edwin Gould Svcs., N.Y.C., 1976-79; v.p. fin. instns. and global markets Bankers Trust Co., N.Y.C., 1979-92; v.p. compensation human resources Chase Manhattan Bank, 1992-96; pres. Loodie Prodns., Inc., 1996; instr. mgmt. Adelphi U. Grad. Sch. Bus. Adminstrn., 1981—; notary pub. State N.Y., 1978—. Mem. Human Resource Planning Soc., Assn. MBA Execs., Am. Compensation Assn., Wall St. Compensation and Benefits Assn. (chmn. 1994-96, pres. 1993-94), N.Y. Compensation Assn., Adelphi U. Businesswomen's Alumni Assn. (pres. 1980-82).

PARKS, JAMES WILLIAM, II, public facilities executive, lawyer; b. Wabash, Ind., July 30, 1956; s. James William and Joyce Arlene (Lillibridge) P.; m. Neil Ann Armstrong, Aug. 21, 1982; children: Elizabeth Joyce, Helen Frances, James William III. BS, Ball State U., 1978; JD, U. Miami, 1981. Bar: La. 1981, Fla. 1982, U.S. Dist. Ct. (ea. dist.) La. 1981, U.S. Dist. Ct. (mid. dist.) La. 1982, U.S. Ct. Appeals (5th cir. and 11th cir.) 1981. Atty. Jones, Walker, Waechter, Poitevent, Carrere et al., New Orleans, 1981-83, Foley & Judell, New Orleans, 1983-88, McCollister & McCleary, pc, Baton Rouge, 1988-95; pres., CEO La. Pub. Facilities Authority, Baton Rouge, 1995—. Mem. AICPA, Nat. Assn. Bond Lawyers, La. State Bar Assn., Fla. Bar Assn., Assn. for Gifted and Talented Students, Baton Rouge (treas. 1994-96, pres.-elect 1996-97, pres. 1997-98), Soc. La. CPA (govt. acctg. and auditing com. 1994-95), Nat. Assn. Higher Edn. Facilities Authorities (bd. dirs. 1996—, v.p. 1997-99, pres. 1999—). Avocations: travel, computers. Home: 5966 Tennyson Dr Baton Rouge LA 70817-2933 Office: La Pub Facilities Authority 2237 S Acadian Thruway Ste 650 Baton Rouge LA 70808-2380

PARKVALL, STEFAN, electrical engineer, researcher; b. Stockholm, July 31, 1967; s. Ulf and Britta (Axelsson) P. MScEE, Royal Inst. of Tech., Sweden, 1991, PhD, 1996. Rsch. asst. Royal Inst. of Tech., Sweden, 1992-96, rsch. assoc., 1996-97, asst. prof., 1997—; vis. scholar U. Calif. San Diego, 1996, vis. rschr., 1997-98; rschr. Ericsson Rsch., Sweden, 1999—; cons., tchr. in field, 1993—; organizer, founder Ann. Swedish Workshop on CDMA, 1995—. Contbg. author: CRC Comprehensive Dictionary of EE terms; contbr. articles to profl. jours. Recipient Saab-Scania award Saab, 1995; Hans Werthen postdoctoral award Royal Swedish Acad. of Engring. Sci., 1996, Hans Werthen award Royal Swedish Acad. of Engring. Sci., 1997. Mem. IEEE (chmn. student br. 1992-94, chmn. VT/COM Soc. Sweden sect. 1999—). Avocations: hiking, culture, scuba diving. Home: Sigtunagatan 18, 11322 Stockholm Sweden Office: Ericsson Rsch, 164 80 Stockholm Sweden

PARLE, BERTHA IBARRA, writer short stories, poetry; b. El Paso, Tex., Nov. 14, 1947; d. Arnulfo and Bertha (Soto) Ibarra; m. Dennis Jerome Parle, Aug. 16, 1969; children: Joseph, Mónica, Angélica. BA in French, Spanish, U. Tex., El Paso, 1968; MA in Spanish, U. Kans., 1970, H.S. tchg. cert., 1971; postgrad. courses in French, U. Houston, 1990-95. Bilingual tchr. Kansas Remedial Edn. Program, Sharon Springs, 1967, 71, 72; Spanish tchr. Ottawa (Kans.) H.S., 1971-74; ESL instr. North Harris Coll., Houston, 1977-83; fgn. lang. prof. N. Harris Montgomery C.C. Dist., Houston, 1983-97, head lang. inst., 1997—; cultural cons., sponsor Hispanic students North Harris Coll. and Montgomery Coll., 1983-97, organizer Hispanic cultural events, 1983—, sponsor Cath. Newman Club, 1985-95; lectr., slide show The Nahua Mexica Legacy, 1994-96; participant in field seminars; NEH and Fulbright Ecuador field experience. Poetess; Spanish poetry publ. in Tejidos, Grito al Sol, 1972-94. Hispanic leader St. Leo's Cath. Ch., Houston, 1982-92. Recipient Tchg. Excellence award North Harris Coll., 1997, Excellence award Nat. Inst. for Staff and Orgn. Devel., 1998; Am. Coun. Tchrs. Fgn. Langs. summer scholar U. Montreal, 1999. Mem. AAUW, Am. Coun. Tchrs. Fgn. Langs., Computer Assisted Lan. Instruction Consortium, Am. Assn. C.C. Women, Tex. Fgn. Lang. Assn., Inst. Hispanic Culture., North Harris United Faculty. Avocations: creative writing, study of indigenous language cultures, Hispanic students and Hispanic issues in the community. Office: Montgomery Comty Coll 3200 College Park Dr Conroe TX 77384-4500

PARMAN, SETYAMARTANA, engineering educator; b. Semarang, Indonesia, June 19, 1963; parents Parman Partodidjojo and Woro Duryatini Parman; m. Yulia Indarsih Setyamartana Moch Besar, Jan. 2, 1992; 1 child, Ksatriya Anantayutya. Insinyur, Bandung Inst. Tech., Indonesia, 1990; D of Engring., Nagaoka (Japan) U. Tech., 1999. Asst. prof. Bandung Inst. Tech., 1990—. Contbr. papers to profl. jours. Avocations: traveling, drawing, reading. Fax: 62 22 2534164. E-mail: smp@aero.pauir.itb.ac.id. Home: Cibiru Indah V/a, Bandung 40393, Indonesia Office: Bandung Inst Tech, Jalan Ganesha 10, Bandung 40132, Indonesia

PARMANAND, NARI (LARRY), textile company executive; b. Hyderabad, India, July 30, 1937; s. Parmanand and Motalbai (Bhagwanti) P.; m. Mita N. Parmanand, Nov. 4, 1963; children: Vanita, Dilip. Grad. parochial sch., Kowloon, Hong Kong. Asst. mgr. Royal India Tailors, Kowloon, 1953-59, mgr., 1959-74, mng. dir., 1974—; chmn. Parmanand (HK) Ltd., Kowloon, 1974—, Chantilly (HK) Ltd., Kowloon, 1974—. Bd. dirs. Hong Kong Tourist Assn., 1983-85; pres. India Assn., Hong Kong, 1988—. Mem. India Club (pres. 1986-88), Royal Hong Kong Jockey Club, Kowloon Club (house com., mem. exec. bd.), Rotary (pres. Kowloon club 1982-83). Office: 310-312 Hankow Ctr, 5-15 Hankow Rd, Tsimshatsui Kowloon, Hong Kong

PARMAR, BALRAJ SINGH, chemistry educator; b. Hoshiarpore, India, Sept. 30, 1944; s. Sunder Singh and Parvati Devi (Jaswal) P.; m. Titiksha Thakur, Nov. 26, 1973; children: Geetika, Puneet. MS, Punjab Agrl. U., 1965; PhD, Indian Agrl. Rsch. Inst., Delhi, 1970. Pool officer Indian Agrl. Rsch. Inst., Delhi, 1970-72, scientist, chemist, 1972-78, sr. scientist, 1979-84, prin. scientist, 1985—, head dept., 1987-93, 98—, prof., 1993-98. Author, editor 8 books; editor Neem Newsletter, 1984—, Pesticide Rsch. Jour., 1995-99; inventor in field. Recipient Indian Coun. Forestry Rsch. & Edn. Neem award, 1996, Recognition award Nat. Acad. Agr. Sci., 1999. Fellow Nat. Acad. Agrl. Sci. (convenor Delhi chpt. 1994-97), Soc. Pesticide Sci. Avocations: Yoga, gardening, sports, music. Home: 337 Mandakini Enclave, New Delhi 110019, India Office: Indian Agrl Rsch Inst, Divsn Agrl Chems, New Delhi 110012, India

PARMEGGIANI, LUCA, asset management company executive; b. Milan, Mar. 23, 1962; arrived in Switzerland, 1962; s. Luigi and Renata (Bossi) P.; m. Annalea Stettler, Sept. 8, 1995. Degree in econs., U. Geneva, Switzerland, 1984, M in Econometrics, 1986. Cert. EFFAS fin. analyst. Tchg. asst. U. Geneva, 1984-87; biometrician Area Serono, Geneva, 1987-89; asst. to CEO Galenica, Bern, Switzerland, 1989-92; fund mgr. Lombard Odier & Co., Geneva, 1992-97; head of internat. equities Vontobel, Zürich, Switzerland, 1997—. Co-author: Regression et Donnees Atypiques, 1988. Office: Vontobel Asset Mgmt, Tödistrasse 27, 8002 Zürich Switzerland

PARMELEY, JERRY PAUL, software support specialist; b. St. Louis, Sept. 27, 1971; s. Jerry Paul and Sherry Nadine P.; m. Tricia Dawn Clarke, Nov. 1, 1997; 1 child, Katelynn. Cert. of Paramedicine, East Cen. Coll., Union, Mo., 1994. Cert. paramedic, Mo. Paramedic Boone Hosp. Ctr., Columbia, Mo., 1995—; support specialist PDS, Columbia, 1999—. Alderman Ward One, City of Centralia, Mo., 1998—. With USAF, 1989-93. Republican. Avocations: computers, model rockets. E-mail: jparmeley@hotmail.com. Office: PDS 1400 Forum Blvd Columbia MO 65203-1997

PARMENTER, TREVOR REGINALD, education educator; b. Lismore, Australia, May 2, 1934; s. Reginald George and Gladys May (Leslie) P.; m. Marie Edna Smith, Aug. 27, 1955 (dec. Feb. 1984); 1 child, Jacqueline; m. Marie Louise Yazbeck, Oct. 26, 1986; children: Natalie, Sophie. BA, U. New Eng., 1972; PhD, Macquarie U., 1984. From tchr. to prin. Dept. Edn., New South Wales, 1953-73; from sr. tutor to professorial fellow Macquarie U., Sydney, Australia, 1974-97; prof., found. chair devel. disability Sydney U., 1997—; exec. mem. Australian Catholic Social Welfare Commn., 1986-88, Internat. Labour Orgn. Global Applied Disability Rsch. Network, 1997-98; dir. Ctr. Devel. Disability Studies Australia, 1997—. Author: Vocational Training for Independent Living, 1980, Bridges from School to Working Life, 1986; editor: Preparation for Life, 1986; contbr. chpts. to books, articles to profl. jours. Fellow Australian Coll. Edn., Am. Assn. Mental Retardation, Internat. Assn. Scientific Study of Intellectual Disabilities; mem. Internat. Assn. Sci. Study Intellectual Disabilities (pres. 1996—), N.Y. Acad. Scis., Coun. Exceptional Children, Acad. Mental Retardation. Roman Catholic. Avocations: gardening, reading, classical music. Home: 53 Church St, 2154 Castle Hill NSW, Australia Office: Ctr Devel Disability Study, 59 Charles St, 2112 Ryde NSW, Australia

PARMENTIER, GUILLAUME, strategic expert, educator; b. Paris, Sept. 26, 1953; s. Michel and Simone Marie (Dumas de Saignemonteil) P.; m. Lucie Anne Carswell, June 23, 1990; children: Quentin, Daphné. Diploma, Inst. Polit. Sci., Paris, 1974; MLitt, Cambridge (Eng.) U., 1977; Doctoral degree, Sorbonne, Inst. Polit. Sci., Paris, 1980. Asst. prof. Inst. Polit. Studies Sec. to French Assn. of Polit. Sci., Paris, 1977-80, assoc. prof., 1980-90; dir. civilian affairs com. North Atlantic Assembly, Brussels, 1983-90; dep. dir., head of external rels. NATO hdqs., Brussels, 1990-94; advisor French Min. of Def. Charles Millon, Paris, 1995-97; dir. studies and rsch. Found. for Def. Studies, 1997—; prof. U. Paris II, 1995—; bd. dirs. Ctr. for Analysis of European Security; founder Ctr. U.S. and France, Brookings Inst., Washington, 1999; founder, head French Ctr. on U.S., IFRI, 1999—. Author: Le Retour de l'Histoire; Strategie et Relations internationales pendant et apres la guerre froide, 1993; contbr. numerous articles and reports to profl. publs. Mem. Internat. Inst. for Strategic Studies, French Inst. Internat. Rels., Royal Inst. for Internat. Affairs (assoc.). Gaullist. Roman Catholic. Avocation: fencing. Home: 9 Ave Constant Coquelin, 75007 Paris France Office: French Ctr on US IFRI, 27 rue Procession, 75740 Paris Cedex 15, France

PARMER, DAN GERALD, veterinarian; b. Wetumpka, Ala., July 3, 1926; s. James Lonnie and Virginia Gertrude (Guy) P.; m. Donna Louise Kesler, June 7, 1980; 1 child, Dan Gerald; 1 child from previous marriage, Linda Leigh. Student, L.A. City Coll., 1945-46; DVM, Auburn U., 1950. Gen. practice vet. medicine, Galveston, Tex., 1950-54, Chgo., 1959-83; veterinarian in charge Chgo. Commn. Animal Care and Control, 1974-88; med. dir. food protection divsn., disease outbreak control Chgo. Dept. Health, 1988-93, ret., 1993; dir. Cook County Dept. Animal Control, 1998—; chmn. Ill. Impaired Vets. Com., 1985-93; mem. Ala. Impaired Vets. Com., 1993-98; chmn. Ill. Wellness Com., 1998—; tchr. Highlands U., 1959; humane officer Elmore County, 1994—; dir. sales for south, southeast and lower midwest Am. Vet. Identification Devices, Norco, Calif., 1993-98, nat. dir. companion animal divsn., 1996—. Pres. Elmore County Humane Soc. Served with USNR, 1943-45, PTO, USAF Vet. Corps, 1954-59. Decorated 9 battle stars; recipient Vet. Appreciation award U. Ill., 1971, commendation Chgo. Commn. Animal Care and Control, 1987. Mem. VFW, AVMA (nat. com. for impaired vets., coun. pub. health and regulatory medicine 1990—, nat. com. animal welfare), Ill. Vet. Medicine Assn. (chmn. civil def. and package disaster hosps. 1968-71, Pres.' award 1986), Chgo. Vet. Medicine Assn. (bd. govs. 1969-72, 74-81, pres. 1982, treas. 1999, Lifetime Merit award 2000), South Chgo. Vet. Medicine Assn. (pres. 1965-66), Am. Animal Hosp. Assn. (dir.), Ill. Acad. Vet. Practice (pres. 1994), Nat. Assn. Professions, Am. Assn. Zoo Vets., Am. Assn. Zool. Parks and Aquariums, Elmore County Humane Soc. (pres. 1994-98), Midlothian Country Club, Valley Internat. Country Club, Masons, Shriners, Kiwanis, Ill. Acad. Vet. Medicine (pres.-elect 2000). Achievements include discovery of Bartonellosis in cattle in N.Am. and western hemisphere, 1951; co-development of bite-size high altitude in-flight feeding program USAF, 1954-56. Home: 5704 W 89th St Oak Lawn IL 60453-1222 Office: Cook County Animal Control 10220 S 76th Ave Bridgeview IL 60455-2427

PARNAS, JOSEF STEFAN STANISLAW, psychiatrist; b. Lublin, Poland, Apr. 24, 1950; arrived in Denmark, 1969, naturalized, 1977; s. Joseph and Zofia (Mijal) P.; m. Annick Urfer, Sept. 22, 1994; children: Josephine, Marie, Valentine. MD, U. Copenhagen, 1974, DMed. Scis., 1986. Specialist in psychiatry, Nat. Health Svc. Denmark, 1983. Intern State Hosp., Nykobing Sjaelland, Denmark, 1974-77; resident in psychiatry Kommunehospitalet, Copenhagen, 1977-79, rsch. assoc. dept. psychiatry, 1979-81, first resident in psychiatry, 1981-84, acting cons. in psychiatry, 1984-86, cons. in psychiatry, 1986—; asst. prof. psychiatry U. Copenhagen, 1979-86, assoc. prof., 1986—; sr. rsch. assoc. Psykologisk Inst. Kommunehospitalet, 1981-86, dir., 1986—; vis. prof. psychology U. So. Calif., 1988; vis. prof. psychiatry Lausaane U., Switzerland, 1995. Contbr. articles on Epileptology to profl. jours., 1978—, on schizophrenia to profl. jours., 1982—, on phenomenology, 1992—, on philosophy and phenomenology to profl. jours. Home: Strandvejen 187, 2900 Hellerup Denmark Office: Kommunehospitalet, Univ Dept Psychiatry, Copenhagen Denmark

PARNELL, CHARLES L., speechwriter; b. Myrtis, La., Feb. 13, 1938; s. Forrest L. and Dorothy D. (Jones) P. BA, Rice U., 1960; M Bus. and Pub. Adminstrn., Southeastern U., 1977. Commd. ens. USN, 1960, advanced through grades to comdr., 1975, ret., 1987; speechwriter Mead Data Cen., Dayton, Ohio, 1987-89, Nationwide Ins. Co., Columbus, Ohio, 1989-90; exec. speechwriter Miller Brewing Co., Milw., 1990-96; speechwriter, Milw., 1996-98; exec. speechwriter, Dallas, 1998—. Contbr. articles to profl. jours. Mem. U.S. Naval Inst., Ret. Officers Assn., World Future Soc., Pub. Rels. Soc. Am. Avocations: reading, writing, travel. Home and Office: 1311 Brittany Ln Mansfield TX 76063-4013

PARNELL, MICHAEL JOHN, medical products executive; b. London, July 8, 1940; s. Herbert Henry and Constance (Turner) P.; m. Freda Jenifer Wood, Feb. 19, 1971 (dec. July 2000); children: Claire Patricia Anne, Sarah Katie Louise, Lucinda Felicity Jayne. Licentiate Royal Soc. Chem. Student scientist May & Baker Ltd., Dagenham, Eng., 1958-63, head of electrochemistry rsch., 1963-73; head of med. devel. planning Rhone-Poulenc, Dagenham, Eng., 1973-90; dir. bus. devel. Rhone-Poulenc Rorer Ltd., Eastbourne, Eng., 1990-94; prin. cons. Mike Parnell Assocs., High Easter, Eng., 1994—. Author papers on pesticide sci. Churchwarden Ch. of England, High Easter, 1995—. Mem. Assn. for Project Mgmt., M & B Club (vice chmn. 1985—). Mem. Ch. of England. Avocations: rugby, travel, steam trains. Home and office: Mike Parnell Assocs, Old Post Office High Easter, Chelmsford Essex CM1 4QW, England

PARNES, EDMUND IRA, oral and maxillofacial surgeon, educator; b. Pitts., Apr. 16, 1936; s. David E. and Sara (Engelberg) P.; m. Elizabeth Cameron, Nov. 27, 1977; children: Dana, Mara, Lauren. Student, Vanderbilt U., 1954-55, U. Miami, 1955-56; DMD, U. Pitts., 1960. Diplomate Am. Bd. Oral and Maxillofacial Surgery. Oral surgery intern Jackson Meml. Hosp., Miami, Fla., 1960-61; resident, tchr. fellow in anesthesiology Presbyn. Univ. Hosp., Pitts., 1963-64; sr. resident in oral surgery Ben Taub Gen. Hosp., HOuston, 1964-65; pvt. practice oral and maxillofacial surgery, Miami, 1965—; interim assoc. chief oral surgery Jackson Meml. Hosp., Miami, 1970-72; clin. assoc. prof. U. Miami, 1975—; lectr. in field. Capt. U.S. Army, 1961-63. Fellow Am. Coll. Dentists, Am. Assn. Oral and Maxillofacial Surgeons (com. on legis. 1972-73, com. sci. sessions 1979-86, trustee 1991-94, pres.-elect 1994-95, pres. 1995-96), Internat. Coll. Dentists; mem. ADA, Fla. Soc. Oral and Maxillofacial Surgeons (pres. 1974-75), Fla. Dental Assn. (ho. of dels., trustee 1982-95, v.p. 1996, pres.-elect 1998, pres. 1999-2000), S.E. Soc. Oral Surgeons, East Coast Dist. Dental Soc. (chmn. coms. 1980-84, pres. 1981-82), North Dade Dental Soc. (pres. 1971-72), Am. Soc. Dental Anesthesiology (pres. Fla. chpt. 1970), Alpha Omega (pres. 1977-78, regent 1983), Hist. Assn. South Fla. (trustee, bd. dirs. Hist. Mus. South Fla.). Jewish. Office: 8700 N Kendall Dr Ste 221 Miami FL 33176-2206

PARNEVIK, JESPER BO, professional golfer; b. Stockholm, Sweden, Mar. 7, 1965; m. Mia Parnevik; children: Ida Josetin Peg, Penny, Phillipa. Student, Palm Beach Jr. Coll., graduated in 1993. Professional golfer PGA, 1986—; mem. Dunhill Cup team, 1993, 94, 95, 97, World Cup team, 1994, 95, Ryder Cup team, 1997, 99. Winner Odense (Sweden) Open, 1988, Raklosia Open, Sweden, 1988, Swedish Open, 1990, Scottish Open, 1993, Scandinavian Masters, 1995, 98, Trophee Lancome, 1996, Johnnie Walker Super Tour, 1997, Phoenix Open, 1998, Greater Greensboro Chrysler Classic, 1999; 2d pl. Phoenix Open, 1997, Buick Invitational, Freeport, 1997, Mc Dermott Classic, 1997, MCI Classic, 1997, Brit. Open Championship, 1997; 3d pl. Bob Hope Chrysler Classic, 1997, 2000, GTE Byron Nelson Classic, 2000. Office: PGA of America Box 109601 100 Ave of Champions Palm Beach Gardens FL 33410

PARNHAM, MICHAEL JOHN, pharmacologist; b. London, Mar. 13, 1951; arrived in Croatia, 1998; s. Walter and Sheila Jean (Horsman) P.; m. Elaine Cordelia Whitehead, Aug. 9, 1975; children: Philip, Joanna, Ian, Simon. BSc, London U., 1973; PhD, Bristol (Eng.) U., 1976; Habil. in Pharmacology and Toxicology, Frankfurt (Germany) U., 1990. Rsch. fellow Erasmus U., Rotterdam, The Netherlands, 1976-80; rsch. scientist A. Nattermann & Cie. GmbH, Cologne, Germany, 1980-82, head immunopharmacology, 1982-85; dir. gen. biology Rhône-Poulenc, Cologne, 1985-90, internat. project mgr., 1985-90; founding pres. Parnham Adv. Svcs., Bonn, Germany, 1990-98, FIRE GmbH, Bonn, 1992-97; dir. pharmacology and toxicology PLIVA, Zagreb, Croatia, 1998—; adj. prof. Goethe U., Frankfurt/Main, Germany, 1990—. Editor: (book series) Discoveries in Pharmacology, 1983-86, Progress in Inflammation Research, 1996—, Milestones in Drug Therapy, 1997—; mng. editor Inflammation Rsch., 1991—; news editor Experientia, 1992-95; co-inventor EBSELEN. Elder, Bible sch. tchr. Christliche Gemeinde Köln, 1986-97; deacon Zagreb Bapt. Ch., 1999—. Recipient Gosling prize Dutch Rheumatology Assn., 1980, Galenus prize German Med. Assn., 1990. Mem. Brit. Pharmacol. Soc., Inst. of Biology (U.K.), German Soc. for Pharmacology and Toxicology, European Inflammation Soc. (sec. 1980-88, 95-99), Internat. Assn. Inflammation Socs. (com. mem. 1992—). Avocations: church activities, T.V., cinema, walking, photography. E-mail: michael.parnham@pliva.hr. Office: PLIVA Rsch & Devel, Prilaz baruna Filipovica 25, HR-10000 Zagreb Croatia

PARNICHKUN, MANUKID, technology educator; b. Phetchabun, Thailand, Nov. 6, 1970; s. Marnas and Bencharong Parnichkun; m. Rieko Nishijima, Jan. 19, 1997; 1 child, Rom. B Engring., Chulalongkorn U., Bangkok, Thailand, 1991; M Engring., U. Tokyo, 1993, PhD, 1996. Asst. prof. Asian Inst. Tech., Pathumathani, Thailand, 1996—; assoc. faculty mem. Sirindhorn Internat. Inst. Tech., Pathumthani, 1997. Contbr. articles to profl. jours.; designer/builder robots. With Royal Thai Army, 1986-88. Monbusho scholar, 1991-96; grantee U. Tokyo, 1996, Nat. Sci. and Tech. Devel. Agy., Thailand, 1999. Buddhist. Avocations: reading, building equipment. Home: 11/434 Klong 5, Klongluang 12120, Thailand Office: Asian Inst Tech, PO Box 4, Klongluang 12120, Thailand

PARNIERE, PAUL, automotive company executive; b. Clermont-Ferrand, France, Apr. 4, 1943; s. Henry and Maria (Dupuy) P.; m. Genevieve Beaugeix, Apr. 26, 1967; children: Bruno, Stephane. Grad. in engring., Nat.

Higher Sch Arts and Bus., Paris, 1966; DSc, U. Orsay, France, 1978. Rschr. Inst. Recherche Siderurgie Francaise, St. Germain en Laye, France, 1969-72; head dept. Cen. Rsch. Lab. of French Iron and Steel Industry, St. Germain en Laye, 1972-82; dep. dir. rsch. Renault, Boulogne Billancourt, France, 1982-88, dir. strategy, 1988-92, exec. v.p., exec. sec., 1992-98, v.p. purchasing strategy, 1998—; mem. Nat. Com. Sci. Rschr., 1995-00. Mem. French Acad. Scis. (application coun. 1993). Home: 5 bis rue Maurice Denis, 78100 St Germain en Laye France Office: Renault, 49 Quai Le Gallo, 92109 Boulogne Billancourt France

PARO, GEORGIJ, performing company executive; b. Čačak, Yugoslavia, Apr. 12, 1934; s. Frane and Ana (Zwezdin) P.; m. Marija Aljinovic, July 20, 1961; 1 child, Aljoša. MA, Faculty of Philosophy, Zagreb, 1961; MFA, Acad. Dramatic Arts, Zagreb, 1965. Dir. Radio Zagreb, 1956-57; dir. drama Croatian Nat. Theatre, Zagreb, 1959-72, 84-86, theatre mgr., 1992—; artistic mgr. Sterija Theatre, Novisad, 1972-76; dramaturge Zora-Film, Zagreb, 1957-59; artistic mgr. drama program Dubrovnik Festival, 1976-84; prof. Acad. Dramatic Arts, Zagreb, 1986—; artistic dir. Jadran Film, Zagreb, 1987-91; dir. Croatian Nat. Theatre, Zagreb, 1992—; adj. prof. U. La Verne, Calif., 1993—. Author: From My Experience, 1981, Made in USA, 1990, Theatralia Disjecta, 1996, Conversation with Stjepan Miletić, 1999. Recipient award Town of Zagreb, 1950, Vladimir Nazor award Republic of Croatia, 1973, Dubravko Dujsin award Daily Newspaper Vjesnik, 1985, Croatian Theatre award Croatian Assn. Performing Artists, 1993, 95, Judita award Split Summer Festival, 1994, 95, Tito Strozzi award, 1996. Roman Catholic. Avocation: travel. Office: Hrvatsko Narodno Kazaliste, Trg Marsala Tita 15, 10000 Zagreb Croatia

PARODI, ANDRÉ LAURENT MARIE, veterinary medicine educator; b. Sidi-Bel-Abbès, Algeria, Aug. 6, 1933; m. Monique Blanchard-Gaillard; 2 children. DVM, Pasteur Inst.; D hon. causa, U. Cordoba, U. Bucharest. Prof. vet. pathology Nat. Vet. Sch., Alfort, France, 1977—, dean, 1992-98; mem. sci. com. on animal health European Union. Decorated chevalier Ordre Nat. Merite, officer Ordre Palmes Academiques, officer Ordre Merite Agr. (France), chevalier Ordre Legion d'honneur. Mem. World Assn. Vet. Pathologists (pres. 1986-98), Internat. Assn. for Comparative Rsch. on Leukemia and Related Diseases, European Coll. Vet. Pathologists (pres. 1999—), Vet. Acad. France (pres. 2000), Nat. Acad. Medicine, Am. Soc. Toxicol. Pathology, Am. Coll. Vet. Pathologists. E-mail: parodi@vet-alfort.fr. Office: Ecole Nat Vet, Dept Anat-Path, F-94704 Maisons-Alfort France

PARODI, RENATO AUGUSTO, dentist, researcher; b. Genova, Liguria, Italy, July 27, 1939; s. Emilio and Brunilde Italia Bianchi; m. Vilma Maestrale, Dec. 29, 1979; 1 child, Parodi Diego. Degree in surgery, Genova, Italy, 1964, degree in odontology, 1968. lectr. and essayist in field. Recipient sci. merits Amdi, Genova, 1997. Mem. AIC, ICD, SIDP. Office: Studio Parodi, Via Acquarone 3/29, 16121 Genova Liguria, Italy

PAROISSIEN, LEON FRANCIS, editor, art historian, curator; b. Gisborne, Victoria, Australia, Mar. 5, 1937; s. Victor Sydney and Emma Frances (Lennox) P.; m. Lucy Margaret Morris, May 17, 1958 (div. 1978); children: Karen, David. Trained secondary tchrs. cert., U. Melbourne, Australia, 1956, BA, 1968; diploma in Art, Caulfield Inst. Tech., Melbourne, 1964. Secondary tchr. Australia and U.K., 1957-68; lectr. Melbourne Tchrs. Coll., 1969-71; sr. lectr. Tasmanian Coll. Advanced Edn., Australia, 1972-73; dir. visual arts bd. Australia Coun., 1974-80; ind. writer, editor, curator Australia, 1980-84; curator Power Gallery Contemporary Art, U. Sydney, Australia, 1984-89; dir. Mus. Contemporary Art, Sydney, 1989-97; editor Visual Arts and Culture, St. Leonards, Australia, 1998—; dir. Biennale of Sydney, 1983-84; trustee Wollongong (Australia) City Gallery, 1986-90; mem. bd. Internat. Com. Museums and Collections Modern Art, 1986-97; mem. design rev. panel Olympic Coordination Authority, Australia, 1996—, chair pub. art adv. com., 1997—. Editor Australian Art Rev., 1981-82, Art and Australia, 1987-92, Visual Arts and Culture, 1998—; contbr. articles to profl. jours.

PAROMTCHIK, IGOR EUGENE, computer engineer, researcher; b. Minsk, Belarus, Nov. 5, 1963; s. Eugene Ivan and Ariadna Nikolai (Jilinskaya) P. BS, Sch. No. 19, Minsk, 1980; MS, Belarussian State U., Minsk, 1985, PhD, 1990. Asst. prof. Belarussian State U., 1988-95; expert engr. INRIA-Nat. Inst. Computer Sci. and Control, Grenoble, France, 1995—; vis. rschr. U. Karlsruhe, Germany, 1992-94, RIKEN-Inst. Chem. and Phys. Rsch., Tokyo, 1997—. Contbr. numerous articles to sci. jours., also chpts. to books; patentee in field. German Acad. Exchange Svc. fellow, 1992, NATO Sci. fellow Natural Scis. and Engring. Rsch. Coun., Can., 1995, Sci. and Tech. Agy. fellow Japan Internat. Sci. and Tech. Exch. Ctr., 1997. Avocations: jogging, skiing, languages. Office: INRIA Rhône-Alpes, 655 Ave de l'Europe, 38330 Montbonnot Saint Martin France

PAROT, FRANCOISE MARIE, psychology educator, researcher; b. Montereau, France, Apr. 22, 1947; d. Roger and Denise (Lottier) P.; 1 child, Jeanne Mengal. Doctorate, U. Paris V, 1975; Habilitation, U. Paris XI, 1993. Asst. U. Paris V, 1970-78, prof. psychology, 1978—. Co-author: Dictionnaire de Psychologie, 1990, Introduction à la Psychologie, 1992; author: L'Homme Qui Ré Ve, 1995; editor: Pour une Psychologie Historique, 1996. Sect. pres. Human Rights League, Verrières, France, 1997-99. Office: U Paris V UFR Psychology, 75 Ave Ed Vaillant, 92774 Boulogne Cedex, France

PARPALA-SPÅRMAN, TEIJA MIRJAMI, surgeon, urologist; b. Kemi, Finland, Apr. 30, 1965; d. Reijo Topias and Lea Marja (Vittaniemi) Parpala; m. Kari Juhani Spårman, Sept. 2, 1995; children: Santeri, Sonja. Grad. in Medicine, Oulu (Finland) U. Hosp., 1990, grad. in Surgery, 1996, PhD of Urology, 1998. Resident in surgery Länsi-Pohja Hosp., Kemi, Finland, 1991-94; resident in surgery Oulu U. Hosp., 1994-96, resident in urology, 1996-98, urologist, 1998—. Contbr. articles to profl. jours.; patentee in field. Mem. Finnish Assn. Urologists. Avocations: cross country and downhill skiing, hunting, fishing, sports. Office: Oulu Univ Hosp, Kajaanintie 50, 90220 Oulu Finland

PARPAZOV, ARKADI SOLOMON, limnologist, researcher; b. Verkhoturye, Sverdlovsk, USSR, Nov. 17, 1943; arrived in Israel, 1990; s. Solomon Lev and Sophia Lazar (Kaminskya) P.; m. Rosa Moisei Khvoinitskaya, 1967; children: Anna, Sofia. Grad. phys. dept., U. Dniepropetrovsk, USSR, 1967; PhD in Hydrobiology and Limnology, U. Minsk, USSR, 1980. Scientist Inst. To Save Coal Miners, Donetsk, USSR, 1967-69; sr. engr. Elecotech. Inst., Torez, USSR, 1969-74; scientist Sevan (USSR) Hydrobiol. Sta., 1974-75, sec. scis., 1975-87, leading scientist, 1987-90; scientist Yigal Allon Kinneret Limnological Lab., Tiberias, Israel, 1990—; lectr. Yerevan (USSR) U., 1978-80; reviewer Obshchei Biologii, 1975-85. Grantee Soc. Com. on Sci. and Technics, 1980, Israel Ministry Scis., 1991, BMBFA, 1994. Office: Kinneret Limnological Lab, PO Box 345, 14102 Tiberias Israel

PARR, WENDY V., science educator; b. Waverley, Taranaki, New Zealand, June 23, 1951; d. Philip John Parr and Nancy Jackson; m. Thomas James Edhouse; m. Philip George Simpson. BA, Victoria U. Wellington, New Zealand, 1982, BA with honors, 1983; PhD, Otago U., Dunedin, New Zealand, 1988. Registered nurse, midwife, New Zealand. Nursing supr. Hutt Hosp., Wellington, 1976-84; sr. lectr. Victoria U. Wellington, 1988—; dir. Isis Group Seminars Ltd., New Zealand, 1986-90; cons. psychologist New Zealand Olympic and Commonwealth Games Assn., 1989-91. Contbr. articles to profl. jours. Recipient New Zealand Psychol. Soc. Ann. award for best student conf. paper, 1986, Royal Soc. New Zealand Young Scientist award, 1988; PhD scholar New Zealand Univ. Grants Com., 1985. Mem. New Zealand Assn. Scientist, Psychonomic soc. Avocation: wine science. Fax: 064 3 325 3851. E-mail: parrw1@lincoln.ac.nz. Home: 28 Roblyn Pl, Lincoln Canterbury New Zealand Office: Lincoln U, Lincoln Canterbury New Zealand

PARRA-ARANGUREN, GONZALO, judgeInternational Court of Justice; b. Caracas, Venezuela, Dec. 5, 1928. Degree, Ctrl. U. Venezuela, Inter-Am. Law Inst., NYU, Ludwig-Maximilians U., Munich. Prof. Ctrl. U. Venezuela, Caracas, 1956—, Andrés Bello Cath. U., Caracas, 1957—; judge 2d Ct. of 1st Instance Fed. Dist. and State of Miranda, Caracas, 1958-71; 1st assoc. judge Chamber of Cassation Supreme Ct. of Justice, Caracas, 1988-92; alt. judge Supreme Ct. of Justice, 1992; kidge Internat. Ct. Justice, The Hague, The Netherlands; mem. nat. group for Venezuela Permanent Ct. of Arbitration, The Hague, 1985—; arbitrator, Venezuela and abroad; mem. legal adv. com. Ministry of Fgn. Affairs, 1984—, Nat. Congress, 1990—; mem. Acad. Polit. and Social Scis. of Caracas, 1966—, pres., 1993-95; mem. Inst. of Internat. Law, 1979—; Venezuelan rep. several sessions of The Hague Conf. on Pvt. Internat. Law. Author books in field; contbr. articles to profl. jours. Office: Internat Ct of Justice, Peace Palace, 2517 KJ The Hague The Netherlands*

PARRA-MEJIA, TULIO E., surgeon; b. Pamplona, Colombia, Aug. 27, 1950; s. Jose D. and Florentina (Mejia) P. B.S., Colegio Carmelitano, Pamplona, 1968; M.D., U. Nacional de Colombia, Bogota, 1976. Cert. cardiovascular and thoracic surgeon Colombia. Intern and resident U. Nacional, Bogota, 1979-82; surgeon Hosp. Regional, Villavicencio, Colombia, 1982-83, chmn. dept. surgery, Duitama, Colombia, 1983-84; mem. dept. thoracic and cardiovascular surgery Hosp. Militar Central, Bogota, 1985—; dir. intern program Villavicencio, 1982-83. Contbr. articles to profl. jours. Mem. Sociedad Colombiana de Cirugia, Asociacion de Antiguos Alumnos de Medicina U. Nacional, Soc. Internationale de Chirurgie, Sociedad Colombiana de Cardiologia, N.Y. Acad. Scis. Home: Apartado Aereo, 42813 Bogota Colombia

PARREIRA, CARLOS ALBERTO, soccer coach; b. Rio de Janeiro, Mar. 25, 1943; m. Leila Parreira; children: Vanessa, Danielle. Diploma in phys. edn., Fed. U., Rio de Janeiro, 1966. Coach Novo Mexico, Brazil, 1965, Sao Cristovao, Brazil, 1966-67, Nat. Team, Ghana, 1967, Kotoko, Ghana, 1968; phys. preparation mgr. Vasco, Brazil, 1969, Flumenise and Brazil's Nat. Team, 1970-74; coach Flumenise, 1974, 84, coach, phys. preparation mgr., 1975; coach Nat. Team, Kuwait, 1976-83, Brazil, 1983, 91-94, United Arab Emirates, 1984-88, 90, Saudi Arabia, 1988-89; coach Bragantino, Brazil, 1991, Valencia, Spain, 1994-95, Fenerbahce, Turkey, 1995-96, Sao Paulo, Brazil, 1996, N.Y./N.J. Metro Stars, Secaucus, N.J., 1996-97, Saudi Arabia Nat. Team, 1997-98; coach, mgr. Atletico Mineiro. Recipient World Cup, Saudi Arabia, 1998, Mercosur Cup, 2000. Avocations: painting, rug collecting. *

PARRESOL, BERNARD ROSS, research biometrician, statistician; b. Washington, Sept. 15, 1953; s. Thomas and Rita Delores P.; m. Lisa Leigh Morton-Barbé, May 5, 1995; children: Sarah Marie Barbé, Christine Pamela Barbé. BS with honors, Mich. State U., 1977; M of Applied Stats., La. State U., 1983, PhD, 1998. Reg. forester, N.C. Br. mgr. James M. Vardaman & Co. Forestry Cons., Shreveport, La., 1977-80; rsch. assoc. dept. explt. stats. La. State U., Baton Rouge, 1983-86; math. statistician USDA Forest Svc., New Orleans, 1986-95, Asheville, N.C., 1996—; stats. cons. Internat. Inst. Tropical Forestry, Rio Piedras, P.R., 1987—; guest lectr. Nanjing (China) Forestry U., 1994, 97, U. de Tras-os-Montes e Alto Douro, Portugal, 1998; adj. prof. U. Fla., 1999—. Assoc. editor Forest Sci., 1999—; contbr. articles to profl. jours. Officer La. Indian Heritage Assn., 1988-92. Scholar Rockefeller Found., 1990; grantee Smithsonian Tropical Rsch. Inst., Panama, 1992, U.S. Office Internat. Coop. and Devel., Chile, 1993. Mem. Am. Statistical Assn., Soc. Am. Foresters, Internat. Soc. Tropical Foresters. Avocation: Am. Indian culture. Fax: 828-257-4840. E-mail: bparresol@fs.fed.us. Office: USDA Forest Svc PO Box 2680 Asheville NC 28802-2680

PARRETTE, LESLIE JACKSON, lawyer; b. Mt Pleasant, Mo., Aug. 25, 1961; s. Leslie Jackson and Janet Parrette. AB, Harvard Coll., 1983; JD, Harvard Law Sch., 1986. Assoc. Hale & Dorr, Boston, 1986-89, Watson Ess Marshall & Enggas, Kansas City, Mo., 1989-91, Bryan Cave, Kansas City, Mo., 1991-92; ptnr. Blackwell Sanders Peper Martin, Kansas City, Mo., 1992—; mem. adv. com. Ctr. for Internat. Bus., U. Mo., Kansas City. Vice chmn., dir. Kansas City Boys Choir, 1996—; dir. The Eye Found., 1996—, Big Brother Phillips Brooks House, Cambridge, Mass., 1980—; bd. dirs. Internat. Trade Club Greater Kansas City; commr. Sister City Commn., 1999—. Office: Balckwell Sanders Peper Martin LLP 2300 Main St Ste 1100 Kansas City MO 64108-2416

PARRICK, GERALD HATHAWAY, communication and marketing executive; b. Cushing, Okla., Oct. 27, 1924; s. Gerald H. and Phyllis A. (Sheppard) P. BJ, U. Mo., 1948; m. Gail V. Straney, Dec. 5, 1984; children: Gerald Hathaway III, Candace Anne. Creative account exec. George Knox & Assoc., Oklahoma City, 1948-51; account exec. Batten, Barton, Durstine & Osborn, San Francisco, 1952-60; account dir. McCann-Erickson, Los Angeles, 1960-67, v.p., Portland, Oreg., 1967-72; dir. communications Pacific Power Co., Portland, 1972-77, spl. asst. to chmn. bd., 1977-79; pres. Entreepublic Communications, West Linn, Oreg., 1979—, Bailey/Parrick, Inc., Portland, 1981-84, Parrick/Milpacher, Inc., Portland, 1984-85, The Laugh Clinic, Inc., Portland, 1984-90, K-KOR, Inc., 1990-93. Author: A 20th Century Miracle, 1981, Touched by a Miracle, 1997. Mem. Oreg. Advt. Rev. Bd., 1974-75. Served to capt. AUS, 1943-45, 51-52, ETO. Named Oreg. Advt. Man of Yr., Oreg. Advt. Club, 1971. Mem. Am. Advt. Fedn. (chmn. edn. western region 1973-74), Portland Advt. Fedn. (pres. 1974-75), Toastmasters (pres. 1966-67) (Encino, Calif.), Kappa Tau Alpha. Home: 3950 Elmran Dr West Linn OR 97068-1509

PARRILLO, THOMAS MATTHEW, secondary education educator; b. Chgo.; s. Robert William and Emma Mae P.; m. Jeanine Marie Parrillo, June 25, 1993; 1 child, Sophia Marie. BA in English, Colo. State U., 1991; MA in English Edn., Adams State Coll., 1999. Cert. secondary English, Colo. English tchr. Steamboat Springs (Colo.) H.S., 1992-99, Ft. Collins (Colo.) H.S., 1999—. Fulbright grantee U.S. Info. Agy., 1995. Mem. Nat. Coun. Tchrs. English. Republican. Roman Catholic. E-mail: tparrill@psd.k12.co.us. Home: 516 S Monterey Ave Villa Park IL 60181-2717 Office: Ft Collins HS 3400 Lambkin Way Fort Collins CO 80525

PARRINDER, JOHN PATRICK, English literature educator, literary critic; b. Wadebridge, Eng., Oct. 11, 1944; s. Eric Reginald and Eileen Dorothy (Skeffington-White) P.; divorced; children: Anna Christina, Lisa Monica. MA, U. Cambridge, 1965, PhD, 1969. Fellow King's Coll., Cambridge, 1969-74; lectr. U. Reading, Eng., 1974-80, reader, 1980-86, prof., 1986—; vis. prof. U. Ill., Urbana-Champaign, 1978-79, U. Calif., Santa Barbara, 1989. Author: H.G. Wells, 1970; Science Fiction: Its Criticism and Teaching, 1980, James Joyce, 1984, The Failure of Theory, 1987, Authors and Authority, 1991, Shadows of the Future, 1995; editor: H.G. Wells: The Critical Heritage, 1972, Learning from Other Worlds, 2000. Mem. H.G. Wells Soc. (v.p. 1989—), Sci. Fiction Found. Avocation: ornithology. Office: Dept English U Reading, PO Box 218, Reading RG6 6AA, England

PARRIS, MARK ROBERT, ambassador; b. Mpls.; m. Joan Elizabeth Gardner; 2 children. BS magna cum laude, Georgetown U., 1974. With Fgn. Svc., 1972-77; polit. counselor Fgn. Svc., Moscow, 1982-85, dir. Office Soviet Union Affairs, 1985-88; dep. chief mission U.S. Embassy, Tel Aviv, 1989-92; spl. asst. pres., sr. dir. Nat. Security Coun., Washington, 1995-97; amb. to Turkey Ankara, 1997—. Mem. policy bd. Una Chapman Cox Found., U.S.-Israel Edn. Found. Phi Beta Kappa. Office: Am Embassy Ankara Turkey Dept State Washington DC 20521-0001

PARRISH, DAVID WALKER, JR., legal publishing company executive; b. Bristol, Tenn., Feb. 8, 1923. BA, Emory & Henry Coll., 1948, LLD, 1978; BS, U.S. Merchant Marine Acad., 1950; LLB, U. Va., 1951. Pres. The Michie Co., Charlottesville, Va., 1969-89, vice chmn., 1989-96; pub. cons., 1996—. Home: 114 Falcon Dr Charlottesville VA 22901-2013 Office: 300 Preston Ave Ste 103 Charlottesville VA 22902-5044

PARRISH, LORI NANCE, county commissioner; b. Evansville, Ind., July 31, 1948; m. Geoffrey Cohen; children: Gary Brown, Brandi Schmidt. Student, Fla. Atlantic U., 1969, Nova/Davie Cmty. Sch., 1974-75, Broward C.C., Davie, Fla., 1980, Clemson U., 1982, Fla. Atlantic U., 1986, Fla. Atlantic U., 1988; LHD (hon.), Keiser Coll., 1996; postgrad., U. Ctrl. Fla., 1996—. Toll operator So. Bell Telephone Co., 1966-68; adminstrv. asst. Appraisal and Cons. Loan Dept. Hollywood Fed. Savings and Loan Assn., 1968-72; acct., qualifying agt. Victor Purdo Painting Co., 1972-81; fin. mgr. CRG, Inc., 1982-83; bookkeeper I county and vocational Sch. Bd. Broward County South Plantation H.S., 1983-84; commr. dist. 5 Broward County, Fla., 1988-98; chair Broward County, 1990-91, vice chair, 1989-90, 96—; spl. projects coord. Davie/Cooper City C. of C.; adminstrv. asst. to bldg. ofcl. City of Cooper City; landscape contractor, owner Earthy Interiors; Lake Shore Motel and Swap, Inc. (dba Margate Swap Shop), 3290 Sunrise Investments, Inc., 3291 Sunrise Investments, Inc., Fla. Drive-In Theater Mgmt., Inc. (dba Fort Lauderdale Swap Shop). Mem. Broward County Libr. Adv. Bd., 1979-85, Mommas and Poppas of Cooper City High, 1982-90, Broward C.C. Women's Programs Adv. Com., 1981-82; chair Cooper City Elem. Sch. Adv. Com., 1980-82, sec., 1979-80; chair South Ctrl. Area Adv. Com., 1982-83, sec., 1981-82; legis. chair Broward County Libr. Adv. Bd., 1982-84; mem. Broward County Sch. Bd., 1984-88, vice chair, 1987, chair, 1988; bd. dirs. Pembroke Pines Human Resource Ctr. Adv. Com., 1984-88, and numerous others. Recipient of numerous awards including Legislator of Yr. award Broward County Fire Fighters and Paramedics, 1994, Humanitarian of Yr. award Soref Jewish Cmty. Ctr., 1995, award Manatee Survival Found., 1996, Dream Maker award Jr. League Greater Fort Lauderdale, 1996, Jesse Portis Helms award Dolphin Den Club, 1996, Par Excellence award Miramar High Cmty. Sch., 1997, Ray Lisanty Meml. award GUARD, 1999, Gracias award Hispanic Unity, 1999, Polit. Leader of Yr. award The Vanguard Chronicle, 1999; named to Broward County Women's Hall of Fame, 1997. Mem. ALA, Southeastern Libr. Assn., Davie/Cooper City Friends of Libr. (founder), Fort Lauderdale Friends of Libr., Broward County Friends of Libr., and numerous others. Office: Office County Commr Govtl Ctr 115 S Andrews Ave Ste 421 Fort Lauderdale FL 33301-1801

PARRISH, MATTHEW DENWOOD, psychiatrist; b. Washington, Apr. 1, 1918; s. Forrest Denwood and Alice Lorena (Flynn) P.; m. Virginia John Bennet, Sept. 24, 1944 (div.); children: Denwood, John, Stephen; m. Marilyn Kay Arney, May 29, 1978; children: Megan, Maxwell. BA, U. Va., 1939; MD, George Washington U., 1950. Diplomate Am. Bd. Psychiatry. Intern Letterman Hosp., San Francisco, 1950-51; resident in psychiatry Walter Reed Hosp., Washington, 1951-54; commd. 2d lt. U.S. Army, 1941, advanced through grades to col., 1967, ret., 1971; chief tng. Ill. Dept. Mental Health, Chgo., 1972-74; supt. Singer Mental Health Ctr., Rockford, Ill., 1974-85, med. dir., 1985-93; child and adolescent psychiatrist, 1986-95, ret., 1996; clin. prof. psychiatry U. Ill., Chgo., 1972-76; clin. asst. prof. psychiatry Coll. Med., Rockford, 1976—. Editor in chief: U.S. Army Vietnam Medical Journal, 1967-68. Decorated Legion of Merit (2). Fellow Am. Psychiat. Assn. (life); mem. Soc. Med. Cons. in Armed Forces, Assn. Mil. Surgeons U.S. Avocations: writing, photography, painting, linguistics, electronics.

PARRISH, MAURICE DRUE, museum executive; b. Chgo., Mar. 5, 1950; s. Maurice and Ione Yvonne (Columns) P.; m. Gail Marie Sims, Sept. 2, 1978; children: Theodore, Andrew, Brandon, Cara. BA in Arch., U. Pa., 1972; MArch, Yale U., 1975. City planner City of Chgo., 1975-81; architect John Hiltscher & Assocs., Chgo., 1981-83, Barnett, Jones & Smith, Chgo., 1983-84; zoning adminstr. City of Chgo., 1984-87, bldg. commr., 1987-89; dep. dir. Detroit Inst. of Arts, 1989-97, interim dir., 1997-99, exec. v.p., 1999—. Bd. dirs. Arts League of Mich., Detroit, 1994-97, Mosaic Youth Theatre Detroit, 2000—; co-chmn. Mayor's Affordable Housing Task Force, Chgo., 1984-89; chmn. Chgo. Elec. Commn., 1988-89; mem. Chgo. Econ. devel. Commn., 1987-89; pres. St. Philip Neri Sch. Bd., Chgo., 1981-85, South Shore Commn., Chgo., 1982-84. King Chavez Parks fellow U. Mich., 1991, H.I. Feldman fellow Yale U., 1972; Franklin W. Gregory scholar Yale U., 1974, Nat. Achievement scholar U. Pa., 1968. Mem. Am. Assn. Mus., Am. Assn. Mus. Adminstrs., Constrn. Specifications Inst., Lambda Alpha. Avocations: golf, chess, reading, astronomy. Office: Detroit Inst of Arts 5200 Woodward Ave Detroit MI 48202-4094

PARRISH, NORMAN CHARLES, technical consultant, mechanical engineer; b. Los Angeles, Feb. 28, 1912; s. George Cornelius and Estella Nancy (Lay) P.; m. Margaret Pierce Smith (div. Nov. 1969); 1 child, Candace Parrish Peterson; m. Dorothy Dalley Caswell, Jan. 16, 1976; stepchildren: Thomas Caswell, James Caswell, Dennis Caswell. AA, Los Angeles City Coll., 1933; BSME, U. So. Calif., 1942, MS, 1965. Rsch. engr. Lockheed Aircraft Co., Burbank, Calif., 1937-42; dir. Parlin Engring. Co., Hawthorne, Calif., 1943-46; field tech. cons. So. Calif. Edison Co., L.A., 1946-48; preliminary design engr. Northrop Aircraft Co., Hawthorne, 1947-54; research engr. Lockheed Missiles & Space Co., Sunnyvale, Calif., 1955-60; mem. tech. staff Hughes Aerospace Co., El Segundo, Calif., 1960-65; staff scientist Lawrence Berkeley (Calif.) Lab, 1966-81; tech. cons., 1981—; adj. prof. Monterey Inst. Internat. Studies, 1992-96, ret., 1997; cons. U.S. Dept. Energy, 1975-80, Nat. Bur. Standards, 1975-80, SEC, San Francisco, 1979-80; chmn. Nat. Def. Exec. Res., San Francisco, 1979-81; chief engr. animal in space program U. Calif., Berkeley. Author: Micro Diaphragm Pressure Transducers, 1964, Proc. Hawaii Inventors Conf., 1978, Successful Inventing, 1989; co-author: Inventors Source Book, 1978. Mem. Am. Soc. for Metals, Nat. Congress Inventor Orgns. (pres. 1983-92), Inventors of Calif. (bd. dirs. 1979-92). Home: 215 Rheem Blvd Moraga CA 94556-1513

PARRISH-ST. JOHN, FLORENCE TUCKER, writer, retired government official; b. Greenville, Miss., Nov. 12; d. Victor Amos and Martha Buchannan (Binkley) Denslow; m. Joseph Nathaniel Tucker Jr., Nov. 9, 1946 (dec. Dec. 1955); children: Joseph Nathaniel III, Frederick Steven, James Denslow; m. Noel Francis Parrish, June 25, 1983 (dec. Apr. 1987); m. Adrian St. John, Jan. 29, 1998. Diploma in piano, Ward-Belmont Coll., Nashville, 1945; studied piano with Michael Field, N.Y.C., 1945-46; B of Music Edn., Delta State U., Cleveland, Miss., 1960; MS in Counseling, U. So. Miss., 1971; EdD in Human Resources, George Washington U., 1983. Tchr. music Gulfport (Miss.) Pub. Schs., 1959-63; recreation therapist VA Hosp., Gulfport, 1964-70; edn. counselor USAF, Miss. and Japan, 1971-74; edn. svcs. officer, 1974-75, asst. dir. sr. tng. CAP nat. hdqrs., 1975-77; EEO officer D.C. Dept. Labor, 1977-80; bur. chief complaints processing and adjudication Office EEO, U.S. Geol. Survey, Reston, Va., 1980-82; mgr. human resources Dept. Interior, 1982-84; internat. forum coord. Inspire 85 Pres.'s Com. on Employment of Handicapped, 1985; commr. Alexandria Commn. on Aging, Va., 1985-88, chmn. edn. and cultural affairs com., 1985-88; sec. Alexandria Commn. on Aging, 1987-88; lead scholar pilot project Nat. Coun. Aging; vis. prof. Kunsan Tchrs. Coll., Kunsan Jr. Coll., 1974-75; apptd. mem. del. People-to-People Internat. Amb. Program, Beijing, Peoples Republic China and Hong Kong, 1988; mem. steering com. Va. Home Care Alliance, 1990-92; mem. exec. bd. Washington Opera Guild, 1992-94; chmn. Night in Old Vienna benefit ball Embassy of Austria, Washington, 1993, co-chair, 1994; mem. adv. bd. Inst. Conflict Analysis and Resolution George Mason U., 1993—, vice chair, 1995-97, chmn., 1998-2000; del. to Arms Ctrl. Negotiations in the Middle East, Athens, Greece, 1994; mem. ofcl. delegation 8th Internat. Helicopter Olympic Competition, Moscow, 1994; workshop leader, cons. and lectr. in field; bd. dirs. Wake Assocs., Ltd., Washington, 1980-84. Columnist on aging issues, Alexandria Gazette-Packet, feature writer, 1986-92; contrb. articles to profl. jours. Organizer, pres. Gulfport chpt. Parents-Without-Ptnrs., 1962-64; charter mem. Westminster Presbyn. Ch., Gulfport, 1961; active Nat. Coun. on Aging, Military Classics Seminar; officer, bd. dirs. Stonehurst IV Homeowners Assn., 1994-96. Recipient Outstanding Vis. Prof. award Kunsan Tchrs. Coll., 1974, Kunsan Jr. Coll. award for promoting tchr. exch. program, also certs. of commendation, Brigadier Gen. Noel F. Parrish award The Nat. Tuskegee Airmen, Inc., commendation for organizing Young at Art art show Alexandria Commn. on Aging. Mem. Women in Comm., Washington Opera Guild, USAF Assn. (v.p. for cmty. programs Gen. Charles Gabriel chpt. 1991-98, Woman of Distinction award Thomas Anthony chpt., Pres.'s award 1998), NATO Def. Coll. Anciens Assn., Am. Inst. Wine and Food, World Affairs Coun., Va. Assn. on Aging, Nat. Press Club (events and oral history coms., chmn. oral history com., sr. rep. NPC trip to China and Hong Kong 1998, Vivian award 1998, 99, 2000), Miss. Soc. Washington, Ret. Officers Assn., Friends of Kennedy Ctr., Smithsonian Assocs., The Nat. Tuskegee Airmen Inc. Orgn. Home: Stonehurst 9302 Arlington Blvd Fairfax VA 22031-2503 also: 9110 Belvoir Woods Pkwy Apt 118 Fort Belvoir VA 22060-2717

PARR-JOHNSTON, ELIZABETH, academic administrator; b. N.Y.C., Aug. 15, 1939; d. Ferdinand Van Siclen (dec.) and Helene Elizabeth (Ham) Parr (dec.); m. David E. Bond, Dec. 28, 1962 (div. July 1975); children: Peter V.S., Kristina Aline; m. Archibald F. Johnston, Mar. 6, 1982; children: James, Heather, Alexandra, Margaret. BA, Wellesley Coll., 1961; MA, Yale U., 1962, PhD, 1973; postgrad., Harvard U., 1986. Various positions Govt. of Can., Ottawa, Ont., 1973-76, INCO Ltd., Toronto, 1976-79; chief of staff,

sr. policy advisor Ministry of Employment and Immigration, Govt. of Can., 1979-80; various positions Shell Can. Ltd., Calgary, Alta., 1980-90; pres. Parr-Johnston & Assocs., Calgary, 1990-91; pres., vice-chancellor Mt. St. Vincent U., Halifax, Nova Scotia, N.S., 1991-96, The U. New Brunswick, Fredericton, Can., 1996—; instr. U. Western Ont., London, Ont., 1964-67, U. B.C., Vancouver, 1967-71; vis. scholar Wesleyan U., Middletown, Conn., 1971-72; acad. rsch. assoc. Carleton U., Ottawa, 1972-73; bd. dirs. Nova Scotia Power, Bank of Nova Scotia, Fishery Products Internat., The Empire Co., Social Rsch. and Demonstration Corp., BioAtlantech Ltd.; spkr. and presenter in field. Mem. editorial bd. Can. Econ. Jour., 1980-83; contbr. articles to profl. jours. Bd. dirs. Dellcrest Home, 1980-84, Calgary S.W. Fed. Riding Assn., 1985-91, The Learning Ctr., Calgary, 1989-91, Halifax United Way, 1991-92, North/South Inst., 1992-96, Coun. for Can. Unity, 1993—, Vol. Planning N.S., 1992-93, Social Sci. Rsch. Coun., 1995-99; planning chmn. John Howard Soc., 1980-84; mem. policy adv. com. C.D. Howe, 1980-85; mem. Ont. Econ. Coun., 1981-84. Woodrow Wilson fellow, 1962. Mem. Assn. Atlantic Univs. (chair 1994-96), Assn. Univs. and Colls. in Can. (bd. dirs., mem. exec. com. 1994-96), Women in Acad. Adminstrn. (adv. bd. 1991-96), Calgary Coun. Advanced Tech. (exec. 1990-91), Can. Econs. Assn., Inst. Pub. Adminstrn. Can., Sr. Women Acad. Adminstrs. Can., Assn. Commonwealth Univs. (former mem. exec. com.), Phi Beta Kappa. Anglican. Avocations: skiing, golf, sailing, travel. Office: U NB Office of Pres, PO Box 4400, Fredericton, NB Canada E3B 5A3

PARROTT, DENNIS BEECHER, retired insurance executive; b. St. Louis, June 13, 1929; s. Maurice Ray and Mai Ledgerwood (Beecher) P.; m. Vivian Cleveland Miller, Mar. 24, 1952; children: Constance Beecher, Dennis Beecher, Anne Cleveland. BS in Econs., Fla. State U., Tallahassee, 1954; postgrad., Princeton U., 1964; MBA, Pepperdine U., 1982. With Prudential Ins. Co. Am., 1954-74; v.p. group mktg. Prudential Ins. Co. Am., L.A., 1971-74; sr. v.p. Frank B. Hall Cons. Co., L.A., 1974-83; v.p. Johnson & Higgins, L.A., 1983-95; exec. v.p. Arthur J. Gallagher & Co., L.A., 1995-98; ret., 1998; spkr. in field. Chmn. Weekend with the Stars Telethon, 1976-80; chmn. bd. dirs. United Cerebral Palsy/Spastic Children's Found., L.A. County, 1979-82, chmn. bd. govs., 1982-83; bd. dirs. Nat. United Cerebral Palsy Assn., 1977-82, pres., 1977-79; bd. dirs. L.A. Emergency Task Force, 1992; mem. cmty. adv. coun. Birmingham High Sch., Van Nuys, Calif., 1982-85; sect. chmn. United Way, L.A., 1983-84; bd. dirs. The Betty Clooney Found. for Brain Injured, 1986-88; mem. com. to fund an endowed chair in cardiology at Cedars-Sinai Med. Ctr., 1986-88; adv. coun. Family Health Program, Inc., 1986-88; bd. deacons Bel Air Presbyn. Ch., 1990-92, chmn., 1991-92, elder, 1993-96; mem. adv. coun. Blue Cross Calif., 1996-98; chmn. Danny Arnold Meml. Golf Classic at Riviera Country Club benefitting John Wayne Cancer Inst., 1997. 1st lt. AUS, 1951-53. Mem. Am. Soc. C.L.U.s., Internat. Found. Employee Benefits, Merchants and Mfrs. Assns. 44th Ann. Mgmt. Conf. (chmn. 1986), Employee Benefits Planning Assn. So. Calif., L.A. Club, Woodland Hills Country Club, Jonathan Club (L.A.). Republican. Presbyterian. Home: 17023 Encino Hills Dr Encino CA 91436-4009

PARROTT, DENNIS BEECHER, accountant; b. Atlanta, Sept. 11, 1957; s. Dennis Beecher and Vivian Miller Parrott; m. Tami Bennett, Apr. 12, 1980; children: Shelby, Beecher, Macy, Haley, Baxter. BA, U. Calif., Santa Barbara, 1979. CPA, Calif., Ky. Mng. ptnr. KPMG LLP, Louisville, 1979—. Pres. U. Calif. Santa Barbara Acctg. Alumni Assn., 1989-91, Orange County Sigma Chi Alumni Assn., Newport Beach, Calif., 1990-93; trustee South Coast Repretory Theatre, Costa Mesa, Calif., 1990-97. Named Acctg. Alumnus of Yr., U. Calif. Santa Barbara, 1993. Mem. AICPA, CSCPA, KSCPA, Jefferson Club, Valhalla Golf Club, Lake Forest Country Club, Young Pres. Orgn. (Bluegrass chpt.). Office: KPMG LLP 400 W Market St Ste 2600 Louisville KY 40202-3357

PARROTT, MICHAEL VERNE, manufacturing company executive; b. Marshall, Minn., Mar. 2, 1940; s. Robert Belgrove and Paula (Verne) P.; m. Kathryn Ann Rue, Dec. 22, 1964; children: Jennifer Rue, Deborah Corinne, Lesleigh Ann. BA, Carleton Coll., 1962; MBA, Stanford U., 1964. Mgr. dist. sales Inland Steel, Detroit, 1964-69; gen. mgr. Essex Machinery Terminals, Ft. Wayne, Ind., 1969-74; pres. Dunbar Furniture Co., Berne, Ind., 1974-75; chmn., pres., chief exec. officer ICON Internat., Inc., Ft. Wayne, 1979—; bd. dirs. Grange Mut. Cos., Columbus, Ohio, Cogeneration Systems, Nashville, Ind. Trustee, founder The Canterbury Sch., Ft. Wayne, 1976; trustee Parkview Meml. Hosp., Ft. Wayne, 1985. Mem. Greater Ft. Wayne C. of C. (chmn. 1988), Quest Club, Bus. Forum, Ft. Wayne County Club. Home: 6730 Mallard Cove Ter Fort Wayne IN 46804-2888

PARROTT, THENA ELIZABETH, nurse educator; b. Amarillo, Tex., Sept. 13, 1950; d. William Duard and Ruth Virginia (Crist) Henry; m. William Jackson Parrott, Dec. 23, 1977; children: William Richard, Cody Spencer. BSN, Baylor U., 1972; MSN, Tex. Woman's U., 1977; PhD in Edn. Curriculum and Instrn., Tex. A&M U., 1993. RN, Tex. Asst. prof. Dallas Bapt. U., 1976-81; part-time charge nurse Dallas Med.-Surg. Hosp., 1979-81; dir. Vocat. Sch. Nursing, Goodall-Witcher Hosp. Found., Clifton, Tex., 1982; part-time home health nurse Girling Health Care, Temple, Tex., 1988-89; faculty/course coord. Ctrl. Tex. Coll., Killeen, 1984-89; staff nurse ICU/CCU, St. Joseph Regional Health Ctr., Bryan, Tex., 1989-97; mem. faculty Blinn Coll., Bryan, 1990-97, ADN program, 1997—, dir. ADN program coord. allied health programs, 1997-2000, divsn. chair, 2000—; cons. reviewer W.B. Saunders Co., Phila., 1999, J.B. Lippincott, Phila., 1999. Contbr. articles to profl. jours. Sunday Sch. tchr., mem. choir, soloist Northview Bapt. Ch., Bryan, 1989—, Christ's Way Baptist Ch., Bryan, 2000—; vol., bd. dirs., program chair, CPR instr.-tr ainer Am. Heart Assn., Bryan, 1975—; mem. Brazos Hist. Commn., Bryan, 1995—. Recipient awards for vol. work. Mem. ANA, Nat. Orgn. for AD Nursing, Nat. League for Nursing, Nat. Soc. DAR (past treas.), Kappa Delta Pi. Republican. Baptist. Avocations: sewing, crafts, gardening, fishing. E-mail: tparrott@acmail.blinncol.ede. Office: Blinn Coll ADN Program PO Box 6030 Bryan TX 77805-6030

PARRY, DAVID JOHNSTON, lawyer; b. London, Aug. 26, 1941; s. Kenneth and Joyce (Burt) P.; m. Mary Harmer, Apr. 20, 1968; children: Andrew, Susanna, Annette, Marita. MA in Law, Cambridge (Eng.) U., 1962. Qualified solicitor, 1969, Eng. Co-sr. ptnr. Dixon Ward (Solicitors), Richmond, Surrey, Eng., 1969-95; chmn. Ind. Appeals Tribunal, 1994-95; advocate Solicitors' Higher Cts. (criminal), Eng., 1994; circuit judge, Eng., 1995—. Freeman, Co. of Merchant Taylors, Eng., 1975, City of London, 1975. Mem. Law Soc. Eng. Avocations: rugby, cricket, sunbathing, music. Office: Dixon Ward Solicitors, 16 The Green, Surrey Richmond TW9 1QD, England

PARRY, MARINA ANGELICA ANA, biochemist; b. Buenos Aires, Aug. 26, 1964; d. Robert A. and Ethel C. (Ambroggi) P. BA in Biochemistry, U. Buenos Aires, 1991; PhD, Cambridge (Eng.) U., 1995. Postdoc. Max Planck Inst., Munich, 1995-99; group leader structural biology Actelion Ltd., Basel, Switzerland, 1999—; rsch. asst. U. Buenos Aires, 1988-90; tchg. asst. U. Cambridge, 1993-94; trainer biochem. students U. Tuebingen, Germany, 1995-98. Co-author: (chpt.) Design of Synthetic Inhibitors of Thrombin, 1993, Thrombosis and Haemostasis, 1994; contbr. articles to Jour. Biol. Chemistry, Applied Biochemsitry Biotech., Biochem. Jour., Biochemistry, Structure, Nature Structural Biology, Jour. Molecular Biology, Trends in Biochem. Scis.; patentee in field. Tng. scholar Lab. Clin. Analysis, Argentina, 1985-86, E. Merck, Darmstadt, Germany, 1987; Internat. Assn. Exch. Students Tech. fellow Friedrich Mischer Inst., Basel, Switzerland, 1991; recipient Young Investigator award Internat. Soc. Thrombosis and Haemostasis, 1999, 15th Congress Meml. award Internat. Soc. Fibrimolysis and Proteolysis. Mem. N.Y. Acad. Sci., Cambridge Philos. Soc. (life). Office: Actelion Ltd, Gewerbestrasse 16, 4123 Allschwil Switzerland

PARRY, ROBERT TROUTT, bank executive, economist; b. Harrisburg, Pa., May 16, 1939; s. Anthony C. and Margaret R. (Troutt) P.; m. Brenda Louise Grumbine, Dec. 27, 1956; children: Robert Richard, Lisa Louise. BA magna cum laude, Gettysburg (Pa.) Coll., 1960; MA in Econs., U. Pa., 1961, PhD, 1967. Asst. prof. econs. Phila. Coll. Textiles and Sci., 1963-65; economist Fed. Res. Bd., Washington, 1965-70; v.p., chief economist Security Pacific Nat. Bank, Los Angeles, 1970-76, sr. v.p., chief economist, 1976-81, exec. v.p., chief economist, 1981-86; pres., chief exec. officer Fed. Res. Bank San Francisco, 1986—; bd. dirs. Nat. Bur. Econ. Rsch.; mem. adv. bd. Pacific Rim Bankers Program; mem. policy adv. bd. Ctr. for Real Estate and Urban Econs., U. Calif., Berkeley, mem. exec. com. Inst. Bus. and Econs. Rsch.; bd. dirs. San Francisco Bay Area Coun.; mem. Bay Area Econ. Forum; lectr. Pacific Coast Banking Sch., 1976-78; mem. adv. coun. SRI Internat. Mem. econ. vis. com. U. Pa.; mem. exec. bd. Boy Scouts Am., 1993—; bd. dirs. United Way, 1995. NDEA fellow, 1960-63. Mem. Nat. Assn. Bus. Economists (pres. 1979-80), Am. Econ. Assn. Home: 2 Ellis Ct Lafayette CA 94549-2600 Office: Fed Res Bank San Francisco 101 Market St San Francisco CA 94105-1579*

PARRY, ROBERT WALTER, chemistry educator; b. Ogden, Utah, Oct. 1, 1917; s. Walter and Jeanette (Petterson) P.; m. Marjorie J. Nelson, July 6, 1945; children: Robert Bryce, Mark Nelson. BS, Utah State Agr. Coll., 1940; MS, Cornell U., 1942; PhD, U. Ill., 1946; DSc (hon.), Utah State U., 1985, U. Utah, 1997. Rsch. asst. NDRC Munitions Devel. Lab. U. Ill., Urbana, 1943-45, tchg. fellow, 1945-46; mem. faculty U. Mich., 1946-69, prof. chemistry, 1958-69; Disting. prof. chemistry U. Utah, 1969-97, prof. emeritus, 1997; indsl. cons., 1952—; chmn. bd. trustees Gordon Rsch. Conf., 1967-68. Founding editor Inorganic Chemistry, 1960-63. Recipient Mfg. Chemists award for coll. tchg., 1972, Sr. U.S. Scientist award Alexander Von Humboldt-Stiftung, West Germany, 1980, First Govs. medal of Sci., State Utah, 1987. Mem. AAAS (chmn. chemistry sect. 1983), Internat. Union Pure and Applied Chemistry (chmn. U.S. nat. com., chmn. com. tchg. chemistry 1968-74), Am. Chem. Soc. (past chmn. inorganic divsn. and divsn. chem. edn., bd. editors jour. 1969-80, dir. 1973-83, pres.-elect 1981-82, pres. 1982-83, Disting. Svc. to Inorganic Chemistry award 1965, Disting. Svc. to Chem. Edn. award 1977, Utah award Utah sect. 1978, Priestly medal 1993), Sigma Xi. Achievements include research and publications on some structural problems of inorganic chemistry and incorporation results into theoretical models, chemistry of phosphorus, boron and flourine. Home: 5002 Fairbrook Ln Salt Lake City UT 84117-6205 Office: U Utah Dept Chemistry 315 S 1400 E Rm 2020 Salt Lake City UT 84112-0850

PARRY, ROGER GEORGE, entrepreneur; b. London, June 4, 1953; s. George and Margharita (Mitchell) P.; m. Johanna Waterous, Dec. 22, 1990; 1 child, Benjamin. MLitt, Oxford U., 1976; BSc with honors, Bristol (Eng.) U., 1973. Prodr., presenter BBC TV, London, 1979-84; cons. McKinsey & Co., London, 1984-88; group v.p. Aegis Group, London, 1988-94; CEO More Group Plc, London, 1995-98, Clear Channel Internat., 1998—; founder London Radio, 1993; bd. dirs. Future Network Plc, Jazz FM Plc, Johnston Press Plc, Internet Indirect PLC, iTouch cpl. Author: People Businesses, 1991; co-author: City and the Single Market, 1991. Dir. Internat. Globe Ctr., London, 1988—. Recipient Gold award N.Y. Film and TV Festival, 1984. Mem. Marylebone Cricket Club, Oxford and Cambridge Club. Office: Clear Channel Internat, 33 Golden Square, London WIR 3PA, England

PARRY, THOMAS HERBERT, JR., school system administrator, educational consultant; b. Detroit, June 28, 1928; s. Thomas Herbert Sr. and Isabel Constance (Brinsmead) P.; m. Frances Ellen Coley, Aug. 15, 1956; children: Virginia Gilkeson, William Thomas, Robert Brinsmead. BA in Edn., U. Fla., 1950; MEd, U. Va., 1958, EdD, 1967. Lic. profl. supr. of counselors; nat. cert. counselor. Tchr. Broward County Pub. Schs., Ft. Lauderdale, Fla., 1950-51, 54-62; instr. Mary Baldwin Coll., Staunton, Va., 1965-66; psychologist McGuffey Reading Ctr., Charlottesville, Va., 1966-67; prof. Clemson (S.C.) U., 1967-86; pres. Ednl. Horizons, Inc., Clemson, 1986-89, Poquoson, Va., 1989—; cons. Sch. Desegregation Ctr., Columbia, 1970; cons., counselor Advocacy Bd. S.C., 1980-82; exec. sec. S.C. Pers. and Guidance Assn., Columbia, 1980-81; founder S.C. Assn. Measurement and Evaluation in Guidance, 1974-75. Co-author: Developing a Leisure Learning Program, 1980, Beyond the Book: Activities to Correlate with the Virginia Young Readers, 1990-91, Bibliocounseling with Contemporary Children's Literature: A Resource Book for the Clinical Setting, 1996; editor S.C. Pers. and Guidance Newsletter and Jour., 1969-74; founder, editor S.C. Pers. and Guidance Assn. Jour., 1972-74; contbr. articles to profl. jours. Bd. dirs. Peninsula Agy. on Aging, Inc., 1994—. Recipient Svc. award S.C. Pers. and Guidance, 1968-81, Nat. Award for Excellence State Publs. and Guidance Assn., 1971, Meritorious Svc. award Am. Pers. and Guidance Assn., 1973, Award of Merit for Svc. to Youth Boy Scouts Am., 1975. Mem. APA, Am. Counseling Assn., S.C. Counseling Assn., Kiwanis (bd. dirs., chmn. community svc. com. 1991—, disting. sec. 1994-96, Kiwanian of Yr. 1995-96, life capital dist. Kiwanis Found., Inc. 1995), Ft. Benning Lodge # 579, Kappa Delta Pi, Phi Delta Kappa. Presbyterian. Avocations: walking, gardening, photography. Home and Office: 1 Ebb Tide Lndg Poquoson VA 23662-1334

PARRY, VICTOR THOMAS HENRY, retired librarian; b. Newport, U.K., Nov. 20, 1927; s. Thomas and Daisy (Nott) P.; m. Mavis Russull, May 16, 1959; children: Richard, Matthew, Katharine. BA, Oxford (Eng.) U., 1948, MA, 1954; postgrad., Univ. Coll., London, 1953. Asst. libr. Manchester (U.K.) Pub. Librs., 1950-56, Colonial Office and Commonwealth Rels. Office, U.K., 1956-60; libr. Nature Conservancy, U.K., 1960-64; dep. libr. Brit. Mus. Natural History, U.K., 1964-74; chief libr., archivist Royal Botanic Gardens, Kew, U.K., 1974-78; libr. Sch. Oriental and African Studies U. London, 1978-82; dir. ctrl. libr. svcs., Goldsmiths' libr. U. London Libr., 1982-88; ret., 1988; lectr. Manchester Sch. Librarianship, 1954-56; chmn. Cir. of State Librs., 1966-68; mem. Standing Conf. of Nat. and Univ. Librs., U.K., 1978-88; mem. adv. com. Brit. Libr., 1983-90. Editor: Conservation of Threatened Plants, 1976; editor Jour. Soc. for Bibliography of Natural History, 1975-78; dir. ann. bibliographies Kew Record of Taxonomic Literature, 1974-78, Internat. African Bibliography, 1978-82. Mem. coun. Sir Anthony Panizzi Found., 1983-89; chmn. Newport Borough Youth Coun., 1945, Friends of U. London Libr., 1998—. Fellow Royal Soc. for Arts, Royal Asiatic Soc. for Gt. Britain and Ireland, Libr. Assn. (sr. examiner 1959-68, founder, chmn. govt. librs. group 1977-78). Avocations: reading, bridge, ball games, railways. Home: 69 Redway Dr, Twickenham London TW2 7NN, England

PARRY-SOLÁ, CHERYL LEE, critical care nurse; b. Bristol, Pa., Oct. 27, 1960; d. Edmund H. and F. Renee (Platt) P. ADN, Bucks County C.C., 1982. RN, N.J.; CCRN. Formerly asst. head nurse Deborah Heart and Lung Ctr., Browns Mills, N.J.; staff nurse Holy Spirit Hosp., Camp Hill, Pa., 1995—. Office: Holy Spirit Hosp Med ICU 503 N 21st St Camp Hill PA 17011-2288

PARSHALL, GEORGE WILLIAM, research chemist; b. Hackensack, Minn., Sept. 19, 1929; s. George Clarence and Frances (Virnig) P.; m. Naomi B. Simpson, Oct. 9, 1954; children: William, Jonathan, David. B.S., U. Minn., 1951; Ph.D., U. Ill., 1954. Research chemist E.I. duPont de Nemours & Co., Wilmington, Del., 1954-65, research supr., 1965-79, dir. chem. sci., 1979-92, cons., 1992—, mem. com. on environ. mgmt. techs., 1994-97; mem. chem. stockpile disposal com. NRC, Washington, 1992-98, mem. non-stockpile com., 1998-99; bd. chem. sci. NRC, Washington, 1983-86; Reilly lectr. Notre Dame U., 1980; Ipatieff lectr. Northwestern U., 1994. Author: Homogeneous Catalysis, 1980, 2d rev. edit. 1992; editor: Inorganic Syntheses, 1974, Jour. Molecular Catalysis, 1977-80. Recipient Ballar Inorganic Chemistry medal U. Ill., 1976. Mem. NAS, Inst. Chemists (Chem. Pioneer award 1992, Gold medal award 1995), Am. Chem. Soc. (award in inorganic chemistry 1983, award for leadership in chem. rsch. mgmt. 1989), Am. Acad. Arts Scis., Guild Episcopal Scholars (treas. 1994-99). Episcopalian. Home: 2504 Delaware Ave Wilmington DE 19806-1220

PARSLEY, GEORGE MICHAEL JAMES, retired electrical engineering educator; b. Bokburg, Transvaal, South Africa, May 18, 1943; s. George William and Phyllis Maude (Riddell) P.; m. Edith Mary Warner, June 28, 1978. BSEE, U. Capetown, South Africa, 1975; B in Engring. with honors, U. Pretoria, South Africa, 1989; PhD, U. Witwatersrand, Johannesburg, South Africa, 1995. Registered profl. engr., South Africa. Technician Post Office, South Africa, 1963-71, engr., 1975-77, 80-87; engr. Armscor, South Africa, 1977-79; lectr. U. Pretoria, 1987-97. Contbr. articles to profl. jours. Mem. South Africa Inst. Elec. Engrs. Home: 220 Beckett St, Pretoria 0083, South Africa Office: Pretoria Technikon, Pvt Bag X680, Pretoria 0001, South Africa

PARSONAGE, MAURICE JOHN, neurologist, retired; b. Nantwich, Cheshire, Eng., Apr. 9, 1915; s. John Hodson Parsonage and Florence Sophie Martin; m. Marion Helen Clifton, July 22, 1943; children: John David Roderick, Michael Anthony, Fiona Joy Diane Spiller. BSc, Victoria U. Manchester, Eng., 1936; MB, Victoria U. Manchester, 1939, ChB, 1939. House physician Royal Infirmary, Manchester, 1939-40; asst. med. officer Booth Hall Hosp. Children, Manchester, 1940; sr. registrar dept. nervous diseases Guy's Hosp., London, 1946-51; cons. neurologist Leeds Regional Hosp. Bd., Yorkshire, Eng., 1951-81, dir. neuropsychiatric unit and spl. ctr. for epilepsy, 1954-81; mem. Hosp. Bd. Govs., 1969-72, chmn. com. physicians, faculty of medicine United Leeds Hosp.; sr. registrar dept. applied electrophysiology Nat. Hosp. Nervous Diseases, London, 1947-51; cons. neurology Gen. Infirmary Leeds, Eng., 1951-80; pres. 14th Epilepsy Internat. Symposium, London, 1982; mem. med. adv. com. disorders ctrl. nervous sys. Dept. Transport, London, 1976-94. Contbr. articles to profl. publs. With Internat. League Against Epilepsy, coun. mem. 1971—, pres. Brit. br., 1977-80. Acting Lt. col. Royal Army Med. Corps., 1940-46. Named Amb. for Epilepsy, Internat. Bur. Epilepsy, 1972. Fellow Royal Coll. Physicians (licentiate); mem. Royal Coll. Surgeons, Assn. British Neurologists (past. mem. coun.), Electroencephalographic Soc. Great Britain (past. mem. coun.), Internat. League Against Epilepsy, Brit. Epilepsy Assn., North of Eng. Neurol. Assn. (founding mem., pres. 1968-69). Conservative. Mem. Ch. of Eng. Avocations: reading, music, politics, tennis, badminton. Home: 2 Cornwall Close, North Yorkshire HG1 2NY, England

PARSONS, ANDREW ERNEST, solicitor; b. Norwich, Norfolk, UK, Feb. 5, 1963; s. Ernest Edward and Evelina Ann (Newell) P.; m. Caroline Jane Shaw, June 3, 1989; 1 child, Alice. LLB, Reading U., 1984. Ptnr. Radcliffes, London, 1985—. Author: Tenant Default Under Commercial Leases, 1993, 2d edit., 1996, 3d edit., 2000. Trustee, sec. Queen Elizabeth Hosp. for Children's Rsch. Appeal Trust, 1995—. Mem. Law Soc., Royal Soc. Medicine, Royal Automobile Club, City of Westminster Law Soc. Mem. Ch. of England. Avocations: music, sports, family. Office: Radcliffes, 5 Great College St, SW1P 3SJ London England

PARSONS, ANDREW JOHN, management consultant; b. Kingston, Surrey, Eng., July 22, 1943; came to U.S., 1968; s. S. John and Hylda P. (Wili) P.; m. Carol Ann Iannucci, June 6, 1970; children: Alexandra, Katherine. BA, MA, Oxford U., 1965; MBA, Harvard U., 1970. Acct. exec. Leo Burnett, London, 1965-68; from strategic planning dir. to v.p. mktg. Prestige Group Ltd. div. Am. Home Products, N.Y.C. and London, 1970-76; v.p. mktg. Kurzweil Computer Products div. Xerox Corp., Cambridge, Mass., 1979-80; assoc. McKinsey & Co., Inc., N.Y.C., 1976-82, prin., 1982-88, dir. consumer industries sector, mktg. ctr., sr. ptnr., 1988—; underwriting mem. Lloyds of London, 1986—. Contbr. articles to profl. jours. Adv. bd. Salvation Army, Greater N.Y., 1983—, chmn. adv. bd., 1993-97; bd. dirs. United Way, N.Y.C., 1988—; trustee Sarah Lawrence Coll., Bronxville, N.Y., 1993—. Baker scholar Harvard Bus. Sch., 1970. Mem. Siwanoy Country Club, Watch Hill Yacht Club, Weekapaug Golf Club. Home: 56 Hereford Rd Bronxville NY 10708-5408 Office: McKinsey & Co Inc 55 E 52nd St Fl 18 New York NY 10055-0183

PARSONS, ANTHONY DAVID, gynecology educator; b. Weymouth, Dorset, Eng., Apr. 1, 1948; s. Frederick William John and Audrey Lilla (Bull) P.; m. Katharine Jane Leach, Nov. 17, 1989; children: Luke Anthony, Samuel John, Charles Frederick. MB, BS, King's Coll. Hosp., London, 1971, MA, 1989. Lectr. Birmingham (Eng.) U., 1979-85; sr. lectr. U. Warwick, Coventry, Eng., 1985—; cons. gynecology Rugby N.H.S. Trust, Warwickshire, Eng., 1985—; vice chmn. Brit. Pregnancy Adv. Svc., 1990-93. Co-author: Contraception-The Facts, 2d edit., 1990. Fellow Royal Soc. Medicine; mem. British Menopause Soc. (founder., chmn. 1989-91), European Soc. Contraception, Am. Soc. for Reproductive Medicine, Internat. Menopause Soc. Office: U Warwick, Dept Postgrad Medicine, Coventry CV4 7AL, England

PARSONS, DONALD LEE, telecommunications executive; b. Charleston, W.Va., July 21, 1947; s. Orel Adair and Edith Irene Parsons; m. Jo Lynn Parsons, Aug. 18, 1973; children: Jennifer Elizabeth Parsons Lawrence, Meredith Victoria Parsons Whittington. BS in Edn., W.Va. State U., 1972. Ops. mgr. Bell South, Atlanta, 1973—. State rep. Ga. Ho. of Reps., Cobb County, 1994—. With U.S. Army Res., 1966-87. Mem. Kiwanis Club of Marietta. Republican. United Methodist. Home: 3167 Sycamore Ln Marietta GA 30066-4173 Office: 611 Legislative Office Bldg Atlanta GA 30066

PARSONS, JAMES BOWNE, lawyer; b. Mineola, N.Y., Mar. 21, 1954; s. Edward Finch and Elizabeth (Hubbell) P.; m. Carol Anne Sherfy, Dec. 30, 1977. BA in Polit. Sci., U. Puget Sound, 1976; JD, Lewis and Clark Coll., 1980. Bar: Oreg. 1980, Wash. 1982, Bar of No. Mariana Islands 1990, U.S. Dist. Ct. (we. dist.) Wash. 1986, U.S. Ct. Appeals (9th cir.) 1990, U.S. Dist. Ct. (Oreg.) 1990, U.S. Dist. Ct. (No. Mariana Islands) 1990, U.S. Tax Ct. 1985. Sole practice Oregon City, Oreg., 1980-83; assoc. Copenbarger et al, Seattle, 1983-84, Holman & Monahan, Seattle, 1984-86; pvt. practice Seattle, 1986-90; asst. atty. gen. Commonwealth of the No. Mariana Islands, 1990-92; corp. counsel, pres. Secure Benefits, Inc., 1993-96; mng. ptnr. Parsons Law firm, Bellevue, Wash., 1996—; bd. dirs., sec.-treas., spkr. Eastside Legal Assistance Program. Speaker various non-profit orgns. regarding estate planning, charitable giving and bus. formation. Mem. ABA (real property, probate and trust, bus. law sect., com. on fed. regulation of securities), Wash. State Bar Assn. (spkr., real property, probate and trust sects., bus. sect., com. on interprofl. rels.). Democrat. Episcopalian. Avocations: traveling, skiing, scuba diving, wine, music. Home: 8704 NE 21st Pl Bellevue WA 98004-2440 Office: Parsons Law Firm 500 108th Ave NE Ste 1710 Bellevue WA 98004-5599

PARSONS, JOHN DAVID, electrical engineering educator; b. Ebbw Vale, Gwent, Eng., July 8, 1935; s. Oswald and Doris Anita (Roberts) P.; m. Mary Winifred Tate, July 19, 1969. BSc, U. Wales, 1959; MSc in Engring., U. London, 1967, DSc in Engring., 1984. Engr. GEC Ltd., London, 1959-62; lectr., sr. lectr. Regent St. Polytechnic, London, 1962-69; lectr., reader U. Birmingham, Eng., 1969-82; prof., head dept. U. Liverpool, Eng., 1982-86, 96-98, dean engring., 1986-89, pro vice-chancellor, 1990-96; dir. Freshfield Comm. Ltd., Liverpool, 1989-95, Data Info. Systems Ltd., London, 1989—; UN expert in telecomm., Delhi, India, 1977; cons. several cos. and govt. bodies, 1982—. Author: (with S.M. Bozic and R. Cheng) Electronic and Switching Circuits, 1975; (with J.G. Gardiner) Mobile Communication Systems, 1988; The Mobile Radio Propagation Channel, 1992, 2d edit., 2000. Recipient Paul Adorian Premium Inst. Electronic and Radio Engrs., London, 1983. Fellow Royal Acad. Engring., Instn. Elec. Engrs. (Blumlein-Browne-Williams Premium 1975, Marconi Premium 1982, 92). Avocations: golf, bridge, skiing. Office: U Liverpool Dept Elec Engr, Brownlow Hill, Liverpool L69 3GJ, England

PARSONS, JOHN SEYMOUR, accountant, trading company executive; b. Durban, Kwazulu-Natal, South Africa, Mar. 10, 1941; m. Vivienne Margaret Easton, Aug. 8, 1964; children: Andrew, Trevor, Nola. Chartered acct. Zimbabwe, South Africa. Articled clk. A. Hopewell & Co., Durban, South Africa, 1959-63; ptnr. Ernst & Young, Harare, Zimbabwe, 1964-79; mgr. Ernst & Young, Johannesburg, South Africa, 1980-83; group sec. Hudaco Industries Ltd., Johannesburg, South Africa, 1984-91; dir. Parsen Trading and Sr. Svc., Harare, Zimbabwe, 1992—; dir. finance and pub. rels. Mbizi Game Park, Harare, Zimbabwe, 1992—, Woodhill Safaris, Harare, 1995—. Chmn., vice chmn., treas., Aloe, Cactus and Succulent Soc., Zimbabwe, 1972-79, chmn. 1996-98; com. mem. Nat. Trust Zimbabwe, 1972-79, Conservation Trust, 1973-79. Mem. Inst. Chartered Accts South Africa, Inst. Chartered Accts. Zimbabwe. Baptist. Avocations: reading, gardening, travel. Office: Parsen Trading (pvt) Ltd., PO Box UA 358 Union Ave, Harare Zimbabwe

PARSONS, MARK FREDERICK, college development officer; b. Mpls., Nov. 18, 1950; s. Frederick A. and Margaret C. (Anderson) P. BA, U. Minn., 1972; MDiv, United Theol. Sem., New Brighton, Minn., 1976; JD magna cum laude, William Mitchell Coll. Law, St. Paul, 1987; PhD, U. Minn., 1993. Bar: Minn. 1987; ordained deacon Meth. Ch., 1975, elder, 1978. Assoc. min. First United Meth. Ch., Worthington, Minn., 1976-77; min. Fairfax (Minn.) United Meth. Ch., 1977-78, Gethsemane United Meth. Ch., Lino Lakes, Minn., 1979-83; sr. min. Edgewater Emmanuel United Meth. Ch., Mpls., 1983-92; dir. gift planning Hamline U., St. Paul, 1992—; assoc. atty. Lange & Anderson, P.A., Bloomington, Minn., 1988-91; sabbatical Mission Resource Ctr., Emory U., Atlanta, 1998. Merrill fellow Harvard Div. Sch., Cambridge, Mass., 1992. Mem. Minn. State Bar, Minn. Planned Giving Coun., Phi Kappa Phi. Avocations: hiking, reading, golf,

volunteering, travel. Office: Hamline U 1536 Hewitt Ave Saint Paul MN 55104-1284

PARSONS, MARTIN LESLIE, education educator; b. Reading, England, Nov. 12, 1951; s. Donald and Doreen (Brown) P.; m. Josephine Marina Redgrave, July 19, 1975; two children. BA, Open U., Milton Keynes, England, 1978; PhD, Reading U., 1997. From asst. history tchr. to head lower sch. Theale Green Sch., England, 1973-90; from head history to course dir. U. Reading, England, 1990—, dep. head Sch. of Edn. Author: Foundations Skills History, 1986, vol. 2, 1987, vol. 3, 1987, The History of St. Andrew's Church Bradfield, 1994, A Victorian Village, 1995, Evacuation: Insights Into History, 1996, Essential Dates in History, 1996, History Detective Investigates Local History, 1997, I'll Take That One Civilian Evacuation 1939-45, 1998, History Detective Investigates Evacuation, 1999, History Detective Investigates Air Raids, 1999, History Detective Investigates Women at War, 1999, History Detective Investigates Rationing, 1999, Evacuation: The True Story, 1999, Waiting To Go Home, 1999, Friendly Foe, 2000, Evacuee Memories, The Effect of Civilian Evacuation on Dorset, 1939-43; author (radio series and book) Evacuation, The True Story (Sony Gold award for best radio documentary 1999); author (CD Rom): Operation Pied Piper. Fellow Coll. Preceptors, Royal Hist. Soc. Office: U Reading, Woodlands Ave, RG6 1HY Reading England

PARSONS, RYMN JAMES, lawyer; b. Binghamton, N.Y., Sept. 23, 1955; s. James Edward and Dauna Dee (Robinson) P.; m. Mary Helen Pietro, Apr. 7, 1979; 1 child, Mary Katherine. AB, Eisenhower Coll., 1977; JD, Albany Law Sch., 1981; LLM, George Washington U., 1996. Bar: Conn. 1981, U.S. Dist. Ct. Conn. 1981, U.S. Ct. Mil. Appeals 1986, U.S. Supreme Ct. 1986. Assoc. Ells, Quinlan & Robinson, Canaan, Conn., 1981-83, Cramer & Anderson, New Milford, Conn., 1983-85; commd. lt. USN, 1985; advanced through grades to comdr. USNR, 1999; judge adv. naval legal svc. office USN, Newport, R.I., 1985-88; staff judge advocate Naval Surface Group Four, Newport, 1988-90; command judge advocate USS Dwight D. Eisenhower (CVN 69), 1990-92; mil. judge Navy-Marine Corp. Trial Judiciary, Norfolk, Va., 1992-95; staff judge advocate Submarine Group Two, 1996-99; asst. command counsel Navy Pub. Works Ctr., Norfolk, 1999—. Contbr. articles to profl. jours. Counsel St. Andrew's Soc. Conn. Inc., 1984-85; scoutmaster Boy Scouts Am., Salisbury, Conn., 1985, Sea Exploring advisor, Newport, R.I., 1987-89; bd. dirs. Glenwood Homeowners Assn., Virginia Beach, Va., 1993-94; men's tennis coach U.S. C.G. Acad., 1997-99. Mem. ABA, Am. Judicature Soc. (bd. dirs. 1980-81), U.S. Naval Inst., Am. Judges Assn., U.S. Profl. Tennis Registry (profl. instr. 1999—), Nat. Inst. Trial Advocacy (instr. 1989—). Republican. Office: Navy Pub Works Ctr 9742 Maryland Ave Ste 211 Norfolk VA 23511-3015

PARSONS, WALTER AUBREY, food scientist; b. Johannesburg, South Africa, July 5, 1932; s. Victor and Maria (Du Plessis) P.; m. Alien Parsons, May 5, 1956; 1 child, Genevieve. BSc with honors, London Coll., 1975; postgrad., Technikon, Johannesburg, 1993—. Tech. mgr. Bristol Myers, Johannesburg, 1951-61; R&D mgr. Bush Boake Allen, Johannesburg, 1961-67; tech. dir. Haarmann & Reimer, Johannesburg, 1967-94; mng. dir. W.A. Parsons Cons., Johannesburg, 1994—; part-time lectr. various univs., South Africa, 1960—, U. Zimbabwe, 1985—; invited lectr., India, China, U.K., 1998. Author: Cosmetic Science, 1963; contbr. over 189 articles to profl. jours. Bd. trustees Animal Anti-Cruelty League, 1990—. 2d lt. South African Army, 1950-61. Recipient Rectors Award medal Technikon, 1989; U.K. Flavour Assn. fellow, 1974. Mem. Cosmetic Soc. South Africa (pres. 1987), South African Assn. Food Sci. and Tech. (pres. 1993—), Brit. Parfumery Soc., Inst. Food Technologists, Internat. Cosmetic Sci. Fedn., Aerosol Assn., Internat. Union Food Sci. and Tech. (exec. coun. 1998—). Avocation: researching essential oils. E-mail: alljoy@iafrica.com; fax: 0117263471. Home: Auckland Park, 23 Lothbury Rd, Johannesburg South Africa Office: W A Parsons Consultants, PO Box 91182, Auckland Park 2006, South Africa

PARSONSON, PETER STERLING, civil engineer, educator, consultant; b. Reading, Mass., Oct. 18, 1934; s. Alfred Horace and Elvera (Moran) P.; m. Marilyn Shepherd, July 6, 1962 (div. Mar. 1984); children: Sheryl Elaine Parsonson Peeples, Ellen Marie Parsonson Milberger, Peter Shepherd; m. Sarah Irby, Oct. 6, 1990. BS, MIT, 1956, MS, 1959; PhD, N.C. State U., 1966. Registered profl. engr., Ga., Fla., Calif. Civil engr. Fay, Spofford and Thorndike, Boston, 1956-57, Ingenieria de Suelos, S.A., Caracas, Venezuela, 1959-61, Tippetts-Abbett-McCarthy-Stratton, N.Y.C., 1961-64; asst. prof. Coll. Engring. U. S.C., Columbia, 1966-69; assoc. prof. dept. civil engring. Ga. Inst. Tech., Atlanta, 1970-82, prof. dept. civil and environ. engring., 1982-2000, prof. emeritus, 2000—, group leader Transp. Engring. faculty, 1995-99; pres. Parsonson and Assocs., Inc., Atlanta, 1976—; cons. hwy.-engring. litigation; instr., rschr. hwy. design, constrn., operation and maintenance; vis. prof. Simón Bolívar U., Caracas, 1994, Nat. U. Colombia, Medellín, 1996; prof. ad honorem U. P.R., Mayagüez, 1995, 96; vis. lectr. on intelligent transp. systems Jiangsu and Hebei Provinces China, 1999; presenter in field. Author: Management of Traffic-Signal Maintenance, 1984, Signal Timing Improvement Practices, 1992; co-author: Traffic Detector Handbook, 1985; contbr. chpts. to books and articles to profl. jours. Fellow Inst. Transp. Engrs. (Marble J. Hensley Outstanding Individual Activity award 1974, Herman J. Hoose Disting. Svc. award, 1984, Karl A. Bevins Traffic Ops. award, 1992); mem. NSPE, Transp. Rsch. Bd., Nat. Acad. Forensic Engrs. Episcopalian. E-mail: peter.parsonson@ce.gatech.edu. Home: 105 Mark Trl NW Atlanta GA 30328-2102 Office: Ga Inst Tech Civil And Environ Engring Atlanta GA 30332-0001

PÄRSSINEN, JANNE HENRIK, research scientist, chemical engineer; b. Helsinki, Finland, June 28, 1974; s. Heikki Tapani and Eila Helena (Kesleinen) P. MSc, U. Tech., Finland, 1997. Trainee Neles Control Oy, Helsinki, 1994-96; process design engr. Fortum Oil and Gas Oy, Finland, 1997-98; vis. scientist U. Western Ontario, Can., 1998—; spkr. in field. Patentee in field. Conf. vol. CSCHE, Can., 1998. Grantee Neste Rsch. Found., Helsinki, 1998-99, U. Tech., Helsinki, 1998-99; recipient Excellence in Physics award ABB Strömberg Drives Oy, Helsinki, 1993. Mem. AAAS. Office: Univ Western Ontario, Dept Chem and Biochem Engrg, London, Canada

PÄRSSINEN, MARTTI HEIKKI, historian, archeologist; b. Kiikka, Finland, Feb. 26, 1956; s. Mauri and Marja Kaarina (Pietilä) P.; m. Heli Kristiina Forsberg, Dec. 26, 1976; 1 child, Viljami. Degree in archeology, U. Helsinki, Finland, 1985; lic., U. Turku, Finland, 1985, PhD in History, 1992; MA in Anthropology, U. Rochester, N.Y., 1988. Asst. prof. U. Turku, 1985, rschr., 1989-92, sr. rschr., 1995-96; jr. rschr. Acad. of Finland, Helsinki, 1992-95; dir. Finnish Iberoamerican Inst., Madrid, 1996-99; prof. dir. Ibero-Am. Ctr., U. Helsinki, 1999—; vis. prof. Ecole des Hautes Etudes en Scis. Sociales, Paris, 1996; dir. hist.-archeol. expedition Chuquisaca, Bolivia, 1993-94, Pacajes, Bolivia, 1989-92, Cajamarca, Peru, 1987; rschr. Indian Archive, Seville, Spain, 1985-86. Author: Tawantinsuyu: The Inca State and its Political Organization, 1992; contbr. articles to profl. publs. Advisor Spanish-Finnish Joing Com. for Ednl. and Cultural Coop., Madrid, 1997; mem. adminstrv. bd. Iberoamerican Found., Finland, 1992-96. Recipient Rsch. awards Found. fo Emil Aaltonen, Finland, 1985-87; U. Rochester fellow, 1987-88. Mem. Am. Anthropol. Assn., Assn. Devel. Rsch. Finland (adminstrv. bd. 1995-96). Avocations: painting, hiking. Home: Ylonojantie 26, FIN38300 Kiikka Finland Office: Ibero-Am Ctr U Helsinki, PO Box 59, FIN00014 Helsinki Finland

PÄRSSINEN, TAHVO OLAVI, ophthalmologist, educator, myopia researcher; b. Vaasa, Finland, Mar. 27, 1945; s. Jalmari and Iida Maria Pärssinen; m. Helena Marjut Leino, Dec. 28, 1968; children: Markus, Heidi, Tuomas. MD, U. Helsinki, 1971; PhD, U. Tampere, Finland, 1986. Dist. physician Municipality of Himanka, Finland, 1972-73; asst. surgeon Univ. Hosp., Tampere, 1973-77; chief surgeon Regional Hosp., Kristiinank, Finland, 1977-79; ophthalmologist Ctrl. Hosp., Jyväkylä, Finland, 1979-94, chief surgeon, 1995—, union rep., 1983-88; chmn., spkr. internat. congresses, Rome, Singapore, Madrid, others, 1986—; Finnish rep. European Contact Lens Soc. of Ophthalmologists, Amsterdam, The Netherlands, 1993-96; chief ophthalmic Surgery Ctrl. Finland, Jyväskylä, 1988-95; vice chmn. Finnish Ophthalmologists, Helsinki, 1987-88. Author: Wearing of Spectacles and Occurence of Myopia, 1986; contbr. numerous articles on myopia to med. jours. Chmn. Deaf Children's Support Ctrl. Finland, 1982-85. Grantee Acad. Finland, 1983-87. Mem. Finnish Contact Lens Soc. (pres. 1992-94, v.p. 1994-96), Med. Assn. Optics and Contact Lenses (v.p. 1994-96), Finnish Opthalmol. Soc. (v.p. 1997-98). Lutheran. Avocations: reading, fishing. Home: Kannaksenkatu 5, 40600 Jyväskylä Finland Office: Ctrl Hosp of Ctrl Finland, 40620 Jyväskylä Finland

PARTEN, PRISCILLA M., medical and psychiatric social worker, educator; b. Lowell, Mass., Dec. 7, 1944; d. Ralph Bailey and Margaret Lillian (McDonagh) Newton; m. Samuel L. Parten, June 27, 1965; children: Delora Parten Power, Edward Bailey, Ethan Rogers. BA, Northeastern U., 1968; MSW, Adelphi U., Burlington, Vt., 1987. Lic. ind. clin. social worker, lic. clin. social worker, Mass.; lic. ind. clin. social worker, N.H.; bd. cert. diplomate NASW. Family support coord. Easter Seal Early Intervention, Derry, N.H., 1988-91; med. and psychiat. social worker Salem (N.H.) Vis. Nurses, 1992-96; home sch. coord. Timberlane Regional Sch. Dist., Plaistow, N.H., 1992—; dir. Priscilla M. Parten, MSW, ACSW, BCD, Londonderry, N.H., 1992—. Spkr., author, presenter in field, interviewed on Nat. Pub. TV. Bd. dirs. Norwich U. Parents' Assn., 1998—, 1st v.p., 1999-00. Recipient commendation Pres.'s Com. on Mental Retardation, 1968. Mem. NASW, Nutfield Exch. Club (bd. dirs. 1994-96). Democrat. Congregationalist. Avocations: skiing, photography, crocheting, gardening. Office: 40 Nashua Rd Londonderry NH 03053-3406

PARTHASARATHY, KODUVAYUR RAMAIYER, mathematician; b. Bombay, India, Dec. 9, 1933; s. Koduvayur V. Ramaiyar and Koduvayur R. Thangammal; m. Koduvayur Parthasarathy Hema, July 14, 1968; children: Subbalakshmi, Sujatha, Sunanda. BA with honors, Vivekananda Coll., Madras, India, 1954; M in Stats., Indian Statis. Inst., Calcutta, 1962; PhD, Indian Inst. Tech., Kharagpur, 1966. Prof. Mil. Tech. Coll., Baghdad, Iraq, 1982-84; lectr. math. Indian Inst. Tech., Madras, 1966-72, asst. prof., 1972-79, prof., 1979-94; head dept. math. Indian Inst. Tech., 1980-82. Author: Basic Graph Theory, 1994; contbr. articles to profl. jours. Sec. Welfare Assn., Narayana Puram, India, 1995. Mem. Am. Math. Soc., Ramanujam Math. Soc. (life), European Math. Soc. Home: 4 II Main Rd IIT Colony, Narayanapuram, Tamil Nadu 601302, India

PARTHASARATHY, RAJAGOPALAN, trade and professional associations administrator; b. Tanjore, Tamil Nadu, India, Nov. 3, 1934; s. Rajagopalan and Shembakam Krishna; m. Neela Ramanuj, June 2, 1944; children: P. Srivatsan, P. Meenakshi. MA, U. Madras, India, 1956; diploma in adminstrv. law, Indian Law Inst., New Delhi, 1980, diploma in corp. law, 1982; diploma in French, Alliance Francaise de Delhi, New Delhi, 1990. Sec. Delhi Mgmt. Assn., New Delhi, India, 1957-60; economist, econ. and mkt. rsch. divsn. U.S. Comml. Dept., New Delhi, India, 1960-64; chief econ. and mktr. rsch. divsn. Fertilizer Assn. India, New Delhi, 1964-74; sec. gen. Associated Cs. of C. and Industry, New Delhi, 1974-93; CEO Indian Chem. Mfrs. Assn., New Delhi, 1987-90; advisor Internat. Fiscal Assn. India Br., New Delhi, 1993-98; cons. internat. bus. Law Firm Vaish Assocs., New Delhi, 1993-97; chief exec. Olympus Mgmt. & Fin. Cons., 1993—; advisor Nat. Sml. Industries Corp., 1998—; award selection com. on energy and conservation Nat. Productivity Coun., New Delhi, 1989, award selection com. on best. environ. practices Ministry Environment and Forests, Govt. of India, New Delhi, 1992; participant tng. conf. on investment promotion World Trade Inst., World Trade Ctr., N.Y.C., 1991, World Intellectual Property Orgn. UN, Geneva, 1992. Editor: Doing Business in India, 1994; editor and publ. (newsletter) Bus. and Legal News, 1994-97; editor Mgmt. Rev. Jour., 1957-60; also contbr. to econ. and tech. reports on indsl. growth and devel. Active several cultural organizations. Mem. Max Mueller Bhavan, Alliance Française Delhi. Avocations: classical music (Indian and western), gardening, travel, photography. Home and Office: B-23 Hillview Apts, Vasant Vihar, New Delhi 110057, India

PARTINEN, MARKKU MIKAEL, neurologist; b. Helsinki, Finland, Dec. 4, 1948; s. Väinö and Kerttu Elisabeth (Havunen) P.; m. Helena Majanen; children: Eemil Väinö E., Eevert Edvard J. MD, Faculty Medicine, Montpellier, France, 1975; DSc in Medicine, Epidemiology, Faculty Medicine, Helsinki, 1982; Docent Neurology, U. Helsinki, Finland. Gen. practitioner Health Care Ctr., Leppavirta, Finland, 1975-76; asst. physician Clinic Neurophysiology and Medicine, Helsinki, 1975-78; resident in neurology U. Helsinki, 1978-82, asst. dept. pub. health sci., 1980-81, asst. prof. neurology, 1981-83, dir. sleep disorders unit, dept. neurology, 1983-84, staff specialist, neurologist, 1987-96; dir. Ullanlinna Sleep Disorders Clinic and Research Ctr., Helsinki, 1984-95, Vaajasalo Hosp., Kuopio, Finland, 1990-91; chief neurologist Kivelä Hosp., 1991-95; head R&D specialized health care Nat. Rsch. and Devel. Ctr. Welfare and Health, 1993-94; dir. Haaga Neurol. Rsch. Ctr., 1996—; sr. researcher epidemiology, Inst. Occupational Health, Helsinki, 1983-85; research fellow Sleep Disorders Ctr., Stanford, Calif., 1985-86; vis. lectr. Coll. Nurses, Helsinki, 1979-83; docent U. Helsinki, 1987. Spl. editor Annales Clin. Research (Sleep), 1985; editorial adv. bd. Jour. Sleep, 1986—; assoc. editor Jour. Sleep Rsch.; contbr. articles to profl. jours. Served to sub lt. medicine, Finnish Armed Forces, 1976-77. Sleep and Heart Found. fellow Cardiovascular Research Finland, 1980, internat. research fellow Fogarty Internat. Pub. Health Service-NIH, Stanford, Calif., 1985-86; grantee Paavo Nurmi Found., 1983-84, Miina Sillanpaa Found., 1983-87. Mem. Finnish Neurol. Soc., Finnish Brain Rsch. Soc., Scandinavian Sleep Rsch. Soc. (exec. bd. 1982—, pres. 1988—), European Sleep Rsch. Soc. (sci. com. 1986-90, v.p. 1992-94), Sleep Rsch. Soc. U.S., Finnish Sleep Rsch. Soc. (pres. 1988—), World Fedn. Sleep Rsch. Socs. (coordinating sec. 1996—). Evangelist Lutheran. Avocations: skiing, golf, fishing, painting, wines, tennis. Office: Haaga Neurol Rsch Ctr, Makipellontie 15, 00320 Helsinki Finland

PARTNER, PETER DAVID, writer, journalist, educator; b. Little Heath, Herts, Eng., July 15, 1924; s. David and Bertha E. (Partridge) P.; m. Leila May Fadil, Oct. 24, 1953; children: David Michael, Simon Christopher, Sumaya Mary. BA, Oxford U., Eng., 1950, MA, DPhil, 1955. Asst. master Winchester Coll., 1955-86; mem. Inst. Advanced Study Princeton U., N.J., 1976-77. Author: Papal State under Martin V, 1958, Lands of St. Peter, 1972, Renaissance Rome, 1976, Murdered Magicians, 1981, Arab Voices, 1988, The Pope's Men, 1990, God of Battles, 1997, Two Thousand Years, 1999. Served to lt. Royal Naval Res., 1943-46. Fellow Soc. Antiquaries of London; mem. Soc. Italian Studies. Club: Athenaeum (London). Home: 17 Clausentum Rd, Winchester SO23 9QE, England

PARTNOW, SUSAN LEE, consultant; b. L.A., Feb. 20, 1947; d. Abraham and Jeanette (Bernstein) P.; m. Barry Douglas Ganapol, Sept. 16, 1967 (div. Sept. 1978); m. James Albert Peckenpaugh, Oct. 29, 1979; children: Jessica Leigh, Tyler James. BA, U. Calif., Berkeley, 1968, secondary tchg. credential, 1969; MA, Northwestern U., 1976. Tchr. Partnow John Swett Sch. Dist., Rodeo, Calif., 1969-70; tchr. ESL Societe Ednl. de Comm. Indsl., Paris, 1971-74; speech/lang. specialist Tucson Sch. Dist. #1, 1976-78; co-dir. Nat. Inst. Health Grant project U. Ariz., Tucson, 1978-79; clinic dir., speech pathology Profl. Speech and Counseling Svcs., San Diego, 1979-81; speech pathologist Group Health Cooperative, Seattle, 1982-83; comm. disorders specialist Shoreline Pub. Schs., Seattle, 1983-84; organizational devel. and tng. cons. Partnow Comm., Seattle, 1983—. Author: Everyday Speaking for all Occasions, 1998. Founder Families for Peace, Seattle, 1983-90; citizen diplomat Middle East Listening Project, 1992, Peace Trees Vietnam, 1998; pres. Kadima Cmty. Sch., Seattle, 1993-95; pres. bd. Earthstewards, Bainbridge Island, Wash., 1998-99. Recipient Commendation for Excellence in Tng., U.S. Army Corps Engrs., Seattle, 1992; named Associated Students U. Wash. Exptl. Coll. Honored Instr., U. Wash., Seattle, 1992; Rearwin fellow Northwestern U., Evanston, Ill., 1974-76. Mem. ASTD (project dir. and initiator matching profls. with pub. schs. for pro bono consultation 1998-99), Am. Speech and Hearing Assn. (cert. clin. competence, co-chair 1980 dirs. conf.), Orgn. Devel. Network. Jewish. Avocations: languages, peacemaking, study of whole systems change. E-mail: Susan4ps@aol.com and PartnowCom@aol.com. Fax: 206-782-7786. Office: Partnow Comm 4425 Baker Ave NW Seattle WA 98107-4352

PARTOKUSUMO, KARKONO KAMAJAYA, writer; b. Surakarta, Java, Indonesia, Nov. 23, 1915; d. Saminu and Sudarmi Partosentono; m. Sri Murtiningsih, 1968 (div. Apr. 1993); 1 child, Sasi Karini. Student, Tamansiswa Nat. Inst., 1933-34. Corr. Utusan Indonesia, Yogyakarta, 1932-33; journalist Penyebar Semangat, Surabaya, Indonesia, 1934-35; editor Pustaka Timur, Yogyakarta, 1938-39; chief editor Percaturan Dunia and Film, Jakarta, Indonesia, 1939-42; mem. edit. bd. Asia Raya, Jakarta, 1942-43; dir. Cahaya Timur Drama, Jakarta, 1943-45, UP Indonesia Pub. Co., Yogyakarta, 1949—; editor Berita Umum, Jakarta, 1939-42; proprietor Silver Shop, Yogyakarta, 1949-82; chairperson Centhini Found., Yogyakarta, 1984—, Lembaga Javanology, Yogyakarta, 1984-97. Author: Kebudayaan Jawa Perpaduannya dengan Islam, 1995, (drama, novel and film) Solo Diwaktu Malam, 1950, (novel, film) Perawan Desa, 1981; translator Serat Centhini, 1974-91. Recipient Art Appreciation award Provincial Govt. Yogyakarta, 1992, Bintang Jasa Pratama award Pres. Republic Indonesia, 1992, Satyalancana Pioneer of Freedom Movement award, 1996, Javanese Lit. award Rancage Cultural Found., 1995. Mem. Indonesia-India Found., Panunggalan Cultural Found. (chairperson), Indonesia Publ. Assn. (chairperson). Islamic. Avocations: drama, football, tennis. Home: Gg Bekisar UH V/716 E-1, Yogyakarta 55161, Indonesia

PARTON, KEVIN ANTHONY, agricultural economics educator, consultant; b. Middlesbrough, Yorkshire, Eng., Aug. 24, 1951; arrived in Australia, 1974; arrived in Can., 1999; PhD in Agrl. Econs., U. New Eng., Armidale, Australia, 1980. Dir. Ctr. for Health R & D U. New Eng., 1995-99; prof. and chair dept. agrl. econs. and bus. U. Guelph, Ont., Can., 1999—; cons. N.W. Health Svc., Tamworth, Australia, 1994-98. Author: Cost of the Common Agricultural Policy, 1982, Price Policy in Indonesia, 1993, Dryland Farming and Catchment Care, 1997. Asst. treas. St. Mark's Chapel, U. New Eng., 1995-97. Recipient Sir John Crawford award Govt. of Australia, 1992. Avocations: orienteering, soccer. Office: Univ of Guelph, Dept Agrl Econs & Bus, Guelph, ON Canada N1G 4V3

PARTONEN, TIMO TAPIO, physician, researcher; b. Helsinki, Aug. 29, 1965; s. Tapio and Ritva Ilona (Jalonen) P.; m. Jarna Maarit Moilanen, May 21, 1994. B, Laajasalo Lyceum, Helsinki, 1984; MD, U. Helsinki, 1990, PhD in Medicine, 1996. Lic. physician Nat. Bd. Welfare and Health, 1991; specialized psychiatrist U. Helsinki, 1997. House physician Kellokoski Hosp., Tuusula, Finland, 1992-93; trainee U. Ctrl. Hosp., Helsinki, 1994-95; asst. prof. U. Helsinki, 1996-99; sr. rschr. Nat. Pub. Health Inst., Helsinki, 1999—. Author: Seasonal Affective Disorder, 1995; editor-in-chief: Medisiinari, Helsinki, 1988-90; editor: Annals of Medicine, 1996—; contbr. articles to profl. jours. Mem. Finnish Med. Soc. DUODECIM, Finnish Med. Assn., Finnish Psychiat. Assn., Finnish Sleep Rsch. Soc., Soc. Light Treatment and Biol. Rhythms, European Sleep Rsch. Soc. Avocations: poetry, soccer. Office: Nat Pub Health Inst, Mannerheimintie 166, Fin00300 Helsinki Finland

PARTRIDGE, LLOYD DONALD, physiologist, educator; b. Cortland, N.Y., Dec. 18, 1922; s. Bert James and Marian (Rice) P.; m. Jean Marie Rutledge, Aug. 6, 1944; children: Lloyd Donald, David Lee, Gayle Ann Partridge Kneller Spence. B.S., U. Mich., 1948, M.S., 1949, Ph.D., 1953. Instr. U. Mich., Ann Arbor, 1953-56; asst. prof. physiology, research assoc. in neurology Yale U., New Haven, 1956-62; assoc. prof. neurophysiology U. Tenn., Memphis, 1962-70; prof. U. Tenn., 1970-94, dep. chmn. physiology, 1965-73; cons. neurophysiology and bioengring. Conn. State Hosp., 1957-62, Boelter Bioengring. Ctr., UCLA, 1982-87, Acad. Sci. Sofia, Bulgaria, 1981; cons. U. So. Calif., 1992; vis. prof. U. We. Ont., 1981, 82, Med. Coll. Ohio, Toledo, 1985; vis. prof. Memphis State U., 1985, adj. prof. math., 1989-91, adj. prof. biomed. engring., 1993—; adj. prof. biomed. engring. U. Memphis, 1993—; vis. scientist Acad. Sci. USSR, 1987, Pavlov Physiology Soc., USSR, 1989; vis. prof. physiology U. Vt., 1965, 66. Author: The Nervous System, Its Function and Interaction with the World, 1993; assoc. editor: Trans Bio. Med. Engring., 1973-81; assoc. Behavior Brain Rsch., 1981—; sect. editor Annals Biomed. Engring., 1985-94; contbr. chpts. to books, articles to profl. jours. Served with AUS, 1944-46. Mem. Internat. Brain Research Orgn., Am. Acad. Neurology, Am. Physiol. Soc. (editorial bd. 1976-81), Biomed. Engring. Soc. (adminstrn. com. 1977-79), Biophysics Soc., Engring. Medicine and Biology Soc. (bd. dirs. 1985-89), IEEE, Neurosci. Soc., Sigma Xi. Fax: 701 678-5281. E-mail: lpartrdg@latte.memphis.edu. Home: 3061 Dumbarton Ave Memphis TN 38128-5107 Office: Dept Biomed Engring U Memphis Memphis TN 38152-0001

PARTRIDGE, TERENCE ANTHONY, medical researcher, educator; b. London, Aug. 5, 1940; s. Leslie William Partridge and Ivy Frances Swain; m. Joan Lesley Melling, July 6, 1968; children: Joshua Miles, Julius Simon. BSc in Zoology, U. Coll. London, 1962, PhD, 1970. Rsch. asst. Nat. Mus. Natural History, Paris, 1965-66; lectr. U. Glasgow, Scotland, 1967-70; rsch. asst. Charing Cross Med. Sch., London, 1970-75, sr. lectr., 1978-89; reader Charing Cross and Westminster Med. Sch., London, 1989-92, prof. exptl. pathology, 1992-93; prof., head muscle cell biology group Med. Rsch. Coun., London, 1994—; cons. Cell Based Delivery, Providence. Editor: (textbook) Molecular and Cell Biology of Muscular Dystrophy, 1993; (CD) Multimedia Methods in Molecular Biology, 1996. Avocations: alpine gardening, judo, running. Fax: 44-181-383-8264263. Home: 20, Loveday Rd, London W13 9JS, England Office: Hammersmith Hosp, Du Cane Rd, London W12 0NN, England

PARU, MARDEN DAVID, fundraising executive; b. Belmar, N.J., Nov. 18, 1941; s. Isaac and Edith (Rubin) P.; m. Joan Ellen Kemeny, June 5, 1966; children: Victor Milan, Elana Fay. BA, U. Tulsa, 1963; MA, U. Chgo., 1965; postgrad., Syracuse U., 1968-69, Brandeis U., 1970-73. Dir. spl. svcs. Young Men's Jewish Coun., Chgo., 1965-67; asst. dir. Jewish Community Ctr., Syracuse, N.Y., 1967-68; exec. dir. Onondaga County Assn. for Retarded Citizens, Syracuse, 1968-70; lectr., dir. admissions Hornstein program Brandeis U., Waltham, Mass., 1972-74; exec. dir. Jewish Edn. Coun., Montreal, Que., Can., 1974-76, Jewish Fedns. Poughkeepsie-Kingston (N.Y.), 1976-79; exec. v.p. Jewish Fedn. Greater Clifton (N.J.)-Passaic, 1979-82, Cin. Jewish Fedn., 1982-85; dir. N.Y. met. region Am. Technion Soc., N.Y.C., 1985-87; nat. campaign dir. Am. ORT Fedn., N.Y.C., 1987-92; dir. devel. Global Hunger Project, N.Y.C., 1992-93; exec. v.p. Keren-Or, Inc. Jerusalem Ctr. for Multi-Disabled Blind Children, N.Y.C., 1993-96; exec. dir. Jewish Fedn. Rockland, Rockland County, N.Y., 1997-99; fund-raising cons. Nyack, N.Y., 1999—; CEO Marden Paru & Assocs., Inc., 1999; cantor synagogues, Boston, Cin., N.Y. State, Okla., 1960—; cons. on aging pvt. nursing homes, Mass., 1970-74; cons. pvt. Havurot groups, Framingham, Mass., 1970-74. Mem. NASW, Assn. Jewish Community Orgn. Pers. (v.p. 1984-89), Jewish Communal Svc. Assn., Nat. Soc. Fundraising Execs., Acad. Cert. Social Workers, Rotary. Democrat. Avocation: writing poetry. E-mail: mardenparu@juno.com. Home: 4 Salisbury Pt Apt 6B Nyack NY 10960-4730

PARUI, RAMEN KUMAR, airport executive, astrophysicist; b. Calcutta, July 2, 1957; s. Ahi Bhuson and Anima (Pandit) P.; m. Tapati Gayen, Mar. 13, 1991; 1 child, Rajarshee. BSc, Calcutta U., 1977; MSc, Manipur U., Imphal, India, 1988, PhD, 1993. Guide lectr. Birla Indsl. and Tech. Mus., Calcutta, 1979-80; asst. West Bangal State Coop. Mktg. Fedn., Calcutta, 1980-83; asst. mgr. Airports Authority of India, Silchar, 1983—; project scientist Inter Univ. Ctr. for Astronomy and Astrophysics, Pune, India, 1993-94. Mem. Indian Assn. for Cultivation of Sci. (life), Astron. Soc. India. Avocations: exchange of scientific journals, friendship with foreign researchers, collecting astrophysical journals and documents. Office: Aero Communication Station, ACS Bilchar Airport, Silchar 788109, India

PARUSZEWSKI, RYSZARD, pharmacist, researcher; b. Warsaw, Poland, Jan. 1, 1935; s. Zenon and Józefa (Witkowska) P.; m. Bożena Wysocka, Aug. 28, 1966; 1 child, Grażyna. Faculty Pharmacy, Med. U., Warsaw, 1958, PhD in Pharmacy, 1966, D Habilited in Pharmacy, 1973. Asst. dept. pharm. chemistry Med. U., Warsaw, 1958-66, lectr. dept. pharm. chemistry, 1966-73, assoc. prof. pharm. chemistry, 1973-92, prof. pharmacy, 1979—, grad. rsch. prof. pharm. chemistry, 1992—; vis. prof. U. Wis., Madison, 1986-87. Coauthor: Chemical Analysis of Drugs, 1975; contbr. articles to profl. jours.; patentee in field. Postdoctoral fellow Cleve. Clinic Found., 1974-75; grantee Polish State Com. for Sci. Rsch., Warsaw, 1993, 95. Mem. Am. Peptide Soc., European Peptide Soc., Polish Pharm. Soc., Polish Pharmacol. Soc. Avocations: basketball, editing, touring. Home: 6 Brazylijska Str /31, 03-946 Warsaw Poland Office: Med U Dept Drug Chemistry, 1 Banacha Str, 02-097 Warsaw Poland

PARUTHIKAL, LOUIS MATHEN, surgeon, consultant; b. Pulincunnoo, Kerala, India, Feb. 28, 1936; s. Mathen and Mariamma Mathen (Pattom) P.; m. Thankamma Louis Chittilapilly, Nov. 14, 1964; children: Mathen Louis, Simon L., Mary Ann. BSc, Madras (India) U., 1955; BSc, BChir, Kasturba

Med. Coll., Manipal, India, 1960. Diplomate Am. Bd. Surgery. Surg. resident St. Alexis Hosp., Cleve., 1962-66; resident in thorasico-vascular surgery St. Francis Hosp., Pitts., 1966-67; chief of surgery Queens Gen. Hosp., Liverpool, Can., 1973-76; cons. Poruthiyil Narayanan Vydiar Meml. Hosp. and Rsch. Ctr., Cochin, India, 1976-80; head dept. trauma U. W.I., Kingston, Jamaica, 1980-81; asst. prof. thoracic surgery U. Bengazi, Libya, 1981-82; chief surgeon Govt. Belize, 1982-83; chief of surgery Kunjalus N.H., Cochin, 1983-86, Royal Oman Police Hosp., 1986-87; cons. surgeon Ernkulam Med. Ctr., 1980-81. Chief author: Disaster Management, 1989, Trauma Management Centers, 1991, Medical Problems of Senior Citizens, 1998, Management of Chronic Geriatric Problems by Ayurvedic System, 1999. Chief advisor Rural Med. Svc. Vallarpadam, Kerala, India, 1988-93; chief coord. Kerala Dutch Social and Cultural Soc., 1998, World Citizens, Cochin, 1991; ex officio pres. Keral Norwegian Friendship Soc., 1999. Fellow ACS, Royal Coll. Surgeons (Can.), Internat. Coll. Surgeons; mem. Lotus Club (Cochin) (exec. com. 1984). Avocations: tennis, shuttle badminton, bridge. Home: Kalavath Rd, Partuhikal House, Cochin 682025, India Office: Paruthikal Consultancy, Kalavath Rd Palariva Ttom, Kerala 682025, India

PARVATHAM, RAJAGOPALAN, mathematician, educator; b. Madras, India, Sept. 14, 1945; d. Rajagopalan K. and Meeenakshi R. BS, Stella Maris Coll., Madras, 1967, MS, 1969; PhD, Ramanujan Inst., U. Madras, 1975. Rsch. assoc. Inst. Fourier, Grenoble, France, 1975-78, 1980; lectr. Madurai Kamaraj U., India, 1979, Anna U., Madras, 1981-82; lectr. U. Madras, 1982-85, reader, 1985-91, prof., 1991—. Editor Jour. of Analysis, 1993—; contbr. articles to profl. jours. Fellow Forum Analysis; mem. Indian Math. Soc., Am. Math. Soc., Ramanujan Math. Soc., AMTI (sec., editor 1993—). Office: Ramanujan Inst, U Madras, TamilNdu Madras 600 005, India

PARVATHY, USHA, surgeon, educator; b. Ernakulam, Kerala, India, June 1, 1962; d. Raman Thiagarajan and Bhagyam; m. Kapilamoorthy, Aug. 23, 1992. MBBS, Calicut (India) Med. Coll., 1986, MS in Gen. Surgery, 1990; MChir in Cardiovasc. Thoracic, Sri Chitra Tirunal Med. Ctr., Trivandrum, India, 1993. Med. diplomate. Tutor in gen. surgery Calicut Med. Coll., 1990; sr. registrar cardiac surgery Medwin Hosp., Mahawir Hosp., Hyderabad, India, 1994; tutor in cardiothoracic surgery Sri Ramachandra Med. Coll., U. Hosp., Chennai, India, 1994-95; asst. prof. cardiovasc. thoracic surgery Sri Ramachandra Med. Coll., U. Hosp., Chennai, 1995—; presenter in field. Mem. Indian Assn. Cardiovasc. and Thoracic Surgeon (life). Avocations: playing and listening to music, reading books, swimming, playing games, creative work on computers. Office: Sri Ramachandara Med Coll, Ramachandra Nagar, Chennai Porur 600116, India

PARVEZ, MOHAMMAD MASUD, plant biologist, researcher; b. Dhaka, Bangladesh, Jan. 1, 1965; s. Mohammad Abdul Azim and Rabiul Fatima; m. Syeda Shahnaz Parvez; children: Shakib Azim Parvez. BS in Agr. with honors, Bangladesh Agrl. U., 1989, MS in Agronomy, 1991; DSc, Osaka (Japan) City U., 1997. Program officer Uniconsult Internat. Ltd., Dhaka, 1989-90; lectr. Bangladesh Agrl. Inst., Dhaka, 1990—; vis. scientist Japan Internat. Rsch. Ctr. Agrl. Scis., Tsukuba, 1997—, project mem., 1997—. Contbr. articles to Physiologia Plantarum, Bangladesh Jour. Agrl. Sci., Plant Cell Physiology. Recipient Gold medal Krishibid Found. '65, 1989, cert. and trophy Profl. Induction Tng., Bangladesh Agrl. Rsch. Inst., 1991; Merit scholar Govt. Japan, 1993, scholar Sci. and Tech. Ag., Govt. Japan, 1999—. Mem. Bangladesh Soc. Agronomy (life mem.), Japanese Soc. Plant Physiologist, Molecular Biology Soc. Japan, Am. Soc. Plant Physiologists, Botan. Soc. Japan. Avocations: soccer, stamp and currency collecting. Office: Japan Internat Rsch Ctr, 1 2 Ohwashi, Tsukuba Ibaraki 305 8686, Japan

PARVEZ, SAEED, mechanical engineer; b. Gujrat, Punjab, Pakistan, Dec. 28, 1941; d. Saeed Ullah Khan and Iqbal Begum; m. Firoza Razzaque, Oct. 24, 1980; children: Nadia Parvez, Faiza Parvez, Raza Parvez, Zaka Parvez. BSC, Zamindar, Gujrat, 1960. Chief ordnance officer Karachi, Pakistan, 1971-83, P.N. Torpedo Dept., Pakistan; sgt. United Arab Emirates Navy, Abu Dhabi, 1984—. Avocations: hockey, gardening, reading. Home: C-25 Block 13-D-1, Gulshun-E-1QBal, Karachi Pakistan

PARVEZ, SIMONE MARAZZATO, science educator; b. Dremil Lafage, France, July 19, 1944; d. Auguste and Huguette (Chadebec) Marazzato; m. Hasan Parvez, July 31, 1970; children: Salima, Alexandre, Natacha. PhD, U. Paris, 1973, DSc, 1975. Assoc. prof. U. Paris, 1968-89; prof. U. Reims, France, 1989—. Author 17 books; editor internat. jour.; contbr. numerous rsch. papers to internat. jours. Mem. City Coun. Orsay. Mem. internat. biomed. socs. Avocations: gardening, classical music, painting. Home: 11 Str Aristide Briand, 91400 Orsay France Office: URCA, 51687 Reims Cedex 2, France also: CNRS, 91190 Gif France

PARVIAINEN, PEKKA EINO OLAVI, mathematician, educator; b. Turku, Finland, Dec. 4, 1954; s. Kauko Olavi and Kaisa Margareta (Kuonanoja) P.; m. Tarja Maria Jalo, May 9, 1981; children: Anna Maria, Hanne Pilvi Pauliina. MS, Turku U., 1979, Phil. Lic., 1991. Researcher Turku U., 1979-81, asst. prof., 1981-83, 84-92, lectr., 1983-84, sr. lectr. Applied Math. Dept., 1996—; owner Polar Image, 1995—; cons. U. Calif., Los Alamos Nat. Lab., 1988-92. Contbr. articles to profl. jours., photographs to publs. and books. Avocations: astronomy, fishing, photography. Home: Jösse Sakonkatu 8 as 86, 20610 Turku Finland

PARYS, JEAN-BAPTISTE THERESE GASTON, molecular physiologist; b. Brussels, Nov. 11, 1958; s. Karel Wilfrid Hendrik Parys and Marguerite Marie Gaston Debbaudt; m. Rita Van Ginderdeuren, Jan. 18, 1986; children: Elke, Wouter, Sandra. Candidate in Scis., Cath. U. Leuven, Belgium, 1976-78, lic. in Scis., 1980, lic. in Med. Sci., 1982; PhD, Cath. U. Leuven, 1986. Rsch. asst. Cath. U. Leuven, 1980-86; asst. prof. and head dept. genetics Univ. des Scis. et de la Technologie Houari Boumedienne, Algiers, Algeria, 1986-89; asst. prof. Cath. U. Leuven, 1989-90, 97-99; assoc. prof. Leuven, 1999—; rsch. assoc. Cath. U. Leuven, 1992-93; sr. rsch. asst. Nat. Fund for Sci. Rsch., Leuven, 1993-96, rsch. assoc., 1996—; vis. prof. Univ. des Scis. et de la Technologie Houari Boumedienne Algiers, 1990; rsch. assoc. Howard Hughes Med. Inst., Iowa City, Iowa, 1990-92. Contbr. more than 80 articles to sci. jours. including: Jour. Biol. Chem., Biochem. Jour., Pflugers Arch., Cell Calcium, Biochim. Biophys. Acta, Am. Jour. Physiol., Devel. Biol., Biol. Reproduction. Leader Chirojeugd, Anderlecht, Belgium, 1975-77. Recipient award from Schamelhout-Koettlitz Fund, Royal Acad. Medicine, Belgium, 1994. Mem. Belgian Soc. Fundamental and Clin. Physiology and Pharmacology, Biophys. Soc. (U.S.), Calcium Club (European chpt.), N.Y. Acad. Scis., Am. Soc. for Biochemistry and Molecular Biology, Belgian Biophys. Soc., Dutch Biophys. Soc., Belgian Soc. for Cell Biology. Achievements include the purification, localization and functional role of calcium transporting proteins (PMCA, SERCA and InsP3R). Home: Egide Alenusstraat 9, B3290 Diest Belgium Office: Univ Leuven Physiology Lab, Campus Gasthuisberg, B-3000 Leuven Belgium

PAS, HERMAN GERARD, judge; b. Londerzeel, Belgium, Aug. 31, 1931; m. Margaretha Lambrechts, July 9, 1960; 6 children. JD, U. Leuven, Belgium, 1956. Barrister Antwerp, Belgium, 1958-70; judge Labour Ct., Antwerp, 1970-89; justice Labour Ct. of Appeal, Antwerp, 1989-91, pres., 1991-99; tchr. family law Inst. for Family Studies, Brussels, 1974-97. Editor: Vive la Difference?. . . . Co-chmn. Internat. Commn. on Marriage and Interpersonal Rels., London and Paris, 1984; bd. dirs. League of Gt. and of Young Families, Brussels, 1960-99; chmn. High Inst. Family Studies, Brussels, 1978, 88, Flemish Coun. Publicity & Sponsoring Radio & TV, 1993-98; mem. Magistrate Commn. Regularisation Etrangers, 2000. E-mail: herman.pas@antwerpen.be. Home: Kapucinessen Straat 7, B-2000 Antwerp Belgium

PASAVA, JAN, geologist; b. Kolin, Czech Republic, Aug. 26, 1957; s. Frantisek and Alena (Brixova) P.; m. Ludmila Lukasova, Oct. 3, 1981; children: Barbora, Jan. MS, Charles U., 1981, cert. of French lang., 1987; PhD, Acad. Scis., Prague, 1990. Jr. rsch. worker Czech Geol. Survey, Prague, 1981-89, sr. rsch. worker, 1990—; leader Internat. Geol. Correlation Program 254, 357 and 429. Co-editor: Mineral Deposits: From Their Origin to Their Environmental Impacts, 1995, Economic Geology, vol. 91, no. 1, 1996, Mineralium Deposita, vol. 26, no. 2, 1991. Izaak Walton Killam postdoctoral fellow Dalhousie U., 1991-93; Japan Soc. for Promotion of Sci. fellow Tsukuba U., 1998—. Mem. Soc. for Geology Applied to Mineral Deposits (v.p. 1996—, exec. sec. 1998—, Paul Ramdohr medal 1995), Czech IGCP Nat. Com. (pres. 1994—), Czech Commn. for UNESCO. Avocations: collecting minerals, hiking, skiing, travel, football. Office: Czech Geol Survey, Klarov 131, 118 00 Prague Czech Republic

PASCAL, ROBERT ALBERT, lawyer; b. Fort Lauderdale, Fla., Sept. 29, 1965; s. Albert and Maria Pascal. BA, Loyola U., 1987; JD, Nova Southeastern U., 1991. Bar: Fla. 1991. Pvt. practice Fort Lauderdale, Fla., 1991—. Editor E-Mag., 1997, Ibl.com.. Vol. Broward Lawyers Care, Ft. Lauderdale, 1992-97, Lawyer for Arts, Ft. Lauderdale, 1993-98; v.p. Quantum Resource Mgmt. Internat., Ft. Lauderdale, 1992—. Avocations: cycling, swimming, travel, linguistics. Home: 1506 SE 12th St Fort Lauderdale FL 33316-1410 Office: Pascal L Proff Offices 300 Ave of Arts Fort Lauderdale FL 33316

PASCALE, JANE FAY, pathologist; b. New Haven, Conn., May 20, 1932; d. John Adam and Madeline J. (Pompano) P.; m. Joseph H. Kite Jr., Aug. 6, 1970. BA, Mount Holyoke Coll., 1954; MD, U. Chgo., 1959. Cert. anat. and clin. pathology Am. Bd. Pathology; diplomate Nat. Bd. Med. Examiners. Intern, resident in pathology Yale-New Haven Hosp., 1959-63; NIH-NCI spl. fellow dept. microbiology Yale U. Sch. Medicine, 1963-64; NIH-NCI spl. fellow Inst. de Recherches Scientifiques sur le Cancer, Villejuif, France, 1964-66; asst. in pathology Mass. Gen. Hosp. and Harvard Med. Sch., Boston, 1966-68; asst. prof. clin. pathology Yale U. Sch. Medicine, New Haven, 1968-69; attending pathologist Erie County Med. Ctr., Buffalo, N.Y., 1969-95; clin. asst. prof. pathology SUNY, Buffalo, 1969-90, clin. asst. prof. microbiology, 1991—; mem. scientific adv. bd. Infectech, Inc., Sharon, Pa., 1995—; scientific del. Citizen Amb. Program People-to-People Internat. Contbr. articles to profl. jours. Recipient Physician's Recognition award AMA, 1981-99. Fellow Am. Soc. Clin. Pathologists, Coll. Am. Pathologists; mem. AMA, N.Y. Acad. Scis., Am. Soc. Cytology, Assn. Clin. Scientists. Methodist. Achievements include research in immunopathology of tuberculosis and autoimmune disease. Home: 108 Chasewood Ln East Amherst NY 14051-1888 Office: SUNY Dept Microbiology 3435 Main St Buffalo NY 14214-3099

PASCALL, STEPHAN CHRISTIAN, engineer, government official; b. Serres, Macedonia, Greece, Apr. 18, 1946; arrived in Belgium, 1986; s. Christos Stephanos and Angeliki Athanasia (Michalousis) P.; m. Marie Eva-Lott Lantz, Apr. 28, 1985; children: Alexander, Olympia. BSc, City U., London, 1971; PhD, Polytechnic of Ctrl. London, 1975. Chartered Engr., Eng. Exec. engr. Brit. Telecom. Rsch. Ctr., Martlesham Heath, 1975-76; exec. engr. Brit. Telecom. Internat., London, 1976-80, head of unit, 1980-86; prin. adminstr. European Commn., Brussels, 1986-94, head of sector, 1994-99, dep. head of unit, 1999—. Co-author: Commercial Satellite Communications, 1997, (with others) Electronic Engineers Reference Book, 1996, Digital Communications Reference Book, 1995. Mem. Inst. Elec. Engrs. (Eng.). Home: Clos St Georges 12, B-1150 Brussels Belgium Office: European Commn, Rue de la Loi 200, B-1049 Brussels Belgium

PASCALLON, PIERRE, economist, educator; b. Gap, France, Nov. 12, 1941; s. Julien and Denise (Derbez) P.; m. Laurette Gaulin, Dec. 21, 1968 (dec.); 1 child, Nathalie; m. Christine-Claire Fourgeaud, Apr. 17, 1999. Licence, U. Aix en Provence, France, 1967, Doctorat, 1970. Prof. econ. scis. Faculte de Sciences Economiques, Clermont-Ferrand, France, 1970—, adj. dir., 1970-76, v.p., 1976. Contbr. articles to profl. jours. Mayor, Issoire, 1989—; counselor-gen. Puy de Dome, 1992—, dep., 1986-88, 93-97; regional counselor, Auvergne, 1992-93. Decorated Order Palmes Academiques (France), Chevalier dans l'Ordre de la Legion d'Honneur, 1999. Mem. Rotary Club, Club Participation et Progres (pres. 1992—), Club 89 (pres.). Mem. R.P.R. Party. Home: 9 Place Saint-Avit, Issoire 63500, France Office: Faculte Scis Econ BP 54 41, bd François Mitterrand, 63000 Clermont-Ferrand France

PASCHALIDIS, NICKOLAS M., lawyer, writer; b. Thessaloniki, Greece, Mar. 17, 1936; s. Menelaus and Aphrodite (Kargiotakis) P.; m. Helen Hatsiasemidis, Feb. 25, 1967 (div. June 1975); 1 child, Menelaus; m. Marianna Asimakopoulos, Apr. 14, 1985. Law Degree, U. Thessaloniki, 1959. Lawyer Bar Assn., Thessaloniki, 1963-67, Ct. of Appeal, Thessaloniki, 1967-80, Supreme Ct., Athens, Greece, 1980—; legal collaborator High Commr. UN for Refugees, 1971-80. Author: Nomopsychosis, 1980, Labyrinth, 1981, Trap for Sophists, 1985, Macedonian Roulette, 1993 (award Thessaloniki Municipality 1993), Code: Agent Macedonian, 1995 (award Thessaloniki's Bar Assn. 1996), The British Commander Nicholas Hammond, 1995 (award Met. Lions 1995), Konstantin Armenopoulus, The Byzantine Guardian of law and Justice of Thessaloniki, 1996, The British Conflict and the Greek Resistance, Anatomy of a Riddle, 1997 (award Thessaloniki Municipality Ctr. of History 1997). Recipient awards Greek-Am. C. of C., 1995, Assn. Pubs. No. Greece, 1995, Assn. Greek Writers, 1995. Mem. Soc. for Macedonian Studies, Soc. Writers Thessaloniki, Greek-Am. C. of C., Assn. Jurists No. Greece. Fax: 543297. Office: 13 Frangon St, 54626 Thessaloniki Greece

PASCHKE, FRITZ, electronics engineer; b. Graz, Austria, Mar. 2, 1929; s. Eduard and Stefanie (Mittellehner) P.; m. Gertrud Kutschera, July 8, 1955; children: Else, Ulrike. Diploma in engr., Tech. U. Vienna, 1953, DSc, 1955; DSc (hon.), Tech. U. Budapest, 1974. Asst. Tech. U. Vienna, 1953-55; cons. U.S. Govt., N.Y.C., 1955-56; staff RCA, Princeton, N.J., 1956-61; chief engr. Siemens A.G., Munich, Germany, 1961-66; prof. elec. engring. Tech. U. Vienna, 1965-97, prof. emeritus, 1997—. Home: Kahlenberger Str 35, A 1190 Vienna Austria Office: Tech U Vienna, Gusshaus Str 27-29, A-1040 Vienna Austria

PASCHKE, JERRY BRYAN, lawyer; b. Palmdale, Calif., Aug. 6, 1965; s. Donald Joseph and Diana Marie (Scott) P. BS, St. John's U., Collegeville, Minn., 1988; JD, Hamline U., St. Paul, 1991. Bar: Minn. 1991, Army Ct. Mil. Rev. 1992, U.S. Magistrates Ct. 1993. Commd. 1st lt. U.S. Army, 1992, advanced through grades to capt., 1992; post judge advocate U.S. Army-Sierra Army Depot, Herlong, Calif., 1992-94; brigade trial counsel U.S. Army-Camp Stanley, Uijongbu, South Korea, 1994-95; legal instr. U.S. Army-Ft. Huachuca, Sierra Vista, Ariz., 1995-97, chief criminal law, 1997-98, mil. magistrate, 1995-97; acct. Accts.-On-Call, Mpls., 1998—; adminstrv. law officer USAR, Ft. Snelling, Minn., 1998—. Mem. landlord-tenant hotline Minn. Pub. Interest Rsch. Group, Mpls., 1989; advisor DeMolay, Reno, 1992-94. Decorated Army Commendtion medal, Meritorious Svc. medal. Mem. Masons, Order St. Barbara. Avocations: hiking, chess, travel, bowling. Home: 4450 Minnetonka Blvd Apt 103 Saint Louis Park MN 55416-5816

PASCHOUD, FRANÇOIS, university educator; b. Bern, Switzerland, Jan. 11, 1938; s. Maurice and Nelly (Suter) P.; m. Anne-Marie Chêne, July 24, 1978; children: Jerôme, Urbain. Lic. Letters, U. Lausanne, 1960, Litt.D., 1967. Mem. Swiss Inst., Rome, 1962-64; Wissenschaftlicher Mitarbeiter Thesaurus linguae Latinae, Munich, Fed. Republic of Germany, 1965-67; prof. extraordinarius, ordinarius U. Geneva, Switzerland, 1969-74, 1974—; vis. mem. Inst. for Advanced Study, Princeton U., N.J., 1976-77, 83-84. Author: Roma aeterna, 1967; Translation, Commentary of Zosimus I, 1971, II 1 and II 2, 1979, III 1, 1986, III 2, 1989. Historia Agusta, V 1, 1996. Mem. Internat. Fedn. of Socs. of Classical Studies (sec. gen. 1974—), Soc. Latin Studies Paris, Groupe Romand des Etudes Grecques et Latines (pres. 1978-81), Fondation Hardt pour l'étude de l'antiquité Vandoeuvres Geneva (pres.), Real Academia Barcelona (corr. mem.).

PASCHUK, SERGEI ANATOLYEVICH, physicist, educator; b. Yuzno-Sakhalinsk, Russia, Mar. 21, 1956; s. Anatoliy Yulianovich and Inna Petrovna Paschuk; m. Anna Vadimovna Milostanova, June 30, 1976 (div. Oct. 1998); children: Artem Sergeevich, Ekaterina Sergeevna; m. Janine Nicolosi Correa. BSc, Kharkov (Ukraine) U., 1977, MSc, 1979, PhD, 1989. Technician, dept. physics and tech. Kharkov State U., 1975-78, leading technician, nuclear physics dept., 1980-89, sci. rschr. nuclear physics dept., 1989-95, leading rschr., 1989-95; vis. prof. Physics Inst., U. Sao Paulo, Brazil, 1992-95; vis. prof. dept. physics Fed. Ctr. Technol. Edn., Curitiba, Brazil, 1995-98, assoc. prof. dept. physics, 1998—; cons. Nuclear Physics Inst., Nat. Ukrainian Rsch. Ctr., Kharkov, 1994—; advisor dept. postgrad. edn. Fed. Ctr. Technol. Edn., 1998—. Contbr. articles to profl. jours. Recipient awards. Mem. Ukrainian Phys. Soc., Brazilian Phys. Soc., Am. Phys. Soc. Christian Orthodox. Avocations: history of science and technology, world history, literature, music. E-mail: sergei@mail.cefetpr.br. Office: CEFET-PR Dept Physics, Ave Sete de Setembro 3165, Curitiba 80230901, Brazil

PASCOA, MARIO RUI, economics educator; b. Lisbon, Portugal, Sept. 21, 1958; s. Mario Jose and Maria Guilhermina (Miranda) P.; m. Celia Costa Cabral, Sept. 7, 1991; children: Tomas, Filipe. MA in Econs., UCLA, 1983, PhD in Econs., 1986. Teaching asst. U. Nova, Lisbon, Portugal, 1981-82, UCLA, L.A., 1983-86; asst. prof. U. Pa., Phila., 1986-92; asst. prof. U. Nova, 1992-96, assoc. prof., 1996-2000, prof., 2000—; vis. rschr. IMPA, Rio de Janeiro, 1991-92, 97-98, U. Carlos III, Madrid, 1992-94. Contbr. articles to profl. jours. Human Capital and Mobility fellow European Commn., 1993-94. Mem. Portuguese Soc. Rsch. Econs., N.Y. Acad. Scis., Econ. Soc. Office: U Nova Lisboa, Travessa Estevao Pinto, Lisbon 1099-032, Portugal

PASCOE, ARTHUR WILLIAM, motivational speaker, writer; b. Sydney, Australia, July 4, 1935; s. Henry Vincent Pascoe and Carmen Cassie Brown; m. Vicki Adele Prior. Student in social sci., Mitchell Coll. Advanced Edn., Bathurst, 1981; tchr. cert., U. Sydney, 1958, diploma in edn., 1961; diploma in applied psychology, Coll. Applied Psychology, London, 1958; B of Med. Sci., Tokyo Med. Ctr., 1975, D of Psychosomatic Medicine; MS with honors, N.Y., 1976. Various tchg. positions, 1979-82, part-time pvt. practice behavioral cons., therapist, 1975-90; vis. cons., psychologist Australian Def. Forces, NSW and Fed. Police Forces, 1975-90; pvt. practice counselor, 1986-91, ret., 1991-94; coord. sports health Century Health Svcs., Coffs Harbour, Australia, 1995; motivational speaker, cons. Novotel Opal Cove Resort, Coffs Harbour, 1996; pvt. practice lectr., writer, cons. in Zen Shiatsu Coffs Harbour, 1997—. Author: Was That the Bell, 1982, Yesterday's Child Tomorrow, 1986, (textbooks) Zen Shiatsu Therapy, 1999. Mem. Spkrs. Network Internat., N.Y. Acad. Scis. Avocations: music, fishing, travel, sports, gardening. Fax: +02-66527681. E-mail: pascoea@optusnet.com.au.

PASCOE, MICHAEL WILLIAM, conservation consultant; b. Rotherham, U.K., June 16, 1930; s. William Joseph Thomas and Daisy (Farlow) P.; m. Janet Clark, Mar. 24, 1956 (div. Dec. 1974); children: Katherine Jane, Joanna Mary, Madeline Bridget; m. Brenda Hale Reed, Dec. 23, 1974; 1 child, Josephine Lucy. BA, Selwyn Coll., Cambridge, Eng., 1948, PhD, 1955. Med. physicist Mt. Vernon Hosp., Northwood, U.K., 1956-57; tech. officer Brit. Nylon Spinners Ltd., Pontypool, U.K., 1957-60, ICI Paints Divsn., Slough, U.K., 1960-67; lectr. materials Brunel U., Uxbridge, U.K., 1967-75; dir. rsch. Latterly Keeper of Conservation Brit. Mus., London, 1975-80; head sci. for conservation Camberwell Coll., London, 1980-90; tutor counsellor Open U.; vis. lectr. Internat. Ctr. for Conservation, Rome; mem. hist. wrecks com. Coun. for Care of Chs.; cons. Mary Rose Trust, Madame Tussauds, Crafts Coun., Sci. Mus., Pub. Record Office, Parliament of Guyana, States of Jersey, Cultural Instns. Guatemala; vis. prof. Brunel U., 1995, 99; lectr. at various internat. confs. Sch. gov., Ickenham, Eng., 1976-80. Fellow Royal Soc. Arts, Internat. Inst. for Conservation, Brit. Assn. for Advancement of Sci. Avocations: pictoral art, theater, music, literature.

PASCOE, NIGEL SPENCER KNIGHT, Queen's counsel, recorder of Crown Court; b. Barton-On-Sea, Hampshire, England, Aug. 18, 1940; s. Ernest Sydney and Cynthia (Holtom) P.; m. Elizabeth Anne Walter, 1964; children: Gillie Caroline, Hallam James Spencer, Tristan John Marfrey, Jemma Tresillian Mary, Dimity Jane Eleanor, Miranda Lucy Kate. Educated, Epsom Coll., 1959, Inns of Ct. Sch. of Law, 1966. Recorder of the Crown Ct., 1979—; Queen's counsel Queen's Counsel, 1988—; bencher of the Inner Temple, 1998, leader of the Western Cir., 1995-98; chmn. Bar Public affairs com., 1997-98. Author: Trial of Penn and Mead, 1994, (play) The Nearly Man, 1994, (play) Pro Patria, 1996, (play) Who Killed William Rufus?, 2000; founder, 1st editor All Eng. Quarterly Law Cassettes; chmn. editl. bd. of counsel, 1999—; contbr. articles to profl. jours. Councillor Hampshire County, 1979-83; chmn. Bar Pub. Affairs Com., 1997—. Mem. Garrick Club. Ch. of Eng. Avocations: theatre, cricket, acting, writing, presenting, compiling anthologies with Elizabeth Pascoe. Office: Chambers of Guy Boney QC, 3 Pump Ct Temple, London EC4 Y7AJ, England also: Chambers of Guy Boney QC, 31 Southgate St Winchester, Hampshire SO23 9EE, England

PASCU, OLIVIU, medical educator; b. Codlea, Brasov, Romania, May 6, 1939; s. Gheorghe and Nina (Platon) P.; m. Cornelia Potîrcă, July 10, 1976; 1 child, Titel. MD, U. Medicine and Pharmacy, Cluj-Napoca, Romania, 1963, PhD, 1974. Med. diplomate. Resident Inst. Hygiene, Cluj-Napoca, 1963-66; med. practitioner Local Unit, Bistrita-Bîrgiului, Romania, 1966-68; prep. asst. 3rd Med. Clinic, U. Medicine and Pharmacy, Cluj-Napoca, 1968-71, asst., 1971-82, lectr., 1982-90, assoc. prof., 1990-91, prof., 1991—, head dept. internal medicine, 1995—; dean Faculty Medicine, Cluj-Napoca, 1990-92; rector U. Medicine and Pharmacy, Cluj-Napoca, 1992—. Author: Upper Digestive Endoscopy, Treaty of Internal Medicine, Preventive Gastroenterology, 1994, Gastroenterological Emergencies, 1995, Treaty of Clinic Gastroenterology, 1995-96; mem. editl. bd. Acta Endoscopica, Romanian Jour. Gastroenterology; contbr. articles to profl. jours. Fellow Royal Soc. Physicians Edinburgh; mem. Polish Med. Acad., Romanian Med. Acad., Italian Soc. Gastroenterology, Romanian Soc. Endoscopy and Gastroenterology (v.p.). Avocations: music, sports. Office: U Med & Pharmacy 3d Med Cl, Croitorilor St 19-21, 3400 Cluj-Napoca Romania

PASCUA, REYNALDO V., education educator; b. Candon, The Philippines, Sept. 20, 1939; s. Lazaro R. and Enriqueta (Villarba) P.; m. Glenda E. Escobar, Feb. 14, 1965; children; Maria Victoria Pascua-Del Rosario (dec.), Maria Theresa Pascua-Dean, Marissa Regina. Instr., placement officer Poly. U. of the Philippines, Manila, 1961-68; payroll supr. Westinghouse Electric Supply Co., Chgo., 1968-74; adminstrv. asst. DePaul U., Chgo., 1974-77; instr., former dept. chair Regina Dominican H.S., Wilmette, Ill., 1978—; assoc. prof., dean faculty liaison Northwestern Bus. Coll., Chgo., 1989—; part-time instr. Cosmopolitan Prep Sch., Chgo., 1970-72, Bryant & Stratton Coll., Chgo., 1972-74, Oakton C.C., Des Plaines, Ill., 1978-91; reviewer textbook McGraw Hill Pub. Co., Chgo., 1977; chmn. bus. edn. dept. North Ctrl. Accreditation and Evaluation, St. Viator H.S., Arlington Heights, Ill., 1980, St. Edwards H.S., Elgin, Ill., 1980. Recipient Centennial award, Candon, 1998, Golden award of Merit, Candon Nat. H.S., Hall of Fame award Philippine Rev. TV and Via Times Newspaper, Excellence in Edn. and Svc. award Chgo. Area Bus. Edn. Assn., 1997, Most Outstanding Filipino in Midwest award Cavite Assn. Am. Mem. Nat. Bus. Edn. Assn., Nat. Cath. Ednl. Assn., Ill. Bus. Edn. Assn., Nat. Cath. Bus. Edn. Assn. (past v.p.), Greater Midwest Cath. Bus. Edn. Assn. (past pres.), Candonians of the Midwest (past pres., adviser), Filipino-am. Profls. (past pres.), Northshore Filipino Assn. (past pres.), Internat. Assn. Adminstrv. Profls., Chgo. Area Bus. Educators Assn. (past pres.), Pace Inst. Internat., Lions Club Internat. (past dist. gov.), Chgo. Bayanihan Lions Club (past pres.), Delta Pi Epsilon. Avocations: swimming, reading, health club. Home: 150 Ashland Ave Evanston IL 60202-3759

PASCUAL, CARLOTA, painter; b. Cartagena, Murcia, Spain, Feb. 2, 1947; came to U.S., 1990; d. Carlos Pascual and Lucia Garcia; divorced; children: Eva Pineda, Carlos Pineda; m. Guillermo Saez. Student, Inst. Parramont Barcelona, Spain, 1971, Mus. Picasso, Barcelona, 1977, Mus. Modern Art, Barcelona, 1977, Dali Mus. Figueras, Spain, 1978, U. Complutense, Madrid, 1980, Mus. Prado, Madrid, 1980, Mus. Modern Art, Madrid, 1980. Represented by Ward Nasse Gallery, N.Y.C., 1997—; creative cons. R.A. Jaquez Assocs., N.Y.C., 1995-97. Creator art style Fantastic Expressionism (copyright 1996); exhibited in group shows at Ariel Gallery, N.Y.C., 1992 (prize E), Agora Gallery, N.Y.C., 1994 (Soho Internat. Competition prize 1992, 94), Fla. Mus. Hispanic and L.Am. Art, Miami, 1995-96, Ward-Nasse Gallery, 1997-98, Internat. Salon 197, 1997; one-woman shows include Nat. Ctr. Visual Art and Spanish Embassy, Buenos Aires, 1986, Sec. of Culture, Municipality of Buenos Aires, 1987, Immaculate Conception Ctr., Douglastown, N.Y.C., 1999; contbr. cover illustration to Palabras, 1994, Shame: Emotion that Limits Latinos, 1996, Trento, Italy; contbg. artist: New Art International, 1997; featured in Art in America Annual 1998-99 Guide to Museums, Galleries, Artists. Recipient Talent Spectrum Competition prize, Artis Spectrum Mag., N.Y., 1996; named Author of the Yr., Trento, Italy, 1999. Roman Catholic. Avocations: writing poetry, sculpture, theatrical performance. Home: 79 Sherman Ave Apt 5E New York NY 10040-1085

PAŠEK, JOSEF, chemistry educator, researcher; b. Mrtník, Plzeň N, Czechoslovakia, July 11, 1930; s. Václav and Božena (Patejdlová) P.; m. Daniela Cihlářová), Feb. 14, 1953; 1 child, Olga. Ing., Inst. Chem. Tech., Prague, 1952, PhD, 1958. Chem. Engrng. Asst. prof. Inst. Chem. Tech., Prague, 1952-63, assoc. prof., 1963-87, prof. chemistry, 1987—; cons. UCB, Ghent, Belgium, 1998, BCH-MCHZ, Ostrava, Czech Republic, 1980, bd. trustees, 1991-94; owner Cons. Co. Pašek, 1991—. Author: Design of Chemical Reactors from Laboratory Data, 1978, French edit., 1980, English edit., 1981. Recipient State Prize Tech. Pres. of Republic, 1969, 83. Mem. Czech Chem. Soc. Avocations: history. Home: Bělohorská 137, 169 00 Prague 6, Czech Republic Office: Inst Chem Tech, Technická 5, 166 28 Prague 6, Czech Republic

PASETTA, VESNA, mathematical economics educator; b. Ljubljana, Slovenia, Aug. 2, 1949; s. Franc and Toncka (Kroselj) P.; m. Andres Knezevic; m. Miroslav Knezevic, Sept. 20, 1975; 1 child, Sonja. PhD, Belgrade U., 1982. Prof. Belgrade U., Ithaca, N.Y., 1976-90; fulbright fellow Cornell U., Ithaca, N.Y., 1991-92, vis. prof., 1993-98; founder, pres. Econ. Proe[perty Rights Assn., Ithaca, N.Y., 1999—. Author: Economic Property Rights Theory, 1999; contbr. articles to profl. jours. Named Fulbright Teaching Rsch. fellow, 1991. Economic Property Rights Assn. (founder), Assn. of Women in Math., Soc. for Promotion of Econ. Theory. E-mail: vp11@cornell.edu. Office: Econ Property Rights Assn PO Box 4242 Ithaca NY 14852-4242

PASHAYEV, HAFIZ MIR JALAL, diplomat, physics educator; b. Baku, Azerbaijan, May 2, 1941; s. Mirjalal Ali and Pusta (Kazymova) P.; m. Rena Musa Aliyeva, Apr. 8, 1967; children: Mirjamal, Jamila. M Physics, Baku (Azerbaijan) State U., 1963; PhD in Physics, Inst. Atomic Energy, Moscow, 1971; DSc, Acad. Scis., Baku, 1984. Researcher Inst. Physics, Baku, 1963-75; PhD fellow Inst. Atomic Energy, Moscow, 1967-71; postdoctoral fellow U. Calif., Irvine, 1975-76; head metall. physics lab. Acad. Scis., Baku, 1976-92; amb. to U.S.A. from Azerbaijan Washington, 1993—. Author 3 books in physics; co-author 2 dictionaries, 1991-92; contrb. articles to phys. jours. and mass media. Avocations: drawing, sports. Office: Embassy of Azerbaijan 927 15th St NW Ste 700 Washington DC 20005-2335

PASHER, EDNA, management consultant; b. Tel-Aviv, July 29, 1942; d. Aharon Menachem and Haya Rachel (Rubin) Anglister; m. Joseph Ben-Zion Pasher, Feb. 13, 1962; children: Rachel, Dror, Yaron. BA, Tel-Aviv U., 1968; MA, Hebrew U., 1978; PhD, NYU, 1981. Tchr. Beit Yerach High Sch., Israel, 1966-74; head extracurricular activities Denmark High Sch., Israel, 1974-78; prof. Adelphi U., N.Y., 1980; mgmt. cons. Israel, 1981—; tchr. Hebrew U., Jerusalem, 1984—. Tel-Aviv U., 1996—; founding ptnr. Status, Tel-Aviv, 1990—; chmn. Amitim Forum, Tel-Aviv, 1993—; founder Knowledge in Action Internat. Confs. Sgt. Israeli Def. Forces, 1960-62. Mem. Internat. Comm. Assn., Acad. Mgmt., Strategic Mgmt. Soc. E-mail: edna@pashner.co.il. Office: 31 Zohar Tal St, Herzliyya 46741, Israel

PASHKO, VALERY ALEXANDER, marketing director; b. Orenburg, Russia, June 17, 1954; s. Alexander Ivan and Albina Ivan (Semenova) P.; m. Lidia Mike (Khramova), Sept. 22, 1981; 1 child, Alexander. Grad., Aircraft Coll., Vuzan, Russia. Engr. Hazan Helicopters, Russia, 1977-92; mgr. Hazan Helicopters, 1992-98. Office: Kazan Helicopters, Tetsevskaya Str 10, 420085 Kazan Russia

PASIC, SELIM, physics educator, researcher; b. Maglaj, Bosnia and Herzegovina, Sept. 23, 1963; p. Dzemaludin and Nasiha (Hadzemujic) P. MS, U. Zagreb, Croatia, 1994; PhD, U. Zagreb, 1997. Cert. engrng. of physics. Rschr. dept. physics U. Zagreb Faculty of Sci., 1990—. Contbr. articles to profl. jours. Mem. Internat. Radiation Physics Soc., Croatian Phys. Soc. Avocations: dancing, body building. E-mail: spasic@phy.hr. Fax: 385 1 4680 336. Home: Palmoticeva 18, 10000 Zagreb Croatia Office: Dept Physics U Zagreb, Bijenicka 32, 10000 Zagreb Croatia

PASINI, EVASIO, physician; b. La Spezia, Italy, June 20, 1957; s. Oreste and Franca (Bordone) P. MD, Univ. Bologna, Bologna, Italy, 1984. Rschr. fellow Univ. London, 1990; researcher Univ. Brescia, Italy, 1984-92; researcher Found. S. Maugeri, Pavia, Italy, 1992—, also bd. dirs. V.p. Quality Commn., Brescia, 1994—. With Parachutist Corp., 1983-84. Name Best Researcher award Italian Soc. Cardiology, 1985. Mem. European Soc. Cardiology, N.Y. Acad. Scis., Internat. Soc. Heart Rsch. Avocations: scuba diving, parachuting. Home: S Castello, 19017 Riomaggiore Italy Office: Foundation S Maugeri, Via Pinidolo, 25064 Gussago Italy

PASKAI, LÁSZLÓ CARDINAL, archbishop; b. Szeged, Hungary, May 8, 1927. Grad. high sch., Szeged. Joined Franciscan Order, Roman Cath. Ch., 1949, ordained priest, 1951. Episcopal liturgist Szeged, 1952-55; prof. philosophy Theol. Acad., Szeged, 1955-65; lectr., then prof. philosophy Theol. Acad., Budapest, Hungary, 1965-78; apptd. titular bishop of Bavagaliana, apostolic gov. of Veszprem, 1978; diocesan bishop of Veszprem, 1979, coadjutor with right succession to archbishop of Kalocsa, 1982, archbishop of Esztergom, 1987-93, archbishop of Esztergom-Budapest, 1993—, created cardinal, 1988; prefect Sem. Szeged, 1955-62, spiritual, 1962-65, spiritual Cen. Sem. Budapest, 1965-69, rector, 1973-78; chmn. Hungarian Cath. Bench of Bishops, 1986-90; primate of Hungary, 1987—. Office: Uri U 62, H-1014 Budapest Hungary

PASKAWICZ, JEANNE FRANCES, pain specialist; b. Phila., Mar. 3, 1954; d. Alex and Lillian (Pyluck) P. BSc, Phila. Coll. Pharmacy; MA, Villanova U., 1973; postgrad., St. Joseph U., 1979; PhD, Kensington U., 1984. Mem. anesthesiology staff Einstein Med. Ctr., Phila., 1990-94, Temple U. Hosp., 1994—; mem. detox./rehab. staff Presbyn. Med. Ctr., Phila., 1984—; house officer Tenet Hosps., Elkins Park, Pa., 1990—; mem. psychiatry staff Hahnemann U. Hosp., Phila., 1984-90; hostage negotiator Office of Mental Health, Phila., 1984-90; mem. surgery/anesthesiology staff Mt. Sinai Hosp., Phila., 1989-91. Bd. dirs. Phila. Coll. Pharmacy, St. Joseph U. Mem. NAFE, Am. Pain Soc., Nat. Parks Conservation Assn., North Shore Animal League, Amvets, DAV Comdrs. Club, Lambda Kappa Sigma.

PASKIN, NANCY C., rehabilitation education director; b. Dearborn, Mich., 1947; d. Carl E. and Ruth H. (Olds) Miller; m. Samuel M. Paskin, June 1973. BA, Western Mich. U., 1969, MA, 1971. Rehab. tchr. Cen. Assn. for the Blind, Utica, N.Y.; dir. rehab. svcs. Ctr. for Ind. Living., N.Y.C.; dir. rehab. teaching svcs. Westchester Lighthouse, White Plains, N.Y.; dir. vision rehab. therapies The Lighthouse, Inc., N.Y.C.; dir. rehab. tchg. agy.-wide Lighthouse Internat., N.Y.C.; adj. instr. grad. program tchr. edn. Hunter Coll.; adj. instr. Dominican Coll., Blauvett, N.Y., UALR rehab. teaching, 1994. Author: Sensory Development: An Instructor's Manual, 1979; co-author: Whatever Works, 1994. Recipient Charlyn Allen award Mid-Am. Conf. Rehab. Tchrs., 1996, N.Y. State Assn. Edn. and Rehab. of Blind and Visually Impaired Rehab. Tchr. of the Yr. award, 1997. Mem. AER (charter membership N.Y., bd. dirs., cert. rehab. tchr. of the blind, chair nat. cert. com. divsn. 11 1994, bd. dirs. N.Y. chpt. 1995, Meritiroius Achievement award 1994, Bruce McKenzie Lifetime Achievement in rehab. therapy award 1996), Access to Art/Mus. Address: 3771 Valleyview St Mohegan Lake NY 10547-1034

PASMANTER, RUBÉN ALBERTO, physicist, researcher; b. Buenos Aires, Jan. 28, 1945; arrived in The Netherlands, 1975; s. Abraham and Rosa (Schuvaks) P. Msc, U Buenos Aires, 1965; PhD in Theoretical Physics, Weizmann Inst., Rehovot, Israel, 1972. s. Rsch. assoc. MIT, Cambridge, 1974-75; postdoctoral fellow Lorentz Inst., Leiden, The Netherlands, 1975-77; sr. scientist R.W.S., The Hague, The Netherlands, 1977-90, Royal Meteorol. Inst., De Bilt, The Netherlands, 1991—; vis. scientist Weizmann Inst., 1973-74, 83-84, Kyoto (Japan) U., 1992; PhD thesis adviser U. Amsterdam, The Netherlands, 1989—; program adviser NSF, The Netherlands, 1990-91; participant Isaac Newton Inst., Cambridge, Eng., 1996. Contbr. articles to sci. jours., including Phys. Rev., Physics of Fluids, Physica A, Physics Letters, also festschrifts and congress procs. Founding mem. Jewish-Palestinian Dialogue, The Netherlands, 1984—. Mem. Am. Phys. Soc., European Geophys. Soc. (session convenor 1995, 96). Avocations: films, languages, music, molecular biology, anthropology. Home: Egelantiersgracht 392, 1015 RR Amsterdam The Netherlands Office: Royal Dutch Meteorol Inst, PO Box 201, 3730 AE De Bilt The Netherlands

PASPATIS, MIHALIS, research biologist; b. Mytilini, Greece, Jan. 23, 1963; s. Ioannis and Penelope (Magos) P.; m. Dimitra Maragoudaki, Oct. 24, 1998; 1 dau. BS, U. Athens, 1984, MS in Oceanography, 1987; PhD, U. Crete, Heraclion, Greece, 1992. Rschr. Inst. Marine Biology of Crete, Heraclion, 1994—. Contbr. articles to profl. jours. Mem. Geotech. Soc. Greece. Christian Orthodox. Avocations: diving, climbing, travel, photography. Office: IMBC, PO Box 2214, GR-71003 Heraclion Greece

PASQUINI, ANTONIO, sculptor, painter; b. Carrara, Toscana, Italy, Aug. 17, 1944; arrived in Sweden, 1965; s. Bruno and Andreina (Ussi) P.; m. Siv Inger Andersson, Apr. 20, 1968; children: Fredrik, Maria, Robert; m. Aniela Wojdyno, Feb 15, 1991. Student, Art Coll., London, 1964-65. Marble builder Bull Ltd., Eng., 1960-65; mgr., artist Ekeby (Sweden) Stenhuggeri, 1972-82; artist Atelje, Stidsvig, Klippan, Sweden, 1972—; cons., Klippan, 1991—. Exhibitions-shows include Southend-on-Sea, Eng., 1964-65, Getinge, Sweden, 1967, 68, 70, Steninge, Sweden, 1968, Bjuv, Billesholm, Ekeby, Sweden, 1976-82, Bjuv, 1982-85, Italienska kultur vecka, Helsingborg, 1984-85, Nordvikens trädgårdar, Båstad, Sweden, 1983-91, Galleri Råå, Helsingborg, 1984-85, SDS konsthall, Malmö, Sweden, 1984, Internat. marmo e macchine, marina di Carrara, Italy, 1984-89, 91-92, 96, Skand-Expo, Åstorp, Sweden, 1984, Eslövs (Sweden) Kommunal hus, 1986, Landskrona (Sweden) konsthall, 1985, Svalöv (Sweden) kommunal hus, 1986, Herrevadskloster, Lyungbyhed, Klippan, 1985, Galleri G, Helsingborg, 1985-90, Kulturen, Lund, Sweden, 1986, Kulturhallen, Kvidinge, Sweden, 1986, Internat. skulptur symposium, Carrara, Italy, 1986, Piazza Alberica, Carrara, 1986, 89, Marina di Carrara, 1987, Internat. skulptur symposium, Mortarola/Carrara, 1987-88, Kultur träff, Firenze, Italy, 1987-88, Konsthall, Laganland, Ljungby, Sweden, 1987, Art Fair Konst mässan, Stockholm, 1988-90, Alvesta (Sweden) kommun, 1988, Galeria Dolna Volta, Warsaw, Poland, 1989-90, Galeria BWA, Skierniewice, Poland, 1989-90, Skulptur symposium, Oronsko, Poland, 1990, Skulptur och Mäleri symposium, Boleslawow, Poland, 1990, Bulowska Galleriet, Malmö, Sweden, 1990, Galeria Monetti "il Matrimonio", Warsaw, 1991, Galleri Monelli, Helsingborg, 1991, Galleri Pilgränden, Ystad, Sweden, 1991-92, Boalt, Glimåkra, Sweden, 1991-92, Spanien, Costa del Sol, Spain, 1991-92, Galleri Smedbyn, Huskvarna, Sweden, 1992, Galleri gamla stan, Helsingborg, 1991-92, Motala konstfö. Bd. dirs. Svenska Konstnärsförbundet, Göteborg, Sweden, 1986—. Served with Swedish mil., 1969. Recipient 1st prize Simposio Internat. Scultura, Carrara, Italy, 1986, Culture prize Bjurs Coun., Sweden, 1983, Vuxenskolans, Helsingborg, Sweden, 1988, Klippans Kommun Culture prize, 1999. Home and Studio: Studio Artistcoupel, Stidsvigsvägen 47, 26470 Klippan Sweden

PASQUINO, GIANFRANCO, political science educator, columnist; b. Trana, Italy, Apr. 9, 1942; s. Emanuele and Gabriella (Molinatti) P.; divorced, 1990; children: Sara, Emanuele. Laurea, U. Turin, Italy, 1965; MA, Sch. Advanced Internat. Study, Washington, 1967; PhD in Polit. Sci. (hon.), U. Buenos Aires, 1996. Asst. prof. polit. sci. Bologna (Italy) U., 1969-73, Florence (Italy) U., 1970-73; assoc. prof. polit. sci. Bologna U., 1973-75, Florence U., 1973-75; full prof. polit. sci. Bologna U., 1975—, dir. dept. polit. sci., 1983; adj. prof. politics, Bologna Ctr. Johns Hopkins, 1973—; vis. prof. Coll. of Europe, 1995, 97, 98, UCLA, 1998. Author: L'opposizione, 1995, La classe politica, 1999; co-editor: Politics in Italy, 1992, 93, 94, The End of Postwar Politics in Italy, 1994. Senator of the Italian Rep., 1983-87, 87-92, 94-96; chmn. Conf. Group on Italian Politics, 1979-81. Recipient Premio Fiuggi for best essay on Instnl. Analysis, 1988, First prize FIUGGI Founds. Mem. Am. Polit. Sci. Assn., Assn. Il Mulino. Mem. Party of the Democratic Left. Office: Bologna Ctr Johns Hopkins, Via Belmeloro 11, I-40126 Bologna Italy

PASS, CHRISTOPHER LAURENCE, economics educator; b. Bradford, W Yorkshr., England, Mar. 30, 1942; s. Norman and Mary (Hainsworth) P.; m. Averil Dyson; children: Simon, Stephen. BSc in Econs., Hull (Eng.) U., 1963; MPh in Econs., Bradford U., 1976; PhD in Internat. Bus., Bradford (Eng.) U., 1992. Economist Metal Box, London, 1963-64, Barclay Bank, Leeds, Eng., 1964-65; reader, prof. Mgmt. Ctr. Bradford (Eng.) U., 1965—. Author: Servicing International Markets, 1992, Business and Microeconomics, 1994, Companies and Markets, 1994, Canada-UK Bilateral Trade and Investment Relations, 1995, Dictionary of Economics, 3d edit., 2000, Dictionary of Business, 2d edit., 1996, Business and Macroeconomics, 1996, International Business, 2000. Avocations: fgn. travel, reading, snooker. Office: U Bradford Mgmt Ctr, EMM Ln, W Yorks Bradford BD9 4JL, England

PASSAKOS, CONSTANTINOS GEORGE, emeritus psychology educator, researcher; b. Kallithea, Fokidos, Greece, June 23, 1926; s. George Constantinos and Paraskevy George (Asfakianou) P.; m. Penelope Constantinos Mandreka, July 16, 1961; children: George, Demetrios, Paraskevy, Christos. Diploma in edn., Pedagogical Acad., Athens, Greece, 1948; diploma in lit. and philosophy, U. Athens, 1971; MEd, U. Edinburgh, Scotland, 1958; PhD in Psychology, U. Salonica, Greece, 1974. Tchr. primary edn. various pub. schs., Greece, 1950-65; tchr. edn. and psychology Coll. Edn., U. Athens, 1965-70; prin. Pedagogical Acad., Lamia, 1970-73; vice prin. Sch. of In-Svc. Edn., Athens, 1973-76; sr. advisor Nat. Pedagogical Inst., Athens, 1976-85; sch. counselor pvt. primary and secondary sch., Athens, 1986-91; prof. psychology U. Athens, 1991-93, prof. emeritus, 1994—. Author: Psychology of Individual Differences, 1975, 2d edit., 1978, Introduction to Educational Psychology, Vols. I & II, 1980, The Person in the Process of Becoming: The Fundamentals of Personality Psychology, 1994, 2d edit., 1997, Life-long Learning-an Urgent Challenge for Today and Tomorrow, 1996; contbr. numerous articles to profl. jours. Officer Army of Greece, 1949-50. Mem. Christian Assn. Tchrs. Athens. Greek Orthodox. Avocations: reading, climbing, gardening. Home: 20 Pegassus St, 15125 Athens Amarous, Greece Office: U Athens Dept Prim Sch Edn, Navarinou 13A, Athens Greece

PASSANO, E. MAGRUDER, JR., corporate philanthropist; b. Balt., Oct. 2, 1942; s. Edward M. and Mildred P. (Nelson) P.; m. Helen C. Marikle, Sept. 4, 1971; children: Catherine, Tammy, Sarah. BS, Johns Hopkins U., 1967, MA, 1969. With Waverly Inc., Balt., 1965-98, salesman, 1970-73, v.p., 1973-75, v.p. adminstrn., sec., 1975-90, vice chmn., sec., 1990-98; pres., CEO One Waverly LLC, Balt., 1998—. Pres. Passano Found., Balt., 1982—. Am. Lung Assn., Md., 1982-84; mem. exec. com. Vol. Coun. Equal Opportunity, Balt., 1978—, chmn., 1995—; bd. dirs. Combined Health Appeal Am., 1994-97; pres. (CHA) Combined Health Agys., Md., 1985-87, chmn. exec. com., 1987-95; pres. 12:30 Club Balt., 1981-83; mem. exec. com. Balt. City Life Mus., 1982-93, v.p. 1987-93; trustee emeritus, 1993-98; mem. adv. coun. Johns Hopkins U. Sch. Continuing Studies, 1984—, exec. chair alumni chpt., 1986-89, chair edn. cmty. devel. iniative, 1995—; mem. Md. Gov.'s Commn. on High Blood Pressure and Related Cardiovascular Risk Factors, 1986—; bd. govs. Md. New Directions, Inc., 1987-94; bd. dirs., mem. exec. com. YMCA Ctrl. Md., 1988-96; bd. dirs., chair edn. com. Pride of Balt., 1990—; bd. dirs. Ind. Coll. Fund Md., 1994—; bd. vis. Towson State U., 1994—, chmn. 1997—, Sch. Medicine U. Md., 1995—; mem. planning com., bd. vis. Md. Bus. Responsive Govt., 1994—. With USN, 1963-65. Recipient Prince Hall Bicentennial award Masons, 1975; citations Mayor of Balt., 1976, City of Balt., 1977, Vol. of Yr. award for outstanding svc. to CICHA, 1984-85, Presdl. award for outstanding svc. to Am. Lung Assn. Md., 1985, Outstanding Vol., 1988, Disting. Svc. award Soc. Profl. Journalists, 1987, Outstanding Svc. award Am. Heart Assn., 1988, Outstanding Vol. Svc. award Balt. Assn. Retarded Citizens, 1990, Vol. of Yr./Outstanding Leadership and Dedication award Combined Health Agys., 1991-92. Mem. Purchasing Mgmt. Assn. Md. (chmn. com. 1968-70), Balt. Jaycees (v.p. 1974-76, internat. senator 1975), Greater Balt. Minority Purchasing Coun. (Svc. award 1978), Soc. Colonial Wars (chpt. gov. 1989-91), Johns Hopkins U. Alumni Assn. (pres. Balt. 1984-86, Univ. Heritage award 1987). Democrat. Episcopalian. Home: 3925 Linkwood Rd Baltimore MD 21210-3001 Office: One Waverly LLC 100 N Charles St Ste 640 Baltimore MD 21201-3805

PASSANTINO, BENJAMIN ARTHUR, medical marketing executive; b. Bklyn., Feb. 26, 1956; s. Anthony Frank and Ann Marie (Ruggerio) P.; m. Jane Ellen Collins, Nov. 26, 1983; children: Blythe Ann, Paige Ellen. BA, Drew U., 1978; BSBA, Pace U., 1979. Mgr. pub. rels. AT&T, N.Y.C., 1978-82, mgr. mktg. comm. and new techs., 1982-84; pres. B. Arthur Comm., Morristown, N.J., 1984-89; sr. v.p. bus. devel. IMEDIA Creative Corp. Mktg., Morristown, 1989-94, also dir.; mng. ptnr., CEO., Tribeca Global, Inc., Hackettstown, N.J., 1994-99; dir. media and comms. onProject.com, Morristown, 2000—; vice-chair Avid Records, Inc., N.Y.C.; chief mktg. officer Avid Listener, Inc., N.Y.C.; bd. dirs. Dieknowlogist, Inc., N.Y.C., One World Botanicals, Inc., Red Bank, N.J., Lasercomb Am., Inc., N.Y.C., The Perfect Supply Co., Inc., N.Y.C., Imedia, Morristown, N.J., 1990-94. Co-author: One with the Flame, 1985, NFL Quarterbacks, 1987; contbr. articles to mags. Bd. dirs. Am. Cancer Soc., Morristown, 1986—, Jr. Achievement, Basking Ridge, N.J., 1979—; mem. Washington Twp. (Morris County) Planning Bd., chairperson econ. devel. com.; trustee Drakestown United Meth. Ch. Mem. IEEE, Internat. Assn. Bus. Communicators, Am. Mktg. Assn., Bus. Profls. of Advt. Assn., Conf. Bd. Office: 108 High St Ste 2D Hackettstown NJ 07840-1936

PASSARELLA, DANIEL, professional soccer coach, former player; b. 1953. Player, capt. Argentina Nat. Team; winner World Cup, 1978; player River Plate Football Club, Argentina, Fiorentina Football Club, Inter Milan Football Club; coach River Plate Football Club; winner League Titles; coach Argentina Nat. Team, Uruguay Team, 2000—. Recipient World Cup, Argentina, 1998. Office: Assn Del Futbol Argentina, Viamonte 1366/76, 1053 Buenos Aires Argentina Address: Assn Uruguay de Futbol, Guayabo 1531, 112000 Montevideo Uruguay*

PASSARELLO, ESPEDITO, political organization executive; b. Bagnara, Italy, Oct. 1, 1946; s. Francisco and Anunciata (Mangione) P.; m. Ana Maria Marro, July 18, 1968; children: Marcos, Julieta, Selva. License in computer sci., U. Buenos Aires, 1971, M in sys. engring., 1973; postgrad., Cath. U. Argentina, 1975; M in policy culture, I.N.A.P., Argentina, 1993. Dir. S.C.D. Argentine Ministry of Econs., 1970-74; dir. studies Bolivian Ministry Pub. Adminstrn., 1975; dir. informatics Argentine Ministry of Planning, 1976-78; dir. projects UN, Uruguay, 1979, Deutsche Bank, Argentina, 1980-82, Cargill S.A., Argentina, 1983-86, Price Waterhouse, Argentina, 1987-90; dir. tech. Argentine Ministry of Edn., 1990-92; dir. Argentine Inst. Politics, Buenos Aires, 1993—. Author: Electronic Data Processing, 1987; contbr. articles to profl. jours. Mem. Libr. Found., Argentina, 1992, Asociacion Dessarrollo Technologico, Argentina, 1983; pres. Nat. Commn. Informatics, Argentina, 1977-80, Engr. Ctr., Argentina, 1978-84, Informatics Soc., Argentina, 1978-86, Consulting O.E.A. and UNESCO, 1996. Mem. Gimnasia y Esgrima Buenos Aires. Avocations: chess, tennis, swimming, yachting. Home and Office: Arcos 3174, 1429 Capital Federal Argentina

PASSERIN D'ENTREVES, LODOVICO, health association administrator; b. Courmayeur, Aosta, Italy, July 2, 1941; m. Emanuela Gianotti; children: Francesco, Margherita. Degree in law, U. Turin, 1969. Asst. to dep. gen. Toro Assicurazioni, Turin, 1975, head pub. rels., 1987; head comms. IFIL-Finanziaria di Partecipazioni, Turin, 1986; chmn. Internat. Ctr. Right-Soc.-Economy, Courmayeur, 1992, Inst. for Cancer Rsch., Candiolo, 1998; v.p. pub. rels. office Inst. Fin. Indsl.-IFIL Agnelli Group, Turin, 1995. Com. chmn. Turin Internat. Project, 1999. Lt. Italian Mountain Troops. Mem. Galleria Sabauda Friends Assn. (chmn.). Avocations: skiing, iconography of Valle d'Aosta. Office: IFI, Corso Matteotti 26, 10121 Turin Italy

PASSERONE, ALBERTO, chemical engineer; b. Perinaldo, Italy, Aug. 23, 1943; s. Maurizio and Flora (Laura) P.; m. Silvia Giordano, June 4, 1969; two children. BS, U. Genova, 1967; DSc, U. Grenoble, 1981. From rschr. to dir. ICFAM CNR, Genova, Italy, 1970—, dir. rsch.; chmn. ESA MAC, 1997-2000; prin. investigator space rsch. programs Spacelab, Eureca 1, Maser, Texus; lectr. in field. Editor books; contbr. articles to profl. jours., chpts. to books. Mem. European Acad. of Arts, Sci. and Humanities (corrs. mem.), European Low Gravity Rsch. Assn. (v.p. 1994-97), Italian Space Agy. (scientific adv. com. 1999—). Office: ICFAM CNR, Via de Marini 6, 16149 Genoa Italy

PASSEY, MARK LYMAN, sports association executive; b. Healdsburg, Calif., Mar. 4, 1947; s. Lyman E. and Lois L. (Marcantonio) P.; m. Charlene A. Carlsen, Jan. 26, 1968; children: Allison Edmondson, Hilary Walton. Student, Utah State U., Logan, 1965-68. Mgmt. (various) Smith's Mgmt. Corp., Salt Lake City, 1966-85; exec. dir. Utah Golf Assn., Salt Lake City, 1985-90; mgr. regional affairs U.S. Golf Assn., Salt Lake City, 1990—; bd. directors Utah Jr. Golf Association, 1985-90, Univ. Hosp. Utah Open, 1985-90, Showdown at Jeremy Ranch PGA Sr. Tour, 1985-90. Bd. dirs. Alliance for the Varied Arts, Logan, 1980-85. Avocations: arts, skiing, music. E-mail: mpassey@usga.org. Office: US Golf Assn 1121 Loch Lomond Way Salt Lake City UT 84117-4974

PASSI, INDER BIR SINGH, mathematics educator; b. Bilaspur, Haryana, India, Aug. 20, 1939; s. Hukam Chand and Jasmer Kaur P.; m. Surinder Sehgal, May 12, 1963; children: Monica, Erica. BA with honors, Panjab U., Chandigarh, India, 1958, MA, 1960; PhD, U. Exeter, Eng., 1966. Lectr. Nat. Coll., Sirsa, India, 1960-61; lectr. Kurukshetra (India) U., 1961-67, reader, 1967-75, prof. math., 1975-79; prof. math. Panjab U., 1979—; chmn. dept. math. Panjab U., 1984-87, dean fgn. students, 1991-92, dean alumni rels., 1990-91, dean faculty sci., 1995-96, dean univ. instrn., 1997-99; mem. Nat. Bd. Higher Math., India, 1989—. Editor Jour. Indian Math. Soc., 1985-91; author: Group Rings and Their Augmentation Ideals, 1979, also 5 other books; contbr. over 40 articles to math. jours. Recipient S.S. Bhatnagar prize Coun. Scientific Indsl. Rsch., New Delhi, 1983, Maghnad Saha award rsch. in theoretical scis. Univ. Grants Commn., New Delhi, 1988, Indo-Am. Fellowship award, 1987. Fellow Indian Nat. Sci. Acad., Indian Acad. Scis., Nat. Acad. Scis. India. Home: 381 Sector 38A, Chandigarh 160036, India Office: Panjab U, Dept Math, Chandigarh 160014, India

PASSLACK, MATTHIAS, electrical engineer, researcher; b. Dippoldiswalde, Saxony, Germany, May 24, 1959; came to U.S., 1993; s. Guenter and Christa (Klemm) P.; m. Gudrun Schwartz, Feb. 16, 1985; children: Katrin, Jessica. MS in engring., Tech. U. Dresden, Germany, 1984, D. in Engring., 1988. Asst. prof. U. Dresden, 1989-91; vis. scientist U. Ulm, Germany, 1992, AT&T Bell Labs., Murray Hill, N.J., 1993-95; sr. principal staff engr. Motorola PCRL, Tempe, Ariz., 1995—. Contbr. articles to IEEE Trans., Applied Physics Letters. Grantee German Rsch. Assn., 1992. Mem. IEEE (sr.), Am. Phys. Soc. Achievements include patents and patents pending in field; pioneer in field of GaAs metal-oxide-semiconductor technology. Office: Motorola Semiconductor Products Sector 2100 E Elliot Rd # 720 Tempe AZ 85284-1806

PASSLOF, PAT, artist, educator; b. Brunswick, Ga.; m. Milton Resnick. Student, Black Mountain Coll., 1948, Willem de Kooning, 1948-50; BFA, Cranbrook Coll., 1951. Prof. art Coll. of Staten Island, CUNY, 1972—. One woman show Elizabeth Harris Gallery, 1993, 96, 98, 2000. Fellow John Simon Guggenheim Meml. Found., 1999-00. Address: 80 Forsyth St New York NY 10002-5101

PASSMANN, JOHN WALTER, management consultant; b. Wesel, Germany, Nov. 14, 1926; s. Konrad Bernhard and Frieda Anna (Heine) P.; m. Ellen Lüchau, May 11, 1984; 1 child, Gisela. Degree in indsl. adminstrn., Vocat. Sch., Kleve, Germany, 1943; interpreter cert., Cologne, Germany, 1958. Mgr. sys., audits and cost acctg. Ford, Caltex, Avon, Germany, 1956-65; sys. mgr. Marathon Oil, Frankfort and Munich, Germany, 1966-68; mgr. fin. and adminstrn. Somaltex, Bala'ad, Somalia, 1968-70; sys. and pers. mgr. Wilkhahn, Eimbeckhausen, Germany, 1970-73; fin. controller, mng. dir. Rank Strand Electric, Wolfenbüttel, Germany, 1974-76; pvt. practice Rehlingen, Germany, 1977—. Author: Dictionary of Mineral Oil Terms, 1964, Value Analysis Guidelines and Handbook, 1982. With German Army, 1944-45. Mem. Ency. Brit., Nat. Geog. Soc. Avocations: history, geography, English lang., travel, horseback riding.

PASSONI DELL'ACQUA, ANNA MARIA, religious studies educator; b. Milan, Lumbardy, Italy, July 22, 1949; d. Giovanni and Graziella (Raynaud) Passoni; m. Angelo Dell'Acqua, May 19, 1973; children: Andrea, Marco. B in Classical Letters, Cath. U., Milan, 1972, PhD in Oriental Studies, 1974. Cert. biblical philologist, papyrologist. Asst. Ministry Pub. Instrn. Cath. U., 1973-1980, rschr., 1980—, prof., 1994—. Author: Il Testo del Nuovo Testamento, 1994; contbr. Introduzione alla Bibbia, 1994, Il 3 Maccabei, in Apocrifi dell'Antico Testamento, 2000. Mem. Assn. Internat. de Papyrologues, Internat. Orgn. for Septuagint and Cognate Studies, Assn. Biblica Italiana. Avocations: painting, photography, cooking, bricolage. Home:

viale Toscana 11, 20136 Milan Lumbardy, Italy Office: Catholic U, largo Gemelli 1, 20123 Milan Lumbardy, Italy

PASTEN, LAURA JEAN, veterinarian; b. Tacoma, May 25, 1952; d. Frank Larry and Jean Mary (Slavich) Brajkovich. Student, Stanford U., Davis, 1970; BA in Physiology, U. Calif., Davis, 1970, DVM, 1974; postgrad., Cornell U., 1975. Veterinarian Nevada County Vet. Hosp., Grass Valley, Calif., 1975-80; pvt. practice vet. medicine, owner Mother Lode Vet. Hosp., Grass Valley, 1980-96; veterinarian for Morris the 9-Lives cat (of TV comml. fame), 1985-94; veterinarian for Morris the 9-Lives cat (of TV comml. fame) 1985-94; lectr. in field; spokesperson Nat. Cat Health Month; guest Today Show on wildlife. Author: Malignant, Tarantula Whisperer; pub. video How Smart is Your Puppy?. Bd. dirs. Sierra Svcs. for the Blind. Mem. AVMA (ethics com.), AOPA, Calif. Vet. Med. Assn. (exec. com., del., Don Low fellowship selection com.), Mother Lode Vet. Assn., Am. Animal Hosp. Assn. (Mother Lode Hosp. cited for excellence), Nat. Ophthalmol. Soc., Nat. Pygmy Goat Assn., Nat. Llama Assn., Internat. Assn. for Arabians, Nat. Assn. Underwater Instrs., Denver Area Med. Soc., Internat. Vet. Med. Assn. Am., Nevada County C. of C. (bd. dirs.), Ninety-Niners Pilots Assn., Mensa, Endurance Riding Soc., Grass Valley Bus. Women. Republican. Lutheran. Home and Office: 5125 Paso Venado Carmel CA 93923-9477

PASTERNAC, ANDRÉ, cardiologist; b. Toulouse, France, July 22, 1937; came to Can., 1971, naturalized, 1978.; s. Jacques and Règine P. Adv. math., Lyceé Henri IV, Paris, 1956; BA in Polit. Sci., Toulouse U., 1963, MD Med. Sch., 1968. Intern Toulouse Univ. Hosp., 1962-63, resident, 1963-64; resident Edouard-Herriot Hosp., Lyon, France, 1965-66; Fulbright scholar in cardiology Harvard U., 1968-71; research fellow Peter Bent Brigham Hosp., Boston, 1968-69; Milton fellow Children's Hosp., Boston, 1969-71; fellow in cardiology Toronto (Ont., Can.) U., 1971-72; staff cardiologist Montreal (Que., Can.) Heart Inst., 1972—; asst. prof. medicine U. Montreal, 1972-78, clin. assoc. prof., 1978—, clin. prof. medicine, 1994—; vis. lectr. U. Liège (Belgium), 1977, U. Madrid, 1977, U. Warsaw, 1979, 83; cons. Harley St. Clinic, Cromwell Hosp., Wellington Hosp., Heart Hosp., London. Contbr. articles to profl. jours. Bd. dirs. Heart-Brain Rsch. Found. Inc., N.Y.C. Am. Field Svc. grantee, Oreg., 1954-55. Mem. French Cardiac Soc., European Soc. Cardiology, Canadian Cardiovasc. Soc., Am. Coll. Cardiology, Am. Heart Assn., Internat. Soc. Heart Rsch., Am. Fedn. Clin. Rsch., N.Y. Acad. Scis. Research in stress-related myocardial ischemia and dysfunction, mitral valve prolapse, cardiovascular drugs, cardiomyopathies, catecholamines, neuroendocrine control of the heart, stress and the heart, prevention. Home: 4175 Ste Catherine St W Apt 304, Westmount, PQ Canada H3Z 3C9 Office: Montreal Heart Inst, 5000 Belanger E, Montreal, PQ Canada H1T 1C8

PASTERNACK, ROBERT HARRY, school psychologist; b. Bklyn., Nov. 30, 1949; s. William and Lillian Ruth (Levine) P.; m. Jeanelle Livingston, Apr. 10, 1980; children: Shayla, Rachel. BA, U. South Fla., 1970; MA, N.Mex. Highlands U., 1972; PhD, U. N.Mex., 1980. Dir. Eddy County Drug Abuse Program, Carlsbad, N.Mex., 1972-73; adminstrv. intern U.S. Office Edn., Washington, 1975-76; exec. dir. Villa Santa maria, Cedar Crest, N.Mex., 1976-78; clin. dir. Ranchos Treatment Ctr., Taos, N.Mex., 1978-79; sch. psychologist N.Mex. Boys Sch., Springer, 1980—, supt., 1991; pres. Ensenar Health svcs., Inc., Taos, 1980—; CEO Casa de Corazon, Taos, N.Mex., 1994-98; state dir. spl. edn. N.Mex. State Dept. Edn., Santa Fe, 1998—; instr. N.Mex. Highlands U., Las Vegas, 1980—, U. N.Mex., Albuquerque, 1980—; cons. N.Mex. Youth Authority, Santa Fe, 1988—, N.Mex. Devel. Disabilities Bur., Santa Fe, 1986—, various sch. dists.; state dir. spl. edn., N.Mex., 1998—. Author: Growing Up: The First Five Years, 1986; contbr. articles to profl. publs. Pres., bd. dirs. Children's Lobby, N.Mex., 1978, N.Mex. Spl. Olympics, 1986-88, Child-Rite, Inc., Taos, 1990; mem. Gov.'s Mental Health Task Force, Albuquerque, 1988—. Mem. Nat. Assn. Sch. Psychologists, Correctional Edn. Assn., Nat. Alliance Mentally Ill, N.Mex. Coun. on Crime and Delinquency. Avocations: tennis, racquetball, skiing, cooking. Home and Office: Enseñar Inc PO Box 3126 Taos NM 87571-3126 Office: NMex State Dept Edn Spl Edn Office 300 Don Gaspar Ave Santa Fe NM 87501-2752

PASTERNAK, SHAI SAM, physician, nutritionist; b. Jerusalem, June 10, 1967; s. Avshalom and Anna (Bachi) P.; m. Ronit Malka Hammer, Aug. 30, 1992; children: Ella, Amos, David. BSc in Med. Sci., Hadassah Med. Sch., Jerusalem, 1993; MD, Technion, Haifa, Israel, 1997. Physician Carmel Hosp., Haifa, 1997—; nutritionist Pvt. Clinic, Haifa, 1995-98. Med. officer Israeli Def. Forces Res., 1993-98. Mem. Israeli Assn. Food Sci. Israeli Labor Party. Jewish. Avocations: dungeons & dragons, travel, ayurvedic and herbal medicine. Home: 46 Harduf St, Tirat-Carmel Israel

PASTIN, MARK JOSEPH, association executive; b. Ellwood City, Pa., July 6, 1949; s. Joseph and Patricia Jean (Camenite) P.; m. Joanne Marie Reagle, May 30, 1970 (div. Mar. 1982); m. Carrie Patricia Class, Dec. 22, 1984 (div. June 1990); m. Christina M. Brecto, June 15, 1991. BA summa cum laude, U. Pitts., 1970; MA, Harvard U., 1972, PhD, 1973. Asst. prof. Ind. U., Bloomington, 1973-78, assoc. prof., 1978-80; founder, bd. Compliance Resource Group, Inc., 1983—; chmn., CEO, pres. Coun. Ethical Orgns., Alexandria, Va., 1986—; prof. mgmt., dir. Ariz. State U., Tempe, 1988-92, prof. emeritus, 1996—; chair Health Ethics Trust, 1995—; mem. adv. bd. Aberdeen Holdings, San Diego, 1988-90; dir. Learned Nicholson, Ltd., 1990-91; bd. Japan Am. Soc. Phoenix, Found. for Ethical Orgns.; cons. GTE, Interim Healthcare, 1997—, Tex. Instruments, MicroAge Computers, Med-Tronic, Blood Sys., Inc., Opus Corp., GTE, NyNex, Am. Express Bank, Kaiko Bussan Co., Japan, Arex Co., Japan, Century Audit Co., Japan, Scottsdale Meml. Hosp., Consanti Found., Lincoln Electric Co., Tenet Healthcare Corp., The Williams Co.; vis. faculty Harvard U., 1980; invited presenter Australian Inst. Mgmt., Nippon Tel. & Tel., Hong Kong Commn. Against Corruption, 1984, Young Pres.'s Orgn. Internat. U., 1990, Nat. Assn. Indsl. & Office Parks, 1990, ABA, 1991, Govt. of Brazil, 1991. Author: Hard Problems of Management, 1986 (Book of Yr. Armed Forces Mil. Comtrs. 1986, Japanese edit. 1994), Power by Association, 1991, The Hotline Handbook, 1996, Planning Forum, 1992; editor: Public-Private Sector Ethics, 1979; mem. editl. bd. Report on Medicine Compliance; pub. Pastin Report on Healthcare Compliance, 1998—, Guerin Lect. on Philanthropy, 1996. Founding bd. mem. Tempe Leadership, 1985-89; bd. mem. Ctr. for Behavioral Health, Phoenix, 1986-89, Tempe YMCA, 1986—, Valley Leadership Alumni Assn., 1989-92; mem. Clean Air Com., Phoenix, 1987-90. Nat. Sci. Found. fellow, Cambridge, Mass., 1971-73; Nat. Endowment for the Humanities fellow, 1975; Exxon Edn. Found. grant, 1982-83. Mem. Am. Soc. Assn. Execs. (invited presenter 1987-97), Bus. Ethics Soc., Found. Ethical Orgns. (chmn. 1988, pres.), Golden Key, Harvard Club D.C., Univ. Club of D.C., Phi Beta Kappa. Avocations: golf, running. Home: 7206 Park Terrace Dr Alexandria VA 22307-2035 Office: 214 S Payne St Alexandria VA 22314-3530

PASTINICA, NICOLAE, career officer; b. Stoenesti, Arges, Romania, Sept. 17, 1945. Grad., High Mil. Sch. Active Officers, Romania, 1967; D in Mil. Scis., 1995; Grad., Mil. Acad., Romania, 1977, Post Academic Course, Romania; postgrad., Def. Nat. Coll., Romania, 1993. Cadets platoon comdr. Mil. Sch. for Active Officers, Romania, 1967, cadets co. officer, 1970, cadets batallion chief of staff, 1973, comdr. cadets battalion, 1977-81; comdr. Mechanized Regiment, Romania, 1982-85; chief of sect. Romanian Gen. Staff, Romania, 1992-93; chief ops. sect. Army, Romania, 1985, army comdr., 1994-95, chief of staff, 1995-97; inspector gen. of the Armed Forces Ministry of Def., Romania, 1997—, divsn. gen., 1997—; dep. chief of staff Romanian Navy, 1990—. Author: Contribution to the Troops' Training and Education, 1985, The Operational Area Defense Strategy, 1995, The Military Actions Theatre of National Interest, 1997, The Rapid Action in the XXth Century Force, 1998. Mem. Nat. Def. Coll. Found., Friends of Canadian Forces Assn. (pres. 1999), Acad. Men of Sci. Avocations: jogging. Home: 65 Unirii Blvd, Bucharest Romania Office: Ministry of Def, 13-15 Izvor St, 70642 Bucharest Romania

PASTOR, JAVIER LOPEZ, marketing consultant; b. Madrid, July 20, 1952; s. Feliciano Lopez Ceballos and Eusebia Pastor Jimenez; m. Maria Teresa De Cossio Diaz, July 6, 1981; 2 children. Mktg. analyst Smith Seecham, Madrid, 1979; market rsch. mgr. Glaxo Wellcome Plc, Madrid, 1984; product mgr. Antibioticos Pharmacia, Madrid, 1985, U.S. Surg. Corp. Auto Suture, Madrid, 1991; mktg. devel. and formation mgr. Bristol Myers Squibb, Madrid, 1991; cons. Sintra Union Mktg., Madrid, 1999—; lectr. Inst. de Empresa, Madrid, 1994-96, Inst. for Internat. Rsch., Madrid, 1994. With Spanish Artillery, 1975. Avocations: sports, reading. Home: Nuestra Seno Ra de lablanca, 28022 Madrid Spain

PASTOR, STEPHEN DANIEL, chemistry educator, researcher; b. New Brunswick, N.J., Feb. 15, 1947; s. Stephen and Irene (Bors) P.; m. Joan Ordemann, Apr. 3, 1971 (div. 1979); 1 child, Melanie; m. Joanne Behrens, July 13, 1985 (div. 1990). BA in Chemistry, Rutgers U., 1969, MS in Chemistry, 1978, PhD in Chemistry, 1983. Chemist Nat. Starch and Chem. Corp., Bridgewater, N.J., 1972-79; rsch. group leader CIBA-Geigy Corp., Ardsley, N.Y., 1979-84, rsch. mgr., 1985-87; group leader Cen. Rsch. Labs. CIBA-Geigy Ag, Basel, Switzerland, 1987-89; rsch. fellow CIBA-Geigy Ag, Ardsley, 1989-90, rsch. mgr., 1990-97, sr. rsch. fellow, 1998—; asst. adj. prof. PACE U., Pleasantville, N.Y., 1984—, assoc. adj. prof., 1989-93, adj. prof., 1994—. Contbr. articles to profl. jours.; 97 patents in field. 1st lt. U.S. Army, 1969-71. Mem. Am. Chem. Soc. (Westchester sect. Disting. Scientist award 1997). Achievements include research on organophosphorous and organosulfur chemistry, organometallic chemistry, asymmetric synthesis, homogeneous catalysis. Home: 27 Crows Nest Ln Unit 4F Danbury CT 06810-2005

PASTORELLI, GIANNI, gynecologist, medical administrator; b. Lugano, Ticino, Switzerland, Oct. 13, 1953; s. Roberto and Loredana (Tappi) P.; m. Thérèse Zingg, May 29, 1992; 1 child, Giulia. Student, Coll. Lugano, 1973; MD, U. Zurich, 1981, FMH in Gynecology and Obstetrics, 1991. Asst. Univ. Clinic Zurich, 1985-91; head of clinic Hosp. San Giovanni Bellinzona, 1991-93; aide, chief ob-gyn. Hosp. Ciuico Lugano, 1994—. Contbr. articles to profl. jours. Soldier Swiss Army, 1973-95. Mem. Swiss Assn. Gynecologic/Obstetrics, Swiss Assn. Senology, Swiss Assn. Sterility and Fertility, N.Y. Acad. Sci., Rotary Club Lugano. Democrat. Roman Catholic. Avocations: reading, skiing, tennis. Home: Ever Green Park, 6945 Origlio Ticino, Switzerland Office: Via Franscini 1, 6900 Lugano Ticino, Switzerland

PASTRANA, RONALD RAY, Christian ministry counselor, Biblical theology educator, former school system administrator; b. N.Y.C., Sept. 5, 1939; s. Anthony and Mildred Pastrana; m. Josephine Pastrana; children: Christine, Therese. BA in History/Sci. Edn., Queens Coll., 1963; advanced sci. cert., Pace U., 1964-68; MS in Counseling Edn., St. John's U., 1967; diploma, U.S. Acad. of Health Sci., 1975, U.S. Army Command and Gen. Staff Coll., 1979; D Ministry, Sch. Bible Theology Sem., 1996, ThD, 2000. Lic. min. Pentecostal Assemblies of God of Am.; cert. life support sys. in internat. space NOAA, NASA. Tchr. sci. Marie Curie Jr. High Sch., Bayside, N.Y., 1963-68; guidance counselor Half Hollow Hills High Sch., Dix Hills, N.Y., 1969-71; guidance counselor Walt Whitman High Sch., Huntington Station, N.Y., 1968-69, coord. occupational svcs., 1971-74; guidance coord. Dutchess County Bd. Coop. Ednl. Svcs. Tech. Edn. Ctr., Poughkeepsie, N.Y., 1974-86; coord. guidance and related acads. Dutchess County BOCES Tech. Edn. Ctr., Poughkeepsie, N.Y., 1986-96; asst. dir. Reach Out Sch. of Ministry, Hyde Park, N.Y., 1996—; prof. Biblical theology Sch. Bible Theology Sem., San Jacinto, Calif., 1999—; ednl. cons. N.Y. State Edn. Dept., Albany, 1975-83, Armed Forces Vocat. Testing Group, Dept. of Def., Washington, 1975-77; cert. educator Lunar Edn. Project, NASA, 1986-87, Asteroids, Lunar Rocks, Meteorites Edn. Projects, 1999—; sci., math. and tech. cons., 1998; pub. Reach Out Ministries. Author: Career Guidance in the Classroom, 1974, A Curriculum Guide to the Study of the Seven Dispensations and Eight Covenants, 1996, Dispensational Theology, 1997, Pentecostal Doctrine and Theology, 1998, Student Guide to the Seven Dispensations and Eignt Covenants, 1999, The Greek Fathers of the Early Christian Church, 2000, The Latin Fathers of the Early Christian Church, 2000. Lt. col. USAR, ret. 1992. NSF sci. study grantee, 1964-68, grantee NASA and Nat. Ocean. and Atmos. Adminstrn., 1999; recipient: Dutchess County Counselor of the Year award, 1995; decorated Joint Svc. Commendation medal, Army achievement medal, Selective Svc. Meritorious medal, Army Res. Components Achievement medal, Nat. Def. Svc. medal, N.Y.S. medal for Meritorious Svc., Meritorious Svc. award for civilian svc. USN, 2000. Mem. Am. Counselors Assn., Am. Mental Health Counselors Assn., Nat. Career Devel. Assn., Am. Assn. Christian Counselors, N.Y. Acad. Scis., N.Y. State Assn. for Counseling and Devel., Sch. Adminstrs. Assn. N.Y. State, Dutchess County Counseling Assn. (exec. bd. 1989-96), Phi Delta Kappa. Avocations: rock and mineral collecting, fitness activities, canoeing, hiking. Home: 26 Greentree Dr S Hyde Park NY 12538-2132 Office: Reach Out Sch of Ministry PO Box 2035 251 Crum Elbow Rd Hyde Park NY 12538-2703

PASTRAVANU, OCTAVIAN CEZAR, engineering educator; b. Iasi, Romania, May 16, 1957; s. Emilian Decebal and Mariana P. Baccalaureate Diploma, C. Negruzzi Coll., Iasi, Romania, 1976; MS in Control and Computer Engring., Tech. u. Gh. Asachi, Iasi, 1982, PhD, 1992. Rsch. asst. Nat. Inst. Rsch. in Automation, Bucharest, Romania, 1982-86; tchg. asst. dept. electric drives and automation Tech. U. Gh. Asachi, Iasi, 1986-90, asst. prof. dept. automatic control and indsl. informatics, 1990-92, assoc. prof. dept. automatic control and indsl. informatics, 1994-98, prof. dept. automatic control and indsl. informatics, 1998—; vis. researcher dept. automation and control engring. U. Ghent (Belgium), 1992-93, Automation and Robotics Rsch. Inst. U. Tex., Arlington, 1993-94. Author: book; co-author: 2 books; contbr. articles to profl. jours., chpts. to books; reviewer Zentralblatt fuer Mathematik, 1984—; mem. editl. bd., reviewer Romanian Newsletter of Informatics and Automation, 1994—. 2nd lt. Romanian Army, 1976-77. Rsch. grantee Belgian Govt., 1992-93, World Bank and Romanian Govt., 1998—. Mem. Internat. Fedn. Automatic Control. Avocations: literature, philosophy. Office: Tech U Gh Asachi Dept Automatic Control, Blvd Mangeron 53 A, Iasi 6600-RO, Romania

PASTRÉ, JEAN-MARC, Medievalist, educator; b. Lyon, France, Feb. 2, 1940; s. Andrè and Noelle (Tricou) P.; m. Cecile Rivet, July 25, 1975. Agregation, Paris, 1965; D es Lettres, Manterre, Nanterre, France, 1975. Asst. U. Paris Sorbonne, 1969-72; prof., dir. dept. Medieval studies U. Rouen, France, 1972—. Author: Précis de Langue et Littérature, 1975, Grammaire Allemande, 1976, Rhétorique et Adaption, 1979, La Quête du Graal, 1993. Dep. mayor Clamart, 1983—; pres. Republicain Parti, Clamart, 1989; mayor Commune Libre de Clamart, 1996. Named grand master Confrerie Clos de Clamart, 1986; deputee Republic of Montmartre, 1994. Mem. Arthurian Soc., Soc. for Beast Epics, Inst. Nat. Def. Home: 34 Rue Georges-Huguet, F-92140 Clamart France Office: U Rouen, Boite Postale 32, F-76130 Mont-Saint-Aignan France

PASTUCH, BORIS MAX See MAX, BUDDY

PÁSZTOR, KÁROLY, plant breeder, researcher; b. Sófalva, Romania, Jan. 25, 1924; s. Márton and Zsuzsanna (Varga) P.; m. Ilona Elek, Aug. 8, 1953; 1 child, Tamás. Degree in agronomy engring., U. Agr. Sci., Budapest, 1952; DSc, U. Agr. Sci., Gödöllö, Hungary, 1959; PhD, Acad. of Sci., Budapest, 1978. Demonstrator U. Agr. Sci., Budapest, 1949-50; asst. prof. U. Agr. Sci., Gödöllö, 1952-55; 1st asst. U. Agr. Sci., Debrecen, 1955-64, lectr., 1964-79, prof. genetics and plant breeding, 1979-92; with Agr. Co. Ltd., Debrecen, 1992—; pres. Nat. Park of Hortobágy, 1973-75. Contbr. articles to profl. jours. Recipient awards Govt. of Hungary, 1969, 72, Ministry of Culture, 1962. Mem. Hungarian Biol. Soc. of Budapest, Fedn. of Tech. and Sci., Sci. Soc. Biometrics. Avocations: gardening, travel. Home: Kolonia 1-4, H-4034 Debrecen Hungary Office: Agr Co Ltd, Pf 104, 4001 Debrecen Hungary

PASZTOR, LASZLO, spatialist, researcher; b. Budapest, Hungary, Nov. 28, 1964; s. Joachim and Klara (Vegh) P.; m. Zsuzsanna Bauer, Apr. 29, 1989; children: Gergely Balazs, Eszter Szederke, Marcell Sebestyen. MS in Physics, Eötvös U., Budapest, 1989, MS in Astronomy, 1989, PhD in Physics, 1993. Rsch. assoc. Rsch. Inst. for Soil Sci. and Agrl. Chemistry, Budapest, 1989-93, rsch. fellow, 1993-95, sr. rsch. fellow, 1995—; lectr. Eötvös U., Budapest, 1990-91. Contbr. articles to profl. jours. including Astrophysics and space Sci., Astronomy and Astrophysics, Remote Sensing of environment, Water Science and Technology, GIS Europe. Recipient award for youth Hungarian Acad. Scis., 1991, 97. Mem. N.Y. Acad. Scis. Avocations: bicycling, theatre, novel of the 20th century. Home: Kenez Utca 27, H-1161 Budapest Hungary Office: Hungarian Acad Scis, Herman Otto Ut 15, H-1022 Budapest Hungary

PATAKI, BÉLA, management educator; b. Budapest, Hungary, Dec. 6, 1956; s. Béla Pataki and Erzsébet Sebestyén. MSEE, Budapest U. Tech., 1981, MSc in Engring. Mgmt., 1987, DrUniv in Sys. Analysis, 1990, PhD in Engring. Mgmt., 1999. Process devel. engr. Remix Co., Budapest, 1981-88; lectr. dept. indsl. mgmt. and bus. econs. Budapest U. Tech., 1988-91, sr. lectr. dept. indsl. mgmt. and bus. econs., 1991-2000, prin. lectr., 2000—; co-founder Euro-Contact Bus. Sch., Hungarian br. The Open U., Bus. Sch., Budapest, 1989; co-founder, co-editor Harvard Bus. Mgr., 1999—. Author: (book) Managing Technological Change, 1999. Sgt. Hungarian Air Def., 1975-76. Recipient Best Paper award Hungarian Soc. for Telecomm., 1985, 88. Mem. IEEE, Internat. Assn. for Mgmt. of Tech., Acad. Mgmt. (county rep. for Hungary of tech. and innovation 1998—), Soc. for Advancement of Mgmt., N.Y. Acad. Scis. Avocations: kung-fu, hiking. Fax: 36 1 463 1606. E-mail: pataki@imvt.bme.hu. Office: Budapest U of Tech, 9/T Müegyetem rp, Budapest 1111, Hungary

PATAKI, NÁNDOR, engineer; b. Salgótarján, Hungary, Jan. 8, 1930; s. Nándor and Irma Mária (Kozalik) P.; m. Elisabeth Pálovits, June 25, 1971. Civil engr., Tech. U. Budapest, 1952, dr. hydraulic engring., 1968. Cert. engr. Tech. mgr. Enterprise for Mineral & Water Prospecting & Drilling, Várpalota, Hungary, 1952-54; chief of dept. Geol. Authority, Budapest, 1954-57; chief engr. Enterprise for Water Prospecting and Drilling, Budapest, 1957-70; chief of expedition, gen. mgr. Transing and Export Co. for Hydraulic Engring. Products, 1970-76; gen. mgr. Water Prospecting and Drilling Co., 1976-80; asst. prof. Tech. U. of Miskolc, 1980—; asst. prof. UNESCO, Budapest, 1970—; expert in hydrogeology, 1990—; scientific and mktg. expert 16 countries; lectr. in field. Author 6 books; editl. bd. Kőolaj és Földgáz; contbr. articles to profl. jours. Recipient Dionyza Stura Commemorative medal Tchécoslovaquie, 1978, Zsigmondy W. Commemorative medal Hungarian Mining and Metallurgical Soc., 1988, Medal Internat. Thermal Affair, 1990, Medal Pro Facultate Rerum Metalicarum, Miskolc U., 1995. Mem. Hungarian Hydrol. Soc. (sect. of hydrogeology, Bogdánfy Ő Commemorative medal 1987, Dr. Schafarzik Ferenc Commemorative medal 1998), Hungarian Mining and Metallurgical Soc. (dep. pres. oil, gas and water sect. 1975—, chmn. water well dept. oil, gas and water sect.). Avocations: gardening, swimming, archeology. Home: Csáktornya park 4, 1142 Budapest Hungary Office: Hungarian Hydrological Soc, Fo utca 68, 1027 Budapest Hungary

PATASSE, ANGE FELIX, president of Central African Republic; b. Jan. 25, 1937. Student, French Equatorial Coll. Agrl. inspector Govt. of Ctrl. African Republic, 1959-65, dir. agr., 1965, min. devel., 1965, min. state for transport and power, min. state for devel. and tourism, 1969-70, min. state for agr., stock-breeding, waters and forests, hunting, tourism, transport and power, 1970, min. state for devel., 1970, min. state for transport and commerce, 1970-72, min. state for rural devel., 1972-73, min. health and social affairs, 1973-74, min. state for tourism, waters, fishing and hunting, 1974-76, prime min., 1976-78, keeper of seals, 1976; arrested, 1979, escaped, recaptured, detained, 1979, candidate for pres., 1981, took refuge in French Embassy, 1982, fled to Togo, 1982; elected pres. Govt. of Ctrl. African Republic, 1993—; v.p. Coun. Ctrl. African Revolution, 1976; leader Mouvement pour la libération du peuple centrafricain. Office: Office of Pres, Palais de la Renaissance, Bangui Central African Republic*

PATE, JOHN GILLIS, JR., financial consultant, accounting educator; b. Chattanooga, Jan. 27, 1928; s. John Gillis Pate and Iona Estelle (Bowman) Pate Ketchman; m. Daphne Mae Davis, Feb. 8, 1946; children: John Gillis III, Daphne Iona, Donna Gay. Student, U. Tampa, 1947-48; AA with highest honors, U. Fla., 1950; BS cum laude, Fla. State U., 1953, MS, 1958; PhD, Columbia U., 1968. Cert. cost analyst, CPA. Mgr. Grocery Concession, Albany, Ga., 1944-45, Variety Store, Panama City, Fla., 1946-47; asst. to CPA Standard Brands, Inc., Birmingham, Ala., 1951-53; acctg. supervisory trainee Birmingham, Ala., 1953-54; grad. asst. Fla. State U., Tallahassee, 1957-58; asst. to CPA Pensacola, Fla., 1956-58, CPA, 1958; asst. prof. U. Ga., Athens, 1958-60; lectr. Columbia U., N.Y.C., 1961-64; asst. prof. Bernard M. Baruch Coll. of CUNY, 1963-69; prof. acctg. U. Tex.-El Paso, 1969-85, U. S.C., Spartanburg, 1988-93; cons. resource pers fin. and human resources Charles Lea Ctr., Spartanburg, 1988—, dir. Internal Audit and Spl. Projects, 1994—. Author: Index C.P.A. Exams and Unofficial Answers, 1974-81; co-author: Accounting Trends and Techniques, 1967-88, Index to Accounting and Auditing Services, 1971; contbr. articles to ann. profl. publs. Tither, Coronado Bapt. Ch., El Paso, 1969-86, Buck Creek Bapt. Ch., Spartanburg, 1987—; cons. Alderman of El Paso, 1982, County Councilman of Spartanburg, 1991-98. With lt. j.g. USN, 1955-56. Columbia U. fellow, 1960; Earhart Found. fellow, 1960, Am. Acctg. Assn. fellow, 1960, Found fellow, 1961-62; recipient Haskins and Sells award, 1960. Mem. AICPA (cons. 1961-88), Am. Acctg. Assn., Moose, Masons, Shriners, Beta Alpha Psi, Beta Alpha Chi. Republican. Home and Office: 106 Lori Cir Spartanburg SC 29303-5527

PATE, STEPHEN ROBERT, professional golfer; b. Ventura, Calif., May 26, 1961; m. Sheri Pate; children: Nicole, Sarah. Degree in Psychology, UCLA, 1984. Profl. golfer, 1983—; finished top 10 MasterCard Colonial, Motorola We. Open, Canon Greater Hartford Open, Buick Challenge; winner S.W. Classic, 1987, MONY Tournament of Champions, 1988, Shearson Lehman Hutton Andy Williams Open, 1988; runner-up Internat., 1990; lost playoff to Corey Pavin BellSouth Atlanta Classic, 1991; winner Honda Classic, 1991, Buick Invitational Calif., 1992, Nike Olympia Open, 1996, CVS Charity Classic, 1998; finished top 10 Phoenix Open, Buick Invitational, Tucson Chrysler Classic, 1998; mem. nat. team Kirin Cup, 1989, Ryder Cup, 1991, Dunhill Cup, 1991; mem. PGA Tour charity team Buick Open, 1999, Ryder Cup Team, 1999. Avocation: fishing. Office: So Calif Sect of PGA 601 Valencia Ave Ste 200 Brea CA 92823-6300*

PATEL, BHAGWANDAS MAVJIBHAI, research scientist; b. Surat, Gujarat, India, Nov. 24, 1938; came to U.S., 1984; s. Mavjibhai Khushalbhai and Diwalibahen (Mavjibhai) P.; m. Manjula Patel, May 13, 1964; children: Deepti, Varsha, Tejas. BSc, Gujarat U., India, 1961, MSc, 1963; PhD, U. Bombay, India, 1980. Rsch. and devel. scientist Bhabha Atomic Rsch. Ctr., Bombay, Maharashtra Sta., India, 1963-84; vis. scientist U. Fla., Gainesville, Fla., 1971-72; postdoctoral rsch. assoc. dept. chemistry U. Fla., Gainesville, 1984-87, rsch. cons. dept. food sci. and human nutrition, 1987-89, rsch. scientist, 1989-90; rsch. scientist dept. R & D Texaco Inc., Port Arthur, Tex., 1991-98; sr. staff rsch. chemist Equilon Enterprises LLC., Houston, 1998—; adj. postdoctoral rsch. scientist U. Fla. Dept. Chemistry, Gainesville, 1987—. Author: (with others) Trace Analysis, 1983, Lube Base Stocks, 1994; contbr. numerous articles to profl. jours. Sec. Patel Pragati Mandal Ednl. and Cultural Orgn., Bombay, 1968-84. Recipient Internat. Atomic Energy Agy. Fellowship award, Vienna, Austria, 1971, postdoctoral Rsch. Fellowship, U. Fla., Gainesville, 1984-87. Fellow Indian Chem. Soc.; mem. Am. Chem. Soc., Soc. for Applied Spectroscopy, Indian Soc. of Analytical Scis. Avocations: reading, writing, travelling, music, movies. Fax: 281-544-8727. Home: 1003 Burchton Dr Sugar Land TX 77479-5962 Office: Equilon Enterprises LLC W Hollow Technology Ctr 3333 Hwy #6 S Houston TX 77082-3101

PATEL, BHARAT, financial executive; b. Wednesbury, West Midlands, Eng., Oct. 29, 1965; came to U.S., 1981; s. Maganbhai and Shantaben Patel; m. Naynitaben Bharatbhai, Feb. 14, 1990; children: Pritesh, Kunal. AS, Heald Bus. Coll., San Francisco; BS, Golden Gate U. Chmn. bd. dirs. API San Francisco, 1993—; CEO Patelco Investments, Brit. V.I., 1990—. Contbr. articles to profl. publs. Law enforcement cadet Calif. Peace League Activities, San Francisco, 1986; mem. coun. Calif. Dem. Assn., Modesto, 1998. Recipient award Internat. Fedn. for Bus., 1987, Amateur Athletic Assn., Eng., 1998. Mem. Golden Gate Hotel Assn. (bd. dirs. 1989-94). Avocations: travel, reading, playing cricket, movies, teaching. Office: 760 Market St Ste 827 San Francisco CA 94102-2303

PATEL, CHANDRA KUMAR NARANBHAI, communications company executive, educator, researcher; b. Baramati, India, July 2, 1938; came to U.S., 1958, naturalized, 1970; s. Naranbhai Chaturbhai and Maniben P.; m. Shela Dixit, Aug. 20, 1961; children: Neela, Meena. B.Engring., Poona U., 1958; M.S., Stanford U., 1959, Ph.D., 1961. Mem. tech. staff Bell Telephone Labs., Murray Hill, N.J., 1961-93, head infrared physics and electronics rsch. dept., 1967-70, dir. electronics rsch. dept., 1970-76, dir. phys. rsch. lab., 1976-81, exec. dir. rsch. physics and acad. affairs div., 1981-87, exec. dir.

rsch., materials sci., engring. and acad. affairs div., 1987-93; trustee Aerospace Corp., L.A., 1979-88; vice chancellor rsch. UCLA, 1993-2000, prof. dept. physics and astronomy, dept. chemistry, 2000—, prof. dept. elec. engring., 2000—; mem. governing bd. NRC, 1990-91; bd. dirs. Newport Corp.; chmn. bd. Calif. Accuwave Corp., 1994-98; founder, chmn. bd. Pranalytica, Inc., Santa Monica, Calif.; co-founder Photuris, Inc. Contbr. articles to tech. jours. Chmn. Calif. Biomed. Found., 1994—; mem. exec. bd. Calif. Healthcare Inst., 1995—; mem. L.A. Regional Tech. Alliance, 1997—. Recipient Ballantine medal Franklin Inst., 1968, Coblentz award Am. Chem. Soc., 1974, Honor award Assn. Indians in Am., 1975, Founders prize Tex. Instruments Found., 1978, award N.Y. sect. Soc. Applied Spectroscopy, 1982, Schawlow medal Laser Inst. Am., 1984, Thomas Alva Edison Sci. award N.J. Gov., 1987, William T. Ennor Manufacturing Technology award ASME, 1995, Nat. Medal of Sci., 1996. Fellow AAAS, IEEE (Lamme medal 1976, medal of honor 1989, Millennium medal 2000), Am. Acad. Arts and Scis., Am. Phys. Soc. (coun. 1987-91, exec. com. 1987-90, George E. Pake prize 1988, pres. 1995), Optical Soc. Am. (Adolph Lomb medal 1966, Townes medal 1982, Ives medal 1989), Indian Nat. Sci. Acad. (fng.); mem. NAS (coun. 1988-91, exec. com. 1989-91), NAE (Zworykin award 1976), Gynecol. Laser Surgery Soc. (hon.), Am. Soc. for Laser Medicine and Surgery (hon.), Third World Acad. Scis. (assoc.), Calif. Biomed. Found. (pres. 1994-2000), Calif. Healthcare Inst. (exec. com. 1995-2000), Sigma Xi (pres. 1994-96). Home: 1171 Roberto Ln Los Angeles CA 90077-2302 Office: UCLA Dept Physics Astronomy 6 130H Knudsen Hall Los Angeles CA 90095-1547

PATEL, CHIMANBHAI REVADAS, petrochemical company executive; b. Sunda, Kaira, India, Nov. 9, 1942; s. Revadas Nagjibhai and Jadavben Revadas Patel; m. Madhuben Chimanbhai, May 30, 1975; children: Rakshit, Keyur. Diploma in elec. engring., M.S. U., Baroda, India, 1965, diploma in mech. engring., 1966. Maintenance and ops. engr. M/S. Power Cables, Bombay, 1966-67; jr. engr. M/S. Calico Chems., Bombay, 1967-72; technician Indian Petrochems. Ltd., Baroda, India, 1972-75, chargeman, 1975-76, asst. elec. engr., 1976-82, sr. elec. engr., 1982-87, dep. project mgr., 1987-92, maintenance mgr. elec. and inst., 1992—. Avocations: indoor games, music. Home: 11 Urmi Soc, Productivity Rd, Vadodara Gujarat 390007, India Office: M/S Indian Petrochems Corp, PO Petrochemicals, Vadodara Gujarat 391 346, India

PATEL, JYOTINDRA DAHYABHAI, botany educator; b. Uttersanda, India, Oct. 11, 1944; s. Dahyabhai Avichaldas and Ganga Dahyabhai P.; m. Sushila Jyotindra, May 13, 1971; children: Shamik, Tapusi. BS, Gujarat U., India, 1965; MS, Sardar Patel U., India, 1967, PhD, 1971. Lectr. genetics Sardar Patel U., India, 1977-84, reader environ. botany, 1984-92, prof., 1992-97; chmn. Avichal Press (P) Ltd., 1996—, Avichal Dairy Farm Products (P) Ltd., 1996—, Avichal Biotech (P) Ltd., 1996—; cons. in field. Contbr. articles to profl. jours. Postdoctoral fellow Sadar Patel U., 1971-77. Fellow Indian Bot. Soc. (life, councillor); mem. Indian Bot. Contactor (life), Internat. Soc. Plant Morphologists (life), Avichal Sci. Found. (life). Avocations: stamp collecting, writing, art. Office: Avichal Press Ltd, 703/2 GIDC Estate, Vitthal Udyognagar 388 121, India

PATEL, KANUPRASAD DAHYALAL, chemistry educator, researcher; b. Fagodia Vilage, India, Aug. 5, 1964; s. Dahyalal Maganlal and Divaben Dahyalal Patel; m. Sudhaben Kanuprasad, May 8, 1985; children: Vishal, Jinal. BSc, Sardar Patel U., Vallabh Vidyanagar, India, 1984, MSc, 1986, PhD, 1990. Lectr. Arts Sci. & Commerce Coll., Pilvai, India, 1991; lectr. V.P. & R.P.T.P. Sci. Coll., Vallabh Vidyanagar, 1991-96, sr. lectr., 1996—. Contbr. articles to profl. jours. Avocations: music, cricket, volleyball, chess. Home: 8 Gomtivas Nana Bazar, Vallabh Vidyanagar 388 120, India Office: VP & RPTP Sci Coll, Chemistry Dept, Vallabh Vidyanagar 388 120, India

PATEL, KETAN, research engineer; b. Nadiad, Gujarat, India, Apr. 12, 1970; s. Gordhanbhi Bhikhabhai and Pushpaben (Gordhanbhai) P. BS in Indsl. Chemistry, V.P. Sci. Coll., Vidyanagar, India, 1993, M of Indsl. Chemistry, 1995; postgrad., G.H. Patel Inst Materials Sci., Vidyanagar. Rsch. engr. Materials and Electrochem. Rsch. Corp., Tucson, 1998—. Avocations: reading, travel, sports, music. E-mail: kgp12@yahoo.com. Home: 8110 E Speedway Blvd Apt 5250 Tucson AZ 85710-1788 Office: Materials and Electrochems Rsch Corp 7960 S Kolb Rd Tucson AZ 85706-9237

PATEL, MADHU PURUSHOTTAM, engineering executive; b. Karamsad, India, Mar. 3, 1936; s. Purushottam Narandas and Maniben Purushottam. MS in Engring., Century U., Calif., 1980, DSc in Engring., 1982. Mng. dir. Patels Analog and Digital Measurement Co. Ltd., Pune, India, 1967—. Fellow Inst. Engrs., Inst. Electronic and Telecomm. Enrs.; mem. IEEE (sr.). Avocations: Yoga, health, machine design. Office: Patel's Analog Digital Meas, A-6 Electronic Estate MIDC, Pune 411020, India

PATEL, MAHENDRA, chemist; b. Rajkot, India, June 17, 1953; s. Shantilal Gopalji and Parvati Devji (Pansuriya) P.; m. Taralika Trivedi, June 25, 1981; 1 child, Anand. BSc, H & HB Kotak, 1973; MSc, Dept. Chemistry, 1975, PhD, 1980. Rsch. fellow CSIR, Delhi, 1976-77, sr. rsch. fellow, 1978-79; rsch. chemist Deepak Nitrite, Baroda, 1979-82; rsch. officer GNFC, Bharuch, 1982-85, sr. rsch. officer, 1982-85, mgr. process devel., 1990-97, sr. mgr., 1997—. Inventor redox catalyst for sulphur recovery; contbr. articles to profl. jours. Fellow Soc. for Advancement of Electrochem. Sci. and Tech. Avocations: painting, photography, electronics. Home: Street 33/B-4/ Narmadanagar, Dist Bharuch 392 015, India Office: GNFC Ltd, PO Narmadanagar, Bharuch 392 015, India

PATEL, MANUBHAI DARUBHAI, retired banker; b. Awakhal, India, Apr. 6, 1942; s. Darubhai and Surajben P.; m. Jashodaben Manubhai. BSc, M.S. Univ., Baroda, India, 1962, MSc, 1964. Dep. chief officer Res. Bank India, Mumbai, 1965-84; CEO Kalupur Comm. Coop. Bank Ltd., Ahmedabad, India, 1984-2000; ret., 2000. Office: Kalupur Comml Coop Bank, Ashram Rd, Ahmedabad 308 014, India

PATEL, MARTIN KUMAR, researcher; b. Donaueschingen, Germany, Jan. 28, 1966; s. Mahendrakumar Rajeshwar and Alice (Schreiber) P. PhD, Utrecht U., The Netherlands, 1999. Fellow Fraunhofer Inst., Karlsruhe, Germany, 1993-2000; project mgr. Energy and Environ. Policy Studies, Utrecht, The Netherlands, 2000—; vis. rschr. ENEA, Italy, 1996. Contbr. articles to profl. jours. German Acad. Exch. Svc. scholar, Bonn, 1996, European Commn. scholar, Brussels, 1998-99, vis. rsch. scholar Utrecht U., 1996. Office: Fraunhofer Inst, Kanaalweg 16-G, 3526 KL Utrecht Netherlands

PATEL, MRUGANK MAGANBHAI, engineer, consultant; b. Valsad, Gujarat, India, Nov. 1, 1972; s. Maganbhai Kalidas and Gulabben (Maganbhai) Patel Gulabben Vallabhbhai. Diploma in Electronics and Telecomms., MSPM Polytechnic, 1994; Degree in Computer Application, The Oxford Computer Inst., Valsad, 1995. Registered engr., India. Lectr. Inst. Engring. and Tech., Valsad, 1994, admissions counselor, 1994-95, Centre head, 1995—; dir. Sont GM Patel's Inst. Technician Engring., 1996-97; cons. Inst. Engring. and Tech., Valsad, 1987-94; dir. Smt. G.M. Patel I.T.-Engring., 1996—; exec. dir. G.M. Patel Mechatronics Pvt. Ltd., 2000—. Mem. ASME, Inst. Engring. and Tech. (Best Profl. award 1996). Avocations: public relations, visiting foreign countries, consulting in engineering. Office: Inst Engring and Tech, Navchetan Bldg, Halar Rd, Valsad Gujarat 396001, India

PATEL, MUKUND RANCHHODLAL, electrical engineer, researcher; b. Bavla, India, Apr. 21, 1942; came to U.S., 1966; s. Ranchhodlal N. and Shakariben M. Patel; m. Sarla Shantilal, Nov. 4, 1967; children: Ketan, Bina, Vijal. BEng, Sardar U., Vidyanagar, India; MEng with honors, Gujarat U., Ahmedabad, India; PhD in Engring., Rensselaer Poly. Inst., 1972. Registered profl. engr., Pa.; chartered mech. engr., U.K. Lectr. elec. engring. Sardar U., Vidyanagar, India, 1965-66; sr. devel. engr. GE, Pittsfield, Mass., 1967-76; mgr. R & D, Bharat Bijlee (Siemens) Ltd., Bombay, 1976-80; fellow engr. Westinghouse R & D Ctr., Churchill, Pa., 1980-84, mem. senate, 1982-84; pres. Induction Gen., Inc., Pitts., 1984-86; prin. engr. rsch. and devel. Space Divsn. GE, Princeton, Pa., 1986-96; disting. vis. prof. elec. power systems U. Minn., Duluth, 1996—; cons. Nat. Productivity Coun., New Delhi, 1976-80. Assoc. editor IEEE Insulation Mag.; contbr. articles to nat. and internat. profl. jours. Fellow Instn. Mech. Engrs.; mem. IEEE (sr.), Am. Soc. Sci. Rsch., Elfun Soc. Vols., Tau Beta Pi, Eta Kappa Nu, Omega Rho. Achievements include patents and invention awards on electromechanical design of superconducting generators; NASA award for research on space power systems; international authority in the area of electromechanical design of large power. Office: Power Systems Engring 1199 Cobblestone Ct Yardley PA 19067-4751

PATEL, PRAVIN CHATURBHAI, physician, consulting surgeon; b. Pij, Gujarat, India, Oct. 3, 1949; s. Chaturbhai Somabhai and Chanchalben Chaturbhai (Patel) P.; m. Nayana Pravinbhai, July 22, 1973; children: Nirav, Sonal. MB, BChir, U. Gujarat, India, 1973. Intern surgery, ob-gyn., medicine, 1971-72; sr. house officer SHO, gen. surgery New Civil Hosp., Ahmedabad, India, 1973-74, registrar gen. surgery, 1974; clin. attachment in gen. surgery St. Mary's Hosp., Eastbourne, Sussex, Eng., 1974; sr. house officer SHO, A&E, orthopedic surgery Leicester (Eng.) Royal Infirmary, 1975-76, sr. house officer SHO ENT, 1976, sr. house officer SHO gen. surgery, 1976-77; sr. house officer rotating SHO, A&E dept. with hand surgery, orthop. surgery with pediat. orthop. and gen. surgery with peripheral vascular surgery West Hill Hosp., Joyce Green Hosp., Dartford, Kent, Eng., 1977-78; registrar gen. surgery Kent Hosp., W. Hill Hosp., Dartford, Eng., 1978-79; registraar gen. surgery N. Oxfordshire sector Horton Gen. Hosp., Banbury, Oxon, Eng., 1980-82; registrar gen. surgery Victoria Hosp., Blackpool, Eng., 1982-84; specialist grade 1 gen. surgery King Faisal Hosp., Taif, Saudi Arabia, 1984-87; cons. surgeon, sr. registrar, registrar in gen. Medi-Call Locum Agy., Eng., 1987-88; dep. dir. surg. directorate depts. surgery, anesthesia & renal unit, cons. surgeon Armed Forces Hosp. so. region, Khamis Mushayt, Saudi Arabia, 1988-96; pvt. practice Middlesex, Eng., 1996—; mem. day surgery user's com., theatre user's com., med. exec. com., OR com., disaster planning com.; presenter in field. Contbr. numerous articles to profl. jours. Fellow Royal Coll. Surgeons. Home: 507 Kenton Rd, Kenton-Harrow HA3 04L, England HA3 04L Office: Armed Forces Hosps Program, PO Box 101, Khamis Mushayt Saudi Arabia

PATEL, PULINKUMAR, chemistry educator; b. Kavitha, Gujarat, India, Jan. 2, 1971; s. Navinbhai Gordhanbhai and Sushilaben Navinbhai Patel; m. Ritaben Pulinkumar Patel, Mar. 2, 1996; 1 child, Nayan. BSc in Indsl. Chemistry, Vitthalbhai Patel Sci. Coll., Vallabh Vidyanagar, India, 1991, MSc in Indsl. Chemistry, 1993, PhD in Indsl. Chemistry, 1999. Lectr. in applied chemistry N.V. Patel Coll. Pure and Applied Chemistry, Vallabh Vidyanagar, 1998—. Contbr. articles to profl. jours. Avocations: reading, light music, organizing college activities, participating in science seminars. Home: 26 Parth Yamuna Park, Panchayat Hospital Rd, Vallabh Vidyanagar 388 120, India Office: NV Patel Coll Pure and Applied Sci, Mota Bazaar, Vallabh Vidyanagar 388 210, India

PATEL, SHARIF AHMED, food executive, consultant; b. Asna, Gujerat, India, Feb. 22, 1965; arrived in Eng., 1966; s. Ibrahim and Khatija Patel; m. Hawabu Ghanchi, Sept. 21, 1987; children: Mohamed-Ashraf, Yusuf, Adam, Zaheer. Degree in bus. and fin., Bradford (Eng.) U., 1989. Various positions Fox's Biscuits, Batley, Eng., 1983—. Gov. Field Ln. Sch., Yorkshire, 1995—; mem. com. Kirklees Talkback, Kirklees, 1994—. Islam. Avocations: golf, photography, travel, environment, snooker. Home: 6 Talbot St, Batley West Yorkshire WF17 5AW, England

PATEL, VINOD MOTIBHAI, accountant; b. Kilosha, Tanzania, Mar. 1, 1944; came to U.S., 1971; s. Motibhai R. and Lalitaben M. (Lalitaben C.) P.; m. Surekha J. Patel, Dec. 6, 1969; children: Chirag, Roshni. BComm., U. Baroda, India, 1964. Chartered acct., India; CPA, Md. Acct. Dalal, Desai & Kumana, Bombay, India, 1964-70, Bellman, Atlas & Co., London, 1970-71, Garbelman, Winslow & Co., Upper Marlboro, Md., 1971-79; prin. Vinod M. Patel, CPA, Potomac, Md., 1979—; hon. auditor Shri Mangal Mandir, 1981—, Gujarati Samarj, 1999—. Mem. AICPA, Md. Assn. CPA's, Inst. Chartered Accts. India. Hindu. Home and Office: 9644 Reach Rd Potomac MD 20854-2856

PATEL FÜRSTENBERG, CARIN MAYA, steel company executive; b. Punta del este, Uruguay, Sept. 20, 1965; arrived in Argentina, 1970; d. Pravin Bhoghibai and Evelyne Josephine (Furstenberg) Patel. B, Lycee Francais, Buenos Aires, 1983; MD, U. Buenos Aires, 1991. Med. diplomate. Fin. analyst Batory Srl, Buenos Aires, 1990-93, steel trader, 1993—. Avocations: interior design, philosophy. E-mail: cmpatel@mbor.servicenet.com.ar. Home: Virrey del Pino 2180 p11, 1426 Buenos Aires Argentina

PATELL, MAHESH, pharmacist, researcher; b. Ahmedabad, Gujarat, India, June 14, 1937; came to U.S., 1962.; s. Kantilal K. and Maniben K. Patell; m. Rajeshvari S. Amin, Sept. 6, 1967; children: Milan, Rupel. BS in Pharmacy, L.M. Coll. of Pharmacy, Ahmedabad, 1960; MS in Pharmacy, St. Louis Coll., 1964. Rsch. pharmacist Rexall Drug Co., St. Louis, 1968-74; mgr. tech. info. svcs. Cord Labs., Bloomfield, Colo., 1974-77; rsch. investigator K.V. Pharms., St. Louis, 1977-79; assoc. dir. worldwide consumer medicine Bristol Myers-Squibb, Hillside, N.J., 1979—. Mem. Am. Assn. Pharmaceutical Scientists, Controlled Release Soc., Pa. Mfg. Confectioners Assn. Hindu. Achievements include patents for enteric coated tablet and process of making, uniquely designed capsule shaped tablets, taste masking pharmaceutical agents and enteric coated aspirin granules and process for preparation, stable gelatin coated aspirin tablet. Home: 4 Farrington St Edison NJ 08820-1921 Office: Bristol Myers Squibb 1350 Liberty Ave Hillside NJ 07205-1891

PATERSON, IAIN MACKENZIE, surgeon, consultant; b. Banff, Scotland, Oct. 31, 1952; arrived in Eng., 1983; s. William and Alexandrina Morag (MacKenzie) P.; m. Alyson Myra Gordon, Dec. 23, 1976; children: Murray Gordon, Lindsey Jane. MB ChB with distinction in surgery, Aberdeen U., Scotland, 1976; PhD, Aberdeen U., 1984. Fellow Royal Coll. Surgeons (Edinburgh, examiner). House officer Aberdeen Royal Infirmary, 1976-77; rsch. fellow Aberdeen U., 1978; registrar Inverness Hosps., 1980; sr. registrar St. Georges Hosp., London, 1985-91; clin. fellow Queen Mary Hosp., Hong Kong, 1987; cons. surgeon Frimley Park Hosp., Surrey, Eng., 1991—; program dir. South Thames (West) Surg. SpR Rotation. Contbr. articles to profl. jours. Mem. Brit. Soc. Gastroenterology, Assn. Surgeons Great Britain and Ireland. Avocations: hill walking, cycling, reading, wining and dining. Home: 14 Middle Ave, Farnham Surrey GU9 8JL, England Office: Frimley Park Hosp, Portsmouth Rd, Frimley Surrey GU16 5UJ, England

PATERSON, JOHN KIRKPATRICK, retired physician, author; b. Bangalore, Madras, India, Mar. 23, 1921; arrived in France, 1990; s. David Stanley and Margaret Hume (Chidson) P.; m. Mary Frances Berry, Aug. 29, 1946; children: Margaret Tamsin, David Kilner, Penelope Mary, Alison Frances, Sarah Joanna, John Stewart. MB BS, St. Thomas's Hosp., London, 1950. Med. diplomate. Casualty officer St. Thomas's Hosp., 1951; trainee in gen. practice Paddington, London, 1951; asst. in gen. practice Alconbury, Huntingdonshire, Eng., 1951-52; prin. Alconbury Hosp., Huntingdonshire, Eng., 1952-75; pvt. practice musculoskeletal medicine London, 1975-89; clin. retired; tchr. West Middlesex Univ. Hosp.; chmn. sci. adv. com. Internat. Fedn. Manual Medicine, 1993-97. Author: Vertebral Manipulation-A Part of Orthodox Medicine, 1995, Shouted, Sung of Whispered, Can You Hear Me?, 1997, Mostly True, Ordered Thoughts & Yarns, 1998, 20th Century Housey Doctors, 1998, Within Earshot, 1999; co-author: An Introduction to Medical Manipulation, 1985, Examination of the Back: An Introduction, 1986, Back Pain: An International Review, 1990, Musculoskeletal Medicine, The Spine, 1990. Lt. Royal Signal Corps., 1939-45, India and Burma. Recipient Claire Wand prize British Med. Assn., 1956, 57, Butterworth gold medal, 1958. Fellow Royal Soc. Medicine, Brit. Inst. Musculoskeletal Medicine (hon.); mem. Brit. Assn. Manual Medicine (tutor, hon. sec. 1978-86, pres. 1986-89), The Pain Soc. Avocations: gardening, writing. Home: L'llot Les Fitayes, La Roque D'Antheron 13640, France

PATERSON, PAUL CHARLES, private investigator, security consultant; b. Bethlehem, Pa., Dec. 31, 1927; s. Thomas and Ida (Weiss) P.; m. Estelle Marie Nabors; children: Linda Ann, Thomas Scott, Terry Maurice Leard. Grad., Inst. Applied Sci., Chgo., 1950. Jr. credit analyst Bethlehem Steel Corp., Pa., 1947-50; inspector claim spec., claim dir., field supr. Equifax Svcs., Inc., Allentown, Pa., 1953-61; field claim supr. Equifax Svcs., Inc., St. Louis, 1961-63; regional claims mgr. Equifax Svcs., Inc., Phila., 1963-71; spl. claim sales, sales exec.-claims Equifax Svcs., Inc., Atlanta, 1971-89; pvt. investigator, pres. Paterson Investigations, Inc., Douglasville, Ga., 1989—. Editor CFE newsletter The Ga. Examiner, 1994-95. With U.S. Army, 1950-53. Mem. VFW, Am. Legion, Life, Accident and Health Claims Assn. Phila. (life, pres. 1969-70), Mktg. Ins. Claims Assn. (life, v.p. 1985—, pres. 1989-90), So. Loss Assn., Nat. WWII Meml. Assn. (charter), Atlanta Claims Assn., Am. Soc. Indsl. Security, Internat. Narcotic Enforcement Officers Assn., Ga. Assn. Profl. Pvt. Investigators (chair ethics com. 1999, treas. 2000), Assn. Cert. Fraud Examiners (cert., past pres. Ga. chpt. 1990, 93, bd. dirs. 1991-92, faculty 1995-96, bd. regents 1996, Disting. Achievement award 1994, 95, Regent Emeritus, life mem.), Criminal Investigation Divsn. Agts. Assn. Inc., Ga. Assn. Chiefs of Police (profl.), Ga. Sheriffs' Assn., Ga. Claims Assn., Ga. Fire Investigators Assn., Ret. Mil. Police Assn. (assoc.), Am. Legion, Chapel Hills Golf Club. Republican. Avocations: golf, music, swimming, physical conditioning. Home: 6703 Live Oak Ln Douglasville GA 30135-1625 Office: Paterson Investigations Inc PO Box 5063 Douglasville GA 30154-0002

PATERSON, TONY RALPH, sculptor, educator; b. Albany, N.Y., Dec. 17, 1934; s. Ralph Duncan and Mary Rose P.; m. Eleanor Cohen, Nov. 13, 1962; children: Robert, David. Grad. diploma, Sch. Mus. Fine Arts, 1966, diploma, 1983; attended, U. Guadalajara, Mex., 1953, MIT, La Grand Chaumiere Sch., Paris. Prof. SUNY, Buffalo, N.Y., 1968—; head sculpture dept. SUNY, Buffalo, 1995—, dir. Casting/Welding Inst., 1996—. One-man shows include William and Mary Coll., Williamsburg, Va., Tragos Gallery, Boston; group exhbns. include over 100 nat. and internat. shows; represented in permanent collections Brandeis U., Kalamazoo Inst. Arts, Sch. Mus. Fine Arts, Boston. Dir. Rumsey Restoration project, Buffalo, 1968—; overseer restorations for City of Buffalo Arts Commn., 1968—; bd. dirs. Ashford Hollow Found., 1999—. MacDowell Colony fellow; fellow Sch. Mus. Fine Arts, Boston; recipient award NAD, N.Am. Sculpture Exhbn.. E-mail: arp3@acsu.buffalo.edu. Home: 530 Norwood Ave Buffalo NY 14222-1319 Office: SUNY Art Dept 202 Center For The Arts Buffalo NY 14260-6000

PATHAK, KAILASH CHANDRA, manufacturing executive; b. Firozabad, India, Dec. 15, 1964; s. Bangali Bhushan and Gyan (Devi) P.; m. Pushpa Jah, Nov. 28, 1985; children: Anjali, Rahul. BSc, Agra U., 1981, MSc in Chemistry, 1983; MPhil in Chemistry, Panjab U., Chandigarh, 1993; LLB, Delhi U., 1990. Asst. chemist Hilton Rubbers, Sonepat, 1983-85; prodn. chemist Cipham Orgn., Sonepat, 1985-90; sr. officer prodn. Mosepon Labs., Parwanoo, 1990-93; mgr. prodn. Orchid Chems., Chennai, 1993-95, sr. mgr. planning and prodn., 1995-97, asst. gen. mgr. planning and prodn., 1997—. Contbr. articles to profl. jours. Fellow Indian Chem. Soc.; mem. Royal Soc. Chemistry, Instn. Chemists India, Indian Mgmt. Assn. Avocations: photograpy, music, social work, reading. Home: 17/1 Teachers Colony, Adyar Chennai 60020, India Office: Orchid Chems and Pharms Ltd, 1 6th Fl, 34 Cathedral Rd, Chennai Tamil Nadu 600086, India

PATHAK, KARE NARAIN, physicist, researcher; b. Bargaon Chaukhari, India, July 30, 1941; s. Mata Badal and Kunti (Shukla) P.; m. Kulwanti Dubey, June, 1953; children: Vimla, Geeta, Usha, Sanjay, Vindhya. BSc, Agra (India) U., 1960; MSc, Allahabad (India) U., 1962; PhD, Indian Inst. Tech., Kanpur, 1966. Lectr. Indian Inst. Tech., Mumbai, 1966-67; rsch. assoc. Northwestern U., Evanston, Ill., 1969-70; reader Panjab U., Chandigarh, India, 1970-71, chmn. physics dept., 1989-92, dean univ. instrn., 1993-95, dean sci. faculty, 1996-99, prof., 1977—, dir. IIPP cell, 1995—; postdoctoral rsch. fellow NRC, Ottawa, Ont., Can., 1967-69; Sr. Alexander Humboldt fellow Tech. U., Munchen, Germany, 1992; assoc. mem. Internat. Ctr. Theoretical Physics, Trieste, Italy, 1972-76; vis. prof. Lakehead U., Ont., Can., 1985-85. Recipient nat. fellowship award U. Grants Commn., 1991, sr. assoc. award Abdus Salam, Internat. Ctr. Theoretical Physics, 1992, Meghnad Saha award U. Grants Commn., 1996. Fellow Nat. Acad. Scis., Indian Acad. Scis.; mem. Soc. Sci. Values. Home: T-1/6 Sector 25, Chandigarh 160 014, India Office: Panjab U, Dept Physics, Chandigarh 160 014, India

PATHAK, RAKESH RANJAN, internist; b. Nov. 23, 1970. MB, BChir, 1997, MD, 2000. Sr. resident dept. pharmacology Inst. Med. Scis., Banaras Hindu U., Varanasi, India. Contbr. articles to profl. jours.; hon. editor Vangmaya series, 70 vols. Mem. N.Y. Acad. Scis., Internat. Brain rsch. Orgn. (France), Indian Pharmacol. Soc., Am. Diabetes Assn. Home: c/o Shree Radhakant Pathak, Vill PO Derhgoan Via Hasanbazar, Rohtas (Bihar) 802 204, India Office: Plot 47-48, Nandnagar Colony, Karaundi Varanasi 221 005, India

PATHAK, SATISH RAMNARAYAN, pesticide company executive; b. Tarvada, Gujarat, India, Nov. 9, 1951; s. Ramnarayan Nagardas and Narbdaben Ramnarayan (Rao) P.; m. Urmila Satish Bhatt, Feb. 20, 1979; children: Kavita, Toral, Rajal. BSc in Agr., Inst. of Agr., India, 1975, MSc in Agr., 1977; PhD, Bhavnagar U., India, 1992. Agrl. officer Coll. Agr., Junagarh, 1977-82, asst. prof., 1982-85; sr. officer Excel Industries Ltd., Bhavnagar, 1985-92, exec., 1992-95, sr. exec., 1995-98, mgr., 1998—. Contbr. articles to profl. jours. Recipient Vijya Shree award India Internat. Friendship Soc., 1997; U.S.-Asia Environment Programme fellow, 1996. Mem. Indian Assn. Environ. Mgmt. (life), Gujarat Assn. Agrl. Sci. (life). Avocations: reading, gardening, swimming, playing. Home: Sardarnagar, 1959 B nr Sindhi Sch, Bhavnagar 364 002, India Office: Excell Industries Ltd, 6/2 Ruvapari Rd, Bhavnagar 364 005, India

PATHANASOPHON, PORNPEN, civil service officer; b. Chachoengsao, Thailand, Oct. 3, 1953; parents Sompoch Wilaiphan and Cha-orn Sintara; m. Suwich Pathanasophon, Aug. 5, 1979; children: Supornpat, Jirawut. BSc in Animal Sci., Kasetstart U., Bangkok, 1976, D of Vet. Medicine, 1978; PhD in Animal Sci., Tokyo U. Agr., 1995. Vet. rsch. officer vet. rsch. Dept. Livestock Devel., Bangkok, 1979-88, vet. officer Nat. Inst. Animal Health, 1988—; com. mem. Nat. Antimicrobial Resistance Surveillance Ctr., Bangkok, 1997—, Collaboration Ctr. for Salmonellosis Control, Bangkok, 1998—. Inventor in field. Recipient JSPS Ronpaku Program award Japan Soc. for Promotion of Sci., 1994-95, Exch. Rsch. award, 1993, Tng. award Japan Internat. Coop. Agy., 1989-90. Mem. Thai Vet. Medicine Assn. (life, editl. bd. jour. 1998—), Ctr. for Antimicrobial Resistance Monitoring in Food-born Pathogens. Buddhist. Avocations: gardening, movies, sightseeing, meditating. Fax: (02) 5798918-19. E-mail: supornpa@khotmail.com. Office: Nat Inst Animal Health, Kasetklang Jatuchak, Bangkok 10900, Thailand

PATHER, SANDY, consultant; b. Durban, Natal, South Africa, July 10, 1966; came to U.S., 1990; m. Trevor I. Naidoo, May 22, 1992. BA, Fordham U., 1997, MBA, 1999. Mktg. asst. Durban Publicity Assn., 1986-90; mktg. analyst South African Tourism Bd., N.Y.C., 1990-94; bus. cons. Polo Ralph Lauren, Lyndhurst, N.J., 1999; intern tax KPMG, N.Y.C., 1998; sr. cons. Am. Express, N.Y.C., 1999—; sr. cons. Am. Express, N.Y.C., 1999-2000, Cap Gemini, Ernst & Young, N.Y.C., 2000—. Mem. exec. com. Women's Bur. South Africa, Durban, 1989-90. Mem. NAFE, AAUW. Episcopalian. Avocations: reading, short story writing, watercolor painting, swimming. E-mail: sandypather@hotmail.com. Home: 32 Elizabeth Ave Teaneck NJ 07666-4708 Office: Cap Gemini Ernst & Young 750 7th Ave New York NY 10019-6834

PATHI, VIVEK LAKSHMI, cardiothoracic surgeon; b. Madras, India, July 30, 1961; arrived in Scotland, 1971; s. Thiruvellore and Sulochana (Gopal) Lakshimipathi; m. Claire Mangan, May 26, 1995. BMSc with honors, Dundee Med. Sch., 1982, MBChB, 1985. Lectr. anatomy U. Leeds, Eng., 1986-87; sr. house officer Health Bd., Leeds, 1987, Manchester, Eng., 1988-90; sr. house officer Harefield, London, 1990-91; registrar cardiothoracic surgery Health Bd., Glasgow, Scotland, 1992-95, sr. registrar, 1995-99; cons. cardio-thoracic surgeon Western Infirmary, Glasgow, 1999—. Contbr. articles to profl. jours. Fellow Royal Coll. Surgeons (master), Assn. Cardiothoracic Surgeons Gt. Britain. Avocations: water gardening, martial arts. Office: Western Infirmary Dept Surg, Dumbarton Rd, Glasgow G11 6NT, Scotland

PATHRAPANKAL, JOSEPH, theology educator; b. Kottayam, Kerala, India, Sept. 29, 1931; s. Abraham Chacko and Mariamma Pathrapankal. M

Theology, Athaeneum, Pune, India, 1959; M Biblical Studies, Biblican Inst., Rome, 1962; D Theology, Gregorian U., Rome, 1964; D Theology (hon.), U. Uppsala, Sweden, 1997. V.p. Dharmaram, Bangalore, India, 1976-79, pres., 1979-85, dean, 1985-91; mem. Biblical Commn., Rome, 1984-89; v.p. Cocti, 1987-93; mem. SNTS, 1975—; pres. Theol. Publis., 1989—. Author: Text and Context, 1993, The Christian Program, 1999; contbr. articles to profl. jours. Roman Catholic. Home: Dharmaram PO, Karnataka Bangalore 560029, India Office: Dharmaram Vidya Kshetram, 560029 Bangalore Karnataka India

PATIL, JAWAHAR GOVINDAPPA, molecular geneticist; b. Mirji, Karnataka, India, Dec. 22, 1965; s. Govindappa S. and Sarojini G. (Basannavar) P.; m. Rasanthi Mangalika Gunasekera, Nov. 20, 1996. BFSc, Coll. of Fisheries, Mangalore, India, 1987, MFSc, 1989; PhD, Nat. U., Singapore, 1996. Rsch. assoc. Asian Fisheries Soc., Mangalore, 1989-90; merit tchg. fellow Coll. of Fisheries, Mangalore, 1990-91; rsch. scholar U. Singapore, 1991-95; rsch. worker Nat. U., Singapore, 1995-96, rsch. fellow, 1996-98; rsch. scientist divsn. marine rsch. Commonwealth Sci. and Indsl. Rsch. Orgn., Hobart, Australia, 1998—. Coord.: (newsletter) Coll. of Fisheries Alumni Assn., 1990-91. Gen. sec. Coll. of Fisheries Alumni Assn., 1990-91; pres. Student's Assn., Mangalore, 1988-89. Recipient two Rank awards Govt. of Karnataka, India, 1987, 89. Mem. AAAS, Asian Fisheries Soc. Avocations: reading, horseback riding, swimming, basketball, cricket. Office: Divsn Marine Rsch, GPO Box 1538, Hobart TAS 7001, Australia

PATIL, JAYSINGRAO BHAUSAHEB, bank executive; b. Ozarde, India, Apr. 1, 1937; s. Bhausaheb Raoji and Krishana Bhausaheb (Mane) P.; m. Maya Jaysingrao Chavan, May 9, 1965; children: Aditi, Vaishali, Devadata. BA in Econ., Willingdon Coll., Sangli, 1959; B of Commerce, Brihan Maharashtra Coll., 1960; MA in Econ., U. Pune, 1963. From office supt. to mng. dir. Sangli Dist. Ctrl. Coop. Bank Ltd., 1960-96; sec. cum mng. dir. Vishwas Co-Operative Sugar Factory Ltd., Shirala, Sangli, 1969-70; employees rep. On Co-Operative Industries Banking Wage Bd., Bombay, 1982-90; joint sec. Dandekar Com. on Drought Prone Area, Sangli, 1974-75; rep. Nat. Co-Operative Union India, New Delhi, 1973; cons. in field. Chmn. J.B. Patil Pratishtan, Islampur, 1995—; trustee Lokseva Vishavast Nidhi, Sangli, 1990; com. mem. Shikshan Mandal Maratha Samaj, 1982-83. Recipient Best Performance in Rural Devel. Program, Zilla Parishad, Sangli, 1991-92, Udyog Ratna award Indian Econ. R & D Assn., New Delhi, 1996. Hindu. Avocations: reading, writing.

PATIL, NAISHADH PRABHAKAR, otolaryngologist; b. Bombay, India, Sept. 8, 1960; s. Prabhakar Babaji and Vimla (Gersoppa) P.; m. Anita Vishwas Barde, Dec. 25, 1991; children: Anish, Aishan. CM, G.S. Med. Coll., Bombay, India, 1986; MD, U. Wurzburg, Germany, 1988. Approved Alien Extraordinary Ability, U.S. Immigration and Naturalization Svc. Clin. fellow U. Tubingen, Germany, 1987, U. Wurzburg, Germany, 1987-88; clin. tutor otolaryngology U. Galway, Ireland, 1993-99; lectr. otolaryngology Royal Coll. Surgeons, Dublin, Ireland, 1999—; pres. Club Mac, Bombay, 1989, No. Ireland Mac User Group, Belfast, 1991; internet rev. CME-H/N Bull., Eng., 1997—; internat. rev. ENT News, 1995—. Co-author: (monograph) Sensory Changes in the Elderly, 1990, (textbook) Clinical Atlas of ENT, 1992; asst. editor: Proceedings XI and XII/XIII Internat. Congresses of the NES, 1988; mem. editl. bd. Indian Jour. Otolaryngology, 1989-90. Intercollegiate fellow Otorhinolaryngology-Head & Neck Surgery, 1998. Fellow Royal Coll. Surgeons (Edinburgh); mem. Neurotological & Equilibriometric Soc., Politzer Soc. Hindu. Avocations: med. informatics, langs., health and nutrition, writing.

PATINKIN, DEBORAH, hematologist, developmental biologist; b. Chgo., Apr. 19; d. Isaiah and Rose (Goodman) Trossman; m. Don Israel Patinkin (dec. Aug. 1995); children: Naama, Aran, Ilana, Tmira. BSc, U. Chgo., MSc; PhD, Hebrew U. Sch. Medicine, 1974. Rsch. asst. Hebrew U. Sch. Medicine, Jerusalem, 1965-75, lectr. in anatomy, 1975-77; rsch. assoc. biochemistry U. Chgo., 1977-80; rsch. scientist microbiology Einstein Med. Ctr., Bronx, N.Y., 1981-82; lectr. hematology Hadassah Med. Sch., Jerusalem, 1982-87; rsch. scientist bone marrow transplantation Hadassah U. Hosp., Jerusalem, 1996—; lectr. biol. chemistry Life Sci. Inst., 1988-95. Contbr. articles to profl. jours. Mem. AAAS, Am. Soc. Hematology, Israel Soc. Hematology. Avocations: swimming, tennis, hiking, classical music, art. Office: Hadassah U Hosp Bone Marrow, Transplant PO Box 12000, Jerusalem Israel

PATKÓS, ANDRÁS, physics educator, researcher; b. Budapest, May 12, 1947. MSc, Eötvös U., 1970; PhD, Hungarian Acad. of Sci., 1978. Asst. Eötvös U., Budapest, 1970-80, assoc. prof. physics, 1980-88, prof., 1989—; head dept. Ministry of Edn., Budapest, 1996-98; postdoctoral fellow Niels Bohr Inst., Copenhagen, 1981-82, cons., 1983, 85, 93, Rutherford Lab., U.K., 1989, 91; vis. scientist CERN, Geneva, 1984, 90, 95; vis. prof. U. Bonn, Germany, 1986, U. Strasbourg, France, 1999. Contbr. articles to profl. jours. Mem. Hungarian Acad. Sci. (dr.), Hungarian Phys. Soc., Found. for Hungarian Sci. and Edn. (exec. dir. 1997-98).

PATLAZHAN, STANISLAV ABRAMOVICH, physicist; b. Dnepropetrovsk, Ukraine, Aug. 31, 1949; s. Abram and Gulsum (Suleimanova) P.; m. Vera Patlazhan, Jan. 20, 1978; 1 child, Alexei. PhD, Inst. Electronic Technology, Moscow, 1978; DSc, Russian Acad. Scis., Chernogolovka, 1997. From rsch. scientist to leading rsch. scientist Inst. Problems Chem. Physics Russian Acad. Scis., Chernogolovka, 1978—; vis. prof. Ecole des Mines de Paris, 1993-94, U. Pitts., 1995-96. Grantee Russian Found. Basic Problems Rsch., 1996, Inst. Charles Sadron CNRS, 1998, 99, 2000, Ecole Europeenne de Chimie, Polymeres et Materiaux de Strasbourg, 2000. Mem. N.Y. Acad. Scis. Avocations: windsurfing, mountain tourism. Office: Inst Chem Physics, Chernogoovka Moscow, Russia 142432

PATMAN, PHILIP FRANKLIN, lawyer; b. Atlanta, Nov. 1, 1937; s. Elmer Franklin and Helen Lee (Miller) P.; m. Katherine Sellers, July 1, 1967; children: Philip Franklin, Katherine Lee. BA, U. Tex., 1959, LLB, 1964; MA, Princeton U., 1962. Bar: Tex. 1964, U.S. Supreme Ct. 1970, U.S. Dist. Ct. (so. dist.) Tex. 1971, U.S. Dist. Ct. (we. dist.) Tex. 1975. Atty. office of legal adviser Dept. State, Washington, 1964-67; dep. dir. office internat. affairs HUD, Washington, 1967-69; pvt. practice Austin, Tex., 1969—. Contbr. articles to legal jours. Ofcl. rep. of Gov. Tex. to Interstate Oil Compact Commn., 1973-83, 87-91. Woodrow Wilson fellow, 1959. Fellow Tex. Bar Found. (life); mem. ABA, Tex. Bar Assn., Tex. Ind. Prodrs. and Royalty Owners Assn., Tex. Oil and Gas Assn., Tex. Law Rev. Assn., Austin Club, Headliners Club, Westwood Country Club, Rotary, Phi Beta Kappa, Phi Delta Phi. Office: Patman & Osborn 515 Congress Ave Ste 1704 Austin TX 78701-3503

PATODIA, KRISHAN KUMAR, import export company executive; b. Calcutta, India, May 26, 1945; s. Brij Lal and Shakuntala Devi (Patodia) P.; m. Rani Potadia, Mar. 4, 1967; children: Rajiv, Supriya, Siddharth. BSc in Textiles, Tech. Inst. Textiles, Bhiwani, India, 1963. Chmn. Shree Janardana Mills Ltd., Coimbatore, India, BLP Super Spinners, Borgaon, India, Eurospin Industries Ltd., Calicut, India, PBM Polytex Ltd., Petlad, India, Eurotex Industries & Exports Ltd., Kolhapur, India, Patodia Syntex Ltd., Bombay, India; bd. dirs. Rajiv Holdings Pvt. Ltd., Bombay, Sambhu Investments Pvt. Ltd., Bombay, Thrust Investment and Mgmt. Cons. Pvt. Ltd., Bombay, Eurotex Leasing & Fin. Ltd., Bombay. Mem. Cricket Club India, Garware Club House, P.J. Hindu Gymkhana. Avocations: reading, music, sports, travel. Office: Patodia Syntex Ltd 12th Fl, Raheja Chambers 213 Nariman, Bombay 400 021, India

PATOLE, SANJAY KESHAV, pediatrician; b. Aug. 19, 1957. Rsch. asst. in neonatology Rsch. Soc., Grant Med. Coll. JJ Hosp., Bombay, 1985-87; cons. neonatologist NICU, Akshaya Hosp. and Rsch. Ctr., Bombay, 1986-90; fellow in neonatology Children's Hosp., Camperdown, NSW, Australia, 1990-91; sr. fellow in neonatology Royal Women's Hosp., Paddington, NSW, Australia, 1991-94, Royal Alexandra Hosp., Edmonton, 1994-95, U. of Alberta Hosp., Edmonton, 1995; staff specialist in neonatology Kirwan Hosp. for Women, Townsville, QLD, Australia, 1996—; hon. sr. lectr. dept. pub. health and tropical medicine James Cook U., Townsville, 1997—. Contbr. articles to profl. publs. Rameshwardasji Birla Smarak Kosh scholarship, 1990, Ichalkaranji Ednl. Endowment Fund scholarship, 1989. Fellow Royal Australasian Coll. Physicians; mem. Indian Acad. of Pediatrics. Office: Kirwan Hosp for Women, PO Box 187, Thuringowa Ctrl QLD 4817, Australia

PATON, DAVID, ophthalmologist, educator; b. Balt., Aug. 16, 1930; s. Richard Townley and Helen (Meserve) P.; m. Diane Johnston Brokaw, Mar. 9, 1985; 1 child from previous marriage, D. Townley. BA, Princeton U., 1952, DSc (hon.), 1985; MD, Johns Hopkins U., 1956; DSc (hon.), Bridgepopt U., 1984. Diplomate Am. Bd. Ophthalmology. Intern Cornell Med. Sch.-N.Y. Hosp., 1956-57; rsch. fellow in ophthalmology NIH, Bethesda, Md., 1957-59; resident Wilmer Inst., Johns Hopkins Sch. Medicine, Balt., 1959-64; assoc. prof. Wilmer Inst., 1964-71; asst. prof. Johns Hopkins Sch. Medicine, 1964-71; prof., chmn. dept. ophthalmology Baylor Coll. Medicine, Houston, 1971-82, prof. emeritus ophthalmalogy, 1998—; med. dir. King Khaled Eye Specialist Hosp., Riyadh, Saudi Arabia, 1982-84; chmn., chief med. officer OcuSystems, Inc., Greenwich, Conn., 1985-87; prof. Cornell U. Coll. Medicine, 1986-92; chmn., program dir. dept. ophthalmology Cath. Med. Ctr. of Bklyn. and Queens, 1986-92; founder Project ORBIS, Inc., N.Y.C., 1971, med. dir., 1971-87; founder, bd. pres. The EXCEL Found., 1989-99; mem. com. med. sci. USIA, 1991-94; bd. dirs. Eye Bank for Sight Restoration, N.Y.C., One World Sight Project, Southhampton Hosp., 1998—, East Hampton Healthcare Found., 1998—; bd. pres. World Eye Orgn., Hong Kong, 1999—; mem. med. adv. bd. Johns Hopkins Sch. Pub. Health, 1988-2000. Author of several books; contbr. articles to profl. jours. Recipient Royal Decoration 3d Order, Royal Decoration 2d Order (Jordan), Pres.'s Citizen medal, 1987, Legion of Honor (France); Markle scholar in acad. medicine, 1967-72. Fellow Am. Acad. Ophthalmology (sec. continuing edn. 1977-82, 1st v.p. 1982, Honor award 1975, Sr. Honor award 1992), ACS (bd. govs. substitute 1972-73); mem. Am. Bd. Ophthalmology (chmn. 1982), Assn. Univ. Profs. Ophthamology (trustee 1978-81), Md. Ophthalmol. Soc. (pres. 1969-70), Pan Am. Assn. Ophthalmology (coun. 1973-75). Home: PO Box 5015 East Hampton NY 11937-6096

PATON, LENNOX MCLEAN, lawyer; b. Kuala Lumpur, Malaysia, Mar. 19, 1928; s. Robert and Morag (McLean) P.; m. Cheryl Lee Williams, Oct. 17, 1959 (dec. 1977); 1 child, Michael Lennox; m. Lydie Sheelan Milne, Mar. 25, 1978 (div. 1985); 1 child, Charles Robert Matthew; m. Dorinda Ann Moore, June 15, 1991; 1 stepchild, Jessica Nonet. BA, Cambridge U., Eng., 1951, LLB, 1952, MA, 1953; LLM, Cambridge U., 1989. Bar: Singapore 1955, Malaysia 1957, Bahamas, 1967, Eng. Supreme Ct. 1954. Assoc. Donaldson and Burkinshaw, Singapore, 1954-57, Linklaters and Paines, London, 1957-58, Higgs and Johnson, Nassau, Bahamas, 1958-68; dir. Slater, Walker and Withers Ltd., Nassau, 1968-71; prin. Lennox Paton & Co., 1971-72; ptnr. Paton Toothe and Co., Nassau, 1973-74, Paton, Alexiou and Co., Nassau, 1974-79, Toothe, Paton and Co., Nassau, 1980-86; prin. Lennox Paton, Nassau, 1986—. Served to 2d lt. Royal Engrs., 1946-49. Mem. Law Soc. of Eng. and Wales, Bahamas Bar Assn. Office: Ft Nassau Centre, Marlborough St, Nassau Bahamas

PATON WALSH, JILL, author; b. London, England, Apr. 29, 1937; d. John Llewelyn and Patricia (Dubern) Buss; m. Antony Edmund Paton Walsh, Aug. 5, 1961; Children: Edmund, Margaret, Clare. Author: Hengest's Tale, 1966, The Dolphin Crossing, 1967, Fireweed, 1969, (World Book Festival award 1970), Wordhoard, 1969, Goldengrove 1972, Farewell Great King, 1972, Toolmaker, 1973, The Dawnstone, 1973, The Emporer's Winding Sheet, 1974 (Whitbread prize 1974), The Huffler, 1975, The Island Sunrise: Preshistoric Culture in the British Isles, 1975, Unleaving, 1976 (Boston Globe, Horn Book award 1976), Children of the Fox: Crossing to Salamis, 1977, The Walls of Athens, 1978, Persian Gold, 1978, A Chance Child, 1978, The Green Book, 1981, Babylon, 1982, Parcell of Patterns, 1983 (Universe prize 1984), Lost and Found, 1984, Gaffer Samson's Luck, 1984 (Smarties Grand prix 1984), Lapsing, 1985, A School for Lovers, 1989, Birdy and the Ghosties, 1990, "Grace", 1991, Matthew and the Sea Singers, 1992, When Grandma Came, 1992, The Wydham Case, 1993, Knowledge of Angels, 1994, A Piece of Justice, 1995, Connie Came to Play, 1995, Thomas and the Tinners, 1995, The Serpentine Cave, 1997, When I Was Little Like You, 1997, (with Dorothy L. Sayers) Thrones, Dominations, 1998. Fellow Royal Soc. of Lit. (CBE award 1996). Address: care David Higham Assocs, 5-8 Lower John St, Golden Sq London W1R 3PE, England

PATPONG-PIBUL, KITTI, banking executive; b. Samutsakorn, Thailand, Sept. 10, 1945; s. Sod and Sonpit Patpongpibul; m. Vipavaden Luerumrung; 1 child, Soivipa. BSc in Econs., Queens U., Belfast, Ireland. Chartered acct. Eng., Wales. Min. fin. Comptroller Gen. Dept., 1974-75; dep. mgr. H.O. credit dept. Krungthai Bank, Bangkok, Thailand, 1975-81; mng. dir. Govt. Housing Bank, Bangkok, 1981-89, 1st Pacific Asia Securities Ltd., Thailand, 1990-91, Nakornthon Bank Pub. Co. Ltd., Bangkok, 1991-98; dep. gov. Bank of Thailand, 1999—; dir. Urban Cmty. Devel. Office Nat. Housing Auth. Mem. Housing Fin. Assn. (chmn., vice-chmn. ral estate fin. com.), Valuers Assn. Thailand (bd. dirs.). Office: Bank of Thailand, 273 Samsen Rd, Bangkhunprom 10200, Bangkok

PATRA, BHAGABAN CHANDRA, gynecologist; b. Balasore, Orissa, India, Feb. 2, 1943; s. Raghunath and Anadamayee Patra; m. Annapurna Jena; children: Indubhusan, Indira Priyadarshini. MS, SCB Med. Coll., Cuttack, India; MB BChir, VSS Med. Coll., Burla, India. Med. officer Govt. of Orissa, Balasore, 1968-70; resident med. officer Med. Coll., Cuttack, 1970-73; jr. tchr. Cancer Inst., Cuttack, 1973-75; specialist in gynecology Gen. Hosp., Behbehan, Iran, 1975-80; lectr. in gynecology Med. Coll. Berhampor, India, 1980-83; specialist in gynecology Gen. Hosp., Balasore, 1983-89; pvt. practice Balasore, 1989—. Mem. Fedn. Obstet. and Gynecol. Socs. India. Office: Patra Clinic, Sahadevkhunta, 756001 Balasore Orissa, India

PATRA, ELENI, personnel administrator, educator, mediator; b. Athens, Greece, Sept. 18, 1958; d. Lucas P. and Iphigenia (Raptopoulos) P.; m. George P. Bassios, Jan. 28, 1989. BA in Econs., U. Thessaloniki (Greece), 1980; MS in Indsl. Rels. and Human Resources, Rutgers U., 1983. Intern CETA, N.J., 1983; project assoc. AMS Internat., mgmt. cons., Athens, 1983-84; human resource asst. Mobil Oil Hellas A.E., Athens, 1984-85, buyer, 1984-89; pers. adminstr. Shelman Swiss-Hellenic S.A., Athens, 1989-90; prof. The Am. Coll. of Greece, Athens, 1990—; adj. instr. European div. U. Md., Athens, 1984—; human resource specialist Stedima Ltd., mgmt. cons., Athens, 1987-88; mediator Orgn. for Mediation and Arbitration of Greece, 1998—. Contbr. articles to profl. jours. Inst. State Scholarships Greece scholar, 1979, Inst. U. Internat. scholar, 1981. Mem. Internat. Indsl. Rels. Assn., Econ. Chamber Greece. Home: 11 Eptanissou St, GR-11257 Athens Greece Office: Am Coll of Greece, 6 Gravias Str, GR-15342 AG Paraskevi Attikis Greece

PATRAWALLA, ASPI ERUCH, manufacturing executive; b. Bombay, Dec. 7, 1946; s. Eruch Aderji and Aloo Eruch (Daruwalla) P.; m. Dilnavaz Phiroze Aspi Kothawalla, Nov. 12, 1979; children: Behzad Aspi, Nezhat Aspi. Student, Nat. Def. Acad., Kharakvasla, India, 1965; MS, Madras U., 1981; postgrad., Def. Svcs. Staff Coll., Wellington, New Zealand, 1981. Qualified air traffic controller, forward air controller Air HQs, flying instr. FIS AF Tambaram, category A flying instr., CAT/Instrument rating "A". Commd. flying br. Indian Air Force, 1967, from air traffic controller to chief logistics officer, 1969-89; chief mgr. customer svc., outstations Hindustani Aeronaut. Ltd., Bangalore, Karnataka, India, 1989-94; chief mgr. engine overhaus shop Hindustani Aeronaut. Ltd., Bangalore, 1993-94, chief mgr. Kiran aircraft, 1994, dep. gen. mgr., 1994-98, addl. gen. mgr. corp. office, 1998, addl. gen. mgr. overhaul, 1998—. Decorated Commednations Chief of Staff Indian Air Force, 1978, 85, Exemplary Flying badge, 1983. Fellow Aeronaut. Soc. India (Dr. Ghatge award 1994). Avocations: yachting, golf. Home: Rustam Bagh Hal Rd, 560 017 Bangalore Karnataka, India Office: Hindustan Aeronaut Ltd, PO Vimanapura, 560 017 Bangalore Karnataka, India

PATRI, ERWIN, human resources professional; b. Bad Cannstatt, Germany, Feb. 26, 1957; s. Johann and Gertrud (Siegl) P. Abitur, Leibniz-Gymnasium, Stuttgart, 1976; Diploma, Verwaltungswirt Fachhochschule, der Bundesanstalt fur Arbeit/Mannheim, Germany, 1982. Human resources mgr. Dept. of Unemployment, Stuttgart, 1982-87, 1987-93, human resources revisor, 1993—. Avocations: music, biking, swimming, travel, hiking. Office: Vorprufungsamt Bundesanstaltr fur Arbeit, Jaegerstr 14-18, 70174 Stuttgart Germany

PATRICK, ALAN JAMES, physicist; b. Kettering, U.K., Sept. 29, 1947; s. Joseph James and Gertrude Mabel (Thompson) P.; m. Maria Luisa Appleby, July 10, 1971; children: Gareth James, Neil Jonathan. Grad., Polytech of South Bank, 1972. Process scientist Unilever Rsch., Bedford, U.K., 1966—. Mem. Inst. Physics (chartered physicist), Nat. Phys. Lab. Thermal Properties Awareness Club. Avocations: model engring., target shooting. Office: Unilever Rsch Colworth Lab, Sharnbrook, Bedfordshire MK44 1LQ, England

PATRICK, CHARLES WILLIAM, JR., lawyer; b. Monroe, N.C., Oct. 9, 1954; s. Charles William and Louise (Nisbet) P.; m. Celeste Hunt, June 5, 1976; children: Laura Elizabeth, Charles William III. BA magna cum laude, Furman U., 1976; JD, U. S.C., 1979. Bar: S.C. 1979, U.S. Dist. Ct. S.C. 1981, U.S. Ct. Appeals (11th cir.) 1981, U.S. Ct. Appeals (10th cir.) 1983, U.S. Ct. Appeals (4th cir.) 1986. Law clk. to presiding judge 9th Cir. Ct. State of S.C., Charleston, 1979-80; assoc. Ness, Motley, Loadholt, Richardson and Poole and predecessor firm Blatt and Fales, Charleston, 1980—; assoc. Motley, Loadholt, Richardson and Poole and predecessor firm Blatt and Fales, Charleston, 1980-84, ptnr., 1984—. Exec. editor S.C. Law Review, 1978; contbr. articles to profl. jours. Mem. ABA, Assn. Trial Lawyers Am., S.C. Assn. Trial Lawyers, Trial Lawyers for Pub. Justice, Phi Beta Kappa. Democrat. Presbyterian. Avocations: boating, skiing, jogging. Home: 38 Church St Charleston SC 29401-2742 Office: Ness Motley Loadholt Richardson & Poole 151 Meeting St PO Box 879 Charleston SC 29402-0879

PATRICK, DANE HERMAN, lawyer; b. San Antonio, Oct. 18, 1960; s. Kae Thomas and Joyce Lynn (von Scheele) P.; m. Kelly Marie Carlson, May 17, 1986. BA in Econs. with honors, U. Tex., 1983; JD, So. Meth. U., 1987. Assoc. Law Office of Earl Luna, Dallas, 1987-88, Veitch & Davis, San Antonio, 1988-91; pvt. practice, San Antonio, 1991—. Mem. ATLA, San Antonio Trial Lawyers Assn. (bd. dirs.), San Antonio United Shareholder Assn. (chmn. 1988-92). Democrat. Methodist. Avocations: weight lifting, hunting, martial arts. Office: 111 Soledad St Ste 300 San Antonio TX 78205-2298

PATRICK, GEORGIA O'BRIEN LAKAYTIS, communications executive; b. Dallas, July 2, 1945; d. Jack Dallas and Jane (Childs) O'Brien; m. Thomas Donald Patrick, Oct. 23, 1981. BJ, U. Mo., 1967. Tech. writer Mo. Regional Med. Programs, Columbia, Kansas City, 1967-69; with Ctr. for Student Life, U. Mo., Columbia, 1969-76; comm. dir. Am. Assn. Family and Consumer Sci., Washington, 1976-81; exec. v.p. The Communicators, Inc., Washington, 1981-92, CEO, 1992—; founder Internat. Managed HealthCare Inst., 1996; Washington office dir. NetCertification; cons. and leader seminars and workshops for nat. and internat. orgns.; expert on Internet relevance to nat. assns. Contbr. articles to profl. jours. Mem. Am. Soc. Assn. Execs., Nat. Orgn. Competency Assurance. Office: The Communicators Inc 10072 Vista Ct Myersville MD 21773-8138

PATRICK, H. HUNTER, judge; b. Gasville, Ark., Aug. 19, 1939; s. H. Hunter Sr. and Nelle Frances (Robinson) P.; m. Charlotte Anne Wilson, July 9, 1966; children: Michael Hunter, Colleen Annette. BA, U. Wyo., 1961, JD, 1966. Bar: Wyo. 1966, U.S. Dist. Ct. Wyo. 1966, Colo. 1967, U.S. Supreme Ct. 1975. Mcpl. judge City of Powell (Wyo.), 1967-68; sole practice law Powell, 1966-88; atty. City of Powell, 1969-88; justice of the peace County of Park, Wyo., 1971-88; bus. law instr. Northwest Community Coll., Powell, 1968-98; dist. judge State of Wyo. 5th Jud. Dist., 1988—; mem. Wyo. Dist. Judges Conf., sec.-treas., 1993-94, vice chair, 1994-95, chair, 1995-96. Editor: Bench Book for Judges of Courts of Limited Jurisdiction in the State of Wyoming, 1980-90. Dir. cts. Wyo. Girls State, Powell, 1982-85, 89-98; elder, deacon, moderator of deacons Powell Presbyn. Ch., 1997; mem. Wyo. Commn. Jud. Conduct & Ethics, 1997—. Recipient Wyo. Crime Victims Compensation Commn. Judicial award, 1995. Fellow Am. Bar Found., Wyo. Jud. Adv. Coun.; mem. ABA (Wyo. state del. to ho. of dels. 1994—, Wyo. del. judicial adminstrn. divsn., exec. com. nat. conf. trial ct. judges representing Wyo., Colo., Kans., Nebr., N.Mex. 1996-2000, Pub. Svc. award for ct.-sponsored Law Day programs 1990, 92), Wyo. Bar Assn. (Cmty. Svc. award 1999, Am. Pub. Svc. award 1999), Colo. Bar Assn., Park County Bar Assn. (sec. 1969-70, pres. 1970-71), Wyo. Assn. Cts. Ltd. Jurisdiction (pres. 1973-80), Am. Judicature Soc., Nat. Coun. Juvenile and Family Ct. Judges, Nat. Conf. Trial Ct. Judges (exec. com., rep. Wyo., Colo., Nebr., and Kans. 1997—). Avocations: photography, travel, fishing, camping, bicycling. Home: PO Box 941 Powell WY 82435-0941 Office: PO Box 1868 Cody WY 82414-1868

PATRICK, KEITH IAN, art critic, exhibition curator; b. Leicester, England, Feb. 23, 1952; s. Hubert Eric and Edna May (Hart) P.; m. Maite Lorés, Nov. 11, 1989; stepchildren: Fabian Hutchinson, Anna Nuria Smythe. BEd, Hockerill Coll., 1974; BA with honors, Camberwell Sch. Art, London, 1982. Freelance critic, curator, 1983—; guest editor Studio Internat., London, 1983; editor Art Line Internat., London, 1990-96, Contemporary Visual Arts, 1996—. Contbr. articles to profl. jours. Mem. Internat. Assn. Art Critics (pres. Brit. chpt. 1991-94, internat. v.p. 1993-96). Home and Office: 49 Priory Gardens, London N6 5QU, England

PATRICK, MARTY, lawyer; b. N.Y.C., May 10, 1949; s. Harry and Evelyn (Beroza) P.; m. Yolande Andree Sylvain, Feb. 26, 2000; 1 child, Jason. BS, L.I. U., 1971; cert., Inst. for Leadership Devel., Jerusalem, 1974; JD, Nova Southeastern U., 1981. Exec. dir. Zionist Orgn. Am., Miami Beach, Fla., 1975-78; prse. Enigma Enterprises, Inc., Miami, Fla., 1978-82; ptnr. Martin Howard Patrick, P.A., Miami Beach, 1982—; pres. Patrick Law Ctr., Miami Beach, 1983-89; pres. First Fla. Title & Abstract Co., Miami, 1983—; chief exec. officer Atlantic Coast Title Co., 1989—; CEO Laughing in the Dark Prodns., 1994—. Contbr. articles to profl. jours. Horovitz scholar, 1980. Mem. ABA, Ga. Bar Assn., Fla. Bar Assn., Mensa. Office: 1141 Kane Concourse Bay Harbor Is FL 33154-2012

PATRICK, MICHELE MARY, government official; b. Phila., Apr. 18, 1963; d. George Robert and Mary Elizabeth (Pristic) P. BA with honors in Econs., La Salle U., 1985; M in Govt. Adminstrn., U. Pa., 1990. Intern Phila. Water Dept., 1987; intern, asst. to exec. dir. Global Interdependence Ctr., Phila., 1988-89; intern, asst. to dep. dir. Phila. Fin. Dept., 1989, asst. to fin. dir., 1990; asst. mng. dir. City of Phila., 1990-91, 93-96; speechwriter to U.S. Senator Frank R. Lautenberg, 1996-97; speechwriter to Hon. Donna Shalala U.S. Sec. Health and Human Svcs., 1997—; speaker in field. Author: Haunted Prague; co-author: sect. of Municipal Dept. Handbook; trivia writer Merit Inds., Bensalem, Pa., 1993-95; monthly columnist Global Stamp News, 1994-96. Recipient Fulbright fellowship, U.K., Bd. Fgn. Scholarships, Washington, 1985, Nat. Resource fellowship, Pacific-Asian Mgmt. Inst., U. Hawaii, 1984, Lindback award, La Salle U., Phila., 1985, Pa. Forensic Assn., State Championships, 1982, 83, 85, Nat. Forensic Assn. Nat. championship, 1985, Meyerson fellowship, U. Pa., Phila., 1987, Pres. Classroom scholarship, Pres. Classroom for Young Ams., Washington, 1982, James and Helen Hovorka scholarship, Coun. Higher Edn., Brookfield, Ill., 1982, 83, 84. Mem. Amnesty Internat., Am. Friends of Czech Republic, Fulbright Alumni Assn., Omicron Delta Epsilon. Avocations: historical travel, classical music, British and Russian studies.

PATRICK, ROBERT HERBERT, JR., economist, educator. BA magna cum laude, Blackburn Coll., 1978; PhD in Econs., U. N.Mex., 1985. Mgr. Burroughs Corp., Fairbanks, Alaska, 1978-80; rsch. assoc. Purdue U., West Lafayette, Ind., 1985-87; asst. prof. Colo. Sch. Mines, Golden, 1987-91, assoc. prof., 1991-93; project mgr. Electric Power Rsch. Inst., Palo Alto, Calif., 1992-94; vis. scholar Stanford (Calif.) U., 1992-94, assoc. prof. Rutgers U., 1994—; reviewer U.S. EPA, U.S. Dept. Energy, Calif. Energy Commn., NSF, N.Y. Mec. Exch.; coun. of acad. policy advisors N.J. Legis. Contbr. articles to profl. jours. and chpts. to books.; mem. editorial bd. Jour. Regulatory Econs., Jour. Environ. Econs. and Mgmt. Grantee Elec. Power Rsch. Inst., 1994-98, NSF, 1994-96, Gas Rsch. Inst., 1991-92, 90-91, EPA, 1989-92, USDA, 1987, 85-87. Mem. Am. Econ. Assn., Assn. Environ. and Resource Econs., Econometric Soc., Internat. Assn. for Energy Econs. (v.p. Rocky Mountain chpt. 1992, bd. dirs. 1990-91), Mineral Econs. and Mgmt. Soc. (bd. dirs. 1992), N.J. Coun. Acad. Policy Advisors. Home: 7805 Wagon Mound Ct NW Albuquerque NM 87120-2870 Office: Grad Sch of Mgmt Rutgers U Newark NJ 07102

PATRICK, YURI LEV, translator, researcher; b. Leningrad, Russia, Nov. 28, 1945; s. Lev Gersh and Galina Nikifor (Zhdanovskaya) P.; m. Kira Alexander Yepifanova, Sept. 8, 1971; children: Elizabeth, Eva. MSc, U. Kharkov, Ukraine, 1968; MA, Pedagogical Sch., Penza, russia, 1974; PhD, U. Odessa, Ukraine, 1988. Lectr. Mil. H.S., Penza, 1968-78; info. expert, translator Textile Plant, Penza, 1978-85; tchr. Poly. Inst., Penza, 1985-87; lectr. Engring. Inst., Penza, 1987-89; editor-in-chief Semantics Processing Ltd., Tel-Aviv, 1990-91; translation dept. mgr. N.C.Mor-Carmi Ltd., Israel, 1991-95; free-lance translator Tel-Aviv, 1996—. Editor Translators' Procs., 1983-89; editor: Proceedings of translators Meetings, 1983-89, Israel Visionen und Wirklichkeit, 1993; author: German-Russian Dictionary in Computer Science, 1985. Mem. Translation Orgn. (head 1981-89), Israel Translators Assn., Gesellschaft für Angewandte Linguistik. Avocations: music, tennis. Home: 9 Recanati, 69494 Tel-Aviv Israel

PATROCÍNIO, LÉCIO LUÍZ AMARAL, cardiologist; b. Macaé, Brazil, May 5, 1956; s. João Baptista and Edith (Amaral) P.; children: Nina, Yan, Arthur. Degree in medicine, Faculty of Medicine, Teresópolis, Brazil, 1980; MS in Cardiology, Pontificia U. Cath., Rio de Janeiro, 1986. Physician Inst. Estadual de Cardiologia Aluísio de Castro, Rio de Janeiro, 1984-92, Cardiolab, Rio de Janeiro, 1986-95; physician Labex, Macaé, Brazil, 1995—, dir.; cons. Clínica São Lucas, Macaé, 1998—. Mem. N.Y. Acad. Scis., Rotary. Avocations: music, videos, film, soccer. Home: Rua Prefeito Moreira, Neto 85, 27913090 Macaé Brazil Office: Labex, Rua Conde de Araruama 440, Macaé Brazil

PATRYLAK, KAZYMYR IVANOVYCH, chemist, researcher; b. Village Nagorzany, Poland, Dec. 16, 1938; s. Ivan Mykhaylovych and Maria Mykhaylivna (Lenio) P.; m. Nadiya Mykhaylivna Martyshko, Dec. 4, 1970; children: Bohdan Kazymyrovych, Lyubov Kazymyrivna, Ivan Kazymyrovych. Engr.-Technologist, Poly. Inst., Lviv, Ukraine, 1961; PhD, Inst. Petrochem. Processes, Acad. Scis. Azerbaijan, Baku, 1969, D of Chemistry, 1986. Engr. Inst. Macromolecular Chemistry, Acad. of Sci. Ukraine, Kyiv, 1961-69, jr. rsch. worker, 1969-72, sr. rsch. assoc., 1972-77; sr. rsch. assoc. Inst. Physico-Organic and Coal Chemistry Acad. Sci. Ukraine, Kyiv, 1977-82, head alkylation lab., 1982-86, head dept. physico-tech. problems of petrochemistry, 1986-89; head dept. catalytic synthesis Inst. Biorganic Chemistry/Petrochemistry, Acad. Sci. Ukraine, Kyiv, 1989—; cons. to industry, 1972-85; dep. dir. Inst. Physico-Organic Chemistry and Coal Chemistry, Acad. Sci. Ukraine, 1984-87; cons. to refineries, 1989—. Author: Inclusion Compounds and Some Problems of Heterogeneous Equilibria, 1987, (with others) Alkylation on Zeolites, 1991; contbr. chpts. to books, numerous articles to sci. publs. Recipient award Govt. Commn. of USSR, 1987, 88, award Presidium Nat. Acad. Sci. of Ukraine, 1998; grantee CRDF, 1996, INTAS, 1997. Mem. Ukrainian Oil and Gas Acad., Ukrainian Inst. Petroleum Processing (sci. coun. 1995—). Ukrainian Catholic. Avocations: belles lettres, poetry, travel. Office: Inst Biorganic Chem/Petro, 1 Murmans'ka vul, 02094 Kyiv Ukraine

PATSIS, PANOS A. (ARGYRIOS PATSIS), astrophysicist; b. Athens, Greece, Aug. 7, 1961; arrived in Germany, 1989; p. Argyrios P. and Georgia (Skopelitou) P.; m. Aikaterini Papakonstantinou, Dec. 26, 1992. BS, U. Athens, 1985, PhD, 1991. Cert. astrophysics. Postdoctoral fellow European So. Obs., Munich, 1992-94; vis. astronomer Obs. de Marseille, France, 1994-95; rschr. Max Planck Inst. for Astronomy, Heidelberg, Germany, 1995-99, Rsch. Ctr. for Astronomy, Acad. Athens, 1999—. Author: The Neighbors, 1987 (second prize Greek Ministry of Youth 1989); contbr. articles to profl. jours. Cpl. Greek Army, 1990-91. Recipient studentship European Astrophys. Doctoral Network, 1989; postdoctoral fellow European Union Project: Human Capital and Mobility, 1994; grantee Ctr. Nat. de la Rsch. Sci., 1995. Mem. Greek Math. Soc., Greek Astron. Soc., N.Y. Acad. Scis. Avocations: painting, sketching, caricature, cinema, film direction. E-mail: patsis@mpia-hd.mpg.de. Fax: 30 1 36 34 667. Office: Rsch Ctr Astronomy Acad Athens, Anagnostopoulou 14, GR-10673 Athens Greece

PATSTONE, CHERYL, public relations executive; b. Boston, May 4, 1955; d. Harold E. and Anna M. Brown; m. Walter Patstone, Nov. 10, 1979. BA in Econs. and French, Tufts U. Sr. economist, editor electronic bus. forecast Cahners Pub. Co., San Jose, Calif., 1977-87; mgr. pub. rels. Nat. Semiconductor Corp., Santa Clara, Calif., 1987-91, Marcom team leader bus. and comm. group, 1991-96, dir. product pub. rels., 1996-99, dir. strategic Marcom programs, 1999—; v.p. comm. Autoweb.com, Inc., Santa Clara, 2000—. Mem. Internat. Assn. Bus. Communicators, No. Calif. Bus. Mktg. Assn. (bd. dirs., v.p. Programs 1999—). E-mail: cheryl.patstone@autoweb.com. Office: Autoweb.com 3270 Jay St Santa Clara CA 95054-3309

PATT, ADAM LLEWELYN, insurance executive; b. London, Mar. 30, 1960; s. Ian and Diana Jane (Llewelyn Owens) P.; m. Sarah Elizabeth Jackson, Aug. 2, 1986 (div. June 1999); children: Olivia, Alexandra. Student, N.C. State U., 1979; MA, U. St. Andrews, 1983. Asst. master Eton Coll., Windsor, England, 1984-88; exec. Sun Alliance Inc., London, 1988-91; mng. dir. Kay Hockman & Patt, London, 1991—; dir. Layton Blackham Ins. Brokers Ltd., 1998—. Mem. Ch. of England. Avocations: wine, opera, travel. Office: Kay Hockman & Patt, 36 St Georges Wharf, London 8EI 2YS, England

PATT, HERBERT JACOB, lawyer; b. Chgo., Feb. 12, 1935; s. Abraham and Esther Blanch (Kuchinsky) P.; m. Yvonne Phyllis Shavell, Oct. 9, 1958 (dec. Mar. 1986); children: Alon Wayne Patt, Bradley Earl, Colette Emile; m. Lynn Cheryl Feingold, December 26, 1993. BA, Northwestern U., 1956, JD, 1958. Bar: Ill. 1959, U.S. Dist. Ct. (no. dist.) Ill. 1959, U.S. Supreme Ct. 1977, Calif. 1986, U.S. Dist. Ct. (ctrl. and so. dists.) Calif. 1987, U.S. Ct. Appeals (9th cir.) 1987. Assoc. Andres & Andres, Santa Ana, Calif. Pres. Jewish Nat. Fund Orange Co., Santa Ana, 1994-95, chmn., 1996-98, nat. bd. dirs., N.Y., 1994-98; pres. Temple Judea, Laguna Hills, Calif., 1992-93. Office: Andres & Andres 322 W 3rd St Santa Ana CA 92701-5297

PATTABI, MANJUNATHA, materials science educator, researcher; b. Napoklu, Coorg Karnataka, India, Oct. 1, 1961; s. Bhimeshwara and Devamma Bhat; m. Rani Rajamma, Nov. 18, 1988; children: Akshay, Ashitha. BS, Mysore (India) U., 1981; MS, Mangalore (India) U., 1983; PhD, Indian Inst. Tech., Madras, 1988. Lectr. Mangalore (India) U., 1988-95, reader, 1995—; vis. prof. Universidad Nacional Autonoma de Mexico, 1999—; vis. assoc. inter-univ. consortium Dept. of Atomic Energy Facilities, Indore, India, 1995—. Contbr. numerous articles to scientific jours. Avocation: photography. Office: Mangalore U, Materials Sci Dept, 574 199 Mangalagangotri Karnataka, India

PATTANAYAK, DEBASIS, research scientist; b. West Bangal, India, Aug. 6, 1967; s. Hrishikesh and Nanibala (Pradhan) P.; m. Manjushri Dutta, June 13, 1994; 1 child, Chandrayee. BSc in Agr. with honors, Bidhan Chandra Krishi Viswavidyalaya, West Bengal, 1989; MSc in Biochemistry, Indian Agrl. Rsch. Inst., New Delhi, 1992, PhD in Biochemistry, 1997. Scientist Ctrl. Potato Rsch. Inst., Shimla, India, 1995—. Contbr. articles to profl. jours. Scholar Govt. of India, 1983; recipient Nat. Associateship award Govt. of India, 1998. Mem. Soc. for Plant Biochem. Biotech (life), Indian Potato Assn. (life). Avocations: reading, music, football, cricket. Home: Village & PO Putputia, Midnapur West Bengal 721651, India Office: Divsn Crop Physiol & Bioche, Ctrl Potato Rsch Inst, Shimla Himachal Pradesh 171001, India

PATTE, DOMINIQUE MARIE, university administrator, physician; b. Poitiers, France, Dec. 23, 1931; s. Etienne and Elisabeth (Vielliard) P.; m. Françoise Marie Durand, June 27, 1937; children: Ehenne, Marie Odile, François Xavier. MD, Faculte Medicine Paris, 1963. Extern Hosp. Paris, 1953-57, intern, 1957-63; asst. Hosp. Necker, Paris, 1963-70; prof. internal medicine U. Poitiers, Poitiers, 1970-98; dean of med. sch. U. Poitiers, 1979-83, first v.p., 1979-82. Mem. Assn. for Home Dialysisof Ioitou-Charentes (pres. 1975-99). Home: 25 rue des Carmes, Poitiers France Office: AURA-PC, BP 82, 86003 Poitiers France

PATTEN, BEBE HARRISON, minister, chancellor; b. Waverly, Tenn., Sept. 3, 1913; d. Newton Felix and Mattie Priscilla (Whitson) Harrison; m. Carl Thomas Patten, Oct. 23, 1935; children: Priscilla Carla and Bebe Rebecca (twins), Carl Thomas. D.D., McKinley-Roosevelt Coll., 1941; D.Litt., Temple Hall Coll. and Sem., 1943. Ordained to ministry Ministerial Assn. of Evangelism, 1935; evangelist in various cities of U.S., 1933-50; founder, pres. Christian Evang. Chs. Am., Inc., Oakland, Calif., 1944—, Patten Acad. Christian Edn., Oakland, 1944—, Patten Bible Coll., Oakland, 1944-83; chancellor Patten Coll., Oakland, 1983—; founder, pastor Christian Cathedral of Oakland, 1950—; held pvt. interviews with David Ben-Gurion, 1972, Menachim Begin, 1977, Yitzhak Shamir, 1991; condr. Sta. KUSW world-wide radio ministry, 70 countries around the world, 1989-90, Stas. WHRI and WWCR world coverage short wave, 1990—. Founder, condr.: radio program The Shepherd Hour, 1934—; daily TV, 1976—, nationwide telecast, 1979—; Author: Give Me Back My Soul, 1973; Editor: Trumpet Call, 1953—; composer 20 gospel and religious songs, 1945—. Mem. exec. bd. Bar-Ilan U. Assn., Israel, 1983; mem. global bd. trustees Bar-Ilan U., 1991. Recipient numerous awards including medallion Ministry of Religious Affairs, Israel, 1969; medal Govt. Press Office, Jerusalem, 1971; Christian honoree of yr. Jewish Nat. Fund of No. Calif., 1975; Hidden Heroine award San Francisco Bay coun. Girl Scouts U.S.A., 1976, Golden State award Who's Who Hist. Soc., 1988; Ben-Gurion medallion Ben-Gurion Rsch. Inst., 1977; Resolutions of Commendation, Calif. Senate Rules Com., 1978, 94, Disting. Leadership award Ch. of God Sch. of Theology, 1996; hon. fellow Bar-Ilan U., Israel, 1981; Dr. Bebe Patten Social Action chair established Bar-Ilan U., 1982. Mem. Am. Assn. for Higher Edn., Religious Edn. Assn., Am. Acad. Religion and Soc. Bibl. Lit., Zionist Orgn. Am., Am. Assn. Pres. of Ind. Colls. and Univs., Am. Jewish Hist. Soc., Am.-Isreal Pub. Affairs Com. Address: 2433 Coolidge Ave Oakland CA 94601-2630

PATTEN, CHRISTOPHER FRANCIS, government official; b. May 12, 1944; m. Lavender Thornton, 1971; 3 children. Grad., Balliol Coll., Oxford, Eng. With Conservative Party Rsch. Dept., 1966-70, dir., 1974-79; apptd. to Cabinet Office, 1970; with Home Office, then personal asst. to party chair Lord Carrington, 1972-74; M.P. from Bath dist., 1979-92; parliament pvt. sec. to leader Ho. of Commons, 1979-81; to sec. social svcs., 1981-83, parliament under-sec. for No. Ireland, 1983-85, min. of state for edn., 1985-86, min. of overseas devel., 1986-89, sec. of state for environment, 1989-90; chancellor Duchy of Lancaster, London, 1991-92; gov. gen. Hong Kong, 1992-97; external affairs min. European Union, Brussels, 1999—; apptd. to the privy coun. in the Queen's Birthday Honours List, 1989; chmn. Ind. Police Chancellor of Newcastle Univ., 1999—; Commn. for No. Ireland, 1998. Author: East and West, 1998. Named Companion of Honor, 1998; Hon. Fellow Royal Coll. Physicians Edinburgh. Address: Coutts & Co, 440 Strand, London WC2R OQS, England*

PATTEN, RICHARD E., personnel company owner; b. Seattle, May 17, 1953; s. Donald Wesley and Lorraine Louise (Kienholz) P.; m. Monica Rose Bourg, Mar. 20, 1976; children: Richard Douglas, Wesley Bourg, Melinda Rose. BA, U. Wash., 1976. Exec. v.p. Microfilm Svc. Co., Seattle, 1976-84, gen. mgr., 1985-87, chmn. bd., 1988-90; pres. Express Pers. Svcs., Seattle, 1990—. Candidate for U.S. Ho. of Reps., 1982; deacon Bethany Bapt. Ch., Seattle, 1983-86; co-chmn. fin. com. Wash. State Billy Graham Crusade, 1990-91; chmn. Wash. State Coalition toEliminate Death Tax. Mem. Nat. Micrographics Assn. (pres. N.W. chpt. 1979-80, bd. dirs. 1978-79), Assn. Image and Info. Mgmt. (chmn. svc. co. 1987), Assn. Records Mgrs. and Adminstrs., Wash. Athletic Club, Rotary (bd. dirs. 1996-98). Republican. Baptist. Home: 7012 NE 161st St Kenmore WA 98028-4265 Address: Express Pers Svcs 2401 4th Ave Ste 150 Seattle WA 98121-1438

PATTERSON, ALAN BRUCE, obstetrician, gynecologist; b. Indpls., Apr. 23, 1953; s. Samuel S. and Eunice Selma (Brenner) P. BS, Tulane U., 1975; MD, Ind. U., Indpls., 1979. Diplomate Am. Bd. Ob-Gyn. Resident in ob-gyn St. Vincent Hosp., Indpls., 1979-83; mem. staff Metro Health., Indpls., 1983-91; pvt. practice Pompano Beach, Boca Raton, Fla., 1991—; mem. staff, cons., instr. Meth. Hosp., Indpls, 1983-91; instr. Nurse Pitocin Cert. Course, 1985; cons. Indpls. Planned Parenthood, 1982-83, United Parcel Service, Indpls., 1982-83. Recipient Outstanding Citizens award DAR, 1971. Fellow Am. Coll. Ob-Gyn; mem. Palm Beach County Med. Soc., Fla. Med. Assn., Am. Cancer Soc., Boca Raton C. of C., Phi Beta Kappa, Phi Eta Sigma, Beta Beta Beta. Jewish. Avocations: jogging, swimming, wine collecting, photography, golf. Home: 19090 Fox Landing Dr Boca Raton FL 33434-5154 also: 1000 NW 9th Ct Ste 202 Boca Raton FL 33486-2268 also: 1500 N University Dr Ste 106 Coral Springs FL 33071-6071

PATTERSON, CHRISTOPHER NIDA, lawyer; b. Washington Courthouse, Ohio, Apr. 17, 1960; s. Donis Dean and JoAnne (Nida) O.; m. Vicky Patterson; children: Travis, Kirsten. BA, Clemson U., 1982; JD, Nova U., 1985. Bar: Fla. 1985, U.S. Dist. Ct. (mid. dist.) Fla. 1985, U.S. Ct. Mil. Rev. 1986, U.S. Ct. Mil. Appeals 1987, U.S. Dist. Ct. (ea. dist.) Va. 1987, U.S. Supreme Ct. 1990, U.S. Ct. Appeals (11th cir.) 1992, U.S. Dist. Ct. (no. dist.) Fla. 1992, U.S. Dist. Ct. (so. dist.) Tex. 1995; cert. criminal trial lawyer Fla. Bar. and Nat. Bd. Trial Advocacy. Pros. Fla. State Attys. Office, Orlando, Fla., 1985; spl. asst. U.S. Atty. U.S. Dist. Ct. (ea. dist.) Va., 1987-90; ptnr. Patterson & Hauversburk, Panama City, Fla., 1992—; adj. prof. law Gulf Coast Coll.; family law mediator, dependency law mediator Fla. Supreme Ct. Author: Queen's Pawn, 1996, Treasure Trove, 1997; contbr. Nat. DAR Mag., Fla. Defender mag. Chancellor St. Thomas Episcopal Ch. Capt. JAGC, U.S. Army, 1986-92, Desert Storm. Recipient Guardian ad litem commendation Fla. Supreme Ct., 1999. Mem. ABA, ATLA, Fed. Bar Assn., SAR, NACDL (life), Fla. Assn. Criminal Def. Lawyers, Acad. Fla. Trial Lawyers, Assn. Fed. Def. Attys., Fla. Acad. Profl. Mediators, Fla. Bar Spkrs. Bur. (criminal law sect., mil. law standing com., del. 11th cir. jud. conf. 1999, Pro Bono Svc. award, nominee Jefferson award for pub. svc. 1999), Bay County Bar Assn., The Ret. Officers' Assn., Christian Legal Soc., Am. Legion, Fellowship of Christian Athletes, Nat. Triathlon Fedn., Soc. Colonial Wars. Episcopalian. Avocations: athletics, triathlons. Office: PO Box 1368 1021 Grace Ave Panama City FL 32401-2420

PATTERSON, D. BRUCE, legal assistant; b. Lexington, Va., Jan. 2, 1951; s. Edward Nelson Patterson and Agnes Morton Lackey; m. Sharon Lynn Bartley, July 23, 1977; children: William, Christopher, Scott. BS, Va. Tech., 1974; MS, Va. Commonwealth U., 1978. Cert. cir. ct. clk., Va. Auditor First Nat. Bank Lexington, 1973-77; clk. Rockbridge County Cir. Ct., Lexington, 1978—; judicial sys. adv. com. Supreme Ct. Va., Richmond, 1987—. Bd. dirs. Rockbridge County Dem. Com., Lexington, 1969—, Rockbridge Area Housing Corp., 1999—; dist. gov. Natural Bridge (Va.) Ruritan Dist., 1987; pres. Am. Heart Assn. Unit, Rockbridge County, Va., 1985. Mem. Va. Ct. Clks. Assn. (pres. 1991-92, v.p., adv. bd. dirs. 1993-98), Va. Assn. Local Elected Officers, Ruritan Club (pres. Brownsburg chpt. 1985, 94, Outstanding Club Pres. 1985, Garland Gray award 1996, 98, Brownsburg Ruritan of Yr. 1997). Democrat. Presbyterian. Office: Rockbridge County Cir Ct 2 S Main St Lexington VA 24450-2523

PATTERSON, DAVID, academic administrator, educator, scholar, retired; b. Liverpool, Eng., June 10, 1922; s. Louis and Sarah (Marshak Davis) P.; m. Josephine Lovestone, Nov. 19, 1950; children: Deborah, Louise, Daniel, Benjamin. BA, U. Manchester, U.K., 1949, MA, 1954; MA, U. Oxford, U.K., 1956; PhD, U. Manchester, 1962; D of Hebrew Letters (hon.), Balt. Hebrew U., 1988; DHL (hon.), Hebrew Union Coll., 1989. Lectr. U. Manchester, 1953-56, U. Oxford, 1956-89; fellow St. Cross Coll., Oxford, 1965-89; prof. Cornell U., 1966-71; founding pres. Oxford Ctr. for Hebrew and Jewish Studies, 1972-92; prof. Mt. Holyoke Coll., 1987-88; emeritus pres., hon. fellow Oxford Ctr. for Hebrew and Jewish Studies, 1993—; vis. prof. Northwestern U., 1983, 85, 93, Sydney (Australia) U., 1993, Smith Coll., 1994, 95, Hampshire Coll., 1996; hon. fellow Ctr. for Jewish Studies, U. Manchester, 1998—. Author: Abraham Mapu, 1964, The Hebrew Novel in Czarist Russia, 1964, 1999, A Phoenix in Fetters, 1988; editor: Tradition and Trauma, 1994; translator: The King of Flesh and Blood, 1965, Out of the Depths (Brenner), 1992, Random Harvest (Bialik) with E. Spicehandler, 1999. Chmn. adult edn. com. B'nai B'rith, Gt. Britain, 1969-73; coun. mem. World Union Hebrew Studies, Jerusalem, 1979—; mem. bd. regents Internat. Ctr. for Tchg. Jewish Civilisation, Jerusalem, 1982-92; mem. senate Hochschule für Jüdische Studien, Heidelberg, Germany, 1992-99. Recipient Brotherhood award Nat. Conf. Christians and Jews, 1979, Stiller prize for literature Balt. Hebrew U., 1988, Webber prize for translation Oxford Ctr. for Hebrew and Jewish Studies, 1989, Remembering for the Future award, 2000. Mem. Brit. Assn. for Jewish Studies (pres. 1984), United Oxford and Cambridge Club London, European Assn. for Jewish Studies, Lotos Club N.Y. Jewish. Avocations: music, reading, walking. Home: 35 Hayward Rd, Oxford OX2 8LN, United Kingdom

PATTERSON, DENIS W., economic development official; b. Mannheim, Germany, Dec. 5, 1956; s. George W. III and Elisabeth Patterson. BA, U. Conn., 1979; MLA, So. Meth. U., 1982; M in Internat. Mgmt., Am. Grad. Sch. Internat. Mgmt., 1984. With Gen. Reinsurance, Dallas, 1979-83; with Am. Express, Madrid, 1976, Phoenix, 1983-84; prin., ptnr. P.L.Z., Inc., Stamford, Conn., 1984-89; dir. mktg. Dusseldorf Trade Shows, N.Y.C. and Chgo., 1989-94; sr. exec. office of econ. devel. City of Stamford, Conn., 1997—; project cons./owner d/b/a Am. Traders Co., Greenwich, Conn., 1990—. Rep. dist. 8 Town Meeting, Greenwich, Conn., 1985-91, 95-97; bd. dirs. Chgo. Area Project, 1992-94. Named Col. La. State Militia, Gov. Edwards. Mem. SAR, Chgo. Coun. on Fgn. Rels., Univ. Club Chgo., Young Grand Old Party, Mayflower Soc., Sigma Chi (Carlisle scholar 1979, Balfour nominee 1979), Landmark Club (Stamford, Conn.). Republican. Avocations: travel, literature, civic affairs, vineyard. Home: 1435 Bedford St Apt 12A Stamford CT 06905-5289

PATTERSON, EDWARD PALMER, retired physical scientist; b. Kansas City, Kans., Sept. 5, 1921; s. Sidney Edward and Dura (Palmer) P.; m. Eula Mae Bennett, Oct. 15, 1945; children: Nona Marie, Wilma Jean Patterson Graham. BS in Metall. Engring., U. Mo., Rolla, 1944, MS in Metall. Engring., 1947, prof. degree of engring., 1957. Registered profl. engr., Kans. Instr. Nat. Sch. Aeronautics, Kansas City, Mo., 1947-50; metall. engr. Boeing Airplane Co., Wichita, Kans., 1950-51; sr. rsch. engr. GM Corp., Kansas City, Kans., 1951-52; sr. staff engr. White Motors Co., Cleve., 1952-54; sr. engr. Westinghouse Elec. Co., Kansas City, Mo., 1954-59; sr. staff rschr. Cessna Aircraft Corp., Wichita, 1959-60; project engr., project leader Bendix Corp./Allied Signal Corp., Kansas City, Mo., 1960-87; ret., 1987. Vol. Hospice Mesquite Med. Ctr., 1997-98, Nat. Hospice Orgn., Dallas, 1998. With USAF, 1944-46. Mem. AIME, Am. Soc. Materials Internat., Am. Rocket Soc., Phys. Soc., Am. Phys. Soc., Masons (master, York Rite Cross of Hon. & Red Cross of Constantine, High Priest), Knights of Kadosh (comdr. 1968). Republican. Mem. LDS Ch. Achievements include discovery that the so called gravitational constant is not a constant; all properties are related by one or more universal constants; there are numerous equations of the type E=MC2. Avocations: travel, reading, genealogy, computing, family gatherings. Home: 3513 Bermuda Dr Rowlett TX 75088-5364

PATTERSON, JEFFERY ALLEN, business owner; b. Albertville, Ala., Sept. 17, 1961; Children: Tamara Jesse, Madeline Paige and Victoria Autumn (twins). Founder, pres. Marshall County Young Dem., Albertville, 1996; exec. com. mem. Marshall County Democratic Club, 1999; Masons; v.p. Lions Club, Albertville, 1999, pres., 2000; mem. Albertville C. of C., Guntersville C. of C., Boaz C. of C., Sand Mt. Saddle Club, Beulah vol. Fire Dept., Marshall County Bd. of Realtors; Albertville Future Farmers of Amer. (pres. 1978-79); Marshall County Bd. of Realtors; pres. Albertville Jaycees, 2000; elected constable Marshall County, 1996; formed Marshall County Sheriffs Posse, CAP, 2000. Recipient Senate award, 1997, Alabama Jr. C. of C. Outstanding Young Alabamian award, 1998, commendation Marshall County Citizen of Yr. Com., 1997, Knights of Kings Heroes, DAR award, 1999. E-mail: jpatterson@go.com. Home: 107 Auburn Ave Albertville AL 35951-7437

PATTERSON, KERRY DAVID, economist; b. Ilford, Essex, Eng., Oct. 6, 1947; s. David Turnbull and Constance Elizabeth (O'Brien) P.; children: Corin David, Ella Rosemary, Colette Anna. BA with honors, U. Essex, Eng., 1972; PhB in Econs., U. Oxford, Eng., 1974. Economist, econometrician Bank of Eng., London, 1975-78; univ. lectr. U. Reading, Berks, Eng., 1978-87, reader, 1987-91; prof. U. Reading, 1991—. Author, editor: The Measurement of Capital, 1978; editor Economic Modelling at the Bank of England, 1991, An Introduction to Applied Econometrics, 2000; contbr. articles to profl. jours. Grantee Econs. Social Research Council U. Reading, 1987-89. Mem. Royal Econ. Soc. E-mail: K.O.Patterson@reading.ac.uk. Office: White Knights Park, Reading RG6 6AA, England

PATTERSON, MARK ALLAN, musician; b. Highland Park, Ill., Apr. 8, 1960; s. Dale Richard and Elisabeth Ann (Milton) P.; m. Patricia Jean Schultz, June 20, 1987; 1 child, Margaret Clara. BA summa cum laude, U. Denver, 1982. Trombonist Central City (Colo.) Opera Orch., 1982-85; music copyist, transcriber Wedo's Music, N.Y.C., 1983-87; freelance trombonist with various jazz orchs., Broadway shows, concerts, N.Y.C., 1984—; trombonist, libr. N.Y. Pops Orch., N.Y.C., 1985—; trombonist, arranger Rainbow Rm. Orch., N.Y.C., 1990-98; substitute trombonist Vanguard Jazz Orch., N.Y.C., 1993—; mem. BMI Jazz Composers' Workshop, N.Y.C., 1990—. Composer (jazz compositions for big band) Reflections,1990, Just Found Joy, 1995, First Light, 1996, Margaret's World, 1999; performing on jazz rec. Tomorrow's Reflections, 1995; performer, bandleader Jazz Quartet, 1990—; soloist Ridgefield Symphony Orch., 1994. Wichita Jazz Festival scholar at Berklee Sch. Music, 1977. Mem. Am. Fedn. Musicians. Avocations: bicycling, cross-country skiing.

PATTERSON, PERCIVAL JAMES, prime minister of Jamaica; b. Hanover, Apr. 10, 1935; s. Henry and Ina (James) P.; 2 children. BA, U. West Indies, 1958; LLB, U. London, 1963; LLD (hon.), Northeastern U., 1994; JD (hon.), Brown U., 1998. Bar: Middle Temple, London 1963, Jamaica 1963, Queen's counsel 1984. Various positions People's Nat. Party, 1958—, v.p., 1969-80, chmn., 1983-92; mem., opposition spokesman on youth-sports, cmty. devel. Jamaican Senate; mem. parliament for ctrl. Westmoreland Jamaican Ho. of Reps., 1970-80, 89—; min. industry and tourism Govt. of Jamaica, Kingston, 1972-77, min. fgn. affairs, fgn. trade, and tourism, 1978-80, dep. prime min., 1978-80, 89-92, min. devel., prodn., and planning, 1989-90, min. finance, devel., and planning, 1990-92, prime min., min. def., 1992—, min. info., devel., and social planning, 1993—; chmn. Caricom, 1997, sub-com. on external negotiations, group of 15, 1998-99. Recipient Order of Aguila Azteca, Mex., 1990, Order of Liberator Simon Bolivar (First Class), Venezuela, 1992, Great Cross of the Order of Bernardo O'Higghins, Chile, 1992, Order of San Marti Jiminez de Quesda, Colombia, 1994, Order of Fransisco Morzan in the rank of Gran Cruz Placa de Oro, Honduras, 1994, Order of Jose Marti, Cuba, 1997. Office: Office Prime Min, 1 Devon Rd POB 272, Kingston 6, Jamaica*

PATTESON, CHARLES LYNN, musician, retired music educator; b. Dallas, Mar. 20, 1923; s. James Nelson and Eula Lee (Jolly) P.; children: Lisa Ann Patteson Kennedy, Charles Lynn Jr. BA, Tex. Christian U., 1948. Band dir. Poly. High Sch., Ft. Worth, 1948-50, Handley High Sch., Ft. Worth, 1948-50; owner TV store Ft. Worth, 1951-61; band dir. McLean Middle Sch., Ft. Worth, 1961-84; leader Charlie Patteson Dance Orch., Ft. Worth and Dallas, 1950-98; leader Charlie Patteson Dance Orch., Dallas/Ft. Worth. Composer (band music) March 200, 1974, (orch. music) Two Minute Waltz, 1976, Fantasy, 1991, Paris In June, October in London, November in Rome, numerous other compositions and arrangements. With USAF, 1943-46. Recipient 1st place Concert Competition award (dir. McLean Middle Sch. Band), Ft. Worth., 1974-84. Mem. Am. Fedn. Musicians, Musician's Fed. Credit Union (v.p.), Lions, Elks, Masons, Shriners (1st chair clarinet in band 1950-91). Republican. Avocations: water skiing, recording, music arranging. Home: 5101 Westhaven Dr Fort Worth TX 76132-2036

PATTISON, GRAHAM ANTHONY, horticulturist; b. Carshalton, Surrey, Eng., Oct. 31, 1944; s. Gilbert Anthony and Violet Daisy (Samson) P.; married, May 14, 1970; children: Andrew, Robert. Diploma, Royal Botanic Gardens Kew, Richmond, Surrey, 1968. Garden supr. Royal Botanic Gardens KEW, 1968-81; dir./curator Inst. Nat. Investigation Sobre Recursus Bioticus, Xalapa, Vera Cruz, Mex., 1981-86; hort. advisor Nat. Coun. for the Conservation of Plants and Gardens, Woking, Surrey, 1986—; advisor Brit. Coun. Inst. Ecologia Xalapa, Vera Cruz, 1986—; hort. cons. Fellow Inst. Horticulture, Kew Guild. Home: 200 Uxbridge Rd, Hampton Hill, Middx TW12 1BG, England

PATTISON, NEIL SPENCER, obstetrics educator, researcher; b. Auckland, New Zealand; s. Ronald Matthew and Dawn Patricia Pattison; m. Jules Margaret (Twigge) Pattison; children: Ian, Sarah, Max. BSc, Auckland

Med. Sch., 1970, MB, ChB, 1973, MD, 1989; FRCOG, FRNZCOG, M. Med. Sch., 1998. Registrar in obstetrics St. Mary's Hosp., Manchester, Eng., 1979-80; rsch. fellow dept. ob. Nuffield Hosp., Oxford, Eng., 1980-81; assoc. prof. ob. Auckland Sch. Medicine, 1981—. Fellow Royal Coll. Ob-Gyn., Royal Australian & New Zealand Coll. Ob-Gyn. Office: Dept Ob-Gyn, Auckland Sch Medicine, Auckland New Zealand

PATTON, BRUCE M., law educator, management consultant; b. Terre Haute, Ind., Oct. 14, 1956; s. William Eugene and Carol Ann P.; m. Diana McLain Smith, Oct. 21, 1994. AB, Harvard U., 1977, JD, 1984. Bar: Mass. Co-founder, assoc. dir. Harvard Negotiation Project, Cambridge, Mass., 1979-84, dep. dir., 1984—; co-founder, assoc. dir. Program on Negotiation at Harvard Law Sch., Cambridge, Mass., 1983—; co-founder, ptnr. Vantage Partners, LLC, Cambridge, 1997—; co-founder, prin. Conflict Mgmt. Inc., Cambridge, 1984—; co-founder, dir. Conflict Mgmt. Group, Cambridge, 1984—; Thaddeus R. Beal lectr. Harvard Law Sch., Cambridge, 1985-99. Co-author: The Mainstream of Algebra and Trigonometry, 2d edit., 1980, Getting To Yes, 2d edit., 1991, Difficult Conversations, 1999; contbr. articles to profl. jours. Avocations: squash, hiking. E-mail: bpatton@post.harvard.edu. Office: Harvard Negotiation Project Harvard Law Sch Pound Hall 524 Cambridge MA 02138 also: Vantage Ptnrs 1030 Mass Ave Cambridge MA 02138-5388

PATTON, GEORGE SMITH, military officer; b. Boston, Dec. 24, 1923; s. George Smith, Jr. and Beatrice Banning (Ayer) P.; m. Joanne Holbrook, June 14, 1952; children: Margaret, George, Robert, Helen, Benjamin. BS, U.S. Mil. Acad., 1946; M in Internat. Affairs, George Washington U., 1965. Commd. 2d lt. U.S. Army, 1946, advanced through grades to maj. gen., 1973; parachutist Germany, 1947-51; assigned Armor Br., 1949; instr. tank offense sect. Armored Sch. Fort Knox, Ky., 1952-53; comdr. Co. A, 140th Tank Bn. Korea, 1953, exec. officer I Corps Reconnaissance Bn., 1953-54; co. tactical officer dept. tactics U.S. Mil. Acad., 1954-56; officer exec. dept. U.S. Naval Acad., 1956-57; assigned Command and Gen. Staff Coll., Fort Leavenworth, Kans., 1957-58; a.d.c. comdg. gen. 7th Army and comdr. in chief U.S. Army, Europe, 1958-60; exec. officer 1st squadron 11th Armored Cav. Regt. Straubing, Germany, 1960-61; assigned Armed Forces Staff Coll. Norfolk, Va., 1961-62; assigned U.S. Army War Coll. Carlisle Barracks, Pa., 1964-65; spl. forces ops. officer Mil. Assistance Command Vietnam, 1962-63; comdr. 2/81 Armor, 1st Armored Div. Fort Hood, Tex., 1963-64; chief Mainland S.E. Asia br. Far East-Pacific div. Office Dep. Chief Staff for Mil. Ops., Dept. Army, 1965-67; chief force devel. div. U.S. Army, Vietnam, 1967-68; comdg. officer 11th Armored Cav. Regt. Vietnam, 1968-69; assigned U.S. Army Primary Helicopter Ctr., Ft. Wolters, Tex., 1969-70, Ft. Rucker, Ala., 1969-70; asst. div. comdr. for support 4th Armored div. Hdqrs. U.S. Army, Europe, 1970-71; comdt. U.S. Army Armor Sch. Fort Knox, 1971-73; dir. security assistance Hdqrs. U.S. European Command, 1973-74, comdr. Army Readiness Region, 1974-75; comdr. 2d Armored Div. Fort Hood, 1975-77; dep. comdg. gen. U.S. VII Corps, 1977-79; dir. readiness Hdqrs. Dept. Army Materiel Devel. and Readiness Command Alexandria, Va., 1979-80; ret., 1980; instr. history U. Md., 1960-61. Mem. West Point Fund, Alexandria, Va.; trustee Essex Agrl. and Tech. Inst., Hathorne, Mass. Decorated D.S.C. with oak leaf cluster, Silver Star with oak leaf cluster, Legion of Merit with two oak leaf clusters, D.F.C., Bronze Star with oak leaf cluster, Purple Heart; Cross of Gallantry with gold, silver and bronze stars Vietnam; Army Forces Honor medal 1st class. Mem. Assn. U.S. Army, Armor Assn., Blackhorse Assn., Ducks Unltd., N.E. Farm Bur., Legion of Valor, Am. Legion. Home: 650 Asbury St South Hamilton MA 01982-1321

PATTON, JAMES RICHARD, JR., lawyer; b. Durham, N.C., Oct. 27, 1928; s. James Ralph and Bertha (Moye) P.; m. Mary Margot Maughan, Dec. 29, 1950; children: James Macon, Lindsay Fairfield. AB cum laude, U. N.C., 1948; postgrad., Yale U., 1948; JD, Harvard U., 1951. Bar: D.C. bar 1951, U.S. Supreme Ct. 1963. Attache of Embassy; spl. asst. to Am. ambassador to, Indochina, 1952-54; with Office Nat. Estimates, Washington, 1954-55; atty. Covington & Burling, Washington, 1956-61; founding ptnr., chmn. exec. com. Patton Boggs, LLP, Washington, 1962—; Lectr. internat. law Cornell Law Sch., 1963-64, U.S. Army Command and Gen. Staff Coll., 1967-68; Mem. Nat. Security Forum, U.S. Air War Coll., 1965, Nat. Strategy Seminar, U.S. Army War Coll., 1967-70, Global Strategy Discussions, U.S. Naval War Coll., 1968, Def. Orientation Conf., 1972; mem. Com. of 100 on Fed. City, Washington; mem. adv. council on nat. security and internat. affairs Nat. Republican Com., 1977-81; bd. dirs. Security Nat. Bank (Wash.), Signet, N.A., Madeira Sch., Greenway, Va., 1975-81, Lawyers Com. for Civil Rights Under Law, Washington, Legal Aid Soc. Washington; mem. Industry Policy Adv. Com. for Trade Policy Matters, 1984-87; mem. visiting com. Ackland Art Mus. U. N.C., 1987—, Nat. Coun. Anderson Ranch Arts Ctr., 1987—. Adv. coun. mem. Johns Hopkins U. Sch. Advanced Internat. Studies, 1989-92; nat. bd. dirs. Aspen Mus., 1987-90; nat. coun. mem. Whitney Mus., 1992—; bd. dirs., exec. com. Nat. Mus. Natural History, Smithsonian, 1992—; bd. dirs. Smithsonian Nat. Bd., 1999—; trustee Aspen Music Festival and Sch., 1993—. Fellow U.N.C. Wilson Library, 1996—. Mem. ABA (past com. chmn.), Inter-Am. Bar Assn. (past del.), Internat. Law Assn. (past com. chmn.), Am. Soc. Internat. Law (treas., exec. coun.), Washington Inst. Fgn. Affairs, Nat. Gallery (collectors com. 1988-91), Gerrard Soc., Met. Club (Washington), Phi Beta Kappa, Alpha Epsilon Delta.

PATTON, JEFFREY, plastics company executive; b. Blyth, Eng., Jan. 14, 1964; arrived in The Netherlands, 1994; s. Ronald and Catherine Patricia (Beresford) P.; m. Janet Rosalind Moss, Dec. 28, 1988. BSc with hons., Manchester (Eng.) U., 1986. Logistics specialist GE Plastics, Sale, Eng., 1986-88, mktg. specialist, 1988-89, sales exec., 1989-92, sales mgr., 1992-94; purchasing mgr., cons. GE Plastics, Boz, The Netherlands, 1994-96, dir. comml. svcs., human resources cons., 1996-97, bus. process leader, 1997-99, gen. mgr. ABS bus., 1999—. Mem. Elfun Soc., Cannock AA. Mem. Conservative Party. Anglican. Avocations: athletics, soccer, golf, art, photography. Office: GE Plastics BV, Plastics Laan 1, 4600 AC Bergos Op Zoom The Netherlands

PATTON, MICHAEL ALEXANDER, medical geneticist; b. Enniskillen, Northern Ireland, Apr. 15, 1950; s. Harry Alexander and Margery Murray (Drennan) P.; m. Jacqueline Heidi Pickin; children: Alistair Patrick, Rebecca Louise. M.B.Ch.B., Edinburgh (Scotland) U., 1974, MSc, 1976; MA, Cambridge (Eng.) U., 1975. Med. rsch. coun. studentship U. Edinburgh, 1975-77; registrar Royal Alexandra Hosp., North Wales, 1977-79; rsch. fellow Univ. Hosp. Wales, 1980-82; family medicine trainee Gloucester, Eng., 1982-83; sr. registrar Great Ormond St. Hosp., 1983-86; cons. in clin. genetics and read med. genetics St. Georges Hosp. Med. Sch., London, 1986-98; prof. med. genetics, 1998—; med. dir. Birth Defect Found., U.K., 1989—; inspector Human Fertilization and Embryology Authority, U.K., 1990-95. Editor: The Contact a Family Directory of Specific Conditions and Rare Syndromes, 1992; contbr. articles to profl. jours. Mem. Noonan Syndrome Soc. (pres. 1987—), Genetic Interest Group U.K. (mem. com. 1989—), Jenner Soc. (treas. 1992-94). Avocations: skiing, sailing, watercolor painting. Home: Little Bookham, 126 Woodlands Rd, Surrey KT23 4HS, England Office: St George Hosp Med Sch, Med Genetics Dept Cranmer Ter, London SW17 0RE, England

PATTON, PETER MARK, lawyer; b. Chgo., Dec. 23, 1955; s. James T. and Dorothy R. Patton; m. Anne E. Castimore, Oct. 12, 1985; 1 child, William James. AB, Harvard Coll., 1977; JD, U. Calif., Berkeley, 1985. Bar: Pa. 1987, U.S. Dist. Ct. (ea. dist.) Pa. 1987, U.S. Ct. Appeals (4th cir.) 1986, U.S. Ct. Appeals (3rd cir.) 1988. Law clk. U.S. Ct. Appeals (4th cir.), Richmond, Va., 1985-87; assoc. Galfand, Berger, Phila., 1987-93, ptnr., 1993—. Committeeman Dem. Orgn., Delaware County, 1998. Reciient Profl. Responsibility award Am. Jurisprudence, 1985. Mem. Pa. Trial Lawyers Assn., Phila. Trial Lawyers Assn., Million Dollar Advocates Forum. Avocation: running. Office: Galfand Berger 1818 Market St Ste 2300 Philadelphia PA 19103-3648

PATTON, WARREN ANDRE, public relations executive, journalist; b. Chgo., Oct. 15, 1954; s. Willie Roosevelt and Adriana Ultima (Rhodes) P.; m. Annie Yolanda Thomas, Nov. 19, 1981 (div. May 1988); 1 child, Thomas; m. Olga Enid Ostalaza, July 31, 1993 (div. May 1996); children: Rafaela, Jennifer, Christopher, Michael. B in Criminal Justice, Chaminade U., 1986; MBA, Chadwick U., 1992; MPA, Troy State U., 1993. Enlisted USN, 1978, advanced through grades to chief, 1991; journalist USN, 1978—. Fundraiser Combined Fed. Campaign, Pensacola, Fla., 1991, Waterfront Mission, Pensacola, 1993. Mem. ASPA, Nat. Assn. Black Journalists, Coun. of Minority Pub. Adminstrs., Fleet Res. Assn., Hannibal Masonic Lodge No. 1. Avocations: reading, bowling, chess, poetry, jogging. Office: Navy Recruiting Area Eight 1301 Clay St Oakland CA 94612-5217

PATTOO, SRINIVASAN, finance company executive; b. Madras, India, Oct. 6, 1936; s. Srinnasan and Janaki P.; m. Shanthi Ganesan, Sept. 11, 1964; 2 children. BA with honors, Vivekenanda Coll., Madras, 1957, MA, 1958; ML, Govt. Law Coll., Madras, 1959. Law apprentice Menon & Pai, Kochi, India, 1959-61; mid. mgmt. Bank of India, 1961-77; mgr. Bank of Credit & Commerce, Libreville, 1978-80; sr. mgr. Bank of Credit & Commerce, Abidjar, 1980-84; country mgr. Bank of Credit & Commerce, Freetown, Sierra Leone, 1984-87; chief tech. adv. UNIDO, Freetown, Sierra Leone, 1987-92; mng. ptnr. Profinman Enterprises Internat., Madras, 1993—; mng. dir. Profinman Svcs. Internat., Singapore, 1993-99; chmn. K. Fastners & Engrs. Ltd., Rajkot, India, 1993-97; cons. in field. Founder, pres. Wecare Found., Madras, 1993—; sec. Rotary, Hospet, India, 1967-69, bd. dirs., Freetown, 1984-92. Mem. British Inst. Mgmt., First City Madras Country Club. Hindu. Avocations: social service, reading, music, sports. Fax: 91-44-4430439. E-mail: pattoo99@yahoo.com. Home: 19 New Beach Rd Bayview Apt, 600041 Madras India

PATTY, CHARLES EDGAR, JR., physicist, educator; b. Anniston, Ala., Aug. 29, 1946; s. Charles Edgar and Velma Doris (Roper) P.; m. Stephanie Ruth Carter, May 8, 1971; children: Charles Edgar III, Kira Dawne. BS, Jacksonville State U., 1969; MS, U. Ala., 1977, PhD, 1983. Rsch./tchg. asst. U. Ala., Huntsville, 1974-79; dir. Redstone Arsenal (Ala.) Br. Columbia Coll. Extended Studies Divsn., 1979-82; electronics engr. U.S. Army Missile Lab., Redstone Arsenal, 1982-84; sr. systems analyst Teledyne Brown Engring., Huntsville, 1984-2000, Teledyne Solutions, Inc., Huntsville, 2000—; mem. adj. faculty Columbia Coll., Redstone Arsenal, 1978—. Author: Introduction to Experimental Physics, 1975, Experiment and Knowledge, 1986. Block capt. Neighborhood Watch., 1982-83; chmn., founding mem. Coun.Sci. Students, U. Ala., Huntsville, 1976; chmn. bd. Bingham Mountain Landowners Assn., 1984-85. Served as officer with USAF (SAC), 1969-74. Mem. Sigma Xi, Sigma Pi Sigma. Baptist. Home: 1820 Cross Creek Rd SE Huntsville AL 35802-3971 Office: Teledyne Solutions Cummings Research Park Huntsville AL 35805

PATTYN, ETIENNE JEROME STEVE, small business owner; b. Ieper, Belgium, May 20, 1937; s. Leon Pattyn and Maria Magdalena Lamerant; m. Bertha Cornelia Bondue, June 6, 1959; children: Frankie Leon, Heidi Raymonda. Meat processor, 1959-89, chmn. mfg. moldings and frames, 1983-95, owner art gallery framing svc., painter, 1995—, fin. broker, 1995—. Mem. Blue Liberal Party. Roman Catholic. Avocations: painting, reading, cycling. Office: Interart BVBA, Koekoekstraat 68 A, 8793 Waregem Belgium

PATWA, RAJEN MUKUNDLAL, electrical company executive; b. Madhavnagar, India, Oct. 23, 1949; s. Mukundlal Taraklal and Ansuyaben Mukundlal Patwa; m. Diptiben Rajenbhai; children: Rahil R., Nidhi R. BE, M.S. U. Baroda, India, 1972; MS in Electronics, Poly. Inst. N.Y., 1975. Project leader Atira, Ahmedabad, India, 1975-78; ptnr. Patwa Kinarivala Elec. Ltd., Baroda, 1978-96, dir., 1996—. Recipient spl. recognition award Best Entrepreneur Gujarat Govt. of India, 1984, TOYP award Banyan City Jaycees, 1988, award for best performance in indsl. electronics Nat. Productivity Coun., 1987-88, award for excellence in instrumentation and indsl. electronics Hon. Prime Min. Shri. P.V. Narshima Rao, 1991, award for excellence FGMI, 1994, Shri. G. D. Birla award 36th Joint Techol. Conf., 1995, Nat. Award Outstanding In-House R & D Achievements DSIR, 1996. Mem. IEEE, Textile Inst. U.K., Diners Club. Avocations: tennis, music, social work. Home: Opp Vasna Octavi Noika B/L, 390007 Baroda Gujarat, India Office: Patwa Kinarivala Elec Ltd, Ajwa Rd, 390019 Baroda Gujarat, India

PATWARDHAN, VILAS SHRIDHAR, chemical engineer, consultant; b. Thane, India, Oct. 13, 1947; s. Shridhar Prabhakar and Prabhavati Shridhar (Pavgi) P.; m. Meena Vilas (Limaye) P., May 18, 1975; children: Manjiri, Parag. B of Tech., Indian Inst. Tech., Bombay, 1969; MS, Purdue U., 1971, PhD, 1974. Scientist Nat. Chem. Lab., Pune, India, 1974-86; asst. dir. Nat. Chem. Lab., Pune, 1986-91, dep. dir., 1991-97; proprietor Opsim Software, Pune, 1997—; cons. various cos., 1976-97; rsch. guide Pune U., 1981-91; vis. scholar, rsch. assoc. Syracuse (N.Y.) U., 1982-83; vis. fellow Bombay U., 1987-88. Contbr. chpts. to books. Fellow Indian Nat. Acad. Engring., Indian Acad. Scis.; mem. Indian Inst. Chem. Engrs. (assoc., Amar Dye Chem award 1981, Mrs. Chinnamaul Meml. prize 1981, Herdillia award 1991, ICICI Tech. of Yr. award, 1998). Avocation: music, reading, chess. E-mail: vspatw@vsnl.com. Office: Opsim Software, 3 Vibha Heights Sane Wadi, Baner Rd Aundh Pune 411007, India

PATY, DONALD WINSTON, neurologist; b. Peking, China, Sept. 25, 1936; s. Robert Morris and Katherine (Behenna) P.; m. Jo Anne Haymore, Dec. 28, 1958; children: Morris Britten, Beverly Behenna, Breay Winston, Donald Blake. B.A., Emory U., 1958, M.D., 1962. Intern Duke U., 1962-63; resident in medicine and neurology Emory U., 1965-70; fellow in immunology MRC Demyelinating Diseases Unit, U. Newcastle-upon-Tyne, Eng., 1970-72; asst. prof., then prof. neurology U. Western Ont. (Can.) Med. Sch., 1972-80; prof. neurology, head div. U. B.C. Med. Sch., Vancouver, 1980-96; sec.-gen. XV World Congress of Neurology, Vancouver, B.C., 1993; advisor London (Ont.) chpt. Multiple Sclerosis Soc. Can., 1972-80; sec. exec. com., med. adv. bd. Internat. Fedn. Multiple Sclerosis Socs., 1980—; mem. WHO working Group in Multiple Sclerosis, 1998. Author articles in field.; Mem. editorial bds. profl. jours. Bd. dirs. London Symphony, 1978-80; chmn. grants rev. com. Multiple Sclerosis Soc. of Can.; mem. exec. com. med. adv. bd., chmn. med. mgmt. com. Internat. Fed. Multiple Sclerosis Soc., 1983-97. With USPHS, 1963-65. Fellow Can. Life Ins. Assn., 1972-77; grantee Multiple Sclerosis Soc. Can.; grantee Med. Rsch. Coun. Can.; recipient John Dystel Rsch. award Multiple Sclerosis Soc./Am. Acad. Neurology, 1995, Sir Richard Cave award Multiple Sclerosis Soc. Gt. Britain and No. Ireland, 1995, Charcot award Internat. Fedn. of Multiple Sclerosis Socs., 1995. Fellow ACP, Royal Coll. Physicians and Surgeons Can. (chmn. com. in neurology 1982-86), Am. Acad. Neurology; mem. Can. Neurol. Soc. (pres. 1989-90), Am. Neurol. Assn., Brit. Assn. Neurologists (hon.), World Fedn. Neurology (Can. rep. coun. of dels., chmn. multiple sclerosis rsch. group 1993-98, mem. pub. awareness com.), Alpha Omega Alpha. Unitarian. Home: 3657 W 24th Ave, Vancouver, BC Canada V6S 1L7

PATZAKIS, MICHAEL J., orthopaedic surgeon, educator; b. Campbell, Ohio, Nov. 6, 1937; married; four children. BA, Ohio State U., 1959, MD, 1963. Diplomate Am. Bd. Orthopaedic Surgery. Intern L.A. County-USC Med. Ctr., 1963-64, resident, 1964-68; fellow rheumatoid surgery U. Colo. Med. Ctr., 1968-69; instr. U. So. Calif. Sch. Medicine, 1967-68, asst. prof., 1969-75, assoc. prof., 1975-88, prof., 1988—, interim chmn., 1990-91, chmn., 1991—, The Vincent and Julia Meyer chair, 1996—; instr. U. Colo., 1968-69; vis. prof. U. Calif., Irvine, 1969, 70, Case Western Res. U., 1976, Cleve. Clinic, 1976, U. Tex., Dallas, 1977, UCLA, 1977, Northwestern U., 1981, Stanford U., 1981, Northeastern Ohio Sch. Medicine, 1983, U. Calif., San Diego, 1985, Drew Med. Sch., L.A., 1988, Martin Luther King Drew Med. Sch., 1989, Athens Hellenic Trauma Soc., 1990, Walter Reed Army Med. Ctr., Washington, 1996, U. Thessalia, Greece, 1998, many others; mem. med. and sci. com. Arthritis Found. So. Calif., 1974-80; lectr., presenter, cons. in field. Assoc. editor Jour. Clin. Orthopaedics and Related Rsch., 1979—, guest editor, 1983, 84; assoc. editor, mem. editl. bd. Contemporary Orthopaedics, 1980—;. Mem. festival com. St. Anthony's Greek Orthodox, Pasadena, Calif., 1970—, festival chmn., 1971, dir. youth program, 1971-84, mem. ch. bldg. com., 1976-81; basketball commr. Greek Orthodox Youth League So. Calif., 1984-84; active AXIOS Found. of Worthiness-Greek Ams. So. Calif., 1984—; bd. dirs. L.A. Concert Open, 1994—. Named Greek Orthodox Person of the Yr., So. Calif. St. Nectarios Ch., Covina, Calif., 1986; rsch. grantee Am. Arthritis Found., 1968-69, Eli Lilly and Co., 1970-71, 71-72, 72-73, 73-74, 76-77, Bristol Myers Co., 1971-72, Galaxo, 1984, Merck-Germany, 1984, Merrell-Dow, 1987-88, Miles Lab., 1990, R.W. Johnson, 1994, Genetics Inst., 1993-94, 94-95, Abbott Labs., 1996—, Merck Rsch. Labs., 1998-99, Synercid, 1998—, 98—, 99—, others. Mem. AAUP, Am. Acad. Orthopaedic Surgeons (faculty summer inst. 1980-84, mem. com. on evaluation 1986—), Am. Orthopaedic Assn., Assn. Bone and Joint Surgeons, Am. Rheumatism Assn., Western Orthopaedic Assn. (program chmn. 1983-84), Hellenic-Am. Med. Soc. (bd. dirs. 1982-86), Acad. Orthopaedic Soc (mem.-at-large 1995-97), Musculoskeletal Infection Soc. (pres. 1992-93), Calif. Orthopaedic Assn., Calif. Med. Assn., Hippocratic Orthopaedic Soc., L.A. County Med. Assn., U. So. Calif. Grad. Orthopaedic Soc. (program chair 1977-86, pres. 1988-89), Wilson Bost Interurban Club (com. mem. So. Calif. chpt. 1992—), Alpha Epsilon Delta (pres. 1958-59). Office: LA County & USC Med Ctr GNH 3900 1200 N State St Los Angeles CA 90033-1029

PAUL, BINOD BIHARI, engineering educator, researcher; b. Murakari, Shyllet, Bangladesh, Nov. 1, 1943; arrived in India, 1947; s. Banamali and Bindubashi P.; m. Arati Paul, Apr. 17, 1971; children: Bikramjit, Arijit, Debjit. BS in Physics with honors, Presidency Coll., Calcutta, India, 1965; B in Tech., Inst. Radio, Physics & Elec., Calcutta, 1967, M in Tech., 1968, PhD, 1975. Lectr. Inst. Radio, Physics & Elec., 1971-79; reader Banaras Hindu U., Varanasi, India, 1979-86; prof. Banras Hindu U., Varanasi, India, 1986—, chmn. dept. elec. engring., 1988-90, coord. Ctr. Advanced Study dept. elec. engring., 1996; mem. adv. coms. internat. confs.; lectr. in field. Guest editor: Jour. Electronics and Telecomm. Engring.; contbr. numerous articles to profl. publs. including IEEE Transactions on Electron Devices, Jour. Applied Physics, Optical Engring.; mem. editl. bd. sci. jours. Founder, mem. Bengali Soc., 1992—; life mem. Nikhil Bharat Banga, 1995—. Recipient Mometos award Internat. Indian Defense Conf., 1985, 95, Secular India Harmony award, 2000, Millennium medal of honor, 2000, Outstanding Man of the 20th Century, 2000. Mem. Optical Soc. India (life), Semiconductor Soc. India (life, founder, v.p. 1989-93, founder Varanasi chpt., chmn.). Avocation: writing Bengali poetry. Home: Old E/3 BHU Campas, UP Varanasi 221005, India Office: BHU Inst Tech, Dept Elec Engring, UP Varanasi 221005, India

PAUL, CATHERINE J. MORRISON, agricultural educator; b. Champaign, Ill., June 17, 1953; d. Stanley Roy and Phyllis May Morrison; m. Ernst R. Berndt, Jan. 4, 1985 (div. Apr. 1992); m. David J. Paul, Nov. 22, 1998. BA, U. B.C., Vancouver, 1977; MA, U. B.C., 1978, PhD, 1982. Instr. NYU, N.Y.C., 1981-82; from asst. prof. to prof. Tufts U., Medford, Mass., 1982-95; prof. dept. agr. and resource econs. U. Calif., Davis, 1995—; rsch. economist Bur. of Labor Stats., Internat. Affairs and Activities, Divsn. Productivity and Tech., 1981, Nat. Bur. Econ. Rsch., 1983-86, rsch. assoc., 1986-92; guest prof. U. Mannheim, Germany, 1985; vis. scholar Uppsala U., Sweden, Spring 1986, 88, 89; assoc. Conf. on Rsch. in Income and Wealth, 1988—; vis. prof. Bilkent U., Ankara, Turkey, 1989; resident scholar Fed. Res. Bd., 1992; mem. vis. com. to evaluate grad. program Northeastern U., 1993; hon. vis. prof. U. N.S.W., 1996-99. Assoc. editor Jour. of Productivity Analysis, 1984—, Am. Jour. Agrl. Econs., 1996—; contbr. numerous artices to profl. jours.; author: A Microeconomic Approach to the Measurement of Economic Performance: productivity growth, capacity utilization, and related performance indicators, 1992, Cost Structure and the Measurement of Economic Performance: productivity, utilization, cost economies and related performance indicators, 1999. Rsch. grantee NSF, 198386, Mellon Found., 1984, Resources for the future Small Grants Program, 1985, US Dept. Labor, 1994-95, Giannini Found., 1995-96, 97-98, USDA, 1996-97, 98-99; recipient Career Advancement award NSF, 1987-88, Faculty Summer Rsch. award Tufts U., 1989; Can. Coun. fellow, 1977-78, 78-79, Can. Coun. Doctoral fellow 1979-80, 80-81. Office: Univ of Calif-Davis Dept Agrl & Resource Econs One Shields Ave Davis CA 95616

PAUL, DARRELL FREDERICK, state trooper; b. Cairo, Ill., Sept. 26, 1949; s. Alvin Luther and Gertrude (Jones) P.; m. Sandra Justine Merideth Paul, Aug. 7, 1970; 1 child, Darrell F. Paul Jr. AA, Eastern Ky. U., 1981, BS, 1997. Sr. trooper Ky. State Police, Frankfort, 1973—; fire arms instr.; officer survival instr.; police use of force instr. Lance cpl. USMC, 1968-74. Decorated Purple Heart. Mem. Ky. Peace Officers Assn., Ky. State Police Profl. Assn. Baptist. Avocations: target shooting, travel. Home: 1024 W Hebron Ln Shepherdsville KY 40165-7418 Office: Ky State Police PO Box 1297 Elizabethtown KY 42702-1297

PAUL, FRANK ALLEN, physician; b. Joshua Tree, Calif., Oct. 30, 1958; s. Louis Marion and Vivian Anne Paul. AA in Pharmacy and Marine Biology, Fullerton Coll., Calif., 1979; BA in Biochemistry and Biology, Calif. State U., Fullerton, 1982; DO, U. New Eng., 1990. Bd. cert. physician emergency medicine. Store mgr. Alpha Beta Markets, La Habra and Industry, Calif., 1977-81; constrn. supr. Louis M. Paul Constrn. Co., La Habra, 1977-82; co-owner Finecraft Jewelers, Claremont, Calif., 1978—; tchg. fellow U. New Eng., Biddeford, Maine, 1988-89; intern Mt. Clemens (Mich.) Gen. Hosp., 1990-91, resident in emergency medicine, cons. staff, 1991-94; rsch. dir. Herpetol. and Ichthyol. Infectious Disease Rsch. Assocs.; clin. faculty mem. U. New Eng. Coll. Osteo. Medicine, 1994—; dir. edn. and rsch. staff St. Johns Hosp., Springfield, Ill., 1997-2000; clin. asst. prof. So. Ill. U. Sch. Medicine, 1997—, problem based learning tutor; EMS med. dir., staff physician Tucson Heart Hosp., 2000—; med. dir. Ill. Soc. for Respiratory Care, 1998—. Contbr. articles to profl. jours. Recipient Fellowship award Am. Coll. Emergency Physicians (FACEP), 1999, Fellowship award Am. Coll. Osteo. Emergency Physicians (FACOEP), 1999. Mem. Am. Osteo. Assn., Am. Acad. Osteopathy, Am. Coll. Emergency Physicians, Am. Coll. Osteo. Emergency Physicians. Republican. Roman Catholic.

PAUL, JULIAN BRAITHWAITE, media and entertainment company executive; b. Chester, Cheshire, U.K., May 18, 1945; s. Michael Braithwaite and Patricia Elisabeth Ann (Mumm) P.; m. Diana Davies, Nov. 3, 1973; children: Arabella Lucy, Henrietta Charlotte, Rupert Benedict. BA in Philosophy, Politics & Econs., St. John's Coll., Oxford, Eng., 1966, MA, 1969. Trainee acct. Arthur Andersen & Co., U.K., 1966-71; banker Citibank N.A., London and N.Y.C., 1971-74; dep. mng. dir. Banco Hispano Americano Ltd., U.K. and Hong Kong, 1974-87; mng. dir. Guinness Mahon & Co. Ltd., London, U.K., 1987-90; dep. chmn. Castle Comm. PLC, London, U.K., 1991-97; non-exec. chmn. Tele-Cine Cell Group PLC, U.K., 1994-98, Tiger Books Internat. PLC, U.K., 1994-99, Entertainment Rights plc, 1996—; dep. chmn. Eagle Rock Entertainment Plc, U.K., 1997—; non-exec. chmn. Argonaut Games plc, 2000. Pres. Oxford U. Conservative Assn., 1965; county councillor Kent County Coun., 1985-93. Fellow Inst. Chartered Accts.; mem. Carlton Club, Pilgrim's Soc. Avocations: politics, travel. Home and Office: The Mount House, Brasted, Westerham Kent TN16 1JB, England

PAUL, K-LYNN, psychiatric administrator; b. Fergus Falls, Minn., June 14, 1937; s. Lynn and Lettie Ririe Paul; m. Carla Blake, June 17, 1965 (dc. May 1994); children: Richard, William, Robert, John, Kathryn, Eileen; m. Karen Rita Paul, Aug. 23, 1996; 1 stepchild, Kim. Psychiatrist, Okla. U. and Vet. Hosp., Oklahoma City, 1973-86; dir. psychiatric residency tng., U. South Dakota Sch. Med., Sioux Falls, S.D., 1986—; med. dir., Southeastern Behavioral Healthcare, Sioux Falls, S.D., 1989—. Lic. psychiatrist. Psychiatrist Okla. U. and Vets. Hosp., Oklahoma City, 1973-86; dir. psychiat. residency tng. U. S.D. Sch. Medicine, Sioux Falls, 1986—; med. dir. Southeastern Behavioral Healthcare, Sioux Falls, 1989—. Bishop Ch. of Jesus Christ of Latter-day Saints, Sioux Falls, 1999. Maj. U.S. Army, 1971-73. Fellow Am. Psychiat. Assn. (rep.); mem. Am. Assn. of Dirs. of Psychiat. Residency Tng. Mormon. Avocations: hunting, music, church work. E-mail: skueter@usd.edu. Office: U SD Dept Psychiatry 800 E 21st St Sioux Falls SD 57105-1016

PAUL, MAŁGORZATA MARIA, parasitologist, immunologist; b. Swiebodzin, Poland, Aug. 9, 1967; d. Jerzy and Anna (Chrzaszcz) P. Physicial profl. degree, U. Med. Scis. Faculty Medicine, 1992; MD, U. Med. Scis., Poznań, Poland, 1997. Asst. dept. med. microbiology Inst. Microbiology and Infectious Diseases, U. Med. Scis., Poznań, 1997—; mem. European Rsch. Network on Congenital Toxoplasmois, Copenhagen, 1995—; Polish coord. European Multictr. Study on Congenital Toxoplasmosis, London, 1997—. Contbr. articles to profl. publs. Bd. dirs. Found. of the Humanitarian Aid, Poznań, 1994-97. Scientific scholarship U. Grenoble, 1993; rsch. grants Polish Rsch. Com., 1997-99, 99—. Mem. Medicus Munoh Internat., Polish Parasitological Soc. (sec. Poznań sect. 1995—), N.Y. Acad. Sci., Nat. Geog. Soc. Roman Catholic. Avocations: mountain climbing, guide of excursions abroad. Home: Konstytucji 3 Maja 2/93, 63-100 Srem

Poland Office: Inst Microbio/Infect Dis, Wieniawskiego 3, Poznań 61-712, Poland

PAUL, NORMAN LEO, psychiatrist, educator; b. Buffalo, N.Y., July 5, 1926; s. Samuel Joseph and Tannie (Goncharsky) P.; m. Betty Ann Byfield, June 6, 1951 (dec. May 1994); children: Marilyn, David Alexander. MD, U. Buffalo, 1948. Fellow pharmacology U. Cin. Coll. Medicine, Ohio, 1949-50; resident psychiatry Mass. Mental Health Ctr., Boston, 1952-55; fellow child psychiatry James Jackson Putnam Children's Ctr., Boston, 1957-59, Mass. Gen. Hosp., Boston, 1958-59; chief psychiatrist Day Hosp. Mass. Mental Health Ctr., Boston, 1960-64; dir. conjoint family therapy Boston State Hosp., 1964-65, cons. in family psychiatry, 1965-70; assoc. clin. prof. dept. neurology Boston U. Sch. Medicine, 1977—; cons. Mental Health Ctr., Alaska Native Hosp., Anchorage, 1967-68; cons. in family psychiatry Boston VA Hosp., 1967-71, Mass. Soc. for the Prevention of Cruelty to Children, Boston, 1993—; vis. family therapist St. George's Med. Sch., London, 1996-97; lectr. in psychiatry Harvard Med. Sch., Boston, 1976—; faculty assoc. Mgmt. Analysis Corp., Cambridge, Mass., 1979-82; presenter paper Internat. Conf. on Telemedicine and Telecare, London, 1996. Family therapist: (tv documentary) PBS-Trouble in the Family, 1965 (George Foster Peabody award 1965); co-author A Marital Puzzle, 1977, 86, German edit., 1987, French edit., 1995, Chinese edit., 1997. Sponsor Mass. Orgn. to Repeal Abortion Laws, Boston, 1965-70; chair Audio Unit of Child Devel. and Mass Media, White House Conf. on Children and Youth, Washington, 1970; bd. trustees Cambridge (Mass.) Coll., 1977-89; bd. dirs. Let's Face It, 1990—, Ctr. for Family Connections, 1998—. Capt. USAF, 1950-52. Recipient Edward A. Strecker, M.D. award for young psychiatrist of yr., 1966, Cert. of Merit, Mass. Coun. on Family Life, Boston, 1967, Cert. of Commendation, Mass. Assn. for Mental Health, Boston, 1967, Disting. Achievement award Soc. for Family Therapy and Rsch., Boston, 1973, Lifetime Achievement award Mass. Assn. for Marriage and Family Therapy, 1998, Disting. Svc. award Physician Health Svcs., 1998. Fellow Royal Soc. Medicine, Am. Psychiat. Assn. (life); mem. Am. Assn. Marriage and Family Therapy (bd. dirs. 1983-86), Am. Family Therapy Assn. (v.p. 1982-83, Disting. Contbn. award 1984), Assn. for Rsch. in Nervous and Mental Disorders, Group for the Advancement Psychiatry (chair com. on the family 1982-84). Avocations: study of codes, travelling. Office: 394 Lowell St Ste 6 Lexington MA 02420-2549

PAUL, PETER ANDREW, academic administrator; b. Holland, Mich., Oct. 3, 1964; arrived in Japan, 1990; s. Daniel L. and Joan C. (Ten Hoeve) P. AB summa cum laude, Hope Coll., Holland, 1989; student in Politics, Tchrs. Coll. Columbia Univ., 1997. Cert. elem. tchr., Mich., N.Y. Intern Adminstrv. Office U.S. Cts. & D.C. Pub. Defender Svc., Washington, 1989; substitute tchr. Holland and Grand Haven (Mich.) Schs., 1989; tchr. ESL NCA Schs., Shiraoi, Hokkaido, Japan, 1990; acad. dir. NCA Schs., Tomakomai, Hokkaido, Japan, 1991-93; pres. NCA Internat. Schs., Tomakomai, 1994—; grad. intern Tchrs. Network, N.Y.C., 1998; tchr. N.Y.C. Pub. Schs., 1998-99; program assoc. The Tchrs. Network, N.Y.C., 1999-00; asst. dir. The Tchrs. Network, 2000—; pub. spkr./cons. Northern Japan. Named Outstanding Coll. Student Am., 1989; awarded membership Nat. Polit. Sci. Honors Soc., 1989; selected as participant UNESCO regional conf., Hokkaido, 1998—; fellow (hon.) Nat. Tchr. Policy Inst., 1999; named Outstanding Person of 20th Century Internat. Biographical Ctr., England, 2000. Home: 350 Richmond Ter Apt 5H Staten Island NY 10301-1524 Office: NCA Internat Schs, 3 Chome 2 Omotemachi NCA, Tomakomai 053, Japan

PAUL, ROBERT, physician; b. Helsinki, Finland, Nov. 2, 1953; s. Per-Edvard and Vera (Henriksson) P.; m. Riitta Saarinen, 1979; children: Johan, Maria, Henrik, Anna, Emilia. Cand.med., Turku U., Finland, 1975, MD, 1986. Asst. physician Eskilstuna Ctr. Hosp., 1978; asst. physician Turku U. Ctr. Hosp., Finland, 1979-89, sr. physician, 1989-94, sr. lectr., 1993-94; clin. rsch. physician Lilly, Finland, 1994-95, med. dir., 1995-98; med. advisor Novartis, Finland, 1998-99; clin. trial dir. BioTie Therapies, 2000—. Editor Finnish Med. Jour., 1979—; columnist Turun Sanomat, 1997—. Avocations: singing, folk music.

PAUL, ROCHELLE CAROLE, special education educator; b. East Liverpool, Ohio, July 8, 1951; d. Homer Neil and Dolores Elizabeth (Seiler) P. BS, Clarion State Coll., 1973; MS, Clarion U., 1987; MDiv, Trinity Luth. Sem., Columbus, Ohio, 1992. Cert. tchr., Pa., Ohio. Spl. edn. tchr. Dorchester County Bd. Edn., Cambridge, Md., 1973-78, Forest Area Sch. Dist., Tionesta, Pa., 1979-88; edn. coord. juvenile-probate divsn. Common Pleas Ct. of Licking County, Newark, Ohio, 1993-95; instr. Ctrl. Ohio Tech. Coll., Newark, 1994—, program dir. for early childhood assoc. degree, 1999—; prevention specialist Ctr. Alternative Resources, Newark, 1996-98; program dir. early childhood devel. Ctrl. Ohio Tech. Coll., Newark, 1999—. Rep. Pres.'s adv. bd. Trinity Luth. Sem., 1991-92; active St. Paul's Evang. Luth. Ch., Newark, Ohio; mem. LEADS Heart Start Cmty. Assessment Com., 1999—. Mem. ASCD, AAUW, Coun. Exceptional Children (chpt. pres. 1972-73, 98—), Nat. Assn. Edn. of Young Children, Alcohol and Drug Abuse Prevention Assn. Ohio, Ohio Coalition of Assoc. Degree Early Childhood Programs. Avocations: Tai Chi, reading, writing, vocal and instrumental music, travel. Home: 164 Newton Ave Newark OH 43055-4758 Office: Central Ohio Tech Coll 1179 University Dr Newark OH 43055-1766

PAUL, SIGRID, retired social sciences/anthropology educator; b. Leipzig, Sachsen, Germany, Sept. 30, 1929; d. Herbert Friedrich and Anna Marie (Waligora) P. BA, U. Uppsala, Sweden, 1957, PhD, 1962; habilitation, U. Salzburg, Austria, 1978. With h.s. and adult evening schs., Sweden, 1956-62; rsch. asst. Social Psych. Rsch. Ctr. Devel. Planning, Saarbruecken, 1963-69; asst. prof. Inst. Cultural Sociology/U. Salzburg, Salzburg, 1969-78, 1978-85, prof., 1985-90, ret. prof., 1990—; trustee, cons. Found. for Advancement Sci. Rsch., Vienna, 1985-89; cons. univ. entrance without h.s. diploma U. Salzburg, 1985-89. Author: Afrikanische Puppen, 1970, Begegnungen Zur Geschichte Persoenlicher Dokumente in Ethnologie, Soziologie und Psychologie, 1979; editor: Ethnomedizin und Sozialmed. in Tropisch Afrika, 1975, Kultur.Begriff und Wort in China und Japan, 1982; contbr. articles to profl. jours. Recipient scholarship Ohio Wesleyan U., 1954-55; fellowship Alexander von Humboldt Stiftung, 1966-68, 70. Mem. Internat. African Inst., German Assn. Anthropologists, Frobenius Soc. Roman Catholic. Avocations: travelling, hiking, family history research, volunteer social work. Home: Mitterhausen 4, D-94424 Arnstorf Bavaria, Germany Office: Ist Kultursoziol U Salzburg, Rudolfskai 42, A-5020 Salzburg Austria

PAUL, SINDY MICHELLE, preventive medicine physician; b. Phila., Feb. 13, 1957; d. Gerson Stanly and Phyllis (Ostrum) P.; m. Oren Leonard Friedman, Mar. 8, 1986; children: Melissa, Rebecca. AB in Biology hons., magna cum laude, Bryn Mawr (Pa.) Coll., 1979; MD with hons., Temple U., 1983; MPH, N.J. Grad. Program Pub. Health, Piscataway, N.J., 1993. Diplomate Am. Bd. Gen. Preventive Medicine and Pub. Health. Med. dir. N.J. Dept. Health and Sr. Svcs., Trenton, 1988-96, residency program dir., 1995—; asst. clin. prof. U. Medicine and Dentistry N.J., Piscataway, N.J., 1995—; clin. cons. state labs. N.J. Dept. Health and Sr. Svcs., Trenton, 1995—, med. dir., 1996—; mem. exec. com. preventive medicine, pub. health sect. Coll. Physicians of Phila., 1995-97, exec. com. n.e. regional infection control course N.J. chpts. APIC, 1989—. Editor and co-author: (books) Infection Control for Long Term Care Facilities, 1992, HIV/AIDS, 1997; contbr. 150 chpts., abstracts and articles to profl. jours.; mem. editl. adv. bd. (jour.) Infection Control and Hosp. Epidemiology, 1985—, N.J. Medicine., Nursing Spectrum, 2000. Divsn. rep. United Way Campaign, Trenton, N.J., 1988-89. Grantee Ctrs. for Disease Control and Prevention, Atlanta, 1994-98. Mem. Am. Coll. Prevention Medicine (chair joint coun. of residency program dirs.), Assn. for Profls. in Infection Control and Epidemiology, N.J. Pub. Health Assn. (pres.-elect, v.p 1996-2000, mem. exec. bd., pres. elect Ezra Mundy Hunt award, Pres. award for Tb, Pres. award for pub. health), Soc. Healthcare Epidemiology Am. (working group 1995—), Ctrs. for Disease Control and Prevention (5 working groups, 1996—). Office: NJ Dept Health and Sr Svcs 50 E State St Ste 4 Trenton NJ 08608-1715

PAUL, WILLIAM GERALD, educational psychologist; b. Phila., Nov. 27, 1948; s. Walter Michael and Sylvia (Schultz) P. BA in Psychology, Temple U., 1971, MEd in Ednl. Psychology, 1972, PhD in Ednl. Psychology, 1978; postgrad., NYU, 1972-73. Rsch. assoc., statistician Family Ct., 1972; teaching asst. Temple U., Phila., 1976-78; testing and evaluation specialist Sch. Dist. Hamilton Twp., Hamilton Square, N.J., 1979—; part-time rsch. evaluator Child Psychiatry Ctr. St. Christopher's Hosp. for Children, Phila., 1979-82. Mem. Am. Psychol. Assn., Am. Ednl. Rsch. Assn., Nat. Assn. Test Dirs., N.J. Prins. and Suprs. Assn. Home: 1448 Windsor Park Ln Havertown PA 19083-2706 Office: Hamilton Twp Sch Dist 90 Park Ave Hamilton NJ 08690-2024

PAULE, MERLE GALE, pharmacologist; b. Sacramento, June 28, 1952; s. Loren Frenthrup Paule and Edith Anna (Coppin) Lewis; m. Candee Hope Teitel, Jan. 9, 1982; 1 child, Maxwell. AA in Fine Arts, Sacramento City Coll., 1974; BS in Biochemistry, U. Calif., Davis, 1976, PhD in Pharmacology and Toxicology, 1983. Lab. asst. U. Calif., Davis, 1975-77, teaching asst., 1977-78, lab. technician, 1978-81, assoc. in pharmacology, 1981-82; post-doctoral fellow U. Ark. for Med. Scis., Little Rock, 1982-83, instr., 1983; staff fellow Nat. Ctr. for Toxicological Research, Jefferson, Ark., 1983-86, pharmacologist, 1986—. Contbr. articles to sci. and scholarly jours. Mem. Am. Soc. Pharmacology and Experimental Therapeutics, Am. Soc. Primatologists, Behavioral Pharmacology Soc., Neurobehavioral Teratology Soc., Behavioral Toxicology Soc., British Brain Research Assn., European Brain and Behavior Soc., N.Y. Acad. Scis., Soc. Neuroscience, Sigma Xi. Democrat. Avocations: sailing, home video, fishing, outdoor activities, photography. Office: DHHS FDA NCTR Primate Research Facil Jefferson AR 72079

PAULEY, SHIRLEY STEWART, religious organization executive; b. Boston, Sept. 13, 1938; d. Charles Norris and Nellie Consuelo (Yorke) Stewart; m. Edward Haven Pauley, May 29, 1964; children: David Stewart, Deborah Jeanne. BA, Gordon Coll., 1960; postgrad., Ariz. State U., 1961, Boston U., 1963. Sec./receptionist Atwell Co., Boston, summer 1956; sec., typist Kelley Girl, Boston, 1956-60; asst. office mgr. Radiator Chem. Corp., Scottsdale, Ariz., 1960-62; sec., clerical worker GM, Westwood, Mass., 1962-64; v.p. Truth Alive Ministries, Dallas, 1995—. Spkr. At Large, Boston, 1956-60; Sunday sch. tchr. Blaney Meml. Bapt. Ch., Boston, 1956-60; choir dir. Sherwood Bapt. Ch., Phoenix, 1961-62, co-youth dir., 1961; co-youth dir. Blaney Meml. Ch., Boston, 1964-66; mem. book store com. Prestonwood Bapt. Ch., Dallas, 1994—; messenger Bapt. Gen. Conv. Tex., Ft. Worth, 1996. Republican. Avocations: photography, reading, music. Office: Truth Alive Ministries PO Box 794945 Dallas TX 75379-4945

PAULI, JOSEF, computer scientist; b. Hintereben, Bavaria, Germany, Apr. 10, 1960; s. Anton and Maria (Grünberger) P. Dipl.-inform, Tech. U., Munich, 1986, Dr., 1992; Dr.habil., U. Kiel, Germany, 1999. Scientist Tech. U., Munich, 1987-92, U. Kiel, 1993—; project leader U. Kiel, 1993—, tchr. 1993—. Contbr. articles to profl. jours. Mem. Assn. Informatik, Image Graphics Soc. Shanghai. Roman Catholic. Avocation: playing clarinet.

PAULLEY, JOHN WYLMER, gastroenterologist; b. Hastings, Eng., Mar. 2, 1918; s. John and Elisabeth (Green) P.; m. Deirdre Gavin Jones, Mar. 22, 1941 (dec. 1994); four children. MBBS, Middlesex Hosp. Med. Sch., London, 1939, MD, 1944; DSc, U. Buckingham, 1983. House physician Middlesex Hosp., London, 1939-40; flying officer, med. specialist, acting wing comdr. RAF Med. Br., Eng., 1940-46; cons. Ipswich Hosps., Eng., 1949-83; pvt. practice Ipswich, 1983—. Office: Suffolk Nufield Hosp at Christchurch Park, 57-61 Fonnereau Rd, Ipswich IP1 3JN, England

PAULSEN, HARALD, biochemist, researcher; b. Bremen, Germany, Apr. 26, 1953; m. Melinda K. Hoyt, Sept. 4, 1988. Diploma in chemistry, Göttingen (Germany) U., 1978; D in Natural Scis., U. Munich, 1983, Habilitation, 1992. Postdoct. U. Harvard, Cambridge, Mass., 1985-88; tchg. fellow, leader rsch. group U. Munich, 1988-96; prof. U. Mainz, Germany, 1996—; assoc. editor Photochemistry and PhotoBiology, 1996—. Contbr. over 70 articles to sci. publs. Grantee/fellow Studienstiftung des Deutschen Volkes, 1973-80. Office: Univ Mainz Inst Botany, Müllerweg 6, D-55099 Mainz Germany

PAULSEN, REIDAR, pastor; b. Kristiansand, Norway, June 18, 1938; s. Gunnar and Kari (Loge) P.; m. Astrid Sola, July 13, 1963; children: Erik, Kari Anne, Siri, Geir. Tchg. cert., Tchr.'s Coll., Kristiansand, 1961; degree in theology, Free Theol. Faculty, Oslo, Norway, 1967; D in Ministry, Fuller Theol. Sem., Pasadena, Calif., 1981. Pastor Evangelical Lutheran Free Ch., Oslo, 1967-70; sr. pastor Evangelical Lutheran Free Ch., Bergen, Norway, 1970-94, Christ Ch., Bergen, 1994—; nat. denominational bd. Evang. Free Lutheran Ch. of Norway, 1975-81; pres. Ch. Growth Forum Norway, 1981. Author: Filled by the Holy Spirit, 1970, Commentary to Prophets Amos-Malachy, 1971, We Belong Together, 1981, The Salt of the Earth-- The Light of the World, 1989; author, editor: Revival Today, 1972; author: The Same Yesterday and Today, 1989; editor Vision monthly mag., 1991—; contbr. articles to profl. jours, pop. press. Mem. Norwegian Non-Fiction Writers and Translators Assn., Internat. Coalition of Apostles. Home: Ibsensgate 91, N-5052 Bergen Norway Office: Christ Ch, N-5826 Bergen Norway

PAULSON, HENRY MERRITT, JR., venture capitalist, investment banker; b. Palm Beach, Fla., Mar. 28, 1946; s. Henry Merritt and Marianna (Gallaeur) P.; m. Wendy Judge, Sept. 6, 1969; children—Henry Merritt III, Amanda Clark. B.A. in English, Dartmouth Coll., 1968; M.B.A., Harvard U., 1970. Staff asst. to the asst. sec. def. (comptroller) Pentagon, Dept. Def., Washington, 1970-72; staff asst. to the Pres. Domestic Council, The White House, Washington, 1972-73; assoc. Goldman Sachs & Co., Chgo., 1974-77, v.p., 1977-82, ptnr. investment banking dept., 1982—, ptnr. in charge investment banking Midwest region, 1984-90; mgmt. com. co-head investment banking div., vice chmn., COO; CEO, chair Goldman Sachs & Co., Chgo., 1999—. Trustee Chgo. Symphony Orch.; dir. The Peregrine Fund Inc.; adv. bd. J.L. Kellogg grad. sch. of mgmt. NCAA Scholar Athlete, 1967; named to 1st team All-Ivy, All New Eng., All-East; New Eng. Football Coaches' Selection as Outstanding Coll. Lineman, Div. I, New England, 1967. Mem. The Commercial Club (Chgo.), The Econ. Club (Chgo.), Chgo. Club, Phi Beta Kappa. Republican. Mem. Christian Science Ch. Avocations: skiing; fishing; canoeing; tennis. Home: 101 W 67th St Apt 50A New York NY 10023-5952 Office: Goldman Sachs Group 85 Broad St New York NY 10004-2434*

PAULSON, RAYMOND ARNOLD, engineering executive; b. Eagle Rock, Calif., Dec. 29, 1921; s. Arnold Edwin and Clara (Martin) P.; m. Beverly Doris, Sept. 21, 1941; children: Larry, Jerry, Celeste. JD, Calif. Coll. Law; postgrad., Citrus Coll., Nat. Inst., U. S.C. Law instr. U.S. Armed Forces Inst.; dir., mgr. nat. maj. mfr., prodr. tactical army missile The Corporal, 1959; sales mgr., asst. dir. So. Calif. Credit. Bur.; engr., designer radiation and chem. evaluation test labs. USAF; dir., mgr. electro-mech. bus.; founder Calif. Coll. Law; pres. chmn. bd. Paulson Internat. Corp., 1971-90, ret., hon. chmn., 1990—; pres. World Trust Agy. (div. Paulson Devel. Corp.); founder Paulson Products Co.; sole proprietor Paulson Co.; established pvt. trust Paulson Trust; established Guatemala Pvt. Sector Country Trust Fund; devel., instr. exec. leadership tng. program dept. adult edn. Baldwin Pk. Schs. Talent locator "I Love Lucy Show"; designer, assoc. dir. World Internat. Air and Space Show, 1995, Sky Harbor and McCarron Airports, Hdqs. World Air and Space Tours; assoc. designer thermal batter and developer 1st semi-perpetual electric vehicle; pioneered color telecasting; joint originator USMC Christmas program for underprivileged kids Toys for Tots; surveyor, designer U.S. Canal, Brownsville, Tex.; designer Fly by Wire Flight Control Sys.; mfr. 1st all composite single engine two place jet spacecraft in world; designer, developer VAC-PAC All Purpose Shipping Container for ship, rail and truck; designer, prodr. semi-perpetual self-contained charging sys. for electric vehicle battery sources. Leadership tng. dir. Boy Scouts Am., Monte Vista dist. With USAAF, WWII. Recipient Merit award, div. rsch. and sci. guidance L.A. County Supt. Schs. Mem. TV Acad. Arts and Sci. (originator, life assoc. mem.). Fax: 626-332-3436. Office: Paulson Co Internat PO Box 4369 Covina CA 91723-4369

PAULSON-ELLIS, JEREMY DAVID, investment management executive; b. Horley, Surrey, Eng., Sept. 21, 1943; s. Christian William and Vivien Joan (Stevenson) P.-E.; m. Carol Peace (div. 1969); m. Jennifer Jill Milne, Apr. 27, 1973; children: Vivien Louise, Nicholas Jeremy Bruce, Matthew Harry. G-rad. high sch., Sherborne, Eng. Analyst Vickers da Costa, London, 1964-70, ptnr., dir., 1970-85, chmn., 1985-88; chmn. Genesis Investment Mgmt., Ltd., London, 1989—, Genesis Holdings Internat., Ltd., Bermuda, 1989—; mem. adv. coun. Korea Internat. Trust, 1982-87, Seoul Internat. Trust, 1985-87, Thailand Fund, Bangkok, 1986-88; bd. dirs. Japan and Far Ea. Securities Trust Mgmt., Ltd., Hong Kong, 1982-88, The Korea Asia Fund Ltd., 1990-95, The Vietnam Fund, Ltd., Fleming Japanese Investment Trust, Plc; chmn. bd. dirs. Genesis Chile Fund, Ltd., Genesis Malaysia Maju Fund Ltd., Genesis Emerging Markets Fund Ltd. Mem. Heathrow Airport Consultative Com., London, 1984-88. Mem. Ch. of Eng. Home: Broomlands, Langton Green, Kent, Tunbridge Wells TN3 0RA, England Office: Genesis Investment Mgmt, 21 Knightsbridge, London SWIX 7LY, England

PAULU, FRANCES BROWN, international center administrator; b. Hastings, Minn., June 22, 1920; d. Thomas Andrew and Florence Ida (Tuttle) Brown; m. Burton Paulu, June 29, 1942; children: Sarah Leith Paulu Boittin, Nancy Jean Paulu Hyde, Thomas Scott. BA magna cum laude, U. Minn., 1940. Case worker Family Welfare Assn., Mpls., 1943-45; interviewer Cmty. Health and Welfare Coun., Mpls., 1963; sch. social worker Project Head Start, Mpls., 1966; program dir. Minn. Internat. Ctr., Mpls., 1970-72, exec. dir., 1972-89; mem. tourism adv. com. City of Mpls., 1976-83; mem. adv. coun. Minn. World Trade Ctr., 1984-86. Pres. UN Rally, 1970-72; chmn. Mpls. Charter Commn., 1972-74; bd. dirs. Urban Coalition of Mpls., 1967-70; dir. Minn. World Trade Week, 1977-81; participant Intercultural Comm. Project, Japan, 1974; mem. mgmt. team Minn. Awareness Project, 1982-89; dir. Elder Learning Inst., 1995-00; del. Nat. Coun. World Affairs, Taipei-Manila, 1988; coord. Voices from Around the World, 1996—. Recipient Nat. People to People Disting. Membership award, 1987; DeWitt Jennings Payne scholar, 1939-40; fellow U. Minn. Sch. Social Work, 1942-44. Mem. Nat. Coun. Internat. Visitors (officer, mem. exec. com. 1975-81, leader fact-finding team North Africa, Middle East, India 1978, conf. chair 1989), People to People Internat., LWV (pres. Mpls. chpt. 1967-69), UN Assn. Minn. (adv. coun. 1979-92, 96—, sec. 1994-96), Mpls.-St. Paul Com. on Fgn. Rels., Alliance Française (bd. dirs. 1991-94), U. Minn. Women's Club (pres. 1992-94), Phi Beta Kappa, Alpha Omicron Pi, Lambda Alpha Psi. Home: 4300 W River Pkwy Apt 444 Minneapolis MN 55406-3681

PAULUS, CHRISTIAN, maxillofacial plastic surgeon; b. Freiburg, Germany, Sept. 29, 1958; arrived in france, 1979; s. Felix Paulus and Sieglinde Gramlich; m. Sylvie Giraud, July 18, 1986; children: Mathias, Arthur, Carl. MD, U. St. Etienne, 1985. Diplomate specialist in maxillofacial surgery in plastic surgery,. Resident in surgery U. Lyon, France, 1986-91, chief resident, 1991-93; head Hosp. Debrousse, Lyon, 1993—; pvt. practice, Lyon, 1993—. Contbr. articles to med. jours., including French Rev. Stomatology, Annals Plastic Surgery, French Jour. Otorhinolaryngology. Avocations: skiing, playing cello. Office: Hopital Debrousse, 5 Rue Soeur Bouvier, F-69005 Lyon France

PAULUS, WILFRIED GOTTFRIED, chemist; b. Euskirchen, Germany, Jan. 5, 1929; s. Wilhelm and Maria Katharina (Naekel) P.; m. Holde Jänsch, Dec. 27, 1961; children: Anke, Marc. D Natural Sci., U. Bonn, Germany, 1960. Chem. diplomate. Rschr. Inst. Exptl. Ophthalmology, U. Bonn, 1959-60, Chem. Inst. U. Zürich, Switzerland, 1961-62; rschr. devel. and application of microbicides Bayer AG, Germany, 1963-94; cons. biocide application, 1995—. Author: Microbicides for the Protection of Materials, 1993; co-author: Mikrobielle Materialzerstörung und Materialschutz, 1995, Microbially Influenced Corrosion of Materials, 1996; co-editor profl. jours.; contbr. articles to profl. jours.; patentee in field. Mem. German Chem. Soc., German Soc. Naturalists and Physicians, Internat. Biodeterioration Soc., Internat. Biodeterioration Rsch. Group (nat. rep., pres. 1991-92, hon. fellow 1993). Avocations: tennis, travel, sailing, gardening. Home and Office: Deswatines Str 90, 47800 Krefeld Germany

PAUMGARTNER, GUSTAV, hepatologist, educator; b. Neumarkt, Styria, Austria, Nov. 23, 1933; s. Gustav and Grete (Egghart) P.; m. Dagmar List, June 24, 1963 (dec. 1988); m. Christel Köchert, June 26, 1993. Student, Princeton U.; MD, U. Vienna, 1960. Fellow in pharmacology U. Vienna, 1961-63; resident in internal medicine U. Vienna Hosp., 1963-65; fellow in medicine N.J. Coll. Medicine, 1965-66; assoc. dir. dept. clin. pharmacology U. Berne, Switzerland, 1974-79; prof. medicine, chmn. dept. medicine U. Munich, Germany, 1979-99; prof. emeritus, 1999—; chmn. ethics com., med. faculty U. Munich, Germany, 1999—. Author: The Liver, Quantitative Aspects of Structure and Function, 1973; editor Jour. Hepatology; contbr. articles to profl. jours. Fellow Royal Coll. Physicians; mem. European Assn. Study of LIver (sec. 1971-73, pres. 1989), German Soc. Gastroenterology (pres. 1992), German Assn. Study of Liver (pres. 1995). Home: 13 Tassilostrasse, D-82166 Graefelfing Germany Office: U Munich, Klinikum Grosshadern, D-81377 Munich Germany

PAUN, GHEORGHE, mathematician, researcher; b. Cicanesti, Arges, Romania, Dec. 6, 1950; s. Vasile and Floarea (Toma) P.; m. Anisoara Ionescu, Aug. 25, 1974; children: Andrei, Radu. Grad., U. Bucharest, 1974, PhD in Math., 1977; Dr h.c., Internat. Acad. Info., 1998. Programmer Computer Ctr., Bucharest, Romania, 1974-78; rschr. U. Bucharest, 1978-87, 1987-90; rschr. Romanian Acad., Bucharest, 1990—. Author: Generative Mechanisms of Economic Processes, 1980, Matrix Grammars, 1981, Contextual Grammars, 1982, Recent Results in Formal Language Theory, 1983, From the Show of Mathematics, 1983, Between Mathematics and Games, 1986, Mathematics? A Show!, 1988, Introduction to GO, 1985, Solutions for 50 Solitaires, 1987, Two Person Games, 1989, others; (fiction) The Parallel Sphere, 1984, The Generous Circles, 1989, Nineteen Ninety-Four, 1993, Moving Mirrors, 1994, Anghilla Hotel, 1995, Marcus Contextual Grammars, 1997, Grammar Systems: A Grammatical Approach to Distribution and Cooperation, 1994, (with otners) DNA Computing. New Computing Paradigms, 1998, Computing with Cells and Atoms, 2000, others; editor: Mathematical Aspects of Natural and Formal Languages, 1994, Mathematical Linguistics and Related Topics, 1995, Artificial Life: Grammatical Models, 1995, Computing with Bio-Molecules: Theory and Experiments, 1998, Jewels are Forever, 1999, Finite Versus Infinite, 2000, Recent Topics in Mathematical and Computational Linguistics, 2000, others; author articles. Mem. Romanian Soc. Math., Am. Math. Soc., Romanian Writers Assn., Romanian Acad. (corr. mem.). Christian Orthodox. Avocations: logical games, popularization of science. Office: Inst of Math, Po Box 1-764, 70700 Bucharest Romania

PAUNCZ, RUBEN REZSÔ, chemistry educator; b. Szoreg, Hungary, Aug. 8, 1920; s. Ferenc and Sarolta (Popper) P.; m. Miriam Jakabovits, Apr. 20, 1949 (dec. 1984); children: Shmuel, Avraham; m. Kata Heller, Oct. 24, 1985. PhD, Univ. Szeged, 1944, hon. doctorate, 1996. Lectr. Univ. Szeged, 1948-56; sr. lectr. Technion, Haifa, Israel, 1956-60, asst. prof., 1960-62, prof., 1962-88; emeritus, 1988—. Author: Alternant Molecular Obrital Method, 1967, Spin Eigen Functions, 1979, The Unitary Group in Quantum Chemistry, 1981, The Symmetric Group in Quantum Chemistry, 1995. Recipient Excellent Lectr. award Min. of Edn. Hungary, 1956. Mem. Israel Chem. Soc., Royal Soc. Chemistry, Hungarian Acad. Scis., Internat. Acad. Quantum Molecular Sci., European Acad. Arts, Scis. and Humanities. Home: Horeb 48, 34342 Haifa Israel Office: Techion Univ Dept Chem, 32000 Haifa Israel

POUPARD, PAUL CARDINAL, archbishop; b. Aug. 30, 1930. ordained Roman Cath. Ch., 1954. Titular bishop Usula, 1979, archbishop, 1980, proclaimed cardinal, 1985; priest St. Praxedes; pres. Pontifical Coun. Culture, 1988. Address: 00120 Citta del Vaticano, Piazza San Calisto 16, 00153 Rome Italy

PAUREAU, JEAN JULIEN, mechanical engineer; b. Tourlaville, France, May 29, 1940; s. Julien Alfred and Jeanne Marie Paureau; m. Catherine Suzel Chauvet, Dec. 18, 1982; children: Pierre-Jean, Vincent. Engrs. Degree, E.N.S.E.M., Nancy, France, 1964; BSc, U. Marseille, France, 1966; DrIng, U. Grenoble, France, 1971. Draftsman STUDAL, Maxéville, France, 1959-62; engr. Manufacture Française des Pheumatiques Michelin, Clermont-Ferrand, France, 1966-67, Centre Nat. de la Recherche Scientifique, Grenoble, 1967-79, European So. Obs., Geneva, also Munich, Germany, 1979-85; engr., rschr. Inst. Nat. de Recherche et de Sécurité, Vandoeuvre, France, 1985—. Holder several patents. Avocations: cycling, cross-country skiing, mountaineering, reading. Office: INRS, Ave de Bourgogne BP 27, F-54501 Vandoeuvre France

PAUS, RALF, dermatologist; b. Muenster, Germany, Sept. 10, 1960; s. Johannes and Eva-Maria (Urban) P.; m. Silvia Bulfone, June 10, 1990; children: Anna, Lisa, Leo. MD, Freie U., Berlin, 1987. Lic. MD, Berlin. Intern U. Hosp. of Basel, Zurich, Switzerland, 1986; postdoctoral fellow Sch. Medicine Yale U., New Haven, 1987-90; resident dermatology, rsch. assoc. Freie U., 1990-95; dermatologist, asst. prof., head hair rsch. group Humboldt U., Berlin, 1996-99; prof., vice chmn. dept. dermatology U. Hamburg, 1999—. Mem. AAAS, N.Y. Acad. Sci., Ea. Soc. Dermatol. Rsch., Soc.

Invest Dermatol., European Hair Rsch. Soc., Arbeitsgemeinschaft Dermatologische Forschung, Japanese Soc. Investigative Dermatolgy. E-mail: paus@uke.uni-hamburg.de. Home: Bei der Pulvermühle 25B, D-22453 Hamburg Germany Office: U Hosp Eppendorf, Dept Dermatology, D-20246 Hamburg Germany also: Univ Hautklinik und Polikli, Martinistr 52, 20246 Hamburg Germany

PAUW, ANTON, biologist, photographer; b. Cape Town, We. Cape, South Africa, Nov. 5, 1970; s. Charl Cilliers and Jennifer P. BS, U. Cape Town, 1991, BS with honors, 1992, postgrad., 1992—. Field asst. natural history unit BBC, Bristol, 1994-95, scientific advisor, asst. prodr. natural history unit, 1996-98; cons. Struik Publs., Cape Town, 1998. Author, photographer: Tabel Mountain: a natural history, 1999. Recipient Young Scientist award South African Assn. Botanists. Office: U Cape Town, Dept Botany Pvt Bag, Rondebosch 7701, South Africa

PAUW, DIRK ANTON, Greek and Latin studies educator; b. Petauke, Zambia, Apr. 1, 1943; s. Jacobus Christoff and Elizabeth Murais (Van Velden) P.; m. Marianne Alel Hunter, Dec. 7, 1968; children: Rykie, Elmavie, Anton. BA with honors, U. Pretoria, 1965, MA, 1967; Drs. Litt et Phil, U. Leiden, The Netherlands, 1970, D. Litt et Phil, 1972. Cert. lectr. and prof. in Greek, Latin, ancient history. Jr. lectr. U. Pretoria, 1967; lectr. U. South Africa, 1968-70; sr. lectr. Rand Afrikaans U., Johannesburg, South Africa, 1970-80; prof. Rand Afrikaans U., Johannesburg, 1981—. Author: (book) Die Dramatiese Elemente in de Antieke Geskiedskungwing, 1986. Sgt. South African Def. Force, 1969-77. Avocations: gardening, jogging. Home: 40 Soutpans Ave, 2195 Johannesburg South Africa Office: Rand Afrikaans U, PO Box 524 Auckland Park, 2006 Johannesburg South Africa

PAVANELLI, JAMES PAOLO, business executive, financial adviser; b. Migliarino, Italy, Sept. 17, 1946; s. Battista and Gina Lucia (Mazzini) P.; m. Sarah Jane Duncan, June 5, 1966 (div. Mar. 1986); children: Alice Lara, Emma. Student, Internat. House, London, 1965, LSE, London, 1966-67, CNRS, Paris, 1980-81. Interpreter Peruvian Embassy, London, 1964-65; clk. C.I.T. Travel, London, 1965-66; mgr. Kabsiena Ltd., London, 1966-69, pres., 1969-70; fin. adviser S.M.C. Ltd., Geneva, 1971-73; mgr. Keiruse Mcht. Bank, Beirut, 1973-75; fin. dir. Lanerossi Eni Group, Paris, 1976-77; CEO J.P.P. Internat., Paris, 1977-80, First Fin. Corp., Paris, 1981-85, Gruppo Triad-FFC S.A., Torino, Italy, 1986—; v.p. Credito Mercantile SA, Torino, 1996—; Author and speaker in field. Orgn. planner Democrazia Christiana, Genoa, Italy, 1970-75; adviser Italian Cath. Ch., London, 1988-89. Mem. K.M. (fin. adviser). Roman Catholic. Avocations: languages, politics, classical music, travel. Office: Gruppo Triad-FFC SA, Via A Gramsci n 12, 10123 Turin Italy also: Credito Mercantile SA, Piazza Carlo Felice 7, 10123 Torino Italy

PAVAROTTI, LUCIANO, lyric tenor; b. Modena, Italy, Oct. 12, 1935; s. Fernando and Adele (Venturi) P.; m. Adua Veroni, Sept. 30, 1961; children—Lorenza, Cristina, Giuliana. Diploma magistrale, Istituto Magistrale Carlo Sigonio, 1955; studies with, Arrigo Pola, Ettore Campogalliani. Formerly tchr. elem. schs.; salesman ins. Debut as Rodolfo in La Bohème, Reggio Emilia, Italy, 1961; roles include Edgardo in debut Lucia di Lammermoor, Amsterdam, 1963, the Duke in debut Rigoletto,Carpi, 1961, Rodolfo in La Bohème, Covent Garden, 1963, Tonio in debut The Daughter of the Regiment, Covent Garden, 1966, appeared in Lucia di Lammermoor, Australia, 1965, Am. debut, Miami, Fla., 1965; numerous European performances including Italy, Vienna Staatsoper, Paris; performed with San Francisco Opera, 1967, debut, Met. Opera, N.Y.C., 1968; appeared in The Daughter of the Regiment, Met. Opera, 1971, Elisir d'Amore, Met. Opera, 1973, La Bohème, Chgo. Opera, 1973, La Favorita, San Francisco Opera, 1973, Il Trovatore, San Francisco Opera, 1975, Bellini I Puritani, Met. Opera, 1976, Ponchielli La Gioconda, San Francisco Opera, 1979, Aida, San Francisco Opera, 1981, Mozart, Idomeneo, Met. Opera, 1982, Verdi, Ernani, Met. Opera, 1983, Tosca, Met. Opera, 1995; numerous internat. performances including La Scala, Milan, Hamburg, Teatro Colon, Buenos Aires, Australian Opera, Sydney; concert series of Am. and internat. cities, including Carnegie Hall, 1973, Buenos Aires, Moscow, Beijing, Hong Kong, Tokyo, including arena concerts, Madison Square Garden, 1984, and major cities in America, Europe, South America; appeared in film Yes, Giorgio, 1983; established Opera Co. of Philadelphia/Luciano Pavarotti Vocal Competition, 1980; rec. artist on Winner Concorso Internationale, Reggio Emilia, 1961, Amore, 1992, Pavarotti and Friends, 1993, Ti Amo-Puccini's Greatest Love Songs, 1993, Pavarotti and Friends 2, 1995; appeared in PBS TV spl. (with Placido Domingo & Jose Carreras) The Three Tenors, 1994. Named Artist of Yr. Gramophone, 1992; recipient Grammy award, 1981, 1988. Office: care Herbert Breslin 119 W 57th St New York NY 10019-2303

PAVCNIK, DUSAN, researcher, educator; b. Ljubljana, Slovenia, Apr. 24, 1948; s. Leopold and Danica Kovac P.; m. Martina Basin, July 10, 1971; children: Nina, Maja. MD, Sch. Medicine, Ljubljana, 1973; PhD, U. Ljubljana, 1989. Resident in radiology Inst. Roentgenology, Ljubljana, 1976-80; radiologist Hosp. Dr. Franc Dergane, Nova Gorica, Slovenia, 1980-83; asst. prof. radiology Sch. Medicine, Ljubljana, 1983-89, assoc. prof., 1989-93, prof., 1993-95; rsch. fellow Harvard Med. Sch., Boston, 1984-85; vis. scientist MD Anderson Cancer Ctr., Houston, 1990-91; rsch. prof. Dotter Internventional Inst. Oreg. Health Sci. U., Portland, 1995—; collaborative scientist Oreg. Primate Rsch. Ctr., Portland; mem. adv. bd. Jour. Radiology and Oncology, Ljubljana. Inventor square stent based devices, venous valve, large vessel occluder, drum occluder stent graft for treatment of abdominal aortic aneurysms and monodisk; editor Radiologia Yugoslavica, 1981-91 (diploma award 1987). Pres. Slovenian Soc. Radiology, 1982-95. Recipient Cardiovasc. and Interventional Radiology Rsch. and Edn. Found. award, 1998; grantee Cook Inc., Bloomington, Ind., 1999, Copenhagen, 1996; Gianturco rsch. fellow, 1990-91. Fellow Cardiovascular and Interventional Radiol. Soc. Europe (cert. recognition 1996, 97, Best Poster award 1999). Avocations: running, hiking, reading, gardening.

PAVELKA, ELAINE BLANCHE, mathematics educator; b. Chgo.; d. Frank Joseph and Mildred Bohumila (Seidl) P.;. BA, MS, Northwestern U.; PhD, U. Ill. With Northwestern U. Aerial Measurements lab., Evanston, Ill.; tchr. Leyden Cmty. H.S., Franklin Park, Ill.; prof. math. Morton Coll., Cicero, Ill.; invited prof. Internat. Congress on Math. Edn., Karlsruhe, Germany, 1976. RecipientSci. Talent award Westinghouse Electric Co. Mem. Am. Edn. Rsch. Assn., Am. Math. Assn. 2-Yr. Colls., Am. Math. Soc., Assn. Women in Math., Can. Soc. History and Philosophy of Math., Ill. Coun. Tchrs. Math., Ill. Math. Assn. C.C., Math. Assn. Am. Math. Action Group, Ga. Ctr. Study and Tchg. and Learning Math., Nat. Coun. Tchrs. Math., Sch. Sci. and Math. Assn., Northwestern U. Alumni Assn., U. Ill. Alumni Assn., Am. Mensa Ltd., Intertel, Sigma Delta Epsilon, Pi Mu Epsilon. Home: PO Box 7312 Westchester IL 60154-7312

PAVENTI, SAVERIO, anesthesiologist; b. Rome, Jan. 27, 1964; s. Michele Antonio Paventi and Filomena Di Bella; m. Maria Annunziata Parafati, June 14, 1996. Med. diploma, U. La Sapienza, Rome, 1993, PhD in Cardiology, 1996. Assoc. physician Sandro Pertini Hosp., Rome, 1993-96; chief physician Clinica Latina, Rome, 1996-98, assoc. echocardiographer, 1995-98; assoc. physician Emergency Dept. 118, Rieti, Italy, 1996-97; chief resident in anesthesiology U. Cattolica del Sacro Cuore, Rome, 1998—; expert in medicine Law Ct. Rome, 1996-99; med. cons. Ente Nazionale Energia Electrica, Rome, 1993-96, Vatican City State, 1998. Fellow Italian Soc. Cardiology, Italian Soc. Anesthesiology and Intensive Care; mem. European Soc. Anesthesiology. Roman Catholic. Avocations: swimming, tennis, painting, reading, travel. Office: U Cattolica del Sacro Cuore, Largo A Gemelli 8, 00100 Rome Italy

PAVER, WILLIAM KENNETH, dermatologist; b. Sydney, NSW, Australia, May 24, 1920; s. William Amedee and Rebeca Gertrude (Harper) P.; m. Elaine Kathleen Kerr, May 15, 1948; children: Graham, Robert, Philip, Ian, Catherine. MB, BChir, U. Sydney, Australia, 1952, diploma in dermatol. medicine, 1964. Resident med. officer Royal North Shore Hosp., Sydney, Australia, 1952-53; gen. practitioner Merrylands, Sydney, 1953-62; cons. physician pvt. practice, Parramatta Dist. Hosp., Sydney, 1958-62; cons. dermatologist pvt. practice, St. Vincent's Hosp., Sydney, 1964-87; co-founder Merryland gen. practice edn. faculty, 1955-61; sr. cons. rehab., Commonwealth of Australia, Sydney, 1961-65; lectr. dermatology, U. New South Wales, Sydney, 1966-76; chmn. dept. dermatology, St. Vincent's Hosp., Sydney, 1966-76; chmn. Skin and Cancer Found., Sydney, 1978-86. Contbr. numerous articles to profl. jours.; creator of A system of Diagnosis used in tchg. med. students and gen. practitioners; initiator of changes in basic tng. of dermatologists to include mechanism of the diseases; pioneered subspecialization into dermatology. Founder Skin and Cancer Found. for charity dermatology treatment, Psoraisis Assn. of New South Wales in Sydney, life mem. and patron, 1990. Capt. AIF 1939-45, Australia. Decorated mem. Order of Australia, Queen; recipient medal Brit. Assn. Dermatologists, 1964, Molesworth prize, 1983, FRATADD prize U. New S. Wales, Sydney, 1983; Ken Paver medal given to outstanding student by Australian Coll. Dermatologists, 1986—. Fellow Royal Australian Coll. Physicians; mem. Securities Inst. Australia (assoc.). Achievements include pioneering of puva and supspecialisation in dermatology into Australia. Avocations: historic writings, woodwork. Home: 61 A Albany St, East Gosford NSW 2250, Australia

PAVIČIĆ, MLADEN, physicist, educator; b. Zagreb, Croatia, July 4, 1948; s. Dragutin and Mira (Zec) P.; m. Dubravka Ravlić, 1981; 1 child, Karlo Ivan. Degree in Physics Engring., U. Zagreb, 1973, DSc in Physics, 1981; PhD in Physics, U. Belgrade, Yugoslavia, 1986. Asst. Inst. Rudjer Bošković, Zagreb, 1973-74; asst. U. Zagreb, 1979-81, main asst., 1982-89, asst. prof., 1990-95, assoc. prof., 1996—, sr. sci. assoc., 1994—; head sci. project Ministry of Sci., Zagreb, 1991-96, head sci. project Quantum Computation and Quantum Comm., Ministry of Sci., Zagreb, 1996—; vis. prof. U. Md., Balt., 1999-2000. Author: Solved Problems in Physics, 1982, 2d edit., 1984; contbr. articles to profl. jours. Grantee Alexander von Humboldt Found., Cologne, 1988-90, Berlin, 1993, 95, 96, French Ministry Sci., Reims, 1992, Austrian Ministry of Sci., Vienna, Austria, 1993, 94, 95, 96, Erwin Schroedinger Inst., Vienna, 2000; Fulbright sr. scholar, Balt. 1999-2000. Mem. Internat. Quantum Structures Assn. (co-founder, nominating com. 1992-94), European Phys. Soc., Optical Soc. Am., Croatian Phys. Soc., Croatian Math. Soc. Achievements include proof of Pauli Non-Uniqueness, discovery of an interaction-free destruction of atom interference pattern, discovery of polarization correlation between beams of unpolarized light, discovery of a nondistributive model for classical logic and co-discovery of a non-orthomodular model for quantum logic; co-discovery of a second infinite class of equations of infinite dimensional Hilbert Space; use of non-spin preparation to preselect independent particles into a pure spin superposition state; co-formulation of a resonator interaction free detection. Office: Univ Zagreb, Kačićeva 26 Box 217, HR-10001 Zagreb Croatia

PAVITT, WILLIAM HESSER, JR., lawyer; b. Bklyn., Dec. 9, 1916; s. William Hesser and Elsie (Haring) P.; m. Mary Oden, June 19, 1937; children: William, Howard, Gale, Bruce. BA, Columbia U., 1937; JD, 1939. Bar: N.Y. 1939, Philippines 1945, Md. 1946, D.C. 1947, Ohio 1955, Calif. 1958. Law clk. to judge N.Y. Ct. Appeals, 1939-40; assoc. Spence, Windels, Walser, Hotchkiss & Angell, N.Y.C., 1940-44; contracting officer Office of Rsch. and Inventions (now Office of Naval Rsch.), Washington, 1946-48; assoc. Richard Whiting, Whiting and Pavitt, Washington, 1948-54, Toulmin & Toulmin, Dayton, Ohio, 1954-57, Smyth & Roston, L.A., 1957-59; ptnr. Smyth, Roston & Pavitt, L.A., 1960-81; sr. ptnr. Beehler & Pavitt, L.A., 1981—. Mem. L.A. Intellectual Property Law Assn. (pres. 1969-70, chmn. Calif. state bar patent sect. 1971-72). Office: 100 Corporate Pointe Ste 300 Culver City CA 90230-7612

PAVLAKOS, ELLEN TSATIRI, sculptor; b. Athens, May 25, 1936; d. Andrew and Katherine (Fliskanopoulou) Tsatiri; m. Andrew George Pavlakos, Nov. 2, 1952; children: James, John Andrew. Student, Arsakeion, Athens, 1952, Norton Sch. Art, West Palm Beach, Fla., 1975-79, Nat. Acad. Design, N.Y.C., 1980-81. Solo shows include Brevard Art Mus., 1981, Hess Galleries, Allentown, Pa., 1983, Cultural Ctr. Athens, 1990, 5th Ave. Art Gallery, Melbourne, Fla., 1994, 98; group shows include Le Salon des Nations, Paris, 1984, Nat. Exhbn. of Contemporary Realism in Art, Springfield, Mass., 1984, Springville Mus. Art, Utah, 1985, Capitol Gallery, Fla. Dept. Cultural Affairs, Tallahassee, 1988, Outstanding Am. Women Artists Invitational, Sarasota, 1993, Chamber of fine Arts and Min. of Edn. and Civilization Symposium, Nicosia, Cyprus, 1994, Mus. of Art and Sci., Melbourne, 1996, Appleton Mus. Art, Ocala, Fla., 1997, Sculpture '97, Thessaloniki, Greece, 1997, Dunedin (Fla.) Fine Arts Ctr., 1998, Orlando City Hall Gallery, 1998, 621 Gallary, Tallahassee, Fla., 1999, Lee County Alliance of the Arts, Fort Myers, Fla., 1999; bronze sculpture commd. The Harry T. Moore Monument, Titusville Social Svcs. Ctr., 1985, wall relief Knowledge, Brevard Libr., 1993, bronze sculpture Mother Earth, Penakotheke, Athens, 1990, painting Interlude, Penakotheke, Hydrostone sculpture The Flame Keeper, Kennedy Space Ctr., Fla., 1992, Stephen Girard relief Girard Coll., Phila., 1999. Recipient best of Show award Brevard Art Mus., 1980; grantee Brevard County Art in Pub. Places, 1990, 93. Mem. Acad. Artists Assn., Medalic Sculpture Assn., Chamber of Visual Arts in Greece, Nat. League of Am. Pen Women, Ten Women in Art. Greek Orthodox. Avocation: art collecting, gardening. Fax: 407-773-2266. Studio: 331 Coral Way W Indialantic FL 32903-4401

PAVLE PATRIARCH, STOJCEVIC GOJKO, head religious order; b. Kucanci, Donji Miholjac, Serbia, Sept. 1, 1914. Grad., U. Sarajevo, Yugoslavia, 1936, U. Belgrade, Yugoslavia, 1940; postgrad., U. Athens, Greece, 1956; PhD (hon.), U. Belgrade, 1988, St. Vladimir's Theol. Acad., N.Y., 1993. Catechist Serbian Orthodox Ch., Banja Koviljaca, 1944; monk Serbian Orthodox Ch., Raca, 1948, hieromonk, 1954; archimadrite Serbian Orthodox Ch., Belgrade, 1957, bishop of Raska-Prizren, 1957; patriarch Serbian Orthodox Ch., 1990—; pres. Commn. Revision of New Testament, Serbia, 1968-84. Author: Clarifications on Some Questions of Our Faith, 1998; editor Serbicon; editor liturgical books; contbr. articles to profl. jours. Office: Serbian Orthodox Ch, PO Box 182 Kralja Petra 5, 11001 Belgrade Yugoslavia

PAVLICEK, TOMAS, biology researcher; b. Oucmanice, Czech Republic, Nov. 9, 1961; s. Josef and Marie (Lnenicka) P. MSc, T.G. Masaryk U., 1986; RNDr., Charles U., 1987; PhD, Czech Acad. Scis., 1991. Postdoctoral Inst. of Evolution, U. Haifa, Israel, 1991-93, 94-97, associated rschr., 1997—; rschr. Inst. of Entomology, Czech Acad. Scis., 1993-94. Avocations: entomology, traveling, science-fiction, philosophy, history. Office: Inst Evolution U Haifa, Mt Carmel, 31 905 Haifa Israel

PAVLICHENKOV, IGOR MIKHAILOVITCH, physicist, researcher; b. Reutov, Russia, Dec. 4, 1934; s. Mikhail Ivonovitch and Mariya Alekseevna (Muravleva) P.; m. Olga Sergeevna Yavorskaya, Nov. 11, 1972; 1 child, Andrey Igorevitch. Grad. in physics, Moscow U., 1958; Candidate of Physics, Joint Inst. Nuclear Rsch., Dubna, Russia, 1964; D Physics, Kurchatov Inst. Atomic Energy, Moscow, 1982. From jr. rschr. to leading rschr. Kurchatov Inst. Atomic Energy (now Russian Rsch. Ctr.), Moscow, 1958-93; prin. rschr. Russian Rsch. Ctr., Moscow, 1993—; assoc. prof. Engring.-Phys. Inst., Moscow, 1979-90; mem. Russian Nuclear Rsch. Program Com., Moscow, 1986-90; vis. prof. physics U. Littoral, Dunkerque, France, 1995. Contbr. articles to profl. jours. including Jour. Exptl. Theoretical Physics, Phys. Reports, Phys. Rev. C. Recipient I.V. Kuzchatov ann. prize, 1988, 94; Soros grant Internat. Sci. Found., N.Y.C. and Moscow, 1994-95. Avocation: mountain climbing. Office: Russian Rsch Ctr Kurchatov Inst, Kurchatov Sq 1, 123182 Moscow Russia

PAVLIK, IVO, microbiologist, veterinarian researcher; b. Domažlice, Czech Republic, Dec. 29, 1961; s. Ivo and Marie (Plšková) P.; m. Hana Hakenova, Oct. 24, 1987; children: Eliška, Hana. DVM, Vet. U., Brno, Czech Republic, 1986, CSc, 1993. Doctoral student Vet. Rsch. Inst., Brno, Czech Republic, 1989-92, postdoctoral, 1993-94, head unit, 1995—, assoc. prof., 2000—; head Ctr. for Tuberculosis, Paratuberculosis and Mycobacterioses for State Vet. Adminstr., Vet. Rsch. Inst., Brno, 1996. Contbr. numerous articles to profl. jours. Head Ciconia-Club-Ornithology, Brno, 1992—. Grantee Grant of the Czech Republic, Prague, 1993-95, 95-97. Avocation: ornithology. Home: Sumavska 38, 60200 Brno Czech Republic Office: Vet Rsch Inst, Hudcova 70, 621 32 Brno Czech Republic

PAVLIN, ZDENKO, forestry educator, researcher; b. Sisak, Croatia, Feb. 16, 1929; s. Franjo and Paula (Zecic) P.; m. Ana Stankovic, Apr. 26, 1961; 1 child, Mirna. Diploma in timber industry engring., U. Zagreb, Croatia, 1954; MSc, U. Zagreb, 1967, DSc, 1975. Asst. Design Orgn. of Timber Industry, Zagreb, 1954-56; investigator Rsch. Inst. for Timber Industry, Zagreb, 1956-58; asst. faculty of forestry U. Zagreb, 1958-75, asst. prof., 1975-80, assoc. prof., 1980-85, prof., 1985-95; asst. prof. U. Ljubljana, Slovenia, 1975-80; assoc. prof. U. Ljubljana, 1980-85, prof., 1985-95; assoc. dean faculty of forestry U. Zagreb, 1978-82, dean of faculty, 1988-90, mem. univ. coun., 1990-94. Inventor in field. Mem. Internat. Union of Forestry Rsch. Orgns. (working party for wood drying 1972-96). Roman Catholic. Avocations: tennis, skiing, swimming. Home: Panciceva 3, 10000 Zagreb Croatia

PAVLOSKI, VERONICA THERESA, corporate communications specialist; b. Bklyn., June 23, 1966; d. John W. and Veronica Theresa (Bartelotti) P. BA magna cum laude, Seton Hall U., 1988. Lic. FCC operator. Rsch. analyst Katz Comm., Inc., N.Y.C., 1988; rsch. assoc. CMRA, Emerson, N.J., 1990—; staff, engr. WSOU-FM, South Orange, N.J., 1986. Computer graphics exhbns. include Images '88 Communication Arts Festival, 1988. Avocations: sketching, videography, claymation, reading, French cooking. Office: CMRA 134 E Ackerman Ave Emerson NJ 07630-1923

PAVLOV, ALEKSANDR, Kazakhstani government official; b. Pavlodar, Jan. 1, 1953. Grad., Byelorussian Inst. Nat. Econ. Min. finance Govt. Kazakhstan, Almaty, 1994—, dep. prime min. Office: Ministry of Finance, pl Respubliki 4, Almaty 480090, Kazakhstan*

PAVLOV, ALEXANDER VLADIMIROVICH, optics scientist; b. Leningrad, Russia, June 1, 1957; s. Vladimir Grigor'ievich and Irina Nikolaevna (Konushkova) P. Engr.-rschr. in optics, Inst. Fine Mechanics & Optics, Leningrad, 1980; PhD in Opto-Electronics, S.I. Vavilov State Opt. Inst., St. Petersburg, Russia, 1996. Probationer-rschr. S.I. Vavilov State Optical Inst., Leningrad, 1980; sr. rschr. S.I. Vavilov State Optical Inst., St. Petersburg; sr. scientist in opto-electronic devices S.I. Vasilov State Optical Inst., St. Petersburg, 1998; organizer spl. session Internat. Conf. on Neural Info. Processing, Dunedin, New Zealand, 1997, mem. Progr. Comm. of Int. Conf. Neural Computations, 2000. Contbr. articles to profl. jours. Mem. European Optical Soc. Mem. Russian Orthodox Ch. Avocation: Newfoundland dogs. Home: 353 Fontanka 2, 191187 Saint Petersburg Russia Office: SI Vavilov State Opt Inst, 12 Bizgevaya Line, 199034 Saint Petersburg Russia

PAVLOV, DETCHKO, chemical engineer; b. Chipka, Bulgaria, Sept. 9, 1930; s. Pavel Detchkov Milev and Ekaterina Dimitrova Pinteva Mileva; m. Svetla Raicheva, Apr. 7, 1957. Chem. Engr., Higher Inst. of Chem. Tech., Sofia, Bulgaria, 1953; DSc, Cen. Lab. of Electrochem., Power Sources/Bulgarian Acad. Scis., 1984. Asst. prof. Higher Inst. of Chem. Engring., Sofia, 1953-61; rsch. assoc. Inst. of Phys. Chem./Bulgarian Acad. of Scis., Sofia, 1961-67; rsch. assoc. Cen. Lab. Electrochem. Power Sources/Bulgarian Acad. Scis., 1967-70, assoc. prof., 1970-85, prof. electrochemistry, 1986-89, corrs. mem., 1989-97, full mem., 1997—, sr. rsch. scientist, 1986—; head of lead-acid battery dept., Cen. Lab. Electrochem. Power Sources, Bulgarian Acad. Scis., 1967—, dep. dir., 1972-93; chmn. LABAT Internat. Conf., 1989, 93, 96, 99. Author: (books) Power Sources for Electric Vehicles, 1984, 91; contbr. articles to profl. jours.; patentee in field; editor: 5 Vols. Jour. of Power Sources. Lt. chem. troops Bulgarian Army, 1954. Recipient Rsch. award Australian-European Com., Fed. Ministry of Edn., Australia, 1980, Rsch. award U.S. Electrochem. Soc., 1984, Gaston Plante medal Bulgarian Acad. Scis., 1994. Mem. Bulgarian Acad. Scis., Electrochem. Soc., Internat. Alpha/Beta soc. Avocations: classical music, photography. Home: 81/B, Frederick Joliot-Curie Blvd, Sofia 1113, Bulgaria Office: Bulgarian Acad Scis, Acad G Bonchev St Block 10, Sofia 1113, Bulgaria

PAVLOV, DIMITRI ALEXANDROVICH, biologist; b. Moscow, Sept. 25, 1951; s. Alexandr Efimovich and Tsetsilia Vladimirovna (Riskind) P.; m. Alexandra Vasil'evna Morozova, Mar. 20, 1981; 1 child, Efim. Degree in biology-ichthyology, Moscow State U., 1974, PhD, 1979. Lab. worker Moscow State U., 1974-75, rsch. biologist, 1975—. Author: Salmonids (Biology of Reproduction and Development), 1989; patentee method for insemination of wolffish. Mem. Fish Ontogeny Network Europe (assoc.). Home: Lenin Prospect 68, 47, 117296 Moscow Russia Office: Moscow State Univ, Dept Biology, Lengory, MGU, 119899 Moscow Russia

PAVLOV, MIKHAIL, electrochemist, researcher; b. Moscow, Sept. 9, 1966; came to U.S., 1993; s. Yury and Elena Pavlov; m. Alexandra Pavlova, Nov. 30, 1992; 1 child, Valerie. BS in Metallurgy, Moscow Inst. Steel and Alloys, 1988, MS in Electrochemistry, 1991. R & D electrochemist Ginalmazzoloto, Moscow, 1988-93, ECI Tech., East Rutherford, N.J., 1993—. Contbr. articles to profl. jours. Recipient award R & D 100 Mag., 1994. Mem. Am. Soc. Electroplaters and Surface Finishers, Electrochem. Soc., N.Y. Acad. Scis. Avocations: skiing, swimming. Home: 24 Day St Apt C24 Clifton NJ 07011-2552 Office: ECI Tech 1 Madison St East Rutherford NJ 07073-1605

PAVLOV, VALERIY ARKADJEVICH, chemist; b. Kazan, Tatarstan, Russia, Nov. 4, 1949; s. Arkadiy Aleksandrovich Pavlov and Anastasija Stepanovna Zorova; m. Rausa Samigullina, Sept. 24, 1971; children: Oleg, Igor. BSc in Organic Chemistry, Kaszan Inst. Chem. Tech., Russia, 1972, PhD in Organophosphorus Chemistry, 1978, DSc in Organoelement Chemistry, 1999. Rschr. dept. organic chemistry Kazan Inst. of Chem. Technology, 1972-74, post-doctoral rschr., 1978-79, asst. prof., 1979-84, assoc. prof., 1985-89, rsch. prof., 1989-99; rsch. prof. dept. chemistry UCLA, Loma Linda U. Sch. Medicine, 2000—; head of dept. internat. rels. dept. Kazan U. Tech., 1989-91; postgrad. fellow Moscow State U., 1976-77; postdoctoral fellow Queen Elizabeth Coll./U. London, 1984-85; vis. prof. chemistry Inst. Organ Chemistry, U. Gottingen, Germany, 1997. Author: Practical Organic Chemistry, 1993; patentee in field; contbr. papers to profl. jours. Recipient Soros award Internat. Sci. Found., Washington, 1993, 99, INTAS award Internat. Assn., Brussels, 1995; named Soros prof. Internat. Soros Sci. Edn. Program, Washington, 1999. Mem. Am. Chem. Soc., N.Y. Acad. Scis. Avocations: touring, football, skiing. Home: 1325 E Citrus Ave Apt 5A Redlands CA 92374-4079 Office: Lab Chem Endocrinology Sch Medicine Loma Linda Univ Loma Linda CA 92350-0001

PAVLOV, VLADIMIR KUZMICH, oceanographer; b. St. Petersburg, Russia, Mar. 26, 1949; s. Kuzma Semenovich and Anna Akimovna (Veykova) P.; m. Olga Alexandrovna Razumova, Dec. 11, 1992; children: Pavel, Natalya. PhD in Phys. Oceanography, Arctic/Artarctic Rsch. Inst., 1981. Rsch. scientist Arctic and Antarctic Rsch. Inst., St. Petersburg, 1972-80, sr. scientist, 1980-99; rsch. scientist Norwegian Polar Inst., Tromsø, 1999—. Contbr. articles to profl. jours. Mem. Russian Geog. Soc., Am. Geophys. Union. Home: Kristofferjord, Ramfjordbotn, 9027 Tromsø Norway Office: Norwegian Polar Inst, Polar Environ Ctr, 9296 Tromsø Norway

PAVLOVIC, DRAGAN, researcher, sports medicine physician, anaesthesiologist; b. Vranje, Serbia, Yugoslavia, Aug. 4, 1949; arrived in France, 1985; naturalized, 1997; s. Vojislav and Radmila (Sekulic) P. MD, Belgrade (Yugoslavia) U., 1976; diploma in sports medicine, London Hosp., 1984. Gen. practice, Koper, Slovenia, 1977-78; anesthesiologist Gen. Hosp., Marl, Germany, 1978-79, Stuttgart, Germany, 1981-83; rsch. fellow Med. Faculty Xavier Bichat, Paris, 1985-2000, rsch. dir. smooth muscle unit, 1988-2000; rschr., dir. Ernst-Moritz-Arnt U., Greifswald, Germany, 2000—. Editor-in-chief: Dialogue, 1992—; contbr. numerous articles on skeletal muscle and smooth muscle physiology, physiology of respiration and pharmacology to internat. med. jours. including Jour. Applied Physiology; inventor tracheal smooth muscle rsch. model, theory of permanent dialogue for social conflicts resolution, intentional theory of art. Rsch. grantee Found. for Med. Rsch., 1988, French Assn. for Myopathies, 1990, 95. Mem. Soc. Pneumologie d'Ile France, Mind Assn. Avocations: swimming, karate, painting, philosophy. Office: Klinik Poliklihik Anaesthesiologie Intensive Medizin, F Loefler Str 23B Ernst Moritz Arndt U, 17487 Greifswald Germany

PAVLOVIĆ, DRAŠKO, physician; b. Osijek, Croatia, Nov. 13, 1951; s. Aleksandar and Marta (Marjanovic) P.; m. Milenka Jauković, May 10, 1953; children: Nikola, Ivana. MD, U. Zagreb, Croatia, 1975, MSc, 1981, PhD, 1996. Diplomate Am. Bd. Internal Medicine, postgrad. diploma in nephrology. Pvt. practice Zagreb, 1976-78; resident internal medicine Gen. Hosp. Sveti Duh, Zagreb, 1978-83; resident nephrology Med. Faculty, Zagreb, 1984-85; nephrologist Sveti Duh Hosp., Zagreb, 1985—. Contbr. articles to profl. jours. Mem. European Dialysis Transp. Assn., European

Renal Assn., Internat. Soc. Nephrology, Croatian Med. Assn., Croatian Soc. Nephrology, Dialysis, Transplantation, Croatian Soc. Calcified Tissue. Avocation: mountaineering. Home: Kačićeva 6, 10000 Zagreb Croatia Office: Sveti Duh Hosp, Sveti Duh 64, 10000 Zagreb Croatia

PAVLOWITCH, STEVAN K., historian; b. Belgrade, Yugoslavia, Sept. 7, 1933; s. Kosta St. and Mara (Dyoukitch) P.; m. France Raffray, 1967; 1 child, Kosta. Licence ès Lettres in History, Sorbonne U., Paris, 1956; BA with honors in History, U. London, 1956, MA in History, 1959. Univ. tchr. Eng., 1965-96; emeritus prof. U. Southampton, Eng., 1996—. Author: Anglo-Russian Rivalry in Serbia, 1961, Yugoslavia, 1971, Bijou d'Art, 1978, Unconventional Perceptions of Yugoslavia, 1940-45, 1985, The Improbable Survivor, Yugoslavia: 1918-88, 1988, Yugloslavia's Great Dictator, Tito, 1992, A History of the Balkans, 1804-1945, 1999. Fellow Royal Hist. Soc. Office: Univ of Southampton, Dept History, U Southampton, Southampton S017 1NJ, England

PAVLUCH, JIRI, physicist, researcher; b. Prague, Czech Republic, Oct. 23, 1953; s. Lev and Maria (Kloboucnikova) P.; m. Jana Jenickova, July 5, 1977; children: Lukas, Marek, Vojtech. Degree, Charles U., Prague, 1978, PhD, 1984. Rsch. fellow Charles U., Prague, 1982-92, prin. rsch. fellow, 1992—; invited rschr. U. Erlangen-Nurnberg, Germany, 1988-89, U. B. Pascal, Clermont-Ferrand, France, 1995, 96, 97. Co-author: Methods of Surface Analysis, 1990; contbr. more than 15 articles to profl. jours. including Surface Sci. Grantee Charles U., 1993-99, Bd. Edn. Prague, 1992, 99; Copernicus grantee European Cmty., 1996—. Roman Catholic. Avocations: music, philosophy, languages, photography. Homer: Cernokostelecka 107, 10000 Prague Czech Republic Office: Charles U Fac Math & Phys, V Holesovickach 2, 18000 Prague Czech Republic

PAVLYUK, YURY, aerospace engineer; b. Litin, Ukraine, May 20, 1939; s. Stepan and Anna (Laievskaia) P.; m. Svietlana Chesnokova, Sept. 20, 1959; 1 child, Aleksey; m. Olga Komissarova, Mar. 15, 1991. PhD, Tech. U. Chelyabinsk, 1967; DSc, Tech. U. Moscow, 1985. From lectr. rocket tech. to dean aerospace faculty Tech. U. Chelyabinsk, 1960—. Author: Statistical Problems of Dynamics, 1984; contbr. articles to profl. jours. Avocations: music, painting, photography, theatre, poetry. Home: Apt 23 78a Lenin ave, 454080 Chelyabinsk Russia Office: State Tech U Chelyabinsk, 76 Lenina Ave, 454080 Chelyabinsk Russia

PAVONE, GERARDO PIERO, advertising company executive; b. Milan, Jan. 26, 1952; arrived in Belgium, 1997; s. Tommaso and Margherita (Dondi) P.; m. Fabrizia Begozzi, June 2, 1988; 2 children. Copywriting degree, Istituto Europeo, 1973. Exec. creative dir. Roncaglia & Wijkander, Rome, 1981-82, McCann-Erickson, Rome, 1983-88, Saatchi & Saatchi Rome, Rome, 1989-90, Lintas Italy, Milan, 1991-94; ptnr. Pavone and Marinari Advt., Milan, 1995-96; chmn., exec. creative dir. FCB Worldwide, Brussels, 1997—; sr. copywriter FCB-Rome, 1979-80; copywriter Compton-Dupuy, Rome, 1974-78, Promos-BBDO, Rome, 1973, Publinter WPT, Rome, 1971-72. Mem. Italian Art Dirs. Club, Creative Club of Belgium. Office: FCB Worldwide Brussels, Rue Gulledelle 98, 1200 Brussels Belgium

PAVŠIČ, MATEJ, physicist; b. Ljubljana, Slovenia, Feb. 24, 1946; s. Vladimir and Nada (Osojnik) P.; m. Mojca Vizjak, Dec. 9, 1978; children: Tjasa, Katja. Degree in physics, U. Ljubljana, 1971, MS, 1975, PhD, 1979. From rsch. asst. to rsch. collaborator Jožef Stefan Inst., Ljubljana, 1971-93, higher rsch. collaborator, 1994—; vis. scientist Inst. di Fisica Teorica, Catania, Italy, 1976-77; vis. prof. Inst. Math. Stats. and Sci. Computation, Campinas, Brazil, 1993-94; prin. investigator Jožef Stefan Inst., Ljubljana, 1994. Contbr. articles to profl. jours. Boris Kidrič Fund grantee Slovenian Rsch. Coun., Ljubljana, 1974. Mem. Internat. Assn. for Relativistic Dynamics, Slovenian Math. Phys. Soc., Am. Math. Soc. Avocations: skiing, mountain climbing, classical music. Office: Jožef Stefan Inst, Jamova 39, SI-1000 Ljubljana Slovenia

PAWELCZYK, TADEUSZ KAZIMIERZ, biochemist, researcher; b. Poznan, Poland, Sept. 26, 1952; s. Zbigniew and Henryka (Alejska) P.; m. Bozena Stasiak, Apr. 18, 1980; children: Marcin, Anna. MSc, A. Mickiewicz U., Poznan, 1979; PhD, Med. U. Gdansk, Poland, 1984, DSc, 1994; postgrad., U. Tex., San Antonio, 1986-88. Asst. Med. U. Gdansk, 1984-85, assoc. rsch., 1988-89, asst. prof., 1993-94, prof. biochemistry, 1996—, chmn. dept. molecular medicine, 1999—; sr. rschr. Brandeis U., Waltham, Mass., 1990-92; vis. prof. Duke U. Durham, N.C., 1995; cons. Med. Rsch. Ctr. Polish Acad. Sci., Warsaw, Poland, 1999—; mem. clin. analytical com. Polish Acad. Sci., Warsaw, 1997-99, mem. clin. biochem. com., 1997-98. Grantee State Com. Sci. Rsch., Poland, 1998, 99, 2000. Mem. Am. Soc. Biochemistry and Molecular Biology, Polish Biochem. Soc. Mem. Solidarity. Avocations: fishing, art history, gardening, dogs, music. Office: Med U Gdansk Dept Mol Med, Debinki 7 paw 29, 80-211 Gdansk Poland

PAWLAS, KARL RUDOLF, periodical editor, weaponry consultant; b. Bielitz-Beskiden, Poland, Jan. 1, 1926; s. Adolf and Marie Antonia (Wicha) P.; m. Frieda Küffner, Oct. 10, 1948 (div. Dec. 1951); 1 child, Peter; m. Ingeborg Alice Busch, May 20, 1955. Founder, owner Archiv Pawlas, Nuernberg, Germany, 1956—; weaponry cons., Ebern, 1980—. Autor, editor (periodical) Waffen-Revue, 1971—; author numerous books (in German), including: International Collector's Guide, 1968, International Weapons Identification Guide, 24 vols., 1969-71, Pistol-Digest, 9 vols., 1970-89, Cartridge Headstamp Guide, 1970, 86, Weapons Handbook, 1973, Ammunition Handbook, 1973, 95, The NSU Tracked Motorcycle, 1973, The First Turbojet Bomber Arado 234, 1976, Transport-Glider Me 321 and 323 "Gigant", Combat- and Transport-Glider DFS 230 and DFS 331, Assault- and Transport-Gliders Go 242, Go 244, Go 345, P 38, ka 430, German Aircrafts 1914-1918, 1976, Ammunition Guide 1, Artillery Fuses, 1977, 87, Ammunition Guide 2, Military Cartridges from 10 mm On, 1977, 87, Ammunition Guide 3, German Bombs, 1977, 87, others. Home: Am Kirschrangen 9, D-96106 Ebern Germany

PAWLEY, RAY LYNN, zoological park and environmental consultant; b. Midland, Mich., Nov. 7, 1935; s. Lynn Richard and Alice Marie (Skelton) P.; m. Ethel Marie Condon, Feb. 19, 1955 (div. 1974); children: Ray Allyn, Shanna Sue, Cynthia Ann, Dawn Marie, Brandon Earl, Dareen Joy; m. Hedda P. Saltz, Mar. 16, 1997. Student, Mich. State U., 1954-57. Asst. curator, lectr. Black Hills Reptile Gardens, Rapid City, S.D., summers 1952-53; owner, adminstr. Reptile Exhibit, St. Ignace, Mich., 1957-59; animal coord. Marlin Perkin's Wild Kingdom (Don Meier Prodns.), Chgo., 1961-62; zoologist Lincoln Park Zool. Gardens, Chgo., 1961-64; curator Brookfield (Ill.) Zoo, 1964-97; ret., 1997; assoc. dept. zoology Field Mus. Natural History, Chgo.; internat. zoo and conservation cons., Russia, Latvia, Mex., Kenya, China, Ecuador, Czechoslovakia; past instr. herpetology Field Mus., Coll. of DuPage, Triton Coll.; assoc. zoologist Moscow Zool. Pk., Russia; info. resource for fed. and state wildlife agys.; lectr., cons. in field. Contbr. over 80 articles to profl. jours. and popular mags.; co-creator money bench Chgo. Children's Mus. Past v.p. Ill. Endangered Species Protection Bd., Springfield; liaison Endangered Species Tech. Adv. Com., Springfield. Mem. Am. Zoo Assn. (3d Outstanding Svc. awards), Chgo. Acad. Scis. (life), Chgo. Herpetological Soc. (life), Mensa. Avocations: hiking, archaeology, art, mechanics, paleontology. Home: PO Box 218 Hinsdale IL 60522-0218

PAWLIGER, CARYN R., think tank executive; d. Richard and Nancy Pawliger. BA in Spanish & Social Psychology magna cum laude, Tufts U., 1992. Program specialist Am. Diabetes Assn., Alexandria, Va., 1992-95; dir. program devel. Pub. Affairs Coun., Washington, 1995—; cons. Women Govt. Rels., Washington. Vol. Greater D.C. Cares, 1995—; chairperson Washington Tufts Alliance, 1997-2000. Mem. Am. Soc. Assn. Execs., Tufts U. Alumni Assn. (mem. alumni coun. 2000—), Greater Washington Soc. Assn. Assn. Execs. Avocation: photography. Fax: 202-835-8343. Office e-mail: cpawliger@pac.org. Office: Pub Affairs Coun 2033 K St NW Ste 700 Washington DC 20006-1019

PAWLIKOWSKI, TADEUSZ, entomologist; b. Inowroclaw, Bydgoszcz, Poland, Sept. 18, 1947; s. Edmund and Jolanta (Szubinska) P.; m. Elizabeth Palasz, Sept. 10, 1976; children: Christopher, Agnes. MS, Copernicus U., Torun, Poland, 1974, PhD, 1981, DSc, 1992. Asst. Copernicus U., Torun, 1974-81, adj., 1981-93, prof., 1993—. Author: (books) Structure of Bee Communities, 1992 (Rector prize 1993), Social Bees of Poland, 1996, 99; editor: Polish Jour. of Entomology, 1996. Fellow Polish Entomol. Soc.; mem. Internat. Soc. Hymenopterists, N.Y. Acad. Scis., Bees Wasps Ants Recording Soc. Avocations: lit., electronic rock music, turist activities. Home: Buszczynskich 13 M2, PL-87100 Toruń Poland Office: Copernicus Univ, Inst Ecol/Gagarina 9, PL-87100 Toruń Poland

PAWLOWSKI, BOGUSLAW ZBIGNIEW, science educator; b. Prudnik, Poland, June 8, 1962; s. Andrzej Pawlowski and Maria Pikula; m. Bozena Piatek, Aug. 8, 1987; 1 child, Bogna. MSc, Tech. U. Wroclaw, Poland, 1986, U. Wroclaw, Poland, 1989; PhD of Biology, U. Wroclaw, Poland, 1996. Cert. biomed. engr., biologist. Asst. U. Wroclaw, 1990-96, sr. lectr., 1996—. Contbr. articles to profl. jours. Mem. European Anthropol. Assn., N.Y. Acad. Scis., Human Behavior and Evolution Soc. Avocations: chess, traveling. E-mail: bogus@antropo.uni.wroc.pl. Home: Wejherowska 17/10, Wroclaw 54-239, Poland Office: U Wroclaw, Kuznicza 35, Wroclaw 50-138, Poland

PAWLUS, PAWEL PIOTR, mechanical engineering educator, researcher; b. Rzeszów, Poland, Nov. 1, 1961; s. Witold and Barbara (Kazmierczyk) P.; m. Ewa Jasionowicz, Jun 19, 1960; 1 child, Zuzanna. MSc, Rzeszów U. of Tech., Poland, 1986, PhD, 1993. Car mechanic PP Polmozbyt, Rzeszów, Poland, 1986, car master, 1987; asst. Rzeszów (Poland) U. Tech., 1987-93, asst. prof., 1993—. Contbr. articles to profl. jours., 1992—. Mem. Solidarity, RzeszóW, 1990—. Recipient Brit. Coun. fellowship, Warwick U., Eng., 1994, 95; grantee: PHARE, Rzeszów, 1997. Roman Catholic. Avocation: travel. Home: Bohaterów 48, 35-112 Rzeszów Poland Office: Rzeszow U Tech, UL W Pola 2, 35-959 Rzeszów Poland

PAWSON, KENNETH VERNON FRANK, farmer, former hotel company executive; b. Morley, Yorkshire, Eng., Sept. 24, 1923; s. Arnold Gilderdale and Freda Eunice (Woodhead) P.; m. Nicolette Vivian Thoresby, June 15, 1950; children: Nicholas Charles Thoresby Pawson, Caroline Vanessa Thoresby Robertson, Francesca Louise Thoresby Lockyer. BA, Cambridge (Eng.) U., 1948, MA, 1953. Cert. barrister. Mng. dir. Joseph Hobson & Son Ltd., Leeds, Eng., 1949-76; chmn. Gale Lister & Co. Ltd., Leeds, 1974-95; dir., co. sec. Mt. Charlotte Investments Plc., Leeds, 1974-95; farmer, 1995—. Mem. Bar Assn. for Commerce, Fin. and Industry. Anglican. Avocations: shooting, fishing, old cars. Home: Haggas Hall, Weeton Near Leeds LS17 0BH, England

PAXTON, GLENN GILBERT, composer; b. Chgo., Dec. 7, 1931; s. Glenn G. and Florence A. (Nosek) P.; m. Leslie H. Davis, Dec. 8, 1962; children: Alexandra, Eben. BA, Princeton U., 1953. Freelance composer Broadway, opera, TV and film, 1959—. Composer: (theater prodns.) First Impressions, 1959, The Adventures of Friar Tuck, 1983 (Pulitzer prize nomination 1984), (opera) Monticello, 2000, (film) When the Legends Die, 1972, (concert pieces) Four Character Pieces for Piano, 1962, The Evening Sing, 1981, Harmonizing, Ca. 1940, 1986, (TV movies) Charlie and the Great Balloon Chase, 1981, Vital Signs, 1986, Dark Night of the Scarecrow, 1981, Isobel's Choice, 1981, The Two Worlds of Jenny Logan, 1979, The Clone Master, 1978, (TV shows) Amazing Stories, 1986, Willa Cather's America, 1976, Andy Rooney Takes Off, 1983, An American Christmas: Words and Music, 1971, The Hill Country: Lyndon Johnson's Texas, 1967, The Stately Ghosts of England, 1968, Barry Goldwater's Arizona, 1968, New World Visions, 1984, The American Image, 1969, others; (multi-media) Walking Home, 1991; (CD) Prairie Indigo, 1995. Served to lt. (j.g.) USCG, 1953-56. Mem. ASCAP, Dramatists Guild, Am. Music Ctr., Am. Fedn. Musicians. Home and Office: 230A Saddle Ln Ojai CA 93023-4204

PAXTON, JUANITA WILLENE, retired university official; b. Birmingham, Ala.; d. Will and Elizabeth (Davis) P. AB, Birmingham So. Coll., 1950; MA, Mich. State U., 1951; EdD, Ind. U., 1971; postgrad., U. Tex., summer 1965. Dormitory dir. Tex. Tech U., Lubbock, 1951-53; counselor Mich. State U., East Lansing, summer 1951; dir. univ. ctr. and housing SUNY, Fredonia, 1953-56, assoc. dean of students, 1956-57; asst. dean of women U. N.Mex., Albuquerque, 1957-63; dean of women East Tenn. State U., Johnson City, 1963-68, 70-78, dir. Counseling Ctr., 1978-93; tng. dir. CONTACT Teleministries, Tenn., 1984-92, chmn. bd. dirs., 1986, 95. Chmn. social concerns Munsey United Meth. Ch., 1989-92, sec. adminstrv. bd., 1980-84, vice chairperson, 1993, chair, 1994, mem. coun. on ministries, 1980-94, chair stewardship campaign, 1995, chair promotion and publicity subcom. building campaign, 1996—, chair scholarship com., 1997—. U.S. Ednl. Profl. Devel. Act grantee, 1968-69. Mem. Am. Coll. Pers. Assn. (mem. media com. 1977-79, newsletter editor com. XVI 1977-79), Asbury Retirement Ctrs. Tenn. and Va. (bd. dirs. 1991-96, policy com. 1991-96, chair 1995-96, mem. fin. com. 1996, mem. nomination com. 1994-96), Univ. Women's Club (pres. 1994-96), Tenn. Coll. Pers. Assn. (legis. chair 1974), Tenn. Assn. Women Deans Counselors (pres. 1966-68), Gen. Federated Womans Club, Monday Club Aux. (pres. 1980-81, 88-89, 95-96, 99-2000, v.p. 1993-95, 96-99, corr. sec. 1979-80), Watauga Pers. and Guild Assn. (pres.-elect 1967-68, chair ETEA guidance divsn. 1968), Delta Kappa Gamma Soc. Internat. (internat. chair rules com. 1992, mem. exec. bd. 1989-91, internat. rsch. com. 1982-84, constn. com. 1992-94, state rec. sec. 1975-77, state v.p. 1977-79, state pres. 1989-91, chpt. pres. 1972-74, chair state nominating com. 1979-81, chair state ad hoc com. to study feasibility exec. sec. 1987-89, mem. pers. com. 1995-97, chair 1997-99, mem. archives com. 1999—, State Achievement award 1987), E. Tenn. State U. Retiree's Assn. (bd. dirs. 1993-2000, program com. 1994, 95, pres. elect 1995, pres. 1996, sec. 2000). Avocations: reading, bridge, travel, needlework.

PAYÁ-BERNABEU, JORDI, educator, researcher; b. Alcoy, Alicante, Spain, Feb. 20, 1964; s. Manuel Paya and Concepción Bernabeu; m. Josefa Roselló, Oct. 31, 1993; 1 child, Jordi. Bachelor, LaSalle, Alcoy, 1981; univ. degree, U. Valencia, Spain, 1986, doctorate, 1990. Rsch. fellow U. Valencia, 1987-89; assoc. prof. U. Politecnica de Valencia, 1989-95, prof., 1995—; dir. rsch. group Giquima, Valencia, 1990—, Chemistry of Bldg. Materials Unit, Valencia, 1996—. Contbr. articles to profl. jours. Mem. Spanish Cactophile Soc. Avocations: philately, cacti and other succulents. E-mail: jjpaya@cst.upv.es. Office: U Politenica de Valencia, c/Camino de Vera, E-46071 Valencia Spain

PAYATAKES, ALKIVIADES CHARIDEMOS, chemical engineering educator; b. Athens, Greece, Aug. 22, 1945; s. Charidemos and Zenovia (Bitrou) P.; m. Chrysoula Tsitoura, Aug. 28, 1968; children: Alexander Harris, George Jason, Zenia Christie. Diploma in chem. engring., Nat. Tech. U. of Athens, 1968; PhD, Syracuse U., 1973. Registered chem. engr., Greece, U.S.A. Postdoctoral fellow Syracuse (N.Y.) U., 1973; rsch. engr. tech. products divsn. Brunswick Corp., Skokie, Ill., 1973-74; asst. prof. U. Houston, 1974-77, assoc. prof., 1977-80, prof., 1980-81; prof. chem. engring. U. Patras, Greece, 1981—; cons. Commn. of European Communities, Brussels, 1989—, also numerous corps., U.S., 1974-91; A.P. Colburn lectr. U. Del., Wilmington, 1981, R.W. Vaughan lectr. Calif. Inst. Tech., Pasadena, 1982; mem. adv. panel advanced study insts. program NATO, 1998, mem. phys. and engring. sci. and tech. panel, 1999—; mem. phys. and engring. sci. and tech. panel, 1999—; dir. ICE/HT-FORTH, FORTH. Contbr. articles to profl. jours. Chmn. Hellenic Project for Wider Application of R & D, Athens, 1991—; dir. Innovation Relay Ctr. Help Forward, 1995—. Recipient Suttle award Filtration Soc., London, 1975. Mem. AIChE (Best Fundamental Paper award South Tex. sect. 1979, 80), Internat. Consortium of Filtration and Separation Researchers, Found. for Rsch. and Tech., Hellas. Greek Orthodox. Avocations: literature, classical music, hiking. Office: U Patras, Dept Chem Engring, GR 26500 Patras Greece

PAYE, JEAN-CLAUDE, diplomat; b. Longué, Aug. 26, 1934; s. Lucien and Suzanne (Guignard) P.; m. Laurence Jeanneney, 1963; 4 children. Student, Inst. Etudes Politiques, Ecole Nat. Admin. Head pvt. office Mayor of Constantine, 1961-62; sec. Embassy Algiers, 1962-63; with Ministry of Fgn. Affairs, 1963-65; spl. advisor Office Sec. of State for Sci. Rsch., 1965, Office Min. Social Affairs, 1966; head pvt. office M. Barre V.p. Commn. European Communities, 1967-73; counsellor Bonn, 1973-74; dep. head Office Min. Fgn. Affairs, 1974-76; counsellor Prime Min. Raymond Barre, 1976-79; sec. gen. Interministerial Com. for European Economic Coop., 1977-79; dir. econ. and fin. affairs Min. for External Rels., 1979-84; sec. gen. OECD, 1984-96; state counselor Govt. of France, 1996-2000. Min. Plénipotentiaire hors classe, 1986; chevalier Légion d'honneur; comdr. Ordre Nat. du Mérite.

PAYENS, BERNARDUS THEODORUS, electrical engineer, administrator; b. Edam, The Netherlands, Apr. 9, 1927; s. Rumoldus Johannes and theresia Maria (Eeltimk) P.; m. Theresia Maria Lemm, July 23, 1931; children: Ruud, Arthur, Mike. Elec. Engr., ETS, Amsterdam, 1949. Engr. Gasworks, Beverwyk, The Netherlands, 1949-50; engr. Petrogas, Rotterdam, The Netherlands, 1950-56, v.p., 1956-64, ptnr., comml. dir., 1964-76, mng. dir., 1976-92; sr. advisor Petrogas, Gouda, The Netherlands, 1992—. Contbr. articles to profl. jours. Mem. Royal Assn. of Dutch Gas Industry (mem. com. for setting up Dutch/European regulatoins 1973—), Probus Alexander Club. Mem. Christian Dem. Party. Avocations: pike fishing, tennis, sea fishing.

PAYEVSKY, VLADIMIR ALEXANDROVICH, zoologist; b. Leningrad, Russia, Apr. 29, 1937; s. Alexander Vladislavovich and Tamara Ivanovna (Neparidze) P.; m. Yelena Borisovna Bobkova, Oct. 15, 1966 (div. Aug. 1984); 1 child, Vitaly; m. Lydia Demianovna Karelina, June 26, 1986. PhD, Leningrad U., Russia, 1968; DSc, Russian Acad. Scis., Leningrad, 1987. Jr. rschr. biol. sta. Russian Acad. Scis., Kaliningrad, Russia, 1961-65, rschr., 1968-77, sr. rschr. zool. inst., 1977-90, leading rschr., 1990—. Author: Bird Migration Ecological Factors, 1973 (Zool. Inst. award 1973), Sex/Age Indentification of USSR Bird Fauna, 1976, Population Ecology of Chaffinch, 1982, Demography of Birds, 1985 (Menzbier Ornithology Soc. award 1986). Grantee INTAS, 1993, Internat. Soros Sci. Found., 1995, Russian Found. Fundamental Scis., Moscow, 1998. Fellow Am. Ornithologists Union, Menzbier Ornithology Soc. Russia. Avocation: poetry. Office: Russian Acad Sci Zool Inst, Universitetskaya nab 1, 199034 Saint Petersburg Russia

PAYNE, ANTONY JOHN, retired academic administrator; b. Bridport, England, June 7, 1931; s. Arthur and Marjorie (Wyatt) P.; m. Heather Joyce Collins, Aug. 9, 1960; children: Russell Manley, Neville Lawrence, Anita Carolyn. Diploma, Carnegie Coll., 1954. Sportsmaster Hinchley Wood Sch., Kingston, England, 1954-56, Jamaica Coll., Kingston, 1956-59; sportsmaster, asst. housemaster Royal Comml. Travellers Sch., Pinner, England, 1960-66; sports dir. Ealing Coll., England, 1966-96, Thames Valley U., to 1996; ret., 1996. Pres. So. Eng. Students Sports Assn., Middlesex Basketball League. Mem. So. England Students Sports Assn. Avocations: golf, travel, skiing, tennis umpiring.

PAYNE, GEORGE FREDERICK, educational administrator; b. Summerville, S.C., Jan. 29, 1941; s. Fred N. and Lota (Griffith) P.; m. Kay Martin, June 23, 1963; children: John F., Mark C., Janet E. Student, Ga. Inst. Tech., 1959-60, U.S. Naval Acad., 1960-62; BS, U. S.C., 1963, MA, 1966; MRE, Luth. Theol. Sem., 1968; postgrad., U. Ga., 1969-71; LLD (hon.), Lincoln Meml. U., 1988. From instr. to asst. prof. Ga. So. Coll., Statesboro, 1966-78; dir. admission Brewton-Parker Coll., Mt. Vernon, Ga., 1978-80; v.p. for devel. North Greenville Coll., Tigerville, S.C., 1980-86; pres. Limestone Coll., Gaffney, S.C., 1986-91, dir. various grants, 1976-91; spl. agt., registered rep. Prudential Fin. Svcs., 1991-92; dir. ITT Tech. Inst., Greenville, S.C., 1992-95; exec. dir. Inst. Adv. Greenville Tech. Coll./ Greenville Tech. Found., 1996—. Author: An Introduction to the Principles of Geography: Facts, Skills, Concepts, and Models, 1973; also articles. Active Leadership Greer, S.C., 1980-81, regent, 1982-84; active AACTion Consortium, 1980-82, Leadership Greenville, S.C., 1982-83; bd. dirs. Greenville County unit Am. Cancer Soc., 1985-86; advisor Cherokee County Arts Coun., 1986-91, bd. trustees Rolling Green Village Continuing Care Ret. Cmty., 1996—, sec. 1998—. With USN, 1960-62. Recipient Disting Svc. award Brewton-Parker Coll., 1980, Disting. Svc. award North Greenville Coll., 1986. Mem. Coun. for Advancement and Support Edn., Greater Greer C. of C. (bd. dirs. 1981-84). Baptist. Lodge: Rotary. Avocation: reading. Office: Greenville Tech Coll PO Box 5616 Greenville SC 29606-5616

PAYNE, GREGG ALAN, communications consultant, educator; b. Phoenix, Aug. 20, 1941; s. Maynard and Carol Marie (McKiernan) P.; m. M. Carolyn Payne, Feb. 2, 1963; children: Wendy Alain, Gregg Martin. BA in Journalism, U. Ariz., 1963; MS in Mass Comm., San Diego State U., 1987; PhD in Comm., U. Utah, 1995. Asst. dir. Upward Bound, dir. news bur. Ariz. Western Coll., Yuma, 1965-66; editl. dir., asst. mgr. San Diego Area Instrnl. TV Authority, 1966-72; budget analyst San Diego Unified Sch. Dist., 1972-82; pub. rels. account exec. L.J. Cella Co., San Diego, 1982-83; assoc. pub., editor-in-chief Rancher Publs., San Marcos, Calif., 1983-84; v.p., pub. Hare Publs., Carlsbad, Calif., 1984-90; editor., pub. rels. assoc. Western Growers Assn., Newport Beach, Calif., 1991-92; pres. Quantum Comm., Inc., Monarch Beach, Calif., 1992—; mem. adj. faculty U. Calif., Irvine, Chapman U., U. Phoenix, Salt Lake City C.C.; tchg. fellow U. Utah, U. Wash.; presenter in field. Contbr. articles to profl. jours. Recipient 7 Maggie awards Western Publs. Assn. Mem. Pub. Rels. Soc. Am., Internat. Issue Mgmt. Coun., Internat. Assn. Bus. Communicators, Internat. Comm. Assn., Healthcare Pub. Rels. and Mktg. Assn., Nat. Agri-Mktg. Assn. (comm. and issues forum com.), Assn. for Edn. in Journalism and Mass Comm., U. Ariz. Alumni Assn., Phi Kappa Phi, Kappa Tau Alpha, Sigma Delta Chi. Office: Quantum Comm Inc 51 Palm Beach Ct Monarch Beach CA 92629-4526

PAYNE, JOHN D., art educator, sculptor, consultant; b. Pontotoc, Miss., Sept. 17, 1929; divorced; children: Ricardo, Cindy, Marcia. BA, Beloit (Wis.) Coll., 1959; MS, U. Wis., 1961; postgrad., Kans. U., 1969-66; MFA, U. Wis., 1969. Art dir. WKOW TV, Madison, Wis., 1960-61; head dept. fine arts Langston (Okla.) U., 1961-63; mem. faculty art So. U., New Orleans, 1963-65; assoc. prof. 3-D design So. U., Baton Rouge, 1966-71; dir., coord. new art programs Govs. State U., University Park, Ill., 1971-73, 75-79, prof. sculpture, sculptor in residence, 1971—; dir. Sculptor Campus and the Prairie Govs. State U., 1976-81; chair dept. visual arts George Mason U., Fairfax, Va., 1973-74; head art dept. George Mason U., 1976-81; head dept. art, CEO art Western Mich. U., Kalamazoo, 1988-89; owner/pres. Sculpture Commns./Consignment, Crete Twp., Ill., 1981—; vis. artist juror all student show Western Mich. U., Kalamazoo; Martin L. King, Rosa Parks, Cezar Chavez vis. artist Western Mich. U., Kalamazoo, 1988-89. Exhibited at Vedanta Gallery, 1997, Navy Pier, Chgo., 1999; prin. works include sculpture Navy Pier, Chgo., U. Western Mich., 1969, Kellogg Co., Battle Creek, Mich., 1987, Western Mich. U., 1989. Judge cmty. art fairs, 1976-81, 97. Recipient spl. outstanding alumni citation Beloit Coll., 1979; grantee Ill. Arts Coun., 1976, 77, Nat. Endowment for Arts, Washington, 1972, 73, 74, rsch. grantee Danforth Found., 1968-69. Mem. Internat. Sculpture Ctr., Artists Round Table (treas./bus. mgr. 1983-94). Office: 25645 Western Ave Park Forest IL 60466-3417

PAYNE, JOHN PHILIP, German educator; b. Nottingham, Eng., Sept. 5, 1942; s. John Howard and Lucy (Myers) P.; m. Simone Anne Coles, Aug. 12, 1967; children: Emma Clare, Thomas Christopher, Harry George, Jack William. BA, Cambridge (Eng.) U., 1964, MLitt, 1974, PhD, 1989. Asst. lectr. German U. Reading, Eng., 1967-69; asst. prof. German U. Toronto, Can., 1969-73; lectr. German U. Lancaster, Eng., 1973-89, sr. lectr. German, 1989-93, prof. German, 1993—. Editor: Germany Today, 1971; author: Robert Musil's Works 1906-1924, 1987, Zeitungen in der Bundesrepublik Deutschland, 1988, Robert Musil's The Man Without Qualities, 1988. Recipient Robert Musil medal City of Klagenfurt, Austria, 1989. Mem. Assn. Univ. Tchrs. German. Avocations: rowing, sailing. Office: U Lancaster, Lonsdale Coll, Lancaster LA1 4YN, England

PAYNE, KAREN SUZANNE, music educator; b. Topeka, Kans., Mar. 19, 1975; m. Denis Aaron Payne. BMusEd, Kans. State U., 1997. K-12 music tchr. USD 386, Madison, Kans., 1997-99; PK-2nd music tchr. Pembroke-Hill, Kansas City, Mo., 1999—; vocal festival dir. Lyon County League, Emporia, Kans.; music festival dir. Madison Invitational Music Festival, Kans. Ministry intern Emporia Ch. of the Nazaren, 1997-99; children's ch. music dir. Antioch Ch. of the Nazarene, Overland Park, Kans., 1999—; mem. Manhattan Cmty. Band, Kans., 1995-97, sect. leader, 1998. Mem. Kans. Music Tchrs. Assn., Music Educators Nat. Conf., Kans. Music Nat. Assn., Kans. Music Tchrs. Nat. Assn. Avocations: music, volleyball, crafts. E-mail: Kpayne@pembrokehill.org. Office: Pembroke-Hill 400 W 51st St Kansas City MO 64112-2316

PAYNE, MALCOLM D., real estate broker, financial advisor; b. Chgo., Oct. 8, 1970; s. Henry Warren Murray and Deloris Ann Payne; m. Dartavia Payne. Student, DeVry, Columbus, Ohio. Crew leader Wendy's, Toledo, 1992-93; supr. Bergstrom, Rockford, Ill., 1993-99; broker, owner Payne

Realty, Rockford, 1999—; mentor Cmty. Devel., Rockford. Mem. NAR, IAR, RAAR. Avocation: pool. Home: 910 Garfield Ave Rockford IL 61103-6028 Office: Payne Realty and Appraisal 402 E State St Rockford IL 61104-1015

PAYNE, MARY LIBBY, judge; b. Gulfport, Miss., Mar. 27, 1932; d. Reece O. and Emily Augusta (Cook) Bickerstaff; m. Bobby R. Payne; children: Reece Allen, Glenn Russell. Student, Miss. U. for Women, 1950-52; BA in Polit. Sci. with distinction, U. Miss., 1954, LLB, 1955. Bar: Miss. 1955. Ptnr. Bickerstaff & Bickerstaff, Gulfport, 1955-56; sec. Guaranty Title Co., Jackson, Miss., 1957; assoc. Henley, Jones & Henley, Jackson, Miss., 1958-61; freelance rschr. Pearl, Miss., 1961-63; solo practitioner Brandon, Miss., 1963-68; exec. dir. Miss. Judiciary Commn., Jackson, 1968-70; chief drafting & rsch. Miss. Ho. Reps., Jackson, 1970-72; asst. atty. gen. State Atty. Gen. Office, Jackson, 1972-75; founding dean, assoc. prof. Sch. Law Miss. Coll., Jackson, 1975-78, prof., 1978-94; judge Miss. Ct. Appeals, Jackson, 1995—; bd. disting. alumnae Miss. U. Women, 1988-99. Contbr. articles to profl. jours. Founder, bd. dirs. Christian Conciliation Svc., Jackson, 1983-93; counsel Christian Action Com. Rankin Bapt. Assn., Pearl, 1968-92; advisor Covenant Ministerial Fellowship, 1995—. Recipient Book of Golden Deeds award Pearl Exch. Club, 1989, Excellence medallion Miss. U. Women, 1990, Susie Blue Buchanan award Women in the Profession Com. of Miss. Bar, 2000; named Woman of Yr. Miss. Assn. Women Higher Edn., 1989, Power of One honoree Miss. Govs. Conf., 1996, Miss. Coll. Lawyer of the Yr., Mis. Coll. Sch. Law Alumni Assn., 1998, Outstanding Woman Lawyer, Miss. Women Lawyers Assn., 1999. Fellow Am. Bar Found.; mem. Miss. Bar Found., Christian Legal Soc. (nat. bd. dirs. 1992—, regional membership coord., Skeeter Ellis Svc. to Law Students award 1999), Margaret Brent League. Baptist. Avocations: public speaking, travel, needlepoint, sewing, reading. Office: Ct Appeals PO Box 22847 Jackson MS 39225-2847

PAYNE, MEREDITH JORSTAD, physician; b. St. Louis, Feb. 7, 1927; d. Louis Helmar and Cleone Gladys (Branian) Jorstad; m. Spencer Payne, 1948 (div. 1959); m. James McGarity, 1965 (div. 1977); children: Maureen Meredith, James Louis. AB, Washington U., St. Louis, 1947, MD, 1950; MBA, Lindenwood U., 1999. Diplomate Am. Bd. Surgery, Am. Bd. Plastic Surgery. Intern gen. surgery St. Louis City Hosp., 1950-51, asst. resident surgery, 1951-54; chief surg. resident Roswell Park Meml. Hosp., Buffalo, 1954-55; chief plastic surgery resident Allentown (Pa.) Gen. Hosp., 1955-57; clin. instr. surgery Washington U. Med. Sch., 1957-70; vis. surgeon Homer G. Phillips Hosp., St. Louis, 1957-70; staff St. Luke's, St. Louis and Bethesda, 1957 , St. Mary's, 1988 ; chief plastic surgery Vets. Hosp., 1986-98; assoc. prof. plastic surgery (clin.) St. Louis U. Sch. Medicine, St. Louis, 1986—; med. dir. Unity Cleft Palate Clinic. Contbr. articles to profl. jours. Fellow ACS; mem. AMA, Am. Soc. Plastic and Reconstructive Surgery, Mo. Med. Assn. (del., councillor 1988), St. Louis Met. Med. Soc. (councillor 1983-86, sec. 1998-99, v.p. 1999-00), Am. Cleft Palate Assn., Roswell Park Surgery Assn., So. Med. Assn., Washington U. Med. Alumni Assn., Am. Geriatrics Soc., Midwestern Assn. Plastic Surgeons, Pan Am. Med. Assn., City Hosp. Alumni Assn., Soc. Head and Neck Surgeons, St. Louis Area Soc. Plastic Surgeons (pres. 1990-93), City Hosp. Alumni Assn. (v.p. 1995-97, pres. 1997), Mo. Assn. Plastic and Reconstructive Surgery (treas. 1995 , v.p. 1997, pres. 1998), St. Louis Surg. Soc. (v.p. 1998), AMWA (treas. St. Louis chpt. 1995), Order Eastern Star, Zonta (St. Louis pres. 1968-69), College Club (bd. dirs. St. Louis 1983-85). Avocations: skiing, tennis, sewing, knitting, gardening. Home: 7314 Westmoreland Dr Saint Louis MO 63130-4240

PAYNE, MONICA ANNE, psychology educator, researcher; b. London, May 15, 1948; d. Charles Thomas Leonard and Joan Mary (Coates) P. BSc with honors, U. Coll. North Wales, Bangor, 1970; PhD, U. Durham, Eng., 1976. Edn. officer Ministry Edn., Kano, Nigeria, 1974-76; lectr. Bayero U., Kano, Nigeria, 1976-80; lectr., sr. lectr. U. West Indies, Cave Hill, Barbados, 1980-91; sr. lectr. U. Waikato, Hamilton, New Zealand, 1991—. Author: (with others) International Encyclopedia of Education, 2d rev. edit, 1994, Caribbean Portraits: Essays on Gender Ideologies and Identities, 1998; contbr. articles to profl. jours. Fellow Brit. Psychol. Soc. (assoc.); mem. APA (fgn. affiliate), Internat. Assn. for Cross-Cultural Psychology. Avocations: opera, tennis. Office: U Waikato Dept Edn Studies, Pvt Bag 3105, Hamilton New Zealand

PAYNE, RICHARD HAROLD, university research administrator; b. Lowell, Mass., Apr. 30, 1941; s. Calvin Lee and Helen Josephine (Hennessey) P.; m. Harriett Gean Rowan, Feb. 4, 1961 (dec. Feb. 1977); children: James Richard, Deloria Linn; m. Kathy Leigh Freydenfeldt, Mar. 20, 1978. ABJ, U. Ga., 1965, MA, 1966, PhD, 1970. Asst. prof. polit. sci. The Citadel, Charleston, S.C., 1966-72; prof. polit. sci. Sam Houston State U., Huntsville, 1972—, chair dept., 1972-99, assoc. v.p. rsch. and grad. studies, 1999—. Editor Tex. Jour. Polit. Studies, 1988-90; contbr. articles to profl. jours. Bd. dirs. Tex. Rsch. Inst. for Environ. Studies, Huntsville, 1991-97; mem., vol. positions Boy Scouts Am., Huntsville and Houston, 1974-94. memMem. Aubudon Soc. (pres. Huntsville chpt. 1978-79, 84-85), Tex. Ornithol. SocOkla. Ornithol. Soc., Am. Birding Assn. (bd. dirs. 1998—, pres. 1999—), Ecotourism Soc., Nat. Coun. Univ. Res. Adminstrs., Policy Studies Orgn., S.W. Assn. for Can. Studies, Western Social Sci. Assn., Wildlife Mgmt. Inst., Watchable Wildlife, Inc. (vice chmn. bd. dirs. 1999—), Phi Kappa Phi, Pi Sigma Alpha, Kappa Tau Delta, Phi Eta Sigma. Avocations: birding, camping, hiking. Office: Sam Houston State U Office Rsch and Sponsored Huntsville TX 77341-2448

PAYNE, R.W., JR., lawyer; b. Norfolk, Va., Mar. 16, 1936; s. Roland William and Margaret (Sawyer) P.; m. Gail Willingham, Sept. 16, 1961; children: Darrell, Preston, Darby, Clinton. BA in English, U. N.C., 1958, LLB, 1961; LLB, Stetson U., 1962. Bar: Fla. 1963, U.S. Dist. Ct. (so. dist.) 1964, U.S. Ct. Appeals (11th cir.) 1965, U.S. Supreme Ct. 1970. Assoc. Roney & Beach, St. Petersburg, Fla., 1963-64, Nichols, Gaither, Beckham, Colson & Spence, Miami, Fla., 1964-67; ptnr. Spence, Payne, Masington, Miami, 1967-95, Payne, Leeds, Colby & Robinson, P.A., Miami, 1995-97; pvt. practice Miami, 1997, 98; ptnr. McLuskey, McDonald & Payne, P.A., Miami, 1999—; presenter numerous profl. convs. and seminars. Contbr. articles to legal jours., legal edn. books. Mem. Ottawa Roughriders, Can. Football League, fall 1958; capt. football team U. N.C., 1957, bd. dirs., v.p. alumni bd., 1984-92, bd. dirs. ednl. found., 1988-92; bd. dirs. Chem. Dependency Tng. Inst.; past pres. Coral Gables (Fla.) Sr. H.S. Athletic Boosters Club; past bd. dirs. Coral Gables War Meml. Youth Ctr., bd. trustees 1st United Meth. Ch. Coral Gables; past mem. gov.'s coun. on phys. fitness and sports, Fla.; past assoc. mem. Jr. Orange Bowl Com. With USMC, 1959. Fellow Am. Coll. Trial Lawyers, Internat. Acad. Trial Lawyers; mem. ABA, ATLA, Am. Bd. Trial Advocates, Fla. Bar Assn., Acad. Fla. Trial Lawyers (past mem. bd. govs.), Dade County Bar Assn. (past bd. dirs.), Dade County Trial Lawyers Assn. (founder, past pres.), Bankers Club, Miami Club, Univ. Club, Coral Reef Yacht Club, Order of Golden Fleece, Order of Old Well, Sigma Chi, Phi Delta Phi. Avocations: boating, golf, diving. Office: McLuskey, McDonald & Payne PA Two Datran Ctr 19th Flr 9130 S Dadeland Blvd Miami FL 33156-7818

PAYNE, SIDNEY STEWART, retired archbishop; b. Fogo, Nfld., Can., June 6, 1932; m. Selma Carlson, 1962; children: Carla Ann, Christopher Stewart, Robert Clement, Angela Marie Louise. BA, Meml. U., St. John's, Nfld., 1958; lic. of theology, Queen's Coll., St. John's, 1958; BDiv, Gen. Synod, 1968; DDiv (hon.), King's Coll., Halifax, N.S., Can., 1981. Ordained priest Anglican Ch., 1958, bishop, 1978, archbishop, 1990. Deacon Mission of Happy Valley, Goose Bay, Labrador, Nfld., Can., 1957-65; rector Parish of Bay Roberts, Nfld., Can., 1965-70, Parish of St. Anthony, Nfld., 1970-78, 1976-78; bishop Diocese of Western Nfld., 1978-90, archbishop of Western Nfld. and Met. Eccles. Province of Can., 1990-97; ret., 1997; pres. Diocesan Synod, chmn. exec. com., mem. ex-officio diocesan coms.; pres. Provincial Synod, Provincial Coun.; chair Provincial House of Bishops; mem. long range planning com., ministry com., mem. nat. exec. coun. Partners in World Mission, Stewardship and Fin. Devel. Com.; mem. Anglican/Roman Cath. Bishops' Dialogue, Can.; active Provincial and Nat. House of Bishops. Mem. Internat. Grenfell Assn. (past bd. dirs.). Avocations: reading, walking, gardening, cross-country skiing. Home: PO Box 2255, R R 1 Stn Main, Corner Brook, NF Canada A2H 2N2

PAYNE, WINFIELD SCOTT, national security policy research executive; b. Denver, Jan. 20, 1917; s. Winfield Scott and Mildred (Hulse) P.; m. Barbara P. Reid, Nov. 18, 1945; children: Judith P. Beland, Patricia P. Dominguez. AB, U. Colo., 1939, MA (grad. scholar), 1941; postgrad. (fellow) Syracuse U., 1942; MPA, Harvard U., 1948, PhD, 1955. Economist, Bur. Budget, Washington, 1944-46; staff Inter-Univ. Case Program, Washington, 1948-50; indsl. analyst Pres.'s Materials Policy Commn., Washington, 1950-52; project leader Ops. Research Office, Johns Hopkins U., Bethesda, Md., 1952-63; sr. research staff, panel dir. Inst. for Def. Analyses, Arlington, Va., 1963-72; asst. to pres. System Planning Corp., Arlington, 1972-86; cons. 1986-88; adj. rsch. staff Inst. Def. Analyses, 1989-98; assoc. prof., lectr. George Washington U., Washington, 1963-65; cons. Def. Advanced Research Project Agy., 1972-76; guest lectr., various univs. Mem. Cabin John (Md.) Fire Bd., 1955-65. Served with USMC, 1942. Littauer fellow, 1946-48. Mem. AAAS, Cosmos Club, Phi Gamma Delta, Pi Gamma Mu. Contbr. articles to profl. jours.; contbr.: Public Administration and Policy Development: A Case Book, 1951. Home: 8820 Walther Blvd Apt 1304 Parkville MD 21234-9038

PAYNE-JAMES, JOHN JASON, physician; b. Ipswich, Eng., Dec. 14, 1956. MB, BChir, Royal London Hosp. Med. Coll., 1980, LLM, 1994. Forensic med. examiner London, 1990; sr. clin. rsch. fellow Cen. Middlesex Hosp., London, 1990—; freelance med. writer; bd. dir. Forensic Healthcare Svcs., Ltd. Author: Penguin Book of Symptoms and Early Warning Signs, 1993, Key Facts in Clinical Nutrition, 1994, Artificial Nutrition Support in Clinical Practice, 1995, Medicolegal Essentials of Healthcare, 1996, Symptoms and Signs of Substance Misuse, 1996; editor Jour. of Clin. Forensic Medicine, 1993, Current Med. Lit.-Clin. Nutrition. Fellow Royal Coll. Surgeons Eng., Royal Coll. Surgeons Edinburgh, Licentiate Assn. Lawyers; mem. Assn. Police Surgeons, Royal Soc. Medicine (mem. coun. sect. clin. forensic medicine 1993), Acad. Experts, Expert Witness Inst., Soc. of Aultas (med. writer grey com.). Office: Forensic Healthcare Svcs, 19 Speldhurst Rd, London E9 7EH, England

PAYNTER, VESTA LUCAS, pharmacist; b. Aiken County, S.C., May 29, 1922; d. James Redmond and Annie Lurline (Stroman) Lucas; m. Maurice Alden Paynter, Dec. 23, 1945 (dec. 1971); children: Sharon Lucinda, Maurice Alden, Doyle Gregg. BS in Pharmacy, U. S.C., 1943. Lic. pharmacist. Owner, pharmacist Cayce Drug Store, S.C., 1944-52, Dutch Fork Drug Store, Columbia, S.C., 1955-60, The Drug Ctr., Cayce, 1963-81; pharmacist Lane-Rexall, Columbia, 1952-55; dist. pharmacist S.C. Dept. Health and Environ. Control, Columbia, 1983-90, ret., 1990. Vol. pharmacist Free Med. Clinic, Columbia, 1987-90; mem. Amaranth Trinity Ct. #6, West Columbia, S.C., Am. Legion Aux., Cacye Post. Named Preceptor of Yr., Syntex Co./Student Body of U. S.C., 1981. Fellow S.C. Pub. Health Assn., S.C. Pharm Assn., 5th Dist. Pharm. Assn.; mem. CBI VA Assn. (assoc.), 14th Air Force Assn. (assoc.), Order Eastern Star, White Shrine of Jerusalem, Amaranth Trinity Ct. # 6, Am. Legion Aux. (Post 130). Baptist. Avocations: travel, art. Home: 2351 Vine St Cayce SC 29033-3000

PAYTON, GARY DWAYNE, professional basketball player; b. Oakland, Calif., July 23, 1968; m. Monique Payton; children: Raquel, Gary Dwayne. Grad., Oreg. State U., 1990. Drafted NBA, 1990; guard Seattle Supersonics, 1990—. Named mem. All-Am. First Team, The Sporting News, 1990, Pacific-10 Conf. Player of Yr., 1990, NBA All-Star, 1994, 95, NBA Player of the Week; named to NBA All-Def. 1st Team, 1994, 95. Office: Seattle Supersonics 351 Elliott Ave W Seattle WA 98119-4101

PAYTON, PATRICK HOWARD, lawyer, educator; b. N.Y.C., July 3, 1945; s. Ethel A. P.; m. Carol L. Trickey, Aug. 5, 1968 (div.); children: Anastasia Payton, Katheryn Anderson, Stephanie Harrington, Felicia Moss, Tiffany Payton; m. Adella Mae Payton, July 3, 1994; 1 child, Elizabeth Bailey. BA, JD, Drake U., 1964-71; BS, Upper Iowa U., 1987; PhD, Iowa State U., 1999. Tchr. Des Moines Independent Cmty. Sch., Des Moines, 1968-70; pvt. practice Des Moines, 1971—; instr. Des Moines Area C.C., Ankeny, Iowa, 1969-82, Drake U., Des Moines, 1972, U. Osteo. Medicine, Des Moines, 1978-80; adj. prof. William Penn Coll., West Des Moines, Iowa, 1997—; bd. dirs. Occupl. Safety and Health Adv. Coun., Des Moines. City atty. City of Pleasant Hill, Iowa, 1979-84. Mem. KC. Office: 414 E Grand Ave Des Moines IA 50309-1920

PAYTON, ROGER LOUIS, consultant; b. London, Oct. 18, 1930; s. Leonard Joseph and Vera Mary (Crepin) P.; m. Geraldine Eyre Farley, May 10, 1958; children: Jane Geraldine Lyons, Christopher Charles. LLB, London U., 1958. Solicitor. Mgr. corp. fin. dept. Baring Bros. & Co. Ltd., London, 1958-69; dir. Baring Bros. Co. Ltd., London, 1969-84; cons. Roger Payton Assoc., London, 1984—; chmn. Jarvis Plc, Hertford, Eng., 1994-2000, Richardsons Westgarth Plc, Worcestershire, Eng., 1988-2000, Rothsay Holdings Ltd., Surrey, Eng., 1993—; dep. chmn. Great Portland Estates Plc, London, 1990-2000. Chmn. Met. Pub. Gardens Assn., Surrey, 1991—; master Worshipful Co. of Gardeners, London, 1981-82, 98; pres. Bishopsgate Ward Club, London, 1982-83; trustee City Parochial Found., London, 1984—. Fellow Royal Soc. Arts, Inst. Dirs.; mem. Law Soc. Avocations: gardening, tennis. Home and Office: Little Bedwell Essendon, Hatfield AL9 6JA, England

PAZ, YEHUDAH, university administrator; b. Bklyn., Sept. 27, 1930; arrived in Israel, 1950; m. Ruth Lindenfield, Oct., 1950; children: Amos, Avigail, Talia, Michael. BSc in Econs., U. London, 1972, MSc in Sociology, 1978; PhD in Social Philosophy, Jewish Tchrs. Inst., 1986. Founding mem. Kibbutz Kissufim, Negev region, 1951—, treas., 1961-62, tchr. and headmaster sch., 1963-67, gen. sec., 1971, 1997-98, export and sales mgr. MLM Optical Co., 1979; lectr., mem. directorate Efal Edn. and Rsch. Inst. United Kibbutz Movement, 1958-60, chmn. divsn. higher edn., culture and info., 1969-71; dir. gen. youth and Heehalutz dept. Jewish Agy., 1967-69; dep. dir., acting dir. Van Leer Jerusalem Inst., 1972-75; headmaster Maalc Habcsor Regional Comprehensive H.S., 1975-78; dir., prin. Internat. Inst. for Devel., Labor and Coop. Studies, 1980-93; dir. and prin. Internat. Inst., 1994-97; chmn., acad. dir. Negev Inst. Strategies of Peace and Devel., Negev Coll., 1997—; dir. internat. relations Ctrl. Union of Coop. Socs., 1997—; acad. dir. The Coop. Coll., 1997—; sr. cons. Peres Ctr. for Peace, 1999—; lectr. Ben Gurion U., Negev Coll., Efal Edn. and Rsch. Ctr., United Kibbutz Movement; cons. Bernard van Leer Found., The Hague, Switzerland, 1971-93, Internat. Labor Office, Geneva, 1983-95; mem. bd. Internat. Coop. Alliance, vice chmn. Asia-Pacific region, chmn. global human resource devel. com., mem. panel of experts, coop. br.; vis. lectr. various univs. U.S., Can., Australia, Ireland, russia, China, Japan, Korea, Denmark, Spain, India, G.B., others. Contbr. numerous studies, monographs, articles to profl. jours.; editl. bd. Devel. jour. Mem. ctrl. com. Israel Labor Party, chmn. Asia-Pacific-Africa com., internat. dept.; mem. exec. com. Asia-Pacific Socialist Org., Socialist Internat.; co-chmn. Internat. Ctr. for Peace in the Middle East, 1991-95; presidium mem. Coun. of Israeli Coops.; mem. coun. Ctrl. Union of Coop. Socs., Israel; mem. ctrl. com. United Kibbutz Movement; mem. directorate Yad Tabenkin Rsch. Inst.; mem. exec. com. World Zionist Orgn.-Jewish Agy., Hechalutz; gen. sec. Habonim-Dror youth movement, N.Am.; del. numerous Zionist congresses, labor and other confs. Israel, abroad. Mem. AAAS, N.Y. Acad. Scis., Soc. for Internat. Devel. (exec. com. governing coun. to 1995), Assn. of Ams. and Canadians in Israel (pres.). Avocations: playing oboe, reading, research and lecturing on the American civil war. Fax: 972-76806371. E-mail: nisped@post.makash.ac.il. Home: Kibbutz Kissufim, Doar Na, 85130 Negev Israel Office: Negev Inst Strategies Peace, Doar Na Hof Ashkelon, 79165 Negev Israel

PAZANDAK, CAROL HENDRICKSON, liberal arts educator; b. Mpls.; d. Norman Everard and Ruth (Buckley) Hendrickson; m. Bruce B. Pazandak (dec. 1986); children: David, Bradford, Christopher, Eric, Paul, Ann; m. Joseph P. O'Shaughnessy, May 1991 (dec. Feb. 2000). PhD, U. Minn., 1970. Asst. dir. admissions U. Minn., Mpls., 1970-72, asst. dean liberal arts, 1972-79, asst. to pres., 1979-85, office of internat. edn., acting dir., 1985-87, asst. prof. to assoc. to prof. liberal arts, 1970-96, prof. emerita, 1996—; ptnr. Hollrad-Pers. Consulting, Reykjavik, Iceland, 1999—; vis. prof. U. Iceland, Reykjavik, 1984, periods in 1983, 86-99; vis. rsch. prof. U. Oulu, Finland, 1993; exec. sec. Minn.-Iceland Adv. Com., U. Minn., 1984—; cons. U. Iceland, 1983-98; co-chair Reunion of Sisters-Minn. and Finland Confs., 1986-98; sec. Icelandic Assn. of Minn., 1995-97. Editor: Improving Undergraduate Education in Large Universities, 1989. Past pres. Minn. Mrs. Jaycees, Mpls. Mrs. Jaycees; formerly bd. govs. St. John's Preparatory Sch., Collegeville, Minn.; former bd. trustees Coll. of St. Teresa, Winona, Minn.. Recipient Partnership award for contbn. to advancing shared interests of Iceland and Am., 1994; named to Order of the Falcon, Govt. of Iceland, 1990, Coll. Liberal Arts Alumna Notable Achievement, 1995, Pres.'s Club, U. Minn., 1996. Mem. Am. Psychol. Assn., Soc. Advancement of Scandinavian Studies, Soc. for Disability Studies. Home: 1361 Prior Ave S Saint Paul MN 55116-2656 Office: U Minn N 218 Elliott Hall 75 E River Rd Minneapolis MN 55455-0280

PAZ-ANDRADE, MARIA INMACULADA, physics educator, researcher; b. Pontevedra, Galicia, Spain, Nov. 14, 1928; d. Jose Paz and Maria Andrade. Degree in scis., U. Santiago, Spain, 1955; MSc, U. Santiago, 1956, DSc, 1963; MSc, U. Marsilles, France, 1964. Head dept. applied physics U. Santiago de Compostela (Spain), 1986-93, prof. applied physics, prof. emeritus, 1999; vis. rsch. prof. U. Manchester, 1979; mem. presdl. coun. EUROSTAR, European Soc. Thermal Analysis, Calorimetry Thermodynamics and Chem. Reactivity. Contbr. articles to profl. jours. Pres. Secion de Galicia R.S.E.F., Santiago, 1992. Pres. Thermodynamics Group Real Sociedad Española Fisica, Madrid, 1992—. Rsch. fellow U. Manchester, 1974-75; recipient Gold Medal of Physics Real Sociedad Espanola de Fisica, Madrid, 1992; named Best Rschr. of Galicia, Encuentros '90 Vigo, 1993. Mem. Royal Soc. Chemistry, Real Soc. Espanola Fisica, Real Soc. Espanola Quimica, Soc. Portuguesa Quimica, Soc. Portuguese Fisica, Internat. Conf. Thermody. Solution Non-Electrolytes, European Molecular Liquids Group, Am. Chem. Soc., Spanish Royal Soc. Physics, Acad. Ciencias Granada (academic), Premio Galicia. Avocations: tennis, collecting antiques, collecting stamps, collecting coins, music. Home: Fernando III-9, 15706 Santiago de Compostela Spain Office: Univ Santiago de Compostela, Campus Sur, 15070 Santiago de Compostela Spain

PAZDUR, ANNA, physicist; b. Jawornik Polski, Poland, Feb. 12, 1946; d. Tomasz and Maria (Makarska) Zak; m. Mieczyslaw Franciszek Pazdur, May 11, 1969 (dec. May 11, 1995); children: Natalia, Wojciech, Karol. M in Physics, Jagellonian U., 1968; PhD in Physics, U. Siesia, 1978; PhD, Acad. Mining & Metallurgy, Cracow, Poland, 1990. Meteorologist Inst. Meteorology, Katowice, Poland, 1968-69; from asst. to prof. Inst. Physics Silesian U. of Tech., Gliwice, Poland, 1969—. Co-author: Geochronology of the Poland Upper Quaternary in the Light of Radiocarbon and Luminescence Dating, 1994; contbr. articles to profl. jorus. Mem. Polish Acad. Scis. Avocations: literature, poetry, excursions. Office: Inst Physics, Krzywoustego 2, 44-101 Gliwice Poland

PAZOS, WALTER ADRIAN, marketing specialist; b. Buenos Aires, Argentina, May 14, 1971; came to U.S., 1995; s. Primitivo and Olag Maria (Malaspina) P.; m. Elizabeth Anne Payne, Jan. 23, 1998; 1 child, Samantha Katelyn. Degree in advt., U. John F. Kennedy, Buenos Aires, 1994; postgrad., U. Wis., Whitewater, 1999—. Comml. rep. Argencard-Mastercard, Buenos Aires, 1994-95; mktg. cons., cons. asst. Govt., Buenos Aires, 1995, 97; coord. desk Marriott Internat., Fort Belvoir, Va., 1996-97; mktg. coord. Editl. Medica Panamericana, Buenos Aires, 1997; cashier officer fin. dept. Interam. Bank, Washington, 1998—. Mem. Am. Mktg. Assn. Home: 2536 Chadwick Ct Woodbridge VA 22192-2037

PÁZSIT, IMRE, physicist, researcher; b. Budapest, Hungary, Feb. 14, 1948; arrived in Sweden, 1983; s. Imre and Eleonora (Tolgyesi) P.; m. Maria Kordelyos Pázsit, May 11, 1974; 1 child, Raymond. MS in Physics, Eötvös Loránd U. Scis., Budapest, 1971; PhD, U. Scis., Budapest, 1975; DSc, Acad. Scis., Budapest, 1985. Fellow Inst. Atomic Energy, Budapest, 1972-75, from rsch. assoc. to head theory group, 1975-83; from sr. rschr. to dep. group head at reactor Studsvik Energiteknik AB, Nykoping, Sweden, 1983-91; prof., head of dept Chalmers U. Tech., Goteborg, Sweden, 1991—; cons. EuroSim AB, Nykoping, Sweden, 1992; mem. OECD NEA Nuc. Sci. Com., Paris, 1992—; bd. dirs. Ctr. for Fusion Sci., 1992—, Energy Tech. Ctr., 1993—, dir., 1997-98, Chalmers U., Goteborg, Sweden, Swedish Ctr. for Nuc. Tech., 1999—; vis. scholar Kyoto U. Rsch. Reactor Inst., 1999. Contbr. over 100 articles to profl. jours. Recipient First prize for Young Rschr., Inst. Physics, Budapest, 1979, Rsch. fellowship, Internat. Atomic Energy Agy, 1979; fellow Japan Soc. for Promotion of Sci., 1990. Mem. Am. Nuclear Soc., Swedish Phys. Soc., Swedish Nuc. Soc., Environmentalists for Nuclear Power. Avocations: table tennis, guitar music. Home: Klappegatan 9, 43169 Molndal Sweden Office: Chalmers U Technology Dept Reactor Physics, Gibraltargatan 3, 41296 Göteborg Sweden

PBERKOWITZKY, GEOFF, writer, educator; b. N.Y.C., Sept. 24; s. George and Spiedie Pberkowitzky. PhD, Rice U., 1995. Tchr. Scranton (Pa.) Coll., 1996-98. Author: There You Are, 1996. Mem. Kiwanis (pres.). Republican. Avocation: chess. Home and Office: Pb Enterprises 201 Main St Vestal NY 13850-1520

PCHELKIN, BASIL PETER, chemist, researcher; b. Moscow, Mar. 14, 1953; s. Peter Maxim and Valentina Joanna (Petroff) P.; m. Natalia Theodora Luts, Dec. 27, 1986; 1 child, Elisabeth. Diploma in engring., Inst. Fine Chem. Tech., Moscow, 1976. Probationer-rschr. Inst. Plant Physiol., Moscow, 1976-78, minor rsch. worker, 1978-89, rsch. worker, 1989—. Contbr. articles to profl. jours. Grantee Internat. Sci. Found., 1993. Mem. N.Y. Acad. Sci. Office: Inst Plant Physiology, 35 Botanicheskaya, 127276 Moscow Russia

PEACE, WILLIAM HENRY, III, management consultant; b. Phila., Aug. 14, 1938; s. William Henry II and Louisa (Bright) P.; m. Susan Lord, Apr. 20, 1963 (div. Apr. 1990); children: Susan Elizabeth, Catherine Gilpin, William Lord; m. Anna Venturi, May 26, 1990. BS in Physics, Yale U., 1960. Sales engr. Westinghouse Electric Corp., N.Y.C., 1964-69, sales mgr., 1969-76; gen. mgr. Westinghouse Electric Corp., Phila., 1976-80; gen. mgr. synthetic fuels div. Westinghouse Electric Corp., Madison, Pa., 1980-84; v.p., gen. mgr. KRW Energy Systems Inc., Madison, 1984-86; sr. v.p. indsl. refrigeration Carrier Corp., Syracuse, N.Y., 1986-87, pres. European transcontinental ops., 1987-89; ind. cons., 1990-91; dir., exec. cons. Doctus Consulting Europe, London, 1991-93; mgmt. cons., owner Achievement, Great Kings Hill, Eng., 1993—. Served to lt. USN, 1960-64. Republican. Ch. of England. Avocations: making furniture, running, needlepoint. Home and Office: Orchard Cottage, Cockpit Rd, Great Kings Hill HP15 6ER, England

PEACH, DONALD FREDERICK, medical educator; b. Modbury, Devon, Eng., Oct. 17, 1954; s. Douglas and Doreen (Bridgen) P. Diploma coll. radiographers, Plymouth Sch. Radiography, 1975; higher diploma coll. radiographers, Nottingham Sch. Radiograph, 1983; tchrs. diploma coll. radiographers, Oxford Regional Sch., 1984; dip.H.E., Oxford Brooks U., 1990; MSc, U. Oxford, 1991. Rsch. asst. Beechams Rsch. Labs., Worthing, Eng., 1973; radiographer Plymouth Hosps., Eng., 1975-79, Kummunahospitalet, Copenhagen, 1979; sr. radiographer Derbyshire Royal Infirmary, Derby, Eng., 1980-83; supt. radiographer Derby City Hosp., Derby, 1983; tchr. John Radcliffe Hosp., Oxford, 1983-92; lectr. Cranfield U., Shrivenham, Eng., 1992—; external assessor U. Oxford, 1996—; cons. Oxford Intelligent Visualisation and Analysis, 1999—. Reviewer RAD Mag., Harlow, Eng., 1992—; contbr. articles to profl. jours. Treas. Shrivenham United Charities, 1998—. Avocations: falconer, taxidermist, pilot. Home: 9 Charlbury Rd Shrivenham, Oxfordshire SN6-8EQ, England Office: Cranfield U, Shrivenham, Oxfordshire SN6-8LA, England

PEACOCK, GRAHAM REX, business, financial consultant; b. London, Apr. 20, 1938; arrived in Greece, 1982; s. Reginald Coleridge and Hilda Ivy Lilian (Pulman) P. Chartered acct. Articled clk. to audit mgr. Hartleys, Wilkins & Flew, London, 1956-63; fin. acct. Assoc. Motor Cycles Ltd., London, 1964-66; chief acct. Norton Villiers Ltd., London, 1966-68; fin. controller Matthews Holdings Group, Surrey, Eng., 1968-78; fin. dir. Black, Sivalls & Bryson, Surrey, 1979-80; group dir. fin. Dale Keller & Assocs., London and Athens, Greece, 1980-84; cons. London and Athens, 1984—; gen. mgr. Sigma Consult Ltd., Athens and Dublin, Ireland, 1988-93; dep. chief exec. officer Delta Enterprises Group, U.K., Greece, 1989-93, Sigma Ltd., U.K., 1990-93; bd. dirs. various cos. in U.K., France, Holland, and Gibraltar. Bd. dirs. Byron Coll. Ltd., London, 1986-88; gov. Byron Coll., Athens, 1986-88; dir. Byron Ednl. Found., London, 1987-91. Fellow Inst. Chartered Accts. Eng. and Wales; mem. British Hellenic C. of C., Commonwealth Gen. Mgrs., British Humanist Assn. Avocations: jazz, impres-

sionist art, food, travel. Home and Office: Hatzichristou 11 Acropolis, GR117 42 Athens Greece

PEACOCK, MOLLY, poet; b. June 30, 1947; d. Edward Frank and Pauline Ruth (Wright) P. BA magna cum laude, Harpur Coll., Binghampton, N.Y., 1969; MA with hons., Johns Hopkins U., 1977. Adminstr., lectr. in english SUNY, Binghamton, 1970-76; lectr. Johns Hopkins U., Balt., 1977-78; instr. english Friends Sem., N.Y.C., 1981-92; poet-in-residence Bucknell U., 1993-94, Cathedral St. John the Divine, 2000. Author: And Live Apart, 1980, Raw Heaven, 1984, Take Heart, 1989, Original Love, 1995, Paradise, Piece by Piece, 1998, How To Read A Poem and Start A Poetry Circle, 1999; contbg. writer House and Garden mag., 1996; contbr. poems to The New Yorker, The New Republic, The Nation. Danforth Found. fellow, 1970, Yaddo fellow, 1980, 82, 89, Ingram Merrill Found. fellow 1981, 86, New Va. Rev. fellow 1983, Lila Wallace/Woodrow Wilson fellow 1994, 95, 96, 2001; grantee Creative Artists Pub. Svc. Program, 1977, N.Y. Found. for Arts, 1985, NEA, 1991; Regents scholar U. Calif., Riverside, 1998. Mem. PEN, Poetry Soc. Am. (governing bd. 1988—, pres. emeritus). Home: 505 E 14th St Apt 3G New York NY 10009-2903 also: 229 Emery St E, London, ON Canada N6C 2E3

PEACOCKE, CHRISTOPHER ARTHUR BRUCE, philosopher, educator; b. Birmingham, Eng., May 22, 1950; s. Arthur Robert and Rosemary (Mann) P.; m. Teresa Anne Rosen, Jan. 3, 1980; 2 children. BA, Oxford (Eng.) U., 1971, BPhil, 1974, DPhil, 1979. Jr. rsch. fellow in philosophy The Queen's Coll., Oxford, 1973-75; vis. lectr. U. Calif., Berkeley, 1975-76; fellow All Souls Coll., Oxford, 1975-79; fellow, lectr. in philosophy New Coll., Oxford, 1979-85; Stebbing prof. King's Coll., London, 1985-88; Waynflete prof. metaphys. philosophy Oxford U., 1989-2000, Leverhulme Trust personal rsch. prof., 1996-2000; prof. philosophy NYU, N.Y.C., 2000—; vis. assoc. prof. U. Mich., 1978, UCLA, 1981, NYU, 1996-98. Author: Holistic Exploration, 1979, Sense and Content, 1983, Thoughts, 1986, A Study of Concepts, 1992. Pres. Mind Assn., Eng., 1986. Fellow Brit. Acad., 1990, Ctr. for Advanced Studies in Behavorial Scis., Stanford, 1983-84. Avocations: music, visual arts. Office: NYU Main Bldg Dept Philosophy 100 Washington Sq E New York NY 10003-6688

PEAK, GEOFFREY HAROLD, lawyer; b. Auckland, New Zealand, Mar. 1, 1936; s. Leicester and Lois (Worsley) P.; m. Patricia Mary Briggs, Feb. 20, 1960; children: Raewyn, Malcolm, Alastair, Rosalind. LLB, Auckland U., 1960. Solicitor Brookfield Prendergast Schnauer & Smytheman, Auckland, 1956-59; ptnr. Peak Rogers, Auckland, 1960-90; ptnr. Cairns Slane, Auckland, 1990—, now sr. ptnr.; dir. Kwan Holdings Ltd., Fund Mgrs. Auchland Ltd., Royce Holdings Ltd., Heathcote Holdings Ltd.; trustee Auckland Mortgage Trust.; mem. several charitable bds. Legal adviser Meth. Ch., New Zealand, 1977—. Mem. Auckland Law Soc., Maungakiekie Golf Club. Avocations: golf, sailing, beach activities, gardening. E-mail: ghpeak@cairnsslane.co.nz. Home: 12 Wayne Pl Mt Roskill, Auckland 1004, New Zealand Office: Cairns Slane, 156 Vincent St PO Box 6849, Auckland 1036, New Zealand

PEAKALL, DAVID BEAUMONT, environmental chemist; b. Purley, Surrey, Eng., Mar. 17, 1931; s. Ernest Victor and Majory (Smith) P.; children: Beth, Susan, Jonathan, Megan. BSc with honors in Chemistry, U. London, 1952, PhD, 1956, DSc, 1979. Sci. officer Ministry of Supply, Porton, Eng., 1956-57; postdoctoral fellow SUNY, Alfred, 1957-59; chemist Distiller's Co., Banstead, Eng., 1959-60; rsch. assoc. SUNY, Syracuse, 1960-68; sr. rsch. assoc. Cornell U., Ithaca, N.Y., 1968-75; chief toxicology divsn. Can. Wildlife Svc., Ottawa, Ont., 1975-91; sr. rsch. fellow King's Coll., London, 1991-99; del. ecotoxicology expert group OECD, Paris, 1978-88, chmn. environ. effects group, Paris, 1980-82; mem. adv. bd. Wildlife Toxicology Fund, Toronto, Ont., 1984-91, Mount Desert Island Biol. Lab., Bar Harbor, Maine, 1984-92; rsch. fellow Am. Heart Assn., 1966-70; mem. exec. com. Sci. Group for Safety Evaluation of Chems., 1981-92; mem. nat. com. Sci. Problems of Environment, 1982-92. Author: Methods for Estimating Risk of Chemical Injury, 1985, Animal Biomarkers, 1992, Biomarkers/NATO, 1993; editor in chief Ecotoxicology, 1991—. Mem. Am. Ornithology Union (exec. mem. 1962—), Soc. Environ. Toxicologists and Chemists, Brit. Trust for Ornithology, N.Y. State Fedn. Bird Clubs (pres. 1968-69). Avocations: bird watching, gardening, visiting art galleries. Home: 17 St Mary's Rd, Wimbledon, London SW19 7BZ, England

PEAR, CHARLES E., JR., lawyer; b. Macon, Ga., June 18, 1950; s. Charles Edward and Barbara Jane P.; m. Linda Sue King; children: Jennifer Sue, Charles Edward III, Stephanie Sue. BA, U. Hawaii, 1972 with honors; JD, U. Calif., Berkeley, 1975. Bar: Hawaii 1976, Fla. 1977, Colo. 1994, U.S. Ct. of Appeals (9th cir.). Assoc. Rush, Moore, Craven, Sutton, Morry & Beh, Honolulu, 1976-77, of counsel, 1987-90; assoc., ptnr. Carlsmith & Dwyer, Honolulu, 1977-82; ptnr. Burke, Sakai, McPheeters, Bordner & Gilardy, Honolulu, 1983-87; vis. prof. law and computers U. British Columbia, 1990-93; of counsel Holland & Hart, Denver, 1993-96; counsel, ptnr. McCorriston, Miller, Mukai, MacKinnon, Honolulu, 1996—; mem. Hawaii Real Estate Commn. com. on condominium and resort real estate legis., 1978-79; spl. counsel to consumer protection com. Hawaii State Ho. of Reps., 1981-82; chair real property and fin. svcs. sect. Hawaii State Bar Assn., ABA. Editor-in-Chief Hawaii Conveyance Manual II, 1987; editor Hawaii Commercial Real Estate Manual, 1988; bd. editors Hawaii Inst. of Continuing Legal Edn.; co-author: Nat. Assn. of Real Estate Licensing Law Officials and Nat. Timesharing Coun. Model Timesharing Act, 1981-82; contbg. author: Winning With Computers, 1992, Hawaii Real Estate Manual, 1997; lectr. in field, 1981—. Mem. ABA (document assembly interest group, expert sys. interest group, hypermedia interest group).

PEARCE, CHRISTOPHER JONATHAN, clinical biochemist, consultant; b. Leeds, Eng., Feb. 10, 1948; s. Budge and Bettie (Dalton) P.; m. Christine Mary Horton, Sept. 10, 1981. BM, BChir, Oxford U., 1972. House physician Middlesex Hosp., London, 1972-73; resident med. officer Westminster Hosp., London, 1974-75, med. registar, 1975-77; med. registrar Northwick Park Hosp., Harrow, U.K., 1978-80; sci. officer Clin. Rsch. Ctr., Harrow, 1980-85; sr. registrar Liverpool (U.K.) U., 1985-90; cons. The Ipswich (U.K.) Hosp., 1990—. Contbr. articles to profl. jours. Fellow Royal Coll. Physicians, Royal Coll. Pathologists, British Endocrine Soc., Thyroid Club, Assn. Clin. Biochemists. Avocations: golf, windsurfing, music. Office: The Ipswich Hosp, Clin Biochemistry, Ipswich England

PEARCE, GILLIAN, astrophysicist, physician, educator; b. Wednesbury, Eng., Sept. 8, 1956; d. George Arthur and Phyllis Gwendoline Violet (Simkins) P. BSc in Physics with honors, Wolverhampton U., Eng., 1980; PhD in Astrophysics, Keele U., Staffordshire, Eng., 1983; BM BCh, Oxford (Eng.) U., 1997; BSc in Biomed. Scis. with honors, Wolverhampton U., Eng., 1995; postgrad., Internat. Space U., 1990, 91. Cert. open water diver. Rsch. fellow in astrophysics Durham (Eng.) U., 1984-85, Birmingham (Eng.) U., 1985-87; sr. rsch. fellow in astrophysics (Atlas fellow) Oxford U., 1987-92; lectr. Open U., Milton Keynes, Eng., 1990—; rsch. astrophysicist Wolverhampton U., Eng., 1993—; lectr. in astrophysics St. Anne's Coll., Oxford U., 1993-94, vis. rsch. fellow astrophysics St. Johns Coll., Oxford U., 1992; continuing edn. lectr. Bilston Coll., Eng., 1993-96, Oxford U., 1989—; astronaut candidate for Anglo-Soviet space mission Juno, 1988; presenter in field. Contbr. numerous rsch. papers to profl. jours. Vol. Royal Brit. Legion, Walsall, Eng., 1985—, St. John's Ambulance, Wednesbury, 1984-87; mem. congregation and convocation Oxford U., 1987-92; mem. sr. common rm. St. Aidan's Coll., Durham U., 1985—, Jesus Coll., Oxford U., 1987-92. Recipient Churchill-Livingstone Med. Essay 2d prize, 1994; Westminster fellow, Brit. Media fellow BBC World Svc., London, 1993, Snell-Newlands vis. fellow Glasgow U., 1991-92; Brit. Nat. Space Ctr. scholar, 1990; Internat. Collaborations in Rsch. travel grantee Royal Soc., 1993; Hilda Martindale Exhibitioner, Hilda Martindale Ednl. Trust, 1993-95. Mem. Royal Astron. Soc. (mem. coun. 1991-94). Mem. Ch. of England. Avocations: classical music, hill walking, art, diving. Home: 10 Kings Hill Fields, Wednesbury, West Midlands WS10 9JF, England Office: Wolverhampton U Astrophys, Dept Computing/Info Tech, West Midlands England

PEARCE, GRAHAM LLOYD, petroleum engineer; b. Airedale, United Kingdom, Apr. 27, 1949; s. William John and Joy Elizabeth (Hover) P.; m. Ann Dorothy Burton, Oct. 8, 1983; children: Wanda, Holly-Joy, Jasper. BA, Wadham Coll., Oxford U., 1970; PhD, Univ. Coll., London, 1980. Tchr. Vol. Svc. Overseas, Singapore, 1970-71, Hornsey Sch., London, 1973-74; demonstrator Univ. Coll., London, 1978-80; petroleum engr. U.K. Atomic Emergy Auth., Dorchester, 1980-83; sr. petroleum engr. Exploration Cons. Ltd., Henley-on-Thames, 1983-88; mgr. of cons., tech. dir. ECl-Intera, Henley-on-Thames, 1988-91; petroleum engr. Henley-on-Thames, 1991-95; dir. Pearce Energy Cons. Ltd., Henley-on-Thames, 1995—. Avocations: bridge, squash. Fax: 44 1491 628054. E-mail: gpearce@pecl.freeserve.co.uk. Office: Pearce Energy Cons Ltd, 23 Stevens Ln, Rotherford, Peppard Henley-on-Thames RG9 5RG, United Kingdom

PEARCE, JOAN DELAP, research company executive; b. Oakland, Calif., June 13, 1930; d. Robert Jerome and Wilhelmina (Reaume) DeLap; m. Gerald Allan Pearce, June 18, 1953; 1 child, Scott Ford. Student, U. Oreg., 1948-55. Rsch. assoc. deForest Rsch., L.A., 1966-78, assoc. dir., 1978-92; dir. rsch. Walt Disney Prodns., Burbank, Calif., 1978; pres., bd. dirs. Joan Pearce Rsch. Assocs., 1992—; lighting dir. Wilcoxen Players, Beverly Hills, Calif., 1955-60, Theatre 40, L.A., 1960-66. Bd. advisors Living History Ctr., Marin County, Calif., 1982-89, bd. dirs., 1989-94. Mem. Am. Film Inst. Democrat. Avocations: photography; travel; theater; swimming. Home: 2621 Rutherford Dr Los Angeles CA 90068-3042 Office: Joan Pearce Rsch Assocs 8111 Beverly Blvd Ste 308 Los Angeles CA 90048-4525

PEARCE, JOHN BARBER, psychiatry educator; b. Shrewsbury, England, Oct. 27, 1940; s. Arnold Porteus and Ruth (Parry) P.; m. Jean Mary Bogle, June 25, 1966; children: Rachel, Clare, Anna. MB, BChir, U. Coll., London, 1965; MPhil, Inst. Psychiatry, London, 1974. Diploma of child health. House officer Univ. Coll. Hosp., London, 1965-66; pediatric sr. house officer Jenny Lind Hosp., Norfolk, 1966-67; registrar St. Bartholomews Hosp., London, 1967-71; sr. registrar Maudsley Hosp., London, 1971-75; cons. Guys Hosp., London, 1975-87; sr. lectr. Leicester (Eng.) U., 1987-91; prof. Nottingham (Eng.) U., 1991—; examiner Royal Colls. Psychiatry and Physicians, Eng., 1983-94; advisor NHS, Eng., 1986—. Author, co-presenter (book and tv series) Kids Work Out, 1986; author: Bad Behaviour, 1989 (Red House Book of the Month 1989), Thorsons Child Care Series, 1989-94; editor Current Opinion, 1990-93. Team mem. Exploring Parenthood, London, 1991—; lectr. Kidscape, London, 1992—. Fellow Royal Coll. Physicians, Royal Coll. Psychiatrists (sec. child adolescent exec. com., acad. sec. 1990-93, sec. child psychiatry sect. 1993—, mem. parliamentary liaison com. 1995—); mem. Brit. Paediatric Assn., Assn. Child Psychologists-Psychiatrists, Joint Commn. Higher Psychiatrie Tng., Brit. Med. Assn. Avocations: sailing, cello playing, restoring things. Office: The Thorneywood Unit, Porchester Rd, Nottingham NG3 6LF, England

PEARCE, JOHN Y., lawyer; b. New Orleans, Mar. 26, 1948; s. John Young II and Marina (Harris) P.; m. Marjorie Pamela Doyle, May 22, 1971 (div.); children: Andrea Elizabeth, Roger Wellington. BA, La. State U., 1973, JD, 1976. Bar: La. 1977, U.S. Dist. Ct. (ea., mid. and we. dists.) La., U.S. Ct. Appeals (5th and 11th cirs.). Assoc. Doyle, Smith & Doyle, New Orleans, 1977-79, ptnr., 1979-80, mng. ptnr., 1980-84; ptnr. Montgomery, Barnett, Brown, Read, Hammond & Mintz, New Orleans, 1984—. Sgt. U.S. Army, 1969-71. Mem. ABA (ho. dels. 1998-2000), La. Bar Assn. (chmn. mineral law coun. 1994-95), New Orleans Bar Assn. (exec. com., pres. 1997-98). Republican. Episcopalian. Office: Montgomery Barnett Brown Read Hammond & Mintz 1100 Poydras St New Orleans LA 70163-1101

PEARCE, JOSEPH HUSKE, industrial engineer; b. Sarasota, Fla., Mar. 7, 1941; s. Joseph Huske and Lola (Smelcer) P.; m. Victoria Lee Georgie (div. Aug. 1976); children: Sherri Lynn, Lara Ann. BSEE, U. Fla., 1968. Elec. engr. trainee guided missiles range div. Pan Am. World Airways, Patrick AFB, Fla., 1964-65; asst. base ops. mgr. trainee Pan Am. World Airways, Freeport, The Bahamas, 1965-66; installation engr. safeguard anti ballistic missile project Western Electric Co., Winston-Salem, N.C., 1968-73; design and test engr. Western Electric Co., Madison, N.J., 1973-74; indsl. engr. AT&T, Rolling Meadows, Ill., 1974-91; cons. engr. Cen. Office Equipment, 1991—. Petty officer 2d class USN, 1959-63. Republican. Lutheran. Avocations: American and Civil War history, fishing, hunting, classic literature. Office: PO Box 140335 Gainesville FL 32614-0335

PEARCE, PATSY BEASLEY, elementary education educator; b. Dunn, N.C., Apr. 13, 1945; d. Marvin Franklin and Christine (Bryant) Beasley; m. Robert Michael Cole, Aug. 15, 1970 (div.); 1 child, Matthew Bryant Cole; m. Elwood Glenn Pearce, Mar. 1, 1980. BSEd, E. Caroline U., 1966. Cert. collegiate profl., Va. Primary tchr., 1st and 2d grade Va. Beach (Va.) City Schs., 1966-75; primary tchr., 1st. and 3rd grade Jasper County Schs., Hardeeville, S.C., 1976-78; tchr., 4th grade Campbell County Schs., Lynchburg, Va., 1979; kindergarten tchr. Aesop Acad., Portsmouth, Va., 1981-84; primary tchr., 1st grade Chesapeake (Va.) City Schs., 1984—; mem. social studies adoption com. Chesapeake City Schs., 1996-98, colleague mentor, 1997-98, Book It chairperson, 1997—; United Way chair, 1995-97, chairperson Pizza Hut's Book It, 1997—; sch. rep. Chesapeake Reading Coun., 1986-95, colleague mentor, 1988-90; equity tutor Camelot Elem. Sch., Chesapeake, 1994, grade level chmn., 1990-95, coop. tchr., 1990-91; mem. tech. tng. Va. Stds. Learning Tng., 1999-2000. Sunday sch. tchr. Cradock United Meth. Ch., Portsmouth, Va., 1982, worship com. chmn. 1990-91, Acolyte chmn., 1984-89; vacation Bible sch. tchr. Thail United Meth. Ch., Virginia Beach, 1969; com. chmn., treas. Cub Scout Pack 251, Portsmouth, Va., 1980-91; roundtable commr. Merrimac Dist. Boy Scouts Am., Portsmouth, 1989-90, dist. chmn. Scouts Ann. Mall Show and Pinewood Derby Race, 1987-89; children's choir dir. Kempsville Ch. of Christ, Virginia Beach, 1979-80. Named Camelot's Tchr. of Yr., 1995-96. Mem. NEA, Va. Edn. Assn., Chesapeake Edn. Assn., Chesapeake Reading Coun., Internat. Reading Coun., PTA (corr. sec. 1997-98). Avocations: gardening, needlework crafts, travel, granddaughter. Home: 2233 Ferndale Rd Chesapeake VA 23323-5016 Office: Camelot Elem 2901 Guenevere Dr Chesapeake VA 23323-2704

PEARCY, MARK JOHN, engineering educator; b. London Colney, Hertford., Eng., June 28, 1953; s. John Frederick and Jane Margaret (Whitaker) P.; m. Patricia Joy Hosking; children: Luke John Hosking Pearcy, Josh Robert Hosking Pearcy. BSME, U. Bristol, 1974; PhD in Bioengring., U. Strathclyde, U.K., 1979. CPEng. Inst. of Engrs., Australia, CEng., U.K. Rsch. bioengr. Oxford Orthopaedic Engring. Ctr., U.K., 1979-84; lectr. in bioengring. U. Durham, U.K., 1984-90; chief hosp. scientist Royal Adelaide Hosp., Australia, 1990-94; assoc. prof. Flinders U. of South Australia, 1994-96; prof. biomed. engring. Queensland U. of Technology, Australia, 1996—. Contbr. articles to profl. jours. Recipient Tribology award Inst. Mech. Engrs., U.K., 1987, rsch. prize Spine Soc. of Australia, 1992. Fellow Inst. Engrs. Australia. Avocation: Aikido. Office: Queensland U Tech, GPO Box 2434, Brisbane QLD, Australia

PEARINCOTT, JOSEPH VERGHESE, educator, physiologist; b. Travancore, India, May 26, 1929; s. George F. and Elizabeth (Kottakaram) P.; B.Sc., Travancore U., 1949; M.Sc., Aligarh U., 1951; Ph.D., Fordham U., 1959; m. Michaeleen Ferrara, May 1, 1958; 1 son, George Joseph. Came to U.S., 1952, naturalized, 1959. Instr. biology Fordham U., N.Y.C., 1952-56; postdoctoral fellow Columbia Coll. Physicians and Surgeons, N.Y.C., 1959-61; research asso., dept. physiology and pharmacology N.Y. Med. Coll., N.Y.C., 1961-62; asst. prof. biology Northeastern U., Boston, 1962-68, asso. prof. biology, 1968—. Mem. N.Y. Acad. Scis., AAAS, Am. Soc. Zoologists, Entomol. Soc. Am., AAUP, Sigma Xi. Home: 61 Webb St Lexington MA 02420-2245 Office: 360 Huntington Ave Boston MA 02115-5005

PEARL, ALEXANDRA, editor; b. Berlin, Sept. 15, 1967; d. Geoffrey and Judith Nances (Franklin) P. BSc in Biology, Southampton U., 1992; MSc in Biomed. Sci., London U., 1994. Editor Up-date Med. Pub., Athens, 1996-98, Turret Rai, London, 1999, Miller Freeman, London, 1999—. Avocations: scientific philosophy, arts and crafts. Office: City Rd Millharbour 5, Greenwich View Pl, London E14 9NN, England

PEARLMAN, LOUIS JAY, aviation and entertainment company executive; b. Flushing, N.Y., June 19, 1954; s. Herman and Reenie (Nevler) P. BA, Queens Coll., 1976; MBA, Century U., 1980; Degree in Sales Mgmt., SUNY, Buffalo, 1980; PhD in Bus. Adminstrn., Century U., 1983. Pres. Commuter Helicopter Corp., N.Y.C., 1974-75; pres., COO Trans Continental Airlines, Inc., N.Y.C., 1975—, Trans Continental Records, Orlando, Fla., 1991—; gen. mgr. U.S. Westdeutsche Luftwerbung GmbH, N.Y.C., 1976-85; chmn., pres., CEO Airship Internat. Ltd., N.Y.C., 1982—, bd. dirs., 1985—; pres., CEO Trans Continental Records, Inc., 1992—; pres. Backstreet Boys, Inc., 1993—; CEO Chippendales, Inc., 1996-2000, Entertainment Internat. Ltd., 1997—, Planet Airways Inc., 1998—, bd. dirs.; cons. Queens Coll., CUNY, 1977—. Author: Survey and Analysis of the Airline Industry, 1983; song writer. Active Mitchell-Linden Civic Assn., Flushing, 1980-82, Kissimmee (Fla.) Mcpl. Airport, 1985—. Recipient Govs. award NARAS, 2000. Mem. U.S. Power Squadron, Wings Club (disting., recipient Lighter-than-Air award 1987), Lighter-than-Air Soc. (hon.), Young Entrepreneurs Am., Young Millionaires Club, Internat. Air Transport Assn., Blimp Port U.S.A. (pres. 1987—), Friar's Club (N.Y.C.). Avocations: flying airplanes, helicopters and blimps, swimming, bowling, music, boating. Office: Trans Continental Cos Inc 7380 Sand Lake Rd Ste 350 Orlando FL 32819-5257

PEARLMAN, PETER STEVEN, lawyer; b. Orange, N.J., June 11, 1946; s. Jack Kitchener and Tiela Josephine (Fine) P.; m. Joan Perlmutter, June 19, 1969; children: Heather, Christopher, Megan. BA, U. Ill., 1967; JD, Seton Hall U., 1970. Bar: N.J. 1970, U.S. Dist. Ct. N.J. 1970, U.S. Tax Ct. 1973, U.S. Supreme Ct. 1974, U.S. Ct. Appeals (2d cir.) 1981, U.S. Ct. Appeals (3d cir.) 1983, U.S. Ct. Appeals (7th cir.) 1985, U.S. Ct. Appeals (D.C. cir.) 1998, U.S. Ct. Appeals (4th cir.) 1999; cert. civil trial atty., 1982. Assoc. Cohn & Lifland, Esquires, Saddle Brook, N.J., 1970-72; ptnr. Cohn, Lifland, Pearlman, Herrmann & Knopf, Saddle Brook, 1972—; lectr. Nat. Inst. Trial Advocacy, Hempstead, N.Y., 1988—; active trial advocacy program Weidner Law Sch.; adj. faculty mem. trial advocacy program Hofstra Law Sch.; master C. Willard Heckel Inn of Ct.; guest lectr. appellate advocacy Roger Williams Law Sch., 1995—; mem. panel arbitrators Am. Arbitration Assn.; lectr. for Inst. Continuing Legal Edn. for State of N.J. Mem. ABA, ATLA, N.J. Bar Assn. Home: 9 Harvey Dr Short Hills NJ 07078-1122 Office: Cohn Lifland Pearlman Herrmann & Knopf 1 Park 80 Plz W Ste 4 Saddle Brook NJ 07663-5808

PEARN, JOHN HEMSLEY, pediatrician, Australian military officer; b. Brisbane, Australia, Mar. 18, 1940; s. James Owen and Elizabeth Helen (Shaw) P.; m. Vena Beatrice White, Dec. 1, 1966; children: Owen Edward, Nigel John, Susan Cicely. BSc, U. Queensland, Australia, 1962, MB, BChir, 1964, MD, 1969. Registered med. practitioner, Queensland; cert. clin. geneticist; specialist cons. pediatrician physician, and doctor-soldier. Resident med. officer Royal Brisbane Hosp., 1965; clin. lectr., sr. lectr. and reader Royal Children's Hosp., Brisbane, 1968-85; sr. rsch. fellow U. London, Hosp. for Sick Children, 1971-72, Regional Neurol. Ctr., Westgate Hosp., Newcastle, Eng., 1973-74; clin. lectr. U. Queensland, 1966-67, prof., chmn. dept. child health, 1986—; commd. maj. gen. Australian Def. Force, 1998—; vis. scholar Green Coll. U. Oxford, Eng., 1995; mem. med. ethics com. Australian Def. Force, 1990—. Author 20 books in field, including In the Capacity of A Surgeon, 1988, Venoms and Victims, 1988, Preventive First Aid, 1989, Fevers and Frontiers, 1990, New Horizons, 1992, Milestones of Australian Medicine, 1994, Of Heart and Mind, 1999; co-author: The Science of First Aid, 1996, Arms and Aesculapius, 1996; contbr. articles to profl. jours. Nat. dir. tng. St. John Ambulance Australia, Brisbane, 1990-99; councillor Australian Resuscitation Coun., 1987-93; exec. Child Accident Prevention Found., Melbourne, 1979-90, Pediat. Rsch. Soc., Australia, Melbourne, 1976; med. ethics com. Australian Def. Force, 1990—. Col. M.C. Royal Australian Army, 1965-96, nat. hon. col., 1997-98; apptd. surgeon gen. Australia, Def. Force, 1998—. Decorated Order of Australia, Res. Forces; decorated knight Order of St. John, 1996; Florey fellow Royal Soc. London, 1971-74; recipient Bancroft Oration award, 1991, Herbert Moran Oration award, 1991, Ashdown Oration medal Australasian Coll. of Tropical Medicine, 1995, citation Australia Med. Assn., 1995, Vincent Read medal Australian Numismatic Soc., 1997, Ramsay medal Ramsay Soc. (U.K.), 2000; Kenneth Russell orator Royal Australasian Coll. Surgeons, 1996, John Thomson medal Royal Australian Army M.C., 1998; hon. fellow Green Coll., Oxford, 1997. Fellow Royal Australian Coll. Physicians, Royal Coll. Physicians, Royal Coll. Physicians Edinburgh, Am. Coll. Tropical Medicine, Royal Hist. Soc. Queensland (v.p. 1989—), Royal Life Saving Soc. Australia, Royal Australian Coll. Med. Adminstrn. (hon.); mem. Human Genetics Soc. Australas (nat. pres. 1981-83), Parachute Regtl. Assn., United Svc. Inst., Australia Coll. Pediat. (chmn. Queensland 1993-96); Australian Soc. Hist. of Medicine (hon. life mem., pres. 1995-97), Australian Coll. Tropical Medicine. Avocations: medical history, medical philately, ancient stone-tool cultures. Home: 121 Banks St, Brisbane Queensland 4051, Australia Office: Royal Childrens Hosp, Herston, Brisbane Queensland 4029, Australia

PEARSON, ALAN WILFRED, management educator; b. Liverpool, Eng., July 13, 1934; m. Irene Henwood, Nov. 28, 1959 (dec. Aug. 1986); children: Carol, Michael, John, Mark; m. Marianne TidestrÖm, Sept. 21, 1991. BSc, U. London, 1960; PhD (hon.), U. Kiel, Germany, 1993. Chartered physicist. Chemist Pilkington Plc., Eng., 1951-61; R&D project mgr. Simon Engring. Plc., Eng., 1961-64; lectr. U. Manchester, Eng., 1964-67; dir. rsch. & devel. unit Manchester Bus. Sch., 1967—, dir. MBA program, 1985-88, dean, 1992-94; vis. prof. U. Kiel, 1989, U. Twente, 1999—; adj. staff Ctr. for Creative Leadership, 1982-90. Co-author: Mathematics for Economics and Business, 1992; editor R&D Mgmtm. Jour., 1970—. Recipient Centennial medal IEEE, 1984, Max Planck Rsch. award Alexander Von Humboldt Found., Germany, 1991. Fellow Inst. of Physics; mem. Royal Instn., Internat. Soc. for Innovation Mgmt. (exec. com.), Brit. Inst. Mgmt. (coun.). Office: Manchester Bus Sch, Booth St W, Manchester M15 6PB, England

PEARSON, APRIL VIRGINIA, lawyer; b. Martinsville, Ind., Aug. 11, 1960; d. Clare Grill and Sheila Rosemary (Finch) Rayner; m. Randall Keith Pearson, Dec. 10, 1988; children: Randall Kyle, Austin Finch, Autumn Virginia. BA, Calif. State U., Long Beach, 1982; JD, Pepperdine U., 1987. Bar: Calif. 1987, Idaho 1993, D.C. 1989; cert. indsl. fire brigade, HAZWOPER Tex. A&M U. Assoc. counsel Union Oil Co. of Calif., L.A., 1988—; v.p. Pa's Bier, Long Beach, Calif., 1988-98; bd. dirs. Ammonia Safety Tng. Inst., sec., 1995-98, gen. counsel, 1997—; mem. pub. works commn. City of Chino Hills, 1999—. Mem. Women Lawyers of Long Beach (v.p. 1990-93), Am. Corp. Counsel Assn., Chem. Industry Coun. Calif. (chair regulatory affairs com. 1995). Avocations: running, tae kwon do. Office: Union Oil Co of Calif 376 S Valencia Ave Brea CA 92823-6356

PEARSON, BARRIE, finance executive; b. Selby, Yorkshire, Eng., Aug. 22, 1939; s. Albert James and Mary (Burton) P.; m. Georgina Ann Dix, Apr. 23, 1962 (div. 1984); children: Philippa Jane Antonia Pearson, Gavin Charles Livingstone Pearson; m. Catherine Campbell Scutcher, Dec. 17, 1984. BS in Chemistry with honors, Nottingham (Eng.) U., 1960. Line mgr. Dexion Comino Internat., Eng., 1960-67; with dept. corp. fin. The Plessey Co., Eng., 1967-71; fin. contr. Plessey Microelectronics, Eng., 1971-74; group comml. devel. exec. The DeLaRue Co., Eng., 1974-76; exec. chmn. Livingstone Guarantee PLC, London, 1976—. Author: Common Sense Business Strategy, 1989, Common Sense Time Management for Personal Success, 1988, Realising the Value of a Business, 1989, Successful Acquisition of Unquoted Companies, 4th edit., 1998, The Profit Driven Manager, 1990, Manage Your Own Business, 1991, The Shorter MBA, 1991, How To Buy and Sell a Business, 1995, Boost Your Company's Profits, 1998. Fellow Chartered Inst. Mgmt. Accts. Avocations: food and wine, theatre, ballet, 20th century art and sculpture, live music. Office: 15 Adam St, London WC2N 6RJ, England

PEARSON, CLARENCE EDWARD, management consultant; b. Chgo., Apr. 22, 1925; s. Edward and Irene (Silander) P.; m. June Waldhe, Apr. 21, 1951 (dec. 1967); 1 child, Scott; m. Laurie Norris, Apr. 25, 1995. BS, No. Ill. U., 1950; MPH, U. N.C., 1952. Instr. Mt. Prospect (Ill.) Pub. Schs., 1950-51; dir. health edn. DuPage County Health Dept., Wheaton, Ill., 1952-55; chief health edn. St. Louis Health Dept., 1955-57; dir. health and hosps. Health and Welfare Council, St. Louis, 1957-61; dir. health and safety Met. Life Ins. Co., N.Y.C., 1961-87; prof. edn. Columbia Tchrs. Coll., 1975—; pres. Universal Health Concepts, N.Y.C., 1984-87; Coun. Internat. Health, Washington, 1981-84; bd. dirs. Health Info. Co., Nat. Coun. Internat. Health, Washington, 1981-84; chmn. Profl. Exam. Svc., N.Y.C., 1996-99; v.p. Peter Drucker Found. for Nonprofit Mgmt., 1994-96; mem. adv. bd. C. Everett Koop Inst.; bd. overseers Dartmouth Med. Sch., 1992-96, 99—; adj. prof. cmty. health Robert Wood Johnson Med. Sch., 1996—; pres., CEO Nat. Ctr. for Health Edn., 1997—; sr. adv. The Who office, U.N. Co-author: Managing Health Promotion, 1982; co-editor: (with C. Everett Koop) Crit-

ical Issues in Global Health, 2000; contbr. chpts. to books in field. Co-chmn. Scandinavian-Ams. for Rockefeller presdl. campaign, N.Y., 1968; co-dir. Salzburg Seminar Spl. Session: Critical Issues in Global Health. Served as staff sgt. U.S. Army, 1943-46. Recipient Disting. Career award Am. Pub. Health Assn., Washington, 1981, Gold Medal for Achievement, Columbia U., N.Y.C., 1984, Internat. Health award Asia Pacific Consortium, Honolulu, 1984, Porter Prize, Pitts. Health Ctr., 1986. Fellow Am. Pub. Health Assn. (governing council 1970-78), The Univ. Club (N.Y.C.). Home: 530 E 23rd St New York NY 10010-5022 Office: WHO at the UN 2 UN Plz New York NY 10017

PEARSON, COLIN BAMFORD, information systems specialist; b. Birmingham, Eng., Nov. 27, 1943; s. Arnold and Phyllis May (Bamford) P.; m. Gwyneth Anne Bloor, Sept. 7, 1968; children: Clare, Timothy. BA with honors, U. Cambridge, Eng., 1963, MA with honors, 1969. Chartered engr. Sr. analyst/programmer BARIC, Stoke-on-Trent, Eng., 1966-73; prin. engr. Internat. Computers Ltd., Stoke-on-Trent, 1974-81; cons. PPS Ltd., Stoke-on-Trent, 1981—, also bd. dirs.; project mgr. Imperial Chem. Industries, Runcorn, Eng., 1995; support cons. OCS, London, 1996; information tech. specialist, counselor Bus. Link, Staffordshire, Eng., 1997-98; bd. dirs. Puddlemaster Ltd., Stoke; cons. Smarts Ltd. Mem. Brit. Computer Soc., Inst. Data Processing Mgmt., Chartered Inst. Arbitrators (assoc.), Soc. Expert Witnesses, Staffordshire Bus. Club (chmn. 1981-92, pres. 1993—), Assn. Cricket Umpires and Scorers (chmn. tng. bd. 1981-97, v.p. 1998—). Fax: 01782-720-798. E-mail: ppsltd@a-b.co.uk. Home: 167 Nuntwich Rd, Audley Stoke-on-Trent ST7 8DL, England Office: Smarts Ltd, 18 Boundaries Rd, Balham SW12 8HU, England

PEARSON, CONRAD E., financial services executive; b. Edmonton, Alta., Can., Sept. 1, 1951; came to U.S., 1960; s. Hilding A. and Elva Rose (Land) P.; m. Barbara Anne Schroeder; children: Cameron, Nicole, Morgan, Everett. Cert. in Mid. East Studies, Portland State U., 1973, BA in Polit. Sci., 1973; MA in Internat. Affairs, Johns Hopkins U., 1975. Polit. risk analyst Shell Oil, Houston, 1977-78; mgr. Chase Manhattan Bank, N.Y.C., 1979-80; pres. Risk Insights, N.Y.C., 1980-82; co-owner Pearson Fin. Group, Portland, Oreg., 1982—. Pres. Tigard (Oreg.) Coalition Chs., 1983—. Mem. Tigard C. of C. (chmn. bd. dirs. 1994-95), Rotary (pres. Tigard club 1992). Lutheran. Avocation: poetry writing. Home: 1719 Lake Front Rd Lake Oswego OR 97034-4617 Office: Pearson Fin Group 5665 SW Meadows Rd Ste 120 Lake Oswego OR 97035-3130

PEARSON, DAVID GEORGE, journalist; b. Stirling, Scotland, Apr. 17, 1949; arrived in France, 1970; s. George Wilson and Agnes (Marshall) P.; m. Renee Balit Pearson, Apr. 28, 1978; children: Kevin, Christopher, Angela. Journalist Internat. Herald Tribune, Paris, 1970-75, Assoc. Press, Paris, 1975-81; bur. chief Dow Jones Newswires, Paris, 1981-97, columnist, 1997—. Decorated chevalier Ordre Nationale de Merite (France). Mem. Anglo-Am. Press Assn. (pres.). Avocation: private pilot flying. Office: Dow Jones Newswires, 17 Rue Surene, 75008 Paris France

PEARSON, DAVID SADLER, management consultant; b. Chesterfield, Eng., Feb. 20, 1945; s. Wilfred and Dorothy Walker (Sadler) P.; m. June Horbury, Oct. 25, 1970; children: Leigh, Jesse. BSc in Engring., Imperial Coll., London, 1967; MSc in Mgmt. Studies, Loughborough U., Eng., 1978. Chartered engr. Sect. leader RB211 enging Rolls-Royce Plc, Derby, Eng., 1972-74, chief measurement engr., 1974-80, resource and methods mgr. for devel., 1980-84, ops. planning mgr.-exptl., 1984-88; contr. bus. systems Rolls-Royce Plc, Derby, 1988-96, tng. mgr., 1996-98; founder Pearson McCreadie Assocs., 1998—; vis. lectr. Nottingham (Eng.) U., 1993—. Contbr. articles to profl. jours.; patentee in field. Indsl. tutor Inst. Mech. Engrs./Local Edn., East Midlands, 1978-88; steward Meth. Ch., Derby, 1986—. Recipient Nat. Tng. award Ctrl. Govt., London, 1988, Regional Tng. award, 1995. Mem. Instn. Mech. Engrs. (James Clayton prize 1978). Methodist. Avocations: sailing, music, classic cars and motorcycles, travel, photography. Home: 32 Windley Crescent, Derby DE22 1BY, England

PEARSON, DENNIS LEE, optometrist; b. Portland, Oreg., June 21, 1951; s. Alvin Wesley and Pharaby Iva (Barnett) P.; m. Corinne Elaine Boggs, Aug. 27, 1972; children: Kathleen Erin, Erik Edward. BS in Chemistry, Portland State U., 1974; OD, Pacific U., Forest Grove, Oreg., 1978. Optometrist Drs. Diederich & Pearson, St. Helens, Oreg., 1979-83; pvt. practice Lebanon, Oreg., 1983—; adv. panel mem. managed care Vision Svc. Plan, Rancho Cucamunga, Calif., 1995—; adv. panel mem. laser refraction Laser Vision Ctr. at Pacific U., Portland, 1995—; clin. examiner Nat. Bd. Examiners in Optometry, 1994—. Sch. bd. mem. Sodaville Sch. Dist., Oreg., 1989-93; bd. dirs. Lebanon Boys & Girls Club, 1989-91, 93-94; elder Lebanon Presbyn. Ch., 1992-97. Fellow Am. Acad. Optometry; mem. Am. Optometric Assn., Oreg. Optometric Assn. (bd. dirs. 1988-96, past pres.), Kiwanis Club of Lebanon, Lebanon C. of C. Avocations: skiing, sailing, kayaking, reading, mountain biking. Office: Mid-Valley Eye Ctrs 90 Market St Ste 20 Lebanon OR 97355-2396

PEARSON, JENNIE SUE, retired government administrator; b. Washington, Jan. 26, 1928; d. Orville Louis and Jennie (Rogers) Ganbin; m. Eugene Ryder Pearson, Feb. 3, 1945 (div. 1955); 1 child, Ronald Eugene. AA, Frederick (Md.) C.C., 1987. Title examiner Md. Motor Vehicle Adminstrn., Glen Burnie, 1970-74, title advisor, 1975-80, title supr., 1980-84, asst. br. mgr., 1984-91; ret., 1991. Pres. Rebekah Assembly Md., 1968-69, Internat. Assn. Rebekah Assemblies, Winston-Salem, N.C., 1973-74; v.p. Citizens Nursing Home Aux. Vols., 1997-98, pres., 1999—; vice chmn. bd. dirs. Md. Odd Fellows Home, 1991-92; mem. Srs. and Law Enforcement Together Coun.-Frederick City Police Dept.; mem. adv. bd. Inst. Learning in Retirement Frederick Cmty. Coll.; bd. dirs.; trustee Schuyler Colfax Mus., Winston Salem, N.C. Recipient Outstanding Alumni award for significant contbns. Coll. Mission and Alumni Assn., 1991, 98; inductee Md. Sr. Citizens Hall of Fame, Inc. Mem. AARP (pres. Frederick chpt. 1997-99), Frederick C.C. Alumni Assn. (pres. 1991-98), Montgomery County Agrl. Ctr., Inc. (life), Frederick County Commn. for Women, Rebekah Lodge (past noble grand mem. 1997-98, Meritorious Jewel award 2000), Frederick Woman's Civic Club, Inc. (mem. com. 1992-98). Republican. Methodist. Avocations: volunteer work, travel, ice skating, walking. Home: 30 Vienna Ct Frederick MD 21702-3907

PEARSON, JIM BERRY, JR., human resources specialist; b. Wichita Falls, Tex., Sept. 25, 1948; s. Jim Berry and June Louise (Young) P.; m. Cynthia Ann Medlin, Nov. 9, 1985 (div. Jan. 1999). Cert. mediator. Community organizer VISTA, Pitts., 1969-71; youth dir. East Liberty YMCA, Pitts., 1971-72; aide, therapist technician Austin (Tex.) State Sch., 1972-80; labor organizer Comm. Workers Am., Austin, 1980-90; employee resource officer Austin State Hosp., 1990-96; human resource dir. Capital Area State-Operated Cmty. MHMR Svcs., Austin, 1996-97; human resources dir. Bluebonnet Trails Cmty. Mental Health/Mental Retardation Ctr, Round Rock, Tex., 1997—; exec. bd. rep. Communications Workers Am./Tex. State Employees Union, Austin, 1987-90; trustee Austin Cen. Labor Coun. AFL-CIO, Austin, 1983-84. Vol. AFL-CIO Polit. Action Com., 1980—; del. founding conv. Labor Party, 1996. Recipient Vols. in Politics award Nat. ALF-CIO, Washington, 1984, Peacemaker award Travis County Dispute Resolution Ctr., 1993. Mem. Comm. Workers Am./Tex. State Employees Union Local 6186 (founding mem.). Avocations: pre-Colombian archaeology. Home: 1118 Mclain St Taylor TX 76574-2343 Office: Bluebonnet Trails Cmty MHMR Ctr 555A Round Rock Dr W Round Rock TX 78681-5000

PEARSON, JOHN R. ANTHONY, oil service consultant; b. Cairo, Sept. 18, 1930; arrived in Eng., 1944; s. Charles Robert and Olive (Nock) P.; m. Emma Margaret Anderson, Jan. 1, 1930; children: Henry James, George Alexander, Mark Anthony, Sophie Emma. BA, Cambridge (Eng.) U., 1953; AM, Harvard U., Cambridge, Mass., 1954; PhD, Cambridge U., 1957, ScD, 1975. Tech. officer Imperial Chem. Industries Ltd., Welwyn, Eng., 1953-59; rsch. scientist Metal Box Co. Ltd., Eng., 1959-60; asst. dir. rsch. dept. chem. engring. Cambridge U., 1960-72; fellow, dir. studies in math. Trinity Hall, Cambridge, 1962-73; prof. chem. engring. Imperial Coll., London, 1973-82; head math. modelling Schlumberger Cambridge Rsch., Cambridge, 1982-86, scientific advisor, 1986-95; sci. cons., 1996—; ptnr. Corp. Devel. Cons., London. Author: Mechanical Principles of Polymer Melt Processing, 1966, Mechanics of Polymer Processing, 1985. 2d lt. Royal Corps of Signals, 1948-50. Recipient Gold medal Brit. Soc. Rheology, 1984. Fellow Plastics and Rubber Inst. (Silver medal 1964); mem. Instn. Chem. Engrs., Nat. Acad. Engring. (fgn. assoc.). Avocations: tennis, sports. Home: 25 Chaucer Rd, Cambridge CB2 2EB, England

PEARSON, PATRICIA KELLEY, marketing representative; b. Carrollton, Ga., Jan. 21, 1953; d. Ben and Edith (Kelley) Rhudy; m. Ray S. Pearson, June 4, 1976; children: Chad, Jonathan, Kelly. BA in Journalism, Ga. State U., 1974; BSN, West Ga. Coll., 1990. RN Fla. Pub. rels. asst. Grady Meml. Hosp., Atlanta, 1974-77; editorial asst. Childers & Sullivan, Huntsville, Ala., 1977-78; sales rep. AAA Employment Agy., Huntsville, 1978-80; editor Wright Pub. Co., Atlanta, 1980-82; elect./electronic drafter PRC Cons., Atlanta, 1980-87; researcher Dept. Nursing at West Ga. Coll., Carrollton, 1989-90; med./surg. nurse Tanner Med. Ctr., Carrollton, Ga., 1989-90, Delray Community Hosp., Delray Beach, Fla., 1990-91; sales rep. Innovative Med. Svcs., 1991-94; with staff devel., employee rels. Beverly Oaks Rehab. and Nursing Ctr., 1994-95; sales rep./pub. rels. rep. Columbia HCA, Melbourne, Fla., 1996-99; bus. writer/pub. rels. cons. Cocoa Beach, Fla., 2000—. Vol. Project Response, Brevard County Sexual Assault Victim Svcs. All-Am. scholar U.S. Achievement Acad., 1990, recipient Nat. Coll. Nursing award, 1989. Mem. NOW, Space Coast Bus. Writer's Guild, Omicron Delta Kappa. Democrat. Home: 560 Capri Rd Cocoa Beach FL 32931-3094

PEARSON, SELA, poet, speaker; b. Bklyn., Aug. 10, 1952; d. Thomas Turner and Thelma (Brown) Razor; m. Nassar Anwar Jonathan. BS, St. Joseph's Coll., Bklyn., 1988. LPN. Psychiat., pediat. nurse Syosset (N.Y.) Hosp., 1974-78; sales agent Combined Life Ins. Co. N.Y., Albany, 1978-80; med., surg. nurse Bapt. Med. Ctr., Bklyn., 1980-86; nurse counselor Riker's Island Prison Hosp., Queens, N.Y., 1986-88; clinic nurse St. Christopher Ottilie, Queens, 1988-90; intensive case mgr. AIDS Ctr. Queens County, 1990-92; quality assurance, utilization rev. nurse Vanderbilt U. Med. Ctr., Nashville, Tenn., 1992-94; program dir. Boys and Girls Club, Franklin, Tenn., 1994-95; spkr., writer, nurse Akanke Creations, Brentwood, Tenn., 1996—; ind. health contractor Clayton County Crisis Unit, 1997-98; nurse Phoenix Program FHC of Nashville, 1998-99; nurse Murci Homes, 1999—; cons. Murphy Alternative Ctr., Nashville, 1996, Serendipity House, Nashville, 1996, Family and Ednl. Adv. Assocs., Inc., Nashville, 1996, Growing In Grace Leadership Sch., Nashville, 1996; storyteller, presenter poetry recitals; ind. contractor Crisis Group Home, Riverdale, Ga. Author: New York Poetry Foundation Anthology, 1986, Beyond the Stars, 1995 (Editors Choice 1995), Sela's Sounds of Silence, 1995; performer (video) A Soulful Journey, 1995, The Magic of Peace, 1996, Our Voices, 1996; contbr. articles, poetry to jours., mags. Vol. Williamson County Libr., Franklin, 1995—, Boys and Girls Club, Franklin, 1996—; bd. dirs. Nashville Peace Action, 1996—; mem. New Gospel Singers Choir, 1995—; storytelling del. to South Africa People to People Amb. Programs, invited Women in Soc. rep., Egypt, 2000—. Recipient Vol. Svc. award Berksheire Nursing Ctr., West Babylon, N.Y., 1977, icluson of poem Faith to Wm. Kings Regl. Art Ctr., 1999. Mem. Brentwood Early Risers Toastmasters (v.p. membership 1996—, recipient various awards), Tenn. Writers Alliance, Harpeth Storytelling Group, Nat. Storytelling Assn., Internat. Soc. Poets (Poets Choice award 1995, Internat. Poet of Merit award 1995), Tenn. Writers Group Franklin, Tenn. Assn. Perpetuation Preservation Storytelling, Ga. Writers Group, Creative Artists Tenn., Tenn. Spkrs. Assn. Avocations: piano playing, travel, reading. E-mail: akanke@akanke.com. Address: PO Box 111341 Nashville TN 37222-1341

PEARSON, SUSAN ROSE, psychotherapist, fine arts educator, artist; b. Elmhurst, Ill., June 14, 1950. BA in Psychology, Calif. State U., 1992, MS in Ednl. Psychology & Counseling, 1995. Cert. pupil pers. svcs., cert. hypnotherapists. Art tchr., master artist Susan Rose Fine Art Gallery, Santa Rosa, Calif., 1979—; therapist Lifestyle with Dignity, Canoga Park, Calif., 1985-93; author, speaker, cons., inventor. Mem. ACA, Am. Sch. Counselor Assn., Calif. Assn. Marriage and Family Therapists, Nat. Bd. for Cert. Clin. Hypnotherapists (cert. diplomate), Internat. Soc. Speakers, Authors and Cons., Am. Hypnosis Assn., Internat. Platform Assn., Psi Chi (life). Home and Office: PO Box 15235 Santa Rosa CA 95402-7235

PEARSON, TIMOTHY ALFRED, newspaper circulation executive; b. Meriden, Conn., May 29, 1955; s. Howard Lukens and Fran (Felchner) P.; m. Nancy Marie Zachary, May 10, 1986 (div. June 1989); children: Daniel, Andrew, Kevin, Shellie, Kelly. BS, So. Ill. U., Carbondale, 1977. Ind. cons. Fla., Mont., Colo., 1989-92; circulation mgr. motor rt. and single copy sales The Columbian, Vancouver, Wash., 1992-94; dir. circulation The Sentinel, Howard Publs., Carlisle, Pa., 1994-95; mgr. sales devel. Ctrl. Maine Newspapers divsn. Guy Gannett Inc., Augusta, 1995-96; sales and mktg. mgr. So. Conn. Newspapers divsn. Times-Mirror, Stamford, 1996-98; circulation sales mgr. Hartford (Conn.) Courant, 1998; dir. mem. sales and svc. Seacoast divsn. Dow Jones, Inc., Portsmouth, N.H., 1998—; contbr., spkr. Anti-Defamation League World of Differnce Diversity Project, New Haven, 1996—. Mem. Dem. Nat. Com., Washington, 1972-2000. Mem. Nat. Wildlife Fedn., Nature Conservancy, Sierra Club, New Eng. Assn. Circulation Execs. Episcopalian. Avocations: travel, history, Native American studies. Home: 11B Cedarbrook Vlg Rochester NH 03867-4420 Office: Seacoast Newspapers 111 Maplewood Ave Portsmouth NH 03801-3772

PEARSON, TODD, olympic athlete; b. Geraldton, Australia, Nov. 25, 1977. Mem. swim team Australia; 1st pl. in 200 meter freestyle World Cup, Malmo, 1999; winner gold in 4x100 meter freestyle relay WSCC, Hong Kong; mem. world record breaking 4x200 meter freestyle relay team Short Course, 1999; fifth pl. in 100 meter freestyle Telstra Selection Trials, 2000, sixth pl. in 200 meter freestyle, 2000; winner gold in 4x200 meter freestyle Olympics, Sydney, 2000. Avocations: spring races, golf. Office: Australian Swimming Inc, PO Box 940, Dickson ACT 2602, Australia*

PEASE, RENDEL SEBASTIAN, physicist; b. Cambridge, Eng., Nov. 2, 1922; s. Michael Stewart and Helen (Wedgwood) P.; m. Susan Spickernell, Aug. 9, 1952 (dec. 1996); children: Rosamund, Sarah, Christopher, Roland, Rowan; m. Jean Francis White, 1998 (dec. 2000). BA, Nat. Sci. U., Cambridge, 1942; MA, U. Cambridge, 1947, ScD, 1964. Sci. officer operational rsch. dept. RAF Bomber Command, High Wycombe, U.K., 1942-46; sci. officer Ministry of Supply, Harwell, 1947-64; dir. Culham Lab. UKAEA, Abingdon, 1967-81; dir. fusion rsch. UKAEA, London, 1981-87; cons. Pease Ptnrs., Newbury, 1988—; vis. scientist Princeton (N.J.) U., 1964-65; chmn. Internat. Fusion Rsch. Coun., Vienna, 1976-84; chmn. Brit. Pugwash Group, London, 1988; coun. mem. Pugwash Confs. on Sci. and World Affairs, 1992—; vis. prof. U. NSW, Australia, 1988, 91. Editor: Controlled Thermonuclear Reactions, 1965, (with Hill Peierls, Rotblat) Does Britain Need Nuclear Weapons?, 1995; contbr. articles to profl. jours. Councillor w. Ilsley Parish Coun., 1988-2000. Fellow Inst. Physics (v.p. 1973-77, pres. 1978-80), Inst. Elec. Engrs., Royal Soc. (v.p. 1986-87), Am. Inst. Physics, European Nuclear Soc. (hon. fellow), Inst. Nuclear Engrs. Avocation: music. Home: The Poplars, West Ilsley, Newbury Berks RG20 7AW, England

PEATFIELD, RICHARD CROMPTON, neurologist; b. London, Sept. 3, 1949; s. Ronald and Ruth Peatfield; m. Susan Jean Charles; children: Helen, John. BA, Cambridge (Eng.) U., 1970, MB BChir, 1973, MD, 1982. Specialist neurologist. Sr. house officer Nat. Hosp., London, 1974-75; med. registrar Cen. Middlesex Hosp., 1975-79; rsch. fellow Charing Cross Hosp., 1979-81; sr. registrar in neurology Leeds, 1981-89; cons. neurologist Charing Cross Hosp., London, 1989—. Contbr. chpts. to books and papers to profl. jours. Recipient Harold G. Wolff award Am. Assn. Study of Headache, 1981. Fellow Royal Coll. Physicians London. Home: 23 Mount Park Rd, Ealing London W5 2RS, England Office: Charing Cross Hospital, London W6 8RF, England

PEAUCELLIER, PATRICK, French Polynesian government official. Min. finance Govt. of French Polynesia, Papeete. Office: Terr Govt of French Polynesia, BP 2551, Papeete French Polynesia*

PÉBEREAU, MICHEL JEAN DENIS, bank executive; b. Paris, Jan. 23, 1942; s. Alexandre and Yvonne (Raybaud) P.; m. Agnès Faure, Nov. 9, 1962; children: Alexandre, Jérôme, Iris, Sarah. Student, École Polytech., 1961-63, École Nationale d'Administration, 1965-67. Inspector gen. fin. Govt. France, 1967, dep. office gen. inspection fin., 1969-70, from dep. to tech. advisor cabinet Valéry Giscard d'Estaing, min. economy and fin., 1970-74, from dep., under-dir., asst. dir. to head sect. fin. and monetary affairs dept. treasury, ministry economy and fin., 1971-82, dir. cabinet René Monory, min. economy and fin., 1978-80, dep. to office René Monory, 1980-81; v.p. bd. dirs., pres., chmn. indsl. holding Crédit Comml. France, 1986, pres., chmn., 1987-93, hon. pres., 1993—; pres. Banque Nationale de Paris, 1993—, chmn. bd. dirs., CEO, 1993—; chmn. Paribas, 1999; chmn., CEO BNP Paribas, 2000, also bd. dirs.; bd. dirs., Lafarge Coppée, Bancque Nat. Paris, Soc. Anonyme des Galeries Lafayette, Lafarge Coppée, Saint-Gobain, Renault, BNP UK Holdings Ltd., Total Fina; conf. master Inst. Polit. Studies Paris, 1967-78, prof., 1980—, mgmt. coun., 1984—; conf. master École Nationale de la Statistique et de l'Administrn. Économique, 1968-78; recorder to commn. for study of export appropriation, 1970, commn. mkt. stocks, 1971; sec. gen. interministerial com. development indsl. structures, 1974-76; substitute auditor gen. coun. Bank France, 1980-82, inspector gen. fins., 1987; mem. supervisory bd. AXA, Dresdner Bank AG, Banexi. Author: La Politique Économique de la France: les Instruments, les Objectifs, les Relations Financières et Internationales, 3 vols.; dep. chmn. Commn. Control Cinema Films, 1981-85; chmn. Commn. Selective Assistance for films distbn., 1987-88; contbr. articles to profl. jours. Substitute pres. film control commn., 1981-85; pres. commn. selective assistance in film distribution. Named Chevalier Legion Honor, Officier Nat. Order Merit. Avocation: piano. Home: 14 bis rue Mouton-Duvernet, 75014 Paris France Office: BNP Paribasde Paris, 3 rue d'Antin, 75002 Paris France

PECHAN, JIRI VIKTOR, retired neurologist; b. Banska Bystrica, Czechoslovakia, Mar. 8, 1927; arrived in Germany, 1984; s. Antonin and Marie (Tringlerova) P. MD with distinction, Masaryk U., Brno, Czechoslovakia, 1950; Candidatus Scientiarum, Charles U., Prague, Czechoslovakia, 1969. Rsch. worker Charles U., Prague, 1968-73; head dept. neurology Rehab. Ctr., Kladruby, Czechoslovakia, 1973-77; extraordinary lectr. Charles U., Prague, 1978-82; rsch. attachement Bioengring. Ctr. U. Coll. London, 1982-84; dep. head Rehab. Ctr., Bad Driburg, Germany, 1984-87, Bad Oeynhausen, Germany, 1987-92; ret., 1993; cluster headache rsch., 1994-98. Author of four books; contbr. articles to profl. jours. Recipient award for treatment of Bell's Palsy by Local Cortisonoid Adminstrn., Ministry of Nat. Health, Czechoslovakia, 1982. Avocations: piano, organ, cycling, swimming. Home: Ernst-Wigand 2, D-32547 Bad Oeynhausen Germany

PECHMANN, CORNELIA ANN RACHEL, marketing professional; b. Binghamton, N.Y., May 22, 1959; d. Karl and Helen (Guley) P. BA, Bucknell U., 1981; MS, Vanderbilt U., 1985, MBA, 1985, PhD in Mktg. Mgmt., 1988. Asst. prof. mktg. Calif. State U., Fullerton, 1986-88; asst. prof. mktg. U. Calif., Irvine, 1988-95, assoc. prof. mktg., 1995—; rsch. asst. Vanderbilt Diabetes Rsch. & Tng. Ctr., Nashville, 1982-83, Neighborhood Housing Svcs., Nashville, 1982-83, Nashville Cons. Group, 1984-86. Contbr. articles to profl. jours. Recipient Alden G. Clayton Doctoral Dissertation award Mktg. Sci. Inst., 1987; grantee Tobacco Related Disease Rsch. Program. Mem. Assn. for Consumer Rsch., Am. Mktg. Assn., Am. Acad. of Advt., Soc. for Consumer Psychol., Phi Beta Kappa, Beta Gamma Sigma. Democrat. Office: U Calif Grad Sch Mgmt 350 Gsm Irvine CA 92697-3125

PECHMANN, JAMES (WILLIAM) CHRISTOPHER, seismologist; b. Binghamton, N.Y., July 22, 1954; s. Karl and Helen (Guley) P.; m. Judith Burt, Aug. 26, 1978; children: George Karl, Jessica Mary. BA in Geology, Hamilton Coll., 1976; MS in Geophysics, Calif. Inst. Tech., 1979, PhD in Geophysics, 1983. Rsch. assoc. U. Utah, Salt Lake City, 1983-84, rsch. asst. prof., 1984-89, rsch. assoc. prof., 1989—. Contbr. articles to profl. jours. Mem. Am. Geophys. Union, Seismol. Soc. Am., Sigma Xi, Phi Beta Kappa.

PECHSTEIN, CLAUDIA, Olympic athlete. Winner Gold medal women's 3000 meter speedskating XVII Winter Olympic Games, Lillehammer, Norway, 1994; winner Gold medal women's 5000 meter speedskating, 1st place winner women's 5000 meter final XVIII Winter Olympic Games, 1998. Office: care Deutsche Eisschnellauf-Gemeinschaft, Menzinger Str 68, D-80992 Munich Germany*

PECHT, SHUNIA, computer professional; b. Chernovitz, Ukraine, Jan. 11, 1954; s. Shimon and Buzia (Rubinger) P.; m. Zila Martinovsky, Aug. 8, 1977; children: Eyal, Naama, Yaron. BSc in Computer Sci., Technion U., 1981, postgrad. in bus. mgmt., 1989; system engring., Lahav-Tel Aviv U., 1992, project mgmt., 1996. Systems devel. and analysis dept. mgr. Govt. Unit, Tel Aviv, 1981-86, computer ops. mgr., 1986-89, CIO dep., 1989-94; sys. integration project mgr. IBM Israel, Tel Aviv, 1994-97; sys. integration tech. and quality assurance team mgr. IBM Israel, 1998; mgr. SI Bus. Ops. and Resources, 1999; infrastructure dir. CC&B divsn. Amdocs (Israel) Ltd., 2000—. Mem. Project Mgmt. Inst., Israeli Info. Processing Orgn., Israel Chamber of Info. Systems Analysts. Home: Ha Galil Str 88, 55900 Ganey-Tiqwa Israel Office: 16 Aba-Hillel Silver St, 52506 Ranat Gan Israel

PECK, CHARLES EDWARD, retired construction and mortgage executive; b. Newark, N.J., Dec. 1, 1925; s. Hubert Raymond and Helen (White) P.; m. Delphine Murphy, Oct. 15, 1949; children: Margaret Peck Iovino, Charles Edward, Katherine Peck Koustmer, Perry Anne Peck Flanagan. Grad., Phillips Acad., 1943; student, MIT, 1944; BS, U. Pa., 1949; PhD in Pub. Svc. (hon.), Univ. Md. Univ. Coll., 1995. With Owens-Corning Fiberglas Corp., 1949-81; from sales mgr. home bldg. products to exec. v.p. Owens-Corning Fiberglas Corp., Toledo, 1975-81; bd. dir. Owens-Corning Fiberglas Corp.; co-chmn. The Ryland Group, Columbia, Md., 1981-82; chmn., CEO The Ryland Group, Columbia, 1982-91; dir. The Delaware Group of Funds, 1991—; sec. Enterprise Homes, Inc., 1992-2000, New Homesby Enterprise, Inc., 2000—; mem. statutory vis. com. U.S. Nat. Bur. Standards, 1972-77; mem. adv. com. Fed. Nat. Mortgage Assn., 1977-78, 85-86; mem. vis. com. MIT-Harvard Joint Ctr. for Urban Studies; chmn. Prodrs. Adv. Forum, 1977-81. Vis. com. Harvard U. Grad. Sch. Design, 1981-86; chmn. Howard County United Way Campaign, Md., 1987, chmn. Cmty. Partnerships, 1991-94; bd. dirs. Nat. Inst. for Urban Wildlife, 1986-90, United Way Ctrl. Md., 1987-91, Howard County Gen. Hosp., 1988-94, Columbia Festival, Inc., 1988-91, NAHB Rsch. Found., 1989-92, Alliance to End Childhood Lead Poisoning, 1990-93; adv. bd. U. Md. Engring. Sch., 1990—, Continuing Edn. Johns Hopkins U., 1988-91; policy adv. bd. Harvard Joint Ctr. Housing Studies, 1984-94; mem. Chancellor's Adv. Comm. U. Md. Sys., 1988—, chmn., 1988-99; chmn. Univ. Md. Found., 1990-94, bd. dirs., 1990—; exec. fellow Kennedy Sch., Harvard U., 1990-92; chmn. Affordable Housing Initiative, Columbia, Md., 1990-92; bd. overseers U. Md., College Park, 1994-97; bd. visitors Sch. Law U. Md., Balt., 1996—; mem. vis. com. U. Md. Univ. Coll., 1997—; bd. dirs. Ctr. for Grant Devel., 1994-98, Victory '94 com. Md. State Rep. party, chmn. election inquiry funding com., 1994-95; chmn. Children of Separation and Divorce Ctr., 1995—; pres. adv. coun. Washington Coll., Chestertown, Md., 1997—; mem. commn. on future Howard C.C., 1999—; mem. Howard County Delta Project; pres. Peck Family Found., 1992—. 2d lt. USAAF, 1944-46. Mem. U.S. C. of C. (bd. dirs. 1975-81), Ohio C. of C. (bd. dirs. 1975-81), Depression and Related Affective Disorders Assn. (pres. 1986-89, bd. dirs. 1986—, pres. 1993-94), Rotary, Talbot Country Club, City Club, Ctr. Club, Caves Valley Golf Club, Phi Gamma Delta. Home and Office: 6855 Pea Neck Rd Saint Michaels MD 21663-2725

PECK, ELLIE ENRIQUEZ, retired state official; b. Sacramento, Calif., Oct. 21, 1934; d. Rafael Enriquez and Eloisa Garcia Rivera; m. Raymond Charles Peck, Sept. 5, 1957; children: Reginaldo, Enrico, Francisca Guerrero, Teresa, Linda, Margaret, Raymond Charles, Christina. Student polit. sci., Sacramento State U., 1974. Tng. svcs. coord. Calif. Divsn. Hwys., Sacramento, 1963-67, tech. and mgmt. cons., 1968-78; expert examiner Calif. Pers. Bd., Sacramento, 1976-78; tng. cons. Calif. Pers. Devel. Ctr., Sacramento, 1978; spl. cons. Calif. Commn. on Fair Employment and Housing, Sacramento, 1978; cmty. svcs. rep. U.S. Bur. of Census, No. Calif. counties, 1978-80; spl. cons. Calif. Dept. Consumer Affairs, Sacramento, 1980-83; project dir. Golden State Sr. Discount Program, 1980-83; dir. spl. programs Calif. Lt. Gov., 1983-90; ret., 1990; pvt. cons. Sacramento, 1990—; project dir. SSI/QMB Outreach Project, 1993-94; cons., project dir. nat. sr. health issues summit Congress Calif. Srs. Edn. and Rsch. Fund, 1995; project dir. various post-White House Conf. on Aging seminars and roundtables, 1995-97, coord. Calif. Sr. Legis., 1995-97, exec. dir. SMART Coalition Calif., 1997—. Author: Calif. Dept. Consumer Affairs publ., 1981, U.S. Office Consumer Edn. publ., 1982, Diabetes and Ethnic Minorities: A Community at Risk.

Bd. dirs. Sacramento/Sierra Am. Diabetes Assn., 1989-90; trustee Stanford Settlement, Inc., Sacramento, 1975-79; bd. dirs. Sacramento Emergency Housing Ctr., 1974-77, Sacramento Cmty. Svcs. Planning Coun., 1987-90, Calif. Advs. for Nursing Home Reform, 1990-96, Calif. Human Devel. Corp., 1995—; campaign workshop dir. Chicano/Latino Youth Leadership Conf., 1982—; v.p. Comision Femenil Nacional, Inc., 1987-90; del. Dem. Nat. Conv., 1976; mem. exec. bd. Calif. Dem. Cen. Com., 1977-78, mem., 1997—; chairperson ethnic minority task force Am. Diabetes Assn., 1988-90; steering com. Calif. Self-Esteem Minority Task Force, 1990-93; del. White House Conf. Aging, 1995. Recipient numerous awards including Outstanding Cmty. Svc. award Comuicaciones Unidos de Norte Atzlan, 1975, 77, Outstanding Svc. award, Chicano/Hispanic Dem. Caucus, 1979, Vol. Svc. award Calif. Human Devel. Corp., 1981, 98, Dem. of Yr. award Sacramento County Dem. Com., 1987, Outstanding Advocate award Calif. Sr. Legis., 1988, 89, Calif. Assn. of Homes for Aging, Advocacy award, 1989, Resolution of Advocacy award, League Latin-Ams. Citizens, 1989, Meritorious Svc. to Hispanic Cmty. award Comite Patriotico, 1989, Meritorious Svc. Resolution award Lt. Gov. of Calif., 1989, Cert. Recognition award Sacramento County Human Rights Commn., 1991, Tish Sommers award Older Women's League/Joint Resolution Calif. Legislature, 1993, Latino Eagle award in govt. Tomas Lopez Meml. Found., 1994; named Outstanding Advocate on Aging Issues, Calif. State Senate, 1998. Mem. Hispanic C. of C., Older Women's League, Congress Calif. Srs., Sacramento Gray Panthers, Latino Issues Forum, Latino Dem. Club Sacramento County (v.p. 1982-83). Home and Office: 2667 Coleman Way Sacramento CA 95818-4459

PECK, FRED NEIL, economist, educator; b. Bklyn., Oct. 17, 1945; s. Abraham Lincoln and Beatrice (Pikholtz) P.; m. Jean Claire Ginsberg, Aug. 14, 1971; children: Ron Evan, Jordan Shefer, Ethan David. BA, SUNY, Binghamton, 1966; MA, SUNY, Albany, 1969; PhM, NYU, 1984; PhD, Pacific Western U., 1984; MS in Edn., Coll. New Rochelle, 1993. Lectr. SUNY, Albany, 1969-70; research asst. N.Y. State Legislature, Albany, 1970; sales and research staff Pan Am. Trade Devel. Corp., N.Y.C., 1971; v.p., economist The First Boston Corp., N.Y.C., 1971-88; mng. dir. Sharpe's Capital Mkt. Assocs. Inc., N.Y.C., 1988-89; pres., chief economist Hillcrest Econs. Group, N.Y.C., 1989-93; dir. edn. The Ednl. Advantage, Inc., New City, N.Y., 1990-95; adj. prof. Hofstra U., Hempstead, N.Y., 1975; lectr. NYU, 1982; mem. faculty New Sch. for Social Rsch., N.Y.C., 1974-94; coord. ednl. tech. N.Y.C. Bd. of Edn., 1990—. Author, editor: (biennial publ.) Handbook of Securities of U.S. Government, 1972-86. Mem. ASCD, Am. Econ. Assn., Ea. Econ. Assn., Econometric Soc., Nat. Assn. Bus. Economists, Am. Statis. Assn., Doctorate Assn. of N.Y. Educators, Beta Gamma Sigma (hon. soc.), Phi Delta Kappa. Democrat. Jewish. Lodges: Knights Pythias, Knights Khorassan. Office: Robert F Kennedy Acad 420 E 12th St New York NY 10009-4019

PECK, GEORGE HOLMES, public relations executive; b. Altoona, Pa., May 11, 1946; s. George Heckler and Regina (Jackson) P.; m. Barbara Ann Izydorczak, Feb. 21, 1970; children: Mark David, Heather Anne. BA, U. Montana, 1968; MA, Ball State U., 1978. Staff announcer KDRG Radio, Deer Lodge, Mont., 1963-66; staff announcer, producer KUFM Radio-TV, Missoula, Mont., 1965-68; commd. 2d lt. USAF, 1968; info. officer 4621st Air Base Group, Niagara Falls, N.Y., 1968-70; film writer, editor Aerospace Def. Command, Colorado Springs, 1970-72; chief info. Incirlik Common Def. Inst., Adana, Turkey, 1973-75; sr. pub. affairs rep. Camp New Amsterdam, Soesterberg, The Netherlands, 1975-78; dir. pub. affairs Wurtsmith AFB, Oscoda, Mich., 1978-80; spl. asst. pub. affairs Strategic Sys./B-1B Sys. Program, Dayton, Ohio, 1980-84; asst. to vice cmdr. HQ Air Force Sys. Command, Washington, 1984-86; dir. pub. affairs Aeronautical Sys. Divsn., Dayton, Ohio, 1986-88; chief media and civil affairs Hqrs. Strategic Air Command, Omaha, 1988-91; dep. pub. affairs officer UN Command, Seoul, South Korea, 1991-92; dir. pub. affairs Lowry Tng. Ctr., Denver, 1992-94; dir. pub. rels. Lowry Redevel. Authority, Denver, 1994-96; dir. cmty. rels. Columbia Presbyn./St. Luke's Med. Ctr., Denver, 1996-98; dir. pub. affairs and mktg. The Med. Ctr. of Aurora, Aurora, Colo., 1998-2000; v.p. Aurora C. of C., 2000—. Author: Understanding the Media, 1991. Bd. dirs. Aurora (Colo.) Edn. Found., 1991—, Leadership Aurora, 1991-98; bd. mgrs. Aurora YMCA, 1992-96. Mem. Pub. Rels. Soc. Am. (accredited), Air Force Assn., Aurora Press Coun., Aurora Rotary, Aurora C. of C. (bd. dirs. 1999-2000). Roman Catholic. Avocations: jogging, hiking, skiing. Home: 13250 E Center Ave Aurora CO 80012-3514 Office: Aurora C of C 562 Sable Blvd Ste 200 Aurora CO 80011-0809

PECK, GREGORY (ELDRED GREGORY PECK), actor; b. La Jolla, Calif., Apr. 5, 1916; m. Greta Rice, 1942 (div. 1949); m. Veronique Passani; 5 children. Student, U. Calif. Mem. Nat. Council on Arts, 1965—. Actor: (plays) including Sons and Soldiers, (films) including: Keys of the Kingdom, 1945, Valley of Decision, 1945, Spellbound, 1945, The Yearling, 1946, Duel in the Sun, 1947, The Macomber Affair, 1947, Gentlemen's Agreement, 1947, The Paradine Case, Yellow Sky, The Great Sinner, 1948, Twelve O'Clock High, 1949, The Gunfighter, 1950, Captain Horatio Hornblower, 1951, Only the Valiant, 1951, David and Bathsheba, 1951, Snows of Kilamanjaro, 1952, Roman Holiday, 1953, Night People, Man With a Million, Purple Plains, Moby Dick, 1954, Man in the Grey Flannel Suit, 1956, The Designing Woman, 1956, The Bravados, 1958, Pork Chop Hill, 1959, Beloved Infidel, 1959, On The Beach, 1959, Guns of Navarone, 1961, To Kill a Mockingbird (Acad. award as best actor 1962), Cape Fear, 1962, How the West Was Won, 1963, Captain Newman, M.D, 1963, Behold a Pale Horse, 1964, Mirage, 1965, Arabesque, 1966, Mackenna's Gold, 1967, The Chairman, 1968, The Stalking Moon, 1968, Marooned, 1969, I Walk the Line, 1970, Shootout, 1971, Billy Two-Hats, 1972, Amazing Grace and Chuck, 1987, Old Gringo, 1989, Cape Fear, 1991, Other People's Money, 1991; co-producer, star: (films) The Big Country, 1958; producer, star: (films) The Omen, 1976, MacArthur, 1977, The Boys from Brazil, 1978, The Sea Wolves, 1981, The Scarlet and Black, 1983, (TV miniseries) The Blue and the Gray, 1982, The Portrait, 1993, Sinatra: 80 Years My Way, 1995, A Salute to Martin Scorsece, 1997, Moby Dick, 1998; voice: (TV miniseries) Baseball, 1994; rec.: (audio cassette) The New Testament, 1985-86. Nat. chmn. Am. Cancer Soc., 1966; founder, prodr. La Jolla Playhouse, 1947-52. Recipient Presdl. Medal of Freedom, Jean Hersholt Humanitarian award, 1968, Life Achievement award Am. Film Inst., 1989, Career award Cannes Film Festival, 1989, Kennedy Ctr. Honors, 1991, Lifetime Achievements award Lincoln Ctr., N.Y.C., 1992, Legion d'Honneur, France, 1993. Mem. Acad. Motion Picture Arts and Scis. (gov., pres. 1967-70), Am. Film Inst. (founding chmn. bd. trustees 1967-69).

PECK, JOHN FREDERICK, poet, English language educator; b. Pitts., Jan. 13, 1941; s. Clarence Erwin and Louise Bertha (Sayenga) P.; m. Ellen Margaret McKee, Sept. 1, 1963 (div. Dec. 1981); 1 child, Ingrid Louise. AB, Allegheny Coll., Meadville, Pa., 1962; PhD, Stanford U., 1973; diploma in analytical psychology, C. G. Jung Inst., Zurich, Switzerland, 1992. Instr. English Princeton (N.J.) U., 1967-70, vis. lectr. writing, 1972-75; from asst. to assoc. prof. English Mt. Holyoke Coll., South Hadley, Mass., 1977-82; vis. prof. English U. Zurich, 1985-92, Skidmore Coll., Saratoga, N.Y., 1995-97; lectr. MIT, 2000. Author: Shagbark, 1972, The Broken Blockhouse Wall, 1978, Poems and Translations of Hi-Lö, 1991, Argura, 1993, Selva Morale, 1995, M and Other Poems, 1996, Collected Shorter Poems 1966-1996, 1999. Recipient Arts & Letters award Nat. Inst. Arts & Lit., N.Y.C., 1975, Prix de Rome, 1978, Delmore Schwartz award NYU, 1995; Guggenheim fellow, 1981, Ingram Merrill fellow, 1995. Mem. Internat. Assn. Analytical Psychology. Home: 331 Broadway Cambridge MA 02139-1803

PECK, MALCOLM CAMERON, educational exchange specialist; b. Boston, Apr. 4, 1939; s. Wilfred Cameron and Ruth Lorriaux (Murdoch) P.; m. Adelaida Boquilon Ravelo, Dec. 30, 1972; 1 child, John Cameron. AB, Harvard U., 1961, AM, 1966; MA, Tufts U., 1963, MALD, 1964, PhD, 1970. Instr. U. Chattanooga (now U. Tenn.), 1967-68; postdoctoral fellow Harvard U., Cambridge, Mass., 1969-70; asst. to the pres., dir. programs Middle East Inst., Washington, 1970-81; Arabian peninsula affairs analyst U.S. Dept. State, Washington, 1981-83; program officer Meridian Internat. Ctr., Washington, 1984—; pres., bd. dirs. nat. com. to Honor the 14th Centennial of Islam, Washington, 1979-83. Author: The United Arab Emirates: A Venture in Unity, 1986, Historical Dictionary of the Gulf Arab States, 1997; contbr. articles to profl. jours. Pres. Ch. of the Holy City, 1998-00. NDFL fellowship U.S. Govt., 1964-65; postdoctoral fellowship Harvard U., 1969-70. Mem. Middle East Studies Assn., Middle East Inst. (resident fellow 1983), Philippine Arts, Letters, and Media Coun. (sec. 1995—), Soc. for Gulf Arab Studies (co-founder, sec. 1987—). Democrat. Avocations: bicycling, music, reading. Home: 3118 1st St N Arlington VA 22201-1053 Office: Meridian Internat Ctr 1624 Crescent Pl NW Washington DC 20009-4004

PECK, MIRA PASZKO, lawyer; b. Minsk, USSR, Mar. 31, 1946; d. Wolf and Zofia (Wlaznik) Paszko; m. David O. Peck, May 15, 1971; children: Lena Ruth, Benjamin Jay. BSChemE, Melbourne U. Tech., Australia, 1972; MS in Indsl. Adminstrn., Union Coll., 1976; JD, Rutgers U., 1984. Bar: N.J. 1984, U.S. Dist. Ct. N.J. 1984. Tchr. sci. Victoria Edn. Dept., 1971-72; process engr. GAF Corp., Rensselaer, N.Y., 1974-77; design engr. BASF Corp., Parsippany, N.J., 1977-80, product mgr., 1980-86, mgr. corp. strategic planning, 1986-92; v.p. tech. purchasing BASF Corp., Mount Olive, N.J., 1993-2000; pvt. practice Denville, N.J., 1984—. Mem. counsel Protect Wildlife Water and Woods, Denville, 1987—; mem. Mus. Modern Art, N.Y.C. Mem. ABA, NOW, N.J. Bar Assn., Am Inst. Chem. Engrs., Am. Humanist Assn., Amnesty Internat., Simon Wiesenthal Ctr., So. Poverty Law Ctr. Democrat. Avocations: art, reading, music, hiking, bicycling. Office: BASF Corp 3000 Continental Dr Mount Olive NJ 07828-1234

PECK, RAYMOND CHARLES, SR., driver behavior research specialist and research consultant; b. Sacramento, Nov. 18, 1937; s. Emory Earl and Margaret Helen (Fieberger) P.; m. Ellie ruth Enriquez, sept. 5, 1957; children: Teresa M. Pack Montijo, Linda M. Peck Heisler, margaret V. Peck Henley, Raymond C., Christina M. Peck Reich. BA in Exptl. Psychology, Calif. State U., Sacramento, 1961, MA in Exptl. Psychology, 1968. Rsch. analyst Calif. Dept. Motor Vehicles, Sacramento, 1962-71, sr. rsch. analyst, program mgr., 1971-80, rsch. program splst. II, 1980, 81-84, acting, chief rsch., 1980-81, chief rsch., 1984-2000; pres. R.C. Peck & Assocs.; dir. R.C. Peck & Assocs., Sacramento, 2000—; statis. cons. to pvt. and pub. orgns., 1970—; chmn. com. on operator regulation Transp. Rsch. Bd., NAS, 1976-82. Past em. editl. adv. bd. Traffic Safety Evaln. Rsch. Review; mem. editl. bd. Jour. Safety Rsch., Accident Analysis and Prevention; contbr. articles to profl. jours. Recipient Met. Life award of Honor., Nat. Safety Coun., 1970, Met. Life cert. of comendation Nat. Safety Coun., 1972, A.R. Lauer award Human Factor Soc., 1981, Award of Honor, Award of Merit, Nat. Hwy. Traffic Safety Adminstrn., 1982. Mem. APHA, AAAS, Am. Statis. Assn. Am. Assn. Automotive Medicine, Internat. Coun. Alcohol, Drugs and Traffic Safety, Human Factors Soc., N.Y. Acad. Scis., Soc. Epidemiologic Rsch. Democrat. Home and Office: 2667 Coleman Way Sacramento CA 95818-4459

PECKER, DAVID J., magazine publishing company executive; b. N.Y.C., Sept. 24, 1951; m. Karen Balan, Oct. 31, 1987. BBA, Pace U., postgrad. CPA, N.Y. Sr. auditor Price Waterhouse & Co.; mgr. fin. reporting Diamandis Communications, Inc., N.Y.C., 1979; dir. fin. reporting Diamandis Communications, Inc., dir. acctg., asst. contr., 1983; COO, CFO, exec. v.p. pub. Hachette Mags., Inc., N.Y.C., 1990-91, pres., COO, 1991-92, pres. and CEO, 1992-99; chmn., CEO Am. Media Inc., 1999—; pres., CEO, COO Am. Media Inc., Lake Worth, Fla., 1999—; mem. Fashion Group's Internat. Adv. Bd., The N.Y. City Partnership Com.; mem. bd. dirs. The Madison Square Boys & Girls Club. Bd. dirs. Pace U., N.Y.C., Drug Enforcement Agents Found., 1995—. Mem. Am. Mgmt. Assn. Office: Am Media Inc 600 East Coast Ave Lake Worth FL 33464-0001*

PECKER, JEAN-CLAUDE, astronomer, educator, author; b. Reims, Marne, France, May 10, 1923; s. Victor Noel and Nelly Catherine (Herrmann) P.; m. Charlotte Wimel, Sept. 14, 1947 (div. 1964); children: Martine Kemeny, Daniel, Laure; m. Anne-Marie A. Vormser, Dec. 14, 1974. Student Lycée de Bordeaux, U. Grenoble and Paris (Sorbonne); Agrégr. des Scis. Physiques, Ecole Normale Superieure, Paris, 1946; DSc, CNRS, Paris, 1950. Rsch. asst. CNRS, 1946-52; assoc. prof. U. Clermont-Ferrand, 1952-55; assoc. astronomer Paris Obs., 1955-62, astronomer, 1962-65; dir. Nice Obs., 1962-69; prof. Coll. de France, Paris, 1963-88; dir. Inst. Astrophysics, Paris, 1972-79; sec. gen. Astron. Internat. Union, Nice, 1964-67; chmn. Nat. Com. for Sci. and Tech. Culture, 1985-87; chmn. adv. com. Mus. LaVillette, Paris, 1983-85; v.p. commn. nt. UNESCO, 1991-95. Author: (with P. Couderc and E. Schatzman) L' astronomie au jour le jour, 1954, (with E. Schatzman) Astrophysique générale, 1959, Le ciel, 1959, L'astonomie expèrimentale, 1969, Les laboratoires spatiaux, 1969, Papa, dismoi: L'astronomie, qu'est-ce que c'est?, 1971; editor L'astronomie nouvelle, 1971, Clefs pour l'Astronomie, 1981, Sous l'Etoile Soleil, 1984; editor Astronomie Flammarion, 1985, L'avenir du Soleil, 1990, le Promeneur du ciel, 1992, le Soleil est une ètoile, 1992; co-author, co-editor Le dèbat sur le paranormal, 1997, The Mars Effect, 1997, Remembering Edith A. Müller, 1998, Understanding the Heavens, 2000. Sec.-gen. Human Rights Com., Acad. Scis., Paris, 1978-81. With French Army, 1944-45, France. Decorated comdr. Palmes acadèmiques; comdr. Lègion d'honneur, grand officer Ordre Nat. du Mèrite; recipient prix Forthuny, Inst. de France; mèdaille d'Argent, CNRS, 1956; mèdaille Janssen, Astron. Soc. France, 1967; prix Jean Perrin, Soc. Française de Physique, 1973, prix Lodèn, Soc. Astron. Uppsala, 1997; others. Mem. Acad. Scis. (Paris), Acad. Royal Scis. (Brussels), European Acad. Scis., Fine Arts and Humanities, Internat. Acad. Humanism (sec. 1989—), Acad. Europaea (coun. mem., v.p. 1989-92), Sociètè Philomathique (Paris) Club. Office: Collège de France, Annexe 3 rue d'Ulm, 75231 Paris Cedex, France

PECKHAM, COLIN NEIL, academic administrator, minister, lecturer; b. Pietermaritzburg, Natal, South Africa, June 20, 1936; arrived in Eng., 1982; s. Ivan Herbert and Doris Annie (Gladwin) P.; m. Mary Johanna Morrison, Apr. 12, 1969; children: Colin, Heather, Christine. Diploma in theology, Africa Evang. Band Bible Coll., Cape Town, South Africa, 1959; diplomate in agr., Cedara Coll. Agr., Natal, South Africa, 1955; BA in Theology, U. South Africa, Pretoria, 1973, BTh with honors, 1978, MTh, 1983; DTh, Trinity Theol. Sem., Newburgh, Ind., 1990; LTh with honors, Bapt. Theol. Coll., Johannesburg, South Africa, 1982. Ordained to Bapt. Ministry, 1974. Farmer Natal, 1956-58; evangelist African Evang. Band, Cape Town, 1960-68, youth leader, 1969-71, tutor Bible Coll., 1972-74, prin., 1974-82; prin. Faith Mission Bible Coll., Edinburgh, Scotland, 1982-99, prin. emeritus, 1999—. Author: Heritage of Revival, 1987, (poetry) Scattered Pearls, 1982, Youth Challenged, 1982, The Authority of the Bible, 1999, Resisting Temptation, 1999; editor Life Indeed, 1983—. Avocations: walking, reading.

PECKITT, NINIAN SPENCELEY, surgeon; b. Rotherham, England, Aug. 31, 1951; parents Kenneth Ivan Peckitt and Jane Angela (Lala) Gillan; m. Foong Meng Lau, Feb. 4, 1984; children: Robin, Katie. BDS, Dental Sch., Edinburgh, Eng., 1974; MBChB, Med. Sch., Sheffield, Eng., 1979. Demonstrator in anatomy U. Bristol Med. Sch., Eng., 1980-81; SHO in accident and emergency Bristol Royal Inf., Eng., 1981; SHO in plastic surgery Frenchay Hosp., Bristol, Eng., 1981-82; SHO rotation orthopaedics, neurosurgery, gen. surgery United Bristol Hosps., Eng., 1982-84; dir. dental surgery Min. Health, Ha'il, Saudi Arabia, 1984-85; registrar in oral and maxillofacial surgery North Wales Hosps., 1985-88; sr. registrar in oral and maxillofacial surgery Rotation South Wales Hosps., 1988-94; cons. oral and maxillofacial surgery Doncaster Royal Inf. and Mantagu NHS Trust, 1994—; dir. ComputerGen Implants Ltd., Doncaster; cons. oral and maxillofacial surgeon Park Hill Hosp., Doncaster. Contbr. articles on stereoscopic lithography and orofacial reconstruction with computer generated implants to profl. jours. Fellow Brit. Assn. Oral and Maxillofacial Surgeons, Royal Coll. Surgeons (Edinburgh), Royal Coll. Surgeons (Ireland), Royal Coll. Surgeons (Eng.). Avocation: music. Fax: 44 0 1977 658988. E-mail: peckitt@maxfac.com. Home: St Chad's House, Hooton Pagnell, Doncaster DN5 7BW, England Office: Doncaster Royal Inf, Armthorpe Rd, Doncaster DN2 5LT, England

PEČMAN, RUDOLF, musicologist, aesthetist; b. Staré Město, Frydek, Czechoslovakia, Apr. 12, 1931; s. Vladimír and Otilie (Jarošová) P. MA, Masaryk U., Brno, Czechoslovakia, 1955, PhD, 1966, Docent, 1984, DSc, 1989, Ordinary Prof., 1990. Asst. Philosophy Faculty Masaryk U., Brno, Czechoslovakia, 1955-62, sr. asst. Philosophy Faculty, 1962-84, docent (habil.) Philosophy Faculty, 1984-90, ordinary prof. Philosophy Faculty, 1990—; gen. sec., chmn. Musicol. Com., 1966-67; co-founder Internat. Music Festival, Brno, Czechoslovakia, 1966-76; pres. musicol. commn. Union of Composers, 1972-90, Czech Music Soc.; mem. musicol. congresses Germany, Austria, Poland, Italy, USA, Cuba, Russia; lectr. in field. Author: Josef Mysliveček und sein Opernepilog, 1970, Beethoven dramatik, 1978, Beethovens Opernplane, 1981, Josef Mysliveček, 1981, Georg Friedrich Handel, 1985 (award Ministry of Culture 1986), Stage Works of Ludwig van Beethoven, 1986, Essays about Martinu, 1989, F.X. Richter und seine "Harmonischen Belehrungen", 1991, Style and Music 1600-1900, 1991, 2nd edit., 1996, The Attack on Antonín Dvořák, 1992, Stage Works of Ludwig van Beethoven, 1999; contbr. 300 articles to profl. jours. Recipient Smetana award Ministry of Culture, 1974, Janáček award, 1984, Mozart award, 1987, Nummo Memoriali Ateneo rector of Masaryk U., Brno, 1995. Mem. Soc. Music Friends (chmn. 1994—, hon.). Avocations: literature, philosophy. Home: Loosova 12, CZ638 00 Brno Czech Republic Office: Masaryk U Dept Musicology, Arna Nováka 1, 660 88 Brno Czech Republic

PECORI GIRALDI, FRANCESCA, endocrinologist, researcher; b. Florence, Italy, Feb. 8, 1963; d. Alvise and Giovanna (Bulgarini d'Elci) Pecori G.; MD, U. Milan, Italy, 1987. Intern, resident endocrinology Inst. Auxoldgico Italiano, Milan, 1987-91; rschr. Inst. Auxologico Italiano, Milan, 1994—; rsch. assoc. U. Cin., 1991-92, U. Ill., Chgo., 1992-93. Mem. Endocrine Soc., Italian Endocrine Soc. Office: Inst Auxologico Italiano, Via Spagnoletto 3, 20149 Milan Italy

PÉCSI, MÁRTON, geographer; b. Budapest, Hungary, Dec. 29, 1923; s. Dani and Róza (Simon) P.; m. Éva Donáth, July 18, 1954; 1 child, Dora. PhD, Pazmany Peter U., Budapest, 1948; cand. geog. scis., Hungary Acad. Scis., 1958, DSc of Geography, 1962. Asst. geography dept. Pazmany Peter U., Budapest, 1949-54; rschr., dir. Inst. of Geography Hungary Acad. Scis., Budapest, 1954-58, 63-90; assoc. prof. geography Eotvos L. U., Budapest, 1958-62, prof., 1966—; rsch. prof. Geography Inst. Hungary Acad. Scis., Budapest, 1991—. Editor-in-chief Geog. Bull. of Hungarian Geog. Soc., 1958-90, (series) Studies in Geography in Hungary, 1964—; co-author, editor: Landscapes of Hungary, 6 vols., 1967-88, National Atlas of Hungary, 1989 (Szechenyi prize, 1990); author: Quaternary and Loess-research, 1993 (award 1995), Landform Evolution of Hungary, 1999. Recipient State prize Govt. of Hungary, 1975, Alexander Korosi de Csoma medal Hungarian Geog. Soc., 1983, World Lifetime Achievement award, 1993. Mem. Hungarian Acad. Scis., Austrian Acad. Scis., Germany Acad. scis., Gottingen Acad. Scis., Slovenia Acad. Scis., Poland Acad. Scis., N.Y. Acad. Scis. Avocation: photography. Home: Dozsa u 7, 2747 Tortel Hungary Office: Hungary Acad Sci Geog Inst, Budaörsi ut 43-45, 1112 Budapest Hungary

PECULEA, MARIUS SABIN, retired engineering executive, educator; b. Cluj, Romania, Apr. 13, 1926; s. Marius and Sabina (Simu) P.; m. Eleonora Schrauder, Oct. 9, 1949; children: Georgina, Marius. Engr., Poly. Inst., Timisoara, Romania, 1949, PhD, 1966, Docentur, 1974; Dr h.c., U. Cluj, 1995, U. Bucharest, Romania, 1996, U. Craiova, Romania, 1996. Engr. Technofrig, Cluj, 1949-54; asst. Poly. Inst., Cluj, 1954-59; leader Lab. of Isotope Separation, Romanian Acad. Scis., Cluj, 1959-70; dir. "G" Factory, Romanian Acad. Scis., Ramnicu Valcea, 1970-91, dir. Cryogenics and Isotopes Separation,, 1991-94; sec. gen. Romanian Acad. Scis., 1994-99, ret., 1999. Author 6 books; contbr. over 200 articles to profl. publs.; patentee in field. Home: Breaza 7 Bl V22A, 77744 Bucharest Romania Office: Romanian Acad, Calea Victoriei 125, 77102 Bucharest Romania

PEDDIE, PETER CHARLES, retired solicitor; b. Street, Somerset, Eng., Mar. 20, 1932; s. Ronald and Vera (Nicklin) P.; m. Charlotte Elizabeth Ryan, June 25, 1960; children: Emma, Andrew, Rachel, Jonathan. BA, St. John's Coll., Cambridge, Eng., 1954, MA, 1977. Articled clk. Freshfields, London, 1954-57, asst. solicitor, 1957-60, ptnr., 1960-92, cons., 1992; adviser to govs. and head legal unit Bank of Eng., London, 1992-96. Decorated comdr. Brit. Empire apptd. Queen's Counsel, 1997. Mem. Law Soc., City of London Club, Athenaeum Club. Avocations: gardening, foreign travel.

PEDE, RON, film critic; b. Sleidinge, Belgium, May 13, 1950; s. Gabriel Pede and Irma De Fleurquin; m. Marie-Christine Borgonjon, Aug. 26, 1978; children: Klaas, Jeroen, Mitze, Lize. Degree in translating, Mercator/Piho, Ghent, Belgium, 1972. Freelance writer Film En Televisie, Brussels, 1973-76, jr. editor, 1977-89, editor-in-chief, 1990—; programmer Film Festival, Ghent, 1979-88; v.p. Filmarchive, Leuven, Belgium, 1990—, v.p., 1997—; bd. dirs. Beroepsbond Belgische Filmpers, Brussels; Belgian liaison Internat. Fedn. Film Critics, 1993—. Author: Film in België, 1990, (film study) Daens, 1994; co-author: Film en Vriendschap, 1997. Roman Catholic. Avocations: collecting film posters, cards. Home: Wippelgemdorp 121, 9940 Evergem Belgium Office: Film En Televisie, Cellebroersstraat 16 Bus 2, 1000 Brussels Belgium

PEDERSEN, ERLING B., physician, medical educator; b. Broerup, Denmark, July 14, 1946; s. Aksel K. and Sigrid M. (Hansen) P.; m. Birthe D. Moeller; children: Michael, Henrik, Hanne, Martin. MD, Aarhus U., 1975, D in Medicine, 1979. Chief physician dept. medicine U. Hosp., Aarhus, 1987-95; prof. medicine Aarhus U., 1990-97, head lab. nephrology & hypertension, 1995-98, prof. nephrology, 1997—; chief physician, head dept. medicine Holstebro Hosp., 1997—. Office: Holstebro Hosp, Dept Medicine, DK-7500 Holstebro Denmark

PEDERSEN, JAN ANDERS, amusement park manager; b. Halmstad, Halland, Sweden, Feb. 10, 1969; s. Bent Hessellund and Gun-Britt Siv (Jönsson) P. Grad. high sch., Skene, Sweden, 1988. Acct., artist Nordisk Tivoli Park, Horred, Sweden, 1988-92, mgr., owner, 1992—. Author: The Value of Extra-Terrestrial Garbage Recycling, 1992, Codex-X European Adventure, 1996, (radio plays) Irresponsolution of The Individual, 1993, Promotion, 1993, Stupidus Regina, 1993. Pvt. Swedish Army, 1990-91. Mem. Nat. Geog. Soc. Avocations: astronomy, philosophy, literature, kayaking. Office: Sundholmen, 510 10 Horred Vastergd, Sweden

PEDERSEN, LISS, metallurgist; b. Mosjøen, Vefsn, Norway, May 19, 1965; d. Oddbjørn Kristian and Bodhild Lucie (Frydenlund) P. BSc, Trondheim IngeniørHogskole, Norway, 1988; MSc, Norges Tekniske Hogskole, Norway, 1995; PhD, Norges Teknisk-Naturvitenskap., Univ., 1999. Lab. engr. Elkem Aluminium, Mosjøn, 1988-93; process engr. Elkem Aluminium, Farsund, Norway, 1999—. Avocations: literature, embroidery. Office: Elkem Aluminum Lista, Lundevågen S, Farsund 4551, Norway

PEDERSEN, MICHAEL, research scientist; b. Holbaek, Denmark, Nov. 29, 1969; s. Ib and Anne (Christensen) P. MSc, Tech. U. Denmark, Lyngby, 1993; PhD, U. Twente, Enschede, The Netherlands, 1997. Cert. elec. engring. Rsch. asst. Micro Electronics/Materials Engring/Sensors/Actuators Inst., Enschede, 1993-97; rsch. engr. Knowles Electronics, Rolling Meadows, Ill., 1997-2000; MEMS designer Ctr. Nat. Rsch. Initiatives, Reston, Va., 2000—. Contbr. articles to profl. jours. Mem. IEEE, Acoustical Soc. Am. Avocations: reading, music, sports.

PEDERSEN, MICHAEL STANLEY, chemical engineer, researcher; b. Naestved, Denmark, Nov. 22, 1967; s. Freddy and Lis (Johansen) P. BSc in Chem. Engring., Danmark Ingenirakademi, Lyngby, Denmark, 1990; MSc, Tech. U. Denmark, Lyngby, 1993, PhD, 1996. Rsch. engr. Tech. U. Denmark, Lyngby, 1993-96, J.C. Hempels Skibsfarvefabrik, Lyngby, 1996—. Contbr. articles to profl. jours. Avocations: music, tennis. Home: Mariendalsvej 48 B 4TV, 2000 Frederiksberg Denmark Office: JC Hempels Skibsfarvefabrik, Lundtoftevej 150, 2800 Lyngby Denmark

PEDERSEN, NIELS TINGGAARD, hematopathologist; b. Nakskov, Lolland, Denmark, Sept. 7, 1941; s. Sofus Tinggaard and Vera (Rasmussen) P.; m. Kirsten Ehlers; children: Susanne, Carsten, Jeannette. MD, U. Copenhagen, 1969, DMSc, 1976. Rschr. dept. anatomy U. Copenhagen, 1969-75; sr. registrar The Nat. Hosp., Denmark, 1977-80, Finsen Hosp., CPH, Denmark, 1980-82; chief dept. pathology Odense Univ. Hosp., Denmark, 1982—; assoc. prof. Odense U., 1982. Author: (textbooks) Hematology and Haematopathology, 1989, 92, 96; contbr. articles to profl. jours. Recipient awards U. Odense, 1990, William Nielsen's Found., 1992; grantee Rotary, 1991. Mem. Danish Soc. Hematology, Danish Soc. Pathology and Cytology, Danish Soc. Cancer Rsch. Office: Dept Pathology, Odense Univ Hosp, DK-5000 Odense C, Denmark

PEDERSEN, NORMAN ARNO, JR., retired headmaster, literary club director; b. Harvey, Ill., May 27, 1927; s. Norman Arno and Helen Baker

(Reeves) P.; m. Isabel Whitla Braham, June 24, 1950; children: Selina, Norman A. III, Laura. AB, Princeton U., 1949; MA, U. Buffalo, 1958. Tchr., coach Nichols Sch., Buffalo, N.Y., 1954-69; headmaster Brunswick Sch., Greenwich, Conn., 1969-88; interim headmaster Erie (Pa.) Day Sch., 1989-90, ret., 1989; dir. Chautauqua (N.Y.) Lit. and Sci. Cir., 1992-96; mem. adv. bd. Braitmeyer Found., Boston, 1987-91. Cmty. divsn. chair United Way Campaign, Greenwich, Conn., 1986-87; bd. dirs. Greenwich Coun. on Youth and Drugs, 1979-88; elder First Presbyn. Ch., Greenwich, 1971-74. Fulbright summer grantee, 1961. Mem. Country Day Sch. Headmasters Assn., Acad. Sr. Profls. at Eckerd Coll., Exec. Svc. Corp. of Manasota. Avocations: reading, fly-fishing, golf, swimming, bicycle riding. Home: 3702 Sun Eagle Ln Bradenton FL 34210-4236

PEDERSEN, SVEN, chemical engineer, researcher; b. Helsingør, Denmark, July 26, 1949. MSc, Tech. U. Denmark, Lyngby, 1973, PhD, 1978. Rsch. assoc. U. Wis., Madison, 1978-79; chemist Niro Atomizer, Gladsaxe, Denmark, 1979-82; rsch. assoc. Tech. U. Denmark, Lyngby, 1982-83; chemist Novo Nordisk A/S, Bagsvaerd, 1983-91, mgr., 1991—. Author: Immobilized Biocatalysts, 1995; editor: (with S.B. Petersen and B. Svensson) Carbohydrate Bioengineering, 1995; contbr. articles to profl. jours.; patentee in field. Mem. European Fedn. Biotech. (working party applied biocatalysis 1987—), Dansk Ingeniørforening. E-mail: svp@novo.dk. Office: Novo Nordisk A/S, Novo Allé, Bldg 8P, 2880 Bagsvaerd Denmark

PEDERSEN, WESLEY NIELS M., public relations and public affairs executive; b. South Sioux City, Nebr., July 10, 1922; s. Peder Westergaard and Marie Gertrude (Sorensen) P.; m. Angeline Kathryn Vavra, Oct. 17, 1948; 1 son, Eric Wesley. Student, Tri-State Coll., Sioux City, Iowa, 1940-41; BA summa cum laude, Upper Iowa U.; postgrad., George Washington U., 1958-59. Editor, writer Sioux City Jour., 1941-50; corr. N.Y. Times, Life, Time, Fortune, 1948-50; editor Dept. State, 1950-53; fgn. svc. officer Dept. State, Hong Kong, 1960-63; fgn. affairs columnist, roving corr., counselor summit meetings and fgn. ministers confs. USIA, 1953-60, chief, worldwide spl. publs. and graphics programs, 1963-69; chief Office Spl. Projects, Washington, 1969-78, Office Spl. Projects, Internat. Comm. Agy., 1978-79; v.p. Fraser Assocs., pub. rels., Washington, 1979-80; dir. comm. and pub. rels. Pub. Affairs Coun., Washington, 1980—; lectr. creative comm. Upper Iowa U., 1975; chmn., Europe, Ambassadorial Internat. Affairs Seminar, Fgn. Svc. Inst., 1975; lectr. internat. pub. rels. Pub. Rels. Inst., Am. U., 1976; lectr. bus. and mgmt. divsn. NYU, 1976, 77, 78; cons. pub. rels., editl. and design; del. founding sessions 1st Amendment Congress, Phila. and Williamsburg, Va., 1980, mem. exec. com., 1980. Columnist: (as Paul L. Ford) The World Today, 1952-60; (as Benjamin E. West) Behind the Curtain, 1952-60; White House Report, 1966-69 (as Wesley Pedersen), Pub. Rels. Jour., 1980-85; author: Mr. President: Lyndon B. Johnson, 1964, Legacy of a President, 1964, Journey to the Pacific, 1965, Mr. President: Richard M. Nixon, 1969, American Heroes of Asian Wars, 1969; co-author: Effective Government Public Affairs, 1981; editor: The Imam's Story, 1961, Escape at Midnight and Other Stories (Pearl S. Buck), 1962, Exodus From China (Harry Redl), 1962, Macao, 1962, The Dividing Line (Arturo Gonzalez), 1962, China's Men of Letters (K.E. Priestley), 1963, Children of China (Pearl S. Buck and Margaret Wylie), 1963, Destination the Moon (William Howard), 1964, Man on the Moon, 1964, Nine From Little Rock, 1964, To the Moon and Beyond, 1965, Bounty From the Land, 1965, Workers Paradise Lost (Eugene Lyons), 1967, The Americans and the Arts (Howard Taubman), 1969, The Dance in America (Agnes de Mille), 1969, Getting the Most From Grassroots Public Affairs Programs, 1980, Computer Applications in Public Affairs, 1984, Cost-Effective Management for Today's Public Affairs, 1984, Making Community Relations Pay Off: Tools and Strategies, 1988, Winning at the Grassroots: How to Succeed in the Legislative Arena by Mobilizing Employees and Other Allies, 1989, Leveraging State Government Relations, 1990, Managing the Business-Employee PAC, 1992, Adding Value to the Public Affairs Function, 1994, The Corporate PAC Handbook: A Complete Guide to Successful Fundraising (Peter Kennerdell), 1999, Public Affairs Review, 2000, Winning at the Grassroots (Tony Kramer), 2000; Pub. Affairs Rev. Mag., 1980-86, 2000, Impact newsletter on nat. and internat. pub. affairs, 1980—; contbr. to The Commissar, 1972, Informing the People: A Public Affairs Handbook, 1981, The Practice of Public Relations, 1984, Anna 0, 2000; mem. editl. bd. Pub. Rels. Quar., 1975—, Washington correspondent, Pub. Rels. quarterly, 1998—, Fgn. Svc. Jour., 1975-81; mem. adv. bd. Pub. Rels. News, 1991—; contbr. articles to profl. jours. Founding chmn. bd. dirs. Nat. Inst. for Govt. Pub. Info. Rsch., Am. U., 1977-80. Served with USAAF, 1943-46. Recipient 2 awards A.P. Mng. Editors Assn., Iowa, 1949, Meritorious Svc. award USIA, 1963, Superior Svc. award USIA, 1964, Presdl. commendation, 1964, 70, 1st prizes Fed. Editors Assn., 1970, 74-75, Agy. Dir.'s citation USIA, 1974, 1st prizes Soc. Tech. Comm., 1974, 75-76, Gold award Internat. Newsletter Conf., 1982, Silver award, 1985, Eddi award for design excellence Editor's Workshop, 1983, Gold Circle award for outstanding comm. Am. Soc. Assn. Execs., 1983-89, 97, 98, 99, 2000, Editors' Forum award, 1988-90, 94, 95, 96, Assn. Trends award, 1989-2000, 1st ann. Great Assn. Communicator award, Assn. Trends, 1999, Grand prize Internat. Ann. Report Conf., 1989, Gold award 1997, Comm. Concepts awards, 1989—, Grand awards, 1992, 2000, MerComm awards, 1990-2000, Nat. Media Conf. award, 1989, 90, Internat. Acad. Comm. Arts and Scis. award, 1994, 95, 96, 97, 98, 2000, Grand prize, 1995, awards Printing and Graphic Assn., 1987, 91, 96, 97, 2000, Excell award Soc. of Nat. Assn. Publishers, 2000, Judges award 2000; named Most Outstanding Info. Officer in Exec. Br. Govt. Info. Orgn., 1975, Ky. Col. and Adm. Nebr. Navy, 1984. Mem. DAV, Am. Fgn. Svc. Assn., Am. Legion, Internat. Assn. Bus. Communicators (Communicator of Yr. Washington chpt. 1978, various awards 1973, 76-78, 84, 90, 94, 95, 96, 97, 98, 99, 2000, Winner Circle awards dist. III 1996-2000), Nat. Assn. Govt. Communicators (pres. 1978-79, Communicator of Yr. 1977, Disting. Svc. award 1978), Pub. Rels. Soc. Am. (mem. Counselor's Acad. 1980—, chmn. 1st Amendment task force 1980-81, co-recipient Thoth award 1980, 81, 94, recipient twin Thoth awards 1995, 96, 97, 3 Thoth awards 1998, 2 Thoth awards 1999, Thoth award 2000, Bronze Anvil award 2000), World Affairs Coun., Soc. of Profl. Journalists, The Acad. Polit. Sci., Fgn. Svc. Club, Nat. Press Club, Overseas Press Club. Episcopalian. E-mail: wpedersen@pac.org. Home: 4701 Willard Ave Apt 1007 Chevy Chase MD 20815-4622 Office: Pub Affairs Coun 2033 K St NW Ste 700 Washington DC 20006-1019

PEDLAR, ARTHUR PETER, accountant; b. Kokstad, S. Africa, Nov. 5, 1961; s. William James and Annie Wilhelmina (Scheepers) P.; m. Sandra Joanna Hendricks, Aug. 23, 1986; children: Cindy, Peter-John, Paul. B Comm., U. Western Cape, Bellville, S. Africa, 1990; BA with Honors, U. Stellenbosch Grad. Sch. Bus, Bellville, S. Africa, 1993; Diploma in Treasury Mgmt., Euromoney Inst. Fin., Johannesburg, 1994. Treasury acct. Gen. Motors, 1984-86; sr. bus. adv. Small Bus. Devel. Corp., Cape Town, 1987-88; corp. auditor Engen Petroleum, Ltd., Cape Town, 1988-95; fin. mgr. Boltt Removals, Cape Town, 1996; analyst S. African Reserve Bank, Pretoria, 1997; mgr. fin. Ariel Technologies, Pretoria, 1998—; freelance bus. cons., Cape Town, 1989—. Editor: (mag.) Zapp, 1994. Mem. UWC Cmty. sub-com., Bellville, 1981; exec. mem. Civic Assn. of Rondebosch E., Cape Town, 1989-92. Recipient scholarship, Small Bus. Devel. Corp., Cape Town, 1981. Mem. Inst. Comml. and Fin. Accts. So. Africa, Black Mgmt. Forum, Chartered Inst. of Mgmt. Accts. Meth. Avocations: running, poetry, reading, table-tennis. Phone: 083-677-1299. Home: PO Box 633, 0154 Rooihuiskraal South Africa

PEDLEY, JULIAN ERIC, public health physician, consultant; b. Lanchow, Kansu, China, Feb. 10, 1943; s. Cecil James and Betty Irene (Norrish) P.; m. Ella Siglinde Fischer, Jan. 30, 1971; children: Andrew C.J., Jennie C. MB BS, London U., 1967; MSc, London Sch. of Hygiene, 1976, diploma in tropical pub. health, 1970; MA in Med. Law and Ethics, London U., 1998. Med. officer Overseas Devel. Adminstrn., W.I., 1971-74; sr. med. officer Commonwealth Devel. Corp., Swaziland, 1977-81; pub. health cons. Aylesbury and Milton Keynes, 1982-84; dir. pub. health Milton Keynes, 1984-96; dist. gen. mgr. Milton Keynes, Health Authority, 1985-93; chief exec. Bucks Health Authority, Buckinghamshire, 1992-95; cons., medico-legal adviser Med. Protection Soc., London, 1996—. Editor Health of Milton Keynes, 1988-92. Chmn. Willen Hospice, Milton Keynes, 1992—, Hope Outreach Ministries, South Asia, 1993—; vice chmn. Milton Keynes Forum, 1986-90. Fellow Royal Coll. Physicians, Publ. Health Medicine; mem. Inst. Health Svcs. Mgmt., Brit. Med. Assn., Medico-Legal Soc., Christian Med. Fellowship, Assn. Pub. Health. Avocations: christian medical missions, current affairs, bible teaching. Home: 4 Andrewes Croft, Milton Keynes MK14 5HP, England Office: Med Protection Soc, 33 Cavendish Sq, London W1 0PS, England

PEDLEY, LAWRENCE LINDSAY, lawyer; b. Hopkinsville, Ky., May 27, 1932; s. Gracean McGoodwin and Elizabeth Lindsay Pedley; m. Ellen Mack, Oct. 9, 1957 (div. 1981); children: Lawrence Lindsay Jr., David M., Joan Elizabeth, Jill Katharine; m. Wanda Polk, Feb. 3, 1995. BA, The Citadel, S.C., 1955; JD, Yale U., 1959. Bar: Ky. 1959, Fla. 1980, U.S. Dist. Ct. Ky. 1959, U.S. Ct. Appeals (6th cir.), 1975, U.S. Supreme Ct. 1981. Prin. atty. Ky. Dept. of Hwys., Frankfort, 1960; v.p. Nat. Industries, Louisville, 1964-66; gen. counsel, v.p., dir. Life Ins. Co. Ky., Louisville, 1966-69; ptnr. Goldberg & Pedley, Louisville, 1970-80, Pedley, Zielke, Gordinier & Pence, Louisville, 1980—; ptnr. Hardin Properties Group, Louisville, Pedley Ptnrs., Louisville; owner Exec. Express, Louisville, 1969-80. Capt. JAGC, 1967. Mem. ABA, Ky. Bar Assn., Fla. Bar Assn., Filson Club, Harmony Landing Country Club, Pendennis Club. Office: Pedley Zielke Gordinier & Pence 455 S 4th St Ste 1150 Louisville KY 40202-2512

PEDLEY, TIMOTHY ASBURY, IV, neurologist, educator, researcher; b. Phoenix, Aug. 31, 1943; s. Timothy Asbury Pedley III and Mary Adele (Newcomer) Melis; m. Barbara S. Koppel, Mar. 17, 1984. BA, Pomona Coll., 1965; MD, Yale U., 1969. Cert. neurology, electroencephalography, clin. neurophysiology; diplomate Am. Bd. Psychiatry and Neurology. Intern Stanford U. Hosp., 1969-70; resident in neurology Stanford U., 1970-73, postdoctoral fellow, 1973-75, asst. prof. neurology, 1975-79; from assoc. prof. neurology to prof., vice chmn. Columbia U., 1979-98, Henry and Lucy Moses prof., chmn. neurology, 1998—; neurologist-in-chief Columbia-Presbyn. Med. Ctr., N.Y.C., 1998—; dir. comprehensive epilepsy ctr. Columbia-Presbyn. Med. Ctr., 1983-97. profl. adv. bd. Epilepsy Found Am., 1984-98, chmn. profl. adv. bd., 1985-87, pres. bd. dirs., 1991-93, chmn. 1993-95. mem. rev. com. NIH Nat. Inst. Neurol. and Chronic Diseases and Strokes, 1985-89, chmn., 1988-89; various adv. coms. NIH/NINDS, 1990-2000; vis. fellow in exptl. neurology Inst. Psychiatry, London, 1978; mem. merit rev. bd. neurobiology rsch., VA, 1992-96, chmn., 1995-96. Contbr. articles to profl. jours.; editor-in-chief Epilepsia, 1994—. Fellow Am. Acad. Neurology, Am. Electroencephalographic Soc. (pres. 1989-90, bd. dirs. 1981-85); mem. Am. Neurol. Assn. (coun. 1992-94, treas. 1995-98), Am. Epilepsy Soc. (treas. 1980-83, pres. 1991-92), Soc. for Neurosci., Internat. League Against Epilepsy (mem. exec. com. 1994—), Yale Club, Met. Opera Club, Shenorock Shore Club (Rye, N.Y.), Alpha Omega Alpha. Office: The Neurological Inst 710 W 168th St New York NY 10032-2603

PEDLEY, TIMOTHY JOHN, mathematics educator; b. Leicester, U.K., Mar. 23, 1942; s. Richard Rodman and Jean Mary Mudie (Evans) P.; m. Avril Jennifer Martin Uden, July 10, 1965; children: Jonathan Richard, Simon Grant. BA, Cambridge U., 1963, MA, PhD, 1967, ScD, 1982. Postdoctoral rschr. Johns Hopkins U., Balt., 1966-68; lectr. Imperial Coll., London, 1968-73; lectr. Cambridge U., 1973-89, reader in biol. fluid dynamics, 1989, G.I. Taylor prof. fluid mechanics, 1996—; prof. applied math. Leeds U., 1990-96; fellow Gonville Caius Coll., Cambridge, 1973-89, 96—. Author: (with others) The Mechanics of the Circulation, 1978, The Fluid Mechanics of Large Blood Vessels, 1980; editor: Scale Effects in Animal Locmotion, 1977, (with C.P. Ellington) Biological Fluid Dynamics, 1995; assoc. Siam Jour. Applied Math., 1980-83, Jour. Fluid Mechanics, 1983—, Jour. Biomech. Engring., 1983-89, Jour. Fluids & Structures, 1997, Quar. Jour. Mech. and Applied Math., 1994—; contbr. articles to profl. jours. Fellow Inst. Math. and Its Applications (assoc. editor Jour. Applied Math. 1980—), Royal Soc.; mem. Cambridge Philos. Soc., U.S. Nat. Acad. Engring. (fgn. assoc.). Avocations: bird-watching, running, reading. Office: Dept Applied Math/Theo Phys, Silver St, Cambridge CB3 9EW, England

PEDRERO, JOSÉ I., engineering educator, researcher; b. Madrid, Aug. 1, 1959; s. Jose I. Pedrero and Pilar Moya; m. Begoña de la Puente, Mar. 2, 1991; children: María, Belén, Ignacio. Degree in Indls. Engring., Poly. U., Madrid, 1982; PhD in Mech. Engring., Nat. U. Distance Edn., Madrid, 1987. Engr. WAT, Madrid, 1982-85; asst. prof. mech. engring. UNED, 1985-89, assoc. prof., 1989-93, prof., 1996—; prof. mech. engring. U. Murcia, Cartagena, Spain, 1993-95; del. ISO, 1998—. Author: (book) Exercises of Machine Design; contbr. articles to sci. jours.; tech. editor: Iberoamerican Jour. Mech. Engring. Mem. Spanish Assn. Mech. Engring., Am. Gear Mfrs. Assn. (acad.). Roman Catholic. Avocations: tennis, classical music. Fax: +34 913 986 536. E-mail: jpedrero@ind.uned.es. Office: UNED, Apdo 60149, 28080 Madrid Spain

PEDRETTI, ANTHONY D., information systems specialist; b. Maywood, Ill., Aug. 12, 1976; s. Dennis Andrew and Gail Ann Pedretti. AS, Morton Coll., 1996, A in Liberal Studies, 1997; BS, Ill. State U., 1999. Microcomputer support specialist Morton Coll., Cicero, Ill., 1996-99; tech. support specialist Ill. State U., Normal, 1997-99; PC/LAN technician Trans Union Corp., Chgo., 1999-2000, LAN architect, 2000—; reverse mentor Trans Union Corp. Mem. Mortar Bd. (Chgo., life). Avocation: personal fitness. Fax: 312-466-7978. E-mail: ynotp@juno.com. Home: 3726 S 58th Ave Cicero IL 60804-4205 Office: Trans Union Corp 555 W Adams St Fl 10 Chicago IL 60661-3696

PEDRINI, DANIELE, physicist, researcher; b. Milan, Italy, Jan. 18, 1956; d. Ivano and Anna (Agazzi) P.; m. Elena Paltrinieri, Dec. 5, 1983; 1 child, Irene. Laurea, State U., Milan, 1980. Cert. physicist. Rschr. I.N.F.M., Milan, 1986—. Contbr. papers to profl. jours. Soldier Italian Aeronautics, 1980-81. Home: Piazza Adigrat 6, 20133 Milan Italy Office: INFN, Via Celoria 16, 20133 Milan Italy

PEDROSO, IVAN, Olympic athlete; b. Havana, Dec. 17, 1972. Winner long jump World Championships, 1995, 97, 99; winner Gold medal long jump Sydney, 2000. First non-Am. to win long jump at World Championships; first man to win three long jump titles at World Championships; ranked world's no. 1 long jumper, 1998. Office: Fedn Cubana Atletismo, 13 y C Vedado 601, Ciudad Habana ZP 4, Cuba*

PEEBLES, ALLENE KAY, manufactured housing company executive; b. Waukegan, Ill., Feb. 9, 1938; d. Allan Laverne and Kathryn Bernice (McGill) Sedlmayr; m. William Ross Peebles, July 9, 1960; children: Ross William, Robb Allan, Raymond John, Renda Kay (Mrs. Christopher Sivak). BS with high honors, U. Wis., 1960, MS, 1967; grad., Realtors Inst., 1968. Cert. home economist. Tchr. Horicon (Wis.) High Sch., 1960-61, Oconomowoc (Wis.) High Sch., 1961-67; freelance writer, 1967-70; v.p. Luxury Homes, Inc., Watertown, Wis., 1970-93, Land Devel. Plus Devel. Inc., Watertown, 1970—; co-developer Hidden Meadows Condominium Community, Watertown, 1976-96; gen. ptnr. W and A Elderly Housing Ltd. Partnership, Watertown, 1988—; pres. Housing Am., Inc., 1991—; gen. ptnr. Sunrise Housing Ltd. Ptnrship., 1990—; builder new and rehab low-income housing, 1983—. Del. Wis. Rep. Conv., 1997—; mem. Wis. Gov.'s Conf. on Family, 1980, mem. long range planning team, 1996—; chmn. adminstrv. bd. United Meth. Ch., Oconomowoc, 1974-77, 96-99, lay leader, 2000—; chmn. family ministry Wis. Conf., United Meth. Ch.; membership chmn. Boy Scouts Am., 1984-90; chmn. Ams. Abroad Am. Field Svc., Oconomowoc, 1982-87. Recipient Dist. award of Merit Potawatomi Area coun. Boy Scouts Am., 1986. Mem. NAFE, AAUW (pres. Oconomowoc 1983-85), Am. Home Econs. Assn., Wis. Home Econs. Assn. (parliamentarian 1988-90), Nat. Home Economists in Bus. (internat. com. 1985-87, regional U.S. advisor 1990-92), Nat. Assn. Home Builders, Internat. Profl. and Bus. Women, Wis. Home Economists in Bus. (internat. rep. 1998—, state chmn. 1987-88, Home Economist in Bus. of Yr. 1987), Nat. Assn. Realtors, Am. Assn. Family & Consumer Scis., Am. Assn. Univ. Women (pres. Oconomowoc br. 1981-83, officer's bd. 1984-93, fin. advisor 1995—), Wis. Assn. Realtors, Waukesha Bd. Realtors, Wis. Builders Assn., Wis. Manufactured Housing Assn. (bd. dirs. 1979-90, chmn. bd. 1985-88, Mem. of Yr. award 1986), Internat. Fedn. of Home Economists (USA internat. del. 1997—), Met. Builders Assn. Greater Milw., Wis. Assn. Family and Consumer Scis. (state bd. 1999—, state housing chmn. 2000—), Phi Kappa Phi, Phi Upsilon Omicron, Kappa Omicron Nu, Phi Lambda Theta. Republican. Avocation: writing. Home: 37788 Mapleton Rd Oconomowoc WI 53066 Office: Housing Am Inc W1140 Marietta Ave Ixonia WI 53036-9748

PEEK, GILES JOHN, cardiothracic surgeon, researcher, educator; b. Pembury, Kent, Eng., Jan. 14, 1966; s. Rodney Ernest and Judith Elizabeth (Andrews) P.; m. Sally Jayne Torkington, July 7, 1990; children: Alexander Joseph, Isabelle Jessica. MB, BS, Kings Coll. Hosp., London, 1990; MD, U. Leicester, Eng., 1998. Resident surg. officer Brompton Hosp., London, 1992; sr. house officer in cardiothoracic surgery Groby Road Hosp., Leicester, 1994; resistrar in cardiothoracic surgery Glenfield Hosp., Leicester, 1994, rsch. fellow in cardiothoracic surgery and ECMO, 1994-98; specialist registrar in cardiothoracic surgery No. Gen. Hosp., Sheffield, Eng., 1998; lectr. cardiac surgery and ECMO Glenfield Hosp.-U. Leicester, 1999—. Contbr. articles to med. jours., including Injury, Annals Thoracic Surgery, Lancet, Chest, ASAIO. Jr. rsch. fellow Brit. Heart Found., 1995. Fellow Royal Coll. Surgeons. Avocations: white water canoeing, skiing. E-mail: ycq57@dial.pipex.com. Office: Glenfield Hosp ECMO Office, Groby Road Dept Cardiothor, Leicester LE3 9QP, England

PEERS, MICHAEL GEOFFREY, archbishop; b. Vancouver, B.C., Can., July 31, 1934; s. Geoffrey Hugh and Dorothy Enid (Mantle) P.; m. Dorothy Elizabeth Bradley, June 29, 1963; children: Valerie Anne Leslie, Richard Christopher Andre, Geoffrey Stephen Arthur. Zert.dolm., U. Heidelberg, Germany, 1955; BA, U. B.C., Vancouver, 1956; Licentiate in Theology, Trinity Coll., Toronto, Ont., 1959, DD (hon.), 1977; DD (hon.), St. John's Coll., Winnipeg, Man., 1981, Wycliffe Coll., Toronto, 1987, Kent U., Canterbury, Eng., 1988, Montreal Diocesan Coll., Que., Can., 1989, Coll. of Emmanuel and St. Chad, Sask., Can., 1990, Thorneloe U., 1991; DCL (hon.), Bishop's U., Lennoxville, Que., 1993; DD (hon.), Huron Coll., London, Ont., 1998. Ordained to ministry Anglican Ch. as deacon, 1959, as priest, 1960, consecrated bishop, 1977. Asst. curate St. Thomas Ch., Ottawa, 1959-61; chaplain U. Ottawa, 1961-66; rector St. Bede's Ch., Winnipeg, 1966-72, St. Martin's Ch., Winnipeg, 1972-74; dean of Qu'Appelle, Regina, Sask., 1974-77; bishop Qu'Appelle, 1977-82, archbishop, 1982-86; now primate of Anglican Ch. Can., Toronto, Ont.; instr. Ottawa Tchrs. Coll., 1962-66, St. Paul's High Sch., Winnipeg, 1967-69; pres. Coun. Coll. Emmanuel, St. Chad, Saskatoon, 1979-83. *

PEET, CAROLINE LINDA, artist; b. Haarlemmermeer, The Netherlands, Mar. 3, 1960; d. H.Q. Peet. Exhbns. include Avv in elicottero Lugano, 1992, Rocca Paolina, Perugia, 1993, Solfe-Duphar, Weesp, 1994, Europ-Art, Anvers, 1995, An Exposition by catalogue, 1996. Home: Javastraat 63 I, 1094 HA Amsterdam The Netherlands

PEET, HOWARD DAVID, English educator, writer; b. Fargo, N.D., Oct. 7, 1930; s. Howard Morrison and Beatrice Katherine (Gunness) P.; m. Jacquelyn Marie Hegge, June 20, 1953; children: Terry H., Pamela Peet Astrup. BA, Macalaster Coll., St. Paul, 1956; BS, Moorhead State U., 1965, MS, 1965; postgrad., U. Minn., 1970. Ride trumpet Ray Palmer Orch., Chgo., 1950-52; lead trumpet Kliff Riggs Orch., Omaha, 1954-55; ins. investigator Retail Credit Assn., St. Paul, 1955-60; prof. English N.D. State U., Fargo, 1965-86, prof. emeritus, 1986—, dir. concentrated approach program, 1970-80. Author and co-author 70 books including The English Book: A Complete Course, 1980, Wordskill for The Micro Computer, 1982, MacMillan Spelling, 1983, Vocabulary for College Reading and Writing, 1984, Linguistics For Teachers, 1993, Wordskills, 1993, (audio tapes) Words to Success, 1998; co-author lang. arts grad courses for the Internet, N.D. State U., 1999. Pres. Young Reps., Wilkin county, Minn., 1970's, PTA, Barnesville, Minn., 1970's; treas. Presbyn. Ch., Deerhorn, Minn., 1970's. With USN, 1952-54, Korea. Named Red River Valley Educator, Red River Valley Heritage Soc., 1992. Mem. Nat. Coun. Tchrs. English, Writers of the Purple Sage, Am. Legion, La. Soc. Des 40 Hommes Et 8 Chevaux. Avocations: music, reading, traveling, writing poetry and short stories. Home: 25 Prairiewood Xing Fargo ND 58103-4667

PEET, RICHARD CLAYTON, lawyer, consultant; b. N.Y.C., Aug. 24, 1928; s. Charles Francis and Florence L. (Isaacs) P.; m. Barbara Jean McClure, Mar. 17, 1956 (div. July, 1988); children: Victoria Clementine, Alexandra Constance, Elizabeth Erica, Clarissa Barbara. JD, Tulane U., 1953. Bar: La. 1955, D.C. 1955. Law clk. Melvin M. Belli, San Francisco, 1954; with The Calif. Co., Standard Oil of Calif., 1955; atty. appellate sect. Lands div. Dept. Justice, Washington, 1956; asst. to dep. gen. counsel Dept. Commerce, 1957; legis. asst. Republican policy com. U.S. Senate, 1958; legis. asst. U.S. Senate minority leader William F. Knowland, 1958; asso. counsel House Judiciary Com., 1959-62; asso. minority counsel House Pub. Works Com., 1969-74; pres. Citizens for Hwy. Safety, 1978-84; practiced in Washington, 1962-68; prin. Richard Clayton Peet & Assos., 1972—; ptnr. Anderson, Pendleton, McMahon, Peet & Donovan, 1977-80, Anderson, Peet & Co., 1980-84; pres., mng. dir. Lincoln Rsch. Ctr., 1965-72; v.p. Oil East Corp., 1978-83. Author: Goals for a Constructive Opposition, 1966; contbg. editor: Congressional Digest, 1960-61, Jour. Def. and Diplomacy, 1983-86, Senate Rep. Week, 1991; (weekly radio show) Across the Aisle, 1992; composer: song Stand Up For America, 1971 (George Washington medal Freedom's Found. 1971), A Monologue With God, 1996, Remembrance House. Chmn. bd. Workshop Library on World Humor; Rep. candidate Pres. of U.S., 1999-2000. With U.S. Army, 1946-47, with USAFR, 1950-55. Nominated for Rockefeller Public Svcs. Awd. Mem. Phi Delta Phi, Pi Kappa Alpha. Achievements include conceiving Highway Safety Act of 1973 with Cong. Wm. Harsha, OH, establishing road safety improvement programs, created (with congress) Natl. Bicentennial Highway Safety Year to promote, organized and chaired (with Pres. Ford) White House Conf. on Highway Safety, 1976, Rep. candidate for U.S. Pres., 1999-2000. Home: PO Box 971 Mc Lean VA 22101-0971

PEET, VICTOR ELLART, physicist, researcher; b. Temirtau, Kazakhstan, Jan. 1, 1956; arrived in Estonia, 1962; s. Ellart Ernst and Nina Vitaly (Rogova) P.; m. Nadia Ostap Lyzhnik, June 20, 1977; 1 child, Alexandr. BSc, U. Tartu, Estonia, 1978; PhD, Inst. Gen. Physics, Moscow, 1988. Engr. Inst. Physics, Tartu, 1978-80, jr. scientist, 1982-88, scientist, 1988-90, sr. scientist, 1990—; vis. lectr. U. Tartu, 1991-95. Referee Jour. Optics Comm., Optics Letters, 1996—; contbr. articles to profl. jours. With Soviet Infantry, 1980-82. Grantee Internat. Sci. Found., 1993, Estonian Sci. Found., 1994—. Avocations: astronomy. Office: Inst Physics Univ Tartu, Riia 142, Tartu 51014, Estonia

PEETERMANS, WILLY EDUARD, physician; b. Mol, Antwerp, Belgium, Jan. 13, 1958; s. Frans and Margaretha (Kinnaer) P.; m. Marianne Vermeulen, July 29, 1983; children: Marijke, Bart. MD, K.U. Leuven Cath. U., Belgium, 1983, internist, 1988; infectiologist, U. Leiden, Netherlands, 1989; PhD, K.U. Leuven, 1994. Resident U. Leiden, 1989; assoc. chief Univ. Hosp. Leuven, Belgium, 1990—; prof. medicine K.U. Leuven, Belgium, 1994—. Author books & sci. articles. Lt. Med. Svc., 1990-91, Belgium. Address: Univ Hosp KU Leuven, Herestraat 49, B-3000 Leuven Belgium

PEETERS, WILLEM JOHANNES MARIA, German language and literature educator; b. Weert, Limburg, The Netherlands, Dec. 8, 1945; s. Jan P. J. and Jozefien A. B. (Segers) P.; m. Louise D. S. de Wijs, Oct. 21, 1977; children: Aernout, Sytze, Reinier (dec.), Jurriaan. BA in German Lang. and Lit., Utrecht U., The Netherlands, 1971, MA in German Linguistics & Dialectology, 1973, PhD in Phonetics, 1991. Asst. lectr. Utrecht U., 1971-73, asst. prof., 1973—, sec. governing bd. dept. German, English and Celtic, 1993-98. Corp. first class The Netherlands N.G., 1992-97. Recipient Hon. German Lang. award German Embassy, 1966. Mem. Netherlands Reformed Ch. Avocations: classical music, motorcycling, hiking, wine. Home: Tuinstraat 70, 3732 VM De Bilt (Utrecht) Utrecht, The Netherlands Office: Utrecht U Rsch Inst Lang & Speech, Trans 10, 3512 JK Utrecht The Netherlands

PEEV, GEORGI ANGELOV, chemical engineering educator, researcher; b. Sozopol, Bulgaria, Feb. 23, 1935; s. Angel Doinov and Nadejda Georgieva (Popova) P.; m. Lili Borisova Popova, Aug. 12, 1962; children: Ludmila, Borislav. Diploma in engring., Inst. Chem. Tech., Sofia, Bulgaria, 1958, PhD, 1970, DSc, 1980. Sr. chemist Rosen Mining, Bourgas, Bulgaria, 1958-59; head lab. Hemus Enterprise, Bourgas, 1959-60; asst. prof. Inst. Chem. Tech., 1960-72, assoc. prof., 1972-82, dean Organic Faculty., 1980-87, head dept., 1984-92, vice-rector, 1987-89; prof. U. Chem. Tech and Metallurgy, Sofia, 1983—; invited prof. S.W. U., Blagoevgrad, Bulgaria, 1995—; expert univ. accreditation Bulgarian Ministry of Edn., 1999—; mem. rsch. bd. advisors Am. Biog. Inst., 1999—. Mem. editl. bds. Ciela Pub. House, Sofia, 1997—. Scholar Brit. Coun., London, 1967; grantee European Commn., Brussels, 1992. Mem. Bulgarian Soc. Chem. Engring., Bulgarian Soc. Rhe-

ology. Office: U Chem Tech and Metallurgy, Kl Ohridski 8, 1756 Sofia Bulgaria

PEEV, TODOR MICHAILOV, chemist, educator; b. Bourgas, Bulgaria, Dec. 21, 1937; s. Michail Peev and Anastassia Ivanova (Djakova) Andreeva; m. Vasja Georgieva, July 5, 1964; children: Michail, Gergana. Diploma in chemistry, Sofia (Bulgaria) U., 1963; PhD in Chemistry, Sofia U. Tech., 1977; DSc, Bulgarian Acad. Sci., Sofia, 1991. Tchr. secondary sch., Bourgas, 1963-65; asst. Higher Inst. Chem. Tech., Bourgas, 1965-82, assoc. prof. chemistry, 1982-92, prof. chemistry, 1992—; head dept. chemistry Assen Zlatarov U. (formerly Higher Inst. Chem. Tech.), Bourgas, 1994-97; prof. chemistry dept. chemistry South-West U., Blagoevgrad, 1997-98, vice-dean faculty of math. and natural scis., 1998—; dean Higher Inst. Chem. Tech., 1981-89, chancellor, 1992-93. Mem. Sci. Union, Bulgarian Electrochem. Soc., Bulgarian Catalysts Club. Avocations: classical and opera music, drawing. Home: 10-A Shipchenski prohod, 1113 Sofia Bulgaria Office: 66 Ivan Michailov, 2700 Blagoevgrad Bulgaria

PEH, KWEE LIM, laboratory technologist; b. Singapore, June 18, 1948; s. Pay Chew Chwee and Lim Ah Phong. Tech. diploma in elec. engring., Singapore Poly. U., 1979; diploma in supervisory mgmt. studies, Inst. Supervisory Mgmt., U.K., 1982; diploma in adminstrv. mgmt., Inst. Adminstrv. Mgmt., U.K., 1983; diploma in mgmt., Assn. Bus. Execs., U.K., 1984. Cert. in quality control; City and Guilds of London Inst, 1981. Lab. technologist Nat. U. Singapore, 1965-81, sr. lab. technologist, 1981-94, prin. lab. technologist, 1995—; mem. Inter-Univ. Coun., St. Bartholomew's Hosp. Med. Coll., 1976; adminstr. rsch. labs., rschr., presenter, organizer workshops, seminars in field. Contbr. numerous articles to profl. jours. Recipient Boehringer-Mannheim award, 1994. Fellow Inst. Sci. Tech. U.K., Singapore Assn. for Med. Lab. Scis. (asst. sec., treas., mem. com., internal auditor 1974-90, editl. bd. Jour. Med. Lab. Scis. 1990-93), Australasian Coll. Biomed. Scientists; mem. Inst. Biology (chartered biologist), Inst. Mgmt. Specialists (life), Ob-Gyn. Soc. Singapore (assoc.), Biomed. Rsch. and Exptl. Therapeutics Soc. Singapore (assoc.), Assn. Bus. Execs., Inst. Indsl. Engrs., Inst. Adminstrv. Mgmt., Inst. Supervisory Mgmt., Inst. Engrs. and Technicians (assoc.), Singapore Assn. Clin. Biochemists (assoc.). Home: # 03-04, 237 Tembeling Rd, Singapore 423721, Singapore Office: Nat U Hosp Dept Ob-Gyn, Lower Kent Ridge Rd, Singapore 119074, Singapore

PEH, WILFRED CHIN GUAN, radiologist, researcher; b. Singapore, Apr. 21, 1958; s. Eng-Teck and Libby (Tin) P.; m. Angeline Yue, July 28, 1988; children: Fraser, Austin, Laura. MBBS, Nat. U. Singapore, 1982; MD, U. Hong Kong, 1999. Med. officer Singapore Gen. Hosp., 1984-87, Tan Tock Seng Hosp., Singapore, 1987-88; registrar Western Infirmary and Royal Infirmary, Glasgow, Scotland, 1988-90; sr. registrar West Midlands Regional Health Authority, U.K., 1990-91; lectr. U. Hong Kong, 1991-93, sr. lectr., 1993-96, assoc. prof., 1996-97, prof., 1997-99; sr. cons. radiologist, dep. head Singapore Gen. Hosp., 2000—; clin. head radiology Duchess of Kent Children's Orthopaedic Hosp., Hong Kong, 1992—; hon. cons. radiologist Hosp. Authority, Hong Kong, 1993—; vis. fellow Mallinckrodt Inst. Radiology, St. Louis, 1993, 94. Author: 101 Years of a New Kind of Rays, 1996, Clinics in Diagnostic Imaging, 1998; mem. editl. adv. bd. Hong Kong Practitioner, 1996—, Diagnostic Imaging Asia Pacific, 1996—, Hong Kong Radiographers Jour., 1997—, Asian Oceanian Jour. Radiology, 1998—, Jour. Hong Kong Coll. Radiologists, 1998—, Radiology, 1999—, Brit. Jour. Radiology, 2000—, Singapore Med. Jour., 2000—, SGH Procs., 2000—, Am. Jour. Orthopedics, 2000—; contbr. over 250 articles to profl. jours., chpts. to books; editor-in-chief Jour. Hong Kong Coll. Radiologists, 1998-2000. Capt. Singapore Armed Forces, 1976-77, 83—. Rsch. grantee Hong Kong Rsch. Grant Coun., 1996. Fellow Royal Coll. Radiologists, Hong Kong Coll. Radiologists, Hong Kong Acad. Medicine, Acad. Medicine Singapore; mem. Brit. Inst. Radiology, Radiol. Soc. N.Am. (editl. fellow 1998), Am. Roentgen Ray Soc., Internat. Skeletal Soc., Royal Coll. Physicians and Surgeons of Glasgow, World Assn. Med. Editors. Avocations: horseback riding, golf. Home: 3 Ascot Rise, Singapore 289815, Republic of Singapore Office: Singapore Gen Hosp, Dept Radiology Outram Rd, 169608 Singapore Republic of Singapore

PEHLKE, HELMUTH BRUNO, theology educator; b. Zitzmin, Pomerania, Germany, Nov. 15, 1943; s. Bruno and Emma (Zilz) P.; m. Lore E.O. Zander, May 8, 1970; children: Samuel, Stefan, Thomas. ThM, Dallas Theol. Sem., 1978, ThD, 1985. Tchr. German Bible Inst., Seeheim, Germany, 1970-75; prof. German Theol. Sem., Giessen, Germany, 1983—; dir. Christian svcs. German Bible Inst., Seeheim, 1972-75; Old Testament dept. chmn. German Theol. Sem., Giessen, 1988—; chmn. Facharbeitsgruppe Altes Testament, Tübingen, Germany, 1990-97. Editor: (42 vols.) Edition C AT, 1998—; editor book revs.; contbr. articles to profl. jours. William M. Anderson scholarhip Dallas Sem., 1985. Mem. Evang. Theol. Soc., Arbeitsgemeinschaft für Evanelikale Theologie, Am. Schs. Oriental Rsch., Soc. Bibl. Lit. Avocations: fishing, mountain climbing. Office: Freie Theol Acad, Schiffenberger Weg 111, D-35394 Giessen Hesse, Germany

PEI, IEOH MING, architect; b. Canton, China, Apr. 26, 1917; came to U.S., 1935, naturalized, 1954; s. Tsu Yee Pei and Lien Kwun Chwong; m. Eileen Loo, June 20, 1942; children: T'ing Chung, Chien Chung, Li Chung, Liane. BArch, MIT, 1940; MArch, Harvard U., 1946; DFA (hon.), U. Pa., 1970, Rensselaer Poly. Inst., 1978, Carnegie Mellon U., 1980, U. Mass., 1980, Brown U., 1982, NYU, 1983, Dartmouth Coll., 1991, Northeastern U.; LLD, Chinese U., Hong Kong, 1970, Pace U.; LHD, Columbia U., 1980, U. Colo., 1982, U. Rochester, 1982, U. Hong Kong, 1990, Am. U., Paris, 1990. Practice architecture N.Y.C., 1939-42; asst. prof. Harvard Grad. Sch. Design, 1945-48; dir. archtl. div. Webb & Knapp, Inc., 1948-55; with Pei Cobb Freed & Partners (formerly I.M. Pei & Ptnrs., I.M. Pei & Assos.), N.Y.C., 1955-96; now ind. architect N.Y.C., 1996—. Prin. projects include Mile High Ctr., Denver, Nat. Ctr. Atmospheric Rsch., Boulder, Colo., Dallas City Hall, John Fitzgerald Kennedy Libr., Boston, Can. Imperial Bank Commerce Complex, Toronto, Overseas Chinese Banking Corp. Ctr., Singapore, Dreyfus Chemistry Bldg. MIT, East-West Ctr. U. Hawaii, Honolulu, Mellon Art Ctr. and Choate Rosemary Hall Sci. Ctr., Wallingford, Conn., Univ. Plz. NYU, Johnson Mus. Art Cornell U., Ithaca, N.Y., Washington Sq. East, Phila, Everson Mus. Art, Syracuse, N.Y., Nat. Gallery Art, East Bldg., Washington, Wilmington Tower, Raffles City, Singapore, West Wing Mus. Fine Arts, Boston, expansion and modernization of Louvre Mus., Paris, Morton H. Meyerson Symphony Ctr., Dallas, MIT Arts and Media Ctr., Jacob K. Javits Conv. Ctr., N.Y.C., Fragrant Hill Hotel, Beijing, Tex. Commerce Tower, Houston, Bank of China, Hong Kong, Creative Artists Agy., Beverly Hills, Calif., Guggenheim Pavilion, Mount Sinai Med. Ctr., N.Y.C., Rock n' Roll Hall of Fame and Mus., Cleve., Mus. Modern Art, Athens, Greece, Miho Mus. of Art, Shiga, Japan, Bilbao (Spain) Estuary Project, Four Seasons Hotel, N.Y.C., others; planning projects include S.W. Washington Redevelopment Plan, Govt. Ctr. Redevelopment Plan, Boston, Oklahoma City Downtown Redevelopment Plan, Bedford Stuyvesant Super Block, Bklyn., master plan Columbia U. Mem. Nat. Def. Rsch. Com., Princeton, N.J., 1943-45, Nat. Coun. Humanities, 1966-70, Nat. Coun. on Arts, 1981-84. MIT traveling fellow, 1940, Wheelwright fellow Harvard, 1951; Thomas Jefferson Meml. medal for Architecture, 1976, gold medal for architecture Am. Acad. Arts and Letters, 1979, Nat. Arts Club Gold medal of honor, 1981, Mayor's award of Honor for Art and Culture, N.Y.C., 1981, La Grande Medaille D'or L'Académie d'Architecture, 1981, Pritzker Architecture prize, 1983, Medal of Liberty, 1986, Medal of French Legion of Honor, 1988, Nat. Medal of Art, 1988, Praemium Imperiale Japan Art Assn., 1989, UCLA Gold medal, 1990, Colbert Found. first award for Excellence, 1991, Excellence 2000 award, 1991, Freedom medal, 1993. Fellow AIA (Medal of Honor N.Y. chpt. 1963, Gold Medal 1979); hon. fellow ASID; mem. Nat. Inst. Arts and Letters (Arnold Brunner award 1961), Am. Acad. Arts and Scis., Am. Acad. and Inst. Arts and Letters (chancellor 1978-80), Royal Inst. Brit. Architects, NAD, Urban Design Council. Office: care Pei Cobb Freed & Ptnrs 600 Madison Ave New York NY 10022-1615

PEI-ING WU, agricultural economics educator; b. Kaohsiung, Taiwan, Jan. 5, 1959; d. Ching-Liang Wu and Deng-Mei Liu; m. Cheng-Feng Shih; children: Ietsym Shih, Bunsym Shih. BS, Nat. Taiwan U., Taipei, 1981; MS, U. Ill., 1986; PhD, Ohio State U., 1991. Rsch. asst. dept. agrl. econs. Nat. Taiwan U., Taipei, 1981-84, assoc. prof., 1991-99; rsch. asst. dept. agrl. econs. U. Ill., Urbana, 1984-86, rsch. asst. Inst. for Environ. Studies, 1984-86; rsch. assoc. dept. agrl. econs. & rural socs. Ohio State U., Columbus, 1987-90; survey design analyst WTP Inc., Columbus, 1990-91; prof. Nat. Taiwan U., 1999—; sec. gen. Rural Econs. Soc. China, Taipei, Taiwan, 1994-95, 98-99, bd. dirs., 1996-97. Contbr. articles to profl. jours. Hon. rsch. grantee Nat. Sci. Coun., Taipei, 1992-98; fellowship Ohio State U., 1986. Mem. Am. Agrl. Econs. Assn., Am. Econs. Assn., Assn. Environ. & Resource Economists, Gamma Sigma Delta, Phi Kappa Phi. Avocations: music, reading, gardening. Office: Nat Taiwan U Dept Agrl Econ, No 1 Sec 4 Roosevlet Rd, Taipei 106, Taiwan

PEINADO, ARNOLD BENICIO, JR., consulting engineer; b. El Paso, Tex., Oct. 22, 1931; s. Arnold Benicio Sr. and Themis Irene (Molina) P.; m. Rosa de la Torre, July 12, 1954; children: Arnold B. III, Stephen Anthony, Melissa Ann. BS in Engring., Johns Hopkins U., 1952; MS, MIT, 1953. Registered profl. engr., Calif., N.M., Tex. Job supt. Home Constrn. Co., El Paso, 1953-54; staff engr. Simpson & Strata, San Francisco, 1956-59; pres. A. B. Peinado & Sons, Cons. Structural Engrs., El Paso, 1959-71, Peinado, Peinado & Navarro, Cons. Engrs., El Paso, 1971-80; exec. v.p. AVC Devel. Corp., El Paso, 1975-89; pres. AVC Wood Products, Inc., El Paso, 1979-89, Coronado Wood Products Internat., Inc., El Paso, 1988—; exec. v.p. Coronado Engrs. Internat., Inc., El Paso, 1988—; bd. dirs. El Paso br. Fed. Res. Bank of Dallas, 1976-81. Mem. Inter City Group El Paso and Juarez, Mex., 1983—, Tex. bd. advisors Mountain States Tel. & Tel.; vice chmn., bd. dirs. Sierra Med. Ctr. and Hosp., El Paso, 1979-84; state bd. dirs. Cons. Engrs. Coun., Austin, Tex., 1974-76; bd. dirs. Devel. Bd. U. Tex. El Paso, 1984-89; bd. dirs., pres. Pan Am. Contractors Assn., 1971-74. With U.S. Army, 1954-56. People of Vision honoree Tex. Soc. to Prevent Blindness, 1982; named Mem. of Yr. Pan Am. Contractors Assn., 1974. Fellow Tau Beta Pi; mem. ASCE (pres. El Paso chpt. 1971-72), Tex. Soc. Profl. Engrs. (Young Engr. of Yr.1966, Engr. of Yr. 75, pres. El Paso chpt. 1969-70), El Paso Assn. Builders (v.p. 1986-89), Nat. Soc. Profl. Engrs., Granaderos de Galvez (gov. 1986), El Paso Renaissance 400 (bd. dirs.), El Paso C. of C. (bd. dirs., v.p., pres.), Rotary. Avocations: hiking, camping, tennis, archaeology. Home: 5729 Mira Grande Dr El Paso TX 79912-2005 Office: Coronado Engrs Internat Inc 299 Shadow Mountain Dr El Paso TX 79912-4704

PEIRIS, GAMINI LAKSHMAN, Sri Lankan government official; b. Colombo, Sri Lanka, Aug. 13, 1946; s. Glanville S. and Lakshmi C. (Salgado) P.; m. Savitri N. Amarasuriya, 1971; 1 child. Student, St. Thomas' Coll., U. Ceylon, Oxford U. Prof. law U. Colombo, 1979—, dean faculty law, 1982-88, vice chancellor; dir. Nat. Film Corp. Sri Lanka, 1973-88; commr. Law Commn. Sri Lanka, 1986—; min. justice and constitutional affairs Govt. of Sri Lanka, Colombo, 1994—, also dep. min. for finance; vis. fellow All Souls Coll Oxford U., 1980-81; Butterworths vis. fellow Inst. Advanced Legal Studies U. London, 1984; disting. vis. fellow Christ's Coll., Cambridge, 1985-86; Smuts vis. fellow commonwealth studies U. Cambridge, 1985-86; chmn. Com. Vice Chancellors of Univs. Sri Lanka; mem. Securities Coun. Sri Lanka, 1987—. Author: Law of Unjust Enrichment in South Africa and Ceylon, 1971, General Principles of Criminal Liability in Ceylon, 1972, Offences under the Penal Code of Sri Lanka, 1973, The Law of Evidence in Sri Lanka, 1974, Criminal Procedure in Sri Lanka, 1975, The Law of Property in Sri Lanka, 1976, Landlord and Tenant in Sri Lanka, 1977; contbr. numerous articles to profl. jours. Vice chair Janasaviya Trust Fund; mem. Pres. Com. Youth Unrest, 1989; mem. Nat. Edn. Com., exec. com. Assn. Tchrs. and Rschrs. in Intellectual Property Law; bd. govs. Inst. Fundamental Studies. Recipient Presdl. award, 1987. Mem. Internat. Acad. Comparative Law (assoc.), Inc. Soc. Legal Edn. Avocation: walking. Office: Ministry of Justice, Superior Cts Complex, Colombo 12 Sri Lanka*

PEIRSON, GEORGE EWELL, film producer, writer, art director, educator; b. L.A., May 16, 1957; s. Malcolm Alan and Beth (Wanlass) P. BFA, Art Ctr. Coll. of Design, Pasadena, Calif., 1986. Photographer Griffith Park Observatory, L.A., 1981-84; owner, art dir. Peirson to Peirson Studio, Winnetka, Calif., 1983—; pres. Anubis Prodns., Inc., Las Vegas, 1997—; instr. Art Workshops, L.A., 1988-89, Learning Tree U., Chatsworth, Calif., 1990-93. Art dir., films include Valentine's Day, 1986, Private Demons, 1986, The Courtyard, 1987, Hope of the Future, Escape from Lethargia, 1988, Time Scrambler, 1988, Star Quest, 1988, Star Runner, 1989, The World of Early Bird, 1989, The Deadly Avenger, 1991, Hell Comes to Frogtown II, 1991, The Minister's Wife, 1991, Eye of the Stranger, 1992, Star Runners, 1992, Monty, 1992, Guyver, Dark Hero, 1993, Tiger Mask, The Star, 1994, Dragon Fury, 1994, Arizona Werewolf, 1994, Drifting School, 1994; prodr., films include Jurassic Women, 1994, Wolves Carnival, 1995, King of Hearts, 1995, Rollergator, 1995, Lord Protector, 1996, Lancelot: Guardian of Time, 1997, The Gift, 1998, Blade Sisters, 1999, Hell Dawgs, 1999; writer, films include Shalakan, 1997, Final Game, 1997. Mem. Assn. for Astron. Arts (bd. mem., v.p. 1987-89), Costumers Guild West, Assn. of Sci. Fiction and Fantasy Artists. Republican. Avocations: computers, skiing, running, bicycling, scuba diving. Office: Peirson to Peirson Studio 7657 Winnetka Ave Ste 301 Canoga Park CA 91306-2677 Corp Office: Anubis Prodns Inc 3305 Spring Mountain Rd # 60A Las Vegas NV 89102-8609

PEISAKHOVICH, YURI GRIGORIEVICH, physicist; b. Tomsk, Russia, 1947; s. Grigori Abramovich and Rose Grigorievna (Pecherskaya) P.; m. Lubov Aleksandrovna Marchenko, July 10, 1973; children: Vladislav, Elena. Physicist, U. Novosibirsk, 1970; postgrad., Acad. Scis. USSR, Novosibirsk, 1977; BS, Inst. Physics, Krasnoyarsk, 1977. Investigator Rsch. Inst. Inorganic Chemistry, Novosibirsk, 1970-72, scientist, 1975-78; docent State Pedagogical U., Novosibirsk, 1978-89, holder chair of theoretical physics and astronomy, 1990—. Contbr. numerous articles to profl. jours. Home: Sibiriakov, Gvardeitsev St 22 Kv 75, 630048 Novosibirsk Russia Office: Novosibirsk State Ped U, Vilyuiskaya St 28, 630126 Novosibirsk Russia

PEITSCH, WERNER KARL, surgeon, researcher; b. Hildesheim, Germany, Nov. 2, 1945; s. Ewald August Georg and Magdalena (Hilgendorf) P.; m. Maria Regina Kruse Peitsch, 1971; children: Wiebke, Anna Lena, Lennart. MD, U. Goettingen, 1971; degree in Dental Surgery, 1972. Surgeon dept. surgery U. Goettingen, 1972-79; resident U. Tex., Houston, 1979-80; head physician U. Goettingen, 1982-86; prof., 1986-89; dir. St. Josef Hosp., Essen-Werden, Germany, 1989—. Author: Gastrin Receptors in Gastrointestinal Tract in Ulcer and Cancer Patients, 1984, Gastrin Receptor Development and Regulation in Rats, 1983; editor: Diagnostic and Therapy of Malignant Lymphomas, 1992. Grantee Deutsche Forschungsgemeinschaft, U. Houston, 1979-80, U. Goettingen, 1980-85. Mem. German soc. Surgery, Rotary Club Essen-East. Home: Plattenweiler 14, D-45239 Essen Germany Office: Catholic St Joseph Hosp, Propsteistr 2, D 45239 Essen Germany

PEITZMAN, ANDREW BERTRAM, surgeon; b. Phila., Feb. 3, 1949; m. Debra Shaffer; children: Elizabeth, Jonathon, Emily, David. BS, U. Pitts., 1971, MD, 1976. Intern U. Pitts., 1976-77, resident, 1977-79, 81-84; fellow Cornell Med. Ctr. N.Y. Hosp., 1979-81; asst. prof. surgery U. Pitts., 1984-89, assoc. prof., 1989-96, prof. surgery, 1996—; dir. trauma and emergency svcs. U. Pitts. Med. Ctr., 1984—, med. dir. referral communication ctr., 1989—, chief divsn. gen. surgery; co-dir. trauma/neurosurg. ICU Presbyn. U. Hosp., Pitts., 1992—; dir. surg./critical care fellowship U. Pitts., 1992-96. Author: Trauma, 1993, Pathophysiologic Foundations of Critical Care Medicine, 1993; editor: UPMC Trauma Manual, 1994, The Trauma Manual, 1998. Recipient Nat. Rsch. Svc. award NIH, 1980-81. Fellow ACS; mem. Assn. for Acad. Surgery, Soc. Critical Care Medicine, Soc. Univ. Surgeons, Surg. Infection Soc., Ctrl. Surg. Assn. Shock Soc. Office: U Pitts Med Ctr A1010 Presbyterian Univ Hos Pittsburgh PA 15213

PEIXOTO FILHO, JOSE ULISSES, agronomist, educator; b. Fortaleza, Ceara, Brazil, Feb. 21, 1959; s. Jose Ulysses and Maria Izoloa Cartaxo (Teles Cartaxo) P.; m. Renalvia Leandro Brito, Dec. 23, 1983; children: Jose Ulisses, Gabriela Leandro, Davi Leandro. Grad., Union Coll., Recife, Brazil; degree in agron. engring., Pernambuco Fedn. Rural U., Recife, Brazil, lic. in agron. engring. Agrl. engr. Ematerce, Aurora, 1982-83; agrl. instr. Agrl. Coll. Crato, 1984-87, rural bldg. tchr., 1988-94, rural sociology instr., 1995—, adminstrn. dept. dir., 1994-95, pedagogy and didactic support dir., 1995-96. Author: Himanthantus Articulata on Araripe Untafin. Recipient gold medal Agronomist Engring. Assn., 1982. Avocations: farming, teaching, public relations. Home: Rua Coronel Secundo 167, 63100000 Crato Ceara, Brazil Office: Agrl Coll Crato, Aluecegas Farm, 6310000 Crato Ceara, Brazil

PEIXOTO NETO, JOSE ULYSSES, internist, researcher; b. Crato, Ceará, Brazil, Aug. 29, 1930; s. Adérito de Aquino Silva and Adelite Alencar Peixoto; m. Maria Isolda Teles Cartaxo, May 23, 1958; children: Jose Ulysses Peixoto Filho, Eunice Ulysséia Peixoto Maia, Jorge André Cartaxo Peixoto. 1st degree, State Coll. Goias, Brazil, 1942, postgrad., 1942-49; 2d degree, St. John Coll., Fortaleza, Brazil, 1949; postgrad., Fed. U., Recife, Brazil, 1955; Laurel, Cearense Med. Ctr., 1994. Med. resident St. Michael Hosp., Rio de Janeiro, 1956; intern St. Anthony Hosp., Iguatú, Ceará, 1957; founder Social Providence, Crato, Ceará, 1958-64; attendent St. Frances Hosp., Crato, 1958-69; founder St. Michael Hosp., Crato, 1967-93, pres., dir., 1983-93, internist, researcher, 1993—; founder Faculty of Law, Crato, 1977-78; lectr. faculty of medicine The Fed. U. of Ceará, 1976—. Recipient Good Svc. award Lyons Club, 1992, Laurel Cearense Med. Ctr., 1994, Cert. Merit Health Care Profls. Juaziero North Profl. Health Assn., 1998, Gold Medal of Profl. Merit, Ceara Estate Regional Coun. Medicine, 1999. Fellow Brazilian Med. Assn. (specialist); mem. AAAS, ACP, Brazilian Soc. Clin. Medicine (specialist), N.Y. Acad. Sci. Roman Catholic. Avocations: reading, walking in woods, cinema, farming.

PEKER, ELYA ABEL, artist; b. Moscow, June 15, 1937; came to U.S. 1972; s. Aba Z. and Frieda I. (Warshavsky) P.; m. Katrina Friedman, May 19, 1977; 1 child, Benjamin E. Diploma of Artist for Theater Decoration, Art Inst., Moscow, 1956. Comml. artist N.Y.C., 1972-88. One-man shows include Nakhamkin Fine Art Gallery, N.Y.C., 1980-85; exhibited in group shows in Basel, Switzerland, Hong Kong, others; represented in permanent collections of Kennedy-Onassis family, Emil Wolf, Frank L'Angella, Campbell family, Benjamin family, others; contemporary flower and still-life poster series published 1991, reproductions published worldwide. Mem. Am. Biog. Inst. (dep. gov., order internat. ambs., Gold Record Achievement 1995, 20th Century Achievement award 1995, Internat. Cultural Diploma Honor 1996), Internat. Platform Assn., Licensing Industry Merchandiser's Assn. Address: 1673 E 16th St Ste 164 Brooklyn NY 11229-2901

PEKIN, AHHMET VASFI, manufacturing executive; b. Izmir, Turkey, Nov. 24, 1955; s. Ertugrul Mustafa and Fitnet (Akan) P.; m. Gulseren Kordöv, Aug. 17, 1954; children: Bora, (twins) Deniz and Meltem. BS, Bosphorus U., Istanbul, Turkey, 1979. Inventory planning engr. Akgimento TAS, Istanbul, 1982-86, project mgr., 1986-92; works and planning dir. Sabanci Holding Cement Group, Istanbul, 1992-95, strategy and devel. dir., 1998—; gen. mgr. Gimentas TAS, Izmir, 1995-98; bd. dirs. Akcansa, Istanbul, Nigde (Turkey) Gimento. Asst. lt. Gen. Hdqrs. Turkish Mil., 1981-82. Mem. Turkish Cement Mfgs. Assn. (tech. com. 1999—). Avocations: tennis, sailing, scuba diving, horseback riding. Office: Sabana Holding Cement Group, Kule 2 Rat 18 Levent, 80745 Istanbul Turkey

PEKKANEN, TUOMO ANTERO, Latin educator; b. Saari, Finland, July 16, 1934; s. Matti and Aino Maria (Rantonen) P.; m. Inna Anna-Lea Lahdenpera, Feb. 1, 1959 (div. 1976); children: Sirkku, Matti, Marja; m. Virpi Leena Seppälä, Dec. 17, 1976; 1 child, Mikko. PhD, Helsinki U., Finland, 1968. Asst. Roman lit. Helsinki U., 1962-69; dir. Inst. Romanum Finland, Rome, 1969-72; sub. prof. Roman lit. Helsinki, 1973; prof. Latin Jyväskylä U. (Finland), 1975-99. Contbr. articles to profl. jours.; author: Kalevala Latina, 1986. Officer Chevalier of the Order of the Svc. of Republic of Italy, 1971, Chevalier of the Order of the White Rose of Finland, 1991. Fellow Acad. Tiberina, Finnish Acad. Scis., Academia Latinitati Favendae (v.p. 1998—). Home: Adolf Lindforsin tie 9 A 34, 00400 Helsinki Finland

PEKKARINEN, JUSSI OLAVI, physicist, quality manager; b. Turku, Finland, Sept. 4, 1954; s. Aimo Ilmari and Liisa Talvikki Karki (Hedlund) P. BSc, U. Helsinki, 1979, MSc, 1981; PhD, U. Kuopio, Finland, 1989. Qualified indsl. hygienist. Sect. chief, dep. Inst. Occup. Health, Turku, Finland, 1989-90; rschr. Inst. Occup. Health, Helsinki, 1980-89, sr. rschr., 1990-92, asst. departmental dir., 1993-95, mem. sci. bd., 1993-95; quality mgr. Nokia Telecomms., Helsinki, 1995—; vis. scientist Nat. Inst. for Occup. Safety and Health, Cin., 1992-93; docent lectr. U. Kuopio, 1990—; sci. evaluator Acad. of Finland, Helsinki, 1995—. Contbr. chpts. to books, more than 120 articles to internat. and nat. sci. jours. Grantee Emil Aaltonen Found., 1988, Acad. Finland and Academia Sinica Beijing, 1987; Finnish Inst. Occup. Health rsch. exch. grantee, 1992. Mem. Acoustical Soc. Finland (sec. 1981-86, bd. dirs. 1986-89), Audio Engring. Soc., Finnish Radioamateur Assn., Finnish Boating Club (Helsinki). Avocations: sailing, photography, oil painting, amateur radio. E-mail: jussi.pekkarinen@pp.inet.fi. Fax: 358 9 5113 8252. Home: Platinatie 12, 02750 Espoo Finland Office: Nokia Telecoms Oy, Keilalahdentie 4 PO Box 300, FIN-02150 Espoo Finland

PEKKI, SEPPO SAKARI, power plant worker; b. Kouvola, Finland, Aug. 20, 1947; s. Erkki Pekki and Eva (Kiuru) Henriksson. Coal worker PVO Energy Co., Kotka, Finland, 1972—. Avocations: music, reading, astrology, religions. Home: Anjalankatu 2-4 F 66, 48100 Kotka Finland Office: PVO Co, Mussalo MVO Oy PL 108, 48101 Katka Finland

PEKLENIK, JANEZ, engineering educator; b. Trzic, Slovenian, June 11, 1926; s. Joze Peklenik and Marija Primozic; m. Stasa Korbar, July 10, 1954 (dec. Dec. 1966); children: Igor, Ales, Stasa-Marija; m. Marija Caliary, Dec. 8, 1973; 1 child, Damian. Diploma, U. Ljubljana, Slovenia, 1954; D Engring., Tech. U., Aachen, Germany, 1957, Dr.-Ing. Habilitation, 1961. Prof., hon. prof. U. Birmingham, U.K., 1964-72, 73; hon. prof. Aeronautical Inst., Nanjing, China, 1982; rsch. asst. Tech. U., Aachen, 1955-57, asst. prof., 1961-64; prof., head dept. U. Ljubljana, Slovenia, 1972—, dean faculty, 1973-76, rector, 1987-90, prof., dept. head, 1972—; Amb. Rep. of Slovenia in Scis., 1992. Editor: CIRP Jour. on Manufacturing Systems, 1971—; assoc. editor Soc. Mfg. Engrs. Jour. on Mfg. Sys., 1981; contbr. articles to profl. jours. Recipient F.W. Taylor medal Coll. Internat. Rsch. Prodn., Gen. Assembly, Braunschweig, 1959, Soc. Mfg. Engrs., 1981, Georg Schlesinger award Land Berlin and Tech. Univ., 1988, Kidric State award for Rsch., 1974, State award of Slovenia for Rsch., 1996. Fellow Internat. Instn. for Prodn., Engring. and Rsch. (pres. 1979-80), Soc. Mfg. Engrs., Slovenian Acad. Sci. and Art (com. chmn. 1979—), Acad. Europae, Insts. of Mech. Engrs., Engring. Acad. Slovenia (founding pres. 1995—), Internat. Acad. Engring. (Russia), CIRP (hon.). Roman Catholic. Avocations: skiing, hiking, tennis. Home: Rodiceva 3, Ljubljana 1113, Slovenia Office: U Ljubljana, Askerceva 6, Ljubljana 1000, Slovenia

PEKMEZCI, SALIH, physician, educator; b. Sinop, Turkey, May 23, 1962; s. Sati Ali and Semiye Pekmezci; m. Gulperi Uzun, Feb. 6, 1989; children: Yasemin, Yunus. MD, U. Istanbul, Turkey, 1987. Fellow in gen. surgery U. Istanbul, 1994-99, assoc. prof., 1999—. Mem. Nat. Soc. Colon and Rectal Diseases Turkey, Nat. Soc. Traumatology and Emergency Turkey. Avocations: soccer, bridge, music. E-mail: kayasaribey@turk.net. Office: Cerrahpasa Tip Fakultesi, Genel Cerrahi Anabilim Dali, Istanbul Turkey

PELAEZ-HUDLET, JOSE, oceanographer, researcher; b. Mexico City, July 30, 1946; s. José and Odette (Hudlet) Peláez. Diplôme d'Etudes Approfondies, U. d'Aix-Marseille, France, 1976; MS, U. Calif., San Diego, 1978, PhD, 1984. Rsch. asst. Scripps Instn. Oceanography, La Jolla, Calif., 1977-84; collaborator U. de Paris VI, 1986-87, Inst. Français Recherche de la Mer, Brest, France, 1986-87; vis. scientist Joint Rsch. Ctr. European Union, Ispra, Italy, 1988-91; dir. Inst. Oceanografía Satelital, Cuernavaca, Mexico, 1991—; collaborator Inst. de Ciencias del Mar y Limnología, Mazatlán, Mex., 1992—, Universidad Nacional Autónoma de Mex., Mexico City, 1992—. Contbr. sci. articles to profl. jours. Participant civil rights activities. Mem. AAAS, Am. Geophysical Union, Am. Soc. Limnology and Oceanography, N.Y. Acad. Scis. Avocations: sailing, rowing, water sports. Office: Inst Oceanografia Satelital, Ajusco 33 Rancho de Cortés, 62120 Cuernavaca Morelos, Mexico

PELANT, IVAN, physicist, educator; b. Uherské Hradiště, Czech Republic, Dec. 12, 1944; s. Josef and Emilie (Pozdilkova) P.; m. Alena Beresova, Aug. 9, 1980; children: Irena, Dita. MSc, Charles U., 1967, PhD, 1976, DSc, 1990. Lectr. Charles U., Prague, 1973-83; rsch. asst. Latvian Stat U., Riga, 1971-72; postdoctoral fellow Ecole Normale Superieure, Paris, 1976; assoc. prof. Charles U., Prague, 1983—, head dept. chem. physics, 1990-93; rsch.

scientist Louis Pasteur U., Strasbourg, France, 1991-92, Acad. of Scis., Prague, 1994—; cons. TESLA KP, Roznov, 1985-90. Co-author: Structural and Optical Properties of Porous Silicon Nanostructures; contbr. articles to sci. and profl. jours.; patentee in field. Mem. Soc. Czech Mathematicians and Physicists, Internat. Soc. Optical Engring. Avocations: sports, music, history of railways. Home: Moravska 11, 12000 Prague Czech Republic Office: Inst Physics Acad Scis, Cukrovarnicka 10, 16253 Prague Czech Republic

PELAVIN, SOL HERBERT, research company executive; b. Detroit, Dec. 16, 1941; s. Norman J. and Alice A. (Levinson) P.; m. Diane Christine Blakemore, Aug. 14, 1966; children: Shayna Beth, Adam Blake. BA in Math., U. Chgo., 1965, MAT in Math., 1969; MS in Stats., Stanford U., 1974, PhD candidate in mathematical models of edn. research, 1975. Tchr. pub. schs., 1965-70, teaching rsch. asst. Stanford (Calif.) U., 1972-74; cons. Rand Corp., Santa Monica, Calif., 1975; policy analyst SRI Internat., Menlo Park, Calif., 1975-78; exec. officer NTS Research Corp., Durham, N.C., 1978-82; pres. Pelavin Assocs., Inc., Washington, 1982-94; exec. v.p., COO Am. Inst. Rsch., 1994—; dir. Data Analysis and Tech. Support Ctr., Washington, 1989-93, Policy Analysis Support Ctr., Washington, 1993—; expert witness to U.S. Congress, 1977, 79, Cabinet briefing, 1983; cons. Frank, Bernstein, Conway and Goldman, Balt., 1980-81; dir. Ednl. Analysis Ctr., Washington, 1982-85. Author: (with others) Investigation of the Impact of the Emergency School Assistance Programs on Black, Male 10th Grade Student Achievement, 1975, (with P. Barker) A Study of the Generalizability of the Results of Standardized Achievement Tests, 1976, (with J.L. David) Research on the Effectiveness of Compensatory Education Programs: A Reanalysis of Data, 1977, (with others) Federal Expenditures for the Education of Children and Youth With Special Needs, 1981, (with D.C. Pelavin) An Evaluation of the Fund for the Improvement of Postsecondary Education, 1981, 83, (with others) Evaluation of the Commodity Supplemental Food Program, 1982, An Evaluation of the Bilingual Education Evaluation, Dissemination and Assessment Centers, 1984, A Study of a Year-Round School Program, 1978, An Evaluation of the Indian Education Act, Title IV, Part C, Education for Indian Adults, 1984, Teacher Preparation: A Review of State Certification Requirements, 1984, Analysis of the National Availability of Mathematics and Science Teachers, 1983, Minority Participation in Higher Education, 1988, Changing the Odds, 1990, others; contbr. articles to profl. jours. NSF fellow U. Chgo., 1968-69; Cuneo fellow Stanford U., 1973. Mem. AAAS, Am. Ednl. Research Assn., Am. Psychol. Assn. Democrat. Jewish. Office: American Inst Rsch 3333 K St NW Ste 300 Washington DC 20007-3500

PELECHANO, VICENTE, psychologist, educator, researcher; b. Algemesi, Valencia, Spain, June 18, 1943; s. Vicente and Consuelo (Barbera) P. Psychologist, Sch. Psychology Madrid, 1968; behavior therapist, Max Planck Inst. Psychiatry, 1971; PhD of Philosophy, Faculty of Philosophy Madrid, 1972. Lectr. psychology U. Complutense, Madrid, 1968-69, 71-74; prof. psychology U. La Laguna, Spain, 1974-77, U. Valencia, Spain, 1977-83, U. La Laguna, Tenerife, Canary Islands, Spain, 1983—. Patentee in field; editor, contbr. Analysis and Behavior Modification Jour., 1975—; editor Psychologemas Jour., 1987—; contbr. chpts. in books and articles to profl. jours. Mem. APA, Spanish Soc. Psychology (exec. com. 1972-75, Jose Germain award 1968, Luis Simarro award 1970, Pilar Sangro award, 1972), Internat. Soc. for Personality and Individual Differences, Valencian Soc. Behavior Analysis (pres. 1980-82, editl bd.), LaLaguna Personal Disorders Unit Svc. (head), Spanish Soc. of Psychopathology and Clin. Psychology(hon.), Spanish Soc. of Individual Differences (hon.), European Congress Behavioral and Cognitive Therapies (hon. pres.). Office: U La Laguna Psychol Dept, Campus de Guajara, Tenerife Canary I, Spain

PELEG, BEZALEL, mathematician; b. Afula, Israel, Feb. 25, 1936; s. Moshe and Malka Peleg; m. Zmira Madorski, July 1, 1965; children: Gad, Avner, Orith. MSc, Hebrew U., Jerusalem, 1961, PhD, 1964. Asst. Hebrew U., Jerusalem, 1962-63, instr., 1963-64, lectr., 1964-65, 66-69, sr. lectr., 1969-71, assoc. prof., 1971-76, prof., 1976—; asst. prof. U. Mich., Ann Arbor, 1965-66; rsch. fellow Ctr. Econ. Rsch. Tilburg U., The Netherlands, 1993-94; vis. prof. dept. econs. Va. Poly. Inst. and State U., 1986, U. Bielefeld, Germany, 1996; vis. rsch. prof. Copenhagen Bus. Sch., 1998, Inst. Econs., U. Copenhagen, 1999; vis. rsch. prof. dept. equantative econs. U. Maastricht, 2000. Author: Game Theoretic Analysis of Voting in Committees, 1984. Fellow Econometric Soc.; mem. Am. Math. Soc. Office: Hebrew U, Inst Maths, 91904 Jerusalem Israel

PELEKASSIS, CONSTANTINE EUSTATHIUS, retired agricultural educator; b. Zante Island, Greece, Sept. 6, 1917; s. Demetrius and Angelica (Dragonas) P.; m. Julia Carvellas, Oct. 17, 1943; children: Angelica, Elizabeth. Diploma in Agr., Aristotelian Univ. of Salonica, 1940, PhD, 1962; MSc in Entomology, U. Calif., Berkeley, 1957. With agrl. experiment sta. Min. of Agr., Athens, 1942-44, civil servant, 1942-68; lab asst. Benaki Plant Pathology Inst./Kiphisia, Athens, 1959-44, chief of the olive pests Lab., 1956-61, head of entomology and zoology dept., 1964-68; assoc. prof. agr. zoology and entomology Agr. U. of Athens, 1964-65, prof., 1966-85, elected rector, 1977-79; mem. Superior Coun. for Agrochems., Min. Agr., 1968-85, State Lab. for Drugs, 1968-73; mem. exec. com. Commis Intern Lutte Biologique, France, 1961-73; pres. Consultative Coun., Benaki Plant Pathol. Inst., 1990-92; presenter in field on TV, radio and Hellenic confs. for the protection of natural environment, biotopes, and various ecosystems. Author/co-author about fifty scientific rsch. publs. and reports on various destructive phytophagous species of insects and mites in Greece; contbr. articles to profl. jours. in field, coll. text books and catalogues in field. Decorated Croix de Guere Min. of Def., Greece, 1948. Mem. Entomol. Soc. of Greece (pres. 1979—).

PELIKANOVA, TEREZIE, endocrinologist; b. Rumburk, Czech Republic, Oct. 9, 1954; d. Ladislav and Terezie (Habel) Csatlos; m. Pavel Pelikan, Dec. 29, 1977; two children. MD, Charles U., 1980, PhD, 1990; DSc, 2000. Physician Hosp. Na Frantisku, Prague, Czech Republic, 1981-83; sr. rsch. worker IKEM, Prague, 1983-96, head diabetes ctr., 1996—; assoc. prof. internal medicine, 1999—. Office: Inst Clin & Exptl Medicine, Videnska 1958/9, 14021 Prague Czech Republic

PELIKANT, ADAM, electric researcher and educator; b. Lodz, Poland, Dec. 17, 1960; s. Jan Zdzislaw and Halina (Ziolkowska) P.; m. Justyna Janina Laskiewicz, Aug. 31, 1991; 1 child, Magda. MSc, Tech. U. Lodz, 1984, PhD, 1991. Asst. Tech. U. Lodz, 1983-86, sr. asst., 1986-91, adj., 1991; lectr. Coll. Computer Sci., Lodz, 1991—; lectr. Coll. of Computer Sci., Lodz. Contbr. articles to Archiv für Electrotechnik, COMPEL, Compumag, others. Polish Acad. Sci. grantee, 1994. Avocation: data bases, computer graphics and animation. Office: Tech U Lodz Elec Mach/Transf, Stefanowskiego 18/22, 90-924 Lodz Poland

PELINOVSKY, DMITRY EFIM, mathematics educator; b. Nizhny Novgorod, Russia, Mar. 4, 1969; s. Efim N. and Valentine M. (Balabina) P.; children: Marta, Paulina; m. Anna Mikhalchenko, 2000. BS, N. Novgorod (Russia) State U., 1993; PhD, Monash U., Melbourne, Australia, 1997. Rsch. scientist Inst. Applied Physics, N. Novgorod, 1992-94; vis. fellow Australian Nat. U., Canberra, Australia, 1995-97; fellow U. Cape Town, South Africa, 1997; NATO sci. fellow U. Toronto, Ont., Can., 1998-99; asst. prof. McMaster U., Hamilton, Ont., Can., 2000—. Contbr. articles to profl. jours. Avocations: travel, hiking, canoeing. Office: McMaster U Dept Math, 1280 Main St West, Hamilton, ON Canada L8S 4K1

PELIZA, SIR ROBERT JOHN, former Gibraltar government official; b. Nov. 16, 1920; s. Robert Peliza; m. Irma Risso, 1950; 7 children. Grad., Christian Brothers Coll., Gibraltar. Advanced through the grades to maj. Royal Gibraltar Regiment, 1939-61; founder, first leader Integration with Brit. Party, 1967; apptd. following gen. elections to chief min., 1969-72; leader Opposition, 1972-73; speaker House Assembly, Gibraltar, 1989-96; mem. House of Assembly. City councillor, 1945-48; founder European Movement Coun. in Gibraltar, 1976, patron, 1995. Recipient Efficiency Decoration, Freedom of City of Gibralter award, 1998; named hon. col. Gibraltar Regiment, 1993; named Officer of Order Brit. Empire, Knight Commdr. of Brit. Empire, 1997. Mem. Commonwealth Parliamentary Assn. (pres. Gibraltar br., 1989-96). Avocations: painting, reading, rowing, jogging, internet. E-mail: rjpeliza@pelizar.freeserve.co.uk. Fax: 0044-020-8952-1712. Home: 125 Beverley Dr, Edaware Middlesex HA8 5NH, United Kingdom

PELLAT, BERNARD, dean; b. Orleans, France, Oct. 10, 1946; s. Maurice and Monique (Parcollet) P.; m. Christine Gillot, May 18, 1974; children: Emmanuelle, Marine. DDS, U. Paris V, 1973, PhD, 1989. Asst. prof. U. Paris V, 1973-83, master, 1983-90, prof. dept. odontology, 1990—, dean Faculty of Dental Surgery, 1998—, chief dept. biochemistry, 1990—, dir. lab. of biochemistry, 1990—. Author: Abrege de Biochimie, 1983. Coun. mem. U. Paris V, 1998—. Capt. Mil. Health svc., 1973-74. Mem. Internat. Assn. for Dental Rsch. Avocation: classical music. Office: U Paris V Fac Dental Surg, 1 Rue Maurice Arnoux, 92120 Montrouge France

PELLAUD, BRUNO FRANCIS, consultant; b. Martigny, Valais, Switzerland, Oct. 20, 1937; s. André and Francoise (Travelletti) P.; m. Marie-Claire Bieri, July 6, 1962; children: Katia, Diego, Stéphane. MS in Nuclear Physics, Swiss Fed. Inst. Tech., Zurich, 1961; cert. in nuclear postgrad. engring., Swiss Fed. Inst. Tech., Lausanne, 1962; MA in Econs., U. Lausanne, 1963; PhD in Nuclear Engring., NYU, 1967. Staff engr. Consolidated Edison Co., N.Y.C., 1963-66; mgr. physics Gen. Atomics, San Diego, 1967-70; sci. adviser Swiss Fed. Office Energy, Berne, 1970-72; mng. dir. Gen. Atomic Europe, Zurich, 1972-82; v.p. Electrowatt Engring. Svcs., Zurich, 1982-93; dep. dir. gen. Internat. Atomic Energy Agy., Vienna, Austria, 1993-99; exec. cons. Nat. Coop. Disposal Radioactive Waste, Wettingen, Switzerland. Author, editor: An History of Nuclear Energy in Switzerland, 1991; contbr. articles to profl. jours.; contbr. Domaine Pub. Polit. Weekly Mag. Mem. Swiss Nuclear Soc. (pres. 1984-91), European Nuclear Soc. (com. chmn. 1978-92), Inst. Nuclear Materials Mgmt. (disting. svc. award 1999). Fax: 41-27-483 11 74. E-mail: pellauds@bluewin.ch. Home: Chalet San Diego, CH-1977 Icogne Switzerland

PELLEGRINI, ALFREDO, management consultant; b. Milan, Feb. 27, 1937; s. Ulisse and Emilia Ester (Bigolotti) P.; m. Paola Adele Alessandri, Nov. 29, 1975. Grad., U. L. Bocconi, Milan, 1965. Contr. Impresa Farsura Spa, Milan, 1970-78, CEO, 1978-81; CEO MACO srl Mgmt. Cons., Milan, 1982—; dir. Roccon Ltd., Lagos, Nigeria, 1973-79, Zanussi Farsura spa, Pordenone, Italy, 1978-81; mng. dir. Geotecna Progetti spa, Milan, 1993-95, Ambitus srl Ingegneria Ambientale, Milan, 1987-95. Contbr. articles to profl. jours. Mem. Assn. Profession de Italiana Consulentiali Direzione e Organ. (tng. officer 1996—), Assn. Italian Cost Engring., Assoconsult Lombardia (bd. dirs. 1995-97). Avocations: painting, designing, sculpture, bioagriculture, biological building. E-mail: alfpell@tin.it. Office: MACO 3, Via S Pellico 14, 20050 Lesmo Italy

PELLEGRINI, VINCENT D., JR., orthopaedic surgeon; b. Providence, Dec. 27, 1954; m. Lisa Marie Giosa (dec. Apr. 1998); children: Gina Marie, Carla Lynne, Cristina Elaine. BA summa cum laude, Dartmouth Coll., 1977, MD, 1979. Diplomate Nat. Bd. Med. Examiners, Am. Bd. Orthop. Surgery (oral examiner 1997—), Am. Bd. Hand Surgery. Intern in gen. surgery Hartford (Conn.) Hosp., 1979-80, resident in gen. surgery, 1980-81; resident in orthop. Strong Meml. Hosp., U. Rochester, N.Y., 1981-84; chief resident Strong Meml. Hosp., U. Rochester, 1983-84, mem. limb replantation team, 1981-85; instr. dept. orthop. and plastic surgery U. Rochester, 1984-85, asst. prof. orthop. sch. medicine and dentistry, 1986-90, assoc. prof., 1990-92; asst. prof. orthop. divsn. hand, uper extremity and orthop. Stanord (Calif.) U. Med. Sch., 1985-86; chief upper extremity clinic Monroe Cmty. Hosp., U. Rochester, 1986-88; Michael and Myrtle Baker prof., chmn. dept. orthop. Milton S. Hershey Med. Ctr. Pa. State U., Hershey, 1992—, chmn. dept. rehab., 1995—, chief orthop. and rehab., 1997—; emergency rm. physician Newark-Wayne Cmty. Hosp., 1981-84; team physician Rochester Ams. AHL Hockey Team, 1981-85, Greece Athena H.S. Football Team, 1981-84, N.Y. State sect. V H.S. Football Playoffs, 1981-84; physician Regional Golden Gloves Boxing Comptetitions, 1981-84; orthop. cons. San Francisco 49ers NFL Football Team, 1985-86, Children's Disability Clinic, U. Rochester, 1986-92; cons., scientific adv. bd. Orthomet, Inc., 1992-94, Advanced Tissue Scis., Inc., 1992-95; rehab. steering group Pa. State U. Hosps., 1992-95, task force ctr. sports medicine, 1993-95, med. policy bd., 1993-97, coun. clin. svcs., 1993-97, integrated delivery sys., 1997; cons. Wright Med., Inc., 1994-97, DePuy, Inc., 1995—, Zimmer, Inc., 1998—; rehab. coun. Geisinger Health Sys., 1994—, dir. arthritis, bone and joint ctr. coun., 1996—, acad. adv. coun., 1997—, exec. med. coun., 1999—, chair fin. com., 1999—; specialist site visitor panel Accreditation Coun. Grad. Med. Edn., residency rev. com. orthop., 1998—; spkr., presenter in field. Author: (chpt.) Surgery of the Musculoskeletal System, 2d edit., 1990, Surgery of the Hand and Upper Extremity, 1996, Seminars in Arthroplasty, 1997, Atlas of the Hand Clinics, 1997, Orthopaedic Knowledge Update, 1999; co-author: (chpt.) Unsatisfactory Results in Hand Surgery, 1987, Surgery of the Musculoskeletal System, 2d edit., 1990, Fractures in Adults, 3d edit., 1991, 4th edit., 1996, Complications in Orthopaedic Surgery, 1994, Total Hip Arthroplasty Outcomes, 1998, Hand Secrets, 1998; editor Current Opinion Orthop., 1999—; mem. editl. rev. bd. Contemporary Orthop., 1983-84, Yr. Book Hand Surgery, 1987, 95—, Jour. Arthroplasty, 1992—, Jour. Bone Joint Surgery, 1993—, Clin. Orthop. Related Rsch., 1997—, Proceedings Hip Soc., 1998—; editl. rev. cons. Jour. Bone Joint Surgery, 1992-93, Clin. Orthop. Related Rsch., 1994-97, Jour. Hand Surgery, 1997—, Jour. Orthop. Rsch., 1998—; contbr. over 80 articles to profl. jours. Alumni admissions interviewer Dartmouth Coll., Rochester, 1981-82; class agt. Dartmouth Med. Sch. Alumni Fund, 1993, co-dir., head class agt., 1994, 95; bd. dirs., mem. med. scientific com. Arthritis Found. Ctrl. Pa., 1994—; mem. profl. adv. coun. Pa. Blue Shield, 1996-97; adv. task force Highmark-Blue Cross/Blue Shield, 1997—. U. Rochester, Strong Meml. Hosp. fellow, 1984-85, Mayo Clinic Found. fellow, 1985; NIH Biomed. Rsch. support grantee Stanford U., 1986, NIH Hematology Program Project grantee U. Rochester, 1988-92, Kendall Healthcare Products grantee, 1994-99, Orthop. Rsch. Edn. Found. grantee, 1995-99, Dupont Merck Pharm. Co. grantee, 1997-98, Merck & Co., Inc. grantee, 1998—, Zimmer grantee, 1997—, Innovative Biotechnology Rsch. Fund Seed grantee Pa. State U., 1999—, others. Mem. AMA (Physician's Recognition award 1981-99), Internat. Soc. Orthop. Surgery Trauma, Nat. Osteonecrosis Found., Inc., Am. Acad. Orthop. Surgeons (program com. upper extremity 1994—), Am.oc. Surgery Hand (mem. scientific comml. exhibits com. 1989-90, chmn. 1991-92, program com. annual meeting 1991-92, regional leader Am. Found. Surgery Hand 1991-92, Sterling Bunnell Traveling fellow 1991-92), Am. Assn. Hip Knee Surgeons, Am. Orthop. Assn. (residents' conf. com. 1997—, John J. Fahey Meml. N.Am. traveling fellowship com. 1997—, N.Am. Traveling fellow 1984), Orthop. Rsch. Soc., Osteoarthritis Rsch. Soc., Acad. Orthop. Soc. (membership com. 1999—), Clin. Orthop. Soc., Assn. Bone Joint Surgeons, Hip Soc. (bd. dirs. 1998—, John Charnley award 1996, Frank Stinchfield award 1998), N.Y. State Med. Soc., Pa. State Med. Soc., Pa. Orthop. Soc. (bylaws com. 1996—, bd. dirs. 1996—, program chmn. 1997-98), Hinkle Soc., Ea. Orthop. Assn. (nominating com. 1994-95, Resident/Fellow scholar award 1984), Rochester Acad. Medicine, Monroe County Med. Soc., Dauphin County Med. Soc., Oak Hill Country Club (vol. med. svcs. 1989, 95), Hershey Country Club (dir. med. svcs., all pool swim meet 1995), Phi Beta Kappa, Beta Theta Pi, Alpha Omega Alpha. Home: 1345 Windham Rd Hummelstown PA 17036-9168 Office: Milton S Hershey Med Ctr PO Box 850 Hershey PA 17033-0850

PELLEGRINO, PETER, surgeon; b. Camden, N.J., July 7, 1934; s. Peter and Alice (Alchin) P.; m. Barbara Ann Holdon, June 18, 1960; children: Peter Scott, Kathleen Ann, Lisa Marie. AB in Psychology, Franklin-Marshall Sch., 1956; MD, Hahnemann Med. Coll., 1960. Diplomate Am. Bd. Surgery. Intern, Hahnemann Hosp., Phila., 1960-61, surg. resident, 1961-62, surg. resident, 1965-67, 68, attending surgeon, 1969—; chief dept. surgery Kessler Hosp., Hammonton, N.J., 1969—. Served to capt., U.S. Army, 1962-65. Fellow ACS; mem. Am. Acad. Proctology, Soc. Abdominal Surgeons, AMA, N.J. Med. Soc., Hahnemann Alumni Assn. (1st v.p. 1984). Republican. Home: 3 Stafford Ct Berlin NJ 08009-2209 Office: 777 Profl Ctr Hammonton NJ 08037

PELLETT, JON MICHAEL, lawyer; b. Orlando, Fla., Nov. 16, 1961; s. Milton Francis and Jean Ellen (Avery) P.; m. Karen Walker, July 21, 1984 (div. Sept. 1990). BS in Biology, U. Ctrl. Fla., Orlando, 1984, BS in Stats., 1985; JD, Fla. State U., 1993. Bar: Fla. 1995, U.S. Dist. Ct. (mid. dist.) Fla. 1996. Legal trainee Dept. Bus. and Profl. Regulation, Tallahassee, 1993-95; staff atty. Agy. for Health Care Adminstrn., Tallahassee, 1995-96; assoc. Freeman, Hunter & Malloy, Tampa, Fla., 1996-2000, Barr, Murman, Tonelli et al, Tampa, 2000—; vol. guardian ad litem Guardian ad Litem Program, Tallahassee, 1991-95. Bd. dirs. Friends of Arboretum, Orlando, 1998—. Mem. ABA, ATLA, Hillsborough County Bar Assn. Avocations: racquetball, beach volleyball. Office: Barr Murman Tonelli Et Al 201 E Kennedy Blvd Ste 1750 Tampa FL 33602-5829

PELLI, CESAR, architect; b. Tucuman, Argentina, Oct. 12, 1926; came to U.S., 1952, naturalized, 1964; s. Victor V. and Teresa S. Pelli; m. Diana Balmori, Dec. 15, 1950; children: Denis G., Rafael A. BArch cum laude, U. Tucuman, 1949; MS in Architecture, U. Ill., 1954. Assoc. firm Eero Saarinen & Assocs., 1954-64, Daniel, Mann, Johnson & Mendenhall, 1964-68, Gruen Assocs. Inc., L.A., 1968-77, Cesar Pelli & Assocs., New Haven, Conn., 1977—; dean Sch. Architecture, Yale U., New Haven, 1977-84. Works include Pacific Design Ctr. and Expansion, L.A. (Honor award So. Calif. chpt. AIA 1976, Design award from Progressive Architecture 1987), U.S. Embassy, Tokyo, Mus. Modern Art Expansion, N.Y.C., World Fin. Ctr. and Winter Garden, N.Y.C. (Bard award 1992), Cleve. Clinic (Honor award AIA 1986), Herring Hall, Rice U., Houston (Honor award AIA 1986), Carnegie Hall Tower, N.Y.C. (Honor award AIA 1994, Design award AIA/Conn. 1991), Boyer Ctr. Molecular Medicine Yale U. (Design award AIA/Conn. 1991), Bank of Am. Corp. Ctr., Charlotte, NTT Corp. Hdqrs., Tokyo (Design award AIA/Conn. 1997), New Terminal, Washington Nat. Airport (Design award AIA/Conn. 1998, NE Design award 1999, Design for Transp. award 2000), Aronoff Ctr. for the Arts, Cin. (USITT honor award 1996, Design award AIA/CIN 1996, Design award AIA/Conn. 1997), Petronas Towers, Kuala Lumpur, Malaysia (Design award AIA/Conn. 1999, Honor award AIA 2000), Frances Lehman Loeb Art Ctr. Vassar Coll., Poughkeepsie, N.Y. (Design award AIA/Conn. 1996), Internat. Fin. Ctr., Hong Kong, Nat. Mus. Contemporary Art, Osaka, Japan, Performing Arts Ctr. of Greater Miami, Fla., U.S. Fed. Courthouse Bldg., Bklyn.; bd. govs. Perspecta mag.; editor Yale Seminars on Architecture, 1981-82. Fellow AIA (Firm award 1989, named to top ten list of living Am. archs. 1991, Gold medal 1995, Design award 1996); mem. NAD (Arnold M. Brunner Meml. prize 1978), Am. Acad. Arts and Letters (academician), Internat. Acad. Architecture (academician). Office: Cesar Pelli Assocs Pub Rels 1056 Chapel St New Haven CT 06510-2402

PELLICONE, WILLIAM, artist, sculptor, writer, architect; b. Phila., Apr. 12, 1915; s. Emilio and Amelia (Practico) P.; m. Marle Guzzette, July 1964 (div. 1992); m. Ilka Bartel, Aug. 5, 1992. Student, Temple U., Pa. Acad. Fine Arts. lectr. art Phila. Parkway Mus., Queens Settlement, N.Y., U. Iowa, Iowa City, Delaware Sch. Sys., Converse Coll., S.C., Ednl. Alliance, N.Y. One-man shows include Allen Stone Gallery, N.Y., Beryl Lush Gallery, Phila., Trylon Gallery, Southampton, N.Y., Capricorn Gallery, Bethesda, Md., Opus 127 Gallery, Soho, N.Y.C., Harpers Coll., Binghamton, N.Y., Phoenix Gallery, N.Y., Creighton Univ., Nebr., Gallery East, East Hampton, N.Y., Frederick Spratt Gallery, San Jose, Calif.; group shows include Allan Stone Gallery, N.Y., Egan Gallery, N.Y., Alan Gallery, N.Y., Betty Parsons Gallery, N.Y., Tanager Gallery, N.Y., Phoenix Gallery, N.Y., M & L Gallery of Fine Art, N.Y., Arsenal Gallery, N.Y., Camino Gallery, N.Y., Trylon Gallery, N.Y., March Gallery, N.Y., Capricorn Gallery, Bethesda, Md., Brata Gallery, N.Y., Art Alliance, Phila., Landmark Gallery, N.Y., Tenth St. Days, N.Y., Profile Gallery, N.Y., Noho Gallery, N.Y., Gallery East, East Hampton, N.Y., Marie Pellicone Gallery, N.Y., Parish Mus., Southampton, N.Y., Elaine Benson Gallery, Bridgehampton, N.Y., Belanthi Gallery, A Retrospective, Bklyn., Lombardi Gallery, Retrospective, Austin, Tex., 1997; represented in permanent collections, including Met. Mus. Art, N.Y.C., Boston Mus., Smithsonian Inst., Washington, Am. Broadcasting Collection, Iowa Mus., Iowa City, Bayonne (N.J.) Mus., Martin-Rathburn Gallery, San Antonio. With Merchant Marines, 1943-45, France. Grantee Barnes Found., Temple U., Pa. Acad. Fine Arts, Greek Govt., others. Republican. Avocations: musician, sailing, carpentry, writing. Home and Office: 101 Myers Creek Rd Dripping Springs TX 78620-3302

PELLINIEMI, LAURI JOHANNES, medical educator; b. Tampere, Finland, Apr. 8, 1943. MD, U. Turku, Finland, 1971, Dr.Med.Surg., 1975. Asst. U. Turku, 1967-76, 79-82, acting assoc. prof., 1982-84, assoc. prof., 1984-98, dir. Inst. Microbiology and Pathology, 1991-95; Royal Soc. rsch. fellow Royal Postgrad. Med. Sch., London, 1976-77; NIH rsch. fellow Harvard Med. Sch., Boston, 1977-79; prof. U. Turku, 1998—. Editor: Development and Function of the Reproductive Organs, 1988; contbr. over 300 articles to profl. jours., chpts. to books. Office: U Turku, Kiinamyllynkatu 10, FIN20520 Turku Finland

PELOSI, MARCO ANTONIO, obstetrician and gynecologist; b. Lima, Peru, Oct. 5, 1942; came to the U.S., 1968; m. Luisa Garcia-Pacheco, 1962; children: Marco, Carla, Monica. BS, U. Peruana Mayor de San Marcos, Lima, 1962; MD, U. Peruana Cayetano Heredia, Lima, 1968. Cert. Am. Bd. Ob-Gyn. Intern Navy Med. Ctr., Lima, 1967-68; intern dept. ob-gyn. U. Medicine and Dentistry of N.J., Martland Hosp., Newark, 1968-69; resident dept. ob-gyn. CMDNJ-NJMC/Martland Hosp., Newark, 1969-72, fellow oncology dept. ob-gyn., 1972-74; pvt. practice, 1975—; instr. dept. ob-gyn. UMDNJ-N.J. Med. Sch., Newark, 1972-75, clin. asst. prof., 1975-80, 80—; clin. asst. prof. dept. ob-gyn. Hahnemann Med. Coll. Phila., Pa., 1980—; attending physician dept. ob-gyn. UMDNJ-N.J. Med. Sch., Newark, 1972—, Bayonne (N.J.) Hosp., 1974—, St. Joseph Hosp., Paterson, N.J., 1974—, St. Elizabeth Hosp., Elizabeth, N.J., 1979-87, Meadowlands Hosp., Secaucus, N.J., 1979—, Greenville Hosp., Jerasey City, N.J., 1980—; dir. dept. ob-gyn. Bayonne (N.J.) Hosp., 1987—; presenter; pres. Bayonne Hosp. Med. Staff, 1996—. Contbr. chpts. to books and articles, abstracts to profl. jours. Recipient 1st prize The Female Patient's 1st Annual Photo Contest, The Female Patient Mag., 1988, Physician's Recognition award AMA, 1979, 81, 84, 87, 90, 93, 96, 99, Sci. Exhibit Recognition award, Sci. Exhibit Achievement award 83rd Annual Sci. Assembly, So. Med. Assn., Washington, 1989, Physician's Recognition award Med. Soc. N.J., 1999. Fellow ACS, AGOG (Philip F. Williams award 1972, Continuing Edn. award 1972, 79, 82, 84, 87, 90, 93, 96, 99, 2nd prize winner film festival 1999), Internat. Coll. Surgeons, Am. Fertility Soc., N.J. Ob-Gyn. Soc., Am. Inst. Ultrasound in Medicine; mem. Am. Soc. Profs. Ob.-Gyn., Soc. for Minimally Invasive Surgery, Soc. Laparoendoscopic Surgeons, N.J. Med. Soc., Passaic County Med. Soc., Am. Soc. Cytology, Pan Am. Cancer Cytology Soc., Gynecol. Urology Soc., Med. Collectors Assn., Am. Assn. for the History Medicine, Internat. Soc. Physicians Historians, Am. Assn. Gynecol. Laparoscopists (best surgical videos of 1995-2nd place, 1st place best video prodn., 1st place best surgical videos 1996, winner of golden laparoscope award 1996, 3rd place best surgical videos 1997, first place/golden laparoscope award best surgical video 1998), Royal Soc. Medicine, Med. History Soc. N.J. Office: Pelosi Womens Med Ctr 350 Kennedy Blvd Bayonne NJ 07002-1313

PELOTTE, DONALD EDMOND, bishop; b. Waterville, Maine, Apr. 13, 1945; s. Norris Albert and Margaret Yvonne (LaBrie) P. AA, Eymard Sem. and Jr. Coll., Hyde Park, N.Y., 1965; BA, John Carroll U., 1969; MA, Fordham U., 1971, PhD, 1975. Ordained priest Roman Cath. Ch., 1972. Provincial superior Blessed Sacrament, Cleve., from 1978; ordained coadjutor bishop Diocese of Gallup, N.Mex., 1986-90, bishop, 1990—; nat. bd. dirs. Maj. Superiors of Men, Silver Spring, Md., 1981-86, Tekakwitha Conf., Great Falls, Mont., 1981—. Author: John Courtney Murray: Theologian in Conflict, 1976. 1st native Am. bishop. Mem. Cath. Theol. Soc. Am., Am. Cath. Hist. Soc.

PELTASON, JACK WALTER, foundation executive, educator; b. St. Louis, Aug. 29, 1923; s. Walter B. and Emma (Hartman) P.; m. Suzanne Toll, Dec. 21,1946; children: Nancy Hartman, Timothy Walter H., Jill K. BA, U. Mo., 1943, MA, 1944, LLD (hon.), 1978; AM, Princeton U., 1946, PhD, 1947; LLD (hon.), U. Md., 1979, Ill. Coll., 1979, Gannon U., 1980, U. Maine, 1980, Union Coll., 1981, Moorehead (N.D.) State U., 1980; LHD (hon.), 1980, Ohio State U., 1980, Mont. Coll. Mineral Scis. and Tech., 1982, Buena Vista Coll., 1982, Assumption Coll., 1983, Chapman Coll., 1986, U. Ill., 1989. Asst. prof. Smith Coll., Mass., 1947-51; asst. prof. polit. sci. U. Ill., Urbana, 1951-52, assoc. prof., 1953-59, dean Coll. Liberal Arts and Scis., 1960-64, chancellor, 1967-77; vice chancellor acad. affairs U. Calif., Irvine, 1964-67, chancellor, 1984-92; pres. U. Calif. System, Oakland, 1992-95, Am. Coun. Edn., Washington, 1977-84; prof. emeritus dept. politics and soc. U. Calif., Irvine, 1995—; pres. Bren Found., 1997—; Cons. Mass. Little Hoover

Commn., 1950. Author: The Missouri Plan for the Selection of Judges, 1947, Federal Courts and the Political Process, 1957, Fifty-eight Lonely Men, 1961, Understanding the Constitution, 15th edit., 2000, orig. edition, 1949, (with James M. Burns) Government By the People, 18th edit., 2000, orig. edit., 1952; contbr. articles and revs. to profl. jours. Recipient James Madison medal Princeton U., 1982. Fellow Am. Acad. Arts and Scis.; mem. Am. Polit. Sci. Assn. (council 1952-54), Phi Beta Kappa, Phi Kappa Phi, Omicron Delta Kappa, Alpha Phi Omega, Beta Gamma Sigma. Home: 18 Whistler Ct Irvine CA 92612-4069 Office: U Calif Dept Politics & Society Social Sci Plz Irvine CA 92697-0001

PELTONEN, KEIJO KALERVO, manufacturing executive; b. Lahti, Finland, May 18, 1939; s. Lauri Valdemar and Impi Irene (Lahti) P.; m. Raija-Leena Fagerholm; children: Pia-Irene, Laura-Johanna (div. 1981); m. Raijaliisa Rytinki (div. 1993); 1 child, Juha-Pekka; m. Leila Marjatta Simonen, 1998. Student, U. Helsinki, Finland, 1960-64, Helsinki Flight Acad., 1964. Cert. comml. pilot. V.p. Hämeen Kalustaja, Lahti, 1971-82; export mgr. Finnbo Oy, Lahti, 1982-83; pres. Expoline Oy, Lahti, 1983—; mng. dir. Valtti Kaluste, Helsinki, 1962-76, Finnmeb Oy, Lahti, 1971-73; pres. Lahti-Air Oy, 1980-85, Akvor, Helsinki, 1969—; mgr. mktg. Obaid Trading Establishment, Riyadh, Saudi Arabia, 1985-86. Served to capt. Finnish mil. Mem. Finnish Furniture Exporters Assn. (bd. dirs. 1970-74), Lc Laune Club, KK 54. Home: Salpakankaantie 19 B 6, 15860 Hollola Finland Office: Expoline Oy, Huvilatie 38, 16500 Herrala Finland

PELTTARI, ALPO EINARI, electron microscopist, researcher; b. Pudasjärvi, Finland, Nov. 24, 1942; s. Eino Augusti and Lyydia Katariina (Juntunen) P.; m. Marita Pirjo Leppala, Oct. 17, 1947; children: Mikko, Matti. MSc, U. Oulu, Finland, 1971. Asst. in anatomy U. Kuopio, Finland, 1972-76, head of electron microscopy lab., 1976—. Avocation: painting. Office: Univ Kuopio, PO Box 1627, FI-70211 Kuopio Finland

PELUFFO, ANGEL OCTAVIO, military officer; b. Buenos Aires, Aug. 19, 1970; s. Angel Santiago Peluffo and Maria Ines Beracochea; m. Gordana Plahutnik, Dec. 15, 1997; 1 child, Aleksandar. B of Engring., army officer, Coll. Militar de la Nacion, El Palomar, Buenos Aires, 1992. Platoon leader Army, Magdalena, Argentina, 1993-96, Brod Pustara, Croatia, 1996-97; company XO Army, Magdalena, 1997-98; capt. Armor/Army, Argentina, 1999—; instr. Argentine Armor Sch., Concordia, Argentina, 1999—. Contbr. rsch. articles to mags. Recipient Untaes medal UN, 1997. Mem. Mil. Club. Roman Catholic. Avocations: rugby, horseback riding.

PELUFFO, FRANCO VINICIO, trade company executive; b. Acqui Terme, Italy, Apr. 3, 1940; s. Guido and Teresa (Ivaldi) P.; m. Alma Rosalina Bianchi, Jan. 18, 1969 (dec.); children: Vinicio Guido, Micol. D Engr., Politech. Turin, 1964; M in Mktg., Fribourg U., 1981. Market rsch. L'Oreal, Turin, Italy, 1960-64; br. mgr. LaRinascente Supermarkets, Milan, 1969-75; sales dir. Avon Cosmetics, Como, 1975-77; comml. mgr. Euroclub Italia, Milan, 1977-88; gen. mgr. Vorwerk Group, Milan, 1988-90. Pres. European Fedn. Direct Selling Svcs., 1989-91, Avedisco. Named Cavaliere, 1992. Mem. Assolombarda (bd. dirs.).

PELZ, MANFRED FRANZ-JOSEF, foreign language educator; b. Danzig, Germany, Jan. 27, 1937; s. Franz and Gertrud (Salewski) P.; m. Eva Dora Alt, May 5, 1977; m. Heidrun Ilse Wagner, Mar. 16, 1963 (div. 1977); 1 child, Gesine. PhD, U. Tübingen, Germany, 1961, grad., 1962. Tchr. fgn. lang. secondary schs., Cologne, Germany, 1962-68; prof. fgn. lang. Pedagogical U., Freiburg, Germany, 1969—; chmn. Fachverband Moderne Fremdsprachen FMF Baden-Württemberg, 1987-97. Author: Language Encounter and Language of Encounter, 1999, Learn Your Neighbor's Language, 1989, Viens voir, 1987, Passages, 1999. Mem. Order of Acad. Palms French Govt. Avocations: reading, fitness, travel. Home: Marienstrasse 12, 79356 Eichstetten Germany Office: Pedagogical Univ, Kunzenweg 21, 79117 Freiburg Germany

PEMBER, JOHN SCOTT, poet; b. Jackson Heights, N.Y., June 3, 1940; s. Gordon Franklin and Marion Louise (Burt) P.; m. Patricia Ann Farley, Nov. 10, 1965; 1 child, John Scott Jr. BA, Trenton State Coll., 1963; EdM, Rutgers U., 1979, postgrad., 1979-81, 88; postgrad., U. Va., 1987. Cert. secondary tchr., N.J. Tchr. Hammarskjold Jr. H.S., East Brunswick, N.J., 1963-69, East Brunswick H.S., 1969-94, Rutgers U., New Brunswick, N.J., 1992; vis. poet Geraldine R. Dodge Found., Morristown, N.J., 1994—; tchr. Green Mountain Coll. Acad., Dorset, Vt., 2000—; journalism evaluator Columbia U., N.Y.C., 1993-94; mem. poetry adv. bd. Geraldine R. Dodge Found., 1986-94; panelist Piscataway (N.J.) Pub. TV, 1992; presenter, cons. in field. Author: Rope to the Barn, 1993 (Poetry award), (anthology) Under a Gull's Wing, 1996; contbr. poetry to lit. jours. Docent Pember Mus. Natural History, Granville, N.Y., 1996—. Grantee East Brunswick Bd. Edn., 1972, 90-93; Va. Coun. on Arts fellow, 1987; recipient Gov.'s award for outstanding tchg. N.J. Bd. Edn., 1992. Mem. Acad. Am. Poets, Equinox Poetry Soc. Manchester, Vt., Poets' House. Avocations: philately, golf, reading, cinema, photography. Home: 276 Dorset West Rd Dorset VT 05251-9426 Other: PO Box 185 Dorset VT 05251-0185

PEMBERTON, BRADLEY POWELL, lawyer; b. Ft. Scott, Kans., June 15, 1952; s. Howard Duane and Juanita Lucille (Powell) P.; m. Kathleen Frances Querrey, May 22, 1976 (div. Feb. 1984); m. Lori Scott, June 18, 1994. BSBA, U. Mo., Columbia, 1974; JD, U. Mo., Kansas City, 1977. Bar: Mo. 1977, U.S. Dist. Ct. (we. dist.) Mo. 1981, U.S. Tax Ct. 1981; CPA, Mo. Tax acct. Alexander Grant & Co., Kansas City, Mo., 1977-79; shareholder Polsinelli, White, Vardeman & Shalton, Kansas City, 1979—, also bd. dirs. Active Vol. Atty. Project, Kansas City, 1984—; bd. dirs. Synergy House Inc., Kansas City, 1985-88, Youth Vol. Corps of Am., 1991—, March of Dimes, 1995—. Mem. ABA, Internat. Entrepreneurs Coun. (bd. dirs.), Mo. Bar Assn., Kansas City Bar Assn., AICPAs, Mo. Soc. CPAs, Kansas City C. of C., Entrepreneurs Club of Kansas City (bd. dirs.), KC. Avocations: tennis, golf, water skiing, snow skiing, private aviation. Home: 5806 W 131st St Shawnee Mission KS 66209-3639 Office: Polsinelli White Vardeman & Shalton 700 W 47th St Ste 1000 Kansas City MO 64112-1805

PEMBERTON, GARY, air transportation executive; s. Eric P.; m. Margareet Whitford; 4 children. Student, Fort St. H.S. Joined Brambles Industries Ltd., 1972-82, ceo, 1982-93; chmn. Qantas Airways Ltd., Mascot, NSW, Australia, 1993—, Billabong Internat. Ltd., Burleigh Heads, Australia. Ceo Sydney organizing com. Olympic Games, 1994-95, pres., 1995—. Named Companion of the Order of Australia. Office: Billabong Internat Ltd, 1 Billabong Pl, Burleigh Heads QLD 4220, Australia*

PEÑA, FEDERICO FABIAN, retired federal official; b. Laredo, Tex., Mar. 15, 1947; s. Gustavo J. and Lucille P.; m. Ellen Hart, May 1988. BA, U. Tex., Austin, 1969, JD, 1972. Bar: Colo. 1973. Ptnr. Pena & Pena, Denver, 1973-83; mayor City and County of Denver, 1983-91; pres. Peña Investment Advisors, Inc., Denver, 1991-93; sec. U.S. Dept. of Energy, Washington, 1993-98, U.S. Dept. Transp., Washington, 1993-97, U.S. Dept. Energy, Washington, 1997-98; sr. advisor Vestar Capital Ptnrs., Denver, 1998-00; mng. dir. Vestar Capital Partners, Denver, CO, 2000—; assoc. Harvard U. Ctr. for Law and Edn., Cambridge, Mass.; mem. Colo. Bd. Law Examiners. Mem. Colo. Ho. of Reps., 1979-83, Dem. leader, 1981. Named Outstanding House Dem. Legislator, Colo. Gen. Assembly, 1981. Roman Catholic.

PENA, GUILLERMO ENRIQUE, lawyer; b. Miami Beach, Fla., Aug. 16, 1963; s. Gustavo A. and Rosa Amelia (LeRiverend) P.; m. Jacqueline Torre, Sept. 11, 1993; children: Austin Jake, Allison Lee. BBA, Austin Peay State U., Clarksville, Tenn., 1988; JD, Fla. State U., 1991. Bar: Fla. 1991, U.S. Dist. Ct. (no. and so. dists.) Fla. 1991, U.S. Ct. Appeals (11th cir.) 1991, U.S. Supreme Ct. 1996; cert. in criminal trial law Criminal Trial Law Found., Middle Dist. of Fla., 1998, Dist. of Utah, 1999, Western Dist. of Tex., 1998. Assoc. Boehm, Brown, Rigdon & Seacrest, P.A., Tallahassee, 1990-92, Raia & Preira, Miami Beach, Fla., 1992-95, Jeffrey S. Weiner, P.A., Miami, Fla., 1995-96; pvt. practice Miami, 1996—; guest judge U. Miami Sch. Law-Moot Ct. Camp, 1996-99. Sgt. U.S. Army, 1984-86, ETO. Young pres. Mt. Sinai Hosp., Miami Beach, Fla. Recipient Recognition award Legal Svcs. Greater Miami, 1996, Pro Bono Svc. award Dade County Bar Assn., Miami, 1995, Young Pres. Mt. Sinai Hosp., 1999. Mem. ABA (criminal justice sect.), Cuban Am. Bar Assn. (Pro Bono Project 1996), Nat. Assn. Criminal Def. Lawyers, Am. Judicature Soc., Am. Inns of Ct. (barrister), Fla. Assn. Criminal Def. Lawyers, Fla. Bar (cert. as specialist in criminal law), Young Pres. Club. Office: 444 Brickell Ave Ste 928 Miami FL 33131-2407

PENA, MARIA GEGES, academic services administrator; b. Torrance, Calif., Nov. 27, 1964; d. Nicholas John and Dina Connie (Vengel) Geges; m. Vicente Gregorio Pena, June 22, 1991. AA, El Camino Coll., 1985; BA, U. Calif., San Diego, 1987; MS, San Diego State U., 1989, postgrad.; postgrad., Claremont Grad. Sch., 1990—, Western State U., 1995—. Peer counselor El Camino Coll., Torrance, Calif., 1982-85; peer advisor U. Calif., San Diego, 1985-87, vice chancellor student affirmative action rsch. intern, 1986-87, outreach asst. disabled student svcs., 1986-89; coord. student svcs. Mira Costa Coll., Oceanside, Calif., 1989—. Contbr. articles to profl. jours. Mem. Calif. Assn. Postsecondary Educators of Disabled. Democrat. Greek Orthodox. Avocations: law, education, CD collecting, collecting Beatles memorabilia. Office: Mira Costa Coll 1 Barnard Dr Oceanside CA 92056-3820

PENA, RAYMUNDO JOSEPH, bishop; b. Corpus Christi, Tex., Feb. 19, 1934; s. Cosme A. and Elisa (Ramon) P. D.D., Assumption Sem., San Antonio, 1957. Ordained priest Roman Catholic Ch., 1957; asst. pastor St. Peter's Ch., Laredo, Tex., 1957-60, St. Joseph's-Our Lady of Fatima, Alamo, Tex., 1960-63, Sacred Heart, Mathis, Tex., 1963-67, Christ the King and Our Lady of Pillar Parishes, Corpus Christi, 1967-69; pastor Our Lady of Guadalupe Parish, Corpus Christi, 1969-76; v.p. Corpus Christi Diocesan Senate of Priests, 1970-76; aux. bishop of San Antonio, 1976-80; bishop El Paso, 1980-95, Brownsville, Tex., 1995—; mem. secretariat to Prep. Synod of Bishops for Am., 1996-97, Synodal Father, Synod of Bishops for Am., 1995. Mem. Nat. Conf. Cath. Bishops, U.S. Cath. Conf. (chmn. bishops' com. for hispanic affairs 1987-90, bishops' com. for ch. in L.Am. 1994-97, 2000). Home: Rt 8 Box 629 7600 Old Military Rd Brownsville TX 78522 Office: PO Box 2279 Brownsville TX 78522-2279

PENA-ANDREU, JOSE MIGUEL, psychiatry educator; b. Barcelona, Spain, Feb. 22, 1954; s. Jose and Elena (Andreu) P.; m. Gracia Jimenez, Aug. 25, 1985; children: Jorge, Elena. Lic. in medicine, U. Barcelona, 1977; MD cum laude, U. Malaga, 1984. Resident Hosp. Carlos Haya, Malaga, 1977-81; asst. prof. Sch. Medicine U. Malaga, 1978-86; emergency physician Pub. Health Svc., Malaga, 1981-83, neuropsychiatrist, 1983-84; head of psychiatric unit Hosp. San Jose, Malaga, 1984-86; clin. psychiatrist U. Hosp., Malaga, 1986—; prof. psychiatry Malaga U., 1986—, prof. continuing edn. program, 1984—; vis. scholar Stanford (Calif.) U., 1988-89; sr. researcher Tech. Devel. and Rsch. Group, 1986—. Author: Family and Schizophrenia, 1991; contbr. articles to profl. jours. Mem. Physicians for Human Rights, Boston, 1989. Fellow Prevention Over Treatment of Depression Assn.; mem. AAAS, Am. Psychiat. Assn. (corr.), Am. Soc. Hispanic Psychiatry, Andalousian (Spanish) Soc. Psychiatry, N.Y. Acad. Scis. Avocations: trekking, mountain biking. Office: Malaga U Dept Psychiatry Sch Med, Colonia Sta Ines S/N, 29010 Malaga Spain

PEÑA-BAUTISTA, ROBERTO JAVIER, chemist, researcher; b. Mexico City, Mar. 16, 1950; s. Eduardo Peña and Irene Bautista-Torres; m. Luz Maria Arias-Diaz, Aug. 16, 1974; 1 child, Roberto Javier. BSc, Nat. U. Mexico, Mexico City, 1977; MSc, Kans. State U., 1979; PhD, U. Man., Winnipeg, Can., 1984. Lab. technician Internat. Maize and Wheat Improvement Ctr., Texcoco, Mexico, 1973-77; rsch. asst. Internat. Maize and Wheat Improvement Ctr., Texcoco, 1979-81, postdoctoral fellow, 1984-86, rsch. assoc., 1986-91, scientist, 1992, sr. scientist, 1993—, head wheat quality lab., 1993—. Tech. reviewer Jour. Cereal Sci., 1997—; contbr. chpt. to book and articles to profl. jours. Scholar Nat. Coun. Sci. and Tech., Mexico, 1977, 81. Mem. AACC, Internat. Triticale Assn., N.Y. Acad. Sci. Roman Catholic. Avocations: soccer, listening to music, recreational farming, family gathering. Home: HDA Corralejo, 61 Prado Coapa, 14350 Mexico City Mexico Office: CIMMYT, Apdo Postal 6-641, 06600 Mexico City Mexico

PENACHIO, ANTHONY JOSEPH, JR., psychotherapist, hypnotherapist, behavioral therapist; b. Stamford, Conn., Apr. 3, 1953; 1 child, Ariana. Cert. in psychotherapy, Am. Sch. Med. Hynotherapy, 1978; DD, Aquarian Ch. of Jesus, 1978; PSD, Neotharian Sch. of Philosophy, 1980. Cert. clin. registered med. hypnotherapist, psychotherapist, behavioral therapist, biomed. electronics, psychophysiologist; ordained counseling min. Aquarian Ch.; diplomate Am. Psychotherapy Assn. Counseling min., exec. dir. Inst. Clin. Tricotomy, Stamford, 1978—; lectr., radio and cable TV talk show seminar presenter. Contbr. articles profl. jours. Mem. Am. Coun. Hypnotherapist-Psychotherapist (bd. examiners), N.Y. Acad. Sci. (lectr.).

PENBERTHY, STANLEY JOSIAH, JR., publisher; b. Des Moines, Sept. 3, 1921; s. Stanley Josiah and Beatrice Ann (Voith) P.; m. Dorothea Oehmke, July 7, 1945; 1 child, Robert Bruce. Student, Drake U., Des Moines, 1940-43. Engaged in broadcasting, 1941-56, freelance radio, TV, motion picture, actor, narrator, 1956—; v.p. Fed. 1-D Equipment Corp., Dearborn, Mich., 1951-62; pres. Publishers, Inc., Detroit, 1976-99. Author, prodr., narrator nat. radio series These Were Our Presidents, 1975; contbr. Mich. Sesquintennial hist. articles; author: Living Under Cover, Episodes of Life and other Relatives, Cottage Industry. Past mem. bd. dirs. Sleeping Bear Dunes Citizens Coun., Traverse City, Mich., 1968-72, Cass Park Area Devel. Corp., City of Detroit, 1989; pres. Heritage Village Condominium Assn.; trustee Detroit Masonic Temple Assn.; mem. Founders Soc. Detroit Inst. Arts. Mem. AFTRA (past dir.), Adcraft Club Detroit, Detroit Execs. Assn. (dir.), Am. Film Inst., Detroit Prodrs. Assn., Broadcast Pioneers, Masons (33rd degree), Alpha Tau Omega (past alumni pres.). Home: 35560 Heritage Ln Farmington MI 48335-3136 Office: 500 Temple St Detroit MI 48201-2659

PENCHANSKY, DAVID, religious studies educator; b. Bklyn., Dec. 3, 1951; s. Charles and Mimi (Black) P.; children: Simon Graham, Maia Lucy. BA cum laude, Queens Coll., 1974; MA, Assemblies of God Grad. Sch., 1980; PhD, Vanderbilt U., 1988. Assoc. prof. U. St. Thomas, St. Paul, 1989—. Author: The Betrayal of God, 1990, Storyteller's Companion, vol. 2, 1992, The Politics of Biblical Theology, 1995, "Proverbs," Mercer Bible Commentary, 1995, Politics of Biblical Theology, 1995, What Rough Beast?, 1999; contbr. articles to profl. jours. Mem. Soc. Bibl. Lit., Cath. Bibl. Assn., Phi Beta Kappa, Phi Alpha Theta. Home: 1743 Lafond Ave Saint Paul MN 55104-1714 Office: U St Thomas Mail # 4328 2115 Summit Ave Saint Paul MN 55105-1048

PENCHARZ, PHILIP, lawyer; b. Johannesburg, South Africa, July 30, 1919; s. Morris Barney and Rose (Olswang) P.; m. Eva Anita Nach, Jan. 5, 1958; children: Roslyn, Mark. BA, Witwatersrand U., South Africa. Ptnr. Pencharz & Pencharz, Johannesburg, South Africa, 1943-69, Edward Nathan & Friedland, Johannesburg, South Africa, 1969—; dir. Clinic Holdings Ltd., Johannesburg, 1987-98, SABVEST, Johannesburg, 1990—. Recipient Buckle prize Transvaal Law Soc., 1939. Fellow Assn. Arbitrators. Democrat. Jewish. Avocations: sketching, golf. Office: Edward Nathan & Friedland, 2 Maude St, Sandton 2141, South Africa

PENDAGAST, EDWARD LESLIE, JR., physician; b. Danbury, Conn., Aug. 3, 1932; s. Edward Leslie and Ruth Arlene (Staib) P.; m. Eileen Jean Guerin, Feb. 3, 1968; children: Edward Leslie Pendagast III, Eileen Leslie Pendagast. BS, Yale U., 1954; MD, N.Y. Med. Coll., 1958. Intern St. Vincent's Hosp., Bridgeport, Conn., 1958-59; pvt. practice Bridgeport, 1959-68, pres., St. Vincent's Emergency Physicians, 1969-76; attending emergency physician Norwalk (Conn.) Hosp., 1976-78, courtesy emergency physician, 1979-97, emeritus staff, 1997—; dir., emergency dept. New Milford (Conn.) Hosp., 1978-97, hon. staff, 1997—; dir. health Town of Easton (Conn.), 1972—; asst. med. examiner State of Conn., 1980—, ret., 1997; med. adv. bd. Bridgeport Visiting Nurse Assn., 1962-65; exec. com. New Milford Hosp., 1978—, Core Content Rev. Family Medicine, Bloomfield, Conn., 1984-87. Co-author: Advanced Skills in Emergency Care, 1982, The First Minutes, 1984, 2d edit., 1988; consulting physician: Emergency Handbook, 1980; editl. bd. Reviewing Basic EMT Skills, 1982. Fire commr. Town of Easton, 1972—; mem. Emergency Med. Svc. Commn., Town of Easton, 1972-75. Mem. Am. Acad. Family Physicians, Conn. Acad. Family Physicians (bd. dirs. 1977-82, 91-93, pres. 1983-84), Am. Coll. Emergency Physicians, Conn. Coll. Emergency Physicians (councillor to nat. 1982), Black Rock Yacht Club, Bridgeport. Republican. Roman Catholic. Avocations: gardening, hunting, sailing, fishing. Home: 94 Burr St Easton CT 06612-1616

PENDERECKI, KRZYSZTOF, composer, conductor; b. Debica, Poland, Nov. 23, 1933; s. Tadeusz and Zofia P.; m. Elzbieta Solecka; children: Lukasz, Dominique. Grad., State Acad. Music, Krakow, 1958; student, Arthur Malawski and Stanislaw Wiechowicz; Dr. honoris causa, U. Rochester, St. Olaf Coll., Northfield, Minn., Cath U., Leuven, Belgium, U. Bordeaux, France, Georgetown U., Belgrade U., Madrid U., Spain, Adam Mickiewicz U., Warsaw U., Poland, 1993, U. Catolica Argentina, Buenos Aires, 1994, Acad. Music, Cracow, 1994, Acad. Music, Warsaw, 1994, U. Glasgow, 1995, Beijiung Conservatory, 1998, U. Pitts., 1999. Prof. composition Krakow State Sch. Music, 1959-65, Folkwang Hochschule für Musik, Essen, Fed. Republic Germany, 1966-68; composer-in-residence Sch. Music, Yale U., alternate years; guest condr. London Symphony Orch., Polish Radio Orch., Berlin Philharm. Orch. Composer: Psalms of David for chorus and percussion, 1958, Emanations for 2 string orchs., 1959, Strophes for soprano, narrator and 10 instruments, 1959, Dimensions of time and silence, 1959-61, Anaklasis, 1959-60, Threnody for the Victims of Hiroshima, 1960, Psalmus for tape, 1961, Polymorphia, 1961; Fluorescences, 1961, Stabat Mater, 1962, Canon, 1962, Sonata for cello and orch., 1964, St. Luke Passion, 1965, De Natura Sonoris I, 1966, Dies Irae, 1967, Capriccio for violin and orch., 1967, Capriccio for cello Solo, 1968; opera The Devils of Loudun, 1968-69; Utrenja for double chorus, soloists and orch., 1969-71, Cosmogony, 1970, Utrenja II-Resurrection, 1971, Actions for jazz ensemble, 1971, Partita for harpsichord, 4 solo instruments and orch., 1971-72, Cello Concerto, 1967-72; for double chorus, soloists and orchestra Ecloga VIII for 6 male voices, 1972; Symphony 1, 1972-73, Canticum Canticorum Salomonis for 16 voices and chamber orch., 1970-73, Magnificat, 1973-74, When Jacob Awoke for orch., 1974, Violin Concerto, 1976-77, Paradise Lost (rappresentazione), 1976-78, (Christmas) Symphony No. 2, 1980, Te Deum, 1979-80, Lacrimosa, 1980, Agnus Dei for a cappella chorus, 1981, Cello Concerto No. 2, 1982, Requiem, 1983, Concerto per Viola, 1983, Polish Requiem, 1983-84, The Black Mask, 1986, Der Unterbrochene Gedanke, 1987, Adagio, 1989, Ubu Rex, 1991, Sinfonietta for orchestra, 1990-91, Symphony No. 5 for orchestra, 1991-92, Partita for orchestra, rev. edit., 1991, Flute concerto, 1992-93, Quartet for Clarinet and String Trio, 1993, Divertimento per Cello solo, 1994, Violin Concerto No. 2, 1992-95, Agnus Dei, 1995, Symphony No. 3, Seven Gates of Jerusalem, 1997, Hymn to St. Daniel, 1997, Hymn to St. Adalbert, 1997, Credo, 1998, Sonata No. 2 for violin and piano, 2000, Sextet for violin, viola, piano, clatinet, and french horn, 2000, also other works; prin. guest condr. NDR Symphony Orch., Hamburg, and MDR Symphony Orch., Leipzig; artistic dir. Casals Festival, PR. Recipient 1st prize for Strophes Polish Composers Assn., 1959, UNESCO award, Fitelberg prize and Polish Ministry Culture award all for Threnody, 1960, Krakow composition prize for Canon, 1961, grand prize State N. Rhine-Westphalia for St. Luke Passion, 1966, Pax prize Poland, 1966, Jurzykowski prize Polish Inst. Arts and Scis., 1966, Sibelius award, 1967, Prix d'Italia, 1967-68, Polish 1st Class State award, 1968, Gottfried von Herder prize, 1977, prix Arthur Honegger, 1978, Sibelius prize Wihouri Found., 1983, Wolf Found. prize, 1987, 3 Grammy awards, Gamma prize Acad. Rec. Arts and Scis., 1988, Manuel de Falla Gold medal Accademia de Bellas Artes, Granada, 1989, Das Grosse Verdienstkreuz des Verdienstordens der Bundesrepublik Deutschland, 1990, 2 Grammy nominations, 1992, Grawermeyer Music award, 1992, Österreichische Ehrenzeichen für Wissenschaft und Kunst, 1994, 2 Primetime Emmy awards, 1995, 96, Crystall award, Davos, 1997, 2 Grammy awards, 1999, Musikpreis Duisburg, 1999, Cannes Classical award Composer of Yr., 2000; grantee several founds., govts., insts. Mem. AAAL (hon.), Royal Acad. Mus. London (hon.), Nat. Acad. of Santa Cecilia (Rome) (hon.), Royal Swedish Acad. Music, Acad. of Kuenste West Berlin (extraord. mem.), Nat. Acad. of Bellas Artes (Buenos Aires) (corr.), Internat. Acad. Philosophy and Art (Berne), Nat. Acad. Scis., Belles-lettres et Arts (Bordeaux), Acad. Scientiarium et Artium Europaea (Salzburg), L'Ordre de Saint Georges de Bourgogne (officer, Brussels), Am. Acad. Arts and Letters, Bay. Acad. des Schönen Künste. Achievements include creating original notational system allowing aleatory freedom for performer within sects. of precise duration. Fax: 49-6133/92 63 56. Home: ul Cisowa 22, 30229 Cracow Poland Office: ICM Artists Ltd c/o Jenny Vogel 8942 Wilshire Blvd Beverly Hills CA 90211-1934 also: Panstwowa Wyzsza Szkola Muzyczna, ul Starowislna, 31 038 Cracow Poland also: Am Daubhaus 6, D 55276 Oppenheim Germany

PENDERGRAFT, ROY DANIEL, medical educator, physician; b. Wichita Falls, Tex., Jan. 1, 1954; s. James Daniel and Cyrena Gay (Mays) P.; m. Cherlyn Kathleen Bell, Dec. 17, 1977; children: Victoria, Seth, Lauren. BA, Rice U., 1976; MD, U. Tex., San Antonio, 1981. Diplomate Am. Bd. Family Practice; cert. added qualifications in sports medicine, 1999. Family physician U. Park Clinic, Wichita Falls, 1984-86; asst. prof. med. sch. U. Tex., Houston, 1986-89; regional med. officer U.S. Emb., Tanzania, 1990-92; regional med. officer Argentina, 1992-95, Australia, 1995-97, India, 1998-2000; Singapore, 2000—; clin. dir. dept. family practice med. sch., U. Tex., Houston, 1986-88. State del. Rep. Party, Austin, 1984, 86. Recipient Physician's Recognition award, AMA, 1987-90, 1999—. Fellow Am. Acad. Family Physicians; mem. Soc. Tchrs. Family Medicine, Am. Acad. Med. Ethics, So. Med. Assn., Tex. Med. Assn., Christian Med. Soc. Republican. Office: US Embassy-Singapore Psc 470 Box Rmo FPO AP 96534-0470

PENDLETON, ANDREW H., produce company executive; b. Dallas, Sept. 9, 1965; s. Frederick A. and Patricia A. Pendleton. BA, Tex. A&M U., 1989; MBA, NYU, 1992. Auditor Coopers & Lybrand, N.Y.C., 1989-92; internal auditor Pepsi Co., Purchase, N.Y., Dallas, 1992-95; mgr. fin. reporting Cott Beverages, Dallas, 1995-98; dir. planning and analysis Apio, Inc., Guadalupe, Calif., 1998—. Office: Apio Inc PO Box 627 Guadalupe CA 93434-0627

PENDLETON, MICHAEL DEREK, law educator, barrister; b. Sydney, NSW, Australia, Jan. 31, 1953; s. Derek Van Helen and Moira Frances (Mahony) P.; m. Catherine Jeneh, July 31, 1995; 1 child, Maximillian Michael. LLB, Sydney U., 1976, diploma in jurisprudence, 1978; LLM, U. London, 1981. Cert. solicitor Supreme Ct. New South Wales 1976, Supreme Ct. Judicature Eng. and Wales 1980, Supreme Ct. Hong Kong 1982; barrister and solicitor Supreme Ct. Western Australia 1991; mediator World Intellectual Property Orgn. Geneva 1995. Tutor Faculty of Law, U. Sydney, 1976-79; from lectr. to sr. lectr. Faculty of Law, U. Hong Kong, 1981-90; assoc. prof. Sch. of Law, Murdoch (Australia) U., 1990-96, prof., 1996—, dir. Asia Pacific Intellectual Property Law Inst., 1995-98; vis. prof. Columbia U., N.Y.C., 1994, City U. Hong Kong, 1998; cons. Deacons (now Deacons Graham James), Hong Kong, 1984-87, Alsop Wilkinson, Hong Kong, 1988-90, Blake Dawson Waldron, Australia, 1990-93, Drivers, Australia, 1993—; solicitor Wall & Wall, 1976-79, Bird & Bird, London, 1979-80, Edmund WH Chow & Co., 1982-84; mem. intellectual property com. Law Coun. Australia. Co-author: Law of Intellectual and Industrial Property in Hong Kong, 1984, Intellectual Property Law in the People's Republic of China, 1986, (with Zheng Chingsi) Chinese Intellectual Property and Technology Transfer Law, 1987, Copyright Law in China, 1991, (with Peter Garland and Jared Margolis) Law of Intellectual and Industrial Property in Hong Kong, 1993, 3d edit., 1995; contbr. over 50 articles to profl. publs.; mem. editl. bd. European Intellectual Property Rev. Rsch. grantee Australian Rsch. Coun., Asia Rsch. Ctr., Law of Australia, others. Office: A-P Intellectual Prop Inst, Murdoch U South St, Murdoch WA 6150, Australia

PENDLETON, MILES STEVENS, JR., diplomat; b. Montclair, N.J., Mar. 22, 1939; s. Miles Stevens and Lucille (Bond) P.; m. Elisabeth Morgan, Aug. 13, 1967; children: Constance Morrow, Nathaniel Palmer. BA magna cum laude, Yale U., 1961; MPA, Harvard U., 1967; diploma, Nat. War Coll., 1980. Tchr. Ghana Secondary Sch., Koforidua, 1962-63, Adisadel Coll., Cape Coast, Ghana, 1963-64; vice consul Am. Embassy, Tel Aviv, Israel, 1968-70; polit. and econ. officer Am. Embassy, Bujumbura, Burundi, 1970-72; watch officer Ops. Ctr. Dept. State, Washington, 1972-73, staff officer Secretariat Staff, 1973-74, spl. asst. to Dep. Sec. of State Office Dep. Sec., 1974-76; polit. officer U.S. Mission to NATO, Brussels, 1976-79; dep. dir. Office of No. European Affairs Dept. State, Washington, 1980-82, dir. Office of Israel and Arab-Israel Affairs, 1982-83, exec. asst. to under sec. of state for polit. affairs, 1983-85; min.-counselor for polit. affairs Am. Embassy, London, 1985-89; min., counselor for polit. affairs Am. Embassy, Paris, 1989-93; prof. strategy Indsl. Coll. Armed Forces Nat. Def. U., Washington,

1993-95; dir. Office of Ecology and Terrestrial Conservation Dept. of State, Washington, 1995-97. Mem. Am. Fgn. Svc. Assn., North Haven (Maine) Yacht Club, Met. Club (Washington), Phi Beta Kappa. Avocations: sailing, reading. Home: 3410 Lowell St NW Washington DC 20016-5023

PENDLEY, DONALD LEE, association executive; b. Jersey City, Nov. 5, 1950; s. Donald L. and Loretta M. (Purcell) P.; m. Donna Lynn Meade, Oct. 14, 1984; 1 child, Katelyn. BA, Montclair State Coll., 1972; MA, Syracuse U., 1974. Reporter/rewriter The Herald-News, Passaic, N.J., 1969-72; reporter The Dispatch, Union City, N.J., 1973; writer Keep America Beautiful, Inc., N.Y.C., 1974-75, comm. dir., 1976-78, v.p. comm. program devel., 1979-84; sr. v.p. comm. Greater Newark C. of C., 1985-86; dir. pub. rels. Internat. Coun. Shopping Ctrs., N.Y.C., 1987-92; exec. dir. N.J. Hospice and Palliative Care Orgn., Scotch Plains, N.J., 1993-97, pres., 1997—. Creator, dir. theatre composer series William Carlos Williams Ctr., 1987-91; creator, dir. SRO Cabaret Series, 1991-99. Pres. State Repertory Opera, South Orange, N.J., 1981-85, 92-99, Ars Musica Chorale, Englewood, N.J., 1979-81; mem. steering com. Coun. of States, 1999—, chmn. 2000—; bd. dirs. Nat. Hospice Orgn., 2000—. Recipient Award of Excellence Am. C. of C. Execs. 1986, Gold Key awards, Pub. Rels. News, 1982, 86. Mem. PRSA (accredited, sec.-treas. assn. sec. 1989-90, vice-chmn. assn. sect. 1990-91, chmn. 1991-92), Am. Soc. Assn. Execs. (cert., Gold Circle award 1988, comm. sect. coun. 1994-96, dean Sch. Pub. Rels. 1998—), Am. Mensa, Ltd. (nat. devel. officer 1985-89, 96—, regional tng. officer 1989-93), Intertel. Avocations: music, photography. Home: 32 Hamilton Rd Glen Ridge NJ 07028-1109

PENDRILL, DAVID, accounting and financial management educator; b. London, Sept. 26, 1944; m. Marie-Louise Madeleine, Sept. 26, 1972; 1 child, Philip Richard. BSc in Econs. with honors, London Sch. of Econs., 1966-69, MSc, 1972-74. Fellow Inst. Chartered Accts. in Eng. and Wales, Assoc. Chartered Inst. Taxation, Licentiate Trinity Coll. Music, London. Articled clerk Kingdon Marbeck Antill & Co., London, 1961-66; audit supr. Cooper Brothers, London, 1969-70; project exec. Ctr. for Interfirm Comparison Ltd., London, 1970-71; lectr. in mgmr. studies U. of West Indies, Kingston, Jamaica, 1971-72; lectr. in acctg. London Sch. of Econs., 1972-76; sr. tutor Fin. Tng. Ltd., London, 1976-77; sr. lectr. U. Coll. Cardiff (Wales), 1978-89; Esmée Fairbairn prof. acctg. and fin. mgmt. U. Buckingham (England), 1989—. Author: (with R. Lewis) Advanced Financial Accounting, 6th edit., 2000; contbr. articles to profl. jours. Avocations: amateur pianist, long distance running. Office: Univ of Buckingham, Hunter St, Buckingham MK18 1EG, England

PENDRY, JOHN BRIAN, physics educator; b. Ashton-Under-Lyne, Eng., July 4, 1943; s. Frank Johnson and Kathleen (Shaw) P.; m. Patricia Gard, 1977. BA in Physics, Cambridge (Eng.) U., 1965, MA, 1969, PhD in Solid State Theory, 1969. Rsch. fellow Downing Coll., Cambridge, 1969-73; mem. tech. staff Bell Labs., N.J., U.S.A., 1972-73; sr. asst. rsch. Cavendish Lab., Cambridge, 1973-75; sr. prin. scientific officer, head theory group Daresbury (Eng.) Lab., 1975-81; prof. physics Imperial Coll. Sci., London, 1981—, assoc. head dept., 1984-92; fellow, praelector Downing Coll., Cambridge, 1973-75. Author: Low Energy Electron Diffraction, 1974, Surface Crystallographic Information Service, 1987; contbr. articles to profl. jours. Fellow Royal Soc., Inst. Physics. Avocations: music, gardening, photography. Office: Imperial Coll, Blackett Lab, London SW7 2BZ, England

PENER, MEIR PAUL, biologist; b. Budapest, Hungary, Apr. 2, 1930; s. Miklos and Gizella (Virag) P.; m. Hedva Solomon, July 21, 1959; 1 child, Irit. MSc, The Hebrew U., 1958, PhD, 1963. Vis. scientist Ctr. Overseas Pest Rsch., London, 1971; assoc. prof. The Hebrew U., Jerusalem, 1972-80, prof., 1980—; sr. guest scientist Rsch. Labs. Zoecon Corp., Palo Alto, Calif., 1979-80; rsch. assoc. Internat. Ctr. for Insect Physiology & Ecology, Nairobi, Kenya, 1973. Mem. Orthopterists Soc. (bd. govs. 1993-97), Royal Entomol. Soc., European Soc. Comparative Endocrinology, Entomological Soc. Israel.

PENG, DE-CHUN, computer researcher, educator; b. Shuang Feng Xian, Hunan, China, Oct. 10, 1938; s. Yu Tang Peng and Yu Chun Wang; m. Yunan Qiu, Jan. 30, 1970; children: Li Peng, Le Peng. BS, Wuhan (China) U., 1961. Asst. in math. Wuhan U., 1961-64, asst. in computers, 1965-77, lectr. in computers, 1978-82, assoc. prof., 1983-93, prof., 1993—; mem. Mission of Edn., Ministry of Edn., Beijing, 1980; grad. advisor Wuhan U., 1983—, vice-dean rsch. unit, 1983-93; spl. cons. China Internat. Interchange Press, Beijing, 1997; co-founder: a series of GNB-III mini-computers; leader of a rsch. group, founder/dir. WuPP-80 Distributed Parallel Processing Sys., 1980-82, WuSH-86 Distributed Parallel Computing Sys., 1987-89, Wulor-75/32 Load Sharing Remote Execution Sys., 1986-90, PJVM: Parallel Java Virtual Machine, 1996. Co-author: Introduction to Distributed Parallel Processing Techniques, 1996; co-editor: C Lang. and Multi-Window, 1994; Distributed Parallel Processing System Exploration, 1984; contbr. articles to profl. jours.; inventor in field. Recipient Excellent Acad. Paper awards The City of Wuhan, 1991, Hubei Province, Wuhan, 1992, Hubei Computer Soc., Wuhan, 1994; recipient various computer awards including Nat. Scientific Congress, 1978, Hubei Province 1986, Ministeral prize 1991, others. Mem. IEEE (sr.), IEEE Computer Soc. (sr.), Chinese Computer Fedn. Avocations: sweet or peppery, watching TV, playing chess with computer, walking, bicycling. Office: State Key Lab Software Eng, Wuhan Univ, Wuhan Hubei 430072, China

PENG, FREDERICK CHE-CHING, linguistics educator; b. Fongshan, Taiwan, Republic of China, July 9, 1934; arrived in Japan, 1966; s. Ch'ing Liang and Fang (Lin) P.; m. Carol Virginia Meacham, Mar. 2, 1963 (died Dec. 30, 1999); 1 child, Virginia Mary. BA, Nat. Taiwan U., 1958; MA, SUNY, Buffalo, 1962, PhD, 1964. Teaching fellow SUNY, Buffalo, 1961-62, vis. prof. dept. anat. scis., 1976-77; rsch. assoc. Bur. Applied Social Rsch., Columbia U., N.Y.C., 1964; rsch. assoc. Linguistics Inst., Ind. U., Bloomington, 1964; rsch. assoc., vis. assoc. prof. dept. anthropology Tulane U., New Orleans, 1971-72; asst. prof. linguistics Internat. Christian U., Tokyo, 1966-70, assoc. prof., 1970-74, prof., 1974-2000, founder, dir. Lang. Scis. Summer Inst., 1974-91; founder, dir. Confs. on Sociolinguistics and Pedolinguistics, 1974-86; instr. Toronto (Ont., Can.) Inst. Linguistics, summers 1960, 62, 63; dir. Missionary Orientation Ctr., Stoney Point, N.Y., summers 1962, 63; lang. coord. Peace Corps Tng. Ctr., U. Hawaii, Hilo, 1967; cons. Japan Missionary Lang. Inst., Tokyo, 1968-69; mem. secretariat 1st Internat. Congress for Study Child Lang., 1978; chmn. organizing com. 1st Internat. Conf. on Neurolinguistics, Taipei, 1988, 5th and 6th and Taichung (Republic of China) Conf. Neurolinguistics, 1988; hon. cons. Neurol. Inst., Dept. Neurosurgery, Vets. Gen. Hosp., Taipei. Joint author: Folk Song Style and Culture, 1968, The Ainu: The Past in the Present, 1977; editor-in-chief Lang. Scis., 1978-92; founder, editor-in-chief Jour. Neurolinguistics, 1985-92; editor: Language in Japanese Society, 1975, Development in Verbal and Nonverbal Behavior, 1978, Sign Language and Language Acquisition in Man and Ape, 1978, Hidden Dimensions in Communication, 1979, Varieties of Sign Language, 1981; sr. editor Language in Human Society, 1987, numerous others; contbr. numerous articles to profl. jours. Recipient numerous scholarships, fellowships and grants, 1960—; Am. Learned Soc. fellow, 1962-63; NSF grantee, 1968-69, 72-74, Toyota Found. grantee, 1975-76, Japanese Ministry Edn. grantee, 1975-81, Taiwan Dept. Health grantee, 1989. Mem. Linguistic Soc. Japan, Rsch. Soc. Edn. of Deaf in Japan, AAAS (life), N.Y. Acad. Scis., Internat. Linguistics Assn. (exec. bd. 1972-75, bd. dirs. 1975-76), Linguistic Assn. Can. and U.S. (bd. dirs., founder 1975-92), Internat. Assn. for Study Child Lang. (sec., gen. 1975-78), Internat. Assn. Logopedics and Phoniatrics, Japanese Assn. Logopedics and Phoniatrics, Neuropsychol. Soc. Japan, Aphasia Acad. Japan, Lang. Scis. Assn. Japan (exec. dir. 1987-99), Neurolinguistic Assn. Japan (exec. bd. dirs. 1987-99), Singapore Assn. for Deaf (life). Presbyterian. Avocations: violin, guitar, piano, jogging, yoga. Fax: 81-287-76-3054. Office: 10-4-3-chome Osawa Mitaka, Tokyo 181-0015, Japan

PENG, HENG-CAI, editor, writer; b. Tainmen City, Hubei, China, Dec. 28, 1947; m. Zhing-rong Lin, June 8, 1977; 1 child, Lin. BA, Ctrl. Party Sch. Chinese Communist Party, Beijing, 1992. Chief editor Sci. and Tech. Digest, Beijing, 1994—. Author: A Legend of the Savage, 1980; contbr. articles to sci. jours. Mem. Chinese Press Soc., Sci. Tech. Press Soc. China (bd. dirs., vice sec.), Soc. Oral Lit. (vice dir.-in-chief). Home: 508 Apt No 3 2d Dist, Fang Cheng Yuan Fang Zhuang, 100078 Beijing China Office: Sci and Tech Daily, 15 Fuxing Rd, 100038 Beijing China

PENG, HUAN WU, physicist, educator; b. Changchun, Jilin, China, Oct. 6, 1915; s. Hua Tsing Peng and Si Jing Chen; m. Bing Xian Liu, Dec. 25, 1958 (dec. Oct. 1977); 1 child, Zheng Yu. BSc, Tsinghua U., Beijing, 1935; PhD, U. Edinburgh, Scotland, 1940, DSc, 1945. Asst. prof. Sch. Theoretical Physics Dublin (Ireland) Inst. for Advanced Studies, 1945-47; prof. Yunnan U., Kumming, China, 1947-49, Tsinghua U., Beijing, 1949-52, Inst. Atomic Energy, Beijing, 1950-70, Inst. High Energy Physics, Beijing, 1972-78, Inst. Theoretical Physics, Beijing, 1978—; prof. Beijing U., 1952-55, 56-57, 82, U. Sci. and Tech. China, Beijing, 1962-64, Grad. Sch., U. Sci. and Tech. China, Beijing, 1978-79; dep. dir. 9th Acad., 1961-72. Prin. author: (book) Fundamentals of Theory Physics, 1998; contbr. articles to prof. jours. Recipient 1st class nat. prize natural scis. State Commn. Sci. and Tech., 1982, Sci. and Tech. Achievement award Ho Leung Ho Lee Found., 1995, Liang Dan Yi Xing medal of merit Chinese Govt., 1999. Mem. Royal Irish Acad., Chinese Acad. Scis. Office: Inst Theoretical Physics, PO Box 2735, 100080 Beijing China

PENG, LI, government official; b. Chengdu City, Sichuan, Oct. 20, 1928; s. Zhou Enlai; married; three children. Diploma, Yanan Inst. of Natural Scis., 1945, Zhangiakuo Indsl. Vocat. Sch., 1948, Hydroelectric Engring. Studies, Moscow Power Inst., 1955. Technician Jinchiji Power Corp., Beijing, 1946-48; chmn. Chinese Students Assn. in Soviet Union, 1949-55; chief engr. Fengma (then Faxin) power plants, 1945—; dep. chief engr. Northeast Electric Power Bur., 1955-66; dir. Beijing Power Adminstrn., 1966-79; vice-min. to min. Power Industry, 1979-81, 81-82; vice min. Water Conservancy and Electric Power, 1982-83; mem. CPC CC, 1983—; vice premier, 1983-88; mem. CPC CC Secretariat, 1985-89; min. State Edn. Commn., 1985-87; elected mem., chmn. Nat. People's Congress Politburo, 1985—; acting premier State Coun., 1987-88; chmn. State Commn. on Econ. Restructuring, 1988-90; premier State Coun., 1988—; mem. standing com. Politburo; head of numerous govt. delegations abroad. Mem. Communist Party. Office: Politburo, Chmn Nat Peoples Congress, Zhong Nan Ha/Beijing China*

PENG, LIANG-CHUAN, mechanical engineer; b. Taiwan, Feb. 6, 1936; came to U.S., 1965, naturalized, 1973; s. Mu-Sui and Wang-Su (Yang) P.; diploma Taipei Inst. Tech., 1960; M.S., Kans. State U., 1967; m. Wen-Fong Kao, Nov. 18, 1962; children: Tsen-Loong, Tsen-Hsin, Lina, Linda. Project engr. Taiwan Power Co., 1960-65; asst. engr. Carlson & Sweatt, N.Y.C., 1966-67; asst. engr. Pioneer Engrs., Chgo., 1967-68; mech. engr. Bechtel, San Francisco, 1969-71; sr. specialist Nuclear Services Co., San Jose, Calif., 1971-75; sr. engr. Brown & Root, Houston, 1975; stress engr. Foster Wheeler, Houston, 1976; staff engr. AAA Technologists, Houston, 1977; prin. engr. M.W. Kellogg, Houston, 1978-82; pres., owner Peng Engring., Houston, 1982—; instr. U. Houston; condr. piping tech. seminars. Chmn. South Bay Area Formosan Assn., 1974, No. Calif. Formosan Fedn., 1975. Registered profl. engr., Tex., Calif. Developer: (computer progarams) SIMFLEX; condr. seminars in field. Mem. ASME, Nat. Soc. Profl. Engrs. Buddhist. Home: 3010 Manila Ln Houston TX 77043-1312

PENG, MIN, molecular biology; b. Yujiang, Peoples Republic China, Nov. 24, 1959; s. Wenyu and Laiying (Duan) P.; m. Bo Fu, Oct. 01, 1989; 1 child, Xiwen. MD, Jiangxi Medical Coll., 1985, MSc, 1990; PhD, Shanghai Medical Univ., 1993. Rsch. asst. Jiangxi Medical Inst., Nanchang, Peoples Republic China, 1985-90; lectr., rsch. assoc. Shanghai Medical Unic., Shanghai, 1992-95; postdoctor Tel Aviv Univ., Tel Aviv, Israel, 1995-96; postdoctor Univ. Pa., Pitts., 1996-98, rsch. assoc., 1997-99, rsch. specialist, 1999—. Mem. Assn. for Rsch. In Vision and Ophthalmology, Am. Assn. Advancement of Sci., Assn. for Chinese Biochemistry. Avocations: stamps, computer, chess. E-mail: minp@mail.med.upenn.edu. Fax: 610 622 5239. Home: 4010 Garrett Rd Apt 9 Drexel Hill PA 19026-5122 Office: Univ Pa 415 Curie Blvd CRB 575 Philadelphia PA 19104

PENG, ZHONGHUA, chemistry educator; m. Tian Fu, 1992; 1 child, Helen Peng. BS, U. Sci. & Tech. of China, Hefei, Peoples Republic of China, 1989; M in Engring., Chinese Acad. Scis., Shanghai, Peoples Republic of China, 1992; PhD, U. Chgo., 1997. Postdoc. mem. tech. staff Bell Labs./Lucent Tech., Murray Hill, N.J., 1997-98; asst. prof. U. Mo.-Kansas City, 1998—; panelist Nat. Sci. Found., reviewer Nat. Sci. Found. Author: Chemistry of Materials, 1998-99; inventor: 1995; contbr. articles to profl. jours. U. Mo.-Kansas City Faculty scholar, 2000—. Mem. ACS, AAAS, Materials Rsch. Soc. Fax: 816-235-5502. E-mail: pengz@umkc.edu. Office: U Mo-Kansas City 5100 Rockhill Rd Kansas City MO 64110-2481

PENGELLY, ANDREW WILLIAM, surgeon; b. Winchester, Eng., Apr. 25, 1942; s. Kenneth and Christine Winifred Pengelly; m. Geraldine Christian Pumphery, Aug. 27, 1976; children: Oliver, Victoria, Laurence, Rachel. BA, Oxford (Eng.) U., 1967, MA, 1972, BM BCh, 1969. House surgeon Addenbrookes Hosp., Cambridge, Eng., 1971; med. officer Mission Hosp., Peshawar, West Pakistan, 1972; sr. house officer Gloucester (Eng.) Royal Hosp., 1973-74; registrar Middlesex Hosp., London, 1974-77, sr. registrar, 1977-80; med. dir., cons. urologist Royal Berkshire and Battle Hosps., Reading, Eng., 1980—. Contbr. chpts. to books, articles to profl. jours. Fellow Royal Coll. Surgeons (London), European Bd. Urology, Royal Soc. Medicine (mem. coun. sect. urology 1990-92); mem. Brit. Assn. Urol. Surgeons (mem. coun. 1991-93). Avocations: music, painting, trumpet. Home: Fieldgate House, Hollington, Newbury RG20 9XR, England Office: 72 Berkeley Ave, Reading RG1 6HY, England

PENHALL, GEOFFREY KENNETH, human resources executive; b. Adelaide, Australia, Jan. 6, 1943; s. Wilfred Nicholas and Joyce Edith (Rowett) P.; m. Penelope Ann McRae, Aug. 1966 (div. 1986); children: Lisa Joy, Andrew Geoffrey; m. Metty Tedja Effendi, June 1989; 1 child, Georgina, Ingrid. Advanced diploma in edn., Torrens Coll. Advanced Edn., Adelaide, Australia, 1978; BEd, S.A.C.A.E., Adelaide, 1982. Apprentice Weapons Rsch. Establishment, Salisbury, Australia, 1959-63; jr. tchr. Edn. Dept., Adelaide, 1963-66; tech. tchr. South Australian Edn. Dept., 1967-69; tchr. educator SACAE, 1970-79; lectr. U. South Australia, Adelaide, 1980-93; advisor, team leader AusAID, Jakartaand East Java, Indonesia, 1994-99; cons. World Bank, Jakarta, Indonesia, 1990, AusAID, Tonga, 1993; advisor, tchr. educator Australian Internat. Devel. Assistance Bur., Bandung, Indonesia, 1985-88. Chmn. Tea Tree Gully Sch., South Australia, 1984, Australian/Indonesian Assn., South Australia, 1989; justice of the peace South Australian Govt., 1975—. Mem. Australian Human Resources Inst. (chartered), A Coll. Edn., Sporting Car Club. Avocations: photography, auto restoration, music. Home: 2-3 Clair Crs, Victor Harbor SA 5211, Australia Office: Penhall and Assocs, PO Box 401, Victor Harbor SA 5211, Australia

PENISTON, EUGENE GILBERT, psychologist; b. Osceola, Iowa, June 23, 1931; s. Milton James and Delia B. (Jordan) P.; m. Helen M. Kerr, Oct. 16, 1959; children: Denise R., Eugene Lyle. BA, Cen. State U., Wilberforce, Ohio, 1953; MS, S.D. State U., 1962; EdD., Okla. State U., 1972. Lic. clin. psychologist, S.D.; diplomate Am. Bd. Med. Psychotherapy (fellow 1986—); bd. diplomate Am. Acad. Experts in Traumatic Stress and Pain Mgmt.; diplomate Nat. Registry Bd. Examiners, Nat. Registry Neurofeedback Providers (examiner). Chief psychologist Clarance (N.Y.) Pub. Schs., 1965-69; chief psychology svc. tng. ctr. Va. State Hosp., Petersburg, 1972-75; assoc. prof. Va. State U., Petersburg, 1975-76; mental health cons. HHS, USPHS, Roosevelt, Utah, 1976-79; cons. clin. psychologist Redfield (S.D.) State Hosp., HHS, USPHS, 1976-81; clin. psychologist VA Med. Ctr., Ft. Lyon, Colo., 1981-91, 98—, chief psychology svc., 1991-97; profl. adv. coun., Am. Bd. Med. Psychotherapists, Nashville, 1986—. Editorial cons. and mem. of editorial bd. for jours. and newsletters in field; contbr. articles to profl. jours. Mem. Human Rights Commn. Ark. Valley Community Ctr. for Handicapped and Retarded Persons, Inc., La Junta, Colo., 1988-90. Lt. U.S. Army, 1953-56. Recipient Spl. Contbn. award VA Med. Ctr., Ft. Lyon, 1983, VA Spl. Contbn. award, 1988, Outstanding Performance award VA Med. Ctr., Ft. Lyon, 1990, Cert. of Honor for Contbn. for Nation of Israel, Performance award Va. North Tex. Health Care System, 1997. Fellow Am. Psychol. Soc. (divsn. 17 counseling psychology, 13 cons. psychology), Am. Bd. Med. Psychotherapists and Psychodiagnosticians (diplomate), Nat. Registry Biofeedback Providers (examiner), Am. Acad. Experts in Traumatic Stress; mem. APA (bd. govs., cert. 1996—, Outstanding VA Psychologist award divsn. 18 III 1988-89), Behavior Therapy and Rsch. Soc. (clin. fellow), N.Y. Acad. Scis., Phi Delta Kappa (Outstanding Achievement award 1988, treas. 1984-88). Lutheran. Avocations: golf, running. Office: VA Med Ctr 1201 E 9th St Bonham TX 75418-4059

PENLAND, THOMAS COKE, lawyer; b. Blainsville, Ga., Aug. 22, 1919; s. thomas Gordon and Annie Mae (Hughes) P.; m. Evelyn Adams, April 11, 1943 (dec. 1988); children: Penelope, Deanna; m. Sarah Mae, June 9, 1990. BSA, U. Ga., 1943, LLB, 1948. Bar: Ga. 1947. Pvt. practice Thomasville, Ga., 1948-55; sec., treas. State Bd. Workmen's Compensation, Atlanta, 1955-59; pvt. practice Decatur, Ga., 1959-65; ptnr. Cobb, Cobb & Penland, Decatur, Ga., 1965-90, retired, 1990. Mem. Kiwanis Club, Am. Legion Post 31 (commdr. 1948-55, dept. judge advocate 1961-63). Decorated Purple Heart. Methodist. Avocations: hunting, fishing, sports. Home: 329 Tuxedo Dr Thomasville GA 31792-6764

PENM, JACK HLUNG-WEN, statistician, researcher; b. Taipei, Taiwan, Dec. 27, 1949; arrived in Australia, 1977; s. Frank and Tseng (Kuo) P.; m. Ruth Wang, Jan. 7, 1978; children: Elizabeth, Jonathan. BSc, Taiwan Normal U., China, 1972; M in Physics, U. Pitts., 1975, PhD in Elec. Engring., 1977; M in Computer Sci., Australian Nat. U., 1982. Programmer Australian Nat. U., 1978, sys. analyst, 1979, project leader, 1980-84, rsch. cons., 1985—; vis. fellow Australian Nat. U., 1996—; PCF visitor Pacific Cultural Found., Taipei, 1993. Author: Essays in Economic Forecasting, 1996. Baptist. Avocations: painting, gardening. Office: Australian Nat U Dept Stats, GPO Box 4, Canberra ACT 2600, Australia

PENMAN, DAVID WILLIAM, electrical engineer; b. Auckland, New Zealand, Oct. 30, 1954; m. Mary Joy Penman, Apr. 8, 1978; 4 children. BE, Auckland U., 1976, ME, 1978. Reg. elec. engr., New Zealand; chartered engr. U.K. Elec. engr. New Zealand Electricity Dept., 1977-80; scientist D.S.I.R., Auckland, 1980-92, Indsl. Rsch. Ltd., Auckland, 1992—. Mem. IEE. Office: Indsl Rsch Ltd Box 2225, 24 Balfour Rd Parnell, Auckland New Zealand

PENN, DAWN TAMARA, entrepreneur; b. Knoxville, Tenn., July 22, 1965; d. Morton Hugh and Virginia Audra (Wilson) P. AS, Bauder Fashion Coll., Atlanta, 1984; postgrad., U. Tenn., 1986; grad., Rasnic Sch. Modeling, Knoxville, 1986. Gen. mgr. Merry-Go-Round, Knoxville, 1984-86; mgr., dancer Lady Adonis Inc. Performing Arts Dance Co., Knoxville, 1987-90; owner, pres. Lady Adonis, Inc. Performing Arts Dance Co., Knoxville, 1990—, also chmn.; owner/pres. Penn Mgmt. and Investment Co. Comml. Real Estate, Knoxville, 1989—; deputized bonded rep. Knox County Sheriff's Dept., Knoxville, 1989-90; fgn. dance tours include Aruba, Curacao, Caracas, Barbados, Ont., Que., Montreal, Nfld., Labrador, N.S., New Brunswick; cons. The John Reinhardt Agy., Winston-Salem, N.C., 1987—, Gen. Talent Agy., Monroeville, Pa., 1990—, Xanadu, Inc., Myrtle Beach, S.C., 1991—. Author, editor: Lady Adonis Performing Arts promotional mag., 1988; TV and motion picture credits include: Innocent Blood, 1992, The Phil Donahue Show, N.Y.C., 1989, 91. Coord. bridal fair Big. Bros./Big Sisters Knox County, Knoxville, 1985, 86; judge Southeastern Entertainer of Yr. Pageant, Knoxville, 1992—, Miss Knoxville U.S.A. Pageant, Knoxville, 1990—; active Knoxville Conv. and Visitors Bur., 1993-94. Recipient 1st Pl. award for swimsuit TV comml. and runway modeling Internat. Model's Hall of Fame, 1986, 1st Pl. award for media presentation Modeling Assn. Am. Internat., 1986; nominee The Pres.'s Commn. on White House Fellowships, U.S. Office Pers. Mgmt., 1994-95. Mem. Internat. Platform Assn., Profl. Assn. Diving Instrs. (cert.). Methodist. Avocations: scuba diving, racquetball, horseback riding, piano, theology. Home: 7320 Old Clinton Pike Apt 8 Knoxville TN 37921-1064 Office: Lady Adonis Inc/Penn Mgmt Ste 8 7320 Old Clinton Hwy Knoxville TN 37921-1064

PENN, MAGGIE SCOTT, school counselor, small business owner; b. Columbia, S.C., Jan. 1, 1940; d. Walter Lee and Ruby Lee (Seawright) Scott; m. Luther Penn (dec. Oct. 1977); 1 child: Cydni Charise. BS, Eastern Mich. U., 1963, MA, 1966; PhD, U. San Jose, 1998. Lic. profl. counselor, Mich. Bus. tchr. Highland (Mich.) Park Bd. Edn., 1963-70, sch. counselor, 1971-96, high sch. counselor, mental health therapist, 1999—; pres. Bramblewood Enterprises, Detroit, 1978—; owner Penn Hardware, Detroit; mental health therapist Detroit Ctrl. City Mental Health Agy., 1999—. Sec. Detroit NAACP, 1978-84, bd. dirs. 1978-84; sec. Sr. Citizens of Detroit Com., 1980—, Cotillion Wives Aux., Detroit, 1979-85; mgr. state senate pol. campaign, Detroit, 1980; supervisor Peoples Community Ch. Credit Union, Detroit, 1978-84. Recipient Disting. Service award City of Detroit, 1984, Outstanding Membership award Detroit NAACP, 1970, 80-85, Spl. Tribute award State of Mich., 1987. Mem. Internat. Assn. Counselors and Therapists, Am. Fedn. Tchrs., Nat. Assn. Counselors and Female Execs., Mich. Fedn. Tchrs., Highland Park Fedn. Tchrs., Mich. Guidance Assn., Mich. Career Devel. Assn., Am. Bus. Educators, New Metro Detroit Bus. and Profl. Women (editor newsletter, appreciation award 1982), Landlords Assn. Mich., Tots 'n Teens, Delta Sigma Theta, Phi Delta Kappa. Mem. Peoples Cmty. Ch. Avocations: writing, speaking, organizing, decorating, wedding consulting. Home: PO Box 21010 Coll Park Sta Detroit MI 48221 Office: Penn Hardware 7300 Puritan St Detroit MI 48238-1206

PENNELL, DANNY JOE, social worker; b. Aug. 31, 1945; s. Donald Louis and Lela Geneva (Murray) P.; m. Janis Evelyn Reynolds, Dec. 26, 1984; children: Joel, Jason, Jaime, Chad, Colter. BA, U. Ill., 1970, MSW, 1972. Social worker Dept. Child and Family Svcs., Danville, Ill., 1971-72; social worker supr. Dept. Child and Family Svcs., Rockford, Ill., 1972-74; instr. Rockford Coll., 1977-78; pres., CEO Goldie B. Floberg Ctr., Rockton, Ill., 1974—; exec. dir. Found. Ft. Lewis Coll., Durango, Colo., 1986-87; bd. dirs. Winnebago County Child Protection Assn., Rockford, 1974-76; bd. dirs., mem. legis. affairs com., chmn. mental health devel. disabilities com., spl. edn. com. Child Care Assn. Ill., Springfield, Ill., 1980—; mem. child welfare adv. com. Ill. Dept. Children and Family Services; mem. devel. disabilities adv. com. Dept. Mental Health, mem. children's svcs. subcom.; cons. in field. Grantee Ill. Dept. Children and Family Svcs., 1970-72. Mem. Nat. Soc. Fund Raising Execs. (bd. dirs., sec. 1984-85, v.p. 1986-87), Nat. Soc. Fund Raising Dirs. (pres. bd. dirs. 1988, v.p. 1987, v.p. 1986, bd. mem. various coms. 1984, 85), Am. Assn. Mental Deficiency, Nat. Assn. Retarded Citizens, Coordinating Council for Handicapped Children, Nat. Assn. Devel. Disabilities Mgrs., Roscoe C. of C. (bd. dirs. 2000—). Home: 12080 N Ledges Dr Roscoe IL 61073-9600 Office: Goldie B Floberg Ctr PO Box 346 Rockton IL 61072-0346

PENNELL, DUDLEY JOHN, cardiologist; b. London, Sept. 8, 1958; s. Terence John and Irene Joan (Smith) P.; m. Elisabeth Ann Teo, Mar. 21, 1992. BA, Cambridge (Eng.) U., 1980, MB BChir, 1983, MA, 1984, MD, 1992; MRCP, 1986. Cardiology sr. house officer London Chest Hosp., 1985; renal sr. house officer St. Thomas' Hosp., London, 1986, cardiology registrar, 1988; cardiology registrar St. Peter's Hosp., Chertsey, Eng., 1987; lectr. Royal Brompton Hosp., London, 1988-92, cons., 1992—. Author: Thallium Myocardial, 1992, Nuclear Cardiology: Clinician's Guide, 1995; contbr. articles to profl. jours. Fellow European Soc. Cardiology, Am. Coll. Cardiology, Royal Coll. Physicians; mem. Brit. Nuclear Cardiology Group (pres. 1994-96), Soc. for Cardiovascular Magnetic Resonance (pres. 1998—), Am. Soc. Nuclear Cardiology (UK rep. internat. coun. 1995—). Avocations: classical guitar, golf, skiing, tennis. Office: Royal Brompton Hosp, Sydney St, London SW3 6NP, England

PENNER, STANFORD SOLOMON, engineering educator; b. Unna, Germany, July 5, 1921; came to U.S., 1936, naturalized, 1943; s. Heinrich and Regina (Saal) P.; m. Beverly Preston, Dec. 28, 1942; children: Merilynn Jean, Robert Clark. BS, Union Coll., 1942; MS, U. Wis., 1943, PhD, 1946; Dr. rer. nat. (hon.), Technische Hochschule Aachen, Germany, 1981. Research asso. Allegany Ballistics Lab., Cumberland, Md., 1944-45; research scientist Standard Oil Devel. Co., Esso Labs., Linden, N.J., 1946; sr. research engr. Jet Propulsion Lab., Pasadena, Calif., 1947-50; mem. faculty Calif. Inst. Tech., 1950-63, prof. div. engring., jet propulsion, 1957-63; dir. research engring. div. Inst. Def. Analyses, Washington, 1962-64; prof. engring. physics, chmn. dept. aerospace and mech. engring. U. Calif. at San Diego, 1964-68, vice chancellor for acad. affairs, 1968-69, dir. Inst. for Pure and Applied Phys. Scis., 1968-71, dir. Energy Ctr., 1973-91; bd. dirs. Optodyne Corp.; U.S. mem. adv. group aero. rsch. and devel. NATO, 1952-68, chmn. combustion and propulsion panel, 1958-60; mem. adv. com. engring. scis. USAF-Office Sci. Rsch., 1961-65; mem. subcom. on combustion NACA, 1954-58; mem. rsch. adv. com. on air-breathing engines NASA,

1962-64; mem. coms. on gas dynamics and edn. Internat. Acad. Astronautics, 1969-80; nat. lectr. Sigma Xi, 1977-79; chmn. fossil energy rsch. working group Dept. Energy, 1978-82, chmn. advanced fuel cell commercialization working group, 1993-95; mem. assembly engring. NAE, 1978-82; chmn. NAS-NRC U.S. Nat. Com. IIASA, 1978-82; mem. commn. engring. tech. sys. NRC, 1982-84; spl. guest Internat. Coal Sci. Confs., 1983, 85, 87, 89, 91; mentor Def. Sci. Studies Group, 1985-93; chmn. studies mcpl. waste incineration NSF, 1988-89, Calif. Coun. Sci. Tech., 1992; pub. info. adv. com. Nat. Acad. Engring., 1994-98, Independent Commn. on Environ. Edn., 1995-97, Environ. Literacy Coun., 1998—; sci. adv. com., San Diego County, 1997—. Author: Chemical Reactions in Flow Systems, 1955, Chemistry Problems in Jet Propulsion, 1957, Quantitative Molecular Spectroscopy and Gas Emissivities, 1959, Chemical Rocket Propulsion and Combustion Research, 1962, Thermodynamics, 1968, Radiation and Reentry, 1968; sr. author: Energy, Vol. I (Demands, Resources, Impact, Technology and Policy), 1974, 81, Energy, Vol. II (Non-nuclear Energy Technologies), 1975, 77, 84, Energy, Vol. III (Nuclear Energy and Energy Policies), 1976; editor: Chemistry of Propellants, 1960, Advanced Propulsion Techniques, 1961, Detonations and Two-Phase Flow, 1962, Combustion and Propulsion, 1963, Advances in Tactical Rocket Propulsion, 1968, In Situ Shale Oil Recovery, 1975, New Sources of Oil and Gas, 1982, Coal Combustion and Applications, 1984, Advanced Fuel Cells, 1986, Coal Gasification: Direct Applications and Syntheses of Chemicals and Fuels, 1987, CO2 Emissions and Climate Change, 1991, Commercialization of Fuel Cells, 1995, Advanced Nuclear Techs., 1998; assoc. editor Jour. Chem. Physics, 1953-56; founding editor Jour. Quantitative Spectroscopy and Radiative Transfer, 1960-92, Jour. Def. Rsch., 1963-67, Energy-The Internat. Jour., 1975-98; sect. editor Energy and Power Systems, Ency. Phys. Sci. and Tech., 1998—. Recipient spl. award People-to-People program NATO, pub. svc. award U. Calif., Sn Diego, N. Manson medal Internat. Colloquia on Gasdynamics of Explosions and Reactive Systems, 1979, internat. Columbus award Internat. Inst. Comm., Genoa, Italy, 1981, disting. assoc. award U.S. Dept. Energy, 1990, Edward Teller award for def. of freedom, 1997. Fellow Am. Phys. Soc., Optical Soc. Am., AAAS, N.Y. Acad. Scis., AIAA (dir. 1964-66, past chmn. com., G. Edward Pendray award 1975, Thermophysics award 1983, Energy Systems award 1983), Am. Acad. Arts and Scis.; mem. Nat. Acad. Engring., Internat. Acad. Astronautics, Am. Chem. Soc., Sigma Xi. Home: 5912 Avenida Chamnez La Jolla CA 92037-7402 Office: U Calif San Diego 9500 Gilman Dr La Jolla CA 92093-5004

PENNING, DONALD HENRY, anesthesiologist, obstetrician-gynecologist; b. Montreal, Can., Dec. 23, 1956; s. Tom and Joan Penning; m. Janice L. Henderson, June 28, 1980; children: Marion, Alison, Simon. BSc, Queen's U., Can., 1979, MD, 1983, MSc, 1989. LMCC; cert. NALS instr. Clin. assst. Queen's U., Kinston, Ont., Can., 1987; attending staff Kinston Gen., 1988; assoc. staff St. Joseph's Health Ctr., London, Can., 1988-90; asst. prof. Queen's U., Kingston, 1990-92, U. Iowa Hosps., Iowa City, 1992-96; asst. prof. Duke U. Med. Ctr., Durham, N.C., 1996—, chief divsn. women's anesthesia, 1996—. Prodr., author: (video) Permission to be Pain Free, 1999. Recipient BB Sankey Anaesthesia Advancement award U. Western Ont., 1989. Fellow RCPC; mem. Soc. Obstet. Anesthesia and Perinatology (bd. dirs. 1998—, mem. sci. com. 1998—), mem. Am. Soc. Anesthesiologists, Can. Anaesthetist Soc., Soc. for Obstet. Anesthesiology and Perinatology, Assn. Univ. Anesthesiologists. Fax: 919 681-7022. E-mail: penni008@mc.duke.edu. Home: 2807 Wade Rd Durham NC 27705-5622 Office: Duke U Med Ctr Box 3094 RP4 Bldg Rm 119 Research Dr Durham NC 27710

PENNINGS, ENGELBERTUS CASPAR MARIA, engineering executive; b. Sassenheim, The Netherlands, Nov. 3, 1960; s. Albertus Johannes and Johanna Jacoba (Zwetsloot) P. MS in Applied Physics cum laude, U. Groningen, The Netherlands, 1986; PhD in Elec. Engring., Delft U. Tech., The Netherlands, 1990. Mem. tech. staff Bellcore, Redhill, U.S.A., 1990-92; rsch. scientist Philips Rsch., Eindhoven, The Netherlands, 1992-94; cons. Philips, Redhill, U.K., 1994-95; sr. devel. engr. Philips Optoelectronics, Eindhoven, 1995-97; group leader JDS Uniphase, Eindhoven, 1997-99, prod. line mgr., 1999—; bus. devel. mgr. Zetfolie, Groningen; Presenter in field. Contbr. over 60 articles to profl. jours. Chair Caux Conf. Bus. and Industry-Jr. Round Table, Caux, Switzerland, 1997-99. Mem. IEEE (treas. Lasers and Electro-Optics Soc. chpt. 1996-99), Optical Soc. Am.

PENNINGTON, BEVERLY MELCHER, financial services company executive; b. Vermillion, SD, Feb. 8, 1931; d. Cecil Lloyd and Phyllis Cecelia (Walz) M.; m. Glen D., Sept. 1, 1965 (dec. Aug. 1986); 1 child, Terri Lynn. BS, U. S.D., Vermillion, 1952. Enrolled agt. cert. IRS 1989. Sec. budget dept. Bur. of Indian Affairs, Aberdeen, S.D., 1952-53, pvt. sec., 1953-54; pvt. sec. U.S. P.H.S. Indian Health, Aberdeen, 1954-55; adminstr. asst. U.S. Pub. Health Svc., Anchorage, 1955-58, U.S. Pub. Health, Dental Pub. Health, Washington, 1958-61; grant adminstr. Dental Pub. Health, Washington, 1961-65; co-owner Penn Mel Marina, Platte, S.D, 1965-74; co-owner Pennington Tax Service, Platte, 1974-86, owner, 1986-93; pres., CEO, White Tiger Fin. Svc., Inc., Platte, 1994—. Contbr. articles to profl. jours. Mem. Platte Women's Club, sec., 1965-68, pres., 1968-70, 89-91; mem. Libr. Bd., Sec., 1982-85, treas., 1995—. Fellow Am. Soc. Tax Profls. (sec. 1989-91, 2d v.p. 1995, 1st v.p. 1996, pres. 1997); mem. NAFE, Platte C. of C. (v.p. 1989, pres. 1990), Lyric Theatre Mus. Soc. (pres. 1988-92), U.S. C. of C., Washington Dakota Cen. Com. Republican. Presbyterian. Avocations: collecting jewelry, reading, dress designing, gourmet cooking. Office: White Tiger Fin Svc Inc 420 Main St Platte SD 57369

PENNINGTON, D. GLENN, surgeon; b. Meridian, Miss., Oct. 25, 1940; s. Edward and Emma L. Pennington; m. Dorothy J., Jan. 21, 1967; children: Andrew, Jennifer. BA, U. Miss., Oxford, 1962; MD, U. Miss., Jackson, 1966. Residency Tulane U., New Orleans, 1966-72, residency in thoracic surgical, 1972-73; rsch. fellow Harvard U., MG Hosp., Boston, 1975-73; cardiac surgical fellow Mayo Clinic, Rochester, Minn., 1976-77; prof. St. Louis U., 1977-95; chmn. thoracic surgery Wake Forest U., Winston-Salem, N.C., 1995-2000, chmn. surgery, 1977-99. Contbr. articles to profl. jours. Lt. col. USAF, 1973-75. Recipient of awards Nat. Heart Lung and Blood Inst., 1984, 92. Mem. Am. Assn. Thoracic Surgery (coun. mem. 1995-98), Am. Assn. Artificial Internal Organs (pres. 1990), Thoracic Surgery Dirs. Assn. (exec. com. 1998—), So. Thoracic Surg. Assn. (sec.-treas. 1994-98). Baptist. Avocations: running, playing golf, trout fishing. Office: Wake Forest Univ Sch Medicine Medical Ctr Blvd Winston Salem NC 27157-0001

PENNINGTON, DONALD HARRIS, musician, retired physician; b. Clarksville, Ark., Sept. 13, 1945; s. John Powers and Verna Olive (Harris) P.; m. Susan Myree Snyder, Aug. 27, 1966 (div. Aug. 1982); children: Thomas Walter, Aimee Myree, John Herrick. BA, U. of the Ozarks, 1968; MD, U. Ark., 1972; wine diploma, Calif. Dept. Agr., 1973. Intern St. Vincent Infirmary, Little Rock, 1973; physician, founding ptnr. Clarksville Med. Group, P.A., 1972-93; physician Mercy Med. Svcs., Inc., Ft. Smith, Ark., 1993-98; ret., 1998; cons. family planning svcs. Ark. State Bd. of Health, 1973-93; mem. physician adv. bd. Mercy Med. Group, 1996—. Founding mem., musician Ft. Douglas (Ark.) Backporch Bluegrass Symphony, 1976-91; acoustic double bassist River Valley Jazz Union, Russellville, Ark., 1991-97. Bd. dirs. Johnson County Regional Hosp., Clarksville, 1973-82, Clarksville Planning and Zoning commn.; asst. ch. organist 1st United Meth. Ch., Clarkville, 1968—; full time organist 1st Presbyn. Ch., 1994—; active ACLU, Planned Parenthood Fedn., The League to Make a Difference, Sierra Club Legal Defense Fund, The Nature Conservancy, planning and zoning commn. City of Clarksville; mem. Nat. Trust for Hist. Preservation, 1982—; mem. governing bd. Oakland Cemetery Assn., 1997—; med. vol. United Meth. Com. on Relief. Mem. AMA, Assn. Am. Physicians for Human Rights, Nat. Trust for Historic Preservation, Ark. Med. Soc. (county del. 1972-96), Ark. Acad. Family Practice, Religious Coalition for Abortion Rights, Johnson County Hist. Soc. (life, pres. 2000—), 90-Yr. Old's Friday Bridge Club (chauffeur), Tuesday Culture & Bridge Club. Democrat. Avocations: restoration of historic homes, antiques, family history, music, historical preservation. Home: 317 N Johnson St Clarksville AR 72830-2953

PENNINGTON, MARGARET ANGELA, financial consultant; b. Birmingham, Ala., Sept. 20, 1942; d. George Frederick and Regina Angela (Moreno) Kirchoff; B.A., U. Tenn., 1963; M.S.W., Smith Coll., 1965; m. Gerald Lee Pennington. Faculty dept. psychiatry Emory U., Atlanta, 1966-69; asso. dir. St. Jude's House, Atlanta, 1969-72; asso. dir. public affairs Mental Health Assn., Atlanta, 1972-73; community orgn. cons. Ga. Dept. Human Resources, Atlanta, 1974-75; fine art cons. Rentar Industries, N.Y.C., 1975-85; v.p. Shannsongs, Inc., 1985-95 ; pres. Marpal, Inc., Nokomis, Fla., 1980-86; v.p. Penn-Products, Venice, Fla., 1982-99 . Bd. dirs. New Coll. Music Festival, Sarasota, Fla., 1982-86, Sarasota-Manatee Jewish Family Service, 1986-88; v.p. women's div. Sarasota-Manatee Jewish Fedn., 1986-90; co-chmn. Combined Jewish Appeal, 1986-90, chmn. Womens' Div. 1986-90; charter mem. Venice Jewish Com-Sarasota-Manatee Counties, 1986-90; charter mem. Venice Jewish Community Ctr.; bd. dirs. Manatee Community Coll. Found., 1986-88. Nat. Bd. Coun. Jewish Fedn. 1994-96, Nat. Bd. Govs., A.J.C., 1998—, Highlands Chamber Mus. Festival, 1997—; bd. trustees Highlands-Cashier Hosp., 1998—. Recipient awards, grants: Vocat. Rehab. Adminstrn., Nat. Found., Gen. Tire and Rubber Co., Wallace Silver Co., SCV. Mem. Nat. Assn. Social Workers, Acad. Cert. Social Workers, Am. Craft Council, Nat. Soc. Magna Charter Dames, Smith Coll. Alumnae Assn., DAR, Colonial Dames XVII Century, Women's Am. O.R.T., Pi Beta Phi. Jewish. Clubs: The Oaks, Highlands Falls Country Club. Home and Office: 285 Sugar Mill Dr Osprey FL 34229-9074

PENNINGTON, THERESA SUE, engineer professional; b. Bowling Green, Ky., Aug. 20, 1948; d. James Floyd and Dorenda May (Martin) P. Student, Western Ky. U., 1966-69, Nashville State Area Vocat. Tech. Sch., 1990-92. Mem. automotive dept. staff Sears, Roebuck & Co., Nashville, 1979-80; security officer Cain-Sloan, Inc., Nashville, 1975-76; mem. shipping and receiving staff J & M Terminal, Genesco, Inc., Nashville, 1976-77; welder Aladdin Industries, Inc., Nashville, 1977-80; mem. assembly staff Norton/Sun Electric Corp., Lavergne, Tenn., 1980-82; assembler Avco/Textron Aerostructures, Nashville, 1982-88; bldg. contract supr. Nat. Cleaning Contractors, Inc., Nashville, 1989; asst. engr. maintenance, licensed airframe plant mechanic Opryland USA, Inc., Nashville, 1990-93; engr. Peterbilt Motors Co., Madison, Tenn., 1993—. Mem. Internat. Assn. Machinists and Aerospace Workers. Republican. Baptist. Avocations: coin collecting, writing poetry. Home: 177 Beeler Ave Smiths Grove KY 42171-8203 Office: Peterbilt Motors 430 Myatt Dr Madison TN 37115-3000

PENNINGTON, THOMAS HUGH, bacteriology educator; b. Lancaster, Eng., Apr. 19, 1938; s. Thomas Wearing and Dorothy (Gardner) P.; m. Carolyn Ingram Beattie, Apr. 14, 1966; children: Jane, Catherine. MB BChir with honors, U. London, 1962, PhD, 1967; DSc, U. Lancaster, Eng., 1999. GMC registered. Casualty officer, house physician St. Thomas's Hosp., London, 1962-63; from asst. lectr. to lectr. St. Thomas's Hosp. Med. Sch., London, 1963-67; postgrad. fellow U. Wis., 1967-69; sci. staff Med. Rsch. Coun., Glasgow, Scotland, 1969-70; from lectr. to sr. lectr. U. Glasgow, 1970-79; prof. bacteriology U. Aberdeen, Scotland, 1979—; chmn. Pennington Group Enquirer into the 1996 Cen. Scotland E. Coli Outbreak, 1996-97; mem. adv. bd. Med. Rsch. Coun., London, 1999; gov. Rowett Rsch. Inst., Aberdeen. Contbr. chpts. to books; contbr. papers to peer-reviewed jours., mags., and newspapers. Recipient Consumer Advocate award Caroline Walker Trust, 1997, John Kershaw Meml. prize Royal Inst. Pub. Health and Hygiene, 1998, Silver medal Royal Scottish Soc. Arts, 1998; named Scottish Power List 14th Most Powerful Person in Scotland, Observer Newspaper, Channel 4 TV, 1999. Fellow Royal Coll. Pathologists, Royal Soc. Edinburgh, Acad. Med. Scis., Royal Soc. Arts. Avocations: collecting old books, dipterology. Home: 13 Carlton Pl, Aberdeen AB15 4B3, Scotland Office: U Aberdeen, Forester Hill, Aberdeen AB25 2ZD, Scotland

PENNISI, LIZ, women's health nurse; b. Bklyn., Nov. 20, 1953; d. Alexander and Marjorie (Soviero) Perillo; m. Stephen Crain Pennisi, Jan. 17, 1976; children: Stephen, Scott, Greg. Diploma, Beth Israel Sch. Nursing, N.Y.C., 1974. RN, N.Y.; cert. ambulatory women's health nurse. Staff nurse Montefiore Hosp., Bronx, N.Y., 1974-75; mem. staff Beth Israel Med. Ctr., N.Y.C., 1975-77; office nurse Martin Kurman, M.D., N.Y.C., 1977-80, Adam Romoff, M.D. and Suzanne Yale, M.D., P.C, 1984—. Mem. NAACOG. Avocations: tennis, horseback riding, reading. Office: Drs Romoff and Yale 768 Park Ave New York NY 10021-4153

PENNISTEN, JOHN WILLIAM, computer scientist, linguist, actuary; b. Buffalo, Jan. 25, 1939; s. George William and Lucy Josephine (Gates) P. AB in Math. and Chemistry with honors, Hamilton Coll., 1960; postgrad., Harvard U., 1960-61, U.S. Army Lang. Sch., 1962-63; MS in Computer Sci. with honors, N.Y. Inst. Tech., 1987; cert. in taxation, NYU, 1982; cert. in profl. banking, Am. Inst. of Banking of Am. Bankers Assn., 1988.; cert. Asian Langs., NYU, 1992. Actuarial asst. New Eng. Mut. Life Ins. Co., Boston, 1965-66; asst. actuary Mass. Gen. Life Ins. Co., Boston, 1966-68; actuarial assoc. John Hancock Mut. Life Ins. Co., Boston, 1968-71; asst. actuary George B. Buck Cons. Actuaries, Inc., N.Y.C., 1971-75, Martin E. Segal Co., N.Y.C., 1975-80; actuary Laiken Siegel & Co., N.Y.C., 1980; cons. Bklyn., 1981—; timesharing and database analyst banklink corp. cash mgmt. div. Chem. Bank N.Y.C., 1983-85; programmer analyst Empire Blue Cross and Blue Shield, N.Y.C., 1986-88, Mt. Sinai Med. Ctr., N.Y.C., 1988-89, French Am. Banking Corp. (subs. Banque National de Paris), N.Y.C., 1989; sr. programmer analyst Dean Witter Reynolds, Inc., N.Y.C., 1989-92; computer specialist for software N.Y.C. Dept. Fin., 1992-97; sr. cons. Pinkerton Computer Cons., Inc., N.Y.C., 1997-99; tech. officer J.P. Morgan Chase & Co., N.Y.C., 1999—; enrolled actuary U.S. Fed. Pension Legis. Bklyn., 1976—. Contbr. articles to profl. jours. With U.S. Army, 1961-64. Mem. AAAS, MLA, Soc. Actuaries (fellow), Assn. Computing Machinery, IEEE Computer Soc., Am. Assn. Artificial Intelligence, Linguistic Soc. Am., Assn. Computational Linguistics, Am. Math. Soc., Math. Assn. Am., Nat. Model R.R. Assn. (life), Nat. Ry. Hist. Soc., Ry. and Locomotive Hist. Soc. (life), Bklyn. Heights Assn., Met. Opera Guild, Am. Friends of Covent Garden, Harvard Grad. Soc., Am. Legion, Phi Beta Kappa, others. Home: 135 Willow St Brooklyn NY 11201-2255

PENN-TONKIN, LEWIS MONTAGUE, retired solicitor; b. Melbourne, Australia, Aug. 17, 1920; s. Frederick Montague and Caroline (Goudy) P.; m. Judith Priscilla Stevens, Sept. 20, 1928; children: Roslyn, Craig, Janet, Susan. B of Laws, Melbourne U., 1946. Ptnr. Davies, Campbell & Piesse, Australia, 1949-82; cons. Freehill, Hollingdale & Page, Australia, 1982-91; chmn. Bendix Consol. Industries Ltd., Australia, 1959-65; dir. Via Ltd., Australia, 1968-76, Marfleet & Weight Ltd., Australia, 1971-75, Holderbank Australian Ltd., Australia, 1977-87, Holderbank New Zealand Ltd., 1977-87, Richardson Pacific Ltd., Australia, 1982-92; mem. comml. law com. Law Inst. of Victoria, 1960-82. Lt. Australian Imperial Forces, 1941-45. Mem. The Australian Club, Royal Melbourne Golf Club, Frankston Golf Club. Home: Unit 2 58 Kooyong Rd, Armadale 3143, Australia

PENNY, RALPH JOHN, Spanish language educator; b. London, July 31, 1940; s. Edward John and Grace Edith (Anderson) P.; m. Anne Beveridge, Apr. 13, 1963; children: Richard, Kate. M.A. with honors, Edinburgh U., Scotland, 1962; Ph.D., Edinburgh U., 1967. Asst. lectr. Spanish Magee Univ. Coll., Derry, No. Ireland, 1965-66; lectr. in Spanish Westfield Coll., London, 1966-81, reader in Spanish, 1981-86, prof. Spanish, 1986—. Author: El Habla Pasiega, 1970, Estudio Estructural del Habla de Tudanca, 1978, A History of the Spanish Language, 1991, Variation and Change in Spanish, 2000. Mem. Assn. Hispanists Gt. Britain and Ireland, Philol. Soc. Asociación Internacional del Hispanistas, Asociación de Historia de la Lengua Espanñola. Home: 8 Garston Ln, Garston, Watford, Hertfordshire WD2 6QL, England Office: U London, Queen Mary and Westfield Coll, London E1 4NS, England

PENNY, SUSAN CAROLINE VOELKER, investment manager; b. N.Y.C., July 26, 1949; d. Friedrich and Anna Voelker; m. Ralph E. Penny, Aug. 31, 1974 (div. 1989); m. Radomir Stevanovic, Mar. 14, 1992. BA, Syracuse U., 1970; MBA, Columbia U., 1972. CFA. Securities analyst Shearson, Hammill & Co., Inc., N.Y.C., 1972-73; investment analyst, v.p. The Equitable Life Assurance Soc. of the U.S., N.Y.C., 1973-85; mng. dir. Equitable Capital Mgmt. Corp., N.Y.C., 1985-91, sr. v.p., 1991-93; sr. v.p. Alliance Corp. Fin. Group, Inc., N.Y.C., 1993-96; prin. August Ptnrs., LP, N.Y.C., 1996-98, corp. fin. cons., 1998-2000; mng. ptnr. Associated Mezzanine Investors LLC, New Canaan, 2000—. Vice-chair trustees Syracuse U., N.Y., 1997—, chair trustees investment and endowment com., 1996—, trustee exec. com., 1994—, acad. affairs com., 1995-2000, mem. adv. bd. Maxwell Grad. Sch. of Citizenship and Pub. Affairs, 1991—. Mem. AIMR. Republican. Lutheran. Avocations: reading, hiking, opera. Office: 436 Frogtown Rd New Canaan CT 06840-4411

PENSINGER, JOHN LYNN, lawyer; b. Hagerstown, Md., June 5, 1949; s. Linford Snider and Marguerite Joan (McNeal) P.; m. Eileen Sue Howard, Nov. 7, 1972. BA, U. Md., 1971; JD, U. Balt., 1976; LLM, George Washington U., 1987. Bar: Md. 1976, D.C. 1977, U.S. Ct. Claims 1977, U.S. Tax Ct. 1977, U.S. Dist. Ct. Md. 1978, U.S. Dist. Ct. D.C. 1978, U.S. Ct. Appeals (4th cir.) 1978, U.S. Ct. Mil. Appeals 1978, U.S. Ct. Appeals (D.C. cir.) 1978, U.S. Customs Ct. 1979, U.S. Supreme Ct. 1980, U.S. Ct. Internat. Trade 1981, U.S. Ct. Appeals (fed. cir.) 1982, U.S. Ct. Appeals (5th cir.) 1986, U.S. Ct. Appeals (3d cir.) 1988, U.S. Army Ct. Mil. Rev. 1989. Mgr. E.M. Willis & Sons, Washington, 1977-79; pvt. practice Rockville, Md., 1978-79; atty. Amalgamated Casualty Ins. Co., Washington, 1979-86; asst. gen. counsel Legal Svcs. Corp., Washington, 1986-88, sr. litigation counsel, 1988-95; atty. Office Justice Programs, U.S. Dept. Justice, 1995-96, assoc. gen. counsel, 1996—. Mem. ABA, Am. Soc. Internat. Law, Fed. Bar Assn., Med. Bar Assn. Roman Catholic. Home: 4 Stratton Ct Rockville MD 20854-6227

PENTECOST, ERIC JOHN, economics educator; b. Rochester, Eng., Jan. 12, 1956; s. Herbert Edward and Annie Eileen (Perkins) P.; m. Gillian Margaret Nichols, Sept. 3, 1983; children: John Edward, Anne Margaret. BA, Thames Poly., London, 1977; MA, Warwick U., Coventry, Eng., 1977-78; PhD, London U., 1981. Lectr. Thames Poly., 1981-85; rsch. analyst Bank of Eng., London, 1985-87; lectr. in econs. Loughborough (Eng.) U., 1987-96, reader econs., 1996—; cons., Open U., Milton Keynes, 1988-89. Contbr. articles to econs. publs. Mem. Royal Econ. Soc., Am. Econ. Soc. Office: Dept Econs Loughborough U, Loughborough LE11 3TU, England

PENTELÉNYI, THOMAS JOHN, neurosurgeon; b. Budapest, Hungary, Feb. 25, 1939; s. László and Anna Maria (Bohuniczky) P.; m. Mary P. Pálfalvy, Dec. 19, 1947; children: Marianne, Kinga. MD, Semmelweiss Medical Sch., Budapest, 1963, specialist of surgery, 1967; specialist of neurosurgery, Haynal Imre Univ., Budapest, 1974; PhD, Hungarian Acad. of Scis., 1978. Resident of surgery Szovetség Hosp., Budapest, 1964-66, Bajcsy Hosp., Budapest, 1966-68; resident of neurosurgery Nat. Inst. of Traumatology, Budapest, 1968-73, scientific co-worker, 1974-86, head of neurosurgery, 1986-96; prof., chmn. of neurosurgery Nat. Inst. of Traumatology, Haynal Imre Univ., Budapest, 1987-96; head, chmn. dept. neurosurgery Nat. Inst. of Traumatology, Budapest, 1986—; prof. of neurotraumatology Semmelweis U., Budapest, 1986—; pres. Internat. Conf. on Lumbar Fusion and Stabilization/ICLFS Movement, Budapest, 1995—; mem. internat. adv. bd. Paraplegia and Spinal Cord, 1992—, mem. editorial bd. Clinical Neuroscience, 1992—; vis. prof. Univ. Chgo. Medical Sch., 1990, Univ. Tenn., 1989, Temple U., Phila., 1990, Thomas Jefferson U., Phila., 1990, U. Calif., Davis, 1990, U. Calif., Sacramento, 1990, U. Xaveriana, Bogota, Columbia, 1990; coord. Ctrl.-European Internat. Brain Injury Data-Base, 1997—; sr. cons. bd. Memphis Neuroscis. Ctr., 1989-96. Hungarian coord. Ctrl. European Internat. Brain Injury Data Base. Recipient Highest Medical Profl. award Min. of Health, 1987, Budapest, Felicitation Medalist of Indian Neurology Soc., 1994. Mem. WHO (steering com.), World Fedn. Neurosurg. Socs. (neurotraumatology com., chmn. subcom. edn.), Internat. Med. Soc. of Paraplegia, Scientific Program Com. (coun. mem.), European Fedn. Neurol. Soc. (scientist panel 1994—), Euroacad. Multidisciplinary Neurotramatology (exec. com.), Hungarian Spine Soc. (pres. 1993-95), U. Padova (hon.), Purkinje Med. U. (hon.), N.Y. Acad. Scis. (diploma), Indian Neurology Soc. (hon.). Avocations: music, philosophy, fine arts, history of family, ethical problems. Office: Nat Inst of Traumatology Dept Neurosurgery, VIII Fiumei ut 17, 1081 Budapest Hungary

PENTERIANI, VINCENZO, ornithology researcher, educator; b. Rome, Italy, Apr. 25, 1964; s. Stefano and Assunta (Dragone) P.; m. Hélène Cazassus, July 10, 1993; children: Giulia, Félix. D of Natural Scis. in Ornithology, U. La Sapienza, Rome, 1992; DSc, U. Burgundy, Dijon, France, 1999. Sci. cons. Abruzzi nat. Park, Pescasseroli, Italy, 1985-96, Multidisciplinary Assn. Environ. Biologists, Raismes, France, 1993—, Natural Park of Luberon, Apt, France, 1994—, NEMORA s.n.c.-Wildlife and Habitats Mgmt., Rome, 1993—; instr. flycasting T.L.T. Flycasting H.S., various locations, 1996—. Contbr. articles to profl. jours. Mem. Fedn. of Flyfishers, Italian Soc. Natural Scis., Italian Sta. for Ornithol. Studies, Wildlife Soc. Avocations: flyfishing, flytying, birdwatching, photography. Home and Office: La Grande Montagne, Frénois France 21120

PENTIN, DAVID JOHN, accountant, financial advisor; b. Canterbury, Kent, Eng., June 26, 1935; s. Sydney Edward and Amelia Pentin; m. Alicia Henrietta Rodney, June 11, 1960; children: Caroline Louise, John Mark, Richard Harley, Edward Michael. LLB, London U., 1963. Articled clk. Pentin Neame & Co., Canterbury, Eng., 1953-59, ptnr., 1961-85; sr. ptnr. Pentins, Canterbury, 1985-96. city councillor Canterbury City Coun., 1983-99, chmn. fin. com., 1985-90, dep. leader of coun., 1987-90, leader of coun., 1990-91, lord mayor, 1995-96; treas. Canterbury (Eng.) Festival, 1997—. With Royal Air Force, 1959-61. Fellow Inst. Chartered Accts. Eng. and Wales; mem. Forest of Blean Rotary (hon. mem., founder, pres.). Conservative. Anglican. Avocations: walking, cycling, skiing, cricket, music. Home: 16 St Dunstan's Ter, Canterbury Kent CT2 8AX, England Office: Pentins, Lullingstone House 5 Castle St, Canterbury Kent CT1 2FG, England

PENTTINEN, HANNU KALEVI, humanitarian educator; b. Tuusula, Finland, Sept. 17, 1948; s. Kalevi Gunnar and Ina Marjatta (Pensala) P.; m. Merja Kaarina Mäkinen, Sept. 3, 1983; children: Milja, Samu, Viivi. MD, U. Helsinki, 1974, DrMedSci, 1981. Cert. Ednl. Commn. Fgn. Med. Graduates. Asst. U. Helsinki, 1972-77; med. officer Helsinki Health Bur., 1978-89, assoc. sr. physician, 1984-86; mng. dir. Med. Adv. Svc. Ltd., Helsinki, 1989—; dir. Aseman Lapsetry, Helsinki, 1993—; chief editor Citari Mag., Helsinki, 1993—. Mem. Fedn. Family Care Assn. (pres. 1988-91). E-mail: hannu.penttinen@asemanlapset.fi. Address: Ayriaisenk 6B, 01490 Vantaa Finland

PÉNZES, LÁSZLÓ GÉZA, retired biologist, educator; b. Budapest, Hungary, July 14, 1930; s. Antal József and Gizella Mária (Stefanovits) P.; m. Ilona Csáky, Nov. 15, 1951; 1 child, Tamás. Degree in agrl. engring., Univ. Agrl. Scis., Gödöllő, Hungary, 1955, Doctorate, 1960; PhD, Hungarian Acad. Scis., Budapest, 1960, DSc in Biol. Sci., 1982. Trainee Ministry for Food Industry, Budapest, 1955-56; postgrad. Inst. for Animal Husbandry, Budapest, 1956-59, sci. rschr., 1959-66; chief scientist, sci. adviser, vice dir. Gerontology Ctr. Semmelweis U. Medicine, Budapest, 1966-98; ret.; nat. rep. Hungarian Assn. Gerontology, Budapest, 1966-84; guest prof. Bologna (Italy) U., 1993; TEMPUS coord. Joint European Project, 1991-94. Co-author: The Ageing, 1984, Centenarians in Hungary, 1990, Gerontopsychiatry, 1992; contbr. articles to profl. jours.; mem. editorial bd. various scientific jours. Recipient Humboldt Univ. medallion U. Berlin, 1985, Ferdinand medal U. L'Aquila, Italy, 1995, Diploma of Merit, Semmelweis U. Medicine, 1993; UN scholar Internat. Atomic Energy Agy., Vienna, Austria, 1961-62. Mem. Hungarian Assn. Gerontology (pres. 1985-89), Hungarian Acad. Scis. (pub. body 1994—). Achievements include Habilitation at Budapest Univ. (ELTE), 1996. Avocations: tourism, classical music. Home: Madách Imre ut 2-6, 1075 Budapest Hungary

PENZIAS, ARNO ALLAN, astrophysicist, technology consultant, research scientist, information systems specialist; b. Munich, Germany, Apr. 26, 1933; came to U.S., 1940, naturalized, 1946; s. Karl and Justine (Eisenreich) P.; m. Sherry Chamove Levit, Aug. 2, 1996; children: David Simon, Mindy Gail, Laurie Shifra. BS in Physics, CCNY, 1954; MA in Physics, Columbia U., 1958, PhD in Physics, 1962; Dr. honoris causa, Observatoire de Paris, 1976; ScD (hon.), Rutgers U., 1979, Wilkes Coll., 1979, CCNY, 1979, Yeshiva U., 1979, Bar Ilan U., 1983, Monmouth Coll., 1984, Technion-Israel Inst. Tech., 1986, U. Pitts., 1986, Ball State U., 1986, Kean Coll., 1986, U. Pa., 1992, Ohio State U., 1988, Iona Coll., 1988, Drew U., 1989, Lafayette Coll., 1990, Columbia U., 1990, George Washington U., 1992, Rensselaer Univ., 1992, U. Pa., 1992, Bloomfield Coll., 1994, Rankin Tech. U., 1997, Hebrew Union Coll., 1997. Mem. tech. staff Bell Labs., Holmdel, N.J., 1961-72, head radiophysics rsch. dept., 1972-76; dir. radio research lab. Bell Labs., 1976-79, exec. dir. rsch., communications scis. div., 1979-81, v.p. rsch., 1981-95; v.p., chief scientist Lucent Technologies, 1995-98, sen. tech. adv., 1998—; venture ptnr. New Enterprise Assocs., 1998—; bd. dirs. A.D. Little, LCC Internat., Alien Tech. Corp.; sr. advisor New Enterprise Assoc., 1997-98, adj. prof. earth and scis. SUNY, Stony Brook, 1974-84, Univ. Disting. lectr., 1990;

lectr. dept. astrophys. scis. Princeton U., 1967-72, vis. prof., 1972-85; rsch. assoc. Harvard Coll. Obs., 1968-80; Edison lectr. U.S. Naval Rsch. Lab., 1979; Kompfner lectr. Stanford U., 1979; Gamow lectr. U. Colo., 1980; Jansky lectr. Nat. Radio Astronomy Obs., 1983; Michelson Meml. lectr., 1985; Grace Adams Tanner lectr., 1987; Klopsteg lectr. Northwestern U., 1987; grad. faculties alumni Columbia U., 1987-89; Regents' lectr. U. Calif., Berkeley, 1990; Lee Kuan Yew Disting. vis. Nat. U. Singapore, 1991; mem. astronomy adv. panel NSF, 1978-79, mem. indsl. panel on sci. and tech., 1982-92, disting. lectr., 1987, affiliate Max-Planck Inst. for Radioastronomy, 1978-85, chmn. Fachbeirat, 1981-83; rschr. in astrophysics, info. tech., its applications and impacts. Author: Ideas and Information Managing in a High-Tech World, 1989 (pub. in 10 langs.), Harmony-Business, Technology and Life After Paperwork, 1995; mem. editl. bd. Ann. Rev. Astronomy and Astrophysics, 1974-78; mem. editl. bd. AT&T Bell Labs. Tech. Jour., 1978-84, chmn., 1981-84; assoc. editor Astrophys. Jour., 1978-82; contbr. over 100 articles to tech. jours.; several patents in field. Trustee Trenton (N.J.) State Coll., 1977-79; mem. bd. overseers U. Pa. Sch. Engring. and Applied Sci., 1983-86; mem. vis. com. Calif. Inst. Tech., 1977-79; mem. Com. Concerned Scientists, 1975—, vice chmn., 1976—; mem. adv. bd. Union of Couns. for Soviet Jews, 1983—; bd. dirs. Coun. on Competitiveness, 1989-92. With U.S. Army, 1954-56. Named to N.J Lit. Hall of Fame, 1991; recipient Herschel medal Royal Astron. Soc, 1977, Nobel prize in Physics, 1978, Townsend Harris medal CCNY, 1979, Newman award, 1983, Joseph Handleman prize in the scis., 1983, Grad. Faculties Alumni award Columbia U., 1984, Achievement in Science award Big Brothers Inc., N.Y.C., 1985, Priestly award Dickinson Coll., 1989, Pender award U. Pa., 1992, NJ Sci. and Tech. Medal, 1996, Internat. Eng. Cons. Fell. Award, 1997, Industrial Res. Inst. Medalist, 1998, patents for: auction-based selection of telecom. carriers, participant tracking in conference call, remote card game using ordinary playing cards, computer-based transportation system, fraud prevention in calling cards, identifying telephone extensions in residence environment, double-encrypted identity verification sys. Mem. NAE, NAS (Henry Draper medal 1977), AAAS, IEEE (hon.), Am. Astron. Soc., Am. Phys. Soc. (Pake prize 1990), Internat. Astron. Union, World Acad. Arts and Sci. Office: New Enterprises Assocs 2490 Sand Hill Rd Menlo Park CA 94025-6940

PEONIDIS, FILIMON, philosophy educator; b. London, Sept. 30, 1961; s. Alexandros and Eleni (Mavrocordatos) P. BA, Aristotle U. of Thessaloniki, 1984; MS, London Sch. Econs., 1986; PhD, U. Crete, 1993. Asst. prof. Am. Coll. Thessaloniki, Thessaloniki, Greece, 1991-97; lectr. Aristotle U. Thessaloniki, 1998—. Author: Lying and Morality, 1994; contbr. articles to profl. jours. Active UNICEF, Athens. Mem. Greek Philos. Soc., Am. Philos. Assn. Avocations: kayaking, photography. Home: 6 Papadiamanti St, 55133 Kalamaria Greece Office: Dept Philosophy, Aristotle U Thessaloniki, 54006 Thessaloniki Greece

PEOW, ONG TOON, controller; b. Kuala Terengganu, Malaysia, Mar. 15, 1969; p. Ong See Say and Lim Juah Ya. Diploma in acctg., RIMA, 1992, Chartered Inst. Mgmt. Accts., 1998. Delivery asst. Syarikat Lim Seng, Taman Saraya, Malaysia, 1985; factory operator Syarikat Lim Seng, Taman Saraya, 1986; sales asst. Parkson Grand, Cheras, Malaysia, 1987; waiter Westin Hotel, Raffles Place, Singapore, 1989-90; asst. trainer AIA Life Assurance Bhd, Jalan Ampang, Malaysia, 1990; accts. asst. Malaya Acid Works Bhd, Petaling Jaya, Malaysia, 1993-94; asst. mgr. fin., adminstrn. Mah Sing-Yoshikawa, Port Kelang, Malaysia, 1995-97; fin. mgr. corp. divsn. Nona Roguy Group of Cos., Subang Jaya, Malaysia, 1997—; fin. mgr. Nona Roguy, Mustajab Industries Sdn Bhd, Mustajab Industries, Pandan Intan, Delta Computers & Comms., Delta Meters, Teknoelektrik Industries; group mgr. Integrated Healthcare Mgmt., Sunway, Malaysia, 1998—. Avocations: snooker, table tennis, bowling, golfing. Fax: 603 7329535. E-mail: mike-ong@ppp.nationet.net. Home: Taman Pertama, 17 Jalan Selar 2, Batu 3.5 Cheras 56100, Malaysia Office: Lot 42 44 & 46, Jalan SS 19/1D Subang Jaya, Selangor Darul Ehsan 47500, Malaysia

PEPER, BRAM, government official; b. Haarlem, The Netherlands, Feb. 13, 1940. Degree in social sci., U. Amsterdam, 1965; PhD, Netherlands Sch. Econs., 1972. 2d deputy chmn Labor party, 1975; advisor to min. Ministry Culture, 1974-77; mayor Rotterdam, The Netherlands, 1982-98; min. Ministry Home Affairs, The Hague, The Netherlands, 1998—; lectr., rschr. in field. Office: Ministry Home Affairs, Schedeldoekshaven 200, 2511 EZ The Hague The Netherlands*

PEPER, CHRISTIAN BAIRD, lawyer; b. St. Louis, Dec. 5, 1910; s. Clarence F. and Christine (Baird) P.; m. Ethel C. Kingsland, June 5, 1935 (dec. Sept. 1995); children: Catherine K. Peper Larson, Anne Peper Perkins, Christian B.; m. Barbara C. Pleiter, Jan. 25, 1996. AB cum laude, Harvard U., 1932; LLB, Washington U., 1935; LLM, Yale U., 1937. Bar: Mo. 1934. Pvt. practiced St. Louis; of counsel Blackwell Sanders Peper Martin LLP; lectr. various subjects Washington U. Law Sch., St. Louis, 1943-61; ptnr. A.G. Edwards & Sons, 1945-67; pres. St. Charles Gas Corp., 1953-72; bd. dirs. El Dorado Paper Bag Mfg. Co., Inc. Editor: An Historian's Conscience: The Correspondence of Arnold J. Toynbee and Columba Cary-Elwes, 1986. Mem. vis. com. Harvard Div. Sch., 1964-70; counsel St. Louis Art Mus. Sterling fellow Yale U., 1937. Mem. ABA, Mo. Bar Assn., St. Louis Bar Assn., Noonday Club, Harvard Club, East India Club (London), Order of Coif, Phi Delta Phi. Roman Catholic. Home: 1454 S Mason Rd Saint Louis MO 63131-1211 Office: Blackwell Sanders Peper Martin LLP 720 Olive St Saint Louis MO 63101-2338

PEPERMANS, GUIDO JEAN-MARIE, economics researcher; b. Vilvoorde, Belgium, Mar. 31, 1963; m. Ann Clara Cottens, June 17, 1992; children: Arne, Senne. Lic. trade and fin. scis., Vlekho, Brussels, 1985; lic. actuarial scis., Cath. U. Leuven, 1987, PhD in Econs., 1995. Rsch. asst. econs. dept. Cath. U. Leuven, 1985-93, sr. rsch. econs. dept., 1997—; econs. prof. EHSAL, Brussels, 1993-97. Author: (book) Economie van opgave tot uitkomst, 1997. Recipient Winterthur prize, 1988. Fax: 32 16 32 67 96. E-mail: guido.pepermans@econ.kuleuven.ac.be. Office: Cath U Leuven Econs Dept, Naamsestraat 69, Leuven Belgium

PEPINE, CARL JOHN, physician, educator; b. Pitts., June 8, 1941; s. Charles John and Elizabeth (Hovan) P.; m. Lynn Dives, Aug. 3, 1963; children: Mary Lynn, Anne, Elizabeth. BS, U. Pitts., 1962; MD, N.J. Coll. Medicine, 1966. Intern Allegheny Gen. Hosp., U. Pitts., 1966-67; resident in internal medicine Jefferson Med. Coll. Hosp., Phila., 1967-68; resident in internal medicine naval med. ctr., 1968-69, fellow in physiology and cardiovasc. disease, 1969-71; asst. prof. medicine Jefferson Med. Coll., Phila., 1972-74; asst. prof. medicine U. Fla., Gainesville, 1974-75, assoc. prof., 1975-79, prof., 1979—, co-dir. divsn. cardiovasc. medicine, 1982-88; chief cardiology VA Regional Med. Ctr., Gainesville, 1979-94, chief divsn. cardiovasc. medicine, 1998—; dir. cardiology catheterization lab. Shands Hosp., U. Fla., Gainesvile, 1974-86. Mem. editl. bds. Am. Heart Jour., 1997—, Am. Jour. Cardiology, 1981-94, 97—, Am. Jour. Geriat. Cardiology, 1992—, Geriat. Cardiology, 1996—, Clin. Cardiology, 1995—, Circulation, 1980-83, 93—, Cardiac Chronicle, 1989—, Heart Disease: A Jour. of Cardiovasc. Medicine, 1999—, Hypertension, 1999—, Jour. Am. Coll. Cardiology, 1981-85, 91-95, 98—, Jour. Preventive Cardiovasc. Medicine, 1997—, Preventive Cardiology, 1998-2000; chief med. editor Cardiology Today, 1997—; contbr. articles to profl. jours.; developer catheters to measure blood flow and heart circulation. Comdr. USN, 1968-74. Recipient Raculty Rsch. prize in clin. sci., U. Fla., 1989-90, Piioneer Investigator award Internat. Soc. Holter Monitoring, 1990, Rsch. Achievement awards U. Fla., 1990-93, Paul Dudley whhite award Assn. Mil. Surgeons, 1991; grantee Dept. of Def., 1971-74, VA, 1975-90, NHLBI, 1985—. Fellow Am. Coll. Cardiology (master, trustee 1986-88, 90-95, chmn. cardiac catheterization com. 1990-96, chmn. Fla. chpt. found. 1992—, chmn. bd. govs. 1986-87, chmn. ann. sci. sessions 1990), Am. Heart Assn. (coun. on clin. cardiology and on circulation, bronze award 1983), Am. Fedn. Clin. Rsch., Soc. Cardiac Angiography, Am. Soc. Clin. Investigation; mem. Assn. Univ. Cardiologists, Am. Clin. and Climatol. Assn. (Theodore E. Woodward award 1998), Assn. of Profs. of Cardiology, European Soc. Cardiology, Pi Kappa Alpha, Alpha Omega Alpha. Office: U Fla 1600 SW Archer Rd PO Box 100277 Gainesville FL 32610-0277

PEPOL, ANNA TERESA, librarian; b. Matyszolika, Poland, Nov. 1, 1945; d. Albin and Janina Jackowska Wnukowski; m. Jerry Pepol, Apr. 28, 1973; children: Magdalena, Marek, Stefan. MS, U. Poland. Libr. acquisitions dept. Olsztyn, Poland, 1972-76, libr. serials dept., 1976-83, head dept., 1983-90; with Brit. Coun., Warsaw, 1984-90; with info. dept. Olsztyn, 1990-93, system mgr., 1993—, dep. libr., 1998—. Contbr. articles to profl. jours. Roman Catholic. Avocations: classical music, terroist. Office: Main Libr Warmie/Mesumie Un, 4 Ocraposwkiego Str, 10-957 Olsztyn Poland

PEPONIS, HAROLD ARTHUR, insurance agent, broker; b. Chgo., Dec. 12, 1928; s. Arthur Harold and Ethel (Karambis) P.; m. Toula H. Preketes, Mar. 1, 1952 (dec. Dec. 1984); 1 child, Arthur Harold II; m. Aphrodite E. Stavros, May 26, 1990. BS, Loyola U., Chgo., 1950, postgrad., 1991—. Treas. Plaza Cleaners & Dyers, Inc., Chgo., 1950-58; owner Exch. Cleaners, Chgo., 1958-63, Park West Plaza Cleaners, Chgo., 1963-69; ins. agt. Aetna Life & Casualty, Lisle, Ill., 1969—; ptnr. lecture series/pub. co. Images of Orthodoxy; instr. religion Plato Acad., Chgo., 1998-99; pres. Tesera Assoc., Evanston, Ill., 1973—. Mem. editl. bd. Christianity and Arts mag., 1996-98. Pres. parish coun. United Greek Orthodox Chs. of Chgo., 1963-64, Annunciation Cathedral, 1991-92, 94; archon Order of St. Andrew, Greek Orthodox Ch., state comdr., 1994—; mem. diocesan coun. Diocese of Chgo. Greek Orthodox Ch., 1994—, mem. archdiocesan coun., 1997—; archdiocesan rep. Coun. Hellenes Abroad. Recipient medal of St. Paul, Greek Orthodox Archdiocese, 1999. Mem. Pan Arcadian Fedn. Am. (nat. pres. Chgo. 1963-64), Du Page Life Underwriters Assn.. Home: 2626 N Lakeview Apt 2503 Chicago IL 60614-1821 Office: 2956 Central St Evanston IL 60201-1246

PEPPER, ALLAN MICHAEL, lawyer; b. Bklyn., July 5, 1943; s. Julius and Jeanette (Lasovsky) P.; m. Barbara Benjamin, Aug. 30, 1964; children—Leslie Anne, Joshua Benjamin, Adam Richard, Robert Benjamin. B.A. summa cum laude, Brandeis U., 1964; LL.B. magna cum laude, Harvard U., 1967. Bar: N.Y. 1968, U.S. Dist. Ct. (so. and ea. dists.) N.Y. 1968, U.S. Ct. Appeals (2d cir.) 1968, U.S. Supreme Ct. 1988. Law clk. U.S. Ct. Appeals for 2d Circuit, N.Y.C., 1967-68; assoc. Kaye, Scholer, Fierman, Hays & Handler, N.Y.C., 1968-74, ptnr., 1975—; lectr. in field. Mem. exec. com., assoc. nat. chmn. Brandeis U. Alumni Fund, 1979-82, nat. chmn., 1982-85, chmn. 25th Reunion gift com., 1989, devel. com., trustee, 1982-85, pres., councillor, 1980—, mem. 35th Reunion gift com., 1999; trustee Brandeis U., 1985-95, sec., 1992-93, budget and fin. com., 1988-95, chmn. com. strategic plan, 1990-91, acad. affairs com., 1985-92, student life and phys. facilities com., 1985-89, vice chmn. ad hoc by-laws com., 1988-89, long range planning com., 1989-91, chmn. audit com., 1991-95, exec. com., 1990-91, mem. 35th Reunion gift com., 1999; bd. dirs. Styles Brook Homeowners Assn., 1990—, exec. com., 1994—; nominating com. Edgemont Sch. Bd., 1992-93; trustee Edgemont Sch. Found., 1994—; mem. 30th reunion gift com. Harvard Law sch., 1996-97, class agt., 1998—. Recipient Henry Jones-Golda Meier Bnai Brith Youth Services award, 1986, L.I. Press Valedictory medal, 1960; Felix Frankfurter scholar Harvard U. Law Sch., 1964-65; Louis D. Brandeis hon. scholar Brandeis U., 1964. Mem. ABA, Assn. of Bar of City of N.Y. (mem. law firm mgmt. com. 1987-91, litigation com. 1998—), N.Y. State Bar Assn. (comml. and fed. lit. sect., vice chmn. com. on discovery 1993-97), Brandeis U. Alumni Assn. (exec. com. 1982-87, alumni giving strategic planning com., 1992, Alumni Svc. award 1988), Phi Beta Kappa (L.I. Alumni award 1960). Democrat. Jewish. Lodge: B'nai B'rith (pres. Henry Jones Lodge 1982-84, mem. Westchester-Putnam council 1982-85, bd. govs. dist. 1, 1985-86). Office: Kaye Scholer Fierman Hays & Handler LLP 425 Park Ave New York NY 10022-3506

PEPPER, DOROTHY MAE, nurse; b. Merill, Maine, Oct. 16, 1932; d. Walter Edwin and Alva Lois (Leavitt) Stanley; m. Thomas Edward Pepper, July 1, 1960; 2 children, including Walter Frank. RN, Maine Med. Ctr. Sch. Nursing, Portland, 1954. RN, Calif. Pvt. duty nurse Lafayette, Calif.; staff nurse Maine Med. Ctr., Portland, 1954-56, Oakland (Calif.) VA Hosp., 1956-58; pvt. duty nurse, dir. RN's Alameda County, Oakland. Mem. Profl. Nurses Bur. Registry, Maine Writers and Pubs. Alliance. Avocation: writing.

PEPPER, DOTTIE, professional golfer; b. Saratoga Springs, N.Y., Aug. 17, 1965. Student, Furman University. Top ranked player LPGA Tour, 1992. 3 time NCAA All-American; recipient Rolex Player of the Year Award, 1992; recipient Vare Trophy, 1992; leading money winner LPGA, 1992. Achievements include winning tournaments including Mazda Classic, 1989, Crestar Classic, 1990, Nabisco Dinah Shore, 1992, Sega Women's Championship, 1992, Welch's Classic, 1992, Sun-Times Challenge, 1992, LPGA Leading Money Winner, 1992, Wendy's Three-Star Challenge, 1992, PING/Welch's Championship, 1995, JC Penney/LPGA Skins Game, McCall's LPGA Classic, wom four tournaments: Rochester Internat., ShopRite LPGA Classic, Friendly's Classic and Safeway LPGA Golf Champ., 1996, 24 tournaments earning $293,652, 1997, tied 2nd at Rochester Internat., tied 3rd at Star Bank LPGA Classic, tied fourth at ShopRite LPGA Classic, 1997, Solheim Cup, 1998, Nabisco Dinah Shore, 1999. Address: care LPGA 100 International Golf Dr Daytona Beach FL 32124-1082

PEPPER, GORDON TERRY, research center administrator, educator; b. Sutton Coldfield, Eng., June 2, 1934; s. Harold Terry and Jean Margaret (Furness) P.; m. Gillian Clare Huelin, Aug. 30, 1958; children: Alasdair, Ninna, Harry, Mark. MA, Cambridge U., 1957. Actuarial trainee Equity and Law Life Assurance Soc., London, 1957-60; ptnr. W. Greenwell & Co., London, 1960-86, joint sr. ptnr., 1980-86; chmn. Greenwell Montagu & Co., London, 1986-87; dir., sr. adviser Midland Montagu (Holdings) Ltd., London, 1987-90; dir. Midland Montagu Ctr. for Fin. Markets, City U. Bus. Sch., London, 1988-98, prof. dept. banking and fin., 1987-98; dir. Lombard Steel Rsch. Ltd., 1998—; chmn., 2000—; chmn. Payton Pepper & Sons Ltd., Birmingham, Eng., 1987-97; founder, ditor Greenwell's Monetary Bull., 1972-82, 87-90; hon. vis. prof. City U. Bus. Sch., London, 1987-90, 98—. Author: Money, Credit and Inflation, 1990, Money, Credit and Asset Prices, 1994, Inside Thatcher's Monetarist Revolution, 1998, Monetorism Under Thatcher-Lessons for the Future, 2001. Fellow Inst. Actuaries (prize for paper 1974, Finlaison medal 1987), Reform Club, Royal Ocean Racing Club. Home: Staddleden Sissinghurst, Cranbrook Kent TN17 2AN, England Office: City U Bus Sch, Frobisher Crescent, Barbican, London EC2Y 8HB, England

PEPPER, JOHN ENNIS, JR., consumer products company executive; b. Pottsville, Pa., Aug. 2, 1938; s. John Ennis Sr. and Irma Elizabeth (O'Connor) P.; m. Frances Graham Garber, Sept. 9, 1967; children: John, David, Douglas, Susan. BA, Yale U., 1960; PhD (hon.), Mt. St. Joseph Coll., St. Petersburg (Russia) U., Xavier U. Staff asst. Procter & Gamble Co., Cin., 1963-64, asst. brand mgr., 1964-66, brand mgr., 1966-68, copy supr., 1968-69, brand promotion mgr., 1969-72, advt. mgr. bar soap and household cleaning products divsn., 1972-74, gen. mgr. Italy subs., 1974-77, divsn. mgr. internat., 1977-78, v.p. packaged soap and detergent divsn., 1978-80, group v.p. bar soap and household cleaning products divsn., 1980-81, group v.p. Europe, 1981-84, exec. v.p. U.S. bus., 1984-86, pres. U.S. Bus., 1986-90, pres. internat. bus., 1990-95, chmn. bd., chief exec., 1995-99; chmn. Proctor & Gamble Co., Cin., 1999—, exec. com. of bd., 2000—; bd. dirs. Xerox Corp., Motorola, Inc., Boston Scientific Corp. Chmn. U.S. Advisory Com. for Trade Policy and Negotiations; co-chair Devel. campaign, mem., exec. com. Nat. Underground Railroad Freedom Ctr.; group chmn. Cin. United Appeal Campaign, 1980; bd. trustees Xavier U., 1985-89, mem. exec. com., 1989; trustee Cin. Coun. World Affairs, Cin. Art Mus., Ctr. Strategic & Internat. Studies, Christ Ch. Endowment Fund; fellow Yale Corp.; gen. chmn. United Way Campaign, 1994; mem. Gov.'s Edn. and Bus. Advisory Group, State of Ohio; mem. adv. coun. Yale Sch. Mgmt.; mem. schs. com. Cin. Bus. Com.; co-chmn., mem. exec. com. Cin. Youth Collaborative; mem. Total Quality Leadership steering com.; mem., bd. dirs. United Negro Coll. Fund; former v.p. Am. C. of C., Brussels, Belgium (1981-84); former mem. Cin. Symphony Bd. (1979-81), Cin. Art Mus. Served to lt. USN, 1960-63. Mem. Am. Soc. Corp. Execs., Grocery Mfrs. Am., Nat. Alliance Businessmen (chmn. communication com.), Partnership for a Drug-Free Am., Soap and Detergent Assn. (bd. dirs.), The Bus. Coun., Bus. Roundtable, Yale Club, Queen City Club, Commonwealth Club, Comml. Club (former pres.). Office: Procter & Gamble Co 1 Procter And Gamble Plz Cincinnati OH 45202-3393

PEPPER, JON V., mathematics historian, educator; b. Isleworth, London, Jan. 1, 1936; s. A.J. and Anne (Panian) P.; m. Barbara J. Bamford, Apr. 20, 1963; 1 child, Antony. MA, Oxford (Eng.) U., 1961; MSc, U. Coll., London, 1964, PhD, 1967. Tchr., lectr. Eng., 1959-65; sr. lectr. Royal Naval Coll., Greenwich, Eng., 1965-69; head dept. math. South Bank U., London, 1969-72, U. East London, 1972-88; hon. lectr. dept. math. U. Coll., London, 1988—; mem. governing body U. East London, 1972-75, 83-88; sec. Standing Conf. of Heads of Dept., Eng., 1978-82. Contbr. articles to profl. jours. Mem. Internat. Acad. History of Sci., London Math. Soc. Avocations: hill-walking, poetry, music, chess. Office: U Coll London Dept Math, Gower St, London WC1E 6BT, England

PEPPIATT, NICHOLAS ANTHONY, product designer; b. London, Mar. 29, 1947; s. Henri Camil and Phyllis Elizabeth (Ponsford) P.; m. Christine Gillian Wright, May 22, 1971; children: Andrew James, Jennifer Karen. BSc, U. Bristol, Eng., 1968; PhD, U. Bristol, 1974. Grad. trainee Rolls-Royce Ltd., Derby, Eng., 1968-70, preliminary designer, 1970-71; research assoc. U. Bristol, 1974-77; research engr. Wilkinson Match Research Div., Slough, Eng., 1977-79; sect. leader product devel. Wilkinson Sword Ltd., London, 1979-82; product design mgr. Hallite Seals Internat., London, 1982-87, tech. mgr., 1987—. Contbr. articles to profl. jours; patentee in field. Mem. Instn. Mech. Engrs. Avocation: aeromodeling. Home: 52 Mt Pleasant Close, Lightwater GU18 5TR, England Office: Hallite Seals Internat, Oldfield Rd, Hampton TW12 2HT, England

PEQUEUX, JEAN PIERRE, economist, educator; b. Brussels, Belgium, July 13, 1950; s. Alfred and Bertha (Gils) P.; m. Barbro Gillstrom; 1 child, Nicolas. Degree in polit. sci., U. Brussels, 1973; M in Econs., Cooremans Inst., Brussels, 1980. Lectr. Ceria Inst., Brussels, 1972—; head dept. Haute Ecole L. de Brouckere, Brussels, 1996; vice prin. Inst. A Haulot, Brussels, 1995-99; cons. tourism and hotel mgmt., 1992—. Office: Haute Ecole Lucia de Brouckere, Ave E Gryzon Dept Dietetics, B 1070 Brussels Belgium

PERA, CARLOS ALBERTO, airline pilot; b. Santos, Brazil, Mar. 13, 1947; arrived in Singapore, 1994; s. José and Maria (Guerra) P.; m. Rosemary Fonseca, June 15, 1968 (div. 1980); children: Sergio R.F., Carlos A.F., Marcus V.F.; m. Geuceli de Oliveira, June 13, 1991; 1 child, Ana Paula Oliveira Pera. Student, Coll. Maria Tereza, Niteroi, Brazil, 1965-77. DC3 co-pilot VASP Brazilian Airlines, São Paulo, Brazil, 1967-72, YS11-A capt., 1972-74, B737 capt., 1974-84, B727 capt., 1984-86, A300 capt., 1986-90, MD11 capt., chief pilot, 1990-93; B747-400 capt. Singapore Airlines, 1994—; MD11 check pilot McDonnell Douglas/CAA Brazil, Long Beach, Calif., 1990. Mem. Europa Sailing Club. Roman Catholic. Avocations: aeromodels, computers, playing tennis, sailing. Office: Singapore Airlines, Changi Airport, Singapore 819643, Singapore

PERAHIA, MURRAY, pianist; b. N.Y.C., Apr. 19, 1947; m. Naomi Shohet, 1980; 2 children. MS, Mannes Coll. Music; student, Jeannette Haien, Artur Balsam, Mieczyslaw Horszowski; Doctorate (hon.), U. of Leeds, United Kingdom. Appeared with Berlin Philharm., Chgo. Symphony Orch., English Chamber Orch., Boston Symphony Orch., N.Y. Philharm., Cleve. Orch., Los Angeles Philharm., Phila. Orch., others; performed with Budapest, Guarneri and Galimir string quartets; frequent performer, artistic dir.: Aldeburgh Festival, 1983-89; past participant: Marlboro Music Festival; recital tours in U.S., Can., Europe and Japan; recs. for SONY Classical; 1st Am. to record the Complete Mozart Concertos as condr. with English Chamber Orch., recorded complete Beethoven concertos with Haitink concertgebouw Orch. Recipient Kosciusko Chopin prize, 1965, Avery Fisher prize, 1975, Gramophone Record award, 1997, Grammy award, 1999, numerous maj. rec. awards including Leeds Competition, 1972. Office: care Edna Landau IMG 825 7th Ave New York NY 10019-6014

PERAL FERNANDEZ, FERNANDO, chemistry educator; b. Madrid, Spain, June 9, 1951; s. Teodoro and Julia (Fernandez) P.; m. Isabel Redondo, Mar. 29, 1980; children: Diego, Blanca. MS, U. Complutense, Madrid, Spain, 1973, PhD, 1979. Lab. asst. U. Complutense, Madrid, Spain, 1976-77; asst. prof. U. Nat. Edn., Madrid, Spain, 1977-82, lectr., 1985—, head dept., 1994—; adj. prof. U. Nat. Edn., 1982-85. Author: Asociaciones Moleculares, 1992; co-author: Termodinamica Quimica (6 vols.), 1984-85, Tecnicas Instrumentales Fisicoq, 1990; contbr. articles to profl. jours., papers to scientific jours. 2d lt. Spanish Army, 1972-74. F.P.P.I. fellow U. Complutense, 1974-76. Mem. Royal Soc. Chemistry Spain, Assn. Quimicos Espana, N.Y. Acad. Scis. Roman Catholic. Avocations: photography, painting, gardening, sports. Office: U Nac Edn Distancia, Paseo Senda Del Rey 9, 28040 Madrid Spain

PERALTA, LIONEL, financial executive; b. San Jose, Costa Rica, Nov. 19, 1960; s. Lionel and Olga Marta Peralta; m. Maribel Quiros, Aug. 6, 1983; children: Lionel Enrique, Tatiana, Isabela. BBus, U. Costa Rica, 1981, M in Informatics, 1982; DVM, Nat. U. Heredia, Costa Rica, 1983; MMBA, U. Wis., 1984. Mgr. Pvt. Investment Corp., San Jose, 1984-86; pres., CEO Administradora de Capitales, San Jose, 1985—; bd. dirs. DARE Costa Rica, San Jose, 1990—. Mem. Supreme Tribunal of Elections, San Jose, 1986-90. Roman Catholic. Avocations: jogging, breeding horses. Office: PO Box 8479, San Jose 1000, Costa Rica

PERALTA DE MERIDA, ANA MARIA, parasitologist, researcher; b. Guatemala City, July 14, 1940; d. Arturo and Victoria (Orive) Peralta Azurdia; m. Luis Felipe Merida Izaguirre, May 12, 1963; children: Carmen Lucia, Jose Antonio, Luis Arturo, Ana Maria Susana. Degree, U. del Valle de Guatemala. Asst. prof. biology U. del Valle Guatemala, Guatemala City, 1978, asst. prof. parasitology, 1978-1980, prof. gen. microbiology, 1980-83, dir. program lab. tech. parasitology courses, 1983, prof. gen. parasitology, 1984-85; rsch. asst. leischmaniasis med. entomology rsch. tng. unit Mertu/CDC, Guatemala City, 1987-89, rsch. asst., head lab. parasitology, 1991-94; assoc. rschr., head molecular biology lab. Mertug/CDC. 1993-2000. Mem. Am. Soc. for Microbiology, Rotary. Avocation: swimming. Home: 10A Calle 2-22 Zona 14, Guatemala City Guatemala Office: U del Valle de Guatemala, Apartado Postal 82, Guatemala City Guatemala

PERANI, DANIELA, neuroscientist, researcher, educator; b. Milan, July 18, 1953; d. Placido and Garda (Zamparutti) P.; m. Stefan Cappa, Mar. 10, 1987; 1 child, Tommaso. MA, Lices Clemis, Milan, 1972; D of Medicine, Lices Clemis, 1978, degree in neurology, 1982, degree in radiology, 1986. Rschr. Biomed. Tech., Milan, 1984-87; hon. rschr. Royal Post Grad. Med. Sch., London, 1987-88; rschr. ITBA-CNR, Milan, 1988-92; head rsch. INB-CNR, Milan, 1992—; prof. neurology Univ. Milan, 1989—; prof. psychology HSR Univ., Milan, 1998—; invited lectr. Academic des Sci., Paris, 1997; coord. projects aging CNR, Italy, 1991-96; coord. BIOMED I Projects, Europe, 1993, 96. Author: Hankbook of Clinical and Exp. Neuropsychology, 1999; contbr. articles to jours. Mem. EAG V Framework Program EED, Brussels, 1999. Avocations: painting, walking, skiing. Office: Inst Neurosci CNR, Vie Olgettina 60, 20132 Milan Italy

PERÄSALO, JUHANI OLAVI SAKARI, retired physician; b. Helsinki, Finland, Feb. 24, 1943; s. Olavi Valdemar and Aira Tellervo (Haantie) P.; m. Ritva Ilona Lahti, Nov. 5, 1965; children: Marja, Johanna, Kati, Paula. Licentiate in Medicine, U. Helsinki, 1968, MD, 1973. Diplomate in internal medicine. Asst. physician, 1st dept. medicine Helsinki U. Ctrl. Hosp., 1971-74, asst. tchr., 1976-77; physician-in-chief, dir. Finnish Student Health Svc., 1977-97; ret., 1997. Author: (in Finnish) Internal Medicine for Nurses. Chmn. Suomen Sauna Seura, Helsinki, 1986-90. Decorated knight 1st class Order of the Lion of Finland, 1982. Mem. European Union for Sch. and Univ. Health Medicine (pres. 1991-95).

PERCIVAL, ARTHUR JOHN, environmentalist; b. North Kensington, Eng., Oct. 9, 1933; s. Eric Harman and Kathleen Langridge (Heath) P.; m. Dorothy Salthouse, Mar. 21, 1964; children: 1 child, Helen Clare. BA, Wadham Coll., Oxford, 1956, MA, 1994; DLitt (hon.), U. Kent, 1991. Curator of prints and drawings, rschr. Blue Plaques, County Hall, London, 1956-65; libr. Civic Trust, Eng., 1965-67, liaison officer, 1967-87, asst. dir., 1987-92, cons., 1992-94; hon. dir. Fleur-de-lis Heritage Ctr., Faversham, 1977—; cons. Penang Heritage Trust, Malaysia, 1992—, Nara Machizukuri Ctr., Japan, 1992-93; lectr. Workers Edn. Assn., 1973—, Brit. Coun., Japan, 1989, 92. Author: Heavy Lorries, 1970, Understanding Our Surroundings, 1979, Great Explosion at Faversham, 1986, Old Faversham, 1988, Anthology of Faversham Verse, 1999, Faversham Legends of Crispin and Crispinnus, 1999, Traveller's Joy, 2000; hon. editor Faversham Papers, 1964—, London and Middlesex Archaeol. Soc., 1960-63. Mem. Noise Adv. Coun., U.K., 1970-79. Fellow Soc. of Antiquaries of London; mem. Assn.

for Heritage Interpretation, Faversham Soc., Marlowe Soc. (v.p. 1993—), Japan Nat. Trust (hon.). Avocations: enjoying places, photography, listening to music. Office: Fleur de lis Heritage Ctr, 13 Preston St, Faversham ME13 8NS, England

PERCIVAL, BERNARD S., government official; b. Curaçao, Netherlands Antilles, Aug. 20, 1949; married; 2 children. BA, Iona Coll., New Rochelle, N.Y. Senator Govt. Antigua and Barbuda, 1981-89, minister without portfolio Ministry Edn., Sports, Culture &, 1989-91, minister of edn., culture and youth affairs, 1991-94, minister of tourism, culture and environment, 1994—, minister edn., youth, sports and comml. devel., 1994—, minister health and social improvement. Mem. Antigua Labor Party. Office: Min Hlth & Soc Improvement, Cross St, Saint John's Antigua and Barbuda*

PERCIVAL, RAY SCOTT, philosophy educator; b. Bolton, Lancashire, Eng., Apr. 15, 1956; s. Frank and Grace Scott (Barker) P. BS in Psychology with honors, Bolton Inst. Higher Edn., Eng., 1978; MA in Philosophy, U. Warwick, Coventry, Eng., 1982; PhD, London Sch. Econs., 1992. Dir. Diatron, Ltd., Bolton, 1981-83, StrongMart, Bolton, 1983-85, Mossfield Crystal Rm., Bolton, 1985-86; hist. rschr. London, 1985-86; sci. writer New Scientist, 1986—; faculty mem. Connected Edn., Inc., N.Y.C., 1994—; lectr. U. Lancaster, Eng., 1995-96; web site cons., 1995—; chmn., organizer ann. conf. on philosophy of Sir Karl Popper, London, 1988—; founder, owner, pres. Karl Popper Web, Dublin, 1995—. Founder, editor-in-chief: (jour.) The Critical Rationalist, 1996, (E-mail based philosophy forum) Critical Cafe, 1995; assoc. editor, author: (jour.) Jour. of Social and Evolutionary Systems, 1994, (newsletter) Popper Newsletter, 1993; author: Popper for Beginners, 2000. Postgrad. grantee Econ. and Social Sci. Rsch. Coun., London, 1988; grantee Open Soc. Inst., 1995, 97; recipient Charles R. Lambe fellowship Inst. for Humane Studies, London, 1988, Ency. Britannica Internet Guide award, 2000. Mem. AAAS, Am. Philos. Assn., Royal Inst. Philosophy. Avocations: sci. fiction, cycling, dancing, cinema, musical composition. Home: 70 Hillview Ct, Astley Bridge Bolton BL1 8NU, England

PERCY, RODNEY A., retired circuit judge; b. Alnmouth, Eng., May 15, 1924; s. Hugh James and Gertrude (Mitchell) P.; m. Mary Allen Benbow, Mar. 27, 1948; children—Shian, Duncan Charles and Wendy Sara (twins), Suzanne. B.A. (honors), Oxford U., 1948, M.A., 1951; Barrister, Middle Temple, 1950; ad eundem, Lincoln's Inn 1987; Chambers practice from Newcastle-Upon-Tyne, 1950-79; circuit judge North East Circuit, Eng., 1979-93; dep. coroner North Northumberland, 1957-75; asst. recorder Sheffield Quarter Sessions, 1964; dep. chmn. County of Durham Quarter Sessions, 1966-71; recorder of Crown Ct., 1972-79. Pres. Tyneside Marriage Guidance Council, 1983-88; founder, mem. Conciliation Service for Northumberland and Tyneside, 1982-93. Served as lt. Royal Corps of Signals, 1942-46; Burma, India, Malaya, Java. Editor: Charlesworth on Negligence, 1962 (4th edit.); 1971 (5th edit.), 1977 (6th edit.); Charlesworth and Percy on Negligence, 1983 (7th edit.), 1990 (8th edit.), 1996 (9th edit.). Home: "Brookside", Lesbury Alnwick, Northumberland NE66 3AT, England

PERCZEL, ANDRÀS KRISTÓR, chemist; b. Budapest, Hungary, May 10, 1959; s. Dénes and Dénesné (Perczel) P.; m. Dóra Forintos, Aug. 25, 1984; children: Kristóf, Julia, György. MS, Eötvös Lorand U., Hungary, 1985, PhD, 1989, Habilitation, 1999; DSc, Hungarian Acad. Scis., 1998. Rsch. assoc. ELTE, Budapest, 1985-89, assoc. prof. chemistry, 1992-95; postdoctoral rschr. Brandeis U., Waltham, Mass., 1989-92; vis. scientist Oxford (Eng.) U., 1995—; rsch. prof., 1999—. Recipient Pro Sciencia award Hungarian Acad. Scis., 1993, 95, Zemplén Géza award, 1996, Gold Scientific award Eötvös L. U., 1997, Széchényi prof. Ministry of Edn., Hungary, 1998—. Office: ELTE-TTK-KTCS, Dept Organic Chem POB 32, H-1518 Budapest 112, Hungary

PERDANG, JEAN MARCEL, astrophysicist; b. Remerschen, Luxembourg, May 3, 1940; s. Léandre Eugène and Erica Marguerite (Schneider) P.; m. Esmée Marie-Jeanne Ewert, July 15, 1965; children: Pascale, Paul, Patrick. Licence in Physical Scis., U. Liège, Belgium, 1963, Cert. in Stats. Mechanics, 1968, Doctorat in Physical Scis., 1969. Asst. U. Liège, 1963-64, aspirant, 1964-69, chargé de recherches, 1970-74, maître de conférences, 1978—; rschr., 1974—; chargé de cours extraordinaire U. Officielle du Burundi, Bujumbura, 1971; libero docente U. Padova, Padua, Italy, 1974, 75, 78, 94; vis. prof. U. Fla., Gainesville, 1978, 81, 84, Internat. Sch. for Advanced Studies, Trieste, Italy, 1982; astronomer Observatoire de Paris à Meudon, 1989, 91; rschr. U. Montreal, 1971, Columbia U., 1974, Inst. for Theoretical Physics, U. Calif., Santa Barbara, 1990. Author: Stellar Oscillations: The Asymptotic Approach, 1978; co-editor: Chaos in Astrophysics, 1985, Applying Fractals in Astronomy, 1991, Cellular Automata: Prospects in Astrophysical Applications, 1993; author numerous papers in field. Postdoctoral fellow NSF, 1969, Leverhulme fellow in astronomy, 1972-73, European exch. fellow Royal Soc.-Fonds Nat. de la Recherche Scientifique, Belgium, 1979-80, 83, 85, 86, 87, 88, 89, 90, 91, 94, 95, 96, 97, 98, 99, 2000. Fellow Royal Astron. Soc.; mem. Internat. Astron. Union, Com. Belge d'Astronomie (assoc.), Inst. Grand Ducal Sect. des Scis. (hon.), Société Royale des Scis. de Liège, Belgian Royal Acad. (assoc., Silver medal 1995). Avocations: philosophy and history of science. Office: Inst d'Astrophysique, 5 Avenue de Cointe, B-4000 Liége Belgium

PEREA, EVELIO JOSÉ, microbiology educator; b. Santa Cruz, Spain, Jan. 18, 1944; s. Evelio P. and Amalia B. P.; m. Maria Victoria Borobio, Sept. 8, 1969; children: Esther, Evelio. MB, U. Seville, 1967; M Social Scis., U. Granada, 1968; MD, U. Madrid, 1970, PhD in Microbiology, 1971. Head of sect. Clinica Puerta de Hierro, Madrid, 1973-75; assoc. prof. Autonomous U., Madrid, 1972-75; prof. U. Seville, 1975—, v.p., 1981-84, head of dept., 1992—; dir. Sch. Dentistry, Seville, 1979-81; cons. Nat. Ctr. for Med. Rsch., Madrid, 1971-75; asst. Pasteur Inst., Paris, 1968, 71; expert WHO, 1990-91; chmn. Internat. Soc. Sexually Transmitted Diseases Rsch., 1995-97. Editor: (book) Enfermedades Infecciosas, 1991, Enfermedades de Transmisión Sexual, 1992; editor: European Jour. of Clin. Microbiology, 1990—; editor-in-chief: Review Española de Enfermedades Infecciosas, 1987-92. Lt. Spanish Army, 1965-67. Named Rschr. of Yr. Nat. Health Svc., 1978; recipient 1st prize for rsch. City of Seville, 1984. Mem. Soc. Española Enfermedades Infecciosas Microbiology Clinic (pres. 1982-85), European Soc. Clin. Microbiology Infecciosas Disease (pres. 1990-92), Real Club de Golf Las Brisas (pres. 1994-96). Avocations: golf, modern art, opera. Office: U Seville Sch Medicine, Apdo 914, 41080 Seville Spain

PEREA CARRASCO, RAFAEL, physician, biochemist; b. Bollullos, Huelva, Spain, June 3, 1953; s. Manuel Perea Diaz and Maria Carrasco Infante; m. Rocio Perez Coronel, Nov. 12, 1985; children: Rocio, Rafael, Carlos. Pharm. diploma, U. Granada, Spain, 1977; cert. analytical biochemist, Huelva Hosp., 1982; MD, U. Seville, Spain, 1993, cert. specialist in Chinese medicine, 1997. Resident biochemist State Hosp., Huelva, 1980-82; head dept. Andalusian Health Svc., Riotinto, Spain, 1983—; rschr. in field. Contbr. articles to profl. jours. Mem. Spanish Assn. Med. Biopathology, Spanish Assn. Pharm. Analysis, Andalusian Soc. Biochemistry (provincial rep. 1996—).

PEREBEYNOS, VASILIY VASILEVICH, physicist, researcher; b. Volkovo, Russia, Oct. 1, 1948; s. Vasiliy Andreevich and Natalya Nikiforovna (Jolob) P.; m. Ekaterina Vasilevna Koyukova, Nov. 11, 1972 (div. Aug. 1983); 1 child, Vasiliy. MS, Moscow State U., 1972, PhD, 1976. Jr. rschr. Russian Energy Inst., Moscow, 1975-79; rschr. OKB Granat, Moscow, 1979-90, head dept., 1990. Contbr. numerous articles to sci. publs.; inventor in field. Office: OKB Granat, Volokolamskoe Sh 95, 123424 Moscow Russia

PEREIRA, ARTUR TORRES, medical educator, microbiologist; b. Lisbon, Portugal, Apr. 13, 1924; s. Arthur Torres and Maria Antonieta (Oliveira) P.; m. Natercia Ryder Costa, Jan. 29, 1949; children: Artur, Pedro, Jorge. MD, U. Lisbon, 1948, PhD, 1961. Assoc. prof. hygiene and microbiology U. Lisbon, 1965-68, prof. medicine, 1968-94, prof. emeritus, 1994—, vice rector, 1970-74, pres. sci. coun. faculty medicine, 1986-89; dean faculty of medicine U. Lisbon, 1989-94; dir. Inst. Bacteriology Camara Pestana, 1977-94; chmn. discipline coun. Med. Assn. Portugal, 1984-87; chmn. Nat. Commn. on Med. Edn., Portugal, 1990-94; mem. Internat. Subcom. on Nomenclature and Taxonomy of Staphylococci and Micrococci, 1963-94, Internat. Subcom. for Phage-typing of Staphylococci, 1975-94. Contbr. articles to profl. jours. Pres. Portuguese Family Planning Assn., Lisbon, 1970. Mem. Acad. Scis. Lisbon, Portuguese Acad. Medicine (emeritus), Evaluation Com. Portugese Med. Schs. Social Democrat. Roman Catholic. Home: Gregorio Lopes 1514 Apt 10D, 1400 Lisbon Portugal

PEREIRA, CARMO JOSEPH, chemical engineer and researcher; b. Bombay, India, Nov. 5, 1951; came to U.S., 1974; s. Cajetan Joseph Paixão-Pereira and Mary (D'Souza) Pereira; m. Janice Maria Machado, Sept. 5, 1985; children: Marie Ann, Karen Mary. B.Tech., Indian Inst. Tech., 1974; MS, U. Notre Dame, Ind., 1975; PhD, U. Notre Dame, 1978; MBA, Drexel U., Phila., 1984. Vis. asst. prof. U. Notre Dame, 1978-79; rsch. engr. Mobil R&D Corp., Paulsboro, N.J., 1979-82; sr. rsch. engr. W.R. Grace & Co., Columbia, Md., 1982-85, rsch. assoc., 1985-94, sr. rsch. assoc., 1994-97; prin. cons. Du Pont Engring., Wilmington, Del., 1997—; mem. indsl. adv. bd. CCST-U. Del., Newark, 1989-92; instr. Environex, Inc., Wayne, Pa., 1989-92; adj. prof. U. Md., College Park, 1995—. Editor: Computer-Aided Design of Catalysts, 1993; contbr. articles to profl. jours. including Chem. Engring. Sci., Applied Catalysis, chpts. to books. Vol. Grace Athelton Partnership, Columbia, 1989-91. Named Disting. Young Engr., Md. Acad. Scis., 1989; Arthur J. Schmidt fellow U. Notre Dame, 1977. Mem. AIChE (instr. 1989-93, Engr. of Yr. Md. sect. 1990), Am. Chem. Soc., Air and Waste Mgmt. Assn., Sigma Xi. Roman Catholic. Achievements include 15 patents in new products for pollution control and petroleum processing. Avocations: reading, music. Home: 1912 Middlebridge Dr Silver Spring MD 20906-5819 Office: Dupont Co 88452 1000 Market St # 88452 Wilmington DE 19898-0001

PEREIRA, SIR (HERBERT) CHARLES, agricultural scientist; b. London, May 12, 1913; s. Herbert John and Maud Edith (Machin) P.; m. Irene Beatrice Sloan, 1941; children: David, Julie, Martin, Nigel. BSc, U. London, 1934, PhD, 1940, DSc, 1961; DSc (hon.), U. Cranfield, 1976. From head physics divsn. to dep. dir. East African Agrl. and Forestry Rsch. Orgn., 1952-61; dir. Agrl. Rsch. Coun. Ctrl. Africa, 1961-67, East Malling Rsch. Sta., Maidstone, Kent, Eng., 1969-72; chief scientist Ministry Agr., Fisheries and Food, 1972-77, cons. tropical agrl. and hydrol. rsch., 1978—; chmn. sci. adv. panel Commonwealth Devel. Corp., 1979-93; tech. adv. com. World Bank Cons. Group Internat. Agrl. Rsch., 1971-76. Author: Land Use and Water Resources, 1973, Policy and Practice in Management of Tropical Watersheds, 1989; articles on landuse, soil physics, forest hydrology. Maj. Brit. Army, 1939-46. Created knight bachelor, 1977; recipient Haile Selassie prize, 1966, Rhodesian Nat. Farmers Union prize, 1967. Fellow Royal Soc., Royal Agrl. Soc. Eng., Inst. Biology; mem. Atheneum Club, Alpine Club, Harare Club. Mem. Ch. of Eng. Office: Peartrees Nestor Ct, Teston Maidstone, Kent ME18 5AD, England

PEREIRA, INÊS ANTUNES CARDOSO, biochemist; b. Lisbon, Portugal, May 12, 1966; d. Jose Luis Cardoso Pereira and Maria Lurdes F. Antunes Cardoso; m. João Pedro Fontinha Dantas Martins. DPhil, U. Oxford, 1993. Postdoctoral ITQB/UNL, Lisbon, 1994-99, invited asst. prof., 1999—. Grantee Junta Nat. Investigacao Cientifica Tecnologica/Program Ciência, 1989-93, 93-95, postdoctoral grant Junta Nat. Investigacao Cientifica Tecnologica/Praxis XXI, 1997—. Office: ITQB, Av Republica EAN Apt 127, 2781-901 Oeiras Portugal

PEREIRA, JOÃO LOUIS, plant diseases specialist, scientist; b. Mapuca, Goa, India, Nov. 11, 1941; arrived in Brazil, 1975; s. Gerson Candido and Maria Nathalia Pereira; m. Maria Millicent Da Costa; children: Clinton Thomas, Garrick Cecil. Diploma in tropical agr., Egerton U., Kenya, 1963; MSc in Crop Protection, U. Reading, Eng., 1973; PhD in Plant Pathology, U. Bristol, Eng., 1988. Cert. in agr. Rsch. officer Coffee Rsch. Found., Kenya, 1963-75; rsch. coord. M. Agricolas, Jacto, Brazil, 1975-79; prin. rschr. Cocoa Rsch. Ctr., Itabuna, Brazil, 1979—; Latin Am. rep. FAO Panel of Experts, 1980—, Internat. Plant Pathology Soc., 1989—; chief tech. advisor, cons. FAO, 1973-93; coord. 12th Internat. Cocoa Conf., Brazil, 1996; exec. dir. Found. Pau Brazil, 1997—; pres. Internat. Permanent Working Group on Cocoa Pests and Diseases Internat., 1996—; coord. internat. confs., 1984-91; spkr. in field. Author: (book sect.) FAO Plant Production and Protection Paper, 1992; contbr. articles to sci. publs.; inventor in field. Mem. Soc. Pesticide Application (founder mem. 1996—). Avocations: environmental conservation, sculpture, gourmet cooking, furniture design. Home: Rua Espanha, S/N Cx Postal 193 CEP, 45600000 Itabuna Bahia, Brazil Office: Cocoa Rsch Ctr, Cx Postal 7 CEP, 45600000 Itabuna Bahia, Brazil

PEREIRA, MICHAEL, engineering administrator; b. Fall River, Mass., June 19, 1972. BS, Worchester Poly. Inst., 1994. Sr. devel. engr. North Safety Products, Crauston, R.I., 1994-98; engring. mgr. Item NPD, Providence, 1998—. Mem. AIAA, ASME, Soc. Plastic Engrs. Office: Item NPD 10 Davol Sq Ste 400 Providence RI 02903-4752

PEREIRA, ORLANDO JOSÉ BARREIROS ALMEIDA, civil engineer, educator; b. Lisbon, Portugal, July 14, 1967; s. Orlando Almeida and Emilia Silva Barreiros Almeida (Barreiros) P. BS in Civil Engring., Sch. Engring., Sci., Tech., Lisbon, 1990; MSc, Tech. U. Lisbon, 1993, PhD, 1997. Sr. chartered engr. Asst. lectr. Sch. Engring., Sci. and Tech., Lisbon, 1990-97, lectr., 1997—. Contbr. articles to profl. jours. Roman Catholic. Office: Inst Superior Tecnico, Avenida Rovisco Pais, 1049-001 Lisbon Portugal

PEREIRA, RENATO CLAUDIO COSTA, air transportation executive; b. Varginha, Brazil, Nov. 30, 1936; s. Ismael Costa Pereira and Mercedes de Carvalho Pereira; m. Maria Antonieta Arrojado Lisbôa da Costa Pereira, June 27, 1964; children: Christiano A. L. Costa Pereira, Claudio A. L. Costa Pereira, André A. L. Costa Pereira, Ismael da Costa Pereira Neto. Degree, Air Force Acad., Brazil, 1959; postgrad., USAF, 1963, Brazilian Air Force, 1965, Brazilian Air Force Staff Sch., 1977, F.G.V., Brazil, 1983. Officer Brazilian Air Force, 1954-97; exec., project mgr. Centro Tecnico Aeroespacial, Sao Jose dos Campos, Brazil, 1975-85; officer Air Ministry Cabinet, head Procurement Office Ministry of Aeronautics, Brazil, 1985-89; pres. Latin Am. Civil Aviation Commn., 1993-97; chief negotiator CERNAI, Rio de Janeiro, 1990-97; sec. gen. Internat. Civil Aviation Orgn., Montreal, Que., Can., 1997—. Mem. Club Aeronautica, Planetary Soc. Avocations: reading, tennis, walking. Home: 26 Maplewood, Outremont, PQ Canada H2V 2M1 Office: Internat Civil Aviation Orgn, 999 University St, Montreal, PQ Canada H3C 5J9

PEREIRA MARTINS, CARLOS ALBERTO, banker; b. Viseu, Portugal, Sept. 24, 1951; s. Alberto Martins and Dulce Vasconcelos; m. Maria Teresa Gomes da Cruz, Dec. 24, 1951; 1 child, Nuno Pereira Martins. Grad. in econs., Lisbon (Portugal) U., 1974, M Fins., 1989. Gen. mgr., dir. Banco Fomento Nat., Lisbon, 1974-87; fin. dir. Caixa Econ. Montepio Geral, Lisbon, 1987-95, dir. planning and strategy, 1995-98, internat. dir., 1996—, also mem. gen. bd.; bd. dirs. Property & FIG Funds, Lisbon, EGFI Eurotop, Paris, Soficatra, investment soc., Brussels; mem. suprevisory bd. SGA/Autodromo Estoril, Spain, 1998—. Mem. Portuguese Order Economists (bd. dirs.). Office: CE Montepio Geral, Rua Danta Justa 109, 2o, 1100 Lisbon Portugal

PEREIRA-NETTO, ADAUCTO B., botany educator; b. Maceio, Brazil, Oct. 6, 1962; s. Jose A. and Neuza A. Pereira; m. Ana Paula Almeida, Feb. 6, 1988; 1 child, Guisela. BS, U. Brasilia, Brazil, 1985; MS, Campinas (Brazil) State U., 1988; PhD, U. Wis., 1996. Rschr. Bioplant-Plant Tech., Campinas, 1987-88; prof. Maringa (Brazil) State U., 1988-92, Fed. U. Parana, Curitiba, Brazil, 1992—; cons. Aracruz (Brazil) Cellulose, Ministry Sci. and Tech., Brasilia. Recipient award 15th Internat. Conf. on Plant Growth, Internat. Plant Growth Substances Assn., Mpls., 1995, award 16th Internat. Conf. on Plant Growth, Internat. Plant Growth Substances Assn., Makuhari Messe, Chiba, 1998. E-mail: apereira@bio.ufpr.br. Fax: 55 41 2662042. Office: Dept Botany SCB-UFPR, Centro Politecnico, 81531970 Curitiba Parana, Brazil

PEREIRA PINTO, CARLOS MANUEL AZEVEDO, investment manager, consultant; b. Oporto, Portugal, Mar. 4, 1968; s. Manuel De Jesus and Vivelina Adelaide (Azevedo Freixo) P.P. HND in Transp. Mgmt., Bus., North Brook Fedn., Eng., 1987; BSc in Social Policy and Adminstrn., London Sch. Econs., 1989; M in Internat. Rels., U. Lusiada, Lisbon, 1994; M in Internat. Law, U. Social Sci., Toulouse, France, 1994. Coord., mgr. Operfin, Oporto, Portugal, 1993-96; founder, shareholder, adminstr. Docrasto Constrn., Oporto, 1994—, Gardenia-Green Spaces, Oporto, 1995—, Casinor Real Estate Devel., Oporto, 1995—; co-founder, shareholder, adminstr. CTM Mozambique Transport Co., Mozambique; mgmt. cons. Seoropol, Oporto, Portugal, 1996-98; bus. cons. CTM, Mozambique, 1996—. Mem. London Sch. Econs. Club, Oporto Royal Assn., Oporto Sailing Club. Avocations: horse riding, fencing, sailing, collecting, investing. Home: Rua Duarte Barbosa 37 1H, 4150 Oporto Portugal Office: Docrasto Constrn, Rua Marechal Saldanha 418, 4150 Oporto Portugal

PEREL, MARIANO, finance executive, consultant; b. Buenos Aires, Mar. 21, 1945; s. Vicente L. and Luisa (Goijberg) P.; m. Rosa Berta Golodnitzky, Sept. 28, 1974; children: Jonathan, Valeria. MBA, U. Buenos Aires, 1972, CPA, 1975. Pres., CEO Centro de Computos S.A., Buenos Aires, 1978-83; exec. com. Mercorio Group, Bahamas, Argentina, Uruguay, 1993-97, CEO, 1994-96, also bd. dirs.; exec. v.p. Intermonetary Corp., Buenos Aires, 1997—; sr. v.p. ATM Svc. Ltd., White Plains, N.Y., 2000—; ptnr.-in-charge Spicer & Oppenheim, Latin Am., 1980-90; chmn. Estudio Perel, Buenos Aires, 1972—; bd. dirs. Banco del Buenos Aires, 1983-93; pres., CEO JAC Security Corp., Buenos Aires, 1991—; assoc. producer CBS News, 1964-74; producer Telenoche Investiga, 1994-96; sr. v.p., ATM Svc., Ltd., N.Y.C., 1999—. Columnist, editor Ambito Financiero newspaper, 1976-86. Mem. Argentina Inst. Econ. Scis. Profl. (cert.). Jewish. Avocations: sailing, golf, travel. Home: 36 Greenridge Ave Apt 202 White Plains NY 10605 Office: Intermonetary Corp 424 Madison Ave 9th Fl New York NY 10017

PERENNOU, MARIE, filmmaker, biologist; b. Paris; m. Claude Nuridsany. Film maker: (short film) Looking-Glass Inhabitants, 1984, Microcosmos (5 awards); author: (with Claude Nuridseny) Éloge de L'Herbe, 1988, Microcosmos. Recipient Grand Prize Cannes Film Festival, 1996. Office: Editions de la Martinière, 2 rue Christine, 75006 Paris France*

PERÉNYI, ANDRÁS, psychiatrist; b. Szolnok, Hungary, May 28, 1949; s. György and Magdolna (Kapos) P.; m. Kinga Paulheim, July 11, 1973; 1 child, Eszter. Med. degree, Semmelweis Med. Sch., Budapest, Hungary, 1973; degree in psychiatry, Postgrad. Med. Sch., Budapest, Hungary, 1977, degree in neurology, 1982. Rsch. fellow in psychopharmacology McLean Hosp. and Harvard Med. Sch., Belmont and Cambridge, Mass., 1980; trainee in psychiatry Nat. Inst. for Nervous and Mental Diseases, Budapest, 1973-77, trainee in neurology, 1978-79, 81-82, sr. rsch. fellow, 1983-84, cons. psychiatrist, 1985-87, 90-91; cons. psychiatrist Larundel Hosp., Melbourne, Australia, 1988-89; sr. lectr. Postgrad. Med. Sch., Budapest, 1991; cons. psychiatrist Royal Park Hosp., Melbourne, 1992-93, Northeastern Met. Psychiat. Svcs., Melbourne, 1993-95; assoc. U. Melbourne, 1992-95, Monash Med. Ctr. adult psychiatry, 1995—. Editor: Psychiatria Hungarica, 1990-91, mem. editorial bd., 1992—; contbr. numerous sci. papers to profl. publs. Fellow Royal Australian and New Zealand Coll. Psychiatrists; mem. AAAS, European Coll. Neuropsychopharmacology, N.Y. Acad. Scis. Office: Monash Med Ctr Adult Psychiatry, 246 Clayton Rd, Clayton 3168 Vic, Australia

PERERA, DAYANTHA SHRESHTA, ceramic engineer; b. Colombo, Sri Lanka, June 1, 1943; arrived in Australia, 1989; s. Mervyn and Esther (Peiris) P.; m. Shanthi Balasuriya, May 31, 1967; 1 child, Shevantha. BSc, U. Ceylon, Colombo, 1966; BSc in Tech. with honors, U. Sheffield, Eng., 1973; PhD, U. Newcastle Upon Tyne, Eng., 1976. Prodn. mgr. Ceylon Ceramics Corp., Colombo, 1967-70; rsch. assoc. U. Newcastle Upon Tyne, Eng., 1973-77, rsch. fellow, 1986-88; from leader refractories rsch. to dir. New Zealand Ceramics Rsch. Assn., Wellington, 1977-85; leader engring. ceramics Dept. Sci. and Indsl. Rsch., Wellington, 1988-89; prin. rsch. scientist Australian Nuclear Sci. and Tech. Orgn., Sydney, 1989—. Author: New Technology-Its Impact; contbr. articles to profl. jours. Rsch. fellow Sci. Rsch. Coun., Eng., 1976-77, Ministry Def., 1986-88; recipient Prince and Princess of Wales award Royal Soc. New Zealand, 1986. Fellow Inst. Materials; mem. Australasian Ceramic Soc. (fed. sec. 1995—), Toastmasters Internat. (v.p. 1993, pres. 1997-99). Avocations: travel, photography, public speaking, cooking, swimming. Office: Australian Nuclear Sci & Tech Orgn, PMB 1, 2234 Menai Australia

PERERA, LIYANAGE HENRY HORACE, human rights advocate, educator; b. Yatiyantota, Sri Lanka, 1915; arrived in Switzerland, 1961; s. Henry and Maud Mildred (Sirimane) P.; m. Sita Beatrice Senarat Oct. 17, 1942; children: Carmel, Peter, Assumpta, Bernadette. BA, U. London, 1935; postgrad. diploma in edn. and history, Ceylon (Sri Lanka) U., 1946. Sr. master history and govt. St. Benedict's Coll., Sri Lanka; vis. lectr. Ceylon and Indian History and govt. numerous schs., govt. colls., Sri Lanka, 1946-59; registrar Aquinus Coll., 1959-61; edn. dir. World Fedn. UN Assns., Geneva, 1961-63, dep. sec. gen., sec. gen., 1965-76, spl. asst. for Asia world confederation tchg. profession, 1976-86, acting sec. gen., 1996-2000; sec. Masaryk Study Ctr. UN Studies, 1996—; mem. internat. com. adult edn. UNESCO, 1963-73; mem. Pontifical Commn. Peace and Justice, Rome, 1969-77; pres. Conf. NGO, Switzerland, 1969-75; lectr. in field. Co-author: Indian and Ceylon History 2500 BC to 1500 AD, 1950, Ceylon Under Western Rule 1505-1948, 1954; author numerous study guides on human rights conventions, Ceylon and world history. Recipient William Russel medal, Gold medal Czech. Soc. Internat. Rels., 1974, Internat. Assn. Educators Peace award, 1974. Roman Catholic. Avocations: stamp collecting, documents for European UNA confs. and international issues for Sri Lanka newspapers. Home: 22 Av Luserna, 1203 Geneva Switzerland Office: World Fedn UN Assns, Palais des Nations, 1211 Geneva 10, Switzerland

PERERA, VIMAL MARCELLINE, practicing management consultant, accountant; b. Colombo, Sri Lanka, June 2, 1939; s. Valentine Simon and Louise Mary Mansuetta (De Fonseka) P.; m. Irma Marie Frances Waas, June 5, 1976; 1 child, Lilaya Surani Marianne. BSc with honors, U. Sri Lanka, 1962. Asst. cons., dir. Assoc. Mgmt. Svcs. Ltd., Colombo, 1966-77; fin. contr., dir. Galle Face Hotel, Colombo, 1978-80; mgr. group orgn. and sys. Merc. Credit Ltd., Colombo, 1981-82; fin. contr. Hotel Sofitel Doha, Qatar, 1983-84; asst. Mervyn E Smith & Co., Chartered Accts., London, 1985-86; chief acct., fin. contr. Lanka Oberoi Hotel, Colombo, 1987-90; dep. gen. mgr. corp. affairs Ceylon Glass Co. Ltd., Ratmalana, Sri Lanka, 1990-94; fin. mgr. The Sane Charitable Co. Ltd., The Sane Trading Co. Ltd., Sane-Prince of Wales Internat. Ctr.; sec. The Sane Trading Co. Ltd., bd. dirs. Assoc. Mgmt. Svcs. Ltd., A M S Data Svcs. Ltd., A M S Cons. Ltd., A M S Printing House Ltd., C W Mackie & Co. (NTP) Ltd., C W Mackie & Co. Ltd., Ladyhill Tourist Hotels Ltd., Ceylon Ceramics Corp., Lanka Porcelain Ltd., Lanka Wall Tiles Ltd., Ceylon Ceramics Corp. (actg. chmn.), Galle Face Hotel Co. Ltd.; cons. in gen., pers. and fin. mgmt. Editor Young Ceylon, 1966. Treas. The Ceylon Natl. Chamber of Industries, Sri Lanka Scout Assn.; v.p. Ratmalana C. of C.; mem. PTO. Scholar Small Industries Cons. Advanced Tng. Course, Tokyo, 1973. Fellow Inst. Chartered Accts. Sri Lanka (coun. 1976-77), Inst. Cost and Mgmt. Accts. (U.K., lectr. 1977-78, sec. Sri Lanka br. 1973-75, v.p. 1976, pres. 1977, com. mem. 1978-80), Inst. Mgmt. (com. mem. Kingston br.), Chartered Accts. Student Soc. (pres.), The Sri Lanka United Kingdom Soc. (sec.), Lions Club of Colombo West and Lions Club of Colombo (pres., sec., treas.), Productivity Assn. Sri Lanka (treas.), St. Francis Xavier Soc. (treas.), Assn. for Sri Lankan Chartered Accts. in U.K. (treas., sec.), Knights of St. Columbia Coun. (treas., dep. grant knight), Neigborhood Watch Assn. Kingston (treas.), , Assn. Old Josephians in U.K. (treas.), Royal Borough Kingston Upon Thames Lions Club (sec.), Penhryn Investment Club (sec.). Home: Kestral House 44 Sigrest Sq, Canbury Park Rd, Kingston upon Thames Surrey KT2 6JT, England also: 32/3 Skelton Rd, Colombo 5, Sri Lanka

PERES, GIOVANNI, astrophysics educator; b. Palermo, Sicily, Italy, Apr. 12, 1952; s. Andrea and Maria Adele (Privitera) P.; m. Maria Di Giacomo, Sept. 15, 1981; children: Aurora, Chiara. Laurea in Fisica, U. Palermo, Italy, 1976. Ricercatore universitario U. Palermo, 1981-89; astronomo associato Osserv di Catania, Catania, Italy, 1989-93; prof. associato U. Palermo, 1993—; assoc. Harvard U., Cambridge, Mass., 1975-88. Contbr. articles to profl. jours. Mem. Internat. Astron. Union, European Astron. Socc., Socc. Astronomica Italiana, Soc. Italiana di Fisica. Office: Dept Sci Fisiche Astronom, Piazza Parlamento 1, 90134 Palermo Sicily, Italy

PERES, JOSE SERRA DE CARVALHO, economist, educator, consultant; b. Lourengo Marques, Mozambique, Portugal, Dec. 31, 1963; s. Jose De Carvalho and Maria Natalia Do Patrocinio (Serra) P.; children, Nelson Soares Peres, Carolina Passos Peres. MS, U. Nova De Lisboa, 1991; PhD, U. Vigo, Spain, 1996. Univ. prof. Instituto Politecinico de Castelo Branco, Portugal, 1994—; economist IBM Portugal, Lisbon, 1989-94; univ. prof. Universidad Vigo, Spain, 1996—. Author: (book) Estudo Sobe Transferencia De Tecnologia, 1996 (Book award 1996), Estudo Do Emprego Região Norte De Portugal E Galiza, 1996 (Reg. Book award 1996). Official Portuguese Air Force, 1983-85. Avocations: playing chess, painting. Home: 10 ESQ TRAZ, Praceta Da Galiza Lote 172, 4900 Viana Do Castelo Portugal Office: IPVC-ESTG, IPCB-EST, Avenida Do Empresario, 6000 Castelo Branco Portugal

PERES, SHIMON, politician; b. Vishniev, Belarus, 1923; immigrated to Palestine, 1934; s. Isaac and Sarah Persky; m. Sonia Gelman; children: Zvia, Jonathan, Nechemia. Ed., Harvard U. Sec. Working Youth Movement, 1943; mem. Mapai Secretariat, 1947; dir. gen. ministry def., 1953-59; mem. Knesset, 1959—; dep. minister def., 1959-65; founder mem., sec.-gen. Rafi Party, 1965, mem. Labour Party after merger, 1968, chmn., 1977—; minister for econ. dept. in administered areas and for immigrant absorption, 1969-70, minister of transport and communications, 1970-74, minister of info., 1974, minister of def., 1974-77, acting prime minister, 1977; leader of opposition, 1977-84, minister interior and religious affairs, 1984-85, prime minister, 1984-86, vice prime minister, 1986-90, minister fgn. affairs, 1986-88, 92-95; chmn. Yad Ben-Gurion; prime minister, 1995-96; chmn. Labour Party, 1996-97. Author: In Between Hatred and Neighborhood, 1961, The Next Phase, 1965, David's Sling, 1970, Tomorrow is Now, 1978, From These Men, 1979, Entebbe Diary, 1991, The New Middle East, 1993, Reading Diary-Letter to Authors, 1994, Battling for Peace-Memoirs, 1995, For the Future of Israel, 1997, New Genesis, 1998, Le Voyage Imaginaire, 1998; contbr. articles to various jours. Creator Good Fence on Israel's border with Lebanon, 1976; founder Peres Ctr. Peace, 1997. Decorated officer Legion of Honor, 1959, Nobel Peace Prize, 1994. Office: Beit Amot Mishpat, 8 Shderot Shaul Hamelech 9#, 91950 Tel Aviv Israel

PERETZ, CAROL, fashion designer. BFA, Parsons Sch. Design, N.Y.C., 1973. Designer Priscilla of Boston, 1973-74; owner, designer Carol Peretz, New Hyde Park, N.Y., 1974—. Mem. Fashion Group Internat. Avocations: ballet dancer, antiques collector, painter. Office: 121 Lakeville Rd New Hyde Park NY 11040-3003

PERETZ, TAMAR, oncologist; b. Gdansk, Poland, Sept. 10, 1952; d. Eli nad Eugonia (Loss) Yablonski; m. Benjamin Peretz; children: Neta, Alona. MD, Hebrew U., Jerusalem, 1980. Intern Hadassah U. Hosp., Jerusalem, 1979-80, resident in radiation and med. oncology, 1981-86, attending physician dept. oncology, 1986-94, prof., 1995—; acting head Sharett Inst. Oncology/Hadassah U. Hosp., Jerusalem, 1993-94, head, 1994; instr. oncology Hebrew U./Hadassah U. Med. Sch., 1982, lectr. oncology, 1986; sr. lectr. oncology Hebrew U. Med. Sch., 1992; com. for clin. trials, com. for new drugs Ministry of Health,. Mem. editl. bd. Jour. IMAJE. Bd. dirs. Israel Cancer Soc. Meml. Sloan-Kettering Cancer Ctr. fellow, 1987-88, Rsch. fellow, 1988-89; Rsch. grantee Jt. Rsch. Fund Hebrew U./Hadassah U. Hosp., 1984, 86, 90, Israel Cancer Assn., 1986, 88-90, 94-95, Israel Cancer Rsch. Found., 1990-91, Ministry of Health, 1992, Hebrew U., 1998, Mediteranian Cancer Consortrium, 1999, THMRF grant, 1999. Mem. Israel Med. Assn., Israeli Soc. Oncology, Israel Soc. for Medicine and Law, Am. Endocurietherapy Soc., Am. Soc. for Radiation Oncology, The Middle East Cancer Soc., Am. Assn. Cancer Rsch., European Soc. Med. Oncology, European Senology Soc., European Soc. Mastology, Am. Soc. Clin. Oncology. Office: Hadassah Univ Hosp, Oncology Dept, Jerusalem Israel

PEREYRA, NICOLAS ANTONIO, astrophysicist, researcher; b. Caracas, Venezuela, Mar. 23, 1967; s. Bolivar Nicolas Pereyra and Edith Del Carmen Marquez; m. Sijham Ghaleb Bahri, Dec. 17, 1990; 1 child, Gabriel. Licenciad en Fisica, U. Ctrl. Venezuela, Caracas, 1991; MS in Physics, U. Md., 1995, PhD in Physics, 1997. Tchg. asst. U. Ctrl. Venezuela, Caracas, 1988-91; physicist, computer programmer Proservfacica, Caracas, 1990-91; tchg. asst. U. Md., College Park, 1992-93; rsch. asst. Goddard Space Flight Ctr./NASA, Greenbelt, 1993-97, rsch. assoc., 1997-98; postdoctoral rschr. Centro de Astrofisica Teorica, U. de Los Andes, Merida, Venezuela, 1998—. Contbr. articles to profl. jours. Recipient Orden Jose Felix Ribas, Conicit, Venezuela, 1994; Leon Herreid Meml. fellow U. Md./Goddard Space Flight Ctr., NASA, 1995. Mem. Am. Astron. Soc. Home: Apt 03, Calle 14 Res Carreto-PB, 5101 Merida Venezuela Office: U Los Andes Ctr Astrofisica, AP 26, 5101 Merida Venezuela

PEREZ, JOSEPH, civilization educator; b. Laroque d'Olmes, France, Jan. 14, 1931; s. José and Iréne (Belda) P.; m. Germaine Sabardan, Mar. 8, 1954; children: Alain, Cécile. Doctor letters. Prof. U. Bordeaux III, pres., 1978-83; dir. Casa de Velazquez, Madrid, 1989-96. Author: La Révolution des Comunidades de Castille, 1970, Ferdinand et Isabelle, 1988, Charles-Quint, empereur deux mondes, 1994, Histoire de l' Espagne, 1996, d'Espagne de Philippe II, 1999. Named Chevalier de la Legion d Honneur, Officer Ordre Nat. Mérite. Home: 57rue Georges Bizet, Talence France Office: U Bordeaux III, Domaine Univ, 33405 Talence France

PEREZ, JOSEPHINE, psychiatrist, educator; b. Tijuana, Mex., Feb. 10, 1941; came to the U.S., 1960, U.S. citizenship, 1968.; BS in Biology, U. Santiago de Compostela, Spain, 1971, MD, 1975. Nuc. medicine technician, EEG technician, supr. Electrographic Labs., Encino, Calif., 1963-71; clerkships in internal medicine, gen. surgery, otorhinolaryngology, dermatology and venereology Gen. Hosp. of Galicia, Spain, 1972-75; resident in gen. psychiatry U. Miami, Jackson Meml. Hosp. and VA Hosp., Miami, Fla., 1976-78; practice medicine specializing in psychiatry, marital and family therapy, individual psychotherapy Miami, 1979—; emergency room physician Miami Dade Hosp., 1975; attending psychiatrist Jackson Meml. Hosp., 1979—, asst. dir. adolescent psychiat. unit, 1979-83; mem. clin. faculty U. Miami Sch. Medicine, 1979—, clin. instr. psychiatry, 1979—. Mem. AMA (Physicians' Recognition award 1980, 83, 86, 89, 98), Am. Assn. for Marital and Family Therapy (cert. clin. mem., treas. 1982-84, pres.-elect 1985-87, pres. 1987-89), Am. Psychiat. Assn., Am. Med. Women's Assn., Assn. Women Psychiatrists, South Fla. Psychiat. Soc., South Dade Women Physicians Assn. Office: 420 S Dixie Hwy Ste 4A Coral Gables FL 33146-2228

PEREZ, LOUIS ANTHONY, radiologist; b. N.Y.C., June 11, 1939; s. Salvatore Lawrence and Valvadina Rose (Ruscillo) P.; divorced, 1988; children: Lisa, Gregg, Nicole; m. Patricia Ann McVey, May 19, 1990; 1 child, Kelsey. BEE, Manhattan Coll., 1962; MD, SUNY, Bklyn., 1966. Diplomate Am. Bd. Radiology (oral examiner), Am. Bd. Nuclear Medicine. Chief nuclear medicine Misericordia Hosp., Bronx, 1973-75; cons. Manhattan Coll., Radiology Inst., Riverdale, N.Y., 1974-81; chief nuclear medicine Norwalk (Conn.) Hosp., 1975-82; dir. radiology Lawrence Hosp., Bronxville, N.Y., 1982—; asst. clin. prof. radiology Columbia U. Coll. Physicians and Surgeons, N.Y.C., 1995—. Contbr. articles to profl. jours., chpts. to books. Lt. comdr. USN, 1963-77. Grantee, Am. Cancer Soc., 1968-70, USPHS, 1974-75. Fellow Am. Coll. Radiology; mem. Soc. Nuclear Medicine (trustee 1985-89, 92—, chmn. sci. subcom. 1988—, chpt. pres. 1982), Am. Coll. Physician Execs., N.Y. State Med. Soc., Explorers Club, Alpine Club. Republican. Roman Catholic. Office: Diagnostic Imaging Svcs of Bronxville 700 White Plains Rd Ste 244 Scarsdale NY 10583-5063 also: Lawrence Hosp Dept Radiology 55 Palmer Ave Bronxville NY 10708-3403

PEREZ, MAARAVI, theologian, religious studies educator; b. Ben-Gardane, Tunisia, Apr. 16, 1940; arrived in Israel, 1963; s. Nissim and Fortuna P.; m. Simha Aimee Gaziel, Jan. 3, 1968; children: Miriam, Penina, Revital, Efrat, Nethanel. BA, Bar-Ilan U., 1968, MA, 1971, PhD, 1979. From asst. dept. Bible to assoc. prof. dept. Bible Bar-Ilan U., Ramat-Gan, Israel, 1967—; head Bible syllabus com. Min. Edn., Israel, 1989—. Editor: The Commentary of R. Jehuda Ibn Bal'am on Ezekiel, 2000; co-editor: The Commentary of R. Jehuda Ibn Bal'am on Isaiah, 1992; contbr. articles to profl. publs. Pvt. Israeli Def. Army, 1968. Avocations: medieval history, semitic languages. Office: Bar-Ilan U, Dept Bible, 52900 Ramat Gan Israel

PEREZ, PRIEGO MIGUEL ANGEL, educator; b. Cuenca, Spain, Sept. 23, 1946. Dir U. Nat. Edn., Cuenca, Spain, 1994-95, 1989-95, viccerrector, 1995-99. Author: Poesia Femenina En Los Cancioneros, 1990, Teatro Medieval Castilla, 1997, La Edicion De Textos, 1997. Mem. Assn. Hispanica Lit. Medieval (v.p. 989, pres. 1999). Home: Doctor Esquerdo 41, 28028 Madrid Spain Office: UNED, Senda Del Rey s/n, 28040 Madrid Spain

PEREZ, REINALDO JOSEPH, electrical engineer; b. Palm River, Cuba, July 25, 1957; came to U.S., 1975; s. Reinaldo I. and Palminia Ulloa (Rodriguez) P.; m. Madeline Kelly Reilly, Mar. 11, 1989; children: Alexander, Laura-Marie, Richard Kelly, Ella-Dean. BSc in Physics, U. Fla., 1979, MSc in Physics, 1981; MScEE, Fla. Atlantic U., 1983, PhD, 1989. Comms. engr. Kennedy Space Ctr., NASA, Cape Canaveral, Fla., 1983-84; chief reliability engr. jet propulsion lab. JPL Calif. Inst. Tech., Pasadena, 1988—, chief engr. Mars surveyor program, 1994—; instr. engring. UCLA, 1990-94; owner M.R. Rsch. Inc., a telecomm. and aerospace cons. co. Author, editor: Handbook of Electromagnetic Compatibility, 1994, Noise and Interference Issues in Wireless Communications, 3 vols., Wireless Communications Handbook, 1998; contbr. articles to profl. publs. Mem. AAAS, IEEE (sr. mem., book rev. editor 1990—), NSPE, Electromagnetic Compatibility Soc. (assoc. editor jour.), Am. Soc. Physics Tchrs., N.Y. Acad. Scis., Applied Computational Electromagnetic Soc. (assoc. editor jour., chief editor newsletter, bd. dirs., v.p.), Phi Kappa Phi. Republican. Baptist. Avocations: flying, skiing, fishing. Office: JPL Calif Inst Tech 4800 Oak Grove Dr # 301460 Pasadena CA 91109-8099

PEREZ-CRUET, JORGE, physician, psychiatrist, psychopharmacologist, psychophysiologist, educator; b. Santurce, P.R., Oct. 15, 1931; s. Jose Maria Perez-Vicente and Emilia Cruet-Burgos; m. Anyes Heimendinger, Oct. 4, 1958; children: Antonio, Mick, Graciela, Isabelle. BS magna cum laude, U. P.R., 1953, MD, 1957; diploma in psychiatry, McGill U., Montreal, Que., Can., 1976. Diplomate Am. Bd. Psychiatry and Neurology, Nat. Bd. Med. Examiners, Am. Bd. Geriat. Psychiatry; lic. Can. Coun. Med. Examiners; cert. in quality assurance; cert. CHPQ by HQCB92; cert. specialist in psychiatry RCPC. Rotating intern Michael Reese Hosp., Chgo., 1957-58; fellow in psychiatry Johns Hopkins U. Med. Sch., 1958-60, instr., then asst. prof. psychiatry, 1962-73; lab. neurophysiologist and psychomatic lab. Walter Reed Army Inst. Rsch., Washington, 1960-62, cons., 1963-65; rsch. assoc. lab. chem. pharmacology NHI, NIH, Bethesda, Md., 1969-71; adult psychiatry sect. lab. clin. sci. NIMH, Bethesda, Md., 1971-73; psychiatry resident diploma course in psychiatry McGill U. Sch. Medicine, Montreal Gen. Hosp., 1973-76, Montreal Children's Hosp., 1975; prof. psychiatry U. Mo.-Mo. Inst. Psychiatry, St. Louis, 1976-78; chief psychiatry svc. San Juan (P.R.) VA Hosp., pharmacy and therapeutic com., 1978-92; also prof. psychiatry U. P.R. Med. Sch., 1978-92; prof. psychiatry U. Okla. Health Sci. Ctr., Oklahoma City VA Med. Ctr., 1992—; spl. cons. NASA, 1965-69; cons. divsn. narcotic addition and drug abuse NIDA, 1972-73; mem. drug adv. com. FDA/NIDA, 1977-80, mem. pharmacy and therapeutic com., 1992—; local organizer CINP, San Juan, P.R., 1986; spl. advisor mental health P.R. Senate, P.R. sec. health, 1989. Editor: Catholic Physicians Guild Archiocese of Okla., 1997. Capt. M.C. USAR, 1960-62; sr. surgeon USPHS, 1969-71, med. dir., 1971-73. Recipient Coronas award, 1957, Ruiz-Arnau award, 1957, Diaz-Garcia award 1957, Geigy award, 1975, 76, AMA Recognition award 1971, 76, 81, Horner's award 1975, 76, Pavlovian award, 1978, Recognition cert. VA Svc. awards and commendations, 1980-98, Senate of P.R., 1986, Cert. of Merit Gov. of P.R., 1986, Cert. Recognition, Sec. Health, San Juan, Puerto Rico. Fellow Interam. Coll. Physicians and Surgeons, Royal Coll. Physicians and Surgeons Can. (sr., cert.); mem. Am. Psychiat. Assn., Am. Physiol. Soc., Pavlovian Soc., Am. Fedn. Clin. Rsch., Am. Fedn. Med. Rsch., Am. Assn. Geriat. Psychiatry, Am. Soc. Clin. Pharmacology and Therapeutics, Am. Soc. Pharmacology and Exptl. Therapeutics, Am. Soc. Addiction Medicine (cert. 1998), Am. Acad. Addiction Psychiatry, Soc. Neurosci., Nat. Assn. Healthcare Quality, Internat. Soc. Rsch. Aggression, Okla. Psychiat. Assn., Am. Soc. Clin. Psychopharmacology, Menninger Found., Charles F. Menninger Soc., Okla. Assn. Health Care Quality, Alumni, UPR Sch. Med., Johns Hopkins Med. Surg. Inst., NIH, McGill. Roman Catholic. Fax: 405-270-1566. E-mail: jperezcrue@aol.com. Home: 3304 Rosewood Ln Oklahoma City OK 73120-5604 Office: Oklahoma City VA Med Ctr 921 NE 13th St Oklahoma City OK 73104-5007

PEREZ ESQUIVEL, ADOLFO, human rights activist; b. Nov. 26, 1931; m. Amanda E., 1956; 3 children. Grad., Nat. Sch. Fine Arts, Buenos Aires and La Plata, Argentina, 1956. Sculptor, prof. art Manuel Belgrano Nat. Sch. Fine Arts, Buenos Aires, 1956—; prof. faculty arch. and urbanism U. Nat. de la Plata; now rector United Nations U. for Peace, Escalzu, Costa Rica; founder Servico Paz y Justica, 1971, sec. gen., 1974-86; joined Oouddian (Militant Noviolence) group, 1973; founder mag. Paz y Justice; imprisoned for peace activities, 1977-79. Author: Christ in a Poncho: Testimonials of the Nonviolent Struggles in Latin America, 1983. Recipient Pope John XXIII award Pax Christi, 1977; Nobel prize for peace, 1980. Address: SERPAJ CR Paseo de los Estudiantes, Apartido Postal 1190, 1002 San Jose Costa Rica*

PEREZ-FERNANDEZ, MARIA ANGELES, biologist; b. Laguna Dalga, Spain, Aug. 8, 1968; d. Eusebio Perez-Galvan and Cristeta Fernandez-Mayo. BSc, U. Salamanca, 1991, MSc, 1992; M in Environ. Mgmt., Open Internat. U., Malaga, Spain, 1994; PhD, U. Salamanca, 1996. Environ. quality controller IGM, Salamanca, Spain, 1991; sec. of direction U. Salamanca, 1992; scientific advisor European Parliament, Luxembourg, 1992-93; rsch. fellow U. Salamanca, 1993-96, lectr. ecology dept., 1996—; fellow Sch. Environ. Biology Curtin U. Technology, Perth, Australia, 1996-97; cons. Inst. Riojan Studies, Logrono, Spain, 1994—; rsch. fellow Curtin U. Tech., 1996-98, sr. adj. rsch. fellow, 1999; sr. lectr. ecology U. Extremadura, 1997. Mem. Ecol. Soc. Australia. Avocations: teaching, cycling, literature, dancing, scuba diving. Office: U Salamanca Dept Ecology, Calle Espejo s/n, 37007 Salamanca Spain

PEREZ GOMEZ, AUGUSTO, psychology educator, consultant; b. Bogotá, Colombia, May 25, 1947; s. Rafael Perez Paez and Alicia Gomez Barriga; m. Leonor Trujillo Quintero, Mar. 29, 1969; children: Monica, Ingrid. Degree in psychology, Nat. U., Colombia, 1969; Master Degree, U. Louvain, Belgium, 1971, D in Psychology, 1974. Chargé d'enseignement Faculté Libre, Lille, France, 1974-75; asst. prcf. U. Nacional, Bogotá, 1975-76; full prof. U. los Andes, Bogotá, 1977—; expert in group dynamics IHRI, P.R., 1969; dir. grad. U. Andes, Bogotá, 1985-87; dir. La Casa U. of Andes Bogotá; cons. Agy. Internat. Devel., Haiti, 1990-91, Riverside Mental Health Trust, London, 1994-95; vis. prof. U. London, 1994; temporary advisor WHO, Bangkok, 1995; dir. Presdl. Program Against Drug Abuse, 1998—. Author: Clinical Psychology: Basic Problems, 1981, Psychotherapies: Theory, Research and Practice, 1981, Cocaine: Raise and Evolution of a Myth, 1987, La Casa: Supporting the Community on Drugs, AIDS and Suicide, Psychoactive Substances: A History of Drug Consumption in Colombia, 1987, 2d edit., 1994, also papers in field. Fellow APA (internat.); mem. Fedn. Internat. Non-Govtl. Orgns. Contre Drogues (dir. 1990—, v.p. 1993—), S.O.S. Drogue Internat. (sci. com.). Avocations: walking, planting trees, reading, listening to classical music. Home: Apt 302, Carrera 11 #86-86, Bogota Colombia Office: U Los Andes, Calle 18 Cra 1E, Bogota Colombia

PEREZ IPIÑA, JUAN ELIAS, educator; b. Buenos Aires, Argentina, Sept. 21, 1952; s. José Maria and Maria del Rosario (I.; m. Beatriz Bertrand, July 16, 1979; children: Paula, Emiliano, Alejo, Emanuel. Ingeniero Mecanico, U. La Plata (Argentina), 1977. Rsch. asst. U. La Plata, 1977-79; researcher Scientific Rsch. Commn., La Plata, 1981-89; assoc. prof. U. Comahue, Neuquén, Argentina, 1989-90, titular prof., 1990—. Contbr. rsch. papers to profl. pubs. Fellow Scientific Rsch. Commn., La Plata, 1979-81. Mem. ASME, ASTM, AAAS, European Structural Integrity Soc., Sociedad Argentina Metales, Assn. Latinoamericana Metalugia, Assn. Argentina Materiales (pres. 1994-96). Home: Capdevilla #372, Cipolletti, Rio Negro 8324, Argentina Office: Univ Nacional del Comahue, Buenos Aires #1400, Neuquen 8300, Argentina

PÉREZ I POCH, ANTONI, physicist; b. Barcelona, Spain, Oct. 30, 1969; s. Antonio Pérez Font and Dolores Poch González. BSc, U. Barcelona, 1992, MSc, 1996; degree in elec. engring., U. Autonoma, Barcelona, 1997. Rsch. asst. U. Barcelona, 1992-94, U. Poly. Catalunya, Terrassa, Spain, 1995-97; h.s. prof. tech. Maristas Champagnat Sch., Barcelona, 1997-99; assoc. prof. software dept. U. Poly. Catalunya, Barcelona, 1999—; rsch. asst. faculty medicine U. Barcelona, 1999—. Avocations: writing, jogging. Office: EUETIB U Poly Catalunya, c/Urgell 187, EO8036 Barcelona Spain

PEREZ LARAUDOGOITIA, JON, philosophy educator; b. Bilbao, Spain, Apr. 1, 1958; s. Angel Perez Arrieta and Begoña Laraudogoitia Garay; m. Idoia Mardaras Aginaga, June 14, 1990; children: Erik Jon and Gaizka (twins). B of Physics, U. Madrid, 1980; PhD, U. of the Basque Country, Spain, 1985. Asst. prof. U. of the Basque Country, 1983-87, titular prof., 1987—; rschr. in field; mem. rsch. bd. advisors Am. Biog. Inst. Author: Aporias, 1996; contbr. articles to profl. jours. Mem. Alt. for Animal Liberation. Avocation: literature. Home: Calle Blas de Otero # 9A, 48014 Bilbao Spain Office: U of the Basque Country, Calle Paseo Universidad #5, 01006 Vitoria-Gasteiz Spain

PEREZ-LATRE, FRANCISCO J., educator, dean; b. Barcelona, Spain, Mar. 4, 1966; s. Julio and Maria del Carmen (Latre) Perez. BA in Journalism, U. Navarra, Pamplona, Spain, 1989, PhD in Pub. Comm., 1993; MA in Mktg. and Advt., Emerson Coll., Boston, 1993. Prof. U. Navarra, Pamplona, 1994—, asst. to dean students, 1994—, acad. dean students, 1996—; cons., advisor U. Asia and the Pacific, Manila, 1997—; advisor Economy U., Bratslava, Slovakia, 1998—. Author: Centrales de Compra de Medios, 1995, Curso de Medios Publicitarios, 3d edit., 1999, Planificacion y Gestion de Medios Publicitarios, 2000; contbr. articles to profl. jours. Mem. Internat. Advt. Assn., Internat. Assn. Bus. Communicators. Roman Catholic. Avocations: sports, Russian literature, geography. Home: Pedro I S 1o A, 31007 Pamplona Navarra, Spain Office: U Navarra Sch Journalism, Edifico de Ciencias Sociale, 31080 Pamplona Navarra, Spain

PÉREZ-ORDOYO, LUIS IGNACIO, laboratory administrator; b. Gerona, Spain, Dec. 9, 1962; s. Luis Pérez-Ordoyo and Gloria García; m. Elena Ines Bellido, Apr. 29, 1989; 1 child, Alejandro Rodrigo. DMV, Vet. Medicine Sch., Zaragoza, Spain, 1986. Rschr. Vet. Medicine Sch., Zaragoza, 1986-87; analyst Labs. Ovejero, León, Spain, 1988-89, bacteriology mgr., 1989-95, tech. subdir., 1995-96, tech. dir., mgr., 1996—. Avocations: travel, reading, music, sports. Office: Labs Ovejero, PO Box 321, 24080 Leon Spain

PEREZ-OTERMIN, JORGE, diplomat. Perm. rep. of Uruguay to UN N.Y.C., 1995—. Office: Perm Mission of Uruguay to UN 747 3rd Ave Fl 21 New York NY 10017-2803*

PÉREZ-PEÑA, EFRAÍN, medical institute director, educator; b. Sabinas, Mex., Oct. 23, 1945; s. Efraín and Velia (Peña) Péez-Cantú; m. Alma María Corres, Oct. 10, 1970; children: Efraín, Alejandra. MSc, U. Guadalajara, Mex., 1994; DSc, U. Guadalajara, 1999; MD, Mil. Med. Sch., Mexico City, 1998. Diplomate Am. Bd. Ob-Gyn., Mex. Coun. Ob-Gyn., subspecialist in biology of reproductive medicine. Chief dept. ob-gyn. Mil. Hosp., Guadalajara, 1974-90, chief tchg. and rsch. dept., 1986-88; mem. staff ob-gyn. Hosp. Del Carmen, Guadalajara, 1975—; dir. Inst. Reproductive Medicine, Guadalajara, 1988—; examining prof. Med. Coun. Ob-Gyn., Mexico City, 1980—. Author: Infertility, Sterility and Endocrinology of Reproduction, 1981 (1st pl. award Nat. Med. Contest 1980). Recipient commendation for disting. svc. S.D.N., Mexico City, 1982, merit commendation, 1985. Fellow ACS, Am. Coll. Ob-Gyn. (chmn. Mex. sect. 1990-92), Am. Assn. Reproductive Medicine; mem. European Soc. Human Reproductive Embryology, Mex. Assn. Reproductive Medicine (pres. 1995-96), Soc. Ob-Gyn. (pres. 1979-80). Avocations: literature, tennis, travel. E-mail: imergdl@orbitnet.com.mx and epp@prodigy.net.mx. Home: Sur No 115, Av Bosques de San Isidro, 45132 Zapopan Mexico Office: IMER, Domingo Sarmiento 2837-C, 44620 Guadalajara Mexico

PÉREZ-RAMOS, SANTIAGO, microbiology educator; m. Carmen Otero, 1976; children: Elena, Santiago. Grad., lic. medicine and surgery, Cádiz U., Seville, Spain, 1975; asst. prof., 1976, microbiology specialist, 1978; Doctoral Degree, U. Seville, 1980; titular prof., 1983, MPH in Sanitary Adminstrn., 1989. Prof. U. Cadiz, Spain, 1976—; dir. medico Hosp. Mora Provincial of Cadiz, 1985-88; with U. Hosp. Puerto Real: Jefe de Secion de Microbiologia, 1992-95, Jefe de Servivio de los Lab. Clinicos, 1995—. Mem. Am. Soc. for Microbiology, European Soc. Clin. Microbiology and Infectious Diseases, Sociedad Española de Enfermedades Infecciosas y Microbiologia Clinica, Sociedad Española de Microbiologia, Sociedad Española de Quimioterapia, Sociedad Española de Control de Calidad, Sociedad Española de Direccion y Gestion de los Labs. Clinicos, Sociedad Andaluza de Microbiologia y Parasitologia Clinica. Office: Univ Cadiz Faculty Medicine, Plaza Flagela S/N, 11003 Cadiz Spain

PEREZ-RIOS, JOSE, engineering educator; b. La Coruña, Galicia, Spain, July 10, 1948; s. Jose Perez and Hortensia Rios; m. Irene Casares, July 24, 1978; children: Alexandre, Xavier. M in Indsl. Engring., Escuela Tecnica Superior Ingenieros Industriales, Bilbao, Spain, 1973; PhD, U. Poly. Madrid, 1989. Indsl. engr. Wrangler España, S.A., Valladolid, Spain, 1973-77; divsn. engr. Wrangler España, S.A., Valladolid, 1977-86; mfg. dir. Jeans Fashion España, S.A., Valladolid, 1986-89; dir. S9 Consulting, Valladolid, 1989-91; assoc. prof. U. Valladolid, 1989-91, prof., 1991—; cons. Sprint Project, European Commn., Luxembourg, 1994-96; tech. dir. Horizonte 2000, U. Valladolid, 1997-98. Author: Direccion Estrategica y Pensamiento Sistemico, 1992; co-author: (CD-ROM and book) To Be and Not To Be That Is The System: A Tribute to Stafford Beer, 1997; contbr. chpt. to books and articles to profl. jours. Grantee Rsch. Devel. Plan, 1998. Mem. Am. Soc. Quality, World Futures Studies Fedn., Soc. for Computer Simulation, Inst. Indsl. Engrs., Sys. Dynamics Soc., Assn. Española d Econ. Regional, Sociedad Española de Sistemas Generales. E-mail: joperrio@offcampus.es. Office: Campus Miguel Delibes, Edificio Tecnologias Info, 47011 Valladolid Spain

PÉREZ-RIVERA, FRANCISCO, writer; b. Vertientes, Cuba, Oct. 3, 1938; came to U.S., 1968, naturalized, 1974; s. Francisco Daniel Pérez and María Eloísa Rivera. BA, Camagüey Coll., Cuba, 1955; MA in Romance Langs., U. Munich, 1967. Newsman, script writer Bavarian Radio, Munich, 1964-68; newsman AP, N.Y.C., 1968-92, arts and entertainment editor, 1992—; dir. Spanish programs for lang. labs., 1987. Author: (poetry) Construcciones, 1979, (novel) Las sabanas y el tiempo, 1986, (short stories) Cuentos cubanos, 1992, (short stories) Varadero y otros cuentos cubanos, 1998; co-author: Introducción a la literatura española, 1982; short stories in the anthologies New Cuban Storytellers, 1961, Cuba: Nouvelles et contes d'aujourd'hui, 1985, Narrative and Liberty: Cuban Tales of the Dispersion, 1996, Prosa moderna del mundo hispánico, 1997. Grantee German Academic Exchange Svc., Munich, 1961-67; fellow Cintas Found., N.Y., 1980; 1st prize Círculo de Escritores y Poetas Latinoamericanos Short Story Contest, N.Y., 1997, 1st prize Círculo de Cultura Panamericano Short Story Contest, N.J., 1997. Home: 212 E 77th St Apt 1G New York NY 10021-2111 Office: AP 50 Rockefeller Plz New York NY 10020-1605

PÉREZ-SALGADO, IGNACIO, management consultant, educator; b. Ujo, Spain, May 26, 1931; arrived in Chile, 1949; s. Ignacio and Lila Pérez-Salgado; m. Catalina Caldentey, Mar. 1959; children: Ignacio, Esteban, Alejandro. BA in Pub. Acctg. and Econs., U. Chile, 1957, BA in Comml. Engring., 1957; MBA, UCLA, 1963. Dean faculty econs. U. Concepcion, Chile, 1963-67; project mgr. UN, Montevideo, Uruguay, 1968-71; CEO Soquimic, Santiago, Chile, 1972-73; s.t.a. in pub. adminstrn. UN, N.Y.C., 1973-83; resident rep. UNDP, Honduras, 1983-85; chief country programs UNDP, N.Y., 1985-88; resident rep. UNDP, Argentina, 1988-91; cons. pub. mgmt. UNDP, Santiago, 1991-95; cons. Nat. Health Fund, Santiago, 1996—; pres. Corp. Devel. Pub. Mgmt., Santiago, 1991-93; prof. mgmt. and pub. policy U. Santiago, Chile, 1993—, dir. pub. mgmt., 1995—; hon. prof. Ctrl. Am. Inst. Pub. Adminstrn., 1984. Pres. Spanish Socialist Party, N.Y., 1980-85. Recipient Gold Pin, Comml. Engr. Assn., 1963. Mem. Am. Soc. Public Adminstrn., Acad. Mgmt., Engring. Assn., Beta Gamma Sigma. Freemason. Avocations: jogging, tennis, bridge. Home: San Crescente 280 Apt 1001, Santiago Chile Office: U Santiago, Alameda 3363, Santiago Chile

PERFILIEVA, IRINA, mathematics educator, researcher; b. Moscow, Apr. 10, 1953; d. Grigori and Valentina Perfilieva; m. Vilem Novak, Nov. 27,

1999; 1 child, Vitali. MSc, Moscow State U., 1975, PhD, 1980. Asst. Moscow State Acad. of Instrument-Making and Informatics, 1978-82, docent, 1982-96, prof., 1996-98; docent U. Ostrava, Czech Republic, 1999—; dir. CAMAR, Ltd., Moscow, 1993-95; vice dir. KONON, Ltd., Moscow, 1995-96; vice head dept. math. modeling Moscow State Acad. of Instrument-Making and Informatics, 1997. Author: Mathematical Principles of Fuzzy Logic, 1999, Fuzzy Set Theory and Applications, 1990; editor: Discovering the World With Fuzzy Logic, 2000. Avocations: mountain skiing, tennis, fashion. Fax: 420-69-6120-478. Office: U Ostrava, 30 Dubna, 70103 Ostrava Czech Republic

PÉRGOLA, FEDERICO MIGUEL, medical educator; b. Buenos Aires, June 6, 1931; s. Nicolás and Ana Maria (Tettamanti) P.; m. Maria Matilde Nelson; children: Graciela Matilde, Silvina Liliana, Laura Andrea. Diploma in Medicine, U. Buenos Aires, 1955, MD, 1961. Physician U. Buenos Aires, 1955—, prof. internal medicine, 1983—; prof. cons., 1998—; hon. ptnr. Soc. Brasileira of Geriatry and Gerontology; correspondent Acad. Nat. Sci. Buenos Aires, 1993, Counsel of Direction mag. Jano, 1981-84, acad. advisor Faculty of Medicine Buenos Aires, 1991-95; dir. mag. Practice Geriatry, 1991-95; ethics com. Hosp. de Clinicas, Buenos Aries, 1994—. Author: Introduction to Seminology, 1982, History of Medicine, 1985, Shamans and Would-Be Physicians in the Origins of Argentina, 1986 (honor band of Soc. of Argentina Writers 1986)., History of the National Academy of Science of Buenos Aires, 1995, Atlas of Body's Disease, 1999. Recipient 1st reward of lit. Centenary of Hosp. de Clinicas Buenos Aires, 1978, 4th reward Found. Jewess-Argentina Gerontology, Buenos Aires, 1979, Dr. Ignaz Nascher reward Argentina Found. Gerontology and Geriatry, 1987. Mem. Argentina Titular Soc. of Cardiology, Argentina Soc. History of Medicine (pres. 1969-70), Argentina Soc. Gerontology and Geriatry (pres. 1977-78), Venezolana Soc. Gerontology and Geriatry (hon.), Nat. Argentina Soc. History of Medicine (hon.), Neurogeriatrics Argentine Assn. (pres. 1998-99). Avocation: painting. Home: Ramon Freire 2211, 1428 Buenos Aires Argentina Office: Montaneses 2214 PB A, 1428 Buenos Aires Argentina

PERHAM, RICHARD NELSON, biochemist; b. London, Apr. 27, 1937; s. Cyril Richard and Helen Harrow (Thornton) P.; m. Nancy Jane Lane, Dec. 22, 1969; children: Temple, Quentin. BA, U. Cambridge, 1961, PhD, 1965, ScD, 1976. Helen Hay Whitney fellow Yale U., 1966-67; Univ. lectr. U. Cambridge, U.K., 1969-77, reader in biochemistry, 1977-89, prof. structural biochemistry, 1989—; fellow St. John's Coll., Cambridge, 1964—, pres., 1983-87; chmn. Cambridge Ctr. for Molecular Recognition, 1988-92; dir. Cambridge Bacteriophage Tech. Ltd., Cambridge, 1992—. Contbr. articles to profl. jours. Gov. Latymer Upper Sch., London, 1991—; mem. exec. coun. CIBA Found., London, 1989—. With Royal Navy, 1956-58. Fogarty Internat. scholar NIH, Bethesda, Md., 1990-93; recipient Max Planck prize Max Planck Soc., Munich, 1993. Fellow Royal Soc. Arts, Royal Soc. London; mem. European Molecular Biology Orgn., The Biochem. Soc. (Novartis medal and prize 1997), Acad. Europaea. Avocations: gardening, theatre and opera, rowing in Lady Margaret Boat Club. Home: 107 Barton Rd, Cambridge CB3 9LL, England Office: U Cambridge Dept Biochemistry, 80 Tennis Ct Rd, Cambridge CB2 1GA, England

PERIER, PHILIPPE, communications executive; b. Paris, May 29, 1950; s. Jean-Claude and Paulette (Naudot) P. Diploma, Inst. d'Etudes Politics, Paris, 1974, CFJ, Paris, 1975. Journalist Europe 1, Paris, 1975-88, Quotidien of Paris, 1988-89; comm. exec. Natexis Group, Paris, 1989—. Mem. Entreprises et Medias. Home: 53 Rue Meslay, 75003 Paris France Office: Groupe Banques Populaires, 5 rue Leblanc, 75015 Paris France

PERIN, ROMEO VITTORIO, research scientist; b. Manerbio, Brescia, Italy, June 16, 1935; arrived in Switzerland, 1963; s. Antonio and Iole (Cenzi) P.; m. Silene Bruna Rasia, Dec. 1, 1962; children: Maria-Iole, Antonio, Giovanni. advisor ESO, Munich and La Silla, Chile, 1985, IGNITOR, Turin, Italy, 1982-88; sci. advisor U.S. Dept. Energy, Washington, 1989-95; prof. Poly. U. Turin, 1989-90. Direction jr. asst. Montedison, Milan, 1961; sect. leader SNAM-Progetti, ENI, Milan, 1962-63; sect. leader CERN European Orgn. Nuclear Rsch., Geneva, 1963-68, dep. group leader, project leader, 1969-71, group leader, project leader, 1972-89, head magnet group, chief designer large hadron collider superconducting magnets, 1990-96, head supplies, procurement and logistics divsn., 1997—; chmn. Internat. Conf. on Magnet Tech. MT-17, 2000-01. Contbr. sci. articles, reports, monographs to profl. publs. Mem. Associazione Sviluppo Scientifico e Tecnologico Piemonte (sci. com. 1989), European Phys. Soc., Italian Order Acad. Engrs. Office: CERN, European Orgn Nuclear Rsch, 1211 Geneva 23, Switzerland

PERINA, JAN, physicist; b. Mestec Kralove, Nymburk, Czechoslovakia, Nov. 11, 1936; s. Jan and Bozena (Hamplova) P.; m. Vlasta Caganova, Apr. 11, 1964; children: Pavlina, Jan. PhD, Palacky U., Olomouc, Czechoslovakia, 1966, RNDr, 1967, Prof., 1990; DSc, Charles U., Prague, Czechoslovakia, 1984. Rschr. Palacky U., Olomouc, 1964-90, prof., 1990—; dir. Joint Lab. of Optics, Olomouc, 1990; head dept. optics, Palacky U., 1990-94. Editl. bd. Optics Letters, 1982-90, Acta Physica Polonica, 1976-91, Jour. of Modern Optics, 1984-98, Quantum and Semiclassical Optics, 1993-97, Progress in Optics, 1993—, Czechoslovak Jour. of Physics, 1991—, Acta Physica Slovaca, 1993—, Optics and Fine Mechanics, 1995—; author: (books) Coherence of Light, 1972, 74, 85, Quantum Statistics of Linear and Nonlinear Optical Phenomena, 1984, 87, 91; co-author: Quantum Optics and Fundamentals of Physics, 1994, Phase in Optics, 1998; editor: Photon Statistics and Coherence in Nonlinear Optics, 1991. I.I. Rabi award Columbia U., N.Y., 1983; recipient medal/1st degree Union of Math. and Physicists, Prague, 1988, prize Ministry of Edn., Prague, 1991, Ilkovic medal, 1996. Fellow Optical Soc. of Am., Soc. for Sci. of Czech Rep.; mem. Internat. Commn. for Optics (v.p. 1987-90). Avocation: garden activities. Home: Kmochova 3, 779 00 Olomouc Morovia, Czech Republic Office: Palacky Univ, Svobody 26, Moravia 771 46 Olomouc Czech Republic

PERISSICH, RICCARDO, manufacturing executive; b. Milan, Italy, Jan. 24, 1942. Dep. fgn. policy editor Il Punto, Rome, 1962; cons. Italconsult, S.p.A., Rome, 1962-64; from chief European cmty. studies to dep. dir. Inst. Affari Internat., Rome, 1966-70; cabinet chief for Altiero Spinelli, Commr. Euro. Communities Indsl. Policy, Brussels, 1970-76; dir. directorate A, Energy Savings and Forecasts Commn. European Communities,, Brussels, 1977-81; cabinet chief for Mr. Antonio Giolitti, Commr. European Communities Regional Policy, Coord. Funds., Brussels, 1981-84; dir. responsible for overall coord. of works related to implementation of White Paper on completion of Internal Mkt., Brussels, 1986-90; dir. gen. Directorate for Industry, Brussels, 1990-94; mem. bd. dirs., dir. pub. and econ. affairs Pirelli SpA, Milan, 1994—; v.p. Assolombarda, Milan, 1995—; v.p. Assonime, Rome, 1999—. Contbr. articles to profl. jours. Named Chevalier des Artes et des Lettres of the Republic of France. Mem. Internat. Inst. for Strategic Studies (London), Inst. Affairs Internat. (Rome), Aspen Inst. Italy (Rome), Assn. Italian Elec. Industries (v.p.). Office: Pirelli SpA, Viale Sarca 222, 20126 Milan Italy

PERISSIN, ALDO ARRIGO, scientific instruments company executive; b. Monfalcone, Italy, July 18, 1938; s. Giulio and Angela (Pelizzari) P.; m. Sara Giulini Neri, Oct. 1, 1983; children from previous marriage: Robert, Barbara. Student, Leeds U., 1960-61. Mktg. specialist Varian Assocs., Zug, Switzerland, 1962-63; resident rep. Quickfit & Quarts Ltd., Stone, Stafordshire, Eng., 1963-67; project mgr. U.O.P., London, 1967-68; gen. mgr. Packard Instruments, Inc., Milan, 1968-77, Extracorporeal, Milan, 1977-78; mng. dir. Beckman Instruments, Milan, 1978—; pres. Superchrom Italy, Milan, 1978—, High Tech. Trade, Milan, 1985—, Sensormedics Italy, Milan, 1984. Home: Corso Plebisciti 9, 20129 Milan Italy Office: Sensormedics Italia Srl, Via Balzaretti 15, 20131 Milan 10, Italy

PERJÉS, ZOLTÁN ISTVÁN, physicist; b. Budapest, Hungary, Aug. 16, 1943; s. Zoltán Károly Babirád and Olga (Rubik) P.; m. Ildikó Császár, Feb. 20, 1971; children: Pamëla, Fruzsina. MA, R.Eötvös U., Budapest, 1966, BA, 1972; PhD, Hungarian Acad. Sci., Budapest, 1984. Sci. advisor KFKI Rsch. Inst. for Particle and Nuclear Physics, Budapest, 1966—; vis. fellow U. London, 1972-73, U. Tokyo, 1983-84; asst. prof. Dublin (Ireland) Inst. Advanced Study, 1978-79; co-chmn. Internat. Ctr. for Workshops in Theoretical Physics, Budapest, 1986-88; group leader Internat. Theoretical Group, Budapest, 1991-94. Editor: Relativity Today, 1988, 4th edit., 1997. Deutsche Akademische Austauschdienst scholar Max-Planck Inst. Astrophysik, Germany, 1987, Internat. Rsch. and Exch. Bd. scholar Calif. Inst. Tech., Pasadena, 1990-91, Fulbright scholar U. Calif., Santa Barbara, 1994-95. Mem. Internat. Soc. Gen. Relation and Gravitation, R. Eötvös Phys. Soc. (Bródy I. award 1971). Avocation: mathematical recreations. Office: KFKI Rsch Inst Partcl & Nucl Physics, Konkoly ut, H-1525 Budapest 114 Hungary

PERK, CEM, veterinarian, educator; b. Mudanya, Bursa, Turkey, Jan. 5, 1963; s. Kemal and Müeyyet (Tugcu) P.; m. Aynur Sit, Sept. 22, 1989; 1 child, Irem. Diploma in vet., U. Istanbul, Turkey, 1986, PhD, 1992. Head anesthesiology and reanimation dept. U. Istanbul, 1998—. Editor, pub. coord. Pet and Wild Sci. Mag., 2000—. Mem. Turkish Vet. Surgeon Assn. Office: U Istanbul, Dept Surgery, Istanbul 34840, Turkey

PERKALSKIS, BENJAMIN, science educator; b. Ukmerge, Lithuania, Mar. 17, 1929; arrived in Israel, 1991; s. Shabtai Ber and Bella Shmuel (MarK) P.; m. Mina Chaim Golomb, Jan. 5, 1965; 1 child, Sofia. MS, Vilnius State U., Lithuania, 1950; PhD, Tomsk State U., Russia, 1974. Tchr. physics, math. Vilnius, Lithuania, 1948-55; sr. laborant Tomsk State U., Russia, 1955-56, asst., 1956-63, lectr. exptl physics, 1963-64, asst. prof., 1964-75, prof., 1975-82, head dept. exptl. physics, 1982-91; prof. Jerusalem Coll. Tech., 1991—. Author: Demonstration in Physics Using Electronic Oscilloscope, 1960, Using of Modern Science Methods in Demonstration of Physics, 1966, 2d, edit., 1971, Wave Effects in Physical Demonstrations, 1984; contbr. articles to profl. jours.; patentee in field. Recipient Soviet Culture Achievements Exhbn. Golden medal, 1987. Jewish. Avocations: history, geography, literature. Office: Jerusalem Coll Tech, 21 Havaad Haleumi St, 91160 Jerusalem Israel

PERKIN, GEORGE DAVID, neurologist, consultant; b. Leeds, Yorkshire, Eng., Aug. 16, 1941; s. Alan Spencer and Vera (Taylor) P.; m. Louise Ann Boston, July 11, 1964; children: Michael Richard, Emma Josephine, Matthew Christopher. BA, Cambridge U., Eng., 1963, MB, BChir, 1966; MRCS, LRCP, London U., 1966. MRCP, FRCP. Sr. house officer Hammersmith Hosp., London, 1969-70; sr. house officer Nat. Hosp., Queen Sq., 1970, registrar, 1972-74; registrar Whittington Hosp., London, 1971-72; sr. registrar Univ. Coll. Hosp., amd Maida Vale Hosp., London, 1974-77; cons. neurologist Charing Cross Hosp., London, 1977—. Author: Optic Neuritis and Its Differential Diagnosis, 1977, A Slide Atlas of Neurology, 1986, 2d rev. edit., 1993, Basic Neurology, 1986, Diagnostic Tests in Neurology, 1988, Clinical Examination, 1993, 2d edit., 1997, Color Atlas and Text of Neurology, 1998, An Atlas of Parkinson's Disease and Related Disorders, 1998, Neurology and Medicine, 1999; dep. editor Jour. Neurology, Neurosurgery and Psychiatry, 1997—; mem. editl. bd. Jour. Neurology, Neurosurgery and Psychiatry, 1990-94. Fellow Royal Soc. Medicine, Royal Coll. Physicians (mem. part 2 examining bd.). Avocations: reading, bridge, music. E-mail: d.perkin@ic.ac.uk. Home: 29 Dalmore Rd, London SE21 8HD, England Office: Charing Cross Hosp Dept Neurology, Fulham Palace Rd, London W6 8RF, England

PERKINS, JAMES WINSLOW, international business consultant, builder, contractor; b. Southington, Conn., Sept. 15, 1955; s. Robert Winslow and Florence Corinne (Angelone) P. Student, Tunxis C.C., Farmington, Conn., 1973-75. Owner Town & Country Club, Smithfield, R.I., 1975-80, Ad Mark of Mass, Inc., Ludlow, Mass., 1980-84, Car Stereo Distbrs., Inc., West Palm Beach, Fla., 1983-85, Internat. Imports, Lauderdale Lakes, Fla., 1985-88, Modern Sectional Homes, Inc., Southington, Conn., 1989-93. Mem. Nat. Assn. Realtors, Cen. Conn. Bd. Realtors, Mayflower Soc., 100 Club Conn. Republican. Avocations: sailing, water skiing. Home: 2587 Meriden-Wtby Rd Marion CT 06444 Office: Modern Sectional Homes PO Box 153 Marion CT 06444-0153

PERKINS, JOHN HELM, college administrator, educator; b. Phoenix, July 15, 1942; s. Henry Helm and Bessie Eulalia (Speir) P.; m. Barbara Dodge Bridgman, Sept. 15, 1968; 1 child, Ivan Bridgman. BA, Amherst Coll., 1964; PhD, Harvard U., 1969. Peace intern Am. Friends Svc. Com., Cambridge, Mass., 1968-70; postdoctoral fellow Harvard U., Cambridge, 1970-71; staff officer Nat. Acad. Scis., Washington, 1971-74; asst. prof., assoc. prof. Miami U., Oxford, Ohio, 1974-80; sr. acad. dean, mem. faculty Evergreen State Coll., Olympia, Wash., 1980-86, mem. faculty, 1986—; dir. grad. program in environtl. studies Evergreen State Coll., Olympia, 1999—; mem., lead analyst com. on plant protection world food and nutrition study Nat. Acad. Scis., 1976-77; cons. editor Environment, 1980-92. Author: Insects, Experts, and the Insecticide Crisis, 1982, Geopolitics and the Green Revolution: Wheat, Genes and the Cold War, 1997; author, editor: Pest Control: Cultural and Environmental Aspects, 1980, Contemporary Pest Control Practices and Prospects, 1975; contbr. numerous articles to profl. publs. NSF rsch. grantee, 1976-80, 86-91. Mem. AAAS, Am. Soc. for Environ. History (exec. com. 1976-81, v.p. program 1981-82), Nat. Assn. Environ. Profls. (editor-in-chief jour.), Environ. Practice, Sigma Xi (nat. lectr. 1984-86, 87-88). Office: Evergreen State Coll Olympia WA 98505-0001

PERKINS, ROGER ALLAN, lawyer; b. Port Chester, N.Y., Mar. 4, 1943; s. Francis Newton and Winifred Marcella (Smith) P.; m. Katherine Louise Howard, Nov. 10, 1984; children: Marshall, Morgan, Matthew, Justin, Ashley. BA, Pa. State U., 1965; postgrad., U. Ill., 1965-66; JD with honors, George Washington U., 1969. Bar: Md. 1969, Mass. 1975. Trial atty. Nationwide Ins. Co., Annapolis, Md., 1969-72; assoc. Arnold, Beauchemin & Huber, PA, Balt., 1973; from assoc. to ptnr. Goodman & Bloom, PA, Annapolis, 1973-76; ptnr. Luff and Perkins, Annapolis, 1976-78; pvt. practice Anapolis, 1978—; temp. adminstrv. hearing officer Anne Arundel County, 1984-99; asst. city atty., Annapolis, 1980-82; atty. Bd. Appeals of City of Annapolis, 1986—; mem. Appellate Jud. Nominating Commn., 1995—. Editl. adv. bd. Daily Record, 1996-97. Mem. Gov.'s Task Force on Family Law, 1991-94; adv. coun. on family legal need of low income persons MLSC, 1991; coach youth sports. Fellow Am. Acad. Matrimonial Lawyers, Am. Bar Found., Md. Bar Found. (bd. dirs. 1992-95); mem. ABA (ho. dels. 1991-93, 94-96, standing com. on solo and small firm practitioners 1993-97, chair 1996-97), Md. State Bar Assn. (pres. 1992-93, treas. 1988-91, bd. govs. 1985-87, chair spl. com. on lawyer profl. responsibility 1994-95, family and juvenile law sect. coun. 1983-89, chair 1987-88), Anne Arundel County Bar Assn. (pres. 1984-85). Republican. Methodist. Home: 503 Bay Hills Dr Arnold MD 21012-2001 Office: The Courtyards 133 Defense Hwy Ste 202 Annapolis MD 21401-8907

PERKINSON, DIANA AGNES ZOUZELKA, interior design firm import company executive; b. Prostejov, Czechoslovakia, June 27, 1943; came to U.S., 1962; d. John Charles and Agnes Diana (Sincl) Zouzelka; m. David Francis Perkinson, Mar. 6, 1965; children: Dana Leissa, David. BA, U. Lausanne (Switzerland), 1960; MA, U. Madrid, 1961; MBA, Case Western Res. U., 1963; cert. internat. mktg. Oxford (Eng.) U., 1962. Assoc. Allen Hartman & Schreiber, Cleve., 1963-64; interpreter Tower Internat. Inc., Cleve., 1964-66; pres. Oriental Rug Importers Ltd., Cleve., 1979—; pres. Oriental Rug Designers, Inc., Cleve., 1980—; pres. Oriental Rug Cons., Inc., Cleve., 1980—; chmn. Foxworthy's Inc., Ft. Myers, Naples, Sanibel, Fla.; bd. dir. Beckwith & Assocs., Inc., Cleve., Secura Inc., Dallas, Dix-Bur Investments, Ltd. Trustee, Cleve. Ballet, 1979, exec. com., 1981; mem. Cleve. Mayor's Adv. Com.; trustee Diabetes Assn. Greater Cleve.; mem., chmn. grantsmanship Jr. League of Cleve., 1982; mem. mem. Cleve. Found.-Women in Philanthropy, 1982; trustee Ft. Myers Symphony, 1990. Mem. Women Bus. Owners Assn., Oriental Rug Retailers Am. (bd. dir. 1983), Cleve. Racquet Club, Recreation League, The League Club (Naples, Fla.), Hillbrook Club, Univ. Club (Ft. Myers, Fla.), Captiva Yacht Club. Republican. Roman Catholic. Home: Ravencrest 3511 Bonita Bay Blvd Bonita Springs FL 34134-1624 Office: Foxworthys Inc 2430 Periwinkle Way Sanibel FL 33957-3207 also: 17001 Captiva Rd Captiva Island FL 33924 also: 3522 Bonita Bay Blvd # 2 Bonita Springs FL 34134-1623

PERKO, WALTER KIM, computer engineer, songwriter, poet; b. Mpls., Dec. 8, 1950; s. Eero Nestor and Margie (Hanson) P. Computer Sci./Aeronautics, MIT, 1975. With USN, 1968-72, Korea and Vietnam. Lutheran. Avocations: songwriting, flying, computer network interactivity.

PERL, MARTIN LEWIS, physicist, engineer, educator; b. N.Y.C., June 24, 1927; children: Jed, Anne, Matthew, Joseph. B.Chem. Engring., Poly. Inst. Bklyn., 1948; Ph.D., Columbia U., 1955; ScD (hon.), U. Chgo., 1990. Chem. engr. Gen. Electric Co., 1948-50; asst. prof. physics U. Mich., 1955-58, asso. prof., 1958-63; prof. Stanford, 1963—. Author: High Energy Hadron Physics, 1975, Reflections on Experimental Science, 1996; contbr. articles on high energy physics and on relation of sci. to soc. to profl. jours. Served with U.S. Mcht. Marine, 1944-45; Served with AUS, 1945-46. Recipient Wolf prize in physics, 1982, Nobel Prize in Physics, 1995. Fellow Am. Phys. Soc.; mem. Nat. Acad. Scis., Am. Acad. Arts & Scis. Home: 3737 El Centro Ave Palo Alto CA 94306-2642 Office: Stanford U Stanford Linear Accelerator Ctr Stanford CA 94305

PERLEA, PAULA, dentistry educator; b. Bucharest, Romania, Sept. 21, 1969; d. Ioan Ciprian and Paraschiva (Turtureanu) P.; m. Mihai Tudor Baltac, June 29, 1996; children: Paul, Robert. MD, U. Medicine and Pharmacy, Bucharest, 1993; postgrad. diploma in implantology, Frialit Co., Mannheim, Germany, 1996; PhD magna cum laude, Ruprecht Karl U., Heidelberg, Germany, 1997. Med. diplomate in conservative dentistry, endodontics, dentistry for children. Univ. lectr., educator, rschr. faculty dentistry U. Medicine and Pharmacy Carol Davila, Bucharest, 1993—; asst. prof. conservative dentistry dept. U. Heidelberg Ruprecht Karl, 1993-97; med. diplomate, mng. dir. Unitech-Dental Divsn.-SRL, Bucharest, 1995—; cons. for Romania, Heraeus-Kulzer Gmbh, Dormagen, Germany, 1997—. Editor Romanian Dental Jour., 1998—; contbr. articles to profl. jours. Local coord. Student Union, Bucharest, 1989-93; mem. orgn. staff, sci. sec. 12th and 13th Internat. Dentistry Congress, Bucharest, 1998, 99. Recipient German Dentist Chamber Dentsply prize, 1996; grantee Internat. Coll. Dentists, Case Western Res. U., Cleve., 1993, Deutscher Akademische Austauschdienst, Heidelberg, Germany, 1993-94, Baden-Würtenberg Land, Heidelberg, 1995-97. Mem. Nat. Union Dentistry Orgns. (founder), Romanian Soc. Dentistry, N.Y. Acad. Sci., Alumni Assn. Student Clinicians ADA. Avocations: classical music, cars. Home: Str Levantica 57, 74328 Bucharest Romania Office: Faculty Dentistry, Str Calea Plevnei 19, Bucharest Romania

PERLESS, ROBERT L., sculptor; b. N.Y.C., Apr. 23, 1938; s. Meyer and Ethel (Glassman) P.; m. Ellen R. Kaplan, July 2, 1965. Student, U. Miami, Fla., 1955-59. One-man exhbns. include Bodley Gallery, N.Y.C., 1968, 70, Galerie Simonne Stern, New Orleans, 1969, Bernard Danenberg Gallery, N.Y.C., 1970-72, Bonino Gallery, N.Y.C., 1976; group exhbns. include Bodley Gallery, 1970, Whitney Mus., 1970, Forum Gallery, N.Y.C., 1975, Bonino Gallery, 1975, Houston Gallery, 1976, Aldrich Mus., Ridgefield, Conn., 1978, Taft Mus., Cin., 1980, Stamford (Conn.) Mus., 1989, Bruce Mus., Greenwich, Conn., 1989, Andre Emmerich's Top Gallant Farm, 1991, 92, 93, 94, 95, 96, Aldrich Mus., Ridgefield, 1987, 94, 97, 98; represented in permanent collections at Whitney Mus., Aldrich Mus., Chrysler Mus., Norfolk, Va., Everson Mus., Syracuse, N.Y., Okla. Art Ctr., Oklahoma City, Phoenix Art Mus., Stamford (Conn.) Mus., Bard Coll. Annandale-on-Hudson, N.Y. Address: 37 Langhorne Ln Greenwich CT 06831-2611

PERLET, HELMOT, insurance company executive. Assoc. chmn. Allianz Versicherungs AG, Munich, Germany, now chmn.; mem. mgmt. bd. controlling, acctg., tax Allianz AG, Munich. Office: Allianz AG, Koeniginstrasse 28, 80802 Munich Germany*

PERLETH, CHRISTOPH, psychologist, educator; b. Bad Konigshofen, Bavaria, Germany, May 12, 1958; s. Josef and Maria (Ziegler) P.; married; 2 children. Doctorate, Ludwig-Maximilians U. Munich, 1992, habilitation, 1998. Postgrad. rsch. asst. Ludwig-Maximilians U. Munich, 1986, exec. head project, 1987-88, lectr., scientist, 1988-92, asst. prof., sr. rschr., 1992-99; prof. chmn. U. Rostock, Germany, 1999—; partnership tng. Inst. Communication Therapy, Munich, 1988-94; lectr. State Bavarian Acad. for tchr. tng., Dillinger, Germany, 1993-99; counselor Counseling Ctr. of Inst. Edn. Psychology of Germany the Ludwig-Maximilians U. Munich, 1993-99; editing assst. Psychologie in Erziehung und Unterricht (sci. jour. 1994-98). Contbr. to more than 60 books; contbr. articles to profl. jours. Mem. Deutsche Gesellschaft Psychology, European Assn. for Rsch. in Learning and Instruction, Landesverband Bayerischer Schul Psychologen. Office: Inst Edn Psychology U Rostock, Aug-Bebel Str 28, Rostock 18051, Germany

PERLICK, RICHARD ALLAN, steel company executive; b. Chgo., June 23, 1947; s. Allan Arthur and Lorraine Perlick; m. Sharon Behrendt, Mar. 29, 1969; children: Jill Sharon, Timothy Richard, David Matthew. BS in Metall. Engring., Mich. Tech. U., 1969. Corrosion engr. CarTech Specialty Steel Corp., Reading, Pa., 1969-71; nondestructive test engr. CarTech Specialty Steel Corp., Union, N.J., 1971-75; quality control sr. engr. heavy products AlTech Specialty Steel Corp., Watervliet, N.Y., 1975-78; gen. supt. bar finish AlTech Specialty Steel Corp., Dunkirk, N.Y., 1978-79, sr. supr. metallurgist rod mill, 1979-86, mgr. product metallurgy, 1986-87, wire mill supt., 1987-89, sr. product metallurgist, 1989-90; gen. mgr. Techalloy Co.-Union (Ill.) Wire Plant, Ill., 1990-94; dir. corp. metall. svcs. Techalloy Co., Inc., Union, Ill., 1994-96, v.p. metallurgy, process and quality depts., 1997—; pub. spkr. and trainer on metallurgy of stainless steels; expert in field. Author, patentee in field. Cubmaster, scoutmaster Boy Scouts Am., Fredonia, N.Y., 1982-90; mem. ch. choir St. Paul Luth., Dunkirk, 1980-82. Recipient Pres.'s Scoutmaster's award Boy Scouts Am., 1988. Mem. Am. Soc. for Materials, Wire Assn. Internat., Am. Soc. Surface Finishing, Kiwanis. Republican. Avocations: vegetable gardening, woodworking, fishing, golfing, family camping. E-mail: Tecaloymet@aol.com, reperlick@techalloy.com. Home: 1758 Woodhaven Dr Crystal Lake IL 60014-1940 Office: Techalloy Co Olson And Jefferson St Union IL 60180

PERLIK, FRANTIŠEK, pharmacologist, educator; b. Prague, Czech Republic, Aug. 12, 1940; s. František and Emilie (Brabcová) P.; m. Iva Kovaříková, Oct. 17, 1968; children: Martin, Vít, Aleš. MD, Charles U., 1963; PhD, Czechoslovak Acad. Scis., 1972. House physician Dist. Hosp., Kladno, Czech Republic, 1963-67; sci. worker Inst. Pharmacology, Czech Acad. Scis., Prague, 1968-77, Inst. Rheumatology, Prague, 1976-83; chief clin. pharmacologist 1st dept. medicine Charles U., Prague, 1983—, mem. ethical com., 1995—; cons. State Inst. Drug Control, Prague, 1994—; mem. exec. com. European Drug Utilization Rsch. Group, 1996—; chmn. clin. pharmacology of Postgrad. Med. Sch., Prague, 1997—. Author: Therapeutic Drug Monitoring, 1989, Clinical Pharmacology of Antirheumatic Drugs, 1984, Pharmacotherapy in the Elderly, 1990, Clinical Pharmacology in Practice, 1999; contbr. articles to profl. jours. Inst. Rheumatology of Paris scholar, 1974-75. Mem. Czech Soc. Clin. Pharmacology (sci. sec. 1995—). Avocations: languages (Czech, English, Russian, French, German), music. Home: Zelená 14, 160 00 Prague 6, Czech Republic Office: Charles U Clin Pharm Unit 1st Dep, U nemocnice 2, 128 08 Prague 2, Czech Republic

PERLMAN, EDWIN FRANCIS, retired aeronautical engineer; b. Chgo., Nov. 4, 1931; s. Philip Clarence and Belle Irene (Letchinger) P.; m. Elka Aharoni, Aug. 8, 1974 (dec. Feb. 18, 1992). BS, U. Ill., 1953; postgrad., UCLA, 1955-59, U. Ill., 1961-64; MS, U. Ill., 1963. Engr. Douglas Aircraft, Santa Monica, Calif., 1953-61, McDonnell Douglas, Long Beach, Calif., 1964-71. Author reports pertaining to stress analysis and external, internal loads. Vice pres. Temple Beth Shalom Men's Club, Long Beach, 1967, bd. dirs., 1968; mem. congl. cabinet U. Judaism, L.A., 1968; bd. dirs. United Synagogue of Am., 1968. Fellow honor U. Judaism, 1968-70. Mem. AIAA (sr.), IEEE Computer Soc., Assn. for Computing Machinery, U. Ill. Alumni Assn., UCLA Alumni Assn., Assn. Am. and Canadians in Israel, Assn. of Engrs., Architects and Grads. of Technol. Scis. in Israel. Democrat. Jewish. Home: PO Box 22162, Tel Aviv 61221, Israel

PERLMAN, GARY ALESSANDRO, construction company executive; b. Johannesburg, South Africa, Nov. 27, 1962; s. Gustav and Loredana Gemma Therese (Marcon) P. Grad., St. David's Coll., Johannesburg, 1980. Divsn. mgr. Pan African Group, Gaberone, Botswana, 1983-85; gen. mgr. Logaro Constrn. (Pty) Ltd., Johannesburg, 1985-88, CFO, 1988-91, CEO, 1991-94; chmn., CEO Pemexco Corp., Johannesburg, 1994-97, Euro-Africa Hotels (Pty) Ltd., Johannesburg, 1996—; CEO Pemexco Hotels & Mgmt. Ltd., Durban, South Africa, 1994—; bd. dirs. Hortico Constrn., Durban, Langham Investments (pty) Ltd.; cons. Golden Tulip World Wide Hotels, London, 1996; dir. i Travel the World Ltd., i Travel Africa.com, 2000. Mem. South Arican Masters Swimmers Assn. (South Africa champion 1996, 97), Wanderers Club, Aero Club of South Africa (divsn. first 1991). Avoca-

tions: swimming, tennis, reading, flying, art collection. Office: Euro Africa Hotels, PO Box 41336, Craighall 2024, South Africa

PERLMUTTER, JACK, artist, lithographer; b. N.Y.C., Jan. 23, 1920; s. Morris and Rebecca (Schiffman) P.; children: Judith Faye, Ellen. MA, PhD in Fine Arts. Staff Dickey Gallery, D.C. Tchrs. Coll., 1951-68, dir., 1962-68, prof. art; prof. art, chmn. printmaking dept. Corcoran Gallery Art, Washington, 1960-82; resident artist St. Olaf Coll., Minn., Gibbs Art Gallery, Charleston, S.C., Mus. Sch. Art, Greenville, S.C.; vis. prof. art U. Costa Rica, San Jose, 1983; Fulbright research prof. painting and printmaking Tokyo U. Arts, 1959-60; art cons. Pres.'s Com. to Hire Handicapped; curator exhibits Cosmos Club, Washington. NASA artist for: 1st Saturn V moon rocket, Apollo 6, Apollo 16, Orbiter Columbia (space shuttle), Voyager II; contbg. editor: Art Voices South, 1979-80, Art Voices, 1980-82; one-man shows include Balt. Mus. Art, Brandeis U., Corcoran Gallery Art, Dintenfass Gallery, N.Y.C., Makler Gallery, Phila., Smithsonian Inst., Yoseido Gallery, Tokyo, C. Troup Gallery, Dallas, Nat. Acad. Scis., 1981, Arts Club Washington, 1981, Annapolis, Md., 1982, and galleries in Amsterdam, Rotterdam, The Hague and Costa Rica; exhibited in group shows in U.S., Switzerland, Yugoslavia, Europe, S.Am., Can.; represented in permanent collections Bklyn. Mus., Cin. Mus. Art, Carnegie Inst. Art, Corcoran Gallery Art, Library Congress, Met. Mus. Art, N.Y.C., Nat. Gallery Art, Washington, Phila. Mus. Art, Walker Gallery, Mpls., Nat. Mus. Modern Art, Tokyo, U.S. Embassies in Bucharest, Budapest, Bonn, Dublin, London, Prague, Tokyo, others. Recipient awards for paintings and prints from Balt. Mus. Art, Libr. Congress, Corcoran Gallery Art, Butler Inst. Arts, Smithsonian Inst., Soc. Am. Graphic Artists, First Internat. Exhbn. Fine Arts in Saigon, Mus. Fine Arts in Saigon, Mus. Fine Art, Boston, others. Fellow Internat. Inst. Arts and Letters; mem. Soc. Am. Graphic Artists. Club: Cosmos (Washington; curator paintings and prints). Achievements include having prints, drawings and biog. data in Art Archives Am. Fax: 202-483-5666. E-mail: perltone@aol.com. Studio: 2511 Cliffborne Pl NW Washington DC 20009-1511

PERLMUTTER, LYNN SUSAN, neuroscientist; b. N.Y.C., Oct. 12, 1954; d. David Louis and Audrey Marilyn (Cherkoss) P.; m. Howard Jay Deiner, May 30, 1976; 1 child, Jocelyn Rae Perldeiner. BA with highest honors, SUNY, Stony Brook, 1976; MA, Mich. State U., 1980, PhD, 1984. Postdoctoral fellow U. Calif., Irvine, 1984-87; asst. prof. neurology and pathology U. So. Calif., L.A., 1987-94, sec. med. faculty assembly, 1990-92, assoc. prof. neurology and pathology, 1994; sci. coord. U. So. Calif. Bravo Med. Magnet H.S. Partnership, 1993-94; staff scientist pharm. divsn. Inst. Dementia Rsch., Bayer Corp., West Haven, Conn., 1994-97; mgr. med. edn. Bayer Corp., West Haven, Conn., 1997—; ad hoc reviewer John Douglas French Found., L.A., 1988, 91, Calif. Dept. Alzheimer's Disease Program, Sacramento, 1990, 92, Alzheimer's Assn., 1999; mem. neurology rev. panel NIH, 1993, 94; chmn. blood-brain barrier session Internat. Conf. Alzheimer's Disease, Italy, 1992; organizer internat. symposium at Soc. Neuroscientists Africa, 1995; invited spkr. Internat. Alzheimer's Disease Conf., Israel, 1997. Contbr. articles to sci. jours. Coach Conn. state champions problem I, divsn. I, Odyssey of the Mind program, 1996. Travel fellow Internat. Conf. on Alzheimer's Disease, 1990, 92. Mem. AAAS, Soc. Neurosci., Electron Microscopy Soc. Am., Internat. Platform Assn., N.Y. Acad. Scis., Med. Faculty Women's Assn. (chmn. membership 1989-91), Phi Kappa Phi. Democrat. Jewish. Avocations: folk festivals, early and world music, films. Office: Bayer Corp Pharm Divsn Nat Sales Tng Dept 400 Morgan Ln West Haven CT 06516-4175

PERLOFF, JEAN MARCOSSON, lawyer; b. Lakewood, Ohio, June 25, 1942; d. John Solomon and Marcella Catherine (Borngen) Marcosson; m. Lawrence Storch, Stpe. 8, 1991. BA magna cum laude, Lake Erie Coll., 1965; MA in Italian, UCLA, 1967; JD magna cum laude, Ventura Coll. Law, 1976. Bar: Calif. 1976, U.S. Dist. Ct. (cen. dist.) Calif. 1978. Assoc. in Italian U. Calif.-Santa Barbara, 1967-70; law clk., paralegal Ventura County Pub. Defender's Office, Ventura, Calif., 1975; sole practice Ventura, 1976-79; co-prin. Clabaugh & Perloff, A Profl. Corp., Ventura, 1979-82; sr. jud. atty. to presiding justice 6th divsn. 2d Dist. Ct. Appeals, L.A., 1982-97; instr. Ventura Coll. Law, 1976-79. Pres., bd. dirs. Santa Barbara Zool. Gardens, 1987-88; bd. dirs. Montecito Found., 1999—; trustee Lake Erie Coll., 1993—. Named Woman of Yr., 18th Senatorial dist. and 35th Assembly dist. Calif. Legislature, 1993; recipient Disting. Alumnae award Lake Erie Coll., 1996. Mem. Calif. Bar Assn. (appellate ct. com. 1993-95), Fiesta City Club, Kappa Alpha Sigma. Democrat. Avocations: tennis, jogging, biking, reading, music. Home: 1384 Plaza Pacifica Santa Barbara CA 93108-2877

PERLOFF, ROBERT, psychologist, educator; b. Phila., Feb. 3, 1921; s. Myer and Elizabeth (Sherman) P.; m. Evelyn Potechin, Sept. 22, 1946; children: Richard Mark, Linda Sue, Judith Kay. AB, Temple U., 1949; MA, Ohio State U., 1949, PhD, 1951; DSc (hon.), Oreg. Grad. Sch. Profl. Psychology, 1984; DLitt (hon.), Calif. Sch. Profl. Psychology, 1985. Diplomate Am. Bd. Profl. Psychology. Instr. edn. Antioch Coll., 1950-51; with pers. rsch. br. Dept. Army, 1951-55, chief statis. rsch. and cons. unit., 1953-55; dir. R & D Sci. Rsch. Assos., Inc., Chgo., 1955-59; vis. lectr. Chgo. Tchrs. Coll., 1955-56; mem. faculty Purdue U., 1959-69, prof. psychology, 1964-69; field assessment officer univ. Peace Corps Chile III project, 1962; Disting. Svc. prof. bus. adminstrn. and psychology U. Pitts. Joseph M. Katz Grad. Sch. Bus., 1969-90, Disting. Svc. prof. emeritus, 1991—; dir. rsch. programs U. Pitts. Grad. Sch. Bus., 1969-77; dir. Consumer Panel, 1980-83; bd. dirs. Book Ctr.; cons. in field, 1959—; adv. com. assessment exptl. manpower R & D labs. Nat. Acad. Scis., 1972-74; mem. rsch. rev. com. NIMH, 1976-80, Stress and Families rsch. project, 1976-79. Contbr. articles to profl. jours.; editor Indsl. Psychologist, 1963-65, Evaluator Intervention: Pros and Cons; book rev. editor Personnel Psychology, 1952-55; co-editor: Values, Ethics and Standards Sourcebook, 1979, Improving Evaluations; bd. cons. editors Jour. Applied Psychology; bd. advs. Archives History Am. Psychology, Psychol. Svc. Pitts., Recorded Psychol. Jours.; guest editor Am. Psychologist, 1972, Edn. and Urban Soc., 1977, Profl. Psychology, 1977; adv. editor Contemporary Psychology, 1994—. Bd. dirs., v.p. Sr. Citizens Svc. Corp., Calif. Sch. Profl. Psychology; bd. dirs. Greater Pitts. chpt. ACLU, sec., 1997-98; chmn. nat. adv. com. Inst. Govt. and Pub. Affairs, U. Ill., 1986-89, sec. nat. adv. com., 1997—. Decorated Bronze Star; Robert Perloff Grad. Rsch. Assistantship in Inst. Govt. and Pub. Affairs, U. Ill., named in his honor, 1990; Robert Perloff Career Achievement award Knowledge Utilization Soc., named in his honor, 1991. Fellow AAAS, APA (mem.-at-large exec. com. divsn. consumer psychology 1964-67, 70-71, pres. divsn. 1967-68, mem. coun. reps. 1965-68, 72-74, chmn. sci. affairs com., divsn. consumer psychology 1968-69, edn. and tng. bd. 1969-72, chmn. finance com., treas. 1975-84, dir. 1974-82, chmn. investment com. 1977-82, pres. 1985, mem. adv. bd., mem. bd. sci. affairs 1994-96, mem task force intellegence and Intelligence Tests, author column Standard Deviations in jour., pres. address selected as one of 50 over 50 yrs.), Ea. Psychol. Assn. (pres. 1980-81, dir. 1977-80); mem. Am. Psychol. Soc., Internat. Assn. Applied Psychology, Pa. Psychol. Assn. (Disting. Svc. award 1985), Assn. for Consumer Rsch. (chmn. 1970-71), Am. Psychol. Found. (v.p. 1988-89, pres. 1990-92, trustee 1995-98, Lifetime Achievement in Psychology Gold Medal award 2000), Am. Evaluation Assn. (pres. 1977-78), Soc. Psychologists in Mgmt. (Disting. Contbn. to Psychology Mgmt. award 1989, pres. 1993-94), Knowledge Utilization Soc. (pres. 1993-95), Sigma Xi (pres. U. Pitts. chpt. 1989-91), found. alumnus, Coun. of Sci. Soc. Pres., 1998—. Home: 815 Saint James St Pittsburgh PA 15232-2112

PERLSHTEIN, GUEORGUI ZAKHAROVICH, geocryology researcher; b. Moscow, Oct. 5, 1937; s. Zakhar Mikhailovich Perlshtein and Pevzner Acia Iosifovna; m. Levashova Svetlana Vasilievna; 2 children. PhD, Moscow State U., 1968, DSc, 1982. Jr. rschr. Moscow State U., 1960-68; sr. rschr. All-Union Rsch. Inst. of Gold and Rare Metals, Magadan, Russia, 1968-74, chief of lab., 1974-89; chief of dept. North-Ea. Dept. Permafrost Inst., Magadan, 1989; prof. geocryology and hydrogeology Inst. Mining Engrs. Skill Improvement, Magadan, 1971-88; prof. engring. geology and hydrogeology Magadanian Poly. Inst., 1991-95. Author: Water-heat Melioration of Frozen Ground in the North-East of the USSR, 1979; co-author: Techniques of Frozen Ground Preparation to Excavation, 1978, Thermophysical Researches of Syberia's Cryolithozone, 1983, Geocryology of the USSR, vol. 4, 1989, Fundamentals of Geocryology, vol. 5, 2000; contbr. articles to profl. jours. Named Honored Sci. Worker of Russia, 1988. Mem. Nat. Com. Russian Geocryologists, Internat. Acad. Mineral Resources. Home: apt 15 74 Proletarskaya St, Magadan 685030, Russia Office: 12 Gagarin Str, Magadan 685024, Russia

PERLSTEIN, ABRAHAM PHILLIP, psychiatrist, educator; b. N.Y.C., Apr. 15, 1926; s. Benjamin William and Pauline (Gittler) P.; m. Shirley Anne Rubenstein, July 10, 1949; children: Judith Paula, Susan Carol, Bernard William. BS, U. Oreg., 1949; MD, NYU, 1953. Diplomate Am. Bd. Psychiatry and Neurology with added qualifications in Geriat. Psychiatry. Cons. alcoholism dir. SUNY, Bklyn., 1958—, clin. asst. prof. psychiatry, 1957—; med. dir. Peninsula Counseling Ctr., Woodmere, N.Y., 1973-78, psychiat. cons. geriatrics, 1978-90; pvt. practice Elmont, N.Y., 1957-90; assoc. psychiat. dir. Frankling Gen. Hosp., Valley Stream, N.Y., 1980-82; clin. assst. prof. psychiatry Oregon Health Scis. U., Portland, 1997—; attending psychiatrist Kings County Hosp. Ctr., Bklyn., 1957-90, SUNY, U. Hosp. Bklyn., 1963-90, Franklin Gen. Hosp., Valley Stream, 1969-90; adj. clin. asst. prof. psychiatry Cornell U. Med. Coll., N.Y.C., 1978-90; assoc. attending psychiatrist North Shore U. Hosp., Manhasset, N.Y., 1978-90; clin. asst. prof. psychiatry Oreg. Health Scis. U., Portland, 1997—. Sgt. U.S. Army, 1944-46. Fellow Am. Psychiat. Assn. (life). Avocations: music, art, literature, sports. Office: Columbia River Mental Health Svcs PO Box 1337 Vancouver WA 98666-1337

PERLSTEIN, WILLIAM JAMES, lawyer; b. N.Y.C., Feb. 7, 1950; s. Justin Sol and Jane (Goldberg) P.; m. Teresa Catherine Lotito, Dec. 20, 1970; children: David, Jonathan. Student, London Sch. Econs., 1969-70; BA summa cum laude, Union Coll., 1971; JD, Yale U., 1974. Bar: Conn. 1974, D.C. 1976, U.S. Dist. Ct. D.C. 1977, U.S. Ct. Appeals (D.C. cir.) 1978, U.S. Supreme Ct. 1993, N.Y. 2000. Law clk. to judge Marvin Frankel U.S. Dist. Ct., N.Y.C., 1974-75; assoc. Wilmer, Cutler & Pickering, Washington, 1975-82, ptnr., 1982—, mem. mgmt. com., 1995—, chmn., 1998—. Mng. editor Yale Law Jour., 1973-74; contbg. author The Workout Game, 1987. Dir. Neighborhood Legal Svcs. program. Mem. ABA (bus. bankruptcy com. 1983—, vice-chmn. executory contracts subcom. of bus. bankruptcy com. 1988-90, bankruptcy cts. subcom. 1990-97, chmn. legislation subcom. 1997—), Am. Bankruptcy Inst. (chmn. legis. com. 1986-89, bd. dirs. 1989-93, 97—), Am. Law Inst., Am. Coll. Bankruptcy (at-large regent), Am. Bar Found., Phi Beta Kappa. Jewish.

PERMUT, STEVEN LARRY, lawyer; b. Chgo., June 28, 1950; s. Martin and Florence (Kout) P.; m. Linda Fried, Feb. 16, 1975; children: Benjamin, Elisa, David. BA, U. Ill., 1972, BS in Physics, 1977; JD, DePaul U., 1975. Bar: Ill. 1976, Mich. 1976, registered with U.S. Patent and Trademark Office, 1977. Assoc. McGarry & Waters, Grand Rapids, Mich., 1975-78; staff atty. Ford Motor Co., Dearborn, Mich., 1978-82; assoc. patent counsel Masco Corp., Taylor, Mich., 1982-90; mem. Reising, Ethington, Barnes, Kisselle, Learman & McCulloch, Troy, Mich., 1991—. Mem. ABA, Mich. Bar Assn. (chairperson intellectual property law sect. 1992-93), Mich. Patent Law Assn.

PERNA, GIAMPAOLO ROBERT, psychiatrist, researcher; b. Hartford, Conn., Nov. 16, 1964; s. Enrico Roberto Perna and Teiko Ikeda; m. Manuela Holzammer, May 29, 1993; 1 child, Alessandro John. MD, State U. Milan, 1990, PhD in Psychiatry and Behavioral Scis., 1996. Resident in psychiatry State U. Milan, 1997-98, asst. prof. psychiatry, 1998—; Med. diplomate. Avocations: tennis, computers. Fax: +39-2-26433265. E-mail: perna.giampaolo@hsr.it. Office: San Raffaele Hosp, Via Stamira d'Ancona 20, 20127 Milan Italy

PERNAK, JULIUSZ, industrial engineering and chemistry educator; b. Wrzesnia, Poznan, Poland, Mar. 20, 1949; s. Marian and Ewa (Jasek) P.; m. Iwona Jablonska, Dec. 17, 1950; children: Agnieszka, Anna. MSc, Tech. U. Gliwice, Poland, 1971; PhD, Tech. U. Poznan, 1975; Habilitation, Tech. U. Wroclaw, Poland, 1983; postgrad., U. Fla., 1989-91. Assoc. prof. engring. chemistry Poznan Tech. U., 1984-92, prof., 1992-94, full prof., 1994—, dean faculty of chem. tech., 1993-99. Mem. Polish Chem. Soc., Am. Chem. Soc., Internat. Union Pure and Applied Chemistry. Roman Catholic. Avocations: travel, gardening. E-mail: juliusz.pernak@put.poznan.pl. Office: Poznan U Tech, Sklodowskiej-Curie 2, Poznań 60-965, Poland

PERNER, JOSEF, psychology researcher, educator; b. Radstadt, Salzburg, Austria, May 1, 1948; s. Bernhard and Josefine (Klima) P.; m. Anne Cosette Wilson, Dec. 30, 1978; children: Hannah Rosamonde Perner-Wilson, Jacob Bernhard Perner-Wilson. MA, U. Toronto, 1974, PhD, 1978. Wissenschaftlicher Asst. U. Basel, Switzerland, 1978-79; lectr. U. Sussex, Brighton, Eng., 1979-91, sr. lectr., 1991-92, reader, 1992-93, prof. exptl. psychology, 1993-94; prof. Allgemeine Psychologie U. Salzburg, Austria, 1995—; A. von Humboldt rsch. fellow Max-Planck Inst. for Psychol. Rsch., Munich, 1988-89, vis. prof., 1993-94. Author: Understanding the Representational Mind, 1991; co-author: Kognitionspsychologie, 1979. Wachtmeister Jagdkommando, 1967-68. Mem. European Soc. Philosophy and Psychology (pres. 1999—). Avocations: hiking, skiing, volleyball, tennis, folkdancing. Home: Vorberg 355, A-8972 Ramsau Austria Office: U Salzburg, Hellbrunner Strasse 34, A-5020 Salzburg Austria

PERNG, CHIN-LIN, gastroenterologist; b. Hsinchu, Taiwan, Oct. 15, 1957; s. Yun-Huan and Cha-Mai (Shu) P.; m. Hsiao-Feng Chung, Nov. 18, 1988; children: Hsiao-Wen, Shao-Hsuan, Hannah. B of Medicine, Nat. Yang-Ming U., Taipei, Taiwan, 1983. Resident Vets. Hosp., Chutung, Taiwan, 1986-88; resident Vets. Gen. Hosp., Taipei, Taiwan, 1988-92, chief resident, 1992-93, attending physician, 1995—; clin. instr. Nat. Yang-Ming U., Taipei, 1991—, instr. medicine, 1994—; clin. instr. Nat. Defense Med. Ctr., Taipei, 1991—. Contbr. articles to profl. jours. Rsch. fellow Vets. Gen. Hosp., 1993-95, postdoctoral fellow Baylor Coll. Medicine, Houston, 1996-97; recipient 2d prize publ. Nat. Sci. Instn., 1996. Mem. Gastroenterological Soc. Taiwan, Digestive Endoscopy Soc. Taiwan, Soc. Ultrasound Medicine Taiwan. Avocations: harmonica, jogging. Office: Vets Gen Hosp, Shih-Pai Rd, Taipei 11217, Taiwan

PERNICIARO, CHARLES VINCENT, dermatologist, educator, entrepreneur; b. New Orleans, June 15, 1957; s. Ernest Gabriel and Phereby Sheppard (Eagan) P.; children: Jamie Lynn, Kelly Gabrielle. BS, U. La., Lafayette, 1979; MD, La. State U., 1983. Diplomate Am. Bd. Dermatology, Am. Bd. Dermatology and Pathology. Staff physician Ochsner Clin. of Baton Rouge, La., 1987-90; sr. assoc. cons. and staff dermatologist Mayo Clinic, Jacksonville, Fla., 1990-93, cons., staff dermatologist and dermatopathologist, 1993-99; pvt. practice dermatology Brunswick, Ga., 1999—, Jacksonville, Fla., 1999—; pres., CEO Holiday Lighting Concepts, Inc., 1996-2000; lectr., presenter in field; adj. clin. assoc. prof. pathology U. Fla. Shands Jacksonville Med. Ctr., 1999-2000. Contbr. articles to profl. jours. Founder, bd. dirs. S.W. La. Skin Cancer Found., 1987. Recipient Resident-in-Tng. award So. Med. Assn., 1994, Outstanding Paper award Noah Worcester Dermatol. Soc., 1993, First Place Poster award 17th Internat. Colloquium Dermatopathology, 1996. Fellow ACP, Am. Acad. Dermatology (adv. coun. 1995—, environ. coun. 1994-96, com. on preventive dermatology 1988-90, task force on dermatologic oncology 1990-93), Jacksonville Dermatology Soc. (sec.-treas. 1995, pres. 1996), Fla. Soc. Dermatology (bd. dirs. 1998—, chair membership com. 1999-2000), Lions (charter, bd. dirs. Ponte Vedra Beach 1997-98). Avocations: tennis, computers. Home: 317 2d St Neptune Beach FL 32266 Office: Brunswick Dermatology Clinic 3008 E Park Ave Brunswick GA 31520-4241

PERNICKA, ERNST JOSEF, chemist, researcher; b. Vienna, Austria, Feb. 5, 1950; arrived in Germany, 1979; s. Ernst Friedrich and Gertrude (Pohl) P.; m. Evelyn Raidl, Mar. 12, 1976 (div. Apr. 1981); m. Gabriele Helene Felicitas Ober, Apr. 7, 1982; children: Cosima, Laura, Lorenz. PhD in Chemistry, U. Vienna, 1976; privatdozent, U. Heidelberg, Germany, 1986, prof., 1995. Rsch. asst. U. Vienna, 1973-76; fellow Max-Planck-Inst. for Kernphysik, Heidelberg, 1976-77; rsch. asst. U. Vienna, 1977-79; sr. rschr. Max-Planck-Inst. for Kernphysik, Heidelberg, 1979-97; prof. archaeometallurgy TU Bergakademie, Freiberg, 1998—; vis. prof. U. Calif., L.A., 1986-87, U. Vienna, 1991, 93, 95. Editor: Old World Archaeometallurgy, 1989, Archaeometry '90, 1991; contbr. articles to profl. jours. Student rep. U. Vienna, 1970-74. Early metallurgy in Cen. Balkans grantee Volkswagen Found., 1987, tech. and prodn. of Trojan ceramics grantee Deutsche Forschungsgemeinschaft, 1990, early metallurgy in Mesopotamia grantee, Volkswagen Found., 1991. Mem. Hist. Metallurgy Soc., Soc. Archaeol. Scis., Assn. German Chemiker, Deutsches Archaologisches Inst. (corr. mem. 1997). Avocations: tennis, skiing, chess, family activities. Office: TU Bergakad Archaeometrie, Gustav-Zeuner Str 5, D-09596 Freiberg Germany

PERNIČKA, MIROSLAV ENGELBERT, import/export executive; b. Tupesy, Czech Republic, Nov. 7, 1920; s. Tomáš and Anděla (Heliová) P.; m. Františka Matyskevičová, Dec. 7, 1946 (div. 1952); 1 child, Tomáš. Clk. various firms, Czech Republic, 1939-46; customs and tariff clk. Our and Internat. Transport, Ostrava, Czech Republic, 1947-80. Honor award Czech Astron. Soc., 1992. Mem. Czech Astron. Soc. (agent, recorder), Planet Soc. Avocations: golf, philately, astronomy, cosmology, planetary communication. Home: Vyškovická 174, 70030 Ostrava-Jih Czech Republic

PERNY, GUY CHARLES-MARIE, retired physicist, educator; b. Sarreguemines, Moselle, France, June 7, 1923; s. Charles-Marie and Florentina (Sandrino da Pino) P.; m. Marilène Paulus, Aug. 2,1949; children: Chantal, Geneviève, Michel. Cert. higher diploma, École Nat. d'Ingénieurs, Strasbourg, 1947; PhD in Phys. Scis., U. Strasbourg, France, 1957. Asst. prof. edn., 1948-52; rsch. fellow Ctr. Nat. Recherche Sci., 1952-57; prof. physics École Nat. Supérieure de Chimie, Mulhouse, France, 1957-59; assoc. prof. Faculty of Scis., Strasbourg, 1959-63, prof., 1964-77; prof. U. de Haute-Alsace, 1977-85; dir. Ctr. Nat. Conservatory of Arts and Crafts, Mulhouse-Colmar, 1959-61; dir., founder U. Inst. Tech., Mulhouse-Colmar, 1968-71, Physics-Chemistry Lab. of Thin Films, Mulhouse, 1957; co-founder Spectroscopy and Optics Lab. for Solid State, U. Strasbourg, 1952-57. Author: Aspects du Haut Moyen Age Alsacien, 1995, Sur la prééminence des Alsaciens, 1997, Nouvelles Recherches sur la Fondation de l'Ordre des Hospitaliers de Saint Jean de Jérusalem, 1999; contbr. numerous sci. articles to profl. publs. Coll. Pres. Pierre Pflimlin; collaborator Liberation Com. With French Resistance, 1940-45. Recipient Medal of Honor, City of Colmar, 1993, Hungarian Acad. Scis., 1995, several mil. medals; named Citizen of Honor, City of Andlau, 1994. Mem. AAAS, French Soc. Physics, Divsn. Atomic and Molecular Physics (mem. bur. 1984-88), Hist. Soc. France, N.Y. Acad. Scis. (emeritus), Acad. Stanislas, Nat. Acad Metz., Acad. Alsace (chancellor 1984-87). Home: 6 ave de la Marseillaise, Strasbourg France

PERO, MARGARETHA IDA LENA, child and adolescent psychiatrist; b. Norrköping, Sweden, June 27, 1949; d. Wiggo Theodor and Brita Siv Eleonora (Wahlquist) Lund; m. Ronald William Pero; children: Ida, Ebba; stepchildren: Hayley, Amity, Heather. BA, Lund U., 1973, MD, 1987, PhD, 1995. Child psychologist Child and Youth Psychiat. Clinic, Helsingborg, Sweden, 1973-80; med. rsch. asst. Lund U., Sweden, 1982-84, Strang Clinic, N.Y.C., 1984-90; med. intern Lund U., Sweden, 1990-93, med. rsch. asst., 1993-95, resident of child and youth psychiatry, 1995-2000. Me. Swedish Physicians Against Nuclear War. Mem. AAAS, Swedish Med. Assn., Swedish Assn. of Child and Youth Psychiatry, Swedish Soc. of Medicine, N.Y. Acad. Sci. Lutheran. Avocations: family, music, cross-country skiing, hunting. also: 1651 Rupert Rd Arlington VA 05250 Office: St Larsområdet, Lund Sweden also: 1651 Rupert Rd Arlington VT 05250

PEROMINGO, JOSÉ-ANTONIO DÍAZ, physician, biologist; b. Puebla de Trives, Orense, Spain, Aug. 27, 1966; s. Jaime Díaz González and Laudelina Peromingo Alonso; m. María-Teresa Amboage Paz, July 11, 1992. MD, U. Santiago, Spain, 1991, degree in biology, 1997. Diplomate Spanish Bd. Internal Medicine. Resident C.H. Arquitecto Marcide, El Ferrol, Spain, 1992-96, internist, 1998; internist Hosp. Provincial, Pontevedra, Spain, 1997; med. area chief F.P. Hosp. da Barbanza, Riveira, Spain, 1999—; co-worker botany dept. Sch. Pharmacy, Santiago, 1998—. Contbr. articles to profl. jours. Avocations: music, painting, art, botany. Office: F P Hosp da Barbanza, Oleiros S/N, 15993 Riveira Spain

PEROSCH, TONY ANTHONY GEORGE, corporate executive, consul; b. Zagreb, Croatia, Jan. 21, 1930; arrived in Venezuela, 1948; s. Ante Perosch; m. Maria Rosaria De Stefano De Spagna, Aug. 6, 1969; 1 child, Albert. Student, Cen. U. Venezuela, 1959. V.p. Yard, C.A., Caracas, Venezuela, 1959-66; dir. Salta, C.A., Caracas, 1966-83; v.p. Aero Charter, C.A., Caracas, 1972-83; pres. Omni Aviation, C.A., Caracas, 1978-84; chmn. bd. Gruppo Omni, Caracas, 1984—; hon. consul R.S.F. of Yugoslavia, Monte Carlo, Monaco, 1989—; bd. dirs. Fabrica De Aviones, C.A., Caracas. Bd. dirs. Fed. Sec. Nat. Def., Belgrad, 1983, Fed. Dir. Supply and Procurement. Recipient Golden Star, Govt. of Yugoslavia, 1988. Mem. Caracas Country Club, Aero Club. Democrat. Roman Catholic. Avocations: tourist pilot, golf, swimming.

PEROTTI, DANIELA, cancer biology researcher; b. Busto Arsizio, Varese, Italy, Sept. 19, 1969; d. Umberto Perotti and Erminia Bertelli; m. Massimo Molinaro, Nov. 9, 1996. Degree in biol. scis., U. Milan, 1993, PhD in Med. Genetics, 1999. Fellow divsn. pediat. oncology Nat. Tumor Inst., Milan, 1992-96, assoc. rschr., 1996-99, assoc. rschr. divsn. exptl. oncology, 1999—; presenter confs. Contbr. articles to med. jours. Mem. Italian Assn. Pediat. Hematology-Oncology. Avocation: basketball. Home: Via Galvani 14, 20040 Usmate Milan, Italy Office: Nat Tumor Inst, Via Venezian 1, 20133 Milan Italy

PERRE, JOS VAN DE, pipeline equipment supply specialist; b. London, June 23, 1957; s. Hugo and Sarah Selma (Velleman) van de P.; m. Sue Ridley, Feb. 22, 1997. Dir. Alexander Cardew Ltd., London, 1985—. Recipient badge Blue Peter, U.K., 1965. Mem. Pipeline Industries Guild, Ferrari Owners Club Gt. Britain (mem. mgmt. com.). Avocations: motor sport, walking. Office: Unit 27, Chelsea Wharf 15 Lots Rd, SW10 0QJ London SW10 0QJ, England

PERRÉE, HANS GERARD, editor; b. Veghel, The Netherlands, Nov. 10, 1952; s. Piet Gerard and Luus Maria (Vanderburgt) P. DRS, U. Amsterdam, The Netherlands, 1985. Rschr. Cebeon, Amsterdam, 1976-78; H.S. tchr. Amsterdam, 1979-82; programmer Volmac, Utrecht, The Netherlands, 1986-89, Twinsoft, Vianen, The Netherlands, 1989-94; sys. editor newspaper Algemeen Dagblad, Rotterdam, The Netherlands, 1994—. Editor-in-chief Rowing Mag.; contbr. articles to profl. publs. Recipient Press prize Royal Dutch Rowing Assn., Amsterdam, 1992, Golden medal of Honour. Mem. Labor Party. Avocations: rowing, running, writing. Home: Javakade 106, 1019 RV Amsterdam The Netherlands Office: Algemeen Dagblad, Marten Meesweg 35, 3068 AV Rotterdam The Netherlands

PERRET, CLAUDE HENRI, internist; b. Pontarlier, Doubs, France, Oct. 22, 1930; s. Rene and Suzanne (Fonlupt) P.; m. Anne Zbinden, Aug. 28, 1958; children: Jacques, Francois, Florence. MD, U. Lausanne, 1955, cert. internist, 1965. Med. asst. Inst. Physiology, Lausanne, Switzerland, 1956-57; resident U. Lausanne Med. Clinic, 1958-60, Hosp. Necker Nephrology Clinic, Paris, 1960-61; prof. pathophysiology faculty medicine U. Lausanne, Switzerland, 1968-96, head intensive care unit, 1973-96, dean faculty medicine, 1992-96; cons. Signal Processing Lab. Swiss Fed. Inst. Tech., Lausanne, Switzerland, 1997—. Fellow Am. Coll. Chest Physicians, Am. Coll. Critical Care Medicine; mem. Acad. Nat. Medicine (Paris fgn. corr.). Avocations: sailing, golf. Home: Joliette 6, 1006 Lausanne Switzerland

PERRET, GERARD ANTHONY, JR., orthodontist; b. New Orleans, Feb. 13, 1959; s. Gerard A. and Marie M. (Gamino) P.; m. Catherine J. McMahon, 1996; 1 child, Caroline Marie. BS in Chemistry, U. N.C., 1981; DDS, La. State U., 1986, cert. orthodontics, 1989. Clin. asst. prof. La. State U. Sch. Dentistry, New Orleans, 1986-87; pvt. practice dentistry Lakeside Dental Group, Metairie, La., 1986-87; pvt. practice orthodontics Jacksonville, Fla., 1989-91, Tampa, Fla., 1991—; founder, pres. Orthogap, Inc., Tampa, 1993—. Patentee in field. Active New Tampa Cmty. Coun. Mem. ADA, Am. Assn. Orthodontists, Fla. Assn. Orthodontists, Hillsborough County Dental Soc., Hillsborough County Dental Rsch. Clinic, So. Assn. Orthodontists, Rotary (pres. New Tampa chpt. 1997-98), Omicron Kappa Upsilon. Avocations: sailing, fishing, music, golf. Office: 14201 Bruce B Downs Blvd Ste 2 Tampa FL 33613-3913

PERRETT, JOHN EDMUND, motel owner, farmer, butcher; b. Roma, Queensland, Australia, Nov. 11, 1932; s. John Sealy and Francis Mary (Vanaglia) P.; m. Marcelline Ellen Maloney, May 12, 1958; children: Leigh, Judy, Kim. Student, St. Joseph's Sch., Queensland, Australia, St. George's Sch., Queensland, Australia. Cert. butcher. Butcher St. George Butchery,

Australia, 1948-52, mgr., 1952-56; owner, mgr. J.E. Perrett Co., Toowoomba, Australia, 1956-64; grain farmer, grazier J.E. Perrett & Co. Darling Downs, Cecil Plains, Australia, 1964-71; butchery owner, mgr. Perretts' Meats, Beaudes Ert, Australia, 1971-84; owner, mgr. grain, dairy, tourism Woollahra Farm World, Beaudes Ert, Australia, 1984-87; owner, mgr. Oasis Motel J.E. Perrett & Co., Kingaroy, Australia, 1987-90; owner, mgr. Gympie (Australia) Motel J.E. Perrett & Co., 1991-95; owner, mgr. Waltzing Matilda Motor Inn J.E. Perrett & Co., Charleville, Australia, 1994—. Author: Growing Up in the Bush, from the 1930's to the 1960's, 1999. Pres. St. Mary's Parents Friends, Kingaroy, Australia, 1966, art gallery, 1966, Marymount Coll. Parents Friends, Beaudesert, Gold Coast, Queensland, 1972-84; active mem., candidate Nat. Australian Pty., Gold Coast, Queensland, 1968—. Mem. Knights of So. Cross (chmn., sec., past pres.), Lions (com. mem.), Beewah Golf Club. Mem. Nat. Australian Pty. Roman Catholic. Avocations: tennis, golf, guitar playing, writing, shooting. Home and Office: 17 Burgess St, Caloundra QLD 4551, Australia

PERRIN, CHARLES JOHN, banker; b. Exeter, Devon, Eng., May 1, 1940; s. Michael and Nancy (Curzon) P.; m. Gillian Hughes-Thomas, Apr. 16, 1966; children: Felicity Margaret, Nicola May. MA in Jurisprudence, New Coll., Oxford, 1962. With Hambros Bank Ltd., London, 1963-98; exec. dir. Hambros Bank Ltd., 1979-86, dep. chmn., 1986-98, chief exec., 1995-98; chmn. bd. Hambro Pacific Ltd., Hong Kong, 1983—; non-exec. dir. Harland & Wolff PLC, Belfast, No. Ireland, 1984-89; bd. dirs. Hambros PLC, London. Vice chmn. UNICEF U.K. Com., London, 1972-91; gov. Queen Anne's Sch., Berkshire, 1981—, London Hosp. Med. Coll., 1991-95; vice chmn. Royal Brompton and Harefield NHS Trust, 1998—; mem. coun. U. London, 1994—; hon. treas. Queen Mary and Westfield Coll., 1999—. Hon. fellow New Coll. Mem. Royal Coll. Physicians (hon.), Athenaeum. Office: Hambros Bank Ltd, 41 Tower Hill, London EC3N 4HA, England

PERRIN, JOHN ROBIN, economics educator, retired; b. L.A., July 6, 1930; arrived in Eng., 1956; BS, UCLA, 1951, MBA, 1954; PhD, London Sch. Econs., 1958. Asst. prof. Mount Allison U., New Brunswick, Can., 1959-61; sr. lectr. U. Nottingham (Eng.), 1962-68; prof. U. Lancaster (Eng.), 1968-74, U. Warwick, Coventry, Eng., 1974-85; prof. and fellow U. Exeter (Eng.), 1985, ret., 1998; rsch. consulting Nat. Health Svc., Eng., 1977-98. Mng. editor: Jour. Bus. Fin. and Acctg., 1974-85, Fin. Accountability and Mgmt., 1985-97; author: Resource Management in the National Health Service, 1988; co-author: Public Sector Accounting and Financial Control, 1983, 3d rev. edit., 1992; co-author: Accounting for Managers, 1994, 2d rev. edit., 1998. Mem. Coventry Health Authority, Eng., 1979-83. Mem. Healthcare Fin. Mgmt. Assn. Avocations: gardening, rural studies, architecture, local history. Home: Dunnings, Western Rd Ashburn, Newton Abbot Devon TQ13 7ED, England

PERRIN, LOUIS FRANÇOIS, allergist-immunologist, medical educator; b. Lyon, France, Mar. 22, 1921; s. Félix and Jeanne Françoise (Jacquet) P.; m. Michèle Emilie Labry, Apr. 20, 1963; 1 child, Patrick J. MD, Faculty Medicine Lyon, France, 1950; PhD, Faculty Medicine Paris, 1962. Resident med. officer Lyon Hosps., 1946-50; head respiratory physiology lab. U. Lyon Faculty Medicine, 1959-63; prof. exptl. medicine U. Grenoble (France) Faculty Medicine, 1962-72; prof. physiology U. Catholique Faculty Scis., Lyon, 1989-95; mem. Com. Mktg. Authorization of New Drugs, Ministry of Health, Paris, 1987-90. Author: Allergologie pratique, 1984, Immunopathologie clinique, 1990, L'aspirine, 1991, Le systéme immunitaire, 1997. Recipient Nat. Order of Merit, Pres. of France, 1974. Mem. Am. Acad. Allergy, Asthma and Immunology, N.Y. Acad. Scis. Roman Catholic. Avocations: skiing, windsurfing. Home: 2 rue Alphonse-Fochier, F-69002 Lyon France Office: Univ Catholique, Faculté des Sciences, Lyon France

PERRIN, MICHAEL WARREN, lawyer; b. Cameron, Tex., Nov. 10, 1946; s. Frank W. and Mary Ann (Green) P.; m. Melinda Elizabeth Hill, Aug. 9, 1969; children: Elizabeth, Carter, Hunter. BS, U. Tex., Austin, 1969, JD, 1971. Bar: Tex. 1972, U.S. Dist. Ct. (no., ea., we. and so. dists.) Tex., U.S. Ct. Appeals (5th and 11th cirs.), U.S. Supreme Ct. Assoc. Vinson & Elkins, Houston, 1972-73; assoc. Fisher, Roch & Gallagher, Houston, 1973-76; ptnr. Fisher, Gallagher, Perrin & Lewis, Houston, 1976-91; sole practice Houston, 1991-96; ptnr. King & Spalding, Houston, 1996—. Fellow Am. Coll. Trial Lawyers, Internat. Acad. Trial Lawyers, Internat. Soc. Barristers; mem. Am. Bd. Trial Advocates, Am. Bar Found., Houston Young Lawyers Assn. (sec. 1974-75), Tex. Young Lawyers Assn. (dir. 1976-78, chmn. bd. 1978-79), Houston Trial Lawyers Assn. (pres. 1987-88), Tex. Trial Lawyers Assn. (pres. 1989-90), Tex. Bar Found. (Houston chpt.), U. Tex. Devel. bd. Methodist.

PERRIN, RONALD FREDERIC, retired humanities educator; b. Montpelier, Vt.; s. Rene George and Ella (Williamson) P.; m. Alexandrine Koutovsky, Sept. 17, 1960; 1 child, Sasha. BA, Northwestern U., 1965; MA, U. Calif. San Diego, 1967, PhD, 1971. Prof. Philosophy U. Mont., Missoula, 1979-81, prof. Polit. Theory, 1981-97, prof. Philosophy emeritus, 1997—. Author: (book) Max Scheler's Concept of the Person, 1992. Chair Mont. Com. for the Humanities, 1984; mem. bd. dirs. Nat. Fedn. of State Humanities Couns., 1985-88. Hon. Woodrow Wilson fellow Woodrow Wilson Found., 1965; vis. fellow Va. Ctr. for Humanities & Pub. Policy, 1987. Mem. Phi Kappa Phi. Home: 302 Pattee Canyon Dr Missoula MT 59803-1625 Office: Philosophy Dept U Mont Missoula MT 59812-0001

PERRIN-PELLETIER, FRANCOIS JEAN CHARLES, insurance executive; b. Firminy, France, Feb. 21, 1930; s. Georges and Marie Aubounette Josephine Perrin-Pelletier; m. Anne Chapuls, Sept. 8, 1955; children: Luc, Eric, Fanny, Blandineo. Directories chmn. Talbot Automobile, 1978; sec. Com. des Constructeurs Automobiles du Mardié Cmty., 1983-92; chmn. Groupement d'Entreprises de Transports de Franche Cmtuy., Cornbevoi, 1985-94, Gaipare Assn., Paris, 1992—, Groupement des Grandes Entreprises de Transport, 1992-95; vice-chmn. Union Routiere, Paris, 1992—; exec. v.p. Automile Peugeot, 1996—. Mem. Paris C. of C. (hon.), Automobile Club France. Avocations: golf, bridge. Home: 4 rue de General Lanrecac, 75017 Paris France Office: Gaipare Assn, Gaipare Assn, 20 rue le Peltier, 75009 Paris France

PERRONI, CAROL, artist, painter; b. Boston, July 28, 1952; d. Michael John and Mary Agnes (Collett) P.; m. John Richard Mugford, May 23, 1987; 1 child, Jonathan Perroni. Student, Boston Mus. Sch., 1970-71; BA in Art, Bennington Coll., 1976; student, Skowhegan Sch. Painting and Sculpture, 1978; MFA in Art, Hunter Coll., 1983. Studio asst. for artist Isaac Witkin, Bennington, Vt., 1973-74; libr. asst. Simmons Coll. Libr., Boston, 1977-78; studio asst. for artist Mel Bochner, N.Y.C., 1979; bookkeeper Internat. House, N.Y.C., 1979-80; studio asst. for Lee Krasner, East Hampton, N.Y., 1980; rsch. asst. Art News Mag., N.Y.C., 1981; intern Greenespace Gallery, N.Y.C., 1982-83; tech. asst. Avery Architectural and Fine Arts Libr. Columbia U., N.Y.C., 1981-83; libr., rechr. Kennedy Galleries, Inc., N.Y.C., 1984-86; program specialist, art tchr. Swinging Sixties Sr. Citizen Ctr., Bklyn., 1986-87; with Arts in Edn. Program, R.I., 1993-96. One-woman shows include Boston City Hall, 1978, Hunter Coll. Gallery, N.Y.C., 1983, Ten Worlds Gallery, N.Y.C., 1986, Gallery X, New Bedford, Mass., 1993-94, Hera Gallery, Wakefield, R.I., 1995, 98, AS220, Providence, R.I., 1996, C.C. of R.I., Lincoln, 1996, Boyden Libr., Foxboro, Mass., 1997; group shows include Salem State Coll., Mass., 1978, Fuller Mus. Art, Brockton, Mass., 1989-90, Danforth Mus. Art, Framingham, Mass., 1989, Attleboro Mus., Mass., 1989, Gallery One, Providence, 1992, Gallery X, New Bedford, Mass., 1992-98, Grove St. Gallery, Worcester, Mass., 1993, Bell St. Chapel, Providence, 1994-95, AS220, Providence, 1994, 98, Hera Gallery, Wakefield, R.I., 1993-99, 2000, St. Andrew's Sch., Barrington, R.I., 1994, McKillop Gallery, Salve Regina U., Newport, R.I., 1995, North River Arts Soc., Marshfield Hills Village, Mass., 1995, Providence Art Club, 1995, The Sarah Doyle Gallery, Brown U., Providence, 1995-96, R.I. Watercolor Soc. Slater Meml. Park, Pawtucket, 1995, Fed. Reserve Bank, Boston, 1996, Art Advisory/Boston, Quincy, Mass., 1996, Rotch-Jones-Duff Mus., New Bedford, Mass., 1997, Dryden Galleries, Providence, 1997, Renaissance Gallery, Fall River, Mass., 1997, 98, Island Arts Gallery, Newport, 1997, Harwood Art Ctr., Albuquerque, 1998, Branigan Cultural Ctr., Las Cruces, N.Mex., 1999, 2000, Atrium Gallery, Providence, R.I., 2000; represented in permanent collection at R.I. Hosp. Art Collection and pvt. collections. Bd. dirs. Hera Ednl. Found., 1994—. Grantee Artists Space, 1986, Flintridge Found., 1993, fellow Vt. Studio Ctr., Johnson, 1990, Dorland Mountain Arts Colony, 1993. Mem. SOHO 20 Gallery (nat. affiliate mem.), Am. Acad. Women Artists. Home: 2089 Plaza Thomas Santa Fe NM 87505-5438

PERRONNE, BRUCE L., sales executive; b. July 4, 1943. BSME, U. Wis., 1966. Program dir. IBM, White Plains, N.Y., 1998—. Home: 21 Katrina Cir Bethel CT 06801-3310

PERROT, CHARLES, theologist, educator; b. Gannat, France, Feb. 16, 1929; s. Marcel and Therese (Montillier) P. D in Theology, U. Lyon, 1958. Prof. Cath. Faculty Lyon, 1960-69, Cath. Inst. Paris, 1969-94. Author: Jesus et L'Histoire, 1979, Jesus Christ et Seigneur des Premiers Chretiens, 1998. Home: 43 rue de Paris BP 836, 03008 Moulins cedex France

PERRY, ANDRÉ, recording industry executive; b. Verdun, Que., Can., Feb. 12, 1937; s. Armand Perrotte and Juliette Martineau; m. Yaël Brandeis; children from previous marriage: Nathalie, Fabienne. Founder André Perry Prodns., Que., 1968-70, Son Québec, 1970-73; pres., founder Le Studio Morin Heights (Can.) Inc., Que., 1974-88, Groupe André Perry, Morin Heights, Washington, and San Francisco, 1984-88, André Perry Video, 1980-88, André Perry Assocs. Comm. Cons., 1988—; founder, pres. Premiere (Bahamas) Inc., 1994—; founder, bd. dirs. Que. Assn. Record and Entertainment Industry, Can. Ind. Record Producers Assn. Can.; mktg. cons. audio and visual industries. Music co-ordinator, producer Montreal Olympic Games, 1976; producer John Lennon, Wilson Pickett, Charles Aznavour; producer, dir. many French-Can. and Can. rec. artists. Bd. dirs. Syntphonika, 1994—. Mem. Audio Engring. Soc., Pro-Can., Composers, Authors and Pubs. Assn. of Can., Can. Rec. Industry Assn., Societe d'Auteurs, Compositeurs, et Editeurs de Musique. Pioneer in the Can. rec. industry. Home and Office: PO Box CB-13038, Nassau Bahamas

PERRY, BLANCHE BELLE, physical therapist; b. New Bedford, Mass., Sept. 2, 1929; d. Joseph Rudolph and Beatrice (Faria) Andrews; BS, Ithaca (N.Y.) Coll., 1951; MA, Assumption Coll., Worcester, Mass., 1978; m. Louis Perry, Nov. 26, 1953; (dec. 1980); children: Marcia, Susan, Tracey, Evelyn (dec.). Office and hosp. phys. therapist, Mass. and N.Y., 1961-65; dir. rehab. svcs. St. Luke's Hosp., New Bedford, 1967-89; ret, 1989; profl. adv. com. Vis. Nurse Assn. Wareham, 1980; mem. faculty continuing edn. Newbury Coll., 1986; corporator New Bedford Five Cents Savs. Bank, Compass Bank for Savs. Chmn. Mattapoisett Sch. Com., 1970; vice chmn. Mass. Sch. Commn. Area IV, 1972-75; sec. Old Colony Regional Vocat. Sch. Com., 1973—; trustee Abner Pease Scholarship Found.; chmn. com. opportunity ctr. CARF, New Bedford, 1987; pres. St. Luke's Hosp. Retirees, 1996. Grantee Elks Nat. Found., 1965. Mem. Am. Phys. Therapy Assn., Nat. Rehab. Adminstrs. Assn., Delta Kappa Gamma. Republican. Club: Mattapoisett Women's (pres. 1996). Home: 41 Aucoot Rd Mattapoisett MA 02739-2401

PERRY, CHARLES EDWARD, journalist, food historian; b. L.A., Aug. 5, 1941; s. Douglass Brill Perry and Mary Elizabeth Corbaley. Student, Princeton U., 1959-61, Mid. East Ctr. for Arab Studies, Shimlan, Lebanon, 1962-63; AB in Near Ea. Langs., U. Calif., Berkeley, 1964. Editor, staff writer Rolling Stone mag., San Francisco, 1968-76; freelance writer L.A., 1976-90; staff writer L.A. Times, 1990—. Author: The Haight-Ashbury: A History, 1984; prin. author: Medieval Arab Cuisine, 2000; mem. editl. bd. Petits Propos Culinaires, London, 2000—. Mem. So. Calif. Culinary Historians. Office: LA Times 142 S Broadway Los Angeles CA 90012-3114

PERRY, CHRIS, professional golfer; b. Edenton, N.C., Sept. 27, 1961; s. Jim P.; m. Katharine Perry; children: Andrew Christopher, Emily Ann, Natalie Kay. Student, Ohio State U. Profl. golfer, 1984—; finished top 10 Kemper Open, 1987, Canon Greater Hartford Open, 1990; winner Mexican Open, 1994, NIKE Utah Classic, 1994; finished top 10 B.C. Open, 1997, winner, 1998; finished top 10 Greater Milw. Open, 1998, Buick Challenge, 1998, Buick Classic, 1998; PGA tour title, 1998; 19th pl. Spring Internat.; missed cut Nat. Car Rental Golf Classic at Walt Disney World Resort, 1998; mem. PGA Tour charity team Buick Classic, 1999. Recipient Player of Yr. honors NIKE Tour, 1994; named one of only three non-exempt players to earn fullpaying privileges, 1997; 2nd place Buick Open, 2000. Avocations: all sports, college football, snow skiing. Office: So Ohio Sect of PGA 2186 Gateway Dr Fairborn OH 45324-6356*

PERRY, ELAINE KING, neurochemist; b. Edinburgh, Scotland, Sept. 15, 1944; d. James Cyril King and Ella Elizabeth (Walker) Miller; m. Robert Henry Perry, June 5, 1971; children: Jonathan James, Nicolette Sarah Louise. BSc, St. Andrews U., 1967; PhD, Cambridge U., 1972, DSc, 1993. Non-med. biochemist Newcastle (England) Health Authority, 1975-79; rsch. assoc. U. Newcastle, 1979-86; scientist Med. Rsch. Coun., Neurochem. Pathology Unit, Newcastle, 1987-90, sr. scientist, 1991-95, spl. appointment, 1995; prof. neurochem. pathology U. Newcastle, 1995—, dir. Medicinal Plant Rsch. Ctr., 1996—. Sect. editor Neurobiology of Aging Jour., 1993—; contbr. over 200 articles to profl. jours. Kellogg Internat. scholar, U. Mich.; recipient Luigi Amaducci Meml. award for rsch. in neurodegenerative diseases, 1999. Mem. Internat. Soc. Neurochemistry, European Soc. Neurochemists. Avocations: plant medicine, herb cultivation. Home: Dilston Mill House, Corbridge NE45 5QZ, England Office: Newcastle Gen Hosp, Med Rsch Coun Neurochem Pathology Unit, Newcastle Upon Tyne NE4 6BE, England

PERRY, GEORGE WILSON, oil and gas company executive; b. Pampa, Tex., July 18, 1929; s. Frank M. and Ruth (Ingersoll) P.; m. Patricia Carberry Bowen, 1950; children: Sally, Jett Perry Pemrick, Susan Jeanne Perry Bynder-Schrier, Virginia Anne Perry Haynie, Tobe Jackson Perry. BS in Petroleum Engring., U. Tulsa, 1952. Registered profl. engr., Tex. Engr. Stanolind Oil & Gas Co., Oklahoma City, 1952-53, Parker Drilling Co., Tulsa, 1953-54, Holm Drilling Co., Tulsa, 1954-55; drilling engr. Mobil Oil, Victoria, Tex., Lake Charles, La., Paris, France, 1955-79; drilling mgr. Anaco, Venezuela, N.Y.C., Tehran, Iran, Stavanger, Norway, New Orleans, La., 1955-79; exec. v.p. Loffland Bros. Co., Tulsa, 1979-89; pres., CEO Gas Well Properties, Inc., Dallas, 1989—. Mem. Delta Tau Delta. Office: Gas Well Properties Inc PO Box 795302 5995 Summerside Dr Dallas TX 75248-9992

PERRY, IAN CHARLES, physician; b. Apr. 18, 1939; s. Sidney Charles and Marjorie Ellen (Elliott) P.; m. Janet Patricia Watson, July 27, 1963; children: Johanna Elizabeth, Helen. Diploma in aviation medicine, RAF Inst. Aviation Medicine. Intern Guy's Hosp., London, 1957; resident Highlands Hosp., London, 1958, med. surg. intern, 1963-64; commd. 2d lt. RAMC, 1963, advanced through grades to major, ret., 1973, resident, 1965-72; pvt. practice aviation and occupational med. practice, 1973—; med. dir. Internat. Aviation Med. Ctr., London; sr. cons. Avimed Ltd., Mi2g Ltd.; cons. in occupational medicine Winchester NHS Trust; hon. cons. IAOPA, Brit. Helicopter Adv. Bd.; cons. Twinings Tea, Joint Aviation Authority Med. Group. Contbr. articles to profl. jours. Former chmn. Grateley PTA. Fellow Aerospace Med. Assn., Royal Aero. Soc., Inst. Occupational Health and Safety, Inst. Mgmt.; mem. Internat. Acad. Aviation and Space Medicine, Army Air Corps Mus. Friends, Preservation of Rural England, Nurdling Assn. England (sec.), Freeman City of London, Liveryman Worshipful Co of Gunmakers, Guild of Air Pilots and Navigators (past master), Calvary and Guards Club, Tidworth Golf Club. Avocations: orchids, golf, shooting. E-mail: ian@ianperry.com. Home: The Old Farm House, Grateley SP11 8JR, England Office: 19 Cliveden Pl, London SW1 W8HD, England

PERRY, J. WARREN, health sciences educator, administrator; b. Richmond, Ind., Oct. 25, 1921; s. Charles Thomas and Zona M. (Ohler) P. BA, DePauw U., 1944, DSc (hon.), 1998; postgrad., Harvard U., 1948-49; MA, Northwestern U., 1952, PhD, 1955; DSc (hon.), D'Youville Coll., 1990, Med. Coll. Ohio, 1996, DePauw U., 1998. Instr. St. John's Mil. Acad., Delafield, Wis., 1944-47; counselor, asst. prof. psychology U. Ill.-Chgo., 1953-56; dir. prosthetic-orthotic edn., asst. prof. orthopaedic surgery Northwestern U. Med. Sch., 1957-61; lectr. psychology U. Chgo., 1957-61; asst. chief div. tng. Vocat. Rehab. Adminstrn., HEW, 1961-64, dep. asst. commr. research and tng., 1964-66; prof. health scis. adminstrn. SUNY-Buffalo, 1966-85, founding dean Sch. Health Related Professions, 1966-77, dean and prof. emeritus, 1985—; Mary E. Switzer Meml. lectr. Dallas, 1977, Lexington, 1991; mem. task force for Legislation for Allied Health Professions, 1966-67; com. edn. allied health professions and svcs., coun. med. edn. AMA, 1968-73; nat. adv. com. Am. Dietetic Assn., 1970-75, chmn., 1972-75; nat. rev. com., regional med. programs HEW, 1969-72; mem. Inst. Medicine, NAS, 1973—, steering com. on manppower policy for primary care, bd. health promotion and disease prevention, 1981-83, sr. advisor, com. to study the role allied health, com. to study med. manpower in VA, 1988-91; spl. med. adv. com. VA, 1974-77; task force on manpower for prevention Fogarty Internat. Inst., NIH, 1975-76; acad. planning com. Mass. Gen. Hosp. Founding editor: Jour. Allied Health, 1972-78, editor emeritus, 1985—; contbr. articles to profl. jours. Bd. dirs., dir. com. opera edn. Lyric Opera Guild, Chgo., 1957-61; chmn. acad. divsn. dr., coun. trustees Buffalo Philharm. Orch., 1987-93; bd. dirs. Goodwill Industries Buffalo, 1969-76; trustee Cmty. Music Sch. Buffalo, 1977-80; adv. bd., v.p. Sisters of Charity Hosp., Buffalo, 1969-87, pres., 1986-88; bd. visitors U. Pitts., 1977-80; coun. trustees D'Youville Coll., Buffalo, 1978-88, trustee emeritus, 1989-95; bd. dirs. Am. Lung Assn. Western N.Y., 1975-92, pres., 1983; bd. dirs. ARC, Buffalo, Artpark State Performing Arts Ctr., Lewiston, N.Y., 1986-96; Am. Lung Assn. N.Y. State, 1981-85, exec. com., 1989-92; chmn. N.Y. State Coalition Smoking or Health, Albany, N.Y., 1987-91; trustee Theodore Roosevelt Inaugural Site Found., 1987, pres., 1991-94; bd. advisors Buffalo Coun. on World Affairs, 1987-88; trustee Buffalo Opera Co., 1989-94, chmn. opera adv. coun., 1995-97; mem. Legacy Soc.; charter mem. Cmty. Found. for Greater Buffalo, 1998—; patron of the arts Coun. of Buffalo and Erie County, 2000. Recipient Sustained Superior Svc. award HEW, 1965, Disting. Svc. award Am. Orthotics-Prosthetics Assn., 1966, Buffalo Opera Co., 1995, Chancellors award for adminstrv. svc. SUNY, 1977, 1st Allied Health Leadership award, 1988, Disting. Author award Jour. Allied Health, 1978, Cert. of Merit, AMA, 1979, Pres. Cir. PIN, Buffalo State Coll., 1993, 50th Anniversary Alumni citation De Pauw U., 1994, Outstanding Svc. award Theodore Roosevelt Inaugural Site Found., 1994, Theodore Roosevelt Exemplary Citizenship award, 1997, Brotherhood/Sisterhood award in health NCCJ Western N.Y., 1995, Christmas Seal Hall of Fame award ALA N.Y. State, 1995, Disting. Citizenship award Mayor of Buffalo, 1995, Patron of the Arts award ARts Coun. of Buffalo and Eric County, 2000, Alumni Achievement award SUNY-Buffalo, 2000, Wisdom Award of Honor 1999, Wisdom Hall of Fame fellow Wisdom Soc., 1999; named Outstanding Individual Philanthropist, Nat. Soc. Fundraising Execs. Western N.Y., 1992, Ky. Col., 1969, Nebr. admn., 1964; J. Warren Perry Disting. Author award named in his honor Jour. Allied Health, 1984—, J. Warren Perry Meml. lectr. named in his honor SUNY, Buffalo, 1990—, J. Warren Perry Outstanding Vol. Leadership award named in his honor Western N.Y. chpt. ALA, 1994—; Perry Scholarships presented in his honor U. Buffalo Found., 1991—. Fellow Assn. Schs. of Allied Health Professions (pres. 1969-70, cert. of merit 1977, Pres.'s award 1978, Honors of Society 1984); mem. APA, Am. Dietetics Assn. (hon.), Am. Personnel and Guidance Assn., Nat. Rehab. Assn., Phi Beta Kappa, Phi Delta Kappa (pres. 1955), Delta Tau Delta (Alumni Achievement award 2000). Home: 83 Bryant St Apt 5A Buffalo NY 14209-1831

PERRY, JOE NELSON, biometrician; b. Croydon, England, Aug. 17, 1951; s. Jack and Sadie (Nelson) P.; m. Susan Mary Woodward, June 21, 1980; 1 child, Sophie. BSc in Math., Lanchester Polytech., 1973; MSc in Biometry, U. Reading, 1975, DSc, 1989. Lectr. Polytech. of the South Bank, London, 1975-76; rsch. biometrician Rothamsted Exptl. Sta., Harpenden Herts, 1976—; vis. prof. biometry U. Greenwich, London, 1994—. Editl. adv. bd. Jour. of Animal Ecology, Ecol. Entomology; editor Biometric Bull., 1988-92; contbr. articles to profl. jours. Recipient Disting. Stats. Ecologist award Internat. Assn. Ecology, 1998. Fellow Royal Entomol. Soc., Royal Statis. Soc.; mem. Internat. Biometric Soc. (exec. com. 1988-92), British Ecol. Soc. Achievements include development of spatial analysis by distance indices, the Adés family of frequency distributions; research of measurement of range of attraction of pea moth sex pheromone; design of U.K. government's field-scale evaluation of genetically modified crops. E-mail: joe.perry@bbsrc.ac.uk. Office: Dept Ent & N, Rothamsted Exptl Sta, Herts Harpenden AL5 2JQ, England

PERRY, JOHN GRENVILLE, civil engineering educator, education director; b. Stoke-on-Trent, Eng., May 21, 1945; s. Frederick and Elsie (Till) P.; m. Ruth Katharine Forrester, Apr. 20, 1968; children: Jonathan Mark, Timothy Joshua David. B in Engring., U. Liverpool, Eng., 1966, M in Engring., 1967; PhD, U. Manchester, Eng., 1985. Engr. Costain Ltd., Eng., 1968-70; project engr. Imperial Chem. Industries Ltd., Eng., 1970-74; lectr./sr. lectr. Univ. of Manchester, Inst. Sci. and Tech., Eng., 1974-88; prof. U. Birmingham, Eng., 1988—; dep. dean of engring. U. Birmingham, 1995-97; cons. in field, 1978—. Contbr. articles to profl. jours. Fellow Instn. Civil Engrs.; mem. Assn. Project Mgrs. (chartered engr.). Avocations: tennis, golf, photography, reading. Office: U Birmingham, Sch Civli Engring, Birmingham B15 2TT, England

PERRY, JON ROBERT, lawyer; b. Kane, Pa., May 14, 1965; s. James Felix and Judith Rose (Zelina) P.; m. Joni Lee Detrick, Aug. 10, 1991; children: Alex Joseph, Trevor James. BA summa cum laude, Pa. State U., 1987; JD magna cum laude, Duquesne U., 1991. Bar: Pa. 1991, U.S. Dist. Ct. (we. dist.) Pa. 1991, U.S. Ct. Apppeals (3d, 6th, 7th and fed. cirs.). Assoc. Reed Smith Shaw & McClay, Pitts., 1990-94; ptnr. Betts & Perry, Pitts., 1994-97, Meyers Rosen Louik & Perry, Pitts., 1998—; bd. dirs. Flying Pig Theatre, Pitts., J's Place, Inc., Kane, RBCI, Inc., Cranberry, Pa., CDS, Inc., Pitts. Exec. editor Duquesne Law Rev., 1991. Vol. mentor/spkr. elem. and high schs., Pitts., 1992—. Mem. ATLA, Pa. Trial Lawyers Assn., Pa. Bar Assn., Allegheny County Bar Assn., Allegheny County Acad. Trial Lawyers, Phi Beta Kappa. Office: Meyers Rosen Louik and Perry 437 Grant St Pittsburgh PA 15219-6002

PERRY, LEWIS CHARLES, emergency medicine physician, osteopath; b. La Plata, Mo., Apr. 22, 1931; s. Lewis C. and Emily B. Perry; m. M. Sheryl Gupton, Oct. 30, 1953; children: David, Susan, Stephen, John. BS, U. Mo., 1958; postgrad., Louisville Presbyn. Sem., 1958-60; DO, Kirksville Coll. Osteo. Medicine, 1967. Intern Midcities Meml. Hosp., Arlington, Tex.; parish min. Presbyn. Bd. Nat. Missions, Canada, Ky., 1960-62; intern Mid Cities Meml. Hosp., Arlington; pvt. practice, Ingleside, Tex., 1968-72, Tucson, 1972-81; emergency physician Tucson Gen. Hosp., 1981-88, pres. med. staff, 1978-79, clin. instr., 1981-88; emergency physician Meml. Med. Ctr. East Tex., Lufkin, 1988—; clin. instr. Osteo. Coll. Pacific, Pomona, Calif., 1985-88. Pres. Helping Hands, Ingleside, 1969-72; bd. dirs., pres. Salvation Army, Tucson, 1978-81; commr. Cub Scouts Am., Tucson, 1975-76; bd. dirs. Unity of Tucson, Inc., 1986-88; pres. bd. dirs. Unity of Nacogdoches, 1993-94. 1st lt. USAF, 1952-56. Named Physician of Yr., Tucson Gen. Hosp., 1978; recipient God and Country award Boy Scouts of Am., 1960. Mem. Am. Legion, Rotary (recipient God and Country award), Masons, Scottish Rite, Shrine. Avocations: cooking, gardening. Home: 1 Columbia Ct Lufkin TX 75901-7212

PERRY, SIR MICHAEL (SYDNEY), industrialist; b. Eastbourne, Sussex, U.K., Feb. 26, 1934; s. Sydney Albert and Jessie Kate (Brooker) P.; m. Joan Mary Stallard, Oct. 8, 1958; children: Carolyn Clare, Deborah Anne, Andrew John William. MA, St. John's Coll., Oxford, U.K., 1957. Various positions Unilever PLC, London, 1957—, chmn., 1992-96; dep. chmn. Bass PLC, 1991—; non-exec. dir. Bass Plc, London; chmn. Japan Trade Group, London, 1985-98, Centrica PLC, 1997—, Dunlop Slazenger Group Ltd., 1996—; non exec. dir. Marks & Spencer Ltd., 1996—; chmn. Shakespeare Globe Trust, 1993, chmn.; v.p., then pres. Liverpool (Eng.) Sch. Tropical Medicine, 1993—; non exec. dir. Brit. Gas, 1992, 1997; mem. supervisory bd. Royal Ahold; pres. Mktg. Coun. Decorated Knight Bachelor, 1994; recipient C.B.E., The Queen of England, 1990. Mem. Oriental Club. Avocations: golf, music. Office: Centrica Plc Head Office, Charter Ct 50 Windsor Rd, Slough Berks SL1 2HA, England

PERRY, NANCY ESTELLE, psychologist; b. Pitts., Oct. 30, 1934; d. Simon Warren and Estelle Cecelia (Zaluski) Reichard; children: Scott, Karen, Elaine. BS, Ohio State U., 1956, MA in Psychology, 1969, PhD in Psychology, 1973. Nurse various locations, 1956-63; psychologist Pub. Schs., Columbus, Ohio, 1970-72; human devel. specialist Madison County (Ohio) Schs., 1972-75; pvt. practice clin. psychology; cons. psychology Worthington, Ohio, 1975-80; tchr. U. Wis. Sch. Nursing, Milw., 1980-88, Milw. Devel. Ctr., 1980-83; pvt. practice Assoc. Mental Health Svcs., 1983-87, Glendale Clinic for Stress Mgmt. and Mental Health Clinics, 1987-98,

Cambridge Group, 1999—; pvt. practice life transactions therapy Milw. and Santa Fe, 1999—; mem. faculty Wis. Profl. Schs.; adj. faculty U. Wis., Milw. Ohio Dept. Edn. grantee, 1973-76. Bd. dirs. Youth Shelters & Family Svcs., Santa Fe. EPDA fellow Ohio State U., 1973; Ohio Dept. Edn. grantee, 1973-76. Fellow Internat. Soc. Study of Dissociation (sec.-treas. 1995-98), Wis. Psychol. Assn.; mem. APA, Am. Soc. Clin. Hypnosis, Am. Assn. Marriage and Family Therapists. Home: 568 Los Nidos Dr Santa Fe NM 87501-8356 Office: 110 Delgado St Santa Fe NM 87501-2781 also: 6110 N Port Washington Rd Milwaukee WI 53217-4308

PERRY, NELSON ALLEN, radiation safety engineer, radiological consultant; b. Louisville, Mar. 26, 1937; s. Leslie Irvin and Sue Helen (Harris) P.; m. Sarita Sue Cornn, Apr. 28, 1956; children: Melody S. Doyle, Kimberly D. Horne. AS, Campbellsville (Ky.) Coll., 1954; BS, U. Louisville, 1961; MS, U. Okla., 1966. Cert. hazard control mgr., hazart material mgt.; lic. med. physicist, Tex. Assoc. prof. Ind. Christian U., Indpls., 1974-76; asst. prof. Ind. U., Indpls., 1971-75; instr. Ind. Voc. Tech. Coll., Indpls., 1968-76; health physicist Michael Reese Hosp., Chgo., 1966-68; radiation safety officer St. Francis Hosp., Beech Grove, Ind., 1968-76, Ind. U., Indpls., 1971-74; radiation safety officer U. South Ala., Mobile, 1976—, assoc. prof., 1981—; radiol. cons. Perry Radiol. Cons., Inc., 1974—; radiol. cons., 1974—. Contbr. articles to profl. jours. Named Ky. Col., 1964; USPHS trainee, 1965-66. Mem. Am. Assn. Physicists in Medicine, Health Physics Soc., Ala. Health Physics Soc. (sec. 1977-79, pres. 1980-81). Republican. Baptist. Avocation: collecting miniatures. Office: U South Ala 257 Csab Mobile AL 36688-0001

PERRY, PETER JOHN, geography educator; b. Sherborne, Dorset, Eng., Dec. 22, 1937; arrived in New Zealand, 1966; s. Leslie John and Marjorie Florence (Baker) P.; m. Rachel-Mary Stewart Armitage, Dec. 9, 1973; children: George, Diana, Timothy. MA, PhD, Clare Coll., Cambridge, Eng., 1963; diploma in theology, London U., 1975. Lectr. in geography Canterbury U., Christchurch, New Zealand, 1966-70; sr. lectr. Canterbury U., Christchurch, 1970-75, reader, 1975—; dean Faculty of Arts, Canterbury U., 1977-80, 92-96. Author: British Farming in the Great Depression, 1870-1914, 1974, A Geography of 19th Century Britain, 1975, Political Corruption and Political Geography, 1997; editor: Studies in Political Geography, 5 vols., 1980-85. Lay canon Christchurch Cathedral, 1990-92; New Zealand rep. Transparency Internat., 1993-99. Anglican. Avocations: gardening, campanology, swimming. Office: Dept Geography, U Canterbury, Christchurch New Zealand

PERRY, RANDALL A., business executive; b. Furstenfeldbruk, Germany, Nov. 18, 1955; s. Norman Francis and Elfriede Dorothea (Wachter) P.; m. Donna A. Perry, Apr. 9, 1994; 1 child, Christopher; m. Helen A. Perry, Dec. 11, 1977 (div. Dec. 1992); children: Lea, David, Jonathan, Timothy. BSBA, Kennesaw U., 1981. Dir. reimbursement and legis. affairs Healthdyne, Inc., Marietta, Ga., 1983-85, Abbey Health Care, Inc., Fountain Valley, Calif., 1985-88; dir. reimbursement devel. Genentech, Inc., South San Francisco, Calif., 1988-93; biotech. industry rep. Am. Legis. Exchange Coun., Washington, 1990-93; dir. customer devel. Janssen Pharm., Titusville, N.J., 1993-94; v.p. reimbursement Mckesson/HDS, Scottsdale, Ariz., 1994-96; v.p. bus. devel. Bergen Brunswig/ICS, Addison, Tex., 1996-99; prin. Med. Comm. Techs., Atlanta, 1999—. Author: Biopharmaceuticals in Transition, 1990. With USAF, 1973-75. Mem. Nat. Assn. of Med. Equipment Suppliers (bd. dirs. 1983-88), Health Industry Distributors Assn. (co-chmn. health care reform com. 1985-88), Biotech. Industry Orgn. (co-chmn. health care reform com. 1989-93),. Republican. Avocations: snow skiing, mountain biking, rollerblading. Home: 234 Picketts Lake Dr Acworth GA 30101-4787

PERRY, ROBERT TERRELL, JR., nuclear engineer, consultant; b. Paris, Tex., July 19, 1938; s. Robert Terrell and Eleanor Cordia (Endsley) P.; m. Elisabeth Irmina Scherf, July 1, 1976. BS, Tex. A&M U., 1961, MS, 1967, PhD, 1974. Registered prof. engr., Wis. Sr. engr. EG&G Inc., Las Vegas, 1976-78; scientist Interatom Gmbh, Bensberg, Germany, 1972-75; sr. engr. Battelle Lab, Richland, Wash., 1976-79; scientist U. Wis., Madison, 1979-81; asst. prof. Tex. A&M and Pa. State U., Coll. Sta., Univ. Park, 1981-86; tech. staff Los Alamos (N.Mex.) Nat. Lab., 1987—; vis. sci. Princeton (N.J.) U., 1975-76, Max Planck Inst., Garching, Germany, 1975; adj. prof. nuclear engring. Tex. A&M U., College Station, 1998—. Contbr. over 200 articles to profl. mags., jours., reports. 1st Lt. U.S. Army, 1961-63, Korea. Recipient Best Tech. Article award Tex. A&M U., 1979. Mem. NRA, Nat. Soc. Profl. Engrs., Am. Nuclear Soc. (co-chair RP&S tech. program com. 1996—, chair stds. com. 1996—, pres.), Los Alamos Soc. Profl. Engrs., Internat. Radiation Physics Soc., Am. Legion, Masonic Lodge. Libertarian. Mem. Universal Life. Avocations: sailing, exploration. Home: 394 Catherine Ave Los Alamos NM 87544-3565 Office: Los Alamos Nat Lab Mse 541 Los Alamos NM 87545-0001

PERRY, SARAH HOLLIS, artist, archivist; b. Framingham, Mass., Mar. 24, 1934; d. Hollis Stratton and Mary (Norris) French; m. John Curtis Perry, Sept. 14, 1957; children: Elizabeth, Margaret, Rachel, Lyman, Maria. BA, Smith Coll., 1956; diploma, Sch. Mus. Fine Arts, Boston, 1999, cert., 2000. Syss. svc. rep. IBM, Boston, 1956-57; photographic aide Polaroid, Cambridge, Mass., 1957-74, asst. to chmn., 1974-82; asst. to dir. rsch. Rowland Inst., Cambridge, 1982-92, artist in residence/archivist, 1992—; mem. teaching faculty Sch. Mus. Fine Arts, Boston, 1999—. Recipient Jurors award Hera Gallery, Providence, 1996, 97, Erector Sq. Gallery, New Haven, 1998, Atlanta Paper Mus., 1999-2000; named winner of competition to create sculpture Tufts U. Libr. Lobby, 1997; Travelling fellow Sch. Mus. Fine Arts, 2000. Mem. Phi Beta Kappa (Zeta of Mass. chpt.). E-mail: perry@rowl-and.org. Office: Rowland Inst 100 Edwin Land Blvd Cambridge MA 02142-1297

PERRY, STUART WILLIAM, electrical engineer, researcher; b. Sydney, NSW, Australia, Mar. 18, 1972; s. Clifford William and Anne Lynette (James) P.; m. Ada Mei-Tak Chan, Aug. 16, 1997. B of Elec. Engring., U. Sydney, 1995, PhD, 1999. Rsch. asst. Commonwealth Sci. and Indsl. Rsch. Orgn., Sydney, 1993-94; rsch. scientist Def. Sci. and Tech. Orgn., Sydney, 1998—. Contbr. articles to profl. jours. Mem. IEEE, Internat. Soc. for Optical Engring., Australian Pattern Recognition Soc. Avocations: astronomy, history.

PERRY, THOMAS AMHERST, English literature and language educator; b. Beaver City, Nebr., Apr. 26, 1912; s. Thomas Charles and Mable Laura (Avis) P.; m. Lora Margaret Turner, June 20, 1937; children: Laura E. Massie, Robert Thomas, Timothy T., Charles Lee. Student pub. schs., Bayamón, P.R.; BA with honors, Park Coll., 1934; MA, U. Iowa, 1936, PhD, 1943; postgrad., Oxford (Eng.) U., 1964. Prin. grade sch., Des Moines, N.Mex., 1934-35; asst. prof. English, Park Coll., Parkville, Mo., 1936-42; instr. U. Iowa, Iowa City, 1943; prof., dept. head Ctrl. Meth. Coll., Fayette, Mo., 1943-63; Fulbright lectr. Am. lang. and lit. U. Bucharest, Romania, 1963-64; Hermann Brown prof. English, Southwestern U., Georgetown, Tex., 1964-65; prof. English, Tex. A&M U. (formerly East Tex. State U.), Commerce, 1965-80, head dept., 1969-72, prof. emeritus lit. and langs., 1980—; vis. prof. English, U. Mo., Columbia, 1951-52, U. Autónoma Estado Mex., Toluca, 1959, N.E. Mo. State U. (now Truman State U.), Kirksville, summer 1965; mem. com. on doctorate in English, Fedn. North Tex. State Univs., 1972-75; mem. com. on Variorum Glossary, World Shakespeare Congress, Vancouver, B.C., Can., 1970-71; mem. steering com. Romanian Studies Congress, Auckland, New Zealand, summer 1973. Author: A Bibliography of American Literature Translated into Romanian, 1984, From These Roots and Other Poems, 1996; co-author: Romanian Poetry in English Translation: an Annotated Bibliography, 1989, with supplement An Update with Over 60 Newer Poets, 1997; contbr. articles and criticsmm to profl. jours., poems and poem transls. to lit. mags. and anthologies. Past mem. Fayette Libr. Bd.; past mem. local bd. Salvation Army, Commerce; mem. exec. com. Hunt County Rep. Party, Greenville, Tex., 1970-80; past mem. adminstrv. bd. Meth. Ch., Fayette; past mem. adminstrv. bd. 1st Meth. Ch., Commerce. Recipient Disting. Alumnus award Park Coll., 1984; Smith-Mundt grantee, Toluca, Mexico, 1959, award of excellence N.E. Tex. Area Coun. Tchrs. English, 1980, Disting. Faculty award East Tex. State U., 1979; Rsch. Assocs. travel grantee U. Bucharest and U. Cluj, 1968, Am. Coun. Learned Socs. rsch. grantee, Romania, 1978. Mem. MLA (sr. bibliographer 1969—), Comparative Lit. Assn. Am., Shakespeare Assn. Am., Am. Lit. Translators Assn., Internat. Comparative Lit. Assn., Internat. Shakespeare Assn., Am. Romanian Acad. Arts and Scis., Romanian Studies Assn. (exec. bd. 1976-78), Soc. Romanian Studies, Tex. Assn. Coll. Tchrs., Tex. Folklore Soc., Omicron Delta Kappa. Avocations: numismatics, photography, travel. Home: 214 Brookhaven Ter Commerce TX 75428-2002 Office: Tex A&M U - Commerce Dept Lit and Langs Commerce TX 75428

PERRY, WAYNE, endocrinologist, consultant; b. London, June 30, 1944; s. William and Margery Rideley (Wilson) P.; m. Siew Mui Lee, Aug. 8, 1980. MD, U. Birmingham, Eng., 1968. Cert. specialist physician gen. medicine/metabolic medicine, cert. higher specialist tng. Royal Coll. Physicians London. Registrar Kings Coll. Hosp., London, 1971-74; sr. med. registrar Royal Nat. Orthop. Hosp., London, 1974-79; cons. physician King Fahd U., Dammam, Saudi Arabia, 1979-83, London, 1984-88; cons. endocrinologist Endocrine Centre, London, 1989—; med. dir. Arterial Disease Clinics, London, 1985. Contbr. articles to profl. jours. Recipient Sir Herbert Seddon gold medal Inst. Orthpaedics, U. London, 1978; gold medals King Fahd U., Saudi Arabia, 1983. Fellow Royal Soc. Medicine; mem. Brit. Med. Assn., Am. Coll. Advancement Medicine, Royal Coll. Physicians. Avocations: poetry, France, Arcadian landscapes, violocello. Home: Old Hall Farm, Ch Ln Earl Soham, Woodbridge 1P13 7SP, England Office: 57a Wimpole St, London WIM 7DF, England

PERRY, WILLIAM JAMES, educator, former federal official; b. Vandergrift, Pa., Oct. 11, 1927; s. Edward Martin and Mabelle Estelle (Dunlap) P.; m. Leonilla Green, Dec. 29, 1947; children: David, William, Rebecca, Robin, Mark. BS in Math, Stanford U., 1949, MS, 1950; PhD, Pa. State U., 1957. Instr. math. Pa. State U., 1951-54; sr. mathematician HRB-Singer Co., State College, Pa., 1952-54; dir. electronic def. labs. GTE Sylvania Co., Mountain View, Calif., 1954-64; pres. ESL, Inc., Sunnyvale, Calif., 1964-77; tech. cons. Dept. Def., Washington, 1967-77, under sec. def. for research and engring., 1977-81; mng. dir. Hambrecht & Quist (investment bankers), San Francisco, 1981-85; chmn. Tech. Strategies & Alliances, Menlo Park, Calif., 1985-93; prof., co-dir. Ctr. for Internat. Security and Arms Control Stanford U., 1989-93; apptd. Dep. Sec. Def. Pentagon, Washington, 1993-94, appt. Sec. Def., 1994-97; prof. engring.-econ. sys. and ops. rsch. Stanford (Calif.) U., 1997—. Served with U.S. Army, 1946-47. Recipient Def. Disting. Svc. medal U.S. Govt., 1980, 81, Achievement medal Am. Electronics Assn., 1980, Forrestal Medal, 1994, Henry Stimson medal, 1994, Arthur Bueche medal NAE, 1996, Eisenhower award, 1996, Presdl. Medal Freedom, 1997, Outstanding Civilian Svc. medals U.S. Army, 1997, USN, 1997, USAF, 1997, USCG, 1997, NASA, 1997, Def. Intelligence Agy., 1997; Sr. fellow Inst. Internat. Studies, Stanford U., 1997—. Fax: 650-725-0920. E-mail: wjperry@stanford.edu.

PERRY, WILLIAM JOHN, solicitor; b. Bexley, Kent, England, Nov. 19, 1952; s. William Hubert and Margaret Bennett (Annear) P.; m. Jane Ann Sherlock, July 15, 1978; children: Alexandra, Caroline, Michael. BA, Oxford U., 1973, MA, 1977, PhD, 1993. Articled clk. Norton, Rose, Botterell, Roche, London, 1974-77, asst. solicitor, 1977-85; ptnr., head litigation Pickering, Kenyon, London, 1986-95, sr. ptnr., 1990-95; ptnr. Charles Russell, London, England, 1995—; chmn. bd. dirs. Spencer Hill Mgmt. Ltd., London, 1978-81. Contbr. articles to profl. jours. Bd. dirs. London Handel Soc. Ltd., 1990-95. Named Hon. Solicitor Royal Soc. Musicians of Great Britain, 1990-95. Fellow Royal Soc., Arts; mem. City of London Solicitors Co., Law Soc., Holborn Law Soc., Inst. of Mgmt., Chartered Inst. of Arbitrators (assoc.), Carlton Club. Anglican. Avocations: ballet, opera, oenology, political history, walking. Office: Charles Russell, 8-10 New Fetter Lane, EC4A London 1RS, England

PERSCHBACHER, PETER WESLEY, environmental scientist, educator; b. Davenport, Iowa, Nov. 15, 1946; s. Wesley Adolph and Margaret Pohly P.; m. Virginia Brady, Feb. 14, 1986. BS, U. Mich., 1968; MS, Auburn U., 1975; PhD, Tex. A&M U., 1985. Rsch. assoc. U. N.C. Inst. Marine Sci., Morehead City, N.C., 1975-79; grad. rsch. asst. Tex. A&M U., Baytown, 1980-85; Aquaculture Trainer-Peace Corps Rsch. Planning Inst., Ft. Pierce, Fla., 1983; aquaculture biologist Caribbean Marine Rsch. Ctr., Lee Stocking Island, Bahamas, 1985; aquaculture advisor Harza Engring. Internat., Mymensingh, Bangladesh, 1986-87; rsch. biologist Agrl. Rsch. Svc., USDA, Tishomingo, Okla., 1989-93; assoc. prof. U. Ark., Pine Bluff, 1993—; cons. KTAADIN, Newton, Mass., Norwegian Govt., Trondheim, Norway. Author: (bibliography) Recirculation-Aeration Bibliography for Aquaculture, 1993; contbg. author: Third National Reservoir Symposium, 1997; contbr. article to N.Am. Jour. of Aquaculture, 1998 (named to top ten papers of 1998), others. Chair Clean and Beautiful Commn. Bd., Pine Bluff, 2000; mem. Racial Harmony Task Force, Pine Bluff, 1996-98; organizer and co-chair Environ. Fair Grace Episcopal Ch., Pine Bluff, 1997, 99; organizer and chair Waste Mgmt. and Specialty Animal Prodn. Workshops, U. Ark., 1999. Grantee Mgmt. of Environmentally-Derived Off-Flavors in Warmwater, USDA, Stoneville, Miss., 1995-2000, USDA-CSRS, 1999-2004. Mem. Am. Fisheries Soc., Am. Inst. Fisheries Rsch. Biologists, World Aquaculture Soc., Asian Fisheries Soc., Sigma Xi, Xi Sigma Pi. Democrat. Episcopalian. Avocations: native orchids, palms. E-mail: pperschbacher@uaex.edu. Office: Univ Ark at Pine Bluff Mail Slot 4912 Pine Bluff AR 71601

PERSCHE, HENRY-PETER, art consultant, artist; b. Bklyn., Nov. 21, 1940; s. Henry-Peter and Marie (Gramegna) P. BFA, U. Buffalo, 1973, postgrad., 1973-74; postgrad., Coll. St. Rose, 1993-94. Installation dir. for artist Ellsworth Kelly Spencertown, N.Y., 1966-93; archivist, asst., 1966-93; installation cons. for artist Ellsworth Kelly exhins. at Sidney Janis Gallery, Loe Castelli gallery, Blum/Helman gallery, N.Y.C., 1996-93, Mus. Modern Art, N.Y.C., 1973, Mus. Nat. d'Art Moderne, Paris, 1980, Stedelijk Mus., Amsterdam, 1979, Kunsthalle, Baden Baden, Germany, 1979, Mus. Nat. d'Art Moderne, Paris, 1980. Exhibited in group shows Albany (N.Y.) Inst. Art, 1973, Albright-Knox Art Gallery, Buffalo, N.Y., 1973. Poll inspector Dem. Party, Ghent, N.Y., 1994-95. With fin. corps. U.S. Army, 1963-66. Mem. Mus. Modern Art (N.Y.C.), Met. Mus. Art, Guggenheim Mus., Whitney Mus. Am. Art, Gottschee Heritage Assn., Gottscheer Relief Assn. Democrat. Roman Catholic. Avocations: collecting art publications, stamps, and photographs, travel, music. Home: 4811 NW 47th Ave Tamarac FL 33319-3735

PERSEGATI, WALTER ANGELO, museum director, educator; b. Verona, Italy, July 3, 1920; s. Pietro and Adele (Begali) P.; m. Silvana Santiccioli, Sept. 12, 1952; children: Chiara, Francesca. BBA, A.M. Lorgna, Verona, 1940; LLD (hon.), St. Francis Xavier U., Antigonish, N.S., Can., 1985, Trinity Coll., Hartford, Conn., 1999. Cert. adminstrn.-mgmt. Office mgr. Ing. y. Polin DC, Verona, 1941-46; sec. gen. Italian Cath. Youth Orgn., Rome, 1946-51, Internat. Fedn. Cath. Youth Orgn., Rome, 1951-54; dir. Chgo. office Am. Com. Italian Migration, 1954-57; asst. permanent observer of the Holy See FAO of UN, Rome, 1958-70; sec. gen., treas. Vatican Mus., Vatican City, 1970-90, coord. emeritus patrons of the mus., lectr., 1990—. Author: Vademecum for Museum Guards, 1976, 89; editor, author The Vatican Museums Reporter, 1984-93; contbr. articles to profl. jours. Decorated knight comdr. Pontifical Order St. Silvester, knight comdr. Pontifical Order St. Gregory (Vatican City). Mem. bd. dirs., Latinitas Found., Vatican City State, 1975—. Roman Catholic. Avocations: lecturing, photography, hiking. Office: Patrons Vatican Museums, Cortile del Pappagallo, I-00120 Vatican City Italy

PERSHIN, ALEXANDER FEDOROVICH, geneticist, researcher, sunflower breeder; b. Tikhoretsk, Krasnodar, Russia, Aug. 10, 1957; s. Fedor and Raisa (Kolyada) P.; m. Irina Zinow'eva, June 10, 1982; children: Andrey, Juliana. MS, Kuban State U., Krasnodar, Russia, 1979; PhD, Vavilov's Inst. Plant Industry, St. Petersburg, Russia, 1988; sr. rschr., High Attestation Commn., Kiev, Ukraine, 1995. Cert. geneticist. Jr. rschr. Krimsk Breeding Sta. Vir, Krasnodar, 1979-89; head of lab. Inst. Oil Seed Crops Ukrainian Acad. Agrl. Scis., Zaporozhye, 1989—. Author: (book) Descriptor of Castor-bean, 1995; contbr. rsch. articles to profl. jours. E-mail: pershin@eos.zp.ua. Home: AB Box 6117, UA 69093 Zaporozhye Ukraine Office: Inst Oilseed Crops, Settl Solnechny, UA332110 Zaporozhye Ukraine

PERSHINA-NAEGELE, VALERIA GEORGIEVNA, chemist, researcher; b. Chelyabinsk, Russia, Sept. 9, 1953; arrived in Germany, 1990, became German citizen, 1997; d. Georgii Petrovich and Rimma Andreevna (Fartusova) Pershin; m. Jochen Rainer Naegele, June 12, 1992. Diploma in engring., Mendeleev U. Chemistry & Tech., Moscow, 1977; PhD, Inst. Phys. Chemistry, Moscow, 1983, habilitation, 1994. Rschr. Inst. Phys. Chemistry, Moscow, 1977-88, sr. scientist, group leader, 1988-98, dep. head quantum chemistry lab., 1982-90; vis. scientist, rschr. Kassel (Germany) U., 1990-95; rschr. Gesellschaft für Schwerionenforschung, Darmstadt, Germany, 1995-99, Mainz (Germany) U. Inst. Nuc. Chemistry, 1999—; cons. Commn. European Union, Brussels, 1996, U.S./FSU Workshop on Nuc. Safety and Environment, Livermore, Calif., 1995, Laser-Optic-Tech. Co., Darmstadt, 1988—; co-organizer Internat. Conf. Actinides-89, Russia, 1989; invited lectr. to internatl. confs. "Actinides", 1993, 1997, and "Transactinides", 1999, Inst. Curie, Paris, 1988, Göteborg (Sweden) U., 1995, Berkeley (Calif.) Nat. Lab., 1992, 93, 99, Oak Ridge (Tenn.) Nat. Lab., 1992, Inst. Nuc. Physics, Orsay, France, 1994, 99, Inst. Radiochemistry, Rossendorf (Germany) Forschungszentrum, 1995, others. Co-author: (with G.V. Ionova and V.I. Spitsyn) Electronic Structure of the Actinides, 1986; contbr. chpts. to books, over 60 articles to profl. jours. W.E. Heraeus Stiftung fellow, Hanau, Germany, 1993, Deutsche Forschungsgemeinschaft fellow, Bonn, 1994-95, 1999—. Mem. German Chem. Soc. Avocations: music, piano, art. Office: Ges fur Schwerionenforsch, Planckstr 1, D-64291 Darmstadt Germany

PERSICO, ANTONIO MARIA, psychiatrist, physiologist; b. Augusta, Siracusa, Italy, Jan. 23, 1962; s. Andrea P. and Ivana Favarato; m. Patrizia Del Buono, Oct. 28, 1989; 1 child, Matteo. Med. Degree, Cath. U., Rome, 1986; Splst. in Psychiatry, Cath. U., 1990. Med. diplomate. Vis. fgn. fellow ARC/NIDA/NIH, Balt., 1990-93; postdoct. S. Raffaele Hosp., Milan, 1994; asst. prof. U. Campus Bio-Medico, Rome, 1995—; with smoking cessation program Food and Agr. Orgn. U.N., Rome, 1997. Contbr. chpt. to book; co-inventor transporter for encoding human dopamine, receptor for encoding human mu opiate; patentee in field. Served with Italian Navy Med. Corps., 1988-89. Fellow European Coll. Neuropharmacology; mem. Italian Psychiat. Assn., Italian Physiol. Assn., Soc. Neurosci. Roman Catholic. Avocations: music, Roman history and archeology. Home: Via Antonio Serra 83, I-00191 Rome Italy Office: Lab Neurosci UCBM, Via Longoni 83, I-00155 Rome Italy

PERSICO, JOSEPH EDWARD, author; b. Gloversville, N.Y., July 19, 1930; s. Thomas Louis and Blanche (Perrone) P.; m. Sylvia La Vista, May 23, 1959; children: Vanya, Andrea. B.A., SUNY-Albany, 1952, PhD (hon.), 1996; postgrad., Columbia U., 1955. Writer on staff of gov. N.Y. State, Albany, 1955-59; commd. fgn. service officer USIA, 1959; served in USIA, Buenos Aires, Argentina, Rio de Janeiro, Brazil, 1959-62; speechwriter Commr. N.Y. State Health Dept., Albany, 1963-66; chief speechwriter for gov. N.Y. State, Albany, 1966-74; speechwriter for v.p. U.S., Washington, 1975-77. Author: My Enemy My Brother: Men and Days of Gettysburg, 1977; (novel) The Spiderweb, 1979, Piercing the Reich: The Penetration of Nazi Germany by American Secret Agents during World War II, 1979 (Nat. Intelligence Study Ctr. prize for best book on intelligence 1979), The Imperial Rockefeller: A Biography of Nelson A. Rockefeller, 1982, Murrow: An American Original, 1988, Casey: William J. Casey, From the OSS to the CIA, 1990, Nuremberg: Infamy on Trial, 1994; collaborater: Colin Powell: My American Journey, 1995. Served to lt. (j.g.) USN, 1952-55. Recipient Disting. Alumnus award SUNY-Albany, 1982. Mem. Authors Guild, Inc. Home and Office: 222 Heritage Rd Guilderland NY 12084-9314

PERSONS, W. RAY, lawyer, educator; b. Talbottan, Ga., July 22, 1953; s. William and Frances (Crowell) P.; m. Wendy-Joy Mottley, Sept. 24, 1977; children: Conrad Ashley, April Maureen. BS cum laude, Armstrong State Coll., 1975; JD, Ohio State U., 1978. Bar: Ga. 1979, U.S. Dist. Ct. (so. dist.) Ga. 1980, U.S. Dist. Ct. (no. dist.) Ga. 1986, U.S. Ct. Appeals (11th cir.) 1986. Assoc. Troutman, Sanders, Lockerman & Ashmore, Atlanta, 1978-79; atty. Nat. Labor Rels. Bd., Atlanta, 1980-82; legis. counsel U.S Ho. Reps., Washington, 1983-86; atty. Mack & Bernstein, Atlanta, 1986-87; ptnr. Arrington & Hollowell, Atlanta, 1987-95, Swift, Currie, McGhee & Hiers, Atlanta, 1995-99, Hunton and Williams, Atlanta, 1999—; adj. prof. litigation Ga. State U., Atlanta, 1989—; spl. asst. atty. gen. State of Ga., Atlanta, 1988—. Master Am. Inns of Ct. (Lamar chpt.); mem. ABA, ATLA, Internat. Soc. Barristers, Am. Bd. Trial Advocates, State Bar Ga., Atlanta Bar Assn., Lawyers Club of Atlanta. Republican. Roman Catholic. Office: Hunton and Williams 600 Peachtree St NE Ste 4100 Atlanta GA 30308-2217

PERSOW, MEYER JOSEPH, federal official; b. St. Louis, July 22, 1958; s. Harold S. and Harriet Lee (Persow) Kadovitz; life ptnr. Daniel S. Meloy. BA in Polit. Sci., U. Denver, 1980, BA in Secondary Edn., 1980; postgrad., El Paso Community Coll., 1985. Legis. aide Office of the Gov., Denver, 1975; tchr. Sebastian High Sch., Denver, 1977-79; press sec. Barragan for Congress Com., Thornton, Colo., 1980; pvt. practice tutor Denver, 1981-83; adminstrv. asst. Tracks, Internat., Inc., Denver, 1986-87; customer svc. mgr. Continental Airlines, Denver, Washington, 1987-88; program analyst U.S. Office Pers. Mgmt., Washington, 1988-99, treasury and overseas liaison officer, 1999—. News editor: The Denver Clarion, 1978-79, author polit. commentary, 1978-80. Vice chmn. North High Campus Concept. Com., Denver, 1976-77; committeeman Dem. Party Cen. Com., Denver, 1976-83; candidate Denver (Colo.) Bd. Edn., 1977, 79; mem. Dem. Party Exec. Com., Denver, 1978-81. Sgt. U.S. Army, 1983-86. Decorated Army Achievement medal U.S. Army, El Paso, 1985, Dir's. award for Excellence U.S. Office of Personnel Mgmt., 1995, Double Bronze medalist in cycling Gay Games IV, 1994. Mem. Internat. Platform Assn., Mortar Bd., Fed. Club (human rights campaign), Zeta Beta Tau. Avocations: reading, bicycle racing. Office: US Office Pers Mgmt 1900 E St NW Washington DC 20415-0001

PERSSON, BJORN MAURITZ, orthopaedist; b. Boden, Sweden, Jan. 23, 1937; s. Mauritz P.; m. Liselott Forsberg; children: Ylva, Torun, Mons, Tove, Max. MD, U. Lund, Sweden, 1963; PhD, U. Lund, 1968. Chief orthopaedics Ctrl. Hosp., Helsingborg, Sweden, 1984-99, U. Hosp. of Lund, Lund, Sweden, 1999—. Contbr. over 150 articles to med. jours. Mem. Swedish Orthopaedic Assn. (pres. 1987-90), Internat. Soc. Prosthetics and Orthotics (pres. 1998-01). Avocations: sailing, tennis. Home: Vikhog 469, 24632 Loddekoping Sweden Office: Univ Hosp, Lund Sweden

PERSSON, BO N.J., physicist, researcher; b. Hässleholm, Sweden, May 18, 1952. MSc in Engring., Chalmers U. Tech., Göteborg, Sweden, 1975, PhD, 1980. Rsch. scientist Forschungszentrum Jülich, Germany, 1980—. Author: Sliding Friction: Physical Principles and Applications, 1998; editor Physics of Sliding Friction, 1996; contbr. over 130 articles to profl. jours. Recipient Walter-Schottky prize Germany Phys. Soc., 1996, John Yarwood Meml. medal Brit. Vacuum Coun., 1997, Volvo prize, 1981, NATO Nanoscale Sci. award, 1996. Office: Forschungszentrum Jülich, D-52425 Jülich Germany

PERSSON, GORAN, Swedish government official; b. Vingaker, Sweden, Jan. 20, 1949; m. Gunnel Persson; 2 children. Attended, Orebro U., Sweden. Chair Katrineholm Edn. Authority, 1977-79, mcpl. commr., 1985-89; M.P. Parliament of Sweden, 1979-84; min. for schs. and edn. Ministry of Edn. and Cultural Affairs, 1989-91; min. fin. Govt. of Sweden, 1994-97, prime min., 1998—; vice chair bd. Oppunda Savs. Bank, 1976-89. Vice chair bd. Nordic Mus., 1983-89. Mem. Sodermanland Cooperative Soc. (chair 1976-89, chair bd. edn. 1982-89), Swedish Cooperative Wholesale Soc. (acct. 1988-89). Office: Office of Prime Minister, Rosenbad 4, S-103 33 Stockholm Sweden*

PERSSON, HANS ÅKE, ecologist, researcher; b. Lännäs, Örebro, Sweden, Mar. 23, 1942; s. Anders and Valborg (Larsson) P. Univ. degree, Uppsala (Sweden) U., 1968, PhD, 1975. Sec. Internat. Biol. Program Swedish Nat. Rsch. Coun., Stockholm, 1968-69; rsch. asst. Uppsala U., 1969-72, Swedish Agrl. U., Uppsala, 1972-84; rsch. leader Swedish Agrl. U., 1984-90, asst. prof., 1990—. Editor: Plant Roots and Their Environment, 1991, Root Ecology and Its Practical Application, 1992, Plant Root Systems and Natural Vegetation, 1996. Recipient Linné prize Royal Soc. Scis., Uppsala, 1981. Mem. Internat. Soc. Root Rsch. (pres. 1982-88, 88-96, 96—), Brit. Ecol. Soc., Internat. Assn. Ecology. Avocations: landscape painting, philately, ceramics. Home: Björkbacken, Läby-Österby, S-75592 Uppsala Sweden Office: Swedish U Agrl Scis, Dept Ecology & Environ Rsch, S-75007 Uppsala Sweden

PERSSON, JONAS KARL ERIK, physician, researcher; b. Stockholm, Sweden, Sept. 19, 1961; s. Erik and Elsa Karin Helena (Svensson) P.; m. Helena Katarina Karman, Aug. 27, 1988; children: Magnus Kjell Jonas, Mattias Per Erik, Sofia Anna Helena. MD, Karolinska Inst., Stockholm,

1987, PhD, 1995. Demonstrator dept. anatomy Karolinska Inst., 1987-93; internship Huddinge Univ. Hosp., Stockholm, 1993-96, residency in clinical neurophysiology, 1996-2000; cons., researcher Nat. Def. Rsch. Establishment, Stockholm, 1995—.

PERSSON, MATS KURT UNO, international heavy machinery dealer; b. Ekeby, Närke, Sweden, June 29, 1955; s. Malte Kurt Uno and Asta Maria (Ericsson) P. Degree in engring., Sweden, 1973. Pres. MPS Internat., Sweden, 1979-87; mng. dir. World Contracting Establishment, Vaduz, Lichtenstein, 1987-92, Machine Tool Internat. Ltd., U.S. and Sweden, 1992—; Swedish state authorized dealer in gold and precious metals, 1979—; founder Fundacja Zabytki i Obiekty Kultury, Polen, 1989—. Sgt. Swedish mil., 1974-75. Mem. Odd Fellows. Avocation: antique cars. E-mail: mps.int@helsingborg.se. Home: Villa Villerkulla PO Box 180, 26522 Astorp Sweden Office: Machine Tool Internat Ltd, Svang 8, 26533 Åstorp Sweden

PERSSON, ROLAND S., psychologist; b. Vastra Frolunda, Gothenburg, Sweden, Oct. 7, 1958; s. Sven O. F. and Karin G. (Backlund) P. MFA, Ingesund Coll. Music, Sweden, 1982; PhD in Psychology, U. Huddersfield, U.K., 1993. Head tchr. Uddevalla Pre-Conservatoire, Sweden, 1986-90; rschr., lectr. U. Huddersfield, 1990-93; assoc. prof. Jonkoping (Sweden) U., 1994—; bd. regents Ingesund Coll. Music, 1994-98; nat. rep. European Coun. for High Ability, 1994—, World Coun. for Gifted and Talented Children, 1998; bd. dirs. Ctr. for Psychology, Jonkoping. Author: Formal Writing and Personal Style, 1996, Psyche, Stress and Artistic Freedom, 1996, In a Different Land: The Psychology of High Ability, 1997, Handbook of Supervising Research, 1999, Differences or Deficits!, 2000; editor-in-chief High Ability Studies, 1998. Mem. APA, BPS, ECHA, WCGTC, SRPMME. Avocations: civil aviation, botany, philosophy. Office: Jonkoping Univ, PO Box 1026, S-55111 Jönköping Sweden

PERSSON, STEN ERIK BERTIL, member of parliament, physician; b. Malmö, Sweden, May 20, 1937; s. G. Bertil and Ruth I. (Fredriksson) P.; m. Tove C. Hulgaard, Apr. 13, 1963; children: Thomas B.A., Annika T.M. MD, Lund U., 1967; Dr in Medicine, Malmo/Lund U., 1982; Dr in Odontology honors causa, Malmo U. Coll., 1999. Cert. specialist internal medicine, specialist cardiology. Intern and resident Malmö Gen. Hosp./Lund U., 1968-76; chmn. Conservative Studens Union of Sweden, 1962-64; head physician Med. Clinic Gen. Hosp., Malmö, 1982; city commr. hosps., med. health svcs., social welfare City of Malmo, 1986-88; mem. standing com. fgn. affairs Parliament, Sweden, 1988—, mem. standing commn. for med. and social ins., 1988-89; mem. standing com. on law Parliament, 1991-94, mem. standing com. on social affairs, 1994—; chmn. Faculty of Odontology, Malmo U. Coll., 1999—; bd. dirs. Swedish Internat. Devel. Agy., Swedish Com. for Global Devel. Contbr. articles to profl. jours. Chmn. Moderate Party, Malmö, 1989-96; chmn. Swedish Com. for Xenotransplantation, 1997-99; mem. Nat. Com. for Biotech., 1997—; bd. dirs. Swedish Nat. Banks Tri centennial Found., 1992-98, Swedish Med. Products Agy., 1990—. Mem. Nat. Bd. Med. Ethics, Nat. Bd. Genetic Tech., Coun. Interparliamentary Union, Swedish Inst. Med. Tech. (bd. dirs. 1986-90), Ideon Sci. Park Malmo (vice chmn. 1986-90). Conservative. Lutheran. Avocations: tennis, horse sports. Home: Forridargatan 11, Malmo Sweden S 21621 Office: Swedish Parliament, Riksgatan 1, Stockholm Sweden S10012

PERTEET, ICY D., secondary education educator; b. Kosciusko, Miss., Nov. 28, 1952; d. Claude Sr. and Katie Joiner; m. Ray Kenny Perteet, Sept. 17, 1971; children: Kenny De Von, Iginar De Mentria. AA, Holmes C.C., Goodman, Miss., 1973; BS, Miss. U. for Women, 1976. Vocat. preperation tchr. Choctaw County Sch., Ackerman, Miss., 1976-83; family and consumer sci. instr. Choctaw County Sch., Weir, Miss., 1983-97; family and consumer sci./career discovery instr. Attala County Sch., McAdams, Miss., 1997—; advisor Family Career, Cmty. Leader of Am., McAdams, Miss., 1997-2000; pres. Tech. Prep Adv. Bd., McAdams, 1999—. Book reviewer: Family Today, 1999. Life Attala County Youth Choir, Kosciusko, 1990-91; life mem., troop leader Girl Scouts, Kosciusko, 1991-2000; mem. adv. bd. Partnership for a Health Attala County, Kosciusko, 1997-2000. Mem. NEA, Miss. Assn. Family and Consumer Sci. Educator (pres. 1996-97), Coun. Christian Women (pres. 1987-2000), Attala County Assn. Educators (bldg. contact person 1998-2000), Phi Upsilon Omicron (sec. 1975-2000), Gamma Beta Phi. Baptist. Avocations: reading, collecting angels, gardening, traveling. Home: RR 1 Box 232C Sallis MS 39160-9753 Office: Attala County Sch Dist RR 1 Box 2320 Sallis MS 39160-9801

PERTENECE, JOSE PAULO SEPULVEDA, legal administrator. Pres. Supreme Fed. Tribunal, Brasilia, Brazil. Office: Supreme Tribunal Fed, SAS Praca dos Tribunais Super, 70095-900 Brasilia DF, Brazil*

PERTHUISOT, JEAN-PIERRE, science educator; b. Dijon, France, Oct. 27, 1943; s. Louis and Frida (Vallotton) P.; m. Michèle Barusseau, Aug. 5, 1967 (div. 1996); children: Christophe, Nicolas, Isabelle, Sébastien; m. Sabine Castanier, July 6, 1996. Student, Normale Supérieure, Paris, 1963, degree in natural scis., 1967, DS, 1975. Fellow Ecole Normale Supérieure, 1963-67; asst. prof. Ecole Normale Supérieie, 1968-73; 2d class prof. U. Nantes, France, 1983-89, 1st class prof., 1989—, dir. lab. biogeology and microbiogeology, 1983—; expert FAO, Rome, 1983-86, Nat. Inst. Guaranteed Vintage, Paris, 1989—. Author: La Sebkha el Melah de Arzis, 1975 (De Lamothe prize 1981); co-author: Le Domaine paralique, 1983, Brines and Evaporites, 1989; contbr. articles to profl. jours. With French armed forces, 1967. Named Knight Acad. Palms, 1985, Officer Acad. Palms, 1990. Mem. AAAS, Coastal Edn. Rsch. Found., N.Y. Acad. Scis. Avocation: postal history. Office: Faculty Sci & Tech, 2 La Houssiniere, 44072 Nantes 03, France

PERUTZ, MAX FERDINAND, molecular biologist; b. May 19, 1914; s. Hugo and Adele Perutz; m. Gisela Peiser, 1942; 1 son, 1 dau. Ed., U. Vienna; Ph.D., U. Cambridge, 1940. Dir. Med. Research Council Unit for Molecular Biology, 1947-62; chmn. European Molecular Biology Orgn., 1963-69; reader Davy Faraday Research Lab., 1954-68, Fullerian prof. physiology, 1973-79; chmn. Med. Rsch. Coun. Lab. Molecular Biology, 1962-79. Author: Proteins and Nucleic Acids, Structure and Function, 1962, Is Science Necessary and Other Essays, 1989, Stereochemical Mechanisms of Cooperativity and allosteric Regulation in Proteins, 1990, Protein Structure: New Approaches to Disease and Therapy, 1992, Science is No Quiet Life, 1997, I Wish I'd Made You Angry Earlier, 1998. Recipient Nobel Prize for Chemistry, 1962. Fellow Royal Soc. (Royal medal 1971, Copley medal 1979), Royal Coll. Physicians (hon. fellow 1993); mem. Royal Soc. Edinburgh, Am. Acad. Arts and Scis. (hon.), Austrian Acad. Scis. (corr.), Am. Philos. Soc. (fgn.), Nat. Acad. Scis. (fgn. assoc.), Royal Netherlands Acad. (fgn.), French Acad. Scis., Bavarian Acad. Scis., Nat. Acad. Scis. Rome (fgn.), Accademia dei Lincei (Rome) (fgn.), Pontifical Acad. Scis. Office: MRC Lab Molecular Biology, Cambridge CB2 2QH, England

PERVEZ, YAQUB RAZIQ, telecommunications engineer; b. Peshawar, Pakistan, Dec. 15, 1961; s. Yaqub Masih and Alice (Bibi) Y.; m. Kiran Raziq Gill, Nov. 9, 1989; children: Anita Raziq, Monica Raziq. BSc, U. Peshawar, Pakistan, 1981; BSc in Engring. with hons., N.W. Frontier Province U. Engring & Tech., Peshawar, 1985, MSc. with hons., 1993; PhD, Keio U., Yokohama, Japan, 1998. Aircraft engr. Pakistan Internat. Airlines, Karachi, Pakistan, 1986-87; shift engr. Pakistan Water & Power Devel. Authority, Peshawar, 1987-88; asst. divisional engr. Pakistan Telecomm. Corp., Peshawar, 1988-98; rsch. engr. Nokia Rsch. Ctr., Tokyo, 1998-99; asst. mgr. DDI Corp., Japan, 1999—; vis. rschr. Rikkyo U., Tokyo; tech. advisor Initiatives N.W.F.P. Pakistan for Hearing Impaired Children, Pehswar, 1991-93; participant, presenter IEEE Internat. Symposium on Info. Theory and its Applications, Victoria, Can., 1996, IEEE Internat. Conf. Comm., Montreal, 1997, Asia Pacific Symposium on Info. and Telecom. Tech., Vietnam, 1997, Internat. Conf. Telecomm., Melbourne, Australia, 1997, IASTED Applied Informatics, Garmisch, Germany, 1998, Global Summit 3d Generation Mobile Comms., Japan, 1999, Internat. Symposium Computers and Comms., Red Sea, Egypt, 1999, Vehicular Comm. Techs., Houston, Amsterdam, 1999, IEEE Vehicular Tech. Conf., Amsterdam, 1999, Internat. Workshop on Distributed Computing and Comms., Pakistan, 2000; chmn. group 1 Mobile Wireless Internat Forum. Contbr. rsch. papers to profl. jours. and conf. proceedings; editor, writer English newspaper Keio U., Tokyo, 1994-95. English tchr. YMCA, Minami Jr. High Sch. Tsurugashima, Saitama, Japan, 1995-98; mem. Anglican Ch. Peshawar, Pakistan. Recipient scholarship Ministry of Edn., Govt. of Japan, 1996-98, Keio U., 1995-96, Rikkyo U., Tokyo, 1993-95. Mem. IEICE, Christian Student Fellowship Pakistan (sec. 1986-93). Anglican. Avocations: teaching, writing articles. Home: 835-1 Fujigane, 1-207 Green Heights, 350-2206 Tsurugashima Japan

PEŠÁK, JOSEF, biophysics educator; b. Olomouc, Czech Republic, May 21, 1942; s. Josef and Věra (Dočekalová) P.; m. Eva Utěšená, Nov. 13, 1965; children: Daniel, Dagmar Flynt, Dita, Perrier. Msc, Palacky U., 1966, Doctorate, 1968; PhD, Tech. U., Brno, Czech Republic, 1985. Researcher Meopta/Tesla, Přerov and Litovel, Czech Republic, 1966-67, 67-74; sr. lectr. NS UP Olomouc, 1974-88, scientist neurol. clin. med. faculty, 1988-92, asst. prof. dept. biophysics med. faculty, 1992—. Contbr. articles to profl. jours. Mem. Union of Czech Mathematicians and Physicists, Czech Med. Soc., N.Y. Acad. Scis., Czech Acoustical Soc. Avocation: folklore activities. Home: 63 Roosevelt St, Olomouc 777 00, Czech Republic Office: UP Olomouc Med Fac Dept Biophysics, 3 Hnevotinska St, Olomouc 775 15, Czech Republic

PESARAN, MOHAMMAD HASHEM, economist, educator; b. Shiraz, Fars, Iran, Mar. 30, 1946; s. Jamal and Effat (Firoozabadi) P.; m. Marian Fay Swainston, Aug. 10, 1969; children: Bijan, Jamal, Evaleila, Natasha, Hassan Ali. BS in Econs., U. Salford, 1968, D of Letters (hon.), 1992; PhD in Econs., Cambridge (Eng.) U., 1972. Asst. to vice gov. Ctrl. Bank of Iran, 1973-74, head econ. rsch., 1974-76; undersec. Ministry of Edn., Iran, 1977-78; tchg. fellow Trinity Coll., Cambridge, 1979-88; lectr. in econs. Cambridge U., 1985-88, prof. econs., 1988—; professorial fellow Trinity Coll., 1988—; prof. econs., dir. applied econometrics U. Calif., L.A., 1989-92. Author: (with L.J. Slater) Dynamic Regression: Theory and Algorithms, 19809; editor: (with T. Lawson) Keynes' Economics: Methodological Issues, 1985, The Limits to Rational Expectations, 1987, (with T.S. Barker) Disaggregation in Econometric Modelling, 1990, (with B. Pesaran) Microfit: An interactive econometrics software package, 1987, 91, (with Simon Potter) Non-Linear Dynamics, Chaos and Econometrics, 1993, (with M. Wickens) Handbook of Applied Econometrics, Vol. 1, 1995, (with P. Schmidt) Vol. II, 1997, (with B. Pesaran) Working with Microfit 4.0—Interactive Econometric Analysis, 1997, (with R.P. Smith and T. Akiyama) Energy Demand in Asian Developing Economies, 1998), (with C. Hsao, K. Lahiri and L.F. Lee) Analysis of Panels and Limited Dependent Variables, 1999. Served to 1st lt. Iran Army, 1976-78. Fellow Econometric Soc.; mem. Royal Econ. Soc. Home: 283 Hills Rd, Cambridge CB2 2RP, England Office: Trinity Coll, Cambridge CB2 1TQ, England

PESCARMONA, ENRIQUE M., entrepreneur; b. Mendoza, Argentina, Nov. 16, 1941; s. Luis Menotti and Teresa Ana (Peña) P.; m. Lucy Elisabeth Pujals; children: Lucas, Sofia, Luis, Lucila. Degree in engring., U. Nacional de Cuyo, 1965; MBA, U. de Navarra, Spain, 1967. Pres. Corporacion IMPSA, Industrias Metalurgicas Pescarmona S.A.; v.p. Henri Lagarde SA, Mendoza; pres. IMPSAT Fiber Networks, Del.; bd. dirs. Bodega Lagarde SA, Mendoza, ICSA, Mendoza, La Mercantil Andina CIA, de Seguros, SA, Buenos Aires, TCA SA, Buenos Aires. Bd. visitors Pitts. U. Recipient Condecoracion de Comendacion al Merito de la Republica Italiana, 1994, Orden Nacional al Merito en El Grado de Gran Ofcl. Gobierno de Colombia, 1994, Ordem do Rio Branco No Grau de Commendador Gobierno de Brasil, 1995, Orden Francisco de Miranda en su Primera Clase Govt. Venezuela, 1997, Condecoracion de la Orden de San Carlos en el Grado de Commendador Govt. Colombia, 1999, Condecoracional Merito Laboral Govt. Ecuador, 1999. Mem. Consejo Profl. de Ingenieria, Consejo Empresario Mendocino (past pres.), Consejo de Administracion de la fundacion Exoprt-ar (pres.), Consejo de Administracion de la Universidad del Congreso. Roman Catholic. Avocations: hunting, fishing, skiing, biking. Office: Corporacion IMPSA, Av E Madero 940 Piso 19, 1106 Buenos Aires Argentina

PESCE, CESARE, priest missionary; b. Novi Ligure, Italy, Sept. 26, 1919; s. Michelangelo Pesce and Ernestina Montessoro. Degree in Theology, Pontifical Inst. Fgn. Missions, Milan, 1942; diploma, Pastorale/Pontificia U. Latranensis, Rome, 1970. Asst. parish priest Cath. Ch., Voghera, Italy, 1943-48; dir. Cath. Missions, Ruhea and Thakurgaon, Pakistan, 1950-69; gen. sec. Manitese, Milan and Rome, 1969-71; dir. Catechetical Ctr., Dinajpur, Bangladesh, 1972-79, Cath. Missions, Pathorghata and Khalisha, Bangladesh, 1979-99; rector St. Mary Shrine, Dinajpur, Bangladesh, 2000—. Author: Strade Della Vita, 1981, rev. edit., 1989, Bangladesh Zindabad!, 1995, others. Recipient Golden Tower of Novi Ligure, 1998. Office: St Mary Shrine, PO Shekhpura, Dinajpur 5200, Bangladesh

PESCE, MARIA ESTER, medical educator; b. Santiago, Chile, Oct. 16, 1943; d. Jose and Olga Alvarez H.; m. Humberto E. De La Cuadra, Apr. 26, 1969; children: Maria Carolina, Humberto. Cert., Ministry of Edn., Santiago, 1962; diploma in nursing, Pontificia U. Catolica Chile, 1969; diploma in pharmacology, U. Chile, Santiago, 1974. Clin. nurse Hosp. Barros Luco Trudeau, 1967-73; pharmacology trainee U. Chile Ctrl. Br., Santiago, 1974-76; instr. in pharmacology U. Chile South Br., Santiago, 1977-87; instr. prof. U. Chile North Br., Santiago, 1988-95; asst. prof. U. Santiago, 1996—; pharmacology prof. U. Chile, 1975-95; vis. prof., 1992-95. Contbr. articles to profl. jours. Recipient DTI project grants U. Chile, 1993, 96. Roman Catholic. Avocations: gardening, antiques, interior decorating.

PESCOD, MAINWARING BAINBRIDGE, environmental engineering consultant; b. Leadgate, Eng., Jan. 6, 1933; s. Bainbridge and Elizabeth (Brown) P.; m. Mary Lorenza Coyle, Nov. 16, 1957; children: Duncan Warren, Douglas James. BSc in Civil Engring., U. Durham, Eng., 1954; SM in San. Engring., MIT, 1956. Chartered engr., U.K. Teaching and rsch. assoc. MIT, Cambridge, Mass., 1954-56; rsch. assoc. U. Durham/King's Coll., Newcastle upon Tyne, 1956-57; lectr. in engring. Fourah Bay Coll., Freetown, Sierra Leone, 1957-61; asst. engr. Babtie, Shaw & Morton, Glasgow, 1961-64; prof. environ. engring. Asian Inst. Tech., Bangkok, 1964-76; prof. environ. control engring. U. Newcastle upon Tyne, 1976-98; chmn., mng. dir. Environ. Tech. Cons., Motherwell Bridge Group, Tyne and Wear, Eng., 1988—; chmn. M.B. Tech. (Malaysia) Sdn, Bhd, 1996—; non-exec. dir. Northumbrian Water Group PLC, Newcastle-upon-Tyne, 1989-97, Motherwell (Scotland) Bridge Envirotec, 1991-95. Editor: Urban Solid Waste Management, 1991; co-editor: Water Supply and Wastewater Disposal in Developing Countries, 1971, Treatment and Use of Sewage Effluent for Irrigation, 1988. Mem. Northumbrian Water Authority, Newcastle upon Tyne, 1986-89. Decorated officer Order Brit. Empire. Fellow Instn. Civil Engrs., Chartered Instn. Water and Environ. Mgmt. (mem. coun. 1987—), Inst. Wastes Mgmt. Avocations: squash, golf, reading, advising in developing countries. Home: Tall Trees, High Horse Close Wood, Rowlands Gill NE39 1AN, England Office: Environ Tech Cons, Gateshead NE11 0HF, England

PESCOSOLIDO, PAMELA JANE, arts and craft supply store owner, graphic designer; b. Chgo., Dec. 28, 1960; d. Carl Albert Jr. and Linda Clark (Austin) P.; m. Larry Carl Vangroningen, Mar. 5, 1994 (div.); 1 child, Harley Austin. BA, Scripps Coll., 1983; JD, Vt. Law Sch., 1990. Bar: Maine 1990. Office mgr., asst. chef The Elegant Picnic, Stockbridge, Mass., 1983; receptionist, sec. Sequoia Orange County, Exeter, Calif., 1983-84; A/R clk. Tropicana Energy Co., Euless, Tex., 1984-85; owner, calligrapher Calligraphic Arts, Great Barrington, Mass., 1986-87; legal intern Pine Tree Legal Assistance, Augusta, Maine, 1989, Office of the Juvenile Defender, Montpelier, Vt., 1990; bookkeeper Badger Farming Co., Exeter, 1991—; owner, legal drafter and researcher Legal Rsch. Svc., Visalia, Calif., 1990—; owner, graphc designer Hourglass Prodns., Visalia, 1995—; owner, mgr. The Angel Within, Artists, Supplies and Gallery, Exeter, Calif.; rsch. editor Vt. Law Rev., Vt. Law Sch., South Royalton, 1989-90. Designer, graphic artist polit. propaganda for Libertarian Party of Calif.; contbr. poetry to Nat. Coll. Poetry Rev. Mem. county cen. com., chair Valley Libertarians, Libertarian Party of Calif., Visalia, 1996—; candidate Libertarian Party Dist. 19, Calif. U.S. Congress, 1996; candidate Libertarian Party Calif. State Contr., 1998. Chase scholar Vt. Law Sch., 1989. Mem. ACLU, AAUW (newsletter editor 1994-96), ABA, Nature Conservancy. Avocations: artistic endeavors of all kinds. Office: The Angel Within LLC 137 North E St Exeter CA 93221-1728

PESEC, DAVID JOHN, data systems executive; b. Cleve., Apr. 19, 1956; s. Rudolph J. and Martha C. (Kessler) P. BS, Cleve. State U., 1988; MBA, U. Phoenix, 1999; PhD, Trinity Coll., 2000. Pvt. practice cons. Cleve., 1976-78; programmer Champion Svc. Corp., Cleve., 1978; sr. sys. programmer United Tel. of Ohio, Mansfield, 1978-89; dir. devel. Broderick Data Sys., Mansfield, 1989-97; prin. cons. Keane, Inc., Independence, Ohio, 1997-2000; pres. Pesec Creative Mgmt., Inc., Mansfield, Ohio, 2000—; bd. dirs. Park Ave. Pets, Inc. Bd. dirs. ARC, Mansfield, 1989—, Mansfield Emergency Svc., 1986; assoc. pastor Cornerstone Grace Brethren Ch., 1995—; life mem. Rep. Nat. com., 1991—, Rep. Senatorial Inner Circle, 1991—. Recipient Senatoral medal of freedom, 1996. Mem. Am. Mgmt. Assn., Assn. Computing Machinery, Intercity Radio Club (pres. 1987-90), NRA, Gideons (v.p. 1992), Profl. Photographers. Republican. Mem. Grace Brethren Ch. Avocations: flying, auto racing. Office: Pesec Creative Mgmt Inc 1633 Hickory Ln Mansfield OH 44905-2945

PESEK, JIRI VACLAV, economic geology educator; b. Prague, Czech Republic, Apr. 19, 1936; s. Vaclav and Bozena (Tetourova) P.; m. Jarmila Dobiasova, June 1, 1963; children: Dana, Helena. PhD, Fac. of Sci., 1966, RNDr, 1967, DSc, 1988. Geologist Geol. Exploration Inst., Prague, 1959-60; technician Faculty of Sci., Prague, 1961-62, asst. prof., 1965-87, assoc. prof., 1987-91, prof., 1991—. Editor: Coal Bearing Formations of Czechoslovakia, 1988, European Coal Geology and Technology, 1997; author: Fossil Fuel Deposits, 1985, Paleogeographic Atlas of Late Paleozoic Czech Republic, 1998. Mem. Subcom. of Carboniferous Stratigraphy, Australia, 1971—. Recipient Gold medal Faculty of Sci., 1993, Comemor medal Charles U., 1998. Mem. Czech Geol. Soc. Avocations: music, theatre, collecting stamps. Home: Zelivecka 30, 10600 Prague 10, Czech Republic Office: Faculty of Sci, Albertov 6, 12843 Prague 2, Czech Republic

PESERIK, JAMES E., electrical, controls and computer engineer, consultant, forensics and safety engineer, fire cause and origin investigator; b. Beloit, Wis., Sept. 30, 1945; s. Edward J. and G. Lucille Peserik; m. Elaine L. Peserik, May 6, 1972. BSEE, U. Wis., 1968; MS, St. Joseph's U., 1990. Registered profl. engr., registered profl. land surveyor; cert. fire and explosion investigator, cert. fire investigation instr.; diplomate Am. Coll. Forensic Examiners. Development and instrumentation engr. Square D Co., Milw., 1968-71; product engr. I-T-E Imperial Corp., Ardmore, Pa., 1971-72; project engr. Harris-Intertype Corp., Easton, Pa., 1972-74; elec. engr. Day & Zimmerman, Inc., Phila., 1974-76; pvt. practice Coopersburg, Pa., 1976—; sr. elec. engr. S.T. Hudson Engrs., Inc., Phila., 1980-81; mem. adv. coun. Swenson Skills Ctr., Phila., 1990-95. Treas. Salford-Fraconia Joint Parks Commn., Montgomery County, Pa., 1980-83. Mem. IEEE (sec. indsl. applications group Phila. chpt. 1980, chmn. 1981, chmn. Lehigh Valley computer sect. 1999—), NSPE, Pa. Soc. Profl. Engrs., Del. Assn. Profl. Engrs. (external affairs com. 1995—), Nat. Fire Protection Assn., Internat. Assn. Arson Investigators, Nat. Assn. Fire Investigators. Office: PO Box 181 Coopersburg PA 18036-0181

PESKOV, VLADIMIR DMITRIEVICH, physicist, educator, consultant; b. Karaganda, Russia, Jan. 30, 1947; s. Dmitri S. and Olga D. (Petrova) P.; m. Tatiana R. Zabotina, May 3, 1973; children: Dmitri, Tatiana. MS in Physics, Phys. and Tech. Inst., Moscow, 1971; PhD in Physics, USSR Acad. Sci., Moscow, 1976, DSc, 1981. Rschr. Inst. Phys. Problems, Moscow, 1971-76, sr. rschr., 1976-97, leading scientist, 1981-97, prof., 1998; assoc. scientist European Ctr. for Nuclear Rsch., Geneva, Switzerland, 1986-92; application physicist II Fermi Nat. Accelerator Lab., Batavia, Ill., 1992-95; invited prof. Coimbra (Portugal) U., 1995-98; NRC sr. rsch. assoc. Marshall Space Ctr., Huntsville, Ala., 1995-98; guest prof. Royal Inst. Tech., 1998—; dir. rsch. Inst. Applied Mechanics Russian Acad. Sci., 1998—; mem. adv. bd. several internat. confs.; org. com. Internat. Conf. Imaging 2000, Stockholm; mem. TOF experiment CERN. Contbr. more than 100 articles to profl. jours. including Nuclear Instruments and Methods, Soviet Physics JETF, Jour. Physics. Participant Internat. Meeting on Chem. Disarmament, Rome, 1989, Internat. Forum di Amore, Italy, 1991, Internat. Meeting Our Nature, Italy, 1991. Recipient Prize of World Fedn. of Scientists, World Lab./Italian Physics Soc., 1991. Mem. Am. Phys. Soc., Italian Phys. Soc. Achievements include invention of device for magnetic field measurement of landing spacecraft, position sensitive gas scintillating detector; invention of new detector and methods for radiation measurement; some of them, for example detectors with gaseous and solid photocathodes are now widely used in experimental techniques; discovery of new type of plasma instability, connected to accumulation of excited atoms and molecules, a flux-induced breakdown cathode erecitation effect. Office: C/O D Peskov 306 E Lee St Plano IL 60545-1356

PESOLA, WILLIAM ERNEST, restaurant management executive; b. Marquette, Mich., Mar. 2, 1945; s. Ernest Ensio and Janice Mary (LeDuc) P.; m. Kathleen Mary Deschaine, July 9, 1966; children: Christie Lynn, Laurie Anne. BS, No. Mich. U., 1968, MS, 1971. Route driver Coca Cola Co., Marquette, 1963-68; tchr. Gwinn (Mich.) Schs., 1968-78, pub. Sch. News,, 1969; pres. Pesola Mgmt., Marquette, 1974—, Humboldt Ridge, Marquette, 1977—; treas. Elite Bar, Inc., Marquette, 1978—; v.p., dir. Marquette Cablevison, 1981-85; pres. Upper Peninsula Big Boy, Marquette, 1990—; cons. cable TV, 1985—, Bresnan Comm., 1984—. Pres. Gwinn Edn. Assn., 1975-77; regional pres. Upper Peninsula Edn. Assn., 1977-78; mem. Marquette City Commn., 1977-81. Mem. NEA, Marquette Econ. Club, Mich. Edn. Assn., Marquette C. of C. (Exemplary Citizen award 1990), Rotary. Roman Catholic. Home: 1026 N Front St Marquette MI 49855-3514

PESONEN, ERKKI JUHANI, pediatric cardiology educator; b. Helsinki, Finland, Mar. 29, 1943; arrived in Sweden, 1996; s. Heikki K. and Annikki Anita (Schulz) P.; m. Irma T. Vesalainen; children: Juha, Marjut. MD, Helsinki U., 1970, D in Med. Scis., 1974. Resident in pediatrics U. Helsinki, 1974-76, 78-80; pediatric cardiology fellow U. Calif., San Francisco, 1976-77, Northwestern U., Chgo., 1976-77; cons. pediat. cardiology U. Hosp., Helsinki, 1980-93, docent in pediat. cardiology, 1984—, chief pediat. cardiology, 1993-96; prof. pediat. cardiology Lund (Sweden) U., 1996—. Co-editor: Cardiology for a Pediatrician, 1992, 2d edit., 1993; co-editor: Echocardiography, 1989, Youth Cardiology, 1997. Recipient Young Investigators award Finnish Cardiac Soc., 1973, medal for successful rsch. in cardiology U. Turku, Finland, 1993. Mem. Finnish Cardiac Soc. (asst. sec. 1989-90, sec. 1992-93), Assn. European Pediatric Cardiology (coun. 1997-00). Avocation: marathon running. Office: Dept Pediat, Lund Univ Hosp, 221 85 Lund Sweden

PESQUET-POPESCU, BEATRICE, research engineer; b. Bucharest, Romania, Sept. 23, 1971; arrived in France, 1994; d. Nicolae-Sorin and Angela (Stan) Popescu; m. Jean-Christophe Pesquet, Aug. 31, 1996. Degree in engring., U. Politehnica, Bucharest, 1995; DEA, U. Paris XI, 1995; PhD with honors, Ecole Normale Superieure Cachan, 1998. Tchg. asst., rsch. scientist Lab. des Signaux et Sys./U. Paris Sud, 1998-99; rsch. engr. Philips, 1999—. Contbr. articles to profl. jours. including Signal Processing and Fractals in Engring., IEEE Trans. on Info. Theory. Recipient Best Student Paper award European Assn. for Signal Processing, 1997, Young Investigator award French Phys. Soc. Mem. IEEE. Office: Philips, 22 Ave Descartes, 94453 Limeil Brevannes France

PESSA, MARKUS VILJO, physicist, researcher; b. Nikel, Petsamo, Finland, Nov. 21, 1941; s. Viljo E. and Linnea E. (Sysimetsä) P.; children: Kristiina, Alexander. MA, U. Oulu, Finland, 1966; PhD, U. Turku, Finland, 1971, Docent in Physics, 1973. Assoc. prof. Tampere (Finland) U. Tech., 1976-86, prof., 1987—; mem. Acad. Finland, Helsinki, 1992-94. Contbr. over 300 articles to profl. jours. Referee EU Esprit Tech. Programs, Brussels, 1995—, Soros Found., 1994—, and severals sci. jours., 1985—. Mem. Internat. Union for Vacuum Sci., Tech. and Applications (rep. 1982—). Achievements include pioneering the development of compound semiconductor technology and industry in Finland; founder and present director of optoelectronics research centre Tampere University of Technology. Home: Miekka katu 13C11, FIN33530 Tampere Finland Office: Tampere Univ Tech, Kanslerin katu 1, FIN33101 Tampere Finland

PESSES, MARVIN, metal products executive, consultant; b. Bklyn., July 18, 1923; s. I. Aaron and Ann (Deines) P.; m. Elaine Barbara, Oct. 13, 1931; children: Lawrence, Ian, Paul, Michael. BS, Purdue U., 1944; MS, U. Ill., 1946; student, U. Iowa, 1946-48; DSc (hon.), London Coll. Eng., 1966. Registered profl. engr. V.p. Alloy Metal Products, Davenport, Iowa, 1950-

64; pres. Mercer Alloys, Greenville, Pa., 1964-71; CEO, chmn. The Pesses Co., Pepper Pike, Ohio, 1971-80; CEO Pentad Group, Boca Raton, Fla., 1980—; dir. Stainless & Alloy Corp., Greenville, Pa., 1964-1971, Quinten Ptrs., Solon, Ohio, 1971—. Patentee in field. Pres. Tent-at-the-Tower, Moline, Ill., 1960-64. Mem. Am. Soc. Metals (chmn., dir. 1952-68), Am. Foundrymen's Soc. (dir.), Ductile Iron Soc. (dir. 1960-68). Avocations: bicycling, horseback riding, target shooting, hunting, photography. E-mail: labelsaver@aol.com. Home: 6430 Via Rosa Boca Raton FL 33433-6432

PESTELL, GEORGE STANLEY, retired surgeon, consultant; b. Perth, Subiaco, Australia, Mar. 17, 1921; s. George and Lilian May (Parker) P.; m. Texa Berry Marum, April 3, 1954; children: Mark, Richard, Jane. MB BS, U. Melbourne, 1945. Resident med. officer Alfred Hosp., Melbourne, 1945-46, Royal Perth Hosp., 1946-49, King Edward Meml. Hosp., London, 1949-50, Harlow Wood Orthopaedic Hosp., Mansfield, England, 1950-52, Rooksdown House Plastic Unit, Basingstoke, England, 1952-53; dep. med. supt. Royal Perth Hosp., 1953-54, asst. surgeon, 1954; clin. lectr. U. Dept. Surgery, Perth, 1957-77; emeritus cons. surgeon Royal Perth Hosp., 1977; dir. surg. studies St. John of God Hosp., Perth, 1977-89; ret., 1990; cons. surgeon Repatriation Vets. Commn., 1986; chmn. clin. staff Royal Perth Hosp., 1974. Author: The Pestell Saga, 1995. Mem. med. adv. com. Hollywood Vets. Hosp., Perth, 1965; active Med. Bd., Perth, 1964. Fellow Royal Coll. Surgeons (England), Royal Coll. Surgeons (Australia); mem. Australasian Coll. Surgeons (chmn. West Australia br. 1970), Soc. Head and Neck Surgeons, Weld Club, Wyvern Soc. (life). Avocations: electronics, astronomy, photography, classical piano. Home: 29 Cygnet Crescent, Dalkeith 6009, Australia

PESUT, DANIEL J., nursing educator; b. DeKalb, Ill., Dec. 12, 1951; s. George D. and Donna M. Pesut; m. Susan E. Ziel, Aug. 28, 1981; children: Elliott, Erin. BSN, No. Ill. U., 1975; MSN, U. Tex., San Antonio, 1977; PhD, U. Mich., 1984. RN, Ind.; cert. specialist. Assoc. prof. U. Mich. Sch. Nursing, Ann Arbor, 1978-81; dir. nursing William S. Hall Psychiat. Inst., Columbia, 1984-87; assoc. prof. U. S.C., Columbia, 1987-93; prof., dept. chair environ. health Ind. U. Sch. Nursing, Indpls., 1997—. Author: Clinical Reasoning: The Art and Science of Critical and Creative Thinking, 1999. Fellow Am. Acad. Nursing; mem. Sigma Theta Tau (Creativity award 1993). Avocations: piano, travel, reading. E-mail: dpesut@iupui.edu. Home: 14144 Blue Heron Dr Carmel IN 46033 Office: Ind Univ Dept Environ Health Sch Nursing Indianapolis IN 46204

PESUT, TIMOTHY SCOTT, investment advisor, professional speaker, consultant; b. Gary, Ind., June 30, 1956; s. Anton and Virginia Udean (Carahoff) P.; m. Michelle Angela Durdov, May 25, 1985; children: Ariel Fay, Caitlin Michelle. AAS in Elec. Engring. Tech., Purdue U., 1978, AAS Supervision, BS Elec. Engring. Tech., 1980. CFP Coll. Fin. Planning; cert. funds specialist, trust and estate planning advisor, investment mgmt. cons.; registered investment advisor. Cardiology clin. rsch. assoc. Cordis Corp., Miami, Fla., 1980-82, neurosurg. specialist, 1982; investment broker A. G. Edwards Sons, Merrillville, Ind., 1982-86, Shearson Lehman, Sarasota, Fla., 1986-88; portfolio mgr. Prudential Securities, Inc., Venice, Fla., 1988-91; registered investment advisor Wealth Mgmt., Sarasota, Fla., 1991—; v.p., resident mgr. First Southeastern Securities Group, Sarasota, 1995-2000; pres. Money Dr., LLC, 2000—; arbitrator Am. Arbitration Assn., 1992-99; founder Inst. of Cert. Estate Planners. Columnist Money Talks, 1985, Money Mgmt., 1995. Guardian ad litem 12th Dist. Ct., Sarasota, 1985; bd. dirs. Jr. Achievement of Sarasota County; founding mem. Anthony Robbins Found., 1990; fundraising chmn. Jr. Achievement of Sarasota County. Cpl. USMC, 1974-76. Mem. Profl. Assn. Diving Instrs. (Divemaster), Nat. Speakers Assn., Toastmasters Internat. (yr. 2000 conv. chmn., lt. gov. mktg. 1996-97, dist. treas. 1995-96, lt. gov. edn. and tng. 1997-98, dist. 47 gov. 1998-99, Area Gov. of Yr. 1994, Excellence in Edn. and Tng. award 1997-98, Dist. Dist. Gov. award 1998-99, yr. 2000 conv. chmn.). Republican. Methodist. Avocations: scuba diving, skiing, sailing, woodworking, fine arts. Office: Money Dr LLC 7061 S Tamiami Trl # 208 Sarasota FL 34231-5559

PESZKE, MICHAEL ALFRED, psychiatrist, writer; b. Deblin, Poland, Dec. 19, 1932; s. Alfred Bartlomiej and Eugenia Halina (Grebocka) P.; m. Alice Margaret Sherman, Sept. 20, 1958; children: Michele Halina Olender, Michael Alexander. BA, Trinity Coll., Dublin, Ireland, 1956; MB, BCh, BAO, Dublin U., 1956. Bd. cert. psychiatrist. Staff psychiatrist Yale Student Health Svc., New Haven, 1961-64; asst. prof. sch. medicine U. Chgo., 1964-68; cons. psychiatrist Wesleyan U., Middletown, Conn., 1968-70; asst. prof. Sch. Medicine U. Conn., Farmington, 1970-73, assoc. prof., 1973-80, prof. psychiatry, 1980-90; clin. prof. U. Md. Sch. Medicine, Balt., 1991-99; chief Psychiatry Svc. Perry Point (Md.) VA Med. Ctr., 1990-98, co-coord. R&D, 1998-99; dir. psychiat. clin. svcs. John Dempsey Hosp., U. Conn. Health Ctr., Farmington, 1983-87; chief VA Med. Ctr., Newington, Conn., 1987-90; ind. rschr., 1999—. Author: Involuntary Treatment of the Mentally Ill: The Problem of Autonomy, 1975, Battle for Warsaw, 1939-44, 1995, Poland's Navy: 1918-1945, 1999; co-author: (edited by L.A. Pervin, L.R. Reik, W. Dalrymple) The College Drop-out and the Utilization of Talent, 1966, (edited by J. Zusman, E. Bertsch) The Future of Psychiatric State Hospitals, 1975; contbr. articles to profl. jours.; book reviewer Univ. Chgo. Law Rev., 1968, Conn. Law Rev., 1976, Am. Jour. Psychiatry, 1976-99; rschr. in schizophrenia. Mem. Conn.'s Jud. Law Revision Com., 1982-86, Whiting Forensic Adv. Bd., 1975-87; co-chair Commr. Mental Health's Com. to Re-write Conn. Civil Commitment Statutes, 1976-77. WHO travel fellow, United Kingdom, Denmark, Poland, 1977; U. Conn. Research grantee, 1972-87. Fellow APA (life); mem. Am. Coll. Psychiatrists, Soc. for Mil. History, Royal United Svcs. Inst. (London).

PETCHENEV, ALEX, scientist; b. St. Petersburg, Russia, May 3, 1956; arrived in the U.S., 1993; BS, Poly. U., St. Petersburg, 1977, MS, 1979, PhD, 1987. Engr. Mekhanobr-Tekhnika, St. Petersburg, 1978-85, scientist, 1985-92; engr. Bently Nevada Corp., Minden, Nev., 1993-94; scientist Bently Nevada Corp., Minden, 1994—. Mem. ASME, Russian Engring. Acad. (fgn.). E-mail: alex.petchenev@bently.com. Office: Bently Nevada Corp 1711 Orbit Way Bldg 1 Minden NV 89423-4114

PETELENZ, TADEUSZ KAROL, cardiologist; b. Cracow, Poland, Apr. 15, 1925; s. Ignacy and Zofja P.; m. Teresa Wanda Slominska, Aug. 25, 1951; children: Thomas, Michael. Physician, U. Jagiellonica Med. Sch., Poland, 1952; MD, Silesian Med. Sch., Poland, 1961, PhD, 1966. Physician in mil. svc. Poland, 1952-57; chmn. dept. of internal medicine 1st City Hosp., Zabrze, Poland, 1969-75; chmn. cardiol. dept. specialistic Hosp. No 2, Katowice, Poland, 1975-78; prof., chmn. III Clinic of Cardiology Silesian Med. Sch., Ochojec, Poland, 1978-95; chmn. Silesian Cardiol. Ctr. Found. in Katowice-Ochojec, Poland, 1995—; adj. in Clinic of Internal Diseases, Silesian Med. Sch., Zabrze, Poland, 1958-68; chmn. outpatients multispecialists dept. for Dist. Katowice, 1962-75; cons. prof. for cardiology Dist. Czestochowa, Poland, 1977-82, Dist. Katowice, Poland, 1983-91, Silesian Cardiol. Ctr in Katowice, 1995—. Contbr. 420 articles to profl. jours. Recipient prize of 4 World Congress of Cardiology in Mexico City, 1962, Sci. award Polish Cardiol. Soc., 1994, Pres. of Silesian Med. Sch., 1993-94, award for Didactics, 1994, 95. Mem. Polish Med. Soc., Cardiol. Soc. Dist. Katowice (pres. bd. dirs. 1996—), N.Y. Acad. Sci., IEEE. Roman Catholic. Avocations: tennis, sailoring, skiing, swimming, tourism. Office: Silesian Cardiol Ctr, 46 Ziolowa Str, 40635 Katowice Ochojec, Poland

PETER, AGNES, English educator; b. Budapest, Hungary, Aug. 25, 1941; d. Janos and Margit (Czegledy) P.; m. Gabor Gacs; children: Andras, Anna, Zsofia. MA, Eotvos L. Univ., 1964, PhD, 1980. Author: Keats's Concept of Poetry, 1970, Keats Vilaga, 1989, An Awful Rainbow, 1996. Avocations: playing piano, cycling. Home: Bosnyak U 16/A, H-1145 Budapest Hungary Office: Dept English Studies, Ajtosi DS 19, H-1146 Budapest Hungary

PETER, CHRISTIAN, computer company executive; b. Vienna, Austria, Oct. 26, 1956; s. Kurt and Erika Peter; m. Ursula Janeschitz, Apr. 26, 1980; children: Barbara, Andreas. Advanced maintenance devel. engr. IBM, Raleigh, N.C., 1984-86; product mgr. IBM PCs IBM, Vienna, 1991-93, team leader PC brand mgmt., 1994-95, mgr. PC co. product sales and support, 1996, region mgr. PSG tech. support Austria, Cen. Europe, & Russia, 1997, mgr. Netfinity Sys. sales, 1998, mgr. midrange sys. sales, 1998, mgr. sys. sales, 2000—. Avocations: singing, computing. Fax: 43 1 21145 3102. E-mail: christian peter@at.ibm.com. Office: IBM, Obere Donaustrasse 95, A-1020 Vienna Austria

PETER, GERNOT, chemist, researcher; b. Linz, Austria, Apr. 26, 1942; s. Franz and Gerta (Weselsky) P.; m. Agnes Moutsina, July 28, 1968; children: Sascha S., Vanessa. Diploma in chemistry, Johann-Wolfgang-von-Goethe U., Frankfurt, Germany, 1973, Dr.phil.nat., 1977. Sci. asst. Ctr. Biol. Chemistry Johann-Wolfgang-von-Goethe-U., 1973-81; sci. asst. inst. lab. diagnostics Dr. G.-W. Orth., Giessen, Germany, 1973-78; head lab. pharmacokinetics ASTA Medica AG, Frankfurt, 1981-90, head group nonclin. pharmacokinetics, 1990—, sr. scientist dept. biochemistry, 1997—; mem. panel Internat. Pharm. Aerosol Consortium on Toxicity Testing. Contbr. numerous articles and abstracts to profl. publs.; patentee in field. Mem. parents' coun. elem. sch., Nidderau, Germany, 1982-84, St. Lioba Gymnasium, Bad Nauheim, Germany, 1984-93. Mem. Soc. German Chemists, German Cancer Soc., N.Y. Acad. Sci., Soc. Lab. Animal Sci., Assn. German Natural Scientists and Physicians, European Soc. Autoradiography. Mem. Social Dem. Party of German. Avocations: classical music, reading, motor boating, electronics, travel. Home: Dr-Carl-Henss-Str 28, D-61130 Nidderau Germany Office: Asta Medica AG, Weismuellerstr 45, D-60314 Frankfurt Germany

PETER, MIHALY, Russian philologist, educator; b. Budapest, Nov. 8, 1928; s. Hugo and Maria (Biro) Popper; m. Ilona Ilma Boros, Aug. 15, 1962; children: Eva, Zsuzsanna. BA, U. Leningrad, 1954; Dr, U. Budapest, 1959, DSc, 1988. Asst. dept. Russian philology U. Budapest, 1954-59, sr. asst., 1959-67, lectr. dept. Russian philology, 1967-85, prof. dept. Russian philology, 1985—, head dept. Russian philology, 1981-91, prof. dept. East Slavonic and Baltic philology, 1992-99, prof. emeritus, 1999—. Author: Historical Grammar of the Russian Language, 1969 (award Hungarian Text Book Pub. 1970), The Poetic Language of Tvardovsky, 1970, Means and Devices of the Expression of Emotions in Language, 1991, Pushkin's Novel in Verse Eugene Onegin in the Light of its Hungarian Translations, 1999; editor: The Structure and Semantics of the Literary Text, 1977. Recipient Pushkin medal Internat. Assn. Tchrs. Russian Lang. and Lit., 1999. Mem. Hungarian Soc. Linguistics (chmn. Slavic sect. 1986-96, gen. and applied linguistics sect. 1996—), Internat. Com. of Slavicists (subcom. stylistics and poetics 1968—). Home: Buday Laszlo u 7, H 1024 Budapest Hungary Office: Eotvos Lorand U, Eotvos Lorand U, Puskin u 5/7, H 1088 Budapest Hungary

PETER, PHILLIPS SMITH, lawyer; b. Washington, Jan. 24, 1932; s. Edward Compston and Anita Phillips (Smith) P.; m. Jania Jayne Hutchins, Apr. 8, 1961; children: Phillips Smith Peter Jr., Jania Jayne Hutchins Stone. BA, U. Va., 1954, JD, 1959. Bar: Calif. 1959. Assoc. McCutchen, Doyle, Brown, Enerson, San Francisco, 1959-63; with GE (and subs.), various locations, 1963-94; v.p. corp. bus. devel. GE (and subs.), 1973-76; v.p. GE (and subs.), Washington, 1976-79, v.p. corp. govtl. rels., 1980-94; counsel, head govt. rels. dept. Reed Smith Shaw & McClay, Washington, 1994—; chmn. bd. govs. Bryce Harlow Found., 1990-92, bd. dirs. Mem. editl. bd. Va. Law Rev., 1957-59. Trustee Howard U., 1981-89; bd. dirs., exec. com. Nat. Bank of Washington, 1981-86; v.p. Fed. City Coun., Washington, 1979-85; bd. dirs. Carlton, 1987-90, 95-98, pres., 1995-96; bd. dirs. Tudor Place Found., 1999—. With transp. corps U.S. Army, 1954-56. Mem. Calif. Bar Assn., Order of Coif, Wee Burn Club, Ea. Yacht Club, Farmington Country Club, Ponte Vedra Club, Lago Mar Club, Landmark Club, Congl. Country Club, Georgetown Club, Chevy Chase Club, Pisces Club, F Street Club, Fairfax Club, Carlton Club (bd. dirs. 1990-98), Coral Beach and Tennis Club, Johns Island Club, The Windsor Club, Omicron Delta Kappa. Episcopalian. Home: 10805 Tara Rd Potomac MD 20854-1341 also: Johns Island 1000 Beach Rd & 690 Ocean Vero Beach FL 32963-3429

PETER, RALF UWE, dermatologist, radiobiologist; b. Dillenburg, Germany, Feb. 10, 1959; s. Friedrich Werner and Marianne Christa (Geier) P.; m. Anette Hanne Niepoth, Oct. 26, 1984; children: Manuel, Leon, Elena, Anna. Abitur, Wilhelm-von-Oranien, Dillenburg, 1978; MD, U. Giessen, Germany, 1984, U. Giessen, Germany, 1986. Resident in dermatology, surgery Fed. Armed Forces Hosp., Giessen, Germany, 1984-86; chief medical unit artillery bataillon Germany Army, Giessen, 1986-87; prin., investigator Inst. Radiobiology Fed. Armed Forces Medical Acad., Munich, 1987-88; resident in dermatology, allergy U. Munich, 1989-92, cons. dept. dermatology, 1992-96; prof. and chmn. dept. dermatology U. Ulm and Armed Forces Hosp., Germany, 1997—; cons. habilitation U. Munich, 1996. Author: (with R.U. Peter and G. Plewig) Radiation Therapy of Dermatologic Diseases, 1996, (with H.C. Korting, P. Gottlober, M. Schmidt) An Atlas of Ultrasound in Dermatology, 1999; assoc. editor Pigment Cell Rsch., 1995-99. Lt. col. Army, 1979-99, col. Army, 1999—. Mem. Radiation Rsch. Soc., European Soc. Dermatol. Rsch., European Soc. Pigment Cell Res. (treas.), German Soc. Wound Healing (pres. 1999-2000), Am. Soc. Therapeutic Radiology and Oncology, Nat. Liberal Club, Lions Club (London and Ulm). Lutheran. Avocations: double bass, guitar, classical, jazz. Office: U Ulm Dept Dermatology, Oberer Eselsberg 40, 89081 Ulm Germany

PETER, ROLAND, biologist and educator; b. Vienna, Austria, Mar. 13, 1940; s. Franz and Maria (Haberhauer) P.; m. Hedwig Kocko, Mar. 25, 1972. PhD, U. Vienna, 1971. Asst. prof. dept. genetics and gen. biology U. Salzburg, Austria, 1972-81, assoc. prof., 1982—. Contbr. articles to profl. jours. Mem. N.Y. Acad. Scis., Freshwater Biol. Assn. U.K., Austrian Biochem. Soc. Office: U Salzburg Dept Genetics, Hellbrunnerstrasse 34, A-5020 Salzburg Austria

PETER, SEBASTIAN AUGUSTINE, endocrinologist; b. St. Georges, Grenada, Jan. 20, 1944; came to U.S., 1975; s. Sidney Augustine and Cisly (Scoon) P.; m. Angela Missouri Sherman, July 18, 1970; children: Sebastian Augustine Jr., Senaka Akalbi. MBBS, U. W.I., 1969. Intern U. W.I., Nassau, 1970; resident in medicine Dalhousie U., Halifax, N.S., Can., 1971-72; resident in medicine U. Ottawa, Ont., Can., 1972-74, resident in endocrinology, 1974-75; fellow in endocrinology SUNY Health Sci. Ctr., Bklyn., 1975-76, assoc. clin. prof. medicine, 1992—; chief of endocrinology St. Mary's Hosp., Bklyn., 1992—. Contbr. articles to profl. jours. Recipient Community award Grenada Ex-Students Assn., 1991. Democrat. Avocations: music, jazz, playing musical instrument, reading. Home and Office: 1717 Ditmas Ave Brooklyn NY 11226-6603

PETERKIN, ALBERT GORDON, retired education educator; b. Phila., May 25, 1915; s. Albert Gordon and Eleanor Frances (Fricke) P.; m. Helen Webster, June 14, 1947; children: Eleanor Fricke, Scott Boddington, Mark Webster. BA, U. Pa., 1936; MAT, Harvard U., 1946; EdD, Columbia U., 1954. Cert. sch. adminstr., N.J., Conn., Ill. Tchr. Arms Acad., Shelburne Falls, Mass., 1938-39, Park Sch. of Buffalo, Snyder, N.Y., 1939-41; asst. prof. Lehigh U., Bethlehem, Pa., 1948-55; founding supt. Watchung Hills Regional H.S., Warren, N.J., 1955-60; supt. Westport (Conn.) Pub. Schs., 1960-70, Winnetka (Ill.) Sch. Dist. 36, 1971-77; prof. edn. Vanderbilt U., Nashville, 1977-81; ret., 1981; cons. Nat. Assn. Sch. Bus. Officers, Washington, 1968-70, Tenn. State U., Nashville, 1980-81; advisor Coun. Basic Edn., Washington, 1975; trustee Country Sch., Madison, Conn., 1985-91; chmn. master's program Iranian Sch. Devel., 1978-80, assessment instrument devel., 1974; initiator Cooperative Individualized Reading Project, U.S. Office Edn., 1970-73. Initiator Urban Coalition Sch. Study, Bridgeport, Conn., 1969-70; pres. Friends of Libr., Madison, 1984-85; prodr. cmty. TV, Madison, 1984-90; mem. Madison Inland Wetlands Commn., 1985—, chmn., 1990-92. Lt. comdr. USNR, 1941-45. John Hay fellow Greenwood Found., 1965; Kettering Found. fellow, 1966, 69; Whitehead fellow Harvard Sch. Edn., 1970-71; named to Supt.'s Hall of Fame Sch. Mgmt. Study Group, 1973. Mem. Am. Assn. Sch. Adminstrs., Suburban Sch. Supts., Madison Beach Club, Phi Delta Kappa. Mem. Religious Soc. of Friends. Avocations: garden design, travel, home video, golf, music. Home: 88 Notoh Hill Rd Apt 282 New Branford CT 06471-1851

PETERLE, LOJZE, Slovenian politician; b. Čužnja Vas, Slovenia, July 5, 1948; m. Branka Berkopec; children: Neža, Ožbej, Meta. Degree in econs., U. Ljubljana, Slovenia, 1972, degree in history and geography, 1975. Rschr. Town-Planning Inst., Ljubljana, 1975-86; counselor Nat. Planning Inst., Ljubljana, 1986-89; prime min. Govt. of Slovenia, 1990-92, min. fgn. affairs, 1993-94; freelance worker, 1990. Editor Revija 2000, 1971-86; editor-in-chief Tretji Dan, 1985-89. Pres. Christian-Dems. Party, Slovenia, 1989-2000; v.p. European Union Christian Dems., Vienna, 1993-99; chmn. parliamentary com. European affairs, 1997-2000, min. fgn. affairs, 2000—. Recipient Preseren Student award Govt. of Slovenia, 1975, Internat. award Kiwanis Soc., 1991, Golden Sign of Honour, Govt. of Slovenia, 1992; named Knight Pius Order with Great Cross, Pope, 1993. Roman Catholic. Avocations: aviation, climbing, bee-keeping, cycling. Office: Min Fgn Affairs, Gregorčičeva 25, SI-1000 Ljubljana Slovenia

PETERMAN, ZELL E., geologist; b. Cass County, Iowa, Nov. 29, 1934; s. Lloyd Sydney and Clara Edna (Hudson) P.; m. Gladys Irene Hendry, Mar. 4, 1960; chldren: Bruce Doyle, Brian James. Geol. Engr., Colo. Sch. Mines, 1957; MS in Geology, U. Minn., 1959; PhD in Geology, U. Alta., Can., 1962. Registered profl. engr., Colo. Rsch. geologist U.S. Geol. Survey, Washington, 1962-64; rsch. geologist U.S. Geol. Survey, Denver, 1964-71, chief isotope geology br., 1971-76, project chief, 1976-90, chief environ. sci. team, 1990—. Contbr. numerous articles to profl. jours. Recipient Meritorious Svc. award Dept. of Interior, 1982. Fellow Geol. Soc. Am., Mineral. Soc. Am., Soc. Econ. Geologists; mem. Am. Geophys. Union., Geochem. Soc. Republican. E-mail: zpeterman@compuserve.com. Home: 9795 W Ohio Dr Lakewood CO 80226-4062 Office: US Geol Survey MS 963 DFC Denver CO 80225

PETERMANN, FRANZ KARL, clinical psychologist; b. Weinheim, Germany, Sept. 28, 1953; s. Karl and Elisabeth Anna (Mitsch) P.; m. Ulrike Franziska Hasslinger, Feb. 1, 1978. Diploma in psychology, U. Heidelberg, 1975; PhD, U. Bonn, 1977, priv.doz, 1980. Univ. lectr. U. Heidelberg, 1975-76; univ. assoc. U. Bonn, 1976-80, prof., 1985-91; prof. Tech. U., Berlin, 1980-82, Aucher, 1982-85; prof. U. Bremen, 1991—; dir. Ctr. of Rehab. Rsch., 1995—; cons. Nat. Inst. Health, Germany, 1991. Author books; contbr. numerous articles to profl. jours. Recipient Deutsche Diabetes-Gesellschaft, 1992. Mem. European Acad. of Health (pres. 1991-93). Roman Catholic. Avocation: music. Office: U Bremen Ctr Rehab Rsch, Grazerstr 2, D-28359 Bremen Germany

PETERMANN, HANS JÜRGEN, research scientist; b. Vienna, Austria, Feb. 2, 1942. MA in German, Calif. State U., 1971; PhD in Physics, 2d Phys. Inst., Vienna, Austria, 1976; PhD in Botany (hon.), Bot. Inst., Berlin, Germany, 1980. Prof. phys. scis. Coll. of Desert, Palm Desert, Calif.; rsch. scientist Palm Springs, Calif., 1991—; lectr. in field. Author: Curiosities of Plant Kingdom, 1980, Gravitation and Space Travel, 1997, The Prehistory of Humanity, 1999; patentee in field. With U.S. Army, 1963-66. Avocations: hiking, tennis, scuba diving, mountain climbing, swimming. Office: PO Box 4513 362 N Palm Canyon Dr Apt 6 Palm Springs CA 92263-4513

PETERMANN, JÜRGEN, chemical engineering educator; b. Niederstriegis, Germany, Feb. 14, 1942. Diploma in physics, Göttingen U., 1968, PhD in Solid State Physics, 1970. Rsch. assoc. Bochum U., 1970-72, Gothenburg (Sweden) Tech. U., 1972-74, Saarbrücken (Germany) U., 1974-76; vis. scientist U. Del., 1976; prof. Tech. U. of Hamburg-Harburg, 1982-93; prof. Dortmund (Germany) U., 1993—, chmn. materials sci., 1993—; vis. prof. Guangzhou Inst. of Chemistry, China, 1993. Contbr. articles to profl. jours. Mem. German Phys. Soc., German Soc. for Materials Sci. Office: Dortmund U Lehrstuhl Werkst, Fachbereich Chemietechnik, D-44221 Dortmund Germany

PETERS, ANDREA JEAN, artist; b. Boston, Dec. 27, 1947; d. Andrew A. and Mary M. (Badessa) De Francesco; m. Mark Douglas Peters, Aug. 9, 1970; children: Melissa J., Christine M. Cert. of completion/diploma, Vesper George Sch. Art, 1966; student, Mass. Coll. Art, 1966-68. drawing and painting tchr. Tewksbury (Mass.) Fine Art Ctr., 1975-76, Wilmington, Mass., 1975-79. Gallery representation Art 3, Inc., Manchester, N.H., 1985—, Diana Levine Fine Art, Boston, 1988—, Gleason Fine Art, Boothbay Harbor, Maine, 1992—, Sandwich Art Gallery, Mass., 1994—, Granite Shore Gallery, Mass., 1997—; (cover illustrations) Community Connection Phone Book, 1993, 94. Recipient Daniel V. Hoye Meml. award Permanent Collection of Hoyt Inst. Fine Art, New Castle, Pa., 1986, Jurors award Whistler Mus., Lowell, Mass., 1987, Madlyn-Ann Woolwich award Pastels 1996 Pastel Soc. of No. Fla., 1996. Mem. Pastel Soc. Am. (master pastelist, Pearl Paint award 1987, J.G. Sher award 1988), Copley Soc. Boston (Jurors award 1988), North Shore Arts Assn. (J.S.G. Saunders Meml. award 1984), Am. Artist Profl. League, Allied Artists Am., Maine Coast Artists. Home: Boothbay Shores PO Box 245 East Boothbay ME 04544-0245

PETERS, ANN LOUISE, accounting administrator; b. Knoxville, Tenn., Jan. 26, 1954; d. William Brown and Louise (Emerson) Nixon; m. Raymond Peters, July 11, 1975. BBA, Miami U., Oxford, Ohio, 1976; MBA, Xavier U., 1985. Cert. internal auditor. Acctg. officer Soc. Bank (formerly Citizens Bank), Hamilton, Ohio, 1977-85; internal auditor Procter & Gamble Co., Cin., 1985-86, audit sect. mgr., 1986-88, sr. cost analyst, beauty care, 1988-90; plant fin. mgr. Procter & Gamble Mfg. Co., Phoenix, 1990-92; sr. fin. analyst, beauty care Procter & Gamble Co., Cin., 1992-93, group mgr., gen. acctg., 1993-96, group mgr. R&D fin., 1996-99, group mgr., global fin., paper divsn., 1999—. Mem. Inst. Internal Auditors, Inst. Mgmt. Accts. Republican. Congregationalist. Avocations: golf, swimming. Home: 7889 Ironwood Way West Chester OH 45069-1623 Office: Procter & Gamble Co PO Box 599 Cincinnati OH 45201-0599

PETERS, ANNE LOUISE, ophthalmology educator; b. Port Elizabeth, South Africa, Feb. 25, 1945; d. Colin Ingersoll and Florence Thora (Bergh) P.; m. Colin Michael Reardon, April 3, 1969; children: Timothy, Delia, Stephen. MB ChB, U. Capetown, South Africa, 1968; MMeD in Ophthalmology, U. Natal, South Africa, 1982. Cert. ophthalmologist. Specialist ophthalmologist, lectr. U. Natal, Durban, South Africa, 1982-84, sr. specialist, sr. lectr., 1984-87, prof., dept. head, 1987—; medical adv. bd. Retinitis Pigmentosa Found., South Africa, 1988. Editorial bd. Ophthalmic News Jour., 1994; contbd. articles to profl. jours. Mem. South African Med. and Dental Coun., Coll. Medicine South Africa, Vitreo retinal Soc., Club Jules Gonin. Avocations: languages, walking. Office: U Natal Med Sch, Umbilo Rd, 4001 Durban Kwa Zulu/Natal, South Africa

PETERS, D. STEFAN, research scientist; b. Gleiwitz, Germany, June 5, 1932; s. Wilhelm and Anna (Gorlich) P.; m. Margarete Mosch, Sept. 3, 1957; children: Winfried, Christiane, Bettina. MSc, U. Wroctaw, Poland, 1956; Dr. phil. nat., U. Frankfurt, 1961, privat dozent habil., 1979. Asst. U. Zool. Inst., Wroclaw, 1956-58; tchr. Secondary Sch., Hanau, Germany, 1961-64; asst. Forschunginst. Senckenberg, Frankfurt, 1964-87, head dept. vertebrates, 1987-97, vice dir., 1987-97; assoc. prof. U. Frankfurt, 1988—; mem. gov. bd. Senckenbergische Naturforschende Gesellschaft, Frankfurt, 1985-97, Ungerer Found., Frankfurt, 1987-97; treas. Deutsche Ornithologen Gesellschaft, Germany, 1980-85; expert for birds CITES, Bonn, Germany, 1978-93; mem. standing com. Ornithological Nomenclature, 1993—. Editor of periodical: Natur und Mus., 1965-68; co-editor: Morphologie und Evolution, 1994, Evolutionstheorie und ethische Fragestelluungen, 1981. Active Mcpl. Coun., Liederbach. Mem. AAAS, N.Y. Acad. Scis., Deutsche Zoologische Gesellschaft. Roman Catholic. Avocations: classical music, history of art. Office: Forschungsinst Senckenberg, Senckenberganlage 25, D-60325 Frankfurt am Main Germany

PETERS, DOUGLAS ALAN, nurse, insurance appeals analyst; b. Portsmouth, Va., Oct. 4, 1968; s. Terrance Gene and Pamela (Haffner) P. BA in Philosophy, Va. Poly. Inst. and State U., 1992; BSN summa cum laude, James Madison U., 1995; postgrad., Johns Hopkins U., 1997, U. Md., Balt., 1998—. RN, Va. Photojournalist CVNI/The Greene County Record, Stanardsville, Va., 1992; nursing asst. Rockingham Meml. Hosp., Harrisonburg, Va., 1993-95; clin. nurse Bapt. Hosp., Pensacola, Fla., 1995-96; neurology nurse Tallahassee Meml. Regional Med. Hosp., 1996; nurse mgr./quality assurance Escambia County Jail Infirmary, Pensacola, 1996-97; case mgr. U.R. Total Health Care, Balt., 1997-98; case mgr. Blue Cross/Blue Shield of Md., Balt., 1998-2000, appeals analyst, 2000—; quality control team advisor Bapt. Health Care, Pensacola, 1995. Vol. hospice unit Rockingham Meml. Hosp., 1994-95; vol. tourette Syndrome Assn., 1996—. Mem. ABA (student mem.), Nat. League for Nursing, Alpha Chi Sigma, Phi Sigma Pi, Sigma Theta Tau, Phi Delta Phi. Avocations: biomedical ethics, photography.

PETERS, ELLEN ASH, trial referee, retired state supreme court justice; b. Berlin, Mar. 21, 1930; came to U.S., 1939, naturalized, 1947; d. Ernest Edward and Hildegard (Simon) Ash; m. Phillip I. Blumberg; children: David Bryan Peters, James Douglas Peters, Julie Peters Haden. BA with honors, Swarthmore Coll., 1951, LLD (hon.), 1983; LLB cum laude, Yale U., 1954, MA (hon.), 1964, LLD (hon.), 1985; LLD (hon.), U. Hartford, 1983; Georgetown U., 1984; LLD (hon.), Yale U., 1985, Conn. Coll., 1985, N.Y. Law Sch., 1985; HLD (hon.), St. Joseph Coll., 1986; LLD (hon.), Colgate U., 1986, Trinity Coll., 1987, Bates Coll., 1987, Wesleyan U., 1987, DePaul U., 1988; HLD (hon.), Albertus Magnus Coll., 1990; LLD (hon.), U. Conn., 1992; LLD, U. Rochester, 1994. Bar: Conn. 1957. Law clk. to judge U.S. Circuit Ct., 1954-55; assoc. in law U. Calif., Berkeley, 1955-56; prof. law Yale U., New Haven, 1956-78, adj. prof. law, 1978-84; assoc. justice Conn. Supreme Ct., Hartford, 1978-84, chief justice, 1984-96; judge trial referee Superior Ct., Hartford, 2000—. Author: Commercial Transactions: Cases, Texts, and Problems, 1971, Negotiable Instruments Primer, 1974; contbr. articles to profl. jours. Bd. mgrs. Swarthmore Coll., 1970-81; trustee Yale-New Haven Hosp., 1981-85, Yale Corp., 1986-92; mem. conf. Chief Justices, 1984—, pres., 1994; hon. chmn. U.S. Constl. Bicentennial Com., 1986-91; mem. Conn. Permanent Commn. on Status of Women, 1973-74, Conn. Bd. Pardons, 1978-80, Conn. Law Revision Commn., 1978-84; bd. dirs. Nat. Ctr. State Cts., 1992-96, chmn., 1994, Hartford Found., 1997—. Recipient Ella Grasso award, 1982, Jud. award Conn. Trial Lawyers Assn., 1982, citation of merit Yale Law Sch., 1983, Pioneer Woman award Hartford Coll. for Women, 1988, Disting. Svc. award U. Conn. Law Sch. Alumni Assn., 1993, Raymond E. Baldwin Pub. Svc. award Quinnipiac Coll. Law Sch., 1995, Disting. Svc. award Conn. Law Tribune, 1996, Nat. Ctr. State Cts., 1996; named Laura A. Johnson Woman of Yr. Hartford Coll., 1996. Mem. ABA, Conn. Bar Assn. (Jud. award 1992, Spl. award 1996), Am. Law Inst. (coun.), Am. Acad. Arts and Scis., Am. Philos. Soc. Fax: 860-548-2887. Office: Superior Ct 95 Washington St Hartford CT 06106-4431

PETERS, EVELYN JOAN, artist; b. Anchorage, Alaska, Mar. 25, 1927; d. Algernon Sidney Jones and R. Lee (Bartholf) Jones-Lange; m. Curtis Gordon Chezem, Sept. 29, 1945 (div. Oct. 1956); children: Joanne Lee Chezem, David Gordon Chezem; m. Frederick William Peters Jr., May 30, 1958. Student, U. Oreg., 1945-50, Oreg. State Coll., 1955-56. Pvt. sec. Pub. Svc. Commn., Las Vegas, Nev., 1957-58; tech. sec. Los Alamos (N.Mex.) Nat. Lab., 1958-70; sr. sec. EG&G, Los Alamos, 1970-71; chmn. bd. dirs. Buchanan Arts and Crafts, Inc., Buchanan Dam, Tex., 1980, 86. One woman show at Frame Corner Gallery, Farmington, 1996, San Juan Coll., Farmington, 1998; exhibited in shows at Inn of Loretto, Santa Fe, 1982, Capital Rotunda, Austin, Tex., 1983, Golub Gallery, Steamboat Springs, Colo., 1985, Safari Park Hotel, Nairobi, Kenya, 1990 (Artistic Expressions award 1990, Gold medal 1990, St. John's Coll., Cambridge, Eng., 1992 (Bronze medal 1992), Western N.Mex. U., Silver City, 1993, Sixth Bear River Western Hist. Art Exhbn., Craig, Colo., 1994, Fed. Hall Mus., N.Y.C., 1994, 97, Ann. COGAP Exhbn., Governor's Island, N.Y., 1994 (George Gray Award, 1993), St. Francis Newman Ctr., Silver City, 1994, Apples, Aspen and Art, Cedaredge, Colo., 1995 (Most Popular Painting), Western and Wildlife Art Show, Estes Park, Colo., 1995, Sheraton-on-the Park Hotel, Sydney, Australia, 1995, Colo. Indian Market, Denver, 1995, Art Concepts Gallery, Tacoma, Wash., 1997, Keble Coll., Oxford, Eng., 1997, Sunwest Bank, Farmington, 1997, Rotunda Canon Office Bldg., U.S. Ho. of Reps., Washington, 1997, Durham Art Gallery, Eng., Arts for the Parks, 2000; represented in permanent collections at Aviation Heritage Mus., Anchorage, Daystar Found., Oklahoma City, Eleanor Bliss Ctr. Arts, Steamboat Springs, Colo., Marble Falls Depot Mus., Mus. N.W. Colo., Craig, Nat. Gallery Rural Art, Bonner Springs, Kans., Pioneer and R.R. Mus., Temple, Tex., USCG; paintings appeared in numerous mags., books, calendars and catalogs. Pres. Highland Arts Guild, Marble Falls, Tex., 1977, 90, 2d v.p., 1989; sec. Highland Lakes Arts Coun., Marble Falls, 1986. Recipient Marine Safety award Olin-Matheson, 1968, cert. of appreciation USCG Aux., 1969, 70, 1st and purchase award Kiwanis Art Competition, Granbury, Tex., 1983, 2d Pl. award Tex. Women Western Artists Show, Cresson, Tex., 1983, 2d and 3d pl. awards Llano Rodeo Art Show, 1986, 1st pl. award 9th Nat. Small Painting Western Show, 1987, 1st and purchase award Gt. Am. Art Competition, 1988, Most Popular Painter award 3d Ann. Invitational Art Show, Waco, Tex., 1988, Best of Show award Bear Valley Hist. Art Show, Craig, 1989, Highland Lakes Arts Competition, Kingsland, Tex., 1991, Internat. Woman of Yr. in art Internat. Biog. Ctr., 1991-92, Most Popular Painting award Western Colo. Ctr. for Arts, 1996, Purchase award NWNMAC, Farmington, 1997, Ouray Coll. 39th Ann. Art Exhibit, 1999, choice award 8th Ann. Nat. Christian Art Show, San Juan Coll., Farmington, N.Mex., 2000, Top 200 Arts for the Parks, 2000, numerous others. Mem. N.Mex. Arts Coun., signature mem. Nat. Acrylic Painters Assn. (US/UK, cover award 5th Internat. Open Exhibit 2000), official Coast Guard Artist, 1987—, Salmagundi Club, 1989-95, World Found. of Successful Women (charter mem.), Am. Biog. Inst. Rsch. Assn. (life, dep. gov. 1989, Gold Cup 1993, Medal of Honor 1992, Woman of Yr. 1994, 95), World Inst. of Achievement (life, Excellence as Painter award 1988), N.W. N.Mex. Arts Coun. (acting exec. dir. 1999—). Avocations: gardening, photography, reading, travel. Studio: Evelyns Studio 3706 San Medina Ave Farmington NM 87401-2328

PETERS, JACQUELINE MARY, secondary education educator; b. Milw., Oct. 6, 1947; d. Arnold Martin and Rosalie Ellen (Mulherin) Fladoos; divorced; children: Casey Martin, Ann Marie. Student, Clarke Coll., Dubuque, Iowa, 1965-67; BA, Calif. State U., Long Beach, 1970; MA in History and Tchg., LaVerne (Calif.) U., 1973. Reading tchr. Chaffey H.S., Ontario, Calif., 1971-78, tchr. phys. edn., 1976-78, English tchr., 1978-90, tchr. history, 1990—; mentor AAUW, cmty. schs., 1997-99. State rep. Trans Nat. Golf Assn., 1963-75; bd. dirs. Cmty. Challenge Grants, Ontario, 1996-00. Named to Sports Hall of Fame, Dubuque Sr. H.S., 1996; Med-Cal grantee, 1996, Project Yes grantee, 1997-99. Mem. AAUW (bd. dirs., br. pres. 1995-99, Edn. Foun. Gift Honoree 1998), Calif. Tchrs. Assn. Republican. Roman Catholic. Avocations: golf, fly fishing, pysanka, poetry, bridge. Home: 320 W 21st St Upland CA 91784-1413 Office: Chaffey HS 1245 N Euclid Ave Ontario CA 91762-1923

PETERS, JOSEPH DONALD, filmmaker; b. Montebello, Calif., Mar. 7, 1958; s. Donald Harry and Anna Lucia (Suarez) P. BA in Comm., U. So. Calif., L.A., 1982. Filmmaker Renaissance Prodns., Ltd., San Dimas, Calif., 1986—. Writer, prodr., dir. films, TV, Seniors and Alcohol Abuse, 1986, Eskimo Ice Cream Shoes, 1990 (Gold award 1991), Rachel, 1994 (Silver and Bronze award 1995), The Adventures of Sam and Kathy, 1998, Emotions, 1999 (Gold and Honorable Mention award 1999). Nominated Internat. Man. of Yr. Internat. Biog. Ctr., 2000. Mem. Am. Film Inst., Ind. Feature Project/West, Cinewomen. Avocations: reading film books, collecting videos, sporting events. Office: Renaissance Prodns Ltd Ste 48 301 N San Dimas Canyon Rd San Dimas CA 91773-2734

PETERS, LEROY RICHARD, materials management consulting company executive; b. Milw., June 26, 1943; s. LeRoy Edwin and Eleanor Hedwig (Bensing) Peters; m. Barbara Jean Hackney, Nov. 18, 1964 (div. July 1970); 1 child, Neal; m. Nancy Elizabeth Till, July 17, 1971; children: Richard, Brenda, Eric, Linda. BS, U. Wis., 1966; Grad., U.S. Army/Command and, Gen. Staff Coll., Ft. Leavenworth, Kans., 1977. Cert. fellow in prodn. and inventory mgmt. Inventory supr. Bucyrus Erie, Erie, Pa. and Pocatello, Idaho, ach3-76; inventory mgr. Am. Microsystems, Pocatello, 1976-78; prodn. mgr. Worthington Compressor, Buffalo, N.Y., 1978-80; mfg. mgr. St. Regis WPM Div., Denver, 1980-82; materials mgr. Robinson Brick Co., Denver, 1982-86; prodn. mgr. Merritt Equipment Co., Denver, 1986-89; instructional designer Martin Marietta, Denver, 1989-90; sr. cons. J.D. Edwards, Denver, 1990-93; sr. cons. mgr. AMX Internat., 1993-97; v.p. The Thompson Group, 1997-98; CEO, Enterprise Resource Mgmt., Inc., 1998—. Editorial com.: Aerospace and Defense Dictionary, 1990; contbr. articles to profl. jours. Scoutmaster Boy Scouts Am., Denver, 1989, cubmaster, 1988, outdoor chmn., Denver, 1990; dist. capt. Adams County Colo. Reps., Denver, 1986. Col. U.S. Army, 1966-94, Vietnam, Desert Storm. Decorated Legion of Merit, Bronze Star, Meritorious Svc. medal, Army Commendation medal. Fellow Am. Prodn. and Inventory Control Soc. (bd. dirs. region VI 1990—, pres. Colo. chpt. 1989-90); mem. Am. Def. Preparedness Assn., Moose. Lutheran. Avocations: fishing, reading, music, photography, geology. Home: 1468 W 111th Ave Northglenn CO 80234-3397

PETERS, MELANIE MARIA, federal official; b. Geleen, The Netherlands, Oct. 26, 1965; d. Austin John and Maria Petronella (Bijlmakers) P. MSc, Wageningen (Netherlands) U., 1990; PhD, U. London, 1993. Registered Recognized Toxicologists Netherlands. Rsch. fellow U. Wageningen, 1988-89, Bibra Inst., Carlshalton, U.K., 1989-90, U. London, 1990-93; postdoctoral fellow U. Tex., Austin, 1993-95; rsch. toxicologist Shell Chems., Amsterdam, The Netherlands, 1995-97; sr. policy officer Ministry Agr., The Hague, The Netherlands, 1998—; Dutch del. leader WHO/FAO, Codex Alimentar, 1998—, European Cmty. Vet. Drug Policy, 1998—; account mgr. Dutch Vet. Drug Registration, 1998—. Contbr. articles to profl. jours. Recipient award European Sci. Found., 1992. Mem. Soc. Toxicology, Dutch Toxicology Soc. (3rd prize 1996, 1st prize 1997). Home: Sarphatistraat 44-D, 1018 GN Amsterdam The Netherlands

PETERS, MICHAEL JOSEPH, paramedic instructor; b. Decatur, Ill., Jan. 19, 1965; s. Keith Edward and Josephine Peters; m. Belinda Gay Klein, Apr. 5, 1997; children: Ryan Klein, Jessica Klein. BS in Pers. Adminstrn., Quincy (Ill.) Coll., 1987. Nat. registered paramedic; lic. paramedic, Mo.; cert. paramedic instr., coord., examiner, Mo.; cert. vocat. instr., Mo. Firefighter, EMT Boone County Fire Protection Dist., Columbia, Mo., 1987-90; fire capt., tng. officer South Met. Fire Protection Dist., Raymore, Mo., 1990-92; paramedic, team leader Medevac Emergency Med. Svcs., Kansas City, Kans., 1992-93; dir. EMS edn. EPI/MAST Ambulance, Kansas City, Mo., 1993-96; paramedic instr. Met. Cmty. Colls., Kansas City, Mo., 1996—; adj. mem. paramedic faculty Met. Cmty. Colls., 1992-96; part-time edn. coord. The Children's Mercy Hosp., Kansas City, Mo., 1999—; part-time paramedic U. Mos. Hosps. and Clinics, Emergency Med. Svcs., Columbia, 1999—; lectr., presenter in field. Instr. ACLS, BCLS, PALS Am. Heart Assn., Topeka, Kans.; mem. Troop 11 com. Boy Scouts Am., Belton, Mo., 1995-99, summer camp scoutmaster, 1997, merit badge counselor, 1995—; vol. firefighter, paramedic Belton Emergency Svcs. Dept., 1998-2000. Recipient Red Stethoscope Lifesaving award Met. Ambulance Svcs. Trust, Kansas City, Mo., 1993. Mem. Mo. Emergency Med. Svcs. Assn., Firefighters' Assn. of Mo. Roman Catholic. Avocations: fly fishing, fly tying, collecting fire service insignia, camping, canoeing.

PETERS, RALPH, writer; b. Pottsville, Pa., Apr. 19, 1952; s. Ralph Heinrich and Alice Catherine (Parfitt) P.; m. Katherine McIntire, June 4, 1994. MA in Internat. Rels., St. Mary's U., 1988. Commd. U.S. Army, 1976; advanced through grades to lt. col., intelligence officer, 1980-98, novelist, essayist, 1981—. Author: Red Army, Flames of Heaven, Twilight of Heades, The Devil's Garden, 1997, Traitor, 1999, Fighting for the Future, 1999. Decorated Legion of Merit U.S. Army, 1998. Mem. Army and Navy Club. Avocations: adventure travel, languages, hiking, Shakespeare. Home: 5831 Green Springs Dr Warrenton VA 20187-9324

PETERS, RALPH EDGAR, architectural and engineering executive; b. Harrisburg, Pa., Feb. 20, 1923; s. George Edward and Rebecca Flavia (Michener) P.; m. Roberta Jane Shaffer, June 12, 1948; children: Sheila Jane, Gail Marie, Ralph Jr., Bret Edward. Student, U. Pa., 1942; BA in Bus. Adminstrn., Pa. State U., 1948. From payroll supt. to asst. budget supr. Pa. State U., 1948-52; chief acct., pers. officer Haller, Raymond & Brown, State College, Pa., 1952-54; from contr. to CEO and chmn. bd. Benatec Assocs., Inc. (formerly Berger Assocs., Inc.), Camp Hill, Pa., 1954—. Chmn. bd. advisors Pa. State U., Harrisburg, 1979—; chmn. bd. dirs. Holy Spirit Hosp., Camp Hill, 1982—; past pres. Tri-County United Way, Harrisburg, 1978—; chmn. Pvt. Industry Coun., Harrisburg, 1982-87. With U.S. Army, 1943-45, ETO, 1952-53, Korea. Recipient Comty. Svc. award Salvation Army, 1980, Disting. Pennsylvanian award Greater Phila. C. of C., 1981, Catalyst award Capital Region Econ. Devel., 1992, James Skelly award for exceptional svcs. to the hwy. program Associated Constructors of Pa., 1993, Alexis de Tocqueville Humanitarian award United Way, 1999; named Transp. Adv. of Yr., Pa. Hwy. Info. Assn., 1994; finalist Cen. Pa. Entrepreneur of Yr., 1996; Paul Harris fellow Rotary Internat., 1997. Mem. Pa. C. of C. (bd. dirs., transp. com. chmn. 1972-90), Harrisburg Area C. of C. (pres., chmn. 1979-83), Ams. for Competitive Enterprise Sys. (pres. 1981-83), Cumberland County Transp. Authority, Susquehanna Valley Regional Airport Authority, Lions, Masons, Pa. Jaycees (pres. 1955-56, nat. v.p. 1956-57), Delta Sigma Pi. Lutheran. Office: Benatec Assocs Inc 200 Airport Dr New Cumberland PA 17070-2467

PETERS, RICHARD JONATHAN, lawyer, manufacturing company executive; b. Janesville, Wis., Jan. 6, 1927; m. Ingrid H. Varvayn, 1953; 1 dau., Christina. BS in Chemistry, U. Ill., 1951; JD, Northwestern U., 1954. Bar: Ill. 1954. Chief patent counsel Englehard Industries, 1972-82, Kimberly-Clark Corp., Neenah, Wis., 1982-85; gen. counsel Lanxide Corp., Newark, Del., 1985-87; pvt. practice Chgo., 1985—. Served with CIC, U.S. Army, 1955-57. Patentee in field. Mem. ABA, Am. Intellectual Property Law Assn., Lic. Execs. Soc., Assn. Corp. Patent Counsel, North Shore Golf (Menasha, Wis.), Masons, Scottish Rite, Shriners.

PETERS, RITA PUTINS, political scientist, educator; b. Rezekne, Latvia; came to U.S., 1951; BA in Polit. Sci. & Fine Arts, U. Conn., 1961; MA in Polit. Sci., Boston U., 1965, PhD, 1973. Lectr. Boston U., 1968-70, 79-80, Simmons Coll., 1973, Boston State Coll., 1978-78, 81, U. Mass., Boston, 1982—; vis. lectr. U. Latavia, Riga, 1990, 1993, 1995, Estonian Sch. Diplomacy, Tallin, 1996; cons. U. Latavia, 1993, 1995, Polit. Candidates & others, Riga, 1998, 1999. Author: (with others) The Baltic In International Relations, 1988; book reviewer Choice, 1987—, contr. to Encyclopedia Americana, 1993,94,97 and to profl. jours. Vol. Foster Care Rev. Program, Boston, 1990—; bd. dirs. Baltic Am. Soc. of New England, Boston, 1980—. Fellow Wm. Joiner Ctr. Study of War U. Mass., 1986, grantee Internat. Rsch. & Exch. Bd., 1992, U. Mass., 1993, 1995. Mem. Harvard U. Davis Ctr. Russian Studies (assoc.), Am. Assn. for Advancement Slavic Studies, Assn. for Advancement Baltic Studies (life). Avocations: skiing, designing hand-knit clothing. Office: U Mass Polit Sci Dept 100 Morrissey Blvd Boston MA 02125-3300

PETERS, ROBERT JAMES, SR., draftsman; b. St. Louis, Dec. 20, 1946; s. Lewis Nathaniel and Thelma (Hudson) P.; m. Sharon Loretta Anderson, May 6, 1963 (div. Apr. 1992); m. Sharon Ann Dungy, July 21, 1992; children: Kimberly Rachele Peters Beck, Robert James Jr., Kelly Yusef. AA in Bus. Adminstrn., Forest Park Coll., St. Louis, 1968; BS in Indsl. Safety, Cen. Mo. State U., 1983; MBA, Lindenwood U., 1999. Polyphase tester AmerenUE, St. Louis, 1972-77, safety coord., 1977-79, safety supr., 1979-86, pers. supr., 1986-89, chief draftsman, 1989—; bd. dirs. Electro Savings Credit Union, 2000. Exec. bd. dirs. United Way, St. Louis, 1997—, St. Louis chpt. Am. Red Cross, mem. exec. com., chmn. vols., 1999; exec. bd. dirs. Nat. Conf. Cmty. and Justice; chmn. spkrs. bur. ARC, St. Louis, 1998; mem. spkrs. bur. Alzheimer's Assn., St. Louis, 1998; bd. pres. Wesley House Assn., St. Louis, 1998; bd. dirs. Nat. Conf. Cmty. and Justice, 1999, Do The Right Thing, 1999. With U.S. Army, 1970-72, Vietnam. Recipient Cerman F. Mathews award Mathews-Dickey Boys Club, 1994, Exceptional Vol. Svc. award ARC, 1994, Clara Barton award, 1996, Partnership award, 1996. Mem. Nat. Spkrs. Assn. (Gateway chpt.), Powermasters Toastmasters (pres. 1988-89, DTM award 1995), Optimist Club St. Louis (pres. 1985-86). Assemblies of Yahweh. Avocations: racquetball, cycling, running, public speaking. Home: # 12 Bellerive Acres Saint Louis MO 63121 Office: AmerenUE 1901 Chouteau Ave Saint Louis MO 63103-3003

PETERS, THEODORE, JR., research biochemist, consultant; b. Chambersburg, Pa., May 12, 1922; s. Theodore and Miriam (Lenhardt) P.; m. Margaret Campbell, June 9, 1945; children: Theodore D., James C., Melissa Peters Barry, William L. BS in Chem. Engring., Lehigh U., 1943; PhD in Biol. Chemistry, Harvard U., 1950. Diplomate Am. Bd. Clin. Chemistry. Grad. asst. MIT, Cambridge, 1943-44; rsch. fellow Harvard Med. Sch., Boston, 1948-50; instr. U. Pa. Sch. Medicine, Phila., 1950-51; biochemist U.S. VA Hosp., Boston, 1953-55; rsch. biochemist Mary Imogene Bassett Hosp., Cooperstown, N.Y., 1955-88, rsch. scientist emeritus, 1988—; vis. scientist Carlsberg Laboratorium, Copenhagen, Denmark, 1958-59; guest worker NIH, Bethesda, Md., 1971-72; vis. rsch. prof. U. Western Australia, Perth, 1982; chmn. classification panel FDA, Washington, 1976-79; bd. dirs. Nat. Com. for Clin. Lab. Standards, Villanova, Pa., 1986-87. Author: All About Albumin, Biochemistry, Genetics, and Medical Applications, 1996; chmn. bd. editors Clin. Chemistry, 1979-84; contbr. articles to profl. jours. Chmn. Sewer Bd., Cooperstown, 1975—; mem. Water Bd., Cooperstown, 1973—; chmn. lake com. Otsego County Conservation Assn., Cooperstown, 1972-78. Comdr. USNR, 1944-47, 51-53. Recipient Gold medal Biol. div. Electron Microscope Soc. Am., 1966. Fellow Am. Assn. Clin. Chemistry (pres. 1988, awards 1976, 77, 91); mem. Am. Chem. Soc., Am. Soc. Biol. Chem. Molecular Biology (emeritus), Am. Soc. for Cell Biology (emeritus), Protein Soc., Nat. Acad. for Clin. Biochemistry (diplomate), Acad. Clin. Lab. Physicians and Scientists, Phi Beta Kappa. Avocations: tennis, hiking, music. Home: 85 Lake St Cooperstown NY 13326-1038 Office: Mary Imogene Bassett Hosp Atwell Rd Cooperstown NY 13326-1038

PETERS, TIM, library administrator; b. Elkhorn, Wis., May 26, 1964; s. John M. and Dorothy Anne (Miller) P.; m. Timi Petrice Griffin, May 1, 1992 (div. Sept. 1998); 1 child, Andrew Griffin Peters. BS, U. Wis., Stevens Point, 1986; MLIS, La. State U., 1989. Catalog libr. So. U., Baton Rouge, 1990-91; library dir. Southwestern Mich. Coll., Dowagiac, 1991—. Mem. ALA, Mich. Library Assn. E-mail: tpeters@smc.cc.mi.us. Office: Southwestern Mich Coll Library 58900 Cherry Grove Rd Dowagiac MI 49047-9726

PETERS, TIMOTHY JOHN, biochemistry educator, pathologist, physician; b. Manchester, Eng., May 10, 1939; s. Stanley Frederick and Paula (March) P.; m. Judith Mary Bacon, Sept. 21, 1965. MB ChB with honors, U. St. Andrews, Scotland, 1964, MSc, 1967; PhD, U. London, 1970; DSc, U. St. Andrews, 1985. Med. Rsch. Coun. rsch. fellow Royal Postgrad. Med. Sch., London, 1967-70; MRC traveling fellow Rockefeller U., N.Y.C., 1970-72; lectr. to sr. lectr. to reader dept. medicine RPMS, London, 1972-79; head of divisn. clin. cell biology MRC Clin. Rsch. Ctr., Harrow, Eng., 1979-88; dir. pathology Kings Coll. Hosp., London, 1992—; sub-dean rsch. and higher degrees Kings Coll. Sch. Medicine and Dentistry, 1992—; assoc. dean flexible tng. U. London; vis. prof. biochemistry Chelsea and Kings Coll., U. London, 1980-88. Editor: Alcohol Misuse: A European Perspective, 1996, Subcellular Pathology of Systemic Disease, 1987, The Cell Biology of Inflammation in the Gastro Intestinal Tract, 1990; co-editor: (with G. Edwards) Brit. Med. Bull., Vol. 50, 1994; editor-in-chief: Addiction Biology, 1994—. Fellow Royal Soc. Physicians London, Royal Coll. Physicians Edinburgh, Royal Coll. Pathologists, Royal Coll. Arts. Avocation: Baroque recorders. Office: Kings Coll Sch Medicine, Bessemer Rd, London SE5 9PJ, England

PETERS, WILLIAM, ambassador; b. Morpeth, Eng., Sept. 28, 1923; s. John William and Louise (Woodhouse) P.; m. Catherine Bertha Bailey, Jan. 1, 1944. BA with honors in Lit. Humaniores, Oxford U., 1942, MA with honors in Lit. Humaniores, 1948. Devonshire I certs. London Sch. Econs., Sch. Oriental and African Studies. Brit. civil svc. duties including sec. regional com. North Ghana/Ghana Govt., Tamale, 1950-59; prin., 1st sec., counsellor Fgn. & Commonwealth Office, London, Dhaka, and Nicosia, Cyprus, 1959-67; asst. sec. of state London, 1967-69; dir. internat. affairs divsn. Commonwealth Secretariat, London, 1969-71; head chancery, Brit. High Commn. Brit. Diplomatic Svc., Canberra, Australia, 1971-73; dep. high commr. Brit. Diplomatic Svc., Bombay, 1974-77; amb. Brit. Diplomatic Svc., Montevideo, Uruguay, 1977-80; high commr. Brit. Diplomatic Svc., Lilongwe, Malawi, 1980-83; adviser internat. fin. Trafalgar House Group, London, 1984-88; vice chair exec. com. South Atlantic Coun., London, 1996—. Author: Diplomatic Service, Formation and Operation, 1972, The Crisis of Poverty and Debt in the Third World, 1999; reviewer Army Quarterly & Defence Rev., 1985-94, AsianAffairs, 1987—. Chmn. Lepra, London, 1984-92, Tibet Soc. U.K. and Tibet Fund, London, 1986-93; mem. Debt Crisis Network, 1993—; co-chair Jubilee 2000, 1993-95, v.p., bd. mem. Jubilee 2000 Coalition, 1996—; gov. Walmer (Deal, Kent, Eng.) Sch., 1996-2000; pres. Downs Br. Royal Brit. Legion, Dela, 1985—; chmn. coun. and exec. com. United Soc. Propag. Gospel, 1990-93. Capt. Brit. Army, 1942-46. Decorated Mem. Order Brit. Empire, Ghana, 1959, Lt. Royal Victorian Order, East Pakistan, 1961, Companion Order of St. Michael and St. George, Malawi, 1982. Fellow Brit. Inst. Mgmt., Royal Soc. for Arts; mem. United Oxford and Cambridge Club, Royal Soc. Asian Affairs (editl. bd. 1990—). Anglican. Avocation: Third World debt relief, music. Home: 12 Crown Ct Middle St, Deal CT14 1AG, England Office: United Soc for Propagation of Gospel, 157 Waterloo Rd, London SE1 8XA, England

PETERSDORF, ROBERT GEORGE, physician, medical educator, academic administrator; b. Berlin, Feb. 14, 1926; s. Hans H. and Sonja P.; m. Patricia Horton Qua, June 2, 1951; children: Stephen Hans, John Eric. BA, Brown U., 1948, DMS (hon.), 1983; MD cum laude, Yale U., 1952; ScD (hon.), Albany Med. Coll., 1979; MA (hon.), Harvard U., 1980; DMS (hon.), Med. Coll. Pa., 1982, Brown U., 1983; DMS, Bowman-Gray Sch. Medicine, 1986; LHD (hon.), N.Y. Med. Coll., 1986; DSc (hon.), SUNY, Bklyn., 1987, Med. Coll. Ohio, 1987, Univ. Health Scis., The Chgo. Med. Sch., 1987, St. Louis U., 1988; LHD (hon.), Ea. Va. Med. Sch., 1988; DSc (hon.), Sch. Medicine, Georgetown U., 1991, Emory U., 1992, Tufts U., 1993, Mt. Sinai Sch. Medicine, 1993, George Washington U., 1994; other hon. degrees. Diplomate Am. Bd. Internal Medicine. Intern, asst. resident Yale U., New Haven, 1952-54; sr. asst. resident Peter Bent Brigham Hosp., Boston, 1954-55; fellow Johns Hopkins Hosp., Balt., 1955-59; chief resident, instr. medicine Yale U., 1957-58; asst. prof. medicine Johns Hopkins U., 1958-60, physician, 1958-60; assoc. prof. medicine U. Wash., Seattle, 1960-62, prof., 1962-79, chmn. dept. medicine, 1964-79; physician-in-chief U. Wash. Hosp., 1964-79; pres. Brigham and Women's Hosp., Boston, 1979-81; prof. medicine Harvard U. Med. Sch., Boston, 1979-81; dean, vice chancellor health scis. U. Calif.-San Diego Sch. Medicine, 1981-86; clin. prof. infectious diseases Sch. Medicine Georgetown U., 1986-94; pres. Assn. Am. Med. Colls., Washington, 1986-94, pres. emeritus, 1994—; prof. medicine U. Wash., 1994—, disting. prof., sr. advisor to dean, 1998—; disting. physician Vets. Health Adminstrn., Seattle, 1995-98, sr. physician, 1998—; cons. to surgeon gen. USPHS, 1960-79; cons. USPHS Hosp., Seattle, 1962-79; mem. spl. med. adv. group VA, 1987-94. Editor: Harrison's Priciples of Internal Medicine, 1968-90; contbr. numerous articles to profl. jours. Served with USAAF, 1944-46. Recipient Lilly medal Royal Coll. Physicians, London, 1978, Wiggers award Albany Med. Coll., 1979, Robert H. Williams award Assn. Profs. Medicine, 1983, Keen award Brown U., 1980, Disting. Svc. award Baylor Coll. Medicine, 1989, Scroll of Merit Nat. Med. Assn., 1990, 2d Ann. Founder's award Assn. Program Dirs. in Internal Medicine, 1991, Flexner award Assn. Amer. Med. Coll., 1994; named Disting. Internist of 1987, Am. Soc. Internal Medicine. Master: ACP (pres. 1975-76, Stengel award 1980, Disting. Tchr. award 1993, Laureate award Wash. chpt.), fellow: AAAS, Execs. Assn. (hon.); mem. Inst. Medicine of NAS (councillor 1977-80), Assn. Am. Physicians (pres. 1976-77, Kober medal 1996), Cosmos Club, Rainier Club. Home and Office: 1219 Parkside Dr E Seattle WA 98112-3717

PETERSEN, BARRY REX, news correspondent; b. Norfolk, Va., Jan. 14, 1949; s. Kermit and Mavis Lucille (Sutton) P.; m. Sandra H. Petersen, June 7, 1971 (div. Dec. 1984); children: Emily Jensine, Juliette Rose; m. Jan Chorlton, Feb. 14, 1985. BS in Journalism, Northwestern U., 1970, MS in Journalism, 1972. Sports columnist Sidney (Mont.) Herald, 1964-66; city hall reporter Arlington Heights (Ill.) Day, 1968-69; columnist, copy editor Chgo. Today, 1970-71; pub. Daily Northwestern, Evanston, Ill., 1970-71; reporter Milw. (Wis.) Jour., 1971-72; investigative reporter Sta. WITI-TV, Milw., 1972-74; reporter, anchor Sta. WCCO-TV, Mpls., 1974-78; corr. CBS News, L.A., 1978-81, San Francisco, 1981-85, Tokyo, 1986-88, Moscow, 1988-90, London, 1991-95, Tokyo, 1995—; pres. AFTRA, Milw., 1973-74; Josephine B. and Newton N. Minow vis. prof. in communications Northwestern U., Evanston, Ill., 1991. Recipient Investigative Reporting award Wis. Press Assn., 1973, Nat. Emmy award, 1994, 97, World gold medal radio breaking news N.Y. Festivals, 1999. Mem. Fgn. Corrs. Club Japan. Lutheran. Avocations: sailing, travel, internat. real estate. Office: CBS News/Tokyo 524 W 57th St New York NY 10019-2924 also: CBS News, 5-3-6 Akasaka Minato-ku, Tokyo 107, Japan

PETERSEN, BENTON LAURITZ, paralegal; b. Salt Lake City, Jan. 1, 1942; s. Lauritz George and Arleane (Curtis) P.; m. Sharon Donnette Higgins, Sept. 20, 1974 (div. Aug. 9, 1989); children: Grant Lauritz, Tashya Eileen, Nicholas Robert, Katrina Arleane. AA, Weber State Coll., 1966, BA, 1968; BA, Weber State Coll., 1968; M of Liberal Studies, U. Okla., 1980; diploma, Nat. Radio Inst. Paralegal Sch., 1991; JD, Monticello U., 1999. Registered paralegal. Announcer/news dir. KWHO Radio, Salt Lake City, 1968-70, KDXU Radio, St. George, Utah, 1970-73, KSOP Radio, Salt Lake City, 1973-76; case worker/counselor Salvation Army, Midland, Tex., 1976-84; announcer/news dir. KBRS Radio, Springdale, Ark., 1984-86; case worker/counselor Office of Human Concern, Rogers, Ark., 1986-88; an-

nouncer KAZM Radio, Sedona, Ariz., 1988-91; paralegal Benton L. Petersen, Manti, Utah, 1991—; cons. Sanpete County Srs., Manti, 1992—. Award judge Manti City Beautification, 1992-96; treas. Manti Destiny Com., 1993-98; tourism com. Sanpete County Econ. Devel., Ephraim, Utah, 1993-96. Served with U.S. Army N.G., 1959-66. Mem. Nat. Assn. Federated Tax Preparers, Nat. Paralegal Assn. Mem. LDS Ch. Avocation: reading. Home: 470 E 120 N Manti UT 84642-0011

PETERSEN, DOUGLAS ARNDT, financial development consultant; b. Albert Lea, Minn., Sept. 18, 1944; s. Arndt H. and Helen L. (Slater) P.; m. Winnifred K. Taylor, Aug. 14, 1964 (div. July 1970); children: Scott, Jennifer; m. Cynthia L. Schnabel, June 14, 1975; 1 child, Christopher. BS in Edn., Mankato State U., 1966, postgrad., 1966-68. Youth dir. Mankato (Minn.) YMCA, 1965-68; tchr. Mankato State U., 1965-68; exec. dir. YMCA Camp Christmas Tree, Mound, Minn., 1968-72; asst. exec. dir. West Suburban YMCA, Minnetonka, Minn., 1968-72; exec. dir. Eastside YMCA, Mpls., 1972-75; program/fin. devel. dir. Eastside Neighborhood Svc., Mpls., 1975-79; asst. exec. dir. Mpls. Red Cross, 1979-89; dir. major/planned gifts ARC Nat. Staff, Mpls., 1989-91; pres./chief exec. officer/cons. D.A. Petersen Assocs., Mpls., 1992—. Mem. St. Anthony/New Brighton Found. (chair 1988-92), YMCA Am. (pres. APD 1974), ARC (pres. MFDDC 1988-89). Lutheran. Avocations: travel, community service, scuba, canoeing, backpacking. Home: 3216 Skycroft Dr Minneapolis MN 55418-2552 Office: PO Box 18411 Minneapolis MN 55418-0411

PETERSEN, EDWARD SCHMIDT, retired physician; b. Chgo., Nov. 19, 1921; s. William F. and Alma C. (Schmidt) P.; m. Zoe Andre Bakeeff, June 11, 1944; children: Catherine Petersen Mack, Edward B. Student, Harvard U., 1942, MD, 1945. Diplomate Am. Bd. Internal Medicine. Intern St. Luke's Hosp., Chgo., 1945-46, med. practice, 1951-53; resident in medicine U. Chgo., 1948-51; asst. dir. profl. svcs. VA Rsch. Hosp., Chgo., 1953-54; from asst. to assoc. dean, assoc. prof. Northwestern U. Med. Sch., Chgo., 1954-72, asst. dir. to dir. divsn. undergrad. med. edn., AMA, 1972-88, ret., 1988. Chair Midwest group on student affairs Assn. Am. Med. Colls., Washington, 1967-69; pres. Inst. Medicine, Chgo., 1976; chair com. on hosps. and clinics Ill. Dept. Pub. Aid,Chgo., 1961-70; bd. dirs. Hull House, Chgo., 1962-70; mem. sci. adv. com. Mcpl. TB Sanitarium, Chgo., 1970-74. Capt. Med. Corps., AUS, 1946-48. Fellow ACP; mem. AMA (co-sec. liason com. on med. edn. 1976-87), Geneva Lake Assn. (bd. dirs. 1975-99). Lutheran. Avocations: environmental and historical restoration. Home: W4268 Southland Rd Lake Geneva WI 53147-3957

PETERSEN, GEORGE BOUET, retired biochemistry educator; b. Palmerston N, New Zealand, Sept. 5, 1933; s. George Conrad and Elizabeth Stella (Cairns) P.; m. Patricia Jane Egerton Cau ghey, Apr. 16, 1960; children: Anna, Carola, Tessa Alice. MS, U. Otago, Dunedin, New Zealand, 1956; PhD, U. Oxford, England, 1959; MA by decree, U. Oxford, 1962, DSc, 1993. Scientist Dept. Scientific & Indusl. Rsch., New Zealand, 1959-61, 64-67; demonstrator dept. biochemistry U. Oxford, England, 1962-64; prof. biochemistry U. Otago, Dunedin, New Zealand, 1968-99; head dept. biochemistry U. Otago, Dunedin, 1968-91; dep. dean Otago U. Med. Sch., Dunedin, 1991-95; emeritus prof. biochemistry U. Otago, Dunedin, 1999. Contbr. articles to profl. jours. Pres. New Zealand Inst. Chemistry, 1985-86, Acad. Coun. Royal Soc. New Zealand, 1997—; mem. Coun. Royal Soc. New Zealand, 1987-90, 97—; officer New Zealand Order of Merit, 1997. Recipient Marsden medal, New Zealand Assn. Scientists. Fellow New Zealand Inst. Chemistry, Royal Soc. New Zealand; mem. Internat. Coun. Scientific Unions, Lottery Health Rsch. Com. (chmn. 1992—). Avocations: music, literature, books. Office: Dept Biochemistry, U Otago PO Box 56, Dunedin New Zealand

PETERSEN, GLADYS, accounting clerk, writer; b. Guayaquil, Ecuador, June 3, 1941; d. Ezio and Rebeca (Ratti) Bellettini; m. Ronald Petersen, July 4, 1965. Grad. in med. secretarial, Nat. Sch, L.A., 1987; student, Los Angeles Valley Coll., 1992. With accounts receivable/accounts payable So. Calif. Wholesales Co., L.A.; acctg. clk. Prudential Ins. Co., L.A. Mem. World of Poets (3 awards). Home: 330 N Cordova St Burbank CA 91505-3412

PETERSEN, HENNING, air transportation executive; b. Kolding, Denmark, Sept. 23, 1930; s. Martinus and Astrid Cecilie (Jensen) P.; m. Elsebet Rasmussen, Apr. 20, 1974. Mem. Free Masons.

PETERSEN, HENNING, museum laboratory director, curator, researcher; b. Odense, Denmark; s. Thorvald and Anna (Smith Andersen) P.; m. Ingelise Nygaard Kristensen, May 10, 1964. MSc, U. Copenhagen, 1965. Lectr. U. Copenhagen, 1965-67; scientist, curator Natural History Mus., Aarhus, Denmark, 1967-78; head field lab., chief curator, sr. lectr. Natural History Mus., 1978—; sec. Danish com. for internat. biol. program, 1970-74; external lectr. U. Aarhus, 1977-95; project leader pesticide rsch. Danish Environ. Protection Agy., 1992-97, Rsch. Ctr. for Organic Farming, Foulum, Denmark, 1996—. Contbg. author, editor: Quantitative Ecology of Microfungi and Animals in Soil and Litter, 1982; contbr. articles to profl. jours. Chmn. local com. Danish Soc. for Conservation of Nature, 1977—; bd. dirs. Solstice Found., Copenhagen, 1986—. Avocation: painting. Home: Skellerupvej 2, DK8420 Knebel Denmark Office: Mols Lab Natural History Mu, Strandkaervej 6-8 Femmøller, 8400 Ebeltoft Denmark

PETERSEN, IB DAMGAARD, historian, educator; b. Birkeroed, Denmark, Oct. 31, 1933; s. George Emil Julius and Paula Kathrine (Lauridsen) P.; m. Bitten Vecht, 1961 (div. 1974); 1 child: Louise; m. Jonna Lund, Mar. 8, 1980 (dec. Feb. 1992); 1 child, Mads. M in History and French, U. Copenhagen, Denmark, 1961, PhD, 1979. Archivist Royal Archives, Copenhagen, Denmark, 1961-63; kandidatstipendiat U. Copenhagen, 1963-66, sr. stipendiat, 1966-69; amanuensis Inst. Political Sci./U. Copenhagen, 1969-72, sr. lectr., 1972-89, docent, 1989—; dir. Copenhagen Political Studies Press, 1979—. Author: (book) The World War Pattern, 1999, Comprehensive Security in East Asia, 2000. Recipient scholarship, Boursier d etat de France, 1956-57, Kandidatstipendiat, 1963-66, Wolfson scholarship, British Acad., 1975; fellow U. Sydney, 1988-89, U. Canterbury, New Zealand, 1989. Social-Liberal. Luth. Avocations: sculpting, painting. Home: Staerevej 8, DK-2970 Hoersholm Denmark Office: U Copenhagen Inst Pol Sci, Rosenborggade 15, DK-1130 Copenhagen Denmark

PETERSEN, JENS LYNG, theoretical physicist, educator; b. Sollerød, Copenhagen, Denmark, Feb. 3, 1942; s. Karl Christian and Agnes (Hansen) P.; m. Annette Kock, Mar. 21, 1964; children: Mette Lyng Tjareborg, Jakob Lyng. Candidate Sci., U. Copenhagen, 1966. Rsch. stipendiate U. Copenhagen, 1966-67; rsch. fellow Nordita, Copenhagen, 1967-69, asst. prof., 1972-75; rsch. assoc. U. Copenhagen, 1969-72, assoc. prof., 1975—; Vis. scientist CERN, Geneva, Switzerland, 1970-72, 88-89, group leader, 1999. Contbr. 75 articles and rsch. papers to profl. jours. including Nuclear Physics B, Physics Letters B, 1969—. Avocation: piano. Home: Fyrremejsevej 14, DK-2600 Glostrup Denmark Office: Niels Bohr Inst, Blegdamsvej 17, DK-2100 Copenhagen Denmark

PETERSEN, JILL RENEE LEKAWA, chemical engineer; b. Jeannette, Pa., July 19, 1968; d. Marion Henry Jr. and Joyce Ann Lekawa; m. Kenneth Robert Petersen, Dec. 19, 1990; 1 child, Sean William. BS in Chem. Engring., U. Ariz., 1990. Intern Dow Corning Corp., Midland, Mich., 1989, Dow Chem., Freeport, Tex., 1990; rsch. engr. Exxon Chem., Baytown, Tex., 1990-92, optimization engr., 1992-93; ops. svcs. engr. Enterprise Products Operating L.P., Mont Belvieu, Tex., 1993-98, process engr., 1998—. Sci. fair judge Stafford Indep. Sch. Dist., 1997, 99; violinist Clear Lake Symphony, Houston, 1991-98. Scholar Flinn Found., 1986-90, Nat. Merit Scholar, 1986-90. Mem. AIChE, Tau Beta Pi. Roman Catholic. Avocations: walking, gourmet cooking, reading, playing violin. E-mail: jpetersen@eprod.com. Office: Enterprise Product Operating LP 10207 FM 1942 Mont Belvieu TX 77580-0573

PETERSEN, KITT MIA FALCK, medical scientist; b. Neastved, Denmark, Mar. 30, 1958; came to the U.S., 1990; d. Bjarne Peter Falck and Jytte Sonja Petersen; m. Gerald Israel Shulman, July 4, 1994. BS, N. Zahle's Gymnasieskole, Copenhagen, 1978; MD, U. Copenhagen, 1985. Turnus kandidat U. Hosps. Copenhagen, 1985-87; kandidat stipendiat U. Copenhagen, 1987-89; postdoctoral fellow Yale U., New Haven, 1989-92, assoc. rsch. scientist, 1992-97, rsch. scientist, 1997-98; asst. prof. Yale U. Sch. Medicine, New Haven, 1998—; dir. Magnetic Resonance Ctr. Rsch. Ctr., Yale U., New Haven, 2000. Recipient Kandidat stipendium U. Copenhagen, 1986, Sr. stipendium U. Copenhagen, 1989, Henry Christian award, 1997, 98. Mem. Am. Fedn. for Med. Rsch., Am. Physiol. Soc., Am. Diabetes Assn. (Rsch. award 2000), Danish Med. Soc., Soc. for Patient Related Rsch., Juvenile Diabetes Assn. Avocations: ballet, photography, writing. E-mail: kitt.petersen@yale.edu. Office: Yale U Sch Medicine Fitkin 104 333 Cedar St New Haven CT 06510-3289

PETERSEN, KRESTEN RUBECK, gynecologist; b. Copenhagen, Denmark, Oct. 12, 1955; s. Bent and Inger P.; m. AnnaGrethe Andreasen; three children. MD, U. Copenhagen, 1983. Resident ob-gyn. Herlev Hosp., Denmark, 1983-85; resident in surgery Hvidovre Hosp., Denmark, 1986-88; cons. ob-gyn. Hvidovre Hosp., 1994-96; sr. resident ob-gyn. Copenhagen Hosp., 1989-93; cons. ob-gyn. Hvidovre Hosp., 1994-96, Hillerod Hosp., Denmark, 1997—. Office: Dept Ob-Gyn, Helsevej 2, DK 3400 Hillerød Denmark

PETERSEN, LARS CHRISTIAN, biochemist; b. Middelfart, Denmark, July 27, 1945; s. Herluf Christian and Anna Norvang (Larsen) P.; m. Birthe Moller, June 24, 1967; children: Nana, Mette Boel. MSc, U. Copenhagen, 1973, DSc, 1982; PhD, Odense U., 1976. Stipendiate Odense (Denmark) U., 1973-79; rsch. chemist dept. clin. chemistry Hvidovre Hosp., Copenhagen, 1979-86; rsch. chemist Novo Nordisk A/S, Copenhagen, 1986-92, mgr., 1992—; censor Odense U., 1985—, Aarhus Roskilde and Copenhagen U, 1994—. Office: Novo Nordisk Pk, Tissue Factor, DK-2760 Maaloev Denmark

PETERSEN, MARTIN ROSS, public affairs executive; b. Bakersfield, Calif., Aug. 14, 1944; s. Peter Arthur and Valerie A. (Swink) P.; m. Geri Gottuso, Nov. 12, 1987; children: Kaitlin Jean, Alexander Ross. BA in Govt., Calif. State U., Sacramento, 1969. Asst. dir. govtl. affairs Calif. State U. and Colls., Sacramento, 1967-72; adminstr. divsn. consumer svcs. Calif. Dept. Consumer Affairs, Sacramento, 1972-75; dir. Office External Liaison The White House Office Consumer Affairs, Washington, 1975-77, 83-85; pres. Knauer & Assocs., Inc., Washington, 1977-83; dir. corp. pub. affairs and N.J. ops. adminstrn. Playtex Products, Inc., Allendale, 1985—; exec. v.p. Trade Net, Washington, 1981-85; chmn. Washington Legis. Group, 1984-85; mem. bus. adv. commn. Ramapo (N.J.) State Coll., 1999—. Editor: Auto Imports, 1979; founding editor Customer Relationship Mgmt., 1980-82. Pub. mem. Voluntary Effort To Contain Health Care Costs in Am., Chgo., 1977-80; sec. subcom. on consumer affairs Rep. Nat. Com., Washington, 1979-80; mem. transition team and inaugural com. Reagan-Bush White House, Washington, 1981; v.p. Nat. Coalition for Consumer Edn., Washington, 1981-91; v.p. Oakland (N.J.) Rep. Club, 1990; councilman Borough of Oakland, 1991—; vol. in pub. svc. Product Safety Commn., 1977. With USAF, 1962-66. Mem. Soc. Consumer Affairs Profls. in Bus. (nat. bd. dirs. 1979-83, 98—, exec. com. 1980-83, 99—, pres. D.C. chpt. 1977-78, Outstanding Leader of Yr. award 1985), Am. League Lobbyists, Govt. Affairs Profls. (N.Y.C.), Am. Soc. Quality, Internat. Facility Mgmt. Assn. Avocation: horseback riding. E-mail: martin.petersen@usa.net. Home: 10 Wichita Path Oakland NJ 07436-3818 Office: Playtex Products Inc 75 Commerce Dr Allendale NJ 07401-1600

PETERSEN, MAUREEN JEANETTE MILLER, management information consultant, former nurse; b. Evanston, Ill., Sept. 4, 1956; d. Maurice James and M. Joyce (Mielke) Miller; m. Gregory Eugene Petersen, July 7, 1984; children: Trevor James, Tatyana Brianne. BS in Nursing cum laude, Vanderbilt U., 1978; MS in Biometry and Health Info. Systems, U. Minn., 1984. Nurse U. Iowa Hosps. and Clinics, Iowa City, 1978-82; research asst. Sch. Nursing, U. Minn., Mpls., 1982-83; mgr. Arthur Andersen/Andersen Cons., Mpls., 1984—. Mem. Mensa. Methodist. Avocation: travel. Home: 1050 County Rd C2 W Roseville MN 55113-1945 Office: Andersen Cons 333 S 7th St Minneapolis MN 55402-2414

PETERSEN, NIELS HELVEG, Danish government official; b. Odense, Denmark, Jan. 17, 1939; s. K. Helveg and Lilly P. LLB, U. Copenhagen, 1965, Stanford (Calif.) U., 1961. Mem. Danish Parliament Folketing Social-Liberal Party, 1966-74, 77—, cabinet chief Danish commn. European Commn., 1974-77, chmn. parliamentary group, 1978-88; minister econ. affairs Govt. of Denmark, Copenhagen, 1988-90, mem. parliament, 1990-93, minister fgn. affairs, 1993—. Office: Ministry Fgn Affairs, Asiatisk Plads 2, 1448K Copenhagen Denmark

PETERSEN, OLE SVENSTRUP, engineering educator, researcher; b. Thorup, Denmark, Feb. 18, 1958; s. Svend and Karen (Svenstrup) P.; m. Britta Jepsen, June 29, 1992. MSCE, Aalborg (Denmark) U., 1987, PhD in Engring., 1992. Rsch. asst. Aalborg U., 1992-93, asst. prof., 1993-96, assoc. prof., 1996—; scientist Environment Can., Toronto, 1992-93; rschr. Can. Ctr. for Inland Waters, Burlington, Ont., Can., 1992, Internat. Rsch. Ctr. for Computational Hydrodynamics-DHI Inst. for Water and Environ., 1993-98; sr. cons. engr. Danish Hydraulic Inst., 1997—. Author: Turbulence Models, 1992; contbr. articles to profl. jours. Danish Nat. Rsch. Coun. for Tech. Sci. grantee, 1992. Mem. Dansk Ingenior for Engring., Internat. Asssn. for Hydraulic Rsch., Am. Geophys. Union. Home: Dianas Have 43, DK 2970 Hørsholm Denmark Office: DHI Inst Water & Environ, Agern Allé 16, DK 2970 Horsholm Denmark

PETERSLUND, NIELS ANKER, infectious disease physician, hematologist; b. Copenhagen, Denmark, Dec. 11, 1941; s. Peter Martinus and Marie Christine (Petersen) P.; m. Kirsten Vilsgaard, Mar. 11, 1966; children: Peter, Esther. MD, U. Aarhus, 1971. Resident Aarhus Mcpl. Hosp., 1971-77; resident dept infectious disease Marselisborg Hosp., Aarhus, 1977-78, sr. resident dept. infectious disease, 1979-83; sr. resident Clin. Chemistry and Immunology, Randers, Denmark, 1978-79; sr. resident internal medicine and microbiology Aarhus U. Hosp., 1983-87, sr. resident dept. hematology, 1987-92, cons. physician dept. hematology and internal medicine, 1992—, head dept., 1997—. Mem. Am. Soc. Microbiology, N.Y. Acad. Scis., Hosp. Infection Soc., Danish Soc. Mycology (chmn.). Achievements include research on antiviral treatment of shingles, biochemical markers in infectious diseases. Home: Ørøvanget 7, DK 8381 Mundelstrup Denmark Office: Aarhus U Hosp Hematology, Tage Hansens Gade, DK-8000 Århus Denmark

PETERSON, BARBARA ANN BENNETT, retired history educator, television personality; b. Portland, Oreg., Sept. 6, 1942; d. George Wright and Hope (Chatfield) Bennett; m. Frank Lynn Peterson, July 1, 1967. BA, BS, Oreg. State U., 1964; MA, Stanford U., 1965; PhD, U. Hawaii, 1978; PhD (hon.), London Inst. Applied Rsch., 1991, Australian Inst. Coordinated R, 1995. Prof. history U. Hawaii, 1967-95, prof. emeritus history, 1995—, chmn. social scis. divsn., 1971-73, 75-76; asst. dean U. Hawaii, Honolulu, 1973-74; prof. Asian history and European colonial history and world problems Chapman Coll. World Campus Afloat Semester At Sea, 1974, European overseas exploration, expansion and colonialism U. Colo., Boulder, 1978, Modern China, Modern East Asia, U. Pittsburgh, The West in the World, 1999; assoc. prof. U. Hawaii-Manoa Coll. Continuing Edn., 1981; Fulbright prof. history Wuhan (China) U., 1988-89; Fulbright rsch. prof. Sophia U., Japan, 1978; rsch. assoc. Bishop Mus., 1995-98; lectr. Capital Spkrs., Washington, 1987—; prof. Hawaii State Ednl. Channel, 1993-97; adj. fellow East-West Ctr., Honolulu, 1998—; prof. history U. Pitts. Semester at Sea, fall 1999; adj. prof. Hawaii Pacific U. Co-author: Women's Place is in the History Books, Her Story, 1962-1980: A Curriculum Guide for American History Teachers, 1980; author: America in British Eyes, 1988; editor: Notable Women of Hawaii, 1984, (with W. Solheim) The Pacific Region, 1990, 91, American History: 17th, 18th and 19th Centuries, 1993, America: 19th and 20th Centuries, 1993, John Bull's Eye on America, 1995, Notable Women of China, 2000, Hawaii in the World, 2000; assoc. editor Am. Nat. Biography, 1998 (Dartmouth medal); contbr. articles to profl. publs. Participant People-to-People Program, Eng., 1964, Expt. in Internat. Living Program, Nigeria, 1966; chmn. 1st Nat. Women's History Week, Hawaii, 1982; pres. Bishop Mus. Coun., 1993-94; active mem. Hawaii Commn. on Status of Women; fundraiser local mus. and children's activities. Fulbright scholar, Japan, 1967, China, 1988-89; NEH-Woodrow Wilson fellow Princeton U., 1980; recipient state proclamations Gov. of Hawaii, 1982, City of Honolulu and Hawaii State Legis., 1982, Outstanding Tchr. of Yr. award Wuhan (China), U., 1988, Medallion of Excellence award Am. Biog. Assn., 1989, Woman of Yr. award, 1991; inducted into the Women's Hall of Fame, Seneca Falls, N.Y., 1991; co-champion Hawaii State Husband and Wife Mixed Doubles Tennis Championship, 1985. Fellow World Lit. Acad. (Eng.); mem. AAUW, Am. Hist. Assn. (mem. numerous coms.), Am. Studies Assn. (pres. 1984-85), Fulbright Assn. (founding pres. Hawaii chpt. 1984-88, mem. nat. steering com. chairwomen ann. conf. 1990), Am. Coun. on Edn., Maison Internat. des Intellectuals, France, Hawaii Found. History and Humanities (mem. editl. bd. 1972-73), Hawaii Hist. Assn., Women in Acad. Adminstrn., Phi Beta Phi, Phi Kappa Phi. Avocation: writing, cooking, fund raising for charity and children's organizations and museums, gardening, travel. Office: East West Ctr Burns Hall 1601 East West Rd Honolulu HI 96848-1601

PETERSON, BONNIE LU, mathematics educator; b. Escanaba, Mich., Jan. 19, 1946; d. Herbert Erick and Ruth Albertha (Erickson) P. AA, Bay de Noc C.C., 1966; BS, No. Mich. U., 1968, MA in Math., 1969; EdD, Tenn. State U., 1989. Tchr. Lapeer (Mich.) High Sch., 1969-70, Nova High Sch., Ft. Lauderdale, Fla., 1970-79, Hendersonville (Tenn.) High Sch., 1979—; adj. faculty Vol. State C.C., Gallatin, Tenn., 1989—; chair Sumner County Schs. Tchrs. Insvc., Gallatin, 1990-92; mem. math. specialist team State of Tenn., 1991-93; reader for advanced placement calculus exam. Coll. Bd., 1994, 95, 96, 97, 98, 99; chair equipment com. Tchrs. Tchg. with Tech., 1998; spkr. in field. Mem. edn. com. Vision 2000-City of Hendersonville, 1993-94. Recipient State-Level Presdl. award, 1994, 95, 96, 98, Nat. Presdl. award for Excellence in Math. and Sci. Tchg., 1998; Tenn. State Bd. grantee, 1989-92; Woodrow Wilson fellow, 1993; Tandy scholar, 1995. Mem. ASCD, Nat. Coun. Tchrs. Math. (chair workshop support com. 1990), Tenn. Math. Tchrs. Assn. (v.p. for secondary schs.), Mid. Tenn. Math. Tchrs. Assn. (past pres.), Tenn. Alliance Presdl. Awardees (treas. 2000—, Tenn. co-coord. Presdl. award in Math. 2000—), Phi Delta Kappa (past pres.). Avocations: cooking, counted cross stitch. Home: 1081 Coon Creek Rd Dickson TN 37055-4014

PETERSON, CLARK C., announcer, writer; b. Pine City, Minn., Dec. 27, 1947; s. Carl A. and Bernice C. Peterson. AA, U. Minn., 1967, B Econs., 1969; A in Bible, Grace Bible Coll., 1993; LittD (hon.), Evangel Christian U. Am., Monroe, La., 2000; DLitt (hon.), Omega Bible Inst. and Sem., Swartz, La., 2000. Announcer Sta. KOLM/KWWK Radio, Rochester, Minn., 1974-84; pub. affairs specialist U.S. Army, Oklahoma City, 1985-97; announcer, writer Power Zone Wresting Fedn., Oklahoma City, 1992-98; corr. Pro Wrestling Illustrated Mag., 1992-97; announcer, writer Mid-South Wrestling Fedn., Oklahoma City, 1998—; corr. The Wrestling Tribune, 1993—; parade announcer Mora's (Minn.) Centennial, 1983; announcer Richards-Gebaur AFB Open House, Kansas City, Mo., 1973, Nat. Drum and Bugle Corps Contest, Stillwater, Minn., early 1980's; announcer, entertainment Rochester's (Minn.) 125th Anniversary, 1983; announcer, writer, entertainment Korn & Klover Karnival, Hinckley, Minn., 1973-87, 90-91; judge Miss Teen Minn. Pageant, St. Paul, 1984. Author: The Great Hinckley Fire, 1978, Blasted Unto a Pile of Rubble, 1995; co-author: In Their Name, 1995, We Will Never Forget, 1996, Forever Changed, 1998; contbg. author: Wrestling Title Histories, 2000. Mem., survivor Apr. 19, 1995 Oklahoma City Bombing, Family and Survivors United, 1995—; pub. rels. and advt. advisor Rep. campaign for Minn. Senate, 2000. Served with USAF, 1970-74. Recipient Best Coverage of a Local Story in the U.S., AP, 1978, scholarship Fairfax U., 1988, Civil Svc. Achievement medal U.S. Army, 1997, 14 New Idea/Suggestion awards, One of the highest numbers in U.S. Civil Svc., 1997, 5th prize World-Wide Christmas Outdoor Lighting Display Contest, 1997; named among 25 winners Turner Broadcasting Wrestling Announcing Contest, 1992; inducted Profl. Wrestling's Wall of Fame, 1998. Avocations: outdoor Christmas lighting display, state and city flag collections, coin collecting.

PETERSON, DANIEL RAYMOND, emergency management administrator, career officer; b. Faribault, Minn., Apr. 20, 1944; s. George Everett and Adeline (Agnes) P.; m. Katie Dee Overholt, September 5, 1964; children: Jesse, Matthew. BA in Psychology, U. Minn., 1966. Cert. comml. pilot. Col. USAF, Offutt AFB, Nebr., 1966-91; sr. mktg. mgr. Chrysler Techs., Waco, Tex., 1991-96; dir. Sarpy County Emergency Mgmt. & Comms. Agy., Papillion, Nebr., 1996—. Decorated Legion of Merit USAF, Air medal with twelve oak leaf clusters; recipient DFC USAF, Def. Meritorious Svc. medal OJCS Pentagon, 1981. Exptl. Aviation Assn. (flight advisor), Chpt. 31 Vintage Aircraft Assn. (pres.), Quiet Birdmen. Republican. Avocation: general aviation. Fax: 402-593-2319. Home e-mail: SAC55CMDR@AOL.COM.; office e-mail: Dan@sarpy.com. Home: 4506 Anchor Mill Rd Omaha NE 68108 Office: Sarpy County Emergency Mgmt Agy 1210 Golden Gate Dr Papillion NE 68046-3088

PETERSON, DONALD ROBERT, magazine editor, vintage automobile consultant; b. Sandstone, Minn., Apr. 1, 1929; s. Martin Theodore and Margaret Mildred (Dezell) P.; m. Lois Taylor, Dec. 31, 1951 (div. 1975); children: Wyatt A., Winston B., Whitney C. (dec.), Westley D., Webster E.; m. Edie Tannenbaum, Aug. 31, 1975; 1 child, Ryan Kerry. Student, U. Minn., 1947-50; B.S., Gustavus Adolphus Coll., 1952. Asst. underwriter Prudential Ins. Co. Am., Mpls., 1953-64; chief health underwriter North Central Life, St. Paul, 1964-66; pres. 1st State Bank Murdock, Minn., 1967-73, EDON, Inc., Roswell, Ga., 1974—; editor Car Collector mag., Roswell, 1977-91, editor emeritus, 1992—; v.p., dir. Classic Pub. Inc., Atlanta, 1979-97. Contbr. chpt. to book. Councilman, City of Murdock, 1968-72, mayor, 1972-74; del. State Republican Conv., 1970-72; treas. Swift County Rep. Com., 1970-73. Served with U.S. Navy, 1946-47. Recipient citation for disting. service Classic Car Club Am., 1965. Mem. Internat. Soc. Philos. Enquiry, Swift County Bankers Assn. (pres. 1970-73), Soc. Automotive Historians, Am. Legion, Mensa (pres. Ga. chpt. 1976-78), Milestone Car Soc., Classic Car Club Am. (chpt. pres. 1959, 60, 63, nat. bd. dirs. 1978-81, 97—), Rolls-Royce Owners Club, Antique Automobile Club, Vet. Motor Car Club Am., Packard Club, Cadillac-La Salle Club, Lincoln and Continental Owner's Club, Horseless Carriage Club Am. Republican. Avocations: automobile collecting, internat. traveling. Home: 1400 Lake Ridge Ct Roswell GA 30076-2869

PETERSON, DOROTHY LULU, artist, writer; b. Venice, Calif., Mar. 10, 1932; d. Marvin Henry and Fay (Brown) Case; m. Leon Albert Peterson, June 21, 1955; 1 child, David. AD, Compton (Calif.) Coll., 1950. Artist Moran Printing Co., Lockport, N.Y., 1955—; caricature artist West Seneca and Kenmore Creative Artist Socs., 1973-86; commd. artist in pvt. practice, 1996—; comml. artist Boulevard Mall, Kenmore (N.Y.) Arts Soc., 1974—. Works include portraits of Pres. and Mrs. Reagan in Presdl. Libr. Collection, also portraits of Geraldine Ferraro, Presidents Clinton, Bush, Nixon, Ford, also Bette Davis, Lucille Ball, Bing Crosby, Elizabeth Taylor, 1971-94; sculpture of Pres. Bush, Princess Diana; caricature sculpture of Joan Rivers; author articles. Recipient awards West. Seneca Art Soc., 1975, Kenmore Art Soc., 1982, 86. Recipient Editors award Nat. Poetry Soc., 1997, Editors Choice award Nat. Libr. of Poetry, 1998. Democrat. Baptist. Home: 247 Pryor Ave Tonawanda NY 14150-7407

PETERSON, DOUGLAS PETE (PETE PETERSON), ambassador, former congressman; b. Omaha, Nebr., June 26, 1935; m. Carlotta Ann Neal (dec.); children: Michael, Paula, Douglas (dec.); m. Vi Peterson. Grad., Nat. War Coll., 1975; BA, U. Tampa, 1976; postgrad., U. Ctrl. Mich., 1977. Commd. USAF, 1954, advanced through grades to col., ret., 1980; exec. CRT Computers, 1984-90; mem. faculty Fla. State U., 1985-90; mem. 101st-104th Congresses from 2nd Fla. Dist., 1991-96; mem. appropriation com.-energy and water, agrl., amb. to Vietnam, 1996—. Prisoner of war, Vietnam. Mem. DAV, VFW, Am. Legion, Elks. Roman Catholic. Office: 7 Lang Ha Rd, Hanoi Ba Denh District, Vietnam

PETERSON, DOUGLAS ROBERT, music educator; b. Marshall, Minn., Feb. 8, 1926; s. Wilbur Carl and Emily (Graham) P.; m. Martha Jeanne Gill, Dec. 26, 1956 (dec. May 1984); children: David Scott, Robert Carl, Carolyn Janet, John Douglas (dec.). BA in Psychology, Grinnell Coll., 1950; B Music Edn., Fla. State U., 1951; MA in Music, U. Iowa, 1954, D in Vocal Pedagogy & Choral Performance, 1972; studied with, Robert Shaw, Helmuth Rilling, Don Moses, William LaRu Jones, 1950-99. Dir. music Norway

(Iowa) Consol. Schs., 1951-52; dir. band, choir and orch. Elko (Nev.) Sr. H.S., 1952-53; dir. vocal music Columbus (Ind.) Sr. H.S., 1954-56; dir. choral music North Hagerstown Sr. H.S., Hagerstown, Md., 1956-60; instr. music, choral dir., instr. voice Monmouth (Ill.) Coll., 1962-67; assoc. prof. music U. Nev., Las Vegas, 1967—, choral dir., 1967-91; music dir., CEO, So. Nev. Mus. Arts, Las Vegas, 1968—; founder, Antietam Choral Soc., Hagerstown, Md., 1958-60; dir. music 2d Presbyn. Ch., Elko, 1952-53, Evang. and Ref. Ch., Hagerstown, 1956-60, 1st Congl. Ch., Iowa City, 1960-62, 2d Presbyn. Ch., Monmouth, 1962-64, 1st Meth. Ch., Las Vetgas, 1967-70; choir dir. 1st Bapt. Ch., Galesburg, Ill., 1964-67, Cmty. Luth. Ch., Las Vegas, 1976-84, U. Meth. Ch., 1971-72. Music dir. world premieres Winnie Ille Pu (Alice Parker), 1964, Remembering Those Who Fly (Alice Parker), 1995, African Sanctus (David Fanshawe), 1977, Am. premiere performance 3 Te Deums (Haydn), 1969, African Sanctus (Fanshawe), 1977, Von Himmel hoch (Mendelssohn), 1983, Great Organ Mass, (both Carus edits.), 1984. Bd. dirs. Charleston Heights Arts tr., Univ. Opera Assn., 1981-84. With USN, 1944-46. Recipient Gov.'s award for excellence in arts Nev. Coun. on Arts, 1987, spl. commendation as music dir. So. Nev. Mus. Arts, Sen. Richard G. Bryan, Significant Contbn. to Arts in Clark County Clark County Bd. Commrs., 1992, 25 years outstanding svc. Senator Harry Reid, Cmty. Achievement award in arts and entertainment Las Vegas C. of C., 1998, also others. Mem. Am. Choral Dirs. Assn. (Nev. pres. 1969-74, Nev. chmn. 1991-94), Nev. Music Educators Assn. (v.p. 1970-72), Chorus Am., Internat. Fedn. Choral Music. Democrat. Avocations: travel, video filming, photography. Fax: 702-451-0906. E-mail: drdougp@aol.com. Home: 3950 Springhill Ave Las Vegas NV 89121-6223 Office: U Nev 4505 S Maryland Pkwy Las Vegas NV 89154-9900

PETERSON, ELMOR LEE, mathematical scientist, educator; b. McKeesport, Pa., Dec. 6, 1938; s. William James and Emma Elizabeth (Scott) P.; m. Sharon Louise Walker, Aug., 1957 (div. Jan. 1961); 1 child, Lisa Ann Peterson Loop; m. Miriam Drake Mears, Dec. 23, 1966; 1 child, David Scott. BS in Physics, Carnegie Mellon U., 1960, MS in Math., 1961, PhD in Math., 1964. Technician U.S. Steel Rsch. Ctr., Monroeville, Pa., summer 1959; engr. Westinghouse Atomic Power, Forest Hills, Pa., summer 1960; rsch. engr. Atomics Internat., Canoga Park, Calif., summer 1961; physicist Lawrence Radiation Labs., Livermore, Calif., summer 1963; sr. math. Westinghouse R & D, Churchill Boro, Pa., 1963-66; asst. prof. math. U. Mich., Ann Arbor, 1967-69; assoc. prof. math. and mgmt. sci. Northwestern U., Evanston, Ill., 1969-73, prof. math. and mgmt. sci., 1973-77, prof. applied math. and mgmt. sci., 1977-79; prof. math. and ops. rsch. N.C. State U., Raleigh, 1979—; vis. asst. prof. W.Va. U., dept. Math., Morgantown, 1966; vis. assoc. prof. U. Wis. Math. Rsch. Ctr., Madison, 1968-69; vis. prof. Stanford U. Ops. Rsch. Dept., 1976-77. Author: (with others) Geometric Programming, 1967, Russian trans., 1971; contbr. articles to profl. jours. Mobil Found. Rsch. grantee, 1967-69, Air Force Office Sci. Rsch. grantee, 1973-75, 76-78, NSF grantee, 1985-86. Mem. Soc. for Indsl. and Applied Math., Ops. Rsch. Soc. Am., Am. Math. Soc., Math. Assn. Am. Avocations: aerobic exercise, antique furniture. Home: 3717 Williamsborough Ct Raleigh NC 27609-6357 Office: NC State U Hillsborough St Raleigh NC 27695-0001

PETERSON, ERLEND DEAN, dean; b. St. George, Utah, Nov. 24, 1940; s. Dean Andrew and Lyle (Evans) P.; m. Colleen Dawn Keith, Dec. 5, 1968; children: Kristin, Sheri, Deborah, Deanne, Rebecca, Andrew. BS, Brigham Young U., 1967, MS, 1971, EdD, 1985. From registration officer to dean admissions and records Brigham Young U., Provo, Utah, 1968-87, asst. prof. ednl. leadership, 1990—, dean admissions and records, 1990—; LSD mission pres. to Norway, 1988-90; assoc. David M. Kennedy Ctr., 1985—, asst. prof. Ednl. Leadership, 1990—; bd. dirs. Utah Higher Edn. Assistance Authority, Salt Lake City, Am.-Norwegian Hist. Soc., Northfield, Minn., 1996-99; lectr. and cons. in field. Contbr. articles to profl. jours. Chair, bd. dirs. United Way Utah County, Provo, 1991-94 (chair fund raising campaign 1994-95); coord. Utah Statehood Centennial Ambassadorial Visits Program, Utah, 1995-96. Recipient Norwegian Order Merit and Knight First Class award King Harald of Norway, Oslo, 1997. Mem. Am. Assn. Collegiate Registrars Admissions Officers (Utah chpt., Pacific chpt.). Republican. Mem. LDS Ch. Home: 1121 S 350 W Orem UT 84058-6769 Office: Brigham Young U PO Box 21111 Provo UT 84602-1111

PETERSON, FRED MCCRAE, retired librarian; b. Mpls., Dec. 29, 1936. B.A., U. Minn., 1958, M.S., 1960; Ph.D. in L.S., Ind. U., 1974. Asst. to dir. Iowa State U. Library, 1961-64, head catalog dept., 1964-67, asst. dir. library, 1967-69, assoc. dir. library, 1969-70; with Catholic U. Am., Washington, 1970-82, asst. prof., assoc. chairperson, 1973-77, acting dir. libraries, 1977-78, dir., 1978-82; univ. librarian Ill. State U., Normal, 1982-96, univ. libr. emeritus, 1996—. Mem. ALA, Ill. Libr. Assn. (past pes., Libr. of Yr. award 1994). Home: 32792 Via Malaga San Juan Capistrano CA 92675-4455

PETERSON, GERALD JOSEPH, aerospace executive, consultant; b. Decatur, Ill., Oct. 27, 1947; s. Raymond Gerald (dec.) and Mary Louise (Johnson) P.; m. Sarah Kuuipo Fry, June 1, 2000. AA, Lincolnland Community Coll., Springfield, Ill., 1969; student, Schiller Coll., Heidelberg, Germany, 1971, Sangamon State U., Springfield, 1972, U. Minn., 1976. Cert. aircraft pilot, engrng. tech. Author LOGIC IV commodities futures trading program, 1996; patentee in field. Mem. LDS Ch.; served with USAF, 1965, French Foreign Legion, 1979. Mem. U.S. Naval Inst. (life). Mem. LDS Ch. Office: Peterson Aerospace Corp PO Box 1294 Mountain View HI 96771-1294

PETERSON, H. DALE, lawyer; b. Amherst, Wis., Jan. 4, 1951; s. Harold C. and Eva I. (Hansen) P.; m. Julie A. Goplin, Jan. 1, 1995; children: Matt, David, Alex, Ellen. BS with honors, U. Wis., Stevens Point, 1973; JD cum laude, U. Wis., 1978. Bar: U.S. Dist. Ct. (we. dist.) Wis., U.S. Ct. Appeals (7th cir.) Wis. Rsch. analyst U.S. Dept. Justice, Washington, 1973-75; ptnr. Stroud, Willink & Howard, LLC, Madison, Wis., 1978—; dir. Wis. Farm Bur. Svc. Bd., Inc., Madison, 1994—. Co-author: Contract Law in Wisconsin, 1995. Mem. Dane County Bar Assn. (dir./treas. 1987-91). Office: Stroud Willink & Howard LLC PO Box 2236 Madison WI 53701-2236

PETERSON, H(ARRY) WILLIAM, chemicals executive, consultant; b. Yokohama, Honshu Island, Japan, Mar. 9, 1922; came to U.S., 1924; s. Harry William and Alice (Mateer) P.; m. Doris Jane Howe, Apr. 27, 1946; children: Robert, Christine Fitzpatrick, Janet McMillan. BA in Chemistry and Botany, Colgate U., 1946; postgrad., Princeton U., 1949-50, U. Del., 1982-83. Lic. capt. U.S. inland waters U.S. Coast Guard. Researcher, developer ESSO Standard Oil Co., Bayway, N.J., 1946-51; various positions Enjay Chem. Co., N.Y.C., 1951-65; coord. world-wide chem. Gulf Oil Corp., Pitts., 1965-67; gen. mktg. mgr. Gulf Oil-Eastern Hemisphere, London, 1967-71; corp. v.p. chem. mktg., corp. v.p. mktg. Gulf Oil Can. Ltd., Montreal, Que., Can., 1971-77; CEO chems. divsn., corp. v.p. Golfoil Can., Montreal, Quebec, Can., 1971-77; chief operating officer Corpus Christi Chem. Co., Wilmington, Del., 1971—; mng. dir. Food Machinery & Chem. Corp. Internat. Chems., Phila., 1979-80; internat. cons. Bozman, Md., 1980—. Patentee in field. Leader Young Christians Assn., 1st Bapt. Ch., Somerville, N.J., 1948-53; lay speaker, mem. adminstrn. bd. Riverview Charge, United Meth. Ch.; chaplain Mil. Order Purple Heart. With USMC, 1942-46, PTO. Decorated Purple Heart, two battle stars. Fellow Am. Inst. Chemists; mem. Am. Chem. Soc. (emeritus). Avocations: writing, philosophy, religion. Home and Office: Quakerneck Rd Mulberry Pt Bozman MD 21612

PETERSON, JOHN WILLARD, composer, music publisher; b. Lindsborg, Kans., Nov. 1, 1921; s. Peter Ephraim and Adlina Mary (Nelson) P.; m. Marie Alta Addis (Feb. 11, 1944); children: Sandra Lynn Peterson Catzere, Candace Kay Peterson Strader, Pamela Lee Peterson Cruse. Student, Moody Bible Inst., 1947-48; MusB, Am. Conservatory Music, 1952; MusD (hon.), John Brown U., 1967; DD (hon.), West Bapt. Sem., 1970; DFA (hon.), Grand Canyon U., 1979. Radio broadcaster Sta. WMBI, Chgo., 1950-55; editor in chief, pres. Singspiration, Inc., Grand Rapids, Mich., 1955-71; exec. composer Singspiration, Inc., Carefree, Ariz., 1977-83; pres. Good Life Prodns., Scottsdale, Ariz., 1977-83; John W. Peterson Music Co., Scottsdale, 1983-88; bd. dirs. Gospel Films, Inc., Muskegon, Mich. Co-author: (autobiography) The Miracle Goes On, 1976; composer works include numerous cantatas, musicals, gospel songs, hymns and anthems. 1st lt. USAAF 1942-45, CBI. Decorated Air medal; recipient Sacred Music award Nat. Evang. Film Found., 1966, Music Achievement award Christian Artists, 1985; Honor Cert. Freedoms Found., 1975; winner Internat. Gospel Composition of Yr., Soc. European Stage, Authors and Composers, 1986, Ray DeVries Ch. Music award, 1996; inductee Gospel Music Hall of Fame, 1986. Mem. ASCAP, Hump Pilots Assn. Home: 11668 N 80th Pl Scottsdale AZ 85260-5650

PETERSON, LEROY, retired secondary education educator; b. Fairfield, Ala., Feb. 15, 1930; s. Leroy and Ludie Pearl (Henderson) P.; m. Theresa Petite, Apr. 6, 1968 (div. Oct. 1984); children: Leroy III, Monica Teresa; m. Ruby Willodine Hopkins, July 21, 1985 (div. Mar. 1996). Cert. in piano, Bavarian State Acad., Wuerzburg, Fed. Republic Germany, 1954; BS in Music Edn., Miami U., Oxford, Ohio, 1957. Life credential music tchr., Calif. Tchr. music Cleve. Pub. Schs., 1957-62, L.A. Unified Schs., 1963-94; retired, 1994. Song composer. With U.S. Army, 1952-54. Mem. Alpha Phi Alpha, Phi Mu Alpha Sinfonia. Republican. Avocations: amateur concert pianist, composing, photography. Home: 13005 Spelman Dr Victorville CA 92392-7239

PETERSON, LESLIE RAYMOND, barrister; b. Viking, Alta., Can., Oct. 6, 1923; s. Herman S. and Margaret (Karen) P.; m. Agnes Rose Hine, June 24, 1950; children: Raymond Erik, Karen Isabelle. Student, Camrose Luth. Coll., Alta., McGill. U., Can., London U., Eng.; LLB, U. B.C., Can., 1949; LLD, Simon Fraser U., Can., 1965, U. B.C., 1993; EdD, Notre Dame U., Nelson, Can., 1966; hon. diploma tech., B.C. Inst. Tech., 1994. Bar: B.C. 1949; called to Queens Counsel, 1960. Pvt. practice barrister Vancouver, B.C., 1949-52; with Peterson & Anderson, 1952; then with Boughton & Co. (now Boughton Peterson Yang Anderson).; mem. B.C. Legislature for Vancouver Centre, 1956-63, Vancouver-Little Mountain, 1966; min. of edn., 1956-68, min. of labour, 1960-71, atty. gen., 1968-72; bd. govs. U. B.C., Vancouver, 1979-83, chancellor, 1987-93; bd. dirs. Can. Found. Econ. Edn., Inst. Corp. Dirs. Can., West Vancouver Found., Inst. for Pacific Ocean Sci. and Tech., Karay Holdings Ltd.; trustee Peter Wall Inst. for Advanced Studies; chmn. U. B.C. Found., 1990-96. Bd. dirs. Portland unit Shriners Hosp. for Crippled Children, 1994-96; past bd. dirs. Western Soc. of Rehab., YMCA, Victoria B.C.; past pres. Twenty Club; hon. mem. Vancouver Jr. C. of C.; former v.p. Normanna Old People's Home; founding mem. Convocation, Simon Fraser U. and U. Victoria; hon. dep. French Nat. Assembly, Paris; hon. commr. labor State of Okla.; gov. Downtown Vancouver Assn. With Can. Army, 1942-46, ETO. Recipient Disting. Alumnus award Camrose Luth. Coll., 1980. Fellow Royal Soc. Arts; mem. Vancouver Bar Assn., Law Soc. B.C., Internat. Assn. of Govt. Labour Ofcls. (chmn. standing com., Can. mins. of edn. 1965-66), Terminal City Club (pres. 1991—), Scandinavian Bus. Men's Club (past pres.), Hazelmere Golf and Tennis Club (bd. dirs.), Union Club (Victoria), Wesbrook Soc. of U. B.C. (chmn. 1987), Order of St. Lazarus (knight comdr.), Freemason (potentate Gizeh Temple Shrine 1988), Order of B.C., Venerable Order of Saint John (comdr.). Avocations: skiing, golf, fishing, hunting. Home: 814 Highland, West Vancouver, BC Canada V7S 2G5 Office: Boughton Peterson Yang Anderson, 1055 Dunsmuir St PO Box 49290, Vancouver, BC Canada V7X 1S8

PETERSON, LINDA ELLEN, lawyer; b. Kearny, N.J., Feb. 8, 1960; d. Walter Raymond and JoAnn Evelyn Peterson; m. Domenic James Valentine, Oct. 2, 1988 (div. Apr. 1991); m. Nicholas Joseph Mango, Aug. 17, 1996; 1 child, Jessica Lynn Valentine. BA with honors, Rutgers U., 1983; JD, Pace U., 1987. Bar: N.J. 1987. Law clk. to Hon. Bruce A. Gaeta Hackensack, N.J., 1987-88; asst. county counsel Bergen County Counsel, Hackensack, 1988-91; asst. dep. pub. defenders Passaic County Pub. Defenders, Paterson, N.J., 1991-93, Bergen County Pub. Defenders, Hackensack, 1993—. Vol. St. Catherine's Parish, Ringwood, N.J.1995—. Ranking scholar Pace U., 1986. Mem. Nat. Assn. Criminal Def. Lawyers, N.J. State Bar. Methodist. Avocations: dance, yoga, antiques, gardening, moutain biking. Office: Office Pub Defender 60 State St Ste 4 Hackensack NJ 07601-5469

PETERSON, MAX RUPERT, JR., chemist, researcher; b. Sampson County, N.C., May 26, 1945; s. Max Rupert Sr. and Mary Lily (Peterson) P.; m. Bonnie Fay Farrell, July 20, 1969; children: Karen Fay, Kathryn Hope. BS in Chemistry, Campbell U., 1966; PhD in Organic Chemistry, N.C. State U., 1971. Tchg. asst. N.C. State U., Raleigh, 1966-70, vis. assoc. prof., 1980-82; instr. Campbell U., Buies Creek, N.C., 1970-71, asst. prof., 1971-75, assoc. prof., 1975-87; rsch. chemist Research Triangle Inst., Research Triangle Park, N.C., 1987—; cons. Natural Energy Rsch., Inc., Lillington, N.C., 1978-80, Geotech. Engrng., Raleigh, 1975. Contbr. numerous articles to profl. jours. and ency., chpt. to book. Named Outstanding Educator in Am., Acad. Am. Educators, 1974-75. Mem. Am. Chem. Soc., Air and Waste Mgmt. Assn., Sigma Xi, Phi Kappa Phi. Baptist. Achievements include research in chemical method development, evaluation and validation studies related to measurement of pollutants in stationary source emissions, ambient air, indoor air, hazardous and other wastes, and commercial formulations. Avocations: genealogy, Civil War history, astronomy. Home: 116 Braintree Ct Cary NC 27513-3117 Office: Research Triangle Inst 3040 Cornwallis Rd PO Box 12194 Durham NC 27709-2194

PETERSON, PAMELA CARMELLE, English language educator; b. Bakersfield, Calif., Sept. 24, 1954; d. Bob Eugene and Carmelita Denyse (Coodey) York; m. Robert Leroy Peterson, Feb. 9, 1979; children: Aimee, Sara, Matthew, Hannah. Assoc., Bakersfield Coll., 1992; BA in History, Calif. State U., Bakersfield, 1994. Exec. adminstr. Kern Bldg. Materials, Bakersfield, 1973-95; prin. Rosewall Christian Acad., Bakersfield, 1994—; prin., tchr. Dynasty Christian Schs., Bakersfield, 1995-97; instr. ESL, Calif. State U., Bakersfield, 1997—; instr. English, Santa Barbara (Calif.) Bus. Coll., 1998—; pres. bd. Dynasty Christian Schs., 1995; exec. sec. bd. dirs. Kern Bldg. Materials, 1983-95. Mem. Assn. Christian Schs., Inc., Assn. Christian Sch. Adminstrs., Phi Alpha Theta (sec. 1994-95, v.p. 1995-96). Avocations: history, reading, needlework, gardening, baking. Home: 4213 Rosewall St Bakersfield CA 93313-2529 Office: Rosewail Christian Acad 7850 White Ln # E149 Bakersfield CA 93309-7689

PETERSON, RANDALL SCOTT, management educator; b. Fergus Falls, Minn., Apr. 22, 1964; s. David Harold and Betty Louise Peterson. BS, U. Minn., 1986, MA, 1990; PhD, U. Calif., Berkeley, 1995. Asst. prof. Northwestern U., Evanston, Ill., 1995-97, Cornell U., Ithaca, N.Y., 1997—. Contbr. articles to profl. jours. Mem. APA, Am. Psychol. Soc., Acad. Mgmt. Avocation: photography. E-mail: rsp12@cornell.edu. Home: 208 Bald Hill Rd Spencer NY 14883-9608

PETERSON, ROBERT L., meat processing executive; b. Nebr., July 14, 1932; married; children: Mark R., Susan P. Student, U. Nebr., 1950. With Wilson & Co., Jim Boyle Order Buying Co.; cattle buyer R&C Packing Co., 1956-61; cattle buyer, plant mgr., v.p. carcass prodn. Iowa Beef Processors, 1961-69; exec. v.p. ops. Spencer Foods, 1969-71; founder, pres., chmn., chief exec. officer Madison (Nebr.) Foods, 1971-76; group v.p. carcass div. Iowa Beef Processors, Inc. (name now IBP, Inc.), Dakota City, Nebr., 1976-77, pres., COO, 1977-80, CEO, 1980-81, co-chmn. bd. dirs., 1981-82, CEO, CFO, from 1980, chmn., CEO. Served with Q.M.C. U.S. Army, 1952-54. Mem. Sioux City Country Club. Office: IBP Inc IBP Ave 800 Stevens Port Dr Dakota Dunes SD 57049-5005

PETERSON, ROBERT SCOTT, electrical engineer; b. McKeesport, Pa., Mar. 24, 1930; s. William James and Emma Elizabeth (Scott) P.; m. Betty Louise Oleska, Aug. 11, 1962 (dec. 1995). BSEE, Pa. State U., 1952; MSEE, U. Pitts., 1961. Lic. profl. engr., Pa. Sr. application, design engr. Westinghouse Elec., Pitts., 1952-63; devel. engr. Westinghouse Elec., Buffalo, 1963-85, Pitts., 1985-89; devel. engr. AEG Automation Corp., Pitts., 1989-94; cons. engr. CDI-Ctrl. Corp., Pitts., 1994—. Patentee in field. Coach Midget Football League, McKeesport, 1953-55. With U.S. Army, 1955-57. Mem. IEEE, N.Y. Acad. Scis., Assn. Iron Steel Engrs. Avocations: gardening, woodworking, oil painting, dancing, sports. Home: 719 Heathergate Dr Pittsburgh PA 15238-1000

PETERSON, THAGE G., retired Swedish politician; b. Berg, Sweden, 1933. Grad., Coll. Social Studies, 1957. Sec., vice chmn. Social Dem. Youth League, 1964-67; head, mng. dir. bus. activities Community Ctr. Assn., 1967-70; chmn. Stockholm County br. Social Dem. Party, 1974-89, mem. exec., 1975-90; apptd. under sec. state Cabinet Office, 1971; min. without portfolio, 1975, apptd. cabinet min. and min. industry., 1982-88, apptd. min. justice., 1988; mem. The Swedish Parliament, Stockholm, 1970-99; elected speaker Swedish Parliament, Stockholm, 1988-91; chmn. standing com. on the constitution The Swedish Parliament, 1991-94; min. def., 1994-97; min. Prime Min. Office, Stockholm, 1997—. Office: Prime Mins Office, S-103 33 Stockholm Sweden

PETERSON, TRUDY HUSKAMP, archivist; b. Estherville, Iowa, Jan. 25, 1945. BS, Iowa State U., 1967; MA, U. Iowa, 1972, PhD, 1975. With Nat. Archives, Washington, 1968-87, asst. archivist, 1987-93, dep. archivist of U.S., 1993-95, acting archivist, 1993-95; exec. dir. Open Soc. Archives, Budapest, 1995-98, Open Media Rsch. Inst., Prague, Czech Republic, 1996-97; dir. archives UN High Commr. for Refugees, Geneva, Switzerland, 1999—; Fulbright lectr. in Am. studies, 1983-84; commr. U.S.-Russia Joint Commn. on MIA/POWs, 1992-95; sec. Internat. Conf. on Round Table on Archives, 1992-93, pres., 1993-95; mem. European Bd. on Archives, 1995-96; v.p. program support commn. Internat. Coun. on Archives, 1996—. Author: Agricultural Exports, Farm Income and the Eisenhower Administration, 1979, Basic Archival Workshop Exercises, 1982, Archives and Manuscripts: Law, 1985; editor: Farmers, Bureaucrats and Middlemen: Historical Perspectives on American Agriculture, 1980; mem. editl. bd. The Am. Archivist, 1978-81; contbr. articles to profl. jours. Pres. Capitol Hill Restoration Soc., 1987-88. Recipient Order of Arts and Letters Republic of France, 1995, Hancher-Finkbine Medallion, Disting. Alumni award U. Iowa, 1995; named Samuel Lazerow Lectr. Simmons Coll., 1995. Fellow Soc. Am. Archivists (mem. coun. 1984-87, pres. 1990-91, held various offices, Gondos Meml. award 1973, Fellows Posner prize 1987); mem. Agrl. History Soc. (mem. exec. com. 1982-85, pres. 1988-89), Soc. History in Fed. Govt. (mem. exec. com. 1987-89). Office: UN High Commr for Refugees, 94 rue de Montbrillant, CH-1202 Geneva Switzerland

PETERSON, WALTER FRITIOF, academic administrator; b. Idaho Falls, Idaho, July 15, 1920; s. Walter Fritiof and Florence (Danielson) P.; m. Barbara Mae Kempe, Jan. 13, 1946; children: Walter Fritiof III, Daniel John. BA, State U. Iowa, 1942, MA, 1948, PhD, 1951; HHD (hon.), Loras Coll., 1983; LHD (hon.), Clarke Coll., 1991; DHum (hon.), U. Dubuque, 1997. Asst. prof. history, chmn. dept. history Milw. Downer Coll., 1952-57, assoc. prof. history, chmn. social sci. div., 1957-64; assoc. prof. history Lawrence U., Appleton, Wis., 1964-67; prof. history, Alice G. Chapman libr. Lawrence U., 1967-70; pres. U. Dubuque, 1970-90, chancellor, 1990—; regional tng. officer Peace Corps, 1965-68; cons. history Allis-Chalmers Mfg. Co., 1959-75, Secura Ins. Group, 1968-92, Wm. C. Brown Pub. Co., 1981-92, bd. dirs. Editor: Transactions of Wis. Acad. Scis., Arts and Letters, 1965-72, The Allis-Chalmers Corporation: An Industrial History, 1977, A History of Wm. C. Brown Cos., 1994, A History of Hawkeye Bancorporation, 1996. Advisor Templeton Prize for Progress in Religion, 1986-91; bd. dirs. Finley Hosp., pres., 1983-84; chmn. Finley Health Found., 1986-95, Finley Health Found. Hall of Fame, 2000; pres. Grand Opera House Found., 1996—; bd. dirs. Dubuque Symphony Orch., Dubuque Art Assn., Jr. Achievement, Nat. River Hall of Fame, 1984; chmn. Iowa Assn. Coll. and Univ. Pres., 1975-76; chmn. Iowa Coll. Found., 1982-83; chair Grand Opera House Found., 1998—. With USAAF, 1942-45, PTO. Recipient Dubuque 1st Citizen award, 1990, Disting. Civic Svc. award, 1991, Benjamin Franklin award Nat. Soc. Fundraising Execs., 1994, Paul Harris fellowship, Duduque Rotary Club, 1993; named to Dubuque Bus. Hall of Fame, 1990;. Mem. Iowa Assn. Ind. Colls. and Univs. (chmn. 1988-89), Dubuque County Hist. Soc. (bd. dirs.), Dubuque Golf and Country Club, Phi Alpha Theta, Kappa Delta Pi, Phi Delta Kappa. Office: U Dubuque Office of Chancellor 2000 University Ave Dubuque IA 52001-5050

PETERSON, WILLIAM GENE, public affairs executive; b. Vermillion, S.D., Dec. 15, 1950; s. William Henry and Opal Irene (Johnson) P.; m. Sue Kathryn Lucas, June 15,1991; children: Lucas William, Robert William. Student, U. S.D., 1969-74. With Nat. Bank S.D., Vermillion, 1973-79; dir. legislation and rsch. Sioux Falls C. of C., 1979-83; v.p. pub. affairs S.D. C. of C., Pierre, 1983-84; adminstrv. asst. Lt. Gov. Lowell Hansen, Sioux Falls, 1984-86; v.p. mktg. Jack Rabbit Bus Lines, Sioux Falls, 1984-86; account exec. Colle McVoy Advt., Sioux Falls, 1987-88; asst. v.p. pub. affairs Western Surety Co., Sioux Falls, 1988—; mem. S.D. Ho. of Reps., 1997—, majority whip, 1999—; dir. legis. com. Nat. Assn. Ind. Sureties; prof. Kilian C.C., Sioux Falls, 1982-83, 86-89. Mem. Vermillion Planning Commn., 1975-78, chair, 1977-78; bd. dirs. Clay-Union Health Found., 1979, Kilian C.C., 1989-95, chair, 1991-93; bd. dirs. Family Svc., Inc., Sioux Falls, 1989-95, chair, 1993-94; chmn. Minnehaha County Lincoln Day, 1985; co-chairCitizens for Modern City Govt., Sioux Falls, 1994; chmn. Clay County Rep. Party, 1976-80, Minnehaha County Rep. Party, 1995-96, other civic activities. Named to Outstanding Young Men of Am., 1983. Mem. Pub. Rels. Network of Sioux Falls (pres. 1988, Pub. Rels. Person of Yr. 1994), Sioux Falls C. of C. (chair tax coun. 1988-90, chair pub. affairs com. 1988-90), Masons, Shriners, Surety Assn. of Am. (chair govt. affairs com.). Republican. Lutheran. Home: 3808 E Marson Dr Sioux Falls SD 57103-7223

PETERSONS, HARALDS FREDS, mathematics educator, geophysics researcher; b. Riga, Latvia, Jan. 27, 1942; s. Valdemars Vladislavs and Zigrida (Muske) P.; m. Rita Melita Venta, Jan. 29, 1966; children: Martin Robert, Melissa Helen. BSc with hons., U. Sydney, New South Wales, Australia, 1963, MSc, 1964, PhD, 1970. Tchg. fellow U. Sydney, NSW, Australia, 1963-67; lectr. Australian Nat. U., Canberra, ACT, Australia, 1967-2000; ret. vis. fellow Australian Nat. U., Canberra, 2000—; staff rep. on bd. of faculties, Australian Nat. U., Canberra, 1993-5, sub-dean, 1993-95. Contbr. over 27 articles to profl. jours. Chairperson Phillip Coll., Canberra, Australia, 1989. Avocations: chess, bush walking, sailing. Home: 32 Martin St, Curtin ACT 2605, Australia Office: Australian Nat U, Dept Math, The Faculties, Canberra ACT 0200, Australia

PETERSSON, BIRGIT HOLM, educator; b. Faaborg, Denmark, Mar. 14, 1945; d. Holger Holm abd Kirstine Holm (Dalager) P.; m. Preben Wilhjelm, 1970 (div. 1985); 1 child, Thomas; m. Christen Jensen Sorensen, June 1, 1990. MD, U. Copenhagen, 1973. Physician various hosps., Copenhagen, 1973-87; assoc. prof. U. Copenhagen, 1987—. Author: Misundelse, 1992, Sygeliggørelse af Dkvinder, 1995, Klar besked om Overgangsalderen, 1994, Frygten for Fedtet, 1997, Paene piger, 1998, Tilgivelse, 1999. Chmn. Studenterradgivningen, Copenhagen, 1993-99; vice chmn. KUINFO, Copenhagen, 1992-99. Home: Amalievej 11, DK-1875 Frederiksberg Denmark Office: U Copenhagen, Blegdamsvej 3, DK-2200 Copenhagen Denmark

PETERSSON, CARL STURE, scientist, electronics educator; b. Lövånger, Sweden, Sept. 6, 1941; s. Karl and Alida (Rudholm) P.; m. Viveka Vidmark, July 6, 1968; children: Jenny, Åsa. MSc, Uppsala (Sweden) U., 1965, M Engrng., 1969, PhD, 1973. Asst. prof. Uppsala U., 1973-78, 80-83, docent in electronics, 1974; vis. scientist IBM, Yorktown Heights, N.Y., 1978-80; prof. electronics Royal Inst. Tech., Stockholm, 1983—; dept. head, dept. electronics Royal Inst. Tech., 1985-99; vis. prof. Imec, Leuven, Belgium, 1990-91. Editor: Refractory Metals and Silicides, 1991, Radiation Imaging Detectors, 1999; contbr. numerous articles to profl. jours.; patentee in field. Mem. IEEE, Am. Phys. Soc., Am. Vacuum Soc., Electro. Chem. Soc., Böhmische Physics. Home: Sandmovagen 5, 75647 Uppsala Sweden Office: Royal Inst Tech, Dept Electronics, E229 Kista Sweden

PETERSSON, OLOF R., policy studies administrator; b. Göteborg, Sweden, Mar. 10, 1947; s. Sven R. and Marianne T. Petersson; m. Michele M. Micheletti. PhD, U. Göteborg, 1975. Rsch. asst. U. Göteborg, 1971-74; asst. prof. U. Uppsala, Sweden, 1974-78, assoc. prof., 1978-96, prof., 1996-97; rsch. dir. Ctr. Bus. and Policy Studies, Stockholm, 1997—. Author: Swedish Government and Politics, 1994, The Government and Politics of the Nordic Countries, 1994; editor: Democracy the Swedish Way. Office: SNS, Box 5629, S-11486 Stockholm Sweden

PETERZELL, DAVID, psychologist; b. Santa Monica, Calif., Apr. 26, 1961; s. Harry Labe and Joyce Moore P. BA, U. Calif., Berkeley, 1983; MA, U. Colo., 1988, PhD, 1991. Undergrad. tchg. and rsch. asst. U. Calif., Berkeley, 1980-83; accreditation supr. L.A. Olympic Organizing Com., 1984; tchg. and rsch. asst. U. Colo., Boulder, 1984-91; NIH postdoctoral fellow The Smith-Kettlewell Eye Rsch. Inst., San Francisco, 1992-94, U. Wash.,

Seattle, 1994-97, U. Calif. San Diego, La Jolla, 1997-98; psychology intern/clin. svcs. St. Vincent de Paul Village, San Diego, Calif., 1999-2000; intern in psychology U. San Diego Counseling Ctr., 2000—; vis. scholar U. Calif., San Diego, La Jolla, 1998—; lectr. Calif. Sch. of Profl. Psychology, San Diego, 2000—; statis. cons., 1990—. Contbr. articles to profl. jours. Recipient Garland Clay award Am. Acad. Optometry, 1991, Rsch. award NIH, Nat. Eye Inst., 1996-98. Mem. Am. Psychol. Soc., Assn. for Rsch. in Vision and Ophthalmology, Soc. for Rsch. in Child Devel., Internat. Assn. for Cognitive Psychotherapy. Avocations: meditation, yoga, art glass, running. Office: Psychol Dept/U Calif San Diego/9500 Gilman Dr La Jolla CA 92093

PETH, HOWARD ALLEN, lawyer, educator; b. Calif., Apr. 20, 1955; s. Howard Allen and Diane Marie (Munyan) P.; m. Gloria Gene Stockton, Aug. 9, 1992; children: Andrew Howard, Rachel Gloria. BA, U. Calif., San Diego, 1980; MD, U. Santiago, 1984; JD, U. Mo., 1991. Bar: Calif. 1993, U.S. Ct. Appeals (9th cir.) 1993, U.S. Ct. Claims, U.S. Ct. Appeals (fed. cir.) 1993, U.S. Dist. Ct. (so. dist.) Calif. 1993, U.S. Supreme Ct. 1997; diplomate Am. Bd. Internal Medicine, Am. Bd. Emergency Medicine; lic. physician, Calif., Mo., Wis. Asst. prof. U. Mo. Sch. Medicine, Columbia, 1997—. Fellow Am. Coll. Legal Medicine; mem. AMA, ABA (health law sect.), ACP, Am. Coll. Emergency Physicians. Republican. Episcopalian. Office: U Mo Hosp and Clinic One Hospital Dr Columbia MO 65212

PETITAN, DEBRA ANN BURKE, educator, education counselor, design engineer, writer, author; b. Chgo., Mar. 12, 1932; d. James Marcellus and Susan Florence (Hines) Burke; m. Kenneth Charles Petitan, Aug. 9, 1952; 1 child, Susan Florence. AA, Wilson Jr. Coll., Chgo., 1951, N.Y. Inst. Photography, 1952; BS in Primary Edn., Chgo. State U., 1956, MS in Indsl. Edn., 1967; DSc in Applied Sci. and Tech., London Inst. Tech., 1971; postgrad., U. Wis., Bradley U., U. Calif., U. Ill.; grad., Inst. Children's Lit., West Redding, Conn., 1991; cert. in Childrens' Portraiture, North Light Art Sch., 1997. Tchr. Chgo. Bd. Edn., 1958-71, guidance counselor, 1976-84, now tchr., cons.; nat. dir. edn. Nation of Islam, 1971-75; design engr. Fed. Sign and Signal Corp., Chgo., 1975-76; nat. adv. bd. Nat. Right to Work Orgn., 1976-85; cons. ednl. devel., 1978; computer libr. cons.; owner, CEO, Fayzah's Fin. Svcs., Fayzah's Creative Projects, Inc.; participant summer writing festival U. Iowa, 1991. Photographer VISTA News, 1969-70; writer children's lit.; author curriculum introducing computer-aided design techniques in the pub. schs., 1965. Dir. Christian Edn. Trinity United Ch. Christ, Chgo., 1978-81, family counselor, 1978-81, organizer, leader family counseling ministry, lic. lay Eucharistic minister Episcopal Ch. St. Edmund, Chgo. Epis. Diocese, 1989; chmn. Career Women for Johnson/Humphrey, Chgo., 1965; cmty. svc. recording sec. 9600 Blcok Club. Navigator, pub. rels. officer IL Wing, Squadron 8, capt. Civil Air Patrol, 1953-56. Named Woman of Yr. Iota Phi Lambda, 1978; recipient 250 Hr. medal Ground Observer Corps, 1952, 25 Yr. Service medal Chgo. Bd. Edn., 1987. Mem. Off-Campus Writer's Workshop (editor newsletter), Soc. of Children's Book Writers, Am. Contract Bridge League, Am. Bridge Assn. (life master, rec. sec.), Children's Reading Roundtable, Green River Writers, Epsilon Pi Tau. Achievements include introduction of CAD curriculum to field of edn. Avocations: computer science, canoeing, water color painting, tournament bridge, lapidary. Office: Chgo Bd Edn 1839 W Pershing Rd Chicago IL 60609-2317

PETITO, MARGARET L., public relations executive, consultant; b. Dallas, Sept. 28, 1950; d. Jacob Charles and Eileen (Shank) Loehr; m. John Haven Petito, 1978 (div. 1984); children: John Christian Robert, David Nelson. BA, So. Meth. U., 1972. Mem. Action/Vista Program U.S. Govt., Middlesex, N.Y., 1972-74; prin. Petito & Assocs., Washington, 1994—; dir., curator Oliver House Mus., Penn Yan, N.Y., 1975-77; staff asst. Williams & Jensen, P.C., Washington, 1986-89; dir. fed. rels. Chambers Devel. Co., Inc., 1989-92; dir. fed. affairs DSSI-U.S. Biotech., Washington, 1992-94; cons., dir. pub. affairs Embassy Ecuador, Govt. Ecuador, Washington, 1994-96; prin. Petito & Assocs., 1994—; dir. external events Internat. Cancer Alliance, Bethesda, Md., 1996-97, Sch. of Bus. U. Georgetown, Washington, 1998-99. Dir. Marshall House Mus., Lambertville, N.J., 1980-82; spl. legis. advisor Drugwatch Internat., Chgo., 1993—; bd. dirs., Nyumbani Orphanage for Kenyan Children with AIDS, Africa, Washington, 1989—; mem. Women's Coun. Energy and Environ., Washington, 1990—; mem. task force Women in Govt. Rels., Washington, 1990—; founder, co-chair Forum for the Environ., Washington, 1989-91; pres. Cultural Parthersnip of the Ams., Washington, 1999—. Mem. Tex. State Soc., Tex. Breakfast Club. Roman Catholic. Avocations: squash, needlepoint, fishing. Fax #: 202-362-2414. Home: 6008 34th Pl NW Washington DC 20015-1607

PETIZON, YVES PIERRE, civil engineer; b. Toulouse, France, May 27, 1936; s. Pierre Louis and Marie-Antoinette (Chassang) P.; m. Hélène Wiktorowicz, Aug. 8, 1959; children: Thierry, Laurent, Sophie. MSc, U. Lyon, France, 1954; Civil Engr., Ecole Centrale, Paris, 1959; MBA, Inst. d'Adminstrn. des Entreprises/Sorbonne, Paris, 1960, M Civil Engring., 1960. Lic. civil engr. Gen. mgr. Chaufour Dumez, Dakar, Senegal, 1969-71; area mgr. Africa Dumez, Paris, 1971-82, gen. mgr., 1982-90; gen. mgr. Lyonnaise Eaux, Paris, 1990-93; chmn. Thion-Soccram, Paris, 1993-95; cons. World Bus. Inc., Washington, 1995-97; sr. advisor European Bank, London; chmn. Bus. Advisors & Cons.; advisor to the pres. Salon d'Automne Grand Palais, Paris, 1997—. Constructor Nigeria Bridge, 1962-68, Cairo Metro, 1987, Channel Tunnel, France, 1990. 1st lt. Art. French Mil., 1960-62. Recipient Grosverno, Inst. D'Adminstrn. Des Entreprises/Sorbonne, Paris, 1994. Mem. Golf St Nom. Avocations: golf, motorboating, painting. Home: Domaine du Vallon, 18 Rue des Erables, 78450 Chavenay France Office: Salon D'Automne Grand Palais, Porte HAve Winston Churchill, 75008 Paris France

PETKOV, IVAN GOSPODINOV, oil industry executive; b. Bisser, Haskovo, Bulgaria, Aug. 6, 1934; s. Gospodin Ivanov and Slava Valcheva (Kolemanova) P.; m. Leja Vladimirovna Guner, Jan. 8, 1960; children: Dimitri Ivanovich, Tatiana Ivanova. Degree in engring., Oil U., Moscow, 1958. Dist. engr. Geol., Prospecting and Planning Enterprise, Varna, Bulgaria, 1958-64; chief tech. dep. GPP, Varna, Bulgaria, 1964-70, 78-83, chief innovation dep., 1970-76, offshore drilling engr., 1983-88; chief engr. Bulgargeomin, Libya, 1976-78, 88-90; mng. dir. Black Sea Oil Svcs., Varna, 1991—. Author: Fishing in Well Drilling, 1981; patentee turbo drill. Avocations: sea fishing, excursions. Home: Bolgrad # 8 B, 9010 Varna Bulgaria Office: Black Sea Oil Svcs, Saltanat 55 PO Box 168, 9010 Varna Bulgaria

PETKOV, KIRIL TODOROV, physicist, researcher; b. Dolna Beshovitza, Vratza, Bulgaria, May 12, 1943; s. Todor Petkov and Nena Nikolova Getchovsky; m. Anelia Dilova Natova, July 10, 1966; children, Tony, Alexander. Grad., U. Sofia, Bulgaria, 1968; PhD, Bulgarian Acad. Scis., Sofia, 1988. Physicist Ctrl. Lab Photoprocesses, Sofia, 1968-73, rsch. assoc., 1973-95, sr. rsch. assoc., 1995—. Contbr. over 60 articles to sci. publs. in the field of thin film technology. Sgt.-maj. Bulgarian armed forces, 1962. Mem. Union Scientists Bulgaria, N.Y. Acad. Scis. Avocations: books, music, trade union activities. Home: Komplex Mladost Bl 87 Ent 9, 1797 Sofia Bulgaria Office: Ctrl Lab Photoprocesses, Acad G Bonchev Str Bl 109, 1113 Sofia Bulgaria

PETKOV, ORLIN, physiologist, researcher; b. Sofia, Bulgaria, Mar. 11, 1946; s. Vesselin Draganov and Emilia Philipova (Kurdova) P.; m. Liliana Kirilova Ivanova, Mar. 26, 1967 (div. 1976); 1 child, Vesselin Orlinov. Degree, Med. Acad., Sofia, 1972. Asst. prof. Med. Acad., Sofia, 1974-76, 77-87; rsch. fellow Chem. Pharm. Rsch. Inst., Sofia, 1987—; mem. Internat. Soc. for Heart Rsch. (European sect.), 1983-92, Bulgarian Physiol. Soc., 1975-90, Bulgarian Soc. Young Med. Scientists (pres. 1978-80). Contbr. articles to profl. jours. Mem. Bulgarian Scientific Soc. Pharmacology, Bulgarian Union of Scientists (bd. dirs. 1990-94), Bulgarian League of Hypertension (bd. dirs. 1992—), N.Y. Acad. Scis. Avocations: classical music, fiction. Home: Hemus Block 62 A Apt 46, 1574 Sofia Bulgaria Office: Chem Pharm Rsch Inst, Kliment Ohridsky 3, 1797 Sofia Bulgaria

PETKOVA, KRISTINA GEORGIEVA, social psychologist, educator; b. Nova-Zagora, Sliven, Bulgaria, Nov. 24, 1949; d. Georgi Dinev and Stanka Stoyanova (Radulova) P. MA, U. Sofia, 1974; PhD, Bulgarian Acad. Scis., 1979. Postgrad. Inst. Sociology, Sofia, 1976-79, rschr., 1980-87, assoc. prof., 1988—. Author: The Limits of Scientific Risk - Problem Choice in Science, 1990; co-editor: Sociol. Problems, 1995—; contbr. articles to profl. jours. Scholarship Fulbright Commn., 1991-92. Democrat. Ea. Orthodox. Avocations: basketball, tennis, bridge. Office: Inst Sociology, 13A Moskovska, 1000 Sofia Bulgaria

PETLYUK, FELIX BORIS, chemical engineer, researcher; b. Kasan, Tatarstan, Russia, Jan. 17, 1934; s. Boris Natan Petlyuk and Sofia Abram Kaplinskaya; m. Janna Alexander Bril, Mar. 21, 1961; 1 child, Sofia. PhD, Mendeleev U. Chem. Engring., Moscow, 1965; DSc, Lomonosov State Acad., Moscow, 1982. Engr. State Chem. Machine-Bldg. Inst., Moscow, 1957-61; sr. rschr. State Rsch. Inst. Organic Synthesis, Moscow, 1961-69; head lab. Rsch. & Design Inst. for Oil Refining & Petrochem. Industry, Moscow, 1969-92; sr. expert ECT Svc. Rsch. and Engring. Co., Moscow, 1992—. Author: Multicomponent Distillation: Theory and Calculations, 1983; contbr. articles to profl. jours. Achievements include patents in field. E-mail: felix@dataforce.net and ect@rinet.ru. Fax: 095 288 42 45.

PETNIŪNAITE-NAVAKAUSKIENE, RŪTA, biochemist, researcher; b. Vilnius, Lithuania, June 29, 1965; d. Povilas and Genovaite (ŽiŪraite) Petniūnas; m. Dalius Navakauskas, July 16, 1993; 1 child, Aiste. Diploma, Vilnius (Lithuania) U., 1988; PhD, Inst. Biochemistry, Vilnius, 1992. Rsch. assoc. Inst. of Biochemistry, Vilnius, Lithuania, 1992—; postdoctoral fellow Linköping U., Sweden, 1995-97. Recipient Lithuanian Govt. Stipend, 1994. Mem. Lithuanian Biochem. Soc. (treas. 1994-97), Lithuanian Cell Culture Soc. Fax: (370-2) 729196. E-mail: Ruta.Navakauskiene@bchi.lt. Home: Konarskio 6-39, 2009 Vilnius Lithuania Office: Inst Biochemistry, Mokslininku 12, 2600 Vilnius Lithuania

PETRAK, MICHAEL JOHANNES, biologist, educator; b. Klein-Bulten/Peine, Lower Saxony, Germany, Oct. 27, 1956. Diploma, U. Giessen, 1982, PhD, 1983. Asst. U. Giessen, 1982-86, tchr., 1984-89; cons. Hesse Orgn. for Nature Conservation, Frankfurt, 1986-88; head LÖBF Rsch. Ctr. Wildlife Northrine-Westfalian Office Agrl. Devel., Bonn, 1989—; chmn. Bd. Examiners for Hannover, 1982—, U. Goettingen, 1990—. Author Ecology and Behaviour of Red Deer (Cervus Elaphus Linné, 1758), 1982, 84, Ecology of Fallow Deer (Cervus Dama Linné), 1987, others. Mem. German Soc. for Mammalogy, Internat. Union for Game Biologists, Hessian Orgn. for Ornithology. Office: LOBF, Puetzchens Chaussee 228, 53229 Bonn Germany

PETRAKOVSKII, GUERMAN ANTONOVICH, research scientist, educator; b. Anjero-Sudjensk, Kemerovs, Russia, June 19, 1937; s. Anton Antonovich and Nadezda Stepanovna (Pomogaeva) P.; m. Eleonora Antolievna Novikova, July 17, 1961 (div. Sept. 1987); children: Oleg, Yurii; m. Tamara Vasilievna Drokina, Oct. 9, 1987; children: Sergei, Aleksandr. Grad., State U. Tomsk, 1959; postgrad., Staet U. Tomsk, 1962-63; PhD, Inst. Physics, Krasnoyarsk, Russia, 1972. Jr. scienist Phys. Tech. Inst., Tomsk, 1962-65; jr. scienist Inst. Physics, Krasnoyarsk, 1965-71, head lab., 1971—; head radio physics chair State U., Krasnoyarsk, 1981—. Author: Physics of Ordered Magnetic Matters, 1976, Metal-Dielectric Transmition in 3d Metal, 1983; contbr. more than 200 articles to profl. jours. 2d lt. Russian Mil. Mem. Coun. on Magnetism. Office: Inst Physics, Akademgorodok, 660036 Krasnoyarsk Russia

PETRÁNSKY, LUDOVÍT, art history educator; b. Brezno, Slovak Republic, Nov. 22, 1943; s. Ludovít and Mária (Filadelfy) P.; m. Lívia Kolínska, Oct. 4, 1980; children: Ludovít, Petra, Martin, Ján. Magister of History of Art, Philos. Faculty Comenius U., Bratislava, Slovakia, 1971; PhD, U. Jan Evangelista Purkyně, Brno, Czech Republic, 1974; DOC, Acad. Fine Arts, Bratislava, 1978; DrSc, Slovak Acad. Scis., Bratislava, 1985; PhD, Czechoslovak Acad. Scis., Prague, 1977. Prof. Acad. Fine Arts, 1970-90, rector, 1989-90; prof. faculty architecture Slovak Tech. U., Bratislava, 1990—, vice-dean, 1997—; curator of expositions Nat. Gallery, Prague, 1987, La palais de l'Europe, Strasbourg, 1998, Internat. Monetary Fund, Washington, 1998-99, Galeries d'Art, Montreal, 1999, UN Hdqs., N.Y.C., 1999; lectr. FA ČVUT, Prague, Czech Republic, 1985, 96. Author: Letter and Picture, 1972, Seurat and Neoimpressionizm, 1976, Principles of Modern Arts, 1988 (Prize of Zsvu 1989), Modern Slovak Graphics, 1989 (Nat. Prize of Slovak Republic 1989), Theory and Methodology of Design, 1994, Vincent Hložník, 1997. Mem. Evang. Ch. Avocations: fishing, skiing, tennis, philately, photography. Home: Vansovej 2, 811 03 Bratislava Slovakia Office: FA STU, Nám Slobody 19, 812 45 Bratislava Slovakia

PETRÁŠ, PETR ENRICO, microbiologist, researcher; b. Prague, Feb. 25, 1942; s. Jaroslav and Emilie (Giráškova) P.; divorced; children: Petr, Tereza. Dr., Charles U., Prague, 1966, PhD, 1972. Rschr. Nat. Inst. of Pub. Health, Prague, 1970—, head of lab., 1980—, head rsch. dept., 1989—, dep. head ctr. epidemiology and microbiology, 1994—; cons. LACHEMA, Brno, Czech Republic, 1992—; tchr. Inst. of Postgrad. Edn., Prague, 1995—. Dir.-in-chief (jour.) Zpravy CEM News Bulletin of CEM, 1996. Min. of Pub. Health rsch. grantee, 1994. Mem. N.Y. Acad. Scis., Czech Chem. Soc., Czech Microbiology Soc. Roman Catholic. Avocations: classical music, genealogy, history, photography, volleyball. Home: Jankovcova 29, 170 00 Prague 7, Czech Republic Office: Nat Inst Pub Health, Šrobárova 48, 100 42 Prague 10, Czech Republic

PETRASCU, CATALINA-OANA, physics researcher; b. Brasov, Romania, Nov. 2, 1965; d. Aurel and Elena (Ignat) Curceanu. BSc, Faculty of Physics, Bucharest, Romania, 1988, MSc in Physics, 1989; PhD in Physics summa cum laude, Inst. of Atomic Physics, Bucharest, Romania, 1999. Scientific rschr. Inst. Physics and Nuc. Engring. of Atomic Physics, Bucharest, 1989—; postdoctoral fellowship Lab. Nat. di Frascati Istituto Nazionale di Fisica Nucleare, Italy, 1994-96; sci. rschr. LNF-INFN Lab. Naz. N Frascati, Italy, 1996—; contractor DIRAC CERN Collaboration, Geneva, Switzerland, 1995-96, DEAR (LNF-INFN) Collaboration, Frascati, 1994—, responsible with Monte Carlo simulations, 1995—. Contbr. articles to profl. jours. Avocations: ice skating, travel, lecturing. Office: LNF-INFN, Via E Fermi 40, 00044 Frascati Italy

PETRÁŠEK, JAN VÁCLAV, medical educator; b. Vráto, Czech republic, Sept. 8, 1929; s. Jan Josef and Marie Anna (Jiráčková) P.; m. Drahomira Ljubov Hulíkova, June 12, 1954; 1 child, Vít. MD, Charles U., Prague, Czech Republic, 1953. Physician Č. Krumlov, Czech republic, 1953-56, Univ. Hosp., Prague, 1956-59; asst. Faculty Medicine, Charles U., Prague, 1959-75, assoc. prof., 1975-83, prof., 1983—, prof. cons., 1996—; fellow of qualification commn. Med. Faculty, Charles U., 1978-90. Editor-in-chief Jour. Czech Physicians, 1985—; author 5 textbooks, 2 monographs; contbr. over 200 articles to profl. jours. Recipient Commemorative medal Med. Sch., Charles U., 1979, 89. Fellow Czech Med. Soc. Roman Catholic. Avocations: music, plastic arts and painting. Office: Med Sch of Charles Univ, U Nemocnice 1, 128 08 Prague Czech Republic

PETRASOVITS, GEZA LASZLO, geotechnical engineering educator; b. Torokszentmiklos, Hungary, Sept. 24, 1928; s. Dezsö Imre an Dezsone Erzsebet (Szilagyi) P.; m. Gezane Anna Szegedi, Aug. 2, 1953; children: Anna Judit, Erzsebet Agnes. MSCE, U. Transp., St. Petersburg, Russia, 1952; PhD, Hungarian Acad. Scis., Budapest, 1963, DS, 1973; D of Civil Engring (hon.), Moscow, 1991. Chief civil engring. Enterprise Underground Constrn., Budapest, Hungary, 1952-54; rschr. Hungarian Acad. Scis., Budapest, 1954-58; asst. prof. Tech. U., Budapest, 1958-62, assoc. prof., 1962-74, prof., 1974-93; scientific advisor Hungarian Acad. Scis., 1993—; head applied mechs. rsch. group, Hungarian Acad. Scis., 1971-92, geotech. dept. Tech. U. Budapest, 1983-86; scientific sec. divsn. tech. sci., 1959-78. Author: Underground Structures in Urban Areas, 1992. Mem. Internat. Soc. Soil Mech. & Found. Engring. (Hungarian nat. com. 1974-83, pres. 1983-93), Brit. Geotech. Soc. Office: Tech U Budapest, Muegyeten rkp 1-3, 1111 Budapest Hungary

PETRATOS, STEVEN, neuroscientist; b. Athens, Greece, Nov. 1, 1969; arrived in Australia, 1972; s. Achilleus and Krystalia (Vamvakis) P.; m. Andrea Nicolaou, Apr. 24, 1993; 1 child, Elizabeth. BS with honors, Melbourne U., Australia, 1993, PhD, 1999. Lab. asst. Pennisula Pathology, Melbourne, Australia, 1989-93; lectr. anatomy RMIT U., Melbourne, Australia, 1997-98; rsch. asst. Melbourne U., 1998-99; rsch. officer Monash U., Melbourne, 1999-2000; rsch. officer Walter and Eliza Hall Inst. Med. Rsch., The Royal Melbourne Hosp., 2000—. Contbr. articles to profl. jours. Rsch. grantee and scholar Dept. Health Housing and Cmty. Svcs., 1993-96. Mem. Australian & New Zealand Soc. Neuropathology, Australian Soc. HIV Medicine, Australian Neurosci. Soc. Avocations: golf, tennis, football, chess. Office: Walter & Eliza Hall Inst, Royal Melbourne Hosp, Melbourne 3050, Australia

PETREK, MARTIN, immunogeneticist; b. Olomouc, Moravia, Czech Republic, May 4, 1963; s. Josef and Anna (Krcmarova) P.; m. Jana Petrujova, Nov. 28, 1987; 1 child, Zuzana. MD, Palacky U., Czech Republic, 1987; PhD, Masaryk U., Brno, Czech Republic, 1993. Diplomate in medical microbiology, allergy and clin. immunology. Rsch. fellow Med. Faculty/Palacky U., Olomouc, Czech Republic, 1989-93; lectr. in immunology Med. Faculty/Palacky U., 1993-98; European Community Rsch. fellow Nat. Heart and Lung Inst., London, 1993; Tempus fellow Imperial Coll. of Sci., Technology and Medicine, London, 1994; staff physician U. Hosp., Olomouc, 1994-98; assoc. prof. Immunology Med. Faculty/Palacky U., 1999—; dir. Tissue Typing Lab. U. Hosp., Olomouc, 1999—; chmn. immunogenetic com., Czech Transplant, Prague, 1997-98. Contbr. articles to profl. jours. Mem. Czech Soc. for Immunology (sec. regional br. 1996—), Brit. Soc. for Immunology, World Assn. Sarcoidosis, European Fedn. Immunogenetics, Am. Thoracic Soc. Avocations: classical music, literature, skiing. Office: Palacky U and Univ Hosp Olomouc, Dept Immunology, 775 20 Olomouc Czech Republic

PETRENKO, ALEXANDER YURIEVICH, biochemist, researcher; b. Khrkov, Ukraine, Mar. 7, 1954; s. Yuri Ilich and Hasya Michailovna (Serebrianikova) P.; m. Irina Grigorievna Margulis, Jan. 17, 1975; children: Peter, Yuri. MSc, U. Kharkov, 1976; Cand Sci., Inst. Cryobiology, Kharkov, 1984, PhD, 1993; diploma, Nat. Acad. Sci. Ukraine, Kiev, 1986. Engr. U. Kharkov, 1976-77, prof., 1995-96; jr. scientist Inst. Cryobiology, 1977-84, sr. scientist, 1984-95, chief scientist, 1996-99, head dept., 1999—; vis. scientist U. Edmonton, Alta., Can., 1992-95, cons. Drug Tech. Inst., Kharkov, 1994-97. Contbr. articles to sci. jours., including Analytical Biochemistry, Cryobiology, Biochemistry. Recipient award MRC (Can.), 1992, Paladin award of Nat. Acad. Sci. (Ukraine), 1999. Fellow Soc. for Cryobiology; mem. Biochem. Soc. Avocations: travel, sports. Home: 93 Mironositski St Apt 23, 310023 Kharkov Ukraine Office: Inst Cryobiology, 23 Pereyaslavskaya St, 310015 Kharkov Ukraine

PETRĖTIS, BRONIUS, physicist, researcher; b. Kedainiai, Lithuania, Mar. 28, 1940; s. Mykolas and Viktorija (Daunoraite) P.; children: Vilius, Paulius. M in Physics, Vilnius (Lithuania) U., 1968, PhD, 1976; Habil dr., Inst. Applied Physics, Kishinev, Moldovia, USSR, 1989. Chief dept. Self-Govt., Ignalina, Lithuania, USSR, 1960-63; asst. Vilnius (Lithuania) U., 1968-71, scientific researcher, 1971-85; scientific researcher, chief dept. Inst. Electrography, Vilnius, 1985-90; scientific researcher Inst. Physics, Vilnius, 1990—, dep. dir., 1990-92, chief dept., 1992—; chief dept. Contbr. numerous articles to profl. jours.; patentee in field. Recipient Premium The Best Invention in Lithuania, 1982. Roman Catholic. Home: Rinktines 21-42, 2051 Vilnius Lithuania Office: Inst Physics, Savanoriu 231, 2028 Vilnius Lithuania

PETRI, CARL AXEL, former Swedish government official; b. Ronneby, Sweden, Aug. 12, 1929; s. Carl and Maud (Wrede) P.; m. Brita Petri, June 19, 1953; children: Johan, Maud. MS, U. Lund, Sweden, 1953. Pres. adminstrn. Sweden, 1976-87; with Ct. Appeals., Sweden; minister of energy Sweden, 1979-81, minster of justice, 1981-82; pres. Gotha Ct. Appeal, Sweden, 1987-96. Address: Narvavägen 51, 55312 Jönköping Sweden

PETRIC, ERNEST, Slovenian ambassador; b. Trzic, Slovenia, 1936; married; 3 children. D of Internat. Law, U. Ljubljana, Slovenia, 1960; student, U. Vienna, 1962-63. Min. sci. and tech. Republic of Slovenia, 1967-72; prof., dean faculty of sociology, polit. sci. and journalism U. Ljubljana, 1972-83, 86-89; prof. internat. law U. Addis Ababa, Ethiopia, 1983-86; Yugoslavian amb. to India and Nepal, Yugoslav Embassy, New Delhi, 1989-91; Slovenian amb. to U.S. and Mex., Slovenia Embassy, Washington, 1991-97; dep. fgn. min. Republic of Slovenia, 1997-2000; Slovenian amb. to UN and Brazil, UN, N.Y.C., 2000—; chmn. Yugoslav Assn. for UN, 1987-88. Author: International Protection of Minorities, 1977, Right to Self Determination, 1984, From Emperor to Leader, 1987, others; contbr. numerous articles to internat. law and internat. rels. jours. Mem. Internat. Law Assn. (human rights com.). Home: Na Rebri 4a, Bled Slovenia

PETRIĆ, IVO, composer, artistic director; b. Ljubljana, Yugoslavia, June 16, 1931; s. Vinko and Mara (Šiška) P.; children: Nina, Irena. Diploma, Music Acad., Ljubljana, 1958. Sec. Composers Union, Ljubljana, 1970-79; editor-in-chief Editions of Composers Union, Ljubljana, 1970—; also bd. dirs.; artistic dir. Slovene Philharm., Ljubljana, 1979-95. Composer orchestral, chamber, and solo music including Sonata for Violin Solo, 1975 (Wieniawski award 1976), Contacts Between Clarinet and Percussion, 1979 (Uwharie Duo Contest award 1979), The Picture of Dorian Gray, 1983 (Oscar Espla award 1984). Recipient Prešern Found. award for compositions and conducting, 1971, Župančić award for compositions City of Ljubljana, 1977. Home: Bilecanska 4, 1000 Ljubljana Slovenia

PETRIC, NEDJELJKA, chemical engineering educator, researcher; b. Vis, Croatia, May 15, 1928; d. Ante and Filomena (Ruljancich) Radisić; m. Bartul Petric, Sept. 15, 1952 (dec. Mar. 1994); children: Dragomir, Nabojsa. BS in Engring., U. Zagreb, Croatia, 1954, PhD in Chemistry, 1972. Chief chem. lab. Dalmacija, Dugi Rat, Croatia, 1954-62, chief of prodn., 1962-64; asst. Faculty of Tech.-U. Split, Croatia, 1964-73; asst. prof. Faculty of Tech.-U. Split, 1973-79, assoc. prof., 1979-84, prof., 1984—, vice-dean, 1978-83, dean, 1983-87. Contbr. articles to sci. jours. Mem. Croatian Chem. Soc., Croatian Soc. Chem. Engring., N.Y. Acad. Scis. Office: U Split Fac Tech, Teslina 10, 21000 Split Croatia

PETRICHKO, MIKHAIL IVANOVICH, urologist, nephrologist; b. Lvov, Ukraine, USSR, Oct. 11, 1945; s. Vasily Stepanovich and Sofya Ivanovna (Petrochko) Alekseyevich; m. Nina Mikhailovna Baksheyeva, Sept. 31, 1967; children: Marina Mikhailovna, Andrei Mikhailovich. MD, Far Eastern State Med. U., Khabarovsk, Russia, 1968, Candidate Med. Scis., 1979, D Med. Scis., 1989. Surgeon Mcpl. Hosp., Komsomolsk-na-Amurc, 1968-71; resident Far Eastern State Med. U., 1971-73, mem. faculty dept. urology, 1976-79, asst. prof., 1979-89, prof., 1989—, head dept. urology and nephrology, 1998—, vice rector sci. work, 1994—; head dept. hemodialysis Regional Hosp., Khabarovsk, 1973-76, dir. urolnephrological ctr., 1998—. Author: Acute Renal Failure and Spontaneous Ruptures of Kidneys in Patients with Hemorrhagie Fever with Renal Syndrome, 1979, Phelonephritis in Pregnant, 1997; contbr. over 125 articles to profl. jours.; chief editor Far Eastern Med. Jour., 1995—; inventor in field. Named Excellent Worker, Pub. Health Svcs., 1992; recipient medal, 1995. Mem. Regional Med. Assn. (pres. 1995—), Regional Soc. Urologists (chmn. 1997 Khabarovsk region 1997—). Office: Regional Hosp Dept Urology, Krasnodarskaya 9, 680009 Khabarovsk Russia

PETRIE, BRUCE INGLIS, lawyer; b. Washington, Nov. 8, 1926; s. Robert Inglis and Marion (Douglas) P.; m. Beverly Ann Stevens, Nov. 3, 1950 (dec. Oct. 1993); children: Laurie Ann Roche, Bruce Inglis, Karen Elizabeth Medsger. BBA, U. Cin., 1948, JD, 1950. Bar: Ohio 1950, U.S. Dist. Ct. (so. dist.) Ohio 1951, U.S. Ct. Appeals (6th cir.) 1960, U.S. Supreme Ct. Assoc. Kunkel & Kunkel, Cin., 1950-51; assoc. Graydon, Head & Ritchey, 1951-57, ptnr., 1957—. Exec. prodr. (sch. video) Classical Quest, 2000; contbr. articles to legal jours. Mem. bd. Charter Com. Greater Cin., 1952—; pres. Charter Rsch. Inst., 2000; mem. bd. edn. Indian Hill Exempted Village Sch. Dist., 1965-67, pres., 1967; mem. adv. bd. William A. Mitchell Ctr., 1969-86; mem. Green Areas adv. com. Village of Indian Hill, Ohio, 1969-80, chmn., 1976-80; mem. Ohio Ethics Com., 1974-75; co-founder Sta. WGUC-FM; mem. WGUC-FM Cmty. Bd., 1974—, chmn., 1974-76; bd. dirs. Murray Seasongood Good Govt. Fund, 1975—, pres., 1989—; bd. dirs. Nat. Civic League, Cin. Vol. Lawyers for Poor Found., Linton Music Series, Amernet Chamber Music Soc.; founder parents as tchrs. Metro Housing Authority Commn., 1991—; elder, trustee, deacon Knox Presbyn. Ch.; a prin. advocate merit selection judges, Ohio; pres. Charter Rsch. Inst., 2000. Recipient Pres.'s award U. Cin., 1976, Disting. Alumnus award, 1995. Fellow Am. Bar Found.; mem. ABA, Ohio Bar Assn., Cin. Bar Assn. (pres. 1981, Trus-

tee's award 2000), Am. Judicature Soc. (Herbert Lincoln Harley award 1973, dir.), Nat. Civic League (Disting. Citizen award 1985, coun. 1984—), Am. Law Inst., Ohio State Bar Assn. Found. (Outstanding Rsch. in Law and Govt. award 1986, Charles P. Taft Civic Gumption award 1988, Ohio Bar medal 1988), Cincinnatus Assn., Order of Coif, Lit. Club, Univ. Club, Cin. Club. Avocations: tennis, squash, woodworking, writing, horticulture, music. Home: 2787 Walsh Rd Cincinnati OH 45208-3428 Office: Graydon Head & Ritchey 1900 Fifth 3d Ctr 511 Walnut St Ste 1900 Cincinnati OH 45202-3157

PETRIK, GERD, pharmaceutical executive; b. Brno, CSR, Czechoslovakia, Apr. 13, 1943; came to U.S., 1993; s. Wilhelm and Ingeborg (Bittner) P.; m. Feli Schueller, July 10, 1971; children: Sharon, Wendy. Pharmacist, Free U. Berlin, 1968. Pres. Dr. Will Inc., Karlsruhe, Germany, 1968-70; product mgr. Pfizer, Illertissen, Germany, 1970-73; head rsch. Helopharm, Berlin, 1973-85, pres., owner, 1985—; pres. Berlin Pharm. Assn., 1990-93. Inventor chem. compounds. Pres. Harness Racing Assn., Berlin, 1992-96. Named hon. consul Bangladesh, 1986-90, hon. gen. consul, Panama, 1990-94; scholar Columbia U., 1995-97. Roman Catholic. Avocations: harness racing (German champion, world record holder), golf, tennis, classic car collector. Home: 1538 N Casey Key Rd Osprey FL 34229-9770

PETRINI, BJÖRN SVEN, bacteriologist, researcher; b. Danderyd, Stockholm, Sweden, Apr. 29, 1942; s. Sven Julius and Elisabeth (Papp) P.; m. Christina Alice Svanborg, Nov. 12, 1965; children: Sara, Johan, Emma. B of Medicine, Karolinska Inst., Stockholm, 1964, MD, 1969, PhD, 1977, assoc. prof. (hon.), 1982. Cert. clin. bacteriology. Asst. physician Stockholm County Coun., 1969-79, chief physician, 1979—. Editor Scandinavian Jour. Infectious Diseases, 1995; contbr. over 150 articles to profl. jours. Avocation: gastronomy. Office: Karolinska Inst & Hosp, Dept Clin Microbiology, SE-17176 Stockholm Sweden

PETRO, JAMES MICHAEL, lawyer, politician; b. Cleve., Oct. 25, 1948; s. William John and Lila Helen (Janca) P.; m. Nancy Ellen Bero, Dec. 16, 1972; children: John Bero, Corbin Marie. BA, Denison U., 1970; JD, Case Western Res., 1973. Bar: Ohio 1973, U.S. Dist. Ct. (no. dist.) Ohio 1974, U.S. Ct. Appeals (6th cir.) 1981. Spl. asst. U.S. senator W.B. Saxbe, Cleve., 1972-73; asst. pros. atty. Franklin County, Ohio, 1973-74; asst. dir. law City of Cleve., 1974; ptnr. Petro & Troia, Cleve., 1974-84; dir. govt. affairs Standard Oil Co., Cleve., 1984-86; ptnr. Petro, Rademaker, Matty & McClelland, Cleve., 1986-93, Buckingham, Doolittle & Burroughs, Cleve., 1993-95. Mem. city coun. Rocky River, Ohio, 1977-79, dir. law, 1980; mem. Ohio Ho. of Reps., Columbus, 1981-84, 86-90; commr. Cuyahoga County, Ohio, 1991-95; Auditor of State of Ohio, 1995—. Mem. ABA, Ohio State Bar Assn., Cleve. Bar Assn. Republican. Methodist. Home: 1933 Lake Shore Dr Columbus OH 43204-4963 Office: 88 E Broad St Columbus OH 43215-3506

PETROCHILOS, ELIZABETH A., writer, publisher; b. Blytheville, Ark., Aug. 11, 1943; d. James Alfred Clark and Macie Lee Burris; m. Cleomenis Matheos Petrochilos, Oct. 26, 1961 (div. Mar. 1966); children: Matthew C., Raquel D. Grad., Fresno H.S. Cashier Family Owned Markets, Fresno, 1961-64; med. receptionist Dr. Floyd E. Lee, Lemoore, Calif., 1964-65; pub., author E.A. Prodns., Fresno, 1965—; Author: (poetry) Stone the Poet, 1964. Avocations: books, music, antiques, swimming. Home: 1155 E Bullard Ave Apt 206 Fresno CA 93710-5527

PETROGIANNIS, KONSTANTINOS, psychologist; b. Athens, June 29, 1966; s. Georgios K. and Panagiota N. (Kappa) P.; m. Triantafyllia P. Patsia. B of Edn., Joannina, Greece, 1989; MS, Glasgow, Scotland, 1991; PhD, Cardiff, Wales, 1995. Tutor U. Wales, Cardiff, 1994; rschr. U. Athens, 1996-98; tutor U. Joannina, Greece, 1996-99, U. Panteion, Athens, 1998; lectr. U. Joannina, 1999—. Mem. Brit. Psychol. Soc. (chartered psychologist), Hellenic Psychol. Assn. Avocations: basketball, computers. Office: U Joannina Psychology, 45110 Joannina Greece

PETROIANU, ANDY, surgeon, educator; b. Brăila, Romania, Sept. 2, 1952; arrived in Brazil, 1962; s. Jac and Sonia (Laurian) P.; 1 child, Larissa P.G. Petroianu. Student in philosophy, Fed. U. Minas Gerais, Belo Horizonte, Brazil, 1972-75, MD, 1976, MS in Surgery, 1981, PhD, 1985, MS in Physiology, 1983, PhD, 1997. Specialist in surgery, docent in surgery. Intern in emergency svc. João XXIII Hosp., Belo Horizonte, 1973-76; intern in cardiovasc. surgery svc. Felicio Rocho Hosp., Belo Horizonte, 1974-76; resident surgery Fed. U. Minas Gerais, Belo Horizonte, 1979, clin. instr. surgery, 1978-81, asst. prof., 1981-85, assoc. prof., 1985-94, prof., 1994—, chief rsch. group in medicine, 1987—, dir. internship in surgery, 1995—; surg. rsch. fellow SUNY, Bklyn., 1986-87; prof. surgery Fed. U. São Paulo, Brazil, 1990, U. São Paulo, Ribeirão Preto, Brazil, 1992; rschr. Nat. Coun. Rsch., 1983—; rsch. fellow, clin. instr. Health Scis. Ctr., Bklyn., 1986-87; dir. surg. group Hosp. of Clinics, 1984—; dir. assessoy in medicine Nat. Coun. Rsch. Brasilia, 1996—; presenter in field. Editor books of surgery, including: Clinical and Technics, 1984, 92, 94, 96, 97, Geriatric Surgery, 1997, Clinical and Surgical Geriatry, Surgical Anatomy, Surgical Decision Making, Surgical Deontology, 1998-99, Ethics in Medicine, Tubes and Drains, Endorcinology and Surgical Endocrinology, 2000, others; contbr. over 150 articles to profl. jours. Mem. Brazilian Assn. Medicine (sec. 1979-85), Brazilian Assn. Univ. Profs., Brazilian Coll. Surgeons (Best Rschr. in Surgery 1987). Avocations: literature, swimming, tourism, writing. Home: Apto 1901, Avenida Afonso Pena 1626, 30130005 Belo Horizonte Brazil Office: Med Sch Fed U Minas Gerais, Avenida Alfredo Balena 190, 30130100 Belo Horizonte Brazil

PETRONI, ANNA, pharmacologist, educator; b. Rome, Italy, May 15, 1953; d. Mario Petroni and Luigia (Germondari) P.; m. Paolo Grossi; children: Laura, Stefano. Degree in biol. scis., U. Milan, 1978. Fellow Inst. Pharm. Scis., Milan, 1978-80, Swedish U. Agrl. Sci., Uppsala, 1981-82; rschr. faculty pharmacy U. Milan, 1981—. Mem. Italian Soc. Pharmacology, Internat. Soc. Neuroscis. Avocations: canoeing, skiing. Office: U Milan Faculty Pharm, Via Balzaretti 9, 20133 Milan Italy

PETROPOULOS, JOHN HERCULES, research chemist, educator; b. Cairo, Egypt, July 1, 1935; parents Greek citizens; s. Hercules J. and Despina (Antoniou) P. BSc with honours, London U., 1955; PhD, Manchester (Eng.) U., 1959. Rsch. fellow Imperial Coll., London, 1959-62; group leader Democritos Nat. Rsch. Ctr., Athens, 1962-97; vis. assoc. chemist Brookhaven Nat. Lab., Upton, N.Y., 1963-64; vis. prof. Tokyo Inst. Tech., 1975, 80, N.C. State U., Raleigh, 1978, U. Wash., Seattle, 1986; alt. mem. Nat. Adv. Coun. for Rsch., Athens, 1988-90, mem., 1994-97; lectr. in field. Mem. editl. bd. Jour. Membrane Sci., 1976—; contbr. chpts. to books, articles to profl. jours. Recipient Tsouflis Chemistry award Acad. Athens, 1970. Mem. European Membrane Soc. (mem. coun. 1982-96), Assn. Greek Chemists, N.Y. Acad. Sci. Greek Orthodox. Achievements include development and application of novel approaches for elucidation of the structure of non-homogeneous membranes; description of micromolecular transport in glassy polymers or in porous solids. Home: Massalias No 3, 10680 Athens Greece Office: Democritos Nat Rsch Ctr, Aghia Paraskevi, 15310 Athens Greece

PETROPOULOS, STATHIS, advertising company executive; b. Athens, Greece, Mar. 9, 1953; s. Demetrios and Panagiota (Spala) P.; m. Manina Menidiati, Oct. 24, 1998. Degree in econs., Athens Law Sch., 1975. Media dir. Ted Bates Advt. Agy., Athens, 1985-87, Geo Y&R Advt. Agy., Athens, 1987-89, Lintas Advt. Agy., Athens, 1989-90; media and rsch. dir. Bates Hellas Advt. S.A., Athens, 1990-96, dep. gen. mgr., media and rsch. dir., 1996-98, gen. mgr., media and rsch. dir., 1998—; lectr., advisor Eurocentre, Athens, 1994—; bus. ptnr. Alko Rsch. Co., Athens, 1992—, Promotional Svcs. Co., Athens, 1997—. Contbr. articles to profl. jours. Mem. Hellenic Positions, Athens, 1996—. With Airforce, 1971-75. Mem. Esomar, Greek Inst. of Mktg., Assn. of CEOs. Office: Bates Hellas Advt SA, 11B Konitsis St, 15125 Maroussi Athens, Greece

PETROU, MARIA, researcher, educator; b. Thessaloniki, Greece, May 17, 1953; d. Costantinos and Dionisia (Voziki) P.; m. Philip Lindsay Palmer, July 4, 1981; 1 child, Costas Alexander Palmer. BSc in Physics, U. Thessaloniki, Greece, 1975; postgrad., U. Cambridge, U.K., 1977, PhD in Astronomy, 1981. Rsch. asst. U. Thessaloniki, Greece, 1975-76; lectr. U. Athens, Greece, 1981-83; rsch. asst. in theoretical physics U. Oxford, Eng., 1983-86; rsch. fellow in geography U. Reading, Eng., 1986-87; rsch. fellow Rutherford Appleton Lab., Eng., 1987-88; lectr. U. Surrey, Eng., 1988-93, sr. lectr., 1993-96; reader U. Surrey, 1996-98, prof., 1998—. Author: (with others) Advances in Electronics, 1994, Image Processing: The Fudamentals (with P. Bosdogianni, John Wiley), 1999; editor (newsletter) Internat. Assn. of Pattern Recognition, 1994-98; assoc. editor IEEE Transactions Image Processing; contbr. over 200 articles to profl. jours. Amelia Earhart fellow Zonta Internat., 1979-80, Fulford Rsch. fellow Somerville Coll., U. Oxford, 1984, Atlas Rsch. fellow Saint Hilda's Coll., U. Oxford, 1987; Rsch. grantee Alexandros Onasis Pub. Benefit Found., 1979. Fellow IEEE (chartered engr.); mem. British Machine Vision Assn. (chmn.), Internat. Assn. Pattern Recognition (chmn. tech. com. 7 for remote sensing). Avocations: walking, reading, international affairs. Office: Sch Elec Engring, U Surrey, Guildford GU2 5XH, England

PETROU, SOTIRIS A., economist; b. Agridaki, Cyprus, Apr. 9, 1961; arrived in England, 1991; s. Andreas Petrou and Eleni Andrea (Christodoulou) P.; m. Angela Kyriacou, Sept. 10, 1994. BA cum laude, SUNY, 1987; MA, U. Calif., Santa Barbara, 1988. Quantity surveyor J&P Ltd., Nicosia, Cyprus, 1981-82; land surveyor J&P Ltd., Muscat, Sultanate of Oman, 1982-83; adminstrv. mgr. The Cyprus Popular Bank Ltd., Nicosia, 1989-91; head of spl. loans unit The Cyprus Popular Bank Ltd., London, 1992-93; acting gen. mgr. Valentina Group, London, 1993-95; mgr. cost control Orantenez Clothing Co. Ltd., London, 1996—. Sgt. maj. Nat. Guard of Cyprus, 1979-81. Recipient Partial scholarship award Cyprus-Am. scholarship program, 1995. Mem. Am. Econ. Assn. Greek Orthodox. Avocations: soccer, traveling, hunting. Home: 26 Woodfield Way, London N11 2PH, England

PETROUKHIN, ANDREY SERGEEVICH, pediatric neurologist, educator; b. Moscow, Nov. 7, 1944; s. Sergey Ivanovich Petroukhin and Olga Filipovna Sidorova; Natalia Ivanovna Obreimova, Aug. 14, 1966; children: Anton, Daria. Degree, Russian State Med. U., Moscow, 1968; postgrad., Russian State Med. U., 1968-70, MD, 1972, MD, PhD, 1989. Asst. prof. dept. neurology Med. Inst., Vladivostok, Russia, 1973-75; sr. rschr. dept. pediat. neurology Russian State Med. U., Moscow, 1975-91, prof. dept. med. genetics, 1991-94, head, prof. dept. pediat. neurology, 1994—; head pediat. neurologist Russian Fedn. Ministry of Health, Moscow, 1995—. Author: Child Epileptology, 1999. Mem. Internat. Pediat. Neurology Assn., Russian Neurol. Assn. Avocation: gardening. Office: Russian State Med U, Pozharsky Pereulok 9a, 119034 Moscow Russia

PETROV, NICOLAS, dance educator, choreographer; b. Novia Sad, Serbia, Yugoslavia, Dec. 13, 1933; came to U.S., 1967; s. Sergie Nicolas and Iren Rehorovic (Roboz) P.; m. Marion Freyda Brookes, Apr. 11, 1956. Ed., Govt. Theatrical Acad., Novi Sad, 1945-51; apsolvent, Drzavne Pozorisne Skole Baletski, Otsek, 1951; ed. State Ballet Acad. of Belgrade, Yugoslavia, 1951-54, Belgrade Govt. U. Fgn. Langs., 1951-55, U. de Paris à Sorbonne, 1956-58. Dancer Nat. Popular Theatre Serbi, Belgrade, 1951-54, Ballet de France de Janine Charrat, Paris, 1954-56; prin. dancer Theatre d'Art du Ballet, Paris, 1957-59, Balletto Europeo di Nervi, Genova, Italy, 1960-62; dancer, choreographer Radio TV France, Paris, 1960-67; from asst. prof. to prof. dance Point Park Coll., Pitts., 1968-78, prof., 1978—, dir. fine, applied and performing arts dept. and dance div., 1975-87; founder, artistic dir. Ballet Russe de Nicolas Petrov, Paris, 1962-67, Pitts. Ballet Theatre, Inc., 1967-77, Am. Dance Ensemble, Pitts., 1977-87; choreographer Pitts. Opera, 1967-73, 77-89; guest dancer Leonide Massine Festival, Goteberg, Sweden, 1956-57; guest dancer and actor Theatre de Vervie Belgium, 1956-57; guest star dancer Opera Mcpl. de Marseille, Paris, 1960-62. Appeared in ballets, including Scheherazade, Swan Lake, Romeo and Juliet, Le Carnaval, Nutcracker, Legend of Ohrid, La Valse, Noir et Blanc, Beethoven's 7th Symphony, Blue Danube, Les Amadas de Tervel, Laudes Evangelii, Barber of Seville, Choriartium, many others; choreographer (operas) Aida, Pitts., 1967-68, Carmen, Pitts., 1967-68, 80-81, La Traviata, Pitts., 1977-78; (ballets) Romeo and Juliet, Pitts., 1971-72, Rite of Spring, Pitts., 1971-72, Swan Lake, Pitts., 1971-72, Beethoven's 9th Symphony, Pitts., 1972-73, Cinderella, Pitts., 1973-74, Steel Symphony, Pitts., 1975-76, Fantasia, Pitts., 1976-77, Prince of the Pagodas, Pitts., 1977-78, Nutcracker, Pitts., 1978-79, Bolero, Pitts., 1982-83, Merry Widow, Pitts., 1987-88, Coppelia, Pitts., 1991-92, numerous others; director dance films including Alice in Wonderland, 1972, Carmina Catulli, 1973-74, Romeo and Juliet, 1975; author: The Dance Method, 1967. Asst. mayoral elections, Pitts., 1968, 77; vol. Pitts. Ballet Theatre. Recipient choreography award Nat. Steel Corp., 1976. Mem. AAUP, Am. Guild Music Artists, Rotary, French Masons (N.Y.C.). Avocations: building renovations, skiing, golf, boating. Home: 39 Dilworth St Pittsburgh PA 15211-1913 Office: Point Park Coll 201 Wood St Pittsburgh PA 15222-1984

PETROV, VALERY DANILOVICH, physicist, educator; b. Moscow, Feb. 13, 1946; arrived in Hungary, 1991; arrived in Germany, 1992; s. Valentina Vasilievna (Petrova) Budaeva. Honored diploma in electronic engring., Moscow Inst. Energetics, Moscow, 1970. Jr. rschr. All-Union Rsch. Inst. Cinematography and Photography, Moscow, 1973-75, sr. rschr., 1975-77; chief sci. dept. Ctrl. Rsch. Inst. Technics and Economy in Device Contrn., Moscow, 1977-79; cons. Moscow, 1979-83; sr. engr. All-Union Rsch. Inst. of Tech. Info., Moscow, 1983-90; cons. Ulm, Germany, 1992—. With Soviet Army, 1970-71. Mem. European Optical Soc. Avocations: books, art, sports. Home: Postfach 3350, D-89023 Ulm Germany

PETROVA, JORDANKA, chemistry educator, researcher; b. Kotel, Bourgas, Bulgaria, Nov. 14, 1939; d. Peter Ivanov and Sabka (Stavreva) P.; m. Slavtscho Kunev Ivanov, Mar. 12, 1961; children: Kuni, Peter. Grad. in chemistry, U. Sofia, Bulgaria, 1963, PhD in Chemistry, 1973. Asst. U. Sofia, 1965-69, sr. asst., 1969-73, chief asst., 1973-86, asst. prof. chemistry, 1986—. Author: Manual for Analysis of Toxic Substances, 1994; contbr. over 50 articles to sci. jours., including Phosphorus, Sulfur and Silicon, Jr. Coordinating Chemistry, Synthesis; inventor synthesis of pesticides, complexes and additives. Mem. syndical Com., 1978-88. Grantee Ministry of Fgn. Affairs-France Gen. Direction of Cultural, Sci. and Tech. Rels., 1975, Trans-European Mobility Scheme for Univ. Studies, U.K., 1992. Avocations: music, books, travel. E-mail: jorpetrova@chem.uni-sofia.bg. Home: 7 Nezabrevka Str, 1113 Sofia Bulgaria Office: U Sofia St Kl Ochridski, 1 J Bourchier Ave, 1164 Sofia Bulgaria

PETROVIC, ALEXANDRE GABRIEL, physician, physiology educator, medical research director; b. Belgrade, Yugoslavia, July 10, 1925; naturalized French citizen; s. Gabriel M. and Maria S. (Miskovic) P.; m. Suzanne Durry, Feb. 25, 1956; 1 child, Nicole Gasson. MD, Strasbourg Med. Sch., 1954, DSc, 1961; postgrad., McGill U. Med. Sch., 1961-62. Assoc. staff physician, asst. prof. Northwestern U. Med. Sch., Chgo., 1965-68; prof. U. Montreal Med. Sch., 1970-71; dir. rsch. Nat. Inst. Health and Med. Rsch., Strasbourg, 1968-94; prof. human physiology U. Louis Pasteur Med. Sch., Strasbourg, 1976-90; lectr. in biomed. rsch., methodology, 1989-96, also mem. sci. coun.; vis. rsch. scientist Ctr. for Human Growth and Devel., U. Mich., Ann Arbor, 1976-78; vis. prof. La. State U. Med. Ctr., New Orleans, 1979-97; van der Klaauw prof. U. Leiden, Netherlands, 1985; prof. U. Cattolica del Sacro Cuore, Rome, Italy, 1992-96; prof. honoris causa U. Camilo Castelo Branco, São Paulo, Brazil; charge of French med. missions to USSR, 1969, Yugoslavia, 1969, 74, 76, 78, 81, Argentina, Peru, Brazil and Chile, 1974, U.S., 1977, 78, 82, Cuba, 1986. Recipient prize Vlès, Strasbourg Med. Sch., 1954, prize Laborde, Biol. Soc., 1961, E. Sheldon Friel award European Orthodontic Soc., 1976, Calvin Case award for orthodontic rsch., 1984, Disting. Sci. Craniofacial Biology Rsch. award Internat. Assn. Dental Rsch., 1994, Medalha de Merito Sociedade de Ortodoutia, Brazil, 1998. Mem. Acad. of ALSACE, Soc. Cryobiology (charter), Acad. Medicine (Belgrade, hon. mem.), Academia Ibero-Latino-Am. de Disfunction Craneomandibular (hon. mem.), Club Internat. de Morphologie Faciale, Assn. des Physiologistes, European Tissue Culture Soc., Greek Orthodontic Soc. (hon.), Italian Orthodontic Soc. (hon.), Medalla de Merite in ortodontia, others. Achievements include contbg. author various books and sci. papers on a cybernetic theory of the mechanisms of craniofacial bone growth, on cytopathogenesis of craniostenosis and on philosophy of biomed. research; discovered feasibility of orthopedically stimulating the growth of the mandible; described new ways in orthodontic decision making; pioneer research studies on treatment of otospongiosis by sodium fluoride and disphosphonates, on theory of auto-immune origin of otospongiosis; new classification of bone tumors; discovered possibility of prefecondatory hereditary male contribution by penetration of spermatozoary DNA into intraovarian ovocytes. Home: 2 rue de Rome, 67000 Strasbourg France Office: Inst Nat la Sante et la Rsch Med, 2 Rue de Rome, 67000 Strasbourg France

PETROVIC, MIRKO, geriatrician, consultant; b. Belgrade, Yugoslavia, Oct. 9, 1959; arrived in Belgium, 1992; s. Slobodan Petrovic and Latinka Perovic; m. Ivana Teodorovic, Apr. 20, 1985; children: Milica, Nikola. Grad., Med. Faculty, Belgrade, Yugoslavia, 1983, MSc, 1989. Sr. house officer Clin. Hosp. Zemun, Belgrade, 1983-84, physician, 1984-85; physician City Hosp., Belgrade, 1985-91; cons. physician City Hosp., Belgade, 1991-93; registrar Univ. Hosp., Ghent, Belgium, 1993-98, geriatrician, cons. physician, 1998—. Contbg. author: The Kidney in Pregnancy, 1990, Gastroenterology II, 1990, Gastroenterology III, 1991; contbr. numerous articles, abstracts and procs. to med. publs., including Periodicum biologorum, Archives Gastroenterohepatology, Exptl. Clin. Endocrinology, Serbian Archives Medicine, European Jour. Clin. Microbiol. Infectious Diseases, Acta Clinica Belgica, Internat. Jour. Geriatric Psychiatry, European Jour. Internal Medicine. Mem. European Dialysis and Transplantation Assn., European Renal Assn., European Fedn. Socs. Ultrasound in Medicine and Biology, N.Y. Acad. Scis. Avocations: reading, swimming. Office: Univ Hosp Dept Int Medicine, De Pintelaan 185, 9000 Ghent Belgium

PETROVSKY, VLADIMIR FYODOROVICH, United Nations administrator; b. Stalingrad, Russia, Apr. 29, 1933; s. Fyodor and Anna (Khritinina) P.; m. Myra Mukhina; 1 child. Degree, Moscow Inst. Internat. Rels. With Ministry of Fgn. Affairs, U.S.S.R., 1957—; staff mem. U.S.S.R. mission UN, 1957-61; mem. Office of Fgn. Min. Ministry Fgn. Affairs, U.S.S.R., 1961-64; mem. secr. UN, 1964-71; with dept. planning of fgn. policy Ministry of Fgn. Affairs, U.S.S.R., 1971-78, head dept. planning of fgn. policy, 1978-79; head dept. internat. orgs, 1979-86, dep. min., 1986-91, first dep. min., 1991, rep. of Russia to Coun. Cooperation of NATO, 1992; under sec. gen. UN Dept. Pol. Affairs, 1992, 93—; dir. gen. UN office Geneva, 1993—; sec.- gen. Conf. on Disarmament, pers. rep. of sec.- gen., 1994—; prof. Acad. Natural Scis. of Russian Fedn., Internat. Acad. Informational Process and Tech.; bd. dirs. Stockholm Internat. Peace Rsch. Inst., Geneva Inst. Affaires étrangères. Author: The Foreign Service of Great Britian, 1958, The Diplomacy of 10 Downing Street, 1964, US Foreign Policy Thinking: Theories and Concepts, 1976, The Doctrine of National Security in US Global Strategy, 1980, Disarmament: Concepts, Problems, Mechanisms, 1983, Security in the Era of Nuclear and Outer Space Technology, 1985. Office: UN Geneva Office, Palais des Nations, 1211 Geneva 10, Switzerland

PETRUCCIANI, MARIO, Italian literature educator; b. Caserta, Italy, Feb. 23, 1924. Prof. history of modern Italian lit. U. Rome La Sapienza; pres. Istituto Nazionale di Studi Romani. Office: Istituto Naz di Studi Rom, Piazza Cavalieri Malta 2, 00153 Rome Italy

PETRUKHIN, ANATOLY AFANASIYEVICH, physics educator; b. Moscow, May 22, 1935; s. Afanasiy Antonovich and Elizaveta Pavlovna Gruzdeva P.; m. Adelina Ivanovna Rubtsova, Dec. 22, 1977; children: Kristina, Angelina. Diploma Engring. Physics, MEPhI, Moscow, 1959, Candidate Physics, Math., Sci., 1966, D Physics, Math., Sci., 1975. Engr. MEPhI, 1959-61, postgrad., 1961-64, sr. engr., 1964-67, lectr., 1967-76, prof., 1976—; head of exptl. complex NEVOD, 1990—. Author: (textbooks) Cross Sections for Electromagnetic Processes of Charged Particle Interaction, 1987, Parity Non-Conversation in Weak Interaction, 1991; editor: (in Russian) Background Light in the Ocean, 1990; contbr. articles to profl. jours. and publs. Scientific sec.-in-chief Coun. of Rectors of Univs., Moscow, 1972-92. Recipient Badge of Honour, Supreme Soviet of USSR, 1981, The Order of People's Friendship, 1986, Pres. Prize in Edn., Pres. of Russia, 1998. Mem. Sci. Coun. on Cosmic Rays/Russian Acad. Sci., Sci. Coun. on Neutrino Physics/Russian Acad. Sci. Avocations: mountaineering, skiing, travels. Office: Moscow Engring Physics Inst, Kashirskoye Shosse 31, 115409 Moscow Russia

PETRUNOV, BOGDAN NIKOLOV, medical educator, allergologist; b. Sofia, Bulgaria, Sept. 1, 1936; s. Nikola Georgiev and Ljuba Dimitrova (Jordanova) P.; m. Svetla Stephanova Slavova, Apr. 2, 1961; 1 child, Ljuba Bogdanova. MD, Higher Med. Sch., Sofia, 1960, PhD, 1968; DSc, Med. Acad., Sofia, 1978. Cert. med. doctor, 1960, specialist in immunology, 1967, specialist in clin. allergology, 1970. Gen. practitioner Rural Med. Ctr., Sevlievo, Bulgaria, 1961-62, County Hosp., Sevlievo, 1962-63; rsch. fellow Nat. Ctr. Infectious Diseases, Sofia, 1963-72, head Lab. Allergy, 1972—, vice-dir., 1985-93, dir., 1993—; assoc. prof. medicine Higher Med. Sch., Sofia, 1972-85, prof. medicine, 1985—; mem. specialized counsel of immunology Nat. Accreditation Commn., Sofia, 1985—; mem. Nat. Adv. Com. of Fogarty Found., 1990—; mem. sci. counsel Insts. Immunology and Microbiology, Bulgarian Acad. Scis., Sofia, 1991—; mem. High Med. Counsel of Bulgaria, Sofia, 1992—. Author: Allergens, 1970; editor-in-chief Problems of Infectious and Parasitic Diseases, 1980—, Infectology, 1989—; patentee in field. Named Hon. mem. Cuban Soc. Allergology, Havana, 1986. Mem. Bulgarian Soc. Allergology, Union Scientists in Bulgaria. Avocations: swimming, jogging, music, literature. Home: 30 Buzludja St, 1606 Sofia Bulgaria Office: Nat Ctr Infectious Diseases, 26 Yanko Sakazov Blvd, 1504 Sofia Bulgaria

PETRUSEVICH, YURIY MIHAILOVICH, biophysicist, researcher; b. St. Petersburg, Russia, Apr. 5, 1935; s. Mihail Nikolaevich Petrusevich and Ludmila Ivanovna Kazik; m. Tatyana Vasilyevna Bondarenko, Mar. 25, 1968; 1 child, Vladislav. Student, Moscow State U., 1952-58, BS, 1965, DSc, 1990; postgrad., Inst. Phys. Problems, Moscow, 1958-61. Engr. Inst. Phys. Problems, Moscow, 1958-63; sr. tchr. biol. faculty Moscow State U., 1963-65, asst. prof., 1965-82, asst. prof. phys. faculty, 1982-90, sci. dir., 1990—; lectr. Blokhin Cancer Ctr., Moscow, 1997—. Author: Biophysics, 1968, Ultraweak Hemiluminescence of Biological Systems, 1967, Spectral & Correlative Methods of Molecular Physics and Biophysics, 1997; patentee in field. Mem. Univ. Trade Union (chmn. 1965-70), Phys. Soc. Russia. Avocations: jazz, radioelectronics. Home: Apt 69 Bldg 3, 51 Sevasopolsky Prospect St, 113209 Moscow Russia Office: Moscow State U Phys Fac, Vorobyevy Gory, 119899 Moscow Russia

PETRUSHKINA, ELENA ALEXEEVNA, chemist, researcher, educator; b. Moscow, June 16, 1955; d. Alexei Stepanovich and Zoja Jakovlevna (Kolesnikova) P. Masters degree, M.V. Lomonsov Acad., Moscow, 1978; PhD, Russian Acad. Scis., Moscow, 1992. Rsch. fellow A.N. Nesmeyanov Inst. Organo-Element Compounds Russian Acad. Scis., 1978-88, rschr., 1988-93, sr. scientist, 1993—; vis. prof. Kyungpook U., Taegie, Republic of Korea, 1997-98. Contbr. articles to sci. jours.; patentee in field. Internat. Sci. Found. grantee, 1993, travel grantee, 1993, 96. Mem. NAS. Russian Orthodox. Home: 13A, 15, Prospekt 50th October, 142080 Moscow Klimovsk, Russia Office: AN Nesmeyanov INEOS RAS, Vavilov Str 28, 117813 Moscow Russia

PETRUSHOVA-MARTINOVA, OLGA VIKTOROVNA, chemist, educator; b. Ushgorod, Ukraine, Sept. 19, 1958; came to U.S., 1995.; d. Viktor Michaylovich and Valentina Andreevna (Gerasimova) P.; m. Oleg Sergeevich Martinov, Feb. 11, 1993; children: Martinova, Anastasiya. BS, Uzhgorod, Ukraine, 1978, MS, 1980; PhD, Uzhgorod, 1994. Lab. tch. Uzhgorod State U., Ukraine, 1975-79; engr. Uzhgorod State U., 1982-85, jr. rschr., 1985-89, scientific rschr., 1989-93, sr. scientific rschr., 1993-95; leader lab. semi-conductors Inst. Physics and Chemistry, Uzhgorod, 1993-95; chemist Touro Coll., Brooklyn, 1995—. Author: (book) Chemistry of Semiconductors, 1995; Editor: The Soviet Young Scientists, Uzhgorod State U.; contbr. articles to profl. and sci. jours. Mem. N.Y. Acad. Sci., Am. Assn. Advancement of Sci., Assn. Engrs. and Scientists for New Americans. Avocations: tennis, mountaineering, fencing. E-mail: o martinoff@hotmail.com. Home: 1934 Bath Ave Brooklyn NY 11214-4704

PETRY, WINFRIED JAKOB, physics educator; b. Trier, Germany, June 3, 1951; s. Matthias and Margarette Maria (Monz) P.; m. Josephina Maria Claes; children: Jens, Sarah. Diploma in Physics, Tech. U. Munich, 1976; PhD, Free U., Berlin, 1981; habilitation, Ludwig Maximilians U., Munich, 1992. Scientist Tech. U. Munich, 1976-77, prof., 1992—, dean faculty of Physics, 1996-98, chmn. bd. FRM II, 1999—; scientist Hahn Meitner Inst.,

Berlin, 1977-82; scientific staff mem. Inst. Lane Langevin, Grenoble, France, 1983-92; senator Tech. U. Munich, 1996-98. Editor: Dynamics of Disordered Materials, 1989. Mem. German Mus., German Physics Assn. Avocation: skiing. Office: Technische U München Physics Dept E13, James Franck Str, 85748 Garching Germany

PETRZILKA, HENRY See FILIP, HENRY

PETRZILKA, VACLAV, physicist, journal editor; b. Prague, Czech Republic, Sept. 6, 1941; s. Vaclav and Marie (Volcova) P.; m. Jolanta Lyskova, Apr. 11, 1967; 1 child, Jan. MS, Charles U., Prague, 1964, DSc, 1985; PhD, Czech Acad. Sci., Prague, 1967. Scientist Inst. Plasma Physics, Prague, 1964—. Chief editor Czech Jour. Physics, 1992-97; contbr. over 100 articles to profl. jours. Recipient grants for rsch. Avocations: literature, philosophy. Office: Inst Plasma Physics, Za Slovankou 3 PO Box 17, 18200 Prague 8, Czech Republic

PETSIAVAS, DEMETRE N., industrial company executive; b. Athens, Jan. 17, 1926; s. Nicolas D. and Pelagia (Sfetsos) P.; m. Anna Theodoridou, June 21, 1951; children: Christine, Margaret. BS Engring., Columbia U., 1950, MS Chem. Engring., 1951. Rsch. bio-chem. engring. Merck, Sharp & Domme, Rahway, N.J., 1951-58; sales mgr. Jeannoutsikos Petsiavas S.A., Athens, 1958-61; sales mgr. N. Petsiavas S.A., Athens, 1961-77, pres., 1977—; pres. Polykem S.A., Athens, 1990-98, Thermac S.A., Salonica, 1990—, Domikem S.A., Athens, 1991—. Mem. Am. Hellenic C. of C. (pres. 1974-98). Greek Orthodox. Office: N Petsiavas SA, 21 Ag Anargyron St, K Kifissia 14564, Greece

PETTEE, DANIEL STARR, retired neurologist; b. N.Y.C., Feb. 15, 1925; s. Allen Danforth and Helen Marien (Starr) P.; m. Dimetra Marie Peters, June 24, 1961; children: William, Margaret, Allen. BA, Yale U., 1951; MD, Columbia U., 1955. Diplomate Am. Bd. Psychiatry and Neurology, 1965, Am. Bd. Clin. Neurophysiology, 1984. Rotating internship Strong Meml. Hosp. U. Rochester, N.Y., 1955-57, residency neurology, 1957-62; neurologist pvt. practice, Rochester, N.Y., 1962-96; clinic dir. Rochester (N.Y.) Area Multiple Sclerosis Chpt., Rochester, N.Y., 1962-76; assoc. clin. prof. neurology U. Rochester (N.Y.) Sch. Medicine, 1978-96, emeritus assoc. clin. prof., 1996-97, emeritus clin. prof. neurology, 1997—; clin. assoc. dept. neurology Strong Meml. Hosp., Rochester, 1978-96; head neurology div. dept. medicine The Genesee Hosp., Rochester, 1972-96; pres. Genesee Neurol. Assocs., Rochester, 1974-96; mem. bd. dirs. Rochester (N.Y.) Area Multiple Sclerosis Chpt., 1970-76. Contbr. articles to profl. jours. Mem. and singer Oratorio Soc., 1955-78; bd. dirs., 1960-61, Rochester, N.Y. Recipient Purple Heart, Bronze Star U.S. Army, 1944, Bronze Hope Chest for Svc. award Rochester (N.Y.) Area Multiple Sclerosis Chpt., 1976. Mem. N.Y. Acad. Sci., Rochester Acad. Sci. (astronomy sect. 1989-98, bd. dirs. astronomy sect. 1993-94). Home: 1141 S Gaylord St Denver CO 80210-1826

PETTERSEN, JAN SOMMERFELT, physician; b. Oslo, Norway, Apr. 12, 1958; s. Thorleif and Lulli Sommerfelt (Knudtzon) P.; m. Sigrund Grindheim, Nov. 2, 1985; children: Hella, Oda, Nina. MD, U. Bergen, 1984. Surgeon comdr., chief med. instr. Royal Norwegian Navy, Bergen, 1993—; gen. practitioner Bergen Med. Ctr., 1988—; cmty. medicine instr. U. Bergen, 1990—. Editor (newsletter) Documentum Navale, 1995—, Ideer om Frihet, 1984-92, Stetoscopet, 1993-97. Mem. Norwegian Assn. Maritime Medicine (pres. 1997—). Avocations: medical history, naval history, genealogy. Home: PO Box 1134 Sentrum, N-5809 Bergen Norway Office: Naval Tng Establishment, PO Box 5 Haakonsvern, N-5886 Bergen Norway

PETTERSEN, THOMAS MORGAN, accountant, finance executive; b. Poughkeepsie, N.Y., Nov. 9, 1950; s. Olsen Thomas and Reva Frances (Palmer) P. BS, U. Albany, 1973. CPA, N.Y. Sr. acct. Arthur Andersen and Co., N.Y.C., 1973-76; sr. ops. auditor Gulf and Western Inc., N.Y.C., 1977, fin. analyst, 1978; adminstr. auditing NBC, N.Y.C., 1979; mgr. auditing NBC, Burbank, Calif., 1980, dir. auditing, 1981-88, dir. acctg. systems and ops. analysis, 1988-90; v.p. fin. and adminstrn. Data Dimensions, Inc., Culver City, Calif., 1991-92; cons. Westwood One, Inc., Culver City, 1992-93; CFO Computer Image Sys., Inc., Torrance, Calif., 1993-97; dir. corp. fin. DeCrane Aircraft Holdings, Inc., El Segundo, Calif., 1997—. Mem. AICPA, Fin. Execs. Inst. Republican. Roman Catholic. Avocations: sports, travel. Home: 217 1st Pl Manhattan Beach CA 90266-6503 Office: DeCrane Aircraft Holdings Inc 2361 Rosecrans Ave El Segundo CA 90245-4916

PETTERSEN, TOR ARVE, graphic designer; b. Trondheim, Norway, Jan. 24, 1940; arrived in England, 1962; s. Odd and Cally Agathe (Andersen) P.; m. Joan Lilian Rooke, Oct. 5, 1968; children: Nicholas Tor, Joanna. Diploma in design, London Coll. Printing, 1965. Trainee artist Ekko Reklamebyra, Trondheim, Norway, 1956-59; art dir. asst. Alfsen & Becker A.S., Oslo, 1961-62; designer Caps Design, Ltd., London, 1965-66; designer, prin. Lock Pettersen Ltd., London, 1966-88; prin. Tor Pettersen & Ptnr. Ltd., London, 1988—. Home: 20 Castle Rd, Weybridge England Office: Tor Pettersen and Ptnrs Ltd, 56 Greek St, London W1V 5LR, England

PETTERSON, MARGO, artist; b. L.A., Jan. 12, 1944; d. Edmund and Helen Smolinski; m. Richard M. Petterson, Apr. 14, 1962; 1 child, Sandra. AA, San Bernadino Valley Coll., 1981; student, Cuesta Coll., 1982-83. Asst. libr. San Bernadino County, Big Bear Lake, Calif., 1975-81; med. records clk. San Luis Obispo (CAlif.) Gen. Hosp., 1981-83; adminstrv. asst. Donez Real Estate, Big Bear Lake, 1984-90; owner Petterson's Bear Valley Saw Shop, Big Bear Lake, 1983—; artist Margo Petterson/The Feminine West, Big Bear Lake, 1986—; instr. Beverly Hills (Calif.) Art Guild, 1997-98, Orange (Calif.) Art Guild, 1998, Corona (Calif.) Art League, 1999, Huntington Beach (Calif.) Art Guild, 1999. Pub. limited edit. lithographs, 1990—; contbr. painting to Art of American West, 1998. Sec. City Spirit, Big Bear Lake, 1977; pres. Big Bear Lake Art Assn., 1977-78, treas., 1979-80, 84-86; fundraiser United We Stand Am., Big Bear Lake, 1992; bd. dirs. Friends of the Libr., Big Bear Lake. Recipient 3d Pl. award George Phippen Meml., 1989, Best of Show, 1st Pl. Big Bear Lake Art Assn., 1992, Excellence in Artisty Ed and Maxine Runci Meml. award, 1993, Best of Show award Snake River Showcase, 1995. Mem. Calif. Art Club, Women Artists of the West, Oil Painters of Am., Soroptimist Internat. Avocations: reading, camping, cooking.

PETTERSSON, ANDERS, Swedish literature educator; b. Karlshamn, Blekinge, Sweden, Jan. 21, 1946; s. Axel and Gulli (Abrahamsson) P.; m. Kristina Wallander, July 25, 1974; children: Mats Petter, Kerstin. BA, Lund (Sweden) U., 1967, MA, 1968, PhD, 1975. Univ. tchg. qualification. Sr. lectr. U. Bergen, Norway, 1975-81; lectr. Umeå U., Sweden, 1982-95, prof., 1995—. Author: Realism as a Terminological Problem (in Swedish), 1975, The Concept of a Literary Work (in Swedish), 1981, A Theory of Literary Discourse, 1990. Home: Borgvägen 27 E, 904 20 Umeå Sweden Office: Umeå U, 901 87 Umeå Sweden

PETTERSSON, CHRISTINA, lawyer; b. Stockholm, July 18, 1966; d. Stig Lennart and Marie-Louise (Côte) P. LLM, Stockholm U., 1991. Law clk. County Adminstrv. Ct., Blekinge, Sweden, 1991-93; reporting clk. Adminstrv. Ct. of Appeal, Jönköping, 1993-94; asst. judge County Adminstrv. Ct., Örebro, Sweden, 1994-95; reporting clk. Ct. Appeal, Stockholm, 1995; assoc. judge Adminstrv. Ct. Appeal, Jönköping, 1995-96; assoc. Delphi Law Firm, Stockholm, 1996-99; mem. Swedish Bar Assn., 1998-99; sr. mgr. KPMG Legal, Stockholm, 2000—. Avocations: squash, skiing. Office: KPMG Legal, PO Box 16106, SE-10323 Stockholm Sweden

PETTERSSON, GÖRAN, aeronautical engineer; b. Södertälje, Sweden, June 28, 1966; s. Lars-Ola and Inga-Lill (Berg) P. MSc, Royal Inst. Technology, Stockholm, 1992; postgrad., Internat. Space U., 1995. Flight test engr. trainee Fokker Aircraft BV, Schiphol, The Netherlands, 1993-94; test engr. Saab AB, Linköping, Sweden, 1995—. patentee in field. Mem. Royal Swedish Automobile Club. E-mail: goran.pettersson@saab.se. Office: Baldersvagen 3, 151 60 Sodertalje Sweden

PETTERSSON, GOSTA BENGT, thoracic surgeon; b. Uddevalla, Sweden, June 23, 1944; came to the U.S., 1999; s. Frank Henry Algot and Maerta Sofia (Martinsson) P.; m. Ingegaerd Junie Bolmstrand, Aug. 7, 1971; children: Malin, Pontus, Lisa. MD, U. Gothenburg, Sweden, 1971; PhD, U. Gothenburg, 1979. Cert. specialist gen. surgery, thoracic surgery, Sweden, Denmark. Intern U. Gothenburg Affiliated Hosp., County Hosp., 1969-72, resident in gen. surgery, 1972-76; resident in thoracic surgery Sahlgrenska Hosp., U. Gothenberg, 1977-81, cons. surgeon dept. thoracic cardiovasc. surgery, 1981-90; prof., chief surgeon dept. cardiothoracic surgery Rigshospitalet, Copenhagen U. Hosp., 1990-98; staff surgeon dept. cardiothoracic surgery Cleve. Clinic Found., 1999—; guest prof. dept. thoracic surgery Huddings (Sweden) Hosp., 1996, Fourth Mil. Med. U. Second Affiliated Hosp., Xian, China, 1996, Albany (N.Y.) Med. Ctr., 1996, Med. Direction Ctr. Cardiovasc. Diseases, Open Heart Found., Bucharest, Romania, 1997. Co-author: (chpt.) Kirurgi, 1983, 1986, Medicinsk Kompendium 14, 1994, Kirurgisk Kompendium 2, 1996, Trauma Care-An Update, 1996, Textbook of Thoracic and Vascular Surgery, 1996, Lung Transplantation, 1996; mem. editl. bd. European Jour. Cardiothoracic Surgery, 1993—, Cardiovasc. Engring., 1996—, Scandinavian Cardiovasc. Jour., 1996—; contbr. over 90 articles to profl. jours. U. Ill. fellow, 1979-80; recipient Generalkonsul Ernst Carlsens Fond's prize, 1992, Hon. Gift William Nielsen Fond, 1993, Winterthur Legate, 1993, Heart Friend of Yr., Danish Heart Patients Assn. Chilern's Club, 1993, Simonsen Weel prize, 1994, Richard Faltin medal Finland, 1994. Fellow European Bd. of Cardiothoracic Surgery; mem. Finnish Surg. Soc. (hon.), Lithuanian Soc. Cardiothoracic Surgery (hon.), Romanian Sci. Acad. (hon.), Romanian Med. Acad. (hon.), European Assn. Cardiothoracic Surgery, Am. Assn. Thoracic Surgery, Warren H. Cole Soc., Scandinavian Assn. Thoracic Surgery, Danish Soc. Surgery, Danish Soc. Thoracic Surgery, Danish Soc. Cardiology, Danish Soc. Lung Medicine, Danish Soc. Transplantation, Danish Soc. Thrombosis Hemostasis, Internat. Soc. Heart Lung Transplantation, Internat. Soc. Cardiothoracic Surgeons, Ross Soc., Pete's Club, European Congenital Heart Surgeons Club. Avocations: hunting, sailing, skiing. Fax: 216-445-3294. Office: Cleve Clinic Found Thoracic and Cardiovasc Sur 9500 Euclid Ave # Deskf25 Cleveland OH 44195-0001

PETTERSSON, HOLGER TAGE ARTHUR, radiologist, educator; b. Uddevalla, Sweden, Apr. 2, 1942; s. Carl Arthur and Karin Alfrida Ingeborg (Berndtsson) P.; m. Grethe Abelsen, Nov. 1, 1968; children: Christina, Anders. MD, U. Lund, Sweden, 1970, PhD, 1976. Resident dept. radiology Univ. Hosp., Malmo, Sweden, 1972-76, asst. prof., 1976-80, 81-82; clin. asst. dept. radiology Hosp. for Sick Children, Toronto, Ont., Can., 1980-81; assoc. prof. dept. radiology Univ. Hosp., Lund, 1982-89, prof. radiology, 1989—, chmn. dept. radiology, 1986-92, dep. med. dir., 1989-95; chief county radiologist County Malmöhus, 1995-98; regional chief physician Region of Scania, 1998—; vis. prof. radiology U. Fla., Gainesville, 1984-85; dir. WHO Collaborating Ctr. for Radiol. Edn., Lund, 1993—; sci. and ednl. dir. Nicer Inst., Lund and Oslo, 1990—. Author, editor: A Global Textbook of Radiology, 1995 (English, Spanish, Russian and Chinese edits.), The Encyclopaedia of Medical Imaging, 12 other books in field; contbr. over 200 articles to sci. jours. Capt. Swedish Army, 1962-87. Recipient Jacques Lefevbre Meml. award European Assn. Pediatric Radiology, 1978, Prix Internationale, World Fedn. Haemophilia, 1986, Ture Sjogren award Swedish Med. Soc., 1990, Aggarwal award Indian Radiol. and Imaging Assn., 1994. Fellow Am. Coll. Radiology (hon.); mem. Internat. Soc. Radiology (Antoine Beclère medal 1998), European Soc. Skeletal Radiology (pres. 1993-95), Internat. Skeletal Soc. (pres. 1996-98), Scandinavian Soc. Radiology (gen. sec.), European Assn. Radiology (bd. dirs. 1993-97), Russian Soc. Radiology (hon.), European Congress of Radiology (v.p. 1997—), Internat. Commn. on Radiologic Edn. (chmn. 1998—). Office: Univ Hosp, Dept Radiology, S-22185 Lund Sweden

PETTERSSON, OLLE, agricultural researcher; b. Halmstad, Sweden, Oct. 23, 1942; s. Sven and Valborg (Jönsson) P.; m. Gullevi Engqvist, July 12, 1969; children: Magnus, Maria, Mattias. Degree in agronomy, Swedish U. Agrl. Scis., Sweden, 1970, PhD, 1976. Extension specialist Swedish U. Agrl. Scis., Uppsala, 1977-81, 87—, advisor univ. bd., 1985-87; first sec. govts. com. Sweden, 1982-85. Contbr. chpts. to agrl. textbooks. Mem. Enköping City Parliament, 1974-2000, spkr., 1994-98, mem. city govt., 1988-94. Mem. AAAS, Soc. for Environ. Geochemistry and Health, Royal Swedish Acad. of Agr. and Forestry, 1995—. Social Democrat. Avocations: reading, polit. writing, carpentry. Home: Bergsvagen 29, S-74082 Orsundsbro Sweden Office: Swedish U Agrl Scis, Box 7058, S-75007 Uppsala Sweden

PETTIGREW, ANTONIO, Olympic athlete; b. Macon, Ga., Dec. 3, 1967. Winner Gold Medal World Championship, 1997, placed 2nd nats., 1998, placed 5th 400 meter final World Championships, 1999; co-winner Gold Medal 4X400 relay Sydney, 2000. Office: USA Track and Field Team One RCA Dome Ste 140 Indianapolis IN 46225*

PETTIGREW, PIERRE S., politician, member of parliament; b. Quebec City, Can., Apr. 18, 1951. BA in Philosophy, U. Que., Trois-Rivères, 1972; M in Philosophy in Internat. Rels., Balliol Coll., Oxford, 1976. Dir. polit. com. NATO Assembly, Brussels, 1976-78; exec. asst. to the leader Que. Liberal Party, 1978-81; fgn. policy advisor Prime Min. Can., 1981-84; v.p. Samson Bélair Deloitte & Touche Internat., Montreal, 1985-95; co-chair First Nat. Reform on Can. Internat. Rels., 1994; M.P. for Papineau-St. Denis, 1996—; min. human resources devel. Can. House of Commons, 1996-99; min. for internat. trade Can. Ho. of Commons, 1999—. Author: The New Politics Confidence, 1999; contbr. articles to profl. jours. Office: House of Commons, Min for Internat Trade, Ottawa, ON Canada K1A 0A6 Office: 515 S Ho of Commons, Rm 359 West Block, Ottawa, ON Canada K1A 0A6

PETTIGREW, THOMAS FRASER, social psychologist, educator; b. Richmond, Va., Mar. 14, 1931; s. Joseph Crane and Janet (Gibb) P.; m. Ann Hallman, Feb. 25, 1956; 1 son, Mark Fraser. AB in Psychology, U. Va., 1952; MA in Social Psychology, Harvard U., 1955, PhD, 1956; DHL (hon.), Governor's State U., 1979. Rsch. assoc. Inst. Social Rsch., U. Natal, Republic South Africa, 1956; asst. prof. psychology U. N.C., 1956-57; asst. prof. social psychology Harvard U., Cambridge, Mass., 1957-62, lectr., 1962-64, assoc. prof., 1964-68, prof., 1968-74, prof. social psychology and sociology, 1974-80; prof. social psychology U. Calif., Santa Cruz, 1980-94, rsch. prof. social psychology, 1994—; prof. social psychology U. Amsterdam, 1986-91; adj. fellow Joint Ctr. Polit. and Econ. Studies, Washington, 1982—; mem. adv. bd. women's studies program Princeton (N.J.) U., 1985—; vis. prof. Westfaelishe Wilhelms-U., Germany, 1993, Philipps U., Germany, 2000; disting. vis. prof. Flinders U., Australia, 1997. Author: (with E.Q. Campbell) Christians in Racial Crisis: A Study of the Little Rock Ministry, 1959, A Profile of the Negro American, 1964, Racially Separate or Together?, 1971, (with Fredericksen, Knobol, Glazer and Veda) Prejudice, 1982, (with Alston) Tom Bradley's Campaigns for Governor: The Dilemma of Race and Political Strategies, 1988, How to Think Like a Social Scientist, 1996; editor: Racial Discrimination in the United States, 1975, The Sociology of Race Relations: Reflection and Reform, 1980; (with C. Stephan & W. Stephan) The Future of Social Psychology: Defining the Relationship Between Sociology and Psychology, 1991; mem. editorial bd. Jour. Social Issues, 1959-64, Social Psychology Quarterly, 1977-80; assoc. editor Am. Sociol. Rev, 1963-65; adv. bd. Integrated Edn, 1963-84, Phylon, 1965-93, Edn. and Urban Society, 1968-90, Race, 1972-74, Ethnic and Racial Studies, 1978-95, Rev. of Personality and Social Psychology, 1980-85, Community and Applied Social Psychology, 1989—, Individual and Politics, 1989-93, Jour. Ethnic and Migration Studies, 1994—, 21st Century Afro Rev., 1994—; contbr. articles to profl. jours. Chmn. Episcopal presiding Bishop's Adv. Com. on Race Relations, 1961-63; v.p. Episcopal Soc. Cultural and Racial Unity, 1962-63; mem. Mass. Gov.'s Adv. Com. on Civil Rights, 1962-64; social sci. cons. U.S. Commn. Civil Rights, 1966-71; mem. White House Task Force on Edn., 1967; mem. nat. task force on desegregation policies Edn. Commn. of States, 1977-79; trustee Ella Lyman Cabot Trust, Boston, 1977-79; mem. Emerson Book Award com. United Chpts. Phi Beta Kappa, 1971-73. Guggenheim fellow, 1967-68, NATO sr. scientist fellow, 1974, fellow Center Advanced Study in Behavioral Scis., 1975-76, Sydney Spivack fellow in intergroup relations Am. Sociol. Assn., 1978, Netherlands Inst. Advanced Study fellow, 1984-85, NRC fellow, 1985-88; recipient Kurt Lewin Meml. award Soc. for Psychological Study of Social Issues, 1987, (with Martin) Gordon Allport Intergroup Rels. Rsch. prize, 1988, Faculty Rsch. award U. Calif., Santa Cruz, 1988; Bellagio (Italy) Study Ctr. resident fellow, Rockefeller Found., 1991. Fellow APA, Am. Sociol. Assn. (council 1979-82); mem. Soc. Psychol. Study Social Issues (council 1962-66, pres. 1967-68, Disting. Svc. award 1998), European Assn. Social Psychology. Home: 524 Van Ness Ave Santa Cruz CA 95060-3556

PETTINARO, GIOVANNI COSIMO, robotics and artificial intelligence researcher; b. Corigliano Calabro, Italy, Sept. 27, 1966; arrived in Sweden, 1997; s. Francesco and Elvira (Sammarro) P. Laurea, U. Milan, 1989; MSc, U. Edinburgh, Scotland, 1992; PhD, U. Edinburgh, 1996. Cons. ABB Robotics, Västerås, Sweden, 1997; rschr. ABB Corp. Rsch., Västerås, 1997—. Served with Italian mil., 1990-91. Mem. IEEE, Assn. Computing Machinery, Tex User Group, N.Y. Acad. Scis. Avocations: collecting coins and bank notes, music. Office: ABB Corp Rsch Dept Sys Engr, Gideonsbergsgatan 2, S-721 78 Vösterås Sweden

PETTIS, FRANCIS JOSEPH, JR., electrical engineer; b. Portland, Maine, Oct. 2, 1930; s. Francis Joseph and Mida (Pedersen) P. BSEE, U. Maine, 1960. Electronic technician CAA, Burlington, Vt., 1957, CAA/FAA, New Bedford, Mass., 1958-59; electronic engr. FAA, Portland, 1960-65, Boston, 1965-68, N.Y.C., 1968-69; electronic technician FAA, Bangor, Maine, 1969-79; gen. engr. FAA, Washington, 1979-94, program mgr., 1994-97, gen. engr., 1997—. Cpl. U.S. Army, 1953-54. Mem. IEEE, AAAS, AIAA. Achievements include numerous contributions to the development and improvement of the National Airspace System (NAS). Office: FAA 800 Independence Ave SW Washington DC 20591-0001

PETTIT, JOHN DOUGLAS, JR., management educator; b. Alice, Tex., Aug. 19, 1940; s. John Douglas and Vivian Iola (Beaman) P.; m. Suzanne McLeod, Aug. 23, 1964; children: Melanie Ann Wilson, David Bryant. BBA, U. North Tex., 1962, MBA, 1964; PhD, La. State U., 1969. Instr. mgmt. Miss. State U., Starkville, 1964-65; grad. asst. La. State U., Baton Rouge, 1965-67, instr. mgmt., 1967-68; asst. prof. bus. Tex. Tech. U., Lubbock, 1968-69; assoc. prof. mgmt. U. North Tex., Denton, 1969-78, prof. mgmt., 1978-95; chair excellence in free enterprise Austin Peay State Univ., Clarksville, Tenn., 1995-96; cons. various orgns., 1969-98; mgr., co-owner Pettit's Cleaners/Hatters, Alice, 1992-96; vis. prof. mgmt. Wichita State U., Kans., 1994-95. Co-author: Business Communication: Theory and Application, 7th edit. 1993, Report Writing for Business, 10th edit. 1998, Lesikar's Basic Business Communication, 8th edit. 1999; mem. editl. bd. Organl. Comm. Abstracts, 1980-85; mem. editl. bd. Jour. Bus. Comm., 1987-90, mng. editor, 1990-94. Mem. choir St. Andrew Pres. Ch., Denton, 1985—, diaconate bd. mem., 1988-91; actor, singer Denton Cmty. Theater Summer Prodn., 1988-95. Recipient Master's Degree award Chgo. Bd. Trade, 1963. Fellow Assn. Bus. Comm. (pres., 1st v.p., exec. dir., 1990-94); mem. Southwestern Fedn. Adminstrv. Disciplines (pres., v.p.), Acad. Mgmt., Denton Country Club (bd. dirs.), Blue Key Nat. Hon. Fraternity, Beta Gamma Sigma (hon.), Phi Kappa Phi (hon.), Delta Sigma Pi. Presbyterian. Avocations: music, tennis. Home: 9122 David Fort Rd Argyle TX 76226-2953

PETTIT, PHILIP NOEL, philosopher, educator; b. Ballinasloe, Ireland, Dec. 20, 1945; arrived in Australia, 1983; s. Michael Antony and Bridget Christina (Molony) P.; m. Eileen Theresa McNally, July 1, 1978; children: Rory Conor, Owen Patrick. BA with honors, Nat. Univ. Ireland, Dublin, 1966, MA with honors, 1967, DLitt (h.c.), 2000; PhD, Queen's U., Belfast, Ireland, 1970. Lectr. Queen's U., 1967-68, University Coll., Dublin, 1968-72, Univ. Coll., Dublin, 1975-77; research fellow U. Cambridge, Eng., 1972-75; prof. philosophy U. Bradford, Eng., 1977-83; professorial fellow. Inst. Advanced Studies Australian Nat. U., Canberra, 1983-88, prof., 1989—; vis. prof. Columbia U., N.Y., 1997—. Author: The Concept of Structuralism, 1977, Judging Justice, 1980, The Common Mind, 1993, Republicanism, 1997; co-author: Semantics and Social Science, 1981, Not Just Deserts, 1990. Fellow Acad. Social Scis. Australia., Australian Acad. of Humanities. Office: Australian Nat U, Rsch Sch Soc Scis PO Box 4, Canberra 0200, Australia

PETTMAN, BARRIE OWEN, international institute executive; b. Hessle, Eng., Feb. 22, 1944; m. Norma Edwards, Apr. 10, 1987 (dec. 1991); m. Maureen Crowther, 1992. BSc, Hull Tech. Coll., 1966; MSc, PhD, City U., London, 1970; DLitt, Internat. Mgmt. Centres, 1991. Asst. lectr., lectr. U. Hull, Eng., 1970-82; dir. manpower unit U. Rhodesia, 1978-79; registrar Internat. Mgmt. Ctr. from Buckingham, 1983—; mng. dir. Emmasglen Ltd., 1970—; dir. MDB Unv. Press Ltd., 1974—; ptnr. Barmarick Publs., 1980—; vis. prof. Can. Sch. mgmt., 1983—; hon. v.p. Br. Soc. Commerce, 1975—; chmn. Inst. of Sci. Bus., 1972-79, Ints. of Tng. and Deve., Humberside Br., 1990—. Editor: Internat. Jour. Social Econs. 1973-79, Internat. Jour. of Manpower, 1980-84, Mgmt. Rsch. News, 1981—, Equal Opportunities Internat. 1981—, Internat. Jour. Sociology and Social Policy, 1984—, Internat. Jour. of New Ideas, 1992—, others; author: Training and Retraining, 1973, Labour Turnover and Retention, 1975, Equal Pay, 1975, Manpower Planning Workbook, 1976, 84, Industrial Democracy, 1984, Discrimination in the Labour Market, 1980, Management: A Selected Bibliography, 1983, The New World Order, 1996, Social Economies in Transition, 1996, Self Development, 1997, The Internationalisation of Franchising, 1998, The Ultimate Entrepreneur's Book, 1999, other publs. Fellow Brit. Soc. Commerce (hon. v.p.), Inst. of Mgmt., Internat. Inst. Social Econs., Royal Geog. Assn., Royal Soc. Arts, Inst. Pers. and Devel., Inst. Mfg., Inst. Mgmt. Specialists; mem. Internat. Inst. Social Econs. (pres. 1972—), Brit. Univs. Indsl. Rels. Assn., Internat. Indsl. Rels. Assn., Royal Econs. Soc., Am. Econ. Assn., Assn. for Social Econs., Western Econs. Assn., Assn. Evolutionary Econs., New Econ. Soc., Brit. Social. Assn., Internat. Sociol. Assn., Am. Sociol. Assn., Human Resource Planning Soc. Fax: 01274 785200. Office: Enholmes Hall, Patrington Hull HU12 0PR, England Office: MCB Univ Press, 62 Toller Ln, Bradford/Yorkshire England

PETTOELLO-MANTOVANI, MASSIMO, pediatrician, educator, microbiologist, researcher; b. Milan, Dec. 21, 1956; came to U.S., 1989; s. Luciano and Clara (Ghirardi) P.; m. Ida Giardino, July 15, 1985; children: Luciano, Clara. BA, St. John Evangelist Coll., Rome, 1975; MD, La Sapienza U., Rome, 1983; PhD in Pediat. Scis., Federico II U., Naples, Italy, 1989; PhD, State U., Turin, Italy, 1989. Assoc. Albert Einstein Coll. Medicine, N.Y.C., 1990—; rsch. assoc. dept. pediat. Federico II U., Naples, 1984-85, sr. med. staff assoc. dept. pediat., 1987-89; co-dir. biohazard viral culture and animal study sect. Ctrs. AIDS Rsch., Yeshiva U., N.Y.C., 1994—; cons. Consulate of Italy, N.Y.C., 1996—; prof. pediat. U. Naples, 1997-99, assoc. prof. pediats., 2000—; exec. v.p. Found. Sci. and Tech. Edn. and Rsch., F.O.S.T.E.R. Sci., N.Y., 1998; mem. exec. com. World Health Policy Forum, 2000. Contbr. articles to Lancet, Jour. Immunology, Jour. Exptl. Medicine, Jour. Pediat., Gastroenterology, others. Pres. Villa Contarini Sci. Art Cultural Cr. GHIRARDI Found., Padua, Italy, 1997-98. Recognized as outstanding prof. U.S. Dept. State, 1994; fellow Cath. U. Sacred Hart, 1986; grantee Coun. Nat. Rsch., 1990, Italian NIH, 1992, U.S. NIH, 1996. Fellow Royal Soc. Tropical Medicine Hygiene; mem. N.Y. Acad. Scis., Internat. Soc. Infectious Diseases, European Soc. Clin. Microbiology, Am. Acad. Italian Scientists (v.p. 1996). Achievements include development of a modified humanized-animal model for the study of human immunological diseases and drug development; definition of the role of cryptococco polysaccharide in HIV-1 infection. Office: Albert Einstein Coll Medicine Forch Bldg Rm 401 1300 Morris Park Ave Bronx NY 10461-1926

PETTOROSSI, ALBERTO, computer science educator; b. Portorecanati, Italy, Oct. 21, 1947. Degree in electronic engring., Rome U., 1971; M in Computer Sci., SUNY, Syracuse, 1978; PhD in Computer Sci., Edinburgh U., 1984. Rsch. asst. Rome U., 1971-75, prof. theoretical computer sci., 1988—; rsch. worker CNR, 1975-88. Author Lecture Notes on Informatics, 19991; contbr. more than 100 articles to profl. jours. and confs. With Italian Air Force, 1972-73. Recipient prize Polish Math. Soc., 1990. Mem. Assn. Computing Machinery. Roman Catholic. Office: IASI-CNR, Viale Manzoni 30, 00185 Rome Italy

PETTY, ELIZABETH MARIE, geneticist; b. Chgo., July 13, 1959; d. Ralph David and Joyce Elizabeth (Carlson) P.; life ptnr. Karen Kay Milner, Dec. 15, 1985. BA, Clarke Coll., 1981; MD, U. Wis., 1986. Diplomate Nat. Bd. Med. Examiners, Am. Bd. Pediats., Am. Bd. Med. Genetics, Molecular Genetics and Clin. Genetics. Pediat. intern and resident U. Wis., Madison, 1986-89; genetics fellow Yale U., New Haven, Conn., 1989-93; assoc. prof. U. Mich., Ann Arbor, 1994—, med. dir. genetic counseling program, 1996—, dir. med. genetics outpatient clinic, 1996—; expert witness DNA testing in State of Ohio and Mich., 1995—; presenter regional, nat. and internat. confs. on genetics, 1991—. Contbr. chpt. to books, articles, editls. to profl. jours.;

peer reviewer various jours., 1994—. Participant Gay and Lesbian Health Group, Ann Arbor, 1994—; apptd. to State of Mich.'s Gov.'s Commn. on Genetic Privacy and Progress, 1997-98. Recipient Clin. Investigator award NIH-NCI, 1995-2000, RO1 award, 1997—, Am. Cancer Rsch. Fund award, 1997-98. Fellow Am. Soc. Human Genetics, Am. Coll. Med. Genetics; mem. AMA, Am. Acad. Scis., European Soc. Human Genetics, Human Genome Orgn., Alpha Omega Alpha. Democrat. Roman Catholic. Avocations: flutist, photographer. Office: U Mich 4301 MSRB III Ann Arbor MI 48109-0638

PETTY, JAMES ALAN, mathematics educator, consultant; b. Dublin, Ind., Dec. 27, 1954; s. Orris Delmar and Blanche Irene Petty; m. Soranee Holasuit, May 17, 1980; 1 child, Krissada Holasuit Petty. BS in Math. and Econs., Ball State U., 1977, MS in Math., 1978; PhD, Purdue U., 1996. Instr. math. U. Guam, Mangilao, 1989-92, asst. prof., 1992-94; instr. math./statistics U. Md.-Asia, Andersen AFB, Guam, 1990-94; tchr. educator Western Ky. U., Bowling Green, 1994-95; asst. prof. math. Ind.-Purdue U., Ft. Wayne, 1995-97; asst. prof. edn. U. Tenn., Martin, 1997-00; v.p. mktg. FPA Ednl. Consulting, Martin, 1995-00. Contbg. author: Epistecybernetics, 1997; contbr. articles to profl. jours. Mem. Math. Assn. Am., Nat. Coun. Tchrs. Math., Navy League U.S., Psychology Math. Edn.-N.Am., Tenn. Assn. Math. Educators, Phi Delta Kappa (program coord. N.W. Tenn. chpt. 1998-00). Republican. E-mail: jpetty@utm.edu. Home: 18 University Ct # J Martin TN 38237-4049 Office: U Tenn 240 J Gooch Hl Martin TN 38238-0001

PETTY, PRISCILLA HAYES, writer, columnist, producer; b. Nashville, Aug. 22, 1940; d. Anderson Boyd and Margaret Louise Hayes; m. Gene Paul Petty, Jan. 10, 1961; children: Eric, Damon, Boyd. BA in English, Vanderbilt U., 1962; postgrad., Lang. Inst., Dartmouth Coll., 1965. Cert. tchr. Ohio. Tchr. English Cin. Suburban Pub. Schs., 1962-65, head dept. English, tchr., 1971-79; newspaper columnist Cin. Enquirer, 1978-89; also syndicated newspaper columnist Gannett News Svc., Washington, 1982-89; cons. Arthur Andersen & Co., 1981-82; writer United Western Corp., 1982; exec. producer, on camera interviewer national TV documentary, 1992; commentator nat. bus. TV show, 1992; pres., owner, Petty Cons. Prodns., producer Total Quality Tng. Tapes. speaker W. Edwards Deming Seminars; cons. in field. Author: History of a Boardsman (oral history), 1979, Under a Lucky Star: The Story of Frederick A. Hauck, 1986, What's in It for You and the Firm: CEOs and Presidents Look at Community Involvement. Mem. Cin. Coun. World Affairs; chmn. Cin. Media-Bus. Exch., 1983; founder, pres., bd. trustees Cin. Oral History Found., 1984—. Named Outstanding Tchr., Project Teach, Ohio Edn. Assn., 1978; recipient WICI Great Lakes Regional Communicators' award; Pulitzer Prize nominee for Harvard U. Bus. Rev. article. Mem. Women in Comms. (Outstanding Communicator of Yr. 1985), Oral History Assn., Soc. Profl. Journalist. Home: 229 Oliver Rd Cincinnati OH 45215-2638

PETTY, SCOTT, JR., rancher; b. San Antonio, Apr. 10, 1937; s. Olive Scott and Edwina (Harris) P.; m. Marie Louise James, June 10, 1959 (dec. Dec. 1981); children: Joan Louise Petty, Susan Harris Arnim, Scott James; m. Eleanor Oliver, Apr. 30, 1983; children: Tim A. Weed, Richard Oliver Weed. BS in Petroleum Engring., U. Tex., 1960, MS in Petroleum Engring., 1961. Profl. engr. Tex., La. Asst. to pres. Petty Geophys. Engring., 1961-63, v.p., 1963-65; pres., exec. officer Petty Labs., 1965-67; pres., dir. Petty Geophys. Engring., 1967-73; exec. v.p. Petty-Ray Geophys., 1973-74; cons. Geosource Internat., 1974-76; chmn. bd. C.H Guenther & Son, Inc., San Antonio, 1982—, White Lily Foods Co., Knoxville, Tenn. Mem. chancellor's coun. U. Tex., Austin, devel. bd., San Antonio; bd. dirs. Tex. and Southwestern Cattle Raisers, Ft. Worth, Nat. Cattleman's Beef Assn., N.Am. Deer Farmers Assn. Mem. Am. Assn. Petroleum Geologists, Am. Inst. Mining, Metall. & Petroleum Engrs., Assn. Profl. Engrs., Geologists & Geophysicists of Alberta, Geophys. Soc. Houston, Internat. Assn. Geophys. Contractors, Internat. Oceanographic Found., Soc. Exploration Geophysicists, Soc. Petroleum Engrs., South Tex. Geol. Soc., Tex. Soc. Profl. Engrs., Explorers Club. Republican. Episcopalian. Home: 202 La Jara Blvd San Antonio TX 78209-4444 Office: Petty Ranch Co 711 Navarro St Ste 235 San Antonio TX 78205-1710

PETTY, THOMAS LEE, physician, educator; b. Boulder, Colo., Dec. 24, 1932; s. Roy Stone and and Eleanor Marie (Kudrna) P.; m. Carol Lee Piepho, Aug. 7, 1954; children: Caryn, Thomas, John. BA, U. Colo., 1955, MD, 1958. Intern Phila. Gen. Hosp., 1958-59; resident U. Mich., 1959-60, U. Colo., Denver, 1960-62; pulmonary fellow U. Colo., 1962-63, chief resident medicine, 1963-64, instr. medicine, 1962-64, asst. prof., 1964-68, assoc. prof., 1968-74, prof. medicine, 1974—; pres. Presbyn./St. Luke's Ctr. for Health Scis. Edn., 1989-95; practice medicine, specializing in internal medicine, pulmonary medicine Denver, 1962—; prof. medicine Rush Univ., 1992—; Cons. Vencor Hosp., 1991—. Author: For Those Who Live and Breathe, 1967, 2d edit., 1972, Intensive and Rehabilitative Respiratory Care, 1971, 3d edit., 1982, Chronic Obstructive Pulmonary Disease, 1978, 2d edit., 1985, Principles and Practice of Pulmonary Rehabilitation, 1993, Enjoying Life With COPD, 1995, 3d edit., others; contbr. articles to profl. jours. NIH and Found. grantee, 1966-88. Master ACP, Am. Coll. Chest Physicians (pres. 1982); mem. Assn. Am. Physicians, Assn. of Pulmonary Program Dirs. (founding pres. 1983-84), Am. Bd. Internal Medicine (bd. govs. 1986-92), Am. Thoracic Soc. (chmn. nat. lung health edn. program 1995—, Disting. Achievement award), Am. Soc. Internal Medicine, Phi Beta Kappa, Phi Delta Theta, Alpha Omega Alpha, Phi Rho Sigma (pres. 1976-78). Home: 1940 Grape St Denver CO 80220-1353 Office: Presbyn Hosp Dept Internal Medicine Denver CO 80218

PÉTURSSON, GÍSLI RAGNAR, accountant, consultant; b. Reykjavik, Iceland, Dec. 8, 1937; s. Pétur Sigurdsson and Kristín (Gísladóttir) P.; m. Védis Elsa Kristjánsdóttir, 1961 (div. 1972); children: Elsa Dorothea, Kristján Einar. Grad., Comml. Coll. Iceland, 1956. Clk. USAF, Keflavik, Iceland, 1955; transport mgr. Iceland Product Inc, N.Y.C., 1957-58; acct. Co Op, Reykjavik, 1959-60; gen. mgr. Co Op, Thorshöfn, Iceland, 1961-69; chief acct., asst. fin. mgr. Veltir hf (Volvo) and Gunnar Asgeirsson hf, Reykjavik, 1970-75; pvt. practice Reykjavik, 1976-78; chief acct. Hafskip hf, Reykjavik, 1979-82; cons. worker bldg. dams Hagvirki hf, 1983; dockworker Samskip Co. Op., 1984-85; fin. cons. Iceland State Housing Inst., 1986; mgr. Fin. & Co Op, Kopasker, Iceland, 1987-88; acct. Mcpl. Social Svc., Reykjavik, 1989—; founder, sole owner Pétursson ehf acctg. and mktg. co., 1994—. Pres. study body Comml. Coll. Iceland, 1954-55. Mem. Ch. LDS. Home: Kelduland 7, 108 Reykjavik Iceland

PETURSSON, HANNES, psychiatry educator; b. Reykjavik, Iceland, Dec. 30, 1947; s. Petur Hannesson and Gudrun Arnadottir; m. Juliana Sigurdardottir; children: Solveig Gudrun, Kristin Inga, Thorunn. MD, U. Iceland, Reykjavik, 1975; PhD, U. London, 1983. Med. dir. dept. psychiatry Reykjavik Hosp., 1982-98; assoc. prof. psychiatry U. Iceland, 1988-98, prof., 1998—; dir. dept. psychiatry Landspitalinn U. Hosp., Reykjavik, 1998—; advisor WHO, Geneva, 1983—; mem. com. Icelandic Rsch. Coun., Icelandic Health Authority. Co-author: Dependence on Tranquillizers, 1984; contbr. numerous articles to med. and sci. jours. Fellow Royal Coll. Psychiatrists, Icelandic Sci. Soc., others. Office: Dept Psychiat Lanspitalinn, Univ Hosp PO Box 10, 121 Reykjavik Iceland

PETZ, DÉNES, mathematician, educator; b. Budapest, Hungary, Apr. 8, 1953; s. Dénes and Maria Stöhr; m. Maria Stifter, Dec. 19, 1980. PhD in Math., Eötvös U., Budapest, Hungary, 1979; Postdoct. in Math., Hungarian Acad. Scis., 1982, D. in Math., 1989. Researcher Math. Inst. Hungarian Acad. Scis., Budapest, 1979-92; prof. Tech. U. Budapest (Hungary), 1993—; chmn. dept. math. analysis Tech. U. Budapest (Hungary) (now Budapest U. Tech. and Econs.), 1996—; vis. prof. Cath. U. Leuven (Belgium), 1989, U. Heidelberg (Germany), 1991, Kyoto (Japan) U., 1993. Author: An Invitation to the Algebra of Canonical Commutation Relation, 1996, Quantum Entropy and Its Use, 1993, The Semicircle Law, Free Random Variables and Entropy, 2000. Mem. Am. Math. Soc., János Bolyai Mathemat. Soc., Internat. Assn. Mathemat. Physics. Office: Budapest U Tech and Econs, Mathematical Inst, H-1521 Budapest Hungary

PETZEL, FLORENCE ELOISE, textiles educator; b. Crosbyton, Tex., Apr. 1, 1911; d. William D. and A. Eloise (Punchard) P. PhB, U. Chgo., 1931, AM, 1934; PhD, U. Minn., 1954. Instr. Judson Coll., 1936-38; asst. prof. textiles Ohio State U., 1938-48; assoc. prof. U. Ala., 1950-54; prof. Oreg. State U., Corvallis, 1954-61, 67-75, 77; prof. Oreg. State U., Corvallis, 77, prof. emeritus, 1975—, dept. head, 1954-61, 67-75; prof., divsn. head U. Tex., 1961-63; prof. Tex. Tech. U., 1963-67; vis. instr. Tex. State Coll. for Women, 1937; vis. prof. Wash. State U., 1967. Author: Textiles of Ancient Mesopotamia, Persia and Egypt, 1987; contbr. articles to profl. jours. Effie I. Raitt fellow, 1949-50. Mem. Met. Opera Guild, Greenville County Mus. Art, Sigma Xi, Phi Kappa Phi, Omicron Nu, Iota Sigma Pi, Sigma Delta Epsilon. Home: 150 Downs Blvd Apt A206 Clemson SC 29631-2043

PETZELT, JAN, physicist; b. Prague, Czechoslovakia, Mar. 16, 1941; s. Friedrich and Maria Luisa (Dub) P.; m. Hana Teklá, Nov. 19, 1970; children: Helena, Hana. MS in Physics, Charles U., Prague, 1963; PhD, Acad. Sci., Prague, 1972, DSc, 1992. Asst. Inst. of Physics Czech. Acad. Sci., Prague, 1963-72, scientist, 1972-76, sr. scientist, 1976-91, head dept. dielectrics, 1993—. Contbr. over 210 articles to profl. jours. Mem. European Phys. Soc. Avocations: sports, hiking. Home: Pirinská 3242, 14300 Prague Czech Republic Office: Inst Physics Czech Acad Sci, Na Slovance 2, 18040 Prague Czech Republic

PETZOW, GÜNTER EDMUND, materials scientist, researcher; b. Nordhausen, Germany, July 8, 1926; s. Edmund and Margarethe (Fillbrandt) P.; m. Helen Amalie Mohring, Jan. 28, 1958; children: Heinz, Günter. B in Chemistry, U. Stuttgart, Germany, 1953, MS in Engring., 1956, PhD in Natural Scis., 1959; hon. doctorate, Tokyo Inst. Tech., 1981; DEng (hon.), Hanyang U., Seoul, Korea, 1984; D of Mining Engring. (hon.), Montanistische U. Leonen, Austria, 1989; DEng (hon.), Tech. U. Dresden, Germany, 1992; D of Indsl. Chemistry (hon.), U. Genova, Italy, 1992; hon. doctorate, U. Cluy-Napoca, Romania, 1993, Acad. Sci., Slovakia, 1995. Rsch. assoc. Max-Planck-Inst. Metals Rsch., Stuttgart, 1960-65, head powder lab., 1965-94, dir., 1973-94, dir. gen., 1989-92; prof. U. Stuttgart, 1957-60, emeritus hon. prof., 1994; mem. internat. adv. bd. Kanagawa Acad. Sci. and Tech., Yokohama, Japan, 1987—; Schlumberger prof. U. Mich., 1978; hon. prof. Tech. U. Berlin, 1986, Shanghai Inst. Ceramics, 1988, Inst. Metals Acad. Sinica, China, 1994; ASM-IMS Disting. lectr. on metallagraphy, U.S., 1989. Author: Metallographisches, Keramographisches, Plastographisches Ätzen, 6th edit., 1995; editor Ternary Alloys, 15 vols., 1992-94; contbr. articles to profl. jours. including Preparation of Advanced Ceramics (Best Paper award, 1992), others. Trustee Fraunhofer Inst. Silicate Rsch., Würzburg, Germany, 1980—; chmn. COST (European Action), Brussels, 1984-95; vice-chmn. Ministry of Sci., Ljubljana, Slovenia, 1994—; reviewer, advisor Ministry of Sci. and Tech., Bonn, Germany, 1978-92. Recipient Hume-Rothery prize Inst. of Metals, London, 1982, First Class Order of the Pres. of Germany, Bonn, 1990, Order of Rising Sun, Japanese Emperor, Tokyo, 1995. Fellow ASM (hon.), Am. Ceramic Soc. (hon.); mem. German Ceramic Soc. (bd. dirs. 1985-88), German Soc. Material (pres. 1989-91), Acad. Sci. Artium Europaea (Austria), European Acad. Sci. and Arts (London), Internat. Acad. Ceramics (bd. trustees 1988), Internat. Metallography Soc. (Pres's. award 1995), Korean Soc. Ceramics (hon.), Japan Inst. Metals (hon.), Indian Inst. Metals (hon.), Japanese Materials Rsch. Soc. (hon.), Powder Metallurgy Assn. India (hon.), Korean Soc. Metals (hon.). Avocations: hiking, reading, writing, Japanese gardens, dogs. Home: Tannenweg 7, D 70771 Leinfelden Echterdningen Baden-Wurttemberg, Germany Office: Max Planck Inst PML, Heisenbergstr 5, D 70569 Stuttgart BadenWrt, Germany

PEUGEOT, ROLAND, automobile and holding company executive; b. Valentigney, Mar. 20, 1926; s. Jean-Pierre Peugeot and Colette Boillat-Japy; m. Colette Mayesky, Dec. 21, 1949; children: Jean-Philippe, Eric. Ed., Lycees Janson-de-Sailly, St. Louis Paris, Harvard. Pres. Peugeot Frères, 1959—; v.p. gen. mgr. Peugeot S.A., 1964, pres. bd. surveillance, 1972—; v.p. bd. dirs. Automobiles Peugeot, from 1965, v.p. bd. surveillance, from 1973; hon. chmn. supervisory bd. PSA Peugeot Citroen S.A.; bd. surveillance S.K.F., co. for mech. applications; adminstr. Chambre Syndicale des Constructeurs d'Automobiles. Decorated Legion of Honor of Arts and Letters. Mem. Fédération Française de Golf (bd. dirs.), Golf de Prunevelle à Dampierre-Sur-Le-Doubs (pres.), L'Academie des Sports, L'Automobile-Club de France, Saint-Cloud Country Club, Golf de Chantilly. Office: PSA Peugeot Citroen, 75 Ave de la Grande Armee, 75116 Paris Cedex, France*

PEUS, JOSEPH CARL, orthopedic surgeon; b. Berlin, Germany, Oct. 9, 1936; came to U.S., 1950; s. Carl Joseph and Gerda Eva (Fischer) P.; m. Karen Elaine Peus, Aug. 22, 1964; children: Eric, Brent, Craig, Kristina. BS, U. So. Calif., 1959, MD, 1963. Diplomate Am. Bd. Orthopedic Surgery. Intern L.A. County USC Med. Ctr., 1963-64; pvt. practice family physician L.A., 1964-67; resident L.A. County USC Med. Ctr., 1967-71; total hip surgery fellowship Wrightington, Eng., 1971; orthopedic surgeon Peus, Smith, Birch, Kahmann & Gallivan, Santa Barbara, Calif., 1971—; bd. dirs. Casa Dorinda Retirement Home, Santa Barbara, 1982-90; mem. dir. orthopedic dept. Santa Barbara Cottage Hosp., 1998. Contbr. articles to profl. jours. Maj. U.S. Army, 1964-70. Mem. Am. Assn. Hip and Knee Surgeons, Am. Acad. Orthopedic Surgeons, Calif. Orthop. Assn. Avocations: golf, skiing. Office: 2324 Bath St Santa Barbara CA 93105-4330

PEVEAR, ROBERTA CHARLOTTE, retired state legislator; b. Bethel, Maine, July 4, 1930; d. Frank Albert Sr. and Thirza Estella (Hickford) Gibson; m. Edward Gordon Pevear, Aug. 21, 1971. Diploma in Comml. Art, Gould Acad., 1947. Sec. Wilner Wood Products, South Paris, Maine, 1947-50; sec. export dept. Whitaker Cable, North Kansas City, Mo., 1951-56; sec. br. and dist. Anheuser-Busch, Inc., Kansas City, Mo., 1957-59; legal sec. Johnson & Johnson, New Brunswick, N.J., 1960-65, St. John, Ronder & Bell, Kingston, N.Y., 1966; sec., adminstrv. asst. Sears-Roebuck & Co., Overland Park, Kans., 1967-70, Exeter, N.H., 1971-77; salesman Avon Products, Hampton Falls, N.H., 1978-86; mem. ho. reps. State of N.H., 1979-88, ret., 1988; Commr. Rockingham Planning Commn., N.H., 1979-88, N.H. Planning Com., 1985-88; clk. Environment and Agrl. Com. N.H. Ho. Reps., 1983-88; del. mem. Rockingham County, 1979-88, exec. bd., 1984-88; chmn. Rockingham County Home, 1987-88. Civil Def. dir., Hampton Falls, N.H., 1980-88. Recipient Community Citizen award Hampton Falls Grange, 1982, Seacoast Retired Sr. Service award, 1985. Mem. Nat. Order Women Legislators, N.H. Order of Women Legislators, DAR. Avocations: writing, genealogy, travelling.

PEYERIMHOFF, NORBERT, mathematician, researcher; b. Giessen, Hessen, Germany, Feb. 29, 1964; s. Alexander and Isolde (Schmid) P. PhD, U. Augsburg, Germany, 1993. Rsch. asst. U. Augsburg, 1988-90, 92-94; PhD stipendiate Studienstiftung des Deutschen Volkes, 1990-91; postdoctoral rschr. Forschungsgemeinschaft, N.Y., 1994-96; rsch. asst. U. Basel, Switzerland, 1996-97, U. Bochum, Germany, 1997—; tchr. Rudolf-Diesel-Technikum, Augsburg, Germany, 1992-93; adj. lectr. Lehman Coll. CUNY, 1995-96. Author: (with M. Hüttenhofer and M. Lesch) Mathematik in Anwendung mit C++, 1994. Mem. Deutsche Mathematiker Vereinigung, Am. Math. Soc. Roman Catholic. Avocations: cooking, sailing. Office: Ruhr U Bochum Inst Math, Universitatsstr 150, 44780 Gebaude NA 5/32 Bochum, Germany

PEYMAN, MICHAEL ANTHONY, medical researcher; b. Farnham, Surrey, Eng., Apr. 7, 1925; s. Anthony Leonard and Kathleen Beatrice (Dawes) P. BA, MA, Oxford (Eng.) U., 1945, BM BCh, 1948, MD, 1957. House resident in gen. medicine and pediatrics St. Thomas' Hosp., London, 1948-50; sr. med. registrar in gen. medicine Charing Cross Hosp., London, 1954-57; Evans med. rsch. fellow New Eng. Ctr. Hosp., Boston, 1957-59; clin. rsch. fellow med. professorial dept. New Charing Cross Hosp., London, 1959-61; cons. physician, med. adviser various cos. and orgns., U.K., 1962-92; researcher on blood viscosity. Contbr. articles to med. jours. Maj. Med. Corps, Royal Army, 1952-53. Gosse scholar, 1961-62. Mem. Royal Coll. Physicians, Royal Soc. Medicine. Avocations: collecting modern first editions, 18th and 19th century English watercolors. Office: 37 B New Cavendish St, London W1M 8JR, England

PEYRELEVADE, JEAN, insurance executive; b. Marseille, France, Oct. 24, 1939; s. Paul and Mathilda (Benveniste) P.; m. Anne Chavy, June 12, 1962; children: Pierre, Catherine, Jérôme, Benjamin. Student, Polytech. Sch. Sci.; Degree, Sch. Econs., Paris; Degree in Engring. Civil Aviation. Chief engr. of civil aviation Ministry of Transport, France, 1961; mgr. internat. agy. then mgr. of dept. of external trade couns. by Prime Minister Credit Lyonnxai, France, 1970-81; chmn. Compagnie Financiere de Suez, France, 1983-86, Stern Bank, France, 1986-89, L'Union des Assurances de Paris, France, 1988-93; pres. la conseil d'administration du Crédit Lyonnais, 1993—; dir. gen., CEO Credit Lyonnais (CL) SA. Author: La Mort du Dollar, 1974, L'economie de Speculation, 1978, Economie de L'entreprise, 1989, Pour in capitalisme intelligent, 1993. Avocations: tennis, skiing. Home: 61 ave Charles de Gaulle, 92200 Neuilly-sur-Seine France Office: Crédit Lyonnais, 19 bd des Italiens, 75002 Paris France*

PEYRUSEIGT-MARTI, PIERRE, electronics executive; b. La Feuillie, France, Nov. 18, 1956; s. Jean-Marcel P. and Odette Collemare; married; children: Charles, Edouard. Diploma, Ecole Supérieure des Sciences et Technologie, Nancy, Ecole Nat. Supérieure des Industries Chimiques; M of Bus., Hautes Etudes Commls., 1982; diploma, Centre de Perfectionnement aux Affaires. Mgmt. cons. JMP & Assocs., Paris, 1982-84; sales and mktg. mgr. Digital Equipment Corp., Paris, 1984-91; dir. Western Europa Area GE FIS, Paris, 1991-93; dir. network acquisitions Global One, Paris, 1993-97; mng. dir. Telxon, Paris, 1997—. Mem. Internat. Fin. Assn., Golf Club. Home: 9 rue des Tilleuls, 78350 Les Loges en Josas France

PEYSER, MICHAEL JOHN, chemical engineer; b. Berlin, Nov. 12, 1935; s. Paul and Edith Erna Charlotte Peyser; m. Pauline Margaret Cowley, Apr. 4, 1961; children: Paul Michael, John Martin, Katie Samantha. BSc in Chem. Engring., Loughborough U., England, 1958. Grad. engr. then sales engr. Newton Chambers Engring. Ltd., Sheffield, 1958-64; sales engr. Horseley Piggott Ltd., West Midlands, 1964-69; head heat transfer CJB Ltd., Portsmouth, 1969-70; sales mgr. APV Spiro Gills Ltd, Pulborough, 1970-84, GEA Spiro-Gills Ltd., Stafford, England, 1984-98; cons. SES, Waterlooville, England, 1999—; cons. Stourhall Engring. Svcs. MJP, West Midlands, 1965—. Trustee Deverell Hall, Purbrook, 1985-93; chmn. bd. govs. Purbrook Park Secondary Sch., 1978-85. Mem. ASME, Inst. Chem. Engrs. Avocations: golf, table tennis. Home: 14 Lancaster Way, Waterlooville PO77NG, England

PEYTON, CAROL, social worker; b. Laurel, Miss., Apr. 7, 1966; d. Frankie Delane and Erminia (Harrington) P. AA, J.C.J.C., Ellisville, Miss., 1986; B in Sociology, U. So. Miss., 1989, B in Social Work, 1993. Lic. social worker. Recreation aide Ellisville State Sch., 1990-93, social worker, 1998—; case mgr. Weems Mental Health Ctr., Meridian, Miss., 1994-96, Multi-County Cmty. Agy., Meridian, 1996-97. Mem. NASW, Miss. Conf. Social Welfare, U. So. Miss. Alumni Assn., J.C.J.C. Alumni Assn. Baptist. Avocations: reading, computer skills, typing, sewing.

PFAENDLER, HANS RUDOLF, organic chemistry educator; b. St. Gallen, Switzerland, May 30, 1945; s. Fritz and Nelly (Staehelin) P. Student, U. Basel, 1964-68, DrRerNat, 1971; postgrad., Shionogi Rsch. Lab., Osaka, Japan, 1971-72. Rsch. chemist Woodward Rsch. Inst., Basel, 1973-80, Ciba-Geigy & Co., Basel, 1980-82; prof. organic chemistry U. Munich, 1982—. Contbr. articles to profl. jours.; patentee in field of betalactam antibiotics. Mem. German Chem. Soc., Am. Chem. Soc. Office: U Mich Dept Chemistry, Butenandtstrasse 5-13, 81377 Munich Germany

PFAFF, GERHARD, chemist, researcher; b. Meiningen, Thuringia, Germany, Oct. 19, 1953; s. Manfred and Ilse (Arnold) P.; m. Gisela Engelmann, Aug. 1, 1975; children: Daniela, Matthias. Diploma, F. Schiller U., Jena, Germany, 1978, D of Natural Scis., 1983; Docent, Tech. U., Darmstadt, Germany, 1997. Asst. F. Schiller U., 1983-87, superior asst., 1987-91; lab. mgr. Merck KGaA, Darmstadt, 1991-93, group mgr., 1993-94, head dept., 1994—; lectr. F. Schiller U., 1985-91, Tech. U., 1993—. Author: Pearlescent Pigments, 1997, Special Effect Pigments, 1998; contbr. chpts. to books and articles to profl. jours.; 50 patents in field. Mem. German Chem. Soc. (bd. mem.). Office: Merck KGaA, Frankfurter Str 250, D-64271 Darmstadt Germany

PFAFFENROTH, PETER ALBERT, lawyer; b. Mineola, N.Y., Mar. 29, 1941; s. Albert and Genevieve Astrid (Anderson) P.; m. Sara Ann Beekey, June 26, 1966; children: Elizabeth Cartwright, Peter Cyrus, Catherine Genevieve. BS in Engring., Princeton U., 1963, dipl. in European Civilization, 1963; JD, U. Mich., 1966; LLM in Taxation, NYU, 1972, LLM in Corp., 1976, LLM in Internat. Law, 1998. Bar: N.J. 1966, U.S. Dist. Ct. (N.J. dist.) 1966. With Daimler-Benz, Stuttgart, Fed. Republic Germany, 1961, B.P. Benzin & Petroleum, Hamburg, Fed. Republic Germany, 1962, Office of Internat. Affairs, U.S. Treasury Dept., Washington, 1963, Office of Export Control, U.S. Commerce Dept., Washington, 1964, Commrs. Office, U.S. Patent Office, Washington, 1965; atty. McCarter & English, Newark, 1966-68, Kentz & Gilson, Esqs., Summit, N.J., 1968-69; corp. counsel Tex. Plastics, Maine Sugar Industries, Robbinsville, N.J., 1969-70; atty. c/o Lewis Stein, Esq., Netcong, N.J., 1970-71; pvt. practice Chester, N.J., 1971—. Avocations: antiques, foreign languages, travel, wine. Home: Route 24 At Twin Brooks Trail Chester NJ 07930

PFANDER, HANSPETER, chemistry educator; b. Bern, Switzerland, Apr. 21, 1940; s. Franz and Martha (Soltermann) P.; m. Regula Joss, Sept. 15, 1967; children: Marc, Babette. Lic. Phil. Nat., U. Bern, 1965, D of Phil. Nat., 1968; D (hon.), U. Agrl. Scis., Cluj-Napoca, Romania, 1994; D h.c., U. Med. Sch. Pecs, Hungary, 1997. Asst. prof. U. Bern, 1980-84, assoc. prof., 1984-94, prof., 1994—, dean faculty of sci., 1996-97. Editor: Key to Carotenoids, 1987, (series) Carotenoids, 1995/96. Col. Swiss Mil. Mem. N.Y. Acad. Scis., New Swiss Chem. Soc., Bernese Chem. Soc. Office: U Bern Chem-Biochem Dept, Freiestrasse 3, 3012 Bern Switzerland

PFANNER, NIKOLAUS, biochemist, educator; b. Simmerberg, Germany, Sept. 10, 1956; s. Anton and Martina (Heim) P.; m. Anita Rapp, May 9, 1981; children: Dominik, Raphael. MD, U. Munich, 1985, Habilitation, 1990. Postdoctoral fellow U. Munich, 1985-86, group leader, 1987-92; rsch. fellow Princeton (N.J.) U., 1988-89; prof., chair biochemistry dept. U. Freiburg, Germany, 1992—. Contbr. articles to profl. jours. Mem. Gesellschaft für Biologische Chemie, Fedn. European Biochem. Socs., European Molecular Biology Orgn. Achievements include research in mechanisms of protein sorting, functions of heat shock proteins. Office: U Freiburg Inst Biochem, Hermann-Herder-Str 7, 79104 Freiburg Germany

PFANSTIEL PARR, DOROTHEA ANN, interior designer; b. San Antonio, Nov. 10, 1931; d. Herbert Andraes and Ethel Missouri (Turner) Pfanstiel; m. Thurmond Charles Parr, Jr., Sept. 15, 1951; children: Thurmond Charles, III, Richard Marshall. AA, Coll. San Antonio, 1951. Asst. dean evening divsn. Alamo C.C., San Antonio, 1951; tchr., cons., dir. Humpty Dumpty Early Childhood Devel. Ctr., San Antonio, 1951-58; exec. sec., cons. Thurmond C. Parr, Jr. & Co., San Antonio, 1960-61; founder, pres. Creative Designs, Ltd., San Antonio, 1962—; liaison, coord. Internat. Students Lang. Sch., Lackland AFB, San Antonio, 1959-65. Adv., cons. Urban Renewal Inner City San Antonio, 1959-61. Named Notable Woman of Tex., Awards and Hons. Soc. Am., 1984-85. Republican. Presbyterian. Avocations: travel, swimming, reading, studying, walking. Office: Creative Designs Ltd PO Box 6822 San Antonio TX 78209-0822

PFEFFER, CYNTHIA ROBERTA, psychiatrist, educator; b. Newark, May 22, 1943; d. Edward I. and Ann Pfeffer. BA, Douglas Coll., 1964; MD, NYU, 1968. Assoc. dir. child psychiatry inpatient unit Albert Einstein Coll. Medicine, Bronx, N.Y., 1973-79; chief child psychiatry inpatient unit N.Y. Hosp. Cornell Med. Ctr., White Plains, N.Y., 1979-95; assoc. prof. clin. psychiatry Cornell U. Med. Coll., N.Y.C., 1984—; prof. psychiatry Cornell U. Med. Coll., 1989—; pres. N.Y. Coun. on Child and Adolescent Psychiatry, N.Y.C., 1989—. Author: The Suicidal Child, 1986, Difficult Moments in Child Psychotherapy, 1988; editor: Youth Suicide: Perspectives on Risk and Prevention, 1989, Intense Stress and Mental Disturbance in Children, 1996. Recipient Erwin Stengel award Internat. Assn. Suicide Prevention, 1987, Wilford Hulse award N.Y. Coun. on Child & Adolescent Psychiatry, 1989, Sigmund Freud award Am. Soc. Psychoanalytic Physicians, 1994. Fellow Am. Psychiat. Assn., Am. Acad. Child and Adolescent Psychiatry (councillor-at-large 1989—, Norbert Rieger award 1988), Am. Psychopathological Assn.; mem. Am. Assn. Suicidology (pres. 1987, Young Contbrs. award 1981, 82). Office: NY Hosp Westchester Div 21 Bloomingdale Rd White Plains NY 10605-1504 also: 1100 Madison Ave New York NY 10028-0327

PFEFFER, ROBERT, chemical engineer, academic administrator, educator; b. Vienna, Austria, Nov. 26, 1935; came to U.S., 1938, naturalized, 1944; s. Joseph and Gisela (Aberbach) P.; m. Marcia Borenstein, Dec. 24, 1960; children—Michael, Jacqueline. B.Ch.E., N.Y. U., 1956, M.Ch.E., 1958, D.Eng.Sc., 1962. Mem. faculty CCNY, 1957-92, asst. prof. chem. engring., 1962-66, assoc. prof., 1966-71, prof., 1971-92, chmn. dept. chem. engring., 1973-87, Herbert Kayser prof., 1980-92, dean grad. studies and research, dep. provost, 1987-88, provost, v.p. acad. affairs, 1988-92; v.p. rsch. and grad. studies, prof. chem. engring. N.J. Inst. Tech., Newark, 1992-97, disting. prof. chem. engring., 1997—; vis. prof. Imperial Coll., London, 1969; Fulbright scholar Technion-Israel Inst. Tech., 1976-77; cons. in field. Contbr. articles to tech. publs. Fulbright Hays awardee, 1976-77; DuPont faculty fellow, 1962; NASA faculty fellow, 1964-65. Mem. AIChE (Particle Tech. Forum Nat. award 1995, Tomas Baron Nat. award 2000), Am. Soc. Engring. Edn., Sigma Xi, Tau Beta Pi, Phi Lambda Upsilon. Jewish. Office: NJ Inst Tech Ste 1200 323 Dr Martin Luther King Jr B Newark NJ 07102-1892

PFEFFER, RUBIN HARRY, publishing executive; b. Bklyn., Oct. 9, 1951; s. Martie and Idell (Treiber) P.; m. Lurie Horns; children: Stephanie, Ian, Rebecca, Vaughn. BFA in Graphic Design, Carnegie-Mellon U., 1973. Dir. art Harcourt Brace Jovanovich, San Diego, 1979-84; corp. art dir. Harcourt Brace Jovanovich, Orlando, Fla., 1984—; dir. children's books Harcourt Brace Jovanovich, San Diego, 1984-85; pres. Harcourt Brace & Co. Trade Books, San Diego, 1985-98, Harcourt Online, San Diego, 1998—, 1998—. Bd. dirs. Calif. Ballet Co., San Diego, 1986-87, Easter Seal Soc., San Diego, 1988—. Avocation: painting. Office: Harcourt Online North Tower 6th Floor 200 Wheeler Rd Burlington MA 01803-5501

PFEIFENBERGER, WERNER, political science educator; b. Salzburg, Austria, Oct. 23, 1941; s. Hans and Anne (Stanic) P. LLD, U. Vienna, Austria, 1963; PhD, U. Salzburg, 1970; diploma, Bologna Ctr. Johns Hopkins U., Italy, 1965, U. Oslo, 1971. Legal trainee Dist. Ct. Salzburg, 1966; rsch. asst. Internat. Rsch. Ctr., Salzburg, 1967-70; lectr., asst. prof. U. Salzburg, 1970-72; prof. polit. sci. U. Münster, Fed. Republic Germany, 1973—; prof. internat. law U. Grenoble, France, 1975-78; dir. Austrian Inst. Polit. Edn., Vienna, 1977-83; head dept. U. Stellenbosch, South Africa, 1983-85; holder Tamkang chair Tamkang U., Taipei, Republic of China, 1986. Author: Die Verenten Nationen, 1971 (Kunschak award 1973), Die Und Politik Der Volksrgpublik China, 1978, Beside The Europeanism, 1987, Kuvistogteen Kolonialisme, 1977. Polit. advisor Austrian People's party, Vienna, 1987, 88. Mem. Internat. Polit. Sci. Assn., Internat. Assn. Human Rights, German Assn. Internat. Rsch. (chmn. 1989—). Mem. Conservative party. Roman CAtholic. Avocations: sailing, mountain climbing, chess. Home: Schalk-Strasse 4, A-5020 Salzburg Austria Office: U Münster, Von-Esmarch-Strasse 157, D-4400 Münster NRW, Federal Republic of Germany

PFEIFER, HOWARD MELFORD, mechanical engineer; b. St. Louis, Aug. 23, 1959; s. Howard William and Ruth Joyce P. BS in Applied Sci. and Tech., Charter Oak State Coll., 1990; BSME, U. Hartford, 1991; MBA, Rensselaer Poly. Inst., 1997. Engr. in tng., Conn. Engr. asst. Pratt & Whitney, East Hartford, Conn., 1984-89; devel. engr. Chromalloy Rsch. and Tech. Divsn., Orangeburg, N.Y., 1991-93; process devel. engr. Howmet Corp., North Haven, Conn., 1993-95; process engr. Windsor Airmotive, The Barnes Group, East Granby, Conn., 1995-98; sr. engr. Pratt & Whitney, 1998—; mem. U. Hartford Engring. Alumni Adv. Bd., Bloomfield, Conn., 1992-98, chmn., 1996-98; founder, prin., treas. WEMBA5 Investments LLC, Conn. Mem. NSPE, Sigma Xi (assoc.). Republican. Achievements include research, design and construction of a human powered helicopter, and research to map acoustical soundboard characteristics in a Steinway Grand Piano. Home: 83 Buckley Hill Rd Colchester CT 06415-1712 Office: Pratt & Whitney 400 Main St East Hartford CT 06108-0968

PFEIFER, JOHAN PETER, urban planner, architect, sculptor; b. Helsinki, Finland, Dec. 9, 1949; s. Hans Peter Pfeifer and Mara Liisa Aaltonen; m. Armi Anneli Naukkarinen, June 6, 1987; children: Meri-Aurea, Tuuli Marea. M in Social Sci., U. Helsinki, 1973; MArch, Tech. U. Tampere (Finland), 1974; Lic. Tech., Tech. U., Helsinki, 1979. Arch., city planner Office of Prof. Olli Kivinen, Helsinki, 1973-76; city planner City of Vantaa (Finland), 1976-81; head city planning dept. City of Porvoo (Finland), 1981—; arch., city planner pvt. archtl. firm, Helsinki, 1974-86, Porvoo, 1974—. Author; City Models, 1979; exhibns. in Finland, Sweden, Lithuania, Denmark; prin. works include 2 pub. sculptures. Res. officer Finnis Army, 1975-76. Lutheran. Avocations: sailing, alpine skiing. Office: City Planning Dept Porvoo, Rihkamatori B, 06100 Porvoo Finland

PFEIFER, JOHANN GOTTFRIED, surgeon; b. Graz, Styria, Austria, Nov. 17, 1957; s. Josef and Gertrude (Furtner) P.; m. Anneliese Maria Dusleag, Sept. 16, 1988; children: Christian, Michael, Elisabeth. MD, U. Graz, 1983. Resident Land Steiermark, Graz, 1983-86; surg. resident KAGES Krankenanstaltengesellschaft, Feldbach, Austria, 1986-92; staff surgeon U. Graz, 1992-94, 95—; rsch. fellow Cleve. Clinic Fla., Ft. Lauderdale, 1994-95; lectr. Nurses Sch. Medicine, Graz, 1993-94; course dir. U. Graz, 1994—, lectr., 1995-99; pvt. practice Arztekammer für Steiermark, Graz, 1998—. Contbr. articles to profl. jours. With Austria Army, 1976-77. Mem. Am. Soc. of Colorectal Surgeons (Rsch. award South Fla. chpt. 1995), Internat. Soc. of Univ. Colon and Rectal Surgeons, Soc. of Am. Gastrointestinal Endoscopic Surgeons. Roman Catholic. Avocations: reading, traveling, music. Office: U Med Sch Dept Gen Surgery, Auenbruggerplatz 29, 8036 Graz Styria, Austria

PFEIFER, PETER MARTIN, physics educator; b. Zurich, Switzerland, Apr. 19, 1946; came to U.S., 1986; s. Max and Eva (Korrodi) P.; m. Therese M. Abgottspon, June 13, 1980; children: Anne, Helen. MS in Chemistry, Swiss Fed. Inst. Tech., 1969, PhD in Natural Scis., 1980. Rsch. and tchg. asst. Swiss Fed. Inst. Tech., Zurich, 1970-75, rsch. assoc., instr., 1975-80; rsch. fellow Hebrew U. Jerusalem, 1981-82; asst. prof. chemistry U. Bielefeld, West Germany, 1982-86, habilitation, 1986; assoc. prof. physics U. Mo., Columbia, 1986-95; vis. prof. physics Swiss Fed. Inst. Tech., 1993-94; vis. scientist Ecole Poly., Palaiseau, France, 1994; prof. physics U. Mo., Columbia, 1995—; mem. adv. bd. Symposium on Probability Methods in Physics, Bielefeld, 1984, Symposium on Small Irregular Particles, Cuernavaca, Mex., 1988, Conf. on Fractals in Natural Scis., Budapest, Hungary, 1993, 22d Midwest Solid-State Theory Symposium, Columbia, 1994, 2d Internat. Symposium on Surface Heterogeneity, Zakopane, Poland, 1995, 3d conf. Fractals in Engring., Arcachon, France, 1997; spkr. in field. Mem. editl. bd. Internat. Jour. Fractals, 1992—, Heterogeneous Chemistry Reviews, 1992—; contbr. over 75 articles to profl. jours. Recipient Gränacher Grad. fellowship Found. of Swiss Chem. Industry, 1970-71, fellowship for jr. scientists Swiss Nat. Sci. Found., 1981-82, Outstanding Rsch. prize U.Bielefeld, 1986, Rsch. Coun. fellowship U. Mo., 1986; grantee: Petroleum Rsch. Fund, 1987-98, Rsch. Leave award U. Mo., 1993-94. Mem. Am. Phys. Soc., Materials Rsch. Soc. Achievements include development of fractal analysis in surface science; discovery of first fractal materials and of numerous structure-function relationships (diffusion, scattering, wetting and transport properties); fundamental research in quantum theory: discovery of chiral superselection rule in molecules, unified framework for reduced quantum dynamics, generalized time-energy uncertainty relations, variational bounds for transition probabilities. Office: Univ Mo Dept Physics Columbia MO 65211-0001

PFEIFFER, DIDIER, insurance executive; m. Maryse Bloch, Sept. 27, 1961; 3 children. Diploma, Inst. of Polit. Studies, Paris, JD. Civil adminstr. Ministry of Econs. and Fin., Govt. of France, Paris, 1966-68; chargé de mission au cabinet Ministry of Econs. and Fin., Govt. of France, 1968-71; attaché fin. French Ambassador to U.S., 1971; adminstr. Banque Mondiale, 1972; chargé de mission, fin. ops. UAP, 1973-76, dir. gen. investments dept., 1976-84, dir. gen., 1984-91, adminstr.-dir. gen., 1991-94, v.p., dir.-gen., 1994-96; CEO UAP, Paris; chmn., CEO Groupe des Assurances Nationales SA; pres. Conseil de surveillancede GAN, 1998, v.p. exec. com. Groupama-GAN; v.p. Conseil de Surveillance de CIC, Union Européenne; mem. Conseil de Surveillance Largardère Groupe; pres. of fin. Sorema, 1999. Mem. Groupe des Assurances Nationales (pres. 1996-98), Groupement des Assurances de Personnes (pres. 1990-97), Bur. de Fedn. Française des Soc. d'Assurances. *

PFEIFFER, ERNA, educator, literary translator; b. Graz, Styria, Austria, May 10, 1953. MPhil., U. Graz (Austria), 1975, PhD, 1982. Lectr. U. Graz, 1978—, asst. prof., 1983—; literary translator Edit. Suhrkamp, Frankfurt, German Fed. Republic, 1986—. Author: Literarische Struktur und Realitätsbezug im kolumbianischen Violencia-Roman, 1984, Territorium Frau 1998; contbr. articles to profl. jours. Candidate for municipal council Alternative Liste Graz, 1983. Investigation grantee ICETEX, Bogotá, Colombia, 1977, Austrian Ministry Sci., St. Gallen, Switzerland, 1978. Office: Inst Romanistik, Inst Romanistik, Merangasse 70, A-8010 Graz Austria

PFEIFFER, JOHAN FREDRIK, company official; b. Helsingborg, Sweden, Jan. 22, 1965; s. Claes Hakan Fredrik and Gunilla Pfeiffer; m. Lydia Margret Corkadel, Sept. 14, 1998; 1 child, Fredrika Louise. Diploma in material sci. engring., Swiss Fed. Inst. Tech., Lausanne, 1989; MBA, MA in Internat. Studies, U. Pa., 1993. Tech. svc. and devel. engr. Dow Chem., Horgen, Switzerland, 1989-91; summer assoc. L.Am. mgr. Boston Cons. Group, Munich, 1992; bus. planner FMC Corp., Phila., 1993-94, product mgr., 1994-95, industry mgr., 1995-97; bus. mgr. for L.Am. FMC Corp., Houston, 1997-98; mgr. L.Am. FMC Corp., Caracas, Venezuela, 1998-99; dir. customer support FMC Corp., Bergen, Norway, 1999—; bd. dirs. Kongsberg (NorwY) Offshore AS, AESA, N.Y.C. Fax: 011-47 56 32 32 35. E-mail: johan pfeiffer@fmc.com. Office: FMC Kongsberg Subsea, CCB Base, Agotnes Norway

PFEIFFER, LEONARD, IV, executive recruiter, consultant; s. Leonard Jr. and Felicia Pfeiffer; m. Anna Gunnarsson. BA, Harvard U., MBA. Mktg. mgr. Am. Express, N.Y.C., 1970-72; project dir. S.T.I., N.Y.C. and San Francisco, 1972-74; v.p. R. Olivier & Assocs., N.Y.C., 1974-76, A. Kane & Assoc., N.Y.C., 1976-78; v.p., mng. dir. Korn/Ferry Internat., Washington and N.Y.C., 1978-98; ptnr., group leader Heidrick & Struggles, Washington, 1998—. Bd. dirs. Cmty. Found., Washington, 1982-84, Nat. Ctr. for Missing Children, 1989—, Nat. Blood Found., 1995-97, Nat. Bldg. Mus., 1998—; founding mem. jr. bd. dirs. Washington Opera, 1983-93; mem. men's com. Project Hope; mem. devel. com. Nat. Head Injury Found., Choral Arts Soc., Nat. Symphony Orch. Lt. U.S. Army, 1968-70. Schepp Found. scholar, 1968-70. Mem. Am. Soc. Assn. Execs., Greater Washington Soc. Assn. Execs., Congl. Country Club, Harvard Club (activities com., admissions com. N.Y.C. chpt. 1975-81, 1st v.p. bd. dirs. Washington chpt. 1985-87). Avocations: water and snow skiing, power and sail boating, tennis. Office: Heidrick & Struggles 1301 K St NW Ste 500E Washington DC 20005-3362

PFEIFFER, MICHAEL, orthopaedic surgeon, educator; b. Wanne-Eickel, Westfalen, Germany, June 29, 1960. MD, Philipps U., Marburg, Germany, 1985. Jr. house officer St. Josefs Hosp., Olsberg, Germany, 1985-86; jr. house officer dept. trauma surgery Phillips U., Marburg, 1986-87, sr. house officer dept. orthop. surgery, 1987-93, registrar, 1994-97, assoc. prof., cons., 1998—; rsch. fellow Deutsche Forschungsgemeinschaft dept. biomed. engring. U. Iowa, Iowa City, 1993-94; advisor, cons. various patient based pub. health orgns.; orthopaedic cons., sports medicine, physiotherapy, 1999—. Mem. editl. bd. Spine Mag., 1994—, European Spine Mag., 2000—; contbr. articles to profl. jours., chpt. to book. Recipient fellowship Coordinating Com. Orthop. Socs. European Common Market, 1990, fellowship grant Deutsche Forschungsgemeinschaft, Bonn, 1993-94. Mem. Assn. of Orthopaedic Surgeons in Europe (v.p. 1992—), European Orthop. Rsch. Soc., Deutsche Gesellschaft fuer Orthopaedie, Berufsverband der Aerzte fuer Orthopaedie. Office: Philipps U Hosp Dept Orthop, Baldingerstrasse, 35033 Marburg Hessen, Germany

PFEIFFER, MICHELLE, actress; b. Santa Ana, Calif., Apr. 29, 1957; d. Dick and Donna P.; m. Peter Horton (div.); 1 adopted child, Claudia Rose; m. David Kelley, Nov. 13, 1993. Student, Golden West Coll., Whitley Coll. Actress: (feature films) Falling in Love Again, 1980, Hollywood Knights, 1980, Charlie Chan and the Curse of the Dragon Queen, 1981, Grease II, 1982, Scarface, 1983, Ladyhawke, 1985, Into the Night, 1985, Sweet Liberty, 1986, Amazon Women on the Moon, 1987, Witches of Eastwick, 1987, Married to the Mob, 1988, Tequila Sunrise, 1988, Dangerous Liaisons, 1988 (Acad. award nominee 1989), The Fabulous Baker Boys, 1989 (Achievement award L.A. Film Critics Assn. 1989, D.W. Griffith award Nat. Bd. Rev. 1989, N.Y. Film Critics award 1989, Nat. Soc. Film Critics award 1990, Golden Globe award 1990, Acad. award nominee 1990), The Russia House, 1990,Frankie & Johnny, 1991, Love Field, 1992 (Acad. award nominee 1993), Batman Returns, 1992, The Age of Innocence, 1993, Wolf, 1994, Dangerous Minds, 1995; (TV movies) The Solitary Man,1979, Callie and Son, 1981, The Children Nobody Wanted, 1981, Splendor in the Grass, 1981, (TV series) Delta House, 1979, B.A.D. Cats, 1980, Up Close and Personel, 1996, To Gillian on her 37th Birthday, 1996, One Fine Day, 1996, A Thousand Acres, 1997, Privacy, 1997, The Prince of Egypt (voice), 1998, The Story of U.S., 1998, A Midsummer's Night Dream, 1999, Deep End of the Ocean, 1999, Being John Malkovich, 1999. Named Woman of the Yr., Harvard's Hasty Pudding Theater Club, 1995. Office: care ICM 8942 Wilshire Blvd Beverly Hills CA 90211-1934

PFEILER, WOLFGANG F.W., educator; b. Erfurt, Germany, May 6, 1931; s. Horst and Hildgard (Chall) P.; m. Gisela Ritter; 1 child, Evelyn. Dr.phil, Bonn Univ., Bonn, Germany, 1971, Dr.habil, 1981, prof., 1987. Asst. prof. Bonn Univ., 1972-82, lectr., 1975-82; rsch. fellow Bonn Sankt Augustin, 1982-87, UCLA, 1982; prof. Bonn Univ., 1987-96, Univ. Greifswald, Germany, 1992-97; lectr. in political edn., 1967—. Author: Deutsc landbilder, 1972, Viermacht Optionen, 1991, Deutschlandpolitische Options, 1988; contbr. articles to profl. jours. Del. Christian Dem. Union, 1972-77. Recipient rsch. fellow Konrad-Adenauer Found., 1982-92. Mem. Deutsche Gesellschaft Ausw Polit. Home: Aufdem Stephansberg 2, D 53340 Meckenheim Germany Office: Univ Koblenz/Landau, Rheinau 1, D 56075 Koblenz Germany

PFEISTER, RAYMOND LYNN, diversified financial services company executive; b. Cape Girardeau, Mo., May 31, 1946; s. Herman Joe and Imogene Elsie (Groseclose) P.; B.S., U. Ill., 1969, M.B.A., 1971; Ph.D., Baruch Coll., City U. N.Y., 1978; m. Susan Jane Selby, July 1, 1969; children—Joseph Robert, John Charles. Sales analyst Koppers Co., Magnolia, Ark., 1969-70; instr. bus. U. Ill., Urbana, 1971; spl. agt. Prudential Ins. Co. Am., Champaign, Ill., 1971, div. mgr., Balt., 1971-74, mktg. specialist, mgr. group pension, Newark and N.Y.C., 1974; account exec. Alexander & Alexander Inc., N.Y.C., 1974-76, asst. v.p., 1976-78, v.p., 1978-80; v.p. Johnson & Higgins, N.Y.C., 1980-83; founder, chmn. bd., chief exec. officer Pfeister Barter Inc., N.Y. Reciprocal Trade Exchange, 1979-87; founder, chmn., pres. Pfeister Corp., Wilmington, Del., 1977—; co-founder, pres., treas. Chattan Group, Ltd., N.Y.C., 1983—; co-founder, pres., chief exec. officer Sheffield Assocs., Ltd., N.Y.C., 1985—; co-owner Ceramic Design Ltd., Greenwich, Conn., 1987—; dir. U.S. Ceramic Tile Corp, Canton, Ohio, London Pacific Life Ins. Co., Calif.; lectr., cons. in field. Pres. Jr. Achievement, Denver, 1963-64; active Boy Scouts Am., 1964—, United Fund, 1973. Named outstanding young man Am., U.S. Jaycees, 1977. Mem. Acad. Mgmt., Am. Psychol. Assn., Nat. Eagle Scout Assn., Soc. Am. Foresters, Forest Products Research Soc., Nat. Life Underwriters Assn., Nat. M.B.A. Assn., U. Ill. Alumni Assn. (life)(v.p. 1974—), Sigma Iota Epsilon. Clubs: Siwanoy Country, Campfire Club of Am., Union League Club. Author: The Strategic Planning Process for Alexander & Alexander Services, Inc. and Subsidiaries, 1980; contbg. author: The Practice of Planning-Strategic, Administrative and Operational, 1981. Home: 22 Valley Rd Bronxville NY 10708-2224 Office: Fred Alger Mgmt 1 World Trade Ctr Fl 93 New York NY 10048-0202

PFENDT, HENRY GEORGE, retired information systems executive, management consultant; b. Frankfurt, Germany, Sept. 19, 1934; s. Georg and Elisabeth K. (Schuch) P.; m. Jane Ann Gossard, July 15, 1961; children: Katherine Ann, Henry G. Jr., Karen Jane. BS, U. Rochester, N.Y., 1972, postgrad., 1972; postgrad., U. Mich., 1986. Dir. No. info. ctr. Eastman Kodak Internat., Göteborg, Sweden, 1972-73; sr. project mgr. Eastman Kodak Internat., Stuttgart, Fed. Republic of Germany, 1973-75; dir. adminstrv. svcs. Kodak Australasia Party Ltd., Coburg, Australia, 1975-77; dir. customer svcs. div. Kodak Australasia Party Ltd., Coburg, 1977-81; dir. mktg. Eastman Kodak Co. for Asia, Africa and Australia, 1981-84; dir. architecture devel. Eastman Kodak Info. Systems, Rochester, 1984-86, dir. corp. info. systems, 1986-93; ret., 1993, bus. and info. mgmt. cons., 1993—; bd. dirs. client adv. coun. Compu Ware, Detroit. Creator concepts and mgmt. processes in field. Mem. indsl. devel. agy. adv. bd. Zoning Bd. Appeals; elected town councilman Town Bd. of Barrington, 1999; charter mem. adv. bd. Rochester Inst. Tech. Sch. Computer Sci. and Tech., 1987; bd. dirs. YMCA of Maplewood, Rochester, 1989—; mem. Rep. Nat. Com. With USAF, 1955-59. Recipient Industry Visionary award of 25 Most Influential Communications Execs., 1991, Lectr. of Yr. award Australian Computer Soc., Editor's Choice award Nat. Libr. Poetry. Mem. Soc. for Info. Mgmt., Coun. of Logistics Mgmt., Ctr. for Info. Systems Rsch., Strategic Mgmt. Soc., Internat. Platform Assn., Interact Network (assoc.), C. of C., Am. Legion. Lutheran. Avocations: reading, golf, gardening, jogging, travel. Home: 968 E Lake Rd Dundee NY 14837-9749

PFERSMANN, OTTO, science educator; b. Vienna, Austria, Dec. 3, 1954; s. Hans Juergen and Sophie Madelaine (Karasek) P.; m. Dorothea Schmitz, Sept. 2, 1983; 1 child, Isabel. JD, Vienna (Austria) U., 1978, PhD, 1982; postgrad., U. Aix en Provence, France, 1992. Rsch. fellow Fonds sur Fonderureg der Wissenscha/Glicken Forschung, Vienna, 1981-85; atty. Vienna, 1985-86; scientific sec. Internat. Social Sci. Coun., Vienna, 1986-90; chargé de recherche Coun. Nat. Recherche Sci., Aix en Provence, France, 1991-94; prof. U. Lyon (France) Jean Moulin, 1994-98, U. Paris I Pantheon-Sorbonne, 1998—; mem. Coun. Nat. Rsch. Sci., Paris, 1995-2000, dep. dir. Inst. Comparative Law, 2000—. Author: (with Louis Favoreu et al) Droit Constitutionnel 3rd edit. Dalloz, Paris, 2000, (with F. Koja) Frankreich-Osterreich, Vienna Bohlau, 1994, (with Assn. Francaise des Constitutionnalistes, La revision de la Constitution, Economica, Pars, 1993. contbr. articles to profl. jours. Recipient Bronze medal for sci. rsch. CNRS, 1994. Avocations: literature, classical music, sports. Home: 9 Rue Vavin, F-75006 Paris France Office: U Paris I, 12 Place du Pantheon, F 75005 Paris France

PFEUFFER, DALE ROBERT, secondary school social studies educator; b. Pitts., May 23, 1955; s. Francis Jerome and Dorothy Jean (Hankey) P.; m. Mary Elizabeth Hunter, June 4, 1983 (div. 1992); 1 child, Elberta Hunter. AA, C.C. Allegheny County, 1976; BA, U. Pitts., 1977, MEd, 1983. Cert. tchr. secondary comprehensive social studies, Pa. Tchr. secondary social studies Sto-Rox Sch. Dist., McKees Rocks, Pa., 1980-81, Avonworth Sch. Dist., Pitts., 1983-84, Harford County Sch. Dist., Bel Air, Md., 1984-86; tchr. of homebound Penn Hills Sch. Dist., 1979-80, Sto-Rox Sch. Dist., McKees Rocks, Pa., 1980-84, 86-87, Avonworth Sch. Dist., Pitts., 1983-84. Fund raiser Community Redevel. Fund, Ethnic Festival Sponsor, ARC, 1980-81; sponsor Speech and Debate Club, Harford County Sch. Dist., 1985-86. Mem. NEA, Nat. Coun. Social Studies, Assn. Undergrad. Edn. (subcom. student rsch. grants), Pa. State Edn. Assn., Md. State Tchrs. Assn., Coun. Grad. Students Edn., Nat. Geograph. Soc., Nat. Trust Historic Preservation, The Smithsonian Assocs. Democrat. Roman Catholic. Avocations: racquetball, golf, volleyball, softball, swimming. Home: 5703 Kingfish Dr Apt C Lutz FL 33549-5932

PFEUFFER, THOMAS HANS, biochemist, researcher; b. Schweinfurt, Germany, Feb. 11, 1938; s. Leo and Sophie (Pröschel) P.; m. Elke Pichler. Pharm. Chemist U., Würzburg, Germany, 1963; PhD, Univ. Würzburg, Germany, 1966. Capt. German Army, 1966-67; asst. prof. U. Würzburg, Germany, 1968-80, assoc. prof., 1980-91; full prof., dept. head U. Düsseldorf, Germany, 1991—. Mem. Brit. Bio-Chem. Soc., German Soc. Biol. Chemistry. Home: Espenstr 99, 41470 Neuss Germany Office: Heinrich-Heine Univ Inst, Universitätsstr 1, 40225 Düsseldorf Germany

PFISTER, HERBERT JOHANNES, virology educator; b. Nürnberg, Bavaria, Germany, Aug. 12, 1950; s. Karl Christian Pfister and Rosa Pfister-Keck; m. Gudrun Margarethe Drechsel, Aug. 3, 1974; children: Roman, David, Saskia. Diploma in biology, U. Erlangen, Germany, 1973, PhD, 1974. Assoc. prof. Freiburg (German) Med. Sch., 1980-82; prof. Erlangen Med. Sch., 1982-94; chmn. Inst. Virology, prof. Köln Med. Sch., 1994—. Editor: Papillomaviruses and Human Cancer, 1990, Genital Papillomavirus Infections, 1990; contbr. numerous articles to sci. jours. Heisenberg scholar Deutsche Forschungsgemeinschaft, 1981-82; recipient German Cancer award German Cancer Soc., 1994. Mem. Am. Soc. Microbiology, Polish Dermatologic Soc. (hon. corr. mem.), N.Y. Acad. Scis. Office: Inst Virology, Fürst-Pückler-Str 56, 50935 Cologne Germany

PFISTER, LAUREN FREDERICK, Chinese studies educator, researcher, philosopher; b. Denver, Nov. 8, 1951; s. Frederick and Elsie Mabel (Ogilvie) P.; m. Mirasy Miranda, Nov. 5, 1977; children: Athania Kamell, Xavier Pascal. BA cum laude in American Studies, U. Denver, 1973; MDiv with honors, Denver Conservative Bapt. Seminary, 1978; MA in Philosophy, San Diego State U., 1982; PhD in Comparative Philosophy, U. Hawaii, 1987. Lic. minister, Calif. Prof. Biblical Languages Asian Theol. Sem., Manila, 1976-77; prof. Biblical langs., Ethics, Church History Internat. Coll. Grad. Sch. Theology, Honolulu, 1982-86; spl. acad. editor Academia Quarterly, Shanghai, China, 1995—; asst. editor Jour. Chinese Philosophy, Honolulu, 1990-97, assoc. editor, 1997—; from asst. to assoc. prof. religion and philosophy dept. Bapt. U., Hong Kong, 1987—; rsch. collaborator philosophy dept. Nanjing U., 1988, NEH, 1992-96, United Bd. for Christian Higher Edn., Hong Kong, 1989-90, Hong Kong Bapt. U.; translator, collaborator New History Chinese Philosophy, Hong Kong, 1996—; cons. China Acad. Consortium Edn. Resources and Referrals-China, Beijing, 1996—; mem. rsch. program Christianity in East Asia, 1997—; rschr., collaborator North Atlantic Missiology Project, 1997—; assoc. prof. Hong Kong Bapt. U., 1999—. Author, coord. editor: Critical Edition of James Legge's Chinese Classics, 1997—; contbr. to various dictionaries and encys., articles to profl. jours., chpts. to books on Chinese philosophies and religions, traditional and 19th-20th centuries. Campus min. Campus Ambs., Denver, 1974-76; Cantonese/English church leader Baptist Churches, Calif., Calif., Hong Kong, 1978—; tchr., trainer religion & ethics Edn. Divsn. Hong Kong Govt., 1991-92; public speaker, preacher various chs. and univs., 1987—. Mem. APA, Am. Acad. Religion, Internat. Soc. Chinese Philosophy. Democrat. Baptist. Avocations: singing, running, hiking, numismatics, philatelics. Office: Hong Kong Baptist U Dept Religion & Philosophy, 224 Waterloo Rd, Kowloon Hong Kong China

PFISTER, MANFRED MAX, English literature educator; b. Landshut, Bavaria, Germany, Aug. 19, 1943; s. Max and Regina (Mittermeier) P.; m. Elfi Karolina Gehring, Apr. 26, 1969; 1 child, Dominik. Dr phil, U. Munich, 1972, Dr phil habil., 1978. Tutor U. Munich, 1969-70, asst. lectr., 1970-76, assoc. prof., 1978-80; vis. lectr. U. Sussex, Norwich, Eng., 1976-77; prof. English lit. U. Passau, Germany, 1980-91, Free U. Berlin, 1991—. Author: The Theory and Analysis of Drama, 1988, The Fatal Gift of Beauty 1996, Venetian Views, Venetian Blinds, 1999. Home: Wullenweberstrasse 11, D-10555 Berlin Germany Office: U Munich Inst English Phil, Gosslerstrasse 2-4, D-14195 Berlin Germany

PFLUG, GEORG C., statistician, educator; b. Vienna, Austria, June 10, 1951; s. Guenther and Christiane (Eichinger) P.; m. Esther Füzi; children: Natalie, Denise, Dominik. MA in Law, U. Vienna, 1974, PhD, 1975. Assoc. prof. U. Giessen, 1981-89; asst. prof. U. Vienna, 1975-81, prof., 1989—. Author: Stochastic Approximation and Optimization of Random Systems, 1992, Optimization of Stochastic Models, 1996. Rsch. scholar Internat. Inst. for Applied Sys. Analysis, 1988—. Mem. Austrian Soc. Ops. Rsch. (pres. 1994-96), Bernoulli Soc. (coord. European program 1996-98). Office: U Vienna Dept Stats, Universitaetsstrasse 5, A-1090 Vienna Austria

PFLUM, WILLIAM JOHN, physician; b. N.Y.C., July 30, 1924; s. Peter Arthur and Caroline (Schmidt) P.; m. Roseann Sarah Stubing, Oct. 13, 1956; children: Carol Jean, Jeanine, Suzanne, Denise, Peter. BS, Georgetown U., 1947; MD, Loyola U., Chgo., 1951. Diplomate Am. Bd. Allergy & Immunology. Intern St. Vincent's Hosp, N.Y.C., 1951-52; resident in internal medicine NYU div. Goldwater Meml. Hosp., N.Y.C., 1952-53; resident in allergy Inst. Allergy Roosevelt Hosp., N.Y.C., 1956; attending internist allergy & immunology Overlook Hosp., Summit, N.J., 1958—; assoc. attending Inst. Allergy, Immunology and Infectious Diseases, Roosevelt Hosp., N.Y.C., 1957-92; pvt. practice medicine, specializing in allergy and immunology, Summit, 1957-92; ret.; cons. in field. Participant in Boston Marathon, 1971-96. Served with USAAF, 1943-45; ETO. Decorated Purple Heart, air medal with two clusters, POW medal. Fellow Am. Acad. Allergy, Am. Coll. Allergists, Am. Assn. Clin. Immunology and Allergy; mem. Summit Med. Soc., Am. Assn. Clin. Immunology and Allergy (pres. Mid-Atlantic region 1975-76), Disabled Am. Ves., Mil. Order Purple Heart, Am. Ex-Prisoners of War, 8th Air Force Hist. Soc., World Marathon Runners

Assn., Robert A. Cooke Allergy Alumni Assn. Home: 16 Packer Ave Rumson NJ 07760-2028

PFOUTS, RALPH WILLIAM, economist, consultant; b. Atchison, Kans., Sept. 9, 1920; s. Ralph Ulysses and Alice (Oldham) P.; m. Jane Hoyer, Jan. 31, 1945 (dec. Nov. 1982); children: James William, Susan Jane Pfouts Portman, Thomas Robert (dec.), Elizabeth Ann Pfouts Klenowski; m. Lois Bateson, Dec. 21, 1984 (div.); m. Felicia Sprincenatu, 1993 (div.). B.A., U. Kans., 1942, M.A., 1947; Ph.D., U. N.C., 1952. Rsch. asst., instr. econs. U. Kans., Lawrence, 1946-47; instr. U. N.C., Chapel Hill, 1947-50, lectr. econs., 1950-52, assoc. prof. econs., 1952-58, prof. econs., 1958-87, chmn. grad. studies dept. econs. Sch. Bus. Adminstrn., 1957-62, chmn. dept. econs. Sch. Bus. Adminstrn., 1962-68; cons. econs. Chapel Hill, 1987—; vis. prof. U. Leeds, 1983; vis. rsch. scholar Internat. Inst. for Applied Systems Analysis, Laxenberg, Austria, 1983; prof. Cen. European U., Prague, 1991. Author: Elementary Economics-A Mathematical Approach, 1972; editor: So. Econ. Jour, 1955-75; editor, contbr.: Techniques of Urban Economic Analysis, 1960, Essays in Economics and Econometrics, 1960; editorial bd.: Metroeconomica, 1961-80, Atlantic Econ. Jour, 1973—; contbr. articles to profl. jours. Served as deck officer USNR, 1943-46. Social Sci. Research Council fellow U. Cambridge, 1953-54; Ford Found. Faculty Research fellow, 1962-63. Mem. AAAS, Am. Statis. Assn., N.C. Statis. Assn. (past pres.), Am. Econ. Assn., So. Econ. Assn. (past pres.), Atlantic Econ. Soc. (v.p. 1973-76, pres. 1977-78), Population Assn. Am., Econometric Soc., Math. Assn. Am., Phi Beta Kappa, Pi Sigma Alpha, Alpha Kappa Psi, Omicron Delta Epsilon. Home and Office: 127 Summerlin Dr Chapel Hill NC 27514-1925

PFULG, MICHEL EDMOND, plastic and aesthetic surgeon; b. Fribourg, Switzerland, Feb. 17, 1950; s. Edmond and Agnes (Sonney) P.; m. Maria de Saxe, 1975; children: Fabrice, Florence, Joel. MD, U. Geneva, 1976. Registrar in gen. surgery and plastic surgery Zurich U., 1976-83; sr. registrar U. Innsbruck, Austria, 1983; cons. plastic surgeon Cantonal Hosp. Fribourg, 1988-92; head dept. plastic and aesthetic surgery Clinique Valmont, Switzerland, 1992-2000; cons. aesthetic surgeon Clinique La Prairie, Switzerland, 2000—; head dept. aesthetic surgery Clinique de Collonge, Montreux, Switzerland, 1999—. Roman Catholic. Avocations: modern and contemporary art, skiing, golf. Office: Clinique de Collonge, Av de Collonge 43, 1820 Montreux-Territet Switzerland

PHADKE, UDAY, mechanical and electrical engineer; b. Kampala, Uganda, July 7, 1952; arrived in U.K., 1972.; s. Prabhakar and Mangala (Modak) P.; m. Wendy Mersh, July 14, 1989; children: Leela Jane, Jamie Krishan. M in Engring., Trinity Coll., Cambridge, England, 1976; PhD, U. Sussex, England, 1982. Bus. devel. mgr. Smith Assocs., Cobham, Surrey, England, 1983-85; chief exec. Meta-Generics, Cambridge, 1989-95; mng. dir. Informed Sources, London, 1995-97; exec. chmn. Cartezia Group, Cambridge, 1997—; dir. media & telecomm. PA Cons., Western Europe, 1985-88; dir. Generics Group, England, 1992-95. Contbr. articles to profl. jours. Rsch. fellow U. Sussex, 1980-83, Vis. fellow, 1983-88. Mem. IEEE (assoc.), Inst. Elec. Engring., Inst. Mech. Engring., Reform Club. Avocation: racquet sports. Office: The Cartezia Group, Cambridge England

PHAM, DUC CHINH, mechanical engineering; b. Namdinh, Vietnam, May 13, 1958; s. Van Tan and Thi Thuc (Tran) P.; m. Thi Thuy An Nguyen; 1 child, Thu Giang Pham. MSc in Solid Mechanics, Belarussian State U., USSR, 1981; PhD, Inst. Mechs., Hanoi, Vietnam, 1995, DSc, 1996. Vis. scholar U. Sydney, Australia, 1996—; rsch. assoc. U. Bochum, Germany, 1992; Humboldt rsch. fellow, U. Aachen, Germany, 2000. Mem. Am. Maths. Soc. E-mail: phamduch@hotmail.com. Home: 222 F/12 Doi Can, Hanoi Vietnam Office: RWTH Aachen, Templergraben 64, 52072 Aachen Germany

PHAM, HOANG, engineering educator, researcher; b. Vietnam, Nov. 8, 1960; came to U.S., 1980; m. Michelle Pham, June 17, 1989; children: Hoang Jr., David. BS in Computer Sci., BS in Math., Northeastern Ill. U., 1982; MS in Stats., U. Ill., 1984; MS in Indsl. Engring., SUNY, Buffalo, 1988, PhD in Indsl. Engring., 1989. Sr. specialist engr. Boeing Co., Seattle, 1989-90; sr. engring. specialist Idaho Nat. Engring. Lab., Idaho Falls, 1990-93; assoc. prof. Rutgers U., Piscataway, N.J., 1993—. Author: Software Reliability, 1999; editor: Software Reliability and Testing, 1995; editor-in-chief: Internat. Jour. Reliability, Quality and Safety Engring. Recipient Guest Editor award IEEE Comms. Soc., 1994. Mem. IEEE (sr.), Inst. Indsl. Engrs. (sr., divsn. dir. 1997-98, quality control and reliability achievement award 1998). Achievements include contributions to software reliability engineering, leadership in the field of reliability engineering. Fax: 732-445-5467. Office: Rutgers U Coll Engring Dept Indsl Engring 96 Frelinghuysen Rd Piscataway NJ 08854-8018

PHAM, KIM, aesthetician; b. Hai Phong, Vietnam, Sept. 9, 1953; came to U.S., 1973; d. Ta and Hong (Vu) P.; m. Thiet Pham, Apr. 24, 1977; children: Anthony, Kimberly, Kamie. Diploma in skin care, Cidesco Internat., Europe. Owner Kim's Perfect 10 Salon, Burlingame, Calif. Home: 209 Hazelwood Ave San Francisco CA 94127-2109 Office: Kims Perfect 10 Salon 1205 Capuchino Ave Burlingame CA 94010-3403

PHAM, KINH DINH, electrical engineer, educator, administrator; b. Saigon, Republic of Vietnam, Oct. 6, 1956; came to U.S., 1974; s. Nhuong D. (dec.) and Phuong T. (Tran) P.; m. Ngan-Lien T. Nguyen, May 27, 1985; children: Larissa, Galen. BS with honors, Portland State U., 1979; MSEE, U. Portland, 1982; postgrad., Portland State U., 1988-90. Registered profl. engr., Oreg., Calif., Ariz., Fla., Wash., Mass., Conn., R.I. Elec. engr. Irvington-Moore, Tigard, Oreg., 1979-80; elec. engr. Elcon Assocs., Inc., Beaverton, Oreg., 1980-87, from sr. elec. engr., assoc. ptnr., 1987-96, v.p., 1996—; adj. prof. Portland (Oreg.) Community Coll., 1982—; mem. adv. bd. Mass Transit System Compatibility, 1994. Consulting tech. editor Rsch. and Edn. Assn., 1998—; contbr. articles to profl. jours. Recipient Cert. Appreciation Am. Pub. Transit Assn. and Transit Industry, 1987. Mem. IEEE, N.Y. Acad. Scis., Mass Transit Sys. Compatibility Adv. Bd, Eta Kappa Nu. Buddhist. Avocations: reading, teaching; profl. interests include traction power systems simulation, analysis and design, computer systems simulations, other computer-related systems. Office: Elcon Assocs Inc 12670 NW Barnes Rd Portland OR 97229-9001

PHAM, LOI VU, mathematician, educator; b. Hanoi, Vietnam, July 7, 1934; s. Phong Ich and Van Thi (Nguyen) P.; m. Huyen Thi Nguyen, July 31, 1967; children: Thi Van Lan, Thi Huyen Dung, Vu Nam. B Math. Sci., State Kharcov (Ukraine) U., 1966; Candidate Physics Math. Sci., Inst. Math., Kiev, Ukraine, 1973, D Physics Math. Sci., 1983. Asst. State U., Vietbac, Vietnam, 1966-70; chief rschr. Inst. Earth's Scis., Hanoi, 1974-79; head dept. calculation methods, fgn. rschr. Inst. Math., Kiev, 1980-83; high ranking rschr., head dept. phys. math. methods Inst. Mechanics, Hanoi, 1983—; high ranking rschr. Nat. Ctr. Natural Sci. and Tech., 1983—; prof. Ctr. Master and Doctorate Edn. of Mechanics, Hanoi, 1983—; mem. Sci. Coun. Mechanics, Hanoi, 1983—. Contbr. articles to profl. jours. Recipient nat. medal scics. and tech. Ministry Scis., Tech. and Environ, 1996. Mem. Nat. Geographic Soc., N.Y. Acad. Scis. Home: No 1 A5 Khu Tap The Lap May, Phuong Cong Vi Ba Dinh, Hanoi Vietnam Office: Vien Co Hoc Inst Mechanics, 264 Doi Can St, Hanoi Vietnam

PHAN, BINH CONG, electrical engineer; b. Vietnam, Aug. 1, 1950; s. Dong Van Phan and Chu Xia Trinh; m. Loan Ngoc Chau, Aug. 2, 1981; children: Julie, Derek, Andy. BS, Minh Duc U., 1975; MS, U. Ill., 1980; PhD, So. Meth. U., 1987. Sr. rsch. engr. Motorola, Inc., Fort Worth, Tex., 1979-87; staff engr. Allied-Signal Aerospace, Towson, Md., 1987-88; assoc. prof. George Washington U., 1994-99; program dir. U.S. Postal Svcs., Merrifield, 1988—; v.p. Anacomco, Ind., Columbia, Md., 1989-91. Recipient Achievement award Motorola, Inc., 1979. Mem. IEEE, AAAP, Colesville Tennis Ladder, U. Ill. Alumni Assn. Democrat. Buddhist. Avocations: tennis, dancing, soccer, martial arts. Fax: 301-206-5109. Home: 5661 Gosling Dr Clifton VA 20124-0902 Office: US Postal Svcs 8403 Lee Hwy Merrifield VA 22082-0001

PHAN, SEAMUS CHING-CHIA, technology strategist, educator, consultant, researcher; b. Taipei, Republic of China, Dec. 15, 1964; arrived in Singapore, 1971; s. Siaw-Hong and Tsu-An (Ting) P. Diploma in Fine Arts, Nanyand Acad. Fine Arts, Singapore, 1979; BS, Pacific So. U., 1990; MSc in Info. Tech. and Edn., Greenwich U., 1998, PhD in Bus. Adminstrn., 1999. Tng. officer Seagate Tech., Singapore, 1988; publ. dir. Citibank, Singapore, 1989; head Mktg. Price Waterhouse, Singapore, 1990; sr. cons. Ernst & Young, Singapore, 1992; mktg. mgr. ACS Computer, Singapore, 1994; ptnr. McGallen & Bolden, Singapore, 1994—. Author: Service Quality-The Enlightened Approach, 1994, Internet Webmaster Logbook, 1996, Global Asia, 1995, Villagers at Xenoville, 1996. Named Men and Women of Distinction, 1991. Mem. ASTD, Internat. Soc. for Performance Improvement, Pub. Rels. Soc. Am., Nat. Press Club. Buddhism. Avocations: tennis, photography, writing, computing, saxophone. E-mail: seamus@mcgallen.com. Office: Gold Pine Ind Bldg McGallen & Bolden, 20 Maxwell Rd #04-01F Ste F, Singapore 069113, Singapore

PHAN, VAN KHAI, prime minister; b. Vietnam, Dec. 25, 1933. Student, Plekhanov Inst., Moscow. Chmn. People's Com., Vietnam, 1985-89, State Planning Com., Vietnam, 1989-91; prime minister Govt. Vietnam. Alt. mem. ctrl. com. Communist Party, 1982, mem. 1986, 8th ranked mem. politburo. Office: Office of Prime Minister, Hoang Hoa Thum Str, Hanoi Vietnam*

PHANG, JACOB C.H., engineering educator; b. Singapore, Singapore, Oct. 6, 1953; s. Ah Seong and Siam Chuan (Lim) P.; m. Jennifer W.K. Chan, May 31, 1981; 4 children. BA with honors, Cambridge U., 1975, PhD, 1979. Lectr. Nat. U. of Singapore, 1979-83, sr. lectr., 1983-90, assoc. prof., 1990-98, prof., 1998—; dir. Image Transforms Pte Ltd., Singapore, 1992—. Recipient Nat. Young Scientist and Engr. award Nat. Sci. and Tech. Bd., 1988, Achievement award in R&D Asean Bus. Forum, 1995, Public Adminstrn. award Pres. of Singapore, 1996. Office: Office Univ Rels Nat U, 10 Kent Ridge Crescent, Singapore 119260, Singapore

PHANJOO, ANDRÉ LUDOVIC, psychiatrist, educator; b. Port Louis, Mauritius, Sept. 29, 1937; came to Eng., 1959; s. Andrew and Noelle (Seerungen) P.; m. Barbara Elizabeth Darwell, July 27, 1963; children—Claire, Anna, Ralph. M.B., Ch.B., 1966. Medical diplomate. Registrar Royal Edinburgh Hosp., 1967-69, sr. registrar, 1970-71, cons., 1972—; hon. sr. lectr. U. Edinburgh, 1975—. Contbg. author: Companion To Psychiatry Studies, 1977. Contbr. articles to profl. jours. Fellow Royal Coll. Psychiatrists; mem. Brit. Med. Assn., Brit. Assn. for Psychopharmacology. Social Democrat. Mem. Ch. of England. Home: 29 Blacket Pl, Edinburgh EH9 1RJ, Scotland Office: Royal Edinburgh Hosp, Dept Psychiatry Morningside Park, Edinburgh EH10 5HF, England

PHAN-TAN, TAI, materials scientist, researcher, educator; b. Kien-Giang, Vietnam, July 7, 1939; arrived in Fed. Republic Germany, 1960; s. Van-To Phan and Thi-Ngai Nguyen; m. Thanh-Van Do, Nov. 8, 1968; children: Thanh-Thao, Thanh-Thu, Thanh-Uy. Diploma in engring., Tech. Coll. Engring., Aachen, Fed. Republic Germany, 1966; postgrad., French Inst. Indsl. Freezing, Paris, 1966-68; D of Engring., U. Hannover, Fed. Republic Germany, 1982. Head of sect., Material Rsch. Inst. U. Hannover, 1984-86, lectr., head sect. corrosion dept. properties of material, 1992—. Contbr. articles to profl. publs. Mem. Verein Deutscher Eisenhuttenleute, Verein Deutscher Korosionfachleute, The Minerals, Metals and Materials Soc. Office: Univ Hannover, Appelstrasse 11 A, 30167 Hannover 1, Germany

PHAROAH, PETER OSWALD DERRICK, epidemiologist educator; b. Ranchi, Bihar, India, May 19, 1934; s. Oswald Higgins and Phyllis Christene (Gahan) P.; m Margaret Rose McMinn, May 17, 1960; children: Fiona, Paul, Mark, Timothy. BS, U. London, 1958, MD, 1972, MSc, 1974. House office Nat. Health Svc., London, 1958-63; med. officer Dept. Pub. Health, Papua, New Guinea, 1963-74; sr. lectr. U. London, 1974-79; prof. U. Liverpool, Eng., 1979-97, emeritus prof., 1997—. Editor Internat. Jour. Epidemiology, 1990-99. Avocations: philately, fell walking.

PHAT, VU NGOC, mathematician, researcher; b. Namdinh, Vietnam, May 19, 1952; s. Vu Ngoc and Bui Thi (Ty) Chan; m. Nguyen Thi Mo; children: Dat V.Q., Phuong V.L. BS, Azerbaizan U., 1975, PhD, 1984; DSc, Inst. Math., Warsaw, Poland, 1995. Rschr. Inst. Math., Hanoi, 1976-83, 84-90, sr. rschr., 1990—, prof. math., 1992—, head dept., 1992—; vis. scientist Azerbaizan U., 1981-83; postdoctoral fellow Computing Ctr., Moscow, 1988-89; vis. rschr. Indian Inst. Sci., Banglore, 1991; vis. prof. Tokyo Inst. Tech., 1993, Pusan Nat. U., 1998, Chiangmai (Thailand) Nat. U., 1999, U. West Australia, 2000; assoc. rschr. Internat. Ctr. for Theoretical Physics, Trieste, Italy, 1995-2000. Author: Constrained Control Problems, 1996; assoc. editor Internat. Math. Jour. Optimization, 1997—, Nonlinear Functional Analysis Applications, 1999—; Acta Math. Vietnamica, 2000—. Mem. Am. Math. Soc., Soc. Indsl. Applied Math., N.Y. Acad. Scis., Wordl. Sci. Engring. Soc. Avocation: teaching. E-mail: vnphat@hanimath.ac.vn. Office: Inst of Math, PO Box 631, Bo Ho 10000 Hanoi Vietnam

PHELAN, JOHN DENSMORE, insurance executive, consultant; b. Kalamazoo, Aug. 31, 1914; s. John and Ida (Densmore) P.; m. Isabel McLaughln, July 31, 1937; children: John Walter, William Paul, Daniel Joseph. BA magna cum laude, Carleton Coll., 1935. Reporter New Bedford (Mass.) Std.-Times, 1935-36; with Hardware Mut. Ins. Co., Stevens Point, Wis., 1936-45; with Am. States Ins. Co. (name now Safeco Ins.), Indpls., 1945-90, pres., 1963-76, chmn., 1976-79, also bd. dirs. numerous subs.; bd. govs. Internat. Ins. Soc. Author: Business Interruption Primer, 1949, also later edits; contbr. articles to profl. jours. Past pres. Marion County Assn. Mental Health; chmn. emeritus CPCU-Harry J. Loman Found. Named to Hon. Order Ky. Cols., Sagamore of Wabash. Mem. CPCU Soc. (past nat. pres.), CLU Soc., Woodland Country Club (Indpls.), El Conquistador Country Club, Phi Beta Kappa. Presbyterian. Home: 6501 17th Ave W Apt W206 Bradenton FL 34209-7806

PHELAN, THOMAS, clergyman, academic administrator, educator; b. Albany, N.Y., Apr. 11, 1925; s. Thomas William and Helen (Rausch) P. A.B. (N.Y. State Regents scholar 1942, President's medal 1945), Coll. Holy Cross, Worcester, Mass., 1945; S.T.L., Catholic U. Am., 1951; postgrad., Oxford (Eng.) U., 1958-59, 69-70. Ordained priest Roman Cath. Ch., 1951; pastor, tchr., adminstr. Diocese of Albany, 1951-58; resident Cath. chaplain Rensselaer Poly. Inst., Troy, N.Y., 1959-72, prof. history, 1972—, dean Sch. Humanities and Social Scis., 1972-95, inst. historian, inst. dean, sr. adviser to pres., 1995—; chmn. architecture and bldg. commn. Diocese Albany, 1968—; cons. in field. Author: Hudson Mohawk Gateway, 1985, Achieving the Impossible, 1995; author monographs, articles, revs. in field. Treas. The Rensselaer Newman Found., 1962—; pres. Hudson-Mohawk Indsl. Gateway, 1971-84, bd. dirs. exec. com. 1984—; mem. WMHT Ednl. Telecomm. Bd., 1966-77, 84-90, chmn. 1973-77; chmn. Troy Hist. Dist. and Landmarks Rev. Commn., 1975-86, chmn. hist. adv. com., 1987—; v.p. Preservation League N.Y. State, 1979-82, mem. trustees coun., 1982-87, 89—, pres. 1987-89; sec. and bd. dirs. Ptnrs. for Sacred Places, 1989—; bd. dirs. Hall of History Found., 1983-87; trustee Troy Pub. Libr., 1992—. With USN, 1943-46. Recipient Paul J. Hallinan award Nat. Newman Chaplains Assn., 1967, Ann. award Albany Arts League, 1977, Disting. Cmty. Svc. award Rensselaer Poly. Inst., 1979, Edward Fox Demers medal Alumni Assn. Rensselaer Poly. Inst., 1986, Disting. Svc. award Hudson-Mohawk Consortium of Colls. and Univs., 1988; named Acad. Laureate of the SUNY Found. at Albany, 1988; Danforth Found. fellow, 1969-70; grantee Homeland Found., 1958-59, Dorothy Thomas Found., 1969-70. Fellow Soc. Arts, Religion and Contemporary Culture; mem. Ch. Soc. Coll. Work (dir., exec. com. 1970—), Am. Conf. Acad. Deans, Liturgical Conf., Soc. Indsl. Archaeology, Assn. Internat. pour l'Etudes des Religions Prehistoriques et Ethnologiques, Cath. Campus Ministry Assn., Cath. Art Assn., Assn. for Religion and the Intellectual Life (bd. dirs. 1987—), Soc. History of Tech. Clubs: Ft. Orange, Troy Country; Squadron A (N.Y.C.). Home: 5 Whitman Ct Troy NY 12180-4732 Office: Rensselaer Poly Inst Troy NY 12180

PHELAND, EILEEN HOPE, writer; b. Bklyn., July 22, 1965; d. Bernard and Phyllis (Halpern) P. Writer, publ. Happy Hour Newsletter, N.Y.C., 1999—. Author: The Truth About Being Homeless, 1998. Home: PO Box 121647 San Diego CA 92112-1647

PHELIP, XAVIER ANDRÉ, rheumatologist, educator; b. Lyon, France, Mar. 4, 1936; s. Edme and Elisabeth Jeanne (Delore) P.; m. Jacqueline Damienne Ross, Apr. 15, 1966; children: Pierre-Yves, Jean-Marc, Catherine, Elisabeth. PhD, J. Fourier U., Grenoble, France, 1961. Intern U. Hosp., Grenoble, 1961-66, cons., 1966-71, chief cons., 1971—, prof. rheumatology, 1971—, chief dept. rheumatology, 1981—; cons. med. commn. Univ. Hosp., Grenoble, 1980-84; adminstrv. counselor Uriage (France) Hosp. of Rheumatology, 1986—; prof. rheumatology Grenoble Health Dept.; organizer congresses in field. Contbr. articles to profl. jours. Hon. pres. French Thermal Soc., 1980, French League Against Rheumatism, 1984. Capt. French Health Svc., 1963-80. Mem. French Soc. Rheumatology (adminstrv. counselor, 1988, v.p. 1998), French League Against Rheumatism (adminstrv. counselor 1984—, hon. pres. 1994, sec. gen. 1988-94), Interdisciplinary Group Against Backache (founding pres. 1997), Rotary. Avocations: tennis, skiing, mountain touring, swimming. Office: Univ Hosp, BP 217, 38043 Grenoble Cedex Isere, France

PHELPS, CAROL JO, neuroendocrinologist; b. Sendai, Japan, Apr. 20, 1948; d. Harry J. and Helen I. (Davies) P.; m. James B. Turpen, June 13, 1969 (div. Apr. 1982); children: J. Matthew Turpen, John A. Turpen; m. David L. Hurley, Oct. 12, 1985. BS in Zoology, U. Denver, 1969; PhD in Anatomy, La. State U. Med. Ctr., 1974. Postdoctoral fellow NIH, U. Rochester, N.Y., 1974-76; rsch. assoc. Pa. State U., Univ. Park, 1976-77; instr. Pa. State U., 1977-80, postdoctoral scholar, 1980-82; asst. prof. neurobiology U. Rochester, 1982-90; assoc. prof. anatomy Tulane U. Sch. Medicine, New Orleans, 1990-94; prof., 1994—; nat. scientific adv. coun. Am. Fedn. Aging Rsch., N.Y.C., 1988—; rev. coms. Nat. Inst. on Aging, Bethesda, Md., 1993-97; editl. bd. Neuroendocrinology, Paris, 1994—, Endocrinology, 1996—, Jour. of Andrology, 1996-99. Com. sec., chair Otetiana Coun. Pack 10 Boy Scouts Am., Honeoye Falls, N.Y., 1987-89. NIH fellow, 1974-76; grantee NIH, 1983—. Mem. Am. Assn. Anatomists, Soc. Exptl. Biology and Medicine, Endocrine Soc., Soc. Neurosci. (chpt. pres. 1995-96). Avocations: antique restoration, photography. Office: Tulane U Sch Medicine Dept Anatomy 1430 Tulane Ave New Orleans LA 70112-2699

PHELPS, CHARLES ELLIOTT, economics educator; b. N.Y.C., Apr. 20, 1943; s. McKinnie L. and Carolyn (McCleery) P.; m. Dale L. King, Sept. 2, 1967; children: Darin, Teresa. BA in Math., Pomona Coll., 1965; MBA, U. Chgo., 1968, PhD, 1973. Economist RAND Corp., Santa Monica, Calif., 1973-84; prof. econs. U. Rochester, N.Y., 1984—; provost U. Rochester, 1994—; cons. JUREcon, Inc., L.A., 1977-86; pvt. cons., Rochester, N.Y., 1986—. Author: Health Economics, 2d edit., 1997; also over 70 articles. Fellow Nat. Bur. for Econ. Rsch.; mem. Inst. Medicine, Am. Econ. Assn., Nat. Acad. Social Ins., Soc. for Med. Decision Making (trustee 1991-93), Assn. for Pub. Policy Analysis (sec. 1982-91). Avocations: photography, archery, astronomy, canoeing. Office: Office of the Provost U Rochester 200 Wallis Hall Rochester NY 14627-0001

PHELPS, CHARLOTTE DEMONTE, economics educator; b. East Orange, N.J., Jan. 26, 1933; d. Robert William and Marian Ethel (Page) DeMonte; m. Edmund Strother Phelps, 1957 (div. 1969). BA magna cum laude, Radcliffe Coll., 1955; MA, Yale U., 1956, PhD, 1961. Instr. Conn. Coll., New London, 1961; rsch. staff economist Cowles Found. and Econ. Growth Ctr., Yale U., 1963-65; postdoctoral rsch. felow com. on econ. stblzn. Social Sci. Rsch. Coun., 1965-68; asst. prof. dept. econs. Temple U., Phila., 1967-68, assoc. prof., 1969-97, prof., 1998—; cons. Hay/McBer, 1999—. Author: Unconscious Motivation and Economic Choice, 1981; mem. editl. bd. Jour. Behavioral Econs., 1987-90, Jour. Econ. Behavior and Orgn., 1998—; contbr. articles to profl. publs. Mem. Phila. Cmty. Coordinated Child Care Coun., 1970-72; mem. schs. and scholarships com. Harvard-Radcliffe Clubs Phila., 1977-82. Vis. fellow Yale U., 1998-99; predoctoral grantee Commn. on Money and Credit, 1959-60, grantee Murray Rsch. Ctr., Radcliffe Coll., 1998-2000, Smith Richardson Found., 1998-2000. Mem. Am. Econ. Assn., Cosmopolitan Club Phila., Yale Coun. Phila., Assn. Yale Alumni (del. 1994-97), Yale Club Phila., Phi Beta Kappa. Home: 1420 Locust St Apt 25B Philadelphia PA 19102-4215 Office: Temple U Dept Econs 879 W Ritter Annex Philadelphia PA 19122

PHELPS, DENNIS LANE, minister, educator, author; b. Monroe, La., July 23, 1955; s. Vaughn Lavelle and Vestal (Humphreys) P.; m. Robbin Jean Loewer, May 27, 1979; children: Kristen Lane, David Loewer. BA, La. Coll., 1978; MDiv, New Orleans Bapt. Theol. Sem., 1981; PhD, Southwestern Bapt. Theol. Sem., 1990. Ordained to ministry Bapt. Ch., 1978; cert. intern supr. Coord. ch. ministries La. Moral and Civic Found., Baton Rouge, 1973-79; staff evangelist Dennis Phelps Evangelistic Ministries, 1979—; pastor Brownfields Bapt. Ch., Baton Rouge, 1981-82; grader/teaching fellow Southwestern Bapt. Theol. Sem., Ft. Worth, 1982-87; pastor St. Francis Village Protestant Fellowship, Crowley, Tex., 1986-88; assoc. prof. of preaching Bethel Theol. Sem., St. Paul, 1988-99; assoc. tchg. pastor, exec. adminstr. Severns Valley Ch., Elizabethtown, Ky., 1998—; v.p. Global Horizons, Inc., 1994—. Editor Jour. of Am. Acad. Ministry, 1995-98. Mem. strategy coun. AD2000: Mission Twin Cities, 1994-98; bd. dirs. Youth Connection, Inc., 1997—. Named Outstanding Young Men of Am., U.S. Jaycees, 1983-85, 89, Southwesterner of the Yr. Minn.-Wis. S.W. Bapt. Theol. Sem. Alumni, 1994. Mem. Inst. of Bibl. Rsch., Religious Speech Communications Assn., Acad. of Homiletics, Am. Assn. of Religion, Soc. Bibl. Lit., Assn. Practical Theology, Am. Acad. Ministry (charter), Nat. Storytelling Assn., Evang. Homiletics Soc. (charter), Rotary Club Internat. Office: Severns Valley Ch PO Box 130 Elizabethtown KY 42702-0130

PHELPS, DOROTHY FRINK, civic worker; b. Macon, Ga., June 15, 1906; d. James Richard and Alma (Hall) Frink; m. John Grady Phelps, Feb. 18, 1929 (dec. Oct. 1981); children: Judith Ann Phelps Austin (dec.), John Richard Phelps. Cert. in bus. law, commerce, Fla. State Coll. Women, Tallahassee. Sec. Dir. Pub. Health and Welfare, Miami, 1925-39; ret., 1939. Editor Ch. News Notes, 1st United Meth. Ch., former offices held include chmn. Christian edn.; pres. Silver Bluff Elem. PTA, 1948; v.p. Shennandoah Jr. H.S. PTA; mem. exec. bd., pres. Miami Sr. H.S. PTA; vol. mentor program Milam Elem. Sch., Hialeah, Fla. Recipient award for 76 years serving in Christian edn., 1st United Meth. Ch., 1996. Mem. DAR, Miami Women's Panhellenic Assn. (pres. 1930-31), Miami Woman's Club, Delta Delta Delta Mother's Club, Delta Zeta. Democrat. Home: 5300 W 16th Ave Apt 310 Hialeah FL 33012-2104

PHELPS, GERRY CHARLOTTE, economist, minister; b. Norman, Okla., Oct. 15, 1931; d. George and Charlotte LeNoir (Yowell) P.; 1 child, Scott. BA, U. Tex., 1963, MA, 1984; MDiv, San Francisco Theol. Seminary, 1981. Cert. tchr., Calif. Lectr. in econs. U. Houston, 1966-69; pastor United Meth. Ch., Kelseyville, Calif., 1980-82; sr. pastor Bethel United Methodist Ch., Bakersfield, Calif., 1982-84; founding exec. dir. Bethany Svc. Ctr., Bakersfield, 1982-84; pres., founding exec. dir. Concern for the Poor, Inc., San Jose, Calif., 1985-92; pastor United Meth. Ch., Flatonia, Tex., 1993-97; founding exec. dir. CRISES, Austin, 1994-98, v.p. devel., 1998-99; pvt. practice cons. poverty issues, 1999—; cons. to programs helping people out of poverty. Author: Nutrition for Better Living, 1999, Budgeting for Better Living, 1999. Mem. Task Force on the Homeless, San Jose, 1987, Santa Clara County, 1991. Recipient commendation Mayor of Bakersfield, 1984, Santa Clara County Bd. Suprs., 1992. Avocations: Latin American studies, refugee assistance, homeless assistance, study of connections between economic and social problems. Fax: 512-926-6222. E-mail: gphelps@austin.rr.com.

PHIEU, LE KHA, government executive; b. Thanh Hoa, Vietnam, Dec. 27, 1931; married; 3 children. Grad., Mil. U., Vietnam. Gen. sec. Communist Party Vietnam, 1997—. Office: Communist Party Vietnam, 1 Hoang Van Thu, Hanoi Vietnam*

PHILBIN, DANIEL JUDE, television newswriter; b. L.A., July 24, 1965; s. Regis Francis and Catherine Francis Philbin; m. Lila Jean Bakke, Oct. 18, 1997. BA, Calif. State U., Northridge, 1993; MA, Cath. U. Am., Washington, 1996. Cert. Pub. Affairs Officer course, U.S. Dept. Def. Info. asst. U.S. Dept. Def., Washington, 1993-97; nat. security policy analyst Sci. Applications Internat. Corp., McLean, Va., 1997-98; pub. affairs officer USN, Washington, 1998-99; edit. asst. Fox News Channel, Washington, 1999—. E-mail: philbin@foxnews.com. Office: Fox News Channel 400 N Capitol St NW Ste 550 Washington DC 20001-1502

PHILIP, PRINCE (DUKE OF EDINBURGH), Prince of United Kingdom of Great Britain and Northern Ireland, Earl of Merioneth, Baron Greenwich; b. Corfu, June 10, 1921; renounced right of succession to Thrones of Greece and Denmark; naturalized British subject, 1947, adopted surname of Mountbatten.; s. Prince Andrew of Greece and Denmark and Princess Alice of Battenberg; m. Princess Elizabeth (now Queen Elizabeth II), Nov. 20, 1947; children: Charles Philip Arthur George, Anne Elizabeth Alice Louise, Andrew Albert Christian Edward, Edward Antony Richard Louis. Grad., Cheam Sch., Salem Sch., Gordonstoun Sch., Royal Naval Coll., Dartmouth; LLD (hon.), Wales, London, Edinburgh, Cambridge, Karachi, Malta; DCL (hon.), Durham, Oxford; DSc (hon.), Delhi, Reading, Salford, Southampton, Victoria; hon. degree, Eng. U., Lima, Peru; D in Law (hon.), UCLA. Personal A.D.C. to King George VI, 1948-52, P.C., 1951—; chancellor U. Wales, 1948-76, U. Edinburgh, 1952—, U. Cambridge, 1977—, Salford U., 1967-91; vis. R.C.A, 1967—; privy councillor of Can., 1957—. Author: Birds from Britannia, 1962 (with James Fisher) Wildlife Crisis, 1970, The Environmental Revolution: Speeches on Conservation 1962-77, 1978, Men, Machines and Sacred Cows (speeches and essays), 1984, Down to Earth, 1988, Living off the Land, 1989. Patron, chair of trustees Duke of Edinburgh's Award Scheme, 1956—; pres. English-Speaking Union of the Commonwealth, 1952—, R.S.A., 1952—, Commonwealth Games Fedn., 1955-90, Royal Agrl. Soc. of the Commonwealth, 1958—, Brit. Med. Assn., 1959-60, Wildlife Trust, 1960-65, 72-77, World Wildlife Fund Brit. Nat. Appeal, 1961-81, Coun. for Nat. Acad. Awards, 1965-75, Scottish Icelandic Assn., 1965—, Maritime Trust, 1969—, Nat. Coun. Social Svc., 1970-73, Australian Conservation Found., 1971-76, World Wildlife Fund for Nature Int., 1981-96, pres. emeritus, 1997—, others. With Brit. Pacific Fleet, S.E. Asia, PTO, 1939-45; Adm. of Fleet, F.M., Marshal of RAF, 1953—, Adm. of the Fleet RNZN, 1958, Field Marshal N.Z. Army, 1978, Adm. of the Fleet Australian Mil. Forces, 1954—, Adm. of the Fleet Royal Australian Navy, 1954—, Marshal of Royal Australian Air Force, 1954—. Recipient numerous awards and decorations worldwide. Office: Buckingham Palace, London SW1A 1AA, England

PHILIP, A. G. DAVIS, astronomer, editor, educator; b. N.Y.C., Jan. 9, 1929; s. Van Ness and Lillian (Davis) P.; m. Kristina Drobavicius, Apr. 25, 1964; 1 dau., Kristina Elizabeth Elanor. B.S., Union Coll., 1951; M.S., N.Mex. State U., 1959; Ph.D., Case Inst. Tech., 1964. Tchr. physics, math. and chemistry Brooks Sch., 1954-59; instr. Case Inst. Tech., 1962-64; asst. prof. astronomy U. N.Mex., 1964-66; asst. prof. astronomy SUNY-Albany, 1966-67, assoc. prof., 1967-76, mem. exec. com. Arts and Scis. Coun., 1975-76; rsch. prof. astronomy Union Coll., Schenectady, 1976—, astronomer Dudley Obs., 1967-81, Frank L. Fullam chair astronomy, 1980-81, editor Dudley Obs. Reports, 1977-81; astronomer Van Vleck Obs. Wesleyan U., 1982-94; editor contbns. VVObs., 1982-94; pres. Inst. for Space Observation, 1986—; 76, 86, Acad. Scis. Lithuania, 1973, 76, 79, 86, Stellar Data Ctr., Strasbourg, France, 1978, 79, 80, 82, 85, 86; vis. astronomer Moletai Obs., 1988, 94, 99, ; bd. dirs., sec.-treas. N.Y. Astron. Corp., 1969—; pres., treas. L. Davis Press, Inc., 1982—; trustee, mem. Grants award com. Fund Astrophys. Rsch., 1985—; dir. Shapley Vis. Lectureships Program, 1994—; rsch. bd. advisors Am. Biog. Inst., 1996. Exhibited: 2d Ann. Photography Regional, Albany, 1980; author: (with M. Cullen and R.E. White) UBV Color - Magnitude Diagrams of Galactic Globular Clusters, 1976; (with A. Robucci, M. Frame, K.W. Philip) Mm, Fractal Series, Vol. 1, Midgets on the Spike, 1991; editor: The Evolution of Population II Stars, 1972, (with D.S. Hayes) Multicolor Photometry and the Theoretical HR Diagram, 1975, (with M.F. Mc Carthy) Galactic Structure in the Direction of the Galactic Polar Caps, 1977, (with D. H. DeVorkin In Memory of Henry Norris Russell, 1977, (with Hayes) The HR Diagram, 1978, Problems in Calibration of Multicolor Systems, 1979, (with M.F. McCarthy and G.V. Coyne) Spectral Classification of the Future, 1979, X-Ray Symposium, 1981, (with Hayes) Astrophysical Parameters for Globular Clusters, 1981, (with A.R. Upgren) The Nearby Stars and the Stellar Luminosity Function, 1983, (with Hayes and L. Pasinetti) Calibration of Fundamental Stellar Quantities, 1985, (with D.W. Latham) Stellar Radial Velocities, Horizontal-Branch and UV-Bright Stars, 1985, Spectroscopic and Photometric Classification of Population II Stars, 1986, (with J. Grindley) IAU Symposium No. 126, Globular Cluster Systems in Galaxies, 1987, (with Hayes and Liebert) IAU Colloquium No. 95, The Second Conference on Faint Blue Stars, (with Hayes and Adelman) New Directions in Spectrophotometry, 1988, Calibration of Stellar Ages, 1988, (with A.R. Upgren) Star Catalogues; A Centennial Tribute to A.N. Vyssotsky, 1989, (with P. Lu) The Gravitational Force Perpendicular to the Galactic Plane, 1989, (with D.S. Hayes and S.J. Adelman) CCDs in Astronomy. II. Precision Photometry: Astrophysics of the Galaxy, 1991, (with Robucci, Frame and Philip K.) Midgets on the Spike, vol. I, 1991, (with A.R. Upgren) Objective-Prism and Other Surveys, 1991, N.Y. State Astronomy, 1992, (with B. Hauck and A.R. Upgren) Workshop on Databases for Galactic Structure, 1993, (with K.A. Janes and A.R. Upgren) IAU Symposium No. 167, New Developments in Array Technology and Applications, 1995, (with V. Straizys) Photometric Systems and Standard Stars, 1996, 30 Years of Astronomy at Van Vleck Observatory, 1997, (with Peter Boyce) Electronic Publishing: Now and the Future, 1997, (with J. Liebert and R. Saffer) The Third Conference on Faint Blue Stars, 1997, (with W. van Alterna and A. Upgren) Anni Mirabiles: A Symposium Celebrating the 90th Birthday of Dorrit Hottleit, 1999, The Kth Reunion, 2000; mem. editl. bd., co-editor, Baltic Astronomy, 1995—, Astrometric and Photometric Group, Wesleyan U., 1997—; lectr. tours (with K.W. Philip) An Introduction to the Mandelbrot Set, 1988-91; contbr. chpts. to books, articles to profl. jours.; worked with Dr. Irving Langmuir on "The Pathology of Science", 1950—. Served with AUS, 1951-53. Yale U. vis. fellow, 1976; rsch. grantee Rsch. Corp., NSF, NASA, Nat. Rsch. Lab., NAS, Am. Astron. Soc. Fellow AAAS, Royal Astron. Soc., Am. Phys. Soc.; mem. Am. Astron. Soc. (Harlow Shapley lectr. 1973—, interviewed Neil Armstrong 1973, auditor 1977, 79-85), Am. Math. Soc., Can. Astron. Soc., Internat. Astron. Union (chmn., sec. various coms. and commns., pres. commn. 30 1982-85, chmn. working group on spectroscopic and photometric data 1985-94, chmn. sci. organizing com. symposium # 167), N.Y. Acad. Scis., Astron. Soc. Pacific, Astron. Soc. N.Y. (sec.-treas. 1969—, editor newsletter 1974—), Capital Computer Club (bd. dirs. 1990—, v.p. 1993—), Sigma Xi. Achievements include being 1st U.S. observer Soviet 6M telescope, 1980. Home: 1125 Oxford Pl Schenectady NY 12308-2913 Office: Union Coll Physics Dept Schenectady NY 12308

PHILIPP, ELLIOT ELIAS, consulting gynecologist; b. London, July 20, 1915; s. Oscar Isaac and Clarisse (Weil) P.; m. Lucie Ruth Hackenbroch, Mar. 22, 1939 (dec. July 1988); 2 children. M.B.B.Ch., Cambridge U., 1947. Resident Middlesex Hosp., 1939-40, 46-47, U. Coll. Hosp., 1947-49, St. Thomas's Hosp., 1949-50, Royal Free Hosp., 1950-52; cons. gynecologist Romford, Eng., 1952-64, North London, 1964-80; hon. cons. London, 1980-97; cons. Royal No. Hosp. and Whittington Hosp., 1964-80. Contbr. articles to profl. jours.; editor: Scientific Foundations of Obstetrics and Gynecology, 4 edits., 1970-94, History of Obstetrics and Gynecology, 1994; author of textbook. With Royal Air Force, 1940-46. Chevalier Legion D'Honneur, Govt. of France, 1971. Fellow Royal Coll. Surgeons, Royal Coll. Ob-Gyn., Royal Soc. Medicine (past pres. sect. history medicine), Royal Coll. Physicians, Med. Soc. London (pres.), Hunterian Soc. (pres.). Mem. Liberal Party. Jewish. Avocation: walking. Home: 166 Rivermead Ct, London SW6 3SF, England

PHILIPPE, BAGROS, nephrologist; b. Paris; s. Bagros Michel and Toutain Odile; m. Dominique Bagros Martin (div. 1975); children: Veronique, Caroline, Cyril; m. Helene Bagros Tirbach; children: Julie, Guillaume. MD, Paris, 1965. Chef de svc. nephrology/hemodialysis transplant Hosp de Tours, 1972. Editor: (book) Introduction Aux Sciences Humaines en Medicine, 1993. Home: Le Petit Vouvray, 37210 Vouvray France Office: Hosp Bretonneau, 2 Bd Tonnelle, 37044 Tours France

PHILIPPON, MARC JOSEPH, orthopaedic surgeon; b. Quebec City, Can., May 9, 1965; came to U.S., 1990; s. Pontien Aderville and Micheline (Lortie) P.; m. Senenne Catalina Reid, Mar. 25, 1995; children: Michéle, Marc-Christophe. BA with honors, Fla. Atlantic U., 1987; MD, McMaster U., Hamilton, Ont., Can., 1990. Lic. physician, Fla.; diplomate Am. Bd. Orthopaedic Surgery. Orthopaedic surgeon Holy Cross Hosp., Ft. Lauderdale, Fla., 1995—, chief orthopaedic surgery, 2000; chief orthopaedic surgeon humanitarian mission to Ukraine Kiev Orthopaedic Inst., 1997; orthopaedic surgeon Broward Gen. Hosp., Ft. Lauderdale, 1998—; cons. Howmedica Inc., Rutherford, N.J., 1996-97, Smith & Nephew Inc., Memphis, 1998-99; clin. adv. bd. Oratec Interventions, Inc., Menlo Park, Calif., 1998—; cons. Zimmer (Bristol-Myers Squibb); presenter in field. Patent pending for orthopaedic surgery instrument and devices. Bd. dirs. Svc. Agy. for Sr. Citizens, Ft. Lauderdale, 1996, 97, 98, 99, 2000. Farquharson scholar Can. Med. Rsch. Coun., 1989. Fellow Internat. Coll. Surgeons; mem. AMA, So. Med. Assn., So. Orthopaedic Assn., Fla. Med. Assn., Broward Med. Assn., Am. Acad. Orthopaedic Surgeons, Phi Kappa Phi. Roman Catholic. Avocations: skiing, tennis, sailing, hockey, soccer. Office: Orthopaedic Ctr 4725 N Federal Hwy Fort Lauderdale FL 33308-4603

PHILIPPOUSSIS, MARK, pro tennis player; b. Melbourne, Victoria, Australia, Nov. 7, 1976. Mem. ATP Tour, 1994—; winner Indian Wells, 1999, San Jose Open, 2000. Office: ATP Tour 201 ATP Tour Blvd Ponte Vedra Beach FL 32082*

PHILIPPOVA, OLGA EVGENIEVNA, chemist, educator; b. Moscow, Aug. 27, 1959; d. Evgenii Vladimirovich and Nonna Alexandrovna Philippova; m. Alexander Gennadievich Doubitchev, Jan. 2, 1986; 1 child, Alexander. PhD, M.V. Lomonosov Moscow State U., 1985; DSc, Inst. Chem. Physics, Moscow, 1999. Cert. chemist. Rschr. Inst. Immunology, Moscow, 1985-89; rschr. physics dept. Moscow State U., 1990-94, sr. rschr., 1994-96, assoc. prof., 1996—. Contbr. articles to profl. jours. Grantee Internat. Sci. Found., 1993, or-95, Russian Found. Basic Rsch., 1996—, European Commn. Inco-Copernicus, Brussels, 1997—. Office: Moscow State U Physics Dept, Vorobievy Gory, 117234 Moscow Russia

PHILIPSEN, FLEMMING, management consulting executive; b. Roedding, Denmark, Mar. 7, 1948; s. Thorvald and Betty (Hansen) P.; m. Karin Pagh Nielsen, Oct. 19, 1974; children: Linda, Sandie. Cert. prodn. engring., State Engring. Coll., Odense, Denmark, 1974; BS in Bus. Econs., U. Odense, 1980. Cert. mgmt. cons. Motor mechanic Vulcan A/S, Silkeborg, Denmark, 1965-70; regional mgr. Dansk Datasvcs. A/S, Ballerup, Denmark, 1975-77; divsn. mgr. A/S Regnecentralen, Copenhagen, 1977-81; sales mgr. Jacobs Kaffe A/S, Odense, Denmark, 1981-83; mgmt. cons. Mgmt. Ptnrs. A/S, Copenhagen, 1983-89; mng. dir. Mgmt. Ptnrs. A/S, Munkebo, Denmark, 1989-2000; chmn. bd. dirs. Gjaerlov & Moller A/S, Naestved, Denmark, 1993—, AJ Coating, Naestved, 1993—; bd. dirs. Odense Airport, Denmark, 1998—, Ugerloese Sawmill A/S, Danmark, Joergen Pallisgaard A/S, Denmark; mng. dir. KAPA Cons., 20006. Home: Boegevaenget 2, 5330 Munkebo Denmark

PHILIPSEN, HENRICUS JOHANNES, chemist; b. Boxmeer, The Netherlands, Aug. 28, 1965; s. Johan Hendrik and Anna Cornelia (Gyzen) P. BSc, Hogesch. Venlo, The Netherlands, 1987; PhD, Eindhoven U. Tech., The Netherlands, 1998. Cert. analytical chemist. Rsch. asst. Océ Techs., Venlo, 1987-93, rsch. scientist, 1994—, group coach chem. analysis dept., 1996—; rsch. scientist Eindhoven U., 1994—; chmn. discussion group separation methods of polymers, The Netherlands, 1997—; mem. bd. group separation methods Royal Dutch Chem. Soc., 1998—. Contbr. articles to profl. jours. Home: Opwettensemolen 292, NL-5612 Eindhoven The Netherlands Office: Océ Technologies, PO Box 101, NL-5900 Venlo The Netherlands

PHILLIP, CLYDE HERMAN, electrical and electronic engineer educator; b. San Fernando, Trinidad and Tobago, Mar. 28, 1954; s. Andrew and Johanna (Friday) P.; m. Judy Barclay, Aug. 10, 1985; children: Dale, Kafi, Jason, Jenessa, Jevon. BSEE with honours, U. W.I., Trinidad, 1979, MSc in Electronics and Instrumentation, 1984; diploma in mgmt., Coll. Profl. Mgmt., Eng. Chartered engr., U.K.; registered engr., Trinidad and Tobago; lic. FCC; cert. adminstr. Internat. Soc. Cert. Engring. Technicians; approved employer and assessor continuous profl. devel. activities Instn. Mech. Engrs. Automatic exch. technician Telecom. Svcs. Trinidad and Tobago (formerly TELCO), 1973-76, network engr., 1979-83, sr. rsch. engr., 1984-88, ag. mgr. sys. devel., 1988-93, exec. asst. gen. mgr. engring., 1993-94; founder, prin. Phillip's Comprehensive Ednl. Inst., Carapichaima, Trinidad and Tobago, 1994—; tutor in radio and TV, repair and servicing adult edn. program Ministry Edn., 1973-76; lectr. indsl. electronics San Fernando Tech. Inst., 1979-85; sr. lectr. electronics Hazelwood Sch. Electronics, 1984-86; chmn. electronics com. Nat. Tng. Bd., Trinidad, 1990-93; chmn. Phillip's & Assocs., Trinidad, 1993—. Mem. IEEE, Instn. Elec. Engrs., Audio Engring. Soc., Assn. Profl. Engrs. Trinidad and Tobago, Soc. Engrs. U.K., Rotary (sec., bd. dirs. Chaguanas, Trinidad 1990-91). Home: LP 9 Bucarro Rd, St Mary's Village, Carapichaima Trinidad and Tobago Office: Philip's Comprehen Edn Inst, St Mary's Junction, Carapichaima Trinidad and Tobago

PHILLIPPS, IAN HUGH, retired civil engineer; b. London, Nov. 15, 1924; s. Fredrick Alfred and Gwendolen Herbert (Smith) P.; m. Jennifer Robinson, Oct. 14, 1958; children: Victoria, Vere, Christina. BA, Trinity Coll., Cambridge, Eng., 1945, MA, 1949. With wartime engring. rsch. Ministry of Supply, U.K., 1944-45; design engr./mgr. Humphreys & Glasgow Ltd., London, 1945-60, sales dir., 1960-67; dir. Tube Investments Plc., London, 1970-81, chmn., chief exec. domestic appliance div., 1970-74; chmn., chief exec. Raleigh Industries Ltd., Nottingham, Eng., 1974-81; dir. Chamberlain Phipps Plc., Northants, Eng., 1982-89; chmn. Wests Group Internat. Plc., Cheshire, Eng., 1983-86, The BSS Group Plc., Leicester, Eng., 1986-95. Chmn. of coun. Soc. Brit. Gas Industries, London, 1970-72; pres. of coun. Bicycle Assn. Gt. Britain, Coventry, 1977-79; mem. Nat. Pay Rev. Body for Nursing and Professions Allied to Medicine, U.K., 1984-91; mem. coun. U. Nottingham, 1979-96; chmn. Industry Yr. '86 East Midlands, 1986; gov. Welbeck Coll., Notts., 1987-94; pres. Brit. Assn. for Cricketers with Disabilities, 1992-95. Named Dep. Lt., County of Nottinghamshire, 1990—, High Sheriff of Nottinghamshire, 1992. Fellow Royal Acad. Engring., Instn. Civil Engrs., Instn. Gas Engrs., Coun. Confed. Brit. Industry (chmn. East Midlands region 1983-84). Anglican. Avocations: fishing, rowing, brass bands. Home: Grange Farm Rempstone, Loughborough LE12 6RW, England

PHILLIPS, BETTY LOU (ELIZABETH LOUISE PHILLIPS), author, interior designer; b. Cleve.; d. Michael N. and Elizabeth D. (Materna) Suvak; m. John S. Phillips, Jan. 27, 1963 (div. Jan. 1981); children: Bruce, Bryce, Brian; m. John D.C. Roach, Aug. 28, 1982. BS, Syracuse U., 1960; postgrad. in English, Case Western Res. U., 1963-64. Cert. elem. and spl. edn. tchr., N.Y. Tchr. pub. schs. Shaker Heights, Ohio, 1960-66; sportswriter Cleve. Press, 1976-77; spl. features editor Pro Quarterback Mag., N.Y.C., 1976-79; freelance writer specializing in books for young people, 1976—; interior designer residential and comml.; bd. dirs. Cast Specialties Inc., Cleve. Author: Chris Evert: First Lady of Tennis, 1977; Picture Story of Dorothy Hamill (ALA Booklist selection), 1978; American Quarter Horse, 1979; Earl Campbell: Houston Oiler Superstar, 1979; Picture Story of Nancy Lopez, (ALA Notable book), 1980; Go! Fight! Win! The NCA Guide for Cheerleaders (ALA Booklist), 1981; Something for Nothing, 1981; Brush Up on Your Hair (ALA Booklist), 1981; Texas ... The Lone Star State, 1989, Provençal Interiors—French Country Style in America, 1998, French by Design, 2000; also contbr. articles to young adult and sports mags. Mem. Soc. Children's Book Writers, Internat. Interior Design Assn. (profl. mem.), Am. Soc. Interior Designers (profl. mem., cert.), Delta Delta Delta. Republican. Roman Catholic. Home: 4278 Bordeaux Ave Dallas TX 75205-3718

PHILLIPS, CARYL, writer; b. St. Kitts, West Indies, Mar. 13, 1958. BA with honors, The Queen's Coll., Oxford, Eng., 1979; AM (hon.), Amherst (Mass.) Coll., 1995; DUniv (hon.), Leeds Metro. U., 1997. Writer in residence Factory Arts Ctr. Arts Coun. Great Britain, London, 1980-82; writer in residence U. Mysore, India, 1987, U. Stockholm, 1989; vis. writer Amherst Coll., 1990-92, writer in residence, 1992—, co-dir. creative writing ctr., 1994-97, prof. English, writer-in-residence, 1994-98; prof. English, Henry R. Luce prof. migration and social order Barnard Coll., Columbia U., N.Y.C., 1998—; vis. lectr. U. Ghana, 1990, U. Poznan, 1991; vis. writer Humber Coll., 1992, 93; writer-in-residence Nat. Inst. of Edn., Singapore, 1994; vis. prof. English, NYU, 1993; vis. prof. humanities U. W.I., 1999-2000; arts coun. Great Britain Drama Panel, 1982-85, prodn. bd. Brit. Film Inst., 1985-88, Bush Theatre bd., 1985-89, The Caribbean Writer bd., U.S. V.I., 1989; hon. sr. mem. U. Kent, 1988; cons. editor Faber & Faber, Inc., 1992-94, Caribbean series editor, 1996—; participant, keynote spkr. 12 ann. cons. German-speaking countries New Lits. in English, Giessen, Germany, 1989; resident writer Hull (Eng.) Internat. Lit. Festival, 1992; instr. writing Arvon Found., summers, 1983—; reader, lectr. in field. Author: The Final Passage, 1985 (Malcolm X prize for lit. 1985), A State of Independence, 1986, Higher Ground, 1989, Cambridge, 1991, Crossing the River, 1993 (James Tait Black meml. prize), The Nature of Blood, 1997, The European Tribe, 1987 (Martin Luther King meml. prize 1987), The Atlantic Sound, 2000; editor: Extravagant Strangers: A Literature of Belonging, 1997, The Right Set: A Tennis Anthology, 1999; (plays) Strange Fruit, 1981, Where There Is Darkness, 1982, The Shelter, 1984; (TV documentary screenplays), Welcome to Birmingham, 1983, The Hope and Glory, 1984, The Record, 1985, Lost in Music, 1984, Darker Than Blue: Curtis Mayfield, 1995; (film) Playing Away, 1986, The Final Passage, 1996; (radio plays) The Wasted Years, 1984 (Best Radio Play of Yr. award BBC 1984), Crossing the River, 1985, The Prince of Africa, 1987, Writing Fiction, 1991; (radio documentaries) St. Kitts (Pride of Place), 1983, Sport and the Black Community, 1984, No Complaints: James Baldwin at Sixty, 1985; contbr. to documentary programs, including Black on Black, London Weekend TV, 1983, Bookmark, 1984; contbr. articles to periodicals. Recipient Young Writer of Yr. award London Sunday Times, 1992, Lannan Literary award, 1994; named U. of W.I. Humanities Scholar of Yr., 1999; Guggenheim fellow, 1992; 50th Anniversary fellow Brit. Coun., 1984. Office: Gillon Aitken Assocs, 29 Fernshaw Rd, London SW10 OTG, England Office: Barnard Coll English Dept 3009 Broadway New York NY 10027-6501

PHILLIPS, CHRISTOPHER HALLOWELL, diplomat; b. The Hague, The Netherlands, Dec. 6, 1920; s. William and Caroline A. (Drayton) P.; m. Mabel B. Olsen, May 11, 1943 (dec. May 1995); children: Victoria A. Phillips Boyd, Miriam O. Phillips Eley, David W.; m. Sydney Watkins Osborne, Nov. 29, 1997. A.B., Harvard U., 1943. Reporter, Beverly (Mass.) Evening Times, 1947-48; mem. Mass. Senate, 1948-53; spl. asst. to asst. sec. UN affairs Dept. State, 1953; later dep. asst. sec. of state for internat. orgn. affairs; apptd. U.S. Civil Service commr.; vice chmn. U.S. Civil Service Commn., 1957; U.S. rep. on UN Econ. and Social Council, 1958-61; Chase Manhattan Bank rep. for UN affairs, 2d v.p., mgr. Canadian div., 1961-65; pres. U.S. council Internat. C. of C., 1965-69; ambassador, dep. U.S. rep. UN Security Council, 1969-70; ambassador, dep. permanent U.S. rep. to UN, 1970-73; pres. Nat. Council for U.S.-China Trade, Washington, 1973-86, now hon. mem. bd. dirs.; U.S. ambassador to Brunei Darussalam, 1989-91; presdl. appointee to bd. U.S. Inst. Peace, 1992-97; trustee Am. Inst. in Taiwan, 1995—; mem. adv. coun. Sch. Advanced Internat. Studies, Johns Hopkins U. Mass. dist. del. Rep. Nat. Conv., 1952, 60. Served to capt. USAAF, 1942-46. Mem. UN Assn. U.S.A., Coun. Fgn. Rels., Asia Soc., Mass. Hist. Soc., Coun. Am. Ambs., Met. Club Washington. Episcopalian. Home: 2801 New Mexico Ave NW Apt 924 Washington DC 20007-3938

PHILLIPS, DOROTHY REID, retired medical library technician; b. Hingham, Mass., Apr. 21, 1924; d. James Henry and Emma Louise (Davis) Reid; m. Earl Wendell Phillips, Apr. 22, 1944; children: Earl W., Jr., Betty Herrera, Carol Coe. Cert., Durham Vocat. Sch., 1952; B.S. in Comml. Edn., N.C. Central U., 1959; postgrad. U. Colo., 1969; M.Human Relations, Webster Coll., 1979; postgrad. Grad. Sch. Library Sci., U. Denver, 1983. Vocat. nurse Meml. Hosp., U. N.C., Chapel Hill, 1955-59; vol. work, Cairo, Egypt, 1965-67; library technician Base Library, Lowry AFB, Colo., 1960-65, Fitzsimons Med. Library, Aurora, Colo., 1976-93; ret. 1993; mem. Denver Mus. Natural History, Denver Art Mus., Mariners. Mem. AARP, NARFE, AAUW (chpt. community rep. 1982-83, state chmn. edn. found. 1982-84, pres. Denver br. 1984-86), Altrusa Internat. (corr. sec. Denver 1982-83, bd. dirs. 1984-85, pres. Denver chpt. 1988), Friends of Library, Peace Links, Colo. Coordinating Coun. of Womens Orgn., Inc. (pres. coun.), Colo. Library Assn., Council Library Technicians, Federally Employed Women, Delta Sigma Theta (corr. sec. Denver 1964-66), Women's Assn. of Peoples Presbyn. Ch., League of Women Voters, Denver Urban League. Democrat. Presbyterian. Home: 3085 Fairfax St Denver CO 80207-2714

PHILLIPS, GENEVA FICKER, academic editor; b. Staunton, Ill., Aug. 1, 1920; d. Arthur Edwin and Lillian Agnes (Woods) Ficker; m. James Emerson Phillips, Jr., June 6, 1955 (dec. 1979). BS in Journalism, U. Ill., 1942; MA in English Lit., UCLA, 1953. Copy desk Chgo. Jour. Commerce, 1942-43; editl. asst. patents Radio Rsch. Lab. Harvard U., Cambridge, Mass., 1943-45; asst. editor adminstrv. publs. U. Ill., Urbana, 1946-47; editl. asst. Quar. of Film, Radio and TV UCLA, 1952-53; mng. editor The Works of John Dryden, Dept. English UCLA, 1964—; Bd. dirs. Univ. Religious Conf., L.A., 1979—. UCLA teaching fellow, 1950-53, grad. fellow 1954-55. Mem. Assn. Acad. Women UCLA, Friends of Huntington Libr., Friends of UCLA Libr., Friends of Ctr. for Medieval and Renaissance Studies, Samuel Johnson Soc. So. Calif., Assocs. U. Calif. Press, Conf. Christianity and Lit., Soc. Mayflower Descendants. Lutheran. Home: 213 First Anita Dr Los Angeles CA 90049-3815 Office: UCLA Dept English 2225 Rolfe Hall Los Angeles CA 90024

PHILLIPS, GRETCHEN, clinical social worker; b. Erie, Pa., July 14, 1941; life ptnr. Beverly Campbell, June 10, 1989. BA, Mercyhurst Coll., 1966; MSW, Yeshiva U., 1972; postgrad., Advanced Ctr. Psychotherapy, 1972-73, Washington Sq. Inst., 1973-77. Diplomate clin. social work; cert. social worker, N.Y. Psychiat. social worker, forensic social worker Creedmoor Psychiat. Ctr., Queens Village, N.Y., 1972-80; Med. social worker Bellevue Hosp. Ctr., N.Y.C., 1980-83; intake probation officer N.Y.C. Probation, Family Court, Bklyn., 1983—. Mem. NASW, Am. Group Psychotherapy Assn., Internat. Soc. for Traumatic Stress Studies (N.Y. chpt.). Home: 125 Radford St Apt 3C Yonkers NY 10705-3014 Office: Probation Intake Kings Family Ct 283 Adams St Brooklyn NY 11201-2804

PHILLIPS, J(OHN) TAYLOR, judge; b. Greenville, S.C., Aug. 20, 1921; s. Walter Dixon and Mattie Sue (Taylor) P.; m. Mary Elizabeth Parrish, Dec. 18, 1954; children: John Allen, Susan, Linda-Lea, Julia. AA, Glenville State Coll., 1952; JD, Mercer U., 1955; LLD, Asbury Coll., 1992. Bar: Ga. 1954, U.S. Supreme Ct. 1969. Mem. Ho. of Reps. State of Ga., Atlanta, 1959-62, Senate, 1962-64. With USMC, 1942-51. Methodist. Home: 1735 Winston Dr Macon GA 31206-3241 Office: State Ct Bibb County PO Box 5086 Macon GA 31213-0001

PHILLIPS, JOSEPH DANIEL, geophysicist, oceanographer; b. Woodbury, N.J., Sept. 11, 1938; s. Joseph Francis and Katherine Cecelia (Browne) P.; m. Gwendolyn Williams, 1961; children: Julia Kear, Stephanie Morgan, Joseph Williams. BA, Rutgers U., 1961; MS in Engring., Princeton U., 1963, MA, 1964, PhD, 1966. Engr. trainee Mobil Oil Co., N.Y.C., 1957, N.Y. Shipbuilding Corp., Camden, N.J., 1958-60; engr. mgmt. trainee N.J. Bell Tel. Co., Newark/Camden, N.J., 1961; rsch. asst. Princeton (N.J.) U., 1962-65; asst. scientist Woods Hole (Mass.) Oceanographic Inst., 1965-68, assoc. scientist, 1968-77; staff rsch. scientist MIT, Cambridge, 1977-79; sr. rsch. scientist U. Tex., Austin, 1978-96; chief scientist World Geoscience Corp., Houston, 1996-1999; chief scientist, dir. tech. svcs. Fugro Airborne Surveys, Houston, 1999-2000, Integrated Geophysics Corp., Houston, 2000—; cons. Mobil Oil Corp., Dallas, 1969, Exxon Corp., Houston, 1977, Bell Tel. Labs., Whippany/Murray Hill, N.J., 1976-78; vis. scholar U. Cambridge, Eng., 1974-75; adj. prof./instr. marine geophysics, seismics and geomagnetism, oceanography, acoustics and potential fields, faculty advisor MIT, Woods Hole Oceanographic Inst., U. Tex., 1968-96; cons. airborne/marine archeology Nat. Underwater and Marine Archeologic Agy., 1997-98. Contbr. articles to Jour. Geophys. Rsch. Sci., Geol. Soc. Am., Am. Petroleum Geologist, Ency. Brittanica. Fellow Explorers Club; mem. Am. Soc. Naval Engrs., Am. Geophys. Union, Soc. Exploration Geophysicists, AAAS, Marine Lodge, Phi Beta Kappa, Sigma Xi. Achievements include research in use/design of lock-in amplifiers for rock magnetometers, USN multi-beam sonar for seafloor geology, acoustically navigated vehicles for seafloor studies, vertical seismic profiling aboard deep ocean drilling project ships, aeromagnetic location of archeologic targets, pipeline and wellhead surveying. Home: 18331 Fern Trail Ct Houston TX 77084-5698 Office: Fugro Airborne Surveys Inc 18000 Groeschke Rd Houston TX 77084-5675

PHILLIPS, KENNETH JOHN HERBERT, solar astrophysicist, researcher; b. Isleworth, Middlesex, Eng., May 16, 1946; s. Kenneth Verdun and Mabel Vera (Harding) P. BSc, Univ. Coll., London, 1967, PhD, 1972. NRC postdoctoral fellow Goddard Space Flight Ctr., NASA, Greenbelt, Md., 1972-75; NSF postdoctoral fellow U. Hawaii, Honolulu, 1975-76; rsch. scientist Rutherford Appleton Lab., Eng., 1977—; prin. investigator XRP Instrument on NASA Solar Max Satellite, 1986-89; hon. prof. Queen's U.,

Belfast, Ireland, 1997—. Author: Guide to the Sun, 1992; contbr. articles to profl. jours. Fellow Royal Astron. Soc.; mem. Internat. Astron. Union. Anglican. Mem. Metropolitan Community Church. Avocations: running, music, lecturing.

PHILLIPS, KIMBERLY SANDRA, artist; b. Royal Oak, Mich., July 18, 1966; d. David William Purdie and Jill Sandra Gantz; m. Shawn Lee Phillips, June 14, 1997. Student, Univ. Sch., Birmingham, Mich., 1984, Mich. State U., 1984-85; student graphic arts program, Lansing C.C., 1987-90. Clk. Mich. Dept. Natural Resources, Lansing, Mich., 1986-88; shipping receiving Burlington Coat Factory, Lansing, 1988-91, Modern Hardware, Grand Rapids, Mich., 1991-97; artist Grand Rapids, 1997—. Exhibited in group shows Midland Summer Art Fair, 1999, Arts, Beats & Eats, Pontiac, Mich., 1999, Detroit Festival of the Arts, 1999, Sugarloaf Mountain Works Art Festivals, 2000, others, also pvt. commns. Mem. Am. Craft Assn., Mich. Guild Artists and Artisans (assoc. mem.). Republican. E-mail: ksp4@excite.com. Home: 759 Eleanor St NE Grand Rapids MI 49505-4221

PHILLIPS, LEO HAROLD, JR., lawyer; b. Jan. 10, 1945; s. Leo Harold and Martha C. (Oberg) P.; m. Patricia Margaret Halcomb, Sept. 3, 1983. BA summa cum laude, Hillsdale Coll., 1967; MA, U. Mich., 1968, JD cum laude, 1973; LLM magna cum laude, Free U. of Brussels, 1974. Bar: Mich. 1974, N.Y. 1975, U.S. Supreme Ct. 1977, D.C. 1979. Fgn. lectr. Pusan Nat. U., Korea, 1969-70; assoc. Alexander & Green, N.Y.C., 1974-77; counsel Overseas Pvt. Investment Corp., Washington, 1977-80, sr. counsel, 1980-82, asst. gen. counsel, 1982-85; asst. gen. counsel Manor Care, Inc., Gaithersburg, Md., 1985-91, asst. sec., 1988-99, assoc. gen. counsel, 1991-99, v.p., 1996-99; vol. Peace Corps, Pusan, 1968-71; mem. program for sr. mgrs. in govt. Harvard U., Cambridge, Mass., 1982. Contbr. articles to legal jours. Chmn. legal affairs com. Essex Condominium Assn., Washington, 1979-81; deacon Chevy Chase Presbyn. Ch., Washington, 1984-87, moderator, 1985-87, supt. ch. sch., elder, trustee, 1987-90, pres., 1988-90, mem. nominating com., 1995-96. Recipient Alumni Achievement award Hillsdale Coll., 1980; Meritorious Honor award Overseas Pvt. Investment Corp., 1981, Superior Achievement award, 1984. Mem. ABA (internat. fin. transactions com., vice-chmn. com. internat. ins. Law), Am. Soc. Internat. Law (Jessup Internat. Law moot ct. judge semi-final rounds 1978-83, chair corp. counsel com. 1993-97), Internat. Law Assn. (Am. br.; com. sec. 1982), D.C. Bar, N.Y. State Bar Assn., Royal Asiatic Soc. (Korea br.), State Bar Mich., Washington Fgn. Law Soc. (sec.-treas. 1980-81, bd. dirs., program coord. 1981-82, v.p. 1982-83, pres.-elect 1983-84, pres. 1984-85, chmn. nominating com. 1986, 88), Washignton Internat. Trade Assn. (bd. dirs. 1984-87), Assn. Bar City N.Y., Hillsdale Coll. Alumni Assn. (co-chmn. Washington area 1977-90), Univ. Club (N.Y.C.). Home: 4740 Connecticut Ave NW Apt 702 Washington DC 20008-5632

PHILLIPS, MARK ANTHONY PETER, British official; b. Tetbury, Eng., Sept. 22, 1948; s. Peter W. G. and Anne (Tiarks) P.; m. Princess Anne, Nov. 14, 1973; children: Peter Mark Andrew, Zara Anne Elizabeth; m. Helen Sanford Pflueger, Feb. 1, 1997; 1 child, Stephanie Noelani. Ed., Marlborough Coll., 1963-66, Sandhurst, 1967-69; student, Royal Agrl. Coll., Cirencester, 1978-79. Joined 1st Queen's Dragoon Guards, 1969; regimental duty, 1969-74, co. instr. Royal Mil. Acad. Sandhurst, 1974-77; army tng. directorate, 1977; personal aide de camp to Queen, 1974—; mng. dir. Gleneagles Mark Phillips Equestrian Centre, 1988-92; chmn. Brit. Equestrian Olympic Fund, 1989—; mem. U.K. World Champion equestrian team, 1970, Olympic Gold medallist team, Munich, 1972, Olympic Silver medallist team, Seoul, 1988; Liveryman Farriers Co., Farmers Co.; hon. yeoman Saddlers' Co.; freeman Loriners Co., City of London; v.p. Minchinhampton Cricket Club; chief d' equipe, trainer Spanish Olympic Team, 1992; chief d' equipe USA 3 day event team; course advisor Am. Horse Shows Assn., 1993—, tech. advisor, 1993—. Mem. Royal Caledonian Hunt, Hunters Improvement and Nat. Light Horse Soc. (life), Royal Agrl. Soc., Gloucestershire Trust Nature Conservation, Brit. Dressage Group Horse Trials Assn., Melton Hunt Club, Brit. Field Sports, Beaufort Hunt.

PHILLIPS, MICHAEL ROBERT, psychiatrist; b. Toronto, Can., Sept. 28, 1949; m. Marlys A. Bueber, June, 1990; children: Jessica, Jennifer. BSc, McGill U., Montreal, Can., 1971; MD, McMaster U., Hamilton, Can., 1974; MA in Anthropology, U. Washington, 1985, MPH in Epidemiology, 1985. Cert. psychiatrist. Intern Auckland (New Zealand) Pub. Hosp., 1974-75, sr. house officer, 1975-76, sr. house officer psychiatry, 1978-79; resident psychiatry U. Wash., 1980-83, Robert Wood Johnson rsch. fellow, 1983-85; Exch. scholar Hunan Med. Coll., Changsha, China, 1985-87; dir. Rsch. Ctr. Clin. Epidemiology Shashi (Hubei, China) Psychiat. Hosp., 1987-94, Beijing Hui Long Guan Hosp., 1994—; vis. prof. Peking Union Med. Coll., 1996—; China liaison Internat. Clin. Epidemiology Network, 1991-99; assoc. prof. dept. social medicine Harvard Med. Sch., 1995—; conjoint assoc. prof. Newcastle U., Australia, 1998—. Author: Scales for Assessment of Positive and Negative Symptoms in Psychiatric Patients, 1990; editor: Clinically Applied Health Social Science, 1997; editor Psychiat. Rehab. in China, 1994. Recipient W.H.R. Rivers prize Assn. Med. Anthropology, 1984, Outstanding Achievement award Hubei Provincial Govt., 1995, Great Wall Friendship Awd., Beijing Municipal Govt., 1999; New Zealand Exchange scholar to China, Beijing Langs. Inst., 1976-77, Nanjung U., 1977-78. Mem. Am. Psychiat. Assn., Chinese Psychiat. Assn. (hon. coun. mem. 1994—). Avocations: jogging, swimming. Home and Office: Beijing Hui Long Guan Hosp, 100096 Beijing China

PHILLIPS, OLIVERIO MICHELSEN, retired chemical engineer; b. Fusagasuga, Colombia, June 6, 1928; s. Oliverio M. and Yolanda V. (Villaveces) P.; m. Yolanda M. Villaveces, Mar. 25, 1950; children: Jorge, Gustavo, Yolanda, Roberto, Francis, Alberto, Jose, Carolina. BS, MIT, 1948, MS, 1950, DSc, 1957. Indsl. cons. Bogota, 1968-95; cons. UN OAS, N.Y.C., Washington, 1972-76; pres. Corp. Nal. Investigacion Forestal, Bogota, 1978-81; project mgr. Arinco S.A., Bogota, 1982-87, gen. mgr., 1987-92; ret., 1997. Bd. dirs. Corp. Financ. Popular, Bogota, 1968-71, Colciencias, Bogota, 1969-77, Ingeominas, Bogota, 1976-82. Mem. Inst. Colombiano de Normas Tecnicas, Inst. Investigaciones Tecnologicas (bd. dirs. 1983-87), Fedesarrollo (bd. dirs. 1969-95), Cooperacion Tecnica Internat. (bd. dirs. 1992-95), MIT Club (pres. 1966-68), Soc. Colombiana de Ciencias Quimicas (pres. 1962), N.Y. Acad. Scis. Roman Catholic. Avocations: music, reading, walking. Home: 6804 Chesterbrook Ct Apt 304 Raleigh NC 27615-7815

PHILLIPS, PATRICIA JEANNE, retired school administrator, consultant; b. Amarillo, Miss., Jan. 13, 1935; d. William Macon and Mary Ann (Cawthon) Patrick; m. William Henry Phillips, June 22, 1962; 1 child, Mary Jeanne. BA, Millsaps Coll., 1954; MA, Vanderbilt/Peabody U., 1957; EdD, U. So. Miss., 1978. Tchr. Jackson (Miss.) Pub. Schs., 1954-73, prin., 1973-75, asst. prin., 1975-77; dir. ednl. program Eden Prairie (Minn.) # 272, 1977-80; dir. elem. edn. Meridian (Miss.) Pub. Schs., 1980-91, asst. supt. curriculum, 1991, ret., 1991; prof. Miss. Coll., Clinton, part-time 1977, Miss. State U., Meridian, 1981-2000, ret. 2000; ednl. cons. in field. Co-author: (testing practice) Test Taking Tactics, 1987; developer tng. materials Best Practices; contbr. articles to profl. jours. pres. Meridian Symphony Orch., 1987, 2000—; v.p. Meridian Coun. Arts, 1986; bd. dirs. Meridian Art Mus. Named Boss of Yr., Meridian Secretarial Assn., 1985, Arts Education of Yr., Meridian Coun. Arts, 1991; recipient Excellence award Pub. Edn. Form, 1993. Mem. ASCD, Miss. ASCD, Miss. Assn. Women (pres.), Rotary, Phi Kappa Alpha, Phi Delta Kappa (pres. 1986-87), Alpha Delta Kappa Gamma (pres. 1962). Republican. Methodist. Avocations: grant writing, computers, heirloom sewing, golf. Home: 322 51st St Meridian MS 39305-2013 Office: Miss State Univ Meridian Campus 1000 Highway 19 S Meridian MS 39301-8205

PHILLIPS, ROBERT ALLAN, scientist, administrator; b. St. Louis, July 2, 1937; s. Allan B. and Mildred (Fandrich) P.; m. Corley F. Hamill, June 12, 1959; children: Kristin, Michael, Scott. BA, Carleton Coll., 1959; PhD, Washington U., St. Louis, 1965. Scientist Ont. Cancer Inst., 1967-86; prof. U. Toronto, 1967—, chair dept. med. biophysics, 1981-86; scientist Hosp. for Sick Children, Toronto, 1986-96, head divsn. cancer rsch., 1990-96; exec. dir. Nat. Cancer Inst. Can., 1996—, pres., 1994-96. Author more than 200 sci. papers; editor meeting reports. Bd. dirs. nat. Cancer Inst. Can., 1991-96, Can. Cancer Soc., 1990-96. Named Citizen of Yr., Civitan, Can., 1973. Mem. Phi Beta Kappa, Sigma Xi. Home: 66 Collier St, Toronto, ON Canada Office: Nat Cancer Inst Can, 10 Alcorn St Ste 200, Toronto, ON Canada

PHILLIPS, ROBERT DERRICK, psychiatrist; b. Laurinburg, N.C., Dec. 2, 1925; s. James Dickson and Helen Shepherd Phillips; m. Frances Dana Fulcher Olson, July 28, 1951 (div. Dec. 1974); children: Robert, Stuart, Helen, Jane, Anna, Betsy, Frances; m. Dorothy Jean Andersen, Oct. 17, 1997. BS, Davidson Coll., 1948; MD, U. Pa., 1952. Diplomate Am. Bd. Psychiatry, Am. Bd. Surgery. Surg. resident Med. Coll. S.C., Charleston, 1952-56, chief surg. resident, 1956-57; staff surgeon Presbyn. Med. Ctr., Chonju, Korea, 1957-59; psychiat. resident U. N.C. Meml. Hosps., Chapel Hill, 1960-63; pvt. practice psychiatry Chapel Hill, 1963-95; clin. asst. prof. psychiatry Duke U., Durham, N.C., 1972-95; clin. prof. psychiatry U. N.C. Sch. Medicine, Chapel Hill, 1974-95; ret., 1995; exec. com. Com. of Responsibility to War-Injured and Burned Vietnamese Children, Boston, 1964-67. Author: The Recovery of the True Self, 1995, (monograph) Structural Symbiotic Systems, 1975. Trustee Union Theol. Sem., Richmond, Va., 1965-67; chmn. Human Rels. Commn., Chapel Hill, 1962-63; founder All Races Coalition with Native Am. People, Chapel Hill, 1991 . Ens. USNR, 1943-46, ATO. Recipient Martin Luther King award Orange County Black Caucus, 1987, Founders' Cir., Buffalo Trust, 1999. Mem. Am. Psychiat. Assn., Am. Coll. Surg.; mem. N.C. Psychiat. Soc. Democrat. Avocations: Native American network support, golf, hiking, workshop leading. Home: 1767-3 Harborage Dr SW Ocean Isle Beach NC 28469

PHILLIPS, ROBERT JAMES, JR., lawyer, corporate executive; b. Houston, Aug. 4, 1955; s. Robert James and Mary Josephine (Bass) P.; m. Nancy Norris, Apr. 24, 1982; 1 child, Mary Ashton. BBA, So. Meth. U., 1976, JD, 1980. Bar: Tex. 1980. Vp., gen. counsel Aegis Shipping Ltd., London, 1980-81; assoc. Bishop, Larrimore, Lamsens & Brown, 1981-82; pres. Phillips Devel. Corp., Ft. Worth, Tex., 19825; pvt. practice Ft. Worth, 1982-87, 895; assoc. Haynes and Boone, Ft. Worth, 1988-89; sr. v.p. Am. Real Estate Group, 1989-93, Am. Savs. Bank, N.A., New West Fed. Savs. and Loan Assn., 1989-93, Am. Savs. Bank, Ft. Worth, 1991-92; chmn., CEO creative risk control Environ. Risk Mgmt. Inc., Ft. Worth, 1992-94; pres., CEO Pangburn Candy Co., 1996-99; exec. v.p. Ancor Holdings, 1999—; chmn., CEO Am. Staff Resources Corp., 1999—; bd. dirs. Tex. Heritage, Inc.; chmn., CEO Am. Staff Resources Corp., 1999—. Bd. dirs., exec. com. Ft. Worth Ballet Assn., 1984-85, Van Cliburn Found.; v.p. planning, bd. dirs., exec. com. Ft. Worth Symphony Orch., 1984-85; bd. dirs. Mus. Modern Art, 19865; bd. dirs., exec. com., chmn. investment com. Tex. Boys Choir, 1983-85. Mem. ABA, Tex. Bar Assn., Ft. Worth Bd. Realtors, Crescent Club, Phi Delta Phi, Kappa Sigma, Beta Gamma Sigma. Clubs: River Crest Country, Ft. Worth. Avocations: hunting, fishing, photography. Home and Office: PO Box 470099 Fort Worth TX 76147-0099

PHILLIPS, ROBIN KENNETH STEWART, colorectal surgeon; b. Eng., Nov. 18, 1952; s. John Fleetwood Stewart and Mary Gordon (Shaw) P.; m. Janina Fairley Nowak, June 14, 1975; children: Eva Elizabeth, Henry Elliot. MBBS, Royal Free U., London, 1975; MS, U. London, 1984. Intern Royal Free Hosp., 1975-76; surg. tng. St. Mary's Hosp. Med. Sch., 1979-87; cons. surgeon St. Mark's Hosp., Harrow, Eng., 1987—, chmn. dept. surgery, 1994-97; dean St. Mark's Acad. Inst., 1997—; sr. lectr. St. Bartholomew's Hosp., 1987-90; cons. surgeon Homerton Hosp., 1990-93; dir. polyposis registry Imperial Can. Rsch. Fund, 1993—; hon. adminstrv. dir. Leeds Castle Polyposis Group, 1994—; hon. prof. colorectal surgery Imperial Coll. Sch. Medicine, 2000—. Editor: Modern Coloproctology, 1993, Familial Adonomations Polyposis, 1994, Anal Fistula, 1996, Colorectal Surgery, 1998. Fellow Royal Soc. Medicine (v.p.), Royal Coll. Surgeons Eng. Office: St Marks Hosp, Northwick Pk Watford Rd, Harrow HA1 3UJ, England

PHILLIPS, ROGER, software engineering educator; b. Rhyl, Wales, Oct. 25, 1947; s. Charles Embery and Norah (Jones) P.; m. Anne Wyn Edwards, Aug. 16, 1969; children: Jonathan Andrew, James Edward, Justin Oliver, Laura Anne. BS, Manchester U., 1970, MS, 1978, PhD, 1985. Software engr. ICL, Manchester, England, 1970-73; exptl. officer Manchester U., 1973-76, lectr., 1976-85, 85-90; prof. U. Hull (England), 1990—; subject quality assessor HEFCE, England, 1994. Contbr. articles to profl. jours. Grantee European Commn., 1991, Sci. and Enging. Rsch. Coun., 1993, Brit. Orthopaedic Assn., Dept. Health, 1996. Mem. British Computer Soc. (external examiner 1987-94, accreditation panel 1990—, IT award 1995), Enging. Coun. (chartered). Office: U Hull, Dept Computer Sci, Hull HU6 7RX, England

PHILLIPS, RONALD EDWARD, artist, sales executive; b. Clovis, N.Mex., Apr. 10, 1937; s. Rodney Vernon and Ethel Edna (Huff) P.; m. May Frances Willingham, Aug. 27, 1957; children: Rhonda Louise, Russell Kent, Teresa Gail; m. Janet Irene Johnsonbaugh Smith, July 4, 1972; stepchildren: Steven, Gregg, Laura. Student, Ea. N.Mex. U., 1955-56, U. N.Mex., 1957, Famous Artist Schs., 1963-64, North Light Art Sch., 1989-90. Group merchandiser women's fashions J.C. Penney Inc., Albuquerque, 1957-64; chem. salesman Take Over Products, Clovis, N.Mex., 1964-65; with International Auto Leasing, Albuquerque, 1965; salesman Pennsalt Chems., N.Mex. div., Albuquerque, 1965-67; N.Mex. sales rep. W.W. Grainger Inc., Chgo., 1967-72; founder Pueblo Arts, Inc., Albuquerque, 1972—; mgr. Dairy Queen, Santa Rosa and Lovington, N.Mex., 1982-85; owner, mgr. Western Pit n Grill & Food Gallery, Lovington, 1985-88; owner Pueblo Arts Inc./Trailwest Gallery, Albuquerque, 1988—; tchr. quick draw, continuous line drawing, 1990; artist, guide Pueblo Arts Inc. Trailwest Paintouts, Guide for Artists, 1990-92; ind. sales cons. SWEPCO Bldg. Projects, 1993—. Artist, author sketchbooks Traveling Man's Old Town Sketchbook, 1990, The Shooting of Wyatt Earp, 1994, others; movie extra Whitesands, 1991, Next Fire on Earth, 1992, Wyatt Earp, 1993, Desperate Trails, 1993, Buffalo Girls, 1995, East Meets West, 1995, Lazarus Man Premier, 1995-96. Pres. Albuquerque Wildlife and Conservation, 1963-64; active Albuquerque Conf. & Vis. Bur., 1988—, Albuquerque Arts Alliance, 1994-95, Tourism Assoc. of N.Mex., Albuquerque Film Commn. With N.Mex. Air Nat. Guard, 1955-61. Mem. N.Mex. Art League (hon. life, pres. 1964-65, instr., bd. arts after sch. project 1995-96), Indian Arts and Crafts Assn. (ethics com. 1973-74), Albuquerque Arts Alliance, Guild of Albuquerque Artist Models (advisor, bd. dirs. 1994-98). Republican. Avocations: art, sales and marketing. E-mail: ronpuebloarts@juno.com.

PHILLIPS, SIAN, actress; b. Bettws, Wales; d. D. and Sally P.; m. D.H. Roy, 1957 (div. 1960); m. Peter O'Toole, 1960 (div. 1979); 2 children; m. 2d, Robin Sachs, 1979 (div. 1992). Grad. with honors, U. Wales, 1955, DLitt (hon.), 1983. Newsreader, announcer, drama rep., mem. Repertory Co. BBC, 1953-55; toured for Welsh Arts Coun. with Nat. Theatre Co., 1953-55; mem. bd. govs. Welsh Coll. of Music and Drama, 1992, hon. fellow, 1992. London stage appearances: Hedda Gabler, 1959, Ondine and the Dutchess of Malfe, 1960-61, The Lizard on the Rock, 1961, Gentle Jack, Maxibules and the Night of the Iguana, 1964 (nominated Best Actress), Ride a Cock Horse, 1965, Man and Superman (nominated Best Actress), Man of Destiny, 1966, The Burglar, 1967, Epitaph for George Dillon, 1972, A Nightingale in Bloomsburg Square, 1973, The Gay Lord Quex, 1975, Spinechiller, 1978, You Never Can Tell, Lyric Hammersmith, 1979, Pal Joey, 1980 (nominated Best Actress of Musical), Half Moon and Albery Theatres, 1980, 81, Dear Liar, 1982, Major Barbara, 1983, Peg GiGi, 1985, Thursday's Ladies, 1987, Brel, 1988, Paris Match, 1989, Vanilla, 1990, The Manchurian Candidate, 1991, Painting Churches, 1992, Ghosts (nominated Welsh Artist of Yr.), Lion in Winter, 1994, An Inspector Calls, Broadway, 1995, A Little Night Music, 1996 (Olivier nomination 1995-96), Marlene, London (Olivier nomination), South Africa, Paris, 1997-98; films include Becket, 1963, Goodbye Mr. Chips (Critics Circle award, N.Y. Critics award, Famous Seven Critics award 1969), Laughter in the Dark, 1968, Murphy's War, 1970, Under Milk Wood, 1971, The Clash of the Titans, 1979, Dune, 1983, A Painful Case, 1984, Return to Endor, 1985, Valmont, 1988, The Age of Innocence, 1992, House of America, 1996 (BAFTA nomination), Alice Through the Looking Glass; TV appearances include: Shoulder to Shoulder, 1974, How Green Was My Valley (BAFTA award), 1975, I, Claudius (Royal TV Soc. award, BAFTA award 1978), 1976, Heartbreak House, 1977, The Oresteia of Aeschylus, 1978, Crime and Punishment, 1979, Tinker, Tailor, Soldier, Spy, 1979, Sean O-Casey, 1980, Churchill: The Wilderness Years, 1981, How Many Miles To Babylon, 1982, Smiley's People, 1982, Shadow of the Noose, 1988, Snow Spider, 1988, (Bafta nomination), Vanity Fair, (TV series) Emlyns Moon, 1991, The Chestnut Soldier, 1991 (Bafta nomination), Perfect Scoundrels, 1991, Tonight at 8:30, 1991, Royal TV Soc. Ann. Lectr., 1992, Intent to Kill (also Welsh lang.), 1994, (TV musical) Nearest and Dearest, 1994, (also Welsh lang. version); (TV series) The Borrowers, (film) Heidi (Disney), The Vacillations of Poppy Carew (TV serial), 1995, Scolds Bridle, 1997, Le Femme Nikita, 1998, The Aristocrats, 1998, Cabaret, I Wish You Love (Israel), 1999, Marlene (Broadway, nominated Best Actress in musical Drama Desk and Tony), Magicians House (Canada), 1999, Cinderella (TV), 1999, Nikita (TV, Can.), 1999; author: Sian Phillips', Needlepoint, 1987, Private Faces, vol. I autobiography Pub Hodder, 1999, General Journalism; albums include Pal Joey, GIGI, Peg, Single, Bewitched, Bothered and Bewildered, I Remember Mama, A Little Night Music, Marlene, 1997; Middle East Tour in Concert, 1999, U.K. concert tour, 2000, T.V. Magician's House, Can., 2000, Cabaret at the Firebird Cafe, N.Y.C., 2000. Hon. fellow Cardiff Coll., U. Wales, 1981, Poly. Wales, 1988, U. Swansea, 1998, Trinity Coll. Carmarthen, 1998. Office: Lindy King, c/o Peters Fraser & Dunlop, London WC2 B5HA, England

PHILLIPS, THOMAS EDWORTH, JR., financial advisor, senior consultant; b. Danville, Va., July 7, 1944; s. Thomas Edworth Sr. and Jean (Worley) P.; m. Claudia Mitchell, July 23, 1966; children: Kelly Marie, Melissa Joyce. BS in Econs., Va. Tech., 1966; cert. in investments, N.Y. Inst. Fin., 1969; MS in Bus., Va. Commonwealth U., 1973; postgrad., U. Pa., 1989. Cert. investment mgmt. analyst; registered investment adviser. Edn. coord. Prince William County Schs., Manassas, Va., 1966-67; investment broker Conrad and Co., Richmond, Va., 1967-68; investment exec. Paine Webber, Inc., Richmond, 1968—, divisional v.p., 1980-99, sr. v.p., 2000—; registered prin. NYSE, NASD, 1987—; access program nat. com. PaineWebber, N.Y.C., 1989-90, mem. dir.'s coun., 1987-88, managed accounts nat. adv. bd., 1991-93; mem. mut. fund Nat. Adv. Coun., 1996—, pres.' council, 1997—; bd. dirs. Madison Group, Inc., Richmond, Meadowbrook Assocs., Inc., Richmond; speaker in field. Bd. dirs. Va. Non-Profit Housing Coalition, pres., 1992—; chmn. bd. deacons. Mt. Olivet Ch., Hanover, Va., 1984-85; trustee Hanover Acad., Ashland, Va., 1980-84. Rotary Found. fellow, 1989. Mem. Investment Mgmt. Cons. Assn., Capital Soc., Melody Hills Property Owners Assn. (bd. dirs. 1980—), Va. Tech. Alumni Assn., VCU Alumni Assn., Rotary, Bull and Bear Club, Omicron Delta Epsilon. Baptist. Avocations: horses, tennis, golf. Home: 15058 Melody Hills Dr Doswell VA 23047-2075 Office: 1021 E Cary St Ste 1800 Richmond VA 23219-4000 also: PaineWebber Inc PO Box 430 Richmond VA 23218-0430

PHILLIPS, VICKY L., distance learning specialist; b. Bedford, Ind., Nov. 17, 1958; d. Marlin Dean and Reva June P. BA magna cum laude, Depauw U., 1981; MA, Antioch U., 1985. CEO Geteducated.com, Waterbury, Vt., 1989—; virtual edn. expert for leading media sources, including The N.Y. Times, CNN Fin. News, Dow Jone's Nat. Bus. Employment Weekly, Home Office Computing, Money Mag., U.S. News & World Report, Time, Forbes, others. Author: Best Distance Learning Graduate Schools: Earning Your Degree Without Leaving Home, Never Too Late to Learn: The Adult Student's Guide to College, 2000; pub. Virtual Univ. Gazette (electronic newsletter), The Virtual Univ. Bus. Digest (newsletter). E-mail: vicky@geteducated.com.

PHILLIPS, WALTER MILLS, III, psychologist, educator; b. N.Y.C., Sept. 29, 1947; s. Walter Mills and Grace Mary (Mullen) P.; m. Anne Marie Boyle, July 3, 1971; children: Jonathan, Elizabeth. BS, Fordham U., 1970; MA, U. S.D., 1973, PhD, 1975. Lic. clin. psychologist, Conn.; diplomate Am. Coll. Forensic Examiners, Am. Bd. Disability Evaluators, Am. Bd. Disability Analysts; cert. sr. disability analyst. Adolescent resident counselor Hawthorne (N.Y.) Cedar Knolls Sch., 1970-71; NIMH tng. fellow, 1971-75; clin. psychology intern Inst. of Living, Hartford, Conn., 1974-75; clin. staff psychologist Inst. of Living, Hartford, 1975-79, sr. staff psychologist, 1979-82, asst. dir. dept. clin. psychology, 1980-82, dir. clin. psychology tng., 1980-82; co-dir. outpatient psychiatry U. Conn., Farmington, 1982-88; asst. prof. psychiatry, dir. psychiatry evaluation svc. U. Conn. Health Ctr., 1982-88, dir. Anxiety Rsch. and Treatment Ctr., 1985-88; pvt. practice psychotherapy Hartford, 1976—; dir. adolescent/young adult svc. Grandview Psychiat. Resource Ctr., Waterbury, Conn., 1988-90; dir. psychology Waterbury Hosp., 1990-98; pvt. practice clin. psychology Waterbury, 1990—; asst. clin. prof. psychiatry Sch. Medicine Yale U., New Haven, Conn., 1988—; mem. psychology exec. com. Sch. Medicine Yale U., New Haven. Contbr. articles to profl. jours. Mem. APA, Am. Psychotherapy Assn. (diplomate), Conn. Psychol. Assn., Soc. Psychotherapy Rsch., Soc. Personality Assessment, Conn. Hosp. Assn. (chmn., dir. psychology conf.), N.Y. Acad. Scis., Sigma Xi. Home: 70 Beverly Dr Avon CT 06001-3528 Office: 60 Westwood Ave Ste 115 Waterbury CT 06708-2460

PHILLIPS, WALTER RAY, lawyer, educator; b. Democrat, N.C., Mar. 19, 1932; s. Walter Yancey and Bonnie (Wilson) P.; m. Patricia Ann Jones, Aug. 28, 1954; children: Bonnie Ann, Rebecca Lee. A.B., U. N.C., 1954; LL.B., Emory U., 1957, LL.M., 1962, J.D., 1970; postgrad., Yale U., 1965-66. Bar: Ga. 1957, Fla. 1958, U.S. Supreme Ct. 1962, Tex. 1969. With firm Jones, Adams, Paine & Foster, West Palm Beach, Fla., 1957-58; law clk. to chief judge U.S. Dist. Ct., Atlanta, 1958-59; with firm Powell, Goldstein, Frazer & Murphy, Atlanta, 1959-60; bankruptcy judge U.S. Cts., Atlanta, 1960-64; prof. law U. N.D., 1964-65; teaching fellow Yale U., 1965-66; prof. law Fla. State U., 1966-68, Tex. Tech. U., Lubbock, 1968-71; Disting. vis. prof. law Baylor U., 1971; atty. Commn. on Bankruptcy Laws of U.S., Washington, 1971-72; dep. dir., adminstrv. officer, 1972-73; prof. Sch. Law, U. Ga., 1973—, assoc. dean, 1975-83, acting dean, 1976, Joseph Henry Lumpkin prof., 1977-94, also dir. univ's self. study, 1978, Herman E. Talmadge prof., 1994-2000; Chapman disting. vis. prof. law U. Okla., 1985-86; vis. prof. law U. Okla., 1990, U. Mo., Columbia, 1993, 94; reporter Gov.'s Legislation for Ga., 1973; v.p., dir. Killearn Estates, Inc.; mem. Conf. on Consumer Fin. Law; prof. London Law Consortium, 1999. Author: Florida Law and Practice, 1960, Encyclopedia of Georgia Law, 1962, Seminar for Newly Appointed Referees in Bankruptcy, 1964, Damages: Cases and Materials, 1967, (with James William Moore) Debtors' and Creditors' Rights, Cases and Material, 1966, 5th edit., 1979, The Law of Debtor Relief, 1969, 2d edit., 1972, supplement, 1975, (with James William Moore) Rule 6, Moore's Federal Practice, 1969, Adjustment of Debts for Individuals, 1979, 2d edit., 1981, supplement, 1982, 84, 85, Liquidation Under the Bankruptcy Code, 3d edit., 1988, supplement, 1989, 90, 91, 92, 93, 94, Cases and Materials on Corporate Reorganization, 1983, 3d edit., 1986, 4th edit., 1988, 5th edit., 1990, 7th edit., 1996, 8th edit., 1998, Family Farmer and Adjustment of Individual Debts, 1987, supplement, 1988, 89, 90, 91, 92, 93, 94, A Primer of Chapters 12 and 13 of the Bankruptcy Code, 1995. Bd. dirs. Lubbock Day Nurseries, 1969, pres., 1970-71. Served with USAF, 1950. Mem. ABA (consumer bankruptcy com. 1973—, chmn. 1986-90), Fed. Bar Assn., Fla. Bar Assn., Tex. Bar Assn., Western Circuit Bar Assn., Ga. Bar Assn. (vice chmn. publs. com. 1977-89, com. on profl. responsibility 1983—), Am. Judicature Soc., Am. Trial Lawyers Assn., Phi Alpha Delta (chief tribune). Baptist. Home: 3800 Wakefield Dr Columbia MO 65203-5630

PHILLIPS, WILLIAM DANIEL, physicist; b. Wilkes-Barre, Pa., Nov. 5, 1948; s. William Cornelius and Mary Catherine (Savine) P.; m. Jane Van Wynen, June 20, 1970; children: Catherine, Christine. BS, Juniata Coll., Huntingdon, Pa., 1970; PhD, MIT, 1976. Rsch. asst. MIT, Cambridge, 1970-76, Chaim Weizmann fellow, 1976-78; physicist Nat. Inst. Stds. and Tech., Gaithersburg, Md., 1978-90, group leader, 1990-95, fellow, 1995—; vis. prof. Ecole Normale Supérieure, Paris, 1989-90; adj. prof. physics U. Md., College Park, 1991—. Editor/author: Laser Manipulation of Atoms and Ions, 1992; contbr. articles to profl. jours. Named Outstanding Young Scientist, Md. Acad. Sci., 1982; recipient Gold medal U.S. Dept. Commerce, 1993, Albert A. Michelson medal Franklin Inst., 1996, Gold medal Pa. Soc., 1999; co-recipient Nobel prize for physics, 1997, Schawlow prize in laser sci., APS, 1998. Fellow Am. Phys. Soc., Optical Soc. Am., Am. Acad. Arts & Scis.; mem. NAS. Achievements include demonstrated laser cooling of atomic beams; electromagnetic trapping of neutral atoms; discovered subdoppler laser cooling; produced sub-microkelvin 3D kinetic temperatures. Office: Nat Inst Stds & Tech PHY A167 100 Bureau Dr Stop 8424 Gaithersburg MD 20899-0003

PHILLIPS, WINFRED MARSHALL, dean, biomedical researcher, mechanical engineer, educator; b. Richmond, Va., Oct. 7, 1940; s. Claude Marshall and Gladys Marian (Barden) P.; children: Stephen, Sean. BSME,

Va. Poly. Inst., 1963; MA in Engring., U. Va., 1966, DSc, 1968. Mech. engr. U.S. Naval Weapons Lab., Dahlgren, Va., 1963; NSF trainee, tchg., rsch. asst. dept. aerospace engring. U. Va., Charlottesville, 1963-67, rsch. scientist, 1966-67; asst. prof. dept. aerospace engring. Pa. State U., University Park, 1968-74, from assoc. prof. to prof., 1974-80, assoc. dean rsch. Coll. Engring., 1979-80; head Sch. Mech. Engring., Purdue U., West Lafayette, Ind., 1980-88; dean Coll. Engring., U. Fla., Gainesville, 1988-99, assoc. v.p. engring., 1989-99, v.p. rsch., dean Grad. Sch., 1999—; chmn. bd. dirs. then bd. dirs. North Fla. Tech. Innovation Corp., 1995—, dir., 1999—; bd. dirs. First Union Bank, Gainesville, 1998—; vis. prof. U. Paris, 1976-77; bd. dirs. Tokheim Corp.; chmn. Fla. Tech. Devel. Bd., Southeastern Coalition for Minorities in Engring., vice chmn., 1995—; mem. adv. com. Nimbus Corp., 1985-90, Hong Kong U. Sci. and Tech., 1990-93; co-founder, v.p., CEO Inc., 1990—; mem. acad. adv. coun. Indsl. Rsch. Inst., 1990-93; mem. sci. adv. com. Electric Power Rsch. Inst., 1994-99; mem. adv. com. AvMed Inc.; bd. dirs. Accreditation Bd. on Engring. and Tech., 1989-96, mem. exec. com., 1991-96, mem. internat. revs. for univs. in Saudi Arabia, USSR, The Netherlands, Kuwait, pres., 1995-96. Sect. editor Am. Soc. Artificial Internal Organs Jour.; contbr. more than 165 articles to profl. jours., chpts. to books. Bd. dirs. Ctrl. Pa. Heart Assn., 1974-80, U. Fla. Found., 1989-91, 95-99; mem. Ind. Boiler and Pressure Vessel Code Bd., 1981-88. Named Disting. Hoosier Ind., 1987, Sagamore of the Wabash, 1988, Am. Assn. Engr.Socs., 1999; recipient Career Rsch. award NIH, 1974-78, NIH Surgery and Bioengring. Study sect., 1988-91, Fla. High Tech. and Industry Coun., 1990-94, So. Tech.Coun., 1991—, Natl. Engring. award. Fellow AAAS, AIAA, AAES (sec.-treas. 1999-2000), ASME (sr. v.p. edn. 1986-88, bd. dirs. 1995-2000, pres. 1998-99), N.Y. Acad. Scis., Am. Astron. Soc., Am. Inst. Med. and Biol. Engring. (founding fellow, chair coll. fellows 1994-95, pres. 1996-97), Am. Soc. Engring. Edn. (past chmn. long range planning soc. awards 1990-92, vice chmn. engring. deans coun. 1991-93, chair 1993—, bd. dirs. 1994-98, 1st v.p. 1994-95, pres. 1996-97), Royal Soc. Arts; mem. Am. Soc. Artificial Internal Organs (trustee 1982-90, sec.-treas. 1986-87, pres. 1988-89, adv. bd. 1998—), Nat. Assn. State Univs. and Land-Grant Colls. (com. quality of engring. edn.), Univ. Programs in Computer-Aided Engring., Design and Mfg. (bd. dirs. 1985-91), Am. Phys. Soc., Biomed. Engring. Soc., Internat. Soc. Biorheology, Fla. Engring. Soc., Cosmos Club, Fla. Blue Key, Rotary (pres. Lafayette 1987-88), Sigma Xi, Phi Kappa Phi, Phi Tau Sigma, Sigma Gamma Tau, Tau Beta Pi (eminent engr.). Achievements include development of artificial heart pumps; research on reentry aerodynamics, on blood rheology, on modelling blood flow, on fluid dynamics of artificial hearts, on the use of smooth blood contacting surfaces, on prosthetic valve fluid dynamics and on laser Doppler studies of unsteady biofluid dynamics. Home: 4140 NW 44th Ave Gainesville FL 32606-4518 Office: U Fla Rsch and Grad Programs 223 Grinter Hall Gainesville FL 32611

PHILLIPSON, ROBERT HENRY LAWRENCE, linguistics educator; b. Gourock, Great Britain, Mar. 18, 1942; arrived in Denmark, 1973; s. A. Henry and Jane (Robathan) P.; m. Helle-Vibeke Larsen, July 7, 1967 (div. Nov. 1979); children: Caspar, Thomas, Louise; m. Tove Skutnabb-Kangas, Jan. 8, 1983. BA, U. Cambridge, Eng., 1964, MA, 1967; MA, U. Leeds, Eng., 1969; PhD, U. Amsterdam, 1990. Mem. Brit. Coun., U.K., 1964-73; prof. U. Roskilde, Denmark, 1973-2000, Copenhagen Bus. Sch., 2000—; part-time lectr. U. Copenhagen, 1973-77. Author: (book) Linguistic Imperialism, 1992; editor: (book) Linguistic Human Rights, 1994, Language, a Right and a Resource, 1999, Rights to Language, 2000; contbr. scholarly articles to profl. jours. Bd. dirs. Danish Ctr. for Human Rights, 1993—. Avocation: ecological farming. Home: Trønning Mose 3, 4420 Regstrup Denmark Office: Copenhagen Bus Sch, Dalgas Have 15, 2000 Frederiksberg Denmark

PHILLIS, JOHN WHITFIELD, physiologist, educator; b. Port of Spain, Trinidad, Apr. 1, 1936; came to U.S., 1981; s. Ernest and Sarah Anne (Glover) P.; m. Pamela Julie Popple, 1958 (div. 1968); children: David, Simon, Susan; m. Shane Beverly Wright, Jan. 24, 1969. B in Vet. Sci., Sydney (Australia) U., 1958, D in Vet. Sci., 1976; PhD, Australian Nat. U., Canberra, 1961; DSc, Monash U., Melbourne, Australia, 1970. Lectr./sr. Monash U., 1963-69; vis. prof. Ind. U., Indpls., 1969; prof. physiology, assoc. dean rsch. U. Man., Winnipeg, Can., 1970-73; prof., chmn. dept. physiology U. Sask., Saskatoon, Can., 1973-81, asst. dean rsch., 1973-75; prof. physiology Wayne State U., Detroit, 1981—, chmn. dept. physiology, 1981-97; mem. scholarship and grants com. Can. Med. Rsch. Coun., Ottawa, Ont., 1973-79; mem. sci. adv. bd. Dystonia Med. Rsch. Found., Beverly Hills, Calif., 1980-85, Curtis Rsch. Inst., Risingsun, Ohio, 1998-2000; mem. sci. adv. panel World Soc. for Protection of Animals, 1982-98; Wellcome vis. prof. Tulane U., 1986; mem. acad. scholars Wayne State U., 1995. Author: Pharmacology of Synapses, 1970; editor: Veterinary Physiology, 1976, Physiology and Pharmacology of Adenosine Derivatives, 1983, Adenosine and Adenine Nucleotides as Regulators of Cellular Function, 1991, The Regulation of Cerebral Blood Flow, 1993, Novel Therapies for CNS Injuries: Rationales and Results, 1996; editor Can. Jour. Physiology and Pharmacology, 1978-81, Progress in Neurobiology, 1973-97. Mem. grants com. Am. Heart Assn. of Mich., 1985-90, mem. rsch. coun., 1991-92, mem. rsch. forum com., 1991-96, chair, 1992-93; mem. Brain/Stroke Consortium Study Group, Am. Heart Assn., 1998. Wellcome fellow London, 1961-62; Can. Med. Rsch. Coun. grantee, 1970-81, rsch. prof., 1980; NIH grantee, 1983-2000. Mem. Brit. Pharmacol. Soc., Physiol. Soc., Am. Physiol. Soc., Soc. Neurosci., Internat. Brain Rsch. Orgn. Office: Wayne State U Dept Physiology 540 E Canfield St Detroit MI 48201-1928

PHILO, GORDON CHARLES GEORGE, retired diplomat; b. London, Jan. 8, 1920; s. Charles Gilbert and Nellie (Pinnock) P.; m. Mavis Ella Galsworthy, Sept. 10, 1952 (dec. Sept. 1986). MA, Oxford (Eng.) U., 1947; postgrad., Sorbonne U., France, 1948-49; diploma in Russian, Cambridge (Eng.) U., 1952. Lectr. Wadham Coll., Oxford, 1949-50; founding mem., lectr. St. Antony's Coll., Oxford, 1950-51; officer Fgn. Office, London, 1951-52, counselor, 1970-78; 3d sec. Brit. Embassy, Istanbul, 1954-56; 2d sec. Brit. Embassy, Ankara, 1957-58; 1st sec. Brit. High Commn., Kuala Lumpur, 1963-67; consul-gen. Brit. Consulate Gen., Hanoi, North Vietnam, 1968-69; ret., 1978; assessor Civil Svc. Commn., U.K., 1978-90. Co-author: (as Charles Forsyte) Diplomatic Death, also numerous mystery stories, lit. criticisms, articles. Capt. Brit. Airborne Forces Svc., 1940-46. Decorated Mil. Cross, King George VI of Eng., 1944, Hon. Kesatria Mangku Negara, Malaysian Govt., 1968, Companion of Most Disting. Order of St. Michael and St. George, Queen Elizabeth II of Eng., 1970. Mem. Kipling Soc. (chmn. coun. 1986-88, 97-99), Dickens Fellowship, Athenaeum Club. Avocations: travel, writing, history, literature, walking.

PHILP, IAN, academic administrator, consultant physician; b. Edinburgh, Scotland, Nov. 14, 1958; s. Thomas and Agnes Calder (Yule) P.; m. Elizabeth Anne Boyd, Mar. 16, 1984; children: Hannah Louise, Emily Kathryn, Alexander Thomas. Cert. Gen. Med. Coun. Registrar in medicine Glasgow (Scotland) Royal Infirmary, 1985-86; trainee gen. physician Alva Med. Practice, 1986; BGS Nuffield fellow U. Minn., Mpls., 1989; sr. registrar Ninewells Hosp. Med. Sch., Dundee, 1986-90; cons. sr. lectr. in geriatric medicine U. Southampton, Eng., 1990-94; dep. dean, dir. Sheffoeld Inst. for Studies on Aging, Eng.; prof. health care for elderly people U. Sheffoeld, 1994—; cons. WHO, Denmark, 1994—; advisor EC, Belgium, 1997—, Prix Galien Award, U.K., 1997—; faculty mem. Lundbeck Internat. Neurosci. Found., Denmark, 1997—; chair external ref. group Nat. Svc. Framework on Aging. Creator: (assessment sys.) Easy Care, 1997; editor: (book) Assessing Elderly People in Hospital and Community Care, 1994; group leader: (ednl. CD-ROM) DEP Relief, 1997. Recipient David Wallace medal Australian Gerontology Soc., 1996, Insight award, 1989, Cove of the Elderly award, 1998. Fellow Royal Coll. Physicians Edinburgh, Royal Coll. Physicians London. Avocations: European travel, swimming, salsa dancing, theater. Office: U Sheffield Comty Scis Ctr, No Gen Hosp, SS 7AU Sheffield England

PHILPOTTS, PAUL BARRINGTON, public relations consultant; b. Swindon, Wiltshire, Eng., July 22, 1957; s. Raymond Dennis and Ruby Elizabeth (Richards) P.; m. Joanna Stephanie Hearley, May 22, 1982; 1 child, Alexandra. BSc, Durham U., Eng., 1979. Engring. Asst. editor Control & Instrumentation, Eng., 1979-81, Computer Syss., Eng., 1981-82; editor Food Processing, Eng., 1983; mktg. mgr. Techpress Pub., Eng., 1983-85; account group dir. Hill & Knowlton, Eng., 1986-88; sr. cons. Shandwick Conss., Eng., 1988-89; Mktg. dir. IML Group PLC, Eng., 1989-92; dir. Shandwick Cons., Eng., 1992-94; mng. dir. corp. and fin. comms. Burson-Marsteller, Eng., 1994-96, mng. dir. corp. and fin. comms. Europe, 1996-98; dir. Burson-Marsteller, Europe, 1996-98; mng. dir. Burson-Marsteller, Eng., 1996-98; pres. Ogilvy Pub. Rels. Europe, London, 1998-2000; ptnr. Square Mile Comms., Eng., 2000—. Mem. Am. C. of C. (chmn. European affairs com. 1996-98). Avocations: opera, computers, fast cars. Home: Grey Cedars Station Rd, Woldingham Surrey CR3 7DD, England

PHINN, STUART ROSS, geographer, educator; b. Belfast, No. Ireland; s. Ross Angus and Alison Mary (Maver) P. BSc with honors, U. queensland, 1991; PhD, San Diego State U., 1997. Mgr., asst. Australian Key Ctr. in Land Info., Brisbane, 1990-92; rsch./tchg. assoc. San Diego State U., 1992-97; lectr. U. Queensland, Brisbane, 1997—. Recipient U. Queensland medal, 1991; Fulbright scholar, 1992-94. Office: Univ of Queensland, Dept Geog Scis & Planning, Brisbane 4072 QLD, Australia

PHIPARD, NANCY MIDWOOD, retired educator, writer; b. Boston, Jan. 31, 1929; d. William Henry and Jean Estelle (Dubbs) McAdams; m. Kenneth E. Brown, June 17, 1949 (div.); children: Christopher M., Jennifer Prigodich, Michael H., Jeffrey D.; m. Arnold J. Midwood, Jr., July 2, 1980 (dec.); m. Harvey F. Phipard, Jan. 14, 1998. Student, Mt. Holyoke Coll., 1946-48; BA, Wellesley Coll., 1973; MEd, Boston Coll., 1975. Dir. confs. and insvc. tng., chmn. bd. Mass. Assn. for Children with Learning Disabilities, Waltham and Framingham, 1969-75; chmn. core edn. teams, cons. to spl. programs, grant writer Needham (Mass.) Pub. Schs., 1974-79; ret. Needham (Mass.) Pub. Schs., Wellesley, Mass., 1979; pres., feature writer S.D. Assocs., Inc., Wellesley, Mass., 1980-81; dir. pub. rels., women's career conf. Babson Coll., Wellesley, Mass., 1982; mem. program evaluation team Mass. Dept. Edn., Quincy, 1978. Contbr. poetry to Portraits of a Life, 1996, Fields of Gold, 1996, Ever-Flowing Stream, 1997, Best Poems of 1998, 1998, Colors of the Past, 2000, Echoes of Yesteryear, 2000, America at the Millennium, The Best Poems and Poets of the 20th Century, 2000, Memories of Tomorrow, 2000, Journey to Infinity, 2000. Bd. dirs., chair cmty. rels. Lincoln Child Ctr., Oakland, Calif., 1983-85; docent Calif. Hist. Soc., San Francisco, 1982-87; bd. dirs., fund raiser Hospice of Palm Beach County South, Palm Beach, Fla., 1993-97; bd. dirs. La Coquielle Villas, Inc., Manalapan, Fla., 1994-98. Recipient 4 Editor's Choice awards Internat. Libr. of Poetry, 1996, 98, 2000. Mem. Internat. Soc. Poets (disting. mem.), Phi Beta Kappa. Avocations: tennis, travel, duplicate bridge. Home: 1630 Lands End Rd Manalapan FL 33462-4762

PHIPPS, LYNNE BRYAN, interior architect, clergywoman, educator; b. Chapel Hill, N.C., Sept. 23, 1964; d. Floyd Talmadge and Sandra Patricia (McLester) Bryan. BFA, RISD, 1986, B Interior Architecture, 1987; cert. in parent edn., Wheelock Coll., Boston, 1989; MDiv, Andover Newton Theol. Sem., 1997. Nat. cert. interior arch. Apprentice Thompson Ventulett Stainback, Atlanta, 1983-85; jr. designer Flansberg & Assocs., Boston, 1986-87; sr. designer Andrew Samataro & Assocs., Boston, 1986-87; prin. Innovative Designs, Duxbury, Mass., 1987—; ptnr. Synergy Unlimited, 1997—; parent educator Families First, Cambridge, Mass.; youth min. St. Andrew's Episcopal Ch., Hanover, Mass., 1992-95; youth and family min. St. Stephen's Episcopal Ch., Cohasset, Mass., 1993-96; co-founder Synergy Inc., 1997—; guest lectr., jurist Auburn (Ala.) U., 1988, RISD, Providence, 1990; assoc. prof. Mass. Bay C.C., Wellesley, 1987-88; guest jurist Wentworth U., Boston, 1988-89; pastor Kingston Congl. Ch. UCC; guest lectr. Architectural and Family Issues; guest jurist U. Memphis, 1995. Designer furniture. Mem. Internat. Interior Design Assn., Internat. Platform Assn. Avocations: sailing, tennis, antique boats. Office: Innovative Designs Synergy Inc 4220 South Rd Wakefield RI 02879

PHOCAS, GEORGE JOHN, international lawyer, business executive; b. N.Y.C., Dec. 1, 1927; m. Katrin Gorny, Feb. 26, 1966; 1 child, George Alexander. A.B., U. Chgo., 1950, J.D., 1953. Bar: N.Y. 1955, U.S. Supreme Ct. 1962. Assoc. Sullivan & Cromwell, N.Y.C., 1953-56; counsel Creole Petroleum Corp., Caracas, Venezuela, 1956-60; internat. negotiator Standard Oil Co. N.J. (Exxon), 1960-63; sr. ptnr. Casey, Lane & Mittendorf, London, 1963-72, counsel, 1972-76; exec. v.p. Occidental Petroleumm Corp., Los Angeles, 1972-74; adv., U.S. del. UN, ECAFE, Teheran, 1963. Trustee Assn. Naval Aviation, Washington, Owl's Head Aviation Mus., Maine; mem. vis. bd. U. Chgo. Law Sch.; bd. visitors U. Chgo. Law Sch. Capt. U.S. Army. Mem. ABA, Law Soc. London, Brit. Inst. Comparative Law, Am. Soc. Internat. Law, Assn. Bar City N.Y.; Clubs: Boodles (London), Met. (N.Y.C.). Home: 28 Aubrey Walk, London W87JG, England also: 1605 Middle Gulf Dr 102 Sanibel FL 33957-7601

PHOENIX, DAVID ANDREW, biochemistry educator; b. Manchester, Eng., Feb. 26, 1966; s. Derek and Edna Marion (Tate) P.; m. Stephanie Jayne Bailey, Aug. 6, 1994; children: Adam John, Lauren Aimee. BSc in Biochemistry, U. Liverpool, 1987, PhD, 1991; BA in Math., Open U., 1994, MA in Edn., 1999. Chartered biologist, chemist, mathematician. Rsch. asst. U. Liverpool, 1987-91; rsch. fellow U. Utrecht, Netherlands, 1991-92; biochemistry lectr. U. Ctrl. Lancashire, Preston, 1992-94, sr. lectr., 1994-98, reader in biochemistry, prin. lectr., 1998-2000, prof. biochemistry, 2000—, head forensic sci., 2000—; assoc. lectr. in higher edn. practice Open U., 1998—; cons. SmithKline Beecham Pharms., U.K., 1993-95; vis. specialist Preston Health Authority, 1993-96; vis. cons. in biochemistry Preston Health Authority, 1996—; vis. prof. Moscow State Inst. of Physics and Engring., 1996-00; vis. fellow U. Liverpool, Eng., 1996-99; univ. specialist reviewer molecular biosci. Quality Assurance Agy., 1997—; U.K. rep. European Com. Biol. Assns., 2000—, mem. commn. for biotech., 2000—. Author: Inductory Math for Life Scientists; editor: Protein Targeting and Translocation, 1998; assoc. editor Life Sci. Ednl. Computing, 1998-2000; editl. adv. bd. Molecular Membrane Biology, 1995—, Cell and Membrane Biology, 1998—; editl. bd. Biologist, 1994—; editor Cell. and Molecular Bioscis., 1997—; editor Jour. biol. Edn., 1998—; chmn. edtl. bd. Biologist, 1997—; contbr. numerous articles to profl. jours. Named Young Biologist Focus mag., 1995; awarded European Chemist title, 1994; fellowship European Molecular Biol. Orgn., 1991, 92; recipient grants Royal Soc., EMBO, BBSRC, EPSRC, Wellcome, Smith Kline Beecham. Fellow Inst. of Math and Its Applications (assoc.); mem. Inst. of Biology (mem. N.W. br. 1992-96, coun. 1997—, edn. and tng. bd. 1998—, pub. rels. bd. 1997—), Royal Soc. of Chemistry, Inst. of Math. and Its Applications, European Com. Biol. Assn. (U.K. rep.; commr. for biotech. 2000—), Forensic Sci. Soc. (mem. acad. and edn. com. 2000—), Brit. Assn. (mem. com. X gen sci. 2000). Office: U Ctrl Lancashire, Preston PR1 2HE, England

PHONANAN, TANYA, human resources manager; b. Bangkok, Thailand, June 28, 1946; s. Rachai and Wanna (Phanthawes) P.; m. Pantipaya Suwanjinda, 1972 (div. 1981); m. Taratip Niyomka, 1982 (div. 1994); children: Komkyo Tira-one, Ryochan Tira-two; m. Kwanrudee Phiromsawat, Aug. 27, 1994; children: Kaokwan, Kaokla. Student, Osaka (Japan) U. Fgn. Studies, 1971, Hitotsubashi U., Tokyo, 1971-73; MBA, Sophia U., Tokyo, 1975; BSc in Econs., Kasetsart U., Bangkok, 1968. Mgr. Exec. Resources Thailand, Bangkok, 1984-85; asst. v.p. Bank of Ayudhya, Bangkok, 1985-90; pers. mgr. Muramoto Electron (Thailand), Bangkok, 1990; adminstrn. mgr. Yanmar S.P., Bangkok, 1990-91; dir. human resources Triumph Internat. (Thailand), Samutprakarn, 1992-96; group human resources mgr. Thomson TV (Thailand), Pathumthani, 1996—. Author: (fiction) Road to the Cloud, 1972, 96, (nonfiction) Blood Stain in Korea, 1984; compiler: (books) Human Resources Glossary, 1994, Road to Singapore, 1994, 96. Mombusho scholar Japanese Govt., 1970-73, scholar Tokyo Found. for Inbound Students, 1974-75. Mem. Electronic and Computer Employers' Assn. (v.p. 1997-98), Fedn. of Thai Industry (mem. subcom. for labor mgmt. 1995-96), Pers. Mgmt. Assn. (v.p. 1994-96, advisor 2000—), Tech. Promotion Assn. (exec. dir. 1997—), Soc. for Human Resources Mgmt., Assn. South East Asia Nations Human Resources Mgmt. Fedn. (pres. 1996-97), Writers' Assn. of Thailand (exec. dir. 1999—). Avocations: stamps, coins, photography, mind mappings. E-mail: buzanthai@hotmail.com. Home: 176/381 Ratanawalai Laksi, See Gun Don Muang, Bangkok 10210, Thailand Office: Thomson TV Thailand Co Ltd, 141 Moo 5 Tiwanon Rd, Pathumthani 12000, Thailand

PHULÉ, PRADEEP PRABHAKAR, engineering educator; b. Pune, India, Mar. 14, 1960; s. Prabhakar P. and Pratibha P. (Joshi) Fulay; m. Jyotsna D. Pangrekar, Dec. 28, 1990; children: Aarohee, Suyash. B in Tech. with honors, IIT Bombay, 1983, M in Tech. with honors, 1984; PhD, U. Ariz., 1989. Trainee engr. Sandvik Asia, India, 1980-81; trainee engr. Mahindra Sintered Products, India, 1981-82; rsch. asst., dept. metallurgical engring. IIT, Bombay, 1983-84; teaching asst., dept. chemistry Brigham Young U., Provo, Utah, 1985; grad. rsch. and teaching asst, dept. materials sci. engring. U. Ariz., Tucson, 1985-89; asst. prof. materials sci. and engring. U. Pitts., 1989-92, William Kepler Whiteford faculty fellow, asst. prof., 1992-94, assoc. prof. materials sci. and engring., 1994-99, prof. materials sci. and engring., 1999—, William Kepler faculty fellow, 1999—. Contbr. numerous articles to profl. jours. Presenter in field. Recipient NSF, Alcoa Found., Am. Chem. Soc., U. Pitts. Ctrl. Rsch. Devel. Fund, Internat. Soc. for Hybrid Microelectronics, Ben Franklin Tech. Ctr., Air Force Office Scientific Rsch. grants. Mem. AAAS, Materials Rsch. Soc. (v.p. Greater Pitts. sect. 1990-91, bd. dirs. 1992-93, sec. 1990), Am. Ceramic Soc. (assoc. editor jour. 1995—, electronics divsn.-edn. com. 1992-93, 93-94), Am. Soc. for Engring. Edn., Internat. Soc. for Hybrid Microelectronics, Am. Chem. Soc. Achievements include rsch. in chem. synthesis of advanced electronic and optical ceramic materials. Avocations: tennis, swimming. Office: U Pitts 848 Benedum Hall Pittsburgh PA 15261-2208

PHUMIPHON ADULYADEJ, HIS MAJESTY, King of Thailand; b. Cambridge, Mass., Dec. 5, 1927; s. Prince and Princess Mahidol of Songkhla; m. Mom Rajawongse Sirikit, Apr. 28, 1950; children: Princess Ubol Ratana, Crown Prince Maha Vajiralongkorn, Princess Maha Chakri Sirindhorn, Princess Chulabhorn. Ed., Bangkok and Lausanne (Switzerland). Succeeded brother King Ananda Mahidol (dec.), 1946; coronation ceremony, May 5, 1950. Address: Office of His Majesty The King, The Grand Palace, 10200 Bangkok Thailand*

PIA, PAUL DOMINIC, corporate lawyer; b. Edinburgh, Scotland, Mar. 29, 1947; s. Joseph and Louise Maria Pia; m. Anne Christine Argent; children: Camilla F., Roberta A., Sophie L. LLB in Law and Econs. with honors, U. Edinburgh, 1968; diploma in Italian, U. Perugia, Italy, 1969. Law apprentice Lindsays WS, Edinburgh, 1968-70; solicitor Law Office of Burness Edinburgh and Glasgow, Edinburgh, 1970-74, ptnr., 1974—; coun. mem. Soc. of Writers to Her Majesty's Signet, Edinburgh, 1993-96. Author: Care, Diligence and Skill: Handbook for Directors, 1986. Chmn. Japanese Garden, Edinburgh, 2000; dir. Scottish N.Am. Bus. Coun., 2000. Fellow Inst. Dirs.; mem. ABA (assoc.), Law Soc. Scotland, Japan Soc. Scotland (coun. mem. 1990-96, chmn. 1996—). Avocations: cycling, travel, hill walking. Home: 67 Woodfield Park, Edinburgh EH13 0RA, Scotland Office: Burness 50 Festival Sq, Lothian Rd, Edinburgh EH3 9WJ, Scotland Office: 242 W George St, Glasgow G2 4QY, Scotland

PIACENTINI, RUBEN DARIO, physicist, educator; b. Bigand, Santa Fe, Argentina, May 25, 1943; s. Juan Bautista and Maria (Erceg) P.; m. Noemí Carmen Silva, Nov. 4, 1968; children: Diego, Ariel, Silvina. Licenciado en Fisica, Instituto Balseiro, Bariloche, Argentina, 1966; Docteur d'Université, U. Paris, 1970, Docteur d'Etat, 1972. Rschr. Observatoire de Paris, 1968-71; prof. physics U. Rosario, Argentina, 1971—; rschr. CONICET, Rosario, 1978—, mem. adv. coun., 1984-86; dir. Obs. and Planetarium, Rosario, 1984-99; founder, 1st dir. Exptl. Sci. Mus., Rosario, 1987-99; vis. prof. U. Bordeaux, France, 1976-77; vis. rschr. U. Fla., Gainesville, 1980, Kans. State U., Manhattan, 1992. Author numerous sci. articles. Mem. Fundación Planetario de Rosario, 1984-99. Decorated Chevalier Palmes Academiques, France, 1987; named Citizen of Yr., Rotary Club of Rosario, 1989. Mem. Inst. of Physics (U.K.), Internat. Astron. Union. (CONAE Argentina rep. TOMS/NASA sci. team 1996—, mem. ozone assessment 1998). Roman Catholic. Avocation: soccer. Office: Observatorio Astronómico, Inst de Fisica Rosario, 27 de Febrero Llobis, 2000 Rosario Argentina

PIACITELLI, JOHN JOSEPH, county official, educator, pediatrician; b. Providence, Sept. 1, 1936; s. Joseph A. and Elsie (Mignacca) P.; m. Carol Ann Keirn, Aug. 19, 1961; 1 child, James. BS, U. R.I., 1958; MA, SUNY, Buffalo, 1963; MD, Creighton U., 1964. Diplomate Am. Bd. Pediatrics. Intern Buffalo Gen. Hosp., 1964-65; pediatric resident Children's Hosp. of Buffalo, 1965-67; pediatrician East Nassau Med. Group, North Babylon, N.Y., 1969-79; dir. Charlotte County Health Dept., Punta Gorda, Fla., 1980—; asst. clin. instr. SUNY, Buffalo, 1965-67, instr. in clin. pediatrics, L.I., 1972-79, asst. prof. pediatrics, 1979. Contbr. articles to profl. jours. Mem. health adv. com. Charlotte County Sch., 1981-96; mem. local planning orgn. adv. com., Charlotte County, Fla., 1986-87; mem. Indigent Health Care Adv. Bd., Charlotte County, 1988—; chmn. Charlotte County AIDS Task Force, 1988-91; chmn. adv. com. Head Start Health Svcs., 1991-94. Maj. M.C., U.S. Army, 1967-69. Fellow Am. Acad Pediatrics (cert.); mem. Nat. Assn. County and City Health Ofcls., Fla. Pub. Health Assn., Fla. Assn. County Health Officers, Fla. Med. Assn., Fla. Pediatric Soc., Charlotte County Med. Soc., Fla. Soc. for Preventive Medicine. Office: Charlotte County Health Dept 514 E Grace St Punta Gorda FL 33950-6121

PIANA, ZENÓRIO, agricultural engineer; b. Concórdia, Brazil, Apr. 20, 1952; s. Pedro and Analice M. (Smaniotto) P.; m. Arlete Maria Garcia, Oct. 18, 1980; 1 child, Matheus Garcia. BSc, Pelotas (Brazil) Fed. U., 1975, MSc, 1980; PhD, São Paulo U., Piracicaba, Brazil, 1994. Extensionist Santa Catarina Agrl. Ext. Orgn., Chapecó, Brazil, 1976-78; rschr. Santa Catarina Agrl. Rsch. Enterprise, Lages, Brazil, 1980-87; rschr. coord. Santa Catarina Agrl. Rsch. Enterprise, Florianópolis, Brazil, 1987-91; from rsch. mgr. to dir. Santa Catarina Rsch. and Ext. Co., Florianópolis, Brazil, 1995-97; state agrl. sec. asst. Santa Catarina State Agrl. Sec., Florianópolis, Brazil, 1998. Author: Forage Seeds Production, 1986; contbr. articles to profl. jours.; inventor in field. Counselor Regional Coun. for Engring., Arch. and Agronomy Santa Catarina, 1998-2000. Mem. Agronomist Engrs. Assn. Santa Catarina (tech. dir. 1990-92, polit. dir. 1996-98, v.p. 1998-2000). Roman Catholic. Avocations: tennis, chess, soccer. Home: João Carlos Maurer 220, 88037120 Florianópolis Brazil Office: Santa Catarina Rsch Ext Co, PO Box 502, 88034901 Florianópolis Brazil

PIASECKI, JERZY, chemist, educator; b. Turzno, Poland, Feb. 1, 1926; s. Wladyslaw and Zofia (Przybylowska) P.; m. Alfreda Bartnik, Dec. 10, 1955; 1 child, Wojciech. MSc, Nicolaus Copernicus U., 1952; PhD, U. Agriculture, Szczecin, Poland, 1963, DSc, 1966. Sr. asst. Tech. U. Szczecin, 1953-54; from asst. prof. to prof. Univ. Agriculture, 1954-96; prof. emeritus, 1996—; head dept. gen. chemistry Univ. Agriculture, 1967-96, pres., 1984-90, v.p., 1969-72, dean agrl. faculty, 1967-69; chmn. Coun. Pres. Univs., Szczecin, 1984-90. Co-author: Quantitative and Qualitative Chemical Analysis, 1996; contbr. articles to profl. jours. Mem. Szczecin Scientific Soc. (sec. gen. 1978-81), Polish Chem. Soc., Polish Soil Soc. Avocation: sightseeing. Office: U Agriculture Dept Gen Chemistry, ul Slowackiego 17, 71-434 Szczecin Poland

PIASEK, MARTINA, physician, researcher; b. Zagreb, Croatia, Nov. 3, 1955; d. Gustav and Ljubica Piasek. MD, U. Zagreb, 1980, MSc in Biomedicine, 1986, PhD in Med. Scis., 1990. Intern in gen. medicine Med. Ctr. Varadin, 1980-82; physician Med. Ctr. Varazdin, 1982-86; postgrad. rschr. in biomedicine Inst. for Med. Rsch. and Occupl. Health, Zagreb, 1982-86, rsch. asst., 1986-90, rsch. assoc., 1990-98, sr. rsch. assoc., 1998—; vis. scientist USEPA, Research Triangle Park, N.C., 1991-92, 93-94; lectr., mentor postgrad. study natural scis. U. Zagreb, 1991—. Dep. editor-in-chief, mem. editl. bd. Archives Indsl. Hygiene and Toxicology, 1990—; contbr. over 50 articles to profl. jours. and chpts. to books. Mem. Croatian Physiology Soc., Croatian Med. Assn., Croatian Toxicology Assn., Croatian Assn. for Lab. Animal Sci. Roman Catholic. Avocations: philately, theatre, classical music. Office: Inst Med Rsch & Occupl Hlth, PO Box 291, HR-10001 Zagreb Croatia

PIASETZKY, ELIAZER, physics educator; b. Tel Aviv, Israel, Feb. 9, 1953; s. Refael and Adina (Klideman) P.; m. Clarisa Haimshon; children: Iftah, Michal, Jonatan. BSc, Tel Aviv U., 1974, MSc, 1978, PhD, 1981. Postdoctoral fellow Los Alamos (N.Mex.) Nat. Lab., 1981-82, staff mem., 1982-84; asst., then assoc. prof. physics Tel Aviv U., 1984-92, prof., 1992—, chmn. nuclear physics dept., 1996—; vis. physicist Brookhaven Nat. Lab., N.Y., 1992. Contbr. over 50 articles to sci. jours. Maj. Israeli Def. Force, 1975-84. Recipient Helena and Philip Spitzer award Israel Acad., 1997. Office: Tel Aviv U, Dept Physics, 69978 Tel Aviv Israel

PIAZZA, MICHAEL JOSEPH, professional baseball player; b. Norristown, Pa., Sept. 4, 1968. Student, Miami (Fla.)-Dade C.C. Catcher Los Angeles Dodgers, 1992-97, New York Mets, 1998—; mem. Nat. League All-Star Team, 1993-96. Named Nat. League Rookie Player of Yr., Sporting News, 1993, Catcher on the Sporting News N.L. All-Star Team, 1993-96, N.L. Silver Slugger Team, 1993-94, named to Nat. League Slugger Team,

1993; named Nat. League Rookie of Yr., Baseball Writers Assn., 1993. Office: New York Mets Shea Stadium 123-10 Roosevelt Ave Flushing NY 11368

PIBULSONGGRAM, NITYA, diplomat; b. Bangkok, June 30, 1941; s. Field Marshal P. and Lady La-iad (Bhandhukravi) P.; m. Patricia Osmond, July 3, 1965. AB in Govt., Dartmouth Coll., 1964; AM in Polit. Sci., Brown U., 1967. With fgn. news div. of info. dept. Ministry Fgn. Affairs Govt. of Thailand, Bangkok, 1968, with SEATO div. of internat. orgns. dept., 1969-72, with policy and planning div. Office of Permanent Sec. and Office of Minister of Fgn. Affairs, 1973-75, head polit. dept. S.E. Asia div., 1975-76, dep. dir. gen. info. dept., 1980, dep. dir. gen. polit. dept., 1981, amb.-at-large Fgn. Ministry, 1982, dir. gen. internat. orgns. dept., 1983-87; 1st sec. permanent Thai mission to UN Govt. of Thailand, N.Y.C., 1976-78, dep. permanent rep. Thai mission to UN, 1978-80, amb., permanent rep. to UN, 1988-96; amb. to U.S., 1996—. Decorated Knight Grand Cross (1st class) of Most Exalted Order of White Elephant, 1984, Spl. Grand Cordon of Most Noble Order of Crown of Thailand, 1988. Mem. Royal Bangkok Sports Club, Dartmouth Club (pres. Bangkok chpt. 1986-88). Buddhist. Avocations: skiing, golf, tennis. Home: 2145 Decatur Pl NW Washington DC 20008-1923 Office: Royal Thai Embassy 1024 Wisconsin Ave NW Washington DC 20007-3668

PICACHE, JOSEFINA REYES, travel service company executive, marriage counselor; b. Bulacan, Philippines, June 19, 1945; came to U.S., 1970; d. Cesar Garcia and Leona (Pilao) Delos Reyes; m. Danilo Sabal Picache, Oct. 20, 1968; children: Beverly Reyes, Abigail Reyes. BS in Edn.-Guidance and Counseling, U. Philippines/East, 1967; MS in Edn. Adminstrn./Supervision, Old Dominion U., 1980. Guidance counselor Torres High Sch., Manila, 1967; asst. dir. Philippine Soc. for Prevention of Cruelty to Animals, Manila, 1968; adminstrv. asst. to alumni dir. Old Dominion U., Norfolk, Va., 1976-83; pres./owner Picache Internat. Travel, Virginia Beach, Va., 1983—; pres., CEO, owner Freedom Travel, Inc., Va. Beach, Va.; owner JRP Travel, Missouri City, Tex., 1990—. Recipient Achievement award Atlantic Filipino News, Norfolk, 1980, Recognition award Old Dominion U. Alumni Assn., Norfolk, 1984. Fellow Nat. Assn. Female Execs.; mem. Better Bus. Bur., Hampton Road C. of C., Womens' Network. Avocations: tennis, basketball, reading, traveling. Home: 5224 Hancock Ct Virginia Beach VA 23464-2517

PICARD, DENNIS J., retired electronics company executive; b. 1932. BBA, Northeastern Univ., 1962. With RCA, 1954-55; elec. engr. Raytheon Co., 1955-59, design engr., 1959-61, sect. mgr., 1961-69, dir. equipment div., data acquisition systems directorate, 1969-76, asst. gen. mgr. ops., equipment div., 1976-77, asst. gen. mgr. ops., equipment div., also corp. v.p., 1977-81, v.p. equipment div., 1981-1985, sr. v.p., gen. mgr. missile systems div., 1985-89, pres., 1989-90, chmn. bd., CEO, 1990-99, also bd. dirs. Mem. Def. Policy Adv. Com. on Trade; mem. Pres.'s Export Coun.; mem. Pres.'s Nat. Security Telecomms. Adv. Coun. Served with USAF 1951-53. Mem. NAE, AIAA, IEEE, Mass. Bus. Roundtables, The Bus. Coun. Home: 1373 Monument St Concord MA 01742-5328 Office: Raytheon Co 141 Spring St Lexington MA 02421-7899

PICARD, JACQUES JEAN, retired business development executive; b. Paris, Mar. 10, 1934; s. Aime Jean and Simone Marie (Rosset) P.; m. Anne Lise Nifenecker; children: Lucie, Olivier, Jean-Thomas, Nicolas. Prof. engr., Arts & Metiers, Paris, 1956, Institut Francais Petrole, Rueil, France, 1957; MSc in Naval Architecture, MIT, 1964. Project engr. Institut Oceanographique (headed by Capt. J.Y. Cousteau), Monaco, 1960-67; dir. Technocean, Paris, 1967-69, Ocean-Structures, Paris, 1969-73; bus. devel. dir. CFEM, Paris, 1973-83; bus. devel. dir. Framatome, Paris, 1984-95, ret., 1995. Inventor laboratory buoy, diving saucer and submarines, offshore platforms and numerous others. Mem. MIT Club. Home: 32 rue du Belvedere, 78750 Mareil-Marly France

PICARD, LAURENT A(UGUSTIN), retired management educator, administrator, consultant; b. Quebec, Que., Can., Oct. 27, 1927; s. Edouard and Alice (Gingras) P.; m. Therese Picard; children: Andre, Marc, Robert (dec.), Denys, Jean-Louis, François (dec.). BA, Laval U., Quebec, 1947, BS, 1954; DBA, Harvard U., 1964. Prof. U. Montreal, Que., Can., 1962-68, dir. bus. adminstrn. dept., 1964-68; exec. v.p. Can. Broadcasting Corp., Ottawa, Ont., 1968-72, pres., CEO, 1972-75; joint prof. McGill U. and U. Montreal, 1977-78; dean faculty mgmt. McGill U., Montreal, 1978-86, prof., 1986-97; ret.; mem. Royal Commn. on Newspapers, Royal Commn. on Econ. Union and Devel. Prospects for Can.; conciliation commr. Maritime Employers Assn., Prot of Montreal; bd. dirs. Lombard-Odier Trust Co., Jean Coutu Group, Dorel Ind. Inc.; cons. to industry; guest speaker at internat. meetings. Contbr. articles to profl. jours. Chmn. Nat. Book Festival, 1978-79; chmn. jury Prix Gerin Lajoie, Ministry Cultural Affairs, 1982. Recipient 125th Anniversary medal Can., 1992; decorated companion Order of Can., 1977. Mem. Commonwealth Broadcasting Assn. (1st pres.). Home: 5602 Wilderton Ave, Montreal, PQ Canada H3T 1R9

PICARDI, GERARD A., publisher; b. Boston, Apr. 24, 1949; s. Antonio Sabine and Jane Elizabeth Picardi. BA in English Lit., St. Michael's Coll., 1970. Office mgr. Love's Furniture Co., Stoneham, Mass., 1970-75; sec. Little, Brown & Co., Boston, 1975-76, prodn. asst., 1976-79, asst. prodn. mgr., 1979-84; prodn. coord. Harvard U. Press, Cambridge, Mass., 1984-92, prodn. supr., 1992-97, asst. prodn. mgr., 1997—. Named Harvard U. Hero, 1999. Mem. Bookbuilders Boston (mem. fall roundtable com. 1988-90, cochair 1990-91, mem. publicity com. 1990-91, chair 1991-93, mem. advanced seminar com. 1992-95, bd. dirs. 1991-94, sec. 1993-94, mem. nominations com. 1993-95, mem. edn. com. 1994-95, chair endowment fund com. 1994-95, 1st v.p. 1994-95, pres. 1995-96, chair Dwiggins award com. 1996-97, judge New Eng. book show 1998-99), Am. Assn. Univ. Presses, Am. Inst. Graphic Arts. Roman Catholic. E-mail: gerard_picard@harvard.edu. Home: 350 Sumner St East Boston MA 02128-2218 Office: Harvard U Press 79 Garden St Cambridge MA 02138-1423

PICASSO, MARIA ISABEL, artist; b. Buenos Aires, July 22, 1954; d. Alberto Picasso and Maria Isabel Casas Elia; m. Jorge Pierrestegui, Dec. 21, 1978; 1 child, Jorge. Bachelor's degree, Michael Ham, Buenos Aires, 1971; art degree, Santa Ana, Buenos Aires, 1977. Tchr. Santa Ana, Buenos Aires, 1980-88; artist, painter, photographer Buenos Aires, 1979—. Avocation: photography. Office: Taller, Reconquita890, Buenos Aires Argentina

PICCHI, FRANCO, lawyer; b. Viareggio, Lucca, Italy, Dec. 23, 1922; s. Giovanni and Angelica (Poli) P.; m. Lina Genovesi, May 2, 1946; children: Luca, Alessandro, Eugenia. LLB, Pisa (Italy) U., 1945. Asst. Pisa U., 1945-61; atty. Pisa, 1947-50, atty.-at-law, 1950—; prof. legal subjects secondary schs., Lucca, Italy, 1971-80; pres. Lucca Criminal Ct., 1973-88; coun. mem. Ct. Lucca Bar Assn., 1972-81; hon. vice judge Ct. of First Instance, Viareggio, Italy, 1978-87; pres. Lucca Profl. Rolls, 1980—; pres. Lucca Pisa Massa Carra Arbitration Ct. Lucca, 1985-90; commr. Lucca Second Instance Tax Commn., 1989-97. Recipient gold medal Coun. Ct. Bar Assn., Lucca, 1987, silver medal, 1997. Office: Picchi Lawyers Office, 4 Armando Diaz Dist, 55049 Viareggio Lucca, Italy

PICCIONE, TAL P., insurance company executive; b. N.Y.C., Feb. 9, 1948; s. Patric Francis and Maria Rose (Scandariato) P.; m. Lena Marie Tamburello, Feb. 22, 1970; children: Michael John, Marc Patric. AAS, Pace Coll., 1971; BBA, Pace U., 1973. V.p. Guy Carpenter & Co., Inc., N.Y.C., 1972-87; chmn., CEO U.S. RE Cos., Inc., N.Y.C., 1987—; bd. dirs. Internat. Ins. Coun., Washington; chmn. CNSR Found., N.Y.C., Legatus. Asst. scout master Boys Scouts Am., Bergen County, N.J., 1988-92. Mem. NRA, Columbus Citizens Found., India House, Nippon Club, Safari Club Internat., Sloane Club (London). Avocations: fishing, hunting, boating, opera. Office: US Re Companies Inc 99 Park Ave New York NY 10016-1601

PICCOLI, HUMBERTO CAMARGO, engineering educator, researcher; b. Rio Grande, Rio Grande do Sol, Brazil, Oct. 24, 1954; s. Humberto Canary and Etelvina (Camargo) P.; m. Maria Da Graca Edom, Dec. 2, 1978; children: Carolina, Humberto. Diploma in Indsl. Engring., Furg, Rio Grande, 1977; MS, USP, Sao Carlos, Brazil, 1982; PhD, Unicamp, Campinas, Brazil, 1994. Rschr. Furg, Rio Grande, 1977-82, head dept., 1979-80, asst. prof., 1982-85, head dept., 1983-84, assoc. prof., 1985-99, head dept., 1995-97, dir. grad. courses, 1998-99; head divsn. Furg, Rio Grande, 1986-1987. Pres. Aprofurg, Rio Grande, 1983. Mem. ASME. Roman Catholic. Avocations: sports, music. Home: Paulo Sergio Pegas 362, 96208470 Cassino Brazil Office: Furg, Alfredo Huch 475, 96201900 Rio Grande Brazil

PICCONATTO, EVELYN CLARA, accountant; b. Milw., Mar. 22, 1974; d. John Arthur and Judy Marie Picconatto. BBA, Coll. William & Mary, 1996. CPA, Minn. Acct. Coopers & Lybrand LLP, Mpls., 1995, 96-97, Lurie, Beikof, Lapidus & Co. LLP, Mpls., 1998—. Mem. AICPA, Minn. Soc. CPAs. Roman Catholic. Avocations: outdoor activities, arts & crafts, photography. Office: Lurie Besikof Lapidus and Co LLP 2501 Wayzata Blvd Minneapolis MN 55405-2139

PICHAIWONGSE, CHAKORN, lawyer; b. Muang, Thailand, Jan. 12, 1962; s. Paiboon and Auyporn (Ratarasarn) P. LLB, Thammasat U., Thailand, 1982; LLM, Am. U., 1988. Cert. in Advanced English Studies, Georgetown U., 1987. Atty. Bangkok Ins. Co., 1982-86; trainee Alagia, Day, Marshall, Mintmire & Chauvin, U.S., 1989; assoc. Kanung-Prok Internat. Law Office, Thailand, 1990, Kanung & Ptnrs. Law Office, Thailand, 1990-92; adj. lectr. Bangkok U., 1991-92; atty. Environ. Law Ctr., Thailand, 1992; assoc. Tilleke & Gibbins, Thailand, 1994; sr. assoc. Freshfields, Thailand, 1995; sr. lawyer Clifford Chance Ltd., Bangkok, 1996—. Mem. ATLA. Home: 149/3 Soi Prasatsuk, Yenarekas Rd Khwaeng Chongnonsri, Khet Yannawa Bangkok Thailand Office: Clifford Chance Ltd, 130-132 Wireless Rd Tower 3, Pathumwan, Bangkok 10330, Thailand

PICHAT, LOUIS JEAN, retired research director; b. Lyon, France, Nov. 28, 1926; s. Louis and Lucienne (Buscazzo) P.; m. Raymonde Galedeck, July 29, 1950; children: Christian, Philippe. Degree chem. engring., ESCIL, 1946; PhD, Faculte des Scis., Lyon, 1948. Lab. asst. ESCIL PRJ. Colonge, Lyon, France, 1946-48; postdoctoral rschr. chemistry dept. U. Coll., London, 1948-49; chem. engr. Commissariat Energie Atomique, CEN Saclay, France, 1949-59, chief labeled compounds sect., 1959-65, head labeled compounds dept., 1965-85, dir. rsch., 1985-89, ret.; lectr. Nat. Inst. Nuc. Scis., Saclay, 1960-81; invited lectr. Internat. Isotope STY Confs., Kansas City, 1982-85, 88, Toronto, 1991. Co-editor Jour. of Labelled Compounds and Radio Pharms., 1987-96, editor emeritus, 1998—; co-author: The Chemistry of the Cyano Group, 1970; contbr. over 246 articles to profl. jours. Decorated chevalier Nat. Order of Merit, chevalier Order Palmes Academiques (France); recipient Louis Bonneau Prize Acad. of Scis. France, 1971, IIS award, 1991. Mem. Am. Chem. Soc., N.Y. Acad. Scis. Office: CEA Cen Saclay, 91191 Gif-sur-Yvette France

PICHEREAU, VIANNEY JEAN DENIS, microbiologist, educator; b. Lorient, France, June 27, 1970; s. Camille and Marie-Claude (Segalen) P.; m. Solenn Anne Marie Chiche, June 22, 1996; 1 child, Aristide. Lic. in chemistry and Plant Biology, U. Rennes, France, 1993, M Chemistry and Plant Biology, 1994, DEA in Agronomy, 1995, PhD in Microbiology, 1998. Rschr. U. Rennes, 1994-98; lectr. U. Caen, France, 1998-99; lectr. Inst. Food Scis. and Biotech. U. Caen, Inst. U. Profl. Agro-Alimentaire, France, 1999—; rschr. in field. Contbr. numerous articles to profl. jours. Home: 20 rue du Bessin, 14740 Bretteville France Office: U Caen Lab Microbiol/Envir, Esplanade de la Paix, 14032 Caen France

PICHLER, J(OHANN) HANNS, economics educator; b. Aspach, Austria, May 12, 1936; s. Franz and Berta (Mayr) P.; m. Hannelore M. Haslinger v.d. Linden, Sept. 1963; children: Adelheid, Regine, Markus. M of Bus. and Econs., U. Econs. Vienna, Austria, 1958; D of Econs., U. Econs. Vienna, 1960, D habil., 1965; MSc in Econ., U. Ill., 1963; D (hon.), Cath. U., Brussels, 1994. Mem. faculty U. Econs., Vienna, 1960-65; lectr. U. Ill., Urbana, 1962-63; sr. economist World Bank, Washington, 1965-71; res. rep. World Bank Group, Islamabad, Pakistan, 1971-74; prof. polit. economy, internat. econs. & devel. U. Econs., Vienna, 1974—; head faculty econs. U. Econs., 1975-97, vice dean internat. programs, 1997—; cons. World Bank, UNIDO, ICOMP, ICSID; bd. dirs. Austrian Latin Am. Inst., Schumpeter Soc. Vienna, Oeko-Forum Austria, Soc. Rsch. History of Parliamentarism; chmn. Austrian Inst. Small Bus. Rsch., Ges. fuer Ganzheitsforschung, Vienna; vice chmn. Austrian Devel. Found.; pres. Internat. Coun. Small Bus.; mem. adv. bd. Europa Treuhand/Ernst & Young, Vienna, Afro-Asian Inst., Vienna; European Coun. Small Bus. dean (class: social scis., law & econs.) European Acad. Scis. and Arts. Author books, contbr. to profl. publs.; editl. bd. several internat. scientific jours. Decorated Austrian Cross of Honor for Sci. and Arts 1st class; recipient Austrian Chamber of Labor Prize 1960, Card. Innitzer Sci. award, 1966, Univ. Econs. Prize, 1982, L. Kunschak Prize, 1990; Schumpeter fellow Harvard U., 1990. Mem. Am. Econ. Assn., Ges. Wirtschafts-U. Sozialwiss., List Ges., Rencontres de St. Gall, Internat. Coun. Mgmt. Population Programs, Am. Biog. Inst. Roman Catholic. Avocations: philosophy, astronomy, skiing, internat. travel. Office: U Econs, Augasse 2-6, A-1090 Vienna Austria

PICHLER, JOSEPH ANTON, food products executive; b. St. Louis, Oct. 3, 1939; s. Anton Dominick and Anita Marie (Hughes) P.; m. Susan Ellen Eyerly, Dec. 27, 1962; children: Gretchen, Christopher, Rebecca, Josh. BBA, U. Notre Dame, 1961; MBA, U. Chgo., 1963, PhD, 1966. Asst. prof. bus. U. Kans., 1964-68, assoc. prof., 1968-73, prof., 1973-80; dean U. Kans. Sch. Bus., 1974-80; exec. v.p. Dillon Cos. Inc., 1980-82, pres., 1982-86; exec. v.p. Kroger Co., Cin., 1985-86, pres., COO, 1986-90, pres., CEO, 1990, chmn., CEO, 1990—, also bd. dirs.; spl. asst. to asst. sec. for manpower U.S. Dept. Labor, 1968-70; chmn. Kans. Manpower Svcs. Coun., 1974-78; bd. dirs. Cin. Milacron Inc., Federated Dept. Stores, Inc., Catalyst. Author: (with Joseph McGuire) Inequality: The Poor and the Rich in America, 1969; contbg. author: Creativity and Innovation in Manpower Research and Action Programs, 1970, Contemporary Management: Issues and Viewpoints, 1973, Institutional Issues in Public Accounting, 1974, Co-Creation and Capitalism: John Paul II's Laborem Exercens, 1983; co-editor, contbg. author: Ethics, Free Enterprise, and Public Policy, 1978; contbr. articles to profl. jours. Bd. dirs. Cin. Opera, 1987-96, adv. mem., 1996—; nat. bd. dirs. Boys Hope, 1983-96, Tougaloo Coll., 1986—; mem. Nat. Alliance of Bus. Bd., 1988-95, chmn., 1991-93; mem. fellow adv. com. Woodrow Wilson Found., 1990-93: mem. adv. bd. Salvation Army Sch. for Officers Tng., 1994-2000; mem. Cin. Bus. Com., 1991—, chmn., 1997-98. Recipient Disting. Svc. citation U. Kans., 1992, Disting. Svc. award Nat. Conf. Cmty. Justice, 2000; Woodrow Wilson fellow, Ford Found. fellow, Standard Oil Indsl. Rels. fellow, 1966; named Disting. Alumnus U. Chgo., 1994, William Booth award The Salvation Army, 1998, Horatio Alger award, 1999. Mem. Bus. Roundtable, Catalyst Bd., Queen City Club, Comml. Club of Cin. Office: Kroger Co 1014 Vine St Ste 1000 Cincinnati OH 45202-1100

PICHLER, PETER JOHANN, electrical engineer, researcher; b. Wiener Neustadt, Austria, June 20, 1958; came to Germany, 1986; s. Johann and Theresia Rosina (Tremmel) P.; m. Juliana Kordula Seydel, Oct. 18, 1996; children: Carsten, Friederike. Dipl.-ing., Tech. U. Vienna, Austria, 1982, dr. techn., 1985. Rschr. Fraunhofer-Institut für Integrierte, Schaltungen, Erlangen, Germany, 1986-88, group mgr., 1988—. Editor: Simulation of Semiconductor Devices and Processes, Vol. 6, 1995; author,programmer: (software) PROMIS, ICECREM; contbr. articles to conf. procs., periodicals. Mem. IEEE, The Böhmische Phys. Soc., Materials Rsch. Soc. Avocations: opera, reading, programming. Office: Fraunhofer-Institut für Integrierte Schaltungen, Schottkystrasse 10, 91058 Erlangen Germany

PICHUGIN, YURY A., geophysicist; b. St. Petersburg, Russia, Aug. 13, 1955; s. Alexander and Valentina (Kiselev) P.; m. Irina Dolotov, Jan. 28, 1983; 1 child, Nika. Degree in math., St. Petersburg State U., 1981; PhD, Voeikov Ctrl. Geophysics Obs., 1993. Engr., programmer A.I. Voeikov Ctr. Geophysics Obs., St. Petersburg, 1982-89, jr. rschr., 1989-93, rschr., 1993-97, sr. rschr., 1997—. Contbr. articles to profl. jours. Sr. lt. Russian Army Res. Mem. N.Y. Acad. Scis. Avocations: literature, Chinese medicine, philosophy. E-mail: pichugin@JP4974.spb.edu. Home: 21-2-166 Komendantsky Ave, 197371 Saint Petersburg Russia Office: Ctrl Geophysics Obs, 7 Karbyshev St, 194021 Saint Petersburg Russia

PICK, EDGAR, immunologist; b. Lugoj, Romania, Feb. 15, 1938; s. Erwin and Barbara (Gal) P.; m. Leora Syrkin, Mar. 21, 1965; children: Anat, Dana. MD, Hebrew U., 1965; PhD, U. London, 1970. Rsch. fellow Scripps Rsch. Found., La Jolla, Calif., 1965-67; rsch. assoc. Inst. Dermatology, London, 1967-70; from sr. lectr. to prof. Tel Aviv U. Med. Sch., 1970—; dir. Miverva-Cohnheim Ctr. Phagocyte Rsch., head Sackler Inst. Molecular Med., 1997-2000; head Kodesz Inst. of Host Def. Against Infectious Diseases, 1999—. Mem. editorial bd. Immunobiology, 1980—, Internat. Jour. of Immunopharmacology, 1985—, J. Leukocyte Biology, 1996—. Fellow Am. Assn. Immunologists, Internat. Soc. Immunopharmacology, Soc. for Leukocyte Biol., Am. Soc. Biochem. and Molecular Biol. Jewish. Avocations: literature, architecture, art history, philosophy, science history. Home: 75 Einstein St, 69102 Tel Aviv Israel Office: Tel Aviv U, 69978 Tel Aviv Israel

PICK, MILOŠ, surveyor, educator; b. Luže, Bohemia, Czech Republic, Sept. 1, 1923; s. Viktor and Marie (Špičková) P.; m. Božena Kasalová, Sept. 18, 1957; children: Luboš, Martin. Degree in engring., Tech. U., Prague, Czech Republic, 1950, PhD, 1959, DSc, 1963. Rsch. worker Geophys. Inst., Prague, 1950-63, chief rsch. worker, 1963-90, cons., 1990—; prof. of the Higher Geodesy, 1994; dir. Geophys. Inst., Praha, 1961-70. Author: (monograph) Theory of the Earth's Gravity Field, 1973, (textbook) Study of the Earth's Gravity Field, 1973, Advanced Physical Geodesy and Gravimetry, 2000; contbr. articles to profl. jours. Maj. Mil. Geographical Inst., 1950-53. Avocations: water sports, tourism, photography. Home: Hrusicka 30, Prague 4 14100, Czech Republic Office: Geophys Inst Czech Acad Sci, Bocni II, Prague 4 14131, Czech Republic

PICK, ROBIN ALEXANDER, accountant; b. Worcester, Eng., Apr. 27, 1944; s. Eric Edward and Josephine Mary (Rosenthal) P.; m. Linda Margaret Cox, Jan. 29, 1972; children: Alexander Charles, Caroline Sarah, James Edward. Chartered acct., cert. acct., Eng.; lic. pvt. pilot. Prospective ptnr. Johnson Ralph & Co., London, 1970-71, Howell Wade & Co., London, 1971-72; propr., founder R.A. Pick & Co., London, 1972—; dir. Warwick Ct. Ltd. Fellow Inst. Chartered Accts. in Eng. and Wales, Chartered Assn. Cert. Accts. Avocations: flying light aircraft, gliding, sailing, classical music. Fax: 020 7831 5398. Office: RA Pick & Co Chartered Acct, Cobham House 9 Warwick Ct, London WC1R 5DJ, England

PICK, ŠTĚPÁN, physicist; b. Prague, Czech Republic, Dec. 26, 1949; s. Bohumil and Ludmila (Zamrazilová) P. Degree, Charles U., Prague, 1973, D Natural Scis., 1976; Candidate Scis., Czechoslovak Acad. Scis., 1981. With J. Heyrovský Inst. Phys. Chemistry Acad. Scis. Czech Republic, Prague, 1974—, sr. rschr., 1986—; vis. prof. U. Nancy I, France, 1992. Contbr. articles to profl. jours. Mem. Union Czech Mathematicians and Physicists, Czech Union Nature Conservation. Office: J Heyrovsky Ins Phys Chemistry, Dolejškova 3, CZ-18223 Prague 8, Czech Republic

PICKENS, WILLIAM STEWART, cardiologist; b. Bentonville, Ark., Dec. 16, 1940; s. William Craig and Mary Elizabeth (McFarland) P.; children from previous marriage: Holly, Heather, Brian; m. Wanda J. Godwin. BS, U. Ark., Fayetteville, 1962; MD, U. Ark., Little Rock, 1966. Diplomate Am. Bd. Internal Medicine (subspecialty cardiovascular diseases); cert. nuc. cardiologist. Rotating intern Tampa (Fla.) Gen. Hosp., 1966-67; resident in radiology U. Fla. Med. Ctr., Gainesville, 1970-72; resident in internal medicine, then fellow in cardiology U. South Fla. Med. Ctr., Tampa, 1972-75; fellow in cardiovascular radiology U. Fla. Med. Ctr., 1974; staff physician VA Hosp., Tampa, 1974-75; practice medicine specializing in cardiology Pensacola, Fla., 1976—; mem. staff Bapt. Hosp., Sacred Heart Hosp.; asst. prof. radiology and internal medicine U. Ark., Little Rock, 1975-76 clin. assoc. prof. medicine Tulane U., 1983—; v.p. ECG Systems Inc.; bd. dirs. Mobil Diagnostics, 1985—; trustee Peer Rev. Orgn. State Fla., 1986-91; bd. trustees Bapt. Healthcare. Benefactor Pickens Found. for Edn., 1990, Pickens Computer Lab., Dept. Edn., U. West Fla. Served as officer M.C., USAF, 1967-72; maj. Res. Rockefeller scholar, 1958-59; U. Ark. Alumni scholar, 1958-60; Edn. Found. scholar, 1958-62; Barton Found. scholar, 1965; C.V. Mosby scholar, 1966. Fellow Am. Coll. Cardiology, Am. Coun. on Clin. Cardiology; mem. Am. Soc. Nuc. Cardiology (founder, cert. coun. nuc. cardiology), Sigma Xi (assoc.), Alpha Omega Alpha, Phi Eta Sigma, Alpha Epsilon Delta. Republican. Episcopalian. Office: 1717 N E St Ste 331 Pensacola FL 32501-6335

PICKERELL, BLAIR CHILTON, investment management executive; b. Oakland, Calif., Dec. 3, 1956; s. Albert George and Betty Jean Pickerell; m. Sandy Lien, July 1984; children: David, Heather. BA, Stanford U., 1979, MA, 1979; MBA, Harvard U., 1984. Gen. mgr. Jardine Fleming Taiwan Ltd., Taipei, 1985-88; pres. Taiwan Internat. Securities Corp., Taipei, 1988-90; dir. devel. Mandarin Oriental Hotel Group, Hong Kong, 1990-92; dir. Jardine Fleming Holdings Ltd., Hong Kong, 1992-93; dir. Jardine Pacific Ltd., Hong Kong, 1994-95, mng. dir., 1995-99; mng. dir. JF Asset Mgmt., Hong Kong, 1999—. Bd. dirs. Cmty. Chest, Hong Kong. Office: JF Asset Mgmt, 47/F 1 Connaught Pl Jard Ho, Hong Kong China

PICKERING, AVAJANE, specialized education facility executive; b. New Castle, Ind., Nov. 5, 1951; d. George Willard and Elsie Jean (Wicker) P. BA, Purdue U., 1974; MS in Spl. Edn., U. Utah, 1983, PhD, 1991. Cert. spl. edn. Co-dir. presch. for gifted students, 1970-74; tchr. Granite Community Edn., Salt Lake City, 1974-79; tchr. coordinator Salt Lake City Schs., 1975-85; adminstrv. dir., owner Specialized Ednl. Programming Svc., Inc., Salt Lake City, 1976—; mem. Utah Profl. Adv. Bd.; adj. instr. U. Utah, Salt Lake City, 1985-97; instr. Brigham Young U., 1993-98. Rep. del. Utah State Conv., also county conv.; vol. tour guide, hostess Temple Square, Ch. Jesus Christ of Latter-Day Saints, 1983-88. Mem. Coun. for Exceptional Children, Coun. for Learning Disabilities, Learning Disability Assn., Ednl. Therapy Assn. Profl., Learning Disabilities Assn. Utah (profl. adv. bd.), Attention Deficit Coalition Utah (treas.), Hadassah, Delta Kappa Gamma, Phi Kappa Phi. Home: 1595 S 2100 E Salt Lake City UT 84108-2750 Office: Specialized Ednl Programming Svcs 1760 S 1100 E Salt Lake City UT 84105-3441

PICKERING, BRIAN THOMAS, university official; b. London, May 24, 1936; s. Thomas and Dorothy May (Rourk) P.; m. Joan Perry, Sept. 4, 1965; children: Francesca, Veronica. BSc, U. Bristol, Eng., 1958, PhD, 1961, DSc, 1974; MD (hon.), U. Medicine and Pharmacy, Bucharest, Romania, 1994. Rsch. biochemist U. Calif., Berkeley, 1961-63; scientist Med. Rsch. Coun., London, 1963-65; lectr. then reader U. Bristol, 1965-78, prof. anatomy, 1978-92, dean medicine, 1985-87, dep. vice-chancellor, 1992—; chmn. animal grants bd. Agr. and Food Rsch. Coun., Eng., 1990-94; non-exec. dir. UBHT Nat. Health Svc. Trust, Bristol, 1990-98; mem. gov. bd. Inst. Animal Health, 1991-98; soc. rev. lectr. Anat. Soc. Gt. Britain, Ireland, 1983. Contbr. articles to profl. jours. Mem. European Soc. Comparative Endocrinology (sec.-treas. 1971-77, pres. 1990-94), Soc. Endocrinology (hon. editor proceedings 1972-77, Soc. Medal 1977), Physiol. Soc., Biochem. Soc. Office: U Bristol, U Bristol, Tyndall Ave, Bristol BS8 1TH, England

PICKERING, KIM LOUISE, materials science, engineering educator; b. Leicester, Eng., June 3, 1966; arrived in New Zealand, 1994; d. Walter Pickering and Beryl (Owen) Peatfield; m. Tim Hunt, Mar. 5, 1994. BSc in Engring. Metallurgy and Materials, U. London, 1987; PhD, Surrey (Eng.) U., 1993. Rsch. scientist Plessey Rsch. Caswell, Northants, U.K., 1987-90; lectr. U. Waikato, Hamilton, New Zealand, 1994—. Patentee in field. Recipient Rsch. award New Zealand Lottery Grants Bd., 1995. Mem. Materials Inst. Avocations: orienteering, tramping, watercolor painting.

PICKERING, PETER EDGAR, psychotherapist; b. Melbourne, Victoria, Australia, Apr. 10, 1944; s. Edgar Lawrence and Phyllis May (Probert) P.; m. Elaine Beryl Churches, Jan. 29, 1966; children: Joel Ben, Eran Ben, Ari Ben, Melita Lainie. B Social Sci., Royal Melbourne Inst. Tech. U., Melbourne, 1974; Assoc. degree, Royal Melbourne Inst. Tech. U., 1977; diploma in ednl. tech., Deakin U., Melbourne, 1980; PhD, Monash U., Melbourne, 1990; diploma in reproductive science, Monash U., 1991; diploma in behavioral medicine, Harvard U., 1992. Lectr. Prahran Coll. Advanced Edn., Melbourne, 1973-75; head dept. libr. studies Swinburne U., Melbourne, 1975-80; cons./rschr. various, Australia, 1980-86; med. counsellor, 1986-93; dir. Australian Coll. of Behavioral Medicine, Melbourne, 1993—; examiner higher degrees RMIT U., 1993—; bd. dirs. Faith Chems. Co., Melbourne, 1980—, Alphega Prodns. Co., Melbourne, 1985—. Fellow Internat. Coll. Psychosomatic Med., mem. APA, Am. Fertility Soc., Internat. Soc. Behavioral Medicine. Christadelphian. Avocations: tennis, golf, boating, video prodns., performing arts. Office: ACBM, PO Box 300, Somerton 3062, Australia

PICKERING, POLLYANNA, artist; b. Leeds, Yorkshire, Eng., July 30, 1942; d. Johnathon and Mabel (Wells) Pollard; m. Kenneth Albert Pickering, Apr. 25, 1963 (dec. 1979); 1 child, Anna-Louise. Nat. diploma in design, Cen. Sch. of Arts, London, 1963. Cert. N.D.D. Head dept. Warwick County High Sch., Warwickshire, Eng., 1963-64; owner Pollyanna Pickering Gallery, Derbyshire, Eng., 1980—; exec. producer Highbank Film Co., Surrey, Eng., 1986—. One-woman shows include Peter Simmonite Gallery, Sheffield, 1981, Pentameters Gallery, Hampstead, London, 1989, Derby Mus. and Art Gallery, 1999; exhibited in group shows including Tryon and Moorland Gallery, London, 1980, Royal Acad., London, 1983, Halcyon Gallery, Birmingham, 1989, Soc. Wildlife Artists, Mall Galleries, London, 1991; illustrator: (book) Giant Pandas and Sleeping Dragons, 1996. Prin. Brookvale Bird Rescue (Conservation), Derbyshire, 1980—; pres. (hon.) Hearing Dogs for Deaf, Derby, 1996—, Royal Soc. for Prevention of Cruelty to Animals, Derby, 1997—; amb. Hosp. Radio Link, 1999-2000; mem. ct. U. Derby; patron Raptor Rescue, 1999—, NatureWatch, 2000—. Recipient Silver Palette award Derby Mus. & Art Gallery, Derbyshire, 1983. Mem. Derbyshire Wildlife Trust (patron 1985—), World Wide Fund for Nature (commd. work 1991, 99), Royal Soc. for the Protection of Birds (commd. work 1983, 84, 98, 99), Zoocheck (exhbn. 1991), Royal Soc. for the Protection of Animals (Hong Kong, commd. work 1991-99). Avocations: conservation, theatre. Home and Office: Brookvale House, Oaker DE4 2JJ, England

PICKERING, THOMAS REEVE, diplomat; b. Orange, N.J., Nov. 5, 1931; s. Hamilton R. and Sarah C. (Chasteney) P.; m. Alice J. Stover, Nov. 24, 1955; children: Timothy R., Margaret S. A.B., Bowdoin Coll., 1953; M.A., Fletcher Sch. Law and Diplomacy, 1954, U. Melbourne, Australia, 1956. Joined U.S. Fgn. Svc., 1959; fgn. affairs officer ACDA, 1961; polit. adviser U.S. del. 18 Nation Disarmament Conf., Geneva, 1962-64; consul Zanzibar, 1965-67; counselor of embassy, dep. chief mission Am. Embassy, Dar es Salaam, Tanzania, 1967-69; dep. dir. Bur. Politico-Mil. Affairs, State Dept., 1969-73; spl. asst. to Sec. of State, 1973-74; exec. sec. Dept. State, 1973-74; U.S. amb. to Jordan, 1974-78; asst. sec. for Bur. Oceans, Internat. Environ. and Sci. Affairs, Washington, 1978-81; U.S. amb. to Nigeria, 1981-83, U.S. amb. to El Salvador, 1983-85, U.S. amb. to Israel, 1985-88, U.S. permanent rep. to UN, 1989-92, U.S. amb. to India, 1992-93, U.S. amb. to Russia, 1993-96; pres. Eurasia Found., 1996-97; undersec. of state for polit. affairs Dept. of State, Washington, 1997—. Served to lt. comdr. USNR, 1956-59. Mem. Council Fgn. Relations, Internat. Inst. Strategic Studies, Phi Beta Kappa. Address: 2318 Kimbro St Alexandria VA 22307-1822 Office: Dept of State 2201 C St NW Washington DC 20520-0001

PICKERING, WILLIAM HAYWARD, physics educator, scientist; b. Wellington, N.Z., Dec. 24, 1910; s. Albert William and Elizabeth (Hayward) P.; m. Muriel Bowler, Dec. 30, 1932 (dec. Mar. 1992); children: William B., Anne E.; m. Inez Chapman, July 28, 1994. BS, Calif. Inst. Tech., 1932, MS, 1933, PhD in Physics, 1936; hon. degrees, Clark U., 1966, Occidental Coll., 1966, U. Bologna, 1974. Mem. Cosmic Ray Expdn. to India, 1939, Mexico, 1941; faculty Calif. Inst. Tech., 1940—, prof. elec. engring., 1946-80, prof. emeritus, 1980—, dir. jet propulsion lab., 1954-76; Mem. sci. adv. bd. USAF, 1945-48; chmn. panel on test range instrumentation (Research and Devel. Bd.), 1948-49; mem. U.S. nat. com. tech. panel Earth Satellite Program, 1955-60; mem. Army Sci. Adv. Panel, 1960-64; dir. rsch. inst. U. Petroleum and Minerals, Dharan, Saudi Arabia, 1977-79; pres. Pickering Rsch. Corp., 1980-91; pres. Lignetics, Inc., 1983-94, chmn., 1994—. Decorated Order of Merit Italy, 1966, knight comdr. Order Brit. Empire, 1975; recipient James Wyld Meml. award Am. Rocket Soc., 1957, Columbus medal Genoa, 1964, Prix Galabert for Astronautics; Goddard trophy Nat. Space Club, 1965, NASA Disting. Svc. medal, 1965, Army Disting. Civilian Svc. award, 1959, Spirit of St. Louis medal, 1965, Crozier medal Am. Ordnance Assn., 1965, Man of Yr. award Indsl. Rsch. Inst., 1968, Interprofl. Coop. award Soc. Mfg. Engrs., 1970, Marconi medal Marconi Found., 1974, Nat. Medal of Sci., 1976, Fahrney medal Franklin Inst., 1976, award of merit Am. Cons. Engrs. Coun., 1976, Francoix-Xavier Bagnoud Internat. award, 1993, Japan prize Sci. and Tech. Found. of Japan, 1994. Fellow AIAA (pres. 1963, Louis W. Hill Transp. award 1968, Aerospace Pioneer award 1986), AAAS, NAE, IEEE (Edison medal 1972); mem. NAS, Am. Geophys. Union, Internat. Astronautical Fedn. (pres. 1965-66). Home: 294 Saint Katherine Dr Flintridge CA 91011-4109

PICKETT, GEORGE BIBB, JR., retired military officer; b. Montgomery, Ala., Mar. 20, 1918; s. George B. and Marie (Dow) P.; BS, U.S. Mil. Acad., 1941; student Nat. War Coll., 1959-60; m. Beryl Arlene Robinson, Dec. 27, 1941; children: Barbara Pickett Harrell, James, Kathleen, Thomas; m. Rachel Copeland Peeples, July 1981. Commd. 2d lt. U.S. Army, 1941, advanced through grades to maj. gen., 1966; instr. Inf. Sch., Fort Benning, Ga., 1947-50, instr. Armed Forces Staff Coll., Norfolk, Va., 1956-59; comdg. officer 2d Armored Cav. Regt., 1961-63; chief of staff Combat Devel. Command, 1963-66; comdg. gen. 2d inf. divsn., Korea, 1966-67; ret., 1973; field rep. Nat. Rifle Assn., 1973-85. Decorated Purple Heart with oak leaf cluster, D.S.M. with two oak leaf clusters, Bronze Star with two oak leaf clusters and V device, Silver Star, Legion of Merit with two oak leaf clusters, Commendation medal with two oak leaf clusters. Mem. SAR (pres. Ala. Soc. 1984), Old South Hist. Assn. Episcopalian. Club: Kiwanis. Author: (with others) Joint and Combined Staff Officers Manual, 1959; contbr. articles on mil. affairs to profl. jours. Home: 3525 Flowers Dr Montgomery AL 36109-4719 Office: PO Box 4 Montgomery AL 36101-0004

PICKETT, HARRY ELDON, mathematician; b. Kansas City, Mo., Nov. 14, 1930; s. Orvil Samual and Jennie May (Linendoll) P.; m. Rosyln Nannette Hirsch, Oct. 5, 1952 (div. Feb. 1962); children: Leonard Brandon, Bradley Lawrence; m. Mary Louise Whalen, Aug. 25, 1963; children: Jonathan Edward, Karen. BS, Ariz. State U., 1952; MS, N.Mex. State U., 1954; PhD, U. Calif., Berkeley, 1964. Mathematician GS-7 White Sands Missile Range, Las Cruces, N.Mex., 1952-54; rsch. mathematician Chevron Rsch. Co., Richmond, Calif., 1960-68; sr. math engr. Aerospace Corp., El Segundo, Calif., 1968-70; sr. mathematical cons. Computer Aided Design and Mfg. Cons. Svc. Inc., Irvine, Calif., 1970-74; sr. rsch. cons. Pattern Analysis Recognition, N.Y.C., 1976-78; sole proprietor Pickett Enterprises, Irvine, Calif., 1974—. Contbr. articles to profl. pubs. With U.S. Army Signal Corp, Md., 1954-56. Mem. Pasteur Soc., Tempe, Ariz. Avocation: mathematics. Home: 2760 Kelvin Ave Apt 3118 Irvine CA 92614-5880

PICKETT, JOHN ANTHONY, research chemist, biological and ecological chemistry educator; b. Leicester, Eng., Apr. 21, 1945; s. Samuel Victor and Lilian Frances (Hoar) P.; m. Ulla Birgitta Skålén, July 11, 1970; children: Hilda, Erik. BSc in Chemistry with honors, U. Surrey, U.K., 1967, PhD in Organic Chemistry, 1971; DSc, U. Nottingham, U.K., 1993. Chartered chemist. Postdoctoral fellow U. Manchester (Eng.) Inst. Sci. and Tech., 1970-72; sr. scientist Brewing Rsch. Found., Redhill, Surrey, 1972-76; prin. sci. officer Rothamsted Experimental Sta., Harpenden, Herts, Eng., 1976-83, head dept., 1984—; spl. prof. U. Nottingham, 1991—; chmn. adv. com. Sch. Applied Chemistry, U. North London, 1993-95; external examiner MSc course in pest mgmt. Imperial Coll., Silwood Park, U.K., 1992-95, Environ. Sci. U. Sussex, 1997-2000; hon. mem. acad.staff U. Reading, 1995—. Mem. editl. bd. Jour. Chem. Ecology, 1991—. Recipient Disting. Lecture in Life Scis. award Boyce Thompson Inst. for Plant Rsch., Cornell U., 1991, Alfred M. Boyce Lectr. award U. Calif., Riverside, 1993, Rank Prize for Nutrition and Crop Husbandry, 1995. Fellow Royal Soc. Chemistry U.K., Royal Entomol. Soc.; mem. Internat. Soc. Chem. Ecology (pres. 1995), Soc. Chem. Industry, Am. Chem. Soc., Royal Inst., Royal Soc. Working Group on Sites of Special Scientific Interest (chmn. 2000). Avocation: jazz trumpet playing. E-mail: john.pickett@bbsrc.ac.uk. Home: 53 Parkfield Cres, Kimpton Near Hitchin SG4 8EQ, England Office: IACR, Rothamsted, Harpenden AL5 2JQ, England

PICKETT, STEPHEN WESLEY, university official, lecturer and consultant; b. Billings, Mont., May 27, 1956; s. Wesley William and Carol Ann (Bollum) P. BA, Houston Bapt. U., 1980; MS, U. North Tex., 1988. Cert. elem. tchr., rehab. counselor, Tex. Hosp. tchr. Houston Ind. Sch. Dist., 1981-85; asst. to assoc. dean of students U. North Tex., Denton, 1988-90, asst. coord. disabled student svcs., Office Student Devel., 1990-91, dir. Office Disability Accommodation, 1991—, univ. mentor/advisor, 1992—. Coauthor: curriculum guide The Newspaper as a Student Communicator, 1982 (winner Exxon Found.'s Impact Two award for creative teaching). Chair Mayor's Com. on Employment of Persons with Disabilities, Denton, 1990; mem. coun.-at-large Sam Houston Area Coun. Boy Scouts Am., Houston, 1975—; grad. Denton C. of C. Leadership Program, 1992; pub. rels. chair leadership Denton Steering Com., 1993-94; mem. ad. bd. city of Denton Transit, 1990—; exec. bd. Svc. provision for Aging Needs, a United Way Agy., 1997—; mem. U. of North Tex. Adv. Bd. for ADA Access, 1992—, co-chair UNT ADA adv. com., 2000—; mem. budget com. Denton County United Way, 1998—. Recipient Cmty. Svc. award U. North Tex., 1992, award for svcs. to persons with disabilities North Tex. Rehab. Assn., 1993, Disting. Alumnus award Houston Bapt. U., 1994, Outstanding Alumnus award Ctr. for Rehab. Studies, U. North Tex., 1995. Mem. Assn. Higher Edn. and Disability, Nat. Assn. Student Pers. Adminstrs., Tex. Assn. Coll. and Univ. Student Pers. Adminstrs. (chair multicultural com. 1994-95, v.p. 1995-96, co-chair endowment found. com. 1996-97), Tex. Assn. Higher Edn. and Disabilities (sec. 1998-99, conf. co-chair 1999). Presbyterian. Avocations: reading, travel, stamp collecting. Fax: 940-369-7969. E-mail: stevewp@worldnet.att.net. Office: U North Tex Office Disabili Ste 324 PO Box 305358 Denton TX 76203-5358

PICKFORD, DAVID MICHAEL, surveyor, business executive; b. London, Aug. 25, 1926; s. Charles Aston and Gladys Ethel (May) P.; m. Elizabeth Gwendoline Hooson, July 21, 1956; children: Penelope Anne, Elizabeth Jane, Charles John Norcliffe. Student, Coll. of Estate Mgmt., London, 1943-48. Chartered surveyor. Trainee surveyor Hillier Parker May & Rowden, London, 1943-46; acquisition surveyor London County Coun., 1946-48; dir. London Investment and Mortgage Co., 1948-58; mng. dir., chmn. Haslemere Estates Plc, London, 1958-86; chmn. Compco Holdings Plc, London, 1986—; chmn. Lilliput Property Unit Trust, 1983—; chmn. Gulliver Devels. Property Unit Trust, 1989—. Chmn. London City YMCA 150th Anniversary Appeal, Swift Balanced Property Unit Trust, Wigmore Property Investment Trust Plc, Drug and Alcohol Found., 1985-90; trustee, bd. dirs. CARE, Youth with a Mission; trustee Prison Fellowship Eng. and Wales, chmn., 1989-93; hon. life pres. The Boys' Brigade London Dist.; pres. Christians in Property. Fellow Royal Instn. of Chartered Surveyors, Inst. of Dirs. Avocations: farming, gardening, youth work. Home: Elm Tree Farm, Mersham, Ashford Kent TN25 7HS, England Office: 33 Grosvenor Sq, London W1X 9LL, England

PICKL, OTHMAR, economist, educator; b. Baden, Austria, Sept. 11, 1927; s. Friedrich and Elisabeth (Schwindhackl) P.; m. Gertrude Feidl; children: Wernhard, Astrid. PhD, U. Graz, Austria, 1950, Habilitation, 1966. Tchr. in German and History Graz (Austria) H.S., 1952-69; prof. U. Graz, 1969-95. Author: Geschichte d.Papierzeug i.d. Stmk., 1963, Das älteste Geschäftsbuch Österr., 1966, 800 Years Styria and Austria, 1192-1992, 1992, 100 Years Historical Province Commission for Styria 1892-1992, 1992; editor serials Osterr. Stadtebuch, 1983—, Berichte der Histor, Landeskom., 1957—. Gen. Sec. Hist. Province Commn. for Styria, Graz, 1957—; socio straniero Deputatione di Storia Patria per la Venezia Guilia, Trieste, Italy, 1978—. Served German Army, 1943-45. Decorated Grosses Goldenes Ehrenzeichen d. Landes Steiermark, 1st class Ehrenkreuzwissenschaft und Kunst, Grosses Silbernes Ehrenzeichen Austria (Austria); knight of Holy Grave Jerusalem; recipient history prize Province of Stiria, 1965, Cardinal Innitzer prize, 1966. Mem. Austrian Acad. Sci. Home: Steyrergasse 34/10, 8010 Graz Austria

PICKLE, ROBERT DOUGLAS, lawyer, footwear industry executive; b. Knoxville, Tenn., May 22, 1937; s. Robert Lee and Beatrice Jewel (Douglas) P.; m. Rosemary Elaine Noser, May 9, 1964. AA summa cum laude, Schreiner Mil. Coll., Kerrville, Tex., 1957; BSBA magna cum laude, U. Tenn., 1959, JD, 1961; honor grad. seminar, Nat. Def. U., 1979; hon. grad., U.S. Army JAG Sch., U.S. Army Logistics Mgmt. Sch.; grad., U.S. Army Inf. Sch., Army Command-Gen. Staff Coll. Bar: Tenn. 1961, Mo. 1964, U.S. Ct. Mil. Appeals 1962, U.S. Supreme Ct. 1970. Atty. Brown Shoe Co., Inc., St. Louis, 1963-69, asst. sec., atty., 1969-74, sec., gen. counsel, 1974-85; v.p., gen. counsel, corp. sec. Brown Shoe Co., Inc. (formerly Brown Group, Inc.), St. Louis, 1985—; indiv. mobilization augmentee, asst. army judge adv. gen. civil law The Pentagon, Washington, 1984-89. Provisional judge Municipal Ct., Clayton, Mo., summer 1972; chmn. Clayton Region attys. sect., profl. div. United Fund Greater St. Louis Campaign, 1972-73, team capt., 1974-78; chmn. City of Clayton Parks and Recreation Commn., 1985-87; liaison admissions officer, regional and state coordinator U.S. Mil. Acad., 1980—. Col. JAGC, U.S. Army, 1961-63. Decorated Meritorious Svc. medal; 1st U. Tenn. Law Coll. John W Green law scholar; recipient Cold War Recognition cert. Sec. Def. Fellow Harry S. Truman Meml. Library; mem. ABA, Tenn. Bar Assn., Mo. Bar Assn., St. Louis County Bar Assn., Bar Assn. Met. St. Louis, St. Louis Bar Found. (bd. dirs. 1979-81), Am. Corp. Counsel Assn., Am. Soc. Corp. Secs. (treas. St. Louis regional group 1976-77, sec. 1977-78, v.p. 1978-79, pres., mem. Quarter-Century Club 1979-80), U. Tenn. Gen. Alumni Assn. (pres., bd. dirs. St. Louis chpt. 1974-76, 80-84, bd. govs. 1982-89), U.S. Trademark Assn. (bd. dirs. 1978-82), Tenn. Soc. St. Louis (bd. dirs. 1980-88, treas., sec., v.p. 1984-87, pres. 1987-88), Smithsonian Nat. Assocs., World Affairs Coun. St. Louis, Inc., Am. Legion, University Club (v.p., sec. St. Louis chpt. 1976-81, bd. dirs. 1976-81), Stadium Club, West Point Soc. St. Louis (hon. mem., bd. dirs. 1992—), Conf. Bd. (coun. chief legal officers), Fontbonne Coll. Pres.'s Assocs. (O'Hara and Tower Socs), St. Louis U. Billiken Club, St. Louis U. DuBourg Soc. (hon. v.p.). Republican. Presbyterian. Avocations: reading, spectator sports. Home: 214 Topton Way Saint Louis MO 63105-3638 Office: Brown Shoe Co Inc 8300 Maryland Ave Saint Louis MO 63105-3693

PICÓ-ARACIL, FRANCISCO, cardiologist; b. Alicante, Spain, Apr. 5, 1947; s. Jose Picó-Barberá and Consuelo Aracil-Picó. MD, U. Valencia, Spain, 1971; PhD, U. Murcia, Spain, 1989. Pre-registration house officer Cardiovasc. Hosp., Alicante, 1971; house officer, sr. house officer Cardiology, Arrixaca-Murcia, 1972-75; asst. med. dr. congenital cardiopathies U. Paris, 1975; asst. med. dr. Arrixaca Hosp., Murcia, 1975-76, U. Lausanne, Switzerland, 1977; head hemodynamics unit Arrixaca, Murcia, 1977—; assoc. prof. U. Murcia, 1986—. Author: Introduccion Al Estudio Hemodinamico de las Cardiopatias Adquiridas, 1977, also 9 book chpts.; contbr. papers and articles to profl. jours.; mem. editl. com. Cardiovasc. Intervention, 1997, Cardiovasc. Investigation, 1978. Mem. ethical com. Univ. Hosp., Arrixaca, 1996—; mem. health com. Health Dept., Murcia, 1998. Mem. Cardiology Soc. (pres. 1996-97). Avocations: classical music, guitar, mountain walking. Office: Hosp Virgen Arrixaca, Unidad de Hemodinamica, 30120 El Palmar Murcia, Spain

PIDD, MICHAEL, management science educator, consultant; b. Sheffield, Yorkshire, Eng., Aug. 3, 1948; s. Ernest and Marion (Clark) P.; m. Sally Anne Nutt, Feb. 1, 1971; children: Karen Elizabeth, Helen Louise. B.Tech., Brunel U., London, 1970; M.Sc., Birmingham U., 1971. Team leader in operational research Cadbury Schweppes Ltd., Birmingham, 1971-74; lectr. operational research Aston U., Birmingham, 1974-79; lectr. operational research Lancaster U., Eng., 1979—, head dept. mgmt., 1997—; cons. mgmt. scis. Lancaster, 1979—. Author: Computer Simulation in Management Science, 1984, 4th edit., 1989, Tools for Thinking, 1996; contbr. articles on operational research and mgmt. sci. to profl. jours. Econ. and Social Research Council and teaching company scholar grantee, Birmingham, Lancaster, 1978, 83. Mem. Operational Research Soc., Inst. Mgmt. Sci., Operational Research Soc. (pres. 2000—). Mem. Ch. of Eng. Avocations: Christian work; family life. Office: U Lancaster, Dept Mgmt Sci, Lancaster Bailrigg LA1 4YX, England

PIDGEON, JOHN ANDERSON, headmaster; b. Lawrence, Mass., Dec. 20, 1924; s. Alfred H. and Nora (Regan) P.; children: John Anderson, Regan S., Kelly; m. Barbara Hafer, May 1986. Grad., Phillips Acad., 1943; B.A., Bowdoin Coll., 1949; Ed.D., Bethany Coll., 1973; D.Litt., Washington and Jefferson Coll., 1979. Instr. Latin, adminstrv. asst. to headmaster Deerfield Acad., 1949-57; headmaster Kiskiminetas Springs Sch., Saltsburg, Pa., 1957—; dir. Saltsburg Savs. & Trust. Trustee Winchester-Thurston Sch. Served as ensign USNR, 1943-46. Mem. New Eng. Swimming Coaches Assn. (pres. 1956-57), Cum Laude Soc., Delta Upsilon. Home and Office: Kiski Sch 1888 Brett Ln Saltsburg PA 15681-8951

PIËCH, FERDINAND, automotive executive; b. Vienna, Austria, Apr. 17, 1937; s. Anton P. and Louise (Porsche) P. Degree in engring., Swiss Tech. U., Zurich, 1962; D (hon.), Tech. U., Vienna, 1984, Ben Gurion U., Beer-Sheva, Israel, 1997. Clk. engine testing dept. Porsche KG, 1963-66, mgr. testing ops., 1966-68, mgmt. Porsche devel., 1968-71, tech. mgr., 1971-72; sr. dept. mgr. for spl. duties divsn. tech. devel. Audi Nsu Auto Union AG divsn., 1972-73, mgr. divsn. gen. testing, 1973; tech. devel. mgr. Audi Nsu Auto Union AG divsn., Ingolstadt, 1974; mem. bd. mgmt. Audi Nsu Auto Union AG divsn., 1975-83, vice chmn. bd. mgmt., 1983; chmn. bd. mgmt. Audi AG divsn., 1988-92; chmn. bd. mgmt. Volkswagen AG, 1993—, with dept. R&D, 1995—, with dept. prodn. optimization and purchasing, 1991—, Now CEO. Recipient Austrian Dist. Svc. class I medal for contributions in the fields of sci. and art, 1984. Office: Volkswagen AG, Brieffach 1848-2, 38436 Wolfsburg Germany*

PIEKARSKI, HENRYK CZESŁAW, chemistry educator; b. Konstantynów, Poland, June 26, 1945; s. Józef and Czesława (Skibińska) P.; m. Alina Krystyna Kołodziejska, Dec. 17, 1966; 1 child, Janusz. M of Chem. Sci., U. Lodz, 1967, D of Chem. Sci., 1975. Asst. U. Lodz, Poland, 1967-75, adj., 1975-88, from asst. prof. to assoc. prof., 1988-97, prof., 1997—, head of dept. of phys. chemistry, 1993—, vice dean of the faculty of physics and chemistry, 1996-99, dean faculty physics and chemistry, 1999—. Sci. adv. bd. Jour. of Thermal Analysis, 1996-2000; editor calorimetry Jour. Thermal Analysis and Calorimetry, 2000—; contbr. articles to profl. jours. Recipient Award of Ministry of Sci. and Higher Edn., 1975, Bene Merenti medal U. Regensburg, 2000; grantee Free U. of Amsterdam, 1979, 86, 90, Tempus, Pavia, Turin, Italy, 1993; rsch. grant Nat. Swiss Scientific Found., U. Fribourg, Switzerland, 1995, DAAD, U. Regensburg, 1995. Mem. Polish Soc. of Calorimetry and Thermal Analysis (pres. 1994-2000, v.p. 1991-94). Roman Catholic. Office: U of Lodz Dept Phys Chem, 165 Pomorska, 90-236 Lodz Poland

PIELA, LUCJAN, chemist, researcher; b. Sokolow, Poland, Jan. 2, 1943; s. Stanislaw and Zofia (Czosnek) P.; m. Barbara Konik, July 5, 1975; children: Piotr, Marcin. M in Chemistry, U. Warsaw, Poland, 1965, PhD in Chemistry, 1970. Asst. U. Warsaw, 1966-70, habilitation, 1976, prof., 1977; dep. dir. Inst. Basic Problems of Chemistry U. Warsaw, 1976-78, dean dept. chemistry, 1993-96. Served with Polish Army. Recipient award Polish Acad. Scis., 1979. Fellow Polish Chem. Soc.; mem. Acad. Royale des Scis., des Lettres et des Beaux-Arts de Belgique. Roman Catholic. Avocation: painting. Office: U Warsaw, Pasteura 1, 02 093 Warsaw Poland

PIELAK, GRZEGORZ FRANCISZEK, national investment fund executive; b. Olsztyn, Poland, Dec. 4, 1949; s. Stanislaw and Apolonia (Dobraszkiewicz) P.; m. Elzbieta Henryka Kiela, Aug. 12, 1974; children: Tomasz, Marek. MsC, Mil. Acad. Tech., Warsaw, Poland, 1976; PhD, Inst. Tech. Physics, Warsaw, 1986; MBA, European Cmty. PHARE Program, 1995. Lab. mgr. Mil. Acad., Warsaw, 1976-79; chief of staff UNEF, Suez, Egypt, 1979; OPS officer UNDOF, Damascus, Syria, 1984; lab. mgr. Inst. Tech. Physics, Warsaw, 1980-84, 1985-87; dept. mgr. Inst. Plasma Physics and Laser Microfusion, Warsaw, 1987-92; strategic planning dept. mgr. FSO-Motor Co., Warsaw, 1992-94; logistics coord. GM-Poland, Warsaw, 1994-95; sr. mgr. Raiffeisen Atkins Fund Mgmt., Warsaw, 1996-98; pres. mgmt. bd. NFI "Progress" S.A., Warsaw, 1998-2000; v.p. mgmt. bd. PZU NFI Mgmt., Warsaw, 1999-2000; pres. mgmt. bd. KFA Armatura S.A., Krakow, 2000—; mgr. optical fibres dept. Mil. Acad. Tech., Warsaw, 1976-84; mgr. selfoc lenses dept. Inst. Tech. Physics, 1984-87; mgr. optoelectric dept. Inst. Plasma Physics, 1987-92; chmn. bd. dirs. Zelmot S.A., Warsaw, Transbud S.A., Krakow, PZZ S.A., Krakow, PKRE S.A., Warsaw, FAMEG S.A., Radomsko; vice chmn. bd. dirs. Biaform S.A., Bialystok, Fenes S.A., Siedlce, GPD S.A., Gdánsk, Huta Buczek S.A., Sosnowiec, PPS Tymbark S.A., PFM S.A., Pietrkow. Contbr. some 30 articles to sci. jurs.; holder 5 patents. Mem. SPIE, Optical Soc. Am. Avocations: sports, collecting stamps and coins. Home: Kreta 3/16, 00-759 Warsaw Poland Office: KFA Armatura SA, Zakopianska 72, 30-418 Krakow Poland

PIELE, PHILIP KERN, education infosystems educator; b. Portland, Oreg., May 14, 1935; s. Theodore R. (dec.) and Helen D. (Hanson) P.; m. Sandra Jean Wright, Aug. 10, 1963; children: Melissa, Kathryn. BA, Wash. State U., 1957; student, U. Wash., 1960, San Jose State U., 1964; MS, U. Oreg., 1963, PhD, 1968. From asst. prof. to prof. ednl. policy and mgmt. U. Oreg., Eugene, 1968—, mem. faculty applied info. mgmt. program, 1989-99, dir. numerous ednl. orgns. and coms. Coll. Edn., 1968—, dir. Edn. Resources Info. Ctr. (ERIC) clearinghouse on ednl. mgmt., 1969—, assoc. dir. Ctr. for Ednl. Policy and Mgmt., 1973-76, head dept. ednl. leadership, tech. and adminstrn., 1997-99; vis. lectr. U. Western Australia, Monashe U., U. New S. Wales, and several other Australian Univs., 1973; vis. prof. Ontario Inst. for Studies in Edn., U. Toronto, 1974; vis. scholar Stanford U., 1984; exec. sec. Oreg. Sch. Study Coun., 1980-97; dir. Networks and Comms. Ctr. for Advanced Tech. in Edn., 1984-92. Author numerous books, chpts., monographs; editor numerous books; contbr. articles to profl. jours. Bd. dirs. Oreg. Bach Festival, Eugene, 1980-83, Oreg. Mozart Players, Eugene, 1995-97. Mem. Nat. Orgn. in Legal Problems in Edn. (pres. 1977-78), Nat. Sch. Devel. Coun. (pres. 1985-86), Am. Ednl. Rsch. Assn. (sec. adminstrn. divsn. 1991-93). Home: 2026 Morning View Dr Eugene OR 97405-1632 Office: U Oreg ERIC Clearinghouse on Ednl Mgmt 1787 Agate St Eugene OR 97403-1923

PIEMONTESE, DAVID STEFANO, pharmaceutical scientist; b. Paterson, N.J., July 9, 1965; s. Gennarino and Alba (Reis) P. BS in Biology, William Paterson Coll., 1988; MS in Pharm. Sci., St. John's U., Jamaica, N.Y., 1997. Asst. scientist Hoffmann-LaRoche, Inc., Nutley, N.J., 1988-95; analytical chemist Estee Lauder, Inc., Melville, N.Y., 1995-97, Sciarra Labs. Inc., Hicksville, N.Y., 1996-97; rsch. scientist, stability coord., bioanalytics coord. Nastech Pharm. Co., Inc., Hauppauge, N.Y., 1997-99; pres. Jerry & Son S.R.L., 1999—; presenter in field. Contbr. chpts. to books and articles to profl. jours. Mem. Am. Assn. Pharm. Scientists (nasal drug delivery group), Am. Chem. Soc. (analytical chemistry divsn.). Avocations: travel, bicycling, music, reading. Home: Via Lorenzo Panciatichi No 27, Rome 00135, Italy

PIENINKEROINEN, ILKKA, neurologist, researcher; b. Valkeala, Finland, Oct. 12, 1957; s. Valtter and Elli (Nakko) P.; m. Ritva Savolainen, July 4, 1987; children: Kaarle, Rebecca. MD, Helsinki (Finland) U., 1982, postgrad., 1991. Gen. practice medicine Kouvola, Finland, 1984-85; intern in medicine Helsinki City Hosp., 1985-87; intern in neurology Helsinki U. Med. Sch., 1987-91, cons. neurologist, 1991-92; intern detoxification unit Magnus Huss Clinic Karolinska Hosp., Stockholm, 1992-93, cons. neurologist detoxification unit, 1993-94; cons. neurologist Kymenlaakso Ctrl. Hosp., Kotka, Finland, 1994-99; chief neurologist Porvoo (Finland) Hosp., 1999—. Contbr. articles to med. jours. Mem. Finnish Med. Assn., Finnish Neurol. Soc. Office: Porvoo Hosp, Sairaalantie 1, FIN06200 Porvoo Finland

PIENOVI, ALBERTO DANIEL, sports medicine physician, educator; b. Buenos Aires, Oct. 6, 1950; s. Aroldo Pienovi and Maria Cambiaso; m. Cecilia Davel, Apr. 22, 1986. Bachelor Degree, Escuela Argentina Modelo, Buenos Aires, 1968. Orthopaedic specialist, 1979—, arthroscopy specialist, 1982—, sports medicine specialist, 1983—, orthopaedic prof., 1985—, all Argentina. Staff surgeon Hosp. Italiano, Buenos Aires, 1976-85, Instituto Rehab., Buenos Aires, 1985-92; dir. Sports Medicine Ctr., San Isidro, Argentina, 1985—, Centro de Trauma Tologia San Isidro, Argentina, 1980—. Dir., editor Jour. of Orthopaedic San Isidro, 1985—; editor Arthroscopy Jour., 1994; author some 176 sci. publs., contbr. 138 conf. procs. Mem. Argentine Arthroscopy Assn. (bd. dirs. 1986—, pres. 2000—), Argentine Medicine Assn., Argentina Assn. Sports Medicine (bd. dirs. 1990—), Argentine Orthopaedic Assn. (bd. dirs. 1986-88), Internat. Soc. Arthroscopy, Knee Surgery and Orthopedic Sports Medicine (bd. dirs. 1996-98, 99—). Roman Catholic. Avocations: farming, sailing, golfing, skiing, swimming. Office: Centro de Traumatologia, Ar Libertador 16 664, 1642 San Isidro Argentina

PIEPENBRING, MEIKE, botanist, mycologist; b. Wuppertal, Germany, Dec. 26, 1967; d. Eberhard and Inge (Krull) P. Lic. des scis. naturelles, U. Blaise Pascal, Clermont-Ferrand, France, 1990; Master's, U. Cologne, Germany, 1991; PhD, U. Tübingen, Germany, 1994, habilitation, 1999. Sci. asst. U. Tübingen, 1996—; guest tchr., Tegucigalpa, Honduras, 1997, David, Panama, 2000. Contbr. articles to profl. jours. Mem. Soc. for Threatened People, Germany. German Acad. Rsch. postdoctoral grantee, Ctrl. Am., 1993, 95. Mem. Latin Am. Assn. Mycology, German Bot. Soc., Soc. Biol. Systematics. Avocations: playing music, sports, archeology, ethnobotany, karate. Home: Philosophenweg 79/205, 72076 Tübingen Germany Office:

Spezielle Botanik Mykologie Bot Inst, Auf der Morgenstelle 1, 72076 Tübingen Germany

PIEPER, DAROLD D., lawyer; b. Vallejo, Calif., Dec. 30, 1944; s. Walter A. H. and Vera Mae (Ellis) P.; m. Barbara Gillis, Dec. 20, 1969; 1 child, Christopher Radcliffe. AB, UCLA, 1967; JD, USC, 1970. Bar: Calif. 1971. Ops. rsch. analyst Naval Weapons Ctr., China Lake, Calif., 1966-69; assoc. Richards, Watson & Gershon, L.A., 1970-76, ptnr., 1976—; spl. counsel L.A. County Transp. Commn., 1984-93, L.A. County Met. Transp. Authority, 1993-94; commr. L.A. County Delinquency and Crime Commn., 1983-94, pres., 1987-94; chmn. L.A. County Delinquency Prevention Planning Coun., 1987-90. Contbr. articles to profl. jours. Peace officer Pasadena (Calif.) Police Res. Unit, 1972-87, dep. comdr., 1979-81, comdr., 1982-84; chmn. pub. safety commn. City of La Canada Flintridge, Calif., 1977-82, commr. 1977-88; bd. dirs. La Canada Flintridge Coordinating Council, 1975-82, pres. 1977-78; exec. dir. Cityhood Action Com., 1975-76; active Calif. Rep. Party, Appellate Circle of Legion Lex U. So. Calif.; chmn. Youth Opportunities United, Inc., 1990-96, vice-chmn. 1988-89, bd. dirs. 1988-96; mem. L.A. County Justice Systems Adv. Group, 1987-92; trustee Lanterman Hist. Mus. Found., 1989-94, Calif. City Mgmt. Found., 1992—. Recipient commendation for Community Service, L.A. County Bd. Suprs., 1978, Commendation for Svc. to Youth, 1996. Mem. La Canada Flintridge C. of C. and Cmty. Assn. (pres. 1981, bd. dirs. 1976-83), Navy League U.S., Pacific Legal Found., Peace Officers Assn., L.A. County, UCLA Alumni Assn. (life), U. So. Calif. Alumni Assn. (life), L.A. County Bar Assn., Calif. Bar Assn., ABA, U. So. Calif. Law Alumni Assn. Office: Richards Watson & Gershon 333 S Hope St Fl 38 Los Angeles CA 90071-1406

PIEPER, PATRICIA RITA, artist, photographer; b. Paterson, N.J., Jan. 28, 1923; d. Francis William and Barbara Margareth (Ludwig) Farabaugh. Student, Baron von Palm, 1937-39, Deal (N.J.) Conservatory, 1939, 40, Utah State U., 1950-52; m. George F. Pieper, July 1, 1941 (dec. May 3, 1981); 1 child, Patricia Lynn; m. Russell W. Watson, Dec., 9, 1989. One-woman shows include Charles Russell Mus., Great Falls, Mont., 1955, Fisher Gallery, Washington, 1966, Tampa City Libr., 1977-81, 83, 84, Ctr. Pl. Art Ctr., Brandon, Fla., 1985; exhibited in group shows Davidson Art Gallery, Middletown, Conn., 1968, Helena (Mont.) Hist. Mus., 1955, Dept. Commerce Alaska Statehood Show, 1959, Joslyn Mus., Omaha, 1961, Denver Mus. Natural History, 1955, St. Joseph's Hosp. Gallery, 1980, 82, 84-86; represented in pvt. collections. Pres. Bell Lake Assn., 1976-78, 79. Winner photog. competition Gen. Tel. Co. of Fla., 1979; recipient Outstanding Svc. award Bell Lake Assn., 1987, Meml. award Land O' Lake Bd. of Realtors, 1989, Appreciation award Southwest Fla. Water Mgmt. Dist., 1993, finalist, Awds. of Excellence, Photographers Forum Mag., 1996, 97, 98; photography winner in top 100 out of 8,000 Nat. Wildlife Fedn. competition, 1986; 1st place photography MacDill AFB, 1991. Mem. Pasco County (Fla.) Water Adv. Coun., 1978—, chmn., 1979-82, 83-84, 86-88, 92—; gov.'s appointee to S.W. Fla. Water Mgmt. Dist., Hillsborough River Basin Bd., 1981-82, 84-87, sec., 1988-91, vice chmn. 1992; active Save Our Rivers program, 1982-84, 85-86, 92—; ad hoc chmn., 1991-92; mem. adv. bd. Fla. Suncoast Expwy., 1988-90; pres. Bell Lake Assn., 1986, 87; mem. adv. bd. Tampa YMCA, 1979-80. Mem. VFW (life), Nat. League Am. Pen Women (v.p. Tampa 1976-78, Woman of Yr. award 1977-78), Tampa Art Mus., Ret. Officer's Wives Assn., Land O' Lakes C. of C. (bd. dir. 1981-82, Outstanding Svc. award 1980), Fla. Geneal. Soc., West State Archaeol. Soc. (distaff mem.), Ret. Officer's Assn., MacDill AFB, 1982—, Lutz Club, Land O' Lakes Women's Club, Moose. Home and Studio: 3304 E Derry Dr Sebastian FL 32958-8577

PIEPER, PETER (ERWIN-HANS), archaeologist, fencing master; b. Bochum, Germany, Apr. 16, 1953; s. Erwin and Irene (Sylka) P.; m. Petra Meier, Dec. 14, 1979 (div. June 1991); children: Rebecca Catharina Pelagia, Katharina Wolff. PhD, U. Göttingen, Germany, 1989. Cert. fencing tchr., fencing master. Sci. assoc. in archaeology U. Göttingen, 1978-79; sci. rschr. forensic medicine U. Düsseldorf, 1990—, head dept. archaeology, anthropology and criminology; cons. U.S. Army Meml. Affairs Activity, Europe, 1998—, Acad. of the Art of Fencing in Germany, 1989—, League of Fencing Masters, Germany, 1989—. Contbr. articles to profl. jours. Grantee founds. in Germany and Switzerland. Mem. Optics Within Life Scis., Internat. Assn. Forensic Scis., N.Y. Acad. Scis. Avocations: arts, badminton, criminalistics, cinema. Office: Inst Forensic Medicine, Heinrich-Heine-U, Düsseldorf D-40225, Germany

PIERALISI, VIRNA See LISI, VIRNA

PIERARD, RICHARD VICTOR, history educator; b. Chgo., May 29, 1934; s. John Perkins and Diana Florence (Russell) P.; m. Charlene Burdett, June 15, 1957; children: David, Cynthia. BA, Calif. State U., L.A., 1958, MA, 1959; PhD, U. Iowa, 1964. Prof. history Ind. State U., Terre Haute, 1964—; vis. prof. Greenville (Ill.) Coll., 1972-73, Free Theol. Acad., Seeheim, Fed. Republic Germany, 1971, 78, Regent Coll., Vancouver, B.C., Can., 1975, Trinity Evang. Div. Sch., Deerfield, Ill., 1982, No. Bapt. Theol. Sem., Lombard, Ill., 1987, Fuller Theol. Sem., Pasadena, Calif., 1988, 91, Moscow Theol. Sem., 1997, 99, Gordon Coll., Wenham, Mass., 2000-2001; Fulbright prof. U. Frankfurt, Fed. Republic Germany, 1984-85; Fulbright prof. U. Halle, German Dem. Republic, 1989-90, Gordon Coll., Wenham, Mass., 2000—; mem. nat. adv. coun. Ams. United for Separation of Ch. and State, 1985—; pres. Greater Terre Haute Ch. Fedn., 1987-88; del. Lausanne II Congress on World Evang., Manila, Philippines, 1989; mem. Bapt. Heritage Study Commn., Bapt. World Alliance, 1990—. Author: The Unequal Yoke: Evangelical Christianity and Political Conservatism, 1970, Bibliography on the Religious Right in America, 1986; co-author: Twilight of the Saints: Biblical Christianity and Civil Religion, 1978, Civil Religion and the Presidency, 1988, Two Kingdoms: The Church and Culture through the Ages, 1993, The Revolution of the Candles: Christians in the Revolution of the German Democratic Republic, 1996, The New Millennium Manual, 1999; contbr. articles to religious and hist. publs. Del. White House Conf. on Librs., Washington, 1979, Ind. Dem. Party Convention, Indpls., 1980, 88; precinct committeeman Dem. Party, Terre Haute, 1978-80, 90—; mem. Ind. Gov.'s Adv. Com. on Librs., 1980-81. With U.S. Army, 1954-56. Recipient Terre award for cmty. svc., Terre Haute, Ind., 1991; Fulbright scholar U. Hamburg (Fed. Republic Germany), 1962-63; rsch. fellow U. Aberdeen (Scotland), 1978; Chavanne scholar Baylor U., 1988. Mem. Conf. on Faith and History (sec.-treas. 1967—), Evang. Theol. Soc. (pres. 1985), Am. Hist. Assn., Am. Soc. Ch. History, Ind. Assn. Historians, Am. Soc. Missiology, Internat. Assn. Mission Studies, Soc. for Encouragement and Preservation of Barbershop Quartet Singing in Am., Am. Bapt. Hist. Soc. (bd. mgrs. 1993—). Democrat. Home: 633 Hollowbrook Ct Terre Haute IN 47803-2478 Office: Dept History Ind State U Terre Haute IN 47809-0001

PIERCE, CHARLES ANDREW EVAN, geography educator, writer; b. Nottingham, Eng., Oct. 28, 1940; arrived in Vanuatu, 1971; s. Clifford Evan and Olive Rosemary (Foulsham) P.; m. Barbara Anne Morgan, Dec. 18, 1971; children: Daniel, Sam. BSc with honors, Bristol U., Eng., 1961, Postgrad. Cert. in Edn., 1962. Tchr. Monks Park Comprehensive Sch., Bristol, Eng., 1963-66; asst. geologist Geotechnics, Perth, Australia, 1967-68; tchr. Cannington Sr. H.S., Perth, 1969-70; prin., tchr. Nur Baha'i Sch., Port Vila, Vanuatu, 1971; asst. statistician Govt. of Vanuatu, 1972-79; tchr. Malapoa Coll., 1979-99; tchr., trainer Vanuahi Tchrs. Coll., 1999—; tng. officer Vanuatu Nat. Census, 1989-90; cons. C.S.I.R.O., Australia, 1991-95; researcher Economist Intelligence Unit, Eng., 1989—; exam. cons. S.P.B.E.A., Suva, Fiji, 1995—. Author, editor: sch. textbooks, 1980-89; author, researcher: Vanuatu Population Atlas, 1990. Mem. Baha'i Faith, 1968—; sec. Nat. Spiritual Assembly of the Baha'is of Vanuatu, 1976-81, 94—, treas., 1989-94. Recipient Disting. Svc. medal Govt. of Vanuatu, 1996. Mem. Vanuatu Cricket Assn., Geograph. Assn. (Eng.). Avocations: playing keyboard and guitar, singing, walking, cricket, swimming. Home: Malapoa Estate, Port Vila Vanuatu Office: Vanuata Tchrs Coll, Port Villa Vanuata

PIERCE, DONALD SHELTON, orthopedic surgeon, educator; b. Castine, Maine, May 21, 1930; s. Frederick Ernest and Jeannie (Emmet) P.; m. Janet Ten Broeck, Dec. 29, 1956; children: Donald Shelton, Stanton ten Broeck, Frederick Ernest, Jennifer Emmet. AB cum laude, Harvard U., 1953, MD, 1957. Diplomate Am. Bd. Spine Surgery, Am. Bd. Orthopedic Surgery. Intern U. Hosp., Cleve., 1957-58, resident, 1958-62; rsch. assoc. Biomechanics Lab., U. Calif., San Francisco, 1962-64; practice medicine specializing in orthopedic surgery San Francisco, 1962-64; instr. orthopedic surgery U. Calif. Med. Sch., San Francisco, 1962-64, Harvard Med. Sch., 1964-66; clin. and rsch. assoc. J.P. Kennedy Jr. Meml. Hosp., Brighton, Mass., 1964-66; clin. assoc. in orthopedics Harvard Med. Sch., 1966-67, clin. asst. prof. orthopaedic surgery, 1979-87, clin. assoc. prof., 1987—; chief dept. rehab. medicine Mass. Gen. Hosp., Boston, 1965-72, assoc. orthopedic surgeon, 1969—, vis. orthopedic surgeon, 1969—; lectr. dept. mech. engring. MIT, 1970-72. Co-author: Amputees and Their Porstheses, 1971; author: The Total Care of Spinal Cord Injuries, 1977; contbr. articles in field to profl. jours. Pres. Wellesley (Mass.) Friendly Aid Assn., 1965-67, dir., 1967-70; dir. Family Svc. Counseling Region West, Wellesley, 1965-67; exec. com., task force chmn., adv. bd. Mass. State Rehab. Planning Commn., 1966-68. With USAF, 1951-52. Fellow ACS, Am. Acad. Orthopedic Surgeons, Royal Soc. Health, Pan Am. Med. Assn., Soc. Internat. Chirurgerie, Ortopaedie et Traumatologie; mem. Othopedic Rsch. Soc., Am. Orthopaedic Assn., NRC (musculosbeletal com.), Cervical Spine Rsch. Soc. (pres. 1986), Fedn. Spine Assns. (pres. 1987), N.E. Med. Assn. (pres.). Home: 22 Lathrop Rd Wellesley MA 02482-7012 Office: Mass Gen Hosp 15 Parkman St Boston MA 02114-3117

PIERCE, FRANCIS CASIMIR, civil engineer; b. Warren, R.I., May 19, 1924; s. Frank J. and Eva (Soltys) Pierce; m. Helen Lynette Steinouer, Apr. 24, 1954; children: Paul F., Kenneth J., Nancy L., Karen H., Charles E. Student, U. Conn., 1943-44; BS, U. R.I., 1948; MS, Harvard U., 1950; postgrad., Northeastern U., 1951-52. Registered profl. engr. Conn., N.H., Mass., R.I., Vt.; registered profl. land surveyor R.I. Instr. civil engring. U. R.I., Kingston, 1948-49, U. Conn., Storrs, 1950-51; design engr. Praeger-Maguire & Ole Singstad, Boston, 1951-52; chief found. engr. C.A. maguire & Assocs., Providence, 1952-59, assoc., 1959-69, v.p., 1969-72; sr. v.p. C.E. Maguire, Inc., 1972-76, officer-in-charge Honolulu office, 1976-78, exec. c.p., corp. dir. ops., 1975-87; dir. The Maguire Group, Inc., 1979—; gen. mgr. East Atlantic Casualty Co. Ltd., 1987-88; also dir.; pres. Magma, Inc., tech. ops. svc. co., 1986-88; lectr. found. engring. U. R.I., 1968-69, trustee, 1987—; mem. Coll. Engring. adv. coun., 1986—, U.S. com. Internat. Commn. on Large Dams; mem. register of expert witnesses in the constrn. industry ABA. Contbr. articles to profl. jours. Vice chmn. Planning Bd. East Providence, R.I., 1960-73; bd. dirs. R.I. Civic Chorale and Orch., 1986-90. With AUS, 1942-46. Recipient Commendation Min. of Pub. Works Rep. Venezuela, 1970, Geotech. award ASCE sect. Boston Soc. Civil Engrs., 1979, USCG Meritorious Pub. Svc. award, 1987, Chester H. Kirk Disting. Engr. award U. R.I. Coll. Engring., 1987, Acad. of fellows Am. Mil. Engr., 1996; named Coll. of Engring. Hall of Fame U. R.I., 2000. Fellow Soc. Am. Mil. Engrs., ASCE (life, chpt. past pres., dir.); mem. NSPE (life) Am. Arbitration Assn., R.I. Soc. Profl. Engrs. (nat. dir., engr. of yr. award 1973), ASTM, Am. Soc. Engring. Edn., Soc. Marine Engrs. and Naval Architects, Am. Soc. Planning Ofcls., harvard Soc. Engrs., Scientists, Providence Engrs. Soc., R.I. Soc. Planning Agys (past pres.), U. R.I. Alumni Assn. (S.W. Fla. Gators chpt. 2000—). Home: 3830 St Girons Dr Punta Gorda FL 33950-7870 Office: 225 Foxborough Blvd Foxboro MA 02035-2854

PIERCE, JOHN GERALD (JERRY PIERCE), lawyer; b. Winter Haven, Fla., Jan. 12, 1937; s. Francis E. and Margaret (Butler) P.; m. Kathleen E., Dec. 1, 1989; children: Kathleen M. Cooke, Nancy A., John Gerald Jr., Michael J. B in Chem. Engring., U. Fla., 1959, JD with honors, 1965. Bar: Fla. 1966, U.S. Dist. Ct. (mid. dist.) Fla. 1966, U.S. Ct. Appeals (11th cir.). Assoc. Anderson & Rush, Dean & Lowndes, Orlando, Fla., 1966-68, Arnold, Matheny & Eagen, Orlando, 1968-70; ptnr. Pierce, Lewis & Dolan, Orlando, 1970-74; sole practice Orlando, 1974—. Served to 1st lt. U.S. Army, 1959-62. Mem. ABA, Fla. Bar Assn., Orange County Bar Assn. Republican. Roman Catholic. Avocations: golf, boating, skiing. E-mail: jerryaty@aol.com. Home: 605 Fox Valley Dr Longwood FL 32779-2417 Office: 800 N Ferncreek Ave Orlando FL 32803-4127

PIERCE, LISA MARGARET, telecommunications executive, product and market development manager, lecturer; b. Nyack, N.Y., June 2, 1957; d. William and Elizabeth Pierce. BA with honors, Gordon Coll., Wenham, Mass., 1978; MBA, Atkinson Sch., Salem, Oreg., 1982. Campaign mgr. Carter/Mondale, Manchester, Mass., 1976; investigator Dept. Social Svcs., Nyack, 1977-78; paralegal Beverly, Mass., 1978-79; campaign mgr. Reagan Presdl. Primary, Rockland County, N.Y., 1980; cons. Sidereal, Portland, Oreg., 1981-82; performance analyst Dept. Social Svcs., Pomona, N.Y., 1982; market analyst Momentum Techs., Parsippany, N.J., 1983; cons. Booz Allen & Hamilton, Florham Park, N.J., 1984, Deloitte-Touche, Morristown, N.J., 1985; market researcher, forecaster AT&T, Bedminster, N.J., 1985-87, asst. pvt. line product mgr., 1987-89, Integrated Svcs. Digital Network product mgr., 1989-93; dir. Telecom. Rsch. Assocs., St. Marys, Kans., 1994-98; v.p., rsch. leader Giga Info. Group, Cambridge, Mass., 1998—; panelist, contbr. TeleComms. Assn., San Diego, Internat. Comm. Assn., Atlanta, Ea. Comm. Forum, N.Y., Nat. Engring. Consortium, Chgo.; contbr. N.Y. State ISDN/Internat User's Group; feature commentator Nat. Pub. Radio (All Things Considered), 1999, Pub. Broadcasting Svc. (Nightly Bus. Report), 1999, 2000, MSNBC and CNBC, 1999, Radio Wall Street, 2000. Grantee in field. Mem. IEEE, Am. Mktg. Assn. (profl.), Am. Mgmt. Assn.

PIERCE, MARY, professional tennis player; b. Montreal, Que., Can., Jan. 15, 1975; d. Jim and Yannick Pierce. Profl. debut, 1989; 4th ranked woman USTA, 2000. Victories include Futures, York, Pa., 1989, New Braunfels, Tex., 1990, Palermo, 1991, Cesena, Palermo, P.R., 1992, Filderstadt, 1993, Australian Open, Tokyo, 1995, Italian Open, 1997, Paris Indoors, Amelia Island, Moscow, Luxembourg, 1998, Linz, 1999, (doubles with M. Hingis) Pan Pacific, 2000, French Open (singles and doubles), 2000. Office: IMG Ctr 1360 E 9th St Ste 100 Cleveland OH 44114*

PIERCE, SAMUEL RILEY, JR., government official, lawyer; b. Glen Cove, L.I., N.Y., Sept. 8, 1922; s. Samuel R. and Hettie E. (Armstrong) P.; m. Barbara Penn Wright, Apr. 1, 1948; 1 child, Victoria Wright. AB with honors, Cornell U., 1947, JD, 1949; postgrad. (Ford Found. fellow), Yale U., 1957-58; LLM in Taxation, NYU, 1952, LLD, 1972; various other hon. degrees including LL.D., L.H.D., D.C.L., Litt.D. Bar: N.Y. 1949, Supreme Ct. 1956. Asst. dist. atty. County N.Y., 1949-53; asst. U.S. atty. So. Dist. N.Y., 1953-55; asst. to under sec. Dept. Labor, Washington, 1955-56; assoc. counsel, counsel Jud. Subcom. on Antitrust U.S. Ho. Reps., 1956-57; pvt. practice law, 1957-59, 61-70, 73-81, 89—; sec. HUD, 1981-89; faculty N.Y. U. Sch. Law, 1958-70; guest speaker colls., univs.; judge N.Y. Ct. Gen. Sessions, 1959-61; gen. counsel, head legal div. U.S. Treasury Dept., Washington, 1970-73; cons. Fund Internat. Social and Econ. Edn., 1961-67; chmn. impartial disciplinary rev. bd. N.Y.C. Transit System, 1968-81; chmn. N.Y. State Minimum Wage Bd. Hotel Industry, 1961; mem. N.Y. State Banking Bd., 1961-70, N.Y.C. Bd. Edn., 1961, Adminstrv. Conf. U.S., 1968-70, Battery Park City Authority, 1968-70, N.Y.C. Spl. Commn. Inquiry into Energy Failures, 1977; mem. nat. adv. com. Comptroller of Currency, 1975-80; adv. group commr. IRS, 1974-76; mem. Nat. Wiretapping Commn., 1973-76; dir. N.Y. 1964-65 World's Fair Corp. Contbr. articles to profl. jours. Trustee Inst. Civil Justice, Mt. Holyoke Coll., 1965-75, Hampton Inst., Inst. Internat. Edn., Cornell U., Howard U., 1976-81; bd. dirs. Tax Found. U.S. del. Conf. on Coops., Georgetown, Brit. Guiana, 1956; mem. panel symposium Mil.-Indsl. Conf. on Atomic Energy, Chgo., 1956; fraternal del. All-African People's Conf., Accra, Ghana, 1958; mem. Nat. Def. Exec. Res., 1957-70; mem. nat. exec. bd. Boy Scouts Am., 1969-75; mem. N.Y.C. U.S.O. Com., 1959-61; mem. panel arbitrators Am. Arbitration Assn. and Fed. Mediation and Conciliation Service, 1957—; Bd. dirs. Louis T. Wright Meml. Fund, Inc., Nat. Parkinson Found., Inc., 1959-61; sec., dir. YMCA Greater N.Y., 1960-70; Mem. N.Y. State Republican Campaign Hdqrs. Staff, 1952, 58; gov. N.Y. Young Rep. Club, 1951-53. With AUS, 1943-46; as 1st lt. J.A.G.C. Res., 1950-52. Recipient N.Y.C. Jr. C. of C. Ann. Disting. Svc. award, 1958, Alexander Hamilton award Treasury Dept., 1973, Disting. Alumnus award Cornell Law Sch., 1988, Disting. Svc. Medallion Nassau County Bar Assn., 1988, Reagan Revolution Medal of Honor, 1989, Presdl. Citizens medal, 1989, Salute to Greatness award Martin Luther King Jr. Ctr., 1989; selected mem. of L.I. Sports Hall of Fame, 1988. Fellow Am. Coll. Trial Lawyers; mem. ABA, Assn. of Bar of City of N.Y., Cornell Assn. Class Secs., Telluride Assn. Alumni, Cornell U. Alumni Assn. N.Y.C. (gov.), C.I.D. Agts. Assn. (gov.), N.Y. County Lawyers Assn., Inst. Jud. Adminstrn., Phi Beta Kappa, Phi Kappa Phi, Alpha Phi Alpha, Alpha Phi Omega. Methodist (former mem. commn. on interjurisdictional relations United Meth. Ch.).

PIERCE, SIDNEY K., JR., biology educator, department chair; b. Holyoke, Mass., Sept. 19, 1944; s. Sidney K. and Mary Elizabeth Pierce; m. Christine Elizabeth Pierce, Aug. 5, 1974; children: Alisa, Michael. EdB, U. Miami, Fla., 1966; PhD, Fla. State U., 1970. Asst. prof. U. Md., College Park, 1970-73, assoc. prof., 1973-78, prof. dept. biology, 1978-99, prof., chmn. dept. biology, 1997-99; prof. emeritus, 1999—; prof., chmn. dept. biology U. South Fla., Tampa, 2000—; program dir. NSF, Washington, 1987-89; assoc. dir. agrl. exptl. sta. U. Md., 1987-89. Co-author: Illustrated Invertebrate Anatomy, 1985; mem. editl. bd. Biol. Bull., Marine Biology, Jour. Exptl. Zoology, News in Physiologic Sci., Comparative Biochemistry and Physiology. Fellow AAAS; mem. Am. Physiol. Soc., Soc. Integrative and Comparative Biology. Office: Dept Biology SCA 110 U South Fla 4202 E Fowler Ave Tampa FL 33620-8000

PIERCE KORTE, THRESIA (TISH PIERCE), primary school educator; b. Maize, Kans.; d. Herman and Marie Adeline (Lubbers) Korte; children: Judith, John, Mark. BS, Friends U., 1955; MS, U. Nev., Las Vegas, 1978. Cert. tchr., Nev., Nev. Life Ins. lic. Office worker Internat. Trust Co., Denver, Colo., 1951, Motor Equipment Co., Wichita, Kans., 1952-53; tchr. Wichita Pub. Schs., 1960-69, Clark County Sch. Dist., Las Vegas, Nev., 1970—. Author numerous short stories; contbr. articles to profl. jours. Senator Clark County Edn. Assn., Clark County Classroom Tchrs. Mem. NEA, Epsilon Sigma Delta (v.p. 1962). bd. dirs. Kansas Newman U., Wichita, 1966-68. Home: 3105 Cardinal Dr Las Vegas NV 89121-2204

PIERGUIDI, GIULIANO FRANCESCO LUCIANO, logistic services and record management executive; b. Milan, Jan. 13, 1967; s. Luciano and Franca (Maccabruni) P. Degree in polit. sci., U. Milan, 1993. Sales mgr. INA-Assitalia, Milan, 1994; comml. dir. Seris SPA, Milan, 1994-95; CEO, Seris Spazio SRL, Milan, 1995—. Cpl. Italian Mil., 1993-94. Mem. Sales and Mktg. Mgrs. Assn. Roman Catholic. Avocations: soccer, music, travel. Office: Seris Spazio SRL, Viale Stelvio 5, 20159 Milan Italy

PIERIDES, DEMETRIOS ZENO, shipping company executive, entrepreneur; b. Platres, Limassol, Cyprus, June 30, 1937; s. Zeno and Theodora (Phoeniefs) P. B Econs. and Law, U. Lausanne, Switzerland, 1960. Dir. Amazon Group Cos., Larnaca, Cyprus, 1957—; pres. Z.D. Pierides (1860) Ltd., Larnaca, 1967—, Iophon Shipping S.A., Athens, Greece, 1990—; chmn. Francoudi & Stephanou (1895) Ltd., Limassol, 196i—; dir. Bank of Cyprus Ltd. (1899), Nicosia and Athens; chmn. or bd. dirs. 26 shipping, hotel, travel and automobile importing cos., Cyprus and Greece; v.p. U. Cyprus, 1998. Found., Pierides Found., 1974, Pierides Archaeol. Mus., Larnca, Pierides Hist. and Folk Art Mus., Larnca, Tornaritis-Pierides Mcpl. Mus. Paleontology, Larnaca, Pierides Mus. Contemporary Art, Athens, Nicosia Mcpl. Arts Ctr., Tornaritis-Pierides Marine Life Mus., Aghia Napa, Cyprus, Pierides Libr. on History Art, Nicosia; bd. govs. European Cultural Found., 1985-98. Decorated comdr. Royal Order Polar Star and knight 1st class Royal Order Vasa (Sweden), recipient Highest Awd. of Merit by the Acad. of Scis., Acad. of Athens, Gold Medal for contrbn. to Culture by the pres. of the Rep. of Cyprus. Mem. Rotary (hon.). Greek Orthodox. Avocations: collecting antiquities and contemporary painting and sculpture. Home: 4 Zeno Kitiefs Str, Larnaca Cyprus Office: ZD Pierides Ste 415/416, 16 Archbishop Makarios Ave, 6017 Larnaca Cyprus

PIERIK, ENGELBERTUS G.J.M., surgeon, researcher; b. Terborg, Netherlands, Mar. 29, 1960; s. Oscar T.G. and Ann M.J. (van der Heyde) P.; m. Paula J.M. de Graaff, Dec. 17, 1997; 1 child, Floris. Degree in Phys. Therapy, SVF, Breda, Netherlands, 1983; MS cum laude, U. Rotterdam, Netherlands, 1987; PhD, U. Rotterdam, 1997. Diplomate in gen. surgery, laparoscopic surgery. Resident in surgery Univ. Hosp., Rotterdam, 1987-95; fellow in laparoscopic surgery AZ, Nieuwegein, Netherlands, 1995-97; cons. Isala Clinics, Zwolle, Netherlands, 1997—; sec. Bd. Laparoscopic Surgery, Amsterdam, 1996—. Author: Subfascial Endoscopic Perforating Vein Surgery, 1997; mem. editl. bd. NTVH, 1995-97; contbr. articles to profl. jours. Mem. Internat. Soc. Oxygen Transport to Tissue, Internat. Coll. Surgeons (bd. dirs. 1999), Dutch Soc. Gen. Surgery, European Soc. Laparoscopic Surgery, Rotary (bd. dirs. 1998). Avocations: golf, literature. Office: Isala Clinics, Groot Weezenland 20, 8000 GM Zwolle Netherlands

PIERIK, MARILYN ANNE, retired librarian; b. Bellingham, Wash., Nov. 12, 1939; d. Estell Leslie and Anna Margarethe (Onigkeit) Bowers; m. Robert Vincent Pierik, July 25, 1964; children: David Vincent, Donald Lesley. AA, Chaffey Jr. Coll., Ontario, Calif., 1959; BA, Upland (Calif.) Coll., 1962; cert. in teaching, Claremont (Calif.) Coll., 1963; MSLS, U. So. Calif., L.A., 1973. Tchr. elem. Christ Episcopal Day Sch., Ontario, 1959-60; tchr. Bonita High Sch., La Verne, Calif., 1962-63; tchr., libr. Kettle Valley Sch. Dist. 14, Greenwood, Can., 1963-64; libr. asst. Monrovia (Calif.) Pub. Libr., 1964-67; with Mt. Hood CC, Gresham, Oreg., 1972-98, reference libr., 1983-98, chair faculty scholarship com., 1987-98; campus archivist Mt. Hood C.C., Gresham, 1994-98; ret., 1998; mem. site selection com. Multnomah County (Oreg.) Libr., New Gresham br., 1987, adv. com. Multnomah County Libr., Portland, Oreg., 1988-89; bd. dirs. Oreg. Episcopal Conf. of Deaf, 1985-92. Bd. dirs. East County Arts Alliance, Gresham, 1987-91; vestry person, jr. warden St. Luke's Episc. Ch., 1989-92; vestry person St. Aidan's Episcopal. Ch., 2000—; founding pres. Mt. Hood Pops, 1983-88, orch. mgr., 1983-91, 93—, bd. dirs., 1983-88, 91—. Recipient Jeanette Parkhill Meml. award Chaffey Jr. Coll., 1959, Svc. award St. Luke's Episcopal Ch., 1983, 87, Edn. Svc. award Soroptimists, 1989. Mem. AAUW, NEA, Oreg. Edn. Assn., Oreg. Libr. Assn., ALA, Gresham Hist. Soc. Avocations: music, reading. E-mail: pierikm@teleport.com.

PIERLUISI, PEDRO R., lawyer; b. San Juan, P.R., Apr. 26, 1959; s. Jorge A. and Doris (Urrutia) P.; children: Anthony, Michael, Jacqueline, Rafael. BA, Tulane U., 1981; JD, George Washington U., 1984. Bar: D.C. 1984, U.S. Dist. Ct. D.C. 1985, U.S. Ct. Appeals (D.C. cir.) 1985, P.R. 1990, U.S. Supreme Ct. 1990, U.S. Dist. Ct. P.R., 1990, U.S. Ct. Appeals (1st cir.), 1993. Assoc. Verner, Liipfert, Bernhard, McPherson & Hand, Washington, 1984-85, Cole, Corette & Abrutyn, Washington, 1985-90; ptnr. Pierluisi Pierluisi & Mayol-Bianchi, San Juan, 1990-93; atty. gen. Govt. of P.R., 1993-96; ptnr. O'Neill & Borges, San Juan, 1997—. Mem. ABA (ho. of dels. 1995-96, standing com. on substance abuse 1995-98, coordinating com. on gun violence, 1998—), Nat. Assn. Attys. Gen. (chair eastern region 1996), George Washington U. Internat. Law Soc. (pres. 1982-83), Phi Alpha Delta (hon., Munoz chpt.), N.Y. Stock Exch. (arbitrator), Nat. Assn. Securities Dealers, (arbitrator) 1998—, Am. Arbitration Assn. (arbitrator). Avocation: jogging. Office: O'Neill & Borges 250 Ave Munoz Rivera Am Internat Plz San Juan PR 00918-1808

PIERONI, ROBERT EDWARD, internist, educator, military officer; b. Portland, Maine, June 20, 1937; s. Ansel Kirby and Agnes Mary (Dumais) P.; m. Dorothy Louise McDonnell, Oct. 3, 1970; children: Michelle Kirby, Robert Francis. BS, Boston Coll., 1959; MD, Pa. State U., 1971. Diplomate Am. Bd. Internal Medicine, Am. Bd. Family Practice, Am. Bd. Allergy and Immunology, Am. Bd. Quality Assurance, Am. Bd. Geriatric Medicine. Chemist Mass. Dept. Pub. Health, Boston, 1962-71; sr. bacteriologist Mass. Dept. Pub. Health, 1971-74; asst. prof. internal medicine U. Ala., Tuscaloosa, 1974-76, assoc. prof. dept. internal medicine and family practice, 1976-81, prof. internal medicine and family practice, 1981—; enlisted U.S. Army, 1961, advanced through grades to maj., 1961-81, col., 1981—; prior cons. VA Hosp., Tuscaloosa, T. Hardin Med. Facility and Partlow State Hosp., Tuscaloosa, 1974—, FDA. Contbr. more than 250 textbooks, articles, chpts. and abstracts; mem. editl. bd. various jours. Decorated Bronze Star, 1991, Commendation for Valor; recipient Golden Stethoscope award, 1982, Faculty Recognition award, 1986, Ala. Golden Eagle Humanitarian award Ala. Sr. Citizens Hall of Fame, 1988 and Physicians award, 1998, Wright A. Garner award Ala. Acad. Sci., 1997. Mem. AMA, ACP, Am. Coll. Allergy, Asthma and Immunology, Am. Geriatric Soc., Gerontol. Soc. Am., Am. Acad. Family Physicians, Physicians for Human Rights, VFW, Am. Legion. Democrat. Roman Catholic. Avocations: mountain trekking, scuba diving, studying medical and military history. Home: 398 Riverdale Dr Tuscaloosa AL 35406-1814 Office: U Ala Dept Internal Medicine PO Box 870326 Tuscaloosa AL 35487-0001

PIERPONT, ROSS Z., retired surgeon; b. Woodlawn, Md., Sept. 7, 1917; s. Edwin Lowell and Ethel Celeste (Zimmerman) P.; m. Grace Schmidt, Feb. 5,

1942; 1 child, Christine Pierpont von Kiencke; m. Hippold von Kiencke. BS in Pharmacy, U. Md., 1937, MD, 1940. Diplomate Am. Bd. Surgery. Intern Md. Gen. Hosp., Balt., 1940-41; resident in surgery Balt. City Hosps., 1941-44, U. Iowa, Iowa City, 1944-45; asst. clin. prof. emeritus U. Md.; pres. PSCI Internat. Healthcare; cons. pres. Gempro Internat. Mfg. of Healthcare Supplements. Author: Indicted, 1982, Towson & The Tax Cap, 1991, Health Care System for USA "Its Not the Health Care it's the Health Care System Stupid", 1999, Never Never Ever Give Up, 2000. Bd. dirs. Heritage Found., Washington, 1995; mem. Empower Am., Washington, 1996; Rep. nominee U.S. Senate (Md.), 1998; chmn. adv. bd. Rep. Nat. Com.; active Rep. Senatorial Inner Cir. Fellow Am. Coll. Surgeons; mem. AMA, Soc. Am. Gastrointestinal and Endoscopic Surgeons, Kiwanis Internat. Republican. Methodist. Home: 215 Belmont Forest Ct Unit 408 Timonium MD 21093-7792

PIERQUIN, BERNARD, oncologist; b. Paris, Oct. 21, 1920; s. Jean and Francoise (Vassal) P.; m. Jeanne Touraine, Mar. 31, 1948; children: Odile, Anne, Beatrice. MD, U. Paris, 1953. Intern Hopitaux de Paris, 1949-53; chef de l'unite de radiotherapie interstitielle Inst. Gustave/Roussy, Ville Juif, France, 1960-70; dir. dept. cancerologie Hopital Henri Mondor, Creteil, France, 1970-88; prof. de cancerologie Faculte Paris XII, Creteil, 1973-88; conseiller med. Ligue Contre Le Cancer, Paris, 1988—; hon. prof. Faculté de Médecine de Tianjin, China, 1987. Author: Que Faire devant un Cancer, 1972, Precis de Curietherapie, 1964, Journal d'un étudiant-parisien sous l'occupation (1939-45), 1983, Modern Brachytherapy, 1987, Manuel Pratique de Curietherapie, 1992, En Luttant Contre Le Cancer, 1995, Practical Manual of Brachytherpay, 1997, Un ami d'Arthur Rimbaud: Louis Pierquin, 1997; editor: Jour. de Radiologie, 1974-80, Jour. Europeen de Radiotherapie, 1980-87. Recipient Breur medal, 1982, Medaille du Centre Antoine Beclere, 1996. Fellow Am. Coll. Radiology; mem. Groupe Europeen de Curietherapie Paris. Avocation: making leaded glass windows. Home: 37 Rue de Turenne, 75003 Paris France

PIERRE, BITOUN, pediatrician, geneticist; b. Casablanca, Morocco, Jan. 29, 1950; arrived in France, 1951; s. Helen Theresia Bachmann; children: Samuel, Olivier, Anais. BA in Chemistry, U. Rochester, 1970; MD, U. Paris 13, 1979; Pediatrician, Tufts U., 1982; Geneticist, Paris U., 1994. Pediatric geneticist Jean Verdier Hosp., Bondy, France, 1983—, Sidva 91, Savigny, France, 1984—. Recipient Outstanding Recognition award AMA, Boston, 1985. Fellow Am. Acad. Pediatrics; mem. European Soc. Human Genetics. Office: Hop Jean Verdier, Ave du 14 Juillet, 93143 Bondy France also: 6 rue de Jarente, 75004 Paris France

PIERRE-BENOIST, JEAN (BARON DE VAUBUZIN), retired international trade specialist; b. N.Y.C., July 22, 1947; s. Yves Maurice and Madeleine (Maillet) P.; m. Matilde Eugenia Pefaur Fernández, Sept. 8, 1973; children: Angélique Madeleine, Jean-Louis Réginald, Paul-Michel Théodore. BA, Am. U., 1973, MA, 1982. Analyst C.W.W., Inc., Alexandria, Va., 1977-80; staff economist U.S. Dept. Agr., Washington, 1980-82; internat. trade analyst U.S. Internat. Trade Comm., 1982-99; retired, 1999; v.p., dir. mktg. intelligence Latin Am. Cons., Inc., 1984-85; with PBM Enterprises, Vienna, Va., 1970-92. Contbr. articles to profl. jours. Project leader and sec. 4-H, 1985-88; scoutmaster, mem. com. French Speaking Scouts of Washington, 1975-89, St. Dominic's Ch.; eucharistic minister 3d Order of Preachers, mem. coun. French-speaking Parish of Washington, 1984-87. With USAF, 1964-68, Vietnam. Mem. NRA (life), VFW (life), Am. Legion, Isaak Walton League. Republican. Roman Catholic. Avocations: fishing, hunting, archery, motorcycling. E-mail: jpierre-benoist@ids2.id.online.com. Home: 103 Elmar Dr SE Vienna VA 22180-5803

PIERSON, AL See PIZZAMIGLIO, ALBERT THEODORE

PIERSON, R. WARREN, retired surgeon, farmer; b. York, N.D., June 9, 1926; s. Ralph Jedda and Evangeline B. (Sandven) P.; m. Wilma Jean Kuenild; children: Rosemary, Susan, David, Karoline, Stephen. BA, Concordia Coll., 1950; BS in Medicine, U. N.D., 1952; ND, U. Ill., Chgo., 1954. Surgeon Quoin Ramstad Clin., Bismarck, N.D., 1955-64, Med. Arts Clin., Minot, N.D., 1971-97; resident and fellow surgery Mason Clin., Seattle, 1967-71; ret.; farmer, rancher. Contbr. chpts. to books and articles to med. jours. Mem. Rep. Nat. Com.; pres. task force Nat. Cancer Soc.; archivist 1st Luth. Ch., 1976—. Surgeon M.C., USN, 1956-68. Fellow Am. Coll. Surgeons; mem. AMA, N.D. Med. Soc., Am. Legion, Elks. Lutheran. Avocations: history, gardening. Home: 211 Souris Dr Minot ND 58701-5030

PIERSON, WAYNE GEORGE, trust company executive; b. L.A., Nov. 5, 1950; s. Norman Einar and Annabelle Florence (McLay) P.; m. Margaret Aileen Boyle, Mar. 18, 1972; children: Heather, Dawn, Mark, Michael. BS in Bus. Adminstrn. with honors, Calif. State U., Northridge, 1973. CPA, Oreg., Calif. Audit supr. Ernst & Whinney (now Ernst & Young), L.A. and Portland, Oreg., 1973-80; treas. Gregory Affiliates, Beaverton, Oreg., 1980-82; CFO, treas. Meyer Meml. Trust, Portland, 1982—; mem. adv. com. New Enterprise Assocs., Roanoke Venture, Veta Ptnrs. Investment com. Columbia Cascade Scout Coun. Mem. AICPA, Inst. Chartered Fin. Analysts Fedn., Assn. for Investment Mgmt. and Rsch., Oreg. Soc. CPAs, Portland Soc. Fin. Analysts, Found. Fin. Officers Group (steering com.). Avocations: tennis, scouting, travel. Office: Meyer Meml Trust 1515 SW 5th Ave Ste 500 Portland OR 97201-5450*

PIERSON, WILLARD JAMES, geophysics educator, researcher; b. Manhattan, N.Y., July 7, 1922; s. Willard James and Mary Abagail (Hand) P.; m. Joy Mary Kell, July 3, 1954 (dec. July 1999); children: Mary Jean, Arthur, Mark. BS, U. Chgo., 1944; PhD, NYU, 1949. From asst. prof. to assoc. prof. NYU, N.Y.C., 1949-61, prof., 1961-73; prof. CUNY, N.Y.C., 1973-92, rsch. prof., 1992—. Co-author: HO Pub 603, 1957, Principles of Phyical Oceanography, 1966. Capt. USAF, ret. Recipient Exceptional Sci. Achievement medal NASA, 1980, cert. of appreciation Soc. Naval Arch. Marine Engrs., 1973. Fellow AAAS, IEEE, Am. Geophys. Union (Sverdrup gold medal), Am. Meteorol. Soc. Methodist. Achievements include early research on remote sensing and ocean waves, radar scatterometry, radar altimetry, ship motions. Home: 103 Oakland Ave West Hempstead NY 11552-1924 Office: CCNY-CUNY Convent Ave at 138th St New York NY 10031

PIERZYNOWSKI, STEFAN GRZEGORZ, educator; b. Strzegocin, Poland, Feb. 12, 1951; s. Wladyslaw and Stansilawa (Ratanska) P.; divorced; children: Lukasz, Kacpr, Filip. PhD, Warsaw Agrl. U., Poland, 1982, Lund U., Sweden, 1991; habiltation, Warsaw Agrl. U., 1995; docent, Lund U., 1995. Asst. prof. Warsaw Agrl. U., Poland, 1982-89; asst. prof. Lund U., Sweden, 1992-95, assoc. prof., 1995-99, prof., 1998—; sr. rschr. Danish Inst. Agrl. Sci., Denmark, 1997-98; mgr. rsch. & devel. Gramineer Internat. AB, Sweden, 1998—; vis. prof. Langston U., 1992; expert European Union, Poland, 1995, 96-97. Editor: Biology of Pancreas in Growing Animals, 1999; series editor Biology of the Growing Animals, 2000. Mem. European Pancreatic Club, Am. Assn. Animal Production, European Assn. Animal Production, IPVS. Avocation: skiing. E-mail: stefan.pierzynowski@swipnet.se. Office: Lund U Dept Animal Physiol, Helgonavagen 3 b, SE-22362 Lund Sweden

PIETERSE, JAN KAREL, process engineer; b. 's Gravenmoer, The Netherlands, Dec. 2, 1961. Degree in engring., Christelijke Hogere Tech. Sch., Hilversum, 1984. Rsch. asst. DSM Rsch., Geleen, 1985-96; process engr. DSM Solutech BV, Geleen, 1996—. Patentee thin self-supporting inorganic green compacts and process for the preparation of such green compacts. Served with Netherlands Med. Troops, 1984-85. Office: DSM Solutech BV, PO Box 18, 6160 MD Geleen The Netherlands

PIETKAINEN, IIJA SISKO INKERI, science educator, researcher; b. Lemi, Finland, Aug. 12, 1930; d. Antti Vilhelm and Tyyne Sivia (Hanninen) Pajula; m. Juhani Pietikanen, Nov. 1, 1958; children Panu Lauri, Anna Iia Maria. MS, Helsinki U. Technology, 1957, Lic. in Science, 1970, DS, 1973. Rsch. worker Kudeneule, Finland, 1957-60; dept. mgr. Suomen Silkkikutomo, Finland, 1961-62; rsch. asst. Helsinki U. Technology, Finland, 1967-70; rschr. The Acad. Finland, 1970-80; dir. rsch. project Tampere U. Technology, Finland, 1981-82; acting prof. U. Helsinki, Finland, 1982-86, sr. lectr., 1986-90; prof. U. Joensuu, Finland, 1990-95; pensioner, 1996—; Technical Docent Tampere Univ. Tech., Tampere, Finland, 1979—; referee U. Helsinki, Helsinki, Finland, 1995, 98, 2000; dir. rsch. project U. Joensuu, Savonlinna, Finland, 1996-97. Author: (book) Technical Research Ctr. Finland, 1970, Acta Polytechnica Scandinavica, 1973, Helsinki U. Technology, 1975; contbr. articles to sci. jours.; patentee in field. Fellow The Textile Inst. Mem. Evangelic-Lutheran Ch. Avocations: research, exercise, gardening. Home: Rauduntie 11 H, FIN02130 Espoo Finland

PIETKIEWICZ, ANDRZEJ, electrical engineer; b. Ketrzyn, Olsztyn, Poland, June 11, 1951; arrived in Switzerland, 1991; s. Wladyslaw and Aleksandra (Puzynkiewicz) P.; m. Grazyna Jolanta Podstolska, Nov. 20, 1975; children: Katarzyna, Malgorzata. Engr., Tech. U. Gdansk, 1973, MSc, 1974, PhD, 1989. Tchg. asst. Tech. U. Gdansk, Poland, 1975-79; rsch. fellow Tech. U. Gdansk, 1979-89; rsch. assoc. Calif. Tech. Inst., Pasadena, 1989-91; project leader Ascom Energy Sys., Berne, Switzerland, 1991—. Contbr. articles to profl. jours. Fellow Fulbright Commn., 1989-91; recipient Rsch. award Min. Edn. Poland, 1989. Roman Catholic. Avocations: skiing, hiking, swimming. Home: Kirchbergstrasse 98, 3400 Burgdorf Berne, Switzerland Office: Ascom Energy Sys, Belpstrasse 37, 3000 Bern 14, Switzerland

PIETKIEWICZ, JERZY JAN, biotechnologist, educator; b. Gorowo, Poland, May 1, 1950; s. Jan and Maria (Krzywicka) P.; m. Izabella Ewa Raczynska, Aug. 21, 1976; two children. MSc in Engring., Inst. Food Chem. Tech, Wroclaw, Poland, 1973; PhD, Engring. Inst. Food Chem. Tech, Wroclaw, Poland, 1979. From asst. to rsch. tutor food biotechnology Inst. Food & Chem. Tech., Wroclaw, 1973—; cons. in field. Author: Food Processing Technology, 1995; patentee in field; contbr. articles to profl. jours. Mem. Polish Food Technologists Soc. Office: Dept Food Biotechnology, Komandorska 118/120, PL-53345 Wrocław Poland

PIETRO, JEREMY, finance company executive; b. L.A., Jan. 12, 1950; m. Jane Elizabeth Crawford. BBA, U. Calif., 1968. Mgr. Investicare, Santa Barbara, 1970-78; exec. dir. Richardson & Co., Santa Barbara, 1978-85; CEO Werik, Inc., Washington, 1985—. Contbr. to fin. articles. Mem. AIM. Roman Catholic. Avocations: reading, painting. Office: Werik Inc 7826 Eastern Ave NW Ste 410 Washington DC 20012-1324

PIETROBON, STEVEN SILVIO, electronic engineer, researcher; b. Naracoorte, Australia, Oct. 5, 1963; s. Mario and Margherita Maria (Mondin) P. B of Engring., South Australian Inst. Tech., 1986, M of Engring., 1989; PhD, U. Notre Dame, 1991. Rsch. fellow U. South Australia, Adelaide, 1990-96; propr. Small World Comm., Adelaide, 1997—. Contbr. articles to profl. jours. Recipient South Australian Inst. Tech. medal, 1986, Rsch. assistantship NASA, 1988, Postdoctoral Rsch. fellowship Australian Rsch. Coun., 1993. Mem. IEEE (sr., editor IEEE Transactions and Comm. 1996-99), Brit. Interplanetary Soc., Australian Space Rsch. Inst. Avocations: classical guitar. Office: Small World Comm, 6 First Ave, Payneham South SA 5070, Australia

PIETROKOVSKI, JAIME, dental services administrator, educator; b. Caracas, Venezuela, Mar. 29, 1933; s. Shmuel A. and Lena (Kusnizcky) P.; m. Fany Cohen, Apr. 28, 1939; children: Ruth, Shmuel, Yoav. B of Odontologia, U. San Marcos, Peru, 1955, Cirujano Dentista summa cum laude, 1956; MS, U. Ill., Chgo., 1964. Dental surgeon Municipality of Miraflores, Lima, Peru, 1955-57; instr. faculty dentistry Hebrew U., Jerusalem, 1958-62, dir. removable prosthodontics, 1964-88; dir. dental svcs., dental adv. Hasaf Harofe Med. Ctr., Zrifin, Israel, 1991—; vis. prof. Tufts U., Boston, 1974-76, U. Toronto, Can., 1993, U. Calif., San Francisco, 1994; dir. Dental Project for Elderly, Israel, 1989-94; mem. Nat. Bd. Dental Examiners, Ministry of Health, Jerusalem; cons. gerodontology, Ministry of Health, Jerusalem, 1992—; Disting. vis. scientist U. San Marcos, 1992. Author: Manual Removable Prosthodontics, 1987 (Best Seller 1996), Manual on Complete Dentures, 1991; mem. editl. bd. European Jour. Prosthodontics, 1990—; contbr. articles to profl. jours. Mem. Internat. Coll. Prosthodontics, Am. Assn. Dental Rsch., Internat. Assn. Gerodontology, Israel Dental Assn. (sec. 1964-67), Alpha Omega (pres. 1979-83), Israel Soc. Oral Rehab. (pres. 1979-84), Israel Soc. Geriat. Dentistry (pres. 1988-93). Avocations: active sports, tennis, jogging, light and classic music. Home: Haeshel 9, 90725 Moshav Nir Zvi Israel Office: Hasaf Harofe Med Ctr, Dental Svcs, 70300 Zerifin Israel

PIETROPAOLO, ANIELLO, surgeon, ophthalmologist; b. Naples, Campania, Italy, June 28, 1958; s. Ciro Pietropaolo and Giuseppina Di Sarno; m. Loredana Cardinale Rubino, June 24, 1991; children: Gaia, Lara. MD, U. Naples, 1983, specialization in ophthalmology, 1987; lic. ship dr., Ministry of Health, Rome, 1996. Resident U. Naples, 1983-87; dir., physician Ministry of Health, 1987-90; asst. ophthalmologist S.S.N. Santobono Hosp., Naples, 1990-94, ophthalmologist level 1, 1994—; cons. Ct. of Naples, 1987—; ship physician Costa Cruises, Naples, 1997—. Contbr. articles to profl. publs. Vol. surgeon WOPSEC, Cucuta, Colombia, 1996. Mem. Med. Assn. Italy, Gen. Med. Coun., Ordine Medici-Chirurghi della Provincia di Napoli. Avocations: soccer, chess, travel. Office: Ospedale Santobono, Via M Fiore 5, 80127 Naples Campania, Italy

PIETRUSIEWICZ, KAZIMIERZ MICHAŁ, chemistry educator; b. Białaczów, Poland, Sept. 10, 1946; s. Stanisław and Zofia (Kassyk) P.; m. Małgorzata Henryka Wojciechowska, Mar. 8, 1969; children: Joanna, Mateusz, Jędrzej. MSc, Tech. U., Łódź, Poland, 1969; PhD, Polish Acad. Scis., Łódź, 1976; DSc, Tech. U., Łódź, 1989. Cert. prof. chemistry. Rschr. Polish Acad. Scis., Łódź, 1969-76; postdoctorate U. N.C., Chapel Hill, 1977-78; sr. rschr. Polish Acad. Scis., Łódź, 1979-89, docent, 1989-94; prof. Marie Curie Sklodowska U., Lublin, Poland, 1994—, Inst. Organic Chemistry, Polish Acad. Scis., Warsaw, 1999—; mem. rsch. coun. Ctr. Molecular and Macromolecular Studies, Polish Acad. Scis., Łódź, 1989—, mem. rsch. coun. Inst. Organic Chemistry, Polish Acad. Scis., Warsaw, 1995—; head dept. organic chemistry Marie Curie Sklodowska U., Lublin, 1994—; cons. Com. for Sci. Rsch., Warsaw, 1997—. Co-author: (monograph series) Topics in C-13 NMR Spectroscopy, 1979; contbr. papers and revs. to profl. publs. Humboldt fellow, 1981, Fulbright fellow, 1983. Mem. Polish Chem. Soc. (com. head 1994—), Am. Chem. Soc. Office: Marie Curie Sklodowska U, ul Gliniana 33, 20-614 Lublin Poland

PIETRUSKA, ALEXANDER MICHAEL, investment banker; b. Passau, Germany, Mar. 19, 1959; m. Ann Shirley Hunter, June 7, 1986. MA in Econs., U. Colo., 1986; MBA, INSEAD, Fontainebleau, France, 1991. Fgn. exch. analyst Mfrs. Hannover Trust, N.Y.C., 1987-88; asst. v.p. Fgn. Exch. Concepts, N.Y.C., 1988-90; sr. engagement mgr. McKinsey & Co. Inc., London and Zurich, 1992-97; exec. dir. UBS Warburg, London, 1997-2000; mng. dir. ABN Amro Corp. Fin. Ltd., London, 2000—. Fulbright scholar Fulbright Commn., 1984; Quadrille Ball scholar Germanistic Soc. of Am., 1985; scholar INSEAD, 1991. Avocation: skiings, yoga. Office: McKinsey & Co Inc Warburg Dillon Read, ABN Amro Corp Fin Ltd, 250 Bishopsgate, London EC2M 4AA, England

PIETRUSZKA, MICHAEL F., judge; b. Buffalo, Oct. 20, 1956; s. Walter J. and Dorothy (Lutomski) P.; m. Patricia Ann Joyce, July 19, 1986. BA magna cum laude, Canisius Coll., 1978; JD cum laude, Syracuse U., 1981. Bar: N.Y. 1982, U.S. Dist. Ct. (we. dist.) N.Y. 1982, U.S. Ct. Internat. Trade 1985, U.S. Supreme Ct. 1986. Pvt. practice law Buffalo, 1982-87; asst. corp. counsel City of Buffalo, 1983-86, dir. parking enforcement div., 1986-87; gen. counsel Buffalo Mcpl. Housing Authority, 1987; judge City Ct. of Buffalo, 1988-98, Erie County Ct., Buffalo, 1999—; competition judge N.E. Regional Jessup Internat. Moot Ct., 1996; mem. faculty N.Y. State Assn. Jud. Seminar; mem. exec. com. Nat. Conf. Spl. Ct. Judges, ABA jud. sect., 1997—. Exec. editor Syracuse Jour. Internat. Law and Commerce, 1980-81; legal columnist Am-Pol Eagle, 1982-83, Metro Cmty. News, 1990, Polish Am. Jour., 1993—; author: Polonia Connections, 1997. Active Buffalo Urban League; dir. Floss Ave. Men's Choir, East Buffalo Civic Assn., 1984-87, N.W. Buffalo Cmty. Ctr.; pres. Forest Dist. Civic Assn., Monsignor Healy Found. Scholarship Com.; pres. Western N.Y. chpt. Kosciuszko Found., mem. nat. adv. com.; bd. dirs. Buffalo-Rzeszow Sister City Com.; dir. Gen. Pulaski Assn. of Niagara Frontier; nat. dir. Polish Am. Congress; mem. Polish Am./Jewish Am. Coun. Western N.Y.; hon. dir. Polish Cadets Buffalo, 1998. Recipient Jurist Citation of Honor award Nat. Columbus Day Com., 1988, Martin Luther King Human Rels. award Erie County So. Christian Leadership Conf., 1990, N.W. Buffalo Cmty. Svc. award, 1991, Pres.'s award Buffalo-Rzeszow Sister Cities Inc., 1993, Cert. of Spl. Congl. Recognition, 1996, Civic Recognition award Forest Dist. Civic Assn., 1996, others; named Man of Yr., Pulaski Police Assn., 1989, Am.-Pol Citizen of Yr., 1991. Mem. NAACP, N.Y. State Bar Assn. (cert. of honor 1992, 93, 94), Erie County Bar Assn., Am. Judges Assn., Polish Cadets, Profl. and Businessmen's Assn., K.C., Advocates Club (sec. 1990, v.p. 1991, pres. 1992, Pres.'s award 1993), YMCA Greater Buffalo Century Club, 100 Club Buffalo, Buffalo Canoe Club, Polish Union Am., St. Joseph's Guild, Chopin Singing Soc. Democrat. Roman Catholic. Avocation: travel, computers, website. E-mail: pietruszka@aol.com. Office: Erie County Ct 92 Franklin St Buffalo NY 14202-3902

PIETRZAK, JERZY ANTONI, physicist, educator; b. Barcin, Pomeran, Poland, Apr. 1, 1928; s. Antoni and Teodozja (Kierzkowska) P.; m. Stefania Ratajczak, June 25, 1954 (dec. Aug. 1996); children: Jacek, Hanna. MS in Physics, U. Poznan, 1952; PhD of Physics, Adam Mickiewicz U., 1962. Asst. prof., assoc. prof. Adam Mickiewicz U., Poznan, 1967-91, prof., 1991—; postdoctoral fellow St. Petersburg (Russia) U., 1963-64, Inst. Organoelements Compounds Acad. Sci. Moscow, 1968. Inventor in field of magnetic resonance; contbr. rsch. articles to scientific profl. jours. Recipient Golden Cross of Merit Pres. State Warsaw, 1974, Medal of Nat. Edn. Commn., 1978, Cross of Knight of Order of Renaissance Poland, 1981. Mem. Polish Phys. Soc. (chmn. Poznan br. 1973-78), European Phys. Soc., Internat. Elec. Paramagnetic Resonance, Soc. (Polish sect.), N.Y. Acad. Scis. Avocations: gardening, travel. Office: A Mickiewicz U Inst Physics, Umultowska 85, 61-614 Poznan Poland

PIETRZAK, ZBIGNIEW, obstetrician-gynecologist; b. Łódź, Poland, Feb. 6, 1950; s. Josef and Halina Pietrzak; m. Wlazlo, May 19, 1973; children: Adam, Michal. Physician, Med. Acad., Łódź, 1974; PhD, Mil. Acad. Lodz, 1988. Gen. practitioner Wolsztyn, Poland, 1975-77, Szprotawa, Poland, 1977-84; ob-gyn. Jordan Hosp., Łódź, 1984-88; head dept. Polish Mother's Meml. Inst., Łódź, 1988—, physician, 1988—. Lt. Stargard Szczecinski, Poland, 1974. Mem. Polish Gynecol. Soc., Polish Soc. Gynecol. Oncology. Avocations: computer programming, bicycling, skiing. E-mail: zbigniewpietrzak@klienci.pkobp.pl. Office: Polish Mothers Meml Inst, Rzgowska 281/289, 93-338 Łódź Poland

PIETRZYKOWSKI, JERZY, research scientist, civil engineer; b. Lublin, Poland, June 5, 1920; s. Witold and Anna (Sieklucka) P.; m. Emilia Grzybowska, June 16, 1951. Degree in civil engring, Poly. Coll., Warsaw, Poland, 1947; DS, Polish Acad. Sci., Warsaw, 1961. Asst. lectr. Poly. Coll., Warsaw, 1948-54; builder Robot, Warsaw, 1947-50; cons. Polish Normalization Com., Warsaw, 1950-54; scientist Inst. Polish Acad. Sci., Warsaw, 1953—; vis. prof. U. Southampton, 1963; rschr. Cambridge (Eng.) U., 1962, Brookhaven (N.Y.) Nat. lab., 1978, 88; UNESCO expert civil engr. U. Damascus, Syria, 1964-70, U. Colombo, Ceylon, 1971-73, U. Kampala, Uganda, 1980-86; presenter seminars in field. Author: Central Heating, 1951, also handbooks for civil engring. depts. of various univs.; contbr. over 60 articles to profl. jours. chmn. Tchrs. Trade Union, Polish Acad. Sci., 1955-57; leader social com. Inst. Policy Acad. Sci., 1957-60, chmn. pensioners, 1995. Cpl. Polish Home Army, 1944. Recipient Silver Cross, Polish Scouting Union, 1992, Warsaw Insurrection Cross, Polish Republic, 1995. Mem. Cambridge U. Engring. Assn. (life), Internat. Assn. for Bridge Constrn. Engring., Am. Concrete Inst., Fed. Internat. Beton, N.Y. Acad. Scis. Roman Catholic. Avocations: music, travel, sports. Home: Hoza St 5/7 Ap 74, 00 528 Warsaw Poland

PIETSCHMANN, HERBERT VICTOR, physicist, educator; b. Vienna, Austria, Aug. 9, 1936; s. Victor and Margarete (Keldorfer) P.; m. Edeltraud Sicka, mar. 3, 1960; children: Werner, Dieter, Brigitte. PhD, U. Vienna, 1960, Habilitation, 1966, Prom. sub auspiciis (hon.), 1961; Docent, Tech. U., Sweden, 1966. Rschr. U. Vienna, 1961-64, prof. physics, 1968—; rschr. U. Va., 1964-65; docent Tech. U., Göteborg, Sweden, 1966; vis. prof. U. Bonn, 1967-68; cons. Research Ctr., Seibersdorf, 1970-96; dir. Inst. High En. Phys. Austrian Acad. Sci., 1972-75; vis. prof. NORDITA, Göteborg, 1975; Austrian del. CERN Council, 1972-75; mem. faculty Hernstein Internat. Mgmt. Inst., 1978—. Author: Formulae and Results in Weak Int., 1974, Ende Naturwissenschaft Zeitalters, 1980, Weak Int.-Formulae, Results, and Derivations, 1983, Welt die Wir uns Schaffen, 1984, Electroweak Interactions, 1988, Die Wahrheit liegt nicht in der Mitte, 1990, Die Spitze des Eisbergs, 1994, Gespräche über Konstruktiven Realismus, 1994, Phänomenologie der Naturwissenschaft, 1996, Aufbruch in neue Wirklichkeiten, 1997, Gottwollte Menschen, 1999, E. Schrodinger u.d. Zukunftd Naturwissenschaft, 1999. Recipient Eotvos medal Hungarian Phys. Soc., 1976, Sci. and Tech. prize City of Vienna, 1996, Gold medal Math. and Physics, U. Bratislava, 1996. Mem. Austrian Phys. Soc., Austrian Acad. Sci. (corr.), European Phys. Soc., Gesellschaft Deutsche Naturforscher Arzte, Soc. Social Responsibility Sci., Humboldt Gesellschaft, Hungarian Phys. Soc. (hon.), N.Y. Acad. Sci. Roman Catholic. Home: Arbeiterg 13/18, A1050 Vienna Austria Office: Inst Theoretical Physics, Boltzmanng 5, A1090 Vienna Austria

PIETSCHMANN, PETER, internal medicine educator, rheumatologist; b. Vienna, Austria, May 13, 1960; s. Helmut and Edith (Sachs) P.; m. Flavia Leissinger, Dec. 7, 1983. MD, U. Vienna, 1984. Cert. specialist in internal medicine and rheumatology. Fellow U. Tex., Dallas, 1991-92; intern, resident U. Vienna, 1984-90, fellow, 1990-91, assoc. prof. internal medicine, 1992—. Contbr. over 60 articles to med. jours. Recipient Paracelsus award Austrian Soc. Internal Medicine, 1986, young investigator award World Congress Osteoporosis, 1996. Mem. Am. Soc. Bone and Mineral Rsch., Internat. Bone and Mineral Soc., Austrian Soc. Bone and Mineral Rsch. (bd. dirs.). Avocations: sports, photography, travel. Home: Technergasse 35/16, A-1180 Vienna Austria Office: U Vienna Dept Pathophysiol, Währinger Gurtel 18-20, A-1090 Vienna Austria

PIETZSCH, MICHAEL EDWARD, lawyer; b. Burlington, Iowa, Aug. 1, 1949; s. Walter E. and Leanna (Moore) P.; children: Christine E., Catherine M. AB, Stanford U., 1971; JD, U. Chgo., 1974. Bar: Ill. 1974, Ariz. 1976. Assoc. Schwartz & Freeman, Chgo., 1974-75; ptnr. McCabe & Pietzsch, Phoenix, 1975-90, Pietzsch & Williams, Phoenix, 1990-95, Polese, Pietzsch, Williams & Nolan, Phoenix, 1995—. Contbr. articles to profl. jours.; speaker at profl. confs. Del. White House Conf. Small Bus., Washington, 1986, White House Savs. Summit, 1998; chmn. bd. trustees Ariz. Sci. Ctr., 1994-98; pres. The Group, Inc., 1995-98. Fellow Am. Coll. Tax Counsel, Am. Coun. on Tax Policy; mem. ABA (chmn. personal svc. orgns. com. tax sect. 1986-90), Stanford Phoenix Club (pres. 1982-84). Home: 3101 E Marshall Ave Phoenix AZ 85016-3722 Office: 2702 N 3d St Ste 3000 Phoenix AZ 85004-4607

PIGANIOL, PIERRE GUY ALBERT, science and development policies consultant; b. Chambery, France, Jan. 10, 1915; s. Andre Felix Piganiol and Germaine Blanchard; m. Monique Françoise Mossé, Aug. 19, 1942; children: Catherine, Raymond, Helene, Bertrand. Agrege es Scis. Physiques, Ecole Normale Superieure, Paris, 1938. Cert. chem. engr. Asst. prof. Paris U., 1940-47; dir. rsch. Cie St. Gobain, Paris, 1947-58; délégué gen. recherche scientifique et technique Govt. of France, 1958-62; sci. advisor to the pres. Cie St. Gobain, 1962-71; sci. cons. Paris, 1971—; cons. UNO, UNESCO, OECD, Africa, S.Am., 1962—; chmn. sci. coun. Lab. Cen. Ponts et Chausses, Paris, 1983-91; mem. sci. coun. bldg. rsch. Ctr. Sci. et Tech. du Bariment, 1991—; mem. sci. coun. civil works Lab. Cen. Ponts et Chausses, 1986—. Author: Acetylene, 1942, Macromolécules, 1947, Le Verre, Histoire et Technique, 1965, 4000 ans d'Art du Verra, 1966, Maitriser le Progres, 1966, Du Nid a la Cite, 1969, la Recherche Mal Menee, 1988, Parlons Japonais, 1998. Mem. coun. for radio and TV Office Radio and Television France, Paris, 1964-67; chmn. coun. agrl. rsch. INRA, Paris, 1964-72. Maj. French Fgn. Legion, 1938-45. Decorated Legion d'Honneur, French Govt., King's Medal of Courage, English Govt., Croix de Guerre Belge, Belgian Govt. Fellow Am. Chem. Soc., Soc. Francaise de Chimie, Royal Soc. Chemistry; mem. N.Y. Acad. Scis., French Alpine Club, Club Alpin Francais, Club of Rome (founder), Nat. Park des Ecrins (bd. dirs.). Avocations: mountain climbing, violin. Home and Office: 5 Rue le Dantec, F75013 Paris France

PIGNOTTI, ALBERTO, theoretical physicist; b. Buenos Aires, Nov. 3, 1936; s. Gino and Josefina (Crosti) P.; m. Maria Rosa Pistol, Jan. 11, 1961

(dec. Aug. 1994); children: Maria Laura, Carmen, Gabriela; m. Mercedes Gamboni, Feb. 20, 1999. Lic. in physics, U. Buenos Aires, 1959, D in Physics, 1964. Lectr. physics U. Buenos Aires, 1964-66, prof., 1971-74; postdoctoral fellow U. Calif., Berkeley, 1966-68, Santa Barbara, 1968-69; asst. prof. U. Wash., Seattle, 1969-71, assoc. prof., 1971-72; sect. and dept. head TECHINT, Buenos Aires, 1975-88; dept. head SIDERCA, Campana-Buenos Aires, 1988-89; sr. rsch. scientist, head physics dept. Fundación Para el Desarrollo Tecnológico, Buenos Aires, 1989—; reviewer Phys. Rev., Phys. Rev. Letters, Nuovo Cimento, ASME Jour. Heat Transfer, also others, 1967—. Contbr. numerous articles to sci. jours. Recipient sci. and tech. award Konex Found., Buenos Aires, 1993. Fellow Nat. Acad. Exact Phys. and Natural Scis., Third World Acad. Scis.; mem. Am. Soc. for Nondestructive Tesing, Argentine Physics Assn. (bd. dirs. 1995-98), Argentine Soc. for Info. and Ops. Rsch. (bd. dirs. 1977). Office: FUDETEC, L Alem 1067, 1001 Buenos Aires Argentina

PIGORSCH, CHRISTIAN, physicist, researcher; b. Lutherstadt Eisleben, Germany, Nov. 21, 1971; s. Klaus D. and Waltraud H. Pigorsch; m. Steffi U. Burghardt, Sept. 4, 1998. MA, Martin Luther U. Halle, Germany, 1995. Mem. faculty, rschr. Martin Luther U., Halle, 1996-98, 99—, SUNY, Albany, 1998-99. Mem. German Phys. Soc., Am. Phys. Soc. Avocations: computer sciences, genealogy, soccer. Office: Martin Luther U Physics Dep, Selkestrasse 9, Halle 06099, Germany

PIGOTT, JOHN DOWLING, geologist, geophysicist, geochemist, educator, consultant; b. Gorman, Tex., Feb. 2, 1951; s. Edwin Albert and Emma Jane (Poe) P.; m. Kulwadee Lawwongngam, May 28, 1994. BA in Zoology, U. Tex., 1974, BS in Geology, 1974, MA in Geology, 1977; PhD in Geology, Northwestern U., 1981. Geologist Amoco Internat., Chgo., 1978-80; sr. petroleum geologist Amoco Internat., Houston, 1980-81; asst., then assoc. prof. U. Okla., Norman, 1981—; vis. prof. Mus. Natural History, Paris, 1988, Sun Yat Sen U., Kaohsiung, Taiwan, 1991; rsch. dir. 5 nation Red Sea-Gulf of Aden seismic stratigraphy and basis analysis industry consortium, 1992—; internat. energy cons., 1981—; instr. I.H.R.D.C., Boston, 1987-91, O.G.C.I., Tulsa, 1991—; energy advisor Ministry of Oil and Mineral Resources, Republic of Yemen, 1998—; advisor Prime Min. Rep. Yemen, 1998—. Mem. editl. bd. Geotectonica et Metallogenin Jour., 1992—. Mem. Am. Assn. Petroleum Geologists, Soc. Exploration Geophysicists, Soc. Petroleum Engrs., Geol. Soc. Am., Indonesian Petroleum Assn., Sigma Xi. Roman Catholic; Theravada Buddhist. Achievements include discovering relationship between global CO2 and natural tectonic cycles on the scale of millions of years showing previous greenhouse times during the Phanerozoic, processing first three-dimensional amplitude variation with offset seismic survey to quantify rocks, fluids, and pressures in rocks, processing and displaying first ground penetrating radar survey as a seismic section for ultrahigh resolution sequence stratigraphy, developing tectonic subsidence analysis as a practical tool for investigating the comparative anatomy of a sedimentary basins, their tectonic history, and evolving hydrocarbon potential, and constructing first paleo-heatflow maps of the Red Sea for the past 25 ma. Office: U Okla Sch Geology & Geophysics 100 E Boyd St Norman OK 73019-1000

PIGROVA, GALINA DMITRIEVNA, physicist, educator; b. Birsk, Russia, Nov. 27, 1938; d. Dmitrij Fedorovich and Vera Dmitrievna (Konovalova) Goldin; m. Konstantin Semenovich Pigrov, Mar. 2, 1961; children: Konstantin, Nadezhda, Elena. Physicist, State U. St. Petersburg, 1961; postgrad., Lvov State U., 1967-71; cand. tech. sci., Ctrl. Boiler Turbine Inst., 1972; DS, Tech. U. St. Petersburg, 1993. Engr. physicist Ctrl. Boiler and Turbine Inst., St. Petersburg, 1961-64, leader phase analysis group, 1964—; prof. North-West Polytech. Inst., St. Petersburg, 1995—; acad. sec. Acad. Coun. St. Petersburg, 1992—. Author: Modern Methods in Study of Materials Structure, 1997; inventor in field; contbr. articles to profl. jours. Grantee Soros Fund, 1993, 94. Mem. Russian Metallurgists Assn., Commn. Phase Analysis. Avocation: travel. Home: Kaznacheyskaya 3 Apt 4, 190 031 Saint Petersburg Russia Office: Ctrl Boiler & Turbine Inst, Polytechnicheskaya 24, 194 021 Saint Petersburg Russia

PIGUET, CHARLES, publishing company executive, consultant; b. Lausanne, Switzerland, June 2, 1930; s. Robert and Julie Oulevey P.; m. Jacqueline Koechlin, July 14, 1958; 1 child, Etienne. Permanent del., Moral Re Armament Internat. Network, Congo, Zaire, 1948—, pub. cons., 1996—. Author: The World at the Turning, 1982, Freedom for Africa, 1996; editor: A Listening Ear, 1984. Mem. Swiss Pubs. Assn. (treas. 1987-95), Internat. Pub. Assn. (mem. exec. com., treas. 1995—). Avocations: walking, gardening. Home: Av Eugene Rambert, CH 1815 Clarens Montreux Vaud, Switzerland Office: Caux Edition, Rue Du Panorama Mountain Ho, CH 1824 Caux Vaud, Switzerland

PIGUET, CLAUDE, chemist; b. Geneva, Switzerland, Apr. 4, 1961; s. Alfred and Janine (Merminod) P.; 1 child, Dworak Vincent. MS in Chemistry, U. Geneva, 1986, PhD in Chemistry, 1989. Asst. U. Geneva, 1985-89, maitre asst., 1991-94, asst. prof., 1996-99, prof., 1999—; postdoctoral fellow U. Strasbourg, France, 1989-90, U. Lausanne, Switzerland, 1995. Contbr. articles to profl. jours. Pres. Libr. Commn., Geneva, 1997-2000. Recipient Gillet award, 1980, Werner medal, 1995. Mem. Geneva Chem. Soc., Swiss Chem. Soc. Avocations: musician (oboe), mountain cheveller. Office: U Geneva Inorganic Chem, 30 quai E-Ansermet, 1211 Geneva Switzerland

PIHL, OVE G., publisher; b. Stockholm, Sweden, May 2, 1938; s. Gunnar E. and Lillie I. (Sjoberg) P.; m. Marianne E. Lundell, 1964 (div. 1980); children: Sarah, Johan; m. Birgitta M. Orne, 1994. Student, Enskede Coll., Stockholm, 1952-57, Anders Beckman Sch. Design, Stockholm, 1957-59, Sch. Visual Arts, N.Y., 1961-63. Art dir. Svenska Telegrambyrån Advt., Stockholm, 1960-61; graphic designer Lippincott & Margulies, N.Y.C., 1961-62; art dir. McCann-Ericsson, N.Y.C., 1962-63, Ervaco Advt., Stockholm, 1963-67; art dir., ptnr. Arbman Advt., Stockholm, 1967-70; pres., founder, ptnr. Falk & Pihl Advt., Stockholm, 1970-81; pres., founder, creative dir. Falk & Pihl/Doyle Dane Bernbach, Stockholm, 1981-84; founder, ptnr. Atlantis Pub., Stockholm, 1974-88; pres., founder, ptnr. Page One Pub., Stockholm, 1990—, Concept Pub. Internat., London, 1998—; tchr. advt. design and concept Berghs Sch. Advt., Stockholm, 1988-92. Jury mem. Excellent Swedish Design, 1984, Internat. Posters, Berlin, 1988, Clio Exec. Jury, San Francisco, 1996; chmn. jury Swedish Golden Egg awards, 1994. Bd. dirs. Beckman Sch. Design, 1975-80, Bergs Sch. Advt., 1988-92, Royal Swedish Coll. Art, 1994-96. Active Swedish Air Force, 1959-60. Recipient Pour le Merite Gastronomique, Sandahl Found., 1992, Diploma award The Acad. of Gastronomy, 1998; inductee Hall of Fame, Swedish Art Dirs. Club, 1986. Mem. Platima Acad., Sallskapet Club. Avocations: gastronomy, western riding, flying. Home: Gumshornsgatan 12, 11460 Stockholm Sweden Office: Page One Pub, Gumshornsgatan 15, 11460 Stockholm Sweden

PIHLSTRÖM, SAMI JOHANNES, philosopher, researcher, educator; b. Helsinki, Dec. 27, 1969; s. Esko Erkki Johannes and Ulla-Maija (Akkanen) P.; m. Marianna Elina Soini, 1998; 1 child, Meeri Elvira. MPhil, U. Helsinki, 1993, Licentiate in Philosophy, 1994, PhD, 1996. Tchr. philosophy U. Helsinki, 1993—, rsch. fellow dept. philosophy, 1994-98, docent in theoretical philosophy, 1998—; docent in philosophy U. Turku, 1998—; prof. philosophy U. Kuopio, 1998-99; post-doctoral rsch. fellow Acad. Finland, 1999—; docent in philosophy U. Kuopio, 2000—. Mem. editl. bd. niin & näin, 1993—, Facta Philosophica, 1998—, (book series) Studies in Pragmatism and Values, 1999—; contbr. articles to profl. jours. Recipient Charles S. Peirce essay prize, 1997. Mem. Philos. Soc. Finland (editor Ajatus 1996—, bd. dirs. 1996—), Soc. Finnish Skeptics, Am. Philos. Assn., Finnish Assn. Sci. Editors and Journalists. Avocations: literature, chess. Office: Dept Philosophy U Helsinki, Unioninkatu 40 B PO Box 24, FIN00014 Helsinki Finland

PIIPER, JOHANNES, physiologist; b. Tartu, Estonia, Nov. 11, 1924; arrived in Germany, 1944; s. Johannes and Elwine (Ounapuu) P.; m. Ilse Pfundt, Dec. 28, 1957; children: Hilja, Johanna, Albrecht. MD, U. Göttingen, 1954; Dr. h.c. (hon.), U. Fribourg, 1990, U. Tartu, 1994. Rsch. asst. Max Planck Inst. Exptl. Medicine, Göttingen, Germany, 1953-71; dir. Max Planck Inst. Exptl. Medicine, Göttingen, 1971-92, emeritus dir., 1992—. Editor: Respiratory Function in Birds, 1978, (with P. Scheid) Gas Exchange Function of Normal and Diseased Lungs, 1980. Mem. Am. Physiol. Soc. (hon.), Estonian Acad. Scis. (fgn.). Office: Max Planck Inst Exptl Medicine, Hermann-Rein Str 3, D-37075 Göttingen Germany

PIKAS, ANATOL, education educator; b. Viljandi, Estonia, Nov. 29, 1928; arrived in Sweden, 1944; s. Jaan and Marta (Rosenberg) P.; m. Anna-Lena Delin, June 9, 1962; children: Anders, Martin, Robert. PhD, Uppsala (Sweden) U., 1965. Sr. lectr. Uppsala U., 1968; vis. prof. peace edn. U.S., Can., Germany. Author: Abstraction and Concept Formation, 1966, Barn och Föräldraauktoritet, 1961, Så Stoppar vi Mobbning, 1975, Bekämpar vi Mobbning I skolan, 1987, Gemensamt-Bekymmer-Metoden: Handbok for ett Paradigmskifte i Behandling av Skolmobbning, 1998; founder Shared Concern Method homepage website. E-mail: Anatol.Pikas@ped.uu.se. Office: Dept Edn, Uppsala U, S-750 02 Uppsala Sweden

PIKE, CHARLES JAMES, employee benefits consultant, financial planner; b. Montreal, Apr. 9, 1914; s. Andrew and Frances Alicia (Webster) P.; m. Lois R. Bennet, Dec. 26, 1953 (dec. Aug. 1963); m. Marjorie H. Murdoch, Nov. 25, 1977. Grad. high sch., Montreal. CLU, chartered ins. broker, CFP, registered fin. planner, chartered administr. Subscription sales mgr. Hearst Orgn., then Maclean Hunter, Can., 1932-39; sales mgr. Hires Root Beer, Que., 1939-41; from group rep. to group mgr. Sun Life Can., 1941-48; asst. br. mgr. Sun Life Can., Edmonton, Montreal, 1948-54; pvt. group welfare cons. Montreal, 1955—; pres. Fin. and Estate Planning Coun., Montreal, 1954, Life Underwriters Assn. Montreal, 1955; founding pres. Que. chpt. Can. Assn. Fin. Planners, 1982. Ins. editor, weekly columnist Fin. Times Can., 1950-56. Co-founder mktg. execs. course U. Western Ont., London, 1952; pres. Montreal (Que.) Boys' and Girls' Assn., 1960-63; coun. mem. The Montreal (Que.) Bd. Trade, 1970-72. Mem. Life Underwriters Assn. Can. (life), Million Dollar Round Table (life), Montreal Bd. Trade (life), Que. Assn. Fin. Planners (planner emeritus), Can. Alpine Masters Racing Group (life), JB Ski Club Inc. (past pres.), Beaconsfield Golf Club (life), Montreal Hunt Club (past pres.), Montreal Amateur Athletic Assn. (past coun. mem.). Avocation: golfing. Office: Pike Vezina Assurance, 800 Blvd Rene-Levesque O, Montreal, PQ Canada H3B 1X9

PIKE, EDWARD ROY, physics educator; b. Perth, Australia, Dec. 4, 1929; arrived in Eng., 1932; s. Anthony and Rosalind Irene (Davies) P.; m. Pamela Sawtell, July 23, 1955; children: Martin, Alison, Sarah. BSc in Math., U. Wales, Cardiff, 1953, BSc in Physics, 1954, PhD, 1957. Chartered mathematician, physicist, U.K. Fulbright scholar MIT, Cambridge, Mass., 1958-60; sr. scientific officer to chief scientific officer Royal Signals and Radar Establishment, Malvern, U.K., 1986-91; Clerk Maxwell prof. theoretical physics King's Coll., London, 1986—, head Sch. Phys. Scis. and Engring., 1991-94; non-exec. dir. Richard Clay plc, 1984-86; vis. prof. math. Imperial Coll., London, 1984-86; v.p. Inst. Physics, U.K., 1981-85; chmn. Adam Hilger Ltd., Bristol, U.K., 1981-85; mem. coun. European Phys. Soc., Geneva, 1981-84; chmn. Stilo Tech. Ltd., 1996—, Stilo Internat. plc, 2000—. Co-editor: Frontiers in Quantum Optics, 1986, Chaos, Noise and Fractals, 1987, Photons and Quantum Fluctuations, 1988, Squeezed and Non-Classical Light, 1989; co-author: The Quantum Theory of Radiation, 1995; hon. editor Jour. Physics A, 1973-78, Optica Acta, 1978-82, Quantum Optics, 1989-94; co-editor: Photon Correlation and Light Beating Spectroscopy, 1974, High Power Gas Lasers, 1975, Photon Correlation Spectroscopy and Velocimetry, 1977, Photon Correlation Spectroscopy and Light Scattering, 1997. Mem. Confrèrie St. Etienne, Alsace, France, 1980—; With Royal Corps of Signals, 1948-50. Recipient MacRobert award Confedn. of Engring. Instns., 1977, Ann. Achievement award Worshipful Co. of Sci. Instrument Makers, 1978, Ann. award Com. on Awards to Inventors, 1980, Guthrie medal and prize Inst. Physics, 1996. Fellow Inst. Math. and Its Applications, Inst. Physics, Royal Soc. (Charles Parsons medal 1975). Avocations: music, languages. Home: 8 Bredon Grove, Malvern WR14 3JR, England Office: King's Coll, Strand, London WC2R 2LS, England

PIKIS, GEORGHIOUS M., judge. Pres. Supreme Ct., Nicosia, Cyprus. Office: Min of Justice & Pub Order, Char Mouskos St, Nicosia Cyprus*

PILACZYŃSKA-SZCZESNIAK, ŁUCJA, scientist, researcher; b. Niewiery, Poland, Feb. 8, 1945; d. Michał and Emilia (Sosnowska) P.; m. Stefan Szcześniak, May 18, 1968; 1 child, Aleksandra. Master, U. Adam Mickiewicz, Poznań, Poland, 1968; doctor's degree, U. Sch. of Phys. Edn., Poznań, Poland, 1978. Asst. engr. Med. Sch., Poznań, 1968-74; asst. rschr. U. Sch. of Phys. Edn., Poznań, 1974-79, dr. rschr., 1979-95, prof., 1995—; head of chair U. Sch. of Phys. Edn., 1981—, prodean, 1990-96, head of dept., 1999—. Mem. Polish Soc. of Physiology (asst. mgr. br. Poznań), Soc. of the Friends of Scis. of Poznań (pres. 1996—), Polish Soc. of Nutrition, N.Y. Acad. Sci. Roman Catholic. Avocation: tourism. Office: U Sch of Phys Edn Str 27/39, Królowej Jadwigi, 61-871 Poznań Poland

PILAR, L. PRUDENCIO R., financial services executive; b. Bacarra, Philippines, Sept. 12, 1943; came to U.S., 1977; s. Francisco and Maria (Raralio) P.; m. Vivien Ruth Narciso, Aug. 20, 1967; children: Prudencio Rex Jr., Diogene Ruthard, Keith N., Xydia Vida Ruth N., Benedict. BS in Edn., No. Luzon Tchrs. Coll., Laoag City, Philippines, 1964; MA in Adminstrn. and Supervision, No. Luzon Tchrs. Coll., 1972. CLU, ChFC. Prin., tchr. Bur. of Pub. Schs., Solsona, Philippines, 1964-77; agt. The Equitable, Honolulu, 1978-95; pres. Pilar Fin. & Tax Strategies, Inc., Honolulu, 1995—. Pres. St. Anthony Sch. Parent-Tchrs. Guild, Honolulu, 1987, 88, 89, 94. Fellow Life Underwriter Tng. Coun.; mem. Internat. Assn. for Fin. Planning, Nat. Assn. Life Underwriters, Diocesan Congress of Filipino Cath. Clubs, Oahu Coun. Filipino Cath. Clubs, KC. Democrat. Roman Catholic. Avocation: giving seminars. Office: Pilar Fin & Tax Strategies 33 S King St Ste 108 Honolulu HI 96813-4319

PILARCZYK, DANIEL EDWARD, archbishop; b. Dayton, Ohio, Aug. 12, 1934; s. Daniel Joseph and Frieda S. (Hilgefort) P. Student, St. Gregory Sem., Cin., 1948-53; PhB, Pontifical Urban U., Rome, 1955, PhL, 1956, STB, 1958, STL, 1960, STD, 1961; MA, Xavier U., 1965; PhD, U. Cin., 1969; LLD (hon.), Xavier U., 1975, Calumet Coll., 1982, U. Dayton, 1990, Marquette U., 1990, Thomas More Coll., 1991, Coll. Mount St. Joseph, 1994, Hebrew Union Coll.- Jewish Inst. Religion, 1997. Ordained priest Roman Catholic Ch., 1959; asst. chancellor Archdiocese of Cin., 1961-63; synodal judge Archdiocesan Tribunal, 1971-82; mem. faculty Athenaeum of Ohio, St. Gregory Sem., 1963-74; v.p. Athenaeum of Ohio, 1968-74, trustee, 1974—; also rector St. Gregory Sem., 1968-74; archdiocesan dir. ednl. services, 1974-82, aux. bishop of Cin., 1974-82, vicar gen., 1974-82, archbishop of Cin., 1982—; bd. dirs. Pope John Ctr., 1978-85; trustee Cath. Health Assn., 1982-85, Cath. U. Am., 1983-91, 97—, Pontifical Coll. Josephinum, 1983-92; v.p. Nat. Conf. Cath. Bishops, 1986-89, pres., 1989-92, chmn. Com. on Doctrine, 1996-2000; U.S. rep. Episc. Bd. Internat. Commn. on English in Liturgy 1987-97; chmn., 1991-97. Author: Praepositini Cancellarii de Sacramentis et de Novissimis, 1964-65, Twelve Tough Issues, 1988, We Believe, 1989, Living in the Lord, 1990, The Parish: Where God's People Live, 1991, Forgiveness, 1992, What Must I Do?, 1993, Our Priests: Who They Are and What They Do, 1994, Sacraments, 1994, Lenten Lunches, 1995, Bringing Forth Justice, 1996, 99, Thinking Catholic, 1998, Practicing Catholic, 1999, Believing Catholic, 2000. Ohio Classical Conf. scholar to Athens, 1966. Mem. Am. Philol. Assn. Home and Office: 100 E 8th St Cincinnati OH 45202-2129

PILARCZYK, KRYSTIAN WALENTY, engineering company executive, consultant; b. Ogorzelczyn, Poland, Feb. 14, 1941; arrived in The Netherlands, 1971; s. Jozef and Helena (Wisniewski) P.; m. Marianne Wilma Uijlen, Dec. 20, 1967; children: Yvonne, Michael. MSc in Hydraulic Engring., Gdansk (Poland) Tech. U., 1964. Rsch. engr. Inst. Hydroengring., Gdansk, 1964-66, 68-70, Delft Hydraulics, The Netherlands, 1966-68; project engr. Delta Project, The Hague, The Netherlands, 1971-85; head hydraulic rsch. Pub. Works Dept., The Netherlands, 1985-92; mgr. R & D, hydraulic engring. divsn. Pub. Works Dept., Delft, The Netherlands, 1992—. Author: Geosynthetics and Geosystems, 1999; editor, author: Dikes and Revetments, 1998; co-author: River Training Techniques, 1995, Offshore Breakwaters, 1996. Mem. Permanent Internat. Assn. Navigation Congresses, Internat. Assn. Hydraulic Engring. and Rsch., Dutch Assn. Engrs., Internat. Geosynthetics Soc. Liberal. Roman Catholic. Avocations: sailing, gardening. E-mail: K.Pilarczyk@wxs.nl. Home: Nesciohove 23, NL2726BJ Zoetermeer The Netherlands Office: Hydraulic Engring Divsn, Van den Burghweg 1, NL2628CS Delft The Netherlands

PILBEAM, PAMELA MAY, history educator; b. Stoke-on-Trent, Eng., Aug. 30, 1941; d. Sidney and May (Filcher) Cartlidge; m. Stephen Pilbeam; children: Ashka, Rhys, Llewellyn. BA with 1st class honors, U. London, 1962, PhD, 1966. Lectr. dept. history U. London, 1965—, prof. French history, 1995—; vis. assoc. prof. U. Toronto, Ont., Can., 1971, U. York, Ont., 1972-73, U. Br. Columbia, 1993; Inst. Hist. Research fellow, 1964-65. Author: The Middle Classes in Europe 1789-1914, 1990, The 1830 Revolution in France, 1991, Republicanism in France, 1995, Themes in Modern European History, 1995, The Constitutional Monarchy in France 1814-1848, 1999, French Socialists Before Marx: Workers, Women and the Social Question in France, 2000. Recipient rsch. award Govt. France, 1985. Office: Dept History, Royal Holloway and Bedford New Coll, Egham Surrey, England

PILCH, JÓZEF, cytogeneticist; b. Ksiaznice, Poland, Mar. 15, 1947; s. Benedykt and Julia (Lech) P. PhD, Plant Breeding and Acclimatization Inst., 1977, habilitation, 1989. Head of cytogenetic lab. Poland, 1981-90, 99—, head of statis. and biometric lab., 1989-90; head of genetic and breeding of cereals lab., 1991—; sec. of com. in agrl. adv. ctr. Poland, 1992—, scientific com. in plant breeding, 1992—, com. for registration cereal varieties, 1997—; mem. sect. 3.1.1. Genetics Applied of Plants of Scientific Rsch. Com., 1992-95; mem. internat. com. rye chromosome nomeclature and homoeology relationships, The Netherlands, 1982—. Recipient Silver Cross of Merit Agrl. Ministry, 1989. Mem. Polish Genetic Assn., EUCARPIA, Assn. of Engrs. and Technics in Agronomy. Roman Catholic. Avocations: fishing, photography. Home: Slomiana 2/25, 30-316 Cracow Poland Office: Plant Breeding/Acclimatizaion Inst, Zawila 4, 30-423 Cracow Poland

PILCH, YOSEF HAYIM, physician, retired educator; b. Chgo., Aug. 4, 1935; arrived in France, 1997; s. Judah and Bernice Frances (Shapary) P.; m. Patricia Ann Moncrief, Feb. 15, 1980. BA, U. Wis., 1951; MD, Johns Hopkins U., 1955. Diplomate Am. Bd. Surgery. Intern U. Chgo., 1959-60; resident Albert Einstein Coll. Medicine, 1964-67; sr. surgeon USPHS, Bethesda, Md., 1961-64; sr. surgeon Surgery Br. NCI NIH, Bethesda, Md., 1967-71; asst., assoc. prof. surgery UCLA, 1971-76; prof. surgery U. Calif., San Diego, 1976-86; prof. surgery U. Ill., Chgo., 1986-97, ret., 1997. Author, editor: Surgical Oncology, 1984; contbr. articles to profl. jours. Avocations: music, travel. Home: 33 rue Poussin, 75016 Paris France

PILCHER, ALAN RODNEY, chartered surveyor; b. Town Gosport, Hampshire, Eng., July 3, 1954; s. Walter Alan William and Thelma Doreen (Ellerton) P. Trainee surveyor Hall Pain & Foster, Portsmouth, Hampshire, Eng., 1973-77; investment surveyor, head fund mgmt. sect. Healey & Baker, London, 1977-85, ptnr., 1985—. Fellow Royal Inst. Chartered Surveyor, Royal Geog. Soc. Avocation: hill walking. Office: Healey & Baker, Hanover Sq 29 St George St, London W1A 3BG, England

PILCHER, JAMES BROWNIE, lawyer; b. Shreveport, La., May 19, 1929; s. James Reece and Martha Mae (Brown) P.; m. Lorene Pilcher; children: Lydia, Martha, Bradley. BA, La. State U., 1952; JD summa cum laude, John Marshall Law Sch., 1955; postgrad., Emory U., 1957. Bar: Ga. 1955. Legal aide to Spkr. of Ho. of Reps. Ga., 1961-64; assoc. city atty. City of Atlanta, 1964-69; pvt. practice law Atlanta, 1969—. Exec. committeeman Dem. Exec. Com. of Fulton County, Ga., 1974-86; bd. dirs. Whitehead Boys Club, 1961-89; trustee Ga. Inst. Continuing Legal Edn., 1988-89. Fellow Lawyers Found. Ga., 1996—. Mem. ABA, State Bar Ga. (chmn. 1988-89, gen. practice and trial sect., chmn. criminal law sect. 1986-87), Ga. Assn. Criminal Def. Lawyers (pres. 1980-82), Ga. Trial Lawyers Assn. (life), Ga. Claimants Attys. Assn. (pres. 1983-84), NACDL (bd. dirs. 1980-85), Ga. Inst. Trial Advocacy (bd. dirs. 1986-89), South Fulton Bar Assn. (pres. 1987-88), Am. Bankruptcy Inst., Nat. Assn. Consumer Bankruptcy Attys., Trial Lawyers for Pub. Justice, Kiwanis (Peachtree, Atlanta pres. 1983-84, gov. Ga. dist. 1992-93), Sierra Club of Am. (life). Presbyterian. E-mail: pilcher@mediaone.net. Home: 1195 W Wesley Rd NW Atlanta GA 30327-1407 Office: One Northside 75 Atlanta GA 30318-7715

PILE-SPELLMAN, JOHN MARTIN, radiology and neurosurgery educator; b. Sioux City, Iowa, Jan. 12, 1951; s. George Geneser and Mary Carol (Dwight) Spellman; m. Eliza R. Pile, June 2, 1973; children: Megan, Katherine, Julian. BS, U. S.D., 1976; MD, Tufts U., 1978. Diplomate Am. Bd. Radiology. Resident radiology Mass. Gen. Hosp., Boston, 1980-83, fellow neuroradiology, 1983-85; interventional fellow neuroradiology NYU Med., N.Y.C., 1986; prof. radiology and neurosurgery Med. Sch. Columbia U., N.Y.C.; attending radiologist, neurosurgeon Columbia U., N.Y.C.; radiologist Columbia Presbyn. Med. Ctr. Hosp., N.Y.C., 1992—; adj. prof. radiology and neurosurgery Med. Sch. Cornell U.; vice chmn. radiology for rsch. Columbia U.; attending radiologist and neurosurgeon N.Y. Hosp., N.Y.C., 1997—. Mem. Soc. Cardiovasc. Radiology, Alpha Omega Alpha. Office: CPMC Milstein Hosp 8 South Knuckle 177 Fort Washington Ave New York NY 10032-3713

PILHEU, JORGE ALBERTO, internal medicine educator; b. Juarez, Argentina, May 11, 1919; s. Francisco and Raquel (Gatto) P.; m. Maria Salomé Saavedra, Nov. 30, 1970; 1 child, Maria Salomé. MD, U Buenos Aires, 1945. Intern, resident pneumonology ward Muñoz Hosp., 1945-63; prof. lung diseases U Buenos Aires Sch. Medicine, 1963—; head dept. Muñiz Hosp., Buenos Aires, 1979-84; v.p. Argentine League Against Tb, Buenos Aires, 1987—; pres. World Congress Tobacco or Health, Buenos Aires, 1992. Editor Revista Argentina del Tórax, 1987-93. Fellow Govt. of France, 1950, Am. Coll. Chest Physicians, 1952, Govt. of The Netherlands, 1956. Mem. Soc. Argentina Tisiología (pres. 1968), Soc. Medicina Interna (pres. 1990), Argentine Med. Assn. (hon.), Argentine League Against TB (pres. 1996—). Home: Las Heras 2131, 1127 Buenos Aires Argentina Office: Argentine League Against Tb, Santa Fe 4292, 1425 Buenos Aires Argentina

PILICK, ECKHART RUDOLF, clergyman, editor; b. Cologne, Germany, July 4, 1937; s. Ernst Gustav and Elisabeth Sophia (Weingarten) P.; m. Elisabeth Pia Oberacker, June 28, 1959; m. Gabina Demes (div. 1987); 1 child, Stephanie. PhD, U. Cologne, 1969. Tchr. Folkuniversitetet, Malmö, Sweden, 1968-69, Tchrs. U., Heidelberg and Karlsruhe, Germany, 1974-2000; coun. mem. Internat. Assn. Religious Freedom, 1976-81; rep. Internat. Humanist and Ethical Union, European Parliament, 1976-81. Editor, author: Freie Religion, 1974-91; editor: Wege ohne Dogma, 1992-2000, Gottesbilder heute, 1979, Philosophischer Briefwechsel, 1995, Lexikon Freireligioeser Personen, 1998; author: Interlinguistic Hellesland, 1958? Avocations: book collector. Home: Amthausstr 3, D-76227 Karlsruhe Germany Office: Freireligiöse, Landesgemeinde Baden T6 26, D-68161 Mannheim Germany

PILKAMA, EERO ILMARI, broadcast executive; b. Helsinki, Feb. 3, 1943; s. Kaarlo Juhana Jalmari and Impi Maria (Snäll) P.; m. Inkeri Marjatta Peltola, Oct. 5, 1968; children: Juhana, Santeri. MSc, Helsinki U., 1968. Sales mgr. Kesko Oy, Helsinki, 1968-71, Kemira Oy, Helsinki, 1972-75; mng. dir. Strymer Oy, Kulloo, Finland, 1975-77; dir. Kemira Oy, Helsinki, 1977-80, adminstrn. dir., bd. dirs., 1982-84; mng. dir. Valvilla Oy, Turku, Finland, 1980-82; CEO MTV3 Finland, Helsinki, 1984-99; exec. v.p. Alma Media, Helsinki, 1998—; bd. dirs. TV4 Sweden, Stockholm. Mem. Internat. Inst. Comm. (trustee, treas.), Internat. Assn. Advt., European Film and TV Forum, Rotary. Office: MTV3 Finland, Ilmalantori 2, 00240 Helsinki Finland

PILKERTON, ARTHUR RAYMOND, JR., surgeon, educator; b. Washington, Mar. 27, 1935; s. Arthur Raymond and Mary Rose (Ginechesi) P.; m. Sally Ann Madden, Aug. 6, 1966; children: A. Raymond III, Joseph A., Mary, Christopher, Jeanne Marie. BS in Biology, Georgetown U., 1952-56, MD, 1960. Diplomate Am. Bd. Opthalmology. Intern. U. Pitts., 1961; fellow retina surgery Wills Eye Hosp., Phila., 1964-65; resident ophthalmology Georgetown U. Med. Ctr., Washington, 1961-64, asst. prof., 1965-70, assoc. prof., 1971-78, clin. prof., 1978—; asst. clin. prof. George Washington U., Washington, 1985—; chief ophthalmology Veteran's Adminstrn. Hosp., Washington, 1965-82; chmn. ophthalmology cons., Veterans Adminstrn., Washington, 1978-82. Served with U.S. Army, 1961-70. Named Knight of Malta, Knight Comdr. Holy Sepulchre. Fellow Am. Acad. Ophthalmology, Am. Coll. Surgeons; mem. Retina Soc. U.S., Uitreous Soc. Republican. Roman Catholic. Office: Retina Group Washington 5454 Wisconsin Ave Suite 1540 Chevy Chase MD 20815

PILKINGTON, MARY ELLEN, stockbroker, trader; b. N.Y.C., Feb. 16, 1955; d. Charles Arthur Bertrand and Mary (Lynch) Perez; m. Scott Douglas Ballin (div. 1986); m. John J. Pilkington, Aug. 19, 1994. BA in Polit. Sci., Mt. Vernon Coll., Washington, 1976. Dir. materials ctr. Gen. Fedn. of Women's Clubs, Washington, 1978-80; broker, asst. to the chmn. Folger Nolan Fleming Douglas, Washington, 1980-85; broker, account exec. Rose & Co., N.Y.C., 1985-86; trader Bear Stearns, N.Y.C., 1986-88; trader, broker Robyns Capital, N.Y.C., 1988-89; trader, v.p. trading Jessop Capital Corp., N.Y.C., 1989-91, Kidder Peabody, 1992-94, Dean Witter, 1994-95, Gabelli & Co., 1996—. Trustee Mt. Vernon Coll., Washington, 1999. Roman Catholic. Avocations: golf, skiing, tennis, squash, photography.

PILKUS, JOSEPH EDWARD, III, career officer; b. Phila., Oct. 28, 1967; s. Joseph Edward and Florence Ellen P.; m. Nicole Shelly Pilkus, Dec. 21, 1996; 1 child, Katerina Anne. BA in History, LaSalle U., Phila., 1994; MS in Internat. Rels., Troy (Ala.) State U., 1999; postgrad., Fgn. Svc. Inst., Russia. Closing agt. Commonwealth Land Title Ins. Co., Phila., 1986-88; closing officer Keystone Abstract, Phila., 1988-89; assoc. v.p. NVR Homes, Phila., 1989-91; pres. Profl. Settlement Svcs., Phila., 1991-94; chief military personnel flight 100th Mission Support Squadron, RAF Mildenhall, U.K., 1995-96; squadron sect. commdr. 100th Maintenance Squadron, RAF Mildenhall, U.K., 1996-97; logistics group exec. officer 100th Logistics Group, RAF Mildenhall, U.K., 1998-99; chief global skills devel. Air Force Attache Affairs Office, Rosslyn, Va., 1999—. Hist. rschr.: Christianity and the maghreb Region, 1993. Recipient Acad. Excellence award Christian Bros., Phila., 1992, Daniel Webster Briefing award, USAF, Maxwell, Ala., 1995; named Personnel Mgr. of Yr. USAF, 1997-98, Logistics Group Co. Grade Officer of Yr., USAF, 1998. Mem. Co. Grade Officer's Coun. (v.p., 1997-98, sec. 1996-97). Republican. Roman Catholic. Avocations: chess, Russian language, travel, reading. E-mail address: joseph.pilkus@pentagon.af.mil. Fax: (703) 588-6396. Office: AFAAO 1500 Wilson Blvd Ste 900 Arlington VA 22209-2404

PILLA, ANTHONY MICHAEL, bishop; b. Cleve., Nov. 12, 1932; s. George and Libera (Nista) P. Student, St. Gregory Coll. Sem., 1952-53, Borromeo Coll. Sem., 1955, St. Mary Sem., 1954, 56-59; B.A. in Philosophy, John Carroll U., Cleve., 1961, M.A. in History, 1967. Ordained priest Roman Cath. Ch., 1959. Assoc. St. Bartholomew Parish, Middleburg Hts., Ohio, 1959-60; prof. Borromeo Sem., Wickliffe, Ohio, 1960-72; rector-pres. Borromeo Sem., 1972-75; mem. Diocese Cleve. Liturgical Commn., 1964-69, asst. dir., 1969-72; sec. for services to clergy and religious personnel Diocese Cleve., 1975-79; titular bishop Scardona; and aux. bishop of Cleve. and vicar Eastern region Diocese of Cleve., 1979-80, apostolic adminstr., from 1980; bishop of Cleve., from 1981; pres. Nat. Conf. Cath. Bishops, 1995-98; trustee Borromeo Sem., 1975-79, Cath. U., 1981-84; trustee, mem. bd. overseers St. Mary Sem., 1975-79; mem. adv. bd. permanent diaconate program Diocese of Cleve., 1975-79, hospitalization and ins. bd., 1979;. Bd. dirs. NCCJ, 1986—. Mem. Nat. Cath. Edn. Assn. (dir. 1972-75), U.S. Cath. Conf., Nat. Conf. Cath. Bishops, Cath. Conf. Ohio., Greater Cleve. Roundtable (trustee from 1981). Home and Office: Chancery Office Diocese of Cleveland 1027 Superior Ave E Ste 300 Cleveland OH 44114-2503

PILLAI, C.K.S., scientist; b. Mavelikara, Kerala, India, Dec. 26, 1945; s. N. Krishna Pillai and K. Easwari Amma; m. B. Radhamony, Aug. 30, 1975; chiodren: R. Vidya Jothy, S. Manuprakash. BSC, Kerala U., Thiruvanathapuram, India, 1966, MSc, 1968; PhD, Indian Inst. Sci., Bangalore. Postdoctoral fellow Indian Inst. Sci., Bangalore, 1975-76; scientist Vikram Sarabhai Space Ctr., Thiruvananthapuram, 1976-78; scientist Retional Rsch. Lab., Thiruvananthapuram, 1979-95, scientist, dep. dir., 1995—; Brit. Coun. fellow Strathclyde U., Glasgow, Scotland, 1990-91. Contbr. over 100 articles to profl. jours., chpts. to books. Recipient Independence Day Invention award Nat. Rsch. and Devel. Corp., New Delhi, Gold medal World Intellectual Property Orgn. Mem. Soc. for Polymer Sci. (joint sec. local chpt. 1997—, life), Materials Rsch. Soc. India (treas. local chpt. 1990-96, life), soc. for Biomaterials and Artificial Organs (life). Home: Amrutham NP-8/675 Karumom, Thiruvananthapuram 695 002, India Office: Regional Rsch Lab, Thiruvananthapuram 695 019, India

PILLAI, PALANIKKUMAR AYASAMY, advertising executive; b. Singapore, Feb. 19, 1967; s. Ayasamy Annamalai and Rethinam (Ayakannu) P.; m. Krishnakumari Veerasamy, Jan. 31, 1998. BBA, Nat. U. Singapore, 1992; grad. diploma, Mktg. Inst., Singapore, 1996; MBA, Curtin U., Perth, Australia, 1997. Account exec. EURO RSCG, Singapore, 1993-94, account dir., 1995-96, sr. account dir., 1996-97, group account dir., 1997-98; account mgr. Monsoon Advt., Singapore, 1994-95; dep. mng. dir. Lowe & Ptnrs./Monsoon Advt., Singapore, 1998—. Home: Blk 471, Sembawang Dr 12-425, Singapore 750471 Singapore Office: Lowe & Ptnrs Monsoon Advt, 60 Martin Rd #07-23/26, Singapore 239065, Singapore

PILLAI, PARMESHWARAN GOVINDA, private detective; b. Kottayam, Kerala, India, May 26, 1937; s. Govinda Gopalan and Sarojani Govinda P.; m. Lalita Parmeshwaran, May 3, 1952. Bsc, Kerala U., 1958. Cert. security and safety cons. Security and safety officer German Remadies, Ltd., Bombay, 1969-75; CMD Guj Indl. Security Svcs., Ltd., India, 1977-96; CEO Hawk Secret Svcs., Ahmedabad, India, 1988—; founder, pres. Security Assn. of Guj, 1985—, v.p. 1993-98. Dir. social svcs. Lions Club, 1997; trustee social and edn. trust Asia Charitable Trust, 1997; security cons. in field. Capt. Assam Rifiles/Indian Army, 1960-68. Office: Hawk Secret Svcs, Rm 3 1st Flr Ravi Chambers, 380 001 Ahmedabad Gujarat, India

PILLAI, RAVEENDRAN K., cytologist, researcher; b. Kummil, India, June 1, 1960; s. Kuttan G. and Gomathy P. (Amma) P.; m. I.G. Premkala, Jan 26, 1992; children: Kavya, Arjun. BSc in Zoology, U. Kerala, India, 1981, MSc in Zoology, 1984, PhD in Biochemistry, 1995. Trainee in cancer cytology Regional Cancer Ctr., Trivandrum, Kerala, India, 1985; cytologist Regional Cancer Ctr., Trivandrum, 1986—; rsch. guide Kerala U., Trivandrum, 1995—; PhD thesis examiner Calicut U., Kerala, 1995—. Contbr. articles to profl. jours. Cancer Awareness programmer, Kerala, 1986—. Recipient Dr. Satya Monga award Indian Acad. Cytologists, 1994; Nat. Cancer Ins. fellow, U.S., 1996. Mem. Kerala Acad. Scis. (exec. mem.), Indian Assn. Biomed. Scientists. Socialist Party. Avocations: reading, writing, drawing, football, cinema. Home: Kunnath Veedu, Kummil, 691536 Kollam, Kerala India Office: Reginoal Cancer Ctr, Trivandrum, 695011 Trivandrum, Kerala India

PILLANS, CHARLES PALMER, III, lawyer; b. Orlando, Fla., Feb. 22, 1940; s. Charles Palmer Jr. and Helen (Scarborough) P.; m. Judith Hart, July 6, 1963; children: Charles Palmer IV, Helen Hart. BA, U. Fla., 1962, JD, 1966. Bar: Fla. 1967, U.S. Dist. Ct. (mid. dist.) Fla. 1967, U.S. Ct. Appeals (2d cir.) 1968, U.S. Supreme Ct. 1971, U.S. Ct. Appeals (3d cir.) 1976, U.S. Ct. Appeals (5th and 11th cirs.) 1981. Assoc. Bedell, Bedell, Dittmar, Smith & Zehmer, Jacksonville, Fla., 1966-70; asst. state atty. 4th jud. cir. Jacksonville, 1970-72; asst. gen. counsel City of Jacksonville, 1972; ptnr. Bedell, Dittmar, DeVault Pillans & Coxe, P.A., Jacksonville, 1972—; mem. Fla. Bd. Bar Examiners, Tallahassee, 1979-84, chmn., 1983-84; mem. Jud. Nominating Commn., 1988-92, chmn., 1990-91, 1st Dist. Ct. Appeal, Tallahassee, 1988-92, chmn., 1990-91. Master Chester Bedell Inn of Ct.; fellow Am. Coll. Trial Lawyers, ABA; mem. Am. Bar Found., Fla. Bar Assn. (chmn. profl. ethics com. 1998—, chmn. 1998-99). Methodist. Home: 10 Buck Thorne Dr Amelia Island FL 32034-6518 Office: Bedell Dittmar DeVault Pillans & Coxe PA Bedell Bldg 101 E Adams St Jacksonville FL 32202-3303

PILLAY, KUMAREN, optometrist; b. Umkomaas, South Africa, Apr. 17, 1969; s. Nadasen Marimuthoo and Devi Pillay. B of Optometry, U. Durban, Westville, South Africa, 1991; diploma in herbalism, South African Coll. Herbalism, 1993; cert. advanced study, New Eng. Coll. Optometry, 1996; dip. primary healthcare, complimentary med., Technikon, South Africa, 1998; doctor of med., altern. med., Med. Coll. of Altern. Med., India, 1999. reg. Alternative Medical Practitioner, Counc. of Alternative Systems of Meds. Optometrist in pvt. practice Port Shepstone, South Africa, 1992, 94—; optometrist eye clinic Vision Care, Transkei, South Africa, 1992, Ofakim Eye Clinic, Israel, 1993; cons. Rural Primary Health Care, 1992-93, Eye Care Train, 1997; clin. examiner U. Durban, Westville, South Africa, 1995, Natal Blind and Deaf Soc., 1997. Pres. Earthlife Africa, 1991. Mem. Indian Optometric Assn., South African Naturopaths and Herbalists Assn. Avocations: gym, hiking, horse riding, beach, cultural activities. Home: 6 Seagull Rd PO Box 1021, 4240 Kwa Zulu Natal South Africa Office: Clear Vision Optometrists, Aiken & Robinson St PO 1021, Port Shepstone South Africa

PILLAY, MARRIMUTHOO, nuclear medicine consultant; b. Benoni, Transvaal, South Africa, June 15, 1949; arrived in The Netherlands, 1979; s. Dhurmealingo Soobyah and Munimah Vengetasamy; m. Berosh Tavaria, June 11, 1980; children: Janesh, Darsin, Zoran. MSc, U. London, 1984, PhD, 1990. Cons. nuc. medicine Dr. Daniel den Hoed Cancer Ctr., Rotterdam, The Netherlands, 1980—. Editor: The Clinical Application of SPET, 1994; contbr. articles to sci. jours.; patentee in field. Mem. European Assn. Nuc. Medicine, Brit. Soc. Nuc. Medicine, Dutch Soc. Med. Physics, Dutch Soc. Nuc. Medicine, South African Soc. Nuc. Medicine, Dutch Soc. Radiation Hygiene, Health Physics Soc., Am. Soc. Physicists in Medicine. Avocations: reading, jogging, squash. Office: Dr Daniel den Hoed Cancer Ctr, St Clara Hosp PO Box 9119, 3007 AC Rotterdam The Netherlands

PILLET, GONZAGUE J., economist, educator, consultant; b. Riaz, Switzerland, Nov. 15, 1948; s. Louis P. Pillet and Jacqueline M. Dupasquier; m. Cécile Bianchi, Jan. 28, 1972; children: Rachel L., Mathilde E. M of Econs., U. Fribourg, Switzerland, 1971, PhD in Econs., 1975; Postdoc. Scis., U. Geneva, Switzerland, 1982; Agregation Environ. Econs., U. Fribourg, Switzerland, 1986. Rsch. asst. U. Fribourg, 1971-75, 86; economist Swiss Coun. Sci., 1975-77; sr. economist U. Geneva, 1978-82; rsch. assoc. U. Fla., Gainesville, 1983-84; lecturing prof. U. Fribourg, 1986—; co. exec. ECOSYS, Inc., Switzerland, 1988—; head rsch. program Paul Scherrer Inst. Tech., Switzerland, 1990-92, 93-95; prof. U. Senghor, Alexandria, Egypt, 1992-95; mem. rsch. team European Sci. Found., Strasbourg, France, 1990-92, 97; lead author Intergovtl. Panel on Climate Change, Working Group III/Decision Making Framework, 1993-95; expert, Swiss Fed. Bur. Stats., 1996—. Author: E3-Energy, Ecology, Economy, 1987, Environmental-Economic Account, 1992, Ecological Economics, 1993, Le nomade et l'éboueur, 1997, L'Efficace, le Juste et l'Ecologique, 2000, (with K.J. Arrow and J. Parikh) Decision Making Frameworks, 1996; editor: Les Donneurs de Temps, 1981, Environmental Economics, 1987, Steps Toward a Decision Making Framework to Address Climate Change, 1994, (with X. Oberson) Réforme fiscale écologique, 2000. Chmn. Alachua County Sch. Bilingual Program, Gainesville, Fla., 1983-84. Recipient Latsis prize Latsis Internat. Found., U. Geneva, 1986. Fellow Soc. for Study on Entropy Japan; mem. Swiss Environ. Protection Soc. (bd. dirs. 1995—, v.p. 1999—). Office: ECOSYS, Inc, 27 Rue de la Filature, CH-1227 Geneva Switzerland

PILLING, ANITA RANDALL, educator; b. Houston, Aug. 29, 1943; d. Marion Leon Randall and Ruth Kathryn Lorraine; m. Jerald D. Pilling, June 2, 1964; children: Matthew, Jacob, Rachel, Justin, Benjamin, Andrew. BA, Brighman Young U., 1964; MA, Sam Houston State U., 1983. Tchr. Houston Ind. Sch. Dist., 1964-65, Abilene (Tex.) Ind. Sch. Dist., 1965-67, Tucson Pub. Schs., 1967-69; tchg. fellow Sam Houston State U., Huntsville, Tex., 1982-83; rsch. asst. Sam Houston Meml. Mus., Huntsville, 1982-83; tchr. Willis (Tex.) Ind. Sch. Dist., 1983-95, The John Cooper Sch., The Woodlands, Tex., 1995—; participant numerous seminars and workshops in field; presenter in field; grant writer Tex. Coun. for the Humanities, 1999. Contbr. articles Historical Dictionary of the New Deal, 1985, Historical Dictionary of Imperialism, 1990. Recipient Leadership scholarship Brigham Young U., 1961-64, Powell scholarship Sam Houston State U., 1982-83, Excellence in Tchg. award Coll. of Edn., U. Tex., Austin, 1991, others. Mem. Nat. Coun. Social Studies, Tex. Coun. for Social Studies, Nat. Coun. Geography Edn., Tex. Alliance for Geography Edn., Friends of Geography, nat. Coun. for History Edn., Tex. Coun. for History Edn., World History Assn. Avocations: worldwide travel, backpacking and canoeing, parenting. Office: The John Cooper Sch #1 John Cooper Dr The Woodlands TX 77381

PILLOT, GENE MERRILL, retired school system administrator; b. Canton, Ohio, Apr. 13, 1930; s. John D. Pillot and Vera R. Granstaff; m. Beverly Ann Shaw, June 4, 1982; children: Vera Kathleen Martin, Michael Gene, Patrick Merrill. BS in Math., Ohio State U., 1952; MEd in Adminstrn. and Supvervision, Kent State U., 1957; EdD in Adminstrn. and Supervision, U. Fla., 1970. Asst. prin. North Royalton (Ohio) High Sch., 1959-61, prin., 1961-63; asst. prin. Sarasota (Fla.) Sr. High Sch., 1963-64, prin., 1964-68; dir. staff development Sarasota Dist. Schs., 1968-70, asst. supt., 1970-71, supt., 1971-80; dir. human resources Sarasota Meml Hosp., 1980-83; owner, broker Pillot Realty, Sarasota, 1986-90; commr. Sarasota City, 1989—, vice mayor, 1992-93, 96-97, 99-2000, mayor, 1993-94, 97-98, 2000—; prof. Am. Assn. Sch. Adminstrn., Nat. Acad. Sch. Execs., 1969-73; adj. prof. U. South Fla., Tampa, 1978-81; pvt. cons. edn. orgns., 1969-76. Author (chpt.) Differentiated Staffing, Strategies for D.S., 1971; contbr. articles to profl. jours. Trustee Fla. Sch. Deaf/Blind, St. Augustine, 1980-89, chmn. bd. trustees, 1986-89; bd. dirs. Riverview Found., 1985-94, Girls Club, Sarasota, 1985-89, Hospice Found., Sarasota Opera Assn., Hispanic Am. Alliance; mem. Civil Svc. Bd. Sarasota, 1984-89; mem. adv. bd. Cath. Social Svcs., 1987-89. Mem. Sara Bay Country Club (Sarasota), Phi Delta Kappa (Educator of Yr. 1980). Republican. Roman Catholic. Avocations: writing, genealogy, ballroom dancing. Home: 1212 Hillview Dr Sarasota FL 34239-2020

PILLSBURY, PENELOPE DELAIRE, library director; b. Bristol, Conn., Jan. 5, 1949; d. Edward William and Ellen Caroline (Jewett) DeLaire; m. Keith Anthony Pillsbury, Aug. 3, 1973; children: Ellen Kathleen Elizabeth, Caleb Edward Marshall. BA in History, U. Vt., 1971; MALS, U. Mich., 1973. Reference libr. U. Vt. Bailey/Howe Libr., Burlington, 1973-80, Fletcher Free Libr., Burlington, 1980-83; dir. N.W. Regional Libr. Dept. of Librs., Georgia, Vt., 1983-86; dir. Brownell Libr., Essex Junction, Vt., 1986—. Author: Essex, Vermont, An Annotated Bibliography to Sources, 1992; author essays and articles. Jr. h.s. youth leader Cathedral Ch. St. Paul, Burlington, 1998—; sec. Christian edn. com. Episcopal Diocese of Vt., 1996—; mem. programs com. Bishop Booth Conf. Ctr., Burlington, 1995—; dir. Rock Point Summer Conf. Bd., Burlington, 1996—. Mem. Vt. Libr. Assn. (pres. coll./spl. libr. sect. 1978-79, assn. pres.), New Eng. Libr. Assn. (bd. dirs.), Essex Rotary Club (pres. 1999-2000), Mortar Board, Phi Beta Kappa, Delta Delta Delta (scholar 1970). Democrat. Avocations: reading, bicycling, singing, cross country skiing, gardening. Email: essex jct@aol.state.vt.us. Home: 25 University Ter Burlington VT 05401-3527 Office: Brownell Libr/ Village of Essex Junction 6 Lincoln St Essex Junction VT 05452-3154

PILOT, TACO, dentist, educator; b. Soest, The Netherlands, July 30, 1936; s. Jan and Geesje (Tyink) P.; m. Anita Landré, Nov. 25, 1961; children: Duco Jan, Wiebeke K. DDS, U. Utrecht, The Netherlands, 1960, PhD, 1972. Clin. instr. dentistry U. Utrecht, 1960-71; periodontologist Bilthoven, The Netherlands, 1968-73; prof. periodontology U. Groningen, The Netherlands, 1971-94, chmn. dept. clin. dentistry, 1977-81, dean dental faculty, 1981-85, cons. WHO, 1985—, dir. collaborating ctr. for oral health svcs. rsch. WHO, 1987-96, acting dean dental faculty, 1999—. Contbr. numerous articles to profl. jours., chpts. to books. Avocations: sailing, playing golf. Office: WHO Collab Ctr Oral Health, U Groningen, 9461 EB Gieten The Netherlands

PILOTTO, ALBERTO, geriatrician; b. Schio, Vicenza, Italy, June 4, 1957; s. Giovanni and Gina (Cazzola) P.; m. Adele Scarpari, Apr. 4, 1983; children: Andrea, Davide. D Medicine and Surgery, U. Padua, Italy, 1982; postgrad., U. Padua, 1986, 90. Postdoctoral rsch. fellow U. Padua, 1982-85; asst. Mil. Hosp., Padua, 1984-85; registrar geriatrician Civil Hosp., Schio, Italy, 1985-93; sr. registrar geriatrician Gen. Hosp., Vicenza, 1993—; cons. endoscopist Civil Hosp., Schio, 1986-92; cons. gastroenerologist dept. geriatrics Gen. Hosp., Vicenza, 1993—; vis. faculty mem. East Caroline U., Greenville, N.C., 1990; cons. geriatrician Interdisciplinary Group for Ulcer Study, 1985—, Interdisciplinary Group for Cholelithiasis Study, 1988—; prof. gastroenterology Sch. of Geriatric Medicine, U. Padua, 1998—. Author: (with C.F. Azzini) Digestive Diseases in the Elderly, part 1, 1989, part 2, 1990, (with G. Del Favero) Gallstones in the Elderly, 1994, (with F. DiMario) Peptic Ulcer in the Elderly, 1995, the Elderly in the 2000's, 1997, NSAID-Related Gastroduodenal Damage in the Elderly, 1999. Mem. Italian Gastroenterology Soc. (grantee 1985), Italian Gerontology-Geriatric Soc. (grantee 1992), Italian Geriatric Soc. (grantee 1995), N.Y. Acad. of Scis. Roman Catholic. Avocation: music. Office: S Bortolo Hosp Dept Geriatr, Via Rodolfi 37, 36100 Vicenza Italy

PILÓ-VELOSO, DORILA, chemistry educator, researcher; b. Belo Horizonte, Brazil, Oct. 4, 1944; d. Raimundo Veloso and Maria Idalina (Oliveira) Piló-Veloso; m. Waldo Silva; children: André, Iara. B in Chemistry, Inst. Scis. Exatas, 1966; PhD in Chemistry, U. Fed. Minas Gerais, Belo Horizonte, Brazil, 1973; D Scis. and Physics, Sci. and Med. U. Grenoble, France, 1978. Instr. U. Fed. Minas Gerais, Belo Horizonte, 1969-73, asst. prof., 1973-78; assoc. prof. Univ. Fed. de Minas Gerais, Belo Horizonte, 1979-90, prof., 1991—; stagiaire de recherche Grenoble (France) Ctr. for Nuclear Studies, 1973-78, post-doctoral fellow, 1978-79; post-doctoral fellow U. East Anglia, Norwich, E Anglia, Eng., 1980; adv. bd. Secretariat de Estado de Ciencis and Tech., Belo Horizonte, 1987, Commn. Rels. Internat. Reitoria de U. Fed. Minas Gerais, 1987-89; cons. Fundação Ezequiel Dias, Belo Horizonte, 1988-98; pro-rector rsch. U. Fed. Minas Gerais, 1994-98. Contbr. articles to Jour. Chem. Rsch., Jour. Phys. Chemistry, Jour. Brazilian Chem. Soc., Holzforschung, Jour. Nat. Prodn., Jour. Chem. Soc., Perkin Trans. I, Química Nova, others. Fellow Ministry Fgn. Affairs, France, 1973-77, Joliet-Curie Found., France, 1978; grantee Nat. Coun. Sci. Devel., Brasilia, 1979, 90-98, Found. Amparo Pesquisa de Minas Gerais, Belo Horizonte, 1983-96, Financiadora Estudos Projetos, Rio de Janeiro, 1983-96. Mem. Regional Coun. of Chem. (Sci. Merit award 1992, Santos Dumont Silver medal 1994), Brazilian Soc. Chemistry, Am.Chemical Soc., Brazilian Soc. for the Advance of Scis. Achievements include research in organic and wood chemistry, natural products, organic synthesis. Office: U Fed Minas Gerais Dept Quimica, ICEX UFMG Cidade Univ Pampulha, 31270901 Belo Horizonte MG, Brazil

PILZ, UWE, medical computer scientist; b. Leipzig, Sachsen, Germany, Oct. 20, 1958; s. Friedhelm and Isolde (Voigtländer) P.; m. Anett Pietschmann, Apr. 18, 1986; children: Ulrike, Florian. Electroplater, univ. entrance qual., Galvanotechnik, Leipzig, 1978; diploma in elec. engring., Technische Hochschule Ilmenau, 1985, PhD in Electrochemistry, 1991. Qualified as univ. lectr. Devel. engr. Lokomotivbau, Hennigsdorf, 1985-89; med. computer scientist U. Leipzig, 1990—. Author: Numerical Simulations of the electrical field and the mass transfer for applications in the electrochemical metal deposition, 1995 (with Lothar Engelmann) Integrations of Medical Knowledge in an Expert System for Use in Intensive Care Medicine, 1999; patentee in field; contbr. articles and essays to profl. publs. Avocations: canoeing, astronomy. Office: U Leipzig, Johannis allee 32, 04103 Leipzig Sachsen, Germany

PIMENTA, SIMON IGNATIUS CARDINAL, retired archbishop; b. Bombay, Mar. 1, 1920. Ordained to priest Roman Cath. Ch., 1949. Elected to titular Ch. of Bocconia, 1971; consecrated bishop, 1971, coadjutor archbishop, 1977, archbishop of diocese, 1978, created cardinal, 1988, ret., 1997. Address: Archbishops House, 21 Nathalal Parekh Marg, Maharashtra Bombay 400001, India

PIMENTEL, MÁRCIA MATTOS GONÇALVES, human geneticist, educator; b. Rio de Janeiro, Feb. 8, 1958; d. José Antonio Gonçalves and Dora de Jesus Mattos Gonçalves; m. Carlos Antonio de Abreu Pimentel Filho, Feb. 5, 1983; children: Augusto Cezar Matto Gonçalves de Abreu Pimentel, Júlio Cezar Mattos Gonçalves de Abreu Pimentel. Biologist, Fed. U. Rio de Janeiro, 1979, Master's degree, 1982, PhD, 1987. Cert. dr. of sci. Rschr. Fed. U. Rio de Janeiro, 1988-90; prof. genetics U. of State of Rio de Janeiro, 1991—; dir. Human Genetics Svc., Rio de Janeiro, 1996—; asst. chief dept. cell biology and genetics U. of State of Rio de Janeiro, 1994-95, advisor sci. initiation program, 1995—. Contbr. sci. articles to profl. jours. Recipient Moyse's Feldman award Pedro Ernesto Hosp., 1994; grantee for sci. project FAPERJ, 1997, 99. Fellow Brazilian Genetics Soc., Biology Regional Coun. Roman Catholic. Avocations: reading, walking, traveling, listening to music, writing poetry. E-mail: pimentel@verj.br. Office: U of State Rio de Janeiro, Rua São Francisco Xavier, 20550013 Rio de Janeiro Brazil

PIMENTEL-GOMES, FREDERICO, retired engineering educator, editor; b. Piracicaba, Brazil, Dec. 19, 1921; s. Raymundo and Sylvia Souza (Gomes) P.; m. Mary Lee Fonseca de Bem, Nov. 8, 1941; children: Marli de Bem Gomes, Valquíria de Bem Gomes, Vangri de Bem Gomes. Dr. Agronomy, U. São Paulo, Brazil, 1948, Agronomy Engr., 1943. Asst. prof. U. São Paulo, 1944-58, prof., 1958-59, Cathedratic prof., 1959—; dir. Escola de Engenharia de Piracicaba, 1970-73; dir. Revista de agricultura, Piracicaba, 1968—, editor, 1988—; vis. scholar N.C. State U., 1952-53; vis. prof. U. Buenos Aires, 1983, U. La Plata, Argentina, 1983, 96; sci. cons. Pesquisa Agropecuária Brasileira Jour., 1966—; cons. Instituto de Pesquisas e Estudos Florestais, Piracicaba, 1990-95. Author: Curso de Estatística Experimental, 13th edit. 1990, Iniciação à Estatística, 6th edit., 1978, A Estatística Moderna na Pesquisa Agropecuária, 3d edit., 1987, others; co-author: Experimentos de Adubacão: Planejamento e Análise Estatística, 1987, Análise Matemática, 2d edit., 1980; contbr. numerous articles to profl. jours. Recipient Medal of Bicentenary of Piracicaba, Municipality of Piracicaba, 1967, Medal Prudente de Morais, Hist. and Geog. Inst. of Piracicaba, State of São Paulo, 1995. Home: Rua do Vergueiro 514 ap 51, 13400770 Piracicaba Brazil Office: Revista de agricultura, Caixa Postal 60, 13400770 Piracicaba Brazil

PIMPARKAR, BHALCHANDRA DATTATRAYA, gastroenterologist, educator; b. Vairag, India, June 30, 1923; s. Dattatraya Narhar and Laxmi (Diwakar) P.; m. Deshmukh Kusum Vinayak, June 15, 1947; children: Vivek, Sandhya, Aruna, Neeta. MB BS, Seth G.S. Med. Coll., Bombay, India, 1950; DSc, U. Pa., 1960. House physician TN Med. Coll., Bombay, India, 1950; resident Freedmen's Hosp., Howard U., Washington, 1954-57; instr. U. Pa., Phila., 1957-60; hon. asst. prof. Seth G.S. Med. Coll., Bombay, 1963-70, prof. medicine, 1970-81, prof. emeritus, 1981—; hon. physician Bombay Hosp., 1965-81, hon. dir., 1978-81; hon. physician Nanawati (India) Hosp., 1961—; hon. physician to gov., Govt. Maharashtra, Bombay, 1972—. Contbg. author: (textbook) Gastroenterology, 1964, 74, 84. Recipient fellowship World Congress of Gastroenterology, Copenhagen, 1972. Fellow Nat. Acad. Med. Sci. (India), Indian Coll. Physicians, Am. Coll. Gastroenterology; mem. Indian Soc. of Gastroenterology (pres. 1981). Avocations: farming, gardening, reading. Home: 708 Cumballa Crest, 42 Peddar Rd, Bombay 400026, India Office: Laud Mansion, M Karve Rd, Bombay 400004, India

PIMPINELLA, RONALD JOSEPH, retired surgeon; b. Utica, N.Y., Sept. 27, 1935; s. Joseph and Josephine (Payne) P.; B.A. magna cum laude, Syracuse U., 1956; M.D., U. Rochester, 1960; children: Andrea, Giancarlo. Intern, Albany (N.Y.) Med. Center, 1960-61; resident in ear-nose-throat Columbia Presbyn. Med. Ctr., 1962-65; chief ENT, Martin Army Hosp., Ft. Benning, Ga., 1965-67; practice medicine specializing in otolaryngology and facial plastic surgery, Torrington, Conn., 1967-88; ret.; chief otolaryngology Charlotte Hungerford Hosp. Capt. U.S. Army, 1965-67. Fellow Am. Assn. Ophthalmology and Otolaryngology, Am. Acad. Facial Plastic and Reconstructive Surgery, ACS; mem. AMA, Conn. Med. Soc. (pres. otolaryngology sect. 1978-83). Roman Catholic. Contbr. articles to med. jours. Home: Laurel Run 1900 SE Clatter Bridge Rd Ocala FL 34471

PINA DE SILVA, FERNANDO ANTONIO, tribology educator, researcher; b. Lisbon, Portugal, Nov. 9, 1946; s. Fernando Cerqueira and Maria Salette (Ribeiro) Silva; m. Sara Figueira de Sousa, Sept. 7, 1972; 1 child, Paulo Fernando. Diploma Mech. Engring., Lisbon Tech. U., 1971; diploma, Imperial Coll., London, 1979, PhD, 1979. Rsch. engr. Ford Portugal, Azambuja, 1972; chief engr. Carris, Lisbon, 1979-80; asst. lectr. tribology Higher Tech. Inst., Lisbon Tech. U., 1971-76, asst. prof., 1977-87, assoc. prof., 1988-99, v.p. sci. coun., 1988-91; dir. Assn. Devel. J.S.T., Liston, 1989; gen. sec. Portuguese Soc. Materials, Lisbon, 1994-98. Mem. Table Elector Coun., London, 1975. Grante Calouste Gulbenkian, Lisbon, 1971; fellow NATO, Brussels, Lisbon, 1998. Fellow Instn. Engrs. (bd. dirs. 1996-99); mem. Am. Soc. Lubrication Engrs. Roman Catholic. Avocations: model making, oil painting. Office: Lisbon Tech U Inst High Tec, Ave Rovisco Pais, 1096 Lisbon Codex Estrema, Portugal

PINAULT, LOUIS PIERRE, veterinarian, educator; b. Menigoute, France, July 6, 1942; s. Elie Fernand and Suzanne (Marcireau) P.; m. Danielle Jacqueline Rousseau, July 16, 1966; 1 child, Laurent. Degree, Grad. Vet.

Sch., Alfort, France, 1965; DVM, Medicine Faculty, Paris, 1966; MS, U. Paris, 1972. Prof. asst. Vet. Sch., Alfort, 1967-78; prof. Vet. Sch., Dakar, Senegal, 1978-79; prof. Vet. Sch., Nantes, France, 1979—, dean, 1985-87, dept. head, 1994—; expert F. Pharmacopoeia, Paris, 1976-83, Ministry of Agriculture, Paris, 1986-93; cons. Vet. Medicine Labs., 1978-99; dir. Animal Anti-Poison Ctr., Nantes, 1992-99; French gFARAD access Ctr., 1999. Contbr. articles to profl. jours. Mem. (chmn.) French Commn. Mktg. Authorization for Vet. Medicine, Com. Animal Nutrition, French Toxicology Soc. Roman Catholic. Avocations: travel, music, boating. E-mail: pinault@vet-nantes.fr. Home: 152 Rue Paul Bellamy, 44000 Nantes France Office: Ecole Nationale Veterinaire, La Chantrerie BP 40706, 44307 Nantes Cedex 03, France

PINCHER, (HENRY) CHAPMAN, investigative writer, novelist, journalist; b. Ambala, India, Mar. 29, 1914; s. Richard Chapman Pincher and Helen Foster; m. Constance Sylvia Wolstenholme; children: Patricia, Michael. BS with honors, London U., 1936; grad., Mil. Coll. Sci., Shrivenham, U.K., 1943; LittD (hon.), Newcastle U., Newcastle-upon-Tyne, U.K., 1979. Staff dept. biology Liverpool (Eng.) Inst., 1936-46; def., sci. and med. editor Daily Express, London, 1946-79, asst. editor, freelance writer. Author: Breeding of Farm Animals, 1946, A Study of Fishes, 1947, Into the Atomic Age, 1947, Spotlight on Animals, 1950, Evolution, 1950, (with Bernard Wicksteed) It's Fun Finding Out, 1950, Sleep, and How to Get More of It, 1954, Sex in Our Time, 1973, Inside Story, 1978, Their Trade is Treachery, 1981, Too Secret Too Long, 1984, The Secret Offensive, 1985, Traitors-the-Labyrinths of Treason, 1987, A Web of Deception, 1987, The Truth about Dirty tricks, 1991, One Dog and Her Man, 1991, (autobiography) Pastoral Symphony, 1993, A Box of Chocolates, 1993, Life's a Bitch!, 1996, Tight Lines!, 1997; author: (novels) Not with a Bang, 1965, The Giantkiller, 1967, The Penthouse Conspirators, 1970, The Skeleton at the Villa Wolkonsky, 1975, The Eye of the Tornado, 1976, The Four Horses, 1978, Dirty Tricks, 1980, The Private World of St. John Terrapin, 1982, Contamination, 1989; contbr. numerous articles to sci., agrl. and sporting jours.; rschr. in genetics. Served to capt. Royal Armored Corps, 1940-46. Recipient Journalist of Yr. award Granada TV, 1964, Reporter of Decade award Granad TV, 1964. Fellow King's Coll. London. Avocations: fishing, shooting. Home and Office: Church House, Church House 16 Church St, Kintbury Hungerford RG17 9TR, England

PINCHESON, EDWARD, economic consultant, analyst; b. London, Aug. 21, 1938; s. Boris and Olga (Shakaroff) P.; m. Denise Barda, Sept. 14, 1987; children: Dorian. BA in Geography, London Sch. Econs., 1961; diploma in Urban Planning, Birmingham Sch. Art, 1963, Univ. London, 1979. Planning asst. Gerald Eve & Co. Cons., London, 1963-65; town planning officer Greater London Coun., London, 1965-71; planning asst. France, Switzerland, Israel, 1971-75; ind. cons. London, 1975—; tech. translator Inst. d'Amenagement et d'Urbanisme de la Region Ile-de France, Paris, 1963-79; vis. lectr. Polytech. South Bank, London, 1976-97; asst. prof. City Univ., Richmond Coll., The Am. Coll. London; econ. cons. London, 1975—. Author: Business Opportunities in Spain, 1986, Business Opportunities in Turkey, 1987, Madrid-A European Investment Region, 1991, The East European Automotive Sector, 1994, Textiles and Clothing in Eastern Europe: An Industry in Transition, 1995; contbr. articles to profl. jours. Mem. Royal Inst. Internat. Affairs, Royal Town Planning Inst., Royal Geographical Soc. Avocations: photography, skiing, travel, writing. Office: Eastern Profiles, 67/68 Hatton Garden Ste 50, London EC1N8JY, England

PINCKAERS, SERVAIS THÉODORE, theologian; b. Liège, Belgium, Oct. 30, 1925; s. Théodore and Elisabeth (Charlier) P. Lic. in Theology, Dominican House Study, Huy, Belgium, 1952; ThD, Angelicum, Rome, 1953. Prof. moral theology Dominican House Study, Huy, Belgium, 1953-67, U. Fribourg, Switzerland, 1973-96; emeritus prof. Albertinum, Fribourg; dean studies dept. theology U. Fribourg, 1989-91; internat. theol. commn. Cath. Ch., Rome, 1993-97. Contbr. articles to profl. jours. Recipient Magister in Theologia award Dominican Order, 1991. Roman Catholic. Avocation: hiking. Home: Sq Des Places 2, 1700 Fribourg Switzerland

PINDER, ERIC JAMES, archivist; b. Wakefield, Yorkshire, Eng., Mar. 10, 1942; s. George and Elsie (Grace) P.; m. Susan Kay Smith, Sept. 14, 1963; children: John, Timothy, Lisa. Degree in elec. engring., Leeds Coll. Tech., Yorkshire, 1963; higher nat. cert. in elect. engring., Doncaster Coll., Yorkshire, 1970; cert. in tech. edn., Huddersfield Coll., Yorkshire, 1974. cons. on weights and measures, Doncaster, 1971. Apprentice Ctrl. Electricity Generating Bd., Eng., 1958-63, elect. fitter, 1963-67; lectr. Doncaster Coll., 1967-90; archive supr. Filey (Eng.) Town Coun., 1999—. Author: (series) Electricity in Dancaster, 1997-2000. Recipient City and Guilds Full Technol. cert. C&G London. Mem. Soc. for the History Tech., Brit. Soc. for the History Sci., South Yorkshire Indsl. History Soc. Avocations: chess, model engineering, programming computers, bowling. Home: 1 St Martins Villas Flat 2, South Crescent Ave, No Yorks Filey YO14 9JW, England

PINDYCK, BRUCE EBEN, lawyer, corporate executive; b. N.Y.C., Sept. 21, 1945; s. Sylvester and Lillian (Breslow) P.; m. Mary Ellen Schwartz, Aug. 18, 1968; children: Ashley Beth, Eben Spencer, Blake Michael Lawrence. AB, Columbia U., 1967, JD, 1970, MBA, 1971. Bar: N.Y. 1971, Wis. 1987. Assoc. Olwine, Connelly, Chase, O'Donnell & Weyher, N.Y.C., 1971-80; asst. gen. counsel Peat, Marwick, Mitchell & Co., N.Y.C., 1980-82; ptnr. Hollyer, Jones, Pindyck, Brady & Chira, N.Y.C., 1983-87; pres., CEO Meridian Industries, Inc., Milw., 1985—; also chmn. bd. dirs. Meridian Industries, Inc.; CEO Majilite Corp., Dracut, Mass., 1987—; also chmn. bd. dirs. Majilite Corp.; mem. capital campaign com. Columbia U., 1984-87. Bd. dirs. Harambee Cmty. Sch., 1991-96, Milw. Ballet Co., 1993-97, Milw. Pub. Mus., 1994-98. Mem. Columbia Coll. Alumni Assn. (regional dir. 1988-94, v.p. 1994-98, exec. com., 1994-98), World Pres.'s Orgn. Address: 100 E Wisconsin Ave Milwaukee WI 53202-4107

PINE, BESSIE MIRIAM, social worker, editor, columnist; b. Toronto, Jan. 6, 1919; d. Moses and Annie (Rosenberg) Hadler; m. Kurt Pine, Mar 24, 1943 (dec. May 1962); children: Alfred Marc, Annie Laurie Reuveni. BA in Psychology, U. Toronto, 1939; M in Social Work, U. Pitts., 1944. Lic. social worker, N.Y. Br. dir. YM-YWHA, Toronto, 1940-42; case worker Family Svc. of Greater New Haven, Conn., 1944-47, Jewish Family Svc., Phila., 1947-49; divsn. unit supr. Ednl. Alliance, N.Y.C., 1949-51; older adult supr. Kings Bay YM-YWHA, Bklyn., 1955-59; editor pers. reporter Jewish Comty Ctr. Program Aids, dir. part time pers. bur., N.Y.C., 1962-67; assoc. dir. pers. svcs. Jewish Comty. Ctrs. Assn., N.Y.C., 1967-93. Editor: (booklet) Viewpoints on Social and Social Work Issues, 1965; author: (rsch. study) Making Retirement Count: Options and Opportunities, 1989; author: (publ.) Looking Back and Looking Forward: A 75 Year Retrospective on the Assn. of Jewish Center Workers, 1993. Recipient Florence G. Heller award Jewish Comty. Ctrs. Assn., N.Y.C., 1994. Mem. Com. to Strengthen Group Work in Jewish Comty. Ctrs. (co-chair 1992-99), Assn. of Jewish Ctr. Profls. (columnist Ask Bessie 1994—, Profl. of Yr., Phila. 1990, Tikkun Olam award Balt. 1993), Nat. Assn. Social Workers (cert. social worker). Home: 150 Beaumont St Brooklyn NY 11235-4119

PINE, MARTIN E., management consultant, technology consultant; b. Washington, 1955; s. Irvin and Doris Pine. BS in Bus. and Mgmt. (Fin. and Mktg.), U. Md., 1978, BS in Computer Sci., 1981. Sys. analyst Advanced Sys. Tech., 1979-82; sr. con. Price Waterhouse, 1982-83; pres., chief tech. officer, prin. cons. Pine Sys., 1983-98; CEO, chmn. Methodplex, 1998—; mng. dir. Internat. Consortium Time-Oriented Cons., 1998—; writer, presenter numerous info. sys. modeling courses, workshops, and seminars. Editor-in-chief, pub. (E-zine) The Eleventh Hour, 1998—; co-writer: (TV) Father's Day, Courtroom Instruction; creator: (computer aided software engring. tool) Demand Users Environment, (analytical modeling) Time-Oriented Technology, (requirements engring.) Time-Oriented Methodolgies, Computational Paradigm, SST (Strategy-Strategic Theory), SIMPLE (Strategic Info. Modeling and Process Logic for Enterprises), Hyperabstraction, Enterprise Evolution, Quality-Centric Modeling, Process Continuum Framework, Strategic Enterprise Model, TOTAL (Time-Oriented Technology for Accurate Logic), ALIVE (Autonomous Logic for Interactive Virtual Environments), EVOLVE (Engineering Volital Oporations and Logic for Virtual Enterprises), UTOPIA (Universal Time-Oriented Process for Intelligent Analysis); writer numerous stories; voice-over work in TV. Campaign advisor Charles Janus 7th cir., Circuit Ct. Judge contender, Md., 1994. Mem. Software Maintenance Assn., Java Developer Connection, Netpreneur, Delta Sigma Pi, American Soc. for Quality (mem. Quality Mgmt. Divn., Cmty. Quality Coun., Product Safety and Liability Interest Group). E-mail: mpine@methodplex.com. Office: Methodplex PO Box 2452 Gaithersburg MD 20886-2452

PINE, WILLIAM CHARLES, foundation executive; b. Canton, Ill., Nov. 4, 1912; s. William Charles and Katherine Pauline (Prichard) P.; m. Virginia Rae Keeley, June 14, 1945; children: William Charles, Barry Scott, Nancy Katherine Pine McMahon. BS, Monmouth Coll., Ill., 1939; DHL (hon.), Southwestern at Memphis, 1961; Dr.Laws (hon.), Mercy Coll. Detroit, 1966. Asst. dir. admissions Monmouth Coll., 1939-42; spl. agt. FBI, 1942-45; assoc. dir. Am. City Bur., N.Y.C. and Chgo., 1945-47; dir. pub. relations Lake Forest (Ill.) Coll., 1947-48, v.p., 1948-51; dir. scholarship prog. Ford Motor Co. Fund., Dearborn, Mich., 1951-72; asst. dir. Ford Motor Co. Fund., 1972-75; prog. dir. The Collins Found., Portland, Oreg., 1976-79; exec. v.p. The Collins Found., 1979-97; grant advisor Providence St. Vincent Med. Found., 1997—. Contbr. articles to profl. jours. Mem. Historic Records Adv. Bd., Salem, Oreg., 1984-87. Mem. Soc. Former Spl. Agts. of FBI. Avocations: reading, mail order bus. Office: Providence St Vincent Med Found 9205 SW Barnes Rd Portland OR 97225-6603

PINEAU-VALENCIENNE, DIDIER, industrialist; b. Paris, Mar. 21, 1931; s. Maurice and Madeleine (Dubigeon) P.-V.; m. Guillemette Rident; 4 children. Student, U. Dartmouth; postgrad. in bus., Harvard U.; diploma, Ecole des Hautes Etudes Commerciales. Mgmt. attaché Banque Parisienne Pour l'Industrie, 1958-62, sec. mgmt., 1962-64, dir., 1964-67, gen. dir., administrator, 1969-71; pres., CEO Société Carbonisation et Charbons Actifs Ceca, 1972-74, Société Resogil, 1975-76; dir. gen. Société Celogil, 1975-76; dir. mgmt. control and strategic planning Rhône-Poulenc S.A., 1976-77, dir. gen. divsns. polymers and petrochemicals, mem. exec. com., 1978; pres., CEO Schneider S.A. and Schneider Elec. S.A., 1981—; hon. chmn. Schneider Electric SA; bd. dirs. Société Industrielle et Agricole de Pointe à Pitre, Rhône Poulenc, Compagnie Générale d'Industrie et de Participations, Equitable, Sema Group Plc; mem. European adv. bd. Bankers Trust Co.; mem. supr. bd. AXA-UAP, Banque Paribas; mem. adv. bd. Banque de France, Booz Allen & Hamilton. Bd. dirs. Univ. Tech. Compiègne, 1992—. Decorated Officer de la Légion d'Honneur Nat. Order Merit; named Mgr. of Yr. Le Nouvel Economiste, 1991. Mem. Inst. Bus. (hon. pres. 1993—), Alumni Assn. Ecole des Hautes Etudes Commerciales (head). Home: 12 rue des Pins, 92100 Boulogne Billancourt, France Office: Schneider SA, 43-45 Blvd Franklin-Roosevelt, F-92500 Rueil-Malmaison France*

PINEDA, ANSELMO, neurosurgery educator; b. Lima, Peru, Apr. 3, 1923; s. Anselmo Vicente and Juana (Munayco)P.; m. Monique Yvonne Martin, Mar. 15, 1955; children: Patricia M., Richard A., Gilbert V., Katherine A. MD, San Marcos U., Lima, 1951; MS, Northwestern U., 1962. Diplomate Am. Bd. Neurol. Surgery. Rotating intern Loayza Hosp., Lima, 1950-51; head histology sect. Leprosy dept. Ministry Pub. Health, Lima, 1951; asst. pathologist Nat. Inst. Neoplastic Diseases, 1952; vol. asst. lab. normal and path. histology nervous system San Marcos U. Sch. Medicine, 1953; rotating intern Augustana Hosp., Chgo., 1954, resident in gen. surgery, 1955; jr. asst. resident in neurosurgery U. Chgo., 1955-56, sr. asst. resident in neurosurgery, 1956-57, chief resident in neurosurgery, 1957-58; assoc. instr. neurosurgery U. Tex., 1958-61; assoc. neurosurgeon John Sealy Hosp., Galveston, Tex., 1960-61, attending neurosurgeon, 1961; acting chief neurosurgery VA Hosp., Long Beach, Calif., 1962-63; asst. clin. prof. dept. biology UCLA, 1963-82, assoc. clin. prof. divsn. neuro-biology, 1982—; cons. VA Hosp., Long Beach, 1966-67. NIH spl. fellow in Neuroanatomy Northwestern U., 1961-62. Fellow ACS, Am. Coll. Angiology, Royal Soc. Medicine; mem. AAUP, AAAS, AMA, Congress of Neurol. Surgeons, World Med. Assn., Am. Assn. Neurol. Surgeons, Calif. Med. Assn., Orange County Med. Assn., Am. Acad. Neurology, Am. Assn. Neuropathologists, Internat. Coll. Surgeons, Am. Assn. Anatomists, Am. Assn. Trauma, Am. Soc. Stereotaxic and Functional Neurosurgery, N.Y. Acad. Scis., Internat. Assn. Study Pain, Sigma Xi. E-mail: mp128@aol.com. Home: 16571 Carousel Ln Huntington Beach CA 92649-2115 Office: 2880 Atlantic Ave Long Beach CA 90806-1714

PINEDA, ROSEMARIE DEL ROSARIO, communications executive; b. Manila, The Philippines, Sept. 8, 1954; d. Bernardo and Maria Luisa (Manlangit) del Rosario; m. Rafael Antonio Pamatmat Vera, Sept. 17, 1981 (annulled 1986); m. Leonardo Pontecilla Pineda, Dec. 7, 1996; children: Rudolph Leonard, Rachel Larisse, Roberto Rafael. BS in Food Tech., U. of the Philippines, 1977, postgrad., 1978. Quality control lab. asst., mktg. asst. Purefoods Corp., Manila, 1977-82; product mgr. Kimberly Clark, Manila, 1982-86; sr. product mgr. Bristol Myers Squibb, Manila, 1986-88; mktg. mgr. First Pacific Metro Corp., Manila, 1989-91; dir. mktg. svcs. Pepsi Cola Products Philippines, Inc., Manila, 1992-96; v.p. internat. long distance mktg. Bayan Telecom. Inc., Manila, 1996—. Avocations: travel, swimming, bowling, reading, playing the piano.

PIÑEIRO, ENRIQUE LUIS, dairy company executive; b. Buenos Aires, June 29, 1934; s. Enrique Alberto and Lia Rosa (Pagliere) P.; m. Carolina E. Barros, Mar. 1975; children: Patricia, Marcela, Florencia, Dolores, Carolina, Marcela. Ingeniero Agrónomo, U. Buenos Aires, 1957; MS, La. State U., Baton Rouge, 1960. Prodn. mgr. La Vacongada SA, Buenos Aires, 1967-82, La Martona SA, Buenos Aires, 1967-82; prodn. dir. Interglas SA, Sevilla, Spain, 1982-85; prodn. mgr. Mastellone Hnos SA, Buenos Aires, 1985-90, also bd. dirs.; CEO CONTEC, Buenos Aires, 1989—; hon. joint prof. U. Buenos Aires, 1967-69; prof. Food and Agrl. Orgn., Brazil, 1972, 74, U. E. de Campinhas, Brazil, 1974; mem. Com. Tech. Lactea Centro de la Industria Lechera, Buenos Aires, 1975—. Contbr. articles to profl. jours. Pvt. Argentina Air Force, 1955. Scholar U. Buenos Aires, 1958, C. de Inves C. y Tecnicas, 1958, FAO, 1966, 73, 76, ACTIM, 1975. Mem. Soc. Argentina de Tecnologia Lactea (pres. 1970-75). Avocations: horses, farming, carpintry, bicycle. Office: Contec, San Martin 987 5 Office D, 1004 Buenos Aires Argentina Home: Av Libertador 2602 6to C, 1425 Buenos Aires Argentina

PINERI, RICCARDO, Italian literature and philosophy educator; b. Cesana, Turin, Italy, Aug. 27, 1948; arrived in France, 1973; s. Angelo and Pia (Audisio) P.; m. Ilda Sanquer, Apr. 13, 1977; 1 child, Teiva. PhD, U. Turin, 1973, U. Montpellier, France, 1979; Docteur d'Etat ès-Lettres, U. Montpellier, France, 1989. Lectr. U. Toulouse, France, 1973-81, asst. prof., 1981-90; assoc. prof. U. Montpellier, 1990-93, prof., 1993—; seminar dir. Aesthetics and Italian Philosophy, U. Montpellier, 1993. Editor: Île Matière de Polynesie, 1992, Leopardi Le Retrait de la Voix, 1994, Presence de G.B. Vico, 1996, A.H. Gouwe, Peintre de Polynésie, 1998. Mem. Soc. Etudes Oceaniennes. E-mail: pineri@smr1.univ-montp3.fr. Office: U Paul Valéry, Montpellier 3, 34032 Montpellier France

PINES, WAYNE LLOYD, public relations counselor; b. Washington, Dec. 31, 1943; s. Jerome Martin and Ethel (Schnall) P.; m. Nancy Freitag, Apr. 16, 1966; children: Noah Morris, Jesse Mireth. BA, Rutgers U., 1965; postgrad., George Washington U., 1969-71. Reporter, city editor Middletown (N.Y.) Times Herald-Record, 1965-68; copy editor Reuters News, 1968-69; assoc. editor FDC Reports, Washington, 1969-72; chief Consumer Edn. and Info., FDA; also editor FDA Consumer, 1972-74; exec. editor Product Safety Letter and Devices and Diagnostics Letter, Washington, 1974-75; dep. asst. commr. for pub. affairs, chief press rels. FDA, Rockville, Md., 1975-78, assoc. commr. pub. affairs, 1978-82; spl. asst. to dir. NIMH, 1982-83; sr. v.p., sr. counselor Burson-Marsteller, 1983-87, exec. v.p., dir. med. issues, 1987-93; pres. regulatory svcs. APCO Assocs., Washington, 1993—; dir. crisis com. APCO Assocs.; sr. counselor Grey Healthcare Group, 1993—; mng. dir. Comms. Ptnrs. and Assocs., 1999—; adj. prof. Washington Public Affairs Ctr., U. So. Calif., 1980-81; instr. N.Y.U. Sch. Continuing Edn., 1982-84; instr. Profl. Devel. Inst., 1983-85; mem. adv. bd. Nat. Orgn. Rare Disorders, Orphan Med.; mem. corp. adv. bd. ANA; chmn. Therametrix Inc., 1999—; columnist WebMD, 1999—, Med. Advt. News, 1985-90. Author: The Sermons of Jerome Martin Pines, FDA Advertising and Promotional Manual, When Lightning Strikes: A How-to Crisis Manual, A Practical Guide to Food and Drug Law and Regulation, How to Work with the FDA; contbr. numerous articles in field to profl. jours. Home: 5821 Nevada Ave NW Washington DC 20015-2547 Office: APCO Assocs 1615 L St NW Washington DC 20036-5610

PINET, JEAN MAURICE, aeronautics consultant; b. Toulouse, France, Sept. 13, 1929; s. André and Suzanne (Pascal) P.; m. Claudine Pierrette Rouat, Mar. 28, 1955; children: Marie-Laure, Marie-Annick, Jean-Yves, Marie Helene. Diploma in engring., ENSAM, 1949; diploma in civil aeronautical engring., ENSAE, 1952. Pilot missiles flight tests Centre d'Essais-en-Vol, Bretigny-Sur-Orge, France, 1956-61, Erprobungs Stelle 61 der Bundeswehr, Manching, Germany, 1962-65; pilot Concorde flight tests Sud-Avation/Aerospatiale, Toulouse, France, 1965-84; pilot airbus flight tests Airbus Industrie, Toulouse, 1973-89; pilot flight tng., pres. Aeroformation, Toulouse, 1971-94; cons. pvt. practice, Toulouse, France, 1994—; pres. EURISCO Inst.; co-chmn. Icarus Com. Contbr. articles to profl. jours. Lt. French Air Force, 1955-56. Mem. Terre D'Envol, Soc. Exptl. Test Pilots, French Acad. Air and Space (past pres.). Achievements include being the first pilot to fly a transport aircraft beyond Mach 1. Home: 20 Rue Sainte-Ursule, 31000 Toulouse France Office: SEDITEC, AEROCONSEIL, 3 Rue Dieudonne Costes BP75, 31703 Blagnac France

PING, JEAN, Gabonese government official. Former min. mines, energy and hydraulic resources Gabonese Republic, former min. fgn. affairs and coop., former min. del. of finance, min. of planning, now min. of fgn. affairs and cooperation. Mem. Parti Démocratique Gabonais. Office: Min of Fgn Affairs and, Cooperation BP 2245, Libreville Gabon*

PING, XIN QIAO, economics educator, researcher; b. Zhe Jiang, China, May 12, 1954; s. Zhang Gen Ping and Lai Xia Sheng; divorced; 1 child, Ting-yu. Diploma, East China Normal U., Shanghai, 1973; MA, Peking U., Beijing, 1985, Cornell U., 1996; PhD, Cornell U., 1998. Asst. prof. East China Normal U., 1973-78; lectr. Peking U., 1986-89, assoc. prof.; assoc. prof. econs., dep. head dept. Tsinghua U., Beijing, 1998—. Author: Public Finance and Comparative Finance System, 1992, Investment, Cash Flow and the Problem of Soft-budget Constraint in the Market Transition of China, 1998. Avocation: swimming. Office: Tsinghua U, Sch Econs and Mgmt, Beijing 100084, China

PINHEIRD, PATRICIA RODRIGUEZ, science educator; b. Fortaleza, Brazil, Dec. 7, 1956; d. Simplicio Messias and Maria Eugenia Rodriguez (Carvalho) P. Degree in fishery engring., Fed. U. Ceará, Fortaleza, Brazil, 1980; MSc in Biology, Nat. Inst. for Amasonian Rsch., Manaus, Brazil, 1985, PhD in Biology, 1996. Rschr. INPA, 1985-86; prof. Fed. U. Ceará, 1996—; presenter in field. Contbr. chpt. to book. Mem. Am. Soc. Limnology and Oceanography, Coastal Edn. Rsch. Found., N.Y. Acad. Scis. Roman Catholic. Avocation: nature photography. Office: U Fed Ceara Dept Engenharia, Caixa Postal 12168, 60455760 Forttaleza Cerá, Brazil

PINHEIRO FILHO, JOAO DE DEUS, physics educator, researcher; b. Ico, Ceara, Brazil, Aug. 5, 1947; s. Joao De Deus and Lais Castelo (Branco) Pinheiro; m. Polly Maria Japuhy, Aug. 3, 1985; children: Anderson, Rafael, Samuel, Lais. Lic. in Physics, U. Fed. Rio de Janeiro, 1970; MSc, Ctr. Brasileiro Pesquisas Fisicas, Rio de Janeiro, 1976, PhD, 1983. Tchr. physics Liceu, Fortaleza, Brazil, 1966-67, Moderna Assn. Brasileira Ensino, Rio de Janeiro, 1968; assoc. prof. U. Fed. Fluminense, Niteroi, Brazil, 1971-97, dir. physics inst., 1987; prof. Instituto Militar de Engenharia, Rio de Janeiro, 1998; tchr. physics Colegio Indsl. Leao XIII, Itaborai, Rio de Janeiro, 1998—, Centro Educacional Marica, J.B. Rangel, Marica, Rio de Janeiro, 1999—; asst. meteorologist Inst. Telecom. Aeronauticas Soc. Anonima, Rio de Janeiro, 1968-70; tchr. math. Assn. Crista Mocos, Rio de Janeiro, 1971; vis. prof. Lab. N. Frascati/U. di Rome, 1986, 1988, 1990; cons. Com. Mcpl. Medicina Nuc., Niteroi, 1988-89; assoc. rschr. U. Calif., Berkeley, 1994-97; spkr. in field. Contbr. articles to profl. jours. Sec. local cmty. Agrobrasil, 1989-92. Grantee Fundacao Amparo Pesquisa Rio de Janeiro, 1988-90, Fin. Projetos, 1988-97, Cons. Nac. Pesq., 1988-96. Mem. Soc. Brazilian Progresso Ciencia, Soc. Brazilian Fisica, Assn. Brazilian Energy Nuc. Roman Catholic. Avocations: soccer, travel, backgammon, walking. Home: Rua 27 S/N Agrobrasil, CX Postal 98302, 28695-000 Rio de Janeiro Brazil

PINHO, RUI ANTONIO, engineering executive; b. Porto, Portugal, Dec. 13, 1949; s. José Fernandes Pinho and Idalina Silva Cruz; m. Maria Candida, Sept. 8, 1973. Licenciatura, Porto U., 1974. Prodn. mgr. Sid. Nacional, Maia, Portugal, 1978-91; planning mgr. Ferfor, S.A., Porto, 1991-95; plant mgr. Fico Cables, Limitada, Maia, 1995-96, mng. dir., 1997—; asst. conv. U. Porto, 1979-92. Furrel mil. Army, 1970-74. Avocations: sailing. Office: Fico Cables Lda, Rua do Cavaco 115, P-4470 Maia Portugal

PINILLOS ASHTON, LUIS V., radiologist, educator; b. Lima, Peru, Feb. 1, 1945; s. Luis V. Pinillos Ganoza and Elsie E. Ashton de Pinillos; m. Teresa G. Casabonne; children: Patricia, Mariana, Luis Felipe. MD, U. Cayetano Heredia, Lima, 1970; diploma in med. radiotherapy, U. Manchester, Eng., 1973. Radiotherapist level V Nat. Cancer Inst., Lima, 1973—, gen. dir., 1985-90; prof. U. Cayetano Heredia, Lima, 1973—, head acad. dept. radiology, 1993-96; min. of health Ministry Health, Lima, 1988-89; pres. Oncosalud, Lima, 1991—. Authro: La Salud En El Peru, 1998, Problematica Del Sector Salud, 1999, Un Año de Gestion, 1999; contbr. chpt. to book. Pres. Commn. Nacional Permanente du Lucha Antitabáquica, Peru, 1988-99, Com. L.Am. Coord. Actividades contra le Tabaquismo, S.Am., 1990-96; regional chmn. Union Internat. Contra el Cancer, L.Am., 1995-99. Recipient Daniel A. Carrion award Peru Govt., 1988, Hipolito Unanue award Peru Govt., 1988, Paho medal Paho, L.Am., 1990. Fellow Royal Coll. Radiologists Eng.; mem. Peruvian Cancer Soc. (pres. 1987-88), Am. Soc. Ther Radiology and Oncology, Peruvian Radiol. Soc. (pres. 1987-88). Office: Inst Enfermedades Neoplasic, Av Angamos Este 2520, Surquillo Lima, Peru

PINKER, BRIAN WINDEN, publisher; b. Worthing, Sussex, Eng., Oct. 1, 1947; s. Gordon M. and Joan Pinker; m. Wendy Sawyer; children: Jennifer, Samantha. BSc in Horticulture with honors, U. Reading, Eng., 1971. Registered marketer, Chartered Inst. Mktg. Workstudy officer Geest Mgmt. Svcs., 1971-72; account exec. Geest Hort. Group Ltd., 1972-74, project mgr., 1974-77, divsn. mgr., 1977-85; Sainsbury account mgr. Geest Industries, Ltd., Spalding, 1985-86; mng. dir. Burall Floraprint Ltd., Wisbech, 1986—; bd. dirs. Burall Ltd., Wisbech; mem. exec. com. Floraprint Internat. Est., Vaduz, Liechtenstein. Freeman, City of London. Mem. Hort. Trades Assn. (v.p., hon. treas.), Brit. Pot Plant Growers Assn. (vice chmn. 1979-80), The Workshipful Co. of Horners (liveryman 1973—), Inst. Dirs. Avocations: gardening, landscaping. Office: Burall Floraprint Ltd, Oldfield Ln, Wisbech Cambridgeshire PE13 2TH, England

PINKER, ROBERT ARTHUR, social administration educator; b. London, May 27, 1931; s. Joseph and Dora Elizabeth (Winyard) P.; m. Jennifer Farrington, June 14, 1955 (dec. Nov. 1994); children: Catherine, Lucy. Cert. in Social Sci., London Sch. Econs., 1959; BSc in Sociology, U. London, 1962, MSc in Econs., 1965. Probation officer London Probation Svc., 1955-58; rsch. worker London Sch. Econs., 1958-62; lectr. North Western Poly., London, 1962-64; head sociology dept. Goldsmiths Coll., London, 1964-72, Lewisham prof. social adminstrn., 1972-74; prof. social studies Chelsea Coll., London, 1974-78; prof. social work studies London Sch. Econs., 1978-93, prof. social adminstrn., 1993-96, emeritus prof., 1996—; pro-dir. London Sch. Econs., 1985-88; pro-vice chancellor U. London, 1989-90; coun. mem. Advt. Stds. Authority, London, 1988-95; privacy commr., mem. Press Complaints Commn., London, 1991—; editor Jour. Social Policy, 1977-81, chmn. bd., 1981-85; mem. Barclay com. Role & Tasks of Social Workers, London, 1981-82; chmn. editl. bd. Ageing & Soc., London, 1981-91; mem. Direct Mail Accreditation and Recognition Ctr., 1995-97. Author: English Hospital Statistics, 1966, Social Theory and Social Policy, 1971, The Idea of Welfare, 1979, Social Work in an Enterprise Society, 1990. Lt. Army, 1950-52, with Res., 1952-54. Hon. fellow Goldsmiths Coll., London, 1999—. Avocations: gardening, travel, Scrabble. Home: 76 Coleraine Rd, London SE3 7PE, England Office: London Sch Economics, Houghton St, London WC2A 2AE, England

PINKERTON, HARRY, volcanologist, lecturer; b. Hamilton, Scotland, Mar. 23, 1948; s. Andrew and Janet (Hall) P.; m. Gillian Margaret Ellis; children: Helen Jane, Anne Kirsty. BSc, Strathclyde U., Glasgow, 1969; PhD, Lancaster (Eng.) U., 1978. Rsch. fellow Lancaster U., 1973-75, lectr., 1975-94, sr. lectr., 1994-99, prof., 2000—, dir. Grad. Sch. Sci. and Engring., 1994-97. Contbr. articles to profl. jours. Fellow Geol. Soc. London; mem. Am. Geophys. Union, European Union Geoscis. Home: Highways, Clapham

Old Rd, Ingleton, Carnforth Lancaster LA6 3JA, England Office: Environ Sci Divsn, Lancaster U, Dept Environ Sci, Lancaster LA1 4YQ, England

PINKERTON, JAMES SAUNDERS, travel company executive, consultant; b. Naracoorte, Australia, July 21, 1940; s. Thomas Peter and Ruth Constance (Saunders) P. Cert., Scotch Coll., Adelaide, Australia, 1955; tourism diploma, Fgn. U., Perugia, Italy, 1976; advanced fares diploma, Lufthansa Sch., Germany, 1982. Stockman Dalgety & Co., Naracoorte, Australia, 1957-60; real estate clk. Saunders & Co., Adelaide, Australia, 1960-63; traveling edn., 1963-64; travel cons. TAA, Adelaide, Australia, 1964-68; co. dir. Travel Assocs., Sydney, Australia, 1972-88; exec., mgr. Wentworth Travel, Sydney, Australia, 1988-97; mem. Panam Travel Agt. Adv. Bd., Sydney, Australia, 1982-85, Australian Inst. Internat. Affairs, Sydney, Australia, 1975-82. Com. Young Liberals, Naracoorte, 1958-60. Fellow Australian Inst. Travel & Tourism; mem. Sydney Swans Football Club. Mem. Ch. of Eng. Achievements include opening Vietnam to Australian tourists in 1977; organization of first tour group to Vietnam after war ended. Avocations: reading, model railways, horse racing, golf, stamp collecting. Office: Wentworth Travel, 203 New South Head Rd, Sydney 2027, Australia

PINKERTON, ROBERT BRUCE, mechanical engineer; b. Detroit, Feb. 10, 1941; s. George Fulwell and Janet Lois (Hedke) P.; m. Barbara Ann Bandfield, Aug. 13, 1966; 1 child, Robert Brent. BSME, Detroit Inst. Tech., 1965; MA in Engring., Chrysler Inst. Engring., 1967; JD, Wayne State U., 1976. From mech. engr. to emissions and fuel economy planning specialist Chrysler Engring. Office Chrysler Corp., Highland Park, Mich., 1967-80; dir. engring. Replacement div. TRW, Inc., Cleve., 1980-83; v.p. engring. TRW Automotive Aftermarket Group, 1983-86; v.p. engring. and rsch. Blackstone Corp., Jamestown, N.Y., 1986-89; pres., CEO Blackstone Corp., Jamestown, 1989-90, Athena Corp., Beaufort, S.C., 1990—, Cedar Crest Corp., Beaufort, S.C., 1990—, Value Built Homes, 1998—; chmn., CEO Beaufort Land Co., 1998—; pres., CEO Classic Custom Homes, Hilton Head, S.C., 1999—; bd. dirs. VRI, LLC, Coastal Banking Co., Inc., Low Country Nat. Bank. Bd. dirs. Village Renaissance, Inc., 1994—, Carpenters Hall, 1996—, Coastal Banking Co., Inc., 1999—, Lowcountry Nat. Bank, 1999—; exec. com. Beaufort Schs. Oversight Com., 1995-99, Pvt. Industry Coun., 1996—. Mem. Gtr. Beaufort C. of C. (bd. dris. 1997—), Rotary (asst. dist. gov. 1997—) Beaufort Roundtable. Presbyterian. Home: PO Box 2417 Beaufort SC 29901-2417 Office: PO Box 2115 128 Castle Rock Rd Beaufort SC 29906-9047

PINKHAM, FREDERICK OLIVER, foundation executive, consultant; b. Ann Arbor, Mich., June 16, 1920; s. Frederick Oliver and Leah Winifred (Hallett) P.; m. Helen Kostia, June 20, 1943; children: Peter James, Gail Louise, Steven Howard. AB, Kalamazoo Coll., 1942, LLD (hon.), 1958; MA, Stanford U., 1947, EdD, 1950; LLD (hon.), Lawrence Coll., 1957; DSc (hon.), Ripon Coll., 1990. Tchr., counselor Sequoia Union High Sch., Redwood City, Calif., 1947-49; researcher Stanford (Calif.) Consultation Service, 1949-50; asst. to pres. George Washington U., 1950-51; exec. sec. Nat. Commn. on Accrediting, 1951-55; pres. Ripon (Wis.) Coll., 1955-66; dir. The Yardstick Project, Cleve., 1966-67; v.p., dir. Western Pub. Co., 1967-70; founder, pres. Edn. Mgmt. Services, Inc., 1970-76; asst. adminstr. for population and humanitarian affairs AID, Dept. State, 1976-77; chmn., pres. Population Crisis Com., 1977-87; assoc. dir. Inst. for Population and Resource Studies, Stanford U., 1987-90; program officer David and Lucile Packard Found., 1988-92; cons. for population David and Lucile Packard Found., Los Altos, Calif., 1993—; cons. True North Found., Portland, Oreg., 1993-97, Compton Found., Menlo Park, Calif., 1993-97, Mgmt. Scis. for Health, 1995-97, Poptech, Washington, 1995; v.p., dir. rsch. Ednl. Recs. Bur., Darien, Conn., 1970-72; founder, pres. Edn. Mgmt. Svcs., Inc., 1970-76; v.p., co-founder World Bus. Coun., 1970-77; pres. Capital Higher Edn. Svc., 1975-76; pres., dir. The Omni Group, 1977-83; treas., co-founder Monterey Peninsula coll. Found., 1994-00; cons. Program for the Topical Prevention of Conception and Disease Chgo. Rush U., 1999—. Chmn. Wis. adv. com. Nat. Commn. on Civil Rights; bd. visitors Air U.; pres. Wis. Found. of Ind. Colls.; chmn. Assn. colls. Midwest, Midwest Coll. Council; sec., trustee, mem. exec. com. Young Pres.'s Found.; chmn. task force on fgn. assistance Pres.'s Pvt. Sector Survey on cost Control (Grace Comm.); chmn. bd. Global Tomorrow Coalition, 1985-89; bd. dirs. Internat. Human Assistance Programs, N.Y.C., 1984-87, Mineral Fibre Internat. and Kings Mills Internat., 1986-90, Mgmt. Scis. for Health, 1997—; v.p. Big Sur Land Trust, 1990-00; founder Inst. Reproductive Health, Calif., 2000—. Served with AUS, 1942-45, ETO. Decorated Bronze Star, Purple Heart. Mem. Young Pres. Orgn. (nat. sec., dir., exec. com.), Soc. Internat. Devel., Nat. Heritage Soc. watchkeeper, bd. govs. Old Capital Club Monterey, Calif. (gov.). Home and Office: 8 Skyline Crst Monterey CA 93940-4111

PINKS, MARK DOUGLAS, social studies educator, musician; b. Lima, Ohio, Jan. 16, 1961; s. Oakie and Juanita P. BS, The Ohio State U., 1984; MS, Fla. Internat. U., 2000. Tchr. Ridgemont High Sch., Ridgeway, Ohio, 1985-87, Dade County Schs., Miami, Fla., 1987—. With USANG, 1979-85. Mem. Nat. Coun. for Social Studies. Avocation: old-time fiddle player. Home: 13715 SW 66th St Apt 210A Miami FL 33183-2235

PIN-MEI, IGNATIUS KUNG (GONG) CARDINAL See KUNG (GONG) PIN-MEI, IGNATIUS CARDINAL

PINNA, GRAZIANO, biologist, researcher; b. Oristano, Sardinia, Italy, Feb. 18, 1968; p. Michele Pinna and Luigina Vaccargiu. PhD in Neuropharmacology, U. Cagliari, Italy, 1993; M in Neuroendocrinology, Free U. Berlin, 1996, specialist in pharmacology, 2000. arrived in Germany, 1993;. Rschr. Schering AG, Berlin, 1993-94; rsch. scientist Free U. Berlin, 1994—; vis. scholar U. Ill., Chgo., 1997-98; cons. U. Naples (Italy) Federico II, 1997-98; advisor Clarke Inst. Psychiatry, Toronto, Can., 1998-99, Columbia U., N.Y.C., 1999-2000. Contbr. articles to profl. jours. Active Donazioni Latino Am., Italy, 1997—, AIDS-Hilfe, Berlin, 2000. Grantee Comett-Europian Cmty., Brussels, 1993, U. Cagliari, 1994, Deutsche Forschungsgemeinschaft, Germany, 1994, 97, Regione Sardegna, Sardinia, Italy, 1996, Human Frontiers Sci. Program Orgn., Strasbourg, France, 1998. Mem. German Assn. for Neurowissenschaft, Soc. for Neurosci. Roman Catholic. Achievements include invention of methods for hormones extraction and quantification in CNS. Avocations: sports, arts. Fax: 49 30 8445 2700. E-mail: gpinna@cipmail.ukbf.fu-berlin.de. Office: Free Univ Berlin, Hindenburgdamm 30, 12200 Berlin Germany

PINNER, STEPHEN JOHN, stockbroker; b. Aug. 23, 1951; s. Ronald Wilfred and Pamela Ethel (Goodacre) P.; divorced; children: Simon Edward, Hayley Jane; m. Ivy Murphy, Mar. 22, 1997. Dir. Extel, London, 1983-87; assoc. dir. Hoare Govett, London, 1985-87; dir. Fin. Clearing and Svcs. U.K. Ltd., London, 1985-87; mng. dir. Soc. Gen. Security Settlements, London, 1987-90; dir. City Cons., London, 1991-95, 1998; mng. dir. City Deal Svcs., London, 1993-97; dir. Summerson Goodacre, London, 1998—; mgr. Ctr. File Ltd., London, 1970-83; Strauss, London, 1967-90. Mem. S.I.O.M.C. (com. mem.), Securities Inst. Avocation: football. Office: Summerson Goodacre, 34 Artillery Lane, London E1 7LS, England

PINNISI, MICHAEL DONATO, lawyer, educator; b. Buffalo, N.Y., Oct. 12, 1960; s. Frank Joseph and Dolores Ann Pinnisi; m. Donna Lynn Heilweil, July 13, 1986; children: Kerry Lynn, Rose. AB cum laude, Cornell U., 1982, JD, 1985. Bar: N.Y. 1986, U.S. Dist. Ct. (so. dist.) N.Y. 1987, U.S. Dist. Ct. (no. dist.) N.Y. 1991, U.S. Dist. Ct. (we. dist.) N.Y. 1993, , U.S. Ct. Appeals (2d. cir.) 1988, U.S. Ct. Appeals (fed. cir.) 1998. Trial atty. honor program U.S. Dept. of Justice, Washington, 1985-87; assoc. atty. Shearman & Sterling, N.Y.C., 1987-88; asst. U.S. atty. U.S. Atty., So. Dist. N.Y., N.Y.C., 1988-91; assoc. atty. Cleary, Gottlieb, Steen & Hamilton, Washington, 1991-92; prin. atty. Pinnisi, Wagner et al, Ithaca, N.Y., 1992-97, Brown, Pinnisi and Michaels, Ithaca, 1997—; adj. prof. law Cornell Law Sch., Ithaca, 1992—; cert. arbitrator U.S. Dist. Ct. No. Dist. N.Y., 1993—; gen. counsel Kionix Inc., 1999—; spkr. in field. Dir. Ithaca Cmty. Childcare, 1993-94, F.I.R.S.T., Phila., 1996-97. Mem. ABA, N.Y. State Bar Assn., Tompkins County Bar Assn., Phi Delta Phi. Office: Brown Pinnisi & Michaels PC 400 M & T Bank Bldg 118 N Tioga St Ste 400 Ithaca NY 14850-4343

PINNIX, JOHN LAWRENCE, lawyer; b. Reidsville, N.C., Oct. 8, 1947; s. John Lawrence and Esther (Cobb) P.; m. Sally Auman, June 15, 1985; children: Jennifer Elizabeth Haigwood, William C. Haigwood. BA, U. N.C., Greensboro, 1969; JD, Wake Forest U., 1973; MA, U. N.C., Greensboro, 1975. Bar: N.C. 1973, D.C. 1981; U.S. Dist. Ct. (ea. dist.) N.C. 1977, U.S Dist. Ct. (mid. and we. dists.) N.C. 1981; U.S. Ct. Appeals (4th cir.) 1981; U.S. Supreme Ct. 1981. Assoc. Fagg, Fagg & Nooe, Eden, N.C., 1973-74; spl. counsel Adminstrv. Office of the Cts., Morganton, N.C., 1975-76; ptnr. Allen and Pinnix (formerly Barringer, Allen & Pinnix), Raleigh, N.C., 1977—; adj. N.C. Ctrl. U. Sch. Law, 1997; sr. lecturing fellow Duke U. Sch. Law, 1999—. Contbr. articles to profl. jours. Alt. del. Dem. Nat. Conv., Miami, 1972, mem. rules com., Washington and Atlanta, 1988; bd. dirs. Farmworkers Legal Svcs., Raleigh, 1990-92. Mem. Am. Immigration Lawyers Assn. (founding mem. Carolinas chpt. 1980, chpt. chair 1984-85, 87-88, nat. bd. govs. 1993-2000, sec. nat. exec. com. 1997-99, 2d v.p. 1999-2000, 1st v.p. 2000—), Am. Immigration Law Found. (trustee 1992-97, vice chair 1994-97), N.C. Bar Assn. (chmn. immigration and nationality law com. 1989-91), N.C. State Bar (bd. cert. immigration specialist, immigration law specialty com. bd. legal specialization 1996—), U. N.C. Greensboro Alumni Assn. (bd. dirs. 1975-76, bd. dirs. Excellence Found. 1995-97), Internat. Focus Inc. (bd. dirs. 1998-99), N.C. Bar Assn. (internat. law sect. coun. 1999—). Baptist. Avocations: photography, film, reading. Home: 125 Ammons Dr Raleigh NC 27615-6501

PINNOCK, TREVOR, conductor, harpsichordist; b. Canterbury, Kent, Eng., Dec. 16, 1946; s. Kenneth and Joyce (Muggleton) P. Degree, Royal Coll. Music, London, 1965; hon. degree, Royal Acad. Music, London, 1986; hon. doctorate, U. Ottawa, 1993. Joint founder Galliard Harpsichord Trio, London, 1966-71; harpsichordist, freelance condr., 1966—; mus. dir., founder The English Concert, London, 1972—; artistic dir., prin. condr. Nat. Arts Ctr. Orch., Ottawa, Can., 1991-96; artistic advisor Nat. Arts Ctr. Orch., Ottawa, 1996-97. Decorated comdr. Order Brit. Empire; recipient Edison prize, 1979, 80, 81, 83, 85, 87, Deutscher Schallplattenpreis, 1981, 92, Grande Prixe du Disque, 1984, 91, Grand Prix Nat., 1985, 91, Ritmo prize, 1987. Office: Askonas Holt Ltd Lonsdale Chamb, 27 Chancery Ln, London WC2A 1PF, England*

PINO-ICHAZO, RAUL OMAR, lawyer, educator; b. La Paz, Bolivia, Dec. 29, 1946; s. Sanchez Omar Pino-Ichazo and Bertha Maria Terrazas; m. Pilar Maria Estenssoro, Apr. 21, 1979 (div. June 1983); 1 child, Moira Pino-Ichazo Estenssoro. BS, La Salle U., La Paz, 1964, U. Munich, 1967; LLD, U. St. Andrews, La Paz, 1996. Diplomate atty., aeronautical right diplomate. Sales promotion officer Iberia Airlines, La Paz, 1969-72, sales mgr., 1972-76, gen. mgr., 1976-95; pres. Bolivian Aeronautical Inst., La Paz, 1993—; prof. Cath. U., La Paz, 1997—; bd. dirs. El Diario, La Paz. Author: Passengers Manual, 1985, Five Rights of the Air, 1987, Bilateral Contracts, Aviation Update, Aeronautical Legislation in America, 1992, Farewell to Drugs, 1999. Cons. Civic Com. of La Paz, 1996—. Diploma and honour medaille Aeronautical Ministry, La Paz, 1990, Aeronautical Sec., 1993, Ministry of Industry, Madrid, 1990. Mem. Aeronautical Inst., Skal Club. Roman Catholic. Avocation: writing.

PINON, ERIC MARIE DANIEL, finance company executive; b. Paris, May 1, 1959; s. Bernard Pinon and Françoise Pinon Bernier; m. Béatrice Le Vavasseur, Sept. 13, 1986; children: Axelle, Julie, Quentin. Bachelor's, Massillon U., Paris, 1979; Lic. Econ. Scis., Sorbonne, Paris, 1982, MS de Gestion, 1983. Responsable table Matif, Paris, 1986-88, gerant sicav, 1984-87; gestionnaire Soc. Bourse Puget Mahe, Paris, 1987-90; pres., dir. gen. Europe Egide Fin., Paris, 1990—. Avocation: golf. Fax: 01 53 45 10 30. E-mail: euregifi@worldnet.fr. Home: 6 Sq de la Tour Maubourg, 75007 Paris France Office: Europe Egide Fin, 22 Pl Vendôme, 75001 Paris France

PIÑON, NÉLIDA CUIÑAS, author, educator; b. Rio de Janeiro, May 3, 1937; d. Lino and Olivia Carmen (Cuiñas) P. Grad., Faculty of Philosophy, Pontificia Univ. Católica, Rio de Janeiro; PhD (hon.), Rutgers U., 1988, Fla. Atlantic U., 1996, U. Poitiers, France, 1997, U. Santiago de Compostela, 1998. Asst. editor Cadernos Brasileiros, 1966-67; v.p. Writers Union, Rio de Janeiro, 1978, interim pres., 1989; dir. dept. cultural dissemination Prefeitura of Rio de Janeiro, 1979-80; Dr. H.K. Stanford chair in humanities U. Miami, Fla., 1991—; lectr. U. Buffalo, 1970, CUNY, 1971, U. Pitts., 1978, Yale U., 1980, U. de Palma, 1984, U. do Porto, 1985, U. Fed. Lisboa, 1985, Duke U., 1986, NYU, 1986, The Am. U., 1986, Georgetown U., 1986, Catholic U. of Lima, 1987, Sorbonne, 1987, U. Urbana, 1988, The Johns Hopkins U., 1988, U. Albany, 1989, U. del Pais Vasco, 1990, U. Ga., 1991, U. Fla., 1991, U. Colo., 1992, U. Miami, 1992, Fla. Atlantic U., 1993-94; mem. lit. office Afrânio Coutinho, OLAC, 1979; active internat. jury orgns. and numerous internat. seminars and confs. Author: Guia mapa de Gabriel Arcanjo, 1961, Madeira feita cruz, 1963, Tempo das frutas, 1966, Fundador, 1969 (Walmap award 1970), A casa da paixão, 1972 (Mario de Andrade Best Fiction Book award Assn. Art Critics of Sao Paolo 1973), Sala de armas, 1973, Tebas do meu coração, 1974, A força do destino, 1977, O calor das coisas, 1980, A republica dos sonhos, 1984 (pub. as The Republic of Dreams, 1989; Best Fiction Book award Pen Club 1985, Best Fiction Book award Assn. Art Critics of Sao Paolo 1985), A doce canção de Caetana, 1987 (pub. as Caetana's Sweet Song, 1992; José Geraldo Vieira award Brazilian Union of Sao Paulo Writers 1987), A pão de cada dia, 1994, A Roda Do Vento, 1996 (Juan Rulfo Internat. L.Am. Lit. award 1995); numerous short stories in internat. anthologies and mags.; mem. editl. bd. Avenir Pub., 1980; mem. editl. coun. L.Am. Image, 1993; mem. rsch. coun. Impressions, 1987, Pedagogue and Cultural Workbooks, 1993; mem. editl. rev. adv. bd. L.Am. Lit. and Arts. Mem. coun. Pro-book, 1981; mem. coun. curators Rio Found., 1979; active Assn. Friends of House of Culture Laura Alvim, 1987-89, Nat. Coun. Cultural Politics, Brazil. Decorated Ordem do Cruzeiro do Sul, Lazo de Dama de Isabel La Católica; recipient Galicia medal, Manuel Bandeira medal U. Campina Grande, 1986, Bienal Nestle, 1991, Gold Golfinho award Govt. of State of Rio de Janeiro and State Coun. of Culture, 1990, Castelao medal Galician Parliament, 1992; named One of Ten Women of Yr., Sector Lit., 1979. Mem. Brazilian Acad. (v.p., Personality of Yr. 1989, pres.), Pen Club of Brazil, Brazilian Inst. Hispanic Culture, Acad. Brazilian Acad. Letters (1st woman pres. 1996), Nat. Coun. Woman Dirs., Conselho Estadual de Cultura, Phi Beta Delta (Beta Theta chpt.). Office: Av Epitácio Pessoa, 4956 8o andar Lagoa, 22471-001 Rio de Janeiro Brazil also: Academia Brasileira De Letras, Av Presidente Wilson 203, Rio de Janeiro 20030-021, Brazil*

PINSCHOF, THOMAS, flutist, conductor; b. Vienna, Austria, Feb. 14, 1948; s. Karl and Susanne (Leitmaier) P. Grad. diploma Conservatorium of Vienna, 1972; postgrad. Hochschule für Musik, Freiburg, W.Ger., 1972-75, Ind. U., 1975-76. First pub. appearance, Brahmssaal Wien, 1965; appeared at Tanglewood Festival, U.S.A., 1969; mem. Vienna Symphony Orch., 1971-72; founder ENSEMBLE I, Internat. Chamber Group, 1971; founder, artistic dir. flute orch. ENSEMBLE ZAUBERFLOETE, 1981-98; mng. dir. Magic Flutes Internat., Australia, 1996—; artistic dir. Mozart Orch., Melbourn, 1998—; artist-in-residence Victorian Coll. of Arts, Melbourne, Australia, 1976-78, lectr., 1979-88, head woodwind dept., 1983-84; founder, artistic dir. Mozart on the Mountain Ann. Festival and Master Course, Mt. Buller, Australia; rec. and concert artist. Contbr. articles to music publs. and editions of music. Inventor of Pinschofon, a new type of bass-flute, first presented at the Internat. Frankfurt Fair, 1971. Bd. dirs. Carl Ludwig Pinschof Found. Recipient 2d prize Internat. Flute competition Severino Gazzelloni, 1975; Koussewitzky scholar, Tanglewood, 1969, Austrian Govt. scholar, 1971, 72; Alban-Berg Found. grantee, 1971; Australia Council Music Bd. grantee, 1983. Mem. Gewerkschaft für Kunst und freie Berufe (Austrian Musicians Union), ACT Flute Soc. (pres. 1978-80), Verein der Freunde des ENSEMBLE I (chmn.), Victorian Flute Guild (hon.), Mercedes Benz Club of Victoria. E-mail: pinschof@magicflutes.net.eu. Office: PO Box 101 Doncaster East, Victoria 3109, Australia

PINSKY, MICHAEL RAYMOND, internist, educator, critical care physician; b. N.Y.C., June 7, 1949; s. Bernard and Katherine June (Collins) P.; m. Janis Marshal, June 6, 1982; children: Daniel Alexander, Stephanie Laine, Jill Olivia. BS in Molecular Genetics, Psychology, McGill U., Montreal, Quebec, 1971, MD, CM, 1974. Diplomate Am. Bd. Internal Medicine, Am. Bd. Pulmonary Diseases, Am. Bd. Critical Care Medicine; lic. Md. Dept. Health and Mental Hygiene, Pa. Bd. Med. Examiners, Calif. Bd. Med. Quality Assurance. Intern, jr. resident Stanford (Calif.) U. Med. Ctr., 1974-76, fellow pulmonary medicine, 1976-78; sr. resident in medicine Orlando (Fla.) Regional Med. Ctr., 1978-79; fellow pulmonary medicine, environ. physiology Johns Hopkins Med. Insts., Balt., 1979-81; dir. med. ICU, VA Med. Ctr., Pitts., 1981-83, rsch. assoc., 1985—; asst. prof. medicine and anesthesiology U. Pitts. Sch. Medicine, Pitts., 1981-85, asst. prof. anesthesiology and medicine, 1985-86, assoc prof. anesthesiology and critical care medicine, 1986-91, prof. anesthesiology and critical care medicine, 1991—; investigator Internat. Resuscitation Rsch. Ctr., Pitts., 1987—; dir. rsch. divsn. critical care medicine U. Pitts., 1990—; tenured prof. anesthesiology and critical care medicine U. Pitts. Sch. Medicine, Pitts., 1994—; dir. rsch. dept. anesthesiology and critical care medicine Presbyn.-U. Hosp., Pitts., 1985—; prof. associé U. Paris V, 1998—. Editor: (book) Pathophysiologic Foundations of Critical Care, 1993; contbr. over 300 articles to prof. jours. and chpts. to books; editor Jour. Critical Care, 1990-96. Recipient VA Career Devel. award, 1980, Rsch. fellowship award, 1986, Max Harry Weil Internat. Lecture prize, U. So. Calif., 1994, Gregory Mark Taubin lectr., Children's Nat. Med. Ctr. 1996, Fritz Holstrom Meml. lectr. U. Tex. Health Sci. Ctr., San Antonio, 1996, Internat. Rsch. Svc. Recognition, Vincenza, Italy, 1998. Fellow Am. Coll. Chest Physicians, Coll. of Critical Care Medicine; mem. AAAS, Am. Thoracic Soc., Soc. Critical Care Medicine, Undersea Med. Soc., DaVinci Soc. for Bronchial Blood Flow, Am. Heart Assn. (cardiopulmonary coun. mem.), Shock Soc., Pa. Soc. Critical Care Medicine, Organ Failure Acad, Trieste, Italy, Vincenza Med. Soc. (hon.), European Soc. Intensive Care Medicine. Avocations: sailing, scuba diving, photography, wine tasting. Fax: 412-647-8060. Office: U Pitts 606 Scaife 3550 Terrace St Pittsburgh PA 15261-0001

PINSON, JOHN DENNIS, real estate broker; b. Quansette Point, R.I., July 14, 1963. Student, U. Tampa, Guildford, U.K., 1981-83, Palm Beach Atlantic Coll., 1983-84, 91, U. Surrey, Guildford, U.K., 1984-86, Johns Hopkins U.; grad., Realtors Inst. Cert. internat. property specialist, residential specialist. Broker Merrill Lynch Real Estate, Palm Beach, Fla., 1987-91; broker Prudential Fla. Real Estate, Palm Beach, 1991-95, mng. broker, 1995-99; mng. broker Arvida, Palm Beach, 1999—; v.p. U.S. chpt. Fedn. Internat. Real Estate Scholarship Found., Washington, 1998-2000; v.p. Palm Beach Bd. Realtors, 1999-2000. Mem. Palm Beach Civic Assn., Palm Beach C. of C., Palm Beach Rep. Club (dir. 1999-2000). E-mail: john@pinson.com. Fax: 561-366-1075. Home: PO Box 3386 Palm Beach FL 33480-1586 Office: Arvida 340 Royal Poinciana Way Palm Beach FL 33480-4048

PINTER, NICHOLAS, geologist; b. Palma, Mallorca, Spain, July 27, 1964. BA, Cornell U., 1986; MS, Penn State U., 1988; PhD, U. Calif., Santa Barbara, Calif., 1992. Exploration geologist Mobil Oil, Bakersfield, Calif., 1989, Mobil New Exploration Ventures, Dallas, 1990; rsch. asst. Penn State U., University Park, Pa., 1986-88; rsch., teaching asst. U. Calif., Santa Barbara, 1988-92, rschr., lectr., 1992-93; postdoctoral rschr. Yale U., 1995-96; asst. prof. Southern Ill. U., 1996—. Co-author: Active Tectonics, 1996; contbr. numerous articles to profl. jours. Recipient Dissertation fellowship U. Calif., 1991, Rsch. fellowship White Mtn. Rsch. Sta., 1991, 92, Mathias Rsch. award U. Calif. Natural Res. System, 1990, Pacific Rim fellowship, 1990, fellowship Fulbright Found., 2000—, fellowship Charles A. Lindbergh Found., 1999—. Mem. AAAS, Geol. Soc. of Am., Ill. State Acad. Sci., Sigma Xi. Office: Southern Ill U Dept Geology Carbondale IL 62901-4324

PINTO, CLAUDIO IVAN, anesthesiologist; b. Punia Arenas, Chile, June 28, 1965; s. David Pinto and Blanca Zulema Muñoz; m. Patricia T. Trocoso; children: Florencia, Margarita. B Medicine, U. Austral, Valdivia, Chile, 1988, MD, 1991; MBA, IEDE, Santiago, Chile, 1999. Resident in anesthesia U. Catolica, Santiago, 1991-94, chief resident, 1993-94, staff anesthesiologist, 1994-95, mem. staff surg. ICU, 1994-95; staff pediat. anesthesiologist Hosp. Calvo Mackenna, Santiago, 1995; staff anesthesiologist Hosp. Iquique, Chile, 1995—, chief anesthesia emergency rm., 1999—; med. dir. Clinica Iquique, 1997—. Recipient award Chilean Med. Assn., 1991. Mem. Chilean Anesthesia Soc., N.Y. Acad. Scis. Roman Catholic. Avocation: computers. Home: Ave Costanera 3524 Casa 52, Iquique Chile Office: Chilica Iquique, O'Higgins 103, Iquique Chile

PINTO, EDUARDO DOS SANTOS, marketing consultant; b. Viseu, Portugal, May 14, 1947; s. Eduardo Alfonso and Modesta Pereira (dos Santos) P.; m. Maria Teresa Tomaz Gomes, Nov. 27, 1976; children: Gisela Andreia, Maria Inês, Joana. Complementary Sch., L.N. Viseu, Portugal, 1969. System analyst Marconi, Lisbon, Portugal, 1973-80; support mgr. Datinfor, Lisbon, Portugal, 1980-84; bd. dirs. In Software, Lisbon, Portugal, 1984-90, Time Sharing, Lisbon, Portugal, 1990-92, Marconi/SVA, Lisbon, Portugal, 1991-92; pres. T.S.I., Barcelona, Spain, 1991-93, Softlog, Lisbon, 1991-93; bd. dirs. Marconi, S.I., Lisbon, 1991-93, Interinfo, Lisbon, 1994-95; mktg. mgr. RTP, Lisbon, 1997—; v.p. A.P.I., Lisbon, 1988-90; commn. mem. GATIE, Lisbon, 1990-92; mem. direction APPSTVA, Lisbon, 1994-96. Author: (software package) Documenta, 1984; contbr. articles to profl. jours. Sgt. Army, Lisbon, 1969-70, Guinea, Bissau, 1970-72. Recipient Wang Achievers Club award, 1982; named Tom Master Cons., 1984. Mem. Mem. Associação Portuguesa de Informática, Associação Portuguesa S. Infomação, Associação Portuguesa Qualidade, Forum Administradores Empresas, Associação Portuguesa Mgmt., Club dos Executivos de Informática. Avocations: tennis, music. Home: Estrada da Luz 61 1 Esq, 1600 Lisbon Portugal

PINTO, MARIA CRISTINA ROSAMOND, internal medicine and genetics educator; b. Goa, Ex-Portuguese Colony, Aug. 30, 1950; d. Carlos Eufemiano and Maria Lucy Thelma (Secco) P.; m. João Paulo Aboim Borges, Dec. 23, 1983 (dec. Dec. 1986). BSc, Tech. Sch. Scis., Lourenzo Marques, Mozambique, Ex-Portuguese Ter., 1967; MD, U. Lisbon, Portugal, 1978; MSc, U. Lisbon, 1984, PhD in Med. Genetics, 1988; PhD in Med. Genetics; PhD in Molecular Biology, U. Miami, 1988. Cert. European Bd. Genetics. Lab. technician Univ. Hosps., Mozambique, 1967-74; fellow in medicine Univ. Hosps., Lisbon, 1978-80, fellow in endocrinology, 1980-84; rsch. technician U. Lisbon, 1974-78, asst. instr. genetics and medicine, 1978-83, prof., 1988—, dir. Endocrinology Lab., 1981-84; cons. to genetics coord. Portuguese Ministry Health, Lisbon, 1989; cons. Bds. Sci. and Tech., Lisbon, 1989, Support Group for Mental Deficients, Lisbon, 1995—, European Gene Therapy Group, Lisbon, 1996—; com. assoc. European Alliance Genetic Support Groups, The Netherlands, 1990—. Recipient Pfizer award Pfizer Sci. Com., 1981; spl. grantee Tech. Superior Sch. Health, 1967, grantee NIH, Bethesda, Md., 1984-88; Gulbenkian Found. postdoctoral fellow U. Miami, 1984-88. Fellow Portuguese Soc. Human Genetics (founding), Am. Coll. Med. Genetics (founding); mem. Portuguese Acad. Med. Scis. (yr. rsch. prize 1981). Avocations: piano, classical guitar, soprano singer, tennis, swimming. Office: U Lisbon Dept Human Genetic, Rua Amilcar Cabral 21-RC 4, 1700 Lisbon Portugal

PINTO, OLAVO DE CAMPOS, JR., psychiatrist; b. Sao Paulo, Mar. 22, 1955; s. Olavo de Campos and Clelia Goncalves de Campos Pinto; m. Flavia Marques de Campos Pinto, Mar. 20, 1987; children: Pedro, Fernando, Gabriel. MD, Fed. U. Rio De Janeiro, 1979. Resident in psychiatry U. Calif., San Diego, 1995-97; psychiatrist Georgetown U., Washington, 1994-95; prof. psychiatry U. Calif., San Diego, 1995—; head Bipolar Disorders Clinic, U. Calif., San Deigo, 1996—; physician Gifford Clinic U. Calif. San Diego, 1998—, rschr. psychopharmacology unit dept. of psychiatry, 1998—. Contbr. articles to profl. jours. Mood Disorders fellow U. Calif., 1996-98, fellow U.S. Psychiatry Congress Eli Lilly, 1996; named Resident of Yr. Pfizer Inc. USA, 1997. E-mail: opinto@ucsd.edu. Address: PO Box 2607 Del Mar CA 92014-5607

PINTO ARAYA, JOHN, marketing executive; b. San Jose, Costa Rica; s. John Pinto Sasso and Jenny Araya, July 10, 1999. B of Gen. Studies, U. Miami, 1996. Bus. cons. Hispanic Adv. Group, Miami, 1995-96; product specialist Baxter Healthcare Internat., Mexico City, 1996-97; nat. media coord. Coca-Cola Co., Mexico City, 1998-99, nat. media mgr., 1999—. Fax: (525) 262 2008. E-mail: jpinto@la.ko.com. Office: Coca-Cola Co, Ruben Dario 115, Mexico City 11580, Mexico

PINTO DE ABREU, CARLOS ALBERTO RIBEIRO, lawyer; b. Caldas da Rainha, Portugal, June 12, 1967; s. Carlos Alberto Chambel and Maria do Carmo Vieira (Ribeiro) Pinto de Abreu; m. Cristina Sacadura Santos Silva, Oct. 3, 1992; children: Madalena, Joana. Degree in law, Cath. U., Lisbon, Portugal, 1990, M Criminal Law, 1994. Jr. asst. in labor law Classical U. Lisbon, 1992-93; prof. Câmara dos Solicitadores, Lisbon, 1995-96; jr. asst. in criminal law Internat. U., Lisbon, 1990-95, sr. asst., 1996-99; dir. Germano Marques da Silva and Associados-Sociedade de Advogados.

Author: Prática Judiciária e Jurisprudência Crítica, 1996, Estratégia Processual, 1999; editor Communitas, 1984-90, Veritas, 1998; also articles. Mem. European Lawyers Union, Order Lawyers, Assn. Old Alums Cath. U. (founder, v.p. 1997-99), Acad. Assn. Cath. U. (founder), Lawyers Golf Club, Med. Golf Club. Avocations: golf, classical and jazz music, collecting canes. E-mail: carpa@mail.telepac.pt. Office: Av da República 64 8o, 1050-197 Lisbon Portugal

PINTO-PEREIRA, BERARDO FRANCISCO, financial consultant, management consultant; b. Margão, Goa, India, Sept. 27, 1943; arrived in Trinidad and Tobago, 1989; s. António Vicente and Maria Jovita (Pereira) P.-P.; m. Lexley Maureen Da Silva, Dec. 29, 1978; children: Tarun, Snehal, Rushil. B in Philosophy, Papal Athenaeum, Pune, India, 1968; BSc, U. Pune, 1971, EdB, 1973, MEd, 1975; MA in Pers. Mgmt. and Indsl. Rels., Tata Inst. of Social Scis., Bombay, 1977. Cert. trainer corp. mgmt. devel. tng., Johnson & Johnson, New Brunswick, N.J. Vice prin. Loyola H.S., Margão, 1971-72, St. Vincent's Night H.S., Pune, 1972-74; exec. asst. Lee & Muirhead (Pvt.) Ltd., Bombay, 1977; pers. officer Tata Group of Electric Cos., Bombay, 1977-82; plant pers. mgr. MRF Ltd., Goa, 1982-83; tng. mgr. Johnson & Johnson Ltd., Bombay, 1983-89; gen. mgr. human resources Caribbean Ispat Ltd., Trinidad and Tobago, 1989-91, Ispat Mexicana S.A. de C.V., Lazaro Cardenas, Mex., 1991-92; prin., dir. Applied Tech. Consultants, Trinidad and Tobago, 1992-95; cons. Mondial Internat. Fin. Svcs., Trinidad and Tobago, 1995—; cons., mem. acad. staff Xavier's Inst. of Mgmt. Studies, Bombay, 1977-79; cons., trainer Bharat Petroleum, Bombay, 1979-80, R C Fertilizers, Bombay, 1979-81; cons. total quality mgmt. systems Colonial Life Ins. Co. (Trinidad) Ltd., 1992-94, Cariflex Ltd., Trinidad and Tobago, 1991-94; cons. human resource info. systems U. W.I., Trinidad and Tobago, 1992-94; cons. total quality mgmt. and ISO 9000 systems Trinidad and Tobago Bur. Stds., 1994; cons. Inter Am. Devel. Bank, Washington, 1993, Mondial Internat. Fin. Svcs., 1995. Contbr. articles to profl. jours.; mem. editl. bd. Indian Jour. Tng. and Devel., New Delhi, 1984-87. Pres. Assn. Lyceum Academics, Goa, 1961-63, Christian Youth Coun. St. Xavier's Coll., Goa, 1968-69; chmn. Youth Camp, Goa, 1969, assoc. chmn., 1970; chmn. Youth Camp, Ahmednagar, India, 1971; mem. FEEL Social Svc. Orgn., Trinidad and Tobago, 1996—; bd. dirs. Habitat for Humanity Trinidad and Tobago Ltd., 1997—. Mem. Indian Soc. Tng. and Devel. (life, cert. trainer, editor Sampak quar. rev. 1982-86), Inst. Pers. Profls., Human Resource Mgmt. Assn. of Trinidad and Tobago. Roman Catholic. Avocations: bridge, gardening, reading, electronic entertainment. Home: 29 Stone St, Port of Spain Trinidad and Tobago Office: 135 Bretton Hall, 16 Victoria Ave, Port of Spain Trinidad and Tobago

PIOLINE, CEDRIC, pro tennis player; b. Neuilly, Seine, France, June 15, 1969. Mem. ATP, 1989—, ranked 11th, 2000; winner Monte Carlo Open, 2000, ABN/AMRO World Tennis Tournament, Rotterdam, The Netherlands, 2000. Office: ATP Tour 201 ATP Tour Blvd Ponte Vedra Beach FL 32082*

PIOMBINO, ALFRED ERNEST, law consultant, writer; b. Poughkeepsie, N.Y., Oct. 9, 1962; s. Alfred Raymond and Barbara Jean (Elmendorf) P. AS, Dutchess Community Coll., Poughkeepsie, 1983; BS, Marist Coll., 1986, MPA, 1988. Notary pub., Fla., N.J., N.Y., Maine. Instr. Ulster Community Coll., Stone Ridge, N.Y., 1986-88; pres. Piombino Corp., Poughkeepsie, 1987-94; commr. of deed for Conn. in N.Y., 1991-94, for Fla. in N.Y., 1992-94; mem. Acad. of Legal Studies in Bus.; adj. faculty L.I. U., 1988-94, Pratt Inst., 1989-93; Dedimus Justice, State of Maine, 1995—; founder, chmn. Maine Magistrate's Coun.; fair hearing officer City of Portland, Maine, 1997—; civil svc. commr. City of Portland, 1999—. Author: Notary Public Handbook: A Guide for New York, 2000, Notary Public Handbook: A Guide for New Jersey, 1991, Notary Public Handbook: A Guide for Maine, 1992, Notary Public Handbook: A Guide for Florida, 1993, Notary Public Register and Recordkeeping Protocols, 1993, Notary Public Handbook: A Guide for Vermont Notaries, Commissioners and Justices of the Peace, 1995, Notary Public Handbook: A Guide for California Notaries and Commissioners, 1997, Notary Public Handbook: Principles, Practices & Cases, nat. edit., 1997. Mem. faculty Am. Heart Assn., Dutchess County, N.Y., 1983-88; bd. dirs. ARC, Dutchess County, 1977-82; trustee Nat. Multiple Sclerosis Soc. (Maine chpt.); Ky. Col. Gubernatorial Commn., 1997; mem. Maine Dem. Party State com., 2000—, Cumberland County Dem. com., 2000—, Portland City Dem. com., 2000—. Master, U.S.C.G. lic. officer Merchant Marine. Recipient Nat. First Aid award Johnson & Johnson, 1978, Vt. Sec. of State Commendation, 1995, Ark. Traveler Gubernatorial award, 1996. Mem. ABA (jud. adminstrn. divsn., info. security com.), ASPA (v.p. Dutchess County chpt. 1979-86), Am. Soc. Notaries (life, bd. dirs., cybernotary com.), Nat. Spkrs. Assn., Nat. Judges Assn., Nat. Assn. Parliamentarians, Am. Inst. Parliamentarians, Nat. Conf. Adminstrv. Law Judges, N.Y. State Assn. Notaries Pub. (founder, pres.), Northeastern Regional Acad. Legal Studies in Bus., Nat. Conf. Adminstrv. Law Judges, Italian Heritage Ctr. Portland, Propeller Club of U.S. Democrat. Roman Catholic. Avocations: amateur radio, traveling, private pilot, boating, maritime history and lighthouse preservation. Fax: 800-366-6302. E-mail: piombino@abanet.org. Office: PO Box 778 Portland ME 04104-0778

PIONTEK, HEINZ, writer; b. Kreuzburg, Silesia, Germany, Nov. 15, 1925; s. Robert and Marie P.; m. Gisela Dallmann, July 14, 1951. Student Philosophy and Theology, Hochschule, Dillingen, Germany. Author: (lyrik) Die Furt, 1952, Die Rauchfahne, 1953, Wassermarken, 1955, Mit einer Kranichfeder, 1962, Klartext, 1966, Tod oder lebendig, 1971, Gesammelte Gedichte, 1976, Wie sich Musik durchschlug, 1978, Vorkriegszeit: Ein Gedicht, 1980, Was mich nicht loslaesst, 1981, Helldunkel, 1987, Morgenwache, 1991; (prose) Vor Augen, 1955, (essays) Buchstab-Zauberstab: Ueber Dichter und Dichtung, 1959, (radioplay) Weisser Panther, 1962, Kastanien aus dem Feuer: Erzaehlungen, Kurzgeschichten, Prosastuecke, 1963, Windrichtungen, 1963, Hinweise, Erlaueterungen, Proben, (bio-bibliography) Daten, 1966, (novel) Die mittleren Jahre, 1967, Aussenaufnahmen, 1968, Liebeserklaerungen in Prosa, 1969, Maenner, die Gedichte machen: Zur Lyrik heute, 1970, Die Erzaehlungen, 1950-1970, 1971, German: From Language to Literature, 1972, Helle Tage anderswo: Reisebilder, 1973, Leben mit Woerten: Zum 50, 1975, Dichterleben, 1976, 96, Das Schweigen ueberbruecken: Meditationen, Gedichte, Szenen, Erzaehlungen, 1977, Wintertage, Sommernaechte: Gesammelte Erzaehlungen und Reisebilder, 1977, Trauemen, Wachen, Widerstehen: Aufzeichnungen aus dieser Jahren, 1978, Dunkelkammerspiel: Spiele, Szenen und ein Stuek, 1978, (essays) Das Handwerk des Lesens: Erfahrungen mit Buechern und Autoren, 1979, (novel) Juttas Neffe, 1979, Die Zeit einer Frau: Sechs Erzaehlungen, 1984, (autobiography vol.1) Zeit meines Lebens, 1984, Damals, damals und jetzt: Heinz Piontek zum 15. November 1985, 1985, (autobiography vol. 2) Stunde der Uberlebenden, 1989, Nach Markus, (erzaehlung) 1991, (non-fiction novel) Goethe unterwegs in Schlesien, 1993; (omnibus editions) Werke in Sechs Baenden (6 vols.), 1981-85, Werkauswahl in zwei Baenden (2 vols.), 1990; editor: Aus meines Herzens Gruende: Evangelische Lyrik aus vier Jahrhunderten, 1959, Neue deutsche Erzaehlgedichte, 1964, Augenblicke unterwegs: Deutsche Reiseprosa unserer Zeit, 1968, Ensemble: Internationales Jahrbuch fuer Literatur, 1969-79, Deutsche Gedichte der sechziger Jahre, 1972, Muenchner Edition: Lyrik, Prosa, Essays, (50 vols.) 1980-86, Lieb, Leid und Zeit und Ewigkeit: Deutsche Gedichte aus tausend Jahren, 1981, Ja, mein Engel: Die besten deutschen Kurzgeschichten, 1981; translator: John Keats, Gedichte: Auswahl (Poems: Selection), 1960, 69, 82, 96, William Butler Yeats: Selected Poems, 1977, Gerard Manley Hopkins: Selected Poems, 1982, W.H. Auden: Selected Poems, 1982, Robert Lowell: Selected Poems, 1982. Recipient Berlin prize for Lit., 1957, Andreas Gryphius prize, Esslingen, 1957, Rom prize, Villa Massimo, 1960, Munchner Lit. prize, 1967, Eichendorff prize, 1971, Tukan prize, 1971, Lit. prize des Kulturkreises in BDI, 1974, Georg-Buchner prize, 1976, Werner-Egk prize, 1981, Oberschlesischer Kultur prize, 1983, Grosser Kulturpreis Schlesien des Landes Niedersachsen, 1991, Bundesverdienstkreuz 1st Class, 1985, Bayerischer Verdienst-Orden, 1993. Mem. Bavarian Acad. Fine Arts Muenchen, Ctrl. PEN of Fed. Republic Germany, German Acad. to Lang. and Poetry.

PIOTROVSKAYA, ELENA MICHAILOVNA, chemist; b. Leningrad, Russia, Sept. 18, 1947; d. Michail Ilich and Kseniya Ivanovna (Drosdova) Fefelov; m. Levon Borisovich Piotrovsky, Aug. 20, 1969; 1 child, Marina. BS, Leningrad State U., Russia, 1970, PhD, 1975; DS, St. Petersburg U., Russia, 1995. Rschr. dept. chemistry Leningrad State U., Russia, 1970-82, sr. rschr., 1983-91; asst. prof. dept. chemistry St. Petersburg U., Russia, 1992-95, prof. dept. chemistry, 1995—. Author: Thermodynamics of Fluid-Vapor, 1989; contbr. articles to profl. jours. Grantee Internat. Sci. Found., N.Y.C., 1993, INTAS, Brussels, 1993, 97. Mem. Russian Chem. Soc. Avocations: reading, visiting museums, gardening, hiking. Office: St Petersburg U Dept Chem, Universitetsky pr 2, 198904 Saint Petersburg Russia

PIOVANELLI, SILVANO CARDINAL, archbishop of Florence; b. Feb. 21, 1924. ordained Roman Cath. Ch., 1947. Consecrated bishop Titular Ch. Tubune, Mauritania, 1982; archbishop Florence, Italy, 1983—; proclaimed cardinal, 1985. Address: Arcivescovado, Piazza S Giovanni 3, 50129 Florence Italy

PIPAL, ANIL KUMAR, electronics engineer; b. Jaipur, Rajasthan, India, Sept. 3, 1964; s. Omprakash Pipal and Prem Lata Devi; m. Madhu Gangte Lamboi; Apr. 13, 1991; 2 children. B in Engring., Dharam Singh Desai Inst. Tech., Nadiad, India, 1986. Sales, svc. engr. Systronics, Ahmedabad, India, 1987-88; engring. asst. TV station, Jaipur, India, 1988-89; design engr. CEDT, Imphal, India, 1989-91; scientist D Ministry Info. Tech., New Delhi, 1991—. Hindu. Avocations: chess, music, reading. Office: Ministry Info Tech, 6 CGO Complex, New Delhi 110003, India

PIPCHICK, MARGARET HOPKIN, clinical specialist psychiatric nursing, therapist, consultant; b. Bklyn., Dec. 14, 1942; m. Robert Pipchick, June 13, 1971; children: Christine, Kevin. BSN, Seton Hall U., 1968; MA, NYU, 1974; grad., Blanton Peale Grad. Inst., N.Y.C., 1981; postgrad., The Union Inst., 1998—. Cert. clin. specialist child-adolescent-adult. psychiat. nursing; lic. marriage and family therapist, N.J. Various staff positions hosps., N.Y./N.J.; teaching asst. Seton Hall U., South Orange, N.J., 1971-72; staff therapist, faculty Blanton-Peale Counseling Ctr., Cranford, N.J., 1974-90; pvt. practice individual, couple and family therapy Cranford, 1981—; adj. faculty Fairleigh Dickenson U., Teaneck, N.J., 1989-93, Kean Coll., 1994, 95. Contbr. chpt. to Foundations of Psychiatric Mental Health Nursing. mem. ANA, N.J. State Nurses Assn., Am. Assn. Marriage and Family Therapists, Soc. Cert. Clin. Specialists (treas.), Sigma Theta Tau.

PIPER, FREDESSA MARY, school system administrator; b. Monroe, La., June 19, 1945; d. Floyd Preston and Zona Mary (Jones) P.; m. Robert John Parks, Mar. 20, 1969 (div. 1980); m. Zebedee Taylor Jr., Dec. 1996. BS, Ill. State U., 1964; MEd with distinction, DePaul U., 1972; EdD, Loyola U., Chgo., 1984. Cert. tchr., gen. adminstr., sch. supt., Ill. Tchr. secondary schs. Chgo. Pub. Schs., 1964-73, staff asst., 1974-76, coord., 1977-83, tchr., coord., 1984-87; asst. supt. Ednl. Svc. Region Cook County, Chgo., 1987-95; project coord. Malcolm X City Coll., Chgo., 1973-74; coord. Athletes for Better Edn., Chgo., 1975-77; cons. Community Reading is Rewarding Program, Chgo., 1989—; author radio scripts, speeches. Project coord. Local Ward Back to Sch. Fun-Fest, Chgo., 1983—; program coord. Pre-Thanksgiving Day Srs. Dinner, Chgo., 1983—; asst. to chmn. Re-election Campaign, Chgo., 1986, 88; promotional dir. Unity in Community Boat Cruise, Chgo., 1987—. Mem. ASCD, Nat. Alliance Black Sch. Educators, Am. Assn. Sch. Adminstrs., Phi Delta Kappa, Delta Epsilon Sigma. Democrat. Baptist. Avocations: cooking, writing, computers, public speaking.

PIPER, KIMBERLY A., bank cost analyst; b. Billings, Mont., Jan. 30, 1962; d. Eugene Carl and Iline Margaret Rehling; m. Blake David Piper, June 10, 1995; 1 child, Jordan. BSBA, Ea. Mont. Coll., 1987. Cert. fin. svcs. auditor. Staff auditor Hamilton Misfeldt, Havre, Mont., 1988; sr. bank examiner State of Mont., Billings, 1989-95; internal auditor Security Bank, FSB, Billings, 1996; audit officer First Interstate Banc Sys., Billings, 1996-99, cost analyst-best practices, 1999—. Vol. youth campaign YMCA, Billings, 1998, 99, 2000; bd. dirs. Coll. of Bus., Mont. State U., Billings, 2000. Democrat. Methodist. Avocations: crafts, reading, cross stitch, traveling. E-mail: KPiper1@Fib.com. Office: First Interstate Banc Sys 401 N Thirty 1 St St Billings MT 59116-0001

PIPER, LLOYD LLEWELLYN, II, engineer, government and service industry executive; b. Wareham, Mass., Apr. 28, 1944; s. Lloyd Llewellyn and Mary Elizabeth (Brown) P.; m. Jane Melonie Scruggs, Apr. 30, 1965; 1 child, Michael Wayne. BSEE, Tex. A&M U., 1966; MS in Indsl. Engring, U. Houston, 1973. Registered profl. engr., Tex.; diplomate hazardous waste mgmt. Am. Acad. Environ. Engrs. With Houston Lighting & Power Co., 1965-74; project mgr. Dow Chem. Engring. & Constrn Svcs., Houston, 1974-78; project mgr. Ortloff Corp., Houston, 1978, mgr. engring., 1979-80, v.p., 1980-83; pres., chief exec. officer Plantech Engrs. & Constructors, Inc. subs. Dillingham Constrn. Corp., Houston, 1983-86; pres. The Delta Plantech Co., Houston, 1985-86; dir. on-site tech. devel. Chem. Waste Mgmt., Inc., Oak Brook, Ill., 1986-88; mgr. projects Chem. Waste Mgmt., Inc., Houston, 1988-94, dir. facility devel., 1994-95; asst. mgr. Richland (Wa.) Ops. U.S. Dept. Energy, 1995-96, dep. mgr., 1996-99, adminstr., 1999—; bd. dirs., pres. Harris County Water Control and Improvement Dist., 1973-83; bd. dirs. Environ. Sci. and Tech. Found., 1997-99; bd. dirs. United Way, 1998—, exec. com., 1998—, treas., 2000—; Ponderosa Joint Powers Agy. Harris County, 1977-83, pres., 1977-83; pres. bus. and industry adv. coun. North Harris Montgomery C. C. Dist., 1991-92. Contbr. articles to profl. jours. Recipient Disting. Svc. award Engrs. Coun. Houston, 1970, Outstanding Svc. award Houston sect. IEEE, 1974; named Tex. Young Engr. of Yr., 1976, Nat. Young Engr. of Yr., 1976. Mem. IEEE, Nat. Soc. Profl. Engrs. (chpt. pres. 1978, nat. chmn. engrs. in industry div. 1977, nat. v.p. 1977, chmn. nat. polit. action com. 1979-82, vice chmn. nat. engrs. week 1988-92, nat. trustee edn. found. 1988-90), Nat. Wildlife Fedn., Nature Conservancy, Audubon Soc., Project Mgmt. Inst., Phi Kappa Phi, Tau Beta Pi. Home: 129 Mountain View Ln Richland WA 99352-7652 Office: Dept Energy PO Box 550 Richland WA 99352-0550

PIPER, SAMUEL O'DELL, engineer; b. Greenville, S.C., Feb. 13, 1951; s. Samuel Turrentine and Mary Ellen (O'Dell) P.; m. Betha Louise Roper, June 8, 1974; 1 child, Mark Samuel. BS in Physics with high honors, Ga. Inst. Tech., 1973, MS in Elec. Engring., 1976; postgrad., U. South Fla., 1980-85. Asst. rsch. scientist Ga. Tech. Engring. Exp. Sta., Atlanta, 1973-77, rsch. engr., 1977-78; sr. engr. Sperry Microwave Electronics, Clearwater, Fla., 1978-80, sr. staff engr., 1980-86; sr. rsch. engr. Ga. Tech. Rsch. Inst. Sensors and EM Applications Lab., Atlanta, 1986—, assoc. lab. dir., 1989-93, branch head, 1993—; cons. LTV, Dallas, 1987, Hercules Def. Electronics Systems, Inc., Clearwater, Fla., 1987, Cyber Engring. Svcs., Inc., Dover, N.J., 1997, Dragoon Techs., Inc., Gilbert, Ariz., 1998. 1st Lt. U.S. Army Res., 1973-81. Mem. IEEE (sr., Atlanta sect. sec. 1991-92), Assn. Old Crows, Phi Kappa Phi, Omicron Delta Kappa, Phi Eta Sigma. Methodist. Avocations: sailing. Office: Ga Inst Tech Ga Tech Rsch Institute Atlanta GA 30332-0001

PIPER, THOMAS SAMUEL, minister, consultant; b. Racine, Wis., Feb. 26, 1932; s. Wallace William and Margaret Alice (Lahr) P.; m. Mary Alice Smith, Mar. 12, 1955; children: Daniel Thomas, David Michael, Grace Susan Piper Gonzales. BS, Lawrence U., 1954; ThM, Dallas Theol. Sem., 1969. Ordained to ministry Christian Ch., 1982. Mng. editor Good News Broadcaster mag., Lincoln, Nebr., 1969-82; pastor adminstrn. and edn. Faith Bible Ch., Sterling, Va., 1982-86; pres., cons. Ministries in Sync, Sterling, 1986—; mem. writers conf. faculty Mt. Hermon (Calif.) Christian Conf., 1978-80, Christian Writers Inst., Wheaton, Ill., 1980; mem. pres.'s coun. Loudon County, Good News Jail and Prison Ministry, Arlington, Va., 1984-86; pres. local chpt. Christian Ministries Mgmt. Assn., Washington, 1987, 88; mem. Christian Mgmt. Assn., 1989-90, Nat. Assn. Ch. Bus. Adminstrs., 1986-90. Contbr. numerous articles to profl. jours. Team leader, coach hosp./home visitation McLean (Va.) Bible Ch., 1996-99. With USN, 1956-58. Mem. Voice of Bibl. Reconciliation (bd. dirs. 1991-93), Dallas Theol. Sem. Assn. (pres. local chpt. 1991-93), Internat. Assn. Bus. Communicators (life, pres. local chpt. 1977-79), Greater Washington Christian Edn. Assn. (program chmn., coord. 1997—, exec. editor 1998—, dir. conv. 1999—, bd. dirs. 1999—, chmn. planning com. 1999—). Republican. Home and Office: Ministries in Sync 1307 E Holly Ave Sterling VA 20164-2614

PIPIC, NEDIM, plastic surgeon; b. Sarajevo, Bosnia and Hercegovina, Feb. 7, 1950; arrived in Austria, 1991; s. Ramiz and Sena (Tabakovic) P.; m. Alma Trobradovic, Mar. 11, 1978; children: Nedim, Hano, Elisabeth. Degree, Med. U. Zabreb, Croatia, 1977, M Biol. Sci., 1983, PhD, 1983, Dr.med.sci., 1988. ENT fellow in facial plastic surgery Zagreb, 1980-90, SMZ Hosp., Vienna, Austria, 1991—, U. Hosp., Vienna, 1991—. Contbr. numerous articles to profl. jours. Recipient EMT award Croatia, 1990. Mem. Am. Acad. Facial Plastic and Reconstructive Surgery, Am. Acad. Otorhinolaryngology, Facial Plastic Surgery Europe (v.p. 1996-97). Avocation: music. Home: Arndtgasse 4, 2700 Wr Neustadt Austria Office: SMZ Hosp, Langobarden Str 139, 1220 Vienna Austria

PIPITONE, PHYLLIS L., psychologist, educator, author; b. Chg.; m. Joseph Pipitone, Aug. 28, 1948 (dec.); children: Guy, Daniel, Paul; m. Thomas A. Cox, Jan. 3, 1980. Student, Chgo. Conservatory Music, 1941-44, Peabody Conservatory Music, Balt., 1945, Chgo. Tchrs. Coll., 1946-47, So. Meth. U., 1951-52; MA, U. Akron, 1967; PhD, Kent State U., 1974. With B.S. and H. Advt. Agy., Chgo., 1974; instr. piano and theory Music Acad. Chgo.; psychologist, instr. U. Akron and Kent State U., 1970-79; pvt. practice psychology Akron, 1967—; lectr. in field in U.S and abroad. With WAC, AUS, 1944-46. NIMH grantee, 1974, HEW Child Devel. fellow, 1974. Mem. APA, Nat. Assn. Sch. Psychologists, Mensa, Coun. Exceptional Children, Am. Hypnosis Soc., Kent Psi Rsch. Group Assn. Study/Dreams, Am. Soc. Psychical Rsch., Tues. Musical Club, Weathervane Theatre Women's Bd., Akron Women's City Club, Wadsworth Women's Club, Phi Delta Kappa. Home: 224 Pheasant Run Wadsworth OH 44281-2344

PIPPEN, SCOTTIE, professional basketball player; b. Hamburg, Ark., Sept. 25, 1965. Student, U. Ctrl. Ark., 1983-87. With Seattle Super Sonics, 1987; guard/forward Chgo. Bulls, 1987-98, Houston Rockets, 1998-99, Portland Trailblazers, 1999—; player NBA Championship Team, 1991, 92, 93, U.S. Olympic Basketball Team, 1992. Named to All-Star team, 1990, 92-93, NBA All-Defensive First team, 1992, 93, 94, All-Defensive second team, 1991, NBA All-Star Team, 1992-94, NBA All-Star MVP, 1994, All-NBA First Team, 1994; mem. NBA championship team, 1991-93, 96. Office: Portland Trailblazers One Ctr Ct Ste 200 Portland OR 97227

PIPPERT, JOHN MARVIN, sociology educator; b. Ft. Riley, Kans., Oct. 13, 1954; s. Donald Marvin and Doris Elizabeth Pippert; m. Katherine Sue Ellis, Feb. 10, 1996; children: Justin, Nathan, Anna, Eric, Richard, Anne, Cynthia. BS, James Madison U., 1977; MS, Va. Poly. Inst. and State U., 1979, PhD, 1985. Asst. prof. Longwood Coll., Farmville, Va., 1985-87; asst. prof. Roanoke Coll., Salem, Va., 1987-93, assoc. prof., 1993-98; assoc. prof. sociology North Ga. Coll. and State U., Dahlonega, 1998—; cons. Roanoke (Va.) Times and World News, 1990, Lewis Gale Hosp., Salem, 1990-91, Lavitch and Assocs., Atlanta, 1991, Yankolovich, Clancey Scott, Salem, 1991. Contbr. articles to profl. jours., including Social Sci. Jour., African Am. Ency., Tchg. Sociology. Vol. Roanoke Area Ministries, 1987-98, Food Pantry, Dahlonega, 1999; Grantee NSF, 1995-96, 99, Roanoke Coll., 1997. Mem. Rural Sociol. Soc., Population Reference Bur., Assn. Christian Tchg. Sociology, So. Sociol. Soc., Ga. Sociol. Assn. Baptist. Avocations: camping, backpacking, fishing, family. E-mail: jmpippert@ngcsu.edu. Office: North Ga Coll and State U Dept Psychology Sociology Dahlonega GA 30597-0001

PIPPIN, JAMES ADRIAN, JR., middle school educator; b. Rockingham, N.C., Aug. 6, 1954; s. James A. Sr. and Essie Juanita (Rorie) P. BS, Appalachian State U., 1976; MEd, Columbus Coll., 1982. Tchr. Eddy Jr. H.S., Columbus, Ga., 1976-89; dir. N.C. Agrl. Extension Svc., Penn 4-H Ctr., Reidsville, 1980-89, Millstone 4-H Camp, Ellerbe, N.C., 1993; tchr. Arnold Mid. Sch., Columbus, Ga., 1989-99, Rockingham (N.C.) Jr. High Sch., 1999—; mem. multicultural curriculum com., sick leave bank com., textbook adoption com. and tech. com. MCSD; tchg. program participant Found. Internat. Edn., Inverness, Scotland, 1986, Dunedin, New Zealand, 1989; curriculum devel. program participant Ga. Dept. Edn., Germany, 1989, 91; adv. com. Deutsche Welle Video, 1992, 95; internat. edn. adv. com. Ga. Dept. Edn., 1993—; tchr. cons. N.C. Geographic Alliance. Author: The Physiological and Psychological Effects of Space Flight Environments on Blood Glucose and Circadian Rhythms of the Human Body; contb. author: (curricuums) World Studies, Germany and Georgia: The Search for Unity, Education in Thailand, Germany Unity and Disunity: Ubersichten; Overview of the Federal Republic of Germany, Images of Germany: Past and Present, The Olympic Spirit; A Worldwide Connection, Vol. III. Mem. discovery gallery com. Columbus Mus. Arts & Scis., curriculum devel. com. Atlanta Com. for Olympic Games. Named Ga. Tchr. Yr., 1986, Ga. State Semi-Finalist NASA Tchr. Space Program, 1985; named to USA Today All-U.S.A. 1st Tchr. Team, 1998; recipient Project award TV Worth Tchg., CBS, 1987; Fulbright Study-Tour scholar, Taiwan and Thailand, 1992. Mem. ASCD, NEA (congl. contact team), Columbus Social Sci. Alliance (bd. dirs.), Ga. Assn. Educators, Nat. Coun. Social Scis., Ga. Coun. Social Scis. (bd. dirs.), Musogee Assn. Edn. (v.p., 2d v.p., chmn. policies and grievences com., legis. com., chmn. officer nominating com.), Columbus Hist. Soc., Columbus Hist. Dist. Preservation Soc. (bd. dirs.), Chattahoochee Valley Archaeol. Soc., Phi Alpha Theta, Phi Delta Kappa.

PIPPIN, RONALD GENE, artist; b. L.A., Aug. 6, 1943; s. Elmer Lee and Estelle Katy Pippin; m. Christine McKenna Leigh, Apr. 7, 1997. Student, Harbor Coll., L.A., 1962-64, Inst. de Gnosologia, Arica, Chile, 1970, Chouinard Art Inst., L.A., 1964-68. One-person shows include Cochise Fine Arts Gallery, Bisbee, Ariz., 1980, Shakti Gallery, Long Beach, Calif., 1983, Thinking Eye Gallery, L.A., 1987, Univ. Art Mus., Calif. State U., Long Beach, 1988, Loma Linda U., Sherry Frumkin Gallery, Santa Monica, Calif., 1990, 92, 93, 97, 99, 2000, El Camino Coll., Torrance, Calif., 1991, Redlands (Calif.) U., 1994, Friesen Gallery, Seattle, 1996, 96, Calif. State U., Stanislaus, 1997; exhibited in group shows U. Kyoto, Japan, 1963, L.A. Mcpl. Art Gallery, 1979, Long Beach Artists, 1982, Tucson Mus. Art, 1984, Thinking Eye Gallery, L.A., 1987, 88, Chapman Coll., Calif., 1991, Art Inst. So. Calif., Laguna Beach, 1993, Steele Works Gallery, Hermosa Beach, Calif., 1994, Riverside (Calif.) Art Mus., 1996, Oceanside (Calif.) Mus. Art, 1997, Torrance Cultural Arts Ctr., Joslyn Art Gallery, 1999, others; represented in permanent collections Yountsville (Calif.) VA Hosp., Balboa Bldg., Santa Barbara, Calif., D-Zone Studio, Smithsonian Instn., Washington; featured in publs. Art Connoisseur Mag., L.A. Times, Art Scene Mag. Recipient award Ariz. Crafts Biennial, Tucson Mus. Art, 1981, Ariz. Designer Craftsmen for Jurors Best of Show, 1981; Calif. Arts Coun. fellow, 1990.

PIQUÉ, FERNANDO RAFAEL, international art dealer; b. Havana, Cuba, Oct. 24, 1952; came to U.S., 1961; s. Arturo Raimundo and Arthemis (Serru) P.; m. Christine Diaz, Nov. 15, 1981 (div. July 1984); m. Joan Dee Bennett, July 23, 1985; 1 child, Nicole Erin. Grad. high sch., Miami, Fla. Dist. mgr. EHP, Inc., Pompano Beach, Fla., 1970-76; internat. account exec. to Africa, Europe, Mid. East, N.Am., South America Am. Beverage Machinery, Inc., Miami, 1976-78; salesman new car dealerships, Miami, 1978-81; account exec. Heath and Co., Dallas, 1981-83; founder, chief exec. officer Emporium Enterprises, Inc., Dallas, 1983—, You Name It-We Frame It, Dallas, 1984—, Emporium Art and Frames, Dallas, 1986—, Club Emporium, Dallas, 1988—; cons., broker frame shops and galleries, 1983—. Mem. Profl. Picture Framers Assn. (adv. bd. North Tex. chpt. 1989), Profl. Assn. Divers International, Nat. Assn. Underwater Instrs. Republican. Roman Catholic. Avocations: coin and stamp collecting, scuba diving, underwater photography, sailing, flying. Office: Emporium Enterprises Inc 235 Preston Forest Vlg Dallas TX 75230-2747

PIQUE I. CAMPS, JOSEP, Spanish government official; b. Vilanova i La Geltru/Barcelona, Feb. 21, 1955; m. Margarita Montaner Amoros; 3 children. Degree in econs. and bus. sci., U. Barcelona, doctorate in econs. and bus. sci., degree in law. Dir. gen. industry Catalan Autonomous Govt., 1986-88; pres. EMESA Trefileria S.A., 1988-89; gen. mgr. corp. strategy, bd. dirs. Ercros S.A., 1989-91, mng. dir., 1991—; min. industry and energy Spanish Cabinet, 1996—, min. fgn. affairs; lectr. U. Barcelona; advisor Catalan Govt.; mem. study svc. Caja de Pensiones; chmn. Erkimia S.A., Fertilizantes Espanoles S.A.- Empresa Nacional de Fertilizantes S.A.; bd. dirs. Rio Tinto Menera S.A. Mem. Econ. Circle (pres. 1995—). Avocations: cycling, tennis, reading. Office: Ministry Fgn Affairs, Plaza de la Provincial, 28012 Madrid Spain*

PIRARD, JEAN-PAUL EMMANUEL, chemistry educator; b. Brussels, Nov. 16, 1947; s. Paul Edouard Pirard and Cecilia Clerebouldt; m. Anne Froidebise, Feb. 16, 1974; children: Martin, Sophie, Florence. Degree in chem. engring., Liege (Belgium) U., 1970, PhD in Chem. Engring., 1974. Rsch. fellow Belgian Nat. Sci. Rsch. Found., Brussels, 1970-75; asst. Liege U., 1975-78, asst. prof., 1978-81, assoc. prof., 1981-91, prof. chemistry,

1992—. Contbr. articles to profl. jours.; patentee in field. Recipient Fréderic Swarts prize Belgian Royal Acad. Sci., 1976; decorated officer of Order of Léopold II (Belgium), comdr. of Order of Crown (Belgium). Mem. Chem. Soc. Belgium. Avocation: classical music. Home: 68 Rue de Gaillarmont, B-4032 Liege Belgium Office: U Liege, Inst Chemistry B6, B-4000 Liege Belgium

PIRELLI, LEOPOLDO, industrialist; b. Varese, Italy, Aug. 27, 1925; s. Alberto and Ludovica (Zambeletti) P.; children: Cecilia, Alberto. Degree in mech. engring., Milan Poly., 1950. Chmn., ptnr. Pirelli & C.A.p.A., Milan, 1957-99; dep. chmn. Soc. Internat. Pirelli, Basel, Switzerland, 1979-99; pres. (hon.) Pirelli & C.A. apa., Milan, 1999—; chmn. Pirelli S.p.A., Milan, 1965-96. Mem. Confindustria (exec. coun. 1957—, dep. chmn. 1974-80, bd. dirs. 1974-82). Office: Pirelli & C ApA, via Gaetano Negri 10, 20123 Milan Italy

PIRES, JOSE GUILHERME PINHEIRO, pharmacologist, educator; b. Vitoria, Brazil, Feb. 16, 1952; s. Manoel and Therezinha Pinheiro Pires; m. Neusa Moreira Aguilar, July 16, 1988; children; Tathyana, Guilherme, Christine. MD, Fed. U. Espirito Santo, Vitoria, 1975; MSc in Pharmacology, São Paulo U., Ribeirao Preto, Brazil, 1978, DSc in Pharmacology, 1983. Assoc. prof. Biomed. Ctr. Fed. U. Espirito Santo, Vitoria, 1983—, vice-chancellor for rsch. and postgrad. studies, 1990-92, dean Biomed. Ctr., 1992-96; hon. lectr. Royal Free Hosp. Sch. Medicine, London, 1988-89. Contbr. articles to profl. jours. Post-doctoral studentship Brazilian Ministry Edn., London, 1988. Mem. Brit. Pharmacol. Soc., Soc. for Neurosci. (fgn.). Roman Catholic. E-mail: jgppires@npd.ufes.br. Fax: 55 27 335-7330. Home: Apt 201, R Ludwik Macal, 29060030 Vitoria Brazil Office: CBM-UFES Dept Physiol Scis, Ave Marechal Campos 1468, 29040090 Vitoria Brazil

PIRES DA SILVA, JOÃO MANUEL, chemist, educator; b. Lisbon, Portugal, July 31, 1963; s. Serafim Maria and Maria Manuela Pires; m. Maria João Dias Rua Ferreira, Apr. 9, 1994; one child: João Daniel. Lic., U. Lisbon, 1986, PhD in Chemistry, 1993; MS, Tech. U., Lisbon, 1989. Asst. Tech. Inst., Lisbon, 1986-87; asst. Faculty of Scis., Lisbon, 1987-93, aux. prof. chemistry, 1993—; rschr. in field. Contbr. articles to profl. jours. Mem. Portuguese Chem. Soc. Avocations: literature, bricolage. Office: Fac Scis Dept Chem, Campo Grande Ed C8 Piso 6, 1749-016 Lisbon Portugal

PIRES-NETO, MARIO ARY, physician, medical educator; b. Rio de Janeiro, Apr. 15, 1961; s. Ruy and Sonia Maria (Bernardes) de Ary P. MD, Faculdade Souza Marques, Rio de Janeiro, 1985; MS in Neurosci., U. Fed. Rio de Janeiro, 1991, PhD in Neurosci., 1998. Asst. prof. neuroanatomy dept. neurology and neurosurgery Pontificia U. Catolica Rio de Janeiro, 1987-91; asst. prof. anatomy dept. anatomy U. Fed. Rio de Janeiro, 1993-98, assoc. prof. anatomy dept. anatomy, 1998—. Recipient Eduardo de Moraes award Nat. Acad. Medicine, Rio de Janeiro, 1985, 86. Mem. Brazilian Soc. Neurosci., Soc. Neurosci. (USA), Brazilian Soc. Anatomy, Panam. Soc. Anatomy. Roman Catholic. Avocations: books, computer sci. Home: Ap 701, Praia de Botafogo 280, 22250040 Rio de Janeiro RJ, Brazil Office: U Fed Rio de Janeiro/CCS, Av Brig Trompowski S/N, 21949900 Rio de Janeiro RJ, Brazil

PIRIE, DAVID TARBAT, screenwriter, journalist, critic; b. Dundee, Scotland, Dec. 4, 1946; s. Halyburton Berkeley and Joyce Elaine (Tarbat) P.; m. Judith Leslie Harris, June 21, 1983; 1 child, Alice Jack. BA, U. York, Eng., 1968. Film editor Time Out Mag., London, 1978-86. Screenwriter films Rainy Day Women, 1984 (N.Y. Film and TV Festival), Black Easter, 1995 (Gold plaque award Chgo. Internat. Film Festival 1995); screenwriter TV miniseries Never Come Back, 1990 (Best Network Series, Chgo. Film and TV Festival 1990), The Woman In White, 1997 (Brit. Acad. award nomination). Avocation: running. E-mail: nick@curtisbrown.co.uk. Office: Curtis Brown, Haymarket House, London England

PIRINCCIOGLU, NECMETTIN, education educator; b. Derik, Mardin, Jan. 1, 1966; s. Cemil and Zini (Acer) P. BSc in Chemistry, Ege U., Izmir, Turkey, 1988; PhD in Chemistry, U. Kent at Canterbury, Eng., 1996. With Uppsala (Sweden) U., 1996-97; lectr. Dicle U., Diyarbakir, Turkey, 1997—; vice-chmn. chemistry Dicle U., Diyarbakir, 1997—. Contbr. articles to profl. jours. Mem. Am. Chem. Soc., Royal Soc. Chemistry. Office: Univ Dicle Dept Chemistry, Fen-Kimya, 21280 Diyarbakir Turkey

PIRJEVEC, JOZE, history educator; b. Trieste, Italy, June 1, 1940; s. Miroslav and Ottilia (Oswald) P. Dr.Phil., U. Trieste, 1966; postgrad. diploma, Scuola Normale Superiore, Pisa, Italy, 1969; diploma, Diplomatische Acad., Austria, 1971; D History, U. Ljubljana, Slovenia, 1976. Assoc. prof. U. Pisa, Italy, 1971-77; assoc. prof. U. Trieste, 1977-86, full prof., 1996—; full prof. U. Padova, Italy, 1986-96; rschr. Acad. Scis., Moscow, 1976, Alexander von Humboldt-Stiftung, Munich, 1976-93, Kennan Inst., Washington, 1981. Author: Niccolo' Tommaseo Tra Italia & Slavia, 1977, Storia Della Russia Del XIX Secolo, 1984, Tito, Stalin e L'Occidente, 1985 (Kidric prize 1988), Jugoslavia 1918-1992, 1995, History of the Slovene Minority in Italy 1866-1998, 1998. Pres. Slovene Libr., Trieste, 1984—, Slovene Theatre, Trieste, 1987-91. Fellow Nobel Inst., Oslo, 1994. Mem. Slovene Acad. Scis. Roman Catholic. Avocations: travel, sailing, gardening, collecting art objects. Home: Via Commerciale 76, 34135 Trieste Italy Office: U Trieste Faculty Letters, Via Lazzareito Vecchio 6, 34134 Trieste Italy

PIRK, JAN, cardiac surgeon; b. Prague, Czechoslovakia, Apr. 20, 1948; s. Otto and Jitka (Hrabová) P.; m. Blanka Navrátilová, June 9, 1970; children: Jiri, Tomas. MD, Charles U., Prague, 1972; DSc, Czech Acad. Sci., Prague, 1988. Surgeon Country Hosp., Nymburk, Czech Republic, 1972-74; surgeon Inst. Clin. and Exptl. Medicine, Prague, 1974-83, cardiac surgeon, 1984-90, head of cardiovasc. surgery dept., 1991—; prof. surgery Charles U. Inst. Clin. and Exptl. Medicine, Prague, 2000; fellow in cardiac surgery Ochsner Hosp., New Orleans, 1983-84; cons. Univ. Hosp., Odense, Denmark, 1990-91; counselor EACTS, London,, 1998—. Mem. Soc. Thoracic Surgeons USA, N.Y. Acad. Scis., Czech Soc. Cardiovascular Surgery (com.), Internat. Soc. Cardio-Thoracic Surgeons Japan, European Assn. Cardio-Thoracic Surgery London (councillor). Avocation: sports. Fax: 420 2 4721362. Home: V Domově 28, 130 00 Prague 3, Czech Republic Office: Inst Clin Exptl Medicine, Vídeěská 1958/9, 140 21 Prague 4, Czech Republic

PIRKL, JAMES JOSEPH, industrial designer, educator, writer; b. Nyack, N.Y., Dec. 27, 1930; s. James and Ida Bertha (Gigrich) P.; m. Sarah B. W. Woolsey, June 8, 1974; children: Theo, James, Philip. Cert. advt. design, Pratt Inst., 1951, B of Indsl. Design cum laude, 1958. Design staff Gen. Motors Corp., Warren, Mich., 1958-65; sr. designer Gen. Motors Corp., 1961-64, asst. chief designer, 1964-65; instr. indsl. design Center for Creative Studies, Detroit, 1963-65; faculty dept. design Syracuse (N.Y.) U., 1965-92, assoc. prof., 1969-73, prof. indsl. design, 1974-92, prof. emeritus, 1992—, coord. indsl. design program, 1979-84, chmn. dept. design, 1985-91; exec. council chmn. Sch. Art, 1976-78, 80-81; sr. rsch. fellow All-U. Gerontology Ctr., 1990-92; prin. James J. Pirkl/Design, 1965—; cons. Brownlie Design, Inc., 1972-96, Rolland Co., 1993, Am. Soc. on Aging, 1995, Arthritis Found., 1993-96, GE Appliances, 1994, ProMatura Group, 1994-95, Prince Corp., 1991, Ford Motor Design Ctr., 1992, Loretto Geriatric Ctr., Sage Marcom Inc., 1988-90, Hazard Mgmt. Co., 1985, Marcom Switches Inc., 1977-82, Cazenovia Abroad Ltd., 1973-81, Holistic Mgmt. Group, Inc., 1981, Pulos Design Assocs., 1972-80, Beck Assocs., 1976, Fed. Prison Industries, 1974, Gen. Electric Co., 1967-70, Genesee Labs., Inc., 1968, N.Y. State Council on Arts, 1968-69, Stettner-Trush, Inc., 1972-78, Strathmore Chem. Coatings, Inc., 1969, 72, Village of Cazenovia, 1979-93, Xerox Corp., 1975, Age Wave, Inc., 1993-96; chmn. accreditation council Design Found., 1982-84, adv. to universal kitchen product R.I. Sch. Design, 1996-98; interviewed on Nat. Pub. Radio, 1998; invited lectr. All Union Rsch. Inst., Moscow, 1974, The Bauhaus, Desseau, Germany, 1976, Royal Coll. Art, London, 1993, 95, Netherlands Design Inst., Amsterdam, 1993, 95, Inst. for Gerontech., Eindhoven, 1995, Nat. Coll. Art and Design, Dublin, Ireland, 1995, U. Art and Design, Helsinki, 1995, China Instnl. Design Assn., Taiwan, 1990, Korea Indsl. Design Soc., Taijon, 1992. Author: Transgenerational Design: Products for an Aging Population, 1994; co-author: Guidelines and Strategies for Designing Transgenerational Products, 1988; co-editor: State of Art and Science of Design, 1971; co-designer: Gen. Motors Futurama Exhbn., N.Y. World's Fair, 1964-65; contbr. articles to profl. jours. including Jour. Am. Soc. Aging, Design Mgmt. Jour., Jour. Indsl. Designers Soc. Am., Bus. Adminstrn. Jour., Design News, Design Perspectives, Indsl. Design. Mem. Everson Mus. Art, 1977-85; chmn. planning commn. Town of Cazenovia, N.Y., 1988-93; mem. senate Syracuse U., 1973-80; mem. adv. bd. SEARS Project, 1989-91; chmn. chancellor's citation com., 1988-92; mem. exhbns. com. Syracuse Cultural Resources Coun., 1992-93; coord. Tylenol/Arthritis Found. Student Design Awards Program, 1993-95. With SeaBees USN, 1951-55. Recipient Gold Indsl. Design Excellence award Indsl. Designers Soc. Am. and Bus. Week Mag., 1994. Fellow Indsl. Designers Soc. Am. (chmn. universal design com. 1991-94, chmn. NASAD liaison com. 1984-88, mem. archives com. 1988-92, nat. bd. dirs. 1977-81, chmn. Cen. N.Y. chpt. 1977-78, v.p. Mid-East region 1978-80, dir., chmn. edn. com. 1980-81, U.S. rep., del. Internat. Congress Socs. Indsl. Design 1989, mem. edn. com. 1989); mem. The Design Found. (chmn. accreditation coun. 1982), Nat. Assn. Schs. Art and Design (accreditation evaluator 1985-95), Nat. Ctr. for a Barrier Free Environment (adv. task force 1981), Human Factors Soc. (life mem.), Am. Soc. Aging (contbr. articles to jour.), Author's Guild. Achievements include patent for 4-way handle. Home: 9739 Village Green Dr NE Albuquerque NM 87111-5854

PIRKLE, ESTUS WASHINGTON, minister; b. Vienna, Ga., Mar. 12, 1930; s. Grover Washington and Bessie Nora (Jones) P.; m. Annie Catherine Gregory, Aug. 18, 1955; children: Letha Dianne, Gregory Don. BA cum laude, Mercer U., 1951; BD, MRE, Southwestern Bapt. Sem., 1956, ThM, 1958; DD, Covington Theol. Sem., 1982. Ordained to ministry So. Bapt. Conv., 1949. Pastor Locust Grove Bapt. Ch., New Albany, Miss.; spkr. Camp Zion, Myrtle, Miss. Author: Wintertime, 1968, Preachers in Space, 1969, Sermon Outlines Book, 1969, Are Horoscopes All Right?, 1971, I Believe God, 1973, Who Will Build Your House?,1978, The 1611 King James Bible: A Study by Dr. Estus Pirkle, 1994; prodr. religious films: If Footmen Tire You, What Will Horses Do?, 1973, The Burning Hell, 1975, Believer's Heaven, 1977, Percy ray - A Ray for God, 1998. Home and Office: PO Box 80 Myrtle MS 38650-0080

PIRNER, MIROŠ, civil engineer, researcher; b. Prague, Czech Republic, Sept. 11, 1928; s. Karel and Marie (Jelínková) P.; m. Helena Mündlová, June 14, 1957; children: Viktor, Jan. Degree in civil engring., Tech. U., Prague, 1953, DSc in Civil Engring., 1982; PhD, Tech. U. Transport, Žilina, Slovakia, 1960. Bridge designer State Design Bur. Transport, Prague, 1952-53; tchg. asst., assoc. prof. U. Transport, Prague, 1953-70; sr. rsch. fellow Inst. Theoretical Applied Mechanics Acad. Sci., Prague, 1970-75, chief static and dynamics Tech. Rsch. and Testing Inst., 1975-90, dir. Inst. Theoretical and Applied Mechanics, 1990—; prof. civil engring. Tech. U., Prague, 1990-98; mem. sci. coun. U. Transport, Žilina, 1993—; mem. editl. bd. Fluid Abstracts, Amsterdam, 1995-99. Author: Dynamic Effect of Fluctuation in Civil Engineering, 1981, Aeroelasticity of Cylinder, 1990; co-author: Wind Effects on Civil Engineering Structures, 1983, Dynamics of Guyed Masts, 1987. Chmn. bd. local reps. Civil Engring. Com., Prague, 1989—. Mem. Acad. Civil Engring. Mem. Dem. Party. Home: U Sokolovny 262, 16400 Prague 6, Czech Republic Office: Acad Scis Czech Republic, Prosecká 76, 190 00 Prague Czech Republic

PIRODSKY, DONALD MAX, psychiatrist, educator; b. Freeport, N.Y., Feb. 2, 1945; s. Max and Doris Geilhard (Biedermann) P.; m. Gail Giufre Pallotta, Jan. 4, 1997; children: Laura Anne, Jason Donald. BA, Hofstra U., 1966; MD, SUNY, Syracuse, 1970. Diplomate Am. Bd. Psychiatry and Neurology, Nat. Bd. Med. Examiners. Intern Northwestern U. Med. Ctr., Chgo., 1970-71; resident in psychiatry Strong Meml. Hosp., Rochester, N.Y., 1973-74, U. Ariz. Med. Ctr., Tucson, 1974-76; instr. psychiatry SUNY Health Sci. Ctr., Syracuse, 1976-78, attending psychiatrist, 1976-91, asst. prof. psychiatry, 1978-85, mem. exec. com. of med. coll. assembly, 1979-82, clin. assoc. prof., 1985—, adj. attending psychiatrist, 1991—; pvt. practice Syracuse and Fayetteville, N.Y., 1976—; staff psychiatrist, dir. consultation/liaison svc. Syracuse VA Med. Ctr., 1976-87, chmn. pharmacy rev. and therapeutic agts. com., 1980-86; psychiat. cons. Ariz. Sch. for Deaf and Blind, Tucson, 1975-76, Syracuse Devel. Ctr., 1977—, Rochester Sch. for Deaf, 1978-81; ex-officio mem. Family Counseling Agy., Tucson, 1975-76; adj. attending psychiatrist SUNY Health Sci. Ctr., Syracuse, 1991—. Author: Primer of Clinical Psychopharmacology: A Practical Guide, 1981, (with Jerry S. Cohn) Clinical Primer of Psychopharmacology: A Practical Guide, 2d edit., 1992; contbr. articles to profl. jours., chpts. to med. books. Lt. comdr. USPHS, 1971-73. Fellow Am. Psychiat. Assn. (mem. ctrl. N.Y. dist. br.); mem. Am. Psychosomatic Soc., Am. Assn. Mental Retardation, Med. Soc. State of N.Y., N.Y. State Psychiat. Assn., Onondaga County Med. Soc. Episcopalian. Avocations: sports, collecting baseball cards and other sports memorabilia. Office: 7000 E Genesee St Fayetteville NY 13066-1131

PIROLA, CARLOS JOSÉ, research scientist, consultant; b. Sarmiento, Argentina, May 12, 1955; s. Eladio Nicasio and Lacy Maria del Valle (Ringlestain) P.; m. Monica, Ines Strgacich, Sept. 4, 1981; children: Malena, Facundo Carlos. Biochemist, Buenos Aires U., 1979, PhD in Biochemistry, 1984. Rsch. scientist CONICET, Argentina, 1979—, Cedars-Sinai Med. Ctr., L.A., 1991-93; cons. Lab of Medicine, Argentina, 1984—. Author 40 sci. papers and more than 100 sci. comms. With Argentine Inf., 1980-81. Recipient various grants. Mem. AAAS, InterAm. Soc. Hypertension, Am. heart Assn. (v.p. 1996—). Home: 25 de Mayo 104, 1852 Burzaco Argentina Office: Inst Inv Med A Lanari, Combatientes Malvinas 3150, 1427 Buenos Aires Argentina

PIRONTI, LAVONNE DE LAERE, developer, fundraiser; b. L.A., Jan. 11, 1946; d. Emil Joseph and Pearl Mary (Vilmur) De Laere; m. Aldo Pironti, May 21, 1977. BA in Internat. Rels., U. So. Calif., L.A., 1967. Commd. ensign USN, 1968-91, advanced through grades to comdr., 1979; pers. officer Lemoore (Calif.) Naval Air Sta., 1972-74; human rels. mgmt. specialist Human Resource Mgmt. Detachment, Naples, Italy, 1975-78; comms. staff officer Supreme Hdqrs. Allied Powers Europe, Shape, Belgium, 1979-83; dir. Navy Family Svc. Ctr. Sigonella Naval Air Sta., Sicily, 1983-85; exec. officer Naval Sta. Guam, Apra Harbor, 1985-87; comms. staff officer NATO Comm. and Info. Sys. Agy., Brussels, Belgium, 1987-89; polit. officer for Guam, trust Territories Pacific Islands Comdr. Naval Forces Marianas, Agana, Guam, 1989-91; store mgr. Sandal Tree, Lihue, Hawaii, 1991-92; CEO, exec. dir. YWCA of Kauai, Lihue, 1992-2000; chair adv. com. State Child Welfare Svcs., 1998-2000. Mem. Kauai Children's Justice com., Lihue, 1993—; bd. dirs. Hawaii Health and Human Svcs. Alliance, Lihue, 1993-99; chair Kauai County Family Self Sufficiency Program Adv. Bd., Lihue, 1993-2000. Decorated Navy Commendation medal, Meritorious Svc. Medal with 1 star, Def. Meritorious Svc. Medal with 2 stars, others; named Fed. Woman of the Yr. Comdr. Naval Forces Marianas, 1986-87. Roman Catholic. Avocations: racquetball, reading, aquacise.

PIROZYNSKI, JAN, historian, librarian, educator; b. Tarnów, Poland, Mar. 7, 1936; s. Boleslaw and Helena (Jarosz) P.; m. Czeslawa Ochal, June 7, 1960; 1 child, Magdalena Joanna. MA, Jagiellonian U., Kraków, 1957, D in History, 1968, Habilitation, 1987. Archivist State Archive, Kraków, 1958-59; libr. Jagiellonian Libr., Kraków, 1959-65, sr. libr., 1965-67, adj., 1967-72, cert. custodian, 1972-73, sr. cert. custodian, 1973-88, asst. prof., 1988—, dep. dir., 1978-81, dir., 1981-93; prof., head dept. modern history Jagellonian U., 1991-93, prof. librarianship and info. sci., 1993-96, prof. modern history Inst. History, 1996—; mem. exam. com. for diploma'd librs., Warsaw, 1984—; mem. scientific com. Nat. Libr., Warsaw, 1981—. Author: Warsaw Sjem 1570, 1972, Cracow Printing of the 15th-16th Century, 1975, Princess of Brunsvick Sophia Jagello, 1986, The News from Poland as Colected in the Pamphlets of Johann Jakob Wick in Zürich, 1560-1587, 1995; contbr. articles to profl. jours. Mem. Solidarity Party, 1980—. Recipient Golden Merite, Cross State Coun., Warsaw, 1979, award of the Min. of Sci. Rector's Coun. for Awards and Honours, 1973, 83. Mem. Polish Librs. Assn., Polish Hist. Assn., Gutenberg-Gesellschaft, Leibniz-Sozietät. Roman Catholic. Avocations: touring, skiing. Home: Na Blonie 9a/87, Pl 30-147 Cracow Poland Office: Inst History Dept Modern History, Jagiellonian U ul Gotebia 13, Pl31-004 Cracow Poland

PISAREV, MARIO ALBERTO, endocrinologist, medical researcher; b. Buenos Aires, Mar. 17, 1941; s. Jaime and Rosa (Demb) P.; m. Diana L. Kleiman, Dec. 17, 1964; children: Daniela Paula, Andrea Florencia. MD, Buenos Aires U., 1963. Fellow U.S.-USPHS-NIH, Boston and Chgo., 1968-69; vis. prof. U. Libre Brussels, 1973, 82; rsch. asst. prof. SUNY, Buffalo, 1977-79; asst. prof. biochemistry U. Buenos Aires, 1981-82; prof. biochemistry, 1995—; fellow Argentine NRC, Buenos Aires, 1964-68, established rschr., 1970—; chief divsn. nuclear biochemistry Argentine Atomic Energy Commn., Buenos Aires, 1981-96, head dept. radiobiology, 1996—; secret exec. in pharmacology State Secret Sci. Tech., Argentina, 1983-89; cons. med. scis. Argentine NRC, 1983-88, 95, hon. mem. Found. on Iodine Deficiency Disorders, Venezuela, 1993; vis. rschr., John S. Guggenheim Meml. Found. fellow NIH, Bethesda, Md., 1986-87; vis. rschr. U. Munich, 1990, Sch. Medicine Yale U., New Haven, 1994. Co-author 9 books; contbr. numerous rsch. articles to sci. publs. Prize recipient 10th Internat. Thyroid Conf., The Hague, The Netherlands, 1991. Mem. Argentine Soc. Biology (v.p.), Argentine Endocrine Soc. (pres. 1994-95, prize 1965), L.Am. Thyroid Soc. (pres. 1990-93), Argentine Fed. Endocrine Soc. (pres. 1995-97). Jewish. Avocations: fishing, tennis, music. Home: Av Benavidez 566, 1621 Buenos Aires Argentina Office: Argentine AEC, Ave Libertador 8250, 1429 Buenos Aires Argentina

PISCHINGER, FRANZ FELIX, engineer, researcher; b. Waidhofen, Austria, July 18, 1930; s. Franz and Karoline (Bentz) P.; m. Elfriede Pischinger-Goessler, 1957; children: Gerhard, Martin, Stefan, Thomas, Alice. Diploma in Engring., Tech. U., Graz, Austria, 1952, DR in Internal Combustion Engines, 1954, Habilitation degree, 1958, Dr. (hon.), 1994. Asst. Tech. U., Graz, 1953-58; head rsch. dept. Inst. Internal Combustion Engines (AVL), Graz, 1958-62; leading positions in rsch., devel. Kloeckner-Humboldt-Deutz AG, Cologne, Germany, 1962-70; dir. Inst. Applied Thermodynamics RWTH, Aachen, Germany, 1970-97; pres. FEV Motorentechnik, Aachen, 1978—; v.p. Deutsche Forschungsgemeinschaft, Bonn-Bad Godesberg, Germany, 1984-90. Contbr. articles to profl. jours. Decorated Ehrenring Sub asupiciis praesidentis republicae (Austria), 1954, Bundesverdienstkreuz 1st class (Germany), 1978; recipient Herbert Akroyd Stuard award Inst. Mech. Engrs., 1962, Carl-Engler-Medaille DGMK, Deutsche Wissenschaftliche Gesellschaft Erdöl, Erdgas Kohle, Hamburg, 1990, Austrian cross of Honor for Sci. and Art First Class, 1998. Fellow Soc. Automotive Engrs. U.S.A.; mem. ASME Internat., NAE (USA) (fgn. assoc.), Verein Deutscher Ingenieure (medal of honor 1993, decoration of honor 1997), Deutsche Gesellschaft Mineralölwissenschaft U. Kohlechemie, Rheinisch-Westfälische Akademie Wissenschaften, Aachen-Frankenburg Club, Rotary. Office: FEV Motorentechnik, Neuenhofstrasse 181, 52078 Aachen Germany

PISCIONERI, JAMES D., physician assistant; b. Paterson, N.J., Jan. 10, 1957; s. Joseph D. and Ruth E. P.; m. Lori, July 16, 1995; children: James, Anna, Darik. Student, Chaffey Coll., 1976-77, Crafton Hills Coll., 1977-88, U. Wash., 1989-90. Cert. physician asst.; cert. orthopedic technician, paramedic, firefighter, Calif. State, ACLS, advanced trauma life support, Helitac; trained S.W.A.T. mem. FBI. Emergency orthopedic technician San Antonio Hosp., Upland, Calif., 1975-80; E.M.T. chief paramedic B & B Medevac, Pasadena, Calif., 1975-80; res. firefighter Montclair (Calif.) Fire Dept., 1980-81; firefighter, paramedic City of Redlands (Calif.) Fire Dept., 1981-83, City of Ontario (Calif.) Fire Dept., 1983-87; physican assoc. We. Wash. Med. Group, Everett, 1990—. Mem. Am. Acad. Physician Assts., Nat. Registry Emergency Med. Techicians, Nat. Commn. Physician Assts., Wash. Acad. Physician Assts., Wash. State Med. Assn. Home: 3913 241st St NE Arlington VA 98223 Office: We Wash Med Group Providence Health Care Ctr 12800 Bothell Everett Hwy Everett WA 98208-6629 also: We Wash Med Group 4301 Hoyt Ave Everett WA 98203-2316

PISEDDU, ANTIOCO, bishop; b. Senorbi, Italy, Sept. 17, 1936; s. Joseph and Jane (Lecis) P. Degree in theology, U. Cagliari, Italy, 1978. Lit. tchr. Seminary, Cagliari, 1960-70; asst. tchr. U. Cagliari, 1967-73; sec. to archbishop Cagliari, 1969-73; priest St. Ann's Ch., Cagliari, 1973-81; bishop Diocese of Lanusei, Italy, 1981—; pres. Religious Scis. Inst., Lanusei, 1984—, Regional Coun. Cultural Goods, Cagliari, 1990—; del. Regional Del. Migration, Cagliari, 1982—. Author: Giuseppe Lonis Scultore Sec. XVIII, 1974, Senorbi', Storia di un Paese, 1981 Francesco Desquivel Arciv. Cagliari, 1995; editor L'Ogliastra, 1982; reviewer Studi Ogliastrini, 1998. Sec. Confrenza Episcopale Della Sardegna, 1999. Named Chaplain, The Holy See, 1973, Conventual Chaplain, Supreme Order of Malta, 1984. Home and Office: Diocese of Lanusei, Via Roma 102, 08045 Lanusei Italy

PISHCHIK, VERONIKA NIKOLAEVNA, microbiologist, researcher; b. St. Petersburg, USSR, Sept. 5, 1965; d. Nikolai Stepanovich and Ludmila Sergeevna (Bol'shakova) P. MS in Agrochemistry and Soil Sci., State U., St. Petersburg, USSR, 1988; PhD, Rsch. Inst. Agrl. Microbiology, St. Petersburg, USSR, 1991; postdoctoral, DCTP, Trieste, Italy, 1996. Engr. Rsch. Inst. Agrl. Microbiology, St. Petersburg, USSR, 1988-92; rschr. bacterial collection Rsch. Inst. Agrl. Microbiology, St. Petersburg, Russia, 1992-94; rschr. lab. biol. nitrogen Rsch. Inst. Agrl. Microbiology, St. Petersburg, 1994—. Contbr. articles to profl. jours. Office: All Russia Rsch Inst Agrl, Sh Podbelsky 3, 189620 Saint Petersburg Pushkin 8, Russia

PISKIN, AYSE KEVSER ÖZDEN, scientist, educator; b. Izmir, Turkey, Aug. 21, 1953; d. Ali Riza and Suat (Ozden) O.; m. Erhan Piskin, Oct. 24, 1974 (div. 1989); 1 child, Melis. BS, Hacettepe U., Ankara, Turkey, 1976; MS, McGill U., Montreal, 1981; PhD, Hacettepe U., 1981. Rsch. asst. Hacettepe U., Ankara, Turkey, 1976-86, asst. prof., 1986-90, assoc. prof., 1990-99, prof., 1999—. Inventor in field. Mem. Friends of Presdl. Symphony Orch., Ankara, 1997. NATO fellow, 1979-81, postdoctoral fellow Fred Hutchinson Cancer Rsch. Ctr., Seattle, 1988, UCLA, L.A., 1993; AFS scholar, 1971. Mem. Turkish Biochem. Soc. (gen. sec. 1994-96), Fedn. European Biochem. Soc., Internat. Union Biochem. & Molecular Biology. Avocations: tennis, classical music, swimming. Office: Hacettepe U Faculty Medicine, Hacettepe U Fac Medicine, Biochemistry Dept, 06100 Ankara Turkey

PISPAS, ASTERIOS, chemist, researcher; b. Athens, Attiki, Greece, Oct. 16, 1967; s. Ioannis and Anna (Kourtis) P.; m. Charikleia Tserepa, Nov. 1, 1992. BS in Chemistry, U. Athens, 1989, PhD of Chemistry, 1994. Postdoctoral fellow Chemistry Dept. U. Ala. Birmingham, 1994-95; rsch. assoc. Inst. Electronic Structure and Laser Forth, Heraklion, Greece, 1996; rsch. assoc. Chemistry Dept. U. Athens, 1997—. Contbr. articles to profl. jours. Mem. Greek Chemists Assn., Greek Polymer Soc. Avocations: reading, gymnastics, mountain hiking. Office: Univ Athens, Panepistimiopolis, 15771 Zografoy Athens, Greece

PISSAKAS, SOTIRIS, civil engineer; b. Rhodes, Greece, May 3, 1953; s. John and Mary Pissaka. BSc in Civil Engring, Nat. Tech. U. Athens, 1976; MSc in Soil Mechanics and Found. Engring., U. Birmingham, Eng., 1977. Registered profl. engr., Greece. Candidate European MP for Greece Democratic Ctr. Party, 1981, 89; with tech. chamber of Greece, Dodecanese, 1985-87. With Greek Navy, 1978-80. Home: Voriou Ipirou 7, Rhodes Greece

PISSARIDES, CHRISTOPHER ANTONIOU, economics educator; b. Nicosia, Cyprus, Feb. 20, 1948; arrived in U.K., 1965; s. Antonios and Evdokia (Georgiadou) P.; m. Francesca Cassano, July 24, 1986; children: Antony Giulio, Miranda Olympia. BA in Econs., U. Essex, Colchester, Eng., 1970, MA in Econs., 1971; PhD in Econs., London Sch. Econs., 1974. Rsch. economist Cen. Bank Cyprus, Nicosia, 1974; lectr. in econs. U. Southampton, Eng., 1974-75; lectr. London Sch. Econs., 1976-82, reader, 1982-86, prof., 1986—; vis. prof. Harvard U., Cambridge, Mass., 1979-80, Princeton (N.J.) U., 1984, U. Calif., 1990-91; rsch. dir. Centre for Labour Econs., London, 1985-90; vis. scholar World Bank, 1995; cons. to World Bank, European Commn., OECD, Paris; mem. Coun. Royal Econs. Soc., 1998—. Author: Labour Market Adjustment, 1976, Equilibrium Unemployment Theory, 1990, 2d edit. 2000; editor: Jour. Economica, 1980-83; contbr. articles to profl. publs.; mem. editl. bd.: Rev. Econ. Studies, 1983-92, Economica, 1997—. Grantee Econ. and Soc. Rsch. Coun., 1980—, Dept. Employment, 1980-90; Houblon-Norman fellow Bank of Eng., 1994. Fellow Econometric Soc.; mem. Royal Econ. Soc., European Econ. Assn. Greek Orthodox. Home: Willow House, Willow Rd, London NW3 1TP, England Office: London Sch Econs, Houghton St, London WC2A 2AE, England

PISTOLESI, MASSIMO, medical educator; b. Pisa, Tuscany, Italy, Aug. 1, 1948; s. Vasco and Valeria (Bertini) P.; m. Germana Allescia, June 8, 1996; 1 child, Valeria; m. Vanna Ciampalini, Feb. 23, 1974 (wid. July 1988); 1 child,

Paola. MD, Cath. U., Rome, 1973; Diploma in Respiratory Diseases, U. Pisa, 1975, Diploma in Nuclear Medicine, 1977. Resident in respiratory medicine U. Pisa, 1973-75; career investigator Nat. Rsch. Coun. of Italy, Pisa, 1975-88; assoc. prof. respiratory medicine U. Rome, 1988-91, Pisa, 1991-97; prof. respiratory medicine U. Florence, Italy, 1997—; head respiratory intensive care, U. pisa, 1991-97; dir. sect. of respiratory medicine, U. Florence, 1997—. Author: (book) Reading the Chest Radiograph: A Physiologic Approach, 1993; contbr. articles to profl. jours. Recipient Luigi Pigorini Meml. award Italian Soc. Radiology, 1987, Manfredi del Buono Meml. award U. Zurich, 1988. Mem. Fleischner Soc. for Chest Diagnosis, European Respiratory Soc., Italian Assn. of Respiratory Medicine. Office: Univ Florence Dept Resp Med, Viale Morgagni 85, 50134 Florence Tuscany, Italy

PISTONE, DANIELE, musicologist, educator; b. Belfort, France, Dec. 1, 1946; d. Eugène and Marie-Louise (Sarazin) Colle; m. Silvestro Pistone, Nov. 22, 1969; 1 child, Pascal. Master de Lettres, U. Besançon, France, 1969; PhD, U. Paris IV, 1973. Asst. U. Paris, Sorbonne, 1973-74, head asst., 1974-81, prof. musicology, 1981—, dir. faculty music and musicology, 1990-95; conseiller Mission Scientifique et Technique, 1994-97, Min. Edn. and Rsch.; dir. Collection Musique-Musicologie Ed Champion, France, 1975—; dir. dir. music rev. Internat. Music, France, 1980—; dir. music obs. U. Paris, Sorbonne, 1989—. Author: Le piano dans la littérature française des origines à 1900, 1975, La musique en France de la Revolution à 1900, 1979, 19th Century Italian from Rossini to Puccini, 1995. Chevalier, Order National du Mérite, 1994, Ordre des Palmes Académiques, 1989. Office: Univ of Paris-Sorbonne, 1 rue Victor-Cousin, 75005 Paris France

PIŠTORA, JAROMÍR, physics educator; b. Pardubice, Czech Republic, Mar. 20, 1953; s. Jaromír and Anna (Vernisová) P.; m. Lenka Prokešová, Sept. 1, 1979; children: Michal, Radek. Diploma in engring., Czech Tech. U., Prague, 1977; PhD in Exptl. Physics, Charles U., Prague, 1984. Rschr. Charles U., 1981-83; asst. lectr. physics Tech. U. Ostrava, Czech Republic, 1983-91, sr. lectr., 1991-96, prof., 1996—, vice head dept., 1991-99. Contbr. articles to profl. jours. including Jour. Applied Physics, IEEE Trans. on Magnetism, Jour. Magnetism and Magnetic Materials. Grantee Grant Agy. Czech Republic, 1998-00, Barrande, France and Czech Republic, 1997-99. Mem. IEEE, Internat. Soc. Optical Engring., N.Y. Acad. Scis. Achievements include invention of magnetic defectoscope. Avocations: radio controlled models, stamp collecting, literature. Office: Tech U Ostrava Dept Physics, 17 Listopadu 15, 708 33 Ostrava Czech Republic

PITAYATARATORN, JANEWIT, international business consultant; b. Bangkok, Thailand, Dec. 18, 1950; arrived in Austria, 1970; s. Peng Hui and Saikim (Tae) Tang; m. Brigitte Bauer; children: René, Denise, Aline. M of Econs., Kyiv State U. Culture and Arts, Kiev, Ukraine, 1998; DSc Open Internat. U., Complementary Medicines, 1999. Gen. acct. Bank of Am. NT & SA, Vienna, 1971-75; fin. officer UNIDO, Vienna, 1975-96; mng. dir. Virtual Enterprises Assn., Vienna, 1994—; pres. Virtual Tech. Ctr., 1996—, Vitrual Design Inst., Kaufbeuren, Germany, 1996—; mng. dir. Asian Biometrics, 1998—; internat. bus. cons., 1995—; bd. dirs., treas. Internat. Inst. for Info. Design, Vienna, 1996—; chmn. Joint Austria-Thai Com. on Environ. Tech., 1995—; coord. Virtual Inc., 1997—; spl. advisor various ministries and C. of C.s on new economy, vitual economy issues, 2000—; speaker in field. Named Hon. Citizen, State of Tex., 1970. Office: Virtual Enterprises Assn, Frankenberggasse 9/10, A-1040 Vienna Austria

PITCHFORTH, ROGER JOHN, educator, dispute resolutions administrator, arbitrator, mediator; b. Eng., Apr. 30, 1942; arrived in New Zealand, 1948; s. John and Mina Pitchforth; m. Joan Marion Pigney, May 16, 1970; children: Mathew, Benjamin, Daniel. LLB, Victorian U., Wellington, New Zealand, 1969; MBA, Massey U., Palmerston North, New Zealand, 1984, BA, 1999. Cert. barrister, solicitor High Ct. New Zealand. Clk. Cts. (Justice Dept.), New Zealand, 1959-62; law clk. Stacey Smith & Gibson, Wellington, New Zealand, 1962-68; solicitor Taverner Keys & Pitchforth, Carterton, 1969-79; sr. lectr. Massey U., 1979-95, dir. Dispute Resolution Ctr., 1995—; arbitrator, mediator, New Zealand, 1992. Author: Meetings-Practice, Procedure, 1991, 94. Chmn. Across (Social Svcs.), Palmerston North, 1995-97; lay reader Anglican Ch., 1970—. Fellow Arbitrators' and Mediators' Inst. New Zealand (coun. 1994—, v.p. 1998—), Toastmasters Internat. (dist. gov. 1977-78); mem. Awapuni Rotary (pres. 1993-94). Avocation: croquet. Home: 68 Rangitane St, Palmerston North New Zealand Office: Massey Univ Dispute Res Ctr, Pvt Bag 11222, Palmerston North New Zealand

PITCHIKA, PRASADA RAO VIGNANANDA VARA, anatomist, educator; b. Pandillapalli, India, Aug. 5, 1947; s. Veeraiah and Yellamandamma (Gutti) P.; m. Kumari Vani Gutti, Aug. 19, 1977; 1 child, Ravi. BSc, Andhra U., Waltair, India, 1968; MSc, Madras (India) U., Madras, India, 1972; PhD, U. Ibadan, Nigeria, 1981. Lectr. Dr. V.M. Med. Coll., Shivaji U., Sholapur, India, 1972-75; lectr., sr. lectr. U. Ibadan, Nigeria, 1975-90; sr. lectr. U. Zimbabwe, Harare, 1991—. Contbr. articles to profl. jours. Mem. Anat. Soc. Gt. Britain and Ireland, Anat. Soc. So. Africa. Avocations: gardening, photography. Office: U Zimbabwe, PO Box MP 167, Mt Pleasant, Harare Zimbabwe

PITCOCK, JAMES ALLISON, retired pathologist; b. Little Rock, Sept. 13, 1929; s. Radford Bolling and Anne (Whitelaw) P.; m. Cynthia Jean Dehaven, June 18, 1954; children: Allison P. Mays, James Dehaven. BS, MIT, 1951; MD, Washington U., 1955. Diplomate Am. Bd. Pathology. Intern Vanderbilt U., Nashville, 1955-56; resident Barnes Hosp., St. Louis, 1956-59, 61-62; asst. pathologist St. Vincents Hosp., Little Rock, 1963; asst. pathologist Bapt. Meml. Hosp., Memphis, 1964-75, asst. dir. labs., 1975-87, dir. labs., 1987-95; ret.; vol. faculty U. Tenn. Med. Sch., Memphis, 1965-96, acting chair pathology, 1986-89; com. chair, mem. Am. Heart Assn., Memphis, 1976-84, exec. com., 1983-87, pres., 1985-86. Contbr. chpts. to books and articles to profl. jours. Capt. USAF, 1959-61. Mem. Alpha Omega Alpha, Sigma Xi. Episcopalian. Achievements include experimental and scholarly work in experimental hypertension and surgical pathology.

PITELIS, CHRISTOS, economic educator, researcher, consultant; b. Kavala, Greece, Nov. 10, 1957; arrived in Eng., 1979; s. Nicholaos and Eleni Pitelis; m. Ioanna Glykou, Sept. 12, 1981; children: Eleni Eleanna Nemessis, Alkis Theonas. BA in Pub. Mgmt. 1st class, Pantion U., Athens, Greece, 1979; diploma in Pub. and Indsl. Econs., Newcastle Upon Tyne (Eng.) U., 1980; MA in Econs., Warwick (Eng.) U., 1982, PhD in Econs., 1984. Lectr. U. Nottingham, Eng., 1984-89, U. St. Andrews, Scotland, 1989-91; assoc. prof. econs. Athens U., 1997—; dir. studies, fellow in econs. Queens' Coll. Cambridge (Eng.) U., 1991—, Barclays Bank lectr., Judge Inst., Cambridge U., 1991—, dir. Ctr. of Internat. Bus. and Mgmt., 1997—, assoc. dir., 1993-97; cons. UN, Brazil; advisor to Greek Govt., Ministry Industry, 1994-95, Ministry Devel., 1995—, coord. Future of Greek Industry project; mem. steering com. Cambridge-Harvard Project on Brit. Competitiveness; cons. various orgns., including European Cmty.; mem. Europe 12 Group, and St. Andrews Mgmt. Inst.; organizer workshops and seminars, invited spkr. in field; judge Inst. Cambridge U., 1992-96. Author: Corporate Capital: Control, Ownership, Saving and Crisis, 1987, Market and Non-Market Hierarchies: Theory of Institutional Failure, 1993, Industrial Strategy: For Britain, in Europe and the World, 1994; editor: (with R. Sugden) The Nature of the Transnational Firm, 1991, Transaction Costs, Markets and Hierarchies, 1993, (with T. Clarke) The Political Economy of Privatization, 1993, (with J. Groenewegen and S.E. Sjöstrand) On Economic Institutions, Theory and Applications, 1994, (with M. Milgate) Frontiers of Political Economy; contbr. numerous chpts. to books, articles and revs. to sci. and profl. jours. and conf. procs.; editor rschr. papers on mgmt. studies, 1991-96;. With Greek Army, 1988. Grantee Greek Govt. 1994-97, European Union 1994-96, 91-93, European Cmty. 1995-97. Mem. European Assn. Evolutionary Polit. Economy (area coord. 1993-96). Avocations: reading, music. Office: U Cambridge Queens' Coll, Silver St, Cambridge CB3 9ET, England and: U Athens Dept Economics, 5 Stadiou St, Athens Greece

PITMAN, SIR BRIAN (IVOR), bank executive; b. Dec. 13, 1931; s. Ronald Ivor and Doris Ivy (Short) P.; m. Barbara Mildred Ann Darby, 1954; 3 children. DSc (hon.), City U., London, 1996. With Lloyds Bank, 1952—, joint gen. mgr., 1975-76; exec. dir. Lloyds Bank Internat., 1976-78, dep. chief exec., 1978-82; dep. group chief exec. Lloyds Bank Plc, 1982-83, chief exec., dir., 1983-97, chmn., 1997—; group chief exec. dir. Lloyds TSB Group Plc, 1995-97; chmn. Lloyds TSB Group plc, 1997—; gov. Ashridge Mgmt. Coll., 1997—; dir. Carlton Comm. PLC, 1998—; chmn. NEXT PLC, 1998—; dir. Tomkins PLC, 2000—; pres. Brit. Bankers' Assn., 1996-97. Knighted for svcs. to banking, 1994. Fellow Chartered Inst. Bankers (pres. 1997-98). Avocations: golf, cricket, music. Office: Lloyds TSB Group plc, 71 Lombard St, London EC3P 3BS, England

PITMAN, GARY ROBERT, oil company executive; b. Sandys, Bermuda, Oct. 18, 1948; s. Robert Knoll and Patricia Anne (Howes) P.; m. Martha Jean MacKenzie, May 27, 1972; children: Rebecca, Megan. BBA, U. N.B., Can., 1971. Cert. Gen. Acct., Can. Supr. internat. investments Bank of Bermuda Ltd., Hamilton, 1972-75; mgr. acctg., asst. sec. Kupan Internat., Hamilton, 1975-77; comptr. Kupan Internat. Ltd., Hamilton, 1977-79; asst. treas. Kupan Internat. & Insco Ltd., Hamilton, 1979-80, v.p., treas., 1980-85; sr. v.p., treas. Chevron Internat. Ltd., Hamilton, 1985-90, pres., 1990—; mem. parliament, 1998—; dir. 50 Chevron subs. worldwide; shadow min. Environment, Planning and Natural Resources, 1998—. Former dep. chmn. bd. govs. Warwick Acad., Bermuda, 1987-96; chmn. United Bermuda Party, 1993-98; senator Bermuda Govt., 1994-97, parliamentary sec., 1994-97, justice of the peace, 1995, cabinet minister, govt. senate leader, 1997; chmn. Bermuda Bd. Immigration, 1989-98; pres. U. New Brunswick Bermuda Alumni Chpt., 1997-99; former Senate spokesman for Tourism and Marine Svcs. Ministry, Works, Engring. Parks and Housing Ministry, Info. and Tech. Ministry. Mem. Cert. Gen. Accts. Assn. (pres. 1992-93), Sandys Rotary Club (pres. 1994-95). Roman Catholic. Avocations: deep sea fishing, gardening, travel. Home: 3 Leith Hill Ln, Warwick WK 03, Bermuda Office: Chevron Internat Ltd, 11 Church St POB HM 2082, Hamilton HM HX, Bermuda

PITONIAK, SCOTT MICHAEL, sports columnist; b. Rome, N.Y., Apr. 10, 1955; s. Andrew Edward and Edna (Holloway) P.; m. Susan Ingison, June 9, 1984; children: Amy Leigh, Christopher Drew. BS in Pub. Communication magna cum laude, Syracuse U., 1977. Baseball writer Evening Times, Little Falls, N.Y., 1977; sportswriter Daily Sentinel, Rome, N.Y., 1977; sportswriter, columnist Observer-Dispatch, Utica, N.Y., 1978-84; pro football writer Dem. & Chronicle, Rochester, N.Y., 1985-90, sports projects writer, 1990—; corr. Gannett News Svc., 1982—, Sporting News, 1982—; voter Heisman Trophy Award, 1981—; journalism prof. St. John Fisher Coll., 1995—. Author: The Buffalo Bills Official Trivia Book, 1989, 92; co-author: Silver Seasons: The Story of the Rochester Red Wings, 1996, Playing Write Field, 1997; contbr. articles to mags., newspapers, news svcs. including Sport, Sporting News, USA Today, Washington Post, Phila. Inquirer, AP, UPI, others; co-host TV show Time Warner Comms., 1994-96. Vol. Alzheimer's Assn., Rochester, 1991—. Recipient Disting. Health Journalism award Gold medal 1st Pl. newspaper div., 1991, 1st Pl. sports N.Y. State AP Writing Contest, 1995, 2nd Pl. features, 1993, 2d Pl. sports, 1991, 2d Pl. columns Prof. Football Writers Am., 1st Place Enterprise Reporting 1999, Best of Gannett award, 1996, 97, 98, others; work cited in Best AM. Sportswriting, 1992; Regents scholar; inductee Rochester Sports Walk of Fame, 1999, Syracuse U. Journalism Hall of Fame, 2000; named One of Am.'s Top 10 Sports Columnist APSE 2000. Mem. Profl. Football Writers Am., Coll. Football Writers Assn. Am. (bd. dirs.), Basketball Writers Am., Kappa Tau Alpha, Phi Kappa Phi. Roman Catholic. Avocations: distance bicycle riding, reading, softball, sports memorabilia collecting. Home: 35 Western Pine Dr Rochester NY 14616-5014 Office: Gannett Rochester Newspapers 55 Exchange Blvd Rochester NY 14614-2001

PITR, KAREL, physician; b. Plzen, Czech Republic, May 24, 1957; s. Karel and Jindriska (Vraštilova') P.; m. Gabriela Boskova'; 1 child, Gabriela. MD, Charles U., Prague, Czech Republic, 1983, postgrad., 1986, grad. in phys. medicine and rehab., 1990. House surgeon Faculty Hosp., Plzen, Czech Republic, 1983-86, resident surg. officer, 1986, house physician rehab. dept., 1986-89, resident med. officer, cons., 1990-96, head physician pvt. rehab. dept., 1996—; tchr. phys. therapy and kinesiology Sch. for diploma Physiotherapists, Plzen, 1994—, Charles U. Med. Faculty, Plzen, 1999—; mem. Commn. for Electromagnetism, European Union, 1993. Mem. Soc. Phys. and Rehab. Medicine of Czech Republic, Soc. Myoskeletal Medicine Czech Republic, N.Y. Acad. Scis. Avocations: music, hunting, diving. E-mail: pitrk@volny.cz. Home: Pod Chlumem 14, 31215 Plzen Czech Republic Office: Rehab Ctr, Touzimska' 23, 32335 Plzen Czech Republic

PITSUWAN, SURIN, minister of foreign affairs; b. Nakhon Si Thammarat, Oct. 28, 1949; m. Alisa Ariya. Grad. in polit. sci. cum laude, Claremont Men's Coll., 1972; PhD, Harvard U., 1982. Columnist Nation and Bangkok Post, 1980-92; Congrl. fellow, 1983-84, acad. asst. to dean of faculty of polit. sci.; vice rector for acad. affairs Thammasat U.; min. Ministry of Fgn. Affairs, Govt. of Thailand, 1997—; sec. Spkr. Ho. of Reps., 1986; dep. fgn. min., 1992-94. Decorated Knight Grand Cordon Most Noble Order of the Crown of Thailand, Most Exalted Order of the White Elephant. Islam. E-mail: off0100@mserv.mfa.go.th. Office: Wang Saranrom, Thanon Sanamchai, Bangkok 10200, Thailand*

PITT, GEORGE, lawyer, investment banker; b. Chgo., July 21, 1938; s. Cornelius George and Anastasia (Geocaris) P.; m. Barbara Lynn Goodrich, Dec. 21, 1963 (div. Apr. 1990); children: Elizabeth Nanette, Margaret Leigh; m. Pamela Ann Pittsford, May 19, 1990. BA, Northwestern U., 1960, JD, 1963; hon. grad., U.S. Army Intelligence Sch., Ft. Holabird, Md., 1964. Bar: Ill. 1963. Assoc. Chapman and Cutler, Chgo., 1963-67; ptnr. Borge and Pitt, and predecessor, 1968-87, Katten Muchin & Zavis, Chgo., 1987-97; sr. mng. dir. Banc One Capital Markets, Inc. (formerly First Chgo. Capital Markets, Inc.), 1998-2000; mng. dir. PaineWebber Inc., Chgo., 2000—; conf. chmn. Bond Buyer's 3d Ann. Midwest Pub. Fin. Conf., 1994; conf. co-chmn. Bond Buyer's 8th Ann. Midwest Pub. Fin. Conf., 1999. notes and comments editor Northwestern U. Law Rev., 1962-63. 1st lt. AUS, 1964. Fellow Am. Coll. of Bond Counsel; mem. Ill. State Bar Assn., Univ. Club. Chgo., Michigan City Yacht Club, Ind. Soc. of Chgo., Eta Sigma Phi, Phi Delta Phi, Phi Gamma Delta. Home: 600 N McClurg Ct Chicago IL 60611-3044 Office: PaineWebber Inc 42nd Fl 181 W Madison St Fl 42 Chicago IL 60602-4510

PITT, JOSEPH CHARLES, philosophy educator; b. Hempstead, N.Y., Sept. 12, 1944; s. Louis Antony and Miriam (Baumstein) P.; m. Donna Hanlon Smith, Feb. 25, 1946. AB in Philosophy, Coll. William and Mary, 1966; MA in Philosophy, U. Western Ont., London, Ont., Can., 1968; PhD, U. Western Ont., London, Can., 1972. Instr. Va. Poly. Inst. and State U., Blacksburg, 1971-72; asst. prof. Va. Poly. Inst. and State U., 1972-78; vis. asst. prof. U. Pitts., 1974; assoc. prof. Va. Poly. Inst. and State U., 1978-83, prof. philosophy, 1983—; founding dir. Ctr. for Study of Sci. in Soc., Va. Poly. Inst. and State U., 1980-81, founder, dir. humanities, sci. and tech. program, 1979-89, head dept. philosophy, 1992-98, dir. grad. studies in philosophy, 1998—. Author: Pictures, Images and Conceptual Change, 1981, Galileo, Human Knowledge and the Book of Nature, 1992, Thinking About Technology, 2000; editor: New Perspectives on Galileo, 1978, Theories of Explanation, 1988, New Directions in the Philosophy of Technology, 1995; editor Perspectives on Science: Historical, Philosophical, Social, 1991—; assoc. editor: Techné, The Soc. Philosophy & Tech. Jour., 1996—; mem. bd. editors Philosophy and Tech., 1985-94, Behaviorism, 1985-96, History of Philosophy Quar., 1990—, Sci. and Edn., 1992—; contbr. articles to profl. jours. U. Pitts. Ctr. for Philosophy of Sci. vis. sr. fellow, 1984. Mem. Philosophy of Sci. Assn., Soc. for Philosophy and Tech. (v.p., pres.-elect 1989-91, pres. 1991-93), History of Sci. Soc., Soc. for History of Tech., Am. Philos. Assn., Irish Wolfhound Club Am. (bd. dirs. 1987-95), Sigma Xi. Home: Calyddon Newport VA 24128 Office: Va Poly Inst and State U Dept Philosophy Blacksburg VA 24061

PITT, JUDSON HAMILTON, publisher, author; b. Glen Cove, N.Y., June 7, 1953; s. Gavin Alexander and Eleanore Gaehler (Whiting) P.; m. Elena U. Tokaeva, Dec. 16, 1995. BS in Communications, Ariz. State U., 1977. Resident advisor fraternity Ohio State U., Columbus, 1977-79; supr. student svcs. Loyola U., Chgo., 1979-81; asst. to CEO Flair Communications Agy., Inc., Chgo., 1981—; v.p. Gavin Pitt Assocs., Inc., Chgo., 1986—; pub. Water Tower Pub. House, Chgo., 1989—; dir. ops. Chgo. Marathon, 1984-93. Author: The Official Hard Rock Cafe Pin Collector's Guide, 1997. Mem. Am. Mktg. Assn., Newcomen Soc. U.S., Chgo. Soc. Assn. Execs., Saddle & Cycle Club, Pi Kappa Alpha. Republican. Presbyterian. Home: 5510 N Sheridan Rd Chicago IL 60640-1633 Office: 214 W Erie St Chicago IL 60610-3611

PITT, WILLIAM ALEXANDER, cardiologist; b. July 17, 1942; came to U.S., 1970; s. Reginald William and Una Sylvia (Alexander) P.; m. Judith Mae Wilson, May 21, 1965; children: William Matthew, Joanne Katharine. MD, U. B.C., Vancouver, 1967. Diplomate Royal Coll. Physicians Can. Intern Mercy Hosp., San Diego, 1967-68, resident, 1970-71, assoc. dir. cardiology, 1972-92; resident Vancouver Gen. Hosp., 1968-70, U. Calif., San Diego, 1971-72; with So. Calif. Cardiology Med. Group, San Diego, 1984—; pvt. practice Clin. Cons. Cardiology; pres., med. dir. San Diego IPA, 1997—; bd. trustees San Diego Found. for Med. Care, 1983-89, 91—, pres., chmn. bd. trustees, 1986-88, med. dir., 1991-96; trustee Pacific Found. for Med. Care, 1996—, med. dir., 1996—; bd. dirs. Mut. Assn. for Profl. Services, Phila., 1984-92; pres. Alternet Med. Svcs., Inc., 1992-95; pres. and med. dir. San Diego IPA, 1995—. Fellow Royal Coll. Physicians Can., Am. Coll. Cardiology (assoc.); mem. AMA, Am. Heart Assn., Calif. Med. Assn., San Diego County Med. Soc., San Diego County Heart Assn. (bd. dirs. 1982-88). Episcopalian. Office: So Calif Cardiology Med Group 6386 Alvarado Ct Ste 101 San Diego CA 92120-4906

PITTALUGA, PAUL, cardiologist, consultant; b. Nice, Riviera, France, Oct. 5, 1965; s. Jean-Marie and Evelyne Walker-Rouze P.; m. Helene Thevenin, July 4, 1987 (div. Jan. 1995); 1 child, Thomas; m. Barbara Falkowski, Feb. 3, 1996; 1 child, Charles. BS, U. Nice, 1984, MD, 1995, cert. vascular surgery, 1995. Resident surgery Nice U. Hosp., 1990-95; vascular surgeon Nontes (France) U. Hosp., 1995-96; vascular surgeon Nice U. Hosp., 1996-97, cons. vascular surgery, 1997-98. Contbr. articles to profl. jours. Home: 8 Rue Jean Giono, 06800 Cagnes Sur Mer France Office: Ctr Medico Chirurgical, 10 Ave de Villeneuve, 06800 Cagnes Sur Mer France

PITTARAS, CONSTANTINE, coast guard officer; b. Pyrgos, Ilia, Greece, Jan. 1, 1950; s. John and Magdalene (Papaioannou) P. BSc in Chemistry, U. Athens, Greece, 1973; cert. French lang., U. Sorbonne, Paris, 1973; MSc in Analytical Chemistry, U. Birmingham, Eng., 1975; degree in computer scis., Greek Ministry of Def., Athens, 1988. Rschr. Nuc. Ctr., Saclay, France, 1976; inspector of industry for environment Ministry of Industry, Athens, 1977; tng. in analytical chemistry U. Lyon, France, 1977-78, U. Copenhagen, 1977-78; with Greek Coast Guard, Piraeus, 1979—, advanced through ranks to capt., 1996; dir. Marine Environment Protection divsn. Greek Ministry of Mercantile Marine, Piraeus, 1998—; Greek rep. Internat. Maritime Orgn., London, 1981—, UNEP/REMPEC, Malta, European Union, Brussels. Author numerous regulations of loading and unloading dangerous cargo, chemical safety and safe transport. Battalion of Phoenix, Pres. of the Rep., Greece, 1998, Battalion of Honor, 1998; recipient B-class prize Min. of Mercantile Marines, 1990, 2 awards Hellenic Coast Guard, 1990. Mem. Greek Chem. Soc., Club Coast Guard Officers, U. Birmingham Grads. E-mail: dpthap@mail.yen.gr. Home: 19 Rostan St, 11141 Athens Greece

PITTAS, GEORGE PANAYIOTIS, food products executive; b. Athens, Greece, Oct. 24, 1952; s. Panayiotis G. and Maria (Perri) P.; m. Ismini Lambrinidou, Feb. 14, 1998; children: Maria, Panayiotis. BA, Economic U., Athens, Greece, 1976. Prodn. mgr. Bee Culturing Co. Attiki, Athens, 1972-80, mng. dir., 1980—; hon. cons. C. of C. and Industry, Athens, 1990—. Contbr. articles to mags. Pres. Union Greek Honey Packers, 1983—. Mem. Fedn. Hellenic Food Industries (treas. 1995), Hellenic Mfrs. Assn. (treas. 1995). Avocations: guitar, travel. Home: Sikinou 3, 11361 Athens Greece Office: Bee Culturing Co Attiki, Arcadias 18, 12132 Athens Greece

PITTAWAY, DONALD EDWARD, endocrinology educator, gynecologist; b. Carbondale, Pa., May 8, 1947; s. Clifford Charles and Eleanor Ruth (Schwartztrauber) P.; m. Carmel Celine Imbalzano, June 27, 1970; children: Jennifer, Donald E. Jr. AB, Franklin and Marshall Coll., 1969; PhD, Tenn. U., 1974; MD, La. State U., Shreveport, 1977. Diplomate Am. Bd. Ob-Gyn, Am. Bd. Bioanalysis (high complexity lab. dir.); cert. reproductive endocrinologist. Clin. instr. Sch. Medicine La. State U., 1974-77; instr. Sch. Medicine Vanderbilt U., Nashville, 1981-83; from asst. to assoc. prof. reproductive endocrinology Wake Forest U., Winston-Salem, N.C., 1983-90, prof. endocrinology, sect. head, 1990-98, clin. prof., 1998—; med. adv. bd. Smith Kline Beecham, Pitts., 1993—. Summer fellow NSF, 1971, Rsch. fellow March of Dimes Nat. Found., 1975-76, Ob-Gyn Clin. Rsch. fellow Mead Johnson Am. Coll., 1984-85. Mem. Soc. Gynecol. Investigation, Endocrine Soc., Am. Soc. Reproductive Medicine. Office: Brookview Women's Ctr Ste 105 3333 Brookview Hills Blvd Winston Salem NC 27103-5661

PITTE, JEAN-ROBERT, geography educator, university official; b. Paris, Aug. 12, 1949; s. Jean and Jeanne (Turillon) P.; m. Mayumi Tozuka, July 27, 1978; 1 child, Delphine. Maitrise, Sorbonne, Paris, 1970; Agregation de Geographie, France, 1971; D de 3 Cycle, Sorbonne, 1975; PhD, Etat, Sorbonne, 1986. Prof. Lycee Chaptal, Paris, 1971-72; asst. Ens Nouakchott, Mauritanie, 1972-74; asst., maitre asst. U. Paris-Sorbonne, 1974-88, prof., 1988—, v.p., 1997—. Author: Histoire du Paysage Francais, 2 vols., 1983, Terres de Castanide, 1986, Gastronomie Francaise, 1991, Paris, Histoire d'un ville, 1993, La France, 1997, others. Pres. Com.-Nat. Francais de Geographie, 1992—; charge-de-mission Ministère de l'Enseignement Supérieur, 1993-95. Decorated chevalier de l'Ordre Nat. du Mérite, officier de l'Ordre des Palmes Academiques. Mem. Soc. Geography (v.p. Paris 1995—). E-mail: pitte@easynet.fr. Office: Sorbonne, 1 rue Victor Cousin, 75005 Paris France

PITTENGER, RICHARD FAY, oceanographer; b. Lexington, Nebr., June 1, 1935; s. Ernest James and Margaret Inez Hesser P.; m. Marjorie Andrade, Oct. 14, 1961; children: Elizabeth, Margaret, James, Katherine. BS, U.S. Naval Acad., 1958; M in Physics, Naval Postgrad. Sch., Monterey, Calif., 1965. Commd. officer USN, 1958, advanced through grades to rear adm.; cmdr. of destroyer squadron 26 USN, Norfolk, Va., 1982-84; chief of staff, dep. comdr. US Naval Forces Europe, London, 1984-86; dir. Antisubmarine Warfare Divsn. USN, Washington, 1984-86, oceanographer of the Navy, 1988-90; Arctic rsch. coord. Woods Hole (Mass.) Oceanographic Instn., 1990—, assoc. dir. for marine opers., 1990—. Contbr. articles to profl. jours. and books, including a Commanding Officer's Ref. Book. Mem. naval studies bd. Nat. Acad. of Sci., Washington, 1998-99. Decorated Legion of Merit awards (5) USN, Meritorious Svc. medal, USN, Navy Commendation medal, Superior Pub. Svc. medal. Mem. AAAS, Naval Acad. Alumni, Soc. of Sigma Xi, Oceanography Soc., Marine Technology Soc., Am. Geophys. Union. Avocations: fly fishing, photography. E-mail: rpittenger@whoi.edu. Office: Woods Hole Oceanograph Inst MS-37 38 Water St Woods Hole MA 02543-1055

PITTEWAY, MICHAEL LLOYD VICTOR, computer science educator; b. Ilford, Eng., Feb. 10, 1934; s. Lloyd Sydney and Elsie Maud (Hall) P.; m. Cynthia Ethel Patricia Wilkins, Apr. 2, 1956. BA, Queens Coll., Cambridge, Eng., 1956, MA, 1956, PhD, 1959, ScD, 1972. Fellow Harkness Found., U.S., 1959-61; sr. rsch. fellow Radio Rsch. Sta., 1961-63; computer dir. Nottingham (Eng.) U., England, 1963-67; head. computer sci. dept. Brunel U., Uxbridge, Eng., 1967-85, prof. computer sci., 1985—; assoc. QuantiSci, Henley, Eng., 1991—; civil. dir. Advances Study Inst. NATO, 1985-87. Contbr. articles to profl. jours. Sci. and Engring. Rsch. Coun. grantee, 1969, 90. Fellow: British Computer Soc., Inst. Math. and its Applications, Inst. Physics., Royal Soc. Arts. Avocations: food, wine, music, duplicate bridge, golf, beer. Home: Hedgerows Star Ln, Knowl Hill RG10 9XY, England Office: Brunel Univ, Computer Sci Dept, Uxbridge UB8 3PH, England

PITTHAN, RAINER, physicist; b. Heppenheim, Hessia, Germany, May 15, 1940; came to U.S., 1973; s. Richard Wilhelm George and Hilde Helene (Heiderhoff) P.; m. Cris Carol Ann Oppenheimer; children: Jasmine Sophia Tayabas, Stefanie Helene. BS in Physics, U. Marburg, Germany, 1962; MS in Physics, Tech. Hochschule Darmstadt, Germany, 1967, PhD, 1972. Editor Bibliographisches Inst., Mannheim, Germany, 1963-65; LINAC operator Tech. Hochschule Darmstadt, 1965-67, dir. planning, 1968-70, staff scientist, 1968-73; prof. Naval Postgrad. Sch., Monterey, Calif., 1973-79; dept. head Stanford (Calif.) U., 1979—; assoc. European Ctr. for Nuc. Rsch., Geneva, 1991-92, 99. Contbr. articles to profl. jours. NATO fellow Deutscher Akademischer Austauschdienst, Bonn, Germany, 1973-74; grantee

NSF, 1975-79. Mem. AAAS, Am. Phys. Soc. Avocations: photography, languages, hiking. Office: Stanford U SLAC MS 12 Stanford CA 94309

PITTOCK, MURRAY G. H., literary history educator; b. Jan. 5, 1962; s. Malcolm J.W. and Joan Hornby (Mould) P.; m. Anne G.T.M. Martin, Apr. 15, 1989; 2 children. MA, U. Glasgow, Scotland, 1983; DPhil, Oxford (Eng.) U., 1987. Jr. rsch. fellow Linacre Coll., Oxford U., 1988; Brit. Acad. postdoctoral fellow U. Aberdeen, Scotland, 1988-89; lectr., then reader U. Edinburgh, Scotland, 1989-96; prof., chmn. lit. dept. U. Stratclyde, Glasgow, 1996—, mem. ct., 1998—; mem. adv. com. architecture and design City of Glasgow, 1998-99; coord. for Scotland millennium bid Mus. Brit. History, 1996-97. Author: The Invention of Scotland, 1991, Poetry and Jacobite Politics, 1994, The Myth of the Jacobite Clans, 1995, 2d edit., 1999, Inventing and Resisting Britain, 1997, Jacobitism, 1998, Celtic Identity and the British Image, 1999; editor Scottish Lit. Jour., 1995—. Theme leader for quality of life Glasgow-Strathlyde Scottish Parliamentary Policy Group, 1999—. Recipient Brit. Petroleum humanities rsch. prize Royal Soc. Edinburgh, 1993; 15 rsch. grantes, 1987—. Fellow Royal Hist. Soc. (London), Soc. Antiquaries Scotland; mem. Assn. for Scottish Lit. Studies (coun.). Roman Catholic. Avocations: politics, walking, chess. Office: U Strathclyde, Richmond St, Glasgow G1 1XH, Scotland

PITTS, SADIE TURNER, retired educator; b. Tucson; d. Joe and Sadie (Osborne) Turner; m. William E. Pitts, July 4, 1956; children: William E. II, Allen B., Melissa A. BA in Elem. Edn., U. Ariz., 1955; MA in Elem. Edn., Calif. State Poly., Pomona, 1975. Elem. tchr. Tucson Unified Schs., 1955-62; elem. tchr. Pomona Unified Schs., 1964-72, 90-92, reading tchr., 1972-75, lang. arts specialist, 1975-90; adv. bd. title I, Claremont (Calif.) Unified Sch. Dist., 1976-78; coord. tutorial reading program Alpha Kappa Alpha, Pomona, 1977-79. Author: Sparkle, 1989 (Lorraine Hansberry award 1990), The Tri Bros, 1995 (Pomona Alliance Black Sch. Educators award 1996); (poems) Sons on the Wind, 1995. Spkr. Pomona Schs. Career Day, 1990-94; vol. lang. arts activities Convalescent Care Nursing Home; mem. com. Inland Valley Coun. Chs.; vacation Bible sch. coord. South Hills Presbyn. Ch., Pomona; supt. South Hills Presbyn. Sunday Sch., 1998, Sunday sch. supt., 1996-99; sec. Ch. Women United, Pomona Unit, 1998-99. Recipient Presbyn. Women's Mande E. Pitt award S. Hills Presbyn Ch., Pomona, 1999. Mem. NAACP, Nat. Coun. Negro Women, Soc. Children's Book Writers and Illustrators, Internat. Soc. Poets, Calif. Ret. Tchrs. Assn., Delta Kappa Gamma (pres. 1982-84, Nat. Women's History Mo. award 1995), Alpha Kappa Alpha (treas. 1960—, treas. Epsilon Eta Omega 1996-99). Home: 395 Guilford Ave Claremont CA 91711-5147

PITZ, ECKHART ERNST, physicist; b. Dortmund, Germany, Jan. 26, 1940; s. Norbert and Elisabeth (Savelsberg) P.; m. Kristin Korn, Apr. 15, 1965; children: Anne, Heiner. Vordiplom, U. Erlangen, 1964; diploma, U. Heidelberg, 1966, Dr. rer.nat., 1968. Scientist Landessternwarte, Heidelberg, Germany, 1966-71; trainee Naval Rsch. Lab., Washington, 1970; scientist Max-Planck Inst. Astronomy, Heidelberg; experimenter Desy, Hamburg, 1967-68, co-investigator, Helios Space Probe, 1968-76, principal investigator, Sounding Rocket Expt., 1970-75, project mgr., MPI-A, 1976-98. Contbr. articles to profl. jours. Fähnrich zur See, der Reserve, 1959-60. Avocations: photography, architecture, travel. Office: Max-Planck Inst Astronomie, Königstuhl 17, 69117 Heidelberg Germany

PIVER, M. STEVEN, gynecologic oncologist; b. Washington, Sept. 29, 1934; s. Harry Samuel and Sonia (Bard) P.; m. Susan Myers, June 25, 1958; children: Debra Ellen, Carolyn Jan, Kenneth Stuart. BS, Gettysburg Coll., 1957; MD, Temple U., 1961. Diplomate Am. Bd. Ob-Gyn, Am. Coll. Surgeons. Intern Nazareth Hosp., Phila., 1961-62; resident Johns Hopkins U. Hosp., Balt., 1962; resident ob-gyn. Pa. Hosp., U. Pa., Phila., 1965-68; fellow gynecologic oncology U. Tex., Hosp. and Tumor Inst., Houston, 1968-70; asst. prof. gynecologic oncology U. N.C. Sch. Medicine, 1970-71; assoc. chief gynecologic oncology Roswell Park Cancer Inst., Buffalo, 1972-83, founder, dir. Gilda Radner Familial Ovarian Cancer Registry, 1981—, chief gynecologic oncology, 1984-97; clin. prof., dir. div. gynecologic oncology SUNY, Buffalo, 1986-97, prof. gynecology, 1998—, chair emeritus gynecologic oncology, 1998—. Cons., editor Yearbook of Cancer, 1972-88; assoc. editor Nat. Cancer Inst., PDQ, 1984—; mem. editl. bd. The Female Patient, 1989—, Oncology Reports, 1993—; author: Ovarian Malignancies: Clinical Care of Adults and Adolescents, 1983, Gilda's Disease: Sharing Personal Experiences and a Medical Perspective on Ovarian Cancer, 1996, Myths and Facts About Ovarian Cancer, 1997; editor: Ovarian Malignancies: Diagnostic and Therapeutic Advances, 1987, Manual of Gynecologic Oncology/Gynecology, 1989, Conversations About Cancer, 1990, Handbook of Gynecologic Oncology, 1995; contbr. more than 300 articles to profl. jours. Bd. dirs. United Way of Buffalo and Erie County, 1986-91; chmn. bd. trustees D'Youville Coll., Buffalo, 1989—; pres. Friends of Night People, Buffalo, 1988-97. Capt. USAF, 1962-64. Hon. fellow Phi Beta Kappa, Gettysburg Coll., 1956, Tex. Assn. Obstetricians and Gynecologists, 1983, Alpha Omega Alpha, Temple U. Sch. Medicine, 1995; named Citizen of Yr., Buffalo News, 1989; recipient YMCA Leadership award Buffalo YMCA, 1990, Brotherhood/Sisterhood Award in Medicine (Western N.Y. Region), NCCJ, 1991, St. Marguerite D'Youville Coll. Community Svc. award, 1992. Fellow ACS, Am. Coll. Obstetricians and Gynecologists; mem. Am. Soc. Clin. Oncology, Soc. Gynecologic Oncologists, Soc. Surg. Oncology, Am. Radium Soc., Phi Beta Kappa, Alpha Omega Alpha. Achievements include documentation of hydroxyurea as a radiation sensitizer in cervix cancer that significantly improves cure rate and that ovarian cancer can be inherited. Home: 315 Lincoln Pky Buffalo NY 14216-3127 Office: Sisters Hosp 2157 Main St Buffalo NY 14214-2692

PIVIN, JEAN LOUP, publisher; b. Alger, France, May 28, 1951; s. Jose and Odile (Meyer) P. Diploma in architecture, Ecole Beaux Arts Paris, 1976. Architect Paris, 1976—; dir., pub. Revue Noire, Paris, 1991—; touristic & cultural engr. BICFL, Paris, 1986—. Office: 8 rue CELS, 75014 Paris France

PIVOVAROV, ARKADY SAULOVICH, neurophysiologist, researcher; b. Moscow, Russia, Nov. 27, 1948; s. Saul Iosifovich Pivovarov and Nahama Solomonovna Lyando; m. Svetlana Vladimirovna Slavova; 1 child, Dmitry. Degree, Lomonosov State U., Moscow, 1971, PhD, 1974, DSc, 1995. Jr. scientist Lomonosov State U., Moscow, 1971-86, sr. scientist, 1987-94, head scientist, 1994—; vis. rschr. U. Southampton, 1993, 96, 98. Grantee The Royal Soc., 1993, The Internat. Sci. Found., 1993, 94, The Wellcome Trust, 1996, 98, The Russian Found. for Basic Rsch., 1999. Mem. Internat. Soc. Neurochemistry, European Neuroscience Assn., European Peptide Soc., Internat. Brain Rsch. Orgn. Office: Dept Higher Nervous Activy, Lomonosov State U, 119899 Moscow Russia

PIZA, ARTHUR LUIZ, painter; b. Brazil, Jan. 13, 1928; came to France, 1951; One-man exhbns.: Brazil, Germany, Yugoslavia, U.S., France, Switzerland, Sweden, Spain, Belgium, Italy; represented in permanent mus. and pvt. collections. Decorated Chevalier Des Arts Et Lettres; recipient Purchase prize, 1953; Nat. prize for Prints São Paulo Biennale, 1959, Nat. prize Brazilian critics, 1994; prizes at biennales at Ljubljana, 1961, Santiago, 1966, Venice, 1966, Grenchen triennale, 1961, biennales of Norway and Mex., 1980, biennale San Juan, Puerto Rico, 1990. Address: 16 rue Dauphine, 75006 Paris France

PIZER, MARJORIE, psychotherapist; b. Melbourne, Australia, Apr. 3, 1920; d. Solomon and Ruth (Blashki) P.; m. Muir Beresford Holburn (dec. Nov. 1960); children: Kim Joel, Jo Merri. BA, Univ. Melbourne, 1942. Commonwealth Public Svc., 1941-46; Rsch. Australian Lit., 1947-50; pvt. practice Sydney, 1963—; cons. psychotherapist Leichhardt Women's Cmty. Health Ctr., 1974-81; dir., editor Pinchgut Press, 1975-98. Co-editor: (with Muir Holburn) Creeve Roe, Poems of Victor Daley, 1947, (with Joan Reed) Come Listen, Poetry for Schools, 1966, (with Drusilla Modjeska) Poems of Lesbia Harford, 1985; editor: Freedom on the Wallaby, Poems of the Australian People, 1953, The Men Who Made Australia, Stories and Poems by Henry Lawson, 1957; author: Thou and I, Poems, 1967, To Life, Poems, 1969, Tides Flow, Poems, 1972, Seasons of Love, Poems, 1975, Full Summer, Poems, 1977, Gifts and Remembrances, Poems, 1979, To You the Living, Poems of Bereavement and Loss, 1981, 91, 92, The Sixtieth Spring, Poems, 1982, Selected Poems, 1963-1983, 1984, Equinox, Poems, 1987, Fire in the Heart, 1990, Journeys, 1992, Winds of Change, 1995, Await the Spring, Poems, 1998; co-author: (with Anne Spencer Parry) Below the Surface, Reflections on Life and Living, 1982, 90, 94. Vol. counselor Tranby Aboriginal Coll., Sydney, 2000—. Fellow Australian Writers; mem. Australian Soc. Authors, Assn. Humanistic Psychology, Australian Conservation Found., Nat. Assn. Loss and Grief. Avocations: drawing, painting. E-mail: marjoriepizer@hotmail.com. Home and Office: 6 Oaks Ave, 2090 Sydney Australia

PIZZAMIGLIO, ALBERT THEODORE (AL PIERSON), conductor; m. Nancy Alice Gilman, Mar. 27, 1978; five children. Studied music theory and composition; BA, MA, Ill. State U.; advanced music studies, U. Ill. Condr. Al Pierson Big Band U.S.A., 1975-89, Guy Lombardo's Royal Canadians, Aubrey, Tex., 1989—; nat. youth music dir. Am. Inst. of Cooperation; co-host, owner TV show, Bloomington, Ill.; tchr. high sch. and coll. Musician, composer, arranger, vocalist, band leader; founder Al Pierson & Big Band U.S.A. (Best New Dance Band in the Country 1975, America's Number One Dance Band 1977), performed for fourteen yrs. at numerous famous ballrooms in the midwest and many prestigious pvt. parties, on twenty internat. dance tours including Europe, the Orient, the Middle East, the Caribbean, Mexico, Hawaii, Alaska and Tahiti; released 15 albums; recorded Guy Lombardo music album, 2000, now with Guy Lombardo's Royal Canadians performing throughout the continental U.S. and Can. and 30 other fgn. countries; condr. PBS TV series (past three yrs. and continuing), 1977, PBS TV spls., 1994, 95, 96, 97, 2000, Presdl. Inauguration Festivities, 1994. Recipient Superman award for helping save 32 lives in snowstorm, 1997, 98, 99; inducted into Ballroom Dancers' Hall of Fame, 1976; named amb. Music for World pres. Ill. State U., 1998. Office: Gilman Inc Artists Mgmt RR 1 Aubrey TX 76227-9801

PIZZI, ANTONIO, chemist; b. Rome, May 15, 1946; s. Dino and Luisa Sara (Folena) P.; m. Nellie Edith Napier, Feb. 24, 1973; children: Romain, Michelle, Alexis, Dominique. D of Chemistry, U. Rome, 1969; PhD Chemistry, U. of the Orange Free State, S. Africa, 1978; DSc, U. Stellenbosch, S. Africa, 1985. Rschr. Sentrachem, Johannesburg, South Africa, 1970; works chemist Pretoria Portland Cement, Port Elizabeth, South Africa, 1970-71; rschr. Novoboard, Port Elizabeth, 1971-76; dir. Nat. Timber Rsch. Inst., Pretoria, South Africa, 1977-89; prof., chmn. polymer chemistry U. Witwatersrand, Johannesburg, S. Africa, 1989-95; prof., chmn. indsl. wood chemistry Enstib U. de Nancy, Epinal, France, 1994—; vis. prof. Tsukuba U., Japan, 1997, Nanjing Forestry U., 1995, U. Florence, Italy, 1998, 99; Scuola Normale di Pisa, Italy, 2000; dir., tech. Burmah Adhesives and Sealants, Johannesburg, 1983-84; assessor FAIR programme European Commn., Brussels, 1997, chmn., COST action on Adhesives European Commn., Brussels, 1999, 2000. Editor, author: Wood Adhesives, Vol. 1, 1983, Vol. 2, 1989, Handbook of Adhesive Technology, 1994, Adhesion Promotion Techniques for Advanced Materials, 1999; author: Advanced Wood Adhesives Technology, 1994; mem. editl. bd. profl. and sci. jours.; contbr. articles to profl. jours. Recipient Bark award Forest Products Soc., Boston, 1980, Markwardt Woodbright award, Orlando, 1985, Sci. Achievement award Internat. Union For Rsch. Orgns., Montreal, Can., 1990; named Millennium Acad. lectr., U.S., 2000. Mem. Internat. Acad. Wood Sci. (sec. 1992-95, acad. lectr. 2000). Achievements include devel. and industrialization of natural and synthetic wood adhesives, particularly natural environment-friendly products (adhesives and wood preservatives, and environmental friendly non-toxic wood preservatives); novel contributions to polycolonization gel theory. Office: Enstib U de Nancy 1, 27 Rue Du Merle Blanc, Epinal 88000, France

PIZZUTO, EMANUELINA MARIA, concert pianist, composer; b. Trenton, N.J.; d. Paul Emile and Mildred (Corvine) P.; m. Robert Wayne Martin, Apr. 23, 1959. Student, Am. Conservatoire, Fontainebleau, France, 1938-47; studied with Robert Casadesus, Am. Conservatoire, 1947. Piano soloist Sta. WQXR, N.Y.C., 1947-52, Sta. WFIL, Phila., 1948-52; toured with Les Compagnons de la Chanson, U.S., 1954-55, CAMI, U.S., 1955-56; piano soloist Sta. WEEI, Boston, 1948. Composer (songs) Le Chat Dans la Nuit, 1959, Crier de Journaux, 1959, (with Ricet Barrier) Material for Band and Strings; writer (with J. Mayes and R.W. Martin) numerous mus. shows; composer (with Robert Martin) numerous compositions for band and strings; composer (with Judith Mayes and Robert Martin) several musicals. Mem. ASCAP, hon. mem. Sigma Alpha Iota.

PLAČEK, VÍT, chemist, researcher; b. Děčín, Czech Republic, Apr. 29, 1966; s. Karel and Sieghild (Zieger) P.; m. Ivana Hejná, Feb. 16, 1989; children: Martin, Tomáš. Degree in engring., U. Chemistry and Tech., Prague, Czech Republic, 1989; D of Natural Scis., U. Leipzig, Germany, 1995. Rschr. Nuc. Rsch. Inst., Řež, Czech Republic, 1989-92, Řež, 1995—; rschr. Inst. Surface Modification, Leipzig, 1992-94. Rsch. fellow Internat. Atomic Energy Agy., Vienna, Austria, 1996—. Fellow German Soc. Thermal Analysis; mem. Internat. Electrotech. Commn. (corr.). Avocation: white water canoeing (Czech nat. team 1987, 92). Office: Nuc Rsch Inst, Řež plc, 250 68 Řež Czech Republic

PLAČKOVIĆ, RATKO, engineer; b. Zagreb, Croatia, Jan. 8, 1948; s. Milivoj and Zora P.; m. Marija, Sept. 5, 1970; children: Dean, Saša. BSEE, U. Zagreb, Croatia, 1971, MSc, 1975; MSEE, U. Ill., 1978. Engr. rsch. & devel. Končar-Electrotech. Inst., Zagreb, Croatia, 1970-77; rsch. asst. U. Ill., Urbana, 1977-78; head power plant conrol systems devel. dept. Končar-Electrotech. Inst., 1988-90; project mgmt. Koncar Power Plant and Electric Traction Engring. Inc., 1990—. Avocations: gardening, skiing, literature. Office: Končar-KET, Fallerovo šet 22, 10001 Zagreb Croatia

PLADEVALL, TOMÀS, cinematographer, educator; b. Sabadell, Spain, Nov. 25, 1946; s. Francesc Pladevall and Concepció Fontanet. Grad., Tech. Engrs. Sch., Terrassa, Spain, 1969; dir. of photography, Escuela Oficial Cinematografia, Madrid, 1972. Cinematographer, 1972—; assoc. prof. audiovisual comm. studies U. Pompeu Fabra, U. Barcelona, Spain; films include Warsaw Bridge, Actrices, Train of Shadows, Tic Tac, The Pianist, Leo; photographer over 400 commercials, documentaries, others; lighting designer plays; lighting dir. ceremonies 1992 Barcelona Olympic Games; bd. dirs. Spanish Acad. Found. Arts and Scis. in Cinematography. Author: (dictionary) Video Terminology, 1984. Recipient Best Technician prize Catalan Motion Picture Industry, 1986, 87, Prisma AEC prize for Best Spanish Photography, 1998, Critics' Sant Jordi prize XLIII edit. for contribution to Spanish Motion Picture Industry During 1998. Mem. Assn. Española de Autores de Fotografía Cinematográfica, Spanish Assn. Cinematographers, European Fedn. Dirs. Photography. Avocation: linguistics. E-mail: tpladevall@bcn.servicom.es.

PLAEGER, FREDERICK JOSEPH, II, lawyer; b. New Orleans, Sept. 10, 1953; s. Edgar Leonard and Bernice Virginia (Schiwetz) P.; m. Kathleen Helen Dickson, Nov. 19, 1977; children: Douglas A., Catherine E. BS, La. State U., 1976, JD, 1977. Bar: La. 1978, Tex. 1999, U.S. Dist. Ct. (ea. dist.) La. 1978, U.S. Ct. Appeals (5th cir.) 1981, U.S. Supreme Ct. 1989. Law clk. U.S. Dist. Ct. (ea. dist.) La., New Orleans, 1977-79; assoc. Milling, Benson, Woodward, Hillyer, Pierson & Miller, New Orleans, 1979-85, ptnr., 1985-89; v.p., gen. counsel, corp. sec. La. Land and Exploration Co., New Orleans, 1989-97; v.p., gen. counsel Burlington Resources Inc., Houston, 1997—. Bd. dirs. New Orleans Speech and Hearing Ctr., 1985-91, pres., 1988-90; bd. dirs. Children's Oncology Svcs. La. (Ronald McDonald House of New Orleans), 1987-90; selected mem. Met. Area Com. Leadership Forum, 1986; bd. dirs. Soc. Environ. Edn., La. Nature and Sci. Ctr., 1992-94; bd. dirs. New Orleans City Park Assn., 1996-97. Recipient Service to Mankind award Sertoma, 1989. Mem. ABA, La. Bar Assn., Am. Corp. Counsel Assn. (bd. dirs. New Orleans chpt. 1995-98), Am. Petroleum Inst. (mem. gen. commn. law), Univ. Club, Lakeside Country Club. Republican. Avocations: golf, hunting, fishing. Home: 5105 Longmont Dr Houston TX 77056-2417 Office: Burlington Resources Inc 5051 Westheimer Rd Ste 1400 Houston TX 77056-5686

PLAG, INGO, linguistics educator; b. Bad Honnef, Germany, Aug. 2, 1962; m. Claudia Gelb; children: Jonas, Hannah. MA, U. Marburg, Germany, 1989, PhD, 1993. Rsch. asst. U. Marburg, 1989-95, asst. prof., 1995-99; prof. English linguistics U. Hannover, Germany, 1999-2000, U. Siegen, Germany, 2000—. Author: Sentential Complementation in Sranan, 1993, Morphological Productivity, 1999; co-editor: Creolization and Language Change, 1994; mem. editl. bd. Jour. Pidgin and Creole Langs., 1997—; editor-in-chief: Zeitschrift fur Sprachwissenschaft, 1998—. Mem. German Linguistics Soc. (chmn. program com. 1997), Linguistic Soc. Am., Soc. Pidgin and Creole Linguistics. Office: FB Sprach-und Lit wiss, U-GHS Siegen, D-57680 Siegen Germany

PLAINE, LLOYD LEVA, lawyer; b. Washington, Nov. 3, 1947; d. Marx and Shirley P. Leva; m. James W. Hill. BA, U. Pa., 1969; postgrad., Harvard U.; JD, Georgetown U., 1975. Bar: D.C. 1975. Legis. asst. to U.S. Rep. Sidney Yates, 1971-72; with Sutherland, Asbill & Brennan, Washington, 1975-82, ptnr., 1982—. Fellow Am. Bar Found., Am. Coll. Trust and Estate Counsel (past regent), Am. Coll. Tax Counsel; mem. ABA (past chmn. real property, probate and trust law sect.). Office: Sutherland Asbill & Brennan 1275 Pennsylvania Ave NW Ste 1 Washington DC 20004-2415

PLAISANT, PAOLA, microbiologist researcher; b. Alghero, Sassari, Italy, Aug. 29, 1956; s. Giampaolo and Jolanda (Toso) P. Bachelor, Lic. Classic "G. Manno", Sassari, Italy, 1975; MSc, U. Sassari, 1983; PhD, Cath. U., Rome, 1987. Assoc. biologist Università Cattolica, Rome, 1988-92; vis. investigator The Scripps Rsch. Inst., La Jolla, Calif., 1993; biologist Università Cattolica, Rome, 1994—, prof. Microbiology Sch., 1992—. Mem. Italian Sailing Assn. (master instr. 1975—). Avocation: sailing. Office: Ist Microbiol U Cattolica, Largo F Vito 1, I 00168 Rome Italy

PLAISTED, JOAN M., diplomat; b. St. Peter, Minn., Aug. 29, 1945; d. Gerald A. and Lola May (Peters) P. Student, U. Grenoble, France, 1965-66, U. Calif., Berkeley, 1966; BA in Internat. Rels., Am. U., 1967, MA in Asian Studies, 1969; graduate, Nat. War Coll., 1988. Korea desk officer Commerce Dept., Washington, 1969-72, Japan desk officer, 1972-73; commercial officer Am. Embassy, Paris, 1973-78; internat. economist Orgn. Econ. Cooperation & Devel., Paris, 1978-80; econ. officer Am. Consulate Gen., Hong Kong, 1980-83; trade negotiator White House Office of Spl. Trade Rep., Geneva, 1983-85; deputy dir. China desk State Dept., Washington, 1985-87; acting dep. dir., chief econ./comml. sect. Am. Inst. in Taiwan, Taipei, 1988-91; chargé d'affaires, deputy chief of mission Am. Embassy, Rabat, Morocco, 1991-94; dir. Thai and Burma affairs Dept. of State, Washington, 1994-95; sr. advisor U.S. Mission to UN N.Y.C., 1995; amb. to Republic of Marshall Islands and Republic of Kiribati, 1996—. Recipient Lodestar award Am. U., 1993. Mem. Am. Fgn. Svc. Assn., Hong Kong Wine Soc. (founding). Avocations: wine tasting, gastronomy, history, skiing, scuba diving. Address: PO Box 1379 Majuro MH 96960-1379

PLAISTOWE, WILLIAM IAN DAVID, accountant; b. Oxhey, Eng., Nov. 18, 1942; s. David William and Julia (Ross Smith) P.; m. Carolyn Anne N. Wilson, June 1, 1968; children: Richard, Peter, Nicola. MA, Cambridge (Eng.) U., 1964. Ptnr. Arthur Andersen, London; chmn. Auditing Practices Bd., London, 1994—. Contbr. articles to legal jours. Mem. Inst. Chartered Accts. in Eng. and Wales (pres. 1992-93). Avocations: golf, tennis, skiing, gardening. Home: Heybote, Ellesborough, Aylesbury HP17 0XF, England Office: Arthur Andersen, 1 Surrey St, London England

PLAKHINA, INNA NIKOLAYEVNA, physicist, researcher; b. Moscow, June 7, 1946; d. Melnikov Nikolai Fyedorovich and Anna Konstantinovna Molyavova; m. Evgenii Aleksandrovich Plakhin, Nov. 17, 1967; 1 child, Aleksander Evgen'yevich. MS, Moscow Phys. Tech. Inst., 1970, PhD, 1974. Jr. scientist A.M. Obukhov Inst. Atmospheric Physics-Russian Acad. Scis., Moscow, 1974-75, scientist, 1975-91, rsch. scientist, 1991—. Contbr. articles to profl. jours. Grantee Soros Found., 1995, 96-97. Orthodox. Avocations: swimming, gymnastics, theater, travel, needlework. E-mail: lakhina@omega.ifaran.ru. Fax: 7-095-9531652. Office: Inst Atmospher Physics RAS, Pyzhevskii per 3, 109017 Moscow Russia

PLAKIDA, NIKOLAI MAKSIMILIANOVICH, physicist, educator; b. Riazhsk, Russia, June 7, 1937; s. Maksimilian Eduardovich and Elena Anatolievna (Illarionova) P.; m. Marina Ashotovna Ambartsoumian, Apr. 12, 1944; children: Sergei, Karina. BS, Moscow State U., 1954, MS, 1960; PhD, Math. Inst., Moscow, 1966; DSc, Kiev (Ukraine) U. Rschr. Joint Inst. Nuc. Rsch. (JINR), Dubna, Russia, 1966-70, sr. rschr., 1970-87, prof. physics, head of dept., 1987—. Author: High-Temperature Superconductivity, 1995; co-author, editor: Neutron Scattering by Ferroelectrics, 1989; contbr. over 180 articles to profl. jours. Avocations: mountaineering, skiing. E-mail: plakida@thsun1.jinr.ru. FAX: 7-09621-65084. Home: 17 Pontecorvo St # 802, 141980 Dubna Russia Office: Joint Inst Nuc Rsch (JINR), Theoret Lab, 141980 Dubna Russia

PLAKS, LIVIA BASCH, foundation executive; b. Baia Mare, Romania, Apr. 29, 1947; came to U.S., 1964; naturalized, 1969; d. Kalman and Cecilia (Freund) Basch; m. Andrew H. Plaks, June 9, 1968; children: Jason, Eric. AB, Rutgers U., 1969; AM, NYU, 1971. Exec. assoc. Internat. Rsch. and Exch. Bd., Princeton, N.J., 1986-92; assoc. dir. Project on Ethnic Rels., Princeton, 1992-94, exec. dir., 1994—; rapporteur Orgn. Security Cooperation in Europe on Roma issues, Warsaw, Poland, 1994; mem. U.S. Task Force on Romania, 1990-92; mem. mediation team between Romanian Govt. and Dem. Union of Hungarians in Romania, 1992—; mem. Coun. for Ethnic Accord, 1992—; mem. mediation team between Slovak and ethnic Hungarian Parliamentary parties of Slovakia, 1995—; mem. mediation team Serbs and Albanians of Kosovo, 1995-2000; testified to and for Commn. on Secutity and Cooperation in Europe on issues of Roma/Gypsies, 1994, 98. Recipient Certificate of Merit Pres. Romania, 1996, Govt. Hungary, 1996, Govt. Slovakia, 1998. Mem. AAAS. Avocations: travel, reading. Office: Project on Ethnic Rels 15 Chambers St Princeton NJ 08542-3707

PLANCHER, ROBERT LAWRENCE, former manufacturing company executive; b. N.Y.C., Feb. 21, 1932; s. Murray Leon and Pearl P.; m. Ellen Roslyn, Feb. 14, 1954; children: Kevin, Daryn. B.B.A., CCNY, 1954. With American Brands, Inc., N.Y.C., 1963—; asst. tax dir. American Brands, Inc., 1967, tax dir., 1971, controller, 1978, dir., v.p., controller, 1981-86, sr. v.p., chief acctg. officer, 1986-97; bd. dirs. ACCO World Corp., Acushnet Co., Am. Brands Internat. Corp., Am. Tobacco Internat. Corp., Jim Beam Brands Co., Gallaher Ltd., MasterBrand Industries, Inc.; chmn. bd. 1700 Ins. Co. Ltd., dir. JBB Worldwide, Inc.; mem. Mid Atlantic Metro regional adv. bd. Arkwright Mut. Ins. Co. Served with U.S. Army, 1954-56. Mem. Fin. Execs. Inst., Tax Execs. Inst., Inst. Mgmt. Accts. Office: Fortune Brands Inc 300 Tower Pkwy Lincolnshire IL 60069-3640

PLANKL, JOHANN, physicist; b. Lappersdorf, Bavaria, Germany, July 31, 1961; s. Johann and Therese (Klein) P.; m. Gabriele Stadler, Mar. 1, 1991; 1 child, Julia. Diploma, U. Munich, 1987, PhD, 1990. Rsch. asst. U. Munich, 1987-90; project leader BASF AG, Ludwigshafen, Germany, 1991-93, rsch. scientist, 1993-95; prof. physics Deggendorf (Germany) U. Applied Scis., 1995—, dean, 1995-96; sci. sec. Max Planck Inst. Physics, Munich, 1988; lectr. Med. Sch. Klinikum Ludwigshafen, 1991-95. Contbr. or co-contbr. articles to sci. publs. Scholar, Studienstiftung des Deutschen Volkes, Bonn, Germany, 1988-90. Mem. Initiativ Kreis Bio Regio Regensburg/Ostbayern. Roman Catholic. Avocations: literature, music, family, computer science. E-mail: johann.plankl@fh-deggendorf.de. Office: Deggendorf Univ Appl Scis, Edlmairstrasse 6 und 8, 94469 Deggendorf Bavaria, Germany

PLANO, JACK CHARLES, writer, retired educator; b. Merrill, Wis., Nov. 25, 1921; s. Victor James and Minna Ida (Hass) P.; m. Ellen Louise Ruehlow, June 25, 1954; children: Jay Charles, Gregory Victor, Vicki Lynn. BA, Ripon Coll., 1949; MA, U. Wis., 1950, PhD, 1954. Prof. Western Mich. U., Kalamazoo, 1952-87; ret., 1987. Author, editor: ABC-CLIO Political Dictionary series, 1982; author: American Political Dictionary, 11th edit., 2000; co-author: The United Nations, 3d edit., 2000, Latin American Dictionary. Sgt. U.S. Army, 1942-45, ETO. Ford Found. grantee Emory U., 1957; fellow U. Sussex, 1972-72. Home: 705 Weaver Cir Kalamazoo MI 49006-5551

PLANT, GORDON TERENCE, neurologist; b. Harrogate, Eng., July 4, 1952; s. Thomas Edmund and Sheila May (Atkinson) P.; m. Marilyn Jane Dirkin, Apr. 29, 1978; children: Eleanor Margaret, Emma Louise, Katharine Elizabeth. BA, Cambridge U., Eng., 1974, MB, BChir, 1977, MD, 1987. House physician St. Thomas' Hosp., London, 1977-78; sr. house physician Westminster Hosp., London, 1978-80; registrar Addenbrooke's Hosp., Cambridge, Eng., 1980-83; rsch. assoc. physiol. lab. Cambridge U., 1983-86; registrar in neurology Nat. Hosp. for Nervous Diseases, London, 1986-87; sr.

regsistrar in neurology Nat. Hosp. for Nervous Diseases, Univ. Coll. and Maida Vale Hosps., London, 1987-89; med. rsch. coun. traveling fellow Smith Kettlewell Inst., San Francisco, 1989-91; cons. Nat. Hosp. Neurology, Queen Sq., Moorfields Eye Hosp., London, 1991—, St. Thomas' Hosp., 1991—. Editor: Optic Neuritis, 1986; contbr. numerous articles in neurology of visual disorders to profl. jours. Scholar Downing Coll., 1974; named exhibitioner St. Thomas' Hosp., 1975. Fellow Royal Coll. Physicians (cert.), Royal Soc. Medicine. Avocations: music, clarinet, basset horn, water color painting. Office: Nat Hosp for Neurology, Queens Square, London WC1N 3BG, England

PLANT, WILLIAM JAMES, research scientist; b. Wichita, Kans., Sept. 18, 1944; s. George William and Ruth Elizabeth P.; m. Catherine Blanche Plant, Jun 7, 1964 (div. Dec. 1973); children: Kimberly Ann, Karin Marie; m. Silvia Jeanne Angelika, Sept. 11, 1991; 1 child, Larissa Ingeborg Wright. BS in Physics, Kans. State U., 1966; MS in Physics, Purdue U., 1968, PhD in Physics, 1972. Postdoctoral fellow Nat. Rsch. Coun., Washington, 1971-73; rsch. physicist Naval Rsch. Lab., Washington, 1973-88; sr. scientist Woods Hole (Mass.) Oceanographic Instn., 1988-91; prin. rsch. scientist U. Wash., Seattle, 1991—; affil. prof. U. Wash., Seattle, 1991—, U. Miami, 1997—; vis. scientist Max-Planck Inst. for Meteorologie, Hamburg, Germany, 1994-95. Assoc. editor Jour. of Geophys. Rsch., Washington, 1985-99; editor: (books) Surface Waves and Fluxes, 1990, The Air-Sea Interface, 1996. Mem. IEEE (Disting. Achievement award), Oceanography Soc., Am. Geophys. Union, Union of Radio Scientist Internat. E-mail: plant@apl.washington.edu. Office: Applied Physics Lab/U Wash 1013 NE 40th St Seattle WA 98105-6606

PLANTEY, ALAIN GILLES, French government official, writer; b. Mulhouse, France, July 19, 1924; s. Robert and Marguerite (Stehelin) P.; m. Christiane Wioland, July 23, 1955; children: Marie Agnes, Marie Laure, Marie-Eve, Marie Cecile. Lic es Lettres, U. Bordeaux, France, 1944; DLaw, U. Paris, 1949. Coucillor of State French Govt., Paris, 1949—; French del. to UN, N.Y.C., 1951-53; legal adviser to OECD, Paris, 1955-56; mem. Gen. DeGaulle's Cabinet, Paris, 1959-67; French amb. to Madagascar, 1967-72; sec. gen. Western European Union, Paris and London, 1972-82; pres. Internat. Arbitration Ct., 1989-96. Author: La Formation et le Perfectionnement des Fonctionnaires, 1954, Traité Pratique de la Fonction Publique, 1955, 3d edit., 1972, Fonction Publique Internationale (award 1982), 1980-84, International Civil Service, 1981, La Fonction Publica International y Europea, 1982, De la politique entre les Etats (Principles of Diplomacy, 1987, 92, La Function publique, traité général, 1992, Tratado de derecho diplomatico, 1992, La négociation internationale, 1994. Decorated Gt. Officer Legion of Honor, comdr. Arts and Letters; named laureate Bordeaux U., 1941-43, laureate U. Paris, 1950, laureate Acad. des Scis. Morales et Politiques, Paris, 1978, laureate Acad. Française, Paris, 1982. Mem. Assn. Former Students Ecole Nationale d'Adminstrn. (pres.), French Acad. Moral and Polit. Scis. (past pres.), Internat. Law Inst. (pres.), Am. Acad. Polit. and Social Scis., Soc. Gens de Lettres, Acad. Arts of the Street, Charles de Gaulle's Inst., Internat. Coun. Arbitration for Sport, Internat. Coun. for Comml. Arbitration. Home: Ave Sully Prudhomme 6, 75007 Paris France Office: Inst de France, 23 quai de Conti, F-75006 Paris France

PLAPPERT, STANLEY WARREN, insurance company executive; b. East St. Louis, Ill., Aug. 2, 1962; s. John Steven and Mary Helen (Badger) P.; m. La Donna Sue Pummill, May 21, 1983. BSBA, Ill. Wesleyan U., 1984; MBA, Ill. State U., 1988. CPCU; assoc. in marine ins. mgmt. Self employed Bloomington, Ill., 1983-85; with ins. sales Ch. Mut. Ins., Merrill, Wis., 1985-90; entrepreneur Midwest Tool and Supply, Inc., Bloomington, Ill., 1986-90, Midwest Tool Repair, Inc., Bloomington, Ill., 1986-90; with Gibson Ins. Agy., South Bend, 1990-99; owner, pres., CEO Collier Ins. Svcs. Inc., Naples, Fla., 1999—. Precinct committeeman Normal (Ill.) Rep. Com., 1985-91, South Bend, Ind., 1991-2000; bd. dirs., chmn. fin. com. Habitat for Humanity St. Joseph County, 1990-95; sec.-treas. Mich. World Affairs Coun., 1991-93. Mem. Soc. CPCU's (pres. Michiana subchpt. 1991-93). Mem. Pentecostal Ch. Home: 180 Lambton Ln Naples FL 34104-6512 Office: Collier Ins Svcs Inc 2335 Tamiami Trl N Ste 401 Naples FL 34103-4458

PLASKACZ, EDWARD JOHN, computational scientist, engineer; b. Chgo., Jan. 21, 1959; s. John T. and Pauline H. Plaskacz; m. Elizabeth Ellen Prindiville, July 14, 1990. BS, Ill. Inst. Tech., Chgo., 1981, MS, 1982; PhD, Northwestern U., 1990. Engr. in tng. City of Chgo. Dept. of Water, 1979-81; engring. intern Sargent & Lundy Engrs., Chgo., 1981-82, engring. analyst, 1982-85; rsch. asst. Northwestern U., Evanston, Ill., 1985-90; computational scientist Argonne (Ill.) Nat. Lab., 1990—. Contbr. numerous articles to profl. jours. Recipient Letter of Commendation Chgo. Dept. Water, 1980, Clinton Strycker award Ill. Inst. Tech., 1981, Atanasoff award Second Symposium on Parallel Computational Methods for Large-Scale Structural Analysis and Design, 1993, Exceptional Performance award Argonne Nat. Lab., 1995, 97. Mem. AAAS, Nat Geographic Soc., Nat. Trust Historic Preservation, Colonial Williamsburg Found., U.S. Assn. for Computational Mechanics, Sigma Xi, Tau Beta Pi, Chi Epsilon. Office: Argonne Nat Lab 9700 Cass Ave Argonne IL 60439-4803

PLASSCHAERT, ALPHONS JOHANNES MARIE, dental educator, academic administrator, foundation executive; b. Helmond, Netherlands, Jan. 3, 1942; s. Arthur Prudent and Francisca Alida (van Schijndel) P.; m. Pauline Louise van Lommel, June 4, 1966; children: Véronique, Alain, Sabine, Nicole. DDS, U. Utrecht, Netherlands, 1966; PhD, U. Nijmegen, Netherlands, 1972. Clin. instr. U. Nijmegen, 1967-69, sr. lectr., 1969-76, prof., chmn. dept. cariology, 1976-89, 1995—, dean Dental Sch., 1986-89, vice-chancellor, 1990-94; pres. Found. for Blind, Theofaan, The Netherlands, 1992—, Found. Edward Schillebeeckx, 1994—; chmn. dental sect. Orgn. Cooperating Dutch Univs., Utrecht, 1986-89; pres. Justitia et Pax Commn., The Netherlands, 1999—. Author: Preventieve Maatregelen, 1972; editor: Ergonomie in de Tandheelkunde, 1981, Cariology and Endodontology, 1976-86, 1989; asst. editor Jour. Caries Rsch., 1983-89; pres. Found. Dental Jour., Amsterdam, 1987—; contbr. to numerous profl. publs. Concertmaster Nijmeegs Chamber Orch., 1981—; leader Animato String Quartet, Nijmegen, 1981-93, Valkhof String Quartet, Nijmegen, 1993—. Fulbright scholar, 1984, 94. Mem. Internat. Assn. Dental Rsch., Acad. Operative Dentistry (pres. European sect. 2000—). Roman Catholic. Avocations: violin playing and making, tennis, running. Home: Witsenburgselaan 56, 6524 TL Nijmegen The Netherlands

PLASSER, FRITZ, political science educator; b. Vienna, Sept. 22, 1949; m. Gunda Plasser, Aug. 25. PhD, U. Vienna, 1974. Dir. Ctr. for Applied Polit. Rsch.; prof. U. Innsbruck, 1993. Author, co-editor 18 books; contbr. numerous articles to profl. publs. Mem. Am. Polit. Sci. Assn., Internat. Polit. Sci. Assn. Office: Ctr Applied Polit Rsch, Reisnerstr 40, Vienna A-1030, Austria

PLASTER, GEORGE FRANCIS, Roman Catholic priest; b. Lafayette, Ind., Dec. 6, 1950; s. Robert Lee and Ann Elizabeth (Klinker) P. BS in Econs. and Fin., St. Joseph's Coll., Rensselaer, Ind., 1973; MDiv, Sacred Heart Sch. of Theology, Hales Corners, Wis., 1980. Ordained Roman Cath. Priest, 1980. Bank examiner dept. fin. instns. State of Ind., Indpls., 1973-76; deacon, assoc. pastor St. Patrick Ch., Kokomo, Ind., 1979-82; assoc. pastor Our Lady Mt. Carmel (Ind.), 1982-86, St. Charles Ch., Peru, Ind., 1986-88, St. Joan of Arc Ch., Kokomo, 1988-89; hosp. chaplain St. Vincent's Hosp., Indpls., 1989—; spiritual counselor Jonah Ctr., Wabash, Ind., 1987-88; clin. pastoral educator Ctrl. State Hosp., Indpls., 1989-90, 91-92, 94-95. Mem. Nat. Right to Life, Washington, 1973—. Mem. Nat. Assn. Cath. Chaplains, KC (chaplain 1980-82, 84-85), Indpls. Cursillo (chaplain 1984, 89, 92, 96, 99). Avocation: playing organ and piano. Office: St Vincent Hosp 2001 W 86th St Indianapolis IN 46260-1991

PLAT, FRANCIS RAYMOND, pharmaceutical company executive; b. Paris, Sept. 8, 1957; came to U.S., 1997; s. Edouard and Suzanne (Lipchitz) P.; m. Catherine Grandjean; children: Caroline, Emilie. Bachelor degree, Coll. Stanislas, Paris, 1976; MD, U. Paris VI, 1984; degree in cardiology, Hosp. Broussais, Paris, 1990; degree in mgmt./comm., Eric Krauthamer SA, Paris, 1992. Cardio. dir. Bristol-Myers Squibb, Paris, 1989-91, exec. dir., 1994-96; exec. dir. Bristol-Myers Squibb, Brussels, 1996-97, Princeton, N.J., 1997—. Home: 2 Seminole Rd Skillman NJ 08558-2325 Office: Bristol-Myers Squibb 206 Province Line Rd Princeton NJ 08543

PLATE, ERICH J., civil engineering educator; b. Hamburg, Germany, July 14, 1929; s. Ferdinand and Johanna (Mack) P.; m. Gabriele Waldraff, Nov. 20, 1956; children: Petra, Marcus, Konradin. MS, Colo. State U., Ft. Collins, 1957; Diplomingenieur, U. Stuttgart, Germany, 1958, Doktoringenieur, 1966; Doktoringenieur (hon.), U. Hannover, Germany, 1993. Rsch. asst. U. Stuttgart, 1957-59; from asst. prof. to prof. Colo. State U., 1959-69; rsch. scientist Argonne (Ill.) Nat. Lab., 1969-70; prof. civil engring. U. Karlsruhe, Germany, 1970-97, emeritus prof., 1997—. Author: Aerodynamic Characteristics of Atmospheric Boundary Layers, 1971, Statistik F. Bauing, 1993; editor: Engineering Meteorology, 1982; contbr. numerous articles to profl. jours. Fulbright fellow, 1954; recipient German-Japanese award Japan Soc. Promotion Sci., 1988. Mem. ASCE, Inst. Hydraulic and Water Conservancy Beijing (hon. fellow), Internat. Assn. Hydraulic Rsch. (hon., pres. 1985-89).

PLATH, JENNIFER LYNN, marketing manager; b. Boston, Sept. 29, 1964; d. Warren Joseph and Margaret (Wetzel) P.; m. C. William Kraus, Oct. 12, 1997. AB magna cum laude, Dartmouth Coll., 1986; MBA, Harvard Bus. Sch., 1994. Asst. editor Faber and Faber Ltd., London, 1986-88, Farrar, Strauss & Giroux, N.Y.C., 1988-89; assoc. features editor Elle mag., 1989-90, assoc. editor, 1990-92; intern direct mail mktg. H.F. du Pont Winterthur Mus., Inc., Del., 1993; assoc. program mgr. MBI, Inc., Norwalk, Conn., 1994-96, program mgr., 1996-99, sr. product devel. mgr., 1999—. Mem. Phi Beta Kappa.

PLATIN, BULENT EMRE, mechanical engineering educator; b. Istanbul, Turkey, Sept. 9, 1947; s. Ihsan and Nesibe (Ararat) P.; m. Nurgun Ilgen, Oct. 20, 1978; 1 child, Mehmet Levent. MSc in Mech. Engring., Istanbul Tech. U., 1969, MIT, Cambridge, 1972; ScD in Mech. Engring., MIT, Cambridge, 1978. Rschr. Sci. and Tech. Rsch. Coun. Turkey, Istanbul, 1969-70; instr. Middle East Tech. U., Ankara, Turkey, 1978-79, asst. prof., 1979-84, assoc. prof., 1984-91, prof., 1991—, vice-chair mech. engring. dept., 1990-92, assoc. dean engring., 1992-97; vis. assoc. prof. U. Conn., Storrs, 1988-90. Recipient NATO sci. fellowship Sci. and Tech. Rsch. Coun. Turkey, 1970, Fulbright sr. rsch. award, 1988. Mem. ASME (mem. exec. com. Turkey sect. 1997—). Office: Middle East Tech U, Mech Engring Dept, 06531 Ankara Turkey

PLATIS, CHRIS STEVEN, educator; b. East Chicago, Ind., May 21, 1926; s. Sam and Myra (Theodore) P.; m. Jeanette Brown. BS in Phys. Edn., Ind. U., 1955, MS in Edn., 1964, postgrad., 1965-68. Gen. foreman Cast Armor, Inc., East Chicago, 1951-53; tchr. East Chgo. and Ind. Pub. Schs., 1955—; asst. sports editor East Chgo. Calumet News, 1973-78; asst. dir. No. Ind. State Sports Mus., 1984-95, 96, 97, 98, 00. Appearances include (films) A Bridge Too Far, The Longest Day, Bridge at Remagan, D-Day, The Battle of the Bulge; author: Teaching Kids of Tomorrow, 1978, Are Teachers Adequate for Today's Students?, 1997. Master Boy Scouts Am., East Chicago, 1965-87; asst. recreational dir. North Twp., Northern Ind., 1993; All-Pacific Army, Football, Basketball, Track, 1946. With U.S. Army, 1944-46. Named to East Chgo. Hall of Fame All Am. Amateur Baseball Congress, 1955, 56, 57, Ind. Amateur Baseball Hall of Fame, 1962, U.S. Masters Track and Field All Am., 1995-98 (ranked 8 times # 1 and 2 in the country in masters track and field, 8 times ranked # 1 and 2 in the world in masters track and field, 1996-98), 20 individual Indiana Hooster State Games Regional Medals, 20 individual Indiana Hooster State Games Final Medals, 1996, 97, 98, 2000; Nat. Sr. Olympic track and field qualifier, 1997-99; 90 Yr. Greatest Athletes in East Chgo.'s History; recipient 12 league batting titles, 11 MVP awards, 16 times Ind. All State in Baseball, 21 times League Mgr. of Yr., Nat./European Tchr. of Yr., 1984; mem. team won 53 league championships, 54 playoff championships, 40 Ind. State baseball championships, 7 world regional titles, 5 world finalists, 2 runner-up world championships, Nat. C.I.O. baseball championship, 1949 Big Ten Baseball Champions, Ind. U.; conf. baseball champions, 1942, 43, 44; all-conf. team, 1942, 43, 44, capt., 1942, 43, 44; Ind. State Jr. Legion champions, all-state, Midwest All-Star team, 1942, Ind.-Ill. Bi-State champions, 1950, Most Valuable, Batting Champion, Best Infielder award. Fellow VFW (charter mem. World War II Meml. 1998), Am. Legion, Normandy Invasion Club, Nat. Assn. of Basketball Coaches, Nat. Wildlife Assn. Republican. Avocations: reading, writing, baseball, tennis, golf. Home: 427 Fisher St Munster IN 46321-2330

PLATIS, JAMES GEORGE, secondary school educator; b. Detroit, Mar. 23, 1927; s. Sam and Myra (Theodore) P.; m. Mary Lou Campbell, Aug. 16, 1974. BS in Physical Edn., Ind. U., 1955, MS in Edn., 1965; postgrad., Ind. State U., 1967. Cert. physical edn. tchr., Ind. Foreman Cast Armor, Inc., East Chicago, Ind., 1951-53, Youngstown Sheet & Tube, East Chicago, 1953-54; dir., tchr. East Chicago Pub. Schs., 1955—; sports editor East Chicago Globe/Calumet News, 1973-78, Herald Newspapers, Merrillville, Ind., 1973-78; asst. dir. No. Ind. State Sports Mus., 1984-99. Contbr. articles to newspapers, jours. Founder East Chicago Hall of Fame, 1975, Little Olympics, East Chicago, 1956; pres. Ind. Am. Amateur Baseball Congress, 1954-57, commr., 1984-98; dir. No. Ind. State Sports Mus., 1988-00. With AUS, 1945-47, ETO. Named to Ind. Amateur Baseball Hall of Fame, 1962, East Chicago Hall of Fame, 1976, All-Am. Amateur Baseball Congress, 1955, 56, The Athletic Congress Masters All-Am., 1986-98, 99, 2000; selected to 90 Yr. Greatest Athletes in East Chicago History, Nat. Athletic Congress, 1990; named Amateur Coach of Yr., U.S. Baseball Fedn. Ind., 1990, Amateur Runner-up Coach of Yr., 1988; recipient 47 World and 55 Nat. No. 1 track rankings, Athletic Congress Masters, 1989-98, 2000, 14 League Batting Titles, 12 MV League Players awards; Ind. Jr. Legion State Champions, All-State Batting Champions, MVP in tournament, Conf. Baseball Champions, 1943, 44, 45, All-Conf. Team, 1944-45, Conf. Batting Champion, 1944, Team Cptn., 1945, All-Midwest team, Best Outfielder, 1944; 18 times Ind. all-state team; Ind. Nat. Baseball State Champions; mem. team won 53 League Championships, 54 Playoff championships, 40 Ind. State Baseball Championships, 5 Ind. State Champions Runner Up, 7 World Regional Titles, 5 World Finalists, 2 runner-up World Champions, Big Ten baseball champions Ind. U., 1949, Best Outfielder Congress All-State team, Ill., Ind. Bi-State Champions, 1950, Nat. C.I.O. Baseball Championship, 1951, 12 Times League Mgr. Of The Year, 1982-96; Big Ten Baseball Champions, Ind. U., 1936-2000; named Athlete of Yr. Ind. Masters Track and Field, 1992, World Sr. Olympic Masters Track & Field Champion, Spain, 6 gold medals, 3 Masters Track & Field World Records, 1992, Fla. Masters Track and Field Athlete of Yr., 1994-97; recipient 74 State Ind. Track and Field individual medals, 1983-99, 2000, 74 Ind. state regional individual medals, 1983-98, 2000, 291 All Am. Masters Track and Field Certs., 1986-99, 39 Ill. Grand Prix individual titles, 1989-92, 45 Mid-West Track and Field individual titles, 1989-92, 5 gold medals, silver medal World Sr. Olympic Masters Track & Field, 1996, Ga., 5 Masters Track & Field World Records, 1997, 2 Masters Track & Field World Records, 1998, Nat. Senior Olympics Qualifer, 1991, 93, 95, 97, 99, 4 Gold medals, 2 World Records Nat. Sr. Olympics, 7 gold medals World Svc. Olympic Masters Track and Field, Sydney, Australia, 2000; named Internat. Man of the Yr. in Edn., 1991-92, 93, Professional of the Yr. in Edn., 1991, others. Fellow Nat. Assn. Basketball Coaches, Am. Assn. Health, Phys. Edn. and Recreation; mem. Athletic Dirs. Assn. Sportswriters Guild, VFW, Am. Legion, WWII Meml. (82nd Airborne Divsn., 1st Inf. Divsn. 1998), Mens Club Ind. U. Republican. Avocations: reading, running, baseball, writing. Home: 427 Fisher St Munster IN 46321-2330 Office: East Chicago Pub Schs 2700 Cardinal Dr East Chicago IN 46312-3150

PLATONE, LODO, psychologist, researcher, consultant; b. Pietrasanta Lucca, Italy, May 15, 1930; d. Cesare Lodo and Fernanda Margherita Guidi; m. Vittorio Platone (div.); children: Gloria, Marco, Laura. Degree in psychology, Ctrl. U. Venezuela, Caracas, 1965, MS in Psychology, 1980; EdD, U. Mass., 1984; postgrad., Consejo Nat. Sci. & Tech., Caracas, 1994. Asst. prof. Ctrl. U. Venezuela, 1966—, head psychology dept., 1970-74, dir. postgrad. program in group dynamics, 1976-90, rschr. Psychology Inst., 1995—; cons., rschr. Ctr. Ednl. Rsch., Fundatebas, Caracas, 1995—; cons. Orgnl. Devel. Assn., Caracas. Author: Familia y Sociedad. El Enfoque Sistémático del Cambio, 1999; editor: La Familia: Trama, Escenario y Drama de los Barrios Populares en Venezuela, 1998; contbr. articles to profl. jours. Forum moderator Venezuelan Young Pres. Assn., Caracas. Fellow Venezuelan Social Psychology Assn. (founder), Venezuelan Sch. Psychology Assn. (founder); mem. APA (fgn. affiliate), Federación de Psicólogos de Venezuela. Roman Catholic. Avocations: sculpture, arts and crafts, tennis, jogging. Fax: (58) (02) 662 29 49. Home: Calle El Bosque Res Balvi, 2 piso apt 21 La Castella, Caracas 1060, Venezuela Office: Ctrl U Venezuela Cen Com los Chaguaramos, Inst Psicologia Piso 2, Caracas 1041-A, Venezuela

PLATONOV, ANDREW YURIYEVICH, chemist, educator; b. Leningrad, USSR, Apr. 5, 1948; s. Yurii Nikolaevich and Natalia Andreyevna (Vorokhobova) P.; m. Galina Alexandrovna Galigarova, Feb. 25, 1971; 1 child, Natalia Andreyevna. Cert. chem. technologist, Techol. Inst. Pulp & Paper, Leningrad, 1971, PhD, 1981, cert. assoc. prof., 1991. From engr. to asst. Leningrad Technol. Inst. Pulp and Paper Industry, 1971-88; assoc. prof. St. Petersburg (Russia) State Technol. U. Plant Polymers, 1988—. Contbr. articles to sci. publs., including Russian Jour. Gen. Chemistry, Russian Chem. Bull.; inventor in field. Grantee Russian Base Rsch. Fund, 1994-95, Fed. Target Sci. and Tech. Program, 1996-99, Internat. Competition on Sci. Projects, 1999. Mem. Internat. Union of Pure and Applied Chemistry, Internat. Coun. Main Group Chemistry. Avocations: bicycling, skiing. Home: Nevsky 146 109, 193024 Saint Petersburg Russia Office: State Tech U Plant Polymers, Ivan Chernykh 4, 198095 Saint Petersburg Russia

PLATONOV, IGOR ALEKSANDROVITCH, pharmacology educator; b. Vilandi, Estonia, Russia, Feb. 20, 1948; s. Aleksandr Fedotovitch Platonov and Taisia Fedorovna Nikolaenkova. MS, State Med. Inst., Smolensk, Russia, 1983, DM, 1995. Physician intern State Med. Inst., Smolensk, 1966-73; psychiatrist Cen. Dist. Hosp., Yartsevo, Russia, 1972-74, Regional Psychiatric Hosp., Smolensk, 1974-79; sr. tutor, lectr. pharmacology dept. State Med. Inst., 1979-94, prof. of pharmacology, 1994—; cons. physician Psychiat. Hosp., Smolensk, 1979—; bd. dirs. in field. Editor: Health Strengthening Problems, Prevention and Treatment, 1995, Physical Exercise as a Factor to Strengthen Your Health: Prevention and Treatment, 1996, Pharmacology, 1997; author: Medicobiological Statistics, 1997, Pharmacology in Figures and Tables, 1999; contbr. articles to profl. jours. Active Physicians for Peace Movement, 1987—. Mem. Soc. Neurologists and Psychiatrists, Soc. Pharmacologists, Assn. of Inventors (chmn. regional br. 1985—). Avocations: chess, computer programming. Office: State Med Acad Smolensk, Krupskaya st 28, 214019 Smolensk Russia

PLATONOVA, GALINA ALEXANDROVNA, chemist, researcher; b. Kizlyar, Dagestan, USSR, Apr. 3, 1947; d. Alexandr Alexeevich Galigarov and Vera Dmitrievna (Rubets) Galigarova; m. Adnrew Yriyevich Platonov, Feb. 25, 1971; 1 child, Natalia Andreyevna. Diploma in chemistry, Leningrad (USSR) Tech. Inst. of Pulp & Paper Industry, USSR, 1971; PhD, Russian Acad. Scis., Leningrad, 1987. Lab. asst. Inst. Macromolecular Compounds Russian Acad. Scis., Leningrad, 1971-79, engr., 1979-83, jr. sci. rschr., 1983-89; sci. rschr. Russian Acad. Scis., St. Petersburg, Russia, 1989—. Coauthor: Synthesis, Structure and Properties of Polymers, 1989; contbr. articles to profl. jours. Recipient Hilton honor, 1998-00; grantee Russian Base Rsch. Fund, 1997-99. Mem. Russian Chem. Soc., Russian Biochemical Soc. Avocations: bicycle, table tennis, skiing, swimming. Office: Inst Macromolecular Compnds, Bolshoy pr. 31, 199004 Saint Petersburg Russsia

PLATT, LEWIS EMMETT, retired electronics company executive; b. Johnson City, N.Y., Apr. 11, 1941; s. Norval Lewis and Margaret Dora (Williams) P.; m. Joan Ellen Redmund, Jan. 15, 1983; children: Caryn, Laura, Amanda, Hillary. BME, Cornell U., 1964; MBA, U. Pa., 1966. With Hewlett Packard, Waltham, Mass., 1966-71, engring. mgr., 1971-74, ops. mgr., 1976-77, div. gen. mgr., 1974-80, group gen. mgr., Palo Alto, Calif., 1980-84, v.p., 1983-85, exec. v.p., 1987-92, pres., CEO, chmn., 1993-99; ret.; Trustee Waltham Hosp., 1978-80, Wharton Sch. Bd. Overseers, 1993; mem. Mid-Peninsula YMCA, 1980—, bd. couns. YMCA-USA, 1993—, Cornell U. Coun., 1992—, Computer Sys. Policy Project, 1993—, Calif. Bus. Roundtable, 1993-95, Bus. Coun., 1993—, Bay Area Coun., 1993—, Bus. Roundtable, 1993—; vice chmn. Y Coun., 1989, mem. bd. dirs. Joint Venture, Silicon Valley, 1996. Recipient Red Triangle award Min-Peninsula YMCA, 1992, Internat. Citizens award World Forum Silicon Valley, San Jose, Calif., 1994, outstanding alumnus, Wharton Alumni Honor Roll, Wharton Schl. Business, Univ. Pa., 1994-95, award for bus. excellence U. Calif. Sch. Bus. Adminstrn., 1996, Tree of Life award Jewish Nat. Fund, 1996, Leadership and Vision award San Francisco Chpt. French-Am. C. of C., 1997. Mem. IEEE, Sci. Apparatus Mfg. Assn. (dir. 1978-80).*

PLATTARD, SERGE, nuclear physicist, administrator; b. Berne, Switzerland, Aug. 8, 1947; s. Yves Claude Plattard and Denise Joseph-Joigny; m. Sylvie Marguerite Marie Dupont-Fauville, June 22, 1984; children: Jean, Francois, Antoine, Emmanuel, Sophie. MS in Physics, U. Paris VI, 1969; PhD in Nuc. Physics, U. Paris XI, 1973. Nuc. physicist French Atomic Energy Commn. (CEA), Bruyeres-le-Chatel, France, 1973-80; officer, policy planning staff Ministry External Rels., Paris, 1981-82; long-term planning and forecasting officer French Atomic Energy Commn., Paris, 1983-86; dep. counsellor, sci. and tech. French Emb., New Delhi, 1987-89; dep. dir. scientific and tech. cooperation Ministry Fgn. Affairs, Paris, 1990; counsellor, sci. and tech. French Emb., Tokyo, 1990-94, Washington, 1994-98; dir. internat. rels. French Space Agy. (CNES), Paris, 1998—; asst. prof. nuc. physics, Faculty of Scis., Orsay, France, 1976-86; mem. Sci. Def. Coun., Paris, 1998—; lectr. Ecole Supérieure des Sciences Economiques et Commerciales, Cergy, France, 2000—; lectr., U. Dauphine, Paris, 1984-85. Co-author: Nucléaire, merveille ou menace?, 1984; contbr. numerous articles to profl. jours. and conf. procs. Knight, French Legion of Honor, 1998; honored Golden Rays of the Order of the Sacred Treasure, Imperial Ho., Tokyo, 1994. Mem. Am. Phys. Soc. (life), European Assn. Promotion of Sci. and Tech. (founding mem.). Roman Catholic. Avocations: swimming, Alpine skiing, cycling, reading, photography. E-mail: serge.plattard@cnes.fr or serge.plattard@free.fr. Home: 56 Bd des Etats-Unis, F-78110 Le Vesinet France Office: CNES, 2 Place Maurice Quentin, F-75001 Paris France

PLATTHY, JENO, cultural association executive; b. Dunapataj, Hungary, Aug. 13, 1920; s. Joseph K. and Maria (Dobor) P.; m. Carol Louise Abell, Sept. 25, 1976. Diploma, Peter Pazmany U., Budapest, Hungary, 1942; PhD, Ferencz J. U., Kolozsvar, Hungary, 1944; MS, Cath. U., 1965; PhD (hon.), Yangmingshan U., Taiwan, 1975; DLitt (hon.), U. Libre Asie, Philippines, 1977. Lectr. various univs., 1956-59; sec. Internat. Inst. Boston, 1959-62; adminstrv. asst. Trustees of Harvard U., Washington, 1962-85; exec. dir. Fedn. Internat. Poetry Assns., 1976—; pub. New Muses Quar., 1976—. Author: Winter Tunes, 1974, Ch'u Yuan, His Life and Works, 1975, Springtide (opera), 1976, Bamboo, Collected Poems, 1981, The Poems of Jesus, 1982, Holiness in a Worldly Garment, 1984, Ut Pictures Poeta, 1984, European Odes, 1985, The Mythical Poets of Greece, 1985, Book of Dithyrambs, 1986, Asian Elegies, 1987, Space Ecologues, 1988, Cosmograms, 1988, Nova Comoedia, 1988, vols. II-III, 1992, Bartok: A Critical Biography, 1988, Plato: A Critical Biography, 1990, Near-Death Experiences in Antiquity, 1992, Celebration of Life, 1992, Idylls, 1992, Elegies Asiatiques, 1992, Paeans, 1993, Rhapsodies, 1994, Prosodia, 1994, Visions, 1994, Prophecies, 1994, Epyllia, 1994, Budapesttol Tokyoig, 1994, 2d edit., 1995, Walking Two Feet Above the Earth, 1995, Dictionarium Cumanico Hungaricum, 1996, Emblems, 1996, Epodes, 1996, Aeolian Lilts, 1996, Transformations, 1996, Inexpressions, 1996, Songs of the Soul, 1996, Sacrifices, 1996, Gifts with Poetic Horizons, 1997, Imperceptions, Hermeneutics of Poetry, 1997, From Silence to Silence, New Perspectives in Poetry, 1997, Lincoln the Poet, an Epic Poem, 1997, Looking Away, 1998, Commitments, 1998, The Duino Elegies of Rilke, 1999, Symmetries with Poetic Discoveries, Part I, 1999, Cosmos Flowers with Poetic Discoveries, Part II, 1999, Dreamtide with Principia Spiritualia I (Discoveries III), 2000, Demonstrations with Principia Spiritualia II-III (Discoveries IV-V), 2000, Pictorial Bio-Bibliography, 2000, also numerous others, also translations; editor-in-chief Monumenta Classica Perennia, 1967-84. Named Poet Laureate 2d World Congress of Poets, 1973; recipient Confucius award Chinese Poetry Soc., 1974, Yunus Emre award 12th Internat. Congress of Poets, Istanbul, Turkey, 1991, Jacques Raphael-Leygues prize Société des Poètes Français, 1992, French Ordre des Arts et des Lettres (officer), 1992. Mem. PEN, ASCAP, Internat. Soc. Lit., Die Literarische Union, Internat. Poetry Soc., Acad. Am. Poets, Assn. Lit. Scholars and Critics, 3d Internat. Congress Poets (pres. 1976, poet laureate 1976). Office: Fedn Internat Poetry Assns 961 W Sled Cir Santa Claus IN 47579-6251

PLATTI, RITA JANE, educator, draftsman, writer, inventor; b. Stockton, Calif., Aug. 29, 1925; d. Umbert Ferdinand and Concettina Maria (Natoli) Strangio; m. Elvin Carl Platti, July 27, 1955; 1 child, Kimberley Jane. Student, Dominican Coll., 1943-45; AB in Math, U. Pacific, 1947,

postgrad., 1947-52, 68. Farmer, almond grower Escalon, Calif., 1943—; tchr. math St. Mary's High Sch., Stockton, 1947-49, 52, 54; chem. analyst Petri Winery, Escalon, 1949; draftsman Kyle Steel Co., Stockton, 1950-52; pvt. practice as draftsman Stockton, 1952-66; tchr. math Montezuma Sch., Stockton, 1956-57, Davis Elem. Sch., Stockton, 1957-58; with rental bus., 1958-81; tchr. math Amos Alonzo Stagg High Sch., 1961-80, Humphreys Coll., 1981-83, Hamilton Jr. High Sch., 1984-90; owner, involved in prodn. and mktg. R.J. Creations, 1991—; farm realtor Century 21, Escalon, Calif., 1996-97; spkr. workshops Stanislaus State U., 1992, Calif. Math. Coun., Fresno State U., 1992, Nat. Sci. Found. Conf., 1993; spkr. math./sci. conf. Calif. State U., Bakerfield, 1994-96; evaluator Math. Framework (K-12) Calif. State Dept. Edn. Author: Math Proficiency Plateaus, 1979, Preparing Fundamentals of The Use of Sound in the Teaching of Mathematics, 1994; author, pub. series, 1979-86; 3 patents in field. Mem. NEA, Calif. Tchrs. Assn. Democrat. Roman Catholic. Avocations: inventing, mathematics theoretical development, poetry, piano, environmental clean up.

PLATUS, LIBBY, artist, sculptor, speaker; b. L.A., Aug. 18, 1939; d. Benjamin Lyon and Gertrude Goldman; children: Julie Linda, Diana Lisa. BA, UCLA, 1961. lectr., condr. workshops numerous internat., nat., regional meetings and meetings in all 50 states, including World Craft Conf., Kyoto, Japan, 1978, Vienna, Austria, 1980, Glasgow (Scotland) Sch. Art, 1980, 84, Loughborough Coll. Art, Eng., 1980, 84, R.I. Sch. Design, 1982, Parsons Sch. Design, N.Y.C., 1982, Arrowmont, Gatlinburg, Tenn., 1978, 83, 87, Konstfackskolan, Sweden, 1984, Goldsmith's Coll., Eng., 1984, Taideteo Llinen Korkeakoulo, Finland, 1984, Savannah (Ga.) Coll. Art and Design, 1987, 89, 90, 92, 94, 99, East N.C. U., Greenville, 1989, 92, 97, 2000, Navajo C.C., Shiprock Reservation, N.Mex., 1992, World Wildfowl Carving Exhbn., Ward Found., Md., 1990, Kansas City Art Inst., 1990, 92, So. Ute Tribal Hdqrs., Ignacio, Colo., 1993, U. Western Sydney design dept., 1993, Sydney Coll. Art, 1993, Victorian Coll. Art, Melbourne, Australia, 1993, U. South Australia, Underdale, 1993, Australian Nat. U., Canberra, 1993, Small Bus. Devel. Ctr. Northland Pioneer Coll., Hollbrook, Ariz., 1994, N.Y. State Coll. Ceramics, Alfred U., 1994, 96, Bus. Dept., 2000, Tlingit-Gold Belt Corp., Juneau, 1993, Seneca Nation Econ. Devel. Corp., Jamestown, N.Y., 1996, Assiniboine/Sioux/Gros Ventre-Tribal Bus. Info. Ctr., Ft. Belknap Reservation, Harlam, Mont., 1996, Nat. Home Based Bus. Conf. U. Wis.-Whitewater, Milw., 1996, 10th nat. conf. U.S. Assn. Small Bus. Entrepreneurship, Atlanta, 1996, So. Meth. U., Dallas, 1996, 99, New Orleans Jazz and Heritage Festival, 1994, Small Bus. Devel. Ctr., Binghamton (N.Y.) U., 1996, Small Bus. Devel. Ctr. and N.Mex. Main St. Program, Carlsbad, 1997, So. Ill. U., Carbondale, 1999, Fla. Craftsmen and Pinellas County Art Coun., St. Petersburg, 1997, Oreg. Coll. Art and Craft, Portland, 1999, Montgomery Mus. Art, Ala., 1997, Syracuse (N.Y.) U., 1997, Va. Commonwealth Univ., Richmond, 1999,, Towson Univ., Towson, MD, 1988, 99, Atlantic County Office of Cultural and Heritage Affairs, NJ, 1988, 91, 95, 98, 00, Bear Paw Devel. Corp., Havre, Mont., Riverbend Art Ctr., Dayton, Ohio, 1998, 99, Pride of Dakota, Dept. Agr., N.D., 1999, Utah Heritage Industry Conf., Utah Divsn. Bus. and Econ. Devel., Ephriam, 1999, Keynote, Montpelier, 1999, Wyo. Dept. Employment Vocat. Rehab., Casper, Sheyenne, Sheridan, Rock Springs, 2000, Native Am. Shoshone/Northern Arapahoe, Wind River Reservation, Wyo., 2000, Hand Made in Am., Asheville, N.C., 2000, numerous others; cons. Millstream Arts Festival Coll. St. Benedict, St. Joseph, Minn., 1992, Mountain State Art and Crafts Festival, Cedar Lakes, W.Va., 1992, Grand Junction area C. of C., Home Based Bus. Trade Fair, Colo., 1992, Yavapai Coll. Creative Comm. Convergence, Sedona, Ariz., 1995, Mont. Food and Gift Show Made in Mont. Program, Mont. Dept Commerce, Great Falls Mont., 1999; juror regional exhbn. Fairbanks Art Assn., Alaska, 1984; juror, judge, Greater Gulf Coast Art Festival, Pensacola, Fla., 1999; judge Millstream Arts Festival, Coll. St. Benedict, St. Joseph, Minnesota, 1992; participant Charmin Care TV comml., 1989, Rotary Internat. Group Study Exchange, Bangalore, India, 1998. Group shows include Richmond (Calif.) Designer Craftsmen, 1971, E.B. Crocker Gallery, Sacramento, 1973, Comsky Gallery, Beverly Hills, Calif., 1973, Galeria del Sol, Santa Barbara, Calif., 1973, Laguna Beach (Calif.) Mus. Art, 1973, Riverside (Calif.) Art Ctr., 1974, Calif. State U. Northridge, L.A., 1974, Calif. State U., Fullerton, 1974, Calif. Design '76, L.A., 1976, Cleve. Mus. Art, 1977; represented in collections: Tex. Christian U., Faberge Hdqrs., N.Y.C., numerous other pub. and pvt. collections; commd. works: Big Canyon Country Club, Newport Beach, Calif., Carolando Hyatt Hotel, Orlando, Fla., McCulloch's Silver Lakes Resort Hotel, Victorville, Calif., Blue Cross So. Calif., L.A. Mem. L.A. Olympics 1984 Cultural and Fine Arts Commn., 1980-84, citizens adv. commn., 1980-84; adv. bd. Crafts Report Edn. Fund, 1985-88. Recipient Graphic Achievement award Fox River Paper Corp., 1974; winner Tex. Christian U. Nat. Invitational Fiberwork Competition, 1977. Mem. Artists Equity (adv. bd. L.A. chpt. 1981-87). Home and Office: PO Box 55026 Sherman Oaks CA 91413-0026

PLATZ, OLE, research scientist, consultant; b. Lemvig, Denmark, Oct. 31, 1938; s. Arthur Mouritz and Kamma Meta (Thagaard) P.; m. Bente Guldbrand, Nov. 24, 1962; children: Henrik, Morten. PhD, Århus Univ., 1974. Rschr. Århus U., 1969-73; with Risø Nat. Lab., Roskilde, Denmark, 1973-87, Danish Meat Rsch. Inst., Roskilde, 1987-88, Platz Consult Aps, Svebølle, Denmark, 1988—. Contbr. articles to profl. jours. including Phys. Rev. and Letters, IEEE Transactions on Reliability Jour. of Applied Probability. Home and Office: Aunsøgårdsallé 2, 4470 Svebølle Denmark

PLATZ, THOMAS FRANZ, physician, researcher; b. Landau, Rheinland-Pfalz, Germany, July 22, 1962; s. Werner and Elisabeth (Weisbrod) P.; m. Carolin Fein, Sept. 29, 1990; children: Lukas Imanuel, Maike Makena. Diploma epidemiology and biostat., McGill U., 1997; postgrad., Duke U. Med. Ctr., 1988; MD, U. Heidelberg, Germany, 1989. Resident Klinik Berlin/Free U., 1989-94, 96, cons., 1997; resident Wenckebach Hosp., Berlin, 1993-94; clin. asst., rschr. Inst. of Neurology, London, 1995. Recipient Foedor Lynen award von Humboldt Stiftung, 1995; edn. grant Deutscher Akademischer Austauschdienst, 1996, 97. Mem. European Brain and Behavior Soc., European Neurosci. Assn., Berliner Gesellschaft Neurologie und Psychiatrie, Deutsche Gesellschaft Neurologisch Rehab., Deutsche Gesellschaft Neurologie. Roman Catholic. Avocations: piano. Office: Klinik Berlin, Kladower Damm 223, 14089 Berlin Germany

PLAVINSKAYA, ANNA DMITRIEVNA, artist; b. Moscow, Nov. 26, 1960; came to U.S., 1989, naturalized, 1995; d. Dmitri Petrovich and Nina Nicolaevna; m. Gennady Ioffe, Jan 9, 1988 (div. July 1993). Diploma in Costume Design, Theatrical Art Coll., Moscow, 1976-80. Costume designer Evgeny Vahtangov Theater, Moscow, 1980-82; artist freelance Moscow, 1983-89; art restorer pvt. studio, N.Y.C., 1990-93; artist freelance N.Y.C., 1993—. Exhibited in group shows at art colls., Moscow (hon. mention 1977), Gallery of Moscow Artists, 1983, Ctrl. Exhbn. Hall, Moscow, 1984, 88, Kuznetzky Most Gallery, Moscow, 1985, Tbilisi Acad. of Art, Georgia, 1986, Tallinna Moepaevad '87, Tallinn, Estonia, 1987 (hon. mention), Remizovo St. Gallery, Moscow, 1988, Pushkin Sq. Gallery, Moscow, 1988, The Textile Art Ctr., Chgo., 1991, The Russian Nobility Assn., N.Y.C., 1991, 11th Cleveland Internat. Drawing Biennale, Middlesbrough, Eng., 1993 (2nd prize award), BWA Gallery, Wroclaw, Poland, 1994, BWA Gallery, Lublin, Poland, 1994, Elblag (Poland) Gallery, 1994, Tatranska Gallery, Poprad, Tatry, Slovakia, 1994, State Gallery, Ostrova, Czech Republic, 1994, Botanica '94, Port Royal Mus. Gallery, Naples, Fla., 1994, Art Addiction Gallery, Stockholm, 1996 (hon. mention), 97 (cert. of merit), 98, Art Addiction Gallery, Venice, Italy, 1998, Internat. Platform Assn., 1998, 99; represented in permanent collections Cleveland Contemporary Art Collection, Middlesbrough, Eng., Zimmerli Art Mus., Norton and Nancy Dodge Collection, N.J. Mem. Internat. Platform Assn. (first place award Best of Show 1998, First place award 1999). Russian Orthodox. Avocations: fashion design, antique textile restoration, tennis. Home: 815 W 181st St Apt 3E New York NY 10033-4530

PLAVNIK, ISAK, nutritionist; b. Lepel, Beloruss, Sept. 23, 1940; arrived in Israel, 1972; s. Solomon and Elizabeth (Melnikov) P.; m. Lilia Klipcan, Mar. 25, 1962. MS, Vet. Sch., Vitebsk-Beloruss, 1962; PhD, Vet. Acad., Moscow, 1967. Scientist Animal Inst., Minsk, 1962-67; dept. head Rsch. Sta., Minsk, 1967-72, Volcani Rsch. Ctr., Bet-Dagan, Israel, 1972—; dir. Israeli Poultry Bd., Tel-Aviv, 1986—; dept. head poultry sci., Bet-Dagan, 1986—. Contbr. articles to profl. jours. Mem. World Poultry Sci. Assn., Turkey Working Group. Office: Volcani Rsch Ctr, PO Box 6, Bet Dagan 50-250, Israel

PLAVSIC, MARK ZELIMIR, veterinary virologist; b. Crni Vrh, Yugoslavia, Oct. 26, 1960; came to U.S., 1997; s. Radojica and Mileva Plavsic; m. Ljiljana Andjelic, Aug. 27, 1988; 1 child, Sonja. DVM, Vet. Faculty, Belgrade, Yugoslavia, 1984, DSc, 1992. Diplomate Am. Bd. Vet. Microbiology. Vet. virologist Specialist Vet. Inst., Kraljevo, Yugoslavia, 1985-93; vet. insp. New Zealand Ministry Agr. & Fisheries, Hamilton, 1994; tech. dir. Life Techs., Inc., Auckland, New Zealand, 1995-97; sr. scientist Life Techs., Inc., Grand Island, N.Y., 1998-99, prin. scientist, 1999, dir., R&D, 2000—. Mem. Yugoslavian Vet. Soc., Australian Soc., Microbiology, Am. Assn. Vet. Lab Diagnosticians, Am. Soc. Microbiology, N.Y. Acad. Scis. Achievements include inventor of Q Fever Diagnosis, Virus Inactivation, vaccine adjuvants, blood stabilizing buffer, TSE Risk Assessement. Avocations: martial arts, photography, travel. Office: Life Techs Inc 3175 Staley Rd Grand Island NY 14072-2028

PLAWSKA-JACKIEWICZ, KRISTINA, sculptor; b. Dynesburg, Latvia, Aug. 1, 1932; d. Kazmir and Jadwiga (Miklaszewicz) P.; m. Wiktor Jackiewicz, Sept. 28, 1959; 1 child, Michael. MA, Art Acad., Wroclaw, Poland, 1958. Free-lance sculptor Poland, 1958-72, Yugoslavia, 1972-79, Poland, 1979—. Mem. Polish Art Assn. Roman Catholic. Avocation: swimming. Home: Dereniona 18, 53008 Wrocław Poland

PLAX, KAREN ANN, lawyer; b. St. Louis, June 29, 1946; d. George J. and Evelyn G. Zell; m. Stephen E. Plax, Dec. 19, 1968; 1 child, Jonathan. BA magna cum laude, U. Mo., St. Louis, 1969; JD with distinction, U. Mo., Kansas City, 1976. Bar: Mo. 1976, U.S. Supreme Ct. 1980. Atty. Thayer, Gum & Wickert, Grandview, Mo., 1976-84, Plax & Cochet, Kansas City, Mo., 1984-87; pvt. practice Kansas City, 1987—; past chair divsn. 3, region IV Mo. Supreme Ct. Com. to review ethical conduct of attys., 1997-98. Author: Missouri Bar Practical Skills, 1998; asst. editor: Racial Integration in the Inner Suburb, 1990; contbr. articles to profl. jours. Recipient Pub. Svc. award U. Mo. Kansas City Law Found., 1998, Woman of Yr. award Assn. Women Lawyers of Greater Kansas City, 1999. Fellow Am. Acad. Matrimonial Lawyers (pres. Mo. chpt. 1999-2000); mem. ABA (family law sect. 1976-99), Kansas City Met. Bar Assn., Mo. Bar Family Law (legis. chair 1997-98, v.p. 1999-2000, Spl. Commendation for Legis. Role in Family Law 1998). E-mail: kaplax@swbell.net. Office: 1310 Carondelet Dr Kansas City MO 64114-4803

PLAYER, GARY JIM, professional golfer, businessman, golf course designer; b. Johannesburg, South Africa, Nov. 1, 1935; s. Francis Harry Audley and Muriel (Ferguson) P; m. Vivienne Verwey, Jan. 19, 1957; children: Jennifer, Marc, Wayne, Michele, Theresa, Amanda. Ed., King Edward Sch., Johannesburg; LLD (hon.), St. Andrews U., Scotland, 1995. Profl. golfer, 1953—; with PGA, 1957-85; profl. golfer Sr. PGA, 1985—; chair Gary Player Group. 3rd man in history to win Grand Slam of Golf; winner over 150 internat. golf tournaments, 22 Sr. Tour tournaments; named Christian Athlete of Yr. So. Bapt. Conv., 1967, Sportsman of the Year in South Africa, 1955, 56, 59, 61, 63, 65, 72, 74, 78, South African Sportsman of the Century, 1990; Richardson award Golf Writers Assn. Am., 1975; named to World Golf Hall of Fame, 1974; hon. mem. R&A, 1994, Skills Challenge, 1994. Won East Rand Open, South Africa, 1955-56, Egyptian Mathchplay, 1955, South African Open, 1956, 60, 65-69, 72, 75-77, 79, 81, Dunlop Tournament, Eng., 1956, Ampol Tournament, Australia, 1956, 58, 61, Australian PGA, 1957, Coughs Harbour Tournament, Australia, 1957-58, Natal Open, South Africa, 1958-60, 62, 66, 68, Australian Open, 1958, 62-63, 65, 69-70, 74, Transvaal Open, South Africa, 1959, 60, 62, 63, 66, South African PGA, 1959-60, 69, 79, 82, Western Province Open, South Africa, 1959-60, 68, 71-72, Dunlop Masters, South Africa, 1959-60, 63-64, 67, 71-74, 76-77, Brit. Open, 1959, 68, 74, Victoria Open, 1959, Yomiuri Open, Japan, 1961, Masters Tournament, 1961, 74, 78, Sponsored 5000, South Africa, 1963, Liquid Air Tournament, South Africa, 1963, Richelieu Grand Prix, Capetown, 1963, Johannesburg, 1963, NTL Challenge Cup, 1965, World Cup Internat., 1965, World Series of Golf, 1965, 68, 72, Picadilly World Match Play, Eng., 1965, 66, 68, 71, 73, Australian Wills Masters, 1968, 69, Dunlop Internat., Australia, 1970, Gen. Motors Open, South Africa, 1971, 73, 74, 75, 76, Japan Airlines Open, 1972, Brazilian Open, 1972, 74, Rand Internat. Open, South Africa, 1974, Gen. Motors Internat. Classic, South Africa, 1974, Ibergolf Tournament, Spain, 1974, La Manga Tournament, Spain, 1974, Gen. Motors Classic, 1975, ICL Transvaal, South Africa, 1977, World Cup Individual, The Philippines, 1977, Knonenbrau Masters, South Africa, 1979, Sun City, South Am., 1979, Chilean Open, 1980, Trophee Boigny, Ivory Coast, 1980, Australian Tooth Gold Coast Classic, 1981, Johnnie Walker Trophy, Spain, 1981; recipient PGA tour victories (21) Ky. Derby Open, 1961, Lucky Internat. Open, 1961, Sunshine Open 1961, PGA Championship, 1962, 72, San Diego Open, 1963, Pensacola Open, 1964, 500 Festival Open, 1964, U.S. Open, 1965, Tournament of Champions, 1969, 78, Greater Greensboro Open, 1970, Jacksonville Open, 1971, Nat. Airlines Open, 1971, New Orleans Open, 1972, So. Open, 1973, Danny Thomas Memphis Classic, 1974, Houston Open, 1978, (Sr. PGA tours) (19) Quadel Sr. Classic, 1985, Gen. Foods PGA Srs. Championship, 1986, 88, 90, United Hosps. Sr. Golf Championship, Denver Post Champions of Golf, Mazda Sr. Tournament Players Champion, 1987, Northville Srs., 1987, U.S. Sr. Open, 87, 88, PaineWebber World Srs. Invitational, Aetna Challenge, 1988, Southwestern Bell Classic, 1988, USGA Srs., 1988, Sr. Brit. Open, 1988, 90, 97, GTE North Classic, The RJR Championship, Royal Caribbean Classic, 1991, Bank One Classic, 1993, 95, Northville Long Island Classic, 1998. Avocations: thoroughbred horse breeding, farming, fitness, health, diet. Office: Gary Player Group 3930 Rca Blvd Ste 3001 West Palm Beach FL 33410-4291 Office: Senior PGA PO Box 109601 100 Ave of The Champions Palm Beach Gardens FL 33410

PŁAŻEK, AGNIESZKA MARIA, plant physiologist, researcher, educator; b. Krakow, Poland, Mar. 7, 1959; d. Zenon Henryk and Maria Alicja (Bobowska) K.; m. Stefan Feliks Płażek, Dec. 16, 1981; children: Jan, Jadwiga. MSc, Agrl. U. of Krakow, 1982, PhD, 1997. Engr. Plant Breeding and Acclimation Inst., Krakow, 1983-91, asst., 1991-96; sr. scientist Agrl. U. of Krakow, 1997—. Contbr. articles to profl. jours. Roman Catholic. Avocations: chess, skiing, crosswords, puzzle. Office: Agrl U Plant Physiology, W Podłuzna 3, 30-239 Krakow Poland

PLAZL, IGOR, chemical engineering educator; b. Celje, Slovenia, Feb. 6, 1959; s. Joze and Vida (Cilensek) P.; m. Jasna Pecnik, Aug. 9, 1986; children: Domen, Gaja. Diploma in engring., U. Ljubljana, Slovenia, 1985, MS, 1989, PhD, 1993. Asst. chem. engring. divsn. U. Ljubljana, 1985-92, asst. prof., 1993—. Avocations: basketball, skiing, badminton. Office: U Ljubljana, Askerceva 5, 1000 Ljubljana Slovenia

PLCH, JOSEF, otorhinolaryngologist, educator; b. Brno, Moravia, Czech Republic, Oct. 26, 1944; s. Josef and Vítězslava (Rosáková) P.; m. Milena Kocmanová, June 14, 1969 (div. 1996); children: Eva, Michaela. MD, Masaryk's U., 1969; PhD, Charles' U., 1992. Cert. otorhinolaryngologist; lic. head dept. Doctor, resident, specialist Hosp. Kolíště, Brno, 1969-82, head ORL dept., 1982—; assoc. prof. Palacky's U., 1996; lectr. med. faculty Masaryk's U., Brno, 1965-68; tchr. ORL Inst. Advanced Med. Man Edn., Brno, 1980—. Author: (textbook) ORL for Nurses, 1995; mem. consulting bd. Jour.: Head and Neck Diseases, 1991—; contbr. articles to profl. jours. Mem. exec. com. Czech Med. Soc. for ORL and Head and Neck Soc., Prague, 1990—. Mem. Yacht Club Brno. Avocations: yachting, travel, card playing. Office: Hospital Kolíště, Kolíště 43, 65774 Brno Czech Republic

PLEASANTS, BEN, writer, poet, playwright, educator; b. Weehauken, N.J., Aug. 6, 1940; s. Ben and Mary Frances Pleasants; m. Pamela Walley, Dec. 23, 1961 (div. Nov. 1979); 1 child, Alexandra Pleasants Costa; m. Paula Gail Pleasants, Nov. 10, 1991. BA, Hofstra U., 1962; postgrad., UCLA, 1966. Cert. tchr., Calif. Spl. arts editor L.A. Free Press, 1975-76; arts editor L.A. Vanguard, 1976; book rev. editor Books West, L.A., 1977-78; contbg. editor L.A. Mag., 1994; book and theater reviewer L.A. Times, 1966-82; tchr. L.A. City Schs., 1968-98; asst. to story editor TV Guide, Hollywood, Calif., 1976-80; poetry editor Calif. Quar., Eagle Rock, 1976-80. Author: (poetry) 53 Stations of the Tokaido, 1972, Airmail from Oblivion, 1977; (drama) Winter in Mongolia, 1979, Hemingway/Dos Passos Wars, 1997. Recipient Best Plays of 1997 award Dramalogue, L.A. Mem. United Tchrs. L.A. (chpt. chair 1996-98), UCLA Alumni Assn., Sierra Club, Audubon Soc. Avocation: hiking in the Sierra. E-mail: bpleasants@aol.com. Home: 245 Tavistock Ave Los Angeles CA 90049-3228

PLEH, CSABA, psychologist, linguist; b. Sarisap, Hungary, Nov. 29, 1945; s. Viktor Pleh and Ilona Ökos; m. Judit Grozdits, Aug. 2, 1970 (div. Mar. 1986); 1 child, Daniel; m. Ottilia Boross, Nov. 17, 1988; 1 child, Kamilla. MA in Psychology, Eötvös U., Budapest, Hungary, 1969, PhD in Psychology, 1970, MA in Linguistics, 1973; DSc, Hungarian Acad., Budapest, 1996. From asst. to assoc. prof. Eötvös U., Budapest, 1969-98; with U. Szeged, Hungary, 1998—; vis. Hungarian chair Ind. U., Bloomington, 1991-92; fellow Ctr. for Advanced Studies, Stanford, Calif., 1996-97. Author: History of Psychology, 1992; editor: When East Meets West, 1995. Mem. Hungarian Acad. (corr.). Avocation: running. E-mail: pleh@edpsy.u-szeged.hu. Home: Zichy P U 4, 2092 Budakeszi Hungary Office: SZTE Dept Psychology, Petofi Sgt 30, 6722 Szeged Hungary

PLEKHANOV, ANTON YOURIEVIČ, biologist, researcher; b. Leningrad, USSR, June 28, 1966; s. Youri Viktorovič and Margarita Vassilievna (Parikova) P. MSc in Biology, Leningrad State U., 1988; cert. rschr., Leningrad Nuclear Phys. Inst., 1991; cert. psychologist, St. Petersburg Tech. U., 1995. Rschr. Petersburg Nuclear Physics Inst., Gatchina, Russia, 1988—. Contbr. articles to profl. jours. Lt. chief Russian Mil. Forces, 1997—. Grantee St. Petersburg Magistracy, 1997, 99, Internat.-UNESCO-Internat. Confedn. of Scientific Unions, 1999, Fedn. of European Biochem. Socs., 1999, Pres. of Russia, 1997—. Jewish. Office: Peterburgskij Inst Jadernoj, Fiziki Gatchina, 188350 Leningradskoj Oblast Russia

PLEROU, VASILIKI, physicist; b. Halkida, Greece, Aug. 4, 1969; s. Ioannis Konstantinou and Ekaterini Christou (Triantafyllou) P. BS in physics, Univ. Athens, 1994; MA in physics, Boston Univ., 1996; PhD, Boston Coll., 2000. Rsch. asst. Ctr. for European Nuclear Rsch. CERN, Geneva, 1994-95; teaching fellow Boston Univ., Boston, 1994-96; rsch. asst. Boston Coll., Chestnut Hill, Mass., 1997-99; rsch. assoc. Boston Univ., 1999—. Contbr. articles to profl. jours. Mem. Am. Physical Soc. E-mail: plerou@cgl.bu.edu. Fax: 617 975 0342.

PLESAN, AIDA, neurologist; b. Bucharest, Romania, Jan. 17, 1963; d. Aurel and Ioana (Tudor) P. MD, U. Medicine, Bucharest, 1987; postgrad., Karolinska Inst., Sweden, 1998-99. Gen. practitioner Clin. Hosp., Tg. Mures, Romania, 1987-90, resident in anesthesiology, 1991-94, sr. anesthesiologist, 1994-98; guest rschr. Swedish Inst., 1996. Contbr. articles to profl. jours. Avocations: classical music, travel. Home: Apt 153, Karusellvägen 11 5, 151 37 Sodertalje Sweden Office: Anestesiehn Sodertalje, Rosenborgsgatan 6-10, 152 86 Sodertalje Sweden

PLESCH, PETER HARIOLF, physical chemistry educator; b. Frankfurt, Fed. Republic Germany, Feb. 14, 1918; s. Janos and Melanie (Gans) P.; m. Billy Wild, 1945 (div. 1958); m. Traudi Hayek, 1963. MA, U. Cambridge, England, 1940, Sc.D., 1970; PhD, U. Manchester, England, 1946. Asst. lectr. U. Manchester, 1946-50; from lectr. to prof. personal chair physical chemistry U. Keele, Newcastle-under-lyme, England, 1951-85, prof. emeritus, 1985—. Contbr. more than 150 articles and papers to profl. jours.; editor and author of numerous books. Mem. Royal Soc. Chemistry London, Soc. Chem. Industry London (Leo Baekeland lectr. 1994), Oriental Ceramic Soc. London, Circle Glass Collectors London. Avocations: glass collecting, Chinese and Korean antiquities collecting. Home: 19 Sutherland Dr, Newcastle under Lyme ST5 3ND, England Office: U Keele Chemistry Dept, Staffordshire, Newcastle under Lyme ST5 5BG, England

PLEŠEK, JAROMÍR, chemist, educator, researcher; b. Hostašovice, Moravia, Czech Republic, Sept. 21, 1927; s. František and Aloisie (Horáková) P.; m. Alena Zobáčová, July 24, 1951; children: Marta, Jiří, Eva. MS in Engring., Inst. Chem. Tech., Prague, 1950, Dr., 1952, PhD, 1965. Asst. prof. Inst. Chem. Tech., Prague, 1950-52, assoc. prof., 1952-58; rsch. chemist DENTAL, Prague, 1959-60, Inst. Inorganic Chemistry, Řež, 1961—. Co-author: (monographs) Aldolisations and Related Reactions, 1960, Sodium Hydride and Its Uses, 1968; contbr. over 220 articles to profl. jours.; 62 patents in field. Lt. Czech Army, 1952. Recipient Votoček Gold medal Inst. Chem. Tech., 1993. Fellow Czech Learned Soc.; mem. Czech Chem. Soc., Czech Acad. Scis. (com. for sci. degrees 1990—, Heyrovsky Gold medal 1992). Roman Catholic. Avocations: general physics, astronomy, astronautics, ecology. E-mail: plesek@iic.cas.cz. Home: Patočkova 97, 16900 Praha Czech republic Office: Inst Inorganic Chem, Acad Scis of Czech Rep, 25068 Řež Czech Republic

PLESKO, IVAN, oncologist; b. Selpice, Slovakia, June 13, 1930; s. Stefan and Klementina (Cerna) P.; m. Anna Holoskova, Oct. 21, 1954; children: Denisa, Iveta. MD, Comenius U., Bratislava, Slovakia, 1955, PhD, 1964; DSc, Slovak Acad. Scis., Bratislava, 1987. Lectr., rsch. asst. med. faculty Comenius U., 1955-59, sr. rsch. asst., 1959-68, asst. prof. epidemiology, 1968-76; asst. prof. epidemiology U. Constantine, Algery, 1971-73; head dept. epidemiology Cancer Rsch. Inst., Slovak Acad. Scis., Bratislava, 1976—; head Nat. Cancer Registry, Nat. Cancer Inst., Bratislava, 1996—; cons., sr. rsch. assoc. European Inst. Oncology, Milan, Italy, 1998. Author: Atlas of Cancer Occurence in Slovakia, 1989; editor, co-author: Epidemiology of Lung Cancer, 1990; co-editor, co-author: Atlas of Cancer Mortality in Central Europe, 1996; contbr. over 100 articles to profl. jours. Gen. sec. League Against Cancer of Slovakia, 1990-95; mem. various comms. for conferring sci. degrees, 1986—. Recipient Jesenius medal for rsch. in med. scis. Slovak Acad. Scis., 1980, Golden medal for rsch. and art Slovak Acad. Scis., 1990, prize for establishment of Cancer Registry, Min. of Health, 1984, gold health promotion award, Warsaw, 1998; named Personality of Yr., Slovakia, 1995, Golden medal Slovak Med. Soc., 2000. Mem. Internat. Assn. Cancer Registries (Europe and Mid. East rep. 1988-92), Czech Nat. Registry (hon. mem. sci. coun.). Roman Catholic. Avocations: bicycling, diving, cross-country skiing. Home: Pri Suchom Mlyne 62, 81104 Bratislava Slovakia Office: Nat Cancer Registry, Klenova 1, 833 10 Bratislava Slovakia

PLESKOV, VLADIMIR MIKHAILOVITCH, biochemist, researcher; b. Usviaty, Pskovskaya, USSR, Feb. 25, 1942; s. Mikhail Alexandrovitch and Efrosinya Mikhailovna (Sapunova) P.; m. Natalya Ivanovna Lysova, Sept. 22, 1970; 1 child, Yulia Vladimirovna. MD, 1st State Med. Inst., Leningrad, Russia, 1965; PhD, Inst. Exptl. Medicine, Leningrad, Russia, 1970. Cert. biochemist. Rsch. scientist Inst. Exptl. Medicine, Med. Acad., Leningrad, 1970-76, sr. scientist, 1976-87; chief clin. lab. Marine Hosp., Health Ministry, Leningrad, 1987-89; sr. scientist Influenza Rsch. Inst., RAMS, St. Petersburg, 1989—. Co-author: Myocard's Distrofies, 1971; inventor in field; author experimentally argumented hypothesis of pathogenesis of autoimmune demielinizating diseases of nervous system, mechanism of viral persistence in cells of organism and of the data concerning the problem of tumor cells growth rate decreasing based on the restriction of transport into cells of some metabolites which take part in cell membranes formation. Mem. Nat. Geog. Soc., N.Y. Acad. Scis. Avocations: submarine sport, hunting, fishing. Home: Ispytatelei pr 11-164, 197341 St Petersburg Russia Office: Influenza Rsch Inst, Prof Popova Str 15/17, 197346 St Petersburg Russia

PLESKOV, YURI VIKTOROVICH, chemist; b. Moscow, Russia, Feb. 22, 1933; s. Viktor and Yudif (Vainshtein) P.; m. Maria Monoszon, July 5, 1957. Grad., Moscow U., 1955; PHD, Frumkin Inst. Electrochemistry, Moscow, 1960, Dsc, 1967. From jr. rschr. to prin. rschr., prof Frumkin Inst. Electrochemistry, 1950—. Author: Electrochemistry of Semiconductors, 1965, Rotating Disk Electrode, 1972, Solar Energy Conversion, 1990; co-author: Semiconductor Photoelectrochemistry, 1986. Mem. Internat. Soc. Electrochemistry.

PLESNER, PETER-ULRIK, lawyer; b. Copenhagen, July 20, 1946; s. Mogens and Birgit (Bjerregaard) P.; m. Ulla Secher (div.); m. Marianne Bentzen, Aug. 12, 1977; 1 child, Ditte Marie. Grad., Kildegaard H.S., Copenhagen, 1965. Bar: Supreme Ct. With Gorrissen Lawfirm, Copenhagen, 1971-73; ptnr. Holm-Nielsen & Plesner Lawfirm, Copenhagen, 1973-88, Plesner & Grønborg Lawfirm, Copenhagen, 1989—; bd. dirs. Hartmann Bros. A/S, Copenhagen, Hartmann Bros. Found., Copenhagen, Novartis Healthcare A/S; chmn. bd. dirs. Piet Hein A/S, Gunnar Jensens Found., Eva Denmark A/S, Johan Mangor Holding A/S, Lonborg Madsens Mindelegat, Tytte & Lillemor Faurschous Mindelegat; bd. dirs. Ciba Visions Danmark A/S, Triumph Internat., Bahlsen A/S, Ida Lofbergs Found., Novartis Danmark A/S, Ciba Specialty Chems. A/S, Danish Assn. for the Protection Indsl. Property Rights; chmn. Danish Assn. for the Prevention of Product Piracy. Mem. Assn. Internat. Protection Indsl. Property, Danish

Bar Assn., Internat. Trademark Assn. Office: Plesner & Grønborg Lawfirm, Esplanaden 34, Copenhagen K 1263, Denmark

PLESNICAR, STOJAN JOSIP, oncologist, educator, consultant; b. Gorica, Feb. 5, 1925; arrived in Slovenia, 1934; s. Josip and Luisa (Martelanc) P.; m. Ljudmila Mila Gec, July 15, 1956 (div. 1988); children: Andrew, Tadeusz. MD, U. Ljubljana, Slovenia, 1955. Intern Gen. Hosp., Koper, 1955-57; resident The Inst. Oncology, Ljubljana, Slovenia, 1958-63; asst. prof. The Faculty of Medicine, Ljubljana, Slovenia, 1964-72; rsch. fellow Karolinska Sjukhuset, Stockholm, Sweden, 1973-76; prof. oncology U. Ljubljana, Slovenia, 1976—, chmn., chair oncology, 1982, head dept. tumor biology, 1986-95; lectr. European Sch. Oncology, Milan, Italy, 1985—; vis. prof. U. Nebr. Med. Sch., Omaha, 1981, 82; dir. The Inst. of Oncology, Ljubljana, 1982-86; lectr. Sch. Environ. Scis., Nova Gorica, Slovenia, 1997—. Author: Cancer-A Preventable Disease, 1990 (honorable mention 1994); co-founder, editor-in-chief, mem. editl. bd. Radiology and Oncology, 1990 (recognition of merits Federative Cancer Soc. 1990); editor ESO Challenge newsletter; lectr. in field. Mem. The Djerba Group, 1995. Recipient Golden medal Slovenian Cancer Soc., 1992. Mem. Am. Assn. for Cancer Rsch., N.Y. Acad. Scis., Cancer Rsch. Found. (founder 1993), Acad. Assn. for Third U. in Slovenia (pres.), Lion's Club Ljubljana (gov. 1998-99). Avocations: history of medicine, Templars. Home: Tesarska St No 6, 1000 Ljubljana Slovenia

PLESS, JORGEN EMIL, plastic surgery consultant; b. Apr. 13, 1934; s. Villy Emanuel and Gerda Frederikke (Bork) P.; m. Eva Festersen, May 21, 1961; children: Thomas, Torsten. MD, Copenhagen U., 1960; DDS, Copenhagen Dental Sch., 1969. Intern Sundby Hosp., 1960-61, Odense U. Hosp., Denmark, 1961; intern Svendborg Hosp., 1961-62, resident, 1963, asst. registrar surg. dept., 1962-65; registrar Rigshospitalet Copenhagen, 1965-67; sr. registrar Odense U. Hosp., 1973-76, cons. plastic surgery dept., 1976-98, vice-chmn. med. com., 1982-85, chmn. med. com., 1985-89; com. mem. Inst. Exptl. Surgery, Copenhagen, 1970-73; chmn. med. adv. and ethics com. The Mermaid Clinic Ebeltoft, 1989-95; ednl. inspector Danish Nat. Bd. Health, 1996-2000. Contbr. articles to profl. jours. Founder, vice-chmn. polit. party Fyns Amts Borgerliste, 1999—. Mem. Danish Soc. Plastic and Reconstructive Surgery (pres. 1986-89), Danish Orgn. Plastic Surgery (chmn. 1994-98), Danish Soc. Head and Neck Oncology (sec. 1974-85), Danish Soc. Microsurgery (pres. 1974-78), Scandinavian Assn. Plastic Surgeons (pres. 1986-88), Rotary (Paul Harris fellow 1988). E-mail: jpless@dadlnet.dk. Home: Liljevej 4, DK5700 Svendborg Denmark Office: Odense U Hosp, Sdr Blvd, 5000 Odense Denmark

PLESSKY, VICTOR PETROVICH, physicist, educator; b. Gomel, Belarus, July 2, 1952; arrived in Switzerland, 1991; s. Peter I. and Pauline M. (Goncharova) P.; m. Irina V. Belova, Apr. 7, 1977; children: Vasilii, Olessia. PhD, Moscow Phys. Tech. Inst., 1978; DSc, IRE Acad. Sci., Moscow, 1987; cert. prof., Govt. of Russia, 1995. Jr. scientist Inst. Radio Engring. and Electronics Acad. Sci., Moscow, 1978-82, sr. scientist, 1982-87, head lab., 1987-91; vis. scientist Fed. Inst. Tech., Zürich, Switzerland, 1992; prin. rsch. asst. Advanced Saw Products, Bevaix, Switzerland, 1993-96; projects mgr. Micronas, Bevaix, 1996-97; mgr. surface acoustic waves design bur. Thomson Microsonics, Neuchâtel, Switzerland, 1998—; vis. prof. Helsinki (Finland) U. Tech., 1997. Author: Surface Acoustic Waves in Inhomogeneous Media, Springer, 1995; contbr. articles to profl. jours.; patentee in field. Recipient Young Scientists award Komsomol, 1984. Mem. IEEE. Avocation: gardening. Fax: 41 32 725 2057. E-mail: vplessky@VTX.CH.

PLETCHER, JOHN SHELBY, former insurance company executive, educator; b. Lima, Ohio, Apr. 21, 1925; s. John Fredrick and Harriet Iloe Pletcher; m. Marilyn Lee Pletcher, June 16, 1946; children: John Jeffrey, Robert Craig, Gregory Alan. BSc, Ohio U., 1949; BA, Syracuse U., 1952; MBA, Mich. State U., 1963. Chartered life underwriter Am. Coll., Pa.; lic. series 7 Nat. Assn. Securities Dealers, Md.; cert. tchr. English as 2d lang., Wash. Dir. sys. and programming Marine Bank & Trust, Tampa, Fla., 1970; v.p., data processing mgr. Citrus and Chem. Bank, Bartow, Fla., 1971-76; mgr. strategic planning Martin Marietta Data Sys., Orlando, Fla., 1977-85; pres. Pletcher Fin. Svc., LLC, Bradenton, Fla., 1986-98; tchr. English as Secondary Lang. Bangkok, 2000—. Lt. col. USAF, 1951-70. Mem. Assn. Former Intelligence Officers (charter mem.), Ret. Officers Assn., Sarasota CLU/ChFC Chpt., Bartow Rotary Club (pres. 1975-76), Dr. Phillips Rotary Club (pres. 1982-83, Paul Harris award 1983), Sarasota Shrine Club. Republican. Methodist. Avocations: flying, tennis, traveling, reading. Home: 787 Jacaranda Dr Anna Maria FL 34216

PLETTNER, JEAN-LOUIS GEORGES, angiologist; b. Montelimar, France, May 26, 1939; s. Jules and Simone (Borde) P.; m. Daniele Camille Lalanne, Dec. 11, 1997 (dec.); children: Anne-Laure, Aude. MD, Med. U. Paris, 1970. Pvt. practice angiology Orleans, France, 1971—; cons. Tempo Med., Paris, 1975-84; chmn. Sixth Nat. AFFCA Congress, Angiology and Labour Medicine Meeting, 1999. Mem. Assn. Continuous Formation in Angiology (pres. 1982—), Nat. Syndicate of French Angiologists, Fedn. French Doctors, French Coll. Vasc. Diseases, French Soc. Phlebology, N.Y. Acad. Scis. Phone: 0238542987. Office: 16 rue Pierre 1 de Serbie, 45000 Orleans France

PLEVNIK, DANKO, journalist, columnist; b. Karlovac, Croatia, Mar. 12, 1951; s. Zvonimir and Ana (Hibler) P.; m. Jasna; 1 child, Natko. BA, U. Zagreb, Croatia, 1976, MA, 1979, PhD, 1986; D Info. Scis. Libr. sci. dept. Karlovac City Libr., 1976-84; editor Komunist, Zagreb, 1984-90; columnist Novi List, Rijeka, Croatia, 1990-91, Slobodna Dalmacija, Split, Croatia, 1991—; mem. internat. visitor program USIA, 1992; fellow Salzburg Seminar, Harvard U., Austria, 1996. Author: Information is Communication, 1986, Toward Civilization of Mobile Text, 1988, The Croatian Upheaval, 1993, The Sense of Bosnia, 1997, Slovenes in Croatia, 1998, New NATO or Old Geopolitics, 1999, Europe Viewed From the Balkans, 2000, Their Reckoning with Me, 2000. Named Journalist of Yr. in Croatia Slobodna Dalmacija, Split, 1991. Mem. Internat. Reading Assn., Internat. Fedn. Journalists, Croatian Journalists Assn. (Journalist of Yr. in Croatia 1991, 92), Assn. European Journalists. Avocations: reading, walking, basketball, golf. Home: Kukuljevićeva 9, 47000 Karlovac Croatia Office: Slobodna Dalmacija, Hrvatske mornarice 4, 21000 Split Croatia

PLEVY, ARTHUR L., lawyer; b. N.Y.C., May 26, 1936; s. Louis and Sarah Plevy; children: Scott Eric, Robert Todd. Student, Bklyn. Coll., 1953-57; BEE, CCNY, 1959; LLB, JD, Bklyn. Law Sch., 1967. Bar: N.Y. 1965, N.J. 1970, Ct. Customs and Patent Appeals 1970, U.S. Supreme Ct. 1970. Design engr. IT&T Labs., Nutley, N.J., 1959-60; project engr. Westrex, N.Y.C., 1960-62; sr. mem. tech. staff RCA, N.Y.C., 1962-65; patent counsel RCA Rsch. Ctr., Princeton, N.J., 1965-70; pvt. practice patent law Edison, N.J., 1970-98; sr. ptnr. Plevy & Assocs., Edison, N.J., 1991—; cons. electronic firms; pres. New Ventures, Edison, N.J., 1970—; arbitrator Am. Arbitration Assn. Contbr. numerous articles on electronics, patent and trademark law to profl. jours.; patentee in field of electronics. Mem. ABA, IEEE, CCPA, N.J. Patent Law Scch., Fed. Bar Assn., N.Y. Bar Assn., N.J. Bar Assn., Masons. E-mail: plevyal@bipc.com. Home: 77 Colfax Rd Skillman NJ 08558-2310 Office: Buchanan Ingersoll 650 College Rd E Princeton NJ 08540-6603

PLEVYAK, THOMAS JOSEPH, communications executive; b. Simpson, Pa., Feb. 11, 1938; s. Joseph Bernard and Anna Stasia (Klemak) P.; m. Maureen Naomi Hogan, June 25, 1960; children: Stephen, Laura, Sharon. BS in Nuclear Engring., U. Notre Dame, 1960; MS in Nuclear Engring., U. Conn., 1962; grad. Comm. Devel. Tng. Program, Bell Labs., 1964; MS in Advanced Mgmt., Pace U., 1978. MTS Bell Labs, 1962-70; mgr. gen. depts. AT&T, Holmdel, N.J., 1970-80; mgr. AT&T Network Sys., Holmdel, N.J., 1980-90; dir. internat. standards Bell Atlantic, Arlington, Va., 1990—; vice chair Inter-Am. Telecomms. Commn., Washington, 1994-98. Co-author, co-editor: Telecommunications Network Management into the 21st Century, 1994, Telecommunications Network Management: Technologies and Implementations, 1997; contbr. articles to profl. jours.; holder patents in field. Fellow IEEE Comms. Soc. (bd. govs. 1995-97, pres. 1998-99, past pres. 2000—, Donald W. McLellan award 1995, 3d Millennium medal for outstanding achievements and contbns. 2000). Avocations: travel, reading. Office: Bell Atlantic 1310 N Court House Rd Ste 1 Arlington VA 22201-2586

PLIETH, WALDFRIED JOHANNES LUDWIG, chemistry educator, researcher in electrochemistry; b. Cottbus, Germany, Nov. 7, 1937; s. Erich and Elsa (Heise) P.; m. Hildburg Lassbiegler, 1963; 3 children. PhD, Free U. Berlin, 1963, PhD-Habil., 1970. Prof. Free U. Berlin, 1971-92; prof. Tech. U., Dresden, Germany, 1992—, dir., 1994—. Author more than 250 publs. in chem. journals. Home: Zschonerblick 20, 01462 Ockerwitz, Saxonia Germany Office: Tech U Dresden, 01062 Dresden Germany

PLIEV, TIMUR NIKOLAEVICH, chemistry educator, researcher; b. Vladikavkaz, USSR, Aug. 5, 1930; s. Nicolai Georgievich and Sachti Davidovna (Gikaeva) P.; m. Inessa Pavlovna Shadrina, July 10, 1954; children: Vladimir, Zalina. BS, Mining Inst., Vladikavkaz, USSR, 1950; MS, Mining Inst., Leningrad, USSR, 1951; PhD, Lomonosov State U., Moscow, 1956. Jr. researcher State Aluminum-Magnium Rsch. Inst., Leningrad, USSR, 1951-53; head dept. State U., Jakutsk, USSR, 1956-59; assoc. prof. State U., Jakutsk, 1958; head dept. Rsch. Inst. Chem. Reagents, Donetsk, USSR, 1959-60; sr. researcher Inst. Oil Chemistry, Kiev, USSR, 1960-70; head dept. Med. Acad., Vladikavkaz, Russia, 1970—; prof. chemistry Med. Acad., Vladikavkaz, 1995. Contbr. numerous articles to profl. jours. Mem. N.Y. Acad. Scis. Avocations: literature, art. Home: Butyrina 8/138, 362040 Vladikavkaz Russia Office: Med Acad, Pushkinskaya 40, 362025 Vladikavkaz Russia

PLIMPTON, PEGGY LUCAS, trustee; b. Nov. 3, 1931; d. David Nicholson and Margaret (MacMillan) Lucas; m. Hollis Winslow Plimpton, June 11, 1955; children: Victoria P. Babcock, Priscilla P. Morphy, Hollis Winslow Plimpton III. AB, Duke U., 1954. Trustee Cape Cod Conservatory of Music, 1989—. Bd. trustees Carleton Williard Retirement Home, Bedford, Mass., 1968—, Cape Cod Conservatory Music, 1990—; bd. dirs. Episcopal Ch. Women, 1968-78, Brigham & Women's Hosp., Boston, 1975—; pres. Boston Lying-In Hosp., 1970-72; chmn. Mass. Nat. Cathedral Assn., Boston, 1978-80, 1985-88; pres. bd. trustees Women's Ednl. and Indsl., Boston, 1980-83. mem. New Eng. Farm and Garden Club (bd. dirs. 1965—, pres. 1995—), Chestnut Hill Garden Club (bd. dirs. 1970-74), Jr. League Garden Club (pres. 1981-83), Colonial Dames (bd. mgrs. 1983-89, v.p. 1993-98, pres. 1998—), Vincent Club, Chilton Club. Republican. Episcopalian. Avocations: gardening, golf, bridge, grandchildren.

PLISKA, EDWARD WILLIAM, lawyer, retired judge; b. Rockville, Conn., Apr. 13, 1935; s. Louis Boleslaw and Constance (Dombrowski) P.; m. Luisa Anne Crotti, Nov. 29, 1958; children: Gregory, John, Thomas, Laura. AB, Princeton (N.J.) U., 1956; LLB, U. Conn., 1964; LLD (hon.), San Mateo (Calif.) U., 1975. Bar: Calif. 1965. Dep. dist. atty. Santa Barbara (Calif.) County, 1965; dep. dist. atty. San Mateo County Dist. Atty., Redwood City, Calif., 1965-71, chief trial dep., 1970-71; pvt. practice San Mateo, 1971-72; judge San Mateo County Mcpl. Ct., 1973-86; ptnr. Corey, Luzaich, Manos & Pliska, Millbrae, Calif., 1986—; officer Am. Judges Assn., 1983-86; prodr. and host (TV and Radio show) Justice Forum, 1973-78; prof. criminal and constitutional law San Mateo Law Sch., 1971-76; leader People to People legal delegations to Europe, India, Nepal, 1985, 87, 91. Editor Ct. Rev., 1981-88. Leader People to People Legal Delegations, Europe, India, Nepal, 1985, 87, 91; trustee Belmont (Calif.) Sch. Dist., 1987-91, pres., 1990; chmn. San Mateo County Cultural Arts Commn., 1987-90; mem. Peninsula Comty. Found. Arts Fund, 1988-99; officer Hillbarn Theatre, 1989-99. With U.S. Army, 1957. NEH grantee, 1975, 80. Mem. Calif. Judges Assn., Calif. State Bar Assn., Nat. Assn. Criminal Def. Lawyers, Calif. Attys. for Criminal Justice, San Mateo County Bar Assn., Calif. Pub. Defenders Assn., Bohemian Club. Democrat. Roman Catholic. Avocations: acting and directing plays, reading, sports spectator. Home: 1567 Escondido Way Belmont CA 94002-3634 Office: Corey Luzaich Manos Pliska PO Box 669 700 El Camino Real Millbrae CA 94030-2009

PLITT, ENRIQUE JAVIER, electronic engineer, military officer; b. Buenos Aires, Argentina, Dec. 23, 1971; s. Rodolfo Plitt and Luisa Esther Stevens. Grad., Argengine Air Force Acad., Cordoba, 1994; degree in elec. engring., Air Force U., Cordoba, 1998. Tech. drawer Philips Argentina S.A., Buenos Aires, 1990; commd. lt. Argentine Air Force, Cordoba, 1991, advanced through grades to quality control chief, 1999—; project mgr. Interface Argentina, Cordoba, 1999—; project dir. Flight Control, Buenos Aires, 1999—. Roman Catholic. Avocations: soccer, tennis. Home: Av Cabildo 2134 4 A, 1428 Buenos Aires Argentina

PLOCKINGER, URSULA, endocrinologist, researcher; b. Trostberg, Germany, Aug. 1, 1952; d. Edbert and Edith (Altrichter) P.; m. Hans Jurgen Guabbe. Degree in Pharmacy, Free U. Sch. Pharmacy, Berlin, Germany, 1975; degree in Medicine, Free U. Sch. Medicine, Berlin, Germany, 1982. Cert. internist 1990, endocrinologist 1994, diabetologist 1997. Pharmacist Pub. Pharmacy, Berlin, Germany, 1975-82; internship, residency Univ. Hosp. Benjamin Franklin, Berlin, Germany, 1983-90, sr. resident, 1990-98; with Univ. Hosp. Charité Campus Virclow-Kunikum, 1999—. Mem. Am. Diabetes Assn., Endocrine Soc., Deutsche Gesellschaft für Endokrinologie, Internat. Pituitary Soc., Internat. Growth Hormone Rsch. Soc., Deutsche Diabetes Gesellschaft. Avocations: cycling, opera, gardening, reading, theater. Office: Charite CVK Humbold Univ, Intern Med Hepatol Gastroenterol, 13353 Berlin Germany

PLOGHAUS, ALEXANDER, research scientist; b. Bonn, Germany, June 3, 1969; s. Karl Guenter and Kerstin Elisabeth (Niemoeller) P. BA, Bonn U., 1993, MA, 1996; MSc, Oxford (Eng.) U., 1997. Scholar German Nat. Scholarship Orgn., Bonn, 1990-95, German Acad. Exch. Svc., Oxford, 1992-93; Rhodes scholar Rhodes Trust, Oxford, 1996-99; fellow Merton Coll., Oxford U., 1999—; neuropsychology trainer Neurorehab. Hosp., Bonn, 1989-95. Author: Classical Conditioning and Schizophrenia, 1997; contbr. articles to profl. jours. Staff mem. press office Social Dem. Party, Bonn, 1994-96. Grantee Rhodes Trust, 1998, McDonnell-Pew Found., 1998, Merton Coll., 1999. Mem. MRC Ctr. for Cognitive Neurosci., German Neuropsychology Soc., McDonnell-Pew Found. Avocations: cooking, running, carnivorous plants. Home: Merton St-Merton Coll, Oxford OX1 4JD, England Office: John Radcliffe Hosp, Ctr Functional MRI of Brain, Oxford OX3 9DU, England

PLOKHOI, VLADIMIR VALENTINOVICH, physicist; b. Skomorokhi, Ukraine, Mar. 17, 1939; s. Valentin Vasilyevich and Anfusa Vasilyevna (Mosina) P.; m. Galina Nikolayevna Bychkova, Jan. 29, 1961; children: Elena, Sergey. MS, Kharkov U., Kharkov, Ukraine, 1961; PhD, RFNC-All Rus. Rsch. ITP, Snezhinsk, Russia, 1974. Engr. RFNC-All Russian Rsch. ITP, Snezhinsk, 1961-69, jr. scientist, 1970-73, sr. scientist, 1974-88, leading scientist, 1989—; subproject mgr. Internat. Sci. Tech. Ctr., Moscow, 1997—. Contbr. articles to profl. jours. Office: Russian Fed Nuc Ctr-All, Russian Rsch ITP Vasilyeva St 13, 456770 Snezhinsk Russia

PLONTKE, RAINER KLAUS, physicist; b. Zittau, Saxony, Germany, May 13, 1943; s. Kurt Julius and Anneliese Johanna (Elsner) P.; m. Barbara Margarete Mlynski Ziegenbein, July 5, 1968 (div. 1984); children: Stefan Klaus-Rainer, Robert Arndt Mlynski; m. Annegret Christiane Lüning, May 12, 1989. M in Physics, Tech. U. Dresden (Germany), 1966, Dr. rer. nat., 1974. Scientific fellow Tech. U. Dresden (Germany), 1966-73; scientific fellow Carl Zeiss JENA (Germany), 1973-78, head metrology group e-beam lithography, 1978-84, group mgr., 1984-91; sr. engring. mgr. e-beam lithography Jenoptik GmbH, Jena, 1991-96; project mgr. nano-lithography Leica Lithographie Sys. Jena GmbH, 1996-98, Leica Microsystems Lithography GmbH, 1998—. Contbr. articles to profl. jours.; patentee in field. rep. labor union Carl Zeiss JENA (Germany), 1974-78; mem. Thüringer Entomologenverband e. V. (and precursors), 1958—, Naturschutzbund Deutschlands e.V., 1990—. Recipient Banner der Arbeit German Dem. Republic coun. of state, 1985. Mem. Deutsche Gesellschaft Elektronenmikroskopie, Phantoms Network (assoc.), European Optical Soc. Avocations: entomology, photography, chess. Home: Am Schwemmtümpfel 15, D-99441 Gottern Stadt Magdala Germany Office: Leica Microsystems Litho GmbH, Göschwitzer Str 25, D-07745 Jena Germany

PLORDE, JAMES JOSEPH, physician, educator; b. Brewster, Minn., Feb. 16, 1934; s. James Arthur and Mary Jeanette (Lutz) P.; m. Diane Sylvia Koenigs, Aug. 28, 1964 (div. July 1974); children: Lisa Marie, Michele Louise, James Joshua; m. Jo Ann Gates, Dec. 22, 1986. BA, U. Minn., 1956, BS, 1957, MD, 1959. Diplomate Am. Bd. Internal Medicine, Am. Bd. Pathology. Vol. leader Peace Corps, Gondar, Ethiopia, 1964-66; intern King County Hosp., Seattle, 1959-60; resident U. Wash., Seattle, 1960-62, fellow infectious diseases, 1962-64; chief med. resident King County Hosp., Seattle, 1966-67; asst. prof. medicine U. Wash., Seattle, 1967-71, assoc. prof., 1971-78; fellow clin. microbiology, 1972-73; prof. medicine, lab. medicine U. Wash. Sch. Medicine, Seattle, 1978-98 (ret.), prof. emeritus medicine, lab. medicine, 1998—; head clin. investigation U.S. Naval Med. Research, Addis Ababa, Ethiopia, 1968-71; chief infectious diseases VA Hosp., Seattle, 1973-89, chief clin. microbiology, 1973-98; ret., 1998; instr. U. Wash., 1966-67; cons. WHO, 1975, Suez Canal U. Faculty of Medicine, Ismailia, Arab Republic of Egypt, 1981-85. Contbr. numerous articles to profl. jours., chpts. to books. Fellow Infectious Disease Soc., ACP; mem. AAAS, Am. Soc. Microbiology, Acad. Clin. Lab. Physicians and Scientists. Fax: 206-523-3541. E-mail: jjplorde@u.washington.edu. Home: 3164 W Laurelhurst Dr NE Seattle WA 98105-5346

PLOTCH, WALTER, management consultant, fund raising counselor; b. N.Y.C., July 19, 1932; s. Harry and Belle (Lebowsky) P.; m. Yvette Gabrielle Lambert, Mar. 20, 1957; children: Allison, Jennifer, Adrienne. AB, Queens Coll., 1957; MA, Harvard U., 1959; postgrad., 1959-62. Analyst L.F. Rothschild & Co., N.Y.C. and Boston, 1962-64; cmty. cons., 1964-65; edn. dir. New Eng. Anti-Defamation League B'nai B'rith, 1965-68; nat. edn. dir., 1968-76; v.p. Brakeley, John Price Jones Inc., N.Y.C., 1976-79; sr. v.p., dir., 1979-89; sr. v.p. The Oram Group Inc., N.Y.C., 1989-92; exec. v.p.; pres., CEO Walter Plotch Assocs., Inc., Croton-On-Hudson, N.Y., 1992—; mem. faculty Grad. Sch. Mgmt. and Urban Affairs, New Sch. U.; lectr. Harvard U. Grad. Sch. Edn.; cons. Harcourt, Brace, Plenum Pubs. Co-editor: Pluralism in a Democratic Society, 1977; gen. editor: The Job Corps Intergroup RElations Series, 1974; contbr. articles to profl. jours.; contbg. editor mag., Jour. Sponsored Rsch. Bd. dirs. Schizophrenia Found., 1975-90; nat. bd. dirs. NCCJ, 1980-84, Nat. Charitable Info Bur.,mem. exec. com. 1986-94. Served with USCGR, 1953-55, Korea. Grantee U.S. Office Edn., Dept. Labor, N.Y. Coun. Humanities; tchg. fellow Harvard U., 1959-61. Mem. Princeton Club, Univ. Club, Washington, Phi Alpha Theta. Democrat. Jewish. Office: 39 Furnace Dock Rd Croton On Hudson NY 10520-1406

PLOTKIN, HENRY CHARLES, psychologist, researcher; b. Johannesburg, South Africa, Dec. 11, 1940; s. Bernard Solomon and Edythe (Poplak) P.; m. Victoria Mary Welch Plotkin, July 10, 1975; children: Jessica, Jocelin. BS (hon.), Witwatersrand U., Johannesburg, South Africa, 1963; PhD, London U., 1968. Rsch. scientist Med. Rsch. Coun., London, 1965-72; lectr. U. Coll. London, 1972-88; reader, 1988-93, prof., 1993—, head dept. psychology, 1993-98; sci. dir. ESRC Econ. Learning Social Evolution Rsch. Ctr., 1998—; postdoctoral fellow Stanford U., Palo Alto, Calif., 1971-72. Co-editor: Brain, Behavior and Evolution, 1979; editor: Essays in Evolutionary Epistemology, 1982, The Role of Behavior in Evolution, 1988; author: Darwin Machines and the Nature of Knowledge, 1995, Evolution in Mind, 1997. Grantee Sci. Eng. Rsch. Coun, Med. Rsch. Coun., Eng., Econ. and Social Rsch. Coun., Eng., Ministry for Def., Eng., 1978—. Mem. Experimental Psychology Soc., Assn. for Study of Animal Behaviors. Office: University College London, Gower St, London WCIE 6BT, England

PLOTKIN, STANLEY ALAN, medical virologist; b. N.Y.C., May 12, 1932; s. Joseph and Lee (Fishbein) P.; m. Susan Lannon, Nov. 24, 1979; children: Michael, Alec. BA, NYU, 1952; MD, SUNY, N.Y.C., 1956; MA (hon.), U. Pa., 1974. Diplomate Am. Bd. Pediatrics, Am. Acad. Pediatrics. Intern Cleve. Met. Gen. Hosp., 1956-57; resident pediatrics Phila. Children's Hosp., 1961-62, dir. div. infectious diseases, sr. physician, 1969-90; registrar Hosp. for Sick Children, London, 1962-63; assoc. mem. Wistar Inst., Phila., 1963-74, prof. virology, 1974—; asst. prof. pediatrics U. Pa., Phila., 1966-71, assoc. prof., 1971-74, prof., 1974-91; prof. emeritus, 1991—; assoc. chmn. dept. pediatrics U. Pa., Phila., 1986-88; med. and sci. dir. Pasteur-Mérieux-Connaught Labs. (now Aventis-Pasteur), Marnes-la-Coquette, France, 1991-97; advisor to pres. Aventis Pasteur, Marnes-la-Coquette, France, 19[illegible] Assoc. editor: Am. Jour. Epidemiology, 1967-87, Proc. Soc. Exptl. Biology and Medicine, 1986-85, Pediatric Infectious Disease jour., 1982-87, Vaccine jour., 1983—, Molecular and Cellular Probes jour., 1987—, Clin. Diagnostic Lab. Immunology, 1996—. Served as med. officer USPHS, 1957-60. Joseph P. Kennedy Found. grantee, 1964-66, Hartford Found. grantee, 1971-73, NIH grantee, 1973—; recipient Bruce medal ACP, 1987, Clin. Virology award Pan Am. Group Rapid Viral Diagnosis, 1995; named Disting. Physician Pediatric Infectious Diseases Soc., 1993, Legion of Honor, France, 1998. Mem. Soc. Pediatric Rsch., Am. Pediatric Soc., Infectious Diseases Soc. Am.,Am. Epidemiology Soc., Am. Soc. Microbiology, Am. Acad. Pediatrics (chmn. infectious diseases com. 1987-90). Achievements include pioneering work on vaccine strains for protection against polio, rubella and cytomegalovirus.

PLOTKOWIAK, ZYTA MARIA, pharmacist; b. Poznan, Poland, Aug. 14, 1932; d. Bogdan and Elzbieta (Jeske) Bederski; m. Jan Jerzy Plotkowiak, June 29, 1957; two children. M in Pharm. sci., U. Med. Sci. Poznan, 1955, PhD, 1961. From jr. asst. to prof. pharm. chemistry U. Med. Sci., Poznan, 1954—. Author: Qualitative Chemical Analysis of Drugs, 1971, Quantitative Chemical Analysis of Drugs, 1972, Chemical Analysis of Drugs, 1981; contbr. articles to profl. jours., patentee in field. Mem. Polish Pharm. Soc., Polish Acad. Scis. Home: Przybyszewski Str #45/4, 60-356 Poznan Poland

PLOTNICK, HARVEY BARRY, publishing executive; b. Detroit, Aug. 5, 1941; s. Isadore and Esther (Sher) P.; m. Susan Regnery, Aug. 16, 1964 (div. Apr. 1977); children: Andrew, Alice; m. Elizabeth Allen, May 2, 1982; children: Teresa, Samuel. B.A., U. Chgo., 1963. Editor Contemporary Books, Inc., Chgo., 1964-66; pres. Contemporary Books, Inc., 1966-94; with Paradigm Holdings, Inc., Chgo., 1994—; CEO Molecular Electronics Corp., 2000—. Trustee U. Chgo., 1994—. Office: Molecular Electronics Corp 2 Prudential Plz Ste 3020 Chicago IL 60601-6790

PLOTNIKOV, ALEXEY VITALIEVICH, economist; b. Zaporozhie, Ukraine, June 10, 1965; s. Vitaly and Raisa (Schevchenko) P. BSc, Kiev Econ. U., 1986, PhD, 1991, DSc, 1994, Prof., 1998. Sr. auditor Fin. Bd. City Adminstrn., Kiev, Ukraine, 1986-88; sr. lectr. Kiev Econ. U., 1991-92; from sr. rschr. to head dept. internat. fin. rels. Inst. World Economy & Internat. Rels., Kiev, 1992—. Author: Financial Relations in Market Economy, 1992, Financial Management, 1994, The Problems of Development of Postsocialist Countries, 1995; co-author: Economic Security of Ukraine, 1997, Financial Market in Ukraine, 1998, Dynamics of Foreign Debt of Ukraine, 2000. Avocations: jogging, traveling. Home: 38-109 Predslavinskaja St, 03150 Kiev Ukraine

PLOUGH, CHARLES TOBIAS, JR., retired electronics engineering executive; b. Oakland, Calif., Sept. 7, 1926; s. Charles Tobias Sr. and Miriam Lucille (Miller) P.; m. Jean Elizabeth Rose, June 13, 1950 (div. May 1969); children: Charles III, Cathleen, Mark, Barbara; m. Janet Mary Ansell Lumley, July 5, 1969; children: Mark Ansell Lumley, Simon John Lumley. AB with honors, Amherst Coll., 1950; BSEE with honors, U. Calif., Berkeley, 1953. Mgr. tech. devel. Fairchild Semiconductor, Palo Alto, Calif., 1958-71; v.p. Multi-State Devices, Montreal, Can., 1971-78; mgr. research and devel. Dale Electronics, Norfolk, Nebr., 1978-89, ret., 1989. Patentee in field. Treas. First Unitarian Ch., 1996-99. Mem. Lions (sec. Norfolk 1982-86; pres. Albuquerque chpt. 1999-2000); Leader Albuquerque Interfaith 1993—. Avocation: golf. Home: 2030 Quail Run Dr NE Albuquerque NM 87122-1100

PLOUGONVEN, CHRISTIAN HERVE, semiconductor physics engineer; b. Maray, France, Oct. 6, 1946; s. Francois and Helene (Flohic) P.; m. Claudine D. Frigout, June 27, 1970; children: Brendan, Riwal, Erwan. Physics Engr., Nat. Inst. Applied Scis., Lyon, France, 1968; PhD, Northwestern U., 1972. Staff engr. IBM France, Essonnes, 1976-81, adv. engr., 1981-87, sr. engr., 1987-90, sr. tech. staff, 1990, quality mgr., 1990—; mgr. mfg. engring. dept. IBM, Fishkill, N.Y., 1985-87, Failure Analysis Dept., Essonnes, 1987-90; active IBM Acad. Tech., 1991, Tech. Coun., 1993; v.p. IBM Acad. Tech., 1996-98. Contbr. articles to profl. jours. Mem. IBM Acad. Tech. (council 1993), Sigma Xi. Avocations: tennis, jogging, skiing. Home: 14 Rue De La Brunette, Samois Sur Seine France 77920

PLOUVIER, PHILIPPE ANTOINE, retired management consultant; b. Henin-Beaumont, France, Nov. 25, 1929; s. Daniel Victor and Paulette (Ge-

orges) P.; m. Michele Alfa Bassignot (dec. Aug. 1987); 1 child, Suzanne. BA, Kenyon Coll., 1950; diploma, Inst. d'Études Politiques, Paris, 1952; postgrad., Ecole de Tissage, 1953. Gen. mgr. Tissage Co., 1953-63; fin. mgr. Paulstra, Paris, 1963-70; mng. dir. Pradoval, Sierra Nevada, Spain, 1970-72; cons. Analyses & Liaisons Financières & Adminstrvs., Paris, 1974-98; ret., 1998. City counsellor Mayorship, Conflans sur Lanterne, 1958-63. Mem. Automobile Club de France, Sigma Pi. Fax: 33(0)3 86359298. E-mail: jb.pap.mousseline@wanadoofr. Home: La Mousseline, F-89600 Germigny France

PLOWRIGHT, JOAN ANNE, actress; b. Brigg, Lincolnshire, Eng., Oct. 28, 1929; d. William and Daisy (Burton) P.; m. Roger Gage, 1953 (div.); m. Sir Laurence Olivier, 1961 (dec.); 3 children. Student, Old Vic Theatre Sch. Mem. Old Vic Co., toured S. Africa, 1952-53; 1st leading role in the Country Wife London, 1956; mem. English Stage Co., 1956, Nat. Theatre, 1963-74. Appearances include (plays) The Chairs, 1957, The Entertainer, 1958, Major Barbara and Roots, 1959, A Taste of Honey, 1960 (Tony Best Actress award 1960), Uncle Vanya, 1962-64, St. Joan, 1963 (London Evening Standard Best Actress award 1964), Hobson's Choice, 1964, The Master Builder, 1965, Much Ado About Nothing, 1967, Tartuffe, 1967, Three Sisters, 1967, 68, 69, The Advertisement, 1968, 69, Love's Labour's Lost, 1968, 69, The Merchant of Venice, 1970, 71-72, Rules of the Game, 1971-72, Woman Killed with Kindness, 1971-72, Taming of the Shrew, 1972, Doctor's Dilemma, 1972, Rosmersholm, 1973, Saturday Sunday Monday, 1973, Eden's End, 1974, The Sea Gull, 1975, The Bed Before Yesterday, 1975 (Variety award 1976), Filumena, 1977 (Soc. West End Theatres Best Actress award 1978), Enjoy, 1980, Who's Afraid of Virginia Woolf?, 1981, Cavell, 1982, The Cherry Orchard, 1983, The Way of the World, 1985, The House of Bernada Alba, 1986-87, Uncle Vanya, 1988, Time and The Conways, 1991, If We Are Women, 1995, (films) Much Ado About Nothing, 1969, Equus, 1976, Richard Wagner, 1982, Brimstone and Treacle, 1982, Brittania Hosp., 1983, Revolution, 1985, The Dressmaker, 1987, Drowning By Numbers, 1987, I Love You To Death, 1990, Avalon, 1990, Enchanted April, 1992 (Acad. award nominee Best Supporting Actress, Golden Globe award 1992), Dennis the Menace, 1993, A Pin for the Butterfly, 1993, Last Action Hero, 1993, The Summer House, 1993, Widows' Peak, 1994, Pyromaniacs: A Love Story, 1995, The Grass Harp, 1995, Hotel Sorrento, 1995, Surviving Picasso, 1996, 101 Dalmations, 1996, Mr. Wrong, 1996, The Assistant, 1997, Tea with Mussolini, 1998; (tv films) Merchant of Venice, 1973, Daphne, Laureola, 1977, Saturday Sunday Monday, 1977, The Importance of Being Earnest, 1988, The Birthday Party, 1987, House of Bernarda Alba, A Nightingale Sang, 1989, Stalin, 1992 (Golden Globe Awd. 1992, Emmy nomination, supporting actress - miniseries, 1993), A Place for Annie, 1994, On Promised Land, 1994, Return of the Natives, It Could be the Last Time, 1998, Encore, Encore, 1998, Back to the Secret Garden, 1999, Frankie and Hazel, 1999. Office: ICM care Harriet Robinson, 76 Oxford St, London WIN 0AX, England

PLUCIENNIK, THOMAS CASIMIR, lawyer, former assistant county prosecutor; b. Irvington, N.J., Apr. 8, 1947; s. Casimir Stanley and Helen Victoria (Sienicki) P.; m. Maria Anne Soriano, June 16, 1974. BS in Acctg., Seton Hall U., 1969, JD, 1983; MA in Criminal Justice, CUNY, 1976. Bar: N.J. 1983, U.S. Ct. Mil. Appeals 1986, U.S. Dist. Ct. N.J. 1983, D.C. 1994, U.S. Supreme Ct. 1995, N.Y. 1996, U.S. Ct. Appeals (3rd cir.), U.S. Dist. Ct. (so., ea., fed. dists.) N.Y. 1998; cert. criminal trial atty., mil. trial atty.; lic. pvt. investigator. Mng. ptnr. Joe Bell's Tavern & Restaurant, Newark, 1979; police officer City of Newark, 1972-79; criminal investigator Essex County Prosecutor, Newark, 1980-84, asst. prosecutor, 1984-88; sr. asst. prosecutor Warren County, N.J., 1988-89; atty. Voorhees & Acciavatti Esq., Morristown, N.J., 1989-94; defense atty. Picillo Caruso, 1994-96; assoc. Netchert, Dineen & Hillman, 1996-97; litigator Francis J. Dooley, 1998-99; pvt. practice, 1999—; cert. instr. N.J. State Police Tng. Commn., Trenton, 1984; asst. dir. instruction Officers Candidate Sch. N.J. Mil. Acad., Sea Girt. Committeeman South Orange Republican Club, N.J., 1978-83; treas., founder Tuxedo Park Neighborhood Assn., South Orange, 1977; fin. sec. J. T. Kosciusko Assn., Irvington, N.J., 1979. Served to 1st lt. U.S. Army, 1969-71, maj. (ret.) JAGC, 1985-90. Recipient Class C. Commendations, Newark Police Dept., 1973, 74, 75, Command Citations, 1973, 74, 75, 77, 78. Mem. ATLA, ABA, Worrall F. Mountain Inn of Ct. (master), Trial Attys. N.J., N.J. State Bar Assn., N.J. Def. Assn., Morris County Bar Assn., N.Y. State Bar Assn., Washington D.C. Bar Assn., F&AM Congdon Overlook Lodge 163, Am. Legion, Officers Club (pres. Sea Girt, N.J. 1979-81), Ret. Officers Assn., Picatinny Officers Club, South Orange Lions Club (charter), Polish Univ. Club. Republican. Roman Catholic. Home: 11 Laurel Ln Morris Plains NJ 07950-3216

PLUGIN, ARKADIY NIKOLAEVICH, building materials educator; b. C. Mary, Turkmenistan, Apr. 1, 1941; s. Nicolay Emelianovich and Lidia Ivanovna (Fedorenko) P.; m. Lidia Nikolaevna Kartceva, Nov. 10, 1962; 1 child, Andrey. Grad., Kharkov (Ukraine) Inst. Engrs. of Railway Transport, 1963, Cand. Engring. Sci., 1970; D Chem. Scis., Acad. Scis. Ukraine, Kiev, 1989. Bldg. foreman bldg. assembly train, Kuibyshev, USSR, 1963; foreman concrete shop Factory Reinforced Concrete Constrn. of Dorstroytrest, Kharkov, 1964, chief lab., 1964-67, prin. factory engr., 1967-71; prin. engr. Ukrainian State Design Inst., Kharkov, 1971-76; sr. sci. enployee Kharkov State Acad. Rlwy. Transport, 1976-78, mgr. br. lab. reinforced concrete sleepers, 1978-84, prof., mgr. Faculty Bldg. Materials, Constrn. and Bldg., 1993—, scientific chief, 1996—, chmn. coun. on def. Dc dissertations on bldg. constrn., 1996—; mem. coun. on def. DSc dissertations on bldg. materials and product splty. Kharkov State Tech. U. Constrn. and Architecture, 1991—; Ukraine expert 5th commn. on questions on artificial structures and resource saving techs. Internat. Orgn. Cooperation of Rlwy., Warsaw, Poland, 1996—; mem. sci. and tech. coun. gen. adminstrn. of traveling farm State Adminstrn. Rlwy. Transport Ukraine, Kiev, 1995—. Author: Intensification of Cement Binders Hardening and Concrete, 1987, Statistical Estimation of a Level of Technological Processes of Manufacturing and Quality of Precast Reinforced Concrete Constructions, 1987, Physico-Chemical Mechanics of Building Materials and Construction, 1998, Restoration of Exploitation Properties of Materials and Constrn., 1999; sci. editor. conf. procs., 1996; patentee in field. Mem. Acad. Transp. Scis. Kiev, N.Y. Acad. Scis. Achievements include patents in field. Avocations: gymnastics, drawing, fishing, building country house by hand. Home: Scorohoda 24, f 35, 61093 Kharkov Ukraine

PLULAURELBELLE, ANNA LIVIA See WILLIS, LAUREL EILEEN

PLUM, DAVID ROBERT, educator; b. Gillingham, England, Oct. 8, 1933; s. Robert George and Winifred Florence (Sellen) P.; m. Daphne Marion Walker, Oct. 10, 1959; children: Marion Denise, Fiona Christine, Carolyn Jeanette. BS, London U., 1958; PhD, Manchester U., England, 1972. Engr. Simon-Carves, London, 1958-61, O'Sullivan & Ptnrs., London, 1961-63; assoc. Pell & Ptnrs., London, 1963-67; lectr. U. Manchester, England, 1967-82, U. Newcastle, England, 1982—; cons. in field. Author: Structural Steelwork Design, 1988, Statics and Dynamics, 1996. Fellow Inst. Structural Engring. (br. chmn. 1992-94); mem. Inst. Civil Engrs. Avocations: gardening, model railway. Home: 107 Stockton Rd, Darlington DL1 2RZ, England Office: U Newcastle, Kensington Terr, Newcastle Upon Tyne NE1 7RU, England

PLUMB, SIR JOHN (HAROLD), historian, educator; b. Aug. 20, 1911; s. James P.; B.A. with 1st class honors in History, U. London, 1933; Ph.D., Cambridge U., 1936, Litt.D., 1957; D.Litt. (hon.), U. Leicester, 1968, U. East Anglia, 1973, Bowdoin Coll., 1974, U. So. Calif., 1978, Westminster Coll., 1982, Washington U., St. Louis, 1983, Bard Coll., N.Y., 1988. Ehrman research fellow King's Coll., Cambridge U., 1939-46; with Fgn. Office, 1940-45; fellow Christ's Coll., Cambridge U., 1946—, steward, 1948-50, tutor, 1950-59, vice-master, 1964-68, master, 1978-82, Univ. lectr. history, 1946-62, reader modern English history, 1962-65, prof., 1966, chmn. history faculty, 1966-68; mem. council Brit. Acad., 1977-80; chmn. Ctr. East Anglian Studies, 1979-82; vis. prof. Columbia U., 1960; Disting. vis. prof. NYU, 1971-72, 76; Cecil and Ida Green Honors chair Tex. Christian U., 1974; Disting. vis. prof. Washington U., St. Louis, 1977; Ford's lectr. Oxford U., 1965-66; Saposnekov lectr. CCNY, 1968; Guy Stanton Ford lectr. U. Minn., 1969; Stenton lectr. U. Reading, 1972; George Rogers Clark lectr. Soc. of Cin., 1977. Author: England in the Eighteenth Century, 1950; (with C. Howard) West African Explorers, 1952; Chatham, 1953; Sir Robert Walpole, vol. I, 1956, vol. II, 1960; The First Four Georges, 1956; The Renaissance, 1961; Men and Places, 1962; Crisis in the Humanities, 1964; The Growth of Political Stability in England, 1675-1725, 1967; Death of the Past, 1969; In the Light of History, 1972; The Commercialisation of Leisure, 1974; Royal Heritage, 1977; New Light on the Tyrant, George III, 1978; Georgian Delights, 1980; Royal Heritage: The Reign of Elizabeth II, 1980; contbg. author: Man versus Society in Eighteenth Century Britain, 1968; Churchill Revised, 1969; editor: Studies in Social History, 1955; editor History of Human Soc., 1959—; sr. editor Am. Heritage Co.; hist. adv. Penguin Books, 1960-92; editor Pelican Social History of Britain, 1982—. Trustee, Nat. Portrait Gallery, 1961-82; syndic Fitzwilliam Mus., 1960-77; mem. Wine Standards Bd., 1973-75. Knighted (U.K.). Fellow Royal Hist. Soc., others; mem. Am. Acad. Arts and Scis. (hon. fgn.), Am. Hist. Assn. Home and Office: Cambridge U, Christs Coll, Cambridge CB2 3BU, England Address: British Acad, 10 Carlton House Terrace, London SW1Y 5AH, England

PLUMIDAKIS, NICK KONSTANTINOS, electronic engineer; b. Dec. 17, 1951; s. Konstantinos and Joan (Mamalaki) P.; m. Carol A. Wood; children: Joan-Aphrodite, Mary, Konstantinos-John, Thomas Andrew. Student in telecomm., Atom, Greece, 1971-75. Electronic engr. OTE, Athens, 1974—. Asst. editor SV News, 1983. Mem. RSGB, ARRL, RAAG. Home: Ag Kyriakis NCDXF Barnabas, 19014 Attikis Greece Office: OTE Sa Kifisias Ave, 99 Marousi, Attiki Athens Hellas, Greece

PLUMMER, CHRISTOPHER (ORME) (ARTHUR PLUMMER), actor; b. Toronto, Ont., Can., Dec. 13, 1929; s. John and Isabella Mary (Abbott) P.; m. Tammy Grimes (div.); 1 child, Amanda; m. Particia Audrew Lewis, May 4, 1962 (div.); m. Elaine Taylor. Ed. pub. and pvt. schs., Can.; pupil, Iris Warren, C. Herbertcasari. Stage debut in The Rivals with Can. Repertory Theatre, 1950; Broadway debut in Starcross Story, 1954; London debut in Becket, 1961; leading actor Am. Shakespeare Theatre, Stratford, Conn., 1955, Royal Shakespeare Co., London and Stratford, Avon, Eng., 1961-62, Stratford (Ont.) Shakespeare Festival, 1956, 57, 58, 60, 62, 67, Nat. Theatre Co., London; radio roles include Shakespeare, Canada; plays include Home is the Hero, 1954, Twelfth Night, 1954, 70-71, Dark is Light Enough, The Lark, Julius Caesar, The Tempest, 1955, Henry VI, 1956, Hamlet, 1957, Winter's Tale, 1958, Much Ado About Nothing, 1958, J.B., 1958, King John, 1960, Romeo and Juliet, 1960, Richard III, 1961, Arturo Ui, 1963, The Royal Hunt of the Sun, 1965, Antony and Cleopatra, 1967, Danton's Death, 1971, Amphitryon 38, 1971; (musicals) Cyrano, 1973, The Good Doctor, 1973, Love and Master Will, 1975; Othello, 1982, Macbeth, 1988, No Man's Land, 1993, Barrymore, 1996 (Tony award for Best Leading Actor in a Play, 1997); made TV debut 1953; TV prodns. include Little Moon of Alban, Johnny Belinda, 1958, Cyrano de Bergerac, 1962, Oedipus Rex, After the Fall, 1974, The Doll's House, The Prince and the Pauper, Prisoner of Zenda, Hamlet at Elsinore, BBC, 1964, Time Remembered, Capt. Brassbound's Conversion, The Shadow Box, 1981, The Thorn Birds, 1983, Little Gloria-Happy at Last, A Hazard of Hearts, 1987, Crossings, 1986, Danielle Steele's Secrets, 1992, Liar's Edge, 1992; star TV series The Moneychangers, 1977, Harrison Bergeron, 1995, We the Jury, 1996, The Conspiracy of Fear, 1996, Winchell, 1998; made film debut in 1957; films include Stage Struck, 1957, Wind Across the Everglades, 1958, The Fall of the Roman Empire, 1963, Inside Daisy Clover, 1965, Sound of Music, 1965, Triple Cross, 1967, Nobody Runs Forever, 1969, The Battle of Britain, 1969, The Royal Hunt of the Sun, 1969, Lock up your Daughters, 1969, The Phyx, 1970, Waterloo, 1971, The Man Who Would Be King, 1975, The Return of the Pink Panther, 1975, Conduct Unbecoming, 1975, International Velvet, 1978, Murder By Decree, 1979, Starcrash, 1979, The Silent Partner, 1979, Hanover Street, 1979, Somewhere in Time, 1980, Eye witness, 1981, The Disappearance, 1981, The Amateur, 1982, Dreamscape, 1984, Ordeal by Innocence, 1984, Lily in Love, 1985, The Boss' Wife, 1986, The Boy In Blue, 1986, An American Tail, 1986 (voice), Souvenir, 1987, Dragnet, 1987, Light Years (voice), 1988, Where the Heart Is, 1989, Fire Head, 1991, Star Trek: VI: The Undiscovered Country, 1991, Rock a Doodle, 1992 (voice), Malcolm X, 1992, Wolf, 1994, Dolores Claiborne, 1994, Twelve Monkeys, 1995, Skeletons, 1996, The Arrow, 1997, Hidden Agenda, 1998, The Clown at Midnight, 1998, Winchell (TV), 1998, Blackheart, The Insider, 1999, All the Fine Lines, 1999, Celebrate the Century (TV mini-series), 1999, The Dinosaur Hunter, 2000, Dracula 2000, 2000, Nuremberg (TV mini-series), 2000, American Tragedy (TV mini-series), 2000.. Decorated companion Order of Can., 1968; recipient Theatre World award, 1955, Evening Standard award, 1961, Delia Austrian medal, 1973, 2 Drama Desk awards, 1973, 82, Antoinette Perry award, 1974, Emmy award Nat. Acad. TV Arts and Scis., 1977, Genie award, Can., 1980, Golden Badge of Honor, Austria, 1982, Maple Leaf award Nat. Acad. Arts and Letters. Mem. Theatre's Hall of Fame. Office: c/o Lou Pitt The Pitt Group 9465 Wilshire Blvd Ste 480 Beverly Hills CA 90212-2612*

PLUMMER, GAYTHER L(YNN), climatologist, ecologist, researcher; b. Indpls., Jan. 27, 1925; s. Conley L. and Rowena H. (Huber) P.; m. H. Eileen Barr, June 3, 1950. BS, Butler U., 1948; MS, Kans. State U., 1950; PhD, Purdue U., 1954. Instr. biology Knox Coll., Galesburg, Ill., 1950-51; naturalist Ind. Dept. Conservation, various locations, 1947-52; asst. prof. biology Antioch Coll., Yellow Springs, Ohio, 1954-55; prof. botany U. Ga., Athens, 1955-95, state climatologist, 1978-95; rsch. fellow Oak Ridge (Tenn.) Inst. Nuclear Studies, 1958-62. Author: Georgia Weather Watchers, 1991, Georgia Temperatures, 1993; cartographer 160 vegetation maps of Ga., 1972-74; editor Ga. Jour. Sci., 1977-84; author over 200 rsch. reports. 2d lt. USAAF, 1943-46. Fellow AAAS; mem. Ecol. Soc. Am., Ind. Acad. Sci., Ga. Acad. Sci., Soil Sci. Soc. Am., Crop Sci. Soc. Am., Agron. Soc. Am., Sigma Xi, Phi Kappa Phi. Achievements include research in droughts in S.E. U.S. relating to astrogeophysical processes via geomagnetics; lightning history in Piedmont for over 70 million years etched in Stone Mountain granite. Office: Ga Climatology Assoc Inc 995 Timothy Rd Athens GA 30606-3838

PLUMMER, GRAEME LESLIE, television program director; b. Goulburn, NSW, Australia, July 16, 1943; s. Leslie Albert and Audrey Lillian (Lownes) P.;. BA, U. Western Australia, Perth, 1963. TV program mgr. TVW Channel 7, Perth, 1962-81, Mining TV Network, Perth, 1981-83, Golden West Network, Dianella, Australia, 1983—; TV cons. Graeme Plummer TV Program Svcs., Perth, 1981—. Roman Catholic. Avocations: previewing movies, swimming, football, cricket.

PLUMMER, JOHN LEWIS, medical scientist, researcher; b. Melbourne, Victoria, Australia, Mar. 6, 1951. B of Pharmacy, Victoria Inst. Colls., Melbourne, 1972; MS, Sydney U., 1974, PhD, 1978; grad. diploma in applied stats., South Australia Inst. Tech., Adelaide, 1985. Accredited statistician. Vis. fellow Nat. Inst. Environ. Health Scis., Research Triangle Park, N.C., 1978-80; sr. rsch. officer Flinders U., Adelaide, 1980-85; med. scientist Flinders Med. Ctr., Adelaide, 1985—. Mem. Internat. Assn. for Study of Pain, Statis. Soc. Australia, Australian Pharm. Scis. Assn., Australian Soc. Clin. and Exptl. Pharmacologists and Toxicologists., Am. Statis. Assn. Office: Flinders Med Ctr, Dept Anesthesia, 5042 Bedford Park Australia

PLUNIER, GUY ALBERT, public relations executive; b. Plouha, Brittany, France, July 4, 1930; s. Joseph and Marie (Prevoteau) P.; m. Nicole Irene Ghazi, June 3, 1958; children: Jean-Pierre, Marie-Gabrielle, Danielle. BSBA with honors, Sophia U., Tokyo, 1971, MBA in Internat. Bus., 1973. Salesman Michelin Tires Co., St. Lô, France, 1953; sales rep. Michelin Tires Co., Stanleyville, Belgian Congo, 1954-58; rep. Michelin Tires Co., Teheran, Iran, 1958-61; regional mgr. Michelin Tires Co., Toulouse, France, 1961-64; area mgr. Michelin Tires Co., Colombo, Ceylon, 1964-67; mgr. S.E. Michelin Thailand, Bangkok, 1967-68; Far East del. Michelin Tires Co., Tokyo, 1968-76; gen. del. Compagnie Generale des Establissements (Michelin), Cairo, Egypt, 1976-82, Inst. Econ. de Paris, 1982-86; pub. affairs/rels. dir. Yves Rocher Group, Paris, 1987-90; lectr. internat. mgmt. Author (book reviews) Wall Street Jour. Named Officer, Nat. Order of Merit, 1991, Counsellor of External Trade, Ministry of External Trade, 1970, Col., Ky. State, 1973. Mem. Club de Bretagne XXI (pres. 1990—, sec. gen. 1998—), Tocqueville Found. (pres. 1986—), Club de la Presse de Bretagne (assoc.), The Heritage Found. (pub. policy expert 1988—), Mont Pelerin Soc., Nat. Taxpayers Assocs. (bd. dirs.), Institut de Locarn (bd. dirs., strategic com.). Roman Catholic. Avocations: personal libr., slides collection. Office: Yves Rocher Group, 3 Allée de Grenelle, Issy les Moulineaux 92444, France

PLUNKETT, ROBERT LAWRENCE, lawyer; b. Denver, Dec. 8, 1951; s. Robert Lawrence and Dolores Lorraine; m. Susan Ann Plunkett, Oct. 20, 1984; 1 child, Robert Lawrence. BA, Univ. Calif., 1974; JD cum laude, Loyola Law Sch., 1977. Bar: Calif. 1977. Lawyer Law Offices Robert Plunkett, Lancaster, Calif., 1981—; tchr. Lancaster, Calif., 1996-99; instr. Chapman Univ., Palmdale, Calif., 1999—; faculty mentor S. Calif. Univ., Santa Ana, 1999—; vice dean, prof. Southern Calif. Inst. Law, Ventura, 1992-97; adj. prof. LaVerne Univ. Sch. Law, Woodland Hills, Calif., 1994-95. Contbr. articles to profl. jours. E-mail: robplunkett@mailcity.com. Office: Law Offices of Robert L Plunkett 6752 Teasdale St Lancaster CA 93536-1246

PLUTA, RYSZARD, neuropathologist, educator; b. Biała Podlaska, Poland, Apr. 16, 1952; s. Marian and Antonina (Szarubko) P. Student, Humboldt U., Berlin, 1975, U. Cologne, Germany, 1976; MD, scientist, Med. Acad., Lublin, Poland, 1977; PhD, Polish Acad. Scis., Warsaw, 1983. Intern gynaecology unit State Hosp., Biała Podlaska, 1977; intern dept. pediatry Med. Acad., Warsaw, 1978; intern internal medicine and surgery units Czerniakowski Hosp., Warsaw, 1978; sci. visitor lab. of CNS Resuscitation Pathology, Inst. Gen. Reanimatology, USSR Acad. Med. Scis., Moscow, 1979; sr. rsch. asst. Polish Acad. Sci., Warsaw, 1981-87, asst. prof., 1987-94, assoc. prof., 1994—; postdoctoral fellow NIH, Bethesda, Md., 1986-88; prof. Acad. Phys. Edn., Warsaw, 1995—; resident neurology Med. Acad., Warsaw, 1997; postdoctoral rsch. fellow, vis. prof. N.Y. State Inst. Basic Rsch., Staten Island, 1988-89, 90-91, 93-94, 97; vice-chmn., bd. dirs. State Hosp., Biala Podlaska, 1999-2000; mem. European Stroke Coun., Basel, Switzerland, 1993—; mem. sci. coun. Acad. Phys. Edn., Warsaw, 1995—; mem. senate Acad. Phys. Edn., Warsaw, 1996-99; mem. sci. coun. Inst. Phys. Edn. and Sport, Biała Podlaska, Poland, 1996—. Contbr. articles to profl. jours. Chief Trade Union Solidarność, Med. Rsch. Ctr., Warsaw, 1980-90; chief. Dem. Union, Dist. Biała Podlaska, 1990-94; candidate Polish Parliament, 1991, 93. 2nd lt. Polish mil., 1977. Grantee Polish Com. Sci. Rsch., Warsaw, 1994-2000, St. Batory's Found., Warsaw, 1996, Internat. Brain Rsch. Orgn., Paris, 1997, Alzheimer's Assn., 1998, Fifth Framework Programme European Cmty., 2000—. Mem. European Soc. Clin. Respiratory Physiology, Polish Neurosci. Soc., Internat. Soc. for Brain Edema Rsch., Internat. Soc. Cerebral Blood Flow and Metabolism, Internat. Soc. Neuropathology, N.Y. Acad. Sci., Polish Assn. Neuropathologists (award 1980, 86), Polish Acad. Sci. (Pres.'s award 1982, 89, award med. sect. sec. 1992). Roman Catholic. Avocations: politics, sports, good food, cooking. Office: Med Rsch Ctr Dept Neuropath, Pawińskiego Str 5, 02-106 Warsaw Poland

PLZÁK, ZBYNĚK, chemist; b. Prague, Czech Republic, June 25, 1943; s. František and Libuše (Vernerova) P.; m. Jaroslava Horová, June 11, 1970; children: Markéta, Jan. MS, Prague Inst. Chem. Tech., 1965; PhD, Acad. Scis., Prague, 1970. Rsch. scientist Inst. Inorganic Chemistry Acad. Scis., Rez nr. Prague, 1970—. Contbr. articles to profl. pubs. including Jour. Chromatography, others. Mem. Eurachem (nat. del.). Avocations: gardening, cycling, kynology, library and information sys. E-mail: plzak@iic.cas.cz. Office: Acad Sci Czech Republic, Inst Inorganic Chemistry, 250 68 Rez near Prague, Czech Republic

P'MPOLS, TERESA, geneticist; b. Barcelona, May 3, 1942; d. Hilari and Teresa (Ros) P.; m. Francesc Castells, Aug. 2, 1969; 1 child, Ariadna. PhD, Barcelona U., 1968. Lab. asst. prof. Univ. Autonomous Barcelona, 1969-71; from staff to dir. inst. Biochemistry & Chemistry U. Barcelona, 1969—. Mem. Soc. Study Inborn Errors of Metabolism, Am. Soc. Human Genetics, United Leucodystrophy Found., Internat. Soc. Prenatal Diagnosis, N.Y. Acad. Scis. Office: Inst Biochem & Chem, Corporacis Sanit'ria Clin, Mejma Lequerica 08028, Barcelona Spain

POAD, FLORA VIRGINIA, retired librarian and educator; b. Roanoke, Va., Oct. 8, 1921; d. Thomas Franklin and Ethlind (Wertz) Huff; m. Stanley Theodore Benton, Dec. 24, 1942 (div. Oct. 1983); children: Peggy, Betty, Mary Jo, Lucy; m. James Joseph Poad, June 6, 1986. Student, Radford Coll., 1939-41, Ohio U., 1956-57; BS in Edn., Ohio No. U., 1960; MA in LS, U. Toledo, 1964; postgrad., Kent State U., 1964-66, 71. Reference asst. Roanoke Pub. Libr., 1939-42; catalog asst. Univ. Libr., Emory U., Atlanta, 1942; sec. ARC, Atlanta, 1943; catalog asst. Pickerington (Ohio) Pub. Libr., 1950-51; tchr. Celina (Ohio) Pub. Schs., 1957-62; tchr., libr. Toledo Pub. Schs., 1962-64; libr. supr. Oregon (Ohio) Pub. Schs., 1964-85; instr. U. Toledo, 1970, reference libr., 1971-86; tchr. Sylvan Learning Ctr., Toledo, 1985-92; ret., 1992; mem. evaluation team Ohio Dept. Edn., Columbus, 1973; rep. Ohio Gov.'s Conf. on Librs., Columbus, 1974; chmn., mem. adv. bd. libr. sci. dept. Cmty.-Tech. Coll., 1965-69. Editor Ohio Assn. Sch. Librs. Bull., 1968-71. Vol. Am. Cancer Soc., Toledo, 1946-48, 86-87, Mobile Meals, Toledo, 1986-93, Helping Hands, Toledo, 1994—. Mem. Am. Assn. Ret. Persons, Delta Kappa Gamma, Pi Lambda Theta, Kappa Delta Pi, Phi Kappa Phi. Avocations: reading, walking, crafts.

POBLACIONES, JOSÉ, NATO official; m. Conchita Poblaciones; 7 children. Grad., Naval Acad., 1961. Commd. ensign Spanish Navy, 1961, advanced through grades to vice-adm., 1996, entered Submarine Tng. Ctr., 1963, chief ops. officer SPS Narciso Mounturiol, commdg. officer, comdr. A.G. De Los Reyes; hydrographic officer survey ship Malaspina Spanish Navy, Equatorial Guinea; COO destroyer A. Valdes, exec. officer cestroyer Churruca Spanish Navy, comdr. destroyer Langara, appointed to Ministry of Def., Def. Policy Directorate, NATO, 1989-90; dep. mil. rep. to NATO Hdqrs. Spanish Navy, Brussels, 1990-91, def. counsellor Spanish Delegation, NATO, 1991-93; chief second divsn., Jt. Staff Spanish Navy, Madrid, 1994; head Spanish mil. mission to SACLANT Spanish Navy, 1994-96; Spanish mil. rep. to NATO Mil. Com. Spanish Navy, Brussels, 1996—; instr. Submarine Sch., Naval Acad. Office: NATO Hdqrs, Blvd Leopold III, 1110 Brussels Belgium*

POCH, HERBERT EDWARD, retired pediatrician, educator; b. Elizabeth, N.J., Sept. 4, 1927; s. William and Min (Herman) P.; m. Leila Kosberg, Aug. 27, 1952; children: Bruce Jeffrey, Andrea Susan, Lesley Grace. AB, Columbia U., 1949, MD, 1953. Diplomate Am. Bd. Pediatrics. Intern Kings County Hosp. Ctr., Bklyn., 1953-54; resident Babies Hosp., Columbia-Presbyn. Med. Ctr., N.Y.C., 1954-56; pvt. practice medicine specializing in pediatrics Elizabeth, 1956-92; pres. med. staff, 1989, attending pediatrician Elizabeth Gen. Med. Ctr., 1973, sr. attending pediatrician, 1990, hon. staff, 1993—; attending pediatrician St. Elizabeth Hosp., 1968, chmn. dept. pediatrics, 1971-81, attending pediatrician Monmouth Med. Ctr., 1991-99, emeritus, 1999—, assoc. program dir. pediatrics; instr. pediatrics Columbia U., 1956-72, asst. clin. prof. pediatrics, 1972-91; clin. assoc. prof. pediatrics MCP Hahnemann Sch. Medicine, 1997-99; ret. With AUS, 1945-46. Fellow Am. Acad. Pediatrics; mem. N.J. Med. Soc., Ambulatory Pediatric Assn. Address: 1175 Ocean Ave Long Branch NJ 07740-4518

POCHET, ROLAND, science educator; b. Brussels, Sept. 28, 1947; s. Georges Pochet and Marie-Louise Klein; m. Martine Collignon, Jan. 10, 1971; 1 child, Caroline. BA in Chemistry, U. Libre de Brussels, 1970, MSc in Biochemistry, 1972, PhD in Biochemistry, 1979. Cert. prof. Rschr. U. Libre de Brussels, 1971-79, from asst. prof. to assoc. prof., 1979-91, prof. histology, 1994—; vis. rschr. Hebraic U. Jerusalem, 1974-76; prof. cell biology U. Poitiers, 1992; bd. dirs. Belgian Coop. in Africa, 1997. Editor: (book) Calcium Binding Proteins in Normal and Transformed Cells, 1989, Calcium: The Molecular Basics of Calcium Action in Biology and Medicine, 2000. Decorated officier de l' Ordre de Leopold II, 2000. Mem. European Calcium Soc. (gen. sec. 1997—, mem. steering com. soc. creation 1996), Assn. for Promotion of Alsace (bd. dirs. 1990-99), Belgian Soc. Cellular Biology (bd. dirs. 1997-00). Avocations: tennis, cinema. Fax: 322 55 6285. E-mail: rpochet@ulb.ac.be. Home: Av A Huysmans 28, B-1050 Brussels Belgium Office: U Libre de Brussels, 808 Rte de Lennik, B-1070 Brussels Belgium

POCOCK, STUART JOHN, medical statistics educator, consultant; b. Derby, Eng., July 18, 1946; s. Ernest and Edith (Gregory) P.; m. Lesley Delacourt; children: Ian, Michael, Graham. BA in Math., Cambridge (Eng.) U., 1967; MS in Stats., London U., 1968, PhD in Med. Stats., 1972. Lectr. London Sch. Hygiene and Tropical Medicine, 1969-72; asst. prof. SUNY, Buffalo, 1972-74; rsch. statistician U. Med. Sch., Edinburgh, Scotland, 1974-77; from sr. lectr. to reader to prof. med. stats. Royal Free Hosp. Med. Sch., London, 1978-89; prof. med. stats. London Sch. Hygiene and Tropical Medicine, 1989—; mem. Medicines Commn. U.K., 1996—; cons. biostatistician Harvard Med. Sch., 1996—, New Eng. Rsch. Inst., 1996—. Author:

Clinical Trials: A Practical Approach, 1983; editor: Clinical Trials in Cardiology, 1997; contbr. numerous articles to profl. jours. Mem. Soc. for Clin. Trials (pres. 1997-98), Royal Statis. Soc. (chmn. med. sect. 1989-91, Guy medal 1980), Biometric Soc. (coun. mem. 1991-94, assoc. editor 1985-87). Avocations: tennis, golf, opera, travel, London culture. Office: London Sch Hygiene/Trop Med, Keppel St, London WC1E 7HT, England

POCOSKI, DAVID JOHN, cardiologist; b. Waterbury, Conn., July 15, 1945; s. Edward J. and Stella E. (Kolpa) P.; m. Madelyn M. Pocoski, Sept. 25, 1971; 1 child, Sarah C. BS, U. Conn., 1967; MD magna cum laude, Upstate Med. Ctr., Syracuse, N.Y., 1971. From intern to fellow in cardiology U. Rochester, N.Y.; founder, pres. Osler Clin. of Medicine, Melbourne, Fla.; pres., chief of staff, dir. cardiac rehab. Sea Pines Rehab. Hosp. Commr. Holy Name Jesus Cath. Ch. Maj. USAF, 1974-76. Recipient Outstanding Scientist of the 20th Century award. Fellow Am. Coll. Cardiology; mem. AMA. Republican. Roman Catholic. Avocations: music, art, running, community service. Office: 930 S Harbor City Blvd Melbourne FL 32901-1963

POCSIK, GEORGE, physics educator; b. Kisvárda, Hungary, Aug. 15, 1933; s. István and Erzèbet (Toth) P.; m. Dorottya Pataj, Mar. 2, 1955; children: Eva, Dora. Degree as tchr. secondary sch., U. Szeged, Hungary, 1955; PhD in Physics, Eötvös U., Budapest, Hungary, 1962, D, 1967. Tchr. H.S., Szeged, 1955-58; 1st asst. to prof. Eötvös U., Budapest, 1962-65, lectr., 1966-69, prof., 1969—, dir. grad. sch. particle physics; chmn. particles physics subcom. Acad. Scis., Budapest, 1988-99, chmn. com. sci. qualification, 1995—; mem. Hungarian CERN com., 1992—. Author: Quantum Field Theory and Dispersion Relations, 1977 (prize Acad. Scis. 1982); editor: Standard Model at the Energy of Present and Future Accelerators, 1992, Electroweak Symmetry Breaking, 1995. Recipient R. Schmid prize Hungarian Phys. Soc., 1964, Acad. prize, 1992. Mem. N.Y. Acad. Scis. Avocations: electronic music, walking, touring. Home: Polgar Utca 5, 1033 Budapest Hungary Office: Eötvös Univ, Eötvös Univ, Inst Theoretical Physics, 1518 Budapest Hungary

PODANI, MANUELA, physician, researcher; b. Bucharest, Romania, July 15, 1964; q; d. Constantin Tiberiu and Neacsa (Panghe) P. MD, U. Medicine and Pharmacy, Bucharest, 1988, Specialist in Infectious Diseases, 1995; AFSA in Infectious Diseases/Tropical, Medicine, Paris VI, 1997; AIDS in France and World, Paris XII, 1996. Medical diplomate. Infectious disease specialist U. Hosp. Colentina, Bucharest, 1994-98; fellow CHI Villeneuve/St. George, France, 1996-98; sr. doctor Inst. of Infectious Diseases, Bucharest, 1999—; med. cons. UNHCR - Romania, 1994-96. Contbr. articles to profl. jours. Vol. NGO-SIRDO, 1995-96, Romania, 1998-99. Mem. USSM, GEEP/France. Avocations: mountain climbing, swimming, reading fiction, theater, cinema. Office: Inst Infectious Diseases, 1 Grozovici Str, Bucharest Romania

PODBOY, ALVIN MICHAEL, JR., law library director, lawyer; b. Cleve., Feb. 10, 1947; s. Alvin Michael and Josephine Esther (Nagode) P.; m. Mary Ann Gloria Esposito, Aug. 21, 1971; children: Allison Marie, Melissa Ann. AB cum laude, Ohio U., 1969; JD, Case Western Res. U., 1972, MLS, 1977. Bar: Ohio 1972, U.S. Dist. Ct. (no. dist.) Ohio 1973, U.S. Supreme Ct. 1992. Assoc. Joseph T. Svete Co. LPA, Chardon, Ohio, 1972-76; dir. pub. svcs. Case Western Res. Sch. Law Libr., Cleve., 1974-77, assoc. law libr., 1977-78; libr. Baker & Hostetler, LLP, Cleve., 1978-88, dir. librs., 1988—; instr. Notre Dame Coll. of Ohio, Cleve., 1991—, Am. Inst. Paralegal Studies, Cleve., 1991-96. Mem. editl. adv. bd. Law Tech. News, 1999—. Bd. overseers Case Western Res. U., 1981-87, mem. vis. com. sch. libr. sci., 1980-86, mem. Westlaw adv. bd., 1987-92, bd. govs. law sch. alumni assn., 1992-95, West's Legal Directory Ohio Adv. Panel, 1990-91; mem. adv. com. West's Info. Innovators Inst., 1995-97; chmn. Case Western Res. Libr. Sch. Alumni Fund, 1979-80; Rep. precinct committeeman Cuyahoga County, Cleve., 1981-95, mem. exec. com., 1984-87. 1st lt. USAF, 1972. Mem. ABA, Ohio State Bar Assn. (chmn. librs. com. 1989-91), Cleve. Bar Assn., Am. Assn. Law Librs. (cert., chmn. pvt. law librs. spl. interest sect. 1994-95), Ohio Regional Assn. Law Librs. (pres. 1985), Case Western Res. U. Libr. Sch. Alumni Assn. (pres. 1981), Arnold Air Soc., Am. Legion, KC, Pi Gamma Mu, Phi Alpha Theta. Roman Catholic. Avocation: alpine skiing. Home: 1359 Fox Den Ln # 106 Willoughby OH 44094 Office: Baker & Hostetler LLP 3200 National City Ctr Cleveland OH 44114-3485

PODCAMENI, ABELARDO, engineering educator, researcher; b. Rio de Janeiro, Brazil, Mar. 6, 1941; s. Adolpho and Amalia (Jofe) P.; m. Vera Maria von Bochkor Podcameni, Mar. 6, 1977; children: Pia, Gigi, Ana Paula, Gaby. Degree in Electronics Engring., Puc, Rio de Janeiro, Brazil, 1966, MS, 1969, PhD, 1979. Asst. prof. Puc, Rio de Janeiro, Brazil, 1969-73; sr. engr. Telesp, Sao Paulo, Brazil, 1973-75; asst. prof. Cetuc Puc, Rio de Janeiro, Brazil, 1975-79, assoc. prof., 1979-88; comms. engr. Intelsat, El Segundo, 1988-91; assoc. prof. Cetuc Puc, Rio de Janeiro, Brazil, 1991—; rsch. mgr. ABC-Italtel, Rio de Janeiro, Brazil, 1982-83; treas. Rio de Janeiro Chpt. IEEE, 1992-96. Inventor: 1971; contbr. articles to profl. jours. Mem. IEEE. Avocations: billiards, jogging. Office: PUC-RJ/CETUC, Rua Marques de Sao Vicente, 22453900 Rio de Janeiro Brazil

PODCHERNYAEVA, RAISA JAKOVLEVNA, virologist, researcher; b. Moscow, Feb. 26, 1933; d. Iakov Ivanovich Fomichev and Maria Ivanovna Vorobieva; m. Vladimir Vasilievich Podchernayev, Sept. 11, 1956; 2 children. Degree, Med. Inst. Moscow, 1956. Physician Moscow, 1956-59; physician D.I. Ivanovsky Inst. Virology, Moscow, 1959-64, head group, 1964-86, chief lab., 1986—, prof., 1989—. Author: Genetics and Evolution of Influenza Virus, 1981; contbr. over 230 articles to profl. jours. Mem. Russian Soc. Microbiology, Epidemiology and Parasitology, Russian Assn. Cell Cultures. Avocations: gardening, history of medicine. Home: Rogova Str 7, 123479 Moscow Russia Office: Dr Ivanovsky Inst Virology, Gamaleva 16, 123098 Moscow Russia

PODEA, DELIA MARINA, psychiatrist; b. Arad, Romania, Feb. 20, 1953; d. Toma Micodim and Marina (Marcus) P.; m. Dan Aurel Ilitescu. MD, U. Timisoara, 1972. Resident Hygiene Inst. Timisoara, 1978-80; resident in psychiatry Faculty Medicine Bucuresti, 1980-83; psychiatrist Psychiatry Hosp., Arad, Romania, 1983—; lectr. West U., Arad, 1996-97, reader, 1997—. Author: Panic Disorder, 1997. Mem. IAGP, Psychiat. World Assn. Home: 3 D Bolintineanu Str, 2900 Arad Romania Office: Psychiatry Hosp, 17 O Goga Str, 2900 Arad Romania

PODEMANN SØRENSEN, JØRGEN, religious studies educator; b. Aarhus, Denmark, June 23, 1946; s. Ole and Klara (Svinth) S.; m. Anne-Merete Jensen, May 23, 1996. CandPhil, U. Aarhus, 1972; Mag Art, U. Copenhagen, 1979. Asst. prof., then assoc. prof. U. Copenhagen, 1987-92, 93—. Author, editor: Rethinking Religion, 1989; chief editor Chaos Dansk-Norsk Tidsskrift for Religionshistoriske Studier, 1982-95; contbr. articles to profl. jours. Mem. Danish Assn. History Religions. Avocations: sculpture, bookbinding. Home: Sønderstrupvej 162, DK 4360 Kr Eskilstrup Denmark Office: U Copenhagen Dept Religion, Artillerivej 86, DK 2300 Copenhagen Denmark

PODESTA, ROBERT EDWARD, artist; b. Sept. 7, 1921. BCS, U. Santa Clara, 1943. Prin. R. Podesta & Assocs., San Jose, Calif., 1946-66; owner/mgr. Sta. KREP-FM, Santa Clara-San Jose, 1965-72; cartoonist Honolulu Advertiser, 1991—; lectr. Coll. Bus. Adminstrn., U. Santa Clara, 1948-57. cartoonist San Jose Bus. Jour., Denver Bus. Jour., Ft. Worth Bus. Jour., Pacific Bus. Rev. Home: 100 Sunnycove Dr Santa Cruz CA 95062-4904

PODEWILS, ULRICH, academic administrator; b. Hildesheim, Germany, Sept. 13, 1947; s. Erich and Gisela (Kohne) P.; m. Vaneeta Kumari Khosla, Mar. 9, 1979; 1 child, Indra Sarah. 1st state exam in law, U. Heidelberg, 1972; 2nd state exam in law, State of Baden-Wuerttemberg, 1975. Jr. lawyer State of Baden-Wuerttemberg, Germany, 1972-75; dept. head U. Mannheim, 1975-78; internat. affairs Ministry Sci., Stuttgart, Germany, 1978-83; head pub. rels. Fed. Ministry Edn., Bonn, Germany, 1983-86; sec. gen. Villa Vigoni, Como, Italy, 1986-87; head univ. affairs Fed. Ministry Edn., Bonn, 1987-88; chancellor Tech. U., Berlin, 1988-98; dir. Berlin office, Berlin Artist Program German Acad. Exch. Svc., 1998—. Trustee Friends of Villa Vigoni. Mem. Rotary Club Berlin. Office: DAAD Sci Forum Berlin, Markgrafenstr 37, 10117 Berlin Germany

PODHURST, AARON SAMUEL, lawyer; b. N.Y.C., Apr. 29, 1936; s. Louis and rae (Pomerantz) P.; m. Dorothy Ellen Podhurst, Sept. 7, 1958; children: Karen Beth Dern, Laura Koffsky, Julie Weinberg. BBA, U. Mich., 1957; JD, Columbia U., 1960. Bar: Fla., 1961, N.Y., 1961. Assoc. Nichols, Gaither, Miami, Fla., 1962-67; founding ptnr. Podhurst, Orseck, Josefsberg, Eaton, Meadow, Olin & Perwin, P.A., Miami, 1967—. Vice pres. Miami Coalition for Safe Cmty., 1994—; mem. Orange Bowl Com., Miami, 1996—. Recipient Nat. Medallion award NCCJ, 1994; Harlan Fiske Stone scholar, 1960. Mem. ABA (aviation com.), Internat. Acad. Trial Lawyers (pres. 1990), Acad. Fla. Trial Lawyers (pres. 1978, aviation com.), Am. Coll. Trial Lawyers, Assn. Trial Lawyers Am. (bd. govs., aviation com.), Internat. Soc. Barristers, Inner Cir. of Advocates. Office: Podhurst Orseck Josefsberg Eaton Meadow Olin & Perwin PA 25 W Flagler St Miami FL 33130-1712

PODOLEANU, ADRIAN GH, physics educator; b. Goloasa, Romania, Aug. 6, 1951; s. Gheorghe N. and Elena N. (Alexandrescu) P.; m. Steluta D. Stoian, Aug. 6, 1977; 1 child, Andreea Adriana. PhD, Polytech Inst., Bucharest, Romania, 1984. Engr. Elec. Measurement Instruments Enterprise, Bucharest, Romania, 1975-80; asst. prof. physics Polytech Inst., Bucharest, Romania, 1980-86, lectr., 1986-91, assoc. prof., 1991-92; rsch. fellow physics lab. U. Kent, Canterbury, Eng., 1993—, lectr. applied optics, 1999—. Contbr. articles to profl. jours. Mem. European Phys. Soc. (mem. bd. computational physics group 1990-96), Romanian Soc. Electricity and Bioradiations, European Optical Soc., U.S. Friends in Romania, Soc.Optical Engring. Home: 11 Goudhurst Close, Canterbury CT2 7TU, England Office: U Kent, Physics Lab, Canterbury CT2 7NR, England

PODOLSKI, IGOR YACOVLEVICH, psychobiologist, neuroscientist, researcher; b. Odessa, Ukraine, Apr. 13, 1934; s. Yacov Matveyevich Podolski and Margarita Alexandrovna Morguleva; m. Maria Nickolaevna Rastrepina, Oct. 20, 1953 (div. June 1977); 1 child, Leonid; m. Maria Iosiphovna Pflúger, Oct. 11, 1979; 1 child, Andrey. Diploma with honor, Omsk (USSR) State Med. Inst., 1957; cand. med. scis., USSR Acad. Scis., Moscow, 1970. Intern Regional Clinic, Omsk, 1957-60; jr. sci. rschr. Inst. Higher Nervous Activity & Neurophys. USSR Acad. Scis., Moscow, 1964-68; sci. rschr. Inst. Biol. Physics USSR Acad. Scis., Puschino, USSR, 1968-90; sr. sci. rschr. Inst. Theoretical & Exptl. Biophysics USSR Acad. Scis., Puschino, 1991—, vice-head lab. systemic orgn. of neurons, 1991—; sr. lectr. dept. neurobiology Puschino State U., 1993—. Author: Signal Molecules and Behaviour, 1991; contbr. articles to profl. jours. Coord. Dem. Russia, Puschino, 1993. Mem. Russian Physiol. Soc. (v.p. Puschino sect. 1994—). Mem. Orthodox Church. Avocations: fiction, stage and screen, classical music, mountaineering. Fax: 7 (0967) 790553. E-mail: podolski@venus.iteb.serpukhov.su. Office: Inst Theor/Exptl Biophysics, Russian Acad Scis, 142292 Puschino Moscow, Russia

PODOLSKY, ARNOLD MARK, lawyer, physician; b. Detroit, Oct. 11, 1951. BA, Oakland U., 1972; MD, Wayne State U., 1977; JD, Detroit Coll. Law, 1986. Diplomate Am. Bd. Anesthesiology; Bar: Mich. 1986. Med. cons. Lopatin & Miller PC, Detroit, 1984-86, atty., 1986-91; ptnr. Ravid & Podolsky PC, Southfield, Mich., 1991-93; CEO Podolsky & Assocs. PC, Birmingham, Mich., 1993—. Faculty scholar Detroit Coll. Law, 1983-86. Fellow Am. Coll. Legal Medicine; mem. Mich. Trial Lawyers Assn. (mem. exec. bd. 1991-95), Mich. State Med. Soc., Assn. Trial Lawyers Am., State Bar Assn. Mich. Office: Podolsky and Assocs PC 999 Haynes St Ste 395 Birmingham MI 48009-6775

PODOLSKÝ, JIŘÍ, physicist; b. Mladá Boleslav, Czech Republic, Sept. 28, 1963; s. Jiří and Jaroslava (Jägerová) P.; m. Kateřina Pintová, Sept. 19, 1987; children: Markéta, Tereza. D of Theoretical Physics, Charles U., Prague, 1987, PhD, 1993. Asst. Charles U., Prague, 1991-95, sr. asst., 1995—. Contbr. articles to profl. jours. Visitor grantee Royal Soc. London, 1997, 98, 99, 2000. Office: Charles U Dept Theor Phys, V Holešovickách 2, 180 00 Prague Czech Republic

PODPORKIN, GEORGIJ VIKTOROVICH, engineering executive, educator; b. St. Petersburg, Russia, Aug. 26, 1950; s. Viktor Grigoryevich Podporkin and Irina Vladimirovna Tatarchuk; m. Natalia Borisovna Kozhuhar, Aug. 12, 1981; children: Maria, Polina, Anna. Degree in elec. engring., St. Petersburg Tech. U., 1973, PhD, 1977, DSc, 1990. Rschr. St. Petersburg Tech. U., 1973-79, sr. rschr., 1979-90, fellow rschr., 1990-91; sci. cons. Centro de Pesquisas de Energia Eletrica, Brazil, 1991-95; mng. dir. Streamer Electric Co., Russia, 1995—. Co-author: New Means for Electrical Energy Transmission, 1981, Overvoltage Protection of 6 to 35 KV Power Systems, 1997; contbr. articles to profl. jours.; inventor in field. Mem. IEEE (sr., power engring. soc.). Avocations: skiing, tennis, tourism. Office: Streamer Electric Co, Lomonosova 97 Pargolovo, 194902 St Petersburg Russia

PODSKLAN, JOZEF, geophysicist; b. Oravska Lesna, Czechoslovakia, Apr. 26, 1948; s. Ludovit and Julia (Pacon) P.; m. Maria Zalkova, Sept. 30, 1972 (div. 1991); children: Martina, Peter. MSc, Charles U., Prague, 1972; RNDr, Comenius U., Bratislava, Czechoslovakia, 1977. Rschr. Slovak Acad. Scis., Hurbanovo, Czechoslovakia, 1972-82, scientist, 1982-92, dir. geomagnetic obs., 1986-88; rschr. Rsch. Inst. of Geodesy and Topography, Prague, Czech Republic, 1992-95; Oracle-developer Benzina, A.S., Prague, 1996-99, ANFDATA, 1999—; geophysicist Geologisches Bundesanstall, Vienna, 1991-97. Author, editor: Results of Geomagnetic Observations 1972-1992, others; contbr. numerous articles to profl. jours. Mem. Am. Geophys. Union. Achievements include study of secular variation and its global features on the territory of central Europe. Home: Cernokostelecka 2111, CZ-10000 Praha Czech Republic

PODSKOCHY, ALEXANDER, physician, researcher; b. Tukums, Kurzeme, Latvia, Mar. 5, 1971; arrived in Sweden, 1995; s. Kazimir and Margarita (Gedzune) P. MD, Med Acad. Latvia, Riga, 1995. Physician St. Eriks Eye Hosp., Stockholm, 1995—; rschr. Karolinska Inst., Stockholm, 1996—. Contbr. articles to profl. jours. Recipient grant Hildur Pettersson Found., 1999, Synframjandets Forskningfond, 2000. Mem. Assn. for Rsch. in Vision and Ophthalmology, European Assn. for Vision and Eye Rsch. Home: Tomtrattsvagen 25, 12931 Hagersten Sweden Office: St Eriks Eye Hosp, Polhemsgatan 50, 11282 Stockholm Sweden

POE, RANDALL ELLSWORTH, public relations executive, author; b. Colorado Springs, Colo., Nov. 2, 1935; s. Everett E. and Emilie (Hamburger) P.; m. M. Catherine Ferguson, June 12, 1959 (div. July 1988); 1 child, Andrea Catherine. BA in Journalism, U. Calif., San Jose, 1958. Exec. dir. pub. rels. The Conf. Bd., N.Y.C., 1961-68, news dir., 1968-74, news dir./media mgr., 1974-88, dir. comm., exec. dir., 1988—. Contbr. articles to major mags., chpts. to books. Office: The Conf Bd 845 3rd Ave New York NY 10022-6601

POERTNER, HANS OTTO, zoologist, ecophysiologist, educator, researcher; b. Buende, Germany, Feb. 22, 1955; s. Otto and Irma (Meyer) P.; m. Ursula Berkel, Aug. 19, 1980; children: Daniel, Lisa. PhD in Natural Scis., Heinrich-Heine U., Duesseldorf, Germany, 1983, habil. in zoology, 1990. Rsch. scientist U. Duesseldorf, Germany, 1981-84, 84-92; Heisenberg fellow German Rsch. Coun., Alfred-Wegener Inst., Bremerhaven, 1992-94; prof. Alfred-Wegener Inst., Bremerhaven, 1994—, dep. divsn. head, 1994-99, divsn. head, 1999—; rsch. fellow Max Planck Inst., Goettingen, Germany, 1985-86, Acadia U., Wolfville, Can., 1986-87, Dalhousie U., Halifax, Can., 1987. Guest editor Marine Behaviour and Physiology, 1995; editl. bd. Jour. Comparative Physiology; co-editor (with R. O'Dor and D. Macmillan) Physiology of Cephalopod Molluscs, 1995, (with R. Playle) Cold Ocean Physiology, 1998. Mem. Am. Physiol. Soc., Soc. Exptl. Biology, European Soc. Comparative Physiol. Biochemistry, Deutsch Soc. Zoology. Avocations: photography, bird watching, hiking. Office: Alfred Wegener Inst, Columbusstrasse, 27568 Bremerhaven Germany

POGAČNIK, JOŽE, literature educator; b. Kovor, Slovenia, Mar. 14, 1933; s. Franc and Frančiška (Lombar) P.; m. Nina Aleksandrov; children: Jagna, Ana-Maria. Doctoral degree, Philos. Faculty, Zagreb, Croatia, 1963; student, Slavisches Seminar, Gottingen, Germany, 1975-76, Columbia U., 1981. Cert. in Slavic langs. and lits. Asst. Philos. Faculty, Zagreb, 1959-69, prof., 1969-81; prof. Faculty for Edn., Osijek, Croatia, 1981-90; prof. Faculty for Edn., Maribor, Slovenia, 1990-95, prof. emeritus, 1995—; dean Philos. Faculty, Novi Sad, 1973-75, Faculty for Edn., Osijek, 1990-91, Maribor, 1993-95. Humboldt-Stiftung fellow Slavisches Seminar, 1975-76; Fulbright grantee Columbia U., 1981. Mem. Slovenian Acad., Acad. of Scis. Göttingen. Avocations: recreational activities. Home: Koroška 118, 2000 Maribor Slovenia Office: U Maribor Faculty of Edn, Koroška 160, 2000 Maribor Slovenia

POGANY, DIONYZ, physics and microelectronics researcher; b. Bratislava, Slovakia, Oct. 28, 1963; s. Dionyz and Sarlota (Kowarikova) P.; m. Marta Horobova, Oct. 4, 1997; 1 child, Julia. Diploma in engring., Slovak Tech. U., Bratislava, 1987; PhD in Microelectronics, INSA de Lyon, France, 1994. Rschr. inst. Physics, Slovak Acad. Sci., Bratislava, 1987-90; postdoctoral fellow France Telecom CNET, Grenoble, France, 1994-95; rschr. Inst. Solid State Electronics, Vienna (Austria) Tech. U., 1995—, group leader, 1999; rschr. Inst. Elec. Engring. Slovak Acad. Scis., Bratislava, 1996-99. Contbr. over 50 articles to sci. jours. and conf. procs. Recipient prize Ministry of Edn., 1987. Mem. Assn. Friends of France, Electrostatic Discharge Assn. Lutheran. Avocations: music, art, reading, abstract painting, travel. Office: TU Vienna Inst Solid State, Floragasse 7, A-1040 Vienna Austria

POGGI, LUIGI CARDINAL, archbishop; b. Piacenza, Italy, Nov. 25, 1917. With Sec. of State; ordained titular archbishop Forontoniana, 1965; apostolic del. Ctrl. Africa, 1965; nuncio Peru; head Holy See's Del. Permanent Contact with Govt. of Poland, 1974; nuncio Italy, 1986-92; pro-librarian and pro-archivist Holy Roman Church, 1992-94, archivist and libr., 1994; created and proclaimed cardinal, 1994. Office: Archbishop, 00120 Vatican City Vatican City

POGGI, SILVANO NICOLÓ, communications company executive; b. Calice Ligure, Savona, Italy, Dec. 1, 1939; s. Emilio Poggi and Felice Lucarini; m. Giuseppina Maria Enrico, Aug. 31, 1963; children: Alessandro, Stefania, Paolo Enrico. Student, Navy Acad., Livorno, Italy, 1961; radar specialization, Livorno, Italy, 1965; student, NATO Def. Coll., Rome, 1975. Commd. officer Italian Navy, 1957, advanced through grades to commdg. officer, 1974, ret., 1978; sales mgr. GEC-Marconi Spa, Italy, 1978-91; regional mgr. GEC-Marconi Comm., 1992-96; mng. dir., regional mgr. Marconi Comm., Romania, 1996—. Author: Operations at Sea, 1973. Pres. Sports Assn. Football Club, Albenga, 1979-85. Fellow AFCEA. Social Democrat. Roman Catholic. Avocations: sailing, motor racing, tennis. Home: Via Regione Bagnoli 33, 17036 Leca Algenga Savona, Italy

POGGIANTI, BIANCA MARIA, astronomer; b. Pisa, Italy, Apr. 5, 1967; d. Rimaco and Anna Paola (Giovannini) P.; m. Andrè R.G.H. Cohen, 1999. Degree in physics, U. Pisa, 1991; PhD in Astronomy, Padova (Italy) U., 1995. Rschr., grantee Kapteyn Inst., Groningen, The Netherlands, 1995-96; postdoctoral Inst. Astronomy and Royal Greenwich Obs., Cambridge, Eng., 1996-98; permanent rsch. astronomer Astron. Obs. Padova, 1998—; astron. observer La Palma, La Silla, Gornergrat; invited spkr. and presenter in field. Contbr. articles to profl. jours. and conf. procs., including Astrophys. Jour., Astronomy & Astrophysics; contbr. over 11 articles to books. Rsch. grantee U. Pisa, 1995, Astronomy Coun. Groningen, 1996; Euro. rsch. fellow Network on Galaxy Formation, Cambridge, 1996-98. Avocations: reading, swimming, skiing. Home: Via Mestre 4, Padova 35142, Italy Office: Osservatorio Astronomico, Vicolo Dell'Osservatorio 5, Padova 35142, Italy

POGLIANI, LIONELLO, physical chemistry educator; b. Milan, May 1, 1943; s. Giovanni and Fernanda (Zappa) P. D in Chemistry, U. Firenze, Italy, 1969. Rsch. fellow Ctr. Nuc. Studies, Saclay, France, 1972-74, Tech. U., Berlin, 1974-78, Free U., Berlin, 1978-80; contract prof. U. Siena, Italy, 1981-84, 1985-87; vis. prof. U. Calif., San Francisco, 1984-85; assoc. prof. U. Calabria Rende (Cosenza), Italy, 1987—; vis. prof. U. Lisbon, 1993-94, 95-96. Contbr. more than 100 articles in different fields of phys. chemistry to sci. jours. 2nd lt. arty., Italian Mil., 1970-71. Recipient GM Neural Trauma Rsch. award, San Francisco, 1985. Mem. AAAS. Avocations: foreign languages, literature, music, travel, history of science. Office: U Calabria, Dept Chemistry, 87030 Rende Italy

POGNER, KARL-HEINZ, linguist, researcher; b. Trier, Germany, Nov. 6, 1957; arrived in Denmark, 1988; PhD, Odense (Denmark) U., 1996. Fgn. lectr. Odense U., 1988-96; assoc. prof. So. Denmark Bus. Sch., 1996-98, Copenhagen Bus. Sch., 1998—. Author: Schreiben im Beruf als Handeln im Fach, 1999; editor: At Skrive, Schreiben, Writing, 1992, More About Writing, 1994, Writing: Text and Interaction, 1997; chief editor Odense Working Papers in Lang. and Comm., 1993-96; co-editor Textproduktion: HyperText, Text, KonText, 1999. Mem. Danish Assn. Applied Linguistics, European Assn. for Rsch. on Learning and Instrn. Office: So Danmark Bus Sch, Copenhagen Bus Sch, Dalgas Have 15, DK-2000 Frederiksberg Denmark

POGNONEC, YVES MAURICE, steel products executive; b. Rennes, Bretagne, France, Jan. 21, 1948; came to U.S., 1983; s. Jean P. and Simone J. (Boudot) P. M in Engring., Centrale Paris, 1970; MA in Bus., CPA, Paris, 1982. Cons. Office of Graham Parker, Paris, 1972-75; sales mgr. fittings dept. Vallourec S.A., Paris, 1975-79, mgr. engring. dept., 1980-82; v.p. mktg. and sales Vallourec Inc., Houston, 1983-88, exec. v.p., 1989-97, pres., 1998—; v.p. Vallourec & Mannesmann Tubes Corp., 1997—; advisor French Fgn. Trade Counselors, Houston, 1987—; bd. dirs. Cablofil Inc. Bd. trustees Awty Internat. Sch., Houston, 1997—. Lt. French Air Force, 1970-71. Mem. Assn. Ecole Centrale, Nat. Assn. Steel Pipe Distbrs. (bd. dirs. 1990—). Avocations: pilot, scuba diving, tennis. Office: Vallourec Inc 1990 Post Oak Blvd Ste 1400 Houston TX 77056-3836

POGORELOV, VICTOR IVANOVICH, physicist; b. Moscow, Dec. 15, 1933; s. Ivan Konstantinovich Pogorelov and Sophia Markovna Eisenberg; m. Margarita Azatovna Ter-Zakharyan, Sept. 29, 1962; children: Julia, Nina. Physicist, U. Gorkiy, 1956, PhD, 1964. Rschr. Russian Acad. Scis., Moscow, 1956—. Contbr. articles to profl. jours. Achievements include new method of solutions of differential equations on the basis of Riemannian geometry and its use for the wave equation; the generalization of the well-known Fresnel's formulae for electromagnetic waves near the boundary of two media; the mathematical explanation of the plasmic mechanism for forming polar lights; the relativity variant of the Fermat's principle etc. Home: Perovskaya 46-3-32, 111141 Moscow Russia Office: Inst Applied Geophysics, Rostokinskaya 9, 129128 Moscow Russia

POGREBNOI, ALEXANDER MIKHAILOVICH, physics educator, researcher; b. Zvenigorod, Moscow, Russia, June 29, 1953; s. Mikhail Akimovich and Polina Petrovna (Ryaboshlyk) P.; m. Tatiana Pavlovna Rozukova, July 12, 1977; children: Kirill, Mikhail. Engr., Inst. Chemistry and Tech., Ivanovo, Russia, 1975, PhD, 1981. Cert. in engring.; docent in physics. Jr. rschr. Inst. Chemistry and Tech., Ivanovo, 1975-81, sr. educator, 1981-83, docent dept. physics, 1988—; sr. rschr. Inst. Artificial Leathers and Films, Ivanovo, 1983-88. Contbr. articles to profl. jours. Grantee, Internat. Sci. Found., 1993, 95, 97, 99, Competitive Ctr. of Grants in Field of Fundamental Natural Scis., 1995, 96, 99. Avocation: ice fishing. Home: Radischev St 20 Apt 30, 153035 Ivanovo Russia Office: Ivanovo State U Chem/Tech, Engels St 7, 153460 Ivanovo Russia

POGRIBNY, WLODZIMIERZ, science educator; b. Sahnovschyna, Charkiv, Ukraine, Nov. 19, 1938; s. Alexander A. and Halina P. Pogribny; m. Maria M. Chudak, Dec. 14, 1963 (div. 1975); children: Iryna, Ol'ga; m. Iryna M. Gorbatchova, July 1, 1978; 1 child, Olena. PhD, Inst. Elec. Dynamic Acad. Sci., Kiev, Ukraine, 1970; DSc, Acad. Sci. USSR, Moscow, 1986. Rsch. scientist L'viv (Ukraine) Phys.-Mech. Inst. Acad. Sci., 1960-87; head of chair State U. L'viv Poly., 1987-96; prof. Inst. Telecomms. U. Tech. and Agr., Bydgoszcz, Poland, 1996—; sci. cons. Nat. Sci. Agy., Kiev, 1990—. Author: On-Board Systems of Signals Processing, 1984, Delta Modulation in Digital Signals Processing, 1990; author, editor (with I. Razankivski and Yu. Yurchenko) Principles of Information Processes in Robotics, 1995; contbr. over 250 articles to profl. jours.; inventor in field.

Mem. Internat. Acad. Informatization, Internat. Soc. Optical Engring. Avocations: mountaineering, mountain skiing. Fax: (4852) 3408310. E-mail: pohry@atr.bydgoszcz.pl. Home: 5/35 Jaruzynska, PL85-792 Bydgoszcz Poland Office: Inst Telecomm UTA, 7 Kaliskiego Ave, PL85-791 Bydgoszcz Poland

POGUE, JOHN MARSHALL, physician, editor, researcher; b. Washington, Sept. 21, 1945; s. L(loyd) Welch and Mary Ellen (Edgerton) P. AB with honors, Princeton U.; MD, Georgetown U. Diplomate Nat. Bd. Med. Examiners. Intern/resident Georgetown U. Hosp., Washington; editor, author Bradford Jour., 1983—; historian Gov. Bradford Compact, 1996—, surgeon, 1999—; spkr. in field of cardiology. Designer ofcl. flag Gov. William Bradford Flag, 1987 (New Constellation award Nat. Flag Found., 1996); editor, contbr.: Pogue/Pollock/Polk Genealogy as Mirrored in History, From Scotland to Northern Ireland/Ulster, Ohio, and Westward, 1990 (recipient 7 awards, 5 first-place in genealogy and 2 meritorious in history); assoc. editor: Hereditary Soc. Blue Book, 1997—; author: Herbert Martin Giffin, M.D., A Role Model Physician and a Doctor's Doctor: From Princeton to Johns Hopkins, Mayo Clinic, U.S. Navy and Yater Clinic, 2000; contbr. articles in field of cardiology. Fellow Royal Soc. Medicine, Royal Microscopical Soc. Oxford, Royal Statis. Soc., Royal Geog. Soc., Royal Soc. Arts; mem. AMA, Cardiothoracic Sect. Royal Soc. Medicine, Coun. Clin. Cardiology of Am. Heart Assn., Laennec Cardiovascular Sound Soc., European Soc. Cardiology, Am. Soc. Echocardiography (coun. on cardiac sonography, coun. on intraoperative echocardiography), Internat. Soc. Cardiovasc. Ultrasound, Internat. Cardiac Doppler Soc., Internat. Soc. Electrocardiology (Glasgow U.), Internat. Soc. for Holter and Noninvasive Electrocardiology, Soc. for Cardiovasc. Magnetic Resonance, Heart Failure Soc. Am., Internat. Soc. Cardiovascular Pharmacotherapy (Switzerland), Internat. Soc. Heart Rsch. (Can.), Cardiac Muscle Soc., World Heart Fedn. (Switzerland), Assn. Am. Med. Colls. (individual), Friends of Nat. Libr. Medicine (founding mem.), Friends of McGill U. Osler Med. Libr., Friends of Oxford U. Mus. of History of Sci., Ashmolean Natural History Soc. Oxford, Oxford Hist. Soc., Internat. Shakespeare Assn. Stratford-upon-Avon, Princeton U. Alumni Assn., Princeton Tigertones Alumni, Soc. of Mayflower Descs. D.C. (surgeon 1998—), Order Descs. of Colonial Physicians and Chirurgiens (surgeon gen. 1994-2000, chmn. hon. membership com. 1994—, v.p. 2000—), Provincial Families Maryland, Royal Soc. Medicine Book Club, RSM Music Soc./Royal Soc. Medicine Music Club, The Princeton Univ. Club (Washington), Oxford Bibliogr. Soc. of Oxford U. Bodleian Libr. Avocations: reading Shakespeare, classical music. Home and Office: 5204 Kenwood Ave Chevy Chase MD 20815-6604

POGUE, L(LOYD) WELCH, lawyer; b. Grant, Iowa, Oct. 21, 1899; s. Leander Welch and Myrtle Viola (Casey) P.; m. Mary Ellen Edgerton, Sept. 8, 1926; children: Richard Welch, William Lloyd, John Marshall. AB, U. Nebr., 1924; JD, U. Mich., 1926; SJD, Harvard U., 1927. Bar: Mass., N.Y., D.C., Ohio, U.S. Supreme Ct. Assoc. Ropes, Gray, Boyden and Perkins, 1927-33; ptnr. affiliated firm Searle, James and Crawford, N.Y.C., 1933-38; asst. gen. counsel CAB, 1938-39, gen. counsel, through 1941, chmn. bd., 1942-46; mem., mng. ptnr. Pogue & Neal, Washington, 1946-67; Washington mng. ptnr. Jones, Day, Reavis & Pogue, Washington, 1967-79, ret., 1981; Lindbergh Meml. lectr. Nat. Air and Space Mus., Smithsonian Inst., 1991; presenter essay 50th Ann. Internat. Civil Aviation Orgn., Montreal, 1994; spkr. in field. Author: International Civil Air Transport—Transition Following WW II, 1979, Pogue/Pollock/Polk Genealogy as Mirrored in History, 1990 (1st pl. in Anna Ford Family history book contest 1991, Nat. Genealogical Soc. award for excellence genealogy and family history 1992, William H. and Benjamin Harrison Book award Coun. Ohio Genealogists 1992, Outstanding Achievement award County and Regional History category Ohio Assn. Hist. Socs. and Mus. 1992, 1st pl. award Iowa Washington County Geneal. Soc. 1994, cert. commendation Am. Assn. State and Local History 1994, 1st place award Lake Havasu Geneal. Soc. 1996); contbr. articles to profl. publs. Mem. U.S. dels.: Chgo. Internat. Civil Aviation Conf., 1944; vice chmn. Bermuda United Kingdom-U.S. Conf., 1946; vice chmn. Provisional Internat. Civil Aviation Orgn. Assembly, 1946; active Internat. Civil Aviation Orgn. Assembly, 1947. With AUS, 1918. Recipient Elder Statesman of Aviation award Nat. Aeronautic Assn., Golden Eagle award Soc. Sr. Aerospace Execs., 1st annual recipient of L. Welch Pogue award for Aviation Achievement, McGraw-Hill Orgn.'s Aviation Week Group, 1994; fellow Am. Helicopter Soc., Benjamin Franklin fellow Royal Soc. Arts. Fellow Royal Aero. Soc.; mem. AIAA (hon.), Soc. of Sr. Aerospace Execs. (hon. mem.), Helicopter Assn. Internat. (hon. mem.), Am. Air Mus. in Britain (founding mem.), Can. Aeronautics and Space Inst., Nat. Aeronautic Assn. (pres. 1947), Nat. Air and Space Soc. (founder), Nat. Geneal. Soc., Soc. Sr. Aerospace Execs., New Eng. Hist. Geneal. Soc. (life, former trustee), Ohio Geneal. Soc. (life), Md. Geneal. Soc. (life), Md. Hist. Soc. (life), Provincial Families of Md., First Families of Ohio, Met. Club, Univ. Club, Wings Club (hon., N.Y.C.), Bohemian Club (San Francisco), Cosmos Club, Masons, Order of the First World War (charter), Aero Club of Washington (hon. mem.), Am. Legion (cert. of 80 years continuous membership). Home: 5204 Kenwood Ave Chevy Chase MD 20815-6604 Office: Jones Day Reavis & Pogue 51 Louisiana Ave NW Washington DC 20001-2113

POGUE, MARY ELLEN E. (MRS. L(LOYD) WELCH POGUE), youth and community worker; b. Fremont, Nebr., Oct. 27, 1904; d. Frank Eugene and Mary Nettie (Coe) Edgerton; m. L. Welch Pogue, Sept. 8, 1926; children: Richard Welch, William Lloyd, John Marshall. BFA in Edn. Music, U. Nebr., 1926; studied violin with Harrison Keller, Boston Conservatory of Music, 1926-28; studied violin Kemp Stillings, Violin Master Class, 1935-37. Mem. Potomac String Ensemble, Washington, 1939-80. Compiler, editor: Favorite Menus and Recipes of Mary Edgerton of Aurora, Nebraska, 1963, Family History of Frank Eugene Edgerton and Mary Coe Edgerton of Aurora, Nebraska, 1965. Historian, Gov. William Bradford Compact, 1966—; vice chmn. Montgomery County (Md.) Victory Garden Ctr., 1946-47; pres. Bethesda Cmty. Garden Club, 1946-47; founder Montgomery County YWCA, bd. dirs., 1946-50, 52-55; founder Welcome to Washington Internat. Club Music Group, 1967—; co-founder Group Piano in Montgomery County, Md. schs., 1954. Recipient Gov. William Bradford Compact Cert. of Merit award, 1970, Outstanding Svc. award Bethesda United Meth. Ch., 1984, Bethesda Cmty. Garden Club award, 1985, 93, Devoted Svc. award Mayflower Descendants in D.C., 1985, 89, Welcome to Washington Internat. Club award, 1986, Mortar Board award, 1986. Mem. Gen. Soc. Mayflower Descs., Soc. Mayflower Descs. D.C. (dir. D.C. 1954—, elder 1971-91, elder emeritus 1991—), Nat. Soc. Daus. Founders and Patriots Am., PEO Sisterhood (pres. 1957-59, charter mem. chpt. R, 75 Year Mem. Tribute), Mortar Bd. Alumnae Club (pres. 1965-67, award 1986), Nat. Capitol Area Fedn. Garden Clubs, Nat. Coun. State Garden Clubs, Bethesda United Meth. Women, Nat. Geneal. Soc., New Eng. Historic Geneal. Soc. (life), Ohio Geneal. Soc. (life), Md. Geneal. Soc., Md. Hist. Soc., Conn. Soc. Genealogists, Pilgrim Soc. (life), Plimoth Plantation, Hereditary Order Descs. Colonial Govs., Nat. Soc. Magna Charta Dames, Colonial Order of Crown, Sovereign Colonial Soc. Ams. Royal Descent, Order of Descs. Colonial Physicians and Chirurgiens, Hereditary Soc. Blue Book (perpetual mem.), Nat. Soc. Women Descs. Ancient and Hon. Arty. Co., First Families Ohio, First Families Nebr., Century Families Nebr., Oreg. Trail Pioneers, Sons and Daus. Colonial and Antebellum Bench and Bar 1565-1861 (charter), Welcome to Washington Internat. Club, Ind. Agy. Women (assoc.), Capital Spkrs. Club (Washington), The Plantagenet Soc., Soc. Descs. Knights of Most Noble Order of Garter, DAR, Order Ams. Armorial Ancestry, Saybrook Colony Founders Assn., Soc. Founders Norwich Conn. (cert. desc. Richard Edgerton), Kenwood Country Club, Alpha Phi (75 yr. mem. cert.), Alpha Rho Tau, Delta Omicron Music (life). Methodist. Avocations: genealogy, gardening, music. Home: 5204 Kenwood Ave Chevy Chase MD 20815-6604

POH-FITZPATRICK, MAUREEN B., dermatologist, educator; b. N.Y.C., Feb. 24, 1943; d. Edgar J. and Alice M. (Kennedy) Poh; m. Brian J. Fitzpatrick, Dec. 26, 1970. BS, Siena Coll., 1964; MD, U. Tenn., 1967. Diplomate Am. Bd. Dermatology. Fellow in cardiology Regional Med. Ctr., Memphis, 1968, intern, 1968-69; resident in dermatology Barnes Hosp., St. Louis, 1969-72; asst. Washington U. Sch. Medicine, St. Louis, 1969-72; clin. instr. NYU Sch. Medicine, 1973; from asst. prof. to assoc. prof. dermatology Columbia U. Coll. Physicians & Surgeons, N.Y.C., 1973-86; prof. dermatology and medicine N.Y. Med. Coll., 1987-94; from assoc. prof. to prof. dermatology Columbia U. Coll. Physicians & Surgeons, 1994-98, prof. emeritus, 1998—; clin. prof. medicine U. Tenn. Coll. Medicine, 1998—. Grantee Nat. Inst. Arthritis, Musculoskeletal & Skin Diseases, 1976-98. Fellow Am. Acad. Dermatology; mem. Memphis Dermatology Soc., N.Y. Dermatol. Soc., N.Y. Acad. Medicine. Republican. Roman Catholic. Office: 15 Cedar Lane Ter Ossining NY 10562-2919

POHJOLA, PEKKA TAPANI, systems analyst; b. Jokioinen, Finland, July 3, 1942; s. Urpo and Anni (Konttori) P.; m. Ritva Kaarina Grönlund, Sept. 6, 1970; children: Pia Eviliina, Olli Kaarle Pekka. MSc in Physics, U. Turku, Finland, 1970. Info. mgr. Ovako Oy-Ab, Imatra, Finland, 1970-87; lab. engr. Ovako Oy-Ab, Imatra, 1978-80, project planner, 1987-88; product cons. Carelcomp Forestry, Imatra, 1988, automatic data processing analyst, 1989-98; automatic data processing analyst TietoEnator, Imatra, 1998—. Avocation: singing. Home: Sinikankuja 6, FIN55100 Imatra Finland Office: TietoEnator, Havurinne 3, FIN55800 Imatra Finland

POHJOLA-SINTONEN, SINIKKA HANNELE, internist; b. Lahti, Finland, July 29, 1949; d. Oiva Alvar and Helvi Selma (Jarvi) Pohjola; m. Matti Tapani Sintonen, Dec. 17, 1976; children: Kaarina, Sakari. MD, Helsinki U., 1976, MA, 1997. Registrar in internal medicine Helsinki U. Ctrl. Hosp., 1979-85, cons. in cardiology, 1989-90; rsch. fellow in cardiology Harvard Med. Sch., Boston, 1986-87; asst. chief ICU/CCU Helsinki U. Hosp., 1991-93; asst. chief unit of internal medicine Peijas Hosp., Vantaa, Finland, 1993—; mem. Nat. Agy. of Medicines, Helsinki, 1996—; docent in medicine Helsinki U., 1997—; expert European Agy. for the Evaluation of Med. Products, 1997—. Fellow European Soc. Cardiology; mem. Finnish Cardiol. Soc., Finnish Soc. Internists. Avocation: family. Home: Kruunuvuorenkatu 3A5, 00160 Helsinki 16, Finland Office: Peijas Hosp, Sairaalakatu 1, 01400 Vantaa Finland

POHL, ADOLF LEOPOLD, clinical chemist, quality assurance consultant; b. St. Poelten, Austria, Dec. 14, 1936; s. Adolf Theodor and Cornelia Maria Anna (Moerth) P.; m. Ingrid Maria Antonia Payer, Feb. 24, 1962 (div. Dec. 11, 1975); children: Martin, Ulrike; m. Nanako Tanaka, Mar. 14, 1989; 1 child, Anna Yumi. Grad. in classical studies, Stiftsgymnasium Melk, 1954; BSc, U. Vienna, 1957, MSc, 1965, DPhil, 1968. Rsch. asst. med. dept. I U. Vienna Med. Sch., 1967-69, asst. prof., 1969-85, head erythrocyte enzyme lab. med. dept. I, 1969-85, founder tumor marker lab., 1978, head tumor marker lab., 1984-85, assoc. prof. med. dept. I, dept. chemotherapy, 1985-87, assoc. prof. dept. clin. labs., 1987-97; quality assurance cons. Med. Pharm. Rsch. Ctr., Vienna, 1993—. Mem. editl. bd. Cancer Molecular Biology Jour., 1994—; contbr. articles to profl. jours., chpts. to books. Recipient Austrian Med. Assn. award, 1969. Mem. Am. Assn. for Clin. Chemistry, N.Y. Acad. Scis., IEEE Computer Soc., Drug Info. Assn. Achievements include discovery in human blood serum of a new ADP-ribosyltransferase, implementation of advanced data analysis in clinical chemistry, detection by new micromethods of phospholipid metabolism in red blood cell membranes and study of its abnormalities in hemolytic anemia; research on serum glycosyltransferases as possible cancer markers and critical analysis of galactosyltransferase heterogeneity; leading of 1st foldboat expedition on Tenojoki, 1st behavioral studies of Thai ferret badger. Avocations: botany and wildlife research, humanitarianism, philosophy, poetry. Home: Lambrechtgasse 3/10, A-1040 Vienna Austria

POHL, JÜRGEN ERNST, medicine educator, physician; b. Frankfurt, Germany; arrived in U.K., 1962; s. Ernst Albert and Hildegard Anneliese (Gorschlüter) P.; m. Irene Jean Wickham, Aug. 1963; children: John, Julia, Andrea, David, Deborah. BSc, U. Melbourne, Australia, 1956; MB, BChir, U. Melbourne, 1959. Registered gen. medicine and cardiovascular medicine. Cons. physician clin. pharmacology and medicine U. Manchester, Eng., 1972-76; lectr. in therapeutics U. Manchester, 1972-76; cons. physician medicine and cardiology, sr. lectr. medicine U. Leicester, Eng., 1974—; dir. postgrad. edn. Leicester Gen. Hosp. Trust, 1995—; mem. South Lincolnshire Health Authority, 1982-90, 92-93; expert witness register, 1990—. Sectional editor Jour. Cardiovascular Risk, 1995; contbr. chpts. to books and articles to profl. jours. Fellow Royal Coll. Physicians; mem. Assn. Physicians, Brit. Cardiac Soc., Med. Rsch. Soc., Renal Assn., Mensa. Liberal. Lutheran. Avocations: chess, bridge, reading, languages. Home: 9 Woodland Ave Stoneygate, Leicester LE2 3HG, England Office: Leicester Gen Hosp, Gwendolen Rd, Leicester LE5 4PW, England

POHL, KATHLEEN SHARON, editor; b. Sandusky, Mich., Apr. 7, 1951; d. Gerald Arthur and Elizabeth Louise (Neukamm) P.; m. Bruce Mark Allen Reynolds, June 11, 1982. BA in Spanish, Valparaiso U., 1973; MA in English, No. Mich. U., 1975. Producer, dir. fine arts Sta. WNMU-FM, Marquette, Mich., 1981-82; instr. communications Waukesha County (Wis.) Tech. Inst., 1983; editor Ideals mag., Milw., 1983-85; editor, mng. editor Raintree Pubs., Milw., 1985-87; mng. editor, now exec. editor Country Woman mag., Greendale, Wis., 1987—; exec. editor Country Handcrafts mag., Greendale, 1990-93, Taste of Home Mag., Greendale, Wis., 1993—; editor Talk About Pets, Greendale, 1994-95; exec. editor Quick Cooking Mag., 1998—. Author nature book series, 1985-87; sr. editor: Country Woman Christmas Book, 1996, 97; mng. editor: Irwin the Sock (Chgo. Book Clinic award 1988); sr. editor: Country Woman Christmas Book, 1997; exec. editor Taste of Home's Quick Cooking Mag., 1998—, Down the Aisle Countr Style, 2000. Mem. Nat. Mus. of Women in Arts, Alpha Lambda Delta (hon.). Home: N54 W26326 Lisbon Rd Sussex WI 53089-4249 Office: Country Woman Mag 5400 S 60th St Greendale WI 53129-1404

POHLIT, ADRIAN MARTIN, chemistry educator, researcher; b. Chester, Pa., Feb. 15, 1965; arrived in Brazil, 1989; s. Helmut Martin Pohlit and Barbara Zerbe Macnab; m. Claudéte Inês Kronbauer, June 18, 1994; 1 child: Martina Louise Kronbauer Pohlit. BAs in Chemistry and Film with honors, U. Calif., Berkeley, 1983; PhD in Organic Chemistry, U. São Paulo, Brazil, 1994. Postdoctoral U. Estadua Campinas, Brazil, 1995-97; vis. prof. U. Amazonas, Manaus, Brazil, 1997—. Contbr. articles to profl. jours. Grantee CNPq, Brazil, 1999—. Mem. Am. Assn. Av. Sci., Brazil Chem. Soc., Nat. Geog. Soc. Democrat. Avocation: cinema/film. Office: Univ do Amazonas, Gial Otavio Jordao Ramos, 69000000 Manaus Amazonas, Brazil

POHORECKI, RYSZARD ARTUR, chemical engineering educator, researcher; b. Warsaw, Poland, Feb. 10, 1936; s. Artur and Halina Pohorecki; m. Anna Jakubowska, Apr. 3, 1958; 1 child, Marek. MSc, Warsaw U. Tech., 1959, PhD, 1964, DSc, 1970. From asst. prof. to assoc. prof. Warsaw U. Tech., 1957-80, prof., 1980-87, full prof., 1987—; vis. scholar U. Cambridge, 1965-66; vis. prof. Inst. Poly. Toulouse, France, 1988-89. Author: (books) Thermodynamics and Kinetics of Chemical Engineering Processes, 1977 (Ministry award 1978), Numerical Examples in Thermodynamic and Kinetics of Chemical Engineering Processes, 1979; editor: (book) Heat and Mass Transfer in Gas-Liquid Systems, 1980, (jour.) The Chem. Engring. Jour., 1992. V.p. Alliance of Univs. for Democracy, Knoxville, 1993. Recipient Sci. award Polish Acad. of Sci., 1977, 84. Mem. Cambridge Soc., Polish Acad. Scis. (vice chmn. dept. tech. scis. 1998). Home: Naleczowska 47M68, 02-922 Warsaw Poland Office: Warsaw U of Tech, Warynskiego 1, 00-645 Warsaw Poland

POHTILA, ELJAS HEIKKI PIETARI, forestry researcher, educator; b. Salla, Finland, Aug. 1, 1943; s. Pietari Viljam and Hilja Matilda (Kellokumpu) P.; m. Raili Kaarina Peippo, 1969; children: Tatu, Jukka. MSc in Forestry, U. Helsinki, Finland, 1970, Licentiate of Forestry, 1975; D in Forestry, 1977. Rsch. specialist Finnish Forest Rsch. Inst., Rovaniemi, 1978-80; head officer Dist. Forest Bd. of Lapland, Rovaniemi, 1980-87; mng. dir. R&D dept. for wood procurement and prodn. Finnish Forest Industries Fedn., Helsinki, 1987-88; dir. gen. Finnish Forest Rsch. Inst., Helsinki, 1988—. Author: Reforestation of Ploughed Sites in Finnish Lapland, 1977, Importance of National Forest Inventories in Forestry Research and Practice, 1992. Bd. dirs. Finnish Forest and Park Svc., Vantaa, 1994-97. Capt. Finnish Army, 1963-64. Mem. Royal Swedish Acad. Agr. and Forestry, Internat. Boreal Forest Rsch. Assn. (chmn. 1994-95), Russian Acad. and Agrl. Scis. Avocations: hunting, fishing, reading, music, volleyball. Office: Finnish Forest Rsch Inst, Unioninkatu 40A, SF-00170 Helsinki Finland

POILVET, YANN, magazine editor; b. Landehen, France, Mar. 8, 1927; s. Pierre and Elise (Gicquel) P.; m. Therese Depeix, Nov. 6, 1947; children: Patrick, Helene, Anne-Edith, Yannick, Berc'hed. BA, Coll. Mezeray, France. Chancellor de l'Association des Ecirvain; exec. v.p. de Bretagne Europe; v.p. du Syndicat National de periodique; pres., dir. gen. de la Sapepig; pres. du Cercle Celtique An. Roman Catholic. Avocations: Celtic music and language. Home: Ar Bargodou, 12 rue de la Ville Commault, 22400 Landehen Brittany, France Office: ARMOR Mag, ARMOR Mag, 7 pont st Jacques BP419, 22404 Cedex Lamballe Brittany, France

POINDEXTER, RICHARD GROVER, minister; b. Carthage, N.C., June 9, 1945; s. Romie Dallas and Mollie (Underwood) P.; m. Glenda Joyce Tudor, Feb. 23, 1968; children: Tonya Joyce, Amanda Caroline. BA in Sociology, N.C. State U., 1967; MDiv., New Orleans Bapt. Theol. Sem., 1973. Ordained to ministry So. Bapt. Conv., 1972. Assoc. pastor, youth dir. Amite Bapt. Ch., Denham Springs, La., 1971-72; Sunday sch. cons. Canal Blvd. Bapt. Ch., New Orleans, 1973; pastor First Bapt. Ch., LaGrange, N.C., 1973-77, Anderson Grove Bapt. Ch., Albemarle, N.C., 1977-86, Rankin Bapt. Ch., Greensboro, N.C., 1986-96, First Bapt. Ch., Haw River, N.C., 1996—. State chaplain N.C. Army NG, Raleigh, 1996—; trustee Christian Action League N.C., Raleigh, 1985—. Office: First Bapt Ch 508 E Main St Haw River NC 27258-9652

POIRSON, BRIGITTE, English language educator; b. Dole, France, May 8, 1951; d. Paul and Thérèse (Mittaine) Pernot; m. Patrick Poirson; 1 child, Claire. MA in Arts, Dijon U., 1973, postgrad., 2000—. Asst. High Wycombe Coll., Eng., 1973-74; tchr. high sch. Lycée Dole, 1974-75; univ. lectr. Plymouth Coll., Exeter U., Eng., 1975-76; tchr. high sch. Lycée Franche-Comté, France, 1976-97; probation officer Lure (France) Ct., 1980-82; lectr. C. of C., Vesoul, France, 1995; book translator. Contbr. poetry to various books, 1977—. Mem. Soc. des Gens de Lettres. Home: 1 Bis Pl Calmette, 70 000 Navenne France Office: Lycée le Marteroy, 7 Ave A Briand, 70 000 Vesoul France

POISSONNIER, MARIE-HELENE, obstetrician/gynecologist; b. Paris, June 10, 1949; d. Joseph Achille Alexandre and Arlelte Louise Victorine (Debonnaire) P.; 1 child, Alexandra. MD, U. Paris, 1976, grad. ob-gyn., 1979, grad. sterility and echography, 1980. Hosp. physician St. Vincent de Paul Hosp., Paris, 1988—. Contbr. articles to profl. jours. Mem. European Obstetric and Gynecologist Soc., Soc. de Medecine Perinatale, Club Francophone de Medecine Foetale, Internat. Fetal Medicine and Surgery Soc., Coll. Nat. d'Echographie Foetale, Coll. des Gynecologues et Obstetricien. Avocations: tennis, boat and traveling. Office: D Poissonnier, 20 Boulevard de Republique, Saint Cloud 92210, France

POKORNY, ALEX DANIEL, psychiatrist; b. Taylor, Tex., Oct. 18, 1918; s. John Robert and Olga Frances (Susen) P.; m. Jeanice Brooke Allen, Mar. 13, 1948; children: Martha, Ross, Ellen, Sally. BA, U. Tex., 1939; MD, U. Tex., Galveston, 1942. Diplomate Am. Bd. Psychiatry and Neurology. Psychiatrist VA Hosp., Houston, 1949-55, chief psychiatry and neurology svc., 1955-73; from instr. to prof. psychiatry Baylor Coll. Medicine, Houston, 1949-89, acting chmn. dept. psychiatry, 1968-72, vice chmn. dept. psychiatry, 1972-89; ret. Editor (with others) 7 books, including Phenomenology and Treatment of Anxiety, 1979, Phenomenology and Treatment of Alcoholism, 1980, Phenomenology and Treatment of Psychosexual Disorders, 1983, Phenomenology and Treatment of Psychiatric Emergencies, 1984; editor numerous publs.; contbr. 100 articles to profl. jours. Capt. U.S. Army, 1943-46. Recipient Amersa award for Excellence in Med. Edu. Assn. Med. Edn. & Rsch. Substance Abuse, 1989, Dublin award Am. Assn. Suicidology, 1992. Fellow AAAS, Am. Psychiat. Assn. (life), Am. Coll. Psychiatrists (life); mem. Soc. Psychophysiological Rsch. Home: 813 Atwell St Bellaire TX 77401-4718

POKORNY, JAN, food science educator, nutrition consultant; b. Strmechy, Czech Republic, June 30, 1928; s. Vladimir and Bedriska (Nagyova) P.; m. Vera Chlupova, Aug. 22, 1954; children: Daniel, Paula. MChem, Tech. U., Brno, Czechia, 1951; PhD in Chemistry, U. Chem. Tech., Prague, 1956; DSc, State Com., Prague, 1972. Rschr. oil and fat industry, Usti, Czechia, 1951-55; asst. prof. Inst. Chem. Tech., Prague, 1955-65, assoc. prof., 1965-85, prof., 1985—, dean Faculty Food Biochemistry Tech., 1990-96. Recipient Nat. prize 1st degree in Food Sci., 1973, Balling medal Food Sci. and Tech., 1998, Chevreul medal French Oil Chemistry Soc., 1978, Fachini medal Italian Oil Chemistry Soc., 1974. Mem. Czech Nutrition Soc. (pres. 1994—), Czech Acad. Agr. and Food (chair 1990-96), Czech. Chem. Soc. (hon.; Hanus medal), Polish Acad. Sci. (hon.). Presbyterian. Home: Kapradova 10, 10600 Prague 10, Czechia Office: Vscht Technicka 5, 166 28 Prague 6, Czechia

POKORNY, JAROSLAV, physiologist; b. Prague, Czechoslovakia, Oct. 21, 1945; s. Jaroslav and Lydie (Zverinova) P.; m. Hana Waldhauserova, Apr. 10, 1970; children: Karla, Pavel. MD, Charles U., 1968, DSc, 1995; PhD, Czechoslovak Acad. Scis., 1976. Med. diplomate. Postdoctoral fellow Czechoslovak Acad. of Scis., Prague, 1969-71, rsch. student, 1971-74; asst. prof. Faculty of Medicine/Charles U., Prague, 1974-88; assoc. prof. Faculty of Medicine/Charles U., 1988-97, prof., 1997—. Officer Czechoslovak Army, 1968-69. Mem. Czechoslovak Physiol. Soc., Internat. Soc. Devel. Neurosci., Internat. Brain Rsch. Orgn. Office: Inst Physiology/Charles U, First Faculty Medicine, Albertov 5, 128 00 Prague 2, Czech Republic

POKORNY, LAJOS, radiologist, consultant, educator; b. Orosháza, Hungary, Aug. 17, 1935; s. Lajos and Lenke Pokorny; m. Anna Nöszt, June 8, 1974; children: Anna, Katalin. MD, Albert Szent-Gyorgyi Med. U., Szeged, Hungary, 1959, PhD, 1982. Cert. pathologist; cert. radiologist. Resident in pathology Albert Szent-Gyorgyi Med. U., Szeged, 1959-62, resident in radiology, 1962-64, asst., 1965-70, 1st asst., 1971-79, lectr., sr. lectr., 1980-88, assoc. prof., 1989—; fellow Med. Acad., Erfurt, Germany, 1964-65; cons. Internat. Med. Ctr., Szeged, 1994—. Co-author: Ionische/Nichtionische Kontrastmittel, 1990, 100 Years of Hungarian Radiology, 1996; contbr. artcles to profl. jours. Mem. Soc. Hungarian Radiologists, Soc. International Radiology. Avocations: travelling, skating, rowing. Office: Internat Med Ctr, 6 Semmelweis Str., H-6720 Szeged Hungary

POLAERT, RÉMY HENRI, electrical engineer, researcher; b. Saint André, Nord, France, Apr. 6, 1937; s. Henri Victor and Marie Louise (Taufour) P.; m. Françoise Solange Bearez, Sept. 28, 1963; children: Florence, Hugues, Etienne. Degree in elec. engring., Hautes Etudes Industrielle, Lille, France, 1957; BS, U. Lille, France, 1958, DSc in Radioelectricity, 1961. Rsch. engr. Lab. Electronique Philips, Limeil, France, 1963-69, Nat. Lab.-Philips Laboratorium, Eindhoven, The Netherlands, 1969-70; rsch. engr. Lab. Electronique Philips, Limeil, 1970-78, head photodetection group, 1978-80, head tv projection predevelopment, 1980-87, sr. scientist detection photonics, 1987-91, expert scientist detection photonics, 1991—; Lt. Air Force Res. Contbr. articles to profl. jours. Mem. Soc. des Electriciens et Electroniciens, Soc. des Ingenieurs de l'Automobile. Achievements include contribution and patents in photodetection, secondary emission, tv projection, physical sensors, microwave speedometer, x-ray images, image intensifiers, microchannel plates electron multipliers, high speed photography and related matters, man-made machine interface, touchpad, infra-red remote thermal sensor, fluorescence sensor for dental plaque detection, gas sensors for domestic appliances. Avocation; singing in a choir. E-mail: rpolaert@club-internet.fr. Home and Office: 19 Rue des Merles, 94440 Villecresnes France

POLAJI, SABAJI BHAGWAN, artist; b. Redi, India, Sept. 2, 1943; s. Bhagwan Vishram and Mathura Bhagwan Indumati P.; m. Suchitra Sabaji Ranjana, Nov. 25, 1971; 1 child, Rajendraprasad. Art Master, J.J. Sch. of Art, Bombay, 1968, GD Art, 1977. Art tchr. Tutorial H.S., Shiroda, India, 1961-62, Vidyavihar H.S., Sawantwadi, India, 1963-64, B.L. Ruia H.S., Bombay, 1964-96; hon. art dir. Nat. Soc. for Clean Cities, India, 1979-97; art dir. Bombay. Exhbns. include: Max-Mueller Bhuvan, 1989, Jahangir Art Gallery, 1992, Monsoon Show at Nehru Centre, 1993, Painting Exhbn. at U.S.A. 1993 & 1995, Indian Consulate, U.S.A. N.Y., 1997 (50th Ann. of Indian Independence), Edison, N.J. Expo, 1997, Bank of India, N.Y., 1997, State Bank of India, N.Y., 1997, Nehru Ctr. Art Gallery, 1999, Hotel Sheraton, Phila., 1999, others; paintings collected at Middlesex County Cultural and Heritage Commn., Canara Engring., Gov. of Maharashtra-Shri, Tata Svcs. Ltd., Indian Oil Corp., Consulate of Peru, numerous others. Recipient numerous Best Tchr. awards Lions Club, 1967-69, 71, 73, 74, 75, 88, Bombay Arts and Sports, 1965, 66, 70, 72, 74, 76, 83, 87, 88, others.

POLÁK, STANISLAV, historian; b. Orlová, Czechoslovakia, Jan. 4, 1936; s. Jiří and Marie (Hummelová) P. PhD, Charles U., Prague, 1968. Archivist

Dist. Archive, Příbram, Czechoslovakia, 1960-92; rsch. worker Masaryk Inst. Prague, 1992—. Author: T.G. Masaryk, 1994, enlarged edit., 2000, T.G. Masaryk--His Life in Words in Pictures (text in Czech and English), 2000; contbr. articles to profl. jours. Unitarian. Avocation: classical music. Office: Acad of Scis, Acad of Scis, Masaryk Inst Na Florenci 3, 110 00 Prague Czech Republic

POLÁKOVÁ, JOLANA, philosopher, researcher; b. Prague, Czech Republic, May 14, 1951; d. Václav and Miluse (Prusakova) P. PhD, Charles U., Prague, 1975. Rsch. student Inst. Philosophy and Sociology of Czech Acad. Scis., Prague, 1975-81; editor Avicenum, Prague, 1982-89; rsch. scientist Inst. Philosophy of Czech Acad. Scis., Prague, 1990—. Author: Mental Creativity: A General Theory, 1993, 2d edit., 1997, The Philosophy of Dialogue, 1993, 2d edit., 1996, The Possibilities of Transcendence, 1994, , 2d edit., 1995, 3d edit., 1996, The Perspective of Hope: Search for Transcendence in the Postmodern Era, 1994, 2d edit., 1996, Dialogue with God and Philosophy, 1999. Recipient URAM Award for Excellence in Creative Scholarly Writing, Internat. Soc. for Study of Human Ideas on Ultimate Reality and Meaning, 1993, Tom Stoppard prize Charta 77 Found. Stockholm, 1997. Mem. N.Y. Acad. Scis., European Assn. for Cath. Theology. Home: Hornomlynska 5/1232, 14800 Prague Czech Republic Office: Czech Academy Science, Jilska 1 Ustav Filosoficky, 11000 Prague Czech Republic

POLAND, ANNE SPELLMAN, counselor; b. Woodward, Iowa, June 13, 1922; d. Martin E. and M. Corinne (Geneser) Spellman; m. Philip H. Poland, July 26, 1947 (des. July 1990); children: Margaret, Mary, Suzanne, Patricia, John, Christopher, Eileen, Mark, George, Martha, Stephen, Peter. BS, Marycrest Coll., Davenport, Iowa, 1942; MS, Drake U., Des Moines, 1970; PhD, Iowa State U., 1989. Tchr. home econs. Westside (Iowa) Consol. Sch., 1942-43; tchr. sci. Minburn (Iowa) Sch. Dist., 1943-44; ext. home economist Carroll Farm Bur. and Iowa State Ext. Svc., 1944-47; elem. tchr. Carroll Cmty. Sch. Dist., 1967-74, guidance counselor, 1974—. Author: Global Peace Education, 1989. Office: Carroll Cmty Schs 525 E 18th St Carroll IA 51401

POLAND, SYDNEY WADE, software designer; b. Heflin, La., June 18, 1933; s. Howard Brazil and Helen Lucille (Ryan) P.; m. Evelyn Lucille Miller, Nov. 30, 1956; children: Susan Elizabeth Poland Finch, Stanley Eugene. BS in Physics, La. Tech. U., Ruston, 1955; MS in Math., Tex. Christian U., 1962; MS in Computer Sci., So. Meth. U., 1972. Sci. programmer Temco Aircraft co., Dallas, 1955-58, Chance Vought Aircraft, Dallas, 1958-60; sys. programmer Tex. Instruments Geophys. Svcs., Dallas, 1960-72; sys. designer Tex. Instruments Calculator Divsn., Dallas, 1972-77, Tex. Instruments Equipment Group, Dallas, 1977-80, Tex. Instruments Corp. Engrng. Ctr., Dallas, 1980-82; sr. cons. BP Exploration, Dallas and Houston, 1982-90; sys. designer Tex. Instruments DSP R&D, Stafford, Tex., 1990-95; sr. sys. software designer Tex. Instruments Tech. Tng., Stafford, 1995-98. Author manual and applications notes. Mem. Am. Bonanza Soc., Aircraft Owners and Pilots Assn. Achievements include 26 patents for calculators, digital signal processors, others. Avocations: music, reading, travel. Home: 22309 Prince George Ln Katy TX 77449-2811

POLANYI, JOHN CHARLES, chemist, educator; b. Jan. 23, 1929; m. Anne Ferrar Davidson, 1958; 2 children. BSc, Manchester (Eng.) U., 1949, MSc, 1950, PhD, 1952, DSc, 1964; DSc (hon.), U. Waterloo, 1970, Meml. U., 1976, McMaster U., 1977, Carleton U., 1981, Harvard U., 1982, Rensselaer U., Brock U., 1984, Lethbridge U., Sherbrooke U., Laval U., Victoria U., Ottawa U., 1987, Manchester U. and York U., Eng., 1988, U. Montreal, Acadia U., 1989, Weizmann Inst., Israel, 1989, U. Bari, Italy, 1990, U. B.C., 1990, McGill U., 1990, Queen's U., 1992, Free U. Berlin, 1993, Laurentian U., 1995, U. Toronto, 1995, U. Liverpool, 1995; LLD (hon.), Trent U., 1977, Dalhousie U., 1983, St. Francis-Xavier U., 1984; LLD (hon.), Concordia U., 1990; LLD (hon.), Calgary U., 1994. Mem. faculty dept. chemistry U. Toronto, Ont., Can., 1956—; prof. U. Toronto, 1962—; William D. Harkins lectr. U. Chgo., 1970; Reilly lectr. U. Notre Dame, 1970; Purves lectr. McGill U., 1971; F.J. Toole lectr. U. N.B., 1974; Philips lectr. Haverford Coll., 1974; Kistiakowsky lectr. Harvard U., 1975; Camille and Henry Dreyfus lectr. U. Kans., 1975; J.W.T. Spinks lectr. U. Sask., Can., 1976; Laird lectr. U. Western Ont., 1976; CIL Disting. lectr. Simon Fraser U., 1977; Gucker lectr. Ind. U., 1977; Jacob Bronowski meml. lectr. U. Toronto, 1978; Hutchinson lectr. U. Rochester, N.Y., 1979; Priestley lectr. Pa. State U., 1980; Barré lectr. U. Montreal, 1982; Sherman Fairchild disting. scholar Calif. Inst. Tech., 1982; Chute lectr. Dalhousie U., 1983; Redman lectr. McMaster U., 1983; Wiegand lectr. U. Toronto, 1984; Edward U. Condon lectr. U. Colo., 1984; John A. Allan lectr. U. Alta., 1984; John E. Willard lectr. U. Wis.; 1984, Owen Holmes lectr. U. Lethbridge, 1985; Walker-Ames prof. U. Wash., 1986, John W. Cowper disting. vis. lectr. U. Buffalo, SUNY, 1986; vis. prof. chemistry Tex. A&M U., 1986; Disting. vis. spkr. U. Calgary, 1987; Morino lectr. U. Japan, 1987; J.T. Wilson lectr. Ontario Sci. Ctr., 1987; Welsh lectr. U. Toronto, 1987; Spiers Meml. lectr. Faraday div. Royal Soc. Chemistry, 1987; Polanyi lectr. Internat. Union Pure & Applied Chemistry, 1988; W.B. Lewis lectr. Atomic Energy of Can. Ltd., 1988; Consol. Bathurst vis. lectr. Concordia U., 1988; Priestman lectr. U. N.B., 1988; Killam lectr. U. Windsor, 1988; Herzberg lectr. Carleton U., 1988; Falconbridge lectr. Laurentian U., 1988; DuPont lectr. Ind. U., 1989, C.R. Mueller lectr. Purdue U., 1989; Luther lectr. U. Regina, 1989; Franklin lectr. Rice U., 1990; Laurier lectr. Wilfred Laurier U., 1990; Pratt lectr. U. Va., 1990; Goodrich lectr. Case Western Res. U., 1990; Phillips lectr. U. Pitts., 1991; Albert Noyes lectr. U. Tex., 1992; John and Lois Dove Meml. lectr. U. Toronto, 1992, Fritz London lectr. Duke U., 1993; Castle lectr. U. South Fla., 1993; Linus Pauling lectr. Calif. Inst. Tech., 1994; Hagey lectr. U. Waterloo, 1995; Larkin Stuart lectr. U. Toronto, 1995; Hungerford lectr., 1995, York Club, 1995; disting. lectr. ser. Meml. U., 1995, John C. Polanyi nobel laureate lectr. U. Toronto, 1995, Floyd E. Bartell Meml. lectr. U. Mich., 1996, Christian Culture award lectr. Assumption U., 1996, Liversidge lectr. U. Sidney, Australia, 1996; dist. scientist lectr. Apotex, Inc., 1996; mem. sci. adv. bd. Max Plank Inst. for Quantum Optics, Fed. Republic Germany, 1982-92; mem. nat. adv. bd. on Sci. and Tech., 1987-89; hon. cons. Inst. Molecular Sci., Okazaki, Japan, 1989-94; bd. dirs. Steacie Inst. Molecular Scis., Ottawa, Can., 1991—; founding mem., pres. Can. Com. of Sci. and Scholars; Beam Disting. vis. prof. U. Iowa, 1992, Charles M. & Martha Hitchcock prof. U. Calif., Berkeley, 1994; Young Meml. visitor Royal Mil. Coll., 1994. Co-editor: (with F.G. Griffiths) The Dangers of Nuclear War, 1979; contbr. articles to jours., mags., newspapers; producer: film Concepts in Reaction Dynamics, 1970. Mem. Queen's Privy Coun. for Can., 1992; bd. dirs. Can. Ctr. for Arms Control and Disarmament; founding mem. Can. Pugwash Com., 1960. Decorated officer Order of Can., companion Order of Can., knight grand cross Order St. John of Jerusalem; recipient Marlow medal Faraday Soc., 1962, Centenary medal Chem. Soc. Gt. Brit., 1965, Noranda award Chem. Inst. Can., 1967, award Brit. Chem. Soc., 1971, Mack award and lectureship Ohio State U., 1969, medal Chem. Inst. Can., 1976, Remsen award and lectureship Am. Chem. Soc., 1978, Nobel Prize in Chemistry, 1986, Izaak Walton Killam Meml. prize, 1988, John C. Polanyi award Can. Soc. Chemistry, 1992, Floyd E. Bartell Meml. lectureship U. Mich., 1996, Liversidge lectureship U. Sydney, Australia, 1996, Christian Culture award and lectureship Assumption U., 1996; co-recipient (with N. Bartlett) Steacie prize, 1965, Wolf prize in chemistry, 1982; named Sloan Found. fellow, 1959-63, Guggenheim fellow, 1979-80 Geoffrey Frew fellow, 1996, Dist. Anniversary fellow Australian Nat. U., 1996. Fellow Royal Soc. Can. (founding mem., pres., com. on scholarly freedom, Marshall Tory medal 1977), Royal Soc. London (Royal medal 1989, Bakerian Lectr. and award 1994), Royal Soc. Edinburgh, Royal Soc. Chemistry (hon., Michael Polanyi medal 1989), Chem. Inst. Can. (hon.); mem. NAS (fgn.), Am. Acad. Arts and Sci. (hon. fgn., mem. com. on internat. security studies), Pontifical Acad. Scis., Rome. Office: U Toronto Dept Chemistry, 80 St George St, Toronto, ON Canada M5S 3H6

POLASCIK, MARY ANN, ophthalmologist; b. Elkhorn, W.Va., Dec. 28, 1940; d. Michael and Elizabeth (Halko) Polascik; m. Joseph Ellie, Oct. 2, 1973; 1 dau., Laura Elizabeth Polascik Jr. BA, Rutgers U., 1967; MD, Pritzker Sch. Medicine, 1971. Jr. pharmacologist Ciba Pharm Co., Summit, N.J., 1961-67; intern Billings Hosp., Chgo., 1971-72; resident in ophthalmology U. Chgo. Hosp., 1972-75; practice medicine specializing in ophthalmology Dixon, Ill., 1975—; pres. McNichols Clinic, Ltd.; cons. ophthalmology, Jack Mabley Devel. Ctr., 1976-93; mem. staff Katherine Shaw Bethea Hosp. Bd. dirs. Sinnissippi Mental Health Ctr., 1977-82, Dixon Cmty. Trust Mental Health Ctr., 1989—. Mem. Am. Acad. Ophthalmology, Alpha Sigma Lambda, Galena Territory Club. Roman Catholic. Office: 1700 S Galena Ave Dixon IL 61021-9695

POLAY, ANNA See POLOY, ANNA

POLE, JACK RICHON, historian; b. London, Mar. 14, 1922; s. Joseph and Phoebe Louise (Rickards) P.; children: Ilsa, Nicholas, Lucy. BA, Oxford (U.K.) U., 1949; PhD, Princeton (N.J.) U., 1953; MA, Cambridge (U.K.) U., 1963. Lectr. Am. history U. Coll. London, 1953-63; reader in Am. history and govt. U. Cambridge, 1963-79; Rhodes prof. Am. history and instns. U. Oxford, 1979-89; emeritus fellow St. Catherine's Coll., Oxford, 1989—; vis. assoc. prof. U. Calif., Berkeley; vis. prof. U. Ghana, 1966, U. Chgo., 1969, U. Beijing, 1984; guest scholar Woodrow Wilson Ctr., Washington, 1978-79; Goleib fellow NYU Law Sch., 1990; vis. prof. Marshall-Wythe Sch. Law, 1991; v.p. Internat. Commn. for History of Rep. and Parliamentary Instns., 1990—. Author: Political Representation in England and the Origins of the American Republic, 1966, 2d edit., 1971, The Pursuit of Equality in American History, 1978, 2d edit., 1993, Paths to the American Past, 1979, The American Constitution For and Against, 1987; co-editor: Blackwell Ency. of the Am. Revolution, 1991, A Companion to the American Revolution, rev. edit., 2000, Freedom of Speech: Right or Privilege?, 1998; contbr. to Ency. Britannica 15th edit. Capt. Brit. Army, 1941-46. Recipient Emeritus award Brit. Acad., 1994; Ctr. for Advanced Study in Behavioral Scis. fellow, 1969-70, Commonwealth Fund Am. Studies fellow, 1957, Laverhulme Trust fellow, 1988-92. Fellow Royal Hist. Soc., Brit. Acad.; mem. Marylebone Cricket Club. Avocations: painting, cricket, writing. Home: 20 Divinity Rd, Oxford OX4 1LJ, United Kingdom Office: St Catherine's Coll, Oxford OX13UJ, United Kingdom

POLEDŇÁK, IVAN, musicologist, educator, researcher; b. Velké, Meziříči, Czech Republic, Dec. 31, 1931; s. František and Melanie (Novotná) P.; m. Marie Jandová, June 14, 1961 (div. Apr. 1966); 1 child, Petr; m. Stanislava Kuldová, Dec. 9, 1977. MSc, Masaryk U., Brno, Czechoslovakia, 1956; PhD, Charles U., Prague, Czechoslovakia, 1967, CSc, 1969; DSc, Czech Acad. Scis., Prague, 1989. Lectr. Masaryk U., 1956-59; sci. worker, lectr., head dept. music edn. Inst. for Pedagogical Rsch., Prague, 1959-68; sci. worker Inst. Musicology, Czechoslovak Acad. Scis., Prague, 1968-90, dir., 1990-97; pres. Czech Music Coun., 1993—; mem. Govtl. Accreditation Com. for Univs., 1993-97; prof. Charles U., Palacky U.; participant confs. in Ann Arbor, Mich., Brno, Dijon, France, Innsbruck, Austria, Interlochen, Mich., Lyon, France, Montreal, Que., Can., Moscow, Prague, Stockholm, Tokyo, Vienna, Austria; lectr. U. Pa., Phila., U. Copenhagen. Author or co-author: Czechoslovak Jazz-The Past and Present, 1967, Music and Its Conceptual System, 1981, Psychology for Music Conservatories, 1988, Concise Ency. of Music Psychology, 1984, Jazz Musician Jiří Stivín, 1989, Probes into Pop Music and Rock, 1992, Introduction to the Study of Musicology, 1995; co-editor: Ency. of Jazz and Modern Popular Music, vols. 1-4, 1980-90, Musicology, vols. 1-3, Foundations of Music Semiotics, vols. 1-3, 1992; contbr. numerous articles to profl. jours., including In Theory Only, Internat. Rev. Aesthetics and Sociology Music, Beiträge zur Musikwissenschaft. Recipient various awards for books. Mem. Czech Assn. Musicians and Musicologists (past pres.). Avocations: tennis, bridge, chess. Home: Na Petřinách 2, 162 00 Prague Czech Republic Office: Dept Musicology FF UP, Křizorskeho 8, 77000 Olomouc Czech Republic

POLEMARCHAKIS, HERACLES MICHAEL, social sciences educator; b. Athens, Greece, Oct. 2, 1952; s. Michael and Theodora (Kolymbade) P. AB, Yale U., 1973; PhD, Harvard U., 1977. Assoc. prof. Columbia U., N.Y.C., 1978-80; prof. Columbia U., 1980-90, U. Cath, Louvain, Belgium, 1990—; dir. rsch. Ctr. Planning and Econ. Rsch., Athens, 1987-88; pres. CORE U. Cath., Louvain, 1998—. Fellow Econometric Soc. Home: 25 Ave du General de Gaulle, 1050 Brussels Belgium Office: CORE, 34 Voie du Roman Pays, 1348 Louvain-la-Neuve Belgium

POLEMIS, DEMETRIOS IOANNOU, historian; b. Andros, Cyclades, Greece; s. Ioannis D. and Anthi A. (Balka) P.; m. Maria D. Raissi, Dec. 10, 1960; 1 child, Ioannis. BA, Columbia U., 1960, MA, 1961; PhD, U. London, 1964. Dir. Enomena Shipping Co., Piraeus, Greece, 1970—, Kaïreios Libr., Andros, Greece, 1987—. Author, editor Petalon, Vols. 1-7, 1977-99; editor: (book series) Andriaka Chronika, vols. 17-31, 1988-2000; author: The Doukai, 1968, (hist. album) The Sailing Ships of Andros, 1991 (award Acad. Athens 1992); author many books on Byzantine and Modern Greek history and lit. Greek Orthodox. Home: Apatouria, 845-00 Andros Greece

POLEMITOU, OLGA ANDREA, accountant; b. Nicosia, Cyprus, June 28, 1950; d. Takis and Georgia (Nicolaou) Chrysanthou. BA with honors, U. London, 1971; PhD, Ind. U., Bloomington, 1981. CPA, Ind. Asst. productivity officer Internat. Labor Office/Cyprus Productivity Ctr., Nicosia, 1971-74; cons. Arthur Young & Co., N.Y.C., 1981; mgr. Coopers & Lybrand, Newark, 1981-83; dir. Bell Atlantic, Reston, Va., 1983-97; v.p. corp. auditing Columbia Energy Group, Herndon, 1997—; chairperson adv. coun. Extended Day Care Community Edn., West Windsor Plainsboro, 1987-88. Contbr. articles to profl. jours. Bus. cons. project bus. Jr. Achievement, Indpls., 1984-85. Mem. NAFE, AICPAs, Nat. Trust for Hist. Preservation, Ind. CPA Soc., N.J. Soc. CPAs (sec. mems. in industry com.), Va. Soc. CPAs, Princeton Network of Profl. Women. Avocations: water skiing, tennis. Home: PO Box 2744 Reston VA 20195-0744 Office: Columbia Energy Group 13880 Dulles Corner Ln Herndon VA 20171-4600

POLENAKOVIĆ, MOMIR HARALAMPIE, nephrologist, educator, scientist; b. Skopje, Macedonia, Apr. 26, 1939; s. Haralampie Nikola and Radmila Stojan (Steic) P.; m. Biljana Stavre Filipche, July 10, 1966; children: Radmil, Hari. MD, U. Sts. Cyril & Methodius, Skopje, 1963, D. in Med. Sci., 1977. Cert. specialist interal medicine, nephrology and clin. immunology. Vice dean faculty medicine U. Sts. Cyril & Methodius, 1982-84, co-dir. nephrology, 1982-90, dir. neprhology, 1990—; cons. Aktuality V. Nefrologii; Fulbright vis. prof. in U.S., 1991-92. Advising editor Nephrology Dialysis Transplantation; editor/co-editor 5 med. books; author some 250 articles in field. IREX postdoctoral fellow, 1972-73; WHO fellow, 1983. Mem. Med. Assn. Macedonia (pres. 1984-87, highest awards), Macedonian Soc. Nephrology, Dialysis, Transplantation and Artificial Organs (pres. 1992—), Macedonian Acad. Scis. and Arts, Macedonian-Am. Assn. for Friendship (pres. 1994), Yugoslav Soc. Nephrology (pres. 1985-89), Serbian Acad. Scis. & Arts, European Dialysis and Transplant Assn., European Renal Assn. (ex-officio coun. 1989-91), European Soc. Artificial Organs (gov. 1996). Avocation: collecting stamps. Office: Dept Nephrology Faculty Med, Vodnjanska 17 PO Box 576, 91000 Skopje Macedonia

POLENSKY-KSIĄŻEK, HENRYK, pilot, educator; b. Miechów, Cracow, Poland, Apr. 12, 1953; arrived in Sweden, 1983; s. Jan and Jadwiga (Dzieciot) Ksi—żek; m. Krystyna Bogacz, July 9, 1974 (div. 1986); m. Anna Zachwieja, Jan. 4, 1989; children: Agata Ksiazek, Robert Ksiazek, Artur Polensky. Pilot, Air Force Pilot Acad., Dęblin, Poland, 1974, Am. Flight Acad., Okla., 1992. Lic. airline transport pilot, Poland, U.S., Sweden; lic. instr. fixed wings multiengine jets and helicopters. Pilot-instr. Polish Air Force, Gdańsk, 1974-82; capt. pilot Flygtjänst, Klimpfjäl, Sweden, 1987, Greenland Air Charter, 1988-89, Hal Aviation Inc., Mo., 1989, Euro Flight-Fed. Express, U.S. and Sweden, 1990-93, Florus Air Safaris, Mombasa, Kenya, 1994; mng. dir. Polensky Inc., Sweden, 1994—; also bd. dirs. Polensky Inc.; pilot LOT, Warsaw, 1997—. Author: Kamikaze's Come Back, 1998. Recipient Bronze medal (with Polish Team at World Helicopter Championships). Avocations: karate, music. Home: Solstândsg 30, 415 09 Göteborg Sweden

POLENZ, JOANNA MAGDA, psychiatrist; b. Cracow, Poland, Oct. 20, 1936; came to U.S., 1961; d. Mieczyslaw and Nusia (Goldberger) Uberall; m. Daryl Louis Polenz, July 8, 1962 (div. 1991); children: Teresa Ann, Daryl Philip, Elizabeth Sophia. MD, U. Sydney, Australia, 1960; MPH, Columbia U., 1992. Diplomate Am. Bd. Psychiatry and Neurology. Intern Bklyn. Hosp., 1961-62; resident in psychiatry Mt. Sinai Med. Ctr., N.Y.C., 1962-65; ednl. fellow Mt. Sinai Med. Ctr., 1965-66, rsch. assoc., 1966-67; med. dir. Tappan Zee clin. Phelps Meml. Hosp., Tarrytown, N.Y., 1968-71, dir. dept. psychiatry, 1972-77; sr. attending psychiatrist Meml. Hosp. Ctr., 1972-93; pvt. practice Briarcliff Manor, N.Y., 1971-91; physician Joint Commn. Accreditation of Healthcare Orgns., Oakbrook Terrace, Ill., 1993—; pres. Van Sant Healthcare Assoc. Inc., N.Y.C., 1998—; lectr. in field. Author: In Defense of Marriage, 1981; (with other) Test Your Marriage IQ, 1984, Test Your Success IQ, 1985, The Last Sick Generation, 2000; contbr. articles to profl. jours.; numerous TV appearances including Phil Donahue, 1988, Oprah Winfrey 1984. Grant Found. grant, 1970. Fellow Am. Psychiat. Assn.; mem. AMA, Am. Coll. Physician Execs., N.Y. Acad. Scis., Pan Am. Med. Assn., Westchester Psychiat. Assn. (sec. 1982-85, chmn. fellowship com. 1989-98). Avocations: travel, international affairs. Fax: 212-828-2507. Office: Van Sant Healthcare Assocs 360 E 88th St Ste 37A New York NY 10128-4993

POLESHCHUK, OLEG KHEMOVICH, chemist, researcher, educator; b. Krasnojarsk, Siberia, Russia, Apr. 24, 1947; s. Khema Nakhimovich and Natalia Timofeevna (Anisimova) P.; m. Olga Vladimirovna Zueva, Apr. 24, 1968 (div. June 1983); 1 child, Maria; m. Svetlana Yurievna Ogarkova, June 22, 1983; 1 child, Natalia. MSc, Tomsk (Russia) U., 1970; PhD, Inst. Oil Chemistry, Tomsk, 1976. Jr. rsch. worker Inst. Oil Chemistry, Tomsk, 1970-76, sr. rsch. worker, 1976-80, head of group, 1980-82; sr. tchr. Pedagogical U., Tomsk, 1983-89, docent, dep. dean, 1989-97, prof., head chemistry dept., 1997—; prof. A. Mickiewicz U., Poznan, Poland, 1992—; participant in internat. confs. Contbg. author Ency. of Spectroscopy and Spectrometry; contbr. articles to profl. jours. Chmn. Soviet of sci. Youth, Tomsk, 1980-83. Recipient Tomsk Party Orgn. prize, 1975; grantee Soros Found., 1993, Russian Ministry Edn., 1998-2000, Deutsche Forschungsgemeinschaft, 1998, Fundacja popierania nauki, 1998, 2000, DAAD, 1999, others. Mem. N.Y. Acad. Scis., Best Europe (U.K.). Avocations: reading, computers, skiing, travel. Email: root@polsh.tomsk.su. Home: Vavilova 4/52, 634055 Tomsk Siberia, Russia Office: Tomsk Pedagogical Univ, Komsomolskii 75, 634041 Tomsk Siberia, Russia

POLESKIE, STEPHEN FRANCIS, artist, educator, writer; b. Pringle, Pa., June 3, 1938; s. Stephen Francis and Antoinette Elizabeth (Chludzinski) P.; m. Jeanne Mackin, 1979. B.S., Wilkes Coll., 1959; postgrad., New Sch. for Social Research, 1961. Owner Chiron Press, N.Y.C., 1961-68; instr. Sch. Visual Arts, N.Y.C., 1968; prof. art Cornell U., Ithaca, N.Y., 1969—; vis. critic Pratt Graphic Arts Center, N.Y.C., 1965-68; vis. artist Colgate U., Hamilton, N.Y., 1973, USSR, 1979, Escuela de Bellas Artes, Honduras, 1980, Loughborough Coll. Art and Design, Eng., 1989; vis. prof. U. Calif., Berkeley, 1976. Contbr. short stories to mags. and book; one-man shows include Louis K. Meisel Gallery, N.Y.C., 1978-80, Galerie Kupinski, Stuttgart, Germany, 1979, Palace of Culture and Sci., Warsaw, Poland, 1979, Sky Art Presentation, MIT, 1981, Am. Ctr., Belgrade, 1981, William and Mary Coll., 1983, McPherson Art Gallery, Victoria, B.C., Can., 1984, Studio D'Ars, Milan, 1985, Gallery Flaviana, Locarno, Switzerland, 1985, Il Salatto Gallery, Como, Italy, 1985, Galleria Schneider, Rome, 1987, Mus. Sztuki Lodz, Poland, 1987, Alternative Mus., Lido di Spina, Italy, 1987, Galerie Klaus Lea, Munich, 1987, Patricia Carega Gallery, Washington, 1988, Nine Columns Gallery, Palermo, Italy, 1988, John Hansard Gallery, Southampton, Eng., 1989, Quai Art Gallery, Isle of Wight, Eng., 1989, Lee Art Gallery, Clemson (S.C.) U., 1990, Apogeeairway, N.Y.C., 1991, Nine Columns Gallery, Brescia, Italy, 1991, Glenn Curtiss Mus., Hammondsport, N.Y., 1993, Caproni Mus., Trento, Italy, 1995, Temple U., Rome, 1995, Gallery of Modern Art, Maribor, Slovenia, 1995, Palazzo Communale, Todi, Italy, 1995, Palazzo Della Pretura, Piacenza, Italy; works represented in collections at Met. Mus., N.Y.C., Mus. Modern Art, N.Y.C., Victoria and Albert Mus., London, Whitney Mus., N.Y.C., Walker Art Center, Mpls., Tate Gallery, London, Fort Worth Art Center, Nat. Collection, Washington, others. Am. Fedn. of Arts grantee, 1965; Carnegie Found. grantee, 1967; Nat. Endowment for Arts grantee, 1973; N.Y. State Council on Arts grantee, 1973; Creative Artists Public Service Program grantee, 1978; Best Found. grantee, 1985. Mem. Exptl. Aircraft Assn., Aircraft Owners and Pilots Assn., Polish Acad. Sci. and Art, Internat. Aerobatic Club. Home: PO Box 849 Ithaca NY 14851-0849 Office: Cornell U Tjaden Hall Ithaca NY 14853

POLETIKA, MICHAEL FEDOROVICH, research scientist, educator; b. Nigniy Novgorod, Russia, July 24, 1922; s. Elena Konstantinovna Poletika; m. Polina Nikitichna Kasantzeva, Nov. 18, 1952; children: Irina, Tamara, Lev. MS in Machining, Tomsk (Russia) Polytechnic U., 1946, PhD, 1954; DSc, Aircraft Tech. Inst., Moscow, 1966. Asst. prof. Tomsk Polytech. U., 1949-52, assoc. prof., 1952-63, sr. rschr., 1963-64, prof., 1966-79, 85—, head machining acad. dept., 1979-85, sci. advisor, 1966—; head machining acad. dept. Indsl. Inst., Tjumen, 1964-66. Author: Devices for Cutting Forces Measurement, 1963, Contact Loads on the Tool Cutting Surfaces, 1968; co-author: Development of Cmetal Cutting Science, 1967, Key Engineering Materials: Advanced Ceramic Tools for Machining, 1998. Named Hon. Man in Sci., Russian Fedn., 1994; recipient Labor medal Govt. Russian Fedn., 1970, 93, 95. Mem. Assn. Tech. Scientists. Avocation: gardening. E-mail: push@rac.tpu.edu.ru. Office: Tomsk Polytechnic U, 30 Lenin Av, 634034 Tomsk Siberia, Russia

POLETTO, BERNARD, physician; b. Ecoven, France, Feb. 20, 1946; s. Charles Jean and Olga Odette (Clery) P.; m. Nadine Dintzner, Sept. 6, 1969; children: Bruno, Anne-Yseult. MD, Paris U., 1972, SC, 1974. Project leader RU, France, 1979-85, head med. affairs, 1985-90, mktg. dir., 1990-95; v.p. HMR, France, 1995—; med. cons. U. Paris; lectr. U. Dijon, France, 1978-85; advisor Health Ministry, Paris, 1979-91. Capt. French Health Svc., 1973. Avocations: history, history of music. Home: 16 rue de la Forme, 95460 Ezanville France

POLEY, JANET KATHLEEN, consortium executive; b. Nebraska City, Nebr., Dec. 17, 1945; d. Austin Otto and Kathleen J. (McGowen) Wirth; m. Jeffrey McPherrin Poley, Dec. 23, 1969; 1 child, Lisa Dawn. BS, U. Nebr., Lincoln, 1966, MS, 1971, PhD, 1975. Mem. faculty dept. agrl. comm. U. Nebr., Lincoln, 1966-75; asst. dep. dir. internat. tng. USDA, Washington, 1976-80; project advisor, chief of party USDA/U.S. AID, Tanzania, 1980-86; coord. devel. program Mgmt. Ctr., USDA, Washington, 1986-89; dir. comm., info. and tech. USDA Extension Svc., Washington, 1989-94; pres. ADEC Nat. Consortium, Lincoln, 1994—; speaker in field. Contbr. numerous articles to profl. jours. Internat. Host family; mem. bd. advisors Nat. Agrl. Libr.; mem. Nebr. Agrl. Rels. Coun. Recipient Disting. Alumni award Coll. Home Econs./U. Nebr., 1986, Internat. Svc. award U. Nebr., Lincoln, 1996, numerous others. Mem. Agrl. Communicators in Edn. (award for excellence in computers 1991, award for excellence in distance edn. 1994), Ams. Communicating Electronically, Friends of Tanzania Soc., Smithsonian Instn., Nat. Trust for Historic Preservation, World Future Soc., Rotary Internat., Gamma Sigma Delta, Alpha Epsilon Rho, Alpha Lambda Delta, Omicron Nu, Phi Upsilon Omicron. Avocations: travel, music, technology. Address: ADEC U Nebr C218 Animal Sci PO Box 830952 Lincoln NE 68583-0952

POLI, ALEJANDRO, hospital administrator, accountant; b. Buenos Aires, Nov. 28, 1956; s. Severino and Pilar Asunción (Gonzalvo) P.; m. Lesley Jane Arnott, Mar. 15, 1985; children: Francisco Alejandro, Clara Jane. Grad. pub. acct., Nat. U. Buenos Aires, 1979. Audit mgr. Arthur Andersen, Buenos Aires, 1981-88; contr. BCP, Buenos Aires, 1998-94; pres. Commitment SA, Buenos Aires, 1995-97; gen. dir. Brit. Hosp. Buenos Aires, 1997—. Roman Catholic. Avocations: writing, reading, tennis, travel. Office: British Hosp Buenos Aires, Perdriel 74, 1280 Buenos Aires Argentina

POLIATZKY, NATHAN, physicist, researcher; b. Leningrad, USSR, Apr. 13, 1955; s. Yakar Haskin and Julia Baron Poliatzky; m. Hadassah Gutmann, Oct. 25, 1983; children: Deborah, Chava, Levia, Dina, Scheindel, Sarah, Hanoch, Baruch, Frumet, Rachel. BSc, Technicshe Univ. Berlin, 1979, MSc, 1981; PhD, Weizmann Inst., Rehovot, Israel, 1993. Rschr. Tu Berlin, 1981-86; scientist Fed. Inst. Tech. Inst. Theoretical Physics, Zürich, Switzerland, 1993—. Contbr. articles to profl. jours. Wigner fellow Wigner Found., Berlin, 1987. Fellow N.Y. Acad. Scis. Avocation: music. Office: Fin Rsch Labs, Austrasse 49, CH 8045 Zurich Switzerland

POLICH, JOHN ELLIOTT, marketing consultant, educator, writer; b. Ft. Bragg, Calif., May 18, 1946; s. Aloysius J. and Mildred I. (Johnson) P.; m. Ina Lee Selden, Apr. 23, 1982. BA in Journalism cum laude, Ariz. State U., 1968; MA in Comm., Stanford U., 1974, PhD in Comm., 1976. Reporter Evening Am., Phoenix, 1964-65, Ariz. Rep., Phoenix, 1965-67, KTAR-TV (now KPNX-TV), Phoenix, 1967-68, Express, San Antonio, 1968-72; staff

writer Free Press, Detroit, 1975-76; mgr. Media Divsn. Market Opinion Rsch., 1976-77; mktg. rsch. mgr. N.Y. Times, N.Y.C., 1977-82, group mktg. dir. regional newspapers, 1982-84; pres. Simmons Scarborough, N.Y.C., 1984-86; assoc. dir. freedom forum media studies ctr. Columbia U., N.Y.C., 1986-88; pres. MOR/New York, N.Y.C., 1988-90; global media and visual mktg. prof. Fordham Grad. Sch. Bus. at Lincoln Ctr., N.Y.C., 1990-99; pres. Polich Media Mgmt., N.Y.C., 1991—; mem. faculty New Sch. for Social Rsch., N.Y.C., 1999—; clients include Asia Found., Guangzhou (China) Daily Press Group, CBS TV Network; newspaper rsch. coun. Advt. Rsch. Found., N.Y., 1978-84; readership and mktg. com. Am. Newspaper Pub. Assn., 1979-82; editorial bd. Newspaper Rsch. Jour., 1981—; dean's adv. coun. Newhouse Sch. Pub. Communication Syracuse (N.Y.) U., 1984-89. Co-author: Newspaper Leadership, 1986; travel editl. and art photographer; contbr. articles to profl. jours. Inducted Hall of Fame Walter Cronkite Sch. of Journalism and Telecom. Coll. of Pub. Programs, Ariz. State U., 1998. Mem. Am. Soc. Media Photographers, Advt. Photographers of Am., Overseas Press Club (editor bull. 1990-93, gov. 1993-97, 98—, awards com. 1990—), N.Y. Friars Club.

POLIDORI, GIANCARLO, pediatrician, intensivist; b. Altidona, Ascoli, Italy, Aug. 11, 1939; s. Filippo and Rosa (Del Medico) P.; m. Adriana Podda, Dec. 8, 1971; children: Pierfilippo, Lorenzo. MD, U. Genoa, Italy, 1963. Intern Ospedale S. Martino, Genoa, 1960-63; resident in pediatrics Genoa U., 1963-65; resident in pediatrics Policlinico Gemelli, Rome, 1966-79, assoc. prof. pediatrics, 1983—; neonatologist Rome U., 1975; anesthesiologist Cath. U. Rome, 1979-82, head pediat. intensive care unit, 1992—; head pediat. dept. Schio Hosp., Viconza, 1979-83; head pediat. respiratory dept. Milan Ctr. Auxologico, 1983-88. Contbr. over 200 articles to profl. jours. Roman Catholic. Home: Via B Barbiellini Amidei 97, Rome Italy Office: Cath U Rom, L go A Gemelli 8, 00168 Rome Italy

POLIDORI, PAOLO, veterinarian, researcher; b. Ripatransone, Italy, Sept. 30, 1963; s. Franco and Maria Luisa (Nisi) P. Degree, Fac. of Agr., Milan, 1989; PhD in Animal Husbandry, Fac. of Vet. Medicine, Milan, 1994. Rschr. U. Camerino, Italy, 1993-96, sr. rschr. faculty of vet. medicine, 1996—; vis. scientist U. Wis., Madison, 1995-96, U. Tenn., Knoxville, 1998-99. Co-editor: Quality Control and Requirements of Food of Animal Origin. With Italian Mil. Police, 1989-90. Nat. Rsch. Coun. Rome grantee, 1995, 98, State U. Milan doctoral fellow, 1991. Mem. Italian Soc. Vet. Scis., Sci. Assn. of Animal Prodn. Home: Corso Vittorio Emanuele 14, 63038 Ripatransone Italy Office: Fac of Vet Medicine, Via Circonvallazione 93, 62024 Matelica Italy

POLILLO, ROBERTO, software and information technology executive; b. Milano, Italy, May 27, 1946; s. Arrigo and Nora (Agneta) P.; m. Patricia Caprotti Polillo, July 17, 1981. Diploma in Physics, U. Milano, 1971. Assoc. prof. U. Milano, Italy, 1971—; dir. Etnoteam, Milano, Italy, 1975—, mng. dir., 1996—, CEO, 1999—; cons. European Commn., 1985—, various orgs., 1972—. Co-author: Introduzione Alla Programmazione Strutturata, 1977, Il Software Sulla Scrivania 1985, Dossier, 1983, Un Programma Chiamato Dossier, 1984. Avocation: photography in jazz concerts. Office: Etnoteam, via A Bono Cairoli 34, 20134 Milan Italy

POLIN, ALAN JAY, lawyer; b. N.Y.C., Sept. 5, 1953; s. Mortin and Eleanor (Clarke) P.; m. Sharon Lynn Hirschfeld, Oct. 10, 1976; children: Jay Michael, Meryl Beth. Student, Cornell U., 1971-74; BA cum laude, Seton Hall U., 1978; JD, Nova U., 1981. Bar: Fla. 1981, N.Y. 1990; lic. athlete agt., Fla. Assoc. Berryhill, Avery, Williams & Jordan, Esq., Ft. Lauderdale, Fla., 1981-82, Greenspoon & Marder, P.A., Miami, Fla., 1982-83; pvt. practice Ft. Lauderdale, 1983-86; ptnr. Mousaw, Vigdor, Reeves & Hess, Ft. Lauderdale, 1986-90; pvt. practice Coral Springs, Fla., 1990—; adj. faculty mem. Nova U; mem. grievance com. Fla. Bar, 1989-92, vice chair, 1990-91, chair, 1991-92. Chmn. Broward County Crct. Ct. Handbook, 1988; contbr. chpt. to Bridge the Gap Attorney's Handbook, 1987. Dir. Temple Beth Am., Margate, Fla., 1991-93; mem. Anti-Defamation League, Fla. Regional Bd., 1994—; mem. exec. com. Broward County Dem., 1989-96; vice mayor City of Coral Springs, 1994-96, commr., 1991—; mem. bd. dirs. Fla. Regional Bd. of Anti-Defamation League, 1994—, Children's Cardiac Rsch. Found., Inc., 1996—, The Irving Fryer Found., Inc., 1995-96, Am. Heart Assn., 1997—. Recipient Am. Jurisprudence award Nova U. Law Ctr., 1981, Disting. Pub. Svc. award, Anti-Defamation League, 2000. Mem. Fla. Bar Assn. (bd. govs. young lawyers divsn. 1987-89), Broward County Bar Assn. (exec. com. young lawyers sect. 1986-87), North Broward Assn. Realtors, Inc. (affiliate, std. contract forms com. 1989-95, atty./realtor rels. com. 1989-91), Kiwanis (Key Club advisor 1990-91). Office: 3300 N University Dr Ste 601 Coral Springs FL 33065-4132

POLIRER, DEBRA JOYCE, writer, poet; b. Mt. Kisco, N.Y., June 13, 1962; d. Frank Mathew and Cynthia Claire (Wertheimer) Gasthalter; m. Peter Ian Polirer, June 26, 1988. Student, Georgetown U., 1980-82; BS in Acctg., Mercy Coll., 1987. CPA, N.Y. Sr. proofreader Pennysaver Corp., Yorktown Heights, N.Y., 1983-87; sr. staff acct. Combe Inc., White Plains, N.Y., 1987-94; tax editor H & R Block, Poughkeepsie, N.Y., 1994-95. Author: Secret Journey, Fields of Night, The Invisible Woman, Dark Voyage, Tales from the Tower, The Voice in the Emerald Forest; author poetry anthologies; contbr. articles to profl. jours. Recipient Editor's Choice award Nat. Libr. Poets, 1996, 97, 98, 99. Mem. Internat. Soc. Poets, Delta Mu Delta. Jewish. Avocations: Celtic harp, Irish whistle, creative writing, foreign languages. Home: 186 Spackenkill Rd Poughkeepsie NY 12603-5135

POLISCHUK, VALERY PETROVICH, virologist, educator; b. Irpen, Ukraine, Feb. 5, 1958; s. Petro Ivanovich and Elena Viktorovna (Jakovitskaya) P.; m. Antonina Mikhajlovna Sokolova, Nov. 9, 1979; children: Juna, Anton. MSc, Kiev (Ukraine) State U., 1984; PhD, Inst. Epidemiology, Kiev, 1991. Engr. Inst. Plant Physiology, Kiev, 1984-85; asst. prof. virology Kiev State U., 1988-93, assoc. prof. virology, 1993—; head of lab. Inst. Agroecology, Kiev, 1994-98; prof. Kievo-Mogilanska Akad., Kiev, 1995—; prof. virology Internat. Solomon U., Kiev, 1995—. Author: Monitoring of Phytoviral Disease of Ukraine, 1997, Lectures of General Virology, 1998; contbr. articles to profl. jours. Recipient Zabolotnogo Prize Ukrainian Acad. Sci., 1997. Mem. Am. Phytopathol. Soc., N.Y. Acad. Sci. Avocations: photography, traveling. Office: Dept Virology Kiev State U, 64 Vladimirskaya Str, 252017 Kiev Ukraine

POLISHCHUK, LEONARD V., ecologist, researcher; b. Klintsy, Former USSR, Jan. 12, 1955; s. Vladimir L. and Ginda N. (Katz) P.; m. Elena A. Mnatsakanova, Aug. 22, 1981; 1 child, Sasha. Diploma of higher edn., Moscow State U., 1978, PhD in Biology, 1983. Technician Moscow State U., 1982-86, rsch. scientist, 1986-88, asst. prof., 1988-89, rsch. scientist, 1989—. Author: Dynamic Characteristics of Populations of Planktonic Animals, 1986; co-author: The Quantitative Methods of Estimation of Basic Population Parameters: Static and Dynamic Aspects, 1989; contbr. articles to profl. jours. Fellow Alexander von Humboldt Found., 1991-92, 96-97; grantee Internat. Sci. Found., 1994-95, Acad. of Scis. of The Netherlands, 1998. Mem. Am. Soc. Limnology and Oceanography, N.Y. Acad. Scis. Home: kv 302, Novo-Basmannaya ul dom 4/6, 107078 Moscow Russia Office: M V Lomonosov Moscow State U, General Ecology, 119899 Moscow Russia

POLISI, JOSEPH W(ILLIAM), academic administrator; b. N.Y.C., Dec. 30, 1947; s. William Charles and Pauline (Kaplan) P.; m. Elizabeth Marlowe. BA in Polit. Sci., U. Conn., 1969; MA in Internat. Relations, Tufts U., 1970, MusM, 1973, M of Mus. Arts, 1975; DMA, Yale U., 1980; DHL (hon.), Ursinus Coll., Collegetown, Pa., 1986; MusD (hon.), Curtis Inst. Music, 1990. Exec. officer Yale Sch. of Music, New Haven, 1976-80; dean of faculty Manhattan Sch. of Music, N.Y.C., 1980-83; dean Coll. Conservatory of Music U. Cin., 1983-84; pres. The Juilliard Sch., N.Y.C., 1984—. Performances as bassoonist throughout the U.S.; contbr. articles to various publs. in U.S. and France. Office: Juilliard Sch Office of the Pres 60 Lincoln Center Plz New York NY 10023-6588

POLITE, CARLENE HATCHER, writer, educator; b. Detroit; d. John and Lillian Hatcher; divorced; children: Glynda Morton, Lila Ashaki. Student, Martha Graham Sch. Dance, N.Y.C., 1952-56; diploma, Acad. Leonardo da Vinci, Rome, 1980. Dancer, student Martha Graham Sch., N.Y.C., 1952-56; dancer Alvin Ailey Dance Co., N.Y.C., 1957-58, Edith Stephen Co., N.Y.C., 1958; dancer, actress Vanguard Playhouse, Detroit, 1960-62; prof. English SUNY, Buffalo, 1971—, chair dept. Am. Studies, 1981; prof. emeritus SUNY, 2000; tchr. Golden Dragon Kung Fu Acad., 1974-75, Himalayan Inst. Yoga, 1980-82; panelist NEA, Washington, 1981, N.Y. State Coun. Arts, N.Y.C., 1982, N.Y. Found. Arts, 1983, Seattle Arts in Pub. Places, 1989. Author: The Flagellants, 1966 (Pulitzer Prize nominee 1967, NEA grant 1967, Rockefeller grant 1968), Sister X and The Victims of Foul Play, 1975. Coord. Walk to Freedom with Martin Luther King, Detroit, 1963; del., participant UN-Non-Govtl.Orgns. 4th World Conf. on Women, Beijing, 1995. Recipinet numerous nat. and internat. awards as artist and educator; invited 1st Ann. Conf. African Presence, Paris, 1991, Internat. Educators and Writers Oxford U., 1997. Avocations: T'ai Chi Ch'uan, Hatha Yoga.

POLITES, MICHAEL EDWARD, aerospace engineer; b. Belleville, Ill., Mar. 19, 1944; s. Matthew Charles and Edith Louise (Schwarz) P. BS in Sys. and Automatic Controls, Washington U., St. Louis, 1967; MSEE, U. Ala., 1971; PhD in Elec. Engring., Vanderbilt U., 1986. Aerospace rsch. engr., guidance, navigation and control sys. NASA/Marshall Space Flt. Ctr. Structures & Dynamics Lab, Huntsville, Ala., 1967-95; supervisory chief, instrumentation and control divsn. Astrionics Lab. NASA/Marshall Space Flight Ctr., Huntsville, Ala., 1995-98; dep. dir. astronics lab. NASA/Marshall Space Flight Ctr., Huntsville, 1998-99, dep. mgr. avionics dept., 1999—. 4 patents in field; contbr. numerous articles to profl. jours.; referee various jours. and confs. Mem. adv. bd. Coll. Engring. leadership bd. U. Ala. Recipient 71 NASA awards in the field including NASA-Marshall Co-Inventor of Yr., 1995; U. Ala. Coll. Engring. Disting. fellow, elec. engring. dept. outstanding fellow; named Outstanding Engr., Engrs. Coun., 2000. Fellow AIAA (assoc., guidance navigation and control tech. com. 1990—, digital avionics tech. com. 1996—); mem. IEEE (sr. Outstanding Engr. Huntsville sect. 1995), ASME, Am. Astronautical Soc. (session co-chmn. 1995, 97, 98, 99, 2000, Guidance and Control Conf.), Mensa, Tau Beta Pi, Eta Kappa Nu, Pi Tau Sigma. Office: NASA Marshall Space Flight Ctr Avionics Dept Huntsville AL 35812

POLITO-SHUFFER, ROBIN MARIE, language educator; b. Newark, Oct. 15, 1961; d. Frank Francis and Frederica Marianne Polito; m. Robert D. Shuffer, May 11, 1996 (dec. Apr. 5, 1999); 1 child, Von Francis Holguin. BA, U. Dallas, 1984; M Ednl. Adminstrn., Calif. State U. L.A., 1996. Lang. devel. specialist, bilingual crosscultural lang. and acad. devel., Calif. Tchr. 1st Luth., Northridge, Calif., 1984-88; bilingual tchr. L.A. United Sch. Dist., 1988-97, bilingual coord., 1996-97, elem. LEP program advisor, 1997-99, 2d lang. literacy specialist, 1999—. Author/editor: (handbook) Structured English Immersion Handbook, 1998-99. Mem. Calif. Assn. Bilingual Educators, Nat. Coun. Social Studies, Kappa Delta Pi (Nu Kappa chpt.). Democrat. Roman Catholic. Avocations: reading, walking, travel. E-mail: holpolshuf@earthlink.net. Office: L A Unified Sch Dist 730 E 14th St Los Angeles CA 90021-2114

POLÍVKA, JIŘÍ, physicist; b. Prague, Czech Republic, Apr. 8, 1943; s. Josef and Libuse Bonová Polívka; m. Helena Glaserová, Aug. 8, 1970; children: Jiří, Helena. MSc in Radio Engring., Czech Tech. U., Prague, 1966, PhD, 1975. Rsch. specialist A.S. Popov Rsch. Inst., Prague, 1966-73, Geophys. Inst., Prague, 1973-74; rsch. scientist PTT Rsch. Inst., Prague, 1975-91; dir. experiment # 6 Dubna (USSR)-Intercosmos, 1985-87; invited prof. CINVESTAV-IPN, Mexico City, 1989-90, Monterrey (Mex.) Tech. Inst., 1990; chief comm. lab. PTT Tng. Inst., Prague, 1991-92; invited rschr. Japan Key Technol. Ctr., Tokyo, 1992, UNAM-PUIDE-INAOE, Mexico City, 1993; chief scientist SPACEK Labs., Inc., Santa Barbara, Calif., 1994-96, 98—; rsch. scientist, dielectrics Inst. Physics, Prague, 1997-98; invited lectr. Madrid (Spain) Tech. Inst., 1990. Author: (textbook) Satellite Communication, (in Spanish) 1990, Microwave Radiometry and Applications, (in Spanish) 1993; contbr. over 120 articles to profl. jours. and conf. procs.; patentee in field of microwave components, systems and test methods. Mem. Astron. Union. E-mail: spacek@silcom.com. Office: Spacek Labs Inc 212 E Gutierrez St Santa Barbara CA 93101-1705

POLIZOTTO, MICHAEL JAMES, JR., technology executive, consultant; b. N.Y.C., Mar. 18, 1943; s. Michael James and Helen Polizotto; m. Joan Rita Ann Manzo, Sept. 9, 1967; children: Marc Michael, Ryan Scott. BS in Specialized Mgmt., Kent Coll., 1992; MS in Bus. Adminstrn., La Salle U., 1994. Sr. internal cons. Fiduciary Trust Co. of N.Y., N.Y.C.; asst. dir. sys. and program Boy Scouts of Am., North Brunswick, N.J.; mgr. new design devel. Clark O'Neill, Fairview, N.J.; site mgr., sr. mem. adv. Computer Scis. Corp., Shrewsbury, N.J.; prin. cons. Cap Gemini Am., Iselin, N.J.; exec. v.p. tech. MJMR Infotech., Howell, N.J.; adj. prof. Kent Coll., Mandeville, La., La Salle U., Mandeville. Author: Planning for Success, 1994. Republican. Roman Catholic. Achievements include design and devel. of electronic territory mgmt. to pharma. industry through online mgmt. sys. Avocations: coin collecting, computers, fishing, skiing. Home and Office: 26 Chestnut Hill Rd Howell NJ 07731-1708

POLK, EMILY DESPAIN, conservationist, writer, designer; b. Aberdeen, Wash., July 6, 1910; d. John Dove Isaacs and Constance Ashley (DeSpain) Van Norden; m. Benjamin Kauffman Polk, Aug. 23, 1946. Student, U. Oreg., 1928-29, Oreg. State U., 1929-31, Rudolph Shaefer Sch. of Art, San Francisco, 1931-32. Head display & design V.C. Morris, San Francisco, 1931-37; founder, CEO DeSpain Design, L.A. and N.Y.C., 1937-44, 63-64; ornamental & interior design arch. Benjamin Polk Arch., Calcutta and New Delhi, 1952-63; owner Galeria de San Luis, San Luis Obispo, Calif., 1966-68; founder, CEO Small Wilderness Area Preservation, Los Osos, Calif., 1969-79. Author: Poems and Epigrams, 1959 (All India Book award 1959), Delhi Old and New, 1963, A Wild Part of California, 1991, Rockpool Trilogy, 1995, Shadows: A Giant Tree, Vols. I-II, 1995-96, A Pilgrimage through Time, 1996, A Moment in the Mind, 1997, Invisible Thresholds, 1997, Poems for Drums and Woodwinds, 1999; co-author: (with B. Polk) India Notebook, 1987, (with others) Sri Lanka Buddhist Shrines, 1991; editor (poetry): Calcuttan Magazine, 1961-63; contbr. articles to jours.; designer interior and exhibits Internat. Wool Secretariat, World Trade Fair, New Delhi, 1955; hon. interior designer Pres. of India, New Delhi, 1955, Maharanee of Tripura, Calcutta, India, 1962-63, King of Nepal, Kathmandu, 1962-63, Princess Pema Choki, Gantok, Sikkim, 1963; solo exhbns. paintings and montages India, 1963, U.S., 1963, 75, 89, 91, 98, 99, Eng., 1987, jewelry, U.S., 1948, fashion, India, 1955. Mem. coun. Nat. Mus. Women in the Arts, Washington, 1991-93; del., spkr. Pan Asian Cultural Conf., Calcutta, 1963, India House, N.Y., 1963, The Women's Club, 1964, AAUW, 1998. Recipient Kiwanis Citizenship Plaque Inscription. 1928, Golden Bear Conservation award Calif. Pks. and Recreation, Sacramento, 1972, Nat. Conservation award Am. Motors, 1972. Mem. Soc. Women Geographers (Calif. del., spkr. 50th Anniversary Celebrations 1972, Libr. of Congress Oral History Women of Achievement Program 1995), Small Wilderness Area Preservation, Calif. Hist. Soc., Calif. Oaks Found., Am. Women's Club (pres. 1962), Nat. Indian Assn. Women (pres.), English Speaking Union (bd. dirs.), Gyan Chakra Literary Gp. (founder). Home: 12151 Dale Ave Stanton CA 90680-3889

POLK, GEORGE WASHINGTON, telecommunications executive, entrepreneur; b. Washington, Apr. 21, 1963; s. William Roe and Ann (Cross) P. BA, Harvard U., 1985. Fin. analyst Merrill Lynch Capital Mkts., N.Y.C., 1986-87, asst. to chmn., 1987-88; v.p., corp. devel. Wave Systems Corp., N.Y.C., 1988-90; pres. EP Systems Corp., Rolling Meadows, Ill., 1990-93; sr. v.p., internat. networks Geotek Comm., Montvale, N.J., 1994-98; pres. Global Wireless Holdings (Latin Am.), London, 1998-2000; dir. Colourpath Ltd., London, 1993—. Bd. govs. Middle East Inst., Washington, 1997—; mem. nominating com. George Polk Awards, N.Y.C., 1992—; mem. Coun. on Fgn. Rels. Mem. Internat. Mobile Telecomm. Assn. (vice chmn. 1996-97). Office: 9 Empire House Thurloe Pl, SW7 2RV London England also: Geotek Comm, 6WH 19 Beak St, London WIR 3LB, England

POLK, JAMES RAY, journalist; b. Oaktown, Ind., Sept. 12, 1937; s. Raymond S. and Oeta (Fleener) P.; m. Bonnie Becker, Nov. 4, 1962; children: Geoffrey, Amy; m. Cara Bryn Saylor, June 21, 1980; 1 child, Abigail. BA, Ind. U., 1962. With A.P., Indpls., 1962-65, Milw., 1965, Madison, Wis., 1966-67, Washington, 1967-71; investigative reporter Washington Star, 1971-75; correspondent NBC News, Washington, 1975-92; sr. producer CNN Spl. Assignment, 1992—; pres. Investigative Reporters and Editors, Inc., 1978-80, chmn. bd., 1980-82, nat. coll. chmn., 1983-90. With U.S. Navy, 1955-58. Recipient Pub. Affairs Reporting award, Am. Polit. Sci. Assn., 1961, Raymond Clapper Meml. award, 1972, 74, Pulitzer prize for nat. reporting on Watergate, 1974, Sigma Delta Chi award, 1974, Nat. Headliner award 2d place, 1994, 96, Emmy award for coverage of Oklahoma City bombing, 1996, Ind. U. Disting. Alumni award; named to Ind. Journalism Hall of Fame, 1994. Mem. Phi Kappa Psi. Office: CNN Center Atlanta GA 30348

POLKINGHORNE, JOHN CHARLTON, retired academic administrator, clergyman; b. Weston-Super-Mare, England, Oct. 16, 1930; s. George Baulkwill and Dorothy Evelyn (Charlton) P; m. Ruth Isobel (Martin), Mar. 26, 1955; children: Peter, Isobel Polkinghorne Morland, Michael. MA, Cambridge (Eng.) U., 1956, PhD, 1955, ScD, 1974; DD (hon.), U. Kent, Eng., 1994; DSc (hon.), U. Exeter, Eng., 1994, U. Leicester, Eng., 1995, U. Durham, Eng., 1999. Ordained deacon Ch. of Eng., 1981, priest, 1982. Lectr. U. Edinburgh, Scotland, 1956-58; lectr. U. Cambridge, 1958-65, reader, 1965-68, prof., 1968-79; vicar Blean, Kent, Eng., 1984-86; fellow, dean Trinity Hall U. Cambridge, 1986-89; pres. Queens' Coll. U. Cambridge, 1989-96, fellow, 1996—; fellow Trinity Coll. U. Cambridge, 1954-86. Author: The Quantum World, 1981, One World, 1986, Science and Creation, 1988, Science and Providence, 1989, Rochester Roundabout, 1989, Reason and Reality, 1991, The Faith of a Physicist, 1994, Quarks, Chaos and Christianity, 1994, Serious Talk, 1995, Scientists as Theologians, 1996, Beyond Science, 1996, Belief in God in an Age of Science, 1998, Science and Theology, 1998. Chmn. com. on Rsch. Use of Fetuses and Fetal Material, 1988-89, task force Treatment of Drug Misuses, 1994-96, mem. adv. com. on genetic testing, 1996-99; mem. doctrine commn. Ch. of Eng., 1989-94. Sgt. Army, 1948-49. Hon. fellow Trinity Hall U. Cambridge, 1989, Queens' Coll., Cambridge, 1996. Fellow Royal Soc. Anglican. Avocation: gardening.

POLKINGHORNE, MARTYN NEAL, control engineer, researcher; b. Redruth, Cornwall, Eng., Feb. 26, 1968; s. Michael Stanley and Lilian Mary (Holman) P.; m. Kate O'Neill, Sept. 1, 1990; children: Gideon Ross, Darcy Kate, Marnie Jess, Dylan Jack, Asher Ben. BEng with honors, Poly. Southwest, Plymouth, Eng., 1990; PhD, U. Plymouth, 1994. Engr. ECC Internat. Ltd., St. Austell, Eng., 1988-89; rsch. asst. U. Plymouth, 1990-93, rsch. fellow, 1994-95, sr. mgr. dept. bus. devel., 1996—; project mgr. S.W. Innovation Relay Ctr., 1996—. Author: A Self-Organising Fuzzy Logic Autopilot for Small Vessels, 1994; editor: Applications of Advanced Marine Control, 1996, Applications of Artificial Intelligence for Technological and Business Processes, 1996, Applications of Soft Technologies for Enhanced Manufacture and Management, 1996. Mem. IEE. Anglican. Avocations: music, literature. Office: U Plymouth, Drake Circus, Devon Plymouth PL4 8AA, England

POLKOWSKA, JOLANTA, neuroendocrinologist, researcher; b. Warsaw, Poland, July 9, 1940; d. Stefan and Helena (Kaczorowska) Gieorgica; m. Roman Polkowski, Apr. 8, 1967 (dec. 1982). MSc, U. Warsaw, 1964, PhD in Reproductive Physiology, 1972, habilitation, 1983, Prof. Natural Scis., 1992. Grad. rsch. asst. Kielanowski Inst. Animal Physiology and Nutrition, Jabtonna, Poland, 1968-73, asst. prof. neuroendocrinology, 1973-85, rsch. prof. neuroendocrinology, 1985—, scientific dir., 1992-99. Contbr. articles to profl. jours. Recipient Polish Acad. Scis. award, 1971, 78, 88, 97. Mem. Soc. Endocrinology (Great Britain), Soc. Exptl. Neuroendocrinologie (France). Avocations: skiing, windsurfing, sailing. E-mail: infizyz@atos.warman.com.pl. Home: Przylesie 21A ap 306, 03-153 Warsaw Poland Office: Kielanowski Inst, Animal Physiol Nutrition, 05-110 Jabtonna Poland

POLL, (ERNST) MICHAEL, health facility administrator; b. Graudenz, Germany, Apr. 22, 1941; s. Friedrich Ernst and Friedel (Warmbier) P.; m. Barbara Enders, Aug. 16, 1968; children: Friederike, Karolin, Uta. MD, U. Heidelberg, 1967, venia legendi for internal medicine, 1977. Asst. Mannheim Hosp. Univ. Heidelberg, Germany, 1969-75; head physician Speyererhof Hosp., Heidelberg, 1975-83; med. supt. Hosp. Lubbecke, Germany, 1983—; prof. U. Heidelberg, 1983—; treas. European Assn. Gastroenterology and Endoscopy, 1984-94. Editor: Gastro-Duodenoskopie, 1982; contbr. articles to profl. jours. Mem. German Assn. Internal Medicine, German Assn. Gastroenterology, German Assn. Diabetology, Rotary Club Lubbecke. Avocations: photography, bonsai, classical music. Home: Heidkopfweg 11, 32312 Lübbecke Germany Office: Med Klinik Kreiskrankenhaus, Virchowstrasse 65, Lübbecke 32312, Germany

POLL, RUEDIGER MICHAEL LEANDER, biomedical engineer, educator; b. Koeslin, Germany, Sept. 5, 1944; s. Harald and Franziska (Macht) P.; m. Uta Inge Wunderwald, Nov. 2, 1974; children: Donata, Maria. Specialist in Cardiology, Med. Acad., Dresden, Germany, 1975, MD, 1976; Diplom-Ingenieur, U. Tech., Dresden, Germany, 1981. Qualified to practice as a physician. Physician cardiol. dept. Med. Acad. Dresden, 1970-79, sr. physician, 1979-88; tchg. asst. elec. engring. U. Tech. Dresden, 1988-89, lectr. in biomed. equipment, 1989-92, prof., chmn. med.-technol. systems, 1992—, vice-dir. Inst. Biomed. Engring., 1990—, mem. faculty coun., 1990-94. Patentee in field; contbr. articles to profl. jours. Recipient Humboldt-Medaille, Min. Higher Edn., Berlin, 1983. Mem. IEEE, N.Y. Acad. Sci., Deutsche Gesellschaft für Biomedizinische Technik. Christian Democrat. Avocations: literature, history. Office: Dresden Univ of Tech, Mommsenstrasse 13, 01069 Dresden Saxony, Germany

POLLACK, ANITA JEAN, civil servant, politician; b. Lismore, Australia, June 3, 1946; d. John Samuel and Kathleen (Emerson) P.; m. Philip Stephen Bradbury, June 6, 1986; children: Katherine Louise Pollack Bradbury. BA, London Poly., 1979; MS, London U., 1981. Editor Granada Pub., London, 1971-75; rschr. Barbara Castle MEP, London, 1981-89; head European liaison English Heritage, 2000—; mem. European Parliament, 1989-99. Labour Party. Office: 139 Windsor Rd, London E7 ORA, England

POLLACK, ROBERT WILLIAM, psychiatrist; b. N.Y.C., May 22, 1947; s. George and Esther P.; m. Pam Gregory, Sept. 15, 1984; 1 child, Jessie. BS in Biology, Yale U., 1969; MD, SUNY Downstate Med. Ctr., Bklyn., 1973. Diplomate Am. Bd. Psychiatry and Neurology. Tng. resident U. Fla., 1973-76, chief resident Dept. of Psychiatry, 1975-76; asst. prof. Dept. of Psychiatry U. Fla., Gainesville, 1976-77; clin. asst. prof. dept. psychiatry Shands Hosp., Gainesville, 1977—; chief dept. psychiatry Fla. Hosp., Orlando, 1983, 84; clin. dir. assessment and evaluation team West Lake Hosp., Longwood, Fla., 1984-87, clin. dir. intensive evaluation unit, 1987-89; med. dir. Fla. Psychiat. Assocs., Winter Park, 1989-92, Fla. Psychiat. Mgmt., Winter Park, 1990-97; corp. med. dir. FPM Behavioral Health, 1993-97; co-founder Profl. Quality Analysts, Inc., Casselberry, Fla., 1997—; med. dir. consultation, liaison svc., and spl. med. unit Winter Park Meml. Hosp., 1992; integrated surveyor Jt. Commn. for Accreditation of Healthcare Orgns., 1998-2000, sentinel event, 1999-2000; pres. The Rondo Group, Longwood, Fla., 2000—. Contbr. 4 articles to profl. jours.; author sci. reports. Chmn. Retinitis Pigmentosa Casino Night, Orlando, 1988-92; vice-chmn. nat. championship com. U.S. Blind Golfers Assn., 1991-92, chair 48th ann. championship com., 1992-93; bd. dirs. Tennis with a Different Swing, Orlando, 1988-92; mem. Seminole County Assn. on Domestic Violence, 1998—. Mem. U.S. Blind Golfers Assn. (chairperson, nat. championships 1998, 99, 2000), Alaqua Country Club (bd. dirs.). Achievements include introduction of use of computerized topographical brain mapping as a diagnostic tool in central Florida. Office: Profl Quality Analysts 274 Wilshire Blvd Ste 224 Casselberry FL 32707-5367

POLLACK, STEPHEN J., stockbroker; b. N.Y.C., Aug. 25, 1937; s. Harold S. and Gladys H. P.; m. Barbara Jane Podgur, May 1992. BS in Econs., U. Pa., 1960. V.p. retail sales Drexel Burnham Lambert, N.Y.C., 1960-77; 1st v.p. investments Dean Witter Reynolds Inc., N.Y.C., 1978-98; 1st v.p., fin. advisor Morgan Stanley Dean Witter, N.Y.C., 1998—. pres. B'nai B'rith Gothem, N.Y.C.; exec. v.p. Cosmopolitan League of City of HOpe, v.p. circle mem. Whitney Mus., N.Y.C.; treas. Sutton Pl. Synagogue, pres. Havurah Group. With USAR, 1966. Recipient Double Chai Citation, State of Israel Bonds, 1984, Appreciation award City of Hope, 1984, Kiter Key Club award Franklin Funds, Million Dollar Club Svc. award, B'nai B'rith Internat. award. Mem. Internat. Assn. Fin. Planners, Assn. Investment Brokers (dir.), Youngmen's Philanthropic League (bd. dirs.), Internat.

Study Rsch. Inst., Town Club, Atrium Club, Schuylkill Country Club, Wharton Sch. Club, U. Pa. Club, Yale Club, East River Tennis Club, Fresh Meadow Country Club, Matterhorn Sports Club, East Side Rep. Club, Knickerbokker Rep. Club, Friars Club., Penn. Club (charter). Home: 245 E 40th St Apt 14E New York NY 10016-1714 Office: Morgan Stanley Dean Witter 885 3rd Ave Fl 14 New York NY 10022-4834

POLLACK, SYDNEY, film director; b. Lafayette, Ind., July 1, 1934; s. David and Rebecca (Miller) P.; m. Claire Griswold, Sept. 22, 1958; children: Steven, Rebecca, Rachel. Grad., Neighborhood Playhouse Theatre Sch., N.Y.C., 1954. Asst. to Sanford Meisner, Neighborhood Playhouse Theatre, 1954, instr. acting, 1954-60; exec. dir. West Coast br. The Actors Studio. Appeared in Broadway prodns.: The Dark Is Light Enough, 1954, A Stone For Danny Fisher, 1955; appeared on live TV programs: Alcoa Presents, others; toured in Stalag 17; dir. TV programs: The Chrysler Theatre, Ben Casey, 1962-63, Something About Lee Wiley, 1963-64; Films include: (dir.) The Slender Thread, 1965, This Property is Condemned, 1966, The Scalphunters, 1968, Castle Keep, 1969, Jeremiah Johnson, 1972, Three Days of the Condor, 1975, The Electric Horseman, 1979, The Firm, 1993; (exec. prodr.) Sense and Sensibility, 1995; (dir., prodr.) They Shoot Horses, Don't They?, 1969, The Way We Were, 1973, The Yakuza, 1975, Bobby Deerfield, 1977, Absence of Malice, 1981, Tootsie, 1982 (also actor), Out of Africa, 1985 (Academy Award for Best Picture and Dir.), Havana, 1990, The Firm, 1993, Sabrina, 1995; (prodr.) Songwriter, 1984, Bright Lights, Big City, 1988, The Fabulous Baker Boys, 1989, Presumed Innocent, 1990, Sliding Doors, 1998, The Talented Mr. Ripley, 1999; (exec. prodr.) Honeysuckle Rose, 1980, White Palace, 1990, King Ralph, 1991, Dead Again, 1991, Leaving Normal, 1992, Searching for Bobby Fischer, 1993, Flesh and Bone, 1992, Sense and Sensibility, 1995, Sliding Doors, 1997, Up At the Villa, 1998, The Talented Mr. Ripley, 1998, For Love of the Game, 1998; (actor) The Player, 1992, Death Becomes Her, 1992, Husbands and Wives, 1992, The Firm, 1993, Eyes Wide Shut, 1997, Civil Action, 1998, Random Hearts, 1998, (TV) Mad About You, 1998, Eyes Wide Shut, 1999; dir., prodr., exec. prodr. Random Hearts, 1999. Served with U.S. Army, 1957-59. Recipient Acad. award for best dir. and best picture, 1986. Office: Mirage Enterprises David Lean Bldg #119 10202 Washington Blvd Culver City CA 90232-3119 also: Deloitte & Touche 350 S Grand Ave Los Angeles CA 90071-3406

POLLAK, NORMAN LEE, retired accountant; b. Chgo., Aug. 16, 1931; s. Emery and Helen P.; m. Barbara Zeff, Aug. 21, 1955 (div. 1980); children: Martin Joel, Elise Susan McNeal, Rhonda Louise Wilder. BS, Northwestern U., 1955. CPA, Calif.; lic. real estate agt. Calif. Sr. acct., staff acct., 1952-58, pvt. practice, 1958-88; ret. acct., fin. and mgmt. adv. svcs., pres. Norman L. Pollak Accountancy Corp., Westlake Village; expert witness on domestic dissolution, 1984-87; lectr. profl. orgns.; bus. mgr. for Steven Martin, Nitty Gritty Dirt Band, 1967-77; acct. for Gregg and Howard Allman, 1967, Marion Ross, 1980s. Former pres. Ventura County Estate Planning Coun., 1975-78, 78-79); founder San Fernando Valley Estate Planning Coun., 1962, chpt. pres., 1964-65; founder Ventura Co. Estate Planning Coun.; chmn. Comm. Contest for Hearing Impaired Optimist Club, emergency com. Disaster Preparedness, Oak Forest Mobile Estates Assn.; vol. disaster preparedness plan; coach Braille Olympics for Blind; mem. Conejo Future Found.; bd. dirs. Oak Forest Homeowners Assn., Honokowai Palms Homeowners Assn.; bd. trustees Westlake Cultural Found.; sponsor Code 3 for Homeless Children, 1993. Mem. AICPA (apptd. CPA key person for legis.-polit. program Washington), Calif. Soc. CPAs (former chmn. San Fernando tech. discussion group 1960-61, former mem. com. on cooperation with credit grantors), Nat. Assn. Accts., Westlake Village C. of C., Northwestern U. Alumni Club, Kellogg Sch. Mgmt. Alumni Club, UCLA Alumni Club, Delta Mu Delta. Address: 1930 Village Center Cir #3-428 Las Vegas NV 89134

POLLAK, OLIVER BURT, lawyer, educator; b. London, Nov. 10, 1943; came to U.S., 1953; s. William and Ruth Pollak; m. Karen F. Goldstein; children: Noah, Aaron. BA, Calif. State U., L.A., 1965; PhD, UCLA, 1973; JD, Creighton U., 1982. Bar: Nebr., 1982, Iowa, 1992. Prof. U. Nebr., Omaha, 1974—; atty. Pollak & Hicks, P.C., Omaha, 1983—. Author 4 books; contbr. articles to profl. jours. Mem. Nebr. Humanities Coun., Lincoln, 1981-85, Omaha Jewish Press, 1981-84. Recipient Sandoz award, 1996. Mem. ACLU, Am. Hist. Soc., Am. Hist. Assn., B'nai B'rith. Jewish. Avocations: cycling, reading. Office: U Nebr Omaha History Dept Omaha NE 68182-0001

POLLAND, MADELEINE A(NGELA CAHILL) (FRANCES ADRIAN), children's writer; b. Kinsale, County Cork, Ireland, May 21, 1918; d. Patrick Richard and Christina (Culkin) Cahill; m. Arthur Joseph Polland, June 10, 1946 (dec. Oct. 1987); children: Charlotte Frances, Fergus Adrian. Asst. libr. Letchworth (Eng.) Pub. Libr., 1938-42; guest speaker N.Y. Pub. Libr. Children's Book Fair, 1968. Author: (children's books) Children of the Red King, 1960 (N.Y. Herald Tribune Honor Book 1961), The Town across the Water, 1961, Beorn the Proud, 1961 (N.Y. Herald Tribune Honor Book 1962), Fingal's Quest, 1961, 98, The White Twilight, 1962, Chuiraquimba and the Black Robes, 1962, The City of the Golden House, 1963, The Queen's Blessing, 1963, Flame Over Tara, 1964, Mission to Cathay, 1965, 98, Queen without Crown, 1965, Deirdre, 1967, To Tell My People, 1968, Stranger in the Hills, 1968, Alhambra, 1970, To Kill a King, 1971, A Family Affair, 1971, Daughter of the Sea, 1972 (published in Eng. as Daughter to Poseidon), Prince of the Double Axe, 1976; (adult novels) Thicker Than Water, 1966, Minutes of a Murder, 1967 (published in Eng. as The Little Spot of Bother), Random Army, 1969 (published as Shattered Summer 1970), Package to Spain, 1971, Double Shadow, 1978 (under pseudonym Frances Adrian), Sabrina, 1979, All Their Kingdoms, 1981, The Heart Speaks Many Ways, 1982, No Price Too High, 1984, As It Was in the Beginning, 1987, Rich Man's Flowers, 1990, The Pomegranate House, 1992. With Women's Aux. Air Force, 1942-45. Roman Catholic. Avocations: lawn bowls, travel, museums, art. Home: Edificio Hercules 634, Avenida Gamonal, Arroyo de la Miel Malaga Spain

POLLARD, DAVID WILLIAM, law educator; b. Rugby, Warwick, Eng., Mar. 23, 1939; s. Reginald Arthur and Florence Maud (Godfrey) P.; m. Lorna Cave, Aug. 10, 1963; children: Michael, Elizabeth. LLB, U. Leeds, Eng., 1960. Lectr. U. Hull, Eng., 1962-71; lectr. U. Leicester, Eng., 1971-75, sr. lectr., 1975—, European sec. Faculty of Law, 1995—; vis. prof. U. Strasbourg, France; mem. social security appel tribunal, Leicester, 1980—. Author: Social Welfare Law, 1977, European Community Law, 1994, Constitutional and Administrative Law, 2nd edit., 1997, French Law, 1996. Named chevalier des Palmes Acad., Republic of France, 1992. Mem. Statute Law Soc. (mem. coun. 1985-92). Avocation: mountain climbing. Home: 128 Carisbrooke Rd, Leicester LE2 3PE, England Office: Univ Leicester Faculty Law, University Rd, Leicester LE1 7RH, England

POLLARD, DENNIS BERNARD, lawyer, educator; b. Phila., May 12, 1968. BS in Psychology, Pa. State U., 1990; JD, Ohio State U., 1993; postgrad., U. Mich., 1996. Bar: Ohio 1993, U.S. Dist. Ct. (no. dist.) Ohio 1994, U.S. Ct. Appeals (6th cir.) 1994. Staff atty. The Legal Aid Soc. Cleve., 1993-95; atty. student affairs, student life Pa. State U., 1995-96; acad. adminstrv. intern U. Mich. Law Sch., Ann Arbor, 1996-97; asst. dean student affairs U. Tenn. Coll. Law, Knoxville, 1997-98; program dir. tenants' rights unit Tenants' Action Group of Phila., 1998-99, dir. devel., legis. affairs and spl. projects, 1999—. Mem. ABA, Ohio State Bar Assn., Phi Delta Phi. Avocation: biking. Home: 506 S White Horse Pike Apt D9 Stratford NJ 08084-1550 Office: Tenants' Action Group of Philadelphia 21 S 12th St Fl 12 Philadelphia PA 19107-3610

POLLARD, IRINA, biology and bioscience ethics educator, researcher; b. Ankara, Turkey, Sept. 2, 1939; arrived in Australia, 1949.; d. Pawel and Maria Francesca (Hruby) Lachowicz; m. David Anthony Pollard, May 15, 1965 (div. 1972); 1 child, Morgan; m. Roger George Hiller. BS with honors, U. Sydney, 1962, PhD in Biol. Scis., 1966. Sr. tchg. fellow Monash U., Melbourne, Australia, 1965-67; postdoct. fellow U. Montpellier, France, 1968-69; rsch. fellow Charing Cross Hosp., London, 1970; sr. tutor U. Sydney, 1971-72; assoc. prof. Macquarie U., Sydney, 1973—; tchr. Coll. de France, Paris, U. Oxford, Cambridge U., 1986, U. London, 1996. Author: (textbook) A Guide to Reproduction, Social Issues and Human Concerns, 1994; contbr. over 60 articles to scientific jours. on reproductive biology and bioethics. Commonwealth scholar, 1959-62; grantee Population Coun., 1963-66. Mem. Australian Soc. Teratology, Australian Soc. Reproductive Biology, Australian Inst. Biology, Bioethics Assn., Internat. Bioethics Assn., Greenpeace, numerous others. Avocations: camping, trekking, reading, stained glass, painting. Office: Macquarie U, Dept Biol Scis, 2109 Sydney NSW, Australia

POLLARD, MICHAEL ROSS, lawyer, health policy researcher and consultant; b. Flint, Mich., Apr. 14, 1947; s. Gail Winton Pollard and Evelyn Georgeanna (LeMire) Goplen; m. Penelope Brigham, Aug. 22, 1970. AB in Polit. Sci., U. Mich., 1969; JD, Harvard U., 1972, MPH, 1974. Bar: Mass. 1972, D.C. 1975. Profl. assoc. for program devel. Nat. Acad. Scis. Inst. Medicine, Washington, 1974-77, dir. law and ethics div., 1977-78; atty. advisor Office of Policy Planning, FTC, Washington, 1978-81, asst. dir. Bur. Consumer Protection, 1981-83; dir. Office of Policy Analysis, Pharm. Mfrs. Assn., Washington, 1983-88; exec. dir. Am. Pharm. Inst., Washington, 1988-89; counsel Michaels, Wishner & Bonner, P.C. (now Michaels & Bonner PC), Washington, 1988-89, ptnr., 1989—; cons. Nat. Ctr. for Health Svcs. Rsch., Rockville, Md., 1975-80, Office Tech. Assessment U.S. Congress, 1984-95; dir. Inst. for Health Policy Solutions, 1992—. Contbr. articles to profl. jours. Treas. Nat. Leadership Coalition on AIDS, 1988-93; treas. and dir.-at-large Nat. Commn. on Cert. of Physician Assts., 1991-97, James B. Angell scholar U. Mich., 1967, 68, 69. Mem. ABA, Phi Beta Kappa, Pi Sigma Alpha. Democrat. Avocations: running, cycling, gardening, architectural drawing. Home: 7300 Maple Ave Chevy Chase MD 20815-5108 also: 29 Paradise Lane West Southport ME 04576 Office: Michaels & Bonner 1140 Connecticut Ave NW Ste 900 Washington DC 20036-4009

POLLARD-GOTT, LUCY, writer; b. Endicott, NY, May 20, 1957; d. Frank Trich and Virginia (Claxton) Pollard; m. J. Richard Gott III, June 10, 1978; 1 child, Elizabeth Marjorie. BA summa cum laude, Princeton U., 1978, PhD in Psychology, 1981. Psychology jour. editor Lawrence Erlbaum Assocs., Inc., Mahwah, N.J., 1985-95; writer Carol Pub. Group, N.Y.C., 1995-98; website designer, mgr. pvt. practice, 1998—; admissions cons. Princeton (N.J.) U., 1985-86; abstract preparation cons. ERIC Document Svc., Princeton, 1987. Mem. editl. bd. Discourse Processes, 1983-93; contbr. articles to profl. jours. Nat. Merit scholar, 1974; Pre-doctoral fellow NSF, 1978-81, Postdoctoral fellow USPHS, 1981-82. Mem. Phi Beta Kappa. Avocation: mandolin. Home and Office: 63 Cartwright Dr Princeton Junction NJ 08550-1934

POLLARO, PAUL PHILIP, artist; b. N.Y.C., Aug. 2, 1921; s. Charles and Maria (Aprile) P.; m. Jo Ann Stover, July 16, 1962 (div. Nov. 1979); children: Lauren, Paul Jr.; m. Laura Clayton, Apr. 2, 1985. Student, Art Students League, 1945-48, Pratt Graphic Ctr., 1972. Instr. painting The New Sch. of Social Rsch., N.Y.C., 1964-69; vis. artist Notre Dame U., South Bend, Ind., 1965-67; asst. prof. art, chmn. art dept. Wagner Coll., Staten Island, N.Y., 1970-73; asst. dir. The MacDowell Colony, Peterborough, N.H., 1973-76; pvt. practice Hancock, N.H., 1976—. One-man shows include Jersey City Mus., N.J., 1966 (second prize), S.I. Mus. Art, N.Y., 1973, Manchester Inst. Arts and Scis., Manchester, N.H., 1970-85, Chryser Mus., Norfolk, Va., 1991, numerous others. Sgt. U.S. Army, 1942-45, PTO. Tiffany Found. grantee, N.Y.C., 1967, N.H. State Coun. Arts grantee, 1985; The MacDowell Colony fellow, 1965-69. Roman Catholic. Home: Norway Hill Hancock NH 03449

POLLERT, EMIL, chemist; b. Praha, Czech Republic, May 9, 1938; s. Jaroslav and Karla (Štěpničková) P.; m. Eva Kopřivová, Mar. 17, 1967; children: Veronika, Lukáš, Klára. Engr., Inst. of Chem. Tech., Praha, 1961, PhD, 1972; D in scis., Charles Univ., Praha, 1988; sr. lectr., Inst. of Chem. Tech., Praha, 1991. With Geological Investigation, Praha, 1961-62; with Inst. of Physics, Praha, 1962—, head of lab., 1974—. Contbr. articles to profl. jours. Com. mem. Czech Canoe Union, 1990—; chmn. Civic Dem. Party, Praha, 1991—. Recipient World Champion award Internat. Canoe Fedn., Austria, 1965, prize Czechoslovak Acad. Scis., 1992. Mem. Czechoslovak Assn. for Crystal Growth. Avocations: white water canoeing, skiing. Home: Vodní 4, 150 00 Praha 5 Czech Republic Office: Inst of Physics, Cukrovarnická 10, 16253 Praha Czech Republic

POLLEY, WILLIAM ALPHONSE, retired power systems engineer; b. Milw., Dec. 1, 1942; s. William O. and Florence V. P.; m. Connie A. Pippert, Aug. 28, 1965; children: Christopher, Karen, Craig, Carl. BSME, Marquette U., 1966. Engr. co-op Allis Chalmers, Milw., 1962-66; sales engr. Westinghouse, Duluth, Minn., 1966-79; applications engr. Westinghouse, Appleton, Wis., 1979-88, systems engr., 1988-89; power systems engr. Kimberly-Clark, Neenah, Wis., 1989—. Chmn. St. Michael's Parish Coun., Duluth, 1977-79; scoutmaster Boy Scouts Am., Appleton, 1989-92, scout commr., 19925; exec. couple Nat. Marriage Encounter, Appleton, 1985-87. Mem. IEEE, Instrument Soc. of Am., Assn. Energy Engrs., Internat. Maint. Inst. Avocations: computers, gardening, travel. Home: 1021 E Shady Ln Neenah WI 54956-1225

POLLICOVE, HARVEY MYLES, manufacturing executive; b. Utica, N.Y., May 28, 1944; s. Maxwell Hymen and Carolyn (Vogel) P.; m. Catherine Mary Keady, Aug. 3, 1968; children: Carolyn, Sarah. AAS, Monroe Community Coll., 1968; BS, U. Rochester, 1973. Sr. engr. supr. optics Eastman Kodak Co., Rochester, 1978-82; engring. mgr. optics Eastman Kodak Co., 1982-84, mfg. mgr., 1984-86, mgr. tech. mkts. (internat.), 1986-89; dir. Ctr. for Optics Mfg. U. Rochester, 1989—; U.S. del. (optics) to Internat. Stds. Orgn., 1995—; chmn. Optics and Electro-Optics Standards Coun., 1999—; hon. advisor Hong Kong Photographic and Optics Mfrs. Assn., 2000; lectr. in field. Editorial adv. bd. (optics mag. for mfg.) Laser Focus World, 1990-2000; contbr. articles to profl. jours. Advisor High Tech. of Rochester, 1988-89; advisor tech. applications rev. bd. Strategic Def. Initiative Orgn., 1990-92, Ballistic Missile Def. Orgn., 1993-96; industry advisor Monroe C.C., 1986-97. Recipient Dept. of Def. Mfg. Tech. Achievement award, 1992. Mem. ASME/Optics Stds., Am. Precision Optics Mfrs. Assn. (exec. com. 1987—), Internat. Soc. for Optical Engring., Optical Soc. Am. (hon. mem. Rochester sect. 1996), Optics and Electro-Optics Stds. Coun. Home: 177 Georgian Court Rd Rochester NY 14610-3416 Office: U Rochester Ctr for Optics Mfg 240 E River Rd Rochester NY 14623-1212

POLLMANN, HERBERT JOSEF, mineralogy educator; b. Waldsassen, Bavaria, Germany, June 30, 1956; s. Peter and Elizabeth (Hofer) P.; m. Maria P. Eder; 1 child, Peter. Master Degree, U. Erlangen, Germany, 1980, promotion, 1984, habilitation, 1990. Asst. prof. U. Erlangen, Germany, 1990-94; full prof. U. Halle, Germany, 1994—. Recipient Schlumberger award Cement Additives, 1987, Emmy-Noether award, 1991, Georg Agricola medal German Mineral. Assn., 1994. Office: Univ Halle Mineralogy, Domstr 5, 06108 Halle Germany

POLLMER, JOST UDO, food chemist; b. Himmelpforten, Germany, May 14, 1954; s. Johannes and Ruth (Krugel) P.; m. Doris Ast, Apr. 28, 2000. Staatsprufung fur Lebensmittelchemiker, U. Munich, 1981. Self-employed food chemist, cons., lectr. Gemmingen, Fed. Republic of Germany; sci. dir. European Inst. for Food and Nutrition Scis., 1995. Author: IB und stirb Chemie in unserer Nahrung, 1982, Prost Mahlzeit! Krank durch gesunde Ernährung, 1994, Liebe geht durch die Nase, 1997, Vorsicht Geschmack, 1998, Wohl bekomms, 1998, Lexihon der Populären Forährungsirrtümer, 2000; contbr. articles to profl. jours. Mem. AAAS, Internat. Epidemiol. Assn., Japan Soc. Biosci., Biotech. and Agrochemistry, Behavior Toxicology Soc., Inst. Food Technologists, Am. Chem. Soc., Swiss Soc. Food Environ. Chemistry, Nutrition Soc. (U.K.), Assn. Ofcl. Analytical Chemists, N.Y. Acad. Scis., Internat. Soc. Chem. Ecology, Am. Assn. Cereal Chemists, Am. Diabetes Soc., Am. Soc. Limnology and Oceanography. Home: Eppinger Str 4, D-75050 Gemmingen Germany Office: European Inst for Food & Nutrition Scis, Amselweg 7, D-65239 Hochheim Germany

POLLOCK, BRUCE GODFREY, psychiatrist, educator; b. Toronto, Ont., Can., Aug. 18, 1952; s. Ira Justus and Sheila Joy (Godfrey) P.; m. Judith Arluk, May 18, 1982; children: Debra, Ariel. BS, U. Toronto, 1975, MD, 1979; PhD, U. Pitts., 1987. Chief resident Clarke Inst. Psychiatry, Toronto, 1982-83; fellow U. Pitts., 1983-84, asst. prof. dept. psychiatry, 1984-90, assoc. dir. clin. pharmacology dept. psychiatry, 1987-95, assoc. prof. dept. psychiatry and pharmacology, 1990-96, dir. geriat. psychopharm. dept. psychiatry and pharmacology, 1995—, prof. dept. psychiatry and pharmacology, 1997—. Contbr. over 150 articles to profl. jours.; contbg. author books in field. Centennial fellow Med. Rsch. Coun. of Can., Ottawa, 1983, Merck fellow geriatric clin. pharmacology, Am. Fedn. for Aging Rsch., N.Y.C., 1988; recipient Geriat. Mental Health award NIMH, Bethesda, Md., 1992, Ind. Scientist award, 1997. Fellow Royal Coll. Physicians Can. Home: 7032 Meade St Pittsburgh PA 15208-2429 Office: Western Psychiat Inst/Clin 3811 Ohara St Pittsburgh PA 15213-2593

POLLOCK, GRUSELDA FRANCES SINCLAIR, educator; b. Bloemfontein, South Africa, Mar. 11, 1949; arrived in Can., 1956, Britain, 1962; d. Alan Winston Seton and Kathleen Alexandra (Sinclair) P.; m. Antony Bryant, Oct. 30, 1981; children: Benjamin, Hester. BA with honors, Oxford U., England, 1970; MA, Courtland Inst., London, 1972; PhD, London U., 1980. Lectr. Manchester U., England, 1974-77; lectr. U. Leeds, England, 1977-87, sr. lectr., 1987-90, prof., 1991—, dir. ctr. cultural studies, 1987—; exec. Ctr. for Jewish Studies, 1996—; exec. Ctr. for Jewish Studies, 1996—. Author: Vision and Difference, 1988, Generations and Geographies in the Visual Arts, 1996, Mary Cassatt, 1998, Differencing the Canon, 1999; co-author: Old Mistresses: Women Art and Ideology, 1981, Avant-Gardes & Partisans Reviewed, 1996. Fellow Royal Soc. Arts. Jewish. Avocations: running, tennis, opera, cinema. Office: U Leeds, Dept Fine Art, Leeds LS28 9ND, England

POLLOCK, KAREN ANNE, computer analyst; b. Elmhurst, Ill., Sept. 6, 1961; d. Michael Paul and Dorothy Rosella (Foskett) P. BS, Elmhurst Coll., 1984; MS, North Cen. Coll., 1993. Formatter Nat. Data Corp., Lombard, Ill., 1985; computer specialist Dept. VA, Hines, Ill., 1985—. Lutheran. Avocations: cross-stitch, mystery books, bowling, bicycling, softball.

POLLOCK, LESLIE RONALD, clinical psychologist, researcher; b. Pietermaritzburg, Natal, South Africa, Feb. 22, 1956; s. John Nicolaas and Joan Merial Pollock; m. Ruth Katherine Antoinette Knott, June 3, 1989; children: Nicole Robyne, Danielle Rosa. BA, U. Natal, Durban, 1978, BA with honors, 1979, MA, 1984; PhD, U. Wales, 2000. Cert. psychologist, South Africa, U.K. Clin. psychologist, lectr. U. Natal Med. Sch., Pietermaritzburg/Durban, 1986-91; sr. clin. psychologist Eastbourne (U.K.) Dist. Gen. Hosp., 1991-93; prin. clin. psychologist Powys NHS Trust, Newtown, Wales, 1993—; rsch. fellow Inst. Med. and Social Care Rsch. U. Wales, Bangor, 1993—, clin. supr. psychology doctoral course, 1993—; rsch. assoc. Inst. Rural Health, Powys, 1998-99. Contbr. articles to profl. pubs., chpt. to book. Lt. South African Def. Force, 1981-82. Recipient Gen. Svc. medal South African Nat. Def. Force, 1995. Mem. APA (fgn. affiliate), Brit. Psychol. Soc. (chartered clin. psychologist), N.Y. Acad. Scis., Am. Assn. Suicidology. Avocations: walking, wildlife, travel. Office: Park St Clinic, Psychology Dept, Newtown SY16 1EG, United Kingdom

POLLOCK, MICHAEL JEFFREY, periodical editor; b. Elizabeth, N.J., Sept. 8, 1954; s. Leonard D. and Sara (Weiner) P.; m. Karen Zevin, July 31, 1988; children: Jeremy, Leah. BA in English, Rutgers U., 1976, MBA with high honors, 2000. Reporter The Press of Atlantic City, N.J., 1979-85; assoc. editor editl. page The Press of Atlantic City, 1985-90, editor editl. page, 1990-91; pub. info. officer Casino Control Commn., Atlantic City, 1991-96; editor Gaming Industry Observer, Northfield, N.J., 1996—; adj. prof. Richard Stockton Coll., Pomona, N.J., 1993—. Author: Hostage to Fortune: Atlantic City and Casino Gambling, 1987. Chmn. Domestic Affairs Task Force Jewish Cmty. Rels. Coun. Atlantic and Cape May Counties, Bargaintown, N.J., 1993-97; trustee Fedn. Jewish Agys. of Atlantic and Cape May Counties, 1995-98; organizing sponsor annual Mid-Atlantic Gaming Congress. Three-time recipient Media award N.J. State Bar Assn., 1981-84; 5-time recipient Journalism award N.J. Press Assn., 1983-91; recipient Editl. Writing award Edn. Writers Assn., 1986. Home and Office: 1 Meredith Ct Northfield NJ 08225-1500

POLLOCK, MICHAEL ROBERT, horticulturist; b. Bristol, Eng., Feb. 6, 1938. MS in Horticulture, Royal Horticultural Soc., 1962. Dir. Ministry Agr. Fisheries and Food Rosewarne Exptl. Sta, Camborne, Eng., 1977-89; asst. dir., tech. liaison officer Royal Hort. Soc., Surrey, ENg., 1990-96, head edn., 1996—. Fellow Inst. Horticulture.

POLLOCK, ROBERT ELWOOD, nuclear physicist; b. Regina, Sask., Can., Mar. 2, 1936; s. Elwood Thomas and Harriet Lillian (Rooney) P.; m. Jean Elizabeth Virtue, Sept. 12, 1959; children—Bryan Thomas, Heather Lynn, Jeffrey Parker, Jennifer Lee. B.Sc. (Hons.), U. Man., Can., 1957; M.A., Princeton U., 1959, Ph.D., 1963. Instr. Princeton U., 1961-63; Nat. Research Council Can. postdoctoral fellow Harwell, Eng., 1963-64; asst. prof. Princeton U., 1964-69, research physicist, 1969-70; asso. prof. Ind. U., 1970-73, prof., 1973-84, disting. prof., 1984—, dir. Cyclotron Facility, 1973-79, mem. Nuclear Sci. Adv. Com., 1977-80. Recipient Alexander von Humboldt Sr. U.S. Scientist award, 1985-88. Fellow Am. Phys. Soc. (Bonner prize 1992). Home: 2811 Dale Ct Bloomington IN 47401-2414 Office: Ind U Swain Hall Dept Physics Bloomington IN 47405

POLMEAR, ANDREW FRASER, research fellow; b. Aylesbury, Eng., Apr. 30, 1945; s. Nicholas and Margaret Jean (Dick) P.; m. Margaret West, July 3, 1971. MA in History, U. Cambridge, 1968, MB BChir, 1971. House officer Royal Hants County Hosp., Winchester, 1971-72; sr. house officer Nat. Health Svc., Southampton and London, 1972-74; sr. med. officer United Christian Hosp., Hong Kong, 1974-77; gen. practice trainee Brighton, 1977-78; gen. practice prin. Hove, 1979-96; sr. rsch. fellow U. Sussex, Brighton, 1996—; chmn. Sussex Postgrad. Med. Ctr., Brighton, 1999—; mem. S.E. Regional Sci. Adv. Panel, Eng., 1999—. Co-author: (book) Practical General Practice, 1999; contbr.: (book chpt.) Clinical Guidelines: A Practical Guide. Fellow Royal Coll. Physicians London, Royal Coll. Gen. Practitioners. Avocations: opera, hill walking. Home: 9 Powis Sq, Brighton BN1 3HH, England Office: The Trafford Ctr, U Sussex, Brighton BN1 9RY, England

POLO, OLLI JUHANI, pulmonary physician, physiology educator; b. Alastaro, Finland, Jan. 15, 1959; s. Väinö Abel and Hilkka Helmi Helena (Onnela) P.; m. Magdolna Kovács, Mar. 30, 1990; children: Annabella Ilona, Ákos Marco Alexander. MD, U. Turku, Finland, 1984, PhD, 1992, docent in Physiology, 1995. Lic. of medicine. Rsch. fellow dept. physiology U. Turku, Finland, 1984—, U. Montpellier, France, 1985-87, U. Sydney, Australia, 1992-94; dir. sleep rsch. unit, dept. physiology U. Turku, 1995—. Avocations: classical piano playing, photography. Office: U Turku Dept Physiology, Kiinamyllynkatu 10, 20520 Turku Finland

POLO, RICHARD JOSEPH, engineering executive; b. Barranquilla, Colombia, Oct. 14, 1936; s. Pedro Pastor and Clotilde (Verano) P.; m. Ana Isabel Cepeda, Feb. 1, 1958; children: Richard J. Jr., James Alan. BCE, NYU, 1957; MS in Structural Engring., Iowa State U., 1963, PhD in Structural and Nuc. Engring., 1971; disting. grad., Command and Gen. Staff Coll., Ft. Leavenworth, Kans., 1970; grad., Inter-Am. Def. Coll., Ft. McNair, Washington, 1977; MBA, Marymount U., 1986. Registered profl. engr., Md., Iowa, Fla., Ga., Pa., Conn., N.Y. Commd. 2d lt. U.S. Army, 1957, advanced through grades to col., 1979, various positions, 1957-79; asst. dir. civil works Pacific U.S. Army Office Chief of Engrs., 1979-80; corps engr., engr. brigade comdr. U.S. Army, Ludwigsburg, Fed. Republic Germany, 1980-83; dep. study dir. U.S. Army Office Chief of Staff, Washington, 1984-85; ret. U.S. Army, 1985; v.p. constrn. inspection Kidde Cons. Inc., Balt., 1985, sr. v.p. constrn. inspection, 1986, exec. v.p., 1986-89, corp. sec., 1988-89, also bd. dirs.; v.p. Fla. region CRSS, Miami, 1989-90; CEO, program dir. CRSS/WRJ joint venture, 1989-90; assoc. v.p., dep. divsn. dir. fed. programs Greiner, Inc., Miami, 1991-92; dir. engring. & project ops. CKC (OSC), Miami, 1993-94; dir. L.Am. ops., dir. engring. devel. GeoSyntec Cons., Boca Raton, 1994-96; dir. Miami ops. ICF Kaiser Engrs., Inc., 1996-98, group v.p., 1997-98; mgr. Fla. ops. Stone & Webster Engring., Inc., 1998-2000; sr. v.p. Stone & Webster Transp. Svcs., 1998-2000; pres. Amerint, Miami, 1994—, Am. Enterprises Internat., Inc., Polo Mortgage-Plus, Miami, 1993—; bd. dirs. KCI Holdings, 1988-90. Contbr. articles on mil. and structural engring. to profl. jours. Inventor arcuate space frame. Cmty. comdr. and sr. U.S. rep. Ludwigsburg Mil. Cmty., 1980-83. Decorated Legion of Merit with bronze oak leaf cluster, Bronze Star, others; Fed. Exec. fellow Brookings Institution, 1983-84. Fellow Soc. Am. Mil. Engrs. (bd. dirs. El Paso chpt. 1967-68, pres. Stuttgart chpt. 1980-82); mem. ASCE, NSPE, Md. Soc. Profl. Engrs., Va. Soc. Profl. Engrs. (dir. no. Va. chpt. 1985-89, pres. elect 1988-89), Assn. U.S. Army (pres. Ludwigsburg chpt. 1980-83), Fla. Engring. Soc., Army-Navy Club Coral Gables (dir. 1994-98,

sec. 1995-96, v.p. 1996-97, pres. 1997-98), Greater Miami C. of C. (trustee 1989-92, 97-2000), Country Club Coral Gables (dir. 1997—, sec. 1997-98, v.p. 1999-2000), Rotary, Elks, Sigma Xi, Phi Kappa Phi, Tau Beta Pi, Chi Epsilon, Psi Upsilon (pres. Delta chpt. 1956-57). Republican. Roman Catholic. Avocations: model airplanes, racquetball. Home and Office: Amerint/Am Enterprises Int 430 Sunset Rd Coral Gables FL 33143-6339

POLONYI, JANOS, physics educator; b. Budapest, Hungary, June 1, 1953; s. Janos Polonyi and Julianna Varossy; m. Agnes Janoshazi, Sept. 1, 1979 (div.); children: Eszter, Reka, Anna; m. Marianne Fingberg, July 16, 1999. MS, Eötvös U., Budapest, 1976, PhD, 1977. Rsch. fellow Cen. Rsch. Inst. for Physics, Budapest, 1976-81; postdoctoral fellow Gesellschaft für Schwerionenforschung, Darmstadt, Germany, 1981-82, U. Ill., Urbana, 1982-85; asst. prof. MIT, Cambridge, Mass., 1985-87, assoc. prof., 1987-93; prof. L. Eötvös U., Budapest, 1992—, Luis Pasteur U., Strasbourg, France, 1992—; dir. Lab. Theoretical Physics, Strasbourg, 1992—. Recipient A.P. Sloan fellow Sloan Fellowship, 1986-90, Presdl. Young Investigator award NSF, Washington, 1988-93. Mem. Hungarian Phys. Soc. (Schmidt Rezso award 1988), Am. Phys. Soc. Avocations: psychology, music, history. Office: Luis Pasteur U, 3 rue de l'Universite, Strasbourg Cedex 67084, France

POLOSUKHIN, VASILIY VLADIMIROVICH, anatomist; b. Tsvetnogorsk, Russia, Apr. 22, 1961; s. Vladimir Trofimovich and Tamara Vasiljevna (Kozhurenko) P.; m. Zhanna Anatoljevna Libenko, Oct. 20, 1981 (div. Apr. 1991); 1 child, Maxim; m. Dina Akhatovna Tuganbaeva, Jan. 13, 1994; 1 child, Igor. MD, Tomsk Med. Inst., 1984; PhD, Inst. Clin. Exptl. Medicine, 1991; ScD, Inst. Clin. Exptl. Lymphology, 1998. Rschr. Inst. Clin. and Exptl. Medicine, Novosibirsk, Russia, 1987-91, Inst. Physiology, Novosibirsk, 1991-95, Inst. Clin. and Exptl. Lymphology, Novosibirsk, 1995-99, Univ. Nebraska Med. Ctr., 1999—. Author: Morphogenetic Effects of Laser Induced Treatment in Therapy of Chronic Inflammation of the Bronchi, 1993, Diagnostic Bronchoalveolar Lavage (Ultrastructural Study of the Cell Populations), 1995, Pathological Anatomy of Inflammatory Lung Diseases, 1997, Chronic Bronchitis: Pathogenesis, Diagnosis, Clinical and Anatomic Description, 1998. Grantee Thoracal Laser Ctr., 1991, 92, 93, 94, 95, Pub. Health Siberia, 1996, Bank Khanty-Mansigsk, 1997. Mem. Siberian Soc. Lymphologists, Soc. of Ultrastructural Pathology. Avocations: mushrooming, fishing. Office: Dept Int Med Pulmonary Crit Care Med Sect Univ Nebraska Med Ctr Omaha NE 68198-0001

POLOUJADOFF, MICHEL EUGENE, electrical engineering educator; b. Asnières, France, Apr. 2, 1932; s. Léon and Marguerite Blanche (Guillot) P.; m. Jacqueline Suatton, Mar. 21, 1964; children: Muriel, Marie-Pierre. Degree, Ecole Superieure d'Electricité, Paris, 1955; MS, Harvard U.; DSc in Physics, U. Paris, 1960; Doct.h.c., Liége U., 1983, Budapest U., 1989, Bucharest U., 1996. Prof. U. Grenoble, France, 1961-83, 84-85, U. Pierre et Marie Curie, Paris, 1985—; prof., chair Ecole Centrale, Paris, 1985-96; disting. Hooker vis. prof. McMaster U., Hamiton, Ont., Can., 1983-84. Author: The Theory of Linear Induction Machinery, 1980, Chinese translation, 1985, also 3 tutorial books, 1970, Spanish translations, 1974; mem. editl. bd. 4 internat. revs. in field; contbr. over 200 papers, revs. Sous lt. Armée de l'Air, France, 1960-61. Recipient prix Charles Saulces de Freycinet, Acad. Sci. Paris, 1987. Fellow IEEE (Lamme medal 1994, Nikola Tesla award 1991), N.Y. Acad. Scis.; mem. Soc. Electriciens et Electr. (émérite). Roman Catholic. Avocations: skiing, photography, gardening. Home: 2 Rue Duméril, 75013 Paris France Office: U Paris, 4 Place Jussieu, 75252 Paris France

POLOUKHINE, OLGA, artist; b. Paris, Nov. 1, 1934; came to U.S., 1948; d. Nikita and Sophie (Schidlovsky) Koulomzin; m. Nicolas Poloukhine, Nov. 20, 1960; children: Olga, Michael, Elena. BA, Rutgers U., 1956; MA, Columbia U., 1960. Cert. art tchr. K-12, N.Y. Art tchr. Nyack (N.Y.) Schs., 1957-59, White Plains (N.Y.) Sch. System, 1959-60, Locust Valley (N.Y.) Pub. Schs., 1960-62; represented by Galeria Boriken, Rhinebeck, N.Y. Exhibited in group shows at Wunchs Art Gallery,Taller Galeria Forte, Barcelona, Spain, Richard Gallery, Northea. U., Boston Le Chateau Royal de Collioure, France, Hecksher Mus., N.Y., Nassau County Fine Arts Mus., N.Y., Fine Arts Mus. L.I., Long Beach Mus. Art, numerous others; represented in permanent collection at Zimmerli Art Mus., Rutgers U., other corp. and pvt. collections, including IBM, AT&T, N.Y. Tel. Co., NYNEX, O.C.A. Mem. L.I. Graphic Eye Gallery (founder, pres. 1989-91), Nat. Assn. Women Artists, Nat. Mus. of Women in the Arts (charter), N.Y. Soc. Women Artists. Eastern Orthodox. Home: 83 Skidmore Rd Lagrangeville NY 12540-5033

POLOY, ANNA (ANNA POLAY), dermatologist; b. Ozd, Hungary, July 24, 1942; d. Elemer and Margit (Huszthy) P.; m. Tibor Lakos, Sept. 17, 1982; 1 child, Agnes B. MD, Szeged, Hungary, 1966. Asst. Dermatol. Clinic, Szeged, Hungary, 1966-72; head physician County Hosp., Gyula, Hungary, 1972-96; dermatologist pvt. practice, Gyula, Hungary, 1996—. Contbr. articles to profl. jours. Mem. Internat. Soc. Dermatol. Surgery, European Acad. Dermatology and Venereology, Hungarian Dermatology Soc. Lutheran. Avocations: travel, art history, painting. Home: Budrio 22, 5700 Gyula Hungary Office: County Hosp, Coronella Med Ctr, Nürnbergi str 1, 5700 Gyula Hungary

POLSHAKOV, VLADIMIR IVANOVICH, scientist; b. Saratov, Russia, Mar. 14, 1959; s. Ivan Sergeevich and Yulia Nikolaevna (Bykova) P.; m. Galina Dmitrievna Ermilova, Jan. 12, 1980; 1 child, Anna. BSc, Moscow State U., 1981; PhD, Chem.-Pharm. Rsch. Inst., Moscow, 1988. Cert. in chemistry. Jr. rschr. Chem.-Pharm. Rsch. Inst., Moscow, 1981-88, rschr., 1988-92; rsch. fellow Nat. Inst. for Med. Rsch., London, 1992-94; sr. scientist Ctr. for Drug Chemistry (formerly Chem.-Pharm. Rsch. Inst.), Moscow, 1994—; group leader Ctr. for Drug Chemistry, Moscow, 1996—. Contbr. sci. articles to profl. jours. Fellow Wellcome Trust, 1992; scholar Howard Hughes Med. Inst., 1995; grantee Open Soc. Inst., 1999, internat. grantee Wellcome Trust, 2000. Mem. All-Russia Mendeleev Soc., N.Y. Acad. Scis. Avocations: gardening, tennis. Office: Ctr Drug Chemistry, 7 Zubovskaya Str, 119815 Moscow Russia

POLSTER, ANTON, retired soccer player; b. Mar. 10, 1964. Forward Cologne (Germany) Football Club; center forward Austrian Nat. Team. Address: Deutscher Fussball-Bund, Otto Fleck Schneise 6, D-60528 Frankfurt am Main Germany*

POLSTER, LEONARD H., investment company executive; b. Columbus, Ohio, June 24, 1921; s. Max and Henrietta Polster; m. Constance L. Buderus, Mar. 20, 1948 (dec. Aug. 1967); children: Leonard M., Lance E., Lewis E.; m. Edith Motridge, Nov. 19, 1968. BA, Ohio State U., 1942. Pres. Polster, Inc., 1952-68; pres. real estate and investments co. Polster, Inc., Rancho Santa Fe, 1968—; sr. v.p. PaineWebber Inc., L.A. and Rancho Santa Fe, Calif., 1971-91. Author: Pearls Before Swine, 1994. Pres. Polster Found., Rancho Santa Fe, 1988—; fin. officer, bd. dirs. San Dieguito Boys Club, Solana Beach, Calif., 1991—; bd. dirs. Fairbanks Ranch Cmty. Svcs. Dist., Rancho Santa Fe, 1987-92; pres. Fairbanks Ranch Assn., Rancho Santa Fe, 1985-86, bd. dirs., 1984-86. With USAF, 1942-46. Recipient Commitment to Youth award San Dieguito Boys and Girls Club, 1989; Olympic torch bearer, Apr. 28, 1996. Mem. Scripps Heritage Circle, Fairbanks Ranch Country Club, Phi Alpha Theta. Republican. Presbyterian. Avocations: tennis, reading, music. Home and Office: PO Box 8291 Rancho Santa Fe CA 92067-8291

POLUBESOVA, TAMARA, soil scientist, researcher; b. Yevpatoria, Crimea, USSR, Mar. 29, 1955; d. Aron and Rachil (Cherfus) Pachepsky; m. Guennady Polubesov, Oct. 22, 1977; 1 child, Ira. BS, MS, Moscow State U., 1977; PhD, Inst. Soil Sci., Pushchino, Russia, 1981. Minor rsch. scientist Inst. Soil Sci. Russian Acad. Scis., Pushchino, 1981-89, rsch. scientist Inst. Soil Sci., 1989-93, sr. rsch. scientist Inst. Soil Sci., 1993-94; rsch. scientist Hebrew U. Jerusalem, 1995-98, sr. rsch. scientist, 1998—. Contbr. articles to profl. jours. Grantee NASA, 1993, Min. Sci. and Art, Israel, 1995. Avocations: books, classical music, travel. Home: Weizmann 21B app 17, 76281 Rehovot Israel Office: Hebrew U Jerusalem, Faculty Agr, 76100 Rehovot Israel

POLUBOTKO, ALEKSEY MIKHAYLOVICH, physicist, researcher; b. Leningrad, Russia, USSR, Jan. 11, 1950; s. Mikhail Alekseevich and Evgeniya Sergeevna (Pereliaeva) P.; divorced; 1 child. Degree in radiophysics, Leningrad State U., 1973; PhD, Azerbaidjanskii Inst. Physics, 1983. Sr. engr. dept. radiophysics Leningrad State U., 1973-74; sr. engr. dept. theoretical base of radiotechnic Leningrad Electrotech. Inst., 1974-78; postgrad. rschr. Leningrad Physico-Tech. Inst., Russian Acad. Scis., 1978-82, engr., 1980-83, jr. rschr., then rschr., 1983—; vis. assoc. prof. Tohoku U., Sendai, Japan, 1993; vis. postdoctoral fellow Northwestern U., Evanston, Ill., 1997. Contbr. numerous sci. articles to profl. jours. Home: 5th Soviet St 47 Flat 24, 193024 Saint Petersburg Russia Office: AF Ioffe Physica Tech Inst, Politechnicheskaya 26, 194021 Saint Petersburg Russia

POLUKHINA, VALENTINA PLATONOVNA, Russian studies educator, author; b. Uriup, USSR, June 18, 1936; d. Platon Yevseevich and Pelageya (Innonkentyevna) Borisova; divorced. Student, Pedagogical Coll., Mariinsk, USSR, 1954; BA, Tula (USSR) State U., 1959; MA, Moscow State U., 1972; PhD, Keele U., Newcastle, Eng., 1985. Tchr. Russian Kayakent (USSR) High Sch., 1959-61; lectr. Russian Friendship U., Moscow, 1962-68, 72-73; lang. asst. U. Keele, 1973-76, lectr. Russian studies, 1976—. Author: Joseph Brodsky: A Poet for Our Time, 1989, A Dictionary of Brodsky's Tropes, 1995, Brodsky's Genges, 1995, Joseph Brodsky: The Art of a Poem, 1999; editor: Brodsky's Poetics and Aesthetics, 1990, Brodsky Through the Eyes of his Contemporaries, 1992; contbr. articles to profl. jours. Brit. Acad. grantee, 1979, 87, 90. Mem. Brit. Assn. Slavonic & East European Studies. Russian Orthodox. Office: U Keele, Dept Modern Lang, Newcastle ST5 5BG, England

POLUNIN, NICHOLAS VLADIMIR C., marine ecologist; b. Boston, June 26, 1951; s. Nicholas Polunin; m. Carolyn Lea Polunin; 2 children. BA in Zoology with honors, U. Oxford, Eng., 1972, MA, 1977; PhD in Freshwater Ecology, Cambridge (Eng.) U., 1980. Marine parks warden Seychelles, 1972-74; cons. IUCN/WWF, Indonesia, 1979-82; lectr. marine biology U. PNG, 1982-86; demonstrator, lectr., then reader marine biology U. Newcastle-upon-Tyne, Eng., 1986; pres. Found. Environ. Conservation; cons. in field. Editor: Environmental Conservation; co-editor: Reef Fisheries, 1996; editl. bd. Jour. Exptl. Marine Biology and Ecology, 1988—, Aquatic Living Resources, 1998—; contbr. numerous articles to profl. jours. Mem. BES, ISRS, FSBI, Camb. Phil. Soc. Achievements include research on marine ecology, marine reserves and fishing effects. Office: Univ of Newcastle-upon-Tyne, Dept Marine Scis, Newcastle upon Tyne NE1 7RU, England

POLUNINA, IRINA ALEXANDROVNA, chemist; b. Moscow, Mar. 9, 1951; d. Alexander Vasiljevich and Elena Vasiljevna Krukov; m. Evgenii Vladimorovich, June 1973; 1 child, Konstantin; m. Alexander Vasiljevich Larin, Mar. 17, 1984. MS, Lomonosov State U., Moscow, 1973; PhD, Inst. Phys. Chemistry, Moscow, 1986. Jr. rschr. Inst. Phys. Chemistry, Moscow, 1973-75, sr. rschr., 1975-80, prin. rschr., 1980—; sci. sec. Colloidal Chemistry Coun., Moscow, 1990-98. Contbr. articles to profl. jours. Grantee Russian Found. Fundamental Investigations. Fellow Mendeleev Chem. Soc. (sec. 1986-94). Avocations: sports, philately. Office: Inst Phys Chemistry, Leninskii Prospect 31, 117915 Moscow Russia

PÓLYA, KÁLMÁN, pharmaceutical company executive; b. Kisujszállás, Hungary, Feb. 5, 1932; s. Pólya Kálmán and Irma Pápay; m. Piroska Menyhárt, July 22, 1953; children: Zsófia, Êva. Degree in biology, Kossuth U., Debrecen, Hungary, 1954, MD, 1963; PhD, Acad. Scis., Budapest, Hungary, 1979. Prof. asst. Agrl. U., Debrecen, 1954-56; shift leader BIOGAL Pharm. Works, Debrecen, 1956-58, rsch. engr., 1958-63, chief indoor R&D, dir. dept., 1963-75, chief biotech. R&D divsn., 1975-93, chief consellor, 1993—; counselor Hungarian Tech. Devel. Office, 1997—. Inventor, co-inventor in field; author, co-author books and papers in field. Recipient Order of Work award Hungarian Govt., 1980. Fellow Chemotherapeutical Soc. Budapest; mem. Biotech. Soc. Budapest, Microbiol. Soc. Budapest. Avocations: arranging principles, joinery, basketball. Home: Péchy 9, Debrecen 4032, Hungary Office: BIOGAL Pharm Works, Pallagi 13, Debrecen 4042, Hungary

POLYAKOV, EVGENY VALENTINOVICH, laboratory administrator; b. Sverdlovsk, Urals, July 20, 1953; s. Valentine Efeamovich and Nina Konstantinovna Polyakova; m. Marina Evgenievna Polyakova; 1 child, Konstantine. Degree in Tech. Engring., Urals Poly. Inst., Sverdlovsk, 1977, PhD in Inorganic Chemistry, 1983. Rsch. chemist Urals Poly. Inst., Sverdlovsk, 1977-86, assoc. prof., 1986-87; chief lab. physicochem. methods of analysis Inst. Solid State Chemistry UD RAS, Ekaterinburg, Russia, 1987—; cons. Regional Environ. Protection Com., Ekaterinburg, 1993—. Author: Correlation of Periodicity and Monotony Within Periodic System of Chemical Elements, 1997; co-author: (with Y.N. Makurin, R.N. Pletnev, G.P. Shveikin) Energetic State of Atoms in Molecule and Properties of Chemical Compounds, 1995; contbr. articles to profl. jours. Mem. Internat. Union Radioecology. Achievements include patents in field. E-mail: Polyakov@ihim.uran.ru. Fax: 007 3432 74 44 95.

POLYAKOV, VALERY ARKADIEVICH, researcher in mechanics of composites; b. Jaroslavle, Russia, Feb. 19, 1941; arrived in Latvia, 1948; s. Arkadii Ivanovich and Zinaida Ivanovna (Momotenko) P. Diploma, State U. St. Petersburg, Russia, 1963; CandEngringScis, Acad. Scis., Riga, Latvia, 1971, D of Engring. Scis., 1992. Jr. rschr. Inst. Polymer Mechanics, Latvian Acad. Scis., 1963-72, sr. rschr., 1972-86, leading rschr., 1986-94, group leader, 1994—. Co-author: Properties of Spatially Reinforced Plastics, 1978, Spatially Reinforced Composites, 1987, Spatially Reinforced Composites, 1992; contbr. articles to profl. jours. Recipient awards Latvian Acad. Sci., 1979, 88. Fellow Latvian Sci. Union, Latvian Nat. Com. Mechs. Avocations: poetry, football, running, swimming. Home: 10/1 Caunas Ap 55, LV-1006 Riga Latvia Office: Inst Polymer Mechanics, 23 Aizkraukles, LV-1006 Riga Latvia

POLYANIN, ANDREI DMITRIEVICH, mathematician, researcher; b. Beijing, China, Nov. 1, 1951; s. Dmitry Vasilievich and Mariya Nikolaevna (Shurova) P.; m. Anna Aleksandrovna Melnikova, Apr. 29, 1978 (div. Mar. 1995); 1 child, Dmitry Andreevich; m. Tatyana Alekseevna Koptelova, May 20, 1995. MSc, Moscow State U., 1974; PhD, Inst for Problems in Mechanics, Russian Acad. Sci., 1981, DSc, 1986. Trial rschr. Inst. Problems in Mechanics/Russian Acad. Sci., 1975-76, jr. rschr., 1976-81, rschr., 1981-86, sr. rschr., 1987-92, prof., 1992—; prof. Inst. Gen. Inorganic Chemistry/Russian Acad. Scis., 1997-98; editor book series Overseas Publ. Assn., Amsterdam, 1998—. Author: (with V.V. Dilman) Methods of Modeling Equations and Analogies in Chemical Engineering, 1994, (with V.F. Zaitsev) Discrete-Group Methods for Integrating Equations of Nonlinear Mechanics, 1994, Handbook of Exact Solutions for Ordinary Differential Equations, 1995, (with A.V. Manzhirov) Handbook of Integral Equations, 1998, 18 others; contbr. more than 120 articles to sci. jours.; patentee in field. Recipient Chaplygine prize Russia Acad. Scis., 1991. Mem. Ctrl. House for Scientists. Avocations: chess, skiing, walking in the forest. Office: Inst Problems in Mechanics, Vernadsky Ave 101, Bldg 1, 117526 Moscow Russia

POLYCHRONAKIS, STAVROS ALEXANDER, chemical and environmental engineer; b. Corfou, Greece, Sept. 5, 1950; s. Alexander Stavros and Marie (Kouri) P.; m. Danae Ioanna Maritsa, July 2, 1988; children: Nefeli, Irene. Diploma in Chem. Engring., Nat. Tech. U., Athens, 1973; Diploma, Imperial Coll., London, 1978; PhD, U. London, 1979. Cert. environ. impact statement assessor. Sci. officer Ministry for the Environment, Athens, 1982—. Mem. Tech. Chamber of Greece. Home: 191 Militou St, 16451 Argyroupoli, Athens Greece Office: Ministry for Environment, 11 Alexandras Ave, 11473 Athens Greece

POLYDORIDES, GEORGIA KONTOGIANNOPOULOU, educator; b. Amaliada, Greece, June 29, 1945; d. Euthimios and Alexandra (Markopoulou) Kontogiannopoulou; m. Nicos D. Polydorides; children: Alexandros-Demetrios, Christina. M, Harvard U., 1972, PhD, 1977. Rschr. Harvard Grad. Sch. Design, Cambridge, Mass., 1976-79; sr. rschr. Ministry of Edn., Athens, Greece, 1980-85, Pedagogic Inst., Athens, Greece, 1986-89; assoc. prof. dept. maths. U. Patras, Greece, 1990-95, prof. dept. edn., 1996—; prof. U. Athens, 1991-95; dean sch. humanities & social scis. U. Patras, 1991-94, dir. divsn. sociology edn. & edn. policy, 1991-94, 95, dir. lab. edn. NAL policy analysis, divsn. soc. edn. & edn. policy, 1992-95; dir.. Hellenic coord. ctr. IEA U. Athens, 1996—. Author: Sociological Analysis of Greek Education, 2 vols., 1996, Educational Policy and Practice, 1995. Mem. Hellenic Studiesn Assn., Cambridge, 1971-73. Mem. Internat. Assn. for the Evaluation of Ednl. Achievement (gen. assembly 1989—, standing com. 1994-96), Am. Edn. Rsch. Assn., Tech. Chamber of Greece, Archtl. Assn., Comparative Edn. Soc. Avocations: swimming, gardening, traveling. Home: 50A Rodou St Kifisia, 14562 Athens Greece Office: U Athens, 13A Navarinou St 3d Fl, 10680 Athens Greece

POLYDORIDES, NICOS DEMETRIOU, urban planner, educator; b. Limassol, Cyprus, Mar. 20, 1946; arrived in Greece, 1963; s. Demetrios and Maria (Souliotes) P.; m. Georgia Kontogiannopoulou, Dec. 26, 1969; children: Alexandros, Christina. MArch, Tech. U., Athens, Greece, 1968; M in City Planning, Harvard U., 1973; PhD, U. Calif., Berkeley, 1977. Planning cons. Greece, 1970—; cons. Ministry of Coord., Greece, 1976-80; prof. city and regional planning U. Patras, Greece, 1980—; advisor to Minister of Rsch., Greece, 1994; advisor to commr. EEC, 1986-87, mem. Comett com., 1990-94; mem. interim governing bd. U. Cyprus, 1989-94; chmn. Nat. Documentation Ctr., 1989—. Recipient 1st prize internat. competition for city planning City of Ghent, Belgium, 1971, award internat. competition for new campus U. Brussels, 1970. Mem. Am. Planning Assn., Tech. Chamber of Greece, Harvard Club of Greece (chmn. 1981-82). Avocations: reading, stamps. Home: 50a Rodou St, 14562 Kifisia Athens Greece Office: U Patras, Rion, 261-10 Patras Greece

POLYMENIDIS, ZAFIRIS PANOS, pathologist, immunologist, nephrologist; b. Thessaloniki, Greece, Feb. 26, 1937; s. Panos Zafiris and Polixeni Thomas (Karamitsiou) P.; m. Polixeni Dimitrios Chatzitheoporou, Dec. 26, 1968; children: Panagiotis, Magdalini. Grad., U. Thessaloniki, 1965. Fellow pathology clinic Aristotelian U. of Thessaloniki, 1967-70, asst. prof. pathology, 1970-78, assoc. prof. propedeutic clinic, 1978-85; dir. regional tissue typing lab. Hippokratian Hosp., Thessaloniki, 1985-87, dir., chmn. regional tissue typing lab., 1987—; mem. adminstrn. bd. transplantation com. Min. of Health, 1982-85, Bone Marrow Transplant Assn., 1989-97, Nat. Coun. of Transplantation, 1996-97. Author: Immunological Aspects, 1990-95; contbr. articles to profl. jours.; journalist Athletic News newspaper, 1950-61. Capt. Greek Army, 1966-68. Mem. Hellenic Soc. Immunology (pres. 1996-97), Hellenic Nephrol. Soc., European Found. for Immunogenetics, Balkan Soc. for Histocompatibility Immunogentics, Rotary (establishing mem.), Aristotle Sports Club (establishing mem.). Christian Orthodox. Avocations: fishing, reading, walking. Home: 71 Amalias St, 546 40 Thessaloniki Faliro, Greece Office: Hippokration Hosp, 49 Konstantinoupoulos St, 54692 Thessaloniki Greece

POLYZOGOPOULOS, CONSTANTIN, lawyer, law educator; b. Athens, Greece, Mar. 25, 1950; s. Panayotis and Paraskevi (Morfopoulou) P.; m. Katherine Papadopoulou, July 19, 1979; 1 child, Eva. LLB, U. Athens, 1973; PhD, U. Tübingen, Germany, 1975. Bar: Athens, 1974, Ct. Appeal, 1979, Supreme Ct., 1982. Asst. U. Athens, 1976-82, lectr., 1982-89, asst. prof. law, 1989—; practice Athens. Author: Cross-Examination of the Parties and Oral Affidavits in their Relationship to Each Other, 1976, Execution on Copyright, 1987, Juridical Studies, 1996. Mem. Automobile Club of Greece (pres. disciplinary ct. appeal 1990-96, Medal 1993, 95, v.p. 2000—), Greek Assn. Procedural Law, Internat. Assn. Procedural Law, Assn. Tchg. and Rsch. in Intellectual Property, Internat. Assn. Artistic Literature (treas. Greek section 1982—), Wissenschaftliche Vereinigung für Internationales Verfahrensrecht, U. Tubingen Alumni Assn., German Acad. Exch. Svc. Alumni Assn., German Sch. Athens Alumni Assn., Salzburg Seminar Alumni Assn., Yacht Racing Club Athens. Avocations: sailing, boating. Office: Law Office, Skoufa 60A, GR-10680 Athens Greece

POMBEIRO, ARMANDO JOSE LATOURRETTE, chemistry educator; b. Porto, Portugal, June 9, 1949; s. Armando José Gomes Oliveira Pombeiro and Leontina Latourrette; children: Ana, Henrique, Guilherme. Lic. in chem. engring., Superior Tech. Inst., Lisbon, Portugal, 1971; DPhil, U. Sussex, Brighton, Eng., 1976. Aux. prof. chem. engring. Superior Tech. Inst., 1976-79, assoc. prof. chem. engring., 1979-89, full prof. chem. engring., 1989—; mem. phys. and engring. sci. and tech. panel, NATO Sci. Program, Brussels, 1999, mem. ASI adv. panel, 1995-98; mem. Higher Coun. Sci. and Tech., Ministry Planning and Adminstrn. of Territory, Lisbon, 1995; mem. internat. organizing coms./adv. bds. over 20 internat. confs. and symposia. Author: Techniques and Unit Operations in Laboratory Chemistry, (in Portuguese) 1st edit., 1983, 2d edit., 1991, 3d edit., 1998; editor, co-author: Molecular Electrochemistry of Inorganic, Bioinorganic and Organometallic Compounds, 1993; contbr. 20 chpts. and articles to books, over 220 articles to internat. profl. jours. Fellow Royal Soc. Chemistry; mem. N.Y. Acad. Scis., Portuguese Electrochem. Soc. (co-founder 1983, pres. 1988-89, 94-95, v.p. 1990-91, sec. 1983-87), Acad. Scis. of Lisbon (vice gen.-sec., sec. class of scis. 1998, vice-sec. 1993-98, v.p. class of scis. 1999—, adminstrv. coun. 1998, dir. commn. publs. 1981—), Iberoam. Soc. Electrochemistry (co-founder 1990, nat. rep. 1992-96), Internat. Union Pure and Applied Chemistry (affiliate), Portuguese Chem. Soc., European Soc. Chemistry. Avocation: travel. Office: Inst Sup Tecnico Complexo I, Av Rovisco Pais, P1049-001 Lisbon Portugal

POMBO, MANUEL, pediatric endocrinologist, researcher, educator; b. Sarria, Spain, May 1, 1943; s. Manuel and Natividad (Arias) P.; m. Maria Victoria Suarez, Feb. 24, 1974; children: Manuel, Alejandra. MD, Santiago (Spain) Sch. Medicine, 1968, PhD, 1975. Asst. prof. U. Santiago, 1970-79, assoc. prof., 1979-93, prof. pediatrics, 1993—; sr. register pediatrics Ctrl. Hosp. de Galicia, Santiago, 1978—, head pediat. endocrinology, 1978—; vis. prof. Children's Hosp., Columbus, Ohio, 1991, NIH, Bethesda, Md., 1995; mem. several adv. bds. Editor: Endocrinologia Pediatrica, 1990, Pediatria Practica, 4th edit., 1992, Two Decades of Experience in Growth, 1993, Tratado de Endocrinología Pediatrica, 1997; contbr. over 200 articles to profl. jours. and chpts. to books. Recipient numerous grants and awards. Mem. Spanish Soc. Pediatrics (hon., v.p. 1983-86), Spanish Soc. Pediat. Endocrinology (hon. pres. 1989), European Soc. Pediatric Endocrinology, Lawson Wilkins Pediat. Endocrinology Soc., Growth Hormone Rsch. Soc., N.Y. Acad. Scis. Achievements include research in growth disorders and its treatment. Avocations: writing, collecting antique books. Home: General Pardinas 10-6oD, 15701 Santiago Compostela, Spain Office: Hosp Clin U, Trav de la Choupana S/N, 15707 Santiago Spain

POMERANTZ, SHERWIN BERNARD, economic development consultant; b. N.Y.C., Nov. 18, 1939; s. Sidney and Anna (Simons) P.; m. Barbara Sue Rashbaum (dec. 1989); children: Debi, Shari (dec.); m. Rishona Miner, July 8, 1990. BS in Indsl. Engring., NYU, 1960; MS, U. Ill., 1962; MBA, Northwestern U., 1966. Instr. U. Ill., Champaign, 1960-62; mech. engr. NASA, Cleve., 1962-64; dir. mktg. Masten Corp., Chgo., 1964-66; pres. Controls For Industry, Inc., Chgo., 1966-82; v.p. Luz Industries Ltd., Jerusalem, 1984-90; pres. Atid E.D.I. Ltd., Jerusalem, 1991—. Columnist Chgo. Jewish Post & Opinion, 1974-76. Pres. Maine Twp. Jewish Congregation, Des Plaines, Ill., 1974-76, United Synagogue of Am., Chgo., 1976-79, Bd. Jewish Edn., Chgo., 1979-82, Assn. Ams. & Canadians in Israel, Jerusalem, 1990-92. Capt. U.S. Army Signal Corps, 1962-64, Cleve. Recipient Nehemian Gitelson medallion Alpha Epsilon Pi, 1975. Mem. ASME, Am. Citizens Abroad. Avocations: reading, travel. Home: Hagidud Haivri 6, 92144 Jerusalem Israel Office: ATID ETI Ltd, 5 Kiryat Madda St, 91450 Jerusalem Israel

POMERANZ, FELIX, accounting educator; b. Vienna, Austria, Mar. 28, 1926; s. Joseph and Irene (Meninger) P.; m. Rita Lewin, June 14, 1953; children: Jeffrey Arthur, Andrew Joseph. BBA, CCNY, 1948; MS, Columbia U., 1949; PhD, U. Birmingham, Eng., 1992. Diplomate Am. Bd. Forensic Acctg.; CPA, N.Y., Va., La., N.C.; cert. computer profl., fraud examiner, govt. fin. mgr. Audit staff Coopers & Lybrand, CPAs, N.Y.C., 1949-56; mgr. Marks, Grey & Shron (now Ernst & Young, CPA's), N.Y.C., 1956-58; asst. chief auditor Am.-Standard, N.Y.C., 1958-62; mgr. systems Westvaco Corp., N.Y.C., 1962-66; dir. operational auditing Coopers & Lybrand, CPAs, N.Y.C., 1966-68, ptnr., 1968-85; disting. lectr./dir. Ctr. for Acctg., Auditing, Tax Studies Fla. Internat. U., Miami, 1985-93, prof. acctg., 1993—, assoc. dir. sch. acctg., 1993-99, affil. faculty dept. religious studies, 1996—. Author: Managing Capital Budget Projects, 1984; The Successful Audit: New Ways to Reduce Risk Exposure and Increase Efficiency, 1992; co-author: Pensions-An Accounting and Management Guide, 1976; Auditing

in the Public Sector: Efficiency, Economy, and Program Results, 1976; Comparative International Auditing Standards, 1985; contbr. articles to profl. jours. Emeritus trustee Nat. Ctr. for Automated Info. Rsch.; founding mem. Ctr. for Study of Islam and Democracy. 1st lt. AUS, 1944-46, 51-52. Recipient Spear Safer Harmon faculty fellow Coll. Bus. Administrn., 1987, Coll. Bus. Adminstrn., award for outstanding svc., 1998. Mem. AICPAs, N.Y. State Soc. CPAs, Assn. Systems Mgmt., Acad. Acctg. Historians, Assn. Govt. Accts., N.Y. Acad. Scis., Am. Acctg. Assn., Inter-Am. Acctg. Assn., Assn. Cert. Fraud Examiners, Beta Gamma Sigma, Beta Alpha Psi (Most Disting. and Most Outstanding Prof. awards 1993), Alpha Kappa Psi (Dr. Felix Pomeranz Faculty of Yr. award, Endless Work award). Home: 250 Jacaranda Dr Apt 406 Fort Lauderdale FL 33324-2532 Office: Fla Internat U Sch Acctg University Park Miami FL 33199-0001

POMERENE, JAMES HERBERT, retired computer engineer; b. Yonkers, N.Y., June 22, 1920; s. Joel Pomerene and Elsie Bower; m. Edythe R. Schwenn, Dec. 1, 1944; children: James Bennett, Katherine Ellen, Andrew Thomas Stewart. BSEE, Northwestern U., 1942; postgrad., Princeton U., 1950. Elec. engr. Hazeltine Corp., Little Neck, N.Y., 1942-46; mem. staff electronic computer project Inst. for Advanced Study, Princeton, N.J., 1946-51; chief engr. Inst. for Advanced Study, Princeton, 1951-56; sr. engr. IBM Corp., Poughkeepsie, N.Y., 1956-67; sr. staff mem. IBM Corp., Armonk, N.Y., 1967-76; cons. in field. Patentee in field. IBM fellow T.J. Watson Rsch. Ctr., 1976—. Fellow IEEE (Computer Pioneer award Computer Soc. 1986, Edison medal 1993); mem. NAE, Sigma Xi, Tau Beta Pi. Episcopalian. Home: 403 Bedford Rd N Chappaqua NY 10514-2207

POMEROY, STEPHEN JOHN, electrical engineer; b. Portsmouth, Eng., July 30, 1952; s. Edward John and Nora (Roles) P. BS in Elec. and Electronic Engring. with honors, Portsmouth Poly. Inst., 1975, MS in Electronics, 1981. Design engr. BAE Sys., Portsmouth, 1975—. Editor local history publs. Mem. Inst. Elec. Engrs. (assoc.). Methodist. Avocation: local history. Office: BAE Sys, Brown Ln, Portsmouth Hampshire PO3 5PH, England

POMES, RAMON, physicist, researcher; b. Santiago di Cuba, Cuba, Dec. 5, 1947; s. Ramon and Flora (Hernandez) P.; m. Maria Cobas, Mar. 14, 1970; 1 child, Joanna. BSc, U. Oriente, Cuba, 1970; PhD, U. Leningrad, Russia, 1976; Dr.Habil., U. Humboldt, Germany, 1982; DSc, Ministry of Higher Edn., Cuba, 1982. Faculty U. Oriente, 1970-71, prof., 1977-82; rschr. U. Leningrad, 1971-76; prof., head divsn. Acad. Scis., Cuba, 1982-91, CNIC, Cuba, 1991-94; prof. Centro Nat. de Invest. Cientifi, Mex., 1994—. Contbr. articles to profl. jours. Capt. Cuban Mil. Force, 1964-67. Recipient more than 15 awards, honors, grants Cuba, Russia, Poland, Angola, Mex., Bulgaria. Mem. Cuban Physics Soc., Chem. Assn. Cuba, N.Y. Acad. Scis. Home: Ave Camagvey 11238, Havana Cuba Office: CNIC, PO Box 6880, Havana Cuba

POMFRETT, CHRIS JOHN, neurophysiologist; b. Romford, Essex, Eng., June 3, 1962; s. John and Patricia Pauline (Stockman) P.; m. Veronica Ann Woolgar, May 30, 1987. BS, London U., 1983, PhD, 1987. Rsch. fellow U. Keele, U.K., 1987-89; sr. rsch. asst. U. Manchester, U.K., 1990-94, lectr. in neurophysiology, 1994—. Inventor Depth of Anaesthesia Monitoring, 1991; contbr. articles to profl. publs. Fellow Royal Soc. of Medicine; mem. Physiol. Soc., Anaesthetic Rsch. Soc. Avocation: computer programming. Office: Univ Dept Anaesthesia/Manchester Royal Inf, Oxford Rd, M13 9WL Manchester England

POMIRKO, ROMAN, linguist, educator, researcher; b. Sudova Vychnia, L'viv, Ukraine, May 27, 1942; s. Semen Yossypovych and Kateryna (Ivanivna) P.; m. Zvenyslava-Sofiya Onufrivna Kahuy, Sept. 12, 1971. Postgrad., L'viv State U., 1975-78; DS, Kyiv State U., 1989. Interpreter, lectr. Russian Technol. Inst., Havana, Cuba, 1969-72; Spanish and French lectr. L'viv State U., 1973-75, assoc. prf., 1979-92, prof., 1993—, dean Faculty Fgn. Langs., 1995—; Russian, Ukrainian, and Spanish lectr. U. Angers, 1992, 95; coord. internat. project Tempus-TACIS, 1997-2000. Author: Spanish Language and its Dialects: Variability of a Word, 1996, On the History of Romance Languages, 1992; contbr. articles to profl. jours. Humanitarian aid promoter French-Ukrainian Assn., France, 1992-96; Ukrainian culture acquaintance promoter U. Angers, France, 1993, 96; Ukrainian modern art exhbn. oganizer City Coun. Angers, 1994. Grantee U. Sorbonne, Paris IV, 1984, 87, FIPF, 1994, U. Ministry Culture Spain, 1998. Mem. Alliance Francaise (pres. 1990—), Internat. Fedn. Profs. of French. E-mail: semiv@icmp.lviv.ua. Office: L'viv Ivan Franko Nat U, 1 Universytets'ka st, L'viv Ukraine

POMMÉ, STEFAAN GABRIËL, physicist, researcher; b. Roeselare, W-VL, Belgium, Oct. 4, 1965; s. Marin and Ludwine (Decru) P.; m. Bea Hilda De Sutter, May 18, 1991; children: Sophie, Evelien. Licentiaat Physics, Ghent (Belgium) U., 1987, PhD in Physics, 1992; Kandidat Polit. and Social Scis., U Faculteiten Sint Ignatius, Antwerp, Belgium, 1994; PhD in Chemistry, Ghent U., Belgium, 1999. Scientific researcher Ghent U., 1987-92; postdoct. fellow Inst. for Reference Materials & Measurements, EU, 1992-94; researcher Studiecentrum voor Kernenergie-Centre d'étude de l'énergie nucléaire, Mol, Belgium, 1994—. Contbr. research articles to profl. jours. Office: SCK-CEN GKD, Boeretang 200, B-2400 Mol Belgium

POMMER, HANS JÖRG HELMUTH, economist, management consultant; b. Graz, Styria, Austria, Aug. 13, 1936; s. Wolfgang J. and Paula (Degeler) P.; m. Hannelore B. Zillich, Aug. 1963; children: Marc, Katrin. B in Polit. Sci., U. Paris, 1960; M in Econs., U. Berne, Switzerland, 1964. Analyst and editor Swiss Inst. East European Affairs, Berne, 1962-67; pers. officer IBM Germany, Stuttgart, 1967-71; mgr. human resources IBM Ea. Europe, Vienna, Austria, 1972-75, IBM Germany, various locations, 1976-93; owner Mgmt. and Orgn. Cons., Schoenaich, Germany, 1994—; employee rels. cons. IBM Korea, Seoul, 1989-90. Author: Antisemitism in the Soviet Union, 1963, Politics and Economics in the Soviet Bloc: The Comecon, 1966; (with Laszlo Revesz) Medicine in the Soviet Empire, 1965; contbr. articles to profl. jours. Avocations: classic music, antique clocks and watches, golfing, traveling, hiking. Home and Office: Mgmt & Orgn Cons, Heinrich-Heine-Weg 2, D-71101 Schoenaich Germany

POMMIER, PATRICK, veterinarian; b. Beauchamps, Somme, France, Oct. 11, 1956; s. Gaston and Nelly (Desoutieux) P.; m. Monique Labourdette, July 7, 1990; children: Maïlys, Philémon. DVM, Ecole Nat. Veterinaire, Alfort, France, 1986; diploma in biotechnology, U. Rennes (France) 1, 1989; maitrise de biostatistiques, U. Paris XI, 1992; postgrad., U. Paris 6, 1992, U. Paris 7, 1993. Vet. surgeon Practices, France, 1980-86; in-charge clin. trials CTPA, Ploufragan, France, 1986-93; tech. mgr. CTPA-Zoopôle, Ploufragan, 1993—. Author articles in sci. and profl. jours. Aspirant Svc. de Santé des Armées, France, 1983. Mem. French Assn. Porcine Vet. Medicine, SFB, Biovéto (pres. 1997—). Avocations: jazz, ornithology. Office: CTPA-Zoopôle, BP 7 Rd Point du Zoopole, 22440 Ploufragan France

POMMIER, YVES GEORGES, laboratory administrator; b. Caen, Calvados, France, Apr. 1, 1951; came to U.S., 1988; s. Roger Pommier and Marie-Therese Blais; m. Françoise Champey, Jan. 4, 1988; children: Gabriel, Elie. MS in Pharmacology, U. Paris, 1978, MD cum laude, 1981, PhD, 1986. Cert. radiation safety authorized user NIH. Resident Paris Hosps., 1978-81; pharmacology asst. U. Paris., 1979-81; vis. fellow NIH, Nat. Cancer Inst., Bethesda, Md., 1981-84, vis. scientist, 1984-95, prin. investigator, 1995—, chief lab. molecular pharmacology, 1997—; organizer internat. conf. HIV-1 Integrase Inhibitors, 1996; lectr. in field. Mem. editl. bd. Cancer Rsch., Molecular Pharmacology, Anticancer Drug Design, others; contbr. articles to med. jours.; patentee in field. Recipient Impact Medicin Med. Dr. for Yr. 2000, 1992, Fed. Tech. Transfer award, 1994; competitive tng. grantee French Found. for Biol. Rsch., 1981, NIH intramural grantee AIDS Targeted Antiviral Program of Office of Dir., 1993-94, 95-96, 97-98. Mem. French Soc. Pharmacology, Am. Fedn. for Clin. Rsch., Am. Assn. for Cancer Rsch. (program com. 1996-99, chmn. CaiN award 1998), N.Y. Acad. Scis., NIH Apoptosis Interest Group. Democrat. Avocations: painting, tennis, coaching soccer team. E-mail: pommier@nih.gov. Office: Lab of Molecular Pharmacology Rom 5d02 Nih Bldg 37 Bethesda MD 20892-0001

POMORSKA, BOZENA NERLO, physicist; b. Lodz, Poland, Feb. 5, 1948; d. Henryk and Wanda (Mirowska) Nerlo; m. Krzysztof Roman Pomorski, Sept. 8, 1970; children: Maciej, Agata. Magister of Physics, U. M.C.S. Lublin, Poland, 1970; Habilitated Doctor, U. Lublin, 1981, Prof. Physics, 1996; D Physics, Inst. Nuclear Rsch., Swierk, Poland, 1974. Doctorant Inst. Nuclear Rsch., Swierk, Poland, 1970-74; adj. Maria Curie Skłodowska U., Lublin, 1977-82, docent lectr. physics, 1982-93, extraordinary prof., 1993—; scientist Unified Inst. of Nuclear Rsch., Dubna, 1976; asst. prof. Tech. U., Munich, 1978-80; scientist U.Regensburg, Germany, 1985, Ctr. of Nuclear Rsch., Strasbourg, France, 1993. Contbr. articles to profl. jours. Grantee Polish Com. Sci. Rsch., Warsaw, 1994, 96. Mem. Polish Phys. Soc. Roman Catholic. Avocation: tourism. Home: Lasockiego 17, 20612 Lublin Poland Office: Maria Curie Skłodowska U, Phys Dpt Radziszewskiego 10, 20031 Lublin Poland

POMORSKI, JERZY MIKULOWSKI, sociology educator; b. Katowice, Poland, Jan. 3, 1937; s. Wladyslaw Mikulowski and Barbara Mikulowska (Czaplicka) P.; m. Alina Tarnowska, Mar. 13, 1975. LLM, Jagiellonian U., 1958, M in Sociology, 1963; PhD, Polish Acad. Sci., 1969; dr. habilitus, U. Lodz, 1978; LHD (hon.), Grand Valley State U., 1993; LLD (hon.), U. Teesside, 1995. Asst. Press Rsch. Ctr., Krakow, Poland, 1953-60; editor Magazine Przekroj, Krakow, 1960-61; asst. Cracow U. Econs., Krakow, 1962-69, reader, 1969-78, assoc. prof., 1978-90, prof., 1991-95, ordinary prof., 1995—; pres. Cracow U. Econs., 1990-96, Journalist Found., Krakow, 1990—; trustee Internat. Inst. Communications, London, 1973-84; prof. U. Silesia, Katowice, 1984—. Author numerous books; contbr. articles to profl. jours. Mem. Coun. on Media Pres. of Poland, Warsaw, 1993-96. Recipient Medal Polonie Restituta Pres. Poland, 1991, Prize Polish Journalist Assn., 1981. Mem. Rotary (pres. Krakow club 1997-98). Roman Catholic. Home: 12 Gontyna, 30-202 Cracow Poland Office: Cracow U Econs, 27 Rakowicka, 31-510 Cracow Poland

POMPA, LEONARDO, philosophy educator, university dean; b. Edinburgh, Scotland, Feb. 22, 1933; s. Dominic Albert and Antonia Annunziata P.; m. Juliet Caroline Sich, Aug. 9, 1962; children: Nicholas Dominic, Antonia Elisabeth. MA in History with honors, U. Edinburgh, 1956, MA in Philosophy with honors, 1961, PhD, 1967. Lectr. in logic U. Edinburgh, 1961-77; prof. philosophy U. Birmingham, Eng., 1977-97, dean faculty of arts, 1984-87, 89-92, emeritus prof. philosophy, 1997—; cons. Inst. Vico Studies, N.Y.C. and Atlanta, 1975—; mem. adv. bd. Philosophy of History and Culture, 1988—, Cuadernas Sobre Vico, 1996—; comn. philosophy panel for higher edn. funding coun. Eng.'s Rsch. Assessment Exercise, 1996. Author: Vico: A Study of the New Science, 1975, 2d edit., 1990, Human Nature and Historical Knowledge, 1990; translator, editor: Vico: Selected Writings, 1982; co-editor: Substance and Form in History, 1981; contbr. numerous articles to scholarly publs. Mem. Aristotelian Soc., Nat. Com. Philosophy (com. 1985-99), Brit. Soc. for History Philosophy (com. 1985-92), Storia Antropologia e Sci. del Linguagoio (editorial com. 1990—), Hegel Soc. Gt. Britain (pres. 1989-92), Coun. Royal Inst. Philosophy. Avocations: music, literature, foreign travel, sports, wine.

POMPEI, PIERLUIGI, neuropharmacologist; b. Rome, Italy, Jan. 31, 1960; s. Andrea and Lia (Magni) P. BS in Pharmacy, U. Camerino, 1990; PhD, U. Ancona, 1994. Intern U. Camerino, Italy, 1987-90; postdoctoral rschr. Rockefeller U., N.Y.C., 1991-96; asst. prof. U. Camerino, 1995—. Airman Italian Air Force, 1991-92. Mem. N.Y. Acad. Sci. Avocations: mountaineering, skiing, rock & ice climbing. Home: Berta St, 62030 Camerino Marche, Italy Office: Dept Pharm Sci & Exptl Med, Scalzino St, 63032 Camerino Marche, Italy

POMPEIANO, OTTAVIO, physiologist, educator; b. Faenza, Italy, Sept. 29, 1927; s. Antonio and Maria (Padula) P.; m. Stefi Möller, Sept. 13, 1960; children: Maria, Maria Cristina, Lucia, Antonio. MD, Bologna (Italy) U., 1950. Docent physiology Bologna U., 1958; prof. physiology Med. Sch. Pisa U., 1966—, dir. inst. physiology Med. Sch., 1981-83; acting prof. physiology Rome U., 1962-63; vis. prof. dept. physiology Göteborg (Sweden) U., 1964; acting prof. neurophysiology Scuola Normale Superiore, Pisa, 1968-93; vis. prof. Wash. State U., Pullman, 1985. Author: (with A. Brodal and F. Walberg) The Vestibular Nuclei and Their Connections, Anatomy and Functional Correlations; (with A. Brodal) Basic Aspects of Central Vestibular Mechanisms; (with R. Granit) Reflex Control of Posture and Locomotion; (with C. Ajmone Marsan) Brain Mechanisms of Perceptual Awareness and Purposeful Behavior; (with J.H.J. Allum) Vestibulospinal Control of Posture and Movement; (with C.D. Barnes) Neurobiology of the Locus Coeruleus; editor: Archives Italiennes de Biologie, Pflügers Archiv-European Jour. Physiology, 1970-95, Progress in Brain Rsch., Jour. Vestibular Rsch., Neurol. Psychiat. Brain Rsch., The Cerebellum, Italian Jour. Neurol. Sci. Discovered inhibition of motoneurons during sleep and mechanisms of sensorymotor integration during sleep; developed problems of cen. and reflex control of posture and movements, and brain integration of neck and labyrinth inputs; demonstrated the spatio-temporal response properties of corticocerebellar neurons to labyrinth signals and their changes after neck stimulation; discovered role of cen. noradrenergic system in postural and motor control; demonstrated responses of cen. noradrenergic neurons to stimulation of macular (gravity) and neck receptors and their influences in gain regulation of vestibulospinal and cervicospinal reflexes; discovered adaptive changes of the vestibulospinal reflex and the role that the central noradrenergic system exerts on adaptation of the vestibulo-ocular and the vestibulospinal reflex; described (with A. Brodal) somatotopical organization of efferent projections from cerebellum, lateral vestibular nucleus and red nucleus; demonstrated changes in immediate early gene expression in the rat brain during and after exposure to microgravity, NASA's space-lab mission "Neurolab," April 1998. Rockefeller Found. Rsch. fellow Anat. Inst., Oslo U., 1956-57, Rsch. fellow Nobel Inst. Neurophysiology, Karolinska Inst., Stockholm, 1958-59; Henderson Trust lectr., Edinburgh, Scotland, 1961, Moruzzi lectr., Liège, Belgium, 1981; Decorated Order Cherubino, Pisa U., 1978; NIH grant, 1961-97; recipient Vittorio Emanuele II prize, 1950; E. Cavazza prize Bologna U., 1950; A. Feltrinelli prize for medicine Accademia dei Lincei, Rome, 1974, Edn. Dept. Gold medal Rome, 1979, R. Barany Gold medal for contributions on vestibular physiology, Uppsala U., 1983, P. Caliceti Internat. prize and Gold medal Bologna U., 1984, Disting. Scientist award for contributions on basic mechanisms of sleep Sleep Rsch. Soc., 1999. Mem. N.Y. Acad. Sci., Academia Rodinensis, Academia Europaea, European Neurosci Assn., Italian Physiol. Soc., Am. Neurosci. Soc., Barany Soc., Collegium ORLAS, Internat. Brain Rsch. Orgn. (cen. coun. 1976-86). Home: 46 Strada Statale n 12, 56017 S Giuliano Terme Italy Office: 31 Via S Zeno, 56127 Pisa Italy

POMPIDOU, ALAIN JACQUES, medical educator; b. Paris, Apr. 5, 1942; s. Georges and Claude (Cahour) P.; m. Sophie Gintz, June 7, 1968 (div. 1982); children: Thomas, Romain, Yannick; m. Nicole Duchet, July 9, 1983. MD, U. Paris, 1968, D in Human Biology, 1969, PhD, 1984. Prof. faculty medicine René Descartes U., Paris V, 1986-87; sci. counselor Ministry Rsch., 1987-88; sci. advisor Ministry Health, 1987-88; vice chmn. Hugo Ethics Com., 1992-98; chmn. ethics com. for space UNESCO, 1998-99, mem. French com., 1993—. Contbr. numerous articles to sci. and rsch. publs. Mem. European Parliament, 1989-99; sci. advisor to French Prime Min., 1992-95; mem. nat. com. for univ., 1990—; mem. econ. and social com., France, 1999—. Roman Catholic. Avocations: sculpture, modern art, fishing. Fax: 33-14-05-10-946. Office: Faculty Medicine Cochin, Rue du Faurourg St Jacques, F75014 Paris France

PONCE, ELEANOR HAIGHT, dentist, researcher, educator; b. Sayangan, Atok, The Philippines, Feb. 18, 1963; d. John Tibanban and Prudencia Rilloma (Sibayan) Haight; m. Wilbert Abrera Ponce, Apr. 15, 1989. BS in Biology, U. Baguio, Baguio City, The Philippines, 1982, D in Dental Medicine, 1986; PhD in Dental Sci., Tohoku U., Sendai, Japan, 1999. Rural health dentist Rural Health Unit, Benguet, The Philippines, 1987-88; instr. Pines City Ednl. Ctr., Baguio City, 1988-90; tchg. and clin. instr. U. Baguio, Baguio City, 1990-94, 99—, head endodontics dept., 1999—, rschr., 1999—; dentist, cons. A and A Mktg., Baguio City, 1999—, Benguet Electric Co., Baguio City, 2000—; dentist Haight-Ponce Dental Office, Baguio City, 2000—; rschr. Tohoku U., Sendai, 2000—. Spkr. UNESCO, Sendai, 1997; pres. Filipino Students Group, Sendai, 1998. Scholar Ministry Edn. Japan, 1994-99. Mem. Internat. Assn. Dental Rsch., Japan Dental Assn., Baguio Benguet Dental Assn. Avocations: reading, computer work, tennis, watching movies, singing. Office: U Baguio Coll Dentistry, Gen Luna St, Baguio City 2600, The Philippines

PONCE, VICTOR MIGUEL, civil engineering educator; b. Lima, Peru, July 17, 1946; came to the U.S., 1973; s. Guillermo Ponce and Elsa Campos; m. Jane Vloyantes Ponce, May 22, 1971; children: Miguel Esteban, Christina Jane. BS in Civil Engring., U. Nacional Ingenieria, Lima, 1967; MS in Civil Engring., Colo. State U., 1970, PhD in Civil Engring., 1976. Civil engr. Michelena Assocs., Lima, 1970-73; grad. rsch. asst. Colo. State U., Ft. Collins, 1973-76, asst. prof., 1976-80; assoc. prof. San Diego State U., 1980-83, prof., 1983—, chair civil engring., 1989-92; cons. Orgn. Am. States, Washington, 1979, 86, European Econ. Cmty., Santa Cruz, Bolivia, 1989-90, UN Devel. Programme, Roorkee, India, 1992-93, Hidrovia, Buenos Aires, 1996. Authro: Engineering Hydrology, 1989; contbr. articles to profl. jours. Recipient Alumni and Assocs. award San Diego State U., 1992; grantee in field. Mem. ASCE (Karl E. Hilgard prize 1979). Avocations: travel, photography, exploration. E-mail: ponce@ponce.sdsu.edu. Home: 13386 Samantha Ave San Diego CA 92129-2151 Office: San Diego State Univ 5500 Campanile Dr San Diego CA 92182-0002

PONCE GARCIA, JAIME ALFREDO, bank executive; b. Cochabamba, Bolivia, July 2, 1937; s. Jose Aurelio and Julia Serafine (Garcia Cespedes) Ponce; m. Roxana Cecilia Grundy, Oct. 24, 1972; children: Jaime Augusto Ponce Grundy, Sergio Leonardo Ponce Grundy. BA, Nal Bolivar, 1955; grad. in social sci., U. St. Simon, Bolivia, 1961; MA, U. Louvain, Belgium, 1966; JD, U. St. Andrews, Bolivia, 1970. Dir. social studies Bolivian Inst. Study Sociology, La Paz, 1969-70; prof. Cath. U., La Paz, 1971-72, St. Andrews U., La Paz, 1970-80; fin. adminstrv. mgr. Prudencio Claros y Asociados Ingenieros Consultores, 1976-79, 1981-82, 84-88; gen. mgr. Fidentia, La Paz, 1988—; dir. social planning Ministry of Planning, La Paz, 1974-75; dir. social planning Min. of Planning and Coord., 1980; dir. cmty. devel. Ministry of Urban and Housing, 1971, undersec. of housing, 1972, Ministry of Urban and Housing, 1982-84. Co-author: History of Labour Movement in Bolivia, 1972; contbr. articles to profl. jours. Founder, pres. Inidem, La Paz, 1983-96. Recipient Merit medal Corp. de Desarrollo, Potosi, 1983. Mem. Lawyers Coll. (Merit medal 1995), Ins. Cons. Assn. (pres. 1990-92, 95-97). Roman Catholic. Avocations: classical music, racquet ball. Home: PO Box 3835, La Paz Bolivia Office: Yanacocha 441, La Paz Bolivia

PONCET, DOMINIQUE MATTEO, lawyer, educator; b. Geneva, Aug. 31, 1929; s. Jean Francis and Giuseppina Poncet; m. Eliane Uldry, July 12, 1967; children: Isabelle, Philippe. Licentiate of Laws, U. Geneva, 1951, Doctor of Laws, 1967. With Lord Nathan Oppenheimer's Chambers, London, 1954; lawyer Geneva, 1953—; sr. ptnr. Poncet, Turrettini, Amaudruz & Neyroud, Geneva, 1953—; prof. criminal procedure U. Geneva, 1967-97; dir. various cos.;mem. expert commn. to draft New Swiss Criminal Code; alternate mem. Geneva State Ct. Cassation; pres. Fiat Auto Suisse. Author: L'information contradictoire dans le système de la procédure pénale genevoise, 1967, Droit à l'assistance de l'avocat, 1970, L'extradition et le droit d'asile, 1976, La protection de l'accusé par la Convention Européenne des droits de l'homme, 1977, Le nouveau code de procédure pénale annoté, 1978, Extradition: The European Model, 1986, Le statut du dirigeant d'entreprise en Suisse, 1989, La surveillance des banques étrangères, 1993, Systeme accusatoire: Etats Unis, 1994; ajouter La responsabilité pénale des personnes morales, 2000. Decorated comdr. Order of Merit (Italy). Mem. Swiss Fedn. Lawyers, Geneva Law Soc., Swiss Soc. Jurists, Swiss Soc. Criminal Law, Rotary Club. Mem. Conservative Party. Avocations: golf, skiing, conjuring. Home: 21 route de Pressy, 1253 Vandoeuvres Switzerland Office: Poncet Turr Amaudruz&Neyroud Ass, 8-10 rue de Hesse, 1204 Geneva Switzerland

PONDER, BRUCE ANTHONY JOHN, cancer geneticist; b. Haywards Heath, Sussex, Eng., Apr. 25, 1944; s. Anthony West and Dorothy Mary (Peachey) P.; m. Margaret Ann Hickinbotham, Aug. 2, 1969; children: Jane, Katherine, Rosamund, William. BA, Cambridge U., 1965, MB, BChir, 1968, MA, 1972; PhD, London U., 1977. Clin. rsch. fellow Imperial Cancer Rsch. Fund, London, 1973-77; fellow cancer rsch. campaign Dana Farber Cancer Ctr., Harvard Med. Sch., Cambridge, Mass., 1977-78; sr. registrar and ICRF fellow St. Bartholomews Hosp., London, 1978-80; fellow cancer rsch. campaign Inst. of Cancer Rsch., London, 1980—, sci. staff mem., 1985—, section head human cancer genetics, 1987-89; reader in human cancer genetics U. London, 1987-89; dir. cancer rsch. campaign Human Cancer Genetics Rsch. Group, Cambridge (Eng.) U., Eng., 1989—; cons. physician Addenbrookes Hosp., Cambridge, Eng., 1989—; prof. clin. oncology U. Cambridge, Eng., 1996—; co-dir. Well Being Ovarian Cancer Rsch. Ctr., Cambridge, Eng., 1996—; with Strangeways Rsch. Lab., Cambridge, Eng., 1997—; mem. rsch. adv. com. Cancer Rsch. Campaign, London, 1987—; co-chmn. gene-mapping task force Nat. Neurofibromatosis Found., N.Y., 1987-92; mem. sci. rsch. adv. bd. European Orgn. for Rsch. and Treatment of Cancer, 1989-93; mem. human genetics commn., U.K., 1999—. Co-editor: (book) Biology of Carcinogenesis, 1987; contbr. articls to profl. jours. Named Open Scholar, Cambridge U., 1962, Travelling Fellow, Nuffield Found., Pakistan, 1968, Hon. Cons. Physician, Royal Marsden Hosp., and Guys Hosp., London, 1980, Life Fellow, Cancer Rsch. Campaign, 1989. Fellow Jesus Coll. Cambridge U., Royal Coll. Physicians; mem. Brit. Assn. Cancer Rsch. (treas. 1984-8), Cancer Rsch. Campaign Medullary Thyroid Group (sec. 1983-96), Brit. Soc. Cell Biology, Brit. Soc. Devel. Biology, Am. Soc. Human Genetics, Acad. Med. Scis., Royal Ashdown Forest Golf Club, Royal West Norfolk Golf Club. Avocations: gardening, golf, boardsailing. Office: Dept Oncology, Cambridge Inst Med Rsch Box 193, Hills Rd Cambridge CB2 2QQ, England

PONDER, JAMES ALTON, clergyman, evangelist; b. Ft. Worth, Jan. 20, 1933; s. Leo A. and Mae Adele (Blair) P.; m. Joyce Marie Hutchison, Sept. 1, 1953; children: Keli, Ken. Ordained to ministry Baptist Ch., 1953. Pastor Calvary Bapt. Ch., Corsicana, Tex., 1953-57, First Bapt. Ch., Highlands, Tex., 1957-62, Ridglea West Bapt. Ch., Ft. Worth, 1963-66, First Bapt. Ch., Carmi, Ill., 1966-67; dir. evangelism Ill. Bapt. State Conv., 1968-70, Fla. Bapt. Conv., 1970-81; pres. Jim Ponder Ministries, Inc., 1981—, Life Internat., Inc., 1993-97; dir. Inst. World Evangelism div. Jim Ponder Ministries; preacher Crossroads radio program; fgn. mission bd. evangelist in various countries of Asia, Central Am., Middle East, 1960—; project dir. Korea Major Cities Evangelization Project, 1978-80; evangelist ch. revivals, area crusades and evangelism confs., 1951—; mem. faculty Billy Graham Schs. Evangelism, 1970-2000; co-founder Ch. Growth Inst. Fla., 1976; co-dir. Ch. Growth Crusades, 1978-79; founder, dir. Inst. World Evangelism (I-Owe), 1987—; pres. Conf. Fla. Baptist Evangelists, 1986-87; pres. Fellowship of Bapt. World Ministries, 1992-96, mem. exec. com., 1997-98; mem. Evangelism com. Bapt. World Alliance, 1997-2000; sports announcer Sta. KIYS, Waco, Tex., 1950-54; speaker worldwide missionary radio broadcast Crossroads with Jim Ponder. Author: The Devotional Life, 1970; Evangelism Men...Motivating Laymen to Witness, 1975; Evangelism Men...Proclaiming the Doctrines of Salvation, 1976; Evangelism Men...Preaching for Decision, 1979, The Way to Christ, 1994; author, video tchr. Becoming a Witness; contbr. articles to religious publs.; speaker in field. Mem. Fellowship Christian Athletes, Smithsonian Instn., N.Am. Soc. Church Growth, Acad. Evangelism in Edn., Acad. Evangelism Profs. Republican. Club: Kiwanis. Home: 2000 N Countryside Cir Orlando FL 32804-6914 Office: PO Box 547995 Orlando FL 32854-7995

PONELIS, FRIEDRICH ALBERT, language educator; b. Roodepoort, Gauteng, South Africa, July 28, 1942; s. Frederick Albert Ponelis and Martha Elisabeth Venter; m. Isabella Annanda Broodryk, Dec. 19, 1964; children: Isabel, Frederik, Karlien. BA with honors, U. Potchelstroom, South Africa, 1963; MA, Unisa, Pretoria, South Africa, 1975, PhD, 1969. From lectr. to prof. Unisa, 1964-78; prof. U. Stellenbosch, South Africa, 1979—. Author: Afrikaanse Sintaksis, 1979, The Development of Afrikaans, 1993. Mem. Linguistic Soc. South Africa, Linguistic Soc. Am. Office: U Stellenbosch, Victoria St Pvt Bag XI, Maticland 7602, South Africa

PONG, WAI CHUNG, computer hardware and software research company executive; b. Hong Kong, Hong Kong, Aug. 21, 1956; s. Shing and Yuen Hang (Lau) P.; m. Yuet Han Leung, Sept. 18, 1989; children: Ho Tung, Chung Ling. BS in Engring., U. Hong Kong, 1979, MPhil, 1985. Chartered engr. Staff engr. Hong Kong Coils Ltd., 1979; sr. engr. Electronic Industry Ltd. subs. GE, Hong Kong, 1980-84; dir., gen. mgr. Nam Tai Mfg. Co.,

Ltd., Hong Kong, 1985—; gen. mgr. Bondwell Indsl. Ltd., Hong Kong, 1986-89, HMC Tech. Ltd., Hong Kong, 1989-90; mng. dir. IPL Rsch. Ltd., Hong Kong, 1990—. Mem. IEEE, Instn. Elec. Engrs. (chartered mem.).

PONG, YUEN SUN LOUIS, lawyer; b. Hong Kong, May 5, 1957; s. Che Yue and Leung King (Tam) P.; m. Lai Kuen Grace Brigid Chan, Aug. 5, 1982; children: Sze Ngok Kandor, Sze Lok Portia. BSc, U. Hong Kong, 1979. Qualified lawyer. Asst. solicitor Johnson Stokes & Master, Hong Kong, 1984-88; ptnr. Liau Ho & Chan, Hong Kong, 1988—. Pres. Hong Kong Chinese Family for Christ, 1997—; mem. synod Diocese of Hong Kong and Macao, 1994-98; mem. gen. synod Hong Kong Sheng Kung Hui, 1999—. Mem. Law Soc. Hong Kong. Avocations: couples and family ministry, singing. Home: Flat A 5th fl Avon Ct, 2 Fessenden Rd, Kowloon Tong Hong Kong Office: 6th Fl United Chinese Bank, 31-37 Des Voeux Rd Ctrl, Hong Kong China

PONGPOL, ADIREKSARN, federal official; b. Mar. 23, 1942. BA in Internat. Rels., MA in Internat. Rels. Formerly pres. express transp. orgn.; asst. sec. to min. Ministry of Transport and Comm.; mem. Ho. of Reps., 1983, 92, 95, 96; min. Ministry of Fgn. Affairs, 1992; sec. to leader of opposition, 1993; min. Prime Min. Office, 1995-96, Ministry of Agr. and Coops., Bangkok, 1997—. Writer novels in English. Sec.-gen., Chart Tahi Party. Office: Ministry of Agr and Coops, Thanon Ratchadamnoen Nok, Bangkok 10200, Thailand

PONGRANTZ, INGEMAR GÖRAN, research scientist; b. Quito, Pichincha, Ecuador, Oct. 9, 1966; arrived in Sweden, 1980; s. Göran and Alba (Avilez) P.; m. Katarina Petterson, May 14, 1995. BS, Stockholm U., 1989; PhD, Karolinska Inst., Stockholm, 1996. Asst. prof. Karolinska Inst., 1997—. Mem. jury Huddinge Dist. Ct., Stockholm, 1994-98; bd. dirs. Stockholm So. U., 1994-97. 2nd lt. Swedish Mil. forces, 1992-93. Office: Karolinska Inst, von Eulers väg 3, 177-77 Stockholm Sweden

PONGSIRI, SANGKORN, Thai marine officer; b. Lopburi, Thailand, Apr. 30, 1959; s. Sivasak and Kaleo (Sopon) P.; m. Pornsiri Sopon; 1 child, Purichaya. BS, Naval Acad., Bangkok, 1983; postgrad., Army Command and Staff Coll., Bangkok, 1994, USMC Command and Staff Coll., Quantico, Va., 1997, Def. Resources Mgmt. Sch., Monterey, Calif., 1997. Commd. 1st lt Royal Thai Marine Corps, 1982, advanced through grades to capt., 1997; bn. comdr. Royal Thai Marine Corps, Sattahip, Cholburi, 1994-95, dir. edn., 1997-98, comdr. recruit tng., 1998—. Avocation: golf. Home: 177/23 Paholyothin 51, Bangkok Bangkhen 10220, Thailand Office: Royal Thai Marine Corps, Recruit Tng Marine Edn Ctr, Sattahip Cholburi, Thailand

PONKA, LAWRENCE JOHN, automotive executive; b. Detroit, Sept. 1, 1949; s. Maximillian John and Leona May (Knobloch) P.; m. Nancy Kathleen McNamara, Feb. 20, 1988. AA, Macomb County C. C., Mich., 1974; BS in Indsl. Mgmt., Lawrence Tech. U., 1978; MA in Indsl. Mgmt., Ctrl. Mich. U., 1983, postgrad. in Bus. Mgmt. Cert. internat. cons. Engr.'s asst. Army Tank Automotive Command, 1967-68; with Sperry and Hutchinson Co., Southfield, Mich., 1973, Chrysler Corp., Detroit, 1973, GM Corp., Warren, Mich., 1973-82; coord. engring. staff engring. systems GM Corp., Warren, 1976-82; mfg. engr. Buick-Oldsmobile, Cadillac Group GM Assembly Divsn., Orion Pontiac, Mich, 1982-84; sr. anayst advanced vehicle engring. Chevrolet-Pontiac-Can. group Engring. Ctr., Warren, 1985-86; mfg. planning adminstr. Allanté Detroit Hamtramck Assembly Ctr. Cadillac Luxury Car Divsn., 1986-92, mgr. Cadillac Alante Assembly Ops., 1992—; plant planning adminstr. Cadillac luxury car divsn. Detroit/Hamtramck Assembly Ctr., Cadillac El Dorado, Seville, Deville, Concours, 1993—, sr. mfg. project engr. N. Am. Ops, 1994, Flint, Mich., 1996; advanced mfg. engr. N.Am. ops. mfg. process liaison Cadillac luxury car divsn., 1996-97, total mfg. integration engr. Global Portfolio Devel. Ctr., 1997—; mem. people strategy team on environ. Cadillac Motor Car till 1992; mem. adj. faculty U. Phoenix Grad. Sch. Bus., Mich. campus. With USAF, 1968-72. Elected del Dem. County Conv.;. Decorated Air Force Commendation medal. Mem. DAV (life), Vietnam Vets Assn. (life), Am. Diabetes Assn. Roman Catholic. Home: 35537 Oakdale St Livonia MI 48154-2237 Office: U Phoenix Mich Campus 26999 Central Park Blvd Southfield MI 48076-4174 Other: GM Corp Engring Ctr M/C 480-111-P36 30200 Mound Rd 111 Box 9010 Warren MI 48090-9010

PONNAMBALAM, SIVALINGA GOVINDARAJAN, engineering educator, researcher; b. Tiruvallore, India, Feb. 14, 1954; child of Narasingapuram Muthusamy Govindarajan and Thakkali Ammal Govindarajan; m. Sargunavathi Pulikanti, July 1, 1988; children: Shree Gayathri Ponnamblam, Sandhya Ponnambalam. Degree in mech. engring., Instn. Engrs., India, 1982; M in Indsl. Engring., Madura Kamaraj U., India, 1988; PhD in Indusl. Engring., Bharathiyar U., India, 1995. Lectr. mech. engring. Govt. Poly., Coimbatore, India, 1989-93; asst. prof. Peelmedu Samanaidu Govindsasamy Coll. Tech., Coimbatore, 1993-99; prof. incharge indsl. engring. Peelmedu Samanaldu Govindsasamy Coll. Tech., Coimbatore; prof. incharge indsl. engring. lab. PSG Coll. Tech., Coimbatore; prof. prodn. engring. Regional Engring. Coll., Tiruchirappalli, India, 1999—; lectr. mech. engring. Tamil Nadu Poly., Madurai, 1984-89. Contbr. articles to profl. jours. Fellow Instn. Engrs.; mem. Instn. Mech. Engrs., Operational Rsch. Soc. India, Computer Soc. India. Fax: 91-431-500133. Office: Regional Engring Coll, Tiruchirappalli 620 015, India

PONNÉ, NANCI TERESA, entertainment promoter, writer; b. Chgo., May 10, 1958; d. Joseph Anthony and Irene Theresa (Nasadowski) P.; m. Lee Darrow, Oct. 26, 1996. BA, DePaul U., 1980. Performer, 1961—, dancer, choreographer, 1974—; actress, model Chgo., 1978—; pub. Chgo. Talent Directory, 1985—, Spotlight, 1989; pres./owner Chgo. Talent Enterprises Inc., 1991—; freelance writer, 1992—, graphic designer, 1993—, clairvoyant, 1996—, website designer, 1998—; prodr. VIP Forums on Progress in Chgo. Talent Industry, 1990; speaker in field; mem. Loretta Rozek Dance Co., 1975-79. Prodr.: (radio talk show) The Strange World of Lee Darrow, Sta. WONX-AM, 1993. Dem. vol. to Re-elect Mayor Washington, 1987, Dem. vol. for Clinton/Gore, 1992; Dem. vol. to elect Patrick Quinn to Sec. State, Ill., 1990. Named Miss Chgo., recipient Spl. Judges award Miss America Scholarship Pageant, 1981-82; Goodman Sch. of Drama scholar, 1978. Mem. NATAS, HEREIU, Nat. Assn. Photoshop Profls., Chgo. Conv. and Tourism Bur., Ice Skating Inst. (3 Gold medals World Championships, 1994), Ind. Writers of Chgo., Goldfish Soc. Am. Celtic Catholic. Avocations: competitive figure skating, Star Trek, raising exotic goldfish, metaphysics. Address: 5250 N Broadway St Ste 204 Chicago IL 60640-2304

PONOMARENKO, VASILY PETROVICH, ichthyologist, consultant; b. Poltava, Ukraine, June 4, 1926; arrived in Russia, 1945; s. Petr Mikhailovich Palamarenko and Evdokiya Moiseevna Pokhodun; m. Itta Yakovlevna Lipovich; children: Galina, Sergey. Degree, Moscow State U., 1956; PhD, State U., Petrozavodsk, Russia, 1968; D of Biology, Russian Fed. Rsch. Inst. Fisheries and Oceanography, Moscow, 1996. Jr. scientist Polar Rsch. Inst. Fisheries and Oceanography, Murmansk, Russia, 1956-64; head of Barents Sea Demersal Fish Lab. Polar Rsch. Inst. Fisheries and Oceanography, Murmansk, 1964-74, dep. dir., 1974-76, dir., 1976-82; sr. scientist Russian Fed. Rsch. Inst. Fisheries and Oceanography, Moscow, 1982-93; leading scientist The Inter-Dept. Ichthyological Commn., Moscow, 1993—. Author: (monographs) Main Commercial Fishes of the Barents, Norwegian and Greenland Seas, 1972, Biology and Fishery on Polar Cod of the Barents Sea, 1973; contbr. articles to profl. jours. Avocations: reading, travel, sports, theater, music. Home: Konakovsky Proezd 19-101, 125565 Moscow Russia Office: The Inter Dept Ichthyol Com, 27 Tverskaya St, 103050 Moscow Russia

PONOMAREVA, OLGA VICTOROVNA, epidemiologist; b. Omsr, Russia, Oct. 29, 1959; d. Victor Michailovich and Vera Dmitrievna (Sharapova) Savilov; m. Valeri Vasilyevich Ponomarev, Apr. 15, 1980 (wid. Aug. 1984); 1 child, Anton Valeryevich. MD, 1st Med. Inst., Moscow, 1975; MD category 1, Acad. of Post-Grad., 1987, MD of top category, 1989. Cert. Environ. Health, WMD. Environ. health specialist Cen. San-Epi Surveillance, Moscow, 1983-84; head unit environ. health Russian Republic Info. Analytica, Moscow, 1987-97; head unit environ. health risk assesment Fed. Cen. San-Epi, Moscow, 1997—; dir. Internat. Inst. Health Risk, Moscow, 1995—; mem. work group under Ministry of Pub. Health, Moscow, 1997, software and program expert com., 1998. Recipient Good Practice Intern award, UNCHS, 1998; grantee fo risk assesment, ISC, 1998. Mem. Russian Assn. Hygiene and Epidemology. Avocations: travel, reading, music, fine arts, drama. Office: Cons Cen Health Risk Asses, 19 Warshavscoye Shosse, 113105 Moscow Russia

PONS, JEAN-CLAUDE, obstetrician, gynecologist; b. Riom, Auvergne, France, Dec. 5, 1953; s. Emile and Gisèle (Aubé) P.; m. Laurence Mitéran, Dec. 23, 1976; children: Thibaut, Benjamin, Jessica. DEA, U. René Descartes, 1993. Intern Paris, 1980, doctor, 1983, asst. prof., 1984; praticien Hosp. Paris, 1989, Hosp. Port-Royal, Paris, 1993—; cons. Dept. Ob-Gyn., Paris, 1989-98; prof. ob-gyn. and dir. dept. ob-gyn. CHU, Grenoble, France, 1998—. Author: Les Jumeaux, 1998, Obstetrique, 1995, Jumeaux triplés et plus, 1995, L'Accouchement, 1997, Les Nouvelles Grossesses, 1996, Les Grossesses Multiples, 2000. Mem. Internat. Soc. for Twin Studies, Obstetrician-Gynecologist French Coll., Club Francophone de Médecine Foetale. Avocations: MacIntosh, movies, books, modern art. Office: CHU de Grenoble, BP217, 38043 Grenoble Cedex 09, France

PONS, XAVIER JEAN PAUL, English educator, writer; b. Rodez, Aveyron, France, May 10, 1948; s. Xavier and Paule (Vergnes) P.; m. Geraldine Ribot, May 24, 1980; children: Ariane, Emmanuelle. Liccentiate Letters, U. Toulouse, France, 1968; Maitrise Lettres, U. Toulouse, 1969; D Letters, U. Paris, 1978. Agrégation d'Anglais. Lectr. English U. Toulouse, 1970-81, sr. lectr., 1981-83, prof. English, 1983—; rsch. fellow Flinders U., Adelaide, Australia, 1985; vis. prof. U. NSW, Sydney, Australia, 1990, Queensland U. Tech., Brisbane, Australia, 1994; cons. Ministry Culture, Paris, 1990. Author: L'Australie et ses Populations, 1983, Out of Eden, 1984, A Sheltered Land, 1994, Le Multiculturalisme en Australie, 1996. Mem. European Assn. for Studies on Australia (pres. 1995—), Soc. Francaise d'Etudes Pays du Commonwealth (sec. 1983—), Assn. Culture Franco-Australienne (v.p. 1985—). Avocations: tennis, body building. Home: 3 Rue Richet, 31130 Balma France Office: U Toulouse Le Mirail, 5 Allées Antonio Machado, 31058 Toulouse Cedex, France

PONSONBY, ANNE-LOUISE, public health physician; b. Ithaca, N.Y., Sept. 21, 1961; d. John Leo and Kathy Ellen (Nocan) Madden; m. Michael Ponsonby; children: Thomas, Andrew, James, Stephanie. B in Med. Sci., U. Tasmania, 1982, MB, BChir, 1985, PhD, 1993. Resident Royal Hobart Hosp., Australia, 1986; rsch. officer Menzies Ctr. for Population Health Rsch., Hobart, Australia, 1987, rsch. fellow, 1987-93, dep. dir., 1997, sr. rsch. fellow, 1998—; fellow Nat. Health and Med. Rsch. Coun., Hobart, 1994-97; sr. rsch. fellow U. Sydney, Canberra, Australia, 1998—; sr. lectr. U. Sydney, 1998—. Contbr. articles to profl. jours. Australasian Faculty of Pub. Health Medicine fellow Royal Australasian Coll. Physicians, 1993. Fellow Australasian Epidemiol. Assn. Avocations: fitness, swimming, gardening. Office: Menzies Ctr Population, Health Rsch, Hobart TAS 7000, Australia

PONSONBY, FREDERICK EDWARD NEUFLIZE (10TH EARL BESSBOROUGH), government executive; b. Mar. 29, 1913; s. 9th Earl of Bessborough and Roberte de Neuflize; m. Mary Munn, 1948; 1 child. MA, Trinity Coll., Cambridge, Eng. With W div. Islington (Nat. Govt.), 1935, Sussex (Eng.) Yeomanry, 1936; sec. commn. for refugees League of Nations, 1936-39; second then first sec. Brit. Embassy, Paris, 1944-49; chmn. govs. Brit. Soc. for Internat. Understanding, 1951-71. Author (plays): (with Muriel Jenkins) Nebuchadnezzar, 1939, The Four Men, for Festvival of Britain, 1951, Like Stars Appearing, 1953, The Noon is Night, 1954, Darker the Sky, 1955, Triptych, 1957, A Place in the Forest, 1958, Return to the Forest, 1962, (with Clive Aslet) The Enchanted Forest, 1984; performances include leading roles for Stansted Players, Marlowe Soc., Montreal (Ont., Can.) Repertory, Ottowa (Can.) Little Theatre; contbr. articles and revs. to various publs. Served with Brit. mil., 1939-45. Decorated Chevalier, Legion of Honour. Office: Peer of the Realm, House of Lords, London SW1AOPW, England

PONT, ANTHONY MICHAEL, management consultant, writer; b. Grimsby, Eng., Aug. 1, 1946; s. Leslie Rupert and Monica (Finneran) P.; m. Gillian Margaret Wolsey Pont, Dec. 20, 1969; children: Simon Anthony, Nicholas James. BA (hon.), U. Leeds, 1967; MSc, U. Bradford, 1975; PhD, Internat. Mgmt. Ctrs., 1992. Tchr. Great Horton Sch., Bradford, Eng., 1968-70; lectr. Keighley (Eng.) Coll. of FE, 1970-73; head of ctr. Houghton Regis (Eng.) C.C., 1975-81; area prin. Continuing Edn., Dunstable, Eng., 1981-85; dir. Continuing Edn. MASD #11, Gardiner, Maine, 1982-83; mgmt. devel. mgr. Smithkline & French Labs Ltd., 1985-87; vis. faculty Internat. Mgmt. Ctrs., Buckingham, Eng., 1988-93, Manchester (Eng.) Bus. Sch., 1990-92, Leicester (Eng.) Bus. Sch., 1993-94, U. Lincoln (Eng.), 1996, Cranfield U., 1998-99. Author: Developing Effective Training Skills, 1991, The Role of the Management Development Specialist, 1995, Investing in Training and Development, 1995, Developing Effective Training Skills, 1996, Interviewing Skills for Managers, 1997. Pub. rels. officer Rotary Club, Northampton, Eng., 1992-94. Fulbright Exchange Washington, London, 1981. Avocations: cricket, squash, travel, reading, music. Fax: 751572. E-mail: a.m.pont@btinternat.com. Home: Heyford House, Nether Heyford NN7 3NN, England

PONT, KENNETH GRAHAM, retired education educator; b. Newcastle, NSW, Australia, Apr. 8, 1937; s. Aubrey Clifton and Sylvie Heather Connie (Stein) P. BA with honors, U. Sydney, NSW, 1958; PhD, Australian Nat. U., Canberra, 1965. Lectr. in philosophy U. NSW, 1966-80, sr. lectr., 1980-91, assoc. prof. in liberal and gen. studies, 1992-95; vis. prof. in sci. and tech., 1996-98; vis. assoc. prof. in musicology CUNY, 1973-74; music critic Nation Review, 1974-77; opera critic Nat. Times, 1981; founding convener Symposium of Australian Gastronomy, 1984-88. Co-author: Landmarks of Australian Gastronomy, 1988; contbr. articles to profl. jours. Pres. Musicological Soc. Australia, 1975-77; dir. Univ. Club, 1981-92, 95-96. Rsch. fellow London U., 1963-65; grantee Australian Rsch. Grant Scheme, 1971-73, Australian Rsch. Coun., 1980-90. Mem. Byron Soc. Avocations: cooking, gardening, wine, music, architecture. E-mail: pont@zipworld.com.au. Home: Newtown New South Wales, 41 Forbes St, 2042 Sydney Australia

PONTARA, GIULIANO, philosophy and peace; b. Cles, Trento, Italy, Sept. 9, 1932; arrived in Sweden, 1952; s. Gaetano and Antonia (Dal Lago) P.; m. Aslög Ingegerd Sölvén, Apr. 9, 1963; children: Anders, Tobias, Ellen. Student in philosophy, Rome U., 1956-60; BA, Stockholm U., 1963, MA, 1966, PhD in Philosophy, 1971. Fellow Haverford (Pa.) Coll., 1961-62; tchr. in philosophy Stockholm U., 1963-71, rschr., 1971-75, assoc. prof., 1975-97; vis. prof. U. Siena, Italy, 1984-86; chmn. Internat. U. Peoples' Instn. for Peace, Rovereto, Italy, 1994—. Author: Filosofia Pratica, 1988, Antigone o Creonte, 1990, Etica e Generazioni Future, 1995, M.K. Gandhi: Teoria e Pratica della Nonviolenza, 1996, Breviario per un'etica quotidiana, 1998. Mem. Permanent Peoples' Tribunal, Rome, 1990—. Mem. Acad. Degli Agiati. Avocations: playing violin, tracking, skiing, canoeing. Home: Margaretavägen 62, 12262 Enskede, Stockholm Sweden Office: Stockholm U, Universitetsvägen 10, S 10691 Stockholm Sweden

PONTAROLO, VALERIO, building and hardware company executive; b. S. Daniele del Friuli, Italy, Dec. 23, 1955; s. Giorgio and Enni (Peloso) P.; m. Donatella Sinigaglia, Mar. 26, 1988; children: Luca, Valentina. Diploma in engring., 1976. Exec. Pontarolo S.r.L., Pontarolo Engring. S.a.S., Pontarolo Engring. S.r.L. Pres. Cassa Edile, Pordenone, Italy; bd. dirs. Pordenone Indsl. Assn. Mem. Rotary (organizer Internat. Coun. Human Duties forum). Avocation: horseback riding. Home: 4/D Via Santa Caterina, I-33073 Cordovado Italy

PONTE, CARLOS MANUEL, computer company executive; b. Lisbon, June 14, 1967; s. José Ponte and Beatriz Mendes Silva; m. Maria Elizbete Daniel, Aug. 16, 1990; 1 child, Raquel. BSc in Computer Engring., U. Nova Lisbon, 1990, MBA, 1999. Programmer Easysoft, Lisbon, 1990-91, project mgr., 1992-98, CEO, 1999—. Avocations: running, traveling, reading. Home: rua dos Eucaliptos 8, 1800-200 Lisbon Portugal Office: Easysoft, Av Combatentes 43 11-C, 1600-042 Lisbon Portugal

PONTER, ALAN ROBERT SAGE, civil engineering educator, consultant; b. Abergavenny, Gwent, Wales, Feb. 13, 1940; s. Arthur Tennyson and Margaret Agatha (Boyce-Jones) P.; m. Sonia Valentine, Sept. 12, 1962 (dec.); children: Ruth, David (dec.), Kathryn, Alexandria. BS, U. London, 1961, PhD, 1965; MA, Cambridge (Eng.) U., 1967; MS, Brown U., 1977. Rsch. assoc. Brown U., Providence, R.I., 1964-65; sr. asst. in rsch. Cambridge (Eng.) U., 1966-69, fellow, Pembroke Coll., 1967-69; vis. prof. engring. Brown U., 1976-78; prof. engring. Leicester (Eng.) U., 1978—, pro-vice-chancellor, 1987-91, 93-96; cons. U.K. Atomic Energy Authority, 1972—, vis. prof. engring. U. Calif., Santa Barbara, 1991-92; cons. prof. engring. Chongqing (China) U., 1991—. Editor: Creep of Structure, 1982; contbr. over 120 articles to profl. jours. and books. Originator Nat. Space Sci. Ctr., Leicester, 1994—. Recipient rsch. grants various rsch. couns., 1972—. Home: Peakes Lodge 50 Main St, Burrough on the Hill LE1 2JQ, England Office: Univ Leicester, University Rd, Leicester LE1 7RH, England

PÖNTINEN, PEKKA JUHANI, anesthesiologist, consultant; b. Tampere, Finland, Apr. 5, 1932; s. Otto Edvard and Ellen Margareta (Heiniö) P.; m. Anja Anita Kuukankorpi; children: Anna-Katriina, Juha-Pekka, Riikka-Leena, Hanna-Maaria; m. Irja Tuulikki Ketovuori, Jan. 8, 1976; 1 child, Mika Juhani. B in med., Helsinki U., Finland, 1953; MD, Turku U., Finland, 1957; PhD, Kuopio U., Finland, 1977. Diplomate Finnish Bd. Health Legitimation, Finnish Bd. Anesthesiology. Chief dept. anesthesiology Savonlinna Cen. Hosp., Finland, 1965-69, Kainuu Cen. Hosp., Finland, 1969-75; asst. prof. neurophysiology Kuopio U., Finland, 1974-75; med. dir. Kankaanpää Rehabilitation Ctr., Finland, 1989-92; assoc. prof. anesthesiology Kuopio U., 1978—, Tampere U., Finland, 1980—; chief acupuncture rsch. project Kuopio U., 1976—; cons. dept. neurology Tampere U. Hosp., 1976-93, adv. Ministry of Health & Social Affairs, Helsinki,. 1975—. WHO Com. Standardisation Acupuncture Nomenclature, Geneva, Switzerland, 1989-95uropean Coun. Subcom. Higher Edn., Strassbourg, France, 1990-95. Author: Acupuncture as a Medical Treatment Modality (in Finnish), 1983, Laser as a Medical Treatment Modality (in Finnish), 1988, Low Level Laser as a Medical Treatment Modality (in Swedish), 1991, Low Level Laser Therapy as a Medical Treatment Modality, 1992, Laseracupuncture (in German), 1993, 2d edit., 1998; co-author: TENS Transcutaneous Electrical Nerve Stimulation in Pain Treatment (in German), 1992, 2d edit., 1996, Triggerpoints and Triggermechanisms, 1997 (in German), Alternative and Complementary Therapies in Veterinary Medicine, 1997, Lasers in Medicine and Dentistry, 2000; editor-in-chief Scandinavian Jour. Acupuncture and Electrotherapy, 1987—; editor Acupuncture & Electrotherapeutics Rsch. Internat. Jour., 1981—. AKU, Akupunktur, Theorie und Praxis, 1991-99; mem. sci. com. Internat. Jour. Pain Therapy, 1991-95. Recipient German Promotion award Pain Rsch. and Therapy, 1988. Fellow Internat. Coll. Acupuncture & Electro-Therapeutics Rsch. (vice chmn. coun. 1987—), Acupuncture Found. of India (hon.), Am. Acad. Acupuncture (hon.), Am. Coll. Acupuncture (charter); mem. Am. Pain Soc., Am. Soc. Laser Medicine & Surgery, Brit. Med. Acupuncture Soc. (hon.), German Med. Acupuncture Soc. (hon.), Can. Acupuncture Assn. Can. (hon.), Nordic Acupuncture Soc. (pres. 1980-87, 89—, founding), Internat. Assn. Study of Pain (founding), Phys. Medicine Rsch. Found. (intermultidisciplinary bd. dirs. 1995—), N.Y. Acad. Scis., Società Internazionale di Laserterapia Medico Chirugica (v.p. for Finland 1989—), Finnish Soc. Anesthesiologists (v.p. 1970-71, pres. 1972-73), Finnish Med. Acupuncture Soc. (hon.). Avocations: classical music, fishing, gardening, skiing, ice hockey. Home: Pikkusaarenkuja 4B 77, 33410 Tampere Finland

PONTIUS, DIETER JOHANN JAKOB, chemist; b. Zurich, Switzerland, July 31, 1914; came to U.S., 1957; s. Oswald Herman and Victorina Maria (Torresani) P.; m. Anneliese Alma Mueller, July 7, 1951. MSc, Johann-Wolfgang Goethe U., Frankfurt am Main, Germany, 1947, DSc, 1950. Rsch. scientist endocrine rsch. unit German Scientists' Rsch. Assn., Trier, Fed. Republic Germany, 1951-54; rsch. scientist German Scientists' Rsch. Assn. Univ. Hosp., Hamburg, Fed. Republic Germany, 1954-55, Montreal (Can.) Gen. Hosp., 1956, Clark U., Worcester Found. Biochemistry, Worcester, Mass., 1957-59; rsch. chemist Neuro-endocrine Rsch. Unit, Willowbrook, N.Y., 1959-60, Fairmount Chem. Co., Newark, 1960-69; pvt. researcher N.Y.C., 1970—. Contbr. articles to Klinische Wochenschrift, Zeitschrift Physiologische Chemie, Acta endocrinologica, Analytical Chemistry. Rsch. scholar German Scientists' Rsch. Assn., 1951-55. Fellow Am. Inst. Chemists; mem. Am. Chem. Soc. Achievements include development of four new color reactions for spectrophotometric determination of steroid hormones. Avocations: monster sculpturing, adventure travel, swimming. Home: Waldschmidt Str 6 #5037, 60316 Frankfurt Germany

PONTIUS, JAMES WILSON, foundation administrator; b. Orrville, Ohio, Aug. 29, 1916; s. Howard Taggart and Nova Clementine (Mead) P.; m. Kathryn Jane Sharp, Mar. 12, 1938; children: Howard Garrett, Janne Pettibone, Carolyn Jean, Jon Brewster. BA, Miami U., Oxford, Ohio, 1937. Fin. and taxes GE, Schenectady, N.Y., 1937-47, traveling auditor, 1947-50, cons. electronic data sys., 1953-62; project mgr. internal automation dept. GE, Waynesboro, Va., 1962-64; mgr. advanced info. systems GE, Schenectady, N.Y., 1964-78; retired, 1978; mgr. treasury svcs. GE Supply Corp., Bridgeport, Conn., 1950-53; pres. William Gundry Broughton Charitable Pvt. Found., Inc., Glenville, N.Y., 1992—; mem. adv. com. use of computers in bus. activities U.S. Dept. Def., Washington, 1955-56. Mem. Niskayuna (N.Y.) Sch. Bd., 1965-70, 71-72, 85-86; sec., treas., pres. Schenectady (N.Y.) Rotary Club Found., 1977-80; bd. dirs. Niskayuna (N.Y.) Cmty. Found., 2000—. Republican. Reformed. Avocations: bridge, golf, amateur radio, personal computers, pool. Home: 2009 Garden Dr Niskayuna NY 12309-2309 Office: 133 Saratoga Rd Ste 6 Schenectady NY 12302-4108

PONTOPPIDAN, N. E., judge. Pres. Supreme Ct. Denmark, Copenhagen. Office: Hojesteret, Prins Jorgens Gard 13, 1218 Copenhagen Denmark

PONZANO, GIORGIO ENRICO, mathematical physics educator; b. Alessandria, Piemonte, Italy, Aug. 3, 1939; s. Carlo Luigi and Rosaria Orsola (Beggiato) P.; m. Lucette Boully, May 4, 1968; children: Caterina, Giovanni, Matteo. Grad. in physics, U. Turin, Italy, 1961, specialization, 1964. NATO fellow Palmer Phys. Lab., Princeton (N.J.) U., 1966-67; asst. prof. Inst. for Advanced Study, Princeton, 1967-69, 73-74; asst. prof. math. physics U. Turin, 1962-66, assoc. prof., 1969-73, 74-82, prof., 1982—. Contbr. articles to sci. jours., including Nuovo Cimento, Group Theoretical Methods in Physics, Comm. in Math. Physics, Internat. Jour. Modern Physics B. Decorated ufficiale Ordine al Merito della Repubblica Italiana. Fellow Assn. Mems. Inst. for Advanced Study. Roman Catholic. Avocations: beekeeping, producing mead. Office: U Piemonte Orientale A Avogadaro, Fac Sci MFN Corso T Borsalino 54, 15100 Alessandria Italy

PONZI KAY, MARYLOU, human resources specialist; b. N.Y.C., Oct. 14, 1950; d. Bruno and Constance Louise (DeLuca) P.; m. William J. Kay, Jr., Oct. 24, 1993. BA, SUNY, Geneseo, 1972; MA, U. Iowa, 1974, SUNY, Buffalo, 1979; cert. in advanced study in labor rels., N.Y. Inst. Tech., 1995. Pers. adminstr. Michelin Tire Corp., Lake Success, N.Y., 1978-83; tech. recruiter 1st Data Resources, Lake Success, N.Y., 1983-84; mgr. human resources Chem. Bank, Jericho, N.Y., 1984-87; pers. officer J.P. Morgan Inc., N.Y.C., 1987-89; mgr. employment Am. Express Inc., N.Y.C., 1989-92; dir. human resources RockBottom Stores, Inc., 1992-95; asst. dir. human resources Canon U.S.A., Lake Success, N.Y., 1995-97, dir. human resources, 1997-2000, dir. corp. human resources and devel., 2000; dir. human resources Esselte Ams., Garden City, N.Y., 2000—; adj. prof. human resources N.Y. Inst. Tech., 2000; instr. French and Spanish Amityville H.S. Adult Edn., 1986-96. Editor: New England Guide, 1982, Canada Guide, 1982. Pres. LeBourget Alliance, Amityville, N.Y., 1995-97; pres. bus. adv. coun. Adults and Children with Learning Disabilities, 1994-97, trustee, 1997—. Mem. Soc. Human Resources Mgmt. Roman Catholic. Avocations: languages, travel, cooking, sports. Office: 71 Clinton Rd Garden City NY 11530-4728

POOK, LESLIE PHILIP, mechanical engineering researcher; b. Muswell Hill, Middlesex, Eng., June 12, 1935; s. John Philip and Marianne (Bunting) P.; m. Jean Ann Edmondson, Apr. 18, 1960; children: Stephanie Jean, Adrian Philip. BSc, U. London, 1956; PhD, U. Strathclyde, Glasgow, Scotland, 1969. Chartered engr. Jr. sci. officer Hawker-Siddeley Aviation Ltd., Coventry, Eng., 1956-60; tech. officer Hawker-Siddeley Aviation Ltd., Coventry, England, 1960-63; sr. sci. officer Nat. Engring. Lab., Glasgow, 1963-70, prin. sci. officer, 1970-78; sr. prin. scientific officer, 1978-90; sr. rsch. fellow U. Coll. London, 1990-98, vis. prof., 1998—. Author: The Role of Crack Growth in Metal Fatigue, 1983, Linear Elastic Fraction Mechanics

for Engineers, 2000; co-author: Metal Fatigue, 1974; editor Internat. Jour. Fatigue, 1990-98; contbr. articles to profl. jours. Fellow Inst. of Materials, Instn. Mech. Engrs.; mem. ASTM. Avocations: gardening, enjoyment of the wines, beers and whiskies of the world. Office: Univ Coll London, Dept Mech Engring, Torrington Pl, London WC1E 7JE, England

POOL, DAVID IAN, demography educator; b. Auckland, New Zealand, Nov. 22, 1936; arrived in Can., 1966, 71, in U.S., 1969; s. James and Doris Stewart (Messer) P.; m. Janet Elizabeth Sceats, May 19, 1962; children: Felicity Jane, Jonathan Michael. BA, U. New Zealand, 1957, MA with honors, 1959; PhD, Australian Nat. U., 1964. Asst. lectr. Victoria U. Coll., Wellington, New Zealand, 1960-61; scholar Australian Nat. U., Canberra, 1961-64; lectr. sociology, field rep. Population Coun. (N.Y.) U. Ghana, Accra, 1965-66; vis. fellow London Sch. Econs., 1966; asst. prof. U We. Ont., London, Can., 1966-68; asst. prof. sociology, internat. population program assoc. Cornell U., Ithaca, N.Y., 1968-71; from assoc. prof. to prof. sociology Carleton U., Ottawa, Ont., 1971-78; prof. sociology and anthropology, dir. Population Studies Ctr. U. Waikato, Hamilton, New Zealand, 1978-92, prof. demography, dir. Population Studies Ctr., 1993—; cons. Internat. Statis. Inst. World Fertility Survey, London, 1994-96; invited prof./vis. fellow U. Montreal, Can., 1973, 84, Nat. Inst. Demographic Studies, Paris, 1985, U. Oxford, 1995; cons., sec. Ind. Commn. Population and Quality of Life, Paris, 1994; dir. Inst. Social and Cultural Rsch.; cons. other internat. agencies. Author or co-author 12 books; contbr. numerous articles to profl. jours. Officer Nat. Commn. UNESCO, 1980-82. Fellow Royal Soc. New Zealand; mem. Population Assn. New Zealand (pres. 1981-83, 95—), Internat. Union for Sci. Study of Population (nominating com. 1989-93, sci. commn. age structure and policy 1999—), Population Assn. Am., Internat. Assn. Francophone Demographers. Avocations: walking, swimming, travel, gardening. Office: Univ Waikato, Population Studies Ctr, Hamilton New Zealand

POOL, EUGENE HUNTER, educator, writer; b. N.Y.C., May 9, 1943; s. James Lawrence and Angeline Krech (James) P.; m. Priscilla Jane Choate, Feb. 24, 1968 (div. Sept. 1986); children: Nathan Beekman, Miranda Parrish James; m. Laura Parrish Dobson, Oct. 5, 1986. BA, Harvard U., 1964; MA, Boston U., 1973, MBA, 1984. Tchr. English Browne & Nichols Sch. (later Buckingham Browne & Nichols Sch.), Cambridge, Mass., 1964-67, 68-70, 73-78, head English dept., 1970-71, dean grade 12, 1978-88, acting dean students, 1988-89; dean students, 1989-95; photographer USAR, Ft. Monmouth, N.J., 1967-68; freelance writer Hanover, N.H., 1971-72. Author: The Captain of Battery Park, 1978, The Art of Fairy Tales, 1995; writer poetry; contbr. articles to profl. pubs. Served with USAR, 1967-73. Mem. North Haven (Maine) Casino Yacht Club (pres. 1985-88, sec. 1988-2000). Avocations: athletics, travel. Home: 263 Payson Rd Belmont MA 02478-3426

POOLE, CLIFFORD GEORGE, Anglican priest, secondary school educator; b. Worcester, Eng., Oct. 8, 1936; s. George Ernest and Margaret (Brant) P.; m. Jean Balfour, Jan. 5, 1980; children: Robert, Charlotte. Grad., Keble Coll.; degree in French and German with honours, diploma in Religious Studies, postgrad. cert. in Edn. Ordained priest, 1987. Chaplain to English speaking ch. cmty. Luxembourg, Luxembourg, 1991—; secondary sch. tchr. European Sch., Luxembourg, 1991—. E-mail: clifford.poole@ci.educ.lu. Home and Office: English Speaking Ch Cmty, 89 rue de Muhlenbach, L-2168 Luxembourg Luxembourg

POOLE, PHILIP LESLIE, biochemist, researcher; b. Ilford, England, Jan. 30, 1949; s. Philip Henry and Ivy Lillian (Browning) P.; m. Fiona Alison Carter, Apr. 18, 1981 (div. May 1988). BA, Open Univ., Eng., 1976; PhD, Birkbeck Coll., London, 1983; MRSC, Royal Soc. Chemistry, 1993. Rsch. tech. May and Bakers Chemicals, 1967-70; biochemistry tech. Inst. Laryngology & Otology, 1970-71; biochemistry rsch. tech. Queen Mary Coll., 1971-79; rsch. officer Birkbeck Coll., 1983-87; lectr. Univ. East London, 1987—; symposia organizer British Biophysics, 1983. Editor: Biotechnology Applications of Microinjection, Microscopic Imaging and Fluorescence, 1992; contbr. articles to profl. jours. Recipient rsch. grants Rutherford Appleton Lab., 1993—, Sci. & Engring. Rsch. Coun., 1983. Fellow British Interplanetary Soc.; mem. Royal Institution, N.Y. Acad. Scis., Biochemistry Soc. Mem. Ch. of Eng. Office: U East London, Romford Rd Dept Life Scis, London E15 4LZ, England

POOLE, WILLIAM DANIEL, writer, editor; b. Statesville, N.C., Nov. 3, 1932; s. William Oscar and Edna (Brewer) P.; m. Sandra Ball, June 14, 1980. BA, Wake Forest U., 1955. Reporter Norfolk (Va.) Virginian-Pilot, 1955-57; reporter Washington Star, 1957-61, real estate editor, 1961-71, features editor, asst. mng. editor, 1971-81; v.p. Ins. Info. Inst., N.Y.C., 1981-91; pub. Insurance Rev. mag., N.Y.C., 1986-91. Contbr. articles to profl. jours. Mem. White House Corr. Assn., Nat. Assn. Real Estate Editors (pres. 1970-71), Newspaper Comics Coun. (chmn. 1975-77), Soc. Am. Travel Writers, Mystery Writers of Am., Ins. Mktg. Comms. Assn., Am. Assn. Sunday and Feature Editors, Amateur Comedy Club, Dutch Treat Club, The Players Club (1st v.p.), Nat. Press Club (D.C.), Omicron Delta Kappa, Sigma Phi Epsilon. Republican. Baptist. Home: 139 E 63rd St New York NY 10021-7408

POOLEY, DEREK, retired energy agency executive, consultant; b. Plymouth, Devon, U.K., Oct. 28, 1937; s. Richard Pike and Evelyn (Lee) P.; m. Jennifer Mary Davey, Aug. 26, 1961; children: Michael Bruce, Benjamin John, Miriam Jane. BSc, U. Birmingham, Eng., 1958, PhD, 1961. A.A. Noyes fellow Calif. Inst. Tech., Pasadena, 1961; head materials divsn. Ukaea Harwell, Didcot, U.K., 1976-81; chief scientist U.K. Dept. Energy, London, 1983-86; dir. Winfrith Tech. Ctr., U.K., 1986-91; mng. dir. AEA Tech. Nuclear Group, U.K., 1991-94; chief exec. UK Atomic Energy Authority, Didcot, Eng., 1996-97; ret., 1997; pres. Brit. Nuclear Energy Soc., 1992-94. Author: Real Solids and Radiation, 1975, Shaping Tomorrow, 1981, Energy Technologies for the UK, 1987. Decorated comdr. Order Brit. Empire. Fellow Inst. Physics, Inst. Nuclear Engrs. (hon.). Avocations: walking, gardening, astronomy.

POON, HOH FUN GEOFFREY, chemical company executive; b. Hong Kong, Nov. 21, 1951; arrived in Australia, 1992; s. Tim and Yuet Wah (Cheung) P.; children: Gigi, Vicky, Jason, Vincey. Higher diploma, Hong Kong Polytech., 1978. Jr. engr. Lap Fai Ind Ltd., Hong Kong, 1971-72; sales rep. Medo Corp., Hong Kong, 1972-75; gen. mgr. Funny Corp., Hong Kong, 1975—; mng. dir. Funchem Ltd., Hong Kong, 1986—, Funchem Australia Pty Ltd., 1992—; cons. Golden Ray Trading Co., Hong Kong, 1985—. Sr. rescuer Civil Aid Svcs., Hong Kong, 1969-80. Avocations: singing, fishing, golf, hiking, travel. Office: Funny Corp Unit G 15/F, 173-175 Wo Yi Hop Rd, Kwai Chung Hong Kong

POON, RONNIE TUNG-PING, surgeon, educator; b. Fukien, China, Mar. 22, 1964; s. Shun Yuen and Kam Shau (Ng) P.; m. Peggy Pui-Kei Leung, Mar. 8, 1995; children: Michelle, Calvin, Ian. MB BS, U. Hong Kong, 1989, M of Surgery, 1999. Intern Queen Mary Hosp., Hong Kong, 1989-90, sr. surg. resident, 1994-97; surg. resident Kwong Wah Hosp., Hong Kong, 1990-91; surg. resident St. Vincent's Hosp., Sydney, 1991-92, surg. registrar, 1992-93; asst. prof. U. Hong Kong, 1998—; hon. sr. med. officer Queen Mary Hosp., 1998—, hon. lectr. nursing sch., 1998—; instr. ATLS Am. Coll. of USA, 1998—. Author: (with others) Clinical Nutrition: Parenteral Nutrition, 1999; contbr. articles to profl. jours. Sir Edward Youde Meml. scholarship, 1989, univ. alumni scholarship U. Hong Kong, 1989. Fellow Royal Coll. Surgeons of Edinburgh, Hong Kong Coll. of Surgeons, Hong Kong Acad. of Medicine; mem. AAAS, N.Y. Acad. Sci., Asian Surg. Assn. Avocations: tennis, music. Office: Queen Mary Hosp Dept Surg, Pokfulam Rd, Hong Kong Republic of China

POON, TAK LUN, orthopedic surgeon, photographer; b. Hong Kong. Grad., Munsang/Coll.Kings Coll., Hong Kong, 1975; BS, MB, U. Hong Kong, 1982. Resident Princess Margaret Hosp./United Christian Hosp., 1983; med. officer Queen Elizabeth Hosp., Hong Kong, 1984-85, Kowloon Hosp., Hong Kong, 1986-87, Princess Margaret Hosp., Hong Kong, 1988, Queen Elizabeth Hosp., Hong Kong, 1989; sr. med. officer Queen Mary Hosp., Hong Kong, 1990-97—, cons., 1997—; hon. assoc. prof. Hong Kong U., 1997—; med. officer Hong Kong br. Brit. Red Cross Soc., 1984—; cons. med. officer Hong Kong Red Cross br. Chinese Red Cross Soc., 1997—. Author: (poetry collection) Chu-Ju-Ji I, 1982, Chu-Ju-Ji II, 1984. Fellow Royal Coll. Physicians and Surgeons (Glasgow); mem. Govt. Doctors Assn. Hong Kong (sec. 1990-91), Hong Kong Pub. Doctors Assn. (pres. 1996-99), Hong Kong Aviation Club, Eddy's Magic Club Hong Kong. Avocations: photography, aviation, magic, ancient Chinese zither. Home: F15 Block 6 Site 9, Whampoa Garden, Kowloon Hong Kong Office: Queen Mary Hosp, Pakfulan, Hong Kong Hong Kong

POON, WILSON CHE KEI, physicist, educator; b. Hong Kong, Sept. 26, 1962; arrived in U.K., 1979; s. Chun Pong Poon and Kwan Ying Lui; m. Heidi Ya Heung Lau. BA, Cambridge U., 1984, PhD, 1988. Lectr. Portsmouth Polytech., U.K., 1989; lectr. U. Edinburgh, U.K., 1990-97, sr. lectr., 1997-99; prof. condensed matter physics U. Edinburgh, 1999—. Contbr. articles to profl. jours. Fellow Nuffield Found., 1996-97. Fellow Inst. Physics. Episcopalian. Avocations: piano, painting. Office: U Edinburgh Dept Physics, Mayfield Rd, Edinburgh EH9 3JZ, United Kingdom

POONGUZHALI, KAILASH PALANI, biochemist, educator; b. Chennai, Tamilnadu, India, July 9, 1963; parents: Balasundaram Palani and Velautham Saraswathy; m. Mariappan Kailash, July 7, 1989; 1 child, Priyanka. MSc, Chennai U., Tamilnadu, India, 1985, MPhil, 1987, PhD, 1999. Cert. biochemist, India. Biochemist in charge lab. Childs Trust Hosp., Chennai-Porur, Tamilnadu, India, 1987-88; tutor Sri Ramachandra Med. Coll. & Rsch. Inst., Chennai-Porur, Tamilnadu, India, 1988-93, asst. prof., 1993—; tech. dir. Biogene Diagnostic & Rsch. Ctr., Chennai-ashokknagar, Tamilnadu, India, 1987—. Contbr. articles to profl. jours. Mem. Indian Assn. Biomedical Scientists (life). Avocatons: music, reading, playing keyboard. E-mail: p kuzhali22@hotmail.com. Home: 73 34 Seventh Ave, Chennai-Ashoknagar Tamilnadu, India Office: Sri Ramachandra, Med Coll & Rsch Inst, Porur-Chennai Tamilnadu, India

POOS, JACQUES FRANCOIS, member of European Parliament; b. Luxembourg, June 3, 1935; s. Adolphe and Catherine (Weimerskirch) P.; m. Monique Lorang, July 3, 1969; children: Daniel, Yasmine, Xavier. Dipl. fin. d et sec., Athenee, Luxembourg, 1954; Lic. ès Sc. Ec. et Commn. H.E.C., Switzerland, 1958; Dipl. Sup. Ec. Comparée, U. Internat., Luxembourg, 1960; Docteur ès Sciences Comm. et Ec., U. Lausanne, Switzerland, 1961. Seconded to Ministry of Nat. Economy, 1959-62; mem. Rsch. at Nat. Statis. Office (STATEC), 1962-64; mng. dir. Imprimerie Coopérative and newspaper Tageblatt, 1964-76; mng. dir. Banque Continentale de Luxembourg S.A., 1980-82, Banque PARIBAS, Luxembourg S.A., 1982-84; City counsellor of Esch/Alzette, 1969-76; mem. Parliament, 1974-76, head of Socialist Workers Party Group; v.p. Socialist Workers Party, 1976-95; min. of fin. Luxembourg, 1976-79, v.p. of govt., min. for external trade, coop. min. of economy, min. of treasury, 1984-89, vice prime min., min. of def., min. for fgn. affairs, 1989—, vice prime min., min. fgn. affairs, 1994-99; acting chmn. Coun. European Union, 1985, 91, 97; mem. European Parliament, 1999—. Author: Le Luxembourg dans le Marché Commun, 1961; Le Modèle Luxembourgeois, 1977. Office: European Parliament, Brussels Belgium

POOT, ALLAN ARNOLD, internet financial services company executive; b. Johannesburg, South Africa, Dec. 30, 1956; s. Joop and Aatje (Govers) P. Matric., Hilton Coll., 1974; student elec. engring., U. Witwatersrand, South Africa, 1975-78; dip. BA, Damelin U., 1984. Cert. fin. planner. Personal asst. Orania B.V., Holland, 1979-81; cons. Liberty Life Africa, South Africa, 1983-88; dir. Univ. Fin. Svcs., South Africa, 1988-92, Compass Asset Mgmt. Group, Holland, 1992-2000; gen. mgr. Benelux and Scandinavia Commission Junction, Inc., Holland, 2000—; v.p. Execs. Assn. Southern Africa, 1984-92. With Dutch Mil., 1981-82, UN Mil. in Lebanon. Fellow Inst. Life and Pensions Advisers; mem. European Ind. Fin. Advisors Network, Inst. Dirs., Comml. Anglo Dutch Soc. (mem. com.), Bryanston Country Club. Avocations: fitness training, golf, collecting wine, cooking, windsurfing, skiing, skating. Home: Tesselschadelaan 26, 1399VP Muiderberg The Netherlands

POOT, THEO, bank executive; b. Vlaardingen, Zuid, The Netherlands, May 27, 1951; s. Jan and Agatha Petronella (Kwakkelstein) P.; m. Judith Maria Veen, Mar. 11, 1976. MBA, St. Gallen U., Switzerland, 1974. Dir. Eurohome, France, 1976-82; bank mgr. Bank Mees and Hope, The Netherlands, 1982-87; dir. Pressco Corp., The Netherlands, 1987-91, Chibeco Corp., The Netherlands, 1991-96; bank mgr. ING Bank, The Netherlands, 1996—; bd. dirs. Manuel Beheer BV, The Netherlands, Chibeco BV, The Netherlands, St. C.C.S., The Netherlands. Lt. Dutch Army, 1974-76. Mem. C.B.M.C., F.G.B.F.M.I. C.D.A. Avocations: flying, skiing, parapenting, swimming. Home: Fuchsgasse 12, 8610 Uster Switzerland Office: ING Bank, Glaernisch strasse 36 Zurich, 1000 PA Zurich Switzerland

POP, EMIL, research chemist; b. Tirgu Mures, Romania, Aug. 12, 1939; came to U.S., 1983; s. Victor and Rosalia (Graf) P.; m. Elena Petrina Petri, Apr. 28, 1964; 1 child, Andreea Christina. BS, Babes- Bolyai U., Cluj., Romania, 1961; PhD, Inst. Chemistry, Cluj., and Supreme Coun. for Sci. Titles, Dept. of Edn. B, 1973. Chemist Chem.-Pharm. Rsch. Inst., Cluj, 1962-65; rsch. sci., group leader Chem.-Pharm. Rsch. Inst., 1965-78, prin. rsch. sci., group and compartment leader, 1978-83; rsch. assoc. Dept. Medicinal Chemistry Coll. Pharmacy, U. Fla., Gainesville, 1983-86; rsch. sci. Pharmatec, Inc., Alachua, Fla., 1986-87; group leader Pharmatec, Inc., 1987-89, assoc. dir. chem. devel., 1989-92, dir. chemistry, 1992; dir. chemistry Pharmos Corp., Alachua, 1992-95; sr. dir. chemistry Pharmos Corp., 1995-98; founder, pres., CEO Alchem Labs Corp., Alachua, Fla., 1998—; courtesy prof. Health Sci. Ctr., Ctr. for Drug Discovery, U. Fla., 1998. Contbr. articles to profl. jours.; inventor in field. Inaugural mem. adv. bd. Fla. Ctr. for Heterocyclic Compounds, U. Fla., 1999—. Recipient N. Teclu award Romanian Acad. Sci., 1980. Fellow Am. Inst. Chemists; mem. AAAS, Am. Chem. Soc., Am. Assn. Pharm. Sci., Internat. Union Pure and Applied Chemistry, N.Y. Acad. Scis., Internat. Soc. Quantum Biology and Pharmacology, Assn. de Pharmacie Galenique Industrielle. Greek Catholic. Achievements include design and synthesis of pharmaceutical compounds in particular prodrugs and brain specific chemical drug delivery systems; M.O. calculations. Home: 810 SW 51st Way Gainesville FL 32607-3856

POPA, ALEXANDRU-MIRCEA VASILE, physics engineer; b. Bucharest, Romania, June 3, 1943; Vasile G. Popa and Elena A. Dumitrescu; m. Canstanta G. Stan, Sept. 5, 1974; children: Alexandru-Anton, Bogdan-Ioan. Degree in physics engring., Poly. U. Bucharest, 1966, D in Engring., 1974; MS, U. Calif., Berkeley, 1972. Scientist Semiconductor Rsch. Devel. Ctr., Bucharest, 1968-75; scientist Inst. Atomic Physics, Bucharest, 1975-92, sr. scientist, 1992—. Contbr. articles to profl. jours. Home: St Doamna Ghica No 5 Bl 3, sect 2 Etaj 7 Apt 70, 724041 Bucharest Romania Office: Inst Atomic Physics, Laser Dept PO Box MG 36, 76900 Bucharest Romania

POPA, CONSTANTIN VICTOR, mathematician, educator; b. Bucharest, Romania, Oct. 10, 1956; s. Victor Steliana Popa; m. Cornelia Enachescu; 1 child, Andrii-Vlad. Grad. in math., U. Bucharest, 1981, PhD, 1995. Mathematician I.N.C.R.E.S.T., Bucharest, 1984-87; rschr. Politehnica U., Bucharest, 1987-90; sr. lectr. Ovidius U., Constanta, Romania, 1990-96; assoc. prof. Ovidius U., Constanta, 1996-99, prof., 1999—. Contbr. articles to profl. jours. Grantee Deutscher Akademischer Austauschdiemst, U. Kiel, Germany, 1993, U. Augsburg, Germany, 1998; recipient Anne Abrams Stone fellowship Weizmann Inst. Sci., Israel, 1996-97. Mem. Gesellschaft für Angewandte Mathematik und Mechanik, Romanian Soc. Math. Scis., Romanian Soc. Applied Math. Christian Orthodox. Avocations: good music, travel. Office: U Ovidius Faculty Math, Blvd Mamaia 124, 8700 Constanta Romania

POPA, IOAN, physician; b. Hunedoara, Romania, Nov. 17, 1938; s. Gheorghe and Sofia Popa; m. Zagorca Ostoin, Nov. 17, 1975; children: Alin, Zoran. MD, U. Medicine and Pharmacy, Timisoara, Romania, 1963, Specialist Dr., 1970. Univ. asst. U. Medicine and Pharmacy, Timisoara, 1971, cons. pediatrician, 1979, sr. lectr., 1980-90, prof. pediatrics, 1990—; head Pediatric Clinic II, Timisoara, 1986. Author monographs. Mem. Romanian Cystic Fibrosis Assn., Romanian Assn. for Study of Obesity (v.p.), European Soc. for Human Genetics, Romanian Soc. Med. Genetics (founding mem.). Avocations: poetry, writing. E-mail: cp=bega@mail.sorostm.ro. Office: Pediatric Clinic II, Paltinis 1-3, Timisoara 1900, Romania

POPA, MIHAI EMILIAN, geologist; b. Bucharest, Romania, Aug. 12, 1969; s. Emil and Mihaela (Marchidan) P.; m. Mona Sorana Steriu-Ianulle, Feb. 22, 1998. Degree in geology, U. Bucharest, 1994, PhD, 2000. Jr. asst. prof. U. Bucharest, 1994-97, asst. prof., 1997-2000, lectr., 2000—; cons. Geological Heritage Assessment Group of the Romanian Acad., Bucharest, 1999—. Co-author: Palaeobotany and Palynology, 1997; contbr. articles to profl. jours. Econ. supr. Romanian Info. Ctr., Bucharest, 1997. Maj.-sgt. Ministry of Interior, 1998-99. Rsch. grant Soros Found., 1994, Romanian Acad., 1999. Mem. Soc. for the Preservation of the Geol. Heritage (v.p. 1994—), Geol. Soc. of Romania (treas. 1999—), Internat. Orgn. of Palaeobotany. Avocations: the Gospels, The Old Testament, scuba diving, photography, mountaineering. Home: 74 Popa Savu Str, 71262 Bucharest Romania Office: U Bucharest, 1 N Balcescu Ave, 70111 Bucharest Romania

POPA, MIHAI VASILE, chemist; b. Bucharest, Romania, Apr. 22, 1943; s. Simion and Emilia (Man) P.; m. Elena Secreteanu, July 24, 1965; children: Monica Mihaela, Mihai Florin. Diplomate, U. Bucharest, 1966; PhD, Inst. of Phys. Chemistry, 1978. Asst. rschr. Ctr. of Phys. Chemistry, Bucharest, 1966-69, rschr., 1969-80, scientific sec., 1988-90; sr. rschr. Inst. of Phys. Chemistry, Bucharest, 1980—; assoc. prof. Politech. Inst., Bucharest, 1988—, Oil and Gas Inst., Ploiesti, Romania, 1990-92; dir. Inst. of Phys. Chemistry, 1990—; referee Revue Roumaine de Chimie, Bucharest, 1991—; scientific organizer phys. chemistry confs., Bucharest, 1992—. Author: Protective Coatings and Thin Films, 1996, Organic and Inorganic Coatings for Corrosion Prevention, 1997; contbr. articles to profl. jours.; patentee in field. Grantee NATO, 1996, Ministry of Rsch. and Tech., 1996-98; recipient N. Teclu honor. Mem. Corrosion Commn. of Romanian Acad. (v.p. 1991—), Internat. Corrosion Coun. Manchester (rep. of Romania 1993—), Am. Chemistry Soc. Avocations: swimming, traveling, reading. Home: Str Cringului 9-11 S1, 71298 Bucharest Romania Office: Romanian Acad Inst Phy Chem, Spl Independentei 202, 77208 Bucharest Romania

POPA, SILVIU DANUT, physicist, engineer; b. MEdgidia, Romania, Aug. 5, 1956; s. Ioan and Ecaterina (Stanila) P.; m. Mariana Bulboaca, Dec. 1, 1979; 1 child, Andrei. MS, U. Bucharest, Romania, 1981; PhD, Inst. Atomic Physics, Bucharest, 1994. Engr. "G" Plant, Romania, 1981-83; rsch. scientist Inst. Atomic Physics, Bucharest, Romania, 1983-90, sr. rsch. scientist, 1990—, head rsch. group, 1991—. Contbr. articles to profl. jours. Rsch. grantee UN, 1990. Mem. Romanian Physics Soc., N.Y. Acad. Scis. Avocations: journalism, social communication. Home: Ivan Anghelache, NR 6 BL M26 Ap 41 Sect 5, 76419 Bucharest Romania Office: Inst Atomic Physics, Lab 26, Bucharest Romania

POPE, ANDREW JACKSON, JR. (JACK POPE), retired judge; b. Abilene, Tex., Apr. 18, 1913; s. Andrew Jackson and Ruth Adelia (Taylor) P.; m. Allene Esther Nichols, June 11, 1938; children: Andrew Jackson III, Walter Allen. BA, Abilene Christian U., 1934, LLD (hon.), 1980; LLB, U. Tex., 1937, LLD (hon.), Pepperdine U., 1981, St. Mary's U., San Antonio, 1982, Okla. Christian U., 1983. Bar: Tex. 1937. Practice law Corpus Christi, Corpus Christi, 1937-46; judge 94th Dist. Ct., Corpus Christi, 1946-50; justice Ct. Civil Appeals, San Antonio, 1950-65; justice Supreme Ct. of Tex., Austin, 1965-82, chief justice, 1982-85. Author: John Berry & His Children, 1988; chmn. bd. editors Appellate Procedure in Tex., 1974; author numerous articles in law revs. and profl. jours. Pres. Met. YMCA, San Antonio, 1956-57; chmn. Tex. State Law Libr. Bd., 1973-80; trustee Abilene Christian U., 1954—. Seaman USNR, 1944-46. Recipient Silver Beaver award Alamo council Boy Scouts Am., 1961, Distinguished Eagle award, 1983; Rosewood Gavel award, 1962, St. Thomas More award, St. Mary's U., San Antonio, 1982; Outstanding Alumnus award Abilene Christian U., 1965; Greenhill Jud. award Mcpl. Judges Assn., 1980; Houston Bar Found. citation, 1985; San Antonio Bar Found. award, 1985; Disting. Jurist award Jefferson County Bar, 1985; Outstanding Alumnus award U. Tex. Law Alumni Assn., 1988; George Washington Honor medal Freedom Found., 1988; Disting. Lawyer award Travis County, 1992. Fellow Tex. Bar Found. (Law Rev. award 1979, 80, 81); mem. ABA, State Bar Tex. (pres. jud. sect. 1962, Outstanding Alumnus U. Tex. Sch. of Law 1994, Outstanding Fifty Years Lawyer award 1994), Tex. Bar Found., Order of Coif, Nueces County Bar Assn. (pres. 1946), Travis County Bar Assn., Bexar County Bar Assn., Tex. Philos. Soc., Austin Knife and Fork (pres. 1980), Am. Judicature Soc., Tex. State Hist. Assn., Tex. Supreme Ct. Hist. Soc. (v.p.), Sons of Republic of Tex., Statesmanship award State Bar Tex., 1998, Christian Chronicle Coun. (chmn.), Masons, K.P. (grand chancellor 1946), Alpha Chi, Phi Delta Phi, Pi Sigma Alpha. Mem. Ch. of Christ. Home: 2803 Stratford Dr Austin TX 78746-4626

POPE, FRED WALLACE, JR., lawyer; b. Sanford, Fla., Feb. 9, 1941; s. Fred Wallace and Dorothy (Marshall) P.; m. Jane Laird Miller, Dec. 27, 1962 (div. Oct. 1986); children: Catherine W., Gregory W.; m. Christine R. Fredrick, Jan. 4, 1991. BA in Polit. Sci., U. Fla., 1962, JD with honors, 1969; AM in Internat. Rels., Boston U., 1965. Bar: Fla. 1970, U.S. Dist. Ct. (so., mid. and no. dists.) Fla., U.S. Supreme Ct. 1975, U.S. Ct. Appeals (11th cir.) 1983. Rsch. aide 2d Dist. Ct. Appeal, Lakeland, Fla., 1970; assoc. Trenam, Simmons, Kemker, Scharf & Barkin, Tampa, Fla., 1970-74; ptnr. Johnson, Blakely, Pope, Bokor, Ruppel & Burns, P.A., Clearwater, Fla., 1974—; dir. Citizens Bank Clearwater, 1986-98, First Nat. Bank of Fla., 1998—. Trustee The Fla. Orch., Tampa, 1984—, chmn. bd. trustees, 1991-93; bd. dirs. Pinellas County Arts Coun., Clearwater, 1988-93. Capt. U.S. Army, 1962-67. Mem. ABA (coun. mem. sect. litigation 1983-86, editor, chief Litigation 1979-80), The Fla. Bar (gov. 1982-86), Clearwater Bar Assn. (pres. 1980-81). E-mail: wallyp@jbpfirm.com. Office: Johnson Blakely Pope Bokor Ruppel & Burns PA 911 Chestnut St Clearwater FL 33756-5643

POPE, HARRISON GRAHAM, JR., psychiatrist, educator; b. Lynn, Mass., Dec. 26, 1947; s. H. Graham and Alice (Rider) P.; m. Mary M. Quinn, June 7, 1974; children: Kimberly, Hilary, Courtney. AB summa cum laude, Harvard U., 1969, MPH, 1972, MD, 1974. Diplomate Am. Bd. Psychiatry and Neurology. Resident in psychiatry McLean Hosp., Belmont, Mass., 1974-77, clin. rsch. fellow Mailman Rsch. Ctr., 1977-79, asst. psychiatrist, 1979-84, assoc. psychiatrist, 1984-92, psychiatrist, 1992—, chief biol. psychiatry lab., 1984—; Dupont-Warren rsch. fellow Harvard Med. Sch., Boston, 1976-77; instr. psychiatry Harvard Med. Sch., Boston, 1977-82, asst. prof., 1982-85, assoc. prof., 1985-99, prof. 1999—; staff psychiatrist Hampstead (N.H.) Hosp., 1976-80; vis. fellow The Maudsley Hosp., London, 1977, Hôp. Ste. Anne, Paris, 1977; mem. Am. Psychiat. Assn., 1976-80, adv. com. on schizophrenic, paranoid and affective disorders, 1979, adv. com. on preparation of DSM-III-R, 1984, task force on nomenclature and stats., 1979, 84. Author: Voices from the Drug Culture, 1971, The Road East, 1974, (with J.I. Hudson) New Hope for Binge Eaters: Advances in the Understanding and Treatment of Bulimia, 1984; co-editor: The Psychobiology of Bulimia, 1987, Use of Anticonvulsants in Psychiatry: Recent Advances, 1988, Psychology Astray: Fallacies in Studies of "Repressed Memory" and Childhood Trauma, 1997; The Adonis Complex: The Secret Crisis of Male Body Obsession, 2000; contbr. numerous papers on biol. psychiatry, with emphasis on diagnosis of psychotic disorders, treatment of mood disorders and eating disorders, marijuana abuse, drug abuse by athletes, and false memory syndrome; mem. editl. bd. European Psychiatry, Paris, 1984—, Internat. Jour. of Eating Disorders, 1984—, Jour. Clin. Psychiatry, 1993—. Named one of Outstanding Americans under 40 Esquire mag., 1984; fellow Scottish Rite Schizophrenia Program, No. Masonic Jurisdiction, 1977-81, Charles A. King Trust, Boston, 1977-79. Avocation: weightlifting. Office: McLean Hosp 115 Mill St Belmont MA 02478-1048

POPE, INGRID BLOOMQUIST, sculptor, poet; b. Arvika, Sweden; became U.S. citizen.; d. Oscar Emanuel and Gerda (Henningson) Brostrom; m. Howard Richard Bloomquist, Feb. 14, 1941 (dec. Nov. 1982); children: Dennis Howard, Diane Cecile Connelly, Laurel Ann Shields; m. Marvin Hoyle Pope, Mar. 9, 1985 (dec. June 1997). BA cum laude, Manhattanville Coll., 1979, MA in Humanities, 1981; MA in Religion, Yale U., 1984. Exhbns. include Manhattanville Coll., Purchase, N.Y., Yale Div. Sch., Ch. of Sweden in N.Y.C., Greenwich Arts Coun., Greenwich Arts Soc., First Ch. of Round Hill; author: (books) Musings, 1994, Hosannah, Help Please, 1999. Past bd. dirs. N.Y.C. Mission Soc., Greenwich YWCA, Greenwich Chaplaincy, Greenwich Acad. Mother's Assn., past pres; past trustee First Ch. Round Hill, Greenwich; pres. Ch. Women United, Greenwich, 1989-91. Mem. AAUW, Nat. Assn. Pen Women, English Speaking Union, Nat. Wildflower Assn., Yale Club N.Y.C., Lakeview Club (Austin, Tex.), Acad.

Am. Poets, Nat. Mus. of Women in the Arts, Yale Alumnae Club (Austin and Greenwich, Conn.). Home: 538 Round Hill Rd Greenwich CT 06831-2641

POPE, JOHN WILLIAM, judge, law educator; b. San Francisco, Mar. 12, 1947; s. William W. and Florence E. (Kline) P.; m. Linda M. Marsh, Oct. 23, 1970 (div. Dec. 1996); children: Justin, Ana, Lauren. BA, U. N.Mex., 1969, JD, 1973. Bar: N.Mex. 1973, U.S. Dist. Ct. N.Mex. 1973, U.S. Ct. Appeals (10th cir.) 1976. Law clk. N.Mex. Ct. of Appeals, Santa Fe, 1973; assoc. Chavez & Cowper, Belen, N.Mex., 1974; ptnr. Cowper, Bailey & Pope, Belen, 1974-75; pvt. practice law Belen, 1976-80; ptnr. Pope, Apodaca & Conroy, Belen, 1980-85; dir. litigation City of Albuquerque, 1985-87; judge State of N.Mex., Albuquerque, 1987-92, Dist. Ct. (13th jud. dist.), N.Mex., 1992—; instr. U. N.Mex., Albuquerque, 1983—, prof. law , 1990—; lectr. in field. Mem. state cen. com. Dem. Party, N.Mex., 1971-85; state chair Common Cause N.Mex., 1980-83; pres. Valencia County Hist. Soc., Belen, 1981-83; active Supreme Ct. Jury (UJI civil instructions com., state bar hist. com., bench and bar com.). Recipient Outstanding Jud. Svc. award N.Mex. State Bar, 1996; named City of Belen Citizen of Yr. 1995, Excellence in Tchg. award 1998. Mem. Valencia County Bar, Albuquerque Bar Assn. Avocations: swimming, golf, photography, historical research. Home: 400 Godfrey Ave Belen NM 87002-6313 Office: Valencia County Courthouse PO Box 1089 Los Lunas NM 87031-1089

POPE, LEAVITT JOSEPH, broadcast company executive; b. Boston, Apr. 2, 1924; s. Joseph and Charlotte (Leavitt) P.; m. Martha Pascale, Nov. 20, 1948; children—Joseph, Daniel, Patricia, Elizabeth, Nancy, Maria, Joan, Christopher, Virginia, Matthew, Charles. B.S., Mass. Inst. Tech., 1947. Adminstrv. asst. N.Y. Daily News, N.Y.C., 1947-51; asst. to gen. mgr. Sta. WPIX-TV, N.Y.C., 1951-56; v.p. ops. Sta. WPIX-TV, 1956-72, Sta. WPIX-FM, N.Y.C., 1956-72; sec. WPIX, Inc., N.Y.C., 1958-75; exec. v.p. WPIX, Inc., 1972-75, pres., chief exec. officer, 1975-92, also dir.; sec., exec. v.p. Conn. Broadcasting Co., Bridgeport, 1967-75, pres., chief exec. officer, dir., 1975-87; dir. N.Y. Daily News, 1975-78, Tribune Co., 1978-81; founder Ind. Network News, 1978-89; chair N.Y.C. TV all industry com., advanced TV sys. com. HDTV; chair copyright com. NAB, 1985—. Mem. N.Y. State Regents Ednl. TV Adv. Council, 1958; bd. govs. Daytop Village, 1972—; trustee Catholic Communications Found., St. Thomas Aquinas Coll., 1968-75, Cardinal Cooke Hosp., 1979—, vice chair, 1998—; dir. Archdiocese N.Y. Instructional TV com. 1976—; trustee St. Patrick's Cathedral, N.Y.C., 1992—. Served with Signal Corps U.S. Army, 1942-46. Mem. Assn. Ind. TV Stats. (pres. 1976-78, bd. dirs.), ASME, Internat. Radio and TV Soc., Nat. Assn. Broadcasters (dir. 1982-86), N.Y. State Broadcasters (pres. 1976-78), Sigma Nu, Knight of Malta. Clubs: Univ. (N.Y.C.); Riverbend (Tequesta, Fla.). Home: 173 Dorchester Rd Scarsdale NY 10583-6052

POPE, LENA ELIZABETH, human resources specialist; b. Brookhaven, Miss., Jan. 25, 1935; d. James S. and Elease (Edwards) Smith; m. Roland Van Pope, Dec. 22, 1955 (dec. 1967); children: Nikki D., Ronald V., Ouida. BS, Alcorn A&M Coll., 1955; student, Northwestern U., 1961, DePaul U., 1975-78; MA, Nat. Coll., 1987. Asst. to registrar Alcorn A&M Coll., Lorman, Miss., 1955-57; tchr. Alexander High Sch., Brookhaven, 1957-60, Magnolia High Sch., Moss Point, Miss., 1960-62; asst. student pers. Jackson (Miss.) State Coll., 1962-64; tchr. Chgo. Pub. schs., 1964-65, 78-80; adminstrv. asst. aide U.S. Senator Charles H. Percy, Chgo., 1965-78; tchr. Citywide Colls., Chgo., 1976-79; v.p. human resources Human Resources Devel. Inst., Chgo., 1982—; cons. Foundatin I, Harvey, Ill., 1989—, Safer Found., Chgo., 1990—, Foster Park Community Orgn., Chgo., 1991—. Office mgr. Percy for Senator, Chgo., 1966, 70, 74, 78; transp. dir. Rep. Nat. Conv., Kansas City, Kans., 1976; vol. Thompson For Gov., Chgo.; sec. Oakdale Covenant Ch., 1985-89. Mem. Alcorn State Alumni (sec., con. 1990—), Eta Phi Beta (Soror of Yr. 1987; pres. Alpha Lambda chpt. 1999—). Republican. Avocations: desk top publishing, traveling, reading. Office: Human Resources Devel Inst 222 S Jefferson St Chicago IL 60661-5603

POPE, MARK L., counseling psychologist, educator; b. St. Louis, Apr. 23, 1952; s. Isom Lavern Pope and Ethyle R. (Ray) Enderle. AB, U. Mo., 1973, MEd, 1974; student, Northwestern U., 1977-78; EdD, U. San Francisco, 1988. Nat. cert. counselor; nat. cert. career counselor; lic. psychol., Ill., master addictions counselor, approved clin. supr.; lic. profl. counselor, Mo. Drug abuse counselor Brotherhood Clinic Ill. Drug Abuse Program, Chgo., 1974-75; mental health worker, career counselor adolescent unit Northwestern Inst. Psychiatry, Chgo., 1975-76; career counselor, psychol. test cons. Meth. Youth Svcs., Chgo., 1976-77; rsch. interviewer, drug abuse counselor Cook County Treatment Alternatives to Street Crimes, Chgo., 1977-78; cons., pres. Data Psych Systems, N.Y.C. and San Francisco, 1978-90; computer ops. mgr. Pacific Am. Group, San Francisco, 1981-83; supr. info. systems Bechtel Engring. & Constrn. Cos., San Francisco, 1983-87; software devel. editor Cons. Psychologists Press, Palo Alto, Calif., 1987-89; pres. Career Decisions, San Francisco, 1989—; pres., pub. Cognito Press, San Francisco, 1995-97; dir., founder Horizons Gay and Lesbian Profl. and Peer Counseling Svcs., Chgo., 1975-77; lectr. Cen. YMCA Community Coll. Dept. Psychology, Chgo., 1977-78, Northwestern U. Indsl. Engring. and Orgn. Devel. Dept., 1977-78, John F. Kennedy U. Career Devel. and Planning, Orinda, Calif., 1987-90; adj. prof. Golden Gate U. Grad. Sch. Mgmt. Human Resource Mgmt., San Francisco, 1984-96, psychology dept., 1994-96, U. San Francisco Info. Systems Mgmt., 1986-94, counseling and edn. psychology, 1988-96; counseling San Francisco State U., 1990-96; clin. supr. counseling and health psychology Stanford U., 1990-96; assoc. prof. counseling U. Mo., St. Louis, 1997—; career devel. cons. Pacific Bell, San Francisco, 1988-93; human resources cons. Alpha Computer Svcs., San Rafael, Calif., 1988-91; founder West Coast Counselors With Computers Conf., 1989; program chair Calif. Career Conf., 1989, 95; psychologist Am. Indian AIDS Inst., 1990-94, Native Am. AIDS Project, 1994-96. Author: Experiential Activities for Teaching Career Counseling Classes, 2000; contbr. articles to profl. jours. and chpts. to books. Mem. collaborative planning com. U. San Francisco Sch. Edn., 1987-88, Mo. Gen. Assembly drug abuse adv. com., 1972; bd. dirs. Ill. Civil Liberties Union, Chgo., 1976-78; appointee Mo. Gov.'s Reorganization Commn., 1973. Mem. ACA (mem. couseling software rev. bd. 1987-89, chmn. task force on exhibits 1990-92, mem. com. on gay, lesbian bisexual issues, 1991-92, human rights com. 1995-98, chair 1997-98, gov. coun. parliamentarian 2000-2001), AAAS, APA (mem. divs. 5, 8, 17, 21, 44, 45), APA (divsn. 17, mem. vocational psychology sec., treas., 1996-2000, Gay and Lesbian bisesexual issues sec., chair hospitality suite com. 1997-98, chair special task group on disting. srs. awards 1999-2000, mem. program com. 1999—), Soc. Indian Psychologists, Assn. for Counselor Edn. and Supervision (co-chair internat. network 1988-90, chair subcom. on internat. counselor edn. database 1986-88, mem. counseling and tech. network 1985—, counseling in bus. and industry network 1985—), Assn. for Assessment in Counseling (chmn. interorgnl. affairs com. 1989-90), Bay Area Career Devel. Assn. (co-chair 1987-91), Nat. Mus. Am. Indian (charter), Calif. Assn. for Counseling and Devel. (chair subcom. human rights com. 1986-88, exec. com. 1989-91, chair gay, lesbian, bisexual caucus 1991, conv. program com. 1989-90, chmn. convention program com. 1991-92, mem. exec. com. 1989-91, State Human Rights award, 1996), Calif. Assn. Measurement and Evaluation in Counseling and Devel. (sec., treas. 1988-89, pres. elect 1989-90, pres. 1990-91, past pres. 1991-92), Calif. Assn. Multi-Cultural Counseling, Calif. Career Devel. Assn. (profl. devel. chair 1988-91, no. Calif. regional coord. 1991-93, chair task force to devel. registered career counselor exam. 1991-92, pres.-elect 1993-94, pres. 1994-95, past pres. 1995-96), Am. Counseling Assn. of Mo. (State Human Rights award 2000), N.Y. Acad. Scis., Computers in Psychology, Nat. Career Devel. Assn. (nat. sec. 1992-94, chair pub. rels. com. 1991-92, nat. treas. 1994-97, pres.-elect 1997-98, pres. 1998-99, past pres. 1999-2000, internat. conf. program chair 1997-98, elections com. chair, 1999-2000, eminent career award com. chair 1999-2000, site coord. nat. conf. 1994-95, bd. dirs. exec. com. 1994-2000). Home: 4579 Laclede Ave PMB 436 Saint Louis MO 63108-2103 Office: U Mo Divsn of Counseling 8001 Natural Bridge Rd Saint Louis MO 63121-4401

POPE, ROBERT DANIEL, lawyer; b. Screven, Ga., Nov. 29, 1948; s. Robert Verlyn and Mae (McKey) P.; children: Robert Daniel Jr., Veronica Teres, Jonathan Chase, Byron Christopher, Jessica Victoria. BS in Criminal Justice magna cum laude, Valdosta (Ga.) State Coll., 1975; JD, John Marshall Law Sch., Savannah, Ga., 1980. Bar: Ga. 1981, U.S. Dist. Ct. (no., mid. and so. dist.) Ga. 1983, U.S. Ct. Appeals Ga. 1982. Pvt. practice Cartersville, 1981—; mem. Valdosta Indigent Def. Atty. Panel, 1981-83, Bartow County Indigent Def. Panel, Cartersville, 1987-91, So. Dist. of Ga. Indigent Def. Panel, Brunswick, 1982-84; mem. Cobb County Cir. Defender's Panel for Indigent Criminal Def., Marietta, Ga., 1986—. Recognized as one of most successful criminal def. lawyers Cobb County Cir. Defenders Office, 1994. Mem. Ga. Assn. Criminal Def. Lawyers, Ga. Bar Assn. (criminal law sect.), Am. Criminal Justice Orgn. (Valdosta chpt. pres. 1974-75). Home: 74 Spruce Ln SE Cartersville GA 30121-7643 Office: PO Box 1111 Cartersville GA 30120-1111

POPE, ROBERT DAVID, artist, philosopher; b. Bendigo, Australia, Dec. 9, 1939; s. Ivor Herbert and Mary Matilda (Bussey) P.; m. Rita Marie Müller, Aug. 20, 1966 (div. Jan. 1989); 1 child, Natessa Marie. Educated, Nat. Svc. Balcombe Sch. Survey, Victoria, 1958; part diploma of geology, Royal Melbourne Inst. Tech., 1959. Dir. Pope Art Gallery, Alice Springs, Australia, 1966-68; artist in residence Univ. Adelaide, South Australia, 1978, Univ. Sydney, Australia, 1986; dir. Science Art Centre, South Australia, 1979-92, New South Wales, 1992-95; mng. dir., founder Sci.-Art Rsch. Centre of Australia, Inc., New South Wales, 1995—. Author: Two Bobs Worth, 1989, Creative Physics and a Rigorous Foundation for a Science of Nursing, 1995, Creative Physics: The Science of Life, 1997; work exhibited in galleries of Australia, U.S.A. Dorothy Knox Disting. Persons fellow Dunmore Lang Coll., 1989; recipient sci. rsch. award Inst. Basic Rsch. U.S.A., 1995. Subject of Australian Nat. TV series The Scientists- Profiles of Discovery, 1979. Mem. N.Y. Acad. Scis., Scientific and Medical Network. Avocations: building in stone, chess, model railway, landscape gardening. E-mail: pope@science-art.com.au. Office: Australia Sience Art Rsch Cen, PO Box 733, 2484 Murwillumbah Australia

POPE, RODNEY PETER, physiotherapist, researcher; b. Llandeilo, Wales, Aug. 10, 1967; arrived in Australia, 1972; s. Charles Richard and Sylvia (Kennett) P.; m. Jane Elizabeth De Jong, Nov. 17, 1990; children: Elaine, Kym, Anna, Thomas, Renai. B of Applied Sci. in Physiotherapy, Cumberland Coll. Health Scis., Sydney, Australia, 1988; postgrad. in Biomed. Sci., Charles Sturt U., Wagga Wagga, Australia, 1993—; postgrad. in Psychol. Studies, Deakin U., Melbourne, Australia, 1996—. Registered physiotherapist New South Wales. Physiotherapist Narrandera (Australia) Hosp., 1988-89, Riding for Disabled, Wagga Wagga, 1988-89, Wagga Wagga Base Hosp., 1990-93, Army Recruit Tng. Ctr., Kapooka, Australia, 1990—; injury prevention cons. Army Recruit Tng. Ctr., 1994—. Contbr. articles to profl. jours. Mem. Australian Physiotherapy Assn. Avocation: family activities. Office: Kapooka Med Co, Kapooka 2661, Australia

POPEL, SERGEY IGOREVITCH, physicist, researcher; b. Bostandyk, Tashkent, Uzbekistan, Apr. 14, 1965; s. Igor Sergeevitch Popel and Faina Nikolaevna Tcherkassova. MS with honors, Moscow Inst. Physics and Tech., 1988, PhD, 1991; DSc in Physics and Math., Russian Acad. Scis., Moscow, 1998. Jr. rsch. scientist Inst. Dynamics of Geospheres Russian Acad. Scis., Moscow, 1991-92, rsch. scientist, 1992-96, sr. rsch. scientist, 1996—; head INTAS Project Group Inst. Dynamics of Geospheres Russian Acad. Scis., 1998—; dir., tchr. Moscow Evening Phys.-Tech. Sch. No. 57, Moscow Inst. Physics & Tech., 1983-91; asst. prof. Moscow Inst. Physics & Tech., Dolgoprudny, Russia, 1995—; vis. prof. U. Provence, France, 1999. Author: (with others) Modulational Interactions in Plasmas, 1995; contbr. and reviewer articles to profl. jours. Humboldt rsch. fellow Ruhr U., Bochum, Germany, 1993-95, 96. Mem. Am. Phys. Soc., N.Y. Acad. Scis, COSPAR, Alexander von Humboldt Club. Avocations: history, literature, art, music. Office: Inst Dynamics Geospheres, Leninsky pr 38 Bldg 6, 117979 Moscow Russia

POPENFOOSE, SHARREN E., school counselor; b. Elkhart, Ind., Oct. 27, 1970; d. Charles H. and Sharon R. Smith; m. Brian Lee Popenfoose, Nov. 5, 1994; 1 child, Julia. BA in Psychology/Sociology, Grace Coll., 1993; MA in Counseling Psychology, Ball State U., 1995. Cert. sch. counselor, Ind. Sch. counselor Goshen (Ind.) Cmty. Schs., 1994—, 8th grade volleyball coach. Avocations: scrapbooking, volleyball. E-mail: colts115@bnin.net. Office: Goshen Cmty Schs 721 E Madison St Goshen IN 46528-3521

POPESCU, CHRISTIAN, surgeon; b. Tirgoviste, Dimbovita, Romania, June 5, 1954; arrived in Switzerland, 1983; s. George and Florica (Constantinescu) P.; m. Reynalde Pralong, Feb. 28, 1987; children: Vlad, Victoria, Valériane, Valentin. MD, Bucharest (Romania) U., 1981, PhD, 1996. Med. diplomate. Internal doctor Mcpl. Clin. Hosp. of Bucharest/U. Bucharest, 1980-81; asst. doctor Hosp., Tulcea, Romania, 1981-83, Sion, Switzerland, 1984-85; MD Med. Ctr., Geneva, Switzerland, 1986-89, Sion, 1989-92; MD, PhD Casualty Dept., Geneva, 1993—, Pvt. Surgery, Sion, 1993—; cons. Chantepoulet, Geneva, 1993—. V.p. Union of Patients and Doctors, Lausanne, Switzerland, 1999. Mem. N.Y. Acad. Scis., Charles Darwin Assocs. of N.Y. Acad. Scis., AAAS. Avocations: skiing, shooting, tennis, golf, diving. Home: Rue de Courtille, 1981 Vex Valais, Switzerland Office: Pvt Med Surgery, Rue de la Dixence 6, 1950 Sion Valais, Switzerland

POPESCU, CHRISTINE See PULLEIN-THOMPSON, CHRISTINE

POPESCU, DAN CORNELIU, information science researcher; b. Bucharest, Romania, Dec. 16, 1955; arrived in Australia, 1991; s. Gheorghe and Dina (Stefanache) P. MS in Computer Sci., Poly. Inst. of Bucharest, 1980; PhD in Elec. Engring., Sydney (Australia) U., 1998. Rsch. engr. Poly. Inst. of Bucharest, 1980-90; rsch. scientist Divsn. Math. and Info. Scis. Commonwealth Sci. and Indsl. Rsch. Orgn. Australia, Canberra, 1996—. Contbr. articles to profl. jours. Recipient 1st prize Math. Olympiad Balkan Union Mathematicians, Belgrade, Yugoslavia, 1977, Canon Info. Systems prize for innovative tech. rsch., Canon Australia, Sydney, 1995. Mem. IEEE (signal processing soc., computer soc.). Eastern Orthodox. Avocations: bridge, tennis. Home: 6/2 Carne Pl, Florey 2615, Australia Office: CSIRO Divsn Math & Info Sci, GPO Box 664, Canberra 2601, Australia

POPESCU, GABRIEL-ADRIAN, physician, educator; b. Buzau, Romania, Feb. 19, 1963; s. Constantin and Ioana (Milea) P.; m. Cristina Alexe, July 28, 1995; 1 child, Oana-Carmina. MD/PhD, U. Medicine & Pharmacy, Bucharest, 1988, 99; postgrad., U. Medicine & Pharmacy, 1988; student in polit. scis., U. Bucharest, 1996—. Intern Coltea Hosp., Bucharest, Romania, 1988-89; resident in internal medicine Colentina Hosp., Bucharest, 1989-92, fellowship in infectious diseases, 1992-94; attending physician in infectious diseases Colentina Hosp., 1994-99; sr. physician in infectious diseases Nat. Inst. Infectious Diseases, Bucharest, 1999—; asst. prof. in infectious diseases U. Medicine and Pharmacy, Bucharest, 1992—. Author: (book) Endocarditis - New Trends, 1999; co-author: (book) Infectious Diseases, 1996, Fast Interpretation of Laboratory Findings, 1999; contbr. articles to profl. jours. Recipient 2nd prize nat. math. competition nat. Edn. Dept., Romania, 1980, nat. lit. competition, 1981, 2nd prize in fundamental rsch. at nat. student, 1986. Mem. Romanian Soc. Med. Scis. Avocations: polit. history, tennis, volleyball, travel. E-mail: rnr6@xnet.ro.

POPESCU, MIHAIL ILIE, engineer, researcher, educator; b. Balcesti, Valcea, Romania, Jan. 22, 1936; s. Ilie Ion and Aurelia Savu (Petrescu) P.; m. Rodica-Elena Mihail Serbanescu, June 30, 1978. Engr., Inst. Civil Engring., Bucharest, Romania, 1958, PhD, 1970. Engr. Hydrotechnics Co., Timisoara, Romania, 1958-64; sr. rschr. Hydraulic Engring. Rsch. Inst., Bucharest, 1964-90, Rsch. inst. for Environment, Bucharest, 1990-97; prof. dept. hydraulics U. Costantza, Romania, 1992—. Author: Applied Hydraulics, 1985, Hydroelectric Plants and Pumping Stations, 1987, Selected Problems of Mathematics, 1994, Selected Problems of Geometry, 1997; contbr. articles to profl. jours. Mem. Internat. Assn. for Hydraulic Rsch., N.Y. Acad. Scis., Romanian Assn. Scientists. Home: Bd Iuliu Maniu (Pacii), No 52-72 Bloc 3 ScB Ap 65, 77536 Bucharest Romania Office: U Constantza Fac Engring, Bd Mamaia No 124, 8700 Constantza Romania

POPESCU, THEODOR-DAN, research scientist, educator; b. Rosiori de Vede, Teleorman, Romania, July 4, 1949; s. Aristide I. and Verginia I. (Stănescu) P. MSc, Politehnica U., Bucharest, Romania, 1972, PhD, 1983. Cert. control engring. Engr. Rsch. Inst. Informatics, Bucharest, 1972-77, rschr., 1977-83, sr. rschr. III, 1983-90, sr. rschr. I, 1990—, mem. sci. coun., 1995-97; lectr. Politehnica U., Bucharest, 1975-83, assoc. prof., 1991—; cons. Ctr. for Tng. in Informatics, Bucharest, 1975-85; mem. Romanian Nat. Mem. Orgn. of Internat. Fedn. Automatic Control, Bucharest, 1995-97. Co-author: Adaptive and Flexible Control of Industrial Processes, 1988, Computer-Aided Identification of Systems, 1988, Practice of Time Series Modelling and Forecasting, 1991, Time Sereies Applications in Systems Analysis, 2000; mem. editl. bd. Studies in Informatics and Control Jour., 1992-97. Recipient grants Royal Soc., Lancaster (Eng.) U., 1992, DAAD, Bochum U., Wuppertal U., Germany, 1992, 95, 99, Japan Soc. Promotion of Sci., Tottori U., Kyushu Inst. Tech., 1996, 99, Tudor Tanasescu prize Romanian Acad., 1995. Mem. IEEE, IEEE Control Systems Soc. (tech. com. indsl. process control 1998—), Internat. Fedn. Automatic Control (tech. com. SAFEPROCESS 1996-99—), Former DAAD Gantees Soc. Mem. Orthodox Ch. Avocations: literature, movies, travel, auto. Home: Sos Colentina No 55 Bl 83, Sc A Ap 29, 72247 Bucharest Romania Office: Nat Inst R&D Informatics 8-10, Maresal Alexandru Averescu, 71316 Bucharest Romania

POPESCU, TIBERIU T., business executive; b. Draganesti-Olt, Romania, Mar. 26, 1946; s. Tiberiu M. and Elisabeta I. (Oalea) P.; m. Livia A. Miron, Feb. 19, 1977; children: Alexandru, Andrei-Vlad. Student indsl. mktg., Romanian U., 1991; profl. cert. mgmt., U. London, 1998, profl. diploma mgmt., 1999. Diplomate engr., Bucharest. Jr. engr. SC Mefin S.A., Sinaia, Romania, 1971-74, quality engr., 1975-80, quality dept. head dep., 1980-88, new product devel. engr., 1988-90, export dept. head, 1991-93, gen. mgr., 1995—; mng. dir. SC Trendis Impex SRL, Sinaia, 1993-95; mng. dir. SC Trendis Impex Srl, Sinaia, 1993-95. Mem. Friendship Assn. Athis-Mons (France)-Sinaia, 1998. Mem. Gen. Assn. of Romanian Engrs. (bd. dirs. 1998—), sport and Tourism Promotion Assn., Romanian Ski Fedn., Romanian Baseball Fedn. (v.p.). Mem. Christian-Dem. Paysand Nat. Party. Orthodox. Avocations: sports, tennis, literature, theatre. Office: SC Mefin SA, 41-43 Republicii Blvd, 2180 Sinaia Prahova, Romania

POPESCU, VALERIAN, medical educator, physician; b. Negresti, Romania, Oct. 26, 1912; arrived in France, 1985; s. Constantin D. and Kira M. (Boboc) P.; m. Colette T. Elisievici, Dec. 5, 1943; children: Kira-Cristinel, Qana-Manuela. BS, Basarab, Bucharest, Romania, 1931; D in Medicine and Surgery, Faculty Medicine Bucharest, 1939; specialist in stomatology, Inst. Stomatology, Bucharest, 1943; specialist in maxillo-facial surgery and plastic surgery, Inst. Medicine, Bucharest, 1947, Dr.Docent (hon.), 1960; Dr honoris causa, U. Iassy, 1994, U. Carolus Davilla, 1998. Intern Bucharest's Hosps., 1934-41; resident Maxillo-Facial Surgery Clinic, Bucharest, 1941-48, clin. asst. prof., 1942-49, prof., clinic head, 1949-85, dean faculty stomatology, 1962-76; hon. prof. Med. Inst., Bucharest, 1985; prof. oral-maxillofacial surgery Ecol. U., Bucharest, 1990; expert WHO, Geneva, 1968, Mission WHO in Tunisia, 1972; pres. various internat. congresses, 1970, 72, 81; pres. Romanian Soc. Stomatology, 1948-73, Union Med. Scis. Socs. Romania, 1969-73. Author: Maxillo-Facial Surgery, 1966 (award 1968), Emergencies in Stomatology, 1969, Anesthesia in Stomatology, 1971, Radiodiagnosis in Stomatology, 1973-85, numerous others; editor-in-chief Acta Stomatologica Internationalia, 1980-88, Stomatologia, 1954-90; mem. editorial bd. Maxillo-Facial Surgery, 1972—; contbr. articles, papers in field; originator 12 surgical methods and techniques. Lt. M.C., Romanian Army, 1941-42. Recipient Magitot prize Acad. Medicine France, 1968, Nat. prize Minister of Edn. of Romania, 1968, medal d'Or Acad. Arts; named Internat. Man of Yr., Internat. Biog. Inst., 1992-93, Man. of Yr., Am. Biog. Inst., 1993. Mem. Romanian Acad., Med. Scis. Acad. (pres. 1969), Internat Assn. Stomatology (pres. 1975-79, hon. pres. 1979), Internat. Assn. Maxillofacial Surgery (founding, v.p. 1970), European Assn. Maxillofacial Surgery (founding, counselor 1970), Acad. de Chirurgie Dentaire de France, N.Y. Acad. Scis., Royal Soc. Medicine (fgn.), Fedn. Dentaire Internat. (commn. dental edn and rsch.), European Acad. Implantology (founding, gen sec.). Mem. Orthodox Ch. Achievements include surgical methods and techniques including osteotomie of the ascending rami in the mandibular micrognatia, alveolar ridge reconstruction by autocartilagge, temporo-mandibular arthroplasty in ankilosis, extensive resection in maxillo-facial invasive cancer, transversal-clefts of the face, proprosthetic surgery, surgical techniques in cleft-lip and palate and pharingoplasty in velar oral cancer. Home: 81 Bis Ave Secretan, Paris 75019, France

POPIELA, TADEUSZ, surgeon, educator; b. Nowy Sacz, Poland, May 23, 1933; s. Jan and Bronisława (Chełmecka) P.; m. Mieczysława Werner, Oct. 28, 1955; children: Anna, Tadeusz. Diploma, Jagiellonian U., Kraków, Poland, 1955, doctor's degree, 1961, habilitation, 1965, prof.'s degree, 1972. Specialization in gen. surgery I, specialization in gen. surgery II. Rsch. asst. dept. surgery III dept. Gen. Surgery Jagiellonian U., Kraków, 1955-65, prof. asst., 1965-71, head surg. unit gastroenterology, 1971-76, head 1st dept. gen. and GI surgery, 1976—, rector med. acad., 1972-81; nat. del. Collegium Internat. Chirurgiae Digestivae; exec. office mem., dep. sec. European Assn. for Endoscopic Surgery; head clin. and basic sci. State Com. Sci. Rsch., 1991—; vis. prof. U. Ill., Chgo., 1975, 81, U. Chir. Klinik Wurzburg, 1979, others; presenter in field. Co-author: (with S. Konturek) Clinical Gastroenterology, 1974, (with A. Wojtczak) General Diseases, 1982, (with W. Rudowski and M. Śliwiński) Clinical and Operative Surgery, 1983, (with Gerald M. Larson) Problems in General Surgery, 1993, (with J. Polański) Liver and Bile Ducts Surgery, 1994, numerous others; author: Stomach Cancer, 1987. Recipient Pres. Best Poster prize World Congress CICD, Jerusalem, 1986, 2 1st prizes Internat. Gastric Cancer Congress, Kyoto, 1995. Mem. ACS, Polish Gastroent. Assn. (sect. endoscopic surgery), Am. Gastroent. Assn., European Soc. Surgery, Internat. Gastric Cancer Assn., Internat. Gastro-Surg. Club, Internat. Soc. Surgery, Internat. Coun. Sci. Devel.,World Assn. Hepato-Pancreato-Biliary Surgery, Am. Coll. Gastroenterology, Internat. Coll. Surgeons, N.Y. Acad. Scis., Soc. Polish Surgeons (pres. 1987-89). Home: 47 Walerego St, 30-065 Krakow Poland Office: 1st Dept Gen and GI Surgery, 40 Kopernika St, 31-501 Krakow Poland

POPKIN, ALICE BRANDEIS, lawyer; b. N.Y.C.; d. Jacob H. and Susan Brandeis Gilbert; m. Jordan J. Popkin; children: Susan Cahn, Anne, Louisa. AB magna cum laude, Radcliffe Coll., 1949; JD, Yale U., 1953. Bar: N.Y. 1953, U.S. Dist. Ct. (so. dist.) N.Y. 1956, U.S. Ct. Appeals (2nd cir.) 1959, U.S. Supreme Ct. 1962, D.C. 1972, Mass. 1987. Assoc. Cahill Gordon & Reindel, 1953-61; dir. internat. programs Peace Corps, 1961-63; project co-dir. Georgetown Inst. Criminal Law and Procedure, 1967-72; spl. counsel Senate Sub-Com. to Investigate Juvenile Delinquency, 1972-74; atty., prof. Antioch Sch. Law, 1974-77; assoc. adminstr. EPA, 1977-79; pvt. practice cons. on internat. environ. issues, 1979-81, practicing atty., 1981-87; of counsel Toabe and Riley, Chatham, Mass., 1987—. Fellow Brandeis U.; bd. trustees Radcliffe Coll.; mem. Chatham Harbor Mgmt. Com.; trustee Eldredge Pub. Libr., 1994—. Mem. ABA, Mass. Bar Assn., Barnstable County Bar Assn., Estate Planning Coun. Cape Cod, Planned Giving Coun. Cape Cod. Office: Toabe & Riley Box 707 154 Crowell Rd Chatham MA 02633-2800

POPKOV, YURY SOLOMONOVICH, systems analyst, educator; b. Lugansk, Ukraine, Oct. 16, 1937; s. Solomon Leovich and Gena Moiseevna (Solodkina) P.; m. Elisa Michailovna Kalugina, June 12, 1961; 1 child, Andrew; m. Tatiana Vladimirvna Andreeva, July 30, 1971; children: Eugene, Alex. Degree in Elec. Engring., Moscow Energy Inst., 1960; CandTechScis, Inst. of Control, Moscow, 1964, DSc, 1970. Rschr. Inst. of Control, Moscow, 1960-64, main rschr., 1964-76; head of lab. Inst. for Sys. Analysis, Moscow, 1976-83, head dept., 1983-90, dep. dir., 1990—; prof. Moscow Phys.-Tech. Inst., 1978—, Moscow Inst. Electronics, 1963-85. Author: Optimization and Identification of Nonlinear Dynamic Systems, 1983, System Analysis and Urban Development, 1985, Theory of Macrosystems and Applications, 1995. Mem. N.Y. Acad. Scis. Avocation: skiing. Home: 6 Chelomey St App 92, 117630 Moscow Russia Office: Inst Sys Analysis, 9 Prospect 60 let Octyabrya, 117312 Moscow Russia

POPL, MILAN, chemistry educator, researcher, engineer; b. Caslav, Czechoslovakia, Mar. 10, 1934; s. Frantisek and Vorsila (Modrackova) P.; m. Libuse Stemberkova, July 24, 1955; children: Eva, Ivan. MS, Inst. Chem. Tech., Prague, Czechoslovakia, 1964, PhD, 1969, DSc, 1974. With Inst. Chem. Tech., Prague, 1964—, head analytical dept., 1976-80, prof. analytical chemistry, 1980—; mem. editorial bd. Gas Chromatography Lit., Niles, Ill., 1974. Author: (with others) Analysis of Complex Hydrocarbon Mixtures, 1981, Chromatographic Analysis of Alkaloids, 1990; co-author, co-editor: Instrumental Analysis, 1986; contbr. numerous articles to profl. jours. Mem. Czechoslovak Chem. Soc., Czechoslovak Sci. Tech. Soc. Home:

Treboradicka 1073, 182 00 Prague 8, Czech Republic Office: Inst Chem Tech, Technicka 5, 166 28 Prague 6, Czech Republic

POPLE, JOHN ANTHONY, chemistry educator; b. Burnham, Somerset, Eng., Oct. 31, 1925; s. Herbert Keith and Mary Frances (Jones) P.; m. Joy Cynthia, Sept. 22, 1952; children: Hilary Jane, Adrian John, Mark Stephen, Andrew Keith. BA in Math., Cambridge U., Eng., 1946, MA in Math., 1950; PhD in Math., Cambridge U., 1951. Research fellow Trinity Coll., Cambridge U., Eng., 1951-54, lectr. in math., 1954-58; Ford vis. prof. chemistry Carnegie Inst. Tech., Pitts., 1961-62; Carnegie prof. chem. physics Carnegie-Mellon U., Pitts., 1964-74, J.C. Warner prof., 1974-91; prof. Northwestern U., Evanston, Ill., 1986—. Recipient Wolf Found. Chemistry prize, 1992, Kirkwood medal Am. Chem. Soc., 1994, J.O. Hirschfelder Prize in Theoretical Chemistry, Univ. of Wis., Theoretical Chemistry Inst., 1994, Nobel prize in chemistry, 1998. Fellow AAAS, Royal Soc. London; mem. NAS (fgn.). Office: Northwestern U Dept Chemistry 2145 Sheridan Rd Evanston IL 60208-0834

POPOFF, FRANK PETER, chemical company executive; b. Sofia, Bulgaria, Oct. 27, 1935; came to U.S., 1940; s. Eftim and Stoyanka (Kossoroff) P.; m. Jean Urse; children: John V., Thomas F., Steven M. B.S. in Chemistry, Ind. U., 1957, M.B.A., 1959. With The Dow Chemical Co., Midland, Mich., 1959—, exec. v.p., 1985-87, dir., pres., chief executive officer, 1987-92; chmn., CEO, dir. Dow Chemical Corp., Midland, Mich., 1992-96, chmn., 1996—; exec. v.p., then pres. Dow Chem. Europe subs., Horgen, Switzerland, 1976-85; bd. dirs. Dow Corning Corp., Am. Express, Chem. Bank & Trust Co., Chem. Fin. Corp., Midland. Mem. dean's adv. coun. Ind. U.; mem. vis. com. U. Mich. Sch. Bus.; mem. Pres.' Commn. Environ. Quality. Recipient Internat. Palladium medal, 1994, Société de Chimie Industrielle (Am. Section). Mem. Chem. Mfrs. Assn. (bd. dirs.), U.S. Coun. for Internat. Bus., Bus. Roundtable, Conf. Bd., Am. Chem. Soc. Office: Dow Chem Co 2030 Dow Ctr Midland MI 48674-0001*

POPOLI, MAURIZIO, neuroscientist, pharmacologist; b. Naples, Italy, Nov. 4, 1950; s. Bruno and Adriana (Rossi) P.; m. Nara Rubia Monteiro, Dec. 28, 1995. PhD in Biol. Scis., U. Naples, 1975. Technician U. Naples, 1972-77, rsch. assoc., 1979-80, 83-93; postdoctoral fellow CNR Naples, 1977-79; rsch. assoc. Washington U., St. Louis, 1980-82; asst. prof. U. Milan, 1994—; cons. to pharm. industry, 1994—. Author: Implications of Psychopharmacology to Psychiatry, 1996, Trattato di Farmacologia-Utet vol. 2, 1997; contbr. articles to profl. jours. Mem. Soc. Neurosci., Italian Soc. Neurosci., European Soc. Neurochemistry, European Coll. Neuropsychopharmacology. Office: Univ Milan/Neuropharmacol, Via Balzaretti 9, 20133 Milan Lombardi, Italy

POPOT, JEAN-LUC JACQUES MICHEL, biologist; b. Chartres, France, Oct. 22, 1948; s. Jean and Marie-Thérèse (Milan) P.; m. Jacqueline Barra, May 30, 1991. D D'État, U. Paris XI, 1981. Asst. Coll. de France, 1971-77, maitre asst., 1977-86, maitre de conférences, 1986-89, sous-dir. lab., 1989-96; dir. rsch. CNRS, France, 1996—. Contbr. articles to profl. jours. Recipient Silver medal Soc. D'Encouragement au Progrès, Paris, 1991. Mem. Soc. Française de Biophysique, Com. Nat. Biophysique. Avocations: reading, writing, dining, art, cooking. E-mail: popot@ibpc.fr. Office: Inst Biol Phys-Chem, 13 Rue P & M Curie, F-75005 Paris France

POPOV, BORISLAV NIKOLAEV, economist, journalist; b. Sofia, Bulgaria, June 2, 1965; s. Nikolay Borisov and Dora Doneva (Nedialkova) P. BSc, U. Econs., Sofia, 1990. Programmer Ministry of Trade, Sofia, 1986-87, economist, 1987-90; economist, journalist 168 Hours Ltd., Sofia, 1990-98; editor-in-chief www.Zone168.com, 1999—; CEO Monitor Press Group, 2000—; editor 168 Hours Newspaper, Sofia, 1992-96. Contbr. articles to profl. jours. Recipient Silver medal Deutsche Kanoe Verband, Germany, 1994. Mem. Australian Geog. Soc., Nat. Geog. Soc., Kanoe Fedn. Bulgaria. Avocations: photography, canoeing. E-mail: bobby@monitor.bg. Office: 168 Hours Press Group, Bul Tzarigradsuo Shausse 47, 1504 Sofia Bulgaria

POPOV, EUGENE VLADIMIROVICH, mechanical engineer; b. Nizhny Novgorod, Russia, Sept. 6, 1953; s. Vladimir Fyodorovich and Lilia Bronislavna (Stanevich) P.; m. Tatyana Petrovna Nistratova, May 7, 1977. Degree in engring., Poly. U., Nizhny Novgorod, 1976; PhD in Engring., Izhevsky (Russia) Mech. U., 1987; PhD, Internat. Corp. Grads. Soviet Ednl. Insts., Moscow, 1996. Strength rschr. Shipbuilding Bur., Nizhny Novgorod, 1976-79; head numerical divsn. Rsch. Inst., Nizhny Novgorod, 1979-91; head analysis dept. TRANSAL-AKS Engring. Co., Nizhny Novgorod, 1991-94; major analysis expert JSC Gosincor-NN, Nizhny Novgorod, 1994-96; design and analysis mgr. ALTEX Ltd., Nizhny Novgorod, 1996-97; leader analytic mgr. Indsl. Computer Techs. Co., Nizhny Novgorod, 1997—; sr. specialist SeaTech Ltd., 1998—; lectr. Poly. U., Nizhny Novgorod, 1989—, cons. to PhD students, 1995—; reader Nizhegorodsky Architecture and Bldg. Constrn. U., lectr. to students of descriptive geometry, cons. to PhD students, 1999—. Conbr. articles to profl. jours. Sr. lt. Russian Naval Res., 1982—. Avocations: painting, poetry, traveling, literature, sports. Office: SeaTech Ltd, PO Box 227, 603003 Nizhny Novgorod Russia

POPOV, IGOR ANATOLIEVITCH, physicist; b. Moscow, Apr. 3, 1968; s. Anatoly Igorevitch and Ludmila Alekseevna (Ptchelnikova) P. Degree in electronics engring., Moscow Power Engring. Inst., 1991, PhD in Physics and Math., 1993; PhD in Applied Elect., U. Ghent, Belgium, 2000. With Moscow Power Engring. Inst., 1991-92, asst. prof., 1993-94; scientific coworker U. Ghent, Belgium, 1994—; cons. Rsch. Inst. for Molecular Electronics, Moscow, 1992-94. Contbr. articles to profl. jours. Grand brigand ZAX, N.C., 1994—. Grantee Fed. Svc. for Scientific Policy, Brussels, 1994. Avocations: horseback riding, chess. Office: ELIS-TFCG-IMEC, Sint Pietersnieuwstraat 41, B-9000 Ghent Belgium

POPOV, KANTCHO GEORGIEV, applied mechanics educator; b. Stamovo, Bulgaria, Aug. 30, 1933; s. Georgi Kantchev and Maria (Dimitrova) P.; m. Veneta Borisova, May 25, 1957; children: Georgi, Mihail. PhD, Tech. U., Sofia, Bulgaria, 1978, DSc, 1978. Designer design office Inst. Agrl. Mechanics, Sofia, 1957-58, researcher, 1958-63; asst. prof. Higher Inst. Chem. Tech., Sofia, 1963-70, assoc. prof., 1970-81; univ. prof. Chem. Tech. and Metalurgy U., Sofia, 1981—, Blagoevgrad U. Decorated 1998 French Order Acad. Palms. Mem. Bulgarian Soc. Mechanics, Nat. Com. for New Materials, Sci. Com. for Spl. Polymers, Internat. Francophonic Agy. for Higher Edn. and Rsch. (pres. ctrl. and ea. Europe regional com. 1995—), Cultural Club Tech. U. (pres.), Tennis Club Tech. U. (pres. 1989), Nat. Tennis Assn. (former bd. mem.), Bulgarian Philharm. Soc. Home: Complex Yavorov bl 57A, 1111 Sofia Bulgaria Office: Chem Tech & Metalurgy U, 8 Kliment Ochridski Blvd, 1756 Sofia Bulgaria

POPOV, NICOLAI PAVLOVICH, physicist; b. Leningrad, Russia, Mar. 17, 1934; arrived in Germany, 1990; s. Pavel Nicolaevich and Maria Vladimirovna (Vassilieva) P.; m. Antonina Ivanovna Lazarevich, June 15, 1962; 1 child, Kirill. BS, Leningrad Poly. Inst., 1958; PhD, Ioffe Physico-Tech. Inst., 1966; D of Physics and Math., Leningrad Nuclear Physics Inst., 1984. Jr. scientist Ioffe Physico-Tech. Inst., Leningrad, 1958-71; jr. scientist Leningrad Nuclear Physics Inst., 1971-72, sr. scientist, 1972-87, leading scientist, 1987-90; prof. Ludwig-Maximilians-Univ., Munich, 1992-2000. Contbr. articles to profl. jours. Active Intellectual Unification Perestroika, Leningrad, 1989-90. Grantee Volkswagen-Stiftung, 1996-97. Fellow Internat. Soc. for Human Rights; mem. AAAS, Soc. Sponsors and Friends of Univ. Munich, N.Y. Acad. Scis. Office: U Munich Sektion Physik, Schellingstr 4, 80799 Munich Germany

POPOV, SERGEI YURIEVITCH, research scientist; b. Murmansk, Russia, Apr. 9, 1964. MS, Moscow Inst. Physics and Tech., 1987, Zhukovsky Air Force Acad., 1989; D of Tech., Helsinki U. Tech., 1998. Rsch. asst. Gen. Phys. Inst. Russian Acad. Scis., Moscow, 1984-87; rsch. engr. Zhukovsky Air Force Acad., Moscow, 1987-91; rsch. assoc. Gen. Phys. Inst. Russian Acad. Scis., Moscow, 1991-93; rsch. assoc. Helsinki U. Tech., Espoo, Finland, 1994-98; rsch. fellow Ericsson Telecom AB, Stockholm, 1999—. Contbr. articles to profl. jours. Grantee G. Soros Sci. Found., 1993, CIMO Found., 1994; recipient medal 70th Ann. Soviet Mil. Forces, 1988. Mem. Finnish Optical Soc., Optical Soc. Am., Toastmasters. Avocation: Japanese history and literature. Office: Ericsson Telecom AB, Optical Networks Rsch Lab, 126 25 Stockholm Sweden

POPOV, VADIM PETROVICH, academic administrator, engineering educator; b. Taganrog, Rostov, Russia, Oct. 14, 1940; s. Petr Petrovich and Elena Naumovna (Vischnya) P.; m. Elena Fedorovna Begunova, Sept. 24, 1941; children: Olga, Tatyana. Diploma, Taganrog State U. Radio Engr., 1963, Candidate Sci., 1968; DSc, Inst. Civil Aviation, Kiev, Ukraine, 1975. Cert. radio and elec. engr. Rsch. asst. Taganrog State U. Radio Engring., 1963-65, assoc. prof., 1968-75, prof., dept. chair, 1975-95, vice-rector, 1995—, dean radio engring., 1972-73, 82-86. Author: Circuit Theory, 1985 (2nd prize Russian Higher Edn. 1987), Collection of Problems in Circuit Theory, 1985, Circuits Laboratory, 1986. Named Hon. Educator, Russian Fedn., Pres. Russia, 1997. Mem. IEEE (sr.), Internat. Acad. Informatization. Avocation: yachting. Office: Taganrog State U Radio Engr, 44 Nekrasovsky St, 347928 Taganrog 347928, Russia

POPOV, VICTOR, engineering educator; b. Stavropol, Russia, Nov. 13, 1932; s. Vasily and Daria (Hodeeva) P.; m. Vera Berednikova, Nov. 26, 1957; 1 child, Natalia. MSc, Polytech. Inst. Leningrad, Russia, 1955, PhD, 1962, DSc, 1981; Honored Sci. Worker, St. Petersburg State Tech. U., 1994. Asst. prof. Polytech. Inst., Leningrad, 1955-63, assoc. prof., 1963-83, prof., 1983-86; dean electromech. dept. St. Petersburg State tech. U., 1985-96, chair elec. machines, 1996—; vice dir. Methodical Bd. of Higher Edn., Moscow, 1985—. Author: Electroenergetical Machines, 1990, Thermal Testing of Electrical Machines, 1988. Recipient Award for Successes in Higher Edn., Higher Edn. Min., Moscow, 1984; named Honored Citizen of Hochimin, Govt. Vietnam, 1983; Russian Acad. Sci. grantee, 1994—. Mem. IEEE, Electrotechnics and Energetics sci. Soc. (dir. 1985-92), Russia Electrotech. Acad. Sci., Internat. Energetic Acad. Sci. Social Democrat. Avocations: travel, fishing, house building. Home: Neshinskaya St 4 - 169, 194156 Saint Petersburg Russia Office: St Petersburg Tech Univ, Polytechnitheskaya St 29, 195251 Saint Petersburg Russia

POPOVA, ELIDA NICOLAEWNA, neuromorphologist, researcher; b. Nicolaewskaya, Adigeja, Russia, Sept. 27, 1926; d. Nicolai Fedorovich and Antonina Nicolaewna (Chugreeva) Uschakov; m. Boris Georgievich Popov, Mar. 27, 1954; 1 child, Inena Borisowna. Student, Moscow State U., 1945-50; BS, Moscow State Pedagogical Inst., 1954; PhD, Brain Rsch. Inst., Moscow, 1965. Sr. lab. asst. Morphology Inst., Russian Acad. Sci., Moscow, 1950-51; sr. scientist Brain Rsch. Inst., Moscow, 1956-59, acad. coun. sec., 1959-61, sr. scientist, 1961-76, chief lab., 1976-79, head scientist, 1987—; mem. acad. coun. Brain Rsch. Inst., 1959-79, People Frendsh. U., Moscow, 1980-85. Author: Action of Some Neurotropic Drugs on Brain Structures, 1968, Morphology of Adaptical Changes of Nervous Structures, 1976, Brain and Alcohol, 1984, Brain, Alcohol and Offspring, 1994, Brain Ultrastructure and Dementia, 2000. Avocation: travel. Home: Iwana Babuschkina St 3 251, 117292 Moscow Russia Office: Brain Rsch Inst, Per Obukha 5, 103064 Moscow Russia

POPOVA, ELKA BORISLAVOVA, physiology educator; b. Sofia, Bulgaria, Aug. 29, 1954; d. Borislav Ivanov and Ida Eli (Beracha) Yordanova; m. Pane Lubomirov Popov; children: Lubomira, Iva. MD, Med. U., Sofia, 1979, Speciality in Physiology, 1984. Jr. physician Dist. Hosp., Slivnicha, Bulgaria, 1979-80; asst. prof. dept. physiology Med. U., Sofia, 1980—. Editor: (textbook) Logofetov Handbook for Practical Exercises in Physiology, 1997; contbr. articles to profl. publs. Grantee NIH, Bethesda, 1989. Mem. Bulgarian Physiol. Soc., European Assn. for Vision and Eye Rsch. Avocations: skiing, swimming, mountain climbing. Office: Med Univ/Dept Physiology, 1 G Soffiiski str, 1431 Sofia Bulgaria

POPOVA, JASMINE, diplomat; b. Sofia, Bulgaria, Nov. 8, 1948; d. Nikolas Dimov and Maria Stefaniva (Kilovska) P.; m. Blagoy Savov Guenov; children: Tcholakov, Anguel, Hristov. M in Law, U. Sofia, Bulgaria, 1972; Diplome D- Edudes, Europeennes Centre, Ceu Nancy, France, 1973; PhD in Law, Bulgarian Academie of Scis., Sofia, 1978. Assoc. prof. law U. Sofia, Bulgaria, 1980-89; legal adviser to pres. Bulgaria Office Pres., 1990-91; dep. head Bulgarian Mission to European Union Brussels, 1991-95; sec. on European Integration Coun. of Ministers, Sofia, 1997; dir. European Dept. MFA, Sofia, 1977-78; ambassador of Bulgaria Sweden, Norway and Iceland Stockholm, 1998—; arbiter, Ct. of Arbitration, Bulgarian Chamber for Trade and Industry, 1990-98. Author: (books) The OMR Convention, 1980, Internat. Sale of Goods in the CAEM, 1985, European Community Law, 1977. Bd. trustees, Open Soc. Found., 1990-98, European Movement, 1995—, Cen. European Studies, 1997—. Office: Embassy of Bulgaria, Karlavagen 29, 114 31 Stockholm Sweden

POPOVA, LARISA MICHAILOVNA, chemist, researcher; b. Polevskoy, Sverdlovsk, USSR, Nov. 3, 1955; d. Michail Petrovich Popov and Tamara Konstantinovna Nesterova; m. Andrei Semenovich Poshumensky, Nov. 24, 1978 (div. June 1983). Degree in chemistry, Inst. Tech., Leningrad, USSR, 1979; post-grad., Inst. Qualification Tng., Moscow, 1981, Inst. Tech., Leningrad, 1982; PhD in chemistry, Inst. Tech., 1987; ChD, Inst. Tech., St. Peterburg, Russia, 1999. Cert. design automatization diplomate, in methods quality control. Engr. Inst. Applied Chemistry, Leningrad, USSR, 1979-82, jr. rschr., 1986-89, rschr., 1989-94; sr. rschr. Inst. Applied Chemistry, St. Peterburg, Russia, 1998—. Contbr. articles to profl. jours. Avocations: volleyball, athletics, jazz-ballet, bodybuilding. Office: Rsch Ctr Applied Chemistry, Dobrolyubova Ave 14, 197198 Saint Peterburg Russia

POPOVIĆ, ZORAN VOJISLAV, physicist, educator; b. Arandelovac, Serbia, Yugoslavia, Feb. 23, 1952; s. Vojislav and Draga (Janković) P.; m. Olivera Ranković, June 27, 1976; children: Vuk, Petra. MSc, U. Belgrade, Yugoslavia, 1977; PhD, U. Ljubljana, Yugoslavia, 1984. Asst. prof. Inst. of Physics, Belgrade, 1985-89, prof., 1991—, head dept. for exptl. physics, 1988-92, head dept. solid state physics, 1994—; assoc. prof. Faculty of Elec. Engring., Belgrade, 1991-97, prof., 1997—; dir. Ctr. Solid State Physics and New Materials, rsch. prof. Author: Electrotechnical and Electronic Materials, 1975, 2d edit. 1995; editor: Modern Research in Physics, 1986; contbr. articles to profl. jours. Mem. Am. Phys. Soc., European Phys. Soc., Serbian Phys. Soc. Home: O Župančiča 32v/15, 11070 Belgrade Yugoslavia*

POPP, JOSEPH BRUCE, manufacturing executive; b. Chgo., July 9, 1919; s. Peter Leon and Anna (Chomyz) P.; m. Mabel Lydia Szymanski, Oct. 23, 1941 (dec. Mar. 1993); m. Elinor A. Maves, Jan. 27, 1996; children: Dianne, Lydia, Bruce, Anita, Gregory. Founder, owner Poultry Farm, Westville, Ind., 1941-48, Gary (Ind.) Undercoating Co., 1948-51; survey analyst George S. May Co., Chgo., 1952-54; gen. sales mgr. Maurey Instrument Corp., Chgo., 1958-64; founder, owner Joe Popp Sales Co., North Riverside, Ill., 1964-89, Chart Pool USA Inc., Portage, Ind., 1966—. Inventor hand held berry picker, worldwide bloodhound property security (patents pending). Bd. dirs. YMCA Camp Tecumseh, Brookston, Ind., 1973—. Sgt. U.S. Army, 1942-46. Mem. Nat. Fedn. of Ind. Bus., Greater Portage C. of C., Ind. C. of C., Better Bus. Bur., The Gideons Internat. Republican. Home: 1133 Lincoln St Hobart IN 46342-6039 Office: Chart Pool USA Inc 5695 Old Porter Rd Portage IN 46368-1194

POPP, LILIAN MUSTAKI, writer, educator; b. N.Y.C.; d. Peter and Mae Claire (Cary) Mustaki; m. Robert J. Popp, Dec. 27, 1941. BA, Notre Dame Coll.; postgrad., Columbia U.; MS in Edn., Hunter Coll. Tchr. English McKee Vocat. and Tech. H.S., S.I., N.Y., 1946-63, chmn. acad. studies, 1963-71; prin. William Howard Taft H.S., Bronx, N.Y., 1971-79; adj. prof. Wagner Coll., S.I., 1960-85; instr. Richmond Coll., CUNY, 1968-70; prof. St. John's U., 1991-93; mem. Cmty. Sch. Bd., 1980-93, chmn., 1989-90, chmn. legis. com., 1981-86, chmn. substance abuse and adolescent issues com., 1986—, chmn. pupil pers. svcs. com., 1991-93, chmn. curriculum com.; asst. examiner N.Y.C. Bd. Edn., 1960-85. Author: Journeys in Science Fiction, 1961, Four Complete World Novels, 1961, Gertrude Lawrence as Mrs. A., 1961, Four Complete Modern Novels, 1962, Four Complete Heritage Novels, 1963, Four Complete Novels of Character and Courage, 1964; contbr. articles to profl. jours. Bd. dirs. Staten Island Mental Health Soc.; chmn. vols. N.Y.C. Child Abuse Prevention program, 1984-86; regional dir., mem. exec. bd. dirs. March of Dimes; book discussion leader Snug Harbor Cultural Ctr., 1981—; pres. Com. for a Nuclear-Free Island, 1986-91; v.p. Staten Islanders Against Nuclear Weapons, 1991-95; pres. Brandeis U., Nat. Women's Com., Staten Island chpt., 1996-99; pres., founder Coalition of S.I. Women's Orgns., 1996—; mem. edn. com. Staten Island Cmty. TV; mem. Libr. com. Staten Island Hist. Richmond Town; pres. Staten Island Youth Coun. Recipient Women Helping Women award Soroptimists, 1985, Thomas Wilson award for Substance Abuse Prevention, 1990, S.I. Advance Woman of Achievement award, 1994, Cmty. Hero award S.I. Register, 1996, Woman of Distinction award World of Women, 1998, Paul O'Dwyer Humanitarian award Staten Is. Dem. Assn., 1999; named Outstanding Woman by N.Y. State Sen. Vincent J. Gentile, 1998. Mem. AAUW, Belles Lettres Lit. Soc. (pres.), S.I. Hist. soc., N.Y.C. Assn. Tchrs. English (pres. 1967-71), Nat. Coun. Tchrs. English (bd. dirs. 1968-69), Acad. Pub. Edn., McKee Tchrs. Assn. (pres. 1969), H.S. Prins. Assn. (exec. bd.), Coun. Suprs. and Adminstrs., Arista Hon. Soc. (hon.), Delta Kappa Gamma (pres.), Phi Delta Kappa (v.p. 1990-92). Avocations: travel, reading, photography, jewelry making. Home: 40 Flagg Pl Staten Island NY 10304-1119

POPPER, FELIX, retired conductor, pianist; b. Vienna, Austria, Dec. 12, 1908; s. Ignatz and Margaret P.; m. Doris Jung Crittenden, Nov. 3, 1951; 1 child, Richard. Pvt. study with Hugo Reichenberger, Vienna; student, Staatsakademie Music, Vienna; PhD in Law, U. Vienna, 1930. Condr., music adminstr. N.Y. City Opera, 1949-82; ret.; asst. condr. NBC-TV Opera, N.Y.C., 1953-57; opera coach Mannes Coll. Music, N.Y.C., Curtis Inst., Phila., Acad. Vocal Arts, Phila.; cons. N.Y. City Opera, 1981—. Conducting debut Werner EGK Inspector General N.Y. City Opera, 1960. Master sgt. U.S. Army, 1942-45, ETO. Avocations: collecting opera scores and recordings. Home: 40 W 84th St New York NY 10024

POPRÁDY, GÉZA, librarian; b. Tök, Hungary, Mar. 19, 1940; s. Géza and Ilona (Lugmayer) P.; m. Maria Wéber, July 13, 1963; children: Géza, Judit, Peter. Student, Eötvös Lorand U., Budapest, Hungary, 1958-63. Cert. librarian, tchr. Librarian Architectural Info. Ctr., Budapest, 1963-64, Cen. Rsch. and Design Inst. for Sicicate Industry, Budapest, 1964-83; head dept. Nat. Széchényi Library, Budapest, 1984-90, dep. dir.-gen., 1990-93, acting dir.-gen., 1993-94, dir.-gen., 1994-99, counsellor, 1999—. Author: (book) The Application of Technical Information, 1977, The Systematic Catalogue, 1981, Preservation of Library Materials, 2000; contbr. articles to profl. jours. Recipient Szabó Ervin medal Min. of Culture, 1989. Mem. Assn. Hungarian Librarians (sec.-gen. 1987-90, v.p. 1990-98, award 1988). Avocations: reading, gardening. Home: Buza u 16, H-1033 Budapest Hungary Office: Nat Széchényi Library, Budavári Palota F-épület, 1827 Budapest Hungary

PORAD, FRANCINE JOY, poet, painter; b. Seattle, Sept. 3, 1929; d. Morris H. and Gertrude (Volchok) Harvitz; m. Bernard L. Porad, June 12, 1949; children: Laurie, Bruce, Ken, Constance, Marci, Jeffrey. BFA, U. Wash., 1976. Founder, coord. Haiku NW Poets/Readers, Mercer Isle, Wash., 1988—; editor Brussels Sprout, Mercer Isle, 1988-95; co-editor Haiku Northwest Anthology, Seattle, 1996, Red Moon Press, Berryville, Va., 1996; workshop presenter Haiku Can., Toronto and Alymer, Que., Can., 1992, 95, Haiku N.Am., Calif., Toronto, 1993, 95, Haiku N.Am., Oreg., 1997, Haiku Internat., Tokyo, 1997; judge Internat. Haiku Contest New Zealand Poetry Soc., 1995, People's Haiku & Senryu Contest, Canada, 1999, San Francisco Contest for Haiku Poets of North Calif., 1992, Hawaii Edn. Assn., Honolulu, 1995, 99, Haiku Soc. Am., 1997, PEN Women (Seattle) Internat. Poetry Contest, 2000. Author: Connections, 1986, Pen and Inklings, 1986, After Autumn Rain, 1987, Blues on the Run, 1988, Free of Clouds, 1989, Without Haste, 1989 (Cicada Chapbook award 1990), Hundreds of Wishes, 1990, A Mural of Leaves, 1991, Joy is My Middle Name, 1993, The Patchwork Quilt, 1994 (Haiku Soc. Am. Merit Book 1994), Waterways, 1995 (Haiku Can. Sheet Book series 1995), All Eyes, 1995, Ladies and Jellyspoons, 1996, Extended Wings, 1996, Moon, Moon, 1997, Fog Lifting, 1997, All the Games, 1997, Let's Count The Trees, 1998 (Haiku Can. Sheet Selection 1998), (with M. Mountain) Cur*rent, 1998, The Perfect Worry-Stone, 2000, (with K. Kondo and M. Mountain) Other Rens, 2000, Book Two, 2000, Book Three, 2000. Recipient 1st prize Internat. Tanka competition Poetry Soc. Japan, Tokyo, 1993, Itoen Tea award Haiku Internat., Tokyo, 1996, 98, Cicada award for Haiku sequences by Amelia, 1999, award Mainichi Internat. Haiku Contest, Tokyo, 1999. Mem. Nat. League Am. Penwomen (treas. 1992-94, Owl award 1982, 92, 1st prize state art exhbn. Frye Mus. 1993, 1st pl. Haiku, 1995), Haiku Soc. Am. (pres. 1993, 94, Merit book 1994, judge 1997, Brady Senryu Contest H.M. award 1997), N.W. Watercolor Soc. (treas. 1980-85), Women Painters Wash. (v.p. 1987, bd. 1985-93). Avocations: computer fun, travel. Home: 6944 SE 33d St Mercer Island WA 98040-3324

PORAT, DINA, historian; b. Buenos Aires, Sept. 24, 1943; arrived in Israel, 1950; d. Moshe and Ruth (Gold) Kitron; m. Yehuda Porat, Jan. 1, 1967; children: Iddo, Avichai, Guy. BA, Tel-Aviv (Israel) U., 1968, MA, 1974, PhD, 1984. Mem. staff dept. Jewish history U. Tel Aviv, 1976—, Alfred P. Slaner chair for Study of Anti-Semitism and Racism, 1997—, head Stephen Roth Inst. for the Study of Anti-Semitism and Racism, 1998—, head Jewish History dept., 2000—; mem. adv. com. Yad Vashem, 1984—; fellow advanced studies Hebrew U., Jerusalem, 1984-85, Columbia U., N.Y.C., 1988; lectr. Israel's Staff and Command Army Coll., 1989—; commentator Israeli Radio & TV on Holocaust and anti-semitism, 1982—; mem. Israeli Fgn. Ministry Delegation on Human Rights UN, Vienna, 1993; vis. prof. Harvard U., 1999-2000. Author: The Blue and The Yellow Stars of David, 1990, Beyond the Reaches of our Souls, (in Hebrew) 2000; editor: Surviving the Holocaust, 1990, Anti-Semitism Worldwide, 1994—. With Israeli Def. Forces, 1961-63. Avocation: licensed tourist guide for Israel. Office: Tel Aviv U, Ramat-Aviv, 69978 Tel Aviv Israel

PORATH, DAN, biologist; b. Tel-Aviv, Dec. 20, 1934; s. David Porter and Elisabeth (Engel) Porath; m. Ilana Borowsky, June 11, 1963; children: Nitsan, Etay, Iddo. MS, The Hebrew U., 1963; PhD, Tel-Aviv U., 1973. Rsch. engr. The Weizmann Inst., Rehovot, Israel, 1964-68; rsch. asst. Tel-Aviv U., 1968-73, instr., 1973-75, lectr., 1975-80; lectr. Ben-Gurion U., Sde-Boker, Israel, 1980-85; vis. prof. Carlsberg Rsch. Ctr., Copenhagen, 1978-79; lectr. Upper Galilee Coll., Tel-Hay, 1968-70; rschr. USDA, Beltsville, Md., 1985-86; vis. scientist ARO, Gilat, Israel, 1987-88, Ben-Gurion U., Beer-Sheva, 1990-95. Plant breeder and patentee in field. Pvt. Israel Def. Forces, 1951-54. Recipient the Yaacov Ehrlich award Bnai-Brith, Tel-Aviv U., 1971; rsch. fellow DAAD, The Free U., Berlin, 1972; rsch. grantee Gifrid, Israel, 1977-82. Jewish. Avocations: ancient Jewish folklore, art and its philosophy. Office: Merav Biol Industries Ltd, PO Box 13666, 20179 Tradion Ind Park Israel

PORATH, JAN-ERIK, software engineer; b. Ludvika, Dalarna, Sweden, May 17, 1955. BSc, Polhemsgymnasiet, Göteborg, Sweden, 1975; MSc, Chalmers, Göteborg, Sweden, 1982, PhD, 1991. Engr. ASEA AB, Ringhals, Sweden, 1976-79, Volvo AB, Göteborg, 1982-84; rschr. Chalmers, Göteborg, 1991-93, U. Aalborg, Denmark, 1993-95; pvt. practice JEPtronic, Göteborg, 1995—. Office: JEPtronic, Kvarnbergsgatan 4, S41105 Göteborg Sweden

PORCELLI, GIANFRANCO, language educator; b. Milan, Italy, Feb. 11, 1941; s. Pasquale and Alina (Monfardini) P.; m. Anna Maria Scalise, June 29, 1970; children: Elena, Silvia, Chiara. MA in Langs., U. Cattolica, Milan, 1963. Primary sch. tchr. Italy, 1962-64, secondary sch. tchr., 1964-80; rschr. U. Cattolica, 1980-87, prof., 1990—, head dept., 1996—; prof. U. di Bari, Italy, 1987-90, U. della Svizzera Italiana Lugano, Switzerland, 1997—; tchr. trainer various agys., Italy, 1970—; cons. Ministry Edn., Rome, 1981—; lectr., vis. prof. numerous univs. in Europe, Can. and Argentina. Author over 20 books in applied linguistics and lang. tchr., 1975—; contbr. over 120 articles to profl. jours. Mem. lang. Tchrs. Assn. (nat. v.p. 1986-99). Roman Catholic. Office: U Cattolica, Largo Gemelli 1, 20123 Milan Italy

POREV, VOLODYMYR ANDRIYOVICH, structural engineer, educator; b. Kyiv, Ukrainian, Nov. 1, 1947; s. Andriy Yakovlevich and Vera Semenovna Porev; m. Olena Volodymirivna Dumacheva; children: Gennady, Dmitry. Degree, Kyiv Polytech. Inst., 1986; D, Nat. Tech. U. Ukraine, 1999. Specialist in non-destructive testing. Engr. Sci. Rsch. Inst., Kyiv, 1970-77; lab. chief Kyiv Polytech. Inst., 1977-88, lab chief of spl. devices, 1988—; prof. Nat. Tech. U., Kyiv, 1999—; exec. dir. System, Ltd., Kyiv, 1991-95. Patentee TV device for temperature fields analysis and device for melting parameters analysis; contbr. articles to profl. jours. Capt. Red Army, USSR, 1972-74. Avocation: ping-pong. E-mail: goretz@i.com.ua. Office: Sci Rsch Inst Applied Elect, Politechnichna st corp 16, Kyiv Ukraine

PORKERT, MANFRED (BRUNO), medical sciences educator, author; b. Decin, Czech Repub., Aug. 16, 1933; arrived in West Germany, 1945; s. Bruno and Elfriede (Walter) P.; m. Elisabeth Friederike Herrmann, 1974 (div. 1978); 1 child, Christine Franka; m. Helga Hartung, 1997. PhD, Universite de Paris, 1957. Rsch. fellow Centre Nat. de la Rechereche Sci., Paris, 1955-57, Deutsche Forschungsgemeinschaft, Munich and Bonn, Fed. Republic Germany, 1959-69; dozent Universitat Munich, 1970-75, prof., 1975-78, prof. extraordinary, 1978-95, prof. emeritus, 1996—. Editor, pub.: Acta Medicinae Sinensis, 1980-85; cons. editor Chinesische Medizin, 1986-92; exec. editor-in-chief Internat. Normative Dictionary of Chinese Medicine, 1989—; contbr. numerous articles to profl. jours. Mem. interdisciplinary lectures com. U. Munich, 1975-79, mem. univ. coun., 1977-79, sec. philos. faculty, 1975-77. Mem. Internat. Chinese Medicine Soc. (founder, pres. Munich chpt. 1978-85), Internat. Sci. Chinese Med. Assn. (co-founder 1999—). Avocation: photography. Office: U Munich, Kaulbachstrasse 51a, 80539 Munich Germany

PORRES, ANTONIO, lawyer; b. Cordoba, Mexico, Nov. 22, 1933; s. Antonio Porres; m. Eloisa Blesa; 1 child, Eric. BS, Escuela de Bachilleres, Cordoba, 1951; grad., Escuela Libre de Derecho, Mexico City, 1952-56; postgrad., Diplomatic Sch., Madrid, 1959-60. Legal asst. Banco Cedulas Hipotecarias, Mexico City, 1953-54; atty. Bancomer Banco de Comercio S.A., Mexico City, 1968-87; gen. mgr. Aviculture Co., San Antonio, Mexico City, 1987-91; prof. in labor, civil and tax law Inst. Mex. de Ad Bancaria, 1986-89; tchr. coursesin tax and constl. law Escuela Libre de Derecho, 1974-79. Pers. rep. elections, 1957, Inst. Fed. Electoral rep. elections, 1984, per rep Partido de Accion Nacional, Mexico City's Mayor elections, 1997. Mem. AAAS, N.Y. Acad. Scis., Nat. Geog. Soc. (cert.), Assn. Montañesa de Mex., Assn. Veracruzana Mex. Avocations: reading, research on cosmic physics and medicine, travel, painting, writing. Home: Av San Jeronimo 1568-6, Mexico City 10200, Mexico

PORSCHEN, RAINER, gastroenterologist, clinician; b. Bonn, Rhineland, Germany, May 12, 1954; s. Walter and Irmgard (Bode) P.; m. Beate Halber, July 9, 1982; children: Philipp, Christian. Lic. to practice medicine, U. Aachen (Germany), 1980; MD, Düsseldorf, Germany, 1981; Med. professorship, Tübingen, Germany, 1997. Diplomate in internal medicine and gastroenterology. Vice dir. dept. internal medicine I U. Tuebingen (Germany), 1994—.

PORSTENDORFER, GOTTFRIED, geophysics educator; b. Chemnitz, Saxony, Germany, Nov. 23, 1929; s. Walter and Elsa (Mueller) P.; m. Evamaria Hahn, July 2, 1955; 1 child, Sabine. Diploma in Geophysics, Mining Acad., Freiberg, Germany, 1954, Dr.rer.nat., 1960, Dr.rer.nat.habil., 1964. Scientist VEB Geophysik, Leipzig, Germany, 1954-56; asst. Inst. of Applied Geophysics Mining Acad., Freiberg, 1956-60; assoc. prof. Inst. Applied Geophysics Mining Acad., 1965-66, prof. Inst. Applied Geophysics, 1966-90, prof. emeritus, 1990—; scientific leader dept. practical geophysics Acad. of Scis., Berlin, 1960-66; dep. dir. Dept. Inst. Geodynamics Jena, Freiberg, 1964-66; dep. dean Faculty of Math. and Natural Scis., Mining Acad., 1989-91; curator TU Bergakademie, Freiberg, 1994-99, dep. dir. sect. of geosci., 1968-75, 81-84; officer Internat. Union of Geodesy and Geophysics, 1965, 75-79. Author: (book) Tellurik, 1954, 61, Principles of magneto-telluric prospecting, 1975. Recipient agr. medal Bergakademie Freiberg, 1954, Scientific Univ. award, 1981, Humboldt medal Ministry Coun. Berlin, 1981. Mem. European Assn. of Exploration Geophysicists, German Geophys. Soc., Deutscher Hochschulverband/German Univ. Union. Mem. Evangelistic Reformed. Avocations: sports, piano. Home: Mendelejewstrasse 38, D-09599 Freiberg Germany Office: TU Bergakademie Freiberg Inst Geophysics, Gustav-Zeuner-StraBe 12, D-09596 Freiberg Germany

PORT, ARTHUR TYLER, retired government administrator, lawyer; b. Chgo., Oct. 4, 1916; s. Arthur Christopher and Helen Elizabeth (Brown) P.; m. Aline Helen Gooding, Oct. 21, 1950; children: Cynthia Helen, Christopher Tyler. BA cum laude, Davidson Coll., 1937; JD, Yale U., 1940; LLD, Coll. Advanced Sci., 1962. Bar: N.C. 1940. Law practice Winston-Salem, N.C., 1940-41; radio announcer Sta. WMRF, Lewistown, Pa., 1941-42; civil atty. Judge Adv. div. Hdqrs. European Command, U.S. Army, Frankfurt, Germany, 1946-47; chief policy sect. Mil. Justice Div., 1947-48; legal asst. to spl. advisor to comdr.-in-chief ETO and mil. govt. Germany, 1949; spl. counsel Sec. of Army, 1949-50, spl. asst., 1950-55; dep. dir. office NSC Affairs Office Sec. Def., 1955-56; exec. asst. to asst. sec. def. ISA, 1956-57; dir. office of security policy and dir. indsl. pers. access authorization Office Asst. Sec. Defense, 1957-61; dep. asst. sec. logistics/installatons and logistics Dept. of Army, 1961-67; fgn. ser. res. officer Dept. of State, 1967-73; asst. sec. gen. def. support NATO, Brussels, 1967-73; spl. asst. Asst. Sec. of Army for Energy Policy, 1973-74; dep. for supply, maintenance and transp. Office Asst. Sec. Army, 1974; cons. NATO affairs Stanford Rsch. Inst., Gen. Rsch. Corp., Logistics Mgmt. Inst., 1975-81. With USAAC, 1942-45, USASIGC, 1945-46, ETO, lt. col. USAR, 1946-68. Recipient Meritorious Civilian Svc. award Dept. Army, 1953, decoration for exceptional civilian svc., 1967; Disting. Civilian Svc. award Dept. Def., 1961. Mem. Confrerie de Chevaliers du Tastevin (Cote d'Or, France), Kenwood Golf and Country Club (Bethesda, Md.), Scabbard and Blade, Omicron Delta Kappa, Sigma Upsilon, Eta Sigma Phi, Phi Gamma Delta, Alpha Phi Epsilon. Home: Falcons Landing 20504 Langley Dr Sterling VA 20165-3571

PORTA, CARLO CESARE, publishing company executive; b. Noventa Vicentina, Italy, July 23, 1930; s. Vincenzo and Vera (Spagnol) P.; m. Emilia Milani, Sept. 12, 1959. Degree in Law, U. Pavia, Italy, 1961. Cert. lawyer. Sales mgr. Gardella, Genova, Italy, 1954-56, Lima, Vicenza, Italy, 1956-59; secondary sch. dept. head Casa Editrice Dottor Antonio Milani, Padova, Italy, 1959-65; co-owner Casa Editrice Dottor Antonio Milani, Padova, 1965—. Named Cavaliere ufficiale al merito della Repubblica Italiana, pres. of Republic, 1974, Cavaliere dell'ordine del Santo Sepolcro di Gerusalemme, Roman Catholic Ch., 1983. Mem. Lyons Club Abano-Terme Euganee. Office: C E D A M, via Jappelli 5/6, I-35121 Padua Italy

PORTAL, JEAN-CLAUDE, physicist; b. Villevayre, Aveyron, France, Apr. 2, 1941; s. Antonin and Gabrielle (Davy) P.; m. Rosine Marty, Dec. 17, 1966, (dec. Oct. 1997); children: Gilles, Beatrice, Jerome. Licence in Sci., U. P. Sabatier, Toulouse, France, 1966, PhD, 1969, D ès-Scis., 1975. Asst. prof. solid state physics Inst. Nat. Sci. Appliquees, Toulouse, 1966-69, maitre, 1969-80, prof., 1980-87, prof. 1st class, 1987-97, prof. exceptional class, 1997—; microstructures rsch. group leader Ctr. Nat. Rsch. Sci.-Inst. Nat. Scis. Appliquees, Toulouse, 1975, Grenoble High Magnetic Field Lab., Ctr. Nat. Rsch. Sci., Grenoble, France, 1981, chair mesoscopic physics, sr. mem. Inst. Univ. de France, 1998—; mem. several European rsch. programs. Co-editor: Optical Properties of Narrow Gap Low Dimensional Structures, 1987, Electronic Properties of Multi-layers and Low Dimensional Semiconductors Structures, 1990; mem. editorial bd. Semiconductor Sci. and Tech. Jour., 1990; contbr. book chpts. and over 500 sci. publs. to internat. jours. and confs. Mem. Am. Phys. Soc., Internat. Soc. for Optical Engring., Semiconductors and Advanced Microelectronics Sci. Instrumentation Engrs., Chevalier Palmes Acad. Avocations: music, swimming, walking, reading. E-mail: portal@insa-tlse.fr. Office: Ctr Nat Rsch Inst Nat Sci, 135 Ave Rangueil, 31077 Toulouse cedex 4, France also: Grenoble High Magnetic Field Lab CNRS/MPI, 25 Ave Martyrs BP166, 38042 Cedex 9 Grenoble France

PORTAL, JONATHAN FRANCIS (SIR JONATHAN PORTAL BT.), accountant; b. Winchester, Hampshire, England, Jan. 13, 1953; s. Francis Spencer and Jane Mary (Williams) P.; m. Louisa Caroline Hervey-Bathurst; children: William, Robert, John. B of Commerce, Edinburgh U., Eng., 1972. FCA Binder Hamlyn. Acct. in pvt. practice, freelance fin. dir., Hampshire, Eng., 1984-88; chief acct. Internat. Press Distbrs., 1989-91; fin. dir., subsidiary dir. Herderson Adminstrn. Plc., 1991-93; fin. dir. Grosvenor Ventures Group, 1993; freelance cons. Newton Investment Mgmt. Ltd., 1994—; internat. mgr. Zi Group Plc, 1995-97. Home and Office: Burley Wood Ashe, Basingstoke RG25 3AG, England

PORTA-PUGLIA, ANGELO, plant pathologist, researcher; b. Asmara, Eritrea, Sept. 4, 1942; arrived in Italy, 1953; s. Felice and Lucia (Pasteris) Porta-P.; m. Maria Letizia Prato, July 16, 1973. Degree in scienze agrarie, U. Turin, 1967. Scholar U. Turin (Italy) Inst. Plant Pathology, 1968-69; agrl. officer F.A.O., Algiers, 1971-73; rschr. Istituto Nazionale Piante Legno, Turin, 1970-71, 73-76; H.S. tchr. Istituto Tecnico E. Fermi, Ciriè, Turin, 1974-77; rschr. Istituto Sperimentale per la Patologia Vegetale, Rome, 1977-87, dir. sect. epidemiology and resistance, 1987—; cons. Food and Agriculture Orgn. UN, Comoro Island, 1981, Gabon, 1984, Guinea, 1985, Ethiopia, 1986; mem. cons. coms. Ministry for Agrl., Food and Forest Resources, Italy. Dep. editor: Petria-Giornale di Patologia delle Piante, 1991—; co-editor: Miglioramento Genetico delle Piante per Resistenza a Patogeni e Parassiti, 1993; contbr. articles to profl. jours. Recipient Gold medal Istituto Nazionale per la Prevenzione del Rischio nelle Attività Tecnologiche, 1994. Mem. Mediterranean Phytopathol. Union, European Assn. Grain Legume Rsch. (v.p. 1994-98), Associazione Italiana Protezione Piante (mem. coun. 1993—), Società Italiana di Patologia Vegetale, Società Italiana di Genetica Agraria, Akademio Internacia de la Sciencoj (assoc.). Office: Ist Sperimentale Patologia Vegetale, Via Bertero 22, I-00156 Rome Italy

PORTEANU, MIRCEA JULIAN, electrical engineering educator, consultant; b. Oradea, Bihor, Romania, July 20, 1938; s. Alexandru and Lucia (Ghimicescu) P. MSEE, Poly. Inst., Iasi, Romania, 1960, PhD in Control Engring., 1974. Cert. in elec. engring. Design engr. dept. elec. drives and power sys. IPROMET Inst. Metall. Plants, Bucharest, Romania, 1960-62; sr. design engr. dept. elec. engring. IRME Inst. Power Engring., Bucharest, 1962-70; sr. design engr. dept. control engring. ICPET Inst. Power Equipment, Bucharest, 1970-77; asst. prof. dept. elec. engring. U. Oradea, 1977-82; expert, cons. dept. elec. engring. ICEM Inst. Metallurgy, Bucharest, 1982—; assoc. prof. dept. control and power engring. Constantin Brancusi U., Bucharest, 1994—; assoc. prof. dept. electronic engring. U. Pitesti, 1998—; coord., mgr. for continuing edn. in elec. engring. ICEM Inst. Metallurgy, Bucharest, 1982—; rsch., design, mfg. and start in mgmt. for control of iron and steel works, power stas. and power sys. IMRE Inst. Power Engring., 1962-70 and ICPET Inst. Power Equipment, 1970-77. Author: TTL Integrated Circuits A Practical Guide, 1985; editor, author: Trends in Power Systems and Equipments, 1984, Trends in Electric Machines and Power Electronics, 1984; patentee in field; contbr. numerous articles to sci. jours.; author procs. of confs. and symposia. Grantee Symposium on Electromagnetic Compatibility, Zurich, Switzerland, 1991. Mem. IEEE (sr.). Greek Catholic. Avocations: skiing, swimming, music, traveling. Home and Office: Constantin Brancusi U, PO Box 1-370, 70700 Bucharest Romania

PORTEL, LAURENT, physician; b. Bordeaux, France, May 23, 1966; s. Jean-Pierre and Pierrette (Pavin) P.; m. Marie Caroline Bahougne, Jul. 13, 1992; children: Eva, Heloise, Valentin. Maitrise sci., Bordeaux, France, 1995, diploma, 1996, diploma d'etudes special, 1996. Internship Hosp. De Bordeaux, 1992-96, chief of clinic, 1997-99; asst. of univ. Bordeaux, 1997—; physician Bergerac Gen. Hosp., 2000—; lectr. Nurses Sch., Bordeaux, 1996-99, Mid Wives Sch., Bordeaux, 1997-99, Psychotherapists Sch., 1998-99. Contbr. articles to profl. jours. Avocations: golf, oenology. Office: Centre Hosp, BP 20, F-24108 Bergerac Cedex, France

PORTELA, ANTONIO GOUVEA, retired mechanical engineer, researcher; b. Lisbon, Portugal, Jan. 26, 1918; s. Raul Lello Portella and Esther Gouvea Portela; married, Sept. 29, 1965; 2 children. Engr. degree, Inst. Superior Tecnico, Lisbon, 1960; prof. degree, Inst. Sup. Tecn., Lisbon, 1958. Cert. mech. engring. Contbr. articles to profl. jours. Mem. AAAS, ASME, Am. Nuclear Soc., N.Y. Acad. Scis., Academia de Engenharia of Portugal. Office: Inst Superior Tecnico, Av Rovisco Paes, Lisbon Portugal

PORTELLI, VINCENT GEORGE, business executive, consultant; b. Detroit, Jan. 6, 1932; s. Camillo and Mary (Borg) P.; B.S., U. Detroit, 1953, tchr. cert., 1961; M.A., U. Mich., 1965; postgrad. Harvard Grad. Sch. Bus. Adminstrn., summer 1971; m. Eugenia A. Naruc, Feb. 7, 1959; children: Debra, Mark, David, Anne, James. Mgmt. trainee, cost acct., cost analyst, sr. internal auditor, sr. cost acct. Ford Motor Co., Dearborn, Mich., 1953-60; tchr. Bedford Sch., Dearborn Heights, Mich., 1960-62; bus. mgr., adminstrv. asst. to dir. Wayne State U. Center For Adult Edn., 1962-64; controller, dir. bus. affairs Mercy Coll. of Detroit, 1964-73; sec.-treas. Am. Sunroof Corp., v.p., corp. sec., 1977-81; sec.-treas. Automobile Splty. Corp., Southgate, Mich., 1973-81; pres., dir. Servia, Inc., cons. to mgmt., Livonia, Mich., 1980-81; corp. v.p. ops. Crown Group, Inc., 1981-83; v.p., gen. mgr. Mktg. Displays, Inc., 1983-85; chief exec. officer Physicians Health Plan (United Health Care), Lansing, Mich., 1985-86, Physicians Choice Northwest, Ind. (United Healthcare), Merrillville, 1986-87; exec. dir. Capital Dist. Physician's Health Plan, Albany, N.Y., 1987-92; exec. v.p. Emerald Health Network, Inc., Cleve., 1992-94; pres., CEO Emerald HMO, Inc., 1994-95; gen. mgr. Genesis Health Plans of Ohio, Inc., 1996-97; cons. Managed Health Care, 1995—. Rep. adv. council Livonia Bd. Edn., 1968-71; v.p. Country Homes Estates Civic Assn., 1971-73; commr. Econ. Devel. Corp.; mem. U. Albany Found. Mem. Employers Assn. Detroit, Am. Soc. Tng. Dirs., Am. Arbitration Assn. (mem. nat. panel), Am. Managed Care and Rev. Assn. (founder exec. leadership program), Nat. Found. for Iletitis and Colitis (bd. dir. capital dist. chpt.), Albany Execs. Assn., Group Health Assn. Am., Delta Sigma Pi, Beta Gamma Sigma. Republican. Roman Catholic. Home: 4286 Sabal Pointe Dr SE Grand Rapids MI 49546-8251

PORTER, ANDREW BRIAN, writer; b. Cape Town, South Africa, Aug. 26, 1928; s. Andrew Ferdinand and Vera Sybil (Bloxham) P. BA, MA, Univ. Coll., Oxford, Eng., 1952. Music critic Fin. Times, London, 1950-74, New Yorker, N.Y.C., 1972-92, The Observer, London, 1992-97, Times Literary Supplement, London, 1997—; mem. music panel Arts Council of Great Britain, 1962-74; mem. music adv. panel Brit. Council, 1966-74; vis. fellow All Souls Coll., Oxford, 1973-74; Bloch prof. U. Calif., Berkeley, 1981. Author: A Musical Season, 1974; Wagner's Ring, 1976; Music of Three Seasons, 1978; Music of Three More Seasons, 1981; Wagner's Tristan and Isolde, 1981; Verdi's Macbeth: A Sourcebook, 1984; Musical Events: A Chronicle, 1980-83, 83-86, 87, 89; editor: Musical Times, 1960-67; editorial bd. Opera Mag.; librettist: The Tempest, 1985, The Song of Majnun, 1992, others. Mem. Royal Musical Assn. (v.p.), Am. Musicological Soc. (corresponding mem.), Donizetti Soc. (v.p.), ASCAP, Am. Inst. for Verdi Studies. Office: 9 Pembroke Walk, London W8 6PQ, England

PORTER, DARWIN FRED, writer; b. Greensboro, N.C., Sept. 13, 1937; s. Numie Rowan and Hazel Lee (Phillips) P. BA, U. Miami, 1959. Bur. chief Miami Herald, 1959-60; v.p. Haggart Assocs., N.Y.C., 1961-64; editor, author Arthur Frommer Inc., N.Y.C., 1964-67, Frommer/Pasmantier Pub. Corp., N.Y.C., 1967-86, Prentice Hall Press, N.Y.C., 1987-90, Simon & Schuster, N.Y.C., 1991—. Author: Frommer Travel Guides to: England, 1964, Spain, 1966, Scandinavia, 1967, Los Angeles, 1969, London, 1970, Lisbon/Madrid, 1972, Paris, 1972, Morocco, 1974, Rome, 1974, Portugal, 1968, England, 1969, Italy, 1969, Germany, 1970, France, 1970, Caribbean, Bermuda, the Bahamas, 1980, Switzerland, 1984, Austria and Hungary, 1984, Bermuda and the Bahamas, 1985, Scotland and Wales, 1985, the Virgin Islands, 1991, Scotland, 1992, Jamaica/Barbados, 1992, Puerto Rico, 1992, the Caribbean, 1993, Bermuda, 1993, the Bahamas, 1993, Austria, 1993, Madrid & the Costa del Sol, 1993, San Francisco, 1996, California, 1996, Caribbean Cruises, 1996, Caribbean Ports of Call, 1996, Georgia and the Carolinas, 1996, Charleston and Savannah, 1996, Munich and The Bavarian Alps, 1996, Vienna & the Danube, 1996, Guide to Caribbean Cruises, 1997, Frommer's Europe, 1997, Frommer's Venice, 1997, Barcelona, Madrid & Seville, 1997, Frommer's Portable London, 1998, Frommer's Portable Bahamas, 1998, Frommer's Portable Paris, 1998, Frommer's Portable Berlin, 1999; author: (novels) Butterflies in Heat, 1976, Marika, 1977, Venus, 1982, Razzle-Dazzle, 1998, Blood Moon, 1998, Frommer's Sweden, 1999, Frommer's Denmark, 1999, Midnight in Savannah, 2000. Recipient Silver award Internat. Film and TV Festival N.Y., 1977. Mem. Soc. Am. Travel Writers, Smithsonian Assocs., Nat. Trust for Historic Preservation, Sigma Delta Chi. Home: 75 Saint Marks Pl Staten Island NY 10301-1606

PORTER, DWIGHT JOHNSON, former ambassador, former assistant secretary of state, former electric company executive, foreign affairs consultant; b. Shawnee, Okla., Apr. 12, 1916; s. Dwight Ernest and Gertrude (Johnson) P.; m. Adele Ritchie, Oct. 6, 1942 (dec. Feb. 1997); children: Dwight A., James G., Ellen Jean, Barbara Adele, Joan Anne, Ritchie Johnson. AB, Grinnell Coll., 1938, LLD, 1968; student, Am. U., 1938-40, 46-48, Nat. War Coll., 1957-58. Govt. intern Nat. Inst. Pub. Affairs, Washington, 1938-39; personnel officer U.S. Housing Authority, 1939-41; exec. officer Dept. Agr., San Francisco, 1941-42; asst. personnel dir. Bd. Econ. Warfare, 1942; dir. adminstrv. services Rural Electrification Adminstrn., 1946-48; mgmt. officer Dept. State, 1948; dep. dir. Displaced Persons Commn., 1949; adminstrv. officer U.S. High Commn., Germany, 1949-54; 1st sec. Am. embassy, London, 1954-56; exec. officer econ. area Dept. State, 1956-57; coordinator Hungarian Refugee Relief, 1957, spl. asst. to dep. under-sec., and under-sec. state, 1958-59; counsellor Am. embassy, Vienna, 1959-62; minister Am. embassy, 1962, dep. chief of mission, 1962-63; asst. sec. of state for adminstrn., 1963-65; ambassador to Lebanon, 1965-70; permanent U.S. rep. IAEA, Vienna, 1970-75; v.p. internat. affairs Westinghouse Electric Corp., Washington, 1975-85; fgn. affairs cons., 1986—. Served to maj. USMCR, 1942-45. Recipient alumni award Grinnell Coll., 1958. Address: c/o James Porter 22 Hickory Ave Takoma Park MD 20912-4622

PORTER, GERALD DAVID, English educator; b. Nayland, Suffolk, Eng., Dec. 26, 1946; arrived in Finland, 1970; s. Albert George and Pamela Helen (Whiteley) P.; m. Sirkku Lena Aaltonen; children: Jessica, Emilia, Aliisa. MA in English, U. Oxford, Eng., 1971; PhD in English, U. Umea, Sweden, 1992. Sr. lectr. U. Oulu, Finland, 1970-75, U. Turku, Finland, 1975-77, Abo (Finland) Akademi, 1979-80; rsch. fellow U. Sheffield, Eng., 1986-87; lectr. U. Vaasa, Finland, 1980-86, 87-94; rsch. fellow U. Umea, 1994-98; sr. lectr. U. Vaasa, 1998—. Editor: News That Stays News, 1989, Dangerous Crossing, 1999; author: English Occupational Song, 1992. Mem. English Folk Dance and Song Soc., Finnish Lit. Soc., Greenpeace. Avocation: folk and political song. Home: Kellosepank 19, 65100 Vaasa Finland Office: U Vaasa, Dept English, PL 700 Vaasa Finland

PORTER, HAYDEN SAMUEL, computer science educator; b. Cin., June 2, 1945; s. Hayden Samuel and Thelma (Wulfeck) P.; m. Patricia Maloney, Sept. 28, 1967; children: Hayden, Emily. BS, U. Cin., 1967, PhD, 1973. Postdoctoral fellow U. Fla., Gainesville, 1973-76; sr. mem. tech. staff Computer Sci. Corp., Silver Springs, Md., 1976-79; pres. A2D, Co., Inc., Greenville, S.C., 1981—; Daniel disting. prof. computer sci. Furman U., Greenville, 1979—, chmn., 1986-92. Author: Exploring Macintosh, 1989, Exploring Macintosh Applications, 1989, Exploring Microsoft Works, 1991, Essentials of Lotus 1-2-3 for Macintosh, 1992; contbr. articles to profl. jours. Grantee in field. Mem. Am. Geophys. Union, Am. Phys. Soc., IEEE, Assn. for Computing Machinery (activity monitor 1983-93), Sigma Xi. Avocations: sailing, boating, fishing.

PORTER, JOHN MAURICE, surgeon; b. Catskill, N.Y., Apr. 7, 1959; s. Bernard A. and Mary J. Porter; m. Alebra Lee; children: Jayson Maurice, Jourdan Marie. BS, Davidson Coll., 1981; MD, Johns Hopkins U., 1985. Intern Johns Hopkins Hosp., Balt., 1985-86, resident, 1986-92; trauma and critical care fellow Hosp. U. Pa., Phila., 1992-93; chief trauma, critical care Med. Coll. Hosp., Toledo, 1993-95; mem. med. staff St. Vincent Med., Toledo, 1993-95, Mercy Hosp., Toledo, 1993-95, Toledo Hosp., 1994-95, Lincoln Med. and Mental Health Ctr., Bronx, N.Y., 1995-97; chief divsn. trauma Alameda County Med. Ctr., Oakland, Calif., 1997—, pres.-elect med. staff, 1998—; dir. trauma/critical care St. Elizabeth Health Ctr., Youngstown, Ohio, 1999—. Contbr. articles to profl. jours.; rschr. in field. Trustee Davidson (N.C.) Coll., 1999—; chmn. State of Ohio Policy Panel on Gun Violence, Columbus, 1999—. Capt. U.S. Army, 1989—. Nat. med. fellow Henry J. Kaiser Family, 1985, William and Charlotte Cadbury Scholar, 1984; recipient Lange Med. Publs. award, 1985. Mem. Soc. Critical Care Medicine (mem. pub. policy com. 1998), Ea. Assn. for Surgery of Trauma (violence prevention task force 1993), Nat. Med. Assn., Assn. for Acad. Surgery. Avocation: aikido. Office: St Elizabeth Health Ctr PO Box 1790 Youngstown OH 44501-1790

PORTER, JOYCE KLOWDEN, theatre educator and director; b. Chgo., Dec. 21, 1949; d. LeRoy and Esther (Siegel) Klowden; m. Paul Wayne Porter, June 8, 1980; 1 child, David Benjamin. BA in Speech Edn., U. Ill., 1971; MA in Theatre, Northwestern U., 1972; postgrad., Northeastern U., Chgo., 1980, 89, 98, Ill. State U., 1985-90. Prof. theatre, play dir. Moraine Valley C.C., Palos Hills, Ill., 1972—, acting theatre coord., 1986-87; mem. acad. senate steering com., 1995-97; adj. faculty Columbia Coll., 1988-92; co-owner, tour organizer Chgo. Theatre Arts Tours, Calumet City, Ill., 1988-93; actress, 1972—; text reviewer Harcourt Brace Pub., 1997, Simon & Schuster, 1998, Mayfield, 1999, Martins, 2000. Author: (textbook) Humanities on the Go, 1992, Experiencing the Arts, 2000. Mem. adv. bd. Oak Park (Ill.) Park Dist., 1983; co-chmn. Moraine chpt. Chgo. Area Faculty for nuclear Freeze, Palos Hills, 1985-87; announcer for blind Chgo. Radio Info. Svc., 1982-83; bd. dirs. Festival Theatre, Oak Park, 1989—, sec. 1996-97, pres., 1997-99; mem. play selection com. Village Players of Oak Park, 1992; guest dir. Triton C.C., 2000—. Mem. Assn. for Theatre in Higher Edn., U.S. Inst. for Theatre Tech., Ill. Theatre Assn., C.C. Humanities Assn (presenter midwest conf. 1993, presenter & planning com. nat. conf. 1999), Ill. Fedn. Tchrs., Nature Conservancy, Zeta Phi Eta. Avocations: acting, singing, foreign travel, antiquities and antiques. Office: Moraine Valley CC 10900 S 88th Ave Palos Hills IL 60465-2175

PORTER, MARIE ANN, neonatal nurse; b. St. Paul, June 29, 1961; d. Theodore J. Morrison and Betty Ann Verdick; 1 child, Angela. ADN, Columbia Basin Coll., 1988. RN, Wash.; cert. neonatal resusitation, Neonatal Resuscitation Program instr., ACLS. Staff RN Kennewick (Wash.) Gen. Hosp., 1988-95; legal nurse cons. Richland, Wash., 1995—; owner, pres. Porter Med. Cons.; legal nurse cons. Clearinghouse. Active March of Dimes. Mem. NAFE, Wash. State Trial Lawyers Assn., Nat. Assn. Neonatal Nurses, Richland C. of C.(amb), King County Nurses Assn.

PORTER, ROBERT CARL, JR., lawyer; b. Cin., Sept. 21, 1927; s. Robert Carl and Lavinia (Otte) P.; m. Joanne Patterson, July 5, 1952; children: Robert Carl III, David M., John E. BA with distinction, U. Mich., 1949; JD, Harvard U., 1952. Bar: Ohio 1952, U.S. Dist. Ct. (so. dist.) Ohio 1954, U.S. Ct. Appeals (6th cir.) 1954, U.S. Ct. Mil. Appeals 1956, U.S. Tax Ct. 1980, U.S. Supreme Ct. 1956. Ptnr. Porter & Porter, Cin., 1953-54; sole practice Cin., 1954-63; sr. ptnr. Porter & McKinney, Cin., 1963-88, Porter & Porter, Cin., 1989—; dir. and officer numerous cos. Served with JAGC, USAF, 1952-53. Mem. ABA, Ohio State Bar Assn., Cin. Bar Assn., Cin. Country Club, Univ. Club, U. Mich. Club, Harvard Law Sch. Assn., Masons, Scottish Rite, Shriners, Phi Beta Kappa. Presbyterian. Home: 2365 Bedford Ave Cincinnati OH 45208-2656 Office: Porter & Porter 2100 4th and Vine Tower Cincinnati OH 45202

PORTERFIELD, JAMES STUART, medical virologist; b. Widnes, U.K., Jan. 17, 1924; s. Samuel and Lilian (Gourley) P.; m. Betty Mary Burch, Jul. 15, 1950; children: William James (dec.), Patricia Ann. MB, ChB, U. Liverpool, 1947, MD, 1949. Asst. lectr. in bacteriology U. Liverpool, 1947-49; bacteriologist, virologist Medical Rsch. Coun. Harvard Hosp., Salisbury, Wilts, 1949-51; bacteriologist Royal Air Force Inst. of Pathology & Tropical Medicine, Halton, 1951-53; mem. scientific staff Nat. Inst. Medical Rsch., Mill Hill, U.K., 1953-77; reader in bacteriology Sir William Dunn Sch. of Pathology U. Oxford, 1977-89; fellow Wadham Coll., 1977-89, emeritus, 1989—; seconded to West African Coun. Med. Rsch., 1953-57, chmn. Arbovirus Study Group Internat. Com. on Taxonomy of Viruses, 1967-81. Editor: Multiple Sclerosis Research, 1974, Arboviruses in the Mediterranean Countries, 1980, Andrewes' Viruses of Vertebrates, 1989, Exotic Viral Infections, 1995; contbr. New Dictionary of National Biography and over 100 articles to profl. jours.; editl. bd. numerous jours. With Royal Air Force, 1952-53. Fellow Royal Soc. Tropical Medicine & Hygiene (councillor 1973-76, v.p. 1980-81); mem. Royal Inst. Gt. Britain (sec., v.p. 1973-78), Soc. for Gen. Microbiology (meetings sec. 1972-77). Avocations: hill walking, gardening. Home: Green Valleys, Goodleigh, Barnstaple, Devon EX32 7NH, England

PORTES, RICHARD DAVID, economics educator; b. Chgo., Dec. 10, 1941; s. Herbert and Abra (Halperin) P.; m. Barbara Diana Frank, 1963; children: Jonathan, Alison. BA summa cum laude, Yale U., 1962; MA, Balliol and Nuffield Colls., Oxford, 1965, DPhil, 1969; DSc honoris causa, U. Libre de Bruxelles, 2000. Asst. prof. econs. and internat. affairs Princeton U., 1969-72; prof. econs. U. London, 1972-94; head dept. econs. Birkbeck Coll., 1975-77, 80-83; pres. Ctr. for Econ. Policy Rsch., 1983—; dir. Ecole des Hautes Etudes, Paris, 1978—; prof. econs. London Bus. Sch., 1995—; Disting. Global vis. prof. U. Calif. Berkeley, 1999-2000; assoc. Nat. Bur. Econ. Rsch., Cambridge, Mass., 1980—; vis. prof. Harvard U., Cambridge, 1977-78. Editor, author: Planning and Market Relations, 1971, The Polish

Crisis, 1981, Deficits and Detente, 1983, Threats to International Financial Stability, 1987, Global Macroeconomics, 1987, Blueprints for Exchange Rate Stability, 1989, Macroeconomic Policies in an Interdependent World, 1989, External Constraints on Macroeconomic Policy, 1991, The Path of Reform in Central and Eastern Europe, 1991, Economic Transformation in Central Europe, 1993, European Union Trade with Eastern Europe, 1995, Crisis? What Crisis? Orderly Workouts for Sovereign Debtors, 1995; contbr. numerous articles to profl. jours. Rhodes scholar; fellow Balliol Coll., 1965-69; Guggenheim fellow, 1977-78.. Fellow Econometric Soc.; mem. Coun. Royal Econ. Soc. (exec. com. 1987-92, sec.-gen. 1992—), Econ. Policy (bd. govs., sr. editor 1985—), Coun. on Fgn. Rels., Royal Inst. Internat. Affairs, Franco-Brit. Coun., Commn. Econ. de la Nation (France). Avocation: living beyond my means. Office: London Bus Sch, Regents Park, London NW1 4SA, England

PORTIANSKY, ENRIQUE LEO, veterinarian; b. La Plata, Argentina, Oct. 2, 1958; s. Jim and Nelly Ruth (Fink) P.; m. Carina Judith Scharagrodsky, Sept. 1, 1988; children: Damián Uriel, Tatiana. Degree in vet. sci., Nat. U. La Plata, Buenos Aires, 1982, DVM, 1987, cert. in univ. tchg., 1989; MSc, Weizmann Inst. Scis., Rehovot, Israel, 1984. Students asst. Sch. Vet. Medicine, Nat. U. La Plata, 1978-87, asst. prof., 1987-91, jr. prof., 1991—; rsch. scholar Nat. Coun. Sci. and Tech. (CONICET), Buenos Aires, 1985-91, rsch. fellow, 1991-98, assoc. rschr., 1998—. Author: Bases de Microbiologia e Immunologia Veterinaria, 1996; contbr. many articles to sci. jours., nat. and internat. mags. Jewish. Achievements include patent for new therapeutic uses of known ester and amide compounds; patent for uses of such compounds on tumor and cancerous lesions. Avocations: computer programming, numismatics, ham radio. Office: UNLP Faculty Vet Scis, 60 y 118, La Plata, 1900 Buenos Aires Argentina

PORTILLA, ELISEO, surgical researcher; b. Mexico City, Jan. 20, 1960; s. Jaime Portilla and Maricel de Buen; m. Maria Guadalupe Ramirez, Dec. 12, 1987. Degree in cardiovascular perfusion, Inst. Mex. Seguro Social, Mexico City, 1984; DVM, U. Nat. Autonoma Mex., 1988; M in Med. Scis., U. Colima, 1998. Cert. clin. perfusionist. Perfusionist IMSS, Mexico City, 1982-92; chief surg. rsch. divsn. Western Biomed. Rsch. Ctr. Inst. Mex. del Seguro Social, Guadalajara, 1992—; advisor Cardiovascular Surgery Group, Guadalajara, 1994—. Contbr. articles to profl. jours. Grantee CONACyT, Mex., 2000. Mem. Mex. Nat. Rsch. Sys., Soc. Mex. Perfusion (sec. 1988-90, v.p. 1998-2000, pres. 2000—). Avocations: ship modeling, hiking, philosophy. Office: CIBO IMSS, Sierra Mojada 800, Guadalajara 44340, Mexico

PORTMAN, RONALD JAY, pediatric nephrologist, researcher; b. Portsmouth, N.H., June 8, 1950; s. Harry and Sylvia Rosa (Applebaum) P.; m. Joan Marie Welch, June 29, 1974; children: Wendi Alana, Shayna Matana, Solomon Zachary. BS, Northeastern U., 1973; MD, Dartmouth Coll., 1976. Diplomate Am. Bd. Pediat., Am. Bd. Pediatric Nephrology. Commd. 2d lt. U.S. Army, 1976, advanced through grades to maj., 1981; pediatric house officer Fitzsimons Army Med. Ctr., Denver, 1976-79, pediatric nephrologist, 1983-86; chief dept. pediat. Würzburg (Germany) Army Hosp., 1979-81; fellow in pediatric nephrology Washington U., St. Louis, 1981-83; resigned, Fitzsimmons Army Med. Ctr., U. Colo., 1986; pediatric nepnrologist, assoc. prof. U. Tex. Med. Sch., Houston, 1986-92, dir. divsn. pediatric nephrology and hypertension, 1992—; dir. pediat. spl. care unit and Hermann Chronobiology Ctr., Hermann Hosp., Houston, 1992—; pediatric nephrologist Fitzsimmons AMC, Univ. Colo., Houston, 1983-86; prof. U. Tex. Med. Sch., 1997—; mem. med. adv. bd. Nat. Kidney Found. S.E. Tex., Houston, 1986—; cons. M.D. Anderson Hosp., Houston, 1986—, Chronobiology Ctr. Tel Hashomer, Tel Aviv, 1995—; mem. med. rev. bd. End Stage Renal for Disease Network 14, Dallas, 1992—. Contbr. numerous articles to med. jours., chpts. to books. Bd. dirs. Congregation Brith Shalom, Bellaire, Tex., 1990-94. Recipient svc. award Nat. Kidney Found., 1995; numerous rsch. grants. Mem. Am. Soc. Transplant Physicians, Am. Soc. Pediatric Nephrology, Am. Soc. Nephrology, Am. Soc. Hpertension, Am. Assn. Medical Chronobiology and Chronotherapeutics (sec., treas.), N.Am. Pediatric Renal Transplant Study Group, S.W. Pediatric Nephrology Study Group, Internat. Pediatric Hypertension Assn. (chmn. exec. com.). Jewish. Avocations: chior, baseball umpire, tennis, golf. Office: U Tex Med Sch 7431 Fannin St Houston TX 77054-1901

PORTMAN, VLADIMIR, mechanical engineer, educator, researcher, consultant; b. Khabarovsk, Russia, Dec. 8, 1935; s. Teodor and Shifra (Beresovskaya) P.; m. Alla Vorobjyova, May 20, 1963; children: Svetlana, Bella. MS, Machine Tool Inst., Moscow, 1958; PhD, Rsch. Inst. Machine Tools, Moscow, 1970; DSc, State Supreme Attestation Bd., Moscow, 1988. Designer/group leader Bur. Design and Tech., Moscow, 1958-64; sr. scientist Rsch. Inst. Machine Tools, 1965-79, head lab. machine tools and flexible mfg. systems, 1979-90; rsch. fellow Ben Gurion U. of Negev, Beer-Sheva, Israel, 1991-94, assoc. prof., 1995—; cons. Sharnoa Computerized Machines, Ltd., Tel Aviv, 1990, Temed, Adv. Tech. Ctr., Ltd., Arava, Israel, 1994, Placa, Ltd., Rehovot, Israel, 1999; vis. prof. Keio U., Yokohama, Japan, 1997. Author: Accuracy of Machine Tools, 1986; contbr. articles to profl. jours.; patentee in field. Recipient 1st prize Rsch. Inst. Machine Tools, Moscow, 1976, 1st prize State Com. Sci. and Tech, Moscow, 1988, grant Ministry of Sci. and Tech., Israel, 1992-95. Mem. ASME Internat., CIRP (corr. mem.), N.Y. Acad. Sci., Am. Biographical Inst. (rsch. bd. advs.). Office: Ben Gurion Univ of Negev, Dept Mech Engring PO Box 653, Beer Sheva 84105, Israel

PORTMANN, BERNARD CLAUDE, pathology educator, consultant; b. Ste. Croix, Vaud, Switzerland, Feb. 6, 1940; arrived in Eng., 1973; s. Henri and Emilie (Jaques) P.; m. Elisabeth Hermine Neumann, Sept. 23, 1970; children: Barbara, Jan. Swiss med. diploma, U. Geneva, Switzerland, 1966; MD, Geneva U., 1972. House officer Hosp. Cantonal, Geneva, 1966-67, lectr. pathology dept., 1968-72; rsch. histopathologist liver unit King's Coll. Hosp., London, 1975-78, cons., 1978—; hon. sr. lectr. King's Coll. Med. Sch., London U., 1978-97, prof. hepatopathology, 1997—. Editor: Pathology of the Liver, 1994, The Practice of Liver Transplantation, 1995; assoc. editor Jour. Hepatology, 1995—. Recipient rsch. grant Swiss Acad. Medicine, London, 1972-73, traveling fellowship Brit. Digestive Found., Mt. Sinai, N.Y., 1982. Fellow Royal Coll. Pathologists. Home: Forest Hill, 20 Ewelme Rd, London SE23 3BH, England Office: Kings Coll Hosp Inst Liver, Studies Denmark Hill, London SE5 9RS, England

PORTNOV, BORIS A., urban planner, researcher; b. Odessa, Ukraine, Aug. 15, 1960; arrived in Israel, 1995; s. Adolf A. and Alla M. (Bass) P.; m. Natalia Rudenko, Dec. 3, 1982; 1 child, Alex. MSc in Arch., Poltava Civil Engring. Inst., Ukraine, 1982; PhD, State Inst. Urban Planning, Moscow, 1987; DSc, Moscow Arch. Inst., 1994. Arch. Giprograd, Odessa, 1982-85, chief arch., 1985-87; sr. lectr., prof. Krasnoyarsk Civil Engring. Inst., Krasnoyarski, Russia, 1987-95; sr. rschr. Ben-Gurion U., Sede-Boker, Israel, 1995—; sci. supr. Lab. of Regional Sci. and Urban Planning, Krasnoyarsk, 1990-95. Author: Rational Use of Urban Land, 1992, Renewal of Historical City Districts, 1995, Urban Clustering, 2000; archtl. projects include Dist. Moldavanka-1, Odessa, 1986, Student Dormitory in Norilsk, 1989; editor: Desert Regions: Population, Migration and Environment, 1999. Grantee Soros Found., 1989-94, Russian Ministry of Higher Edn., 1992-93, Fulbright, 1994-95. Mem. Profl. Union Russian Archs., European Network Housing Rsch., Profl. Union Israeli Archs. and Engrs. Avocations: coin collecting, computers. Office: Ben-Gurion U of the Negev, Ctr Desert Arch & Urb Plan, 84990 Sede Boker Israel

PORTO, JARBAS ANACLETO, retired physician; b. Caruaru, Pernambuco, Brazil, Feb. 17, 1921; s. Manoel Rodrigues Porto Filho and Auta Anacleto; m. Leila Gerheim, Apr. 15, 1948; 1 child, Claudio. Diploma, Univ. Coll., Rio de Janeiro, 1940; MD, Fed. Univ., 1946. Intern UFRJ, Rio de Janeiro, 1946, asst. dept. dermatology, 1947, docent, 1959; prof. dermatology U. Severino Sombra, Rio de Janeiro, 1970-72; prof. Fundacao Ednl. Souza Marques, Rio de Janeiro, 1971-77; prof. U. State Rio de Janeiro, 1980-91, chief svc. dermatology, 1980-91, vice dir., 1984-88; sr. clin. instr. U. Mich. Med. Sch., 1958. Founder Rio Dermatologico, 1987. Founder Skin Cancer Campaign, 1988. Recipient Pedro Ernesto medal 2000. Mem. Nat. Acad. Medicine (pres. 1997-99), Assn. Latin Am. Acad. Medicine. (pres. 1997-99), Physicians Sports Club (founder 1959), N.Y. Acad. Scis. Home: R Gen Artigas 54 ap 101, 22450010 Rio de Janeiro Brazil Office: Acad Nacional Medicina, Av Gen Justo 365 7th, 22021130 Rio de Janeiro Brazil

PORTSMOUTH, OWEN HENRY DONALD, physician, consultant, medical ethics educator; b. Swansea, U.K., May 24, 1929; s. Oliver Spencer and Gwendolen (Owen) P.; m. Moira Heloise Sinclair, Sept. 18, 1954 (dec. Aug. 1979); children: Charles, Richard, Andrew, Helen; m. Glennis Weddle, Jan. 3, 1981. MB, BS, U. London, 1953; MA, Keele U., U.K., 1993. Jr. hosp. appointment London, 1953-56; med. specialist Kenya, East Africa, 1956-65; cons. East Birmingham Hosp., U.K., 1966-94; hon. lectr. U. Birmingham, 1994—; vice chmn. Solihull Health Authority, 1982-90; dir. West Midland Inst. Geriatric Medicine, 1975-93; chmn. trustees Solihull Frail Ambulant Unit for Old People, 1992. Recipient Dawson lectureship Queen's U., Kingston, Ont., Can., 1984. Fellow Royal Coll. Physicians, Royal Soc. Tropical Medicine; mem. Brit. Med. Assn. (chmn. Solihull divsn. 1979-80), Brit. Geriatrics Soc. (Pres. medal 1996). Avocations: heraldry, architecture, history, foreign travel. Home: 12 Paddock Dr, Dorridge Solihull B93 8BZ West Midlands, England Office: Univ Birmingham Med Sch, Dept Biomed Ethics Edgbaston, Birmingham B15 2TT, England

PORTUESI, DONNA RAE, psychotherapist, consultant; b. Easton, Pa., Nov. 19, 1949; d. Peter and Alice Lorraine (Hull) Stagnito; m. Sebastian Portuesi, Jr., Nov. 22, 1972 (div. Sept. 1986); 1 child, Christi Noel Buck. AA, No. Seattle C.C., 1987; BA magna cum laude, Western Wash. U., 1989; MSW cum laude, U. Wash., 1992. Registered counselor, Wash. Sec. for Sen. Harry Byrd, Jr. U.S. Senate, Washington, 1970-72; founder Denver chpt. Nat. Found. for Crohn's and Colitis, 1975-79; counselor Mental Health Svcs., Everett, Wash., 1982-84; co-founder Adoption Search and Counseling Cons., Seattle, 1990-96; psychotherapist, cons. ASCC Svcs., Seattle, 1992—; press and speech asst. U.S. Senate, Washington, 1970-72; post adoption cons., Seattle, 1992-96; workshop developer, leader Adoption Search and Counseling, Seattle, 1992-96, exec. dir., 1990-96; ind. search cons. Reunite Adoptees and Birth Parents, 1991—. Contbr. articles to profl. jours. Mem. NASW, Am. Counseling Assn., Am. Adoption Congress. Democrat. Avocations: piano, travel, pets, reading, arts and crafts. Home and Office: 12718 12th Ave NW Seattle WA 98177-4322

PORTWICH, PHILIPP OTTO, physician; b. Kiel, Germany, June 12, 1963; s. Friedrich and Euphemie (Eulenburg) P. Abitur, Gymnasium, Kiel-Altenholz, 1982; MD, Kiel U., 1994. Registrar Dept. Medicine, Neumunster, Germany, 1991-94; rschr. Inst. History Medicine, Kiel, 1994-96, Dept. Psychiatry, Erlangen, Germany, 1997—. Author: Der Arzt Philipp Gabriel Hensler, 1995; asst. editor Fundamenta Psychiatrica, 1997—. Mem. German Assn. Geschichte Medizin. Avocations: tennis, skiing. Home: Burgbergstr 53, D-91054 Erlangen Bayern, Germany Office: Dept Psychiatry, Schwabachanlage 6, D-91054 Erlangen Bayern, Germany Address: U Erlangen Nurnberg, Psychiat Klin & Poliklin, D-91054 Erlangen Germany

PORVAZNIK, PAMELA ANN, public relations specialist; b. St. Louis, Nov. 12, 1942; d. Harry Jack and Rita Gail (Alger) Kreuger; m. Paul R. Porvaznik, Dec. 29, 1967; 1 child, Paul. B in Journalism, U. Mo., 1965. Feature writer, asst. editor The Detroit News Sunday Mag., 1965-70; editor-in-chief The Wichitan Mag., Wichita, Kans., 1976-83; pres., creative ptnr. Think Tank, Inc., Wichita, 1983-88; supr. yearbook & lit. mag. Wichita Collegiate Sch., 1988-90; mktg. dir. in-home respite care Wichita United Meth. Ch., 1988-90; contract writer Steve Reinemond, pres. & CEO Pizza Hut, Inc., Wichita, 1991-94; coord. pub. rels. Pizza Hut, Inc., Wichita, 1994-95; dist. dir. U.S. Congressman Todd Tiahrt, Wichita, 1995—. Exec. com. Friends of Wichita Art Mus., 1998—; bd. dirs. Wichita Ctr. Arts, 1998—, Wichita/Sedgwick County Hist. Mus., 1996-98, Medjugorje Mir Ctr., Wichita, 1999—. Republican. Roman Catholic. Avocations: writing, aerobic exercise, reading, traveling. e-mail: pam.porvaznik@mail.house.gov. Office: US Rep Todd Tiahrt 155 N Market St Ste 400 Wichita KS 67202-1818

PORZENHEIM, CLIFFORD J., business executive; b. N.Y.C., June 6, 1963; s. Christian James and Marian Valerie Porzenheim; m. Michal J. Clements, Mar. 30, 1985; children: Christopher Julian, Mary Jane. BS in Econs., U. Pa., 1985; MMgmt, Northwestern U., 1990. Analyst Securities Data, N.Y.C., 1985-86; assoc. Bank of Am., N.Y.C., 1986-89; strategy cons. A.T. Kearney, Chgo., 1990-93, The Boston COns. Group, 1993-96; dir. corp. devel. GATX, Chgo., 1996-99, v.p. corp. strategy, 1999—. Avocation: bicycling. E-mail: cporzen@gatx.com. Office: GATX Corp 500 W Monroe St Fl 38 Chicago IL 60661-3676

POSADA, JUAN EMILIO, executive; b. Medellin, Colombia, Jan. 27, 1959; s. Guillermo Idem and Helena Idem (Echeverri) P.; m. Denise Webb, Jan. 14, 1984; twins: Maria Antonia and Emilia. BBA, EAFIT, 1981; MBA, Pace U., 1983; postgrad., London Sch. Econs., 1986. Comml. asst. Colcafe, Medellin, Colombia, 1980-81; acting mgr. Bancafe Internat., N.Y.C., 1983-85; credit and fin. mgr. Bancafe Internat., Miami, Fla., 1986-89; internat. v.p. Bancafe, Bogota, Colombia, 1989-91; mgr. precious metals billiton mktg. Dutch Shell, The Hague, The Netherlands, 1992-93; pres. ACES, Medellin, Colombia, 1993—. Roman Catholic. Avocation: horseback riding. Home: Transv 1 84A-29 Apt 701, Bogota Colombia Office: ACES Airlines, Calle 10 Sur 50C-75, Medellin Colombia

POSCH, ROBERT JOHN, JR., lawyer; b. Levittown, N.Y., Feb. 24, 1950; s. Robert John and Maryrose (Finnegan) P.; m. Mary Lou Collins, July 28, 1974; children: Judith Ann, Robert III, Eric. BA, Manhattan Coll., 1972; JD, Hofstra U., 1975, MBA, 1981. Bar: N.Y. 1977, U.S. Ct. Appeals (2d cir.) 1977. Legal asst. Doubleday & Co., Inc., Garden City, N.Y., 1975-77; staff counsel Doubleday & Co., Inc., Garden City, 1977-82, assoc. counsel, 1982-87; sec., counsel Doubleday Book & Music Clubs, Inc., Garden City, 1987-2000; v.p. legal postal and govt. affairs Doubleday Direct, Inc., Garden City, 2000—; sr. v.p. legal postal and govt. affairs BOOKSPAN, Garden City, 2000—; chief compliance officer, sec. BOOKSPAN; instr. Nassau C.C., Hempstead, N.Y., 1984—; mem. adv. bd. real estate symposium Hofstra U.; bd. dirs. Crossings, Inc.; v.p. Literary Express sect. Profl. Book Clubs Inc.; spkr. in field. Author: Direct Marketer's Legal Adviser, 1983, What Every Manager Needs to Know About Marketing and the Law, 1984, Marketing and the Law, 1988, Cumulative Supplement, 1989, 90; (with others) The Direct Marketing Handbook, 1984, 91; columnist: Direct Marketing, 1981—; contbr. articles to profl. jours. Mem. ABA, Am. Corp. Counsel Assn. (newsletter editor 1988-92, bd. dirs. Greater N.Y. chpt.), Postcom (bd. dirs., exec. com.), Direct Mktg. Assn. (privacy, use tax and legal lobbying groups, various coms. 1986—), Continuity Mailers Assn., Christian Legal Soc., Nassau Bar Assn. (com. mem. 1977—, AAP Postal Affairs), L.I. Assn., N.Y. State Bus. Coun., Alpha Mu Alpha, Beta Gamma Sigma. Republican. Home: 3151 Grand Blvd Baldwin NY 11510-4826 Office: BOOKSPAN 401 Franklin Ave Ste 100 Garden City NY 11530-5945

POSCHWITZ, HARTMUT, biologist; b. Leipzig, Sachsen, Germany, Oct. 14, 1950; s. Bruno and Ingeborg (Borchers) P.; m. Silvia Schneider, Sept. 26, 1997. Degree in biology, U. Frankfurt, Germany, 1979; D Geography, U. Mainz, Germany, 1994. Biologist Staatliches Umweltamt, Frankfurt am Main, Germany, 1981—. Author: The Wickerbach, A Small Brook in the Rhine-Main Area Is Used To Show How a Heavily Polluted Stream May Be Reclaimed, 1994. Home: Mariahallstr 15, 63303 Dreieich Germany Office: Staatliches Umweltamt, Frankfurt am Main Germany

POSE, RUDOLF ARTHUR, physicist, researcher; b. Halle, Germany, Aug. 25, 1934; s. Heinz and Luise (Scheunert) P.; m. Antje Roosenstein, May 29, 1963 (dec. Aug. 1998); children: Jascha, Michael. Dr.rer.nat., Humboldt U., Berlin, 1967, Dr.sc.nat., 1970. Engr. Joint Inst. Nuc. Rsch., Dubna, Russia, 1958-61; lab. dir. LCTA Joint Inst. Nuc. Rsch., Dubna, 1990-2000; sci. asst. IfH der AdW, Zeuthen, Germany, 1961-67; divsn. leader IfH der AdW, Zeuthen, 1967-84; dep. sec. dept. math. and info. AdW der DDR, Berlin, 1984-90; adv. dir. Joint Inst. Nuclear Inst., Dubna, 2000—. Author: Rechnergestützte Bildverarbeitung, 1987; editor, author: Einführungyin die Experimentautomatisierung, 1988. Mem. ANS (fgn.), N.Y. Acad. Sci. Home: Friedlander St 60, 12489 Berlin Germany Office: Joint Inst for Nuc Rsch, ul Joliut Curie 6, 141980 Dubna Moscow, Russia

POSEN, ADAM SIMON, economist. AB in Govt. magna cum laude, Harvard Coll.; PhD in Polit. Economy and Govt., Harvard U. Economist Internat. Rsch. Function Fed. Res. Bank N.Y., 1994-97; sr. fellow Inst. Internat. Econs., 1997—. Author: Disciplined Discretion: The German and Swiss Monetary Frameworks in Operation, 1997, Inflation Targeting: Lessons from the International Experience, 1999, Restoring Japan's Economic Growth, 1998. NSF Grad. fellow, 1989-92, Bosch Found. fellow, 1992-93, Okun Meml. fellow Brookings Inst, 1993-94, Short-term Policy fellow Am. Acad. in Berlin, 2000. Mem. Am. Coun. on Germany, Am. Econ. Assn., Brit.-Am. Project, Coun. on Fgn. Rels. (Internat. Affairs fellow 2000-2001), Phi Beta Kappa. Office: Inst Internat Econs 11 Dupont Cir NW Washington DC 20036-1207

POSEY, ELDON EUGENE, mathematician, educator; b. Oneida, Tenn., Jan. 25, 1921; s. Daniel M. and Eva (Owens) P.; m. Christine K. Johnson, Dec. 25, 1943; children—Margaret Posey McQuain, Daniel Marion. B.S., East Tenn. State U., 1947; M.A., U. Tenn., 1949, Ph.D., 1954. Instr. W.Va. U., 1954-55, asst. prof., 1955-59; asso. prof. Va. Poly. Inst., 1959-61, prof., 1961-64; prof. math. U. N.C., Greensboro, 1964-88, prof. emeritus, 1988—; head dept. math. U. N.C., 1964-80. Served to capt. USAAF, 1941-46. Decorated Air medal with 18 oak leaf clusters, D.F.C., Silver Star, Purple Heart. Mem. Am. Math. Soc., Math. Assn. Am., Sigma Xi, Pi Mu Epsilon. Home: 4311 Dogwood Dr Greensboro NC 27410-5611

POSEY, LORAN MICHAEL, pharmacist, editor; b. Albany, Ga., Aug. 22, 1955; s. Loran Willis and Rubye Jane (Lumpkin) P.; m. Teresa Maria McCoy, June 27, 1975 (div. Mar. 1983); m. Cheryl Ann Emerling, Jan. 31, 1989 (div. Mar. 1997); children: Evan Michael, Alan Michael, Loran Michael. BS in Pharmacy, BS in Microbiology, U. Ga., 1979, postgrad., 1992-96. Registered pharmacist, Ga. Sr. editor Am. Soc. Hosp. Pharmacists, Bethesda, Md., 1980-85; pres. PAS Pharmacy/Assn. Svcs., Athens, Ga., 1985-96, PNN Pharmacotherapy News Network, Athens, 1994-97, Pharmacy Editl. and News Svcs., Inc., Athens, 1996—; dir. adminstrv. svcs. Ill. Soc. Hosp. Pharmacists, 1986-92, Va. Soc. Hosp. Pharmacists, 1990-98; exec. dir. Phi Delta Chi Pharmacy Frat., 1983-96, Ga. Soc. Hosp. Pharmacists, 1993-95. Author: Pharmacy Cadence, 1992; editor: Pharmacotherapy: A Pathophysiologic Approach, 1989, 4th edit., 1999; editor The Cons. Pharmacist, 1986-97, Jour. Managed Care Pharmacy, 1995-96, Jour. of Am. Pharm. Assn., 1997—, Pharmacy Today, 1998—, APhA DrugInfoLine, 2000—. Mem. Am. Med. Writers Assn. (chpt. pres. 1988-89, Pres.'s award 1988), Profl. Frat. Assn. (com. chair 1986-90), Am. Soc. Assn. Execs., Ill. Coun. Hosp. Pharmacists (hon.), Phi Delta Chi. Avocations: photography, swimming, reading. Office: PENS Pharmacy Editl and News Svcs Inc PO Box 6565 Athens GA 30604-6565

POSEY, ROBERT B., marketing and human resources executive; b. Lititz, Pa., Apr. 27, 1943; arrived in Switzerland, 1969; s. Robert S. and Beatrice Bomberger P.; 1 child, Mark Robert. BA, Rutgers U., 1965; M in Internat. Law, Cambridge U., Eng., 1967; JD, Duke U., 1969. Ofcl. Internat. Labor Office, Geneva, 1969-77; pub. affairs mgr. Hewlett-Packard Europe, Geneva, 1977-80; pub. rels. mgr. Dow Chem. Europe, Zürich, 1981-85; internat. bus. devel. and mktg. cons., 1985-90; v.p. Exec. Telecard, Nyon, Switzerland, 1990-91, DBM, Geneva, 1991-96; human resources advisor BP Chems., Geneva, 1996-97; founder, pres. Performance Devel. Ptnrs., Geneva, Switzerland. Bd. govs. Aiglon Coll., Villars, Switzerland, 1993-97; chmn. Republicans Abroad, Switzerland, 1996-98, mem. adv. com.; adv. com., Aiglon Coll. Assn. Mem. Swiss Am. C. of C., Execs. Internat. Lausanne, Am. Internat. Club Geneva. Avocations: travel, media, swimming. Home: Residence Bruyere, 40A 1197 Prangins Switzerland Office: ICC Bldg, Box 1887, Geneva Airport Switzerland

POSIN, DANIEL Q., retired physics educator, television lecturer; b. Turkestan, Aug. 13, 1909; came to U.S., 1918, naturalized, 1927; s. Abram and Anna (Izritz) P.; m. Frances Schweitzer, 1934; children: Dan, Kathryn. A.B., U. Cal., 1932, A.M., 1934, Ph.D., 1935. Instr. U. Cal., 1932-37; prof. U. Panama, 1937-41; dean natural scis. U. Mont., prof., 1941-44, chmn. dept. physics and math., 1942-44; staff Mass. Inst. Tech., 1944-46; prof. physics, chmn. dept. N.D. State Coll., Fargo, 1946-55; prof. dept. physics DePaul U., 1956-67; prof. phys. sci. dept. Calif. State U., San Francisco, 1967—; chmn. dept. interdisciplinary scis. Calif. State U., 1969-93; dir. Schwab Sci. Lecture Series, Atoms for Peace exhibit Mus. Sci. and Industry, Chgo.; Chief cons. Borg Warner Sci. Hall and Allied Chem. Sci. Hall, Times Square; scientific cons. CBS-TV. (Recipient 6 Emmy awards for best educator on TV in Chgo., and best ednl. TV programs). Author: Trigonometria, 1937-41, Fisica Experimental, Fisica, 1937-41, Mendeleyev—The Story of a Great Scientist, 1948, I Have Been to the Village, with Introduction by Einstein, 1948, rev. edit., 1974, Out of This World, 1959, What is a Star, 1961, What is Chemistry, 1961, What is a Dinosaur, 1961, The Marvels of Physics, 1961, Find Out, 1961, Chemistry for the Space Age, 1961, Experiments and Exercises in Chemistry, 1961, What is Matter, 1962, What is Electronic Communication, 1962, What is Energy, Dr. Posin's Giants, 1962, Life Beyond our Planet, 1962, Man and the Sea, 1962, Man and the Earth, 1962, Man and the Jungle, 1962, Man and the Desert, 1962, Science in the Age of Space, 1965, Rockets and Satellites, Our Solar System, The Next Billion Years, 1973; contbr. to: Today's Health; sci. cons. Compton's Yearbook; contbr. to: feature articles Chgo. Tribune, (book) After Einstein-Remembering Einstein, 1981; co-contbr. to book The Courage to Grow Old, 1989; appearances, CBS Radio-TV, WTTW-WGN-TV, 1956-67, NET; ABC TV series Dr. Posin's Universe. Chmn. edn. com. Chgo. Heart Assn., 1963-67; Trustee Leukemia Soc. James T. Grady award Am. Chem. Soc., 1972. Fellow Am. Phys. Soc.; mem. A.A.A.S., Phi Beta Kappa, Sigma Xi.

POSKONIN, VLADIMIR VLADIMIROVITCH, chemist, researcher; b. Krasnodar, Russia, Oct. 30, 1955; s. Vladimir Ilyitch Poskonin and Ludmila Grigor'evna Berestovaya; m. Marina Leonidovna Subbotina, June 6, 1981; children: Igor Vladimirovitch, Denis Vladimirovitch. Diploma in higher edn., Krasnodar Poly. Inst., 1977, PhD in Chemistry, 1990; postgrad., Kuban State Tech. U., Krasnodar, 1986-89. Engr. Krasnodar Poly Inst., 1977-81, jr. rsch. worker, 1981-84, rsch. worker, 1984-91; sr. rsch. worker Kuban State Tech. U. (formerly Krasnodar Poly. Inst.), 1991—; asst. dir. for rsch. PSB Ltd., Krasnodar, 1992-95, Rosvuznauka ASB, Krasnodar, 1995—; bd. dirs. Krasnodar Out-of-Budget Rsch. Fund, 1996—. Contbr. articles to profl. jours.; patentee in field. Recipient prize Bashkiria Br. All-Union Mendeleev Soc. for Best Chem. Tech., 1989; rsch. grantee Russian Fund for Fundamental Rsch., St. Petersburg, 1991-92, Krasnodar Territorial Govt., 1997. Mem. Rsch., Introductory and Prodn. Assn. (asst. dir. 1998—). Greek Orthodox. Avocations: spiritual and physical self-improvement, gardening, collecting books, creating literature and music. Home: Apt 99, 70 Let Oktyabrya St 24, 350089 Krasnodar Russia Office: Kuban State Tech U, Moskovskaya St 2 Apt 206, 350072 Krasnodar Russia

POSKROBKO, JAN, chemical engineer, researcher; b. Białystok, Poland, Nov. 12, 1945; s. Piotr and Natalia (Rybak) P.; m. Halina Barbara Postol, Aug. 14, 1971; children: Jolanta, Jakub. MSc, Tech. U., Gliwice, Poland, 1970; PhD, Tech. U., Szczecin, Poland, 1994. Head rsch. devel. lab. Chem. Factory Blachownia, Kedzierzyn, Poland, 1971-75; dept. mgr. Coking Plant, Zdzieszowice, Poland, 1975-76; head quality control, spl. mfg. Welding Inst., Gliwice, 1976-83; specialist Mounting Co. Montochem, Gliwice, 1983-90; head rsch. devel. lab. Inst. Heavy Organic Synthesis, Kedzierzyn, 1990—. Contbr. articles to profl. jours. Avocations: skiing, windsurfing. Home: Partyzantow 14 A/3, 47220 Kedzierzyn Kozle Poland Office: Energetykow 9, 47225 Kedzierzyn Kozle Poland

POŠKUS, DIONIZAS, chemistry researcher; b. Mažeikiai, Lithuania, Dec. 20, 1930; s. Pranas and Rozalija (Rušinaite) P.; m. Regina Tamulyte, Apr. 16, 1955; 1 child, Paulius. PhD, Inst. Phys. Chemistry, Moscow, 1959; DSc, U. Moscow, 1972. Rsch. scientist Inst. Chemistry, Vilnius, Lithuania, 1958-65, head lab., 1965-92, rsch. prof., 1992—; vis. rschr. U. Bristol, U.K., 1970; asst. dir. Inst. Chemistry, 1974-92. Co-author: Adsorption of Gases and Vapours on Homogeneous Surfaces, 1975, Molecular Fundamentals of Adsorption Chromatography, 1986; contbr. over 80 articles to profl. jours. Recipient grant Sci. Rsch. Coun. U.K., 1969, Nat. Prize in Sci., Govt. Lithuania, 1977. Avocations: tourism, fishing. Home: Žirgo 5-20, Vilnius 2040, Lithuania Office: Inst Chemistry, A Goštauto 9, Vilnius 2600, Lithuania

POSNER, REBECCA REYNOLDS, Romance language educator; b. Horden, Durham, Eng., Aug. 17, 1929; d. William and Rebecca (Stevenson) Reynolds; m. Michael Vivian Posner, Aug. 7, 1953; children: Christopher, Barbara. BA with first class hons., Oxford U., 1952, Diploma Comp. Philology with distinction, 1954, DPhil, 1958. Lectr. French Wesleyan U., Conn., 1957-58; fellow Girton Coll., Cambridge, U.K., 1960-63; prof. French studies U. Ghana, 1963-65; prof. Romance philology Columbia U., N.Y.C., 1971-72; reader linguistics U. York, U.K., 1965-78; prof. Romance langs. Oxford U., 1978-96; prof., fellow St. Hugh's Coll., Oxford, 1978-96, hon. fellow, 1996—, prof. emeritus, 1996—; rsch. assoc. Ctr. Linguistics and Philology Oxford U., 1996—; postdoctoral fellow in linguistics Yale U., New Haven, 1957-58; CNRS fellow Sorbonne, Paris, 1956; sr. fellow Princeton (N.J.) U., 1988. Author: Consonantal Dissimilation in the Romance Languages, 1960, The Romance Languages, 1966, The Romance Languages, 1996, Linguistic Change in French, 1997, Las Lenguas Romances, 1997; co-author: Romance Linguistics, 1970; editor/author: Trends in Romance Linguistics, 5 vols., 1980-93. Fellow Oxford Humanities Rsch. Ctr., 1990, fellow London U. Inst. for Romance Studies, 1988—; Leverhulme emeritus fellow, 1997. Mem. Philological Soc. (pres. 1996-2000, v.p. 2000—), Linguistic Soc. Great Britain, Linguistic Soc. Am., Soc. de la Linguistique Romane. Avocations: drama, opera, music, walking, history. Office: Ctr Linguistics Philology, St Hughs Coll, Oxford OX2 6LE, England

POSPISIL, GEORGE CURTIS, biomedical research administrator; b. Thomas, Okla., Aug. 8, 1945; s. George Frank and Zelpha Earline (Hensley) P.; children: Heather Elizabeth, Derek Curtis. Student, Wheaton Coll., 1963-64; BA, U. Okla., 1968; MA, 1971. Tchr. Peace Corps, Maseru, Lesotho, 1973-74; dir. health svcs. fin. project State of Wis., Madison, 1975-76; pub. health advisor USPHS, Rockville, Md., 1972-73, program/policy analyst, 1977-81, 84-86, clin. trials policy adv., 1989-99, contract mgr., 1982-84; dir. Svcs. Crime Victims/Witnesses Project, Tioga County, N.Y., 1986—; guest lectr. U. Wis., Summer Inst., Carthage Coll.; analyst biomed. rsch. program NIH, 1989—; sci. editor The Johns Hopkins U. Krieger Mind/Brain Inst., 1993-95; exec. coun. NIH Recreation and Welfare Assn. Editor: Decde of the Brain, 1990, Maximizing Human Potential: Decade of the Brain, 1991. Mem. Rockville Humanities Commn., 1981-83; spokesperson Neighborhood Planning Com., 1980-82; coordinator mental health svcs. Cuban Refugee Project, Ft. McCoy, Wis., 1980; sec. cmty. adv. com. mental health program Montgomery House, 1982-86; rsch. and tng. adminstr. Cornell U., Itahca, N.Y., 1986-89; bd. dirs. Family Svc. Mongomery County, 1984-86; legis fellow U.S. Senate Labor and Human Resources Com./Health Office, 1991; mem. county Spl. Olympics Com., 1982-86; mem. Citizens' Planning Subcom.; insp. gen. Civil Air Patrol; mem. adv. com. troop 321 Boy Scouts Am.; bd. dirs. Shepherd's Staff Cmty. Svc. program. Office: Nat Inst Neurol Disorders NIH 6001 Executive Blvd Rockville MD 20852-3802

POSPÍŠIL, JAROSLAV, physicist, educator; b. Charvaty, Czech Republic, Feb. 19, 1935. MSc, Palacky U., Olomouc, Czech Republic, 1957, D of Natural Scis., 1968, PhD, 1968, DSc, 1992; MEng, Tech. U., Brno, Czech Republic, 1964. Asst. Palacky U., 1960-85, assoc. prof., 1985-90, prof. exptl. physics, optics and electronics, 1990—; head dept. exptl. physics Palacky U., 1990-93, head dept. applied physics, 1993—; v.p. Czech com. for optics Internat. Com. Optics, 1994-. Contbr. over 210 articles to profl. jours. Fellow Union Czech Mathematicians and Physicists; mem. Internat. Soc. Optical Engring. Avocations: optics, electronics, photonics, tennis, skiing, skating. Office: Faculty Natural Scis, Palacky U Svobody 26, CZ-77146 Olomouc Czech Republic

POSPISIL, LEOPOLD, microbiologist; b. Brno, Moravia, Czech Republic, Mar. 10, 1925; s. Leopold and Hedvika (Muller) P.; m. Dagmar Bernardova, May 15, 1959 (div. 1976); 1 child, Thomas; m. Alena Haklova, Apr. 25, 1986. MD, Masaryk U., Brno, 1949; PhD, Charles U., 1959; Asst. Prof., J.E. Purkynje U., Brno, 1963; DS, Comenius U., Bratislava, 1975; Prof. Microbiol., J.E. Purkynje/U. Brno, 1983; D Vet. Med., Vet. and Pharm. U., Brno, 1995. Cert. med. profession in microbiology and immunology, Czech Med. Chambre. Asst. doctor Regional Hosp., Prerov, Czech Republic, 1949-50, Snct. Anna Hosp., Brno, 1952-56; rsch. scientist Med. Faculty U., Brno, 1956-89; head Inst. Microbiology/U. Brno, 1989-93; rsch. scientist Inst. for Vet. Medicine, Brno, 1993—; pres. Com. for Rsch. of STD, Ministry of Health, Prague, 1983-89. Author: (books) Spezifische Serologie der Lueserkrankung, 1967, Gonorrhoea, 1969, The Lysozyme, 1971. Fellow DAAD, Bonn-Bad Godesberg, 1967. Mem. Czechoslovak Microbiol. Soc. (hon.). Roman Catholic. Avocations: fine arts, tennis. Office: Vet Rsch Inst, Hudcova 70, 62132 Brno Czech Republic

POSPÍŠIL, MILAN, physician, pathophysiology educator, researcher; b. Brno, Czechoslovakia, Mar. 20, 1929; s. Ferdinand and Terezie (Fibichová) P.; m. Jiřina Haladová, Dec. 22, 1956; 1 child, Martin. MD, U. Brno, 1953, PhD, 1956, DSc, 1977; Doctorate (hon.), Šafarih U., Slovak Republic, 2000. Postdoctoral fellow U. Brno, 1953-56, rschr. Inst. Biophysics, 1956—, prof. pathophysiology, 1987—; head dept. radiosensitivity Inst. Biophysics, Czech Acad. Sci., Brno, 1959-90; chmn. intercosmos program Czechoslovak Group for Cosmic Biology and Medicine, 1985-91. Author: (monograph) (with Vácha) Individual Radiosensitivity, 1983; contbr. over 400 articles on pathophysiology, radiobiology and cosmic biology to sci. jours., including Radiation Rsch., Blood. Recipient gold medal for achievements in cosmic biology Czech Acad. Scis., 1987, J.G. Mendel gold medal for achievements in biol. sci., 1989, nat. award for achievements in radiobiology Czech Nat. Coun., 1990. Mem. European Soc. for Radiation Biology, Internat. Acad. Astronautics,, Czech Med. Soc. J.E. Purkyně (hon.). Office: Czech Acad Scis Inst Biophy, Královopolská 135, CZ-61265 Brno Czech Republic

POSPÍŠIL, ZDENĚK, veterinary medicine educator, researcher; b. Vojnice, Olomouc, Czechoslovakia, Nov. 7, 1940; s. Jan and Vlasta (Vacová) P.; m. Jana Čechmánková, Sept. 26, 1964; children: Hana, Richard. DVM, U. Vet. Medicine, Brno, Czech Republic, 1963; PhD, U. Vet. Medicine, 1967, DSc, 1993. Postgrad. Vet. Rsch. Inst., Brno, Czechoslovakia, 1964-67; rsch. officer Vet. Rsch. Inst., 1967-84, sr. rsch. officer, 1984-90; assoc. prof. U. Vet. Sci., Brno, Czech Republic, 1991-93; prof. infectious diseases, vet. epidemiology U. Vet. Sci., Brno, 1993—, head dept. infectious diseases, 1991—; assoc. dean Faculty Vet. Medicine U. Vet. Pharm. Sci., Brno, 1997—; vice rector Univ. Vet. Phamr. Sci., Brno, 2000—. Co-author, editor: (textbook) Infectious Diseases of Dog and Cat, 1996; contbr. 109 articles to profl. jours. With mil. svc., 1963-64. Recipient Medal of the Epidemiologist Abdon Strzysak U. Warsaw, 1997. Mem. Czechoslovak Microbiol. Soc., European Soc. Vet. Virology, Inst. Soc. Vet. Epid. Roman Catholic. Avocations: classical music, gardening, travel. Home: Haškova 2, 638 00 Brno Czech Republic Office: U Vet and Pharm Scis, Palackého 1-3, 612 42 Brno Czech Republic

POSPISILOVA, JANA, physiologist; b. Prague, Czech Republic, May 16, 1940; d. Karel and Marie Sandera; m. Bohus Pospisil, Oct. 17, 1964; children: Skalova Lenka, Podlipna Radka, Pospisil Ondrej. RNDr, Charles U., Prague, 1962; PhD, Acad. Scis., Prague, 1968. Scientist Acad. Scis., Prague, 1968-80, sr. scientist, 1980—; chief bd. dirs. Grant Agy., Prague, 1996-98. Exec. editor: Biologia Plantarum, Prague, 1991—; mem. editl. bd. Photosynthetica, Prague, 1993—; editor: Water-in-Plants Bibliography, Vols. 1-17, 1976-92; contbr. more than 100 articles to profl. jours. Mem. Fedn. European Socs. Plant Physiology. Avocations: nature protection, sports, books, theatre, photography. Home: Kurandove 5, 15000 Prague 5 Czech Republic Office: Inst Exptl Botany, NA Karlovce 1, 16000 Prague 6 Czech Republic

POSSATI, STEFANO, electronic gauge company executive; b. Bologna, Italy, Dec. 23, 1950; s. Mario and Gabriella (Manfredi) P.; m. Benedetta Vittori Venenti, June 4, 1983; children: Francesco, Federico. Baccalaureate, Liceo Galvani, Bologna, 1970. Mem. indsl. rels. staff Marposs, Bentivoglio, Italy, 1974-78; info. system mgr. Marposs, Bentivoglio, 1979-83, gen. mgr., 1984-87, chief exec. officer, 1988-90, pres., 1991—; adv. coun. Bologna Ctr. of Paul H. Nitze SAIS Johns Hopkins U., 1996; bd. dirs. Banca d'Italia, Bologna. Mem. Indsl. Assn. (v.p. 1994-97), Caer (bd. dirs. 1995-97), Soc. Editrice Il Mulino (bd. dirs. 1991, exec. com. 1998). Office: Marposs SPA, Saliceto N 13, 40010 Bentivoglio Bologna Italy

POSSE, MARGARETA G., consulting psychiatrist, researcher, psychoanalyst; b. Sit OLai, Sweden, Oct. 1, 1953; arrived in Eng., 1996; d. Ingemar and Ulla (Gotefors) W.; m. Fredrik N. Posse, June 18, 1980 (div. Dec. 1994); children: Amelie, Caroline, Jacob. BM, U. Gothenburg, Sweden, 1974, Univ. Med. Degree, 1979, lic. neuropsychologist, 1993; diploma psychoanalyst, C.G. Jung Inst., Zurich, Switzerland, 1994; postgrad., Karolinska Inst., Stockholm, 1994—. Lic. psychotherapist, Sweden; cert. specialist in family medicine, Sweden, Denmark, Norway; cert. specialist in gen. adult psychiatry, Sweden, European Union. Rotational scheme for full registration, Skovde, Sweden, 1979-81, rotational scheme as specialist in family medicine, 1982-85, rotational scheme as specialist in psychiatry, 1992-95; gen. practitioner Primary Care Ctr., Tidaholm, Sweden, 1988-92; cons. in adult psychiatry Kernhospital, Skovde, 1996, West Middlesex U. Hosp., Isleworth, Eng., 1996—. Rsch. grantee Inst. Skaraborg, Sweden, 1994. Mem. Gen. Med. Coun., (U.K.), Swedish Soc. Psychiatrists, Med. Soc. Gothenburg, Internat. Assn. Analytical Psychologists, Assn. Grads. in Analytical Psychology Switzerland, Female Acad. Soc. Sweden, Swedish Soc. Cons. Avocations: tennis, equestrian activities, swimming, skiing, reading. Office: West Middlesex U Hosp, Psychiatry Dept Twickenham, Isleworth TW7 6AF, England

POSSE, STEFAN, biomedical physicist, educator; b. Bonn, Germany, July 7, 1961; s. Günther and Renate (Naaf) P.; m. Mary Anthony Jacintha, Oct. 19, 1994; 1 child, Richard Kevin. Diploma in physics, U. Cologne, Germany, 1986; D Natural Scis., U. Berne, Switzerland, 1990; Habilitation, U. Düsseldorf, Germany, 1999. Postdoctoral fellow U. Berne, 1990-91; vis. fellow NIH, Bethesda, Md., 1991-94; head magnetic resonance group Rsch. Ctr. Jülich (Germany) GmbH, 1994-99; asst. prof. dept. psychiatry and behavioral neuroscis. Wayne State U. Sch. Medicine, Detroit, 2000—; affiliate asst. prof. U. Wash., Seattle, 1995—; jour. reviewer Magnetic Resonance in Medicine, 1991—. Contbg. author: Diffusion and Perfusion: MRI, 1995; contbr. articles to Jour. Magnetic Resonance, Radiology, Magnetic Resonance in Medicine, Jour. Computer Assisted Tomography, Jour. Magnetism and Magnetic Materials. Richard Winter Found. scholar U. Fla., 1986-87, Swiss Nat. Sci. Found. scholar, 1987-92; fellow Fogarty Internat. Ctr., 1991-94. Mem. Soc. Magnetic Resonance (reviewer for meetings 1994—), Phi Beta Delta. Achievements include patents and patents pending for quantitative functional MRI, for real time functional MRI, and for PEPSI (proton echoplanar spectroscopic imaging), one of fastest spectroscopic imaging method known for whole body clinical magnetic resonance scanners; introduced functional MR spectroscopic imaging in human brain; research on real time functional magnetic resonance imaging and on advanced short echo time proton magnetic resonance spectroscopic imaging. Avocations: flying, gymnastics, tennis. Office: Wayne State U Sch Medicine Dept Psychiatry-Behav Neuro Univ Health Ctr 9B 18 Detroit MI 48201

POSSELT, MATTHIAS, physicist; b. Dresden, Germany, Mar. 4, 1955; m. Sabine Voigt, May 26, 1984; children: Claudia, Cornelia. PhD, Tech. U. Dresden, 1984. Rsch. scientist Inst. Ion Beam Physics and Materials Rsch. Ctr. Rossendorf, Dresden, 1984—; guest scientist Hahn-Meitner-Inst., Berlin, 1990, Swiss Fed. Inst. Tech., Zurich, 1994, 95, 96, Lawrence Livermore Nat. Lab., 1995. Contbr. numerous articles to sci. jours. Mem. Materials Rsch. Soc., Phys. Soc. Germany. Office: Rsch Ctr Rossendorf, PO Box 510119, 01314 Dresden Germany

POST, GERALD V., business educator; b. Chippewa Falls, Wis., Nov. 27, 1955; s. Vernon Otto and Doris Post; m. Sarah S. Post, Aug. 14, 1982. BA, U. Wis., Eau Claire, 1978; PhD, Iowa State U., 1983. Asst. prof. Oakland U., Rochester Hills, Mich., 1982-89; prof. Western Ky. U., Bowling Green, 1989-99; prof. dept. bus. U. of the Pacific, Stockton, Calif., 1999—; cons. analyst/programmer The Wala Group, Arden Hills, Minn., 1985-99. Author: Database Management Systems, 1999, Management Information Systems, 2000; contbr. articles to profl. jours. Office: Univ of the Pacific 3601 Pacific Ave Stockton CA 95211-0197

POSTACCHINI, FRANCO, orthopaedic surgeon, researcher, educator; b. Fermo, Italy, Oct. 12, 1944; s. Francesco and Giuseppina (Quinti) P.; m. Luciana Lucertini, Feb. 4, 1948; children: Marco, Roberto. Grad., U. La Sapienza, Rome, 1971; specialist in orthopaedic surgery, 1974, specialist in phys. medicine & rehab., 1975. Prof. U. Modena, Italy, 1990-96; from asst. to assoc. prof. U. Rome La Sapienza, 1974-90, prof., 1996—; dir. dept. orthops. U. Rome La Sapienza, Italy, 1998—. Author: The Tendons, 1982, (Bellando Randone prize), Lumbar Spinal Stenosis, 1989, (Bellando Randone prize), Lumbar Disc Herniation, 1998 (Bellando Randone prize); contbr. articles to profl. jours. Mem. Internat. Soc. for the Study of the Lumbar Spine (pres. 1997-98), European Spine Soc. (pres. 1995-96), Soc. Italiana Ortopedia e Traumatologie (v.p. 1998—), Italian Soc. for Shoulder and Elbow Surgery (pres. 1999—). Avocations: swimming, tennis, reading. Home: Via G Curioni 99, 00157 Rome Italy Office: Casa Cura Villa Margherita, Via di Villa Massimo 48, 00161 Rome Italy

POSTAIRE, ERIC R.R., biomedical researcher; b. Cherbourg, France, Mar. 23, 1957; s. Pierre and Janine (Grouille) P.; m. Martine Vigreux, Nov. 13, 1982; children: Benjamin, Romain. PhD, U. Paris XI, 1986. Resident in pharmacology U. Paris XI, Chatenay-Malabry, France, 1980-90, assoc. prof., 1990—. Author: Les Epidemies du XXI e Siecle, 1997; editor: Les Matieres Plastiques, 1992;. Mem. Free Radical Rsch. Soc., N.Y. Acad. Sci. Home: 4 Villa des Nouzeaux, Vanves France F92170 Office: PASTEURMED Inst. Pasteur, 28 rue du D'Roux, F-75015 Paris France

POSTEN, CLEMENS HEINRICH, electrical engineer, researcher; b. Essen, Fed. Republic Germany, Nov. 4, 1955; s. Josef and Elisabeth (Belke) P.; m. Renate E. Suda, Nov. 13, 1987. Abitur, Helmholtz-Gymn, Fed. Republic of Germany, 1974; M in Biology, Ruhr U., Fed. Republic of Germany, 1980; M in Elect Engring., Hannover, Fed. Republic of Germany, 1984; PhD in Elect. Engring., Hannover, 1987. Postdoctoral fellow Tech. U. Hamburg-Harburg, Fed. Republic of Germany, 1987-89; group leader GBF Nat. Rsch. Ctr. for Biotech., Braunschweig, Germany, 1989-95; prof. bioprocess engring. U. Karlsruhe, Germany, 1995—; sr. lectr. Tech. U. Hamburg-Harburg, 1989-95. Co-author: Biological Fundamentals, 1993, Bioprocess Computations, 1993, Bioreaction Engineering-Modelling and Control, 2000; contbr. articles to profl. jours. Active Deutsches Rotes Kreuz, Essen, 1972-85. Mem. Deutsche Gesellschaft fur Chemische Technik und Biotechnologie, Verein Deutscher Ingenieure, Internat. Fedn. of Automatic Control. Avocations: music, traveling, nature. Office: U Karlsruhe, Inst MVM, D-76128 Karlsruhe Germany

POSTGATE, JOHN RAYMOND, microbiology professor; b. London, June 24, 1922; s. Raymond William and Daisy (Lansbury) P.; m. Mary Stewart Oct. 20, 1948; children: Selina Anne, Lucy Belinda, Joanna Mary. BA in Chemistry with honors, Oxford U., Eng., 1945; MA in Chemistry with honors, Oxford U., 1948, PhD, 1960, DSc, 1965; doctorate (hon.), U. Bath, 1990, U. Dundee, 1997. Prin sci. officer Chem. Rsch. Lab., Teddington, Middlesex, Eng., 1948-59; sr. prin. sci. officer Microbiological Rsch. Establishment Ministry of Supply, Salisbury, Eng., 1959-63; asst. dir. Unit of Nitrogenfixation Agr. Rsch. Coun. Queen Mary Coll., London, 1963-65; asst dir. Unit of Nitrogenfixation Agr. Rsch. Coun. U. Sussex, Sussex, Eng., 1965-80; dir. Unit of Nitrogenfixation Agr. Rsch. Coun. U. Sussex, Sussex, 1980-87; prof. of microbiology U. Sussex, 1965-87, emeritus prof. of microbiology, 1987—; vis. prof. U. Illinois, Champaign-Urbana, 1962-63, Oregon State U., Corvallis, 1977-8. Author: A Plain Man's Guide to Jazz, 1973, Microbes and Man, 1969, rev., 2000, Biological Nitrogen Fixation, 1972, Nitrogen Fixation, 1978, rev., 1998, The Sulphate-Reducing Bacteria, 1979, rev., 1984, The Fundamentals of Nitrogen Fixation, 1982, (with Mary Postgate) A Stomach for Dissent, 1994; editor: The Chemistry and Biochemistry of Nitrogen Fixation, 1971; editor 4 symposia, 2 jours. Fellow Inst. of Biology (pres. 1982-84), Royal Soc.; mem. (hon.) Soc. for Gen. Microbiology (pres. 1984-87), Soc. for Applied Bacteriology. Avocations: jazz musician, reviewer, writer. Office: U Sussex, Falmer, Brighton, East Sussex BN1 9NQ, England

POSTLETHWAITE, ROY, retired microbiologist; b. Todmorden, Lancashire, Eng., Apr. 26, 1925; s. Frank and Gladys (Newell) P.; m. Joyce Walker, Mar. 27, 1957; children: Howard, Kevin, Gillian. BSc in Physiology, U. Manchester, 1951, MBChB, 1954, MD, 1959. Resident house officer, clin. pathologist Royal Infirmary, Manchester, Eng., 1954-56; lectr. bacteriology U. Manchester, 1956-61; sr. lectr. bacteriology U. Aberdeen, Scotland, 1961-80; prof. virology U. Aberdeen, 1980-88; ret., 1988; Nuffield fellow U. Mich., Ann Arbor, 1959-60; vis. virologist Nat. Inst. Med. Rsch., London, 1971-72; cons. bacteriology Grampian Health Bd., Aberdeen, 1961-88. Contbr. articles to profl. jours. Lt. U.K. Royal Artillery, 1943-47. Trustee Spongiform Encephalopathy Rsch. Campaign, 1995—. Fellow Royal Coll. Pathologists (examiner virology 1977-88); mem. Soc. Gen. Microbiology, Pathology Soc. Gt. Britain and Ireland, Brit. Soc. Immunology, Brit. Infection Soc. Avocations: travel, walking, swimming, reading, public understanding of science.. Home: 6 Rendcomb Dr, Cirencester GL7 1YN, England

POSTMA, IDS, speed skater; b. Dearsum, The Netherlands, Dec. 28, 1973. Speed skater, 1988—. Recipient Gold medal men's speed skating 1000 meters, 1998, Silver medal men's speed skating 1500 meters, 1998. Office: Dutch Olympic Com, PO Box 302, 6800 AH Arnhem The Netherlands*

POSTMES, TOM THEODOOR, psychology educator; b. Venlo, Limburg, The Netherlands, Jan. 1, 1969; s. Antonius J.M.F. Postmes and Leonie M. van Steenis; m. Rose G.M. Weersink, June 20, 1998. Testamur in psychology with distinction, U. Exeter, Eng., 1992; MSc with distinction, U. Amsterdam, 1992, PhD, 1997. Rsch. trainee dept. social psychology U. Amsterdam, 1992-96, lectr. dept. comm., 1996-97, sr. lectr. dept. comm., 2000—; vis. prof. dept. comm., info., and libr. studies Rutgers U., N.J., 1998; fellow Royal Acad. Arts and Scis., 1998—. Contbr. articles to profl. jours. including Psychol. Bull., Comm. Rsch. Grantee Engring. and Phys. Sci. Rsch. Coun., 1998. Avocations: speed skating, singing. E-mail: postmes@pscw.uva.nl. Office: U Amsterdam Dept Comm, Oude Hoogstr 24, NL1012CE Amsterdam The Netherlands

POSTNOV, KONSTANTIN ALEKSANDROVICH, astrophysicist; b. Moscow, Aug. 19, 1959. Degree in astronomy, Lomonossov Moscow State U., 1983, PhD, 1987; D in Math. Sci., Sternberg Astronomical Inst., Moscow, 1998. From asst. prof to prof. physics Moscow State U., 1987—. Mem. Internat. Astronomical Union. Avocation: skiing, architecture renovation. Office: Sternberg Astronomical Inst, 13 University prospect, 119899 Moscow Russia

POSTOLICĂ, VASILE, mathematics educator, researcher, professor; b. Pastraveni, Neamt, Romania, Feb. 15, 1955; s. Vasile and Ecaterina (Harja) P.; m. Florentina Cucu, July 20, 1981 (div. May 27, 1992); 1 child, Dragos-Florin; m. Steluta Selaru, Nov. 17, 1995. B in Math., Iasi U., Romania, 1979, M in Math., 1980, PhD in Math., 1987. Prof. Gh.Asachi Coll. Piatra Neamt, Romania, 1980-91; prof., cons. expert Didactic House, Piatra Neamt, 1991—; assoc. prof. Petre Andrei Academical Found., Piatra Neamt, 1991—; rsch. prof. PhD Bacău (Romania) State U., 1994—; chief of dept. for improvement of profs. Piatra Neamt, 1991—. Reviewer Zentralblatt für Mathematik, Math. Revs., Optimization and Jota; contbr. numerous articles to profl. jours. Lt. Romanian Mil., 1974-75. Mem. Romanian Acad. Scientists, Romanian Soc. Mathematicians (Jubilee medal 1995), Am. Math. Soc., Internat. Soc. Optical Engring., Internat. Soc. Multi-Criteria Decision Making, The Planetary Soc. Avocations: tennis, cycling, football, basketball, mechanics. E-mail: vpostolica@ub.ro. Home: B-dul Traian Nr 11, bl.A1 sc.A et.4 ap.13, 5600 Piatra Neamt Romania Office: Bacau State Univ, Calea Marasesti Nr 157, 5500 Bacau Romania

POSTON, BEVERLY PASCHAL, lawyer; b. Birmingham, Ala., Aug. 21, 1955; d. Arthur Buel and Nellie Jo (Weaver) P.; m. Richard F. Poston, Aug., 1992. BA with honor, U. North Ala., 1976; JD, Birmingham Sch. Law, 1982. Bar: Ala. 1982, U.S. Dist. Ct. (no. dist.) Ala. 1982, U.S. Ct. Appeals (11th cir.) 1983. Assoc. St. John & St. John, Cullman, Ala., 1982-84; pvt. practice Cullman, 1984-85, 92-96; ptnr. Paschal & Collins, Cullman, 1986-92. Pres. Cullman County Hist. Soc., 1986-87, bd. dirs., 1996—. Named one of Outstanding Young Women Am., 1984; recipient Citiation of Honor, Young Career Women Program, 1989. Mem. ABA, ATLA, Ala. Trial Lawyers Assn., Cullman County Bar Assn. (sec. tres. 1997-98, v.p. 1998-99, pres. 1999-2000), Pilot Club Internat. (Sweetheart award Cullman 1985), Cullman Bus. and Profl. Women's Assn. (young careerist award), Cullman Home Builder Assn. Avocations: horseback riding, rodeos, farming, writing. Home: 1797 County Road 972 Cullman AL 35057-5861 Office: 200 1st Ave SE Cullman AL 35055-3402

POSTREKHIN, YEVGENIY VLADIMIROVICH, physicist, researcher; b. Sverdlovsk, Russia, May 2, 1958; came to the U.S., 1997; s. Vladimir Yevgenievich Postrekhin and Margarita Alexandrovna Cherbakova; m. Diana Arkadievna, Sept. 22, 1983; children: Igor, Regina. PhD, Ural Poly. Inst., Ekaterinburg, Russia, 1992. From sci. rschr. to sr. sci. rschr. Thermophysics Inst., Russian Acad. Scis., Ekaterinburg, 1981-93; fellow T.D. Lee Lab. Fudan U., Shanghai, 1994-97; postdoctoral position U. Cen. Fla., Orlando, 1997-98; rsch. assoc. U. Houston, 1998—. Contbr. articles to sci. publs. Mem. IEEE. Avocation: chess. E-mail: ypostrek@bayou.uh.edu. Home: # 130 5515 Clarewood Dr Apt 130 Houston TX 77081-5342 Office: U Houston Tex Ctr for Supercond Houston Science Ctr Houston TX 77204-0001

POSVAR, JIRI, civil engineer; b. Olomouc, Czech Republic, Sept. 30, 1923; s. Jindrich and Anna (Zapletalova) P.; m. Dagmar Kozlova, July 29, 1934; children: Dagmar, Jiri. Grad., Tech. U., Brno, Czechoslovakia, 1949, DSc, 1963. Asst. Tech. U., Brno, 1949-51; from rsch. worker to leading scientific worker Inst. Traffic, Prague, Czechoslovakia, 1951-80; prof. civil engring. Tech. U., Brno, 1980-91. Co-author: Designing of Carriageways, 1987, Road Laboratory, 1986, National University Textbook, 1989; contbr. articles to profl. jours. Mem. Road Soc. Prague, Tech. Soc. Prague, World Road Assn. (tech. com. 1972-91, corr. mem. tech. com. "Environment" 1992-99, chmn. Czechoslovak nat. com. 1981-2000). Avocations basketball refereeing. Home: Jana Necase 17, 616 00 Brno 16 Czech Republic Office: Tech U Brno, Veveří 95, 662 37 Brno Czech Republic

POSWICK, REGINALD-FERDINAND, Bible and computer scholar; b. Brussels, Jan. 4, 1937; s. Prosper and Geneviève (de Dieudonne) P. B. in Philosophy, St. Louis, Brussels, 1956; B. in Theology, Le Saulchoir, Paris, 1963; lic. in theology, St. Anselmo, Rome, 1964. Benedictine monk Promotion Biblique et Informatique, Maredsous, Belgium, 1975—. Editor, author: (dictionary) Table Pastorale de la Bible, 1974; editor (dictionary database) Dictionnaire Encyclopédique de la Bible, 1987, Concordance de la TOB, 1993, Oeuvres Completes de Jean-Baptiste de La Salle avec Index electronique, 1994, (series) Fils d'Abraham, 1987—, (series) Bible et Vie Chrétienne, 1979—, Spiritual Writings of Abbot Marmion, 1998, Bible Pastorale (pub. 1998, CD-ROM 1999), Data Base and CD-ROM Roi Baudouin, 1998; editor Interface, 1980—, Debora-Doc, 1980-90; editor Telecom-Unio 1989-98; bd. dirs. Cath. Biblical Fedn., 1984-96, OCIC, 1994—, Ecumenical Jury Festival des Films du Monde, Montreal, 1999—; vice-postulator Cans of Abbot Marmion, 2000. Office: CIB Maredsous, B 5537 Denee Belgium

POTEEV, OLEG GENNADY, warehouse executive; b. Perm, Ural, Russia, Oct. 17, 1956; s. Gennady Alexis and Lydmila Borisovna (Salmina) P.; m. Tatjana Vladimirovna Kasjanova, Jan. 1, 1993. Grad., Mil. Coll., Perm, 1980. Cert. engr. of servicing automatic system of flying machines and land equipment. Lab. asst. Mil. Coll., Perm, 1974-75; svc. engr. Computer Sentre, Vitebsk, 1983-85; programmer Dising Office Spectr, Vitebsk, 1985-92; engr. STC Gradient, Vitebsk, 1992-93; gen. mgr. VOTSS Ltd., Russia, Belarus, 1993—. Sr. lt. Military, 1980-83. Mem. Nat. Geog. Soc. Orthodox. Home: P Brovky 26/13-39, 210038 Vitebsk Belarus

POTEKHIN, ALEXANDER YURIEVICH, physicist, researcher; b. Leningrad, Russia, Nov. 5, 1961; s. Yury Andreevich and Nadezhda Dmitrievna (Potekhina) Yappa; m. Marina Olegovna Petrukhina, Mar. 1, 1982; 1 child, Ekaterina. MD, Leningrad State U., 1985; PhD, Vavilov Optical Inst., St. Petersburg, Russia, 1991. Rsch. scientist Vavilov Optical Inst., St. Petersburg, 1985-92; sr. rsch. scientist Ioffe Phys. Tech. Inst., St. Petersburg, 1992—; lectr. St Petersburg State Tech. U., 1993-95. Recipient 1st Sci. award Ioffe Phys. Tech. Inst., St. Petersburg, 1993, Grand Premium of MAIK "Nauka" and Pleiades Pub. Inc., Moscow, 1996. Office: Ioffe Phys Tech Inst, Politekhnicheskaya 26, 194021 Saint Petersburg Russia

POTEMKIN, ALEXEY DMITRIEVICH, botanist; b. Leningrad, Russian Federation, May 13, 1965; s. Dmitry Sergeevich and Lyudmila Vladimirovna Potemkin; m. Natalja Igorevna Belil'nikova, Aug. 30, 1985; children: Pyotr, Kseniya. PhD, V.L. Komarov Bot. Inst., St. Petersburg, Russia, 1990. Jr. rsch. scientist V.L. Komarov Bot. Inst., St. Petersburg, 1990-92, rsch. scientist, 1992-97, sr. rsch. scientist, 1997—; chmn. bryol. com. Russian Bot. Soc., St. Petersburg, 1991—; curator liverwort herbarium V.L. Komarov Bot. Inst. St. Petersburg, 1990—. Contbr. articles to sci. jours. Fax: 7-812-234 4512. E-mail: alexey@ak2348.spb.edu. Office: VL Komarov Bot Inst, 2 Prof Popov St, Saint Petersburg 197376, Russia

POTENKO, VLADIMIR VLADIMIROVICH, science administrator; b. Zhitkovichi, Gomel, Belarus, Sept. 23, 1964; s. Vladimir Fedorovich and Aleksandra Ivanovna (Kuferova) P.; m. Ludmila Michailovna Tsukanova, Jan. 27, 1989; children: Julia, Dmitry. PhD, Belarus Forestry Inst., Gomel, 1991. Rsch. scientist Belarus Forestry Inst., Gomel, 1988-93; chief of genetics lab. Far East Forestry Inst., Khabarovsk, Russia, 1993-95; dep. dir. Breeding Ctr., Sosnogka, Russia, 1995—. Author: Guide to Conifer Species Research, 1989. Soldier Chem. Corps, 1986-88. Grantee Model Forest Gassinsky, Khabarovsk, 1996-98. Achievements include inventor of method of mutation level determination. Home: Flat 6 7 Mir Square, 680555 Sosnovka Russia Office: Breeding & Seed Growing, 12 Nagornaya St, 682305 Sosnovka Russia

POTENTE, EUGENE, JR., interior designer; b. Kenosha, Wis., July 24, 1921; s. Eugene and Suzanne Marie (Schmit) P.; m. Joan Cioffe, Jan. 29, 1946; children: Eugene J., Peter Michael, John Francis, Suzanne Marie. PhB, Marquette U., 1943; postgrad., Stanford U., 1943, N.Y. Sch. Interior Design, 1947; DFA, Carthage Coll., 1970; DLitt (hon.), Concordia U., 1997. Cert. lighting Nat. Coun. on Lighting Qualification. Founder, chmn. Studios of Potente, Inc., Kenosha, Wis., 1949—; pres., founder Archtl. Svcs. Assocs., Kenosha, 1978—, Bus. Leasing Svcs. of Wis. Inc., 1978—; past nat. pres. Inter-Faith Forum on Religion, Art and Architecture; vice chm. Wis. State Capitol and Exec. Residence Bd., 1981—. Sec. Kenosha Symphony Assn., 1968-74; bd. dirs. Ctr. for Religion and the Arts, Wesley Theol. Sem., Washington, 1983-84. With AUS, 1943-46. Recipient Disting. Alumni award Marquette U., 1999. Mem. Am. Soc. Interior Designers (treas., pres. Wis. chpt. 1985-86, 94-95, chmn. nat. pub. svc. 1986), Illuminating Engring. Soc. N.Am. Internat. Interior Design Assn., Elks, Am. Legion (life), Sigma Delta Chi. Roman Catholic. Home: 8609 2nd Ave Pleasant Prairie WI 53158-4720 Office: 914 60th St Kenosha WI 53140-4041

POTGIETER, PIETER CORNELIUS, theologian, educator; b. Bloemfontein, South Africa, Feb. 10, 1940; s. Frederick J.M. and Johanna C. (Olivier) P.; m. Diana Magdalena De Vries, Jan. 23, 1965; children: Frederick, Francois, Cecilia. BA, U. Stellenbosch, Cape Province, South Africa, 1960, BTh, 1964, MTh, 1965, DTh, 1973. Ordained min. Dutch Reformed Ch., 1965. Min. of religion Dutch Reformed Ch., Cape Province, 1966-77; assoc. prof. ethics U. Pretoria (South Africa), 1978-80; prof. systematic theology U. of the Free State, Bloemfontein, 1980—, dean faculty of theology, 1989—; moderator Dutch Reformed Ch. of South Africa, 1990—; convenor com. of theol. ed. and interchange Reformed Ecumenical Coun., Grand Rapids, Mich., 1992—; bd. dirs. Lux Verbi Publs., South Africa. Author: Victory, the Work of the Spirit, 1984, The Power of Prayer, 1996; editor Theol. Forum; contbr. articles to profl. jours. Mem. Internat. Reformed Theol. Inst., South African Acad. Sci. and Arts. Avocations: fishing, hunting, windsurfing, music, mechanics. Home: 63 Albrecht St, Bloemfontein 9301, South Africa Office: Free State U, PO Box 339, Bloemfontein 9300, South Africa

POTIA, ISMAIL FIDAALI, company executive; b. Mumbai, Maharashtr, India, Aug. 29, 1934; s. Fidaali Mohmedali and Ratanbai Fidaali (Nagree) P.; m. Zarina Ismail (Petiwala), June 22, 1954; children: Durriya, Asif, Salim. B in Comm., Sydnaham, 1954. Propr. I.F. Potia & Bros., Mumbai, India, 1958—, Chowpatty Gas, Mumbai, 1962—; mng. dir. Potia Trading, Mumbai, 1964—, B'Bay Compress Gas, Mumbai, 1970—; propr. Zigma Gas Svc., Mumbai, 1972—. Photos exhibited on Nat. Geography Mag., Photographic Soc. Am. Treas. Chhabdi Bazar Niyaze Husein, Mumbai, 1958—, Saify Ambulance, Mumbai, 1960—, Dawoodi Bohra, Mumbai, 1962—, Mcht. Soc., Mumbai, 1970—, Anjumene Muttavin, Mumbai, 1970—. Recipient Gold Medal Photographic Soc. India, 1952, Silver Medal, 1954. Mem. Rotary Club (Bombay chpt.), Radio Club, Royal Western India Turf Club. Office: HL Lakda Bazar, Bellasis Rd, 400008 Mumbai Maharashtra India

POTOCEK, VACLAV, physicist; b. Beroun, Czech Republic, Mar. 5, 1955; s. Vaclav and Jarmila (Hamplova) P.; m. Blanka Fridrichova, Nov. 29, 1978 (div. Sept. 1983); 1 child, Petr; m. Jana Kuklinkova, Apr. 14, 1984; children: Vaclav, Hana. MS, Czech Tech. U., 1979; PhD, Czech Acad. Scis., 1985. Researcher Czech Acad. Scis., Prague, 1980-90, Czech Tech. U., Prague, 1990-94, Commn. L'Energie Atomique, Saclay, France, 1994-95; tech. mgr. GN Resources Internat., Prague, 1996—; scientific sec. Czech Work Group for Remote Sensing, Prague, 1988-90. Contbr. articles to profl. jours.; patentee in field. Lt. Czech Peoples Army, 1979-80. Fellow N.Y. Acad. Scis. Avocations: the Internet, travel, music, history, sports. Home: Renoirova 619, 152 00 Prague 5 Czech Republic Office: CRI, GN Resources Internat, Ve Smečkách 22, 110 00 Prague 1 Czech Republic

POTOCNAK, JOSEPH JAMES, bishop; b. Berwick, Pa., May 13, 1933; arrived in South Africa, 1973; s. John Joseph and Anna (Hunchar) P. Student, U. Nev., 1957-59; BA, Kilroe Sem., Honesdale, Pa., 1963; MDiv, Sacred Heart Sch. Theology, Hales Corners, Wis., 1987; DD (hon.), 1982. Ordained priest Roman Cath. Ch., 1966. Purchasing officer Merck, Phila., 1951-53; vocation dir. Roman Cath. Ch., Gt. Barrington, Mass., 1967-70; rector sem. Roman Cath. Ch., Lenox, Mass., 1970-73; parish priest Roman Cath. Ch., Noupoort, South Africa, 1973-77, De Aar, South Africa, 1977-88, Graaff-Reinet, South Africa, 1988-92; bishop of De Aar Roman Cath. Ch., 1992—; vice chmn. Bishop's Liturgy Commn., Pretoria, South Africa, 1994—. Trustee Good Shepherd Hospice, Middelburg, South Africa, 1992—. Sgt. USAF, 1953-57. Home and Office: PO Box 73, 1 Van Riebeeck St, De Aar 7000, South Africa*

POTSCHKA, MARTIN, biophysical chemist, consultant; b. Vienna, Austria, Jan. 25, 1955; s. Walter and Elizabeth (Wanek) P.; m. Gerlinde Keppl, Feb. 3, 1984 (div. Dec. 1988); m. Zaruhi Kuepcue, Apr. 19, 1996. MS, U. Vienna, 1978, PhD, 1983. Rsch. asst. U. Conn., Storrs, 1978-81; rsch. scientist U. Vienna, 1982-84, Max Planck Inst. Biophys. Chemistry, Göttingen, Germany, 1985-87, Immuno AG, Vienna, 1988-90; cons. Vienna, 1990—; vis. prof. U. Conn., Storrs, 1987-88; vis. scholar Inst. Advanced Studies, Ind. U., Bloomington, 1992. Editor: Strategies in Size Exclusion Chromatography, 1995; contbr. articles to profl. jours. Fellow Internat. Union Pure and Applied Chem.; mem. Austrian Chem. Soc., Am. Chem. Soc., Am. Biophys. Soc. (Harold Lamport award 1981), German Biophys. Soc., Internat. Soc. for Study European Ideas. Avocations: music, culture, travel. Office: Porzellang 19-2-9, A-1090 Vienna Austria

POTTENGER, MARK MCCLELLAND, computer programmer; b. Tucson, Feb. 9, 1955; s. Henry Farmer and Zipporah Herrick (Pottenger) Dobyns. BA, UCLA, 1976, DDiv (hon.), 1998. Data entry operator Astro Computing, Pelham, N.Y., 1976-77; programmer/analyst LA-CCRS, L.A., 1977-80; programmer/analyst cons. L.A., 1977—, R. Gonzalez Mgmt., L.A., 1980—; rsch. dir. Internat. Soc. for Astrol. Rsch., L.A., 1985-95. Editor: Astrological Research Methods, 1995; co-author: Tables for Aspect Research, 1986; editor The Mutable Dilemma, 1977-99; author: (computer programs) CCRS Horoscope program, 1977-92, Frequencies for Aspect Rsch., 1986-92. Recipient Jansky award Aquarius Workshops, L.A., 1989. Mem. Internat. Soc. for Astrol. Rsch., Nat. Coun. for Geocosmic Rsch. Democrat. Mem. Religious Sci. Ch. Avocations: reading science fiction and regencies. Home and Office: 3808 49th St San Diego CA 92105-2101

POTTER, BARRY VICTOR LLOYD, biological and medicinal chemistry educator; b. Brighton, Sussex, United Kingdom, Sept. 29, 1953; s. John Evelyn and Dorothy Josephine (Taylor) P.; m. Erika Katharina Wiesenmüller, Dec. 17, 1993; 1 child, Hannah Sophie. BA in Chemistry, Oxford (Eng.) U., 1977, MA, 1980, DPhil, 1981, DSc, 1993. Rsch. student Dyson Perrins Lab., Oxford, 1977-79, postdoctoral rsch. asst., 1980-81; jr. rsch. fellow Wolfson Coll., Oxford U., 1980-81; Royal Soc. European exch. fellow Max-Planck Inst. Experimental Medicine, Göttingen, Germany, 1981-83; Wissenschaftlicher Mitarbeiter der Max-Planck Gesellschaft, 1983-84; lectr. biol. chemistry, Lister Inst. rsch. fellow U. Leicester, United Kingdom, 1984-90; Lister Inst. rsch. prof., Sch. Pharmacy and Pharmacology U. Bath, United Kingdom, 1990-95, prof. biol. and medicinal chemistry, 1995—; dir. medicinal chemistry Sterix Ltd., 1997—; invited lectr. numerous univs. and internat. scientific confs. Contbr. numerous articles to profl. jours.; patentee in field; open exhibitioner in natural scis. Oxford U., 1973-77. Recipient The Part II Thesis prize in organic chemistry Oxford U., 1977, Worcester Coll. Soc. prize Worcester Coll., Oxford, 1977, Grad. scholarship Wolfson Coll., Oxford, 1980-81; grantee Med., Sci. and Engring. and Biology and Biotech. Rsch. Couns. Cancer Rsch. Campaign, The Wellcome Trust, The Wolfson Found., The Royal Soc., Lister Inst. Preventive Medicine, others. Fellow Royal Soc. Chemistry; mem. Biochem. Soc., Lister Inst. Preventive Medicine. Avocations: music, squash, English morris dancing, skiing. Home: 95 Dovers Park Bathford, Bath BA1 7UE, England Office: U Bath Sch Pharmacy/Pharmacology, Clavertown Down, Bath BA2 7AY, England

POTTER, CLEMENT DALE, district attorney general; b. McMinnville, Tenn., Dec. 22, 1955; s. Johnnie H. and Elnora (Harvey) P.; children: Cory, Sarah, John Warren. BS, Middle Tenn. State U., 1984; JD, U. Tenn., 1987; cert., Tenn. Law Enforcement Acad., 1980. Bar: Tenn. 1987, U.S. Dist. Ct. (ea. dist.) Tenn. 1989. Pvt. practice law McMinnville, 1987-89; city judge City of McMinnville, Tenn., 1988-89; pub. defender 31st Dist. State Tenn., McMinnville, 1989-98, dist. atty. gen., 1999—. Asst. to gen. editor Tools for the Ultimate Trial, 1st edit., 1985. Mem. Leadership McMinnville, 1989, chmn., 1995, 96. Staff sgt. USAF, 1974-80. Named McMinnville Warren County C. of C. Vol. of Yr., 1995; recipient D. Porter Henegar & Fred L. Hoover Sr. Bell Ringer award, 1995, Upper Cumberland award of merit 2000. Mem. ABA, Cheer Mental Health Assn. (dir. 1988—, pres. 1991-96), Harmony House Inc. (dir. 1993-95), Noon Exch. Club McMinnville (dir. 1992-94, sec. 1994, pres.-elect 1995, pres. 1996-97), Kiwanis Club of Warren County (pres. 1986-87), Tenn. Secondary Schs. Athletic Assn. (h.s. football referee 1988—), Am. Legion. Avocations: computers, gardening, coaching youth softball. Office: Dist Atty Gen 31st Dist PO Box 510 455 N Chancery Mc Minnville TN 37111

POTTER, DAVID STONE, Greek and Latin educator; b. Cambridge, Mass., Mar. 15, 1957; s. Harold David and Elizabeth Fleming (Stone) P.; m. Ellen Ann Bauerle, Aug. 18, 1990; children: Claire Penelope, Natalie Sarah Ni Qing. BA, Harvard U., 1979; PhD, Oxford U., 1984. Vis. asst. prof. Greek and Latin Bryn Mawr (Pa.) Coll., 1984-86; asst. prof. Greek and Latin U. Mich., Ann Arbor, 1986-91, from assoc. to prof. Greek and Latin, 1991-96—, dir. Lloyd Hall Scholars program, 1999—. Author: Prophecy and History in the Crisis of the Roman Empire, 1990, Prophets and Emperors: Human and Divine Authority from Augustus to Theodosius, 1994, Literary Texts and the Roman Historian, 1999, Life Death and Entertainment in the Roman Empire, 1999. Recipient Phi Beta Kappa award Harvard U., 1979, Conington prize Oxford U., 1988. Episc. Home: 2377 Timbercrest Ct Ann Arbor MI 48105-9269 Office: Univ Mich Dept Classical Studies Ann Arbor MI 48109-1003

POTTER, GEORGE WILLIAM, JR., mining executive; b. St. Louis, Aug. 5, 1930; s. George William and Fay Marguerite (Finch) P.; m. Emily Louise Withers, Feb. 11, 1956; 1 child, Anne Russ. BA, U. Mo., Kansas City, 1952. Pres. Oritz Mines, Inc., Joplin, Mo., 1962-64, chmn. bd. dirs., 1964-87; chmn. bd. dirs. Nancy Oil & Royalty Co., Joplin, 1981-86; pres., chmn. bd. dirs. Potter Industries, Inc., Joplin, 1981-90; chmn. bd. dirs. Cresset Corp., Joplin, 1986. Art exhibited in one-man shows at Barn Gallery, Kansas City, Mo., 1974, Fountain Valley Sch., Colorado Springs, Colo., 1974, U. Leyden, The Netherlands, 1977, others; author books (under pseudonym E.L. Withers): The House on the Beach, 1957, The Salazar Grant, 1959, Diminishing Returns, 1960, Heir Apparent, 1961, The Birthday, 1962, Royal Blood, 1964; fgn. edits. include Brit., French, Italian, German, Scandinavian, Japanese. Bd. dirs. Winfred L. and Elizabeth C. Post Meml. Art Reference Libr., 1977-82, Kansas City Ballet, 1976-79; trustee Conservatory of Music, Kansas City, 1988—. Recipient Mo. Writers award, 1967. Mem. Authors Guild, Nat. Trust for Hist. Preservation, Soc. Fellows Nelson Gallery Found. (coun. 1988-91), Kansas City Country Club. Home: 1239 W 61st Ter Kansas City MO 64113-1327

POTTER, JAMES VINCENT, association executive; b. Walla Walla, Wash., July 17, 1936; s. James Floyd and Dorothy May (Turner) P.; m. Margaret Mae Fogerson, July 4, 1954 (div. Apr. 1970); children: Deborah Ann, David Allan, Rebecca Lynn, Mary Michelle, Jonathon James; m. Paula Maureen Brutsman, Feb. 28, 1986; stepchildren: Carolyn June, Catherine Doreen, Paul Clayton, Connie Lynn. BA in Bibl. Studies, Logos Bible Coll., 1989; MA in Theology, Logos Grad. Sch., 1989; PhD, Vision Christian U., 1990, postgrad., 1991-95. Diplomate Nat. Assn. Forensic Counselors, Nat. Bd. Addiction Examiners, Am. Coll. Profl. Mental Health Practitioners; lic. clin. pastoral counselor; cert. temperament therapist, doctoral addictions counselor, domestic violence counselor, diplomat clin. hypnotherapist. Lectr., nat. presenter, lit. evang. Seventh-day Adventist Ch., Idaho, 1956-60, Oreg., 1960-61; staff mem. U. of the Nations Family Ministries, Kailua-Kona, Hawaii, 1989; pastor Gospel of Salvation Ministries, 1989-93; dean Coll. Christian Counseling, Vision Christian U., Hilo, Hawaii, 1990-93; pres. Family Care Svcs. Internat., 1990-93; v.p., mem. faculty Vision Christian U., Ramona, Calif., 1991-92, 1998—; adminstr., clinician Hawaii Family Care Ctrs., Hilo, 1989-93; exec. dir. Agape Family Svcs., Inc. and Alliance Recovery Svcs., 1995—; vice chmn. Teen Challenge of Hawaii, 1991-93, govtl. apptd. mem. Hawaii Area Commn. on Mental Health and Substance Abuse, 1991-94; pres., Profl. Assn. Christian Therapists, 1989-94, Internat. Christian Counselors Assn., 1988—; lectr. western states, 1989—; nat. presenter on domestic violence prevention and treatment. Author: Soul Care, 1989, Untwisting Twisted Temperaments, 1991, (book and curriculum), Save Our Families, Pulling Down Strongholds, 1998, Breaking Free, 1998, Discovering Our True Selves, 1999, Mastery Over Anger, 2000, Assertiveness Training, 2000, Beyond Codependency, 2000, Man's Magnificent Mind, 2000, Healing Developmental Wounds, 2000, Reparenting the Self, 2000, Growing Beyond Our Genetcis, 2000, Toxic Shame and the Journey Out, 2000; co-author: Family Care Center Manual, 1991, Christian Character Alignment, 1991; (newsletter) Gem-State Surveyor, 1976. Dem. nominee Idaho State Legis., House Rep., Boise, 1976, 78; vice chmn. Idaho Tech. Adv. Coun., Boise, 1976-83; pres. Idaho Assn. Land Surveyors, Boise, 1976-77; chmn. Western Fedn. Profl. Land Surveyors, 12 western states, 1979-80; nat. dir. Am. Congress Surveying Mapping, Washington, 1981-83; gov. Nat. Soc. Profl. Land Surveyors; state del. Mont./Hawaii State Rep. Conv., Turtle Bay, 1988. With USN, 1953. Am. Congress Surveying Mapping fellow, Washington, 1980. Mem. Nat. Assn. of Forensic Counselors (regional and state dir., cert. ednl. provider), Nat. Bd. of Addiction Examiners, Nat. Bd. Cert. Clin. Hypnotherapists, Am. Assn. Family Counselors, Am. Assn. Christian Counselors, Nat. Christian Counselors Assn (bd. dirs. 1988—), Christian Assn. Psychol. Studies, Am. Assn. Christian Therapists. Office: PO Box 992168 1501 Market Redding CA 96099

POTTER, J(EFFREY) STEWART, property manager; b. Ft. Worth, July 8, 1943; s. Gerald Robert Potter and Marion June (Mustain) Tombler; m. Dianne Eileen Roberb, Dec. 31, 1970 (div. Aug. 1983); 1 child, Christopher Stewart; m. Deborah Ann Blevins, Oct. 20, 1991. AA, San Diego Mesa Coll., 1967. Cert. apartment mgr., apartment property supr., housing adminstr. Sales mgr. Sta. KJLM, La Jolla, Calif., 1964-67; mgr. inflight catering Host Internat., San Diego, 1967-69; lead aircraft refueler Lockheed Co., San Diego, 1969-70; property mgr. Internat. Devel. and Fin Corp., La Jolla, 1970-72; mgr. bus. property BWY Constn. Co., San Diego, 1972-73; mgr. residents Coldwell Banker, San Diego, 1973-74; mgr. Grove Investments, Carlsbad, Calif., 1974-76, Villa Granada, Villa Seville Properties Ltd., Don Cohn, Chula Vista, Calif., 1976-83; gen. mgr. AFL-CIO Bldg. Trades Corp., National City, Calif., 1983—; instr., Cert. Apt. Mgmt. San Diego Apt. Assn., 1995-98. Bd. dirs. San Diego County Apt. Assn., 1995-97, Policy Panel Youth Access to Alcohol, San Diego. Fellow Nat. City C. of C., Founding Families San Diego Hist. Soc., Am. Assn. Retired Persons, San Diego County Apt. Assn. (bd. dirs.), La Jolla Monday Night Club (treas. 1984-89), La Jolla Hist. Soc. Roman Catholic. Avocations: golf, tennis, snow skiing. Office: AFL-CIO Bldg Trades Corp 2323 D Ave National City CA 91950-6730

POTTER, JOHN BUCHANAN, educational association director; b. Salisbury, Eng., Jan. 28, 1938; s. Robert James and Geraldine Elizabeth (Buchanan) P.; m. Celia Rubery, Apr. 18, 1964 (div. 1989); children: Andrew, Alasdair, Tanya; m. Valerie Oliver, Feb. 17, 1990. BA with honors, Politics Philosophy Econ., Oxford, Eng., 1961. Asst. curate Ch. of Eng., Coventry, 1963-66; vicar Ch. of Eng., Writtle, 1970-78; sr. lectr. Warden Hall of Residence, Lanchester Poly., Coventry, 1966-70; canon Derby (Eng.) Cathedral, 1978-85; devel. officer Cmty. Svc. Vols., London, 1985-90, dir., 1990—; dir. Writtle Pastoral Found., Chelmford, Eng., 1974-78; trainer Westminster Pastoral Found., London, 1985-90, 90—; dir. CSV Edn. for Citizenship. Contbr. articles to profl. jours. Gov. Bemrose Sch., Derby, 1979-84; chmn. Assn. Pastoral Care and Counseling, 1993-94. 2d lt. British mil., 1956-58. Fellow Royal Soc. Arts. Avocations: travel, photography, walking. Office: CSV, 237 Pentonville Rd, N19NJ London England

POTTER, JOHN DAVIS, investment banker; b. Mt. Kisco, N.Y., Feb. 3, 1944; s. John Clarkson and Mary Paschall (Davis) P.; m. Lidija Grzac, July 15, 1967 (div. Aug. 1982); children: Philip G., Andrew G.; m. Maria Luisa Herradura Manlulu, May 21, 1983. PhD, U. Paris, Sorbonne, 1972. Mgr. Commerce Union Bank, Nashville, 1973-75; asst. v.p. Wells Fargo Bank, San Francisco, 1975-78; mgr. Wells Fargo Ltd., London, 1978-79; v.p. Am. Express Bank Ltd., Manama, Bahrain, 1979-81; gen. mgr. A.H. Algosaibi & Bros. Co., Alhobar, Saudi Arabia, 1982-84, Algosaibi Investment Holdings, Manama, 1984—; bd. dirs. Saad Investments Co., Manama, S & A Trading and Devel., Inc., Manila, Philippines. Mem. Oriental Club, Am. Assn. of Bahrain (pres.). Office: Algosaibi Investment, PO Box 1736, Manama Bahrain

POTTER, JOHN MCEWEN, retired neurosurgeon and medical educator; b. London, Feb. 28, 1920; s. Alistair Richardson Potter and Mairi Chalmers Dick; m. Kathleen Gerrard, Apr. 21, 1943; children: James Gerrard, Andrew John, Simon Stephen. BA, MB, BChir., U. Cambridge, 1943, MA, 1945; MA, BM, BCh, U. Oxford, 1963, DM, 1964. Lectr. St. Bartholomew's Hosp., London, 1948-50, jr. chief asst. surg. professorial unit, 1950-51; grad. asst. to Nuffield prof. surgery U. Oxford, Eng., 1951-56, dir. postgrad. med. edn., 1972-87; cons. neurosurgeon Manchester (Eng.) Royal Infirmary, 1956-61, Radcliffe Infirmary, Oxford, 1961-87; fellow, professorial fellow, sub-warden Wadham Coll., Oxford, 1969-87, emeritus fellow and dean of degrees; v.p. Fourth Internat. Congress Neurol. Surgery; vis. prof. UCLA, 1967; examiner in medicine Univs. Oxford and Cambridge, 1970-74; bd. govs. United Oxford Hosps., 1973; mem. Gen. Med. Coun., London, 1973-89; lectr. Cairns Trust, Adelaide, Australia, 1974; mem. Oxfordshire Health Authority, 1982-89, hebdomadal coun. U. Oxford, 1983-89, Med. Appeals Tribunal, London, 1987-90. Author: The Practical Management of Head Injuries, 1961, 4th edit., 1984; contbr. articles to profl. jours., chpts. to books. Capt. Royal Army Med. Corps, 1944-47. E.G. Fearnsides scholar U. Cambridge, 1954-56. Fellow Royal Coll. Surgeons (Hunterian Professor 1955); mem. Am. Assn. Neurol. Surgeons (lifetime inactive), Royal Soc. of Medicine (pres. sect. neurology 1975-76), Soc. Brit. Neurol. Surgeons (sr., formerly hon. sec. and archivist), Deutsche Gesellschaft Fur Neurochirurgie (corr.), Sociedad Luso-Espanhola De Neurocirurgia (corr.), Egyptian Soc. Neurol. Surgeons (hon.). Mem. Ch. of Eng. Avocation: fishing.

POTTER, JONATHAN ANDREW, psychologist, educator; b. Ashford, Kent, Eng., June 8, 1956; s. Percy Albert and Mary Diana (Merricks) P. BA, Liverpool U., 1977; MA, Surrey U., 1978; PhD, York U., 1983. Lectr. St. Andrews (Scotland) U., 1985-88; from lectr. to reader Loughborough (Eng.) U., 1988-95; prof. Loughborough (Scotland) U., 1995—. Author: Discourse and Social Psychology, 1987, Discursive Psychology, 1992, Mapping the Language of Racism, 1992, Representing Reality, 1996. Mem. Internat. Comm. Assn., Brit. Psychol. Soc. Avocation: postmodern leisure consumption. Office: Dept Social Scis, Loughborough Univ, Loughborough LE11 3TU, England

POTTER, LILLIAN FLORENCE, business executive secretary; b. Montreal, Que., Can., Oct. 19, 1912; came to U.S., 1934; naturalized citizen.; d. Thomas Joseph and Lily Rose (Robertson) Quirk; m. Theodore Edward Potter, July 20, 1932 (dec. Apr. 1980); children: Peter Edward, Stephen Thomas. Grad. high sch., Montreal, 1929, grad., 1931. Sr. sec. S.D. Warren div. Scott Paper Co., Westbrook, Maine, 1955-69, editor indsl. publ. S.D. Warren div., 1969-72; editor Nat. Antiques Rev. mag., Portland, Maine, 1972-77; exec. sec. Humboldt Portland Litho div. Humboldt Nat. Graphics, Inc., Fortuna, Calif., 1977—; free lance writer Guy Gannett Pub. Co., Portland, 1960-64. Author: (children's book) Once Upon an Autumn, 1984 (state 1st pl. award, nat. 3d pl. award), (antiques and collectibles) A Re-Introduction to Silver Overlay on Glass and Ceramics, 1992; co-author: (textbook, tchrs. manual) Foundations of Patient Care, 1981; asst. editor, N.E. dist. The Secretary mag., Profl. Secs. Internat., 1960-62; editor Maine Chpt. Bull., 1963-64. Recipient George Washington Honors medal Freedoms Found., Valley Forge, Pa., 1964, Sec. of Yr. award Portland chpt. Profl. Secs. Internat., 1967, Outstanding Svc. award State of Maine Sesquicentennial, 1970, Outstanding Svc. award Island Pond (Vt.) Hist. Soc. 1978. Mem. Maine Media Women (pres. 1970-71, Woman of Yr. 1973, Communicator of Achievement plaque and prize 1991), Maine Writers and Pubs. Alliance, Woman's Lit. Union, Portland Lyric Theater, Island Pond Hist. Soc., Jones Mus. Glass and Ceramics, Westbrook Woman's Club, OES (past matron, past pres.). Republican. Episcopalian. Avocations: reading, researching, antiques, swimming, gardening. Home: 80 Payson St Portland ME 04102-2851

POTTER, WILLIAM ALLEN, trade association administrator; b. E. Cleveland, Ohio, July 30, 1947; s. William Allen and Dori Virginia P.; m. Kimberly C., May 24, 1986; children: Mark, Tami, Lisa, Stacie, Rick. BS, George Mason U., 1991. Sales and mktg. mgr. Parts Pro Distributing, Washington, 1971-87; trade assn. exec. Automotive Aftermarket Industry Assn., Chgo. and Bethesda, Md., 1988—. Recipient 1st Pla. Spot News Radio Nat. Motorsports Press Assn., 1976, Edn. award Northwood U., 1979; named Top 25 Aftermarket Influences, 1999. Avocations: auto racing, dogs, snow skiing. Office: AAIA 4600 E West Hwy Ste 300 Bethesda MD 20814-3415

POTTER, WILLIAM JAMES, investment banker; b. Toronto, Aug. 11, 1948; s. William Wakely and Ruby Loretta (Skidmore) P.; m. Linda Lee, Nov. 25, 1972; children: Lisa Michelle, Meredith Lee, Andrew David. AB, Colgate U., 1970; MBA, Harvard U., 1974. With White Weld & Co., Inc., N.Y.C., 1974-75, Toronto Dominion Bank, Toronto (Can.) and N.Y., 1975-78; group mgr. Toronto Dominion Bank, Toronto, 1979-82; 1st v.p. Barclays Bank PLC, N.Y.C., 1982-84; mng. dir. Prudential-Bache Securities, Inc., N.Y.C., 1984-89; pres. Ridgewood Capital Funding Inc., N.Y.C., 1989—, Ridgewood Group Internat. Ltd., N.Y.C., 1989—; advisor Ladenberg Thalman Internat., 1990-92, Laidlaw Holdings, Inc., 1992-93; bd. dirs. 1st Australia Fund Inc., Md., 1st Australia Prime Income Fund Inc., Md., 1st Australia Prime Income Co. Ltd., New Zealand, Impulsora del Fondo Mex., Mexico City, Alexandria Bancorp, Can., Columbus Mills Ltd., Ghana, 1st Commonwealth Fund, Md., E.C. Power Inc. Author: Finance for the Minerals Industry, 1985. Bd. dirs. Glen Ridge (N.J.) Community Fund, 1985—; fin. mem. Glen Ridge Congl. Ch., 1985—; trustee Glen Ridge Ednl. Found., 1994—. Mem. Nat. Fgn. Trade Coun. (bd. dirs., chmn. fin. com.), Harvard Club, Williams Club (N.Y.C.), Nat. Club (Toronto), Glen Ridge Country Club (N.J.), Buck Hill Country Club (Pa.), Internat. Platform Assn., Econ. Club N.Y. Congregationalist. Avocations: golf, tennis. Office: Ridgewood Group Internat Inc 236 W 27th St Fl 3 New York NY 10001-5906

POTTERS, JOHANNES HUBERTUS, geophysicist; b. Tiel, The Netherlands, Apr. 23, 1957; s. Johannes Jacobus Potters and Gerarda Antonia Van Oorsouw; m. Marianne Ricarda Smits, Nov. 20, 1980; children: Jan, Max. MSc in Astrophysics, Rijksuniversiteit, Utrecht, The Netherlands, 1980, PhD in Physics, 1984. Cert. geophysicist, physicist. Rsch. physicist Found. for Fundamental Rsch. of Matter, Nieuwegein, The Netherlands, 1980-84; rsch. geophysicist Shell Rsch., Rijswijk, The Netherlands, 1984-89, Shell Devel., Houston, 1989-90; sect. head geophysics Shell Rsch., Rijswijk, 1990-94; team leader geophysics Petroleum Devel. Oman, Muscat, 1994-98; coord. subsurface integration Shell Tech. Exploration and Prodn., Rijswijk, 1998—; vice-chmn. European Assn. Geoscientists and Engrs., Houten, The Netherlands, 1999-00. Contbr. papers to profl. jours. Organizer Internat.

Astron. Youth Camps, Königswinter, Germany, 1977, Borj-el-Amri, Tunisia, 1978. Mem. European Assn. for Geoscientists and Engrs. (chair 2000—), Soc. Exploration Geophysicists, Am. Geophys. Union. Avocations: astronomy, literature. Office: Shell Tech Expl & Prod, Volmerlaan 6, 2280 AB Rijswijk The Netherlands

POTTHOFF, MATTHIAS, process engineer; b. Frankfurt, Hessen, Germany, Feb. 6, 1961; s. Karl Gustav and Hedwig (Klein) P.; m. Christiane Britta Runge, Oct. 30, 1994; children: Judith Karin, Justus. Diplom, Tech. Hochschule, Darmstadt, Germany, 1987; Dr. Engring., Tech. U., Braunschweig, Germany, 1992. Sci. asst. Tech. U., Braunschweig, 1987-92; rsch. fellow Osaka (Japan) U., 1993-94; sr. process engr. Krupp Uhde GmbH, Dortmund, Germany, 1994—; commissioning mgr. fertilizer complex, Egypt, 2000. Contbr. articles to profl. jours. With German Air Force, 1980-81. Alexander von Humboldt Found. Postdoctoral fellow, 1993. Mem. Verein Deutsche Ingenieure (leader working group 1984), Rowing Club Nassovia. Avocations: rowing, playing violin, literature. Home: Knospenweg 9, 44265 Dortmund Germany Office: Krupp Uhde GmbH, Friedrich-Uhde-Strasse 15, 44141 Dortmund Germany

POTTI, PERIYAMANA KESAVAN GOVINDAN, mechanical engineer, researcher; b. Quilon, Kerala, India, Dec. 24, 1959; s. Periyamana Govindan Kesavan and Kesavan Kamala (Devi) P.; m. Eppurath Vasudevan Soniya, May 3, 1989; children: Vandana, Rohith. BS in Engring., Govt. Engring. Coll., Trichur, India, 1982. Engr. Indian Space Rsch. Orgn., Trivandrum, India, 1982—. Contbr. articles to profl. jours. Mem. Astronautical Soc. India, Indian Assn. for Quality and Reliability (life). Avocation: singer (light and classical music). Home: CHD IV/592, Periyamana Desam PO, Alwaye Kerala 683103, India Office: Vikram Sarabhai Space Ctr, Structural Engring Group, Trivandrum Kerala 695022, India

POTTMEYER, HERMANN JOSEF, theology educator; b. Bocholt, Germany, June 1, 1934; s. Ernst and Hermine (Veelken) P. Lic. in philosophy, U. Gregoriana, Rome, 1957, ThD, 1964; Habilitation, U. Münster, Fed. Republic Germany, 1974; hon. doctor, Papal Theol. Acad. Cracow, 1998. Ordained priest Roman Cath. Ch., 1960. Vicar Diocese of Münster, 1964-67; sci. asst. U. Münster, 1967-72, scholar, 1972-74, univ. lectr., 1974; prof. theology U. Bochum, Fed. Republic Germany, 1974-99; cons. Synod German Dioceses, 1971-75, German Bishops Conf., 1980—, Cen. Com. German Caths., 1987—; Com. Internat. Theologians, Rome, 1992—; vis. prof. U. Gregoriana, Rome, 1989, U. Notre Dame, Ind., 1991, 99. Author: Der Glaube vor dem Anspruch der Wissenschaft, 1968, Unfehlbarkeit und Souveränität, 1975, Towards a Papacy in Communion, 1998, 2000, Die Rolle des Papsttums im dritten Jahrtausend, 1999; editor: Fragen an Eugen Drewermann, 1992, Fides Quaerens Intellectum, 1992, Wozu noch einen Papst, 1993, Kirche im Wandel, 1982, Handbuch der Fundamentaltheologie, 4 vols., 1985-88, Die Rezeption des 2 Vatikanischen Konzils, 1986, Die Bischofskonferenz, 1989, Kirche im Kontext der modernen Gesellschaft, 1989, Festschrift: Kirche sein, 1994. Recipient Quasten award Cath. U. Am., Washington, 1991.

POTTRUCK, DAVID STEVEN, brokerage house executive; b. 1948. BA, U. Pa., 1970, MBA, 1972. Now pres., CEO U.S. Govt., 1972-74; with Arthur Young & Co., 1974-76, sr. cons.; with Citibank N.Am., 1976-81, v.p.; with Shearson/Am. Express, 1981-84, sr. v.p. consumer mktg. and advt.; with Charles Schwab & Co., San Francisco, 1984—; exec. v.p. mktg., br. adminstr. Charles Schwab and Co., Inc.; pres., CEO The Charles Corp., Charles Schwab & Co.; pres., COO The Charles Schwab Corp., pres., co-CEO. Office: Charles Schwab & Co Inc 101 Montgomery St Ste 200 San Francisco CA 94104-4175*

POTTS, BILLIE LUISI, college administrator; b. N.Y.C., Mar. 5, 1940; d. Harold and Esther Malka (Ulano) Meisner; m. Carmen John Luisi, May 18, 1962 (div. Jan. 1972); 1 child, Thecla Luisi. AB, Hunter Coll., N.Y.C., 1962; AM, Fordham U., Bronx, N.Y., 1964. Dir. tng. and tech. assistance Ctr. for Women in Govt., U. Albany, N.Y., 1986-91; dir. devel. Catskill Area Hospice, Oneonta, N.Y., 1994-98, Regents Coll., Albany, 1999—; cons. human resources Developmental Dynamics, Summit, N.Y., 1979—. Author: A First Book of Clay, 1973, Small Scale Goatkeeping, 1979, 84. Winifred Found. grantee, Wainscott, N.Y., 1998. Mem. Kingston Sunrise Rotary (newsletter editor 1997—). Jewish. Avocations: gardening, hiking, sculpture, painting. Home: PO Box 293 Summit NY 12175-0293

POTTS, DANIEL THOMAS, archaeology educator; b. N.Y.C., Feb. 10, 1953; arrived in Australia, 1991; s. Morgan and Virginia Belle (Aal) P.; m. Hildreth Burnett, June 2, 1979; children: Rowena, Morgan, Hallam. BA, Harvard U., 1975, PhD, 1980; DPhil, U. Copenhagen, 1991. Vis. lectr. U. Copenhagen, 1980-81, lectr., 1986-91; lectr. Free U. Berlin, 1981-86; Edwin Cuthbert Hall prof. Mid. Ea. Archaeology U. Sydney, Australia, 1991—; dir. Near Ea. Archaeology Found., Sydney, 1991—; editor-in-chief Arabian Archaeology & Epigraphy Internat. Jour., Copenhagen, 1990—. Author: The Arabian Gulf in Antiquity, 1990, Miscellanea Hasaitica, 1989, The Pre-Islamic Coinage of Eastern Arabia, 1991, Mesopotamian Civilization: The Material Foundations, 1997, The Archaeology of Elam: Formation and Transformation of an Ancient Iranian State, 1999, Ancient Magan: The Secrets of Tell Abraq, 2000. Sydney interviewer of applicants for Harvard Coll., 1991—; mem. Harvard Club Australia, 1994—. Fellow Australian Acad. Humanities, Soc. Antiquaries (London); mem. Am. Oriental Soc., Am. Numismatic Soc. Avocations: music, fishing, rugby union. Home: 29 Henry St, 2024 Queen's Park Australia Office: U Sydney, 2006 Sydney Australia

POTTS, GLENDA RUE, music educator; b. Butler, Ala., Nov. 26; d. Jennings Herschel and Erma Rue (Holdridge) Moseley; m. Billy Wayne Blackwell, June 23, 1963 (div. Aug. 1977); children: William Stephen, Melton Jennings; m. Willis Jones Potts, Jr., July 13, 1985; 1 stepchild, Timothy Brendon. BM in Music, Auburn U., 1963. Organist Beverly Meth. Ch., Birmingham, 1964-65; music tchr. grades 3-8 Birmingham Pub. Schs., 1964-65; music tchr. grades 7-9 Chattanooga Pub. Schs., 1965-66; organist 1st Bapt. Ch., Prattville, 1969-85, 87-93, music asst. dir., 1980-85; pianist, dir. children's choirs, asst. organist Bull St. Bapt. Ch., Savannah, Ga., 1995-99; piano tchr. Kreative Keyboards, Savannah, 1993-99, 1999—; owner piano/organ studio, Prattville, 1967-93. Sec., mem. chair Savannah Symphony Women's Guild, 1993-99; soprano Savannah Symphony Chorale, 1993-94; mem. chair Savannah Newcomer's, 1994-95. Honored as one of Top 400 Women Grads. of Centennial of Admission of Women Students, Auburn U., 1992. Mem. Ga. Music Tchr's. Assn. (pres. Savannah chpt. 1997-99), Music Tchr's. Nat. Assn. (nat. and state cert. tchr. and adjudicator), Nat. Guild of Piano Tchr's. (nat. and state cert. tchr. and adjudicator, Hall of Fame 1990), Am. Coll. Musicians. Republican. Baptist. Home: 2614 Horseleg Creek Rd SW Rome GA 30165-8583

POTTS, WILLIAM FREDERICK, consultant; b. Scarborough, Yorkshire, Eng., Dec. 19, 1935; came to the U.S., 1977; s. William Christopher and Winifred Potts; m. Elaine Lillian Peet, May 7, 1960; children: William Frederick, Christopher Michael, Valerie Rosaline. Student, U. London. Programming methods specialist Air Can., Montreal, 1958-62; programming supr. Robert Simpson Co., Toronto, Can., 1962-64; project analyst IBM Can., Toronto, 1965-68; dir. sys. and programming Ont. Ministry Revenue, Toronto, 1968-69; product mktg. mgr. Memorex, Santa Clara, Calif., 1972-80, Zentec Corp., Santa Clara, 1981-83; dir. internat. market devel. comm. products Novell, Mountain View, Calif., 1983-89; pres., owner WFP Consulting, San Jose, Calif., 1989—; sec. Sys. Planning and Devel. Exch.-IBM Computer Users' Group, Toronto, 1961-69; com. mem. Can. Stds. Assn., Toronto, 1974-77. Author: McGraw-Hill Data Communications Dictionary, 1992, The Simple Modem Book, 1993; contbr. articles to profl. jours. Pres. Toronto Humanist Assn., 1975-77; vol. Planned Parenthood, San Jose, 1996—. Fellow Brit. Computer Soc.; mem. U.S. Metric Assn. (cert. metrication specialist). Avocation: website development. E-mail: wfp@wfpconsulting.com. Fax: 408-972-0161. Office: WFP Consulting 937 Foothill Dr San Jose CA 95123-2628

POTUPA, ALEXANDER SERGEEVICH, physicist; b. Sevastopol, Russia, Mar. 21, 1945; s. Sergej Nicholaevich and Nina (Semionovna) P.; m. Lubov Nilovna Biletnikova, Apr. 20, 1974; children: Elena, Andrej. BS, Lomonosov Moscow State U., 1967; MS, Nat. Acad. Sci. Belarus, 1970; PhD in Info. Techs., Internat. Acad. Info. Process, 1995. Rsch. worker Inst. Physics, Minsk, Russia, 1967-74; sr. rsch. worker Belarussian State U., Minsk, 1974-77; author, expert Minsk, 1978-88; gen. dir. Eridan Pub. and Printing Co., Minsk, 1989-96; dir. Ctr. for Future Studies, Minsk, 1992—, prof., 1995—. Author 12 books, including Discovery of Universe: Past, Present, Future, 1991, Something Unimaginable, 1992, Run for Infinity, 1977, Idealized Measuring Procedures in Quantum Theory, 1970; contbr. articles to profl. jours. Recipient Torch of Birmingham, 1995. Mem. AAAS, Belorussian Human Rights Conv. (chmn. 1997—), Belorussian Assn. Think Tanks (coun. 1997—), Belorussian Union Entrepreneurs (v.p. 1994—), Belorussian Confedn. Industrialists and Entrepreneurs (coun. 1993—), Belorussian Euro-Atlantic Assn. (coun. 1996—), N.Y. Acad. Sci., Internat. Acad. for Leadership in Bus. and Adminstrn., Internat. Acad. Info. Process and Techs., Internat. Inst. Sociology, World Future Soc., Internat. Fedn. Journalists, Internat. Pen Club. Achievements include research in maximum power, principle of futurogenic causality. E-mail: a.potupa@usa.net.

POTVIN, WILLIAM TRACEY, management consultant; b. Milw., June 20, 1951; s. William John and Joan (Wach) P.; m. Louisa I. Vorosmarty, July 23, 1983. BS in Internat. Econs., Georgetown U., 1973; MBA, Am. U., 1975. Investment mgr. GEICO, Washington, 1973-78; mgmt. cons. Touche Ross & Co. (now Deloitte & Touch LLP), N.Y.C., 1978-85, ptnr., 1985—; nat. dir. Fin. Inst. Cons., N.Y.C., 1987-90; mng. ptnr., CEO Deloitte & Touche CIS, Moscow, 1990-96; nat. dir. Deloitte & Touche Actuarial and Ins. Cons. Group, N.Y.C., 1996-99; pres., CEO The ESP Group LLC, Arlington, Va., 1999—; chmn. adv. group to Russian govt. on mass privatization World Bank, 1992-94, acting CFO Russian Privitization Ctr., 1996; speaker to ins. groups, N.Y.C., 1985—. Contbr. articles to profl. jours. Mem. Coll. of Ins. (mem. fin. industries task force 1985-90, lectr. 1985-90). Roman Catholic. Office: The ESP Group LLC Ste 1103 Crystal Gateway Two Arlington VA 22202 also: The ESP Group LLC 76 Chestnut Ridge Rd Armonk NY 10504-3001

POTWOROWSKI, TADEUSZ KRZYSZTOF, accountant; b. Lindern, Germany, Jan. 10, 1947; arrived in Eng., 1947; s. Jan Jozef and Jadwiga Stefania (Jaroszynska) P.; m. Irena Izabella Bninska, Dec. 28, 1974; children: Dominik, Gabriela. Chartered acct. Chief acct. Cato O'Brien, London, 1971-73; sr. ptnr. Potworowski Kinast, London, 1974-95; ptnr. Grant Thornton, London, 1995—; bd. dirs. Potworowski Kinast Grant Thornton, Poland, 1990—, Robinski & Co. Ltd., Eng., 1986-88; mem. supervisory bd. SAN S.A. Poland, 1994—; trustee Fund for Blind of Laski, Eng., 1991—. Fellow Inst. Chartered Accts. in Eng. and Wales; mem. West London Chartered Accts. (chmn. 1986-89), London Soc. Chartered Accts. (com. mem. 1991-95), Polish Chamber of Auditors, West London C. of C., (dir. 1997—). Roman Catholic. Avocations: tennis, skiing, gardening. Office: Grant Thornton, 7 High St Internat House, London W5 5DB, England

POU, PEDRO, bank executive. Pres. Ctrl. Bank Govt. of Argentina, 1996—. Office: Ctrl Bank Argentina, Capital Fed Reconquista 266, 1003 Buenos Aires Argentina*

POUCKOVA, PAVLA MILOSLAVA, biologist; b. Prague, Czech Republic, Apr. 7, 1950; d. Alois and Bozena (Hrdlickova) Kischner; m. Josef Poucek, July 10, 1972; 1 child, Petra. PhD, Mil. Med. Faculty Hradec, 1990. Expert asst. 2d Med. Faculty Prague, 1973-74; expert asst. 1st Med. Faculty Prague, 1974-90, sci. worker, 1990—; bd. dirs. RCD Ltd., Prague; sci. sec. Radiobiol. Soc. Prague, 1990—. Avocations: literature, music, swimming. Home: Americka 632, 2APAD Dobrichovice Prague, Czech Republic Office: Inst Biophysics, Salmovska 1, 120 00 Prague Czech Republic

POULIOT, PHILIPPE, theoretical physicist; b. Montreal, Que., Can., Mar. 29, 1971; s. Roger Pouliot and Muriel Therrien Miller. BSc in Math. Physics, MSc in Physics, U. Montreal, 1992; PhD in Physics, Rutgers U., 1996. Postdoctoral rsch. physicis U. Calif., Santa Barbara, 1996-99, U. Tex., Austin, 1999—. Avocations: flutist, brain and mind sciences. Fax: 512-471-4888. E-mail: pouliot@griffy.ph.utexas.edu. Office: U Tex Physics Dept Theory Group C1608 Austin TX 78712

POULOS, JOAN GRAHAM, lawyer; b. Almena, Kans., June 7, 1936; d. Gilbert W. and Opal Z. Graham; m. John W. Poulos (div. 1978); children: John S., Alexandra J. Poulos Fullerton; m. David C. Lewis, Dec. 29, 1989. BS, U. Kans., 1958; JD, U. Calif., San Francisco, 1962; MA, U. Calif., Riverside, 1978. Bar: Calif. 1963, U.S. Supreme Ct., U.S. Ct. Appeals (9th cir.), U.S. Dist. Ct. (so., ea. and no. dists.) Calif. Pvt. practice Davis, Calif., 1978—; dir. People Resources Inc., Yolo County, Calif., 1994-96. City coun. mem. City Davis, 1972-74, mayor, 1974-76; chmn. juvenile justice com. Mendo County, Ukiah, Calif.; commr. Nat. Commn. Uniform State Law, 1978-86; mem. Davis Chorale; pres. Mental Health Assn. Yolo County. Mem. ABA, Am. Women for Internat. Understanding, Yolo County Bar Assn. Democrat. Office: 1723 Oak Ave Davis CA 95616-1004 also: PO Box 1241 Bodega Bay CA 94923-1241

POULOT, DOMINIQUE PIERRE, history educator; b. Saint Jean D'Angely, Charente, France, Mar. 10, 1956; s. Maurice and Marcelle (De la Maziere) P.; m. Monique Moreau, Oct. 17, 1981; children: Marie-Laure, Suzanne, Cecile. Diploma d'Etudes, EHESS, Paris, 1979; D in History, Sorbonne, Paris, 1989; Habilitation, Grenoble, France, 1993. Asst. prof. U. Grenoble, 1983-90, maitre de conférences, 1991-93, full tenure prof., 1993-97; Jean Monnet fellow European U. Inst. Firenze, Italy, 1990-91; mem. U. Inst. of France, 1992-97; full prof. modern history U. Tours, France, 1997-2000; full prof. modern art history U. Paris, Sorbonne, 2000—; mem. histor com. French Ministry of Culture, 1993—. Mem. editl. bd. Publics et Musées Jour., France, 1992—, Hist. Reflections jour./Alfred U., 1993—, Histoire Urbaine Jour., France, 1999; author: (books) Bibliographie de l'histoire des musées de France, 1994, Surveiller et s'inst., 1996, Musée, Nation, Patrimoine, 1997, Les Lumières, 2000; contbr. articles to profl. jours. Recipient medal French U. Inst., 1993. Mem. Soc. Modern History, Assn. Internat. Sociology of French Lang. Office: Univ Paris 1, Pantheon-Sorbonne 3 rue Michelet, F-75006 Paris France

POULSEN, EMIL, toxicological advisor; b. Ebeltoft, Denmark, July 12, 1921; s. Niels Carl Waldemar Poulsen and Johanne Cecilie Carstensen; m. Ellen Elisabeth Kibaek, Feb. 24, 1945; children: Per, Jorgen, Hanne. DVM, Royal Vet. & Agrl. U., Copenhagen, 1943, D of Medicine Veterinariae, 1957. Asst. in veterinary practice Kolind, Denmark, 1943-44; asst. prof. Royal Vet. & Agrl. U., Copenhagen, 1944-48, 51-64; vet. supr. Pub. Health, Copenhagen, 1948-51; assoc. prof. Dept. State Vet. Medicine, Copenhagen, 1964-68; dir. Nat. Food Agy. Inst. Toxicology, Copenhagen, 1968-86; chief advisor toxicology Ministry of Health, Copenhagen, 1986-91, toxicol. advisor, 1991—. Mem. EU Scientific Com. for Food, 1974-95, pres., 1980-86. Fellow Acad. Toxicology; mem. Toxicology Forum (bd. dirs. 1979-98), Internat. Life Scis. Inst. Europe (bd. dirs. 1989-95). Home: 26 GL Strandvej, DK-3050 Humlebaek Denmark

POULSEN, IB, mass communications educator, researcher; b. Ringkobing, Denmark, Jan. 8, 1949; s. Johannes and Grethe (Rydstrom) P.; m. Gudrun Bodin, Mar. 30, 1982; 1 child, Christian. MA, U. Copenhagen, 1975, PhD, 1982. From asst. prof. to assoc. prof. U. Copenhagen, Denmark, 1976-99; prof. Royal Danish Sch. Ednl. Studies, 1999-2000, Danish Ednl. Univ., 2000—; external examiner Min. Edn., Denmark, 1980; ednl. cons. Danish Broadcasting Corp., 1983-91; mem. Danish Media Commn., 1994-95. Mem. Internat. Assn. Mass Comm. Rsch., Assn. Internat. Linguistique Appliqué. Avocations: traveling, jogging, art. Office: Royal Danish Sch Ednl Studies, Emdupvej 101, 2400 Copenhagen NV, Denmark

POULSEN, JENS KRISTIAN, ultrasonics researcher; b. Thisted, Denmark, Jan. 30, 1966; arrived in Can., 1998; s. Kjeld and Else Marianne Westergaard P. MSEE, Tech. U. Denmark, Lyngby, 1992. Rsch. asst. Radiometer, Copenhagen, 1988; instr. Tech. U. Denmark, 1988-89; rsch. asst. Jydsk Telefon, Aarhus, 1989, Skejby Sygehus, Aarhus, 1992-98; ultrasonics rschr. Toronto U., Ont., Can., 1998—; computer cons. Medistim, Oslo, 1994-97. Inventor in field; contbr. articles to profl. jours. Mem. IEEE/Ultrasonics Ferroelectrics and Frequency Control (student mem.), IEEE/Engring. in Medicine and Biology Soc. (student mem.). Avocations: running, salsa dancing. Office: U Toronto Dept Med Biophys, 2075 Bayview Ave, Toronto, ON Canada M4N 346

POULSEN, JENS MICHAEL, physicist; b. Aarhus, Denmark, Oct. 26, 1953; arrived in Italy, 1982; s. Poul and Anna (Michaelsen) P.; m. Nilda Geronimo Estrada, Mar. 30, 1996; one child, Annalise Gabriella. Grad., U. Copenhagen, 1977; MSc, Danish Space Rsch. Inst., Lyngby, 1980. Asst. tchr. U. Copenhagen, 1976-79; tchr. high sch., Haslev, Denmark, 1981; physicist Danish Space Rsch. Inst., 1981; rsch. fellow European Space Agy., Bologna, Italy, 1982, Tesre-CNR, Bologna, 1983-91; sys. engr. Laben Spa, Milan, Italy, 1992—. Treas. Meth. Ch., Copenhagen, 1976-81. Mem. Evang. Christian Ch. Office: Laben Spa, SS Padana Superiore 290, 200 90 Vimodrone Italy

POULSEN, LARS KAERGAARD, chemical engineer; b. Copenhagen, Denmark, Jan. 29, 1958; s. Poul K. and Inger K. Poulsen; m. Lisbeth E. Mansen. MSChE, Danish Tech. U., 1984; PhD, U. Copenhagen, 1988, D in Med. Sci., 2000; Diploma Bus. Adminstrn., Copenhagen Bus. Sch., 1997. Head lab. Nat. Univ. Hosp., Copenhagen, 1985—; assoc. prof. U. Copenhagen, 1995—; dir. Danish Allergy Rsch. Ctr., 1997—. Contbr. articles to profl. jours. Fellow Johns Hopkins U., 1989. Mem. Danish Soc. Allergology (bd. dirs.). Office: Nat U Hosp Dept 7542, Blegdamsuej 9, DK 2100 Copenhagen Denmark

POULSEN, SVEN, dental educator; b. Elsinore, Denmark, Apr. 12, 1941; s. Otto and Elisabeth (Hansen) P.; m. Annette Tuxen (div. 1988); children: Michael, Christian, Thomas; m. Bodil Birn, Sept. 21, 1997. DDS, Royal Dental Coll., Copenhagen, 1965; PhD, Royal Dental Coll., Aarhus, Denmark, 1970, D in Odontology, 1976. Asst. dentist in pvt. practice Copenhagen, 1965-66; clin. fellow Eastman Dental Ctr., Rochester, N.Y., 1966-67; asst. prof. Royal Dental Coll., Aarhus, 1967-72; chief advisor Danida, Dar es Salaam, Tanzania, 1991-94; dean Royal Dental Coll., Aarhus, 1987-91, prof., 1978—; former advisor WHO, Syria, Cuba, Peru, Beijing; dir. WHO Collaborating Ctr. Oral Health Planning and Rsch. in 3d World Countries, 1997—; cons. Nat. Bd. Health, Copenhagen; external examiner various internat. univs.; cons. Tanzania Dental Jour., 1996—; reviewer The Cochrane Collaboration: Oral Health Group, U. Manchester, Eng., 1997—; mem. internat. editl. bd. Brit. Dental Jour., 1998—; presenter numerous internat. confs. Co-editor: Pedodontics—A Systematic Approach, 1981; contbr. numerous articles to internat. profl. jours. and conf. procs., chpts. to books. Mem. European Orgn. for Caries Rsch., Internat. Assn. for Dental Rsch. (scientific divsn.), Danish Soc. Pediat. Dentistry (pres. 1998—). Home: Hans Broges Gade 25, DK-8000 Århus C, Denmark Office: Royal Dental Coll, 9 Vennelyst Blvd, DK-8000 Århus C, Denmark

POULTERER, WILLIAM TAYLOR, III, river pilot; b. Phila., Sept. 4, 1938; s. William Taylor Jr. and Betty (Bennett) P.; m. Jane D. Fisher, Aug. 23, 1991; children by previous marriage: Stacy P. Thompson, Andrew T. Student, U. Del., 1980-81, U. Richmond, 1983. Lic. first class pilot for Del. Bay and River Commonwealth of Pa., USCG. River pilot Pilots Assn. Bay and River Del., Phila., 1957-99, pres., 1999—. State legislator, mem. Del. Ho. of Reps., Dover, 1970-74; pres. bd. dirs. Edn., Inc., Salina, Kans., 1970-78; bd. dirs. Planned Parenthood, Wilmington, Del., 1972-74; mgr. Del. Franklin P. Hall re-election campaign, Richmond, Va., 1987-89; pres. Chapelcroft Civic Assn., Wilmington, 1968-70, Gates Head Civic Assn., Richmond, 1988-89, Challenge Discovery Projects, Richmond, 1989-91. Named Young Rep. of Yr. New Castle County Young Reps., 1970. Mem. Am. Pilots Assn. (trustee 1994—), Pilots Soc. For Relief of Distressed and Decayed Pilots Their Widows and Children (pres. 1980-94), Phila. Pilots Assn. (bd. dirs.), Masters Mates and Pilots. Avocations: outdoor activities, skiing, tennis, travel. Home: 109 Marina Dr Lewes DE 19958-1279

POUMELLEC, BERTRAND GILBERT, researcher, consultant; b. Enghien les bains, France, June 6, 1955; s. Gilbert Louis and Michelle Genevieve (Jardin) P.; m. Michele Josette Badiolle, July 22, 1978; children: Nathalie, Arnaud, Marie-Anne. Agrégation Phys. Scis., 1975; MSc in Phys. Chemistry, U. Paris Sud, Orsay, 1978, D Geophys., 1980, DSc, 1986. Rsch. assoc. CNRS, Orsay, 1982-86, in charge of rsch., 1986—; optical fibers cons. in field. Mem. Optical Soc. Am. Achievements include patents in field; defect induced optical properties in SiO2-GeO2 based material for optical fiber; simulation of non-exponential kinetics, simulation of K pre-edge structures in X-ray absorption of first row transition metal oxides; uv luminescence spectroscopy. Office: U Paris Sud, Lab Physico-chimie des solides, 91405 Orsay France

POUND, JOHN BENNETT, lawyer; b. Champaign, Ill., Nov. 17, 1946; s. William R. and Louise Catherine (Kelly) P.; m. Mary Ann Hanson, June 19, 1971; children: Meghan Elizabeth, Matthew Fitzgerald. BA, U. N.Mex., 1968; JD, Boston Coll., 1971. Bar: N. Mex. 1971, U.S. Dist. Ct. N. Mex. 1971, U.S. Ct. Appeals (10th cir.) 1972, U.S. Supreme Ct., 1993. Law clk. to Hon. Oliver Seth, U.S. Ct. Appeals, 10th Cir., Santa Fe, 1971-72; asst. counsel Supreme Ct. Disciplinary Bd., 1977-83, dist. rev. officer, 1984—; mem. Supreme Ct. Com. on Jud. Performance Evaluation, 1983-85; bd. dirs. Archdiocese Santa Fe Cath. Social Svcs., 1995—. Contbr. articles to profl. jours. Pres. bd. dirs. N.Mex. Ind. Coll. Fund, Santa Fe; chmn. N.Mex. Dem. Leadership Coun., 1991—; bd. dirs. Santa Fe Boys Club, 1989-92; rules com. N.Mex. Dem. Party, 1982—; v.p. Los Alamos Nat. Lab. Comm. Coun., 1985-90; fin. chmn. N.Mex. Clinton for Pres. campaign, 1992; co-chmn. Clinton-Gore Re-election Campaign, N.Mex., 1996. Fellow Am. Bar Found., Am. Coll. Trial Lawyers, N.Mex. Bar Found.; mem. ABA, Am. Bd. Trial Advocates, N.Mex. Bar Assn. (health law sect. 1987—), Santa Fe County Bar Assn. Democrat. Roman Catholic. Avocations: history, foreign language, literature, swimming, baseball. Office: Herrera Long & Pound PA PO Box 5098 2200 Brothers Rd Santa Fe NM 87505-6903*

POUNDER, NEILL MALCOLM, material scientist; b. Nottingham, Eng., June 7, 1967; s. Keith Albert and Gillian (Benson) P.; m. Jayne Atkinson, Apr. 18, 1992; 1 child, Aidan Benjamin. BSc in Physics, Leeds U., 1988, PhD in Physics, 1991. Chartered physicist. Rsch. scientist Smith Nephew Grc, York, Eng., 1991—. Mem. Inst. of Physics. Avocations: cycling, travel. Office: Smith Nephew, York Sci Pk Heslington, York Y010 5DF, England

POUNDS, GERALD AUTRY, aerospace engineer; b. Boaz, Ala., Mar. 21, 1940; s. C.B. and Pauline (DeBord) P.; m. Linda Lee Lindsey, July 29, 1967; children: Kristina Marie, Alissa Michelle. B in Aerospace Engring., Auburn U., 1963, MS in Aerospace Engring., 1965. With Lockheed Martin Aero. Sys., Marietta, Ga., 1960—, mgr. wind tunnels and aircraft sys. test dept.; lectr. U. Tenn. Space Inst., Tullahoma, 1988-95. Contbr. articles to Jour. Aircraft. Vestry, from jr. warden to sr. warden Christ Episcopal Ch., Kennesaw, Ga., 1974-82; mid. adult retreat coord. Mt. Paran Ch. of God, Atlanta, 1986-91. NSF scholar, 1963-64. Fellow AIAA (assoc., dep. dir. for test, tech. activities com. 1991-97, chmn. Atlanta sect.); mem. Supersonic Tunnel Assn. (com. rep.), Subsonic Aerodynamic Testing Assn. Home: 6 Hastings Dr Cartersville GA 30120-6472 Office: Lockheed Martin Aero Sys D 7358 Z 0605 Marietta GA 30063-0001

POUNDS, KENNETH ALWYNE, physics educator; b. Leeds, Yorks, Eng., Nov. 17, 1934; s. Harry and Dorothy Louise (Hunt) P.; m. Margaret Mary O'Connell, Dec. 29, 1961 (dec. May 1976); children: David Edwin, Jillian Barbara, John Michael; m. Joan Mary Millit, Dec. 10, 1982; children: Michael Andrew, Jennifer Anne. BSc, U. Coll., London, 1956, PhD, 1960; DUniv, U. York, Eng., 1984; DSc, Loughborough U., 1992. Asst. lectr. U. Leicester, Eng., 1960-61, lectr., 1962-69, reader, 1969-73, prof. space physics, 1973—, head physics dept., 1986-93, 98—; chief exec. U.K. Particle Physics and Astronomy Rsch. Coun., Swindon, 1994-98. Contbr. over 170 articles to profl. jours. Decorated Comdr. Brit. Empire. Fellow Royal Soc. of London; mem. U.K. Sci. and Engring. Coun. (chmn. astronomy space and radio bd. 1980-84), Internat. Acad. Astronautics, Academia Europaea, Royal Astron. Soc. (pres. 1990-92, Gold medal 1989). Home: 12, Swale Close, Oadby Leicester England LE2 4GF Office: U Leicester, Dept Physics & Astronomy, Leicester LE1 7RN, England

POUNGUI, ANGE-EDOUARD, former People's Republic of Congo government official; b. Mouyondzi, People's Republic of Congo, Jan. 4, 1942; s. Casimir and Agnes Moungondo; married; 8 children. Student Centre d'Enseignement Superieur, Brazzaville, People's Republic of Congo, law sch., 1969. Legal rep. Bank of Central African States, 1973-76, asst. dir., 1976-79; dir. gen. Congolese Comml. Bank, 1979-84; minister of fin. People's Republic

of Congo, Brazzaville, 1971-73, minister of planning, 1973, prime minister, 1984-89; v.p. State Council, 1972-73; fin. counsel to head of state, 1979—; mem. Nat. Council for Revolution, 1968, mem. directorate, 1969; gov. for People's Republic of Congo at IMF and African Devel. Bank, 1971-73; adminstr. Bank for Devel. of Central African States, from 1976; pres. Nat. Com. for Cellulose. Mem. polit. bur. Parti Congolais du Travail, 1969-75, 84—, elected mem. Parliament, 1993, mem. central com., from 1969; now dir. Ctrl. Bank Congo, 1994—. Mem. Fedn. of Profl. Assns. of Banks of Bank of Central African States (pres. from 1982), Profl. Assn. of Banks of Congo (pres. 1984). Office: Bank Ctrl African States (BEAC), PO Box 126, Brazzaville Congo*

POUNTAIN, RICHARD JOHN, writer, consultant; b. Chesterfield, Eng., Jan. 18, 1945; s. John Waring and Kathleen Vida (Wibberley) P. BSc in Chemistry with honors, Imperial Coll., London, 1966, Diplomate in Biochemistry, 1967. Dir. Dennis Pub., London, 1972-85; mng. editor Personal Computer World, London, 1981-83, Soft mag., London, 1983-84; contbg. editor Byte mag., Peterborough, N.H., 1985-98; real world editor PC Pro mag., London, 1995—; non-exec. dir. Dennis Pub., London, 1985—. Author: Object Oriented Forth, 1987, Tutorial Introduction to OCCAM Programming, 1987, "Cool Rules," 2000. Mem. Scotch Malt Whisky Soc. Avocations: music, motorcycling, botany, hill walking, cooking. Home: 8 Rousden St, London NW1 0SU, England

POUPARD-WALBRIDGE, GLORIA PATRICIA, strategic planning consultant; b. Cota-Bogota, Colombia, July 15, 1946; arrived in France, 1968, New Zealand, 1993.; d. Rafael and Sylvia (Arias) C.; m. Jean-Michel Poupard, May 20, 1968 (div. June 1992); m. Stuart Wilfred Walbridge, Apr. 17, 1993. BA in Econs., U. Melbourne, Australia, 1978; MBA, Victoria U. Wellington, New Zealand, 1990. Mgr. contract rsch. Victoria U. Wellington, 1990-92; mng. dir. European Design Concepts, Wellington, 1992-94; mgr. strategic planning Kiwifruit Mktg. Bd., Auckland, New Realand, 1995; dir. Rsch. Adv. Bur., Auckland, 1996—; cons. Aquatech Farms Ltd., Tampo, New Zealand, 1993-94, Perfect Weddings, Auckland, 1998-99, New Zealand Prawns Ltd., Tampo, 1999. Exhibited in group show Nat. Salon Art, Bolivia, 1982. Sec. Act, polit. party, Auckland, 1995-96. Mem. Rotary (coord. friendship cir. Auckland 1997—). Roman Catholic. Avocations: sailing, scuba diving, skiing, reading, art. Home: 4 St Vincent Ave, Remuera, Auckland New Zealand

POURARYAN, SIAMAK MICHAEL, management consultant; b. L.A., Oct. 27, 1964; s. Siroos Po Pouraryan and Mindo Mozaffari; m. Maryam Pouraryan, Oct. 14, 1998. AA, Pasadena City Coll., Calif., 1985; BA, Calif. State. U., L.A., 1987. Opers. mgr. Advt. Engterprise Solutions, Santa Ana, Calif., 1992—. Democrat. Avocations: stamp collecting, writing, swimming.

POURBEIK, PEYAM, communication engineer; b. Bordeaux, France, Jan. 16, 1971; arrived in Australia, 1980; s. Hossien and Taherah (Tamaddoni) Pourbeik. B in Engring. with honors, U. South Australia, 1992, PhD in Electronic Engring, 1999. Registered profl. engr. Tutor U. South Australia, Adelaide, 1992-96; data comm. engr. Railcom, Sydney, Australia, 1996-98; profl. svcs. engr. Scitec, Adelaide, 1998-99; sr. devel. engr. Argus Comms, Sydney, 1999—. Contbr. articles to profl. jours. Mem. IEEE, Inst. Engrs. Australia, N.Y. Acad. Scis. Bahai. Avocations: history, philosophy, computing, electronics, cricket. Home: Unit 9 9 May St, Hornsby NSW 2077, Australia Office: Argus Comms Level 16, 55 Market St, Sydney NSW 2000, Australia

POURBEIK, POUYAN, applications engineer; b. Apr. 17, 1972. B of Engring. with honors, U. Adelaide, Australia, 1992, PhD in Elec. Engring., 1997. Application engr. GE Co., Schenectady, N.Y., 1997-2000; cons. engr. ABB Power T&D Co., Raleigh, N.C., 2000—. E-mail: pouyan.pourbeik@us.abb.com. Fax: 919-807-5060. Office: ABB Power T&D Company Elec Systems Cons 940 Main Campus Dr Ste 300 Raleigh NC 27606

POUR-EL, MARIAN BOYKAN, mathematician, educator; b. N.Y.C.; d. Joseph and Mattie (Caspe) Boykan; m. Akiva Pour-El; 1 dau., Ina. A.B., Hunter Coll.; A.M., Harvard U., 1951, Ph.D., 1958. Asst. prof. math. Pa. State U., 1958-62, assoc. prof., 1962-64; mem. faculty U. Minn., Mpls., 1964—; prof. math. U. Minn., 1968—; mem. Inst. Advanced Study, Princeton, N.J., 1962-64; mem. coun. Conf. Bd. Math. Scis., 1977-82, trustee, 1978-81, mem. nominating com., 1980-82, chmn., 1981-82; lectr. internat. congresses in logic and computer sci., Eng., 1971, Hungary, 1967, Czechoslovakia, 1973, Germany, 1983, 96, 97, Japan, 1985, 88, China, 1987; lectr. Polish Acad. Sci., 1974; lecture series throughout Fed. Republic of Germany, 1980, 87, 89, 91, Japan, 1985, 87, 90, 93, China, 1987, Sweden, 1983, 94, Finland, 1991, Estonia, 1991, Moscow, 1992, Amsterdam, 1992; symposium held in Pour-El's honor, Kyoto, Japan, 1993; invited hour spkr. nat. meetings Am. Math. Soc., Math. Assn. Am., 1976, 82, 89; mem. Fulbright Com. on Maths., 1986-89; invited spkr. Internat. Congress on Computability and Complexity Theory, Kazan U., Russia, 1997, Workshop on Computability and Complexity in Analysis, held in conjunction with 23rd Internat. Symposium on Math. Founds. of Computer Sci. and Computer Sci. Logic, Brno, Czech Republic, 1998, IEEE Workshop on Real Number Computation, 1998. Author: (with I. Richards) Computability in Analysis and Physics, 1989; author numerous articles on mathematical logic (theoretical computer sci.) and applications to mathematical and physical theory. Named to Hunter Coll. Hall of Fame, 1975; NAS grantee, 1966. Fellow AAAS, Japan Soc. for Promotion of Sci.; mem. Am. Math. Soc. (coun. 1980-88, numerous coms., spkr., orgn. spl. sessions on math. logic), Assn. Symbolic Logic, Math. Assn. Am. (nat. panel vis. lectrs.), Phi Beta Kappa, Sigma Xi, Pi Mu Epsilon, Sigma Pi Sigma. Achievements include research in mathematical logic (theoretical computer science) and in computability and noncomputability in physical theory—wave, heat, potential equations, eigenvalues, eigenvectors. Office: U Minn Sch Math Vincent Hall Minneapolis MN 55455-0488

POURFARZAM, MORTEZA, clinical biochemist; b. Esfahan, Iran, Sept. 21, 1960; s. Ali Akbar and Fakhri (Houshmand) P. BS, EsFahan, 1984; MS, Newcastle U., 1986, PhD, 1990. Rsch. assoc. Newcastle Upon Tyne (Eng.) U., 1990-94, lectr., 1994—. Contbr. articles to profl. jours. Avocations: tennis, jogging, weight tng. Office: Inst of Child Health, U Newcastle upon Tyne, Newcastle upon Tyne NE1 4LP, England

POURNOOR, K. JOHN, scientist; b. Tehran, June 30, 1960; s. Mehdi and Sedigeh Pournoor; m. Rebecca Carolyn Lutt, Aug. 5, 1983; 1 child, Sara. BSChemE, U. Calif., Berkeley, 1982; PhD in Chem. Engring. and Polymer Sci., U. Wash., 1987. Rsch. scientist U. Calif., Berkeley, 1981-83; rsch. engr. Engring. Tech. Lab. Dupong Co., Experimental Station, Del., 1984; vis. scientist materials tech. lab. Boeing Co., Renton, Wash., 1985-86; sr. rsch. scientist Life Scis. Sector Materials Lab. 3M, St. Paul, 1987-91, rsch. specialist Life Scis. Sector Materials Lab., 1991-93; rsch. specialist 3M Health Care, St. Paul, 1993—; co-dir. Infection Prevention Discovery Ctr. 3M, 1997—; advisor 3M-Mayo Clinic Alliance, St. Paul and Rochester, 1998—; rep. U. Calif.-Berkeley Indsl. Liaison Program, Berkeley, 1994—. Contbr. sci. rsch. articles to profl. jours.; patentee in field. Bd. dirs. U. Minn. Inst. Tech. Alumni Soc., Mpls., 1999. Recipient Best Rsch. award Soc. Plastics Engrs., 1986; Genesis grantee 3M Co., 1989, 90, 91; Dupont rsch. scholar, 1983-87. Mem. Am. Phys. Soc. (life). Fax: (651) 736-6747. E-mail: kpournoor@mmm.com. Office: 3M Co 3M Center Bldg 201-2w17 Saint Paul MN 55144-1000

POUSADA, JOSE EDUARDO, mechanical engineer; b. Sao Paulo, Brazil, July 25, 1952; s. Alfredo and Alice (Peixe) P.; children: Marcello, Edoardo, Guilhermo; m. Adriana Spagnolo; children: Marina, Demetrios. BSME, U. Sao Paulo, 1974. Dir. Wormald-Resmat, Sao Paulo, 1975-86; pres. Fire Control Ltd., Sao Paulo, 1986—. Avocations: tennis, football. E-mail: fire.control@tlenet.com.br. Fax: 55 (11) 3746-6194.

POUSADA, LIDIA, physician; b. Mt. Kisco, N.Y., July 21, 1957; d. Manuel and Maria Nieves (Mejuto) P.; m. Andrew Kemper Goodman, June 26, 1983 (div. Sept. 1986); 1 child, Sara Pousada Goodman; m. Wayne William Maibaum, Apr. 11, 1987 (div. July 1993); 1 child, Anna Pousada Maibaum; m. James Paul Kreindler, Mar. 2, 1996; 1 child, Victoria Pousada Kreindler. BS, CUNY, N.Y.C., 1978; MD, N.Y. Med. Coll., 1980. Diplomate Am. Bd. Internal Medicine, Am. Bd. Geriatric Medicine. Student geriatric fellowship NYU Med. Sch., N.Y.C., 1978-80; resident in internal medicine Montefiore Med. Ctr., Bronx, N.Y., 1980-83, dir. geriatric unit, 1986-89; with nat. health svc. North Cent. Bronx Hosp., 1983-84, Morris Heights Health Ctr., Bronx, 1985; instr. City Coll. Med. Sch., N.Y.C., 1982-85; instr. Albert Einstein Coll. Medicine, Bronx, 1983-84, 86-89, asst. prof. medicine, 1988-89; assoc. prof. clin. medicine N.Y. Med. Coll., 1993—; dir. geriatric cons. svc. Montefiore Med. Ctr., 1987-89, assoc. chief divsn. geriatrics, 1988-92; chief divsn. geriatrics and gerontology Sound Shore Med. Ctr., 1992—. Author: Geriatric Diagnostics, 1983, Emergency Medicine for the House Officer, 1986, 2d edit., 1995, Emergency Medicine for Nurses, 1989, Perioperative Medical Care of the Geriatric Patient, 1989, Case Studies in Emergency Medicine for the House Officer, 1993. Physician scholar Nat. Health Svc., 1978-80. Fellow ACP, Gerontol. Soc. Am., Am. Geriatric Soc.; mem. Physicians for Social Responsibility. Office: Sound Shore Med Ctr 16 Guion Pl New Rochelle NY 10801-5503

POUSCHINE, JOHN LAURENCE, private equity investment executive; b. Glen Cove, N.Y., Jan. 28, 1957; s. Ivan and Helen (Carlson) P.; m. Catherine Dana, Nov. 16, 1991; children: Alexander, Anna. BA, Princeton U., 1979; MBA, Harvard U., 1983. Officer's asst. JP Morgan, N.Y.C., 1979-81; assoc. Prudential Securities, Inc., N.Y.C., 1983-85; v.p. Bradford Ventures Ltd., N.Y.C., 1985-88; sr. v.p. Electra Inc., N.Y.C., 1989-96; mng. dir. Pouschine Cook Capital Mgmt., LLC, 1997—; bd. dirs. Russian Children's Welfare Soc., N.Y.C., MasterCraft Boat Co., Inc., Vonore, Tenn., MedPay Corp., Memphis, LIS Corp., Ansonia, Conn. Mem. Nassau Club, Princeton Club of N.Y., Union Club, Bridgehampton Club. Avocation: sports. Office: Pouschine Cook Capital Mgmt 410 Park Ave Ste 810 New York NY 10022-4407

POUSSAINT, ALVIN FRANCIS, psychiatrist, educator; b. N.Y.C., May 15, 1934; s. Christopher Thomas V. and Harriet (Johnston) P. BA, Columbia U., 1956; MD, Cornell U., 1960; MS, UCLA, 1964. Intern UCLA Ctr. for Health Sci., 1960-61, resident in psychiatry Neuropsychiat. Inst., 1961-64, chief resident, 1964-65; So. field dir. Med. Com. Human Rights, Jackson, Miss., 1965-66; asst. prof. psychiatry Tufts U. Med. Sch., 1966-69; assoc. prof. psychiatry, assoc. dean students Harvard Med. Sch., 1969-75, 78—, prof. psychiatry, 1993—, dean students, 1975-78; cons. HEW, 1969-73. Author numerous articles in field. Nat. treas. Black Acad. Arts and Letters, 1969-70, Med. Com. Human Rights, 1966—. Recipient Michael Schwerner award, 1968, Am. Black Achievement award in Bus. and the Professions Johnson Pub. Co., Inc., 1986, John Jay award for Disting. Profl. Achievement Columbia Coll., N.Y., 1987, Medgar Evers Medal of Honor Beverly Hills/Hollywood chpt. NAACP, Hollywood, Calif., 1988, and numerous hon. degrees. Fellow AAAS, Am. Orthopsychiatric Assn., Am. Psychiat. Assn. (mem. com. on Black Psychiatrists 1970-75); mem. Nat. Med. Assn., Am. Acad. of Child Psychiatry, Children's Longwood. Office: Judge Baker Ctr 3 Blackfan Cir Boston MA 02115-5713

POUZAR, VLADIMIR ZDENĚK, organic chemist; b. Prague, Czech Republic, Mar. 26, 1951; s. Vladimír and Věra Anna (Sacherová) P. RNDr, Charles U., Prague, 1974, CSc, 1978. Rsch. worker Inst. Organic Chemistry and Biochemistry, Prague, 1978-90, sr. rsch. worker, 1990—. Author: Manual of Czech Noble Families, 1996, 99; contbr. 90 articles to profl. jours.; editl. bd. Collection of Czechoslovak Chem. Comm., 1986—. Mem. Czech Chem. Soc. Avocation: history. Office: Inst Organic Chem/Biochem, Flemingovo nám 2, CZ 16610 Prague Czech Republic

POVINEC, PAVEL PETER, physicist; b. Ochodnica, Czechoslovakia, Feb. 18, 1942; s. Juraj and Klara (Koptakova) P.; m. Elena Jackova, July 4, 1968; children: Pavol, Peter. MSc, Comenius U., Bratislava, Slovakia, 1965, PhD, 1972. Asst. prof. Comenius U., Bratislava, 1965-73, assoc. prof., 1974-84, prof. physics, 1984, head dept. nuclear physics, 1981-92, vice dean faculty math. and physics, 1981-91; head radiometrics lab. Internat. Atomic Energy Agy., Monte Carlo, Monaco, 1993—; mem. editorial bd. Radiocarbon, 1990—. Editor: Process Low Radioactivities, 1985, Rare Nuclear Processes, 1992, Understanding and Protecting the Marine Environment, (jours.) Process Low Level Counting, 1986, Process Rare Nuclear Decays, 1991. Fellow The European Environ. Rsch. Orgn.; mem. European Phys. Soc. (coun. mem. 1983-88). Avocations: music, protecting the environment. Home: 6 Ave Pierre Weck, 06320 Cap d'Ail France Office: Internat Atomic Energy Agy, 4 Quai Antoine 1er, MC 98000 Monte Carlo Monaco

POVISH, KENNETH JOSEPH, retired bishop; b. Alpena, Mich., Apr. 19, 1924; s. Joseph Francis and Elizabeth (Jachcik) P. A.B., Sacred Heart Sem., Detroit, 1946; M.A., Cath. U. Am., 1950; postgrad., No. Mich. U., 1961, 63. Ordained priest Roman Catholic Ch., 1950; asst. pastorships, 1950-56; pastor in Port Sanilac Mich., 1956-57, Munger, Mich., 1957-60, Bay City, Mich., 1966-70; dean St. Paul Sem., Saginaw, Mich., 1960-66; vice rector St. Paul Sem., 1962-66; bishop of Crookston Minn., 1970-75; bishop of Lansing Mich., 1975-95; bd. consulators Diocese of Saginaw, 1966-70; instr. Latin and U.S. history St. Paul Sem., 1960-66. Weekly columnist Saginaw and Lansing diocesan newspapers. Bd. dirs. Cath. Charities Diocese Saginaw, 1969-70. Mem. Mich. Hist. Soc., Bay County Hist. Soc., Lions Club, KC (pres. Mich. Cath. Conf. 1985-95), Kiwanis.

POVOA, PEDRO MANUEL, physician, consultant; b. Aveiro, Portugal, May 14, 1962; m. Josue Rodrigues and Emilia Jesus (Sarmento) P.; m. Ana Paula Barbosa, May 27, 1989; 1 child, Joao Pedro. MD, U. Lisbon, 1986; diploma in internal medicine, U. London, 1992. House officer Hosp. St. Maria, Lisbon, 1987-88, registrar, 1989-93, cons., 1994-95; cons. Hosp. Garcia d'Orta, Almada, 1995—; rsch. asst. U. Lisbon, 1983-88, 92-95; cons. Infarmed, Lisbon, 1998—. Mem. editl. bd. Revista Portuguesa de Medicina Intensiva, 1998—; contbr. articles to profl. jours. Recipient award Internat. Fedn. Clin. Chemistry-AVL Med. Instruments AG, 1998. Mem. Soc. Portuguesa de Medicina Interna, Soc. Portuguesa de Cuidados Intensivos, European Soc. Intensive Care Medicine (Belgium). Avocations: photography, sailing. Home: R Diogo de Silves 38-B, 1400-107 Lisbon Portugal Office: Hosp Garcia de Orta, Pragal, 2800 Almada Portugal

POVSTENKO, YURIY ZINOVIY, mathematics educator, researcher; b. Myrhorod, Ukraine, May 5, 1949. MS, Lviv U., Ukraine, 1971; Candidate, Inst. Maths., Lviv, Ukraine, 1977; Doctor, Poly. U., St. Petersburg, Russia, 1993, Inst. Applied Problems of Mechanics and Math., Lviv, 1995. Young rschr. Inst. Math., Lviv, 1973-78; young rschr. Inst. Applied Problems of Mechanics and Math., 1978-80, sr. rschr., 1980-93, chief rschr., 1993—; prof. Inst. Applied Problems of Mech. and Math., 1998; asst. prof. Lviv U., 1988-95. Author: Introduction to the Mechanics of Surface Phenomena in Deformable Solids, 1985. Recipient grant Internat. Sci. Found., 1993, 98. Mem. Gesellschaft für angewandte Mathematik und Mechanik, N.Y. Acad. Scis. Avocation: chess. Office: Pidstryhach Inst, Naukova 3b, 79053 Lviv Ukraine

POVZNER, DMITRY MARKOVICH, executive; b. Ivanovo, Russia, Jan. 6, 1953; s. Mark Davidovich and Anna Grigorjavna (Getiskina) P.; m. Valentina Ivanovna Basheva, Jyly 25, 1978; children: Eugene, Kaeniya, Mark. Grad., Inst. Nat. Economy, Russia, 1978. Sr. economist Gen. Bank, Palana, Russia, 1978-79, deputy chief dept., 1979-82; mgr. Ctrl. Bank, Bolsheretsk, Russia, 1982-87; deputy mgr. Agropromhank, Petropavlovsk, Russia, 1987-89, mgr., 1989-90; pres. Kamchatcomagro, Petropavlovsk, Russia, 1990—; ch.n. bd. dirs. Picobank, Russia, 1992—, JS Fish Processing Plant, Russia, 1998—; bd. dirs. Fish Processing Plang #55, Kamachatka, Russia, UTRF, Russia. Mem. bd. guardians Kamchatka Eparchy, Russia, 1999. With Ikraine Mil., 1971-73. Avocations: fishing, skiing, travel, walking. Home: 10 Vitaly Kruchina St, 683000 Petropavlovsk Russia Office: Kamchatcomagroprombank, 683024 Petropavlovsk Russia

POWELL, ALAN, acoustical engineer, aeronautical engineer, mechanical engineer; b. Buxton, Derbyshire, Eng., Feb. 17, 1928; came to U.S., 1956; s. Frank and Gwendolen Marie (Walker) P.; m. June Sinclair, Mar. 28, 1956. Student, Buxton Coll., 1939-45; diploma in aeros., Loughborough Coll., 1948; BSc in Engring. with 1st class honors, London U., 1949; honours diploma 1st class, Loughborough Coll., 1949; D.Tech. (hon.), Loughborough U. Tech., 1980; PhD, U. Southampton, 1953. Chartered engr. Engr. Percival Aircraft Co., Luton, Eng., 1949-51; research asst. U. Southampton, Eng., 1951-53; lectr. U. Southampton, 1953-56; research fellow Calif. Inst. Tech., Pasadena, 1956-57; engr. Douglas Aircraft Co., 1956; assoc. prof. UCLA, 1957-62, prof. engring., 1962-65, head Aerosonics lab., 1957-65; assoc. tech. dir., head acoustics and vibration lab. David Taylor Model Basin, Dept. Navy, Washington, 1965-66; tech. dir. David Taylor Model Basin, Dept. Navy, 1966-67, David Taylor Naval Ship Research & Devel. Center, Bethesda, Md., 1967-85; mem. Undersea Warfare Research & Devel. Council, 1966-76, chmn., 1971-72; mem. council on Fed. Labs., 1972-85; prof. mech. engring. U. Houston, 1985-2000, chmn., 1985-87, prof. emeritus, 2000—; mem. com. on hearing bioacoustics and biomechs. NAS-NRC, 1961-85, exec. coun., 1963-65, chmn., 1965-66, advisor, 1985-95, mem. naval studies bd. 1990-95; mem. various coms. Naval Studies Bd. and Marine Bd., 1990-96; advisor Chinese U. Devel. Project, 1989-91; cons. Douglas Aircraft Co., various aerospace and acoustics cos., 1956-65; mem. adv. coun. Internat. Towing Tank Conf., 1981-85; mem. advisor U.S.-Japan Program Natural Resources, 1987-90, mem. Marine Facilities Panel; gen. chmn. 3d advanced vehicles conf. AIAA and Soc. Naval Archs. and Marine Engrs., 1976; chmn. internat. conf. Computer Aided Design, Manufacture and Ops. in Marine and Offshore Industries, 1987-88; cons. Sci. Applications Internat., Inc., 1987-90; governing bd. Am. Inst. Physics, 1995-97. Contbr. articles to profl. jours. Recipient Navy Meritorious Civilian Service award, 1970; Brit. Empire scholar, 1945; named Meritorious Exec. Pres. of U.S., 1982; Capt. Robert Dexter Conrad gold medal for sci. achievement Sec. Navy, 1984. Fellow Royal Aero. Soc. London (Baden-Powell prize 1948, Wilbur Wright prize 1953), Acoustical Soc. Am. (biennial award 1962, assoc. editor Jour. 1962-67, chmn. edn. com. 1964-66, exec. coun. 1966-69, chmn. medals and awards com. 1978-81, v.p. elect 1981-82, v.p. 1982-83, pres. elect 1989-90, pres. 1990-91, past pres. 1991-92, Silver medal in engring. acoustics 1992, designated Nat. Spkr. in Engring. Acoustics 1994-98), Inst. Mech. Engrs., Inst. Acoustics (U.K.); mem. AIAA (assoc. fellow, Aeroacoustics award 1980), ASME (Rayleigh lectr. 1988, Per Brüel Gold medal 1991), Inst. Noise Control Engrs. (initial mem., dir. 1974-77, Disting. lectr. 1975, 83, v.p. 1981-84, bd. cert. 1993), Acoustics, Speech and Signal Processing Soc. (exec. com. 1969-72, awards com. 1971-73, bylaws com. chmn. 1973-75), Am. Soc. Naval Engrs. (life), Am. Acad. Mechanics, Tau Beta Pi (hon. life). Office: U Houston Dept Mech Engring Houston TX 77204-0001

POWELL, BENJAMIN L., entertainment company executive; b. Boston, Sept. 26, 1970; s. Arthur George and Barbara Schieffelin Powell. AB, Haverford Coll., 1993; MS in Fgn. Sci., Georgetown U., 2000. Journalist The Mexico City News, 1993-94; dist. aide N.Y. State Senator Catherine Abate, N.Y.C., 1994-96; pres., founder City Golf Entretenimiento SA de CV, Puebla, Mexico, 1997—. Editor-in-chief Georgetown Jour. Internat. Affairs, 1999-2000. Del. Trilateral Conf. on NAFTA, Ottawa, Can., 1999. Mem. Nat. Pks. Conservation Assn., Am. Acad. Achievement, Groton Sch. Alumnae Assn. Democrat. Avocations: tennis, travel. E-mail: belopo@hotmail.com. Home: 1545 18th St NW Apt 921 Washington DC 20036-1345 Office: City Golf Entretenimiento, 45 Poniente 1908 La Noria, Puebla Mexico

POWELL, CHARLES DAVID (LORD POWELL OF BAYSWATER), merchant; b. Haywards, Heath, Eng., July 6, 1941; s. John Frederick and Geraldine Ysolda (Moylan) P.; m. Carla Bonardi, Oct. 24, 1964; children: Hugh, Nicholas. BA, New Coll. Oxford, Eng., 1963. Mem. H.M. Diplomatic Svc., London, 1963-83; pvt. sec., adviser fgn. affairs Lady Thatcher and subsequently John Major, London, 1983-91; dir. Jardine Matheson Holdings, 1991—; bd. dirs., chmn. internat. adv. bd. Nat. Westminster Bank, London, 1991-2000; bd. dirs. Louis-Vuitton Moet-Hennessy (LVMH), Paris, Said Holdings Ltd., Bermuda, Brit.-Mediterranean Airways Plc, London; pres. China-Britain Trade Group, 1992—; chmn. Singapore Brit. Bus. Coun., 1994—; mem. internat. adv. coun. Textron Inc., R.I., 1996—; trustee Aspen Inst., U.S.; chmn. bd. trustees Oxford U. Bus. Sch., 1998—; mem. European adv. bd. Rolls-Royce; mem. internat. adv. bd. Barrick Gold. Contbr. articles to profl. jours. Recipient Knigh Comdr., Order of St. Michael and St. George, 1990. Mem. Turf Club. Home: 1 Caroline Close, London W2 4RW, England Office: Matheson and Co, 3 Lombard St, London EC3V 9AQ, England

POWELL, CHRISTOPHER ROBERT, systems engineer, executive, computer scientist; b. Summit, N.J., Feb. 2, 1963; s. Robin Powell and Nancy Mae (Spurling) Gould; m. Bonnie Jean Manning, June 10, 1989; 1 child, Emilie Alyson Grace. BS in Math. and Computer Sci., Clarkson U., 1984; postgrad., Syracuse U., 1984-88, SUNY, Binghamton, 1988-90, U. Wis., Eau Claire, 1998—. Sr. assoc. program IBM Corp., Endicott, N.Y., 1984-90; sr. systems analyst/programmer Supercomputer Systems, Inc., Eau Claire, Wis., 1990-93; systems programmer prin. Network Systems Corp./Channel Networking Strategic Bus. Unit, Brooklyn Park, Minn., 1993-96; sys. engring. mgr. II Sequent Computer Sys., Eau Claire, Wis., 1996-99, IBM Corp., Eau Claire, Wis., 1999-2000; acting v.p., cons. bus. and program mgmt. Tonbu, Inc., Eau Claire, Wis., 2000—. Appt. City of Spring Lake Park Energy Commn., 1995; vice chmn. Energy Commn., 1996; treas. First Baptist Ch., Eau Claire, 2000—. Mem. Assn. for Computing Machinery, Nat. Systems Programmers Assn., NSC Leadership Forum, Alpha Phi Omega (torchbearer 1987-2000), Pi Mu Epsilon, Pi Delta Epsilon. Democrat. Mem. Am. Baptist Ch. Achievements include assisting in Network Systems and Sequent computer systems registration for ISO 9000. Home: 3311 W Country Club Ln Altoona WI 54720-1013

POWELL, DEBORAH ELIZABETH, pathologist; b. Lynn, Mass., Nov. 28, 1939. MD, Tufts U., 1965. Diplomate Am. Bd. Pathology. Intern Georgetown Med. Ctr., Washington, 1965-66; resident in pathology NIH, Bethesda, Md., 1966-69; exec. dean, vice-chancellor clin. affairs U. Kans. Sch. Medicine, Kansas City, 1997—; pres. U.S. & Canadian Acad. Pathology, Inc.; trustee Am. Bd. Pathology. Office: U Kans Sch Medicine 3901 Rainbow Blvd Kansas City KS 66160-0001

POWELL, DURWOOD ROYCE, lawyer; b. Raleigh, N.C., Nov. 21, 1951; s. Albert Royce and Powell; m. Leej Ida Copperfield, Mar. 1, 1980. BS, U. N.C., 1974, JD, 1979; LLM in Taxation, Emory U., 1985. Bar: N.C. 1979, U.S. Dist. Ct. (ea., mid. and we. dists.) N.C. 1981, U.S. Tax Ct. 1981, U.S. Ct. Appeals (4th cir.) 1984, U.S. Ct. Claims 1984, U.S. Supreme Ct. 1984, D.C. 1988, U.S. Ct. Appeals (D.C. cir.) 1988, N.Y. 1989. Mgmt. analyst GAO, Norfolk, Va., 1974-76; tax staff Arthur Andersen & Co., Washington, 1979-80; assoc. Biggs, Meadows, Etheridge & Johnson, Rocky Mount, N.C., 1980-82, Biggs Law Firm, Rocky Mount, 1982-83; prtnr. Maupin, Taylor, Ellis & Adams, Raleigh, N.C., 1985—, also bd. dirs., 1985—; adj. prof. corp. taxation Grad. Sch. Bus., U. N.C., Chapel Hill, 1989-92; faculty Duke U. Tax and Estate Planning Conf., 1991; mem. negotiation project Harvard U., Cambridge, Mass., 1992. Contbr. articles to profl. jours. Tax reform com. Duke U., Washington, 1988. Mem. ABA (tax, corp., banking and securities sects.), N.C. Bar Assn. (tax and corp. sects.), Phi Beta Kappa, Phi Eta Sigma. Home: 7616 Wingfoot Dr Raleigh NC 27615-5485 Office: Maupin Taylor Ellis & Adams 3200 Beech Leaf Ct Ste 500 Raleigh NC 27604-1064

POWELL, ERIC KARLTON, lawyer, researcher; b. Parkersburg, W.Va., July 23, 1958; s. James Milton and Sarah Elizabeth (Gates) P. BA in History, W.Va. U., 1980, BSBA, 1981; JD, Western State U., Fullerton, Calif., 1987. Bar: Ga. 1992, W.Va. 1993, U.S. Dist. Ct. (we. dist.) W.Va. 1993. Reference libr. Western State U., 1984; tchr. acctg. Rosary H.S., Fullerton, 1984-85; law clk. Zonni, Ginnochio Taylor, Santa Ana, Calif., 1986-93; temp. law sch. Gibson, Dunn & Crutcher, Irvine, Calif., 1993; pvt. practice, Parkersburg, 1993—. Asst. scoutmaster Boy Scouts Am., Parkersburg, 1981-83. Mem. ABA, ATLA, W.Va. Trial Lawyers Assn., Nat. Eagle Scout Assn., Elks, Delta Theta Phi. Republican. Presbyterian. Avocations: hiking, reading, canoeing, chess, astronomy. Home: 2002 20th St Parkersburg WV 26101-3606 Office: 500 Green St Parkersburg WV 26101-5131

POWELL, JOHN CONSTANTINE, artist; b. Jamaica, Aug. 17, 1960; s. James and Tressiline (Johnson) P. Degree, U. West Indies Sch. Visual Art, 1990. Tchr. St. Andrew H.S. for Girls, Kingston, Jamaica, 1990-91, Bridgeport Comprehensive H.S., Kingston, 1993—; artist-in-residence Braco Village, 1997. Exhibited in one-man shows at The School of Visual Art, Jamaica, 1990; group exhbns. include Jamaica Cultural Devel. Commn., 1987, 89, 90, 91, 92, 93, Nat. Gallery of Jamaica, 1990, 91, 92, 93, 94, 95, 96, 98, Mut. Life Gallery, 1991, 92, 94, 95, 96, 98-99, The Bay Gallery, 1993, 94, Chelsea Galleries, 1991, Le Meridien Jamaica Pegasus Gallery, 1998, 99.

Mem. Metro. Mus. Art. Avocations: reading, classical music, playing violin. Address: PO Box 1229, Mandeville Jamaica Office: Victor Dixon High Sch, Mandeville, Manchester Jamaica

POWELL, JOHN WILLIAM, mechanical engineer, consultant; b. Bristol, Eng., Aug. 1, 1937; s. Cyril William and Hilda Emily May (Preece) P.; m. Katherine Maureen March, Aug. 27, 1960 (div. Aug. 1990); children: Robin John William, Adrian Edward, Steven Martin; m. Josephine Abena Akom, May 10, 1991; 1 child, Ohema Akosa Brenda. BSc in Engring., U. Southampton, (Eng.), 1960; PhD, U. Southampton, 1963. Chartered engr. Tech. dir. Westwind Air Bearings Ltd., Poole, Eng., 1963-68; sr. sci. officer U.K. Atomic Energy Authority, Winfrith, Eng., 1968-71; sr. lectr. U. Sci. and Tech., Kumasi, Ghana, 1971-72; dir. Tech. Cons. Ctr., Kumasi, 1972-86, GRATIS Project, Tema, Ghana, 1987-92; chief exec. I.T. Ghana, Accra, 1992—; dir. Westwind A.B. Ltd., Poole Dorset, 1968-71, Midway Tech. Ltd., U.K., 1993—; internat. tech. tng. expert UNIDO/MPI, Hanoi, Vietnam. Editor, part author: Gas Lubrication, 1964, Design of Aerostatic Bearings, 1971, The Intermediate Technology Transfer Unit, 1986, 95, The Survival of the Fitter, 1995. Officer Order of Brit. Empire, Queen Elizabeth II, New Year Honours, 1991. Fellow Instn. Mech. Engrs. (London), Ghana Instn. Engrs. Achievements include 12 patents in field of gas lubrication. Office: Intermediate Tech Ghana, PO Box 7894, Accra Ghana

POWELL, LOUISE FOX, real estate developer; b. Hickory, N.C., June 14, 1925; d. Lester Lee and Vesta Boliek Fox; m. Nelson Sherril Powell, May 23, 1953 (dec.); children: Cynthia Louise, Joan Marie, Suzanne Jayne. Grad. in Bus., King's Coll., Charlotte, N.C., 1942. Time study engr. Glenn L. Martin Co., Balt., 1942-44; owner, mgr. Isenhour Fabric Co., Lenoir, N.C., 1949-53; rsch. mgr. Alfred Politz Rsch., Tampa, Fla., 1957-63; cemetary sales mgr. Southea. Advt. and Sales, Hickory and Atlanta, 1954-56; owner, mgr. Louise Powell Realty, Hickory, 1964—; pres., owner Benson-Fox Assocs., Ltd., Hickory, 1986—; owner, mgr. Fairway Shopping Ctrs., Inc., Hickory, 1989—. Leader Girl Scouts U.S., Hickory and Tampa, 1967—; active First United Meth. Ch., Hickory; mem. Hickory Mus. Arts, 1983—, Am. Legion Aux., Hickory, 1973—, Hickory Cmty. Theatre. Avocations: helping others, dolls, quilting, dancing, music. Home: 1235 10th Street Blvd NW Hickory NC 28601-2367

POWELL, MARTIN JOHN, physicist; b. Manchester, England, Dec. 31, 1951; s. Frederick and Betty (Plant) P.; m. Judith Davies, July 4, 1975 (div. 1995); 1 child, Andrew Simon. BA, Cambridge U., 1973, MA, 1977, PhD, 1977, ScD, 1992. Mem. tech. staff Philips Rsch. Labs., England, 1977—; vis. prof. Dundee (Scotland) U., 1991—; mem. electronic materials com. Sci. and Engring. Rsch. Coun., 1991-94. Contbr. articles to profl. jours.; guest editor: IEE Procs. Part G, 1992. Recipient Paterson medal and prize Inst. Physics, 1988. Fellow Inst. Elec. Engrs. (profl. group com. 1992-98), Inst. Physics. Achievements include research in the physics of amorphous silicon thin film transistors; led team which developed first color liquid crystal television in Europe and developed amorphous silicon large area image sensors. Office: Philips Rsch Labs, Redhill, Surrey RH1 5HA, England

POWELL, SIR (ARNOLD JOSEPH) PHILIP, architect; b. Bedford, Eng., Mar. 15, 1921; s. Arnold and Winnifred (Walker) P.; m. Philippa Powell, Jan. 17, 1953; children: Dido, Ben. AA Diploma Sch. Architecture, Epsom Coll. Ptnr. Powell and Moya, London, 1946-91. Prin. works include Churchill Gardens flats, Westminster, 1948-62, Skylon for Festival of Britain, 1951, Chichester Theater, 1962, Brit. Pavilion Expo70, Osaka, Japan, 1970, Mayfield Sch., Putney, 1955, Picture Gallery Christ Ch., Oxford, 1967, Mus. of London, 1977, London and Manchester Assurance HQ, 1978, Queen Elizabeth II Conf. Ctr., 1986, Queen's Bldg., Royal Holloway Coll., Egham and labs., 1986-90; extensions Brasenose Coll., Oxford, 1961, Christ Ch., 1967, Corpus Christi Coll., Oxford, 1969, St. John's Coll. Cambridge, 1967, Wolfson Coll., Oxford, 1974, Queens' Coll., Cambridge, 1976, Hosps. at Swindon, Slough, High Wycombe, Wythenshawe, Woolwich, Maidstone, Hastings, Ashington, Great Ormond Street (London), 1960-92. Mem. Royal Fin. Art Commn., London, 1969-94; trustee Soane Mus., London. Decorated officer Order Brit. Empire, 1957, Companion of Honour, 1984; recipient Royal Gold medal Royal Inst. Brit. Architects, 1974. Mem. Royal Acad. Arts (trustee and treas. 1985-95).

POWELL, SIMON EDWARD MEREDITH, management and business consultant; b. Solihull, Eng., Aug. 31, 1953; s. Geoffrey Meredith and Mary Margaret (Macleod) P. BSc in Bus. Adminstrn. with honors, U. Bath, Somerset, Eng., 1976; MBA, City U., London, 1990, Diploma in Fin. Svcs. Treasury mgr. Natwest Markets, London, 1988-89, sr. corp. fin. exec., 1990-93; head corp. banking Asia Pacific Natwest Markets, Hong Kong, 1993-94; dir. investment banking Natwest Markets, London, 1994-95, head corp. lending svc., 1995-97; mng. dir. CASEwise Systems Ltd., 1997-98; prin. Styal Mgmt. Assocs., 1999—; vis. tutor City U. Bus. Sch., London, 1993—. Bd. govs. Priory Sch., London, 1995-96. Fellow Royal Soc. Arts; mem. Assn. MBAs, Chartered Inst. Bankers (assoc.). Avocations: travel, rugby, tennis, music, theatre. Home: 51 Somerset Rd Wimbledon, London SW19 5RT, England

POWELL, STEPHEN WALTER, judge; b. Hamilton, Ohio, Jan. 25, 1955; s. Walter E. and Bobbi M. (Powell) P.; m. Kathryn Powell; children: Eric R.W., S. Michael; stepchildren: Greggory A., Garrett A. BA, Heidelberg Coll., 1977; JD, U. Dayton, 1981. Bar: Ohio 1981, U.S. Dist. Ct. (so. dist.) Ohio 1982. Referee Common Pleas Ct., Juvenile, Domestic and Probate, Hamilton, 1984-88; ptnr. Powell, Napier, Carmella and Allen, Hamilton, 1986-91; judge Area II Ct., Butler County, Ohio, 1989-91; judge probate div. Butler County Common Pleas Ct., Hamilton, 1991-95; presiding judge Ohio Ct. Appeals, 12th Appellate Dist., Middletown, 1995-97, adminstrv. judge, 1997-98, presiding judge, 1999—; agt. Commonwealth Land Title, Louisville, 1998-90; parliamentarian Judges Assn. Ohio Ct. Appeals, 1995—. Sec. Butler County Rep. Cen. Com., 1982-88; trustee Union Twp., Butler County, West Chester, 1979-88; bd. dirs. United Way Hamilton Area, 1986-90. Named Man of the Day Sta. WMOH, Hamilton, 1986; recipient Meritorious Svc. award Ohio Assn. Probate Judges, 1992, 93, 94. Mem. ABA, Ohio Bar Assn., Butler County Bar Assn. Presbyterian. Office: Ohio Ct Appeals 12th Appellate Dist 1 City Centre Plz # 1009 Middletown OH 45042-1901

POWELL, THOMAS EDWARD, III, biological supply company executive, physician; b. Elon College, N.C., Aug. 1, 1936; s. Thomas Edward, Jr., and Sophia Maude (Sharpe) P.; m. Betty Durham Yeager, June 19, 1965; children: Frances Powell Barnes, Thomas Edward IV, Caroline Powell Rogers. AB in Biology, Va. Mil. Inst., 1957; MD, Duke U., 1961; MA, Harvard U., 1966. Surgeon USPHS, 1966-68; co-founder Biomed. Reference Labs., Inc., Burlington, N.C., 1969, exec. v.p., 1969-75, chmn. exec. com., 1979-82, also dir.; exec. v.p. Carolina Biol. Supply Co., Burlington, N.C., 1968-80, chmn., 1977-80, 94—, pres., 1980-94; pres. Wolfe Sales Corp., Burlington, 1980-84, Waubun Labs. Inc., Schriever, La., 1980—, Bobbitt Labs., Inc., Burlington, 1983-94; bd. mgrs. Wachovia Bank and Trust Co. N.A., Burlington. Contbr. articles to profl. jours. Bd. dirs. United Way Alamance County, Burlington, 1968—; bd. dirs. Elon Coll., N.C., 1968—, sec., 1975—; bd. dirs. Am. Cancer Soc., Burlington, 1971-81; bd. dirs. Burlington Day Sch., 1973—, pres., 1974-78, 80-84; bd. dirs. N.C. Citizens for Bus. and Industry, Raleigh, 1983-87, Nat. Found. for Study of Religion and Econs., Greensboro, 1984-88, Blue Ridge Sch., Dyke, Va., 1985-90. Served to capt. USAR, 1957-66. Recipient Citizens Service award Elon Coll. Alumni Assn., 1980. Mem. Assn. Biology Lab. Edn., N.C. Acad. Sci., Alamance-Caswell Med. Soc., N.C. Med. Soc., Assn. Venture Founders, Newcomen Soc. Democrat. Mem. United Ch. of Christ. Clubs: Alamance Country (Burlington); Capital City (Raleigh, N.C.); Congl. Country (Washington); N.C. Country (Pinehurst); Hope Valley Country (Durham, N.C.); Greensboro City.

POWELL, THOMAS ERVIN, financial consultant, small business owner; b. Trion, Ga., Mar. 19, 1947; s. Ervin and Myrtice (Wike) P.; m. Lana Lois Lang, June 20, 1976; children: Thomas Christopher, Alissa Lynne, Ashley Beth. BS, U. Ctrl. Fla., 1974, MS, 1977; postgrad. studies, U. Fla., 1979. CPA, Fla.; cert. internal auditor. Pub. acct. KPMG Peat Marwick, Orlando, Fla., 1974-75, Arthur Andersen & Co., Orlando, 1975-77; instr. acctg. U. Ctrl. Fla., Orlando, 1977-81; dir. Inst. Internal Auditors, Altamonte Springs, Fla., 1981-95; pres. The Powell Group, Inc., Windermere, Fla., 1996—; dir. of consulting Graham & Cottrill, PA, 1998—; mem. accreditation com. Am. Assembly Collegiate Schs. Bus., 1992-93; adj. prof. Rollins Coll., Winter Park, Fla., 1999—. Author: Examination Writer's Guide, 1978, rev. edit., 1991, 96; mem. editl. bd. Issues in Acctg. Edn. Jour., 1995—. Vice chmn. audit bd. City of Orlando, 1990-95; treas. Christian Endowment Found., 1996—; chmn. Practice Advising Coun.; mem. Orlando/Orange County Airport Zoning Bd., 1997—; chmn. adv. coun. West Orange H.S., 1997-98; mem. West Orange H.S. Found.; mem. strategic dir. com. Orange County Pub. Schs, 1997-98. With USAF, 1967-71. Mem. AICPA, Am. Acctg. Assn. (profl. exam. com. 1986-89, 93-98, audit edn. conf. com. 1990-93, mem. profl. rels. com. 1997-98, v.p. profl. practices 1994-96, chmn. practice adv. coun. 1996—), Inst. Internal Auditors, Fla. Soc. CPAs (edn. com. 1990-93, legis. com. 1991), Beta Alpha Psi (adv. coun. 1993-95, Alumnus of Yr. U. Ctrl. Fla. 1992), Beta Gamma Sigma. Republican. Avocations: guitar, skiing, photography. Home: 1938 Maple Leaf Dr Windermere FL 34786-8003 Office: The Powell Group Inc PO Box 766 Gotha FL 34734-0766

POWELL, WILLIAM ARNOLD, JR., retired banker; b. Verbena, Ala., July 7, 1929; s. William Arnold and Sarah Frances (Baxter) P.; m. Barbara Ann O'Donnell, June 16, 1956; children: William Arnold III, Barbara Calhoun, Susan Thomas, Patricia Crain. BSBA, U. Ala., 1953; grad., La. State U. Sch. Banking of South, 1966. With Am. South Bank, N.A., Birmingham, Ala., 1953—, asst. v.p., 1966, v.p., 1967, v.p., br. supr., 1968-72, sr. v.p., br. supr., 1972-73, exec. v.p., 1973-79, pres., 1979-83, vice chmn. bd., 1983-93, also bd. dirs.; pres. AmSouth Bancorp., 1979—; bd. dirs. AmSouth Bank Fla., AmSouth Bancorp. Bd. dirs. United Way Found., Warrior-Tombigbee Devel. Assn.; life trustee Ala. Ind. Colls., trustee Ala. Hist. Soc., Birmingham Hist. Soc.; past pres. United Way, campaign chmn., 1987; mem. pres.'s coun. U. Ala., Birmingham; life mem. bd. visitors U. Ala. Lt. AUS, 1954-56. Mem. The Club, Mountain Brook, Birmingham Country Club, Hoover Country Club (Birmingham), Birmingham Area C. of C. (life mem. bd. dirs.). Home: 2114 Hickory Ridge Cir Birmingham AL 35243-2925

POWELL, WILLIAM COUNCIL, SR., service company executive; b. Burlington, N.C., Nov. 5, 1948; s. Thomas Edward Jr. and Annabelle (Council) P.; m. Jacqueline Garrison, July 3, 1976; children: William C. Jr., Ashley C. Student, U. S.C., 1968-69; BS, Va. Mil. Inst., 1971; MBA, Wake Forest U., 1974; postgrad., Elon Coll., 1972. Lic. pilot. Lic. real estate broker, N.C. Adminstrv. assoc. Carolina Biol. Supply Co., Inc., Burlington, 1971-91; also bd. dirs.; v.p. Bobbitt Labs., Burlington, 1974-77; pres., 1977-82; owner HEADS, Inc., 1978—, pres., 1984—; owner Ashwil Acres Farm, Mebane, N.C., 1981—; pres. Granite Diagnostics, Inc., Burlington, 1981-84, UST Specialists Inc., 1991—; owner Powell Real Estate, Burlington, 1979—, bd. dirs. Excalibur Lock Co., Inc., Burlington; Warren Land Co., 1990-94, pres., 1994—, Merrymount Property Owners Assn., Inc., pres., 1996—; pres. Merrymount Boat Slip Assn., Inc., 1996—, Stratonet Inc., Burlington, 1996—; v.p. fin., bd. dirs. Environ. Responsible Bus. Inc., 1992-97; mem. Babcock Sch. Alumni Coun. Wake Forest U., 1981-85; bd. dirs. Waubun Labs., Inc., Schriever, La.; mgr. Macon Farm, 1992-95; chmn. bd. Ensci Corp., Inc., 1991-95, ptnr. Port Assocs., 1987—, Port Assocs. II, 1992—; chmn. bd. Netpath Inc., 1995-96; filed for election N.C. Senate, 2000. Bd. advisors Elon Coll. (N.C.), 1984-86, bd. visitors, 1987-92; bd. advisors Duke U. Marine Lab., Beaufort, N.C., 1985-92; nat. adv. coun. Baruch Marine Inst., 1998—; mem. adv. panel Air Quality Compliance Panel State of N.C. Dept. Environ. Health and Natural Resources, 1994—; guardian mem. Boy Scouts Am., Burlington, 1985; trustee Dr. T.E. Powell Jr. Trust, 1989-95; v.p. fin. Cherokee Coun. Boy Scouts of Am., 1990-92, exec. bd., 1990-94, exec. bd. Old N. State Coun., 1994-95; mem. Front St. United Meth. Ch., Burlington, N.C. Capt. USAR, 1971-79. Recipient Bill Fish Cert. State of S.C., 1983, 2 Bill Fish Certs. State of N.C., 1990, Sower's award Duke U., 1985, N.C. Gov.'s Cup for Billfishing, 1991, 3rd Pl., Big Rock Blue Marlin Tourn, 1998. Mem. NRA (life), Newcomen Soc. N.Am. (life mem.), Billiard Congress Am., Am. Angus Assn., Billiard and Bowling Inst. Assn., N.C. Forestry Assn. (legis. affairs com. 1994—), N.C. Wildlife Habitat Found. (life), Ducks Unltd. (area chmn. 1985-87, 97—), N.C. Chpt. Safari Club Internat. (state pres. 1985-88, life mem.), Aircraft Owners and Pilots Assn., Cessna Owner Orgn., Atlantic Coast Conservation Assn. (life), Nat. Soc. of SAR, Alamance Wildlife Club (bd. dirs. 1992-95, pres. 1999—), Rolls Royce Owners Club, N.Am. Hunting Club (life), Found. N.Am. Wild Sheep (life), Chaine des Rotisseurs (chevalier 1991), Brotherhood of the Knights of the Vine (master knight 1991), 10 Point Hunt Club, Am. Angus Assn., Nat. Wild Turkey Fedn., Quail Unltd. (life), N.C. Cattlemans Assn., Nat. Cattlemans Assn., Inc., Internet Users Group Alamance, Debordieu Club, Alamance County Cattleman's Assn., Citation Fishing Team (capt. 1979—), Alamance Country Club, Debordieu Beach Club, Litchfield Carriage House Club. E-mail: wcp@netpath.net. Home: 1109 W Front St Burlington NC 27215-3610 Office: HEADS Inc 2608 NC Hwy 100 Elon College NC 27244-8539 also: Stratonet Inc 2260 S Church St Ste 601 Burlington NC 27215-5380

POWER, DESMOND JOHN, special education educator, consultant; b. Cobden, Victoria, Australia, Mar. 23, 1936; s. John Patrick and Bridget Teresa Power; m. Mary Rose O'Kane; children: Lucy, Benedict, Linus, Peter. BA, U. Melbourne, Victoria, 1968, MEd, 1971; PhD, U. Ill., 1972. Queensland state registered tchr.; Queensland state registered psychologist. Tchr. Victorian Sch. for Deaf Children, Melbourne, 1956-60, Glendonald Sch. for Deaf Children, Melbourne, 1961-72; sr. lectr., dir. of rsch. Inst. Spl. Edn. Burwood State Coll., Melbourne, 1972-77; prof. spl. edn., dir. Ctr. for Deafness Studies and Rsch. Griffith U., Brisbane, Queensland, Australia, 1978—; spl. edn. and disability cons., Australia, 1978—. Named Mem. of Order of Australia, Australian Govt., 1994. Roman Catholic. Avocations: reading, gardening, walking. Fax: 617 3875 5942. E-mail: d.power@mailbox.gu.edu.au. Office: Griffith U, Kessels Rd, Nathan Queensland 4122, Australia

POWER, EDWARD GERARD MARTIN, microbiologist; b. Gibraltar, Mar. 16, 1965; s. Edward and Marie Carmen (Romero) P.; m. Abigail Anne Diaz, Aug. 19, 1988 (div. Sept., 1999); 1 child, Craig Edward; m. Joanne Lee Ravenscroft, Feb. 18, 2000; 1 child, Rebecca Sharon. BSc in Microbiology with Honors, U. Bristol, Eng., 1986; PhD, U. Wales, 1989. Postdoctoral fellow UMDS, London, 1989-91, lectr., 1991-95, 1995-98; asst. dir., microbiology/sr. advisor Smithkline Beecham Internat., 1998—; cons. Ministry of Def., Eng., 1993; editor: Letters in Applied Microbiology, 1993—, jour. od Applied Microbiology. Contbg. author: Introduction to the Principles of Drug Design, 1996, Pharmaceutical Microbiology. Mem. Soc. Applied Bacteriology (com. mem. 1994-97, hon. gen. sec. 1997—, recipient Rsch. award 1992, W.H. Pierce Meml. prize 1995), Soc. Gen. Microbiology, Brit. Soc. Antimicrobial Chemotherapy. Roman Catholic. Avocations: sports, literature, wining and dining, fgn. travel. Office: Smithkline Beecham Internat, SB House Greta West Road, Brentford Middlesex TW8 9BD, England

POWER, JOHN BRUCE, lawyer; b. Glendale, Calif., Nov. 11, 1936; m. Sandra Garfield, Apr. 27, 1998; children by previous marriage: Grant, Mark, Boyd. AB magna cum laude, Occidental Coll., 1958; JD, NYU, 1961; postdoctoral, Columbia U., 1972. Bar: Calif. 1962. Assoc. O'Melveny & Myers, L.A., 1961-70, ptnr., 1970-97; resident ptnr. O'Melveny & Myers, Paris, 1973-75; Sheffelman disting. lectr. Sch. Law, U. Wash., Seattle, 1997; mem. Social Svcs. Commn. City of L.A., 1993, pres., 1993; pres. circle, exec. com. Occidental Coll., 1979-82, 91-94, chair, 1993-94. Contbr. articles to jours. Bd. dirs. Met. L.A. YMCA, 1988—, treas., 1998—; mem. bd. mgrs. Stuart Ketchum Downtown YMCA, 1985-92, pres., 1989-90; mem. Los Angeles County Rep. Ctrl. Com., 1962-63; trustee Occidental Coll., 1992—, vice chmn., 1998—. Root Tilden scholar. Fellow Am. Coll. Comml. Fin. Lawyers (bd. regents 1999—); mem. ABA (comml. fin. svcs. com., com. 3d party legal opinions, UCC com., bus. law sect.), Am. Bar Found. (life), Calif. Bar Assn. (chmn. partnerships and unincorporated assns. com. 1982-83, chmn. uniform commn. code com. 1984-85, exec. com. 1987-91, chmn. bus. law sect. 1990-91, chmn. coun. sect. chairs 1992-93, liaison to state bar commn. on future of legal profession and state bar), L.A. County Bar Assn. (exec. com. comml. law and bankruptcy sect. 1970-73, 86-89), Internat. Bar Assn., Fin. Lawyers Conf. (bd. govs. 1982—, pres. 1984-85), Exec. Svc. Corps (sec. 1985-2000, vice chair 2000—, trustee 1994—), Occidental Coll. Alumni Assn. (pres. 1967-68), Phi Beta Kappa (councilor So. Calif. 1982—, pres. 1990-92). Office: O Melveny & Myers 400 S Hope St Los Angeles CA 90071-2899

POWER, JONATHAN RICHARD A., columnist; b. North Mimms, United Kingdom, June 4, 1941; s. Patrick Baker and Dorothy (Cobham) P.; m. Anne Hayward, Dec. 22, 1964 (div. 1986); children: Carmen, Miriam, Lucy; life ptnr. Jean-Christine Eklund, 1 child, Jenny. BA, Manchester U., 1963; MS, U. Wis., 1966. Agrl. officer Ministry Agr., Dares, Tanzania, 1963-64; freelance writer, filmmaker London, 1966-73; columnist Internat. Herald Tribune, Paris, 1973—; cons. Aspen (Colo.) Inst., 1973, UN Emergency Office for Africa, N.Y.C., Internat. Fund Agrl. Devel., 1991-92. Author: Development Economics, 1967, World of Hunger, 1975, New Proletariat, 1979, Against Oblivion, 1981, A Vision of Hope-The Fiftieth Anniversary of the United Nations, 1995, Like Water on Stone-The Story of Amnesty International, 2001; producer: It's Ours Whatever They Say, 1972. Recipient Silver medal Venice Film Festival, 1972. Mem. Internat. Inst. for Strategic Studies. Roman Catholic. Avocations: walking, cycling, opera. Home and Office: Little House, Lincombe Ln, Boars Hill, Oxford England

POWER, MICHAEL W., physician, consultant; b. Dublin, Ireland, June 25, 1962; s. James F. and Mary B. (Devitt) P.; m. Melanie J. Strickland; 1 child, Eoin. MB BCh, U. Coll. Dublin, 1986. Diplomate in critical care medicine Am. Bd. Internal Medicine. Intern, house officer St. Vincent's Hosp., Dublin, 1986-88; resident in internal medicine Med. Coll. Wis., Milw., 1988-91; registrar Eastern Regional Anaesthetic Tng. Programme, Dublin, 1991-97; fellow faculty anaesthesia Royal Coll. Surgeons in Ireland, Dublin, 1995-97; fellow in multidisciplinary critical care tng. program U. Pitts. Med. Ctr., 1997-99; cons. anaesthetist Beaumont Hosp., Dublin, 1999—. Fellow Royal Coll. Surgeons (Ireland); mem. Intensive Care Soc. Ireland, Soc. Critical Care Medicine. Avocation: Irish language. Office: Beaumont Hosp, Dept Anaesthesia, Dublin 9, Ireland

POWERS, ARLENE JORDON, lawyer; b. Plainfield, N.J., Jan. 23, 1963; d. Walter Matthew and Dorothy Jordon; m. James Francis Powers, Jan. 12, 1961; children: Rachael, Sarah, Olivia. BS ChE, Tufts U., 1985; JD, Suffolk U., 1991. Bar: Mass. 1991, U.S. Dist. Ct. Mass. 1992. Assoc. Samuels, Gauthier & Stevens, Boston, 1991—. Mem. Boston Patent Law Assn. Home: 3 Winnicunnett Way South Easton MA 02375-1464 Office: 225 Franklin St Ste 3300 Boston MA 02110-2898

POWERS, DAVID MURPHY, consumer products company executive; b. Lumberton, N.C., Oct. 27, 1959; s. Russell Hall Powers and Elizabeth Gwyne Atkins; m. Shreita Taylor, June 11, 1988. BA in Econs., BA in Bus. Mgmt., N.C. State U., 1983; MBA, Campbell U., 1988. Field rep. Helms for Senate Com., Raleigh, N.C., 1983-85; real estate rep. Franchise Enterprises, Inc., Rocky Mount, N.C., 1986-88; asst. v.p. facilities So. Nat. Bank, Lumberton, 1988-89; exec. dir. Internat. Shooting and Hunting Alliance, Washington, 1989-91; intergovernmental rels. officer U.S. Dept. Housing and Urban Devel., Washington, 1991-92; dir. state govt. rels. Smokeless Tobacco Coun., Washington, 1993-95, R.J. Reynolds Tobacco Co., Winston-Salem, N.C., 1995—; mem. White House Initiative on Rural Econ. Devel., U.S. Dept. Housing and Urban Devel., Washington, 1991-92. Nat. Conv. alt. Rep. Nat. Com., Rep. Conv., New Orleans, 1988; conv. staff Dole/Kemp 1996, San Diego, 1996; fund raising com. Bush for Pres. 2000, N.C., 1999-2000. Mem. Nat. Rep. Legislators Assn. (policy com. 1999—), Washington Area State Rels. Group. Methodist. Avocations: jogging, reading, hunting, classical and jazz music. E-mail: powersd@rjrt.com. Office: RJ Reynolds Tobacco Co PO Box 2959 Winston Salem NC 27102-2959

POWERS, ELIZABETH WHITMEL, lawyer; b. Charleston, S.C., Dec. 16, 1949; d. Francis Persse and Jane Coleman Cotten (Wham) P.; m. John Campbell Henry, June 11, 1994 (dec. Jan. 1997); m. Henry C. B. Lindh, June 16, 2000. AB, Mt. Holyoke Coll., 1971; JD, U. S.C., 1978. Bar: S.C. 1978, N.Y. 1979. Law clk. to justice S.C. Cir. Ct., Columbia; assoc. Reid & Priest, N.Y.C., 1978-86, ptnr., 1986-97; of counsel LeBoeuf, Lamb, Greene & MacRae, N.Y.C., 1997—. Exec. editor S.C. Law Rev., Columbia, 1977-78. Bd. dirs. The Seamen's Ch. Inst., 1996—, sec., 1999—; vol. N.Y. Jr. League, N.Y.C., 1983—; bd. trustees Ch. Club, 1991-94, 97—, v.p. 1992-94. Mem. ABA, S.C. Bar Assn., Nat. Soc. Colonial Dames of Am. (parliamentarian 1994—), Nat. Soc. Colonial Dames in State of N.Y. (pres. 1992-95). Avocations: bridge, tennis.

POWERS, JOHN HENRY, communications educator; b. Valparaiso, Ind., Oct. 7, 1947; s. Henry Verdell and Mary Helen (Anderson) P.; m. Gwendolyn Gong, Mar. 14, 1987; 1 child, Devereux Gong Powers. BA, Milligan Coll., 1969; MA, U. Denver, 1974, PhD, 1977. Cert. h.s. tchr., Ohio, 1969. H.s. tchr. Orrville (Ohio) Pub. Schs., 1969-70, Rockford (Ill.) Pub. Schs., 1970-73; asst. prof. to assoc. prof. comm. Tex. A&M U., College Station, 1977-93; assoc. prof. comm. Hong Kong Bapt. U., 1993—; vis. assoc. prof. comm. Malaysia Inst. Tech., Shah Alam, 1988; assoc. head dept. comm. Tex. A&M U., 1990-93; acting head dept. comm. Hong Kong Bapt. U., 1994-95. Author: Public Speaking: The Lively Art, 1994; co-editor: (with A.R. Kluver) Civic Discourse, Civil Society and Chinese Community, 1999; contbr. articles to profl. jours. Treas. Shatin (Hong Kong) Jr. PTA, 1997-98. Mem. Nat. Comm. Assn. (Disting. Scholar award 2000), Internat. Comm. Assn., So. States Comm. Assn. Democrat. Avocation: tennis. Office: Hong Kong Bapt U, Dept Comm Studies, Kowloon Tong, Hong Kong

POWERS, JOHN KIERAN, lawyer; b. Schenectady, Aug. 2, 1947; s. Paul Joseph and Anne Marie (Leahy) P.; children: Erin Kelly, Megan Kerry. BS, U. Notre Dame, 1969; JD, Union U., 1972. Bar: N.Y. 1973, U.S. Dist. Ct. (no. dist.) N.Y. 1973, U.S. Dist. Ct. (so., ea. and we. dists.) N.Y. 1982, U.S. Ct. Appeals (2d cir.) 1984, U.S. Supreme Ct. 1985, U.S. Dist. Ct. Vt. 1988. Assoc. Medwin and McMahon, Albany, 1973-77; pvt. practice law Albany, 1973-80; pres. John K. Powers, P.C., Albany, 1980-87; ptnr. Powers and Santola, Albany, 1987—. Contbr. articles to profl. publs. Trustee N.Y. State Lawyers Polit. Action Com., 1983-88, treas., 1989-93, chair, 1993—; trustee ATLA Polit. Action Com., 1995-98. Fellow Roscoe Pound Found. Mem. ABA (sustaining vice-chair, legis. subcom., automobile law com., trial and ins. practice sect., state leader com. on state legis. sect.), Nat. Coll. Adv. (co-founder), ATLA (life, state del. 1990, bd. govs. 1990—, exec. com. 1995—), Am. Bd. Trial Advocates (advocate), N.Y. State Bar Assn. (sustaining, lectr., exec. com. and chmn. legis. com. trial lawyers sect.), N.Y. State Trial Lawyers Assn. (sustaining, bd. dirs. 1983-88, chmn. key person legis. com., chmn. pubs. com., chmn. atty. referral com., exec. com. 1986—, treas. 1988-89, v.p. 1989-91, 1st v.p. 1990-91, pres.-elect 1991-92, pres. 1992-93, award of merit 1990, 94, award of excellence 1991, Pres. award 1995, 96, 98, 99, 2000, dist. svc. award 1997), N.Y. Trial Lawyers Inst. (lectr. and program chmn. 1981—, treas. 1988-89, pres. 1992-93), (life) N.Y. State Head Injury Assn. (co-counsel 1983-85, bd. dirs. 1992-93, 1st v.p. 1993—), Capitol Dist. Trial Lawyers Assn. (bd. dirs. 1979-81, v.p. 1983-85, pres. 1985-86), Pa. Trial Lawyers Assn., Alban County Bar Assn. (lectr.), Chief Judge's Com. to Improve Availability of Legal Svcs., Chief Judge's Pro-Bono Monitoring Com., Civil Justice Found. (guest lectr. Law Sch. NYU, Albany Law Sch., U. Syracuse Law Sch., Albany Med. Coll.), Trial Lawyers for Pub. Justice, Lions (pres. Scotia, N.Y. chpt. 1979-80). Democrat. Roman Catholic. Home and Office: 39 N Pearl St Albany NY 12207-2785

POWERS, KAREN ELIZABETH, medical research administrator; b. Warren, Ohio, Jan. 6, 1955; d. Shannon Curtis and Charlene (MacAtee) P.; 1 child, Elizabeth Sutliffe Grady Powers. BA, Emory U., 1977; MBA, Columbia U., 1980; MA, Boston U., 1995. Asst. treas. The Bank of N.Y., N.Y.C., 1980-87; rsch. asst. Harvard U. Med. Sch., Boston, 1993-95; project coord. Harvard Sch. Pub. Health, Boston, 1996-98, project mgr. The Coll. Alcohol Study, 1998—. Mem. Concord Runners. Episcopalian. E-mail: Kpowers@hsph.harvard.edu. Home: 12 Emerson Gdns Lexington MA 02420-2630 Office: Harvard Sch Pub Health 1633 Tremont St Boston MA 02120-1616

POWERS, ROBERT WILLIAM, biologist; b. Evanston, Ill., Dec. 21, 1968; s. Robert William and Susan Mae Powers; m. Catherine Ann Herman, Oct. 9, 1993. BS, John Carroll U., 1991; PhD, U. Cin., 1996. Rsch. asst. Abbott Labs., Abbott Park, Ill., 1989-91; grad. rsch. asst. U. Cin., 1991-96; postdoctoral fellow Magee-Women's Rsch. Inst., Pitts., 1996—. Contbr. articles to profl. jours. Pres. Regent Square (Pa.) Civic Assn., 1998—, v.p., 2000—; mem. adv. bd. Nine Mile Run, Pitts., 1998—. Recipient Nat. Rsch. Svc. award NIH, 1997-2000. Mem. AAAS, Soc. for Study of Reproduction, Internat. Soc. for Study of Hypertensoin in Pregnancy, Am. Physiol. Soc.

Avocations: puzzles, home brewing, cycling. Fax: (412) 641-1530. E-mail: rsirwp@mail.magee.edu. Home: 50 Holland Rd Churchill PA 15235-5047 Office: Magee-Women's Rsch Inst 204 Craft Ave Pittsburgh PA 15213-3005

POWERS, RONALD GEORGE, management consultant; b. N.Y.C., July 9, 1934; s. Lee Whitney and R. Anne Powers; m. Elizabeth Braislin McClellan, July 24, 1980. Chmn. Boardroom Advisors, Inc., Winter Park and Tampa, Fla., The Strategic Mgmt. Adv. Group, Inc., Winter Park and Tampa, Fla., Human Svc. Technologies, Inc., Orlando, Fla.; adviser to chief execs. of banks, corps. and govts. on strategic mgmt. issues, 1971—. Trustee Trinity Sch., Fla. Symphony Orch. Mem. Interlachen C. of C. Republican. Episcopalian. Home: PO Box 2174 Winter Park FL 32790-2174 Office: PO Box 1922 Winter Park FL 32790-1922

POWERS, RUNA SKÖTTE, artist; b. Anderstorp, Sweden, Oct. 29, 1940; d. Gösta Nils Folke and Kristina Torborg (Andersson) S.; m. David Britton Powers, Mar. 13, 1965; children: Kristina, Davis. Student, Art Inst. So. Calif., 1976-83; BMA, U. So. Calif., 1986. Exhbns. include Newport Festival Arts, Newport Beach, 1980, Costa Mesa Art League, 1980, Orange County Fair, Costa Mesa, 1980, Art Inst. So. Calif., Laguna Beach, 1976-83, Studio Sem Ghelardini, Pietrasanta, Italy, 1983, Design House, Laguna, 1984, Vorpal Gallery, 1983-84, Laguna Beach Mus. Art, 1984, Gallery Sokolov, Laguna Beach, 1985-93, Margareta Sjödin Gallery, Malibu, 1988, Ana Izax Gallery, Beverly Hills, 1988, Envision Art, 1991, Gallery Slottet, Hörle, Sweden, 1990-92, J.F. Kennedy Performing Arts Ctr., Washington, 1991, Internat. Art Expn., L.A., 1985, N.Y., 1986-87, San Bernardino County Mus., 1993. Founder Found. Hörle Manor House, Värnamo, Sweden, 1987—. Avocations: music, reading, cooking, swimming. Home: 1831 Ocean Way Laguna Beach CA 92651-3235

POWERS, WILLIAM EDWARD, emergency physician, educator; b. Atlanta, Sept. 16, 1957; s. Richard Candler and Olive Carol Osburn Powers; m. Nancy Carolyn Freeman, May 17, 1986; children: Nicole, Will. MS in Biomed. Engring., U. Ill., Chgo., 1981; MS in Aerospace Medicine, Wright State U., 1991; MD, Rush U., 1985. Diplomate Am. Bd. Emergency Medicine, Am. Bd. Preventive Medicine. Intern in gen. surgery Orlando (Fla.) Regional Med. Ctr., 1985-86, resident in emergency medicine, 1986-88; resident in aerospace medicine Wright State U., Dayton, Ohio, 1989-91; biomed. engr., rsch. asst. U. Ill., Chgo., 1980-81; chief resident emergency medicine Orlando (Fla.) Regional Med. Ctr., 1987; assoc. dir. emergency medicine Kissimmee (Fla.) Meml. Hosp., 1988-89; asst. med. dir. Martin-Marietta Aerospace, Orlando, Fla., 1988-89; emergency med. physician, clin. instr. Wright State U. Med. Sch., Dayton, Ohio, 1989-91; med. officer, flight surgeon NASA Johnson Space Ctr., Houston, 1991-92; asst. med. dir. Cape Canaveral Hosp., Cocoa Beach, Fla., 1991-93, Twin Cities Hosp., Niceville, Fla., 1991-93; asst. prof. emergency medicine, rsch. dir. U. Tex. Med. Sch., Houston, 1993-95; asst. prof. family medicine, dir. urgent care U. Tex. Med. Br., Galveston, 1995-96; asst. prof. medicine Baylor Coll. Medicine, Houston, 1996—. Contbr. articles to profl. publs. Med. missionary Missionary Ventures, Honduras, 1995, 98. Fulbright Found. grantee U. Vienna, Austria, 1996. Fellow Am. Coll. Emergency Physicians, Aerospace Med. Assn. (assoc. fellow); mem. Soc. for Acad. Emergency Medicine, Exptl. Aircraft Assn. Methodist. Avocations: flying, soccer, basketball, photography, piano. E-mail: WEPowers@aol.com. Office: Baylor Coll Medicine/Meth Hosp 6565 Fannin St # M-196 Houston TX 77030-2704

POWLES, MICHAEL JOHN, diplomat. Rep. to UN Govt. of New Zealand, 1996—. Office: Permanent Mission New Zealand UN 1 U N Plz Fl 25 New York NY 10017-3515*

POWLES, RAYMOND LEONARD, oncologist; b. London, Mar. 9, 1938; s.Leonard William David and Florence (Conolly) P.; m. Louise Jane Richmond; children: Sam, Luke, Ella, Max. BSc, St. Bartholomew's Hosp., 1961, MB BS, 1964. House physician St. Bartholomew's Hosp., London, 1965-66, house surgeon thoracic unit, 1966, registrar in medicine, 1967-68; house physician Brompton Hosp., London, 1966-67; resident med. officer in medicine Royal Marsden Hosp., London, 1967; sr. registrar in psychiatry Addington Hosp., Durban, South Africa, 1967; sr. lectr. in medicine Inst. Cancer Rsch., Sutton, Eng., 1974—; chief clin. svcs. Inst. Cancer Rsch., Sutton, Eng., 1990—; cons. physician med. oncology Royal Marsden Hosp., Sutton, 1974—; physician in charge leukemia & myeloma unit Royal Marsden Hosp., 1978—; prof. haemato-oncology U. London, Inst. Cancer Rsch., 1997—; instr. medicine U. London, 1977-88; clin. tutor Royal Coll. Physicians, 1986—; med. adviser Bud Flanagan Charity Com.; mem. S.W. Thames Regional Negotiating Team Drugs and Supplies; mem. med. rsch. coun. Working Party on Adult Leukemia; mem. London Bone Marrow Transplant Group; mem. adv. adv. com. Internat. Bone Marrow Transplantation Registry. Mem. editorial bd. Human Lymphocyte Differentation, Apheresis, Indian Jour. Cancer Chemotherapy, Leukaemia Rsch., Exptl. Haematology; mem. editorial rev. bd. Bone Marrow Transplantation; conbr. over 300 articles on leukemia and bone marrow transplantation to profl. pubis. Fellow Royal Coll. Physicians London (vis. joint com. on higher med. tng., subcom. on med. oncology); mem. Brit. Assn. Cancer Rsch., Brit. Soc. Haematology, Brit. Transplantation Soc., Assn. Cancer Physicians, European Soc. Med. Oncology (bd. dirs.), Am. Cancer Soc. Sci. Writers Alumni, European Bone Marrow Transplantation Soc., Internat. Soc. Exptl. Hematology, Internat. Transplantation Soc. Avocations: sports, cooking, reading. Home: Little Garratts, 19 Garratts Ln, Surrey England Office: Royal Marsden Hosp, Downs Rd, Sutton Surrey SM2 5PT, England

POWLES, STEPHEN BRUCE, agricultural educator, researcher; b. Brisbane, Australia, Apr. 4, 1950; s. Kildare Powles and Jacqueline Swaab; m. Wendy Margaret Remilton; children: Julia, Amy, Mark. BSc, U. Western Sydney, Australia, 1974; MSc, Mich. State U., 1976; PhD, Australian Nat. U., Canberra, 1979. Fellow Stanford (Calif.) U., 1980-82, U. Paris, 1983; prof. agr. U. Adelaide, Australia, 1984-97, U. Western Australia, Nedlands, 1998—. Author: Herbicide Resistance in Plants, 1994; contbr. over 100 articles to profl. jours. Home: 24 Kilkenny Rd, Floreat WA 6014, Australia Office: U Western Australia, Nedlands WA 6907, Australia

POWLING, CHRIS, children's writer; b. London, Feb. 16, 1943; s. Leonard and Queenie (Richings) P.; m. Janet Smith, Aug. 27, 1966; children: Katie, Ellie. MA, St. Catherine's Coll., Oxford, Eng., 1965; cert. in edn., King's Coll., London, 1966; L.R.A.M., Royal Acad. Music, 1968; advanced diploma in edn., Inst. Edn., London, 1970; MA, U. Sussex, 1984. Tchr. London, 1966-75, head tchr., 1975-85; sr. lect. profl. studies King Alfred's Coll., Winchester, Eng., 1985-95. Author: Daredevils or Scaredycats, 1979, Mog and the Rectifier, 1980, The Mustang Machine, 1981, Uncle Neptune, 1982, The Conker as Hard as a Diamond, 1984, Stuntkid, 1985, The Phantom Carwash, 1986, Flyaway Frankie, 1987, Fingers Crossed, 1987, Bella's Dragon, 1988, Hiccup Harry, 1988, Hoppity-Gap, 1988, Ziggy and the Ice Ogre, 1988, Harry's Party, 1989, The Golden Years of Mother Goose, 1989, A Spook at the Superstore, 1990, ELF 61, 1990, Dracula in Sunlight, 1990, Harry with Spots On, 1990, Butter Fingers, 1991, Old Chap Dragon, 1991, Where the Quaggy Bends, 1992, Wesley at the Water Park, 1992, Harry Moves House, 1993, A Razzle-Dazzle Rainbow, 1993, Phantom Carwash, 1993, It's That Dragon Again, 1993, Kingfisher Book of Scary Stories, 1994, Best of Books for Keeps, 1994, Famous With Smokey Joe, 1995, Harry the Superhero, 1995, Kit's Castle, 1995, Roald Dahl, 1983, Talkback, 1998, Sophies Nu-Pet, 1998, (series) What's It Like to Be; editor: Books for Keeps, 1989-96 (Eleanor Farjeon award for svcs. to children's books 1996), Harry on Holiday, 1997, Story Telling in Schools, 1997, Gorgeous George, 1999, Dick King-Smith, 1999, Quentin Blake, 1999, Shirley Hughes, 1999, My Sister's Name is Rover, 1999, Long John Santa, 1999. Active area PTO. Socialist. Office: 9 Guildford Grove, London SE10 8JY, England

POWRIE, JAMES KENNETH, endocrinologist, consultant; b. Perth, Scotland, Nov. 25, 1958. B of Med. Biology, Aberdeen (Eng.) U., 1979, MBChB, 1982, MD, 1992. Sr. house officer medicine Aberdeen Hosps., 1983-85, registrar in medicine, 1985-87, registrar in endocrinology, 1987-88; clin. rsch. fellow St. Thomas' Hosp., London, 1988-92, lectr., 1992-96; cons. hon. sr. lectr. Guy's and St. Thomas Hosp., London, 1996—. Contbr. articles to profl. jours. Fellow Royal Coll. Physicians; mem. Brit. Diabetic Assn., Royal Soc. Medicine. Avocations: skiing, squash, windsurfing, sailing. Office: Guys Hosp, Saint Thomas St, London SE1 9RT, England

POWRIE, PHILIP PETER, French cultural studies educator; b. Southall, Eng., Nov. 21, 1951; s. Peter James and Colette Marie (Grangier) P.; m.Juliet Ann Horsley, Feb. 20, 1990 (div.); children: Nicholas, Josephine, Manon. BA in Modern Langs. with honors, Oxford (Eng.) U., 1974, DPhil, 1983. Lectr. U. Newcastle Upon Tyne (England), 1978-91, sr. lectr., 1978-95, prof. French cultural studies, 1995—, dir. Ctr. Rsch. Into Film, 1996—. Author: René Daumal and Roger Gilbert-Lecomte, 1988, René Daumal: Etude D'une Obession, 1990, co-author: Contemporary French Fiction by Women: Feminist Perspectives, 1991, French Cinema in the 1980's: Nostalgia and the Crisis of Masculinity, 1997, French Cinema in the 1990s: Continuity and Difference, 1999. Office: U Newcastle Upon Tyne, Sch Modern Langs, Newcastle upon Tyne NE1 7RU, England

POYATO-ARIZA, FRANCISCO JOSÉ, paleontologist, educator; b. Granada, Spain, Aug. 16, 1963; s. Alfonso Poyato and Juana Ariza. Grad. in Biol. Scis., U. Autónoma de Madrid, Spain, 1986, D Biol. Scis., 1991. Postdoctoral rschr. Mus. Natural History/U. Kans., Lawrence, 1993-94, Mus. für Naturkunde der Humboldt U., Berlin, Germany, 1994; rschr. U. Autónoma de Madrid, 1995-97, 97—. Contbr. articles to Sci., Nature, Mesozoic Fishes, Palaeo Ichthyologica, Palaeontology, Paleogeography, Palaeoclimatology, Palaeoecology, others. Mem. Amnesty Internat., Madrid, 1988—; mem. Greenpeace, Madrid, 1988—. Mem. Spanish Palaeontology Soc., Soc. Vertebrate Paleontology, European Paleontological Assn. Avocations: opera, movies, photography, painting and other fine arts. E-mail: francisco.poyato@uam.es. Home: Tres Peces 12, 1-A, Madrid Spain 28012 Office: U Aut Madrid/Paleontology, Cantoblanco, Madrid Spain 28049

POYSER, JOHN, general practice physician; b. Sheffiey, Yorkshire, U.K., Apr. 9, 1952; s. Thomas and Dorothy P.; m. Jean Anne Nelson, July 27, 1976; children: Thomas Edwin, Alexander James. MB, Sheffield (U.K.) U., 1976, MPhil, 1994. Ho. officer Wharncliffe Hosp., Sheffield, U.K., 1976-77; sr. ho. officer accident and emergency Royal Infirmary, Sheffield, Eng., 1977-78; sr. ho. officer gen. surgery and cardiothoracic surgery Royal Hallamshire Hosp., Sheffield, 1978-79, registrar, 1979-80; pvt. practice Sheffield, 1980—; lectr. U. Sheffield, 1985—; chmn. Sheffield W. Primary Care Group, 1999—; non-exec. mem. Family Health Svcs. Authority, Sheffield, 1990-95. Chmn. Local Med. Com., Sheffield, 1992-96. Office: Tramways Med Ctr, 54A Holme Ln, Sheffield S6 4JQ, England

POYSER, NORMAN LESLIE, pharmacology educator; b. Nottingham, Eng., Aug. 9, 1947; arrived in Scotland, 1969; s. George Clifford and Marjorie Ellis (Knight) P.; m. Valerie Lesley Whitehead, Apr. 19, 1976 (dec. Mar. 1985); children: Timothy James, Natalie Claire; m. Moira Anderson Scott, Aug. 16, 1990. B Pharmacy, London U., 1968; PhD, U. Edinburgh, Scotland, 1971, DSc, 1990. Imperial Chem. Industries rsch. fellow dept. pharmacology U. Edinburgh, 1971-73, Med. Rsch. Coun. rsch. fellow, 1973-75, lectr., 1975-87, sr. lectr., 1987—, dept. head, 1995-98, dir. studies, mem. 1981; dept. biomed. scis., 1998—. Author: Prostaglandins in Reproduction, 1981; mem. editl. bd. Internat. Jour. Clin. Pharmacology Rsch., 1981—, Brit. Jour. Pharmacology, 1981-87; editl. advisor Biochem. Jour. U.K., 1996-99; contbr. articles to profl. jours. Mem. Brit. Pharmacol. Soc. (Sandoz prize), Soc. for Endocrinology, Soc. for Study Fertility. Home: 5 Buckstone Close, Edinburgh EH10 6XA, Scotland Office: U Edinburgh Dept Biomed Sci, Robson Bldg, George Sq, Edinburgh EH8 9XD, Scotland

POZA, ERNESTO JUAN, business consultant, educator; b. Havana, Cuba, Mar. 27, 1950; came to U.S., 1961; s. Hugo Ernesto and Carmen (Valle) P.; m. Karen Elizabeth Saum, Oct. 14, 1978; 1 child, Kali Jennette. BS in Adminstrv. Sci., Yale U., 1972; MS in Mgmt., MIT, 1974. Personnel mgr. rsch. Sherwin Williams Co., Chgo., 1974-75; orgn. specialist Sherwin Williams Co., Cleve., 1975-77, dir. orgn. planning, 1977-79; pres., sr. mgmt. cons. E.J. Poza Assoc., Cleve., 1979—; prof. Weatherhead Sch. Mgmt. Case Western Res. U., Cleve., 1996—; advisor Family Firm Inst., 1986; bd. dirs. several privately held firms; vis. lectr. Yale U., U. Chile, MIT, Sloan Sch. Mgmt. Author: Smart Growth: Critical Choices for Business Continuity and Prosperity, 1997, A la Sombra del Roble: La Empresa Privada Familiar y Su Continuidad, 1995, La Empresa Familiar Por Dentro, 1998; contbg. editor Family Bus. Mag.; mem. editl. bd. Family Bus. Rev., 1997—; contbr. articles to profl. jours. Bd. dirs. Neighborhood Health Care, 1980, Family Firm Inst., 1990; program com. United Way, Cleve., 1985, Hispanic Leadership, 1986; founding mem. Family Firm Inst., 1985. Recipient Richard Beckhard Practice award Family Firm Inst., 1996. Mem. Acad. Mgmt. (entrepreneurship div., 1980—, orgn. devel. network, 1975—). Office: EJ Poza Assocs 37300 Jackson Rd Chagrin Falls OH 44022-1922

POŽÁR, LADISLAV, psychologist, educator; b. Znojmo, Czechoslovakia, May 26, 1931; s. František and Ružena (Kravalová) P.; m. Magdalena Alexandrovna Guseva, June 22, 1957; children: Svetlana, Elena. Grad. in Edn., Psychology, U. Leningrad, USSR, 1957; PhD, Comenius U., Bratislava, Czechoslovakia, 1968, Candidate Psychol. Scis., 1968. Asst. in psychology Faculty of Arts, Bratislava, 1957-66, 67-70; with Rsch. Inst. Child Psychology and Pathopsychology, Bratislava, 1966-67, mem., 1976-94; head dept. pathopsychology, social pathology Faculty of Edn., Trnava, Czechoslovakia, 1970—, vice dean, 1972-86, dean, 1986-87, mem. faculty dept. psychology and pathopsychology, 1995-97; head dept. psychology and ethics U. Trnava, 1998—; mem. rsch. coun. Pub. Ctr. of Psychodiagnostic and Ednl. Tests, Bratislava, 1976-86. Author: Pathopsychology of Visually Impaired, 1972; author, editor: Psychology of Personality of Handicapped, 1996, 97, Moral Development of Handicapped Children and Youth, 1990, Psychology of Handicapped Children and Youth, 1996, Pathopsychology of Handicapped Children, 1984, 2d edit., 1987, Pathopsychology, 1975, School Integration of Visually Impaired Children and Youth, 1996 and others; contbr. over 100 articles to profl. jours.; mem. editl. com. Jour. Child Psychology and Patopsychology, 1974—, Jour. Studia Psychologica, 1976-85, Bull. Psychodiagnostika v socialistickych krajinách, 1976-86, Jour. EFETA, 1990—. Named Meritorious Worker Bratislava Ministry of Edn., 1981. Mem. Slovak Lit. Found. (registered translator), Acad. Pedagogical and Social Scis. (Russia). Avocations: literature, traveling. Office: Pedagogicka Faculta, UK Moskovska 3, 813 34 Bratislava Slovak Republic

POZDNYAKOV, DMITRY VICTOROVICH, science educator; b. Orenbourg, USSR, Aug. 31, 1942; s. Victor Leontyevich and Natalya Maphodievna Pozdnyakov; m. Tatyana Adoulovna Mazitova, Sept. 24, 1971; 1 child, Irina. MS, Electrotech. Inst., Leningrad, Russia, 1964; PhD, State U., Leningrad, 1972; DSc, Acad. Scis., St. Petersburg, 1992; prof., Electrotech. U., St. Petersburg, 1992. Cert. in engring. Asst. prof. State U., Leningrad, 1965-83; sr. scientist Inst. for Lakes Rsch., St. Petersburg, 1983-92; leading scientist Nansen Ctr., St. Petersburg, 1992-99, rsch. dir., 1999—. Co-author: (books) Optical Properties and Remote Sensing of Inland and Coastal Waters, 1995, Limnology and Remote Sensing: A Contemporary Approach, 1999; contbr. papers to profl. jours. Avocations: foreign languages, painting. Fax: 7 812 230 79 94. Home: Korablestroiteley 23-1-533, Saint Petersburg 199226, Russia Office: Nansen Inter Environ/Remote, Korpousnaya St 18, Saint Petersburg 197110, Russia

POZO-LORA, RODRIGO, food scientist, educator; b. El Carpio, Spain, Mar. 20, 1925; s. Rodrigo Pozo-Lopez and Rafaela Lora-Romero; m. Escribano Luna Soledad, Sept. 20, 1960; children: Rodrigo, Antonio. BS in Vet. Medicine, Vet. Faculty, Córdoba, Spain, 1948; DVM, Vet. Faculty, Madrid, 1952. Asst. lectr. vet. faculty Univ. Córdoba, 1948-70, prof. food hygiene & food microbiology, 1970-90, emeritus prof. food hygiene and food microbiology, 1990—; rschr. High Coun. Sci. Rsch., Cordoba, 1956-70; gen. sec. U. Córdoba, 1973-74, rsch. vice chancellor, 1977-81, dir. dept. hygiene, inspection & food microbiology, 1978-86, dir. dept. food sci. & tech., 1986-90; adviser Nat. Coun. Univs. of Ministry of Edn. & Sci., 1977-86, Zootechnic Inst., Córdoba, 1986-93; evaluator rsch. projects Ministry Edn. & Sci., 1977—, Govt. Andalucia, 1986—; cons. UN, 1986—; sci. adv. bd., editorial coun. Archivos de Zootecnica, 1971-86, Veterinaria, 1971-76, Microbiologie-Alimentation-Nutrition, France, 1986—. Author: Bases Zoologicas de la Inspeccion de Aves, 1956, Datos Basicos para la Confeccion de Formulas de Piensos Compuestos, 1960, Investigaciones Sobre la Contaminacion por Plaguicidas Organoclorados de la Leche de la Region Sur de España, 1977, Metodos de Analisis para Higiene e Inspeccion de Alimentos, 1981, Metodos de Analisis para Microbiologia de los Alimentos, 1981, Legislación Veterinaria de Alimentos, 1981, El Sistema Linfatico en la Inspeccion de la Carne, 1986; co-author 4 books: El Patronato Alfonso El Sabio En Cifras, 1972, Indice Catalogo De Zooparasitos Ibericos, 1975, Informe Sobre La Investigacion Universitaria, 1978, Una Imagen De Calidad. Los Productos Del Cerdo Iberico, 1984; contbr. over 170 articles to profl. jours. Home: 1o Izda, Avda del Gran Capitan 39, 14008 Cordoba Spain Office: Campus de Rabanales Dept, Bromatol y Tech de los Alimentos, 14005 Córdoba Spain

POZZI, ANGELO, engineering executive, civil engineer; b. Wattwil, Switzerland, Aug. 12, 1932; m. Verena Schubiger; children: Lucia, Monica, Martina, Felice. Grad. civil engring., Swiss Fed. Inst. Tech., Zürich, Switzerland, 1956, D. in Tech. Sci., 1970. Project mgr. different orgns. N.Am., Europe, 1956-67; rsch. fellow Swiss Fed. Inst. Tech., Zürich, 1968-70, prof., 1971-91; CEO Motor-Columbus Ltd., Baden, Switzerland, 1983-84, chmn., CEO, 1985-92, chmn., 1992-93; chmn. Pozzi & Ptnrs. Ltd., Baden, Switzerland, 1993—; chmn. Aare-Tessin Ltd., 1987-99; bd. dirs. Holderbank Ltd.; chmn. Internat. Hightech-Forum. Home: Chesa Prade 9, CH-7503 Samedan Switzerland Office: Pozzi & Ptnrs Ltd, Landliweg 9A, CH 5400 Baden Switzerland

POZZI, MAURIZIO, gynecologist; b. Rome, Italy, Nov. 28, 1938; s. Enrico and Giorgina (Spisani) P.; m. Maria Raffaella Jaccod; children: Pierluigi, Valerio. MD, U. Rome, 1962. Asst. Clin. Ob-Gyn., Rome, 1962-67; asst. Regina Elena Nat. Cancer Inst., Rome, 1967-80, chief asst., 1980-90; chief Outpatient Gyn. Dept. San Gallicano Derm. Inst., Rome, 1990—; pres. Luigi Pozzi s.r.l., Rome, 1980—. Editor: Manual of Gynecological Oncology and Gynecology, 1994; contbr. articles to profl. jours. including Gyn. Oncology and Oncology Reports. Mem. Italian Soc. Gynecology and Oncology, Italian Soc. Obstets. and Gynecology. Avocations: botany, ballet. Home: Viale Bruno Buozzi 51, 00197 Rome Italy

POZZO, RICCARDO, philosophy educator; b. Milan, June 7, 1959; came to U.S., 1996; s. Giancarlo and Carla (Rizzani) P.; m. Annette Popel, Sept. 4, 1992; 1 child, Carlo. Laurea in Philosophy, U. Milan, 1983; Promotion in Philosophy, U. Saarland, Saarbrücken, Germany, 1988; Habilitation in Philosophy, U. Trier, Germany, 1995. Rsch. assoc. U. Saarland, 1984-85; fellow Deutscher Akademischer Austauschdienst, Germany, 1985-97, Herzog August Bibliothek Wolfenbüttel, Germany, 1988-90, Alexander von Humboldt-Stiftung, Bonn, Germany, 1990-98; h.s. tchr. Sch. Superintendency Lombardy, Milan, 1994-96; univ. tchr. Cath. U. Am., Washington, 1996—; lectr. U. Trier, 1991-96. Author: Hegel: Introductio in Philosophiam, 1989, Kant und das Problem einer Einleitung, 1989 (Promotion 1988), El giro kantiano, 1998, Georg Friedrich Meiers Vernunftlehre, 2000; co-editor: (with Karl-Otto Apel) Zur Rekonstruktion der Praktischen Philosophie, 1990, (with Michael Oberhausen) Vorlesungsverzeichnisse der Universität Königsberg 1720-1804, 1999; cons. editor: Longanesi Editore, 1988-89, Feltrinelli Editore, 1988-96. Recipient 6th Study Tour of Japan, Japanese Ministry of Fgn. Affairs, 1984. Mem. Kant-Gesellschaft, Am. Catholic Philosophical Assn., North Am. Kant Soc., Humboldt Assn. of Am., Società Italiana di Studi Kantiani, Deutscher Hochschulverband, Hegel Soc. N.Am. Roman Catholic. Avocations: golf, reading contemporary literature. Office: 112A Mcmahon Hl Washington DC 20064-0001

PRABAKARAN, DANIEL, biochemist, researcher; b. Mel Siviri, Tamil Nadu, India, June 25, 1959; came to U.S., 1989; s. Daniel Chinathambi and Kamala Serkad (Mani) P.; m. Crenie Sarah Paul, Feb. 14, 1992; 1 child, Elizabeth Jane. BSc, U. Madras, India, 1979, MSc, 1982; PhD, All India Inst. Med. Scis., 1989. Asst. rsch. officer All India Inst. Med. Sci., New Delhi, 1984-85, rsch. officer, 1985-88, postdoctoral fellow, 1988-89; postdoctoral fellow Beth Israel Deaconess Med. Ctr./Harvard Med. Sch., Boston, 1989-97, instr., 1998—. Contbr. numerous articles to profl. jours. Indian Coun. Med. Rsch. Jr. Rsch. fellow, 1983; Dept. Sci. and Tech. Travel grantee, 1988. Mem. AAAS, Am. Soc. Cell Biology, Endocrine Soc., N.Y. Acad. Scis. Home: 1 Trudeau Ter Wayland MA 01778-5122

PRABHAKARAN, BALAKRISHNAN, computer science educator; b. Madras, Tamil Nadu, India, June 2, 1965; parents Balakrishnan and Saraswathy B.; m. Rajeswari Sankaran, Oct. 26, 1995; children: Gokul, Divya. B in Engring., Madurai-Kamaraj U., India, 1986; MS, Indian Inst. Tech., Madras, 1990, PhD, 1995. Rsch. faculty U. Md., College Park; asst. prof. dept. computer sci. Nat. U. Singapore, 1997-99. Author: Multimedia Database Management Systems, 1999, Mobile Computing Environments for Multimedia Systems, 1999; editor jour. spl. issues; mem. editl. bd. Multimedia Tools and Applications, 1995-99. Rsch. grantee Nat. U. Singapore, 1998. Mem. IEEE. Avocations: swimming, walking, meditation. Fax: +65-779-4580. E-mail: prabha@comp.nus.edu.sg. Office: Nat U Singapore, Dept Computer Sci, Singapore 117543, Singapore

PRABHU, GIRIDHAR GURUPUR, food products executive; b. Mangalore, Karnataka, India, May 4, 1957; s. Sadananda G. and Rohini S. Prabhu; m. Archana G. Kamath, July 8, 1981; children: Achala, Amitha, Anuja. B in Commerce, St. Aloysius Coll., Mangalore, 1977. Ptnr. Consolidated Cashews, Mangalore, 1977-82; CEO Achal Industries, Mangalore, 1981-92, proprietor, 1992—; dir., CEO Achal Cashews Pvt. Ltd., Turkewadi, India, 1983—. Mem. com. adminstrn. The Cashew Export Promotion Coun. of India, Cochin, 1986-96, vice-chmn., 1996-98; active Indian Cashewnut Devel. Coun., Cochin, 1988-91. Mem. Mangalore Cashew Mfrs. Assn. (hon. sec. 1993-95, pres. 1995-97), Kanara C. of C. and Industry (hon. sec. 1991-93, treas. 1993-95, editor jour. 1991-95). Hindu. Avocations: development economics, reading, writing. E-mail: achalind@hotmail.com. Home: Phalguni, Kadri Kambla Rd, Mangalore 575004, India Office: Achal Industries, 190 Industrial Area, Baikampady 575011, India

PRABHU, SASINDRAN MADHAVA, communications engineer; b. Abiramam, Tamil Nadu, India, Feb. 26, 1961; s. Madhava Srinivasan and Priyothama Madhava Prabhu; m. Asha Ratnakar Bhagath, Jan. 31, 1988; 1 child, Sneha. ME, Anna U., 1985; PGDM, A.I.M.A., New Delhi, India, 1996. Rsch. engr. Ctr. Devel. Telematics, Bangalore, India, 1985-90; program mgr. Ctr. Devel. Telematics, Bangalore, 1991-95, sr. program mgr., 1996—. Mem. IEEE. Home: Jayanagar 9th Blk, 001/B-10 Shanthi Park Apts, Bangalore 560 069, India Office: Ctr Devel Telematics, 71/1 Miller Rd, Bangalore 560 052, India

PRABHU, SURESH, government official; b. 1952. Elected to Lok Sabha, India, 1996; min. Ministry of Industry, India, 1996, Ministry Environment & Forests, India, 1998—; min. chems. and fertilizers. Address: Dr Rajendra Prasad Rd, New Delhi 110 001, India Office: Ministry Environment, Paryavana Bhawan, New Delhi 110 003, India*

PRABU, R.S.K. LAKSHMANAN, business educator; b. Madras, India, Aug. 16, 1969; s. R.S. Kothandaraman and R.S.K. Dhanalaxmi. B in Polit. Sci., Kakatiya U., Warangal, India, 1991, M in Am. Lit., 1993; MBA, newport U., 1993; MPA, U. Madras, India, 1998. Dir. adminstrn. technol. mgmt. M.K. Univ., Tamil Nadu, India, 1991—; rschr. mgmt. studies Madras Christian Coll., Tamil Nadu, 1998—; trustee SRI Rengalatchumi Ednl. Trust, Chennai, India, 1991—; dir. instn. Pacheri Sri Nalla Thangalamman Coll. Engring., 1991—; dir. Nallathangal Inst. Mgmt., Dindigul, 1993—; mem. governing coun. Prescribed AICTE, New Delhi, 1995—. Dir. Human Chain Drug Awareness, Dindigul, 1996, Drug Awareness Camp, Dindigul, 1997, Having Procession in Eradicating Leprosy, Dindigul, 1997, AIDS Awareness Camp, Dindigul, 1997, Blood Donation Camp, Dindigul, 1998-99. Mem. Acad. Ethical Sci., Indian Alumni of World U., League Club, Brit. Coun., Am. Libr., Theosophical Libr. Avocations: portrait painting, swimming, dancing. Home: Murugabhavanam SRLE Trust, 9 O C Pillai Nagar, Dindigul 624 622, India Office: PSNA Coll Engring & Tech, Kothandaraman Nagar, Dindigul 624 622, India

PRACH, KAREL, plant ecologist, researcher, educator; b. Planá, Czech Republic, Oct. 20, 1953; s. Karel and Alena (Dobrovská) P.; m. Eva Medonosová, Feb. 19, 1987; children: Jindřich, Martin. MSc, Charles U., Prague, Czech Republic, 1977, Rerum Naturalium D, 1978; PhD in Biology, Charles U.-Acad. Sci., 1983. Asst. Charles U., 1977-82, sr. lectr., 1989-95; rsch. scientist Czech Acad. Sci., Třebon, 1982-90, sr. rsch. scientist, 1990—, head dept., 1990-92; sr. lectr. biology U. Č. Budějovice, Czech Republic, 1991—, head acad. senate Faculty Biol. Sci., 1992-95, head dept., 1999—; mem. adv. bds. Šumava and Třebon Biosphere Res., 1994,, 95—. Main editor, author:

Floodplain Ecology and Management, 1996; editor, co-author: Succession in Abandoned Fields, 1990; mem. editl. bd. Restoration Ecology Jour., 1993—; contbr. articles to sci. jours., including Jour. Biogeography, Oikos. Founding mem. Civil Forum, Czech Republic, 1989. Darwin initiative grantee Govt. of U.K., 1995-97, biodiversity scheme grantee World Bank, 1995-97. Mem. Czech Bot. Soc. (main com.), Brit. Ecol. Soc., Internat. Assn. for Vegetation Sci. Avocations: history, travel. Office: U C Budejovice Fac Biol Sci, Branišovská 31, CZ-37005 Budějovice Czech Republic

PRACHT, DENIS, radiodiagnostician; b. Strasbourg, France, Jan. 10, 1951; s. Louis and Antoinette (Resch) P.; m. Christiane Jaeger, May 9, 1975; children: Valentine, Benjamin. MD, Med. U. Strasbourg, France, 1984, specialist in radiodiagnostics, 1984. Resident St. Catherine Hosp., Saverne, France, 1975-80; resident Cancer Treatment Ctr., Strasbourg, 1981-84, asst. specialist dr., 1986-90; pvt. practice Illzach, France, 1990—; assoc. tchr. Med. U., Strasbourg, 1985-90; assoc. specialist Gen. Hosp., Mulhouse, France, 1991-98. V.p. Local Union Radiologists, Alsace, France, 1995—. Capt. Mil. Health Svc., 1976-77. Mem. French Radiol. Soc. Roman Catholic. Avocation: trekking. Office: Cab de Radiologie, 8 Pl de la Republique, 68110 Illzach France

PRACHUAP, CHAIYASAN, federal official; b. Udonthai Province, Aug. 28, 1944; married. BA in Polit. Sci., Thammasat U. Adminstr. Planned Parenthood Assn. Thailand, 1972-73; dist. officer Udonthani, 1974-75; project adminstr. ILO, UNDP, 1976; chmn. Slot Internat. Co., Ltd., 1977-83; dep. min. Ministry of Commerce, 1986-88; min. Ministry of Sci., Tech. and Energy, 1988-90, Ministry of Pub. Health, 1991, Ministry of Agr. and Coop., 1994, Ministry of Fgn. Affairs, 1996, Ministry of Univ. Affairs, Bangkok, 1998—, Ministry of State Univ. Bur. Nat. Devel. Party. Office: Khet Rachathewee, 328 Thanon Si Ayutthaya, Bangkok 10400, Thailand*

PRADA, RICARDO BERNARDO, electrical engineering educator, consultant; b. Rio de Janeiro, Apr. 18, 1951; s. Carlos Lourival and Sylvia (Bernardo) P.; m. Ruth de Aquino Araujo, June 1976 (div. July 1982); 1 child, Bruno; m. Ana Teresa Velho, Jan. 7, 1986; children: Julia, Lucas. Degree in engring., Cath. U., Rio de Janeiro, 1975, MSc, 1977; PhD, Imperial Coll., London, 1980. Lectr. Cath. U., 1975-87, assoc. prof., 1983-93, 1997—; acad. visitor Imperial Coll., London, 1988; prof. Fed. U., Maranhão, Brazil, 1994-96; cons. Ctrl. Electricity Generating Bd., London, 1988, Eletrobrás, Rio de Janeiro, 1990-92, Light Elec. Svcs., Rio de Janeiro, 1993, Cepel Elec. Energy Rsch. Ctr., Rio de Janeiro, 1999—. Contbr. articles to profl. publs. Rsch. grantee Brazilian Govt. Rsch. Coun., 1999—, Rio de Janeiro Rsch. Coun., 1999—. Mem. Cigrée-Brazil (mem. adminstrv. bd. 1999—, Best Article award 1993), Automatic Control Brazilian Soc., Brazilian Soc. for Progress of Sci. Avocation: catch and release fishing. Office: Cath U Dept Elec Engring, Rua Marques Sao Vicente 225, 22453900 Rio de Janeiro Gavea, Brazil

PRADAN, DASHO OM, government official; b. Neoly, Bhutan, Oct. 6, 1946; married. BA in History, Delhi (India) U., 1968. Trainee officer Ministry of Trade, Industry and Forests, Bhutan, 1969-70, acting sec., 1970-72, sec., 1972-79, dep. minister, 1979; permanent rep. of Bhutan UN, N.Y.C., 1980-84; amb. to India, Nepal and the Maldives Govt. of Bhutan, 1984-85; dep. minister Ministry of Trade and Industry, Bhutan, 1985; minister Ministry of Trade, Industries and Tourism, Bhutan, 1989—; rep. to the UN N.Y.; chief coord. for settlement of landless people in So. Bhutan, 1976. Recipient Gold medal for meritorious svc. Govt. of Bhutan, 1974. Office: Ministry Trade Industry and Tourism, Thimphu Bhutan Address: 27th Fl 2 United Nations Plaza New York NY 10017*

PRADEEP, SREELATHA, electronics engineer, researcher; b. Trivandrum, Kerala, India, May 27, 1970; s. Padmanabhan and Pushkalambal (Padhanabhan) P.; m.; Pradeepkumar Punathikkandiyil, May 8, 1994. BTech, Coll. Engring., Trivandrum, India, 1991, MTech, 1994. Engr. SB Vikram Sarabhai Space Centre, Trivandrum, 1992-94, engr. SC, 1994-98, engr. SD, 1998—. Hindu. Avocations: reading, gardening, yoga. Office: Vikram Sarabhai Space Ctr, Space Physics Lab, Trivandrum 695022, India

PRADELLA, STEPHAN PAUL, ophthalmologist, physician; b. Frankfurt, Germany, June 14, 1966; s. Paul and Elisabeth (Operhalski) P.; m. Britta Linse, Aug. 15, 1997; children: Luca Paul, Leon Felix. BS, Semmelweis U., 1988; MD, Justus Liebig U., Giessen, Germany, 1992. Sr. physician Martin Luther U. Eye Hosp., Halle, Germany, 1993-96; physician eye hosp. Frankfurt, Germany, 1996-98; physician in pvt. practice with laser ops. Oberursel, Germany, 1999—. Author: Epidemiological and Diagnostic Aspects of Helicobacter Pylori, 1997; contbr. articles to profl. jours. Mem. German Ophthalmology Soc.

PRADELLI, JOHN MAURICIO, physician, gerontologist, translator; b. Mar del Plata, Argentina, Jan. 23, 1957; came to U.S., 1958; s. Ezio Louis and Linda Louisa (Piacentini) P.; m. Mariella Fregni, Jan. 7, 1989; 1 child, Lorenzo Louis. BSEE, SUNY, Stony Brook, 1979; MD, U. Modena, Italy, 1994. Freelance translator, 1980-84; computer programmer Fabbidata, Modena, 1985-90; specialist in geriatrics U. Modena, 1998, data mgr. Geriatric Evaluation Unit, 1998—; attending physician RSA 9 Gennaio; cons. to biotech. cos., Italy, 1980-94. Contbr. articles to sci. internat. jours.; translator, copy editor books and papers in biology, botany and medicine. Species of tardigrade Hypsibius pradellii sp. nov. named in his honor. E-mail: pradelli@unimo.it. Home: Via degli Adelardi 3, 41100 Modena Italy Office: RSA 9 Gennaio, Via Paul Harris 165, 41100 Modena Italy

PRADES, JOAQUIM, physicist; b. Castello de la Plana, Spain, Feb. 3, 1963; s. Joaquin and Francisca (Hernandez) P. Diploma in Physics, Universitat de Valencia, 1988, PhD in Physics, 1991. Assoc. prof. physics Universidad de Granada, 1997—.

PRADHAN, DEVENDRA, lawyer; b. Kathmandu, Nepal, Aug. 3, 1969; s. Rudra and Urmila Pradhan. BL, Nepal Law Campus, Kathmandu, 1990. Assoc. Nepal Law Firm, Kathmandu, 1991-96, Kusum Law Firm, Kathmandu, 1996-97; sr. atty., proprietor Pradhan Assocs., Kathmandu, 1997—. Mem. Internat. Bar Assn., Supreme Court Bar Assn., Nepal Law Soc., Human Rights Orgn. Nepal, Internat. Assn. for the Protection of Indsl. Property, The Southwestern Legal Found. Acad. Alumni Assn. Avocations: reading, traveling, swimming. Home: Chakupat 22, Lalitpur Nepal Office: Pradhan Assocs, GPO Box 11185 Maitighar, Kathmandu Nepal

PRADHAN, GANESH BALLABH, journalist; b. Kathmandu, Nepal, July 1937; s. Purna Ballbh and Govind Kumari Pradhan; m. Hari Badan; children: Shirish Ballabh, Alaka, Jyoti. B in Sanskrit, U. Beneras, India, 1959; MA, U. Kathmandu, 1971. Joint sec. Kathmandu dist. com. Nepali Congress Party, 1960-61; editor Matribhoomi, Kathmandu, 1963-67; editor Janmabhoomi Daily, Kathmandu, 1967-68, chief editor, 1968—; headmaster Adult H.S., Nepal, 1968-72; former chmn. Nepal TV; chmn. Nat. News Agy. Treas. Social Welfare Coun, 1992-93. Mem. Nepal Family Planning Assn., Free Press Soc. Nepal (chmn.). Fax: 9771-262744. E-mail: rss@wlink.com.np. Home: Tahachal, PO Box 3244, Kathmandu Nepal Office: Janmabhoomi Office, Tahachal 3244, Kathmandu Nepal

PRADHAN, KISHORE DWARKANATH, landscape architect, consultant; b. Bombay, Feb. 4, 1944; s. Dwarkanath Ganesh and Prema Dwarkanath (Kulkarni) P.; m. Neeti Gupté, Mar. 2, 1975; children: Kshipra, Samved. BArch, Sir J. J. Coll. Arch., 1966; diploma in landscape arch., Ecole Nat. supèrieure d', Horticulture, 1972. Archtl. and landscape cons. Bombay, 1973—; vis. lectr. Sir J. J. Coll. Arch., Bombay, 1974-90. Prin. works include Hyatt Regency Hotel Delhi, Indira Gandhi Inst. Devel. Rsch., Inter-Univ. Ctr. Astronomy and Astro-Physics, Reliance Petroleum Ltd. Mem. Indian Inst. Archs. (assoc.), Chembur Gymkhana. Avocations: playing indian classical music on flute, history of architecture, French language and culture. Office: A/2 Natraj Apts, Pestom Sagar Rd No. 6, 400 089 Bombay India

PRADHAN, SUNIL, neurology educator, consultant; b. Najibadad, India, Aug. 17, 1957; s. Om Prakash and Om Vati (Saxena) P.; m. Neena Srivastava, Feb. 20, 1990; 1 child, Shikhar. MBBS, King George's Med. Coll., Lucknow, India, 1980, MD, 1983, DM in Neurology, 1986. Sr. resident King George's Med. Coll., 1985-86; sr. registrar Jaslok Hosp. and Rsch. Ctr., Bombay, 1987; scientist pool officer Nat. Inst. Mental Health and Neuro-Scis., Bangalore, India, 1987-88; asst. prof. Nizan's Inst. Med. Scis., Hyderabad, India, 1988-89; asst. prof. neurology Sanjay Gandhi Postgrad. Inst. Med. Scis., Lucknow, 1989-93, assoc. prof., 1993-97, examiner for DM degree, 1996-2000, additional prof., 1997—; cons. neurologist. Contbr. articles to med. jours., including Lancet, Neurology, Jour. Neurol. Scis., Pediatric Neurology, Annals of Neurology, Jour. Neurol. Neurosurg. and Psychiatry, EEG Clin. Neurophysiology, Acta Neurologica Scandinevica; inventor Pradhan's technique for electrophysiol. evaluation of intercostal nerves; discoverer Pradhan sign in Duchenne muscular dystrophy, perilesional gliosis as a risk factor for seizure recurrence, parainfectious conus myelitis as an important cause of unexplained urinary symptoms, Japanese encephalitis virus as a cause for parkinsonism. Recipient S.T. Achar award Indian Acad. Pediat., 1994, 95, H.B. Dingley award Indian Coun. Med. Rsch., 1994, Shakuntala Amir Chand award Indian Coun. Med. Rsch., 1996; Japan Internat. Cooperation Agy. fellow Nagoya (Japan) U. Sch. Medicine, 1991-92. Mem. World Fedn. Clin. Neurophysiology, Indian Acad. Neurology, Neurol. Soc. India. Hindu. Avocations: painting, flute, badminton, poetry. Office: S Gandhi Post Inst Med Scis, Dept Neurology, Lucknow 226014, India

PRADHAN, SURESH CHANDRA, pharamacologist, educator; b. Bamur, Orissa, India, Apr. 3, 1951; s. Achyuta Nanda and Rasabati P.; m. Nirupama Pradhan, May 23, 1981; children: Pritam, Prita. BS, Buxi Jagabandhu Bidyadhar Coll., Bhubeneswar, India, 1970; MBBS, Maharaja Krushna Chandra Gajapati Med. Coll., Berhampur, India, 1975; MD in Pharmacology, Inst. Med. Scis., Banaras Hindu U., Varanasi, India, 1980. Cert. of registration Orissa Coun. Med. Registration. House physician Shambhu Nath Pandit Hosp., Calcutta, 1976-77; jr. resident Inst. Med. Scis., Banaras Hindu U., Varanasi, India, 1977-78; sr. resident Inst. Med. Scis., Banaras Hindu U., Varanasi, 1978-81; lectr. Mahatma Gandhi Inst. Med. Scis., Sewagram, India, 1981-84; asst. prof. Jawaharlal Inst. Post-Grad. Med. Edn. and Rsch., Pondicherry, India, 1984-88, assoc. prof., 1988-92, prof., 1992—; PhD guide Pondicherry (India) U., 1991—. Assoc. editor Indian Jour. Pharmacology, 1992-94, cons. editor, 1994-98; contbr. articles to profl. jours. Recipient Uvnas prize Indian Pharmacol. Soc., 1990. Fellow Indian Coll. Allergy and Applied Immunology, WHO (regional office S.E. Asia); mem. Indian Assn. Med. Jour. Editors, Indian Med. Assn. (Pondicherry br.), Internat. Soc. Infectious Diseases, N.Y. Acad. Scis. Hindu. Avocations: reading, writing, travel, coin collecting. Office: JIPMER, Dept Pharmacology, 605 006 Pondicherry India

PRADO, PATRICK, anthropologist, researcher; b. La Baule, France, Oct. 17, 1940; s. Yves Prado and Monique Thébault; m. Sakuya Sekido, Dec. 20, 1988; 1 child, Louis Natsuki Voltaire. MA in Sociology, U. Paris, 1962. Anthropology rschr. Assn. Marc Bloch, Paris, 1972-75; video dir. Inst. Nat. de l'Audiovisuel, Paris, 1975-77; rschr. Ctr. Nat. de la Rsch. Sci., Paris, 1977—. Author: L'Entrée dans la Ville, 1974, Vivre sa Ville, 1978, La Ville en Partage, 1985, Les Anglais dans nos Campagnes, 1995. Office: MNATP Ctr Nat Recerche, Scientific, 75116 Paris France

PRADZYNSKI, ANDRZEJ HENRYK, chemist; b. Plock, Poland, Jan. 1, 1924; came to U.S., 1969; s. Maurycy and Frania (Goldkind) Nejman; m. Halina Romana Bromberger, Apr. 1, 1946; children: Richard E. Neuman, Zgibniew Jacek. BS, U. Wroclaw, Poland, 1949, MS, 1951. Asst. prof. crystallography, chmn. dept. U. Wroclaw, 1948-51; sect. mgr. materials testing Inst. Aviation, Warsaw, Poland, 1951-57; adj. prof. Polish Acad. Scis., Warsaw, 1957-68; dept. dir. Atomic Energy Commn. Poland, Warsaw, 1959-68; rsch. assoc. IV nuclear reactor U. Tex., Austin, 1969-80; exec. v.p. Halinco Skin Care Products, Inc., Austin, 1980—; cons. IAEA, Vienna, Austria, 1968-69. Author: Industrial Radiography (in Polish), 1957; also over 3o articles in IAEA Conf. Procs., Nukleonika, ISA Trans., also others. Mem. Am. Chem. Soc., Soc. Cosmetic Chemists, N.Y. Acad. Scis. Achievements include patent for method and apparatus for collection and analysis of mercury in the atmosphere; developer method of photo-nuclear activation analysis of copper in ores and concentrates, synthetic standards for EDX-ray analysis, method of collection and analysis of mercury in air, method of nondestructive X-ray analysis of heavy metals in toys. Developed pre-concentration methods of trace elements in water for EDX-ray analysis. E-mail: halandre@fc.net. Office: Halinco Skin Care Products PO Box 9405 Austin TX 78766-9405

PRAENDL, FELIX, lawyer; b. Munich, Germany, Oct. 7, 1959; s. Oskar and Annelies (Kunze) P.; m. Doris Krammer, June 26, 1992; children: Florian, Johannes. JD, Vienna Sch. Law, Austria, 1982; LLM, Tulane U. Sch. Law, 1984; JSM, Stanford Law Sch., 1986. Rsch. fellow Tulane Sch. Law, New Orleans, 1984-85; fgn. assoc. Hancock, Rothert & Bunshoft, San Francisco, 1986; assoc. Schonherr, Barfuss & Torggler, Vienna, 1986-94; ptnr. Brauneis, Klauser, Praendl, Vienna, 1994—. Author: Austrian Competition Law, 1996; contbr. articles to profl. jours. Fulbright grantee, 1983. Mem. Internat. Bar Assn., Austrian Bar Assn. Office: Brauneis Klauser & Praendl, Bauernmarkt 2, A-1010 Vienna Austria

PRAETORIUS, FINN, oral pathology educator; b. Copenhagen, Mar. 31, 1933; s. Wilhelm Alfred and Ina Praetorius (Kromann) Clausen; m. Kirsten Elisabeth Koch, Apr. 5, 1958; children: Henrik, Niels, Christian. Candidatus odontologiae, Royal Dental Coll., Copenhagen, 1957. Cert. specialist in oral pathology Nat. Bd. Health, Denmark. Rsch. assoc. and asst. prof. Sch. of Dentistry, U. Copenhagen, 1961-65, assoc. prof., 1965—; chief Dental Clinic Naval Base Copenhagen, Royal Danish Navy, 1959-91; dental supr. SIRIUS, Greenland, 1959-93; dep. dir. dental svcs. Danish Armed Forces Health Svc., 1991-93; external examiner oral pathology Sch. Dentistry U. Aarhus, Denmark, 1964—, U. Nairobi, Kenya, 1986-87; mem. membership com. Internat. Assn. for Dental Rsch., Washington, 1975-79; vis. prof. Sch. Dentistry, U. Minn., Mpls., 1974-75; sec. EUROMED Working Group Dental Svcs., 1990-93; Danish del. CINCHAN Dental Working Group (NATO), 1992-93; Med. Rsch. Coun. vis. scientist U. Western Cape, South Africa, 1995; Sholem Kay Meml. lectr. South African Head and Neck Oncology Soc., 1995; Pindborg lectr. U. Umea, Sweden, 1988, Elsinor, Denmark, 1999. Co-author, co-editor: (with H. Björn and J.J. Pindborg) Nordic Dictionary of Odontology, 1970; co-author: Oral Diseases in the Tropics, 1992; asst. editor Acta Odontologica Scandinavica, 1959-61; contbr. articles to profl. jours. Surgeon comdr. Royal Danish Navy, 1957-93. Coun. of Europe fellow, Paris, 1962, George C. Marshall Meml. fellow, Mpls., 1972, Lasby Found. fellow U. Minn., Mpls., 1974, Fulbright fellow, Mpls., 1974. Fellow AAAS; mem. Internat. Acad. Pathology (officer Danish divsn. 1995—), Internat. Assn. for Oral Pathologists (charter, pres.-elect 1995-96, pres. 1996-98), Scandinavian Fellowship for Oral Pathology and Oral Medicine (charter, pres. 1977-79), Assn. of Danish Mil. Dentists (hon. mem.). Avocations: genealogy, history, photography, painting, classical music. Home: Nivaavaenge 37, DK-2990 Nivaa Denmark Office: U Copenhagen Sch Dentistry, Noerre Alle 20, DK-2200 Copenhagen Denmark

PRAG, ANDREW JOHN NICHOLAS WARBURG, archaeologist; b. Oxford, Eng., Aug. 28, 1941; s. Adolf and Frede Charlotte (Warburg) P.; m. Kay Wright, July 5, 1969; children: Johnathan R.W., Kate S. BA, Oxford U., 1964, diploma classical archaeology, 1966, MA, 1967, DPhil, 1975. Temp. asst. keeper Ashmolean Mus., Oxford, 1966-67; keeper of archaeology Manchester Mus., Manchester Univ., 1969—; hon. lectr. Dept. History, Manchester Univ., 1977-83, Dept. of Archaeology, Manchester Univ., 1984—; vis. prof. classics McMaster Univ., Hamilton, Ont., Can., 1978; vis. fellow Brit. Sch. of Athens, 1994. Author: The Oresteia, 1985; Making Faces Using Forensic and Archaeological Evidence, 1997 (reprinted 1999); contbr. articles to profl. jours. Fellow Soc. of Antiquaries of London. Avocations: travel, walking, cooking, music. E-mail: john.prag@man.ac.uk. Office: The Manchester Mus, Univ of Manchester, Manchester M13 9PL, England

PRAG, DEREK NATHAN, journalist, retired politician; b. Merthyr Tydfil, Wales, Aug. 6, 1923; s. Abraham Joseph and Edith (Levitt) P.; m. Dora Weiner, Sept. 23, 1948; children: Nicholas Simon, Jonathan Richard, Stephen Julian. Cert. in Russian, Cambridge (Eng.) U., 1947, BA, 1948, MA, 1963; DLitt (hon.), U. Hertfordshire, Eng., 1993. Trainee ctrl. buyer John Lewis, London, 1949-50; sub-editor Reuters Wire Svc., London, 1950-52; econ. corres., bur. mgr. Reuters Wire Svc., Brussels and Madrid, 1953-55; spokesman European Coal and Steel Cmty.'s High Authority, Luxembourg, 1955-58; spokesman, head publs. divsn. European Cmty. Joint Info. Svc., Brussels, 1958-65; dir. European Cmty. Press and Info. Office, London, 1965-73; chmn., mng. dir. Derek Prag Assocs., London, 1973-79; mem. for Hertfordshire European Parliament, 1979-94; editor Fin. Times Bus. Letter from Europe, London, 1975-77; dep. chmn. Brit. Conservative spokesman Instl.l Com., European Parliament, 1989-94, spokesman European Dem. Group on instl. afairs, 1982-84, 87-92, spokesman on Polit. Affairs Com., mem. Subcom. on Human Rights, 1984-87, Subcom. on Security and Disarmament, 1989-94, Transport and Tourism Com., 1992-94, dep. chmn. 1st Com. of Enquiry in to Racism and Fascism in Europe, mem. Israel interparliamentary del., dep. chmn. S.E. Asia interparliamentary del., founder All-Party Disablement Group (now Disability Intergroup), 1980, chmn. 1980-94; founder, mem. Conservative Group for Europe, 1969, dep. chmn. 1974-77, 91-93. Author: Europe's International Strategy, 1976, Foreign Policy and Defence-A Role for Europe, Democracy in the European Union, 1998; co-author: (with E.D. Nicholson) Businessman's Guide to the Common Market, 1973; (with others) Our Future in Europe-The Long-Term Case for Going In, 1970. Chmn. London Europe Soc., 1973-2000, pres., 2000—. Lt. Brit. Army, 1942-47. Recipient Silver medal of European Merit, Found. Mérite Europeen, Luxembourg, 1974; named Hon. Dir. European Commn., Brussels, 1974, Hon. Mem. European Parliament, 1994, Comdr. Order of Leopold II, Kingdom of Belgium, 1995. Mem. Royal Overseas League, Royal Anglo-Belgian Club. Mem. Conservative Party. Avocations: music, theater, swimming, gardening, foreign languages. Home: 47 New Rd, Digswell Welwyn AL6 0AQ, England

PRAHARAJ, SHANTI SHANKAR, neurosurgeon; b. Chakradharpur, Bihar, India, Nov. 18, 1961; s. Sudha Krishna and Usha Rani (Chokroborty) P.; m. Sujata Maitra; 1 child, Sushanto. B Medicine B Surgery, G.R. Med. Coll., Gwalior, India, 1984, MS in Gen. Surgery, 1988, MCh in Neurosurgery, Sree Chitra Trinual Inst., Trivandrum, India, 1992. Diplomate India Nat. Bd. Exams. Resident surg. officer G.R. Med. Coll. Hosp., Gwalior, 1985-88; sr. resident in neurosurgery Sree Chitra Tirunal inst. Med. Sci. and Tech., Trivnadrum, 1989-92; cons. neurosurgeon Sehgal Neurol. Rsch. Inst., New Delhi, 1992-93; asst. prof. neurosurgery St. John's Med. Coll. and Hosp., Bangalore, India, 1993-94, A.I.I.M.S., New Delhi, 1995, N.I.M.H.A.N.S., Bangalore, 1995—; registrar in neurosurgery Newcastle (U.K.) Gen. Hosp., 1994-95; co-organizer Neurosurgery Update '98, Bangalore, 1998, Neuroendoscopy Workshop, Bangalore, 1997; presenter, lectr. in field. Contbr. articles to profl. jours. Mem. Neurol. Soc. India (life, Best paper award 1996), Neuro-otolobical and Equilibriumetric Soc. India (life), Bangalore Neurol. Soc. (life). Avocations: travel, family. Office: Nimhans Dept Neurosurgery, Hosur Rd, Bangalore Karnataka 560 029, India

PRAHM, LARS PHILIPSEN, director general, science institute administrator, atmospheric scientist; b. Aarhus, Denmark, May 1, 1944; s. Hilmar Philipsen and Barbara P.; m. May-Britt Jensen. MSc, Tech. U. Denmark, 1971; DSc, U. Copenhagen, 1979. Rschr. RISQ, Denmark, 1971-72, Danish Meteorol. Inst. (DMI), Copenhagen, 1972-77, Nat. Agy. Environ. Protection, Copenhagen, 1977-83; dir. computing Danish Meteorol. Inst. (DMI), 1983-87, dir. gen., 1987—; coun. mem. European Ctr. for Medium Range Weather Forecasts, Reading, England (ECMWF), 1987—, v.p. 1999-2000; coun. mem. European Orgn. for Exploitation of Meteorol. Satellites, Darmstadt (EUMETSAT), Germany, 1987—; Danish permanent rep. of World Meteorol. Orgn. (WMO), 1987—; pres. Danish Space Bd., Copenhagen, 1996-2000; v.p. European Ctr. Medium Range Weather Forecasts, 1999—. Editor (jour.) Atmospheric Environment, 1980-99, Jour. Atmospheric Chemistry, 1981-90. Mem. (coun.) European Space Agy. (ESA). Office: Danish Meteorological Inst, Lyngbyvej 100, DK 2100 Copenhagen Denmark

PRAIS, DARIO, physician, researcher; b. Buenos Aires, July 27, 1963; s. Isaac and Eva (Rosenberg) P.; m. Paula Wilhelm, Aug. 17, 1986; children: Yogev, Tamar, Yaniv. Physician Rabin Med. Ctr., Israel. Office: Rabin Med Ctr, Belinson Campus, 49100 Petah-Tikua Israel Address: Rabin Med Ctr Dept Neonatal, Beilinson Campus, 49100 Petah Tiqwa Israel

PRAJAPATI, JASHBHAI B., dairy microbiologist; b. Nanikhadol, Gujarat, India, Oct. 31, 1958; s. B.R. and Surajben B. P.; m. Meenaben J. Prajapati; children: Neha, Chintan. BS in Dairy Tech., Gujator Agrl. U./ Anand, India, 1980, MS in Dairy Microbiology, 1984; PhD in Dairy Microbiology, Nat. Dairy Rsch. Inst., Karnal, India, 1990. Agr. officer Gujarat Agr. U., Anand, India, 1982-84, asst. prof., 1984-91, assoc. prof., 1991—; asst. rector Gau, Anand, 1991-94; examiner several univs., India, 1984—; INSA vis. fellow NDRI, Karnal, India, 1993. Author: (book) Fundamentals of Dairy Microbiology, 1995; editor: (newsletter) DSCA News Link, 1997—; contbr. 100 articles to profl. jours. and publs. Recipient Chancellor's gold medal Govt. of Gujarat, 1984, Hari Ohm Ashram award S.P. U., 1987, Prof. J.P. Trivedi award GASS, Ahmedabad, 1993. Mem. Indian Dairy Assn. (life), Indian Sci. Congress Assn., Assn. Food Sci. and Technologists (life), Assn. Microbiologists of India (life). Avocations: tech. writing, social activities, friends. E-mail: jbprajapati@gau.guj.nic.in. Office: Dept Dairy Microbiology, SMC Coll Dairy Sci GAU, Anand/Gujarat 388110, India

PRAKASARAO, ANDRA SURYA, retired aerospace executive; b. Dowlaishwaram, Andhra, India, Sept. 13, 1939; s. Andra Subbarao and Andra Potula Narasaratnam; m. Andra Sarojini Damerla, June 18, 1967; children: Usha, Venu. BSc with honors, Andhra U., Waltair, India, 1958, MSc, 1959; PhD, Phys. Rsch. Lab., Ahmedabad, India, 1970. Jr. lectr. Andhra U., Waltair, 1959-61; elec. engr. Phys. Rsch. Lab., Ahmedabad, 1962-65, rsch. assoc., 1965-71; postdoctoral rsch. staff MIT, Cambridge, 1971-73; group head Isro Satellite Ctr., Bangalore, India, 1973-86, dep. dir., 1984-97. Contbr. articles to profl. jours. Fellow Instn. Electronics and Telecom. Engrs.; mem. IEEE (sr.). Avocations: studies in sustainable development, futures, school education. Home: Vanikrupa 47 2nd Main, Amarjyoti Layout Sanjaynagar, RMVII Ph Bangalore 560 094, India

PRAKASH, KUNJA ADHAVAN, biomedical engineer; b. Vellore, Tamilnadu, India, Aug. 27, 1969; s. Kunja Manickam Prakasam and Prakasam Vairam. Grad. in engring., Madras U., India; postgrad. in med. instrumentation, Bharathiar U., India; postgrad. in biomedicine, Mangalore U., India. sr. lectr. dept. electronics and comms. Arunai Engring. Coll., Tamilnadu, India. Mem. Biomed. Engring. Soc. India. E-mail: adhavan-prakash@hotmail.com. Home: 1/1 Masilamani Mdr Hostel, Vellore Tamilnadu 632001, India Office: Arunai Engring Coll, Tiruvannamalai, 606603 Tamilnadu India

PRAKASH, SWATANTRA, engineering executive; b. Kanpur, India, Aug. 15, 1952; s. Jagat Narain and Ramsundari Devi Dwivedi; m. Nirmala Dwivedi, Feb. 19, 1980; children: Aditi, Vatsa. B of Tech. in Chem. Engring., Inst. Tech. BHU, Varanasi, India, 1974, M of Tech. in Chem. Engring., 1976; PhD in Metall. Engring., Indian Inst. Tech., Kharagpur, India, 1988. Project officer Indian Inst. Tech., Kanpur, 1977-78; sr. process engr. Saurashtra Chems., Parbandar, India, 1978-80; mem. faculty Harcourt Butler Technol. Inst., Kanpur, 1980-81; scientist Nat. Metall. Lab., Jamshedpur, India, 1981-89, asst. dir., 1989-94, joint dep. dir., 1994—; acad. visitor Imperial Coll. Sci., London, 1991-92. Author: Dephosphorisation of Steel and Secondary Steelmaking to Produce Clean Steel, 1991; co-author: Kinetics of Metallurgical Reactions, 1991; editor: Transport Phenomena in Metallurgical Processes, 1996; contbr. articles to profl. jours.; patentee in field. Brit. Govt. fellow Imperial Coll., 1991; Dept. Atomic Energy grantee, Bombay, 1996; CSIR grantee, New Delhi, 1996, 98, grantee Dept. Sci. and Tech., New Delhi, 1996. Fellow Inst. Engrs.; mem. Indian Inst. Metal, Iron and Steel Inst. Japan, Rotary Club, BHU Alumni Assn. (sec. 1984). Avocations: swimming, driving, squash, billiards. Fax: 0091(657) 270527. E-mail: sprksh@yahoo.com. Office: Nat Metall Lab, Jamshedpur 831007, India

PRAKASH, THAZHA PURATHIYATH, research scientist, chemist; b. Menapram, Kerala, India, May 4, 1964; came to the U.S., 1994; s. Raghavan and Janu Kunhi Parambath; m. Smitha Prakash, Mar. 21, 1993; 1 child, Piyush. BS in Chemistry, Calicut (India) U., 1984; MS in Chemistry, Cochin (India) U. Sci. & Tech., 1986; PhD in Chemistry, Nat. Chem. Lab., Pune, Maharashtra, India, 1993. Postdoctoral rschr. U. Calif., Riverside, 1994-96, ISIS Pharms., Carlsbad, Calif., 1996-99; sr. scientist ISIS Pharms., Carlsbad,

1999—. Contbr. articles to profl. jours. Mem. Am. Chem. Soc. Avocations: reading, tennis, volleyball, chess, table tennis. E-mail: tprakash@isisph.com. Home: Kunhi Parambath House, PO Chokli Thalassery, Kerala 670672, India Office: ISIS Pharms 2280 Faraday Ave Carlsbad CA 92008-7208

PRAMANIK, ALADDIN, biophysicist, biochemist, researcher, educator; b. Jamalpur, Bangladesh, July 12, 1955; arrived in Sweden, 1985; s. Mofizuddin and Rahima Khatun (Munshi) P.; m. Catrine Svetlana Alexjevna Sytcheva, Jan. 11, 1983; children: Lotta, Alec. MSc with honors, Moscow State U., 1980, PhD, 1984. Postdoctoral rschr. dept. biophysics Moscow State U., 1984-85; postdoctoral rschr. dept. biochemistry Arrhenius Labs., U. Stockholm, 1985-86, rsch. assoc., 1986-89, cons., 1989-90; sr. rschr. dept. neurosci. Karolinska Inst., Stockholm, 1989-96, assoc. prof. dept biochemistry and biophysics, 1996—; cons. dept. biochemistry Arrhenius Labs., U. Stockholm, 1989-90. Inventor inorganic pyrophosphate dependent protein kinase, c-peptide receptor peptide function; contbr. articles to profl. jours. Scholarship The Swedish Inst., 1985-87; grantee Wenner-Gren Found., 1987-89. Mem. Swedish Univ. Tchrs. Assn., Swedish Soc. Medicine, Soc. for Neurosci., European Coll. Neuropsychopharmacology (award 1991). Islam. Avocations: languages, music, fishing, ice hockey, promenade. Home: Ruddammsvagen 34, 1TR, 114 21 Stockholm Sweden Office: Karolinska Inst, Von Ellers Vägs, 171 77 Stockholm Sweden

PRAMANIK, BIRENDRA N., chemistry researcher; b. Santahar, Bogra, Bangladesh, Jan. 23, 1944; came to U.S., 1970; s. Kanai Lal and Charu Bala Pramanik; m. Nandita Pramanik, Aug. 16, 1964; children: Barnali, Bidyut. MSc, Rajshahi (Bangladesh) U., 1965; MS, Stevens Inst. of Tech., 1973, PhD, 1977. Sr. analytical chemist Richarson-Vicks, Inc., Mount Vernon, N.Y., 1978-80; sr. scientist Schering-Plough Corp., Bloomfield, N.J., 1980-83, prin. scientist, 1984-87; sr. prin. scientist Schering-Plough Rsch. Inst., Bloomfield, N.J., 1987-90; devel. fellow Schering-Plough Rsch. Inst., Kenilworth, N.J., 1990-95, sr. devel. fellow, 1996; sr. rsch. fellow Schering-Plough Rsch. Inst., Kenilworth, 1996—; course dir. Ea. Analytical Symposium, 1996—; vis. scientist Stevens Inst. of Tech., N.J., 1975-77, 96—; spkr. in field. Editor Applied Electrospray Mass Spectrometry, 2000; contbr. chpts. to books and over 90 articles to profl. publs. Recipient Richardson Vick Chmns. award Vicks Chem. Co., 1980. Mem. N.J. Mass Spectrometry (chmn.-elect 1989, chmn. 1990), Am. Soc. of Mass Sepctrometry (oral co-chair 1999). Avocations: gardening, tennis. Home: 3 Tara Dr Parsippany NJ 07054-3312 Office: Schering-Plough Rsch Inst 2015 Galloping Hill Rd Kenilworth NJ 07033-1300

PRAMANN, ROBERT FREDERICK, JR., psychologist; b. Panama City, Fla., July 24, 1954; s. Robert Frederick and Jane Carolyn P.; m. Pebble Lyn Messamore, June 2, 1979; children: Emery Alan, Amber Janene. BA in Psychology, Westmont Coll., 1977; MA in Clin./Counseling Psychology, Western Conservative Bapt.Sem., Portland, 1983; PhD in Clin. Psychology, Western Conservative Bapt.Sem., 1986. Lic. psychologist, Utah; cert. group psychotherapist, Nat. Register Cert. Group Psychotherapists; cert. practitioner of psychodrama, Am. Bd. Examiners in Psychodrama, Sociometry, and group psychotherapy; nat. register for H.S.P. Clin. psychology intern Philhaven Hosp., Mt. Gretna, Pa., 1985-86; postdoctoral intern in psychol. assessment State of Utah, Salt Lake City, 1986-87; psychology resident Mt. Olympus Christian Counseling Ctr., Salt Lake City, 1986-87; psychologist Shepherd's Staff Christian Couns. Ctr., Sandy, Utah, 1989—; clin. dir. Shepherd's Staff Christian Couns. Ctr., Sandy, 1998—; psychodrama workshop trainer Shepherd's Staff Christian Couns. Ctr., 1997—; presentor conferences in field. Author publs. in field. Mem. Internat Soc. Study Dissociation (founder Wasatch chap.), Christian Assn. Psychol. Studies. Avocations: running, skiing, camping, fishing. E-mail: utpramann@aol.com. Office: Shepherds Staff Christian Couns Ctr 731 E 8600 S Sandy UT 84094-6312

PRANADA, MARFRED JANDOC, financial adviser; b. Pleiku, Vietnam, May 17, 1970; s. Alfredo and Magdalena (Jandoc) P. BS in Bus. Econs., U. Philippines, 1991; MBA, Australian Nat. U., 1995. Rsch. asst. to v.p. Philippine Inst. Devel. Studies, Manila, 1991-92; lect., co-officer in charge Ctr. for Rsch. & Comms., Manila, 1992-93; mgr. AusAsean Group Ltd, Manila, Kuala Lumpur, Sydney, Jakarta, 1995-96; v.p. Price Waterhouse Fin. Advisors, Inc., Manila, 1997—; lectr. U. of Asia and the Pacific, Pasig City, Philippines, 1997—. Office: Pricewaterhouse Coopers, 14th Fl Multinat Bancorp Ct, Makati City Manila, Philippines

PRANANTO, BENI, shipping executive; b. Kudus, Indonesia, Jan. 3, 1959; d. Djoni Prananto and Tanti Soewandi; m. Netty Bunyamin, Sept. 6, 1984; children: Lesley, Kenny, Claudia Aristya, Kristy Arysnia. Degree in mktg., Vanier Coll., Montreal, Can., 1979; B of Commerce, Concordia U., Montreal, 1981. Dir. PT Pan Asia Express Lines, Jakarta, Indonesia, 1984—; mng. dir. PT Rama Dinamika Raya, Jakarta, 1985—, PT Fatrapolindo, Jakarta, 1987—, PT Tasikmadu Shipping, Jakarta, 1992—; commr. PT Asia Perintis Contindo, Jakarta, 1994—; mng. dir. PT Mitra Rajasa Tbk, Jakarta, 1994—. Treas. Patra Biru Found., Jakarta, 1984; chmn. Anugerah Kudus Found., Jakarta, 1995. Avocations: sports cars, fishing. Office: PT Mitra Rajasa Tbk, Jl A M Sangaji #12, Jakarta 10130, Indonesia

PRANCE, SIR GHILLEAN TOLMIE, botanical gardens administrator, botanist; b. Brandeston, Suffolk, Eng., July 13, 1937; s. Basil Camden and Margaret Hope (Tolmie) P.; m. Anne Elizabeth Hay, July 13, 1961; children: Rachel Julia, Sarah Elizabeth. BA, Oxford U., 1960, DPhil, 1963, MA, 1965; Fil Dr (hon.), Goteborg U., 1983; DSc (hon.), Portsmouth U., 1994, U. Kent, 1994, Kingston U., 1994, St. Andrews U., 1995, Bergen U., 1996, Sheffield U., 1997, Fla. Internat. U., 1997, CUNY, 1998, Liverpool U., 1998, Glasgow U., 1999, Plymouth U., 1999, Keele U., 2000, Exeter U., 2000. Rsch. asst. N.Y. Bot. Garden, Bronx, 1963-66, assoc. curator, 1966-68, curator Amazonian botany, 1968-75, dir. rsch., v.p., 1975-8l, sr. v.p., dir. Inst. Econ. Botany, 1981-88; dir. Royal Bot. Gardens, Kew, Eng., 1988-99; sci. dir. The Eden Project, 1999—; McBryde prof. Nat. Tropical Bot. Garden, 2000—; adj. prof. CUNY, N.Y.C., 1968-99; vis. prof. Yale U., New Haven, 1983-88, Reading (Eng.) U., 1988—; dir. grad. studies Inst. Nac. Pesquisas Amazonia, Manaus, Brazil, 1973-75. Author more than 17 books and monographs; editor 11 books; contbr. more than 320 articles to sci. jours. and popular publs. Mem. White Plains (N.Y.) Cable TV Commn., 1981-88; trustee Au Sable Inst. Environ, Mancelona, Mich., 1984—, Bd. Rainforest Alliance, 1988-97, Margaret Mee Amazon Trust, Richmond, Eng., 1988-96, Worldwide Fund for Nature Internat., 1989-93, Horniman Mus., 1990-99, Lovaine Trust Co. Ltd., 1990-99; trustee, chmn. Bentham Moxon Trust, Richmond, 1988-99. Created knight bachelor, 1995; decorated grand cross Ordem de Merito Cientifico (Brazil), 1995, Comendador da Ordem Nacional do Cruzeiro do Sul, Brazil, 2000; recipient hon. diploma of merit Inst. Nat. Pesquisas Amazonia, 1978, Disting. Svc. award N.Y. Bot. Garden, 1986, Henry Shaw medal Mo. Bot. Garden, 1988, Linnean medal, 1990, Internat. Cosmos prize Expo '90 Found. (Japan), 1993, Janaki Ammal medal Internat. Soc. Ethnobotany, 1996, Internat. award excellence Botanical Rsch. Inst. Tex., 1998, Asa Gray award Am. Soc. Plant Taxonomists, 1998, Victoria medal of honour Royal Hort. Soc., 1999, Lifetime Discovery award, 1999, Fairchild medal for plant exploration, 2000; named hon. citizen Ft. Worth; hon. fellow Keble Coll., Oxford U., 1993—. Fellow AAAS, Linnean Soc. London (pres. 1997-2000), Royal Geog. Soc. (Patron's medal 1994), Inst. Biology (pres. 2000—), Explorers Club, Royal Soc. of London for Improving Natural Knowledge; mem. Assn. for Tropical Biology (pres. 1979-80), Systematics Assn. (pres. 1988-91), Royal Danish Acad. Scis. and Letters (fgn.), Royal Swedish Acad. Scis. (fgn. mem.), Brazilian Acad. Scis. (corr.), Bot. Soc. Am. (corr.), Economic Botany Soc. (pres. 1996-97), Brit. Ecol. Soc. (hon.). Anglican. Avocation: stamp collecting.

PRANGE, ARTHUR JERGEN, JR., psychiatrist, neurobiologist, educator; b. Grand Rapids, Mich., Sept. 19, 1926; s. Arthur Jergen and Martha Frances (Elliott) P.; m. Sarah Elizabeth Bowen, Feb. 4, 1950; children—Christine Anne, Martha Louise, Laura Beth, David Elliott. B.S., U. Mich., 1947, M.D., 1950. Intern Wayne County Gen. Hosp., Eloise, Mich., 1950-51; resident in psychiatry U. N.C., Chapel Hill, 1954-57; instr. U. N.C., 1957-60, asst. prof., 1960-64, asso. prof., 1964-68, prof. psychiatry, 1968-83, Boshamer prof. psychiatry, 1983—, acting chmn. dept. psychiatry, 1983-85, dir. NIMH Clin. Rsch. Ctr., 1979—; vis. scientist Med. Rsch. Coun. Unit, Epson, Surrey, Eng., 1968-69; chmn. clin. projects rsch. rev. com. HEW, NIMH, 1975-76, chmn. bd. sci. counselors, 1986-87; mem. psychopharmacologic drugs adv. com. HEW, FDA, 1979-82. Editor: The Thyroid Axis, Drugs and Behavior, 74; Contbr. articles to med. jours. Recipient NIMH Career Devel. award 1961-69, Career Scientist award, 1969-95, Gold Medal award Soc. of Biol. Psychiatry, 1992, Exemplary Psychiatrist award Nat. Alliance for the Mentally Ill, 1997, Selo prize Nat. Alliance for Rsch. in Schizophrenia and Affective Disorders, 1997. Fellow Am. Psychiat. Assn. (life, Rsch. in Psychiatry award 1996), Am. Coll. Neuropsychopharmacology (life, pres. 1987, Hoch award 1995); mem. Internat. Soc. Psychoneuroendocrinology (founding mem.), N.C. Neuropsychiat. Assn., Collegium Internationale Neuropsychopharmacologicum, Royal Coll. Psychiatrists (London). Home: 218 Conner Dr Apt 6 Chapel Hill NC 27514-7070 Office: Univ NC Sch Medicine Dept Psychiatry Chapel Hill NC 27599-0001

PRASAD, BRAJ KISHORE, metallurgist, materials scientist, researcher, consultant; b. Bekobar, India, Jan. 24, 1956; s. Mahavir Prasad Modi and Shanti Prasad Modi; m. Meera Prasad, Feb. 9, 1981; 1 child, Neera. B of Sci. Engring. in Metallurgy, Bihar (India) Inst. Tech., 1981; M of Tech. in Metall. Engring., Indian Inst. Tech., 1983; PhD in Metall. Engring., U. Roorkee, India, 1994. Rsch. officer Regional Rsch. Lab., Bhopal, India, 1983-84; lectr. dept. metall. engring. Regional Engring. Coll., Durgapur, India, 1984-85; scientist Regional Rsch. Lab., 1985—; cons. Regional Rsch. Lab., 1990—, rsch. scientist, 1985—; rschr. in field of indsl. problems. Contbr. over 85 articles to profl. jours.; patentee in development of process for synthesis of aluminium alloy, graphite particle composites. Khosla Rsh. Awd., Univ. of Roorke, India, 1997. Mem. Instn. Engrs. India (life), Indian Inst. Metals (life), Materials Rsch. Soc. India (life), Tribology Soc. India (life), Inst. Stds. Engrs. India (life). Office: Regional Rsch Lab, Habibganj Naka, Bhopal 462 026, India

PRASAD, DASIKA HANUMANTHA LAKSHMINATHA, research scientist; b. Kaikalur, India, May 12, 1946; s. Dasika Suryanaryana and Dasika Syamalamba; m. Dasika Vijaya, May 27, 1981; children: Jaya Deepti, Ravinath. B of Tech., Andhra U., Waltair, India, 1967; MS, Indian Inst. Sci., Bangalore, 1971, PhD, 1978. Project aast., rsch. assoc. Indian Inst. Sci., Bangalore, 1978-80; scientist Indian Inst. Chem. Tech., Hyderabad, India, 1980—. Contbr. chpt. to Handbook of Heat and Mass Transfer, 1986; contbr. articles to porfl. jours. Avocations: reading, writing, walking, religion. Office: IICT Chem Engring Lab, Uppal Rd Tarnaka, Hyderabad 500 007, India

PRASAD, KODATI SATYA, electronics and communication educator, researcher; b. Kaja, India, Aug. 5, 1955; s. Kodati Gopala Krishnaiah and Kodati Pushpavathi; m. Kodati Lakshmi, June 21, 1980; children: Sireesha, Sree Rekha. Btech., JNTU Coll. Engring., Anantapur, India, 1977; ME, Coll. Engring, Madras, India, 1979; PhD, Indian Inst. Tech., Madras, 1989. Teaching asst. Regional Engring. Coll., Warangal, India, 1979; lectr. JNTU Coll. Engring., Kakinada, India, 1987-88; asst. prof. JNTU Coll. Engring., Hyderabad, India, 1987-88; asst. prof. electronics and comm. JNTU Coll. Engring., Anantapur, India, 1988-97, prof. electronics and comms. engring., 1997—. Mem. Indian Soc. Tech. Edn. (exec. coun. 1992-94), Instn. of Engrs. Avocations: reading, travel. Office: JNTU Coll Engring, 515 002 Anantapur India

PRASAD, KRISHNA CHANDRA, mathematics educator, consultant; b. Champaran, Bihar, India, Jan. 15, 1946; s. Kamaleshwar and Yogmaya P.; m. Kiran Bala, May 20, 1972; children: Kumar Alok, Kumari Richa, Kumari Ritu, Kumari Nimisha. BSc, Bhagalpur U., Dumka, India, 1963; MSc, Patna (India) U., 1965; PhD, Ranchi (India) U., 1977. Lectr. Commerce Coll., Patna, India, 1965-66, Ranchi (India) Coll., 1966-80; reader Ranchi U., 1980-85, prof., 1985—; head math. dept. Ranchi U., 1994—; editor Ranchi U. Math. Jour., 1989—; reviewer Math. Rev., U.S., 1995—; vis. associateship U. Grants Commn. Panjab U. Chandigarh, 1994-96; reg. coord. Nat. Bd. Higher Math. (atomic energy com.), 2000—. Contbr. over 20 rsch. articles to profl. jours. Coord. Akhil Bhartiya Vidyarthi Parishad, Ranchi, 1969-74; head edn. wing Rashtria Swayamsevak Sangh, Ranchi, 1986-90. Mem. Am. Math. Soc., Indian Math. Soc. (life), Bihar Math Soc. (life, acad. sec. 1994-97). Avocations: letters to editors, yoga, coaching for math. olympiads. Home: Sukhdeo Nager (Hehal), Bihar Ranchi 834 006, India Office: Ranchi U Dept Math, Bihar Ranchi 834 008, India

PRASAD, KRISHNA NANDAN, economist. MA in Econs., Delhi Sch. Econs., 1960; PhD in Econs., Gokhale Inst., Poona, India, 1969. Prof. planning devel. U. Mumbai, India, 1982—; adv. bd. Varta; cons. Planning Commn., 1980-82; mem. internat. adv. bd. STD Forum, Internat. Conf., Karachi, 2000; vis. fellow Econ. Growth Ctr. Yale U., 1998. Co-editor: Input-Output Analysis; mem. editl. bd. Internat. Jour. Devel. Lit.; contbr. articles to profl. jours. A.N. Sinha Inst. fellow, 1970, U. Bombay fellow, 1970-80. Mem. Input-Output Rsch. Assn. India (sec.). E-mail: drknprasad@hotmail.com. Fax: 91 22 611 6707. Address: D-303 Shanti Complex Tunga, Shiv Shakt Nagar Sakivihar Rd, L8T # 7 Powai Mumbai 400 072, India

PRASAD, MOHIT KISHORE, electrical engineer; b. Gaya, Bihar, India, Apr. 16, 1962; s. Gopi Kishore and Madhuri Bhushan P.; m. Faith Marie Stapleton, July 28, 1990; 1 child: Mallika. B in Tech., Indian Inst. Tech., Kanpur, Uttar Pradesh, 1983; MS, SUNY, Buffalo, 1996, PhD. Mem. devel. staff IBM, Tucson, 1990-91, adv. engr., 1991-93; mem. tech. staff Bell Labs., Lucent Techs., Allentown, Pa., 1994-98; staff engr. Sony Wireless, San Diego, 1998-99, sr. staff engr., 1999—. Avocations: reading, jogging, electronics. Home: 9125 Truman St San Diego CA 92129-3631 Office: Sony Corp 16450 W Bernardo Dr San Diego CA 92127-1898

PRASAD, RAHUL RASIK, physicist, researcher; b. New Delhi, Apr. 20, 1961; came to U.S., 1982; s. Devki Nandan and Shirley (Gupta) P.; m. Sharmila Majumdar, Feb. 19, 1985. BSc in Physics with honors, St. Stephen's Coll., New Delhi, 1982; MS in Applied Physics, Yale U., 1984, MPhil in Applied Physics, 1985, PhD in Applied Physics, 1987. Assoc. rsch. scientist Yale U., New Haven, 1987-89; sr. physicist Physics Internat. Co., San Leandro, Calif., 1989-90; sr. rsch. scientist Sci. Rsch. Lab., Alameda, Calif., 1990-94; prin. scientist Alameda Applied Scis. Corp., San Leandro, Calif., 1994—. Contbr. over 35 articles to profl. jours. Mem. IEEE, Am. Phys. Soc. (div. fluid dynamics, gallery of fluid motion award 1987 div. plasma physics), Am. Vacuum Soc., Sigma Xi. Home: 595 Creedon Cir Alameda CA 94502-7795 Office: Alameda Applied Scis Corp 2235 Polvorosa Dr Ste 230 San Leandro CA 94577-2249

PRASAD, RAMON, physicist, mathematics educator; b. London, Apr. 1, 1940; m. Anne Barbara Ramshaw, Sept. 2, 1967. BS in Physics, London U., 1961, MS in Theoretical Physics, 1962, PhD in Theoretical Physics, 1967. Lectr. then sr. lectr. Middlesex U., London, 1967—. Author: (books) Unified Field Theory, 1975, Fundamental Constants, 1981, Elem. Particles, 1984, Interacting Fields, 1993. Avocations: classical paintings, classical music. Home: 21 Nassington Rd, Hampstead London NW3 2TX, England Office: Middlesex U, Bounds Green Rd, London N11 2NQ, England

PRASAD, SHAILENDRA KRISHNA, animal scientist, educator; b. Patna, Bihar, India, Jan. 21, 1942; s. Rameshwar and Sumitra (Devi) P.; m. Kiran Sahai, May 2, 1966; children: Sandeep, Neeraj, Sourabh. B Vet. Sci. and Animal Husbandry, Bihar Vet. Coll., 1965; MSc, Nat. Dairy Rsch. Inst., Karnal, India, 1969; PhD, Panjab U., Karnal, 1978. Cert. vet. and animal husbandry. Asst. lectr. Ranchi (India) Vet. Coll., 1965-71; sr. rsch. fellow Coun. Sci. and Indsl. Rsch., New Delhi, 1971; asst. prof. Nat. Dairy Rsch. Inst., Karnal, 1972-76, assoc. prof., sr. scientist, head, 1976-82; prof., head immunogenetics divsn., scientist S3 Nat. Inst. Animal Genetics, Karnal, 1982-86, prin. scientist, head immunogenetics divsn., 1986-98, dir. Nat. Bur. Animal Genetic Resources, 1992, project coord. blood group and biochem. genetics, 1987—; prin. investigator dept. biotech. Govt. of India, New Delhi, 1999; dir. Nat. Bus. Animal Genetic Resources, 2000. Author: A Practical Approach to Immunogenetics of Farm Animals, 1992, Recent Advances in Immunological Control of Fertility in Farm Animals, 1984, Bovine MHC Class I Antigens, 1986-92, Yak-A Valuable Genetic Resource of Alpine Pastures, 1997; co-author: Applications of Genetic Techniques in Farm Animals. Rsch. fellow UN Devel. Project, Wageningen, Holland, 1973, fellow IAEA, Havana, 1979. Mem. Soc. Conservation Domestic Animal Biodiversity (life), Indian Immunology Soc. (life). Hindu. Avocations: music, reading, gardening.

PRASAD, SUBHASH CHANDRA, engineering educator, researcher, consultant; b. Rusera, Bihar, India, Jan. 2, 1948; s. Mahabir Prasad and Ram Sakhi (Devi) Arya; m. Madhuri Kumari, June 30, 1972; children: Pushp, Shefali. BSc in Engring., Bihar Inst. Tech., Sindri, 1971; MTech, Indian Inst. Tech., Kanpur, 1977, PhD, 1987. Sr. tech. asst. Ctrl. Ground Water Bd., Chandigarh, 1973-74; rsch. asst. Indian Inst. Tech., Kanpur, 1976; civil engring. lectr. Madan Mohan Malviya Engring. Coll., Gorakhpur, 1976-77; civil engring. lectr. Motilal Nehru Regional Engring. Coll., Allahabad, 1977-87, civil engring. reader, 1987-97, prof. civil engring., 1997—; assoc. prof. environ. engring. Arbaminch (Ethiopia) Water Tech. Inst., 1991-92, head environ. engring., 1992-93; chief coord. Indian Tng. Networks Course, Allahabad, 1994-99; expert selection com. Aligarh Muslim U. Mem. Instn. Engrs. (life), Indian Soc. Tech. Edn. (life), Indian Water Works Assn. (life), Indian Assn. Environ. Mgmt. (life), All India Coun. for Tech. Edn. (mem. review com.). Avocations: reading, music, social work. Office: MNR Engring Coll, Dept Civil Engring, 211004 Allahabad 211004, India

PRASAD, VEENA RANI, English language educator; b. Muzaffarpur, Bihar, India, Jan. 10, 1940; d. Lal Bahadur Prasad and Shanti Devi; m. Awadh Kumar Sinha, June 10, 1962. BA with honors and distinction, Bihar U., India, 1958, MA in English, 1960, PhD, 1973. Lectr. MDDM Coll./Bihar U., Muzaffarpur, 1960-75, reader and head, 1975-85, univ. prof., 1985—. Author: (book) Wallace Stevens: The Symbolic Dimension of His Poetry, 1987; contbr. articles to profl. jours.

PRASAD, YAMUNA, English educator; b. Daltongunj, Bihar, India; s. Modi Chhakauri and Devi Rada; m. Devi Maya, May, 5, 1968; 4 children. BA in English with honors, 1965, MA in English, 1967, PhD, 1978. Prof., head dept. English; lectr. in field. Author: E.M. Forster: The Theory and Practice of His Novels, 1980. Avocation: poetry writing in Hindu and English. Home: Cheya Villa, New Colony Korra, Hazaribag Bihar 825301, India Office: Vinoba Bhave U, Dept English, Hazaribag Bihar 825301, India

PRASHAD, HAR, company executive, researcher; b. Garhi Habibullah, India, July 5, 1944; s. Makhan Lal and Veeran Wali H.; m. Darshan Kumari; 2 children. BSc, DBS Coll., India, 1964; MSc, DAV Coll., India, 1965; ME (hons), Moscow, 1970; PhD in Mech. Engring., Hyderabad, India, 1993. Sr. engr. BHEL, Hyderabad, 1974-79, dep. mgr., 1979-83, mgr., 1983-90, sr. mgr., 1990-94, dep. gen. mgr., 1994-99, sr. dep. gen. mgr., 1999—; ASST engr. Bakarosteel, Dhanbad, India, 1971; pool officer Indian Inst. Petroleum, Dehradun, India, 1970. Contbr. over 100 articles to profl. jours.; patentee in field; editor: TSI newsletter, 1997-99. Mem. Tribology Soc. (joint sec. 1997-99, life), STLE. Avocations: reading, spiritual orientation, lectures on religion. Home: Domal Guda 302 Central View, 1-2-319/A Gagan Mahal, Hyderabad 500029, India Office: BHEL Corp R&D, Vikas Nagar, Hyderabad 500029, India

PRASSIANAKIS, IOANNIS NICOLAOS, mechanics educator, researcher; b. Chania, Crete, Greece, July 9, 1941; s. Nikolas Georgios and Eleftheria Leonidas (Kouridaki) P.; m. Maria Christodoulos Sgourou, Sept. 18, 1977; children: Eleftheria, Nicolaos. Physicist, Nat. U. Athens, 1969; PhD, Nat. Tech. U. Athens, 1979. Asst. educator, rschr. Nat. Tech. U. Athens, 1970-82, lectr., 1982-85, asst. prof., 1985-95, assoc. prof., 1996—; vis. prof. Tech. U. Crete, Greece, 1985-88; mem. Hellenic Orgn. for Standardization (ELOT)/Tech. Com. 70 for Non Destructive Testing, 1992—; organizer of 14 seminars on Non Destructive Testing methods of grade level II; participant in internat. and nat. workshops; rschr.; head of testing materials lab, Nat. Tech. U. Athens. Author: Kinematics and Dynamics of Point Particle and Absolutely Solid Body, 1987, Mechanics of Deformed Material-Strength of Materials, 1987, Experimental Strength of Materials (theory), 1988, Experimental Strength of Materials (laboratories and excercises), 1993, Non-Destructive Testing of Materials - The NDT Method of Ultrasounds, 1996, others dealing with materials strengths or testing methods. Fellow Brit. Inst Non-Destructive Testing; mem. Hellenic Soc. Non-Destructive Testing (pres. 1996—), N.Y. Acad. Scis and other profl. and social orgns. Achievements include development of method for axial extension and triaxial loading of concrete, Mohr envelope; experiments in tests including ultrasounds, industrial radiography, Eddy currents, liquid penetrant, magnetic particle, thermography, acoustic emisssion, and visual examination. E-mail address: Prasian@Central.ntua.gr. Home: 23 Nikis St Kalimaki Alimou, GR.17455 Athens Greece Office: NTUAthens Enging Sci Dept, 5 Iroon of Polytech Ave, GR 15773 Athens Greece

PRAT, FREDERIC PIERRE, hepatogastroenterologist; b. St. Mande, France, Feb. 2, 1960; s. Pierre Jacques and Genevieve Anne Marie (Baudry) P.; m. Lydie Nathalie Larquemin, Sept. 10, 1994; children: Thomas, Antoine, Clara, Maxence. Parasitology/Tropical Medicine Master, Lyon 1, France, 1984; MD, Paris XI, France, 1986; Statistics and Epidemiology Master, Lyon 1, France, 1988; Gastroenterologist, Paris XI, France, 1989; PhD, Lyon 1, France, 1993. Cert. digestive oncology. Intern Lyon U. Hosps., France, 1984-89; mission coord. Medecins Du Monde, Guatemala, 1985, S. Africa, 1986; rschr. Nat. Inst. Med. Rsch. (INSERM), Lyon, 1990-91; asst. prof. Paris U. Hosps., 1992-95, cons. endoscopy, 1996—; cons. scientific commn., U. Paris XI, France, 1992-95, scientific com. Nat. Soc. for Digestive Endoscopy, 1999—. Patentee: Ultrasound Applicator for Endoscopic Tumor Destruction, 1998; contbr. articles to profl. jours. Mem. Action for Tobin Tax, France, 1998—, Medecins Du Monde, 1985—. Recipient Ferring Grant for Digestive Rsch., Ferring Corp., 1993, rsch. grants Cancer Rsch. Assn., Paris, 1995-97, Paris U. Hosps., 1997-99. Mem. Am. Assn. Cancer Rsch., Am. Soc. Gastrointestinal Endoscopy, Soc. Nat. Francaise de Gastroenterologie, 1992. Avocations: public health in developing countries, nutritional hazards. Office: Svc Maladies/L'App Digestif, 78 Rue due General Leclerc, 94275 Le Kremlin-Bicêtre France

PRAT, VIVIANE, media company executive; b. Casablanca, Morocco, Mar. 21, 1945; d. Albert and Suzanne (Myare) Assor; m. Jean-Marie Prat, Apr. 12, 1972 (div. 1983); m. Philippe Garnier; 3 children. Grad., Sch. Higher Comml. Studies, Paris, 1968. Media planner Synergie, Paris, 1970-74, media dir., 1975-84; gen. mgr. Zenith-Club Media, Paris, 1984-88; pres. Optimum Media, Paris, 1989-96; pres., CEO Optimum Media Direction (OMD), Paris, 1996—. Home: 28 Blvd Raspail, 75007 Paris France Office: OMD, 15 rue Pasquier, 75008 Paris France

PRATAP, SIDDHARTH, electromechanics researcher, educator; b. Bombay, Dec. 21, 1955; came to U.S., 1981; s. Bharatkumar Dhirajlal and Snehlata Bharatkumar Pratap; m. Swati Siddharth Pratap, Jan. 17, 1985; children: Paulomi S., Mallika S. B in Engring., U. Bombay, 1979; MS, U. Tex., 1982, PhD in Engring., 1996. Grad. engr. Tata Engring. and Locomotive Inc., Bombay, 1979-81; grad. rsch. asst. Ctr. for Electromechanics U. Tex., Austin, 1982-83, rsch. engr. assoc. II, 1983-84, rsch. engr. assoc. III, 1984-86, rsch. engr. assoc. IV, 1986-87, rsch. engr. assoc. V, 1987-90, spl. rsch. assoc., 1990-91, rsch. assoc., 1991-97, rsch. scientist, 1997, chief scientist, 1997—, sr. adj. prof., 1997—, co-prin. investigator, 1998—. Contbr. articles to profl. jours., chpt. to book; patentee in field. Mem. IEEE. Avocations: reading, flying kites, nature trekking. Office: Ctr for Electromechanics U Tex Austin PRC-EME Mail Code R7000 Austin TX 78712

PRATHER, WILLIAM C., III, lawyer, writer; b. Toledo, Ill., Feb. 20, 1921; s. Hollie Cartmill and Effie Fern (Deppen) P. BA, U. Ill., 1942, JD, 1947. Bar: Ill. 1947, U.S. Supreme Ct. 1978. Co-pres. student govt. U. Ill., 1942, asst. dean, 1942-43; atty. First Nat. Bank Chgo., 1947-51; asst. gen. counsel U.S. Savs. and Loan League, Chgo., 1951-59; gen. counsel U.S. League of Savs. Instns., Chgo., 1959-82, gen. counsel emeritus, 1982—; sole practice Cumberland County, Ill., 1981—; sem. lectr. in law, banking. Editor: The Legal Bulletin, 1951-81, The Federal Guide, 1954-81; author: Savings Accounts, 8th edit., 1981; contbr. articles to publs. Lt. Armed Forces, 1943-45. Decorated Bronze Star. Mem. ABA, FBA, Internat. Bar Assn., Ill. Bar Assn., Chgo. Bar Assn., Union Internat. des Avocats, Nat. Lawyers Club Washington, Cosmos Club, Univ. Club Chgo., Kiwanis, Mattoon Golf and Country Club, Exeter and County Club (Eng.), Club de Bonmont Melisande (France), Tennis Club de Beaulieu (France), Soc. Colonial Wars, Phi Delta Phi, Phi Gamma Delta, Phi Eta Sigma, Phi Alpha Chi. Home: Applewood Farm PO Box 157 Toledo IL 62468-0157 Office:

142 Courthouse Sq Toledo IL 62468 also: L'Orangeraie, 42 Av General Leclerc, Villefranche-sur-Mer 06230, France

PRATLEY, DAVID ILLINGWORTH, management consultant; b. London, Dec. 24, 1948; s. Arthur George and Olive Constance (Illingworth) P.; m. Caryn Lois Becker, 1966. LLB, U. Bristol, 1970. Dir. Greater London Arts Assn., 1976-81; regional dir. Arts Coun. Gt. Britain, London, 1981-86; chief exec. Royal Liverpool Philharmonic Soc., 1987-88; mng. dir. Trinity Coll. Music, London, 1988-91; dir. leisure, tourism and econ. devel. City of Bath, U.K., 1992-96; prin. David Pratley Assocs., London, 1996—; chmn. bd. Dance Umbrella Ltd., London, 1990-92. Policy advisor Social Democrat Party, London, 1986-88; chmn. Nat. Campaign for the Arts, London, 1988-92; nat. lottery policy advisor Arts Coun. Eng., 1996—. Fellow Royal Soc. Arts; mem. Brit. Am. Arts Assn. (project advisor 1986-92), Athenaeum. Avocations: arts, landscape gardening, travel. Home and Office: 54 Walnut Tree Walk, London SE11 6DN, England Office: 14 Great Peter St, London SW1, England

PRATLEY, KIMLEIGH GEORGE MONTAGUE, manufacturing and mining company executive; b. Johannesburg, Transvaal, South Africa, Mar. 24, 1954; s. George Montague and Marguerite Joan (Liddon) P.; m. Valerie Naida Wright, Jan. 10, 1980; children: Andrew, Charles. BSc in Engring., U. Witwatersrand, South Africa, 1979; grad. diploma, U. Witwatersrand, 1981, MSc in Engring., 1985. Toolmaker Pratley Mfg. and Engring. Co. Pty. Ltd., Krugersdorp, South Africa, 1979-81, tech. dir., 1982-83; mng. dir. Pratley Group of Cos., Krugersdorp, 1983—; bd. dirs. Chamdor Tng. Ctr., South Africa. Patentee in field. Maj. South African Air Force, 1980—. Named Krugersdorp Businessman of Yr., Chmn.'s award for design Atlas Aircraft Co. Mem. Krugersdorp Industrialists Assn. (chmn.), Krugersdorp Chamber of Bus. (vice chmn.), Krugersdorp Flying Club (vice chmn. 1988-2000). Avocations: flying, geology, science. Office: Pratley Group, Box 3055 Kenmare, Krugersdorp Gauteng 1745, South Africa

PRATT, ALAN JOHN, business and marketing consultant; b. Eng., July 21, 1927; s. Alan Reginald and Ellen Gwendoline (Roff) P.; m. Asako Tsuneyoshi, May 1, 1961. BA in Engnrg., Watford Coll., 1948; MBA, Calif. We. U., 1974; PhD, DBA, 1976. Surveyor Air Registration Bd., Eng. and Hong Kong, 1957-63; pres. Eutectic of Japan, Tokyo, 1963-66; group v.p. Alexander Industries, 1966-69; mgr. Far East Digital Equipment Corp., Japan, 1969-72; dir. for Japan Gen. Insrument Corp., 1972-75; exec. v.p. Klingelnberg Japan Ltd., Tokyo, 1975-79; mng. ptnr. Alan J. Pratt and Assocs., Kailua-Kona, Hawaii, 1979—; v.p. Kosei, Inc., 1979—; pres. Astra-Pacific Internat., Inc., Kailua-Kona; assoc. sr. cons. Adams-Boston Cons. Co., Tokyo, 1964-68; guest lectr. Japan-Am. Inst. Mgmt. Sci., Honolulu. pres. Kona Coffee Festival, 1984-86, Crime Stoppers West Hawaii, 1984-85, 92—, founder pres., 1992—; bd. dirs. Crime Stoppers Internat., chmn. conf., 1994, pres. 1997; bd. dirs. Interquest Inc., pres. 2000. Mem. Am. Mgmt. Assn., Inst. Quality Engrs., Soc. Mfg. Engrs., Am. C. of C. in Japan (chmn. programs com. 1972-74), Royal Aero Soc. Gt. Britain, Brit. Inst. Mgmt., Brit. Mgmt. Assn., Kona Coast C. of C. (chmn. programs and comms. com. 1980, pres. 1981-82, chmn. Japan-Asia-Australia tourist and trade rels. com. 1983-86), C. of C. of Hawaii (dir.). Roman Catholic. Home and Office: PO Box 5186 Kailua Kona HI 96745-5186

PRATT, DAVID BRUCE, industrial engineering educator; b. Oklahoma City, Jan. 6, 1954; s. Harold F. and G. Lahoma (Goyer) P.; m. Jan M. Hussey, Aug. 28, 1976; children: Brian, Kristi. BS in Indsl. Engring. and Mgmt., Okla. State U., 1976, M in Indsl. Engring., 1977, PhD in Indsl. Engring. and Mgmt., 1992. Registered prof. engr., Okla. Ops. rsch. analyst Phillips Petroleum Co., Bartlesville, Okla., 1976-81; sr. ops. rsch. analyst Phillips Petroleum Co., Bartlesville, 1981-85, sect. dir. ops. rsch., 1985-86; sr. prodn. sys. engr. Garrett Turbine Engine Co., Phoenix, 1986-87; mgr. corp. ops. rsch. Internat. Paper Co., Memphis, 1988; asst. prof. Okla. State U., Stillwater, 1992-97, assoc. prof., grad. program dir., 1997—; workshop instr. Inst. Indsl. Engrs., Norcross, Ga., 1991-92, Assn. Energy Engrs., Atlanta, 1994. Co-author: Principles of Engineering Economic Analysis, 1998; contbr. chpt. to book. Rsch. grantee NSF, Washington, 1994, 95. Mem. NSPE (programs v.p., Mathcounts coord. local chpt., state-wide scholarship com.), Am. Prodn. and Inventory Control Soc. (cert. fellow prodn. and inventory mgmt.), Am. Soc. for Quality Control (cert. quality engr.), Inst. Indsl. Engrs. (sr., sys. integration cert. com. 1991-92, sys. integration bd. mem. 1991-92). Fax: 713-968-0499. E-mail: dpratt@okstate.edu. Home: 1909 S Iba Dr Stillwater OK 74074-1334 Office: Okla State Univ 322 Engineering N Stillwater OK 74078-5017

PRATT, GEORGE JANES, JR., psychologist, author; b. Mpls., May 3, 1948; s. George Janes and Sally Elvina (Hanson) P.; m. Vonda Pratt; 1 child, Whitney Beth. BA cum laude, U. Minn., 1970, MA, 1973; PhD with spl. commendation, Calif. Sch. Psychology, San Diego, 1976. Diplomate Am. Bd. Med. Pschotherapists, Am. Acad. Pain Mgmt., Am. Coll. Forensic Examiners; lic. psychologist, CAlif., 1976. Psychology trainee Ctr. for Behavior Modification, Mpls., 1971-72, U.Minn. Student Counseling Bur., 1972-73; predoctoral clin. psychology intern San Bernardino County (Calif.) Mental Health Svcs., 1973-74, San Diego County Mental Health Services, 1974-76; mem. staff San Louis Rey Hosp., 1977-78; postdoctoral clin. psychology intern Mesa Vista Hosp., San Diego, Calif., 1976; clin psychologist, dir. Psychology and Cons. Assocs. of San Diego, 1976-90; chmn. Psychology and Cons. Assocs. Press, 1977-94; bd. dirs. Optimax, Inc., 1985-94; pres. George Pratt Ph.D., Psychol. Corp., 1979—; chmn. Pratt, Korn & Assocs., Inc., 1984-94; mem. staff Scripps Meml. Hosp., La Jolla, Calif., 1986—, chmn. psychology, 1993-95, 2000—; founder La Jolla Profl. Workshops, 1977-81; clin. psychologist El Camino Psychology Ctr., San Clemente, Calif., 1977-78; grad. teaching asst. U. Minn. Psychology and Family Studies divsn., 1971; teaching assoc. U. Minn. Psychology and Family Studies divsn., Mpls., 1972-73; instr. U. Minn. Extension divsn., Mpls., 1971-73; faculty Calif. Sch. Profl. Psychology, 1974-83, San Diego Evening Coll., 1975-77, Nat. U., 1978-79, Chapman Coll., 1978, San Diego State U., 1979-80; vis. prof. Pepperdine U., L.A., 1976-78; cons. U. Calif. at San Diego Med. Sch., 1976-78, also instr. univ., 1978—; psychology chmn. Workshops in Clin. Hypnosis, 1980-84; cons. Calif. Health Dept., 1974, Naval Regional Med. Ctr., 1978-82, ABC-TV; also speaker. Author: Sensory/Progressive Relaxation, 1979, Effective Stress Management, 1979, A Clinical Hypnosis Primer, 1984, 88, Clinical Hypnosis: Techniques and Applications, 1985; co-author: Hypnosis: Questions and Answers, 1986, HyperPerformance, 1987, Release Your Business Potential, 1988, Handbook for Hypnotic Suggestions and Metaphors, 1990, Imagery in Sports and Physical Performance, 1994, Rx for Stress, 1994, Instant Emotional Healing, 2000. With USAR, 1970-76. Fellow Am. Soc. Clin. Hypnosis (cert., approved cons.); mem. Am. Psychological Assn., Nat. Register of Health Svc. Providers in Psychology, Internat. Soc. Hypnosis, Am. Assn. Sex Educators, Counselors and Therapists (cert.), San Diego Soc. Sex. Therapy and Edn. (past pres.), San Diego Soc. Clin. Hypnosis (past pres.), San Diego Psychol. Assn., Soc. Clin. and Exptl. Hypnosis, U. Minn. Alumni Assn., Beta Theta Pi. Office: Scripps Meml Hosp Campus 9834 Genesee Ave Ste 321 La Jolla CA 92037-1216

PRATT, HILLEL, neurophysiologist; b. Haifa, Israel, Aug. 5, 1948; s. Baruch and Mona (Levinson) P.; m. Toby Kirschenbaum, Oct. 20, 1974; children: Gad, Shi. BS, Hebrew U., Jerusalem, 1972, PhD, 1977. Instr. Hebrew U., Jerusalem, 1973-77; postdoctoral fellow U. Calif., Irvine, 1977-79; lectr. Israel Inst. Tech., Haifa, 1979-82, sr. lectr., 1982-88, assoc. prof., 1988-96, prof., 1997—. Cons. editor Jour. Electroencephalography and Clinical Neurophysiology; editl. bd. Audiology, Brit. Jour. Audiology. Mem. Israel Soc. for Clin. Neurophysiology (pres.), Israel Soc. for Auditory Rsch. (exec. bd.), Collegium Otorhinolaryngol. Amicitae Sacrum. Home: PO Box 186, Nofit 36001, Israel Office: Evoked Potentials Lab, Gutwirth Bldg, Haifa 32000, Israel

PRATT, PHILIP CHASE, pathologist, educator; b. Livermore Falls, Maine, Oct. 19, 1920; s. Harold Sewell and Cora Johnson (Chase) P.; m. Helen Clarke Deitz, Feb. 4, 1945; children: William Clarke (dec.), Charles Chase (dec.). A.B., Bowdoin Coll., 1941; M.D., Johns Hopkins U., 1944. Diplomate: Am. Bd. Pathology. Intern in pathology Johns Hopkins Hosp., 1944-45, asst. resident in pathology, 1945-46; pathologist Saranac Lab., Saranac Lake, N.Y., 1946-52; asst. dir. Saranac Lab., 1952-55; instr. Ohio State U., 1955-57, asst. prof. pathology, 1957-62, assoc. prof., 1962-66; assoc. prof. Duke U. Med. Ctr., 1966-71, prof., 1971-90, prof. emeritus, 1991—. Author: (with V.L. Roggli and S.D. Greenberg) Pathology of Asbestos Related Diseases, 1993; contbr. numerous articles to profl. publs. Fellow Am. Coll. Chest Physicians, Coll. Am. Pathologists; mem. AAAS, Am. Thoracic Soc., Am. Soc. Exptl. Pathology, Am. Assn. Pathologists and Bacteriologists, Internat. Acad. Pathology, Royal Soc. Health. Unitarian. Office: PO Box 3712 Durham NC 27710-0001

PRATT, RAYMOND BURL, educator, researcher; b. Detroit, Aug. 5, 1940; s. Raymond Wilson Pratt and Mildred Elizabeth Cross; m. Eleanor R. Hatfield, Dec. 16, 1961 (div. 1979); 1 child, Leah Catherine; m. Sara T. Goulden, June 1, 1989. BA, Mich. State U., 1963, MA, 1965; PhD, U. Oreg., 1968. Asst. prof. Washington U., St. Louis, 1968-71; from asst. prof. to prof. Mont. State U., Bozeman, 1971-91, prof. polit. sci., 1991—. Author: Rhythm and Resistance, 1990, 2d edit. 1994. Nat. Endowment for the Humanities fellow U. Calif., Santa Barbara, 1978-79. Avocations: music lecturer, disk jockey. E-mail: rpratt@montana.edu. Office: Dept Polit Sci Montana State U Bozeman MT 59717-0001

PRATT, SHARON L., secondary and elementary education educator; b. Terrell, Tex., Dec. 5, 1946; d. Cecil and Bobbie Lou (Hodge) Brown; m. John E. Pratt, Aug. 31, 1968; 1 child, Randolph W. BS in Edn., U. North Tex., 1969, MS, 1980; ESL cert., East Tex. U., 1987. Cert. elem., English tchr., reading specialist, ESL tchr., Tex. Tchr. Mesquite (Tex.) Ind. Sch. Dist.; elem. tchr. sci. U.S. Govt., Manama, Bahrain; secondary tchr. McDonald Mid. Sch., Mesquite; tchr. ESL and reading improvement North Mesquite High Sch., 1991-92, 96—; adj. faculty devel. reading Cedar Valley C.C., Lancaster, Tex., 1992-95; secondary tchr. Robert T. Hill Mid. Sch. Dallas Ind. Sch. Dist., 1995-96; ESL and reading tchr. North Mesquite H.S., 1996—; tchr. ESL and adult edn. classes Dallas Ind. Sch. Dist.; instr. ESL class Eastfield Community Coll., Mesquite. Author poems. Mem. TESOL, Internat. Reading Assn., Tex. State Reading Assn. Home: 1001 Villa Siete Mesquite TX 75181-1237 Office: North Mesquite High Sch 18201 Lbj Fwy Mesquite TX 75150-4124

PRATT, WILLIAM FREDERIC, radiomedical scientist; b. Wanganui, New Zealand, Oct. 2, 1929; s. Frederic John and Joan Marion (Strachan) P.; m. Margaret Bethea Ammundsen, Dec. 14, 1957; children: Christine, Alastair, Michael. BA, U. New Zealand, 1951. H.S. tchr. dept. edn. Raurimu Dist. H.S./Wanganui Tech. Coll./Horowhenua Coll., New Zealand, 1952-75; med. scientist New Zealand, 1975—; bd. dirs. Mangaone Holdings, Wanganui, Mangaone Farm, 1967; rschr. with non-orthodox cures for bacteria and viruses, including HIV and Ebola, via Radiomed. Theory which states that the living processes of a bacterium or virus are dependent on the continuation of the organism's chem.-elec. cycle; radiomed. sci. studies include the ability of radio waves to boost immune responses, inactivate some toxic substances in human animal bodies and in the air, water and food chain, correct some neural abnormalities, and neutralize bacterial and viral infections. Fellow Internat. Biog. Assn.; mem. AAAS, N.Y. Acad. Scis., Royal Soc. New Zealand, Royal Astron. Soc. New Zealand. Achievements include successful use of radio waves to neutralize bacterial and viral infections; to boost immune responses and to inactivate some chemical poisons; devel. of a long-range Biological Defense Transmitter, now operational with global capabilities; rsch. interests include: radiomed. sci., interdimensional physics outside the scope of orthodox scientists; involved in the investigation of radio frequencies as a mode of inactivating bacterial and viral infections; experiments with a wide range of infective organisms including HIV, Herpes and Ebola viruses, and carcinomas, working with both low and high power transmitters to determine the optimum power levels necessary to inactivate bacteria and viruses, based on the radiomed. theory that the living processes of a bacterium or virus are dependent on the continuation of its chemical-electrical cycle; the function of his experiments is to disrupt the electrical phase of the cycle through radio transmission, more. Home and Office: Waikupa Rd, Okoia RD 12, Wanganui 5021, New Zealand

PRAUS, PETR, chemist, laboratory director; b. Ústí nad Orlicí, Czech Republic, Mar. 19, 1964; s. Otakar and Marie (Halbrštátová) P.; m. Renata Hrabáková, Apr. 9, 1988 (div. Mar. 1995); 1 child, Adam; m. Hana Krejčová, Sept. 28, 1996. MSc, Inst. Chem. Tech., Prague, Czech Republic, 1987; PhD, U. Pardubice, Czech Republic, 1995. Cert. analytical chemistry. Rschr. Vž Vítkovice, Ostrava, 1988-90; analyst Odra River Basin Co., Ostrava, 1990-94, head lab., 1994-96; head lab. Ostrava Water and Sewerage Co., 1996—; cons. Technical U. Mining and Metallurgy, Ostrava, 1997—. Contbr. articles to profl. jours. Mem. Czech Spectroscopical Soc. Jana Marca Marci, Czech Chem. Soc. Avocations: painting, literature, theatre. Office: Ostrava Water & Sewerage Co, Dvořákova 15, 72971 Ostrava Czech Republic

PRAVDYUK, YURY ALEKSEYEVICH, composer, performer; b. Dikanka, Poltava, USSR, Feb. 7, 1924; s. Aleksey Stepanovich and Yuliya Grigoryevna (Kislaya) P.; m. Ludmila Dmitrievna Tsarihina, Sept. 16, 1950 (div. Feb. 1971); 1 child, Igor Yuryevich; m. Irina Mihaylovna Prischenko, Jan. 16, 1981. Higher edn., Engr.-Bldg. Inst., Kharkov, USSR, 1945-51. Engr. cert. Sr. engr. Electrowire Adminstrn., Kharkov, 1951-69; leader mus. light-painting studio Student's Palace, Kharkov, 1967-92; art leader mus. light-painting concert hall Kharkov, 1969-91; leader tour group Philharm. Soc., various locations, USSR, 1978-87; lectr. mus. light-painting courses Culture Inst., Minsk, USSR, 1987-89; cons., performer mus. light-painting theater Sretozhyvopis, Kharkov, 1993—; developer art synthesis of music and dynamic light-painting; creator concert hall Ctrl. Park of Culture and Leisure, Kharkov, 1969; developer mus. light-painting for psychotherapy Yerino, Podolsk, 1979-85. Composer, performer numerous mus. light-painting plays, USSR, 1967—; author concept visual equivalent of mus. and description of mus. light-painting apparatus; prodr. film about mus. light-painting, 1997-98. Head Svetozhivopis charity soc., Kharkov, 1997—. Recipient diploma of composers Soyuz of USSR, 1985, medal for excellent work Ministry of Culture USSR, 1987, also hon. degrees, laureates, and titles from numerous orgns., 1970—. Avocations: concerts, art exhibitions, museums, nature. Home: Moscovsky prospect 17 ap 12, 310003 Kharkov Ukraine

PRAWER, SIEGBERT SALOMON, author, Germanic language and literature educator; b. Feb. 15, 1925; s. Marcus and Eleanora Prawer; m. Helga Alice Schaefer, 1949; 4 children (1 dec.). MA, LittD, Cambridge (Eng.) U., 1950, Oxford (Eng.) U., 1969, Birmingham, Eng.; PhD, U. Birmingham, 1953; LittD (hon.), Birmingham, 1988; DPhil (hon.), U. Cologne, 1984; Adelaide Stoll rsch. student, Christ's Coll., Cambridge U., 1947-48. Asst. lectr., lectr., sr. lectr. U. Birmingham, 1948-63; prof. German Westfield Coll., London U., 1964-86; fellow Queen's Coll., Oxford, 1968-87, dean of degrees, 1975-93, hon. fellow, 1987—, Taylor prof. German lang. and lit., 1969-86, Taylor prof. emeritus, 1986—; vis. prof. CCNY, 1956-57, U. Chgo., 1963-64, Harvard U., 1968, Hamburg U., 1969, U. Calif., Irvine, 1975, Otago (New Zealand) U., 1976, U. Pitts., 1977, Australian Nat. U., Canberra, 1980, Brandeis U., 1981-82; hon. dir. London U. Inst. Germanic Studies, 1967-69, Charles Oldham Shakespeare scholar, Cambridge U., 1945-46. Author: German Lyric Poetry, 1952; Mörike und seiner Leser, 1960, Heine's Buch der Lieder: A Critical Study, 1960, Heine: The Tragic Satirist, 1962, The Penguin Book of Lieder, 1964, The Uncanny in Literature (inaugural lecture), 1965, Heine's Shakespeare, A Study in Contexts (inaugural lecture), 1970, Comparative Literary Studies: An Introduction, 1973, Karl Marx and World Literature, 1976, Caligari's Children: The Film as Tale of Terror, 1980, Heine's Jewish Comedy: A Study of His Portraits of Jews and Judaism, 1983; editor: (with R.H. Thomas and L.W. Forster) Essays in German Language, Culture and Society, 1969, The Romantic Period in Germany, 1970, Seventeen Modern German Poets, 1971, Frankenstein's Island: England and the English in the Writings of Heinrich Heine, 1986, Israel at Vanity Fair Jews and Judaism in the Writings of W.M. Thackeray, 1992, Breeches and Metaphysics: Thackeray's German Discourse, 1997, W.M. Thackeray's European Sketch Books, 2000; editor (screenplay) Das Kabinett des Dr. Caligari, 1996; co-editor Oxford German Studies, 1971-75, Anglica Germanica, 1973-79; contbr. numerous articles on German, English and comparative lit. to profl. jours. Recipient Goethe medal, 1973, Isaac Deutscher Meml. prize, 1977, Friedrich Gundolf prize German Acad., 1986, German Goethe Soc. Gold medal, 1995; fellow resident Queen's Coll., Oxford U., 1969—, Knox Coll., Dunedin, New Zealand, 1976; hon. fellow Jesus Coll., Cambridge; Charles Oldham Shakespeare scholar Cambridge U., 1946. Fellow Brit. Acad., German Acad. Lang. and Lit., London U. Inst. Germanic Studies (hon.), Brit. Comparative Lit. Assn. (hon., pres. 1984-86); mem. MLA (hon.), English Goethe Soc. (pres. 1990-94, v.p. 1994—). Office: Queen's Coll, Oxford OXI 4AW, England

PRAYAGA, KRISHNA MURAI MOHAN, anesthesiologist, consultant; b. Gotivada, India, July 22, 1938; arrived in Norway, 1987; s. Ramasanyasi Rao and Seethamma (Kandarpa) P.; m. Lakshmi Mohan Garigipati, Aug. 24, 1946; children: Prasantha, Sravani, Sanyasiram. MBBS, Andhra U., Waltair, India, 1965; diploma in Anesthesiology, Osmania U., Hyderabad, India, 1970; diploma, European Acad. Anesthesiology, London, 1990, Indian Acupuncture Ctr., Nagaur, 1993. Med. officer A.P Med. and Health Svcs., Hyderabad, 1966-68; asst. to chief anesthesiology Osmania Gen. Hosp., Hyderabad, 1968-71; specialist anesthesiology Dist. Hosp., Khammam, India, 1971-72; anesthesiologist Port of Spain Gen. Hosp., Trinidad and Tobago, 1972-75, Nat. Health Svc., U.K., 1975-80, Irish Med. Svc., Cork, Ireland, 1980-83; staff anesthesiologist Health Svc., Vejle, Denmark, 1983-88; chmn. anesthesiology Hordaland Health Svcs., Bergen, Norway, 1988-95; sr. anesthesiologist Finnmark Health Svcs., Kirkenes, Norway, 1995-99, Hammerfest, Norway, 1999—; Author: Emergency First-Aid in Traffic Accidents, 1974, Clinical Considerations of Postpinal Headache, 1990; editor Andhra Pratibha, 1976, Indo-European Med. Jour., 1984—. Trustee for many Hindu orgns. in India, U.K., Norway. Mem. European Acad., many profl. orgns. Mem. Bharatiya Janata Party. Hindu. Avocation: writing. Office: Hammerfest Hosp, 9600 Hammerfest Norway

PRCHALOVÁ, LEA, library director; b. Ostrava, Moravia, Czechoslovakia, July 17, 1957; d. Lubomír and Anna (Blažková) Šmrha; m. Miloslav Prchal, Apr. 19, 1980; 1 child, Luboš. Degree in Engring., U. Ednl. Tech. U., Ostrava, Czech Republic, 1981. Cert. sys. engring. Cons. for regional librs. State Rsch. Libr. in Ostrava, 1982-86, head rsch. dept., 1986-95, directress of libr., 1995—; mem. of head libr. coun. Minitry of Culture, Prague, Czech Republic, 1997-99. Mem. Czech Republic Libr. Assn. (mem. of the head 1995—). Home: Krestova 1, CZ-70030 Ostrava Czech Republic Office: State Rsch Libr Ostrava, Prokešovo Námesti 9, CZ-72800 Ostrava Czech Republic

PREBLE, ROBERT CURTIS, JR., insurance executive; b. Oak Park, Ill., Dec. 19, 1922; s. Robert Curtis and Dorothy (Seidel) P.; m. Lidia Blazik, May 29, 1963. BA, Amherst Coll., 1947; MBA, Harvard U., 1949, post-grad., 1971. CLU, Chartered Fin. Cons. Asst. to gen. supt., asst. buyer Carson Pirie Scott & Co., Chgo., 1949-52; with sales dept. Northwestern Mut. Life Ins. Co., Chgo., 1952-53, Nat. Life Ins. Co., Chgo., 1953-59; prin. Preble Assocs., Chgo., 1959—; pres., treas. Savs. Plans Inc., 1980—; cons. Iowa Savs. & Loan League, 1959-82; consul of Colombia, 1981-86, Bolivia, 1965-70; bd. dirs., chmn. fin. com. Guardsman Life Ins. Co., 1962-74; chmn. exec. com. World Book Life Ins. Co., 1974-83; mem. Gov.'s Adv. Bd., Ill. Dept. Ins., 1965-70. Dep. regional chmn. Dem. Nat. Fin. Com., 1952; bd. dirs. McCormick Theol Sem., 1977-83, Sr. Ctrs. Met. Chgo., 1974-77, Chgo. Coun. on Fgn. Rels., 1971-77; deacon 4th Presbyn. Ch. of Chgo., 1967-70. Recipient svc. award Chgo. coun. Boy Scouts Am., 1962. Mem. Soc. Fin. Svc. Profls. (past pres. Chgo. chpt., Huebner scholar 1991, Grauer award 1998), Million Dollar Roundtable, Nat. Assn. Life Underwriters, Assn. Advanced Life Underwriting (founding pres.), Harvard Bus. Sch. Assn. (alumni coun. 1977-82), Harvard Alumni Assn. (dir. 1980-82), Inst. Internat. Edn. (midwest adv. bd., 1979-99), Found. Study Cycles (internat. adv. bd.), Soc. Colonial Wars (coun.), Mil. Order World Wars, Univ. Club, Chgo. Club, Harvard Bus. Sch. Club (past pres.), Amherst Club (past pres.), Oak Park Country Club, Spanish Wells Country Club, Econ. Club Chgo., Chi Psi (past chmn. ednl. trust, pres. 1992-95, Svc. award 1986). Home: 300 N State St Apt 5406 Chicago IL 60610-4870 Office: Savs Plans Inc 10 Trent Jones Ln # 122-109 Hilton Head Island SC 29928-7655

PRECKER, JOSEPH ALEXANDER, psychotherapist, writer; b. N.Y.C., May 15, 1925; arrived in Italy, 1994; s. Louis and Fannie (Trost) P. BSS, CCNY, 1946; MA, Columbia U., 1947, PhD, 1951. Cert. psychologist, N.Y. Asst. prof. Bard Coll., N.Y., 1947-52; dir. adminstrn. Project AFIRM, Columbia U., 1952-53; dir. mktg. rsch. Pfizer, Inc., N.Y.C., 1954-56; rsch. asst. neurophysiology N.Y. State Coll. Medicine, 1956-58; dir. rsch. J. Walter Thompson, Detroit, 1958-60; v.p. planning and rsch. Raymond Loewy, N.Y.C., 1960-63; cons., 1963-65; far east dir. INRA, Tokyo, 1967-72; acting dir. clin. psychol. grad. program U. Hong Kong, 1973-77; vis. prof. Sophia U., Tokyo, 1978-92; vis. prof. Sch. Psychotherapy, Regents Coll., London, 1992-94; pvt. practice N.Y.C., Tokyo, London, Hong Kong, Venice, 1952—; hon. prof. dept. psychiatry U. Hong Kong Med. Sch., 1977—; cons. SARDA, Hong Kong, 1975-77; bd. dirs. Bierer House, N.Y.C., 1961-67; far east dir. fertility study World Health Orgn., 1975-82; vis. prof. Internat. Christian U., Keio U., Aoyama Gakuin. Co-editor Personality: Symposia on Topical Issues, 1948-52, (book) Success in Psychotherapy, 1952; co-translator: Secret Gardens in Venice, 1996; contbr. articles to profl. jours., also poetry and plays. Bd. dirs. group to designate historic buildings, N.Y.C., 1961-67; advisor Hong Kong Police Dept., 1974-77; mem. adv. group Tokyo Cmty. Counseling Ctr., Tokyo, 1978-92; active supporter Phoenix House, N.Y.C., 1965—; cultural dir. Robertos Italian Table: Culinary and Cultural Holidays. Ford Found. scholar Bur. Applied Social Rsch., Columbia U., N.Y.C., 1953-54. Fellow Hong Kong Psycholog. Soc. (pres. 1975-76); mem. APA. Avocations: gardening and garden planning, Chinese painting and caligraphy, music, architectural restoration. Fax: 39 041 714 571. E-mail: bobwilk@tin.it. Home and Office: Dorsoduro 3441, 30123 Venice Italy

PRECLIK, GUENTER WOLFGANG, gastroenterologist; b. Ichenhausen, Germany, Nov. 6, 1955; s. Robert and Marlene (Nussbaum) P.; m. Monika Maria Felkel, Sept. 5, 1981; children: Markus Christian, Tobias Michael. Abitur, Gymnasium, 1975; MD, U. Ulm, 1982. Physician Dept. Internal Medicine, Ulm, Germany, 1984-97; with gastrointestinal endscopy U. Ulm, 1993-97; physician dept. gastroenterology Waldkrankenhaus St. Marien, Erlangen, Germany, 1997—. Mem. Deutsche Ges Verd Stoffw Krankh, Deutsche Ges Inn Med, Deutsche Diabetes Ges.

PREDELEANU, MIRCEA, research science educator; b. Valenii de Munte, Romania, May 10, 1929; arrived in France, 1978; s. Ioan and Floarea (Frates) P.; m. Paulina Berehoi, Aug. 13, 1960; children: Roxana, Andra. BSc, U. Bucharest, Romania, 1953; Engr., Constrn. Inst., Bucharest, 1954; PhD, Acad. Romania, Bucharest, 1961. Rschr. Acad. Romania, 1954-65; asst. prof. Inst. Petrol, Bucharest, 1963-65, assoc. prof., 1965-71, prof., 1971-75, head math. dept., 1967-72; prof. Poly. Inst., Bucharest, 1976-78, rsch. prof. Mechanics and Tech. Lab., 1978-97, rsch. prof. emeritus mechanics, 1997—; dir. Mechanics and Tech. Lab., Cachan, France, 1984-92; chmn. Internat. Conf. on Material Processing Defects, Cachan, 1987, 97, Sieburg, Germany, 1992. Author: Mathematical Methods, 1970; editor: Computational Methods for Predicting Material Processing Defects, 1987, Material Processing Defects, 1995, Advanced Methods in Materials Processing Defects, 1997. Mem. Assn. Univ. Mecanique, Internat. Soc. Boundary Elements (rsch. coun. Paris 1992—). Fax: (33) 147 402785. Office: Ecole Normale Superieure, 61 Ave du President Wilson, 94235 Cachan France

PREDOTA, STANISLAW, foreign language educator; b. Zaczarnie, Poland, July 1, 1944; s. Stanislaw and Ludwika (Czosnyka) P.; m. Irena Swiatlowska, Oct. 22, 1994; children: Janusz, Jerzy. MA, U. Leipzig, Germany, 1967; doctorate, U. Wroclaw, Poland, 1974, habilitated doctorate, 1983. Instr. U. Wroclaw Dept. German Studies, 1967-68, lectr., 1968-70, sr. lectr., 1972-74, reader, 1974-83, asst. prof., 1983-89; prof., Erasmus chair Dutch studies U. Wroclaw, 1989-93, sr. prof., Erasmus chair Dutch studies, 1993—; vice dean Faculty of Langs. and Literature, U. Wroclaw, 1982-87, dept. dir. Dept. German Studies, 1987-89, head Inst. Dutch Studies, 1989-90, head of Erasmus Chair of Dutch Studies, 1990-95, head Inst. Dutch Lang., Erasmus chair of Dutch Studies, 1995—; mem. linguistic sect. State Com. Rsch., 1991—. Author: Die polnisch-deutsche Interferenz im Bereich der Ausssprache, 1979 (Rector's award 1979), Konfrontative Phonologie Polnisch-Niederländisch, 1983 (Rector's award 1983), Klein Nederlands-Pools spreekwoordenboek, 1986 (Rector's award 1987), Kleines deutsch-polnisches Sprichwörterbuch, 1992 (Rector's award 1993); co-author: Podrecznik wymowy niemieckiej, 1982 (Min. of Edn. award 1983), Szkice z literatury niderlandzkiej, 1983, Mowimy po niderlandzku, 1986 (Min. Edn. award 1986), numerous others; translator: Einführung in die experimentelle Phonetik, 1971; joint editor: Neerlandica Wratislaviensia Vol. IV, 1989, Vol. V, 1991, Vol. VII, 1994, Vol. VIII, 1995, Vol. IX, 1996, Vol. X, 1998, Vol. XII, 1999, and numerous others. Recipient medal 40th Anniversary Polish

People's Republic, 1985, Golden Cross of merit Pres. State Coun., 1988, Visser Neerlandia prize Algemeen Nederlands Verbond, 1991; grant State Com. Rsch., 1995, 97. Mem. Soc. Dutch Philology (hon.), Internat. Vereniging voor Neerlandistiek (bd. dirs. 1973-82), Polish linguistic Assn., Societas Linguistica Europaea, Polish Phonetics Assn., Wroclaw Sci. Assn. (vice chmn. philological dept. 1991-93, chmn. philological dept. 1993-95), Internat. Soc. Phonetic Scis., Soc. Polish-Dutch Fiendship, Internat. Phonetic Assn., Stowarzyszenie Germanistow Polskich, Vereniging voor Neerlandici van Middenen Oosteuropa, Internat. Vereinigung Germanistische Sprachund Literaturwissenschaft, Polish Acad. Scis. (sec. Philological Commn. Wroclaw br. 1986—, mem. neophilogical com. 1990—, mem. linguistic com. 1993—). Roman Catholic. Avocations: gardening, travelling. Fax: 48 71 362 87 70. Home: ul Karkonoska 29 m 2, 53-015 Wroclaw Poland Office: Katedra Filologii Niderlandzkiej, ul Kuznicza 21-22, 50-138 Wroclaw Poland

PREECE, PETER FREDERICK WILLIAM, education educator; b. Sheffield, Yorkshire, Eng., June 12, 1941; s. Frederick William and Edna (Wilson) P.; m. Rita Janet Burton, July 13, 1968; children: Catherine Louise, William Michael. BA, Oxford (Eng.) U., 1962, MA, 1967; PhD, Exeter (Eng.) U., 1975. Asst. master Cheltenham Coll., U.K., 1963-67; lectr. St. Johns Coll., York, U.K., 1967-70; from lectr. to reader Exeter U., 1970-96, prof., 1996—; bd. Assoc Examining Bd., U.K., exec. com., 1997—; mem. coun. Assessment and Qualifications Alliance, 1998—. Contbr. articles to profl. jours. Fellow Inst. Physics. Office: Univ Exeter Sch Edn, Heavitree Rd, EX1 2LU Exeter England

PREER, JAMES RANDOLPH, academic administrator, science educator; b. Monahans, Tex., May 22, 1944; s. John R. Jr. and Louise B. (Brandau) P.; m. Jean H. Lyon, June 24, 1967; children: Genevieve L., Stephen R. AB, Swarthmore (Pa.) Coll., 1966; PhD, Calif. Inst. Tech., 1970. Woodrow Wilson teaching intern, 1969-71; asst. prof. chemistry Fed. City Coll., Washington, 1969-73; asst. prof. interdisciplinary sci. U. D.C., 1973-76, assoc. prof. interdisciplinary sci., 1976-79, prof. interdisciplinary sci., 1979-80, acting chairperson, 1979-80, prof. environ. sci., 1980—, asst. provost acad. programs and rsch., 1997-99, assoc. provost acad. programs & rsch., 1999-2000. Co-author: Integrated Science, 1976, 88; contbr. over 25 articles to profl. jours. Asst. scoutmaster Boy Scouts Am., Washington, 1990-93, chmn. troop com., 1993-95; bd. dirs. Beauvoir Sch., Washington, 1983-86. Woodrow Wilson Found. fellow Columbia U., 1965-66, NSF fellow Calif. Inst. Tech., 1966-69, MIT, 1976-77; U. D. C. grantee, 1978-98. Mem. Am. Chem. Soc., Phi Beta Kappa, Sigma Xi. Office: Office of the Provost & VPAA Dept Biol & Environ Scis 4200 Connecticut Ave NW Washington DC 20008-1122

PREGNOLATO, MASSIMO, pharmaceutical chemist, researcher; b. Vigevano, Italy, Sept. 6, 1961; s. Beniamino and Dina (Bergamini) P.; m. Aura Bruna Daneri, July 10, 1993; 1 child, Edoardo Alessandro. Grad. cum laude, U. Pavia, 1988; MS in Chem. Synthesis, Politecnic of Milan, 1991. Expert chemist Ursus Gomma S.p.a., Vigevano, 1982-83; rschr. C.N.R., Milan, Italy, 1989-90; tech. U. Pavia, Italy, 1991-92, rschr., 1992-95, sr. rschr., 1995-97; asst. prof. U. Pavia, 1997—; LAN sys. operator dept. pharm. chemistry U. Pavia, Italy, 1995-97; cons. dept. pharmacology Poly. San Matteo, Pavia, 1993-99; cons. dept. environ. Inst. Mario Negri, Milan, 1994-98; vis. prof. U. Mass. Med. Ctr., 1996-97, Inst. de Catalisis CSIC, Madrid, 1999; evaluator Current Drugs Ltd., 1997—; founder Pharm. Bioatalyses Labs. Contbr. articles to profl. jours. Fellow Consiglio Nazionale Ricerche, 1990, grantee, 1995; grantee Istituto Superiore Sanità, 1996-98, Archimica Group, 1999—, Recordati spa, 1999—. Mem. Soc. Chimica Italiana, Am. Chem. Soc., N.Y. Acad. Scis. Avocations: playing piano, dancing. Home: Cascina Santa Sofia 2, 27020 Torre d'Isola Italy Office: U Pavia Dept Pharm Chemistry, Via Taramelli 12, 27100 Pavia Italy

PREILOWSKI, BRUNO, psychology educator; b. Kassel, Germany, Aug. 6, 1943; m. Myung-Sook Kim, May 26, 1977; children: Stefan Hjon-Ho, Julia Su-Tsin. MS, Tulane U., New Orleans, 1968; PhD, Tulane U., 1970; Dr. habil., Konstanz U., Germany, 1979. Clin. neuropsychologist. Postdoctoral fellow Caltech, Pasadena, Calif., 1970-72; asst. prof. Konstanz U., Germany, 1972-79; prof. Tuebingen U., Germany, 1979—; various guest professorships in clin. and exptl. neuropsychology in U.S. and Asia. Contbr. articles to profl. jours., books. Fulbright fellow Tulane U., 1967-68; McDonnell-Pew fellow U. Calif. San Francisco Med. Sch., 1992-93. Mem. Gesellschaft fur Neuropsychologie (v.p. 1994—), numerous others psychol. and neurosci. socs. Office: Tuebingen U, Reutlinger Str 12, D-72072 Tübingen Germany

PREIS, CARL OTTO, company executive, mechanical engineer; b. Bklyn., Jan. 14, 1927; s. Otto and Madeline Adele Preis; m. Vera Marie Preis, Aug. 2; children: Carl Ernest, Brenda Marie. Student, Cornell U., 1950-51; BME, Poly. U., Bklyn., 1957. Registered profl. engr., N.Y. WTS engr. Republic Aviation, Farmingdale, N.Y., 1951; missile design engr. Missile divsn. Republic Aviation, N.Y.C. and Hicksville, N.Y., 1951-58; engr. Hazeltine Corp., Little Neck, N.Y., 1959; shock and vibration cons. Hazeltine Corp., Green Lawn, N.Y., 1959-64; CEO, Preis Mayer Corp., Baldwin, N.Y., 1965-87, Copace Corp., Baldwin, 1968—; cons. engr., Baldwin, 1955—; operator Timber Hill Farm, Presque Isle, Maine. Editor Atlantic Rock Artisans Newsletter, 1970-80. Night school instr. Baldwin Adult Edn., 1970-80; past pres. Rep. Social Club, Baldwin. With USNR, 1942-46. Mem. Am. Assn. for Artificial Intelligence, N.Y. Soc. Profl. Inventors, Pi Tau Sigma (hon.) Achievements include patent for variable frequency vibration absorber. Home and Office: 2249 Charing Cross Rd Baldwin NY 11510-3048

PREISER, SIEGFRIED HEINZ HELMUT, educational psychologist; b. Görlitz, Silesa, Germany, Mar. 10, 1943; s. Herrmann Oskar and Ilse (Schirrmacher) P.; m. Cornelia Hardtke, Feb. 3, 1967; children: Christoph, Joachim, Michael, Eva-Mareike. Diploma in psychology, U. Erlangen-Nürnberg, Germany, 1966, PhD, 1970, Dr.phil.habil., 1985. Asst. Psychol. Inst. U. Erlangen-Nürnberg, 1966-74; prof. U. Frankfurt/Main, Germany, 1974—; vice-chmn. Sect. Polit. Psychology. Author: (books) Person Perception, 1979, Creativity Research, 1986, Control and Committed Action, 1988, Goal-Oriented Action, 1989, Creativity Training, 1997, Creativity, 2000. Mem. German Soc. for Psychology, Berufsverband Deutscher Psychologen, 1970. Evangelical Lutheran. Home: Kurt-Schumacher-Strasse 1, D-61194 Niddatal Germany Office: Inst Pedagogical Psychology, Post Box 111932, D60054 Frankfurt am Main, Germany

PREISIG, HANS RUDOLF, botany educator; b. Winterthur, Switzerland, May 20, 1949; s. Ernst and Anny Elisabeth (Allenspach) P.; m. Esther Ursula Huber, July 12, 1985; children: Stefan, Daniel, Tobias. Diploma in botany, U. Zurich, Switzerland, 1973, PhD, 1979. Univ. lectr. U. Zurich, 1984—, prof. botany, 1995—. Co-author: The Biology of Free-Living Flagellates, 1991, The Protistan Cell Surface, 1994; contbr. to Progress of Botany, 1998, 99; editor: Nova Hedwigia, 1993—, European Jour. Phycology, 1993—. Mem. Internat. Phycological Soc., Phycological Soc. Am., Swiss Botanical Soc. (treas. 1994-96), Brit. Phycological Soc. (v.p. 1999). Home: Bungertweg 6, CH-8404 Winterthur Switzerland Office: Univ Zurich - Botany, Zollikerstr 107, CH-8008 Zurich Switzerland

PREISS, MITCHELL PAUL, mathematics educator; b. N.Y.C., Nov. 13, 1956; s. Charles and Lucille Rosalyn (Cohen) P. BS in Math., Cooper Union for Advancement of Sci. and Art, 1977; MS in Indsl. and Applied Math., Poly. Inst. N.Y., 1979, PhD in Ops. Rsch., 1986. Teaching fellow Poly. Inst. N.Y., Bklyn., 1977-79, adj. instr. math., 1978-79; instr. math. St. Peter's Coll., Jersey City, 1979-81; adj. instr. math. Baruch Coll., CUNY, 1979; instr. math. York Coll. CUNY, Jamaica, 1981-82; adj. assoc. prof. math. Pace U., N.Y.C., 1978-82, asst. prof., 1982-91, assoc. prof., 1992-97, prof., 1998—. Contbr. articles to profl. jours. Judge N.Y. Met. Math. Fair, 1983—, Jr. Acad. Sci. Rsch. Competition, 1984, 86-88; judge Am. Inst. Sci. and Tech. Sci. Fair, N.Y.C. 1987—. N.Y. State Regents scholar, 1973. Mem. N.Y. Acad. Scis. (life mem.), Am. Math. Soc., Math. Assn. Am., Pi Mu Epsilon, Kappa Mu Epsilon. Democrat. Avocations: tennis, softball, jogging, reading. Office: Pace U 41 Park Row Rm 701 New York NY 10038-1508

PREJMEREAN, CRISTINA ALEXANDRA, research scientist, chemist; b. Cluj-Napoca, Cluj, Romania, Jan. 31, 1959; d. Enea Alexandru and Valentina Doina (Trif) Pop; m. July 30, 1982; 1 child, Ovidiu. Diploma, U. Babes-Bolyai, Cluj-Napoca, Romania, 1984. Reg. chemistry engr. Chemistry engr. Drugs Factory, Cluj-Napoca, 1984-87; chemistry engr. dept. dental composite materials Inst. Chemistry, Cluj-Napoca, 1987-90, rschr., 1990—. Patentee in field. Mem. World Assn. Theoretical Organic Chemists, N.Y. Acad. Scis. Avocations: classical music, nature. Home: B-dul 1 Decembrie 1918 nr24, 3400 Cluj-Napoca Romania Office: Institute of Chemistry, Str Fântânele nr 30, 3400 Cluj-Napoca Romania

PREM, F. HERBERT, JR., lawyer; b. N.Y.C., Jan. 14, 1932; s. F. Herbert and Sybil Gertrude (Nichols) P.; m. Patricia Ryan, Nov. 18, 1978; children from previous marriage: Julia Nichols, F. Herbert III. AB, Yale U., 1953; JD, Harvard U., 1959. Bar: N.Y. 1960. Assoc. Whitman & Ransom, N.Y.C., 1959-66, ptnr., 1967-93, co-chmn. exec. com., 1988-92, chmn., 1993; chmn. Whitman Breed Abbott & Morgan LLP, N.Y.C., 1993-99, of counsel, 2000—; bd. dirs. Fuji Photo Film U.S.A., Inc., Fuji Med. Sys. U.S.A., Inc., Noritake Co., Inc., Seiko Instruments America, Inc., The HealthCare Chaplaincy, Inc. Bd. dirs. Bagaduce Music Lending Libr., Inc. 1988-95, pres., 1989-93; bd. dirs. Cmty. Action for Legal Svc. Inc., 1967-70, treas., 1967-69; bd. dirs. Legal Aid Soc. N.Y.C., 1957-70. Lt. (j.g.) USNR, 1953-56. Mem. ABA, Assn. of Bar of City of N.Y. (sec. 1967-69), N.Y. State Bar Assn., Am. Law Inst. (life) Am. Soc. Internat. Law, Yale Club. Episcopalian.

PREMASATHIAN, DILOK, plastic surgeon; b. Ayuthya, Thailand, Sept. 29, 1935; s. Derm Premasathian and Payom Despratheep; m. Noparatana Tuchinda, June 21, 1968; children: Nalinee, Nol. Degree in premed. sci., Chulalongkorn U., Bangkok, Thailand, 1957; MD, Siriraj Med. Sch., Bangkok, 1964. Diplomate Am. Bd. Plastic Surgery. Resident in gen. surgery VA Hosp., Brookline, N.Y., 1965-68, Ft. Howard, Md., 1965-68; resident in gen. surgery Sacred Heart Hosp., Allentown, Pa., 1965-68, VA Hosp./St. Francis Hosp., Hines, Ill., 1968-72; chief plastic surgery faculty medicine Chiangmai (Thailand) U., 1972-78; chmn. surgery dept. Prince of Songkla (Thailand) U., 1979-85; instr., lectr. Chulalongkorn U., 1985-97; cons. Samitives Hosp., Bangkok, 1985-98, Rama Hosp., Bangkok, 1985-98; asst. sec. Asian Internat. Congress of Plastic Surgeons, Bangkok, 1986; sec. gen. Internat. Congress of Aesthetic Plastic Surgery for Orientals, Bangkok, 1992, 94. Fellow ACS; mem. Thai Soc. Plastic Surgeons, Soc. Aesthetic Plastic Surgeons of Thailand, Soc. Aesthetic Plastic Surgery for Orientals (nat. sec. 1988-97).

PREMI, BR, banking executive; b. Tathyar, India, Jan. 28, 1968; s. Mishru Ram and Durgi (Devi) P.; m. Sohan Bhatti, Jan. 25, 1993; 1 child, Kritika. BSc in Agr., H.P.K.V., Palampur, India, 1989; MS in Horticulture, Parmar UHF, Solan, India, 1992; PhD in Horticulture, Indian Agrl. Rsch. Inst., New Delhi, 1996. Asst. mgr. Nat. Bank for Agr. and Rural Devel., India, 1996—; Recipient Kejriwal award, NA Pandit award, All India Food Preservers Assn. Office: Nat Bank Agrl/Rural Devel, Bandra-Kurla Complex, Mumbai India

PREMINGER, ANER HILLEL, film producer, director, writer; b. Tel Aviv, Jan. 17, 1955; s. Eliezer Erich and Miriam (Kornstein) P.; m. Michal Jacoby, Sept. 17, 1955; children: Matan, Ayana, Tamar. BSc in Physics, Tel Aviv U., 1974, postgrad., 1994—; MFA in Filmmaking, NYU, 1983. Prodn. dir. Beit Zvi Sch. Theater and Cinema, 1984-86; documentary filmmaker Israeli TV, Jerusalem, 1986-90; prof. Film Review U., Jerusalem, 1989—, Tel Aviv U., 1995—; film lectr. Beit Berl Coll. Sch. Art, Israel, 1995—, Hadassah Coll. Tech., Israel, 1996—; script lectr., editor INDIC, Tel Aviv, 1996. Author: Enchanted Screen, 1995; dir., co-prodr., co-writer feature film: Blindman's Bluff, 1993 (Wolgin award for Israeli Best Film, Jerusalem Film Festival, 17th Montreal World Film Festival, 41st Internat. Film Festival of San Sebastian 1993, Antigone D'Or 1st prize 15th Festival Internat. Du Cinema Mediterraneen Montpellier 1993, 8th Ann. Washington Internat. Film Festival 1994, Jaguar Maya De Oro spl. prize 1994); dir., prodr., co-writer: (feature film) Last Resort, 1999; dir., prodr., writer, cinematographer documentary feature film: On My Way to Father's Land, 1995; dir., prodr., writer Front Window, 1990; dir., prodr.: (documentary feature film) Ransom of the Father, 2000. Bd. dirs. Com. in Pub. Coun. for Developing Art Edn., Ministry of Edn. and Culture, 1990—. Maj. Israeli Def. Forces, 1974-79. Mem. Israeli Acad. Motion Pictures (bd. dirs. 1995—), Israel Film & TV Dir. Guild (bd. dirs. 1994—), Peace Now. Home and Office: Neve Shaanan 7, Jerusalem 93708, Israel

PREMO-HOPKINS, BLANCHE LILLIE, university official, philosophy educator; b. Highland Park, Mich., Jan. 20, 1943; d. Charles George and Anna Catherine (Clair) Kolar; m. E. R. Premo, June 24, 1966 (div. Sept. 1976); children: Mary Katharyn, Bianca Caroline; m. Crale DeVaul Hopkins, June 27, 1988. AB in Philosophy magna cum laude, Marygrove Coll., Detroit, 1967; MA in Philosophy, Marquette U., 1969, PhD in Philosophy, 1974. Assoc. prof. philosophy St. Mary's U., Winona, Minn., 1972-78, assoc. dean, 1976, v.p. for acad. affairs, 1976-78; asst. dir. divsn. edn. programs NEH, Washington, 1979-84, dep. dir. divsn. rsch. programs, 1984-88; vice chancellor for acad. affairs U. S.C., Aiken, 1988—, assoc. prof. philosophy, 1988—; professorial lectr. Cath. U. Am. Sch. Philosophy, Washington, 1982-84, Georgetown U., Washington, 1982-84; cons. internat. com. on UNESCO, U.S. Dept. State, 1980-87; mem. bd. S.C. Humanities Coun., 1992-98; mem. adv. com. on acad. affairs S.C. Commn. on Higher Edn.; cons., panelist NEH, 1989, Bicentennial Commn. on U.S. Constn., 1989-91; editorial cons. NEH, 1985-88; bd. mem. USC Bicentennial Commn., 1999—; sponsor Rsch. Adv. Commn., 2000; mem. numerous SACs accreditation teams; panelist NSF. Contbr. articles to profl. jours. Recipient Paderewski medal; fellow NDEA, 1969-71, Alfred J. Schmitt fellow, 1971-73; grantee NEH, 1975, Coun. for Philos. Studies, 1976. Mem. Am. Philos. Assn., Assn. Am. Colls., Kiwanis. Home: 1753 Huckleberry Dr Aiken SC 29803-5813 Office: U SC 471 University Pkwy Aiken SC 29801-6399

PREMOVIĆ, PAVLE ILIJA, chemist, educator; b. Niš, Serbia, Yugoslavia, Dec. 23, 1940; s. Ilija Puniša and Emilija Mihajlo (Glušć) P.; m. Nadežda Svetislav Veljković, July 14, 1964 (div.); children: Miroslav, Dora; m. Ana Branislav Nikolić, Oct. 3, 1993 (div.); m. Ivana Ratomir Tonsa, June 11, 1998. BSc, U. Belgrade, Yugoslavia, 1965; MS, U. Zagreb, Croatia, 1971; PhD, U. Victoria, B.C., Can., 1975. Rschr. Inst. Vinča, Belgrade, 1969-72; rsch. asst. U. Victoria 1973-75, postdoctoral fellow, 1975-76; asst. prof. U. Niš, 1976-79, assoc. prof., 1979-88, prof. chemistry, 1995—; vis. prof. La. State U., Baton Rouge, 1980-81, Pierre and Marie Curie U., Paris, 1997-99, U. Ctrl. Venezuela, Caracas; vis. scientist Med. Coll. Wis., Milw., 1986-87. Contbr. articles to profl. jours. Pres. Dem. Movement of Serbia, Niš, 1991; mem. Fed. Parliament, Belgrade, 1992. Rsch. grantee Ministry of Sci., Yugoslavia, 1981, 86, 91, 96. Mem. Planetary Soc., Internat. Assn. of Geochemistry and Cosmochemistry Can., European Assn. Organic Chemists, Serbian Chem. Soc. (pres. 1978-86). Avocations: soccer, table tennis, mountaineering. Office: U of Niš Faculty Sci, PO Box 91, 18000 Niš Serbia, Yugoslavia

PRENGLE, HERMAN WILLIAM, JR., chemical engineer; b. Pa., Nov. 6, 1919; s. Herman William and Irene (Smith) P.; m. Ruth Hamilton, Dec. 6, 1941; children: Pixie Bernice Irene, Karl William, Scott Hamilton. BS, Carnegie-Mellon U., 1941, MS, 1947, DSc, 1949. Registered profl. engr., Tex. Rsch. engr. Linde Air Products Co., Tonwanda, N.Y., 1941; sr. engr. Shell Oil Co., Houston, 1949-53; assoc. prof. U. Houston, 1953-59, prof., 1959-97, prof. emeritus, 1997—, chmn. chem. engring dept., 1958-61, assoc. dean Cullen Coll. Engring. 1981-85, dir. MChE program chem. engring. dept., 1985-97; vis. scholar chemistry dept. Cambridge (Eng.) U., 1971-72, Corpus Christi Coll., 1988, Darwin Coll., 1990; cons. chem. and petroleum industries U.S. Govt., 1958—; panel mem. peer rev. of rsch. U.S. EPA, Washington, 1975-97. Contbr. articles to profl. jours. Chmn. Charter Commn., Friendswood, Tex., 1970-71; mem. Nat. Rep. Com., Washington, 1980—; mem. Rep. Presdl. Task Force, Washington, 1983—; mem. U.S. Com. Battle Normandy Mus., Caen, France, 1988—. Lt. col. U.S. Army, 1941-46, ETO. Decorated Bronze Star with oak leaf cluster; recipient Kittinger Tchg. award U. Houston Cullen Coll. Engring., 1971, award of Merit, Pollution Engring. Mag., Chgo., 1976, Tchg. Excellence award Haliburton Found., 1989, 92, 94, 96. Fellow Am. Inst. Chemists; mem. AIChE, Am. Chem. Soc., Royal Chem. Soc. (London), Army-Navy Club, Brotherhood of St. Andrew, Sigma Xi, Tau Beta Pi, Phi Kappa Phi. Episcopalian. Achievements include 3 patents (with others) for ozone-UV advanced oxidation prodess for water borne toxic compounds; invention (with other) of ammonium hydrogen sulfate (AHS) and duplex AHS solar energy storage process; invention (with others) of infrared radiometry spectroscopy method process; invention (with others) of infrared radiometry spectroscopy method (IRSM) for remote sensing of temperatures, gradients and pollutant concentrations from stationary emission sources; invention (with others) of hydrogen peroxide-VisUV process (HP/VisUV) for treatment of hazardous water borne substances and gaseous emissions; invention and patent (with others) for improved apparatus for fractional distillation of multi-component hydrocarbon mixtures. Home: 105 Sandpiper Cv Georgetown TX 78628-4809

PRESACAN, CLAUDIA, olympic athlete; b. Sibiu, Romania, Dec. 28, 1979. Mem. gymnastics team Romania; winner third pl. in all-around European Championship, 1998, winner bronze in uneven bars and balance beam, 1998; winner silver in all-around Romanian Internat. Championship, 1999, winner gold in uneven bars, 1999, winner silver in balance beam and floor exercise, 1999, winner bronze in vault, 1999; winner gold team all-around Olympics, Sydney, Australia, 2000. Office: Romanian Gymnastics Ctr Romanian Studies, Ofcl Postal 1 Casuta Postala 108, 6600 Iasi Romania*

PRESCOTT, BARBARA LODWICH, educational administrator; b. Chgo., Aug. 15, 1951; d. Edward and Eugenia Lodwich; m. Warren Paul Prescott, Dec. 2, 1979; children: Warren Paul Jr., Ashley Elizabeth. BA, U. Ill., Chgo., 1973, MEd, 1981; MA, U. Wis., 1978; postgrad., Stanford U., 1983-87. Cert. tchr., learning handicapped specialist, cmty. coll. instr., Calif. Grad. rschr. U. Ill., Chgo., 1979-81; learning handicapped specialist St. Paulus Luth. Sch., San Francisco, 1981-83; grad. rsch. asst. Sch. Edn. Stanford (Calif.) U., 1983-87, writing cons. for law students, 1985-86; learning handicapped specialist/lead therapist Gilroy Clinic Speech-Hearing-Learning Ctr., Crippled Children's Soc., Santa Clara, Calif., 1988-89; ednl. dir. Adolescent Intensive Resdl. Svc. Calif. Pacific Med. Ctr., San Francisco, 1989-95; exec. dir. Learning Profiles, South Lake Tahoe, Calif., 1995—; instr. evening San Jose City Coll., 1988-92. Contbr. articles to profl. jours.; author: Proceedings of Internat. Congress of Linguistics, 1987; editor: Proceedings - Forum for Research on Language and Learning, 1989. Recipient otape: Making a Difference in Language and Learning, 1989. Recipient Frederick Bork Teaching Trainee award San Francisco State U., 1983; Ill. State scholar, 1973. Mem. Calif. Adult Assn. Pvt. Specialized Edn. and Svcs., Phi Delta Kappa (v.p. 1984-86), Pi Lambda Theta (sec. 1982-83), Phi Kappa Phi, Alpha Lambda Theta. Office: Learning Profiles 2145 Harvard Ave South Lake Tahoe CA 96150-4425

PRESCOTT, JOHN, deputy prime minister of Great Britain; b. May 31, 1938; s. John Herbert and Phyllis P.; m. Pauline Tilston, 1961; 2 children. Diploma in econs. and polit. sci., Ruskin Coll., Oxford, Eng.; BSc in Econs., Hull U. Steward Passenger Lines, Merchant Navy, 1955-63; recruitment officer Gen. & Mcpl. Workers Union, 1965; ofcl. Nat. Union of Seamen, 1968-70; mem. staff sec. state Brit. Parliament, 1974-76, opposition spokesman on transport, 1979-81, opposition front bench spokesman regional affairs and devolution, 1981-83, spokesman on transport, 1983-84, 88-93, spokesman on employment, 1984-87, 93-94, spokesman on energy, 1987-88, mem. shadow cabinet, 1983—, mem. NEC, Labour Party, 1989—, dep. leader Labour Party, 1994—; dep. prime min., sec. state for environ., transport, regions Govt. of U.K., 1997—; mem. select com. Nationalized Industries, 1973-79, Coun. of Europe, 1972-75, European Parliament, 1975-79, leader Labour Party Del., 1976-79. Office: Office of Prime Minister, 10 Downing St, London SW1 2AA, England*

PRESCOTT, JOHN BARRY, business executive; b. Oct. 22, 1940; M. Jennifer Mary Louise Cahill; 4 children. BComm in Indsl. Rels., U. NSW, Australia, 1995, DSc (hon.), 1995; LLD (hon.), Monash U., 1994. With Broken Hill Proprietary Co. Ltd. (BHP), 1958-98; various indsl. rels. positions BHP, Newcastle and Whyalla; supt. indsl. rels., shipping and stevedoring BHP, Newcastle and Sydney, 1969-74; asst. mgr. fleet ops. BHP, Newcastle, 1974-79; exec. asst. to gen. mgr. transport BHP, 1979-80, mgr. ops. transport, 1980-82, gen. mgr. transport, 1982-87; exec. gen. mgr., CEO BHP Steel, 1987-91; mng. dir., CEO BHP, Melbourne, Victoria, Australia, 1991-98; exec. chmn. Horizon Private Equity Pty Ltd, 1998—; dir. Normandy Mining Limited, 1999—, Inst. of Pub. Affairs, 1999—; mem. adv. bd. Booz Allen & Hamilton Inc., 1991—; mem. internat. coun. J.P. Morgan; trustee Conf. Bd.; mem. Asia Pacific adv. com. N.Y. Stock Exch., Inc.; mem. Australian Shipping Defence Coun., 1983-87, Defence Industry Com., 1988-93, Stevedoring Industry Consultative Coun., 1983-85; bd. mem. Walter and Eliza Hall Inst. Med. Rsch.; chmn. Australian Mfg. Coun., 1990-95; mem. exec. com. Australian Mining Industry Coun., 1991-95; mem. Transport Industries Adv. Coun., 1982-87, dep. chmn., 1986-87; mem. Maritime Industry Coun. Australia, 1983-87. Bd. dirs. Bus. Coun. Australia, 1995-97, Walter and Eliza Hall Inst. Med. Rsch., 1994-98; mem. internat. coun. Asia Soc.; patron Australian Quality Coun., 1990-99, Australian Am. C. of C., Hawaii, 1995-98; mem. Australia-Japan Bus. Cooperation Com., 1991-98. Fellow Australian Inst. Mgmt., Australian Acad. Technol. Scis. and Energing., Australian Inst. Co. Dirs. Avocations tennis, golf. Address: Horizon Private Equity Mgmt, Level 28 140 William St, Melbourne Victoria 300, Australia

PRESCOTT, JOHN VICTOR, geographer, educator; b. Newcastle-upon-Tyne, Eng., May 12, 1931; arrived in Australia, 1961; s. George and ada Selina (Howell) P.; m. Dorothy Francis Allen, Sept. 12, 1953; children: Margaret, Philip. BSc with honors, Durham (Eng.) U., 1952, MA, 1957, Dip.Edn., 1955; PhD, London U., 1961; MA (hon.), U. Melbourne, Australia, 1969. Lectr. Univ. Coll. Ibadan, Nigeria, 1956-61; lectr. U. Melbourne, 1961-65, sr. lectr., 1966-68, reader, 1969-86, prof. dept. geography, 1986-96, prof. emeritus, 1996—. Author: Maritime Political Boundaries of the World, 1985, Political Frontiers and Boundaries, 1986, (with S. Davis) Aboriginal Frontiers and Boundaries, 1993, (with D. Hancox) Secret Surveys in the Spratly Islands, 1997, The Gulf of Thailand: Limits to Conflict and Cooperation, 1998, others. Lt. U.K. Royal Artillery, 1952-54. Avocations: fishing, reading. Office: Univ of Melbourne, Dept of Geography, Parkville 3052 VIC, Australia

PRESCOTT, WILLIAM BRUCE, minister; b. Denver, Dec. 30, 1951; s. William Rex and Betena Naomi (Fletcher) P.; m. D. Kylene Winters, Nov. 24, 1973; children: William Doyle, Candice Joy. BS in Corrections, U. Albuquerque, 1973; MDiv, Southwestern Bapt. Sem., 1978, PhD, 1986. Ordained minister in Bapt. Ch., 1976. Youth minister Sandia Bapt. Ch., Albuquerque, 1974-75; pastor Clairette (Tex.) Bapt. Ch., 1976-79; instr. philosophy and religion Tarrant County Jr. Coll. NW Campus, Ft. Worth, 1984-86; pastor Easthaven Bapt. Ch., Houston, 1987-98; exec. dir. Mainstream Okla. Baptists, 1998—; adj. prof. Southwestern Bapt. Theol. Sem., HBU Extension, Houston, 1987-90; police chaplain Houston Police Dept., 1987-94; trustee S.E. Area Ministries, Houston, 1988-98, exec. bd. 1997-98, v.p. 1998; mem. exec. bd. Union Bapt. Assn., 1987-98, Bapt. Gen. Conv. Tex., 1993-98, Tex. Bapts. Committed, 1990-98; coord. coun. Coop. Bapt. Fellowship, 1994-97, mem. Tex. exec. com., 1996-98, Tex. steering coun., 1994-98; spkr. confs. in field. Book reviewer to Southwestern Jour. Theology; radio talk show host, Religious Talk, 1999—; editor: The Mainstream Messenger, 1998—. Served on Bapt. Gen. Conv. Tex. Com. Distinctives Com., 1994-98, Exec. Bd. Nominating Com., 1996, Com. on Conv. Arrangements, 1997; CBF Theol. Edn. Ministry Group , 1994-95, Bapt. Principles Ministry Group, 1995-98, Adminstrv. Coun. Structure Com., 1996, Adv. Coun., 1996-98, Info. Systems Mgmt. Project Team, 1996-97, chmn. Bapt. Bapt. Distinctives Partnership Team, 1995-97; trustee San Andres U., San Andres Island, San Andres Found. Named one of Outstanding Young Men of Am., Jaycees, 1984. Mem. ACLU, Am. Acad. Religion. Ams. United for Separation Ch. and State (pres. Houston chpt. 1997-99, nat. adv. coun. 1997—, editor First Amendment Advocate Newsletter, 1999—), So. Bapt. Alliance, Baptists Committed, People for the Am. Way, Concord Coalition, Whitsett Soc., Interfaith Alliance. Democrat. Home: 1706 Kiamichi Rd Norman OK 73026-5924 Office: Mainstream Okla Baptists 205 E Main St Norman OK 73069-1304

PRESCOTT, WILLIAM GLENN, psychiatrist; b. Portland, Oreg., Sept. 24, 1936; s. Glenn Leroy and Willmina (Long) P.; m. Katherine Lee Finnel, June 16, 1960 (div. 1975); children: Tracy K., Erin A., Shannon L., Bryn W., Duncan M.; m. Barbara Ann Carlson, Oct. 19, 1982; children: William G.,

Anna E., Andrew D. BS, Portland State U., 1959; MS, U. Oreg., 1963, MD, 1963; diploma in psychiatry, Harvard U., 1972. Diplomate Am. Bd. Psychiatry and Neurology, specialty in geriatric psychiatry, forensic psychiatry and addictions psychiatry, Am. Bd. Geriatric Psychiatry. Dir. USPHS Clinic, San Juan, P.R., 1972-75; chmn. dept. psychiatry USPHS Hosp., San Francisco, 1975-81; dir. Cuban-Haitian Unit NIMH, Washington, 1981-84; supt. St. Elizabeth's Hosp., Washington, 1984-87; asst. surg. gen. USPHS, 1984-87; med. dir. Brook Ln. Psychiat. Ctr., Hagerstown, Md., 1987-97; consulting psychiatrist Northcote Cmty. Mental Health Ctr., Palmerston North, New Zealand, 1992-93; cons. in field. Contbr. articles to profl. jours. Med. officer CAP, Oreg., Md., Mass., D.C., 1951—. Served to rear adm. (asst. surgeon gen.) USPHS, 1964-87. Decorated Bronze medal of Valor, D.S.M., Meritorious Svc. medal, Outstanding Svc. medal; Selling fellow U. Oreg., 1961-63. Mem. APA (bd. cert. in adminstrv. psychiatry), Md. Psychiat. Soc., Acad. Psychosomatic Medicine, Am. Assn. Psychiat. Adminstrs., Am. Coll. Health Care Execs., Am. Acad. Psychiatry and Law, Am. Coll. Mental Health Adminstrs., Am. Assn. Mental Health Adminstrs., Med. and Chirurg. Soc. Md., Harvard Club at the Nat. Press Club. Methodist. Avocations: music; bicycling; diving. Home: 12909 Old Annapolis Rd Mount Airy MD 21771-7809 Office: Brooklane Psychiatric Ctr PO Box 1945 Hagerstown MD 21742-1945

PRESCOTT THOMAS, JOHN DESMOND, broadcasting executive, media consultant; b. Prestatyn, Clwyd, Wales, May 28, 1942; arrived in Eng., 1960; s. William and Beatrice Isobel (Jones) P. T.; m. Bridget Margaret Somerset-Ward, Oct. 7, 1967 (div. 1993); children: Viveka Ruth, Bronwen Jane; m. Heather Elizabeth Graham, Oct. 14, 1994; step-children: Katherine Elizabeth Mary, Timothy William John, Caroline Marjorie. BA, U. Oxford, Eng., 1963, MA, 1967. Trainee BBC, London, 1963-65, asst. producer sch. TV, 1965-68, producer sch. TV, 1968-76, sr. producer modern languages, European studies sch. TV, 1976-81, head sch. TV, 1981-84; head network production ctr. BBC, Bristol, Eng., 1984-86; head of broadcasting, south and west BBC, Bristol, 1986-90; mng. dir. Westcountry TV, Plymouth, Eng., 1991-95, JPT Media Assocs. Ltd., 1995—; lectr. internat. Univs. and groups., 1984—; vis. prof. faculty art, media and design U. W. of Eng., Bristol; cons. in field. Author (TV Script) Adaptation of The Black Lamp, 1980, also numerous language learning guides and workbooks in French, Spanish and German, 1980-83; producer over 20 radio and TV series; exec. prodr. interactive tng. programs in sound and animation; contbr. articles to language and ednl. jours. Trustee Bath Internat. Festival, 1985-96, dep. chmn. 1989-96; trustee TV Trust for the Environment, London, 1985-89, The Exploratory, Bristol, 1985—, St. George's Music Trust, Bristol, 1987—, Bristol Cathedral Trust, 1988—; chmn. South West Arts, Exeter, 1986-89; dep. chmn., gov. U. W. Eng., 1989—; dep. chmn. The Harbourside Ctr., Bristol, 1997—, trustee, 1999—; dir. Watershed Arts Trust, 1996—; vice-chmn. Channel West, 1996-2000; mem. European bd. CIRCOM Regional, 1997-98; dir. Exeter & Devon Arts Ctr., 1994-98, S.W. Media Devel. Agy., 1996-99. Comdr. Royal Naval Res., 1961-92. Fellow Royal TV Soc. Presbyterian. Avocations: travel, sailing, photography, flying, alto saxophone. Office: JPT Media Assocs Ltd, 30 Royal York Crescent, Clifton Bristol BSB 4JX, England

PRESLEY, KEVIN PATRICK, minister of music; b. Springfield, Mo., June 19, 1964; s. Robert Lee and Darylene Delane P.; m. Robyn Michelle Maloy, Dec. 30, 1989; 1 child, Kirk Ian. BS in Music, S.W. Baptist U., 1986; M in Sacred Music, Southern Meth. U., 1989, M in Music, Voice Performance, 1989. Minister of music First United Meth. Ch., Celina, Tex., 1987-89, Peachtree City (Ga.) United Meth. Ch., 1989-94, Emmanuel United Meth. Ch., Memphis, 1994—; treas. Fellowship of United Meth. in Music, Worship and other arts, North Ga. Conf., 1991-94. Designer, dir. musical program Building the City, 1997, For the Journey, 1998, Honour Bound, 1999, A Generation of Faith, 2000. Singer Atlanta (Ga.) Symphony Chorus, Chamber Chorus, 1991-93; co-leader Metro Memphis Children's Choir Festival, 1995. Mem. Am. Choral Dirs. Assn., Chorister's Guild (exec. bd. mem. 1992-94). Avocations: travel, architecture, desktop publishing-design, health and fitness. Office: Emmanuel United Methodist 2404 Kirby Rd Memphis TN 38119-6621

PRESS, EDWARD, consulting physician; b. N.Y.C., 1913; s. Louis and Anna Press; m. Ruth Scheffer, July 8, 1951; children: Stephen, Phyllis. B.A., Ohio U., 1934; M.D., NYU, 1937; M.P.H., Harvard U., 1947. Diplomate: Am. Bd. Pediatrics, Am. Bd. Preventive Medicine. Intern Beth Israel Hosp., N.Y.C., 1938-40; resident Lincoln Hosp., Bronx, N.Y., 1940; psychiatric resident E.P. Bradley Home, East Providence, R.I., 1940-41; asst. dir. maternal and child health div. W.Va. Health Dept., 1941-42; pediatric cons. Mich. Health Dept., 1946; regional med. dir. U.S. Children's Bur., Chgo., 1947-50; asso. dir. div. services crippled children U. Ill., 1950-55; field dir. Am. Public Health Assn., N.Y.C., 1955-59; dir. Dept. Public Health, Evanston, Ill., 1959-64; med. asst. to dir. Ill. Dept. Public Health, 1964-67; state health officer (Oreg. Health Div.), Portland, 1967-79; public health cons., 1979—; emeritus sec.-treas. Press Internat. Sales Corp., 1978—; asst. prof. preventive medicine U. Ill., 1950-55; asst. prof. pediatrics Northwestern U., 1964-67; clin. prof. pub. health, preventive medicine and pediatrics Med. Sch., Oreg. Health Scis. U., 1967-79, emeritus clin. prof., 1979—; vice chmn. Tech. Adv. Group for Fire Safe Cigarette Act of 1990-93. Mem. editorial adv. com. The Nation's Health, 1989-91; contbr. articles to profl. jours. Organizer Poison Control Ctr., Chgo., 1953; trustee Underwriters' Labs., Inc., 1969-79. Served to maj. USAAF, 1942-46. Recipient Clifford G. Grulee award Am. Acad. Pediatrics, 1961; recognition award Am. Assn. Poison Control Centers, 1975. Mem. AMA, Am. Pub. Health Assn. (founder and pres. Conf. Emeritus Mems. 1986-89, Excellence in Health Admintrn. award 1992), Nat. Soc. Prevention of Blindness, Am. Assn. Public Health Physicians (pres. 1971-72, Bronze medal 1979), Conf. State and Provincial Health Authorities N.Am. (pres. 1971-72), Assn. State and Territorial Health Officers (mem. exec. com. 1972-75, Arthur G. McCormack award 1978), Am. Assn. Sr. Physicians (pres. 1984-86), Oreg. Pub. Health Assn. (Leadership award 1986), Oreg. Med. Assn. (presdl. citation 1980), Am. Acad. Pediatrics, Portland City Club, Multnomah Athletic Club, Rotary. Home: 3100 N Ocean Blvd # 1804 Fort Lauderdale FL 33308-7192

PRESSER, CARY, research engineer; b. Bklyn., June 20, 1952; s. Harry and Regina Deborah (Lieberman) P.; m. Karen Leslie Antonoff, Feb. 27, 1977; children: Yona Ruth, Aliza Miriam. BSc in Aerospace Engring., Poly. U., 1974, MSc in Aero. Engring., 1976; DSc in Aero. Engring., Technion-Israel Inst. Tech., 1980. Tchg. fellow Poly. U., 1974-75; tchg. instr., rsch. asst. Technion-Israel Inst. Tech., Haifa, 1975-80; engr. Nat. Inst. Stds. and Tech., Gaithersburg, Md., 1980—, group leader high temperature processes, 1994-99; group leader thermal and reactive processes Nat. Inst. Stds. and Tech., Gaithersburg, 1999—. Contbr. articles to profl. jours. Recipient Silver medal U.S. Dept. Commerce, 1991, SMART Bonus award, 1992, Sustained Superior Performance award nat. Inst. Stds. and Tech., 1983-89; Lady Davis grad. fellow Technion-Israel Inst. Tech., 1975-76. Fellow AIAA (assoc., Best Paper award terrestrial energy sys. tech. com. 1994, Best Paper award propellants and combustion tech. com. 1987, 89, propellants and combustion tech. com. 1987-90, terrestrial energy sys. tech. com. 1992—, mem. computational fluid dynamics com. on stds. 1997—); mem. AAAS, ASTM (com. on particle size measurements 1991—, chmn. subcom. reference materials 1992-95), ASME (mem. com. heat transfer in energy sys. heat transfer divsn. 1986—, mem. com. acad. and indsl. rsch. fuels and combustion techs. divsn. 1995—), AIChE, Am. Assn. Aerosol Rsch., N.Y. Acad. Scis., Inst. Liquid Atomization and Spray Sys. (mem. diesel and automotive sprays tech. com. 1997—, mem. computational and modeling tech. com. 1997—), Assn. Orthodox Jewish Scientists, Combustion Inst. (interagy. propulsion com., symposium program rev. subcom. 1989—), Instrument Soc. Am., Joint Army-Navy-NASA-Air Force (modeling and simulation subcom. 1999—), Sigma Xi (admissions com. NIST chpt. 1990-93), Sigma Gamma Tau, Tau Epsilon Phi. Office: Nat Inst Stds and Tech 100 Bureau Dr Stop 8360 Gaithersburg MD 20899-8360

PRESSER, STEPHEN LEE, insurance and investment counselor; b. Feb. 19, 1944; s. Broadus Lee and Mary Iola (Pyland) P.; m. Deborah T. Presser; children: Stephanie Diane, Todd Stephen. AA, Sch. of Ozarks, 1964; BS, U. Ark., 1967. CLU, ChFC. Inst. and investment counselor Equitable Fin. Svcs., Inc., Atlanta, 1971-95, Mass. Mut., Atlanta, 1995—. With U.S. Army, 1967-70. Decorated Bronze Star with oak leaf cluster, Purple Heart. Mem. Nat. Assn. Life Underwriters, Ga. Dist. Builder's Club (chmn. 1987-92), Atlanta Assn. Life Underwriters, Am. Soc. Fin. Profls. (bd. dirs. 1998-99, pub. rels. chmn. 1995-97, newsletter editor 1997-98), Million Dollar Roundtable, U. Ark. Alumni Assn. Met. Atlanta (bd. dirs. 1985-91, pres. 1988-90), Kiwanis (bd. dirs., Outstanding Kiwanian 1985, 86, 87, 88, 89, 90, 91, 94, 96, co-chmn. Kiwanis Internat. Holiday, gov. divsn. 1 Ga. dist. 1999-2000). Avocations: Nautilus, swimming. Home: 1988 Bramblewood Dr NE Atlanta GA 30329-1703 Office: 3445 Peachtree Rd NE Ste 300 Atlanta GA 30326-1234

PRESSMAN, JACOB, rabbi; b. Phila., Oct. 26, 1919; s. Solomon David and Dora (Levin) P.; m. Marjorie Steinberg, June 14, 1942; children: Daniel Joseph, Joel David, Judith Sharon. BA, U. Pa., 1940; MHL, Jewish Theol. Sem., 1944, Dr.Hebrew Letters, 1960, Dr. Humane Letters, 1979. Ordained rabbi, 1945. Rabbi Forest Hills Jewish Ctr., N.Y.C., 1944-46, Congregation Sinai, L.A., 1946-50, Temple Beth Am, L.A., 1950—; dir. Bonds of Israel, L.A., 1988-90, city chmn., 1990-91; vice chmn. bd. govs. L.A. Jewish Fedn. Coun., 1988—; founder U. Judaism, L.A. Hebrew High Sch., Herzl Sch., Camp Ramah at Ojai, Akiba Acad., Rabbi Jacob Pressman Acad. Mem. Rabbinical Assembly Western Region (pres. 1954-56), Bd. Rabbis So. Calif. (pres. 1958-61). Office: Temple Beth Am 1039 S La Cienega Blvd Los Angeles CA 90035-2507

PRESSMAN, THANE A., consumer products executive; b. San Diego, June 6, 1945; s. Harold Andrew and Audre Ethelyn (Negus) P.; m. Caroline Hannah Hood Snyder, Nov. 23, 1966; children: Sean, Steven. BS, Springfield (Mass.) Coll., 1967; MS, Syracuse U., 1969. Various to brand mgr. Procter & Gamble Co., Cin., 1968-76, assoc. mgr. advt., 1976-79; v.p. Lamalie Assocs., Inc. Chgo., 1979-81; dir. new products Alberto Culver Co., Melrose Park, Ill., 1981-84; group staff, v.p. Sara Lee Corp., Northbrook, Ill., 1984-85; pres., COO Kitchens of Sara Lee Can., Bramalea, Ont., 1986-88; exec. v.p. Sara Lee Bakery Co., Bramalea and Deerfield, Ill., 1988-90; pres., CEO Crestar Food Products, Inc. (affiliate of H.J. Heinz Co.), Eugene, Oreg., 1991-92, Crestar Food Products Inc. & Crestar Food Products Can. Ltd., Nashville and Mississauga, Ont., Can., 1992-93; pres. Labatt Ont. Breweries, Etobicoke, 1993-95; pres., CEO Labatt U.S.A. LLC., Norwalk, Conn., 1995-98, Tone Bros. Inc., Ankeny, Iowa, 1998—; guest lectr. U. Mich. Grad. Sch. Bus., Ann Arbor, 1977-79; bd. dirs. Brewers Retail Inc., Toronto, ENESCO Group Inc., 2000—; bd. dirs. Brewers of Ont., 1994-95, chmn., 1995. Bd. dirs. Am. Field Svc. U.S.A., N.Y.C., 1986-91, Greater Des Moines Partnership, 2000—; trustee AFS Intercultural Programs, N.Y.C., 1988-93; trustee Springfield Coll., 1988—. Mem. Assn. Governing Bds. Univs. and Colls., David Allen Reed Soc., Food and Consumer Products Mfrs. Can., Grocery Mfrs. Am., Glen Oaks Country Club, Vintage Sports Car Club Am., Vintage Automobile Racing Assn. Can., Vintage Sports Car Drivers Assn., Vintage Drivers Club Am.

PRESSNELL, RAYMOND THOMAS, electronics engineer; b. Dover, Kent, Eng., Sept. 18, 1935; s. Thomas James and Dorothy Maud (Coppard) P.; m. Joan Elaine Hicks, Jan. 31, 1959; children: Colin, Lisa Angela. BA, Open U., Milton Keynes, U.K., 1981. Registered profl. engr. Technician Rediffusion (NW) Ltd., Preston, U.K., 1963-75; tech. mgr. Telarama Rediffusion (Pty.) Ltd., Johannesburg, South Africa, 1975-79; tech. adviser CP Aerials, Morecambe, U.K., 1980-84, tech. adviser and cons., 1990—; electronics supr. Ministry of Def. and Aviation, Jeddah, Saudi Arabia, 1985-86; installation mgr. Johnson Controls, Riyadh, Saudi Arabia, 1987-89; low power TV transmitters and user adviser South African Broadcasting Corp., Johannesburg, 1976-77; cons. BBC/ITV, London, 1980—. Contbr. articles to profl. jours. Fellow Inst. Electrical and Electronic Inc. Engrs., Inst. Diagnostic Engrs.; mem. Inst. Elec. Engrs. (assoc., cons. 1983—). Achievements include patent pending for means to remove dissolved pollution from coastal waters; research on the standing voltage effects of static buildup (pre lightning discharge) on electrical/electronic hardware installed on steep gradients; retro-design of CCTV systems for Moda's multi-radar military installations throughout Saudi Arabia, hydro electricity generator. Avocations: technical writing, electrical and electronic experimentation, environmental solutions, alternate technologies. Home: 30 Limes Ave, Morecambe Lancashire LA3 1HS, England

PRESSOUYRE, LÉON, medieval archeology educator, consultant; b. Bayonne, France, Jan. 27, 1935; s. Ferdinand Pierre and Jeanne Marie (Diharce) P.; m. Sylvia Paule Capitaine, July 29, 1961 (dec. 1987); m. Katérina Stenou, Sept. 9, 1995; children: Karitini, Fivos, Basile. Licence d'Histoire, Université de Bordeaux, 1960, Licence d'Archéologie, 1960; Agrégation d'Histoire, U. Paris, 1963; Doctorat es Lettres, U. Strasbourg, 1979. Mem. Ecole française d'archéologie, Rome, 1964-66; attaché Centre Nat de la Recherche Scientifique, Paris, 1967-70, maître de recherche, 1973-80; mem. Inst. for Advanced Study, Princeton, N.J., 1971-72; prof. medieval archeology U. Paris, 1980—, chmn. dept. art and archaeology, 1987-89, v.p., 1989-97; Focillon fellow Yale U., 1967-68; vis. prof. U. Mich., Ann Arbor, 1979; chmn. medieval sect. Centre Nat. de la Recherche Scientifique, 1980-82; permanent expert Internat. Coun. Monuments and Sites, Paris, 1980-90; spl. adviser to dir. gen. UNESCO, 1996—. Author: Le cloître de Notre-Dame-en-Vaux (French, English, German edits.), 1981, Le rêve cistercien, 1990; mem. editl. com. Archéologie Medévale, Bull. Archéologique, Bull. Monumental, Monuments historiques, Revue de l'art, Arte Medievale; contbr. articles in field to publs. Regional del. for culture Comité Economique et Social, Chalons, 1979-83. Lt. French Armed Forces, 1960-62. Decorated Chevalier des Arts et Lettres, Republic of France, 1970, Chevalier du Mérite Nat., 1978, Officier du Mérite Nat., 1987, Gt. Cross Brasilia Order of Merit, 1988, Chevalier de la Légion d'Honneur, 1990; recipient Pirx Houllevigne, Institut de France, 1957, Prix Lefévre-Pontalis, Société francaise d'archéologie, 1977. Mem. Société Nationale es Antiquaires de France (chmn. 1991), Commn. Nationale de l'inventaire, Comité des travaux historiques et scientifiques (v.p. 1991-93). Roman Catholic. Office: Inst d'Art et d'Archeologie, 3 rue Michelet, 75006 Paris France also: UNESCO, 7 Place de Fontenoy, Paris France

PRESSYANOV, DOBROMIR STEFANOV, physicist, educator, researcher; b. Varna, Bulgaria, Aug. 23, 1960; s. Stefan Pressyanov and Tzanka Ivanova (Dimitrova) Nedev; m. Velimira Savova Dimitrova, Aug. 18, 1985; children: Stefan, Julian. MSc, St. Kliment Ohridski U. Sofia, Bulgaria, 1985, PhD, 1993. Physicist, rsch. fellow IO-REDMET, Sofia, 1985-91; health physicist hygienic and epidemiology inspection Ministry of Health, Sofia-Buhovo, Bulgaria, 1991-94; sr. asst. prof. U. Sofia, 1994-99, assoc. prof., 1999—; cons. Georedmet Ltd., Sofia, 1994-96; mem. Com. on Use Atomic Energy for Peaceful Purposes, Bulgaria. Contbr. articles to profl. publs.; patentee in field. Mem. Bulgarian Soc. Biomed. Physics and Tech., Bulgarian Nuc. Soc., Union Physicists in Bulgaria. Avocation: scuba diving. Office: U Sofia Faculty Physics, 5 James Bourchier Blvd, BG-1164 Sofia Bulgaria

PREST, NICHOLAS MARTIN, company executive; b. Cambridge, Eng., Apr. 3, 1953; s. Alan Richmond and Pauline Chasey (Noble) P.; m. Anthea Joy Elizabeth Neal; children: Clementine Joy Chasey, Frederick George Alan. M.History and Econ., Oxford U., 1974; MBA, U. Bradford, 1979. CEO United Sci. Holdings plc, London, Alvis Ltd., London, Helio Mirror Co. Ltd., London, United Sci. Instruments Ltd., London, Avimo Ltd., London; chmn. bd. Alvis plc; dir. Invertron Simulation Sys. Ltd., Avimo Singapore Ltd. Office: Alvis Plc, 34 Grosvenor Gardens, London SW1W 0AL, England*

PREST, WILFRID ROBERTSON, historian, educator; b. Melbourne, Australia, Aug. 9, 1940; s. Wilfred and Marjorie Wynn (Robertson) P.; m. Cedar Sonnenberg, June 19, 1965 (div. 1983); children: Richard, James; m. Sabina Florence White, May 9, 1984. BA, U. Melbourne, 1961; DPhil, U. Oxford, Eng., 1965. Tutor dept. history U. Melbourne, 1962; asst. prof. dept. history Johns Hopkins U., Balt., 1969-71; lectr. dept. history U. Adelaide, Australia, 1966-69, sr. lectr., reader, 1971-90, prof., 1991—; vis. fellow All Souls Coll., Oxford U., 1975, Davis Ctr./Princeton U., 1980, Clare Hall Cambridge U., 1985, Nat. Humanities Ctr., Research Triangle Park, N.C., 1998-99. Chmn. bd. Art Gallery of South Australia, 1978-85. Fellow Acad. Social Scis. Australia.

PRESTAGE, JEWEL LIMAR, political science educator; b. Hutton, La., Aug. 12, 1931; d. Brudis L. and Sallie Bell (Johnson) Limar; m. James J. Prestage, Aug. 12, 1953; children—Terri, James, Eric, Karen, Jay. B.A., So. U., Baton Rouge, 1951; M.A., U. Iowa, 1952, Ph.D., 1954; LHD (hon.), U. D.C., 1994, Loyola U., Chgo., 1999; LLD (hon.), Spelman Coll., 1999. Assoc. prof. polit. sci. Prairie View (Tex.) Coll., 1954-55, 56; assoc. prof. polit. sci. So. U., 1956-57, 58-62, prof., 1962—, chairperson dept., 1965-83, dean pub. policy and urban affairs, 1983-89; prof. polit. sci. Prairie View U., 1989-90; dean Benjamin Banneker Honors College, Prairie View (Tex.) Coll., 1990-98, prof. political sci., 1998—; chmn. La. adv. com. to U.S. Commn. on Civil Rights, 1975-85; mem., chmn. nat. adv. coun. on women's ednl. programs U.S. Dept. Edn., 1980-82; vis. prof. U. Iowa, 1987-88. Author: (with M. Githens) A Portrait of Marginality: Political Behavior of the American Woman, 1976; contbr. articles to profl. jours. Rockefeller fellow, 1951-52; NSF fellow, 1964; Ford Found. postdoctoral fellow, 1969-70. Mem. NAACP, Am. Polit. Sci. Assn. (v.p. 1974-75), So. Polit. Sci. Assn. (pres. 1975-76), Nat. Conf. Black Polit. Scientists (pres. 1976-77), Nat. Assn. African Am. Honors Programs (pres. 1993-94), Am. Soc. for Pub. Adminstrn. (pres. La. chpt. 1988-89, nat. exec. coun. 1989-90), Links Inc., Alpha Kappa Alpha. Home: 2145 77th Ave Baton Rouge LA 70807-5508 Office: So Univ PO Box 125 Prairie View TX 77446-0125

PRESTANSKI, HARRY THOMAS, public relations executive; b. Zanesville, Ohio, Aug. 31, 1947; s. Joseph Raymond and Della Theresa (Butryn) P.; m. Jeanene LaRee Versaw, Sept. 19, 1970; children: Lisa Jodene, Shari LaRee, Amy Elizabeth. BS in Journalism, Ohio U., 1972; postgrad. U. Dayton, 1973-74. Publs. editor Hobart Brothers, Troy, Ohio, 1972-75; v.p., account supr. Josephson, Cuffari & Co., Montclair, N.J., 1975-77; publicity mgr. Winnebago Industries, Forest City, Iowa, 1977-80; v.p., gen. mgr. CMF & Z Pub. Relations div. Creswell, Munsell, Fultz & Zirbel, Cedar Rapids, Iowa, 1980-88; v.p., mng. dir. Carmichael Lynch Pub. Rels., Mpls., 1988-90; pres. H.P. Communications, Cin., 1990—. Contbr. articles to profl. jours. Fin. chair Senate dist. 41 Minn. Rep. Party, 1993-96, chmn., 1994-96, state del., 1993-96; campaign chair various Minn. Rep. candidates, 1993-96. Served to cpl. USMC, 1966-69. Mem. Pub. Rels. Soc. Am. (pres. Quad cities chpt. 1988, bd. dirs. 1985-88, Counselors Acad.), Minn. Press Club, Indian Creek Nature Ctr. (bd. dirs. 1986-88), Burnsville C. of C., Literacy Network of Greater Cin. (bd. dirs. 1996-99). Republican. Roman Catholic. Office: 6896 Windwood Dr Cincinnati OH 45241-4105

PRESTAR, FRANZ JÜRGEN, neurosurgeon, researcher; b. Recklinghausen, Germany, Jan. 6, 1959; s. Franz and Gertrud (Reiners) P. MD, U. Munich, 1983. Asst. Anat. Inst. U. Munich, 1979-83; resident in neurosurgery U. Aachen, 1983-86; resident in neurosurgery Bergmannsheil Gelsenkirchen-Buer, 1987-89, asst. head physician in neurosurgery, 1990—; specialist in cervical spine surgery, surgery of lumbar spinal stenosis, spinal tumors, minimally invasive spinal surgery. Contbr. articles to profl. jours. including Jour. Neurosurgery, Minimally Invasive Neurosurgery, Zentralblatt für Neurochirurgie, and Chirurgische Praxis. Mem. German Soc. Neurosurgery, Soc. Spine Investigation, German Soc. Spine Surgery. Office: Knappschaftskrankenhaus, Scherner Weg 4, D-45894 Gelsenkirchen Buer, Germany

PRESTON, BRUCE MARSHALL, lawyer, educator; b. Trinidad, Colo., Feb. 24, 1949; s. Marshall Caldwell and Juanita (Killgore) P.; m. Mariannina Erra, Aug. 10, 1974; children: Charles Marshall, Robert Arthur. BS summa cum laude, Ariz. State U., 1971; MA, U. Ariz., 1972, JD, 1975. Bar: Ariz. 1975, U.S. Ct. Appeals (9th cir.) 1976, U.S. Ct. Claims 1983, U.S. Tax Ct. 1983, U.S. Supreme Ct. 1983; cert. fin. planner. Atty. Maricopa County Office of Pub. Defender, Phoenix, 1975-84; ptnr. Simonsen & Preston, Phoenix, 1985-86, Simonsen, Preston, Sargeant & Arbetman, Phoenix, 1986; atty. office of atty. gen. State of Ariz., 1987-90; assoc. Broening, Oberg and Woods, Phoenix, 1989-96, ptnr., 1997—; judge pro tem Mcpl. Ct., Phoenix, 1984-86; licensee in sales Ariz. Dept. Real Estate, Phoenix, 1981-87; adj. faculty Phoenix Coll. for Fin. Planning, Denver, 1984-87, Maricopa County Community Coll. Dist., Phoenix, 1985-87, Ariz. State U. Coll. of Bus., Tempe, 1986-87, Ottawa U., Phoenix, 1986. Chmn. com., treas., pres. bd. dirs. Kachina Country Day Sch., 1982-90; bd. dirs. Family Svc. Agy., Phoenix, 1988—, treas., 1990-91; bd. dirs. Clearwater Hills Homeowners Assn., Paradise Valley, Ariz., 1989—, v.p., 1990, treas., 1991; bd. dirs. Phoenix Boys Choir, 1989-90. Mem. Ariz. Assn. Def. Counsel, Ariz. Bar Assn. (cert. specialist criminal law 1982-84), Maricopa County Bar Assn., Ariz. State U. Coll. Liberal Arts Alumni Assn. (bd. dirs. 1978-80, 87-88), Phi Kappa Phi. Avocations: computers, skiing, boating, running. Home: 7247 N Black Rock Trl Paradise Vly AZ 85253-2802 Office: Broening Oberg & Woods 1122 E Jefferson St Phoenix AZ 85034-2224

PRESTON, CLIVE IAN, palliative medicine consultant; b. Carshalton, Surrey, Eng., Nov. 10, 1952; s. Albert and Margaret Jean (Campion) P.; m. Alison May Rodger, Dec. 29, 1976; children: Matthew James, Rosamunde Elizabeth, Katherine Fiona, Christina Florence. BS in Med. Sci. with honors, Edinburgh (Scotland) U., 1974, MB ChB, 1977, diploma in med. radiotherapy, 1985. House physician, house surgeon Nat. Health Svc., Edinburgh, 1977-78; sr. house officer Nat. Health Svc., Ipswich, Eng., 1978-80; registrar in gen. medicine Nat. Health Svc., Ashington, Eng., 1980-83; registrar in oncology Nat. Health Svc., Edinburgh, 1983-88; sr. registrar in oncology Nat. Health Svc., Cardiff, Wales, 1988-90; cons. in clin. oncology Nat. Health Svc., Hull, Eng., 1991-95; cons. Fife Palliative Care Svc., Kirkaldy, Scotland, 1995—. Contbr. articles to profl. jours. including Brit. Jour. Urology and Clin. Radiology. Mem. Scottish Green Party, 1983—; chmn. Trinity Acad. Sch. Bd., Edinburgh, 1995—. Fellow Royal Coll. Radiologists (London); mem. Assn. Palliative Medicine. Avocations: philately, music. Home: 64 Inverleith Row, Edinburgh EH3 5PX, Scotland Office: Fife Palliative Care Svc, Willow Dr Whytemans Brae, Kirkcaldy Fife, Scotland

PRESTON, LETRICIA ELAYNE, financial planner; b. El Paso, Tex., Oct. 19, 1947; d. Leon A. and Doris (Jones) Curry; m. Elisha I. Preston, May 22, 1965 (div.); children: Rhonda E. Eastman, Stacy A. Milburn. Student, El Paso C.C. Lic. real estate broker. Sec. S.I.C. Fin. Co., El Paso, 1966-67; sec., credit investigator, asst. cashier First City Nat. Bank, El Paso, 1967-79; real estate agt. Allied Agts., El Paso, 1979-80, Coldwell Hovious, El Paso, 1980-83; asst. v.p. First Fin. Savs., El Paso, 1983-86; sec. Kelly Svcs., El Paso, 1986-87; sales-securities br. mgr. First Investors Corp., El Paso, 1987-93; br. mgr. Linsco Pvt. Ledger Corp., El Paso, 1993—. Avocations: dancing, travel, reading, bowling, crossword puzzles. Office: Linsco Pvt Ledger Corp 1790 N Lee Trevino Dr Ste 303 El Paso TX 79936-4525

PRESTON, PAUL, historian educator; b. Liverpool, Eng., July 21, 1946; s. Charles Ronald and Alice (Hoskisson) P.; m. Gabrielle Patricia Ashford-Hodges, Mar. 24, 1983; children: James, Christopher. BA, Oriel Coll., 1968; MA, U. Reading, U.K., 1969; PhD, U. Oxford, 1976. Lectr. U. Reading, U.K., 1973-75; lectr., prof. Queen Mary Coll. U. London, 1975-91; prof. Internat. History London Sch. Econs., 1991—. Author: The Coming of the Spanish Civil War, 1978, 2d edit., 1994, The Triumph of Democracy in Spain, 1986, The Politics of Revenge, 1990, Franco: A Biography, 1993 (Yorkshire Post Best Book of Yr. 1993), Comrades! Portraits from the Spanish Civil War, 1999. Recipient Encomienda de la Orden de Merito Civil King of Spain, 1986; fellow Brit. Acad., 1994. Avocations: modern fiction, classical music, opera, wine. Office: London Sch Econs, Houghton St, WC2A 2AE London England

PRESTON, RONALD HAYDN, theologian, retired educator; b. Bristol, Eng., Mar. 12, 1913; s. Haydn and Eleanor Jane (Knights) P.; m. Edith Mary Lindley, Sept. 6, 1948 (div.); chdlren: Mark, Ann, Barbara; m. Mary Elizaveth Smith, Aug. 14, 1997. BSc, London Sch. Econs., 1935; BA, St. Catherine's Coll., Oxford, Eng., 1940; MA, Oxford U., 1944, DD, 1983. Study sec. Student Christian Movement, U.K., 1943-48; warden St. Anselm Mall, Manchester, Eng., 1948-63; canon theologian The Cathedral, Manchester, 1957-71; prof. social and pastoral theology Manchester U., 1970-80. Author: Religion and the Persistence of Capitalism, 1979, Explorations in Theology, 1981, Church and Society in the Late Twentieth Century, 1983, The Future of Christian Ethics, 1987, Religion and the Ambiguities of Capitalism, 1991, Confusions in Christian Social Ethics, 1994, The Middle War, 2000. Mem. Labour Party. Anglican. Home: 161 Old Hall Ln, Manchester M14 6HJ, England

PRESTON, SEYMOUR STOTLER, III, manufacturing company executive; b. Media, Pa., Sept. 11, 1933; s. Seymour Stotler and Mary Alicia (Harper) P.; m. Jean Ellen Holman, Sept. 8, 1956; children: Courtney J.,

Katherine E., Alicia D., Shelley S. BA, Williams Coll., 1956; MBA, Harvard Coll., 1958. With Pennwalt Corp., Phila., 1961-89; exec. v.p. in charge of chems. and equipment ops., worldwide Pennwalt Corp., 1975-77, pres., COO, 1977-89; pres., CEO Elf Atochem N.Am., Inc. (formerly Atochem N.Am.), Phila., 1990-93; chmn. AAC Engineered Sys. Inc., 1994—; bd. dirs. Scott Specialty Gases, Inc., Albermarle Corp., Tufco Techs., Inc. Trustee Shipley Sch., Bryn Mawr, Pa., 1976-88, Phila. Orch. Assn., 1992-95; trustee Wistar, 1997—, Acad. Natural Scis., 1980—, chmn., 1995-2000, pres., 2000—; bd. mgrs. Franklin Inst., Phila., 1980-92; bd. dirs. Lawrenceville (N.J.) Sch., 1982-99, Wistar Inst., 1997—, Barra Found., 1998—. 1st lt. USAF, 1958-61. Mem. Soc. for Chem. Industry, Greater Phila. C. of C. (bd. dirs. 1979-94), Radnor Hunt Club (Malvern, Pa.).

PRESTON, WILLIAM LEON, family practice; b. Salina, Kans., Nov. 19, 1947; s. Billie Wirth and Mary May Preston; m. Rebecca Cecilia Preston, June 19, 1971; children: William Andrew, Ellen Marie. BA in Physics, Kans. Wesleyan U., 1968; MD, U. Colo., 1972. Diplomate Am. Bd. Family Physicians. Resident West Suburban Family Practice, Oak Park, Ill., 1972-75; assoc. dir. Family Practice Ctr., LaGrange, Ill., 1975-79; med. dir. Wholistic Health Ctr., LaGrange, 1979-80; sr. ptnr. Preston Family Practice, Western Springs, Ill., 1980—; med. dir. St. Thomas Hospice, Hinsdale, Ill., 1980—. Lay leader First United Meth. Ch., Western Springs, 1992—. Fellow Am. Acad. of Family Physicians; mem. Nat. Hospice Orgn., Am. Coll. of Sports Medicine. Republican. Methodist. Avocations: photography, music, martial arts. E-mail: billcmq@aol.com. Office: Preston Family Practice 4479 Central Ave Western Springs IL 60558-1714

PRESTRIDGE, PAMELA ADAIR, lawyer; b. Delhi, La., Dec. 25, 1945; d. Gerald Wallace Prestridge and Louis Baugh and Peggy Adair (Arender) Martin. BA, La. Poly. U., 1967; M in Edn., La. State u., 1968, JD, 1973. Bar: U.S. Dist. Ct. (mid. dist.) La. 1975, U.S. Dist. Ct. (so. dist.) Tex. 1982, U.S. Ct. Appeals (5th cir.) 1982, U.S. Supreme Ct. 1990. Law clk. to presiding justice La. State Dist. Ct., Baton Rouge, 1973-75; ptnr. Breazeale, Sachse & Wilson, Baton Rouge, 1975-82, Hirsch & Westheimer P.C., Houston, 1982-92; pvt. practive, Houston, 1992—. Counselor Big Bros./Big Sisters, Baton Rouge, 1968-70; legal cons., bd. dirs. Lupus Found. Am., Houston, 1984-93; bd. dirs. Quota Club, Baton Rouge, 1979-82, Speech and Hearing Found., Baton Rouge, 1981-82, The Actors Workshop, Houston, 1988-93; active Tex. Accts. and Attys. for the Arts. Recipient Pres.'s award Lupus Found. Am., 1991, cert. of appreciation Assn. Atty. Mediators, 1992, Outstanding Profl. Woman of Houston award Fedn. Profl. Women, 1984. Mem. ABA, La. Bar Assn., Tex. Bar Assn., Houston Bar Assn., Houston Bar Found., Assn. Atty. Mediators (bd. dirs. 1994-96, Citation for Outstanding Mems. 1993), Profl. Atty.-Mediators Coop. (v.p. 1994, bd. dirs. 1994-96, pres. 1995), Phi Alpha Delta. Eckankar. Avocations: acting, ultralite flying. Home: 1701 Hermann Dr Unit 407 Houston TX 77004-7345 Office: 3300 Phoenix Tower PO Box 130987 Houston TX 77219-0987

PRESTWICH, MICHAEL CHARLES, historian, educator; b. Oxford, Eng., Jan. 30, 1943; s. John Oswald and Menna (Roberts) P.; m. Margaret Joan Daniel; children: Robin James, Christopher Michael, Kate Elizabeth. BA, Oxford U., England, 1964, DPhil, 1968. Research lectr. Oxford U., 1965-69; lectr. U. St. Andrew's, Fife, Scotland, 1969-79; reader history U. Durham, Eng., 1979-86, prof., 1986—; pro-vice chancellor, 1992-99. Author: War, Politics and Finance under Edward I, 1972, The Three Edwards, 1980, Edward I, 1988; editor: Documents Illustrating the Crisis of 1297-98, 1980, English Politics in the Thirteenth Century, 1990., Armies and Warfare in the Middle Ages: The English Experience, 1996. Fellow Royal Hist. Soc., Soc. Antiquaries; mem. Surtees Soc. (v.p. 1987—). Office: U Durham, 43 N Bailey, Durham DH1 3EX, England

PRESTWOOD, ALVIN TENNYSON, lawyer; b. Roeton, Ala., June 18, 1929; s. Garret Felix and Jimmie (Payne) P.; m. Sue Burleson Lee, Nov. 27, 1974; children: Ann Celeste Prestwood Peeples, Alison Bennett, Cynthia Joyce Lee Koplos, William Alvin Lee, Garret Courtney. BS, U. Ala., 1951, LLB, 1956, JD, 1970. Bar: Ala. 1956, U.S. Ct. Appeals (6th and 11th cirs.) 1981, U.S. Supreme Ct. 1972. Law clk. Supreme Ct. Ala., 1956-57; asst. atty. gen. Ala., 1957-59; commr. Ala. Dept. Pensions and Security, 1959-63; pvt. practice Montgomery, Ala., 1963-65, 77-82; ptnr. Volz, Capouano, Wampold, Prestwood & Sansone, 1965-77, Prestwood & Rosser, 1982-85, Capouano, Wampold, Prestwood & Sansone, 1986-94, Volz, Prestwood & Hanan, 1995—; chmn. Gov.'s Com. on White House Conf. on Aging, 1961; mem. adv. com. Dept. Health, Edn. and Welfare, 1962; sec. Nat. Coun. State Pub. Welfare Adminstrs., 1962. Mem. editorial bd. Ala. Law Rev., 1955-56; contbr. articles to profl. jours. Pres. Morningview Sch. P.T.A., 1970; chmn. Am. Nursing Home Assn. Legal Com., 1972; bd. dirs. Montgomery Bapt. Hosp., 1958-65; chmn. bd. mgmt. East Montgomery YMCA, 1969; chmn. deacons Cloverdale Bapt. Ch., 1994, 95, 98. Served to 1st lt., inf. AUS, 1951-53. Decorated Combat Inf. Badge.; recipient Sigma Delta Kappa Scholastic Achievement award U. Ala. Sch. Law, 1956, Law Day Moot Ct. award U. Ala. Sch. Law, 1956. Mem. ABA (chmn. com. on jud. performance and conduct 1996, chmn. Judiciary's Image Evaluation Task Force 1996-2000), Ala. Bar Assn. (chmn. adminstrv. law sect. 1972, 78, 83, 97), Montgomery County Bar Assn. (chmn. exec. com. 1971), Farrah Order Jurisprudence, Eleventh Cir. Jud. Conf., Am. Judicature Soc., Kappa Sigma. Home: 1431 Magnolia Curv Montgomery AL 36106-2043 Office: Volz Prestwood & Hanan 350 Adams Ave Montgomery AL 36104-4204

PRETI, ANTONIO, psychiatrist, researcher; b. Cagliari, Italy, Apr. 23, 1958; s. Franco and Elena (Onnis) P.; m. Paola Miotto, Aug. 31, 1998. Univ. degree in medicine, U. Cagliari, 1986; qualification in psychiatry, U. Padua, Italy, 1992. Med. diplomate. Intern Dept. Pharmacology, Cagliari, 1983-86, Dept. Psychiatry, Cagliari, 1987-88; asst. psychiatry br. Dept. Emergency, Padua, 1991-92; cons. Padua, 1993-94, CMG Health Ctr., Cagliari, 1995—; cons. jud. ct., Cagliari, 1995—; dir. Neurobiology of Major Psychoses, Italy, 1995—; sr. lectr. dept. psychology U. Cagliari, 2000. Contbr. sci. articles to profl. jours. including Neurosci. Letters, Psychiat. Genetics, Jour. Affective Disorders, Psychiatry Rsch. Mem. AAAS, Italian Soc. Psychiatry, Soc. for Neurosci., European Soc. Clin. Neuropharmacology, N.Y. Acad. Sci. Avocations: photography, writing novels, music composition. E-mail: antolink@yahoo.it. Office: Genneruxi Med Ctr, Costantinopoli 42, 09129 Cagliari Sardinia, Italy

PRETTYMAN, ALFRED EMERSON, English language and social and behavioral sciences educator, publishing executive; b. Balt., Feb. 15, 1935; s. Edward Augusta and Helen P.; m. Julia Poussaint (div.); children: Meryl, Evan; m. Kathleen Conwell, Dec. 25, 1987 (dec.); m. Susan Stedman, Aug. 17, 1997. BS, Hamilton Coll., 1956; postgrad., Cornell U., 1959, Antioch U. Coll. exec. editor Harper & Row Pub., N.Y.C., 1966-70, sr. editor, trade, 1969-71; founder, pres. Emerson Hall Pub., N.Y.C., 1973-80; asst. prof. Rutgers U., New Brunswick, N.J., 1989-98, Rockland C.C., SUNY, Suffern, N.Y., 1988—; co-founder, pres. Pretty-Steady Prodns., N.Y.C., 1992—; asst. prof. Ramapo Coll. N.J., 1999—; chair bd. The Nyack (N.Y.) Ctr., 1996-98; cons. N.E. Humanities, Washington, 1970-73, N.E. Arts, Washington, 1970-72; elector Nat. Medal Lit., N.Y.C., 1980; co-chair lit. N.Y. State Coun. Arts., 1970; judge Nat. Book Awards, N.Y.C., 1980; exec. dir. Nyack Ctr., 2000—. Editor: U.S.: National Civics in a Mosaic Democracy 1996, 98, U.S.: The Intercultural Nation, 1999; prodr. Ogun's Fire: The Sculpture of Melvin Edwards, 1993; contbr. articles to profl. jours. Recipient Excellence In Comm. award Creative and Editl. Black Achievement, 1983. Mem. Assn. Study Africana Philosophy (co-founder). Avocations: tennis, cooking, gardening, fly-fishing, singing. Home and Office: 215 W 98th St Apt 12-b New York NY 10025-5635

PREUSS, ROGER E(MIL), artist; b. Waterville, Minn., Jan. 29, 1922; s. Emil W. and Edna (Rosenau) P.; m. MarDee Ann Germundson, Dec. 31, 1954 (dec. Mar. 1981). Student, Mankato Comml. Coll., Mpls. Sch. Art. emeritus instr. seminar Mpls. Inst. Arts Speakers Bur.; former judge ann. Goodyear Nat. Conservation Awards Program; founder U.S. Fed. Roger Preuss Waterfowl Prodn. Area, LeSueur County, Minn., 1997; advisor Wildlife Forever Nat. Fish-Art Contest. Painter of nature art; one-man shows include: St. Paul Fine Art Galleries, 1959, Albert Lea Art Center, 1963, Hist. Soc. Mont., Helena, 1964, Brotherhood Fine Arts Ctr., 1965, Bicentennial exhbn., Le Sueur County Hist. Soc. Mus., Elysian, Minn., 1976, Merrill's Gallery of Fine Art, Taos, N.Mex., 1980; exhbns. include: Mpls. Inst. Art Msa exhibit, 1946, Midwest Wildlife Conf. Exhbn., Kerr's Beverly Hills, Calif., 1947, Laguna Art Mus., Calif., 1947, Joslyn Meml. Mus., Omaha, 1948, Hollywood Fine Arts Center, 1948, Minn. Centennial, 1949, Federated Chaparral Authors, 1951, Nat. Wildlife Art, 1951, 52, N.Am. Wildlife Art, dir. exposition, 1952, Ducks Unltd. Waterfowl exhibit, 1953, 54, St. Paul Winter Carnival, 1954, St. Paul Gallery Art Mart, 1954, Harris Fine Arts Center, Provo, Utah, 1969, Galerie Internationale, N.Y.C., 1972, Holy Land Conservation Fund, N.Y.C., 1976, Faribault Art Ctr., 1981, Wildlife Artists of the World Exhbn., Bend, Oreg., 1984, U. Art Mus., U. Minn., Mpls., 1990, Rochester Art Ctr., 1991, Minn. Hist. Soc.-Hill House, Minn., 1992, Bemidji Art Ctr., 1992, Jack London Ctr., Dawson City, Yukon Territory, Can., 1992, Weyerhaeuser Meml. Mus., Little Falls, Minn., 1995, Minn. Valley Nat. Wildlife Refuge Ctr., Bloomington, 1995, Sagebrush Artists Exhbn., Klamath Falls, Oreg., 1995; represented in permanent collections: Demarest Meml. Mus., Hackensack, N.J., Smithsonian Instn., N.Y. Jour. Commerce, Mont. Hist. Soc., Inland Bird Banding Assn., Minn. Capitol Bldg., Mont. State U., Wildlife Am. Collection, LeSueur Hist. Soc., Voyageurs Nat. Park Interpretive Ctr., Krause-Hartig VFW Post, Mpls., Nat. Wildlife Fedn. Collection, Minn. Ceremonial House, U.S. Wildlife Svc. Fed. Bldg., Fort Snelling, Minn., Crater Lake Nat. Park Visitors Ctr., VA Hosp., Mpls., Luxton Collection, Banff, Alta., Can., Internat. Inst. Arts, Geneva, Mont. Capitol Bldg., People of Century-Goldblatt Collection, Lyons, Ill., Harlem Savings Collection, N.Y.C., Weisman Art Mus., Mpls., Minn. Vets. Home, Mpls., Blauvelt Art Mus., Oradell, N.J., Roger Preuss Art Collection, Augustana Ctr. for Western Studies, Sioux Falls, S.D., Minn. Mus. Am. Art, St. Paul, U. Minn. Art Mus., C.M. Russell Mus., Great Falls, Mont., Le Sueur County Courthouse, Le Center, Minn., others, numerous galleries and pvt. collections; designer: Fed. Duck Stamp, U.S. Dept. Interior, 1949, Commemorative Centennial Pheasant Stamp, 1981, Gold Waterfowl medallion Franklin Mint, 1983, Gold Stamp medallion Wildlife Mint, 1983, 40th Anniverary Commemorative Fed. Duck Stamp etching, 1989; panelist: Sportsman's Roundtable, Sta. WTCN-TV, Mpls. (emeritus), from 1953; author: Is Wildlife Art Recognized Fine Art?, 1986; contbr.: Christmas Echos, 1955, Wing Shooting, Trap & Skeet, 1955, Along the Trout Stream, 1979; contbr. Art Impressions mag., Can., Wildlife Art, U.S.; also illustrations and articles in Nat. Wildlife and over 300 essays on North American animals, others.; assoc. editor emeritus: Out-of-Doors mag.; compiler and artist: Outdoor Horizons, 1957, Twilight over the Wilderness, 1972, 60 limited edition prints Wildlife of America, from 1970; contbr. paintings and text Minnesota Today; creator paintings and text Preuss Wildlife Calendar; inventor: paintings and text Wildlife Am. Calendar; featured artist Art West, 1980-84, Wildlife Art; featured in films Your BFA- Care and Maintenance, Black Ducks Along the Border. Del. Nat. Wildlife Conf.; bd. dirs. emeritus Voyageurs Nat. Park Assn., Deep-Portage Conservation Found.; bd. dirs. Wetlands for Wildlife U.S.A.; active Wildlife Am.; co-organizer, v.p., bd. dirs. Minn. Conservation Fedn., 1952-54; mem. U.S. Hospitalized Vets. Venison Program, 1957—; trustee Liberty Bell Edn. Found.; Waseca Arts Coun.; founder, dir. Roger Preuss Conservation Preserve for Study of Nature, 1990—. With USNR, World War II. Recipient Stamp Design award U.S. Fish and Wildlife Svc., 1994, Minn. Outdoor award, 1956, Patron of Conservation award, 1956, award for contbns. conservation Minn. Statehood Centennial Commn., 1958, 1st award Am. Indsl. Devel. Coun., citation of merit VFW, award of merit Mil. Order Cootie, 1963, merit award Minn. Waterfowl Assn., 1976, silver medal Nat. SAR, 1978, Svcs. to Arts and Environ. award Faribault Art Ctr., 1981, Ptnrs. for Wildlife award U.S. Fish and Wildlife Svc., 1994; named Wildlife Conservationist of the Yr., Sears Found.-Nat. Wildlife Fedn. program, 1966, Am. Bicentennial Wildlife Artist, Am. Heritage Assn., 1976; hon. mem. Ont. Chippewa Nation of Can., 1957; named Knight of Mark Twain for contbns. to Am. art Mark Twain Soc., 1978; named to Water, Woods and Wildlife Hall of Fame, named Dean of Wildfowl Artists, 1981, Hon. Ky. Col.; recipient hon. degree U.S. Vets. Venison program, 1980, Western Am. award significant contbns. to preservation arts and history No. Prairie Plains, Augustana Coll. Ctr. for Western Studies, Sioux Falls, S.D., 1992, Pub. Svc. award for outstanding contbns. to Am. conservation and environ. U.S. Dept. Interior, 1996; named creator first signed, numbered photolithographic print pub. in N.Am., 1959; documented Colorado Springs Fine Arts Ctr., 1993, colleague of Frederick R. Weisman Mus., Mpls., 1994; grantee NEH, 1995, Prairie Lakes Arts Coun., 1995. Fellow Internat. Inst. Arts (life), Soc. Animal Artists (emeritus), N.Am. Mycol. Assn., Nat. Wildlife Fedn. (nat. wildlife week chmn. Minn.), Minn. Ducks Unltd. (bd. dirs. emeritus), Minn. Artists Assn. (v.p., bd. dirs. 1953-59), Outdoor Writers Am. (emeritus), Soc. Artists and Art Dirs. (emeritus), Am. Artists Profl. League (emeritus), Mpls. Soc. Fine Arts, Wildlife Soc., Minn. Mycol. Soc. (pres. emeritus, hon. life mem.), Le Sueur County Hist. Soc. (hon. life mem.), Minn. Conservation Fedn. (hon. life), Wildlife Artists World (charter mem., emeritus internat. v.p., chmn. fine arts bd.), Internat. Platform Assn. (emeritus), Great Lakes Outdoor Writers (emeritus), The Prairie Chicken Soc. (patron), Mission Oceanic Arctic, 1992, Beaverbrook Club (hon. life), Minn. Press Club (emeritus), Explorers Club (N.Y.C., emeritus), Silver Lake Sports (hon.). Office: care Wildlife Am PO Box 580004-a Minneapolis MN 55458-0004 Studio: 2224 Grand Ave Minneapolis MN 55405-3412

PREUSSER, F. ALBRECHT, computer scientist, consultant; b. Beerfelden, Germany, May 6, 1949; s. Heinrich and Gertrud Preusser; m. Sung-Hi Youn, Oct. 28, 1977; 2 children. Dipl.-Ing., Technische Hochschule, Darmstadt, Germany, 1972; Dr.-Ing., Tech. U., Berlin, 1977. Sci. asst. Tech. U., 1972-77; referendar Senator für Bau-und Wohnungswesen, Berlin, 1977-78; computing analyst Wissenschaftliches Rechenzentrum/Technische U. Berlin, 1978-85; sr. analyst Fritz-Haber Institut der Max-Planck-Gesellschaft Berlin, 1985—; cons. to software firms, govt., chartered engrs., univ. mems. Author numerous programs for contour drawing in use worldwide; developer mathematical algorithms in use worldwide; contbr. numerous articles to profl. jours. Mem. Numerical Algorithms Group Users Assn., Deutscher Verein für Vermessungswesen. Evangelic Christian. Avocations: humans, nature, sports. Office: Fritz-Haber-Institut MPG, Faradayweg 4-6, D-14195 Berlin Germany

PREVAL, RENE, Haitian president. Prime min., min. nat. def., min. interior Haiti, Port-au-Prince, 1991, pres., 1996—. Office: Office of the Pres, Palais Nat Champ de Mars, Port-au-Prince Haiti*

PREYSZ, SANDRA, music educator. BA, U. Utah, 1973. Cert. piano tchr. Pvt. piano tchr. Salt Lake City, 1977—. Mem. Utah Music Tchrs. Assn. (state bd. dirs., membership chair 1995—), Utah Fedn. Music Club (state bd. dirs., sec. 1997—). Avocations: skiing, sailing, tennis.

PREZZIA, CHARLES PAUL, physician; b. East Liverpool, Ohio, Mar. 6, 1956; s. Paul Dominic and Anna Mae (Colista) P.; m. Karen Long, Sept. 11, 1982; children: Paul, Charles, Anna, John, Marie, Claire, David, Rosemary. BA in Physics, Amherst Coll., 1978; MD, Ohio State U., 1981; MPH, Med. Coll. Wis., 1991. Intern, resident Good Samaritan Hosp. Wright State U., Dayton, Ohio, 1982-85; occupational emergency physician Middletown (Ohio) Regional Hosp., 1984-87, med. dir. occupational health program, 1986-87; med. dir. Immediate Care Ctr., Middletown, 1986-98; physician in charge Maumee (Ohio) Stamping Plant, Ford Motor Co., 1988-98; staff physician Norfolk & So. R.R., 1989-98; physician Toledo Sun Oil Refinery, Oregon, Ohio, 1989-98; med. dir. Clyde (Ohio) divsn. Whirlpool Corp., 1990-98; pres. Occupational Care Cons., Oregon, 1990-98; gen. mgr. health svcs., med. dir. USX/US Steel Group, Pitts., 1998—; cons. physician Libbey Glass, Inc., Toledo, 1990-98. Fellow Am. Coll. Occupl. and Environ. Medicine, Am. Coll. Preventitive Medicine, Royal Soc. Medicine; mem. Am. Indsl. Hygiene Assn., Ohio State Med. Assn. (workers' compensation com. 1991—), Cath. Med. Assn. (pres.). Roman Catholic. Avocations: chess, wine, computers, theology, classical music. Home: 220 Mckenzie Rd Clinton PA 15026-1570 Office: 600 Grant St Rm 4581 Pittsburgh PA 15219-2702

PRIBBENOW, PAUL P., higher education administrator, consultant; b. Decorah, Iowa, Jan. 18, 1957; s. Jerome Carroll and Elsie Mae (Zellmer) P.; m. Ann F. Raney, Sept. 4, 1982 (div. Sept. 1995); m. Abigail G. Crampton, Apr. 27, 1996. BA, Luther Coll., Decorah, 1978; AM in Divinity, U. Chgo., 1979, PhD in Ethics, 1993. Cert. fund raising exec. Dir. devel. Sch. Art Inst. Chgo., 1985-89; assoc. dean Sch. Social Svc. Adminstrn., U. Chgo., 1989-91, Div. Sch., U. Chgo., 1991-93; v.p. Sch. Art Inst. Chgo., 1993-96; dean for coll. advancement Wabash Coll., Crawfordsville, Ind., 1996—; mem. faculty Sch. Art Inst. Chgo., 1993-96, Spertus Coll., Chgo., 1990-96. Contbr. articles to profl. jours. Mem. vis. com. Div. Sch., U. Chgo., 1996—; sec. bd trustees Wabash Coll., 1998—. Mem. Nat. Soc. Fund Raising Execs. (Pres.'s award for profl. leadership 1994), Coun. for Advancement and Support of Edn. Democrat. Lutheran. Avocation: reading. Office: Wabash Coll 511 W Wabash Ave Crawfordsville IN 47933-2421

PŘIBYLOVÁ, HANA, pediatrician, researcher; b. Prague, Czech Republic, Aug. 23, 1928; d. Emil and Maria (Pikart) P.; m. Ladislav Přibyl (dec. Feb. 1990); children: Tomáš, Markéta. MD, U. Medicine, Prague, 1952; degree in pediatrics, Charles U., Prague, 1957, PhD, 1960, DSc, 1992. Pediatrician Hosp., Cheb, Czechoslovakia, 1953-54; rsch. asst. Inst. for Care of Mother and Child, Prague, 1954-57, rschr., 1957-69, 75—, chief neonatology, 1967-74; rschr. dept. pediatrics Karolinska Inst., Stockholm, 1969-70; prof. Internat. Sch. Medicine, Dubrovnik, Yugoslavia, 1981-89, Tatranska Lomnica, Czechoslovakia, 1992. Author: (in Czech) Temperature Regulation and Metabolism in Newborn Infant, 1967, The Infant of the Diabetic Mother, 1982; contbr. numerous articles to profl. publs., chpts. to books. Internal grantee Min. Health Czech Republic, 1990-93, 94-96; recipient Min. prize Czech Republic, 1990. Mem. N.Y. Acad. Scis., Czechoslovak Soc. J.E. Purkyně. Roman Catholic. Home: Nám Sv Čecha 1, 101 00 Prague 10, Czech Republic Office: Inst Care Mother and Child, Pololské nábř 157, 147 10 Prague 4, Czech Republic

PRICE, BETTY JEANNE, choirchime soloist, writer; b. Long Beach, Calif., June 12, 1942; d. Grant E. and Miriam A. (Francis) Sickles; m. Harvey H. Price, Aug. 6, 1975; children: Thomas Neil Gering, Timothy Ray (dec.), Pamela Kay (dec.). Degree in Acctg., Northland Pioneer Coll., Show Low, Ariz., 1977. Youth missionary Open Bible Standard Missions, Trinidad, 1958-59; typographer Joel H. Weldon & Assocs., Scottsdale, Ariz., 1980-89; exec. chief acct. Pubs. Devel. Corp., San Diego, 1991-93; coord. music and worship College Ave. Bapt. Ch., San Diego, 1994-95; ChoirChime soloist, 1986—. Author: 101 Ways to Fix Broccoli, 1994, ABC's of Abundant Living, 1995; co-author: God's Vitamin C for the Spirit, 1995, Bounce Back, 1997, You Can Bounce Back Too, 1998. Mem. Christian Writers Guild, San Diego Cash Flow Assn. (founder), Am. Soc. Notaries.

PRICE, DANIEL MARTIN, lawyer; b. St. Louis, Aug. 23, 1955; s. Albert and Edith S. (Werner) P.; m. Kim Ellen Heebner, July 15, 1984; children: Emma Rachel, Joseph Armin, Joshua Simon. BA, Haverford Coll., 1977; diploma in law, Cambridge U., 1979; JD, Harvard U., 1981. Bar: D.C. 1981, Pa. 1987. Assoc. Drinker, Biddle & Reath, Phila., 1981-82, 86-89; dep. gen. counsel Office of U.S. Trade Rep., Washington, 1989-92; ptnr. Powell, Goldstein, Frazer & Murphy, Washington, 1992—; atty., adviser Dept. State, Washington, 1982-84; dep. agt. U.S. Iran-U.S. Claims Tribunal, Hague, The Netherlands, 1984-86; lectr. Haverford Coll., 1982. Articles editor Harvard Law Rev., 1980-81; contbr. articles to profl. jours. including Am. Jour. Internat. Law, Internat. Lawyer, Internat. Fin. Law Rev., Internat. Banking and Fin. Law, others. Am. Keasbey scholar Cambridge U., 1977-78. Mem. ABA (co-chmn. trade com. on N.Am. Free Trade Agreement), Internat. Bus. Forum (legal adv. bd. 1987-89), Am. Arbitration Assn. (panel arbitrators), Internat. C. of C. (arbitrator), Orgn. for Internat. Investment (counsel), Phi Beta Kappa. Office: 1001 Pennsylvania Ave NW Washington DC 20004-2505

PRICE, DAVID B., JR., manufacturing executive; b. St. Louis, Nov. 9, 1945; s. David B. and Ethyl (Armstrong) P.; m. Joyce Jacobs, Dec. 3, 1966; children: Danyale, Jason. BSCE, U. Mo., Rolla, 1968; MBA, Harvard U., 1976. Structural design engr. Monsanto Co., St. Louis, 1972-74, v.p., gen. mgr. specialty chem. divsn., 1987-90, v.p., gen. mgr. performance products divsn., 1991-93, v.p., gen. mgr. indsl. products group comml. ops., 1993-95, pres. performance materials, 1995-97; exec. v.p. BF Goodrich Co., Richfield, Ohio, 1997—; pres., COO performance materials BF Goodrich Co., Brecksville, Ohio, 1997—; bd. dirs. Tenneco Automotive, Inc., Am. Plastics Coun.; mem. adv. bd. Chem. & Engring. News. Mem. No. Ohio Minority Bus. Coun., Exec. Leadership Coun.; bd. dirs. Cleve. Tomorrow, United Way Svcs. of Cleve., First Tee of Cleve.; trustee Cleve. Playhouse Square Found., Sta. WVIZ-TV, pub. TV. Mem. Chem. Mfrs. Assn. (bd. dirs.). Avocations: golf, music, reading. Office: BF Goodrich 9911 Brecksville Rd Brecksville OH 44141-3247

PRICE, DAVID EDUARDO, lawyer, lobbyist; b. D.C., Feb. 15, 1964; s. Robert Morris and Barbara May Price; m. Yaffa Ranjbaran, Nov. 19, 1997; children: Michael, Adinah. BA, U. Md., 1985; JD, D.C. Sch. Law, 1996. Bar: Md. 1996, U.S. Dist. Ct. DC 1999. Polit. info. officer Israeli Fgn. Ministry, Atlanta and Washington, 1986-89; mem. campaign staff Reelection Com. for Sam Gejdenson, Norwalk, Conn., 1992; atty., lobbyist Law Offices of Price, P.C., Washington, 1995—. Bd. dirs. Mogen DAvid Synagogue. Mem. ATLA, ABA. Jewish. Office: Law Offices of Price PC 1915 Eye St NW Washington DC 20006-2107

PRICE, DAVID GEOFFREY, geography educator; b. Cockermouth, Cumberland, Eng., July 6, 1931; s. Philip Richard and Amy (Hill) P.; m. Patricia Moir, Sept. 7, 1955; 1 child, Helen Ceridwen. BA in Geography with honors, U. Bristol, Eng., 1952, MA, 1960; PhD, London Sch. Econs., 1967. Cert. tchr., Eng. Tchr. Secondary Tech. Sch., Brighton, Sussex, Eng., 1956-60; lectr. Coll. Tech. and Art, High Wycombe, Bucks, Eng., 1960-65, Polytech. Cen., London, 1965-87; ret. Co-author: Changing Geography of Service Sector, 1989; contbr. articles to profl. jours. Served to lt. RAF, 1953-56. Recipient Research award Leverhulme Fund., Dartmoor, Eng. 1977; grantee Internat. Geographical Union, 1981. Fellow Royal Geographical Soc.; mem. Inst. Brit. Geographers, Geographical Assn., Prehistoric Soc. Methodist. Avocations: photography, walking. Home: 339 Desborough Ave, High Wycombe Bucks HP11 2TH, England

PRICE, DAVID HEILBRON, journalist, author; b. Cheshire, U.K.. Author: Books on Robert Schuman: Creator of the European Union Reconciliation, 1999, New Cold War or Common European Home?, 1997, 2d edit., 1998, Russia and the Danger for the European Union, 1995, 2d edit., 2000, Schuman and the Yugoslav Crisis, 2000, Robert Schuman: Jeteur de Jalons de la Paix Mondale, 2000; contbr. articles to profl. jours.

PRICE, DAVID WILLIAM JAMES, money manager, farmer; b. Shanghai, People's Republic of China, June 11, 1947; s. Richard J.E. and Miriam Joan (Dunsford) P.; m. Shervie Ann L. Whitaker, Feb. 27, 1971; children: Hesther, William. Student, Oxford U., 1969. Dep. chmn. Mercury Asset Mgmt., London, 1986-97; chmn. Fgn. and Colonial Mgmt., London, Govett Asian Recovery Trust, Harrington Hall Farms Ltd.; dir. Mercury European Investment Trust, London, Equitable Life Assurance Soc., London, Iceland Group plc, Scottish Am. Investment Co. Councillor Borough of Lambeth, London, 1979-82. Mem. Halifax Bldg. Soc. (London bd. 1991-95). Home: Harrington Hall, Spilsby, Lincs PE 234NH, England Office: Fgn and Colonial Mgmt, Exch House Primrose St, London EC2A 2NY, England

PRICE, EDWARD WARREN, aerospace engineer, educator; b. Detroit, Dec. 6, 1920; s. Frank E. and Elizabeth Alleyne (Rattray) P.; m. Mary Kate Howard, June 21, 1952; children: Douglas Brian, Alison Tamara, Carolyn Louise. BA in Physics, Math, UCLA, 1948. Ballistician Calif. Inst. Tech., Pasadena, 1941-44; physicist U.S. Naval Weapons Ctr., China Lake, Calif., 1946-74; prof. aerospace engring. Ga. Inst. Tech., Atlanta, 1967-68, 74—, v.p. tech. AIAA, mem. Am. Acad. Scis.-Nat. Rsch. Coun. Space Shuttle Booster Redesign Rev. Panel, 1986-89; cons. in field. Contbr. articles to profl. jours. With USNR, 1944-46. Recipient Pub. Svc. award, Astronauts award NASA, 1987. Fellow AIAA (Rsch., Pendrary, Goddard awards 1966, 71, 76); mem. AASS, Nat. Acad. Engring., Combustion Inst., Sigma Xi. Achievements include numerous contributions to science in areas of rocket propulsion and combustion. Home: 5058 Highpoint Rd NE Atlanta GA 30342-2313 Office: Ga Inst Tech 225 North Ave Mail Code 0150 Atlanta GA 30332

PRICE, FRANK, property investment consultant; b. Birmingham, Eng., July 26, 1922; s. George Frederick and Lucy (Bayley) P.; m. Daphne Ling; children: Noel, Clinton. Student, St. Matthias Sch., Birmingham, Vittoria Art Sch., Birmingham. Dir. Murrayfield Real Estate Co., London, 1959-68; mng. dir. Murray Field Real Estate Co., London, 1965-68; chmn. Telford (Shropshire, Eng.) New Town Corp., 1968-74, Wharfholdings, London, 1972-76, M.L. Alcan, London, 1976-77, Price-Brown Partnership, Mojacar, Almeria, Spain, 1985—; chmn. Brit. Waterways Bd., London, 1968-84.

Councillor City of Birmingham, 1949-75, alderman, 1956-75, hon. alderman, 1975—, lord mayor, 1964-65; freeman City of London; mem. Westmidland Econ. Planning Coun., 1965-72, mem. lord chancellor's adv. com., 1967-72; founder, mem. Nat. Exhbn. Ctr., 1970-76; mem. Brit. Nat. Water Coun., 1975-79; mem. English Tourist Bd., 1976-84. Knighted Queen Elizabeth II, U.K., 1966; Queen's Dep. Lt., 1968—. Fellow Royal Inst. Chartered Surveyors, Inst. Valuers, Chartered Inst. Transport, Royal Soc. Arts. Avocations: painting, reading. Home: Mojacar Casa Non Such, Canada of Aguilar 534, 04638 Almeria Spain Office: Price Brown Partnership, Mojacar Playa Apt 534, 04638 Almeria Spain

PRICE, GLANVILLE, writer, French language educator; b. Rhaeadr, Wales, June 16, 1928; s. John Edmond and Bessie Price; m. Christine Winifred Thurston, Aug. 18, 1954; children: Gareth Charles, Christopher Iwan, Eluned Catrin, Steven Trefor. BA, U. Wales, Bangor, 1949, MA, 1952; doctorate, U. Paris, 1956. Lectr. in French U. St. Andrews, Scotland, 1958-64, U. Leeds, Eng., 1965-66; prof. French U. Stirling, Scotland, 1967-72; prof. French U. Wales, Aberystwyth, 1972-92, rsch. prof., 1992-95, prof. emeritus, 1995—; vis. prof. U. Calif., Berkeley, 1982; bd. govs. Ctr. Info. on Lang. Teaching and Rsch., 1971-77; mem. Broadcasting Coun. for Wales, 1980-84. Author: The Present Position of Minority Languages in Western Europe, 1969, The French Language: Present and Past, 1971, (with Kathryn F. Bach) Romance Linguistics and the Romance Languages: A Bibliography of Bibliographies, 1977, The Languages of Britain, 1984, (revision) L. S. R. Byrne and E. L. Churchill, A Comprehensive French Grammar, 1986, An Introduction to French Pronunciation, 1991; editor: William, Count of Orange: Four Old French Epics, 1975, The Celtic Connection, 1991, Encyclopedia of the Languages of Europe, 1998, Languages in Britain and Ireland, 2000; editor: The Yr.'s Work in Modern Lang. Studies, 1972-75, co-editor, 1975-92, (with C. Lupu) Hommages offerts à Maria Manoliu-Manea, 1994. Mem. Soc. for French Studies, Philol. Soc. (coun. 1973-79, 84-87), Modern Humanities Rsch. Assn. (gov. com. 1972—, chmn. 1979-90). Office: Univ of Wales, Dept of European Languages, Aberystwyth SY23 3DY, Wales

PRICE, JAMES MELFORD, physician; b. Onalaska, Wis., Apr. 3, 1921; s. Carl Robert and Hazel (Halderson) P.; m. Ethelyn Doreen Lee, Oct. 23, 1943 (div.); children: Alta Lee, Jean Marie, Veda Michele; m. Charlotte E. Schwenk, Sept. 27, 1986; children: Shirley S. Bunn, Cindy S. Davis, Irene S. McCumber. BS in Agr., U. Wis., 1943, MS in Biochemistry, 1944, PhD in Physiology, 1949, MD, 1951. Diplomate Am. Bd. Clin. Nutrition. Intern Cin. Gen. Hosp., 1951-52; mem. faculty U. Wis. Med. Sch., 1952—, prof. clin. oncology, 1959—, Am. Cancer Soc.-Charles S. Hayden Found. prof. surgery, 1957—; on leave as dir. exptl. therapy Abbott Labs., 1967—, v.p. exptl. therapy, 1968, v.p. corp. rsch. and exptl. therapy, 1971—, v.p. corp. sci. devel., 1976-78; v.p. med. affairs Norwich-Eaton Pharms., 1978—; v.p. internat. R&D, 1980-82; pres. RADAC Group, Inc., 1982-80, Biogest Products, Inc., 1984-88; mem. metabolism study sect. NIH, 1959-62, pathology B study sect., 1964-68; sci. adv. com. PMA Found.; chmn. rsch. adv. com. Ill. Dept. Mental Health; sci. com. Nat. Bladder Cancer program; mem. Drug Rsch. Bd. Nat. Acad. Scis./NRC. Bd. dirs. Grandview Coll., Des Moines, 1977-78. With USNR, 1944-45. Fellow Am. Coll. Nutrition, Royal Soc. Medicine London; mem. Am. Soc. Pharmacology and Exptl. Therapeutics, Am. Assn. Cancer Rsch., Am. Cancer Soc. (com. etiology 1957-61), Pharm. Mfrs. Assn. (chmn. R&D sect. 1974-75), Am. Soc. Biol. Chemists, Am. Inst. Nutrition, Am. Soc. Clin. Nutrition, Rsch. Dirs. Assn. Chgo., Soc. Exptl. Biology and Medicine, Soc. Toxicology. Achievements include research on trytophan metabolism, metabolism vitamin B complex, chemical carcinogenesis; research and development pharmaceutical, diagnostic and consumer products, licensing and business development. Avocation: flying. E-mail: jmp4csp@ascent.net. Home: 6308 County Rd 32 Norwich NY 13815-3551

PRICE, JAMES TUCKER, lawyer; b. Springfield, Mo., June 22, 1955; s. Billy L. and Jeanne Adele Price; m. Francine Beth Warkow, June 8, 1980; children: Rachel Leah, Ashley Elizabeth. BJ, U. Mo., 1977; JD, Harvard U., 1980. Bar: Mo. 1980. Assoc. firm Spencer Fane Britt & Browne, Kansas City, 1980-86; ptnr. Spencer Fane Britt & Browne LLP, Kansas City, 1987—, chair environ. practice group, 1994—, mem. exec. com., 1997—; mem. Brownfields Commn., Kansas City, 1999—; mem. steering com. Kansas City Bi-State Brownfields Initiative, 1997—. Contbr. to monographs, other legal publs. Mem. ABA (coun. sect. environ, energy and resources 1992-95, vice chmn. solid and hazardous waste com. 1985-90, chmn. 1990-92, chmn. brownfields task force 1995-97, vice chmn. environ. transactions and brownfield com. 1998—), Mo. Bar Assn., Kansas City Met. Bar Assn. (chmn. environ. law com. 1985-86), Greater Kansas City C. of C. (co-chair Brownfields Working Group, 1996-98, chmn. energy and environ. com. 1987-89). Office: Spencer Fane Britt & Browne LLP 1000 Walnut St Ste 1400 Kansas City MO 64106-2140

PRICE, JOHN ALEY, lawyer; b. Maryville, Mo., Mar. 7, 1947; s. Donald Leroy and Julia Catherine (Aley) P.; m. Deborah Diadra Gunter, Aug. 12, 1995; children: Theodore John, Joseph Andrew. BS, N.W. Mo. State U., 1969; JD, U. Kans., 1972. Bar: Kans. 1972, U.S. Dist. Ct. Kans. 1972, U.S. Ct. Appeals (10th cir.) 1972, Tex. 1984, U.S. Ct. Appeals (5th cir.) 1984, U.S. Supreme Ct. 1987; cert. civil trial law Tex. Bd. Legal Specialization. Law clk. U.S. Dist. Ct. Kans., Wichita, 1972-74; assoc., then ptnr. Weeks, Thomas and Lysaught, Kansas City, Kans., 1974-82; ptnr. Winstead, Sechrest & Minick, Dallas, 1982-96, litigation sect. coord., 1990-92, intellectual property sect. litigation coord., 1993-95; gen. counsel Travelhost Inc., Dallas, 1996—, Club Co., Inc., 1999—, Umansys, Inc., 2000—; gen. counsel Club Co. Inc., Dallas, 1999—, UMansys Inc., Dallas, 2000—; spl. prosecutor Leavenworth County Office Dist. Atty., 1970-71, Sedgwick County Offce Dist. Atty., Wichita, Kans., 1971-72. Author: Our Boundless Self (A Call to Awake), 1992, A Gathering of Light: Eternal Wisdom for a Time of Transformation, 1993; co-author: Soular Reunion: Journey to the Beloved, 1998; editor (mag.) Academic Analyst, 1968-69; assoc. editor U. Kans. Law Rev., 1971-72, Dallas Bus. Jour.; autor legal publs. Co-dir. Douglas County Legal Aid Soc., Lawrence, Kans., 1971-72; co-pres. Northwood Hills PTA, Dallas, 1984, Westwood Jr. H.S. PTA, 1989-90; founder New Frontiers Found., 1993; co-founder Wings of Spirit Found., 1994, dir., v.p. 1994—. Mem. ABA, Kans. Bar Assn. (mem. task force for penal reform; Pres.'s Outstanding Svc. award 1981), Tex. Bar Assn., Pro Bono Coll., State Bar Tex., World Bus. Acad., Inst. Noetic Scis., UN Assn. (human rights com. Dallas chpt. 1991-93, bd. dirs. 1991-93), Campaign for the Earth (chpt. coord. Global Report 1991-92, coord. govt. and polit. area 1991-92), Blue Key, Order of Coif, Phi Delta Phi, Sigma Tau Gamma (v.p. 1968-69). Mem. Unity Ch. Office: Travelhost Inc 10701 N Stemmons Fwy Dallas TX 75220-2419

PRICE, JOHN EDWARD, religion educator; b. Chgo., Mar. 7, 1942; s. Edward Price and Carolyn Maxine Polachek; m. Julia Valeriyevna Shvartser; children: Larissa Marie, James Thomas, Elizabeth Suzanne. BA, Univ. of St. Mary of the Lake, 1964, STB, 1966, STL, 1968. Lic. dir. religious edn. Tchr. Mother of God Sch., Waukegan, Ill., 1968-69; tchr., chmn. religion dept. Holy Trinity High Sch., Chgo., 1969-70; coord. religious edn. Transfiguration Ch., Wauconda, Ill., 1970-75; dir. religious edn. St. Athanasius Ch., Evanston, Ill., 1975-91, Ch. of St. Mary, Lake Forest, Ill., 1991—; catechist resource person Archdiocesan Office of Religious Edn., Chgo., 1977-80; field supr. Mundelein Coll. and Inst. Pastoral Studies, Chgo., 1979-80, 84; team mem. North Ctrl. Evaluation, Chgo., 1984; presenter, lectr. Archdiocese of Chgo., 1979, 80, 84, 85, mem. Dir. Religious Edn. Cert. Commn., 1997—. Author: (filmstrip) Learning Right and Wrong, 1978, (testing svc.) Religious Education Diagnostic Survey, 1983; contbr. articles to religious publs. Del. Ill. White House Conf. on Librs. and Info. Svcs., Springfield, 1978. Mem. Cath. Theol. Soc. Am., Religious Edn. Assn., Nat. Assn. Parish Coords. and Dirs., Chgo. Assn. Religious Educators (treas. 1979-82, Care award 1983). Avocations: religious art, fishing, scuba diving, bicycling, poetry. Office: St Mary's Religious Edn Ctr 185 E Illinois Rd Lake Forest IL 60045-1915

PRICE, JOSEPH HUBBARD, lawyer; b. Montgomery, Ala., Jan. 31, 1939; s. Aaron Joseph and Minnie Jule (Reynolds) P.; m. Cynthia Winant Ramsey, Sept. 14, 1963 (div. 1980); children—Victoria Reynolds, Ramsey Winant; m. Courtney McFadden, Apr. 26, 1980. A.B., U. Ala., 1961; LL.B., Harvard U., 1964; postgrad. London Sch. Econs., 1964-65. Bar: Ala. 1964, D.C. 1968. Law clerk to justice Hugo L. Black, U.S. Supreme Ct., Washington, 1967-68; assoc. Leva, Hawes, Symington, Martin & Oppenheimer, Washington, 1968-71; v.p. Overseas Pvt. Investment Corp., Washington, 1971-73; ptnr. Leva, Hawes, et. al., Washington, 1973-83, Gibson, Dunn & Crutcher, Washington, 1983—. Mem. CARE Com. Washington; mem. adv. com. Hugo Black Meml. Library, Ashland, Ala. Served to capt. U.S. Army, 1966-67; Vietnam. Decorated Bronze Star; Frank Knox Meml. fellow London Sch. Econs., 1964-65. Mem. ABA, Am. Soc. Internat. Law, Supreme Ct. Hist. Soc., Phi Beta Kappa. Clubs: Metropolitan. Home: 3104 Cathedral Ave NW Washington DC 20008-3419 Office: Gibson Dunn & Crutcher 1050 Connecticut Ave NW Ste 900 Washington DC 20036-5306

PRICE, JOSEPH STERLING, air force officer; b. Rockville Centre, N.Y., June 2, 1954; s. Harold Lloyd and Lola Peele (Talton) P.; m. Karen Lee Peters, Oct. 14, 1978. BS in Indsl. Mgmt., Ga. Inst. Tech., 1976; MS in Logistics Mgmt., Air Force Inst. Tech., 1980. Quality control chemist Jesco Lubricants Co., Atlanta, 1976; commd. 2d lt. USAF, 1976, advanced through grades to lt. col., 1992—. Mem. Ga. Tech. Alumni Assn., Nat. Eagle Scout Assn. (life), Air Force Assn. (life), Nat. Def. Indsl. Assn. (life), Appalachian Trail Conf. Avocations: hiking, history. Office: Def Acquisition Deskbook Program Office Dayton OH 45433

PRICE, LEONTYNE, concert and opera singer, soprano; b. Laurel, Miss., Feb. 10, 1927; d. James A. and Kate (Baker) P.; m. William Warfield, Aug. 31, 1952 (div. 1973). BA, Central State Coll., Wilberforce, Ohio, 1949, DMus, 1968; student, Juilliard Sch. Music, 1949-52; pupil, Florence Page Kimball; LHD, Dartmouth Coll., 1962, Fordham U., 1969, Yale U., 1979; MusD, Howard U., 1962; Dr. Humanities, Rust Coll., 1968. Profl. opera debut in 4 Saints in 3 Acts, 1952; appeared as Bess in Porgy and Bess, Vienna, Berlin, Paris, London, under auspices U.S. State Dept., also N.Y.C. and U.S. tour, 1952-54; recitalist, soloist with symphonies, U.S., Can., Australia, Europe, 1954—; appeared concerts in India, 1956, 64; soloist, Hollywood Bowl, 1955-59, 66, Berlin Festival, 1960; role as Mme. Lidoine in Dialogues des Carmelites, San Francisco Opera, 1957; opera singer, NBC-TV, 1955-58, 60, 62, 64, San Francisco Opera Co., 1957-59, 60-61, 63, 65, 67, 68, 71, as Aida at La Scala, Milan, 1957, Vienna Staatsoper, 1958, 59-60, 61, Berlin Opera, 1964, Rome Opera, 1966, Paris Opera, 1968, recital, Brussels Internat. Fair, auspices State Dept., 1958, Verona Opera Arena, 1958-59, recitals in Yugoslavia for, State Dept., 1958; rec. artist, RCA-Victor, 1958—, appeared Covent Garden, London, 1958-59, 70, Chgo. Lyric Theatre, 1959, 60, 65, Oakland (Calif.) Symphony, 1980, soloist, Salzburg Festival, 1959-63, Tetro alla Scala, Milano, 1960-61, 63, 67, appeared Met. Opera, N.Y.C., 1961-62, 64, 66, 75, 76; since resident mem., until 1985; soloist, Salzburg Festival, 1950, 60, debut, Teatre Dell'Opera, Rome, 1967, Teatro Colon, Buenos Aires, Argentina, 1969, Hamburg Opera, 1970; recordings include A Christmas Offering with Karajani, God Bless America with Charles Gerhardt, Arias from Don Giovanni, Turandot, Aida, Emani, Messa di Requiem, Trovatore, Live at Ordway, The Prima Donna Collection, A Program of Song with D. Garvey, Right as the Rain with André Previn. Hon. bd. dirs. Campfire Girls; hon. vice-chmn. U.S. com. UNESCO; co-chmn. Rust Coll. Upward Thrust Campaign; trustee Internat. House. Decorated Order at Ment Italy; recipient Merit award for role of Tosca in NBC-TV Opera, Mademoiselle mag., 1955, 20 Grammy awards for classical vocal recs. Nat. Acad. Rec. Arts and Scis., citation YWCA, 1961, Spirit of Achievement award Albert Einstein Coll. Medicine, 1962, Presdl. medal of freedom, 1964, Springarn medal NAACP, 1965, Schwann Catalog award, 1968, Nat. Medal of Arts, 1985, Essence award, 1991, others; named Musician of Year, Mus. Am. mag., 1961. Fellow Am. Acad. Arts and Sci.; mem. AFTRA, Am. Guild Mus. Artists, Actors Equity Assn., Sigma Alpha Iota, Delta Sigma Theta. Office: Price Enterprises 1133 Broadway Ste 920 New York NY 10010-7901

PRICE, LEW PAXTON, writer, engineer, scientist; b. Takoma Park, Md., Dec. 19, 1938; s. Raymond Miller and Clarene Pearl (Morris) P.; m. Sherrie Darlene Sellers, June 25, 1960 (div. Apr. 1979); children: Terilyn Ann, Heather Rae, Crystal Alene. BS, U.S. Air Force Acad., Colorado Springs, Colo., 1960. Hon. Ho-O Ryu Bushido 6th Dan Master. Electronics engr. Pacific Telephone, Sacramento, Calif., 1965-66, engrng. coord., bldgs., 1966-85; pres., design engr. Condor Aeroplane Works, Ltd., Sacramento, 1983-85; engrng. coord. Tuttle Engrng. and Constrn. Consultants, El Dorado Hills, Calif., 1989-92; scientist, flute design cons., writer, flutemaker Fair Oaks, Garden Valley, Calif., 1977—; cons. flute design. Author: The Cosmic Stradivarius, 1974, Aquarian Anastasis, 1975, The Music of Life, 1984, Dimensions in Astrology, 1986, Native North American Flutes, 1990, Secrets of the Flute (Math, Physics & Design), 1991, Creating & Using the Native American Love Flute, 1994, Creating & Using Grandfather's Flute, 1995, The Oldest Magic (Prehistory & Influence of Music), 1995, Creating & Using Older Native American Flutes, 1995, Creating & Using Smaller Native American Flutes, 1995, Creating & Using the Native American Concert Flute, 1996, More Secrets of the Flute, 1997, Creating and Using Larger Native American Flutes, 1998, Creating and Using the Largest Native American Flutes, 1998, Creating and Using Very Small Native American Flutes, 1998, Behind Light's Illusion (5 book series), 1999, 2000; author, programmer: (computer program) Flute Design (Native American), 1996. Co-advisor Aviation Explorers, archery/space/sci. merit badge instr./examiner, Boy Scouts Am., North Highlands, Calif., 1968-70; panelist United Crusade, Sacramento, Calif., 1971; rifle/pistol/shotgun safety instr. NRA, Fair Oaks, Calif., 1970-72. Capt. USAF, 1960-65. Mem. No. Calif. Flute Circle (co-organizer 1996), Oreg. Native Am. Flute Circle (hon.). Avocations: flying, singing, flute playing, hiking, archery. Home and Office: PO Box 88 Garden Valley CA 95633-0088

PRICE, LIONEL D.D., economist; b. Birkenhead, Cheshire, Eng., Feb. 2, 1946; s. Harold and Florence M. (Thompson) P.; m. Sara A. Holt, Oct. 19, 1968; children: Matthew W., James R. BA, Corpus Christi Coll., Cambridge, Eng., 1967, MA, 1971. Various positions Bank of Eng., London, 1967-79, head info. div., 1981-84, head internat. div., 1985-90, head econs. div., 1990-97; alt. exec. dir. Internat. Monetary Fund, Washington, 1979-81; mng. dir. Fitch Sovereign Ratings, 1997—. Contbr. articles to profl. jours. Office: Bank of Eng, Fitch Ratings Ltd, 2 Eldon St, EC2M 7UA London England

PRICE, MICHAEL, electricity company executive; b. London, Oct. 22, 1950; s. George Henry and May Lilian (Dolan) P.; m. Helen Anne Brown, Sept. 24, 1951; children: Jonathan Michael, Philip John. BA, Oxford (Eng.) U., 1972, MA, 1975; diploma in mgmt. studies, Mich. U., 1977, grad. Net program, 1989; grad. AMP pgram, Harvard U., 1997. Resources planning mgr. China Light and Power Co. Ltd., Hong Kong, 1978-81, maintenance mgr., 1982-88, fuel supply mgr., 1989-90, power sta. mgr. Castle Peak, 1991-92, gen. mgr. corp. svcs., 1993-95, gen. mgr. generation, 1996-97, chief oper. officer, 1998-99; mng. dir. CLP Power, 1999—; bd. dirs. Castle Peak Power Co., CLP Property, CLP Engring, CLP Power, HK nuc. Investment Co., Guangdon Nuc. Power JV Co., CLP Telecomms. Contbr. articles to profl. jours. Mem. Pilotage Adv. Com., Hong Kong, 1989-95, Hong Kong Govt. Energy Adv. Com., 1994-95; hon. treas. Scouts, Hong Kong, 1992-95. Mem. Instn. Mech. Engrs. (U.K.), Instn. Elec. Engrs. (U.K.), Hong Kong Instn. Engrs. Avocations: golf, squash, sailing. Office: CLP Power Hong Kong Ltd, 147 Argyle St, Kowloon Hong Kong China

PRICE, MICHAEL F., money management executive; b. 1952; div., 3 sons. Graduate, U. Okla., 1975. Rsch. asst., mgr., to CEO Heine Securities, Short Hills, N.J., 1975-97; CEO Franklin Mutual Advs. Inc. (formerly Heine Securities), Short Hills, N.J., 1997—; pres., chmn. bd. dirs. Franklin Mutual Series Fund Inc. Office: Franklin Mutual Advisers Inc 51 John F Kennedy Pkwy Short Hills NJ 07078-2702

PRICE, NICK, professional golfer; b. Durban, South Africa, Jan. 28, 1957; m. Sue Price; children: Gregory, Robyn Frances, Kimberly. Profl. golfer PGA, 1977—. Winner Asseng Invitational, 1979, Canon European Masters, 1980, Italian Open, 1981, South African Masters, Vaals Reef Open, 1982, World Series of Golf, 1983, Trophee Lancome, 1985, ICL Internat. Open, West End South Australian Open, 1989, GTE Byron Nelson Golf Classic, 1991, Canadian Open, Air New Zealand/Shell Open, 1992, PGA Championship, 1992, 1994, H.E.B. Tex. Open, The Players Championship, 1993, Canon Greater Hartford Open, Sprint Western Open, Fed. Express St. Jude Classic, HondaClassic, 1994, Southwestern Bell Colonial, Motorola Western Open, Bell Canadian Open, Alfred Dunhill Challenge Hassan II Golf Trophy, Zimbabwe Open, British Open, 1994, MCI Classic, 1997, Dimension Data Pro-Am, 1997, 97, Suntory Open, 1999; 3rd PGA Tour Money Leader, 1992, PGA Tour Money Leader, 1993, 10 USPGA Tour Victories, 26 World Wide Victories; recipient Vardon Trophy, 1993; named Player of Yr., 1993. Achievements include holding PGA Tournament record for lowest score (269), 1994.

PRICE, ROBERT DEMILLE, lawyer; b. N.Y.C., Oct. 11, 1915; s. Willard DeMille Price and Eugenia Reeve; m. Newell Potter, Aug. 15, 1940 (div. May 1946); 1 child, Jonathan; m. Ruth Bentley, July 5, 1946; children: Katharine, Susannah, Rebecca. AB in Econs. with honors, Cornell U., 1936; JD, Harvard U., 1940; MBA, Clark U., 1973. Bar: Mass. 1940, U.S. Dist. Ct. Mass. 1941, U.S. Ct. Appeals (1st cir.) 1976, U.S. Tax Ct. 1977, U.S. Supreme Ct. 1978. Assoc. Ropes & Gray, Boston, 1940-43, 1946-50; ptnr. Vaughan, Esty, Crotty & Mason, Worcester, Mass., 1950-53, Sibley, Blair & Mountain, Worcester, 1953-70, Corbin, Sarapas, Madaus & Arakelian, Worcester, 1970-73, Price & Madaus, Worcester, 1973-87; pres. Robert D. Price, PC, Holden, Mass., 1987—; dir. Appian Way Pizza, Ltd., Worcester, 1951-61, Food Specialties, Inc., Worcester, 1951-61, James Monroe Wire and Cable Co., S. Lancaster, Mass., 1973—; mem. Fin. Com., Holden, 1989-95, conservation com., 1999—. Moderator (TV series) Am. Bar Assn. Jr. Bar Assn., 1947-50. Bd. dirs., treas. Friends Gale Free Librs. Inc., Holden, 1988—; mem. adv. bd. Met. Dist. Commn., 1990-96; pres. Humanist Chaplaincy at Harvard, 1995—; bd. dirs. Humanist Assn. Mass., 1979—, Am. Humanist Assn., 1991-94; trustee AHA Endowment Fund, 1999—. Lt. USNR, 1943-51. Mem. Mass. Bar Assn., Worcester County Bar Assn., Worcester Club (dir. 1953-56), Boston Athenaeum (propr. 1949—). Avocations: museum and art show, photography, alpine climbing, sailing. Office: 2 Malden St Holden MA 01520-1827

PRICE, ROBIN MURRAY, retired medical librarian; b. Wellington, Eng., May 2, 1932; s. George Murray and Sybil Mary (Harris) P.; m. Julia Violet Northen, 1968 (separated 1981). BA, U. Cambridge, Eng., 1954, MA, 1956; diploma in librarianship, U. London, 1966. Asst. libr. House of Lords, London, 1957-63; asst. prin. Commonwealth Rels. Office, London, 1963-65; asst. libr. Wellcome Inst. for the History of Medicine, London, 1967-73, dep. libr., 1973-96; ret., 1996. Mem. Soc. of Apothecaries London (dir. history medicine diploma course 1990—, sec. history faculty 1985-96), Royal Soc. Medicine (pres. open sect. 1992-94, pres. history sect. 1997-98), Kensington Soc. (com. mem. 1995—, dep. chmn. 1999—), Norland Conservation Soc. (chmn. 1994-99), North Kensington Forum (chmn. 1994—), Harveian Soc. London (pres. 1996-97), Brit. Soc. History Medicine (pres. 1999—). Home: 5/7 Princedale Rd, W11 4PH London England

PRICE, THEODORA HADZISTELIOU, individual and family therapist; b. Athens, Greece, Oct. 1, 1938; came to U.S. 1967; d. Ioannis and Evangelia (Emmanuel) Hadzisteliou; m. David C. Long Price, Dec. 26, 1966 (div. 1989); children: Morgan N., Alkes D.L. BA in History/Archaeology, U. Athens, 1961; DPhil, U. Oxford, Eng., 1966; MA in Clin. Social Work, U. Chgo., 1988; Diploma in Piano Teaching, Nat. Conservatory, Athens, 1958. Lic. clin. social worker; bd. cert. diplomate in clin. social work. Mus. asst. and resident tutor U. Sydney, Australia, 1966-67; instr. anthropology Adelphi U., N.Y.C., 1967-68; archaeologist Hebrew Union Coll., Gezer, Israel, 1968; asst. prof. classical archaeology/art U. Chgo., 1968-70; jr. rsch. fellow Harvard Ctr. Hellenic Studies, Washington, 1970-71; clin. social worker Harbor Light Ctr., Salvation Army, Chgo., 1988-89; therapist Inst. Motivational Devel., Lombard, Ill., 1989-90; caseworker Jewish Family & Community Svc., Chgo., 1989-90; staff therapist Family Svc. Ctrs. of South Cook County, Chicago Heights, 1990-91; pvt. practice child, adolescent, family therapy Bolingbrook, Ill., 1991—; dir. counseling svcs., clin. supr., psychotherapist The Family Link, Inc., Chgo., 1993; staff therapist Cen. Bapt. Family Svcs., Gracell Rehab., Chgo., 1991, 91-92; casework supr., counselor Epilepsy Found. Greater Chgo., Chgo., 1992-93; therapist children, adolescents and families dept. foster care Catholic Charities, Chgo., 1993-94; individual and family therapist South Ctrl. Cmty. Svcs. Individual-Family Counseling Svcs., Chgo., 1994-97; lectr. in field; bd. mem., counselor Naperville Sch. for Gifted and Talented, 1982-84. Author: (monograph) Kourotrophos, Cults and Representations of the Greek Nursing Deities, 1978; contbr. articles to profl. jours. Meyerstein Traveling awardee, Oxford, Eng., 1963, 64; Eleutherios Venizelos scholar, 1962-65. Mem. NASW, Nat. Acad. Clin. Social Workers, Ill. Clin. Social Workers. Avocations: yoga, piano playing, dog training and therapy, hesychasm. Home and Office: 10 Pebble Ct Bolingbrook IL 60440-1557

PRICE, THOMAS FREDERICK, theatre educator; b. Salt Lake City, June 19, 1937; s. Thomas William P. and Caryl Susan Brown; children: Devin, Jennifer. BA in Drama, Pomona Coll., 1960; MA in Theatre, San Francisco State U., 1962; PhD in Drama, Stanford U., 1968; student, Columbia U. Rare Book Sch., 1983. Asst. prof. English U. of the Pacific, Stockton, Calif., 1968-70; asst. prof. drama U.S. Internat. U., Sch. Performing Arts, San Diego, 1970-74; archivist, curator The Philibrick Theatre Libr., Los Altos Hills, Calif., 1975-85; prof. English Tianjin (China) Normal U., 1985-87; adj. prof. theatre So. Oreg. State Coll., Ashland, 1991-92; assoc. prof. English Tanmkang U., Taipei, Taiwan, 1993—; ednl. broadcaster KPFA-FM, L.A., 1959-62 (original staff), KSRO-FM, Ashland, Oreg., 1990-92. Author: Edward Gordon Craig Revisited, 1984, Edward Gordon Craig and the Theatre of the Imagination, 1985, Dramatic Structure and Meaning, 1992, rev. edit., 1999; editor: Critical Edition of the Jealous Wife and Polly Honeycombe by George Colman the Elder, 1997; contbr. articles to profl. jours. Recipient Taiwan Nat. Sci. Found., 1998, Disting. Tchr. award Tamkang U., 1998. Mem. Calif. Scholarship Fedn. (hon. life).

PRICE, WILLIAM ANTHONY, psychiatrist; b. Youngstown, Ohio, Aug. 15, 1959; s. Edward J. and Margaret (Krispli) P.; divorced; children: Matthew, Nicole; m. Pamela R. Gardner, Nov. 18, 1985; 1 child, Andrew A.; m. Sheryl A. Neider, Sept. 23, 1995. BS, Kent State U., 1983; MD, Northeastern Ohio U., 1983. Diplomate Am. Bd. Psychiatry and Neurology, Nat. Bd. Med. Examiners; lic. psychiatrist, Ohio, Pa. Intern U. Health Ctr., Pitts., 1983-85; resident in psychiatry Northeastern Ohio U., 1985-86, chief resident, clin. assoc. prof., 1986-87; psychiatrist Splty. Care Psychiat. Svcs., Boardman, Ohio, 1987—; med. dir. PsyCare, Boardman; med. dir. Belmont Pines Hosp., Youngstown, 1990-91, adult program dir., 2000—; med. dir., clin. dir. NEO-Therapeutic Mgmt. Svcs., Warren, Ohio, 1997—; cons. psychiatrist Pathways Ctr. for Geriatric Psychiatry, 1997—, med. dir., 1999—; co-med. dir. Ivy Woods Manor, 2000—; psychiat. clerkship dir. Youngstown Osteo. Hosp., 1998—; med. dir. Premenstrual Syndrome Program, Parkview Counseling Ctr., Youngstown, 1985-88, Child and Adolescent Diagnostic and Devel. Ctr., Youngstown, 1988-95, Psycare; assoc. med. dir. psychiatry Windsor Hosp., Chagrin Falls, 1989—; clin. asst. prof., Northeastern Ohio U., 1987—; clin. assoc. prof. Ohio U. Coll. Medicine, 1997—; adj. prof. psychiatry Coll. Osteo. Medicine and Sci., 1997—; chief clin. officer, Mahoning County Mental Health Bd, 1990—; clerkship dir. psychiatry, St. Elizabeth Hosp. Med. Ctr., Youngstown, 1987—, Western Res. Care System, Youngstown, 1988-90; regional clerkship dir. psychiatry Ohio U. Coll. Medicine, 1998—, clin. asst. prof. medicine, 1998—; reviewer Jour. Clin. Psychiatry, 1987—, Am. Jour. Psychiatry, 1987—, Psychosomatics, 1987—, lectr. various confs., forums, seminars, 1985—. Author: (with others) Opiate Addiction in the Biological Foundations of Clinical Psychiatry, 1986, Nootropics: Toward the Mind in the Biological Foundations of Clinical Psychiatry, 1986, (audiocassettes) Mitral Valve Prolapse and Bipolar Affective Disorder, 1985, Dealing with PCP, 1985; contbr. numerous articles to profl. publs., poems and 2 short stories to nat. mags. Recipient Founders Day award for Sci. Rsch., Ohio Psychiat. Assn. Edn. and Rsch. Found., 1986, hon. mention Lebenson award, Am. Assn. Gen. Hosp. Psychiatrists, 1987, Founder's award, Am. Assn. Psychiatrists in Alcoholism and Addictions, 1987, fellowship award, Assn. Acad. Psychiatrists, 1987; Laughlin fellow, Am. Coll. Psychiatrists. Mem. Am. Psychiat. Assn., Am. Acad. Clin. Psychiatry, Am. Soc. Clin. Pharmacology, Am. Assn. Psychiatrists in Alcoholism and Addiction, Am. Gen. Hosp. Psychiatrists, Am. Soc. Psychosomatic Ob-Gyn., Am. Coll. Psychiatrists, Am. Assn. Geriatric Psychiatry, Internat. Soc. Psychosomatic Ob-Gyn., Nat. Fedn. Ind. Bus., Assn. Acad. Psychiatrists, Cen. Neuropsychiatric Assn., Soc. Neurosciences, Soc. Menstrual Cycle Rsch., Ohio State Med. Assn., Ohio Psychiat. Assn., Mahoning County Med. Assn., Mahoning County Mental Health Bd., Coun. Chiefs Psychiatry, Parents Supporting Parents (adv. bd. dirs.), Youngstown, Phi Delta Epsilon. Avocations: gourmet

cooking, wine tasting, art collecting, skiing. Office: NEO-Therapeutics Mgmt Inc 1132 High St NE Warren OH 44483-5858

PRICHARD, JOHN ROBERT STOBO, academic administrator, law educator; b. London, Jan. 17, 1949; arrived in Can., 1951; s. John Stobo and Joan Suzanne (Webber) P.; m. Ann Elizabeth Wilson, Dec. 19, 1975; children: Wilson, Kenneth, John. Honors Econs. student, Swarthmore Coll., 1967-70; MBA, U. Chgo., 1971; LLB, U. Toronto, Ont., Can., 1975; LLM, Yale U., 1976. Asst. prof. faculty of law U. Toronto, 1976-81, assoc. prof., 1981-88, prof., 1988—, assoc. Ctr. for Indsl. Rels., 1979—, dean faculty of law, 1984-1990, pres. univ., 1990—; vis. assoc. prof Yale U. Law Sch., New Haven, Conn., 1982-83; vis. prof. Harvard U. Law Sch., Cambridge, Mass., 1983-84; mem. Ont. Law Reform Commn., Toronto, 1986-1990; chmn. Fed., Provincial and Territorial Review of Liability and Compensation on Health Care, Ottawa, Ont., 1987-90; dir. Imasco, Onex, Four Seasons Hotels and Resorts, Tesma Internat., Moore Corp., BioChem Pharma, Visible Genetics, World Bank Inst. Co-author: Canadian Business Corporations, 1977, Canadian Competition Policy, 1979, Choice of Governing Instrument, 1982; co-author, editor: Public Ownership: The Calculus of Instrument Choice, 1983. Mem. Law Soc. Upper Can. Avocation: children, farming. Office: U Toronto, 215 Huron St, Toronto, ON Canada M5S 1A1*

PRIDACHIN, DMITRY, physicist, research scientist; b. Novosibirsk, Siberia, Russia, Oct. 16, 1966; s. Nicolay and Iraida (Moskvicheva) P.; m. Liliya Grishanova, Jan. 1, 1997; 1 child, Valeriya. MS in Engring. and Physics, Electrotech. Inst., Novosibirsk, 1989. Grad. employee Inst. Semiconductor Physics, Novosibirsk, 1989-91, engr., 1991-96, sci. employee, 1996—. Contbr. articles to profl. jours. Soros Fund grantee in physics, 1992-93. Avocations: cars, reading, travel. Office: Inst Semiconductor Physics, Lavrentiev Ave 13, 630090 Novosibirsk Russia

PRIDDLE, ROBERT, international organization director; b. Sept. 9, 1938; s. Albert Leslie and Alberta Edith P.; m. Janice Elizabeth Gorham, 1962; 2 children. Attended, King's Coll. Sch., Wimbledon, Peterhouse, Cambridge U. U.K. minister of aviation, 1960; with Dept. Trade and Industry, 1973, 85-89; with Dept. Energy, 1974—, dep. sec., dir. gen. energy resources, 1989-92; exec. dir. Internat. Energy Agy.; pres. Conf. of European Posts and Telecommunications Adminstrations, 1987-89; chmn. gov. bd. Internat. Energy Agy., 1991-92; mem. Fin. Reporting Coun., 1992-94; exec. dir. Internat. Energy Agy., 1994—. Author: Victoriana, 1959, 2d edit. 1963. Office: Internat Energy Agy, 9 rue de la Federation, 75739 Paris Cedex 15, France*

PRIDEAUX, BRUCE RICHARD, education educator, regional planner; b. Townsville, Australia, Oct. 6, 1953; s. Richard Alfred and Marjory Josephine (Murgatroyd) P.; m. Linda Veronica Hunter, Dec. 18, 1982; children: Jillian Heather, Benjamin Luke, Joshua Samuel, Krystin April, Jeremy Richard. BE, James Cook U., Townsville, Australia, 1976; BA, U. Queensland, Brisbane, Australia, 1979; M in Regional Planning, James Cook U., 1986; PhD, U. Queensland, Australia, 2000. Cert. of edn. Tchr. high sch. Queensland Dept. of Edn., Townsville, Australia, 1974-84; transport analyst Queensland Dept. Transport, Townsville, Australia, 1984-89, actiong regional officer, 1989-91; lectr. U. Queensland, Gatton, Australia, 1992—; prin. BRP Consulting, Gatton, 1994-97. Editor: Asia Pacific Jour. of Transport, 1996—. With Australian Army Res. Recipient Travel grant Australia Korea Found., 1997. Fellow Chartered Inst. of Transport (chmn. 1991), Australian Inst. Tourism and Travel (assoc.), Asia Pacific Tourism Assn. Avocations: travel writing, travel. Home: 19 Tew Ct, Gatton 4343, Australia Office: U Queensland Dept Tourism & Leisure Mgmt, 11 Salisbury Rd, Ipswich Queensland 4305, Australia

PRIDHAM, GEOFFREY FRANCIS MICHAEL, political science educator; b. Guildford, Surrey, Eng., Jan. 29, 1942; s. Clement Edward and Marian Shirley (Seyfang) P.; m. Pippa Anne Mason, June 15, 1974 (div. 1982). BA, Cambridge U., 1964, MA, 1968; PhD, London U., 1969. Rsch. asst. Fgn. Office, London, 1964-67, Inst. Contemporary History, London, 1967-69; lectr., reader in European politics, prof. European politics Bristol U., Avon, Eng., 1969—; bd. dirs. Ctr. Mediterranean Studies U. Bristol, 1987—. Author: Hitler's Rise to Power, 1973, Documents on Nazism, 1974, Christian Democracy in Wetern Germany, 1977, Transnational Paty Cooperation and European Intgration, 1981, The Nature of the Italian Party System, 1981, Nazism 1919-1945: A Documentary Reader, 1983, 84, The New Mediterranean Democracies, 1984, Coalitional Behaviour in Theory and Practice, 1986, Political Parties and Coalitional Behaviour in Italy, 1988; co-editor: Democratisation in Eastern Europe, 1994, Stabilising Fragile Democracies, 1996, The Dynamics of Democratisation, 2000; rev. editor West European Politics, 1982-92. Mem. Polit. Studies Assn., Assn. for Study of Modern Italy, Assn. for Study of German Politics, Societa Italiana di Studi Elettorali, European Consortium for Polit. Rsch., Conf. Group on Italian Politics, Royal Inst. Internat. Affairs, Univ. Assn. for Contemporary European Studies (sec. 1975-77). Avocations: rambling, music, travel, swimming, cinema. Home: 7 Hampton Park, Redland, Bristol BS6 6LG, England Office: U Bristol Dept Politics, 10 Priory Rd, Bristol BS8 1TU, England

PRIDMORE, ELIZABETH ANN, marketing professional; b. Portland, Oreg.. BA in Comm., Denison U., 1990; MA in Comm., U. Denver, 1994. Asst. dir. admissions Denison U., Granville, Ohio, 1990-92; mktg. comm. asst. AM/FM Internat., Denver, 1994-96, Holme Roberts & Owens LLP, Denver, 1996-98; mktg. comm. specialist J. D. Edwards, Denver, 1998-99, ptnr., mktg. mgr., 1999—. Mem. Interant. Assn. Bus. Communicators (bronze quill materials coord. Colo. chpt. 1997-99, pres. 1999-00, past pres. 2000—, award merit 1999). Republican. Avocations: downhill skiing, singing in church choir. Fax: 303-334-4515. Office: J D Edwards 1 Technology Way Denver CO 80237-3000

PRIEBE, CEDRIC JOSEPH, JR., pediatric surgeon; b. N.Y.C., Feb. 7, 1930; s. Cedric Joseph and Mary Martha (O'Beirne) P.; m. Cynthia Amelia Cali, June 11, 1955; children: Diane Marie, Janice Marie, Cedric Joseph III, Catherine Marie, Michael Stephen, Gregory Paul, Marta Marcella. BS cum laude, Fordham U., 1951; MD, Cornell U., 1955. Surg. resident The Roosevelt Hosp., N.Y.C., 1955-60; pediatric surg. resident Ohio State U., Children's Hosp., Columbus, 1965-67; pediatric surgeon, asst. and assoc. prof. The Roosevelt Hosp., Colombia U., N.Y.C., 1967-79; chief pediatric surgery, prof. surgery La. State U., Charity Hosp., New Orleans, 1979-82, SUNY at Stony Brook, U. Hosp., 1982—; sr. clin. trainee in cancer control NIH, Washington, 1963-65. Editl. cons. Jour. of Pediatric Surgery, Phila., 1994—; author: (with others) Neoplasia in Childhood, 1966; contbr. articles to profl. jours. Maj. USAF, 1956-65. Mem. ACS, Am. Burn Assn., Soc. for Surgery Alimentary Tract, Am. Acad. of Pediatrics (publs. com.), Am. Pediatric Surg. Assn. (membership, by-laws, cancer com. 1970—), Children's Oncology Group (cancer control com. 1992—), N.Y. Soc. of Pediatric Surgery (v.p. 1968-79, pres. 1982—). Republican. Roman Catholic. Avocations: tennis, squash racquets, travel. Home: 9 Woodhull Cove Ln Setauket NY 11733-1643 Office: SUNY at Stony Brook Hsc T 19 Stony Brook NY 11794-0001

PRIES, JANISE GOFF, counselor, secondary education educator; b. L.A., Oct. 3, 1949; d. Dean Carlson and Mercedes (Patakas) Goff; m. John T. Evans Jr., June 18, 1971 (div. 1986); children: John D., Jason R., Jacquelyn E.; m. Kim Henry Pries, May 15, 1993. BA, U. Colo., 1970; MEd, U. Tex., El Paso, 1996. Nat. certified counselor; lic. profl. counselor, Tex.; cert. secondary edn., gifted and talented endorsement, Tex. Rector's sec. St. Francis-on-the-Hill Episcopal Ch., El Paso, 1987; music dir., English tchr. St. Clement's Episcopal Parish Sch., El Paso, 1987-93; 8th grade lang. arts tchr. Morehead Mid. Sch., El Paso, 1993-95, humanities tchr., 1996-97; humanities tchr. H.E. Charles Mid. Sch., El Paso, 1995-96; counselor Rusk Elem. Sch., El Paso, 1997—; vol. counselor Jewish Family and Children's Svcs., El Paso, 1996-97. Co-editor: Counselor Connection. Soprano, El Paso Pro Musica, 1990-93; dir. St. Clement's Honors Handbell Chorus, El Paso, 1989-93; aux. charter pres., mem. choir Bruce Nehring Consort, El Paso, 1993-95, 97-98; chmn. bd. deacons 1st Presbyn. Ch., El Paso, 1990-91, elder, 1992-94. Recipient Masons Mirabeau B. Lamar award, 2000. Mem. Am. Counseling Assn., Tex. Classroom Tchrs. Assn., Chi Sigma Iota. Avocations: reading, counted cross-stitch, singing. Office: Rusk Elem Sch 3601 N Copia St El Paso TX 79930-4796

PRIEST, MELVILLE STANTON, retired consulting hydraulic engineer; b. Cassville, Mo., Oct. 16, 1912; s. William Tolliver and Mildred Alice (Messer) P.; m. Vivian Willingham, Mar. 22, 1941 (dec.); m. Virginia Young, Dec. 16, 1983. BS, U. Mo., 1935; MS, U. Colo., 1943; PhD, U. Mich., 1954. Registered profl. engr., Ala., La., Miss. Jr. engr. U.S. Engrs. Office, 1937-39; from jr. to asst. engr. Bur. Reclamation, 1939-41; from instr. to assoc. prof. civil engring. Cornell U., 1941-55; prof. hydraulics Auburn (Ala.) U., 1955-58, prof. civil engring., head dept., 1958-65; dir. Water Resources Research Inst., Miss. State U., 1965-77; UN adviser on hydraulics, Egypt, 1956, 57, 60; Mem. Ala. Bd. Registration Profl. Engrs., 1962-65. Contbr. articles to profl. jours. Fellow ASCE (pres. Ala. 1962, exec. com., pipeline div. 1971-74), Am. Water Resources Assn. (dir. 1973-75), Sigma Xi, Tau Beta Pi, Chi Epsilon, Pi Mu Epsilon. Address: PO Box 541 Starkville MS 39760-0541

PRIEST, ROBERT GEORGE, psychiatrist, educator, author; b. London, Sept. 28, 1933; s. James George and Phoebe (Logan) Young P.; m. Marilyn Baker, June 24, 1955; children: Ian N.R., Roderick J.D. MB, BChir, U. London, 1956, MD, 1970. Lectr. U. Edinburgh, Scotland, 1964-67; exchange lectr. U. Chgo., 1966-67; sr. lectr. St. George's Hosp. Med. Sch., London, 1967-73; prof. Imperial Coll. Sch. Medicine, St. Mary's U., 1973—, chmn. dept. psychiatry, 1973-96; cons. Nat. Health Svc. Gt. Britain, 1967-96; prof. psychiatry U. London, 1973—, chmn. bd. studies in medicine, 1987-90, mem. senate, 1989-93. Author: Insanity, 1977, Anxiety and Depression, 1983, Psychological Disorders in Obstetrics and Gynecology, 1985, Oro och depression, 1987, Trastornos Psicologicos En Obstetrica y Ginecologia, 1987; co-author: Handbook of Psychiatry, 1986, Anxiety and Depression, 1992, 96, Depression in General Practice, 1996; editor: Sleep Research, 1979, Psychiatry in Medical Practice, 1982; contbr. articles to profl. jours., chpts. to books. Served to maj. Brit. Army, 1957-60. Recipient A.E. Bennett award Soc. Biol. Psychiatry, 1965, Doris Odlum prize Brit. Med. Assn., London, 1968, Gutheil von Domarus award Assn. for Advancement of Psychotherapy, 1970. Fellow Royal Coll. Psychiatrists Eng. (registrar 1983-88); mem. Internat. Coll. Psychomatic Medicine (sec. 1981-85, v.p. 1985-87), Soc. Psychosomatic Rsch. (pres. 1980-81), World Psychiat. Assn. (ctrl. com. 1984-93, coun. 1989-93), Brit. Med. Assn. (chmn. mental health group 1982-84), Ctrl. Com. for Hosp. Med. Svcs. (chmn. psychiat. subcom. 1983-87). Avocations: squash, tennis, swimming, foreign languages. Office: Acad Dept Psychiatry, 29 Old Slade Ln Richings Pk, Iver SL0 9DY, England

PRIESTLEY, CLIVE, former management consultant; b. Manchester, Lancashire, U.K., July 12, 1935; s. Albert Ernest and Annie May (Mellers) P.; m. Barbara Anne Wells, Apr. 8, 1961 (div. 1984); children: Alison Virginia, Rebecca Janet; m. Daphne June Loasby, Sept. 7, 1985. BA in History, Nottingham Univ., 1956, MA in History, 1958; postgrad., Harvard U., 1967-68. Harkness fellow Harvard U., Cambridge, Mass., 1967-68; prin. Home Civil Svc., London, 1964-72, asst. sec., 1974-79; under sec. Prime Minister's Office, London, 1979-83; divisional dir. BT plc, London, 1983-88, mgmt. cons., 1988-94. Author: Scrutiny of Royal Opera House and Royal Shakespeare Company, 1983, Arts Funding in Northern Ireland, 1992, British Construction, 1993, Chief Officers of National Institutions, 1994. Mem. Arts Coun. of Gt. Britain, London, 1991-94, Arts Coun. England, 1994-95, 96-97; chmn. London Arts Bd., 1991-97; v.p. St. Bartholomew's Hosp. Med. Coll., 1992-95, trustee, 1996—; gov. Royal Shakespeare Co., Stratford-on-Avon, U.K., 1984—, Trinity Coll. of Music, London, 1997—; mem. coun. Queen Mary U. London, 1995—. Mem. Brit. Soc. Gastroenterology, Army and Navy Club. Ch. of England. Avocations: arts, medical education.

PRIESTLEY, HOLLY, education educator; b. Phila., Dec. 6, 1945; d. Vernard Fenel Delk and Florence Amelia Baker; m. William J. Priestley, May 24, 1986; 1 child from previous marriage, Aaron C. Stout. BS in Sci. Edn., Indiana U. of Pa., 1968; MEd in Sci. Edn., U. Pitts., 1975; EdD, Temple U., 1996. Tchr. Wilkinsburg (Pa.) Sch. Dist., 1971-75; sci. and math. tchr. Sch. Dist. Borough of Morrisville, Pa., 1977-99; instr. Holy Family Coll., Phila., 1985-89, Bucks County C.C., Newtown, Pa., 1989-93, Temple U., Phila., 1994-98, St. Joseph's U., Phila., 1998-99; instr. edn. U. Hawaii, Hilo, 1999—. Co-author assessment tool Inquiry Matrix, 1998. Mem. Am. Edn. Rsch. Assn., Assn. for Edn. of Tchrs. of Sci., Hawaii Sci. Tchrs. Assn., Nat. Assn. Biology Tchrs., Nat. Coun. Tchrs. Math., Phi Delta Kappa. Avocations: greyhound adoption, gardening. Home: 1 W Water St Lock Haven PA 17745-1230

PRIESTLEY, HUGH MICHAEL, investment manager; b. Northaw, Herts, Aug. 22, 1942; s. James Frederick and Honor Purefoy (Pollock) P.; m. Caroline Clarissa Duncan Prendergast; children: Alexandra, Susannah. MA, Worcester Coll., Oxford, 1964. Sub-editor Times Newspaper, London, 1964-66; with Henderson Adminstrn., London, 1966-92; dir. Henderson Adminstrn., 1972-93; investment dir. Rathbone Investment Mgmt., 1993—; mng. dir. Witan Investment Co., London, Henderson Highland Trust plc. Treas. U. Coll., London, 1981-98. Mem. Assn. Investment Trust Cos. (dep. chmn.). Office: Rathbone Investment Mgmt, 159 New Bond St, London W1Y 9PA, England

PRIESTLEY, MAURICE BERTRAM, statistics educator; b. Manchester, U.K., Mar. 15, 1933; s. Jack and Rose (Druker) P.; m. Nancy Nelson, June 24, 1959; children: Ruth N., Michael R. BA, U. Cambridge, Eng., 1954, MA, 1958; PhD, U. Manchester, 1960. Sci. officer Royal Aircraft Establishment, Fairborough, U.K., 1955-56; asst. lectr., then lectr. U. Manchester, 1957-65; sr. lectr. U. Manchester Inst. Sci. and Tech., 1965-70, prof. stats., 1970—; dir. Manchester-Sheffield Sch. Author: Spectral Analysis, 1980, Non-Linear Time Series, 1988; editor: Essays in Prob Theory, 1985. Fellow Royal Statis. Soc., Inst. Math. Stats.; mem. Internat. Stats. Inst. Avocations: amateur radio, high fidelity, music. Office: U Manchester Inst Sci Tech, Sackville St, M60 2QD Manchester England

PRIETO, FABIO ROMAO, engineer, product manager; b. Sao Paulo, Brazil, Sept. 6, 1965; s. Francisco Prieto Santos and Adair Romao Prieto. Degree in Elec. Engring., Fac Engring. Indsl., Sao Bernardo Campo, Brazil, 1988; Degree in Mech. Engring., Fac Tecnologia, Sao Paulo, 1991; MBA, Edinburgh U., 1996. Elec. engr. Ubisys Corp., Sao Paulo, 1986-95; mktg. planning corr. AstraZeneca, Cotia, Brazil, 1996-99, product mgr., 1999—. Avocations: sailing, travel.

PRIETO, VICTOR GERARDO, physician; b. Madrid, Spain, Feb. 14, 1963; arrived in U.S., 1991; MD, Alicante, Alicante, Spain, 1986; PhD, Barcelona, Barcelona, Spain, 1991. Resident pathology N.Y. Hosp., N.Y., 1993-94; fellow pathology Meml. Sloan Kettering, N.Y., 1994-95; fellow dermatopathology N.Y. Hosp. Cornell Med. Ctr., N.Y., 1991-93, 95-96; asst. prof. pathology Duke Univ., Durham, 1996-99; asst. prof., chief dermatopathology Univ. M.D. Tex. Anderson Cancer Ctr., Houston, 1999—; editorial bd. Joun. Cutameous Pathology, 1997—. Contbr. articles to profl. jours. Recipient Fetter award Duke Univ., 1998, Callaway award, 1999. Fellow Am. Soc. Dermatology, Soc. for Investigative Dermatology; mem. U.S. and Canadian Acad. Pathology, Internat. Soc. of Investigative Dermatology, Am. Assn. Advancement Sci. Avocations: guitar, bicycling. E-mail: vprieto@mdanderson.org. Office: Univ Tex Anderson Cancer Ctr Dept Pathology Box 85 1515 Holcombe Blvd Houston TX 77030-4009

PRIETO VIAL, DANIEL, international relations consultant, educator; b. Santiago, Chile, July 16, 1951; s. Hernán Prieto Subercaseaux and María Vial Freire. MBA, Cath. U. of Santiago, Chile, 1977, degree comml. engring., 1978, M in Internat. Rels., 1978. Def. advisor, cons. Min. of Def., Santiago, 1975-84; asst. Chilean Fgn. Investment Com., Santiago, 1977; gen. mgr. Corretajes Internacionales Ltd., Santiago, 1978-80; mktg. dir. Cardoen Industries Ltd., Santiago, 1980-86; dir. project of R&D in electronics and sys. Cath. U., Santiago, 1992-94; dir. Prieto-Vial Cons., Santiago, 1990—; external cons. Chamber of Dipuries and the Senate, Valparíso, Chile, 1990—, cons. Ministry of Def. and Ministry of Fgn. Affairs, Santiago, 1990—; prof. Finis Terrae U., Santiago, 1991-97, Desarrollo U., Concepcion and Santiago, 1993—. Author: The Geopolitical Structure of Chile, The Neighbors and Brazil, 1978, Hacia el Siglo XXI, La Proyeccion Estrategica de Chile, 1989, Defence Chile 2000, 1989, 2d edit., 1990, The Strategic Protection of China, 1998. Dir. Instituto de Investigaciones Historica José Miguel Carrera, Santiago, 1986—, Environtl. Orgn., Santiago, 1997—. Lt. comdr. Naval Res. of the Chilean Navy, 1971-87. Named Knight of Malta Soveran Mil. Order of Malta, 1989. Mem. Club de Golf Los Leones, Club de Polo San Cristobal, Club de la Union. Roman Catholic. Avocations: wild animal life, parachuting, skiing, polo, history. Home: PO Box 132 de Pirgue, Pirgue-Santiago Chile Office: Prieto Vial Cons, Constitucion 9 Bellvista, Santiago Chile

PRIGERSON, HOLLY GWEN, psychiatry researcher, educator; b. Bklyn., Jan. 1, 1962; d. Lowell and Joyce (Puchall) P.; m. Paul Kevin Maciejewski, July 27, 1991; children: Abigail Judith, Zachary Brian. AB, Columbia U., 1984; MA, Stanford U., 1985, MS, 1986, PhD, 1990. Postdoctoral fellow Yale U. Sch. Medicine, New Haven, Conn., 1900-91; from asst. to assoc. prof. psychiatry Yale U. Sch. Medicine, 1997—; postdoctoral fellow Western Psychiat. Inst. & Clinic, Pitts., 1991-93; asst. prof. psychiatry Western Psychiat. Inst. & Clinic, 1993-97. Contbr. articles to profl. jours. Recipient Scientist Devel. award NIH, 1997; grantee Am. Suicide Found., 1996, award, 2000; grantee Pepper Ctr. on Aging, 1998, NIMH, 1999, NIMH ROI, 1999. Democrat. Jewish. Avocations: running, tennis. Home: 833 Mountain Rd Cheshire CT 06410-3305 Office: Yale U Sch Medicine 34 Park St New Haven CT 06519-1109

PRIGMORE, CHARLES SAMUEL, social work educator; b. Lodge, Tenn., Mar. 21, 1919; s. Charles H. and Mary Lou (Raulston) P.; m. Shirley Melaine Buuck, June 7, 1947; 1 child, Philip Brand. A.B., U. Chattanooga, 1939; M.S., U. Wis., 1947, Ph.D., 1961; extension grad., Air War Coll., 1967, Indsl. Coll. Armed Forces, 1972. Social caseworker Children's Svc. Soc., Milw., 1947-48; social worker Wis. Sch. Boys, Waukesha, 1948-51; supr. tng. Wis. Bur. Probation and Parole, Madison, 1951-56; supt. Tenn. Vocat. Tng. Sch. for Boys, Nashville, 1956-59; assoc. prof. La. State U., 1959-64; ednl. cons. Coun. Social Work Edn., N.Y., 1962-64; exec. dir. Joint Commn. Correctional Manpower and Tng., Washington, 1964-67; prof. Sch. Social Work, U. Ala., 1967-84, prof. emeritus, 1984—, chmn. com. on Korean relationships, 1980-84; Fulbright lectr., Iran, 1972-73; vis. lectr. U. Sydney, 1976; cons. Iranian Ministry Health and Welfare, 1976-78; frequent lectr., workshop leader. Author: Textbook on Social Problems, 1971, Social Work in Iran Since the White Revolution, 1976, Social Welfare Policy Analysis and Formulation, 1979, 2d edit., 1986; editor 2 books; contbr. articles to profl. jours. Adv. Com. for Former Prisoners of War VA, 1981-83; chmn. Prisoner of War Bd., State of Ala., 1984-89; state comdr. Am. Ex-Prisoners of War, Ala., 1985-86, nat. legis. officer, 1985—, nat. dir., 1989-92, nat. sr. vice comdr., 1993—, nat comdr., 1994-95; gov.'s liaison U.S. Holocaust Meml. Coun., 1983-89; mem. Ala. Bd. Vets. Affairs, 1986-89, Ala. Bicentennial Commn. on Constn., 1987-90; bd. dirs. Community Svcs. Programs of W. Ala., 1985-89, others in past. Served to 2d lt. USAAF, 1940-45, prisoner of war, Germany, 1944-45; lt. col. Res., ret. Decorated Air medal with oak leaf cluster; recipient Conservation award Woodmen of the World, 1971; Fulbright rsch. fellow Norway, 1979-80. Fellow Am. Sociol. Assn., Royal Soc. Health; mem. Acad. Cert. Social Workers, Nat. Coun. Crime and Delinquency, Tuscaloosa Country Club, Capitol Hill Club, Alpha Kappa Delta, Beta Beta Beta. Home: 63 S Main St Alfred NY 14802-1322

PRIGNOT, JACQUES JULES, retired pneumology educator; b. Ixelles, Belgium, Feb. 2, 1924; s. Louis Joseph Prignot and Marguerite Defoin-Prignot; m. Monique Lucie Van Mechelen, Aug. 2, 1952 (div. Nov. 1980); children: Bernard, Baudouin, Paul, Olivier, Isabelle, Catherine, Charlotte; m. Françoise Marguerite Pouthier-Bernier, Sept. 11, 1982. MD, U. Louvain, Belgium, 1948. Agrégé de L'Enseignement Superieur, U. Louvain, 1959; specialist pneumology, 1952. Lectr. U. Louvain, 1959-67, prof., 1967-89, head pneumology dept., 1973-89, prof. emeritus, 1989—; med. dir. Univ. Clinic Mont-Godinne, Yvoir, Belgium, 1967-89, hon. med. dir., 1989—. Author: (with L. Goncette) Atlas Systematique De Radiodiagnostic, 1980; editor-in-chief IUAT-LD newsletter, Paris, 1991-95; contbr. more than 300 articles to profl. jours. Hon. pres. Found. des affections respiratoires et de l'Edn., Brussels, European Bur. Action Smoking Prevention, 1990-92, Solidarité et Cooperation Med. au Tiers Monde, 1980-99; adminstr. Belgian Com. UNICEF, 1990—. Mem. Belgian Soc. Pneumology (Prix Derscheid 1970, pres. 1981-82). Roman Catholic. Avocation: philately. Home: Rue Du Parc 20, B-5000 Namur Belgium Office: Solidarite & Cooperation Med, Av G Therasse 1, B-5530 Yvoir Belgium

PRIGOGINE, VICOMTE ILYA, physics educator; b. Moscow, Russia, Jan. 25, 1917; s. Roman and Julie (Wichmann) P.; m. Marina Prokopowicz, Feb. 25, 1961; children: Yves, Pascal. PhD, Free U. Brussels, 1941; hon. degree, U. Newcastle, Eng., 1966, U. Poitiers, France, 1966, U. Chgo., 1969, U. Bordeaux, France, 1972, U. de Liège, Belgium, 1977, U. Uppsala, Sweden, 1977, U de Droit, D'Economie et des Scis., d'Aix-Marseille, France, 1979, U. Georgetown, 1980, U. Cracovie, Poland, 1981, U. Rio de Janeiro, 1981, Stevens Inst. Tech., Hoboken, 1981, Heriot-Watt U., Scotland, 1985, Universidad Nacional de Educacion a Distancia, Madrid, 1985, U. Francois Rabelais de Tours, 1986, U. Peking, People's Republic of China, 1986, U. Buenos Aires, 1989, U. Cagliari, Sardinia, Italy, 1990, U. Sienne, Italy, 1990; DS (hon.), Gustavus Adolphus Coll., 1990; Membre d'Honneur, l'Academie Nationale d'Argenti, 1989, l'Academie des Sciences Naturelles de Republique Federale de Russie, 1991; Pres. d'Honneur, l'Acad. Nat. des Scis. de Republique de San Marino, 1991; Membre d'Honneur, l'Academie Chilienne des Scis., 1991, de l'Université de Nice-Sophia-Antipolis, Nice, France, 1991, de l'Univ. Philippines System, Quezon City, 1991, del'Université de Santiago, Chile, del'Université de Tucumán, Argentine, 1991; Docteur Honoris Causa, Université Lomonosov de Moscow, Russie, 1993, L'Univ. de A L.I. Cuza IASI, Iasi, Romania, 1994, U. de San Luis, Argentina, 1994, U. de Palermo, Argentina, 1994, Institut Nat. Polytechnique, Lorraine, France, 1994, SUNY, Binghamton, 1995, Vrije U. Brussel, Brussels, Belgium, 1995, Internat. Assn. U. Pres., Seoul, 1995; Doyen d'honneur Honoris Causa, l'Institut Royal des Elites du Travail de Belgique Albert I, Brussels, 1995; Docteur Honoris Causa, U. Valladolid, Espagne, 1995, l'Universite de Saint-Petersbourg, Saint-Patersbourg, Russia, 1995; Laurea ad honorem in philosophy, U. degli Studi Inst. Filosofia, Urbino, Italy, 1996; Docteur Honoris Causa, U. Salvador, Buenos Aires, 1996, U. Xanthi, Greece, 1996; Hon. Degree in Sci. and Applied Sci., Aristoteles U. of Thessaloniki, Thessaloniki, Greece, 1998; Hon. Degree, Nat. Inst. Astrophysics, Optics & Electronics, Puebla, Mex., 1998; Doctor Honoris Causa, Universidad Nacional Autonomade Mex., Mex., 1998; Hon. Degree, Wesleyan U., Ill., 1998; Doctor Honoris Causa, Wroclaw U. Tech., Wroclaw, Poland, 1998. Prof. Free U. Brussels, 1947—; dir. Internat. Insts. Physics and Chemistry, Solvay, Belgium, 1959—; prof. physics and chem. engring. U. Tex., Austin, 1967—, dir. Ilya Prigogine Ctr. Studies Statis. Mechs./Complex Sys., 1967—; hon. prof. U. Nankin, People's Republic of China, 1986, Banaras Hindu U., Varasani, India, 1988; Ashbel Smith regental prof. U. Tex., Austin, 1984—; Dir.'s Disting. visitor Inst. for Advanced Study, Princeton (N.J.) U., 1993; conseiller spl. Commn. des Communautés Européennes, 1993; internat. advisor de l'Internat. Inst. Advanced Studies, Kyoto, 1994; hon. dir. Inst. Internat. Investigaciones Cientficas U. Salvador, 1996; hon. chmn. Inst. Complex Sys., Thrace, Greece, 1996; mem. adv. bd. Kothari Ctr. Sci., Ethics and Edn. U. Delhi, 1995; mem. Internat. Info. Acad, Moscow, 1996, Académie de Yuste-Fauteuil J.S. Bach, Madrid, 1996; hon. pres. Ctr. Fl No Linear Sistemas Complejos U. Santiago, Chile, 1996—; with Ctr L.Am. Estudios, U. Nacional San Luis, Argentina, 1994, U. Lomonosov, Moscow, 1995, Haute Ecole Libre Ilya Prigogine, Brussels, 1996, Inst. Documentazione Ricerca Sull, Italy, 1996, Opere di Ilya Prigogine, CISST, Brugine, Padova, Italy, 1996; Ilya Prigogine chair philosophy scis. U. Palermo, Argentina, 1996; pres. seminar Penser la Sci., U. Louvain, Belgium, 1997; hon. pres. Inst. Philosophy, Naples, Italy, 1997; Prigogine lectr. U. Lombarde, Como, Italy, 1999. Author: (with R. Defay) Traite de Thermodynamique, conformement aux methodes de Gibbs et de De Donder, 1944, 50, Etude Thermodynamique des Phenomenes Irreversibles, 1947, Introduction to Thermodynamics of Irreversible Processes, 1954, 62, 67, translation: Russian, Serbo-Croatian, French, Italian, & Spanish, (with A. Bellemans, V. Mathot) The Molecular Theory of Solutions, 1957, Nonequilibrium Statistical Mechanics, 1962, (with R. Herman) Kinetic Theory of Vehicular Traffic, 1971, (with R. Glansdorff) Thermodynamic Theory of Structure, Stability and Fluctuations, 1971, (with G. Nicolis) Self-Organization in Nonequilibrium Systems, 1977, From Being to Becoming-Time and Complexity in Physical Sciences, 1980, French, German, Japanese, Russian, Chinese, Italian, Romanian, & Portuguese edits., (with I. Stengers) Order Out of Chaos, 1983, La Nouvelle Alliance, Les Métamorphoses de la Science, 1979, German, English, Italian, Spanish, Serbo-Croatian, Romanian, Swedish, Dutch, Russian, Japanese, Chinese, Portuguese, Bulgarian, Greek, Korean, Polish, Danish, Turkish & Hungarian edits., (with G. Nicolis) Die Erforschung des Komplexen, 1987, Exploring Complexity, 1989, Chinese,

Russian, Italian, French, Spanish & Japanese edits., (with I. Stengers) Entre le temps et l'Eternité, 1988, Dutch edit. 1989, Italian edit. 1989, Spanish edit. 1990, Portuguese edit. 1993, Le leggi del Caos, 1993, Das Paradox der Zeit, 1993, (with I. Stengers), La Nascita del Tiempo, 1998, Les Lois du Chaos, 1994, Die Gesetze des Chaos, 1995, La Fin des Certitudes, 1996, Spanish, Portuguese, Dutch, English, Italian, Korean, Japanese, Greek edits., 1997, Las leyes del caos, 1997, (with D. Kondepudi) Modern Thermodynamics: From Heat Engines to Dissipative Structures, 1998, French edit., 1999; mem. editl. bd. Ukrainian Phys. Jour., 1990. Mem. sci. adv. bd. Internat. Acad. for Biomed. Drug Rsch., 1990; mem. adv. com. Internat. Coun. Human Duties, U. degli Studi di Trieste, Italy, 1996. Fellow RGK Found. Centennial, U. Tex. 1989-90; decorated comdr. Légion d'Honneur, 1989, France, comdr. de l'Ordre de Leopold, 1968, Médaille de la resistance comdr. de l'Ordre Leopold II, 1961, Grande Croix de l'Ordre de Leopold II, 1977, Médaille Civique de Premiere Classe, 1972, comdr. de l'Ordre National du Mérite, France, 1977, comdr. de l'Ordre des Arts et des Lettres, France, 1984, Titulaire de l' Ordre du Soleil Levant, avec Médaille d' Or et d' Argent, Japon, 1990; recipient Prix Franqui, 1955, Prix Solvay, 1965, Nobel prize in chemistry, 1977, Honda Prize, 1983, Rumford gold medal Royal Soc. London, 1976, Karcher medal Am. Crystallographic Assn., 1978, Descartes medal U. Paris, 1979, Prix Umberto Biancamano, 1987, award recipient Gravity Rsch. Found., 1988, Artificial Intelligence Sci. Achievement award Internat. Found. for Artificial Intelligence, 1990, Prix Summa de l'Universite Laval, Can., 1993, Medaille Piotr Kapitza decernee par l'Academie des Scis. Naturelles de Russie, 1996—, Medaille de l'Ecole Normale Superieure, Paris, 1995, Medaille d'honneur de l'Inst. Phys. Chemistry-Polish Acad. Scis., 1996—, others. Fellow NAS India (hon.); mem. Royal Acad. Belgium (pres.), Am. Acad. Sci. (medal 1975), Royal Soc. Scis. Uppsala (Sweden), NAS U.S.A. (fgn. assoc.), Soc. Royale des Scis. Liège Belgium (corr.), Acad. Gottingen Germany, Deutscher Acad. der Naturforscher Leopoldina (Cothenius medal 1970), Osterreichische Acad. der Wissenschaften (corr.), Academie Nationale des Sciences, des Lettres et des Arts de Modene (Italy, hon.), Commn. Mondiale de la Culture et du Devel. de l'UNESCO (hon.), Chem. Soc. Poland (hon.), Internat. Soc. Gen. Systems Rsch. (pres.-elect 1988), Royal Soc. Chemistry Belgium (hon.), N.Y. Acad. Sci., Internat. Acad. Philosophy Sci., World Acad. Arts and Scis., World Inst. Sci., Assemblée Européenne Scis. Tech., Communantés Européenne, Étranger Acad. Scis., Internat. Soc. Theoretical Chem. Physics. (mem. hon. bd.), Soc. Coréenne de Chimie (hon.), Conseil Consultatif Sci. Internat. de l'UNESCO, European Assembly of Sci. and Tech., Acad. of Sci. Belorus, Internat. Soc. for Theoretical Chem. Physics (hon. bd. 1995—), Royal Acad. Medicine (hon. mem.), Consejo Académico, Korean Acad. Sci. and Tech. (hon. fgn. mem.), Internat. Acad. Russia. Address: 67 Ave Fond Roy, 1180 Brussels Belgium Office: Inst Internat Physics & Chem, Campus Plaine ULB CP231, Bld du Triomphe 1050 Brussels Belgium also: U Tex Ilya Prigogine Ctr Robert Lee Moore Hall Studies Statis Mechanics Austin TX 78712

PRIKHODKO, IGOR VLADIMIROVICH, chemist; b. Tomsk, Russia, Apr. 9, 1964; s. Vladimir Alexandrovich and Tamara Victorovna P.; m. Inna Anatolievna Orlova, June 11, 1989 (div. Dec. 1991). M of Chemistry, St. Petersburg State U., Russia, 1986, PhD, 1992. Rsch. fellow St. Petersburg State U., Russia, 1990—, rschr., 1994—; postdoctoral Tech. U., Delft, The Netherlands, 1998-99. Contbr. articles to profl. jours. Mem. Mendeleev's Russian Chem. Soc. Office: St Petersburg State U Dept Chem, Universitetsky pr 2, 198504 Saint Petersburg Russia

PRIKNER, KAREL, geophysicist; b. Kladno, Czechoslovakia, Nov. 17, 1937; s. Karel and Blazena (Durdik) P.; m. Jitka Kovar, Apr. 18, 1963; 1 child. MSc, Charles U., 1960, PhD, 1967. From jr. rschr. to sr. scientist Geophys. Inst. Czech Acad. Sci., Prague, 1960—. Office: Geophys Inst Acad Scis Czech Rep, Bocni II 1401, 14131 Praha 4-Sporilov Czech Republic

PRIKRYL, PETR, mathematician; b. Prague, Czech Republic, May 28, 1942; s. Vladimir and Miloslava (Rulfova) P.; m. Vera Ilkova, Aug. 4, 1967; 1 child, Jan. MS, Charles U., Prague, 1964; PhD, Czechoslovak Acad. Sci., Prague, 1972. Cert. in numerical analysis, computational physics, materials sci. Programmer State Inst. Heat Tech., Prague, 1964-66; rsch. asst. Math. Inst. Acad. Sci., Prague, 1966-72, rsch. worker, 1972-79, sr. rsch. worker, 1979—, dept. head, dep. dir., 1991-99; mem. Interkosmos Working Group, Prague, 1983-89. Author: Numerical Analysis, 1985, 2d edit., 1988, 3d edit., 1994; contbr. articles to profl. jours.; dep. editor jour. Applications of Maths., 1990-99, editor, 2000—. Mem. Union Czech Math. Physicists, European Materials Rsch. Soc. Avocations: music, art, philately, tourism. Home: Na Safrance 13, 101 00 Prague 10, Czech Republic Office: Math Inst Acad Sci, Zitna 25, 115 67 Prague 1, Czech Republic

PRIMAS, VINSON BERNARDI, management consultant; b. Baton Rouge, La., July 9, 1966; s. Isadore and Augustine (Perry) P. BS, Grambing State U., 1988; MS, Rensselaer Poly. Inst., Troy, N.Y., 1992; CSS, Harvard U., 1997. Programmer Dow Jones, Chicopee, Mass., 1988-91; programmer analyst Geary Corp., Pittsfield, Mass., 1992; bus. analyst Motorola ISG, Mansfield, Mass., 1993-97; lectr. Newbury Coll., Brookline, Mass., 1993; project cons. Lucent Tech., Cambridge, Mass., 1997-99; sr. cons. Ernst & Young LLP, Dallas, 1999; ptnr. 80 Legion Pkwy: Capital Ventures, 1999-2000; process solution cons. Bus. Edge Solutions, Dallas, 2000—; ptnr. Smart Investors Investment Trust Co., 1997-2000. Staff asst. Springfield Mass. Mental Health Assn., 1985-99; mem. men's fellowship Messiah Bapt. Ch., Brockton, Mass., 1995-98; bd. dirs. Messiah Bapt. Fed. Credit Union, 1998; laymem. Torn Veil Ch. of God in Christ, Brockton, Mass., 2000—, Messiah Bapt. Cmty. Ctr., Brockton, 2000—. Avocations: reading, solving business issues, sports. Home: 1824 E Peters Colony Rd # 4502 Carrollton TX 75007-3729

PRIMATESTA, RAÚL FRANCISCO CARDINAL, archbishop; b. Capilla del Señor, Argentina, Apr. 14, 1919. Ordained priest Roman Catholic Ch., 1942; formerly tchr. minor and maj. seminaries, La Plata; titular bishop of Tanais, also aux. of La Plata, 1957; bishop of San Rafael, 1961-65; archbishop of Córdoba, 1965—; elevated to Sacred Coll. Cardinals, 1973; titular ch., St. Mary of Sorrowful Virgin; mem. Congregation of Bishops, Congregation of Religious and Secular Insts., Congregation Sacraments and Divine Worship, Commn. Revision Code Canon Law. Address: Arzobispado, Avda Hipólito Yrigoyen 98, 5000 Cordoba Argentina*

PRIMDAHL, SOEREN, chemical engineer; b. Skanderborg, Denmark, July 16, 1967; s. Iver and Grete (Stisen) P.; m. Annette Christina Soeberg, June 10, 1996; children: Katrine, Morten. MSc, Tech. U. Denmark, 1993; PhD, U. Twente, The Netherlands, 1999. Sr. rsch. scientist RISOE Nat. Lab., Roskilde, Denmark, 1993—. Mem. Danish Electrochem. Soc. (chair 1997-98), Danish Ceramic Soc. Home: Åvej 1 St TV, 4000 Roskilde Denmark Office: RISOE Nat Lab Dept Mat Rsch, PO Box 49, 4000 Roskilde Denmark

PRIMEAUX, HENRY, III, automotive executive, author, speaker; b. New Orleans, Nov. 16, 1941; s. Henry Jr. and Ethel (Ritter) P.; m. Jane Cathrine Velcich, July 23, 1960; children: Joann Primeaux Longa, Lisa, Henry Joseph. Student, La. State U., New Orleans, 1959-63. Compt. Jimco, New Orleans, 1965-66; owner, mgr. Picone Seafood, New Orleans, 1966-67; v.p. NADW Inc., Metairie, La., 1967-78, Am. Warranty Corp., L.A., 1978-80; pres. F&I Warranty Corp., Arlington, Tex., 1980-87; exec. v.p. F&I Mgmt. Corp., Arlington, 1980-87; pres., CEO Primco Corp., Arlington, 1987-91; owner Flavors Restaurant, Tulsa, Okla., Primeaux Mktg.; mng. ptnr. Crown Auto World, Brighton; cons., corr. Wards Auto Dealer, Detroit, 1987-95, weekly TV program Automotive Satellite TV Network; cons. Nissan Motor Co., L.A., 1988-89, Convergent div. Unisys, Hunt Valley, Md., 1988-90; cons. Mercedes-Benz N.Am.; cons. Automatic Data Processing; exec. com. Okla. Workforce Investment Bd.; chmn. Tulsa Workforce Investment Bd. Writer Auto Age mag.; author: F&I Handbook. Mem. Rep. Task Force Okla. Workforce Devel. Com.; bd. dirs. John Starks Found., Boy Scouts U.S.; mem. athletic com. Tulsa Pub. Schs.; mem. nat. adv. bd. Automotive Yes Sch. to Work Initiative; mem. Okla. Boxing Commn., Okla. Sch. to Work Commn., bd. mem. Tulsa River Parks Commn. With USN, 1959-61. Mem. Am. Internat. Automobile Dealers Assn., Assn. of F&I Profls. (bd. dirs. 1990—, pres. 1994), Nat. Auto Dealers Assn. (pres. Tulsa chpt. 1994, Time Quality Dealer of Yr. 1994), Okla. Amateur Sports Commn. (chmn.), Met. Tulsa C. of C. (bd. dirs. 1998—). Roman Catholic. Home: 11716 S 66th East Ave Bixby OK 74008-2051 Office: Crown AutoWorld 4444 S Sheridan Rd Tulsa OK 74145-1122

PRIMM, DAVID JOHN, middle school educator; b. Des Moines, June 26, 1950; s. John Gerald and Nora Alice (Williams) P.; m. Linda Kay Huffman, Aug. 5, 1973; children: John, Heather. BS in Edn., Northwest Mo. State U., 1972, MA, 1976. Cert. tchr., Mo. and Iowa. Tchr. Maryville (Mo.) Sch. Dist., 1973—. Mem. Mo. State Tchrs. Assn., Maryville Pride Lions. Methodist. Avocations: reading, camping, restoring old farm tractors, woodworking. Home: 205 E Bentley St Ravenwood MO 64479-9124 Office: Maryville Sch Dist 1429 S Munn Ave Maryville MO 64468-2756

PRIMORAC, MILJENKO, physics educator, researcher; b. Uzarići, SirokiBrij, Bosnia-Herzegovina, Feb. 10, 1944; s. Stanko and Milka (Kraljević) P.; m. Nada Hren, May 2, 1970; children: Martina, Hrvoje, Bariša, Mislav, Koraljka. Grad. in theoretical physics, U. Zagreb, Croatia, 1968, MSc in Chemistry, 1978, PhD in Physics, 1986. Tchr. physics Prvomajska, mech. sch., Zagreb, 1970-80; lectr. physics dept. wood tech. U. Zagreb Forest Faculty, 1980-91, asst. prof., 1991-97, assoc. prof., 1997—; exterior rschr. Ruder Bošković Inst., Zagreb, 1978—; guest prof. U. Mostar, Bosnia-Herzegovina, 1993—; v.p. Labor Union Sci. and Higher Edn., Zagreb, 1990-93. Contbr. articles to sci. jours., including Jour. Physics, Jour. Computational Physics, Jour. Molecular Structure, Phys. Rev. A., Internat. Jour. Quant. Chem. Roman Catholic. Avocations: history, politics, cycling. Office: U Zagreb Forestry Faculty, Svetošimunska 25, HR-10001 Zagreb Croatia

PRINCE, DICK, circuit judge, educator; b. Berwyn, Ill., Aug. 14, 1951; s. Richard Joseph and Dolores Shirley P.; m. Mary Nancy Rouse, July 15, 1977 (div. 1990); m. Lydia Lorraine, Dec. 28, 1990; children: Richard Paul, Caleb Lee, Justin Paul, Teresa Dee. BA in History, Stetson U., 1973, JD, 1976. Bar: Fla., U.S. Dist. Ct. (no. dist.) Fla., U.S. Dist. Ct. (so. dist.) Fla., U.S. Dist. Ct. (mid. dist.) Fla., U.S. Ct. Appeals (5th cir.), U.S. Ct. Appeals (11th cir.). Spl. asst. pub. defender 6th Cir. Pub. Defender, St. Petersburg, Fla., 1976; asst. state atty. 10th Cir. State Atty., Bartow, Fla., 1976-78, chief consumer fraud sect. asst. state atty., 1982-84; sole practitioner Law Office of Dick Prince, Bartow, Fla., 1978-80; ptnr. Prince & Smith, P.A., Winter Haven, Fla., 1980-82; county judge Polk County, Bartow, Fla., 1985-95; circuit judge 10th Judicial Cir., various, Fla., 1995—; dean traffic adjucation sch. Fla. Jud. Conf., 1990-95; prof. Polk C.C., Winter Haven, 1977—, Fla. So. Coll., Lakeland, Fla., 1984; instr. Conf. of County Cir. Judges, Fla., 1986—. Author: (poem) Full Moon In The Days Of The Dog, 1982 (1st prize 1983); contbr. articles to profl. jours. Bd. dirs. Big Brothers of Polk County, Lakeland, 1978-81, Lakeland Rifle and Pistol Club, 1992-94; sunday sch. tchr. St. Thomas Aquinas, Barton, 1979-84; shooting coach Jr. Olympics, Fla., 1992-96. Recipient Disting. Jurist award Justice for Children, 1985, 86, 88, Disting. Judicial award Fla. Coun. on Crime and Delinquency, 1998, Law Enforcement Commendation medal Sons of the Am. Revolution, 1st Annual Dirs. award Police Acad. Polk Cmty. Coll., 1999. Mem. NRA, Fla. Bar, Fla. Dept. Law Enforcement, Fla. Conf. Circuit Judges. Republican. Roman Cath. Avocations: Harley-Davidson motorcycles, clawhammer banjo, dry fly fishing. Office: Polk County Courthouse PO Box 9000 Bartow FL 33831-9000

PRINCE, GREGORY SMITH, JR., academic administrator; b. Washington, May 7, 1939; s. Gregory Smith and Margaret (Minor) P.; m. Toni Layton Brewer; children: Tara Wyndom, Gregory S. III. BA, Yale U., 1961, M in Philosophy, 1969, PhD, 1973; cert. in teaching English as a Second Language, Georgetown U., 1961; DHL (hon.), Amherst Coll., 1991, LLD (hon.), 1991. Instr. New Asia Coll., Kowloon, Hong Kong, 1961-62, Chinese U., Kowloon, 1962-63, Yale China Assn., Kowloon, 1961-63, Woodberry Forest (Va.) Sch., 1963-65; dean summer programs Dartmouth Coll., Hanover, N.H., 1970-72, asst. dean faculty, 1972-78, assoc. dean faculty, 1978-89; pres. Hampshire Coll., Amherst, Mass., 1989—; vice chair coun. on race and ethnic justice ABA; bd. dirs. Mass Ventures. Producer: (film) A Way of Learning, 1988. Trustee Montshire Mus. Sci., Hanover, 1973-89, Washington Campus, 1978—; trustee, chmn. Univ. Press New England, Hanover, 1983-84; trustee, pres. Yale-China Assn., New Haven, 1969-84; bd. dirs., pres. Five Colls., Inc., Amherst, 1989—; bd. dirs. Mass. Internat. Festival for Arts, 1994-98; chmn. bd. dirs. Assn. Ind. Colls. and Univs. Mass., 1994-95; chair commn. on accreditation Am. Coun. Edn.; bd. dirs. Mass. Nature Conservancy, 1996—; bd. dirs. Nat. Assn. Ind. Colls. and Univs., 1999—. Coe fellow Stanford U., 1965, Woodrow Wilson fellow Yale U., 1966, NDEA fellow, 1967-70. Mem. Internat. Assn. of Chiefs Police Found. (bd. dirs. 1991-95), Nat. Assn. of Ind. Colls. and Univs. Democrat. Episcopalian. Home: 15 Middle St Amherst MA 01002-3009 Office: Hampshire Coll 893 West St Amherst MA 01002-3372

PRINCE, LEAH FANCHON, art educator and research institute administrator; b. Hartford, Conn., Aug. 12, 1939; d. Meyer and Annie (Forman) Berman; m. Herbert N. Prince, Jan. 30, 1955; children: Daniel L., Richard N., Robert G. Student, U. Conn., 1957-59, Rutgers U., Newark, 1962; BFA, Fairleigh Dickinson U., 1970; postgrad., Caldwell Coll. for Women, 1973-75, Parsons Sch. of Design, N.Y.C., 1978. Cert. tchr. art, N.J. Tchr. art Caldwell-West Caldwell (N.J.) Pub. Schs., 1970-75; pres. Britannia Imports Ltd., Fairfield, N.J., 1979-89; tchr. religious studies Bohrer-Kaufman Hebrew Acad., Randolph, N.J., 1981-82; co-founder, corp. sec. Gibraltar Biol. Labs., Inc., Fairfield, 1970—; dir., co-founder Gibraltar Inst. for Rsch. and Trng., Fairfield, 1984—; cons. Internat. Antiques and Fine Arts Industries, U.K., 1979-89; cons. in art exhibitry Passaic County Coll., Paterson, N.J., 1989-93; art curator Fairleigh Dickinson U., Rutherford, N.J., 1972-74; curator history of design Bloomfield (N.J.) Coll., 1990-91; lectr. nat. meeting Am. Soc. Microbiology, New Orleans, 1989; spkr. in field. Exhibited in group shows at Bloomfield (N.J.) Coll., 1990, Caldwell Women's Club, N.J., 1991, State Fedn. Women's Clubs Ann. Show, 1992 (1st pl. award 1992), Newark Art Mus., 1992, West (N.J.) Essex Art Assn., 1990, Somerset (N.J.) Art Assn. Ann. Juried Show, 1994, Mortimer Gallery, Gladstone, N.J., 1994 (1st pl. award 1998), Tewksbury His. Soc. (1st pl. award 1994); one-woman shows include Passaic County Coll., N.J., 1990, Caldwell Coll., N.J., 1990; author children's stories. Chair ann. juried art awards Arts Coun. of Essex Bd. Trustees, Montclair, N.J., 1984-90; chair fundraising Arts Coun. Essex County, N.J., 1989. Recipient 1st place award N.J. Tewksbury Hist. Soc., 1994, 98. Mem. AAUW, Soc. Childrens Book Writers & Illustrators, Somerset Art Assn., Nat. Mus. of Women in the Arts, Nat. League Am. Pen Women, Inc., Internat. Platform Assn., Barnegat Light Yacht Club. Republican. Avocations: boating, tennis, opera. Home: 5 Standish Dr Mendham Twp Morristown NJ 07960-3224

PRINCE, STEPHEN, software developer, researcher; b. Nottingham, Eng., Dec. 30, 1959; s. Ronald Arthur and Margaret Lillian (Maltby) P.; divorced; children: Christopher Stephen, Chloe Lee. B in Engring., Swinburne U. Tech., Melbourne, Victoria, Australia, 1982; programming cert., Monash U., Melbourne, Victoria, Australia, 1983; Grad. Dip CS, RMIT U., Melbourne, Australia, 1996. Design engr. L&L Australia, Boronia, Victoria, 1981-82, '83-84, Info. Mechanics Inc., Melbourne, 1982-83; software cons. Micronics, Melbourne, 1984; systems programmer Labtam Ltd., Braeside, Victoria, 1984-90; software mgr. CLC Solutions, Melbourne, 1990-95; tech. dir., 1995-97; sr. developer Phone Ware Comms., Burwood East, 1997-99, sr. developer, product mgr., 1999—; speaker Uniforum Singapore Conf., 1990, FUAA Conf., 1993, Officer Power User Group, Reston, Va., 1996, DRS User Assn., Warwick, Eng., 1996, others; mem. Internet Engring. Task Force. Mem. USENIX Assn., Internet Soc., Assn. for Computing Machinery, Australian Unix Users Group (chmn., coms. 1990-92, pres. Victorian chpt. 1991-94). Avocation: gym, chess, bonsai, golf, music. Home: 62 Nottingham St, Glen Waverley VIC 3150, Australia Office: Phone Ware Comms, 303 Burwood Hwy, Burwood VIC 3151, Australia

PRINGLE, DENNIS GRAHAM, geography lecturer, consultant, researcher; b. Bangor, County Down, No. Ireland, May 25, 1949; s. John Gavey and Ethel Chambers (Graham) P.; m. Rosaleen Josephine Duffy, Aug. 4, 1973; children: James, Andrew, Christine, Gillian. BA, Trinity Coll., Dublin, 1971, MA, 1975; PhD, Queen's U., Belfast, 1978. Rschr. Queen's U., Belfast, No. Ireland, 1971-73, Durham (Eng.) U., 1973-74; lectr. Maynooth U., Ireland, 1974—; sec. Nat. Com. for Geography, Ireland, 1991-95. Author: One Island, Two Nations?, 1985; editor GeoNews, 1988-95. Youth worker Leixlip United AFC, County Kildare, Ireland, 1990-95. Mem. Geog. Soc. Ireland (sec. 1980-86, v.p. 1991-92,, 94-95, pres. 1992-94, membership sec. 1995—), Irish Orgn. for Geog. Info. (exec.). Avocations: travel, camping. Office: Maynooth U, Maynooth County Kildare, Ireland

PRINTZ, LOUIS MARTIN RAHBEK, economist, educator; b. Aarhus, Jutland, Denmark, Nov. 16, 1933; s. Hugo Carl Jørgensen and Gerda Kirstine (Rahbek) P.; m. Henny Jensine Andersen, Nov. 23, 1963; children: Merete, Niels. BSc in Econs., Aarhus Sch. Bus., 1962, MSc in Econs., 1964, PhD in Econs., 1969, Doktor Mercaturae, 1982. Salesman Aarhus Dampvaeveri, 1951-56; maj. lt. Danish Army, 1958-62; cons. Jutland Inst. Tech., Denmark, 1962-63, Regnecentralen, Denmark, 1963-64; asst. prof. Aarhus Sch. Bus., 1964-71, prof., 1971—; mem. adv. bd. EDB Radet, Copenhagen, 1967-71, Dansk Sygehus Inst., Copenhagen, 1975-81; mem. Danish Rsch. Adminstrn., Copenhagen, 1984-92; head govt. rsch. program Danish Food Industry, Copenhagen, 1990-94. Grantee Reinholdt W. Jorck Found., 1983. Mem. Århus City Rotary. Avocations: tennis, painting, music, philosophy, travel. Home: Brovej 7, 8250 Århus Jutland, Denmark Office: Aarhus Sch Bus, Haslegaardsvej 10, DK 8210 Århus Denmark

PRINZ, B. BETH, physician; b. Troy, Ohio, Apr. 30, 1967; d. Robert Mansfield and Bonnie Carol (Stocking) Mills; m. Sascha M. Prinz, July 30, 1995; children: Tristan Alexander, Morgan Elizabeth. BA in Biochemistry/Cell Biology, U. Calif., San Diego, 1990; MD, Med. Coll. Va., Richmond, 1995. Diplomate Am. Bd. Internal Medicine. Resident physician St. Vincent's Hosp., N.Y.C., 1995-98; fellow in pulmonary medicine Hammersmith Hosp., London, 1998—. Republican.

PRIOR, FRANCIS GEORGE RICHARD, pharmacist, researcher; b. Glasgow, Scotland, Mar. 28, 1949; s. Denis Victor and Elenor Mann (Logan) P.; m. Bonnie Gail Moore, June 15. BPharm, U. London, 1971; MSc, Heriot Watt U., Edinburgh, 1975; MBA, Napier U., Edinburgh, 1993; PhD, Welsh Sch. Pharmacy, Cardiff, 1997. Trainee, pharmacist Guys Hosp., London, staff pharmacist; pharmacist Buckland Hosp., Dover, Eng.; chief pharmacist Eastern Gen. Hosp., Edinburgh; founder, dir. Ctr. for Innovation in Healthcare Tech., Glasgow, 1999; lectr. BAPEN, London, 1994—, Queen Margarets Coll., Edinburgh, 1995—; bd. dirs. Pro Rsch., Edinburgh, Integrated Images, Edinburgh. Author: Medical Hypotheses; contbr. articles to profl. jours.; inventor in field; contbr. poetry to New Poets 93, 1993. Mem. Royal Pharm. Soc., Inst. of Biology, Port Edgar Yacht Club (commodore 1989-92). Avocations: sailing, photography, song writing, guitar, writing poetry. Office: Pulse Reverse Osmosis Rsch, 26 Cotlands Park, Longnidory E Lothian EH32 0QX, Scotland

PRIOR, HOWARD GRENFELL, secondary school educator, acupuncturist; b. Balt., Mar. 7, 1954; s. Grenfell and Elizabeth Canter Prior; m. Molly DeBastiani Aston, June 26, 1990; children: William Aston Prior, Samuel Grenfell Aston. BA, St. John's Coll., 1992; MA, Traditional Acupuncture Inst., 1995. Cert. acupuncturist, Md., Washington. Computer programmer Environ. Measurements Inc., Annapolis, Md., 1977-81; English tchr. Shane Englsh Sch., Chiba, Japan, 1985-91, course mgr., 1988-90; pvt. practice acupuncturist Balt., 1995—; assoc. faculty mem. Traditional Acupuncture Inst., Columbia, Md., 1995-99; math. tchr. Balt. City Pub. Schs., 1999—. Mem. Md. Acupuncture Soc. Avocations: Tai Chi, Aikido. E-mail: hprior.charm.net.

PRIOR, LORD JAMES MICHAEL LEATHES, business executive; b. Norwich, Eng., Oct. 11, 1927; s. C.B.L. and A.S.M. P.; m. J.P.G. Lywood, 1954; 4 children. Ed., Cambridge (Eng.) U. M.P. for Lowestoft, 1959-83, M.P. for Waveney, 1983-87; with African Cargo Handling Ltd., 1998—, MSI Cellular Investments BV, 1999—; parliamentary pvt. sec. to Pres. of Bd. of Trade, 1963, to Min. of Power, 1963-64, to Rt. Hon. Edward Heath, 1965-70; vice chmn. Conservative Party, 1965, 72-74; Min. agr., fisheries and food, 1970-72, Lord Pres. of Coun., 1972-74, Conservative spokesman on Employment, 1974-79; Sec. of State for Employment, 1979-81, for No. Ireland, 1981-84; chmn. The Gen. Electric Co. PLC, 1984-98, Royal Vet. Coll., 1990-98, East Anglian Radio, plc, to 1992-96; non exec. dir., chmn. Alders Ltd., to 1994; chmn. Arab-Brit. C. of C., 1996—; chancellor Anglia Poly. U., to 1999, Tenneco European Adv. Coun., to 1997, Am. Internat. Group Adv. Coun., 1988—. Office: Ho of Lords, London SW1A OPW, England also: 6 Belgrave Sq, London SW1X 8PM, England*

PRIOR, ROGER ARNOLD, executive search consultant; b. Temora, NSW, Australia, Mar. 15, 1938; arrived in Singapore, 1980; s. Walter Edward Fredrick and Dorothy Grace (Eady) P.; m. Jane Claire Rose, Mar. 14, 1981; three children. B in Commerce in Econs. with honors, U. NSW, Australia, 1969. Rep. South Brit. Ins., various cities, Australia, 1954-65; mgr. IBM Corp., London and Sydney, Australia, 1966-80; regional mgr. MSA Inc., Sydney and Singapore, 1980-83; mng. dir. Roger Prior Assocs., Singapore, 1984—, YWA-Priority Cons., Singapore, 1988—. Mem. Australian Computer Soc., Singapore Computer Soc. (sr.), Singapore Cricket Club, Tanglin Club (Singapore), Singapore Australia Bus. Coun., Singapore Am. C. of C. Avocation: scuba. Office: Roger Prior Assocs, 111 N Bridge Rd #20-02, Singapore 179098, Singapore

PRIOR, WILLIAM ALLEN, electronics company executive; b. Benton Harbor, Mich., Jan. 14, 1927; s. Allen Ames and Madeline Isabel (Taylor) P.; m. Nancy Norton Sayles, July 7, 1951 (div. Oct. 1971); children: Stephanie Sayles, Alexandra Taylor, Robert Eames, Eleanor Norton; m. Carol Luise Becker-Ehmck, Oct. 30, 1971; children: Michael Becker-Ehmck, Jeffrey Renner. AB in Physics, Harvard Coll., 1950, MBA, 1954. Salesman IBM, Mineola, L.I., N.Y., 1950-52; sales engr. Lincoln Electric Co., Cleve., 1954-57; ptnr. Hammond Kennedy & Co., N.Y.C., 1957-66; v.p. The Singer Co., N.Y.C., 1967-68; pres. Tansitor Electronics, Bennington, Vt., 1969-71, Aerotron Inc., Raleigh, N.C., 1971-82; v.p. J. Lee Peeler & Co., Durham, N.C., 1986-89; pres. Accudyne, Inc., Raleigh, 1990-99; chmn. Royal Blue Capital, Inc., Raleigh; bd. dirs. NeoDyne, Inc., Raleigh. Cpl. USAAF, 1945-46, Germany. Mem. IEEE, North Ridge Country Club (Raleigh), Raleigh Racquet Club, Harvard Club of N.Y.C., 50 Group. Republican. Avocations: tennis, skiing, computer programming. Home: 329 Meeting House Cir Raleigh NC 27615-3133 Office: Accudyne Inc 5800 Mchines Pl Raleigh NC 27616-1839

PRIOR-PALMER DE MARCO, DIANA MARY, writer; b. Loxwood, Sussex, Eng., Apr. 1, 1929; naturalized American citizen, 1965.; d. Otho Prior-Palmer and Barbara Mary Frankland; m. Bruno Rinaldo de Marco. Student, U. Paris, La Sorbonne, 1950-53; studied the gypsies, under Musee de l'Homme, Paris, 1954-55; student, Dante Alighieri Inst. Italian, Studies, Rome and Florence, 1956, Aspen Inst. Humanistic Studies, Colo., 1959, Johns Hopkins Sch. Advanced, Internat. Studies, 1960-64. Editl. asst., photo editor and writer Office of Info., The Marshall Plan, Paris, 1950-54; bilingual asst. in conf. divsn. NATO Hdqtrs., Paris, 1955; publicity dir. European office Ampex Corp., London, 1956-57; with Export Promotion Dept. Ampex Hdqtrs., Redwood City, Calif., 1957-58; freelance assignment Sec. of State George Ball/European Coal and Steel Cmty., 1959; press attache Royal Cambodian Embassy, Cambodian Mission to UN, Washington, 1960-64; U.S. nat. coord. UNESCO Internat. Campaign for Monuments, 1965; dir. pub. rels. Nat. Coun. on the Arts/The White House, Washington, 1965-67; dir. of govt. liaison Nat. Endowment for the Arts/The White House; numerous positions with Nat. Endowment for the Arts; worldwide travel on humanitarian assignments including programme officer for FAO's Freedom from Hunger Campaign, 1971-79, spl. projects officer FAO/UN Hdqs., Rome, 1980-90, others; lectr. in field. Designer, editor: Fighting Hunger & Newslink mags.; contbr. articles to profl. jours.; freelance writer/rschr.: (NBC/Tv's weekly documentary program) David Brinkley's Journal, others. Vol. Stay in Sch. Fund, 1963-64, For Love of Children, Washington, Project Hope, Caritas Earthquake Emergency Ctr., Nocera Umbra, Italy, 1997-98, Albania/Kosovo, 1999, others; founder, organizer St. Kitts Prisoner's Def. Fund, London, 1967, London Barristers, Internat. Commn. Jurists; mem. Amnesty Internat., London, Charter 88, London. Recipient citation of merit Am. Scenic and Hist. Preservation Soc., N.Y., 1965. Mem. Soc. for Internat. Devel. (former v.p.), New Ecns. Found. (London). Episcopalian. Avocations: fluent in French and Italian; knowledge of German, Spanish and Swedish, skiing, sailing, gardening.

PRIPATNANONT, PRISANA, dentist, consultant; b. Chonburi, Thailand, Oct. 14, 1958; d. Prapai and Bunnai Thongnoppakao; m. Choosak

Pripatnanont, May 24, 1986; children: Wichaya, Chanon. BS, Mahidol U., Thailand, 1980, DDS, 1982, grad. diploma in clin. sci., 1985. Diplomate Thai Bd. Oral and Maxillofacial Surgery/Thai Dental Coun. Lectr. Khon Kaen (Thailand) U., 1982-87; lectr. Prince of Songkla U., Hadyai, Thailand, 1987-90, asst. prof., 1990-99, assoc. prof., 1999—. Contbr. rsch. articles to profl. jours. Mem. Internat. Assn. Dental Rsch., Acad. Osseointegration, Thai Soc. Oral and Maxillofacial Surgery, Thai Dental Assn. Thailand. Avocations: gardening, reading books, tennis, listening to music. Fax: 66 74 239243. E-mail: pprisana@ratree.psu.ac.th. Home: 37 Juthiuthis 4 Hadyai, Songkhla 90110, Thailand Office: Prince of Songkla U, Hadyai, Songkhla 90110, Thailand

PRISANT, L(OUIS) MICHAEL, cardiologist; b. Albany, Ga., Dec. 25, 1949; s. Bennie Martin and Mozelle (Cosper) P.; m. Rose Corinth Trincher, June 28, 1975; children: Michelle Elizabeth, Louis Michael. BA, Emory U., 1971; MD, Med. Coll. Ga., 1977. Diplomate Am. Bd. Internal Medicine, Am. Bd. Cardiovascular Diseases, Am. Bd. Geriatric Medicine, Am. Bd. Clin. Pharmacology, Am. Bd. Forensic Medicine, Nat. Bd. Med. Examiners, Am. Bd. Forensic Examiners, Am. Soc. Hypertension; cert. specialist in hypertension. Intern Med. Coll. Ga., Augusta, 1977-78; resident Med. Coll. Ga., 1978-80; chief med. resident, 1979-80; cardiology fellow Med. Coll. Ga., 1980-82, instr., 1982-83, asst. prof. medicine, 1983-89, assoc. prof. medicine, 1989-94, prof., 1994—, dir. cardiology fellowship tng. program, 1996, dir. hypertension unit, 1999; cons. in field; nat. and internat. lectr. in field. Contbr. over 111 abstracts and over 116 articles to profl. jours., 9 chpts. to books; author of 13 monographs; manuscript reviewer med. jours.; mem. editl. bd. Blood Pressure Monitoring, Am. Jour. Clin. Hypertension, Physicians and Computers, Heart Disease: Jour. Cardiovasc. Medicine, Am. Jour. Therapeutics. FOE grantee, 1989, Rorer, 1989, Am. Cyanamid, 1988, Sandoz, 1989-93, Merck, 1990-92, Squibb, 1991, Lorex, 1991, NIH, 1991, 96, Lederle, 1993, Ciba-Geigy, 1995, Omedha, 1997, Smith-Kline-Beecham, 1997, Apothecon, 1998, Bristol-Meyer-Squibb, 1998, Novartis, 1999, HDI, 2000, Searle, 2000. Fellow ACP, AMA (Physician's Recognition award 1982-02), Am. Coll. Cardiology, Am. Coll. Clin. Pharmacology, Am. Coll. Chest Physicians, Am. Coll. Forensic Examiners, Coun. Geriatric Cardiology; mem. AAUP, Internat. Soc. on Hypertension in Blacks, Am. Fedn. Clin. Rsch., Am. Heart Assn., Am. Soc. Echocardiography, Am. Soc. Hypertension, Am. Soc. Internal Medicine, So. Med. Assn., Ga. Heart Assn., Assn. for Advancement Med. Instrumentation, Ga. Med. Care Found., Med. Assn. Ga., Richmond County Med. Soc., Ahlquist Soc. (pres.), Phi Delta Epsilon, Alpha Phi Omega, Tau Epsilon Phi. Jewish. Avocation: computers. Office: Med Coll Ga Sect Cardiology BBR-6515A Augusta GA 30912-3105

PRISCHL, FRIEDRICH CORNELIUS, nephrologist; b. Wels, Austria, Dec. 12, 1956; s. Cornelius and Dorothea (Orth) P.; m. Renate Elisabeth Pöckl, July 8, 1978; children: Clemens, Sophie, Anna, Clara. MD, U. Vienna Med. Sch., 1982. Intern 1st Dept. Medicine U. Vienna, Austria, 1983-89; vis. scientist Nat. Tumor Inst., Milan, Italy, 1984; tng. in nephrology IIIrd Dept. Medicine Hosp. of Wels, Austria, 1990-91; resident, vice head dept. IIIrd Dept. Medicine Gen. Hosp. of Wels, Austria, 1989—; assoc. prof. Med. Sch. U. Vienna, 1998—. Contbr. articles to Circulation, Jour. Am. Soc. Nephrology, Brit. Jour. Hematology, Nephron, Nephrology Dialysis Transplantation, Leukemia and other profl. jours. Grantee Hochschuljubiläumsstiftung der Stadt Wien, Vienna, 1988, Kommission Onkologie, U. Vienna, 1989. Mem. Internat. Soc. Peritoneal Dialysis, Internat. Soc. Nephrology, Austrian Soc. Nephrology, European Dialysis Transplant Assn. Roman Catholic. Office: 3rd Dept Med Div Nephrology, Grieskirchnerstrasse 42, A-4600 Wels Austria

PRISCO, DOUGLAS LOUIS, physician; b. N.Y.C., Nov. 30, 1945; s. Frank James and Isabel (Gaetano) P.; m. Marianne Paula Mangano, Jan. 8, 1972; children: Jennifer Leigh, Douglas Louis, Dana Lauren, Andrew Michael. AB, Georgetown U., 1967; postgrad., NYU, 1967-68; MD, U. Rome, 1974. Diplomate Am. Bd. Internal Medicine, sub-bd. Pulmonary Diseases. Intern Mt. Sinai Svcs., Elmhurst, N.Y., 1974-75, resident in medicine, 1975-77, pulmonary medicine fellow, 1977-79; practice medicine specializing in pulmonary medicine N.Y.C., New Hyde Park, N.Y., 1979-81; clin. asst. in medicine Bklyn. Hosp., 1979-81; pulmonary cons. and admitting physician Booth Meml. Hosp. (now N.Y. Hosp. Med. Ctr. of Queens), Pkwy Hosp., Flushing Hosp. Med. Ctr.; admitting physician L.I. Jewish Hosp., New Hyde Park, Mt. Sinai of Queens, 1999—; chief pulmonary medicine Deepdale Gen. Hosp., 1980-93; clin. asst. Mt. Sinai Sch. Medicine, N.Y.C., 1977-79; physician adviser St. Barnabas Hosp., 1981-82; pres. Met. Pulmonary Assocs., P.C., 1980—, Met. Pulmonary P.C., 1985—; v.p. network devel. Parkway Hosp., 1997—; physician adv. to Queens County Profl. Standards Rev. Orgn., 1979-85; co-chmn. quality assurance com. downstate region Island peer Rev. Orgn., 1990—, vice chmn. pro-tem regional quality assurance com., N.Y., 1993—; bd. dirs. Queens County Profl. Standards Rev. Orgn., 1984-85, Fresh Meadows Med. Care, med. dir., 1997; chief pulmonary diseases Little Neck Cmty. Hosp. (formerly Deepdale Ge n. Hosp.), 1980-93, pulmonary chief, med. dir., 1993-96; pres. Med. Staff Soc., 1992—, mem. med. bd., 1993—; mem., cons. Queens div. Island Peer Rev. Orgn., 1985—; dir. pulmonary svcs. Astoria Med. Group, 1999—; dir. Fresh Meadows Care, 1997. Mem. Rep. Senatorial Inner Cir., 1990. Fellow Am. Coll. Chest Physicians; mem. ACP, Am. Lung Assn. Queens (bd. dirs. 1988—, honoree 1997), Queens County Med. Soc., Port Washington Yacht Club (former chmn. jr. activities 1987-88, fleet surgeon 1991-93, 95-97, bd.d irs. 1995-97), Capitol Hill Club, Integrated Delivery Systems of N.Y. (vice chmn., chmn. 1995-97). Roman Catholic. Address: 3003 New Hyde Park Rd Ste 203 New Hyde Park NY 11042-1214

PRISCO, FRANK J., psychotherapist; b. N.Y.C.; s. Frank J. and Isabel (Gatano) P.; m. August Frances; children: Frank, Christian, Meredith. BS in History, NYU, 1964, MA in History and Psychology, 1972, PsyD in Psychoanalysis, 1980. Diplomate Am. Psychotherapy Assn., Am. Bd. Psychol. Specialties of Am. Coll. Forensic Examiners; cert. psychoanalyst, cert. med. hypnotherapist. Cons., staff therapist Creedmore Psychiat. Ctr.; faculty Psychoanalytic Inst., L.I.; pvt. practice Ctr. for Modern Psychoanalytic Studies; instr. psychology N.Y.C. Bd. Edn.; trainer of trainers Conflict Mgrs. Program, N.Y.C.; discussion leader Gt. Books Found. Eucharistic min. Cath. Ch.; group leader Great Books Found. Recipient Soc. of Emil award. Mem. AAAS, Am. Psychol. Soc., Am. Assn. Guidance and Counseling, N.Y. Acad. Scis., Nat. Assn. Advancement Psychoanalysis, Am. Poetry Assn. (Poet Merit award 1988-90), Soc. Modern Psychoanalysis.

PŘISTOUPIL, TOMÁŠ IVAN, retired biochemist; b. Ústí, Bohemia, Czechoslovakia, Mar. 7, 1928; s. Vladislav and Marie (Divecká) P.; m. Kamila Skurovcová, Apr. 23, 1952; children: Jana, Olga, Ivo. Rerum Naturalium Doctor diploma, Charles U., Prague, Czechoslovakia, 1952; Candidate Chem. Scis. diploma, Masaryk U., Brno, Czechoslovakia, 1959. Analytical biochemist Inst. Hematology and Blood Transfusion, Prague, 1952-54, biochem. rschr. blood substitutes and new analytical micromethods, 1955-67, leading rschr., 1968-90; prof. assoc. U. Nancy, France, 1992; now ret.; mem. organizing com. Fedn. European Biochem Socs. Congress, Prague, 1968. Co-author: (with K. Přistoupilová) Role of Folates in Metabolic Pathways, 1997, Homocysteine, Vitamins, 1999, Hyperhomocysteinemia, S-Adenosylmethionine, 2000; contbr. articles to profl. jours. Mem. Internat. Soc. on Artificial Cells (internat. com. blood substitutes and immobilization tech.), Czech Biochem. Soc., N.Y. Acad. Scis., Nat. Geog. Soc. Avocations: translations, painting, music, gardening, tourism. Home: Na Hřebenkách 19, 150 00 Prague 5, Czech Republic

PRITCHARD, CLAUDIUS HORNBY, JR., retired university president; b. Charleston, W.Va., June 28, 1927; s. Claudius Hornby and Katherine (Ellison) P.; m. Marjorie Walker Pullen, Aug. 9, 1952; children: Virginia Aiken, Katherine Winston, Olivia Reynolds, Claudius V. BA, Hampden-Sydney Coll., 1950; MA, Longwood Coll., 1965; PhD, Fla. State U., 1971. Comml. loan teller Am. Nat. Bank and Trust Co., Danville, Va., 1950-53; asst. cashier Planters Bank & Trust Co., Farmville, Va., 1953-55; asst. to pres. Hampden-Sydney (Va.) Coll., 1955-57, bus. mgr. and treas., 1957-67, v.p. devel., 1967-71; sr. budget analyst-edn. State of Fla., Tallahassee, 1971-72; pres. Sullins Coll., Bristol, Va., 1972-76; v.p. adminstrn. Maryville U., St. Louis, 1976-77, pres., 1977-92, pres. emeritus, 1992—; adv. dir. Commerce Bank of St. Louis, 1982-92. Author: Col. D. Wyatt Aiken (1828-1887) South Carolina's Militant Agrarian, 1970; contbr. articles to profl. jours. Bd. dirs. West St. Louis County YMCA, Chesterfield, Mo., 1985-92; bd. visitors Charleston So. Univ., 1993—. Served with USNR, 1945-46. Fla. State U. fellow, 1969-70, Arthur Vining Davis fellow Am. Council on Edn., 1974. Mem. AAUP, SCV, Am. Assn. Higher Edn., So. Hist. Assn., S.C. Hist. Soc., Mo. Colls. Fund (bd. dirs., chmn. 1987-88), Mil. Order of the Stars and Bars, Ind. Colls. and Univs. Mo., Chesterfield C. of C. (pres. 1987, Chesterfield Citizen of Yr. award 1986), Rotary. Republican. Presbyterian.

PRITCHARD, COLIN, social work educator; b. Bradford, Yorkshire, Eng., Feb. 24, 1936; s. Sydney William and Doris (Barraclough) P.; m. Beryl Harrison, Sept. 15, 1962; children: Rebecca Anne, Claire Elizabeth. Postgrad. Diploma, U. Manchester, Eng., 1965; MA, U. Bradford, Eng., 1970; PhD, U. Southampton, Eng., 1996. Psychiat. social worker West Riding, Eng., 1960-65; sr. prin. psychiat. social worker, 1965-70; lectr. U. Leeds, 1970-76; sr. lectr. U. Bath., Eng., 1976-80; found. chair social work U. Southampton, 1980—; rsch. coord. JVC, London, 1976-80, chmn. SWEC Joint U. Coun. London, 1980-87; mem. CCETSW, London, 1982-87; mem. Southampton Health Authority, 1980-87. Author: Social Work, Reform and Revolution, 1978, Social Work and Adolescence, 1980, The Protest Makers - Anti-Nuclear Movement 1968-78, 1982, Suicide - The Ultimate Rejection, 1995, King David: War and Ecstasy, 2000, others; contbr. articles to profl. jours. and publs. Avocations: squash, family, friends, fell walking. Office: Mental Health, Royal Southampton Hosp, SO 14 099 Southampton England

PRITCHARD, IORWERTH GWYNN, broadcasting executive; b. Ffynnongroew, Wales, Feb. 1, 1946; s. Islwyn and Megan Mair (Lloyd) P.; m. Marilyn Patricia Bartholomew, Oct. 17, 1970 (dec. Nov. 1994); children: Matthew, Nia, Dafydd; m. Althea Sharp, Dec. 18, 1998. MA, King's Coll., Cambridge, 1968. Producer/dir. BBC TV, London, 1969-78; producer/dir. BBC Wales, Cardiff, 1979-82, head of programmes, 1992-97; producer/dir. HTV Wales, Cardiff, 1982-85; commissioning editor Channel 4, London, 1985-88, sr. commissioning editor, 1989-92; head of Welsh broadcast BBC Wales, Cardiff, 1997—; trustee Broadcast Support Svcs., U.K., 1989-92, Nat. Inst. for Adult and Continuing Edn., U.K., 1989-92; U.K. bd. mem. INPUT/Internat. TV Conf., 1988-94, pres. 1992-93. Fellow Winston Churchill Meml. Trust, 1973, Hugh Weldon Broadcasting fellow, U. Bangor, 1990-91, Chevalier de L'Ordre des Arts et Des Lettres, French Govt., 1990. Mem. Brit. Acad. Film and TV Arts, Royal TV Soc., Welsh Writers Trust (trustee 1990—). Avocations: swimming, walking, cinema, reading. Office: BBC Wales, Broadcasting House, Cardiff CF52YQ, Wales

PRITCHARD, JAMES PATRICK, investment company executive; b. Buffalo, Mar. 2, 1960; s. Thomas Stanley and Marylou (Titus) P.; m. Jenny Margaret Howell, Aug. 23, 1986; children: James, Katherine, Laura. BA in Econ., Columbia U., 1982. CFP. Stockbroker Smith Barney, Scottsdale, Ariz., 1982-85; owner Pritchard Investment Mgmt., Durango, Colo., 1986—; CEO, founder Fundsearch.net, 1999, MyPortfolioPlanner.com, 2000, BuildYourOwn401K.com, 2000, iSharesAdvisor.com, 2000. Author: Every Boys Dream, 1998, The Gods, 1998; performer Durango Snowdown Follies, 1999, 2000; pub.: Advantages of Indexing, 2000. Bd. dirs. Medina Meml. Hosp., 1988-93; v.p., bd. dirs. Medina Healthcare Found., 1990-93; pres. Chapman Hill Improvements Assn., Durango, 1993-98. Named to Kenmore East H.S. Athletic Hall of Fame, 1996. Avocations: writing, coaching football, handball, ice hockey, acting. Fax: (970) 259-8909. E-mail: jim@pritchardinvestment.com. Office: Fundsearch 556 Main Ave Durango CO 81301-5439

PRITCHARD, PAUL WILLIAM, environmental management scientist, consultant; b. Northallerton, Yorkshire, Eng., Jan. 15, 1958; s. William Alfred and Dorothy (Sly) P.; m. Charlotte Dwyer, July 29, 1995; 1 child, Olivia Mary. BA in Chemistry, U. York, 1979; PhD in Environ. Chemistry, Newcastle (Eng.) Polytechnic, 1986. Rsch. asst. Newcastle Polytechnic and Northumbrian Water Authority, 1980-83; chemistry lectr. Newcastle Polytechnic, 1984; sect. mgr. water and environ. radiochemistry Lab. Govt. Chemist, London, 1985-88; group mgr. rsch., cons. Thomson Environ. Labs., London and Milton Keynes, 1988-90; prin. scientist environ. mgmt. svcs. Brown and Root Environ., Surrey, 1990-94; tech. dir. Ashdown Environ., Oxon, Eng., 1994-97; group environ. adv. Royal & Sun Alliance, London, 1997—. Author: Managing Environmental Risks and Liabilities, 1992, Environmental Risk Management, 2000; contbr. articles to profl. jours.; inventor device for in-situ remediation of contaminated land. Mem. Royal Soc. Chemistry, Environ. Auditors Registration Assn., Inst. Environ. Scis., Inst. Occupational Safety and Health. Anglican. Avocations: soccer, cricket, Anglo-Saxon history. Home: 3 Millstream Mews, Stanstead Abbotts Herts SG12 8HG, England Office: Royal & Sun Alliance, 30 Berkeley Sq, London W1X 5HA, England

PRITCHARD, ROBERT JEROME, resort owner, retired; b. Mpls., June 8, 1930; s. Raymond James and Eva Ellen (DyBerg) P.; m. Marlys Jeanette Anderson, Sept. 9, 1950; children: Randy, Pamela, Penny, Reed. M Photography. Owner Pritchard Photography, Mpls., 1954-66, Clearwater (Minn.) Forest Resort, 1965-93; cons. SCORE, St. Cloud, Minn., 1980-85; bd. dirs. Coral Harbor, Islamorada, Fla. Author: Minnesota Lake Atlas, 1963, Minnesota Hunting and Fishing Atlas, 1964. Assoc. Royal Photog. Soc. Great Britain. Republican. Avocation: fishing. Winter Home: 88181 Old Hwy Islamorada FL 33036-3068 Summer Home: 8098 Channel View Rd Nisswa MN 56468

PRITCHATT, DIANE JOY, librarian; b. Birmingham, England, May 27, 1960; d. Dennis Harold and Millicent (Davis) P. BLS with honors, U. Loughborough, 1982. Libr. Microelectronics Edn. Program, Newcastle upon Tyne, 1983, Price Waterhouse Office of Local Govt Svcs., Birmingham, 1983-86; info. officer Nat. Coun. for Ednl. Tech., Coventry, 1986-90; libr. Midland Ctr. for Neurosurgery and Neurology, Smethwick, 1990-96; resources mgmt. libr. U. Hosp. Queen Elizabeth Hosp., 1996-98; resources mgr. libr. Queen Elizabeth Hosp. Libr., 1998—; chair Midland Ctr. for Neurosurgery and Neurology Joint Staff Cons. Com., 1993-95. Contbr. articles to profl. jours. Avocations: writing, swimming, gardening, cats, dressmaking and tailoring. Office: Queen Elizabeth Neurosci Med Ctr, U Hosp Birmingham, NHS Trust/Queen Eliz Hosp, Birmingham B15 2TH, England

PRITIKIN, JAMES B., lawyer, employee benefits consultant; b. Chgo., Feb. 18, 1939; s. Stan and Anne (Schwartz) P.; m. Barbara Cheryl Demovsky, Apr. 20, 1968 (dec. 1988); children: Gregory, David, Randi; m. Mary Szatkowski, July 7, 1990; 1 child, Peyton. BS, U. Ill., 1961; JD, DePaul U., 1965. Bar: Ill. 1965, U.S. Dist. Ct. (no. dist.) Ill. 1965, U.S. Supreme Ct. 1985; cert. matrimonial arbitrator. Pvt. practice, Chgo., 1965-68, 1984—; ptnr. Sudak, Grubman, Pritikin, Rosenthal & Feldman, Chgo., 1969-80, Pritikin & Sohn, Chgo., 1980-84, Nadler, Pritikin & Mirabelli, Chgo., 1997—; pres. Prepaid Benefits Plans Inc., Chgo., 1978—; exec. dir. The Ctr. for Divorce Mediation Ltd. Fellow Internat. Acad. Matrimonial Lawyers, Am. Acad. Matrimonial Lawyers (pres.-elect); mem. ABA, Am. Acad. Matrimonial Lawyers (pres. Ill. chpt.), Ill. Bar Assn., Chgo. Bar Assn. (cir. ct. Cook County liaison com.), Chgo. Pub. Schs. Alumni Assn. (v.p. 1984—). Office: 1 Prudential Plz 130 E Randolph Dr Chicago IL 60601-6207

PRITTS, KIM DEREK, state conservation officer, writer; b. Connellsville, Pa., Nov. 18, 1953; s. Harold Blaine and Janet Lorraine (Roth) P.; m. Rosanne Pritts; children: David, Brent, Kelly. BS, Pa. State U., 1978. Cert. mcpl. police tng.; cert. conservation officer. Police officer Royersford (Pa.) Police Dept., 1978-81; state conservation officer Pa. Fish and Boat Commn., Lancaster, 1981—; competition judge Ethnic Minorities Screenwriting Competition, L.A., 1992-97; cons., expert Am. Ginseng. Author: The Mystery of Sadler Marsh, 1993, Ginseng: How to Find, Grow, and Use America's Forest Gold, 1995; author: (screenplay) Outlander (Christopher Columbus Discovery award), 1994. Mem. D.U.I. Coun. of Lancaster County. Cpl. USMC, 1972-74. Finalist, Am.'s Best Writing competition The Writers Found., 1994, 95. Mem. Conservation Officers of Pa., N.Am. Wildlife Enforcement Officers Assn., Pa. Sportsmen for the Disabled (Outstanding Svc. award 1992), Phila. Ind. Film Assn. Mem. Ch. of God. Avocations: hiking, photography.

PRITULA, IGOR MICHAYLOVICH, physicist, researcher; b. Volgograd, USSR, Oct. 8, 1959; s. Mikhail Martynovich and Valentina (Fedorovna) Pritula; m. Elena Leonidovna Kolybaeva, Aug. 2, 1991; children: Vladislav, Evgeniya. MSc, Kharkov State U., USSR, 1981; PhD in Math. and Physics, Nat. Acad. Scis. Ukraine, Kharkov, 1992. Cert. physicist. Engr. Inst. Low Temperature Physics & Engring. Nat. Acad. Scis., Kharkov, 1981-84, rsch. scientist, 1984-93; sr. rsch. scientist, advisor Inst. Single Crystals, Kharkov, 1993-99. Contbr. articles to profl. jours. Grantee Sci. and Tech. Ctr. Ukraine, 1997. Mem. Ukrainian Phys. Soc. Avocations: tourism, photography, music. Fax: 101-707-598-1346. Home: 10 Elizarova Str. Apt 53, 61098 Kharkov Ukraine Office: Inst Single Crystals, 60 Lenin Ave, 61001 Kharkov Ukraine

PRITZKER, ANDREAS EUGEN MAX, physicist, administrator, author; b. Baden, Aargau, Switzerland, Dec. 4, 1945; s. Boris and Alice (Kamer) P.; m. Marthi L. Ehrlich, 1970 (dec. 1998). PhD, Swiss Fed. Inst. Tech., Zurich, Switzerland, 1974. Scientist ETH, Zurich, 1970-75, Alusuisse, Zurich, 1975-77; cons. Motor Columbus, Baden, 1977-80; scientist Swiss Inst. Nuc. Rsch., Villigen, 1980-83; asst. to pres. Bd. ETH, Zurich, 1983-87; head logistics and mktg. Paul Scherrer Inst., Villigen, 1988—. Author: Filberts Undoing, 1990, End of Delusion, 1993, Catch Up With Time, 2000, also several short stories; contbr. articles to profl. jours. Mem. Swiss Writers Assn., Swiss PEN Ctr., Am. Phys. Soc. E-mail: apritzker@bluewin.ch.

PRITZKER, ROBERT ALAN, manufacturing company executive; b. Chgo., June 30, 1926; s. Abram Nicholas and Fanny (Doppelt) P.; m. Mayari Sargent; children: James, Linda, Karen, Matthew , Liesel. B.S. in Indsl. Engring., Ill. Inst. Tech., Chgo., 1946; postgrad. in bus. adminstrn., U. Ill. Engaged in mfg., 1946—; chief exec. officer, pres., dir. Marmon Corp., Chgo., Marmon Indsl. Corp., Chgo.; pres., dir. The Colson Group, Inc.; pres., CEO Marmon Holdings, Inc., Marmon Industries, Inc., Chgo.; bd. dirs. Hyatt Corp., Chgo., Dalfort Corp., Union Tank Car Co.; vis. prof. Oxford U.; chmn. Nat. Assn. Mfrs. Chmn. bd. Pritzker Found., Chgo.; trustee, chmn. Ill. Inst. Tech., Chgo. Symphony Orch.; immediate past chmn. Field Mus. of Natural History; bd. dirs. Rush-Presbyn.-St. Luke's Med. Ctr. Mem. NAE, Nat. Assn. Mfrs. (former chmn.). Office: Marmon Group Inc 225 W Washington St Ste 1900 Chicago IL 60606-3511

PRIVALOVA, IRINA, Olympic athlete. Winner Gold medal 400 meter hurdles Sydney, 2000. Office: All-Russia Athletic Found, Luzhnetskaya Nab 8, Moscow 119871, Russia*

PRIZZI, JACK ANTHONY, investment banking executive; b. Rochester, N.Y., July 5, 1935; s. Samuel Anthony and Mary Ann (Emanuele) P.; m. Geraldine A. Bias, Feb. 16, 1957 (div. 1971); children: Lynne Marie, Michael Vincent, Karen Annette; m. Serafina M. Iacono, Sept. 30, 1995. BS in Chemistry, Va. Mil. Inst., 1956; MS in Phys. Chemistry, U. Va., 1961, MBA, 1963. Chem. engr. E.I. duPont DeNemours & Co., Inc., Niagara Falls, N.Y., 1956-57; engr. Project Mercury, NASA, 1959; mgr. planning and devel. PPG Industries, Pitts., 1963-68; gen. mgr. Process Components Inc., Norfolk, Va., 1968-70; ptrn. Alan Patricof Assocs., N.Y.C., 1970-74, Beacon Ptnrs., N.Y.C., 1974-76, 77-79, Stuart Bros., N.Y.C., 1976-77; v.p. Walter E. Heller & Co.; exec. v.p. Heller Capital Svcs. Inc., N.Y.C., 1979-84; sr. v.p. DnC Am. Banking Corp., N.Y.C., 1984-86; mng. dir. DnC Capital Corp., 1986-89; pres., CEO Jack A. Prizzi & Co., 1989-98; founder, mng. prin. CoE Assocs., L.L.C., N.Y.C., 1998—; spl. ltd. ptnr. Harvest Ptnrs., 1993-97; bd. dirs. The Meridian Resource Corp.; instr. advanced grades N.Y. Power Squadron. Vol. Urban Cons. Group. Capt. U.S. Army, 1958-59. Grantee Office Naval Rsch., 1960, Calif. Rsch. Corp., 1960-61. Mem. Assn. for Corp. Growth, Am. Chem. Soc., Raven Soc., N.Y. Athletic Club. Office: CoE Assocs LLC 156 W 56th St Ste 1400 New York NY 10019-3800

PROBASCO, DALE RICHARD, management consultant; b. Ogden, Utah, July 23, 1946; s. Robert Vere and Dorleen E. (Oppliger) P.; m. Joan Michele Takacs, Dec. 20, 1969 (div.); children: Todd Aaron, Brad Dillon; m. Vivian Jean Bennett, May 21, 1998. BS, Utah State U., 1975; MS, U. Phoenix, 1988. Inventory asst. Moore Bus. Form, Logan, Utah, 1973-75; systems engr. Electronic Data Systems, Dallas, 1975-76; start-up engr. Bechtel Corp., San Francisco, 1976-78; supr. project scheduling Toledo Edison Co., 1978-80; mgr. project controls Utah Power and Light Co., Salt Lake City, 1980-87, mgr. mktg. strategy, 1987-89; pres. Probasco Cons., Inc., West Jordan, Utah, 1989-90; prin. Navigant Cons., Inc., Deerfield, Ill., 1990—. Contbr. articles to profl. publs. Pres. Emery County Little League, Castledale, Utah, 1981-84; coach Little League Baseball, West Jordan, Utah, 1985-86. With USN, 1965-72. Mem. Am. Pub. Power Assn., Nat. Rural Electric Coop. Assn. Lutheran. Avocations: computer programming, softball, basketball, music.

PROBERT, EDWARD WHITFORD, foundation executive, volunteer; b. Orange, N.J., May 27, 1936; s. George Ernest and Ethel Loring (Whitford) P.; m. Ann Schuyler Linen, July 2, 1960; children: Edward Whitford Jr., Leslie P. Sirbaugh, David Linen. BA, Yale U., 1958; LLB, U. Va., 1961. With Morgan Guaranty Trust Co. of N.Y., N.Y.C., 1961-88, v.p., 1970-88; v.p. Fannie E. Rippel Found., Annandale, N.J., 1988-93; pres. Fannie E. Rippel Found., Basking Ridge, N.J., 1994-95; pres., CEO Fannie E. Rippel Found., Basking Ridge, 1996—; sec. Intersearch Inst., Inc., Annandale, N.J., 1989-93; bd. advisors Whitehead Inst. for Biomed. Rsch., Cambridge, Mass., 1996—. Co-chmn. capital campaign Jersey Battered Women's Svc., Morris Plains, N.J., 1996-99; governing bd. solicitor capital campaign Morristown (N.J.) Meml. Hosp., 1996—; mem. Wilks Fund com. St. Peter's Episcopal Ch., Morristown, 1999—. Mem. Royal Dornoch Golf Club, Mountain Lake Club, Morristown Club and Morristown Field Club, Somerset Hills C.C. (bd. govs., golf chmn. 1981-90). Republican. Episcopalian. Avocations: golf, swimming, scuba diving, reading, singing.. Home: Miller Rd New Vernon NJ 07976 Office: Fannie E Rippel Found 180 Mount Airy Rd Ste 200 Basking Ridge NJ 07920-2021

PROBERT, ERIC DAVID, editor, researcher; b. Birmingham, England, Mar. 22, 1939; s. Gilbert Ambrose and Winifred (Buck) P.; m. Jane Ann Reeves, Sept. 16, 1961; children: Clare Stacey Jane, Nigel Charles. BSc with honors, U. Birmingham, 1960; diploma in mgmt., Anglia Poltech. Univ., Chelmsford, U.K., 1968; cert. in genealogy, Univ. of London, 1993. Design engr. Marconi Co. Ltd., Chelmsford, 1960-66; deputy head of elec. Greater London Coun., London, 1966-75, engring. mgr., 1975-86; divsn. engr. Inner London Edn. Authority, London, 1986-90; owner Family History Rsch. Ctr., Chelmsford, 1990—. Author: Company and Business Records for Family Historians, 1994; contbr. articles to profl. jours. Fellow IEE, Soc. Genealogists; mem. Chelmsford Folk Dancers. Avocations: tennis, English folk dancing, world war II aviation. Home and Office: 62 Sidmouth Rd, CM1 6LS Chelmsford United Kingdom

PROBST, MICHEL, physiotherapist; b. Cologne, Germany, Jan. 30, 1954; s. Georges Probst and Jacqueline Sabbe; m. Beatrice Haine, July 10, 1982; children: Steven, Kristiaan, Thomas. MA in Physiotherapy, Cath. U. Louvain, Belgium, 1978, postgrad. in psychomotor therapy, 1979, postgrad. in relaxation therapy, 1982, PhD in Rehab., 1997. Body-oriented therapist in eating disorder unit Univ. Ctr., Kortenberg, Belgium, 1979—; assoc. prof. Cath. U. Louvain, 1998—. Home: Treuveld 8, B-3080 Tervuren Belgium Office: Univ Ctr Sint Jozef, Leuvense Steenweg 517, B-3070 Kortenberg Belgium

PROBSTFIELD, JEFFREY LYNN, cardiology educator, consultant; b. Fargo, N.D., June 27, 1941; s. Margaret Helen (Belgum) P.; children: Erik, Kathryn, Cindy, Dawn, Shannon, Laura. BA, Pacific Luth. U., Tacoma, Wash., 1963; MD, U. Washington Sch. Medicine, Seattle, 1967. Attending physician U. Minn. Hosps., Mpls., 1972-78; asst. prof. medicine Baylor Coll. Medicine, Houston, 1978-84; spl. expert clin. trials branch NHLBI, DECA, Bethesda, Md., 1984-88, med. officer clin. trials branch, 1988-92; clin. prof. medicine Uniformed Svcs. U. Health Scis., Bethesda, Md., 1991-93; cons. physician Fred Hutchinson Cancer Rsch. Ctr., Seattle, 1993—; prof. cardiology medicine U. Washington Sch. Medicine, Seattle, 1994—, dir. clin. trials svc. unit cardiology, 1995—. Contbr. articles to profl. jours. E-mail: jeffp@swog.fhcrc.org. Fax: 206-667-4408. Office: Fred Hutchinson Cancer Rsch Ctr 1100 Fairview Ave N # Mp557 Seattle WA 98109-4417

PROCACCINI, TERESA, composer, music educator; b. Cerignola, Foggia/Puglia, Italy, Mar. 23, 1934; d. Vittorio Procaccini and Maria De Tullio. Piano, V. Giordano Conservatory, Foggia, Italy, 1952; Organ, S. Cecilia Conservatory, Rome, 1957, Composition, 1958, Film Music master class, 1955-56; Composition master class, Accad. Mus. Chigiana, Siena, Italy,

1965. Tchr. organ and composition V. Giordano Conservatory, Foggia, 1959-74, dir., 1972-74; tchr. composition Refice Conservatory, Frosinone, Italy, 1974-78, S.Cecilia Conservatory, Rome, 1978—; tchr. composition master classes Festival delle Nazione, Citta de Castello, Italy, 1976-79, Accademia Mus. D. Respighi, Assissi, 1980-92, Internat. Meisterkursen, Duren, Germany, 1988, Estate Mus. Frentana, Lanciano, 1992-93; artistic dir. Amici della Musica, Foggia, 1972-98. Composer (ballet) La Bella Galiana, 1998, Chanson for soprano, 1998, Miserere mei Deus for orch., 1998, Mystère, 1998, Moments, 1998, Tre liriche for soprano and orch., 199, Tre pezzi facili, 1999, Trio for flute, cello, piano, 1999, La Levataccia for chorus, 1999, Serenata Notturna (Little Seranade), 1999, Moonlight for three guitars, 1999, Trio for clarinett, viola and piano, 1999, Guitargames, 1999, Promenade, 1999, Songs for soprano and quartet, 1999, Vocalizzo, 1999, Concerto Romantico for piano and symphonic band, 1999, numerous other ballets, choreographies, didactic music; operas include La Vendetta di Luzbel, 1970 (Prize for Lyric Opera Cassa Nazionale Assistenza Musicisti 1974), La Prima Notte, 1973, Questione di Fiducia, 1974. Recipient A. Casella prize Accademia Mus. Napoletana, 1970, prize Internat. Competition for String Quartet, 1981. Office: Conservatoria S Cecilia, Via dei Greci 18, Rome Italy

PROCHASKA, CHARLES ROLAND, aerospace engineer; b. Nampa, Idaho, Dec. 8, 1941; s. Roland William Anthony and Dorothy Helen (Harris) P.; m. Patricia Blessing Devlin, May 1, 1965 (div. May 1975); children: Roland Anthony, Meikle John, Peter Henry; m. Judith Diane Armstrong, May 16, 1975; stepchildren: Diane Elayne Petet (dec.), Gregg Andrew Petet. B. Aerospace Engring., U. Mich., 1965. Specialist engr. BCAC/BMS/BAC, Renton, Wash., 1965-79; sr. specialist engr. 767 div. Boeing Co., Everett, Wash., 1979-82; sr. specialist engr. Boeing Marine Systems, Renton, 1982-87; prin. engr. Sea Lance, Boeing Aerospace & Electronics, Kent, Wash., 1987-90; prin. engr. 777 div. Boeing Co. Cargo Systems, Renton, 1990-91; mgr. 777 divsn. Boeing Co. Cargo Furnishings, Everett, 1991-95, 777 divsn. Boeing Co. Insulation, Everett, 1994-95, Payloads, Boeing Co. Insulation-New Process, Everett, 1995-97; option mgmt. Boeing Co., Everett, 1997-98; mgr. Payloads, Boeing Co Emergency Equipment-Narrow Bodies, Everett, 1998-99, prin. engr. emergency equipment, 767 plane cabin interiors, 1999; prin. engr. Payload Concept Ctr., 1999—; master Deer Lagoon Grange, Langley, Wash., 2000—; asst. steward Island County Grange, Wash., 2000—; gen. chmn. 2d Aerospace Structures Design Conf., 1970. Scoutmaster troop 478 Boy Scouts Am., Auburn, Wash., 1983-91, cubmaster pack 478, 1980-83, round table commr. Green River dist., Seattle, 1981-84. Recipient Dist. Award of Merit, Chief Seattle coun. Boy Scouts Am., 1985. Mem. Seattle Profl. Engring. Employees Assn. (councilman 1967-72). Methodist. Achievements include patent for Locking Mechanism. Home: 3499 Smugglers Cove Rd Greenbank WA 98253-9764 Office: Boeing Co PO Box 3707 Seattle WA 98124-2207

PROCHÁZKA, ALES BEDRICH VACLAV, electrical engineer, researcher, educator; b. Prague, Czech Republic, Feb. 27, 1948; s. Emanuel and Marta (Čichová) P. MS, Czech Tech. U., Prague, 1971; PhD, Inst. Chem. Tech., Prague, 1983. Cert. engr. Lectr. Inst. Chem. Tech., Prague, 1971-74, sr. lectr., 1974-90; postdoctoral fellow U. Cambridge, Eng., 1987; assoc. prof. dept. computing and control engring. Inst. Chem. Tech., Prague, 1990-99, prof., 2000—, vice-dean Faculty of Chem. Engring., 1997—, head of dept. of computing and control engring., 1997—; mem. univ. sci. bd. Inst. Chem. Tech., Prague, 1990—, head of tech. sec., 1990-94, mem. acad. senate, 1990-94; mem. univ. exam. bd. Czech Tech. U., Prague, 1993—. Author: (textbook) Computing Methods, 1990; editor: Signal Analysis and Prediction, 1998; contbr. papers to profl. publs. and procs. Grantee TEMPUS/Phare/European Comty., 1991, 94, 98, Grant Agy. of Czech Republic, 1994-96. Mem. Signal Processing Soc. and Computer Soc. IEEE, European Assn. for Signal Processing, Nat. Geographic Soc., N.Y. Acad. Scis. Roman Catholic. Avocations: culture, theater, sports, skiing, traveling. Home: Starého 2168/11, 160 00 Prague 6, Czech Republic Office: Inst Chem Tech Dept Computing and Control Engring, Technická 1905, 166 28 Prague 6, Czech Republic

PROCHÁZKA, JAROSLAV, civil engineering educator, researcher; b. Prague, Czech Republic, May 21, 1934; s. Jaroslav and Ružena (Kratochvílová) P.; m. Jitka Duspivová, Aug. 12, 1967; 1 child, Eva Kulová. Grad. structural engr. with honors, Czech Tech. U., Prague, 1957, PhD, 1969. Design engr. Cons. Office Transport Engring., Prague, 1957-60, cons., 1961-63; asst. prof. civil engring. Czech Tech. U., 1964-88, assoc. prof., 1989-93, prof., 1994—, head divsn. concrete bldg. structures, 1995—; vis. prof. Poly. Milan, 1992, U. Wales Sch. Engring., Cardiff, 1994; chmn. Czech Standardization Com. for Concrete Structures, 1984—; head com. Design Concrete Structures; Czech Republic dep. to European Com. for Standardization, Brussels, 1993—; cons. engr. on design analysis and reconstrn. design of concrete structures. Author: (with L. Janda and V. Křístek) Slender Concrete Structures, 1983, Design of Concrete Structures, 1993, Concise Eurocode and Commentary for Design of Concrete Structures, 1995; co-author, editor: Design Examples of Concrete Structures, 1998, over 15 other textbooks on design of concrete structures; contbr. over 200 articles to tech. jours. and procs. Recipient award for outstanding concrete TV tower Soc. Civil Engrs. Czechoslovakia, 1976, medal for contbn. to new tech. Govt. of Czechoslovakia, 1987; Fulbright scholar U. Ill., Urbana-Champaign, 1990. Fellow Concrete Soc. U.K. (hon.); mem. Am. Concrete Inst. (liaison mem. com. 318 1992-98), Czech Chamber Cert. Engrs., Czech Concrete and Masonry Soc. (vice chmn. 1992—), European Assn. Concrete Socs. Achievements include research on non-linear analysis of concrete structures, slender reinforced columns, prefabricated reinforced concrete frames, design of two-way slabs. Avocations: travel, culture, philately. E-mail: proch@beton.fsv.cvut.cz. Home: Viktorinova 1, CZ-14000 Prague 4, Czech Republic Office: Czech Tech U Fac Civil Eng, Thákurova 7, CZ-16629 Prague 6, Czech Republic

PROCHAZKA, PETR PAVEL, structural mechanics educator; b. Prague, Czechoslovakia, May 29, 1945; s. Paul Hundertmark and Jirina Prochazkova; m. Ivana Linhartova, Jul. 31, 1968 (div. 1979); children: Ivana, Katerina, Eva, Michal. MS, Czech Tech. Univ., Prague, 1968, PhD, 1975; Dr.rer.nat., Charles Univ., Prague, 1976; DS, Czech Tech. Univ., Prague, 1990. From asst. prof. to prof. Czech Tech. Univ., Prague, 1968—; chief analyst Metroprojekt, Prague, 1972-79; head of dept. CAD Cons. Inst. Capital, Prague, 1979-89; prin. sci. officer Acad. Sci. Czech Republic, Prague, 1989-92; prof. Czech Tech. Univ., Prague, 1993—; cons. exec. APPIS, Prague, 1990—; vis. prof. RPI, Troy, N.Y., 1992-93. Author: Be Technology, 1987, 95, Slope Stability, 1993. Recipient rsch. grants. Mem. AMS, Internat. Assoc. Computational Mechs. & Applied Geotechnics, Acad. Sci. Czech Republic. Roman Catholic. Avocations: tennis, volleyball. Home: Kladenská 560/28, 160 00 Prague 6 Czech Republic Office: Czech Tech Univ, Thakurova 7, 16629 Prague Czech Republic

PROCHÁZKA, STANISLAV, plant physiologist, educator; b. Střílky, Czechoslovakia, Nov. 25, 1940; m. Jiřina Maternová, 1963; children: Dagmar, Petra. Engr., U. Agriculture, Brno, Czechoslovakia, 1963, DSc, 1984. Asst. U. Agriculture, Brno, 1965-78, assoc. prof., 1978-85, prof., 1985—, vice-rector, 1985-86, rector, 1986-91, 2000—. Co-author: (book) Experimental Plant Morphology, 1983, 2nd edit., 1992; contbr. articles to sci. jours. Mem. Fedn. European Socs. of Plant Physiology (pres. 1992-94), European Soc. New Methods in Agrl. Rsch. (v.p. 1988—), Soc. Exptl. Biology Czech Republic (chmn. 1992—), Bot. Soc. Am. Office: Mendel U of Agriculture, and Forestry, Zemědělská 1, 61300 Brno Czech Republic

PROCOS, COSTAS, paper company executive; b. Athens, Attiki, Greece, Apr. 20, 1968; s. Evaguelos and Triantafillia (Thravalou) P. Ptychion, U. Athens, 1991; MA, Yale U., 1992, MPhil, 1993. Exec. v.p. E. J. Procos S.A., Infonita, Greece, 1994—. Home: 48 Karaoli Dimitriou St, 145 65 Agios Stefanos Attiki, Greece Office: E J Procos SA, Infonita 320 11, Greece

PROCTOR, MILLICENT CARLÉ, social worker; b. Chgo., Mar. 9, 1944; d. Harry and Erene (Merriweather) Vinée; m. Donald Proctor (div. 1972); m. James Smith (dec. 1995). BA in Polit. Sci. and History, U. Ill.; MSW, Loyola U.; PhD, 1986. Cert. social worker, Ill.; master addiction counselor. Caseworker, case work supr. Cook County (Ill.) Dept. Pub. Aid; social work supr. dept. children and family svcs. State of Ill.; exec. dir. Adler Adoption Agy., Chgo.; dir. pub. health social svc. Chgo. Dept. Health, coord. mental health info. and edn. Contbr. articles to profl. jours. Active women's bd. Wesley Hosp., materials mgmt. vol. Mem. Am. Pub. Health Assn., Chgo. Child Care Soc., Ill. Child Care Soc., Ill. Psychiat. Assn., Blind Assn. Ill., Acad. Cert. Social Workers, Am. Psychologists Assn., Nat. Assn. Forensic Counselors. Office: Adler Adoption Agy 25 E Washington St Ste 1500 Chicago IL 60602-1804

PROCTOR, WILLIAM LEE, college president; b. Atlanta, Jan. 27, 1933; s. Samuel Cook and Rose Elizabeth (Nottingham) P.; m. Pamela Evans Duke; children: Samuel Matthews (dec.), Priscilla Nottingham. BS, Fla. State U., 1956, MS, 1964, PhD, 1968. Tchr. Seminole County Pub. Schs., Longwood, Fla., 1956-57, 58-62, Orange County Fla. Pub. Schs., Orlando, Fla., 1957-58; athletic coach Fla. State U., Tallahassee, 1962-65, asst. dean men, 1965-67, grad. fellow, 1967-68; supt. of schs. Rock Hill (S.C.) Sch. Dist. #3, 1968-69; dean of men U. Ctrl. Fla., Orlando, 1969-71; pres. Flagler Coll., St. Augustine, Fla., 1971—; cons. on higher edn. policy Heritage Found., Washington, 1983—; mem. Commn. on Colls., So. Assn. Colls. and Schs., 1995—; dir. Tchr. Edn. Accreditation Coun. Vice-chmn. Fla. Edn. Stds. Commn., 1995—; bd. dirs. Flagler Health Svcs., Inc., St. Augustine, 1977-95, Penney Farms Retirement Cmty., chmn., 1991—; bd. dirs. Vicar's Landing Retirement Cmty., pres., 1992-95, bd., 1990-96; trustee, chmn. Fla. Sch. for Deaf and Blind, St. Augustine, 1984—; mem. adv. coun. Salvation Army, St. Johns County; mem. devel. coun. First Coast Work Force, 1998—. Recipient Disting. Educator award Fla. State U. Coll. Edn., 1989, Phil Carrol award Soc. for Advancement Mgmt., 1990, Disting. Svc. award Fla. Sch. for Deaf and Blind, 1990, Patrick Henry Medallion patriotic achievement Mil. Order of World Wars, 1991, Stetson S Club Achievement award, 1993, Order of the South So. Acad. Letters, Arts, and Scis., Excellence in Mgmt. award Soc. for Advancement of Mgmt., 2000; named to Fla. State U. Athletic Hall of Fame, 1988. Mem. Am. Assn. Pres. of Ind. Colls., State Hist. Assn., Ind. Colls. and Univs. of Fla. (legis. chmn. 1974-77, vice chmn. 1976-77, chmn. 1978-79), Rotary (pres. 1978-79, govs. dist. 697 1988-89). Republican. Presbyterian. Avocations: history, jogging, karate. Office: Flagler Coll Office of the Pres PO Box 1027 Saint Augustine FL 32085-1027

PRODAN, AUGUSTIN, educator; b. Var-Jibou, Romania, Feb. 4, 1945; s. Gheorghe and Amalia (Munteanu) P.; m. Rodica Burdea, Feb. 13, 1971. D in Math., U. Babes-Bolyai, Romania, 1988. Rschr. Software ITC Inst., Cluj-Napoca, Romania, 1968-71, rschr. degree 3, 1971-88, rschr. degree 2, 1988-91, rschr. degree 1, 1991-95; prof. Juliu Hatieganu U., Cluj-Napoca, Romania, 1995—. Author: Microsoft Office 95, 1996, JAVA Environment for Internet, 1997, Microsoft Office 97, 1998. Recipient award 80 Years of Med. and Pharm. Edn. in Transylvania, 1999. Mem. DECUS Europe. Avocations: trips, gardening, basketry, swimming, reading. Home: Str N Titulescu 14/76, 3400 Cluj-Napoca Romania Office: Juliu Hatieganu U, Str Emil Isac 13, 3400 Cluj-Napoca Romania

PRODI, ROMANO, economist, educator, former prime minister of Italy; b. Scandiano, Reggio Emilia, Italy, Aug. 9, 1939; married; 2 children. Degree in econs. and commerce, Cath. U. Milan, Italy, 1961. Prof. indsl. econs. and policy Dept. Polit. Sci. U. Bologna; dir. Ctr. for Econ. and Indsl. Policy; pres. sci. com. Nomisma, Bologna, 1978-79; minister for industry Govt. of Italy, 1978; pres. Inst. Indusl. Reconstrn., 1982-89, 93-94; mem. Council for Italo-Am. Relations, 1983—; prime min. Govt. of Italy, Rome, 1996-98; pres. European Commn., 1999—. Home: Via Gerusalemme 7, I-40125 Bologna Italy Office: European Commn, 200 rue Loi/Wetstraat 200, B-1049 Brussels Belgium*

PROENÇA, DOMÍCIO, JR., strategic studies educator, consultant; b. Rio de Janeiro, May 3, 1960; s. Domicio Proença Filho and Maria Luiza Ribeiro de Carvalho. Degree in engring., U. Fed. Rio de Janeiro, 1984; MS, Grad. Engring. Ctr./U. Fed. Rio de Janeiro, 1987, PhD, 1994. Prof., pres. strategic studies Grad. Engring. Ctr. U. Fed. Rio de Janeiro (COPPE), 1987—, chmn. group for strategic studies, 1991—; speaker Army Staff Sch., Nat. War Coll., Brazil, Chamber of Reps., Brazil, 1994—, strategy and force planning, Naval War Coll., 1998—; chmn. Arms Industry Symposia, Brazil, 1992-94; researcher N.Am. Studies Ctr./Candido Mendes Univ., Rio de Janeiro, 1995—; cons. Rio Strategic Plan, Rio de Janeiro, 1995—, Navy Staff, Army Gen. Staff, Air Force Gen. Staff, Strategic Affairs Secretariat; mem. Rio de Janeiro State Gov.'s Blue Panel on Pub. Security, 1999; project mgr. Mil. Engring. Inst., 1997. Author/editor: Brazilian Arms Industry, 1993, Brazilian Arms Industry: Essays, 1994, Brazil's Defence Policy, 1998, Guide for the Study of Strategy, 1998, 99; contbr. articles to profl. jours. Mem. Computer Game Developers Assn., Internat. Peace Rsch. Assn., Internat. Inst. Strategic Studies. Avocations: wargaming, science fiction, Sherlock Holmes, cooking, fine cigars. Office: U Fed Rio de Janeiro, Group for Strategic Studies, 68507 Rio de Janeiro 21945947, Brazil

PROFFITT, JOHN RICHARD, business executive, educator; b. Grand Junction, Colo., Sept. 12, 1930; s. Hillus D. and Joy Elaine (Lindsay) P.; m. Claire Boyer Miller, May 8, 1965 (div. 1992); children: Cameron Lindsay, William Boyer. BA in Edn., U. Ky., 1953, MA in Polit. Sci., 1961; postgrad., U. Mich., 1959-65. Asst. dean of men, instr. polit. sci. dept. U. Ky., Lexington, 1957-59; teaching fellow U. Mich., Ann Arbor, 1961-63, 63-65; asst. dir. Nat. Commn. on Accrediting, Washington, 1966-68; dir. accreditation and eligibility staff U.S. Dept. HEW, Washington, 1968-75; dir. divsn. eligibility and agy. evaluation U.S. Dept. Edn., Washington, 1975-80, dir. divsn. instnl. and state incentive programs, 1980-82; pres. The Clairion Corp., Bethesda, Md., 1982-84, Nat. Asbestos Removal, Inc., Beltsville, Md., 1985-90; pres. Commonwealth Environ. Svcs., Inc., Alexandria, Va., 1987-91, also chmn. bd. dirs.; chmn. Internat. Environ. Engrs., Inc., Alexandria, Va., 1991-92; pres. Canterbury Internat., Vienna, Va., 1992-95; cons., 1995-99; v.p. E-Pass Techs., Inc., McLean, Va., 1999—; cons. Conn. State Commn. Higher Edn., Hartford, 1967, Am. Coun. Edn., Washington, 1970; cons. U.S. Dept. Hew, 1967, 68; mem. study steering com. Am. Vocat. Assn., Washington, 1968; exec. sec. Nat. Adv. Com. on Accreditation and Instnl. Eligibility, Washington, 1968-80; mem. gen. com. Nat. Study Sch. evaluation, Alexandria, 1970-78; mem. task force Edn. Commn. of the States, Denver, 1972; subcom. chmn. Fed. Interagy. Com. on Edn., Washington, 1974-76; lectr., presenter profl. confs. Co-author: Accreditation and Certification in Relation to Allied Health Manpower, 1971; contbg. author: Health Manpower: Adapting in the Seventies, 1971, Accreditation in Teacher Education, 1975, Transferring Experiential Credit, 1979; contbr. articles to profl. and govtl. agy. publs., 1968-79. v.p., bd. dirs. Nat. Accreditation Coun. for Agys. Serving the Blind, N.Y.C., 1985; pres., chmn. bd. dirs. Found. for Advancement of Quality Svcs. for the Blind, Alexandria, 1988. 1st lt. USAF, 1953-55, Japan and Korea. Higher edn. fellow Univ. Mich., 1959. Mem. Club Internat. (Chgo.), Island Club (Hobe Sound, Fla.), Thoroughbred Club Am. (Lexington, Ky.), Tower Club (Vienna, Va.), Sigma Nu. Democrat. Episcopalian. Avocations: conservation, animal welfare, travel, antiques, art. Home: 515 Beall Ave Rockville MD 20850-2106

PROFFITT, MICHAEL HERRY, atmospheric scientist; b. Long Beach, Calif., July 2, 1942; s. Wade Leroy and Bertie (Herry) P.; Sept. 1967 (div. Oct. 1984); children: Daniel Wade, Monica Claire; m. Cynthia Mariel De Chana, July 16, 1988; children: Victoria Mariel, Sofia Maria. BA, U. Tex., 1964, MA, 1966, PhD, 1968. Asst. prof. math. SUNY, New Paltz, 1968-71, assoc. prof. math., 1971-72; rsch. scientist physics dept. U. Tex., Austin, 1979-80, Robert A. Welch fellow in chemistry, 1972-76, Robert A. Welch fellow in physics, 1977-79; rsch. assoc./CIRES U. Colo., Boulder, 1980-98; sr. sci. officer World Meteorol. Orgn., Geneva, Switzerland, 1999—. Contbr. more than 100 articles to profl. jours., including Nature and Sci. Jour. Mem. Am. Geophys. Union, Internat. Soc. Optical Engring., Sigma Xi. Achievements include identification of significant ozone loss surrounding Antarctic ozone hole and within Artic vortex from high altitude aircraft data; demonstration that polar ozone loss occurs in mid to early winter, which is earlier than previously believed; responsible for world-wide coordination of ground-based ozone measurements within the Global Atmosphere Watch Network. Office: World Meteorol Orgn AREP, 7 bis Ave de la Paix, 1211 Geneva 2, Switzerland

PROFILLIDIS, VASSILIOS ARISTIDIS, educator; b. N. Petritsi, Greece, Aug. 31, 1957; s. Aristidis L. and Sofia G. (Akritidis) P. BSin Civil Engring., U. Thessaloniki, Greece, 1980; MS, PhD, Ecole Nat. Ponts Chaussées, Paris, 1983; BS in Law and Polit. Sci., U. Thessaloniki, 1987. Advisor Ministry Pub. Works, Athens, Greece, 1991-93; participant rsch. projects European Commn., Brussels, 1991-2000; advisor Ministry Transp., Athens, 1995-96; prof. Democritus U., Xanthi, Greece, 1990-2000; vis. prof. U. Macedonia, Thessaloniki, 1995-99. Author: Transport Economics, 1993, Railway Engineering, 1995, 2000; editor: Modernisation of Airway and Railway Transport, 1995, 2d edit., 2000; contbr. sci. papers to profl. publs. With Greek Corps Engrs., 1996-97. Rsch. fellow Ecole Nat. Ponts Chaussées, 1981-84. Office: Democritus U, Univ Campus, 67100 Xanthi Greece

PROFIT, VERA BARBARA, German language and literature educator; b. Vienna, Austria; came to U.S., 1957; d. Franz Johann and Edith E. (Kratochwil) P. Student, Inst. European Studies, Paris, 1965-66; BA in French and German, Alverno Coll., 1967; postgrad., U. Vienna, 1968-69; MA in Comparative Lit., U. Rochester, 1969, PhD in Comparative Lit., 1974. Instr. St. Olaf Coll., Northfield, Minn., 1974-75; asst. prof. U. Notre Dame, Ind., 1975-81, assoc. prof., 1981-96, prof., 1996—; vis. scholar Harvard U., Cambridge, Mass., 1979-80, Northwestern U., Evanston, Ill., 1984; lectr. in field. Author: Interpretations of Iwan Goll's Late Poetry with a Comprehensive and Annotated Bibliography of the Writings by and about Iwan Goll, 1977, Ein Porträt meiner Selbst: Karl Krolow's Autobiographical Poems (1945-58) and Their French Sources, 1991, Menschlich: Gespräche mit Karl Krolow, 1996. Avocations: photography, alpine hiking. Office: U Notre Dame Dept German Russian Notre Dame IN 46635

PROIETTI, TOMMASO, educator; b. Rome, June 6, 1964; s. Aldo and Maria Concetta (Canepone) P.; m. Angela Lisanti; children: Giulia. BSc in Econs., U. Perugia, 1988; MSc in Stats., London Sch. Econs., 1991; PhD in statistics, Univ. London, 1999. Rschr. U. Perugia, Italy, 1990-98; prof. Univ. Udine, 1998—. Author: (with others) Research on Economic Inequality, 1995; rschr. in field; contbr. articles to profl. jours. Mem. Soc. Italiana di Statistica, Internat. Statis. Assn., Internat. Inst. Forecasters. Home: Via Petarca 16, 33100 Udine Italy Office: Dept di Science Statistiche, Via Treppo 18, 33100 Udine Italy

PROKEŠ, JAROSLAV, toxicologist, educator; b. Praha, Czechoslovakia, Feb. 25, 1930; s. Jaroslav and Anna (Vopěnková) P.; m. Milena Kubánková, Jan. 10, 1953; children: Michal, Tomáš. M Pharmacy, Masaryk U., Brno, Czechoslovakia, 1953; CSc/PhD, Charles U., Praha, 1961, MD, 1965; DSc, Czech Acad. Scis., Hradec Králové, 1992. Indsl. rschr. VCHZ Rybitví (Czechoslovakia)/East Bohemian Chem. Works, 1953-54; rschr. KÚF/Pharm. Controll Inst., Praha, 1954-66; sr. lectr. U. Sci. and Tech., Kumasi, Ghana, 1966-69; assoc. prof. Inst. Toxicology, Charles U., Praha, 1969—, dir., 1990-92. Author: Introduction to Toxicology, 1990; editor, co-author: Principles of Toxicology, 1993, Principles of Toxicology I, 1997, Principles of Toxicology II, 1998. Recipient award Ministry Edn., Praha, 1994. Mem. Internat. Union Pure & Applied Chemistry, Czech Nat. Com. for Chemistry, N.Y. Acad. Scis. Home: V Cibulkách 1, 150 00 Praha 5, Czech Republic Office: Charles U Inst Toxicology and Forensic Chem, Na Bojišti 3, 150 00 Praha 2 Czech Republic

PROKHORENKO, VICTORIA IVANOVNA, space mission situation analyst, researcher; b. Zaporojie, Ukraine, Aug. 12, 1935; d. Ivan Lukianovich and Maria Vasilievna (Naumenko) P.; m. Oleg Vasilievich Starovierov, 1957 (div. 1959). Grad. in Math., Moscow Lomonosov State U., 1957; PhD, Russian Acad. Scis., 1989. Engr. Industry Inst., Moscow, 1957-60; head math. group Ctrl. Inst. Mech. Engring., Moscow, 1960-68; sr. scientist Space Rsch. Inst., Russian Acad. Scis., Moscow, 1968—. Contbr. articles to profl. jours. Recipient Vet. of Labour medal Moscow Mcpl. Coun., 1989, N. Pilugin medal Space Sci. Fedn. Russia, 1989. Mem. Am. Geophysical Union. Avocation: ballroom dancing. E-mail: vprokhor@iki.rssi.ru. Home: Apt 193, Voroncovskie Prudy str 9, 117630 Moscow Russia

PROKHOROV, ALEXANDER OKTYABRINOVYCH, psychologist, educator, psychotherapist, researcher; b. Kazan, Russia, Jan. 6, 1948; s. Oktyabrin Vasilyevich and Anna Philippovna (Andreyeva) P.; m. Farida Akhmetovna Khisamova, Oct. 10, 1974; children: Dina Alexandrovna, Darya Alexandrovna. PhD in Psychology, St. Petersburg (Russia) U., 1981; psychotherapist, Psychoneurol. U., St. Petersburg, 1985; DSc in Psychology, U. St. Petersburg, 1992. Master of Sports, USSR, 1973. Asst. prof. Inst. Phys. Tng., Kazan, 1978-82, dean of faculty, 1982-86, pro-rector, 1986-88; head of dept. State Pedagogical U., Kazan, 1988—, prof. psychology, 1993—; psychologist USSR Combined Team, Kazan, 1982-88; scientific cons. Gymnasia 50, Kazan, 1992-96; scientific supr. postgrad. studies, Kazan State U., 1994—. Author numerous publs. including: Psychological Conditions and Their Displaying During the Studies, 1991, Psychological Conditions and Their Functions, 1994, Unsteady Psychical Conditions, 1997 (Russian laureate 1996), Psychology of Psychical Conditions, 1997 (Russian laureate 1997). Head of Runners' Club, Kazan, 1986—. Capt., Motorized Infantry. Grantee Russian Scientific Fund for the Humanities, 1995-97, Soros Found., 1997. Mem. Internat. Acad. Psychol. Scis. (academician) Internat. Acad. Pedagogical Scis. (academician), Baltic Pedagogical Acad. St. Petersburg (academician), N.Y. Acad. Scis., Petrovsk Acad. Arts and Scis., Acad. Natural Scis., Russian Soc. Psychologists, Profl. Psychoneurol. League, Specialized Bds. for Theses in Psychology adn Pedagogics. Avocations: marathons and supermarathons, bicycle tours, ski races. E-mail: Prokhora@KSPU.KSN.RU; Prokhora@KNET.RU. Home: Khalturin Str 11/10-57, 420032 Kazan Russia Office: Kazan State Pedagogical U, Mezhlauk Str 1, 420021 Kazan Russia

PROKHOROV, DMITRI VALENTINOVICH, mathematician; b. Saratov, Russia, Sept. 11, 1946; s. Valentin Ivanovich and Vera Nikolaevna (Temnova) P.; m. Valentina Ivanovna Teplova, Feb. 23, 1968; 1 child, Michael. Diploma, Saratov State U., Russia, 1968; Philos. Degree, Leningrad State U., Russia, 1974. Engr. Inst. of Geology, Saratov, 1968-69; asst. Saratov State U., 1969-71, assoc. prof., 1974-90, prof., head of sect. of math. analysis, 1990—; head of com. for testing secondary sch. tchrs., Ministry of Edn. of Saratov region govt., 1993-97; head of exam commn. Saratov Pedagogical H.S., 1985-98. Author: (book) Reachable Set methods in Extremal Problems for Univalent Functions, 1993; contbr. articles to profl. jours. Grantee Russian Fund for Basic Rsch., Russian Acad. of Scis., Moscow. Avocations: chess, fishing. Office: Saratov State U/Dept Math, Astrakhanskaya St 83, Saratov 410026, Russia

PROKHOROV, IGOR VASILIEVICH, mathematics educator; b. Dalnerechensk, Russia, Jan. 20, 1966; s. Vasili Vasilievich and Ludmila Nikolaevna Prokhorov; m. Tatyana Viktorovna Aleshina, Jan. 20, 1996; 1 child, Dmitry. M in Math. Sci., Far East U., Vladivostok, Russia, 1988; Candidate Physics and Math. Scis., Far East Br. Acad. Sci., Khabarovsk, Russia, 1995. Math. educator Inst. Applied Math., Far East Br. Acad. Scis., Vladivostok, 1988—, jr. rschr., 1988-92, sr. rschr., 1992—. Contbr. articles to profl. jours. Avocation: sports. E-mail: prh@iam-mail.febras.ru. Home: Apt 509, Kirova 64, 690068 Vladivostok Russia Office: Far East Br Acad Sci Math, Radio 7, 690041 Vladivostok Russia

PROKHOROV, IGOR YURIEVICH, physicist, researcher; b. Perm, Russia, Nov. 30, 1955; s. Yury Ivanovich and Bibisara Faskhutdinovna (Shamsutdinova) P.; m. Alla Nikolaevna Posokhina, Feb. 15, 1958; children: Svetlana, Olga. BSc, Donetsk (Ukraine) State U., 1978; PhD, Donetsk Phys. Tech. Inst., 1991. Engr. Donetsk Phys. Tech. Inst., 1978-87, scientist, 1987-99, sr. scientist, 1999—. Author: Weibull Modulaus and Hydrostatic Pressing of Ceramics, 1991; contbr. articles to profl. jours. Home: app 59, Kievskii prosp 55A, 83054 Donetsk Ukraine Office: Donetsk Phys Tech Inst, R Luxemburg St 72, 83114 Donetsk Ukraine

PROKOF'EVA-MIKHAILOVSKAJA, VALENTINA VLADIMIROVNA, astrophysicist, researcher; b. Leningrad, Russia, Apr. 21, 1929; d. Vladimir Konstantinovich Prokofiev and Lidia Eduardovna Mikhailovskaja; 1 child, Ksenia. Grad., Leningrad State U., 1953, PhD in Physics and Math., 1962, D Physics and Math., 1983. Candidate Crimean (Ukraine) Astrophys. Obs., 1953-56, sci. rschr., 1956-83, leading sci. rschr., 1983—. Author: Television Astronomy, 1974, 2d edit., 1983. Mem. Internat. Astron. Union, European Astron. Soc. Orthodox. Avocation: history. Home: P/O Nauchny 8-3, 98409 Crimea Ukraine Office: Crimean Astrophy Obs, P/O Nauchny, 98409 Crimea Ukraine

PROKOFIEV, ANDREI VASILIEVICH, physico-chemist, researcher; b. Leningrad, Russia, Aug. 20, 1960; s. Vasiliy Alexeevich and Margarita Petrovna (Krichevskaya) P.; m. Irina Mikhailovna Zelenkova, Mar. 13, 1987; 1 child, Mikhail. Diploma in Chemistry, U. St. Petersburg, Russia, 1982, PhD, 1993. Lic. chemist. Engr. Inst. Applied Chemistry, St. Petersburg, 1982-84; with Ioffe Inst., St. Petersburg, 1984-85, sr. rschr., 1985-88, 95—; sr. rschr. Phys. Inst. U. Frankfurt (Germany), 1999-2000. Contbr. articles to profl. jours. Grantee Internat. Sci. Found., Soros, 1993, Russian Basic Rsch. Found., Moscow, 1996. Avocations: Russian and world history. Fax: 812-515-67-47. Office: Ioffe Phys Tech Inst, 26 Polytechnicheskaya, 194021 Saint Petersburg Russia

PROKOFIEV, VLADIMIR VICTOROVICH, zoology educator, researcher; b. Alma-Ata, Kazakhstan, USSR, Feb. 18, 1958; s. Victor Aleeseevich Prokofiev and Mila Aleksandrovna (Andreeva) Prokofieva; m. Marina Lvovna Korneva, Feb. 8, 1980; 1 child, Ekaterina. Diploma in tech., Constrn. Coll., Pskov, Russia, 1978; diploma, U. Leningrad, Russia, 1987, PhD, 1995. Sr. scientist Marine Biology Inst. Russian Acad. Scis., Murmansk, 1987—; assoc. prof. Pskov State Pedagogical Inst., 1996—. Contbr. articles to profl. jours. Dep. Village Counsel, Dalnye Zelentsy Muzmanck Region, 1990-92. Mem. N.Y. Acad. Scis. Avocations: computers, fishing. Home: Grazhdanskaya str 7A apt 18, 180017 Pskov Russia Office: State Pedagog Inst Zoology, Lenin Sq 2, 180000 Pskov Russia

PROKOP, LUDWIG, sports medicine physician, physiologist; b. St. Pölten, Austria, Aug. 6, 1920; s. Ludwig and Elfriede (Worbs) P.; m. Erika Fleischmann, Aug. 11, 1955; children: Eva, Ilse, Klaus. MD, U. Breslau, Germany, 1944; U. Prof. Physiology, U. Vienna, Austria, 1959; PhD, U. Vienna, 1993, Dr. rer. nat., 1996. Asst. physician Hosp. Traumatology, Vienna, Austria, 1944-46; head medicine Dept. Inst. Phys. Edn. U. Vienna, 1946-74, dir. Inst. Sport Scis., 1974-90, dean Faculty Basic Scis., 1978-82; dir. Austrian Inst. Sportsmedicine, Vienna, 1969-92; dir. Sportambulance, Vienna, 1950-76, cons. Ministry for Edn., Vienna, 1954-70; mem. Med. Commn. IOC, Lausanne, Switzerland, 1967—. Author of 32 books in sportsmedicine, nutrition, sport-damages, sauna, wine age; contbr. more than 750 sci. articles to profl. jours. in 13 langs. Mem., pres., hon. pres. Internat. Fedn. Sportmedicine, Rome, Vienna, Rio de Janeiro, 1959-84; pres., hon. pres. Austrian Sauna Fedn., Vienna, 1972-96, Panathlon Internat., Vienna, 1970-94, Austrian Fedn. Sportsmedicine, Vienna, 1949—; mem. Internat. Olympic Com. med. com., 26th Olympic Games. Recipient Philipp-Noel-Baker prize UNESCO, Paris, 1977, Golden Cross of Hon. Rep. Austria, 1964, Cross of Hon. for Sci. and Rsch., 1979, Great Silver Sign of Hon., 1989, Golden Cross of Hon., City of Vienna, 1984; named hon. mem. of 5 European Med. Soc., 1975-87. Mem. N.Y. Acad. Scis., Austrian Olympic Com. Avocations: German and Austrian champion swimming, fencing, pentathlon. Home: Kolingasse 6/34, A-1090 Vienna A 1090, Austria Office: Inst Sportsciences, Auf der Schmelz 6, A-1150 Vienna Austria

PROKOP, OTTO, microbiologist; b. St. Pölten, Austria, Sept. 29, 1921; s. Lüdwig and Elfriede Worbs (Bachmayr) P.; m. Wilhelmine Katharina Karola Cohnen, May 23, 1953; children: Uta, Eberhard. Dr. med., U. Bonn, 1948; Dr. honoris causa, U. Szeged, Ungarn, 1983, U. Leipzig, 1984, Kitasato U., Tokyo, 1989. Asst. prof. U. Bonn, 1948-56; dir. Inst. of Legal Medicine Charité, Berlin, 1957-87; prof. hon. Teikyo U., Japan, 1988; commr., dir. Inst. of Legal Medicine, U. Leipzig, Germany, 1958-61, Inst. of Legal Medicine, U. Halle, Germany, 1959-61. Contbr. over 550 articles to profl. jours., 50 books. With German Wehrmacht, 1941-45. Mem. German Acad. of Scis., German Acad. of Leopoldina, Slovenian Acad., Academia Olimpica. Office: Inst Gerichtsmedizin, Hannoversche Str 6, 10115 Berlin Germany

PROKOPEC, MIROSLAV, anthropologist; b. Prague, Czech Republic, Aug. 6, 1923; s. František Prokopec and Marie (Pálová) Prokopcová; m. Marie Tesařová, July 20, 1965; 1 child, Hana. Student in anthropology, U. Coll. London, 1947-48; MA, Charles U., Prague, 1950, PhD, 1957, DSc, 1969. Asst. dept. anthropology Charles U., 1950-54; sci. worker Nat. Inst. Pub. Health, Prague, 1954-69, leading scientist, 1969-94; assoc. prof. Charles U., Prague, 1994; cons., 1994—; vis. curator South Australian Mus., Adelaide, 1974-75, 82, 90; external lectr. human biology House of Youth, Prague, 1973-90, pedagogical faculty Charles U., Prague, 1960-62, 87-90. Author: Tracing Man's Evolution, 1956, Antropologie, 1967, Physical and Mental Development of the Present Generation of Our Children, 1969 (Kabrhel prize 1969), Growth Surveys and Growth Surveillance in Czechoslovakia, 1989, (mus. exhibition) Descent of Man and Life Work of Dr. A. Hrdlička, 1959, 69, 88; mem. editorial bd. Annals Human Biology, 1973-98, Internat. Jour. Anthropology, 1987—. Recipient Dr. A. Hrdlička medal City of Humpolec, Czech Republic, 1959; Moravian Mus. rsch. fellow, 1969; grantee Indian Statis. Inst., 1964, Wenner-Gren Found. for Anthrop. Rsch., 1965, 68, 73, Australian Inst. of Aboriginal Studies, 1974-75, Smithsonian Instn., 1983, 92-93, 99. Mem. European Anthrop. Assn. (hon., council mem. 1982—), Internat. Assn. for Human Auxology (exec. com. 1979—), Czechoslovak Anthrop. Assn. (founder), Soc. for Study Human Biology, Am. Assn. Forensic Scis., N.Y. Acad. Sci. Avocation: photography. Home: Narcisova 2850, 10600 Prague 10, Czech Republic Office: Nat Inst Pub Health, šrobárova 48, 10042 Prague 10, Czech Republic

PROKOPOVICH, PIOTR, federal official. Past dep. prime minister Govt. of Belarus; chmn. bd Nat. Bank Rep. Belarus, Minsk. Office: Nat Bank Rep Belarus, 20 Skorina Ave, 220008 Minsk Belarus

PROMMERSBERGER, KLAUS HUBERT, mechanical engineer, researcher; b. Wuerzberg, Germany, Feb. 21, 1970; s. Hubert and Theresia (Foerg) P. MS in Engring., U. Karlsruhe, Germany, 1996. Rsch. scientist Inst. Thermal Turbomachinery, Karlsruhe, Germany, 1996—. Contbr. articles to profl. jours. Mem. VDI. Avocations: skiing, hiking, photography. Phone: 49-721 688909. Office: Inst Thermal Turbomachinery, Kaiserstr 12, 76128 Karlsruhe Germany

PRONIK, IRAIDA IVANOVNA, astrophysicist, researcher; b. Balashov, Saratov, USSR, Jan. 17, 1928; d. Ivan Jakovlevich and Nina Ivanovna (Kozlova) Nazarov; m. Vladimir Ivanovich Pronik, May 22, 1957; children: Olga, Ekaterina. Grad., U. Moscow, 1950, MSc, 1961; PhD, U. Bjurakan, Armenia, 1989. Jr. rschr. Crimean Obs., Simeis, USSR, 1950-61; rschr. Crimean Obs., Nauchny, USSR, 1961-75, sr. rschr., 1975-90, leading rschr., 1990—, chief sci. group, 1980—; Contbg. author: Astrophysical Investigation on Cosmic Station "Astron," 1994; contbr. articles to sci. jours., including Astrophys. Jour., Astronomy and Astrophysics. Mem. Internat. Astron. Union, European Astron. Soc. Avocations: badminton, swimming, walking. Office: Crimean Astrophys Obs, Settle, 334413 Nauchny Ukraine

PRONIN, ALEXANDER VASILYEVICH, immunologist, researcher; b. Moscow, Dec. 12, 1953; s. Vasiliy Alekseyevich and Anna Ivanovna (Kanaeyeva) P.; m. Svetlana Petrovna Zakharina, May 31, 1975 (div. Nov. 1995); children: Marina, Tanya; m. Anna Valentinovna Truschina, 1997. Grad. in biology, Moscow State U., 1976; Candidate Biol. Sci., Gamaleya Inst., Moscow, 1981, D Biol. Sci. in Immunology, 1991. Lab. asst. N.F. Gamaleya Inst. for Epidemiology and Microbiology, 1976-80, jr. rschr., 1980-84, sr. rschr., 1984-88, head lab., 1988—, chmn. coun. young scientists, 1984-87; gen. dir. Micro-plus Ltd., Moscow, 1991—. Author: Consequences of the Chernobyl Catastrophe, 1996, Handbook of Infectious Immunology, 1996; patentee for antiviral drug. Judge People's Ct., Moscow, 1981-84. Mem. Russian Soc. Immunologists. Orthodox. Avocation: classical philosophy. Home: Leningradskoye sch 122-92, 125445 Moscow Russia Office: NF Gamaleya Inst Epid-Micro, Gamaleya st 18, 123098 Moscow Russia

PROOS, LEMM ARTUR, pediatrician; b. Tartu, Estonia, Sept. 29, 1943; arrived in Sweden, 1944; s. Artur and Taimi Rhode (Kokamägi) P.; m. Anna-Karin Sjöström, June 14, 1975. Student, Brandeis U., 1965-66; MD, Karolinska Inst., Stockholm, 1971; DMSc, Uppsala (Sweden) U., 1992. Med. dir. Eglise Christ Zaire Swedish Baptist Mission, Zaire, 1971-74; pediatrician Swedish and Internat. Red Cross, Cambodia, 1981; med. coord. Uppsala U., Hanoi, Vietnam, 1983-85; pediatrician, rschr. dept. pediatrics Uppsala (Sweden) U., 1986—; pediatrician ctr. growth and devel. adopted children Children's Hosp. Uppsala U., 1996—; cons. World Health Orgn., Geneva. Contbr. articles to sci. jours. Mem. Swedish Med. Assn., Swedish Pediat. Assn. Office: Uppsala Univ, Dept Pediatrics, S-751 85 Uppsala Sweden

PROPATTO, JUAN CARLOS ALDO, bank executive, educator; b. Buenos Aires, Apr. 8, 1953; s. Juan Carlos and Dorina (Puppin) P.; m. Maria Elena Bosio, Jan. 9, 1982; children: Mercedes, Lucia, Juan Francisco. Degree in econs., U. Buenos Aires, 1975, degree in acctg., 1980. Prof. English Lenguas Vivas Inst., Buenos Aires, 1970; clk. Banco de la Nacion Argentina, Buenos Aires, 1972-75, programming and control profl., 1975-77, budget and costs analyst, 1977-83, head programming and budget area, 1983-87, chief head planning and mgmt. area, 1987-88, chief mgr. planning and mgmt. area, 1988-91, dept. gen. mgr. ops., 1991-92, dept. gen. mgr. mgmt. and sys. area, 1992-93, dir. gen. Madrid br., 1993-95, dept. gen. mgr. planning, mgmt. and sys. area, 1995—; chmn. Bd. Compensadora Electrónica S.A.; economist, expert in nat. accts. UN -CEPAL, Buenos Aires, 1987-92; dir. exec. bd. Argentina C. of C., 1993-95; cons. Nat. Account Dept., 1995—; prof. nat. accts. U. Buenos Aires, 1974-86, assoc. prof., 1986-89, assoc. prof. in charge chair, 1989-99, regular prof., 1999—, titular prof., 1986—, prof. Econ. Master Degree, 2000—, hon. mem. sci. commn., doctorate com. of faculty of econ. scis., 1997-99; regular prof. bus. Argentine U., Buenos Aires, 1986—; assoc. prof. Belgrano U., 1991-97, regular prof., 1997—; econ. cons. pvt. entitles Lorenzo Ezcurra Medrano S.A. and Assocs. Enterprises, Buenos Aires, 1980-87. Mem. Profl. Coun. Econs. Scis. Grads. (mem. com. 1977-78), Pub. Budget Assn., Argentine C. of C. (Spain, dir. exec. bd. dirs. 1993-95), Sci. Commn.-Doctorate Com. of Faculty of Econ. Scis. (hon. mem.). Avocations: reading, travel. Home fax: 1826-2536; office fax: 4347-6435. Home e-mail: jpropatto@ciudad.com.ar; office e-mail: propatto@bna.com.ar. Home: Beruti 3219 - 12a, 1425 Buenos Aires Argentina Office: Banco de la Nación Argentina, Bartolomé Mitre 326 3P Local 358, 1036 Buenos Aires Argentina

PROPOI, VYACHESLAV IVANOVICH, editor-in-chief, physicist, researcher; b. Moscow, Feb. 15, 1945; s. Ivan Mitrofanovich and Antonia Nikolaevna (Kaligina) P.; m. Marina Vasilievna Fomina, June 14, 1968; 1 child, Vladimir Vyacheslavovich. Degree in physics engr., Moscow Physics and Tech. Inst., 1969; candidate of scis., chemistry, Inst. Chem. Physics USSR Acad. Scis., 1981. Jr. rschr. Inst. Chem. Physics, USSR Acad. Scis., Moscow, 1969-81; sr. rschr. Sci. Coun. on Measurement Problems, Moscow, 1981-84; head of advanced tech. editorial office Mir Pub., Moscow, 1984-90, dep. editor-in-chief, 1990-92, editor-in-chief, 1992—. Contbr. articles to profl. jours. Avocations: traveling.

PROSE, JOHN LEE, health care administrator, management consultant; b. Portsmouth, Ohio, Nov. 22, 1955; s. Charles Julius and Margaret Mae (Koenig) P.; m. Gloria Jean Theye, Nov. 26, 1982 (div. Mar. 1989); m. Rita Florence Sclury, May 12, 1990. M of Secondary Edn. Adminstrn., Xavier U., 1981, M of Health and Hosp. Adminstrn., 1983. Dir. ops. Maple Knoll Village, Cin., 1983-85; exec. dir. Amasa Stone Ho., Cleve., 1985-87; gen. mgr. Canton (Ohio) Regency Retirement Cmty., 1987-90, Brighton Gardens, Virginia Beach, Va., 1990, Colonnades Retirement Cmty., Charlottesville, Va., 1991-96; exec. dir. Grandview Terrace Retirement Cmty., Sun City West, Ariz., 1996-97; mgmt. cons. Quest for Quality Consultants, Glendale, Ariz., 1997-99; v.p. Maple Knoll Village Mgmt., Cin., 1999—; mem. adv. bd. Jefferson Area Bd. on Aging, Charlottesville, 1991-96, U. Va. Aging and Rsch. Program, 1991-96; adj. faculty Xavier U. grad. program, 1983-85. Co-chmn. ann. art auction Rotary, Canton, Ohio, 1987-90; vol. Big Brother Assn., Cleve., 1985-87. Fellow Am. Coll. Health Care Adminstrs. (sec. Ohio chpt. 1986); mem. Am. Soc. Quality. Avocations: jogging, hist. rsch., reading, gardening. Office: Maple Knoll Village Cincinnati OH 45246

PROSINECKI, ROBERT, soccer player; b. Schwenningen, Germany, Jan. 12, 1969. Midfielder Red Star, 1987-91, Real Madrid, 1991-94, Real Oviedo, 1994-95, Barcelona, 1995-96, Sevilla, 1996-97, Croatia Zagreb Football Club, 1997-99; coach, capt. Croatia Zagreb FC, 1999—. Office: Croatian Football Fedn, Ilica 31, CRO-1000 Zagreb Croatia*

PROSIŃSKA-KIBLER, MARIA KRYSTYNA, physician, consultant; b. Równe, Wołyń, Poland; d. Mikołaj and Halina Czesława (Koreywo) P.; m. Wojciech Andrzej Kibler, Apr. 1964; 1 child, Tomasz. BSc in Medicine, Warsaw (Poland) Med. Acad., 1961, diploma physician, 1962; MD, Mil. Acad. Medicine, Warsaw, 1978. Cert. specialist in internal medicine I and II degree. Jr. physician Med. Acad. and Ctr. Postgrad. Study, Warsaw, 1961-63; asst. vol. dept. cardiology Ctr. Postgrad. Study, Warsaw, 1964-65; gen. practitioner Cmty. Health Svc., Warsaw, 1965-67; asst. sr. asst., lectr. Inst. Internal Medicine, Warsaw, 1968-77; sr. asst. Ambulance Svc. of Capital City of Warsaw, 1977-80; cons. physician Civil Svc. Commn., Nigeria, 1980-90; gen. practitioner Warsaw, 1990—; head ward on duty Inst. Internal Medicine, Warsaw, 1968-77, cons., 1968-77; cons., head med. depts. Tchg. Hosps., Nigeria, 1980-84; mem. coun., co-editor newspaper Profl. Students' Orgn., Acad. Medicine, 1955-62. Author: Dictionary of Abbreviations Used in Medicine and Cooperating Sciences, 1994; translator: Hypertension, 1997. Mem. Polish Red Cross, Warsaw, 1949—. Mem. Polish Soc. Cardiology, Polish-Nigerian Soc. (mem. coun. 1990—), Soc. 4-Continents. Roman Catholic. Avocations: music, theatre, books, skiing, travel.

PROSNITZ, DAVID J., unemployment cost control company executive; b. Newark, June 27, 1948; s. Henry Marcus and Elaine Esther (Hendricks) P.; m. Lori Kim, July 20, 1986; children: Joseph, Hannah, Miriam. BA, Clark U., 1970; MA, New Sch. Social Rsch., 1973; PhD, U. Chgo., 1978. Rsch. analyst Mayor's Office, Chgo., 1978-81; pres., owner Personnel Planners, Inc., Chgo., 1981—. Coach Am. Youth Soccer Orgn., Skokie, Ill., 1984-86; treas. Friday night group Anske Emet Synagogue, Chgo., 1986-88. Mem. Assn. Unemployment Tax Orgns. Republican. Jewish. Avocations: anthropology of religion, reading, basketball. Office: Personnel Planners Inc 913 W Van Buren St Ste 3A Chicago IL 60607-3528

PROSPERI, CARLOS HUGO, biologist, educator, researcher; b. Cordoba, Argentina, Nov. 29, 1954; s. Rinaldo Alberto and Elsa Angela (Sitano) P.; children: Mariana Elizabeth, Gabriela Mercedes. Bachelor, Monserrat Coll., 1972; Lic. in Philosophy, U. Cordoba, 1978, PhD in Biology, 1984. Rschr. Anctarctic Inst., Buenos Aires, 1978-79, Inst. Phylosophyc Anthropology, 1980-91, Autonomous U. Madrid, 1990-92; prof. U. Cordoba, 1988—; vis. prof. Queen's U., Kingston, Can., 1987; v.p. Can. Cultural Ctr., Cordoba, 1988—; rschr. Nat. Coun. Rsch., 1981—; vice head Dept. Botany, 1988-90; cons. Water Rsch. Jour., Gt. Britain, 1995—. Contbr. articles to profl. jours. Recipient Tchg. award U. Cordoba, 1993, 95. Mem. Argetinian Soc. Botany, Internat. Phycological Soc., N.Y. Acad. Scis. Roman Catholic. Avocations: scuba diving, classical music, militaria collections. E-mail: cprospe@impsat1.com.ar. Home: Velez Sarsfield 272, 5000 Cordoba Argentina Office: Univ Cordoba, Velez Sarsfield 299, 5000 Cordoba Argentina

PROSSER, JOHN MARTIN, architect, educator, urban design consultant; b. Wichita, Kans., Dec. 28, 1932; s. Francis Ware and Harriet Corinne (Osborne) P.; m. Judith Adams, Aug. 28, 1954 (dec. 1982); children: Thomas, Anne, Edward; m. Karen Ann Cleary, Dec. 30, 1983; 1 child, Jennifer. BArch, U. Kans., 1955; MArch, Carnegie Mellon U., 1961. Registered architect, Kans., Colo. Architect Robinson and Hissem, Wichita, 1954-56, Guirey, Srnka, and Arnold, Phoenix, 1961-62, James Sudler Assocs., Denver, 1962-68; ptnr., architect Nuzum, Prosser and Vetter, Boulder, 1969-73; from asst. prof. to prof. U. Colo., Boulder and Denver, 1968—, acting dean, 1980-84, dean, 1984; dir. environ. design U. Colo., Boulder, 1969-72, dir. urban design, 1972-85; cons. John M. Prosser Assocs., Boulder and Denver, 1974—; vis. prof. urban design Oxford Poly., Eng., 1979; vis. critic Carnegie Mellon U., U. N.Mex., Colo. Coll.; pres. Denver chpt. AIA, 1983; prin. investigator Fitsimmons-U. Colo. Health Scis. City Rsch. Study, 1997-99. Author, narrator PBS TV documentary Cities Are For Kids, Too, 1984; prin. works include (with others) hist. redesign Mus. Western Art, Denver (design honor 1984), Vila Italia, Lakewood, Colo., Denver, Auraria Higher Edn. Ctr., Pueblo C.C. campus plan and new acad. facilities, comprehensive campus plan Denver U., Ft. Lewis Coll., Westminster Golf Course Cmty., Denver Botanic Gardens 20-Yr. Concept Plan, Colo. Coll. Historic Preservation Plan, Buffalo Hills Ranch Golf Course Cmty., Fountain Valley Sch., Regional Urban Design and Campus Planning. Bd. dirs. Denver Parks and Recreation Bd., 1987-93, 96—; chmn. design rev. bd. univs. Colo., Boulder, Denver, Aurora, and Colorado Springs, 1981—; mem. archtl. control com. Denver Tech. Ctr., 1984—, Meridian Internat. Bus. Ctr., 1984—, DTC West, 1991—, Denver Internat. Bus. Ctr., 1993—, Nat. Renewable Energy Lab., 1995—, Buffalo Hills Ranch, 1996—; planning cons. Denver Internat. Airport Environs. Devel. Projects, Fitzsimons $5 Billion Redevel. Capt. USAF, 1956-59. Co-recipient 2d place nat. award Am. Soc. Interior Designers, 1984, honor award Colo. Soc. Architects, 1984. Mem. Urban Land Inst., Denver Country Club (bd. dirs. 1984-88, pres. 1986-87). Democrat. Avocation: Arlberg ski. Home: 1620 Monaco Pky Denver CO 80220-1643 Office: U Colo 1200 Larimer St Denver CO 80204-5310

PROSSER, SIR IAN M.G., financial executive; b. July 5, 1943; s. Maurice and Freda Prosser; m. Elizabeth Herman, 1964; 2 children. BComm, Birmingham U. With Coopers & Lybrand, 1964-69, Bass Charrington Ltd. (later Bass PLC), London, 1969—; group mng. dir. Bass PLC, London, 1984-87, vice chmn., 1982-87, chmn., CEO, 1987—, chmn. bd. dirs.; dir. Boots Co., Lloyds Bank; chmn. Stock Exch. Listed Cos. Adv. Com., 1992—. Mem. Brewers and Lic. Retailers Assn. (dir. 1983—), Royal Automobile Club. Avocations: bridge, gardening. Office: Bass Plc, 20 N Audley St, London W1Y 1WE, England*

PROSSINGER, HERMANN RANDALL, physics and computer science educator; b. Salzburg, Austria, Nov. 30, 1948; s. Hermann Anton and Romana (Hochleitner) P.; m. Cynthia Ruth Bearse, Nov. 14, 1978; 1 child, Violetta. DS, U. Vienna, Austria, 1976. Tchr. asst. Inst. Theoretical Physics U. Vienna, 1975-76; secondary sch. tchr. Krems, Austria, 1976-77; tchr. Am. Internat. Sch., Vienna, 1977—; rschr. Argonne (Ill.) Nat. Lab., 1979, Warburg Inst., London, 1982, Nat. Hist. Mus., Vienna, 1985-96, Inst. Human Biology, U. Vienna, 1996—. Contbr. articles to profl. jours., chpts. to books. Osterreichische Nat. Bank grantee, 1999. Mem. Austrian Phys. Soc. Home: Esterhazygasse 11A/19, A-1060 Vienna Austria

PROST-A-LA-DENISE, BERNARD M., financial controller, industrial economist; b. Lyon, France, July 4, 1940; s. Gustave and Lucienne Agnes (Blanc) Prost-a-la-D.; m. Monique Hoffmann, Sept. 11, 1972; 1 child, Maxime. Degree in mgmt., fin., politics and economy, U. Lyon, 1963, 66, U. Lausanne, Switzerland, 1968; IHESI, Paris, 1995. Chief tech. adviser Ministry of France, Abidian, 1968-73; head fin. and econs. Rubber's Industry Assn., Paris, 1977-83; chief tech. adviser World Bank, Abidian, 1983-85; fin. mgr. Bourgeois, Morbier, 1985-87; chief tech. adviser UNIDO, Kinshasa, Zaire, 1987-88; indsl. coord. mgr. IPS, Abidian, 1988-89; sec. gen. Bourgeois SA, Morbier, 1989-91; fin. contr. ICPO/Interpol, Lyon, 1991—; indsl. economist cons., 1985—. Contbr. articles to profl. publs. Decorated Caveliere dell'Ordine al Merito della Republica Italiana, Rome, 1972. Mem. Polit. Economy Soc. Lyon, French Profl. Orgn. Internal Auditors. Avocations: reading, walking, biking. Home: 1 Boulevard des Belges, 69006 Lyon France

PROT, BAUDOUIN, financial company executive. MBA, Hautes Etudes Commls., 1972; MPA, Ecole Nat. d'Adminstrn., 1976. With Inspection Générale Fins., 1976-80; dep. head energy and raw materials Ministry Industry, 1980-83; exec. v.p. Banque Nat. Paris, 1983-92, dep. mng. dir., 1992—, pres., COO, 1996—; pres., COO, exec. dir. BNP PARIBAS, exec. mem., 2000; bd. dirs. Banque Nat. Paris, Banque Nat. Paris Intercontinental, Cetelem, Cofinoga, Compagnie Immobilière France, Pechiney, Petrofigaz; chmn. supervisory bd. Meunier Promotion; mem. supervisory bd. Accor, Pinault-Printemps-Redoute. Decorated Knight of the Nat. Order of Merit, 1996, Knight of the Legion of Honour, 2000. Office: BNP Paribas Group, 16 Bldg des Italiens, 75009 Paris France

PROTHEROE, ALAN HACKFORD, communications executive; b. St. David's, Wales, Jan. 10, 1934; s. Baden Powell and Rose Christina (Hackford) P.; m. Anne Miller, Aug. 18, 1956 (dec. May 1999); children: Christopher, Michael. Grad., The Grammar Sch., Glamorgan, Wales. Reporter The Glamorgan Gazette, Wales, 1951-53; reporter BBC, Wales, 1957-59, indsl. correspondent, 1959-64, editor news and pub. affairs, 1964-70; asst. editor TV network news BBC, London, 1970-72, dep. editor TV news, 1972-77, editor, 1977-80, asst. dir. news and pub. affairs, 1980-82, asst. dir. gen., 1982-87; mng. dir. Svcs. Sound and Vision Corp., Bucks, England, 1987-93; dir. Visnews Internat. Film Agy., 1982-87; lectr. Mil. Staff Colls., Univs., etc. on media, pub. affairs, terrorism; chmn. Europac Group, Chaltec Ltd. Contbr. articles to newspapers, profl. jours. Mem. Mission for Reorganization for Greek TV, 1973; mem. Directing Coun. European Broadcasting Union News Group, 1977-87; chmn. East Wessex Res. Forces, 1991-99; hon. cons. Royal Brit. Legion; dep. lt. Buckinghamshire. 2d lt. Welch Regiment, 1954, col. UK Res. Army. Decorated CBE, TD. Fellow British Inst. Mgmt.; mem. Inst. Pub. Rels., Assn. of British Editors (founder 1984, chmn. 1987), The Royal United Svcs. Inst. (Coun. for Defense Studies 1984-87), Army & Navy Club. Avocations: photography, golf, wine. Home: Amberleigh House, Chapman Ln Flackwell Heath, HP10 9BD Bucks England Office: SSVC Sound & Vision Corp, Narcott Ln, Gerrards Cross SL9 8TN Bucks England

PROTHRO, EDWIN TERRY, psychologist educator; b. Robeline, La., Dec. 11, 1919; Edwin Thomas and Frances Lillian (Terry) P.; m. Dorothy Kenworthy, Apr. 26, 1943 (div. 1967); children: Martha Carol Wells, Edwin Terry Jr.; m. Najla Salman, July 31, 1968; 1 child, Gwendolyn. PhD, La. State U., 1942. Asst. prof. psychology La. State U., Baton Rouge, 1946-49; assoc. prof. psychology U. Tenn., Knoxville, 1949-51; prof. psychology Am. U. Beirut, Lebanon, 1951-85; prof. emeritus, 1994—; fellow Ctr. for Middle East Studies Harvard U., Cambridge, Mass., 1960; dean, provost Am. U. Beirut, Lebanon, 1965-73; dep. dir. Edn. Abroad Program U. Calif., Sant Barbara, 1975-77; v.p. Hariri Found., Washington, 1986-97; cons. Middle East Office Ford Found., Beirut, 1973-75; mem. bd. trustee Am. Community Sch., Beirut, 1970-73; mem. edit. bd. Jour. Social Psychology, 1955-70. Co-author: Psychology: A Biosocial Study of Behavior, 1950, 72; Changing Family Patterns in the Arab East, 1974; contbr. articles to profl. jours. Lt. USNR, 1943-46, WWII. Recipient Order of the Cedars Rep. Lebanon, 1969; Nat. Inst. Mental Health grantee, 1966-70, fellow 1963, 64. Mem. Am. Psychology Soc., La. Psychology Assn. (pres. 1949), Sigma Xi (pres. Beirut chpt. 1955).

PROTO, ARACELI NOEMI, physicist; b. Buenos Aires, Jan. 4, 1944; s. Eusebio Proto and Noemi (Concepcion) Bermolen; divorced; 1 child, Silvana Mabel Otero. Lic., Nat. U. Buenos Aires, 1967; PhD, Nat. U. La Plata, 1974. Asst. physicist dept. physics Comision Nacional de Energia Atómica, Buenos Aires, 1969-73, assoc. physicist, 1973-78, physicist, 1978-86; prin. researcher Comision Investigaciones Cientificas de la Prov Buenos Aires, 1987—; mem. faculty Sch. Physics, U. Buenos Aires, 1966-69; invited prof. Latin Am. Sch. Concrete Tech., La Plata, Argentina, 1980; prof. Sch. Exact Sci. Nat. U. Centro, 1978-85, U. Lujan, 1985-91; gen. sec. Commn. Sci. Investigations Buenos AiresState, 1983-85, v.p. 1985-87; cons. Commn. Nat. Investigaciones Espaciales, 1987-89, Commn. Nat. Actindacles Espaciales, 1998—; dir. Tech. Rsch. Ctr. Nat. Tech. U., 1988-89; cons. R&D Buenos Aires State Congress, 1991—; mem. internat. adv. comn. Internat. Workshop on Condensed Matter Theories, 1991; dir. workshop Indsl. Math. 1988, Adriatico Rsch. Conf. Info. Theory in Classical and Quantum Mechanics, 1995; chairwoman workshop Condensed Matter Theories, 1992, workshop Dyanamics of Social and Econ. Systems, 1998; chairwoman satelite conf. Staphys 17 9, Cataratas del Iguazu 7-10 de Agosto de, 1989. Editor: Nonlinear Phenomena in Complex Systems, 1989, Condensed Matter Theories, Vol. 7, 1992, Proceedings of the Workship on Dynamics of Social and Economic Systems, 1999; contbr. articles to profl. jours. Fellow Latin Am. Physics Ctr., 1968, 84, Comision Nacional de Energia Atomica, 1969, Internat. Ctr. for Theoretical Physics, Spring Coll. on Order and Chaos, 1986, Second Workshop on Math. for Industry, 1987; recipient Teofilo Isnardi Prize, Nat. Acad. Scis., 1975; rsch. grantee Rsch. Com. State Buenos Aires, 1981-86, CONICET, 1982-91, 91-93, Internat. Centre Theoretical Physics, 1987. Mem. Internat. Ctr. for Theoretical Physics (assoc. mem. 1988-93, sr. assoc. 1998-03), Sociedad Cientifica Argentina, Am. Phys. Soc., Assn. Bonaerense de Cientificos (pres. 1997-98, 99—). Home: Gral Paz 1106 11A, 1429 Buenos Aires Argentina Office: Group Complex Systems UBA, DD 15-Suc 1, 1640 Martinez Argentina

PROTOGENOV, ALEXANDER PAVLOVICH, physicist, researcher; b. Vilnus, Lithuania, May 25, 1946; s. Pavel Sergeevich and Mariya Alexandrovna (Shirokova) P.; m. Tat'yana Vadimovna Shtin, Sept. 7, 1976 (div.

Oct. 1978); children: Iliya, Liza; m. Galina Markovna Shmerelson, May 14, 1993. BS in Physics, State U Gorky, Russia, 1968, MA in Physics, 1969, PhD in Physics, 1972, 99. Cert. physicist-rschr. Lectr. Phys. Soc. Znanie, Gorky, 1969-72; rsch. fellow Radio Phys. Rsch. Inst., Gorky, 1972-77, Inst. Applied Physics, Gorky, 1977; assoc. prof. Poly. Inst., Gorky, 1977-92; sr. rschr. Inst. Applied Physics, Nizhny Novgorod, Russia, 1992—; vis. scientist Engring. & Phys. Inst., Moscow, 1981; invited lectr. Inst. Solid State Physics, Chernogolovka, 1991; vis. scientist ICTP, Trieste, 1994-95, SISSA/ISAS, Trieste, 1997. Contbr. articles to profl. jours. Soros Found. grantee APS, N.Y.C., 1993, ISF grantee, N.Y.C., 1994. Mem. ICTP (sr. assoc. condensed matter 1995-99, grantee 1995), Radio Phys. Soc. (vice-chmn. 1974-77). Avocations: PC computing, internet surfing. Office: Inst Applied Physics RAS, 46 Ul'yanov Str, 603600 Nizhny Novgorod Russia

PROUDFOOT, GEORGE WILFRED, hypnotherapy educator, consultant; b. Crook, Durham County, Eng., Dec. 19, 1921; s. Frank and Clara (Smith) P.; m. Margaret Mary Jackson, Nov. 4, 1950; 3 children. Student Scarborough Coll., Yorkshire, Eng., 1935-37. Cert. master practitioner neurolinguistic programming. Mem. Brit. Parliament from Cleveland, Yorkshire, 1959-64, from Brighouse and Spenborough, 1970-74; owner, operator, tchr. Proudfoot Sch. Hypnosis, Scarborough, 1980—; pvt. practice hypnotherapy, 1977—; chmn. Brit. Council Hypnotist Examiners, 1984—. Co-author: The Two-Factor Nation, 1977. Past chmn. Cleveland European Constituency Assn., Scarborough Conservative Assn. Served to sgt. RAF, 1940-45. Mem. Va. Sarir Internat. Network. Mem. Ch. of England. Avocations: travel; public speaking. Office: Proudfoot Sch Hypnosis, Caxton Way Eastfield Park, Scarborough North Yorkshire YO11 3YT, England

PROUT, CAROLYN ANN, controller, personnel administrator; b. Clare, Mich., Jan. 18, 1947; d. Aaron Eugene and Alice Marie (Fall) Prout; m. Stanley George Lyon, July 13, 1968 (dec. May 1971); children: Lori Anne Lyon, Jamie Lynn Lyon; m. Dennis Karl Hunt, Jan. 1975 (div. Nov. 1977); 1 child, Julie Marie Hunt; m. Arthur Roy Przybylowicz, Nov. 3, 1979 (div. Jan. 1998). Cert. acctg., Lansing Bus. U., 1965; BBA, Davenport Coll., 1998. Bank teller Citizens Bank & Trust, Rosebush, Mich., 1965-68; bookkeeper, sec. Doyle & Smith P.C., Lansing, Mich., 1968-74; legal sec. Foster, Swift, Collins & Coey P.C., Lansing, 1974-79; mgr. office ARC, Lansing, 1979-81; controller, personnel adminstr. Mich. Protection & Advocacy Service, Lansing, 1981-88; bus. adminstr. White, Przybylowicz, Schneider & Baird, P.C., Okemos, Mich., 1988-98; faculty sec. Thomas M. Cooley Law Sch., 1998—. Vol. bookkeeper Citizens Alliance to Uphold Spl. Edn., Lansing, 1977-79; coord. bingo IHM Sch., Lansing, 1979-80; mem. St. Casimir Christian Svc., Lansing, 1981-84, chairperson, 1983-84; eucharistic min., 1987—; bd. dirs. Immaculate Heart of Mary Sch., Lansing, 1977-80; vol. Ingham County chpt. Am. Cancer Soc., 1989—, Nokomis Learning Ctr., 1990-97; vol. ARC, 1998—, WKAR-Radio Talking Book, 1999—. Democrat. Roman Catholic. Avocations: sewing, travel, photography. Office: Thomas M Cooley Law Sch 300 S Capitol Ave Lansing MI 48933-2020

PROUT, TIMOTHY, retired genetics educator; b. Watertown, Conn., June 14, 1963; s. Curtis and Edith Prout; m. Marjorie Lester, June 6, 1950; children: Mary Ellen, David Lester. BA, Hobart Coll., 1948; PhD, Columbia U., 1954; DSc (hon.), U. Aarhus, Denmark, 1997. Asst. prof. zoology U. Calif., Riverside, 1954-59, assoc. prof. zoology, 1960-63, prof. zoology, 1964-74; prof. genetics U. Calif., Davis, 1975-88, prof. genetics emeritus, 1988—. Editor Theoretical Population Biology, 1976-87, Am. Naturalist, 1980-85; contbr. articles to profl. jours. Sgt. U.S. Army, 1943-46. Fellow AAAS. Democrat. Episcopalian. Avocation: fly fishing. E-mail: tgprout@ucdavis.edu. Home: 413 Del Oro Ave Davis CA 95616-0418 Office: U Calif Davis Dept Evolution and Ecology 1 Shields Ave Dept And Davis CA 95616-5270

PROVAN, DREW BENJAMIN, hematologist, consultant; b. Glasgow, Scotland, Nov. 20, 1955; s. Lawrence and Margaret (Batchelor) P.; m. Valerie Elizabeth Wilkes, Nov. 6, 1982; 1 child, Fraser. BSc, Leicester U., 1979; MB BChir, Leicester (Eng.) Med. Sch., 1984; MD, Southampton (Eng.) U., 1997. Med. registrar Stobhill Hosp., Glasgow, 1986-88, hematology registrar, 1988-89; hematology registrar Southampton Hosps., 1989-90; sr. registrar hematology Southampton and Bath Hosps., 1990-93; rsch. fellow medicine Dana-Farber Cancer Inst., Harvard Med. Sch., Boston, 1993-94; sr. lectr. hematology Southampton Hosps., 1994—; dir. molecular pathology divsn. Southampton Hosp., 1998—. Author: (books) MCQs in Medicine for MRCP Part 1, 1990, (with others) Clnical Haematology: a Postgraduate Exam Companion, 1997, The Oxford Handbook of Clinical Haematology, 1998, Molecular Haematology, 1999; editor: (with others) ABC of Clinical Haematology, 1998; contbr. to Drug Therapy in Old Age, 1998; contbr. numerous articles and papers to profl. jours., including Brit. Med. Jour., Brit. Jour. Haematology, Rev. Series Oncology. Am. traveling fellow Med. Rsch. Coun. London, 1993. Fellow Royal Coll. Physicians London; mem. Royal Coll. Pathologists London, Am. Soc. Hematology, Brit. Soc. Haematology. Anglican. Avocations: writing, typography, jazz music, cacti and succulents. Home: 5 Crofton Close, Southampton SO17 1XB, England Office: Southampton Gen Hosp, Tremona Rd, Southampton 5016 6YD, England

PROVASEK, EMIL FRANK, JR., small business owner; b. Ft. Worth, Aug. 11, 1957; s. Emil F. and Rema Maxine (Dennis) P. BSEE, U. Tex.-Arlington, 1979. Sr. microwave systems engr. Gen. Dynamics Corp., Ft. Worth, 1979-91; mgr. Causey's Rare Coins, Ft. Worth, 1991—. Pres. ACLU, Fort Worth chpt.; bd. advisors Tarrant County Lesbian and Gay Alliance. Mem. IEEE, ACLU (bd. dirs.), Am. Numismatic Assn., Tex. Coin Dealer Assn. (bd. dirs.), Eta Kappa Nu. Roman Catholic. Avocations: broadcast history, preservation of historical broadcast and electronic equipment. Home: PO Box 150411 Fort Worth TX 76108-0411 Office: 1806 Layton St Fort Worth TX 76117-5437

PROVENCHER-KAMBOUR, FRANCES, public relations executive; b. Exeter, N.H., Apr. 22, 1947; d. Roger Arthur and Josette Marguerite (Camus) Provencher; m. Benjamin C. Ryder, Apr. 12, 1969 (div. Mar. 1979); 1 child, Tiffany Nicholas; m. Edward S. Kambour, Dec. 27, 1988. BA, U. N.H., 1969; exec. MBA (partial, 1990-91) U.N.C. at Chapel Hill. Clk. typist, editorial asst. U.S. Embassy, Moscow, 1964-65; asst. editor Durham (N.H.) Advertiser, 1965-69; assoc. editor Kaman Aerospace Corp., Bloomfield, Conn., 1970-71; pubs. editor The Hartford Ins. Group (Conn.), 1974-76; pub. rels. cons. Fran Ryder Assocs., Farmington, Conn., 1976-78; pub. rels. account exec. Shailer Davidoff Rogers, Inc., Fairfield, Conn., 1978-80; sr. account exec. Creamer Dickson Basford, Inc., Hartford, Conn., 1980-83; account group mgr., account exec. Spiro & Assocs., Phila., 1983-84, v.p., assoc. pub. rels. dir., 1984-85; sr. v.p. pub. rels. LSGE Advt. Inc., Avon, Conn., 1985-87; v.p. corp. communications Wondriska Assocs., Farmington, Conn., 1987-88; pres. The Kambour Co., Raleigh, N.C., 1988-92, dir. pub. rels. & mktg. The PBM Co., Research Triangle Park, N.C., 1993-94; The Kambour Co., Westmoreland, NH, 1994—. Translator: The Cogito in Edmund Husserl's Phenomenology, 1969. Founder, The Art Guild, 1975; bd. dirs. Parent's Assn., Hartford Sch. Ballet, 1982-83, U. Conn. Found., 1986-99, dir. Emeritas, 1999—, Cheshire Med. Ctr./Dartmouth-Hitchcock Clinic Community Adv. Coun., 1997— (trustee, 1999—); incorporator, 1995-97. Recipient Gold Quill awards Internat. Assn. Bus. Communicators, 1974; Natl. Safety Coun. award, 1985, Paul Harris fellow award, Rotary Internat., 1997, Mem. Pub. Rels. Soc. Am. (accredited, bd. dirs. 1980-88, 90—, assembly del. 1987-88, spl. commendation 1985, mem. Counselors Acad. 1982-92, 1994-99, Yankee Chpt. (pres., 1998-99), natl. presdl. citation for leadership, 1993), Elm City Rotary Club, 1995— (bd.dirs., 1995-2000). Republican. Congregationalist. Address: 4 Dutton Rd Westmoreland NH 03467-4201

PROVIS, DOROTHY L(OUISE), artist, sculptor; b. Chgo., Apr. 26, 1926; d. George Kenneth Smith and Ann Hart (Day) Smith Guest; m. William H. Provis Sr., July 28, 1945; children: Timothy A., William H. Jr. Student, Sch. Art Inst., Chgo., 1953-56, U. Wis.-Milw., 1967-68, 69-70. Sculptor Port Washington, Wis., 1963—; pres. bd. dirs. West Bend Gallery of Fine Arts, Wis., 1984-86, bd. dirs., 1987-89; speaker, presenter in field. Co-curated exhbn. West Bend Gallery of Fine Arts, 1992. Author, lobbyist Wis. Consignment Bill, Madison, 1979; presenter Art of Bead Making Charles Allis Art Mus., Milw., 1991, Fimo, polymer clay jewelry techniques Moraine Valley C.C., Palos Hills, Ill., 1992; panelist Women's Caucus for Art Conf., Phila., 1983, Coalition Women's Art Orgn. at Coll. Art Assn. Conf., Seattle, 1993; mem. adv. bd. Percent for Art Pro., 1985-87; mem. adv. bd. Wis. Arts Bd., salary assistance program, 1991; pres. workshop Milw. Art Mus., 1990; conf. panelist Coll. Art Assn., N.Y.C., 1990. Wis. Arts Bd. Designer-Craftsmen grantee, NEA, 1981. Mem. Coalition of Women's Art Orgns. (del. to continuing com. Nat. Women's Conf. 1979, panelist conf. 1981, v.p. for membership/nominations, 1981-83, pres. 1983-85, nat. pres. 1985-87, 89-91, 91-93, 93-95, 95-97, v.p. communications 1987-89, editor CWAO newsletter 1985—, rep. CWAO at Am. Coun. for Arts Advocacy Day, Washington, 1993, panelist Southeastern Coll. Art Conf. 1995), Wis. Painters and Sculptors (life mem., pres. 1982-84, editor newsletter 1982-85), Wis. Women in Arts (legis. liaison 1978-80), Nat. Women's Studies Assn. (conf. presenter 1988), Artists for Ednl. Action (corr. 1979-85), Wis. Designer Crafts Coun. (membership chair 1991-93, editor newsletter 1993-95), Women's Caucus for Art (panelist 1981, 83, 86, 87, conf. com. panelist 1987, presenter 1989), Chgo. Artists Coalition. Home and Studio: 123 E Beutel Rd Port Washington WI 53074-1103

PROVORNY, FREDERICK ALAN, lawyer, educator; b. Bklyn., Sept. 7, 1946; s. Daniel and Anna (Wurm) P.; m. Nancy Ileene Wilkins, Nov. 21, 1971; children: Michelle C., Cheryl A., Lisa T., Robert D. BS summa cum laude, NYU, 1966; JD magna cum laude, Columbia U., 1969. Bar: N.Y. 1970, U.S. Supreme Ct. 1973, D.C. 1975, Mo. 1977, Md. 1987, Calif. 1989; CPA, Md., Mo. Law clk. to Judge Harold R. Medina U.S. Ct. Appeals (2d cir.), N.Y.C., 1969-70; asst. prof. law Syracuse (N.Y.) U., 1970-72; assoc. Debevoise, Plimpton, Lyons & Gates, N.Y.C., 1972-75, Cole & Groner P.C., Washington, 1975-76; with Monsanto Co., St. Louis, 1976-86, asst. co. counsel, 1978-86; pvt. practice Washington, 1986-89; ptnr. Provorny & Jacoby, Washington, 1989-91; counsel Shaw, Pittman, Potts & Trowbridge, Washington, 1991-93; ptnr. Tydings & Rosenberg, Balt., 1993-94; pvt. practice Balt., 1994-95, Washington, 1995-98; Harold R. Tyler prof. of sci. and tech. law and director Sci. and Tech. Law Ctr., Albany (N.Y.) Law Sch., 1998—; lect. Bklyn Law Sch., 1973-74; adj. prof. U. Balt. Sch. of Law, 1996-98; pres. Sci. and Tech. Assocs., Inc., 1986-91. Contbr. articles to profl. jours. Trustee Christian Woman's Benevolent Assn. Youth Home, 1979-83. Mem. ABA, Am. Law Inst., Am. Arbitration Assn. (panel comml. abitrators), Philo-Mt. Sinai Lodge 968, Masons, Beta Gamma Sigma. Jewish. Home: 11803 Kemp Mill Rd Silver Spring MD 20902-1511 Office: Albany Law School 80 New Scotland Ave Albany NY 12208-3434

PROVOST, CHERYL LOUISE WINTERS, account executive; b. Niagara Falls, N.Y., Apr. 25, 1947; d. William Joseph and Virginia Louise (Greene) W.; children: Christopher Chase, Matthew Chase, Richard Chase. AAS, Adirondack Community Coll., 1975; BS, Charter Oak State Coll., 1999. RN. RN critical care St. Clare's Hosp., Schenectady, N.Y., 1975-79; RN ICU Glens Falls (N.Y.) Hosp., 1979-80; sales and svc. rep. Clin. Data, Inc., Brookline, Mass., 1980-82; dir. regional devel. Med-Care Convalescent Supply Co., Inc., Rhinebeck, N.Y., 1982-85; sales mgr. ea. ops. Vortec Health Care, Cin., 1985-86; diagnostic sales rep., tng. assoc. MallincKrodt, Inc., St. Louis, 1986-94; cardiology sales specialist and tng. assoc. Mallinkrod Med., Inc., 1988-94, regional account mgr. New Eng., 1994-96, northeast regional bus. mgr., 1996-98, northeast ultrasound market devel. mgr., 1998-99, sales tng. mgr., 1999—. Mem. Nat. Assn. Female Execs., Am. Heart Assn. Republican. Presbyterian. Avocations: cross-country and alpine skiing, golfing, cooking, sailing, hiking. Home: 7 Horicon Ave Glens Falls NY 12801-2616 Office: Mallinckrodt Inc 675 Mcdonnell Blvd Saint Louis MO 63134-2001

PROWELL, ROY WALTERS, JR., orthodontist; b. Pitts., Oct. 6, 1945; s. Roy Walters and Dorothy Jane (Forney) P.; student U. Calif., Davis, 1963-65, D.D.S. in Orthodontics (Regents scholar), U. Calif., San Francisco, 1969; m. Evelyn Joyce Morgan, Aug. 1, 1971 (div. June 1985); children: Roy Walters III, Ian Morgan; m. Gretchen Fretter, Oct. 17, 1992 (div. July 1999). Assoc., Gordon Osser, D.D.S., Castro Valley, Calif., 1970-71, Willard Collins, D.D.S., Stockton, Calif., 1971-72; practice dentistry specializing in orthodontics, Pittsburg and Antioch, Calif., 1969-76; pres. R. Walt Prowell, D.D.S., Inc., Pittsburg and Antioch, 1976-91; mem. staff Mt. Diablo Rehab. Center, Pleasant Hill, Calif., Delta Meml. Hosp., Antioch; cons. Apples Orthodontix, Inc., 1999—; mem. East Bay (Calif.) Cleft Palate Panel, East Bay Facial Surgery Panel. Pres., U. Calif. Orthodontic Alumni Found., 1978-81, treas., 1981-84; dist. chmn. Boy Scouts Am., 1992-95. Republican. Presbyterian. Lodge: Masons, Rotary. Office: 3107 Lone Tree Way Ste E Antioch CA 94509-4959

PROXIMO, JUAN FERNANDEZ, land developer; b. Iloilo, The Philippines, Mar. 8, 1921; s. Agustin Montero Proximo and Juliana Guancia Fernancez; m. Juanita Bernaldo Santos, May 29, 1960 (dec. July 1977); 1 child, Sonny; m. Rufina Santos Pabalan, May 11, 1979; children: Pablan, Michael. BSC, Far Eastern U., Manila, 1954; LLB, Philippine Law Sch., Pasay, 1982. Pvt. practice real estate broker The Philippines, 1959-84, Chgo., 1984-86; land developer S.F. Proximo Holdings, Manila, 1986—, S.F. Proximo Holdings & Devel. Corp., Manila, 1983—; chmn., owner Internat. Montessori Ctr., The Philippines, 1989-97; lectr. in field. Bd. dirs. OISCA, Japan, 1972-80; pres. Y's Men's Club, Manila, 1979-82; ch. planter, 1983. Recipient Stewardship award Ctrl. Philippine U., 1997. Mem. Cons. and Real Estate Bd. Assn., Shelter and Housing Devel. Assn., Rotary (bd. dirs. 1988-94). Republican. Baptist. Avocations: swimming, billiards, singing. Home and Office: Greenmeadows, # 2 Hornbill St, Quezon City The Philippines

PROZES, ANDREW, publishing executive; b. Jan. 21, 1946. BA in Math, U. Waterloo, Ont., Can.; MBA, York U., Toronto. Former group pres. Southam Inc., Don Mills, Ont., Can.; exec. v.p., COO Westlaw, The West Group (subs. Thomson Corp.), Eagan, Minn., 1997-99; CEO global legal pub. & info. divsn. Reed Elsevier, N.Y.C., 2000—. Office: Reed Elsevier 2 Park Ave Frnt 7 New York NY 10016-5602*

PRUDNIKOV, EVGENIJ DMITRIEVICH, chemist, researcher; b. Leningrad, USSR, Mar. 30, 1937; s. Dmitrij Fjodorovich and Pelageja Stepanovna (Novikova) P.; m. Yunona Semjonovna Shapkina, Feb. 24, 1967; children: Gleb, Evgenij. BSc in Chemistry, Leningrad State U., Russia, 1959, cand. Scis. in Chemistry, 1968, superior sci. worker, 1971. Sci. worker Earth's Crust Inst. Leningrad State U., 1959-71, superior sci. worker, 1971-95, leader flame spectrometry lab., 1971-97; dir. lab. Earth's Crust Inst., St. Petersburg, Russia, 1995—; dir. ecolog. edn.-sci. ctr. St. Petersburg State U., 1995—; vis. prof. U. Santiago, Cuba, 1977, Free Univ., Berlin, 1980, Carleton U., Ottawa, Can., 1984-85, U. Amsterdam, The Netherlands, 1991, 94, U. Mass., Amherst, 1995-96, 97-98, Sheffield U., Eng. 1999; pres. State Exam. Commn., Arhangel'skij (USSR) State Pedagogical Inst., 1989, 90. Coauthor: (book) Spectral Analysis of Pure Substances, 1994; inventor: holds 13 Russian patents; contbr. numerous articles to profl. jours. Mem. Trade Union Bur., Geolog. Dept. Leningrad State U., 1971-87. 94-00, pres. 1982-87; mem. Presidium of Trade Union Com.; mem. sci. coun. geolog. dept. Leningrad State U., 1982-87, pres. Commn. for Protecting Labor, 1987-90; mem. Pub. Children's Commn., Vasileostrovskij Dist., Leningrad, USSR, 1985-89. Recipient of inventor's award Leningrad State U., 1980, Vet. of Work medal, 1989; winner of socialist Competition, 1975, 77, 78, 79; named Shockworker of 10 Piatiletka, 1980, Inventor of USSR, 1982; grantee NATO, 1995-98, grantee Royal Soc. of Chem. 1999. Fellow H.S. Trade Union, Mendeleev All Russian Chem. Soc., Inventor Soc. Russia (USSR), N.Y. Acad. Sci. Avocations: reading, football, volley-ball, skiing, swimming. Office: Earth's Crust Inst State U, Universitetskaja nab 7/9, 199034 Saint Petersburg Russia

PRUEHER, JOSEPH W., military officer; b. Nashville, Nov. 25, 1942. Grad., U.S. Naval Acad., Annapolis, Md., 1964. Commd. ensign USN, advanced through grades to adm.; commdr. in chief U.S. Pacific Command, Camp H.M. Smith, Hawaii, 1996-99; amb. to People's Republic of China Dept. of State, Beijing, 1999—. Office: United States Embassy, 3 Xiu Shui Bei Jie, 100600 Beijing People's Republic of China

PRUESSNER, DAVID MORGAN, lawyer; b. Corpus Christi, Tex., May 13, 1955; s. Harold Trebus and Alma (Morgan) P.; m. Becky McKinney, May 21, 1977; children: Jennifer, Daniel, Heather. BA cum laude, Baylor U., 1977, JD cum laude, 1980. Bar: Tex. 1980, U.S. Dist. Ct. (no. dist.) Tex. 1980, U.S. Ct. Appeals (5th cir.) 1986, U.S. Supreme Ct. 1989. Atty. Coke & Coke, Dallas, 1980-83, Shank, Irwin & Conant, Dallas, 1983-90, Pettit & Martin, Dallas, 1990-92, Fletcher & Springer, Dallas, 1992-99; pvt. practice Law Offfices of David Pruessner, Dallas, 2000—; instr. legal assts. program So. Meth. U., Dallas, 1989-91. Assoc. editor Baylor Law Rev., 1980. Avocations: world religions, history, chess. Fax: (214) 378-7401. E-mail: david@pruessner-shilling.com. Office: Law Offices of David M Pruessner Ste 285 10300 N Central Expy Dallas TX 75231-4363

PRUITT, GEORGE ALBERT, college president; b. Canton, Miss., July 9, 1946; s. Joseph Henry and Lillie Irene (Carmichael) P.; m. Pamela Young; 1 child, Shayla Nicole. BS, Ill. State U., 1968, MS, 1970, DHL (hon.), 1994; PhD, Union Grad. Sch., Cin., 1974; D Pub. Svc. (hon.), Bridgewater State Coll., 1990, MA (hon.), 1990; LLD (hon.), Ill. State U., 1994; DHL (hon.), SUNY Empire State Coll., 1996. Asst. to v.p. for acad. affairs Ill. State U., Normal, 1968-70, dir. high potential students program, 1968-70; dean students Towson State U., 1970-72; v.p., exec. asst. to pres., assoc. prof. urban affairs Morgan State U., 1972-75; v.p., prof. Tenn. State U., 1975-81; exec. v.p. Council for Advancement Experiential Learning, Columbia, Md., 1981-82; pres. Thomas A. Edison State Coll., Trenton, 1982—; commn. on ednl. credit and credentials, labor/higher edn. coun. Am. Coun. on Edn.; advisor group XII, Nat. Fellowship program W.K. Kellogg Found., 1990-94, advisor group XV, 1995-99; bd. dirs. SEEDCO; trustee Ctr. for Analysis of Pub. Issues, Princeton, N.J., 1993—; nat. adv. com. on instnl. quality and integrity U.S. Dept. Edn., 1994—. Trustee Union Inst., Cin., Mercer Med. Ctr., 1989-97; bd. dirs. N.J. Assn. Colls. and Univs., N.J. div. Am. Cancer Soc., 1992-97. Recipient Resolution of Commendation Bd., Trustees Morgan State U., 1975, Outstanding Svc. to Edn. award Tenn. State U., 1981, Gubernatorial citation Gov. of Tenn., 1981, Good Guy award George Washington coun. Boy Scouts Am., 1991, Humanitarian award NCCJ, 1992, Educator of Yr. award Black N.J. Mag., 1993, Disting. Alumni award Ill. State U., 1996; apptd. hon. mem. Gen. Assembly Tenn., 1981, hon. mem. U.S. Congress from 5th Tenn. dist., 1981; named ofcr. of the Most Effective Coll. Pres. in U.S., Exxon Edn. Found. Study, 1986; named to Coll. of Edn. Hall of Fame, Ill. State U., 1995; named Mercer Co. N.J. Citizen of Yr., Mercer Co. C. of C., 1997. Mem. Coun. for Advancement Exptl. Learning, Am. Assn. State Colls.and Univs., Coun. for Advancement and Support of Edn., Am. Coun. Edn., Mid. States Assn. Colls. and Schs. (accreditation evaluator commn. on higher edn.), Mercer County C. of C. (chmn.). Office: Thomas Edison Coll 101 W State St Trenton NJ 08608-1101

PRUITT, STEPHEN WALLACE, finance educator; b. Indpls., Feb. 3, 1957; s. Harry Wallace and Dorothy (Thorp) P.; m. Mary Melinda Settle, Dec. 19, 1981; children: Rebecca Elizabeth, Victoria Barrick. BS in Mgmt., Purdue U., 1979; MBA in Fin., Ohio State U., 1980; PhD in Fin., Fla. State U., 1987. Internat. cash mgr. Marathon Oil Co., Findlay, Ohio, 1980-81; fin. analyst Nat. Svc. Industries, Crawfordsville, Ind., 1981-83; asst. prof. fin. U. Miss., Oxford, 1986-88, Ind. U., Bloomington, 1988-93; assoc. prof. fin. U. Memphis, 1993-96, prof. fin., 1996-2000; Arvin Gottlieb/Mo. chair in bus. econs. and fin. U. Mo., Kansas City, 2000—; cons. in field. Contbr. articles to profl. jours. Bd. dirs. Art Mus. U. Memphis, 1995-2000; founder, pres. Memphis Print Club, 1995-2000. Mem. So. Fin. Assn., Fin. Mgmt. Assn. Republican. Baptist. Avocation: collecting art and antiques. Home: 1367 Pinpointe Dr Collierville TN 38017 Office: U Mo Henry W Bloch Sch Bus & Pub 5100 Rockhill Rd Kansas City MO 64110-2481

PRUKNER-RADOVČIC, ESTELLA, microbiologist, researcher; b. Zagreb, Croatia, May 22, 1955; d. Tomislav and Milada (Nukovic) Prukner; m. Bruno Radovčic, Sept. 29, 1987; children: Lovro, Renata. DVM, U. Zagreb, 1981, MS, 1986, PhD, 1990. Rsch. asst. Croatian Vet. Inst., Zagreb, 1982-86, sci. asst., 1987-91, asst. prof., 1992-94, assoc. prof. microbiology and poultry pathology, 1995—; head bacteriol. lab. Vet. Inst., Zagreb, 1989-91; head Nat. Corr. Lab. Salmonellae, 1990-92. Mem. Croatian Microbiol. Soc. (sec. gen. 1997—), World Vet. Poultry Assn., Poultry Sci. Assn., N.Y. Acad. Scis. Roman Catholic. Home: Krešimirov trg 13, 1000 Zagreb Croatia Office: Dept Poultry Pathol Vet Fac, U Zagreb Heinzelova 55, 10000 Zagreb Croatia

PRUNCKUN, HENRY WALTER, JR. (HANK PRUNCKUN), criminologist; b. Springfield, Mass., July 16, 1954; arrived in Australia, 1977; s. Henry Walter and Ann Marie (Slezak) P.; m. Ann Elizabeth Doolette, Mar. 9, 1978; children: Orren Henry, Naomi Elizabeth, Isobel Ann Doolette-Prunckun. ASc, Springfield Tech. Cmty. Coll., 1975; BSc, Westfield (Mass.) State Coll., 1977; DipSocSc, Flinders U., Adelaide, Australia, 1985; MSocSc, U. South Australia, Adelaide, 1996. Police officer Springfield Police Dept. Aux.; probation and parole officer Dept. Correctional Svcs., South Australia; investigator Dept. Public and Consumer Affairs, South Australia; sr. rsch. officer Police Dept., South Australia; intelligence analyst Nat. Crime Authority, South Australia; chief project officer Courts Adminstrn. Authority, South Australia; prin. rsch. analyst Slezak Assocs., South Australia. Author: Information Security, 1989, Special Access Required, 1990, Shadow of Death, 1995, Operation El Dorado Canyon, 1995; (software) SpyBase, 1990, Index Manager, 1990; contbr. articles to profl. jours. including Conflict & Terrorism, Police Studies, others. Mem. Australian Inst. Profl. Intelligence Officers, Australian and New Zealand Soc. Criminology, Internat. Assn. Law Enforcement Intelligence Analysts (recipient lit. award, 1991, profl. svcs. award, 1992, 96). Avocation: amateur radio operator. Office: Slezak Assocs, 57 Davenport Terr, Wayville SA 5034, Australia

PRUNETI, CARLO A., psychologist, psychotherapist; b. Pomarance-Pisa, Italy, Dec. 21, 1955; s. Benito and Piera (Fabbri) P.; m. Lucia Siracusano (div.); children: Luca, Federico. Degree in Exptl. Psychology, U. Florence, 1979; MS in Differential Psychology, U. Siena, Italy, 1983; MS in Psychodianostics, U. Messina, Italy, 1985; PhD in Psychol. Scis., U. Rome, 1988; MS in Med. Sexology, U. Florence, Italy, 1994. Psychotherapist STA Chiara Hosp., Italy, 1978—; rschr. Inst. Clin. Physiology, Italy, 1985-94; prof. psychology U. Pisa, Italy, 1989-96, U. Florence, Italy, 1997—; dir. Clin. psychol. Ctr., 1988—. Author: Pisa Stress Questionnaire, 1995, Valutazione Stati Depressivi, 1996, Stress Mind-Body Integration, 1996, Pisa Survey for Eating Disorders, 1998, Pisa Survey...Adolescent, 1999. With Italian Navy, 1980-82. Fellow European Assn. Cognitive Behavioral Therapy; mem. Soc. Psychophysiology, Soc. Personality Assessment, Italian Assn. Psychology. Roman Catholic. Avocations: sailboating, climing, hiking, swimming. Home: 52 Via G Galilei, I55049 Viareggio Italy Office: STA Chiara U Hosp NPI Dept, 67 via Roma, I56100 Pisa Italy

PRUSINER, STANLEY BEN, neurology and biochemistry educator, researcher; b. Des Moines, May 28, 1942; s. Lawrence Albert and Miriam (Spigel) P.; children: Helen Chloe, Leah Anne. AB cum laude, U. Pa., 1964, MD, 1968; PhD (hon.), Hebrew U., Jerusalem, 1995, René Descartes U., Paris, 1996; DS (hon.), U. Pa., 1998, Dartmouth Coll., 1999. Diplomate Am. Bd. Neurology. Intern in medicine U. Calif., San Francisco, 1968-69, resident in neurology, 1972-74, asst. prof. neurology, 1974-80, assoc. prof., 1980-84, prof., 1984—, prof. biochemistry, 1988—, acad. senate faculty rsch. lectr., 1989-90; prof. virology U. Calif., Berkeley, 1984—, dir. Inst. for Neurodegenerative Diseases, 1999—; mem. neurology rev. com. Nat. Inst. Neurol. Disease and Strokes, NIH, Bethesda, Md., 1982-86, 90-92; mem. sci. adv. bd. French Found., L.A., 1985—, chmn. sci. adv. bd., 1996—; mem. sci. rev. com. Alzheimer's Disease Diagnostic Ctr. & Rsch. Grant Program, State of Calif., 1985-89; chmn. sci. adv. bd. Am. Health Assistance Found., Rockville, Md., 1986-2000; mem. spongiform encephalopathy adv. com., FDA, 1997—. Editor: The Enzymes of Glutamine Metabolism, 1973, Slow Transmissible Diseases of the Nervous System, 2 vols., 1979, Prions--Novel Infectious Pathogens Causing Scrapie and CJD, 1987, Prion Diseases of Humans and Animals, 1992, Molecular and Genetic Basis of Neurologic Disease, 1993, 2d edit., 1997, Prions Prions Prions, 1996, Prion Biology and Diseases, 1999; contbr. more than 250 articles to profl. jours. Mem. adv. bd. Family Survival Project for Adults with Chronic Brain Disorders, San Francisco, 1982-90, San Francisco chpt. Alzheimer's Disease and Related Disorder Assn., 1985-91; trustee U. Pa., 2000—. Lt. comdr. USPHS, 1969-72. Recipient Leadership and Excellence for Alzheimer's Disease award NIH, 1990-97, Potamkin prize for Alzheimer's Disease Rsch., 1991, Presl. award, 1993, Med. Rsch. award Met. Life Found., 1992, Christopher Columbus Discovery award NIH and Med. Soc. Genoa, Italy, 1992, Charles A. Dana award for pioneering achievements in health, 1992, Dickson prize for outstanding contbns. to medicine U. Pitts., 1992, Max Planck Rsch. award Alexander von Humboldt Found. and Max Planck Soc., 1992,

Gairdner Found. Internat. award, 1993, Disting. Achievement in Neurosci. Rsch. award Bristol-Myers Squibb, 1994, Albert Lasker award for Basic Med. Rsch., 1994, Caledonian Rsch. Found. prize Royal Soc. Edinburgh, 1995, Paul Ehrlich and Ludwig Darmstaedter award Germany, 1995, Paul Hoch award Am. Psychopathol. Assn., 1995, Wolf prize in medicine, 1996, ICN Virology prize, 1996, Victor and Clara Soriano award World Fedn. Neurology, 1996, Pasarow Found. prize in neurosci., 1996, Charles Leopold Mayer prize French Acad. Scis., 1996, Keio Internat. prize for med. rsch., 1996, Baxter award Am. Assn. Med. Colls., 1996, Louisa Gross Horwitz prize Columbia U., 1997, Nobel prize in medicine, 1997, K.J. Zulch prize Gertrude Reemtsma Found., 1997, Benjamin Franklin medal Franklin Inst., 1998, Jubilee medal Swedish Med. Soc., 1998; Alfred P. Sloan Rsch. fellow U. Calif., 1976-78; Med. Investigator grantee Howard Hughes Med. Inst., 1976-81; grantee for excellence in neurosci. Senator Jacob Javits Ctr., NIH, 1985-90. Fellow AAAS, Am. Soc. Microbiology, Am. Acad. Arts & Scis., Royal Coll. Physicians; mem. NAS (Inst. Medicine, Richard Lounsbery award for extraordinary achievements in biology and medicine 1993), Am. Acad. Neurology (George Cotzias award for outstanding rsch. 1987, Presdl. award 1993, Disting. Achievement award 1998), Am. Assn. Physicians, Am. Soc. Neurochemistry, Internat. Soc. Neurochemistry, Am. Soc. Virology, Am. Neurol. Assn., Am. Soc. Clin. Investigation, Am. Soc. Biochemistry and Molecular Biology, Am. Chem. Soc., Soc. Neurosci., Am. Soc. Human Genetics, Genetics Soc. Am., Am. Soc. Cell Biology, Am. Soc. Cellular Biology, Am. Soc. Molecular Biol. Biochemistry, Am. Philos. Soc., Royal Soc. London, Protein Soc. (Amgen award 1997), Concordia Argonaut Club.

PRUSZAK, ZBIGNIEW, scientist; b. Mata Komorza, Bydgoszcz, Poland, Mar. 6, 1947; s. Konrad and Halina (Polum) P.; m. Agnieszka Spaginska, Oct. 8, 1977; 1 child, Marcin. MS, Tech. U., Gdansk, 1970; PhD, Polish Acad. of Scis., Gdansk, 1977, DSc, 1990; Assoc. Prof., Polish Acad. Scis., Gdansk, 1992. Rsch. assoc. Polish Acad. Scis., Gdansk, 1971-75, sr. rsch. assoc., 1975-92, head of dept., 1998—; head of dept. of coast engrng. and dynamics, Gdansk, 1998—. Co-author: (design manual) Effectiveness of Coastal Defence Measures, 1992; author: (book) Dynamics of Beach and Sea Bed, 1998. Arbiter Marine Coldrat, Gdynia, 1996; chmn. local hunting assn., Gdansk, 1982. Roman Catholic. Avocations: hunting, tourism. Office: Polish Acad of Scis, 7 Koscierska, 80-953 Gdansk Poland

PRUT, EDUARD VENIAMINOVICH, health facility administrator, physics educator; b. Gzodekovo, Russia, Mar. 5, 1939; s. Veniamin Davidovich and Olga Grigor'evna (Bezuglaya) P.; m. Galina Borisovna Yavorskaya, July 15, 1961; 1 child, Victoria. Student, Moscow Inst. Physics & Tech., Dolgoprudnyi, Russia, 1956-62, Candidate, 1963. Cert. engrng. physicist. Scientist Inst. Chem. Physics, Russian Acad. Scis., Moscow, 1963—, head lab., 1986—; asst., docent, prof. gen. physics Moscow Inst. Physics and Tech., Dolgoprudnyi, 1968—. Author: High-Pressure Chemistry and Physics of Polymers, 1994, Physics Problems, 1998, 99; contbr. articles to profl. jours. Avocations: book, classical music, chess, traveling. Office: Inst Chem Physics RAS, St Kosygin 4, 117977 Moscow Russia

PRUTER, ROBERT DOUGLAS, editor; b. Phila., July 1, 1944; s. Hugo Rehling and Nancy Lee (Taylor) P.; m. Margaret Franson; 1 child, Robin Franson. BA, Roosevelt U., 1967, MA, 1976; MLS, Dominican U., 2000. Asst. editor New Std. Ency., Chgo., 1969-74, assoc. editor, 1974-79, sr. editor, 1979-96; sr. rsch. assoc. Planning Comms., 1996-97; asst. editor Charles D. Spencer & Assocs., Chgo., 1997-98; assoc. editor Charles D. Spencer & Assocs., 1999—. Author: Chicago Soul, 1991, Doowop: The Chicago Scene, 1996; editor: Blackwell Guide to Soul Recordings, 1993; adv. editor Popular Music and Society, 1995—; rhythm and blues editor Goldmine Mag., 1984—. Mem. adv. com. Chgo. Blues Festival, 1992—. Served U.S. Army, 1967-69, Vietnam. Mem. NARAS, N.Am. Soc. for Sport History, Ill. Hist. Soc., Chgo. Hist. Soc., Soc. Midland Authors (bd. dirs.). Democrat. Avocations: collecting records, sports history rsch. Office: Charles D Spencer & Assocs 250 S Wacker Dr Ste 600 Chicago IL 60606-5892

PRUZANSKY, JOSHUA MURDOCK, lawyer; b. N.Y.C., Mar. 16, 1940; s. Louis and Rose (Murdock) P.; m. Susan R. Bernstein, Aug. 31, 1980; 1 child, Dina Gabrielle. BA, Columbia Coll., 1960, JD, 1965. Bar: N.Y., 1965, U.S. Dist. Ct. (ea. and so. dists.) N.Y., 1968, U.S. Supreme Ct., 1980. Ptnr. Scheinberg, DePetris & Pruzansky, Riverhead, N.Y., 1965-85; ptnr. Greshin, Ziegler & Pruzansky, Smithtown, 1985—, Smithtown, N.Y., 1985—; mem. exec. coun. N.Y. State Conf. Bar Leaders, 1984—, chmn., 1988-89; mem. grievance com. Appellate Divsn. 10th Judicial Dist., 1992-96; mem. adv. bd. Ticor Title Guarantee Co., 1992—; mem. L.I. adv. bd. HSBC Bank, 1995—; dir. N.Y. State Com. for Modern Cts., 1998—; mem. adv. task force N.Y. Dept. State corps., 1998—. Mem. bd. visitors Columbia Law Sch., 1998—; chair bd. visitors Touro Law Sch., 1998—; dir. The Mus. Stony Brook, 1998—. Fellow ABA Found., N.Y. State Bar Found. (bd. dirs. 1994—); mem. ABA (ho. of dels. 1997—, probate and real property sect., standing com. on solo and small firm practitioners 1998-2000, N.Y. state del. Caucus of State Bar Assns.), N.Y. State Bar Assn. (ho. dels. 1982—, pres. 1997-98, exec. com. 1992-99, spl. com. women and law 1986-91, task force on small firms 1991-92, spl. com. on MDP 1999-2000, nominating com. 1999-2000, chair 1999-2000, trusts and estates sect., gen. practice, elder law), Suffolk County Bar Assn. (bd. dirs. 1979-89, pres. 1985-86), N.Y. County Lawyers Assn., Nassau County Bar Assn. Office: Greshin Ziegler & Pruzansky 199 E Main St Smithtown NY 11787-2892

PRYCE, JOHN DERWENT, mathematics educator; b. Bowness, Eng., Jan. 27, 1941; s. Maurice H. Pryce and Susanne Margarethe Born Farley; m. Christine Mary Cannon, Nov. 1988 (div.); children: Nathaniel, Lois, Hugh; m. Kate Ese Iyere, Feb. 23, 1990. BA, Trinity Coll., Cambridge, 1962; PhD, U. Newcastle-upon-Tyne, 1965. Chartered mathematician. Temp. lectr. U. Newcastle-upon-Tyne, 1965; math. tchr. Abingdon (Berks.) Sch., 1966-68; lectr. pure math. U. Aberdeen, Scotland, 1968-72; sr. prog. advisor U. Aberdeen Computing Ctr., 1972-75; lectr. numeric analysis U. Bristol, 1975-88; sr. lectr. numeric analysis Royal Mil. Coll. Sci., Shrivenham, Wilts., 1988—; cons. Republic Packaging Corp., Chgo., 1983-87, Sun Microsys., Inc., 1999—; sr. acad. asst. NAG Ltd., Oxford, 1988-91; co-chair 6th Internat. Conf. Sci. Computing, Benin, Nigeria, 1994. Author: Basic Methods of Linear Functional Analysis, 1974, Numerical Solution of Sturm-Liouville Problems, 1993; co-editor Jour. Comp. Applied Math. Millennium Volumes, 1999-2000. Fellow Inst. Math. and Applics. Avocations: hill walking, woodworking, gardening, music. Office: Royal Mil Coll Sci, Shrivenham Wilts, England SN6 8LA

PRYCE, JONATHAN, actor; b. North Wales, June 1, 1947. Appearences include (stage) Liverpool Everyman, 1972, Nottingham Playhouse-Comedians, Comedians, 1977 (Tony award, Theatre World award), Hamlet (Olivier award), Macbeth, The Caretaker, 1981, Accidental Death of an Anarchist, 1984, Miss Saigon, 1991 (Tony award, Olivier award), Oliver, 1995; (films) Voyage of the Damned, 1976, Breaking Glass, 1980, Loophole, 1981, Praying Mantis, 1982, The Plowman's Lunch, 1983, Something Wicked This Way Comes, 1983, Brazil, 1985, The Doctor and the Devils, 1985, Haunted Honeymoon, 1986, Jumpin Jack Flash, 1986, Hotel London, 1987, Man On Fire, 1987, The Adventures of Baron Munchausen, 1988, Consuming Passions, 1988, The Rachel Papers, 1989, Glengarry Glen Ross, 1992, The Age of Innocence, 1993, Shopping, 1994, A Business Affair, 1994, Carrington, 1996 (Best Actor award Cannes Film Festival 1995), Evita, 1996, Tomorrow Never Dies, 1997, Regeneration, 1997, Ronin, 1998, Stigmata, 1999; (TV movie) Barbarians at the Gate, HBO, 1993 (Emmy nomination, Supporting Actor - Miniseries or Special, 1993), David, 1997. Address: Julian Belfrage Assocs, 46 Albermarle St, London WIX 4pp, England

PRYDE, NEIL FREDERICK, manufacturing company executive; b. Te Aroha, New Zealand, Oct. 19, 1939; s. Neil Middleton and Mavis (Lawn) P.; m. Nina Sui Fun Yuen, July 29, 1967; children: Katherine Anne, Anne Margaret, Michael Lee. Assoc. chartered acct., Auckland U., New Zealand, ž1963. Cert. assoc. chartered acct., New Zealand. Asst. tax assessor Inland Revenue Dept., Auckland, New Zealand, 1957-59; fin. acct. Allied Industries Ltd., Auckland, New Zealand, 1959-63; mng. dir. Rolly Tasker Ltd., Hong Kong, 1963-70, Neil Pryde Ltd., Hong Kong, 1970—. Avocation: yacht racing. Office: 16F Tins Ctr Stage 3, 3 Hung Cheung Rd Tuen Mun, NT Hong Kong China

PRYDZ, HANS PETER BLANKENBORG, medical director, cell biologist; b. Oslo, Sept. 6, 1933; s. Peter B. and Ingebjørg (Øilo) P.; m. Reidunn Svensen, Aug. 4, 1954 (div. 1982); m. Anne-Brit Kolstø, July 11, 1985. MD, U. Oslo, 1957, PhD in Biochemistry, 1965. Various internships Norway, 1958-60; rsch. fellow U. Clinic, Oslo, 1960; rsch. fellow dept. biochemistry U. Oslo, 1961-65, asst. prof. microbiology, 1965-71, prof. med. rsch., 1980—; prof. biochemistry U. Tromsø, Norway, 1971-78; dir. Biotech. Ctr. Oslo, 1989—; mem. Nat. Biotech. Commn., 1991-98; v.p. EMBL Coun., 1988-90. Contbr. over 270 articles to profl. jours. Lt. Med. Corps Norway, 1958. Mem. Norwegian Biochemistry Soc. (hon.), Norwegian Acad. Sci., European Thrombosis Rsch. Orgn. (v.p. 1993-96). Avocations: art, theater, skiing, hiking. Office: Gaustadalleen 21, 0371 Oslo Norway

PRYLUTSKYY, YURIJ IVANOVICH, physicist; b. Shargorod, Vinnitza, Ukraine, May 25, 1965; d. Ivan Olexandrovych and Galyna Grygorivna (Storozh) P.; m. Svitlana Volodymyrivna Grechana, Sept. 24, 1995, 1 child, Tetyana. MS, Kyiv Shevchenko U., Ukraine, 1989, PhD, 1992, DSc, 1998. Sci. worker Kyiv Shevchenko U., 1992-93, asst. prof., 1993-95, doctorant, 1995-98, assoc. prof., 1998—; vice-dean Kyiv Shevchenko U., 1993-95. Contbr. articles to profl. jours. Grantee Soros Found., 1992; recipient Shevchenko prize for scientific rsch., 1997. ISSEP grantee, 1998, grantee INTAS, 1999; Cabinet of Ukraine scholar, 1998, Kasa Mianowskiego of Polish Acad. Scis. scholar, 1999; DAAD grantee, 1999, CR Nato grantee, 1999. Mem. Ukrainian Phys. Soc. (exec. sec. 1993), Am. Phys. Soc. Avocations: football, swimming. Office: Kyiv Nat Shevchenko U/Physics, Volodymyrska Str 64, 01033 Kyiv Ukraine

PRYME, IAN FRASER, biochemistry educator; b. Stockport, Eng., May 31, 1944; arrived in Norway, 1967; s. Harry and Robina Betsy (Atherton) P.; m. Ritha Melchior, July 4, 1969; children: Anita, Veronica, Colin. BS, U. Newcastle upon Tyne, Eng., 1966, MS, 1967; PhD, U. Bergen, Norway, 1981. Rsch. asst. U. Bergen, Norway, 1967-70, lectr. dept. biochemistry, 1972-76, assoc. prof., 1977-91; prof. biochemistry and molecular biology U. Bergen, 1992—; dep. chmn. U. Bergen, 1976-88, 90-95; vis. rsch. assoc. Brown U., Providence, 1971; rschr. Rowett Rsch. Inst., Aberdeen, Scotland, 1987-88, U. Barcelona, Spain, 1996. Co-editor: Protein Synthesis, 1983, Treatise on the Cytoskeleton, Vol. I, 1995, Vol. II, 1996, Vol. III, 1996. Mem. Tissue Culture Assn., Norwegian Biochem. Soc., British Biochem. Soc., Inst. Biology, Nordic Soc. Cell Biology, Old Scarborians. Anglican. Avocations: fishing, skiing, tennis, scottish country dancing. Home: Natlandsfjellet 120, N-5098 Bergen Norway Office: U Bergen Dept Biochemistry & Molecular Biology, Arstadveien 19, N-5009 Bergen Norway

PRYNNE, JEREMY HALVARD, poet, librarian; b. Bromley, Eng., June 24, 1936; s. Halvard Ingram and Sarah Muriel (Andrade) P.; m. Suzanne Elizabeth Furmston; children: Lorna Clare Antoinette, Jessica Margaret Anne. BA with honors, Cambridge (Eng.) U., 1960, MA, 1964. libr., dir. studies in English, Gonville and Caius Coll. Author: Force of Circumstances and Other Poems, 1962, Kitchen Poems, 1968, Day Light Songs, 1968, Aristeas, 1968, The White Stones, 1969, Fire Lizard, 1970, Brass, 1971, Into The Day, 1972, A Night Square, 1973, Wound Response, 1974, High Pink in Chrome, 1975, News of Warring Clans, 1977, Down where changed, 1979, Poems, 1982, The Oval Window, 1983, Bands Around the Throat, 1987, Word Order, 1989, Not-You, 1993, Her Weasels Wild Returning, 1994, For the Monogram, 1997, Red D Gypsum, 1998, Poems, 1999, Pearls That Were, 1999, Triodes, 1999. Avocations: reading and study, music, natural history, sinology, thought. Office: Gonville and Caius College, Cambridge CB2 1TA, United Kingdom

PRYOR, JOHN PEMBRO, uroandrologist, consultant; b. Reading, Berkshire, Eng., Aug. 25, 1937; s. William B. and Kathleen M. (Pembro) P.; m. Marion Hopkins, July 25, 1959; children: Andrew, Damian, Justin, Marcellus. MS, King's Coll., London, 1961. Resident, 1968-69; cons. urologist King's Coll. Hosp., 1974-94, St. Peter's Hosp., 1974-99. Treas. Brit. Jour. Urology, 1992-99. Recipient St. Peters medal British Assn. Urol. Surgeons, 1995; named Hunterian prof. Royal Coll. Surgeons Eng., 1972, 95. Mem. Brit. Soc. Urology, European Soc. Imp Rsch. (pres. 1999—), Brit. Soc. Andrology (1st chmn. 1978-82). Avocations: opera, theatre, birds, wine. Office: Lister Hosp, Chelsea Bridge Rd, London SW1W 8RH, England

PRYOR, WAYNE ROBERT, astronomer; b. Oakland, Calif., May 21, 1961; s. Arthur William and Lila Marie (Carlin) P. AB in Physics and Applied Math., U. Calif., Berkeley, 1983; PhD in Astrophys. Planetary & Atmos. Sci, U. Colo., 1989. Rsch. assoc. Lab. for Atmospheric and Space Physics, Boulder, Colo., 1989—; co-investigator Neptune data analysis program NASA, 1990, Pioneer Venus guest investigator program, 1991, Galileo ultraviolet spectrometer team, 1992-2000, Upper Atmosphere Rsch. Satellite guest investigator program, 1994, NSF Comet Shoemaker-Levy 9 Study, 1995, Hubble Space Telescope Jupiter studies, 1995-2000, Ulysses Guest Investigator Program, 1998-00. Contbr. articles to profl. jours. Methodist. Office: Lab Atmospheric & Space Physics 1234 Innovation Dr Boulder CO 80303-7814

PRYOR, WILLIAM DANIEL LEE, humanities educator; b. Lakeland, Fla., Oct. 29, 1926; s. Dahl and Lottie Mae (Merchant) P. AB, Fla. So. Coll., 1949; MA, Fla. State U., 1950, PhD, 1959; postgrad., U. N.C., 1952-53; pvt. art study with Florence Wilde; pvt. voice study with Colin O'More, Anna Kaskas; pvt. piano study with Waldemar Hille and audited piano master classes of Ernst von Dohnányi. Asst. prof. English, dir. drama Bridgewater (Va.) Coll., 1950-52; grad. tchg. fellow humanities Fla. State U., Tallahassee, 1953-55, 57-58; instr. English U. Houston, University Park, Houston, 1955-59; asst. prof. U. Houston, University Park, 1959-62, assoc. prof., 1962-71, prof., 1971-97, prof. emeritus, 1997; vis. instr. English, Fla. So. Coll., Lakeland, MacDill Army Air Base, Tampa, Fla., summer 1951, Tex. So. U., 1961-63; vis. instr. humanities, govt. U. Tex. Dental Br., Houston, 1962-63; lectr. The Women's Inst., Houston, 1967-72; lectr. humanities series Jewish Cmty. Ctr., Houston, 1972-73; originator, moderator weekly TV and radio program The Arts in Houston on Stas. KUHT-TV and KUHF-FM, 1956-57, 58-63. Contbg. author: National Poetry Anthology, 1952, Panorama das Literaturas das Americas, vol. 2, 1958-60; assoc. editor Forum, 1967, editor, 1967-82; contbr. articles to various jours.; dir. Murder in the Cathedral (T.S. Elliot), U. Houston, 1965; performed in opera as Sir Edgar in Der Junge Lord (Henze), Houston Grand Opera Assn., 1967; played the title role in Aella (Chatterton), Am. premiere, U. Houston, 1970. Bd. dirs. Houston Shakespeare Soc., 1964-67; bd. dirs., program annotator Houston Chamber Orch. Soc., 1964-76; narrator Houston Symphony Orch., Houston Summer Symphony Orch., Houston Summer Symphony Orch., Houston Chamber Orch., U. Houston Symphony Orch., St. Stephen's Music Festival Symphony Orch., New Harmony, Ind.; narrator world premier of the Bells (Jerry McCathern), 1969, U. Houston Symphony Orch., 1969, Am. premier Symphony No. Seven, Antartica (Vaughn-Williams), Houston Symphony Orch., 1967, L'Histoire du Soldat (Stravinski), U. Houston Symphony Orch., 1957, Am. premier Babar the Elephant (Poulenc-Francais), Houston Chamber Orch., 1967, Le Roi David (Honegger), 1979, Voice of God in opera Noye's Fludde (Britten), St. Stephen's Music Festival, 1981; bd. dirs., program annotator Music Guild, Houston, 1960-67, v.p., 1963-67, adv. bd., 1967-70; bd. dirs. Contemporary Music Soc., Houston, 1958-63; mem.-at-large, bd. dirs. Houston Grand Opera Guild, 1966-67; mem. repertory com. Houston Grand Opera Assn., 1967-70; bd. dirs. Houston Grand Opera, 1970-75, adv. bd. 1978-79; mem. cultural adv. com. Jewish Cmty. Ctr., 1960-66; bd. dirs. Houston Friends Pub. Libr., 1962-67, 73-75, 1st v.p., 1963-67; adv. mem. cultural affairs com. Houston C. of C., 1972-75; adv. bd. dirs. The Wilhelm Schole, 1980-98, Buffalo Bayou Support Com., 1985-87, bd. dirs. The Moores Sch. Music Soc., 1998—; charter mem. 1927 Soc. U. Houston, 1998—; bd. dirs. U. Houston Retiree Assn., 1999—, v.p., 2000—. Recipient Master Tchg. award Coll. Humanities and Fine Arts U., Houston, 1980, Favorite Prof. award Bapt. Student Union, U. Houston, 1991. Mem. MLA, Coll. English Assn., L'Alliance Francaise, English-Speaking Union, Alumni Assn. Fla. So. Coll., Fla. State U., Am. Assn. U. Profs., South Ctrl. MLA, Conf. Editors Learned Jours., Coll. Conf. Tchrs. English, Nat. Coun. Tchrs. English, Am. Studies Assn., Phi Beta (patron), Phi Mu Alpha Sinfonia, Alpha Psi Omega, Pi Kappa Alpha, Sigma Tau Delta (citied as an Outstanding Prof. of English U. Houston chpt. 1990), Houston Philos. Soc., Tau Kappa Alpha, Phi Kappa Phi, Caledonian Club (London). Episcopalian. Avocations: tennis, racquetball, swimming, traveling. Home: 2625 Arbuckle St Houston TX 77005-3929 Office: U Houston Dept English U Park 3801 Cullen Blvd Houston TX 77004-2602

PRZHONSKA, OLGA VICTOROVNA, physicist, researcher; b. Dniepropetrovsk, Ukraine, Sept. 18, 1946; d. Victor Fedorovish and Zoya Alexandrovna (Strokatova) Dobrovolsky; m. Anatoly Mikhailovich Przhonsky, Nov. 28, 1970 (dec. Feb. 1991); 1 child, Natalia. Diploma (hon.), Poly. Sch. Kiev, 1964; MSc in Optics (hon.), U. Kiev, 1969; PhD in Physics, Inst. Physics, Kiev, 1979. Rsch. scientist Inst. Physics, Kiev, 1969-84, sr. rsch. scientist, 1985—; vis. scientist BAM, Berlin, 1994, U. Oreg., Eugene, 1995, CREOL/UCF, Orlando, 1996; lectr. U. Rome, 1995. Contbr. articles to profl. jours. Grantee DFG, Berlin, 1995, CIES, Orsay, France, 1996, NSF, 1997. Office: Inst of Physics, Prospect Nauki 46, 252650 Kiev 22, Ukraine

PRZYBOJEWSKA, BARBARA, microbiologist, researcher; b. Sniadowo, Poland, July 15, 1939; d. Emilian and Zofia (Parowska) P. M in Microbiology, Maria Curie Sklodowska U., 1963; DSc in Agrl. Scis., Agrl. Acad., Lublin, Poland, 1972. Rsch. scientist Inst. Occupl. Medicine, Lublin, 1963-73, Med. Acad., Lodz, Poland, 1974-76; mgr. Sanitary Sta., Pabianice, 1977-79; rschr. Inst. Occupl. Medicine, Lodz, Poland, 1980—. Author: Toxic, Genotoxic and Potential Carcinogenic Activity of Azo, Triphenylmethane and Antraquinone Dyes, 1993, Guide to Short-Term Tests for Detecting Mutagenic and Carcinogenic Chemicals, 1993; contbr. numerous articles to profl. jours. Mem. European Environ. Mutagen Soc., Polish Soc. Occupl. Medicine, N.Y. Acad. Sci., Polish Soc. Toxicology. Roman Catholic. Avocations: travel, reading, collecting stamps. Home: Astronautow 5 m 29, 93-533 Lodz Poland Office: Inst Occupl Medicine, 8 St Teresy, 90-950 Lodz Poland

PRZYBYLAK, RAJMUND KRZYSZTOF, climatologist; b. Nakło, Poland, Apr. 21, 1957; s. Zygmunt and Jadwiga (Małek) P.; m. Dorota Bernarda Makuła, Apr. 12, 1986; children: Anna Maria, Julia Dorota. M, Nicholas Copernicus U., Toruń, Poland, 1980, PhD, 1988. Tech. asst. Polish Acad. Sci., Toruń, 1980-82; asst. Nicholas Copernicus U., Toruń, 1982-88, adj., 1988—. Author: The Thermic and Humidity Relations Against a Background of the Circulations Conditions in Hornsund, 1992. Rsch. grantee Com. of Sci. Rsch., 1992-95, 99—. Mem. Polish Geophys. Soc., Am. Geophys. Union, European Geophys. Soc. Roman Catholic. Avocations: skiing, sailing, tennis, volleyball, football. Home: Legionów 165b/7, 87-100 Toruń Poland Office: Nicholas Copernicus U, Danielewskiego 6, 87-100 Toruń Poland

PRZYBYLSKI, MARIUS, physicist; b. Zielona Gora, Poland, July 19, 1953; arrived in Germany, 1983; s. Jerzy and Lidia (Smolenski) P.; m. Margarete Eva Kucharczyk, Mar. 10, 1983; children: Rafael, Dawid. MSc, U. Poznan, Poland, 1977; PhD in Molecular Physics, Polish Acad. Scis., Poznan, 1981. Staff scientist Inst. Molecular Physics Polish Acad. Scis., 1977-83; Alexander von Humboldt Found. rsch. fellow U. Göttingen, Germany, 1983-85; postdoctoral fellow Max-Planck Inst. Polymer Rsch., Mainz, Germany, 1985-87; sr. laser scientist Laser Lab., Gottingen, 1987-90; product mgr. excimer and dye laser Lumonics, Inc., Munich, 1990-94; pres. ATL Lasertechnik Ltd., Wermelskirchen, Germany, 1995—; rsch. fellow Netherlands Energy Rsch. Found./ECN, Petten, The Netherlands, 1979-80, Ctr. d'Etudes Nucleaires de Fontenay aux Roses, Paris, 1983, numerous sci. presentations and lectures. Contbr. numerous articles to profl. jours. Recipient Sci. award for Physics Polish Acad. Scis., 1982. Mem. German Phys. Soc. Avocations: swimming, skiing, travel. Office: ATL Lasertechnik GmbH, Forstring 48, 42929 Wermelskirchen Germany

PRZYTYCKI, JOZEF HENRYK, mathematician; b. Warsaw, Oct. 14, 1953; s. Jakub and Roza (Awrach) P.; m. Teresa Maria Szczepanek, June 19, 1984; children: Tomasz, Pawel. MS, Warsaw U., 1977; PhD, Columbia U., 1981; Habilitation, Warsaw U., 1994. Postdoctoral fellow Toronto U., Ont., 1987-88; mem. Inst. for Advanced Study, Princeton, N.J., 1990; prof. math. George Washington U., Washington, 1999—; adj. prof. Warsaw U., 1982-86; vis. asst. prof. U. B.C., Vancouver, Can., 1986-87, vis. assoc. prof., 1988-89; vis. scholar Mich. State U., East Lansing, 1989; assoc. vis. prof. Univ. Calif., Riverside, 1990-92; vis. assoc. rsch. mathematician U. Calif., Berkeley. Assoc. editor: The Jour. of Knot Theory, 1995—; contbr. articles to profl. jours. Recipient prize of pres. Warsaw U., 1989. Mem. Polish Math. Soc. (Marcinkiewicz prize 1977), Am. Math. Soc., Math. Assn. Am., AAAS. Office: George Washington Univ 2201 G St NW Funger 428 Washington DC 20052-0001

PSAKHIS, BORIS YOSIPOVICH, thermophysicist, researcher; b. Odessa, Ukraine, Feb. 1, 1939; s. Yosip Abramovich P. and Ciliya Moyseevna Clur; m. Lianna Mikhailovna Rouzis, July 12, 1959; children: Renata, Irina. MSc, State Acad. Refrigeration, Odessa, Ukraine, 1962, Habilitation, 1991; PhD, Acad. Scis. USSR, Novosibirsk, Russia, 1974; DSc, Acad. Refrigeration, St. Petersburg, Russia, 1978. Cert. engr. Head designer group Spl. Design Bureau, Odessa, Ukraine, 1962-71; chief engr. Siberian br. Tekhenergochimprom, Novosibirsk, Russia, 1971-86; dir. Odessa br. Tekhenergochimprom, Russia, 1986-90; dir. Water Treatment Engrng. Ctr., Odessa, Russia, 1990—; lab. head Inst. Thermophysics, Siberian Acad. Scis., Novosibirsk, Russia, 1971-86; head of expert group Ministry Sci. and Tech., Moscow, 1978-90; prof., chair State Acad. Refrigeration, Odessa, Ukraine, 1986-97; head tech. experts adv. coun. Gov. Ukraine, Kiev, 1990-96. Author: Methods for Waste Heat Treatment, 1984, Ways of Utilization of Secondary Energy Resources, 1984, Energy Savings in Chemical Industries, 1986. Recipient diplomas All-Union Mendeleef Chem. Soc., Moscow, 1975, 76, 78, gold and silver medals achievements in nat. economy of USSR exhbn. com., Moscow, 1978, 84, first prize All-Union competition for best offer in saving electric & heat energy, 1981. Mem. Acad. Scis. Technol. Cybernetics (chief sci. sec. 1993—). Avocations: poetry, traveling. E-mail: psakhis@paco.net. Home: 4 Osipov St Apt 15, 270011 Odessa Ukraine Office: Engrng Ctr Water Treatment, 37 Pushkinskaya St, 270011 Odessa Ukraine

PSALTIKIDOU, MARIA, hospital engineer; b. Kavala, Greece, July 9, 1962; d. Ioannis and Ariadni Psaltikidou; m. Constantinos Retsos, June 13, 1997. Diploma in elec. engring., Aristotelian U. Thessaloniki, Greece, 1985; MSc, Pa. State U., 1988, PhD, 1992. Rschr. Biotrast V.E.T.P., Thessaloniki, 1992-95, Aristotelian U. Thessaloniki, 1993; seminar tchr. Ctr. Cont. Edn., Thessaloniki, 1995-96; asst. prof. Technol. Inst. Greece, Thessaloniki, 1995-96; engring. programmer, cons. Imaging Arts, Thessaloniki, 1995—; hosp. engr. Theageneèo Anti-cancer Hosp., Thessaloniki, 1997—. Mem. IEEE, Tech. Parliament Greece. Avocations: film, reading books, travel. Office: Theageneèo Hosp, 2 A Symeonidi St, Thessaloniki Greece

PSALTIS, HELEN, medical and surgical nurse; b. Rockford, Ill., Nov. 27, 1931; d. Harry and Martha (Triantafelakis) P. Diploma, St. Margaret Hosp., Hammond, Ind., 1953; BSN, DePaul U., 1961; MS in Health Edn., Purdue U., 1971; MSN, Purdue U., Calumet, Ind., 1988. RN, Ind., cert. sch. nurse, Ind. Sch. nurse Pub. Sch. City of E. Chgo., Ind.; asst. supr., staff nurse, instr. St. Catherine Hosp., East. Chgo., Ind.; instr., head nurse, staff nurse St Margaret Hosp., Hammond. Mem. ANA, Nat. League for Nursing, Sigma Theta Tau. Home: 4303 Ivy St East Chicago IN 46312-3026

PSARIANOS, BASIL, highway engineering educator, consultant; b. Piraeus, Attica, Greece, Sept. 19, 1954; s. Michael and Evangelia (Peraki) P.; m. Panagiota Kapota, June 5, 1994; 1 child. MSc, Nat. Tech. U. Athens, Greece, 1976; DEng in Rural and Surveying Engring., U. Hannover, Germany, 1982. Freelance engr., Athens, 1984-87; lectr. hwy. engring. Nat. Tech. U. Athens, 1987-92, asst. prof., 1992-97, assoc. prof., 1997—; cons. engr., Athens, 1984—. Co-author: Highway Design and Traffic Safety Engineering Handbook, 1999; contbr. articles to Transp. Rsch. Record, Strassen-und Tiefbau. Sgt. Greek Army, 1982-84. Mem. Transp. Rsch. Bd., Forschungsgesellschaft für Strassen-und Verkehrswesen, Deutscher Verein für Vermessungswesen. Greek Orthodox. Home: 148 Kourtidou St, GR-11143 Athens Greece Office: Nat Tech U Athens, 9 Hiroon Polytechniou St, GR-15780 Athens Greece

PSHENICHNIKOV, ALEXANDER FYODOROVICH, physicist; b. Perm Region, Russia, Sept. 16, 1946; s. Fyodor Pavlovich and Marie Andreevna Kotsheeva P.; m. Lidia Nikolaevna Trubina, Sept. 30, 1972; children: Sergei, Yuri. MS, Perm State U., Russia, 1969; PhD, Kazakhstan State U., 1978; DSc, Physcis of Metal Inst., Russia, 1992. Asst. Perm State U., 1969-72, lectr., 1974-83; sr. rsch. scientist Inst. of Continuous Media Mechanics, Perm, 1983-87, leading rsch. scientist, 1987-91, head of lab., 1991—; assoc. prof. Perm State U., 1989-92, prof. physics, 1992—. Editor: (book) Nonequilibrium processes in magnetic suspensions, 1986; contbr. articles to profl. jours. Grantee Internat. Sci. Found., 1994-95, Russian Found. for Basic Rsch., 1993-2001, Russian Acad. of Scis., 1994—; state sci. scholar Presidium of Russian Acad. of Scis., 1994-96, 97-99. Fellow Inst. Continuous Media Mechanics, Scientific Coun. in Mechanics. Office: UB of Russian Acad Scis, Inst Mech/1 Korolyov St, 614013 Perm Russia

PSHENISNOV, KIRILL PAVLOVICH, surgeon, educator; b. Yaroslavl, Russia, Jan. 21, 1960; s. Tamara Fedorovna Peshenisova; m. Inna Yurievna Khlobystova, Aug. 4, 1987 (div. Nov. 1993); 1 child, Artiom; m. Elena Sergeevna Tchenykaeva, Aug. 1, 1997; 1 child, Kirill. MD, Med. Sch., Yaroslavl, 1982, PhD, 1985; PhD, Mil. Acad., St. Petersburg, Russia, 1992. Supreme quality qualification in surgery, 1994. Lectr. Med. Inst., Yaroslavl, 1985-89, asst. prof., 1989-94; assoc. prof. Med. Acad., Yaroslavl, 1994-96, prof., 1996—; dir. Plastic Surgery Ctr., Yaroslavl, 1997—; pres. Northeastern Partnership Plastic and Reconstructive Surgeons, Yaroslavl, 1997—. Contbr. articles to profl. jours.; inventor in field. Dep. of People's Deps. Mcpl. Soviet Coun., Yaroslavl, 1980-82. Lenin's Stipend grantee Ministry of High Edn., Moscow, 1979-82; recipient medal and diploma Acad. Med. Scis., Moscow, 1981, Ministry of High Edn., 1981. Mem. Russian Soc. Plastic, Reconstructive and Aesthetic Surgeons (founder, chmn. com.) Am. Soc. Plastic and Reconstructive Surgeons (corr.), N.Y. Acad. Scis. Avocations: volleyball, swimming, boating, drawing, photography. Office: Med Acad, 5 Revolutsionnaya St, 150000 Yaroslavl Russia

PSIHARIS, NICHOLAS See HARRICE, NICHOLAS CY

PSOMAS, MARSELO IGNATIO, food service executive; b. Mytilene, Greece, July 4, 1957; came to U.S., 1975; s. Ignatio F. and Helen E. (Rallidi) P.; children: Nate, Nicole. AS in Aero. Studies, Embry-Riddle U., 1980, AS Aero. SCi., 1981, BS in Aero Studies, 1982, postgrad., 1982-83. Asst. mgr., maitre'D Sheridan Sq. Restaurant, N.Y.C., 1975-79; asst. gen. mgr., maitre'D Daniels of Daytona, Daytona Beach, Fla., 1979-82; pres., gen. mgr. Athen's Pizza Inn, Inc. (dba Franco's), New Smyrna Beach, Fla., 1982—; pres., chief exec. officer Carlo's Restaurant Concepts, Inc. (holding co. Franco's, Inc. and Franco's Skyline Restaurant and Lounge); cons. Italian cuisine Daytona Beach Community Coll., 1982—. Mem. Wine Inst. Calif., Embry-Riddle Alumni Assn., Chaine De Rottisseries. Republican. Club: Flying (Daytona Beach). Lodge: Rotary. Avocations: tennis, flying, running, bicycling, skiing. Office: Riverview Charlies Seafood Grill Piano Lounge 101 Flagler Ave New Smyrna Beach FL 32169-2634

PSTRUZINA, KAREL, philosopher, educator; b. Ostrava, Moravia, Czech Republic, Jan. 23, 1941; s. Jan and Marie (Cimburova) P.; m. Jaroslava Hurtikova, Nov. 30, 1963 (div. June 1973); 1 child, Jiri. PhDr., U. Charles, Prague, Czech Republic, 1967, PhD, 1979, Doctor, 1981. Asst. dept. philosophy U. Econ., Prague, 1967-81, docent, chair dept. philosophy, 1981—. Author: Introduction to the Methodology, 1972, The World of Modern Thinking, 1985, The Etudes on the Brain and Thinking, 1993, The Place of Man in History, 1996, The World of Cognition, 1998; editor E-LOGOS Jour., 1993—. Recipient Silver medal for pedagogical work Ministry of Edn., Czech Republic, 1985. Mem. Soc. Philosophy, Natural Alternative Philos. Assn. Avocations: theatre, literature, chess, puzzles. Home: Slovinska 8, 101 00 Prague Czech Republic Office: Univ Econ, W Churchilla 4, 130 67 Prague Czech Republic

PSYCHOUDAKIS, ASIMAKIS DEMETRIOS, agricultural economy educator, consultant; b. Ptolemais, Greece, Sept. 22, 1943; s. Demetrios Asimakis and Katerini Ioani (Tsapari) P.; m. Sophia Asimakis Popoutsi, Aug. 22, 1971; children: Demetrios, Vasilis. BSc in agrl., Aristole U., Thessaloniki, Greece, 1968, BSc in econs., 1974; PhD, U. Cambridge, Eng., 1984. Rsch. and teaching asst. Univ. Thessaloniki, 1970-84, lectr., 1985-87, asst. prof., 1988-92, assoc. prof., 1993-99, prof., 1999—. Contbr. articles to profl. jours. Home: N Telloglou 5, 546-36 Thessaloniki Greece Office: Aristoltle Univ of Thessaloniki, 540-06 Thessaloniki Greece

PTASZKOWSKI, STANLEY EDWARD, JR., civil engineer, structural engineer; b. N.Y.C., June 11, 1943; s. Stanley Edward and Elsie Helena (Heihs) P. AAS, Acad. Aeronautics, Flushing, N.Y., 1967; BS in Civil Engring., U. Mo., 1975. Registered profl. engr., Tex., profl. sanitarian, Tex. Engr. Brown & Root, Inc., Houston, Tex., 1975-79; sr. engr. Marathon Marine Engring. Co., Houston, 1979-84, Gen. Dynamics, Ft. Worth, 1984-91, Bridgefarmer & Assocs., Dallas, 1991-93; prin. Pasko Consultants, Arlington, Tex., 1993—; mgr. spl. projects Raytheon Svc. Co., Ft. Worth, 1994—. Mem. NSPE, Tex. Soc. Profl. Engrs., Soc. Profl. Bldg. Designers (cons.). Lutheran. Avocations: lic. pvt. pilot, golf, racquet ball. Home: 2002 Park Hill Dr Arlington TX 76012-1926

PTITCHNIKOVA, GALINA ALEXANDROVNA, architect, educator, researcher; b. Krasnojarsk, USSR, Mar. 1958; d. Alexander Ivanovich and Tamara Grigorievna (Konchevska) P.; m. Alexey Vladimirovich Antuyfeev, June 20. 1987; 1 child, Olga. MArch, Poly. Inst., Krasnojarsk, USSR, 1980; PhD in Arch., Moscow Archtl. Inst., 1985. Asst. tchr. Poly. Inst., Krasnojarsk, 1980-82; chief porject State Project Inst., Volgograd, USSR, 1987-92; prof. State Arch. and Engring. Acad., Volgograd, 1992—; guest rschr. Royal Inst. Tech., Stockholm, 1994-95, 97-98; cons. Town Planning Coun., Krasnojarsk, 1985-87, Volgograd, 1987-92. Author: Town Planning and Architecture of Sweden 1980-2000, 1999 (prize VolgGASA 1999), (text) Town Planning, 1992; contbr. articles to profl. jours. Expert advisor Ecol. Parliament, Volgograd, 1991-96; expert Regional Ctr. Biodiversity, Volgograd, 1999—. Grantee Wenner-Gren Ctr., Stockholm, 1996-97, UNESCO, 1996, Swedish Inst., Stockholm, 1999. Mem. Union Architects of Russia, Union Designers of Russia, Union of Urbanists Russia. Russian Orthodox. Avocations: painting, drawing, landscape design. Home: Tkacheva St 11-144, 400087 Volgograd Russia Office: VolgGASA, Academicheskaya St 1, 400074 Volgograd Russia

PU, HONGJUN, systems architect; b. Ma'anshan, Anhui, China, Aug. 10, 1961; arrived in Germany, 1989; parents Zhihu Pu and Kaifan Zhu; m. Yan Li, July 26, 1986; 1 child, Zhaoxin. BS of Engring., China U. Sci. and Tech., Hefei, 1982, MS of Engring., 1985; D of Engring., U. Wuppertal, Germany, 1997. Asst. China U. Sci. and Tech., Hefei, 1985-87, lectr., 1987-89; rsch. fellow U. Wuppertal, 1990-99; sys. arch. VDO Car Comm., Wetzlar, Germany, 1999—. Author: (book) Compact, Systematic and Complete Robot Dynamics, 1998; contbr. papers to profl. jours. Recipient 2d prize for progress in sci. and tech. Chinese Acad. Scis., 1987. Mem. N.Y. Acad. Scis.

PU, ZENG YUAN, professor of law, consultant; b. Jiading, Shanghai, Nov. 26, 1928; s. Yong and Zu Xuan (Wang) Pu; m. Pei Ti Zhou, Feb. 1, 1957; 1 child, Jun. LLB, Soochow U., Shanghai, 1951. Asst. East China Inst. Polit. Sci. and Law, Shanghai, 1952-56, lectr., 1956-58; lectr., chief acad. secretariat Shanghai Acad. Social Scis., 1958-79; assoc. rsch. prof. Inst. Law, Shanghai Acad. Social Scis., 1980-87, dep. dir., 1981-89, rsch. prof., 1987—; vis. prof. Coll. William and Mary Law Sch., Williamsburg, Va., 1987-88, U. Sydney (Australia) Law Sch., 1991; legis. cons. standing com. Shanghai Mcpl. People's Congress, 1994—. Editor: Constitutional Law, 1982 (award 1986), Highlights of Constitutional Systems and Private Laws in the Countries of the World, 1987 (award 1988). Recipient of Govt. Spl. Allowance, State Coun. People's Republic of China, 1993. Mem Internat. Assn. Constitutional Law (mem. exec. com. 1999—), China Law Soc. (vice-chmn. constitutional law rsch. com. 1985—), Chinese Assn. Polit. Sci. (dir. 1980—), Shanghai Law Soc. (chmn. constitutional law rsch. com. 1984—), Shanghai Assn. Polit. Sci. (v.p. 1984—). Communist. Avocations: poetry, calligraphy, philately. Office: Inst Law Shanghai Acad, 622/7 Huaihai Zhong Rd, Shanghai 200020, China

PUANG, MELVIN KAH WEI, aerospace engineer; b. Singapore, Dec. 4, 1971; s. Robert Chee Loong and Shelagh Ah Moi (Seow) P. BS in Aerospace Engring., U. Md., 1995; MS in Aeronautics, Imperial Coll., Eng., 1997. Progress adminstr. Singapore Armed Forces, 1990-91; aerospace engr. Singapore Air Force, 1997-98; rsch. engr. Nanyang Technol. U., 1998—; math. lectr. Open U., Eng., 1999-2000; remote sensing/satellite imaging assoc. scientist Nat. U. Singapore, 2000—; math. modeling tutor Singapore Inst. of Mgmt., 2000—. Co-author: The Elements of Academic Research, 1996. Mem. AIAA, IEEE, Royal Aeronaut. Soc., Golden Key, Sigma Gamma Tau, Tau Beta Pi. Avocations: aeromodelling, travel, badminton, swimming. Home: Blk 117 Bukit Merah Cen, Bukit Merah Cen # 10-3755, Singapore Singapore

PUCCETTI, LUCA, rheumatologist, researcher; b. Pisa, Tuscany, Italy, Aug. 6, 1957; s. Lorenzo Puccetti and Osanna Rambelli; m. Elda Neri, May 30, 1987; children: Lavinia, Lorenza. MD, U. Pisa, Italy, 1985. Prof. Sch. Rheumatology U. Pisa (Italy), 1995—. Contbr. articles to profl. jours. Mem. Internat. Soc. for Study of Pain, Italian Soc. Rheumatology, Am. Soc. for Bone and Mineral Rsch. Avocations: computer games, gardening, classical music. E-mail: lpuccett@int.med.unipi.it. Home: Via Brogiotti 5, 56011 Calci Pisa, Italy Office: Via Toscoromagnola 1082, S Frediano Cascina, 56021 Cascina Pisa, Italy

PUCHKOV, ANDREW ALEXANDER, architecture educator, writer; b. Kyiv, Ukraine, USSR, Mar. 4, 1970; s. Alexander Anatoly and Nataly Georg (Nazarova) P.; m. Svetlana Victor Simakova, Dec. 17, 1994; 1 child, Nikita. BS Architecture, Kyiv Civil Engr. U., Ukraine, 1993; PhD Architecture, Kyiv Civil Engr. U., 1996. Asst. Kyiv Civil Engr. U., 1993-96, asst. prof., 1996-2000; learned sec. Sci. Rsch. Inst. Theory and History Arch. and Town Planning, Kyiv, Ukraine, 1995—. Author: Theory of Architecture Spatial Surroundings, 1994, Architectonica of the Book, or Bibliograph's Methempsychosis (about I. Rerberg), 1995, Etudes of the Architecturology, 1996, Alexander Gabrichevsky: Architectural Organism Conception in the Mental Process 20-30th, 1997, The Paradox of Antiquity: Artistic and Plastic Corporality as a Principle of Classical Architecture, 1998, Julian Kulakovsky and His Time: From the History of Ancient and Byzantine Studies in Russia, 2000; editor: A. Gabrichevsky. The Theory and History of Architecture: The Selected Works, 1993, J. Kulakovsky. Avitus, bishop of Wiennus (Bourgund.) the School and World Outlook, 1999; contbr. 150 articles to profl. jours. Recipient prize Nat. Acad. Scis. Ukraine, 1995. Mem. Nat. Union Architects Ukraine, Union Urbanists Ukraine. Avocations: investigations, reading and writing books. Home: 32/16 Roussanovskaya Naberejna St, 03147 Kyiv Ukraine Office: NDITIAM, 9 Velika Zhytomirskaya St, 01025 Kyiv Ukraine

PUCHTLER, HOLDE, histochemist, pathologist, educator; b. Kleinlosnitz, Germany, Jan. 1, 1920; came to U.S., 1955; d. Gottfried and Gunda (Thoma) P. Cand. med., U. Würzburg, 1944; Md, U. Köln, 1949; MD, U. Köln, Germany, 1951. Rsch. assoc. U. Köln, 1949-51, resident in pathology, 1951-55; rsch. fellow Damon Runyon Found., Montreal, Que., Can., 1955-58; rsch. assoc. Med. Coll. Ga., Augusta, 1959-60, asst. rsch. prof., 1960-62, assoc. rsch. prof., 1962-68, prof., 1968-90, prof. emerita, 1990—. Assoc. editor Jour. Histotech., 1982-94; mem. editorial bd. Histochemistry, 1977-90. Honored at Symposium on Connective Tissues in Arterial and Pulmonary Diseases, 1980. Fellow Am. Inst. Chemists, Royal Microscopical Soc.; mem. Royal Soc. Chemistry, Am. Chem. Soc., Histochem. Soc. Gesellschaft Histochemie, Anatomische Gesellschaft, Ga. Soc. Histotech. (hon.). Achievements include development of new techniques for light, polarization, visible and infrared flourescence microscopy based on theoretical and physical chemistry and x-ray diffraction data; demonstration of relations between dye configurations and selective affinity for certain components of human tissues, such as collagens, elastin, myosins, neurofibrils, and amyloids; application of molecular orbital theories to histochemistry. Avocations: archeology, history of science, folk medicine, comparative religion. Office: Med Coll Ga Dept Pathology Augusta GA 30912

PUCKETT, C. LIN, plastic surgeon, educator; b. Burlington, N.C., Oct. 19, 1940; s. Harry W. and Lula C. Puckett; m. Florence Elizabeth Loy, June 18, 1961 (div. 1976); children: Loy C., Lisa A., Leslie A.; m. Patricia Louise Wells, June 17, 1984 (div. 1994); 1 child, Harry James; m. Teresa G. Teel, Nov. 24, 1995. MD, Bowman Gray Sch. Medicine, 1966. Assoc. in surgery Duke U. Med. Ctr., Durham, N.C., 1971-73; assoc. prof., head divsn. plastic surgery U. Mo. Med. Ctr., Columbia, 1976-81; prof., head attending plastic surgeon U. Mo. Med. Ctr., Truman VA Hosp., Columbia, 1982—. Mem. editl. bd. Jour. Plastic & Reconstructive Surgery, 1994—; contbr. articles to profl. jours. Fellow ACS (gov. 1992-98); mem. AMA, Am. Assn. Hand Surgery (bd. dirs. 1982-84, chmn. nominating com. 1985, v.p. 1987, pres.-elect 1988, pres. 1988—), Am. Assn. Plastic Surgeons (trustee 1995), Am. Cleft Palate Assn., Am. Soc. Plastic and Reconstructive Surgeons Inc. (bd. dirs. 1985—, asst. sec. 1988, trustee 1990, chmn. bd. trustees 1992, parlamentarian 1993, historian 1994, sec. 1995, v.p. 1997—, pres.-elect 1998, pres. 1999), Am. Bd. Plastic Surgery (cert., bd. dirs. 1988-94, chmn. 1993-94), Am. Soc. Surgery of the Hand, Am. Trauma Soc., Internat. Microsurg. Soc., Mo. Chpt. ACS, Plastic Surgery Rsch. Coun., So. Med. Assn., Assn. Acad. Chmn. Plastic Surgery (bd. dirs. 1985—, pres. 1987-88), Sigma Xi, Alpha Omega Alpha. Republican. Avocation: breeding Quarter horses, angus cattle. Office: U Mo Med Ctr Divsn Plastic Surgery 1 Hospital Dr Columbia MO 65212-0001

PUCKETT, PAUL DAVID, electronics company executive; b. Atlanta, July 31, 1941; s. Jonas Levi and Ovella (Juhan) P.; m. Margaret Ann Straetz, June 29, 1974, (div. Jan. 1984); m. Catherine Marie Ryan, Apr. 5, 1984; children: Shawn Michael, Glen David. BS in Edn., Nyack Coll., 1963; MBA in Mgmt., Pace U., 1988. Mgr. quality Rockland Systems Corp., Blauvelt, N.Y., 1971-75, Electronics for Medicine, Inc., White Plains, N.Y., 1975-77; mgr. ops. Tele-Resources, Inc., Armonk, N.Y., 1977-79; mgr. quality Materials Rsch. Corp., Orangeberg, N.Y., 1979-83; mgr. quality plasma systems div. Perkin-Elmer, Wilton, Conn., 1983-84, dir. ops. plasma systems div., 1984-86, mgr. spl. studies semiconductor group, 1986-87; mgr. quality programs instrument group Perkin-Elmer, Norwalk, Conn., 1987-90; dir. ops. applied sci. div. Perkin-Elmer (sold applied sci. div. to Orbital Scis. Corp.), Pomona, Calif., 1990-93; dir. ops. Pomona (Calif.) ops. Orbital Scis. Corp., 1993—; examiner Malcolm Baldrige Nat. Quality award, Gathersberg, Md., 1989-90, Conn. State Quality award, Stamford, 1988-90, cons., trainer, 1990. Contbr. articles to profl. jours. Mem. Young Reps., New City, N.Y., 1975-76; vol. police officer Rockland County Sheriff's Dept., New City, 1974-83; coach Am. Youth Soccer Orgn., Bethel, Conn., 1984-85. Recipient Conn. State Quality award, 1989. Mem. N.Y. Acad. Sci., Am. Soc. Quality Control, Assn. for Quality and Participation, Am. Electronics Assn. Republican. Episcopalian. Avocations: golf, racing, flying. Home: 1500 Mansfield Ct Upland CA 91784-7963 Office: Orbital Scis Corp Pomona Ops 2771 N Garey Ave Pomona CA 91767-1809

PUCKETT, RICHARD EDWARD, artist, consultant, retired recreation executive; b. Klamath Falls, Oreg., Sept. 9, 1932; s. Vernon Elijah and Leona Belle (Clevenger) P.; m. Velma Faye Hamrick, Apr. 14, 1957 (dec. 1985); children: Katherine Michelle Briggs, Deborah Alison Norton, Susan Lin Rowland, Gregory Richard. Student, So. Oreg. Coll. Edn., 1951-56, Lake Forest Coll., 1957-58, Hartnell Jr.Coll., 1960-70; BA, U. San Francisco, 1978. Acting arts and crafts dir. Ft. Leonard Wood, Mo., 1956-57; arts and crafts dir., asst. spl. svcs. officer, mus. dir. Ft. Sheridan, Ill., 1957-59; arts and crafts dir. Ft. Irwin, Calif., 1959-60, Ft. Ord, Calif., 1960-86; dir. arts and crafts br. Art Gallery, Arts and Crafts Ctr. Materials Sales Store, 1960; opening dir. Presidio Monterey Army Mus., 1968; dir. Model Army Arts and Crafts Program. One-man shows include Seasie City Hall, Ft. Ord Arts and Crafts Ctr. Gallery, 1967, 73, 79, 81, 84, 86, Presidio of Monterey Art Gallery, 1979, So. Oreg. Art Assn., Salinas Valley Art Gallery, Glass on Holiday, Gatlinburg, Tenn., 1981, 82, Del Messa Gallery, Carmel, Calif., 1998; exbns. in Mo., Ill.; also pvt. collections; designed and opened first Ft. Sheridan Army Mus., Presidio of Monterey Mus. Mem. Salinas (Calif.) Arts Coun. Recipient 1st pl. Dept. Army and U.S. Army Forces Command awards for programming and publicity, 1979-81, 83-85, 1st and 3d pl. sculpture awards Monterey County Fair Fine Arts Exhibit, 1979, Comdrs. medal civilian svcs., 1986, other awards, Golden Acad. award, Internat. Man of Yr. award, 1991-92. Mem. Monterey Peninsula Art Mus. Assn., Salinas Fine Arts Assn., So. Oreg. Art Assn., Ft. Ord Alumni Assn., Southern Ore Art Assn., Salinas Valley Art Assn. (pres. 2000—). Home: 210 San Miguel Ave Salinas CA 93901-3021 also: 110 Ashland Ave Medford OR 97504-7523

PUCKETT, ROBERT MARION, clergyman; b. June 17, 1926. BA, Mercer U., 1954; BD, Colgate Rochester Div. Sch., 1957; postgrad., U. Chgo., 1957-58; D Ministry, Princeton Theol. Sem., 1980. Ordained minister Am. Bapt. Ch., 1944, Internat. Coun. of Cmty. Chs., 1944. Min. small rural chs., Ga., Tenn.; small rural chs., Fla., 1947-54, Immanuel Congl. Ch., Ontario, N.Y., 1954-57, 1st Bapt. Ch., East Aurora, N.Y., 1964-67, Norris (Tenn.) Religious Fellowship, cmty. ch., 1967-94; assoc. min. South Ch.-Cmty. Bapt., Mt. Prospect, Ill., 1957-59, Scarsdale (N.Y.) Cmty. Bapt. Ch., 1959-64; min. visitation Tellico Village Cmty. Ch., Loudon, Tenn., 1994—; pres. Internat. Coun. Cmty. Chs., 1987-89; mem. Morehouse Coll. Preachers, Morehouse Coll., 1988. Editor Pastor's Jour., 1984-94, Inclusive Pulpit, 1996—. Faculty fellow Colgate Rochester Divinity Sch., 1957-58, Melvin Jones fellow Internat. Lions Club, 1994. Home and Office: 177 Chahyga Way Loudon TN 37774-2801

PUCKETT, STANLEY ALLEN, consultant, software engineer, business educator; b. Dayton, Ohio, July 21, 1951; s. Russell Elwood and Dorothy Christine (Hoskins) P.; m. Kum Cha Pak, July 28, 1986; children: Thomas Abraham, Jacqueline Sue. BGS, U. Ky., 1974; MSM, Troy State U., Eng., 1983; PhD, Sussex Coll., Eng., 1987. Asst. prof. mktg. Lamar U., Beaumont, Tex., 1987-88; asst. prof. mgmt. Grambling (La.) State U., 1988-93; realtor Tourtelot Bros., Inc., St. Petersburg, Fla., 1994-95, 97, Century 21 Am. Dream Realty, Inc., St. Petersburg, 1995-96; mainframe cons. Decision Cons., Inc., Clearwater, Fla., 1997-99; software engr. Computer Task Group, Tampa, Fla., 1997-98; IT cons. AT&T & SSI Group, 1999; cons. Open-Network Technologies, Clearwater, 2000—, eCommerce, 2000—; edn. cons. Hyundai Mgmt. Devel. Inst., I-chon, Korea, 1986-87; bus. cons. NAF Contracting Office, Ft. Polk, La., 1990; free enterprise fellow Students in Free Enterprise, Inc., Springfield, Mo., 1989-90; admissions liaison USAF Acad., Colorado Springs, Colo., 1989—; adj. prof. Union Inst. Grad. Sch., Tampa Coll., U. South Fla. Author: Social Marketing, 1988; contbg. author: Great Ideas for Teaching Marketing, 1991; editor chpts.: History of the 8th Air Force, 1986, 87-88, 89-92, History of U.S. Central Command, 1992-94. Maj. USAFR (ret), 1975-96. Named to Honorable Order of Ky. Colonels, 1974. Mem. Am. Assn. Individual Investors, Ret. Officers Assn., Air Force Assn., Republican. Mem. Christian Ch. (Disciples of Christ). Avocations: flying, computers, investing, golf, consulting. E-mail: Fantom01@netscape.net. Home and Office: 4500 15th Ave N Saint Petersburg FL 33713-5234

PUDDU, PAOLO EMILIO, cardiologist, educator, researcher; b. Rome, Oct. 7, 1952; s. Claudio Puddu and Maria Antonietta Dantoni; m. Isabella del Balzo di Presenzano, Nov. 29, 1979; children: Antonio Raimondo, Gian Lorenzo, Pier Ludovico, Francesco Simone. MD, Univ. La Sapienza, Rome, 1976, diploma in cardiology, 1979; diploma in hemodynamics, U. Montreal, Can., 1980; Diploma in Exptl. Surgery, U. Marseilles, France, 1983. Rsch. fellow U. Montreal, 1979-80, U. Marseilles, 1980-84; asst. prof. U. Rome, 1984-90; prof. pharmacology Cardiology Sch., Rome, 1990—; dir. lab. cardiovascular pharmacology U. Rome Sch. Medicine, 1991—. Contbr. articles to profl. jours. Lt. Italian Air Force, 1978. Fellow Am. Coll. Cardiology, European Soc. Cardiology; mem. French Soc. Cardiology (fgn.), Italian Soc. Cardiology. Avocations: heraldry, pope history, enthomology. Office: Inst Cardiac Surgery, Viale del Policlinico, 00161 Rome Italy

PUDLIK, WIESLAW WLADYSLAW, mechanical engineer, educator; b. Gdynia, Poland, Aug. 26, 1930; s. Bronislaw and Magdalena (Kleinert) P.; m. Alicja Teresa Wojtczuk, Mar. 23, 1961; 1 child, Marcin. B in Engring., Higher Engring. Coll., Gdansk, Poland, 1954; M in Engring., Tech. U. Gdansk, 1956, DEng, 1966, DSc, 1973. Energy inspector State Dredging Corp., Gdansk, 1950-54; rschr. Inst. Fluid Flow Machinery, Gdansk, 1955-65; educator, rschr. Tech. U. Gdansk, 1966-2000; rschr. Studsvik Energiteknik AB, Nyköping, Sweden, 1979-80; educator Hochschule Bremen, Germany, 1991-95; head dept. Tech. U. Gdansk, 1973-93, 97-2000, vice rector, 1984-87. Author: Heat Transfer, 1980, Thermodynamics, 1993, Problems in Thermodynamics, 2000; contbr. articles to profl. jours. Mem. Polish Soc. Theoretical and Applied Mechs. (bd. dirs. 1988-92), Polish Acad. Scis. (com. thermodynamics and combustion 1981-92). Roman Catholic. Avocations: sailing, swimming, cross-country skiing, classical music. E-mail: wpudlik@due.mech.pg.gda.pl. Home: Morenowa 79, PL 80172 Gdańsk Poland Office: Tech U Gdansk, G Narutowicza 11/12, PL 80952 Gdańsk Poland

PUDLO, FRANCES THERESA, executive assistant; b. Hartford, Conn., Jan. 17, 1948; d. Alexander and Eve Antoinette (Paczkowski) P. AS in Secretarial Sci., U. Hartford, 1974. Sec. United Techs. Corp., East Hartford, Conn., 1966-74; asst., sec. Richard M. Bissell, Jr., Farmington, Conn., 1974-94; adminstrv. officer DeWolfe New Eng., Avon, Conn., 1994-97; exec. asst. to pres. Painting & Decorating, Inc., New Britain, Conn., 1997—. Co-author: Reflections of a Cold Warrior: From Yalta to the Bay of Pigs, 1996. Bd. dirs. Friends of Hill-Stead Mus., Farmington, Conn., 1994—, sec. 2000—, SS Cyril and Methodius Sch., 2000—; mem. World Affairs Coun., 1996—; sec. 100th ann. com. SS Cyril and Methodius Ch., Hartford, 1997—, eucharistic minister, 2000—. Avocations: reading, cooking, gardening, ancient history, travel. Home: 63 Lafayette Ave East Hartford CT 06118-2628

PUENTE, JOSE GARZA, safety engineer; b. Cuero, Tex., Mar. 19, 1949; s. Roque Leos and Juanita Vela (Garza) P.; m. Francisca Rodriguez Estrada, Sept. 7, 1969; 1 child, Anthony Burk. BA, West Tex. A&M U., 1972; postgrad., U. Ariz., 1980; grad., U.S. Army Transp. Courses, 1972, 78, Command and Gen. Staff Coll., 1992; cert. pub. mgr., Ariz. State U., 1997. Cert. U.S. Coun. Accreditation in Occupl. Hearing, Audiometric Technicians of Am. Indsl. Hygiene Assn.; cert. pub. mgr., Ariz. Asst. gen. mgr. Am. Transit Corp., Tucson, 1972-75; pub. transp. supt. City of Tucson, 1975-77, asst. safety coord., 1977-81; safety coord. City of Mesa, Ariz., 1981-88; corp. safety dir. Am. Fence Corp., Phoenix, 1988-89; safety adminstr. Ariz.-ADOT, Phoenix, 1989-98; safety mgr. ADP Marshall, Raleigh, N.C., 1998, ADP Marshall Lucent Tech., Norcross, Ga., 1998-99; svcs. dir. Bell South Projects, Liberty Mut., Norcross, 1999—; owner La Paz Gospel Supplies & Gift shop, Tucson, 1979-80. Mem. Tucson Child Care Assn., 1973-74; mem. citizen task force Sunnyside Sch. Bd., 1977; mem. minority selection for Hispanic seatbelt program vendor Gov.'s Office of Hwy. Safety, 1989—; mem. Mayor's Task Force on Seatbelt Awareness, City of Mesa, 1988-89. Lt. Col. USAR, 1971-99. Recipient Excellence award Ariz. Safety Assn., 1984; fellow Advanced Mgmt. Seminar Urban Mass Transp. Adminstrn., Northeastern U., 1976-77. Mem. Am. Soc. Safety Engrs. (pres. Ariz. chpt. 1990-91, Safety Profl. of Yr. 1984), Inc. Mex.-Am. Govtl. Employees (charter), Ariz. Safety Engrs., Ariz. Mcpl. Safety Assn. (Profl. of Yr. 1986), Nat. Coun. of La Raza), Internat. Order DeMolay (charter), Toastmasters. Republican. Baptist. Fax: 770-831-6504. Home and Office: 5434 Culzean Way Suwanee GA 30024-4129 Office: 1750 Beaver Ruin Rd Ste 500 Norcross GA 30093-2805

PUENTE, YOLANDA, biochemist, allergist; b. Seville, Spain, Oct. 20, 1966; d. Manual Puente and Maria Jesus Crespo. MBBS, Seville U., 1989, MD, 1996. Resident in biochemistry Virgen del Rocio Hosp, Seville, Spain, 1992-95; resident in med. allergy Virgen Macarena Hosp., Seville, 1996-2000. Avocations: travel, reading. Home: Virgen de Lujan, 41011 Seville Spain

PUENTE FONSECA, CLAUDIO JULIO, pediatric surgeon; b. Bayamo, Granma, Cuba, July 1, 1945; s. Claudio and Marina (Fonseca) P.; m. Alina Maury, Dec. 14, 1969; children: Vivian, Liliana. MD, U. Oriente, 1971, 1st grade specialist pediatric surgery, 1975, 2d grade specialist pediatric surgery, 1985. Head pediatric surgery dept. Hosp. Infantil Sur Docente, Cuba, 1982-87, 1989—; pediatric surgeon Muhimbili Med. Ctr., Tanzania, 1987-89; instr. Sch. of Medicine, Cuba, 1975-82, asst. prof., 1982-87, aux. prof., 1987-98, prof. surgery, 1998—. Author: Terminologia ingles-espanol para la practica medica, 1997; contbr. articles to profl. jours. Recipient Medal for Cuban Edn. Ministry of Superior Edn., 1993. Mem. Cuban Soc. of Surgery, Caribbean Med. Assn. Avocations: philately, music, foreign languages. Home: Felix Pena 307 altos, Santiago de Cuba 90100, Cuba Office: Hosp Infantil Sur Docente, Ave 24 de Febrero 402, Santiago de Cuba 90200, Cuba

PUERNER, PAUL RAYMOND, lawyer; b. Milw., Mar. 27, 1927; s. Bertram Harvey and Carmen Marie (Sousa) P.; m. Rae Harriet Smart, Aug. 19, 1950; children: John, Pamela, Thomas, James, Jane, Michael, Susan. BS in Mech. Engring., U. Wis., 1949; JD, Harvard U., 1955. Bar: Ill. 1955, Wis. 1956, U.S. Dist. Ct. (ea. dist.) Wis. 1956, U.S. Ct. Appeals (7th cir.) 1957, U.S. Supreme Ct. 1960, U.S. Ct. Appeals (fed. cir.) 1982. Engr. Lago Oil & Transport Co., Aruba, The Netherlands, West Antilles, 1949-52; atty. Vapor Heating Corp., Chgo., 1955-56; assoc. Michael, Best & Friedrich, Milw., 1956-64, ptnr., 1964-87; pvt. practice Milw., 1987—. Bd. dirs. Mequon-Thiensville (Wis.) Union High Sch. Dist. 1, 1968—. With USNR, 1945-46. Mem. ABA, Wis. Bar Assn., Milw. Bar Assn., Wis. Intellectual Property Law Assn. (pres. 1970-71), Alpha Chi Rho. Methodist. Home: 335 E Antoine Dr Port Washington WI 53074-1398 Office: PO Box 26677 Milwaukee WI 53226-0677

PUGA, ANDRÉ TEIXEIRA, engineering educator; b. Porto, Portugal, June 30, 1961; s. Andres Puga Alvarez and Maria Pacheco Teixeira; m. Maria Ramos Costa, Aug. 8, 1989; 1 child, Clara Ramos. Licenciatura, Oporto (Portugal) U., 1985, MSc, 1991, PhD, 2000. Investigator Inst. Encenharia Sistemas Computadores, Porto, Portugal, 1986—; asst. Faculdade Encenharia U. Porto, Portugal, 1989-99, asst. prof., 2000—. Contbr. articles to profl. jours. Recipient Innovation and Creativity award Endiel, 1990. Mem. N.Y. Acad. Scis., Assn. Portuguesa Recouhecimento Padroes. Office: INESC-Porto Apt 4433, Largo Mompilher 22, 4007 Porto Portugal

PUGACHEVA, GALINA IVANOVNA, physicist, researcher; b. Moscow, Apr. 25, 1939; d. Ivan Antonovich and Antonina Sergueevna (Kukushkina) P.; m. Anatoly Alexandrovich Gusev, Sept. 12, 1972. BS, Moscow Engring.-Phys. Inst., 1962; MS, Russian Acad. Scis., Moscow, 1962; PhD, Moscow State U., 1973. Exptl. nuclear physics engring. Engr. Lebedev Physics Inst. Acad. Sci., Moscow, 1962-67; sr. scientist Nuclear Physics Inst. Moscow State U., 1967-92; rev., chief, opponent master's and PhD theses, 1975—; vis. prof. UNICAMP (U. Campinas (Brazil)), 1993—. Prin. investigator experiments on bd. satellites, 1971—; contbr. numerous articles to space physics jours.; inventor Cerenkov detector of spl. constrn. Head dept./labs. Sindicate of High Edn. Sch. Workers, Moscow, 1980-91. Recipient Medal of State Exposition of Advanced Tech. in Industry and Sci. Coun. Mins., 1974, 79, Medal of Yurj Gagarin Ministry High Edn. and Sci., 1991. Mem. Am. Geophys. Union (life), Soc. Brasileira Fisica. Russian Orthodox. Avocations: tennis, singing, classical music, cooking. Office: UNICAMP/IFGW/DRCC Cidade U, Zeferino Vaz Distrito Barao Geraldo 6165, 13083970 Campinas SP, Brazil

PUGEAT, MICHEL, endocrinologist; b. Lyon, France, Mar. 30, 1947; s. Henri and Simone (Galland) P.; m. Elisabeth Metiffiot; children: Guillaume, Antoine, Florent. MD, UCBL, Lyon, 1976, cert. in human biology, 1982. Physician HCL, Lyon, 1976-84, endocrinologist, 1994—; prof. UCBL, 1984—; rschr. INSERM, 1971-84, chief rschr., 1993—; cons. HCL, 1971—, dir., 1998—. Co-author: Binding Proteins of Steroids Hormones, 1986; contbr. articles to profl. jours. Mem. steering com. Lyon Hosps., 1998—. Grantee Fogarty Ctr., 1978-81, Endocrine Soc., 1999. Mem. AAAS, Endocrine Soc., Soc. Française d'Endocrinologie. Avocation: bicycling. Home: 47 chemin de Fontaniàres, 69350 La Mulatiàre France Office: Hosp Antiquaille, Clinique Endocrinologique, 69321 Lyon Cedex 5, France

PUGH, DAVID JOHN, accountant, company director; b. Cheadle Hulme, Cheshire, Eng., Sept. 17, 1950; s. John Ivor and Dorothy Pearl (Freeborn) P.; m. Martina Hill, Aug. 26, 1978; children: Andrew David, Martin James. B Commerce with honours, Leeds (Eng.) U., 1972. Fin. contr. Cory Oil & Gases, Send, Eng., 1984-87, William Cory & Son Ltd., Send, 1987-89; divsnl. fin. contr. Ocean Group plc, Bracknell, Eng., 1989-90; fin. dir. McGregor Cory, Stratford, Eng., 1990-93; project dir. McGregor Cory, Bracknell, 1993-94; dir. Daymar Ltd., Guildford, Eng., 1995—; sec. JLI Group plc, London, 1996-98; group company sec. Harrington Food Group plc, 1998—; treas. S.E. Petroleum Tng. Fedn., London, 1984-92. Treas. Old Stopfordians, London, 1983—, LL Appeal Fund, Guildford, 1990—. Fellow Chartered Accts. Eng. and Wales, Inst. Mgmt., Inst. Internal Auditors, Assoc. Inst. Logistics (treas. South East region 1995-98), Affiliate Inst. Credit Mgmt. Avocations: golf, sailing. Home: Merrow Park, 15 Partridge Way, Guilford GU4 7DW, England Office: 15 Partridge Way Merrow Pk, Guildford, Surrey GU4 7DW, England

PUGH, KYLE MITCHELL, JR., musician, retired music educator; b. Spokane, Wash., Jan. 6, 1937; s. Kyle Mitchel, Sr. and Lenore Fae (Johnson) P.; m. Susan Deane Waite, July 16, 1961; children: Jeffray, Kari. BA in Edu., East Wash. U., 1975. Cert. tchr., Wash. Tuba player Spokane Symphony Orch., 1958-63; rec. assoc. Century Records, Spokane, 1965-73; tuba player World's Fair Expo '74, Spokane, 1974; bass player Russ Carlyle Orch., Las Vegas, 1976, Many Sounds of Nine Orch., northwest area, 1969-81; band tchr. Garry Jr. High School, Spokane, 1976-79, Elementary Band Program, Spokane, 1979-96; bass player Doug Scott Cabaret Band, Spokane, 1982-91; dept. head Elem. Band Dept., Spokane, 1984-89. Editor (newsletter) The Repeater, 1987 (Amateur Radio News Svc. award 1987); extra in movie Always, 1989. Active in communications Lilac Bloomsday Assn., Spokane, 1977. Served to E-5 USNR, 1955-63. Recipient Disting. Service award Wash. State Commn., 1974, Nev. Hollerin' Champ Carl Hayden Scribe, 1979. Mem. Am. Fedn. Musicians (life), Spokane Edn. Assn. (rec. sec. 1987), Music Educator's Nat. Conf., Am. Radio Relay League (asst. dir. 1987), Ea. Wash. Music Educator's Assn. (pres. 1978-79), Dial Twisters Club (pres. 1979-80), VHF Radio Amateurs (dir. 1980-83), Elks. Avocations: ham radio operator, model railroading, photography. Home: 5006 W Houston Ave Spokane WA 99208-3728

PUGH, REVELLA, executive assistant; b. Clarksdale, Miss., June 16, 1947; d. Steve and Louetta (Underwood) Booker; divorced; children: Lorenzo Jr., Bethany Lynne. M in Mgmt. in Bus., Cambridge Coll., Boston, 1998. Cert. profl. sec. Sec. Joseph T. Ryerson & Son, St. Louis, 1967-76; asst. payroll Hercules Constrn., St. Louis, 1979-80; sec. May Dept. Stores, St. Louis, 1980-82; exec. sec. Olsten Svcs., St. Louis, 1984—; bd. dirs. Ryerson Employees Credit Union, St. Louis, 1974—; mem. pub. rels. com. Ryerson Steel Co., St. Louis, 1974—. Pres. Hazelwood PTA, St. Louis, 1982-83, coun. treas., 1986-87; leader local troop Girl Scouts U.S., 1983-84, cookie chmn., 1984-85; vol. speaker Women's Self Help Ctr., St. Louis, 1990; cert. in CPR by ARC, 1990; treas. Christian Women Fellowship Internat.; pres. Women's Mission Group. Mem. Profl. Sec. Internat. Avocations: church choir, church scouting, being a good aunt.

PUGH, RICHARD FORREST, food product company executive; b. Colwyn Bay, Eng., July 13, 1947; s. William Griffith and Doris (Clarkson) P.; m. Claudia Lacy, Aug. 19, 1978; children: Terry, Rachel. BSc, Liverpool (Eng.) U., 1969, PhD, 1972. Chartered chemist. Lab. mgr. Cadbury, Birmingham, Eng., 1972-74, rsch. mgr., 1974-78; prodn. mgr. Cadbury Typhoo, Liverpool, Eng., 1978-83, gen. mgr., 1983-85; tech. dir. Tesco, Cheshunt, Eng., 1985-95; dir. rsch. and devel. Whitbread Plc, Luton, Eng., 1995-99; CEO Leatherhead Food Rsch. Assn., Eng., 2000—; bd. dirs. Horticulture Rsch. Internat., Wellesbourne, Eng.; mem. exec. com., bd. dirs. Leatherhead Food Rsch. Assn., Eng., 1991-94; mem. rsch. steering com. Meat & Livestock Commn., Milton Keynes, Eng., 1993-95; chmn. tech. com. British Retail Consortium, London, 1992-95; mem. food adv. com. Ministry of Agrl. Fish & Food, London, 1993-97; mem. exec. bd. Brewing Rsch. Found. Internt., Redhill, Eng., 1996-98. Mem. eco-labelling bd. Dept. of Environment, London, 1992-94, nutrition task force Dept. Health, London, 1992-97. Fellow Royal Soc. Chemistry, Royal Soc. Arts, Inst. Food Sci.; mem. Royal Agrl. Coll. Cirencester Eng. (strategy group 1997-99), Inst. Grocery Distbn. Eng. (chmn. nutrition labeling group 1993—). Avocations: fly fishing, cycling, numismatism, food. E-mail: rfpugh@lfra.co.uk. Office: Leatherhead Internat plc, Randalls Rd Leatherhead Surrey KT22 7RY, England

PUGLISI, FILADELFIO, engineer; b. Florence, Italy, Nov. 5, 1943; s. Alfio and Maria (Gulisano) P.; m. Giovanna Michi, Jan. 29, 1975; children: Alfio Timothy, Annalena. Doctorate, U. Pisa, Italy, 1970. Dir. aux. svcs. S. Cabrini Hosp., Montreal, Can., 1972-74; design engr. Montreal Engring. Co., Can., 1974-77; rsch. assoc. U. Montreal, 1977-81; prof. Tech. Inst. L. DaVinci, Florence, Italy, 1981—; head bioengring. unit F.P.J., Florence, 1980—. Author: (book) The Renaissance Flutes of Italy, 1995; contbg. author: Electrophysiological Kinesiology, 1993, Respiratory and Critical Care Medicine, 1996. Lt. Italian artillery, 1970-72. Mem. European Soc. Biomechanics, Am. Soc. Automotive Engring. Roman Catholic. Avocation: early music. Home: Via Pilastri 34, I-50121 Florence Italy Office: Fond Pro Juventute, Via Imprunetana 124, I-50020 Monteoriolo Florence Italy

PUHA, ELENA, humanities educator; b. Dorohoi, Botosani, Romania, Sept. 29, 1937; d. Theodor and Aglaia (Nascu) Chiorescu; m. Ioan Puha, Mar. 28, 1959; 1 child, Ioana. B in History, Faculty of History, Iasi, Romania, 1960; diploma in philosophy, U. Bucharest, Romania, 1966; PhD, 1971. Asst. lectr. U. Al. T. Cuza, Iasi, 1960; lectr. U. Alexandru Ioan Cuza, Iasi, 1966-71, asst. prof., 1971-92, prof., 1992—; vice chancellor U. Al. I. Cuza, 1981-89. Author: 20th Romanian Humanism, 1977, Historical Consciousness, 1989, Introduction in Philosophy, 1993, Philosophical Anthropology Viewpoint, 1995, Philosopy.Concepts.Problems.Topics, 1997; chief editor The Annals of Social Scis., 1984-88. Co-founder Stephen Lupasco Sci. and Cultural Found., 1997. Mem. Romanian Soc. for Feminist Analyses. Avocations: walking, music. Office: U Al I Cuza Faculty Philos, B-dul Copou 11, 6600 Iasi Romania

PUIG, AL A., JR., real estate broker; b. Havana, Cuba, Dec. 29, 1955; m. Janet C., March 31, 1991; children: Leah, Jason, Claire. AA, U. Tex., Arlington, 1975. Cert. residential specialist, residential broker. V.p. ops. Brown Saloon Corp., Houston, 1977-81; pres. Restaurant Concepts, Denver, 1981-83; broker Stadler Assocs., Miami, 1985-90; broker, pres. Re/Max Advance Realty, Miami, 1990—; pres. Realtor Assocs. Dade County, Miami, 1998, sec., treas., 1999. Mem. Nat. Assn. Realtors (dir. 1998, dir. Fla. chpt. 1995-99), Residential Brokerage Coun., Residential Sales Coun., Toastmasters Internat. Avocations: racquet ball, diving, skiing, travel, wine collecting. E-mail: alpuig@miamiremax.com. Office: Re/Max Advance Realty 11010 SW 88th St Ste 200 Miami FL 33176-1216

PUIG, JUAN GARCIA, internist, researcher; b. Madrid, Spain, Feb. 26, 1952; s. Juan Eusebio Garcia and Socorro Puig; m. Pilar Pavia Martin-Ambrosio, Sept. 16, 1976; children: Pablo, Arturo. BS, Recuerdo, Madrid, Spain, 1969; MD, Autonoma, 1975; PhD, 1978. Internship Madrid, Spain, 1976, resident, 1977-79; vis. prof. Ann Arbor, Mich., 1982-83. Contbr. articles to profl. jours. Recipient SEARLE award Hypertension, Madrid, 1989, JANO award, Barcelona, 1991, CEPA award Hypertension, Madrid, 1996. Avocations: sports, music. Office: La Paz Hosp, Paseo de la Castellana 261, 28046 Madrid Spain

PUISIEUX, FRANCIS HENRI ROBERT, chemistry educator; b. Trilbardou, France, Sept. 7, 1934; s. Gaston Louis and Therese Victorine (Delahaye) P.; m. Claude Genevieve Guenand, Nov. 5, 1959; children: Yves, Francois, Alain. Degree in pharmacy, U. Paris, 1957, PhD in Phys. Chemistry, 1960; D (hon.), U. Brussels, 1997, U. Geneva, 1998. Rsch. asst. Nat. Ctr. Sci. Rsch. (CNRS), France, 1959-60, rsch. fellow, 1960-64; asst. prof. U. Caen, France, 1964-68; asst. prof. U. Paris XI, 1968-72, prof., 1972-2000; cons. Ministry Edn., France, 1983-86, Ministry Rsch., France, 1982-83, 89-90; vice dean faculty of pharmacy U. Paris XI, 1973-81, v.p., 1994-98. Co-editor: Les émulsions, 1983, Les liposomes, 1985, Les formes pharmaceutiques nouvelles, 1985, Liposomes, 1995. Recipient Adrian and Moureu awards French Soc. Chemists, 1961, Nativelle and Darolles awards Nat. Acad. Medicine, 1966, 79, Galien award Quotidien Medecin Quotidien Pharmacien, 1990, M.M. Janot award, 1998. Fellow Royal Belgian Acad. Medicin; mem. Nat. Acad. Pharmacy, Am. Assn. Pharm. Scientists. Avocations: travel, photography. Home: 66 rue de Strasbourg, 94700 Maisons-Alfort France Office: Faculty of Pharmacy, 5 rue Jean-Baptiste Clement, 92296 Chatenay-Malabry France

PUISSOCHET, JEAN-PIERRE, judge; b. Clermont-Ferrand, France, May 3, 1936; s. René and Hélène (Brengues) P.; m. Eliane Millet, Aug. 28, 1973; 1 child, Hélène. State counsellor France; dir., then dir.-gen. legal svc. Coun. European Communities, Brussels, 1968-73; dir.-gen. Agence Nationale pour l'Emploi, Paris, 1973-75; dir. gen. adminstrn. Min. of Industry, Paris, 1977-79; dir. legal affairs OECD, Paris, 1979-85; dir. Inst. Internat. d'Adminstrn. Publique, Paris, 1985-87; jurisconsult, dir. legal affairs Min. Fgn. Affairs, Paris, 1987-94; judge Ct. of Justice of European Communities, Luxembourg, 1994—. Author: l'Elargissement des Communautés Européennes, 1973. Officier de la Légion d'honneur et comdr. de l'ordre Nat. du Mérite, Croix de la valeur militaire, Officier du Mérite agricole. Office: Court Justice European Com, Blvd Konrad Adenauer Kirchb, L-2925 Luxembourg Luxembourg

PUKAHUTA, CHARIDA, microbiologist; b. Bangkok, Apr. 10, 1960. BS in Biology, Kasetsart U., Thailand, 1982, MS in Microbiology, 1986, PhD in Biosci., 1996. Rsch. asst. dept. agr. Min Agr. and Coops., Thailand, 1984; rsch. asst. dept. microbiology Kasetsart U., Thailand, 1985-86; resource person Inst. for Promotion Tchg. Sci. and Tech., 1986-97; lectr. dept. biol. scis. Ubon Ratchathani (Thailand) U., 1997—. Recipient rsch. fund. Thailand Rsch. Fund, 1998-2000. Mem. Thai Soc. Biotech., Nature Conservancy Club, Mushroom Grower and Researcher of Thailand. Avocations: reading, travel, cycling, music, mushrooming.

PUKEL, CLIFFORD STUART, physician; b. Bronx, Nov. 15, 1955; s. Bayas William and Pearl (Buchholtz) P.; m. Victoria Perry; children: Zachariah, Jacob. BA in Biology, CUNY, 1979; MD, U. Miami, 1991. Rsch. technician Sloan-Kettering Inst. for Cancer Rsch., N.Y.C., 1980-83, rsch. asst., 1983-85; rsch. assoc. dept. medicine U. Miami, Fla., 1985-87; resident dept. internal medicine U. W.Va., Charleston, 1991-94; fellow hematology, oncology Dartmouth-Hitchcock Med. Ctr., Lebanon, N.H., 1994-97; pvt. practice Wichita, 1997—; vis. scientist Escola Paulista de Medicina, Sao Paulo, Brazil, 1984. Contbr. articles to profl. jours. Free Sons of Israel scholar, 1974, N.Y. State Regents scholar, 1974, U. Miami Med. Sch. scholar, 1990. Jewish. Achievements include patent for Method for Detecting the Presence of GD3 Ganglioside; notable findings on role of gangliosides in human cancer, on role of cytokines in diabetes mellitus. Office: Oak Leaf Hematology/Oncology 1030 Oakbridge Dr Ste 1 Eau Claire WI 54701

PUKKILA, TARMO MIKKO, academic administrator, educator; b. Vähäkyrö, Finland, Mar. 26, 1946; s. Valde Vilhelmi and Laila Maria (Tapio) P.; m. Helena Nykänen, May 21, 1972; children: Elina, Laura. PhD, U. Tampere, Finland, 1977. Asst. in stats. U. Tampere, 1970-71, 73-74, asst. in math., 1971-72; planning mgr. Computer Centre, Tampere, 1974-75; sr. asst. in stats. Dept. Math. Scis. U. Tampere, 1976, acting prof. stats., 1976-80, prof. stats., 1980-93, rector, 1987-93; dir. gen. ins. dept. Min. Social Affairs and Health, 1993—. Sr. lt. Finnish Army, 1972-73. Mem. IEEE, Bernoulli Soc. Math. Statisticians, Am. Statisticians Assn., Inst. Math. Stats., Internat. Statis. Inst. Office: Min Social Affairs & Health, PO Box 33, FIN00083 Valtioneuvosto Finland

PULCHERIOS, ALEX, insurance company executive; b. Nicosia, Cyprus, Dec. 14, 1933; s. Christodoulos and Eleni (Yiangou) P.; m. Evdokia Michaelidou, Jan. 1, 1934; children: Polys, Elena. Office mgr. ins. dept. D. Severis and Sons, Ltd., Nicosia, 1953-70; gen. agt. Aegon Ins. Co., Ltd., Holland, 1970-80; mng. dir. Reliance Ins. Co., Ltd., Nicosia, 1980-86; gen. agt., cons., dir. Paneuropean Ins. Co., Ltd., Nicosia, 1986-93; mng. dir. Ledra Ins., Ltd., 1993—; mng. dir. Pulcherios Ins. Services, Ltd., Nicosia, 1970—; bd. dirs. Glyphos Estate, Ltd., Nicosia, 1964—. Contbr. articles to profl. jours. Mem. Motor Insurers Fund (chmn. 1980-82), Cyprus Hire Risks Pool (bd. dirs. 1970-80, chmn. 1972), Cyprus Ins. Assn. (bd. dirs. 1965-86). Greek Orthodox. Club: Toastmasters (pres. 1977-78), Field. Lodge: Rotary (sec. 1984-85). Avocations: tennis, reading, gardening, swimming. Office: PO Box 23942, Nicosia Cyprus

PULIAEV, SERGEI PALLADIEVICH, astronomer, educator; b. St Petersburg, Russia, June 5, 1954; s. Palladiy Alexandrovich and Anna Petrovna (Vinogradova) P.; m. Galina Nikolaevna Potemkina, Mar. 28, 1978; children: Anna, Ivan. MS, St. Petersburg State U., 1976; PhD, Pulkovo Observatory, St. Petersburg, 1982. Asst. Pulkovo Observatory, St. Petersburg, 1976-81, assoc. rschr., 1981-87, rschr., 1987—, dir. Astron. Mus., 1977-92. Author: (with others) Sea Atlas, 1980; contbr. more than 50 articles to profl. jours. Mem. Nat. Acad. Sci. Bolivia, Astron. Soc. Brazil. Russian Orthodox. Avocations: travel, fishing, sports, music. Home: Rua Alm Tefe 632 AP 911, Niteroi, 24030080 Rio de Janeiro Brazil Office: Observatorio Nacional/CNPq, Rua Gal Jose Cristino 77, 20921400 Rio de Janeiro Brazil also: Pulkovo Observatory, 196140 St Petersburg Russia

PULIAFITO, CARMEN ANTHONY, ophthalmologist, healthcare executive; b. Buffalo, Jan. 5, 1951; s. Dominic F. and Marie A. (Nigro) P.; m. Janet H. Pine, May 19, 1979. AB cum laude, Harvard Coll., 1973, MD magna cum laude, 1978; MBA, U. Pa., 1997. Diplomate Am. Bd. Ophthalmology. Intern Faulkner Hosp., Tufts U. Sch. Medicine, 1978-79; resident Mass. Eye and Ear Infirmary, Boston, 1979-82, retina fellow, 1982-83; instr. Harvard Med. Sch., Boston, 1983-85, asst. prof., 1985-89, assoc. prof., 1989-91; dir. divsn. continuing edn. dept. ophthalmology Harvard Med. Sch., 1989-91; vis. scientist MIT Regional Laser Ctr., Cambridge, 1982—, asst. prof. health scis. and tech. program, 1987-89, assoc. prof., 1989-91; mem. staff Mass. Eye and Ear Infirmary, Boston, 1983; dir. Morse Laser Ctr., Mass. Eye and Ear Infirmary, 1986-91, dir. New Eng. Eye Ctr., 1991—; prof., chmn. dept. ophthalmology Tufts U. Sch. Medicine, 1991—, prof. ophthalmology and health mgmt., 1997—; adj. prof. biomed. engring. Tufts U., 1991—; chmn. med. bd. New Eng. Med. Ctr. Hosps., 1994-95, ophthalmologist in chief, 1991—; assoc. examiner Am. Bd. Ophthalmology, 1990—; sr. v.p. for network devel. Lifespan, 1997—. Author: (with D. Albert) Foundations of Ophthalmic Pathology, 1979, (with R. Steinert) Principles and Practice of Ophthalmic YAG Laser Surgery, 1984, Lasers in Surgery and Medicine: Principles and Practice, 1996, (with M.R. Hee, J.S. Schuman and J.G. Fujimoto) Optical Coherence Tomography of Ocular Diseases, 1996, (with E. Reichel) Atlas of Indocyanine Green Angiography, 1996; editor-in-chief Lasers in Surgery and Medicine, 1987-95, Ophthalmic Surgery and Lasers, 1995—; contbr. about 120 articles to profl. jours. Pres. Am. Soc. for Laser Medicine and Surgery, 1994-95; v.p. Mass. Soc. Eye Physicians and Surgeons, 1994-96; assoc. examiner Am. Bd. Ophthalmology, 1990—; retina trustee Assn. Rsch. in Vision and Ophthalmology, 1995—. Recipient Richard and Hinda Rosenthal award in visual scis., 1994, Man of Vision award Boston Aid to the Blind, 1993, Leon Goldman award Biomed. Optics Soc., 1993, I Migliori award Pirandello Lyceum of Mass., 1994. Fellow Am. Acad. Ophthalmology, Am. Soc. for Laser Medicine and Surgery (pres. 1994-95); mem. Assn. Rsch. in Vision and Ophthalmology (pres.-elect 1998-99, pres. 1999-2000, immediate past pres. 2000—), Mass. Soc. Eye Physicians and Surgeons (v.p. 1994-96). Roman Catholic. Fax: 617-636-4866. E-mail: journalosl@msn.com. Home: 69 Pigeon Hill Rd Weston MA 02493-1641 Office: New Eng Eye Ctr Box 450 750 Washington St Boston MA 02111-1526

PULIDO, MARK A., pharmaceutical and cosmetics company executive; b. 1952. McKesson Drug Co., 1975-88; Exec. v.p. FoxMeyer Drug Co., 1988-89; chmn., pres., CEO Red Line Healthcare Corp., 1989-96; pres., CEO Sandoz Pharmaceuticals Corp., 1994-95; pres., chmn., CEO, dir. McKesson Corp., 1996-99; chmn., CEO BenefitPoint, San Francisco, 2000—. Office: BenefitPoint 801 Montgomery St San Francisco CA 94133-5164

PULIMOOD, BENJAMIN MANI, gastroenterologist, consultant, physician; b. Kottayam, India, Apr. 14, 1935; s. Pulimood Mathai Mani and Anna Mani; m. Ramani Thomas, June 25, 1959; 3 children. MBBS, Trivandrum Med. Coll., India, 1957. Rsch. asst. West Middlesex Hosp., London, 1961-63; lectr. Christian Med. Coll., Vellore, India, 1963, prof. medicine, 1972-95, prin., 1981-87, dir., 1987-94; chmn. Scheflien Leprosy Rsch. Tng. Inst., India, 1996—; found. chmn. bd. studies Med. U., Tamil Nadu, 1988-93; adj. prof. Tulane U. Sch. Pub. Health, New Orleans, 1995-99; adj. faculty BITS, Pilani, India, 1995. Contbr. articles to profl. jours. Mem. World Coun. Chs., Nairobi, 1975. Recipient Ath Vishista Chikalsa award Assn. Chest Physicians India, 1996, Ida Scudder award Scudder Assn., 1993, Honour award Rotary Club of Vellore India, 1993. Fellow Royal Coll. Physicians Edinburgh; mem. Indian Soc. Gastroenterology (life, hon. sec. 1970-75, pres. 1978-79), Assn. Physicians of India (life). Avocations: university- and state-level football. Home and Office: TA Beerankunju Rd, Cochin 682018, India

PULJIC, VINKO CARDINAL, archbishop; b. Prijecani, Banja Luka, Sept. 8, 1945. Archbishop of Vrhbosna Sarajevo, Bosnia-Herzegovina, 1991—, created and proclaimed cardinal, 1994. Office: Nadbiskupski Ordinarijat, Kaptol 7, 71000 Sarajevo Bosnia-Herzegovina

PULJIC, ŽELIMIR, bishop; b. Kamena-Mostar, Croatia, Mar. 7, 1947; s. Ivan and Ana (Ragu ž) P. Student, Theol. Faculty, Split, 1967-70, Urban U., Rome, 1970-74, Salesian U., Rome, 1974-80; M of Theology, Lateran U., Rome, 1980; D of Psychology, Salesian U., Rome, 1983. Doyen theol. faculty Vrhbosanska Katolic. Teol., Sarajevo, Bosnia, 1981-85; rector of theology Vrhbosanska katolic teol., Sarajevo, Bosnia, 1985-89, bishop of Dubrovnik, 1990—; bd. govs. U. Zagreb, Croatia, 1993-95. Author: Selfactualizing People and Synergic Society in the Psychology of A.H. Maslow, 1984, Josip Stadler, 1989, Cristianity of Medioeval Bosnia, 1991, Vatikan and Dubrovnik, 1994, Mato Vodopić, 1995, Thousand Years of Archidiocese of Dubrovnik (998-1998), 1999; contbr. articles to profl. jours. Office: Biskupski Ordinarijat, Poljana Marina Drzica 2, 20000 Dubrovnik Croatia*

PULKKINEN, JYRKI TUOMO JUHANI, structural engineer; b. Paltamo, Finland, Sept. 25, 1963; s. Yrjo Kalle and Aino Johanna Pulkkinen; m. Karen Elaine Brautcheck, Oct. 24, 1993. MCE, U. Oulu (Finland), 1991. Registered profl. engr., Mich., Fla.; Eur. Ing. Structural engr. Makelainen & Raiha Engring., Kajaani, Finland, 1990; rsch. asst. VTT Bldg. Tech., Oulu, 1991; adminstrv. intern City of San Diego, 1992-93; project engr. Interclean Equipment Inc., Ann Arbor, Mich., 1993-94; project mgr. LWS Inc., Ann Arbor, 1994-96, Shimizu Am. Corp., Canton, Mich., 1997-98, Adminstrv. Controls Mgmt., Detroit, 1999—. Mem. Mich. Soc. Profl. Engrs., Assn. Finnish Civil Engrs. Avocations: photography, cars, model cars. Home: 2543 Meade Ct Ann Arbor MI 48105-1304 Office: Gen Motors Corp Argonaut A 485 W Milwaukee St Detroit MI 48202-3220

PULKKIS, PER-GÖRAN BERNHARD, computer engineering educator; b. Helsinki, Finland, Jan. 31, 1945; s. Tor Bernhard and Gretel Harriet (Schultz) P.; m. Anneli Sinikka Jalovaara, May 5, 1973; children: Taisto Viljami, Uljas Voitto. MSc in Engring., Helsinki U. of Tech., 1970, lic. tech., 1976, Dr.Tech., 1983. Tchr. asst. Helsinki U. of Tech., 1968-73, 74-79, labr. engr., 1984-85, lectr. in computer sci., 1986-88; rschr. Finnish Acad. of Sci., Helsinki, 1979-84, Valmet Corp., FMS Group, Tampere, Finland, 1984-85; sr. lectr. in computer engring. Arcada Polytech., Helsinki, 1988—; guest lectr. in field, 1996-99; IT coord. Arcada Polytech., 1997—. Contbr. articles to profl. jours. Ensign Anti-tank forces, 1964. Grantee Finnish Acad. of Scis., 1978, 84. Mem. Assn. of Swedish Engrs. in Finland, 1994—. Avocations: gymnastics, swimming, jogging, skiing, reading. Office: Arcada Polytech, Skogsmansgranden 3, 02130 Esbo Finland

PULLEIN-THOMPSON, CHRISTINE (CHRISTINE POPESCU), children's writer; b. Wimbledon, Surrey, Eng., Oct. 1, 1930; d. Harold James and Joanna Pullein-Thompson; m. Julian John Hunter Popescu, 1954; children: Philip Hunter, Charlotte Vivien, Mark Cannan, Lucy Joanna. Dir. Grove Riding Schs. Ltd., Peppard and Oxford, Eng., 1945-55. Author: We Rode to the Sea, 1948, We Hunted Hounds, 1949, I Carried the Horn, 1951, Goodbye to Hounds, 1952, Riders from Afar, 1954, Phantom Horse, 1955, A Day to Go Hunting, 1956, The First Rosette, 1956, Stolen Ponies, 1957, The Second Mount, 1957, Three to Ride, 1958, The Lost Pony, 1959, Ride by Night, 1960, The Horse Sale, 1960, Giles and the Elephant, 1960, For Want of a Saddle, 1961, The Empty Field, 1961, Giles and the Greyhound, 1961, The Open Gate, 1962, Bandits in the Hills, 1962, The Gipsy Children, 1962, Giles and the Canal, 1962, Homeless Katie, 1963, The Doping Affair, 1963 (published as The Pony Dopers 1968), The Eastmans in Brittany, 1964, Granny Comes to Stay, 1964, The Eastmans Move, 1964, The Boys from the Cafe, 1965, The Eastmans Find a Boy, 1966, The Stolen Car, 1966, Little Black Pony, 1966, A Day to Remember, 1966, The Lost Cow, 1966, Robbers in the Night, 1967, Room to Let, 1968, Dog in a Pram, 1969, Nigel Eats His Words, 1969, Phantom Horse Comes Home, 1970, Riders on the March, 1970, No One at Home, 1972, They Rode to Victory, 1972, Phantom Horse Goes to Ireland, 1972, I Rode a Winner, 1973, The Follyfoot Horse and Pony Quiz Book, 1974, A Pony to Love, 1974, Good Riding, 1975, Mystery at Black Pony Inn, 1976, Riding for Fun, 1976, Pony Patrol SOS, 1977, Strange Riders at Black Pony Inn, 1977, Secrets at Black Pony Inn, 1978,

Prince at Black Pony Inn, 1978, Improve Your Riding, 1979, Pony Patrol, 1979, Black Velvet, 1979, Pony Patrol Fights Back, 1979, Phantom Horse Comes Home, 1979, Phantom Horse Goes to Ireland, 1979, Phantom Horse in Danger, 1980, Ride by Night, 1980, Riders on the March, 1980, Pony Patrol and the Mystery Horse, 1981, Phantom Horse Goes to Scotland, 1981, Father Unknown, 1982, Ponies in the Park, 1982, Ponies in the Forest, 1983, Ponies in the Blizzard, 1985, Wait for Me, Phantom Horse, 1985, A Home for Jessie, 1986, Please Save Jessie, 1986, Stay at Home Ben, 1987, Careless Ben, 1988, The Road Through the Hills, 1988, The Big Storm, 1988, Smoke in the Hills, 1989, Candy Goes to the Gymkhana, 1989, Candy Stops a Train, 1989, Runaway Ben, 1990, Come Home Jessie, 1991, The Long Search, 1993, Horse Stories, 1994; (with sisters Diana Pullein-Thompson and Josephine Pullein-Thompson) It Began with Picotee, 1946, The Impossible Horse, 1957, Black Beauty's Clan, 1975, Black Beauty's Family, 1978, Black Beauty's Family Two, 1982, Riding, 1983, A Treasury of Horse and Pony Stories, 1998 (autobiography) Fair Girl on Grey Horses, 1995; editor: The First Pony Scrapbook, 1972, The Second Pony Scrapbook, 1973, Book of Pony Stories, 1977, Pony Parade, 1978, I Want That Pony, 1993, A Pony in Distress, 1994, The Best Pony for Me, 1995, Horse Haven, 1995, Fair Girls on Grey Horses, 1996, Thundering Hooves, 1996, The Pony Test, 1997, Bedtime Pony Stories, 1997, More Bedtime Pony Stories, 1997, Sundance Saves the Day, 1997, The Pony Picnic, 1998, Adventure Stories From Black Pony Inn, 1998, Magical Pony Tales-Incredible Pony Tales, 1998, More Adventure Stories From Black Pony Inn, 1999, 3-in-1 Pony Stories, 1999, Horse Haven Lives On, 1999, Havoc at Horse Haven, 1999. Mem. Ch. of Eng. Office: The Old Parsonage, Mellis Eye, Suffolk 1PS 8EE, England

PULLEIN-THOMPSON, JOSEPHINE MARY WEDDERBURN (JOSEPHINE MANN), children's writer; b. Wimbledon, Surrey, Eng., Apr. 3, 1924; d. Harold James and Joanna (Cannan) Pullein-Thompson. Student, Wychwood Sch. Former co-owner 2 riding schs.; competitor horse shows and hunter trials; show judge jumping and dressage events. Author: Gin and Murder, 1959, They Died in the Spring, 1960, Murder Strikes Pink, 1963, (under pseudonym Josephine Mann) A Place with Two Faces, 1972, Six Ponies, 1946, I Had Two Ponies, 1947, Plenty of Ponies, 1949, Pony Club Team, 1950, The Radney Riding Club, 1951, Prince among Ponies, 1952, One Day Event, 1954, Show Jumping Secret, 1955, Patrick's Pony, 1956, Pony Club Camp, 1957, The Trick Jumpers, 1958, All Change, 1961 (Ernest Benn award 1961), The Hidden Horse, 1982, How Horses Are Trained, 1961, Ponies in Colour, 1962, Learn to Ride Well, 1966, Ride Better and Better, Blackie, 1974, Star Riders of the Moor, 1976, Race Horse Holiday, 1977, Ride to the Rescue, 1979, Fear Treks the Moor, 1979, Black Nightshade, 1980, Ghost Horse on the Moor, 1980, The No-Good Pony, 1981, Treasure on the Moor, 1981, The Prize Pony, 1982, Pony Club Cup, 1983, Pony Club Challenge, 1984, Mystery on the Moor, 1984, Save the Ponies!, 1984, Pony Club Trek, 1985, Suspicion Stalks the Moor, 1986, Black Swift, 1991, A Job with Horses, 1994; (with Christine Pullein-Thompson and Diana Pullein-Thompson) It Began with Picotee, 1946, Black Beauty's Clan, 1975, Black Beauty's Family, 1978, Black Beauty's Family Two, 1982, Fair Girls and Grey Horses: Memories of a Country Childhood, 1996; editor: Horses and Their Owners, 1970, Proud Riders: Horse and Pony Stories, 1973; contbr. articles to profl. jours. Named to Order of Brit. Empire, 1984. Mem. Soc. Authors, English Ctr. Internat. PEN (gen. sec. 1976-93, pres. 1994-97, ofcl. del. of English Ctr. to PEN Internat. congresses), Pony Club (vis. commr. 1960-68, dist. commr. 1970-76). Mem. Anglican Ch. Avocations: gardening, reading, theatre, travel. Office: 16 Knivet Rd, London SW6 1JH, England

PULLEN, JULIA M., psychiatrist. News corr. Orofino VFW Aux., 1994-97; news cor. Orofino Kiwanis Club, 1994—, neweletter editor, 1994—. Mem. Clearwater County adv. Com. for Commrs., 1965-66; active Clearwater County Dem. Party, 1994—, Twin Ridge Vol. Fire Dept.; mem. Clearwater Hosp. Aux. Mem. Am. Psychiat. Assn. (exec. sec. Western regional meeting 1962), Intermountain Psychiat. Assn. (exec. sec. 1962-66), Clearwater County Mental Health Assn., Idaho Mental Health Assn. (pres. 1963-64), Idaho Am. Assn. U. Women (social concerns com. chair 1963-70, del. biennial nat. conv. 1964, del. nat. ocnv. 1966), Idaho PTA (chair mental health com. 1960-69, sec. 1964, pres. Orofino 1957), Orofino Kiwanis, Clearwater Hist. Soc. (sec. 1997—), VFW Aux. (life).

PULLIAM, FRANCINE SARNO, real estate broker, real estate developer; b. San Francisco, Sept. 14, 1937; d. Ralph C. Stevens and Frances I. (Wilson) Sarno; m. John Donald Pulliam, Aug. 14, 1957 (div. Mar. 1965); 1 child, Wendy; m. Terry Kent Graves, Dec. 14, 1974. Student, U. Ariz., 1955-56, U. Nev., Las Vegas, 1957. Airline stewardess Bonanza Airlines, Las Vegas, 1957; real estate agt. The Pulliam Co., Las Vegas, 1958-68, Levy Realty, Las Vegas, 1976-76; real estate broker, owner Prestige Properties, Las Vegas, 1976—; importer, exporter Exports Internat., Las Vegas, 1984—; bd. dirs. Citicorp Bank of Nev.; mem. adv. bd. to Amb. to Bahamas Chic Hect. Bd. dirs. Las Vegas Bd. Realtors, Fedn. Internat. Realtors, Nat. Kidney Found., Assistance League, Cancer Soc., Easter Seals, Econ. Rsch. Bd., Children's Discovery Mus., New Horizons Ctr. for Children with Learning Disabilities, Girl Scouts, Home of the Good Shepard, St. Jude's Ranch for Homeless Children; pres., bd. dirs. Better Bus. Bur.; chmn. Las Vegas Taxi Cab Authority; pres. Citizens for Pvt. Enterprises. Mem. Las Vegas C. of C. (bd. dirs., developer). Republican. Roman Catholic. Office: 2340 Paseo Del Prado Ste D202 Las Vegas NV 89102-4341

PULLIAM, YVONNE ANTOINETTE, gifted education educator; b. Chgo.; d. Virgil D. Sr. and Velma (Hunter) P. BA in Edn., Lane Coll., 1966; MA in Ednl. Adminstrn. and Supervision, Roosevelt U., 1988. Cert. intermediate tchr. Tchr. Howalton Day Sch., Chgo., 1968-69; actress N.Y.C., 1970-75; tchr. gifted Chgo. Bd. Edn., 1975-78, 81—; tutor Broadway play Raisin, N.Y.C., 1977-78, Annie, N.Y.C., 1980-82; coordinator Adopt-a-Sch. program, Chgo., 1984-85; tchr. rep. PTA O'Keefe Sch., Chgo., 1984-85. cartoonist 1st Nat. Bank Chgo. newsletter 1969; stand-in for Diana Ross In Mahogany, 1976; appeared on All My Children, The Hosp. and indsl. films and voiceovers; assoc. dir.: (TV comedy) From Chicago. Recipient cert. of merit Glamour mag., 1965, award for innovative teaching Bus.Week, 1990; named featured designer V2 Fashions, Chgo., 1967, Essence mag., 1971. Mem. AFTRA, Chgo. Tchrs. Union, Am. Film. Inst., Phi Delta Kappa. Democrat.

PULLIN, ANDREW STUART, conservation biologist, educator; b. Bristol, Eng., Nov. 4, 1958; s. Stuart William and Marjorie Ethel Mary (Cavill) P. BSc in Environ. Scis., U. Warwick, Eng., 1980; MSc in Ecology, U. Durham, Eng., 1981; PhD, Oxford (Eng.) Poly., 1986. Rsch. asst. Oxford Poly., 1982-86; rsch. fellow Leeds (Eng.) U., 1986-89; lectr. Keele U., Eng., 1989-96; sr. lectr. U. Birmingham, Eng., 1996—. Editor: Ecology and Conservation of Butterflies, 1995, Jour. of Insect Conservation, 1997—, NERC, 1997, 98. Rsch. grantee Royal Soc., 1993, Leverhulme Trust, 1995. Mem. Species Survival Commn., Brit. Ecol. Soc., Soc. for Conservation Biology, British Butterfly Conservation Soc. (trustee, coun.). Office: Univ Birmingham, Dept Biosci Edgbaston, Birmingham B15 2TT, England

PULSIFER, EDGAR DARLING, leasing service and sales executive; b. Natick, Mass., Jan. 11, 1934; s. Howard George and Elvie Marion (Morris) P.; m. Alice Minarik, Feb. 16, 1957 (div. Oct. 1979); children: Mark Edgar, Audrey Carol, Lee Howard; m. Barbara Ann Chuhak, Apr. 19, 1980. BSEE, MIT, 1955. With sales and service dept. Beckman Instruments, Fullerton, Calif., 1956-59; regional sales mgr. Hewlett Packard, Palo Alto, Calif., 1959-72, Gen. Automation, Anaheim, Calif., 1973-74; exec. v.p. Systems Mktg., Elk Grove Vlg., Ill., 1975-79; pres. Consol. Funding, Mt. Prospect, Ill., 1979—. Served as 1st lt. U.S. Army, 1956. Mem. MENSA, Coast Guard Auxiliary. Republican. Episcopalian. Clubs: North Shore Country (Glenview, Ill.), Itasca (Ill.) Country. Avocations: coins, stamps, curling, scuba diving, golf. Home: 370 Dulles Rd Des Plaines IL 60016-2755 Office: Consol Funding Corp P O Box 801 Mount Prospect IL 60056-0801

PULTAR, GÖNÜL AYDA, writer, educator; b. Istanbul, Nov. 3, 1943; d. Resid Mazhar and Adile (Arsal) Ayda; m. Mustafa Kubilay Pultar; children: Giray, Eren, Selcuk. BA, Robert Coll., Istanbul, 1967; MA, Middle East Tech. U., Ankara, Turkey, 1986, PhD, 1994. Freelance journalist Ankara, 1968-70, 75-82; fgn. broadcasts specialist Anatolian News Agy., Ankara, 1970-72; chief publs. Middle East Tech. U., 1982, instr., 1982-90; instr. Bilkent U., Ankara, 1992-2000, dep. dir. Ctr. for Turkish Lit., 1998-99, asst. prof., 2000—. Editor: Jour. Am. Studies Turkey, 1995—; author: Dunya Bir Atlikarinca, 1979, Technique and Tradition in Beckett's Trilogy of Novels, 1996, Ellerimden Su Icsinler, 1999. Pres. World League of Tatars, Kazan, Russian Fedn., 1997—; mem. adv. bd. Longfellow Inst., Harvard U., 1998—. Recipient prize Hachette-Larousse (France), 1970; fellow Salzburg Seminar, 1980, Harvard U., 1998. Mem. Am. Studies Assn. Turkey (v.p. 1994-2000), Am. Studies Assn. (internat. com. 1997-2000), Multi-ethnic Lits. of U.S.-Europe (steering com. 1998-2000), MLA (discussion group on Am. Lit. in Langs. Other than English exec. com. 1998—), Group for Cultural Studies in Turkey (chair 1999—), Multi-ethnic Studies Europe Am. (adv. bd. 2000—), Internat. Am. Studies Assn. (charter), Cen. Eurasian Studies Soc., Samuel Beckett Soc. Home: Merkez Lojmanlari 7/5, Bilkent, Ankara 06533, Turkey Office: Bilkent U, Dept English, Ankara 06533, Turkey

PULTORAK, JERZY, electronics engineer, educator; b. Luck, Poland, Jan. 2, 1932; s. Julian and Leontyna (Komarnicka) P.; m. Maria Brodnicka, Jan. 9, 1960; children: Anna, Maciej, Urszula. MS, Warsaw (Poland) Tech. U., 1956; diploma, Imperial Coll. Sci. and Tech., London, 1959; PhD, Inst. Basic Tech. Problems, Warsaw, 1964; DSc, Warsaw Tech. U., 1969. Cert. electronics engr. Head of lab. Inst. Basic Tech. Problems, Warsaw, 1962-66; head of lab. Inst. Electron Tech., Warsaw, 1966-73, head of dept., 1973-77, head of doctorate studies, prof., 1974—, head of lab., 1996—. Author 4 books; contbr. numerous articles to sci. jours.; patentee in field. Recipient State prize State Coun., 1964. Roman Catholic. Avocations: touring, photography, music. Home: ul Zwirki i Wigury 33 m 2, 02-091 Warsaw Poland Office: Inst Electron Tech, al Lotnikow 32/46, 02-668 Warsaw Poland

PULVERER, GERHARD, secondary education educator; b. Klagenfurt, Austria, Mar. 4, 1930; arrived in Germany, 1956; s. Josef and Maria (Glawischnig) P.; m. Rosemarie Walterscheidt, May 31, 1963; children: Klaus, Bernd, Daniela. MD, U. Vienna, 1954. Intern Reg. Hosp., Gmünd, Austria, 1955; postdoc. U. Vienna/Inst. of Pathology, 1955-56; fellow A. von Humboldt Found., Cologne, Germany, 1956-57, Inst. Pasteur, Paris, 1957-58; asst. prof. Inst. of Hygiene, Cologne, 1958-68; prof. Inst. of Hygiene, 1969—; dean med. faculty U. Cologne, 1974-75; v.p. Deutsche Gesellschaft für Hygiene and Mikrobiologie, 1983-85, Deutsche Gastronomische Acad., 1983-87. Exec. editor Internat. Jour. Med. Microbiology, 1989-1999; published over 700 scientific papers. Recipient order of merit (commander class) Republic Poland, 1994, (1st class) Republic Germany, 1995, Ferdinand Cohn-medal (DGHM), 1996, C.F. von Rumohr medal Gastronomische Akad. Deutschlands, 1999, W. Heisenberg medal A. von Humboldt Found., 1999. . Fellow Royal Coll. Pathologists, Royal Soc. of Medicine, numerous other nat./internat. scientific socs.,; corresponding fellow Infectious Diseases Soc. of Am.; mem. Deutsche Acad. Naturforscher Leopoldina, Polish Acad. Scis., Soc. for Japanese Arts/Crafts. Avocations: Japanese art, music, literature. Office: Goldenfelsstrasse 19, Cologne D 50935, Germany

PULZER, PETER GEORGE JULIUS, political science educator; b. Vienna, May 20, 1929; s. Felix and Margaret (Breiner) P.; m. Gillian Mary Marshall, Dec. 8, 1962; children: Matthew, Patrick. BA/MA, Cambridge (Eng.) U., 1950, PhD, 1960; BSc in Econs., U. London, 1951-54. Lectr. Oxford (Eng.) U., 1959-84, Gladstone prof. govt., 1984-96; tutor in politics Christ Church, 1962-84. Author: The Rise of Political Antisemitism in Germany and Austria, 1964, 2d edit., 1988, Political Representation and Elections in Britain, 1967, 2d edit., 1971, 3d edit., 1975, Jews and the German State, 1848-1933: The Political History of a Minority, 1992, German Politics, 1945-95, 1995, Germany 1870-1945: Politics, State Building, and War, 1997; co-author: German-Jewish History in Modern Times, 1999. Avocations: opera, hiking. Office: All Souls Coll, Oxford OX1 4AL, England

PUMARIEGA, JOANNE BUTTACAVOLI, mathematics educator; b. Coral Gables, Fla., May 27, 1952; d. Ciro Charles and Rosaria Frances (Calabrese) Buttacavoli; m. Andres Julio Pumariega, Dec. 26, 1975; children: Christina Marie, Nicole Marie. BA in Math. and Edn. magna cum laude, U. Miami, 1973, MA in Math., 1974; postgrad., U. Houston, 1991-92. Cert. secondary math. tchr., Tex., Fla., Tenn., N.C. Grad. tchg. asst. U. Miami, Coral Gables, 1973-74; substitute tchr. Dade County Pub. Schs., Miami, 1975; math. instr. Miami Dade C.C., 1975-76; math. and G.E.D. instr. Durham (N.C.) Tech. Inst., 1976-77; math. instr. Durham H.S., 1977-78, Durham Acad., 1978-80, Univ. Sch. of Nashville, 1980-83; pvt. practice math. instr. Houston, 1984-86; tutor Clear Lake Tutoring Svc., Houston, 1987-90; pvt. practice, S.A.T, lang. instr. League City, Tex., 1990-92; pvt. practice math. and S.A.T. instr. Johnson City, Tenn., 1996—; lang. instr. Nelson Elem. Sch., Columbia, 1993-96; instr. fgn. langs. and math. Lonnie B. Nelson Elem. Sch., Columbia, S.C.; adj. faculty math. East Tenn. State U., 1999—. Co-author: (with F. Rodriguez & J. Pumariega) HIV/AIDS in Children and Adolscents, 1999. Chair bd. edn. St. Mary Parish, League City, 1988-90, lector, 1992, v.p. coun. Cath. Women, Johnson City, 1997-99; C.C.E. tchr. St. John Neumann Cath. Ch., Columbia, S.C. & Johnson City, Tenn., 1993-95, lector, 1992-96; lector St. Mary's Ch., Johnson City, 1996—; treas. St. Thomas More Women's Club, Houston, 1985-86; v.p., then pres. housestaff med. wives Duke U., Durham, N.C., 1978-80; mem. East Tenn. Med. Auxiliary, 1997—, head pub. rels. 1999—. Mem. Newcomers of Greater Columbia (chmn. pub. rels. chpt. 1993,95), Newcomers of Greater Colo. (com. chair coord. 1994-95), Welcome Neighbors of Bay Area (v.p., program chmn. 1991-92), Washington/Unicoi/Johnson Co. Med. Aux. (chair pub. rels. com. 1999—), Tex. Med. Aux., Med. Aux. Washington County, Bay Area Med. Wives, East Tenn. State U. Women's Club (v.p. 1997-98, pres. 1998-99, parliamentarian 1999—), U. S.C. Faculty Women's Club (v.p. 1993-94, pres. 1994-95, parliamentarian, advisor 1995-96), , Phi Kappa Phi, Kappa Delta Pi, Alpha Lamba Delta (Woman of Yr. 1972). Roman Catholic. Avocations: reading, public speaking, traveling. Home: 2 Round Tree Ct Johnson City TN 37604-1492 Office: East Tenn State U Dept Math PO Box 70663 Johnson City TN 37614-1701

PUMPENS, PAUL, molecular biologist, researcher; b. Riga, Latvia, Oct. 21, 1947; s. Paul and Rozalija (Sidlovska) P. Biochemist, Latvian U., Riga, 1970; cand. in Biology, Latvian Acad. Scis., Riga, 1975; D in Biology, Inst. Molecular Biology, Moscow, 1988; D Habil. in Biology, Latvian Coun. Scis., Riga, 1991. Rsch. fellow Inst. Organic Synthesis, Riga, 1973-89, head labor, 1989-90; head labor Inst. Molecular Biology, Riga, 1990-91; dept. head Biomed Rsch. & Study Ctr., Riga, 1991—; prof. U. Latvia, 1998—; corr. mem. Latvian Acad. Scis., 1990-92. Contbr. over 170 articles to sci. publs. and profl. jours. including Intervirology, Gene, Proceedings of USSR Acad. Sci., Virol. Recipient All-Union Comsomol's prize, Moscow, 1976, Grindel medal, 1997, Cabinet of Ministers prize, 1998. Mem. Latvian Acad. Sci. (Sci. award 1988). E-mail: paul@biomed.lu.lv. Home: Baznicas Str 27/29 21, LV-1010 Riga Latvia Office: U Latvia Biomed Rsch/Study Ctr, Ratsupites Str 1, LV-1067 Riga Latvia

PUMPHREY, JANET KAY, editor, publisher; b. Balt., June 18, 1946; d. John Henry and Elsie May (Keefer) P. AA in Secondary Edn., Anne Arundel C.C., Arnold, Md., 1967, AA in Bus. and Pub. Adminstrn., 1976. Office mgr. Anne Arundel C.C., 1964—; mng. editor Am. Polygraph Assn., Severna Park, Md., 1973-98; owner JKP Publ. Svcs., 1990—, Brooke Keefer Ltd. Eds.; dir. Am. Polygraph Assn. Reference Svc., 1995-98; owner Brooke Keefer Ltd.Editions, 1999—. Editor: (with Albert D. Snyder) Ten Years of Polygraph, 1984, (with Norman Ansley) Justice and the Polygraph, 1985, 2d edit., 1998, A House Full of Love, 1990, Mama, There's A Mouse in My House, 1996; pub. Vergennes, Vermont and The War of 1812, 1999; co-pub.: An Investigator's Guide to Non-Verbal Communication, 2d edit., 2000. Mem. Rep. Nat. Sustaining Com. Mem. NAFE, Am. Polygraph Assn. (hon.), Md. Polygraph Assn. (affiliate), Anne Arundel County Hist. Soc., Alumni Assn. Anne Arundel Community Coll. Republican. Methodist. Avocations: travel, poetry, gardening, mystery writer. Home: 3 Kimberly Ct Severna Park MD 21146-3703 Office: JKP Pub Svcs Brook Keefer Ltd Edits PO Box 1535 Severna Park MD 21146-8535

PUNČOCHÁŘ, PAVEL, limnologist, researcher; b. Pelhřimov, Czechoslovakia, Mar. 20, 1944; s. Vlastimil and Marie (Mištová) P.; m. Marcela Nováková, Aug. 26, 1967. BSc, Charles U., Prague, 1966, MSc, 1969; PhD, Czechoslovak Acad. Scis., Prague, 1972. Rsch. asst. hydrobiology lab. Czechoslovak Acad. Scis., Prague, 1966-72, rsch. officer, 1972-80, sr. rsch. officer, 1980-84; sr. rsch. officer Czechoslovak Acad. Scis., České Budějovice, Czechoslovakia, 1984-86; head dept. microbiology Water Rsch. Inst., Prague, 1986-90; dir. inst. The T.G. Masaryk Water Rsch. Inst., Prague, 1990-97; dir. dept. water mgmt. policy Ministry Agr., Prague, 1998—; chmn. working group Internat. Com. Elbe Protection, Magdeburg, Germany, 1991—; mem. sci. bd. Krkonoše Mts. Nat. Pk. Vrchlabi, Czech Republic, 1993—, Sci. Bd. Inst. Hydrobiology, Č. Budějovice, 1991—, Sci. bd. Water Rsch. Inst., Bratislava, Slovak Republic, 1992—, Sci. Com. Postgrad. Studies, Brno, Czech Republic; mem. sci. bd. Inst. Meliorat. Soil Quality, 1996—, mem. sci. bd. postgrad. studies Hydrobiology Charles U., Prague, 1996; mem. Internat. Com. Elbe Prot., 1996—; external lectr. Faculty Natural History, Charles U., 1994-99; mem. internat. com. Danube Protection, 1999—; mem. nat. com. Internat. Commn. Irrigation and Drainage, 2000. Contbr. articles to profl. jours., inventor. Mem. Czech Republic Limnological Soc. (sci. sec. 1979-82, pres. 1997—), Czech Microbiol. Soc., Czechoslovak Zool. Soc., Nat. Acad. Agrl. Scis. Avocations: bionomy of water mites, sport fishing, gardening. Home: Zitkova 225/3, CS-15300 Prague 5, Czech Republic Office: Ministry Agr Dept Water Mgmt, Tesnov 17, 11705 Prague 1, Czech Republic

PUNDMANN, ED JOHN, JR., automotive company executive; b. St. Charles, Mo., Feb. 24, 1939; s. Ed J. Sr. and Ruth O. (Brehme) P.; m. Dolores Anne Lienau, June 15, 1963 (dec.); children: Mary Ann, Steven A., Susan K. BA, Westminster Coll., 1961. Jr. accountant Peat, Marwick & Mitchell, St. Louis, 1961-62; salesman Pundmann Ford, St. Charles, 1962-82, gen. mgr., 1982-92, pres., 1992—; bd. dirs., chmn. First State Bank; bd. dirs. Mut. Fire Ins., St. Charles; mem. St. Charles City Tax Incremental Financing Commn.; mem. Ford Motor Dispute Settlement Bd., 1993-94. Treas. St. Charles City Charter Commn., 1981; mem. St. Charles City Park Bd., 1981-82; chmn. St. Charles City Econ. Devel. Commn.; mem. St. Charles City Park Found. Bd., 1985—, also past pres.; St. Louis Regional Commerce and Growth Assn.; adv. bd. St. Charles County; mem. Handicapped Facilities Bd. St. Charles County, 1986-94, also past pres. ; active St. Charles County Road Bd., 1996—; past pres. St. John United Ch. of Christ; bd. dirs. Emmaus Homes, 1981-91, Parkside Meadows Retirement Facility, 1982—; chmn. St. Charles City Charter Rev. Commn., 1991; bd. dirs. St. Charles Jaycee Village Retirement Home, 1980-90, Boone Ctr. Workshop, 1982-92; dist. chmn. Boy Scouts Am., 1979-82. Recipient Gov. of Mo. award, 1989, Mo. Time Quality Dealer award, 1995, United Ch. of Christ award, 1993, Jefferson award TV Sta. KSDK, St. Louis, 1996. Mem. Mo. Auto Dealers Assn. (bd. dirs. 1983—, treas. 1997-98, 2d v.p. 1998-99, 1st v.p. 1999-2000, pres. 2000—), Greater St. Louis Ford Dealers Assn. (past pres.), St. Charles C. of C. (past bd. dirs., pres., Citizen of Yr. award 1986), Rotary (past pres.). Lodge: Rotary. Home: 3304 Lennox Dr Saint Charles MO 63301-0632 Office: Pundmann Ford 2727 W Clay St Saint Charles MO 63301-2566

PUNINSKIJ, GENNADIJ EVGEŃEVICH, mathematics educator, researcher; b. Bobrujsk, Belorussia, Russia, Sept. 26, 1961; s. Evgenij Leont'evich and Alla Mikhajlovna (Zubritskaja) P.; m. Vera Aleksandrovna Kuzicheva, Apr. 5, 1986; 1 child, Evgenij. Degree in math., Moscow U., 1983, PhD in Math., 1987, 2d degreein Math, 1996. Asst. Moscow Mendeleev Inst., 1986-93, docent, 1993-96, prof., 1996—; chair dept. Moscow State Social U., 1996—. Contbr. articles to profl. jours. including Siberian Math Jour., Jour. Pure and Applied Algebra, among others. Recipient award Ministry of Sci. Germany, 1994. Mem. Moscow Math. Soc., Acad. Social Scis. Russian Orthodox. Avocations: chess, gardening. Home: Chertanovskaja 1-1-154, 113208 Moscow Russia Office: Moscow State Social U, Losinoostrovskaja 24, 107150 Moscow Russia

PUNKARI, YRJÖ MAUNO, computer software company executive, programmer; b. Vesilahti, Finland, Aug. 10, 1946; s. Vilho Valter and Marja-Terttu (Poukka) P.; m. Aino-Maija Maijala, Feb. 15, 1991; 1 child, Eeva Pauliina. Univ. degree mag. phil., Helsinki (Finland) U., 1973; music tchr. flute, Sibelius Acad., Helsinki, 1975; computer programmer, Helsinki U. Headmaster Music Sch., Vesilanti, 1979-94; computer programmer Narvasoft, Vesilahti, 1985—, exec., 1989—; lectr. history, Lempäälä, 1983—. Composer woodwind music and theater music, other arrangements; contbr. articles on history, philosophy, and anthropology to profl. jours. Avocation: photography. E-mail: ymp@sci.fi. Office: Narvasoft, Punkalaitumentie 8, 37370 Narva Finland

PUNNING, JAAN-MATI, environmental scientist; b. Tartu, Estonia, Mar. 13, 1940; s. Karl and Marta (Madison) P.; m. Karin Raba, Sept. 10, 1963; children: Marika, Herod. Diploma in physics and chemistry, Tartu (Estonia) U., 1963; degree in geology, Estonian Acad. Sci., Tallinn, 1968; D in Geography, Inst. Geography, Moscow, 1981. Engr. Geol. Survey, Tallinn, 1963-72; head lab. Inst. Geology, Tallinn, 1972-87; dep. dir. Inst. Electrophysics, Tallinn, 1987-92; prof. Tartu U., 1989-92, Tallinn Pedagogical U., 1993—; dir. Inst. Ecology, Tallinn, 1992—; cons. Ministry of Environment, Tallinn. Editor: Human Impact on Environment, 1993; guest editor Radiocarbon, 1993; contbr. articles to profl. jours.; inventor in field. Recipient K.E. Baer medal Estonian Acad. Scis., 1990, N. Vavilov medal All-Union Coun. Scis., Russia, 1988, Sci. award Republic of Estonia, 1995, Acad. Sci. Estonia medal, 1998. Mem. Estonian Geog. Soc. (pres. 1985—), Ea. European Assn. of 14C Lab. (steering com. 1992—, chmn. 1992—), Internat. Geog. Union, (working group 1992—), Euroscience. Avocations: literature, art, tourism, sports. Office: Inst Ecology, Kevade 2, EE0031 Tallinn Estonia

PUNTIS, JOHN WILLIAM LAMBERT, pediatrician, consultant; b. West Bromwich, U.K., Jan. 11, 1954; s. Jack and Irene Waverley (Lambert) P.; m. Hilary Jane Admans, Aug. 20, 1982; children: Emma Louise, James Ian, Thomas Jack, Daniel Joseph. BM with honors, U. Southampton Med. Sch., U.K., 1977, D Medicine, 1995. Registrar pediatrics Birmingham Children's Hosp., U.K., 1981-83; rsch. fellow U. Birmingham, U.K., 1983-86, lectr. in pediatrics and child health, 1986-89; cons. pediatrician Leeds United Teaching Hosps. Trust, U.K., 1990—; sr. lectr. dept. child health and pediatrics U. Leeds, U.K., 1990—. Contbr. papers to profl. publs. Sec. Med. Practitioners Union, West Midlands, Birmingham, 1979-85. Named Sheldon Rsch. fellow West Midlands Health Authority, Birmingham, 1984-86. Fellow Royal Coll. Physicians, Royal Coll. Pediatrics and Child Health; mem. Brit. Pediatric Assn., Brit. Soc. Gastroenterology, Brit. Assn. Perinatal Medicine, Pediatric Rsch. Soc., Brit. Soc. Pediatric Gastroenterology and Nutrition. Avocations: politics, history, cycling, music, family. Home: 6 The Avenue Roundhay, Leeds LS8 IDW, England

PUNTONET, CARLOS G., physics educator; b. Barcelona, Spain, Nov. 8, 1960; s. Carlos G. Velasco and Remy Puntonet; m. Elena Gomez Medialdea, June 14, 1991. BSc, U. Granada, Spain, MSc, PhD in Physics, 1994. Titular prof. Univi. Sch. U. Granada, 1986-96; univ. prof. Granada U., 1997—, sec. electronics dept., 1991-94, sec. architecture dpet., 1998—. Contbr. articles to profl. jours.; patentee in field. Serves with Spanish Navy, 1982-84. E-mail: carlos@atc.ugr.es. Office: Granad U/Architecture/Comp, Campus Fuentenueva s/n, Granada 18071, Spain

PUNZALAN, ERIC RUBIA, chemistry educator, consultant; b. Candelaria, Quezon, Philippines, July 15, 1963; s. Eduardo Baon and Bibiana (Rubia) P.; m. Emma Asuncion, May 20, 1994; children: Emmanuel, Cristina. BS, De La Salle U., Manila, 1984; PhD in Chemistry, U. Conn., 1994. Lectr. De La Salle U., 1984-87, instr., 1987-88; rsch. asst. U. Conn., 1988-94; postdoctoral rsch. assoc. U. Chgo., 1994-95; assoc. prof. chemistry De La Salle U., 1996—, dir. Sci. Rsch. Office, 1997—, dir. Environ. Rsch. Ctr., 1997—; cons. U.S. A. Labs., Inc., Cabuyao, Philippines, 1996; environ. impact assessment reviewer Dept. Environment and Natural Resources, Philippines, 1997—. Ind. tech. advisor Senate Com. on Environment, Philippines, 1999. Named Outstanding Young Scientist, Nat. Acad. Sci. and Tech., Manila, 1999. Mem. Chem. Soc. Philippines (pres. 1999—), Organic Chemistry Tchrs. Assn. (pres. 1997—), Am. Chem. Soc. Avocations: scuba diving, fishing, home repair. Office: DeLa Salle U Dept Chemistry, 2401 Taft Ave, 1004 Manila Philippines

PUOLAKKAINEN, PAULI ANTERO, surgeon and educator; b. Helsinki, Finland, Apr. 5, 1959; s. Leo Emil and Anneli Helena (Sampola) P.; m. Mirja Hellevi Raatikainen,May 21, 1983; children: Suvi, Tero, Maria. MD, U. Helsinki, 1984, PhD, 1989. Resident Lahti (Finland) Mcpl. Hosp., 1984-86; resident in surgery Helsinki U. Cen. Hosp., 1986-90; vis. scientist Bristol-Myers Squibb PRI, Seattle, 1990-93, U. Wash., Seattle, 1990-93; asst. prof. surgery Helsinki U. Cen. Hosp., 1993—, sr. lectr. Sch. Nursing, 1987-90; vis. prof. The Hope Heart

Inst., Seattle; cons. surgeon in pvt. clinics, Helsinki, 1986—. Contbr. articles to profl. jours. 2d lt. Finnish Army, 1988-89. Rsch. grantee Finnish Acad. Sci., 1994, Sigrid Juselius Found., 1993. Mem. Finnish Assn. Surgeons, Wound Healing Soc. USA, N.Y. Acad. Sci. Avocations: jogging, downhill skiing, hunting, golf, family. Office: Helsinki U Ctrl Hosp 2nd Dept Surg, Haartmaninkatu 4, 00290 Helsinki Finland

PUPPALA, VIJAYA KUMAR, agroclimatologist; b. Ariba, Orissa, India, Mar. 15, 1958; s. Rama Murty and Savitramma (Allu) P.; m. Annapurna Sundaraneedi; children: Sri Sai, Srujana. BS, Sri Krishna Chandra Gajapati Coll., 1979; MS, Andhra U., 1981. Project asst. Indian Inst. Sci., Bangalore, 1982-83; rsch. scholar Indian Inst. Tech., New Delhi, 1984; scientist Ctrl. Rsch. Inst. for Dryland Agr., Hyderabad, India, 1984-92; sr. scientist Ctrl. Rsch. Inst. for Dryland Agr., Hyderabad, 1992—. Contbr. articles to profl. jours. Mem. Soc. Dryland Agr. and Devel. Avocations: writing, reading, classical music, acting, chess. Home: Sri Sai Sakti Apts, Saleemnagar Malakpet, AP Hyderabad 500 036, India Office: Ctrl Rsch Inst Dryland Agr, Santo Shnagar Saidabad, AP Hyderabad 500 059, India

PURANEN, KRISTINA, retired translator; b. Kuopio, Finland, Aug. 22, 1930; d. Hugo Johannes and Laila Regina (Stålhane) Hukkinen; m. Jouni Herman Puranen, Apr. 4, 1953; children: Ilona Matilainen, Panu Puranen, Kimmo Puranen. MSc in Econs., Helsinki Sch. Econs./Bus. Admi, 1971. Lic. translator. English translator Bank of Finland, Helsinki, 1972-88; entrepreneur Käännöstoimisto Puranen Oy, Espoo, Finland, 1988-99; ret., 1999. Mem. Fedn. of Finnish Translators and Interpreters (auditor 1989—), Fedn. of Finnish Translation Agencies, Fedn. of Finnish Economists. Avocation: violin playing.

PURCELL, DALE, college president, consultant; b. Baxley, Ga., Oct. 20, 1919; s. John Groce and Agnes (Moody) P.; m. Edna Jean Rowell, Aug. 2, 1944; children: David Scott, Steven Dale, Pamela Jean; m. Mary Louise Gerlinger, Aug. 26, 1962; adopted children: Amelia Allerton, Jon Allerton. B.A., U. Redlands, 1948, M.A., 1949; postgrad., Northwestern U., 1951-52; LL.D., Lindenwood Colls., 1974. Topographer U.S. E.D., 1939; U.S. counter-intelligence agt., 1940-42; assoc. prof. Ottawa U., 1953-54, asst. to pres., 1954-58; gen. sec. Earlham Coll., 1958-61; dir. devel. U. So. Fla., 1961-63; pres. MITAC, Inc., Beverly Hills, Calif., 1961-72; exec. dir. Cancer Research Center, Columbia, Mo., 1963-65; pres. Westminster Coll., Fulton, Mo., 1973-76, Dale Purcell Assocs., 1972-92; a founding dir. Am. Sports Medicine Inst., Birmingham, Ala., 1987-92; chmn. Corp. Health Solutions, Arlington, Tex., 1988—; rep. cons. clients Hughston Sports Medicine Found., Columbus, Ga., Berry Coll., Mt. Berry, Ga., Hope Coll., Holland, Mich., William Woods Coll., Fulton, Mo., Eureka (Ill.) Coll., Cranbrook Insts., Bloomfield Hills, Mich., Penrose Hosp., Colorado Springs, Colo., Northwestern Coll., Orange City, Iowa, Centro Medico Docente, Caracas, Venezuela, Wayland Acad., Beaver Dam, Wis., Cen. Coll., Pella, Iowa, U. of Stirling, Scotland, U. Ottawa, Ont., Can., Washington & Lee U., Lexington, Va., Taylor U., Upland, Ind., Menninger Found., Topeka, Kans., Ill. Wesleyan U., Bloomington, Cox Med. Systems, Springfield, Mo., Nat. Council Family Rels. Mpls., Stephens Coll., Columbia, Mo., Hist. Savannah Found., Ga. Bd. visitors Berry Coll. Capt. USMCR, 1942-46, 52-53. Recipient Disting. Achievement award Berry Coll., 1974, medal Pres. of China, 1945, medal Pres. of Korea, 1953. Mem. Pi Kappa Delta (Alpha chpt.). Presbyterian (elder 1964—). Clubs: St. Louis (Clayton), Univ. (St. Louis and N.Y.C.), Litchfield County Ct. Home: Woodlands 120 Belden St Falls Village CT 06031-1124

PURCELL, GEORGE RICHARD, artist, postal employee; b. Clayton, N.Y., May 4, 1921; s. George Thomas and Katherine Eileen (Eagan) P.; m. Mary Sutter, Apr. 3, 1961. BS, Niagara U., 1947; postgrad., Syracuse U., 1952-53, 55-56. With Eagan Real Estate, Syracuse, 1948-49; claims interviewer N.Y. State Divsn. Unemployment Ins., 1949-50, 52; with U.S. Postal Svc., Syracuse, 1957—, cert. classifier of mails, 1975-77, with registry dept., 1977—; tutor in philosophy, 1971—. Exhibited in Ctrl. N.Y. Art Open, 1981, Drake Gallery, Fayetteville, N.Y., 1982, Assoc. Artists Gallery, Syracuse, 1983, 91, Fayetteville Art Festival, 1984, Recreation Generation Art Exhibit, 1982—, DeWitt (N.Y.) Libr., 1986-94, N.Y. State Fair, 1990, Art Telauc WCNY-TV, Syracuse, 1990—, Cazenovia Coll. Art Auction, 1994, N.Y. State Fair Fine Art Exhibit, 1999. Founder, pres. Syracuse chpt. Cath. Med. Mission Bd., 1973-76, rep., 1976—; del. Presdl. Trust, 1992; active Cath. Near-East Welfare Assn., Book Mission Program, New Mems. Art Show Manlius Libr., 1991, Rep. Nat. Com., Heritage Found., Washington; dep. dir. gen. Internat. Biog. Assn. Served with U.S. Army, 1943-46. Decorated Legion de l'Aigle der Mer, Order of Holy Cross of Jerusalem, Order Knight Templars of Jerusalem, knight Order of Holy Grail, knight Lofsensischen Ursinius Orden, baron Royal Order of Bohemian Crown; N.Y. State War Svc. scholar, 1955. Fellow Australian Inst. Coordinated Rsch. (life); mem. Am. Biog Inst. (life assoc., rsch. bd. advisors nat. divsn., apptd. dep. dir.), Internat. Soc. Neplatonic Studies, World Jewish Congress, Soc. Ancient Greek Philosophy, Inst. des Hautes Etudes, Alliance Universelle pour la Pax (hon. prof.), Osterrichische Albert Sweitzer Gesselshaft, Acad. Maison des Internationale Intellectuels. Roman Catholic.

PURCELL, HENRY, III, real estate developer; b. Watertown, N.Y., Dec. 21, 1929; s. John Cecil and Elizabeth (Hathway) P.; m. L. Betty Collier; children: Robert William, Emmy Purcell Reynolds, Jenny Purcell Hawley. BS in Mil. Engring., U.S. Mil. Acad., 1953; MBA in Econs. and Fin., U. Utah, 1975; postgrad., Princeton, 1960-61. Cert. Middle East specialist, Turkish linguist. Commd. 1st lt. U.S. Army, Augsburg, Republic of Germany, 1953; advanced through grades to lt. col. U.S. Army, 1967; commdr. Co. K. 1st regiment, 5th infantry div. U.S. Army, Augsburg, Fed. Republic of Germany, 1955-56; chief translation, U.S. Mil. Mission to Turkey U.S. Army, Ankara, Turkey, 1957-59; batallion commdr., tng. div. U.S. Army, Ft. Ord, Calif., 1965; sr. regimental adv. 7th ARVN regiment, 5th ARVN div. U.S. Army, South Vietnam, 1966, adv. G3 plans, III Corps ARVN, 1966-67; with Middle East Plans div., U.S. Strike Commd. U.S. Army, Tampa, Fla., 1968-70; asst. chief staff, G5 101st Airborne/Ambl div. U.S. Army, I Corps, South Vietnam, 1970; with G3Plans, Iv Corps ARVN U.S. Army, South Vietnam, 1970, sr. regimental adv. 32d regiment, 1971; with war plans div., deputy chief of staff, ops., The Pentagon U.S. Army, 1971; Middle East Specialist U.S. Readiness command U.S. Army, Tampa, Fla., 1972-74; retired U.S. Army, 1974; Middle East specialist U.S. Attache's Office, Ankara, Istanbul, 1961-63; with Spacos, G3 Plans and nuclear weapons employment div. NATO, Izmir, Turkey, 1963-65; pres. Henry Purcell, Inc., Tampa, 1976—, Warn-a-Prowler Inc., Tampa, 1994—; personal interpreter/Turkish translator for Lyndon B. Johnson. Pres. Nat. Sojourners, Tampa, 1969, 70, 72, Wilson Jr. High Sch. PTA, Tampa, 1977; commdr. Heroes of '76, Tampa, Fla., 1969, 70. Decorated DFC, Bronze Star for Valor with two oak leaf clusters, Cross of Gallantry, Gold Star, Silver Star (Vietnam), 10 Air medals, Army Commendation medal for valor with one oak leaf cluster with "V" device. Mem. Unified Constrn. Trades Bd., Nat. Assn. Realtors, Fla. West Coast Roofing Assn., Nat. Builders Assn., Greater Tampa C. of C. (com. of 100 1980—). Office: 825 W Platt St Tampa FL 33606-2251

PURCELL, JAMES NELSON, JR., international organization administrator; b. Nashville, July 16, 1938; s. James Nelson and Mary Helen P.; m. Walda Jean Primm, July 16, 1961; children: Deirdre Ann, Carole Elizabeth. B.A. in Polit. Sci., Furman U., 1961; M.P.A. (Maxwell Grad. Sch. fellow), Syracuse U., 1962. Mgmt. intern U.S. AEC, N.Y.C., Washington, Oak Ridge, 1962; budget analyst U.S. AEC, Oak Ridge, Washington, 1962-66; mgmt. analyst AID, State Dept., Washington, 1966-68; budget preparation specialist Office Mgmt. and Budget/Exec. Office of the Pres., 1968-69, dept. chief budget preparation, 1969-72; sr. budget examiner Internat. Ednl. Exch. program Office of Pres., 1972-74; chief Justice-Treasury br. Office Mgmt. and Budget/Exec. Office of the Pres., 1974-76; chief resources programming and mgmt. div. Bur. Ednl. and Cultural Affairs, Dept. State, Washington, 1976-77; exec. dir. Bur. Adminstrn., Dept. State, Washington, 1978-79; dep. asst. sec. Bur. Refugee Programs, Dept. State, Washington, 1979-82, dir., 1982-87; dir. gen. Internat. Orgn. for Migration, Geneva, 1988-98; internat. cons., 1998—. Mem. Am. Soc. Pub. Adminstrn. Home: 5113 W Running Brook Rd Columbia MD 21044-1522

PURCELL, KATHY ANN, business association administrator; b. Fremont, Nebr., Oct. 28, 1957; d. Samuel Dean Hanen and Goldie Mae Siegfried; m. Bill Purcell, May 17, 197; children: Kimberly, Nicole, Andrew. Grad., Mo. Valley (Iowa) H.S., 1976. Owner, mgr. Kathy's Hallmark, Missouri Valley, Iowa, 1985-92, Confetti Flowers, Blair, Nebr., 1992-94; dir. Missouri Vallley C. of C., 1994—; dir. We. Iowa Tourism Region, Red Oak, 1999-00. Grant writer Missouri Valley Cmty. Found., 1999. Mem. Iowa C. of C. Execs. (dir. 1999-00), Rialto Theater Assn. (treas. 1990—), Midwest Interpretive Assn. (1998—). Avocations: gardening, walking. E-mail: kpurcellmv@aol.com. Home: 2316 Liberty Ave Missouri Valley IA 51555-5010 Office: Missouri Valley C of C PO Box 130 Missouri Valley IA 51555-0130

PURCELL, MARY LOUISE GERLINGER, retired educator; b. Thief River Falls, Minn., July 17, 1923; d. Charles and Lajla (Dale) Gerlinger; m. Walter A. Kuyawski, June 9, 1950 (dec. July 1954); children: Amelia Allerton, Joh Allerton; m. Dale Purcell, Aug. 26, 1962. Student, Yankton Coll., 1941-45, Yale Div. Sch., 1949-50, NYU, summer 1949; MA, Columbia U., 1959, EdD, 1963. Teenage program dir. YWCA, New Haven, 1945-52; dir. program in family rels. Earlham Coll., Richmond, Ind., 1959-62, asst. prof. sociology and psychology, 1959-62, conf. coord. undergrad. edn. for women, 1962; chmn. div. home and cmty. Stephens Coll., Columbia, Mo., 1962-73, chmn. family and cmty. studies, 1962-78; dir. Learning Unltd., continuing edn. for women, 1974-78; head dept. family and child devel. Auburn (Ala.) U., 1978-84, prof., 1978-88, chmn. search com. for v.p. acad. affairs, 1984, spl. asst. to v.p. acad. affairs, 1985-86, prof. emerita, 1988—; developer course The Contemporary Am. Woman, 1962, cons., 1962; vis. prof. Ind. U. Summer Sch., 1970; cons. student personnel svcs. Trenton (N.J.) State Coll., 1958-59, 61. Contbr. articles to coll. bulls., jours. V.p. Falls Village-Canaan Hist. Soc. Alumni fellow Tchrs. Coll. Columbia U., 1959; recipient Alumni Achievement award Yankton Coll., 1975. Mem. AAUW, Am. Home Econs. Assn. (bd. dirs. 1967-69, chair 1st subject matter unit 1969, family rels. and child devel. sect. 1986-89), Groves Conf. on Family, Nat. Coun. Family Rels. (dir., chmn.-elect affiliated couns. 1981-82, chmn. 1982-84, nat. program chmn. 1977, chmn. film awards com., chmn. spl. emphases sect., bd. dirs., Ernest G. Osborne award for excellence in teaching 1979), Housatonic Camera Club (co-pres. 1996-2000), Delta Kappa Gamma. Congregationalist. E-mail: mlgp@discovernet.net. Home: 120 Belden St Falls Village CT 06031-1124

PURCELL, PHILIP JAMES, financial services company executive; b. Salt Lake City, Sept. 5, 1943; m. Anne Marie Mc Namara, Apr. 2, 1964. B.B.A., U. Notre Dame, 1964; M.Sc. in Econs., London Sch. Econs. and Polit. Sci., U. London, 1966; M.B.A., U. Chgo., 1967. Mng. dir., cons. McKinsey & Co., Inc., Chgo., 1967-78; v.p. planning and adminstrn. Sears, Roebuck and Co., Chgo., 1978-82; from pres., CEO, to chmn., CEO Dean Witter Discover & Co., N.Y.C., 1982-97; chmn., CEO, Morgan Stanley, Dean Witter & Co., N.Y.C., 1997—, also vice chmn.; dir. N.Y. Stock Exch., 1991-96; mem. coun. U. Chgo. Grad. Sch. Bus. Trustee U. Notre Dame. With USNR. Mem. Econ. Club Chgo., Chgo. Club, Links. Roman Catholic. Office: Morgan Stanley/Dean Witter & Co 1585 Broadway Ste 39th New York NY 10036-8200

PURCELL, STEVEN RICHARD, international management consultant, engineer, economist. B of Mech. and Indsl. Engring., NYU Coll. Engring., 1950; MS in Indsl. Engring., Columbia U., 1951; EdM, Harvard U., 1968. Registered profl. engr., Can. Lectr. engring. NYU Coll. Engring., N.Y.C., 1948-50; gen. mgr. Dapol Plastics Co., Inc., Boston, 1956-58; gen. div. mgr. Am. Cyanamid Co., Sanford, Maine, 1958-61; sr. prin., mgmt. cons. investment banking Purcell & Assocs., N.Y.C., 1961-66; prof., chmn. Bristol Coll., Fall River, Mass., 1966-68; assoc. dean grad. faculty adminstrv. studies York U., Toronto, Ont., Can., 1969-71; chief economist Dept. Manpower and Immigration, Ottawa, Ont., Can., 1970-71; cons. Treasury Bd., Ottawa, 1971-72; dir. urban and internat. environ. policy Ministry of State for Urban Affairs Internat. Activities, Ottawa, 1973-74; mem. com. on challenges of modern soc. NATO, Ottawa, 1973-74; mem. sci., econ. policy com. OECD UN, Ottawa, 1973-74; prof. Grad. Sch. Bus. Adminstrn. and Econs. Algonquin Coll., Ottawa, 1974-76; advisor, cons. House of Commons, 1976-77; sr. prin. Purcell & Assocs., Internat. Mgmt. Cons., Washington, 1977-80, chmn., CEO, 1981—; chmn., CEO Phoenix Internat. Capital Associates, Washington, 1981—; exec. dir. nat. coastal zone mgmt. adv. com. NOAA U.S. Dept. Commerce, Washington, 1980-81; profl. lectr. Northeastern U. Grad. Sch. Bus. Adminstrn., Boston, 1953-56, U. Toronto, 1968-69, George Washington U. Grad. Sch. Bus. Adminstrn., Washington, 1979; vis. prof. Rensselaer Poly. Inst. Advanced Mgmt. Program, 1967, U. Ottawa Grad. Sch. Bus. Adminstrn., 1971-74; lectr. Council for Internat. Progress in Mgmt., N.Y.C., 1960, Royal Bank Can. Mgmt. Assn., Toronto, Ont., 1970; corp. appointment cons. Harvard U., Cambridge, Mass., 1967-68; cons. Govt. Venezuela, 1967-68, Can. Inst. Bankers, Toronto, 1969-70; internat. sr. adviser NASA, 1985-86, mem. nat. adv. bd. Ctr. for Nat. Policy; dir. Rental Resource Corp., 1986-89. Contbr. articles on indsl. orgn., sci. policy and fin. to profl. jours. Lt. AC, USNR, 1943-46. Mem. UN Assn., Soc. for Advancement of Mgmt. (pres. 1949-50, leadership award 1950), Tau Beta Pi, Alpha Pi Mu (v.p. 1949-50), Columbia Univ. Club (Washington, trustee 1982-84, chmn., sr. trustee 1984-85), Harvard Univ. Club. Office: 12904 Mayflower Ln Bowie MD 20720-3368

PURCELL, STUART MCLEOD, III, financial planner; b. Santa Monica, Calif., Feb. 16, 1944; s. Stuart McLeod Jr. and Carol (Howe) P. AA, Santa Monica City Coll., 1964; BS, Calif. State U., Northridge, 1967; grad., CPA Advanced Personal Fin. Planning Curriculum, San Francisco, 1985. CPA, Calif.; CFP. Sr. acct. Pannell Kerr Forster, San Francisco, 1970-73; fin. cons. Purcell Fin. Services, San Francisco, 1973-74, San Rafael, Calif., 1980-81; controller Decimus Corp., San Francisco, 1974-76, Grubb & Ellis Co., Oakland, Calif., 1976-78, Marwais Steel Co., Richmond, Calif., 1979-80; owner, fin. counselor Purcell Wealth Mgmt., San Rafael, 1981—; guest lectr. Golden Gate U., San Francisco, 1985—; leader ednl. workshops, Larkspur, Calif., 1984; speaker Commonwealth Club Calif., 1989, 91. Contbr. articles to newspapers and profl. jours. Treas. Salvation Army, San Rafael-San Anselmo-Fairfax, Calif., 1987—; chmn. fin. planners div. United Way Marin County, Calif., 1984; mem. fundraising com. Marin County March of Dimes, 1987—, Marin County Arthritis Found., 1988—; mem. Marin Estate Planning Council. Served to lt. (j.g.) USNR, 1968-76. Named Eagle Scout, 1959, Best Fin. Advisor Marin County Independent-Jour. newspaper, 1987, Top Producer Unimarc, 1986; recipient Outstanding Achievement award United Way, 1984; named to The Registry of Fin. Planning Practitioners, 1987. Mem. AICPA, Calif. Soc. CPAs, Nat. Speakers Assn., Internat. Assn. for Fin. Planners (exec. dir. North Bay chpt., San Francisco 1984), Internat. Soc. Pre-Retired Planners, Soc. CPA-Fin. Planners (dist. membership chmn. San Francisco 1986), Registry Fin. Planning Practitioners, Sigma Alpha Epsilon. Presbyterian. Avocations: travel, auto racing, skiing, gardening. Home: 45 Vineyard Dr San Rafael CA 94901-1228 Office: Purcell Wealth Mgmt 1811 Grand Ave Ste B San Rafael CA 94901-1925

PURCHASE, FRANCENA, human resources specialist; b. Milw., Nov. 14, 1960; d. Johnny and Arlene (Roberts) Purchase. AA, Milw. Stratton Coll., 1982; BS in Applied Liberal Studies, Western Mich. U., 1997, postgrad. Investment mgmt. sec. M&I Bank, Milw., 1984-85; cons. United Devel. Corp., Milw., 1986-88; paraprofessional Grand Rapids (Mich.) Pub. Schs., 1990-92; customer svc. rep. kent County Conv. and Visitors Bur., Grand Rapids, 1995; mktg. rschr. Kennedy Rsch., Grand Rapids, 1996-98; pres. Creative Wocks, Grand Rapids, 1988—, F.P. Internat. Honor Soc., Kentwood, Mich., 1999—, F.P. Internat. Applied Studies, Kentwood, 1999—, Purchase Bus. Inst., Kentwood, 1999—; mktg. coord. Mich. Nat. Bank, Grand Rapids, 1980-81; asst. exec. sec. Manpower Internat. Inc., Milw., 1982-84; cons. NASW. Vol. United Way, Grand Rapids, 1990; reading condr. S.E. Neighborhood Assn., Grand Rapids, 1990; mem. literacy coun. Kent County Literacy Coun., Grand Rapids, 1991—; mem. task force Dwelling Pl., Grand Rapids, 1999; bd. dirs. Kent County Cmty. Mental Health, 1999—. Phillip Morris scholar Alverno Coll., 1981; Nontraditional Student grantee Western Mich. U., 1994; Thurgood Marshall Assistanship scholar Western Mich. U., 1998. Mem. Am. Mgmt., Soc. Human Resource Mgmt. Avocations: modern dancing, reading, tennis. Office: Purchase Bus Inst 1486 44th St SE Kentwood MI 49508-4633

PURDEA, IOAN, algebra educator; b. Caseiu, Cluj, Romania, Jan. 24, 1938; s. Gheorghe and Maria Purdea. BSc, Babes-Bolyai U., Cluj-Napoca, Romania, 1961, PhD, 1969. Asst. Babes-Bolyai U., Cluj-Napoca, 1961-68, lectr., 1968-79, reader, 1979-90, prof. algebra, 1990—, head chair algebra, PhD advisor, 1990—. Author: Treatise of Modern Algebra, Vol. I, 1977, Vol. II, 1982. Mem. Romanian Math. Soc. Home: Plopilor 4/26, Cluj-Napoca 3400, Romania Office: Babes-Bolyai U, Kogalniceanu 1, Cluj-Napoca 3400, Romania

PURDON, RICHARD ALAN, food products executive; b. Birmingham, Eng., Nov. 11, 1948; s. Peter Edward and Barbara Mary (Jones) P.; m. Helen Margaret Garside, May 20, 1972; children: Catherine Jane, Andrew Mark, Michael James. Diploma in Mktg. Sci. with distinction, North Staffs Coll., Stoke, Eng., 1976. Cost clk. Cadbury Schweppes, Birmingham, Eng., 1969-70; salesman Cadbury Schweppes, Birmingham, 1970-73; product mgr. Harrison, Birmingham, 1973-74, Scot of Bletchley, Milton Keynes, Eng., 1974-76; nat. account mgr. Scot Bowyers, Amersham, Eng., 1976-77; mktg. mgr. Bowyers, Trowbridge, Eng., 1977-83; gen. mgr. Bowyers, Amersham Bucks, Eng., 1983-86; mng. dir. Robirch, Burton, Staffs, Eng., 1986-90; divisional mng. dir. Kerry (U.K.) Ltd., 1991; prin. Hericam Assocs., 1991—; mng. dir. Baron Meats, 1992—; chief exec. Galley Parks, 1994; site dir. Stocks Covell, 1996-98; mng. dir. Key Coutnry Foods, 1998-99; dir. Freshway Foods. Mem. Brit. Meat Mfrs. Assn., Pork and Bacon Coun., Round Table (treas. Sutton Coldfield 1988-89, pres. 1990-91), Inst. Mktg., 41 Club (chmn. 1999-2000), Buckingham Sports Club (sec. 1976). Mem. Conservative Party. Mem. Ch. of England. Avocations: golf, travel, theatre. Home: 2 Beaconsfield Rd, West Midlands, B74 2NX Sutton Coldfield England Office: Baron Meats Ltd, Stafford Ct, Fordhouses, Wolverhampton WV10 7EL, England

PURDY, JOHN EDGAR, manufacturing company executive; b. Detroit, June 17, 1919; s. William Everett and May Adeline (Fountain) P.; m. Elizabeth Anne Van Dyne; 1 child, Vannessa Anne. Grad. h.s., Mich. Founder, chmn. Dayton (Ohio) Showcase Co., 1947-87. Capt. USAF, 1942-46. Decorated DFC with 2 oak leaf clusters, Purple Heart, Air medal with 6 oak leaf clusters. Mem. Am. Fighter Aces Assn. (pres. 1983-84), Am. Fighter Aces Mus. Found. (chmn. 1984-91), Nat. Aviation Hall of Fame (trustee 1978-86), Nat. Aviation Hall of Fame (bd. dirs. bd. of nominations), P-38 Nat. Assn. (pres. 1999—), Internat. Fighter Pilots Mus. Found. (trustee 1999—). Avocations: golf, aviation historian. Address: 6441 Far Hills Ave Dayton OH 45459-2725 also: 7634 E Bonnie Rose Ave Scottsdale AZ 85250-6825

PUREPONG, WICHIT, company executive, marketing researcher; b. Bangkok, Feb. 28, 1959; m. Nithima Purepong, May 2, 1999. BS in Agr., U. Thailand, 1980; MS in Edn., Ind. U., 1982, PhD in Edn., 1987. Rschr. Prime Min. Office, Thailand, 1987-88; rsch. dir. Prakit/FCB, Thailand, 1989-91, Frank Small and Assocs., Thailand, 1992-93; rsch. mgr. Nestle, Thailand, 1993-94; mng. dir. Corp. Resources Mgmt., Thailand, 1995-97, Rsch. Dynamics Co. Ltd., Thailand, 1997—. Mem. ESOMAR, Thai Market Rsch. Soc. (vice chmn. 1999—), Ind. U. Alumni Assn. (exec. com. 1996-97). Buddhist. Avocations: traveling, tennis. E-mail: rdvcl@ksc15.th.com. Fax: 662-238-0864. Home: 222/90 Onpa Tower, Sirinthorn Rd, Bangkok 10700, Thailand Office: Rsch Dynamics Co Ltd, 109 Surawongse Rd 7th Fl, Bangkok 10500, Thailand

PURETIĆ, ŠTEFANIJA KOŠAK, pediatric dermatologist; b. Prelog, Medjimurje, Croatia, July 2, 1922; d. Dominik and Amalija (Glavina) Košak; m. Božidar Puretič, July 30, 1945 (dec. 1971); children: Zvonimir, Višnja, Milavec. PhD in Dermatovenereology, Zagreb (Croatia) U., 1946. Pediatric diplomate, Croatia. Asst. physician anatomy inst. Zagreb U., 1945-50, asst. pediatrician, rsch. asst. clin. hosp., 1950-80; founder and chief pediatric dermatol. ward Zagreb Med. Sch., 1950-81; chief dermahistol. lab Dermatoven, Zagreb, 1955-66, 97; cons. pediat. dermatology Pediat. Clin. Hosp., Zagreb, 1956—, Hospice of Majka Terezija, Zagreb, 1990—. Contbr. chpts. to textbooks, articles to profl. jours.; author: Puretic Syndrome. Recipient Diplome for Socius honoris causa Croatian Dermatol. Soc., Zagreb, 1993. Mem. Croatian Med. Assn., Croatian Acad. Med. Sci. (senate). Roman Catholic. Avocations: sports, music. Home: Petrova ulica 90, 10000 Zagreb Croatia

PURGATORI, ANDREA, journalist, scriptwriter; b. Rome, Feb. 1, 1953; s. Mirko Purgatori and Luciana Bazzani; m. Nicola Schmitz; children: Edoardo, Ludovico, Victoria. M in Journalism, Columbia U., 1980. Reporter Il Tempo, Rome, 1974-76; reporter, editor met. sect., spl. corr. Corriere Sera, Rome, 1976—; TV anchor Utto Di Motte, 1997-98, Porte Chiuse, 1999—. Author: (novel) La Piovra 5, 1991, A un passo dalla guerra, 1996, (scripts) Spettri, 1987, Maya, 1988, Panama Sugar, 1990, Muro di Gomma, 1991, Continente Nero, 1992, Giudice Razazzino, 1994, Segreto di Stato, 1995, Last Cut, 1996, Vite Blindate, 1998, Iqbal, 1998, Fine Secolo, 1999, La Vita Cambia, 1999. Served with Italian Army, 1980-81.

PURI, ADIP RAMESH, communications company executive; b. Calcutta, India, Dec. 1, 1963; s. Ramesh and Kusum (Kapoor) P. BA in Econs., St. Xavier's, 1983; M in Mktg., St. Jain Inst., 1985. Market devel. mgr. Eureka-Forges, Mumbai, India, 1985-88; client svcs. dir. Ogilvy & Mather, Mumbai, 1989-96; client svcs. dir. Rediffusion Denisu-Young & Rubicam, Mumbai, 1997-99, gen. mgr., 1999—. Home: Union Park Kmar West, Mumbai 400 052, India Office: Rediffusion Denisu, Young & Rubicam, Mumbai India

PURI, BASANT KUMAR, medical researcher, physician; b. London, Feb. 25, 1961; s. Hari Ram and Sarla Rani (Dhir) P. BA with honors, U. Cambridge, 1982, BChir, 1984, MB, 1985, MA, 1986; DipMath, Open U., 2000; MPhil, London U., 2000. House physician Queen Elizabeth Hosp. U. Birmingham, 1985, house surgeon, 1985-86; registrar Addenbrooke's Hosp., Cambridge, Eng., 1986-88; sr. rsch. assoc. neurosci. Peterhouse Cambridge U., 1988-89; sr. registrar, lectr. Charing Cross Hosp., London, 1990-94; rsch. fellow Charing Cross & Westminster Med. Sch. London U., 1995-96; sr. rsch. fellow royal postgrad. medical sch. Hammersmith Hosp. London Univ., London, 1996-97, cons. psychiatrist, sr. lectr., hon. cons. radiology, 1997—. Author: Sciences Basic to Psychiatry, 1992, 2nd edit., 1998, Essentials of Psychiatry, 1995, 2d edit., 2000,Textbook of Psychiatry, 1996, Statistics for the Health Sciences, 1996, Statistics in Practice, 1996, Psychiatry Revision, 1997, Revision Notes in Psychiatry, 1999, Complete MCQs in Psychiatry, 1999, A Psychiatric Vade-Mecum, 1999. Recipient Young Scientist award U. London, 1994, 95, 96, Sr. Scientist award 2000. Mem. Royal Coll. Psychiatrists. Avocation: violin. Home: 63 Caraway Rd, Cambridge CB1 5DU, England Office: Robert Steiner MRI Unit Royal Postgrad Medical Sch, Hammersmith Hosp/ Du Cane R, London W12 OHS, England

PURI, RAJENDRA KUMAR, business and tax specialist, consultant; b. Hoshiarpur, Punjab, India, Dec. 22, 1932; came to the U.S., 1965, naturalized, 1969; s. Harbans Lal and Satya Vati (Jerath) P.; children: Neena, Veena, Ram. BS, Agra U., 1952; diploma in Russian lang. and lit., U. Dehli, 1958; BA, U. Wash., 1968, MBA, 1969; MS in Taxation, Golden Gate U., 1982. Customs officer Govt. of India, New Delhi, 1955-60; asst. treas. Merc. Bank Ltd., New Delhi, 1960-65; mem. staff Peat, Marwick, Mitchell & Co., CPAs, Seattle, 1969-70; state examiner State of Wash., Seattle, 1970-72, asst. supervising state examiner, 1972-74, supervising state examiner, 1974-77; sr. internal auditor Lockheed Corp., Sunnyvale, Calif., 1977-79; sci. programming analyst Lockheed Missile and Space Co., Sunnyvale, 1979-80, data processing specialist, 1980-84, sci. programming specialist, 1984-88; chief acct. Tex. Dept. Health, Austin, 1989-90; dir. internal audit, internal auditor Tex. Workers' Compensation Commn., Austin, 1990-95; bus. and tax cons., 1976—. Del. Wash. State Rep. Conv., 1976, Snohomish County Rep. Conv., 1976; Rep. nominee for state auditor, Wash., 1976; spl. advisor U.S. Congl. Adv. Bd., 1982-83. Mem. AICPA. Home: 2608 Hunlac Cove Round Rock TX 78681-7107

PURI, SANJAY, physicist; b. Rampur, India, Nov. 23, 1961; s. Rabindra Nath and Uma (Anand) P.; m. Bindu Puri, Dec. 7, 1989; children: Nikaash, Akshay. MS, IIT Delhi, New Delhi, India, 1982, U. Ill., Urbana, 1984; PhD, U. Ill., Urbana, 1987. Asst. prof. Jawaharlal Nehru U., New Delhi, 1987-93, assoc. prof., 1993—. Editor: Dynamics of Fluid Phases, 1994, Dynamics of Complex Systems, 1997; contbr. more than 85 papers on nonequilibrium statis. mechanics, 1985-2000. Pres. IIT Delhi Student Orgn., New Delhi, India, 1981-82. Recipient Young Scientist medal Indian Nat. Sci. Acad., New Delhi, 1993, Satyamurthy medal Indian Physics Assn., Bombay, 1995. Home: 1st Fl, 52/8 Chittaranjan Park, New Delhi 110019, India

Office: School of Physical Scis, Sch Phys Scis, Jawaharlal Nehru U, New Delhi 110067, India

PURI, SHAMLAL, news agency executive, editor; b. Nangli, India, July 4, 1951; arrived in Eng., 1975; s. Hussan Chand and Lajya (Devi) P.; m. Manjula Puri, Apr. 26, 1979; 1 child, Samir. BA with honors, Punjab U., Chandigarh, 1973. Corr. Tanzania Standard Newspapers, 1973-75; asst. editor India Weekly, London, 1975-77; sr. editor World Times, London, 1977-79; dir. Harambee, London, 1980-87; mng. editor Newslink Africa, London, 1983—; mng. dir. Newslink Africa Ltd., London, 1984—; dir. Adlink Internat. Ltd., London; bd. dirs. Harambee P.R. Assocs., London; mem. UNESCO Consultative Group Devel. of an Independent Press in Africa. Author: The Twilight, 1976, Best of Matatu, 1987, Press in East Africa, 1988, The Socio-Economic Parameters of a Viable Independent Press in Africa for UNESCO, 1991, Conf. Africa South of the Sahara Annual Guide, 1995; contbr. articles to profl. jours. Mem. Tanganyika African Nat. Union, Kigoma, 1970. Mem. Nat. Union Journalists, Pan African Orgn. Writers and Journalists. Mem. Revolutionary Party of Tanzania. Hindu. Avocations: reading, photography, motor sports, flying, travel. Office: Newslink Africa Ltd, 7-11 Kensington High St, London W8 5NP, England

PURI, SUNIL, forest scientist, researcher, educator; b. Nangal Twp., Punjab, India, Mar. 17, 1953; s. Kishori Lal and Nirmala (Sehgal) P.; m. Geeta Sharma, Nov. 30, 1980; 1 child, Manu. BS with honors, Punjab Agrl. U., Ludhiana, India, 1974; MS with honors, Punjab Agrl. U., 1975; PhD, Guru Nanak Dev U., Amritsar, India, 1979; MS in Forestry, Oxford U., 1986. Asst. prof. forestry U. Horticulture and Forestry, Solan, India, 1979-85; assoc. prof. Haryana Agrl. U., Hisar, India, 1985-94; head forestry dept. Haryana Agrl. U., Hisar, 1988-90; prof., head forestry dept. Indira Gandhi U., Raipur, 1994—. Editor: books, 1988, 93, 94, 97; cons. editor: Kluwer Acad. Publisher, The Netherlands, 1997; contbr. articles to profl. jours. Mem. Indian Soc. of Tree Scientists (mem. govning. body 1992—). Avocations: photography, swimming, cricket, table tennis. Home: Indira Gandhi Agrl Univ, House no F/12, 492 012 Raipur MP, India Office: Indira Gandhi Agrl U, Dept Forestry, 492 012 Raipur MP, India

PURI, VIJAYA RAVINDER, physics researcher, educator; b. Trivandrum, Kerala, India, June 9, 1954; d. Venkatraman and Lakshmi (Narayanan) Krishnamurthi; m. Ravinder Kumar Puri, Nov. 25, 1984; children: Deepika, Rohit. BSc in Physics, Delhi (India) U., 1974, MSc in Physics, 1976; PhD in Physics, Poona (India) U., 1982. Rsch. assoc. Pune U., 1982-85; lectr. Shivaji U., Kolhapur, India, 1985-86; rsch. scientist Shivaji U., Kolhapor, 1988—; lectr. Kolhapur Inst. Tech. Coll., Kolhapor, 1986-87, Warana Coll., Kolhapor, 1987-88. Contbr. over 60 articles to jours. in field. Mem. IEEE, Internat. Soc. Hybrid Microelectronics, Inst. Electronics and Telecomm., Indian Vacuum Soc., Indian Physics Assn. Avocations: stamp collecting, reading. E-mail: vijayapuri@hotmail.com. Office: Shivaji U Dept Physics, Vidya Nagar, Kolhapor 416004, India

PURICELLI, FRANCO, investment company executive; b. Milan, Nov. 26, 1962; s. Romeo and Allesandra (Mauri) P.; m. Alessandra Peviani, Apr. 21, 1990; children: Federica, Enrico. Degree in bus. adminstrn., U. Boccollo, Milan, 1987. Fin. analyst Leonzid Ego. Stockbrokers, Milan, 1987-90; portfolio mgr. Gesticredit, Milan, 1990-94; sr. portfolio mgr. Credido Italiano, Milan, 1994-96; chiev investment officer Aureo Gestioni, Milan, 1996—. Mem. AIAF. Roman Catholic. Office: Aureo Gestioni, Via Caradosso 18, 20100 Milan Italy

PURIŠIĆ, ANKA, radiophysicist, consultant; b. Split, Dalmatia, Croatia, Mar. 2, 1956; d. Jakov and Jakica (Delić) P. Degree in Physics Engring., U. Natural Sci., Zagreb, Croatia, 1981. Tchr. High Sch. for Civil Engring., Zagreb, 1981-88; radiophysicist Clin. Hosp. Rebro, Zagreb, 1988-93, Univ. Hosp. for Tumors, Zagreb, 1993—. Author: Radioterapija, 1996. Fellow Am. Assn. Physicists Medicine. Roman Catholic. Office: Univ Hosp for Tumors, Ilica 197, 10000 Zagreb Croatia

PURISIMA, FIDEL, justice The Philippines Supreme Court; b. San Ildefonso, Ilocos Sur, The Philippines, Oct. 28, 1930; s. Antonio Lazo and Concepcion Purisima; m. Fevi Suerte Felipe Velasquez, Apr. 19, 1959 (dec. Nov. 1989); children: Cesar Antonio, Dalla Purisima-Ponce de Leon, Grace; m. Josefina Chaves Lim, Apr. 6, 1995. LLB, Far Ea. U., Manila, 1953. Bar: The Philippines 1953. Aux. justice of peace, Buayan, Cotabato, The Philippines, 1956-57; mcpl. judge, Buayan, 1958-66; presiding judge br. I, Ct. of First Instance, Malolos, Bulacan, The Philippines, 1976-79; presiding judge br. VIII, Ct. of First Instance, 1979-82; assoc. justice Sandiganbayan, The Philippines, 1982-84, Intermediate Appellate Ct., The Philippines, 1984-86; acting presiding justice Ct. Appeals, Manila, 1994, sr. assoc. justice, 1994-97; acting presiding justice Supreme Ct. The Philippines, Manila, 1997-98, assoc. justice, 1998—. Del. Constl. Conv. The Philippines, 1971; mem. Sr. Provincial Bd., South Cotabato, 1967-70; acting gov. of South Cotabato, 1967-70; mcpl. councilor, Tacurong, Cotabato, 1955-57; pres. Our Lady of Peace and Good Voyage Parish Coun., 1965-67. Recipient Most Outstanding Alumni in Field Judiciary award Far Ea. U., 1995, plaque of recognition Far Ea. U. Law Alumni Assn., 1997. Mem. KC (grand knight), Lions (founder, charter officer Gen. Santos City 1968). Homee: 37 Damortis St, Quezon City 1115 NCR, The Philippines Office: Supreme Ct The Philippines, Padre Faura, Manila 1000 NCR, The Philippines

PURKIS, ANDREW JAMES, memorial fund executive; b. London, Jan. 24, 1949; s. Clifford Henry and Mildred Jeanie (Crane) P.; m. Jennifer Harwood Smith, July 18, 1980; children: Joanna Beatrice, Henry Francis. MA with honors, Corpus Christi Coll., Oxford, Eng., 1970; PhD, St. Antony's Coll., Oxford, Eng., 1978. Civil servant No. Ireland Office, London, 1973-80; head of policy, asst. dir. Nat. Coun. for Vol. Orgns., London, 1980-87; dir. Coun. for Protection of Rural Eng., London, 1987-92; Archbishop's sec. for pub. affairs Archbishop of Canterbury's Office, Lambeth Palace, London, 1992-98; chief exec. Diana Princess of Wales Meml. Fund, London, 1998—. Author: Housing and Community Care, 1982, Health in the Round, 1983. Dir., trustee Contact a Family, London, 1986-93; dir. Green Alliance, London, 1992—; chair Pedestrians Assn., 1999—. Avocations: music, reading, walking. Home: 38 Endlesham Rd, Balham London SW12 8JL, England Office: Lambeth Palace, County Hall, Westminster Bridge Rd, London SE1 7PB, England

PURNELL, CHARLES G., engineering executive; b. Clifton, Eng., July 22, 1943; s. Sidney Tom and Irene Vinter (Procter) P.; m. Mary Kitchen, Mar. 1972; children: Daniel Thomas, Joanna Sarah. MA, Oxford U., Eng., 1966. Cert. engr. Rsch. officer BNFMRA, London, 1966-80; rsch. svcs. supt. BNFMTC, Wantage, Eng., 1980-86; materials devel. mgr. Brico Engring., Coventry, Eng., 1986-89, R&D mgr., 1989-95, tech. dir., 1995-96; R&D dir. T and N Powder Metal Products Group plc, Eng., 1997—. Inventor in field. Mem. Inst. Materials, ASTM, APMI, SAE. Avocations: campanology, gardening. Office: Brico Engring, Fed-Mogul Sintered Products, Holbrook Ln, CV6 4BG Coventry England

PURNELL, ELIZABETH, psychology and linguistics educator; b. Manassas, Va., Jan. 26, 1970; d. Walter Valerian Jr. and Carol Sue Purnell; m. A. Kovach. BA in Linguistics, U. Ill., 1993; MA in Linguistics, Ind. U., 1996; MA in Psychology, U. Pa., 1998. From instr. to assoc. instr. Ind. U., Bloomington, 1995-97, U. Pa., Phila., 1997-98; lectr. Balt. Internat. Coll., 1999; rsch. asst. Rice U., Houston, 2000—; linguistics expert/eGuide www.hungryminds.com. Contbr. articles to books. Cognitive Sci. summer rsch. fellow Ind. U., 1995, 96, 97, Scholar fellow, 1997. Mem. APA, AAUW, Am. Psychol. Soc., Linguistic Soc. of Am., Ind. U. Linguistics Club (v.p. 1994-95), Sigma Delta Epsilon. E-mail: epurnell@psych.upenn.edu. Home: # 8211 1504 N Prospect Ave Apt 205 Milwaukee WI 53202-2313

PURNELL, OLIVER JAMES, III, judge; b. Richmond, Va., Jan. 18, 1949; s. Oliver James Jr. and Margaret Helen (Hodges) P.; m. Cheryl Naomi Williams, June 30, 1973; children: Oliver James IV, Amy Susan. AA, U. Hartford, 1969; AB, Middlebury Coll., 1972; MSLS, Case Western Reserve U., 1976; JD, Western New England Sch. Law, 1982. Bar: Conn. 1982, U.S. Dist. Ct. (fed. dist.) Conn. 1982. Dir., pharmacy libr. U. Conn. Sch. Pharmacy, Storrs, Conn., 1977-81; assoc. Lavitt, Hutchinson & Kaplan, Vernon, Conn., 1981-84, DuBeau & Ryan, Vernon, Conn., 1984-87, Howard, Kohn Sprague & Fitzgerald, Hartford, Conn., 1987-89; pvt. practice Vernon, 1989-92; reference libr. U. Conn. Sch. Law, Hartford, 1992-98; regional info. mgr. Lexis-Nexis, Vernon, 1998-99; judge Ellington Dist. Probate Ct., Vernon, 1999—. Contbr. articles to profl. jours. Scoutmaster Boy Scouts of Am., Rockville, Conn., 1990—. Recipient Eagle Scout award Boy Scouts of Am., 1964. Mem. Am. Assn. Law Libraries, So. New England Law Libr. Assn. (pres. 1998-99), Masonic Lodge, A.F. & A.M. (master Fayette Lodge 1970). Avocations: skiing, camping, hiking, church organist. Office: 6 Forestview Dr Vernon Rockville CT 06066-4807

PUROHIT, DIPAKKUMAR MANILAL, chemistry educator, researcher; b. Bharuch, Gujarat, India, Feb. 21, 1962; s. Manilal Mahashanker and Nirmalaben (Manilal) P.; m. Nayanaben Dipakkumar Nayana, Apr. 27, 1986; children: Hetaben, Swetaben. BSc, S.G. U., Surat, India, 1984, MSc, 1986; PhD, Saurashtra U., Rajkot, India, 1997. Plant operator Indian Oil Co., Ltd., Baroda, 1986-89; tchr. Sch., Bharuch, 1989-90; lectr. Virani Sci. Coll., Rajkot, 1980—; chemistry lectr. Saurashtra U., Rajkot, 1997—. Author numerous books; contbr. articles to profl. jours. Avocations: research, cricket, teaching, learning. Home: Sarva Mangal D-68, Shastrinager Nanamova Main, Rajkot Gujarat 360005, India Office: Shri MN Virani Sci & Yogiji, Kalawad Rd, Rajkot Gujarat 360005, India

PUROL, R.M. SCOTT, psychiatric nurse; b. Phila., Sept. 16, 1946; d. Sylvester Steven and Josephine Veronica (Czarnecka) P.; m. Stephen Chas Hershey, Dec. 27, 1986. Diploma in nursing, St. Joseph's Hosp., 1968; BA, Lone Mtn. Coll., 1974; BSN, U. San Francisco, 1976; M in Nursing, Emory U., 1990. Staff nurse Meth. Hosp., Phila., 1968—; clin. nurse specialist Interdisciplinary Practice, Columbus, 1991-95; found. Health Mentors, Columbus, 1995—. Served in U.S. Army Nurse Corps, 1967-87. Grantee NIH, 1976. Mem. ANA, Am. Psychiat. Nurses Assn., Am. Holistic Nurses Assn., Ga. Nurses Assn. (Dist. Honoree 1996), Internat. Soc. Consultative Liaison Nurses, Assn. Child and Adolescent Psychiat. Nurses, Nat. Registry of Cert. Group Psychotherapists, Am. Group Psychotherapy Assn. (clin.), Am. Coll. Nurse Practitioners, Sigma Theta Tau. Avocations: singing, piano, music therapy research. Home and Office: Health Mentors PO Box 7937 Columbus GA 31908-7937

PURRER, SIEGFRIED, trading company executive; b. Vöcklabruck, Austria, Oct. 17, 1949; s. Josef and Hildegard (Kritz) P.; m. Johanna Knoll, May 19, 1979; children: Siglinde, Christian, Susanna. Dr. Law, J. Kepler U., Linz, Austria, 1972. With purchasing dept. Voest-Alpine AG, Linz, 1974-78; v.p. Voest-Alpine Intertrading, Linz, 1978-85, pres., 1985-90; pres. Coutinho Caro & Co. Trading GmbH, Hamburg, 1990-97; mng. dir. F.J. Elsner & Co. GmbH, Vienna, 1998—. Roman Catholic. Avocations: mountaineering. Home: Mozartstrasse 2A, Mozartstrasse 2A, 4614 Marchtrenk Austria also: Grosse Sperlgasse 7/15, A-1020 Vienna Austria Office: FJ Elsner & Co GmbH, Baumgasse 60B, A-1030 Vienna Austria

PURVEZ, AKHTAR, otolaryngologist, researcher; b. Srinagar, India, Apr. 1, 1958; s. Muzaffar Aazim and Padshah (Jan) Mir; m. Mudhasir Bashir; children: Ana Mir, Sama Mir. MB, BS, Govt. Med. Coll., Srinagar, India, 1981, M of Surgery with honors, 1986. Intern in surgery, ENT, medicine Govt. Med. Coll. Associated Hosps., Srinagar, 1981-82, resident house surgeon ENT, 1982-83, asst. surgeon ENT, 1983-84, postgrad. scholar ENT, 1984-86, registrar ENT, asst. surgeon, 1986-87; asst. surgeon, ENT specialist Kashmir Health Svcs., India, 1987; registrar ENT dept. otorhinolaryngology Hosp. Govt. Med. Coll., 1987-89; ENT surgeon specialist King Fahad Hosp., Tabuk, Saudi Arabia, 1989-90; registrar, otolaryngology Riyadh Al Kharj Mil. Hosps., Saudi Arabia, 1990—. Fellow Internat. Coll. Surgeons, Indian Medicos Soc.; mem. AAAS, Assn. Otolaryngologists India, Indian Med. Assn. Avocations: literature, mountaineering, riding, charities. E-mail: apurvez@hotmail.com. Home: 13 Sherman Rd Chestnut Hill MA 02467-3130

PURVIS, JOHN ROBERT, international business consultant; b. St. Andrews, Fife, Scotland, July 6, 1938; s. Robert William Berry and Vivienne Daphne Elizabeth (Camell) P.; m. Louise Spears Durham, Jan. 1, 1962. MA with honors, U. St. Andrews, 1962. Officer 1st Nat. City Bank (divsn. Citibank N.A.), London, 1962-63, N.Y.C., 1963-65, Milan, 1965-69; treas. Noble Grossart Ltd., Edinburgh, Scotland, 1969-73; mng. dir. Gilmerton Mgmt. Svcs. Ltd., St. Andrews, 1973-86; mng. ptnr. Purvis and Co., St. Andrews, 1986—; mem. for Scotland European Parliament; non-exec. dir. Crown Vantage Ltd., Guardbridge, Scotland, Curtis Fine Papers Ltd., Guardbridge, LeggMason European Utilities Trust PLC, Exeter, Eng.; chmn. Kingdom FM Radio Ltd., 1998—, Belgrave Capital Mgmt. Ltd., 1999—. Contbg. author: Power and Manoeuvrability, 1978. Mem. European Parliament, Strasbourg, France, Brussels, Belgium and Luxembourg, 1979-84, Scotland, 1999—; v.p. Scottish Conservative and Unionist Assn., Edinburgh, 1988-90, chmn. econ. com., 1986-97; chmn. for Scotland Ind. Broadcasting Authority, London, 1985-89; mem. Scottish Adv. Com. on Telecomm., Edinburgh, 1990-97, taxation com. Scottish Landowners Fedn., 1978—. 1st lt. Scots Guards Brit. Army, 1956-58. Named Comdr. Order of the Brit. Empire, 1990. Fellow Inst. Dirs.; mem. Royal and Ancient Golf Club (St. Andrews), Cavalry & Guards Club (London), New Club (Edinburgh). Mem. Ch. of Scotland. Avocations: family history, Italy. Office: Purvis and Co, Gilmerton, St Andrews KY16 8NB, Scotland

PURVIS, STEWART, broadcast executive. BA, U. Exeter, Eng. News trainee BBC, London, 1969; journalist ITN, London, 1972, program editor News at Ten, 1980-83, editor Channel Four News, 1983, dep. editor, 1983-89, editor, 1989-91, editor-in-chief, 1991-95, chief exec., 1995—. Office: ITN, 200 Grays Inn Rd, London WC1X 8XZ, England*

PURWONO, ALBERTUS SOEGIARTO, biologist; b. Purwokerto, Indonesia, June 5, 1945; s. Adi and Gondopujiati P.; m. Ruth Aryani, Dec. 20, 1974; children: Adrian, Debora. D in Biology, U. Kristen Satyawacana, Salatiga, 1974. From staff mem. to head rsch. & devel. lab. PT Air Mancur, Solo, Indonesia, 1974—. Mem. Indonesian Traditional Herbal Soc. Avocations: gardening, swimming, reading. E-mail: researchdev@airmancur.co.id. Home: Melati II AA 80, 57171 Solo Indonesia Office: PT Air Mancur, PO Box 253, 57102 Solo Indonesia

PURYAYEV, DANIIL TROFIMOVICH, optician, university administrator; b. Kulikovo, Russia, Sept. 5, 1934; s. Trofim Ivanovich and Aleksandra Michailovna (Emelyanova) P.; m. Valentina Sergeevna Kashayeva, Sept. 16, 1961; 1 child, Sergey. Engr.-optician diploma, Moscow State Bauman Tech. U., 1958, Candidate of Tech. Sci., 1966, D of Tech. Sci., 1977. Asst. prof. Moscow State Bauman Tech. U., 1966-80, prof., 1980-91, head of dept., 1991—; sci. cons. astronomic optics project Moscow State Bauman Tech. U. and Rubin, 1978-85; sci. dir. projects in optical measurement field Moscow State Bauman Tech. U., 1985-97; sci. cons. cosmic opto- and radiotelescopes project Astrocosmic Ctr., Moscow, 1997—. Author: (book) Methods of Optical Aspheric Surface Testing, 1976 (Univ. prize 1977); inventor in field. Recipient Gold medal Soviet Union Govt., 1952, 6 medals for inventions, 1967-82; prize winner Min. Coun. of Soviet Union, 1982. Mem. Internat. Soc. of Optical Engring. (mem. nat. br.). Avocations: mowing, collecting aphorisms, recitative verses. Home: Apt 36, 27 Srednyaya Pervomaiskaya, 105077 Moscow Russia Office: Moscow State Bauman Tech U, 5 2nd Baumanskaya, 107005 Moscow Russia

PUŞCAŞ, IULIANA CARMEN, internist, gastroenterologist, researcher; b. Simleu Silvaniei, Salaj, Romania, Sept. 24, 1960; d. Ioan and Ecaterina (Boacă) P. Grad. in medicine, U. Cluj, Romania, 1987; MD, U. Timişoara, Romania, 1997. Physician Med. Ctr., Şimleu, 1987-90; advanced postgrad. tng. in gastroenterology Academisch Med. Ctr., Amsterdam, The Netherlands, 1993; young clinician spl. tng. 10th WCOG, L.A., 1994; resident in internal medicine Ctr. for Rsch. and Med. Assistance, Romanian Acad. Scis., Şimleu, 1990-93, chief gastroenterology dept., 1993—. Co-author: Progress in the Pathophysiology of Gastric and Duodenal Ulcers, 1985, Carbonic Anhydrase and Modulation of Physiologic and Pathologic Processes in the Organism Listed in I.S.I., 1994; contbr. articles to med. jours.. Mem. Şimleu Iuliu Maniu Found., Şimleu, 1990; founder, pres. Dr. Puşcaş Found., Şimleu, 1997. Mem. County Orgn. for Children. Mem. Christian Democrat National Party. Orthodox. Avocations: reading, photography, motorcycles, music, painting. Home: Cetatii St 1, 4775 Şimleu Salaj, Romania Office: Romanian Acad Scis, Ctr for Rsch, 37 Dunarii St, 4775 Şimleu Salaj, Romania

PUSCAS, NICULAE TIBERIU, physicist, educator; b. Gherla, Romania, Dec. 13, 1952; s. Nicolae and Iuliana Puscas; m. Liliana Stanescu, July 26, 1980. Degree in physics, U. Babes-Bolyai, Cluj, Romania, 1976; PhD in Physics, Bucharest (Romania) U., 1991. Prof. physics Lyceum 20, Bucharest, 1976-80; asst. Poly. U. Bucharest, 1980-91, lectr., 1991-94, assoc. prof. physics, 1994-98, prof. physics, 1998—. Author: Optoelectronic Devices Physics, 1998; co-author: Lasers and Multiphotonic Processes, 1988, Introduction to Optical Processing, 1999; co-editor (jour.) Optical Engring., 1996. Lt., Transmissions, 1980, Bucharest. Mem. Internat. Soc. Photo-Optical Instrumentation Engring. (pres. Romanian chpt. 2000—), European Phys. Soc., European Optical Soc. Greek Orthodox. Avocations: basketball, football, music. Home: Blvd Corneliu Coposu 32, 70092 Bucharest Romania Office: U Poly Bucharest Phys Dept, Splaiul Independentei 1313, 77206 Bucharest Romania

PUSCAS, VICTOR, judge. Chmn. Supreme Ct Moldova. Office: Supreme Ct of Justice, 70 Mihai Cogalniceanu St, Chisinau Moldova*

PUSCHETT, JULES B., medical educator, nephrologist, researcher; b. Hazelton, Pa., Mar. 13, 1934; m. Diane Puschett; children: Mitchell, Lynne. BA magna cum laude, Lehigh U., 1955; MD, U. Pa., 1959. Intern Jackson Meml. Hosp., Miami, 1959-60; resident, fellow endrocrinology and metabolism Univ. Hosp., Balt., 1963-66; postdoctoral fellow in medicine NIH Inst. Arthritis and Metabolic Disease, Bethesda, Md., 1966-68; fellow, renal-electrolyte sect. U. Pa. Sch. Medicine, Phila., 1966-68; rsch. assoc. VA Hosp., Phila., 1968-70, staff to chief renal-electrolyte sect. dept. medicine, 1968-73, clin. investigator, 1970-73; head renal-electrolyte divsn. Allegheny Gen. Hosp., Pitts., 1973-78; dir. renal-electrolyte divsn. fellowship tng. program U. Pitts. Sch. Medicine, 1976-78; chief renal-electrolyte divsn. dept. medicine U. Ark. for Med. Scis., Little Rock, 1979-80, U. Pitts. Sch. Medicine, 1980-90; interim chief sect. nephrology dept. medicine Tulane U. Sch. Medicine, New Orleans, 1990-92, prof. chmn. dept. medicine, 1990—, asst. dean network affairs, 1996-99, Harry B. Greenberg, MD chair in internal medicine, 1999—; instr. medicine U. Pa. Sch. Medicine 1967-79, assoc. in medicine 1969-70, asst. prof. medicine 1970-73; clin. assoc. prof. medicine U. Pitts. Med. Sch. 1973-78; prof. medicine U. Ark. Med. Scis. 1979-80; prof. medicine U. Pitts. Sch. Medicine 1980-90. Editor: The Diuretic Manual, 1984, Diuretics: chemistry, Pharmacology and Clinical Applications, 1984, Disorders of Fluid and Electrolyte Balance: diagnosis and Management, 1985, Diuretics II: Chemistry, Pharmacology and Clinical Applications, 1986, Diuretics III, 1989, Diuretics IV, 1993; contbr. over 170 articles to profl. jours.; spkr. and presenter in field; editl. bd. Am. Jour. Med. Scis., Am. Jour. Nephrology (sect. editor Physiology for the Nephrologist), Cardiovasc. Risk Factors, Internat. Jour. Artificial Organs, Southern Med. Jour. Chmn. 1st Ann. Kidney Ball, Nat. Kidney Found. of Western Pa., 1988, chmn. 2d Ann. Kidney Ball, 1989. With USN 1960-63. Recipient Gloria P. Walsh award for Tchg. Excellence, Graduating Class/Tulane U. Sch. Medicine, 1998; named Outstanding Tchr. Yr., Owl Club, Tulane U., 1991, 94; Coxe Meml. scholar Lehigh U., 1951. Fellow ACP; mem. AMA, AAAS, Am. Fedn. Clin. Rsch., Am. Soc. Artificial Internal Organs, Am. Soc. Nephrology (chmn. audit com. 1992), Nat. Kidney Found. (pub. policy com. 1989, vol. svc. award 1990), Internat. Soc. Nephrology, Am. Heart Assn. Coun. on the Kidney in Cardiovasc. Disease (chmn. subcom. on scientific confs. 1991-92, exec. com. 1991-95, long-range planning com. 1992-94, vice chair 1998-2000, chair-elect 1999-2000, chair 2000—), Am. Heart Assn. Coun. for High Blood Pressure Rsch., Am. Physiol. Soc., Fedn. Am. Socs. for Exptl. Biology, Am. Geriat. Soc., Ctrl. Soc. for Clin. Rsch., Soc. for Exptl. Biology and Medicine, Am. Soc. Clin. Pharmacology and Therapeutics, Am. Coll. Clin. Pharmacology, Endocrine Soc., Am. Soc. Renal Biochemistry and Metabolism, Am. Soc. Hypertension (Outstanding Tchr. Yr. 1986), Internat. Soc. Nutrition and Metabolism in Renal Disease, Am. Soc. Bone and Mineral Rsch., European Dialysis and Transplant Assn., Nat. Kidney Found. of Western Pa. (med. adv. com. 1981, chmn. 1981-83, Gift of Life award 1991), Nat. Kidney Found. of La. (mem.-at-large, trustee 1991), So. Med. Assn., So. Soc. Clin. Investigation (councilor 1992-94, sec.-treas. 1994-99, pres.-elect 1998-99, pres. 1999-2000), La. State Med. Soc., Orleans Parish Med. Soc. (membership com. 1993, long-range planning com. 1993), La. Soc. Internal Medicine, S.E. Clin. Club, Midwestern Salt and Water Club, Phi Beta Kappa, Alpha Epsilon Delta, Alpha Omega Alpha. Office: Tulane Univ Sch Medicine Dept Medicine SL 12 1430 Tulane Ave New Orleans LA 70112-2699

PUSEP, YURI ALEXANDER, physicist, researcher; b. Novosibirsk, Russia, Feb. 9, 1953; arrived in Brazil, 1994; s. Alexander Ostvald and Olga Pusep; m. Olga Nickolai Nikulinsky, Apr. 6, 1978; children: Stanislav, Serguei. Master's degree, Inst. Electronic Engring., Novosibirsk, 1975; PhD, Inst. Semicondr. Physics, Novosibirsk, 1985. Jr. rschr. Inst. Semicondr. Physics, Novosibirsk, 1975-87, sr. rschr., 1988-92, 93-96; prof. U. Fed. São Carlos, Brazil, 1994—; vis. scientist Max-Planck-Inst., Stuttgart, Germany, 1987-88, Reimsch Westfalishen Technische Hohschule, Aachen, Germany, 1992. Fellow Alexander von Humboldt Found.; mem. Electrochem. Soc., Inc. Brazilian Phys. Soc. Avocations: bicycling, skiing. Home: R Luiz Barbosa de Campos 72, 13562-330 Sāp Carlos Brazil Office: U Fed São Carlos, DF Via Washington Luis, 13565 São Carlos Brazil

PUSEY, MAVIS IONA, artist, educator. Student, Art Students League, 1961-65, Birgit Sch. Workshop, London, 1967-68, Robert Blackburn Workshop, 1969-72, New Sch. for Social Res., 1974, 76, 87. instr. painting New Sch. for Social Rsch., N.Y.C., 1973-88; asst. prof. painting and printmaking SUNY, Stony Brook, 1974-77; instr. intermediate painting Pa. Acad. Fine Arts, Phila., 1974-86; instr. printmaking and painting N.Y. State Summer Sch. of the ARts, 1978-79; instr. etching and painting Drew U., Madison, N.J., 1980-81; instr. studio art, art history and art appreciation Woodberry Forest (Va.) Sch., 1993—; lectr. in field. One-woman shows include Rainbow Art Found., N.Y., 1977, Franklin and Marshall Coll., Pa., 1979, New Sch. Assocs., N.Y.C., 1980, Korn Gallery, Drew U., Madison, 1980, Piedmont Va. C.C., 1993, St. Catherine's Sch., 1995, bozART Gallery, Charlottesville, Va., 1999; group exhbns. include Douglas Coll. Art Gallery, Rutgers U., New Brunswick, 1980, William Penn Meml. Mus., Harrisburg, Pa., 1983, City Gallery/2 Dept. Cultural Affairs, City of N.Y., 1983, Art Students League, 1986, 93, Lamar Dodd Art Ctr., LaGrange, Ga., 1991, Nat. Arts Club, 1993, others; traveling group exhbns. include Greenville (S.C.) Mus. Art, 1984, Metro-Dade Cultural Ctr., Miami-Dade Pub. Libr., 1988, The Artmobile, Miami-Dade Pub. Libr. Sys., 1991, Bronx (N.Y.) Art Ctr. and Gallery, 1992, Hillwood Art Mus., L.I. U., Bronxville, N.Y., 1992, others; represented in permanent collections Citibank, N.Y.C., First Nat. Bank Chgo., Chem. Bank, Tougaloo Coll., Miss., Mus. Modern Art, N.Y.C., numerous pvt. collections. Recipient Bryon Browne Meml. award Art Students League, 1963, Ford Found. Tuition award Art Students League, N.Y., 1964, Louis Comfort Tiffany Found. award, 1972, Louis Comfort Tiffany Found. Purchase award, 1974, Majors Travel Tour award S.I. Mus., 1975, Internat. Woman's Yr. award in recognition of outstanding cultural contbn. and dedication to women and art, 1976.

PUSEY, WALTER CARROLL, III, geologist, consultant; b. Upper Darby, Pa., Feb. 13, 1935; s. Walter Carroll Jr. and Elizabeth Foulke (Sharples) P.; m. Betsy Cantwell, Mar. 30, 1960; children: David, Steven, Anne. BA, Amherst Coll., 1960; PhD, Rice U., 1964. Cert. petroleum geologist. Mgr. worldwide exploration Conoco, Houston, 1964-93; prof. geology ESRI, U. S.C., Columbia, 1994-96, ESRI, U. Utah, Salt Lake City, 1996; cons., pres. Twin Lakes Resources, Houston, 1996—. Author, editor: Belize Shelf Carbonates, Clastics and Ecology, 1995. Served with U.S. Army, 1955-58. NSF grantee, 1959; NSF grad. fellow, 1960-64. Mem. Am. Assn. Petroleum Geologists (Citation of Excellence 1999), Geol. Assn. Am., Soc. Sedimentary Geology, Nat. Speleological Soc., Sigma Xi. Quaker. Achievements include patent and liquid window concept which is widely used in the petroleum industry to describe thermal maturity of oil and gas source rocks. Avocation: photography. Home and Office: 5527 Honor Dr Houston TX 77041-6557

PUSHKAREV, BORIS S., research foundation director, writer; b. Prague, Czechoslovakia, Oct. 22, 1929; came to U.S., 1949, naturalized, 1954; s. Sergei G. and Julie T. (Popov) P.; m. Iraida Vandellos Legky, Oct. 20, 1973. BArch, Yale U., 1954, M.C.P., 1957. Instr. city planning Yale U.,

New Haven, 1957-61; chief planner Regional Plan Assn., N.Y.C., 1961-69, v.p. rsch., 1969-89, sr. v.p., 1989-90; adj. assoc. prof. NYU, 1969-79; chmn. Russian Rsch. Found. Study of Alternatives to Soviet Policy, 1981—; bd. dirs. Russian Solidarists; lectr. New Humanitarian U., Moscow, 1993—. Author: (with Christopher Tunnard) Man-Made America, 1963; (with Jeffrey Zupan) Urban Space for Pedestrians, 1975, Public Transportation and Land Use Policy, 1977, Urban Rail in America, 1982, Russia and the Experience of the West, 1995; editl. bd. POSSEV; contbr. articles to profl. jours. Recipient Nat. Book award (with C. Tunnard), 1964. Mem. Am. Assn. for Advancement of Slavic Studies. Russian Orthodox. Home: 770 Anderson Ave Apt 20F Cliffside Park NJ 07010-2172

PUSHNYKH, VICTOR ALEXANDROVICH, education educator, researcher; b. Tomsk, Siberia, Russia, July 24, 1950; s. Alexander Fedorovich and Olga Yudkovna (Rakhlina) P.; m. Svetlana Andreevna Koshikova, Dec. 4, 1974.; MS in Machining, Tomsk Polytechnic U., 1972, PhD, 1980. Engr. Tomsk Polytech. U., 1972-75, asst. prof., 1978-80, head rsch. dept., 1980-82, head CAD/CAM rsch. dept., 1982-86, dep. head machining acad., 1988-95, dir. Russian-Am. Ctr., 1995-97, dir. Interdisciplinary Ctr. for Continuing Edn. Specialists, 1997—; cons. C. of C. and Industry, 1997—, Bus. Assn. Indsl. Enterprises, Tomsk, 1997—. Author: Cultural Literacy, 1994; co-author: Key Engineering Materials: Advanced Ceramic Tools for Machining, 1998; contbr. more than 45 articles to profl. jours. Grantee Soros Found., 1999. Mem. Brit. Alumni Club. Avocations: reading, driving, walking. E-mail: push@rac.tpu.edu.ru. Office: Inter Ctr Contin Edn Splts, 30 Lenin Ave, 634034 Tomsk Siberia, Russia

PUSHPALAL, GAME KANKANAMGE DINILPREM, research engineer; b. Galle, Sri Lanka, Aug. 18, 1958; s. Game Kankanamge and Somalatha Matilda Ananda (Seneviratne) Samaradasa; m. Inoka Priyadarshana Kumari Wimalasiri, May 25, 1989; children: Hatsuko, Kisako. D of Engring., Toin U. of Yokohama, 1997. Instr. Ministry of Higher Edn., Sri Lanka, 1984-90; rsch. engr. Maeta Techno-Rsch. Inc., Sakata, Japan, 1991-96, sr. rsch. engr., 1997—. Patentee in field. Recipient Best Rsch. Paper in Cement Chemistry Japan Cement Assn., 1997. Mem. Am. Concrete Inst., Materials Rsch. Soc. Home: 15-20 Wakahamacho, Sakata, Yamagata 998-0857, Japan Office: Maeta Techno-Rsch Inc, 6-7 Kamihoncho, Sakata, Yamagata 998-8611, Japan

PUSHPAVANAM, MALATHY, research scientist; b. Villupuram, Tamilnadu, India, Jan. 21, 1948; d. Muthusamy Ramasamy Balachandran and Balachandran Rajalakshmi; m. Subramanian Pushpavanam, July 1, 1970; children: S.P. Ravishankar, S.P. Prabhushankar. BSc, Holy Cross Coll., Trichy, India, 1968; postgrad. degree, Instn. Chemists, Calcutta, 1981; PhD, Panjab U., Chandigarh, India, 1990. Sr. lab. asst. Ctrl. Electrochem. Rsch. Inst., Karaikudi, India, 1968-75, jr. tech. asst., 1975-82, scientist, 1982-94, asst. dir., 1994—; cons. in field; project dir. IGCAR, Kalpakkam, India, 1996—, VSSC, Trivandrum, India, 1997-2000, project team mem. min. of def., aeronautics, agriculture, 2000—. Contbr. over 200 articles to profl. jours.; 15 patents in field of indsl. metal finishing and corrosion sci. and engring. Recipient Ferroguard award Electrochem. Soc. India, 1981, Vaswik award Vividhlaxi Audhyogik, 1989. Fellow Soc. for the Advancement Electrochemical Sci. and Tech. (sec. 1993-94), Assn. Instn. Chemists, Indian Inst. Metals; mem. Computer Soc. India, Electrochem. Soc. India. Avocations: music, cooking, gardening, reading, interior decoration. Home: No 10 4th St S Extension, Subramaniapuram, Karaikudi 630 002, India Office: Ctrl Electrochem Rsch Inst, Karaikudi, Tamil Nadu 630 006, India

PUSKA, PEKKA MATTI, public health institute official; b. Vaasa, Finland, Dec. 18, 1945; s. Sulo Matti and Elin Elli (Hissa) P.; m. Arja Anneli Vornanen, Mar. 21, 1992; children: Eeva Maria, Juha Pekka. M in Polit. Sci., U. Turku, Finland, 1968, MD, 1971; PhD, U. Kuopio, Finland, 1974; PhD (hon.), U. St. Andrews, Scotland, 1999. Prin. investigator North Karelia project U. Kuopio, 1972-78; dept. dir. Nat. Pub. Health Inst., Helsinki, 1978—, divsn. dir., 1992—; ctrl. com. Acad. Finland, Helsinki, 1978-83; pres. Finnish Ctr. for Health Edn., 1989-95; chmn. Internat. Mgmt. Com. WHO Cindi Program, Copenhagen, 1994; academician Russian Acad. Natural Scis., 1997. Contbr. articles to profl. jours. Mem. Finnish Nat. Parliament, Helsinki, 1987-91, City Coun., Joensuu, 1993-97; elector Pres. Rep., Helsinki, 1988. Lt. Finnish mil. res. Recipient Health Edn. award WHO, Geneva, 1990. Office: Nat Pub Health Inst, Mannerheimintie 166, 00300 Helsinki Finland

PUSKARZ, STANLEY JOHN, engineering executive; b. Hartford, Conn., Apr. 6, 1937; s. John and Mary Kathrine (Czertak) P.; m. Shirley Sue Roberts Puskarz, May 24, 1958; children: Stephanie, Kathryn. BSME, Ind. Inst. Tech., Fort Wayne, 1959; cert. in Advanced Mgmt., Washington U., St. Louis, 1979. Sales coord. Ideal Electric and Mfg. Co., Mansfield, Ohio, 1959-62; project engr. Alcoa, Richmond, Ind., 1962-65, field svc. supv., 1965-68; R&D engr. Battle Creek (Mich.) Pkg., 1969-70, Standard Knapp, Portland, Conn., 1970-73; engring. mgr. George J. Meyer Mfg., Cudahy, Wis., 1973-77; dir. engring. Barry Wehmiller Co., St. Louis, 1977-83; v.p. George J. Meyer Mfg., Charleston, S.C., 1983-88; v.p. engring., ptnr. Fowler Products Co., Athens, Ga., 1989—; lectr. U.S. Brewers Assn., Washington, 1980-86; pres. Ga. Soc. Profl. Engrs., NE Ga. Chpt., 1991-97. Inventor: 1970—; contbr. papers in field; patentee in field (9 U.S., 3 internat.). Marriage prep counselor Cath. Ctr. U. Ga., Athens, 1992—; math counts coord. Ga. Soc. Profl. Engrs., Athens, 1994-97. Named Eagle Scout Boy Scouts Am., Bristol, Conn., 1952, Engr. of Yr. in Industry Ga. Profl. Engrs., Atlanta, 1995-96. Mem. Am. SOc. Mech. Engrs., Internat. Soc. Beverage Technologists, Inst. Pkg. Porfls., Ga. Soc. Profl. Engrs. Avocations: boating, target shooting, fishing, ballroom dancing. Office: Fowler Products Co 150 Collins Industrial Blvd Athens GA 30601-1516

PUSKÁS, TAMÁS, radiologist, consultant; b. Pécs, Baranya, Hungary, Oct. 27, 1951; s. Ödön and Erzsébet (Gálos) P.; m. Piroska Lőrincz, July 19, 1980; 1 child, András. MD, U. Med. Sch., Pécs, 1976; Specialist in Radiology, Pécs, 1981. Resident Markusovszky Hosp., Szombathely, Hungary, 1976-81; specialist Markusovszky Hosp., 1981-94, cons., 1994-2000, head Diagnostic Ctr., 2000—. Contbr. articles to profl. jours. Mem. Hungarian Radiol. Soc. Avocations: fishing, travel. Office: Markusovszky Hosp, Markusovszky Str 1-3, 9700 Szombathely Hungary

PUST, LADISLAV, physicist, researcher; b. Prague, Czech Republic, Mar. 3, 1953; s. Ladislav and Marie (Landova) P.; m. Renata Pustova, 1989; children: Daniela, Lucie. MSc in Engring., Czech Technical Univ., Prague, 1976; PhD, Inst. Physics, 1981. Rsch. asst. Rsch. Inst. Elec. Engring., Prague, 1975-76; rsch. fellow Ohio State U., Columbus, 1984-85; physicist Inst. Physics, Acad. of Scis. of Czech Republic, Prague, 1976-97; rsch. scientist dept. physics Wayne State U., Detroit, 1997-98; sr. rsch. staff Seagate Tech. Recording Heads, Mpls., 1998—. Contbr. numerous articles to profl. jours. Recipient scholarship Ohio State U., 1984. Mem. IEEE (sr.), Am. Phys. Soc., European Phys. Soc., Materials Rsch. Soc. Avocations: skiing, hiking. Home: # 2 5695 S Park Dr Savage MN 55378-2821 OFFICE: SEAGATE RECORDING HEADS 7801 Computer Ave Bloomington MN 55435-5489

PUST, LADISLAV, mechanical engineer; b. Prague, Jan. 26, 1927; s. Jaroslav and Josefa (Kamelska) P.; m. Marie Landova, July 23, 1952; children: Libor, Ladislav. Diploma in Engring., Czech Tech. U., 1950, PhD, 1955; DS, Czech. Acad. of Scis., 1968. Rschr. Nat. Mech. Rsch. inst., Prague, 1950-55; scientist Inst. Thermomechanics, Prague, 1955-97, vice-dir., 1969-90; mem. presidium Czechoslovak Acad. of Sci., Prague, 1990-92; lectr. Czech Tech. U., Prague, 1962-90; sec. gen. Internat. Fedn. for the Theory of Machines and Mechanisms, 1988-95, chmn. tech. com., 1995—. Author 6 books on Oscillations, 1960-92; contbr. 158 articles to profl. jours.; editor proceedings in field; co-author: Mechanical Vibration, 1994; patentee in field. Recipient State prize Czechoslovak Govt., Prague, 1966. Mem. European Mechanics Soc., Czech Nat. Com., Internat. Union of Theoretical and Applied Mechanics, Internat. Fedn. for the Theory of Machines and Mechanisms. Mem. Czechoslovak Ch. Avocations: tourism, sports, culture. Office: Inst of Thermomechanics, Dolejskova 5, Prague 18200, Czech Republic

PUTHENKUDY, RAJAN VARGHESE, engineering executive; b. Perumbavoor, Kerala, India, Feb. 18, 1955; arrived in Saudi Arabia, 1978; s. Varghese and Mariyamma Varghese Puthenkudy; m. Jancy Rajan Chemparathymoottil, Jan. 15, 1984; children: Rithu Mary Rajan, Rijususan Rajan. Diploma in elec. engring., G.P.T. Kalamassery Cochin, India. Formen elec. Al Andalus, Sharjah, Dubai, 1977-78; elec. engr. East & West, Dammam, Saudi Arabia, 1978-85; prodn. engr. Remal Electric, Dammam, 1985-87, engring. mgr., 1987—. Mem. IEEE, SME. Office: Remal Electric Factory, PO Box 1498, Al-Khobar 31952, Saudi Arabia

PUTILOV, ARCADY ALEXANDROVICH, chronobiologist, researcher; b. Novosibirsk, Siberia, Russia, Apr. 17, 1954; s. Alexander Antonovich Putilov and Margarira Alexandrovna Purik; m. Galena Sergeevna Russkikh, June 21, 1973 (div. Dec. 1997); children: Julia, Dmitriy. MS, Tomsk State U., Russia, 1976; PhD, Inst. Physiology SB RAMS, Novosibirsk, 1985; D in biol. sci., Siberian Med. U., 1999. Sr. technician Inst. of Physiology, Novosibirsk, 1976-82, jr. rschr., 1982-85, sr. rschr., 1985-88, head lab., 1988-92, lead rschr., 1992-95; cons. sr. rschr. Internat. Sci. Ctr. ARKTIKA FEB RAS, Magadan, 1995—, Ctr. for Social Adaptation, Novosibirsk, 1996—; lead rschr. Inst. for Med. and Biol. Cybernetics SB RAMS, Novosibirsk, 1995—; prof. Siberian Humanitarian U., Novosibirsk, 1993-95, prof. Classical Inst., 1999—; consulting sr. rschr. Inst. for Gen. Pathology and Human Ecology SB RAMS, Novosibirsk, 1995—. Author: System Forming Function of Synchronization, 1987, Owls, Larks and Others, 1997; also articles; mem. editl. bd. Biol. Rhythms Rsch., 1991—, Jour. of Interdisciplinary Cycle Rsch., 1991-94. Pres. English Club in House of Scientists, Akademgorodok, Novosibirsk, 1995—. Mem. European Soc. for Chronobiology, European Sleep Rsch. Soc., Melatonin Club. Avocations: travel, tennis. E-mail: putilov@cyber.ma.nsc.ru. Home: 6/6 Musjy Jalila St, 630055 Novosibirsk Russia Office: Inst for Med and Biol Cyber, 2 Timakova St, 630117 Novosibirsk Russia

PUTIN, VLADIMIR, president of Russia; b. Leningrad, Oct. 7, 1952. Grad., State U., St. Petersburg, 1975. With KGB, Germany, 1975-90; head external rels., then dept. mayor, deputy chief of staff; head Fed. Security Bur., 1998-99; Russia's prime min., 1999-2000; pres. Russia, 2000—. Office: Office of the Pres, 103073 The Kremlin, Moscow Russia*

PUTNAM, JOE B., JR., thoracic and cardiovascular surgeon; b. Franklin, N.C., Sept. 26, 1953; s. Joe B. Putnam; m. Jacqueline Putnam; four children. AB in Zoology, U. N.C., 1975, AB in Chemistry with honors, 1975, MD, 1979. Diplomate Am. Bd. Surgery, Am. Bd. Thoracic Surgery. Surg. intern Johns Hopkins Hosp., Balt., 1979-80, resident in surgery, 1980-81; med. staff fellow, surgery br. Nat. Cancer Inst./NIH, Bethesda, Md., 1981-84; resident and chief resident in surgery U. Rochester (N.Y.) Sch. Medicine, 1984-86; resident in thoracic surgery U. Mich., Ann Arbor, 1986-88; asst. prof. divsn. thoracic and cardiovascular surgery U. Tex. Sch. medicine, Houston, 1988-94; asst. surgeon, asst. prof. surgery U. Tex. M.D. Anderson Cancer Ctr., Houston, 1988-94, assoc. surgeon, assoc. prof. thoracic and cardiovas. surgery, 1994-2000, dep. chmn. dept. thoracic and cardiovascular surgery, 1995—, surgeon, prof. surgery, thoracic & cardiovascular surgery, 2000—. Contbr. articles to profl. jours. Recipient awards and grants in field. Fellow ACS, Am. Coll. Chest Physicians; mem. AMA, Am. Assn. for Cancer Rsch., Am. Assn. for Thoracic Surgery, Am. Soc. for Clin. Oncology, European Assn. for Cardi-Thoracic Surgery, Gen. Thoracic Surg. Club, Soc. Thoracic Surgeons, Soc. Surg. Oncology, So. Thoracic Surg. Assn., Internat. Assn. for Study of Lung Cancer, Tex. Med. Assn., Houston Surg. Soc., Sigma Xi, others. E-mail: putnam@mdanderson.org. Office: U Tex MD Anderson Cancer Ctr 1515 Holcombe Blvd # 109 Houston TX 77030-4009

PUTNAM, ROBERT ERVIN, chemist; b. Northampton, Mass., Oct. 18, 1927; s. Ervin Earl and Mary Gertrude (Connelly) P.; m. Caroline Wright, Aug. 23, 1952; children: David Earl, Mary Caroline, Robert Edward, Andrew Wright. BS in Chemistry, U. Mass., 1950; PhD in Organic Chemistry, U. Ill., 1953. Rsch. chemist E.I. du Pont de Nemours, Wilmington, Del., 1953-59; rsch. supr. E.I. du Pont de Nemours, Wilmington, Del., 1959-65, sr. rsch. supr., 1965-67; sr. rsch. supr. E.I. du Pont de Nemours, Parkersburg, W.Va., 1967-78, rsch. lab. supt., 1978-82, rsch. mgr., 1982-85; adj. faculty Washington State C.C., Marietta, Ohio, 1985-95; pvt. practice Marietta, 1985-95; alumni adv. coun. dept. chemistry U. Mass., Amherst, 1975-78; instr. chemistry Marietta Coll., 1982-89, adv. coun., 1989-95, dir. Inst. for Learning in Retirement, 1995-98. Editor Bull. Am. Friends of Puttenham, 1984—; contbr. over 20 articles to profl. jours. With USNR, 1945-46. NSF fellow, U. Ill., 1952-53. Fellow AAAS; mem. Am. Chem. Soc. (chmn. Ohio Valley sect. 1976-78), Valley Renaissance Consort, Mid-Ohio Valley Aviation Assn. Democrat. Mem. Unitarian Ch. Achievements include patents on fluorine containing polymers and monomers, ion exchange resins; research on industrial processes for nylon, polyacetals, acrylics, rubber toughened plastics, fluorinated plastics. Address: 100 Alden Ave Marietta OH 45750-1138

PUTREVU, UDAY, oceanographer; b. Madras, India, Oct. 7, 1963. B in Tech., Indian Inst. Tech., Madras, India, 1985; MS, U. Deleware, Newark, 1988; PhD, U. Deleware, 1992. Rsch. assoc. Ctr. Applied Coastal Rsch., Newark, Del., 1991-93; rsch. scientist N.W. Rsch. Assocs., Bellevue, Wash., 1993—. Contbr. over 40 articles to profl. publs. Grantee Delaware Sea Grant, 1991. Am. Geophysical Union, Am. Soc. Civil Engrs. E-mail: putrevu@nwra.com. Fax: 425-644-8422. Office: NW Rsch Assocs Inc 14508 NE 20th St Bellevue WA 98007-3713

PUTSEYS, YVAN FRANS LOUIS, retired language educator; b. Heverlee, Brabant, Belgium, Apr. 28, 1936; s. Frans and Maria (Paessens) P.; m. Wilma Elisabeth Jackers, 1962. MA in Germanic Philology, K.U. Leuven, Belgium, 1958, PhD, 1973. Prof. English linguistics K.U. Brussels, 1969-96, ret., 1996; guest lectr. K.U. Leuven, Belgium 1989-96; vis. prof. S.L.U., Baguio City, Philippines, 1971-88. Author: A Modular Approach to the Grammar of English, 1996. Pvt. Tosalisana/Belgian Congo, 1959-60. Avocations: reading, walking, travel, cooking, swimming. Home: Van t Sestichlaan 26, B-3020 Winksele Brabant, Belgium

PUTT, JERRY WAYNE, municipal official; b. Memphis, Mar. 22, 1966; s. Charles Q. and Barbara Jean (Santucci) P. AAS in Adminstrv. Justice with honors, Olney (Ill.) Ctrl. Coll., 1995; BA in Psychology with honors, Ea. Ill. U., 1997; cadet, Ill. State Police Acad., 1999—. Factory worker Snap-On Tools, Mt. Carmel, Ill., 1984-85, machinist, 1987-91; security officer Rend Lake (Ill.) Coll., 1985; water plant operator Village Bone Gap, Ill., 1991-93, water sys. supt., 1993—; sr. security officer McDonald's Corp., Olney, 1993—; dir. pub. works City of St. Francisville, 1998. Inventor solar air heater, 1997, K-9 reel, 1997. Vol. fireman Bone Gap Fire Dept., 1997. With USAR, 1988—. Mem. Machinist Union, Nature Conservancy, Planetary Soc., Smithsonian Inst., 700 Club. Baptist. Avocations: weight training, jogging, hiking, target shooting. Office: Village of Bone Gap Water Dept RR 1 Bone Gap IL 62815-9801

PUTTER, DAVID SETH, lawyer; b. N.Y.C., Mar. 11, 1944; s. Norton Seth and Ruth Crystal P.; m. Lee Dow, Apr. 26, 1987. BA in Biology, Beloit Coll., 1965; student, U. Granada, Spain, 1964; JD, Syracuse U., 1968. Bar: Vt. 1970, N.Y. 1971, U.S. Dist. Ct. Vt. 1970, U.S. Ct. Appeals (2d cir.) 1973, U.S. Ct. Claims 1998. Atty. Putter & Carrington, Arlington, Vt., 1970-73; Bennington County pub. defender State of Vt., Bennington, 1973-76; law clk. to Superior Ct. judges State of Vt., Burlington, 1976-78; asst. atty. gen. State of Vt., Montpelier, 1979-81; assoc. Putter & Unger, Montpelier, 1981-88, Saxer, Anderson, Wolinsky & Sunshine, Montpelier, 1988-2000; pvt. practice Law Offices David Putter, Montpelier, 2000—. Contbr. articles to profl. jours. acting Superior Ct. judge, 1997—; chair legal panel ACLU Vt., 1988—; sponsored advisor on assembly, free press, free speech USIA, Lusaka, Zambia, Kampala, Uganda, 1996. Recipient Jonathan Chase award ACLU Vt., 1991, 97. Avocations: hiking, camping, theater, travel, music (folk and rock). Home: 6 Towne St Montpelier VT 05602-4231 Office: Montpelier VT 05600

PUTTLITZ, DONALD HERBERT, medical microbiologist; b. Kingston, N.Y., Apr. 21, 1938; s. Adalbert Siegfried and Elizabeth Ann (Barthel) P.; m. Barbara Ann Dingman, July 19, 1969; children: Michelle, Brian, Laura. BS with distinction, SUNY, New Paltz, 1959; MS, SUNY, Albany, 1961; PhD, Cornell U., 1965. Diplomate Am. Bd. Med. Microbiology. Assoc. microbiologist Beth Israel Med. Ctr., N.Y.C., 1967-85; supr. microbiology Jamaica (N.Y.) Hosp., 1985-92; instr. physician asst. program Touro Coll., N.Y.C., 1986-88; supr. microbiology Sound Shore Med. Ctr. of Westchester, New Rochelle, N.Y., 1993-97; mem. faculty Mt. Sinai Coll. Medicine, 1972-85. Mem. N.Y.C. Bd. Edn., 1997—. Predoctoral traineeship fellow NIH, 1964-65, postdoctoral traineeship fellow USPHS, 1965-67. Mem. Am. Soc. Microbiology, N.Y.C. Soc. Microbiology. Roman Catholic. Home: 116 Horace Harding Blvd Great Neck NY 11020-1107

PUTTNAM, LORD DAVID TERENCE, film producer; b. London, Feb. 25, 1941; s. Leonard Arthur and Marie Beatrix Puttnam; m. Patricia Mary Jones, 1961; two children. LLD (hon.), Bristol (Eng.) U., 1983; DLitt (hon.), Leicester U., 1986, Leeds U., 1992, U. Bradford, 1993. With advt. firms, 1958-66, photographer's agt., 1966-68, film prodr., 1968—; chmn. Columbia Pictures, 1986-88; vis. prof. films Bristol U.; dir. Anglia TV Survival Anglia. Prodr. films including That'll Be the Day, 1971, Mahler, 1973, Bugsy Malone, 1975, The Duellists (Spl. Jury prize Cannes 1977), 1977, Midnight Express, 1977 (2 Acad. awards), Chariots of Fire (4 Acad. awards and 3 BAFTA awards including Best Film award 1981, 4 Oscars including Best Picture), Local Hero, 1982, The Killing Fields, 1984 (3 Am. Acad. awards, 8 Brit. Acad. awards, BAFTA award for Best Picture), Cal, 1984, The Mission, 1986 (Palme d'Or 1986, Acad. award), Memphis Belle, 1990, Meeting Venus, 1991, Being Human, 1992, War of the Buttons, 1993, The Burning Season, 1994 (Golden Globe award best film for TV), Le Confessional, 1995, My Life So Far, 1999. Chmn. ITEL; founder, pres. Atelier du Cinema European; trustee Nat. Energy Found., Sci. Mus., 1996; hon. fellow The Chartered Soc. Designers, Manchester Poly.; chmn. Nat. Mus. Photography, film and TV com. Knighted, 1995; decorated Officier dans l'Ordre des Artes et des Lettres, 1986, comdr. of the Most Excellent Order of the Brit. Empire, 1982, Kt., 1995; recipient Michael Balcon award for Outstanding Contbn. Brit. Film Industry, BAFTA, 1982, Benjamin Franklin award, 1996, Crystal award World Econ. Forum, 1997. Fellow Royal Soc. Arts, Royal Photographic Soc., Royal Geog. Soc. Address: Enigma Prodns, 29a Tufton St, London SW1P 3QL, England*

PUTVINSKI, SERGEI, physicist; b. Leningrad, Russia, Feb. 22, 1947; came to U.S., 1993; s. Vladimir Putvinski and Ludmila Putvinskaya; m. Nina Kuzmina, Sept. 9, 1971; children: Sergei, Nicolay, Katia. MS, Moscow Physico-Tech. Inst., 1971; PhD, I.V. Kurchatov Inst., Moscow, 1976, DSc, 1990. Rschr. I.V. Kurchatov Inst., Moscow, 1973-81, sr. rschr., 1981-91; vis. scientist Jet Joint Undertaking, Abingdon, England, 1991-93; group leader ITER Joint Ctrl. Team, La Jolla, Calif., 1993-99; sr. scientist Archimedes Tech. Group, Inc., San Diego, Calif., 99—. Author 4 books including Review of Plasma Physics, 1990; contbr. over 80 articles to profl. jours. Achievements include computational modeling of plasma processes in experimental fusion devices, physics of energetic particles in fusion plasmas, plasma stability and transport, tokamak-reactor design. Home: 3940 La Jolla Village Dr La Jolla CA 92037-1418 Office: 5405 Oberlin Dr San Diego CA 92121-1700

PUTZ, BARBARA, computer scientist; b. Warsaw, Dec. 2, 1949; d. Zbigniew and Irena (Radzikowska) Janicki; m. Andrzej Putz, June 15, 1974; children: Joanna, Andrzej. MSc, Warsaw U. Technology, 1973, PhD, 1983. From asst. prof. to prof. Warsaw U. Technology, 1973—. Roman Catholic. E-mail: bputz@mp.pw.edu.pl. Home: Ul Bora Komorowskiego 10M77, 03-982 Warsaw Poland

PUVANESWARY, MURUGASU, radiologist and consultant; b. Seremban, Negri Semb, Malaysia, Aug. 7, 1947; arrived in Australia, 1986; d. Murugasu and Nallamah Kandapoo; m. K.T. Singham, Dec. 3, 1972; children: Shamani, Shahlini. MB BS, U. Malaya, 1972. Intern Univ. Hosp., Kuala Lumpur, Malaysia, 1972-73, med. officer, 1974-76, 78-79, lectr. radiology, 1980-81, 84-86; clin. asst. Royal Infirmary, Glasgow, Scotland, 1977; hon. registrar radiology Univ. Hosp., Nottingham, Eng., 1982; staff specialist Royal Newcastle Hosp., Newcastle, Australia, 1986-91; sr. staff specialist John Hunter Hosp., Newcastle, 1992—. Contbr. articles to profl. jours. Fellow Royal Coll. Radiologists (U.K.); mem. Royal Australasian Coll. Radiologist (ednl. affiliate), Clin. Magnetic Resonance Soc., Radiol. Soc. N.Am., Australian Soc. for Ultrasound Medicine, Am. Roentgen Ray Soc. Avocations: gardening, walking, music.

PUYBASSET, LOUIS JEAN, anesthesiologist, intensivist; b. Paris, July 18, 1964; s. Jean Marie and Michèle (Peretti) P.; m. Odile Marie Launay, May 20, 1989; children: Alexis, Charles, Vincent, Adrien. MD, 1987. Intern Hosp. Paris, 1988, resident in anesthesiology, 1987-995, asst. chief clinic, 1995—, rschr. ICU, 1995—, staff mem., asst. prof., 1998—, head neurointensive care and neuro anesthesia unit, 1999—. Contbr. articles to profl. jours. Mem. European Soc. Anesthesiology, French Soc. Anesthesia and Intensive Care. Home: 11 Rue de la tour, 75016 Paris France Office: Dept Anesthesiology ICU, 83 BD de L'Hopital, 75013 Paris France

PWEDDON, NICHOLAS, academic administrator, educator, researcher; b. Waduku, Adamawa, Nigeria, 1933; s. Soweto Waga and Jantabo Bekum; m. Tonvirwo Buba; children: Pwanokai, Royaudu, Reform, Nadyanga, Kangom, Karonti, Tamwakala, Ngulgeino. BA, Fourah Bay Coll., Sierra Leone, 1964; MA, U. Nebr., Omaha, 1973, U. Wisc., 1975; PhD, U. Wisc., 1977. Headmaster Numan Pr. Sch., Nigeria, 1956-57; prin. Numan Tchr.'s Coll., Nigeria, 1965-71; prin. Hong Sec. Sch., Nigeria, 1978-79, asst. chief inspector edn., 1979; special advisor to gov. Gongola State, Nigeria, 1979-83; chmn. dept. English Univ. y Jos, 1995—; dir. Gongola State Hotels, Ltd., 1984-89; chmn. Christian Pilgrims' Welfare Bd., 1987-90; external examiner U. Abuja, 1997—. Contbr. articles to profl. pubs. Sec. United Middle Belt Cong., Numan Br., 1958-59; mem. Leaders of Thought, Nigeria, 1966-67, Waduku-Tingno Disturbances com., 1988-91; cons. Bwatiye Devel. Assn., 1979—. Recipient Principal's Hat for Math., 1951; named Ngiko Bachama (Pillar of Bachamaland), Chief of Bachama, 1991. Mem. Acad. Staff Union of Univs., Assn. Nigerian Authors, Nigerian Folklore Soc. People's Democratic Party. Lutheran. Avocations: sports, reading fiction. Office: Univ Jos, Dept English, Jos Plateau State, Nigeria

PYCKHOUT-HINTZEN, WIM MAURITS AUGUST, physical chemist, researcher; b. Mechelen, Antwerp, Belgium, May 5, 1959; arrived in Germany, 1986; s. Paul Pyckhout and Susanne Op de Beeck; m. Maria Elisabeth Hintzen, Nov. 11, 1988; 1 child, Michael. PhD in Phys. Chemistry, U. Antwerp, Belgium, 1986. Postdoctoral staff Forschungszentrum, Jülich, Germany, 1986-89; rschr. Forschungszentrum, Jülich, 1989, 90—. Recipient Jan Stas prize Belgian State, Brussels, 1986; postdoctoral fellow Exxon, Annandale, N.J., 1989-90. Avocation: historical guide in Jülich City/Fortress. Home: Lindenstr 1a, D-52445 Titz Germany

PYE, KENNETH, environmental sedimentology educator, consultant; b. St. Helens, Eng., Aug. 24, 1956; s. Leonard and Joyce Pye; m. Diane Cadman; 1 dau., 1 son. BA with honors 1st class, Oxford (Eng.) U., 1977, MA, 1981; PhD in Geomorphology, Cambridge (Eng.) U., 1980, ScD in Earth Scis., 1992. Chartered geologist. NERC rsch. fellow, dept. earth scis. Cambridge U., 1980-82; Sarah Woodhead rsch. fellow Girton Coll., Cambridge, 1980-83; Royal Soc. rsch. fellow, dept. earth scis. Cambridge U., 1983-88; non-stipendiary fellow Girton Coll., 1987-89; lectr. quaternary sedimentology Reading (Eng.) U., 1989-92, reader in sedimentology, 1992-94, prof. environ. sedimentology, 1994-98; prof. environ. geology Royal Holloway U. London, 1999—; founder, dir. Cambridge Environ. Rsch. Consultants, Ltd., 1986-95; ind. cons., writer, expert witness, U.K., 1981—; treas. Brit. Sedimentological Rsch. Group, 1990-93; founder K. Pye Assocs., Wokingham, U.K., 1998—. Author: Aeolian Dust and Dust Deposits, 1987, Aeolian Sand and Sand Dunes, 1990, Backscattered Scanning Electron Microscopy and Image Analysis of Sediments and Sedimentary Rocks, 1998; editor: Chemical Sediments and Geomorphology, 1983, Saltmarshes—Morphodynamics, Conservation and Engineering Significance, 1992, The Dynamics and Environmental Context of Environmental Sedimentary Systems, 1993, Aeolian Sediments Ancient and Modern, 1993, Environmental Change in Drylands—Biogeographical and Geomorphological Perspectives, 1994, Sediment Transport and Depositional Processes, 1994, Coastal and Estuarine Environments — Sedimentology, Geomorphology and Geoarchaeology, 2000; contbr. more than 120 articles to profl. jours. and conf. procs.; mem. editl. bd. Earth Surface Processes and Landforms, 1991—, Jour. Sedimentary Rsch., 1999—. Recipient Gordon Warwick award Brit. Geomorphological Rsch. Group, 1991, Wiley award, 1989, Sedgwick prize Cambridge U., 1984; Leverhulme Trust fellow, 1991-92, Royal Soc. Leverhulme Trust Sr. Rsch. fellow, 1996-97. Fellow Geol. Soc. London, Royal Geog. Soc.; mem. Internat. Assn. Sedimentologists, Soc. Expert Witnesses, numerous others.

Avocations: world travel, historical sites and monuments, rocks and minerals. Office: U London Royal Holloway, Dept Geology, Egham Surrey TW20 OEW, England

PYE, LENWOOD DAVID, materials science educator, researcher, consultant; b. Little Falls, N.Y., May 16, 1937; s. Lenwood George and Elizabeth Marie Pye; m. Constance Lee Lanphere, Sept. 6, 1958; children: DeAnn, Lorie, Lisa, Brien. BS, Alfred U., 1959, PhD, 1968. Rsch. engr. PPG Industries, Pitts., 1959-60; rsch. scientist Bausch & Lomb, Rochester, N.Y., 1960-61, 62-64; prof. glass sci. N.Y. State Coll. Ceramics Alfred U., 1968—, dean N.Y. State Coll. Ceramics, 1996-2000, dir. Inst. Glass Sci. and Engring., 1984-96, dir. Industry-Univ. Ctr. Glass Rsch., 1986-96; pres. Internat. Commn. on Glass, 1997—; bd. dirs. Alfred Tech. Resources, Inc., Schott Glass Technologies. 1st lt. U.S. Army, 1960-62. Recipient Dominick Labino lectr. award 1995, Phoenix award as Glassman of Yr., 1996. Mem. Acad. Ceramics, Am. Ceramics Soc., Optical Soc. Am., U.K. Soc. Glass Tech., Can. Ceramic Soc., German Soc. Glass Technology (hon.). Office: Alfred U Sch Ceramic Engring 2 Pine St Alfred NY 14802-1214

PYE, NORMAN, geography educator; b. Wigan, Lancashire, Eng., Nov. 2, 1913; s. John Whittaker and Hilda Constance (Platt) P.; m. Isabella Jane Currie, Dec. 5, 1940; children: Alistair Grierson, Michael Richard. BA Class 1, U. Manchester, Eng., 1935; Diploma in Edn. Class 1, Manchester U., 1936. Prof. geography U. Leicester, Eng., 1954-79, prof. emeritus, 1979—, pro-vice chancellor, 1963-66; lectr. and sr. lectr. U. Manchester, 1937-54. Editor, contbr.: Leicester and Its Region, 1972; contbr. articles to profl. jours. Gov. Up Holland Grammar Sch., 1953-74; mem. Norhtants C.C. Edn. Com., 1956-74; ct. Nottingham U., 1964-79; schs. coun. 1967-78; mem. coun. RMetS, 1953-56; coun. Inst. of Brit. Geographers, 1954, 55; coun. RGS, 1967-70; coun. Urban Studies Ctrs., 1974-81; mem. Brit. Nat. Com. Geography, 1970-75; mem. Heritage Edn. Group, 1976-90. Fulbright grantee, 1952, Leverhulme grantee, 1944. Fellow Royal Geog. Soc. (hon.); mem. Geog. Assn. (hon., hon. v.p. 1979-83), Geog. Club. Mem. United Reformed Ch. Avocations: gardening, oenology, traveling.

PYFER, JOHN FREDERICK, JR., lawyer; b. Lancaster, Pa., July 25, 1946; s. John Frederick and Myrtle Ann (Greiner) P.; m. Carol Trice, Nov. 25, 1970; children: John Frederick III, Carol Lee. Grad. cum laude, Peddie Sch., 1965; BA in Polit. Sci. and Econs., Haverford Coll., 1969; JD, Vanderbilt U., 1972. Bar: Pa. 1972, U.S. Dist. Ct. (ea. dist.) Pa. 1973, U.S. Tax Ct. 1975, U.S. Supreme Ct. 1975, U.S. Dist. Ct. (mid. dist.) Pa. 1984, U.S. Ct. Appeals (3d cir.) 1986. Law clk. to presiding justice Ct. Common Pleas, Lancaster, Pa., 1972-74; assoc. Xakellis, Perezous & Mongiovi, Lancaster, 1972-76; founding ptnr. Allison & Pyfer, Lancaster, 1976-85; pres. Pyfer & Assocs., Lancaster, 1986-88, Pyfer & Reese, Lancaster, 1988—; prof. para-legal tng. Pa. State Ext. Svc., 1989-93; fed. ct. mediator, 1992—. Contbr. articles to law revs., law treatises. Pres. Lancaster-Lebanon Coun. Boy Scouts Am., 1989-93, coun. commr., 1987-89, mem. nat. com., 1996—, exec. bd. N.E. region, 1998—, area pres. 2000, Eagle Scout with 3 palms, God and Country award, God and Svc. award, Wood Badge, Scouter's Key, Vigil Honor, Order of Arrow, Disting. Commr. award, Silver Beaver and Silver Antelope awards, West fellow, 1910 Soc., Nat. Jamboree, 1960, 64, 85, 89, 93, 97, World Jamboree, 1967, 87, 95, 98, Japan Jamboree, 1990, Can. Jamboree, 1993; bd. dirs. World of Scouting Mus. Fellow Am. Bd. Criminal Lawyers, Lancaster Heritage Ctr.; mem. ABA (First prize Howard C. Schwab Nat. Essay Contest in Writing 1972), ATLA, SAR, Nat. Assn. Criminal Def. Lawyers, Pa. Trial Lawyers Assn., Pa. Criminal Def. Lawyers Assn., Am. Arbitration Assn., Pa. Bar Assn., Lancaster Bar Assn., Inns Ct. (founder, pres. W. Hensel Brown 1993-94), Christian Lawyers Soc., Train Collector Assn. (divsn. pres. 1984), Am. Orchid Soc. (affiliate pres. 1998), Lions Club (pres. 1980-82, 2000) (Willow Street, Pa.), Masons (Lancaster). Republican. United Ch. of Christ (elder, pres. 1989, 95). Home: 1100 Little Brook Rd Lancaster PA 17603-6116 Office: Pyfer & Reese 128 N Lime St Lancaster PA 17602-2951

PYKH, YURI ALEXANDER, ecological modelling, researcher; b. Novosibirsk, USSR, June 3, 1944; s. Alexander David and Evdokia Peter (Baranova) P.; m. Irina German Malkina, 1989. Magister, Poly. Inst., Leningrad, USSR, 1967; DSc, State U., Leningrad, USSR, 1972; prof., Computer Ctr., Moscow, 1982. Prin. investigator Agrophys. Rsch. Inst., Leningrad, 1969-95; pres. Ctr. Internat. Environ. Coop., St. Petersburg, 1989—; Mem. Com. Sys. Analisys, Moscow, 1987—. Author: Equilibrium and Stability in the Models of Population Dynamics, 1983; co-author: Dynamic Theory of Biological Populations, 1974, Dynamic Models of Ecological Systems, 1980, The Method of Response Function in Ecology, 2000; editor Ecol. Indicators. V.p. Green Cross Russia, Moscow, 1993—. Mem. Internat. Soc. Ecol. Modelling. Fax: 7-812-272-42-65. E-mail: inenco@mail.neva.ru. Office: Ctr INENCO, nab Kutuzova 14, 191187 Saint Petersburg Russia

PYLKKÄNEN, KARI EINO K., psychiatrist; b. Jyväskyla, Finland, June 28, 1944; s. Eino and Eila J.M. Mäntylä (Hovilainen) P.; m. Elina Paloneimo, Mar. 10, 1970 (div. 1990); children: Lisa, Kaisa; m. Marja Hannele Taimisto, Aug. 22, 1997. MD, U. Helsinki, 1970; MSc in Cmty. Medicine, Sch. Hygiene and Tropical Med., London, 1982. Lic. psychiatrist, Finland. Resident in psychiatry Hesperia Hosp., Helsinki, 1970-74; med. dir. Veikkola Sanitarium, Keikkonummi, Finland, 1975-79; dir. hosp. Nikkilä Hosp., Sipoo, Finland, 1979-80; nat. mental health dir. Nat. Bd. Health, Finland, 1982-91; pvt. practice Helsinki, 1991-96; chief psychiatrist Student Health Svc., Helsinki, 1996—; cons. psychiatrist Evang. Luth. Ch. Family Guidance, Finland, 1981—, Psychoanalyst Internat. Psychoanalytical Assn., 1981; tng. psychotherapist Psychiat. Assn. Finland, 1987—; temp. advisor WHO, Copenhagen, 1982-91; zonal rep. World Psychiat. Assn., North Europe, 1996—; chmn. task force Innovations in Developing Mental Health Svcs., 1982-96. Author, editor books on adolescent mental health, 1974-81 (State Award on Pub. 1981); contbr. articles to profl. jours. Recipient Christian Sibelius award, 1997, Iciars Knighthood award The White Rose Order, Finland, 1997. Mem. Finnish Psychiat. Assn. (pres. 1990-95), Finnish Mental Health Assn. (pres. 1992—), Assn. of Adolescent Psychiatry of Finland (hon. pres.), Med. Assn. Finland (v.p. 1999—), Union of European Med. Specialists (mem. mgmt. coun. 1994—), European Bd. and Sect. of Psychiatry, Helsinki Finnish Club. Avocations: tennis, playing cards, films. Office: Finnish Student Health, Töölökatu 37A, 00260 Helsinki Finland

PYNCHON, THOMAS RUGGLES, JR., author; b. Glen Cove, N.Y., May 8, 1937; s. Thomas R. Pynchon. BA, Cornell U., 1958. Former editorial writer Boeing Aircraft Co., Seattle. Author: V, 1963 (William Faulkner novel award 1963), The Crying of Lot 49, 1966 (Rosenthal Found. award Nat. Inst. Arts and Letters 1967), Gravity's Rainbow, 1973 (Nat. Book award 1974), Slow Learner, 1984, Vineland, 1989, Deadly Sins, 1994, Mason and Dixon, 1997; contbr. short stories to publs. including N.Y. Times Mag., N.Y. Times Book Rev., Cornell Writer, Saturday Evening Post, Kenyon Rev. Served with USNR. Recipient Howells medal Nat. Inst. and Am. Acad. Arts and Letters, 1975. Office: Penguin Books 200 Madison Ave New York NY 10016-3903

PYNE, DAVID BRUCE, sports scientist, researcher; b. Canberra, Australia, Dec. 3, 1962; s. Stanley Hamilton and Shirley Dorothy (Geeves) P. B in Applied Sci., U. Canberra, Australia, 1985, M in Applied Sci., 1989; PhD, Australian Nat. U., Canberra, Australia, 1995. Cert. Red Cross first aid; flow cytometry operators course; biomed. instrumentation course. Midshipman Royal Australian Army, 1981; rsch. officer Dept. of Health, Canberra, Australia, 1987; scientist Australian Inst. of Sport, Canberra, 1987—; physiologist Australian Swimming Team, 1987—; steward Commonwealth Pub. Sector Union, Canberra, 1991—; cons. Australian Football League, Melbourne, 1996-97; adj. lectr. U. Canberra, 1997—. Contbr. articles to profl. jours. Recipient Coll. scholarship Royal Australian Navy, 1980, Postgrad. Rsch. award Australian Nat. U., 1991, Outstanding Contbn. to Swimming award Australian Swimming Coaches Assn., 1994, 96, 98, Australian Sports medal, 2000. Mem. Am. Coll. Sports Medicine, Internat. Soc. for Exercise Immunology, Australian Swimming Inc. (sports sci. adv. group 1991—). Avocations: sports, reading, current affairs, movies, music. E-mail: david.pyne@ausport.gov.au. Office: Australian Inst Sport, Leverrier Cres PO Box 176, Belconnen ACT 2616, Australia

PYNE, WILLIAM JOSEPH, chemist; b. Boston, Jan. 30, 1923; s. Thomas Francis and Mary (Reidy) P.; m. Martha Ellen Cannon, July 3, 1954 (dec. Oct. 1991); children: Thomas, James, Kevin, Colleen, Patricia, Brian. BS, Boston Coll., 1948, MS, 1950; postgrad., Western Res. U., Cleve., 1953-57, Ohio State U., 1970. Instr. King's Coll., Wilkes-Barre, Pa., 1950-51; rsch. chemist Diamond Shamrock Co., Painesville, Ohio, 1952-66, sr. rsch. chemist, 1966-77, rsch. assoc., 1977-82; sr. rsch. assoc. Quatum Technologies, Twinsburg, Ohio, 1984-85; corp. fellow in synthetic organic chemistry Rex Adv. Svcs., Painesville, 1985—; lectr. in field. Contbr. articles to profl. jours.; patentee in field (20 U.S. and 36 fgn. patents). Mem Cmty. Devel. Com., Painesville, 1978. With U.S. Army, 1943-45. Recipient Squirrel award for patent Diamond Shamrock Co., 1982. Mem. Am. chem. Soc. (chpt. sec. 1976-77). Roman Catholic. Avocations: history, visiting Civil War battle fields. Home and Office: 257 Meriden Rd Painesville OH 44077-3733

PYNZENYK, VICTOR MYKHAYLOVYCH, economist; b. Smolohovytsya, Ukraine, Apr. 15, 1954; s. Mykhaylo Vasylyovych and Maria Ivanivna (Molodtsova) P.; m. Ulyana Dmytrivna Balahurak, Aug. 24, 1975 (div. Feb. 1992); children: Olga, Julia; m. Maria Romanivna Karaman, Nov. 21, 1992; 1 child, Volodymyr Victorovych. PhD in Econs., U. Moscow, 1989. Instr. U. Lviv, Ukraine, 1975-81, asst. prof., 1981-87, sr. scientific rschr., 1987-89, assoc. prof., 1989-91, prof., 1991-92; deputy head econ. bd. State Dumá Ukraine, Kyiv, 1992; min. of economy Cabinet Mins. Ukraine, Kyiv, 1992-93, vice prime min., 1992-93, 94-97; people's deputy Supreme Rada Ukraine, Kyiv, 1991-2000. Author: Prices and Quality of Industrial and Technical Products; editor: The Basics of Economic Calculation, Horses Can't Be Blamed. Reforms or Imitations; contbr. articles to profl. jours. Mem. Ukrainian Found. Promotion Reforms, Inst. for Reforms. Reforms and Order party. Avocations: tennis, music, travel. Office: Supreme Rada Ukraine, Vul Hrushevskogo 7, 01008 Kiev Ukraine

PYOKARI, MAURI KULLERVO, geography educator; b. Johannes, Finland, Jan. 11, 1936; s. Otto and Hilja Josefina (Hyvonen) P.; m. Maire Hellevi Saastamoinen, Aug. 10, 1968; 1 child, Heikki. MS, U. Turku, 1967, Lic. Philosophy, 1973, PhD, 1979. Sr. tchr. high sch. Rovaniemi, Finland, 1968-72, Turku, Finland, 1972-99; researcher U. Turku, 1974, asst., 1975-76, docent in geography, 1982—; mem. working group on dynamics of shoreline erosion Internat. Geog. Union, 1976, commn. on coastal environment, 1979—. Author: Mixed Sand and Gravel Shores in the SW Finnish Archipelago, 1973; editor jour. Publs. Inst. Geog. Univ. Turkuensis, 1976; contbr. articles to profl. jours. Lectr. Worker's Ednl. Inst., Turku, 1975—. Grantee Finnish Nat. Research Council, Helsinki, 1976, Finnish Cultural Found., Helsinki, 1978, Found. of Univ. of Turku, 1988, Finnish Cultural Found., 1979. Fellow Geog. Soc. Finland, Geog. Soc. Turku (bd. 1976-77, 81-82), Astron. Soc. Lutheran. Avocations: nature, travelling. Home: Kuikankatu 7 AS 6, 20760 Piispanristi Finland Office: U Turku, Dept Geography, FIN20014 Turku Finland

PYPE, PATRICK FILIP, electrical engineer, engineering company official; b. Roeselare, Belgium, Feb. 22, 1962; s. Marcel and Monique (Velghe) P.; m. Annick Vanthemsche, Mar. 23, 1996; 1 child, Wotan. Grad. in engring., Cath. U. Louvain, Belgium, 1985, MBA, 1988. Mgr. strategic projects IMEC, Louvain, 1986-96; co-founder, dir. bus. devel. Coware, Louvain, 1996-99; tech. liaison officer Philips, Louvain, 1999—; mgr. DSP Valley, Louvain, 1994-97; expert evaluator European Cmty., Brussels, 1992—; bd. dirs. Omimo, Brussels; participant confs. in field. Contbr. articles to profl. jours., including Tech. Mgmt., Elekronika. Bd. dirs. Vereniging Ingenieurs Leive, Louvain, 1989-92; mem. Friend's Cir., Nat. Opera, Brussels, 1992—, Friend's Cir., Vlaamse Opera, Antwerp, Belgium, 1996—. Lt. Belgian Army, 1989-90. Avocations: opera, model trains, literature, travel. Home: Brusselsesteenweg 261, B-3020 Herent Belgium Office: Philips, Interleuvenlaan 74-76, B-3001 Louvain Belgium

PYROHOVA, VERA, medical educator, dean; b. Drohobych, Lviv, USSR, Oct. 15, 1951; d. Ivan Vladimirovich Pyrohov and Galina Adnreevna Vorobjova; m. Alexandr Kirillovich Shurpyak, Aug. 25, 1972; 1 child, Andrey. MD, Lviv State Med. U., 1974, PhD, 1984; DSc, Nat. Med. U., Kiev, 1995. Staff physician labor dept. Lviv Emergency Hosp., 1975-78; staff physician Regional Hosp., Lviv, 1978-81; from asst. prof. to assoc. prof. Lviv Med. Hosp., 1982-98, prof., 1998-99; dean Lviv State Med. U., 1996—, chief ob-gyn dept., prof., 1999—; cons. Lviv Perinata Ctr., City Maternity Hosp., 1990—. Contbr. articles to profl. jours. Mem. Assn. Obstetricians and Gynecologies Ukraine, European Assn. Obstetricians and Gynecologists, World Assn. Perinatal Medicine, N.Y. Acad. Scis. Avocations: traveling, reading, singing, gardening. Fax: 0322-75-48-43. Office: Lviv Med U, 69 Pekarska Str, 79010 Lviv Ukraine

PYRROS, DEMETRIOS G., orthopaedic surgeon; b. Thessaloniki, Greece, Aug. 14, 1961; s. George D. and Afroditi G. (Hadjianesti) P.; m. Efi V. Laliotou, Oct. 24, 1993; 1 child, George. MD, U. Ioannina, Greece, 1986. Intern surgery dept. 251 Hellenic Air Force Gen. Hosp., Athens, 1987-88; resident pediatric orthopaedic clinic Penteli Children's Hosp., Athens, 1988-89; resident orthopaedic clinic U. Athens, 1991-94; aeromed. evacuation dr. Nat. Emergency Care Ctr., Athens, 1994-95, cons., 1997—; officer humanitarian affairs UN Dept. Humanitarian Affairs, Liberia, 1996; med. officer UN Office of Humanitarian Coord. for Iraq, Baghdad, 1997; med. cons. UN, Monrovia, Liberia, 1991, dispensary physician, Kabul, Afghanistan, 1990, Monrovia, 1993; cons. to med. dir. UN Hdqs., N.Y.C., 1992; cons. and founding mem. Emergencies Rsch. Ctr., Athens, 1992—; cons. Earthquake Planning and Protection Orgn., Athens, 1994—; officer in charge dept disaster medicine Nat. Emergency Care Ctr. for Earthquake, Aegiou, Greece, 1995; active 3d permanent sci. com. Earthquake Planning and Protection Orgn., Greece. Disaster physician Greek Rescue Team, Leninakan, USSR, 1988; exploratory mission physician Medecins Sans Frontieres, Greek Albanian Border, 1991. Lt. Hellenic Air Force, 1986-88. Recipient Spl. medal for rescuers in Armenia, Armenian Govt., USSR, 1990. Mem. World Assn. Disaster and Emergency Medicine, Medecins San Frontieres (Greek sect. v.p., founding mem.), Hellenic Assn. Orthopaedic Surgery and Traumatology, UN Greek Assn., Anatolia Coll. Alumni Assn. Home: Ipirou 39, GR-15341 Paraskevi Greece Office: Medecins San Frontieres, Stournara 57, GR-10432 Athens Greece

PYTELA, OLDŘICH, chemistry educator; b. Ústí nad Orlicí, Czech Republic, Dec. 25, 1950; s. Oldřich and Libuše (Balcárková) P.; m. Miroslava Macková, AUg. 17, 1973; children: Pavel, Martin. MS in Engring., Inst. Chem. Tech., Pardubice, Czechoslovakia, 1974, PhD in Chemistry, 1979. Rschr. Inst. Chem. Tech., 1979-81; asst. prof. U. Pardubice, 1981-90, assoc. prof., 1990-96, vice dean faculty of chem. tech., 1995-97, prof. organic chemistry, 1996—, chancellor, 1997-2000; mem., Czech com. univ. senates, 1994-2000, v.p., 1997-2000; mem. accreditation. commn. Min. of Edn., Youth and Sports of Czech Republic. Author (textbooks): Optimization, 1985, Preliminary Course from Organic Chemistry, 1983; co-author: Organic Chemistry, Part 2, 1991, Chemometrics for Organic Chemists, 1993, 95, 2000; contbr. numerous articles to profl. jours including Organic Reactions, Collective Czech Chem. Cmty., also others. Recipient State prize for chemistry Czech Rep., 1989. Mem. Czech Chem. Soc., Swiss Chem. Soc. Avocations: hiking, chamber music, computational technique. Home: U Hřiště 1351, CZ 56206 Ústí nad Orlicí Czech Republic Office: U Pardubice, Čs Legií 565, CZ 53210 Pardubice Czech Republic

PYTKO, STANISLAW JERZY, mechanical engineering educator; b. Pacanow, Poland, Oct. 19, 1929; s. Wiktor and Aniela (Badyl) P.; m. Krystyna Zasucha, July 2, 1955; children: Jolanta, Pawel. BSc in Engring., Tech. U. Mining & Metallurgy, Kraków, Poland, 1954, DSc in Engring., 1964, prof. Du Sc., 1978. Asst. Tech. U. Mining and Metallurgy, Kraków, 1952-58, adj., 1958-71, asst. prof., 1971-78, prof., 1978—; with Sci. Ctr. for Terotech., Radom, 1990—; v.p. Internat. Tribology Coun., London, 1991—; mem. European adv. bd. Eurometalworking, Italy, 1992—; hon. prof. Autonomous Khakasskoi, Russia, Tech. U., Rybinsk, Russia, Rybinsk State Avio-Tech. Acad. Russia; mem. ASM-HTS Quenchig and Cooling Com. U.S.A. Author: Principles of Tribology, 1984-89; author, editor: Problems of Contact Strength, 1982, Ultrasound Diagnostics of Friction Joints, 1989, Tribology of Cutting Processes of Metal, 1999, Along Rolling Bearings, 1999; editor Exploitation Problem of Machines, 1956—; chmn. editl. bd. Tribologia-Poland, 1992—; mem. editl. bd. Tribologija u Industriji, Yugoslavia, 1990—, Friction and Wear Byloruss, 1995—, Mechanics, Machine-building and Geotechnology, Azerbaijan, 1999, Church of Pacanów, Church in Zborowek; contbr. more than 270 papers on tribology and tech. Recipient Tribology gold medal, 1995. Mem. Polish Tribology Soc. (pres., chmn. 1990—), Acad. Engring. in Poland, Polish Acad. Scis. (com. for mech. engring. 1980—), Transport Acad. Engring. in Ukrainia, Quality Acad. Engring. Russia, Russian Tribology Soc. (hon.), N.Y. Acad. Sci., Am. Biog. Inst. (rsch. bd. advisors), Am. Soc. Tribology and Lubrication Engrs. Roman Catholic. E-mail: s pytko@uci.agh.edu.pl. Home: Orlat Lwowskich 5/1, 31-518 Cracow Poland Office: Tech U Mining & Metallurgy, Al Mickiewicza 30, 30-059 Cracow Poland

PYTKOWSKI, MARIUSZ, cardiologist; b. Warsaw, Poland, Nov. 7, 1961; s. Stanislaus and Halina (Klewek) P.; m. Hanna Grażyna Chrzan, Nov. 20, 1982; children: Marta, Magdalena, Zuzanna. MD, Med. Acad. Warsaw, 1987; PhD in Cardiology, Inst. Cardiology, Warsaw, 1995. Cert. in cardiac pacemaker implantation, automatic cardioverters defibrillators, clin. electrophysiology and catheter ablations of cardiac arrhythmias. Intern Bakoulev Inst. Cardiac Surgery, 1992; resident Duke U. Med. Ctr., 1992, St. Georges Med. Sch. Hosp., London, 1996-97; asst. Inst. Cardiology, Warsaw, 1991-94, sr. asst., 1995-97, head clin. cardiac electrophysiology lab., 1998—. Contbr. articles to profl. jours., procs. in field. Grantee Komitet Badan Naukowych state agy., 1995, 98, Komitet Badan Naukowych and Brit. Coun., 1996. Mem. Polish Cardiac Soc. (mem. young investigators club 1994—). Roman Catholic. Avocations: travel, reading, car racing. Office: Inst Cardiology, Spartanska 1, 02-637 Warsaw Poland

PYTSKY, VICTOR IVANOVICH, allergist, educator; b. Moscow, Apr. 21, 1924; s. Ivan Ermalaevich and Darya Mitrophanovna (Chochlova) P.; m. Helena Gregorevna Bogdanova, Mar. 12, 1934. MD, 2d Moscow State Med. Inst., 1951, postgrad., 1951-54. Asst. chair pathophysiology 2d Moscow State Med. Inst., 1954-62, head chair gen. pathology, 1967-99; rschr. Rsch. Allergologic Lab., Moscow, 1962-67; prof., chair gen. pathology Russian Med. U., Moscow, 1999—; educator 2d Moscow State Med. Inst., 1955—, prof., 1971—; editor-in-chief Allergology sect. Bolshaja Med. Ency., 1980. Author: Allergic Diseases, 3d edit., 1999; author: Corticosteroids and Allergic Processes, 1976; contbr. articles to profl. jours. Recipient honoris causa diploma Assn. Medicorum Bohemoslovacorum. Mem. Interasma (bd. dirs. Russian sect. 1997—), Internat. Soc. on Immunorehabilitation Moscow. Avocations: gardening, collecting art books. Home: Ivana Babushkina Str 3, 117292 Moscow Russia Office: Russian Med U, Ostrovitjanova St 1, 117869 Moscow Russia

PYTTE, AGNAR, physicist, former university president; b. Kongsberg, Norway, Dec. 23, 1932; came to U.S., 1949, naturalized, 1965; s. Ole and Edith (Christiansen) P.; m. Anah Currie Loeb, June 18, 1955; children: Anders H., Anthony M., Alyson C. A.B., Princeton U., 1953; A.M., Harvard U., 1954, Ph.D., 1958. Mem. faculty Dartmouth Coll., 1958-87, prof. physics, 1967-87, chmn. dept. physics and astronomy, 1971-75, assoc. dean faculty, 1975-78, dean grad. studies, 1975-78, provost, 1982-87; pres. Case Western Res. U., Cleve., 1987-99; researcher in plasma physics; mem. Project Matterhorn, Princeton, 1959-60, U. Brussels, 1966-67, Princeton U., 1978-79; bd. dirs. Goodyear Tire & Rubber Co.; A.O. Smith Corp. Bd. dirs. Sherman Fairchild Found. Inc., 1987—; mem. Bretton Woods Co., Accreditation Coun. for Grad. Med. Edn. Mem. Am. Phys. Soc., Phi Beta Kappa, Sigma Xi.

PYYKKÖ, PEKKA, chemistry educator; b. Hinnerjoki, Finland, Oct. 12, 1941. PhD, U. Turku, Finland, 1967. Assoc. prof. Quantum Chemistry åbo Akademi, Turku, Finland, 1974-84; prof. chemistry U. Helsinki, Finland, 1984—; rsch. prof. Acad. Finland, Helsinki, 1995-2000. Author: Relativistic Theory of Atoms and Molecules Vol. I, II, 1986, 93; contbr. over 200 scientific papers on quantum chemistry. Mem. European Acad. Arts, Scis. and Humanities, Finska Vetenskaps-Soc, Suomalainen Tiedeakatemia, The Royal Acad. Arts and Scis., Internat. Acad. Quantum Molecular Scis., Bayerische Akad. Wiss., The Chem. Soc. Finland. Home: Etumetsäntie 14 B, 00620 Helsinki Finland Office: U Helsinki Dept chemistry, PO Box 55, 00014 Helsinki Finland

QADAR, ALI, scientist; b. Azamgarh, India, July 1, 1949; s. Ghirau and Nadira (Begum) Sheikh; m. Salma Nigar, Aug. 9, 1975; children: Sajid, Shehla, Arham. MSc, Aligarh (India) Muslim U, 1971, MPhil, 1982, PhD, 1984. Cert. plant physiology. Lectr. Govt. Postgrad. Coll., Rampur, India, 1975; sr. rsch. asst. Ctrl. Soil Salinity Rsch. Inst., Karnal, India, 1975; scientist S-0 Ctrl. Soil Salinity Rsch. Inst., Karnal, 1975-76, scientist S-1, 1976-82, scientist S-2, 1982-85, sr. scientist, 1986—. Councillor Indian Jour. Plant Nutrition, 1984; cons. editor Indian Jour. Plant Physiology, 1994, 95, 96. Pres. Muslim Welfare Assn., Karnal, 1995—. Fellow Indian Soc. for Plant Physiology (life mem.); mem. Indian Soc. for Plant Nutrition. Avocations: gardening, social work, badminton. Home: E/2 CSSRI Karnal, Karnal 132001, India Office: Divsn Crop Improvement, Ctrl Soil Salinity Rsch Ins, Karnal 132001, India

QASEM, AREF QASEM MOHAMMED, import/export company executive; b. Asira, Nablus, Jordan, Mar. 22, 1942; s. Qasem Mohammed and Mariam Masood (Abdullah) Q.; m. Fakhriyeh M.R. Abdul Rahman, Oct. 1, 1965; children: Rami A., Qasim A., Reema A., Mohammed A., Ahmad A. BS in Commerce and Acctg., Aleppo (Syria) U., 1967, BS in Stats., 1968. Acct. Agr. Materials Co., Damascus, Syria, 1961-62; br. mgr. Agr. Materials Co., Aleppo, Syria, 1963-69; country mgr. Agr. Materials Co., Damascus, 1970-75; area mgr. NZARCO, Abqaiq, Saudi Arabia, 1975-82; gen. mgr. NZARCO, Mubarraz, Saudi Arabia, 1982—; cons. Khalidia Group of Schs., Mubarraz, 1982—; gen. mgr. NZARCO Travel Agy., Mubarraz, 1982—, NZARCO Laundry Svcs., Khafji, Saudi Arabia, 1985—; pres. Arcan-Tech., Tech., Trading, Import & Export, Ont., Can., 1994—; owner rep. Prince Saud Bin Jalawi Hosp., Saudi Arabia, 1985—. Pres. Palestine Students Orgn., Aleppo, 1962-69, Arab Students Orgn., Aleppo, 1962-69; treas. Palestine Club, Aleppo, 1964-69. Mem. Am. Mgmt. Assn. Avocations: table tennis, walking, reading, writing poems, playing chess. Office: Nasser H Al Zarah Est, PO Box 10068, Mubarraz Al Hassa 31982, Saudi Arabia

QASIM, SYED SHAH ABUL, transportation planner; b. Bangalore, Dec. 8, 1925; s. Qazi Syed Ismail and Aesha Bibi; m. Rabia Khanum, Jan. 8, 1953 (dec. Dec. 22, 1986); children: Syed Shahzad, Syed Sartaj, Seema Qasim, Saleha Qasim. BSc, Mysore U., 1945, Staff Coll., Quetta, Pakistan, 1955; MSc, Indonesian Staff Coll., Bandung, 1965. From cadet to brig. gen. Pakistan Army, 1946-76; mng. dir. KTC, Pakistan, 1977-84; CEO Chartered Inst. Transport, Karachi, Pakistan, 1985—; vis. prof. Karachi U., 1985—; cons. World Bank, Karachi, 1987—. Hon. fellow Chartered Inst. Transportation. Mem. Assn. Transport Devel. in India. Islam. Avocations: photography, travel, international affairs, golf.

QAYYUM, MALIK MOHAMMAD, judge, agriculturist; b. Lahore, Punjab, Pakistan, Jan. 18, 1945; s. Malik Mohammad and Ayesha (Sadiqa) Akram; m. Rukhsana Hussain; children: Mohammad Ahmed, Asad, Ahad, Sana. BA, F.C. Coll., Pakistan, 1961; LLB, Univ. Law Coll., Pakistan, 1963. Lawyer Lahore, 1963-88; judge Lahore High Ct., 1988—; sec. dist. bar., Lahore, 1971-77, pres., 1980-81; mem. Punjab Bar Coun., Lahore, 1985-89; dep. atty. gen., Lahore, 1984-88; chmn. Punjab Election Authority, 1996—. Editor Pakistan Supreme Ct. cases. Mem. Punjab Club, Gymkhana Club, Garrison Golf Club. Muslim. Avocations: golf, books, poetry, music. Office: Lahore High Ct, Mall Rd, Lahore Punjab, Pakistan

QAZI, FIRDOUS ANWER, humanities educator; b. Tando Adam, Sind, Pakistan, Sept. 11, 1947; d. Qazi Zakir Hassan and Zubaida Khatoon; m. Anwer Kamal Qazi, Dec. 25, 1964 (dec. May 1988); children: Harris, Afshan, Khakashan. Grad., U. Sind, Jamshoro, Pakistan, 1968; M in Urdu, U. Karachi, Pakistan, 1971; PhD in Urdu, U. Balochistan, Quetta, Pakistan, 1983. Lectr. U. Balcoshistan, Quetta, 1975-85, asst. prof., 1985-90, prof., 1990—, chairperson dept. Urdu, 1993-98; rsch. dir. Allama Iqbal Open U., Islamabad, Pakistan, 1990—; rsch. advisor U. Balochistan, Quetta, 1990—. Author: Khawaboun Ke Basti, 1990 (Best Book Qalam Qabila award 1991); author of short stories and articles. Mem. Qalam Qabella (exec.), Harf-e-Haqait (sr. exec.). Avocations: short story writing and reading, literary criticism. Home: B-1 Univ Colony, Sariab Rd, Quetta Pakistan Office: Dept Urdu, Univ Balochistan, Quetta Pakistan

QAZI, MANZAR MOIN, advertising executive; b. Karachi, Sindh, Pakistan, June 29, 1968; s. Moin Uddin and Dur Shehwar (Shama) Q.; m. Deeba Manzar James, May 18, 1995; 1 child: Arsaz. BSc, Sindh U., 1989; MBA, Internat. U., Sindh, 1992. Account exec. Sasa Advt., Pakistan, 1993-94, The Circuit, Pakistan, 1994-96; account mgr. Circuit/FCB, Pakistan, 1996-97, account dir., 1998—; guest spkr. Indus Valley Sch. Arts, Pakistan, 1998—, Pakistan Inst. Mgmt. & Scis., 1999. Editor daily advt. jour. Recipient awards Lahore Inst. Mgmt. and Sci., 1998, Pakistan Newspapers Soc., 1998. Mem. Inst. Mktg. Mgmt. (assoc., life), Pakistan Advt. Assn. (mem. adv. com. 1998—, award 1997), HRCP, Pakistan Bridge Assn. Avocations: reading, writing, chess, bridge. Home: F-78, Block 5, Scheme 5, Kehkashen Clifton, Karachi 75600, Pakistan

QI, MING, metallurgist, educator; b. Xi'an, China, Nov. 29, 1957; s. Changjia and Kuiying (Wu) Q.; m. Wenjun Wang, Dec. 30, 1984; 1 child, Ji. B in Engring., Xi'an Jiaotong U., 1982, M in Engring., 1987, D in Engring., 1992. Asst. Xi'an (China) Jiaotong U., 1982-87, lectr., 1987-92, assoc. prof., 1992-93; postdoctoral rschr. Shanghai Inst. Metallurgy, 1993-95, prof., 1995-99, deputy dir., 1999—; vis. rschr. Tokyo Inst. Tech., 1990-91; vice gen. mgr. Shanghai Ericsson Simtek Electronics Co., Ltd., 1996-97; asst. dir. Shanghai Inst. Metallury, 1995—; dir. State Key Lab. Functional Materials for Informatics, 1997—. Recipient Silver award R&D Xi'an Jiaotong U., 1993, Gold award, 1995, Silver award R&D Shaanxi Edn. Com., 1995, R&D Chinese Acad. Scis., 1996, Copper award, 1996, Silver award R&D Shaanxi Province Govt., 1996, Copper award Nat. R&D China, 1997, Copper award R&D Shanghai Municipality, 1997. Mem. IEEE. Office: Shanghai Inst Metallurgy, 865 Changning Rd, Shanghai 200050, China

QI, XICHENG, civil engineer, researcher; b. Liyan, Jiangsu, People's Republic of China, Dec. 16, 1956; came to U.S., 1990; s. Shunfa and Hongzhen (Zhang) Q.; m. Xiao Cai, Aug. 8, 1987; 1 child, Dawei. BS, Nanjing Inst. Tech., Jiangsu, 1977; MS, S.E. U., Nanjing, 1986, U. Nev., Reno, 1991; PhD, U. Md., 1992. Registered profl. engr., Va. Lectr. Xian Tech. Inst., Shaanxi, 1982-86; rsch. engr. S.E. U., Nanjing, 1986-87; project engr. Nanjing Engring. Co., 1987-90; rsch. assoc. U. Nev., Reno, 1990-92; rsch. engr. U. Md., College Park, 1992-96; civil engr. Fed. Hwy. Adminstrn., McLean, Va., 1996—; cons. C&Q Info. Technologies, McLean, 1994—, Xian Engring. Svcs., Shaanxi, 1982-86. Author: Building Materials, 1984; contbr. articles to profl. jours. including Jour. Transp. Engring., Jour. Materials in Civil Engring., Transp. Rsch. Record; inventor in field. Mem. ASCE, NSPE, Am. Concrete Inst., Transp. Rsch. Bd., World Rd. Assn., Assn. Asphalt Paving Technologists. Avocations: running, ping pong, reading. Office: HRDI-II FHWA 6300 Georgetown Pike Mc Lean VA 22101

QIAN, BOHAI, statistics and economics educator; b. Taixing, Jiansu, China, May 26, 1928; s. Hanyu and Lishi (Li) Q.; m. Meiying Lin, Jan. 31, 1956; children: Zhenming, Gongming. BS, Fudan U., Shanghai, 1951. Asst. lectr. stats. Xiamen (China) U., 1951-60, dep. dir., lectr. dept. econs., 1960-78, dep. dir., assoc. prof., 1978-83, dir., prof. dept. stats., 1983-87, dean and prof. coll. econs., 1987-93, dir., prof. Inst. Nat. Econs. and Acctg., 1993—; sr. advisor China's Gen. Office for Statis. Affairs, Beijing, 1993—, sr. adv., Info. Assn. Fujian, 1992—; advisor Planning Commn. of Fujian, 1980-92; mem. Econs. & Mgmt. Branch Evaluation Team of Degree Com. in State Coun., Beijing, 1981-97. Author: National Economic Statistics 1982; contbr. 30 monographs & textbooks, over 100 articles to profl. jours. Named Exemplary Tchr., Fujian Provincial Govt. and Xiamen Mcpl. Govt., 1960, 78, Model Worker, 1987, Expert with Outstanding Achievements, Fujian Provincial Govt., 1993. Mem. Assn. of Statis. Edn. (adult edn. on stats. hon. chmn.), Internat. Statis. Inst., Royal Statis. Soc.; v.p. Chinese Statis. Soc., China's Nat. Acctg. Assn.; pres. Fujian Statis. Soc. Avocation: music. Home: Xiamen Univ, PO Box 346, Xiamen 361005, People's Republic of China Office: Dept Statistics, Xiamen Univ, Xiamen 361005, People's Republic of China

QIAN, FANG, software engineer; b. ShiJiaZhuang, HeBei, China; d. Wangming Qian and Qizhen Chen. BSEE, Nanjing U., 1989; MS in Biomed. Engring., Drexel U., 1995. Elec. engr. Inst. Acoustics, Acad. Sinica China, Beijing, 1989-92; rsch. asst. Drexel U., Phila., 1992-96; sys. engr., web master Hamilton Security, Washington, 1996; mem. tech. staff Telogy Networks, Germantown, Md., 1996-97; sr. software engr. Optimus Corp., Silver Spring, Md., 1998—. Calhoun fellow Drexel U., Phila., 1992. Mem. IEEE, Assn. for Computer Machinery, Biomed. Engring. Soc. E-mail: floraqian@hotmail.com and flora.qian@optimuscorp.com. Office: Optimus Corp 8601 Georgia Ave Ste 700 Silver Spring MD 20910-3439

QIAN, FENG, electrical engineer; b. Beipiao, Liaoning, China, Jan. 20, 1964; s. Chengzhang Qian and Sulan Liu; m. Danping Yu, Apr. 12, 1964; 1 child, Songyun. BS, Southeastern U., Nanjing, China, 1985; MS, Beijing Vacuum Electronics Inst., 1987; PhD in Electronics Engring., U. Erlangen-Nurnberg, Germany, 2000. Engr. Beijing Vacuum Electronics Inst., 1987-91, project mgr., 1991-93; dir. Sino-German Vacuum Lab., Beijing, 1993-95; vis. scholar Fraunhofer Inst. Integrated Circuits, U. Erlangen-Nürnberg, 1995—. Contbr. articles to sci. jours.; designer std. temperature lamp and UV-detector. Scholar German Acad. Exch. Svc., 1995. Mem. Chinese Vacuum Soc., German Elec. Engrs. Assn. Avocations: football, swimming, classical music. Office: Pfeiffer Vacuum GmbH, Emmeliusstrasse 33, D-35614 Asslar Germany

QIAN, JIANG, engineering educator, researcher; b. Dandong, Peoples Republic of China, Jan. 22, 1960; s. Rongxi and Wenge (Zhou) Q. BS, U. Sci. and Tech. China, Hefei, China, 1982; M in Engring., 1985, PhD, 1989. Asst. prof. Tongji U., Shanghai, China, 1988-91; assoc. prof., 1991-92; vis. scientist U. Patras, Greece, 1992-93; rsch. fellow Ruhr-Univ. Bochum, Germany, 1993-94; sr. rschr. U. Hong Kong, 1995-96; assoc. prof. Tongji U., Shanghai, China, 1997-98, prof., 1998—. Researcher in field. Recipient Scientific Achievement award, 1992, 97, Outstanding Young Scholar award Shanghai Municipality, China, 1991, 99, Marie Curie Fellowship Commn. of European Communities, 1992, Alexander von Humboldt Fellowship AVH Found., Germany, 1993. Mem. Chinese Soc. Mechanics. Avocations: electrotechnics, photography, travel, reading. Fax: (86)-21-65982668. E-mail: jqian@public1.sta.net.cn. Office: Tongji U Inst Eng Struct, 1239 Siping Rd, Shanghai 200092, China

QIAN, KUN-XI, science and technology educator; b. Wujing, Jiangsu, China, Aug. 10, 1944; s. Wan-Xie Qian and Xiao-Mei He; m. Su-Hua Li; children: Jing, Ying, Rong. BS, Fudan U., Shanghai, 1968; MS, Jiangsu U. Sci. and Tech., Zhenjiang, China, 1980. Vis. scholar Free U., Berlin, 1980-83; project dir. Second Med. U., Shanghai, 1984-88; prin. investigator Aachen (Germany) Tech. U., 1989-92; assoc. prof. Taiwan U., Taipei, 1993-94; prof. Second Mil. Med. U., Shanghai, 1995; prof., dir. Biomed. Engring. Inst. Jiangsu U. Sci. and tech., 1996—; cons. U. Utah, Salt Lake City, 1992. Author: Assisted Circulation 3, 1989, Assisted Circulation 4, 1995; contbr. articles to profl. jours. Grantee Chinese Nat. Natural Scis. Founds., 1985, 96, 2000, Chinese Nat. Commn. Scis., 1997; recipient Gold prizes Einstein Invention Expo Ctr., 1997, Edison Invention Ctr. USA, 1998, Bronze prize sci. and tech. advancements Min. for Edn., 1999. Mem. AAAS, Internat. Soc. Artificial Organs, Am. Soc. Artificial Internal Organs, Chinese Soc. Mech. Engring. (sr.). Home: Luo Yang Villa No 3, PO Box 96 602, 201100 Shanghai China Office: Jiangsu U Sci and Tech, 212013 Zhenjiang Jiangsu China

QIAN, LIANG, neurosurgeon; b. Shenyang City, China, Aug. 5, 1964; s. Fa Xin and Shu Lan (Yan) Q.; m. Yun Kang, Jan. 4, 1990. BS, MD, China Med. U., 1987; PhD, Tokyo Med. & Dental U., 1996. Resident China Med. U., 1986-87, asst., 1987-90; rschr. Kyorin (Japan) U., 1990-91; postgrad. Tokyo Med. & Dental U., 1992-96, posdoctoral rschr., 1996—; cons. AMDA Internat. Med. Info. Ctr., Japan, 1992-96; translator IDEA, Japan, 1992-94; chmn. Liaoning Internat. Exch. Assn. China, 1996—; product mgr. Tokibo Co. Ltd., Japan, 1996—. Author: (book) Marketing Communications Executives Internat., 1995 (Bronze award 1995); contbr. articles to profl. jours. Recipient scholarship Monbasho, Tokyo, 1990. Mem. The China Neurosurg. Soc., The Japan Neurosurg. Soc., Japanese Soc. Neurotraumatology. Avocations: swimming, table tennis, Mac, chess "go". Office: Tokyo Med & Dental U, Bunkyo ku 1-5-45 Yushima, Tokyo T113, Japan

QIAN, QICHEN, Chinese government official; b. 1928. Student, Cen. Youth League Sch., USSR, after 1954. Active Communist Party and Youth League activities, 1940's; 2d sec. Chinese Embassy, USSR, after 1955; dep. head fgn. affairs dept. Higher Edn. Ministry, after 1955; counsellor Chinese Embassy, USSR, after 1972; ambassador to Guinea, after 1974; head info. dept. Ministry of Fgn. Affairs, after 1977; vice-fgn. minister, 1982-88; fgn. minister Chinese govt., 1988—, also vice premier, state coun., 1993—. Office: Office of Premier, State Coun Secretariat, Zhong Nan Hai Beijing 100701, China also: Office Fgn Affairs, 225 Chachei St, Dangsi Beijing China*

QIAN, RENGJI, engineering educator; b. Waigang, Shanghai, Dec. 4, 1938; s. Hanchun and Wanru (Qiu) Q.; m. Nianshi Wang, Oct. 1, 1967; children: Jia, Bing. B, Shanghai Jiaotong U., China, 1961. Asst. Shanghai Jiaotong U., China, 1961-76, lectr., 1977-86, assoc. prof., 1987-97; prof. Shanghai Jiaotong U., 1997—; vice dir. divsn. structural mechanics Sch. Naval Arch. & Ocean Engring., Shanghai Jiaotong U., 1990—; dir. Lab. Structural Mechanics, Shanghai, 1982-86. Author: Fracture and Fatigue Analysis in Ship and Ocean Engineering Structures, 1987, 96, Propagation of Fatigue Crack, 1990, 91, Finite Element Method in Ship Structures, 1996, Applying Strain Energy Density Factor Theory to Propagation Estimating of Surface Crack, 1996, Variational Principle in Shell Structures, 1997, Probabilistic Damage Tolerance Analysis, 1997, 98. Vis. scholar U. Coll. London, 1986-87. Mem. Chinese Soc. Naval Arch. & Marine Engrs., Chinese Ocean Engring. Soc., Chinese Mechs. Soc. Avocations: reading, swimming, music, art. E-mail: rjqian@guomai.sh.cn. Office: Shanghai Jiaotong U, Shanghai Jiaotong U Arch, Ocean Engring 1954 Huashan, Shanghai 200030, China

QIAN, SHINAN, optical engineer, researcher, educator; b. Hong Kong, June 8, 1939; s. Xiaobo Qian and Lianyin Fung; m. Zhiping Zhang, May 18, 1970; children: Jin, Kun. B in Engring., Beijing Tsinghua U., 1962. Tchg. asst. Beijing Tsinghua U., 1962-71; asst. engr. Inst. Cement Equipment Tangshan, China, 1971-73; engr., group head Inst. Optics Fine Mechics Anhui, Acad. Sinica, Hefei, China, 1973-84; rschr., prof., group head U. Sci. Tech. China, Acad. Sinica, Hefei, 1984-91; rschr., group head Sincrotrone Trieste, Italy, 1991-97; rsch. engr. Brookhaven (N.Y.) Nat. Lab., 1997—; scientist Brookhaven (N.Y.) Nat. Lab., 1985-87. Recipient People's Rep. China Sci. Tech. Accomplishment award, 1983; R&D 100 award Rsch. and Devel. Mag., 1993. Achievements include patents for surface profiling interferometer, computerized micro-displacement instrument using interference method, inclination beam interferometer for expansion measuring and equipment, quick vacuum actuator. Office: Brookhaven Nat Lab Bldg 535B Upton NY 11973-5000

QIAN, XUEYU, physicist; b. Wengzhou, China, Aug. 1, 1943; came to U.S., 1980; s. Peichi and Fengjuan (Huang) Q.; m. Ping Zhu; children: Jun, Jiang, Tong. B in Physics, Beijing U., 1968; PhD in Physics, U. Mich., 1987. Head semiconductor divsn. Wenzhou Engring. Sch., Zhejiang, 1970-74; lectr., rschr. U. Sci. and Tech., China, 1974-80; vis. scholar U. Mich., Ann Arbor, 1980-81, rsch. asst., 1981-87; rsch. assoc. U. Calif., Santa Barbara, 1987-88, Berkeley, 1988-90; tech. dir. Applied Materials, Santa Clara, Calif., 1990—. Author: (textbook) The Physics of Magnetic Recording, 1976; contbr. numerous articles to sci. publs.; patentee, inventor in field. Rsch. grantee Dept. Energy, 1981-87, Calif. Micro and Applied Materials, 1988-90. Mem. Am. Vacuum Soc. (No. Calif. chpt., editor plasma etch user's group 1996—). Office: Applied Materials 974 E Arques Ave # Ms81158 Sunnyvale CA 94085-4520

QIAN, ZHENGFANG, research scientist; b. Jingtan, China, July 14, 1959; came to U.S., 1993; s. Huiming and Xihua Qian; m. Wei Zhou, June 18, 1999. BE, Jiangsu Inst. Chem. Tech., Changzhou, China, 1982; M of Engring., Nanjing U. Chem Tech., 1985; PhD, Chongqing (China) U., 1991. Lectr. Wuhan (China) Inst. Chem. Tech., 1985-87, Chinese Acad. Scis., Beijing, 1991-93; postdoctoral fellow U. Iowa, Iowa City, 1993-95; rsch. assoc. U. Md., Baltimore County, 1995-96; rsch. scientist Wayne State U., Detroit, 1997-99, dep. dir. electronic packaging lab., 1998-99; staff engr. Motorola, Schaumburg, Ill., 2000—. Editor: Thermo-Mechanical Characterization of Evolving Packaging Materials and Structures, 1998; contbr. numerous articles to profl. jours. Recipient URP award Ford Motor Co., 1999; NSF grantee, 1999. Mem. ASME, IEEE, AAAS. Avocation: fishing. E-mail: az9ool@email.mot.com. Office: Global Software Group Motorola 1303 E Algonquin Rd Schaumburg IL 60196-4041

QIAN, ZIFEN, artist, researcher; b. Shanghai, Dec. 30, 1957; came to U.S., 1987; s. Mingkong and Xuan Wu (Chen) Q.; m. Li Dai, Mar. 27, 1992; 1 child, Kristin. BA, Shanghai Normal U., 1983; MFA, Portland State U., 1989. Sr. artist Carol Wilson Fine Arts, Portland, 1992—; art instr. Pacific Northwest Coll. Art, Portland, 1989-95, Portland State U., 1987-89; art dir. Classic Clay Concept Inc., 1990-92; art editor Youth and Health mag. WHO, Shanghai, 1983-87; pres. Northwest Chinese Artists Assn., Portland, 1993-95; editor-in-chief World Arts Pub. Co., Portland, 1997—; fine artist: (paintings, art philosophy) The Oregonian newspaper, 1987, Stepping Out Arts mag., 1988, (paintings in a book) Entertaining with Betsy Bloomingdale, 1994, (paintings prints) Carol Wilson Fine Arts, 1992—, (art experience) The Dictionary of World Chinese Artists Achievements, 1994. One-man exhbns. Denise Amato Galleries, 1989-98, Indigo Gallery, 1992, Portland State U. Gallery, 1989 (fine artist award), U.S. Bancorp Towers, 1987; paintings shows Shanghai Fine Arts Acad. Shows, 1982, 84, Across East China Nat. Art Show, 1986; featured in The Washington Post, 1995, The Houston Chronicle, 1995, (book) Always Bright (Paintings From 1970-1999), 1999; painting on cover of book Traditions and Encounters-A Global Perspective on The Past (From 1500 To The Present), 2000; represented in permanent collections at State Senate of Oreg., State House of Oreg., City Hall of Portland, Oreg. Recipient Outstanding Painting award Lucil S. Welch Meml. Found., 1988. Avocations: creating poetry, singing, tennis. E-mail: lzwap@aol.com.

QIANG, WEIGUO, chemist, researcher; b. Changzhou, Jiangsu, China, June 29, 1943; s. Hua Qiang and Yao Ding; m. Hong Xu; 1 child, Zhongjun. BS, Guizhou U., Guiyang, China, 1964. Practician, rsch. fellow Indsl. Health Inst., Chengdu, China, 1964-78, asst. rsch. fellow, 1979-84, assoc. rsch. fellow, 1985-88; vis. scientist FDA, Washington, 1987-88; dir. technologist Sichuan Provincial Inst. Food Sanitation, Chengdu, 1989—; mem. Sichua Lab. Accreditation Com., Chengdu, 1990—; cons. Sichuan Profl. Title Awarding Office, Chengdu, 1992—. Contbr. articles to profl. publs. (Nat. Sci. Congress award 1978, Sichuan Health Dept. award 1981, China Health Ministry award 1984). Recipient Excellent Accrediatation award Sichuan Province Accrediation Com., 1991, Excellent Expert Outstanding Achievement award Sichuan Govt., 1993. Mem. AOAC Internat., Chinese Assn. for Food Sanitation Exam. (v.p. 1992). Avocations: writing, computers, photography. Home: 40 Huaishu St, Chengdu Sichuan 610031, China Office: Sinchuan Provincial Inst, Supervision & Exam Food San, Sichuan 610031, China

QIAO, QING, pediatrician, researcher; b. Qingdao, Shandong, China, Feb. 6, 1959; Arrived in Finland, Nov. 1992; s. Tinglan Qiao and Yumin Li; m. Jinlong Zhang, Dec. 20, 1984; children: Zhang, Nan. MB, Qingdao Med. Coll., 1983; PhD, U. Oulu, 1997. Resident, asst. Qingdao Med. Coll., 1983-87, chief resident, 1987-88, lectr., 1988-92; vis. scholar Children's Hosp. of U. Helsinki, Finland, 1992-93; rschr. dept. pub. health sci. and gen. practice U. Oulu, Finland, 1993-97; rschr. genetic and diabetes unit Nat. Pub. Health Inst., Helsinki, 1997—. Avocations: sports, baking. Office: Nat Pub Health Inst, Mannerheimintie 166, 00300 Helsinki Finland

QIAO, YANXIAO, geologist; b. Shijiazhuang, Hebei, China, Jan. 27, 1954; s. Lufang Qiao and Yuncai Yao; m. Cuifen Yao, Jan. 1, 1983; 1 child, Lei Qiao. B in Engring., Hebei Geol. Coll., Zhangjiakou, China, 1982. Cert. hydrogeology and engring. geology. Asst. engr. No. 9 Geologic Team, Hengshui, China, 1983-89; engr. Remote Sensing Ctr. Hebei Province, Shijiazhuang, 1990-94, sr. engr., 1995—. Author: The Selections of National Achievements in Scientific Research in Period, 1999; contbr. articles to profl. jours. Recipient Third Class award sci. and tech. result Ministry Geology and Mineral Resources China, 1987, 97, Third Class award sci. and tech. result Nat. Planning Com., 1997. Mem. Interpretion Assn. Hebei Province, Geologic Assn. China, Sci. and Tech. Assn. Hebei Province. Home: 9 Zhongnang Lu, Youyibei dajie, Shijiazhuang Hebei, China Office: Remote Sensing Ctr Hebei, 131 Huai Zhong Lu, Shijiazhuang 050021, China

QIAO, ZHI GUI, biophysicist; b. Shanghai, China, Oct. 17, 1945; arrived in Norway, 1985; s. Qing Ming and Jin Hua Qiao; m. Lin Zhen Wang, Sept. 30, 1972; 1 chid, Shuo-Wang. MSc, Tsinghua U., Beijing, China, 1970; PhD, U. Oslo, 1993. Engr. Lingling Radio Factory, Hunan, China, 1970-76, Shanghai No. 2 Radio Factory, 1976-78; lectr. Shanghai Med. Instrumentation Coll., 1978-85; rsch. fellow dept. med. engring. Rikshospitalet, U. Oslo, Oslo, 1985—; rsch. fellow Inst. Surg. Rsch. Rikshospitalet, U. Olso, Oslo, 1985—; head rschr. Rsch. Inst., Dikemark Hosp., Oslo, 1985—; vis.prof. China Acad. Mgmt. Sci., Beijing, 1993—; dir. Beijing Meridian Rsch. Ctr., 1993—; cons. Gullbro Wang's Co., Oslo, 1991—; sr. engr. Nat. Inst. of Occupl. Health, Norway, 1997—; v.p. Norway-Asia Bio-tech (Shanghai) Co., Ltd., China, 1999—. Author: Measurements of Electrodermal and Microcirculatory Activities, 1993, The 3-1-2 Meridian Exercise Programme (Chinese), 1993, (English), 1994; editl. bd. Chinese Jour. med. Elec. Impedance, 1993—; contbr. articles to profl. jours. Chmn. Norway-China Sci. & Culture Exch. Promotion Soc., Oslo, 1992—. Mem. IEEE (computer soc.), Norwegian Soc. Civil Engrs., Nordic Elec. Imdepance Club, Internat. Fedn. Med. and Biol. Engring., N.Y. Acad. Scis. Avocations: Chinese literature, poetry, gardening, cooking, music. E-mail: Qiao.ZG@stami.no. Home: Brusetfaret 42B, N-1395 Hvalstad Akershus, Norway Office: Postbox 8149 Dep, N-0033 Oslo Akershus, Norway

QIN, GUO-WEI, chemist; b. Shanghai, Jiangsu, China, Sept. 18, 1941; s. Zhong-Ying and Qin-Fang Qin; m. Hui-Ying Yuan; 1 child, Zhi-Bi. BS, Shanghai Med. U., 1965. Rsch. asst. Shanghai Inst. Materia Medica, Chinese Acad. Scis., 1965-79, rsch. assoc., 1980-85, assoc. prof., 1988-93, prof., 1994—, chmn. dept. phytochemistry, mem. acad. com., 1992—; postdoctoral fellow Columbia U., N.Y.C., 1986-88; mem. acd. com. Phytochem. Lab. Kunming Inst. Botany, Chinese Acad. Scis.; rep. for China Regional Network for Chemistry of Natural Products in S.E. Asia, UNESCO, 1993—, exec. sec., 1994-98; invited spkr. confs. and sci. activities in U.S.A., Germany, New Zealand, Thailland, Malaysia, Vietnam, Japan, Korea, Hong Kong. Chief editor: Handbook of Identification of Flavoroids, 1981; mem. editl. bd. Acta Botanica Yunnanica, 1999—, Chinese Traditional and Herbal Drugs, 1997—, Inflammophramacology, 1999—, Acta Pharmaceutica Sinica, 2000—; contbr. over 100 articles to profl. jours. Mem. Chinese Soc. Botany (mem. Plant Chemistry Commn. 1989—), Chinese Pharm. Soc. (mem. Traditional Chinese Medicine and Natural Drug Commn. 1997—). Avocations: classical music, art appreciation, travel. Office: Shanghai Inst Materia Medic, 294 Tai-Yuan Rd, Shanghai 200031, China

QIN, LING, orthopedics educator, researcher; b. Suzhou, Jiangsu, China, July 5, 1959; s. Tiangau and Huaizhen (Jin) Q.; m. Xia Guo, May 24, 1987; 1 child, Lai-yin. BEd, Beijing U. Phys. Edn., 1982, MEd, 1987; PhD, German Sports U., 1992. Asst. lectr. Beijing U. Phys. Edn., 1982-85; postdoctoral fellow Arbeitsdembindeschaft Osteosymthese Frgen, Switzerland, 1992-93; rsch. scientist dept. orthopedics Free U. Berlin, 1993-94; sci. officer dept. orthopedics Chinese U. Hong Kong, 1995-96, dir. rsch., 1997—, asst. prof. orthopedics., 1997-2000; adj. prof. Wuhan Inst. Phys. Edn., China, 1996—, Jianghan U., China, 1996—; advisor nat. textbook com. Sports Anatomy, China, 1997—; sr. advisor Guangzhou Rsch. Inst. Traumatology, China, 1999—. Author: (chpt.) The Laureate of the Dragon, 1998, (textbook) Sports Anatomy, 1999. Recipient Sci. Achievement award Wuhan Assn. Sci. and Tech., 1997, Contbn. award Chinese Assn. Sports Medicine, 1998, Traveling award 17th Japanese Soc. Bone Mineral Rsch., 1999. Mem. Chinese Speaking Orthopaedic Soc. (life), Euro Osteoporosis Study Group (bd. dirs.), Arbeitsgembindschaft Osteosymthese Alumni Assn. Avocations: tennis, reading, dancing, singing. Office: Chinese Univ Hong Kong, Dept Orth and Traumatology, Hong Kong China

QIN, QING HUA, mechanical engineer; b. Yongfu, Guangxi, China, Mar. 22, 1958; parents: Yun Lian Qin and Gui Zheng Zhang; m. Yi Xiao, Apr. 23, 1962; 1 child, Xue Rong. BSc, Xian Hwy. Inst., China, 1982; MSc, Huazhong U. Sci. & Tech., Wuhan, China, 1984, PhD, 1990. Lectr. Huazhong U. Sci. & Tech., 1987-94; DAAD/K.C. Wong fellow U. Stuttgart (Germany), 1994; postdoctoral fellow Tsinghua U., Beijing, 1995-96; Queen Elizabeth II fellow U. Sydney, Australia, 1997—. Author: The Trefftz Finite and Boundary Element Method, 2000; contbr. articles to profl. jours. Mem. Chinese Mechanics Soc. Office: U Sydney, Dept Mech Engring, Sydney NSW 2006, Australia

QIN, YONG-MEI, medical sciences educator; b. Beijing, Sept. 16, 1965; s. Xi-Xuan Qin and Guang-fen Tan; m. Qiang Qu, Dec. 20, 1991; 1 child, Man-Di. BSc, Beijing Med. U., 1988; MSc, U. Oslo, 1993; PhD, U. Oulu, Finland, 1999. Rsch. scientist China Rehab. Rsch. Ctr., Beijing, 1988-89. Contbr. articles to sci. and profl. jours. Avocations: classical music, tennis, swimming.

QIN HUASUN, diplomat; b. Jiangsu Province, Sept. 1935. Counsellor, dep. perm. rep. to UN and other internat. orgns. Geneva, 1984-87; perm. rep. to UN office/IAEA UNIDO, Vienna, 1987-90; dir.-gen. dept. internat. orgns. and confs. Ministry of Fgn. Affairs, 1990-93, asst. min. fgn. affairs, 1993-95; perm. rep. to UN, 1995—. Office: Perm Mission of China to UN 350 E 35th St New York NY 10016-3760*

QIU, GUO YU, agircultural engineer; b. Alashan, China, Jan. 18, 1963; s. Shun Mei and Xiu Ying (Lu) Q.; m. Bing Yang, Apr. 3, 1987; children: Shuang, Xu. BS, Forestry U. Inner Mongolia, Huhhot, China, 1984; MS, Chinese Acad. Sci., Lanzhou, China, 1987; PhD, Tottori U., Japan, 1996. Rschr. Chinese Acad. Sci., Lanzhou, China, 1987-89; lectr. Chinese Acad. Sci., Lanzhou, 1989-92; postgrad. Tottori U., Japan, 1993-96; rschr. Nat. Rsch. Inst. Agrl. Engring., Tsukuba, Japan, 1996-99; post doctoral fellow Nat. Inst. Environ. Studies, Tsukuba, 1999—. Contbr. articles to profl. jours. Recipient fellowships Ministry Edn., Sci. and Culture, Tokyo, 1992-96, Environ. Agy. of Japan, 1999—. Mem. Japanese Soc. Irrigation, Soc. Agrl. Meteorology of Japan. Avocations: sports, travel, language. Office: Nat Inst Environ Studies, 16-2 Onogawa, 305-0053 Tsukuba Japan

QIU, HUA, mechanical engineering educator; b. Chengdu, Sichuan, China, Aug. 28, 1954; s. Ming Qiu and Liyang Wen; m. Yumi Kataoka, Apr. 9, 1990; children: Kataoka, Marika.; B in Engring., Chongqing U., China, 1982; M in Engring., Kyushu U., Japan, 1986, PhD in Engring., 1989. Tchr. Chengdu Radio Machinery Coll., China, 1976-78; rsch. asst. Fukuoka U., Japan, 1990-92; assoc. prof. Kyushu Sangyo U., Japan, 1992—. Contbr. articles to profl jours. including JSME Internat. Jour., Tansactions of Soc. Instrument and Control Engrs., Transactions of Japan Soc. Mech. Engrs., Computer Aided Design. Mem. Japanese Soc. Mech. Engrs., Japan Soc. Precision Engring., Robotics Soc. Japan, Soc. Instrument and Control Engrs., Chinese Mech. Engring. Soc. (sr.). Office: Kyushu Sangyo U Dept Mech Eng, 2-3-1 Matsukadai Higashi-ku, Fukuoka 813-8503, Japan

QIU, JU-FENG, materials physicist, engineer, researcher; b. Zhangwu, Liaoning, China, Nov. 15, 1937; s. Gui Qiu and Shi Zhang; m. Ya-Ru Wang, May 16, 1972; children: Dong-Mei, Xiao-Mei. BSc, Northeastern U., Shenyang, China, 1963. Technician Baotou (China) Rsch. Inst. Rare Earths, Ministry Metall. Industry, 1963-79, engr., 1980-86, vice dir. phys. dept., 1984-91, sr. engr., 1986—, vice chief engr., 1994-97, vice dir. acad. com., 1994-97; vis. rschr. Inst. Metal Rsch., Acad. Scis. China, Shenyang, 1965-66; vis. fellow U. NSW, Sydney, 1991-93; cons. China Rare Earth Info. Ctr., Baotou, 1995—; editor of English, Editl. Office Jour. Chinese Rare Earths, Baotou, 1995—. Editor: (with others) Applications of Rare Earths in Iron and Steel, 1987; contbr. articles to sci. jours., including Acta Metallurgica Sinica, Jour. Chinese Rare Earths, Jour. Chinese Electron Microscopy Soc., Measurement Sci. and Tech., Materials Rsch. Bull., Materials Sci. and Engring. B, Jour. Magnetism and Magnetic Materials. Recipient state invention award State Sci. and Tech. Commn. China, 1990. Mem. AAAS (internat.), China Rare Earths Soc., China Soc. Metals. Avocations: learning foreign languages, reading newspapers and classical novels, walking, travel. Home: Neighborhood No 22-19-19, Gangtie St, Inner Magnolia, Baotou 014010, China Office: Baotou Rsch Inst Rare Earth, 129 Tuanjie St PO Box 131, I Mongla Baotou 014010, China

QIU, MING XIN, laser scientist; b. Huangyan, Zhejiang, China, Nov. 5, 1935; s. Xin-Hao Qiu and Hui-Nan Huang; m. Yue-Ming Feng; 1 child, Lili. Grad., Peking U., China, 1962; PhD equivalent, Beijing Inst. Electronics, 1967. Group leader Beijing Inst. Electron, China, 1967-75; group leader Shanghai Inst. Laser Tech., China, 1975-78, rsch. assoc., 1978-80, assoc. prof., 1980-86, prof., 1986—; invited prof. Ecole Poly. Fed. de Lausanne, Switzerland, 1982-83; postdoctoral fellow U. Calif., Davis, 1986-87; vis. prof. Victoria (Australia) U. Tech., 1990-91, U. Zaragoza, Spain, 1991-92, U. Autonoma de Barcelona, Spain, 1996-97, Pisa U., 1996, U. Politecnica Catalunya, Spain, 1999; prof. Kyushu Inst. Tech., Japan, 1997-99, 2000. Author 10 books on laser sci.; contbr. more than 150 articles to profl. jours. Recipient award of Sci. and Tech. Congress of China, 1978, 1st class award of sci. and tech. progress of Acad. of China, 1980, 2d class of progress award of Shanghai Govt., 1981; nominated candidate academician Acad. Sci. in China, 1995. Mem. Optical Soc. Am., Optical Soc. China, Shanghai Laser Soc. (bd. dirs.), Physics Soc. China. Avocations: painting, music. Address: Rm 304 #1 1131 Ln, Changle Rd, Shanghai 200031, China

QIU, SIGANG, telecommunications engineer; b. Jan. 5, 1965; came to the U.S., 1994; s. Jian Shui Qiu and Qin Xiang Xu; m. Feng Zhou, Feb. 19, 1994; 1 child, Waveley Qiu. MS, Qufu (China) Normal U., 1989, U. Conn., 1996; PhD, U. Vienna, Austria, 2000. Cert. engr. N.C. Tchg. asst. U. Conn., Storrs, 1994-97; engr. Cirrus Logic, Raleigh, N.C., 1997-99; sr. engr. Ambient Techs., Raleigh, 1999—; book referee Birkhauser Book Pub., Boston, 1997. Contbr. articles to profl. jours. Mem. IEEE (jour. referee Trans. on Signal Processing 1994—), Soc. Photo-Optical Instrumentation Engrs., Am. Math. Soc. Avocations: walking, basketball, hiking. E-mail: sigang@ieee.org. Office: Ambient Techs 110 Horizon Dr Raleigh NC 27615-4926

QIU, SUNQING, engineering educator; b. Zhouning, Fujiang, China, Oct. 28, 1965; s. Nairen and Demi (Ye) Q.; m. No Wei, Jan. 1, 1989; 1 child, Yu. BS, Fujiang Normal U., Fuzhou, China, 1985; MS, Chinese Acad. Scis., Changchun, China, 1988; PhD, Logistic Engring. Coll., Chongqing, China, 1999. Tchr. Logistic Engring. Coll., Chongqing, 1988-96; prof. S.W. Jiastong U., Chendu, China, 1999—. Inventor in field. Avocations: singing, swimming.

QIU, ZEYUAN, researcher, educator; b. Hubei, China, July 16, 1965; came to U.S., 1993; parents Jinmao Qiu and Shouxiang Liu; m. Mei Fu, June 25, 1993; children: Christina, Jeanna. BS, Ctrl. China Agrl. U., Wuhan, 1986; MS, People's U. China, Beijing, 1989; PhD, U. Mo., 1996. Lectr. People's U. of China, Beijing, 1989-93; rsch. asst. prof. U. Mo., Columbia, 1996—. Contbr. articles to profl. jours. Mem. Am. Agrl. Econs. Assn., Soil and Water Conservation Soc., So. Agrl. Econs. Assn. Office: U Mo 131A Mumford Hall Columbia MO 65211-6200

QU, BAO-KUI, education educator; b. Yixing, Jiangsu, China, Feb. 6, 1923; s. Gu-lan Sun, Mar. 1950; children: Yigu Qu, Erlan Qu, Hong Sun. BS, Fudan U., Shanghai, 1947. High-grade specialist cert. Asst. dept. edn. Fudan U., Shanghai, 1947-51; lectr. dept. edn. East China Normal U., 1953-79, asst. prof. dept. edn., 1980-85, prof. dept. edn., 1986—, advisor doctoral students, 1986—. Chief editor: (books) Anthology of Education, 1986-95 (Nat. Excellence award of Arts and Social Scis. 1995), Series of the Branches of Educational Sciences, 1993—, The Chinese Ency.: The Branches of Education, 1985; editor: Jour. East China Normal U., 1983-95. Recipient award for tchrs. Zeng Xianzi Ednl. Found., 1993, Govtl. Subvention for Specialist, Cen. Govt., 1992—. Mem. The Chinese Soc. of Edn. (v.p. 1992—), Nat. Study Assn. of Theoretical Periodicals on Edn. (chmn. 1995—), Nat. Assn. Edn. (vice-chmn. 1990—), Soc. of Edn. of Shanghai (hon. pres. 1996—). Avocations: reading works of philosophy, history and lit., watching modern drama. Office: Dept Edn, 3663 Zhongshan North Rd, 200062 Shanghai People's Republic of China

QU, CHENGYI, epidemiologist; b. Chengdu, China, Apr. 26, 1943; s. Lianjun and Dehua (Liu) O.; m. Suzhen Hao, Feb. 4, 1970; children: Lu, Hang. B of Biophys., Shanxi Med. Coll., Taiyuan, China, 1962, MD, 1966. Physician Hosp. Constrn. Workers, Changzhi, China, 1966-74; asst. epidemiology Shanxi Med. Coll., Taiyuan, China, 1974-83, lectr. epidemiology, 1983-88, assoc. prof. epidemiology, 1988-95, prof. epidemiology, 1995—; dir. Control Endemic Disease, Taiyuan, 1994—; cons. in field. Author: Test of Learning Aptitude for Deaf, 1994; inventor in field. JIDR-MENCAP fellow, Helsinki, 1996. Mem. Internat. Epidemiology Assn., Internat. Coun. Control Iodine Dificiency Disorders, Nat. Rehab. Assn. Learning Disablility. Avocations: table tennis, accordian. Office: Shanxi Med U, 86 Xinjiannan Lu, Taiyuan 030001, China

QU, HAILIN, hospitality and tourism professional; b. Shanghai, China, Nov. 8, 1951; s. Gengming Qu and Renai Zhuo; m. Weifen Fang, Nov. 22, 1982; 1 child, Yi. AA, Shanghai Inst. Tourism, 1981; cert. mgmt. and microcomputer sci., Shanghai Jiaotong U., 1984; BS, No. Ariz. U., 1987; MS, Purdue U., 1989, PhD, 1992. Lectr. Shanghai Inst. Tourism, 1981-86; asst. prof. Hong Kong Polytechnic U., 1992-96; assoc. prof. San Francisco State U., 1996-99; prof. Okla. State U., 1999—; William E. Davis disting. chair Okla. State U., Stillwater, 1999—; advisor URBIS Travers Morgan Ltd., Hong Kong, 1993-96; vis. fellow Hong Kong Poly. U., 1998, vis. chair prof., 2000—; vis. prof. Ecole Hoteliere, Lausanne, Switzerland, 1999. Editor: Pacific Tourism Rev., Australia, 1996 , Jour. Quality Assurance in Hospitality and Tourism Mgmt., 1999 , Jour. Travel and Tourism Mktg., 1999 , Jour. Tchg. in Travel and Tourism, 1999 ; contbg. author: Tourism and Economic Development in Asia and Australasia, 1997; reviewer Jour. Hospitality and Tourism Rsch.; contbr. articles to profl. jours. Keynote or invited spkr. Asia-Bound Travel Congress, Hong Kong, 1996, China Nat. Tourism Adminstrn. Shanghai, 1993, 95, Hong Kong Peihua Edn. Found., 1995. Hon. lectr. U. Hong Kong, 1996; hon. prof. Beijing Inst. Tourism, 1993, China Tourism Mgmt. Inst., Tianjing, 1993. Mem. CHRIE/Washington, China Tourism Assn., China Hotel Assn., Travel and Tourism Assn. Avocations: reading, travel, classical music, tennis. Office: Okla State U 210 Hes Stillwater OK 74078-6120

QU, PENG, engineer, researcher; b. Hong Kong, Apr. 15, 1963; s. Run Xu and Xian Feng (Jing) Q.; m. Li Ya Zhang Qu, July 22, 1987; 1 child, Fei. BS, Nan-Jing U., 1983, MS, Shanghai Fisheries U., 1990. Cert. engr. Rschr. Shanghai Rsch. Inst. Chem. Ind., 1983-87; dir. first rsch. sect. Shanghai Rsch. Inst. Food Sci., 1990—; dir. Rsch. project Preparation of Thrombin, Preparation of Polysaccrides. Office: Rsch Inst Food Sci, 513 E Wu-Zhong Rd, Shanghai 200233, Peoples Republic of China

QU, QIANG, surgeon; b. Beijing, Aug. 22, 1963; parents TianJin Qu and HongYi Liu; m. YongMei Qin, Dec. 23, 1991; 1 child, Mandi. Bachelor's degree, Beijing Med. U., 1987, MD, 1992; PhD, U. Turku, Finland, 1999. Surgeon U. Hosp. Beijing Med. U., 1987-92, Southampton (Eng.) Gen. Hosp., 1993-94; rsch. asst. U. Turku, 1994-99; surgeon Gen. Post Hosp., Beijing, 1999—. Contbr. rsch. articles to med. jours. Mem. Am. Soc. Bone and Mineral Rsch., European Calcified Tissue Soc. Avocations: bridge, boating. Fax: 86-10-64222727. E-mail: qiangqu@hotmail.com. Home: Liupukang 2-22-3-15, XiCheng Dist, Beijing 100011, China Office: U Turku Dept Anatomy, Kiinamyllynkatu 10, 20520 Turku Finland

QUAAL, WARD LOUIS, broadcast executive; b. Ishpeming, Mich., Apr. 7, 1919; s. Sigfred Emil and Alma Charlotte (Larson) Q.; m. Dorothy J. Graham, Mar. 9, 1944; children: Graham Ward, Jennifer Anne. A.B., U. Mich., 1941; LL.D. (hon.), Mundelein Coll., 1962, No. Mich. U., 1967; L Pub. Service, Elmhurst Coll., 1967; D.H.L. (hon.), Lincoln Coll., 1968, DePaul U., 1974. Announcer-writer Sta. WBEO (now sta. WDMJ), Marquette, Mich., 1936-37; announcer, writer, producer Sta. WJR, Detroit, 1937-41; spl. events announcer-producer WGN, Chgo., 1941-42, asst. to gen. mgr., 1945-49; exec. dir. Clear Channel Broadcasting Service, Washington, 1949-52, pres., chief exec. officer, 1964-74; v.p., asst. gen. mgr. Crosley Broadcasting Corp., Cin., 1952-56; v.p., gen. mgr., mem. bd. WGN Inc., Chgo., 1956; exec. v.p., then pres. WGN Continental Broadcasting Co. (now Tribune Broadcasting Co.), 1960-75; pres. Ward L. Quaal Co., 1975—; dir. Tribune Co., 1961-75; dir., mem. exec. com. U.S. Satellite Broadcasting Co., 1982-2000; bd. dirs. Christine Valmy Inc., Nat. Press Found., chmn. exec. com., dir. WLW Radio Inc., Cin., 1975-81; co-founder, dir. Universal Resources Inc., 1961-86; mem. FCC Adv. Com. on Advanced TV Sys., 1988-96. Author: (with others) Broadcast Management, 1968, rev. edit., 1979, new edit. 1997; co-prodr. (Broadway play) Teddy and Alice, 1988. Mem., Hoover Commn. Exec. Br. Task Force, 1949-59; mem. U.S.-Japan Cultural Exchange Commn., 1960-70; mem. Pres.'s Council Phys. Fitness and Sports, 1983-93; bd. dirs. Farm Found., 1963-73; bd. trustees Hollywood (Calif.) Mus., 1964-78, MacCormac Jr. Coll., Chgo., 1974-80; chmn. exec. com. Council for TV Devel., 1969-72; mem. bus. adv. coun. Chgo. Urban League, 1964-74; bd. dirs. Broadcasters Found., Internat. Radio and TV Found., Sears Roebuck Found., 1970-73; trustee Mundelein Coll., 1962-72, Hillsdale Coll., 1966-72. Served as lt. USNR, 1942-45. Recipient Disting. Bd. Gov.'s award Nat. Acad. TV Arts and Scis., 1966, 87, Freedoms Found. award, Valley Forge, 1966, 68, 70, Disting. Alumnus award U. Mich., 1967, Loyola U. Key, 1970, Advt. Man of Yr. Gold medallion, Chgo. Advt. Club, 1968, Disting. Svc. award Nat. Assn. Broadcasters, 1973, Ill. Broadcaster of Yr. award, 1973, Press Vet. of Yr. award, 1973, Comm. award of distinction Brandeis U., 1973, Founder & Leadership award Broadcast Pioneers Libr., 1991; first recipient Sterling Medal, Barren Found., 1985, Lifetime Achievement award in broadcasting Ill. Broadcasters Assn., 1989, Lifetime Achievement award WGN TV 50th Anniversary, 1998; 1st person named to Better Bus. Bur. Hall of Fame, Council of Better Bus. Burs. Inc., 1975; named Radio Man of Yr. Am. Coll. Radio, Arts, Crafts & Scis., 1961, Laureate in Order of Lincoln, Lincoln Acad. Ill., 1965, Communicator of Yr., Jewish United Fund, 1969, Advt. Club Man of Yr., 1973; named to Delta Tau Delta Disting. Svc. Chpt., 1970; named one of top 100 mems. of Delta Tau Delta who has attained the highest levels of nat. achievement during 20th century, 1999; named to Broadcasting Mag. Hall of Fame, 1991; named one of top 100 contbrs. to broadcasting and cable in 20th century, Broadcasting and Cable Mag., 1999. Mem. NATAS (bd. govs. 1966-76, Silver Circle award 1993), Nat. Press Found. (bd. dirs. 1991-99), Nat. Assn. Broadcasters (bd. dirs. 1952-56), Fed. Comm. Bar Assn., Broadcast Music Inc. (bd. dirs. 1953-70), Assn. Maximum Svc. Telecasters Inc. (bd. dirs. 1952-72), Broadcast Pioneers (pres., bd. dirs. 1962-73), Broadcast Pioneers Libr. (pres. 1981-84), Broadcast Pioneers Ednl. Fund Inc., Broadcasters Found. (chmn. bd. 1996-99). Office: Ward L Quaal Co 401 N Michigan Ave Ste 3140 Chicago IL 60611-5537

QUACK, MARTIN, physical chemistry educator; b. Darmstadt, Germany, July 22, 1948; m. Roswitha, May 24, 1977; children: Till, Niels, Manfred. Vordiplom, TH Darmstadt, Germany, 1969; Diplom, U. Göttingen, Germany, 1971; Dr ès sces techn, Ecole Poly. Federale, Lausanne, Switzerland, 1975. Privatdozent, prof. U. Göttingen, Germany, 1978-82; prof. U. Bonn, Germany, 1982-83; prof. ordinarius ETH Zürich, Switzerland, 1983—; Hinshelwood lectr., Christensen fellow St. Catherine's Coll., Oxford U., 1988; Mulliken lectr. U. Ga., Athens, 1995; Löwdin lectr. Uppsala U., 1996. Author: Molekulare Thermodynamik und Kinetik, 1986; editor Molecular physics, 1984-87; contbr. some 200 sci. articles to profl. jours. Recipient Nernst-Haber-Bodenstein prize, 1982, Otto Klung prize Free U. Berlin, 1984, Otto Bayer prize, 1991. Fellow Am. Phys. Soc.; mem. Deutsche Akademie der Naturforscher Leopoldina, Berlin Brandenburgische Akademie der Wissenschaften (formerly Purssian Acad. Scis.). Office: Lab Physikalische Chemie, ETH Zurich, CH-8092 Zurich Switzerland

QUADRAT, OTAKAR, research scientist; b. Prague, Czech Republic, Nov. 5, 1932; s. Otakar and Marie (Svobodová) Q.; m. Julie Křivinková, Sept. 18, 1958; children: Otakar, Petr. M of Engring., U. Chem. Tech., 1957; PhD, Inst. Macromolecular Chemistry, 1963; DSc, U. Chem. Tech., 1984. Analytical chemist Hosp. Bulovka, Prague, 1957-63; rsch. fellow Inst. of Macromolecular Chemistry, Acad. of Scis., Prague, 1963-75, chief rsch. fellow, 1975-97; head of dept. hydrodynamics Inst. of Macromolecular Chemistry, Acad. Scis., Czech Republic, 1990-97, sr. scientist phys. chemistry, 1998—. Avocations: driving a fast car, angling, concerts classical music, paint galleries. Home: Nad Šárkou 8, 160 00 Prague Czech Republic

QUADRIO, CURZIO ALBERTO, economics educator; b. Tirano, Sondrio, Italy, Dec. 25, 1937; m. Maria Luisa Bottasso, 1964. Degree polit. sci., Cath. U. Milan, 1961; PhD in Econs., 1968. Assoc. prof. econs. U. Caglari, 1965-68; assoc. prof. econs. U. Bologna, 1968-72, prof. econs., 1972-75, chmn. polit. sci., 1974-75; prof. econs. Cath. U. of Milan, 1976—, chmn. polit. sci., 1989—; dir. Ctr. of Econ. Analysis Cath. U. of Milan, 1977—; chmn. scientific com. Fondazione Cariplo Per la Picerca Scientific, Milan, 1991-95; dir. Review Economia Politca, Bologna, 1984—. Author: Noi, L'Economia e L'Europa, 1996; co-author: Risorse, Tecnologie, Rendita, 1996, Rent. Resources Technologies, 1999; co-editor, author: Innovation, Resources and Economic Growth, 1994. Recipient St. Vincent award, 1984, Cortina Ulisse award, 1997. Mem. Accademia Nazionale dei Lincei, Istituto Lombardo, Accademia di Scienze e Lettere, Royal Econ. Soc. Roman Catholic. Avocation: skiing. Office: U Cattouca, Largo Gemelli 1, 20123 Milan Italy

QUAINTANCE, ALICE LYNN, elementary school media specialist; b. Morristown, Tenn., July 20, 1958; d. Celton D. and Mary Lou (Scott) VanCleave; m. David Scott Quaintance, Aug. 2, 1980; children: Jennifer Lee, Allison Marie. BS, East Tenn. State U., 1980. Media specialist Surgoinsville (Tenn.) Elem. Sch., 1980-82; media specialist Clearwood Jr. H.S., Slidell, La., 1982-83, 84-86, tchr., 1983-84; media specialist Rose Park Mid. Sch., Nashville, 1987-88, Hermitage (Tenn.) Elem. Sch., 1988—; owner Just Acquaintances. Publicity chairperson Donelson/Hermitage (Tenn.) Neighborhood Assn., 1995-97; parent rep. Nashville Ballet Friends, 1997-99. Recipient Dalcon Arts in Schs. award Nashville Inst. for the Arts, 1992, Merit award Gov. Tenn., 1993, Acts of Excellence award Mayor of Nashville, 1994, Golden Apple award Metro Nashville Pub. Schs., 1996, Vol. of Yr. award Nashville Ballet, 1998. Mem. NEA, Tenn. Edn. Assn., Met. Nashville Edn. Assn., Delta Kappa Gamma (sec. 1993-97). United Methodist. Avocation: the Arts. Home: 3826 Pacifica Dr Hermitage TN 37076-1926

QUAINTON, ANTHONY CECIL EDEN, diplomat; b. Seattle, Apr. 4, 1934; s. Cecil Eden and Marjorie Josephine (Oates) Q.; m. Susan Long, Aug. 7, 1958; children: Katherine, Eden, Elizabeth. BA, Princeton U., 1955; BLitt, Oxford (Eng.) U., 1958. Research fellow St. Antony's Coll., Oxford, 1958-59; with Fgn. Service, State Dept., 1959-97; vice consul Sydney, Australia, 1960-62; Urdu lang. trainee, 1962-63; 2d sec., econ. officer Am. embassy, Karachi, Pakistan, 1963-64, Rawalpindi, Pakistan, 1964-66; 2d sec., polit. officer Am. embassy, New Delhi, 1966-69; sr. polit. officer for India Dept. State, Washington, 1969-72; 1st sec. Am. embassy, Paris, 1972-73; counselor, dep. chief mission Am. embassy, Kathmandu, Nepal, 1973-76; ambassador to Central African Empire, Bangui, 1976-78, Nicaragua, Managua, 1982-84, Kuwait, 1984-87; dir. Office for Combatting Terrorism, Dept. State, Washington, 1978-81; dep. insp. gen. Dept. State, 1987-89; ambassador Peru, 1989-92; asst. sec. of state for diplomatic security Dept. State, Washington, 1992-95, dir. gen. fgn. svc., 1995-97; exec. dir. Una Chapman Cox Found., 1998-99; vis. lectr. Princeton U., 1998-99; pres., CEO Nat. Policy Assn., 1999—; mem. internat. policy com. U.S. Cath. Conf.; mem. adv. com. Inst. L.Am. Studies, Columbia U. V.p. Washington Lions Found.; v.p. Pub. Diplomacy Found.; adv. coun. Inst. of Latin Am. Studies Columbia U. English Speaking Union fellow, 1951-52; Marshall scholar, 1955-58; recipient Rivkin award, 1972, Herter award, 1984, Disting. Honor award Dept. State, 1997. Mem. Am. Acad. Diplomacy, Coun. on Fgn. Rels., Am. Fgn. Svc. Assn., Lions Internat., Met. Club, Phi Beta Kappa. Home: 3424 Porter St NW Washington DC 20016-3126 Office: 1424 16th St NW Ste 700 Washington DC 20036-2240

QUALE, ANDREW CHRISTOPHER, JR., lawyer; b. Boston, July 7, 1942; s. Andrew Christopher and Luella (Meland) Q.; m. Sally Sterling Ellis, Oct. 15, 1977; children: Andrew, Addison. BA magna cum laude, Harvard U., 1963, LLB cum laude, 1966; postgrad., Cambridge (Eng.) U., 1966-67. Bar: Mass. 1967, N.Y. 1971. Fellow Internat. Legal Ctr., Bogota, Colombia, 1967-68; cons. Republic of Colombia, Bogota, 1968-69; assoc. Cleary, Gottlieb, Steen and Hamilton, N.Y.C., 1969-75; ptnr. Coudert Brothers, N.Y.C., 1975-82, Sidley & Austin, N.Y.C., 1982—; adj. prof. Sch. of Law U. Va., Charlottesville, 1976-88; cons. privatizations World Bank, UN, Harvard Inst. Internat. Devel., 1982—. Contbr. to profl. publs. Pres. Bronxville (N.Y.) Sch. Bd., 1991-93; founder, bd. dirs. Bronxville Sch. Found., 1991-95, 96—; bd. dirs. Coun. The Ams. Mem. ABA, Assn. Bar City N.Y. (chmn. Inter-Am. affairs com. 1982-85), N.Y. State Bar Assn., Colombian-Am. Assn. (v.p., bd. dirs.), Bronxville Field Club, Norfolk (Conn.) Country Club, Doolittle Lake Co. (Norfolk, bd. dirs.). Office: Sidley & Austin 875 3rd Ave Fl 14 New York NY 10022-6293

QUANDOUR, MOHYDEEN IZZAT, financial consultant, author; b. Amman, Jordan, Mar. 6, 1938; s. Izzat Hassan Quandour and Zakia Kassim Shid; m. Diana M. Beauregard, July 16, 1961; 1 child, Inal; m. Raghda Moh'dnur Hassan, June 19, 1981 (div. 1995); children: Murad, Natasha; m. Luba Balagova, Nov. 13, 1998. BA, Earlham Coll., 1960; MA, Claremont Grad. Sch., 1961; PhD, Claremont Univ. Ctr., 1962. Account exec. J. Walter Thompson Co., N.Y.C., 1962-64; product mgr. Bristol Myers Co., N.Y.C., 1964-66; area mgr. Africa-Mid. East Bristol Myers Group Internat., Rome, 1966-70; film prodr., dir. Cintel Prodns., Hollywood, Calif., 1970-73; internat. dir., ptnr. Mktg. & Fin. Cons. Inc., L.A., 1973-76, Photo-Scan Ltd., Ruislip, Eng., 1976-80; pres. Mafcon Internat., London, 1981-88; pres., chmn. bd. Mktg. & Fin. Cons., London, 1988-92; chmn. Kafkas Inkombank, Russia, 1992—; cons. Inkombank, Moscow, 1994—, Mitsui Bank Corp., Tokyo, 1996—. Author 8 hist. novels to date incl. The Kavkas Trilogy, 1992, others; songwriter, classical music composer including Balagova's Requim, 1999. Mem. Internat. Equestrian Fedn., Lausanne, Switzerland, 1994, judge show jumping, 1995; mem. Arab Equestrian Fedn., Doha, Qatar, 1994-96; v.p. Royal Jordanian Equestrian Fedn., Amman, 1994-96. Mem. Internat. Advt. Assn., Am. Mktg. Inst., Internat. Bus. Club. Avocations: classical music, horseback riding. Home and Office: PO Box 404 Khilda, 118-21 Amman Jordan

QUANN, JOAN LOUISE, French language educator, real estate broker; b. Phila., Oct. 14, 1935; d. John Joseph and Pauline Cecelia (Karpink) Q. Diploma, U. Paris, 1963; BA in French, U. Pa., 1976; grad., Temple U. Real Estate Inst., 1988; MEd, Temple U, 1994. Lic. real estate broker. Exec. sec. to chief fgn. corr. Newsweek, Inc., Paris, 1964-70; internat. editorial asst. Newsweek, Inc., N.Y.C., 1971-73; exec. sec., adminstrv. asst. Richard I. Rubin & Co., Inc., Phila., 1977-91; tchr. French and English to speakers of other langs. The Sch. Dist. of Phila., Bd. Edn., 1991—. Judge of elections City of Phila., 1977-81. Mem. AAUW (2d v.p. membership 1985-87, bd. dirs., corr. sec. 1987-91, fin. com. 1993), Alliance Francaise, La Societe Francophone Arts et Loisirs (bd. dirs. 1988—), Am. Coun. on Tchg. of Fgn. Langs., Pa. Acad. Fine Arts, MLA of Phila. and Vicinity, Phila. Mus. Art (Asian adv. group 2000). Republican. Roman Catholic. Avocations: art history, reading, swimming, travel. Office: Sch Dist of Phila Bd Edn 21st St S Of The Pky S Philadelphia PA 19103

QUANN, MEGAN, Olympic athlete; b. Tacoma, Wash., Jan. 15, 1984. Recipient Gold medal 100-meter breaststroke, 4 x 100-meter medley (team) Sydney Olympics, 2000, Silver medal 100-meter breaststroke Pan Pacific Championships, 1999; set Am. record for 100-meter breaststroke U.S. Open Swimming Championships, San Antonio, 1999; winner 100-meter breaststroke title U.S. Spring Nats., 1998, 99. Office: USA Swimming 1 Olympic Plz Colorado Springs CO 80909-5746*

QUANT, HAROLD EDWARD, retired financial services company executive, ranc; b. Aug. 21, 1948; s. Harold Atwell and Dorothy Ann Quant; m. Michelle Bumpers, June 27, 1982; children: Andrew, Angela, Emily. BSBA, San Jose State U., 1976. Account exec. Dun & Bradstreet, San Jose, Calif., 1970-81; pres. Telecredit Collection Svcs., Inc., L.A., 1981-85; v.p. FCA, Arlington, Tex., 1986-90; pres., CEO Creditwatch, Inc., Arlington, 1990-2000, chmn. bd. dirs.; ret., 2000. Sgt. USMC, 1965-70, Vietnam. Decorated Bronze Star, Purple Heart. Mem. City Club. Republican. Mem. United Ch. of God. Avocation: horses.

QUANT, MARY, fashion and cosmetics company executive, designer; b. London, Feb. 11, 1934; d. Jack and Mildred Quant; m. Alexander Plunket Greene, 1957; 1 son. Ed., Goldsmiths Coll. Art, London; hon. degree, Winchester Sch. Art, 2000. Began career in Chelsea London, 1954; co-chmn. Mary Quant Ltd., 1955—; mem. Design Coun., 1971-74; mem. U.K.-U.S.A. Bicentennial Liaison Com., 1973—; mem. adv. coun. Victoria and Albert Mus., 1976-78, dir., Mary Quant Grp. Companies, 1955—, appointed non-exec. dir., House of Fraser, 1997. Retrospective exhbn. of 60's fashion London Mus., 1974. Decorated Order Brit. Empire; recipient Internat. Fashion award Sunday Times, Rex award (U.S.), Piavolo d'Oro (Italy), Hall of Fame award for Outstanding Contbn. to Brit. Fashion, Brit. Fashion Coun., 1969, Award of Brit. Fashion Coun. for Contbn. to Brit. Fashion Industry, 1990; named Royal Designer for Industry, Hon. fellow Goldsmiths U., 1993; sr. fellow Royal Coll. Art, 1991. Fellow Soc. Indsl. Artists and Designers (Ann. Design medal), Royal Soc. for Arts (hon.). Office: Mary Quant Ltd, 3 Ives St, London SW3 2NE, England*

QUARCOO, EMMANUEL AUULEY, language educator, researcher; b. Accra, Ghana, July 1, 1945; s. Onyame Kwaku and Naomi Nartey; m. Emma Baaba Parker-Bennin, Jan. 1988; children: Larteley, Teokor, Nii. BA, U. Ghana, Legon, 1969; MEd, U. Ibadan, Nigeria, 1979; PhD, U. Jos, Nigeria, 1989. Tchr. Mfantsiman Sch., Ghana, 1969-74; rsch. officer Exams Coun., Ghana, 1974-77, sr. asst. registrar, 1978-81, prin. asst. registrar, 1982; lectr. U. Jos, Nigeria, 1982-90, U. Ghana, 1991—. Mem. N.Y. Acad. Scis., Poetics & Linguistics Assn. Avocations: swimming, boxing. Home: PO Box C2054, Accra Ghana Office: U Ghana, Box 129, Legon Ghana

QUARG, GUNTER, librarian; b. Friedberg, Hessen, Germany, Feb. 5, 1943; s. Walter Hermann and Ilse Martha (Sior) Q. Diploma, Tech. U., Darmstadt, Germany, 1969; Doctorate in Chemistry, Deutsches Kunststoff-Inst., Darmstadt, 1972; Libr. for Higher Svc., Bibliothekar-Lehrinstitut, Cologne, Germany, 1975. Asst. Eduard-Zintl-Inst., Darmstadt, 1967-68; postdoctoral fellow Deutsches Kunststoff-Inst., Darmstadt, 1972-73; Candidate for higher libr. svc. U. Libr., Karlsruhe, Germany, 1973-74; libr. for the higher svc. U. and Mpcl. Libr. of Cologne, 1975—; leader Spl. Libr. for Chemistry, U. Cologne, 1975—; libr. for the scis. U. Libr., 1975—. Author numerous publs. including: (books) Naturgeschichte und Naturwissenschaften an der alten Koelner Universitaet, 1996, Deutsche Buchkunst im 20. Jahrhundert, 1995; contbr. articles to profl. jours. Mem. Bibli.-Gesellschaft Koeln, N.Y. Acad. Scis. Avocations: numismatics, musicology, history of the scis. Office: Univ & Stadtbibliothek Koeln, Universitaetsstrasse 33, N Rhine Cologne D-50931, Germany

QUARTA, ROBERTO, manufacturing company executive; b. May 10, 1949; two children. BA, Coll. Holy Cross. Mgmt. trainee David Gessner, 1971-73; mgr. purchasing and prodn. control Worcester Controls Corp., 1973-78, v.p. internat. procurement, 1979-85; mfg. dir., mng. dir., group mgr., CEO Hitchener Mfg. Corp., 1985-89; chief divsnl. exec. BTR, 1989-93; dir., group chief exec. BBA Group, 1993—. Avocations: tennis, music. Office: BBA Group PLC, 70 Fleet St, London EC4Y 1EU, England*

QUASEM, MUHAMMAD ABUL, philosophy educator; b. Ghatla, Noakhali, Bangladesh, Mar. 2, 1940; s. Muhammad Abdul Karim and Musammat Amirunnesa; m. Quazi Quamrunnesa, Apr. 18. 1976; children: Hafsa, Muhammad Shuayb, Muhammad Ibrahim, Muhammad Yusuf, Afra. SSC in Islamic Studies, Ghatla (Bangladesh) Madrasa, 1950; HSC in Islamic Studies, Chwmohani (Bangladesh) Madrasa, 1954; BA in Islamic Studies, Islamiya Madrasa, Noakhali, Bangladesh, 1956; MA in Islamic Studies, Alia Madrasa, Dhaka, Bangladesh, 1958; SSC in Humanities, Dhaka Bd., 1961; HSC in Humanities, Comilla Bd., 1963; BA in Philosophy with honors, U. Dhaka, 1966, MA in Philosophy, 1968; PhD in Islamic Philosophy, U. Edinburgh, Scotland, 1973. Lectr. in philosophy Victoria Coll., Comilla, Bangladesh, 1968; lectr. in philosophy U. Dhaka, 1968, prof. philosophy, 1986—, chmn. dept. philosophy, 1988-91; sr. lectr. in philosophy U. Rajshahi, Bangladesh, 1969; lectr. in philosophy Nat. U. Malaysia, Bangi, 1973-76, assoc. prof. philosophy, 1976-81; assoc. prof. philosophy, chmn. dept. J. Nagar U., Savar, Dhaka, 1985-86; dir. devel. ctr. for philos. studies U. Dhaka, 1994-97; dir. Islamic Found. Bangladesh, 1983-85; founder, dir. of Sch. at BeriBand, Muhammadpur, Dhaka, 1999—. Author: The Ethics of al-Ghazali, 1978, Al-Ghazali on Islamic Guidance, 1979, The Recitation and Interpretation of the Qur'an, 1982, Salvation of the Soul and Islamic Devotions, 1983, The Jewels of the Qur'an, 1983; mem. editl. bd. Bengali Ency. of Islam, Islamic Found. Bangladesh, Sirat Ency., Islamic Found. Bangladesh, Dhaka University Studies, 1997-99, Philosophy and Progress, Dhaka U., 1994-97, Darshan wa Progoti, Dhaka U., 1994-97; contbr. papers to profl. pubs. Commonwealth scholar Assn. Commonwealth Univs., 1969-73, scholar U. Dhaka, 1966-67, 1st Grade Talent scholar and gold medal H.S.C. Edn. Bd.,

1963-66, Bangladesh Madrasa Edn. Bd., 1950-58. Mem. Am. Philos. Assn. (hon., internat. assoc.), Bangladesh Philos. Soc., Dhaka U. Tchrs. Assn., Asiatic Soc. of Bangladesh, B.M. Sufi Soc. Islam. Avocations: study of writings on religions, saints and sufis, visiting places of artistic and architectural importance. Home: Dhaka U Campus, House No 64-A, Dhaka 1000, Bangladesh Office: U Dhaka, Dept Philosophy Faculty Art, Dhaka 1000, Bangladesh

QUATREHOMME, GERALD, pathologist, researcher; b. France, June 20, 1955. MD, Reims, France, 1979; internat. degree, Nice, France, 1984; PhD in Forensic Pathology, Bordeaux, France, 2000. Cert. forensic pathologist. Forensic physician, 1982, neurologist, 1985, expert by the cts., 1986, pharmacokinetics, 1987, forensic pathologist, 1991, dir. rsch. habilitation, 1995; prof. forensic pathology U. Nice, France, 1998—; head dept. forensic pathology U. Nice. Contbr. articles to internat. profl. jours. Fax: 33-492-03-81-48. E-mail: gquatreh@unice.fr. Office: Univ Nice Fac Medicine, Ave de Valombrose, F-06107 Nice Cedex 2, France

QUAY, THOMAS EMERY, lawyer; b. Cleve., Apr. 3, 1934; s. Harold Emery and Esther Ann (Thomas) Q.; divorced; children: Martha Wyndham, Glynis Cobb, Eliza Emery; m. Winnifred B. Cutler, May 13, 1989. A.B. in Humanities magna cum laude (Univ. scholar), Princeton U., 1956; LLB (Univ. scholar), U. Pa., 1963. Bar: Pa. 1964. Assoc. Pepper, Hamilton & Scheetz, Phila., 1963-65; with William H. Rorer, Inc., Ft. Washington, Pa., 1965—; sec., counsel William H. Rorer, Inc., 1974-79, v.p., gen. counsel, sec., 1979-88; v.p. legal planning and adminstrn. Rorer Group, 1988-90; counsel Reed Smith Shaw and McClay, Phila., 1991-93; v.p., gen. counsel Athena Inst., Chester Springs, Pa., 1993—. Bd. dirs. Main Line YMCA, Ardmore, Pa., 1971-73, chmn. bd., 1972-73; editor 10th Reunion Book Princeton Class of 1956, 1966, 25th Reunion Book, 1981—, class sec., 1966-71, class v.p., 1971-81, pres., 1981-86. Lt. (j.g.) USNR, 1957-60. Recipient Svc. Commendation Main Line YMCA, 1973. Mem. ABA, Pa. Bar Assn., Phila. Bar Assn., Pharm. Mfrs. Assn. (chmn. law sect. 1983), Pa. Biotech. Assn. (chmn. legis. com., mem. exec. com. 1991-93), Phila. Drug Exch. (chmn. legis. com. 1975-78), Cannon Club of Princeton U., Sharswood Law Club of U. Pa., Princeton Club of Phila. Democrat. Presbyterian. Office: 601 Swedesford Rd Ste 201 Malvern PA 19355-1573

QUAYE, SAMUEL WILKINSON, manufacturing executive; b. Tema, Ghana, Jan. 19, 1963; s. Mary Amoah. Diploma, Sotech, Somanya, Ghana, 1982. Tchr. Anada Maga, Bankok, Thailand, 1985-87; researcher Tex. Internat., 1977-88; pertain Metal & Rubber Internat., Taipei, Taiwan, 1988—; rep. Polytex, Taipei, Taiwan, 1989-93; tchr. Redmen, Taipei, 1987-91; pertain Lodical, Calif., 1987-90; researcher Jofca, Taipei, 1986-90; dir. ops. SFIAC, ANKOBRA, 1997, Pertain Dansamik Enterprise, 1997; founder SWIQUE Enterprise, 1998; coord. Amuse Ltd., 1999, George & Sam Procurement Agy., Thailand, 2000. Mem. St. Paul's Methodist Men's Fellowship Tema. Mem. Oxford Club. E-mail: swquaye@jancc.africeonline.com.gh. Home: PO Box OS277, OSU Accra Ghana

QUAYLE, DAN (JAMES DANFORTH QUAYLE), former vice president United States, entrepreneur; b. Indpls., Feb. 4, 1947; s. James C. and Corinne (Pulliam) Q.; m. Marilyn Tucker, Nov. 18, 1972; children: Tucker Danforth, Benjamin Eugene, Mary Corinne. BS in Polit. Sci., DePauw U., Greencastle, Ind., 1969; JD, Ind. U., 1974. Bar: Ind. 1974. Ct. reporter, pressman Huntington (Ind.) Herald-Press, 1965-69, assoc. pub., gen. mgr., 1974-76; with consumer protection divn. Office Atty. Gen., State of Ind., 1970-71; adminstrv. asst. to gov. State of Ind., 1971-73; dir. Ind. Inheritance Tax Div., 1973-74; tchr. bus. law Huntington Coll., 1975; mem. 95th-96th Congresses from 4th Dist. Ind., Washington; U.S. Senator from Ind. U.S. Senate, Washington, 1981-89; V.P. of U.S. Washington, 1989-93; founder J.D. Quayle & Co., 2000; author, speaker, corp. bds.; disting. vis. prof. Am. Grad. Sch. Internat. Mgmt., 1997-99. Author: Standing Firm, 1994, The American Family, 1996, Worth Fighting For, 1999. Chmn. Campaign Am., 1995-99. With Ind. Army N.G., 1970-76. Mem. Huntington Bar Assn., Hoosier State Press Assn., Huntington C. of C. Club: Rotary. Office: 2425 E Camelback Rd Ste 1080 Phoenix AZ 85016

QUAYLE, JULIETA M. DE BARROS REIS, clinical psychologist; b. Santos, Brazil, May 18, 1952; d. Sylvio de Barros Reis and Maria Nelly Faria de Barros Reis; m. John Young Quayle, III, Feb. 17, 1978; 1 child, Carolina. Grad., Cath. U. Sao Paulo, 1975, M in Clin. Psychology, 1985, PhD, 1991. Pvt. practice clin. psychology Sao Paulo, 1976—; clin. psychologist Psychiat. Inst. Hosp. Sao Paulo State, 1978-79, chief psychologist, 1979-83, dir. psychology svc., 1983-85, tech. asst. bd. dirs., 1985-87; psychologist obstetric dept. Clin. Hosp. Sao Paulo, 1987-98, rsch. dir. psychology, 1998—. Co-editor: Psychosomatic Obstetrics, 1997; contbr. articles to profl. jours. Mem. APA. Avocations: horses, writing, reading, painting.

QUE, PETER D., JR., banking executive, consultant; b. Manila, Oct. 13, 1956; s. Pei Chan Que and Bee Ley Dy. BSEE, Mapua Inst. Technology, Manila, 1982; M of Computer Sci., Ruhr U., Bochum, Germany, 1986. Technician Computer Lab., Mapua Inst. Technology, 1982-85, programmer, 1983-85, instr., 1984-89, systems analyst, 1986—, cons., 1989—; head network engring. Rizal Comml. Banking Corp., 1989-93, asst. to head divsn. info. tech., 1994-2000, securities cons., 2000; mem. screening com. 2d nat. search for product excellence in info. tech., dept. sci. and tech. and info. tech. Found. of the Philippines, 1998, 3d nat. search, 2000; chmn., CEO Primar Holdings, Inc., Philippines, 1999—; mem. screening com. Third Nat. Search for Product Excellence in Info. Tech., Dept. Sci. and Tech. and Info. Tech. Found. of the Phlippines, 2000; mem. quality assurance team on higher edn. Nat. Capital Region Philippines, 1999-2000. Author publs. Vol. Lighthouse BBS, The Philippines; fire fighter So. Manila Vol. Fire Brigade, 1992-95, dir., 1995—; chmn. telecomm. Philippine Share Guide, Makati, 1992-94; logistics secretariat S.E. Asian Regional Computer Confedn., Makati, 1990; mem. Philippine Share Guide, 1992-98; dir., founder Que Family Found., Manila, 1997. Mem. Philippine Computer Soc. (bd. dirs. 1993-95, 2000, internal auditor 1997-98, treasurer, 1999—, Presdl. award of merit, 1994-95, 99-2000). Avocations: golf, animals, technology. Home: 9 Gov Pascual Ave, Bo Potrero, Malabon MM 1400, The Philippines Office: Rizal Comml Banking Corp, 333 Sen Gil Puyat, Makati MM 1200, The Philippines

QUE, WEN XIU, engineer, researcher; b. Yongding, Fujian, Peoples Republic of China, Sept. 18, 1963; s. Que De Hu and Lai Bao (Ying) X.; m. Ma Xiao Ye, May 21, 1992; 1 child. B degree, No. Jiaotong U., Beijing, 1986, M degree, 1991; PhD, Xi'an Jiaotong U., 1995. Asst. engr. Beijing Heavy Machine Plant, 1986-88; rsch. asst. No. Jiaotong U., Beijing, 1988-90, Beijing Info. Engring. Inst., 1990-92, Tsinghua U., 1992-95; rsch. fellow Xi'An Jiaotong U., 1995-96; postdoctoral fellow Nat. U. Singapore, 1996-98; rsch. fellow Nanyang Technol. U., Singapore, 1998—. Contbr. articles to profl. jours. including Applied Physics Letters, Jour. Materials Rsch., Sci. in China, Jour. of Am. Ceramic Soc., Japanese Jour. Applied Physics. Recipient Devel. Scholarships in the 21st Century of China Student in Univ., Chinese Govt., 1995, Bao Steel Edn. Fund Scholarship of China, 1994, Excellence Grad. and PhD Student, Shaan Xi Province Govt., 1995. Avocations: reading, bridge, music. Office: Nanyang Technol U Elec Eng, Block S1 Photonics Lab, Nanyang Ave 639798, Singapore

QUEEN, DANIEL, acoustical engineer, consultant; b. Boston, Feb. 15, 1934; s. Simon and Ida (Droker) Q.; 1 child, Aaron Jacob. Student, U. Chgo., 1951-54. Quality control mgr. Magnacord, Inc., Chgo., 1955-57; project engr. Revere Camera Co., Chgo., 1957-62; dir. engring. for Amplivox products Perma Power Co., Chgo., 1962-70; prin. engr. Daniel Queen Assocs., Chgo., 1970—; pres. Daniel Queen Labs., Inc., Chgo., 1980—; chmn. Am. Nat. Standards Subcom. PH7-6, 1969-84, mem. com. PH-7; mem. standards com. P8-5 Electronic Industries Assn., 1967-82. Contbr. editor Sound and Communications, 1973—; patentee in field; contbr. papers to profl. jours., also articles to trade and popular jours.; editorial bd. Jour. Audio Engring. Soc., 1978—. Bd. dirs. The Working Theatre. Recipient Technical Emmy award TV Acad. Arts and Scis., 1995. Fellow Audio Engring. Soc. (stds. mgr. 1980—, chmn. tech. coun. 1985-96); mem. IEEE (sr.), ASTM, AAAS, Am. Nat. Stds. Inst. (sec. com. S4 on audio engring.), Acoustical Soc. Am. (chmn. Chgo. regional chpt. 1976-78, mem. engring. acoustics com. 1974-97), Midwest Acoustics Conf. (pres. 1971-72), Chgo. Acoustical/Audio Group (pres. 1969-70), Assn. Ednl. Comms. and Tech., Soc. Motion Picture and TV Engrs. (audio rec./reprodn. com.), Am. Pub. Health Assn., Nat. Coun. Acoustical Cons., Inst. Noise Control Engring. Office: 239 W 23rd St New York NY 10011-2398

QUEEN, NATHANIEL FRANCIS, JR., financial executive, consultant; b. N.Y.C., Feb. 1, 1955; arrived in Eng., 1990; s. Nathaniel Francis and River Lee (McQuitter) Q. BA, Harvard U., 1977. Asst. sec. Chem. Bank, N.Y.C., 1969-79, 1979-81; dir. devel. Nat. Action Coun. for Minorities in Engring., N.Y.C., 1982-86; dir. corp. affairs, non-govtl. del. to UN CARE, N.Y.C., 1986-89; dir. internat. fin. Aquaculture Techs. Ltd., N.Y.C., 1989-90; sr. v.p. T. Barile & Assocs., N.Y.C., 1989-90; sr. mng. dir. T. Barile & Assocs., London, 1990—; bd. dirs. Kingman Films Internat., Dir.-Vive Ltd., Non-Stop Entertainment Co. Chmn., bd. dirs. East Harlem Coll. and Career Counseling Program, N.Y.C., 1985-91; co-chmn. London (Prince of Wales Dist.) St. John Ambulance, Eng., 1987-97; sr. vice chmn. Jr. League of Friends-Royal Marsden Hosp., London, 1996-2000, chmn., 2000—; mem. European steering cm. The Lawrenceville Leadership Campaign, 1993; class sec. The Lawrenceville Sch., 1975—. Named Officer, Most Venerable Order of St. John of Jerusalem (Eng.), 1995. Mem. Harvard Club of London (schs. and scholarship coms. 1995—). Episcopalian.

QUEGAN, SHAUN, mathematician; b. Bolton, England, Apr. 8, 1949; s. Robert and Vedon (Anthony) Q.; m. Susan Margaret Dwyer, Dec. 29, 1976; children: Liam John, Thomas Andrew. BA, U. Warwick, 1970, MSc, 1972; PhD, U. Sheffield, 1982. Tchr. Spinkhill Coll., Eng., 1972-73, Oulder Hill Sch., Rochdale, Eng., 1973-75; head math. dept. Hinde House Sch., Sheffield, Eng., 1975-78; rsch. asst. U. Sheffield, 1980-82; rsch. scientist, group chief Marconi Rsch. Ctr., Chelmsford, Eng., 1982-86; lectr., prof. U. Sheffield, 1986—; dir. Sheffield Ctr. for Earth Obs. Sci., 1993—. Author: Understanding Radar Sys., 1992, Understanding Synthetic Aperture Radar Images, 1998. Mem. IEEE, Remote Sensing Soc. Office: U Sheffield, SCEOS, Hicks Bldg, Hounsfield Rd, Sheffield S3 7RH, England

QUELLA, JAMES ANDREW, management consultant; b. Chgo., Feb. 3, 1950; s. Andrew Sylvester and Mary (Failla) Q.; children: Lindsay V., James S. BA, U. Wis., 1975; MBA, U. Chgo., 1981. Sales dir. Textron, Inc., Dallas, 1975-79; v.p. Strategic Planning Assocs., Washington, 1981-90; vice chmn. Mercer Mgmt. Consulting, N.Y.C., 1990-2000; bd. dirs. Mercer Mgmt. Consulting, 2000—; mng. dir./sr. op. ptnr. DLJ Merchant Banking Ptnrs., 2000—; bd. dirs. Merrill Corp. Co-author: Profit Patterns, 1999; contbr. articles to profl. jours. Vol./contbr. Hale House, N.Y.C., 1996—. Avocations: golf, skiing, biking, art collection, basketball. E-mail: QuellaJ@aol.com. Home: 22 W 66th St # 12 New York NY 10023-6202 Office: DLJ Merchant Banking Ptnrs 277 Park Ave Fl 7 New York NY 10172-3400

QUELLMALZ, HENRY, printing company executive; b. Balt., May 18, 1915; s. Frederick and Edith Margaret (Shaw) Q.; m. Marion Agar Lynch, Aug. 2, 1940; children: Lynn Quellmalz Johnson, Susan Quellmalz Mastan, Jane Quellmalz Carey. . BA with high honors, Princeton U., 1937. Pres. Princeton Advt. Agy., 1936-37; dir. pers. Macy's Men's Store, 1938-40; asst. mgr. Fowlers Dept. Store, Glens Falls, N.Y., 1940-41; pers. dir. U.S. Army Post Exchs., Ft. Meade, Md., 1941-44; with Boyd Printing Co., Albany, N.Y., 1944—, pres., 1952-84, chmn. bd., 1984—; v.p. Q Corp. U.S.; agt. for WHO publs., 1965—. Campaign chmn. ARC, Albany, 1956, 57; bd. govs. Doane Stuart Sch., Albany, 1977-79, treas. bd., 1977-78; vice chmn. Family Svc. Assn. Am. Salute to Families, 1979—, Nat. UN Day com., 1980-82; mem. adv. bd. Ind. Coll. Fund of N.Y., 1971-91, corp. trustees, 1992—; bd. dirs. Am. Assn. World Health, 1977-82, Combined Health Appeal of Capitol Dist., Inc., 1984, Camelot Home for Boys, 1975; trustee St. Peter's Hosp. Found., Albany, 1982—, asst. sec., 1987-89, chmn. bd. dirs., 1989-91. With AUS, 1943. Recipient Pres.'s award Am. Assn. Mental Deficiency, 1976; 25 Yrs. Svc. award N.Y. State Bar Assn., 1983, 34 Yrs. Svc. Award Am. Sociol. Assn., 1985. Mem. Albany Area C. of C., Printing Industry Am. Assn. East Ctrl. N.Y. (pres. 1958), Ft. Orange Club, Hudson Mohawk Assn. of Colls. and Univs. (Spl. award for svcs. 1995, Sr. Svcs. of Albany 3rd Age Achievement award for Bus. 1996). Democrat. Episcopalian. Home: 1 Park Hill Dr Apt 6 Menands NY 12204-2142 Office: 49 Sheridan Ave Albany NY 12210-2735

QUENEAU, PAUL BLAISDELL, metallurgical engineer, educator; b. Rochester, N.Y., Mar. 17, 1941; s. Paul E. and Joan O. Q.; m. Jean M. Brekke, Sept. 5, 1966; children: Renée, Shelly, Paul. BS in Metallurg. Engring., Cornell U., 1964; PhD, U. Minn., 1967. Profl. engr., Colo. Rsch. engr. Kennecott Copper Corp., Salt Lake City, 1967-72; R&D supr. AMAX, Inc., Golden, Colo., 1972-82; cons. metallurg. engr. P.B. Queneau Co., Inc., Golden, 1982-83; prin. metallurg. engr. Hazen Rsch., Inc., Golden, 1983-97; pres. P.B. Queneau & Assocs., Inc., Golden, 1997—; adj. prof. Colo. Sch. Mines, Golden, 1990—, short course organizer, 1992—; plenary spkr. Wadsworth Hydrometallurgy Symposium, 1993. Editor: Symposium on Arsenic Metallurgy: Fundamentals and Applications, 1987, International Symposium on Residues and Effluents Processing, 1991, Third Internat. Symposium on Recycling of Metals and Engineered Materials, 1995; contbr. numerous articles to profl. jours; patents for precipitation of low-sulfur calcium tungstate, 1983, silica control during acid pressure leaching of nickel laterite ore, 1983, recovery of vanadium and nickel from petroleum coke, 1984, stripping of tungsten from organic solvents, 1984, recovery of alumina values from alunite ore, 1986, electrolytic dissolution and control of NiS scale, 1986, apparatus and method to inhibit leaching of lead in water, 1996, numerous others. Mem. Am. Inst. Mining (pres. 1987-88, chmn. AIME-Extraction and Processing Divsn. awards com. 1995-96), Metallurg. and Petroleum Engrs. (pres. Denver sect.), Canadian Inst. Mining and Metallurgy, Tau Beta Pi. Avocations: golf, hiking, fishing, hunting, tennis. Home: 1954 Mt Zion Dr Golden CO 80401-1736 Office: CMRI 5906 Mcintyre St Golden CO 80403-7445

QUÉNEC'HDU, YVES, electrical engineering educator, researcher; b. Paris, July 20, 1941; s. Jean-Baptiste and Odette (Daudu) Q.; m. Claire Bourlaud, July 1, 1965; children: Anne, Sophie, Gaelle, Helene. Diploma in Engring., Ecole Supérieure d'Electricité, Paris, 1966; MSc, U. Paris, 1967. Asst. prof. Ecole Supérieure d'Electricité, 1966-72, prof., head dept., 1972-96; dep. mgr. Ecole Supérieure d'Electricité, Rennes, France, 1996—; auditor Ofcls. Bodies for Planning and Devel., Paris, 1980—; vice chmn. bd. dirs. Geoïde Co., Brest, France, 1988-92; chmn. Sci. Congress, Paris and Brussels, 1992-94. Contbr.: Informatics Education for All Students, 1984; contbr. articles to profl. jours. Mem. Soc. Electriciens Electroniciens (sr., chmn. sect. on control engring. 1986-92), IEEE, Assn. for Rsch. in Automatic Control (bd. dirs. 1980). Avocations: painting (oils, water colors), chairman of an association for arts development. Home: 34 rue du Courtil, 35510 Cesson Sevigné France Office: Ecole Superieure D Elec, Ave de la Boulais, 35510 Cesson Sevigné France

QUENON, ROBERT HAGERTY, retired mining consultant and holding company executive; b. Clarksburg, W.Va., Aug. 2, 1928; s. Ernest Leonard and Josephine (Hagerty) Q.; m. Jean Bowling, Aug. 8, 1953; children: Evan, Ann, Richard. B.S. in Mining Engring., W.Va. U., 1951; LL.B., George Washington U., 1964; PhD (hon.), U. Mo., 1979, Blackburn Coll., 1983, W.Va. U., 1988. Mine supt. Consol. Coal Co., Fairmont, W.Va., 1956-61; mgr. deep mines Pittston Co., Dante, Va., 1964-66; gen. mgr. Riverton Coal Co., Crown Hill, W.Va., 1966-67; mgr. ops. coal and shale oil dept. Exxon Co., Houston, 1967; pres. Monterey Coal Co., Houston, 1969-76; sr. v.p. Carter Oil Co., Houston, 1976-77; exec. v.p. Peabody Coal Co., St. Louis, 1977-78; pres., chief exec. officer Peabody Coal Co., 1978-83; pres., chief exec. officer Peabody Holding Co., Inc., St. Louis, 1983-90, chmn., 1990-91; bd. dirs. Newmont Mining Co., Denver, Ameren Corp., St. Louis, Laclede Steel Co., St. Louis, Miss. Lime Co., Alton. Ill.; bd. dirs., chmn. Fed. Res. Bank St. Louis, 1993-95, dep. chmn., 1990-92; mem. coal industry adv. bd. Internat. Energy Agy., 1980—, bd. chmn., 1984-90; chmn. Bituminous Coal Operator's Assn., 1980-83, 89-91. Trustee Blackburn Coll., Carlinville, Ill., 1975-83, St. Louis U., 1981-91; pres. St. Louis Art Mus., 1985-88. Served with AUS, 1946-47. Recipient Eavenson award Soc. Mining, Metallurgy, and Exploration, 1994, Erskine Ramsay award Am. Inst. Mining, Metallurgy, and Petroleum Engrs., 1985. Mem. Am. Mining Congress (vice-chmn. 1980-91), Nat. Coal Assn. (chmn. bd. 1978-80), U.S. C. of C. (dir. 1982-88). Office: PO Box 11328 Saint Louis MO 63105-0128

QUENTRALL-THOMAS, PETER, civil engineer; b. Hampshire, England, Oct. 22, 1946; s. John and Elizabeth Hester (Young) Q.; m. Sheila Parkinson, Aug. 22, 1966 (div. 1989); children: Lara, Abigail; m. Diane Seukeran, Dec. 27, 1989 (div. 1996); children: Faris, Aasma. Grad., Plymouth U., 1966. Engr. trainee Tor Bay Coun. Borough, 1967-70; civil engr. Christiani Neilson, 1970-72, Ronald Lion Devel. Ltd., 1972-74; project mgr. WIMPEY Internat., 1974-78; gen. mgr. Apex Engring. Ltd., 1978-82; chmn. Quentrall Inds. Ltd., 1982—, The Source, 1986—, Computer & Tech. Books, 1991—. Publisher: The Petroleum Times of Trinidad and Tobago, 1988-90. Chmn. Pt. Lisas Ind. Devel. Corp., 1992-95; pres. South Chamber Ind. Com., San Fernando, 1986-87; mem. Nat. Planning Commn., 1986; dir. The Trinidad and Tobago Bur. Stas., 1989-92. Mem. Assn. Prof. Engrs. Trinidad and Tobago, Masons, Rotary (pres. San Fernando, 1984). Avocations: sailing, flying, computing. E-mail: pqt@sibis.com. Office: Quentrall Inds Ltd, 61 Picton St, Port of Spain Trinidad and Tobago

QUERCIA, FRANCESCA FEDERICA, geoscientist; b. Rome, Aug. 18, 1953; d. Italo Federico and Alessandra (Perali) Q. Geology degree summa cum laude, U. La Sapienza, Rome, 1976; MS in Engring. Geosci., U. Calif., Berkeley, 1980. Rsch. asst. U. Calif., Berkeley, 1978-80; geoscientist AGIP, Milan, Italy, 1980-83; rsch. scientist ENEA, Rome, 1984-94; environ. risk assessor Nat. Environ. Protection Agy., Rome, 1994—; nat. coord. evactions contaminated land assessment and remediation, 1996—; risk assessment/mgmt. expert European Union Environemnt Agy., UNIDO, NATO, WHO. Contbr. articles to profl. jours. Fellowship Fulbright-Hays, 1978-80; grantee Jane Lewis, 1978-80. Mem. Nat. Assn. San. Engring. Office: ANPA, Via V Brancati 48, 00144 Rome Italy

QURESHI, MOHAMMED YOUNUS, psychology educator, consultant; b. Haripur Hazara, Pakistan, Dec. 12, 1929; came to U.S., 1953; s. Mohammed Noor and Meryam Khatoon Q.; m. Nora Jane Knapp, May 27, 1958 (div. Nov. 1979); children: Ahmed, Amna, Shukria, Shawn; m. Farzana Kaukab, May 17, 1980; children: Ajmel, Sabeeha, Azem. PhD, U. Ill., 1958. Lic. psychologist, Wis.; diplomate Am. Bd. Psychol. Spltys. Asst. prof. psychology U. Minn., Duluth, 1960-62, U. N.D., Grand Forks, 1962-64; assoc. prof. psychology Marquette U., Milw., 1964-70, prof., 1970—, chmn. dept. psychology, 1971-77; cons. psychologist. Author: Statistics and Behavior: An Introduction, 1980, 2d edit., 1991; contbr. articles to sci. and profl. jours. Pres. 81st St. Sch. PTA, 1968-70; merit badge counselor Milw. County coun. Boy Scouts Am., 1973-88; pres. Islamic Assn. Greater Milw., 1978-83. NIH grantee, 1962-69; Office of Edn. grantee, 1970-71; TOPS Club grantee, 1969-76. Mem. Am. Psychol. Assn., Psychometric Soc., Sigma Xi. Home: 2759 N 68th St Milwaukee WI 53210-1204 Office: Marquette U Schroeder Health Complex PO Box 1881 Milwaukee WI 53201-1881

QUERLEU, DENIS, obstetrics and gynecology educator; b. Lievin, France, June 10, 1949; s. Pierre and Claudine (Decourcelles) Q.; m. Dorothee Olivier; children: Charlotte, Juliette, Martin, Camille. Baccalaureat, France, 1966; MD, Lille, France, 1974. Chef de clinique Univ. Lille, France, 1976-81, asst. prof., 1982-94, prof., 1994—; chief dept. gynecologic oncology Oscar Lambret Cancer Ctr., Lille; dir. Experimental Rsch. Lab. Sch. Medicine, Lille, 1991-99. Author: La Chirurgie Au Feminin, 1990, Cancers et Grossesse, 1977, Techniques Chirurgicales en Gynecologie, 1995, Laparoscopic Surgery in Gynecologic Oncology, 1999. Mem. Internat. Soc. Gynecologic Endoscopy (bd. dirs. 1992-96), Am. Assn. of Gynecol. Laparoscopists (hon. chair Atlanta meeting 1998). Avocations: jogging, horse riding, painting. Office: Oscar Lambret Cancer Ctr, Chirurgie Gynecologique, 59000 Lille France

QUERRIEN, ANNE, editor, sociology researcher, educator; b. Paris, Dec. 13, 1945; d. Max and Madeleine (Moignet) Q.; children: David, Michael. BA in Sociology, Paris U., 1965, degree in urbanism, 1980; MA in Polit. Sci., Institut D'Etudes Politique, Paris, 1966; degree in sociology, Nanterre U., France, 1967. Editor assessor Institut Nat. Pour la Formation des Adultes, France, 1968-71; editor Assn. lur l'enseignement des érangers, France, 1972-73; rschr. Ctr. d'etudes de Rschrs.et de Formation Institutionnelles, France, 1974-79; rschr. Ministere de l'Equipement du Logement et des Transports, France, 1979-84, editor, 1985—; cons. Ctr. Centre D'Etudes et de Rschs. Architecturales, France, 1978-80; tchr. U. Paris, 1985—. Editor: Education Permanente, 1968-71, Vivre en France, 1972-73, Annales de la Recherche Urbaine, 1985—. Mem. Internat. Assn. Techniciens Experts and Chercheurs, Paris, 1995—, Confederation Francaise Democratique du Travail, Trade Union, Paris, 1979—. Mem. Internat. Assn. Sociology, European Urban Rsch. Assn. Mem. Socialist Party. Avocation: philosophy. Home: 124 Ave du Maine, 75014 Paris France Office: Annales Recherche Urbaine, Arche Nord, 92055 Paris La Defense France

QUERUBIN, POMPEYO UDARBE, lawyer, sugar cane planter; b. Bacolod City, Negros Occidental, Philippines, Oct. 2, 1928; s. Jose and Consuelo (Udarbe) Q.; m. Teresita Luna, Sept. 30, 1929; children: Cecilia, Patricia, Elizabeth, Catherine, Rufino, Tessa. LLB, Philippine Law Sch., 1956. Confidential asst. Dept. of Labor, Bacolod City, Philippines, 1951-54; practicing lawyer, 1954-60, 63-72, 1972-74; asst. br. chief Presdl. Anti-Graft Com., Malacañang, Manila, Philippines, 1960-63; pres. Philippine Nat. Coop Bank, Manila, 1972; pres., gen. mgr. Negros Vets. Security Agy., Inc., Bacolod City, 1976—; adviser Fiscal Econ. Adv. Coun., Bacolod City, Philippines, 1995—; pres. Querubin-Luna Devel. Corp., Bacolod City, 1997—. V.p. Bacolod City (Philippines) Devel. Found., 1997; chmn. Bacolod City Water Dist., 1997. Col. Judge Adv. Gen. Svc., Armed Forces of the Philippines. Recipient AFP Home Def. Badge Armed Forces fo the Philippines, 1984. Mem. Philippine Assn. Detective and Protective Agy. Operators (pres. region VI chpt. 1981—), Am. Soc. Indsl. Security, Metro Bacolod C. of C. and Industry, Philippine Mental Health Assn. (dir. Bacolod City 1996—), Lions (dir. Mt. Kanlandong 1986—, pres. 1994-95, 100% Excellence President 1994, Melvin Jones fellow 1995, area dep. gov. dist. 301-B 1997, dist. vice-gov. 1999—), La Carlota Planters Assn. (sec. gen.), Integrated Bar of the Philippines. Avocations: table tennis, golf. Home: Camia Rd. Espinos Village, 6100 Bacolod City Negros Occidental, Philippines Office: Negros Vets Security Agy, QL 358 Unit 4 Gonzaga St, 6100 Bacolod City Negros Occidental, Philippines

QUESADA, ORLANDO, internist, educator; b. San José, Costa Rica, July 26, 1943; s. Manuel and Violeta (Vargas) Q.; m. Aida Del Vecchio; children: Orlando, Edgar. MD, UNAM, 1967. Intern CCSS, Costa Rica, 1966-67, resident in medicine, 1969-71; instr. in medicine U. Costa Rica, 1972-74, assoc. prof. medicine, 1974-92, prof. medicine, 1992—; fellow in medicine Johns Hopkins, Balt., 1971-72; med. officer KLM, Costa Rica, 1985-99; med. advisor Embassy France, Costa Rica, 1985-88; internal medicine advisor Costa Rica Coll. of Physicians, 1980-84; founder, mem. Nat. Acad. Medicine of Costa Rica. Author/editor: Manual of Medical Emergencies, 1984; editor: Bibliographic Manual in Internal Medicine, 1980, Manual of Clinicopathlogical Conferences, 1992; inventor computarized acid-base program. Mem. ACP, Coll. Physicians Costa Rica, John Hopkins Med. Assn. Roman Catholic. Avocations: jogging, volleyball, basketball. Office: PO Box 5251, San Jose 1000, Costa Rica

QUEST, KRISTINA KAY, art educator, small business owner; b. Fort Atkinson, Wis., Sept. 22, 1952; d. Duane and Kiwa (Kikuchi) Tessman; m. Michael Charles Quest, July 28, 1973; children: Jennifer, Eric, Sarah. BS in Art Edn., U. Wis., 1992. Lic. tchr., Wis. Substitute tchr. various cities, 1993-97, 99—; summer sch. tchr. Ft. Atkinson Sch. Dist., 1993-97; art tchr. 7th and 8th grade St. Peter's Luth. Sch., Helenville, Wis., 1997; tchr., kindergarten day care tchr. 1st Class Presch., Before Sch. Day Care at Prospect Elem., Lake Mills, Wis., 1997-99; owner The Oriental Quest, Oshkosh, Wis., 2000—, Back Acres Mobile Home Park, Oshkosh, Wis., 2000—; past mem. Jefferson Arts Coun., bd. dirs., 1976-90; workshop fine arts fair judge Lakeside Luth. H.S., Lake Mills, Wis., 1991, 92; art fair judge for Fort Fest, Fort Atkinson, Crafters, 1993; owner mobile home park, Before/After Regular/Summer Sch. Day Care, Lake Mills Elem. Sch.; substitute tchr. Lake Mills (Wis.) Sch. Dist., Johnson Creek (Wis.) Sch. Dist. Author/illustrator: (book) Tiannamen Square, China's Dark Hours, 1987 (Juried Art Show 1993). Participant art donator AIDS Wellness Auction, The Globe, Oshkosh, 1999. Recipient art award Wis. Regional Arts Program/Waukesha Creative Arts League, Madison, 1993. Mem. Wis. Art Edn. Assn., Nat. Art Edn. Assn., Women in the Arts Nat. Mus., Japanese Am. Pub. Mus., U. of Wis.-Whitewater Alumni Assn., Student Tchr.'s Assn. Lutheran. Avocations: watercolor, sketching, painting, Japanese Sumi

brushstroke painting, block printing. Office: 105 Aztalan St Johnson Creek WI 53038-9666 Office: The Oriental Quest Retail Store Millennium Mall 558 N Main St Oshkosh WI 54901-4925

QUESTER, PASCALE GENEVIEVE, marketing educator, consultant; b. St. Nazaire, France, Sept. 20, 1961; arrived in Australia, 1991; d. Rene and Huguette (Chagneau) Q.; m. Robert John Langton, Jan. 17, 1990 (div. 1993); m. Nicholas Piers Buchdahl, Aug. 18, 1995; 1 child, Maya. Diplome d'etudes superieures commerciales et adminstrn. fin., Ecole Supérieure de Commerce, France, 1985; MA in Mktg., OSU, 1986; PhD, Massey U., New Zealand, 1991. Cert. practicing marketer. Lectr. Massey U., 1987-91; lectr. U. Adelaide, Australia, 1991-92, sr. lectr., 1992-99, assoc. prof. mktg., 1999—; bd. dirs. Hexagon Mktg., Franco-Australian Ctr. for Rsch. in Mktg. Author: (with McCarthy and Perreaut) Basic Marketing, 2d edit., 1997 (Australian award for excellence in ednl. pub.), (with McCarthy, Wilkerson, Percauld and Lee), Basic Marketing, 1993, (with Hawkins and Neal) Consumer Behavior, 1994, 2d edit., 1998. Mem. Australian Aiding Children, Adelaide, 1995—. Fellow Australian Mktg. Inst.; mem. Am. Mktg. Assn., Assn. for Consumer Rsch., Acad. Mktg. Svcs., Assn. Francaise du Mktg., European Mktg. Acad., Australian and New Zealand Mktg. Acad., Beta Gamma Sigma (life). Avocations: cinema, cuisine, travel. Home: 6 Raymond St, Henley Beach SA 5022, Australia Office: U Adelaide, Sch Commerce, Adelaide SA 5005, Australia

QUEVAUVILLER, PHILIPPE JACQUES, environmentalist, international government official; b. Chatelaillon Plage, France, July 28, 1959; s. Pierre and Annie (Camelot) Q.; m. Sabine Helgen, Aug. 17, 1996; children: Adrien, Louis. Lic. in geology, U. Bordeaux I, Talence, France, 1982, M Oceanography, 1983, PhD in Oceanography, 1987, PhD in Scis., 1991, HDR in Chemistry, 1999. Sci. cooperator Ministry Environ., Lisbon, Portugal, 1984-86, rsch. assoc., 1986-87; rsch. assoc. Ministry Pub. Works, The Hague, The Netherlands, 1988-89; sci. officer European Commn., Brussels, 1989. Editor Measurements and Testing Newsletter, 1992-99, Quality Assurance in Environmental Monitoring, 1995, Monitoring of Water Quality, 1998; assoc. editor Quality Assurance for Environmental Analysis, 1995, Harmonization of Leaching/Extraction Tests, 1997; contbg. editor Jour. Trends in Analytical Chemistry; mem. editl. bd. Jour. Fresenius, Jour. Analytical Chemistry, Jour. Analytical Atomic Spectroscopy, Jour. Environ. Monitoring; contbr. over 200 articles to internat. sci. jours. and 60 abstracts in procs. of internat. confs.; author 60 reports; author: Method Performance Studies for Speciation Analysis, 1998; co-author: Interlaboratory Studies and Certified Reference Materials for Environment Analysis, 1999; mem. editl. bd. Jour. Sed. Soils; series editor Water Quality Measurement. Mem. Internat. Union Pure Applied Chemistry (mem. working group Commn. V2 1995-2000). Avocations: music, judo, skiing, tennis, writing novels. E-mail: philippe.quevauviller@cec.eu.int. Home: Rue Longue 50, 1150 Brussels Belgium Office: European Commn, European Commn/DG Research, Rue de la Loi 200, 1049 Brussels Belgium

QUEVEDO, HERNANDO, physicist, researcher; b. Cachipay, Colombia, Aug. 17, 1958; arrived in Mexico, 1992; s. Nestor Quevedo and Maria Cubillos; m. Natalia Koulikovskaia, Sept. 24, 1982; children: Patricia, Katerina. MS in Physics and Math., Russian Friendship U., Moscow, 1982; MS, U. Cologne, Germany, 1984, PhD, 1987. Rschr. U. Cologne, 1988-90; vis. rschr. U. Mo., Columbia, 1991-92; rschr. U. Mexico, Mexico City, 1992—, head dept. Inst. Nuclear Scis., 1994-96. Contbr. articles to profl. jours. Rsch. grantee Deutsche Forschungsgemeinschat, Germany, 1988, CONACYT, Mexico, 1994. Mem. German Phys. Soc. Avocations: sports, reading. Office: Inst Nuclear Physics UNAM, AP 70-543, 04510 Mexico City Mexico

QUEZADA, ROBERTO A., media specialist, film maker; b. Guatemala City, Guatemala, Feb. 22, 1949; s. Roberto Polanco Quezada and Alba Estela Dardon; m. Rita Marie Lechtenburg (div. Feb. 1978); m. Hillary Beth Gray Bernard, June 18, 1988; children: Melissa, Elizabeth, Lauren, Amanda, Daniela. MFA, UCLA, 1977. Gaffer various cos., L.A., 1978-90; film prodr. Starway Internat., L.A., 1990-96; dir. web site devel. Amnesty Internat. USA, N.Y.C., 1996-98; dir. electronic media Planned Parenthood Fedn. Am., N.Y.C., 1998—. Prodr.: (film) Beastmaster, 1981, Phantasm, 1981. Avocations: writing, graphic art, photography. Office: Planned Parenthood Fedn Am 810 7th Ave New York NY 10019-5818

QUEZADA-EUAN, JOSE JAVIER GUADALUPE, veterinarian, researcher; b. Progreso, Yucatan, Mexico, Oct. 14, 1963; s. Jose and Evangelina (Evan) Q. BSc, U. Yucatan, Merida, Mexico, 1988; MPhil, U. Wales, Cardiff, 1991, PhD, 1997. Rsch. asst. faculty vet. medicine U. Autonoma Yucatan, Merida, 1987-89, jr. rschr., 1991-92, assoc. rschr., 1992-95, titular rschr., 1995—, head dept., 1998—, coord. MSc course, 1998—; cons. coord. Conargen, Mexico City, 1999—; nat. rschr. candidate Conacyt, Mexico, 1995, nat. rschr. I, 1998. Contbr. articles to profl. jours. Mem. IBRA. Avocations: photography, painting, music, beekeeping, body building. Home: Calle 60 No 260, Nueva Hidalgo, 97227 Merida Yucatan, Mexico Office: Faculty Vet Medicine, Apdo Postal 4-116, 97100 Merida Yucatan, Mexico

QUIAMBAO, DALISAY LELAY, dietician, consultant, surveyor; b. Catanduanes, The Philippines, July 10, 1945; came to U.S., 1970; d. Patricio and Concepcion (Aldave) Lelay; m. Enrique Quiambao, Dec. 10, 1967 (div. Aug. 1989); children: Larry, Edwin, Cheryl. BS in Nutrition, Philippine Women's U., Manila, 1966; postgrad., U. N.C., Greensboro, 1976-78. Cafeteria mgr. Durham County Schs., Durham, N.C., 1973-78; dietetic technician Murdoch Ctr., Butner, N.C., 1978-80, clin. dietitian, 1980-84, adminstrv. dietitian, 1984-86; dir. food svc. N.C. Spl. Care Ctr., Wilson, 1986-88; dietitian cons. Granville (N.C.) Med. Ctr., 1985-86; dietitian cons. div. facility svcs. N.C. Dept. Human Resources, Raleigh, 1988—; foodsvc. cons. Classic Food Svcs., Durham, 1989-90; dietary cons. Coordinating Coun. for Sr. Citizens, Durham, 1990-91; dietitian cons. Meals on Wheels, Interim Health Care Corp.; instr. Durham Tech. Community Coll., 1990. Recipient cert. for pub. mgr. program N.C. Office State Pers., 1987, svc. award N.C. Dept. Human Resources, 1988. Mem. Am. Dietetic Assn. (registered), N.C. Dietetic Assn., Am. Heart Assn., Philippine Am. Assn. N.C. Roman Catholic. Avocations: reading, baking, arts and crafts, developing recipes, volunteering. Home: 503 Windcrest Rd Durham NC 27713-6224 Office: NC Dept Human Resources Div Facility Svcs 701 Barbour Dr Raleigh NC 27603-2008

QUIAT, GERALD M., lawyer; b. Denver, Jan. 9, 1924; s. Ira L. and Esther (Greenblatt) Q.; m. Roberta M. Nicholson, Sept. 26, 1962; children: James M., Audrey R., Melinda A., Daniel P., Ilana L., Leonard E. AA, U. Calif., Berkeley, 1942; AB, LLB, U. Denver, 1948, changed to JD, 1970. Bar: Colo. 1948, Fed. Ct. 1948, U.S. Dist. Ct. Colo. 1948, U.S. Ct. Appeals (10th cir.) 1948, U.S. Surpeme Ct. 1970. Dep. dist. atty. City and Co. of Denver, Colo., 1949-52; partner firm Quiat, Seeman & Quiat, Denver, 1952-67, Quiat & Quiat (later changed to Quiat, Bucholtz & Bull, P.C.), 1968; pres. Quiat, Bucholtz & Bull & Laff, P.C. (and predecessors), Denver, 1968-85; pvt. practice Denver, 1985—; bd. dirs., chmn. audit com. Guaranty Bank & Trust Co., Denver; past bd. dirs. and chmn. bd. ROMED, RMD, Inc. Past trustee Holding Co., Rose Med. Ctr., Denver, pres., chmn. bd. dirs., 1976-79; mem. Colo. Civil Rights Com., 1963-71, chmn., 1966-67, 69-70, hearing officer, 1963-71; bd. dirs. Am. Cancer Rsch. Ctr., Denver, chmn. bd., 1991-93; chmn. bd. Am. Med. Ctr., 1993-95; mem. nat. civil rights com., hon. mem. nat. exec. com., hon. nat. commr. Anti-Defamation League, B'nai B'rith, mem. exec. com., chmn. bd. Mountain States region, 1980-82. With inf. U.S. Army, 1942-45. Decorated Combat Infantry Badge, Bronze Star. Mem. ABA, Colo. Bar Assn., Colo. Trial Lawyers Assn. (pres. 1970-71), Am. Legion (comdr. Leyden-Chiles-Wickersham post 1 1955-56, past judge adv. Colo. dept.). Home: 5361 Nassau Cir E Englewood CO 80110-5100 Office: Penthouse Suite 1720 S Bellaire St Denver CO 80222-4304

QUICK, DANNY RICHARD, computer systems engineer; b. Millen, Ga., Aug. 7, 1948; s. John Francis and Olene (Crane) Q.; m. Donna Kay Nobles, Oct. 13, 1973; children: Dexter Brian, Debby Kim. Cert. data processing, Strayer Coll., Arlington, Va., 1989. Enlisted USAF, 1967, advanced through grades to sr. master sgt., 1984; chief Message Processing Br., Orgn. Joints Chiefs of Staff, Pentagon, Washington, 1984-88, ret., 1988; systems analyst Potomac Systems Engrng., Annandale, Va., 1988-89; sr. systems cons. Wang Labs., Inc., Bethesda, Md., 1989-93; prin. systems engr. Computer Scis. Corp., Falls Ch., Va., 1993—; mem. methods & procedures panel U.S. Mil. Comm.-Electronics Bd., Washington, 1984-88, mem. call signs panel, 1984-88. Recipient Defense Meritorious Svc. medal Sec. Defense, Washington, 1987, Meritorious Svc. medal Sec. Air Force, Washington, 1980; named one of 50 Outstanding Airmen of Yr., Airforce Mil. Personnel Ctr., Randolph AFB, Tex., 1983-84. Mem. Am. Legion (exec. com. 1984-86, editor Post-O-Gram, 1983-84). Republican. Methodist. Achievements include the merge of the principal officers e-mail system and the foreign affairs information systems networks; led the CSC test and deploy team intesting and deploying a Lotus Notes locally developed database program, which is installed on a Microsoft Windows NT LAN, for distributing inbound and transmitting outbound diplomatic telegrams, throughout the Department of State and at American embassies and consulates worldwide. Home: 4 Caledon Ct Stafford VA 22554-1608 Office: Computer Sys Corp 7374 Boston Blvd Springfield VA 22153-2804

QUICK, JERRY RAY, academic administrator; b. Gosport, Ind., July 3, 1939; s. Waldo C. and M. Marguerite (Goss) Q.; m. Elizabeth Ahlemeyer, June 10, 1962; children: Patrick, Andrew. BS, Ind. State U., 1961; MS, Ind. U., 1965. Tchr., coach MSD Washington Twp., Indpls., 1961-63; assoc. dir. housing Ind. State U., Terre Haute, 1963-75; asst. v.p. Ctrl. Mich. U., Mt. Pleasant, 1975-85; assoc. vice chancellor for bus. Vanderbilt U., Nashville, 1985-89; v.p. fin. and adminstrn. U. Ala., Huntsville, 1989—; mem. task force U.S. Dept. Edn., Washington, 1981-84; mem. accreditation teams So. Assn. Colls. and Schs., 1993—. Contbr. articles to profl. jours. and chpts. to books. Bd. dirs. Better Bus. Bur., Nashville, 1988-89, Better Bus. Bur., Huntsville, Ala., 1998—; mem. Mayor's Commn. on Efficiency, Nashville, 1988-89. Mem. Nat. Assn. Coll. and Univ. Bus. Officers (editl. bd. 1987-92), So. Assn. Coll. and Univ. Bus. Officers, Nat. Assn. Coll. Aux. Svcs., Ala. Assn. Coll. and Univ. Bus. Officers, Assn. Coll. and Univ. Housing Officers (pres. 1979-80), Huntsville C. of C., Huntsville Rotary Club. Avocations: farming, collecting and restoring antiques, travel, microcomputers. Home: 2513 Garth Rd SE Huntsville AL 35801-1422 Office: U Ala Mdh 131 Huntsville AL 35899-0001

QUICK, JONATHAN DICKINSON, health organization executive; b. Albany, N.Y., June 5, 1951; s. James F. and Olva F. (Faust) Q.; m. Tina L. Burdick, May 1, 1982; children: Janneke C., Katrina F., Kimberly C. AB magna cum laude, Harvard U., 1974; MPH, MD, U. Rochester, 1979. Diplomate Am. Bd. Family Practice, Am. Bd. Preventive Medicine. Resident/chief resident family medicine Duke U., Durham, N.C., 1982; chief of staff USPHS Hosp., Talihina, Okla., 1982-84; dir. drug mgmt. program Mgmt. Scis. for Health, Boston, 1984-89; health svcs. advisor Mgmt. Scis. for Health, Peshawar, Pakistan, 1989-91; health planner Min. of Health, Nairobi, Kenya, 1991-94; med. officer WHO, Geneva, 1995-96, dir. essential drugs, 1996-98, dir. essential drugs and medicines policy, 1999—; adj. assoc. prof. Boston U. Sch. Pub. Health, 1990—; cons. Aga Khan Health Scis., Tanzania, 1982-83. Editor: Managing Drug Supply, 1997; co-editor: Preventive Stress Management in Organizations, 1997; co-author: Stress and Challenge at the Top, 1990, Rhinos in the Rough: A Golfer's Guide to Kenya, 1993; editl. bd. Jour. Occupl. Health Psychology, 1995—. Mem. worship team Crossroads Evang. Ch., Ferney-Voltaine, France, 1996—. Lt. USPHS, 1982-84. Fellow Royal Soc. Medicine, Am. Coll. Preventive Medicine; mem. Am. Acad. Family Physicians, Rotary Interant. (com. mem. 1992-94). Avocations: jazz and rock 'n roll drumming, jogging, snow skiing, writing. Home: 9 les Choulets, F-01220 Sauverny France Office: WHO, 20 Ave Appia, CH-1211 Geneva 27, Switzerland

QUIGLEY, JOHN MARY, chemistry educator, researcher; b. Dublin, Ireland, May 14, 1954; s. William Flannan and Margaret (O'Flaherty) Q.; m. Patricia Geraldine O'Hara, July 16, 1988; children: David John, Niall Joseph. BSc, Nat. U. Ireland, Dublin, 1976, PhD, 1981; MA, Dublin U., 1984. Lectr. Dublin U., 1981—. Contbr. articles to profl. jours. Mem. Inst. Chemistry Ireland. Roman Catholic. Mem. Secular discalced Carmelites.

QUIGLEY, KEVIN F. F., nonprofit organization executive; b. N.Y.C., Dec. 3, 1952; s. Martin S. and Katherine D. Quigley; m. Susan L.Q. Flaherty, Nov. 1, 1986. BA, Swarthmore Coll., 1974; MA, Nat. U. Ireland, Dublin, 1975; MIA, Columbia U., N.Y.C., 1981; PhD, Georgetown U., 1995. Budget examiner Office of Mgmt. and Budget, Office of Pres. of U.S., Washington, 1981-86; legis. dir. for Senator John Heinz U.S. Senate, Washington, 1986-89; dir. policy programs Pew Charitable Trusts, Phila., 1989-95; guest scholar Woodrow Wilson Ctr., Washington, 1995-97; v.p. Asia Soc., N.Y.C., 1997-99; exec. dir. Global Alliance for Workers and Cmtys., Balt., 1999—. Co-author: The Allies and East-West Conflict, 1989; author: For Democracy's Sake, 1997. Vice chmn. Inst. for Sustainable Cmtys., Burlington, Vt., 1999, Adv. Com. on Fgn. Voluntary Aid, Washington, 1990-94. Mem. Coun. on Fgn. Rels. Fax: 410-951-1525. E-mail: kffquigley@iyfnet.org. Home: 1600 N Oak St Apt 808 Arlington VA 22209-2754 Office: Global Alliance for Workers and Cmtys 32 South St Ste 500 Baltimore MD 21202-7503

QUIGLEY, ROBERT CHARLES, insurance industry consultant; b. Phila., Feb. 2, 1949; s. James and Kathrine Regina (Kinckiner) Q.; m. Barbara Jeanne Browne, Apr. 17, 1971; children: Robert J., Michael J., Brian A., Jason T. BS in Acctg., Pa. State U., 1970. CPA, Pa. Sr. acct. Touche Ross & Co., Phila., 1970-72; dir. acctg. policy and rsch. Ins. Co. of N.Am., Phila., 1972-81; asst. treas. Reliance Ins. Co., Phila., 1981-85; v.p., treas. Mutual Fire Marine and Inland Ins. Co., Phila., 1985-86; owner Quigley & Assocs., Hatboro, Pa., 1987—; team leader accreditation Nat. Assn. of Ins. Commrs., Kansas City, 1992—. Author: (with others) Property and Liability Insurance Accounting, 5th edit., 1991. With USMCR, 1967. Mem. AICPA, Soc. of Ins. Fin. Mgmt., Am. Arbitration Assn. (panelist 1987—). Republican. Presbyterian. Avocations: family, reading, writing. E-mail: RCQCPA@aol.com. Office: PO Box 147 Hatboro PA 19040-0147

QUIGLEY, STEPHEN HOWARD, executive editor; b. Boston, May 29, 1951; s. John Joseph Sr. and Anne Margaret (O'Brien) Q.; m. Suzanne Elizabeth Daley, July 21, 1980; children: Benjamin Parker, Theodore Hunter, Margaret Hunter. BA in French and Internat. Rels., Dartmouth Coll., 1973. Sales rep. Addison-Wesley Pub. Co., Inc., Reading, Mass., 1973-75, math. editor, 1975-81, regional sales mgr., 1981-85; sr. math. editor Scott, Foresman and Co., Chgo., Ill., 1985-88, PWS-KENT Pub. Co., Boston, 1988-95; exec. editor math. and stats. sci., tech. and med. pub. div. John Wiley and Sons, Inc., 1995—. Mem. Independence Day Celebration Commn., 1987-88; mem. Eveleth Sch. liaison to Sch. PTA, Marblehead, Mass., 1989-90, vice chair sch. com., 1991-92, chair sch. comm., 1992-93; water safety chmn., bd. dirs. ARC, Greater Lynn chpt., 1978-81; leader Boy Scouts Am., Explorers Group, Marblehead, 1976-79; swim ofcl. Ill. High Sch. Ofcls. Assn., 1984-88; lector Star of Sea Ch., Marblehead, 1988—; dir. Goldthwait Reservation, Marblehead. Recipient Club of Year award Dartmouth Coll., Chgo., 1988, Book award Assn. of Am. Publ., 1999. Mem. ASCD, Am. Math. Soc., Math. Assn. Am., Am. Statis. Assn., Am. Math. Assn. Two-Yr. Colls., Nat. Fedn. Interscholastic Ofcls. Assn., Glenview C. of C. (accreditation team 1988), Nat. Coun. Tchrs. Math., Corinthian Yacht Club (rec. chair, operating com., 1997, 2000, North Shore (Mass.) Dartmouth Club, Chgo. Dartmouth Club (pres. 1988-89), North Shore Friends in Pub. (founder), Rotary (bd. dirs. Boston 1990-95, svc. award 1988). Republican. Roman Catholic. Avocations: computers, swimming, sailing, skiing, tennis. Fax: 781-631-0271. E-mail: squigley@wiley.com. Home: 10 Leicester Rd Marblehead MA 01945-1817 Office: Cooks Corner 3 Pleasant St Marblehead MA 01945-3431

QUIGNEY, THERESA ANN, special education educator; b. East Cleveland, Ohio, June 19, 1952; d. James and Lenora Mary (McDonald) Q.; m. Joseph Carl Lang, July 23, 1983. BA, Notre Dame Coll., 1974; MEd, Cleve. State U., 1980; PhD, Kent State U., 1992. Cert. tchr. handicapped K-12; cert. ednl. adminstrv. specialist edn. of exceptional pupils; cert. ednl. supr.; cert. elem. prin.; cert. h.s. prin. cert. tchr. French K-12, Ohio. Spl. edn. tchr. Newbury (Ohio) Local Schs., 1974-80; county supr., specific learning disabilities and behavior handicaps Geauga County Bd. Edn., Chardon, Ohio, 1980-88; asst. prof. spl. edn. West Chester (Pa.) U., 1992-93; asst. prof. edn. Heidelberg Coll., Tiffin, Ohio, 1993-94; assoc. prof. spl. edn. Cleve. State U., 1994—. Contbr. articles to profl. jours. Vol. cons. Tchrs. for Action Rsch., South Euclid/Lyndhurst (Ohio) Sch. Dist., 1996—; past participant issues task force Ohio Coun. for Exceptional Children; past bd. mem. Camp Sue Osborne, Lake County, Ohio. Grantee Ohio State Supt.'s Task Force on Spl. Edn., 1997, Cleve. State U. Coll. Edn., 1997, Am. Sch. Counselor's Assn.; recipient achievement recognition Assn. for Children and Adults with Learning Disabilities, Ohio, 1980. Mem. CEC, ASCD, Am. Ednl. Rsch. Assn., Learning Disabilities Assn., Mid-We. Ednl. Rsch. Assn., Coun. for Learning Disabilities, Kappa Delta Pi, Phi Delta Kappa, Pi Lambda Theta (vol. cons. Gamma Epsilon chpt. 1996—). Avocations: travel, writing, reading, sketching. Office: Cleveland State Univ Euclid Ave at E 24th St Cleveland OH 44115

QUIJADA, ANGÉLICA MARÍA, elementary education educator; b. Tijuana, Mex., Mar. 22, 1963; came to U.S., 1967; d. Juan José and Paula (Magallanes) Q. AA, L.A. Harbor Coll., Wilmington, Calif., 1985; BA, Calif. State U., Carson, 1990, MA, 1993. Tchr. asst., tutor L.A. Harbor Coll., 1982-85; elem. tchr. asst., tutor Ambler Avenue Sch., Carson, 1985-90; bilingual elem. tchr. Hooper Avenue Sch., L.A., 1991—; mentor tchr. Hooper Avenue Elem. Sch., L.A., 1997—, mem. coordinated compliance rev. team, 1998; Jefferson cluster tchr. trainer dist. stds. L.A. Unified Sch. Dist., 1996—, tchr. trainer early literacy, 1997—; stakeholder Instrnl. Transformation Team, 1995-96; mem. pupil quality rev. team, 1995-96; co-chair local sch. leadership coun., 1998; mentor Latino Tchr. Project, U. So. Calif., 1993—. counselor Pathfinders, Carson Seventh Day Adventist Ch., 1980; treas. Carson Spanish Seventh-Day Adventist Ch., 1994; pianist Harbor City Seventh Day Adventist Ch., 1995-96; mem. ednl. com. Lynwood Seventh Day Adventist Ch., 1999. Mem. TESOL, United Tchrs. L.A. (co-chmn. 1994, chpt. chmn. 1995-98). Democrat. Avocations: playing piano, photography, reading, playing softball, drawing. Home: 320 E 181st St Carson CA 90746-1815

QUILLEN, CECIL DYER, III, lawyer; b. Rochester, N.Y., Aug. 15, 1963; s. Cecil Dyer, Jr. and Vicey Ann (Childress) Q.; m. Mary Stuart Humes, Oct. 20, 1990; children: Caroline, James C.D. AB magna cum laude, Harvard U., 1985; JD, U. Va., 1988. Bar: N.Y. 1989, D.C. 1991, U.S. Ct. Appeals (4th cir.) 1989. Law clk., Sr. Cir. Judge U.S. Ct. Appeals (4th cir.), Richmond, Va., 1988-89; assoc. Sullivan & Cromwell, N.Y.C., 1989-95; assoc. Linklaters, N.Y.C., 1995-96, ptnr., 1996—; ptnr. London office Linklaters, 2000—; spkr. various profl. confs. Notes editor Va. Law Rev., 1987-88. Mem. ABA, N.Y. State Bar Assn., Assn. Bar City of N.Y., Raven Soc., Order of Coif, Phi Beta Kappa. Office: Linklaters, One Silk St, London EC2Y 8HQ, England

QUILLOPE, JOSE PEREZ, pathologist, consultant; b. Caoayan, Ilocos Sur, The Philippines, May 1, 1961; s. Alejandro Quyo Quillope and Ludovica Bautista Perez; m. Josefa Limos Gelido, Sept. 24, 1994; 1 child, Sofia Joy. DVM, U. of the Philippines, 1984; MD, Angeles U., The Philippines, 1989. Diplomate Philippine Soc. Pathologists. Med. officer Jose R. Reyes Meml. Med. Ctr., Manila, 1991-95; cons. pathologist Dr. Jose N. Rodriguez Meml. Hosp., Kalookan City, The Philippines, 1996—; cons. pathologist Amos Gen. Hosp., The Philippines, 1998—. Named Most Outstanding Citizen in Medicine, Municipality of Caoayan, 1998. Mem. Philippine Med. Assn. (life). Avocations: driving, photography, playing flute, computer games, basketball. E-mail: quillope@digitelone.com. Home: Blk 5 Lot 34 Verde Heights, 3 Bulacan Gaya-Gaya, San Jose del Monte The Philippines Office: Dr J N Rodriguez Meml Hosp, Tala, Kalookan City The Philippines

QUINA, MARION ALBERT, JR., lawyer; b. Mobile, Ala., Apr. 18, 1949; s. Marion Albert Sr. and Tallulah (Dunlap) Q.; children: Marion Albert III, Elliott Richardson; m. Jamie Mayhall Curtis, May 2, 1998. BS, U. Ala., 1971; JD, Samford U., 1974. Bar: Ala. 1974, U.S. Dist. Ct. (so. dist.) Ala. 1975, U.S. Ct. Appeals (5th cir.) 1977, U.S. Ct. Appeals (11th cir.) 1981. Assoc. Lyons, Pipes & Cook, Mobile, 1974-77, ptnr., 1978-87; shareholder Lyons, Pipes & Cook, P.C., Mobile, 1988—. Past mem., bd. dirs. Mobile Touchdown Club, Presch. for the Sensory Impaired; mem. United Way, 1989—; mem. adv. bd. Cumberland Sch. of Law, Birmingham; sec., treas., vice chmn., chmn. Southeastern Admiralty Law Inst., Athens, Ga., 1996—. 1st lt. U.S. Army. Mem. ABA, Ala. Bar Assn., Mobile Bar Assn. (chmn. admiralty and maritime law com.), Maritime Law Assn. U.S. (assoc.), Ala. Wildlife Fedn. (past dir.), Mobile Area C. of C. (past vice chmn., gen. counsel), Kiwanis (past dir.), Mobile County Wildlife Assn., Mobile Propeller Club, Mobile Area C. of C. Diplomat Club, among others. Avocations: hunting, fishing. Office: Lyons Pipes & Cook PC 2 N Royal St Mobile AL 36602-3896

QUINLAN, GUY CHRISTIAN, lawyer; b. Cambridge, Mass., Oct. 28, 1939; s. Guy Thomas and Yvonne (Carver) Q.; m. Mary-Ella Holst, Apr. 18, 1987. AB, Harvard Coll., 1960; JD, Harvard U., 1963. Bar: N.Y. 1964, U.S. Dist. Ct. (so. and ea. dists.) N.Y. 1965, U.S. Ct. Appeals (2d cir.) 1967, U.S. Supreme Ct. 1969, U.S. Ct. Appeals (8th cir.) 1973, (10th cir.) 1977, (4th cir.) 1993, (11th cir.) 1995, U.S. Tax Ct. 1977. Assoc. Clifford, Chance, Rogers & Wells, N.Y.C., 1963-70, ptnr., 1970-80, of counsel, 1991—. Past pres. Unitarian Universalist Svc. Com., Yorkville Common Pantry; past pres. Unitarian Universalist Dist. of Met. N.Y.; mem. adv. council on ministerial studies Harvard U. Div. Sch. Mem. ABA, N.Y. State Bar Assn., Fed. Bar Coun., Am. Judicature Soc., Am. Assn. Internat. Commn. Jurists, Lawyers Com. on Nuclear Policy, Harvard Club. Democrat. Office: Clifford Chance Rogers & Wells 200 Park Ave Fl 8E New York NY 10166-0899

QUINLAN, MICHAEL EDWARD, retired civil servant; b. Hampton, Eng., Aug. 11, 1930; s. Gerald A. and Roseanne (Corr) Q.; m. Mary Finlay, Aug. 7, 1965; children: Anthony, Jane, Matthew, Caroline. MA, Merton Coll., Oxford (Eng.) U., 1952. Under-sec. Cabinet Office, U.K., 1974-77; dep. sec. for policy Ministry of Defence, U.K., 1977-81; dep. sec. for industry Treasury, U.K., 1981-82; permanent sec. Dept. of Employment, U.K., 1983-88, Ministry of Defence, U.K., 1988-92; dir. Ditchley Found., U.K., 1992-99; vis. prof. King's Coll., London, 1992-95; trustee Sci. Mus. U.K., 1992—. Author: Thinking About Nuclear Weapons, 1997, also numerous articles on def. and other pub. policy issues. Flying officer RAF, 1952-54. Decorated Knight Grand Cross Order of Bath (U.K.). Roman Catholic. Avocations: golf, sports, music. Office: 3 Adderbury Pk, Banbury Oxon OX17 3EN, England

QUINN, ANTHONY RUDOLPH OAXACA, actor, writer, artist; b. Chihuahua, Mexico, Apr. 21, 1915; naturalized, 1947; s. Frank and Nellie (Oaxaca) Q.; m. Katherine de Mille, Oct. 2, 1937 (div.); children: Christina, Kathleen, Duncan, Valentina; m. Iolanda Addolori, Jan. 1966 (div. Aug. 1997); children: Francesco, Daniele, Lorenzo; m. Katherine Benvin, Dec. 7, 1997; children: Antonia, Ryan. Student pub. schs. Actor in plays including Clean Beds, 1936, Gentleman from Athens, 1947, Street Car Named Desire, Let Me Hear the Melody, Beckett, 1961, Tchin-Tchin, 1963, Zorba, 1983-86; has appeared in over 200 motion pictures including Guadalcanal Diary, 1943, Buffalo Bill, 1944, Irish Eyes are Smiling, 1944, China Sky, 1945, Back to Bataan, 1945, Where Do We Go From Here?, 1945, Tycoon, 1947, The Brave Bulls, 1951, Mask of the Avenger, 1951, World in his Arm, 1952, Against all Flags, 1952, Viva Zapata (Acad. award 1952), Ride Vaquero, 1953, City Beneath the Sea, 1953, Seminole, 1953, Blowing Wild, 1953, East of Sumatra, 1953, Long Wait, 1954, Magnificent Matador, 1955, Ulysses, 1955, Naked Street, 1955, Seven Cities of Gold, 1955, Lust for Life, (Acad. award best supporting actor 1956), La Strada, 1954, Man from Del Rio, 1956, Wild the Wind, 1957, Attila the Hun, 1958, The Wild Party, 1956, The Ride Back, 1957, The Hunchback of Notre Dame, 1957, The River's Edge, 1957, Hot Spell, 1958, Heller with a Gun, Savage Innocents, 1959, The Black Orchid, 1958, Last Train From Gun Hill, 1958, Warlock, 1959, Heller in Pink Tights, 1960, Portrait in Black, 1960, Guns of Navarrone, 1961, Becket, 1961, Barabbas, 1962, Lawrence of Arabia, 1962, Requiem for a Heavyweight, 1963, The Visit, 1963, Behold a Pale Horse, 1964, Zorba the Greek, 1964, High Wind in Jamaica, 1965, Guns for San Sebastian, 1968, The Shoes of the Fisherman, 1968, The Secret of Santa Vittoria, 1969, A Dream of Kings, 1969, Flap, 1970, A Walk in Spring Rain, 1970, R.P.M., 1970, The City, 1971, Jesus of Nazareth, 1971, Across 110th Street, 1972, Arruza, Deaf Smith and Johnny Ears, 1973, The Don Is Dead, 1973, Mohammed Messenger of God, 1977, Caravans, 1978, The Children of Sanchez, 1978, The Greek Tycoon, 1978, The Inheritance, 1978, The Passage, 1979, Lion of the Desert, 1981, High Roll, 1981, Valentina, 1984, The Salamander, 1984, Treasure Island, 1986, Stradivarius, 1987, Revenge, 1990, Ghosts Can't Do It, 1990, A Star for Two, 1990, Jungle Fever, 1990, Only the Lonely, 1991, Mobsters, 1991, The Last Action Hero, 1993, Somebody

to Love, 1994, A Walk in the Clouds, 1995, Project Mankind, 1996, Il Sindaco, 1996, Seven Servants, 1996; appeared in TV prodns. of The Life of Christ, Onassis: The Richest Man in the World, 1988, Old Man and the Sea, 1990, This Can't Be Love, 1994, Gotti, 1996, El Camino de Santiago, 1999; script writer: Metro-Goldwyn-Mayer prodn. The Farm; author: The Original Sin, 1972, Self-Portrait, 1995; artist 13 major exhbns. oil paintings, sculptures and serigraphs, Hawaii, 1982, 87, San Francisco, 1983, N.Y.C., 1984, 89, San Antonio, 1984, Houston, 1984, Washington, 1985, Beverly Hills, Calif., 1986, Mexico City, 1990, Paris, 1990, Zurich, Switzerland, 1990, Vienna, Austria, 1991, Buenos Aires, 1992, Las Vegas, 1993; artist 17 major exhbns., Toronto, Can., Seoul, Korea, 1998.

QUINN, BARRY MICHAEL, marketing educator; b. Lurgan, Armagh, Northern Ireland, Feb. 2, 1968; s. Michael Joseph and Kathleen Jane (Murphy) Q. BA with honors, U. Ulster, Coleraine, Northern Ireland, 1992, PhD, 1997. Lectr. U. Ulster, 1995—. Contbr. articles to profl. jours. Mem. Chartered Inst. of Mktg., European Assn. of Rsch. in the Distributive Trades. Avocations: swimming, football, walking, movies. Office: U Ulster, Cromore Rd, Coleraine BT52 1SA, Northern Ireland

QUINN, DAVID BEERS, retired history educator; b. Dublin, Ireland, Apr. 24, 1909; s. David and Albertina (Devine) Quinn; m. Alison Moffat Oct. 30, 1937 (dec. 1993); children: Nicholas R.K., Roderick E. N., Brigid L.S.A. (Quinn) Wainwright. BA, Queen's U., Belfast, Northern Ireland, 1931, MA, 1957, D Lit, 1958; PhD, U. London, 1934; D Litt, Meml. U., Newfoundland, 1964, New U., Ulster, 1975, Nat. U. of Ireland, 1981; DHL, St. Marys Coll., 1964, MD, 1964; LLD, U. N.C., Chapel Hill, 1980; DHL, William and Mary Coll., 1995. Lectr. U. Coll., Southampton, Eng., 1934-39; sr. lectr. Queen's U. of Belfast, Northern Ireland, 1939-44; prof. U. Wales, Swansea, 1944-57; prof. Modern History U. Liverpool, Eng., 1957-76; visiting prof. Coll. of Willam and Mary, Williamsburg, Va., 1969-70, St. Mary's Coll. of Md., St. Mary's City, 1976-78, '80-82, U. Mich., Ann Arbor, 1979. Editor or co-editor many historical books including: Port Books of Southampton, Edward IV, 1937-39, Raleigh and the British Empire, 1947, 61, 73, Voyages of Sir Humphrey Gilbert, 2 vols., 1940, The Roanoke Voyages, 2 vols., 1955, (with P. Hulton) American Drawings of John White, 1964, North America from Earliest Discovery to First Settlement, 1977, John Derrick, The Image of Ireland, 1986, Explorers and Colonies: America 1500-1625, 1990, Ireland and America, 1500-1640, 1991, (with Alison M. Quinn) Discourse of Western Planting, 1993, European Approaches to North America, 1998; contbr. numerous articles to profl. jours. internationally. Named Leverhulme Rsch. Fellow, 1969-70, Hon. Sr. Fellow U. Liverpool, 1985, Fulbright 40th Anniversary Disting. Fellow, 1986, Hon. Fellow British Acad. 1984, Hon. v.p. Royal Hist. Soc., 1983, visiting scholar British Coun., New Zealand, Hungary, many other honors. Mem. Brit. Acad., Am. Hist. Assn., Royal Hist. Soc., Hakluyt Soc., Royal Irish Acad., Irish Hist. Soc., Soc. for the History of Discoveries, Past and Present Soc., Friends of Liverpool Maritime Mus., Friends of John Carter Brorn Libr. (medallist 1995), Caroliniana Soc., Friends of the Inst. of Early Am. History and Culture, Friends fo the U. Liverpool, Ulster Soc. of Irish Hist. Studies (hon. sec. 1939-44). Mem. British Labour Party. Avocation: collecting books and prints. Home: 9 Knowsley Rd, Liverpool L19 0PF, England Office: Dept History U Liverpool, PO Box 147, Liverpool L69 3BX, England

QUINN, FRANCIS XAVIER, arbitrator, mediator, author, lecturer; b. Dunmore, Pa., June 9, 1932; s. Frank T. and Alice B. (Maher) Q.; m. Marlene Stoker Quinn; children: Kimberly, Catherine, Cameron, Lindsay, Megan, Savannah. BA, Fordham U., 1956, MA, 1958; STB, Woodstock Coll., 1964; MS in Indsl. Rels., Loyola U., Chgo., 1966; PhD in Indsl. Rels., Calif. Western U., 1966. Assoc. dir. Inst. Indsl. Rels. St. Joseph's Coll., Phila., 1966-68; Manpower fellow Temple U., Phila., 1969-74, asst. to dean Sch. Bus. Adminstrn., 1972-78; arbitrator Fed. Mediation and Conciliation Svc., Nat. Mediation Bd., Am. Arbitration Assn., Nat. Assn. Railroad Referees, Dem. Nat. Steering Com.; ; apptd. to Rail Emergency Bd., 1975, to Fgn. Service Grievance Bd., 1976, 78, 80. Author: The Ethical Aftermath of Automation, 1963, Ethics and Advertising, 1965, Population Ethics, 1968, The Evolving Role of Women in the World of Work, 1969, Developing Community Responsibility, 1970; editor: The Ethical Aftermath Series; contbr. articles to profl. jours. V.p. Dem. Nat. Steering Com. 1998-2000; chmn. Hall of Fame com. Internat. Police Assn., 1990—, Tulsa City-County Mayor's Task Force to Combat Homelessness, 1991-92; mem. exec. bd. Tulsa Met. Ministries, 1990-92, Labor-Religion Coun. Okla., 1990—. Named Tchr. of Yr. Freedom Found., 1959; recipient Human Rels. award City of Phila., others; inducted into Hall of Fame, Internat. Police Assn., 2000. Mem. Nat. Acad. Arbitrators (v.p. 1999-2001), Indsl. Rels. Rsch. Assn., Assn. for Social Econs., Soc. for Dispute Resolution, Am. Arbitration Assn. (arbitrator), Nat. Assn. Railroad Refs. (v.p. 1996—, pres. 2000-2002, arbitrator), Internat. Soc. Labor Law and Social Security, Internat. Ombudsman Inst. Democrat. Home: 4213 Blackhaw Ave Fort Worth TX 76109-1618

QUINN, JARUS WILLIAM, physicist, former association executive; b. West Grove, Pa., Aug. 25, 1930; s. William G. and Ellen C. (DuRoss) Q.; m. Margaret M. McNerney, June 27, 1953; children: J. Kevin, Megan, Jennifer, Colin, Kristin. BS, St. Joseph's Coll., 1952; postgrad., Johns Hopkins U., 1952-55; PhD, Cath. U. Am., 1964. Rsch. assoc. physics Johns Hopkins U., 1954-55; staff scientist Rsch. Inst. Advanced Study, 1956-57; rsch. assoc. physics Cath. U. Am., 1958-60, instr., 1961-64, asst. prof., 1965-69; exec. dir. Optical Soc. Am., Washington, 1969-93; governing bd. Am. Inst. Physics, 1973-94; pres. Stellar Focus, Sunnyvale, Calif., 1994-95. Bd. govs. Am. Assn. Engring. Socs., 1990-93. Fellow Optical Soc. Am. (Distinguished Service Award, 1993), mem. Am. Phys. Soc., Am. Soc. Assn. Execs., Coun. Engring. and Sci. Soc. Execs. Home: 357 Fearrington Post Pittsboro NC 27312-8517

QUINN, JOHN MICHAEL, physicist, geophysicist; b. Denver, May 8, 1946; s. Leonard Simon and Winifred Ruth (Doolan) Q.; m. Pamela Dagmar Shield, May 28, 1983. BS in Physics, U. Va., 1968; MS in Physics, U. Colo., 1982. Physicist U.S. Naval Rsch. Lab., Washington, 1967-73; prin. engr. Singer Simulation Products, Silver Spring, Md., 1973-74; rsch. physicist U.S. Naval Rsch. Lab, Washington, 1979-80; geophysicist U.S. Naval Oceanog. Office, Stennis Space Ctr., Miss., 1974-79, 82-85, geophysicist, mathematician, 1985-95; rsch. geophysicist U.S. Geol. Survey, Denver, 1995—; investigator Polar Orbiting Geomagnetic Survey Experiment, 1990-94; prin. investigator Def. Meteorol. Satellite Program Polar Orbiting Geomagnetic Survey Ext., 1991—; chmn. com. on earth and planetary geomagnetic survey satellites Internat. Assn. Geomagnetism and Aeronomy, 1991—, mem. internat. geomagnetic ref. field com., 1989—; U.S. del. UN Internat. Stds. Orgn., 2000—. Author: Epoch World Geomagnetic Model, 1985, 90, 95. With U.S. Army, 1968-71. Mem. Am. Geophys. Union, Am. Math. Soc., European Geophys. Soc., Math. Assn. Am. Achievements include creation of official Department of Defense world magnetic models which are used by military and civilian agencies for navigational purposes and basic rsch. of the earth's magnetic field; project coord. USN Project MAGNET; developed specialized remote geomagnetic sensing/modeling techniques to detect, in the lithosphere, magnetization due to meteorite impact shocks and hotspot basalt flows; engaged in geodynamo research, yielding high-resolution fluid-flow models at the core-mantle-boundary. Home: 2732 S Braun Way Lakewood CO 80228-4954 Office: US Geog Survey Magnetics Group 966 Federal Blvd Denver CO 80204-3215

QUINN, LOCHLANN GERARD, manufacturing executive, bank executive; b. Dublin, Ireland, Nov. 6, 1941; s. Malachi and Julia (Hoey) Q.; m. Brenda Ivers; children: Oisin, Conall, Daragh, Lochlann, Alison, Sarah. B commerce, U. Coll. Dublin, 1962. Fellow Inst. Chartered Accts. in Ireland. Profl. staff Arthur Andersen, London, 1966-69; mgr. Arthur Andersen, Dublin, 1969-76, ptnr., 1976-80; dep. chmn., fin. dir. Glen Dimplex, Dublin, 1980-92, dep. chmn., 1992—; chmn. AIB Bank PLC, Dublin, 1997—. Bd. dirs. Irish Mus. Modern Art, Dublin, 1990-2000, Grad. Bus. Sch. U. Coll. Dublin, 1991—. Avocations: golf, art. Office: Glen Dimplex, 41 Ailesbury Rd, Dublin 4, Ireland

QUINN, MICHAEL DESMOND, diversified financial services executive; b. Balt., Sept. 4, 1936; s. Michael Joseph and Gladys (Baldwin) Q.; m. Mary Annette McHenry, Apr. 11, 1961; children: Cailin A., Maureen K., Patricia B., Marianne P. BA, U. Md., 1970. With Weaver Bros., Inc. of Md., Balt., 1960—, investment v.p., corporate dir. interim loan dept., 1978-86; chmn. bd. Wye Mortgage Co., L.P., 1977—, Christiana Capital Group, Inc.; chmn., chief exec. officer Alliance Recovery Group, Inc., 1990—, Estate Trust Co., Inc.; faculty evening coll. Johns Hopkins U., Essex Community Coll., 1967—. Mem. gov.'s task force Md. Housing Ins. Fund; mem. Md. Health Claims Arbitration Panel; bd. visitors U. Md.; dist. adv. coun. U.S. Small Bus. Adminstrn. With USN, 1956-58. Mem. Md. Mortgage Bankers Assn. (pres. bd. govs.), Real Estate Bd. Greater Balt. (bd. dirs.), Home Builders Assn. Md., Md. Bankers Assn., Balt. Econ. Soc., N.Am. Soc. Corp. Planning, Greater Balt. Com., Ancient Order Hibernians, Balt Jr. Assn. Commerce (Richard Troja Meml. award 1967, Outstanding Young Man of Balt. 1969), Balt. County C. of C. (bd. dirs.). Home: 8207 Robin Hood Ct Baltimore MD 21204-1900 Office: 7400 York Rd Ste 300 Baltimore MD 21204-7502

QUINN, MICHAEL JOHN, surgeon; b. Sydney, Australia, May 15, 1954; s. William Stewart and Madeline Agnes (Bigelow) Q. MB BChir, U. NSW, Sydney, 1979. Plastic surgeon Royal Prince Alfred Hosp., Sydney, 1988—. Fellow Royal Australian Coll. Surgeons. Avocations: yacht racing, skiing, longboarding. Home and Office: 155 Missenden Rd Ste 4, 2042 Newtown NSW, Australia

QUINN, RUAIRI, Irish politician; b. Dublin, Ireland, 1946; married; 2 children; remarried; 1 child. Student, Blackrock Coll., Dublin, 1960-64; Degree in Architecture, Univ. Coll., Dublin, 1969. Jr. architect, 1969-70; lectr. architecture Univ. Coll., Dublin, 1971-82; asst. design architect Burke, Kennedy, Doyle and Ptnrs., 1971-73, ptnr., 1974-82; mem. Dublin City Coun., 1974-77, 91-93, Dail Eireann, Irish Nat. Parliament, 1977-81, 81—; min. of state at environment/urban affairs Govt. of Ireland, 1982-83, min. for labour, 1984-87, min. of pub. svc., 1986-87; pres. Social Affairs Coun., 1984; mem. Coun. Social Affairs Mins. of European Union, 1984-87; prin. Ruairi Quinn & Assoc., 1987-93; opposition spokesperson on fin. and econ. affairs, 1989-93; alderman Dublin City Coun., 1991-93; leader Labour Group on Dublin Corp., 1991-93, Civic Alliance and Dublin City Coun., 1992-93; dep. leader Labour Party, 1989, 97; min. for enterprise and employment Govt. of Ireland, 1993-94; min. for fin. Govt. of Ireland, Dublin, 1994-97, leader labour party, 1997—. Fax: 6184153. Home: 23 Strand Rd, Sandymount, Dublin 4, Ireland Office: Leinster House, Dublin 2, Ireland*

QUINN, TOM, communications executive; b. L.A., Mar. 14, 1944; s. Joseph Martin and Grace (Cooper) Q.; m. Amy Lynn Friedman, Nov. 24, 1982; children: Douglas, Lori, Shelby. BS, Northwestern U., 1965. Reporter, newswriter ABC Radio, Chgo. and L.A., 1965; reporter, prodr. Sta. KXTV, Sacramento, 1966; day editor City News Svc., L.A., 1966-68, chmn., 1980-85; pres. Americom Broadcasting, Inc., L.A., 1985—; pres. Radio News West, L.A., 1968-70. campaign mgr. Jerry Brown for Sec. State, L.A., 1970; dep. sec. state Calif., Sacramento, 1971-74; campaign mgr. Brown for Gov., L.A., 1974; sec. Calif. Dept. Environ. Affairs, Sacramento, 1975-79; chmn. Calif. Air Resources Bd., Sacramento, 1975-79; pres. Reno Radio Reps., 1998—, KFSO Radio, Fresno, 1995-98; dir. Parallel Comms. Co.; dir. Southland News, L.A.; dir. Frightmare, Inc., Reno, Nev., 1999—, Parallel Comms. Co.; chmn. Tom Bradley Mayoral Campaign, 1985. Recipient Headliner of Yr. award Greater L.A. Press Club, 1978, Environ. Protection award Calif. Trial Lawyers Assn., 1979. Democrat. Office: # 1880 1900 Ave of the Stars Los Angeles CA 90067

QUIÑONES, JOSE EDUARDO, lawyer; b. Guatemala City, Guatemala, Mar. 8, 1968; s. Mario R. and O. Yolanda (Leòn) Q. JD, Landivar U., Guatemala, 1992; MBA, U. Rochester, 1995. Ct. officer Guatemala Supreme Ct., Guatemala, 1985-92; ptnr. Quiñones & Quiñones, Guatemala, 1992—; prof. Universidad Francisco, Marroquin, Guatemala, 1996—; dir. Qia Capital Mgmt., Guatemala, 1995—. Mem. AIDA (rep. del. 1997—). Avocation: HAM radio TG9AQL. Office: Quiñones & Ibarguen, 6 calle 5-47 zona 9, 01009 Guatemala Guatemala

QUINT, DAVID PAUL, investment banking executive; b. Independence, Iowa, July 24, 1950; s. Paul Theodore and Mary Ann (Connolly) Q.; m. Kathleen Mary Stern, May 25, 1973; children: Jennifer, Angela, David, Geoffrey. BA in Modern Langs., U. Notre Dame, 1972, JD, 1975. Assoc. Arter & Hadden, Cleve., 1975-82; mng. dir. Belden & Blake, London, 1983-92; pres., CEO RP&C Internat., London, 1992—. Mem. Notre Dame Law Rev., 1974. Rotary Internat. fellow, 1978. Mem. Ohio State Bar Assn. Republican. Roman Catholic. Avocation: travel. Home: Avallon East Rd, KT1 30LF Weybridge England Office: RP&C Internat, 56 Green St, W1Y 3RH London England

QUINTANILLA, ANTONIO PAULET, physician, educator; b. Feb. 8, 1927; came to U.S., 1963, naturalized, 1974; s. Leandro Marino and Edel Paulet Quintanilla; m. Mary Parker Rodriguez, May 2, 1958; children: Antonio Paulet, Angela, Francis, Cecilia, John. PhD, San Marcos U., 1948, MD, 1957. Assoc. prof. physiology U. Arequipa, Peru, 1960-63; assoc. in physiology Cornell U., N.Y., 1963-64; prof. physiology U. Arequipa, 1964-68; assoc. prof. medicine Northwestern U., 1969-80, prof., 1980-2000; ret.; chief renal sect. VA Lakeside Hosp., 1976-90; cons. nephrologist Northwestern Meml. Hosp., Evanston Hosp., 1990-98, sr. attending emeritus; lectr. nat. Ctr. Advanced Med. Edn., Chgo.; mem. adv. bd. Am. Fedn. Clin. Rsch. Contbr. articles on renal disease to med. jours.; author books, poetry, short stories. Fellow ACP; mem. Ctrl. Soc. Clin. Rsch., Internat. Soc. Nephrology, Am. Soc. Nephrology, Am. Physiol. Soc. Home: 650 S River Rd Unit 411 Des Plaines IL 60016-8428 Office: Nephrology Divsn Evanston Hosp 2650 Ridge Ave Evanston IL 60201-1718

QUINTANILLA, EDUARDO RODRIGO, lawyer, educator; b. La Paz, Bolivia, Sept. 21, 1963; s. Eduardo Quintanilla and Graciela Balliviàn. JD, U. Mayor de San Andrès, La Paz, 1987; DSU, U. de Droit, The Sorbonne, Paris, 1989; LLM, Harvard U., 1990. Assoc. Quintanilla & Soria Abodados, La Paz, 1990-93; ptnr. Quintanilla & Soria Abogados, La Paz, 1993—; prof. comml. law U. Mayor de San Andrés, 1991-92, U. Catolica Boliviana, La Paz, 1993-96; prof. IID UCB masters program Harvard U., La Paz, 1996—; mem. cons. com. IID/UCB masters program Harvard U., La Paz, 1993—. Mem. Assn. for Def. of Civil Rights (bd. dirs. 1991—), Colegio Abogados de Bolivia, Circulo de la Unión, Harvard Club of Bolivia (bd. dirs. 1995—). Avocations: literature, music, arts, photography, travel. Home: Obrajes Calle 6 No 614, Casilla La Paz 3143, Bolivia Office: Quintanilla Soria Abogados, Loayza 250 Edif Castilla, Piso 7 Castilla 3143 La Paz, Bolivia

QUINTAO, GERALDO MAGELA DA CRUZ, federal official. Min. of def. Brazil. Office: Ministry of Defense, Esplanada dos Ministerios, Brasilia Brazil*

QUINTON, LORD ANTHONY MEREDITH, academic administrator; b. Gillingham, Kent, Eng., Mar. 25, 1925; s. Richard Frith and Gwenllyan Letitia (Jones) Q.; m. Marcelle Wegier, Aug. 2, 1952; children: Joanna Bateman, Edward Frith. BA, Oxford (Eng.) U., 1949, MA, 1950; LHD, NYU, 1986; DHL, Ball State U., 1989. Fellow All Souls Coll., Oxford, 1949-55; fellow, tutor New Coll., Oxford, 1955-78; lectr. Oxford U., 1950-78; pres. Trinity Coll., Oxford, 1978-87; chmn. bd. Brit. Library, London, 1985-90; gov. Stowe Sch., Buckingham, Eng., 1963-83; fellow Winchester (Eng.) Coll., 1970-85; del. Oxford Univ. Press, 1970-76; mem. Arts Coun. Great Britain, London, 1979-81. Author: The Nature of Things, 1973, Utilitarian Ethics, 1973, Politics of Imperfection, 1978, Thoughts and Thinkers, 1982. Mem. House of Lords, Westminster, 1982, Govt. Com. on Future of Broadcasting, London, 1986. With RAF, 1943-46. Brit. Acad. fellow, 1977. Mem. Beefsteak, Garrick, Brooks's. Conservative. Home: A11 Albany, Piccadilly, London W1V 9RD, England

QUINTOS, JUAN GOMEZ, JR., bank executive; b. Manila, Nov. 24, 1932; s. Juan Dizon and Natalia (Gomez) Q.; m. Lourdes Ejercito, Mar. 2, 1957; children: Emmanuel, John, Victor, Agnes, Carmela. BBA, U. The Philippines, 1953; MS, Columbia U., 1955; diploma in econ. and social adminstrn., London U., 1961. Staff mem. Ctrl. Bank of The Philippines, San Juan, 1955-73, dir., 1973-74, spl. asst., 1974-80, dep. gov., 1980-92, monetary bd., 1999—. Contbr. articles to profl. jours. Bd. dirs. U. of the East, The Philippines, 1989-90; prof. Far Eastern U., The Philippines, 1956-68; cons. Asia United Bank, The Philippines, 1998-99. Mem. Panxenia Internat. Trade Fraternity. Roman Catholic. Avocations: sports, reading, painting. Home: 39 R Lagmay, 1500 San Juan The Philippines

QUIRICI, DANIEL, finance company executive; b. Chelles, France, June 8, 1948; s. Ernest Jean and Candide Albine (Postai) Q.; m. Margaret Louise Mann, Sept. 1972; children: Alexander, Francois, Florence. MA, Sorbonne, Paris, 1970; MBA, Hautes Etudes Commerciales, Jouy, France, 1970; PhD, Stanford U., 1974. Cons. Mgmt. Analysis Ctr. Inc., Cambridge, Mass., 1974-76, Arthur D. Little, Paris, 1976-82; v.p. Credit Commercial de France, Paris, 1983-85; mng. dir. C.C.F.-Laurence Prust Ltd., London, 1986-91; ptnr., CEO Deloitte Touche, London, 1991—; CEO Corp. Fin. Europe, London, 1991—; bd. dirs. Schroder Salomon Smith Barney subs. Citygroup. Mem. Knightsbridge Assn. Traffic Com., London, 1988—. Mem. Royal Automobile Club, Hurlingham Club. Avocations: tennis, golf, antiques, music. Fax: 44-20-79-86-80-90. E-mail: daniel.quirici@ssmb.com. Home: 8 Montpelier Sq, London SW7 1JU, England Office: Citigroup Ctr, 33 Canada Square, Canary Wharf London E14 5LB, England

QUIRK, LORD RANDOLPH, former academy president, educator, consultant; b. Isle of man, U.K., July 12, 1920; s. Thomas and Amy Randolph (Simcocks) Q.; m. Gabriele Stein. BA, U. London, 1947, MA, 1949, PhD, 1951, DLitt, 1961; hon. doctorate, Lund U., Uppsala U., U. Paris, U. Liège, U. Nijmegen, U. Leicester, U. Poznan, Bar Ilan U., U. So. Calif., U. Glasgow, Richmond C., U. Copenhagen, U. Bath, U. Reading, U. Salford, U. Durham, U. Newcastle, U. Prague,, Open U., U. Essex, U. Sheffield, Brunel U., U. London. Postdoctoral fellow Yale U., 1951-52; prof. English, Durham (Eng.) U., 1954-60; prof. English, London U., 1960-81, vice chancelor, 1981-85; Lee Kuan Yew fellow Nat. U. Singapore, 1985-86; pres. British Acad., 1985-89, Coll. Speech Therapists, 1987-91; chmn. Brit. Govt. Inquiry into Speech Therapy Service, 1969-72, chmn. adv. com. Brit. Library, 1984-97, Hornby Ednl. Trust, 1979-93; trustee Am. Sch. in London, 1986-89, Wolfson Found., 1987—; vice chmn. govs. Am. U. London. Author numerous books. Decorated comdr. Order Brit. Empire, 1976, knight, 1985, life peer, 1994. Fellow Brit. Acad., Royal Belgian Acad. Scis., Royal Swedish Acad., Acad. Europea, Finnish Acad. Scis.; mem. Am. Acad. Arts and Scis., Linguistic Soc. Am., Philol Soc. U.K., Athenaeum Club. Office: U Coll, Gower St, London WC1E 6BT, England

QUIROGA RAMIREZ, JORGE FERNANDO, vice president of Bolivia; b. May 5, 1960; married; 3 children . BS in Indsl. Engring. summa cum laude, Tex. A&M, 1981; MBA, U. St. Edward, Austin, Tex., 1986. Asst. prof. calculus Tex. A&M U., College Sta., 1980-81; computer engr. IBM, Austin, Tex., 1981-88; advisor fin. adminstrn. sys. and govt. control project Gen. Auditor of Bolivia, La Paz, 1988-89; adminstrv. mgr. MINTEC, La Paz, 1989-90; econ. advisor Minister of Fgn. Affairs, Bolivia, 1990; undersec. pub. investment and internat. cooperation Ministry of Planning, Bolivia, 1990-91; minister of fin. Bolivia, 1992, nat. chmn. presdl. campaign Gen. Hugo Bánzer Suárez, 1992-93; advisor to pres. Andean Devel. Corp., 1993; v.p. investment project Banco Mercantil, S.A., Bolivia, 1993-97; v.p. Govt. Bolivia, 1997—. Vice chmn. Acción Dem. Nacionalista, 1995-97. Office: Palacio Legislativo, Ayacucho esq Mercado, La Paz Bolivia*

QUIROZ VELASCO, MARIA TERESA, dean, communications researcher; b. Lima, Peru, Mar. 28, 1952; d. Jorge Quiroz R. and Berta Velasco de Q.; m. Mario Alfredo Tejada Ch., Apr. 6, 1973 (div. Jan. 3, 1988); children: Paula Tejada Q., Natalia Tejada Q. B in Social Studies, U. Nat. San Marcos, Lima, Perú, 1973, degree in sociology, 1975; M in Sociology, U. Católica, Lima, Perú, 1979. Asst. Inst. Planification, Lima, Perú, 1973-74; prof. Escuela Bellas Artes, Lima, Perú, 1976-92, U. del Pacifico, Lima, Perú, 1980-85; prof. U. Lima, 1980-97, dir. acad., 1994-96, dean Faculty of Mass Comm., 1996—; dir. Federación Latinoamericana de Facultades de Comunicación Social, Lima, 1986-89, 90-92. Author: Escolares y Medios de Comunicación en Lima Metropolitana, 1992, La Recepción Crítica de Televisión, 1993, Todas las Voces, 1993, Videojuegos o los compañeros Virtuales, 1996. Recipient Rsch. award Bustamente y Rivero, Haya de la Torre. Mem. Asociación Latinoamericana de Investigadores de la Comunicación, Asociación Peruana de Investigadores de la Comunicación, Asociación Peruana para el Fomento de las Ciencias Sociales, Internat. Assn. of Mass Comm. Rsch. Office: U Lima, Av Javier Prado Este s/n, Lima Lima 100, Peru

QURAISHI, MOHAMMED SAYEED, health scientist, administrator; b. Jodhpur, India, June 23, 1924; came to U.S., 1946, naturalized, 1973; s. Mohammed Latif and Akhtar Jahan Q.; m. Akhtar Imtiaz, Nov. 12, 1953; children: Rana, Naveed, Sabah. B.Sc., St. John's Coll., 1942; M.Sc., Aligarh Muslim U., 1944; Ph.D., U. Mass., 1948. Sr. mem. UN, WHO Team to Bangladesh, 1949-51; entomologist Malaria Inst. Pakistan, 1951-55; sr. rsch. officer Pakistan Council Sci. and Indsl. Rsch., 1955-60; sr. sci. officer Pakistan AEC, 1960-64; assoc. prof. entomology U. Man., 1964-66; assoc. prof. entomology N.D. State U., Fargo, 1966-70, prof., 1970-74; chief scientist biology N.Y. State Sci. Svc., Albany, 1974-75; entomologist, toxicologist, chief pest control and consultation sect. NIH, Bethesda, Md., 1976-84; health scientist adminstr., exec. sec. microbiology and infectious disease rsch. com. Nat. Inst. Allergy and Infectious Diseases, Bethesda, Md., 1984-88, sci. rev. adminstr. spl. revs., 1988-96, sci. rev. adminstr. AIDS clin. epidemiol. rsch. rev. br., 1996—; sr. scientist Cen. Treaty Orgn., Inst. Nuclear Sci., Tehran, Iran, 1960-64; program mgr. interdepartmental contract Project THEMIS, Dept. Def., 1968-74; vis. scientist Harvard Sch. of Pub. Health, 1995. Author: Biochemical Insect Control: Its Impact on Economy, Environment and Natural Selection, 1977; mem. editorial bd. Jour. Environ. Toxicology and Chemistry, 1981-84; author numerous sci. papers. Chmn. NIH Asian-Am. Cultural Assn., 1980-81. Recipient Sustained High Quality Performance award, 1980, Merit Pay Performance awards, 1984, 86, 87, Recognition and Appreciation of Spl. Achievement award NIH, 1988, Spl. Recognition award for Svcs. to NIH, Asian Am. Cultural Com., 1989, Appreciation in Recognition of Outstanding Support for Combined Fed. Campaign, 1991. Mem. Am. Chem. Soc., Soc. Environ. Toxicology and Chemistry (mem. publs. com. in charge spl. publs. 1982-84), Sigma Xi, Phi Kappa Phi. Home: 19813 Cochrane Way Gaithersburg MD 20879-1637 Office: NIH 6700 B Rockledge Dr Rm 2103 Bethesda MD 20892-0001

QURAISHI, MUMTAZ AHMAD, chemistry educator, researcher; b. Khandwa, India, July 1, 1951; s. Shakur Abdul Quraishi and Sharifa Begum; m. Rehana Quraishi, May 26, 1952; children: Sarosh, Danish, Ramish Arafat. BSc, Saugur (India) U., 1969, MSc, 1971; MPhil, Kurukshetra (India) U., 1978, PhD, 1986. Lectr. Coll. Arts, Commerce and Sci., Dhamtari, India, 1971-72; asst. prof. Govt. Sci. Coll., Jabalpur, India, 1973-86; prof. Govt. Girls Coll., Bilaspur, India, 1986-90; reader Aligarh (India) Muslim U., 1990—. Contbr. over 75 articles to profl. jours. and books. Recipient Indian Nat. Sci. Acad. award, 1992; Coun. Sci. and Indsl. Rsch. vis. fellow, 1993. Mem. Nat. Assn. Corrosion Engrs. Internat. (regional dir. 1995-99, Excellence award 1997), Soc. Advancement Electrochem. Sci. and Tech. (vice chmn. corrosion group 1995-97), Electrochem. Soc. India. Fax: 91-571-700528. Home: B-9 Med Colony AMU, Aligarh 202002, India Office: Aligarh Muslim U, Applied Chemistry, Aligarh 202002, India

QURESHI, AZHAR K., biostatistician, research scientist; b. Karachi, Sindh, Pakistan, June 12, 1962; came to U.S., 1988; s. Gihulam K. and Saeeda H. (Hashmi) Q.; m. Adriana Rosas Masi, Dec. 27, 1997. MD, Dow Med. Coll., Karachi, 1987; MPH, Calif. State U., Northridge, 1994; DPH, UCLA, 1997. Chief rsch. scientist St. Joseph Health Sys., Orange, Calif., 1997—. Contbr. articles to profl. jours. Mem. Am. Statis. Assn., Inst. Bus. Forecasting, UCLA Alumni Assn. Avocations: weight lifting, running, soccer. Home: 412 N Palm Dr Beverly Hills CA 90210-4054 Office: Saint Joseph Health Sys 440 S Batavia St Orange CA 92868-3995

QURESHI, FAZAL, editor-in-chief, newspaper publishing executive; b. Ambala, British India, Jan. 10, 1933; s. Nazar Mohammad and Amtul Manan Qureshi; m. Mumtaz Khalil-Mumtaz, Mar. 31, 1963; children: Amer, Imran. M Persian, U. Karachi, Pakistan, 1954, M Journalism, 1956. Reporter Pakistan Press Internat. News Agy., Karachi, 1956—, chief reporter, 1960, fgn. corr. in Middle East, 1961-65, mng. dir., chief editor, 1977—; part-time corr. The Times, London, 1966-68, Newsweek, N.Y.C., 1966—. Islam. Avocations: travel, writing, music, photography. Home: G/3 Roomi Gardens, Khyaban Roomi, Chifton POB 3837 Karachi 75600, Pakistan Office: Pakistan Press Internat, PO Box 3837 Chiffon, Karachi Pakistan

QURESHI, GHULAM ALI, bioanalytical chemist, educator; b. Hyderabad, Sind, Pakistan, July 6, 1948; arrived in Sweden, 1978; s. Ziaullah and Hawi Qureshi; m. Ilze Vagals, Apr. 2, 1976; children: Tarik, Omar, Joseph. BSc with honors, Sind U., Jamshoro, Pakistan, 1969, MSc, 1970; PhD, Queen's U., Belfast, Northern Ireland, 1975; diploma in analytical chemistry, Uppsala (Sweden) U., 1972. Rsch. fellow Queens U., Belfast, 1973-75; fellow Aston's U., Birmingham, Eng., 1975-76; asst. prof. El-Fatah U., Tripoli, Libya, 1976-78; rsch. assoc. Linköping (Sweden) U., 1978-80; vis. scientist Max Plank Inst., Mülheim, Germany, 1980-82; rsch. engr. Inst. Renal Medicine Karolinska Inst., Stockholm, 1982-90, biochemist dept. psychiatry, 1990-94, assoc. prof. Clin. Rsch. Ctr. and clin. neurosci. dept., 1994-97; prof. clin. biochemistry dept. Bagai Med. U., Karachi, 1997—. Contbr. articles to profl. jours., chpts. to books. Mem. AAAS, Brit. Soc. Endocrinology, N.Y. Acad. Scis. Avocations: tennis, reading, swimming, mountain climbing, chess. Office: Bagai Med U Dept Biochemistry, PO Box 2407 Tor Plz Super Hwy, Karachi Pakistan

QURESHI, JAHANGIR, mechanical engineer; b. Lahore, Pakistan, Dec. 5, 1958; s. Mohammad and Manzoor (Fatima) Q.; m. Farida Rehman, Oct. 6, 1989; children: Anam, Myra. BSc, U. Engring. & Technology, Lahore, 1980; MSc, U. New Brunswick, 1983. Design engr. Descon Ltd., Lahore, Pakistan, 1980-81; quality control engr. to sr. mgr. engines/diversification Millat Tractors Ltd., Lahore, 1984—. Mem. ASME, Instn. Engrs. Pakistan, Pakistan Engring. Coun. Avocations: badminton, reading, gardening, stamp collecting, international affairs. Home: 202B Phase II A Block, Govt Coop Housing, Lahore 54700, Pakistan

QURESHI, SHAKEEL AHMED, pediatric cardiologist; b. Kotli, Azad Kashm, Pakistan, Mar. 20, 1952; s. Mohammed Aslam and Sara (Begum) Q.; m. Azra Siddique, Dec. 29, 1968; children: Rahila Noreen, Sajid Shakeel, Abid Shakeel, Atif Imran Shakeel. MBChB, U. Manchester, 1976; MRCP, Royal Coll. Physicians, London, 1979. FRCP; cons. pediatric cardiologist. Rsch. fellow Harefield (U.K.) Hosp., 1980-83; cons. cardiologist Armed Forces Inst. of Cardiology, Rawalpindi, Pakistan, 1983-85; rsch. fellow Guy's Hosp., London, 1985-86, cons. pediatric cardiologist, 1988—; sr. registrar Children's Hosp., Liverpool, U.K., 1986-87, cons. pediatric cardiologist, 1987-88. Inventor in field; contbr. articles to profl. jours. Maj. Army Med. Corps, Pakistan Army, 1983-85. Mem. Assn. European Paediatric Cardiologists, Brit. Paediatric Cardiac Assn. (hon. sec. 1991-93), Brit. Cardiac Soc. Avocations: playing cricket, badminton, travel. Office: Guys Hosp Dept Paediatric Cardiology, St Thomas St, London SE1 9RT, England

QURESHI, SOHAIL ASIF, molecular biologist, researcher; b. Lahore, Punjab, Pakistan, May 21, 1963; arrived in Eng., 1995; s. Asif Ali Qureshi and Shamim Asif; m. Romena Gazi, Feb. 1999. Diploma D'études Collégiales, Champlain Coll., Quebec, Can., 1982; MSc, Quaid I. Azam U., Islamabad, Pakistan, 1984; PhD, U. Maine, 1990. Postdoc. fellow Glasgow (Scotland) U., 1990-93; sr. postdoc. fellow Imperial Cancer Rsch. Fund, London, 1993-94, Cambridge (Eng.) U., 1994-97; staff scientist U. Wis., Madison, 1997—. Author: (chpt.) Modular Texts in Molecular and Cellular Biology, 1997; contbr. articles to profl. jours. Named Most Disting. Scholar, Min. Edn., Pakistan, 1982. Muslim. Avocations: chess, travel, bridge, football, hockey. Fax: 608-262-2327. Office: U Wis Dept Neurology MSC Rm 1765 1300 University Ave Madison WI 53706

QURESHY, JAMIL AHMAD, librarian; b. Aligarh, India, Jan. 10, 1938; s. Ahmad Khalil and Khursheed Jehan; m. Malika Jamil Qureshy. BA, Muslim U., 1957, BLS, 1960; MA, JMI U., New Delhi, 1968, PhD, 1993. Asst. libr. JMI U., New Delhi, 1961-75; libr. King Fahd U. of Petroleum and Minerals, Dhahran, Saudi Arabia, 1975—; fellow librarianship and documentation, Holland, 1971-72; convener Libr. Automation, Internat. Indian Sch., Dammam, Saudi Arabia, 1996-98. Contbr. articles to profl. jours. Mem. mng. com. Internat. Indian Sch., 1996-98. Librarianship fellow Govt. Netherlands, 1971-72. Mem. Spl. Librs. Assn. (Arabian Gulf chpt.). Avocations: reading, social service. Office: King Fahd Univ of, Petroleum/Minerals No 1613, 31261 Dhahran Saudi Arabia

QVARNSTROM, MARI JOHANNA, physician; b. Juankoski, Finland, Jan. 29, 1963; d. Ake Verner and Vappu Bertta (Putkonen) Q; m. Markku Ali Ilmari Surakka, June 14, 1986; children: Lasse Verner, Leo Walfrid. Lic. in Medicine, U. Kuopio, Finland, 1988, MD, 1994; Specialistin Phoniatrics, U. Kuopio Hosp., 1995. Physician Kuopio Univ. Hosp., 1989-94, specialist in phoniatrics, 1995—, physician-in-chief dept. phoniatrics, 1996—; lectr. faculty of medicine U. Kuopio, 1993—. Contbr. articles to profl. jours. Mem. Finnish Phoniatricians, Internat. Assn. Logopedics and Phoniatrics, Finnish Otolaryn Soc. Office: Kuopio Univ Hosp, PB 1777, 70211 Kuopio Finland

RAABERG, GLORIA GWEN, literature educator; b. Atlanta, Dec. 31, 1932; d. Lawrence Leslie and Gwendolyn Neff (Ewing) Hill; m. Charles B. Raaberg, Jan. 29, 1955 (div. 1983); children: Charlyn L., Ross W., Valerie R. BA, Col. William & Mary, 1954; MA, Calif. State U., 1971; PhD, U. Calif., Irvine, 1978. Instr. lit. UCLA, 1977-78; Mellon fellow lit. Case Western Res. U., Cleve., 1978-79; asst. prof. U. Tex., Dallas, 1979-85, 87-89; vis. prof. U. Calif., Irvine, 1985-86; Fulbright sr. prof. U. Debrecen, Hungary, 1986-87; prof. English, dir. women's studies Western Mich. U., Kalamazoo, 1989—; fellow Ctr. Humanities U. Calif., 1985-86, U. Va., Charlottesville, 1996; mem. exec. bd. Ctr. Ethics in Soc., Kalamazoo, Mich., 1991—. Author: Toward a Theory of Literary Collage, 1978; co-editor: Surrealism and Women, 1991; contbr. articles to profl. jours. Mem. Women Civic Leaders Network, Kalamazoo, 1989-92. Lilly Found. grantee, 1991-93, NEH grantee, 1983-85. Mem. MLA, Nat. Women's Studies Assn., Am. Studies Assn. Avocations: hiking, art, archaeology. Office: Western Mich U Kalamazoo MI 49008

RAAMACHANDRAN, JAYARAMAN, engineering educator; b. Madras, India, July 31, 1943; s. Thiruvenkadu Swetharanyan Jayaraman and Jayaraman Jayalakshmi; m. Jayanthi Venkatesan, June 6, 1971; 2 children. BSc in Physics, Madras U., 1963, BE in Civil Engring., 1966; MTech., Indian Inst. Tech., Madras, 1971, PhD, 1974. Siddha med. diplomate. Assoc. lectr., lectr. Indian Inst. Tech., Madras, 1971-82, asst. prof., 1982-91, assoc. prof., 1991-93, prof., 1993—; softwarecons. Murugan Valli Enterprise, Madras, 1993—. Author: Strength of Materials, 1980, Plasticity and Plastic Design, 1982, Thin Shells, Theory and Problems, 1993, Boundary and Finile Elements, 2000. Mem. Intenrat. Soc. for Boundary Elements. Mem. Tamil religion, Murugan Cult. Avocations: astrology, Tamil story writing, Iamil music singing. Home: Murugan Illam, 6 Kamakoti Nagar, 600087 Madras India Office: Indian Inst Tech, 600036 Madras India

RAAS, DANIEL ALAN, lawyer; b. Portland, Oreg., July 6, 1947; s. Alan Charles and Mitzi (Cooper) R.; m. Deborah Ann Becker, Aug. 5, 1973; children: Amanda Beth, Adam Louis. BA, Reed Coll., 1969; JD, NYU, 1972. Bar: Wash. 1973, Calif. 1973, U.S. Dist. Ct. (we. dist.) Wash. 1973, U.S. Ct. Appeals (9th cir.) 1975, U.S. Supreme Ct. 1977, U.S. Tax Ct. 1983, U.S. Ct. Claims 1984. Atty. Seattle Legal Svcs, VISTA, 1972-73; reservation atty. Quinault Indian Nation, Taholah, Wash., 1973-76; reservation atty. Lummi Indian Nation, Bellingham, Wash., 1976-97, spl. counsel, 1997—; mem. Raas, Johnsen & Stuen, P.S., Bellingham, 1982—; cons. Falmouth Inst., Fairfax, Va., 1992—, Nat. Am. Ind. Ct. Judges Assn., McLean, Va., 1976-80. Rules chmn. Whatcom County Dem. Conv., Bellingham, 1988, 92, 94, 96; bd. dirs. Congregation Beth Israel, Bellingham, 1985-2000, pres., 1990-92; mem. adv. com. legal asst. program Bellingham Vocat. Tech. Inst., 1985-91; trustee Whatcom County Law Libr., 1978—; pres. Vol. Lawyer Program, 1990-93, bd. dirs., 1988-94; pres. Cliffside Cmty. Assn., 1978-80, bd. dirs., 1977-89; bd. dirs. Friends Maritime Heritage Ctr., 1983-86, Samish Camp Fire Coun., 1988-94, pres. 1991-94, v.p., 1989-91, regional v.p. Union Am. Hebrew Congregations, 1986-93, nat. trustee, 1995—, exec. com., 1995-99, sec. Pacific N.W. region, 1993-95, pres., 1995-99. John Ben Snow scholar, NYU, 1969-70, Root-Tilden scholar, NYU, 1970-72. Mem. Wash. State Bar Assn. (trustee Ind. law sect. 1989-95, Pro Bono award 1991), Whatcom County Bar Assn. (v.p. 1981, pres. 1982, Pro Bono award 1991), Grays Harbor Bar Assn. (v.p. 1976). Home: 1929 Lake Crest Dr Bellingham WA 98226-4510 Office: Raas Johnsen & Stuen PS 1503 E St Bellingham WA 98225-3007

RAB, ABDUR, soil physicist; b. Dhaka, Bangladesh, Mar. 3, 1952; arrived in Australia, 1982; s. Lal Miah and Asia Begum; m. Monowara Begum, Dec. 25, 1977; children: Masum, Rumana. BS with honors, Bangladesh Agrl. U., 1975; PhD, La Trobe U., Melbourne, Australia, 1977; M of Engring., AIT, Bangkok, Thailand, 1979. Lectr. Bangladesh Agrl. U., 1987—; rsch. scientist dept. natural resources and environment; sr. rsch. scientist dept. natural resources Keith Tumball Rsch. Inst., Franston, Australia, 1984. Contbr. articles to profl. jours. Home: 42 Monash Cres, Melbourne 3169, Australia Office: Keith Tumbell Rsch Inst, Bollarto Rd, Frankston 3199, Australia

RABADEAU, MARY FRANCES, protective services official; b. Elizabeth, N.J., July 13, 1948; d. Russell John and Frances (Hanley) R. Student, Union Coll., 1967-69; MEd, Kean Coll., 1976. Officer City of Elizabeth Police Dept., N.J., 1978-82, detective, 1982-83, sgt., 1983-87, lt., 1987-91, capt., 1991-92; dir. City of Elizabeth Police Dept., 1993-95, dep. chief, 1994; chief N.J. Transit Police Dept., Maplewood, 1995—; instr. Union County Police Acad. Trustee Blessed Sacrament Ch., Elizabeth, N.J., 1989-99; bd. acad. advisors N.J. state police grad. studies program Seton Hall U.; bd. trustees Benedictine Acad., Elizabeth, N.J. Named one of Outstanding Young Women in Am., 1983, Woman Leader N.J. Assn. Women Bus. Owners, 1997; recipient John H. Stamler Police Acad. Svc. award, 1992, Cert. of Recognition award YWCA, 1992, Disting. Grad. award Nat. Cath. Ednl. Assn., 1995; honoree Union County Commn. on the Status of Women, 1993, Hispanic Law Enforcement Assn. of Union County, 1995. Mem. NAACP, Internat. Assn. Chiefs of Police, N.J. State Chiefs of Police, Essex County Chiefs Assn., N.E. Assn. Women Police (cert., Merit award), Elizabeth Police Patrolman's Benevolent Assn., Elizabeth Police Superior Officers Assn. (treas. 1983-91, v.p. 1991), Am. Soc. Law Enforcement Trainers, Emerald Soc., Union County Urban League, Italian Law Enforcement Officers Assn., Fellas Inc. (hon.), Union County Men's Svc. Orgn., Nat. Assn. of Women Law Enforcement Execs. Democrat. Roman Catholic. Office: NJ Transit Police Dept 180 Boyden Ave Maplewood NJ 07040-2494

RABANALES, AMBROSIO, linguistics educator, researcher; b. Santiago, Chile, July 11, 1917; s. Inocencio R. and Eloísa Ortiz; m. Lidia Contreras, 1953; children: Gabriel, Ananda. Lic. en Filosofía, U. Chile, 1941, Lic. en Filología Clásica, 1942, D in Filología Románica, 1954. Prof. Castillian U. Chile, Santiago, Chile, 1946—; rector Liceo Nocturno Federico Hanssen, Santiago, Chile, 1948-51; dir. Inst. Filología U. Chile, Santiago, 1970; pres. Ateneo Santiago, 1996-97; invited prof. U. Bonn, U. Augsburgc, U. Heidelberg, U. Bucharest, U. Colonia, U. Nac. Autónoma Mex., U. Nac. San Juan, Argentina, U. Leipzig, U. Basel, U. Nimega, U. Utrecht, The Netherlands. Author: Introducción al estudio del español de Chile, 1953, Determínación del Concepto de Chilenismo, (with Lidia Contreras) Léxico del habla culta de Santiago de Chile, 1987, Métodos probatorios en gramática científica, 1992; editor: (with Lidia Contreras) El habla culta de Santiago de Chile-Materiales para su estudio, 1990; cons. Intercontinental Dictionary Series U. Calif., 1984, (CD Rom) Encarta Ency., Madrid, 1996. Mem. Soc. Ling. Paris, Comité Internat. Scis. Onomastiques Louvain (Belgium, hon.), Internat. Soc. Functional Linguistics, 1979, Real Acad. Española, Acad. Chilena de la Lengua (pres. grammar commn. 1994), Assn. Ling. y Filología Am. Lat. (sec. gen. 1966-77), Soc. Chilena de Linguistics. Avocations: music, painting. Home: La Verbena 3882 Providencia, Santiago Chile Office: U Chile, Casilla 10136, Santiago Chile

RABBANI, KHONDKAR SIDDIQUE-E, physics educator; b. Faridpur, Bangladesh, May 9, 1950; s. Khondkar Lutfi Rabbani and Najmon Nesa; m. Gulshan Ara Begum, Apr. 27, 1980; children: Piul Sanjana, Rhaad Muasir. BS in Physics with honors, U. Dhaka, Bangladesh, 1970; MS in Physics, U. Islamabad, Pakistan, 1972; PhD in Electronics, U. Southampton, 1978. Lectr. Resdl. Model Coll., Dhaka, 1973-74; asst. prof. dept. physics U. Dhaka, Bangladesh, 1978-84, assoc. prof., 1984-88, prof., 1988—; cons. Bangladesh Electronic Projucti Kendro, Dhaka, 1990-93, Bangladesh Innovative Tech. Group, Dhaka, 1993-97; cons. dir. Grameen-Bitek, Ltd., Dhaka, 1997—; pres. Relevant Sci. and Tech. Soc., Dhaka, 1996—; dir. Bangladesh Inst. for Biomed. Engring. and Appropriate Tech., Dhaka, 1996—; vis. prof. IIT Kanpur, India, 1997; invited spkr. X Internat. Conf. Electrical Bio-impedance, Barcelona, Spain, 1998. Patentee in field; photographer: (photographic set) People at Work, 1979 (3d prize Bangladesh Photographic Soc. award 1979), Mosques, 1980 (1st prize - color - Islamic Found./Bangladesh award 1980, 2d prize - black and white). Pres. Cine-Seek Audiovisual Club, Dhaka, 1982—. Recipient Commonwealth scholarship Commonwealth Commn., U.K., 1974; Nat. fellow Asiatic Soc. Bangladesh, 1995-96; grantee for rsch. WHO, Dhaka, 1983-86, Brit. Coun. and Brit. ODA, Dhaka and Sheffield, U.K., 1985-95, numerous others. Mem. IEEE, Bangladesh Phys. Soc. Muslim. Avocations: singing, photography. E-mail: srabbani@dhaka.agni.com. Office: Dept Physics, Univ Dhaka, 1000 Dhaka Bangladesh

RABBITT, PATRICK MICHAEL, psychologist, educator; b. Bombay, Sept. 23, 1934; arrived in Eng., 1948; s. Joseph Bernard and Edna Maud (Smith) R.; m. Adriana Cornelia Habers, Oct. 13, 1955 (div. 1975); children: Adrian, Helen, Jennifer; m. Dorothy Vera Bishop, Dec. 12, 1976. BA in Psychology, Cambridge (Eng.) U., 1957, MA in Psychology, 1961, PhD in Psychology, 1962; MA in Psychology, Oxford (Eng.) U., 1968; MSc in Psychology, Manchester (Eng.) U., 1985. Mem. sci. staff Med. Rsch. Coun., Cambridge, 1961-68; lectr. Oxford (Eng.) U., 1967-82, fellow in Queen's Coll., 1968-82; prof. U. Durham, 1982-83; rsch. prof. U. Manchester, 1983—; rsch. fellow NIMH, Bethesda, Md., 1963-64, 64-68; vis. prof. McGill U., Montreal, Can., 1981-82; adj. chair U. Western Australia, Perth, 1982—; Myers lectr. Brit. Psychol. Soc., 1986. Contbr. articles to profl. jours. Fellow Brit. Psychol. Soc. (hon., chair sci. affairs 1984-87); mem. Exptl. Psychology Soc. (hon., pres. 1991-94, Sir Frederick Bartlett lectr. 1992). Avocations: whisky, nostalgia. Office: U Manchester, Cognitive Performance Rsch, Manchester M13 9PL, England

RABE, ALITA, manufacturing company executive; b. L.A., Sept. 21, 1937; d. Rome and Hortense (Anderson) Durden; m. Paul Joseph Rabe, Sept. 4, 1965. BS in Bus. Adminstrn., U. Redlands, 1987; cert. govt. contracts mgmt., UCLA, 1992. Software contracts mgmt. adminstr. Hughes Aircraft Co., El Segundo, Calif., 1979-89; software contracts mgmt. specialist Hughes Aircraft Co., El Segundo, 1989-92, engring. specialist, 1992-95; project mgr. Raytheon Corp., El Segundo, 1995-98; co-owner Panda Enterprises, Downey, Calif., 1999—. Recipient Award of Acad. Excellence, Cerritos Coll., Norwalk, Calif., 1983, 84. Mem. Valley Collectibles Club (sec. 1999—). Avocations: hiking, traveling, camping, collectibles, reading. E-mail: atilahon1@aol.com.

RABE, HORST, historian; b. Hildesheim, Germany, Aug. 19, 1930; s. Willy and Emmy (Paûl) R.; m. Rena Margarete Brückel, May 23, 1958; children: Markus, Florian. D Theology, U. Göttingen, Germany, 1958; LLD, U. Tübingen, Germany, 1966. Asst. prof. U. Tübingen, 1958-66; prof. U. Konstanz, 1966-95, dean faculty of philosophy, 1969-70, prorector, 1971-72, 79-81. Author: Naturrecht und Kirche bei Samuel von Pufendorf, 1958, Der Rat der Niederschwäbischen Reichsstädte, 1966 (award U. Tübingen 1964), Reichsbund und Interim, 1971, Deutsche Geschichte 1500-1600, 1991; editor: Karl V, Politik und Politisches System, 1996, L. Karl V, Politisdie Korrespondenz, 20 vols., 1999. Mem. Lions Club (pres. 1994-95). Avocations: church music, gardening, mountain touring. Home: Schwanenweg 4, 78465 Konstanz Germany

RABE, RICHARD FRANK, dentist, lawyer; b. Crystal Lake, Iowa, May 19, 1919; s. Otto Henry and Agnes Marie (Juhi) R.; m. Barbara Jean McNeal, Mar. 15, 1946; children: Richard Frank, Mary Elizabeth, Kathleen Ann, Michelle. AA, Waldorf Coll., 1938; DDS, U. Iowa, 1942; JD, Drake U., 1952. Bar: Iowa 1952. Dentist pvt. practice, Des Moines, 1946—, atty., 1952—; cons. Nat. Bd. Dental Examiners, 1955-60; chmn. Iowa Bd. Dental Examiners, 1962-63, Iowa Bd. Nursing Home Examiners, 1980-84; lectr. dental assns. throughout U.S. Contbr. articles to profl. jours. Fellow Am. Coll. Dentists; mem. ABA, ADA (vice chmn. coun. legis. 1977-78), Am. Acad. Dental Practice Adminstrn., Am. Inst. Parliamentation, Iowa Dental Study Club (past pres.), Iowa Dental Assn. (pres. 1972, trustee 1960-71), Iowa Bar Assn., Des Moines Dist. Dental Soc. (past pres.), Milw. Dental Rsch. Group, Ctrl. Regional Dental Testing Agy., Masons, Shriners, Des Moines Gold & Country Club, Psi Omega, Delta Theta Phi. Episcopalian. Avocations: sailing, flying. Home and Office: 5709 N Waterbury Rd Des Moines IA 50312-1337 also: 6527 Bay Club Dr Fort Lauderdale FL 33308-1814

RABEE, HUSSEIN MOHAMMED, surgeon, educator; b. Alexandria, Egypt, June 15, 1961; s. M. M. Rabee and Zinab M. Saud; m. Eman A. Salme, Jan. 15, 1987; children: Salma, Ahmad, Sohila. MBChB, Sch. Medicine, Alexandria, 1984, MD in Surgery, 1989; MD, Ain Shams U., Cairo, 1996. Resident in surgery Alexandria U., 1984-89; specialist in surgery Afghan Refugee Hosp., Beshawer, Pakistan, 1989-90; specialist in vascular surgery Ministry Health, Alexandria, 1990-95; sr. registrar vascular surgery Royal Liverpool (Eng.) Univ. Hosp., 1997-98; asst. prof. vascular surgery King Saud U., Riyadh, Saudi Arabia, 1998—; cons. Med. Syndicate, Alexandria. Fellow Royal Coll. Surgeon Ireland, European Soc. Vascular Surgery; mem. Interant. Soc. Cardiovasc. Surgery. Fax: 9661 4679493. Office: KKUH Vascular Sugery, 37, PO Box 7805, Riyadh 7805, Saudi Arabia

RABER, JACOB, neuroscientist; b. Amsterdam, Oct. 4, 1961; s. Michael and Ann Raber; m. Galit Raber. BSc in Chemistry, Free U., Amsterdam, 1983, MSc in Pharmacochemistry, 1986; PhD in Molecular Genetics and Virology, Weizmann Inst. Sci., Rehovot, Israel, 1991. Postdoctoral rschr. The Scripps Rsch. Inst., La Jolla, Calif., 1991-95; staff rsch. investigator, instr. dept. neurology The Gladstone Molecular Neurobiology Program, U. Calif., San Francisco, 1996-98; staff rsch. scientist, asst. adj. prof. neurology Gladstone Inst. Neurol. Disease, U. Calif., San Francisco, 1998—. Contbr. articles to profl. jours. Alzheimer's Assn. grantee, 1999—. Mem. AAAS, Soc. for Neurosci., N.Y. Acad. Scis., Dutch Chem. Soc. Office: Gladstone Inst Neurol Disease PO Box 419100 San Francisco CA 94141-9100

RABEY, DAVID IAN, theater educator; b. Stourbridge West Midlands, England, Feb. 21, 1958; s. Ken and Roma (Mobberley) R.; m. Charmian Caroline Savill; children: Isabel Morgana, Ryan Jack. BA, U. Birmingham, England, 1978, MA, 1979, PhD, 1982; MA, U. Calif., Berkeley, 1980. Lectr. in English and drama Trinity Coll., Dublin, 1982-84; sr. lectr. in theatre studies U. Aberystwyth, 1985—. Author: British and Irish Political Drama in the Twentieth Century, 1986, Howard Barker: Politics & Desire, 1989, David Rudkin: Sacred Disobedience, 1997, (play) The Back of Beyond, 1996. Office: U Aberystwyth Dept Theatre, Parry Williams Bldg, Aberystwyth SY23 3HA, Wales

RABIN, ALAN ABRAHAM, economics educator; b. N.Y.C., June 16, 1947; s. Sidney and Claire Rabin. BA, Hamilton Coll., 1969; PhD, U. Va., 1977. NSF trainee U. Va., 1970-71, 71-72; intern Coun. Econ. Advisors, 1971; asst. prof. Calif. State U., Northridge, 1973-74, Georgetown U., Washington, summer 1975; asst. prof. econs. U. Tenn., Chattanooga, 1977-81, assoc. prof., 1981-86, prof., 1986—. Contbr. articles to profl. jours. NDEA fellow, 1969-70; U. Tenn.-Chatanooga faculty rsch. grantee, 1982. Mem. Am. Econs. Assn., So. Econs. Assn., Atlantic Econs. Soc., We. Econs. Assn., U. Tenn. Chattanooga Coun. Scholars, Omicron Delta Epsilon. Jewish. Avocations: sports, stamp collecting, bridge. Home: 1175 Pineville Rd Apt 161 Chattanooga TN 37405-2653 Office: U Tenn-Chattanooga Dept Economics Chattanooga TN 37403

RABIN, BRIAN ROBERT, biotechnology company executive, consultant; b. London, Nov. 4, 1927; s. Emanuel and Sophia (Neshaver) R.; m. Sheila Patricia George, Aug. 29, 1954; children: Paul Robert, Carol. BSc, Univ. Coll., London, 1951, MSc, 1952, PhD, 1956. Lectr. enzymology Univ. Coll., 1954-63, reader, 1963-67, prof., 1967-70, head dept., 1970-88, prof. biochemistry, 1988-94, emeritus prof., 1994—, fellow, 1984; found., dir. London Biotech. Ltd., 1985—; founder numerous consultancies; vis. scientist AEC, Berkeley, Calif., 1963-64; mem. cell bd. Med. Rsch. Coun., London, 1974-77; mem. sci. com. Cancer Rsch. Campaign, London, 1971-83; bd. dirs. LBL, London. Numerous patents, including test for carcinogens, biol. test, med. diagnostics detection, enzymic method of detecting analytes; inventor new methodology for cancer treatment. Rockefeller fellow U. Calif., Berkeley, 1956-57. Fellow Zool. Soc. London (sci.), Inst. Biology; mem. European Molecular Biology Orgn., Acad. für Umweltfragen, Athenaeum Club. Avocations: travel, walking, carpentry.

RABIN, OLIVIER PAUL, medical researcher; b. Brest, France, Apr. 7, 1965; s. Auguste Francis and Annick Denise (Duval) R.; m. Carole Florence Fougereux, July 29, 1998; children: Karell, Jade. Cert. of toxicology, U. Coll. London, 1989; MS, U. Paris, 1990, PhD, 1992, degree in biomed. engring., 1995. Rschr. INSERM, Paris, 1991-93, NIH, Bethesda, Md., 1993-96; project mgr. Beaufour-Ipsen, Paris, 1996—; tchr. Med. Sch. Paris, 1996-99; cons. in field. Author: Frontiers in Cerebral Vascular Biology, 1993, Advances in Ginkobiloba Extract Research, 1996, 98, Metals and Oxidative Damage in Neurological Disorders, 1997. Grantee French Ministry Rsch., Paris, 1989-92, NIH, 1991, French Pharm. Industry, 1993-96. Avocations: martial arts, running, teaching science to elementary students. Office: Ipsen Int Ltd, 14 Kensington Sq, London W8 5HH, United Kingdom

RABINOVICH, BORIS ISAAKOVICH, aerospace engineer, researcher; b. Moscow, Russia, June 23, 1924; s. Isaak Moiseevich and Elena Markovna (Zlobinskaya) R.; m. Natalya Alekseevna Sapozhnikova, Nov. 25, 1949; 1 child, Alexander. Degree in engring., Joukowski Mil. Engring. Acad., Moscow, 1948; PhD, Artillery Scis. Acad., Moscow, 1952; DSci, Central Inst. Mech. Engring., Moscow, 1961. Lt. Col. Soviet Army Air Forces, USSR, 1942-60; dept. head Ctrl. Inst. Mech. Engring., Moscow, 1960-74, Rsch. Prodn. Assoc., Moscow, 1974-93; prof. Moscow State Acad. Control Devices Design, Informatics, Moscow, 1993—; lead scientist Space Rsch. Inst. Russian Acad. Scis., Moscow, 1998—; Bd. dirs. Mashinostroenie Pub. House, Moscow. Author: (with Mikishev) Dynamics of a Solid Body with Liquid, 1968, Introduction to Spacecraft Carrier Dynamics, 1983, (with lebedev and Mytarev) Vortex Processes and Solid Body Dynamics, 1994; contbr. articles to profl. jours. Recipient Great Patr. War. Vict. medal Supr. Coun., 1945, Battle Mer. medal, 1957, Yu Gagarin medal Space Sci. Fe., 1987, S. Korolev medal, 1990. Mem. Planetary Soc., Moscow House Scientists chpt. Avocations: scuba diving. Home: Dnepropetrovskaya 39-1 #248, 113570 Moscow Russia

RABINOVICH, EDUARDO JORGE, economics educator; b. Buenos Aires, Mar. 11, 1948; s. Luciano Rabinovich and Esther Levinton. Degree, U. Buenos Aires, 1973, D in Econs., 1983; diploma in internat. export mktg., Trinity Coll., Ireland, 1986; diploma of bus., U. Los Andes, Colombia, 1993. Econ. analyst Ministry of Economy, Argentina, 1969-70, Nat. Devel. Coun., Argentina, 1970-74, Nat. Inst. Econ. Planning, Argentina, 1974-80; economist, chief analyst Ministry of Economy, Office of Fgn. Trade, Argentina, 1980-89; counselor Chamber of Reps., Argentina, 1989-91; counselor of cabinet Ministry of Economy, Office of Industry, Argentina, 1991—; prof. U. Buenos Aires, U. Belgrano, OAS, U. Palermo, Argentine Sch. Bus., European Sch. Bus., Interam. Open U., Assn. Bus. Leaders, Argentine Inst. Polit. and Social Scis., bus. L.Am. Inst.; econ. advisor Interam. Devel. Bank, 1976-92; cons. Nat. Atomic Energy Commn., Argentina, 1978; econs. evaluator Latinoconsult, Argentina and Paraguay, 1980; investigator Argentine Coun. Internat. Rels., 1992—; mem. econ. com. Argentine Gen. Confederacy of Industry, 1994. Author: The New International Economic Order, 1984, The Conditions of Argentine Economic Growth, 1996; contbr. articles to profl. jours. Pres. Latin Am. Congress of Students of Econs., Ecuador, 1969; mem. Radical Civic Union, Argentina, 1982—, Citizen Power Found., Argentina, 1992—. Recipient award Am. Field Svc., U.S. Govt., 1962, Centennial prize Nat. Coll. U. Buenos Aires, 1963, prize of sponsoring bus. coun.. U. Buenos Aires, 1968. Mem. Argentine Scientific Soc., Argentine Assn. for Progress of Scis., Coll. Grads. in Econ. Scis., Argentine Writers Assn. (bd. dirs. 1996—), Soc. for Internat. Devel., Third World Found., Assn. Friends of World Diplomatique, Internat. Soc. Ency. Britannica, Planetary Citizens. Avocations: pianist, philately, music, piloting airplanes. Home: Godoy Cruz 2931, 1425 Buenos Aires Argentina

RABKIN, PEGGY ANN, lawyer; b. Buffalo, Apr. 13, 1945; d. Anthony J. and Margaret G. (Catuzzi) Marano; m. Samuel S. Rabkin, June 29, 1969. BA, SUNY, Buffalo, 1967, MEd, 1970, MA, 1972, JD, PhD, 1975. Tchr. Buffalo Pub. Schs., 1967-69; grad. teaching asst. SUNY, Buffalo, 1969-72; case analyst U.S. Equal Employment Opportunity Com., 1974; dir. affirmative action U. Louisville, 1975-78, asst. prof. of law, 1976-77; atty. office for civil rights HEW, N.Y.C., 1978; sr. atty. for labor and employment Am.

Home Products Corp., N.Y.C., 1978-86, sr. atty., 1986—. Author: Fathers to Daughters, 1980; editor: Buffalo Law Rev., 1974-75; contbr. articles to profl. jours. Commr. Louisville & Jefferson Co. Human Relations Com., Louisville, 1977-78. Recipient Christopher Baldy fellow, SUNY at Buffalo Law Sch., 1974-75, Regents Coll. Scholarship N.Y. State Bd. of Regents, 1963-67. Mem. ABA, Assn. of Bar of City of N.Y., Am. Corp. Counsel Assn., Soc. of Human Resources Mgmt., U.S. C. of C. (labor com. 1991—). Avocations: skiing, reading, cooking, and nutrition. Office: Am Home Products Corp 5 Giralda Farms Madison NJ 07940-1027

RABOCH, JAN, sexologist, educator; b. Prague, Czechoslovakia, Aug. 25, 1917; s. Josef and Rozalie (Vítkovcová) R.; m. Miloslava Říhová, Sept. 30, 1947; children: Pavel, Jiří. MD, Charles U., Prague, 1947, DSc, 1965. Diplomate Czechoslovakian Bd. Medicine. Asst. prof. Charles U., Prague, 1947-64, assoc. prof., 1964-73, prof., head sexological inst., 1973-98. Author over 550 books and articles; mem. editorial bd. Sexualmedizin, 1971, Archives of Sexual Behavior, 1981, Cahiers de Sexologie Clinique, 1984, Jour. Sex and Marital Therapy, 1974. Dep. City of Prague, Czechoslovakia, 1971-76. Recipient Award of Merit, Soc. for Sci. Study of Sex, 1976. Mem. Internat. Acad. Sex. Rsch. (pres. 1976-77), Czechoslovakian Sexological Soc. (chmn. 1971-89), Polish Med. Soc. (hon.), Czechoslovakian Med. Soc. (hon.), East German Dermatol. Soc. (hon.), Lokomotiva Club. Avocations: tennis, piano. Office: Sexological Inst. Karlovo náměstí 32, 120 00 Prague 2, Czech Republic

RABOCH, JIŘÍ, psychiatrist, educator; b. Prague, Czech Republic, Jan. 29, 1951; s. Jan and Miloslava (Říhová) R.; m. Hana Kaiglová, Apr. 9, 1976; children: Tomás, Jan. MD, Charles U., Prague, 1975, DSc, 1989. Lic. psychiatrist, sexologist, psychotherapist; ct. expert. Physician Charles U., Prague, 1975-86, sr. asst., 1986-88, assoc. prof., 1988-92, prof., 1992—; dep. dir. dept. psychiatry Charles U., 1990-98, dir., 1998—; ct. expert psychiatry-sexology, Prague, 1985—; pres. local organizing com. European Psychiat. Conf., Prague. Author, editor: Child Sexual Abuse, 1995, Psychiatry, Practice Guidelines, 1999; contbr. articles to profl. jours. Mem. exec. com. Vondrácek Found., Prague, 1992—. Recipient ann. award Czech Sexological Soc., 1993, Vondrácek Found., 1996. Mem. Czech Psychiat. Assn. (pres. 1993), Czech Sexological Assn. (v.p. 1990—), Assn. European Psychiatrists, Rotary (past pres. Prague Old Town chpt. 1997-98). Avocation: tennis. Office: Dept Psychiatry, Ke Karlovu 11, 128 21 Prague Czech Republic

RABOSKY, JOSEPH GEORGE, engineering consulting company executive; b. Sewickley, Pa., May 20, 1944; s. Mary Helen (Mayer) Rabosky; m. Suzanne Lazzelle, Aug. 23, 1969. BS, Pa. State U., 1966; MS in Engring., W.Va. U., 1969, MSCE, 1973; PhD, U. Pitts., 1984. Registered profl. engr., Pa., Tenn., W.Va., Mo., Ohio. Project engr. Chester Engrs., Coraopolis, Pa., 1969-70, mgr., 1989-92; project mgr. Calgon Corp., Pitts., 1970-73, sect. leader, 1979-85, mktg. mgr., 1985-86; sr. environ. specialist Mobay Chem. Corp., Pitts., 1975-79; project engr. Morris Knowles, Inc., Pitts., 1973-74; project mgr. Penn Environ. Cons., 1974-75; engring. mgr. Baker/TSA, Inc., Pitts., 1986-89; pres. AquaTerra, Inc., Moon Twp., Pa., 1992-95, Rabosky & Assocs., Moon Township, Pa., 1995—; adj. prof. U. Pitts., 1985-88, Pa. State U.-Beaver, McKeesport and New Kensington campuses, 1985—. Mem. Am. Acad. Environ. Engrs. (diplomate, cert. water supply wastewater engr.), Water Environ. Fedn., Pa. Water Environ. Assn. (chmn. rsch. com. 1984-89, 91-92, officer 1994-98, pres. 1996-97), Western Pa. Water Pollution Control Assn. (officer 1984-94, pres. 1992-93), Internat. Water Conf. (mem. exec. bd. 1989-94, gen. chmn. 1992-93). Home: 104 Wynview Dr Moon Township PA 15108-1033

RABSCH, WOLFGANG, bacteriologist, researcher; b. Oschersleben/Bode, Saxony-Anhalt, Germany, May 24, 1951; s. Otto and Ilse R.; m. Susanne Vlach, Sept. 26, 1975; children: Stefan, Cornelius. Dipl. in biology, Martin Luther U., Halle-Wittenberg, Germany, 1973, D in Natural Scis., 1977; D.rer.nat.Dipl.-Biol., Acad. Arztliche Fortbildung, Berlin, 1986. Asst. Inst. Exptl. Epidemiology, Wernigerode, Germany, 1976-86, sr. asst., 1986-90; sr. asst. Robert von Ostertag Inst., Wernigerode, Germany, 1991-94, Fed. Inst. Consumer Health Protection and Vet. Medicine, Wernigerode, Germany, 1994-98, Robert Koch Inst., Wernigerode, Germany, 1999—; with Nat. Vet. Reference Lab. for Salmonella, Wernigerode, 1991-98, Nat. Reference Ctr. for Salmonella and other Enterics, Wernigerode, 1998; adv. bd. Internat. Jour. Med. Microbiology, 2000. Author: (with R. Reissbrodt) Iron Chelators for Clinical Use, 1994, (with H. Tschaepe and R. Helmuth) Salmonella Enterica Serovar Enteritidis in Humans and Animals: Epidemiology, Pathogenesis and Control, 1999; inventor process for using iron chelators as selective growth supplements for microorganisms. Sponsor Hochschule Harz, Wernigerode, 1993. Mem. Internat. Fedn. Enteric Phage Typing, German Assn. Naturforscher und Arzte, Vereinigung for Allgemeine und Angewandte Mikrobiologie, German Assn. for Hygiene and Microbiology. Avocations: table tennis, photography. Office: Robert Koch Inst, Burgstrasse 37, 38855 Wernigerode Saxony-Anhalt, Germany

RABUFFETT, ARMANDO, science administrator, soil science educator; b. Montevideo, Uruguay, Jan. 1, 1942; s. Angel Guido Rabuffetti and Angela Hirigoyen; m. Carmen Avenamar Perdomo, Dec. 22, 1973; children: Mauricio Armando, Federico Augusto, Fiorella Marina. BSc in Agronomy, U. Uruguay, Montevideo, 1965; MSc in Agronomy, Iowa State U., 1967; PhD in Soil Sci., N.C. State U., 1976. Dean Sch. Agronomy U. Uruguay, 1982-85; dir. gen. Nat. Agr. Rsch. Inst., Uruguay, 1986-95; exec. dir. Inter-american Inst. for Global Change Rsch., Sao Jose dos Campo, Brazil, 1995—; cons. FAO, Monte Video, Uruguay, 1985, ISNAR-CGIAR, The Hague, The Netherlands, 1990, IAEA, Santiago, Chile, 1991, IICA, San José, Costa Rica, 1994. Contbr. articles to profl. jours. Recipient Recognition to Svc. in Agr. award Gamma Sigma Delta N.C., Raleigh, 1976. Mem. Internat. Soc. Soil Sci., Am. Soc. Agronomy. Avocations: popular music, playing accordion. Home: 3887 Carlos Vaz Ferreira, 11700 Montevideo Uruguay Office: Interamerican Inst Global, 1758 Ave dos Astronautas, 12227010 Sao Jose dos Campos Brazil

RABUKA, SITIVENI LIGAMAMADA, Fijian government official, army officer; b. Nakobo, Fiji, Sept. 13, 1948; s. Kolinio E.V. and Salote Lomaloma R.; m. Suluweti Camaivuna Tuiloma, 1975; 3 children. Ed., New Zealand Army Schs., 1972-73; postgrad., Indian Def. Svcs. Staff Coll., 1979, Australian Joint Svcs. Staff Coll., 1982. Sr. operational plans officer UNIFIL, Lebanon, 1980-81; chief staff Fiji, 1981; ops. and tng. officer Fiji Army, 1982-83, 85-87; comd. Fiji Bn., Sinai, 1983-85; staged coup, May 1987, adviser on home affairs, head security, 1987, staged 2d coup, declared a republic, Oct. 1987; comdr., head interim mil. govt. Fiji, 1987; comdr. Fiji Security Forces, 1987; min. for home affairs, nat. youth svc. and aux. army svcs., 1987-91; 1st pres. Fijian polit. party Min. Home Affairs, Suva, from 1991; prime min. Fiji, 1992-99; with Commonwealth Sec. Gen.'s Spl. Envoy for Peace, Solomon Islands, 1999—; chmn. Great Coun. of Chiefs, Govt. Bldgs. Box. Author: No Other Way, 1988; subject of biography: Rabuka of Fiji (John Sharpham), 1999. Avocations: golf, rugby. Office: Govt Bldgs Box 2437, Suva Fiji

RABY, KENNETH ALAN, lawyer, retired army officer; b. Dec. 29, 1935; s. Carl George and Helen Josette (Milne) R.; m. Shirley Rae Nelson, June 2, 1957; children: Randolph Carlton, Shelly Ann. BA, U. S.D., 1957, JD, 1960; grad. with honors, Command and Gen. Staff Coll., 1975, U.S. Army War Coll., 1981. Bar: S.D. 1960, Ga. 1988. Commd. 2d lt. U.S. Army, 1957, advanced through grades to col. JAGC, 1979, ret., 1987; dep. staff judge adv. Am. Divsn., Chu Lai, Vietnam, 1968-69; chief legal team U.S. Army Inf. Sch., Ft. Benning, Ga., 1969-71; team chief, acting divsn. chief adminstrv. law divsn. Office JAG, Dept. Army, 1971-74; staff judge adv. Hdqs. 24th Inf. Divsn., Ft. Stewart, Ga., 1974-79; staff judge adv. U.S. Army Armor Ctr., Ft. Knox, Ky., 1979; chief criminal law divsn. Office of JAG, Washington, 1981-84; sr. judge Army Ct. Mil. Rev., Falls Church, Va., 1984-87; law asst. Ga. Ct. Appeals, 1987—; former chmn., mem. Joint Service Com. on Mil. Justice, 1981-84; mem. Mil. Justice Act of 1983 Adv. Commn., 1984-87; army liaison to criminal law sect. ABA, 1981-84; chief mil. def. counsel U.S. vs. Calley. Decorated Legion of Merit, Bronze Star with oak leaf cluster, Meritorious Svc. medal with 2 oak leaf clusters, Joint Svc. Commendation medal, Air medal, Army Commendation medal with oak leaf cluster, Army Achievement medal. Mem. FBA (chmn. law enforcement liaison com. 1986-87), Assn. U.S. Army, Ga. Bar Assn., Order Ea. Star (worthy grand patron, grand chpt. Ga. 1999-2000), Masons, Shriners, Scottish Rite (3d degree), Delta Theta Phi, Theta Xi. Home: 575 Spender Trce Atlanta GA 30350-5017 Office: Staff Atty Ga Ct Appeals Jud Bldg Rm 336 Capitol Sq Atlanta GA 30334-9003

RACAMIER, HENRY, metal products executive; b. Pont-de-Roide, Doubs, France, June 25, 1912; s. Paul and Elisabeth (Mettetal) R.; m. Odile Vuitton, Apr. 27, 1943; two children. Lic. en Droit, Faculté Droit, Paris, 1934; diploma, Ecole Hautes Etudes Commles., Paris, 1934. CPA, Paris. Dep. comml. mgr. Peugeot Steel Co., Paris, 1936-41; head of group Assn. Alloy Steel Producers, Paris, 1941-46; chmn., CEO Stinox, Paris, 1946-77; pres., CEO Louis Vuitton, Paris, 1977-90; gen. dir. Vuitton Investment Gestion, Paris, 1977—; pres. strategic bd., gen. dir. LVMH, Paris, 1987-89; pres., CEO Orcofi, Paris, 1990-93; bd. dirs. Transpacific Fund Luxemburg, Jeanne Lanvin S.A., Champagne Laurent-Perrier, Flavia S.A. Pres. Assn. Orcofi for Opera, Music and Arts, Paris, 1990—; mem. chmn.'s coun. Met. Mus. Art, N.Y.C., 1990—; mem. com., bd. dirs., pres. Assn. pour le Rayonnement de l'Opéra de Paris, 1995-99; bd. dirs. N.Y. Internat. Festival of the Arts, N.Y.C., 1990—, Festival d'Automne a Paris, UCAD. Named Chevalier of the Legion d'Honneur, Officer de l'Ordre Nat. du Mérite, comdr. l'Ordre Arts et Lettres. Mem. Cercle Interallié, Cercle du Bois de Boulogne, Yacht Club de France. Avocations: opera, music, yachting. Office: 39 Bd de Montmorency, 75016 Paris France

RACE, GEORGE JUSTICE, pathology educator; b. Everman, Tex., Mar. 2, 1926; s. Claude Ernest and Lila Eunice (Bunch) R.; m. Annette Isabelle Rinker, Dec. 21, 1946; children: George William Daryl, Jonathan Clark, Mark Christopher, Jennifer Anne (dec.), Elizabeth Margaret Rinker. M.D., U. Tex., Southwestern Med. Sch., 1947; M.S. in Pub. Health, U. N.C., 1953; Ph.D. in Ultrastructural Anatomy and Microbiology, Baylor U., 1969. Intern Duke Hosp., 1947-48, asst. resident pathology, 1951-53; intern Boston City Hosp., 1948-49; asst. pathologist Peter Bent Brigham Hosp., Boston, 1953-54; pathologist St. Anthony's Hosp., St. Petersburg, Fla., 1954-55; staff pathologist Children's Med. Center, Dallas, 1955-59; dir. labs. Baylor U. Med. Center, Dallas, 1959-86; chief dept. pathology Baylor U. Med. Center, 1959-86, vice chmn. exec. com. med. bd., 1970-72; cons. pathologist VA Hosp., Dallas, 1955-71; adj. prof. anthropology and biology So. Meth. U., Dallas, 1969; instr. pathology Duke, 1951-53, Harvard Med. Sch., 1953-54; asst. prof. pathology U. Tex. Southwestern Med. Sch., 1955-58, clin. assoc. prof., 1958-64, clin. prof., 1964-72, prof., 1973-94, prof. emeritus, 1994—, dir. Cancer Center, 1973-76, assoc. dean for continuing edn., 1973-94, emeritus assoc. dean, 1994—; pathologist-in-chief Baylor U. Med. Ctr., 1959-86, prof. biomed. studies Baylor Grad. sch., 1989-94; chmn. Baylor Rsch. Found., 1986-89; prof. microbiology Baylor Coll. Dentistry, 1962-68, prof. pathology, 1964-68, prof., chmn. dept. pathology 1969-73, dean A. Webb Roberts Continuing Edn., 1973-94; spl. advisor on human and animal diseases to gov. State of Tex., 1979-83. Editor: Laboratory Medicine (4 vols.), 1973, 10th edit., 1983; Contbr. articles to profl. jours., chpts. to textbooks. Pres., Tex. div. Am. Cancer Soc., 1970; chmn. Gov.'s Task Force on Higher Edn., 1981. Served with AUS, 1944-46; flight surgeon USAF, 1948-51, Korea. Decorated Air medal. Fellow Coll. Am. Pathologists, Am. Soc. Clin. Pathologists, AAAS; mem. AMA (chmn. multiple discipline research forum 1969), Am. Assn. Pathologists, Internat. Acad. Pathology, Am. Assn. Med. Colls., Explorer's Club (dir., v.p. 1993-2000), Sigma Xi. Fax: 214-526-8607. Home: 3429 Beverly Dr Dallas TX 75205-2928

RACEK, JAROSLAV, clinical chemist, educator; b. Plzen, Czech Republic, July 25, 1951; s. Josef and Marta (Stadlikova) R.; m. Alexandra Peskova Racková, Jan. 9, 1975; children: Sylva, Marika, Martin. Degree in Clin. Chemistry, Inst. Postgrad. Edn., Prague, Czech Republic, 1978, Inst. Postgrad. Edn., Prague, Czech Republic, 1981. Physician Charles U. Hosp., Pilsen, Czech Republic, 1975-91; assoc. prof. Med. Faculty Charles U., Pilsen, Czech Republic, 1991-97, prof., 1997—; cons. Charles U. Hosp., Pilsen, 1991-96, with med. faculty, 1997—; head Inst. Clin. Chemistry Lab. Diagnostics, Inst. Clin. Chemistry, Charles U., 1997—. Inventor: way of creatine kinase determination, 1985, electrone acceptor for lactate determination, 1987, biosensor for lactate determination, 1989; author: Cell-Based Biosensors, 1994, Isoenzymes in Clinical Practice, 1982, Use of Immobilized Enzymes in Medicine, 1986, Clinical Biochemistry, 1999. Mem. Am. Assn. Clin. Chemists, Czech Med. Soc., Clin. Biochemistry Metabolism (mem. editl. bd.), Czech Med. Chamber, N.Y. Acad. Scis. Avocations: botany, mountain tourism, numismatics. Home: Brojova 19, 30704 Pilsen Czech Republic Office: Charles U Hosp, Alej Svobody 80, 30460 Pilsen Czech Republic

RACHIE, CYRUS, lawyer; b. Willmar, Minn., Sept. 5, 1908; s. Elias and Amanda (Lien) R.; m. Helen Evelyn Duncanson, Nov. 25, 1936; children: John Burton Rachie, Janice Carolyn MacKinnon, Elisabeth Dorthea Becker. Student, U. Minn., 1927-28; JD, George Washington U., 1932, William Mitchell Coll. Law, 1934. Bar: Minn. 1934, U.S. Supreme Ct. Atty. Minn. Hwy. Dept., 1934-43; spl. asst. atty. gen. Minn., 1946-50; counsel Luth. Brotherhood (fraternal life ins. co.), 1950-61; pvt. practice law Mpls., 1961-62; v.p., counsel Gamble-Skogmo, Inc., Mpls., 1962-64; v.p., gen. counsel Aid Assn. Lutherans, Appleton, Wis., 1964-70; sr. v.p., gen. counsel Aid Assn. Lutherans, 1970-73; with Rachie & Rachie, 1973-83; pvt. practice, 1983—; part-time spl. master Minn. 4th Jud. Dist., 1977; one of eleven com. mems. planning 1957 Luth. World Fedn. in Mpls. Councillor Nat. Luth. Coun., 1959-66, sec., 1962-64, mem. exec. com., 1965-66; United Luth. Ch. in Am. del. to 4th Assembly Luth. World Fedn., Helsinki, 1963; past pres. Luth. Welfare Soc. Minn.; past chmn. Mpls. Mayor's Coun. on Human Rels.; chmn. finance United Fund drive, 1967-68; past mem. bd. dirs. Mpls. YMCA; trustee emeritus William Mitchell Coll. Law Augsburg Coll. With USNR, 1943-46. Recipient Disting. Alumnus award William Mitchell Coll. Law, 1987. Mem. ABA Minn. Bar Assn., Am. Legion, Minn. Fraternal Congress (past pres.). Lutheran. Club: Rotarian. Home: 7500 York Ave S Apt 101 Minneapolis MN 55435-4736

RACHKOVA, MARIANA ILIEVA, physician, researcher; b. Assenovgrad, Plovdiv, Bulgaria, June 27, 1955; came to U.S., 1993.; d. Ilia Ivanov Rachkov and Ivanka Georgieva (Bakalova) R.; children: Maria I. Nikova, Iliana I. Nikova. MD, Med. Acad., 1979. Cert. clinical biochemistry, Sofia, 1988; specialization immunotherapy of melanoma Nat. Inst. of Cancer, 1990. Staff physician Gen. Hosp., Sliven/Burgas, 1979-82; attendant physician Gen. Hosp.-Emergency, Stara Zagora, 1982-83; chief asst. prof. Med. U., Stara Zagora, 1983-93; med. cons. Jriston Corp., Chgo., 1994-95; scientist Jriston Corp., 1996—; pres. Union of the Young Scientists, Stara Zagora, 1985-93. Contbr. articles to profl. jours. Grantee European Soc. for Pigment Cells Rsch., 1991, project comm. of the European Cmtys., Belgium, 1993; recipient Award Brighton Internat. Melanoma Conf., 1991. Mem. European Soc. for Pigment Cell Rsch., Ill. Coun. for Health-Sys. Pharmicists, Am. Assn. for Cancer Rsch., European Assn. for Cancer Rsch., Internat. Soc. for Pigment Cell Rsch. Democrat. Orthodox. Avocation: iridology as a science; melanoma, AIDS. E-mail: asson93@yahoo.com.

RACHOW, SHARON DIANNE, realtor; b. St. Joseph, Mo., Apr. 12, 1939; d. Norman DeLos Zancker and Sylvia Lavina (Hawkins) Trouel; m. Thomas Eugene Rachow, Oct. 22, 1968; children: Todd A., Tiffany K. Student, So. Ill. U., 1969-72. Sec. Westab, Inc. (now Mead), St. Joseph, 1957-60, Seitz Packing Co., St. Joseph, 1960-66; exec. asst. to v.p., gen. mgr. Kansas City (Mo.) Chiefs, 1972; co-owner, mgr. Pool 'N Patio Plus, St. Joseph, 1973-84; realtor Coldwell Banker Gen. Realtors, St. Joseph, 1984-93, RE/MAX, 1993-99. Trustee Nat. Multiple Sclerosis Soc., Mid Am. chpt., Midland M.S. Express Br., 1993-98. Inducted ReMax Internat. Hall of Fame, 1999. Mem. St. Joseph Regional Bd. Realtors (mem. Multi-List com. 1993-99, mem. forms com. 1994-98, dir. 1994, St. Joseph Top Residential Sales award 1986—, Top 10, grad. Realtor Inst. 1986, cert. residential specialist 1987), Million Dollar Club (life), Re/Max Mid-States Region (Mo. Top 100 1993-98, Hall of Fame), Real Estate Buyer's Agt. Coun. (accredited buyers rep. 1996—). Republican. Lutheran. E-mail: srachow@ponyexpress.net. Home: 4211 Country Ln Saint Joseph MO 64506-2454 Office: RE/MAX of St Joseph Inc 1119 N Woodbine Rd Saint Joseph MO 64506-2434

RACICOVSCHI, VIRGIL DAN, electrical engineering company official; b. Bucharest, Romania, Mar. 5, 1954; s. Alexe and Sabina (Ilasu) R.; m. Iulia Ichim, 1986; 1 child, Ioana. MSEE, Poly. U., Bucharest, 1979; PhD in Elec. Engring., Tech. Mil. Acad., Bucharest, 1996. Cert. in mgmt. and internat. econ. rels. Engr. ICPA SA, Bucharest, 1979-82, rschr., 1982-94, head of dept., 1992-93, program mgr., 1993-94, sci. mgr., 1994-96, 1st degree sr. rschr., 1994—, corp. mgr., 1996—. Author: (books) Electrical Gyromotors and Non-Conventional Gyroscopes, 1986, Electrical Components for Gyro Systems, 1997; (screenplay) Novelties in Electrical Engineering, 1987; patentee in field; contbr. articles to sci. jours. Mem. IEEE, ANCEM, Romanian Scientists Assn. (assoc.). Avocations: movies, mountain trips, stamps, music, football. Home: B-Dul Unirii 14 Sector 4, Bucharest Romania Office: ICPE SA, 313-Splaiul Unirii, 74204 Bucharest Romania

RACINE, ERIC, pharmacology administrator, educator, researcher; b. Quebec City, Que., Can., July 20, 1970; s. Michel Racine and Murielle Blouin-Racine; m. Kristine Carole Sutton, Oct. 13, 1996. BPharm, Laval U., Que., 1993; PharmD, Wayne State U., 1995. Pharmacy intern Christ Roi Hosp., Que., 190-93; clin. specialist Harper Hosp. Detroit Med. Ctr., 1995-98, dir. IAD project, 1998-99, coord. clin. pharmacy svcs. Harper Hosp., 1999—; clin. asst. prof. U. Mich., Ann Arbor, 1999—; adj. asst. prof. Wayne State U., Detoit, 1997—; mem. adv. bd. Dupont Pharm., Wilmington, Del., 2000, Aventis; cons. Cor Pharm., San Francisco, 1998-99. Editor DMC Anticoagulation Svcs. Newsletter, 1997—; contbr. articles to profj. jours.; spkr. in field. Mem. AHA (clin. cardiology and arteriosclerosis thrombosis and vasc. biology couns. 1997—), Am. Soc. Health-Sys. Pharmacists, Am. Coll. Clin. Pharmacy, Mich. Soc. Health Sys. Pharmacists (co-chmn. edn. com. 1999—). Avocations: golf, travel, history. Office: Detroit Med Ctr Harper Hosp 3990 John R St Detroit MI 48201-2018

RACKERS, THOMAS WILLIAM, physicist; b. Ft. Thomas, Ky., Apr. 1, 1955; s. Paul William and Geraldine (Cox) R.; m. Thelma J. Cox, June 18, 1977; 1 child, Teresa Dawn. BA cum laude, Thomas More Coll., Ft. Mitchell, Ky., 1975; MS, Ohio State U., 1977, PhD, 1984. Rsch. assoc. dept. physics Ohio State U., Columbus, 1981-84; rsch. physicist rsch. and technol. dept. Naval Coastal Sys. Ctr., Panama City, Fla., 1984-91; rsch. physicist coastal rsch. and tech. dept. NSWC Coastal Systems Sta., Panama City, 1992—; mem. exec. comms. North Am. Data Gen. Users Group, co-chmn. Cent. Ohio Users of Data Gen. Equipment, Columbus, 1981-84; ind. computer cons. Composed and recorded original music for local cmty. theater prodns., 1994—. Judge Three Rivers Sci. and Engring. Fair, Panama City, 1985-89, 99; vol., actor Kaleidoscope Theatre, Panama City, 1987-97, bd. dirs., 1994-97, Internet Web site adminstr., 1996-97; active mentor program Jr. Mus. Bay County, Fla., 1988-89; guitarist St. John the Evangelist Cath. Ch. Folk Choir, Panama City, 1984—, co-dir., 1990-94, dir., 1995—; sec. Long Glass Youth Bowling League, 1993-94; active sch. enrichment program, NSWC Coastal Systems Station, 1997—; staff instr. Tae Kwon Do Am. Martial Arts, Panama City Beach, Fla., 1998—. Mem. Mensa, Bay Line Model R.R. (Panama City condr. 1987-89), St. Andrews Bay NTRAK (chmn. 1989-90), Sigma Pi Sigma. Roman Catholic. Avocations: computers, electronic and folk music, 2nd degree black belt Tae Kwon Do, model railroading, science fiction. Home: 2012 Pattho Ln Lynn Haven FL 32444-5411 Office: NSWC Coastal Systems Sta Code R13 6703 W Highway 98 Panama City FL 32407-7000

RACKHAM, OLIVER, botanist, historical ecologist; b. Bungay, Suffolk, Eng., Oct. 17, 1939; s. Geoffrey Herbert and Norah Kathleen (Wilson) R. BA, Cambridge (Eng.) U., 1961, PhD, 1964. Fellow Corpus Christi Coll., Cambridge, 1964—; jr. proctor Cambridge U., 1996-97. Author: Trees and Woodland in the British Landscape, 1976, 2d edit., 1990, The History of the Countryside, 1986 (Angel Lit. prize 1986), The Illustrated History of the Countryside, 1994 (Sir Peter Kent Conservation Book prize 1995, Natural World Book prize 1995). Mem. Brit. Ecol. Soc., Bot. Soc. of the Brit. Isles, Landscape History Soc. Anglican. Avocations: archaeology (especially of timber structures), conservation of buildings. Office: Corpus Christi Coll, CB2 1RH Cambridge England

RÁCZ, ISTVÁN, physicist; b. Makó, Hungary, Mar. 21, 1959; s. István and Istánné (Tamás) R.; divorced; children: Zsolt, Orsolya, Zoltán. Diploma in math. & physics, Lajos Kossuth U., Debrecen, Hungary, 1983; postgrad., Hungarian Com. Sci., Budapest, 1989. Tchr. J. Landler Sec. Grammar Sch., Nagykanizsa, Hungary, 1983-86; rsch. assoc. Ctrl. Rsch. Inst. Physics, Budapest, 1989-90, rsch. fellow, 1990-93; sr. rsch. fellow MTA-KFKI Rsch. Inst. Particle & Nuclear Physics, Budapest, 1993—; dep. Theoretical Dept. MTAKFKI Rsch. Inst. Particle & Nuclear Physics, Budapest, 1994—; Soros fellow Soros Found., Chgo., 1991-92. Contbr. articles to profl. jours. Recipient hon. mention Gravity Rsch. Found., 1987, 88; Fellow Japanese Soc. for Promotion Sci., 1997-99. Mem. Am. Math. Soc. Avocations: swimming, reading, gardening, painting. Home: Ady Endre Sétány 36, H-2100 Gödöllö Hungary Office: MTA KFKI Rsch Inst, XII Ken Konkoly Thege 29-33, H-1525 Budapest Hungary

RACZ, JOSEPH GEORGE, psychiatrist, researcher; b. Budapest, Hungary, Apr. 28, 1957; s. Joseph and Anna (Lékai) R.; m. Eva Csom (div. 1992); 1 child, Peter Marton. MD, Semmelweis Med. Sch., Hungary, 1981. Med. diplomate, psychiatrist, psychotherapist. Scholar Inst. for Psychology, Hungarian Acad. Scis., Budapest, 1983-86, jr. rsch. fellow, 1986-91, rsch. fellow, 1991-96, sr. rsch. fellow, 1996—; head dept. addictions Coll. of Health, Semmelweis U., Budapest, 1996—; dir. Blue Point Drug Counseling Ctr., Budapest, 1996—; sci. advisor Nat. Coord. Com. on Drug Affairs, 1999—. Author: Drug Taking Behavior, 1988, Addictions: Symptons and Interventions, 1999. Soros Found. scholar, 1990; Ashoka fellow, 1995. Office: Inst Psychology, Victor Hugo u 18-22, 1132 Budapest Hungary

RACZ, ZOLTAN GABOR, biologist; b. Miskolc, Hungary, Aug. 1, 1945. MS, U. Eötvös, 1970, PhD, 1986. Mem. staff Pharms. Richter, Budapest, 1970-71, Rsch Inst. for Medicinal Plants, Budapest, 1971-74; biologist Nat. Blood Transfusion Svc., Budapest, 1975-99, Diachem Ltd., Budapest, 1999—. Contbr. more than 50 articles to profl. jours.; patentee in field. Avocation: collecting and restoration of antiques. Office: Diachem Ltd, Högyes E u 4, Budapest Hungary

RACZASZEK, JOANNA KAROLINA, psychologist, researcher, journalist; b. Warsaw, Poland, Aug. 26, 1966; d. Krzysztof and Halina (Laudanska) R.; m. Guiseppe Leonardi, July 3, 1999; 1 child, Julia. MA, U. Warsaw, 1990; PhD, Fla. Atlantic U., 1995. Tchg. and rsch. asst. Fla. Atlantic U., Boca Raton, 1990-95, lectr., 1992-93; asst. U. Warsaw, 1995-96, adj. prof., 1996—; sci. editor Daily Zycie, Warsaw, 1996-98. Editor Psychology of Lang. and Comm., 1998—; trans.: Bright Air Brilliant Fire (by G. Edelman); contbr. more than 50 articles to profl. jours. Recipient Polish Found. award, 1997; grantee U. Warsaw, 1996, Sci. Rsch. Com., 1999. Mem. European Soc. for Philosophy in Psychology. Avocation: photography. E-mail: raczasze@sci.psych.uw.edu.pl. Office: U Warsaw/Dept Psychology, ul Stawki 5/7, 00-183 Warsaw Poland

RACZEK, TOMASZ STANISŁAW, magazine editor, film critic; b. Warsaw, Poland, June 15, 1957; s. Ryszard Roman and Krystyna Stanisława (Lipinska) R. MA in Theatre, Acad. Dramatic Arts, Warsaw, 1981. Lit. dir. State Comedy Theatre, Warsaw, 1978-79, Oko, film unit, Warsaw, 1986-87; theatre critic Polityka, weekly mag., Warsaw, 1982-86; film critic Przeglad Tygodniowy, weekly, Warsaw, 1986-89; dep. dir. channel 2, Polish TV, Warsaw, 1989-90; editor-in-chief Pawie Oko, monthly mag., Warsaw, 1990-91; programming dir. Graf Film Internat., Gdansk, Poland, 1991-92; editor-in-chief Polish edit. Playboy, Warsaw, 1992-97, programming dir. Polish edit., 1997-99; co-founder, content dir. Ahoj Internet Portal, Warsaw, 2000—; TV host Polish TV, Warsaw, 1984—; Warsaw corr. The European, 1990-91; talk show anchor Straight Talk About Art, Polish TV, 1985-87, Perly Z Lamusa, Polish TV P, 1990-99, Seven Heaven, Polish Canal Plus TV, 1995-96, 97-98, Na Gape, Polish Canal Plus TV, 1996-97, 98-99, Nigdzie indziej Polish Canal Plus TV, 1998-99; tv columnist Wprost, Pani, Cinema. Author: (with Zygmunt Kaluzynski) Perly do Lamusa?, 1992, Polawiacze perel, 1998, Pies na Telwizje, 1989, Perlowa ruletka, 2000; theatre columnist Polityka, Przeglad Tygodniowy, 1982-89 (Wyspianski award as best critic of yr. Polish Journalists Assn. 1986); editor-in-chief Voyage Monthly, Warsaw, 1999-2000. Recipient Victor award for TV talk show, 1987. Roman Catholic. Avocations: travel, listening to music, reading, home living. Office: MotherShip Poland Internet Holdings, Foksal 3/5, 00-366 Warsaw Poland

RACZKA, TONY MICHAEL, artist; b. Pottsville, Pa., Jan. 16, 1957; s. Albert Joseph and Rosemary Bernadette Raczka; m. Virginia Boone, 1974

(div. 1984); 1 child, Mesika; m. Patricia Martinez, June 20, 1986; 1 stepchild, Cynthia. BFA, No. Ariz. U., 1978; MFA, No. Ill. U., 1980; postgrad., U. Calif., San Diego, 1991-92. Instr. art Southwestern Coll., Chula Vista, Calif., 1981-84, No. Ariz. U., Flagstaff, Ariz., 1983; registrar Mingei Internat. Mus. World Folk Art, San Diego, 1985-86; instr. art San Diego State U., 1987; asst. dir. Quint Gallery, San Diego, 1987; sr. mus. preparator U. Art Gallery, U. Calif., San Diego, 1989-95; presenter in field. One-man shows include Quint Gallery, 1982, 83, Paris Green Gallery, La Jolla, Calif., 1987, Queens Coll. Art Ctr., CUNY, Flushing, N.Y., 1999—; two person shows include Printworks, Chgo., 1982, 84; exhibited in group shows include Butler Inst. Am. Art, Youngstown, Ohio, 1983, 97, The Drawing Ctr., 1994, Meridian Gallery, San Francisco, 1995 (Best of Show 2d place), Coll. William and Mary, 1996, Trenton (N.J.) State Coll., 1996, Laguna (Calif.) Art Mus., 1997, Carnegie Mus. Art, 1997, U. Richmond, Va., 1996, 98, San Jacinto Coll., Houston, 1998 (Merit award), Palm Springs Mus., 1999, Weber State U., Ogden, Utah, 2000; author poetry. Mem. Internat. Soc. Phenomenology and Scis. of Life, San Diego Mus. Art. Home: 4430 42d St # 2 San Diego CA 92116

RACZKOWSKI, JOZEF WOJCIECH, oil industry executive, petroleum engineer; b. Sanok, Poland, Sept. 10, 1930; s. Stanislaw Józef and Bronislawa (Rydzik) R.; m. Olga Anna Sarna, Apr. 25, 1955; 1 child, Marta. MSc, U. Mining and Metallurgy, Cracow, Poland, 1955, DSc, 1963. Cert. mining gen. dir. 1st rank. Asst., sr. asst., lectr. U. Mining and Metallurgy, Cracow, Poland, 1951-58, asst. prof., 1965; designer, chief designer various oil industry projects, Cracow, 1955-87; sr. engr. Geol. Works, Cracow, 1959-61; assoc. prof. U. Mining and Metallurgy, 1972, prof. engring., head inst., dean, 1966-75; gen. dir. Oil and Gas Inst., 1976—, prof., 1979; pres. Łukasiewicz-prize-awarding jury, Cracow, 1996. Author: Big Hole Drilling, 1970, Rheology of Drilling Fluids, 1978, Technology of Drilling Fluids, 1981, Filtration of Drilling Fluids, 1993; chmn. editl. bd. NAFTA-GAZ Jours., Oil and Gas Inst., 1990. Res. lt., Polish Mil., 1978. Recipient prize Min. Head Tech. Progress Office, Warsaw, 1987. Mem. Internat. Energy Found., Soc. Petroleum and Gas Engrs. and Technicians in Poland (Łukasiewicz-prize 1987), Com. Energy, Mining Com. Polish Acad. Scis., Russian Acad. Natural Scis. Roman Catholic. Avocation: travel. E-mail: raczkowski@igng.krakow.pl. Home: ul Królowej Jadwigi 328/6, 30-234 Cracow Poland Office: Oil and Gas Inst, Lubicz 25a, 51-503 Cracow Poland

RACZYNSKI, STANISLAW, engineering educator; b. Krakow, Poland, Oct. 9, 1938; s. Stanislaw and Bronislawa (Gawin) R.; m. Krystyna Tatomir, Nov. 18, 1968; children: Agnieszka, Krzysztof. M Engring., Acad. Mining and Metallurgy, Krakow, 1964, D Tech. Scis., 1969, Habilitated D. Tech. Scis., 1977. Asst. prof. Acad. Mining and Metallurgy, Krakow, 1964-72, assoc. prof., 1976-83; rschr. Internat. Rsch. Group, Moscow, 1973-76; prof. faculty engring. Nat. U. Mexico, Mexico City, 1983-86; prof. Sch. of Engring. Universidad Panamericana, Mexico City, 1986—; head Acad. Computer Ctr., Krakow, 1970-72, Systems Analysis Group, Krakow, 1976-83; internat. dir. Soc. for Computer Simulation Internat., 1994—; mem. Nat. System of Rsch., Mexico, 1994—. Avocations: music, jazz.

RADA, ALEXANDER, university official; b. Kvasy, Czechoslovakia, Mar. 28, 1923; s. Frantisek and Anna (Tonnkova) R.; came to U.S., 1954, naturalized, 1959; M.S., U. Tech. Coll. of Prague, 1948; postgrad. Va. Poly. Inst., 1956-59, St. Clara U., 1966-67; Ed.D., U. Pacific, 1975; m. Ingeborg Solveig Blakstad, Aug. 8, 1953; children: Alexander Sverre, Frank Thore, David Harald. Head prodn. planning dept. Mine & Iron Corp., Kolin, Czechoslovakia, 1941-42; mgr. experimenting and testing dept. Avia Aircraft, Prague, 1943-45; sec.-gen. Central Bldg. Office, Prague, 1948; head metal courses dept. Internat. Tech. Sch. of UN, Grafenaschau, W.Ger., 1949-50; works mgr. Igref A/S, Oslo, 1950-51; cons. engr., chief sect. machines Steel Products Ltd., Oslo, 1951-54; chief engr., plant supr. Nelson J. Pepin & Co., Lowell, Mass., 1954-55; sr. project engr., mfg. supt. Celanese Corp. Am., Narrows, Va., 1955-60; mgr. mfg., facilities and maint. FMC Corp., San Jose, Calif., 1960-62; mgr. adminstrn. Sylvania Electronic Systems, Santa Cruz, Calif., 1962-72; asst. to pres., devel. officer Napa (Calif.) Coll., 1972-88; chief exec. officer NAVCO Pacific Devel. Corp., Napa, 1984-91; pres. NAVCO Calif. Co., 1991—; prof. indsl. mgmt. Cabrillo Coll., Aptos, Calif., 1963-72; mgmt. and engring. cons., 1972—. Pres. ARC, Santa Cruz, 1965-72, bd. dirs., pres., Napa, 1977-88; mem. Nat. Def. Exec. Res., U.S. Dept. Commerce, Washington, 1966—, chmn. No. Calif. region 9, 1981-88; mem. President's Export Council-DEC, San Francisco, 1982—. Recipient Meritorious Service citation ARC, 1972, Etoile Civique l'Ordre de l'Etoile Civique, French Acad., 1985; registered profl. engr., Calif. Mem. NSPE, Calif. Soc. Profl. Engrs., Am. Def. Preparedness Assn., Assn. Calif. Community Coll. Adminstrs., Nat. Assn. Corp. Dirs., World Affairs Council No. Calif., Czechoslovak Foreign Inst., Praha, 1993—, Phi Delta Kappa, Editor-in-chief Our Youth, 1945-48; co-editor (with P. Boulden) Innovative Management Concepts, 1967. Home and Office: 1019 Ross Cir Napa CA 94558-2118

RADÁK, ZSOLT, physical education educator; b. Nagykanizsa, Hungary, Dec. 11, 1961; s. Lajos and Lajosné (Hirku Erzsébet) R.; m. Zsuzsa Kalmár; children: Fanni Sára, Bence Zsombor. D Phys. Edn., Hungarian U. Phys. Edn., Budapest, 1991; PhD, U. Tsukuba, Japan, 1996. Rschr. Budapesti Honved Sport Egysület, Budapest, 1985-89; rschr. Hungarian U. Phys. Edn., Budapest, 1989—, assoc. prof., 1996-2000, prof., 2000—. Editor: Free Radicals in Exercise and Aging, Human Kinetics; contbr. articles to profl. jours. Recipient Bolyai fellowship in sci. medicine award Richter Co.; Rsch. fellow U. Tsukuba, 1991-96, sr. rsch. fellow Toho U., Japan, 1997-98. Mem. Am. Coll. Sports Medicine, Oxygen Soc., Geog. Soc. Avocation: paintings. Home: Dévai u 20/A 3/9, 1134 Budapest Hungary Office: HUPE, Alkotás u 44, 1123 Budapest Hungary

RADCHENKO, ARCADI NICOLAEVICH, information processing specialist; b. Armavir, USSR, Jan. 30, 1929; s. Nicolai L'vovich and Maria Alexeevna Radchenko; m. Larisa Grigorievna Goncharova; 1 child, Larisa; m. Nina Georgievna Petrova, Oct. 24, 1969. Degree in engring., Inst. Avialnstruments, Leningrad, USSR, 1953; DrPh, Acad. Sci. USSR, Leningrad, 1960. Engr. Inst. Automata and Telemechs, Acad. Sci. USSR, Leningrad, 1953-62; codent Inst. Avialnstruments, 1963-69; head robot dept. Poly. Inst., Leningrad, 1969-83; head memory lab. Rsch.-Indsl. Inst. Vector, Leningrad, 1983-90; sr. sci. rschr. Inst. Informatics and Automata, Russian Acad. Sci., St. Petersburg, 1991—. Author: Simulation of the Base Mechanisms of the Brain, 1968, Association Memory. Neural Networks. Optimization of Neuro Processors, 1989; contbr. articles to profl. jours.; inventor info. processing and memory devices. E-mail: radchenko@mail.iias.spb.su. Home: Kurchatov St 6/6 k 34, 194223 Saint Petersburg Russia Office: Inst Informatics RAS, 14-Line 39 Vasilievski Isl, 199178 Saint Petersburg Russia

RADCLIFFE, EDWARD BRUCE, entomologist; b. Rapid City, Can., Oct. 25, 1936; s. Thomas Reid and Helen Louise R.; m. Betty Loraine Pederson, Dec. 20, 1964; children: David Glen, Peter Michael. BSA, U. Manitoba, 1959; MS, U. Wis., 1961, PhD, 1963. Rsch. fellow U. Minn., St. Paul, 1963-64, rsch. assoc., 1964-65, asst. prof., 1965-70, assoc. prof., 1970-76, prof., 1976—. Author numerous scientific publs. Mem. AAAS, Entomol. Soc. Am., Entomol. Soc. Can., Potato Assn. of Am. Office: Dept Entomology/U Minn 219 Hodson Hall 1980 Folwell Ave Saint Paul MN 55108-1037

RADEBE, JEFF T., South African government official; b. Cato Manor, Durban, Feb. 18, 1953; divorced; children: Vukani, Mandisa; m. Bridgette Motsepe. Degree in Internat. Law, Leipzig (Germany) U., 1981; LLM in Internat. Law, Karl Marx U., 1981; student in Law, U. Zululand; LLD (hon.), Chgo. State U., 1996. Journalist African Nat. Congress Radio Freedom, 1977-86; project coord. Nat. Assn. Dem. Lawyers, 1991; Cabinet Min. Pub. Works for Nelson Mandela, 1994; min. of pub. works Govt. of South Africa, Pretoria, 1994—; head policy dept. African Nat. Congress Govt. of South Africa, 1998—; min. Pub. Enterprises Govt. South Africa, 1999—; chancellor Ea. Cape Technikan; founder KwaMashu Youth Orgn.; forerunner Nat. Youth Orgn.; mem. Black Consciousness Movement for polit. activism. African Nat. Congress rep. Tanzania, Zambia, Lesotho, mem. nat. exec. com., mem. head ept., served in elections com., chair manifesto com.; mem. ctrl. com. S.A. Communist Party, 1996—; active participant in politics for unemployed, exploited workers, poorer socs., rural comtys., women and children; chmn. 80th Birthday Com. Pres. Mandela's 80th Birthday Party, Nelson Mandela Millenium Fund. Recipient numerous awards from various insts. and orgns. for his commitment and contbn. to devel. Black Bus. South Africa. Mem. Organizing/Logistics Com. Office: Infotech Bldg Ste 401, 1090 Arcadia St PB X15, Hatfield 0028, South Africa

RÅDEGRAN, GÖRAN, physicist; b. Stockholm, Aug. 14, 1964; s. Kjell and Ann (Seavers) R. MSc in Engring. Physics, Chalmers U. Technology, 1990; postgrad., U. Lund, 2000—. Computer programmer dept. thoracic surgery U. Göteborg, Sweden, 1987; asst. acct. ESAB, 1988; rsch. assoc. dept. surface physics Chalmers U. Technology, Göteborg, 1989-90; rsch. assoc. dept. exptl. rsch. U. Malmö, Sweden, 1991-93; rsch. assoc. Copenhagen Muscle Rsch. Ctr., 1994—; expedition leader high altitude acclimitization project Copenhagen Muscle Rsch. Ctr., Chacaltaya, Bolivia, 1998. Avocations: skiing, mountaineering, sailing, basketball, tennis. Office: CMRC Rigshospitalet S# 7652, Tagensvej 20, DK-2200 Copenhagen N, Denmark

RADEMACHER, DAVID JEFFREY, neuroscientist, psychology educator; b. Coon Rapids, Minn., July 26, 1971; s. Jeffrey Thomas and Diane Mary Rademacher. BA, Hamline U., 1994; MS, U. Wis., 1999. Tchg. asst. U. Wis., Milw., 1996-98, grad. rsch. fellow, 1998—; adj. psychology instr. Carroll Coll., Waukesha, Wis., 1999—. Contbr. articles to profl. jours. Recipient Individual Nat. Rsch. Svc. award Nat. Inst. on Drug Abuse, Bethesda, Md., 1998—; grantee Sigma Xi, Research Triangle Park, N.C., 1997; Presdl. fellow scholar Hamline U., St. Paul, 1994-96. Mem. AAAS, Soc. for Neurosci., Soc. Environ. Toxicology and Chemistry, Phi Kappa Phi. Democrat. Lutheran. E-mail: drad@concentric.net and psychrad@csd.uwm.edu. Fax: 414-229-5219. Home: 813 E Glendale Ave Apt 3 Shorewood WI 53211-1032 Office: U Wis 2441 E Hartford Ave Milwaukee WI 53211-3160

RADEN, KOESTEDJO, surgeon, educator; b. Purbalingga, Indonesia, Aug. 5, 1916; s. Raden Koesmen Wirjosoemarto and Raden Roro Tarsinah; m. Raden Roro Soertiti; children: Koestijowati, Koesprijantono, Koestriastoeti, Koespraptono, Koesoemaningsih. MD, Med. Faculty Batavia, 1944. Pvt. practice Cilacap, Indonesia, 1945-50; resident in surgery Cen. Hosp., Semarang, Jakarta, 1950-56; head surg. dept. Ctrl. Hosp., Bandung, 1957-77; asst. dean Med. Faculty Bandung, 1962-65, prof. surgery, 1965, dean faculty, 1971-72, mem. cancer team, 1981—; lectr. med. faculty U. Padjedjaran, Bandung, 1963-65; med. advisor Found. for Care of Crippled Children, Bandung, 1953-64, Found. for Care of Patients with Hare-lip and Cleft-palate, 1979—; chmn. Indonesian Cancer Soc., 1984—; lectr. in field. Contbr. articles to profl. jours. Capt. Indonesian Army, 1944-50. Mem. Indonesian Med. Assn., Indonesian Surgeons Assn., Indonesian Oncology Assn., Perkumpulan Gerontologi, Bandung Country Club. Islam. Avocations: billiards, walking. Home: Jalan H IR Juanda 68, Bandung 40132, Indonesia Office: Yayasan Kanker Indonesia, Jalan Kejaksaan 43, Bandung Indonesia 40132

RADEN, LOUIS, tape and label corporation executive; b. Detroit, June 17, 1929; s. Harry M. and Joan (Morris) R.; m. Mary K. Knowlton, June 18, 1949; children: Louis III, Pamela (Mrs. T.W. Rea III), Jacqueline (Mrs. Robert Roy). BA, Trinity Coll., 1951; postgrad., NYU, 1952. With Time, Inc., 1951-52; with Quaker Chem. Corp., 1952-63, sales mgr., 1957-63; exec. v.p. Gen. Tape & Supply, Inc., Detroit, 1963-68, pres., CEO, chmn. bd., 1969—. Pres. Mich. Gun Clubs, 1973-77, L.R. Properties, Inc., Southfield, Mich., 1996—; coach Detroit County Day Sch. Varsity Soccer Team, 1965-69; fifth reunion chmn. Trinity Coll., 1956, pres. Mich. alumni, 1965-72, sec. Class of 1951, 1981-86, pres. 1986-91, The McCook Fellow Soc.; trustee, v.p. Mich. Diocese Episcopal Ch., 1980-82, mem. urban evaluation com., 1975-78, chmn. urban evaluation com., 1978, chmn. urban affairs com., 1977-79; vice chmn., bd. dirs. Robert H. Whitaker Sch., Theology, 1983-85; vice chmn. Mich. Diocese Econ. Justice Commn., 1989-96; bd. dirs. Fund Mgmt. Com., 1989—, Poverty and Social Reform Inst., 1992—; founding sponsor World Golf Hall of Fame; trustee Mich. Housing Trust Fund, 1993—. Recipient Person of Yr. award Mich. Diocese Econ. Justice Commn., 1994; inductee Hall of Fame Robert H. Whitaker Sch. Theology, 1996. Mem. NRA (life), Nat. Skeet Shooting Assn. (life, nat. dir. 1977-79, 5 man team world champion award 1977, pres. coun.), Mich. Skeet Assn. (all state team 1975-80, inductee Hall of Fame 1994), Greater Detroit Bd. Commerce, Automotive Industry Action Group, C. of C. U.S.A., Mich. C. of C., Greater Hartford Jaycees (exec. v.p. 1955-57, Key Man award 1957), Detroit Golf Club, Detroit Gun Club (sec. bd. dirs. 1996-97, bd. dirs. 1996—, pres. 1997-2000, chmn. bd. 2000—), Katke-Cousins Golf Club, Midland County Club, Black Hawk Indians Club, Pinehurst Country Club, Oakland U. Pres's Round Table Club, Detroit Sportsmen's Congress Club, Founders Soc. Detroit Inst. Arts, Theta Xi (life, alumni pres. 1952-57, regional dir. 1954-57, Disting. Svc. award 1957). Home: 1133 Ivyglen Cir Bloomfield Hills MI 48304-1236 Office: Gen Tape & Supply Inc 21500 W Eight Mile Rd Southfield MI 48075-5668

RADER, STEVEN PALMER, lawyer; b. Charlotte, N.C., Dec. 30, 1952; s. Alvin Marion Jr. and Shirley Ninabelle (Palmer) R. AB, Duke U., 1975; postgrad., Stetson U., 1975-76; JD, Wake Forest U., 1978. Bar: N.C. 1978, U.S. Dist. Ct. (ea. dist.) N.C. 1979. Assoc. Wilkinson and Vosburgh, Washington, N.C., 1978-81; pvt. practice Washington, 1981-88; spl. asst. to sec. N.C. Dept. Human Resources, Raleigh, 1988-89, asst. dir. office legal affairs, 1989-91, gen. counsel, 1991-93; ptnr. Wilkinson & Rader, P.A., Washington, 1993—; commr. Nat. Conf. Commrs. on Uniform State Laws, 1985-93; gen. counsel N.C. Rep. Party, 1992-97; commr. N.C. Rules Rev. Commn., 1997-99. Mem., sec. City of Washington Human Rels. Coun., 1981-83; chmn. Beaufort County Rep. party, Washington, 1983-87, 1st Congl. Dist. Rep. party, N.C., 1985-92; v.p. East Main St. Area Neighborhood Assn., 1983-85, 1st v.p., Ocean Villas Homeowners Assn., 1999—; del. Rep. Nat. Conv., 1984, 88, 92. Mem. N.C. State Bar, 2d Jud. Dist. Bar, Beaufort County Hist. Soc. (v.p. 1981-85, pres. 1985-86). Lutheran. Avocations: boating, classic automobiles, travel. Home: PO Box 1901 Washington NC 27889-1901 Office: Wilkinson & Rader PA PO Box 732 Washington NC 27889-0732

RADEVSKI, IVELIN VALTCHEV, physician; b. Dobrich, Bulgaria, June 22, 1964; s. Valtcho and Maria (Dimitrova) R.; m. Zdravka Valtchanova, Sept. 26, 1987; 1 child, Peter. MD, U. Varna Med. Sch., 1991. Med. officer F.H. Odendaal Hosp., Nylstroom, South Africa, 1992-94; sr. med. officer Baragwanath Hosp., Johannesburg, 1994-96, dir. rsch. cardiology, 1996—. Mem. Am. Soc. Hypertension, AAAS, N.Y. Acad. Scis. Avocations: music, literature, movies, driving.

RADHA, RAMASWAMY, physics educator, researcher; b. Kumbakonam, Tamil Nadu, India, Apr. 28, 1966; d. Nagarajan Ramaswamy and Ramachandran Gokila. BSc, Bharathidasan U., Kumbakonam, 1986, MSc, 1988; MPhil, Bharathidasan U., Tiruchirapalli, India, 1990, PhD, 1997. Jr. rsch. fellow Bharathidasan U., Tiruchirapalli, 1991-93, sr. rsch. fellow, 1993-96; lectr. in physics Govt. Coll. for Women, Kumbakonam, 1996—; category A Theoretical Physics Sem. Cir. spkr. Dept. of Sci. and Tech., India, 1995-96, 97-98. Inventor induced dromions. Jr. rsch. fellow Coun. of Scientific and Indsl. Rsch., India, 1990; named Young Scientist for Yr. 1999-2000, TNSCST, Internat. Woman of Yr. 2000-01. Avocations: reading, television, gardening, music. Home: 21 Solayappa St, Kumbakonam 612001, India Office: Govt Coll for Women, Kumbakonam 612001, India

RADHAKISHUN, PRETAAPNARAIN, Surinamese government official. V.p. Govt. of Suriname, 1996—. Office: Office of Pres, Office Vice Pres, Dr Saphiew Redmondstraat 11, Paramaribo Suriname*

RADHAKRISHNAN, TARUR VENKATASUBRAMANIAN, research company executive; b. Mumbai, India, Nov. 15, 1946; s. Marayan Venkatasubramanian Subramanian and Peruvemba Ponnammal; m. Radhakrishnan Sitalakshmi, Mar. 29, 1979; children: Shailesh, Sudhir. BSc, Parle Coll., Mumbai, India, 1968; BSc in Tech., UDCT, Mumbai, 1971, PhD in Tech., 1977; DIC (hon.), Imperial Coll., London, 1979. Rsch. assoc. Imperial Coll., 1977-79; v.p. R&D RPG Life Scis. (formerlly Searle India Ltd.), Mumbai, 1979—; part-time vis. faculty mem. UDCT, 1996—, examiner postgrad. studies, 1982—. Patentee in field. Mrs. Soonabhai Trust scholar, 1971. Fellow Royal Soc. Chemistry. Home: A-301 Vaishali Tower, B R Rd Mulund (W), Mumbai Maharashtra 400080, India Office: RPG Life Scis 25 Midc Land, Thane-Belapur Rd, Thane Maharashtra 400705, India

RADHAKRISHNAN, VENKATARAMAN, astrophysicist; b. Madras, India, May 18, 1929; s. C.V. and Lokasundari Raman; m. Francoise Bernard; one child. BSc, Mysore U., 1950; PhD (hon.), U. Amsterdam, 1996. Rsch. scholar Indian Inst. Sci., Bangalore, 1950-51; rsch. assoc. Chalmers Inst. Tech., Gothenburg, Sweden, 1955-58; sr. rsch. fellow Calif. Inst. Tech., Pasadena, 1959-64; prin. rsch. scientist Commonwealth Sci. & Indsl. Rsch. Orgn., Sydney, Australia, 1965-71; dir. Raman Rsch. Inst., Bangalore, 1972-94. Fellow Indian Acad. Scis., Royal Swedish Acad. Scis.; mem. Royal Astron. Soc. (assoc.), Nat. Acad. Scis. Avocations: aviation, sailing. Office: Raman Rsch Inst, CV Raman Ave Sadashivanagar, 560 080 Bangalore India

RADHAKRISHNAN, V.R., chemical engineer, educator; b. Palghat, Kerala, India, Feb. 7, 1940; s. Ramachandra Iyer V.A. and Nagammal P.S. Radhakrishnan; m. Vijayalakshmi Venkatraman, Feb. 4, 1971 (dec. Feb. 1994); children: V.R. Ramachandran, V.R. Venkatraman. BSc, Madras (India) U., 1958; B of Tech. with honors, India Inst. Tech., Kharagpur, 1958, M of Tech., 1966, PhD, 1981. Lectr. India Inst. Tech., Kharagpur, 1966-72, asst. prof., 1972-84, prof., 1984-97; prof. U. Sains Malaysia, Tronoh, Malaysia, 1997—; cons. Indian Explosives, India, 1985-86, Steel Authority, India, 1990-95, Indian Oil, 1992-94. Author: Instrumentation for Chemical, Mineral and Metallurgical Processes, 1998; contbr. articles to profl. jours. Fellow German Acad. Exchange, Germany, 1980-81, Fulbright U. Utah, 1985-86. Mem. Internat. Inst. Chem. Engring. (sec. 1972-76), Internat. Inst. Mineral. Engring. Hindu. Avocations: reading, music, comparative religions. Home: B-141-B Sector 26, Noida 201301, India Office: Sch Chem Engring, U Sains Malaysia, Tronoh 31750, Malaysia

RADHAMOHAN, SAMPRATI KALANIDHI, engineer; b. Rajamundry, India, June 15, 1944; s. Samprati Kalanidhi Madhusudanarao and Sitamma Radhamohan; m. Venkoba Rao Syamala, Jan. 25, 1970; children: Vidyasagar, Venkatesh. BE, Govt. Engring. Coll., Anantapur, India, 1965; ME, Indian Inst. Sci., Bangalore, India, 1967; PhD, Indian Inst. Tech., Kanpur, India, 1971. Dep. head structures divsn. Vikram Sarabhai Space Ctr., Trivandrum, 1975-79, dep. project dir., 1982-89, project dir., 1989-96, group dir., 1996—; mem. adv. com. Internat. Conf. on Engring. Software, 1989. Contbr. articles to profl. jours. including ASME, AIAA Jour., among others. Recipient award ASME, 1980. Mem. Indian Soc. for Advancement of Materials and Process Engring. Avocation: listening to carnatic music. Home: II/7 VSSC, Housing Colony, Trivandrum 695586, India Office: Vikram Sarabhai Space Ctr, ISRO, Trivandrum 695022, India

RADHI, HASSAN ALI, lawyer; b. Sitra, Bahrain, Mar. 21, 1947; s. Ali Ahmed Radhi and Zainab Ali Al Wazeer; m. Mahdiya Mahmood Sharaf, July 6, 1974; children: Saba, Noor, Mona, Layla. Vocat. cert., BAPCO Sch., Manama, Bahrain, 1968; LLB, U. MV, Rabat, Morrocco, 1973; MPhil, SOAS, London, 1986. Bar: Bahrain 1974. Price contr. BAPCO, Manama, 1973; credit analyst, contr. Citibank, Manama, 1973; supr. adminstrn., pres. labor com. BP EA, Manama, United Arab Emirates, 1974; atty., legal advisor in pvt. practice Manama, 1974; sr. ptnr. Hassan Radhi & Assocs., Manama, 1974—; co-chmn. Arab regional forum IBA, London, 1992-96; mem. lawyers disciplinary adv. com. Ministry of Justice, Bahrain, 1995—; mem. Internat. Court of Arbitration of the Internat. C. of C., Paris, 2000; mem. London Court of Internat. Arbitration (LCIA), 1999; vis. lectr., Univ. Bahrain. Editorial bd. (books) Arab Law Quarterly, Middle East Commercial Law Review. Trustee Wisdom Soc. Bahrain, 1992—. Mem. Bahrain Bar Soc. (pres. 1986-87, 89-91), Internat. Bar Assn. (rep. Bahrain chpt., mem. Arab regional forum), coun. mem. Sch. of Oriental and African Studies, Mohammed V, Bahrain Petroleum Company, British Petroleum Company, Eastern Agencies, Internat. Bar Assn. Avocations: poetry writing, squash, table tennis. Office: Hassan Radhi & Assocs, 503 Diplomat Tower PO 5366, Manama Bahrain

RADIĆ, NJEGOMIR, chemistry educator; b. Vrgorac, Dalamatia, Croatia, Sept. 17, 1943; s. Ante and Stana (Mušan) R.; m. Ksenija Vojković, Sept. 19, 1970; 1 child, Mislav. Grad., U. Split, Croatia, 1969; MSc in Chemistry, U. Zagreb, Croatia, 1974, PhD in Chemistry, 1978. Tchg. asst. Faculty of Chem.-Tech. U. Split, Croatia, 1970-79, asst. prof. Faculty Tech., 1979-84, assoc. prof., 1984-96, prof., 1996—, head dept. analytical chemistry, 1979-83, vice dean, 1983-87, dean, 1995-99, pres. coun., 1980-82; vis. prof. dept. chemistry U. Cin., 1981-82. Contbr. articles to sci. jours. Recipient cert. of appreciation dept. chemistry U. Cin., 1982. Mem. Croatian Chem. Soc., Am. Chem. Soc. Achievements include research in potentiometric sensors. Avocation: tennis. Home: Sižgovićeva 20, 21000 Split Croatia Office: Faculty Chem Tech, Teslina 10, 21000 Split Croatia

RADICE, FRANK J., communications executive; b. Washington, Dec. 13, 1949; m. Vida S. Radice, July 4, 1995. Student, U. Md., 1968-72. Film editor WRC/NBC-TV, Washington, 1971-72; film editor ABC News, Washington, 1972, assignment editor, 1976, assoc. producer Good Morning Am., 1978, ops. producer World News Tonight, 1979-80; producer Nightline N.Y.C., 1980-83; program producer The Last Word ABC News, N.Y.C., 1983; field dir. Entertainment Tonight Paramount Motion Pictures, N.Y.C., 1984; producer, developer Live At 5:00 WRC/NBC-TV, Washington, 1985; exec. prodr. Entertainment News, Cable News Network, N.Y.C., 1987-89; InterActive sr. producer/product devel., producer advt. and promotion ABC News, N.Y.C., 1989-91; advt. mgr. WCBS-TV, N.Y.C., 1991; v.p. advt. and promotion NBC Entertainment, N.Y.C., 1996; sr. v.p. The NBC Agy., 2000—; pres. Radice Prodn. Ltd., 1991. Prodr.: A Line in the Sand, War of Peace, War in the Gulf; writer, prodr., 1992; co-exec. prodr. CD, The Best of The Today Show Summer Concerts, Vol. 1, NBC Records, 2000. Recipient award Coll. Emergency Physicians, 1983, Emmy award NATAS, 1984, 1990, 2 N.Y. Festival awards; Alfred I Dupont grantee Columbia U., N.Y.C., 1984, 91, Mobius award, 1998. Mem. Broadcast Music Inc. (writer affiliate), AFTRA, Nat. Assn. Broadcast Employees and Technicians, Internat. Alliance Theatrical and Stage Employees, Writers Guild Am., Dirs. Guild Am., Congressional Country Club, Friars (N.Y.C.). Democrat. Roman Catholic. Office: NBC Ste 1891E 30 Rockefeller Plz New York NY 10112-0002

RADICELLA, RENATO, nuclear chemist, consultant; b. Messina, Italy, July 6, 1934; arrived in Argentina, 1949; s. Salvatore and Giovanna (La Rosa) R.; m. Beatriz Santiago, Dec. 26, 1957 (div. July 1976); children: Juan Pablo, Diego, Marcos; m. Martha Barmasch, July 12, 1977; 1 child, Renato M. BS in Chemistry, U. Tucumán, Argentina, 1955, MS, 1957; postgrad. rsch., U. Oslo, 1958-59; PhD, U. Tucumán, Argentina, 1959. Asst. radiochemistry U. Buenos Aires, 1956-61, prof. radiochemistry, 1961-70; various positions Atomic Energy Commn., Buenos Aires, 1955-90; head L.Am. sect. Internat. Atomic Energy Agy., Vienna, Austria, 1990-97; advisor Atomic Energy Commn., Buenos Aires, 1997—; vis. scientist Atomic Energy Commn., Saclay, France, 1966-67; dir. INVAP Soc. del Estado Bariloche, Argentina, 1980-84, pres., 1984-89; pres., CEO, ENACE Soc. Anónima, Buenos Aires, 1987-89; pres. Interam. Nuc. Energy Commn., 1986-88, v.p., 1984-86, pres. adv. com., 1977-81; mem. nuclear affairs com. Argentine Coun. internat. rels., 1994—. Co-author: Especificaciones y normas de radiofármacos, 1970, Manual de controles radiofarmacéuticos, 1972, Farmacotecnia Teórica y Práctica, 1981, La cooperacion internacional de la Argentina en el campo nuclear, 1998; contbr. over 70 articles to profl. jours. Officer, Order of Merit for Disting. Svc., Peru, 1978, recipient Konex Found. prize for Sci. and Tech., Argentina, 1983, Huesped Distinguido de la Ciudad de La Paz, Bolivia, 1981. Mem. Am. Nuc. Soc. (L.Am. sect., mem. prize com. 1987—), Argentine Soc. Nuc. Biology and Medicine (founder, dir. 1973-74), Argentine Soc. Nuc. Tech. (dir. 1978-84), Argentine Soc. Advancement of Sci. (dir. 1983-90), Argentine Soc. Radiation Protection, Univ. Club Buenos Aires. Avocation: cooking. Home: Juramento 5304, Piso 7 "B", 1431 Buenos Aires Argentina Office: Nat Atomic Energy Commn, Ave del Libertador 8250, 1429 Buenos Aires Argentina

RADIN, SAM, lawyer, estate planner; b. N.Y.C., Aug. 1, 1951; s. Clarence and Marjorie (Rembar) R.; m. Pamela Anderson, Sept. 13, 1981; children: Clarence Anderson, Elizabeth Rebecca. BA, Columbia U., 1973; JD, Boston U., 1976. Bar: N.J. 1976, U.S. Dist. Ct. N.J. 1976, N.Y. 1978, U.S. Dist. Ct. (so. dist.) N.Y. 1978, U.S. Ct. Appeals (D.C. cir.) 1978, U.S. Supreme Ct. 1980. Assoc. Burns, Van Kirk, N.Y.C., 1976-79, Lovejoy Wasson successor to Burns, Van Kirk, N.Y.C., 1979-80; pvt. practice, N.Y.C., 1980-84; v.p., gen. counsel Nat. Madison Group, Inc., N.Y.C., 1984-99, pres., 1999—. Contbg. author: Executive Compensation Answer Book, 1998; contbg.

author, editor: Estate and Retirement Planning Answer Book, 1999; also articles. Bd. dirs. Student Athletes Inc., N.Y.C., 1992-98, Westchester Conservatory Music, White Plains, N.Y., 1995-97; trustee Payomet Performing Arts Charitable Trust, 1999—, Nat. Lighthouse Ctr. and Mus., 2000—. Recipient Nathan Burkan Meml. prize ASCAP, 1975. Mem. ABA (subcom. on life ins. tax sect. 1996—), N.Y. State Bar Assn., Assn. Bar City N.Y. Avocations: salt water fly fishing, collecting books, skiing, running. Home: 71 Greenacres Ave Scarsdale NY 10583-1442 Office: Nat Madison Group Inc 260 Madison Ave New York NY 10016-2401

RADIN, SHULAMITH, materials engineer; b. Moscow, June 25, 1948; came to U.S., 1983; d. Samuel and Debora (Lifshist) Ryzhak; m. Alexander Radin, Aug. 1, 1970; 1 child, Michael. MD in Merallurgy, Moscow U. Steel & Alloys, 1969; PhD in Materials Sci., Nat. Inst. Aerocraft Materials, 1972. Sr. rsch. engr. All-Nat. Inst. Aericraft Materials, Moscow, 1972-75, project dir., 1975-80; rsch. assoc., sr. investigator U. Pa., Phila., 1986—. Inventor in field. Mem. Soc. Biomaterials.

RADINA, ALEJANDRO, airline pilot; b. Mar del Plata, Argentina, Feb. 5, 1964; s. Juan Domingo Alejandro and Neli Rosa (Moraz) R. Ed., Air Force Acad., Cordoba, Argentina, 1983-87. Fighting pilot Air Force, Mendoza, Argentina, 1988, Reconquista, Argentina, 1989-93; instr. pilot Air Force, Cordoba, 1994-97; pilot, capt. flight engring. dept. Southern Winds Air Lines, Cordoba, 1997-2000; mgr. instr. pilots Air Force Acad., Cordoba, 1995-97. Author: Instrumental Flying Theory, 1996. Capt. Argentine Air Force, 1983-87. Named Best Instr. Pilot, Argentine Air Force, 1996. Mem. The Planetary Orgn. Roman Catholic Apostolic. Avocations: electronics, physics, astronomy, astrophysics.

RADKAU, JOACHIM, history educator; b. Oberl, K. Minden, Germany, Apr. 10, 1943; s. G and Ruth (Koch) R.; m. Orlinde Petersen. PhD, U. Hamburg, 1970; Habilitation, U. Bielefeld, 1981. Asst. Pädagogische Hochschule, Bielefeld, 1971-80; prof. U. Bielefeld, 1980—. Author: Die Deutsche Emigration in Den USA, 1971, (with George W.F. Hallgarten) Deutsche Industrie und Politik, 1974, Aufstieg und Krise der deutschen Atomwirtschaft, 1981, Technik in Deutschland, 1989, Das Zeitalter der Nervosität, 1998, Natur und Macht - Eine Weltgeschichte der Umwelt, 2000. Home: Bultkamp 16, 33611 Bielefeld Germany Office: U Bielefeld Fac Hist & Phil, Postfach 100131, 33501 Bielefeld Germany

RADMANN, MICHAEL WOLFDIETER, diplomat, geologist; b. Mexico, May 26, 1964; s. Wolfdieter and Margarita (Ester) R.; m. Virginia Alkis Gregoris, Dec. 5, 1992; 1 child, Barbarita Radmann. BS in Geology, Tex. A&M U., 1986; MBM, Am. Grad. Sch. Internat. Mgmt., Glendale, Ariz., 1991. Commd. fgn. svc. officer. Geologist intern Exxon Co., Houston, 1983-85; groundwater geologist Can. Internat. Devel. Agy./U.S. Peace Corps, Swaziland, S. Africa, 1987-89; bilingual tchr. Houston C.C., 1989-90; asst. office mgr. INROADS/Houston, 1989-90; diplomat USAID, Washington, 1992; diplomat/project devel. officer USAID/Am. Embassy, San Salvador, El Salvador, 1992-96; diplomat, program officer USAID/Am. Embassy, Tirana, Albania, 1997-99; internat. bus. analyst Silver and Baryte Ores Mining Co., Athens, Greece, 2000—. Mem. AFS Assn., Soc. Internat. Devel., Am. Assn. Petroleum Geologists, Nat. Peace Corps Assn., UN Assn. of U.S.A. Roman Catholic. Avocations: windsurfing, scuba diving, snow skiing, photography. Home: Imittou # 45/15561 Holargos, Athens 15561, Greece

RADMER, MICHAEL JOHN, lawyer, educator; b. Wisconsin Rapids, Wis., Apr. 28, 1945; s. Donald Richard and Thelma Loretta (Donahue) R.; children from previous marriage: Christina Nicole, Ryan Michael; m. Laurie J. Anshus, Dec. 22, 1983; 1 child, Michael John. B.S., Northwestern U., Evanston, Ill., 1967; J.D., Harvard U., 1970. Bar: Minn. 1970. Assoc. Dorsey & Whitney, Mpls., 1970-75, ptnr., 1976—; lectr. law Hamline U. Law Sch., St. Paul, 1981-84; gen. counsel, rep., sec. 147 federally registered investment cos., Mpls. and St. Paul, 1977—. Contbr. articles to legal jours. Active legal work Hennepin County Legal Advice Clinic, Mpls., 1971—. Mem. ABA, Minn. Bar Assn., Hennepin County Bar Assn. Club: Mpls. Athletic. Home: 4329 E Lake Harriet Pky Minneapolis MN 55409-1725 Office: Dorsey & Whitney Pillsbury Ctr S 220 S 6th St Ste 2200 Minneapolis MN 55402-1498

RADONJIC, LJILJANA, educator, researcher; b. Belgrade, Yugoslavia, Apr. 14, 1940; d. Miodrag and Desanka Stanisavljevic (Trifunovir) R. Dipl.Ing., Faculty Tech., Belgrade, Yugoslavia, 1964, MS, 1968; PhD, MIT, 1973. Asst. IHTM, Belgrade, 1963-70; asst. prof. Faculty of Tech., Bern, Switzerland, 1973-74; prof. Faculty of Tech., Novi Sad, Yugoslavia, 1974—; cons. Faculty of Tech., Belgrade, 1974-84, Tokyo U., 1981. Author monograph; contbr. articles to profl. jours. Grantee Matsumae Internat. Found., Tokyo, 1981, Sigma, 1975. Mem. Am. Ceramic Soc., Electronic Microscopy Soc. Home: Dr A Neto 84, 11070 Belgrade Yugoslavia

RADOSEVIC-STASIC, BISERKA, physiology, immunology, pathophysiology educator; b. Zagreb, Croatia, Nov. 1, 1940; d. Hanibal and Jelka (Degen) Radosevic; m. Josip Stasic, Feb. 4, 1967; children: Nenad, Nikola. MD, U. Rijeka, Zagreb, 1965; MS, U. Rijeka, Croatia, 1969, PhD, 1975. Physician Clin. Hosp. Ctr., Rijeka, 1965-66; asst. dept. physiology and immunology Med. Faculty, Rijeka, 1966-77, docent dept. physiology and immunology, 1977-81, assoc. prof. dept. physiology and immunology, 1981-86, prof. dept. physiology and immunology, 1986—, head cathedra for physiology, immunology and pathophysiology, 1986-95, dir. postgrad. study clin. pathophysiology, 1990-94, vice dean for edn., 1994-97; postdoctoral fellow Inst. for Cell Biology, Zürich, Switzerland, 1976; mem. organizing and sci. com. Alps Adria Soc. for Immunology and Reproduction, Croatian Immunol. Soc., Med. Faculty-U. Rijeka, Zagreb and Rijeka, 1992, 94, 96, 98; coord. network HR-41 Ctrl. European Exch. Program Univ. Studies, Croatia, Austria, Slovenia and Ungaria, 1996-97. Author 73 sci. publs., 150 abstracts in field of Physiology and Immunology; patentee in field. Mem. Croatian Immunol. Soc. and Transplant Soc. E-mail: Biserka.Radosevic-Stasic@mamed.medri.hr. Home: B Milanovica 12, 51000 Rijeka Croatia Office: Univ Rijeka, B Branchetta 22, 51000 Rijeka Croatia

RADOVANOVIC, ZORAN, epidemiologist; b. Belgrade, Yugoslavia, Apr. 17, 1940; s. Milutin and Danica (Grujic) R.; m. Ruzica Slobodanovic, Oct. 28, 1965; children: Vera, Milutin. M.D., Belgrade Sch. Medicine, 1965, cert. in epidemiology, 1973; Diploma in Tropical Pub. Health, London Sch. Hygiene and Tropical Medicine, 1970; D.Sc., U. Belgrade, 1977. Asst. prof. U. Belgrade, 1967-77, assoc. prof., 1977-83, prof. epidemiology, 1983-88; dir. Inst. Epidemiology, 1983-88; sec.-gen. Yugoslav Med. Assn., 1988; prof. epidemiology Kuwait U., 1988—, chair dept. cmty. medicine, 1991-93, 1999-2000. Co-author (books) AIDS, 1987, Balkan Endemic Nephropathy, 2000; co-author, editor: General Epidemiology, 1979, 1986, 97; co-author: Epidemiology of Infectious Diseases, 1980, 1988, 98; editor (Serbo-Croatian edit.) Dictionary of Epidemiology, 1991. Mem. Royal Soc. Tropical Medicine and Hygiene, Sci. Soc. History of Medicine, Internat. Epidemiol. Assn., Am. Pub. Health Assn., European Assn. for Cancer Research, N.Y. Acad. Scis., Serbian Med. Acad. Home: Sindjeliceva 4/I, 11000 Belgrade Yugoslavia Office: Kuwait U Comm Med Fac Med, PO Box 24923, Safat 13110, Kuwait

RADRIZZANI, IVES, philosophy researcher, writer, educator; b. Zürich, Switzerland, Jan. 21, 1960; s. René and Huguette (Duvoisin) R.; m. Fawzia El Tobgui, July 18, 1991; 1 child, Fabrice. Degree in arts, U. Lausanne, Switzerland, 1982, D, 1992; postgrad., U. Rouen, France, 1993. Qualified asst. U. Lausanne, 1982-88, lectr., 1993—; young rschr. Swiss Nat. Inst. Sci. Rsch., Munich, 1988-90; advanced rschr. Swiss Nat. Inst. Sci. Rsch., Paris, 1990-93; rschr. Swiss Nat. Inst. Sci. Rsch., Lausanne, 1995-98; lectr. U. Bern, Switzerland, 1994-95; permanent collaborator Bavarian Acad. Scis., Munich, 1990—, Jacobi-Briefausgabe, 1990—; co-organizer colloquium for 200th anniversary of Fichte's Wissenschaftslehre, Poitiers, France, 1994; assoc. rschr. Ctr. Hegel-Marx, Nat. Ctr. Sci. Rsch., Poitiers, 1995—, Ctr. d'Histoire de la Philosophie Moderne, Nat. Ctr. Sci. Rsch., 1997—. Author: Vers la fondation de l'intersubjectivité chez Fichte- Des Principes à la Doctrine de la Science Nova Methodo, 1993; editor: Fichte et la France, vols. I-III; editor, translator: Fichte, La Doctrine de la Science nova methodo, Essai d'une nouvelle présentation de la Doctrine de la Science, 1989; editor, author introduction: Maine de Biran, De l'aperception immédiate, 1995; translator, editor introduction: Le Caractère de l'époque actuelle, 1990; co-translator, author introduction: Philosophie de la Maçonnerie- Les Lettres à Constant, 1995; co-editor: Der Grundansatz der ersten Wissenschaftslehre Johann Gottlieb Fichtes- Tagung des Internationalen Kooperationsorgans der Fichte-Forschung in Neapel, 1995; mem. sci. bd. Archives de Philosophie, 1991, Rev. de Théologie et de Philosophie; mem. editl. bd. Fichte-Studien, 1995—, Cités, 1999—; contbr. articles to profl. jours. Mem. Swiss Soc. Philosophy, Novalis Gesellschaft, Internat. Kooperationsorgan für die Fichte-Forschung (co-organizer congress 1995), Internat. Fichte-Gesellschaft (exec. com.). Avocations: reading, art, music, walking, swimming. Home: Keferstr 35a, 80802 Munich Germany Office: Bavarian Acad Scis, Marstallplatz 8, 80539 Munich Germany

RADU, ADRIAN, civil engineer, consultant; b. Iasi, Romania, Sept. 25, 1928; s. Constantin and Natalia (Hatmanu) R.; m. Veronica Cosma, Nov. 5, 1955. Degree in Engring., Tech. U. Iasi, 1951; D. Engring., Tech. U. Cluj, 1969. Cert. Civil Engr. Chief engr. Bldg. Co. Iasi, 1951-58; asst. prof. Tech. U. Iasi, 1955-72, prof., 1972—; head dept. Tech. U. Iasi, 1977-89, dean faculty, 1990-95; mem. perm. conf. bldg. physics, Stuttgart, Germany, 1991—; mem. nat. coun. sci. rsch., Bucharest, Romania, 1992-95; mem. nat. coun. accreditation of universities, Bucharest, 1996—; sci. coord. Tempus and Inco-Copernicus joint European projects; mem. CIB commns. W-040 and W-067. Author: (book) Handbooks of Building; contbr. numnerous articles to profl. jurs. Pres. Acad. Soc. Former Students of Civil Engring. Faculty Tech. Univ. Iasi, Romania, 1991—. Mem. Romanian Acad. Scientists., Assn. Civil Engrs. in Romania, Romanian Acad. Tech. Scis. E-mail: raduadr@theta.ce.tuiasi.ro. Fax: 40-32-233368. Home: St. L. Catargi 46, 6600 Iasi Romania Office: Tech. U. Faculty Constrn., Splai Stang Bahlui 43, 6600 Iasi Romania

RADUCAN, ANDREEA, olympic athlete; b. Birlad, Romania, Sept. 30, 1983. Mem. gymnastics team Romania; winner second pl. in all-around Internat. Team Championship, 1998, winner team title, 1999; winner silver in balance beam European Championship, 1998, winner bronze in floor exercise, 1998; winner team gold World Championship, Tianjin, China, 1999, winner gold in floor exercise, 1999, winner silver in balance beam, 1999; winner gold team all-around Olympics, Sydney, Australia, 2000. Office: Romanian Gymnastics Ctr Romanian Studies, Ofcl Postal I Casuta Postal 108, 6600 Iasi Romania*

RADULESCU, ELENA, hematologist, immunocytochemist, researcher; b. Rosiorii-de-Vede, Teleorman, Romania, May 14, 1927; d. Gheorghe A. and Voica Gh. (Popescu) Radulescu; m. Alexandru A. Matusan, Sept. 2, 1952 (div. Mar. 1969); 1 child, Mircea Radu Matusan. Degree in Medicine, Faculty Gen. Medicine, Cluj, Romania, 1953; MD, PhD in Med. Scis., U. Medicine and Pharmacy, Cluj-Napoca, Romania, 1977; postgrad., Royal Post Grad. Med. Sch., London, 1983, 87, 90. Cert. Univ. Prof. Romanian Med. Scis. Acad., 1999. Lab. physician Oradea Hosp., Romania, 1953-57; lab. specialist CFR Hosp., Oradea, 1957-66; rschr. dept. hematology Oncol. Inst., Ion Chiricuta, Cluj, 1966-91; sr. rschr. Cluj-N. br.Biotehnos S.A., Bucharest, 1991-93, 2d Pediatric Clinic, Cluj, 1993—; specialist in hematology Oncological Inst., Cluj, 1966-78, sr. rschr., 1978-91, 91-96; chmn. Internat. Congress of Histochemistry and Cytochemistry, Helsinki, 1984, Washington, 1988, Paris, 1991, others; pres. Oncological Union, Cluj-Napoca, 1980-82; hon. mem. prof.'s coun. U. Medicine and Pharmacy, Cluj-Napoca. Author: Cancer Malignant Haemopathies, 1982; contbr. articles to profl. jours. Recipient grants, London, 1983, 87, 90. Mem. Internat. Fedn. Rschrs. for Sci. and Tech. (Gt. Britain), World Soc. Cellular and Molecular Biology N.Y., Internat. Soc. Hamatology (European and African divsn.). Mem. Romanian Social Democrat Party. Orthodox. Avocations: sciences, art, music, travel. Home: Unirii No 1 Et III ap 16, 3400 Napoca Romania

RADUTA, APOLODOR ARISTOTEL, physicist, educator; b. Ulmi, Giurgiu, Romania, Mar. 6, 1943; s. Gheorghe and Ioana (Dinca) R.; m. Emilia Ganea, Aug. 16, 1966; children: Alexandru, Cristian. Diploma in physics, Faculty of Physics, Bucharest, Romania, 1965; diploma in math., Faculty of Math., Bucharest, 1972; PhD, Inst. for Atomic Physics, Bucharest, 1972. Physicist-chemist Inst. for Atomic Physics, Bucharest, 1965-68, stagiar rschr., 1968-70; rschr. Joint Inst. Nuclear Rsch., Dubna, Soviet Union, 1970-71; physicist Inst. for Atomic Physics, Bucharest, 1971-75, sr. rschr. rank III, 1975-77; sr. rschr. rank III Inst. Physics and Nuclear Engring., Bucharest, 1977-81, sr. rschr. rank II, 1981-90, sr. rschr. rank I, 1990—; PhD supr. Ministry of Edn. Bucharest, 1982—, prof. theoretical physics, 1994—; sr. fellow Humboldt Found., Frankfort on the Main, Germany, 1975-76; mem. adminstrv. coun., pres. sci. coun. Inst. Physics and Nuclear Engring., 1997-99; dir. 5 internat. summer schs. Contbr. some 140 articles to sci. jours. and procs.; mem. editl. bd.: Romanian Jour. Physics, 1990—. Founding fellow, senate mem. Civic Forum of Romania, 1998. Sgt. Romanian mil., 1965. Recipient Dragomir Hurmuzesu prize Romanian Acad., 1974, rsch. grantee, 1997, 98. Fellow Bolintineanu Found., Scientists Acad. of Romania, Humboldt-Club. Avocations: playing tennis, reading literature, listening to music, hiking. Home: Bl 61-63 ScA et 6 Ap 22, Calea Dorobantilor 61-63, Bucharest Romania Office: Inst Physics/Nuclear Engrin, MG6 Bucharest Romania

RADVANY, JOÃO, neurologist; b. São Paulo, Jan. 30, 1943; s. Karoly Béla and Hedvig Maria (Csendes) R.; m. Edoarda Anna Paron, Aug. 6, 1994. MD, U. São Paulo, 1968. Diplomate Am. Bd. Psychiatry and Neurology. Physician Hosp. Albert Einstein, São Paulo. Fellow Am. Acad. Neurology. Office: Hosp Albert Einstein, Av Albert Einstein 627cj389, 05651901 São Paulo Brazil

RADWAN, ABDALLA GOMAA, pharmacologist; b. El-Bagour, Menofia, Egypt, Dec. 5, 1938; s. Gomaa Yehia Radwan; m. Suhair Mahmoud Al-Witry; children: Samar, Reem, Ahmed. MB, B Ch, Cairo (Egypt) U., 1961; PhD in Pharmacology, London U., 1968. Demonstrator Assiut (Egypt) U., 1963-64; lectr. Al-Azhar U., Cairo, Egypt, 1968-74; asst. prof. Al-Azhar U., Cairo, 1974-79, prof., 1979—, chmn. dept. pharmacology, 1992-99; cons. Memphis Co., Cairo, Egypt, 1973-75; asst. prof. Mosul (Iraq) U., 1975-79; prof. pharmacology, Sanaa (Yemen) U., 1988-92. Editor Al-Azhar Medical Jour., 1972, Jour. Egyptian Soc. Toxicology, 1975. Mem. Egyptian Soc. Toxicology (sec.-gen. 1975), Union African Socs. of Pharmacology (treas. 1983), Arab Socs. Pharmacology (mem. exec. coun.), Egyptian Soc. Pharmacology (dep. pres.), Al-Azhar Med. Soc. (pres. 1998), Al Azhar U. Club, SHAMS Club. Home: 5-Salwa Hegazy St, 11769 Cairo Heliopol, Egypt Office: Al-Azhar U Dept Pharmacol, Faculty of Medicine, 11884 Nasr City Egypt

RADWAN, AHMED ELAZAB, mathematics educator; b. Gharbia, Egypt, Aug. 16, 1953; s. Elazab Ali and Amena Ismael Radwan; m. Samia Said Abdrabow, May 20, 1979; children: Magdy, Marrwa, Mohamed. BSc with honors, Aim-shams U., Cairo, 1975, MSc, 1979, PhD, 1989. Demonstrator faculty of sci. Ain-shams U., 1975-79, lectr., 1979-89, asst. prof., 1989-94, assoc. prof., 1994-99, prof., 1999—; participant internat. math. confs., Belgium, Italy, Japan, Sweden, Egypt, and Bahrain. Contbr. articles to profl. jours. With Egyptian Army, 1975-76. Avocations: sports, reading, fishing. Home: Elmarrwa City, Flat 1001 Bldg 1, Heliopls Cairo Egypt Office: Ain-shams U, Faculty Sci Math Dept, Cairo Egypt

RADWANSKI, KAZIMIERZ, archaeologist; b. Willa-Góra, Poland, Sept. 25, 1924; s. Marian and Helena (Szmoniewska) R.; m. Teresa Lenkiewicz, Apr. 24, 1968. Dr. degree, Warsaw (Poland) U., 1984; DSc, Politech. U., Cracow, Poland, 1985. Specialist in archaeology State Monuments Preservation Office, Cracow, 1955-61; dir. archaeology Archeol. Mus. Cracow, 1961-95; cons. Revalorization Office for Archaeol. and Hist. Monuments of Town of Cracow, 1973-95. Author: Krakow Przedlokacyjny, 1975 (award 1975); contbr. articles to profl. publs. Recipient Sci. award Town of Cracow, 1974, Archaeol. Activities award Voivode of Cracow, 1994. Mem. Polish Nat. Com. of ICOM, Polish Acad. Scis. (com. of pre- and prohist. rsch. 1992-96, Sci. award for archaeol. activities, 1976). Home: ul Szewska 24, 31-009 Cracow Poland Office: Mus Archeology Krakow, ul Senacka 3, 31-002 Cracow Poland

RADWAY, LAURENCE INGRAM, political science educator; b. Staten Island, N.Y., Feb. 2, 1919; s. Frederick and Dorothy (Segall) R.; m. Patricia Ann Headland, Aug. 20, 1949; children: Robert Russell, Carol Sinclair, Michael Porter, Deborah Brooke. B.S., Harvard U., 1940, M.A., 1948, Ph.D., 1950; M.P.A., U. Minn., 1943; M.A. (hon.), Dartmouth, 1959. Jr. economist OPA, 1941; intern U.S. Bur. Budget, 1941-42, Nat. Inst. Pub. Affairs, 1941-42; teaching fellow govt. dept. Harvard U., 1946-50; instr. govt. dept. Dartmouth U., 1950-52, asst. prof., 1952-57, assoc. prof., 1957-58, prof., 1958—, chmn. dept., 1959-62, 70-72, 77-80, dir. Comparative Studies Ctr., 1963-68; cons. ODM, 1952; prof. Nat. War Coll., 1962-63; civilian aide to sec. army, 1962-70; mem. N.H. Ho. Reps., 1968-72. Author: (with John W. Masland) Soldiers and Scholars, 1957, Military Behavior in International Organizations, 1962, Foreign Policy and National Defense, 1969. Chmn. Hanover Democratic Com., 1954-56; mem. N.H. Dem. Com., 1958-60, chmn. Platform Conf., 1959, 60, chmn., 1975-77; chmn. Grafton County Dem. Com., 1956-58; mem. Dem. Nat. Com., 1975-77; Bd. dirs. N.H. World Affairs Council, 1955-81; bd. advisers Indsl. Coll. Armed Forces, 1958-62. Served from pvt. to capt., Transp. Corps AUS, 1943-46. Pub. Adminstrn. fellow U. Minn., 1940-42; Social Sci. Research Council fellow, 1957. Mem. Council Fgn. Relations, Internat. Inst. Strategic Studies, Am. Polit. Sci. Assn. (nat. council 1965-67), Royal Inst. Internat. Affairs, New Eng. Polit. Sci. Assn. (mem. com. 1959-60, pres. 1964-65), Phi Beta Kappa. Presbyn. Home: 29 Pinewood Vlg West Lebanon NH 03784-3119

RADWI, AMER NAEEM, medical educator; b. Makkah, Saudi Arabia, Apr. 9, 1960; s. Naeem Radwi and Sultan Najmi; m. Durre Haroon Najmi. MB BChir, King Abdul Aziz U., Saudi Arabia, 1984. Diplomate in med. oncology Am. Bd. Internal Medicine, Can. Bd. Internal Medicine; cert. spl. competence in med. oncology Royal Coll. Physicians and Surgeons of Can. Demonstrator King Abdul Aziz U., Jeddah, Saudi Arabia, 1985-87; resident dept. medicine U. Ottawa, Ont., Can., 1987-90, fellow in med. oncology, 1990-92; asst. prof. King Abdul Aziz U., Jeddah, 1992—; cons. in internal medicine and med. oncology dept. medicine King Abdul Aziz U., Jeddah, 1992—; cons. med. oncologist King Faisal Specialist Hosp., Riyadh, Saudi Arabia, 1997-99. Fax: 966-2-6408315. Home: PO Box 41579, 21531 Jeddah Saudi Arabia

RADY, MOHAMED RAMADAN, research scientist; b. Giza, Cairo, Egypt, Nov. 17, 1953; s. Ramadan Rady and Hayam (Abbas) R.; m. Aug. 10, 1989; children: Ayah, Ashraf. PhD, Al-Azhar U., Cairo, 1988. Specialist Nat. Rsch. Ctr., Giza, Egypt, 1981-88; researcher asst. Nat. Rsch. Ctr., Giza, 1988, assoc. researcher, 1988-95, researcher, 1995—; expert in agr. State of Sierra Leone, Freetown, 1986. Avocations: football, tennis. Office: Nat Rsch Ctr Plant Cell & Tissue Culture, El-Tahrir St Dokki, Giza Egypt

RADZIEVSKII, GRIGORI VADIMOVICH, mathematician; b. Kharkov, Ukraine, Jan. 14, 1948; s. Vadim Antonovich Radzievskii and Zinaida Dmitrievna Kostjuk; m. Elena Ivanovna Zhukina, Dec. 10, 1997. PhD, Moscow State U., 1973; DSc in Physics and Math., Nat. Acad. Sci., Ukraine, 1980. Asst. Moscow State U., 1971-73; jr. scientist Inst. Math., Kyiv, Ukraine, 1974-78, sr. scientist, 1978-86; prof. Kyiv Poly. Inst., 1982-90; head scientist Inst. Math., Kyiv, 1986—. Contbr. articles to profl. jours. Home: Teremkivska Str 14 Apt 30, 252187 Kiev Ukraine Office: Inst Math Nat Acad Sci, Tereshenkivska Str 3, 252601 Kiev MSP, Ukraine

RADZIKOWSKI, WLADYSLAW, econometrician, researcher; b. Lodz, Poland, Feb. 5, 1929; s. Bronislaw and Stanislawa (Bajer) R.; m. Danuta Eleonora Kielkiewicz Radzikowski, Sept. 27, 1947; children: Pawel, Maciej. M in Econ., Main Sch. Planning & Stat., Warsaw, Poland, 1955; PhD in Math. Programming, 1964; degree in Econometrics, Econ. Acad., Wroclaw, Poland, 1969. Head of dept. Inst. Organ. in Machine-Build. Industry, Warsaw, Poland, 1955-66; deputy dir. rsch. Inst. Industry Econ. and Organ., Warsaw, Poland, 1966-68; head dir. Inst. Organ. in Machine-Build. Industry, Warsaw, Poland, 1968-71; deputy dir. rsch. R&D Ctr. of Informatics, Warsaw, Poland, 1971-73; head of chair Warsaw U., Warsaw, Poland, 1974—; prof. in ordinary Nicolai-Copernicus U., Torun, Poland, 1990—; vis. prof. Fordham U., 1976, 78, 79, Fachhochschule fuer Wirtschaft, 1982, U. Detroit, 1984; supv. tchr. U. Milano, 1991, U. Amsterdam, 1992; v.p. Sci. Soc. for Orgn. and Mgmt., Warsaw, Poland, 1977—; chmn. Sci. Bd., 1981-89. Author: Project Management, 1979, Informatics Systems in Organization and Management, 1981, Development of the School of Management, 1987, Operations Research in Management, 1985, 94, 97. Mem. Polish Acad. Scis. (mem. com. orgn. and mgmt.), Polish Soc. for Ops. and Sys. Rsch., Polish Econ. Soc. (vice chmn. Warsaw divsn. 1971-72, chmn. 1997—), German Soc. for Ops. Rsch., Gesellschaft der Hochschullehrer für Betriebs-Wirtschaft, Inst. for Ops. Rsch. and Mgmt. Scis., Internat. Input-Output Assn. Roman Catholic. Avocations: stamp collecting, canoeing. Home: Marszalkowska 27/35/37, 00-639 Warsaw Poland Office: Warsaw University, Szturmowa 3, 02-678 Warsaw Poland

RAE, MATTHEW SANDERSON, JR., lawyer; b. Pitts., Sept. 12, 1922; s. Matthew Sanderson and Olive (Waite) R.; m. Janet Hettman, May 2, 1953; children: Mary-Anna, Margaret Rae Mallory, Janet S. Rae Dupree. AB, Duke, 1946, LLB, 1947; postgrad., Stanford U., 1951. Bar: Md. 1948, Calif. 1951. Asst. to dean Duke Sch. Law, Durham, N.C., 1947-48; assoc. Karl F. Steinmann, Balt., 1948-49, Guthrie, Darling & Shattuck, L.A., 1953-54; nat. field rep. Phi Alpha Delta Law Frat., L.A., 1949-51; research atty. Calif. Supreme Ct., San Francisco, 1951-52; ptnr. Darling, Hall & Rae (and predecessor firms), L.A., 1955—; mem. Calif. Commn. Uniform State Laws, 1985—, chmn., 1993-94; chmn. drafting com. for revision Uniform Prin. and Income Act of Nat. Conf., 1991-97, Probate and Mental Health Task Force, Jud. Coun. Calif., 1996—. Vice pres. L.A. County Rep. Assembly, 1959-64; mem. L.A. County Rep. Ctrl. Com., 1960-64, 77-90, 2000—, exec. com., 1977-90; vice chmn. 17th Congl. Dist., 1960-62, 28th Congl. Dist., 1962-64; chmn. 46th Assy. Dist., 1962-64, 27th Senatorial Dist., 1977-85, 29th Senatorial Dist., 1985-90; mem. Calif. Rep. State Ctrl. Com., 1966—, exec. com., 1966-67; pres. Calif. Rep. League, 1966-67; trustee Rep. Assocs., 1979-94, pres., 1983-85, chmn. bd. dirs., 1985-87. 2d lt. USAAF, WWII. Fellow Am. Coll. Trust and Estate Counsel; academician Internat. Acad. Estate and Trust Law (exec. coun. 1974-78); mem. ABA, L.A. County Bar Assn. (chmn. probate and trust law com. 1964-66, chmn. legis. com. 1980-86, chmn. program com. 1981-82, chmn. membership retention com. 1982-83, trustee 1983-85, dir. Bar Found., 1987-93, Arthur K. Marshall award probate and trust law sect. 1984, Shattuck-Price Meml. award 1990), South Bay Bar Assn., State Bar of Calif. (chmn. state bar jour. com. 1970-71, probate com. 1974-75; exec. com. estate planning trust and probate law sect. 1977-83, chmn. legis. com. 1977-89; co-chmn. 1991-92; probate law cons. group Calif. Bd. Legal Specialization 1977-88; chmn. conf. dels. resolutions com. 1987, exec. com. conf. dels. 1987-90), Lawyers Club L.A. (bd. govs. 1981-87, 1st v.p. 1982-83), Am. Legion (comdr. Allied post 1969-70), Legion Lex (bd. dirs. 1964-99, pres. 1969-71), Air Force Assn., Aircraft Owners and Pilots Assn., Town Hall (gov. 1970-78, pres. 1975), World Affairs Coun., Internat. Platform Assn., Breakfast Club (law, pres. 1989-90), Commonwealth Club, Chancery Club (pres. 1996-97), Rotary, Phi Beta Kappa (councilor Alpha Assn. 1983—, pres. 1996), Omicron Delta Kappa, Phi Alpha Delta (supreme justice 1972-74, elected to Disting. Svc. chpt. 1978), Sigma Nu. Presbyterian. Home: 600 John St Manhattan Beach CA 90266-5837 Office: Darling Hall & Rae 520 S Grand Ave Fl 7 Los Angeles CA 90071-2600

RAE, SIMON JAMES GRAHAM, lawyer; b. England, Nov. 24, 1956; s. John Graham and Elizabeth Mary (Elston) R. LLB, Aberdeen (Scotland) U., 1979. Trainee solicitor Adam Cochran & Co., Aberdeen, Scotland, 1979-81; solicitor Shepherd & Wedderburn, Edinburgh, Scotland, 1981-85; solicitor Johnson, Stokes & Master, Hong Kong, 1985-90, ptnr., 1990—. Author of numerous articles relating to Hong Kong Taxes in various Tax Jours. Mem. Law Soc. Scotland, Law Soc. Hong Kong (revenue com. 1996—, joint liason com. of taxation), Hong Kong Gen. C. of C. (tax com. 1988—), Internat. Fiscal Assn. (com. mem. Hong Kong br. 1996—), Internat. Tax Planning Assn., Hong Kong Trustees Assn. (mem. exec. com.), Internat. Pacific Bar Assn. (revenue com. deputy chmn. 1998—). Avocations: tennis, travel, reading. Fax: 852-2845-9121. Email: sr@jsm.com.hk. Office: Johnson Stokes & Master 17F, Princes Bldg 10 Chater Rd, Hong Kong China

RAEBURN, JOHN ALEXANDER, medical geneticist, educator; b. Adlington, U.K., June 25, 1941; s. Hugh Adair and Christina Constance (Forbes) R.; m. Patricia Hawco, Aug. 12, 1967 (div. Apr. 1980); children: Elspeth, Alison, Hugh; m. Arlene Rose Conway, May 17, 1980. MB, Edinburgh U., 1964, PhD, 1976. Lectr. in therapeutics Edinburgh U., U.K.,

1968-72; sr. rsch. fellow Leiden U., U.K., 1972-73; sr. lectr. Edinburgh U., U.K., 1973-90; prof. med. genetics Nottingham U., U.K., 1990—; genetic advisor Assn. Brit. Insurers, 1996—; mem. Govt. Genetics and Ins. Com., 1999—. Contbr. over 100 papers to profl. publs. Maj. RAMC, 1966-85. Fellow Royal Coll. Physicians; mem. Scottish Down Syndrome Assns. (past chair), Cystic Fibrosis Rsch. Trust (past chair). Avocations: reading, fishing, music. Home: 3 Grove Farm, Lowdham NG14 7AY, England Office: City Hosp, Ctr for Med Genetics, Nottingham N65 1PB, England

RAEDEKE, LINDA DISMORE, geologist; b. Great Falls, Mont., Aug. 20, 1950; d. Albert Browning and Madge (Hogan) Dismore; m. Kenneth John Raedeke, Dec. 26, 1971 (div. 1982); m. Charles Moore Swift, Jr., Mar. 14, 1992. BA in History, U. Wash., 1971, MS in Geology, 1979, PhD, 1982. Geomorphologist, park planner Corporacion Nacional Forestal and U.S. Peace Corps, Punta Arenas, 1972-75; glacial geologist Empresa Nacional del Petroleo, Punta Arenas, 1972-75; geologist FAO, UN, Punta Arenas, 1974, Lamont-Doherty Geol. Obs., COlumbia U., Tierra del Fuego, Chile, 1974-75; wetlands evaluation project coord. Wash. Dept. Agr., U. Wash., Seattle, 1975-76; curator Remote Sensing Applications Lab. U. Wash., 1976-77; exploration geologist Chevron Resources Co., Denver, 1981-84; rsch. geologist Chevron Oil Field Rsch. Co., La Habra, Calif., 1984-89; sr. compensation analyst Chevron Corp., San Francisco, 1989-90; staff geologist Chevron Overseas Petroleum, Inc., San Ramon, Calif., 1990-91, project leader, 1991-95, new ventures coord. for the far east, 1995-96; sr. staff analyst for planning Chevron Corp., 1996-98; coorr. upstream bus. Chevron Rsch. Tech. Co., 1998-99; group mgr. Integrated Labs., 1999—; mem. adv. bd. Bay Area Earth Sci. Inst., 1999—, Montana State U. Coll. Tech., 2000—. Contbt. articles to profl. jours. Mem. Am. Geophys. Union, Geol. Soc. Am., Am. Assn. Petroleum Geologists (poster chmn. 1987, internat. chmn. 1996 meeting). Office: Chevron Rsch and Tech Co 100 Chevron Way Richmond CA 94801-2016

RAEL, HENRY SYLVESTER, SR., retired health administrator, financial and management consultant; b. Pueblo, Colo., Oct. 2, 1928; s. Daniel and Grace (Abeyta) R.; m. Helen Warner Loring Brace, June 30, 1956 (dec. Aug. 1980); children: Henry Sylvester Jr., Loring Victoria, Thomas Warner Bush. AB, U. So. Colo., 1955; BA in Bus. Adminstrn., U. Denver, 1957, MBA, 1958. Sr. boys counselor Denver Juvenile Hall, 1955-58; adminstrv. asst. to pres. Stanley Aviation Corp., Denver, 1958-61; Titan III budget and fin. control supr. Martin Marietta Corp., Denver, 1961-65; mgmt. adv. services officer U. Colo. Med. Center, Denver, 1965-72; v.p. fin., treas. Loretto Heights Coll., Denver, 1972-73; dir. fin. and adminstrn. Colo. Found. for Med. Care, 1973-86, Tri-County Health Dept., Denver, 1986-96; fin. cons. Denver, 1996—; cons. Clayton Found.-Denver Headstart, 1996, Colo. Dept. Pub. Health & Environ., 1997, Hosp. Shared Svcs., 1997-98, U.S. Dept. Commerce Census, 2000, Census Enumerator, 2000; instr. fin. mgmt., mem. fin. com. am. Assn. Profl. Standards Rev. orgn., 1980-85; speaker systems devel., design assns., univs., 1967-71. Mem. budget lay adv. com. Park Hill Elem. Sch., Denver, 1967-68, chmn., 1968-69; vol. worker Boy and Girl Scouts, 1967-73; bd. dirs. Community Arts Symphony, 1981-83, 85-87; controller St. John's Episcopal Cathedral, 1982-83; charter mem. Pueblo (Colo.) Coll. Young Democrats, 1954-55; block worker Republican Party, Denver, 1965-68, precinct committeeman, 1978-84; trustee Den Astro Soc. Van Nattan Scholarship Fund, 1974-96; bd. dirs. Vis. Nurse Assn., 1977-84, treas., 1982-84. Served with USAF, 1947-53, res., 1954-61. Recipient Disting. Service award Denver Astron. Soc., 1968, Citation Chamberlin Obs., 1985; Stanley Aviation masters scholar, 1957; Ballard scholar, 1956. Mem. Assn. Systems Mgmt. (pres. 1971-72), Hosp. Systems Mgmt. Soc., Budget Execs. Inst. (v.p. chpt. 1964-65, sec. 1963-64), Colo. Pub. Employees Retirement Assn. (bd. dirs. 1993), Denver Astron. Soc. (pres. 1965-66, bd. dirs. 1982-94), Am. Assn. Founds. for Med. Care (fin. com. 1981-82), Nat. Astronomers Assn. (exec. bd. 1965-97), Brandy Chase Homeowners Assn. (bd. dirs. 1997), Whispering pines of Denver Homeowners Assn. (pres., bd. dirs., 1998), Epsilon Xi, Delta Psi Omega. Home: 7755 E Quincy Ave # 57 Denver CO 80237-2312

RAEV, DIMITAR CHRISTOV, cardiologist, educator; b. Russe, Bulgaria, Jan. 28, 1956; s. Christo Dimitrov and Mila Stephanova (Panteva) R.; m. Petja Nikolova Chorozova, Dec. 25, 1982; 1 child, Raev Niki. MD, Med. U., Pleven, Bulgaria, 1982; PhD in Med. Sci., Med. U., St. Zagora, Bulgaria, 1993. Cert. specialist in internal diseases Ministry Pub. Health, cert. specialist in cardiology. Gen. practitioner Pub. Health Office, Russe, 1982-84; asst. prof. Med. U., St. Zagora, 1984-89, head asst. prof., 1989-94; asst. prof. Nat. Ctr. Cardiovasc. Disease, Sofia, Bulgaria, 1994-98, assoc. prof., 1998—; head dept. intensive care Sci. Inst., Ministry of Internal Affairs, Sofia, 1996—; cons. Nat. Ctr. Cardiovasc. Disease, 1994-95, Sci. Inst., Ministry of Internal Affairs, 1996. Patentee computer analysis of echocardiography, handgrip device; contbr. articles to sci. jours. Fellow Am. Heart Assn., European Soc. Cardiology; mem. Internat. Soc. Noninvasive Cardiology, N.Y. Acad. Scis. Avocations: body building, diving. Home: Iavorov 49, 1111 Sofia Bulgaria Office: Ctrl Clin Hosp, Skobelev 79, Dept Intnsv Cr, 1606 Sofia Bulgaria

RAEV, MICHAEL BORISOVICH, immunologist, educator, molecular biologist; b. Sverdlovsk, Ural, USSR, July 18, 1959; s. Boris Solomonovich and Regina Alexandrovna (Hrakovskaya) R.; m. Lyudmila Pavlovna Philippova, Mar. 16, 1979 (div. 1994); 1 child, Elena. Diploma, Sch. No. 12, Perm, USSR, 1976; PhD, VAC, Russia, 1995. Engr. Dept. Ecology and Genteics Microorganisms, Perm, 1981-83, sr. engr., 1983-85, jr. rschr., 1985-90; rschr. Inst. Ecology and Genetics Microorganisms, Perm, 1990-93, sr. rschr., 1993—; asst. prof. Perm State U., 1995—; leading specialist Ctr. Peptons Inst. Bioorganic Chemistry, Moscow, 1991-93; invited adviser Orgenics, Israel, 1994. Author: Streptococci and the Host, 1997. Mem. Russian Soc. Immunologists, N.Y. Acad. Scis. Achievements include patent in method of stereospecific assay and method of conjugate production for stereospecific assay. Avocation: hunting. Home: Komsomolskiy av. 58-50, 614039 Perm Russia Office: Inst Ecol & Genetics Micro, Goleva str., 13, 614081 Perm Russia

RAEVA, SVETLANA NIKOLAYEVNA, neurophysiologist, researcher; b. Tbilisi, Georgia, Sept. 1, 1925; d. Nikolay Mikhailovich Raev and Alexandra Ivanovna (Miagkova) Raeva; widow. MD, Med. Inst., Tbilisi, 1947; D in musicology, Fac. Theory & Composition Conservatoire, Tbilisi, 1948; postgrad., Inst. Higher Nervous Activity and Neurophysiology, USSR Acad. Sci., Moscow, 1954; D in medical sci., Inst Exptl. Medicine, USSR Acad. Med. Scis., Leningrad, Russia, 1977. Intern Psychiat. Hosp., Tbilisi, 1947-50; rschr. Inst. Higher Nervous Activity & Neurophysiology USSR Acad. Scis., Moscow, 1954-68; sr. rschr. Inst. Biology Physics USSR Acad. Scis., Moscow, 1968-75, head lab., 1968-75; head lab. Inst. Biol. Physics, Moscow, 1975-80, Inst. Chem. Physics, USSR Acad. Scis., Moscow, 1980—; vis. sci. Lab. de Physiologie des Centres Nerveux, Faculte de Scis. Univ. Paris, Paris, 1967; head group for use of microelectrode techniques in stereotaxy Inst. Neurosurgery, Russian Acad. Med. Scis., Moscow, 1969—. Contbr. over 200 articles to profl. jours. Mem. Internat. Brain Rsch. Orgn., Pavlov Russian Physiol. Soc., Internat. Basal Ganglia Soc. Avocations: rsch. work, classical music. Office: Inst Chem Physics Russian Acad Scis, Kosygin str 4, Moscow 117977, Russia

RAEZ, MATILDE, psychologist; b. Lima, Aug. 29, 1944; d. Ernesto Raez and Matilde Villa-Garcia; widowed; children: Ramirez Raez Alfredo, Ramirez Raez Matilde, Ramirez Raez Roxana. BA, Pontificia U. Cath., Peru, 1967, Degree in Psychology, 1967; Magister, U. Mayor de San Mrcos, Peru, 1969; PhD, Cath. U. of Nijmegen, The Netherlands, 1998. Mem. Nat. Rehab. Inst., Peru, 1966-67; head of dept. Lima Rehab. Ctr. for the Blind, Peru, 1967-68, Nat. Police, 1969-89; prof. Pontificia U. Cath., 1979—; nat. adviser on mil. psychology, Peru, 1984—; mem. Nat. Mental Health Plan, Peru, 1984-86; nat. advisor on rehab. Min. of Health, 1970; clin. cons. in field, 1980—. Author: (books) Personality Development of Women Leaders, 1998, Identity Study on Organized Women, 1990 (Social Scis. Rsch. award 1989); co-author: (book) Peruvian Women Profile; mem. Internat. Test Commn. Project/Rsch. Study in Peru for Devel. of Stds. for Psychol. Test Use, 1997. Psychology therapist apptd. by Peruvian govt. to work with relatives of Japanese, 1996-97; ambassador residence hostages Min. of Justice, Lime, 1985-98; cons. Min. of Interior Affairs, Lima, 1998-90, Marginal Urban Sectors Sch., Lima, 1992—. Col. Nat. Polic Force, Lima, 1988—. Recipient Nat. prize for health psychology Peruvian Psychologist Assn., Lima, 1997; grantee Cath. U. Nijmegen, 1994. Mem. Peruvian Rorschach Soc. (pres. 1997—), Internat. Rorschach Soc. (Peruvian del. 1998—), APA. Avocations: reading, theatre, films, paintings.

RAFAEL AGUILERA, JULIO CESAR, surgery educator; b. San Isidro, Lima, Peru, July 25, 1951; s. Nazario Segundo Rafael and Amada Felicid Aguilera; children: Cesar Augusto, Fabiola Gisella, Gisella Vanessa. MB, San Marcos Nat. U., Lima, 1977; MD, San Marcos Nat. U., 1977; Gen. Surgeon, Cavetano Heredia Peruvian U., 1982; Oncol. Surgeon, Nat. Inst. of Neoplastic Dis, Lima, 1982. Resident Stella Maris Clinic, Lima, 1976-78, Nat. Inst. Neoplastic Diseases, Lima, 1978-82; staff mem. So. Peru Ilo Hosp., Ilo, 1982-94, Social Security Ilo Hosp., Ilo, 1994-97; dir. Ilo Clinic CBSSP, 1997-98, Es Salud Lima Hosp., 1999—; pres. Ilo Med. Assn., 1995-98; med. dir. Peruvian Union Against Cancer, Ilo Br., 1985-2000; cancer cons. Minero Peru Ilo Hosp., 1983-92; surg. cons. Ilo 2000 Clinic, 1990-97; oncol. cons. Peruvian Health Ministry, Ilo Br., 1983-2000; dir. cultural and sci. programs for TV. Gov. Peruvian Govt., Pacocha, Ilo, 1990-93; industry and tourism councilman Ilo Local Govt., 1996-98; worshipful master Ilo Mason Lodge, 1996-97; pres. Ilo Children Found., 1995-98. Recipient Hipolito Unanue award Hipilito Unanue Med. Inst., Lima, 1980; clin. oncology fellowship U. Wash., Seattle, 1983; Noble Shrine, Peruvian Grand Lodge and Shrine Club, 1997. Fellow Am. Coll. Surgeons, Internat. Coll. Surgeons; mem. AMA, AAAS, N.Y. Acad. Scis., Sicentific Am. Soc., The Planetary Soc., Am. Legion, Internat. Airlane Poassengers Assn., Peruv. Cancer Soc., Ilo Med. Assn., Peruv. Med. Coll. Avocations: running, swimming, martial arts, ecol. preservation. Home: Mariano Cornejo 1928, Pueblo Libra-Lima Peru Office: Ilo Med Assn, Grau 213 Ste 5, Ilo Peru

RAFEL, ENRIQUE, pathologist; b. Barcelona, Spain, Dec. 21, 1938; s. Enrique C. and Remedios C. (Ribas) R.; m. Dahlia To-Ong Quijada, Dec. 11, 1969; children: Cristina, Eugenio. Intern Luth. Hosp. Md., Balt., 1966-67; resident anatomic pathology U. Md., Balt., 1968-72; head section Govt. Hosp., Seville, 1972—. Fellow Coll. Am. Pathologists. Roman Catholic. Avocations: computers, reading, music. Home: Plaza Juan Zaldivar 7, 41007 Sevilla Spain Office: HUVR Anatomia, Manuel Siurot S/N, 41013 Sevilla Spain

RAFFAELLI, MARCELA, psychology educator. BA, Williams Coll., 1982; MA, U. Chgo., 1987, PhD, 1990. Rsch. assoc. Johns Hopkins U., Balt., 1990-92; asst. rsch. prof. Rutgers U., New Brunswick, N.J., 1992-94; assoc. rschr. U. Wis., Madison, 1994-95; asst. prof. U. Nebr., Lincoln, 1995-99, assoc. prof., 1999—; mem. social policy com. Soc. for Rsch. Adolescents, Ann Arbor, Mich., 1997—; mem. internat. planning com., 2d internat. meeting for st. boys and girls Pan Am. Health Orgn., Washington, 1991-92. Co-editor: (monograph) Homeless and Working Youth Around the World, 1999; contbr. articles to profl. jours.; chpts. and revs. to books. Mem. mental health adv. bd. Hispanic Cmty. Ctr., Lincoln, 1999—. B/Start grantee NIMH, 1997-98. Mem. Am. Psychol. Affiliation, Assn. for Women in Psychology, Soc. for Rsch. in Child Devel., Soc. for Rsch. on Adolescence. E-mail: mraffaelli1@unl.edu. Office: U Nebr Dept Psychology 238 Burnett Hall Lincoln NE 68588-0308

RAFFALLI, HENRI CHRISTIAN, retired judge, educator, criminologist; married; 3 children. BA, St. John's U., Bklyn., 1951, JD, 1956; postgrad., CUNY, 1959-64, Columbia U., 1967-68, St. Lawrence U., Canton, N.Y., 1966. Bar: N.Y. 1957. With U.S. Army Mil. Intelligence Svc., Linz an der Donau, 1951-53; pvt. practice atty. Forest Hills, N.Y., 1957-64; mem. N.Y. State Divsn. of Parole, N.Y.C., 1964-87; commr. N.Y. State Bd. of Parole, N.Y.C., 1987-98, adminstrv. law judge, 1998-99, ret., 1999; mem. comm. faculty Am. Inst. Banking, N.Y.C., 1968-70; mem. faculty dept. criminal justice Nassau C.C., SUNY, Garden City, N.Y., 1985—; adj. assoc. prof. dept. criminal justice Sch. Health and Pub. Svc. C.W. Post Ctr. L.I. U., Greenvale, N.Y., 1971-85; lectr. in field. Author: The Battered Child: An Overview of a Medical, Legal and Social Problem, 1970, The Burden of Proof in Parole Violation Cases, 1970, The Fourth Amendment and Search and Seizure in the Parole Process, 1975, Manual for the Inspector General of the New York State Division of Parole, 1986, Code of Conduct for the New York State Division of Parole, 1986, Exercises in Discretionary Release, 1999; contbg. author: Deviance, 1975; editor-in-chief N.Y. State Parole Jour., 1983; contbr. articles to profl. jours.

RAFFEGEAU, JEAN MICHEL, audit and consulting company executive, editor; b. St. Germain en Laye, Yvelines, France, Sept. 24, 1930; s. Louis and Irene (Pithon) R.; m. Nicole Laporte, Jan. 19, 1962; children: Catherine, Brigitte. Diploma in law, Sorbonne U., Paris, 1954; diploma in bus. adminstrn., H.E.C., Paris, 1954. Chartered acct. Commissaire aux Comptes, 1966. Asst. mgr. Banque de Paris et des Pays-Bas, Paris, 1955-57; adminstrv. and fin. mgr. Société Industrielle de Transmissions, 1958-66; chmn., mng. dir. Befec, Paris, 1966-89, Befec-Price Waterhouse, 1989-94; regional mng. pntr. French-speaking Europe and Africa Price Waterhouse, Paris, 1994-96, hon. pres., 1995—; legal expert Court Appeal, Paris, 1979, adminstv. court, Paris, 1982. Co-author: L'Audit Opérationnel, 1993; co-author, editor: Les Comptes Consolidés, 1989, Guide du Financement des Entreprises, 1993, Le Mémento Comptable, 1997. Recipient silver medal Order of Experts Comptables, Paris, 1979, Chevalier de la Légion d'Honneur, Govt. France, Paris, 1995,. Mem. Chartered Accountancy Exams. Jury, Rotary (Paris) (treas. 1987-88), Cercle Union Interalliée. Avocations: reading, cinema, photography.

RAFFER, KUNIBERT, economics educator; b. Bleiburg, Kärnten, Austria, Aug. 8, 1951; s. Kunibert and Hermine Raffer; m. Charlotte Mahrer, July 4, 1981. LLD, M Econs., U. Vienna, Austria, 1974, PhD in Econs., 1977, Habilitation in Econs., 1986. Lectr. dept. econs. U. Vienna, 1975-88, assoc. prof., 1988—; vis. prof. U. Klagenfurt, Austria, 1986-89; vis. fellow Inst. Devel. Studies, Sussex, Eng., 1989; hon. rsch. fellow dept. commerce U. Birmingham, Eng., 1990-93; cons. UNIDO, 1979-80, 83-84; mem. adv. coun. on energy stats. Ctrl. Statis. Office, Vienna, 1982—; mem. adv. coun. on devel. aid Federal Chancellery, 1987-96. Author: Unequal Exchange and the Evolution of the World System, 1987; co-author: The Foreign Aid Business, 1996; co-editor: Trade, Transfers and Development, 1993. Chmn. adv. bd. Austrian North-South Inst., Vienna, 1991-98. Avocations: judo, scuba diving, skiing, gourmet cooking. Office: U Vienna Dept Econs, Hohenstaufengasse 9, A-1010 Vienna Austria

RAFIQUE, MOHAMMAD, philosophy educator; b. Barhan, India, Nov. 11, 1939; s. B. and Haleema Khan; m. Naseem Akhtar Rafique; children: Mohsin Nadeem, Yasmeen Rafique, Seemi Rafique. BA, Aligarh (India) Muslim U., Aligarh, India, 1959; MA, Aligarh (India) Muslim U., 1961, PhD, 1968. Lectr. Shri Aurobindo Degree Coll., Bhopal, India, 1965-66, M.P. Govt., Jabalpur, India, 1966-67; lectr. Aligarh Muslim U., 1967-70, reader, 1978-86, prof., 1986—; mem. subject panel UGC, New Delhi, 1998-01; mem. governing body Indian Coun. Philos. Rsch., 1998-01; mem. exec. coun. Jamia Milla Islamia, New Delhi, 1998-01; dean faculty arts Aligarh Muslim U., 1999-01. Author: (books) Shri Aurobindo and Iqbal: A Comparative Study, 1974, Shri Aurobindo's Ideal of Human Life, 1988, Indian and Muslim Philosophy: A Comparative Study, 1999. Muslim. Home: Barg-E-Gul 4/1322, Aligarh 202002, India Office: Aligarh Muslim U, Faculty of Arts, 202002 Aligarh India

RAFIQUE, SYED FIROZ ALFRED, physician, retired; b. London, Nov. 23, 1930; arrived in India, 1934; s. Syed Ahmad and Margaret Eddy (Hawes) R.; m. Elisabeth Valerie HArtley, May 2, 1958 (div. July 1975); children: Susan, David, Louise, Jonathan; m. Sheila Van Bodegom, Mar. 16, 1991. MBBS, King's Coll., 1960. Apprentice marine engr. Karachi Docks, Pakistan, 1949, N.E. Marine Engring. Co., Wallsend on Tyne, England, 1949-54; house surgeon Royal Victoria Infirmary, Newcastle, England, 1960-2000; house physician Musgrove Pk. Hosp., Taunton, England, 1961; ret., 2000; clin. asst. dermatology Greenwich Dist., 1970-85. Mem. Brit. Am. Photographic Soc. Muslim. Avocations: bridge, chess, badminton, Japanese prints, theatre. Home and office: 19 Foreshore, London SE8 3AQ, England

RAFTER, PATRICK, tennis player; b. Mt. Isa, Australia, Dec. 28, 1972. Prof. tennis player, 1991—, winner U.S. Open, 1998. Avocations: fishing, golf. Office: c/o ATP Tour Internat Hdqrs 201 Atp Tour Blvd Ponte Vedra Beach FL 32082-3211*

RAFTERY, MARGARET MARY, English educator, editor, translator; b. Durban, Natal, South Africa, May 29, 1959; d. James Delamere and Margaret Anne Gordon (Barnes) R. BA first class, U. Natal, Durban, 1980, BA cum laude with honors, 1982, MA, 1986; MPhil, Oxford (Eng.) U., 1986; PhD, U. of the Orange Free State, Bloemfontein, South Africa, 1997. Tchr. Natal Edn. Dept., Durban, 1980-87; lectr. U. of the Orange Free State, Bloemfontein, 1988-89, sr. lectr., 1990—. Editor: Mary of Nemmegen, 1991, Textures, 2000—; dep. editor Acta Academica, 1998—; mem. editl. bd. Acta Academica, 1990—; contbr. articles to profl. jours. including Millennium, Nomina Africana, and So. African Jour. of Medieval and Renaissance Studies. Recipient Emma Smith Overseas scholarship U. Natal, 1983-86, Merit award, 1997, Tchg. and Rsch. award 1997, 98. Mem. MLA, Soc. Internat. Medieval Theatre, Names Soc. So. Africa (sec. Bloemfontein br. 1990—), So. African Soc. Medieval and Renaissance Studies, Internat. Medieval Inst., South African Acad. Sci & Arts. Roman Catholic. Avocations: reading, theater, choral music. Office: U of the Orange Free State, PO Box 339, Bloemfontein 9300, South Africa

RAGAB, RAGAB, research scientist, hydrologist; b. Alexandria, Egypt, Jan. 9, 1949; s. Abou El-Enine and Aziza (Sharaf) R.; m. Nadine Julia Depré, Aug. 1, 1981; 1 child, Hany Ragab. BS, Alexandria U., Egypt, 1970, MSc, 1974; diploma in irrigation, ICAMAS, Bari, Italy, 1976; PhD, U. Leuven, Belgium, 1982. Rsch. asst. dept. soil and water scis. Alexandria U., 1970-74, teaching asst., 1974-77, asst. prof., 1983-85, assoc. prof., 1987-88; rsch. fellow dept. rural engring. U. Leuven, 1977-82; post-doctoral fellow Georg August U., Gottingen, Federal Republic of Germany, 1986-87; vis. scientist dept. of soil scis. Swedish U. of Agrl. Scis., Uppsala, 1988-89; prin. rsch. scientist Inst. of Hydrology, Wallingford, Eng., 1989—; external examiner for PhD, MSc diplomas Newcastle U., U.K.; keynote spkr. various internat. confs., 1997, 98; lectr. internat. postgrad. courses, 1998; cons. IFAD orgn., 1999; mem. panel of specialists on remote sensing European Space Agy., Netherlands; spkr. in field. Author numerous articles, reports and revs. for profl. jours. Recipient New Century award The Baron 500, 2000, European Cmty. fellowship, 1992, Environment Can. fellowship, 1992, Brit. Coun. fellowship U. Murcia, Spain, 1990, vis. fellowship to various univs. and insts. in the U.S., 1980. Awarded State Recognition and Merit prize in Sci., Egypt, 1987. Mem. Acad. Staff of Reading U. (hon.), European Geophys. Soc. (elected), Am. Soc. Agronomy, Soil Sci. Soc. Am., Soil Sci. Soc. West Germany, Brit. Soc. Soil Sci., Internat. Soil Sci. Soc., Internat. Commn. on Irrigation and Drainage (U.K. rep., chmn. com. 1995, chmn. work group 1996), U.K. Irrigation Assn. Office: Inst Hydrology NERC, Wallingford England

RAGAMPETA, SRINIVAS, chemist, researcher; b. Vemulawada, Andhra Pradesh, India, July 28, 1958; s. Lingaiah and Radha R.; m. Samrajayam Kamalavari, March 10, 1985; children: Ravi Chandra, Rajesh. BSc, Osmania U., Hyderabad, India, 1977, MSc, 1979; PhD, Indian Inst. Tech., Madras, India, 1984. Scientist B Indian Inst. Chem. Tech., Hyderabad, India, 1985-89, scientist C, 1989-94, scientist E-1, 1994—; vis. scientist Tech. U., Berlin, 1989-91, 99. Contbr. rsch. papers to chemistry jours. Fax: 91-40-7173757/7173387. E-mail: srini@iict.ap.nic.in. Home: 2-4/2 Kakatiya Nagar St # 2, 500 007 Hyderabad Andhra Pradesh, India Office: Indian Inst Chem Tech Nat Ctr Mass Spectrometry, Uppal Rd, 500 007 Hyderabad Andhra Pradesh, India

RAGAN, ROBERT ALLISON, private investment executive, financial consultant; b. Gastonia, N.C., Aug. 21, 1938; s. Caldwell and Jocelyn (Sikes) R. BS in Bus. Adminstrn., U. N.C., 1961; postgrad., Rutgers U., 1968. V.p. N.C. Nat. Bank (now Bank of Am.), Charlotte, 1961-81; pres., treas. R.A. Ragan & Co., Inc., Charlotte, 1981—; dir. Carolina Mills, Inc., Maiden, N.C., 1977—. Author, pub.: The Ragans of Gastonia (1790-1995), 1995, The Textile Heritage of Gaston County, N.C. (1848-2000), 2000. Trustee, bd. visitors Darlington Sch., Rome, Ga., 1981—; pres. bd. trustees Gaston County Mus. Art and History, Dallas, N.C., 1978-81, 97-99. Mem. Charlotte City Club, DeBordieu Colony Country Club (Georgetown, S.C.), Linville (N.C.) Ridge Country Club. Republican. Presbyterian. Avocations: preservation and recording of local and North Carolina history, especially industrial history, travel. Home: 227 Fenton Pl Charlotte NC 28207-1913 Office: R A Ragan & Co PO Drawer 6158 Charlotte NC 28207-0001

RAGHAVAN, RAMASUBRAMANIAN, quality assurance professional, researcher; b. Villathikulam, India, July 15, 1943; s. S. Ramasubramanian and S. Kamatchi; m. Shanta Ramasamy, Sept. 6, 1970; three children. BS in Chemistry and Physics, U. Madras, 1965; MS in Chemistry, U. Udaipur, 1970; PhD, Mohan Lal Sukhadia U., Udaipur, 1998. Degree equivalent in Metall. Engring. from Indian Inst. Metals, Calcutta, India, 1984. Rsch. asst. Ctrl. Electro-Chem. Rsch. Inst., Karaikudi, 1965-67; jr. scientific asst. Neyveli Lignite Corp., Neyveli, India, 1967-68; asst. chemist Hindustan Zinc Ltd., Udaipur, 1968-71; chemist Rajasthan State Indsl. & Mineral Devel. Corp., Jaipur, India, 1971-74, Hindustan Zinc Ltd., Tundoo, India, 1974-76; sr. chemist Hindustan Zinc Ltd., Visakhapatnam, India, 1978-84; mgr. Hindustan Zinc Ltd., Udaipur, 1984-94, sr. mgr., 1994-96; sr. mgr. Hindustan Zinc Ltd., Visakhapatnam, 1996—; chemist Rajasthan State Indsl. & Mineral Devel. Corp., Jaipur, India, 1971-74. Joint sec./editor tech. jour., 1993-95; contbr. articles to profl. jours. Fellow Soc. Advancement Electrochemical Tech. (chmn. Electrothermics and Metallurgy group, 1999-2001); mem. (life) Indian Assn. Analytical Scientists; mem. Indian Inst. Metals, Computer Soc. of India, Quality Circle Forum of India. Avocations: stamp collecting, swimming. Office: Hindustan Zinc Ltd, Gajuwaka, 530 015 Visakhapatnam India

RAGHAVAN, VENKATESAN V., pharmaceuticals company executive, consultant; b. Devakottai, Tamil Nadu, India, Mar. 1, 1941; s. Srinivas V. Venkatesan and Kamala; m. Mythili Rangaswamy, Jan. 29, 1969; 1 child, Venkat. BS, U. Bombay, 1961, MS, 1965. Lic. pharmacist, mfr. and mktg. Product exec. Johnson & Johnson Ltd., Bombay, 1965-70; plant mgr. JL Morison Ltd., Bangalore, India, 1970-87; exec. dir. Eros Pharma Ltd., Bangalore, 1987—; cons. Resources Internat. Inc., Lexington, Ky., 1994—. Mem. Drug Info. Assn., Pharm. Mfg. Assn., Rotary Internat. (sec., dir. 1974-83). Avocations: traveling, music, nature, wildlife. Home: #7 17A Cross Malleswarm W, 500055 Bangalore India Office: Eros Pharma Ltd, 67/68A VI Cross III Phase, Peenya Bangalore 560058, India

RAGHU NANDAN, KADABA RAMAPATHY, geologist; b. Bangalore, India, Feb. 7, 1937; m. Sunita Iyengar, July 9, 1967; children: Gauri Prasad, Kartik Venkatesh. BS with honors, Ctrl. Coll. Mysore U., Bangalore, India, 1956, MS, 1957. Lectr. geology Indian Sch. Mines, Dhanbad, 1957-60; geologist, engring. geology Geol. Survey India, Calcutta, 1960-64; mining geologist Indian Bur. Mines and Geol. Survey India, Jaipur, 1964-67; tech. sec. Geol. Survey India, Bangalore, 1974-81, dir., 1981-92; deputy dir.. gen. Geol. Survey India, Jaipur, 1992-93, Bangalore, 1993-95; cons. geologist Bangalore, 1995—. Author articles on precious metals and mineralisation in India to profl. publs. Fellow Geol. Soc. India (mem. governing coun. 1992-95). Avocations: classical Indian music, photography, cricket. Home: 787 Venkatadri 7th Cross, M C Lavout, Bangalore 560040, India

RAGLAND, ROBERT ALLEN, lawyer; b. Bartlesville, Okla., Apr. 18, 1954; s. Thomas Martin and Joan Ethel (Murphy) R. BA, U. Md., 1976; JD, George Mason Sch. of Law, 1980. Dir. regulatory reform and govt. orgn. Nat. Assn. Mfrs., Washington, 1979-82, asst. v.p. taxation, 1983-86; mgr. congl. relations The Clorox Co., Oakland, Calif., 1982-83; dir. tax rsch. U.S. C. of C., Washington, 1988-93; chief tax counsel, mng. dir. Nat. Chamber Found., Washington, 1989-93; v.p. Trust First Union Nat. Bank, 1995—, officer, 1995—. Author: Transportation Reform, 1980, Employee Stock Ownership Plans, 1989, Taxation of Foreign Source Income, Distributional Impact of Excise Taxes, 1990; editor: Taxation of Intercorporate Profits, 1990, Jour. Regulation and Social Costs, 1992—, Journal of Regulation, 1992-93. Active Boy Scouts Am., Washington, 1967— (Eagle Scout 1970, bd. dirs. nat. capital area coun.); dep. dir. duPont for Pres., 1987-88; v.p. Nat. Chamber Found. U.S. C. of C., 1989-93, dir., Liz Lerman Dance Exchange, 1993—, dir. Our House, Inc., 1988—. Republican. Roman Catholic. Home: 4100 Cathedral Ave NW Washington DC 20016-3584

RAGLAND, THOMAS EUGENE, osteopath, prison medical director; b. Dunlap, Kans., Sept. 22, 1936; s. Sylvester Ellis and Edna Mae (Cooper) R.;

m. Barbara Jean Royal, Aug. 5, 1961 (dec. June 1977); children: Sheri Elizabeth, Thomas Eugene II, Diedra Elise; m. Tawina Denise Barganier, May 30, 1992. BS, McPherson (Kans.) Coll., 1959; DO, Coll. Osteo. Medicine Surgery, Kansas City, Mo., 1973; doctoral student, Ashland (Ohio) Theol. Sem., 1993—. Cert. med. technologist, Am. Soc. Clin. Pathology, St. Mercy Sch. Med. Tech., Hutchinson, Kans., 1960. Med. intern Youngstown (Ohio) Cafaro Hosp., 1973-74; founder, pres. The Cmty. Health Ctr., Youngstown, 1974—; med. resident Youngstown Hosp. Assn., 1976-77; med. dir. Trumbull Correctional Instn., Warren, Ohio, 1991-93, Belmont Correctional Instn., St. Clairsville, Ohio, 1995—; assoc. med. cons. So. Ohio Correction Facility, Lucasville, 1993-95; health dir. City of Youngstown, 1975-76; spl. med. task force East Ohio Regional Hosp., Martins Ferry; night clinic Hough Norwood Health Ctr., Cleve. Author: The Faces of Fear, 1989, At the Window of Death, 1996, The Exoffended Home, 1996, (documentary) Seven-Seven-Seven: Personal Autobiography of a Prison Physician, 1996; lectr., spkr., host radio talk show (WGFT) A Unique Ministry, Youngstown. Mem. AMA, Am. Osteo. Med. Assn., Nat. Osteo. Med. Assn., State Med. Bd. of Ohio. Mem. Holiness Church of God in Christ. Avocations: basketball, track, tennis, fishing. Address: A Unique Ministry PO Box 6218 Youngstown OH 44501-6218 Office: Community Health Ctr 3025 Market St Youngstown OH 44507-1636

RAGNARSSON, INGEMAR, physicist; b. Hjarnarp, Sweden, June 27, 1945; s. Ragnar and Gurli (Svensson) Johansson; married; children: Carl Johan, Charlotte. M in sci., Lund (Sweden) Inst. Tech., 1969, D in Tech., 1975. Fellow Nordita, Copenhagen, Denmark, 1972-75, Lund Inst. Tech., 1975-85, CERN, Geneva, Switzerland, 1978-80; acting prof. Lund Inst. Tech., 1980-82, assoc. prof., 1985—; sci. assoc. CERN, Geneva, 1986-87. Author: Shapes and Shells in Nuclear Structure, 1995; divsn. assoc. editor Phys. Rev. Letters, 1992-95; contbr. numerous articles to sci. jours. Office: Lund Inst Tech, Dept Math Physics Box 118, S 22100 Lund Sweden

RAGNEMALM, HANS, international justice; b. 1940. D of Law. Prof. pub. law Lund U.; prof. pub. law, dean Law faculty U. Stockholm, Sweden; parliamentary ombudsman Stockholm; judge Supreme Adminstrv. Ct. Sweden, Ct. of Justice of European Cmtys., Luxembourg, 1995—. Office: Ct Justice European Cmtys, Palais de Cour de justice, Kirchberg L-2925, Luxembourg*

RAGO, ANN D'AMICO, university official, public relations professional; b. Pitts., Aug. 24, 1957; d. Jack and Florence (Zappa) D'Amico; m. John Thomas Rago, Aug. 31, 1984; children: Annie J., Emily J., John Henry. BA, Duquesne U., Pitts., 1979, MA, 1987. From communications assoc. to dir. pub. relations Duquesne U., 1979-89, coord. univ. relations, 1989-93, exec. dir. pub. affairs, 1993—, adj. prof. comm. Editor University Record, 1989 (silver medal). Bd. dirs. Support, Pitts., 1989-91; sch. dir. Carylnton Sch. Bd., Pitts., 1989-93, pres. sch. bd., 1990. Recipient Gold award for publs./external prospectus 9th Ann. Admissions Advt. Awards, 1994, Gold award for Total Pub. Rels. Campaign, 10th Ann. Admissions Advt. Awards, 1995, Gold award for Total Pub. Rels. Campaign, 11th Ann. Admissions Awards, 1996, 1st Place award in Category 35, Internal Pub. Rels. Campaign, Pitts. chpt. Women in Comm., Inc., 1996, Bronze Cert. for logo and letterhead for Duquesne U.'s Capital Campaign and cert. merit for Duquesne U.'s internal publ. 14th Ann. Admissions Advt. Awards, 1998. Mem. Pub. Rels. Soc. Am. (1st place award 1993), Internat. Assn. Bus. Communicators (award of excellence 1991, award of honor 1993, award of merit 1994), Am. Mgmt. Assn., Press Club Western Pa., Sigma Delta Chi. Office: Duquesne U 600 Forbes Ave Pub Affairs Office Pittsburgh PA 15282

RAGO, THOMAS ASHTON, physical oceanographer; b. N.Y.C., Jan. 29, 1957; s. Louis Joseph and Dorothy (Ashton) R. BA, Amherst Coll., 1979; MS, U. R.I., 1986. Oceanographer Naval Postgrad. Sch., Monterey, Calif., 1987—. Contbr. articles to profl. publs. Mem. Am. Geophys. Union, Oceanography Soc., Aircraft Owners and Pilots Assn. Avocation: pvt. pilot. Office: Naval Postgrad Sch Code OC/Rg 833 Dyer Rd Bldg 232 Monterey CA 93943-5193

RAGONE, DAVID VINCENT, former university president; b. N.Y.C., May 16, 1930; s. Armando Frederick and Mary (Napier) R.; m. Katherine H. Spaulding, Dec. 18, 1954; children: Christine M., Peter V. S.B., MIT, 1951, S.M., 1952, Sc.D., 1953. Asst. prof. chem. and metall. engrng. U. Mich., Ann Arbor, 1953-57, assoc. prof., 1957-61, prof., 1961-62; asst. dir. John J. Hopkins Lab for Pure and Applied Sci., also chmn. metallurgy dept. Gen. Atomic div. Gen Dynamics, La Jolla, 1962-67; Alcoa prof. metallurgy Carnegie-Mellon U., Pitts., 1967-69; assoc. dean Carnegie-Mellon U. (Sch. Urban and Pub. Affairs), 1969-70; dean Thayer Sch. of Engrng., Dartmouth Coll., 1970-72, Coll. Engrng., U. Mich., 1972-80; pres. Case Western Res. U., Cleve., 1980-87; vis. prof., dept. materials sci. and engring. MIT, Cambridge, 1987-88, sr. lectr. dept. materials sci. and engring., 1988-98; gen. ptnr. Ampersand Ventures, 1988-92, ptnr., 1992—; trustee Mitre Corp.; bd. dirs. Cabot Corp., Sifco Inc. Mem. Nat. Sci. Bd., 1978-84; mem. tech adv. bd. U.S. Dept. Commerce, 1967-75; chmn. adv. com. advanced auto power systems Council on Environ. Quality, 1971-75; Trustee Henry Luce Found. Named Outstanding Young Engr., Engrng. Soc. Detroit, 1957. Mem. Univ. Club (N.Y.C.), Longwood Cricket Club (Boston), Sigma Xi, Tau Beta Pi. Office: Ampersand Ventures 55 William St Wellesley MA 02481-4003

RAGSDALE, RALPH HAIRSTON, electrical engineer; b. Roswell, N.Mex, Jan. 17, 1949; s. Luther Earnest and Mary Naomi (Bates) R.; m. Janet Eve Hettinga, Dec. 16, 1972; children: Carrie Marie, William Ty. BEE, N. Mex. State U., 1973. Registered profl. engr., Tex., N.Mex. Distbr. engr. Southwestern Pub. Svc., Lubbock, Tex., 1973-75; substation design engr. Southwestern Pub. Svc., Amarillo, Tex., 1975-80; sr. design engr. Southwestern Pub. Svc., Amarillo, 1975-84; sr. divsn. oper. engr. Southwestern Pub. Svc., Roswell, N.Mex, 1984-97; mgr. ops. engr. Southwestern Pub. Svc., Roswell, 1997—. Bd. dirs. Amarillo coun. Girl Scouts U.S., 1978-80, Zia coun. Girl Scouts U.S., Artesia, N.Mex, 1993-95, United Way of Chaves Co., Roswell, 1996-98. Mem. NSPE, IEEE. Methodist. Home: 1202 Moore Ave Roswell NM 88201-1172 Office: Southwestern Pub Svc Co PO Box 1937 Roswell NM 88202-1937

RAGULIN, ALEXEI JURIEVICH, engineer, physicist, computer specialist; b. Tomsk, Russia, Apr. 17, 1961; s. Jury Mihailovich and Galina Ivanovna Radulin; m. Marina Vladimirovna, Sept. 22, 1981; children: Dmitriy, Vera, Katerina. Student, Tomsk (Russia) Poly. Inst., 1988-91. Lab. asst. Tomsk (Russia) Poly. Inst., 1980-83, lab. technician, 1983, younger sci. rschr., 1984-88, sci. rschr., 1991-92, sr. sci. rschr., 1992-93, chief lab., 1993-97; dep. dir. Energomashcorp.-Khabarovsk Co. Ltd., Khabarovsk, 1997—; rschr. in field. Contbr. articles to profl. publs. Mem. N.Y. Acad. Scis. Office: Energomashcorp-Khabarovsk, Kim-U-Chen St Office 104, Khabarovsk Russia

RAHARINAIVO, ANDRÉ LÉON, research executive, educator; b. Tananarive, Madagascar, Sept. 1, 1940; arrived in France, 1954; s. Ignace Léon and Marthe (Rasoazanamalala) R.; m. Christiane Martine Laurent, May 7, 1966 (div. June 1994); 1 child, Jacques Yves. Engr. mining and metallurgy, Ecole des Mines, Nancy, France, 1964; degree superior scientific studies, U. Nancy, France, 1964; PhD, U. Compiegne, France, 1982. Cert. engr. Head sect. Lab. Ctrl. Ponts et Chaussées, Paris, 1971-80, dep. head dept., 1980-83, sec. sci. coun., 1983-91, rsch. mgr., 1991—; prof. Ecole Normale Superieure, Cachan, France, 1980, U. Paris-Sud, Orsay, France, 1981; lectr. Ecole Nat. Ponts et Chaussées, Paris, 1977. Author: Fracture Mechanics and Mechanisms, 1990; patentee in field. Capt. Equipment, 1967-69, France. Mem. Ctr. Français Anticorrosion, Nat. Assn. Corrosion Engrs. Avocation: singing Gospel music. Home: 378 rue de Vaugirard, F-75015 Paris France

RAHEEL, MASTURA, textile scientist, educator; b. Lahore, Pakistan, Mar. 1, 1938; d. Sultan Mohamad and Firdous Dean; m. Akbar Javed Raheel, Jan. 25, 1959; children: Seemal, Salman. PhD, U. Minn., 1971; MS, Okla. State U., 1962; PhD, U. Minn., 1971. Asst. prof., head dept. textiles and clothing Home Econs. Coll., Lahore, 1960-77; lectr. textiles and clothing U. Minn., 1977-78; vis. prof. Ind. U., Bloomington, 1978; asst. prof. textile sci. U. Ill., Urbana, 1978-84, assoc. prof., 1984-91, chmn. divsn. textiles, apparel and interior design, 1987-89, prof., 1991—. Contbr. articles to profl. and tech. jours. Recipient Gold medal, 1960; Ford Found. fellow, 1960-62, 68-71, rsch. grantee, 1979—. Mem. ASTM, Internat. Textile and Apparel Assn., Am. Chem. Soc., Am. Assn. Textile Chemists and Colorists, Am. Home Econs. Assn. (Mfr. Fiber Rsch. award 1989), Omicron Nu, Sigma Xi. Home: 2611 Willoughby Rd Champaign IL 61822-7567 Office: U Ill 239 Bevier Hall Urbana IL 61801

RAHIM, BAZLUR, magazine editor; b. Faridpur, Bangladesh, Sept. 27, 1950; s. Khuda and Jobeda (Khatun) Buksh; m. Nasrin Zaman, Nov. 18, 1979; children: Sajidur, Ashiqur. H.S.C., Dhaka Coll., Bangladesh, 1969, BA with honors, 1973, MA, 1974. Rsch. officer Gonoshasthaya, Dhaka, 1976-78; acting editor Gonoshasthaya Mag., Dhaka, 1979-94, editor, 1995—. Translator: (book) Where There is No Doctor, 1983, Where There is No Dentist, 1990, The Childbirth Picture Book, 1990. Avocations: photography, reading, writing, travel. Home: House #99 Rd 11/A, Dhanmandi Dhaka 1209, Bangladesh Office: Gonoshasthaya Kendra, 14E Dhanmandi RA, Dhaka 1205, Bangladesh

RAHIM, M. ABDUR, oncologist; b. Bogra, Bangladesh, Apr. 15, 1933; s. Emamuddin and Hamida (Khatun) Ahmed; m. Rahima Khatoon, June 12, 1960; 3 children. LMF, Dacca Med. Sch., Pakistan, 1953; MB, BChir, Dacca U., 1965, DMRT, 1969. Resident Surgeon Med. Coll., Dacca, Bangladesh, 1967-71; from asst. prof. to prof. radiotherapy Med. Coll. Dacca, 1972-80; dir. Cancer Inst., Dacca, 1980-85, Cancer Epidemiology Rsch. Program, Bogra, Bangladesh, 1972—; vis. physician, prof. Rosewell Park Meml. Cancer Inst., N.Y., 1980; nat. program officer WHO, Delhi, India, 1985-91; adviser radiotherapy Govt. Bangladesh, 1978-91. Author: If I Suffer from Cancer vol. I & II, 1985; editor Bangladesh Cancer Reports, 1972—; mem. editl. bd. Asian Jour. Oncology, 1998—; contbr. articles to profl. jours. Recipient Cancer Chemotherapy Found. medal, Japan, 1978. Fellow Royal Coll. Radiology, Coll. Chest Physicians; mem. WHO, ISPO, IACR, Internat. Assn. Cancer Registry, Internat. Soc. Preventive Oncology (sci. com.), Bangla Acad. (life), Indian Assn. Cancer Chemotherapy, Japan Cancer Soc., Bangladesh Assn. Cancer Svcs., Indian Assn. Pediat. Oncology. Avocations: photography, reading. Home: Daktar Bari Beharhat, Bogra Bangladesh Office: Cancer Epidemiology Rsch Pr, DHORMO PUR, 5800 Bogra Bangladesh

RAHIM, SHEIKH IDRIS ABDEL, psychiatry educator; b. Kosti, White Nile, Sudan, Jan. 1, 1936; s. Abdel Rahim H. Amin and Nafisa Abdel Magid (Faki) R.; m. Suad Mohamed Mustafa; children: Seiza, Nazim, Mohamed, Salma, Sara, Abdel Rahim. MBBS, U. Khartoum, Sudan, 1960; PhD, U. Kharkov, USSR, 1965; MRC in Psychiat., Royal Coll. of Psychiatrists, London, 1973, FRC in Psychiat., 1988. Diplomate Sudan Med. Coun., Consultant Psychiatrist. Consultant psychiatrist Ministry of Health, Sudan, 1966-75, head, dept. of neurosis, 1975-77, dir. psychiat. rsch., 1977-84; prof. and chmn. dept. psychiatry U. Khartoum, Sudan, 1984-88, King Faisal Univ., Damam, Saudi Arabia, 1988-93; prof. of psychiatry King Faisal Univ., Damam, 1993—; mem. Saudi Bd. Psychiatry Coun. Contbr. articlee to profl. jours. including Jour. Child Psychiatry, Brit. Jour. Psyciat. and others. Mem. WHO, Royal Coll. Psychiatrists, World Psychiatric Assn. (mem. subcom.), Saudi Bd. Psychiatry Coun. Home: PO Box 40101, Ea Prov Al-Khobar 31952, Saudi Arabia Office: King Faisal U, PO Box 2208, Al-Khobar 31952, Saudi Arabia

RAHIM, YOUSIF AHMED ABDUL, oil company executive, consultant; b. Muharraq, Bahrain, July 15, 1951; s. Ahmed Abdul Rahim and Halima Abdulla Hassan; m. Aysha Khalil Al-Moayyed, Mar. 19, 1981; children: Fawaz, Ahmed, Feras. BSc with honors, U. Manchester (Eng.), 1975; diploma in advanced mgmt., Henley (Eng.) Staff Coll., 1979. Chartered engr., Eng. Process engr. Bahrain Petroleum Co., Bahrain, 1975-76; project engr. Bahrain Nat. Oil Co., Bahrain, 1976-77, sr. project engr., 1977, coord. mgmt. svcs., then chief engr., 1977-80, mgr. tech. svcs., 1980-81; CEO Heavy Oil Conversion Co., Bahrain, 1981-84; mng. dir. Internat. Mktg. Enterprises, Bahrain, 1984—. Contbr. articles to profl. jours. Fellow Bahrain Soc. Engrs., Inst. Chem. Engrs. (Eng.); mem. AICE, ASME, Inst. Mgmt. (Eng.), European Fedn. of Nat. Engrng. Assns. Avocations: political research, reading, travel, classical music. Office: Internat Mktg Enterprises, PO Box 22983, Manama Bahrain

RAHKONEN, OSSI JUHANI, educator; b. Heinlkola, Finland, Jan. 25, 1952; s. Veikko and Laura (Laurikainen) R.; m. Elina Hemminki. MA in Social Sci., U. Helsinki, 1982, PhD, 1994. Rschr. U. Helsinki, 1983-90, asst. prof., 1990-95, assoc. prof., 1996, sr. lectr., 1996-99, prof., 1999—. Editor: Jour. Social Medicine, 1992—. Mem. Soc. Social Medicine (bd. dirs. 1991—). Avocations: badminton, cross-country skiing. Home: Kiskontie 31, 00280 Helsinki Finland Office: U Helsinki Dept Social Policy, Snellmaninkatu 10, 00014 Helsinki Finland

RAHM, DAVID ALAN, lawyer; b. Passaic, N.J., Apr. 18, 1941; s. Hans Emil and Alicia Katherine (Onuf) R.; m. Susan Eileen Berkman, Nov. 23, 1972; children: Katherine Berkman, William David. AB, Princeton U., 1962; JD, Yale U., 1965. Bar: N.Y. 1966, D.C. 1986. Assoc. Paul, Weiss, Rifkind & Wharton, N.Y.C., 1965-66, 1968-69; asst. counsel N.Y. State Urban Devel. Corp., N.Y.C., 1969-72, assoc. counsel, 1972-75; counsel real estate div. Internat. Paper Co., N.Y.C., 1975-80; ptnr. Stroock & Stroock & Lavan, N.Y.C., 1980-83, sr. ptnr., 1984—; mem. legis. com. Real Estate Bd. N.Y., 1988-92; lectr. Old Dominion Coll., Norfolk, Va., 1967-68, NYU, 1986—; mem. editl. bd. Comml. Leasing Law and Strategy, 1988-95; mem. N.Y.C. bd. advisors Commonwealth Land Title Ins. Co., 1996—. Contbr. articles to profl. jours. Fund raiser corp. com. N.Y. Philharm., N.Y.C., 1980-84; trustee Manhattan Sch. Music, 1989—, treas., 1991-94, chmn., 1994—. Mem. ABA (comml. leasing com. 1987-88, 94—, pub./pvt. devel. com. 1989—, real property sect.), Assn. of Bar of City of N.Y. (housing and urban devel. com. 1977-80, 81-84, real property com. 1989-92), Princeton Club. Democrat. Presbyterian. Avocations: music, reading, travel. Office: Stroock Stroock & Lavan 180 Maiden Ln Fl 17 New York NY 10038-4937

RAHM, SUSAN BERKMAN, lawyer; b. Pitts., June 25, 1943; d. Allen Hugh and Selma (Wiener) Berkman; m. David Alan Rahm, Nov. 23, 1972; children: Katherine, William. BA with honors, Wellesley Coll., 1965; postgrad., Harvard U., 1966-68; JD, NYU, 1973. Bar: N.Y. 1974, D.C. 1988. Assoc. Marshall, Bratter, Greene, Allison & Tucker, N.Y.C., 1973-81, ptnr., 1981-82; ptnr. Kaye, Scholer, Fierman, Hays & Handler, LLP, N.Y.C., 1982—, chair real estate dept., 1993-98, chair internat. practice group, 1999—; N.Y. adv. bd., Chgo. Title Ins. Co., 1995. Editor: New York Real Property Service, 1987. Bd. dirs. Girls Inc., 1989-93; mem. aux. bd. Mt. Sinai Hosp., N.Y.C., 1976-78. Recipient cert. of outstanding svc. D.C. Redevel. Land Agy., 1969, She Knows Where She's Going award Girls' Clubs of Am., 1987, Woman of Yr. award CREW.NY, 1999. Mem. ABA, Assn. of Bar of City of N.Y., N.Y. Bar Assn. (real property law com., co-chmn. real-estate devel. . 1987-91), Am. Coll. Real Estate Lawyers, Comml. Real Estate Women N.Y. (bd. dirs. 1988-94, v.p. 1988-91, pres. 1991-93). Office: Kaye Scholer Fierman Hays & Handler LLP 425 Park Ave New York NY 10022-3506

RAHMAN, ANIS, environmental scientist, researcher; b. Azamgarh, India, Dec. 6, 1945; arrived in New Zealand, 1972; s. Mohammed Yasin and Basrun Nisa; m. Qamar Shamim Qureshi, June 14, 1965; children: Anjum N., Nadeem S., Shadia F. BSc in Agr., U. Gorakhpur, Jaunpur, India, 1963; MSc in Agr., Agra U., Kanpur, India, 1965; MSc, U. Alta., Edmonton, Can., 1968; PhD, U. Sask., Saskatoon, Can., 1971. Profl. agrologist, New Zealand. Rsch. asst. Rockefeller Found., New Delhi, 1965-66, U. Alta. and U. Sask., 1966-71; postdoctoral fellow U. B.C., Vancouver, 1971-72; scientist Ministry of Agr. and Fisheries, Hamilton, New Zealand, 1972-85; group leader plant sci. MAF Tech., Hamilton, 1985-91; group leader plant protection AgRsch., Hamilton, 1991—; tech. adviser New Zealand Pesticides Bd., Wellington, 1988—; pres. New Zealand Plant Protection Soc., Rotorua, 1993-95. Mem. editl. bd. three sci. jours.; contbr. chpts. to books and articles to profl. jours. V.p. Parent-Tchr. Coun., Hillcrest H.S., Hamilton, 1989-94; panel mem. Adult Learning Ctr., Hamilton, 1990—; mem. Inter-Faith Coun., Hamilton, 1990—, Waikato Ethnic Coun., Hamilton, 1994—. Recipeint Rsch. award Monsanto, 1985, Khwarizmi Internat. award, 1999. Mem. Royal Soc. New Zealand, European Weed Rsch. Soc., New Zealand Inst. Agrl. Scis., Internat. Weed Sci. Soc. (bd. dirs. 1993—), Asian-Pacific Weed Sci. Soc. (treas. 1991—), N.Y. Acad. Sci. Muslim. Avocations: cricket, bridge, reading, international traveling, public speaking. Office: AgRsch Ruakura Rsch Ctr, East St PB 3123, Hamilton New Zealand

RAHMAN, IRFAN, biochemist, researcher; b. India, Sept. 5, 1960; s. Mumtaz and Rabia (Ansari) A. BSc, Nagpur U., 1981, MSc, 1983, PhD, 1989. Lectr. S.K.P. Coll., Kamptee, 1985-88, Nagpur U., 1988-89; postdoctoral fellow U. Miami, Fla., 1989-90; rsch. assoc. Georgetown U., Washington, 1990-92; sr. scientist U. Edinburgh, 1993—; vis. scientist Amscot Med. Ctr., Cin., 1995-96; spkr. at internat. confs. Coontbr. articles to profl. jours. Nat. merit scholar Govt. of India, 1981-83; Japanese Sci. fellow, 1994-95; Can. Lung. Found. fellow, 1995, Astra Lung travel fellow, 1996, Brit. Lung Found. fellow, 1996-98, Chest, Heart and Stroke Scotland travel fellow, 1997, 98, BLF/Allen Hanburys fellow, 1999, BLF/Boehringer Ingelheim fellow, 2000. Fellow The Royal Soc.; mem. Brit. Assn. for Lung Rsch., Biochem. Soc. (U.K.), Soc. Biol. Chemistry, Indian Assn. Hypertension (founder mem.), Oxygen Soc. (U.S.). Avocations: travel, trekking. Office: ELEGI Lab Resp Med Unit, U Edinburgh Teviot Pl, Edinburgh EH8 9AG, Scotland

RAHMAN, M. HABIBUR, legal educator, researcher; b. Baniagati, Bogra, Bangladesh, Dec. 12, 1946; s. M.P. Talukder and Delsor Begum; m. Morjina Khatun Bilkis, Nov. 3, 1972; children: Humairath Hilmi, Niath Mahmud, Shariar. MSc, U. Dacca, Bangladesh, 1968, LLB, 1969; LLM, U. Rajshahi, Bangladesh, 1979, U. Wales, 1982; PhD, Nat. Law Sch. India U., Bangalore, 1999. Lectr. in law Rajshahi U., 1970-74, from asst. prof. law to assoc. prof., 1974-92, chmn. dept. law, 1987-90, prof. law, 1992—. Author: (research monographs) Delimitation of Maritime Boundaries with Special Reference to the Bangladesh-India Situation, Deep Seabed Mining Under the Law of the Sea Convention 1982 - With Special Reference to Interests of Developing Countries, (books) Delimitation of Maritime Boundaries, 1991, Muslim Law, vol. I, 1989, vol. II, 1990; contbr. articles on maritime law to legal jours. in Australia, Bangladesh, Germany, Hong Kong, India, Pakistan, U.K. and U.S. Fax: 880-0721-7560064. E-mail: rajucc@citetechco.net. Office: Rajshahi U, Dept Law, Rajshahi Bangladesh

RAHMAN, MAHFUZAR, physician, researcher; b. Rangpur, Bangladesh, June 1, 1966; s. Motiur and Zaharun (Nessa) R.; m. Ireen Akhter Chowdhury, Dec. 4, 1987; 1 child, Saraf Wasia. MBBS, Rajshahi Med. Coll., Bangladesh, 1992; PhD, Linköping (Sweden) U., 1999. Rschr. Linmköping U., 1999—. Contbr. articles to profl. jours. Mem. Bangladesh Med. Assn., Internat. Epidemiol. Assn., Internat. Cancer Assn. Avocation: reading magazines and novels. E-mail: mahfuzar.rahman@ihm.liu.se. Office: Divsn Occupl/Environ Med, 681 85 Linköping Sweden

RAHMAN, MIZANUR, ophthalmologist; b. Chapainawabganj, Bangladesh, Jan. 1, 1948; s. Hai Momtaz Ahmed Mia and Asia Khatun; m. Rokeya Begum Mizan, July 5, 1972; children: Kaniz Arifa, Zahid. MBBS, Rajshahi Med. Coll., Bangladesh, 1972; DO, IPGM&R, Dhaka, Bangladesh, 1980. Asst. surgeon Rajshahi, Dhaka and Barisal Med. Coll. Hosp., Bangladesh, 1972-79; asst. prof. ophthalmology NIO, Dhaka, 1980-84; assoc. prof. ophthalmology Sylhet MAG, Osmani Med. Coll., Bangladesh, 1984-89; prof. ophthalmology Sylhet MAG, Osmani Med. Coll., 1989-93; prin. Rajshahi Med. Coll., 1993-97; dir. Inst. Epidemiology, Disease Control and Rsch., Dhaka, 1997-98; prin. Sir Salimullah Med. Coll., Dhaka, 1998—; dean Faculty of Medicine, Rajshahi U., 1993-97; prin. Rajshahi Med. Coll., 1993-97; mem. syndicate Rajshahi U., 1993-97. Author: (textbook) Chakhu Chikitsa, 1985; contbr. articles to profl. jours. Regtl. med. officer Bangladesh Army, 1971. Recipient Citation award Lions Internat., 1980, 90, 92. Mem. Bangladesh Med. Assn. (life), Ophtal. Soc. Bangladesh (pres. 1991-93, 94-96, v.p. 1997-98). Avocation: shooting. Home: 41-24 Basbari, Block C, Mohammadpur Dhaka 1205, Bangladesh Office: Sir Salimullah Med Coll, Midford, Dhaka Bangladesh

RAHMAN, MOHAMMED SIDDIQUR, environmental engineer, researcher; b. Bogra, Bangladesh, Mar. 22, 1948; came to U.S., 1980; s. Azizar and Samina (Khatun) R.; m. Shahanara Zaman, Aug. 14, 1974; children Sabrina Rahman, Sajedur Amin Rahman. BS, Bangladesh Agrl. U., Mymensingh, 1970; MS, U. of New Castle Upon Tyne, Eng., 1979; PhD, Rutgers U., 1984. Lectr. Bangladesh Agrl. U., Mymensingh, 1972, asst. prof., 1974; rsch. asst. Rutgers U., New Brunswick, N.J., 1980; environ. engr. N.J. Dept. Environ. Protection, Trenton, 1986, rsch. scientist, 1987—. Author, editor: Elevated Radon Area Evaluation Program, 1990. Convener Fedn. Bangladeshi Assns. in N.Am., N.J., 1994; pres. Bangladesh Soc. of N.J., 1992-94. Talent scheme scholar Bangladesh govt., 1964, commonwealth scholar, Eng., 1977. Mem. Conf. Radiation Control Program Dirs. (assoc.), Bangladesh Engrng. Inst. Home: 145 Franklin Corner Rd Lawrenceville NJ 08648-2501 Office: Dept of Environ Protection CN415 Trenton NJ 08625

RAHMAN, MUHAMMAD ABDUR, mechanical engineer; b. Sylhet, Assam, India, Mar. 1, 1930; came to U.S., 1950; s. Haji Sajjad Ali Khan and Momotaj Khanom. BSME, U. Toledo, 1953, MSME, 1968; PhD in Engrng., Calif. Coast U., 1985. Registered profl. engr., Calif. Mech. design engr. various cons. firms, L.A., 1955-61; aerospace engr. Douglas Aircraft Co., Santa Monica, Calif., 1962-63, N.Am. Aviation, Inc., L.A., 1963-64, NASA Manned Spacecraft Ctr. Gemini & Apollo Program Office, Houston, 1964-70; safety engr. U.S. Dept. Labor, OSHA, Washington, 1975-86; invention researcher Arlington, Va., 1987—; Contbr. articles to profl. jours. Mem. N.Y. Acad. Scis. Democrat. Islam. Achievements include patent for solar energy collector, supersonic MHD generator system; copyrights for hypothesis on unified field theory and creation of the universe, on the gravitoenergy in the creation of cosmic matters in the space, on the mechanism of superconductivity, a note of caution for superconductivity in reference to permeability and permitivity, concentration on suggesting methods to build superconductors and biomedical engineering instrumentation for cancer in particular, others. Home and Office: 1805 Crystal Dr Apt 1013 Arlington VA 22202-4407

RAHMAN, MUSTAQUR, travel representative; b. Mymensingh, Bangladesh, Jan. 2, 1954; came to U.S., 1976; s. Mohammad Abdul Bari and Akika Akhtar Khatun. BA with honors, Jahangirnagar (Bangladesh) U., 1974; BS, Western Ill. U., 1978; diploma in journalism, Dhaka (Bangladesh) U., 1975, MA, 1981; diploma in travel and tourism, Parks Coll., Denver, Colo., 1985; cert., Travel Careers Internat., 2000. Field officer in charge Australian Bapt. Missionary Soc., Dhaka, 1974; field officer Coop. Asst. Relief Everywhere, Dhaka, 1976; clk. Talent Tree, Denver, 1984-85; light indsl. dept. Handy Andy, Chgo., 1986-88; shipping asst. Eden Staffing, N.Y.C., 1996; clerical asst. Temps Am., N.Y.C., 1996; clk., quality contr. CTI Ops., N.Y.C., 1997; mgmt. asst. Top Job Personnel, N.Y.C., 1997-98, ITR, Travel Navigator, USA, 1999; travel cons. Travel Helps, Dhaka, 1989-96. Contbr. over 200 commentaries to daily newspapers and weekly mags. Merit scholar Govt. Bangladesh, Dhaka, 1966-68, 68-70, 74-75. Mem. Nat. Consumer Rsch. Assn., Smithsonian Instn., Minister of God The Order of the Holy Spirit. Avocations: stories, travel, photography, sports. Home: PO Box 215 New York NY 10156-0215

RAHMAN, NASEEM, theoretical chemistry educator; b. Dhaka, Bangladesh, Feb. 16, 1943; s. Habibur and Selima (Ali) R.; m. Giuliana de Biasio, Oct. 23, 1965 (dec.); 1 child, Sonya Michele; m. Hilda Alicia Gomez, Dec. 21, 1992. BSc with honors, U. Dacca, Pakistan, 1963, MSc, 1964; MS, U. Md.; PhD, Am. U., Washington. Engr. French Atomic Energy Commn., Saclay, France, 1971-73; wissenschaftliche mitarbeiter U. Bielefeld, Germany, 1973-74; rschr. NRC, Pisa, Italy, 1974-80; assoc. prof. U. Pisa, 1980-86; prof., chmn. U. Trieste, 1986—; coord. Internat. Ctr. Pure & Applied Chemistry, Trieste, 1994-96. Editor: (with C. Guidotti) Photon-Assisted Collisions and Related Topics, 1982, Collisions and Half-Collisions with Lasers, 1984, (with C. Guidotti and M. Allegrini) Photons and Continuum States of Atoms and Molecules, 1986, (with S. Carra) From Molecular Dynamics to Combustion Chemistry, 1992. Dir. Internat. Ctr. Complex Systems; pres. Internat. Ctr. Sci. Tech. and Environ. for Densely Populated Region, 1997—. Grantee for rsch. European Cmty., Brussels. Mem. Italian Chem. Soc. Avocations: golf, tennis, languages, chess. Office: U Trieste, Via Giorgieri No 1, 34100 Trieste Italy

RAHMAN, RAFIQ UR, oncologist, educator; b. Mirali, Pakistan, Mar. 3, 1957; came to U.S., 1985; s. Rakhman and Bibi (Sana) Gul; m. Shamim Ara

Bangash; children: Maryam, Hassan, Haider. BS, MB, U. Peshawar, Pakistan, 1980. Bd. cert. internal medicine, med. oncology, hematology; lic. physician Pa., Ala., Ky. House officer in internal medicine Khyber Teaching Hosp.-U. Peshawar, Pakistan, 1980-81, house officer in gen. surgery, 1981, jr. registrar med. ICU, 1983-84; jr. registrar internal medicine Khyber Teaching Hosp., 1981-82; sr. registrar internal medicine Khyber Teaching Hosp.-Lady Reading Hosp. & Postgrad. Inst., Peshawar, 1984-85; Audrey Meyer Mars fellow in med. oncology Roswell Park Cancer Inst., Buffalo, 1985-86; resident in internal medicine SUNY-Buffalo Gen. Hosp.-Erie County Med. Ctr.-VA Med. Ctr., 1986-88; chief resident in internal medicine SUNY-Buffalo-Erie County Med. Ctr., 1988; fellow in hematology and med. oncology SUNY-Buffalo-Roswell Park Cancer Inst., 1989-90; hematologist, med. oncologist Daniel Boone Clinic and Harlan A.R.H., 1991-92; clin. asst. prof. medicine U. Ky., 1991—; attending physician, hematology/med. oncologist Hardin Meml. Hosp., Elizabethtown, 1993—, chief medicine, 1996; tchr. med. students Med. Sch., SUNY; participant CALGB protocol studies Roswell Park Cancer Inst., investigator. Editor English sect. Cenna mag. Cenna; contbr. articles to profl. jours. Founder Cmty. Uplift Program, Pakistan; founder Venture Fund for Info. Tech., Pakistan. Mem. Pakistan Med. & Dental Coun., Ky. Med. Assn., Hardin-LaRue County Med. Soc. Avocations: traveling, aeromodeling, swimming, studying political science and history. Home: 400 Briarwood Cir Elizabethtown KY 42701-6915 Office: 1107 Woodland Dr Ste 105 Elizabethtown KY 42701-2789

RAHMAN, SHAHID, architect; b. Bahawalpur, Punjab, Pakistan, Mar. 15, 1950; s. Abdur Rahman Khan and Iqbal Begam; m. Kausar Shahzadi, July 22, 1977 (dec. Jan. 1986); children: Rabia, Ali; m. Tehmina Jamil, Jan. 18, 1990; 1 child, Adil. National diploma in Arch., Nat. Coll. Arts, Lahore, Pakistan, 1974. Arch. Pakistan Environ. Planning and Archtl. Cons., Rawalpindi, 1975-79; archtl. engr. Directorate of Mil. Works, Baghdad, Iraq, 1980-81; sr. arch. Pakistan Environ. Planning and Archtl. Cons., Islamabad, Pakistan, 1981-82; sr./prin. arch. Nat. Engring. Svcs. Pakistan, Lahore, 1982—; external examiner U. Engring. and Tech., Lahore, 1987; juror Nat. Coll. Arts, Lahore, 1998-99, Al-Khair U., Lahore, 1999; cons. arch. SL Koch, Saudi Arabia, 1997. Cartoons appear in newspapers, periodicals and TV. Recipient 1st prize competition project Pakistan Ordinance Factor, 1977, Pakistan Sports Bd., Army Welfare Trust, 1989. Mem. Inst. Archs. Pakistan, Pakistan Coun. Archs. and Town Planners. Achievements include patent applied for add-on type shoes design. Avocations: art, sculpting, cartooning, inventing. Home: 13-A St 48 F-8/4, Islamabad Punjab, India Office: Nespak House, 1-C Blk N Model-Town, Lahore Punjab, Pakistan

RAHMAN, SHAIKH MIZANUR, agriculturist, educator; b. Jhikar Gacha, Jessore, Bangladesh, Nov. 1, 1963; s. Shaikh Golam Mostafa and Mosamatt Bagum Nurjahan; m. Firoza Parvin, Jan. 19, 1992. BSc in Botany with honors, Rajshahi U., 1984, MSc in Botany, 1985; MS in Agr., Saga (Japan) U., 1994; PhD in Agr., United Grad. Sch. Agrl. Sci., Kagoshima, Japan, 1997. Rsch. asst. dept. botany Rajshahi (Bangladesh) U., 1989-91, asst. prof. dept. genetics and breeding, 1998—. Contbr. articles to profl. jours. Grantee Ministry of Sci. and Tech., Bangladesh, 1990-91, Ministry of Edn., Japan, 1992-97. Mem. Bangladesh Assn. (pres. 1997), Japan Soc. for Promotion of Sci. Moslem. Avocations: volleyball, singing, running. Home: Bamon Ali, 7400 Jhikar Gacha Jessore Bangladesh Office: Rajshahi U, Dept Genetics and Breeding, 6205 Rajshahi Bangladesh

RAHMAN, SYEDUR A. H., ophthalmologist, consultant; b. Calcutta, Bangladeshi, Mar. 18, 1936; s. Abdur and Umme Salma (Quazi) R.; m. Zerina Khan, Oct. 2, 1958; children: Ashiqur, Mohibur. MBBS, Dhaka Med. Coll., 1962; Diploma in Ophthalmology, Royal Coll. Physicians and Royal Coll. Surgeons, 1969. House officer Ophthalmology unit Dhaka Med. Coll. Hosp., 1962-63, house officer surgical unit, 1963, house officer med. unit, 1963-64; clin. attachment Moorfield Eye Hosp., London, 1964-65; sr. house officer In Ophthamology Royal Surrey Hosp., Guildford, Eng., 1965-70; registrar Ophthalmology Guildford and Godalming Group of Hosps., Eng., 1970-72; locum cons. Ophthamology Guildford and Godalming Group of Hosps., England, 1972; cons. in Ophtholmology Holy Family Red Cross Hosp., 1973-89, Dhaka Nat. Med. Inst. Hosp., 1974-87; cons. Dhaka Eye Hosp. Bangladesh Nat. Soc. for the Blind, 1976-82; cons. in Ophthalmology Dhaka Shisu Hosp., 1978-80; fellow World Health Orgn. at Mehidol U., Bangkok, Thailand, Singapore Gen. Hosp., All India Med. Inst., Delhi; guest lectr. Inst. Postgrad. Medicine and Rsch., 1976-80, Eye Infirmary and Tng. Inst., chittagong, 1980-86, Internat. Agy. for the Prevention Blindness, Singapore, 1979, Nat. Inst. Ophthalmology Dhaka, 1980—; mem. faculty medicine Dhaka U., 1981-82; mem. senate of the Dhaka U., 1974-79; mem. academic coun. Bangladesh Inst. Rsch. and Rehab. Diabetic Endocrine and Metabolic Disorders, 1983—. Author: India, Pakistan, Bangladesh What Next?, 1971, Problems in Western Economy, 1972, Indian-Pacific Ocean and the United States, 1986, Diabetic Retinopathy: and Its Management, 1st edit., 1998; contbr. articles to profl. jours. Sec. Bangladesh Peace Coun., 1973-74; mem. steering com. UN Assn. Bangladesh, 1984—; gen. sec. Bangladesh Afro-Asian Peoples Solidarity Orgn., 1984—. Fellow Coll. Opthalmology, U.K., 1990. Mem. Bangladesh Med. Assn. (pres. 1981-82), Bangladesh Med. and Dental Coun. (v.p. 1980—), Ophthalmological Soc. Bangladesh (gen. sec. 1973-74), Assn. for the Advancement Med. Sci. (v.p. 1978-79), Bangladesh Nat. Coun. for the Blind (v.p. 1981, 82, 83), Nat. Soc. for the Blind (bd. govs. 1976-83), Bangladesh Inst. Child Health (academic coun., 1982). Avocations: reading books, gardening, music. Home: 67/3 Kakrail, Dhaka 1000, Bangladesh Office: Ibrahim Diabetes Ctr, 122 Kazi Nazrul Islam Ave, Dhaka 1000, Bangladesh

RAHMANI, REZA MOSSAVER, writer, retired Iranian Air Force officer, banker, tour operator; b. Tehran, Iran, Jan. 17, 1912; came to U.S., 1963; s. Aliasghar M. and Khadijeh M. R.; m. Behjatmolook Lazgui, 1939 (div. 1947); children: Farhad, Sohrab; m. Poorandokht Amir Fazli, 1949; children: Ali M., Jasmin M. Rahmani Dugan. BS, Mil. Cadet Acad., Tehran, 1934; MS, Air Obs. Acad., Tehran, 1935, Higher Acad. Air Navigation, Cazaux, France, 1949; PhD equivalent, Staff and War Coll., Tehran, 1942; LLB, U. Tehran, 1945; MBA, Columbia U., N.Y.C., 1967. Commd. officer Iranian Air Force, 1948, advanced through grades to col., 1949; tchr., operator 1st Wing Iranian Air Force, Tehran, 1942-45; prof. Mil. Cadet Acad., 1945-46, Staff and War Coll., Tehran, Iran, 1946-48; reorganizer ednl. sys. Iranian Air Force, 1948-52; ret., 1952; air, mil. and naval attache Iranian Embassy, Baghdad, Iraq, 1952-54; mgr. Bank Saderat, Ekbatan, Iran, 1954-55; head internat. dept. Bank Saderat, Tehran, 1955-60; gen. mgr. Bank Saderat, Hamburg, Germany, 1961-63, Paris, 1962-63, London, 1962-63; founder head Persepolis Travel, Ltd., N.Y.C., 1967-91; ret., 1991; ofcl.guest ednl. orgns., U.S., Gt. Britain, France, also aircraft factories in all three countries. Author: The Old Soldier, Vol. 1, 1985, Vol. 2, 1992, Vol. 3, 1993. Active Freedom Party, 1952. Decorated Sci. medal 3, Sci. medal 2 (Iran). Mem. Columbia U. Alumni Assn., Rancho Bernardo Swim and Tennis Club. Democrat. Home: 17199 Prado Pl San Diego CA 92128-2163

RAHMATHULLAH, VIJAYA LAXMI, physician; b. Basra, Iraq, June 19, 1930; d. Venkatajalem and Ponnamma; m. Mohamed Rahmathullah, Mar. 19, 1952 (wid. Feb. 1970); children: Raheem, Tahir. MBBS, Lady Hardling Med. Coll., New Delhi, India, 1957; Diploma in Tropical Pub. Health, London, 1976. Supt. Candonment Hosp., Nilgiris, India, 1965-71; med. advisor United Planters Assn. of South India, Nilgiris, 1971-86; prin. investigator Sight Savers, Madurai, 1987-90; dir. Vitamin A deficiency/Child Devel., India, 1987-89, Aravind Children's Hosp., Madurai, India, 1990—; health cons. Assn. for Sarva Seva Farms, madurai, 1995—. Author rsch. in field. Mem. Indian Govt. Task Force, Family Planning Assn. of So. India, Resource Ctr. (bd. dirs. 1992—). Avocations: reading, gardening. Office: Aravind Ctr Women/Chld/Hlth, 28 Kamarajar St Anna Nagar, 625 020 Madurai/Tamil Nadu India

RAHN, FRIEDRICH JAMES, financial executive and researcher; b. Tzaneen, South Africa, Dec. 10, 1935; s. Friedrich Wilhelm and Mabel Jane (Eckard) R.; m. Heather Joy Sourgen, Nov. 27, 1965; children: Kevin, Chantelle, Sonja. BComm, U. South Africa, 1968; BComm with honors, 1970, MComm, 1971, DComm, 1972. Cert. mine surveyor. Surveyor Durban Deep, South Africa, 1953-60; sect. surveyor Western Deep Levels, South Africa, 1960-64; analyst Anglo Am. Corp., South Africa, 1964-69; mgr. Gen. Mining, South Africa, 1969-82; dir. Anderson Wilson & Part, South Africa, 1983-95, Standard Equities, South Africa, 1996—; cons. various mines, South Africa, 1983-85. Methodist. Avocations: woodwork, golf, birding, hiking. Home: PO Box 69379, Bryanston 2021, South AFrica

RAHTZ, PHILIP ARTHUR, archaeologist, writer; b. Bristol, Eng., Mar. 11, 1921; s. Frederick John and Ethel May (Clothier) R.; m. Mary Hewgill Smith, Sept. 14, 1940 (dec. May 1977); children: Philippa, Nicholas, David, Diana, Sebastian, Matthew; m. Lorna Rosemary Watts, Apr. 7, 1978. MA, U. Bristol, 1964. Lectr. then sr. lectr., reader U. Birmingham, Warwickshire, Eng., 1963-78; prof. archaeology U. York, Yorkshire, Eng., 1978-86; pres. Coun. Brit. Archaeology, London, 1986-89. Author: Ed Rescue Archaeology, 1971, Invitation to Archaeology, 1985, Glastonbury, 1993. Served to sgt. RAF, 1941-46. Fellow Soc. of Antiquaries; mem. Inst. Field Archaeologists (hon.). Avocations: naturism, music, travel, swimming. Home: The Old Sch Harome, Helmsley Yorkshire Y062 5JE, England

RAI, ARTI K., law educator; b. Kanpur, India, Nov. 17, 1966; came to U.S., 1973; d. J.P.Srivastava and Jagdish Bains. AB, Harvard U., 1983-87, JD, 1991; student, Harvard Med. Sch., 1987-88. Bar: Pa. 1993, D.C. 1994. Law clk. to Hon. Marilyn Hall Patel U.S. Dist. Ct., San Francisco, 1991-92; atty. Jenner & Block, Washington, 1992-94, U.S. Dept. Justice, Washington, 1994-95; lectr. law and medicine U. Chgo., 1995-96; faculty fellow Harvard U., Cambridge, Mass., 1996-97; assoc. prof. law U. San Diego Law Sci., 1997—; vis. assoc. prof. U. Pa. Law Sch., fall 2000. Co-author: Law and Mental Health System, 1999; contbr. articles to profl. jours.; bd. editors Am. Jour. Law and Medicine. John Harvard scholar, 1986, 87; Wilson, Sonsini, Goodrich & Rosati Internet scholar, 1998, Nat. Merit scholar. Mem. ABA (vice chair intellectual property com. of adminstrv. law sect.), Am. Soc. Law and Medicine. Office: U San Diego Law Sch 5998 Alcala Park San Diego CA 92110-2476

RAI, GURCHARAN SINGH, physician, educator; b. Ludhiana, Punjab, India, July 30, 1947; s. Gurdev Singh and Kartar (Kaur) R.; m. Harsha Bhatia, Nov. 8, 1977; children: Sandeep Gurdev Singh, Gurdeep Singh. MBBS, U. Newcastle, Newcastle-upon-Tyne, Eng., 1971, MD, 1978; MSc, U. London, 1977. House physician, surgeon Gen. Hosp., Nottingham, Eng., 1971-72; sr. house officer Univ. Hosps., Newcastle-upon-Tyne, 1972-73, registrar, 1974-76, sr. rsch. assoc., 1976-78; sr. registrar Chesterton Hosp., Cambridge, Eng., 1978-80; cons. physician Whittington Hosp., London, 1980—; sr. lectr. geriatric medicine Univ. Coll. Hosp. Med. Sch., London, 1980—; prof. geriatric medicine U. Nijmegen, Netherlands, 1991-92. Author: Databook on Geriatrics, 1980, Case Presentations in Clinical Geriatric Medicine, 1987, Manual of Geriatric Medicine, 1991, Postgraduate Medicine: Revision and Self-Assessment, 1998, Medical Ethics and the Elderly, 1999, Elderly Care Medicine, 2000; contbr. articles to profl. publs. Fellow Royal Coll. Physicians; mem. Brit. Nuc. Medicine Soc., Brit. Geriatric Soc., Brit. Assn. Svcs. for Elderly, Brit. Med. Assn., Am. Geriatric Soc. Home: 22 Northwick Cir, Kenton Harrow HA3 0DY, England Office: Whittington Hospital, Highgate Hill, London NI9 5NF, England

RAI, LALLAN PRASAD, mathematician; b. Azamgarh, India, July 1, 1952; s. Mangala and Subhagi R.; m. Nirmala Singh, May 13, 1968; 1 child, Meenakshi. MSc, Banaras Hindu U., 1974, PhD, 1977. Scientist CSIR, India, 1978—; coordinating scientist, math. modelling group Nat. Inst. Sci. Tech. and Devel. Studies, CSIR. Dep. editor Jour. Mgmt. Sci. and Applied Cybernetics (SCIMA). Mem. Indian Math. Soc. (life), Indian Sci. Congress Assn. (life), Indian Soc. Math. Modelling and Computer Simulation (life), Indian Soc. Indsl. and Applied Math. (life), Soc. Mgmt. sci. and Applied Cybernetics (treas., hon. joint sec.). Avocations: chess, boks. Home: P 139 Sanjay Nagar, 201 001 Ghaziabad UP, India Office: NISTADS, Dr KS Krishnan Rd, 110012 New Delhi India

RAI, VIRENDRA NATH, physicist; b. Ghazipur, India, July 25, 1957; s. Rajendra Prasad and Madan Devi Rai; m. Savita Rai; children: Archana, Richa, Ashutosh Kumar. BSc with honors, Banaras Hindu U., 1975; MSc in Physics, B.H. Univ., 1977, PhD in Physics, 1983. JRF, SRF, PDF Banaras Hindu U., Varanasi, India, 1977-84; rsch. assoc. Inst. for Plasma Rsch., Gandhinagar, India, 1984-87; fellow Inst. for Plasma Rsch., Gandhinagar, 1987-90; scientific officer Ctr. for Advanced Tech., Indore, India, 1990—; prin. collaborator Ctr. for Plasma Studies, Jadavpur U., Calcutta, 1995—. Contbr. articles to profl. jours. Mem. Nat. Lang. Promotion Com., Indore, 1996—. Nat. scholarship Dir. of Edn., 1971. Mem. Plasma Sci. Soc. of India (councillor 1989-91), Laser and Spectroscopy Soc. of India, Indian Laser Assn. Avocations: music, scientific fiction reading, story reading, football. Home: D-8 CAT Colony, Indore 452 013, India Office: Ctr for Advanced Tech, PO CAT, Indore 452 013, India

RAIBLEY, PARVIN RUDOLPH, dentist; b. Boonville, Ind., Nov. 19, 1926; s. Otto Sr. and Hallie Marie (Hedges) R.; m. Mary Helen Holder, Aug. 31, 1946; children: Bruce D., Brian L., Brent A. Student, Purdue U., 1945, U. Evansville, 1946-50; BS in Dentistry, Ind. U., 1951, DDS, 1954. Practice gen. dentistry Evansville, Ind., 1954—; pres. Parvin Raibley Profl. Dental Corp.; bd. dirs. Health Resources Inc., Evansville, 1986-94; dir. Health Resources, Inc. of Ky., 1988-94; dir. Ill. Dental Plans, 1993-94. Served with U.S. Army, 1944-45. Named Dentist of Yr. Ind. Acad. Gen. Dentistry, 1992. Fellow Acad. Gen. Dentistry, Am. Soc. Dentistry Children, Internat. Coll. Dentists, Pierre Fauchard Acad.; mem. ADA, First Dist. Dental Soc., Ind. Dental Assn., Ind. Acad. Gen. Dentistry, Am. Soc. Dentistry for Children, Masons (scouting counselor). Republican. Methodist. Avocations: farming, forestry, fishing, poetry, gardening. Home: 7100 Olive St Evansville IN 47715-3625 Office: 207 S Green River Rd Evansville IN 47715-7334

RAICHEV, IVAN TODOROV, pathologist, consultant, medical educator; b. Assenovgrad, Bulgaria, Jan. 14, 1929; s. Todor Ivanov and Alexandra (Dimitrova) R.; m. Tanija Nenkova Tomova, Apr. 30, 1955; 1 child, Sasha. MD, Med. U. Plovdiv, Bulgaria, 1952; PhD in Medicine, Med. U. Sofia, Bulgaria, 1968; DSc in Medicine, U. Pleven, 1988. Pathologist Ministry of Health, Bulgaria, 1956-59; asst. prof. Med. U., Sofia, 1959-69; sr. rsch. worker Rsch. Inst. Pulmonary Diseases, Sofia, 1969-76; prof., head dept. pathology U. Sch. Med., Pleven, 1976-95, prof., cons. pathology, 1995—. Author: Immunomorphology of the Primary Tuberculosis, 1974. contbr. numerous articles to med. jours. including Archives of Pathology, Bulgarian Medicine, others. Recipient honorable badge Union of Scientists in Bulgaria, 1985. Mem. Bulgarian Sci. Soc. Pathology. Avocations: theatre, concerts, travel, swimming. Home: Liulin 605 St bl 603 apt 35, 1336 Sofia Bulgaria Office: Pleven U Sch Med Pathology, 1 St Kliment Ochridski St, 5 800 Pleven Bulgaria

RAIDA, ZBYNĚK, radioelectronics educator; b. Opava, Czech Republic, Dec. 1, 1967; s. Alois and Hedvika (Lenkova) R.; m. Bohuslava Šenkova, July 20, 1991; children: Vaclav, Anna. MSc in Engring., Tech. U., Brno, Czech Republic, 1991, PhD, 1994. Asst. prof., 1993-98, assoc. prof., 1998—. Author: Electromagnetic Waves and Transmission Lines, 1995, Object Oriented Programming in Pascal, 1997, Analysis and Design of Microwave Structures, 1999. Office: Tech U Brno, Purkyňova 118, 612 00 Brno Czech Republic

RAIKES, DACRE FRANCIS, retired oil company official, civic worker; b. Llandovery, Carmarthen, Wales, Dec. 29, 1925; s. Cecil Dacre Raikes and Katharine Georgina Weld-Forester. DEd (hon.), Srinakharinwirot U., Bangkok, 1996. Sugar planter Booker Bros. McConnel Co., Ltd., Brit. Guiana, 1947-50; forest asst. Borneo Co., Ltd., Chiangmai, Thailand, 1951-55; with timber dept. Borneo Co., Ltd., Bangkok, 1956-59, cosumer marketeer, 1959-63, asst. gen. mgr., dep. mng. dir., then mng. dir., 1964-74; v.p. Triton Oil Co. Thailand, Bangkok, 1975-76; bd. dirs. Metal Box Co. (named changed to Carnaud Metal Box Co.), Thailand; v.p. Bd. Trade Thailand, 1971-73; hon. sec., later vice chmn. Timber Exporters Assn. Thailand, 1956-58. Contbr. articles to Jour. Siam Soc. Advisor Thai classical dance and music group Srinakharinwirot U.; mem., pres. other art related coms.; vol. Nat. Mus. With Brit. Royal Navy, 1943-46. Decorated Most Nobel Order of Crown of Thailand, officer Most Excellent Order Brit. Empire. Mem. Brit. C. of C. (hon., chmn. 1971-73), Siam Soc. (hon., mem. coun., then v.p. 1976-93, lectr.),. Avocations: music, dance and drama of southeast Asia, western classica music. Home: Ban Plu Luang, 127/1 Soi, Soon Vichai 14/6 Petchburi, Bangkok 10310, Thailand

RAIKES, ROBERT TIMOTHY, computer consultant; b. Hammersmith London, Feb. 21, 1953; s. David Robert and Shirley (Brotherwood) R.; m. Yvette Valerie Willis, Oct. 6, 1973; children: Elizabeth, Katherine, Alexandra. Degree, Luton Coll., 1980. Student apprentice Marconi Co. Ltd., Chelmsford, England, 1970-71; with sales dept. Brit. Steel Corp., Manchester, London, 1973-83, DE/DDL, Luton, Ascot, England, 1983-85; sales mgr. Taxan UK Ltd., Bracknell, England, 1985-88; mng. dir. Eizo UK Ltd., Woking, England, 1988-94, Meko Ltd., Camberley, England, 1994—. Mng. editor: Display Monitor, 1994—; U.K. editor: The Peddie Report, 1994—; contbg. editor: Computer Shopper, 1995—, PC Mag., 1995—. Mem. Soc. Info. Display. Avocation: music. Office: Meko Ltd, 134 Upper Chobham Rd, Camberley Surrey GU15 1EJ, England

RAILEY, KEVIN JAMES, English educator; b. Bklyn., Oct. 28, 1954; s. George Anthony and Joan (Bauer) R.; m. Catherine King. BA in English, Albany U., 1977; MA in English, Stony Brook U., 1986, PhD in English, 1990. Prof. English Skidmore Coll., Saratoga Springs, N.Y., 1989-91; prof. English Buffalo (N.Y.) Coll., 1991—, chair dept. English, 1999—. Author: Natural Aristocracy, 1999. Mem. MLA, Faulkner Soc. Office: Buffal State Coll Dept English 1300 Elmwood Ave Buffalo NY 14222-1004

RAILTON, WILLIAM SCOTT, lawyer; b. Newark, July 30, 1935; s. William Scott and Carolyn Elizabeth (Guiberson) R.; m. Karen Elizabeth Walsh, Mar. 31, 1979; 1 son, William August; children by previous marriage: William Scott, Anne Greenwood. BSEE, U. Wash., 1962; JD with honors, George Washington U., 1965. Bar: D.C. 1966, Md. 1966, Va. 1993, U.S. Patent Office 1966. Assoc., then ptnr. Kemon, Palmer & Estabrook, Washington, 1966-70; sr. trial atty. Dept. Labor, Washington, 1970-71, asst. counsel for trial litigation, 1971-72; chief counsel U.S. Occupational Safety and Health Rev. Commn., Washington, 1972-77; acting gen. counsel U.S. Occupational Safety and Health Rev. Commn., 1975-77; ptnr. Reed, Smith, Shaw & McClay, Pitts., 1977—; lectr. George Washington U. Law Sch., 1977-79, seminar chmn. Occupational Safety and Health Act, Govt. Inst., 1979-96; lectr. Practicing Law Inst., 1976-79. Author: (legal handbooks) The Examination System and the Backlog, 1965, The OSHA General Duty Clause, 1977, The OSHA Health Standards, 1977; OSHA Compliance Handbook, 1992; contbg. author: Occupational Safety and Health Law, 1988, 93. Regional chmn. Montgomery County (Md.) Republican party, 1968-70; pres. Montgomery Sq. Citizens Assn., 1970-71; bd. dirs., pres. Foxvale Farms Homeowners Assn., 1979-82; pres. Orchards on the Potomac Homeowners Assn., 1990-92; dir. Great Falls Hist. Soc., 1991-94; scoutmaster Troop 55 Boy Scouts Am., 1993-98. With USMC, 1953-58. Recipient Meritorious Achievement medal Dept. Labor, 1972, Outstanding Service award OSHA Rev. Commn., 1977, elected fell. Coll. Labor and Employment Lawyers, 1998. Fellow Coll. Labor and Employment Lawyers; mem. ABA (mgmt. co-chmn. occupational safety and health law com. 1995-98), Md. Bar Assn., Va. Bar Assn., Bar Assn. D.C. (vice chmn. young lawyers sect. 1971), Order of Coif, Sigma Phi Epsilon, Phi Delta Phi. Home: 10102 Walker Lake Dr Great Falls VA 22066-3502 also: East Tower 1301 K St NW # 1100 Washington DC 20005-3317

RAINA, RAVINDER, botanist, educator; b. Srinagar, Kashmir, India, Mar. 25, 1957; s. Omkar Nath and Sobhagya Rani (Bhan) R.; m. Jyoti Koul, Feb. 14, 1993; children: Manik, Madhuri. BSc, Sri Pratap Coll., Srinager, India, 1977; MSc, Kashmir U., Srinager, India, 1980, MPhil, 1981, PhD, 1985. Lectr. botany Women's Coll., Sopore, India, 1985-89; asst. prof. medicinal plants U. Horticulture and Forestry, Solan, India, 1990—. Editor: Prospects of Medicinal Plants, 1998. Mem. Indian Soc. for Promotion of Medicinal Plants (joint sec. 1998-2000). Hindu. Avocations: nature watching, travel. Home: Saikripa Officers Colony, Kotla Nalla, Solan 173212, India Office: Dept Forest Products, U Hort and Forestry, Solan 173230, India

RAINA, ROSHAN LAL, educator; b. Trichal, India, June 21, 1955; s. Brij Nath and Jai Kishori R.; m. Ratni, July 3, 1983; children: Upasana, Udit. BSc, Kashmir (India) U., 1975, BLS, 1978; MLS, Panjab (India) U., 1979; PhD, Sagar India U., India, 1996. Libr. asst. IMS, India, 1980; libr. EEI (MOA, G&I), India, 1981, WIHG (DST, G&I), Dehra Dun, India, 1981-83; libr. officer CIMAP (CSIR), Luchnow, India, 1983-85; dep. libr. Indian Inst. Mgmt., Lucknow, India, 1985-88, libr., 1988-2000, dep. comm., 2000—; visitor Brit. Coun., New Delhi, 1991; visitorship Brit. Coun., 1991; cons. in field. Author, editor 7 books and 80 articles in field. Recipient Fulbright award USIS, 1990-91, Best Libr. award ILA, 1996, Best. Libr. Yr. award IASLIC, 1999. Mem. UPLA (v.p.), IASLIC (Libr. Yr. award 1991), CLSC, ILA. Avocations: reading, gardening, music. Home: 504-IIML Campus, Sitapur Rd, Lucknow 226013, India Office: Indian Inst Mgmt, Prabandh Nagar, Lucknow 226 013, India

RAINAL, ATTILIO JOSEPH, electronics engineer, researcher; b. Marion Heights, Pa., Feb. 14, 1930; m. Violet Dorothy Robel, June 29, 1957; children: Valery, Eric. BS in Engring. Sci., Pa. State U., 1956; MSEE, Drexel U., 1959; D of Elec. Engring., Johns Hopkins U., 1963. Engr. Applied Physics Lab. Johns Hopkins U., Silver Spring, Md., 1955; engr. Martin Co., Balt., 1956-59; mem. rsch. staff Carlyle Barton Lab. Johns Hopkins U., Balt., 1959-64; mem. tech. staff R & D AT&T Bell Labs., Whippany and Murray Hill, N.J., 1964-83, mem. disting. tech. staff R & D, 1983—. Contbr. more than 40 articles to jours. including Rev. of Sci. Instruments, Electronics, Bell Systems Tech. Jour., Bell Labs. Tech. Jour. With USAF, 1948-52. Mem. IEEE (life), Info. Theory, Component, Hybrids and Mfg. Tech. Achievements include research on noise theory, signal detection and estimation, radiometry, radar, FM, first passage times of random processes, crosstalk, voltage breakdown, current carrying capacity of printed wires, performance limits of electrical interconnections; 12 patents, including balanced interconnections, and laser intensity modulation. Home: 28 Woodruff Rd Morristown NJ 07960-4620

RAINBOW, PHILIP STEPHEN, marine biologist, museum zoologist; b. Khartoum, Sudan, Oct. 21, 1950; s. Frank Evelyn and Joyce May Victoria (Turner) R.; m. Mary Meaken, Aug. 4, 1973; children: James Andrew, Christopher John. BA with honors, U. Cambridge, Eng., 1972; PhD, U. Wales, U.K., 1975; DSc, U. Wales, 1994. Lectr. Queen Mary Coll., U. London, 1975-89; reader Queen Mary and Westfield Coll., U. London, 1989-94, prof., 1994-97; keeper of zoology The Natural History Mus., London, 1997—; mem. exec. com. Field Studies Coun., U.K., 1980-86, 87-93, 95—. Co-author: Biomonitoring of Trace Aquatic Contaminants, 1993; co-editor: Heavy Metals in the Marine Environment, 1990, Exotoxicology of Metals in Invertebrates, 1993; contbr. articles to profl. jours. Fellow Linnean Soc. London (coun. mem. 1987-90, 99—), Zool. Soc. London; mem. Marine Biol. Assn. (U.K.), Marine Biol. Assn. Hong Kong, Estuarine Coastal Sci. Assn. Office: Queen Mary & Westfield Coll, Cromwell Rd, London SW7 5BD, England

RAINES, FRANKLIN DELANO, company executive; b. Seattle, Jan. 14, 1949; s. Delno Thomas and Ida Mae Raines; m. Wendy Farrow, Sept. 11, 1982. BA magna cum laude, Harvard U., 1971, JD cum laude, 1976; postgrad., Oxford U., 1971-73. Assoc. dir. Seattle Model Cities Program, 1972-73; assoc. Preston, Thorgrimson, Ellis, Holman & Fletcher, Seattle, 1976-77; asst. dir. White House Domestic Policy Staff, Washington, 1977-78; assoc. dir. U.S. Office of Mgmt. and Budget, Washington, 1978-79; v.p. Lazard, Freres & Co., N.Y.C., 1979-82, sr. v.p., 1983-84, gen. ptnr., 1985-90, ltd. ptnr., 1990-91; vice chmn. Fannie Mae, Washington, 1991-96; dir. Office Mgmt. and Budget, 1996-98; chmn., CEO designate Fannie Mae, Washington, 1998-99, chmn., CEO, 1999—; bd. dirs. AOL, Pepsico, Pfizer, Inc.. Former pres. overseers Harvard U.; bd. dirs. Nat. Urban League, Enterprise Found., Black Student Fund of Washington, Fannie Mae; chmn. Fannie Mae Found. Rhodes scholar, 1971. Mem. AAAS, Coun. Fgn. Rels., Nat. Acad. Social Ins., Washington State Bar Assn., D.C. Bar Assn. Avocations: running, tennis, golf.

RAINES, LOUIS EDWARD, school administrator; b. Balt., Nov. 24, 1965; s. Clarence William Raines and Nona Ann Raines-Dotson; m. Carmen Benninga, Dec. 29, 1989. BME, Kans. State U., 1994, M of Ednl. Adminstrn., 1996. Cert. instr. grade K-12, Kans.; cert. bldg. level adminstr., Kans. Prin. arranger, composer Frontier, Manhattan, Kans., 1984-89; freelance composer, arranger Manhattan, 1989-94; dir. choral activities Concordia (Kans.) H.S., 1994-98, assoc. prin., 1998-2000, prin., 2000—; state resource specialist Kans. North Cen. Accreditation, Wichita; vis. team chair N. Ctrl. Ac-

creditation, Wichita; mem. legis. liaison com. United Sch. Adminstrs. Kans. Composer: (songs) Country Christmas, 1987; arranger: (mus. medley) Nursery Rhyme Parade, 1992; studio arranger: (sound recs.) Won't Let Love Hurt Me Again, Bed of Roses, Second Wind, Something to Remember You By, 1988; performer with Kans. State Opera Theatre; edn. and polit. editor Open Directory Project. Precinct capt., county level organizer Clay County Dem. Party, Clay Center, Kans., 1997-98; ordained elder, deacon Presbyn. Ch., Louisville, Ky., 1993—; mem. Kans. State Choir, Manhattan, 1986-88, 92-94. Mem. Nat. Assn. Secondary Sch. Prins., United Sch. Adminstrs. of Kans., Kans. Assn. Secondary Sch. Adminstrs., Kans. Music Educators Assn. (choral chairperson no. cen. dist. 1995-97), Golden Key Nat. Honor Soc., Phi Kappa Phi. Democrat. Presbyterian. Avocations: public speaking, coin collecting, writing and arranging music, fishing. Fax: (785) 243-8805. E-mail: raines@dustdevil.com. Office: Concordia H S 436 W 10th St Concordia KS 66901-4122

RAINEY, JOCELYN ELIZABETH, artist, educator; b. Detroit, Nov. 26, 1961; d. Harriett Jacquline Lindsey. BFA, Ctr. Creative Studies, 1996; MA, Wayne State U., 1998. Dir. Bldg. a Village, Detroit, 1996—; art tchr. Loyola H.S., Detroit, 1998—; owner J. Rainey Gallery, Inc., Detroit, 1998—. Apptd. bd. mem. to select dir. Detroit Inst. Arts, 1997-99. Avocations: kick boxing, dancing, skating. E-mail: jr@jraineygallery.com. Fax: 313-259-2282. Home: 5946 Nottingham Rd Detroit MI 48224-3117 Office: JRainey Gallery Inc 1440 Gratiot Ave # 1E Detroit MI 48207-2723

RAINEY, NANCY L., organization executive; b. Madison, Wis., Mar. 13, 1944; d. Earl W. North and Arlyn M. Merritt. BS, U. Wis., 1966. Asst. dir. Dairy Coun., Inc., Indpls., 1967-68, exec. dir., 1968-85; exec. dir. Electric League Ind., Inc., Indpls., 1985-99, Internat. Spl. Events Soc., Indpls., 1999—. Mem. Am. Soc. Assn. Execs. (cert.), Ind. Soc. Assn. Execs. (pres. 1999). Avocations: traveling, reading, computers. E-mail: nrainey@ises.com. Office: Internat Spl Events Soc 9202 N Meridian St Ste 200 Indianapolis IN 46260-1834

RAINEY, TERRY LEE, music educator, director; b. Miami, Fla., June 5, 1967; choir dir. First Presbyn. Ch., Cedartown, Ga., 2000 .; s. Terry Lee Sr. and Olivia Marilyn (Meyers) R.; m. Cindy Renea Bradshaw, Apr. 4, 1992; children: Terry L. III, Randy, Danielle. BS in Music Edn. magna cum laude, U. Ala., 1990; postgrad., Jacksonville State U., 1991; MEd, Ga. So. U., 1997. Cert. music tchr., Ga., Ala. Music instr. U. Ala., Tuscaloosa, 1989-90; dir. bands, music tchr. Wadley (Ala.) H.S. and Elem. Schs., 1990-91; dir. bands Albany (Ga.) Mid. Sch., 1991-92; music tchr., chorus dir. Sixes Elem. Sch., Canton, Ga., 1992-93; dir. bands, head music dept. McIntosh County Acad., Darien, Ga., 1993-98; dir. bands Cedartown H.S., 1988—; choir dir. First Presbyn. Ch., Cedartown, Ga., 2000—; choir dir. Darien United Meth. Ch., 1994-98. Composer vocal music, ch. hymn. Sunday sch. tchr. First United Meth. Ch., Wadley, 1991-92, Canton, 1992-93. U. Ala. scholar, 1987-90. Mem. Ga. Music Educators Assn., Phi Kappa Lambda, Phi Mu Alpha Sinfonia (pres. 1988-90, citation of excellence 1990). Avocations: computer games, travel, home renovation, walking.

RAINIER, PRINCE III (LOUIS HENRI MAXENCE BERTRAND RAINIER), Sovereign Prince of Monaco; b. Principality of Monaco, May 31, 1923; s. Comte Pierre de Polignac and Princesse Charlotte de Monaco; m. Grace Kelly, Apr. 19, 1956 (dec. 1982); children: Caroline (H.R.H. Princess of Hanover), Albert Alexandre Louis Pierre, Stephanie Marie Elizabeth. Ed., Summerfields, Hastings, Eng., Le Rosey, Faculte de Montpellier, Ecole des Scis. Politiques de Paris. Became hereditary Prince of Monaco, June 2, 1944; delegated by reigning prince to administer affairs of the Principality, Apr. 1949; succeeded his grandfather, Prince Louis, II, May 9, 1949. Founder Red Cross of Monaco, 1948; founder Am. Friends of Monaco, 1952, Prix Prince Rainier, III, de Monaco (annual lit. prize for fgn. writers). Served as lt. and col. French Army, 1944-45. Decorated Grand Master of Ordre de Saint-Charles; Grand Cross of Legion of Honor (France); mem. Ordre des Seraphins (Sweden); Grand Cross of Royal Orr. of Geo. 1st of Greece; Grand Cross of Ordre de Leopold de Belgique: Grand Cross of Ordre de Lion d'Or de Nassau (Netherlands); Grand Cross of Ordre Equestre de Saint-Martin (Republic San Marino); Grand Cross of Ordre du Sauveur de Grece; Grand Master Ordre de la Couronne; Grand Master Ordre des Grimaldi (Monaco); mem. Ordre Militaire Pontificial de l'Esperon d'Or, Grand Cordon Ordre du Merite de la Republique Italienne; Grand Cross Ordre de Mohamed Ali; Grand Cross Ordre de l'Etoile de Karageorgevitch; Croix de Guerre (France, Belgium, Italy); others. Address: Palais de Monaco, BP 518, 98001 Monaco Cedex, Monaco

RAININKO, KYÖSTI KALEVI, sugar company administrator; b. Johannes, Finland, Sept. 18, 1934; s. Vilho Henrik and Aliina (Inkinen) R.; m. Sirkka Tuulikki Puolakka, July 2, 1964; children: Tuomo Pellervo, Teppo Juhana, Timo Kalevi. MS, U. Helsinki, Finland, 1960, Lic. in Sci., 1962, PhD, 1968. Asst. U. Helsinki, 1960-64; rsch. asst. Acad. Finland, Helsinki, 1964-68; head fodder plant dept. Hankkiia Plant Breeding Inst., Tuvsula, 1968-74; dept. mgr. product R&D Hankkiia Co., Helsinki, 1974-76; dir. Sugar Beet Rsch. Ctr., Pernio, Finland, 1976—; dir. agr. dept. Sucros Ltd., Salo, Finland, 1995-97; temporary tchr. U. Helsinki, 1969-88; prof. 1994. Mem. editl. bd. Jour. Agrl. Sci. in Finland, 1981-86, 93, editor, 1988-92. Mem. Dist. Coun., Halikko, 1984-88, vice chmn., 1989-92. Fellow Sci. Agr. Soc. Finland, IIRB, Rotary (pres. 1988-89). Lutheran. Avocation: jogging. Home: Toivontie 2, 24800 Halikko Finland Office: Sugar Beet Rsch Ctr, Korvenkylantie 201, 25170 Kotalato Finland

RAINS, GLORIA CANN, environmentalist company executive; b. Atlanta, Feb. 12, 1928; d. Norman Douglas and Jane (McCurdy) Cann; m. John H. Rains Jr., Jan. 15, 1946 (dec. 1983); children: Michael W., Gordon C., Deborah C., John H. III. Freelance writer, cons. Palmetto, 1976—; chmn. ManaSota-88, Inc., Palmetto, 1976—. Home: 5314 Baystate Rd Palmetto FL 34221-8756

RAINSFORD, KIM DRUMMOND, biomedical scientist, educator; b. Adelaide, Australia, Apr. 2, 1941; s. Keith Carr and Ruth Alice (Drummond) R.; m. Marion Jago, June 30, 1968 (div. 1981); children: Miriam Ann Estelle, Andrea Louise Reece; m. Veronica Koechli, Aug. 20, 1983; children: Alexander Keith, William Lawrence. BSc, Australian Nat. U., 1968; PhD, U. London, 1970; MD (hon.), Pecs U. Medicine, 1997. Sr. lectr. U. Tasmania, Hobart, 1972-79; vis. sr. scientist Lilly Rsch. Ctr., Windlesham, England, 1980-81; reader U. Zimbabwe, Harare, 1981-82; Wellcome sr. scientist, sr. assoc. U. Cambridge, England, 1982-88; prof. McMaster U., Hamilton, Ont., Canada, 1988-92, Sheffield Hallam U., England, 1992—; guest prof. U. Basel, Switzerland, 1979-80; chmn. Heads Univ. Ctrs. Biomed. Sci., London, 1999—. Editor Internat. Jour. Inflammapharmacology, 1999—; mem. editl. bd. Jour. Pharmacy & Pharmacology, 1987—, Inflammation Rsch., 1977—. Mem. parish coun. St. Anne's Ch., Baslow, 1993—. Fellow Royal Coll. Pathologists, Royal Soc. Chemistry, Inst. Biology, New Zealand Inst. Chemistry, Inst. Biomed. Sci.; mem. Australian Coll. Edn. Avocations: horticulture, classical music. Office: Sheffield Hallam U, Howard St, S1 1WB Sheffield England

RAINWATER, JOAN LUCILLE MORSE, investment company executive; b. Chattanooga, Mar. 5, 1943; d. Robert Ora and Alma Lucille (Miller) M.; m. Percy Raymond Rainwater (div. 1987); children: Karen Sue, Steven Jay, Robin Rae, Linda Sue. Student, John Robert Powan Sch. Design, 1977-78, Corcoran Sch. Art, 1985-86, Nova U., 1980, 85, 87. Co-owner Rainwater Concrete, Lorton, Va., 1962-87, Undertaking Gallery, Occoquan, 1977-80; cons. in art edn. Occoquan Elem. Sch., Woodbridge, Va., 1969-73; owner Riverside Gallery, Occoquan, 1980-84, Joamen Investments, Occoquan, 1985—. Author: (poems) At Waters Edge, 1995. Founding mem. Hist. Occoquan, 1970, Women's Mus., Washington; pres., v.p. Woodbridge Art Guild, 1980-82. Recipient numerous awards for paintings, various juried shows Washington area, 1977-87. Mem. Unity Ch. Avocations: hiking, reading, esoteric studies. Office: Rainwater Investments 611 Queen St Alexandria VA 22314-2514

RAIS, MARK, composer, musicologist, acoustician; b. Magnitogork, Russia, June 14, 1951; arrived in Estonia, 1972; s. Lev and Ljubov (Kaz) R. Ed., Musical Coll., Magnitogorsk, 1966-70, Conservatory, Tallinn, Estonia, 1972-77. Tchr. mus.-theoretical disciplines and piano Musical Coll., Magnitogorsk, 1970-72; lectr. Music House, Magnitogorsk, 1967-72; tchr. of piano Culture House, Tallinn, 1977-83; pres. Computer Music and Mus. Informatics Assn., Tallinn, 1989-99; freelance composer and musicologist, Tallinn, 1983—; radio journalist Estonian radio, Tallinn, 1977, 94—. Composer: (operas) Tale about the Courteous Robber, 1974, Before the Mirror, 1991, Play for Two, 1996, (cantatas) Provincial Songs, 1978, Memory, 1980, Kaddish, 1998, (symphonic poem) By the Way to the Gallow, 1976, Concerto for Cello and Computer, 1993, (interactive compositions) Anno 5756, 1996, And All People on Earth Will Be Blessed Through You, 1995, also vocal cycles for voice and piano, choral music, chamber music, computer music; author: (books) New Estonian School, Five Silhouettes, Dialogues about Computer Music, Memoires of Eugen Kapp, others; author some 200 broadcasts; contbr. numerous articles to profl. jours. Mem. Meml., Moscow, 1986-88; vice chmn. Memento, Tallinn, 1989-92. Recipient 1st prize Phys.-Math. Olympiad, City of Magnitogorsk, 1966, award Komsomol Com., Magnitogorsk, 1968, award Russian Choral Soc., 1969, 1st prize Competition of Young Composers of Baltic Rep., 1976, prize Competition of Estonian Musicologists, 1978, prize Arts Ctr., Karnolski, Sofia, Bulgaria, 1996; Culture Capital creative grantee, 1996, 99. Mem. ISAST, Estonian Composers' Union, Jewish Cmty. of Estonia. Jewish. Avocations: collecting horoscopes, philately, travel, exhibitions, concerts. Home: Kentmanni 10-16, 10116 Tallinn Estonia

RÄISÄNEN, JYRKI ANTERO, physicist, researcher; b. Helsinki, Jan. 27, 1953; s. Aarne and Lahja L. (Nieminen) R.; m. Pirkko H. Pakarinen, July 17, 1976; children: Juha, Minna. BA, U. Helsinki, 1977, licentiate in physics, 1979, D Physics, 1981, docent, 1983. Insp. Instn. Radiation Safety, Helsinki, 1982; sr. scientist Acad. Finland, Helsinki, 1987-88, 93-94; asst. U. Helsinki, 1980-83, assoc. prof. physics, 1984, 92-93, rschr., 1985, lab. engr., 1986-90, sr. asst., 1991—; prof. U. Jyraskyla, 1998—; vis. prof. JRC, Belgium, 1994-95; referee Phys. Rev. and Phys. Rev. Letters, Am. Phys. Soc., 1988—. Mem. editl. bd. Nuclear Instr. Meth. B; contbr. more than 150 articles to internat. profl. jours., chpt. to ency. Rsch. grantee Acad. Finland, 1987, 93, 2000. Mem. European Microbeam Analysis Soc. (adv. bd. 1987-97). Avocations: ice hockey, music. Office: U Helsinki, U Jyraskyla, PO Box 35, FIN40351 Jyraskyla Finland

RAISER, KONRAD, international organization executive. Gen. sec. World Coun. of Chs., Genéva. Office: World Coun of Chs, 150 route de Ferney PO Box 2100, CH-1211 Geneva Switzerland*

RAISIAN, JOHN, academic administrator, economist; b. Conneaut, Ohio, July 30, 1949; s. Ernest James and Ruby Lee (Owens) R.; m. Joyce Ann Klak, Aug. 17, 1984; children: Alison Kathleen, Sarah Elizabeth. BA, Ohio U., 1971; PhD, UCLA, 1978; LLD (hon.), Albertson Coll. Idaho, 1995. Rsch. assoc. Human Resources Rsch. Ctr., U. So. Calif., L.A., 1972-73; cons. Rand Corp., Santa Monica, Calif., 1974-75, 76; vis. asst. prof. econs. U. Wash., Seattle, 1975-76; asst. prof. econs. U. Houston, 1976-80; sr. economist Office Rsch. and Evaluation, U.S. Bur. Labor Stats., Washington, 1980-81; spl. asst. for econ. policy Office Asst. Sec. for Policy, U.S. Dept. Labor, Washington, 1981-83, dir. rsch. and tech. support, 1981-84; pres. Unicon Rsch. Corp., L.A., 1984-86; sr. fellow Hoover Instn., Stanford, Calif., 1986—, assoc. dir., dep. dir., 1986-90, dir., 1990—; exec. dir. Presdl. Task Force on Food Assistance, Washington, 1983-84. Mem. editorial bd. Jour. Labor Rsch., 1983—; contbr. articles to profl. jours. Advisor Nat. Coun. on Handicapped, Washington, 1985-86, Nat. Commn. on Employment Policy, Washington, 1987-88; chmn. minimum wage bd. Calif. Indsl. Welfare Commn., 1987; mem. nat. adv.com. Student Fin. Assistance, Washington, 1987-89; corp. mem. Blue Shield Calif., 1994-96; bd. dirs. Sentinel Groups Fund, Inc., 1997—; mem. Pacific Coun. Internat. Policy, nat. adv. bd. City Innovation. Recipient Best Publ. of Yr. award Econ. Inquiry, Western Econ. Assn., 1979, Disting. Teaching award U. Houston Coll. Social Scis., 1980, Disting. Svc. award U.S. Dept. Labor, 1983; predoctoral fellow Rand Corp., 1976. Mem. Am. Econs. Assn., Western Econ. Assn. (chmn. nominating com. 1992), Commonwealth Club of Calif., World Affairs Coun., Mont Pelerin Soc., Coun. on Fgn. Rels., Nat. Assn. Scholars, Phi Beta Kappa. Republican. Avocations: wine collecting, sports enthusiast. Office: Stanford U Hoover Hoover Inst War-Rev & Peace Stanford CA 94305-6010

RAISMAN, GEOFFREY, neurobiologist; b. Leeds, U.K., June 28, 1939. MB, Oxford U., U.K., 1964, PhD, 1965, MD, 1974. Lectr. Oxford U. Med. Sch., 1965-74; vis. fellow Harvard U. Med. Sch., Boston, 1968-69; head lab. Nat. Inst. for Med. Rsch., London, 1974—; sci. dir. Norman and Sadie Lee Rsch. Ctr., London, 1988—. Achievements include research in neuronal plasticity; sexual dimorphism of the brain. Office: Nat Inst for Med Rsch, The Ridgeway, Mill Hill London NW7 1AA, England

RAIT, SATWANT KAUR, librarian; b. Hoshiarpur, India, Oct. 29, 1942; d. Ram Singh and Prakash (Kaur) Roop; m. Harbhajan Singh, Oct. 12, 1967; children: Greta, Jasjit Singh. BA, U. Delhi, 1965, MA in History, 1967; MA in Libr. Sci., U. Sheffield, Eng., 1973; MPhil, Leeds Sch. Librarianship, Eng., 1983; postgrad., Leeds Sch. Librarianship, 1970; PhD, U. Longhborough, 1993. Sch. libr. Dir. Edn., Delhi, India, 1961-67; libr. asst. Leeds City Libr., 1974-75; asst. libr. Kirkless Libr. and Mus., Eng., 1975-82; sr. asst. libr. Bradford Met. Libr., Eng., 1982—, race rels. officer, 1986-90; co-coord. Edn. Dept. Leeds, 1990—; rschr. Loughborough U., Eng., 1985—. Author: A Dictionary of Punjabi Name Elements, 1984; contbr. articles to profl. jours. Active edn. dept. translation and interpretation unit Leeds City Coun. Mem. Libr. Assn. U.K. Sikh. Avocations: walking, hill climbing, creative knitting, reading. Home: 23 Vesper Rise, Leeds LS5 3NJ, England Office: Derbyshire County Hq, Matlock Derby England

RAJ, BALDEV, engineering executive; b. Jammutawi, India, Apr. 9, 1947; m. Neeloo Arunakumari; children Hemant Pachnanda, Kunal Pachnanda. B in Engring., Ravishankar U., 1969; postgrad. tng. sch., BARC, Bombay, 1970; PhD, Indian Inst. Sci., 1990. Sci. officer BARC, Bombay, 1970-73; scientist Riso (Denmark) Nat. Lab., 1973-74; group leader, head Radio Metallurgy Lab., IGCAR, Kalpakkam, India, 1974-86; head divsn. for Pie and NDT devel. IGCAR, Kalpakkam, 1986-93, dir. Metallurgy and Materials Group, 1993—, dir. Chem. and Reprocessing Group, 1999—; cons. Indian Dept. Space, Indian Dept. Def., Govt. Mus., Madras, Sri Chitra Tirunal Inst. Med. Sci. and Tech., Inst. Rock Mechanics, Kolar Gold Fields, Indian Dept. Sci. and Tech., Bur. Indian Stds., Nat. Aerospace Labs., Fraunhofer Inst. NDT, Germany, Metal Physics Inst., Sverdelovsk, Russia, Spectra, Moscow. Author of several books; contbr. numerous articles to profl. jours. Fellow Internat. Com. on NDT (hon., pres. 1992-96, pres. 14th World Conf. on NDT 1992-96, chmn. policy and gen. purpose com. 1996—), Brit. Inst. Non-destructive Testing (hon.), Greece Soc. NDT (hon.), Indian Soc. NDT (hon.), Internat. Assn. Quality Practitioners, Indian Nat. Acad. Engring., Indian Instn. Engrs., Indian Inst. Metals (life, G.D. Birla Gold medal for materials rsch. 1996, Nat. Metallurgist Day award 1986), Indian Inst. Welding (chmn. tech. com., v.p., Keith Hartley Meml. award 1992), Acoustical Soc. India (Sir C.V. Raman award 1988, Vasvik award 1994), Tamil Nadu Acad. of Scis., Indian Acad. Scis.; mem. Indian Group Internat. Soc. Stereology (pres. 1990—), Acoustic Emissions Working Group India (past pres., nat. exec. coun., Gold Medal 1994), Asia-Pacific Acad. Materials. Office: Metall Material Grp Indira, Gandi Ctr Atomic Rsch TN, Kalpakkam 603102, India

RAJ, MAHENDRA, business educator; b. Trivandrum, Kerala, India; arrived in U.K., 1996; p. Gangadhar Mahendra and Ponnamma Valsala; m. Nandini Ramkumar Raj; 1 child, Trishna. BS in Mech. Engring., U. Kerala, Trivandrum, 1982; MBA, Baylor U., 1988; PhD in Fin., U. Ariz., 1992. Mech. engr. FACT Ltd., Cochin, India, 1982-86; lectr. U. Ariz., Tucson, 1989-92; sr. lectr. U. Waikato, Hamilton, New Zealand, 1993-96; Aberdeen asset mgmt. prof. internat. fin. Robert Gordon U., Aberdeen, Scotland, 1996—; dir. rsch. Robert Gordon U., Aberdeen, 1996—; cons. Commonwealth of Nations, London, 1998—. Mem. editl. adv. bd. Bus. Jour., 1999—; mem. editl. bd. North Ctrl. Bus. Jour., 1998—, Jour. Global Bus., 1999—, Fin. India, 1999—, Jour. Bus. and Behavioral Scis., 2000—; editor: Studies in Economics and Finance; contbr. articles to profl. jours. V.p. Waikato Tamil Assn., Hamilton, 1993-95; pres. Asian Social and Cultural Assn. Aberdeen, 1998-99; exec. mem. Grampian Racial Equality Coun., Aberdeen, 1999—. Mem. Fin. Mgmt. Assn. Internat. (program com. mem. 1999—), Assn. Global Bus. (exec. com. mem. 1999—), Am. Soc. Bus. and Behavioral Scis. (exec. mem. 1999—), New Eng. Bus. Adminstrn. Assn. (exec. mem. 1999—), Aberdeen Magical Soc. Avocations: magic, chess. E-mail: mahend raj@yahoo.com and m.raj@rgu.ac.uk. Fax: 44 1224-263100. Home: 20 Huxterstone Dr, Kingswells, Aberdeen AB15 8UN, Scotland Office: Aberdeen Bus Sch, Viefield Rd, Aberdeen AB15 7AW, Scotland

RAJA, DHIRENDRA MULJIBHAI, insurance executive; b. Kisumy, Kenya, Africa, Dec. 11, 1939; arrived in Eng., 1974; s. Mulji Jivandas and Diwaliben (Rughani) R.; m. Aug. 17, 1963; three children. Grad. high sch., Kenya. Co-dir. D.M. Raja Ltd., Wembley, Eng., 1974—; dir. D.M. Raja Fin. Ltd., Wembley, 1978—. Office: DM Raja Ltd, 316 Harrow Dr, Wembley HA9 6LL, England

RAJA, IFTIKHAR AHMED, physics educator, environmentalist, researcher; b. Kotnajibullah, Hazara, Pakistan, Dec. 12, 1947; arrived in Eng., 1993; s. Mohammad Fazil and Gulshan (Sultan) R.; m. Shahnaz Parveen Kiyani, Sept. 8, 1956; children: Nauman, Farhan, Amber, Asim. BSc in Physics, Chemistry, and Math., U. Peshawar, Pakistan, 1968, MSc in Physics, 1971; diploma in nuc. engring., Queen Mary Coll., London, 1982; MSc in Nuclear Reactor Sci. and Engring., U. London, 1982; PhD in Solar Energy, U. Strathclyde, Glasgow, 1992. Med. rep. Mars Pharma Ltd., Karachi, Pakistan, 1968-69, Eastern Traders, Karachi, Pakistan, 1972-74; comml. mgr. Awena Traders, Tripoli, Libya, 1974-75; supr. Pan Arabian Trading & Engring. Co., Benghazi, Libya, 1975-81; physics lectr. U. Balochistan, Quetta, Pakistan, 1984-93; lectr. Sheffield Coll., 1993-94; rsch. fellow Sch. Arch. Oxford Brookes U., Oxford, Eng., 1994-98; rsch. fellow U. Portsmouth, Eng., 1999—. Author: Solar Energy Resources of Pakistan, 1996, Thermal Comfort, Time and Posture, 1996, Thermal Comfort Survey in Pakistan II, 1997, among others; contbr. articles to profl. jours. including Renewable Energy, Internat. Energy Jour. Sec. Muslim Welfare House, Oxford, 1994-98. Recipient numerous grants. Mem. Instn. Nuclear Engrs., Pakistan Inst. Physics, Brit. Nuclear Energy Soc., European Nuclear Energy Soc., Internat. Solar Energy Soc., Internat. Energy Found. Mem. Labour Party/Muslim League. Islam. Avocations: community social services, stamp collecting. Achievements include rsch. in renewable energy, energy and the environment, atmospheric pollution and related issues, indoor thermal comfort based on adaptive model with interest in energy efficiency and passive use of solar energy in building; involved in building management systems, and use of ambient endothermic energy for heating/cooling buildings, horticulture, protected crops and desalination. Home: 9 Swinburne Rd, Oxford OX4 4BE, England Office: U Portsmouth Dept Elec, Anglesea Bldg, Portsmouth PO1 3DJ, England

RAJA, RAMESH CHANDRA, radiologist; b. Nairobi, Kenya, Feb. 11, 1947; arrived in Eng., 1984; m. Joytsna Thakrar, Dec. 1, 1973; 1 child, Hemal. MBChB, Makerere Med. Sch., Kampala, Uganda, 1971; MMed, Nairobi Med. Sch., 1973; diploma in med. diagnostic radiology, Royal Coll. Radiology, London, 1977. Fellow Royal Coll. Radiology, London, 1977. Sr. lectr. U. Nairobi, 1979-84, chmn. radiol. divsn., 1981-84; cons. radiologist Rochdale (Eng.) Infirmary, 1984—, clin. dir. radiol. divsn., 1990—; mng. dir. MRI Scanning Highfield, 1993—; advisor in radiology WHO, Brussels, 1981. Radiology editor East African Med. Jour., 1979-83. Pres. Indian Assn. Rochdale, 1989-91. DAAD scholar German Embassy, 1983. Fellow Royal Coll. Radiology London, Brit. Inst. Radiology, Brit. Med. Assn.; mem. Rotary (pres.). Avocations: Indian drama, theater and folk dancing, study of Masais of Kenya, country walks. Home: 7 Beaumonds Way, Bamford Rochdale OL11 5NL, England Office: Rochdale Infirmary, Main XRay Dept Whitehall St, Rochdale OL12 ONB, England

RAJABOV, SAFARALI, Tajik government official. Chmn. nat. assembly Govt. of Tajikistan, Dushanbe; now pres. Tajkistan Supreme Coun., Dushanbe. Office: Supreme Council, Office of President, Dushanbe Tajikistan*

RAJAGOPAL, RATHINAM, electrical and communications engineer, researcher; b. North Panjampatty, India, May 4, 1959; s. Rathinam Duraisamy and Lakshmi Rathinam; m. Mohana Rajaram, June 16, 1989; 1 child, Vivek. Prin. sci. officer, dept. elec. and comms. engring. Regional Engring. Coll., Tiruchirapall, India, 1992-98; mem. sr. rsch. staff Ctrl. Rsch. Lab., Bangalore, India, 1998—; chief investigator Naval Phys. and Oceanographic Lab. Project, Cochin, India, 1997—; cons. Dept. of Electronics Project, New Delhi, 1992-94, 94-97; invited spkr. Stanford U., 1988, Loughborough U., Eng., 1991, Adelaide (Australia) U., 1994. Editor CRL Tech. Jour., Bangalore, Procs. of Symposium on Advanced Techs., Bangalore, 1999. Mem. IEEE, Inst. of Electronics and Telecomms. Engrs., Nat. Geographic Soc., Officer's Club (Regional Engring. Coll.), Sri Vidya Ganapathi Seva Samithi (Regional Coll., pres. 1994-97). Fax: 91-080-8381168. Office: Ctrl Rsch Lab, Jalahalli PO, Bangalore 560 013, India

RAJAGOPAL, SANJEEVI, biologist, researcher; b. Srirengapuram, Tamil Nadu, India, May 14, 1963; arrived in The Netherlands, 1994.; s. Ellappa Perumal and Krishnammal (Narayanasamy) Sanjeevi; m. Vasuki Ayyappan, Feb. 9, 1992; 2 children: Praveen, Kavin. MSc in Zoology, U. Madras, Tamil Nadu, 1986, MPhil in Zoology, 1987, PhD, 1993; DSc, U. Nijmegen, The Netherlands, 1997. Jr. rsch. fellow dept. atomic energy U. Madras, 1987-89, sr. rsch. fellow dept. atomic energy, 1989-90, sr. rsch. fellow coun. indsl. and sci. rsch., 1990-91; lectr. in zoology Madurai (Tamil Nadu) U., Thiagarajar Coll., 1991-94; post-doctoral fellow U. Nimjegen, 1994-95, guest scientist, 1995—; cons. KEMA Power Generation, Arnhem, The Netherlands, 1994—; advisor Grupo Ecologista, U. Misiones, Argentina, 1994—. Contbr. articles to profl. jours. Cultural sec. Washburn Hall, Am. Coll., Madurai, 1983; sec. Thiagarajar Coll. Tchr. Assn., Madurai, 1993. Jr. and sr. rsch. fellow Dept. Atomic Energy, Bombay, 1987, sr. rsch. fellow Coun. Sci. and Indsl. Rsch., New Delhi, 1990, post-doctoral fellow KEMA Environ. Svcs., Arnhem, 1994. Mem. Brit. Ecol. Soc. Avocations: sports, games, classical music. E-mail: raju@sci.kun.nl. Fax: 31 24 365 2134. Home: Kwakkenbergweg 53, 6523 ML Nijmegen The Netherlands Office: U Nijmegen Dept Ecology, Toernooiveld 1, 6525 ED Nijmegen The Netherlands

RAJAGOPALAN, MANI, psychiatrist, consultant, researcher; b. Madras, Tamil Nadu, India, July 12, 1963; s. Madurai Subramaniam and Violet (Sudarsanam) R.; m. Bishakha Bhattacharjya, April 30, 1990; 1 child, Ashray. MBBS, Christian Med. Coll., Vellore, India, 1985, diploma in psychol. medicine, 1991, MD in Psychiatry, 1993. Diplomate Nat. Bd. Psychiatry. Registrar Christian Med. Sch., Vellore, 1989-93, lectr., 1993-95; cons. psychiatrist Ballarat Health Svcs., Australia, 1996—; hon. sr. lectr. Monash U., Melbourne, Australia, 1998; hon. sr. fellow U. Melbourne, 1998. Asst. editor: Indian Jour. Psychiatry, 1993-95; contbr. articles to profl. jours. Fellow Indian Psychiatric Soc. (Jayaram award 1994, Bombay Psychiatric Soc. award 1995), Royal Australian and New Zealand Psychiatrists, Internat. Coll. Psychosomatic Medicine, Royal Australian and New Zealand Coll. of Psychiatrists; mem. N.Y. Acad. Scis. Avocations: theatre, movies, music, cricket, reading. Office: Ballarat Health Svcs, PO Box 577, Ballarat 3350, Australia

RAJAGOPALAN, RAVI, management consultant; b. Palghat, India, Oct. 13, 1963; came to U.S., 1998; s. Perinchery Kullapura and Bhagyalakshmi Rajagopalan; m. Devi Chand Nair, Apr. 18, 1994; children: Reshma, Kieran. Diploma in Marine Engring., Riversdale Inst. Tech., Liverpool, U.K., 1984; B of Bus. with distinction, U. South Australia, 1991. Analyst programmer Coca-Cola, Adelaide, Australia, 1985-89; cons. Nayer Enterprises, Adelaide, Australia, 1989-91; lectr. U. South Australia, Adelaide, Australia, 1990-91; comml. mktg. officer Shell Chems., Melbourne, Australia, 1992-93; property ops. coord. Shell Australia, Melbourne, 1994, state ter. mgr., 1995, sr. bus. process cons., 1996-98; engagement mgr. Cap Gemini Am., Houston, 1998—. Pres. U. Bus. Coun., Adelaide. Mem. IEEE, Assn. Computing Machinery. Avocations: Tai-Chi, yoga, tennis. E-mail: rav.dev@iname.com. Fax: 281-345-4119. Home: 16322 Shining Rock Ln Houston TX 77095-4521 Office: Cap Gemini Am Inc 5847 San Felipe St Houston TX 77057-3000

RAJAH, EASON THURAI, barrister; b. Ipoh, Malaysia, Jan. 18, 1967; came to Eng., 1978; s. Nagalingam Thurai and Gnanambigai R.; m. Ann Elizabeth Collier, Aug. 20, 1993. LLB with honors, Nottingham U., 1988. Reg. Contentious Trust and Probate Specialist. Barrister Gray's Inn, 1988, Bar of Eng. and Wales, 1989-91; adv. and solicitor High Ct. of Malaya,

1991—. Mem. Assn. of Charity Lawyers, Chancery Bar Assn. Office: Chambers of Leolin Price CBE QC, 10 Old Sq Lincolns Inn, London WC2A 3SU, England

RAJAKOVICS, GUNDOLF EMIL VON, retired academic institute director, engineering educator; b. Berlin, Aug. 17, 1937; s. Emil and Erna Maria (Mreule) R.; m. Elisabeth C. Freiin Kotz Dobř, Apr. 10, 1962; children: Paulus, Maria-Regina, Markus, Hemma. Diploma Engring., Tech. U. Graz, Austria, 1962, Docent, 1975; D. of Montanistic, U. Leoben, Austria, 1970; Dr honoris causa, U. Miskolc, Hungary, 1997. Engr. Bohler Bros. Ltd., Austria, 1962-63, head dept., 1964-77; prof., head Inst. Mech. Engring. U. Leoben, 1977-97; ret., 1997; guest scientist Siemens Ltd., West Germany, 1963-64; chmn. Internat. Energy Agy. Exec. Com. on Energy Cascading, Paris, 1976—; cons. mech. engr. Contbr. more than 40 sci. articles to profl. jours.; patentee (30). Recipient Award for Energy Rsch., Fed. Ministry of Austria for Sci. and Rsch., 1979. Mem. Old Order of St. George (mem. capitel, Komtur award 1975). Roman Catholic. Home: Schloss Weissenegg, A-8410 Dillach 16, Austria Office: Franz-Josef Strasse 18, Montanistical U Leoben, A-8700 Leoben Austria

RAJAKUMAR, DESHPANDE VASUDEVARAO, neurosurgeon, consultant; b. Mandya, Karnataka, India, June 1, 1958; s. Deshpande Narasimhamurthyrow and Shantha Vasudevarao; m. Anjana Ramarao, Feb. 23, 1989; 1 child, Shreshta. MB, BChir, Mysore (India) Med. Coll., 1982; MChir, NIMHANS, Bangalore, India, 1989. Sr. resident NIMHANS, Bangalore, 1988-90; ast. prof. M.S.R. Med. Coll., Bangalore, 1991-95, assoc. prof., 1995-97; sr. cons. Manipal Hosp., Bangalore, 1997—. Skull base fellow Wayne State U., Detroit, 1996. Mem. Neurol. Soc. India (life), Skull Base Soc. India (life), Bangalore Neurol. Soc. (life). Avocations: reading, cricket. Home: 315/B 9th Main Rd, Jayanagar 5th Block, Bangalore 560041, India Office: Manipal Hosp, Airport Rd, Bangalore India

RAJAN, MANKUTTIPADATH PISHARATH, environmental scientist; b. Mankuttipadam, India, Apr. 11, 1952; s. V.P. Ramapisharody and M.P. Amminipisharasyar; m. Jayasree Rajan, May 25, 1981; children: Krishnaraj, Keerthana. BSc in Chemistry, U. Calicut, India, 1972; MSc in Chemistry, U. Bombay, India, 1984; PhD in Chem., U. Madras, India, 2000. Supr. Jivan Silk Mills, Bombay, India, 1972-73; scientific officer Bhabha Atomic Rsch. Ctr., India, 1974-99; ofcr. in charge Environmental Survey Lab, Health Physics Divsn., Bhabha Atomic Rsch. Ctr., 1999—. Contbr. articles to profl. jours. Mem. Indian Soc. Rediation Physics (life, exec. com. 1992-94), Assn. Waste Mgmt. & Remediation of Environment (life, exec. com. 1998—). Home: 66 4th St, Kalpakkam 603102, India Office: Environ Survey Lab, Sadras West, Kalpakkam 603102, India

RAJANTIE, ARTTU KALERVO, physicist, researcher; b. Helsinki, Finland, June 17, 1974; s. Jukka Lauri Rajantie and Marjo Hilkka Hannele (Kataja) Tuoriniemi; m. Hanna Katariina Kantanen, June 6, 1998. BS, U. Helsinki, 1995, MS, 1996, PhD, 1997. Rsch. asst. U. Helsinki, 1995-98; rsch. fellow U. Sussex, Eng., 1998-00; rsch. assoc. Cambridge (Eng.) U., 2000—. Contbr. articles to profl. jours.

RAJAONARIVELO, PIERROT J., Madagascar government official; b. Madagascar, June 17, 1945; m. Honorine Renee Razafindralamb; 3 children. MA in Law and Polit. Sci., U. Madagascar, 1973; postgrad. in mgmt. tng., Columbia U., 1974-75; grad. degree in Mgmt., U. Paris, 1980. Comml. attaché Mission of Madagascar to UN, N.Y.C., 1973-77; with econ. and comml. sect. Embassy of Madagascar, Paris, 1978-80; dir. mktg. Société industrielle et commerciale, 1981-83; dir. internal trade Govt. Madagascar, 1983-84, dir. gen. fgn. trade, 1984-88; dir. gen. commerce, ministry commerce Govt. Madagascar, Antananarivo, 1988-89; Madagascaramb. to U.S., Madagascar Embassy, Washington, 1989-97; vice prime min. in charge budget of autonomus provinces Govt. of Madagascar, Antananarivo, 1997—; chmn. bd. govs. Société malgache de Commerce et de distributien, 1983-89; mem. bd. govs. BFV Bank, 1986-89, chmn., 1989. Mem. African Group Ambs. in Washington (chmn. econ. com. 1994—). Office: Office of Prime Minister, Mahazoarivo 101, Antananarivo Madagascar*

RAJAPOV, MATKARIM RAJAPOVICH, foreign government official; b. Tashauz, Turkmenistan, Mar. 3, 1937; s. Rajap Atamuradov and Enejan Orazmetova (Enejan) Orazmetova; m. Bibijan Zhumatova, Feb. 28, 1958; children: Dilaram, Shukhrat, Akhmet, Rashid, Batyr. Engr., Inst. Engrs. Irrigation and Mechanization in Agr., Tashkent, Uzbeckistan, 1959. From engr. to dep. min. Agr. Ministry of Turkmenistan, Ashgabat, 1959-84; head The Ctrl. Stats. Adminstrn. of Turkmenistan, Ashgabat, 1984-87; chmn. State Com. on Stats. of Turkmenistan, Ashgabat, 1987-90; dep. chmn. Coun. Ministers, Gosplan Chmn. Coun. Ministers of Turkmenistan, Ashgabat, 1990-91; dep. govt. head, chmn. com. on econ. issues, pres.'s coun. Govt. of Turkmenistan, Ashgabat, 1991-92; minister Cabinet of Ministers of Turkmenistan, Ashgabat, 1992-93; 1st dep. chmn. State Com. on Stats. of Turkmenistan, Ashgabat, 1993-94; dep. chmn. Cabinet of Mins. of Turkmenistan, Ashgabat, 1994-96; min. of economy and fin. Ministry of Economy and Fin., Ashgabat, 1996—. Contbr. articles to profl. jours. Supreme soviet dep. Supreme Soviet of Turkmenistan, Ashgabat, 1986-90; Mejlis dep. Mejlis of Turkmenistan, 1999—; mem. polit. coun. Dem. Party of Turkmenistan, Ashgabat, 1991—. Recipient Labour Valour medal Supreme Soviet of USSR, 1970, 71, Honour Mark award, 1978, For the Love to Motherland medal, 1996, Galkinish (revival) award, 1997; named Honored Economist Turkmenistan, 1997. Mem. Acad. Agrl. Scis. Avocations: turkmen music, theatre, history, travel. Home: Inzhenernaya 10, 744032 Ashgabat Turkmenistan Office: Min Econ and Fin, N Pomma 4, 744000 Ashgabat Turkmenistan

RAJARAM, GOVINDARAJAN, researcher; b. Madurai, Tamilnadu, India, Aug. 24, 1961; arrived in Spain, 1991; s. Govindarajan Muthuswamy and Dhanalakshmi Kamatchi; m. Lourdes Cavada, Dec. 9, 1995; 1 child, Clara Govindarajan. BS with distinction, Thiagarajar Coll. Engring., Madurai, 1981; BTech with distinction, Madras (India) Inst. Tech., 1984; M of Engring., Asian Inst. Tech., Bangkok, 1987; PhD, Iowa State U., 1991. Accredited lead auditor of quality sys. tng. Registrar Accreditation Bd.-Am. Soc. for Quality. Scientist B VRDE, Ahmednagar, India, 1984-86; floor staff Tesco Internat., Niigata, Japan, 1987-88; rsch. asst. NSTL, USDA, Ames, Iowa, 1989-91; cons., rschr. Univ. Poly., Madrid, 1991-92; dir. ILI, Vigo, Spain, 1992-96; assembly engring. mgr. GKN, Vigo, 1993-95; rschr. U. Vigo, 1996—; dir. products and svcs. EQS, Plymouth, Maine, 1997-99; cons., pres. Best Practices Internat., Vigo, 1999—. Author: (books) QS-9000, 1999, ISO 9000, 1999; patentee in field; referee numerous sci. jours. Vol. Youth & Shelter, Inc., Ames, 1989; fund raiser Iowa State U., Ames, 1990; pres. Internat. Week, Ames, 1990; NGO Vol., India and Mex., 1988—. Recipient Monbosho award Japanese Govt., 1987. Mem. Internat. Soc. Soil Sci., Am. Soc. Agrl. Engrs., Soc. Automotive Engrs. Avocations: writing, meditation, golf, ham radio, traveling. Home: Feliciano Rolan 14, 263 03 Vigo Spain Office: Best Practices Internat, Balaidos 37-2B, 36210 Vigo Spain

RAJARAM, RAMACHANDRAN, electrical engineer, consultant; b. Kanchipuram, Tamil Nadu, India, May 12, 1938; s. Krishnan and Ramachandran (Balaptbal) Ramachandran; m. Rajaram Seethalakshmi. B Engring., Madras U., 1960; Diplome de L'Actim, Actim, Paris, 1970. Scientific officer Bhabha Atomic Rsch. Ctr., Bombay, 1961-76; cons., 1976-86; sr. engr. MHD/BHEL, Trichy, India, 1986-89; mgr. MHD/BHEL, 1989-92, 1992-96, ret., 1996; cons. Chennai, India, 1997—; cons. in vacuum and cryogenics engring.; external examiner MTech, IIT, Bombay; guide for BTech, B CS, Trichy. Designer India's 1st freeze dryer, 1968, India's 1st expansion engine, 1973; contbr. articles to profl. jours. Pres. Lions Club of CBE Siruvani, Coimbatore, India, 1982. Spl. invitee CNRS, Italy, 1991, ASTEF scholar, Paris, 1968-70. Fellow Indian Cryogenic Coun.; mem. Instn. Engrs. (India), Indian Vacuum Soc. (life). Avocations: reading, writing articles, bridge, touring. Home: Jagir Ammapalayam Post, Plot No 33 Vijayaraghavan, Nagar Salem 636302, India

RAJARAMAN, VAIDYANATH, English educator; b. Bombay, India, Apr. 21, 1942; s. Vaidyanath Mozhaiyoke Sambasiya Iyer and Rangam Vaidyanath; m. Lalitha Rajaraman, July 3, 1958. BA in Lit., U. Bombay, 1953, MA in Lit., 1955, MA in Ancient Indian Culture, 1958, LLB, 1964. Head dept. English K.J. Somaiya Coll., Bombay, 1979-92; lectr. U. Kabul, Afghanistan, 1970-72; head dept. English Advanced Tchrs. Coll., Maiduguri, Nigeria, 1977-79; asst. prof. English Asmara Varsity, Ethiopia, 1982-84; prof. Waukesha Coll., Pewaukee, Wis., 1990-91; fellow U. North Malaysia, 1994-95; prof. comms. skills Somaiya Inst. of Mgmt. Studies, Bombay, 1992—; vis. faculty English lit. Bombay U., 1982—; dir. Somaiya Inst. of Journalism, Bombay, 1992—; comms. skills expert Tata Consultancy Svcs., Bombay, 1996—. Hon. editl. bd. Ethiopian Jour. of African Studies; contbr. articles to profl. jours. Avocations: journalism, yoga, Indian classical music, radio talks, travelling. Home: 6 Ram Sadan Plot No 50, Matunga, Bombay 400019, India Office: KJ Somaiya Inst of Mgmt, Vidyavihar, Bombay 400 077, India

RAJARAO, ANANTHARAMIAH, electrical engineer; b. Hubli, India, June 23, 1937; s. C.K. Anatharamiah and C.K. Subbalakshamma; m. Usha Narayanarao, May 11, 1966; children: Ananth, Sunil, Anuradha. B in Engring., U. Mysore, 1957; M in Engring., Indian Inst. Sci., Bangalore, 1959. Design engr. Kirloskar Elec. Co. Ltd., Bangalore, 1959-61; asst. chief engr. Heavy Elecs. Ltd., Bhopal, India, 1961-72; sr. design engr. Bharat Aluminum Co., Korba, India, 1972-75; from mgr. to exec. dir. Bharat Heavy Elecs. Ltd., New Delhi, India, 1975-95; ind. cons. in elec. power and mfg. Bangalore, 1995—. Mem. IEEE (sr.). Home: 471 22d Cross, Banashankari II Stage, Bangalore 560070, India

RAJA RAYAN, RAJ K., dentist; arrived in Eng., 1960; m. Ahila Raja Rayan; 3 children. MSc, U. London, BDS, 1976. Dir. Primary Dental Care/Eastman Dental Inst., London. Mem. editl. bd. Selection Criteria for Radiography, 1998; co-editor: Practical Dentistry Series, 1999; contbr. articles to profl. jours. Decorated Order Brit. Empire. Fellow Royal Coll. Surgeons (Edinburgh) (Eng.), Internat. Coll. Dentists; mem. Dentists Pres. Soc. (dir.), Brit. Soc. Gen. Dental Surgery, Anglo Asian Odontol. Group (past pres.), Gen. Dental Coun. Avocations: bridge, cricket. Office: 46 Harley St, London W1N 1AD, England

RAJA-RAYAN, RAJA-VIGNESHWARAN, computer programmer; b. Colombo, Sri Lanka, Jan. 9, 1970; arrived in U.K., 1985; s. Ramanathan Chelvarayan and Lingamani (Suntharalingam) Rajarayan. B of Engring. with honors, Univ. Coll., London, 1992; MS, Brunel U., Uxbridge, Eng., 1993. Rschr. Ultrasonic Engring. Ltd., London, 1993; computer technician Fletcher Constrn., Hong Kong, 1994; rsch. asst. U. Hong Kong, 1994; cons. Peakward Enterprises (HK) Ltd., Hong Kong, 1994-95; computer developer Cray Sys., Fleet, Eng., 1996; computer programmer PB Computers, Redhill, Surrey, Eng., 1996-97; analyst, programmer Custom Quest Ltd., Billinghurst, Eng., 1997—. Conservative. Hindu. Avocations: badminton, riding, music, flying, sports cars. Home: 34 Cook Rd, Horsham West Sussex RH12 5GG, England

RAJASEKAR, SHANMUGANATHAN, physicist; b. Tuticorin, India, July 15, 1963; s. Alagirisamy and Sundari (Muthiah) S.; m. Sankaralingam Kamakshi, Oct. 25, 1993; 2 children: Dinesh Chander, Rajageethan. BMSc, Bharmathidasan U., Tiruchirapalli, India, 1985, MPhil, 1987; PhD, Bharmathidasan U., 1992. Lectr. in physics M.S. U., Tirunelveli, India, 1993—. Avocations: reading books, watching movies, playing with children. Home: care A Sankaralingam, 3G/3 Reddiar Patti St, Rajanagar, Melapalayam Tirunelveli India 627012 Office: Manonmaniam Sundaranar U, Dept Physics, 627002 Tirunelveli India

RAJASEKARAN, SUNDARAMOORTHY, civil engineering educator; b. Chennai, India, Sept. 18, 1942; s. R. and Indumathi Sundaramoorthy; m. Saraswathi Ramanathan, Nov. 28, 1971; children: Latha, Preetha. BE in Civil Engring., PSG Tech., Tamil Nadu, India, 1963, MSc in Structural Engring., 1965; PhD in Civil Engring., U. Alta., Can., 1971; DSc in Civil Engring., Bharalfiar U., Coimbatore, India, 1999. Postdoctoral fellow U. Alta., Edmonton, Can., 1971-73; lectr. PSG Tech., Coimbatore, 1966-68, asst. prof., 1973-76, prof. civil engring., 1976—; vis. prof. U. Alta., 1979-80, U. Sydney, Australia, 1990, U. Stuttgart, GErmany, 1982-83. Author book; contbr. articles to profl. jours. Named Outstanding Young Person, Jaycees, Coimbatore, 1980; recipinet fellowships. AVH fellow, 1982-83; recipient Outstanding Acad. award ISJE, numerous others. Fellow Instn. Engrs., Inst. of Valuers (India); mem. ASCE, Computer Soc. India. Avocations: philately, numismatics, photography, internet. E-mail: sekaran@hotmail.com. Office: PSG Tech, Peelamedu Coimbatore India 641004

RAJASINGH, JOHN SAMUEL, engineering consulting company executive; b. Nallur, Tamil Nadu, India, June 3, 1932; s. John and Devanesam Samuel; m. Rajasingh Kamala Jesubatham, June 22, 1955 (dec. Sept. 1998); children: Christobel Roberts, R. Ranjitsingh, R. Benjamin. B Engring., Coll. Engring. Guindy, Madras, India, 1954. Chartered engr., India; cert. gazetted valuer, India. Jr. engr. State P.W.D., Madras, 1954-58; head designs Rwys., Madras, 1958-61; engr. Prynne Abbott & Davis, Madras, 1961-63, chief engr., 1964-67; engr. Taylor Woodrow, London, 1963-65; mng. ptnr. Kingsway Cons., Chennai, India, 1967—; ptnr. Rajasingh & Belliappa, Chennai, 1982-92, Alex Charleston & Kingsway Cons., Chennai, 19846. Bd. dirs. YMCA, Chennai, 1970-80, Eclof, Chennai, 1987-96; pres. Cmty. Devel. Info. and Action Ctr., Chennai, 1982—. Recipient Vijay Ratna award Internat. Friendship Soc., 1996. Mem. ASCE, Instn. Structural Engrs. London, Instn. Engrs. India, Coun. Arch. Mem. Ch. of South India. Avocations: fishing, game hunting, tennis, table tennis. Home: 6 Jarret Gardens, Casa Major Rd, Chennai Tamil Nadu 6000 008, India Office: Kingsway Cons, 6 Jarret Gardens Casa Major, Chennai Tamil Nadu 600 008, India

RAJIV, E(DAVAN) P(UTHALATH), corrosion engineer, researcher; b. Kannur, Kerala, India, Dec. 23, 1960; s. Narayanan Nambiar and Savitri Narayanan; m. Amita Iyer, Jan. 18, 1993. BSc with honors, Ranchi (India) U., 1982; Msc, Indian Inst. Tech., Kharagpur, India, 1985; M Tech., Regional Inst. Tech., Jamshedpur, India, 1989; PhD, Indian Inst. Tech., Madras, India, 1993; M in Tech., Regional Inst. Tech., Jamshedpur, India, 1989. Cert. metall. engring. Quality incharge staff Punj Pipe Coaters, Gandhidham, India, 1986-87; rsch. scholar Nat. Metall. Lab., Jamshedpur, India, 1987-89; rsch. assoc. Ctrl. Electrochem. Rsch. Inst., Karaikudi, India, 1993-94; corrosion engr. Gujarat Heavy Chem. Ltd., Veraval, India, 1994-96; tech. mgr. India Lead Zinc Info. Ctr., New Delhi, India, 1996-98; mgr. quality assurance Bhushan Steel & Strips Ltd., Sahibabad, India, 1998—. Contbr. articles to profl. jours. Mem. Indian Inst. Metals. Avocations: music, literature. Home: Savitri Nivas Shankarpur, Jamshedpur 831 002, India Office: Bhushan Steel & Strips Ltd, 23 Site IV Indsl Area, UP Sahibabad 201 010, India

RAJKOVIC, VLADISLAV, management information systems educator; b. Ljubljana, Slovenia, July 20, 1946; s. Velimir and Vera (Pozar) R.; m. Magda Mejak; children: Uros, Tanja. BSc, U. Ljubljana, 1970, MSc, 1975, PhD, 1987. Rschr. J. Stefan Inst., Ljubljana, 1970-80; lectr. Faculty Orgnl. Scis., Kranj, Slovenija, 1980-88; asst. prof. Faculty Orgnl. Scis., Kranj, 1988-93, prof., 1993—, head Lab. for Decision Processes and Knowledge-based Systems, 1996—; cons. in field. Co-author: Compute Science with Program Language Pascal, 1984, Talent Expert System for Advising Children in Choosing Sports, 1997, DEX Decision EXpert Support System, 1999. Recipient B. Kidric award Slovene Rsch. Cmty., Ljubljana, 1988, Informatica Soovene Soc. award, Ljubljana, 1997, Golden Tablet, U. Maribor, 1999. Mem. European Assn. for Audiovisual Media Edn. (IFIP TC3 nat. rep.), Slovene Soc. Informatika, Slovene Assn. for Artificial Intelligence, Assn. for Info. Sys., Soc. for Judgement and Decision Making. Avocations: skiing, scuba diving, golfing. Home: Jakceva 43, SI-1000 Ljubljana Slovenia Office: U Maribor Fac Orgnl Scis, Kidriceva 55A, SI-4000 Kranj Slovenia

RAJNA, PETER, psychiatrist; b. Budapest, Hungary, Jan. 29, 1949; s. Lajos and Magdolna (Kanitz) R.; m. Erika Wagner, July 1, 1972; children: Gabor, Balint, Agnes. MD, Semmelweis U., Budapest, Hungary, 1973. Resident Semmelweis U. Dept Medicine, Budapest, Hungary, 1973-76; asst. prof. Nat. Inst. Mental Diseases, Budapest, Hungary, 1976-86; 1st asst. prof. Semmelweis Med. U., 1986-93, prof., 1993—. Author: Epilepsy, 1996; co-author: Epilepsy, 1989. Mem. EEG Health Found. (bd. dirs. 1992-99), Hungarian EEG Assn., Internat. League Against Epilepsy (chmn. Hungarian chapter 1999—). Avocations: painting, mushrooms, waterpolo. Home: Kalvaria u 13, 2141 Csömör Hungary Office: Semmelweis U Faculty Medicine, Balassa u 6, 1083 Budapest Hungary

RAJOY BREY, MARIANO, Spanish government official; b. Santiago de Compostela, Mar. 17, 1955. JD, U. Santiago Compostela. V.p. regional junta, pres. local junta, mem. parliament, 1981; dir. gen. instl. rels. Xunta de Galicia; mem. AP Permanent Commn.; v.p. Xunta de Galicia, 1986-87; mem. nat. exec. com. Partido Popular, 1989—, dep. gen. sec.; min. pub. adminstrns. Govt. of Spain, Madrid, 1996—, min. edn. and culture; 1st v.p. Min. of the Presidency, Madrid. Office: Palacio de la Moncloa, Edisicio INIA, 28071 Madrid Spain*

RAJPUROHIT, KISHAN SINGH, government official, researcher, consultant; b. Simrakhiya-Purohitan, Rajasthan, India, July 1, 1951; s. Prem Singh and Indira (Kanwar) R.; m. Gomati Kanwar, Apr. 30, 1974; children: Jitendra Singh, Surendra Singh, Hemendra Singh. BS, Jodhpur U., Rajasthan, India, 1973, MA in Geography, 1975, PhD in Biogeography, 1980. Jr. rsch. fellow Jodhpur U., Rajasthan, 1976-78, sr. rsch. fellow, 1979-80, postdoct. fellow, 1980-81; lectr. Tribhuvan U., Pokhara, Gandaki, Nepal, 1981-85; dep. dir. Social Policy Rsch. Inst., Jaipur, Rajasthan, India, 1985-86; rsch. assoc.-C Bangalore U., Karnataka, India, 1986-90; rsch. assoc.-D Wildlife Inst. India, Dehradun, India, 1990—; cons. Narmada Valley Devel. Authority, Bhopal, India, 1990-94; cons. on tiger-human conflict World Wide Fund for Nature-India Tiger Conservation Program, New Delhi, 1999. Editor: Contributions to the Ecology of Halophytes, 1982; contbr. articles to profl. jours. Jr. rsch. fellow Jodhpur U., 1976, sr. rsch. fellow Coun. Scientific and Indsl. Rsch., 1979, postdoct. fellow Coun. Scientific and Indsl. Rsch., 1980. Achievements include research in the fields of halophytes of Indian arid zone, vegetation of the Annapurna Himalayas, Nepal, mangroves of India, environmental impact assessment of large hydro-power and irrigation dams on flora and fauna in India, human-wildlife conflicts in different states of India. Avocations: religious activities, nature explorations, wildlife, spiritual meetings. Home: HIG-1 Phase-II Indira Puram, Majra Dehradun, 248 171 Uttar Pradesh India Office: Wildlife Inst India, Chandrabani PO Box 18, Dehradun Uttar Pradesh 248 001, India

RAJPUT, BALWANT SINGH, physicist; b. Bijnor, India, Jan. 4, 1943; s. Kishori and Saggo R.; m. Prabha Rajput, 1969. BSc, Agra U., 1962, MSc, 1964, PhD, 1971. Lectr. Kurukshetra U., India, 1964-76; reader, head Garhwal U., India, 1976-80; prof., head Kumaun U., India, 1980—; vis. prof. Gutenberg U., Germany, 1983-84; vis. scientist ICIP, Triese, Italy, 1976-77; vice-chancellor Garhwal U., India, 1992-95, Kumaun U., India, 1998—; chmn. U.P. Coun. Higher Edn., 1997—. Author: Mathematical Physics, 1991, Advanced Quantum Mechanics, 1992; contbr. 250 articles to profl. jours. Home: 4B Sleepy Hollow, 263001 Nainital India

RAJU, KANTHI PENMATCH, psychiatrist; b. Hyderabad, AP, India, Oct. 16, 1967; s. Penmatcha Narasimha and Suguna Raju P.; m. Sreenivasa Vegesna, June 24, 1988; 1 child: Meena. BS, Miss. Coll., 1990; DO, UOMHS, Des Moines, 1994. Biomaterials lab tech. U. Miss. Sch. Dentistry, Jackson, 1990; physician resident U. Iowa, Des Moines, 1994-95, U. Tex. Southwestern Med. Ctr., Dallas, 1996-99; triage physician Charter Behavioral Health Care System, Plano, Tex., 1997-98; staff psychiatrist Dallas Metrocare Svcs., 1999—; chief resident dept. psychiatry U. Tex. Southwestern Med. Ctr., Dallas, 1998-99. Contbr. articles to profl. jours. Scholar U. Miss., 1985, Memphis Acad. Arts, 1985. Mem. AMA, Am. Psychiat. Assn., Am. Osteo. Assn., Tex. Med. Assn. Democrat. Avocations: painting, reading. Office: Dallas Metrocare Svcs 4645 Samuell Blvd Dallas TX 75228-6885

RAJU, KONDURU NAGABHUSHAN, mechanical engineer; b. Rayachoty, India, Aug. 1, 1965; s. K.C. Naga Raju and Venkata Lakshmi; m. Dasaraju Sailaja; 1 child. B in Technology, Sri Venkateswara U., 1987; M in Technology, Bharatidasan U., 1989. Cons. engr. Tata Energy Rsch. Inst., Bangalore, India, 1990-93; tech. officer S.K. Univ., Anantapur, India, 1993—. Mem. Instrument Soc. India, Inst. Engrs. India. Office: Sri Krishnadevaraya U, SV Puram, 515003 Anantapur India

RAJWADE, ANANT RAMCHANDRA, mathematician, educator; b. Sangli, India, June 18, 1939; s. Ramchandra Ganpat and Indumati Ramchandra (Patwardhan) R.; m. Nirmala Anant Apte, Feb. 17, 1964; 1 child, Bajirao Anant. Degree in math. Tripus part II, Cambridge (Eng.) U., 1961, degree in math. part III, 1962, PhD in Math., 1966. Lectr. Ctr. Advanced Study in Math. Panjab U., Chandigarh, India, 1967-68, reader, 1968-82, prof. math., 1982—. Author: Squares, 1993; contbr. articles to profl. jours. Indian Nat. Sci. Acad. fellow, 1996. Avocations: playing sitar, badminton, philately, gardening. Home: House 138 Sector 8A, Chandigarh India Office: Ctr Advanced Study in Math, Panjab U, Chandigarh India

RAK, KALMAN, internist; b. Szeged, Hungary, Aug. 20, 1929; s. Kalman Rak and Margit Lantos; m. Anna Macher, Jan. 4, 1963; 1 child, Peter. MD, Univ. Med. Sch., Szeged, 1953; PhD, Hungarian Acad. Scis., Budapest, 1967, DSc, 1984. Specialization in internal medicine and hematology. Resident 1st dept. medicine U. Med. Sch., Szeged, 1953-57, from asst. prof. to assoc. prof., 1958-74, chmn., prof. 2d dept. medicine, 1974-94, prof. medicine, 1994—; head of hematology dept. 2d dept. medicine U. Med. Sch., Debrecen, 1994-2000. Author 30 book chpts. on med. aspects of blood; contbr. numerous articles to med. jours.; mem. editl. bd.: Oncologist, Haematologia, Orvosi Hetilap, Magyar Belorvosi Archivum. Pres. Alexander Koranyi Soc., Budapest, 1982-86, Sci. Coun. of Health, Budapest, 1991—; v.p. regional com. Hungarian Acad. Scis., Debrecen, 1993-99. Recipient Markusovszky prize and medal for articles, 1982, Hetényi medal for lectr., 1973, Korányi medal for lectr., 1986, Fornet medal for lectr., 1993, Endre Högyes medal Sci. Coun. Health, 1990, Szent-Györgyi medal Ministry of Pub. Edn., 1997, Pro Urbe medal Coun. of Debrecen, 1997. Mem. Hungarian Soc. Haematology (pres. 1995-99, Marschalko medal 1993, Eotvos-wreath Laureatus Academiae 1997, Szechenyi prize and medal 2000), others. Avocations: photography, music. Office: Univ Med Sch, 2d Dept Medicine, H-4012 Debrecen Hungary

RAKHA, KARIM AHMED, civil engineer, educator, researcher; b. Cairo, Egypt, Mar. 18, 1966; s. Ahmed Mohamed and Gwyneth Daintre (Astwick) R.; m. Dina Mamdouh El-Deeb, Aug. 6, 1993; children: Maryam, Sara. BSc, Cairo U., 1988, MSc, 1990; PhD, Queens U., Kingston, Can., 1995. Asst. prof. Cairo U., 1996—; guest rschr. ICCH at Danish Hydraulic Inst., 1995-96, 97-98; cons. Ministry Constrn., Cairo, 1996, Egyptian Environ. Affairs Agy., 1998—; sr. coastal engr. Engring. Co. Marine Affairs. Contbr. articles to profl. jours. including Jour. Coastal Engring. Recipient scholarship Queens U., 1991-95. Muslim. Avocations: reading, swimming. Office: Cairo U Dept Irrigation, Fac Engring, Cairo Giza Egypt

RAKHMANOVA, AZA GASANOVNA, physician, educator; b. Baku, Azerbaigdgan, Sept. 17, 1932; s. Gasan Pacha and Hava Gysein (Guseinbekova) R.; m. Nikolay Ivanovich Vinogrado, Jan. 27, 1955 (div. Sept. 1977); m. Evgeny Aleksandrovich Borisov, Dec. 15, 1978. PhD, Baku, Azerbaigdgan, 1964; DSc, Leningrad, St. Petersburg, Russia, 1974. Postgrad. physician Med. Inst., St. Petersburg, 1955-57; microbiologist, infectionist Med. Inst., Semipaltinsk, Kasachstan, Russia, 1958-60; physician, rschr. City Hosp., Baku, 1960-62; asst. Med. Inst., Baku, 1962-65; asst., dozent, prof. Med. Inst., St. Petersburg, 1965-86; head of dept. Med. Acad. Postgrad. Studies, St. Petersburg, 1986—; chief infectionist City Health Com., St. Petersburg, 1974—, head of the scientific-edn. practical union, St. Petersburg and Regions, Order Ministry of Health, Russia, 1992; scientific dir. Russian AIDS Ctr., St. Petersburg, 1994—; chmn. of assn. AIDS, Sex, Health, 1994—; participant confs. in AIDS field, 1991, 96. Author: Hepatic Failure, 1981, 2d. edit. 1986, AIDS, 1991, 3d edit. 1996, various textbooks, Manual on Infections Diseases for GPs, 1995; inventor in field. Adv. bd. Human Right Commn., San Francisco, 1991; mem. Doctors Against Nuclear War, Russia, 1994. Recipient awards in field. Mem. N.Y. Acad. Sci., Acad. Internat. Acad. of Ecology. Avocations: collecting badges, poetry books, coins. Office: Med Acad Postgrad Studies, Kirochnaj 41, 193015 Saint Petersburg Russia

RAKHMONOV, EMOMILI, president of Tajikistan; b. Dangara, Tajikistan, Oct. 5, 1952. Dir. sivkhoz Dangar Region, Tajikistan, 1988-92; chair Kulyab Regional Exec. Soviet, Dushanbe, Tajikistan, 1992-94; pres.

Rep. of Tajikistan, Dushanbe, 1994—. Office: Office of the President, Presidential Palace, Dushanbe Tajikistan*

RAKHSHANI-MOGHADAM, ALI-ESFANDIAR, physics educator; b. Birjand, Khorasan, Iran, Mar. 12, 1947; s. Mohamad-Reza Rakhshani-Moghadam and Bahereh Obahi; m. Sana Abdul-Aziz Madi, Jan. 5, 1957; children: Rasha, Rawa, Sara. BS in Physics, Tehran U., 1969; M Tech. in Physics, Brunel U., Uxbridge, U.K., 1973, PhD in Solid State Physics, 1976. Lectr., chmn. physics dept. Pars Coll./Material & Energy Rsch. Ctr., Tehran, 1976-78; rsch. assoc. Wayne State U., Detroit, 1979-81, Queensland U., Brisbane, Australia, 1981-83; asst. prof. Kuwait U., 1983-90; lectr. U. New South Wales, Sydney, Australia, 1990-92; assoc. prof. Kuwait U., 1992—; reviewer Am. Jour. Applied Physics; rschr. in field of semiconductors, electronic/optoelectronic materials and devices, solar cells. Author booklets on experimental techniques in the the field of semiconductors, 1990, 97; co-author booklet on electricity and magnetism, 1992; contbr. over 40 articles to profl. jours. Officer Iranian Armed Forces, 1969-71. Rsch. grantee Kuwait U., 1995, 97. Avocations: sports, travel, computers, rsch. Office: Kuwait Univ/Physics Dept, PO Box 5969 Safat, 13060 Safat Kuwait

RAKITYANSKY, SERGEY ANATOLJEVICH, theoretical physicist, educator; b. Omsk, USSR, Mar. 31, 1956; s. Anatoly Konstantinovich and maria Pavlovna (Brjukhanova) R.; m. Helena Yurjevna Filatova, Mar. 6, 1981; children: Olga, Anna, Anastassia. MSc, Taskhent (USSR) U., 1978; D of Physics and Math., Joint Inst. for Nuclear Rsch., Dubna, USSR, 1985. Rsch. asst. Joint Inst. for Nuclear Rsch., Dubna, 1978-81, engr., 1981-90, rsch. scientist, 1990-96, sr. rsch. scientist, 1997—; rschr. UNISA, Pretoria, South Africa, 1997-98, lectr., 1999—; invited lectr. Kalinin (USSR) U., 1990; guest rschr. UNISA, Pretoria, 1993, 94, 95, 96. Contbr. sci. articles to Chinese Jour. Physics, Few-Body Systems, Nuclear Physics, Nucleonica, Physics Letters, Soviet Jour. Nuclear Physics, others. Recipient award for theoretical rsch. Joint Inst. Nuclear Rsch., 1986; grantee Soros Found., 1994-95, Russian Found. for Basic Rsch., Moscow, 1996-97, DFG, Germany, 1998-99, NATO, 1999. Russian Orthodox. Avocations: reading, writing. Home: 287 Mears St, Muckleneuk Pretoria 0002, South Africa Address: UNISA Dept Physics, PO Box 392, Pretoria South Africa

RAKO, SUSAN, psychiatrist, author; b. Springfield, Mass., Sept. 4, 1939; d. Robert and Ann (Melnikoff) Mandell; 1 child, Jennifer Sarah. Student, Wellesley Coll., 1957-60; BS, U. Cin., 1961; MS in Film, Boston U., 1988; MD, Albert Einstein Coll. Medicine, 1966. Med. rsch. asst. neuroendocrinology Worcester Found. Experimental Biology, Shrewsbury, Mass., 1959; med. rsch. asst. May Inst., Cin., 1961-62; intern in medicine, surgery Mt. Auburn Hosp., Cambridge, Mass., 1966-67; resident in adult psychiatry Mass. Mental Health Ctr., Boston, 1967-69; tchg. fellow in psychiatry Harvard Med. Sch., Boston, 1967-69; clin. fellow in psychiatry, 1969-70; pvt. practice Newton, Mass., 1970—; clin. instr. psychiatry Harvard Med. Sch., Boston, 1970-75; resident in child and adult psychiatry Beth Israel Hosp., Boston, 1969-70; psychiatrist Mass. Health Ctr., Boston, 1970-77, Newton-Wellesley Hosp., 1982; cons. Cutler Counseling Ctr., Norwood, Mass., 1983, VA Hosp., San Juan, P.R., 1990-94; spkr. in field. Author: The Hormone of Desire: The Truth About Testosterone, Sexuality, and Menopause, 1996, 2d edit., 1999; co-editor: Semrad: The Heart of a Therapist, 1984; film maker Susan and Jenni, 1987. E-mail: susanrako@aol.com.

RAKOVSKY, SLAVTCHO KIRILOV, chemistry researcher, educator; b. Galabnik, Sofia, Bulgaria, May 11, 1947; s. Kiril Slavov and Tzvetanka Krumova (Zareva) R.; m. Rositza Stefanova Katrova, Dec. 30, 1968; children: Tzvetana, Ciril. MS in Engring., U. Sofia, Bulgaria, 1970; PhD, Inst. Chem Physics Acad. Scis., U.S.S.R., 1975; DSc, 1999. Chemist Inst. Organic Chemistry Bulgarian Acad. Scis., Sofia, Bulgaria, 1970-72; rschr. Inst. Catlysis Bulgarian Acad. Scis., Sofia, 1975-85, assoc. prof., 1985-2000, prof., 2000—; group head Inst. Catalysis, Bulgaria Acad. Scis., 1975-86, lab. head., 1986—, dep. dir., 1993-95, sci. sec., 1995-96, deputy dir., 1996—. Co-author: (book) Ozone and Its Reaction with Organic Compounds, 1983 (Bulgarian Acad. Scis. award 1987), Kinetics and Mechanism of the Ozone Reaction in Liquid Phase, 1999. Mem. Bulgarian Catlytic Club, Nat. Ecol. Club. Mem. Bulgarian Social Party. Orthodox Christian. Avocations: theater, literature, tennis, opera. Home: Saborna St 4A, 1000 Sofia Bulgaria Office: Inst Catlysis, Acad G Bonchev St Bl 11, 1113 Sofia Bulgaria

RAKOWER, JOEL A., business appraiser, litigation consultant; b. 1958. BA in Acctg., U. South Fla., 1980. CPA, N.Y., Fla. Ptnr. Goodman, Rakower & Agiato, Commack, N.Y., 1989-93; pres. Fin. Appraisal Svcs. Ltd., Commack, 1993—; testified as expert witness numerous times in N.Y. and Conn.; lectr., seminar presenter to profl. and ednl. orgns. Author: Enhanced Earning Capacity: Understanding the Computations, 1993, Quantifying Celebrity Status, 1995; contbr. articles to profl. jours. Mem. Nat. Assn. Cert. Fraud Examiners (cert.), Fla. Inst. CPAs, Am. Soc. Appraisers, Inst. Bus. Appraisers, N.Y. State Soc. CPAs, Nat. Assn. Forensic Economists. Office: Fin Appraisal Svcs Ltd 366 Veterans Memorial Hwy Commack NY 11725-4387

RAKUSIC, NEVEN, pulmonologist, consultant; b. Veliki Prolog, Dalmatia, Croatia, Apr. 17, 1949; s. Lester and Neda (Jelavic) R.; m. Spomenka Beker, Aug. 23, 1980; children: Nika Margareta, Nevena Ana. Diploma, U. Zagreb, 1972; pulmonologist, Med. Faculty, Zagreb, Croatia, 1979; cons. bronchologist, Pulmonary Clinic, Zagreb, 1981; MS, Med. Faculty, Zagreb, 1987, sci. asst. for medicine, 1989. Dep. gen. medicine, team chief Health Ctr., Zagreb, 1974-75; head pulmonary dept. Clinic for Pulmonary Diseases, Zagreb, 1990—; guest investigator Inst. Nacional Salud Hosp., Madrid, 1990; cons. Respiratory Rehab. Ctr., Lošinj, Croatia, 1979, Talasoterapia, Rab, Croatia, 1983; cons. pulmonologist Otorhinolarngology Clinic, Zagreb, 1994—; cons. bronchologist Thoraco Surgery Clinic, Zagreb, 1985—. Contbg. author: (books) Internal Medicine, 1991, 97; editor: Internal Procedures, 1999; contbr. articles to med. jours. Mem. European Respiratory Soc. (nat. del. 1998—), Croatian Med. Assn., Croatian Pulmonary Soc. (pres. 1996—), Croatian-Irish Soc., European Acad. Clin. Allergology-Immunology. Roman Catholic. Avocations: painting, tennis, enology. Home: Sermageova 4, 10000 Zagreb Croatia Office: Pulmonary Clinic, Jordanovac 104, 10 000 Zagreb Croatia

RAKUSIC, SPOMENKA BEKER, federal agency administrator; b. Zagreb, Croatia, Sept. 12, 1952; d. Robert and Beker-Ana (Crljen) Beker; m. Neven Rakusic, Aug. 23, 1980; children: Nika, Nevena. BS, Faculty Agronomy, Zagreb, Croatia, 1974; MS, Faculty Economy, Zagreb, Croatia, 1997. Chief decoration Hotel Intercontinnental, Zagreb, Croatia, 1975-77; head dept. ASTRA Internat., Zagreb, Croatia, 1977-93; product mgr. Adria Gulf Ltd., Zagreb, Croatia, 1993-95; advisor to min. Min. Economy, Zagreb, Croatia, 1995—; lectr. Econ. Faculty, Zagreb; cons., tchr. in field. Recipient Spl. Achievement medal Pres. Croatia, 1998, Vukovar medal, 1999. Mem. Croatia Ireland Soc., Croatia Mktg. Assn. Roman Catholic. Avocations: ecology, nature, arts.

RALEA, MIHAI F., physicist, educator; b. Ghermanesti, Vaslui, Romania, Aug. 3, 1950; s. Fanica and Elena (Bejan) R.; m. Carmen Maria Costin, Aug. 13, 1980; children: Miruna-Alexandra, Mihai-Ioan. BS, Al i Cuza U., Iasi, Romania, 1973, MS, 1974; PhD, U. Bucharest, 1993. Physics diplomate. Tchr. H.S. # 9, Bucharest, 1974-78; asst. prof. Bucharest Poly. U., 1978-93, assoc. prof., 1993—; postdoctoral fellow Oxford (Eng.) U., 1994; v.p. physics dept. trade union Buch arest Poly. U., 1996—. Lt. Romanian Army, 1978-79. Co-author: (book) Holographic Interferometry Applications, 1999; contbr. articles to sci. jours. Postdoctoral Stage grantee Oxford Colls. Hospitality Scheme for East European Scholars, 1994; project financing Romanian Acad., 1997, 98, Ministry Edn. Project, 1999, World Bank Project, 1999. Mem. Soc. Photo-Optical Instrumentation Engrs., Am. Phys. Soc., Optical European Soc. Avocations: cooking, car and boat restoration, traveling, wine making. Home: Bl 04 Apt 172, 6 Dreptatii Str, 77565 Bucharest Romania Office: Bucharest Poly U, Splaiul Independentei 313, 76206 Bucharest Romania

RALLIS, TIMOLEON STAVROS, veterinary medicine educator; b. Mytiline, Lesvos, Greece, Feb. 16, 1953; s. Stavros and Stela (Kariotis) R.; m. Penelopi Koskidou, Apr. 23, 1982; 1 child, Stela. DVM, PhD, U. Thessaloniki, Greece, 1977; postgrad., U. London, 1989-90. Intern, asst. Sch. Vet. Medicine U. Thessaloniki, 1981-86, lectr. Sch. Vet. Medicine, 1989-92, asst. prof. Sch. Vet. Medicine, 1992-97, assoc. prof. Sch. Vet. Medicine, 1997—. Mem. Nat. Drug Orgn., 1996-99. Mem. European Soc. Comparative Gastoreenterology, Brit. Small Animal Soc. Home: 66 Analipseos St, 552 36 Thessaloniki Greece Office: U Thessaloniki Sch Vet Med, 11 St Voutyra St, 54627 Thessaloniki Greece

RALLO, HARRY, architect, artist; b. N.Y.C., Sept. 28, 1951; s. Angelo and Rose Rallo; m. Bridgette Louise Bruno, May 5, 1979; 1 child, Matthew Henry. Student, CUNY, 1968-69; BS in Architecture, CCNY, 1973, BArch, 1977; student, Palm Beach Armory Art Ctr., 1994-97; studied under Douglas Ferrin, West Palm Beach, Fla., 1997-98. Registered arch., N.Y., Conn., Fla. Project engr. Turner Constrn. Co., N.Y.C., 1973-87; prin. Harry Rallo, Arch., Deerfield Beach, Fla., 1987—; editl. cartoonist Observer, North Broward, weekly newspaper, Deerfield Beach, 1993—. One-man shows include Cultural Arts Com., Lighthouse Point, Fla., 1995, Cultural Com., Deerfield Beach, 1995, Meml. Hosp., Hallandale, Fla., 1997; commns. include Wellington Forum, Fla., 1995, Ft. Lauderdale St. Patrick's Day Com., 1995, Roman Cath. Archdiocese, Miami, Fla., 1996, Fla. Urban Forestry Coun., 1995; contbr. articles to various publs. Recipient 4th pl. prize Nat. Competition, Palm Beach Soc. for Arts. Home and Office: 47 Greenwoods Rd E Norfolk CT 06058-1321

RALLS, KATHERINE, zoologist; b. Oakland, Calif., Mar. 21, 1939; d. Alvin Wallingsford and Ruth (McQueen) Smith; m. Kenneth M. Ralls, June 1958 (div. Sept. 1968); children: Robin, Tamsen, Kristin. AB, Stanford U., 1960; MA, Radcliffe Coll., 1962; PhD, Harvard U., 1965. Guest investigator Rockefeller U., N.Y.C., 1968-70, adj. asst. prof. biology, 1970-76; asst. prof. Sarah Lawrence Coll., Bronxville, N.Y., 1970-73; rsch. zoologist Inst. Rsch. in Animal Behavior, N.Y. Zool. Soc., 1970-73; zoologist Nat. Zool. Park, Smithsonian Instn., 1976—; mem. psychobiology adv. panel NSF, 1982-83; mem. sea otter recovery team U.S. Fish and Wildlife Svc., 1989—, mem. Calif. condor recovery team, 1990—; apptd. Hawaiian monk seal recovery team Nat. Marine Fisheries Svc., 1997. Mem. editorial bd. Signs, 1975-78; contbr. articles to profl. jours. Radcliffe Inst. fellow, 1973-74, Smithsonian Instn. fellow, 1973-76. Fellow AAAS, Animal Behavior Soc.; mem. Am. Soc. Mammalogists (bd. dirs. 1984-87, 2d v.p. 1990-91, 92, C. Hart Merriam award 1996), Internat. Union Conservation of Nature and Natural Resources (captive breeding specialist group 1979—, otter specialist group 1989—), Am. Assn. Zool. Pks. and Aquaria (species survival plan subcom. 1981-88), Soc. Marine Mammalogy (editorial bd., book rev. editor Marine Mammal Sci. 1983-89), Soc. Conservation Biology (bd. govs. 1985-90, Edward T. LaRoe award 1996), Animal Behavior Soc., Assn. Women in Sci., Wildlife Soc. Achievements include research in relationship between mammalian social behavior and other aspects of mammalian biology, conservation biology, genetic problems of small populations, and threatened and endangered mammals. Office: Nat Zoo Smithsonian Instn Washington DC 20008

RALSTON, LUCY VIRGINIA GORDON, artist; b. Washington, Sept. 9, 1926; d. Byron Brown and Lucy (Virginia (Gordon) R. Grad., Finch Jr. Coll., 1942; student, Parsons Sch. Design; studied with, Leon Kroll. Freelance artist Tiffany and Co., 1947-48; designer U.S.S. Constution book Am. Bible Soc. and John Jay and Eliza Jane Watson Found. for presentation Bibles to grads. U.S. Naval Acad., USCG Acad., Marchant Marine Acad., 1953—; art tchr. Sr. Citizens of Pelham, 1948-50. One-woman show Pelham (N.Y.) Meml. High Sch., 1939; exhibited in group shows Westchester Fedn. Women's Clubs, Bronxville, N.Y., 1954, Mt. Vernon (N.Y.) Art Assn., 1955, Allied Artists Am., N.Y.C., 1955, Manor Club, Pelham, 1997—, others; represented in permanent collections Assn. Jr. Leagues Am., N.Y.C. and tour U.S. and Can., John Jay and Eliza Jane Watson Found., Elizabeth, N.J.; executed mural at Westchester Restaurant, Mamaroneck, N.Y.; commd. portraits of Princess Anne and Prince Charles of Eng., Brit. Am. Soc. Vol. numerous civic orgns., 1942-45. Recipient Popular prize Manor Club, 1947, 48, 2d prize, 1958, 1st prize for graphic art, 1957; Popular prize Westchester Assn. Women's Clubs, 1951, Mt. Vernon Art Assn., 1954, 2d prize Met. Mus., Pelham, 1969. Mem. DAR (registrar Knapp chpt. 1961-63, rec. sec. Anne Hutchinson chpt. 1989—), Jr. League Pelham, Daus. of Cin. (registrar 1973-78), Colonial Soc. Ams. Royal Descent, Nat. Soc. Magna Carta Dames, Colonial Soc. Descs. Knights of Garter, Colonial Order Crown, Huguenot Soc. Am., Welcome to Washington Internat. Club. Republican. Episcopalian. Avocations: raising purebred dogs, swimming, sailing. Home and Studio: 4782 Boston Post Rd Apt C2M Pelham NY 10803-3021

RALSTON, STEVEN PHILIP, portfolio manager, financial analyst; b. Trenton, N.J., Mar. 29, 1954; s. George and Edith Martha Ralston; m. Miriam Mercedes Font, July 14, 1979. BS, MIT, 1975. CFA. Account exec. Merrill, Lynch, Pierce, Fenner & Smith, Balt., 1979-80; security analyst Fidelity and Deposit Co. of Md., Balt., 1980-83; security analyst, v.p. First Nat. Bank of Md., Balt., 1983-95; dir. rsch. 1st Nat. Bank of Md., Balt., 1990-95; portfolio mgr., analyst, v.p. Gen. Accident, Phila., 1995-98; equity investment mgr., v.p. BlackRock, Phila., 1998—; instr. Johns Hopkins U., Balt., 1985-87. Mem. Howard County Hist. Soc., Ellicott City, Md., 1969-92; mem. Lake Falls Improvement Assn., 1984-95, treas., 1987, pres., 1988; mem. Northwoods Assn., 1995—, bd. dirs. 1996—; mem. Springfield Twp. Hist. Soc., 1997—. Mem. Inst. Chartered Fin. Analysts, Balt. Security Analysts Soc. (bd. dirs., v.p. 1984-89), Fin. Analysts Phila., Fin. Analysts Fedn., Assn. for Investment Mgmt. and Rsch., Consumer Analysts Group N.Y. Avocation: auctions. Home: 515 Edann Rd Glenside PA 19038-1404 Office: BlackRock 1600 Market St Philadelphia PA 19103-7240

RAM, HARI HAR, vegetable breeder, researcher, educator; b. Azamgarh, India, Feb. 10, 1948; s. Sohit Prasad and H.R. Yadava; m. Chandra Yadava; 2 children. BSc in Agriculture, Sri Durga Ji Degree Coll., Chandesar, India, 1967; MSc, G.B. Pant U., Pantnagar, India, 1969, PhD in Plant Breeding, 1973; postdoctoral, U. Goettingen, Germany, 1978. Asst. prof. Pantnagar U., 1973-83, assoc. prof., 1983-92, prof., head dept. vegetable sci., 1993-96, prf. vegetable breeding, 1992—. Author: Crop Breeding & Genetics, 1994, Vegetable Breeding, 1998, Biotechnology in Crop Improvement, 1996; editor: Crop Breeding in India, 1994; contbr. articles to profl. jours.; released 21 varieties of soybean and vegetable crops. Fellow Indian Soc. Genetics & Plant Breeding, Vegetable Sci. Soc. India (councillor 1996—). Avocations: writing, walking. Office: Dept Vegetable Sci, GB Pant U Agriculture & Tec, Pantnagar 263145, India

RAMA, NATU, dentist, pain management specialist, researcher; b. Auckland, New Zealand, Aug. 10, 1948; s. Rama and Divaliben (Patel) Naranji; m. Vasantiben Dahyabhai Patel, June 26, 1976; children: Anish, Alkesh, Anand, Shilpaben. BS in Biochemistry, U. New Zealand, 1975, DDS, 1975. Locum tenens, U.K., New Zealand, 1975-77; pvt. practice, Auckland, New Zealand, 1977—; lectr. South Pacific Pain Seminars, 1995—; pain mgmt. and rehab. specialist; rschr. in chronic pain and myofascial pain pathways. Contbr. articles to dental jours.; prodr. 3 TV documentaries, 1986. Pres. Dunedin Indian Assn., 1972-73. Fellow Internat. Coll. Craniomandibular Orthopaedics; mem. Am. Acad. Pain Mgmt., Acad. Gen. Dentistry. Fax: 64-09-2762502. E-mail: nr2502@xtra.co.nz. Office: Pain and Rehab Myomed Clin, 42 Hall Ave PO Box 22264, Otahuna Auckland New Zealand

RAMA, RUTH, economics researcher; b. Montevideo, Uruguay, Feb. 25, 1948; d. Carlos Mauel Rama and Judith Dellepiane; m. Gabriel Guzmán-Uribe; children: Manuel, Marcela. B in Econs., U. Paris I, 1970; PhD in Econs., U. Autónoma Barcelona, Spain, 1980. Rsch. asst. UN, Rio de Janeiro, Brazil, 1970-71, Santiago, Chile, 1972-74; lectr. U. Autónoma Mex., Mexico City, 1974-83; fellow Inst. Cooperación Iberoamericano, Madrid, 1984; cons. Orgn. Econ. Coop. & Devel., UN Food & Agrl. Orgn., Paris, 1985-87; sr. researcher Nat. Rsch. Coun., Madrid, 1988—; cons. UN, Mexico City, 1979; assessor Govt. Mex., Mexico City, 1989-82; cons. EEC, Madrid, 1985, Food and Agr. Orgn. (UN), Thailand, 1991-92. Author: Investing in Food, 1992; contbr. articles to profl. jours., chpt. to book. Recipient Award in Econs. Colegio Economistas (Mex.), 1980; named Etudiante Patronée French Govt., 1966. Mem. Assn. Advancement of Sci. Spain (founder, mem. steering com. 1998). Office: Inst Economia y Geografia, Pinar 25, 28006 Madrid Spain

RAMACCIOTTI, CARLA EMILIA, psychiatrist, educator; b. Viareggio, Lucca, Italy, Feb. 25, 1949; d. Carlo Ramacciotti and Mila Malfatti; m. Franco Carmassi, June 15, 1974 (separated); children: Elena, Caterina. MD, U. Pisa, Italy, 1976. Med. diplomate; registered Italian Bd. Endocrinology, 1982, Italian Bd. Pharmacology, 1986, Italian Bd. Psychiatry, 1992. Intern internal medicine endocrinology U. Pisa, 1976-80, fellow pharmacology dept., 1982-89, rschr., 1989—; guest staff NIH, Bethesda, Md., 1980-82; incharged outpatients eating disorders program Pisa U. Psychiatry Bd., 1990—, psychiatry tchr., 1992—. Author: Disordini del Comportamento Alimentare, 1997; contbr. articles to profl. jours. and chpts. to textbooks. Mem. Help for Life, Pisa, 1989—. Mem. Italian Soc. Psychiatry, Italian Soc. Neuropsychopharmacology, Acad. Eating Disorders. Roman Catholic. Avocations: reading, gardening, swimming, meditation and relaxing technique, cats. Office: U Pisa Clinic Psychiatry, Via Roma #67, 56100 Pisa Tuscany, Italy

RAMACHANDRA, TEKKATTE VENKATA RAMANA, environmental science researcher; b. South Kanara, India, Jan. 25, 1961; s. T.R. Venkataramana and T.V. Savithramma Hathwar; m. A.V. Nagarathna. B in Elec. Engring., Bangalore Maha Sreenivaslah Coll. Engring., Bangalore, India, 1985; PhD, Indian Inst. Sci., Bangalore, India, 1995. Sci./rsch. asst. Indian Inst. Sci., Bangalore, 1985-91, tech. officer, 1991-96, sci. officer, 1996—; cons. Karnataka Power Corp. Ltd., Bangalore, 1996—; mem. IISC Ditigal Info. Svc. Ctr.; mem. NRDMS expert com. Karnataka State Coun. for Sci. and Tech.; coord. Karnataka 2000 State of Environment Report. Contbr. articles to profl. jours. Grantee Ministry of Environment and Forests, Govt. of India, 1990—, Dept. Sci. and Tech., India, 1997—. Mem. IEEE (sr.), Internat. Assn. Hydrol. Scis., Solar Energy Soc. of India, Assn. Energy Engrs. (sr.). Avocations: reading, discussions with tribals, forest trekking. Telefax: 91-080-3601428. E-mail: cestvr@ces.iisc.ernet.in. Office: Energy Rsch/Ctr Ecol Scis, Indian Inst Scis, Bangalore 560 012, India

RAMACHANDRACHAR, K., education educator; b. Udipi, Karnataka, India, Apr. 8, 1941; m. Usha Rao, Aug. 31, 1978; children: Raghuram, Geeta. BSc, Veerasaiva Coll., Bellary, India, 1962; EdB, Govt. Coll. Edn., Gulbarga, India, 1965; MEd, Karnatak U., Dharwad, India, 1967; PhD, M.S. U. Baroda, India, 1975; DCPA, Annamalai U., Annamalainagar, India, 1996. Tchr. Govt. Secondary Schs., Harapanahalli, Sedam, India, 1962-68; lectr. St. Ann's Coll. Edn., Mangalore, India, 1971-74, coord. dept. extension svcs., 1974-78; reader postgrad. dept. studies in edn. Karnatak U., 1978-95, reader, chmn. dept., dean faculty, 1989-94, prof., 1995—, prof., chmn. dept., dean faculty, 1996-98; mem. senate Karnatak U., 1990, 92-94, 96—, mem. syndicate, 1993-94, 98, chmn. bd. studies in edn., 1990, 92-98; mem. bd. studies in edn. Bangalore U., Gulbarga U.; mem. subject panel on edn. Univ. Grants Commn., New Delhi, 1994-96; acad. facilitator Nat. Open Schs. Orgn., New Delhi, 1995—; chapt. author staff devel. higher and distance edn. Aravali Internat., New Delhi, 1997. Author: Samparka Yugadalli Shikshana Tantra Shasthra, 1990, (book and test file) Ramachandrachar's Creativity Response Matrices, 1996; editor: Bhugola Bodhane Mattu Rashtriya Samagrathe, 1975, A Plan of Action for Secondary Schools, 1976; chpt. author: Teacher Education in India: A Resource Book, 1990; contbr. chapts.: Criterion References Measurement; Sarthaka Shikshana ed. Vajrakumar Felictatsan Com. Dharwad, 1998; A Comparative Study of the Impact of Three Academic Staff Colleges on Cololege Teacher Perceptions, Media & Tech for HRD, 1999; contbr. articles to profl. jours. Univ. Grants Commn. rsch. scholar, Dharwad, 1967, 68-71, maj. rsch. grantee, 1989; Fulbright fellow, Indo-Am. fellow Fulbright Found. and Univ. Grants Commn., Pa. State U. and U. Wis., Madison, 1991. Mem. Indian Sci. Congress Assn. (life), All India Assn. Ednl. Tech. (life), Coun. for Teacher Edn. (life). Avocations: drawing, painting, Indian classical music, gardening. E-mail: et vidya@satyam.net.in. Office: Karnatak Univ, Rodda Rd, PG Dept Studies in Edn, Dharwad Karnatak 580001, India

RAMACHANDRAPPA, B.K., agronomy educator; b. Davanagere, India, Oct. 1, 1955; s. Mahadevamma Eshwarappa; m. C.V. Manjula. BSc in Agr., Agrl. Coll., Dharwad, India, 1978, MSc in Agr., 1981; PhD, Agrl. Coll., Bangalore, India, 1991. AAO Dept. Agr., Harihara, India, 1981-82; rsch. asst. U. Agrl. Scis., Dharwad, 1982-83; asst. prof. U. Agrl. Scis., Bangalore, 1983-93, assoc. prof., 1993—; referee Indian Soc. Agronomy, New Delhi, Karnataka Jour. Agrl. Scis., Dharwad. Contbr. over 100 articles to profl. jours. including Mysore Jour. Agrl. Scis. Recipient Crop Rsch. award Gaurav Soc., 1997, gold medal U. Agrl. Scis. Mem. Indian Soc. Oil Seeds Rsch., Indian Soc. Agronomy. Avocations: reading, writing, music, television.

RAMADAN, NABIH M., pharmaceutical companyofficial, educator; b. Beirut, Lebanon, Feb. 3, 1960; came to U.S., 1985; s. Manih Fawzi Ramadan and Nadia Shaar; m. Cynthia Ann Ramadan, Mar. 26, 1988. BS in Biology and Chemistry, Am. U. of Beirut, Lebanon, 1980, MD, 1985. Resident in neurology U. Cin., Ohio, 1985-88; fellow in cerebrovascular disease Henry Ford Hosp., Detroit, 1988-90, dir. Ambulatory Headache Clinic, 1990-96, dir. Cerebrovascular Diseases Lab., 1990-96; dir. Cin. Headache Ctr., 1996-99; assoc. prof. neurology U. Cin., 1996-99; med. dir. Eli Lilly & Co., Indpls., 1999, rsch. advisor, 1999—; adj. prof. neurology Ind. U. Med. Ctr., Indpls. Office: Eli Lilly & Co Lilly Corp Ctr Indianapolis IN 46285-0001

RAMADAN, TAHA YASIN, Iraqi government official; b. Mosul, 1938. Grad., mil. coll. Mem. regional coun. Arab Ba'ath Socialist Party; pres. Office of Arab Affairs, 1969; mem. Revolutionary Command Coun., 1970; pres. Spl. Ct., 1970; min. of industry Govt. of Iraq, 1970-72, min. of economy, 1971; pres. High Coun. of Resistance, 1972; mem. regional command Socialist Arab Ba'ath Party, 1974; min. of labor and housing Govt. of Iraq, 1976-77; mem. nat. command Arab Ba'ath Socialist Party, 1977; dep. prime min. Govt. of Iraq, 1979—; v.p., mem. Revolutionary Command Coun.; comdr. People's Army; v.p. Govt. of Iraq, Baghdad. With Iraqi Army. Mem. Arab Ba'ath Socialist Party. *

RAMAKRISHNA, DEVARAKONDA, English educator, researcher; b. Kothapeta, India, May 3, 1940; s. Devarakonda Satyanarayana Murty and Devarakonda Papayamma; m. Devarakonda Varalakshmi, May 22, 1964; 1 child, Satya Srinivas Devarakonda. BA, Andhra U., Waltair, India, 1960; MA, Banaras Hindu U., Varanasi, India, 1962; PhD, Kakatiya U., Warangal, India, 1980. Lectr. in English Banaras Hindu U., Varanasi, 1962-64, A.N.R. Coll., Gudivada, India, 1968-71; assoc. editor Am. Studies Rsch. Ctr., Hyderabad, India, 1971-75; from lectr. to reader in English Kakatiya U., Warangal, 1975-95, prof. English, 1995—; head dept. English Kakatiya U., 1995-97, chmn. bd. studies, 1997—. Author: Close Encounters with the Muse: Essays and Letters on Indian Writing in English, 1986, Explorations in Poe, 1992, The Craft of Poe's Tales, 1998; editor: Indian English Prose: An Anthology, 1980, The American Classics Revisited: Recent Studies of American Literature, 1985, Perspectives on Poe, 1996, Kakatiya Jour. English Studies, 1995-97; assoc. editor Indian Jour. Am. Studies, Hyderabad, 1971-75. Recipient Gold medal Seminar Rsch. Ctr., 1997; Fulbright fellow USIS, USEFI, 1992; Publ. grantee Govt. Andhra Pradesh, 1986. Mem. The Edgar Allan Poe Soc. (hon. life), Am. Studies Rsch. Ctr. (life, postdoctoral rsch. fellow 1989, 91, 95), PEN All-India Ctr. (life). Avocations: photography, creative writing. Home: 2-4-1623 Ashoka Colony, Hanamkonda 506001 Andhra Pradesh, India Office: Dept English, Kakatiya U, Warangal 506009, India

RAMAKRISHNA, SEERAM, engineering educator; b. Cherukupalli, Guntur, India, June 15, 1964; arrived in Singapore, 1999; s. Ranarai abd Sarojini Devi Seeram; m. Susithra Manickam, Nov. 2, 1999. BMetE, Andhra U., Visakhapatnam, India, 1985; MTech in Aircraft Engring., Indian Inst. Tech., Madras, 1988; PhD in Materials Sci., Cambridge (Eng.) U., 1992. Sci. officer Hindustan Aeronautics Ltd., Bangalore, India, 1985-89; vis. lectr. Kyoto (Japan) Inst. Tech., 1993-96; sr. lectr. dept. mech. and prodn. engring. Nat. U. Singapore, 1997-98, assoc. prof., 1999—; asst. dir. Ctr. Biomed. Materials and Tech., Singapore, 1998—; cons. ISO/TC 150 std. com. Productivity and Stds. Bd., Singapore, 1998—. Contbr. articles to sci. jours.; mem. editl. bd. Jour. Sci. and Engring. Compostite Materials, 1998—; guest editor Composites Sci. and Tech., 1999; inventor in field. Recipient Young Investigator award Japan Soc. Artificial Organs, 1997, Best Paper award ASME Asia, 1997; Nehru fellow Govt. of India, 1989, fellow Cambridge Commonwealth Soc., 1992, Lee Kuan Yew fellow Govt. of Singapore, 1996. Hindu. Avocations: travel, movies, philosophy. Fax: +65-779-1459. E-mail: mpesr@nus.edu.sg. Office: NUS Dept Mech & Prodn Eng, 10 Kent Ridge, Singapore 119260, Singapore

RAMAKRISHNAN, ANGARAI GANESAN, electrical engineer, educator; b. Bangalore, Karnataka, India, Feb. 14, 1958; s. K.S. and Radha Ganesan; m. Gowri Kothandaraman, June 27, 1988; children: Vyass, Mohan Shiva, Dhanwanthari. B in Engring. with hons., U. Madras, India, 1980; M in Tech., Indian Inst. Tech., Madras, 1982; PhD, Indian Inst. Tech., 1989. Sr. project officer Indian Inst. Tech., Madras, 1985-88; rschr. BPL India Ltd., Bangalore, 1989-90; posdoc. fellow Fetzer Inst., Kalamazoo, Mich., 1990-91; rsch. assoc. Indian Inst. Sci., Bangalore, 1992-94, asst. prof., 1994-2000, assoc. prof., 2000—; cons. Vivekananda Yoga Rsch. Found., Bangalore, 1995—, Inst. Aerospace Medicine, Bangalore, 1997—; acad. adv. com. Clin. Engring. Ctr., Bangalore, 1996—; bd. advisors for paramedical courses All India Coun. for Tech. Edn., 1998—. Contbr. articles to profl. jours. Vol. Voluntary Income Tax Agy., Kalamazoo, 1991. Recipient Sir Andrew Watt Kay Young Rschr. award RCPS, 1992, Young Scientist award Govt. India, 1994. Fellow Inst. Engrs. India, Instn. Electronics and Telecom. Engrs.; mem. IEEE (sr., Engring. Medicine Biology Soc. club advisor 1995—, Signal Processing Soc.), Biomed Engring. Soc. India (editor 1997—, pres. Bangalore chpt. 2000), Indian Assn. Biomed. Scientists (Thangam Vasudevan award 1985), Internat. Forum for Info. Tech. in Tamil (gen. coun.). Hindu. Avocations: philosophy, singing, music, yoga, relaxation therapy. Home: Hanumantha Nagar, 692 5th Main 6th Cross, Bangalore 560019, India Office: Dept Elec Engring, Indian Inst Sci, Bangalore 560012, India

RAMAKRISHNAN, LAKSHMY, biochemist; b. Trichur, Kerala, India, Nov. 9, 1964; d. Ramakrishnan Narayan and Lakshmy Subramanyan. Postgrad., Osmania U., Hyderabad, India, 1987; doctorate, Nat. Inst. Nutrition, Hyderabad, 1994. Rsch. assoc. All India & Inst. Med. Scis., New Delhi, 1995-98, asst. prof., 1998—; in charge Clin. Biochemistry Lab., CNC, 1998—; mem. HRIDAY (NGO), India, 1999; co-investigator ICMR Project on Risk Factors for Acute MI. Contbr. papers to profl. jours. Jr. and sr. rsch. fellow CSIR, Govt. India, 1987, rsch. associateship, 1995; Nat. Merit scholar Govt. India, 1985. Mem. Endocrine Soc. Office: All India Inst Med Scis, Ansarj Nagar, New Delhi 110029, India

RAMAKRISHNAN, VENKATASWAMY, civil engineer, educator; b. Coimbatore, India, Feb. 27, 1929; came to U.S., 1969, naturalized, 1981; s. Venkataswamy and Kondammal (Krishnaswamy) R.; m. Vijayalakshmi Unnava, Nov. 7, 1962; children: Aravind, Anand. B.Engring., U. Madras, 1952, D.S.S., 1953; D.I.C. in Hydropower and Concrete Tech, Imperial Coll., London, 1957; Ph.D., Univ. Coll., U. London, 1960. From lectr. to prof. civil engring., head dept. P.S.G. Coll. Tech., U. Madras, 1952-69; vis. prof. S.D. Sch. Mines and Tech., Rapid City, 1969-70, prof. civil engring., 1970—, dir. concrete tech. research, 1970-71, head grad. div. structural mechanic and concrete tech., 1971—, program coordinator materials engring. and sci. Ph.D. program, 1985-86, disting. prof., 1996—; emeritus mem. TRB. Author: Ultimate Strength Design for Structural Concrete, 1969; also over 200 articles. Recipient Outstanding Prof. award S.D. Sch. Mines and Tech., 1980, 1st Rsch. award, 1994; Colombo Plan fellow, 1955-60. Mem. Internat. Assn. Bridge and Structural Engring., ASCE (vice chmn. constrn. div. publs. com. 1974), Am. Concrete Inst. (chmn. subcom. gen. considerations for founds., chmn. com. 214 on evaluation of strength test results, sec.-treas. Dakota chpt. 1974-79, v.p. 1980, pres. 1981, Robert Philio Rsch. Excellence award), Instn. Hwy. Engrs., Transp. Rsch. Bd. (chmn. com. on admixtures and curing, chmn. com. on mech. properties concrete), Am. Soc. Engring. Edn., NSPE, Internat. Coun. Gap-Graded Concrete Rsch. and Application, Sigma Xi. Address: 1809 Sheridan Lake Rd Rapid City SD 57702-4219

RAMALINGAM, GANESAN, computer scientist; b. Srivilliputhur, India, Feb. 6, 1966; came to the U.S., 1987; s. R. and Kalavathi Ganesan; m. Rajalakshmi Ramalingam, Nov. 15, 1992; children: Ragini, Ramya. MS in Computer Sci., U. Wis., 1989, MA in Math., 1991, PhD in Computer Sci., 1993. Tchg. asst. U. Wis., Madison, 1987-88, rsch. asst., 1989-93; postdoctoral fellow IBM Rsch. Divsn., Yorktown Heights, N.Y., 1993-95; rsch. staff mem. IBM Rsch. Divsn., Yorktown Heights, 1995—. Author: Bounded Incremental Computation, 1996; contbr. articles to profl. jours. Achievements include patent for object model for Java. E-mail: rama@watson.ibm.com.

RAMALINGAM, SUTHAMALLI K., chemistry educator and researcher; b. Tirunelveli, Tamil Nadu, India, Oct. 5, 1935; s. Krishnaganapathy Vadhyar and Gomathy R.; m. L. Vijayam, Mar. 16, 1977; children: S.R. Anand, B.E., S.R. Arthy. BE, St. Joseph's Coll. U. Madras, Trichy, India, 1955; MSc, Banaras Hindu U., Banaras, India, 1958; PhD, Indian Inst. Sci., Bangalore, India, 1967. Lectr. Thiagarajar Engring. Coll., Madurai, India, 1958-62, 68, Sch. of Chemistry, Madurai-Kamaraj U., India, 1969-84; reader Sch. of Chemistry, Madurai-Kamayaj U., 1984-94, sr. prof., 1994-96, retired, 1996. Contbr. numerous articles to internat. profl. jours.. Recipient Recognition cert. Chem. Abstracts Svc. Am. Chem. Soc., 1974 for an outstanding contrbn. to the advancement of chem. sci. through chem. abstracts. Fellow Indian Chem. Soc.; mem. Electrochem. Soc. India. Home: Lake View Gardens, 40 22 Meenakshi St, Tml Nadu Madurai KK Nagar 625020, India Office: Madurai Kamaraj U, Sch Chemistry, Tml Nadu Madurai 625021, India

RAMAMOORTHY, NARAYANI, biochemist, educator; b. Madras, Tamilnadu, India, May 5, 1966; d. Ramamoorthy and Indhira. BSc, U. Madras, 1987, MSc, 1989, PhD, 1994. Jr. rsch. fellow Ctrl. Leather Rsch. Inst., Madras, 1989-91, sr. rsch. fellow, 1991-94, rsch. assoc., 1995-96; asst. prof. Vinayaka Mission's Med. Coll., Salem, India, 1996-97; reader and head dept. biochemistry Paladugu Nagia Chowdry PNC and Kotha Raguramiah Coll. of PG Courses, Narasa Raopet, India, 1997-98; prof., head biochemistry dept. Sri Ramasami Meml. Dental Coll. and Hosp., Madras, India, 1998—. Contbr. articles to profl. jours.; inventor in field. Jr. rsch. fellow Coun. of Sci. and Indsl. Rsch., New Delhi, 1989, Sr. Rsch. fellow Coun. of Sci. and Indsl. Rsch., New Delhi, 1991, Rsch. assoc. Coun. of Sci. and Indsl. Rsch., New Delhi, 1995. Mem. Soc. for Biomaterials and Artificial Organs (life), N.Y. Acad. Scis. Avocations: classical dance, classical music, writing. Home: West Mambalam, 39/16 Thambia Reddy St, Madras 6000 33, India

RAMAN, NATARAJAN, chemist, educator; b. Meenachiapuram, India, Aug. 8, 1964; s. Nata Rajan Ramasamy and Thangathai Natarajan. BSc in Chemistry, NMSVN Coll., Madurai, Tamilnadu, India, 1985; MSc in Chemistry, Madurai Kamaraj U., 1987, PhD in Inorganic Chemistry, 1992. Rsch. scholar Madurai Kamaraj U., 1988-91; lectr. VHNSN Coll., Virudhunagar, India, 1991—; N.S.S. advisor VHNSN Coll., 1992-95, hostel warden, 1991—, mem. coll. mag. com., 1994-95, program officer 2000. Contbr. articles to profl. jours. Rsch. grantee Univ. Grants Commn., 1994, Tamilnadu Coun. for Sci. and Tech., 1994, young scientist fellowship, 1998; Madurai Kamaraj U. rsch. fellow, 1988. Fellow Indian Chem. Soc., Asian Jour. Chemistry, Indian Coun. Chemists. Avocations: football, tennis, kabaddi, softball, chess. Home: Meenachiapuram Post, Muhavoor Rajapalayam Taluk, Kamarajar Tamil Nadu 626111, India Office: VHNSN Coll, Dept Chemistry, Virudunagar 626001, India

RAMAN, POONDY GOPALRATNAM, medical educator; b. Madras, Tamil Nadu, India, Sept. 12, 1940; s. Poondy Gopalratnam and Gopalratnam Rajalkkshmi; m. Raman Ansuya Saksena, June 3, 1968; children: Manjula, Rajeev. MBBS, Indore U., 1962, MD in Medicine, 1965. Resident med. officer M-Y Hosp., Indore, 1962-65, J.A. Group of Hosp., Gwalor, 1966-67; lectr. medicine S.S. Med. Coll., Rewa, 1962-72, 75-78; Joslin fellow Joslin Clinic, New Eng. Deaconess Hosp., Boston, 1972-74; fellow Lakey Clinic, Boston, 1974-75; lectr. medicine Mahatma Gandhi Meml. Med. Coll., Indore, 1978-82, reader medicine, 1982-91, prof. medicine, 1991-97, head dept. medicine, prof. Med. Coll., 1997—. Author: (books) Short Cases in Medicine, Diabetes Mellitus; contbr. articles to profl. jours. Fellow All India Inst. Diabetes, Coll. Physicians India; mem. Indian Assn. Gastroenterology (life), Geriatric Assn. India (life), Assn. Physicians India (life), Indian Med. Assn. (life). Hindu. Avocations: reading, watching TV. Home: 72 Dhar Kuth, Opp Robert's Nursinghome, Indore 452001, India Office: Mahatma Gandhi Med Coll, Dept Medicine, Indore 452007, India

RAMAN, VENKATA, communications company executive; b. Bangalore, India, Nov. 26, 1943; s. Rao Shama and Venkatalakshmi; m. S. K. Padma, Dec. 5, 1972; children: Kala, Smitha. BS, Nat. Coll. Bangalore, 1963; BS in Engring., Indian Inst. Sci., 1967; BMS, Bhavatidasan U. Sr. engr. Bharat Electronics Ltd., Bangalore, 1973-78, dep. mgr., 1978-85, mgr., 1985-93, dep. gen. mgr., 1993—; lectr. St. Joseph's Coll., Bangalore, 1993—. Avocations: music, the internet, painting. E-mail: bsuraman@usnl.com. Home: 128 3d Cross Jayanauar 2d B, Bangalore India

RAMANANTSOA, COLOMBE, magistrate; b. Antananarivo, Madagascar, Sept. 17, 1941; s. Paul Razafinjato and Albertine Razafindrafara; m. Andriantsoa Rasamoelina, Dec. 24, 1966; children: Riana Samson, Sylvie Lalatiana, Roland, Mamy David. Baccalaureat de l'Enseignement, Lycee Jules Ferry, Antananarivo, 1961; Licence Droit Prive, U. Madagascar, Antananarivo, 1965. Juge Tribunal Instance, Toamasina, Madagascar, 1965-66, Antananarivo, 1966-67; pres. Tribunal Instance, Antsiranana, Madagascar, 1967-70; v.p. Tribunal Instance, Fianarantsoa, Madagascar, 1970-72, Antananarivo, 1972-73; pres. de chambre Cour d'Appel, Antananarivo, 1973-85; avocat gen. Cour Supreme, Antananarivo, 1985—, procureur gen., 1992—. Contbr. articles to profl. jours. Vice pres. Fedn. Nat. des Assns. four le Sauvegarde et la Protection de l'Enfance et de la Jeunesse, Antananarivo, 1989—. Named Officier de l'Ordre Nat. Mologacy, State Chancellor's Office, 1994. Mem. Syndicat des Magistrats de Madagascar. Roman Catholic. Avocations: reading, aerobic. Home: VT-74H Andohanimandroseza, Antananarivo 101, Madagascar Office: Cour Suprême, Palais de Justice, Antananarivo 101, Madagascar

RAMANATHAN, KUMARAN, biochemist, researcher; b. Mumbai, Maharashtr, India, Mar. 2, 1967; s. Radhakrishnan and Bala Ramanathan; m. Alamelu Kumaran Venkatakrishnan, Aug. 26, 1994; 1 child, Ramakrishnan Kumaran. BSc, Bombay U., 1987; MSc, Pune U., 1989; PhD, Indian Inst. Tech., Delhi, 1996. Jr. rsch. fellow Nat. Phys. Lab., New Delhi, 1990-92, sr. rsch. fellow, 1992-94, rsch. assoc., 1994-96; postdoctoral fellow Hebrew U., Jerusalem, 1995-96; guest rschr. in biochemistry Lund (Sweden) U., 1996-2000; assoc. Nat. Rsch. Coun. U.S. Environmental Protection Agency, Las Vegas, Nev., 2000—; cons. ABT AB, Lund, 1996—, Prolight AB, Lund, 1998—, TMS Chem AB, Lund, 1997—; trainee Cancer Rsch. Inst., Tata Meml. Hosp., Bombay, 1987-88. Patentee in field; author reviews. Vol. in health svc. Indian Coun. Med. Rsch., Bombay, 1982-84. Dept. of Biotech., Govt. of India studentship, 1987-89; Coun. of Sci. and Indsl. rsch./Govt. of India fellow, 1990-94, assoc., 1994-95; Hebrew U. postdoctoral fellow, 1995-96, Swedish Inst. fellow, 1996-97. Mem. AAAS, Am. Chem. Soc., Coun. of Sci. and Indsl. Rsch. Hindu. Avocations: reading, travel, inventing. Home: Kämnärsvägen 9K102, S-22646 Lund Sweden Office: USEPA 944 E Harmon Ave Las Vegas NV 89119-6748

RAMANAUSKAS, RIMGAUDAS JUOZAPAS, chemistry laboratory administrator; b. Kaunas, Lithuania, Dec. 3, 1934; s. Juozas and Elena (Januschkevichiute) R.; m. Valentina Ramanauskiene; 1 child, Regina. Engr., Dairy Inst., Vologda, Russia, 1959; postgrad., Inst. Refrigeration, St. Petersburg, Russia, 1961-64; PhD, Dairy Inst., Vologda, Russia, 1967; DSc, Acad. Biotech., Moscow, 1993. Cert. engr. Scientist Food Inst., Kaunas, 1964—, head phys. chemistry lab., 1964—. Author: Relative Humidity in Milk Products, 1969, (with D. Peseckas) New Varieties of Semi-hard Rennet Cheeses, 1974, (with S. Urbiene) Ways to Improve Sour Milk Product Consistency, 1978, (with others) Storage of Rennet Cheese in Industrial Refrigerators, 1978, (with others) Cheese Technology, 1984, (with M. Paserpskiene) Use of Ultrafiltration in Cheese Manufacturing, 1989, (with I. Schalomskiene) Milk Preparing for Cheese Production, 1989, (with others) Milk Product Technology, 1994; patentee in field. Named Internat. Man of Yr., Cambridge, 1997, Man of Yr. A.B.I., 1998; recipient Gold Star award, Cambridge, 1997. Mem. Internat. Acad. Engring., Internat. Acad. Refrigeration, N.Y. Acad. Sci. Office: Food Inst, Taikos 92, Kaunas Lithuania

RAMANAUSKAS, ROMAS, bank executive; b. Vilnius, Lithuania, July 30, 1961; s. Vincas and Grazina (Karaliute) R.; m. Loreta Dzimidaite, Oct. 15, 1982; 1 child, Vilius. MA, Vilnius U., 1984. Dept. head Electrographical Rsch. Inst., Vilnius, 1988-90; dept. head Lithuanian Innovation Bank, Vilnius, 1991-92, v.p., 1992-93; bd. dirs. Lithuanian Innovation Bank, 1994—; dep. gen. mgr. Devin Bank A.S., Bratislava City, Slovakia, 1997—; dir. corp. banking divsn. Hansa Bank Lithuania, Vilnius, 1998; head pvt. banking Nord/LB, Vilnius, 1999—; cons. Banking Inst., Vilnius, 1995-96. Mem. Economists' Club Vilnius. Avocations: table tennis, bowling. Office: Nord/LB, Vilniaus Str 28, 2600 Vilnius Lithuania

RAMANI, K. V., computer and information systems educator; b. Cochin, Kerala, India, May 3, 1949; s. K.P. and Balamani Viswanathan; married; 2 sons. BSc with honors, Kerala U., 1969, MSc, 1971; MS, Cornell U., 1975, PhD, 1977. Prof. Indian Inst. Mgmt., Ahmedabad, India, 1977—; vis. faculty Fla. Internat. U., 1984-86, Nat. U. Singapore, 1991-92, 95-96, Johnson Grad. Sch. Mgmt. Cornell U., 1999; vis. scholar U. Tex., Austin, 1989, Helsinki (Finland) Sch. Econs., 1989, U. Western Sydney, Australia, 1996; presenter seminars, workshops in field. Co-Author: Computers and Information Management: A Primer for Practicing Managers, 1989, 2d edition 1991, Regional Energy Demand Model and Analysis, 1991; contbr. numerous articles to profl. jours. Avocations: sports. E-mail: ramani@iimahd.ernet.in. Office: Indian Inst Mgmt, Ahmedabad 380015, India

RAMAPPA, PUTTARAMAPPA GOWDA, chemistry educator, researcher; b. Arabagatte, India, Sept. 13, 1938; s. Puttaramappa Gowda Mahadevappa and Mallamma Mahadevappa; m. Saroja Ramappa, Nov. 10, 1967; children: Deepak, Preeti. BSc with honors, Ctrl. Coll. Bangalore, India, 1960; MSc, U. Mysore, India, 1961, PhD in Chemistry, 1976. Lectr. U. Mysore, 1961-64, 68-83; reader, vice prin. Sree Siddaganga Coll. Sci., Tumkur, India, 1965-68; reader U. Mysore, 1983-86, prof. chemistry, 1987—; dean faculty sci. and tech., U. Mysore, 1993-95, head dept. chemistry, 1993-95, head dept. computer sci., 1995-96, senate mem., 1993-95, coord. sugar tech., 1993—, mem. acad. coun., 1987—. Co-author: Analytical Chemistry, vols. 1 and 2, 1976; editor Vijnana Karnataka Sci. Jour., 1981-83; mem. editl. bd. Asian Jour. Chemistry, Jour. Mysore U.; contbr. over 100 articles to internat. profl. jours. Rsch. grantee, Mysore. Fellow Indian Chem. Soc. (life), Indian Coun. Chemists (life; pres. inorganic chemistry sect. 1996); mem. Karnataka Assn. Advancement of Sci. (life). Hindu. Avocations: reading science and technology. Home: 107, II Main, IV stage,, T.K. Layout, Mysore 570 009, India Office: U Mysore Dept Chemistry, Manasagangotri, Mysore 570 006, India

RAMARATNAM, SRIDHARAN, neurologist; b. Madurantakam, India; s. Srinivasan and Janakavalli Ramaratnam; m. Kalpana Raghavan, May 20, 1980; 1 child, Kavita. B Medicine B Surgery, Jawaharlal Inst., Pondicherry, India, 1976, MD in Internal Medicine, 1979; DM in Neurology, Inst. Med. Edn. and Rsch., Chandigarh, India, 1981. Cert. Tamilnadu Med. Coun., India. Lectr. in neurology Nat. Inst. Mental Health and Neuroscis., Bangalore, India, 1982-83, Arab Med. U., Benghazi, Libya, 1983-85; cons. neurologist Apollo Hosp., Madras, India, 1986—; hon. assoc. prof. neurology Sri Ramachandra Med. Coll. and Rsch. Inst., Madras, 1999—; hon. rsch. fellow U. Liverpool, Eng., 1999—; dir. Madras Neurodiagnostic and Rsch. Ctr., 1991—. Contbr. articles to profl. jours., chpts. to textbooks. Fellow Am. Acad. Neurology (corr.), Indian Acad. neurology; mem. Nat. Acad. Med. Scis., Neurology Soc. India, Indian Acad. Pediats. Avocations: gardening, photography, computers. Fax: 91-44-8234429. E-mail: ahel@vsnl.com. Home: T Nagar, 57 Thirumalai Pillai Rd, Madras Tamilnadu 600017, India Office: Apollo Hosp, Greams Ln, Madras Tamilnadu 600006, India

RAMASAMY, RAMACHANDRAN, petrologist, researcher; b. Muthulapuram, Tuticorin, India, June 8, 1942; s. Pulamadan Ramachandran and Muthaiah Karuppayammal; m. Gurusamy Saroja, Dec. 6, 1976; children: Kalaiselvi, Pulamadapandiyan. BS in Geology, U. Madras (India), Karaikudi, 1963; MS in Geology, U. Madras (India), Chennai, 1967, PhD, 1974; postdoct., Moscow State U., 1977-80. Sci. tchr. Kalaimagal H.S., Vaiyampatti, India, 1964-65; PhD rsch. fellow Presidency Coll. U. Madras, Chennai, India, 1967-73; petrologist Tamilnadu State Dept. Geology and Mining, Chennai, 1974—; postdoct. fellow Moscow State U., 1977-80; vis. faculty Coll. Engring. Anna U., Chennai, India, 1987-89, co-convener seminar indsl. minerals in nat. economy, 1988, course dir., work book editor, 1989, PhD external guide, 1989—; mem. Pan Indian sci. terminology geology rep. Tamil lang. Ministry Human Resource Devel., New Delhi, 1984—; Lemonosov Meml. lectr. Moscow State U., 1979; chairperson WB03 30th Internat. Geol. Congress, Beijing, 1996. Author: Kanimathettam, 1976; contbr. geology sect. Tamil Sci. Ency., 1986—, over 50 articles to profl. jours. Named Best Field Worker Geologists' Assn. Alagappa Coll., 1962-63, 63. Mem. Indian Geol. Congress U. Roorkee (India, life), Tamilnadu Sci. Congress. Avocations: writing articles in Tamil language. Office: Tamilnadu State Dept Geol, Industrial Estate Guindy, 600032 Chennai India

RAMASESHAN, BALASUBRAMANIAN, marketing educator; arrived in Australia, 1984; PhD, Indian Inst. Tech., Bombay, 1984. Prof. mktg., head Sch. Mktg. Curtin U., Perth, Australia, 1995—. Contbr. articles to profl. jours. Office: Curtin U Tech, Sch Mktg, Perth Australia

RAMASESHAN, SIVARAJ, physicist, researcher, editor, retired educator; b. Calcutta, India, Oct. 10, 1923; s. Sivaramakrishnan and Sitalaxmi; m. Kausalya Sankaran; children: Arati Raman, Sita Sunder, Tara Ramaseshan. MSc, Nagpur (India) U., 1943; AIISc, Indian Inst. Sci., Bangalore, 1949, DSc, 1950. Mem. faculty Indian Inst. Sci., 1945-62, dir., 1981-84; head dept. physics Indian Inst. Tech., Madras, 1962-66; dir. grade scientist Nat. Aerospace Labs., Bangalore, 1966-79; mem. faculty Raman Rsch. Inst., Bangalore, disting. prof. emeritus, 1990—. Author: Crystal Optics Handbuch der Physik, 1961, Pictorial Biography of C.V. Raman, 1988; editor Current Sci., 1989—, Collected Works of C.V. Raman, 6 vols., 1988, Collected Works of Dorothy Crowfoot Hodgkin, 3 vols., 1994; contbr. over 200 articles to profl. jours. Recipient Bhatnagar award Coun. Sci. and Indsl. Rsch., 1966, Arya Bhatta medal Indian Nat. Acad. Sci., MRSI medal, 1990, C.V. Raman award, 1988, C.V. Raman Centennial medal Indian Sci. Congress, 1994, Platinum Jubilee medal Indian Inst. Sci., Padma Bhushan award Govt. of India, others; Nehru fellow. Fellow Indian Acad. Scis. (Bangalore, pres. 1983-85), Indian Nat. Sci. Acad. (New Delhi), Nat. Acad. Scis. (Allahabad chpt.), Collegium Ramazzini (Bologna, Italy), European Acad. Sci. and Arts, Aeronautical Soc. India; mem. Internat. Union Crystallography (v.p. 1981-84). Avocations: science, writing. Home: 7/10 Palace Cross Rd, Bangalore 560 020, India Office: Raman Rsch Inst, CV Raman Ave, Bangalore 560 080, India

RAMA SUBBU, RAJA GOPALAN ARIYUR, surgeon, consultant; b. Sri Rangam, Tamilnadu, India, Aug. 18, 1954; s. Ramaswamy Ariyur Raja Gopalan and Ramaswamy Angarai Jayalaksami; m. Rama Subbu Ariyur Priya, May 19, 1982; children: Ramani Meera, Neeraja. MBBS, Thanjavur Med. Coll., India, 1979, MS in Gen. Surgery, 1986. Cons. surgeon Leonard Hosp., Batlagundu, India, 1986-87, Tatatea Hosp., Munnar, India, 1987-89, Maria Hosp., Kerala, India, 1989-92, King Fahad Hofuf Hosp., Saudi Arabia, 1992-97; sr. cons. surgeon Ch. South India Hosp., Kerala, 1997-98, Carmel Hosp., Nagerkovil, India, 1998—; med. supt. Carmel Hosp., Manalikarai, India, 1998—. Grantee Internat. Fedn. Surg. Colls., 1999, Royal Coll. Surgeons Edinburgh, 1999. Fellow Internat. Coll. Surgeons, Internat. Soc. Surgery; mem. Internat. Assn. Surgery Trauma & Surg. Intensive Cases, Internat. Assn. Endocrine Surgeons. Hindu. Avocations: stamp collecting, coin collecting, music, cricket, travelling. Home: 104, Christopher Nagercoil, Kanyakumari 629003, India Office: Carmel Hosp, Manlikarai, Kanyakumari 629164, India

RAMASWAMI, PANCHAPAKESAN, educational administrator; b. Tiruchi, Tamilnadu, India, Aug. 20, 1936; s. N. Ramaswami Ayyar and Alamelu Seethalaksmi Ammal; m. Vasantha Panchapakesan; children: Ramani, Kannan. BS, Alagappa Coll., Karaikudi, India; LLB, U. Madras, India. Mgmt. trainee Orissa Cement Ltd., Rajgangpur, India, 1959-61; quarry mgr. Dalmia Cement Ltd., Dalmiapuram, India, 1961-65, exec., 1965-67; mng. trustee, sec. Padmabhushan Sri N. Ramaswami Ayyar Ednl. Complex, Tiruchy, India, 1967—; educator Kamokoti Vidyalaya, Savitri Vidyasala, Hindu Girls H.S., Tiruchirapalli; cons. Seethalakshmi Ramaswami Coll., Padmabhushan Sri N. Ramaswami Ayyar Meml. Poly., Srivivasa Computer Ctr., Tiruchirapalli. Pub. Lalitha Sahasranamam. Mem. renovation com. Sri Akilandeswari Temple. Recipient Gnana Viridhi award Madurai Adheenam, 1996, Arappani Semmal award Sri Kanchi Kamakoti Peetam, 1996, Mahalier Kalvipenum award Gupalar Kasu Ninaivu Iliakkia Kuzhu, 1996. Mem. Indian Red Cross Soc., Tiruchirapalli Productivity Coun. Avocation: reading. Home: 77 Butterworth Rd, Tiruchirapalli 620 002, India Office: Padmabhushan Sri Ramaswami, Sankaran Pillai Rd No 349, Tiruchirapalli 620 002, India

RAMASWAMY, MOHAN KRISCHKE, cultural consultant; b. Vienna, Austria, July 25, 1953; s. Kerangudi Venkatarama Ramaswamy and Gudrun Krischke Quatember; m. Annette Kerner; children: Mohini, Timon, Nora, Paul, Marian, Ilja, Anita. PhD, U. Goettingen, Germany, 1977. Lectr. U. Goettingen, 1976-86; information officer Consulate Gen. of India, Hamburg, 1977-78; film editor Inst F Scientific Film, Goettingen, 1979-81; pvt. practice film producer, editor, 1984-89; social and cultural cons., 1990; project cons., 1999; head spkr. W.-E. Barkoff Inst., 1993—. Mem. World Bus. Acad. Home and Office: Duestere-Eichen-Weg 52, D-37073 Goettingen Germany

RAMAY, BILAL AHMAD, pharmaceutical company executive, consultant; b. Lamapind, Pakistan, Oct. 6, 1949; s. Mohammad Abdullah and Rahmat (Bibi) R.; m. Naseem Bilal; children: Awais, Ahmad. BSc, U. Sindh, Pakistan, 1970, MSc in Chemistry, 1972; PhD, Ctr. for Excellence in Analytical Chemistry, Pakistan, 1980. Rsch. fellow Univ. Grants Commn., Pakistan, 1975-80; postdoctoral rsch. fellow Ctr. Excellence in Analytical Chemistry, 1980-81; edn. officer Govt. of Nigeria, 1981-82, mem. continuous assessment com., 1981-89, sr. lectr., head chemistry dept., 1982-89; gen. mgr., co. sec. Opal Pharms. (Pvt.) Ltd., Karachi, Pakistan, 1989—; chmn. curriculum com., mem. acad. bd. Anambra Poly. Nigeria, 1982-84; external examiner for theses and projects evaluaton in univs., govt. agys. in Pakistan and fgn. countries, 1982—; mem. pharmacopea experts com. Govt. of Pakistan, 1997—; mem. bd. studies pharm. chemistry U. Karachi, Pakistan, 1999—; numerous presentations at seminars, confs., workshops for WHO, Drug Info. Agy., Ministry Health, Ministry Edn., govts. of Pakistan and Nigeria; organizer numerous seminars and workshops, Pakistan and fgn. countries. Rsch. grantee Univ. Grants Commn., 1975-80. Fellow Inst. Chartered Mgrs., Inst. Mktg. Mgmt., Pakistan Acad. Pharm. Scis.; mem. Royal Soc. Chemistry (registered analytical chemist, mgmt. and mktg. group 1994—, hon. rep. mgmt. group 1997), Chem. Soc. Pakistan (mem. exec. coun. 1999—), Pakistan Assn. Scientists and Sci. Profession, Joint Pharm. Analysis Group (U.K), Pharm. Profls. Club, Pakistan Pharm. Mfrs. Assn. (mem. environ. com. 1999—). Home: R33 Paradise Homes Sect 13A, Scheme 33, Gulzar-E-Hijri Karachi 75330, Pakistan Office: Opal Labs (Pvt) Ltd, LC-41 LITE Landhi, Karachi 75160, Pakistan

RAMAYAH, VANGAT, advocate, solicitor; b. Singapore, June 13, 1949; s. Chengama Naidu R. and Sivagami Sivasamy; m. Renuga Devi, Feb. 18, 1989. LLB with honors, U. London, 1979; Bar Finals, Inns of Ct. Sch. of Law, 1980; LLM, U. London, 1981; MA, City of London Coll., 1981. Barrister at law, Lincoln's Inn. Magistrate, coroner Singapore, 1983-85; ptnr. Wee Ramayah & Ptnrs., Singapore, 1985—; judge adv. Singapore Armed Forces, 1992-97; notary pub., Singapore, 1997. Mem. Children Aid Soc. (exec.), Zetland in the East (past master). Avocations: astronomy, trekking. Office: UIC Bldg, 5 Shenton Way # 23-01, Singapore 086608, Singapore

RAMAZANOV, RAMIL, neurosurgeon; b. Ufa, Bashkiria, Russia, June 22, 1952; arrived in Portugal, 1996; s. Khaidar Yusupovich and Anuza Mansurovna (Assadulina) R.; m. Talia Gaptoulovna Nureyeva, June 25, 1980; children: Alia, Adelia. Art Degree, Sch. Art, Ufa, 1967; MD, Superior Med. Inst., Ufa, 1975; PhD in Medicine, Burdenko Neurosurg. Inst., Moscow, 1985; Degree in Med. Engring., Bauman Tech. U., Moscow, 1988. Sr. resident surgeon, neurosurgeon Ctrl. Hosp., Ufa, 1975-78, Nat. Ctrl. Inst. for Advanced Med. Tng., Moscow, 1978-80; neurosurgeon, cons. Botquin Hosp., Moscow, 1980-81; neurosurgeon, rschr. Nat. Ctrl. Inst. for Advanced Med. Tng., Moscow, 1981-88; dir. neurosurgery dept., neurosurgeon Ctrl. Hosp., Maputo, Mozambique, 1988-96; cons. Pvt. Clinics, Lisbon, Portugal, 1996—. Contbr. articles to profl. jours. Founder, pres. Students for Health Orgn., Superior Med. Inst., Ufa, 1972-75; adviser New Med. Techniques, Ministry Health USSR, 1985-88; responsible staff Ultrasonic Surgery Devels., Ministry Health, 1985-88. Recipient Diplom, 3 medals All-Union Exhibn. Nat. Econ. Achievements, USSR, 1982-85. Mem. Internat. Soc. for Neurosurg. Instrument Inventors, Acoustics in Medicine, Ordem dos

Medicos. Avocations: painting, photography, antiques. Home: Praça Junqueiro No 5 Dto, 2775-597 Carcavelos Portugal

RAMBABU, KARUMUDI, communications company executive; b. Ongole, India, Sept. 5, 1972; parents Venkateswarlu and Subbamma Karumudi. B of Tech., Nagarjuna U., Guntur, India, 1994; M of Tech., Banaras Hindu U., Varanasi, India, 1996. Cert. in engring. Mem. rsch. staff Cen. Rsch. Lab. Bharat Electronics, Bangalore, India, 1996—. Contbr. articles and papers to profl. jours.; patentee in field. Avocations: playing cricket and badminton. Home: Gudimella Padu, 523262 Ongole India Office: Bharat Electronics, Cen Rsch Lab Jalahalli, 560013 Bangalore India

RAMBAUX, CLAUDE HENRI, Latin educator, researcher; b. St. Quentin, Picardie, France, Sept. 6, 1937; s. Henri and Hélène (Jucker) R.; m. Françoise Martin, July 28, 1979; children: Pascal, Béatrice,. Agrégation in Classic Letters, U. Paris, 1964, D of State, 1976. Asst. prof. U. Montpellier, France, 1966-67, U. Paris, 1967-73, assoc. prof., 1973-81; prof. Latin, U. Limoges, France, 1981—; expert French Ministry Edn., Paris, 1994-98. Author: Tertullien face aux Morales des Trois Premiers Siécles, 1979, Trois Analyses de l'Amour: Catulle, Poésies, Ovide, Les Amours, Apulée, Le conte de Psyché, 1985, Tibulle ou la Répétition, 1997, (memoir) Jésus Dieu: Une Représentation qui Porte la Marque de son Temps?, 1985. Avocation: music. Office: U Limoges Faculty Letters, 39 E Rue Camille Guérin, 87036 Limoges Cedex, France

RAMBIDI, NICHOLAS GEORGE, chemical physics educator; b. Novokuznetzk, Russia, Mar. 12, 1932; s. George Ivan and Maria Alexander (Shatalova) Rambidi; m. Irina Theodore Moskovskaya, July 5, 1955 (div. 1982); 1 child, Helena; m. Galina Gabriel Fedikina, July 23, 1983 (dec. 1985); 1 child adopted, Gregory Nicholas; m. Helena Vladimir Uglova, Oct. 25, 1986 (dec. 1990); m. Marina Lev Shibaeva, Sept. 22, 1990; adopted children: Katharine Nicholas, Vera Nicholas, Stanislav Nicholas. PhD, Moscow State U., 1959, DSc, 1970. Jr. scientific worker, sr. scientific worker Chem. Dept. Moscow State U., 1954-65; sr. scientific worker, head of dept. Inst. for High Temperature, USSR Acad. of Scis., Moscow, 1965-74; head of dept., dir. rsch. inst. Rsch. Ctr., USSR State Com. for Stds., Moscow, 1974-88; head of dept. Internat. Rsch., Inst. for Mgmt. Scis., Moscow, 1988—; prof. Moscow Phys. and Tech. Inst., 1978-95; prof. physical dept. Moscow State U., 1996—; mem. USSR Nat. CODATA Com., Moscow, 1976-94; vice-chmn. State Interdepartmental Coun. for Molecular Electronics, 1985-90, State Interdepartmental Coun. for Measurement Problems, Moscow, 1977-90. Editl. staff Optical Memory and Neural Networks, 1995—, BioSystems, 1996—; author 8 books; contbr. articles to profl. jours. Mem. Internat. Soc. for Molecular Electronics and BioComputing (nominating com. 1991—, chmn. 1994—), Russian Acad. of Natural Scis., Internat. Acad. of Infomatics. Avocations: reading fiction, visiting classic music concerts, traveling, working at the country house. Home: 2 ya Pestchanaya 8-53, 125252 Moscow Russia Office: Internat Rsch Inst Mgmt Sci, 9 Prospect 60-let Octyabria, 117312 Moscow Russia

RAMCHANDER, SANJAY, finance educator; b. Madras, India, July 25, 1968; came to U.S., 1988; s. Ganesan and Chandra Ramchander; m. Jana T., July 5, 1996; 1 child, Naitra. B in Comm., Osmania U., Hyderabad, India, 1988; MBA, St. Louis U., 1990; PhD, Cleve. State U., 1995. Rsch. asst. Cleve. State U., Dept. Fin., 1990-94; asst. prof. Coppin State Coll., Balt., 1994-97, Minn. State U., Mankato, 1997-00; assoc. prof. Marshall U., Huntington, W.Va., 2000—; instr. Cleve. State U., Dept. Fin., 1992-94; presenter in field; mem. dept. curriculum com. Minn. State U., 1998-00, scholar enhancement com., 1998-99, tech. enhancement com., 1998-00, faculty advisor, 1997-00. Ad hoc reviewer Jour. Futures Markets; contbr. articles to profl. jours. Faculty Rsch. grant Minn. State U., 1999. Mem. Fin. Mgmt. Assn., Acad. Econ. and Fin., Am. Acad. Acctg. and Fin., Beta Gamma Sigma. Avocations: reading. E-mail: ramchander@marshall.edu.

RAMDAHL, GUNNAR HALVOR, security services professional; b. Oslo, Norway, Mar. 23, 1944; m. Birgit Taje; children: Paal, Morten, Thomas. M in Bus. Adminstrn., U. Commerce, Bergen, Norway, 1968. Sys. cons. ICL, Oslo, Norway, 1968-70; salesman ICL, Oslo, 1970-73, sales dir., 1973-76; mng. dir. Nixdorf, Oslo, 1976-84; nordic dir. NCR, Oslo, 1984-88, Olivetti, Copenhagen, 1988-95; mng. dir. Advanced Info. Security, Olso, 1995—. Home: Trudvangveien 29, 0363 Oslo Norway

RAMDIN, ALBERT RAMCHAND, Suriname government official, ambassador; b. Suriname, Feb. 27, 1958; s. Boedhram and Roosalia (Madarie) R.; m. Lalita Adhin, Aug. 26, 1984 (div. Nov. 1995); m. Charmaine Baksh, Dec. 1, 1995; children: Kareana-Amy, Anu-Xsitaaz. BSc in Human Geography, U. Amsterdam, The Netherlands, 1984; MSc in Devel. Geography, Free U., Amsterdam, 1987. Policy ofcl. Re-Migraion Found., The Hague, The Netherlands, 1987-91; dir. Co-Fin. Orgn., Oeostgeest, The Netherlands, 1991-93; sr. trade policy adviser Ministry Trade and Industry, Paramaribo, Suriname, 1993-95; mktg. dir. Brit. Am. Tobacco Co., Paramaribo, 1995-97; advisor to fgn. min. Ministry Fgn. Affairs, Paramaribo, 1997; amb., permanent rep. OAS, Washington, 1997-99, vice chmn., chmn. Coun. for integral devel., 1990-99, chmn. permanent coun., 1998; amb., asst. sec. gen. for fgn. and cmty rels. Caribbean Cmty., Georgetown, Guyana, 1999—; non-resident amb. to Costa Rica, Ministry Fgn. Affairs, Paramino, 1999—; mem. bd. supervisory dirs. Port Authority, Paramaribo, 1994-97, mem. Presdl. Com. on Privatization, Paramaribo, 1997; participant confs. on mktg. and strategic mgmt.; mem. Presdl. Coun. for State Enterprises, Suriname, 1996; advisor to min. fin., Suriname, 1997; vice chmn. prep. com. for 2d summit of ministerial exec. coun. assn. Caribbean States; coord. Caribbean Ambs. Caucus, 1999; govt. rep. several confs. and meetings; mem. Suriname del. to Heads of Govts. Confs., Caribbean Cmty., St. Lucia, Suriname, Dominican Republic, Trinidad and Tobago, II Summit of Ames., Chile, Heads of State Meeting, Dominican Republic, II Summit of Assn. Caribbean States, Dominican Republica, 5th African-AfricanAm. Summit, Ghana. Hindu. Avocations: reading, listening to classical Indian music. E-mail: asgfer@caricom.org. Home: Sayside Towers Ste 308, 219-221 Western Main Rd, Port of Spain Trinidad and Tobago

RAMELAN, RAHARDI, government official; b. Sukabumi, West Java, Indonesia, Sept. 12, 1939; s. Mohamad and Sumarsih Ramelan; m. Tumbu Tri Iswari Astiani, Sept. 12, 1969; children: Bastian Kuntoadi, Kunti Sintorini. MSME, Czech Tech. U., Praha, Czechoslovakia, 1964. Head mech. engring. dept. Advanced Tech. div. Pertamina, Jakarta, Indonesia, 1976-78; dir. indls. devel. Agy. for the Assessment and Application of Tech., Jakarta, 1978-82, dep. chmn. for indsl. analyses, 1982—; min. trade and industry; spl. asst. to the pres. dir. Indonesian Weapon and Munition Factory, Bandung, 1985—; vice min. Nat. Devel. Agy., 1993-989; min. rsch. and tech., 1998—, min. industry and trade, head Nat. Logistics Agy., 1998-99; chmn. RR Resources, 2000. Mem. Indonesian Automotive Engring. Assn., Indonesian Soc. Engr. Technicians (vice chmn. 1987—), Indonesian Aircraft Industry, NRC, Nat. Standardization Coun. Avocations: tennis, cross country cycling. Fax: 62-21-73888607. E-mail: ramelan@attglobal.net. Home: Jl Kayu Putih Lima #9, Jakarta 13260, Indonesia Office: Jl Murai II, Blok J-3 No 1 Sektor I, 12330 Jakarta Bintaro Jaya, Indonesia

RAMER, HAL REED, academic administrator; b. Kenton, Tenn., June 8, 1923; s. Claude Orion and Dixie Clayton (Carroll) R. BS, George Peabody Coll., 1947; MSW, U. Tenn., 1952; PhD, Ohio State U., 1963. Asst. dean men Ohio State U., Columbus, 1953-58, dir. internat. house, 1958-60, staff asst. to pres., 1960-62; asst. commr. State Dept. Edn., Nashville, 1963-70; founding pres. Vol. State C.C., Gallatin, Tenn., 1970—; bd. dirs. Sumner Regional Health Sys., Inc. Mem. adv. bd. First Union Bank Mid. Tenn., Hendersonville, Tenn., com. March of Dimes, Gallatin; trustee Nashville United Way, 1970s; bd. advisors Aquinas Coll., Nashville, 1967—; bd. dirs. YMCA; former chmn. Tenn. Fulbright-Hays Sch. Commn. With USAAF, 1943-45; col. Tenn. Def. Force. Recipient Distinctive Svc. award Devel. Coun. Peabody Coll., Nashville, 1960s, Disting. Svc. award Tenn. Dept. Edn., 1970, Outstanding Leader award Vanderbilt U. chpt. Phi Delta Kappa, 1987, Gov.'s Svc. award State of Tenn., 1993, Sertoma Club Svc. to Mankind award, 1995-96, Disting. Alumnus award Peabody Coll., 1996, Disting. Svc. award Tenn. Bd. Regents, 1997, Svc. Awd. Amer. Assn. of Commty. Col., 1999, Otis Floyd Jr. Awd. for Excellence Tenn. COll. Pub. Rels. Assn., 1999; named Rotarian of the Yr., 1979; Paul Harris fellow Rotary Internat., 1981. Mem. Am. Legion, Coun. Pres. C.Cs. (chmn. state Tenn. 1988-89), Tenn. Coll. Assn. (pres. 1985-86), Nat. Alumni Assn. Peabody Coll. (pres. 1970-71, trustee), Tenn. Acad. Sci., Tenn. and Sumner County Hist. Socs. (bd. dirs.), English Speaking Union Internat. (Nashville chpt.), So. Assn. Colls. and Schs., Univ. Club Nashville, Gallatin and Hendersonville C. of C., St. Thomas Aquinas Soc., Torch Club, Alpha Tau Omega, Kappa Phi Kappa, Alpha Phi Omega, Phi Delta Kappa. Methodist. Avocations: antiques, antique cars, photography. Home: 120 Abbottsford Nashville TN 37215-2440 Office: Vol State CC Office of Pres 1480 Nashville Pike Gallatin TN 37066-3148

RAMER, LAWRENCE JEROME, corporation executive; b. Bayonne, N.J., July 29, 1928; s. Sidney and Anne (Strassman) R.; m. Ina Lee Brown, June 30, 1957; children: Stephanie Beryl, Susan Meredith, Douglas Strassman. B.A. in Econs, Lafayette Coll., 1950; M.B.A., Harvard U., 1957; LLD (hon.), Lafayette Coll., 1992. Sales rep., then v.p. United Sheet Metal Co., Bayonne, 1953-55; with Am. Cement Corp., 1957-64; v.p. mktg. div. Riverside Cement Co., 1960-62, v.p. mktg. parent co., 1962-64; vice chmn. bd., chief exec. officer Clavier Corp., N.Y.C., 1965-66; exec. v.p., vice chmn. bd. Pacific Western Industries, Los Angeles, 1966-70; pres., chief exec. officer Nat. Portland Cement Co. Fla., 1975-89; chmn. bd. Sutro Partners, Inc., Los Angeles, 1977-89, Somerset Mgmt. Group, 1975-92, Luminall Paints Inc., Los Angeles, 1972-95; chmn. bd., chief exec. officer Bruning Paint Co., Balt., 1979—, Pacific Coast Cement Co., Los Angeles, 1979-90; pres., chief exec. officer Ramer Equities, Inc., 1990—; chmn. Lee and Lawrence J. Ramer Family Found., 1986—; bd. dirs. Orbis Internat., N.Y.C., The Music Ctr., L.A., Canyon Ranch, Tucson, Music Ctr. Found., L.A.; bd. dirs. Ctr. Theatre Group-Mark Taper Ahmanson Theatres, L.A., pres. and chmn., 1987-97. Chmn. bd. trustees Lafayette Coll., Easton, Pa.; trustee, chmn. bd. trustees Calif. Inst. Arts, Valencia, Calif.; bd. dirs. Non-Traditional Casting Project, N.Y.; nat. bd. govs. Am. Jewish Com., N.Y., assoc. chmn. bd. trustees. Office: Ramer Equities Inc 1999 Ave Of Stars Ste 1090 Los Angeles CA 90067-4612

RAMESH, ATMAKURU, research scientist; b. Nellore, India, Feb. 4, 1966; s. Atmakaru Venkata Narayana Rao and Lakshmi; m. Alladi Venkatesan Shanthi, Feb. 9, 1995; 1 child. BSc, Sri Venkateswara U., India, 1984, MSc, 1987; PhD, Jawaharlal Nehru U., Hyderabad, India, 1991. Lectr. Ratnam Degree Coll., India, 1991-92; scientist Frederick Inst. Plant Protection and Toxicology, Kanchipuram, Tamil Nadu, India, 1992, sr. scientist, 1994—; lectr. in pesticide chemistry. Grantee Univ. Grants Commn. New Delhi, 1988-90. Mem. Royal Soc. Chemistry (London, chartered chemist), Indian Soc. Mass Spectrometry (life), Environ. Soc. India (life), Soc. Pesticide Sci. (life). Fax: 0 91-44-3723387. E-mail: fippat@giasmd01.vsnl.net.in. Home: New No 2, Rangarajapuram Main Rd, Kodambakkam Chennai 600024, India Office: FIPPAT, Padappai, Tamil Nadu 601301, India

RAMESH, JALLIGAMPALA, metals company executive; b. Bhubaneswar, Orissa, India, Mar. 17, 1957; s. Jalligampala Apparao and Jalligampala Kamala; m. Jalligampala Shrilata, May 1982; children: Deepshika J., Harshita J. B of Commerce, Utkal U., Bhubaneswar, 1978. Mgr. Nav Chrome Ltd., Hyderabad, India, 1989-90, gen. mgr., 1991-94, wholetime dir., 1995-96; v.p. Nava Bharat Ferro Alloys Ltd., Hyderabad, 1997—; bd. dirs. Shriharshdeep Aqua Ltd., Hyderabad. Mem. Jubilee Hills Internat. Ctr. (permanent mem.), Secunderabad Club. Avocations: traveling, reading.

RAMESH, K.H., geneticist, researcher; b. Bangalore, Karnataka, India, Feb. 5, 1956; came to U.S., 1986; s. Hanumantha Chetty and Jayalakshimi Shetty; m. Chandrika Sreekantaiah, Feb. 18, 1991; children: Amrita, Brinda. BS, Govt. Sci. Coll., Bangalore, India, 1978; PhD, Bangalore U., 1991, Diploma in Pub. Rels., 1978; MS, Ctrl. Coll., Bangalore, 1980. Cert. clin. cytogenetics Dept. Health N.Y. State. Rsch. affil. Roswell Park Cancer Inst., Buffalo, N.Y., 1986-88; rsch. assoc. S.W. Biomed. Rsch. Inst., Scottsdale, Ariz., 1988-89; prof. rsch. asst. Health Sci. Ctr. U. Colo., Denver, 1989-91; asst. prof. Kidwai Meml. Inst. Oncology, Bangalore, 1991-92; cytogeneticist Genzyme Genetics, Yonkers, N.Y., 1992-94, Long Is. Coll. Hosp., Bklyn., 1994-95; asst. dir. pathology Albert Einstein Coll. Medicine/Montefiore Med. Ctr., Bronx, 1995—; cons. geneticist N.Y. Med. Coll., Valhalla, 1994—; lab. dir. Dept. Health N.Y. State, Albany, 1995—. Rev. Cancer Genetics and Cytogenetics, 1992—, Cell Genetics and Cytogenetics, 1995—; contbr. chpt. to book. Mem. Am. Soc. Human Genetics, AAAS, Am. Mus. Natural History, N.Y. Acad. Scis., Wildlife Conservation Soc. Democrat. Hindu. Avocations: jogging, collecting bottle corks as a reminder of celebrations. Office: Albert Einstein Coll Medicine/Montefiore Med Ctr 111 E 210th St Rm C-321 Bronx NY 10467-2401

RAMESH, SARAF RAJAGOPALAIAHSETTY, zoology educator; b. Chintamani, Kolar, India, Mar. 22, 1954; s. Naduminti Madappa Rajagopalaiahsetty and Naduminti Rajagopalaiahsetty Rathnamma; m. Saraf Ramesh Surya Kumari, Oct. 30, 1980; 1 child, Sandhya Lakshmi. BSc, U. Mysore, Chintamani, India, 1972; MSc, U. Mysore, Mangalore, India, 1974; PhD, U. Mysore, Mysore, 1980. Cert. tchr. Rsch. fellow U. Mysore, 1975-79, lectr. sericulture, 1980-81, lectr. zoology, 1981-94, reader zoology, 1994-99, prof. zoology, 1999—, cons. faculty, 1990-92; postdoctoral fellow German Acad. Exch. Svc., Bochum, 1986-88, vis. fellow, Dusseldorf and Bochum, 1994. Recipient gift equipment Gesellschaft Technische Zsusammenarbeit, Germany, 1989. Mem. Indian Soc. Cell Biology (life), N.Y. Acad. Scis., Arya Vysya Students Welfare Assn. (sec. 1997—), Arya Vysya Ofcls. and Profls. Assn. (bd. dirs. 1999—), Am. Biog. Inst., Inc. (bd. adv. rsch.). Hindu. Avocations: drawing, travel, music, reading, learning of languages. Home: # 696, Vinaya Marg, 10th Cross Siddartha Nagar, Mysore 570011, India Office: U Mysore, Manasagangotri, Dept Studies Zoology, Mysore 570006, India

RAMGOOLAM, NAVINCHANDRA, prime minister of the Republic of Mauritius; b. July 14, 1947; s. Late Sir Seewoosagur and late Lady Sushill R.; m. Veena Brizmonun, 1979. Degree, Royal Coll. Surgeons, Dublin, LRCP, LRCSI; London Sch. Econs.; LLB with honors, Inns of Ct. Sch. of Law; D (hon.), U. Mauritius, 1998, Aligarh Muslim U., 1998. Bar: Inner Temple, 1993. Leader Mauritius Labour Party, 1991—, pres., 1991-92, Member of Parliment, leader of opposition, 1991-95; prime min. Republic of Mauritius, 1995—, also min. def. and home affairs, min. external comm.; mem. internat. adv. bd. Ctr. for Internat. Devel. Harvard U., 1999. Hon. Fellow Inner Temple, 1998. mem. internat. adv. bd. Centre for Internat. Devel., Harvard U., 1999. Avocations: reading, music, water skiing, chess. Home: 37 Riverwalk, Vacoas Mauritius Office: Govt House, Port Louis Mauritius

RAMÍK, JAROSLAV, operations research educator, researcher; b. Frydek, Moravia, Czech Republic, Sept. 28, 1951; s. František and Jarmila (Oborná) R.; m. Eva Molinová, Jan. 20, 1978; children: Jana (dec.), Vojtěch. MSc, Charles U., Prague, Czechoslovakia, 1975, PhD, 1980, Habilitation in Ops. Rsch. and Math., 1991. Rschr. Iron and Steel Rsch. Inst., Dobrá, Czechoslavakia, 1980-85; sr. rschr. Regions and Towns Rsch. Inst., Ostrava, Czech Republic, 1985-90; prof. ops. rsch. Silesian U., Karviná, Czech Republic, 1990—, vice dean Sch. Bus., 1991-97; prof. Tech. U., Ostrava, 1994—; rschr. Inst. for Fuzzy Modeling, Ostrava, 1996—; cons. Inst. Hygienic Studies, Karviná, 1995—. Author: Business Statistics, 1992, Linear Programming with Inexact Coefficients, 1993; editor Ctrl. European Jour. for Ops. Rsch., 1993; patentee for control sys. of blast furnace. Rep. Municipality of Cesky Těšín, Czech Republic, 1992-95. Rschr. grantee Czech Grant Agy., 1996. Mem. Czech Soc. for Ops. Rsch. (v.p. 1993-95, pres. 1995-97), Czech Soc. Mathematicians and Physicists. Avocations: classical music, playing violin, skiing, hiking, tennis. Home: Rakovec 281, CZ-73701 Cesky Těšín Czech Republic Office: Silesian U, University Sq 76, CZ-73340 Karviná Czech Republic

RAMIN, GILLES F., business executive; b. Paris, July 3, 1949; s. Jacques and Wanda (Dunin Wasowicz) R.; m. Anne Bettina Bacot, Sept. 21, 1981; children: Louis-Jacques, Pauline. Baccalaureat, Louis le Grand, Paris, 1968; licence gestion, U. Panthéon, Paris, 1972; sci. politique, I.E.P., Paris, 1973. Attaché Credit Lyonnais, Paris, 1975-76; asst. v.p. Bankers Trust, N.Y., Paris, 1976-84; v.p., gen. mgr. First Chgo., Paris, London, 1984-88; pres. James Capital Corp. Fin., London, 1989-92, Fleming Enterprise, Paris, 1992-94, AKTO, Paris, 1994—; prof. ISA, Paris, 1999. Mem. Club Fin. Internat. of HEC (exec. com.). Avocations: drawing, skiing. Home: 226 Boulevard Saint Germain, 75007 Paris France Office: AKTO, 370 Rue Saint Honoré, 75001 Paris France

RAMIREZ, CARLOS EDUARDO, electrical engineer; b. Puntarenas, Costa Rica, Nov. 28, 1950; s. Cesar Augusto Ramirez and Carmen Maria Mendoza; m. Vilam C. Perez, Dec. 26, 1974; children: Pablo, Roberto, Artur. AS, Compton Jr. Coll., 1972; BS in Elec. Engring., La. State U., 1976, MS in Elec. Engring., 1977; MBA, Inst. Centroamericano Adminstrn. Empresas, Costa Rica, 1999. Prof. Inst. Tech. Costa Rica, Cartago, 1978-82; field svc. engr. Integral Systems, San Jose, Costa Rica, 1981-85; tech. mgr. Soc. Internat. Telecommunications Aeronautiques, San Jose, 1985-88, tech. supr. Central Am., 1988-98, gen. mgr., 1998—. Contbr. articles to profl. jours. Mem. IEEE. Roman Catholic. Avocations: home computers, home security systems, management, finance. Office: Soc Internat Tele Aero, Calle 1 Ave 5 Piso 3, Edificio Banco San Jose Costa Rica

RAMIREZ, FRANK TENORIO, lawyer; b. Fresno, Calif., July 16, 1952; s. Ramon and Connie Ramirez; m. Teresa Gonzales, Apr. 15, 1978; children: Irene, Isabel, Francesca. BS, Calif. State U., Fresno, 1974; JD, U. Calif., Berkeley, 1977. Bar: Calif. 1978, U.S. Dist. Ct. (ea. dist.) Calif. 1978, U.S. Dist. Ct. (so. dist.) Calif. 1983, U.S. Ct. Appeals (9th cir.), 1984. Staff atty. Calif. Rural Legal Assistance, Inc., Madera, 1977-81; regional counsel Calif. Rural Legal Assistance, Inc., Fresno, 1982-84; trustee Calif. Rural Legal Assistance, Inc., San Francisco, 1986-98; pub. defender Fresno County Pub. Defender's Office, Fresno, 1982; ptnr. Hernandez & Ramirez, Fresno, 1984—; trustee Fresno County Law Libr., 1998. Mem. Fresno County Bar Assn., Madera County Bar Assn. (pres. 1996), La Raza Lawyers Assn. (pres. San Joaquin Valley chpt. 1983). Democrat. Roman Catholic. Office: Hernandez & Ramirez 6103 N 1st St Ste 102 Fresno CA 93710-5406

RAMIREZ, JOSE ERNESTO, sociologist; b. Bogota, Colombia, Mar. 28, 1954; s. Jose Antonio and Maria Ines (Pinzon) R.; m. Ligia Ortiz Cepeda, Dec. 3, 1983 (dec.); 1 child, Camilo Ernesto. Magister, Inst. Altos Estudios Para el Desarrollo, U. Externado de Colombia; sociologist, Nat. U. Colombia, 1984. Fellow Dept. Sociology, Bogota, Colombia, 1981; researcher Ctr. Jorge Eliecer Gaitan, Bogota, 1982-83; prof. U. Coop. de Colombia, Bogota, 1984; researcher Cons. and Investigation, Medellin, 1985-87; prof. U. Piloto Columbia, Bogota, 1986-87; researcher Colciencias/ Nat. U., Bogota, 1988-89, Cinep, Bogota, 1990, Found. Ebert of Colombia, Bogota, 1991—; corr. OIT/PREALS, 1993—; co-investigator FORO/ Cogciencids, 1992-94. Author: Poder Economico Y Dominacion Politica, 1984; editor: Intra 1986-1990; contbr. articles to profl. jours. Bd. dirs. Centro de Estudios Camilo Torres Restrepo CECTOR, 1985, Asesor de la CUT, 1991. Mem. Asociacion para el Foueinto de la Educación Tecudógica de Cos Trabejadore, DFETT, 1993. Avocations: camping, rock collecting, triathlon, ecology, computer games. Home: Spartado Séreo 56635, Santafe de Bogota Colombia Office: CECTOR, Avda el Dorado # 46-20 616, Santafe de Bogota Colombia

RAMIREZ, MARTIN RUBEN, architect, engineer, educator, cognitive scientist, consultant; b. San Luis Potosi, Mex., Aug. 17, 1962; s. Victorio Niño and Concepcion (Zuñiga) R.; m. Maureen Therese McDermott, July 27, 1991. BS in Civil Engring., Northwestern U., 1984, MS, 1986, PhD, 1991. Asst. to v.p. engring. Perkins & Will, Chgo., 1980-84; cons. engr. Alfred Benesch & Co., Chgo., 1985-86, Teng & Assocs., Chgo.; asst. prof. engring. Johns Hopkins U., Balt., 1990-94; pres., chief lng. officer Innovative Design Edn. and Assessment Sys., 1994—; cons. Wiss-Jenney Elstner, Northbrook, Ill., 1985-86, Mitsubishi Heavy Industries, Hunt Valley, Md., 1993-94, Synthesis NSF Coalition, U. Calif. Berkeley, 1996—, and to U.S. and fgn. govts., dists. and instns.; founder, Dir. program on engring. edn. Johns Hopkins U., 1993. Reviewer for several jours.; editor Needs Database. Recipient Fazlur Khan Meml. prize, 1986, Young Investigator award NSF, 1993; Lilly fellow, 1992; NSF grad. fellow, 1985. Mem. ASCD, ASCE (assoc.), ASME, Am. Edn. Rsch. Assn., Am. Soc. Engring. Edn. (chair Frontiers in Edn. Conf. 1993), U.S. Assn. for Computational Mechanics, IEEE Computer Soc., Am. Acad. Mechanics, Tau Beta Pi. Achievements include designs of or influence on designs of many major educational curricula and programs. Avocations: bicycling, cars, travel, music. E-mail: mramirez@cris.com. Office: IDEAS 1364 Middleburg Rd Naperville IL 60540-7013

RAMIREZ, NOEL, bank executive. Pres. Banco Central de Nicaragua. Office: Banco de Nicaragua, Kilometro 7 Carreter Sur, Zona 5 Managua Nicaragua*

RAMIREZ, NORBERTO LUIS, public official; b. Buenos Aires, Sept. 16, 1937; s. Luis Maria and Angela (Crespo) R.; m. Catalina Isabel Maria Bund de Ramirez, July 11, 1964; children: Camilo Norberto, Facundo Carlos. Acct., U. Buenos Aires, 1964; D in Adminstrn., UN, Mar del Pleta, 1997. Tchr. U. Mar Del Plata, Argentina, 1965-74, 84—; mcpl. pub. ofcl. Ente Turism Mcpl., 1964-79, 91-97; titular tchr. in chair adminstrn. and turism licentiate Nat. U. Mar Del Plata, 1965-74, also investigation dir.; rschr. mcpl. mgmt., 1999-2000. Mem. Econ. Ciencies Profl. Coun., Mar Del Plata, 1987-89; vice-dean Econs. Ciencie's Faculty, Mar Del Plata, 1988-94, acad. cons., 1988-92; mem. Social Security Prof. Econ. Ciencies, Mar Del Plata, 1991-99. Avocation: film editing. Home: Formosa #2058, 7600 Mar del Plata Argentina

RAMIREZ, RAMON, soccer player. Midfielder Guadalajara (Mex.) Football Club, Tigres; played in 1994 World Cup. Office: Tigres Estudio U Plata 13, San Nicolas de los Garza, CP 66451 Nuevo Leon Mexico*

RAMIREZ, RAMON, database company executive; b. Barcelona, Cataluna, Spain, Jan. 29, 1946; arrived in Venezuela, 1955; s. Antonio Ramirez and Pilar Canela; m. Trina Marquez, Dec. 15, 1973; children: Ramon, Anabella; m. Rosa D'Adamo, Nov. 12, 1995. Student, Miami-Dade C.C., Fla., 1968. Pres. Mailing List de Venezuela, 1986-97; sales mgr. Philips Venezolana, Venezuela, 1989-93; mktg. dir. Diners Club, Venezuela, 1993-97; pres. Latin Am. Mailings, Caracas, Venezuela, 1997—; dir. Mktg. Dir. Venezuela, 1997—. Mem. Gym Tamanaco Hotel, Carenero Yacht Club. Avocations: mountain climbing. Office: Latin Am Mailings, Box 63036, 1067A Caracas Venezuela

RAMIREZ, RICARDO, bishop; b. Bay City, Tex., Sept. 12, 1936; s. Natividad and Maria (Espinosa) R. B.A., U. St. Thomas, Houston, 1959; M.A., U. Detroit, 1968; Diploma in Pastoral Studies, East Asian Pastoral Inst., Manila, 1973-74. Ordained priest Roman Catholic Ch., 1966; missionary Basilian Fathers, Mex., 1968-76; exec. v.p. Mexican Am. Cultural Ctr., San Antonio, 1976-81; aux. bishop Archdiocese of San Antonio, 1981-82; bishop Diocese of Las Cruces, N.M., 1982—; cons. U.S. Bishop's Com. on Liturgy, from 1981; advisor U.S. Bishop's Com. on Hispanic Affairs, from 1981. Author: Fiesta, Worship and Family, 1981. Mem. N.Am. Acad. on Liturgy, Hispanic Liturgical Inst., Padres Asociada Derechos Religiosos Educativos y Sociales. Lodges: K.C; Holy Order Knights of Holy Sepulcher. Office: Diocese Las Cruces 1280 Med Park Dr Las Cruces NM 88005-3239

RAMIREZ DE ARELLANO, CAROLINE MARGARET, export company executive; b. Harare, Zimbabwe, Jan. 13, 1966; d. Maurice David and Heather Escourt (Cutter) Bromley; m. George Francisco Bernard Ramirez de Arellano, Dec. 16, 1989; children: Patricia Teresa, Jacquelyn Nicole. BS in Biology, Averett Coll., 1987. Mng. dir. Ramirez & Cutter, Inc., Manila, 1988—; cons. Sports Values, Inc., Subic, The Philippines, 1994—. Avocation: cooking. Office: Ramirez & Cutter Inc, 88 St Martin St Valle Verde, Pasig City 1600, The Philippines

RAMIREZ-OCAMPO, JORGE, economist; b. Bogotá, Colombia, May 15, 1936; s. Augusto and Mariela (Ocampo) Ramirez-Moreno; m. Magda Botero; children: María José, Enrique. Degree in philosophy, Javeriana, Bogotá, 1961, degree in math., 1961; degree in econs., Andes, Bogotá, 1964; MA in Econs., Williams Coll., 1965. Econ. rsch. dir. Caja Agraria, Bogotá, 1962-66; Colombian govt. del. Internat. Coffee Orgn., London, 1966-74; minister Colombian Govt., Bogotá, 1974-76; pres. CIA Gen. Inmobiliaria, Bogotá, 1976-82; exec. dir. CIA Colombiana Automotriz, Bogotá, 1982-86; cons. Bogotá, 1986—; bd. dirs. Cartón de Colombia, Cali, Banco Sudameris, Clinica Shaio, Museo de Arte Moderno, Prodeco, Bogotá. Author: Indus-

trialización y Comercio Exterior, 1976, Política Cafetera Int, 1983; contbr. articles to mags. Chmn. Sociedad Colombiana Economistas, Bogotá, 1976-79, Fedemol, Bogotá, 1977-84, Fedemango, Bogotá, 1987. Mem. Futuro Colombiano, Instituto de Ciencia Politica, Jockey Club, Country Club. Office: Cra 7 No 72-64 of 215, Bogotá Colombia

RAMIREZ-PORTILLA, CARLOS ALFONSO, architect; b. Guatemala, May 18, 1949; s. Carlos Humberto Ramirez Aldana and Estela Portilla Wright; m. Elisa Sinibaldi Dalton, Nov. 20, 1976; children: Juan Pablo Jose Antonio, Carlos Adolfo. BArch, U. San Carlos, Guatemala City, 1974; postgrad., U. San Carlos; MBA cum laude, U. Francisco Marroquin, Guatemala City, 1985. Exec. architect Comosa, Guatemala City, 1972-78; pres. C.R.P. Assocs. Archs., Guatemala City, 1978—, Showbiz Pizza Place, Guatemala City; dir., chief exec. officer Jett Tours, Guatemala; CEO Performing Arts Internat., Dragon Aviation, Wash. Entertainment Concepts and Seattle Entertainment Concepts. Author: Proyeccion Universitaria Dos Parametros, 1974. Recipient hon. mention Guatemalan Archtl. Mag., 1978, Guatemala C. of C., Book of Houses of Guatemala, 2000. Mem. Interam. Assn., AIA Guatemala, Rotary (past pres.). Roman Catholic. Home: KM 13 Al Salvador, Hacienda El Socorro #3, Puerta Parada Guatemala Office: Boulevard Liberacion, 6-31 z.9, Guatemala City Guatemala

RAMIRO, RENALD PETER TY, college dean, physiatrist; b. Manila, Apr. 27, 1964; s. Salvador Zalameda and Fredezvinda Velasquez (Ty) R.; m. Maria Araceli Avanzado, July 18, 1998; 1 child, Anika Margarita. BS in Biology cum laude, U. Philippines, Diliman, 1986; MD, U. Philippines, Manila, 1991; postgrad., Cebu Doctors' Coll. Diplomate Philippine Bd. Rehab. Medicine. Dean Coll. Rehab. Scis. Cebu (The Philippines) Doctors' Coll., 1996—, chmn. dept. phys. medicine and rehab., 1996—, asst. prof., 1999—; chmn. dept. phys. medicine and rehab Mactan Cmty. Hosp., Cebu, 1996—; head Ormoc Polymedic Rehab. Ctr., Ormoc City, The Philippines, 1998—; physiatrist Mandaue City Rehab. Ctr., Cebu, 1998—, Verano and FAM REhab. Ctr., Maasin City, The Philippines, 2000—. Co-organizer Arthritis Health Fair, Arthritis Found. of the Philippines and Philippine Gen. Hosp. Rehab. Medicine, Manila, 1995; organizer prosthetics update Cebu Doctors' Coll. Rehabilitative Scis. and Philippine Gen. Hosp. Rehab. Med. Alumni Assn., Cebu, 1996, Sports Medicine of Shoulder and Knee, 1998, Motor Delay Rehab., 1999. Mem. Cebu Med. Soc., Philippine Rheumatology Assn., Philippine Acad. Rehab. Medicine, Mu Sigma Phi. Roman Catholic. Avocations: music, snorkeling, dancing, jogging, swimming, biking. Home: Tuscania Townhouse, # 9 Guadalupe, Cebu 6000, The Philippines Office: Cebu Drs Coll Rehab Scis, Osmena Blvd, Cebu 6000, The Philippines

RAMIS, CLEMENTE, meteorologist, educator; b. Llucmajor, Spain, Jan. 5, 1949; s. Sebastian Ramis and Antonia Noguera; m. Margarita Pocovi, Nov. 23, 1948; 1 child, Sebastian. BSc, U. Barcelona, 1972, MSc in Physics, 1976; PhD in Physics, U. Balearic Islands, 1983. Meteorologist Nat. Meteorol. Svc., Spain, 1970-87; from asst. to reader in meteorology U. Balearic Islands, Spain, 1987—. Author: Practical Works in Meteorology, 1996; contbr. articles to profl. jours. Fellow Royal Meteorol. Soc.; mem. Spanish Royal Soc. Physics (sec. group atmospheric & oceanic physics), European Geophys. Soc. Office: U de les Illes Balears, Carretera Valldemossa km7.5, 07071 Palma de Mallorca Spain

RAMIS, HAROLD ALLEN, film director, screenwriter, actor; b. Chgo., Nov. 21, 1944; s. Nathan and Ruth (Cokee) R.; m. Erica Mann; children: Violet, Julian, Daniel. BA, Washington U., St. Louis, 1966, ArtsD (hon.), 1993. Assoc. editor Playboy mag., 1968-70; actor, writer Second City, Chgo., 1970-73, Nat. Lampoon Radio Hour, Lampoon Show, 1974-75; actor, head writer SCTV, 1977-78; producer, head writer Rodney Dangerfield Show, ABC-TV, 1982. Screenwriter (with Douglas Kenny and Chris Miller) National Lampoon's Animal House, 1978, (with Janice Allen, Len Blum and Dan Goldberg) Meatballs, 1979, (with Douglas Kenny, Brian Doyle-Murray) Caddyshack, 1980, (with Len Blum and Dan Goldberg) Stripes, 1981, (with Dan Aykroyd) Ghostbusters, 1984, (with Brian Doyle-Murray) Club Paradise, 1986; co-screenwriter (with Peter Torokvei) Armed and Dangerous, 1986; writer (with Dan Akroyd) Ghostbusters II, 1989; dir. feature films: Caddyshack, 1980, National Lampoon's Vacation, 1983, Club Paradise, 1986; exec. producer, co-screenwriter (with Rodney Dangerfield) Back to School, 1986; film appearances include: Stripes, 1981, Ghostbusters, 1984, Baby Boom, 1987, Stealing Home, 1988, Ghostbusters II, 1989, As Good As It Gets, 1997, American Storytellers, 2000; dir., exec. producer, co-writer Groundhog Day, 1993; dir., co-prodr. Stuart Saves His Family, 1995, Multiplicity, 1996; dir., co-screenwriter (with Peter Tolan and Ken Lonergan) Analyze This, 1999. Mem. AFTRA, SAG, Writers Guild Am., Dirs. Guild Am.

RAMIS, PLA JOAQUIM, communications company executive, consultant; b. Vic, Barcelona, Spain, Aug. 17, 1967; s. Josep and Dolors (Pla) R.; m. Laura Del Hoyo. LLB, U. Barcelona, 1991; MBA, IESE, Barcelona, 1994. Bus. gift mgr. Montblanc Spain, Barcelona, 1994-95; product mgr. internat. Gen. de Confieria, Barcelona, 1995-97; vice gen. mgr. Lorente Eu, Barcelona, 1997; gen. mgr. CP Communication, Barcelona, 1998—. Lt. Spanish Army, 1990-91. Avocations: skiing, sailing, mountain biking, football.

RAMIZ, ALIA, former president of Albania; b. Shkoder, Albania, Oct. 18, 1925. Leader Union of Working Youth, 1948-55; minister of edn. Govt. of Albania, 1955-58; sec. Albanian Workers Party, 1958-61, mem. politburo, 1961-82; chmn. Presidium of the People's Assembly, 1982-91; 1st sec. Albanian Workers Party, 1985-91; pres. Republic of Albania, Tirana, 1991-92—. Office: Office of Pres of Albania, Rruga Gjin Bue Shpata, P9/A/50, Tirana Albania

RAMMOS, KYRIAKOS S., surgeon; b. Thessaloniki, Greece, Aug. 24, 1947; s. Stylianoc and Maria (Apergi) R.; m. Athena-Vasilixi Papaterpou, May 10, 1975; children: Stylianos, Charalambos, Maria-Despina. MD, Aristotle U., Thessaloniki, 1971. Diplomate Am. Bd. Surgery, Am. Bd. Thoracic Surgery. Gen surgery resident Hahnemann U., Phila., 1975-80; thoracic surgery resident Mt. Sinai Hosp., N.Y.C., 1980-82; pediatric cardiac surg. resident Harvard Med. Sch./Children's Hosp., Boston, 1982; cons. thoracic surgery G. Papanikolaou Hosp., Thessaloniki, 1983-85, AHEPA Gen. Hosp., Thessaloniki, 1985-93; lectr. thoracic surgery Aristotle U., Thessaloniki, 1993-97, asst. prof. cardiac surgery, 1997—. Author/editor: Endothelium and Coronary Artery Disease, 1997, Internal Thoracic Artery and Other Bypass Grafts, 1998. With greek Army, 1972-74. Fellow AAAS, Internat. Soc. Cardiovascular Surgeons, Med. Soc. of Thessaloniki; mem. Cardiology Soc. No. Greece, Hellenic Cardiology Soc., Hellenic Surg. Soc., Hellenic Soc. for Cardiac Thoracic and Vascular Surgery. Home: 101 Mitcopoleos St, 54622 Thessaloniki Greece Office: 29 Karolou Diehl St, 54622 Thessaloniki Greece

RAMO, ROBERTA COOPER, lawyer; b. Denver, Aug. 8, 1942; d. David D. and Martha L. (Rosenblum) Cooper; m. Barry W. Ramo, June 17, 1964. BA magna cum laude, U. Colo., 1964, LHD (hon.), 1995; JD, U. Chgo., 1967; LLD, U. Mo., 1995, U. Denver, 1995. Bar: N.Mex. 1967, Tex. 1971. With NC. Fund, Durham, 1967-68; nat. tchg. fellow Shaw U., Raleigh, N.C., 1968-70; mem. Sawtelle, Goode, Davidson & Troilo, San Antonio, 1970-72, Rodey, Dickason, Sloan, Akin & Robb, Albuquerque, 1972-74; sole practice law Albuquerque, 1974-77; dir., shareholder Poole, Kelly & Ramo, Albuquerque, 1977-93; shareholder Modrall, Sperling, Roehl, Harris & Sisk, Albuquerque, 1993—; lectr. in field. Co-author: New Mexico Estate Administration System, 1980; editor: How to Create a System for the Law Office, 1975; contbg. editor: Tex. Probate Sys., 1974; contbr. articles to profl. jours., chpts. to books. Bd. dirs., past pres. N.Mex. Symphony Orch., 1977-86; bd. dirs. Albuquerque Cmty. Found., N.Mex. First, 1987-90; bd. regents U. N.Mex., 1989-94, pres., 1991-93, chmn. presdl. search com., 1990; mem. vis. com. U. Chgo. Law Sch., 1987-90, 96—; mem. steering com. World Conf. Domestic Violence, 1996—; mem. Am. Law Inst. Coun., 1997—, Martindale-Hubbell Legal Adv. Bd., 1997—; chmn. bd. Cooper's Inc., 1999—. Recipient Disting. Pub. Svc. award Gov. of N.Mex., 1993. Fellow Am. Bar Found.; mem. ABA (pres. 1995, bd. govs. 1994-97, chmn. London 2000 com. 1997—, Asia Law Initiatives Coun. 1999—, others), Albuquerque Bar Assn. (bd. dirs., pres. 1980-81), N.Mex. Bar Assn. (Outstanding Contbn. award 1981, 84), Am. Bar Retirement Assn. (bd. dirs. 1990-94), Am. Judicature Soc. (bd. dirs. 1988-91), Law Inst. Coun., Am. Arbitration Assn. (bd. dirs. 1997—, bd. trustees Global Ctr. Dispute Resolution Rsch. 1999—), Greater Albuquerque C. of C. (bd. dirs., exec. com. 1987-91). Address: Modrall Sperling Roehl Harris & Sisk PO Box 2168 Albuquerque NM 87103-2168*

RAMÓN, BAGUR, educational adviser, engineer; b. Mexico City, Dec. 2, 1949; s. Ramón Madrid and Bagur Ayala Teresa; m. Straffon Manzano Lourdes, Sept. 12, 1986. Engr., U. Nat. Autonoma Mex., 1975; Master's degree, ICLE, Mex., 1999. Cert. in engring. Tech. dir. Environ. Undersub-secretary, Mex., 1974-76; sports dir. DDF, Mex., 1977-82, ISSSTE, Mex., 1982-89; bus. with the Mexican abroad SRE, Mex., 1990-93; chief publs. Coordinación de Proyectos Especiales SEP, Mex., 1993-94; edn. adviser SEP, Mex., 1995—; cons. Analítica Consultores S.C., Mex., 1995-99, cons. adviser, 1995-99; adviser SEP, Mex., 1995-99. Author: (book) Los saberes de los Mexicanos, 1999; designer: (invention) Crematory Furnaces, 1984. Sec. sports action PRI, Mex., 1986-89; sec. popular consult CNOP, Mexico City, 1984-86. Recipient Profl. Excellence award Mex. Mech. Engring. Assn., 1993, medal of acad. merit La Salle, 1993, Indivisa Manet award La Salle, 1992. Mem. AIUME, SEFI, Mech. Engring. Assn. (Excellence award 1993), PRI. Roman Catholic. Avocations: running, classical music, karate, old cars. Fax: 5255500054. E-mail: anasaber@mail.internet.com.mx. Home: San Jerónimo 150, 01900 Mexico City Coyoacan, Mexico Office: Analítica SC, Ometusco 7, 06100 Mexico City Condesa, Mexico

RAMOS, CARLOS H.I., scientist, researcher; b. Belo Horizonte, Brazil, Oct. 12, 1967; s. Jose I. Filho and Maria C.A. Ramos. Grad., Minas Gerais Fed. U., Brazil, 1991; PhD, Sao Paulo U., Brazil, 1996. Asst. tchr. Minas Gerais Fed. U., 1989, Sao Paulo U., 1994; postdoctoral fellow Stanford (Calif.) U., 1998; assoc. rschr. Laboratorio Nacional de Luz Sincrotron, Brazil, 1999—. Contbr. articles to Biochemistry, Jour. Biol. Chemistry, Jour. Molecular Biology, others. Pew Charitable Trusts Latin Am. fellow, 1997, Pew Charitable Trusts grantee, 1999, Sao Paulo Sci. Found. grantee, 1999. Mem. Protein Soc., N.Y. Acad. Scis., Brazilian Biochemistry and Moleculat Biology Soc. E-mail: cramos@lnls.br. Office: Lab Nac de Luz Sincrotron, CP6192 Guara 1000, Campinas 13083970, Brazil 13083

RAMOS, HUGO ROBERTO, cardiologist; b. Jujuy, Jujuy, Argentina, May 12, 1958; s. Juan José and Elda Noemi (Benavidez) R.; m. Susana Patricia Navarrete, Nov. 5, 1982; children: Ariel, Esteban, Daniel, Andrea, Belén. Perito mercantil, Nacional de Comercio, Argentina, 1975; medico cirujano, Nat. U. Cordoba, Argentina, 1981; prof. in medicine, Nat. U. Argentina, 1992. Diplomate internal medicine, cardiology. Staff cardiology Inst. Modelo de Cardiologia, Cordoba, 1987-94; chief dept. emergency Hosp. de Urgencias, Cordoba, 1994—; prof. cardiology Cath. U., Cordoba, 1995-96; chief dept. critical care Clinica Caraffa, Cordoba, 1996—, chief clin. cardiology, 1998—; coord. disaster com. Cordoba County, 1998—; instr. Soc. Argentina de Cardiologia, 1989—, ACS, Chgo., 1996—; vis. mem. Disaster Planning, Tokyo, 1997, Chile, 1998. Author: Community Education Project for Prevention Motorcycle Accidents, 1994, Emergency Department Design and Equipment, 1993, Prehospital Emergency System for Cordoba City, 1996. Mem. cmty. edn. project for prevention of motorcycle accidents Cordoba County, 1994; mem. emergency dept. design and equipment Hosp. de Urgencias, Cordoba City, 1993; mem. med. project prehosp. emergency sys. Cordoba County, 1996. Recipient Internal Medicine award Internal Medicine Soc., 1987. Mem. Am. Coll. Emergency Physicians, Soc. Airway Mgmt., Cardiology Soc. Avocations: history, soccer. E-mail: belenr@arnet.com.ar. Home: Obispo Lazcano 2666, 5009 Cordoba Argentina Office: Hosp de Urgencias, Catamarca 441, 5000 Cordoba Argentina

RAMOS, JULIO ANTONIO, ophthalmologist, educator; b. Buenos Aires, July 13, 1939; s. Jose Antonio and Anita (Garcia) R.; m. Martha Beatriz Bueno; children: Diana, Julio, Pablo. MD, U. Buenos Aires, 1961. Cert. Argentine Acad. Medicine. Adj. prof. Faculty of Medicine, Buenos Aires, 1988—; chief of svc. ophthalmology dept. Hosp. Español, Buenos Aires, 1976. Mem. Rotary Club. Roman Catholic. Avocations: computers, golf, scuba diving. Home & Office: Ave de la Riestra 5644, 1439 Buenos Aires Argentina

RAMOS, LILIANA LACAMBRA, information systems specialist; b. Pasay City, The Philippines, Oct. 21, 1956; came to U.S., 1967; d. Carlos Blas and Begonia Ormaechea Lacambra; m. Domingo Carlos Ramos, Aug. 12, 1978; children: Domingo Nicholas, Carlos Jefferey, Benjamin Manuel. AA in Liberal Arts, Evergreen Valley Coll., San Jose, Calif., 1986; AA in Adminstrn., C.C. USAF, 1986. Cert. total quality mgmt., project mgmt., Calif. Enlisted U.S. Air N.G., 1975, advanced through grades to chief master sgt.; supply clk. 60 Mil. Airlift Wing, Travis AFB, Calif., 1975-77; orderly rm. clk., supr., tng. mgr., 1st sgt. 129th Rescue Wing, Moffett Fed. Airfield, Calif., 1977-89; human rels. clk. Lockheed, Sunnyvale, Calif., 1978-84, 87-91; beauty cons. Mary Kay, Milpitas, Calif., 1984-87; project mgr. 129th Res. Wing, Moffett Fed. Airfield, 1991—, quality adminstr., 1997-98, project mgr., info. systems br. chief, 1998—. Contbr. articles to publs.; featured in Philippine News, 1999. Historian Parent Tchr. group, Santa Clara, Calif., 1997-98, v.p., Milpitas, 1995, sec., rm. mother, 1992-94; sec. Parent Tchr. Student Assn., Milpitas, 1999—. Mem. Air Force Assn. (bd. mem. liaison for unit 1999—), NAFE. Avocations: reading, walking, bicycling. Office: 129CF/SCX Stop #23 680 Macon Rd Moffett Field CA 94035

RAMOS, LOPES KLEYDE MENDES, biologist, general practitioner; b. V.da Conquista, Bahia, Brazil, Apr. 18, 1939; d. Miguel Lopes Ferraz and Zenith Mendes; m. Alvanio Machado Ramos, July 12, 1964; children: Illa Blanche Lopes, Ilbert Lopes, Ina Karisia Lopes. Cert. biology tchr., Fed. U. Bahia, Salvador, Brazil, 1961; MD, Cath. U., Salvador, Brazil, 1974. Especialized Lab. of Human Genetics, Salvador, Bahia, Brazil, 1962-64; biologist Biology Inst., Salvador, 1964-65, researcher of genetics, 1965-67; titular prof. Cath. U., Salvador, 1967—; writer Salvador, 1978—; asst. prof. Fed. U., Salvador, 1969-77, orienter prof. 1979-81, adj. prof. 1977—, titular prof. 1991; dir. Inst. Biology, Salvador, 1980-88; coord. Bd. of Dirs. of Med., Salvador, 1977-85. Author: Genetics, 1978, (poetry) A Arte de Amar-te, 1989, Amando Sempre, 1989, Vivendo, 1991, Esperanças, Doce Sertão, 1992, A Luz do Sol, 1993, Outros Caminhos, 1994, O Olodum do Pelourinho, 1995, Mimos do Ceu, 1996; contbr. articles to profl. jours.; presenter at confs. Fellow Rockefeller Found. 1961, Rio Grande Do Sul 1962. Mem. InterAm. Israelense Soc., Latin Am. Genetic Assn., Brazilian Geriatric / Gerontol. Soc., Brazilian Med. Assn., Brazilian Med. Women Assn., Brazilian Soc. to Sci., Brazilian Genetics Soc., Writer and Arts Acad. Salvador. Avocations: poetry, music, mode, farm. Achievements include creating Brazilian Friends' Day, April 18. Home: Av Manoel Dias da Silva 706, 40.000 Salvador Bahia, Brazil Office: Inst Biology, Barao de Geremoabo, 40.000 Salvador Bahia, Brazil

RAMOS, MANUEL, JR., hospital administrator; b. Wichita Falls, Tex., July 25, 1941; s. Manuel Arredondo and Erlinda (Gonzalez) R.; m. Patricia Arlene Ramos, Sept. 4, 1962 (dec. 1979); children—James Howard, Michael Arlie, Timothy Daniel; m. 2d, Emma Ochoa, Aug. 5, 1980. B.S. in Edn., Midwestern State U., 1972, M.S. in Edn., 1973. Tchr., athletic coach various schs., Tex. and Calif., 1962-75; personnel dir. Tex. Dept. Mental Health Retardation, San Antonio, 1975-79, hosp. adminstr., Laredo, 1979-83; hosp. adminstr. Charter Med. Corp., Laredo, 1983-86; hosp. adminstr., chief exec. officer HCA Deer Park (Tex.) Hosp., 1986—; pres., CEO Unified Health Network, LLC., Houston, 1990—; chmn. bd. San Antonio Fed. Credit Union, 1977-79; advisor Kingsville Health Systems Agy. (Tex.), 1979-82. Treas. March of Dimes, Laredo, 1979; chmn. Tex. United Way Campaign, 1982. Served with USMC, 1962-65. Named to Football Hall of Fame, Latin Am. Internat., 1982. Mem. Am. Soc. for Personnel, Nat. Assn. Supts. Pub. Residential Facilities for Mentally Retarded, Am. Assn. Mental Deficiencies. Republican. Roman Catholic. Home: 2322 Donegal Ct Deer Park TX 77536-4065 Office: Unified Health Network LLC 12555 Gulf Fwy Houston TX 77034-4509

RAMOS, PEDRO DE PAULA NOGUEIRA, information science educator; b. Lisbon, Portugal, Nov. 12, 1965; s. Joao Barreto Nogueira and Maria Teresa Cantaxo de Paula (Nogueira) R.; m. Maria Manuela Antones Gomes Silva, May 7, 1993; children: Carolina, Gil and Nuno (twins). Grad., ISCTE, Lisbon, 1988, MS, 1992, PhD, 1999. Assoc. prof. info. sci. U. Social and Bus. Scis., Lisbon, 1988—. Home: Rua do Mirador 41 2o Esq. 1300 Lisbon Portugal Office: ISCTE, Av Forcas Armadas, 1600 Lisbon Portugal

RAMOS, SEVERINO MONTEIRO, engineering executive; b. Gameleira, Brazil, May 15, 1936; s. Pedro Monteiro And Lucinda Ramos; m. Ramos Marcedes Monteiro, May 17, 1959; children: Marise, Fabiola, Lorena. Grad., Comml. Tech. Sch., Maceio, Brazil, 1951, Nobel Tech., Sao Paulo, Brazil, 1965, Politecnico Inst., Sao Paulo, 1971. Mech. sect. head Setal, Sao Paulo, 1974-76, project engr., project mgr., 1976-86, procurement coord., 1986—; project engr. field svcs. Setal, Campos, Brazil, 1990-91. Avocation: tennis. Office: Setal, Av Das Nacoes Unidas 18605, 04795902 Sao Paulo Brazil

RAMOS, TABARE, professional soccer player; b. Montevideo, Uruguay, Sept. 21, 1966; came to U.S., 1976, naturalized, 1988; s. Julian Ramos; m. Amy Ramos; 1 child, Alex Christopher. Edn., N.C. State U., 1984-87. Midfielder Metrostars, Secaucus, N.J., 1995—, U.S. Nat. Team, 1999—. Office: Metrostars 8th Fl One Harmon Plz Secaucus NJ 07094

RAMOS, THEODORE SANCHEZ DE PIÑA, artist, educator; b. Oporto, Portugal, Oct. 30, 1928; s. Guillermo Sanchez de Piña and Patrocinio Ramos Garcia; m. Julia Nan Rushbury, Aug. 17, 1950; children: Julian Sanchez de Piña (dec. 1986), Adrian Henry, Benedict John, Dominic Salvador. Student, No. Poly. London, 1943-45, Hornsey Sch. Art, 1945-47; diploma in fine art, Royal Acad. Schs., London, 1949-54. Freelance portrait painter; advisor on design and graphics Royal Acad. Arts, London; vis. lectr. fine art Royal Acad. Schs., 1954-75, Brighton Coll. Art, 1956-70, Harrow Sch. Art, 1960-69; cons. on graphics to numerous orgns. Illustrator Chinese art for Penguin Classics, poster and catalog design for Royal Acad.; represented in permanent collections Nat. Portrait Gallery, Royal Acad.; portraits include Anita Leslie and Lord Thorneycroft, Sir Henry Rushbury, Her Majesty the Queen, His Royal Highness The Duke of Edinburgh, Prince Charles, The Queen Mother. Recipient Royal Acad. Silver medal, 1953; titular Count of Codevilla. Mem. East India Club (life), Devonshire Club (life), Marylebone Cricket Club. Liberal. Roman Catholic. Home and Studio: Studio 3 Chelsea Farmhouse, Milmans St, London SW10 ODA, England

RAMOS-ALVAREZ, MANUEL, pediatrician, researcher; b. Mexico City, May 24, 1926; s. Manuel Mercado Ramos and Concepcion Arochi Alvarez; m. Maria Eugenia Gomez-Portugal Francia, Dec. 13, 1958; children: Maria Eugenia Ramos Francia, Manuel Ramos Francia, Federico Ramos Francia. MD, Universidad Nacional, Mexico City. Rsch. fellow USPHS, Montgomery, Ala., 1952; rsch. fellow dept. preventive medicine Sch. Medicine Yale U., New Haven, 1953; rsch. fellow pediat. Cleve. City Hosp./Western Res. U., 1953-54; prof. pediat. infectious diseases Universidad Nacional, 1958-86; founder, dir. gen. biol. products, 1961-66; head divsn. infectious diseases Children's Hosp., Mexico City, 1965-86; adviser Sec. Health, Mexico City, 1961-65; head pediat. divsn. Gen. Hosp., Mexico City, 1965-68; med. cons. Pfizer Internat., N.Y.C., 1962-64, Dow Chem. Human Rsch. Devel., Indpls., 1964; sr. investigator Children's Hosp. Rsch. Found. Sch. Medicine U. Cin., 1954-57; cons. dir. biol. stds. USPHS, 1958; invited lectr. Sch. Medicine Yale U., 1958, dept. virology & epidemiology Baylor U., Houston, 1963, U. Buenos Aires, U. Rosario Argentina, 1963; spl. cons. preventive medicine IMSS, Mex., 1959; chief advisor to Min. Health, Mex., 1959-65. Invited previewer Am. Jour. Diseases Children, 1966; contbr. articles to profl. jours. Recipient Premio Nacional Pediatria, 1959, 64, Premio Carnot Medalla Oro ACad. Nacional Medicina, 1962, Medalla Oro Eduardo Liceaga, 1963, Premio Federico Gomez Hosp. Inftantil Mex.; grantee NIH. Home: Blvd Virreyes 1135-PH, 11000 Mexico City Mexico Office: Nueva York 32-301, Mexico City Mexico

RAMOS-CANO, HAZEL BALATERO, caterer, chef, innkeeper, entrepreneur; b. Davao City, Mindanao, Philippines, Sept. 2, 1936; came to U.S., 1960.; d. Mauricio C. and Felicidad (Balatero) Ramos; m. William Harold Snyder, Feb. 17, 1964 (div. 1981); children: John Byron, Snyder, Jennifer Ruth; m. Nelson Allen Blue, May 30, 1986 (div. 1990); m. A. Richard Cano, June 25, 1994. BA in Social Work, U. Philippines, Quezon City, 1958; MA in Sociology, Pa. State U., 1963, postgrad., 1966-67. Cert. exec. chef, Am. Culinary Fedn. Faculty, tng. staff Peace Corps Philippine Project, University Park, Pa., 1961-63; sociology instr. Albright Coll. Sociology Dept., Reading, Pa., 1963-64; research asst. Meth. Ch. U.S.A., State College, Pa., 1965-66; research asst. dept. child devel. & family relations Pa. State U., University Park, Pa., 1966-67; exec. dir. Presbyn. Urban Coun. Raleigh Halifax Ct. Child Care and Family Svc. Ctr., 1973-79; early childhood educator Learning Together, Inc., Raleigh, 1982-83; loan mortgage specialist Raleigh Savings & Loan, 1983-84; restaurant owner, mgr. Hazel's on Hargett, Raleigh, 1985-86; admissions coord., social worker Brian Corp. Nursing Home, Raleigh, 1986-88, food svc. dir., 1989-90; regional dir. La Petite Acad., Raleigh, 1989-90; asst. food svc. mgr. Granville Towers, Chapel Hill, N.C., 1990-92; mgr. trainee Child Nutrition Svcs. Wake County Pub. Sch. System, Raleigh, N.C., 1993-94; food svc. dir. S.W. Va. 4-H Ednl. Conf. Ctr., Abingdon, 1994-95; caterer, owner The Eclectic Chef's Catering, 1995—; innkeeper, owner Love House Bed and Breakfast, 1996—; pres. Ramos-Cano Inc., 1996—; cooking instr. Wake Cmty. Tech. Coll., Raleigh, 1986-92; freelance caterer, 1964-95; chair Internat. Cooking Demonstrations Raleigh Internat. Festival, 1990-93. Pres. Wake County Day Care United Coun., 1974-75, N.C. Assn. Edn. Young Children (Raleigh Chpt.), 1975-76; bd. mem. Project Enlightenment Wake County Pub. Schs., 1976-77; various positions Pines of Carolina Girl Scout Council, 1976-85; chmn. Philippine Health and Medical Aid Com., Phil-Am Assn. Raleigh 1985-88 (publicity chmn.); elder Trinity Presbyn. Ch., Raleigh, 1979-81, bd. deacons, 1993-94; elder, session mem. Sinking Spring Presbyn. Ch., 1997—; treas. Abingdon Newcomers Club, 1997—, Presbyn. Women, Sinking Spring Presbyn. Ch., Abingdon, 1999—; master gardener Va. Tech. Master Gardeners Program, 1998—. Recipient Juliette Low Girl Scout Internat. award, 1953, Rockefeller grant Rockefeller Found., 1958-59, Ramon Magsaysay Presidential award, Philippine Leadership Youth Movement, 1957; Gov.'s Cert. Appreciation State N.C., 1990, Raleigh Mayor's award Quality Childcare Svcs., 1990, Recipient award for keeping hist. Abington beautiful Abington Kiwanis Club, 1997. Mem. Am. Culinary Fedn., Presby. Women, Raleigh, (historian 1975-76), Penn State Dames (pres. 1968-69). Democrat. E-mail: v&ainn@naxs.com. Office: Victoria & Albert 224 Oakhill Inn St Abingdon VA 24210 also: The Lone House Bed and Breakfast 210 E Valley St Abingdon VA 24210

RAMOS-HORTA, JOSE, Indonesian political activist; b. Dili, East Timor, Dec. 26, 1949; s. Francisco Horta and Natalina Ramos Filipe Horta; m. Ana Pessoa, 1978 (div.); 1 child. Student, Hague Acad. of Internat. Law, Inst. of Human Rights, Strasbourg, Columbia U., Antioch U. Journalist, broadcaster, 1969-74; min. for external affairs and info. East Timor, 1975; permanent rep. of Fretilin to UN N.Y., 1976-89; pub. affairs and media dir. Mozambican Embassy, Washington, 1987-88; dir., lectr. diplomacy tng. program U. NSW, from 1990; now v.p. Nat. Coun. East Timor Resistance, Dilli; vis. prof. 1996—; sr. assoc. mem. St. Antony's Coll., Oxford, 1987—. Contbr. articles to profl. publs. Spl. rep. Nat. Coun. of Maubere Resistance, 1991—; mem. bd. East Timor Human Rights Ctr., Melbourne. Recipient Unrepresented Nations and People's Orgn. award 1996; shared Nobel Peace Prize, 1996, Order of Freedom award 1996. Avocation: tennis. Fax: (1) 886-3791. Office: PO Box 2, Dilli East Timor, Indonesia*

RAMOS-MARTÍNEZ, ERNESTO, pathologist; b. Chihuahua, Mexico, Feb. 7, 1948; s. Ernesto and Fabiola (Martínez-Fourzán) Ramos-Avilés; m. Ana Maria Torres-Moye, Aug. 9, 1973; 1 child, Ernest David. MD, Chihuahua U., 1972; degree in anatomic pathology, Mex. U., 1976. Intern Nat. Med. Ctr. Hosps. Mex. Social Security, Mexico City, 1973-74, resident in anatomic pathology, 1974-77; prof. pathology Mex. U., 1975-85; anatomic pathologist Mex. Social Security, Mexico City, 1977-85, Chihuahua, 1985-92; anatomic pathologist Univ. Hosp., Chihuahua, 1992—; prof. histology Chihuahua U., 1986-99, prof. pathology, 1999—; assoc. researcher Mex. Social Security, 1983-85; chief postgrad. sch. Med. U. Chihuahua, 1986-88, sec. rsch. and postgrad. studies, 1988-92. Contbr. articles to profl. publs. Pres. Chihuahua U. Found., 1995-99. Recipient Best Proffered Paper award Soc. Gastroenterology, Chihuaha prize in biology area. Fellow Mex. Soc. Pathologists, Lat. Am. Soc. Hepatology Argentina, Lat. Am. Soc. Pathology, Med. Coll. Chihuahua (pres. 1991-93), Lat. Am. Fedn. Socs. Ob-Gyn; mem. Nat. Acad. Medicine, Chihuahua Soc. Pathology (pres. 1996-97). Roman

Catholic. Avocations: reading, tennis, jogging, movies, golf. Office: Gómez Farías # 115, 31000 Chihuahua Mexico

RAMOS-SOBRADOS, JUAN IGNACIO, engineering educator, researcher; b. Bernardos, Segovia, Spain, Jan. 28, 1953; s. Florentino and Maria (Sobrados) Ramos; m. Mercedes Naveiro, Dec. 1, 1990; children: Juan, Fernando. B.Engring., Madrid Poly. U., 1975, Dr.Eng., 1983; MA, Princeton (N.J.) U., 1979, PhD, 1980. Instr. Carnegie-Mellon U., Pitts., 1979-80, asst. prof., 1980-85, assoc. prof., 1985-89, prof. engring., 1989-93; vis. prof. U. de Malaga, Spain, 1990-91, prof., 1992—; engr. AISA, Madrid, 1976-77; cons. PPG Industries, Pitts., 1982-84, Aerochem Rsch. Labs., Princeton, 1988-91, Gruppo Nazionale por la Vulcanologia, Pisa, Italy, 1991-92; vis. prof. U. di Roma Tor Vergata, Italy, 1988, 89. Author: Internal Combustion Engine Modelling, 1989; assoc. editor Applied Math. Modelling, 1986—; adv. editor Internat. Jour. Heat and Fluid Flow, 1992—; mem. editl. bd. Hybrid Methods in Engring. and Sci., 1997—. 2d lt. Spanish Air Force, 1975-77. Recipient Aero. Engring. medal The King of Spain, 1977, Ralph R. Teetor award SAE, 1981; Van Ness Lothrop fellow Princeton U., 1979-80, Daniel and Florence Guggenheim fellow Princeton U., 1977, 78. Mem. AIAA (faculty advisor), SIAM. Roman Catholic. Avocations: tennis, classical music, reading. Office: Univ de Malaga, ETS Ingenieros Industriales, Plaza el Ejido S/N, 29013 Malaga Spain

RAMOS-ZÚÑIGA, RODRIGO, neurosurgeon, educator; b. Autlan, Jalisco, Mex., July 13, 1962; s. Roberto and Dolores (Zúñiga) R.; m. Rocio Enriquez, Apr. 3, 1993; 1 child, Rodrigo. MD, U. de Guadalajara, 1986, degree in neurosurgery, 1992, MSc, 2000. Tech. asst. U. Guadalajara, 1982-86, prof. physiology, 1986-99, prof. neurosci., 1999—; prof. VGF Hosp., Guadalajara, 1992—; pres. sci. com. med. students U. Guadalajara, 1985, pres. bachelors. Author: Neurophysiology, 1998; editor Neurosciences Jour., 1997; contbr. articles to profl. jours. Recipient Nat. Young award in Scis. from Pres. of Mex., 1987. Mem. Mexican Soc. Exptl. Surgery (v.p.), Mexican Soc. Neurol. Surgeons (sci. advisor), Mexican Surg. Rsch. Soc., Am. Assn. Neurol. Surgeons, Am. Assn. Neurol. (internat. mem. cerebrovascular sect.). Avocations: music, poetry, camping, snorkeling. E-mail: rodrigor@cencar.udg.mx. Office: Univ Guadalajara, Victoria 1531, Guadalajara 44630, Mexico

RAMOVS, PRIMOZ, composer; b. Ljubljana, Slovenia, Mar. 20, 1921; s. Franc and Alba (Zalar) R.; m. Stefanija Schubert, Jan. 17, 1955; children: Klemen, Polona, Ales. Diploma, Acad. Music, 1941; MusD (hon.), Marquis Guiseppe Scicluna Internat. U. Found., Malta, 1988. Libr. Slovene Acad. Scis. and Arts, Ljubljana, 1945-52, libr.-in-chief, 1952-87; prof. Conservatory in Ljubljana, 1948-52, 55-64. Composer 6 symphonies, musiques funèbres, Profils, Symphonic Portrait, Polyptych, Organofonia, 33 concertos for various instruments, symphonie chamber and instrumental music (over 450 opuses). With Naval Inf., 1947. Decorated Order of Work with Golden Wreath, Order of Sainsts Cyrille and Method, Eques Comendator Ordinis Sancti Gregorii Magni; recipient awards Philharm. Soc., 1944, Festival, 1958, Fund of Preseren, 1962, Yugoslav Radio, 1967, 69, 70, 76, diploma Cop, 1971, Internat. Cultural Diploma Honor, 1988, Slovene Philharm., 1978, Chevalier Comdr., 1989, World Decoration of Excellence, 1989. Mem. Soc. Slovene Composers Ljubljana (v.p. 1967-71), Soc. Slovene Librs. Ljubljana, Slovene Acad. Scis. and Arts (Preseren's prize 1983, medal of honor 1986), Slovene Alpine Soc., Slovene Lit. Soc., Croatian Acad. Scis. and Arts, European Acad. Scis. and Arts, World U. (doctoral mem.), Slovene Philharm. (hon.). Roman Catholic. Home: 1 Slovenska cesta, 1000 Ljubljana Slovenia

RAMPACHER, HERMANN HANS, computer science executive; b. Ulm, Germany, Dec. 29, 1934; s. Hermann Alexander and Pauline Katharine (Milch) R.; m. Ursel Hanna Brand; 1 child, Carsten. BS, Coll. Stuttgart, 1954, MSc in Physics, 1962; PhD in Physics, U. Munich, 1968. Rsch. asst. Max Planck Gesellschaft, Munich, 1965-68; asst. prof. U. Tuebingen, 1968-70; systems engr. IBM Deutschland, Stuttgart, 1970-79; rschr. GMD German Nat. Rsch. Ctr. for Info. Tech., Bonn, 1979-81; chief exec. Gesellschaft for Info., Bonn, 1982-99; mng. dir. German Info. Acad. GmbH (DIA), 1997—; bd. dirs. Internat. Conf. and Rsch. Ctr. for Computer Sci., Schloss Dagstuhl, 1995-99; exec. com. Coun. European Profl. Informatics Socs., London, 1996-97. Fellow Br. Computer Soc.; mem. IEEE, Max-Planck Gesellschaft, Allgemeine Gesellschaft for Philosophy in Deutschland, N.Y. Acad. Scis. Avocations: ethics, history, literature, classical music. Office: Deutsche Informatik Akad, Wissenschaftszentrum Ahrstr, D-53175 Bonn Germany

RAMPAL, MARIUS, urologist, surgeon, educator, retired; b. Marseille, France, July 5, 1926; s. Louis and Antoinette (Silvi) R.; m. Madeleine Reineri, Sept. 4, 1951; children: Pierre, Anne, François, Dominique. Grad., Med. U., Marseille, 1946. Asst. 1st degree Marseille Hosp., 1947-50, asst. 2d degree, 1950-56, chief asst. surgeon, 1956-60, prof. gen. surgery, surgeon, 1962-95, prof. urology, 1974-95, ret., 1995; chief surg. svcs. Marseille Hosp., 1974-75. Contbr. over 300 articles to profl. jours. Lt. Nat. Mil., 1951-52. Mem. Exptl. European Surgery, French Transplantation Soc. Avocations: physical training, hunting, sea fishing, skiing. Home: 19 Blvd Sylvestre, 13012 Marseille France

RAMPLEY, DENNIS NEIL, company director; b. Moatlands Brenchley, Kent, Eng., July 29, 1941; s. Arthur and Mary (Murray) R. Rschr., Oxford U.; diploma in freight forwarding, Fedn. Internat. des Assns. de Transitaires et Assimiles, Zurich; licentiateship, City and Guilds London Inst. Rsch. worker Shell Rsch. Ltd., 1963-66, U. London, 1966-72; pvt. practice mgmt. and tech. cons., 1973-77; with Powell Duffryn Shipping Ltd., 1977-87; co. sec. Assoc. Transport Corp. Ltd. (now Anglo European Agys. Ltd.), 1987-91, Deutrans (London) Ltd., 1990-91, Arnessen Global Svcs. Ltd., DSR Lines Ltd.; v.p., dir. Decofreight Internat., Inc., Miami, Fla., 1990-91; pres., dir. Seafast Inc., Miami, 1990-91, Chartered Internat. Assocs. Inc., Miami, 1990—; lectr. graduateship exam. Inst. of Materials Handling, 1969-70; provost Meridian U. Internat., 1991-94; vis. prof. Nova U., Ft. Lauderdale, Fla., 1993; mem. liquidation coms. of inspection, 1977-91; expert witness in field, 1971-91. Freeman City of London, 1995; mem. com. Canterbury Kent, Brit. Inst. Mgmt., 1976-77; pub. rels. officer S.E. divsn. Inst. Materials Handling, 1970-71; chmn. East Kent sect. Inst. Supervisory Mgmt., 1974-75. Fellow Inst. Bus. Adminstrn. (life), Brit. Soc. Commerce (life), Royal Soc. Arts (life), Chartered Inst. Transport, Inst. Chartered Shipbrokers, Inst. Co. Accts., Tech. Surface Coatings (internat. register), Inst. Logistics and Transport; mem. Chartered Inst. Journalists, Chartered Inst. Arbitrators, Royal Sch. Mines Assn. (life), Oxford Soc. Avocations: chess, cooking, driving, gardening, numismatics. Home: 28 Lower Herne Rd, Herne Bay Kent CT6 7NA, England

RAMPOLLA, MAURA SMITH, public health professional; b. Phila., Apr. 12, 1968; d. Gerard Peter and Barbara McInnis Smith; m. Mark Stephen Rampolla, Oct. 3, 1998. BA in Polit. Sci., cert. African studies, Northwestern U., 1990; M in Pub. Health, U. N.C., 1996. Adminstrv. asst. Lassez et Associes, Paris, 1990; translator Project Hope, Quetzaltenango, Guatemala, 1992; placement officer African-Am. Inst., N.Y.C., 1992-95; rsch. asst. Carolina Population Ctr., Chapel Hill, N.C., 1995-96; cons. Internat. Projects Assistance Svcs., Carrboro, N.C., 1996, Rsch. Triangle Inst., 1997; coord. health promotion Le Bonheur Children's Med. Ctr., Memphis, 1997-99; dir. edn. Memphis Regional Planned Parenthood, 1999; ind. cons., 2000—. Maternal and infant health com. mem. Shelby Regional Health Coun., Memphis, 1998-99; grant reviewer Women's Found. of Greater Memphis, 1998-99; advocacy chair, mem. Adolescent Pregnancy Prevention Coun., Memphis, 1997-99. ILAS Field Rsch. and Travel grant Tinker Found., 1996; fgn. lang. and area studies fellowship U.S. Dept. of Edn., 1996. Mem. Am. Pub. Health Assn., Am. Sch. Health Assn. Avocations: scuba diving, hiking, singing. Home: 6400 Poplar Ave Apt E60 Memphis TN 38197-0100

RAMPONE, SALVATORE, computer scientist; b. Benevento, Italy, May 1, 1962; s. Glauco and Emilia (Casamassa) R. Licenza liceale, Liceo Scientifico Grummo, 1981; laurea in computer sci., U. Salerno, 1989. Fellow Alcatel, Salerno and Milan, 1989-90; cons. IIASS, Vietri, Italy, 1990-91; fellow CNR (Nat. Rsch. Coun.), Naples, Italy, 1991-93; prof. U. Salerno, 1992-96, U. Sannio, 1997—; co-organizer Italian Neural Network Soc. Conf., Vietri, 1993—; cons. dept. fisica Teorica e SMSA U. Salerno, 1993-95. Author: Neural Nets, 1995; contbr. articles to profl. jours. Mem. INFN, GRIN, others. Avocation: amateur radio. Office: U Sannio Facoltá Scienze, Via Port'Arsa 11, Benevento 82100, Italy

RAMQVIST, LARS HENRY, communications company executive; b. Grängesberg, Sweden, Nov. 2, 1938; s. Henry Erik and Alice (Södersten) R.; m. Barbro Maria Petterson, Apr. 12, 1962; children: Louise, Martin. PhD, Uppsala U., Sweden, 1969. Head material lab. Stora AB, Stockholm, 1962-65; pres. Axel Johnson Inst., Stockholm, 1965-80; v.p. LM Ericsson, Stockholm, 1980-84; pres. Rifa AB, Stockholm, 1984-86, Ericsson Radio Systems AB, Stockholm, 1988-90; pres., CEO, Telefonaktiebolaget LM Ericsson, Stockholm, 1990-98, chmn., 1998—; bd. dirs. Astra, Svenska Cellulosa Akteibolaget SCA, Volvo, and the Fedn. of the Swedish Industries. Mem. Royal Swedish Acad. Engring. Scis., Royal Swedish Acad. Scis. Office: Telefonaktiebolaget LM Ericsson, Telefonaktiebolaget, S-126 25 Stockholm Sweden*

RAMS, DIETER, industrial designer, architect; b. Wiesbaden, Hessen, Germany, May 20, 1932; m. Ingeborg Kracht Rams. Diploma in Architecture, Sch. Art, Wiesbaden, 1953; Dr., Royal Coll. of Art, London, 1991. With Otto Apel, 1953-55; indsl. designer, dir. design, exec. dir. design Barun AG Kronberg, 1955-95; ret., 1995; prof. Hochschule für Bildende Künste, Hamburg, Fed. Republic Germany, 1981-97, prof. emeritus, 1997—; internat. mem. Jury for the 2d Design Competition, 1984; hon. internat. faculty mem. Ontario (Can.) Coll. Art, 1987—. One-man shows include Internat. Design Ctr., 1980, Phila. Mus. Art, 1983; exhibited in group shows at Biennal of Idnsl. Design, Ljubljana, 1980, Amos Andersen Art Mus., Helsinki, Padiglione d'arte Contemporeana di Milano, Victoria and Albert Mus., London, 1982, Stedeljk Mus., Amsterdam, 1982, Kunstgewerbemuseum, Cologne, 1983. Recipient Interplast award, 1961, 63, Gold Medal Triennale, Phono-Radio-Combination Audio 1, 1964, Internat. "Wiener Möbelsalon" gold medal, 1969, Gute Form award, 1969, 70, 73, 83, Design Ctr. Stuttgart award, 1975, 79, 80, Soc. of the Indsl. Artists and Designers medal, 1978, Rosenthal Studio award, 1978, Busse Longlife Design Award, 1981, World Design medal Indsl. Designers Soc. of Am., 1996; named Hon. Royal Designer for Industry, Royal Soc. Arts, 1968, Fgn. Hon. Academician, Exec. Com. of the Academia Mexicana de Diseno, 1985; Kulturkreis im Bundesverband der Deutschen Industrie, 1960. Mem. German Design Coun. (pres., mem. supervisory bd. 1976—), Assn. German Indsl. Designers, Deutscher Werkbund. Office: Franz Schneider Brakel GmbH, Nieheimer Strasse 38, D-33034 Brakel Germany also: SDRT, Schaevenstr 7, D-50676 Cologne Germany*

RAMSAHOYE, LYTTLETON ESTIL, geophysicist, consultant, educator; b. Fellowship, Demerara, Guyana, Aug. 11, 1930; arrived in Barbados, 1978; s. Edward Jairad and Wilhelmina Alverna (Fenton) R.; m. Elizabeth Mariai Kerry, June 2, 1962; children: Debra, Carol. BSc in Physics with honours, King's Coll., London, 1954; PhD in Geophysics, Imperial Coll., London, 1957; diploma in pub. health engring., U. Minn., 1959. Geophysicist, hydrologist Geol. Survey Guyana, 1957-59; chief Pure Water Supply, Guyana, 1960-62; prof. physics U. Guyana, 1963-78, dean natural scis., dep. vice chancellor, 1964-78; rsch. dir. Caribbean Meteorol. Inst., Christchurch, Barbados, 1978-83; ret., 1983; cons. hydrologist Aubrey Barker Assocs., Guyana, 1963-78. Contbr. articles to profl. jours.; patentee for cement extender. Vol. Queen Elizabeth Hosp. Lab., Barbados, 1987—; mem. parliament Guyana, 1973-78. Scholar Govt. of Guyana, 1949; fellow Pan Am. Health Orgn., 1960. Home: Cardomar, Maxwell Main Rd, Christchurch Barbados

RAMSAHOYE, WALTER ALAN, neurologist; b. Blankenburg, Guyana, Mar. 30, 1942; s. Edward Jairad and Wilhelmina Alverna (Fenton) R.; m. Marion Tessa Gray, Aug. 4, 1973 (div. 1977). BA in Natural Sci., Cambridge U., Eng., 1964, MB, BChir, 1967, MA, 1968; MRCP, Royal Coll. of Physicians, London, 1970. FRCP/London, Edinburgh, Glasgow. House appointments physician St. Thomas' Hosp., London, 1967-68, registrar in dermatology, 1968-69; registrar in dermatology St. John's Hosp. and Inst. of Dermatology, London, 1968-69; registrar in gen. medicine St. Thomas' Hosp., 1969-70, registrar in cardiology, 1970; registrar in dept. neuro-surg. studies The Nat. Hosp. Queen Sq., London, 1970; chmn. Med. Coun. Cuyana, 2000—; acad. registrar The Nat. Hosp. Queen Square, London, 1970-71, registrar in neurology, 1971-74, cons. physician, Georgetown, Guyana, 1974—, cons. neurologist, 1974—. Author: Research on Medical Legislation, 1988, Code of Ethics for Medical Profession, others; contbr. articles to profl. jours. Chmn. Nat. Formulary Com., Guyana, 1987-89; v.p. Queen's Coll. Old Students' Assn., Guyana, 1990-92; chmn. Commonwealth Liaison Unit, Guyana, 1990-92; pres. Guyana Cycling Assn., 1977-82. Govt. of Guyana Cambridge U. schoar, 1961-67; recipient Highest award Order of Giglioli Guyana Med. Assn., 1999. Fellow Am. Acad. Neurology, Royal Coll. Physicians; mem. Guyana Med. Assn. (v.p. 1987-89, pres. 1989-92), Sports Medicine Assn. (chmn. steering com. 1989-92), Cabinet Sub-Com. on Health, Am. Coll. Physicians, Georgetown Cricket Club, Georgetown Club/Guyana. Mem. Ch. of Eng. Avocations: music, drama, reading, internat. affairs, cricket. Office: 11 North Rd/Bourda, Georgetown 4 Guyana

RAMSAY, JAY, poet; b. Guilford, Surrey, Eng., Apr. 20, 1958; s. Donald and Yvonne (Wray) Ramsay-Brown; m. Carole Bruce Landless. BA with honors, Pembroke Coll., Oxford, Eng., 1980. Co-founder, performer, adminstr. Angels of Fire Collective, 1982-89; co-creator workshop The Sacred Space of The Word, 1988; tchr., project dir. Chrysalis, 1990—; asst. to dir. Directory of Social Change, 1984, Think Green, 1986. Author: Psychic Poetry: A Manifesto, 1985, Raw Spiritual: Selected Poems, 1980-85, 1986, Trwyn Meditations, 1987, The White Poem, photographs by Carole Bruce, 1988, The Great Return, books 1-5, 1988, transmissions, 1989, Strange Days, 1990; (with Geoffrey Godbert) For Now, 1991; The Rain, The Rain, 1992, Improvisations, 1994; (with Jenny Davis) Journey to Eden; Kingdom of the Edge, New and Selected Poems, 1980-1998, Alchemy-The Art of Transformation, 1997, Love's Way--The Alchemy of Relationships, 2000; editor: (with others) Angels of Fire: An Anthology of Radical Poetry in the Eighties, 1986, Transformation: The Poetry of Spiritual Consciousness, 1988, In the Gold of Flesh, 1990, Earth Ascending, 1997, Sacred Britain, 1997, Tending Holy Ground, 1997; co-translator Tao Te Ching, 1993-94, I Ching, 1995, (with Martin Palmer) Kuan Yin, 1995; editor (poetry mag.) Third Eye, 1983-84; contbr. poems and reviews to Brit. and European mags. Office: Chrysalis, 5 Oxford Ter Uplands, Glos Stroud GL5 1TW, England

RAMSAY, JOHN GERARD, academic administrator, writer; b. Phila., Oct. 31, 1951; s. Jack and Jean (Duffey) R.; m. Michele Twomey, July 10, 1982; children: Nicholas John, Jacob Joseph, Luke Michael. BA in History, Bucknell U., 1973; PhD in Ednl. Studies, SUNY, Buffalo, 1984. Cert. tchr., N.Y., Laubach Literacy tutor. Tchr. English and history, debate coach Collegiate Sch., N.Y.C., 1981-84; chmn., dir. tchr. edn. Dickinson Coll., Carlisle, Pa., 1984-89; chmn. dept. ednl. studies Carleton Coll., Northfield, Minn., 1989-92, 95-96, coord. Carleton's Perlman Ctr. Learning and Tchg., 1997—, pres. faculty, 2000—. Columnist Talk of the College: Has it Grown Quiet?, 1999. Mem. Northfield Pub. Schs. Bd. Edn., Minn., 1996—, treas., 2000—. Nat. Acad. Edn. fellow, 1987-88, Am. Coun. Learned Studies fellow, 1992-93. E-mail: jramsay@carleton.edu.

RAMSAY, JOHN GRAHAM, geology educator; b. London, June 17, 1931; arrived in Switzerland, 1977; s. Robert William and Kathleen May (Ellis) R.; m. Christine Marden, Aug. 19, 1960 (div. Dec. 1987); children: Ishbel, Alison, Rebecca; m. Dorothee Dietrich, Mar. 5, 1990. BS, London U., 1952, diploma Imperial Coll., PhD, 1954, DSc, 1974; doctorat (hon.), Rennes (France) U., 1978. Lectr. London U., 1957-66, prof., 1966-73; prof., dept. head U. Leeds, Eng., 1973-77, ETH Zürich and U. Zürich, Switzerland, 1977—. Author: Folding and Fracturing of Rocks, 1967, Modern Structural Geology, 1983, vol. 2, 1987, vol. 3, 2000, Poems, Verses and Monologues, 1998. Mem. Natural Environment Rsch. Coun., Eng., 1989-92. Musician Corps of Engrs., 1955-57. Recipient Prestwich medal Société Géologique de France, 1989. Fellow (hon) Geol. Soc. London (coun. 1968-71, Bigsby medal 1973, Wollaston medal 1986), Holmes medal 1991, Trasentes medal 1991, Prix Lataud (acad. sci. France) 1991, Comdr. Order British Empire (CBE) 1992, Royal Soc. London, Geol. Soc. Am. (hon.), Am. Geophysical Union (hon.); mem. U.S. Nat. Acad. Scis. (fgn.), fellow Indian Nat. Sci. Acad. (fgn.). Avocations: chamber music, skiing, writing poetry. Office: Geologisches Inst, ETH Zentrum, 8092 Zürich Switzerland

RAMSAY, LOUIS LAFAYETTE, JR., lawyer, banker; b. Fordyce, Ark., Oct. 11, 1918; s. Louis Lafayette and Carmile (Jones) R.; m. Joy Bond, Oct. 3, 1945; children: Joy Blankenship, Richard Louis. JD, U. Ark., 1947; LLD (hon.), U. Ark., Fayetteville, 1988, U. Ark., Pine Bluff, 1992. Bar: Ark. 1947, U.S. Dist. Ct. Ark. 1947, U.S. Ct. Appeals (8th cir.) 1948, U.S. Supreme Ct. 1952. Of counsel Ramsay, Bridgforth, Harrelson & Starling and predecessor firm Ramsay, Cox, Lile, Bridgforth, Gilbert, Harrelson & Starling, Pine Bluff, Ark., 1948—; pres. Simmons First Nat. Bank, Pine Bluff, Ark., 1970-78, CEO, chmn. bd. dirs., 1978-83; chmn. exec. com., bd. dirs. Blue Cross-Blue Shield of Ark., Usable Life Ins. Co.; chmn. exec. com. Simmons First Nat. Corp. Mem. bd. Econ. Devel. Alliance of Jefferson County; mem. ofcl. bd. First United Meth. Ch. With USAF, 1942-45, maj. Res., 1945-49. Recipient Disting. Alumnus award U. Ark., 1982, Outstanding Lawyer award Ark. Bar Assn./Ark. Bar Found., 1966, 87. Mem. ABA (mem. spl. com. on presdl. inability and vice presdl. vacancy 1966), Ark. Bar Assn. (pres. 1963-64), Ark. Bar Found. (pres. 1960-61, Joint Bar Assn.,-Bar Found. Outstanding Lawyer award 1966, Lawyer Citizen award 1987), Ark. Bankers Assn. (pres. 1980-81), Pine Bluff C. of C. (pres. 1968), Rotary (pres. Pine Bluff 1954-55). Methodist. Office: Ramsay Bridgforth Harrelson & Starling 11th Fl Simmons 1st Nat Bldg 501 S Main St Pine Bluff AR 71601-4327

RAMSAY, TIMOTHY NIGEL, chemist; b. Derby, Derbyshire, Eng., Feb. 27, 1953; s. Norman and Beatrice Dorothy (Higgs) R.; m. Lynne Marjorie Clark, May 29, 1976; children: Jonathan Edward, Abigail. B in Chemistry, Sheffield (Eng.) Hallam U., 1981. Analytical chemist Staveley Chems, Chesterfield, Eng., 1974-77; devel. chemist Staveley Chems, Chesterfield, 1977-80; analytical chemist Rhône-Poulenc Chems, Chesterfield, 1980-86, analytical devel. chemist, 1986-93, sect. mgr. effluents, 1993-96, quality, safety and environ. officer, 1996—; presenter in field. Gov. Derbyshire Schs., Chesterfield, 1990-94, 96—. Mem. Royal Soc. Chemistry (chartered), Chartered Inst. Water Environ. Mgmt. Avocations: walking, swimming, badminton. Fax: 01246 342364. E-mail: tim.ramsay@eu.rhodia.com. Office: Rhodia Eco Svcs, Staveley Works Chesterfield, Derbyshire SH3 2PB, England

RAMSAY, WILLIAM CHARLES, writer; b. N.Y.C., Nov. 6, 1930; s. Claude Barnett and Myrtle Marie (Scott) R.; m. Jane Coutant Evans, July 7, 1997; children from previous marriages: Alice, John, Carol Ramsay Scott, David. BA in English Lit., U. Colo., 1952; MA in Physics, UCLA, 1957, PhD in Physics, 1962. NFS postdoctoral fellow U. Calif., San Diego, 1962-64; asst. prof. U. Calif., Santa Barbara, 1964-67; tech. mgr. Systems Assocs., Inc., Long Beach, Calif., 1967-72; sr. environ. economist U.S. AEC, Bethesda, Md., 1972-75; tech. adviser U.S. Nuclear Regulatory Agy., Washington, 1975-76; sr. fellow Resources for the Future, Washington, 1976-83, Ctr. for Strategic and Internat. Studies, Washington, 1983-85; sr. staff officer NAS, Washington, 1985-86; freelance writer, editor, publ. Washington, 1986—; cons. Vols. in Tech. Assistance, Arlington, Va., 1987-90, 98—, Internat. Resources Group, Washington, 1991. Author: Unpaid Costs of Electrical Energy, 1979, Bioenergy and Economic Development, 1985, (play) Agamemnon, Georgetown Theatre Co., 2000; co-author: Managing the Environment, 1972, Energy in America's Future, 1979; editor, pub. Fiction-Online (electronic lit. jour.). Mem. adv. bd. Nat. Zoo, Washington. Buenos Aires Convention fellow, 1952, NSF fellow, 1962; NATO scholar, 1960, 62. Mem. Am. Phys. Soc., Am. Astron. Soc., Internat. Assn. Energy Economists, Washington Ind. Writers, Writers' Ctr. (bd. dirs.). Avocations: piano, musical composition. Home and Office: 3120 N St NW Washington DC 20007-3413

RAMSDALE, DAVID ROLAND, cardiologist; b. Rishton, Lancashire, Eng., Dec. 3, 1950; s. William and Winifred Ramsdale; m. Bernadette Ann Shaw, Mar. 6, 1976; children: Christopher, Mark, Kathryn. BSc in Anatomy, Manchester (Eng.) U., 1971, MBChB, 1975, MRCP, 1978, MD, 1981. Accreditation cardiology, specialist in interventional cardiology. Rsch. fellow Wythenshawe Hosp., Manchester, 1979-81; sr. registrar in cardiology Sefton Gen. Hosp., Broadgreen Hosp., Liverpool, 1981-86; dir. Cardiac Catherisation Labs., Liverpool, Eng., 1990-95, chmn. dept. cardiology, 1995—. Author: Difficult Concepts in Cardiology, 1993; author, editor Practical Interventional Cardiology, 1996. Fellow Royal Coll. Physicians; mem. Brit. Cardiac Soc., Brit. Cardiovascular Intervention Soc. Avocations: golf, music, theatre. Home: 45 Rodney St, Liverpool L19EW, England Office: Cardiothoracic Centre, Thomas Dr, Liverpool L14 3PE, England

RAMSDELL, RICHARD ADONIRAM, marine engineer; b. Hartford, Conn., Feb. 28, 1953; s. Robert Allen and Irene Ella (Lewis) R.; m. Vicki Lynn Pepin, July 1, 1978 (div. Mar. 1984); children: Eric Charles, Ryan Amber; m. Beverly Jane Tenken; children: Alexander Richard, Matthew Robin. BS in Marine Engring., Maine Maritime Acad., 1975. Plant operator Ga. Pacific, Woodland, Maine, 1975-77; 2d asst. engr. Farrell Lines, Inc., N.Y.C., 1977-83; steam plant foreman Jackson Lab., Bar Harbor, Maine, 1984-86; plant operator Babcock-Ultrapower Jonesboro, Maine, 1986-90; results, environ. engr. Maine Power Svcs., Bangor, 1990-92; plant engr. Babcock-Ultrapower West Enfield, Maine, 1992-95, Ebensburg (Pa.) Power Co., 1995—. Office: Ebensburg Power Co PO Box 845 Ebensburg PA 15931-0845

RAMSDEN, JEREMY JOACHIM, biophysics scientist; b. Amersham, Eng., Aug. 13, 1955; s. Geoffrey Reeve and Dolores Helena Martha (Forster-Müller) R. MA, Cambridge (Eng.) U., 1981; Dr. ès Sci., Ecole Poly. Fédérale, Lausanne, Switzerland, 1985. Rsch. scientist Ilford, Ltd., Warley, Essex, Eng., 1977-81; rsch. assoc. Princeton (N.J.) U., 1985-86; visiting scientist Hungarian Acad. Scis., Bioctr., Szeged, 1986-87; scientist Basel (Switzerland) U., Bioctr., 1987—, privat-docent, 1994—; pres. Inst. Advanced Study, Basel, 1999—; vis. scientist Swiss Nat. Found., Budapest, Hungary, 1985, USSR Acad. Scis., Moscow, 1990. Author: The New World Order, 1991; contbr. articles to profl. jours. Mem. United Oxford & Cambridge Univ. Club, Swiss Biochem. Soc., Math. Assn. Am. Avocations: music, alpine skiing, sailing. Home: Hochstrasse 51, Basel CH-4053, Switzerland Office: Biozentrum der Univ, Klingelbergstrasse 70, Basel CH-4056, Switzerland

RAMSDEN, KAREN MCCOIN, writer; b. Knoxville, Tenn., Sept. 26, 1945; d. Bedford Hamilton Sr. and Kathryn Etolia (Hines) McCoin; m. Richard William Ramsden, Oct. 22, 1976; 1 child, Kathleen Hamilton. Student, Westminster Sch. for Girls, Atlanta, 1963, U. Hawaii, 1963; BS, U. Tenn., 1967, postgrad., 1975-76; postgrad., Edn. for Ministry, Sewanee, Tenn., 1991-92, Precept Bible Study, Marietta, Ga., 1992—. Buyer Athletic House, Knoxville, 1969-70; tutor Minority Students Program U. Tenn., Knoxville, 1974; architectural/interior designer Design/Build, Knoxville, 1976-83; aide pub. rels. Christ the King Sch., Atlanta, 1987-89, also instr. guidance, 1988-89. Author: The Tablet of Destinies, 1988, (newsletters) Hotline, King's Kids, 1987-89; contbr. to newspaper Ga. Bull., 1987-89; editor, pub. (quar.) What's Ahead?, 1988; residential designer Hild House, Thomas House, 1977; contbg. editor, pub. (quar.) Stillpoint, 1990-91; contbg. essayist (quar.) The Direct Line, Johnson Ferry Bapt. Ch. Ministry, 1997—. Dir., vol. Playmobile, Knoxville, 1971-73. Recipient community recognition Knoxville News Sentinel, 1980. Mem. Jr. League Cobb-Marietta, Inc., Nine O'Clock Cotillion, Alpha Lambda Delta, Delta Delta Delta (alumni v.p. 1982). Avocations: phys. fitness, gourmet cooking, gardening, travel, conversation.

RAMSDEN, MICHAEL JOHN, library professional, consultant; b. Leeds, Yorkshire, Eng., Apr. 17, 1935; arrived in Australia, 1971; s. Joseph and Ada (Wilson) R.; m. Sylvia Shirley Brisley, Nov. 28, 1959; children: Philip, Caroline, Patrick. BA with honors, U. Southampton, 1957; M in Social Sci., RMIT, Melbourne, Australia, 1978. Various positions pub. librs. U.K., 1957-71; from lectr. to sr. lectr. Coll. of Librarianship, Aberystwyth, Wales, 1967-71; from lectr. to sr. lectr. dept. librarianship RMIT, 1971-77, head dept. librarianship, 1977-85, dean Faculty of Comm. and Social Scis., 1985-94, pro-vice chancellor acad. programs, 1994-95. Author: A History of the AAL, 1895-1945, 1973, An Introduction to Index Language Construction, 1974, Performance Measurement of Some Melbourne Public Libraries, 1978, Precis: A Workbook for Students of Librarianship, 1981. Councillor Beaumaris H.S. Coun., Melbourne, 1980-83, Libr. Assn. U.K., 1965-70, Libr. Assn. Australia, 1977-78. Fellow Libr. Assn., Australian Libr. and Info. Assn.; mem. Victoria State Opera Soc.; Assn. Asst. Librs. (pres. 1969,

councillor 1961-70). Avocations: cricket, opera, reading. Home: 104 Lakeview Dr, Lilydale Victoria 3140, Australia

RAMSEY, BILL (WILLIAM MCCREERY), singer, actor, composer-lyricist, television executive; b. Cin., Apr. 17, 1931; s. William McCreery II and Olivia (James) R.; m. Erica Moeckli, Dec. 14, 1962 (div. Feb. 1982); 1 son, Joachim.; m. Petra Bock, Aug. 3, 1983. Student, Yale U., 1949-51, Goethe U., Frankfurt/Main, Germany, 1955, 57, U. Cin., 1956-57. guest prof. vocal jazz and presentation in pop and jazz program Hamburg U. Music and Drama, Hamburg, 1983-86. Partime profl. singer, 1949; appeared on Horace Heidt show, Hollywood, Calif., 1951, Eddie Fisher tour, Europe, 1953, Raymond Burr tour, Europe and North Africa, 1954, series jazz concerts, Germany and Am., 1953-55; 1st American to appear at German Jazz Festival, 1955, 1st American jazz vocalist after war to tour Yugoslavia, 1955, 1st TV portrait, Frankfurt/Main, 1955, 1st films in Baden-Baden, Munich, Hamburg, 1955; full-time profl. jazz and pop vocalist, 1957—, numerous recs.; actor numerous films, TV shows; songwriting, disc jockey work with Radio Luxembourg, Europawelle Saar, Radio Salzburg; 1st American jazz singer to tour Poland after war, also appearances Polish Jazz Festival, 1957, 67, Czek Jazz Festival, 1966; 1st pop record hit German version of Purple People Eater, 1958; program dir. Televico AG, Zurich/Gockhausen, Swiss TV and Film Prodn. Co., 1968-72, rec. artist for Polydor, Electrolia, Columbia, Cornet, Warner Bros., Stockfish, Ariola, Dino, Bear Family; in addition to singing, TV moderator on all three German Programs as well as in Austria since 1970. With USAF, 1951-55. Recipient top positions in various jazz polls. Mem. German Authors and Composers Soc. Address: Elbchaussee 118, D-22763 Hamburg Germany

RAMSEY, JOANNE MARIE, data processing executive; b. Long Branch, N.J., Oct. 13, 1945; d. Erwin P. and Erna M. (Green) Forrest; 1 child, Cheryl. BS, Monmouth Coll., 1967; MS, Stevens Inst. Tech., 1971. Mem. tech. staff Bell Telephone Labs., Holmdel, N.J., 1967-71; programmer analyst Cooper Electric Supply Co., Middletown, N.J., 1971-73; sr. programmer Insco Systems Corp., Neptune, N.J., 1973-78; sr. programmer analyst Internat. Flavors and Fragrances, Hazlet, N.J., 1978-79; mgr. Bristol-Myers Squibb Co., Plainsboro, N.J., 1980—. Mem. NAFE, Am. Prodn. and Inventory Control Soc. Home: 424 E Highland Ave Atlantic Highlands NJ 07716-1710 Office: Bristol-Myers Squibb 777 Scudders Mill Rd # P3508 Plainsboro NJ 08536-1615

RAMSEY, JOHN CHARLES, insurance executive; b. Pitts., Nov. 15, 1963; s. Gordon Charles Ramsey and Genevieve Mary McCartney; m. Laura Caine, Nov. 28, 1987; children: Gordon, Elizabeth, Olivia. BS, Robert Morris Coll., 1986; JD, NYU, 1990. Product mgr. The Equitable, N.Y.C., 1984-90; sales mgr. Mut. N.Y., Pitts., 1990-94; pres. Berkshire Ramsey Group, Pitts., 1994-97; mng. dir. Signator Fin. Network, Canfield, Ohio, 1997—; spkr. in field. Trustee Robert Morris Coll., Pitts., 1997-99; mem. new leadership bd. Pitts. Symphony Orch., 1999—; amb. Civic Light Opera. Recipient Nat. Mgmt. award Gen. Acct. Mgrs. Assn., 1998. Mem. Nat. Assn. Life Underwriters, Gen. Agts. and Mgrs. Assn., Harvard Yale Princeton Club (bd. dirs. 1992-96), HYP Pitts. Club (bd. dirs. 1991), Salem Golf Club, Robert Morris Coll. Alumni Assn. (past pres.). Republican. Presbyterian. Avocations: reading, weightlifting. Home: 1787 Pearce Cir Salem OH 44460-1852

RAMSEY, KATHLEEN SOMMER, toxicologist; b. Port Washington, Wis., June 2, 1947; d. Harrison Wilson and June Kathleen (Hansen) S.; m. Glenn A. Ramsey, Oct. 4, 1975; 1 child, David A. BA, Ripon Coll., 1969; PhD, U. Iowa, 1973. Diplomate Am. Bd. Toxicology. Rsch. assoc. U. Wis., Milw., 1969; instr. Baylor Coll. Medicine, Houston, 1973-74, USPHS rsch. fellow, 1974-76; rsch. chemist Shell Devel. Co., Houston, 1976-77; toxicologist Shell Oil Co., Houston, 1977-80; dir., cons. toxicologist Toxicon Corp., Magnolia, Tex., 1980—; mem. nat. adv. rsch. resources coun. NIH, Bethesda, Md., 1974-78; bd. dirs. Reid Road Mcpl. Utility Dist., Houston, 1982-95; guest lectr. U. Tex. Sch. Pub. Health, Houston. Contbr. articles to profl. jours. Paramedic Cy-Fair Vol. Fire Dept., Houston, 1983-87; dir. Harvest Bend Home Owners Assn., Houston, 1984-86. U. Iowa grad. fellow, Iowa City, 1969-73; recipient Nat. Rsch. Svc. award NIH, Bethesda, 1975. Mem. Am. Coll. Toxicology, Assn. Water (bd. dirs.), Am. Chem. Soc., Nat. Sci. Tchrs.' Assn. Office: Toxicon Corp PO Box 130685 The Woodlands TX 77393-0685

RAMSEY, NORMAN F., physicist, educator; b. Washington, Aug. 27, 1915; s. Norman F. and Minna (Bauer) R.; m. Elinor Jameson, June 3, 1940 (dec. Dec. 1983); children: Margaret, Patricia, Janet, Winifred; m. Ellie Welch, May 11, 1985. AB, Columbia U., 1935; BA, Cambridge (Eng.) U., 1937, MA, 1941, DSc, 1954; PhD, Columbia U., 1940; MA (hon.), Harvard U., 1947; DSc (hon.), Case Western Res. U., 1968, Middlebury Coll., 1969, Oxford (Eng.) U., 1973; DCL (hon.), Oxford (Eng.) U., 1990; DSc (hon.), Rockefeller U., 1986, U. Chgo., 1989, U. Sussex, 1990, U. Houston, 1991, Carleton Coll., 1991, Lake Forest Coll., 1992, U. Mich., 1993, Phila. Coll. Pharmacy & Sci., 1995, Colby Coll., 1998. Kellett fellow Columbia U., 1935-37, Tyndall fellow, 1938-39; Carnegie fellow Carnegie Inst. Washington, 1939-40; assoc. U. Ill., 1940-42; asst. prof. Columbia U., 1942-46; assoc. MIT Radiation Lab., 1940-43; cons. Nat. Def. Research Com., 1940-45; expert cons. sec. of war, 1942-45; group leader, asso. div. head Los Alamos Lab., 1943-45; assoc. prof. Columbia U., 1945-47; head physics dept. Brookhaven Nat. Lab. of AEC, 1946-47; assoc. prof. physics Harvard U., 1947-50, prof. physics, 1950-66, Higgins prof. physics, 1966-86, Higins prof. emeritus, 1986—; sr. fellow Harvard Soc. of Fellows, 1970—; Eastman prof. Oxford U., 1973-74; Luce prof. cosmology Mt. Holyoke Coll., 1982-83; prof. U. Va., 1983-84; dir. Harvard Nuclear Lab., 1948-50, 52-53, Varlan Assos., 1963-66; mem. Air Forces Sci. Adv. Com., 1947-54; sci. adviser NATO, 1958-59; mem. Dept. Def. Panel Atomic Energy; exec. com. Cambridge Electron Accelerator and gen. adv. com. AEC. Author: Nuclear Moments and Statistics, 1953, Nuclear Two Body Problems, 1953, Molecular Beams, 1956, 85, Quick Calculus, 1965, Spectroscopy with Coherent Radiation, 1998; contbr.: articles Phys. Rev.; other sci. jours. on nuclear physics, molecular beam experiments, radar, nuclear magnetic moments, radiofrequency spectroscopy, masers, nucleon scattering. Trustee Asso. Univs., Inc., Brookhaven Nat. Lab., Carnegie Endowment Internat. Peace, 1962-85, Rockefeller U., 1977-90; pres. Univs. Research Assocs., Inc., 1966-72, '73-81, pres. emeritus, 1981—. Recipient Presdl. Order of Merit for radar devel. work, 1947, E.O. Lawrence and AEC, 1960, Columbia award for excellence in sci., 1980, medal of honor IEEE, 1983, Rabi prize, 1985, Monte Ferst award, 185, Compton medal, 1985, Rumford premium, 1985, Oersted medal, 1988, Nat. medal of Sci., 1988, Nobel prize for Physics, 1989, Pupin medal Columbia Engring. Sch. Alumni Assn., 1992, Sci. for Peace prize, 1992, Einstein medal, 1993, Vannevar Bush award, 1995, Alexander Hamilton award, 1995; Guggenheim fellow Oxford U., 1954-55. Fellow Am. Acad. Sci., Am. Phys. Soc. (coun. 1956-60, pres. 1978-79, Davisson-Germer prize 1974); mem. NAS, French Acad. Sci., Am. Philos. Assn., AAAS (chmn. physics sect. 1977), Am. Inst. Physics (chmn. bd. govs. 1980-87), Phi Beta Kappa (senator 1979-88, v.p. 1982-85, pres. 1985-88), Sigma Xi. Home: 24 Monmouth Ct Brookline MA 02446-5634 Office: Harvard U Lyman Physics Lab Cambridge MA 02138

RAMSEY, SALLY ANN SEITZ, retired state official; b. Columbus, Ohio, Feb. 15, 1931; d. Albert Blazier and Mildred (Dodson) Seitz; m. Edward Lewis Ramsey, Apr. 11, 1953 (div. 1962); children: Edward Lewis, Sylvia Ann Mitchell. BA, Ohio State U., 1952, MA, 1955, postgrad., 1963-66; postgrad. St. Mary Coll.-Xavier, Kans., 1962. Rsch. engr., then sr. rsch. engr. N.Am. Aviation, Inc., Columbus, Ohio, and Downey, Calif., 1962-67; legis. intern State of Ohio, 1964-65; rsch. and info. officer Ohio Dept. Urban Affairs, Columbus, 1967-68; adminstrv. specialist Ohio Dept. Devel., Columbus, 1968; assoc. planner, then sr. planner Div. State Planning, Fla. Dept. Adminstrn., Tallahassee, 1968-76; econ. analysis supr., then econ. analyst Fla. Dept. Commerce, 1976-93; ret., 1993; congl. campaign cons., 1966. U.S. Econ. Devel. Adminstrn. fellow, 1978-79. Mem. ASPA, DAR, Fla. Econs. Club, Kappa Kappa Gamma, Pi Sigma Alpha. Episcopalian. Home: 3012 Obrien Dr Tallahassee FL 32308-2760

RAMSEY, WILLIAM DALE, JR., marketing and technology consultant; b. Indpls., Apr. 14, 1936; s. William Dale and Laura Jane (Stout) R.; m. Mary Alice Ihnet, Aug. 9, 1969; children: Robin, Scott, Kimberly, Jennifer. AB in Econs., Bowdoin Coll., 1958. With Shell Oil Co., 1958-95; salesman Albany, N.Y., 1960; merchanding rep. Milton, N.Y., 1961-63; real estate and mktg. investments rep. Jacksonville, Fla., 1963-65; dist. sales supr. St. Paul, 1965-67; employee rels. rep. Chgo., 1967-69; spl. assignment mktg. staff-adminstrn. N.Y.C.; recruitment mgr. to sales mgr. Chgo., 1970-75; sales mgr. Detroit, 1975-79; dist. mgr. N.J. and Pa. Newark, 1979-84; Mid-Atlantic dist. mgr. (Md., D.C., Va.), 1984-87; econ. advisor head office Houston, 1987-89, mgr. mktg. concepts head office, 1989-94, mgr. tech. head office, 1984-95; mng. ptnr. Ramsey Cons., 1995—; dir. N.Am. Fin. Svcs., 1971-72; lectr., spkr. on energy, radio, TV appearances, 1972—; guest lectr. on bus. five univs., 1967-72; v.p., dir. Malibu East Corp., 1973-74; prin. Robotics Rsch. Consortium, 1991—; mem. Am. Right of Way Assn., 1963-65. Author: Corp. recruitment and Employee Relations Organizational effectiveness Study, 1969. Active Chgo. Urban League, 1971-75; mem. program com., bus. adv. coun. Nat. Rep. Congl. Com., 1981-87, rep. nat. com., 1994—, nat. Rep. senatorial com., 1997—; mem. Rep. senatorial adv. com., Gov.'s Coun. on Tourism and Commerce, Minn., 1965-67; mem. Founders Soc., Detroit Inst. Arts, 1978-80; bd. dirs. N.J. Symphony Orch. Corp., 1981-85; mem. Nat. Audubon Soc., 1997—; mem. B.R.A.S.S. orgn. Jacksonville Symphony Orch., 1999—. Capt. U.S. Army, 1958-60. James Bowdoin scholar Bowdoin Coll., 1958. Mem. Internat. Svc. Robot Assn., N.J. Petroleum Coun. (exec. com. 1979-84, vice chmn. 1982-84), Midwest Coll. Placement Assn., Md. Petroleum Coun. (exec. com. 1984-87), Nat. Trust Hist. Preservation, Nat. Audubon Soc., Ponte Vedra (Fla.) Club, Bowdoin Alumni Club (Houston), Morris County Golf Club, Kingwood (Tex.) Country Club, Houston Soc. Club, Bethesda (Md.) Country Club. Episcopalian. Achievements include patents in Method for Automated Refueling; Automated Refueling System; Customer Interface for Driver; three patents pending. Office: Ramsey Consulting PO Box 1679 Ponte Vedra Beach FL 32004-1679

RAMSEY LINES, SANDRA, forensic document examiner; b. Detroit, Dec. 8, 1940; d. Henry Alexander and Genevieve Agnes (Pilote) Habeeb; m. Richard Ramsey, Apr. 30, 1960 (div. 1965); children: Theresa L., Richard A., Renee A.; m. Ruskin R. Lines II, Sept. 9, 1998. AA, Scottdale (Ariz.) C.C., 1987; BA, U. Phoenix, 1989. Diplomate Am. Bd. Forensic Document Examiners; cert. pub. mgr. Sch. Pub. Affairs/Advanced Pub. Affairs Exec. Program Ariz. State U. Cert. peace officer, sgt. Cleve. Police Dept., 1973-82; investigator Ariz. Bd. Med. Examiners, Phoenix, 1983-84; cert. peace officer investigator Maricopa County Atty.'s Office, Phoenix, 1984-85; spl. agent cert. peace officer Office of Atty. Gen., Phoenix, 1985-96, forensic document examiner, 1991-96; forensic document examiner Bur. Alcohol, Tobacco and Firearms, Walnut Creek, Calif., 1996-99; pvt. practice as forensic document examiner, Paradise Valley, Ariz., 1999—; mem. tng. com. Ariz. Law Enforcement Coord. Com., Phoenix, 1995; asst. dir. We. States Hazardous Waste Project, Phoenix, 1987-88; com. mem. Sci. Working Group for Document Examiners, FBI, 1998-2000; presenter in field. Contbr. articles to profl. jours. Recipient Resolution for Achievements in Law Enforcement Cleve. City Coun., 1979, Committment and Support plaque Fraternal Order of Police, 1996. Fellow Am. Acad. Forensic Scis. (questioned document sect. 1996), Am. Soc. Questioned Document Examiners, S.W. Assn. Forensic Document Examiners. Republican. Mem. Maronite Cath. Ch. Achievements include being one of 14 women in 1973 to be the first women in uniform patrol and later the first woman in homicide unit of Cleve. Police Dept., establishment of forensic document lab. at Ariz. Atty. Gen.'s office; established and hosted study group meetings for Document Examiners No. Calif.

RAN, RUICHENG, chemist; b. Xuan Han, Sichuan, China, Feb. 7, 1946; came to U.S., 1988; s. Zhengbing Ran and Jicheng Zhang; m. Weiwei Pei, June 20, 1974; 1 child, Xiaosong. BS in Chemistry, Peking U., Beijing, 1970, PhD equivalent in Polymer Sci., 1978. Processing chemist Polysulfone Plant, Beijing, 1970-72; tchg. asst. Peking U., 1973-78, asst. prof., 1978-83, lectr., 1983-87; postdoctoral rsch. asst. Bowling Green State U., Ohio, 1988-89; postdoctoral rsch. asst. Miss. State U., 1988-91, sr. rsch. asst., 1991-95; sr. chemist ChemFirst Fine Chems., Inc., Dayton, Ohio, 1995—. Author: (book chpt.) The Polymeric Materials Encyclopedia, 1996; patentee in field; contbr. articles to sci. jours. Mem. Am. Chem. Soc., Chinese Chem. Soc. Office: ChemFirst Fine Chems Inc 1515 Nicholas Rd Dayton OH 45418-2712

RANA, BHUPENDRA KUMAR, accreditation officer, researcher; b. Amroha, Uttar Pradesh, India, June 13, 1971; s. Shyam Singh and Prakashwati (Singh) Chauhan; m. Seema Singh Rana, Dec. 5, 1997; 1 child, Koshika Rana. MS, Pantnagar (India) U., 1992; PhD, Banaras U., Varanasi, India, 1997, diploma in German, 1995. Scientist Vimta Labs, Ltd., Hyderabad, India, 1998-99; postdoctoral fellow Ctr. for Cellular and Molecular Biology, Hyderabad, 1999; program assoc. Nat. Accreditation Bd. for Testing and Calibration Labs., New Delhi, 1999—. Contbr. articles to profl. jours. Recipient Natural Product Symposium award Chem. Soc. Japan, 1997; jr. and sr. rsch. fellow Univ. Grants Commn., Varanasi, 1993-96, sr. rsch. fellow Banaras Hindu U., India, 1997-98; travel grantee Coun. Sci. and Indsl. Rsch., Munich, 1996. Mem. N.Y. Acad. Scis., Sci. and Humanities Soc. Pantnagar. Avocations: reading, playing badminton. Office: Nat Accreditation Bd, B6 Qutab Hotel New Mehrauli Rd, 110016 New Delhi 110 016, India

RANA, HARMINDERPAL SINGH, lawyer; b. Bombay, July 4, 1968; came to U.S., 1970; s. Baljit Singh and Devinder (Kaur) R.; m. Aasjot Kaur Sidhu, Mar. 8, 1998. BS in Fgn. Svc., cert. in Asian studies, Georgetown U., 1990; JD, honors cert. in internat. law, Rutgers U., Camden, N.J., 1994. Bar: N.J. 1994, U.S. Dist. Ct. N.J. 1994, N.Y. 1995, U.S. Dist. Ct. (so. and ea. dists.) N.Y. 1995. Pvt. practice Warren, N.J., 1994—; assoc. staff analyst N.Y.C. Dept. Mental Health, Bklyn., 1995-97, borough coord., Bklyn. and S.I., 19975; pool atty. family law litigation N.J. Office Pub. Defender, Middlesex and Somerset counties, 19955. Mem. traffic safety com. Warren Twp. (N.J.) Coun., 1997-99. NYU Trustees scholar, 1986, N.Y. State Regents scholar, 1986. Mem. ABA, Assn. Bar City N.Y. (health law com. 19975). Sikh. Avocations: literature, philosophy, world affairs, athletic cross training, public service. Office: 3 Krausche Rd Warren NJ 07059

RANA, KASHIRAM, government official; b. Surat, India, Apr. 7, 1938. B in Commerce, LLB, South-Gujarat U. Mem. Gujarat Legis. Assembly, India, 1975; mayor Surat Mcpl. Corp., India, 1983-84, 87; pres. Gujarat State, India, 1985-87, 93-96; elected mem. lok Sabha, India, 1989—; min. Ministry Textiles, New Delhi, India, 1998—. Office: Ministry Textiles, Udyog Bhawan, New Delhi 110 011, India*

RANA, M. RAMZAN ZIA, lawyer, psychologist; b. Gurdaspur, East Punjab, India, Mar. 1, 1946; arrived in Pakistan, 1947; s. Rana Abdul Hameed and Fazal (Begum); m. Parveen Begum, July 12, 1970; children: Kiran Zia, Tanzila Zia. PhD in Persian Lit., U. Iran, 1975; LLB, U. Karachi, Pakistan, 1980; MD, U. Iran, 1982; LLM, U. Karachi, Pakistan, 1990, MA in English, 1995. Advocate High Ct., Supreme Ct.; med. cons., psychologist. Mem. editorial bd. Law Jour. of Karachi, 1989—, Psychology & Life, 1992—. Contested election for the seat of Mem. Nat. Assembly of Pakistan, 1985, 88, 1993; chmn. Rehab. Assoc. & Trust of Destitutes from Bangladesh. Mem. Internat. Bar Assn., Bar Assn. Karachi, Sindh Bar Coun. Karachi. Mem. Pakistan Peoples Party. Avocation: gradening. Home: R-25 Bostan E Rafi Mair Ext, Karachi Pakistan Office: G-16 Rizvia Society, Nazimabad, 74600 Karachi Pakistan

RAÑADA, ANTONIO FERNANDEZ, physics researcher, educator; b. Bilbao, Vizcaya, Spain, Dec. 1, 1939; s. Antonio Fernandez Rañada and Maria Menendez de Luarca; m. Maria Shaw, Jan. 3, 1969; children: Antonio, Isabel, Ines. Lic. scis., U. Complutense, Madrid, 1963, D in Scis., 1967; D in Theoretical Physics, U. Paris, 1965. Rschr. U. Paris, Orsay, France, 1964-66, Spanish Nuclear Coun., Madrid, 1966-68; prof. physics U. Barcelona, Spain, 1968-70, U. Saragosse, Spain, 1972-76, U. Complutense, Madrid, 1970-72, 76—; dean physics faculty U Complutense, Madrid, 1978-86. Author: (books) Dinamica clasica, 1990, The Scientists and God, 1994, Los muchos rostros de la ciencia, 1995 (Jovellanos Internat. Prize for essays 1994); editor: Revista Española de Fisica, 1987-97. Recipient Rsch. medal Royal Acad. Scis., Madrid, 1977, Golondriz prize Humor Acad., Madrid. Mem. Spanish Phys. Soc. (medal 1985), Internat. Assn. Math. Physics. Avocation: sports. Home: Ministro Ibañez Martin 4, 28015 Madrid Spain Office: U Complutense, Facultad Fisica, 28040 Madrid Spain

RANADE, GEETANJALI GAJANAN, medical safety educator, researcher; b. Ratnagiri, India, Oct. 8, 1965; d. Gajanan Shivhari and Sudha Gajanan R. BSc, Parle Coll., India, 1986; MSc, Cancer Rsch. Inst., India, 1988; PhD, India Inst. Tech., 1994; FRHS (hon.), Indian Bd. Alternative Med., India, 1996, RMP. Cert. aromatherapy, 2000. Jr. resident fellow Indian Coun. Med. Rsch., India, 1988-89; rsch. assoc. India Inst. Tech., 1994-95, vis. prof. medicine, 1996—; vis. prof. medicine Bombay Univ., 1995-96; postdoctoral scientist Nat. Cardiovasc. Ctr., Japan, 1998-99. Contbr. articles to profl. jours. Mem. Asian Soc. Microcirculation, Rural Health Soc. Avocations: painting, music, reading, crafts, teaching the disabled. Office: School Biomed Engring, Powai, Bombay 400076, India

RANAKUSUMA, ASMAN BOEDISANTOSO, physician, medical educator; b. Magelang, Indonesia, Jan. 28, 1946. MD, U. Indonesia, 1970, PhD cum laude, 1986. Intern, resident in internal medicine U. Indonesia, 1971-76; mem. devel. co. for family planning Cipto Mangunkusumo Gen. Hosp., 1979-81, mem. devel. com. for nutrition svc., 1981-85; mem. symposium com. internal med. schs. U. Indonesia, 1984, mem. contuing edn. program, 1985, sec. rsch. and devel. com. medicine, 1986-91, mem. coord. com. tng. and consultation, 1992—, vice rector for acad. affairs, 1994-97, rector, 1998; psychology guest lectr. U. Indonesia, 1992-95, metabolic endocrinology, 1981-96; mem. WHO rsch. project on nutritional diabetes in developing countries Zagreb, Yugoslavia, 1981-85; mem. ASEAN Fedn. Study Group on Diabetes Melitus, 1986—, mem. Fedn. on Endocrine Socs. Study Group on Diabetes Pregnancy, 1990—; coord. organizing com. for carsinoma tiroid-cipto Mangunkusumo Gen. Hosp., 1990—; coord. gangrene diabetic team Cipto Mangunkusumo Gen. Hosp., 1990—; rsch. Makmal Inst. for Immunoendocrinology, U. Indonesia, 1989—. Author 4 books; editor 2 books; contbr. more than 160 articles to profl. jours. Mem. Internat. Diabetes Fedn., Indonesian Assn. Endocrinology, Indonesian Assn. Diabetes Melitus, Indonesian Internists Assn. (Jakarta br.), Indonesian Med. Doctors Assn. Office: U Indonesia US Campus, Rectorate Bldg 2d Fl, Depok 16424, Indonesia*

RANALD, RALPH ARTHUR, former government official, educator; b. N.Y.C., Nov. 25, 1930; s. Josef A. and Pearl R.; m. Margaret Florence Loftus, Feb. 26, 1955; 1 dau., Caroline. AB, UCLA, 1952, MA, 1954; AM, Princeton U., 1958; postgrad. (Carnegie fellow) Law Sch., Harvard U., 1961-62, 76-77, 99-2000; grad., Exec. Program Nat. and Internat. Security, 1978; PhD, Princeton U., 1962; JD, Fordham U., 1997. Bar: N.Y. Teaching asst. UCLA, 1952-54; univ. fellow, rsch. asst. Princeton (N.J.) U., 1956-59; asst. prof. Fordham U. Grad. Sch., N.Y.C., 1959-65; asst. dean acad. affairs, prof. Coll. Arts and Scis. NYU, N.Y.C., 1965-69; prof. CUNY, 1969—; spl. policy asst. HEW, Washington, 1968-69, Office of Mgmt. and Budget, 1976-77; sr. cons. U.S. Dept. Def., 1969-70, 77-78; mem. staffs Dept. Def. and Army Gen. Staff U.S. Govt. Long Com., 1989, U.S. Dept. Def., 1995-96; vis. prof. and cons. univs. including U. So. Calif., summers 1968-74, Calif. State U., UCLA, summers 1985, 98. Author: Management Development in Government, 1979, George Orwell, 1965; contbr. reports, articles to publs. in law, govt. and edn. Treas. N.Y. State Com. for Pub. Higher Edn., 1975-78, mem. com., 1970—. 1st lt. U.S. Army, 1953-56, to col., 1977-78, res., 1978—. Recipient U.S. Legion of Merit, 1983; sr. fellow Am. Soc. Pub. Adminstrn. (selection com. for fellows, 1970-74); mem. Res. Officers Assn. U.S. (life), Harvard U. Law Sch. Assn., Assn. of Princeton U. Grad. Alumni, U.S. Army War Coll. Alumni Assn., John F. Kennedy Sch. of Govt. Alumni Assn., Princeton Club of N.Y., Army and Navy Club, Phi Beta Kappa. Home and Office: 239 Central Park W New York NY 10024-6038

RANALOW, JOHN VIVIAN APLIN, solicitor; b. Barnes, Surrey, Eng., Apr. 17, 1930; Arrived in Portugal, 1969; s. Arthur Vivian and Alfreda Althea (Aplin) R. Degree in law, U. London. Jr. ptnr. Beddington Hughes & Hobart, London, 1956-58; pvt. practice Ranalow, Charles & Co., Hornchurch, Essex, Eng., 1958-69; cons. Ranalow, Charles & Co., Hornchurch, Essex, 1969-72; pvt. practice J.V.A. Ranalow Solicitor, Madiera, Portugal, 1972-92; assoc. SMS Advogadas, Madiera, 1992—; oral examiner in English Cambridge U., Funchal, Portugal, 1982-94. Author: (textbook) Law of Conveyancing, 1984. Sec. Assn. Friends of Conservatory of Music Found., 1994—; lay asst., trustee Holy Trinity Church, Funchal, 1981—; supt. Brit. Cemetary, Madeira, 1983—. Mem. Law Soc., Offshore Inst. Anglican. Avocations: music, reading. Fax: 351-291-776-998.

RANCK, EDNA RUNNELS, academic administrator, researcher; b. Waterville, Maine, Aug. 24, 1935; d. Everett Elias and Edna May (King) Runnels; m. James Gilmour Ranck, June 30, 1971 (dec. May 1979); children: Matthew, Christopher, Joshua Duggan; m. Martin Fleischer, Apr. 19, 1982; stepchildren: Christina, Laura Ranck. BA cum laude, Fla. State U., Tallahassee, 1957; MDiv magna cum laude, Drew U. Theol. Sch., Madison, N.J., 1971, MEd in Edn. Adminstrn., 1978; EdD in Curriculum and Tchg., Columbia U., N.Y.C., 1986. Dir. Collinsville Child Care Ctr., Morristown, N.J., 1971-78; exec. dir. Children's Svcs. Morris County, Morristown, N.J., 1980-84; co-mgr. N.J. Child Care Clearinghouse, Trenton; coord. N.J. Child Care Adv. Coun., Trenton, 1987-92; dir. N.J. Office Child Care Devel., Trenton, 1992; child care coord. N.J. Dept. Human Svcs., Trenton, 1992-98, Nat. Assn. Child Care Resource & Referral Agys., Washington, 1998—; adj. faculty Kean U. N.J., Union, 1983; dir. Sprout House Preschool, Chatham, N.J., 1984-87; mem. Morris County Human Svcs. Adv. Coun., Morristown, N.J., 1986-87, spkr. in field. Author: Dodge Foundation Project, 1984, Young Children, 1987, Our History, Our Vision: A History of the National Association of Child Care Rsource and Referral Agencies, 1997; contbr. articles to profl. jours. Exec. bd. Drew U. Alumni Assn. Theol. Sch., 1986-92; mem. Drew U. Alumni Study Commn., 1993, Non-Govt. Orgn. rep. to UN Internat. Fedn. Educative Cmtys., 1992-99; mem. history/archives panel Nat. Assn. for Edn. of Young Children. Recipient Volpe Commitment in Child Care award, N.J. Child Care Assn., 1991, Essex C.C. Early Childhood award, 1997, Aletha Wright award for Excellence in Early Edn., 1998. Mem. Child Care Action Campaign Panel, Acad. Child and Youth Care Workers, Phi Beta Kappa, Pi Sigma Alpha. Republican. United Methodist. Avocations: writing, travel, swimming, clothing design, art collecting. Home: 4447 Macarthur Blvd NW Washington DC 20007-2564 Office: NACCRRA 1319 F St NW Ste 810 Washington DC 20004-1117

RAND, LAWRENCE ANTHONY, investor and financial relations executive; b. Bklyn., Nov. 19, 1942; s. Gerald M. and Elaine Shirley Rand; m. Madelon L., July 4, 1942; children: Allan, Joshua, Emily. AB with honors, Brown U., 1964; MA, NYU, 1965, PhD, 1998. Lectr. NYU, 1967, CUNY, 1968; analyst CIA, Langley, Va., 1967-68; account supr. Ruder & Finn Inc., N.Y.C., 1968-71; co-founder, sr. v.p. Kekst & Co., N.Y.C., 1971—, also bd. dirs.; chmn., bd. dirs. ALS Assn., L.A., 1987-92. Chmn. ethics com. Village of Rye Brook, N.Y., 1993-2000, trustee, 2000—. Mem. City Athletic Club (bd. govs.), Brown U. Club, Bailiwick Club (Greenwich, Conn.). Office: Kekst & Co 437 Madison Ave 19th Fl New York NY 10022-7195

RANDALL, CATHERINE HORN, advocate; b. Davenport, Iowa, Jan. 5, 1947; d. Frank Walton and Catherine (Castle) Horn; m. Robert Quentin Randall, Dec. 27, 1969. BA, MacMurray Coll., Jacksonville, Ill., 1969. Tchr. North Green Sch. Dist., Whitehall, Ill., 1970-71; substitute tchr. Jacksonville (Ill.) H.S., 1972-73; staff writer MacMurray Coll., Jacksonville, 1973-75; alderman City of Jacksonville, 1987-91; bd. dirs. Convocom. Pres. Jacksonville Theatre Guild, 1984-87; mem. adv. coun. Ill Sch. Visually Impaired, 1986-99; 1st v.p. Nat. Fedn. Blind Ill., 1986-96; mem. coun. Ill. State Libr., 1992-98; mem. alumni bd. MacMurray Coll., Jacksonville, 1993—, trustee, 1993—; treas. Jacksonville Ctr. Ind. Living, 1996-99; sec.-treas. Trinity Ch. Guild, 1996-97; v.p. Ind. Network Ctr., 2000—. Recipient Gwendolyne Williams Meml. award Nat. Fed. Blind Ill., 1991, Alexander J. Skrzybek award Ill. Libr. Assn., 1996. Mem. Friends in Council Literary Orgn., The History Class. Episcopalian. Home: 333 East Ave Quincy IL 62301-4332

RANDALL, ELIZABETH ELLEN, press clippings company executive; b. Maple Hill, Kans., Mar. 21, 1915; d. Edwin and Ann (Scott) Sage; m. George Albert Randall, May 29, 1941; children: Cheryl Ann, Rebecca Lynn. Student, Kans. State U., 1932-34. Tchr. elem. sch Maple Hill, Kans., 1932-34, Dover, Kans., 1934-46; reader Luce Press Clippings, Topeka, 1959-63, supr., 1964, office mgr., 1964-97, sr. staff advisor, 1997-2000; ret. Tchr. Jr. High Ch. Sch., 1949-61; mem. pastoral com. Dover Federated Ch., 1991—. Mem. Dover 4-H Club (leader 1960-62), Dover Rebekah Lodge,

Eastern Star, Am. Leg. Aux., Disabled Am. Vets. Aux., 14th Armored Divsn. Aux. Democrat. Avocations: collecting antiques, plates and dolls, needlework. Home: 7220 SW Asbury Dr Apt 1107 Topeka KS 66614-6048

RANDALL, KAY TEMPLE, accountant, real estate agent, retired; b. Chattanooga, Sept. 23, 1952; d. James H. Temple and Hortense N. (Dailey) Goodner; m. Gary F. Goodner, Feb. 9, 1968 (div. July 1972); 1 child, Jeffrey F. Goodner; m. Rodney B. Randall, Oct. 3, 1987. Student, Chattanooga State Coll., 1970-77, 82-83, Am. Inst. Banking, 1977, 78, 79. Lic. real estate agt.; notary public, Tenn. Ins. rep. Colonial Life Accident and Health, Columbia, S.C., 1980-82; real estate appraiser, agt. Chattanooga, 1983-88; acct. Mr. Transmission of Chattanooga, Inc., 1987—; real estate agt. Chattanooga, 1989—; notary pub. at large Tenn., 1982—; adminstrv. asst. to legal profession, Chattanooga, 1972-75. Mem. adv. bd. United Meth. Ch., Chattanooga, 1979-82, tchr., 1979-83; fellow cen. br. YMCA, Chattanooga, 1977-97. Fellow Walden's Club. Republican. Episcopalian. Avocations: collecting art, grandchildren. Home: 1858 Rivergate Ter Soddy Daisy TN 37379-5947 Office: Mr Transmission of Chattanooga Inc 2022 E 23rd St Chattanooga TN 37404-5822

RANDALL, ROBERT L(EE), ecological economist; b. Aberdeen, S.D., Dec. 28, 1936; s. Harry Eugene and Juanita Alice (Barstow) R. MS in Phys. Chemistry, U. Chgo., 1960, MBA, 1963. Market devel. chemist E.I. du Pont de Nemours & Co., Inc., Wilmington, Del., 1963-65; chem. economist Battelle Meml. Inst., Columbus, Ohio, 1965-68; mgr. market and econ. rsch. Kennecott Copper Corp., N.Y.C., 1968-74, economist, 1974-79, dir. new bus. venture devel., 1979-81; pres., mng. dir. R.L. Randall Assocs., Inc., 1981—; economist U.S. Internat. Trade Commn., Washington, 1983—; founder, pres., exec. dir. The RainForest ReGeneration Inst., 1986—, ind. internat. press corr., 1997—, indsl. panel policy rev. of effect of regulation on innovation and U.S.-internat. competition U.S. Dept. Commerce, 1980-81; participant preparatory com. UN Conf. on Environ. and Devel., Rio de Janeiro, 1991; del. observer internat. negotiating com. UN Framework Conv. on Climate Change, 1991—. Contbg. author: Computer Methods for the 80's; sect. lead author, editor: World Energy Assessment, 2000; pub. reviewer intergovtl. panel on climate change Third Assessment Report; addresser 4th Internat. Greenhouse Gas Tech. conf., Interlaken, Switzerland, 1998; contbr. articles to profl. jours. Mem. Gay Activists Alliance, N.Y.C., 1971-75, chmn. state and fed. legislation com., 1975. Mem. AAAS (organizer ann. meeting Tropical Forest Regeneration Symposium), AIME (econ. coun., mineral econ. subsect.), Internat. Soc. Ecol. Health, Internat. Soc. Ecol. Economists, Am. Econ. Assn., Am. Statis. Assn., Am. Chem. Soc., Soc. Mining Engrs., Marine Biol. Assn. U.K., Chemists Club of N.Y.C., Metall. Soc., N.Y. Acad. Scis., Nat. Econs. Club Washington (sec., reporter), Assn. Environ. and Resource Economists, Marine Biol. Assn. (Plymouth, Eng.), Wanderbirds Hiking Club (hike leader, treas.), Capital Hiking Club (hike leader, Washington). Home: 1727 Massachusetts Ave NW Washington DC 20036-2153 Office: US Internat Trade Com 500 E St NW Washington DC 20436-0003

RANDALL, VERNELLIA, lawyer, nurse, educator; b. Gladewater, Tex., Mar. 6, 1948; d. Ernest and Pauline (Hall) R.; children: Tshaka, Issa. AA, Amarillo (Tex.) Coll., 1968; BS, U. Tex., 1972; MSN, U. Wash., 1978; JD, Lewis and Clark Coll., 1987. Bar: Oreg. 1987. Prof. torts, health care law, women and the law, race/racism U. Dayton, Ohio, 1990, dir. acad. excellence program, 1994—; assoc. Bullivant, Houser, Bailey, Pendergrass & Hoffman, Portland, Oreg., 1987-90; adj. prof. law Lewis and Clark Coll., 1988-90, Wright State Med. Sch., 1990—; vis. prof. Seattle U., 1995. Editor: website: Race and Racism in American Law, Race, Health Care and Law, Students Learning Legal Education, Gender and the Law. Bd. dirs. Oreg. Legal Svcs., 1988-90, Oreg. chpt. Am. Heart Assn., 1988-90, Mary Scott Nursing Home, Inc., 1998—. Mem. ABA (vice chmn. health ins. com. 1988-90, young lawyers health com. religious non-profit orgn.), ANA, Am. Health Care Assn., Am. Assn. Law Schs. (sec. sect. on health care law 1995, sec., chair sect. law and medicine 1996, chmn. sect. health care law 1997, exec. com. sect. on tchg. methods, 1998—, chair-elect 2000, treas.-elect sect. on women and the law), Oreg. Bar Assn., Assn. Oreg. Black Attys., Oreg. Women Lawyers (bd. dirs. 1989-90), Multnomah County Bar Assn. (status of women com.), Thurgood Marshall Legal Soc. (continuing edn. chair 1992). Avocation: computers. E-mail: randall@udayton.edu. Office: U Dayton Sch Law 300 College Park Ave Dayton OH 45469-0001

RANDALL, WILLIAM B., manufacturing company executive; b. Phila., Jan. 8, 1921; s. Albert and Ann (Fine) R.; m. Geraldine Kempson, Aug. 10, 1943; children: Robert, Erica Lynn, Lisa. Student, Rider Coll., Trenton, N.J., 1940-41. Gen. Sales mgr. Lowres Optical Mfg. Co., Newark, 1946-49; pres., founder Rand Sales Co., N.Y.C., 1949-58; gen. mgr. Sea & Ski Co. div. Botany Industries, Inc., Millbrae, Calif., 1958-61; pres., dir. Botany Industries, Inc., 1961-66, v.p., 1961-65; pres. Renauld of France, Reno, 1967-68; chmn. bd. Renauld Internat., Reading, Pa., 1963-65; pres., chief operating officer Renauld Internat., Ltd., Burlingame and Reno, 1966-67; pres., chmn. bd. Randall Internat., Ltd., 1967-68; sr. exec. v.p. Forty-two Prods. Ltd., 1969-71; pres. Exec. Products Internat. Ltd., 1969-71, New Product Devel. Ctr., Carlsbad, Calif., 1971—; pres. Internat. Concept Ctr. Exec. Products Internat. Ltd., Irvine, 1971—, pres. Sun Research Ctr., 1974—; pres. La Costa Products Internat., 1975-86; mng. dir. merchandising La Costa Hotel and Spa, 1986-88; pres., chief exec. officer Randall Internat., Carlsbad, 1989—; bd. dirs. Bank of La Costa, Garden Botanika. Served to 1st lt., navigator USAAF, 1942-45. Mem. Am. Mgmt. Assn., Nat. Wholesale Druggists Assn., Nat. Assn. Chain Drug Stores, Hon. Order Ky. Cols., Baja Beach and Tennis Club (bd. dirs.). Home: 7150 Arenal Ln Carlsbad CA 92009-6701

RANDALL, WILLIAM BRIAN, mortgage banker; b. Bay City, Mich., Oct. 3, 1951; s. William Charles and Ruth Catherine (Soderquist) R.; m. Christie Reed Bailey, July 18, 1987; children: Matthew Charles, Tyler Bailey. Student, U. Toledo, 1969-71; Grad., Jones Real Estate Coll., Denver, 1976. Lic. real estate profl. Sales assoc. Charlton Co. Realtors, Aurora, Colo., 1977-78; loan officer Quadrant Mortgage Co., Denver, 1978-79, Suburban Coastal Corp., Schaumburg, Ill., 1980-82, Norwest Mortgage, Schaumburg, 1982-83, Jersey Mortgage Co., Rolling Meadows, Ill., 1983-84; v.p., div. mgr. West America Mortgage Co., Lombard, Ill., 1984-90; br. mgr. Investors Savs. Mortgage, Oak Brook, Ill., 1990-91; v.p., gen. mgr. First Home Mortgage Corp., Mt. Prospect, Ill., 1991-94; v.p., mng. officer Pinnacle Home Mortgage Co., Lombard, Ill., 1994—; instr. mortgage sch. Ill. Mortgage Bankers Assn., 1996, 1998-99. Contbr. articles to newspapers and profl. jours. Vol. basketball coach Downers Grove Park Dist., 1995-97; chair golf outing com Indian Boundary YMCA, 1998, 99; 5th grade girls basketball coach St. Mary's of Gostyn, 1998-99, 5th grade boys asst. basketball coach, 1999-00, 6th grade girls basketball coach, 1999-00. Mem. Ill. Mortgage Bankers Assn. (mem. Spring conf. planning com. 1991, chmn. progs. com. 1991, bd. dirs. 1992-96, 99-00, officers and bd. nominating com. 1992, long range planning com. 1994, 95, wholesale lending com. 1996, vice chair wholesale lending com. 1997, chair wholesale lending com. 1998-99, chair Midwest lending conf. com. 1999), Northwest Suburban Assn. Realtors (bd. dirs. 1990-91, chmn. affiliate com. Arlington Heights, Ill. 1990-91, Affiliate Mem. of Yr. award 1990), Ill. Assn. Mortgage Brokers (Midwest lending conf. com. 1994-00, named Operations Mgr. Yr. 1997, events planning com. 1992-00, treas. polit. action com. 2000, bd. dirs. 2000, treas. 2000, exec. com. 2000), Home Builders Assn. Greater Chgo. (mortgage fin.com. 1995), Northwest Suburban Assn. Realtors (Member of Yr. 1990, chair affiliate com. 1990, 91, bd. dirs. 1990-91). Avocations: scuba diving, reading, photography, Chicago Cubs baseball fan. Office: Pinnacle Home Mortgage Co Ste 220 55 W 22d St Lombard IL 60148

RANDIVE, RAJUL V., process engineer; b. Rajkot, Gujarat, India, Mar. 18, 1968; came to U.S., 1990; s. Vidyadhar S. and Kokila V. (Parekh) R. M, Gujarat U., Ahmedabad, India, 1990, Clarkson U., 1994; D, Clarkson U., 1998. Process engr. CVC, Rochester, N.Y., 1997—. Mem. Am. Chem. Soc., Soc. Vacuum Coaters, Sigma Xi. Avocations: travelling, reading, photography. Home: 1077 East Ave Apt 4A Rochester NY 14607-2234 Office: CVC 525 Lee Rd Rochester NY 14606-4236

RANDLANE, TIINA, botanical educator; b. Tallinn, Estonia, Sept. 10, 1953; d. Vsevolod and Ellen (Kilstrom) Gruntal; m. Rein Randlane, Aug. 1, 1974 (div. 1987); children: Triin, Marju. BS, U. Tartu, Estonia, 1977, PhD, 1986. Asst. U. Tartu, Estonia, 1977-79, jr. rschr., 1979-87, rschr., 1987-91, sr. rschr., 1992-93, asst. prof., 1993—; coun. mem. Red Data Book Estonia, 1995—; curator Lichenological Herbarium U. Tartu, 1992—. Co-author, coeditor: Macrolichens of Estonia, 1994; co-editor: Jour. Folia Cryptogamica Estonica, 1996—; contbr. articles to profl. jours. Grantee Internat. Sci. Found., 1994-95, Swedish Inst., 1993, Estonian Sci. Found., 1992-2000, Swedish Threatened Species Unit, 1999. Mem. Internat. Assn. Lichenology (exec. coun. 1992—), British Lichen Soc., Estonian Naturalists Soc. Avocation: aerobics. Office: Inst Botany Ecology, Inst Botany Ecology, U Tartu, 51005 Tartu Estonia

RANDLE, ELLEN EUGENIA FOSTER, opera and classical singer, educator; b. New Haven, Conn., Oct. 2, 1948; d. Richard A.G. and Thelma Lousie (Brooks) Foster; m. Ira James William, 1967 (div. 1972); m. John Willis Randle, Dec. 24, 1983. Student, Calif. State Coll., Sonoma, 1970; studied with Boris Goldovsky, 1970; student, Grad. Sch. Fine Arts, Florence, Italy, 1974; studied with Tito Gobbi, Florence, 1974; student, U. Calif., Berkeley, 1977; BA in World History, Lone Mountain Coll., 1976, MA in Performing Arts, 1978; studied with Madam Eleanor Steber, Graz, Austria, 1979; studied with Patricia Goehl, Munich, Fed. Republic Germany, 1979; MA in Counseling and Psychology, U. San Francisco, 1990, MA in Marriage and Family Therapy, 1994, EdD in Internat. Multicultural Edn., 1998. Asst. artistic dir. Opera Piccola, Oakland, Calif., 1990-92; instr. African Am. culture and humanities Mission C.C., Santa Clara, Calif., 1997—; instr. Peralta C.C. Dist., Oakland, 1998—; psychotherapy intern, sr. peer counseling program City of Fremont, Calif., 1999-2000; psychotherapist, marriage family therapist intern Porter Bell Home Behavioral Health and Tng. Ctr., Concord, Calif., 2000—; instr. East Bay Performing Art Ctr., Richmond, Calif., 1986, Chapman Coll., 1986, Las Positas C.C., Livermore, Calif., 1999—. Singer opera prodns. Porgy & Bess, Oakland, Calif., 1980-81, La-Traviata, Oakland, Calif., 1981-82, Aida, Oakland, 1981-82, Madame Butterfly, Oakland, 1982-83, The Magic Flute, Oakland, 1984, numerous others; performances include TV specials, religous concerts, musicals; music dir. Natural Man, Berkeley, 1986; asst. artistic dir. Opera Piccola, Oakland, Calif., 1990—. Art commr. City of Richmond, Calif. Recipient Bk. Am. Achievement award. Mem. Music Tchrs. Assn., Internat. Black Writers and Artists Inc. (life mem., local #5), Nat. Coun. Negro Women, Nat. Assn. Negro Musicians, Calif. Arts Fedn., Calif. Assn. for Counseling and Devel. (mem. black caucus), Nat. Black Child Devel. Inst., The Calif.-Nebraskan Orgn., Inc., Calif. Marital & Family Therapist Assn. (San Francisco chpt.), Black Psychotherpist of San Francisco and East Bay Area, San Francisco Commonwealth Club, Gamma Phi Delta. Democrat. Mem. A.M.E. Zion Ch. Avocations: cooking, entertaining. Home: 5314 Boyd Ave Oakland CA 94618-1112

RANDLE, PETER, communications company executive; b. Warwickshire, Eng., Apr. 16, 1951. BSc with honors, London U., 1973; MSc, Queen's U., Can., 1975. Mng. dir. Global ICT Cons. Ltd.; mitarbeiter, doktorand Max-Planck Inst., Germany, 1975—; head computing Std. Telephones & Cables/ITT Inc., 1982-84; dir. computing and order processing MBS plc, 1985-86; ptnr., prin. Nova Consulting, Germany, 1980-92. Contbr. articles to profl. jours. Mem. Inst. of Math. and its Applications (assoc.), IEEE, Inst. of Dirs. of U.K., British Computer Soc. (chmn. intellectual property com. 1990-91, 96-98, mem. pornography task force, profl. and pub. affairs bd. 1996-98), Inst. of Mgmt. of U.K., Royal Soc. of Chemistry of U.K. (life), Computer Soc. of IEEE, Gesellschaft für Informatik e.V. (Bonn), EURIM (various working parties 1996—), N.Y. Acad. Scis., Can. Info. Processing Soc. Avocations: music, languages, travel, walking, cooking. Voicemail/Fax: +44 7750-299-990. E-mail: peter randle@computer.org. Home and Office: 19 Benson Quay, Wapping London E1W 3TR, England

RANDLE, SIR PHILIP JOHN, clinical biochemistry educator; b. Nuneaton, Warwickshire, U.K., July 16, 1926; s. Alfred John and Nora Annie (Smith) R.; m. Elizabeth Ann Harrison, Sept. 26, 1952; children: Rosalind Jane, Peter John (dec. 1971), Sally Elizabeth, Susan Penelope. BA, Cambridge U., 1947, MA, MB, BChir, 1950, MD, 1964, PhD, 1955. House physician, surgeon Univ. Coll. Hosp., London, 1951; rsch. fellow dept. biochemistry Cambridge U., 1952-55, rsch. fellow Sidney Sussex Coll., 1954-57, lectr. biochemistry, 1955-64, fellow, dir. med. studies Trinity Hall, 1957-64; prof., chmn. dept. biochemistry Bristol U., 1964-75; prof., chmn. dept. clin. biochemistry Oxford U., 1975-93, fellow Hertford Coll., 1975-93, prof. emeritus clin. biochemistry, 1993—, emeritus, 1993—. Contbr. over 200 articles to med. and sci. jours. Knighted by Her Majesty the Queen, 1985. Fellow Royal Soc. (v.p. 1988-89), Royal Coll. Physicians of London; mem. European Assn. for Study of Diabetes (pres. 1977-80). Home: 11 Fitzherbert Close, Iffley Oxford OX4 4EN, England Office: Radcliffe Infirmary, Dept Clin Biochemistry, Woodstock Rd Oxford OX2 6HE, England

RANDMAN, BARRY I., real estate developer; b. Cin., Apr. 1, 1958; s. David I. and Marilyn June (Garfinkel) F. BBA in Fin., U. Denver, 1980. With acctg. dept. Rookwood Pottery & Celestial Restaurants, Cin., 1976-80; asst. to pres., head mktg. and real estate branching Great Am. Banks Inc., Miami, 1980-83; pres. Tower Mgmt. Inc., Cin., 1983-85, bd. dirs.; pres. Ohio Jet Svcs. Inc., Cin., 1983-85; v.p. Home State Fin. Svcs. Inc., Cin., 1984-85; pres. East Hill Devel. Corp., Cin., 1985—, B.I.R. Properties Inc., Cin., 1985—; pres. Golden Devel. Corp., 1988-91, SRB Food Corp., 1988-92, Scarborough Devel. Corp., 1989, Redmont Devel Corp., 1990—, Eastridge, Inc., 1993-99, 613 Roce LLC, Hale Justis, LLC, 1999—. Mem. Jewish Welfare Fund, Cin., 1980. Avocations: skiing, tennis, gardening. Home: 2840 Ambleside Pl Cincinnati OH 45208-3357 Office: 2321 Kemper Ln Cincinnati OH 45206-2610

RANDOLPH, JESSE, III See CASTILE, RAND

RANDOLPH, LEONARD MCELROY, JR., career officer; b. Washington, Sept. 22, 1943; s. Leonard McElRoy and Jessie Marshall (Stockton) R.; m. Linda Fleming Raney, Aug. 1, 1987; children: Nathaniel Randolph, Brion Randolph, Holly Muterspaw-Randolph, Chad Muterspaw, Judd Muterspaw. BS in Biology, Marietta (Ohio) Coll., 1965; MS in Microbiology, Howard U., Washington, 1967; MD, Meharry Med. Coll., Nashville, 1972. Diplomate Am. Bd. Surgery, Am. Bd. Med. Mgmt., Am. Coll. Physician Execs.; cert. physician exec. Grad. tchg. asst. Howard U., Washington, 1966-67; rsch. microbiologist Georgetown U., Washington, 1966-67; chemistry tchr. Ballou H.S., Washington, 1967-68; Commd. 2d lt. USAF, 1972, advanced through grades to maj. gen., 1998; intern USAF, Keesler AFB, Miss., 1972-73, resident, 1973-77; gen. surgeon USAF, Bergstrom AFB, Tex., 1977-78, chief gen. surgery, 1978-80, chief surg. svcs., 1980-83; hosp. cmdr. USAF, George AFB, Calif., 1988-90; forward command surgeon Desert Storm USAF, Riyahd, Saudi Arabia, 1990-91; med. ctr. comdr. USAF, Travis AFB, Calif., 1994-97; asst. prof. surgery Wright State U. Sch. Medicine, Dayton, Ohio, 1983-88; command surgeon U.S. Ctrl. Command, MacDill AFB, Fla., 1991-94, U.S. Transp. Command and Air Mobility Command, Scott AFB, Ill., 1997-99; lead agt. DOD Health Svc. Region 10, 1994-97; spec. asst. to USAF Surg. Gen., 1999, dep. surgeon gen., 1999—; assoc. prof. surgery U. Calif. Dvis Sch. Medicine, 1995-97; assoc. prof. mil. medicine and emergency medicine Uniformed Svcs. U. of Health Scis., 1995—. Contbr. articles to profl. jours. Decorated Def. Superior Svc. medal for Operation Restore Hope, Legion of Merit Operation Desert Storm; selected for Boys State (Georgetown U.); escort for Pres. Dwight D. Eisenhower (Nat. Christmas Tree lighting, laying of wreath at tomb of Unknown Soldier); pres. Student Nat. Med. Assn., 1971-72; named Disting. Alumni of Yr., Nat. Assn. for Equal Opportunity in Higher Edn., 1999. Fellow ACS (bd. govs. 1996—), Am. Coll. Physician Execs. (disting., pres. 2000—), Am. Acad. Med. Adminstrs. (hon.); mem. Soc. Air Force Clin. Surgeons (bd. govs. 1996—), Assn. Mil. Surgeons of the U.S., Air Force Assn. (life), Christian Med. Assn., Aerospace Med. Assn., Alpha Omega Alpha, Beta Kappa Chi, Beta Beta Beta. Avocations: reading, lecturing, sports, writing. Office: Hdqrs USAF Office of the Surgeon Gen 110 Luke Ave SW Ste 400 Bolling AFB DC 20332-5113

RANDOLPH, ROGER BROOKE, manufacturing executive; b. Lancaster, Pa., Mar. 12, 1965; s. Clarence Jefferson and Betty Elizabeth Randolph; m. Debra Ann R., May 23, 1998. BSBA, Kutztown U., 1989; MBA, Lebanon Valley Coll., 1993. Staff acct. H.R. Neidermyer, CPA, Lititz, Pa., 1989-92; plant mgr. Rotadyne, Hartford, Wis., 1993-99, ops. mgr., 1999—. Avocations: racquetball, physical fitness. E-mail: spidermI00@aol.com. Office: RotaDyne 1076 Western Dr Hartford WI 53027-2719

RANDRUP, NILS L., communications executive, business educator; b. Copenhagen, Oct. 17, 1964; s. Levi Randrup and Hanna Ida Littau Nielsen; m. Annika Olufsson, May 30, 1998; 1 child, Marcus. MBA, PhB, Kellogg Sch. Mgmt./CBS, Evanston, Ill., Copenhagen, 1989. Mgmt. assoc. Coco-Cola, Copenhagen, 1989-91; group brand mgr. Unilever, Hedehusene, Denmark, 1991-92; media exec. Leo Burnett, Copenhagen, 1993-95; media dir. MediaCom, Copenhagen, 1995-96; account and media dir. J. Water Thompson, Copenhagen, 1996-98; dir. J. Walter Thompson Interactive, Copenhagen, 1998—; external prof. Copenhagen Bus. Sch., 1991—; cons. Nestli, Copenhagen, 1996-99. Author: The Art and Science of Persuasive Business Presentations, 1996; contbr. articles to profl. jours.; TV host KKR TV, Copenhagen, 1997. Counsellor for deprived children Salvation Army, L.A., 1987-94; counsellor Street Kids Colombia, Bogota, 1995; coach Ejby Soccer Assn., 1987-89. Mem. Internat. Advt. Assn. (diploma, assoc. chpt. pres. 1995-97, v.p. 1997-98). Avocations: mountainbiking, soccer, teaching, helping deprived children. E-mail: nils.annika@post.tele.dk and nils.randrup@jwt.com. Fax: 45 33 70 75 00. Home: Vejdammen 79, 2840 Holte Denmark Office: J Walter Thompson, Store Kirkestraede 1, 1073 Copenhagen Denmark

RANDS, ROBERT LAWRENCE, archaeologist; b. Washington, May 13, 1922; s. John and Una Alice (Clingan) R.; m. Barbara Rathbone Cornett, Aug. 1948 (div. 1977); 1 child, Gordon Phillips; m. Elizabeth Lowry Vaughan, May 26, 1977 (dec. Oct. 18, 1990). BA in Anthropology, U. N.Mex., 1949; MA in Anthropology, U. Calif., L.A., 1949; PhD in Anthropology, Columbia U., 1952. Asst. prof. to prof. U. Miss., University, 1952-63; prof., asst. dir. rsch. lab. anthropology U. N.C., Chapel Hill, 1963-66; prof., curator Mesoamerican archaeology So. Ill. U., Carbondale, 1966-91; rsch. prof. So. Ill. U., Ctr. Archeol. Investigations, Carbondale, 1993—; rsch. assoc. U. Mus., U. Pa., Phila., 1960-82; vis. scholar Dumbarton Oaks, Washington, 1975; rsch. collaborator Smithsonian Instn. Ctr. Materials Rsch. & Edn., Washington, 1987-93, 95—, Brookhaven Nat. Lab. Dept. of Chemistry, Upton, 1974-77, 80-83; ceremicist Proyecto de las Cruces Palenque Pre-Columbian Art Rsch. Inst., San Francisco, 1997-98. Co-editor: Man Across The Sea, 1971; co-author: Maya Sculpture, 1972. Fellow John Simon Guggenheim Found., 1956; grantee Inst. Andean Rsch., 1951, 59, Am. Philos. Soc., 1959, NSF, 1963, 67, 70, 75, Found. Advancement MesoAmerican Studies, 1998. Mem. Soc. Am. Archaeolgy (Excellence in Ceramic Studies award 1998), Am. Anthrop. Assn., Archeol. Inst. Am., Sigma Xi. Achievements include research in ceramic technology as a means of investitaging trade and interaction in ancient Maya society; major archaeological expeditions Chiapas and Tabasco, Mexico. Home: 27898 Old Village Rd Mechanicsville MD 20659-4286

RAND-WEAVER, MARIANN, biochemist; b. Nordfjordeid, Norway, June 10, 1959; d. Oddvin Rand and Ruth (Pettersen) Geitanger; m. Peter Weaver, July 12, 1980; 1 child, Eleanor Ruth. BSc, King's Coll. London, 1982, PhD, 1986. Postdoctoral fellow U. Bergen, Norway, 1986-89; rsch. assoc. Kitasato U., Japan, 1989-91; rsch. fellow Brunel U., Uxbridge, England, 1991-95, lectr., 1995—. Contbr. articles to profl. jours. Mem. Soc. Endocrinology, Soc. Experimental Biology. Office: Brunel Univ, Brunel U, Dept Biol Scis, Uxbridge UB8 3PH, England

RANE, KOYAR SANLO, science educator; b. Karwar, Karnatak, India, Aug. 1, 1948; s. Sanlo Koyar and Gangabai Sanlo (Powar) R.; m. Savitri Kyoar Powar, May 9, 1978; two children. BSc, Karnatak U., Dharwad, India, 1969, MSc, 1971; PhD, Indian Inst. Tech., Mumbai, India, 1976. Doctoral and postdoctoral staff Indian Inst. Tech., Madras, 1971-80; owner Pharm. Firm, Hubli, India, 1980-82; asst. prof. Goute Inst. Tech., Belgaum, India, 1982-87; sr. lectr. Goa U., India, 1987-90; reader Goa U., 1990-96, sr. reader, 1996—. Contbr. articles to profl. jours. Recipient award U. Manchester Inst. Sci. and Tech., 1995; German Acad. Exch. Svc. fellow, 1984-85, 92. Mem. Indian Sci. Congress (life), Indian Coun. Chemists, Indian Thermal Analysis Soc., Indian Materials Rsch. Soc. Avocations: wandering, cycling, reading, watching movies, making friends. Home: Sham Kunj, Near Sirur Park, Hubli Vidyanagar 580021, India Office: Goa Univ, Taleigaon Plateau, Goa 403206, India

RANE, ULHAS, architect, educator; b. Mumbai, India, Sept. 30, 1947. BArch, Jamshedji Jeejibhoy Coll. Arc., Mumbai, 1971; govt. diploma, J.J. Coll., Mumbai, 1971; MA in Sociology, Mumbai U., 1980; postgrad. diploma in environ. & ecology, Indian Inst. Ecology, New Delhi, 1985. Ptnr. The Designers, Mumbai, 1971—; prof. J.J. Coll., 1985—, M.S. Ramaiah Inst. Tech., Bangalore, India, 1997—. Author: Rural/Tribal Architecture, 1997, History of Indian Landscape Design, 1997; editor ednl. booklets: Nisarg Yatra, 1983. Hon. sec. Bombay Natural History Soc., Mumbai, 1990-92; trustee Prince of Wales Mus., Mumbai, 1992-94; pres. Save Sahyadri, Mumbai, 1983—, Ashwattha Trust, Mumbai, 1998—. Sr. under officer Nat. Cadet Corps, 1964-70. Recipient Internat. Photography award Bombay Natural History Soc., Mumbai, 1983; Hon. Wildlife Warden, Govt. of Maharashtra, India, 1987-98. Fellow Indian Inst. Architects, Indian Inst. Valuers; mem. Bombay Natural History Soc. (exec. com. 1983—), W.W.F. (cons.), Nat. Ctr. for Performing Arts, Coun. Arch. E-mail: ulhas-rane@vsnl.net. Home: Brindavan 227 1st Main Rd, Rajmahal Vilas Extn II, Bangalore Karnataka 560094, India

RANGANAYAKULU, SEGU VENKATA, electronics educator, researcher; b. Markapur, India, June 1, 1968; s. Segu Krishnaiah and Venkata Ravikrindi Subbama; m. Konakalla Nalini Kumari, Oct. 15, 1997; children: Sri Harshini, Srikhar. MSc in Physics, Andhra U., India, 1991; MEd, Bharathidasan U., India, 1998; MPhil, Andhra U., Waltair, India, 1998, Phd, 1999. Lectr. Tallakula Jalayya Polisetty Somasundaram Coll., Guntur, India, 1991-93, lectr. postgrad. dept. electronics, 1993—. Author: A Review of Integrated Circuits, Introduction to Mechanics. V.p. Young Men Social Svc. Orgn., Guntur, 1993-96; mem. Guntur Round Table, 1994-95. Mem. IEEE, Indian Sci. Congress Assn., Indian Physics Tchrs. Assn., Ultrasonics Soc. India. Mem. Bharthiya Janatha Party. Rashtriya Swayamsevak Sangh. Avocations: table tennis, chess, badminton. Home: 4th Ln, Krishna Nagar, Guntur 522006, India Office: TJPS Coll, Pattabhipuram, Guntur 522006, India

RANGER, PAUL VICTOR, periodical editor; b. Streatham, London, Eng., June 10, 1933; s. Charles Percival and Dorothy May (Cook) R. Cert. in edn., London U., 1955; diplomas in drama and theatre, Assoc. Drama Bd., 1967; licentiate, Trinity Coll., London, 1963, London Acad. Music & Drama Art, 1963, London Coll. Music, 1964, Guildhall Sch. Music and Drama, 1965, Royal Acad. Music, 1966; BA, Open U., Eng., 1973; MLitt, Bristol (Eng.) U., 1978; PhD, Southampton (Eng.) U., 1984. Tchr. London County Coun., 1955-59, Royal Sch. Deaf Children, Birmingham, Eng., 1959-60, Derbyshire (Eng.) County Coun., 1960-63; headmaster Inner London Ednl. Auth., 1963-67; lectr. King Alfred's Univ. Coll., Winchester, Eng., 1967-83, head faculty theater, 1983-87; adj. prof. Cal. State U., 1973-83; vis. lectr. Cambridge (Eng.) U., 1992—. Author: Experiments in Drama, 1970, The Lost Theatres of Winchester, 1976, A Masterguide to She Stoops to Conquer, 1985, A Masterguide to The School for Scandal, 1986, Performance, 1990, A Catalogue of Strolling Companies, 1990, Terror and Pity Reign in Every Breast, 1991, Meaning, Form and Performance, 1993; co-author and editor: (with Anthony Denning) Theatre in the Cotswolds, 1993, Meaning, Form and Performance, 1995, The Georgian Theatres of Hampshire, 1730-1830, 1997, (with Carol Schroder) The Discussion, 2000; theatre critic Oxford (Eng.) Times, 1985-93; external examiner London Coll. Music and Media; external reader and examiner, English faculty U. London; contbr. articles to profl. jours. Drama advisor Arts Coun. and So. Arts Eng., London, 1980—; examiner drama and speech LAMDA, London, 1984—. Recipient fellowship Trinity Coll. London, 1968. Fellow English Speaking Bd.; mem. Soc. Tchrs. Speech and Drama (chair and exec. coun. officer 1984—, editor Speech and Drama jour.), Nat. Trust (lectr.), Assn. Cultural Exchange (course dir.). Anglican. Avocations: walking, theatre production, writing. Office: Speech and Drama, 4 Fane Rd, Oxford OX3 0SA, England

RANGRA, KAMALJIT, physicist, researcher; b. Hamirpur, India, Jan. 3, 1959; s. Laturia Ram and Janaki Devi Rangra; m. Mithlesh Jaswal, July 27,

1987; children: Subeer, Aarooshee. BSc in Physics with honors, Punjabi U., Patiala, India, 1980, MSc in Physics, 1982; Degree in Micro-Electronics, Birla Inst. Tech. and Sci., Pilani, India, 1991. Scientist B Ctrl. Electronics Engring. Rsch. Inst., Pilani, 1986-91, scientist C, 1991—. Fellow Inst. Electronics and Telecom. Engrs.; mem. Indian Physics Assn. (life, sec. Pilani chpt. 1995-97), Indo-French Tech. Soc. Avocations: photography, music. Home: MITRA-1 Mitra Apts, CEERI Colony, Pilani 333031, India Office: Ctrl Electronics Engring Rsch Inst, Pilani 333031, India

RANI, K. YAMUNA, chemical engineer; b. Secunderabad, India, Sept. 15, 1965; d. K.R. Rao and K. Annapurna. B of Tech., Osmania U., Hyderabad, India, 1986; M of Tech., Indian Inst. Tech., Madras, India, 1988. From rsch. assoc. to scientist B Indian Inst. Chem. Tech., Hyderabad, 1988-95, scientist C, 1995—. Contbr. articles to profl. jours. German Acad. Exch. Svc. fellow, Bonn, 1994-95; recipient Young Scientist award Coun. for Sci. & Indsl. Rsch., India, 1999. Mem. Indian Inst. Chem. Engrs. (life), Indian Inst. Tech. Alumni Assn. Avocations: music, TV, reading, crossword puzzles. Office: Indian Inst Chem Tech, Uppal Rd, 500 007 Hyderabad India

RANI, RAJNI, immunologist, researcher; b. New Delhi, Apr. 4, 1955; p. R.V. Lal and Raj Kumari Sinha; m. Santosh Kumar Sethi, Jan. 11, 1985; children: Surbhi, Stuti. BSc with honors in Anthropology, U. Delhi, 1974, MSc in Anthropology, 1976, PhD, 1982. Asst. rsch. officer Cytology Rsch. Ctr., New Delhi, 1983; vis. fellow NIH, Bethesda, Md., 1983-86; staff scientist II Nat. Inst. Immunology, New Delhi, 1987-92, staff scientist III, 1992-97, staff scientist IV, 1997—; pres. Postgrad. Women's Hostel U. Delhi, 1979-80; vis. fellow Southwestern Med. Ctr., Dallas, 1992, 96, 98. Contbr. articles to profl. jours. Mem. Indian Immunology Soc. (life), Indian Transplantation Soc. (life), Indian Soc. Histocompatibility and Immunogenetics (founder), Assn. Microbiologists India (life). Avocations: drawing, singing. Home: A-4 Nat Inst Immunology, New Delhi 110067, India Office: Nat Inst Immunology, Aruna Asaf Ali Marg, New Delhi 110067, India

RANIERI, MARCO, hydraulic engineer; b. Rome, Feb. 24, 1959; s. Luciano and Anna Maria (Mete) R.; m. Alberta Carboni, June 4, 1994; 1 child, Francesca Ranieri. M of Hydraulic Engring., U. La Sapienza, Rome, 1984; PhD in Sanitary Engring., Milan Poly., 1989. Registered profl. hydraulic and sanitary engr. Design engr. Azienda Commale Energia e Ambiente, Rome, 1985-92; water dept. chief Federgasacqua, Rome, 1992-96; tech. dept. chief Azienda Servizi Pubblici Idraulici e Vari, Venice, Italy, 1996-99; planning and strategies chief Acquedotto Pugliese, Bari, Italy, 1999—; design engr., 1992. 2d lt. Italian Air Force, 1984-85. Avocation: tennis. Office: Aquedotto Pugliese SpA, Via Cognetti 36, 70121 Bari Italy

RANJADAYALAN, KULASEGARAM, cardiologist, physician, consultant; b. Jaffna, No., Sri Lanka, Oct. 5, 1955; arrived in Eng., 1987; s. Thambiah and Subathira (Cumarasooriar) Kulasegaram. MBBS, U. Peradniya, Sri Lanka, 1979; MD, U. Colombo (Sri Lanka), 1986; MPhil in Cardiology, U. London, 1994. Lectr. U. Jaffna (Sri Lanka), 1983-86; registrar in medicine Scunthorpe Gen. Hosp., Eng., 1987; rsch. registrar in cardiology Newham Gen. Hosp., Eng., 1988-92; staff physician in cardiology, chest medicine Newham Gen. Hosp., 1992-95, cons. physician, cardiologist, 1995—, chief coord. clin. audit, divsn. medicine and support svcs., 1997—; examiner human diseases U. London and King's Coll. Hosp., 1995—; lectr. med., dental students Royal London Hosp., 1992—. Contbr. articles to profl. jours. Fellow Royal Coll. Physicians (Edinburgh), Royal Coll. Physicians (London); mem. Royal Coll. Physicians (U.K.), Brit. Cardiac Soc., Brit.Soc. Echocardiology. Avocations: tennis, golf, music, reading. Office: Newham Gen Hosp, Glen Rd Plaistow, E13 8SL London Eastern, England

RANJEVA, RAYMOND, international court of justice judge; b. Antananarivo, Madagascar, Aug. 31, 1942; s. René and Eugénie (Raolosoa) R.; m. Yvette Madeleine R. Rabetafika, June 17, 1967; 5 children. Teaching cert., U. Madagascar, LLD, student nat. sch. adminstrn. Dir. law and polit. sci. U. Madagascar, Antananarivo, 1973-82, pres., dean, faculty law, econs., mgmt. and sociology, 1982-88, rector, 1988-90; judge Internat. Ct. Justice, The Hague, Netherlands, 1991—; CEO, chmn. bd. dirs. bur. consultations JURECO; atty., counsel border dispute Govt. Mali. Author numerous works; editor monthly jour. JURECO, 1988-90. Pub., civil and social com. Coun. Cath. Chs. Madagascar, Antananarivo, 1978-90; active Justitia & Pax, Antananarivo, 1978-90. Recipient award Nat. Assn. Doctors in Law, Nat. Sch. Adminstrn. Madagascar, VI Honneurs, Madagascar; named Comdr. l'Ordre Nat. Malgache, Officier Legion Honneur, Chevalier l'Ordre de Merite Madagascar, l'Ordre National Mali. Mem. Interant. C. of C. (internat. ct. arbitration 1994—), Ct. Arbitration for Sport. Avocations: walking, traditional music. Office: Internat Ct Justice, Palais de la Paix Carnegieplein 2, 2517 KJ The Hague The Netherlands

RANJIT, ARUN, journalist; b. Kathmandu, Nepal, Sept. 27, 1960; s. Ishwar Man and Tulasi Ranjit; m. Gayatri Ranjit, Mar. 27, 1986; children: Abison, Monica. MBA, Tribhuvan U. Inst. Mgmt., Kathmandu, 1987. Assoc. editor quar. Baisakha, Kathmandu, 1980-84; fin. contr. Hotel Amb., Kathmandu, 1984-87; reporter Tribhuvan U., Kathmandu, 1987-88; asst. editor UNICEF South Asia Region, Kathmandu, 1992; assoc. editor Lalitya Fortnightly, Kathmandu, 1979—, The Rising Nepal Daily, Kathmandu, 1988—; editor Maulik (Nepali) Weekly, Kathmandu, 1993—; asst. editor UNICEF's Publs., South Asia office, 1992; bd. dirs. Athaha Pub. Pvt. Ltd.; jury mem. Nepal Selection Com. for Asian Art Show in Japan, 1995. Author: An Organization Structure, 1987, Arts and Artists, 1996, Patan: A City of Arts and Crafts, Bhaktapur: A City of Hollywood's Little Buddha Film Shooting Site, Pashupatinath: Hindus' Holy Temple, Nepalese Small and Medium Industries: Prospects and Problems; editor: Journalism, 1987, The Vol., 1990; advisor-editor Indreni Weekly, 1995—; editl. mem. Nepali Arts and Culture Jour., 1995; press advisor: J Art Gallery. Recipient medal King of Nepal, various medals and prizes. Mem. Internat. Study Ctr. for Mass Media (gen. sec. Nepal br. 1991—), South Asian Assn. for Regional Cooperation Journalists Assn. (exec. mem. 1994—), Internat. Orgn. Journalists, Nepal Press Inst. Alumni Assn. (founding mem.), Internat. Orgn. Journalists Tng. Ctr. (exec. mem. 1992—), Art Critic Journalists' Assn. (pres. 1996), Nepal Press Union, Nepal Journalists Assn. Avocations: literature, sports (football, swimming), social service. E-mail: aroon@geo.wlink.com.np.

RÁNKI, ZSUZSANNA, management consultant; b. Budapest, Hungary, July 26, 1954; d. György and Erzsébet (Váli) R. B Econs., U. Econs., Budapest, 1977, M Econs., 1985; MBA, Ind. U., 1983. Sr. economist Hungarian Fgn. Trade Bank, Budapest, 1978-85; dir. Skála-Coop, Budapest, 1985-87; founder, mng. dir. Internat. Mgmt. Ctr., Budapest, 1987-90; mng. dir. Soros Mgmt. Tng. Programs, Budapest, 1990-99; mng. prin. Egon Zehnder Internat., Budapest, 1992—; mng. dir. Ward Howell Euroselect Ltd., Budapest, 1999—; bd. dirs. Soros Mgmt. Tng. Programs; chmn. Prince of Wales Bus. Leaders Forum, Hungary, 1990—. Bd. dirs. Lauder Sch., Budapest, 1991—. Avocations: cinema, music, social outings, books. Office: Ward Howell Euroselect Ltd, Ady E #8, H-1024 Budapest Hungary

RANKILOR, PETER RICHARD, geotechnical engineer, educator; b. Jabalpur, India, Apr. 3, 1942; arrived in Eng., 1950.; s. Brian Arnold and Ivy (Coates) R.; m. Helen Marjorie Addison, July 25 (div. Oct. 1996); children: Nancy Helen, Penelope Susan, Benjamin Peter; m. Helena Martin, Jan. 18, 1997. BSc, Nottingham (Eng.) U., 1963; MSc, Salford (Eng.) U., 1969, PhD, 1989. Chartered civil engr.; chartered geologist; chartered textile technologist. Engr. Manstock Engring. Co. Ltd., Manchester, 1963-67; lectr. Salford U., 1967-71; assoc. ptnr. Wardell Armstrong, Newcastle, Eng., 1971-74; dir. Manstock Engring. Co. Ltd., Manchester, 1974-76; mng. dir. Manstock Geotech., Manchester, 1976-95; prin. Rankilor Consultants, Macclesfield, Eng., 1995—; founding chmn. Salford U. Convocation, 1970-71; chmn. AEG (U.K.), London, 1975-77; founding chmn. IGS (U.K.), London, 1987-88; vis. prof. Bolton (Eng.) Inst., 1993—. Author: (books) British Palaeogeography, 1972, Membranes in Ground Engineering, 1980, UTF Geosynthetics Manual, 1992, (computer programme) Geosynth, 1994. Fellow Geol. Soc. London, Inst. Civil Engrs., Instn. Geologists, Instn. Mining and Metallurgy. Anglican. Avocations: guitar, keyboard, skiing, computer, motor-caravan. Office: Rankilor Consultants, 9 Blairgowrie Dr, Macclesfield SK10 2UJ, England

RANKIN, CLYDE EVAN, III, lawyer; b. Phila., July 3, 1950; s. Clyde Evan, Jr. and Mary E. (Peluso) R.; m. Camille Cozzone, Aug. 24, 1997; A.B., Princeton U., 1972; J.D., Columbia U., 1975; postgrad. Hague Acad. Internat. Law, 1975. Bar: N.Y., N.J., D.C., U.S. Supreme Ct. Law clk. to judge U.S. Dist. Ct. So. Dist. N.Y., 1975-77; assoc. Debevoise, Plimpton, Lyons & Gates, N.Y.C., 1977-79; assoc. Coudert Bros., N.Y.C., 1979-83, ptnr., 1984—. Trustee The Rensselaerville (N.Y.) Inst., 1989—, Coun. on Fgn. Rels., 1996—. Stone scholar, 1974. Mem. ABA, Assn. of Bar of City of N.Y., N.Y. State Bar Assn., D.C. Bar Assn., N.J. Bar Assn. Roman Catholic. Club: Amateur Comedy (N.Y.C.). Contbr. article to legal jour. Office: Coudert Bros 1114 Ave of Americas New York NY 10036-7703

RANKIN, DAWN CAROL, poet; b. Liverpool, Eng., Dec. 25, 1960; d. Thomas Vincent Williams and Edith Agnes Kerr; m. Paul Rankin, June 29, 1985 (div. Apr. 1989); 1 child, Samuel Paul. Diploma in sociology, Southport Coll., 1980. Lic. gaming, Kingsway Casino. Poet, dir. Rankin & Rankin Originals, 1986—; writer, lyricist World Union Songwriters, U.K., 1996—; dir. poetryshack poetry publ. WWW.poetryshack.co.uk, 1999. Poetry pub. in newspapers, 1984. Matron Guiney Pig Sanctuary, 1988—; active several humanitarian campaigns. Liberal. Roman Catholic. Avocations: animals, collecting oil & water colors paintings, furniture restoration. Home and Office: 6 Raglan Lodge, 23 N Lodge Rd Penn Hill, Dorset BH14 9BA, England

RANKIN, HELEN CROSS, cattle rancher, guest ranch executive; b. Mojave, Calif; d. John Whisman and Cleo Rebecca (Tilley) Cross; m. Leroy Rankin, Jan. 4, 1936 (dec. 1954); children—Julia Jane, Patricia Helen Denvir, William John. A.B., Calif. State U.-Fresno, 1935. Owner, operator Rankin Cattle Ranch, Caliente, Calif., 1954—; founder, pres. Rankin Ranch, Inc., Guest Ranch, 1965—; mem. sect. 15, U.S. Bur. Land Mgmt.; mem. U.S. Food and Agrl. Leaders Tour China, 1983, Australia and N.Z., 1985; dir. U.S. Bur. Land Mgmt. sect. 15. Pres., Children's Home Soc. Calif., 1945; mem. adv. bd. Camp Ronald McDonald. Recipient award Calif. Hist. Soc., 1983, Kern River Valley Hist. Soc., 1983. Mem. Am. Nat. Cattlemen's Assn., Calif. Cattlemen's Assn., Kern County Cattlemen's Assn., Kern County Cowbelles (pres. 1949, Cattlewoman of Yr. 1988), Calif. Cowbelles, Nat. Cowbelles, Bakersfield Country Club, Bakersfield Raquet Club. Republican. Baptist. Office: Rankin Ranch Caliente CA 93518

RANKIN, SIR IAN, BARONET, textile manufacturer, real estate and oil company executive; b. London, Dec. 19, 1932; s. Niall Arthur and Jean Margaret (Dalrymple) R.; m. Alexandra Durlacher, July 2, 1959 (div. 1967); children: Gavin, Zara; m. June Marsham-Townsend; 1 child, Lachlan. Student, Eton Coll., Windsor, Eng., 1946-51; MA with honors, Christ Ch., Oxford, Eng., 1953-57. With Colman Prentis & Varley, London, 1958-61; chmn., dir. I. N. Rankin Sales Ltd., London, 1961—; chmn. bd. I.N. Rankin Oil Ltd., London, 1979—, B.S. Group, Bristol, U.K., 1994; dir. Slumberfleece Ltd., London, New Arcadia Explorations, Ltd., Vancouver; patron Samaritans, Slough, U.K., 1992—. Lt. Scots Guards, 1951-53. Mem. Whites Club, Royal Yacht Squadron. Avocations: chess, skiing, shooting. Home and Office: Rankin House, 97 Elgin Ave, London W9 2DA, England

RANKIN, JIMMIE R., neuroscience nurse; b. Auburn, Calif., May 22, 1941; s. Gilbert O. and Wilma E. (Robertson) R. MSN, U. Calif., San Francisco, 1989; BSN, USNY, 1983; BA, U. Calif., Berkeley, 1969; BS in Psychology, ASN, USNY, Albany, 1977. Staff nurse Neurol. Inst., N.Y.C.; ind. nurse, prin. Dry Bones Nursing BBS, Dry Bones Press, San Francisco; dir. nursing Pacific Coast Hosp., San Francisco. Mem. AANN. Home: PO Box 597 Roseville CA 95678-0597

RANKINE, V.V., sculptor, painter; b. Boston, July 27, 1920; d. Auguste and Hetty (Hemenway) Richard; m. John Magruder, 1945 (div. 1950); 1 child, John Magruder; m. Paul Scott Rankine, 1952 (div. 1969); 1 child, David Scott; m. Rufus King, Nov. 23, 1973. Student, Amedee Ozenfant Sch., N.Y.C., 1940-41, Black Mt. Coll., 1942-43. Dir. dept. art Madeira Sch., Greenway, Va., 1967-70; artist-in-residence Inst. Man and Sci., Rensselaer, N.Y., summer 1968; instr. humanities art Hunter Coll. H.S., N.Y.C., 1970-71; instr. painting and drawing U. Md., College Park, 1979-81. One-woman shows include Fraser's Stable Gallery, Washington, 1978, Corcoran Gallery Art, Washington, 1978, No. Va. C.C., 1978, Women Artists Ea. L.I., East Hampton, N.Y., 1979; group exhbns. include Corcoran Gallery Art, Washington, 1954, 55, 58, 67, Betty Parsons Gallery, N.Y.C., 1966-81, Mus. Modern Art, N.Y.C., 1966, 30th Corcoran Biennial, Washington, 1967-68, Four Americans, Axiom Gallery, London, 1968, Painting and Sculpture Today, Indpls., 1965; work rep. in Nat. Mus. Am. Art, Washington, Corocoran Gallery Art, Washington, Oklahoma City Mus., Indpls. Mus. Art, Woodward Found., Washington, Guild Hall Mus., East Hampton, N.Y. Recipient Painting prize Corcoran Gallery, 1955, Maurice Tuchman Juror award Corcoran Gallery Art, 1978. Home: 3524 Williamsburg Ln NW Washington DC 20008-1207

RANSIL, BERNARD J(EROME), research physician, methodologist, consultant, educator; b. Pitts., Nov. 15, 1929; s. Raymond Augustine and Louise Mary (Berhalter) R. BS, Duquesne U., 1951; PhD in Phys. Chemistry, Cath. U. Am., 1955; MD, U. Chgo., 1964. NRC-NAS postdoctoral fellow Nat. Bur. Stds., Washington, 1955-56; cons. heat div. thermodynamics sect. Nat. Bur. Standards, Washington, 1956-62; cons. NASA exobiology project, Washington, 1962-68; rsch. assoc. and dir. diatomic molecule project, Lab. Molecular Structure and Spectra, physics dept. U. Chgo., 1956-63; intern Harbor Gen. Hosp., UCLA, Torrance, Calif., 1964-65, Guggenheim fellow, 1965-66; from rsch. assoc. in medicine to assoc. prof. in medicine Harvard Med. Sch., Boston, 1966-96; from rsch. assoc. and clin. fellow to clin. assoc. Harvard II and IV Med. Svcs., 1966-74; core lab. scientist Clin. Rsch. Ctr. Thorndike Meml. Lab Boston City Hosp., Boston, 1966-74; asst. physician Beth Israel Hosp., Boston, 1974-96, sr. physician, 1996—; dir. Core Lab. Clin. Rsch. Ctr., 1974-94, Data Analysis Lab., 1989-94; cons., rsch. ops. Beth Israel Hosp., Boston, 1994-96; cons. computational stats. dept. neurology Beth Israel Deaconess Med. Ctr., Boston, 1996—; statis. computing cons. Boston City Hosp. and Beth Israel Hosp., 1966-96; cons. Prophet project NIH, Bethesda, Md., 1971-88, exec. com., 1986-91, Howard Hughes Med. Inst., Boston, 1979-80, Coop. Cataract Rsch. Group, Boston, 1981-83, Mass. Alzheimer's Disease Rsch. Ctr., 1992-94; guest lectr. med. ethics Seton Hall U., 1971—; vis. scientist Rockefeller U., 1985, Scripps Rsch. Found., 1986, Calif. State U., 1986, U. Pitts. Med. Sch., 1987. Author: Abortion, 1969, Background to Abortion, 1979; editor: Life of a Scientist: Autobiography of Robert S. Mulliken, 1989, (videocassettes) Elements of Statistics and Data Analysis, 1985; contbr. biography of R.S. Mulliken to Nobel Laureates in Chemistry, 1973; contbr. numerous articles on computational chemistry, med. topics, computational stats. to sci. jours., also book revs. to Boston Globe, other periodicals, essays and poetry to The Critic. Recipient alumni rsch. award Cath. U. Am., 1969, Duquesne U. centennial award, 1978. Mem. numerous profl. socs. Home: 226 Calumet St Boston MA 02120-3303

RANSMAYR, GERHARD N., neurology educator; b. Linz, Austria, Mar. 22, 1956; s. Gerhard A. and Gertrud M. (Heller) R.; m. Sibylle A. Tepser, May 17,1 986; children: Christine, Johanna, Lucia, Sophia. MD, Innsbruck U., Austria, 1980. Assoc. prof. dept. neurology Innsbruck U., 1997—; cons. Natters (Austria) Hosp., Tirol, 1997—. Mem. Rotary Club. Office: Dept Neurology, Anichstr 35, A-6020 Innsbruck Tirol, Austria

RANSOM, DAVID MICHAEL, retired ambassador; b. St. Louis, Nov. 23, 1938; s. Clifford Fredic and Inez Natalie (Green) R.; m. Marjorie Ann (Marilley) Ransom; children: Elizabeth Inez, Katherine Hope, Sarah Grace. AB, Princeton U., 1960; MA, Johns Hopkins Sch. of Advanced Internat. Studies, 1962; student, The Nat. War Coll., 1982-83. With U.S. Dept. State, Yemen, Iran, Lebanon, Saudi Arabia, 1965-71; nat. security coun. staff White House U.S. Dept. State, Washington, 1971-73; dep. chief mission Am. Embassy, Sana'a, Yemen Arab Rep., 1975-78; dir., dept. dir. near east divsn. internat. security affairs Office of Sec. of Def., U.S. Dept. of Def., Washington, 1978-82; dep. chief mission Am. Embassy, Abu Dhabi, United Arab Emirates, 1983-85; dep. chief of mission Am. Embassy, Damascus, Syria, 1985-88; country dir. Arabian Peninsula-Near East Bur., U.S. Dept. State, 1988-90, country dir. Greece, Turkey, Cyprus-European Bur., 1990-93; amb. to Bahrain, Am. Embassy, Manama, 1994-97; ret., 1997; prin. DM Ransom Assocs., Washington, 1997—. 1st lt. inf. USMC, 1962-65. Mem. Met. Club (Washington). Episcopalian. Avocations: scuba diving, canoeing, skiing. Home: 2269 Cathedral Ave NW Washington DC 20008-1510 Office: 1100 Connecticut Ave NW Ste 310 Washington DC 20036-4136

RANSOM, GAYLORD RICK, structural engineer; b. Redwood City, Calif., Feb. 3, 1953; . Gaylord Pat and Yola Grace (Old) R.; m. Linette Diane Pauls, June 25, 1984 (d ec. Sept., 1992); children: Anna, Brent, Sarah, Kimberly, Amy, Rebecca; m. Karla Jean Lauck, Feb. 7, 1993. BS in Civil Engring., Calif. State U., Fresno, 1977. Civil engr. intern III City of Fresno, Calif., 1973-75; engr. aide II City of Fresno, 1975-76, civil engineer I, 1976-78, structural engr. III, 1978-80, chief structural engr., 1980-83, dep. city engr., 1982-83, asst. dep. dir. inspections, 1980-83; prin. Ransom, Boone & Assocs., Fresno, 1976-83; assoc. William Brooks Assocs., Fresno, 1983-95; pres. Brooks, Ransom & Assocs., Fresno, 1995—. Chmn. CSUF Engring. adv. com., Fresno, 1995—. Mem. Structural Engrs. of Calif. (bd. dirs.), Calif. Soc. Profl. Engrs. (pres. 1981-82), Nat. Soc. Profl. Engrs., Internat. Conf. of Bldg. Officials. Republican. Baptist. Avocations: firearms, hunting, fishing, 4-wheel drive. Office: Brooks Ransom Assocs 155 E Shaw Ave Ste 100 Fresno CA 93710-7619

RANSOM, VICTOR HARVEY, engineering educator; b. King Hill, Idaho, Mar. 23, 1932; s. Harvey Edgar and Edna Jessie (Honess) R.; m. Mary Ann Pierce, July 20, 1975 (div. June 1974); children: JoEllen Kay, Vickie Ann, Darin Victor; m. Delrie G. Gridley, July 6, 1974; children: Jessica Delrie, Natasha Lynn. BSChemE, U. Idaho, 1955; PhD, Purdue U., 1970. Registered profl. engr., Calif. Engr. Rocketdyne Divsn., Canoga Park, Calif., 1955-59; rsch. engr. Aerojet Gen. Corp., Sacramento, Calif., 1959-73; sci. and engring. fellow Idaho Nat. Engring. Lab., Idaho Falls, 1973-90; head sch. of nuclear engring. Purdue U., West Lafayette, Ind., 1990-98, prof. nuclear engring., 1998—; cons. Creare, 1997—, State of Maine, 1996—, Scientech, 1994—, U.S. Nuclear Regulatory Commn., Washington, 1991—, Idaho Nat. Engring. Lab., Idaho Falls, 1990—, Argonne Nat. Lab., Chgo., 1992—. Named to Alumni Hall of Fame U. Idaho, 1991. Fellow Am. Nuclear Soc. (chair T-H divsn. 1988, 1999, tech. achievement award 1999); mem. ASME, ASEE, Sigma Xi, Phi Eta Sigma, Sigma Chi. Achievements include development of the RELAP5 computer code for simulation of the transient response of Nuclear Powerplants under accident conditions. Avocations: skiing, auto mechanics. Home: 3035 Hamilton St West Lafayette IN 47906-1155 Office: Purdue U NUCL 140 Purdue University IN 47907

RANTA, RAIMO OLAVI, science administrator, electronics engineer, researcher; b. Vesilahti, Finland, July 28, 1949; s. Arvo Olavi and Elvi Helena (Teeri) R.; m. Tuula Sanni Marjatta Toivonen, Dec. 30, 1973; children: Miia, Mikko, Jussi, Janne, Riia. MSc, Tampere (Finland) U. Tech., 1977, Lic. Tech., 1989, D Tech., 1997. Rschr. Rsch. Ctr. of Army, Ylöjärvi, Finland, 1977-85, Finnish Meteorol. Inst., Helsinki, 1985-86; rschr. Rsch. Inst. Info. Tech. (now Digital Media Inst.), Tampere, 1986-90, dir., 1990-95, with European Union Project Cooperation, 1995-96; with Def. Forces Materiel Commd. Hdqrs., Tampere, 1997—. Engr. Lit. Finnish Mil., 1975-76. Mem. IEEE. Lutheran. Avocations: music, literature, body building, cars, wandering. Office: Finnish Def Forces Def Mat, PO Box 69, FIN33541 Tampere Finland

RANTAKALLIO, PAULA TUULIKKI, medical educator; b. Kemi, Finland, July 1, 1930; d. Arvid Eelis and Olga Emilia (Lahti) R. Lic. in medicine, Helsinki (Finland) U., 1957; D of Medicine and Surgery, Oulu (Finland) U., 1969. Temporary lectr. in child health U. Manchester, England, 1969; acting assoc. prof. pediatrics U. Oulu, 1969-70, acting prof. pub. health, 1973, assoc. prof. pub. health, 1978-87, prof. pub. health, 1987-96; jr. and sr. rsch. fellow, sr. scientist The Finnish Acad., 1972-78; sec.-gen. and rsch. officer Nordic Coun. Arctic Med. Rsch., Finland, 1977. Author monographs. Mem. Internat. Epidemiol. Assn., European Sci. Found. Office: Dept Pub Health/Gen Pract, Aapistie 1, 90220 Oulu Finland

RANTALA, TAPIO TUOMAS, physics educator; b. Pielisjärvi, Finland, Feb. 16, 1955; s. Leo Alpertti and Pirkko Marjatta (Peltonen) R.; m. Maire Lahja Irmeli Laukka, Feb. 6, 1980; children: Anne-Maria Helena, Mona-Marika Kristiina, Tomi Harri Matias. MSc in Physics, U. Oulu, Finland, 1978, MSc in Engring., 1984, PhD in Physics, 1987. Vis. scientist dept. physics Chalmers U. Tech., Gothenburg, 1984-85; jr. rsch. scientist Acad. Finland, 1987-90; vis. scientist dept. physics SUNY, Buffalo, 1989-90; tchg. asst. dept. physics U. Oulu, 1980-87, asst. prof., 1990-99; prof. physics Tampere (Finland) U. Tech., 1999—. Contbr. over 40 articles to internat. sci. publs. Lt. Finnish mil., 1980. Avocations: squash, soccer, alpine skiing, badminton, orienteering. Home: Multatie 2, 90650 Oulu Finland Office: Tampere Univ Tech, Inst Physics, FIN33101 Tampere Finland

RANTA-MAUNUS, ALPO KALEVI, timber engineering scientist; b. Kuortane, Finland, Aug. 16, 1944; s. Paavo Hermanni and Martta Katariina (Knuuttila) Ranta-M.; m. Aila Kaisu K. Lassila, Dec. 30, 1972. Diploma Engring., Helsinki U. Tech., 1970, D Tech., 1976. Researcher VTT Bldg Tech, Espoo, Finland, 1970-72; rsch. prof. VTT Bldg Tech., Espoo, 1985—; inspector Inst. Nuclear Safety, Helsinki, 1973-74, chief inspector, 1974-82, dep. dir., 1983-85; tchg. asst. Helsinki U. Tech., Espoo, 1968-71; vis. researcher N.W. Univ., Evanston, Ill., 1979-80; docent Helsink U. Tech., 1989—. Mem. editl. bd. European Jour. Wood Tech.; contbr. articles to profl. jours. Fellow Internat. Union Testing & Rsch. Labs. for Materials and Structures (chmn. TC 133 1991-94); mem. ASME, Assn. Finnish Civil Engring. (chmn. timber com. 1988—), European Cost Orgn. (chmn. E15 1999—).

RANTSIOS, APOSTOLOS TRIANTAFYLLOS, military veterinarian, researcher, consultant; b. Nikisiani, Macedonia, Greece, Oct. 9, 1938; s. Triantafyllos Apostolos Rantsios and Fotini Triantafyllos-Dimitrios Rantsiou-Kioupkioli; m. Evangelia Apostolos-Georgios Mountraki, Apr. 17, 1966; children: Fotini, Kalliopi. DVM, Vet. Sch., Thessaloniki, Greece, 1961, PhD, 1972, prof. cert., 1982. With Hellenic Army, Greece, 1962-69; head histology dept. Biol. Rsch. Ctr. Hellenic Army, Athens, 1971-78, gen. staff Med. Corps, 1978-83; chief B corps vet svc. Hellenic Army, Veria, 1983-84; gen. staff Chief Vet. Svc. Hellenic Army, Athens, 1984-87; dir. vet. br. Biol Rsch. Ctr. Hellenic Army, Athens, 1987-88; comdr. Tng. Ctr./Vet. Svc. Hellenic Army, Larissa, Greece, 1988-89; chief Vet. Svc. Hellenic Army, Athens, 1989-92; chmn. W.G. Food Hygiene-Food Technology European NATO Armed Forces, Athens, 1982-92; cons., Athens, 1975—; prof. ex-oficio Aristotelian U., Thessaloniki, 1982—; vis. rschr. U.K. Agr. Rsch. Coun., 1969-71, Bundesamstahlt für Fleischforschung, 1985. Author: Seafood Technology, 1986; contbr. articles to profl. jours. Served with Hellenic Army Vet. Corps, 1962-92, ret. Decorated Cross of Comdr. of the Order of Phoenix, Hellenic Rep. Mem. Hellenic Vet. Med. Soc. (pres. 1987-97), World Vet. Assn. (nat. rep., pres. 1995-99), Am. Inst. Food Technology, Geotechnical Chamber Greece, Hellenic Inst. Food Technologists, Hellenic Soc. Food Hygienists-Technologists, Soc. Macedonian Studies, Internat. Com. Military Medicine. Home and Office: 81 Hlois Rd, GR 15125 Marousi Athens Greece

RANUZZI (DE BIANCHI), PAOLO, bank executive; b. Bologna, Italy, Jan. 24, 1940; m. Cristina Di Carpegna, Dec. 18, 1971; children: Laura, Anna, Giulia. Dr degree, U. Florence, Italy, 1964; PhD, Cornell U., 1967. Prof. U. Bologna, 1970-72, 80-83; economist European Cmty., Belgium, 1972-80; dir. gen. Italian Treasury, Italy, 1983-88; gen. mgr. Fondigest, Milan, 1988-98; gen. mgr., head pvt. banking Intesa Bank, Italy, 1999—; econ. policy com. OECD, working party; coordination group European Cmty. Coun. of Ministries, Brussels. Office: Intesa Bank, Via Romagnosi 5, 20121 Milan Italy

RAO, AKKINEPALLI BADRI NARAYAN, physician, educator; b. Hyderabad, India, Oct. 7, 1923; arrived in Australia, 1973; s. Sita Ram and Rama Chudamma (Rangaraju) R.; m. Norah Janet Gardner, Mar. 22, 1958; children: Priti, Nandita. FSc, Osmania U., 1942, B Medicine B Surgery, 1947. House surgeon medicine, surgery and obstetrics Hyderabad, 1948; house surgeon ear nose and throat Royal Nat. Ear Nose and Throat Hosp., London, 1951-52; registrar ear nose and throat Birmingham and Midland Ear Nose and Throat Hosp., 1952-54; ear nose and throat surgeon Osmania Gen. Hosp. and Med. Coll., Hyderabad, 1954-67, prof. ear nose and throat, 1958-73; cons. ear nose and throat surgeon Birmingham Regional Hosp.,

Eng., 1967-69; sr. ear, nose and throat surgeon Royal Darwin (Australia) Hosp., 1973-97, emeritus ear, nose and throat cons.; emeritus prof. ear, nose and throat Osmania Med. Coll., Hyderabad, India; fgn. collaborant Acta Otolaryngologica, Stockholm; vis. ear, nose and throat specialist Mackay Base Hosp., Queensland, 1997—; lectr., presenter in field. Contbr. articles to profl. publs., chpts. to books. Recipient Citizen of Australia award Australian Day Coun., 1996, Order of Australia, 1997; fellow Internat. Coll. Surgeons, 1957-67. Fellow Royal Soc. Medicine; mem. Royal Commonwealth Soc. Australia (life), Australian Med. Assn. (mem. exec. coun. N.T. sect.), Neuro Equilibriomatic Soc., Prosper Meniere Soc., Assn. Otolaryngologists of India (life), Otolaryngol. Soc. Australia. Avocations: travel, teaching. Home: 57 Pamela St, Mount Waverley VIC 3149, Australia Office: Royal Darwin Hosp, Casuarina, Darwin 0811, Australia

RAO, ANNANGI SUBBA, soil scientist, research administrator; b. Ravulapuram, India, May 1, 1952; s. Tiripalu and Saidamma Annangi; m. Annangi Usha Rani, July 16, 1976 (div. Oct. 1995); children: Saida Subha Prada, Sudeepti; m. Sri Bhulakshmi Devi, Nov. 21, 1996. BSc in Agr., Andhra Pradesh Agrl. U., Bapatla, India, 1973, MSc in Agr., 1976; PhD, Indian Agrl. Rsch. Inst., New Delhi, 1980. Jr. scientist Andhra Pradesh Agrl. U., Amadalavalasa, India, 1980; asst. prof. Andhra Pradesh Agrl. U., Bapatla, 1980-84; soil scientist Potash Rsch. Inst. India, Gurgaon, 1984-89; prin. scientist Indian Inst. Soil Sci., Bhopal, 1989-97, project coord., 1997—. Contbr. articles to profl. jours. Recipient Silver Jubilee award of excellence Fertiliser Assn. India, 1989, award Potash Rsch. Inst. India, 1991, others. Mem. Indian Soc. Soil Sci. (councillor 1991-92). Hindu. Avocations: listening to music, reading, watching TV, gardening. Office: Indian Inst Soil Sci, Nabibagh, Berasia Rd, 462038 Bhopal India

RAO, ARATLA TRIVIKRAMA, veterinary pathologist; b. Paralakhemundi, India, July 21, 1940; s. Aratla and Jaya (Lakshmi) R.; 2 children. B in Vet. Sci., Vet. Coll., Bhubaneswar, India, 1958-62; MVSc, IVRI, Izatnagar, India, 1966; PhD, Vet. Coll., Hissar, India, 1977. Rsch. asst. Icar Rsch. AH Directorate, Cuttack, India, 1962-64; from asst. prof. to prof. Agriculture U., Ouat, India, 1966—. Named Best Tchr. in Vet. Faculty, 1994-95, Best Tchr. in Univ., 1996-97; recipient Dr. Prkiyer Meml. medal, 1992, Dr. Ganti Asastry award 1994, Dr. Cmsingh award 1996, Dr. RR Sukla award 1995, Sri Ramlal Agrawala Nat. award, 1996-97. Fellow Nat. Acad. Agrl. Sci., Nat. Acad. Vet. Sci., Indian Assn. Vet. Pathologists. Office: Vet Coll, Bhubaneswar, 751003 Orissa India

RAO, ARUN P., physician; b. Bangalore, India, Aug. 4, 1962; s. Padmanabha and Sunanda Rao; m. Anita Alwani, Jan. 22, 1999. MB BChir, Govt. Med. Coll., Nagpur, India, 1985. Diplomate Am. Bd. Internal Medicine, specialty in internal medicine, cardiology, cardiac electrophysiology. Intern St. Francis Hosp., Evanston, Ill., 1993-94, resident in medicine, 1994-96, fellow in cardiology, 1996-98; fellow in electrophysiology U. Oklahoma City, 1998-2000; clin. dir. U. Okla. Health Scis. Ctr., Oklahoma City. Home: 7133 S Santa Fe Ave Oklahoma City OK 73139-7513 Office: U Okla Health Scis Ctr 920 S Youngs Blvd Oklahoma City OK 73108-2653

RAO, ATLURI TRIVIKRAMA, geology educator, researcher; b. Seridentakurru, Andhra, India, May 29, 1942; s. Atluri Seshagiri Rao and Atluri Vajramma Cherukuri; m. Vijaya Lakshmi Tottempudi, Feb. 14, 1975; children: Atluri Sri Krishna Prabha, Atluri Lakshmi Madhuri. BSc, Mahakhosal Mahavidyalaya, Jabalpur, India, 1960, MSc, 1962; PhD, Andhra U., Visakhapatnam, India, 1972. Lectr. Andhra U., Visakhapatnam, 1974-84, reader, 1984-92, prof., 1992—. Author: A Crustal Section of Eastern Dharwar Craton-Godavari Rift-Eastern Ghats Mobile Belt, India, 1997, Eastern Ghats and Surrounding Areas Within East Gondwana, 1998, Precambrian Crustal Processes in East Coast Granulite-Greenstone Regions of India and Antarctica within Eastern Gondwana, 1998; editor: India as a Fragment in East Gondwana, 1995, Eastern Ghats Granulites, 1999; contbr. over 165 articles to profl. jours. Recipient Young Scientist award Andhra Pradesh Acad. Scis., 1977. Mem. Geol. Soc. of India, Geol., Mining and Metallurgy Soc. of India, Gondwana Rsch. Group, Sigma Xi. Avocations: reading scientific journals, field work in mountainous terrains. Home: MVP Colony Sector XI, 2-45-8 Mig 46 A U Plots, Visakhapatnam 530017, India Office: Dept Geology, Andhra U, Visakhapatnam 530003, India

RAO, BUTTI SUBRAHMANYESWARA, chemist; b. Rajahmundry, India, Aug. 14, 1955; s. Butti Ramachandra Rao and Butti Gangamamba Rao; m. Butti Suryakumari, Aug. 8, 1982; children: Priyanka, Prathyusha. BS, Andhra U., India, 1975, MS, 1977; PhD, Indian Inst. Tech., Delhi, 1982. Rsch. assoc. Indian Inst. Tech., Delhi, 1983-85; fellow U. Pierre Et Marie Curie, Paris, 1985-87; pool officer Nat. Chem. Lab., Pune, India, 1987-89; scientist org. coatings & polymer divsn. Indian Inst. Chem. Tech., Hyderabad, India, 1990—; vis. rsch. assoc. U. Pitts., 1989-90. Author: Polymer Sciences-Recent Advances, 1994, Macromolecules Current Trends, 1995. Postdoctiral fellow U. Pierre Et Marie Curie, Paris, 1985-87. Mem. Oil Techs. Assn. India. Avocations: chess, table tennis, music. Office: Org Coatings & Polymer Divs, Indian Inst Chem Tech, Hyderabad 500 007, India

RAO, CHINTAMANI NAGESA, academic administrator, chemistry educator; b. Bangalore, Karnataka, India, June 30, 1934; s. Hanumantha Nagesa and Nagamma Nagesa R.; m. Indumati Rao, May 15, 1960; children: Suchitra, Sanjay. MS, Banaras Hindu U., Uttar Pradesh, India, 1953; PhD, Purdue U., 1958; DSc, Mysore U., Karnataka, 1961; DSc (honoris causa), other univs., India, France, Poland, Russia, U.S., U.K. Head Dept. Chemistry Indian Inst. Tech., Kanpur, Uttar Pradesh, 1963-77; chmn. Solid State and Structural Chemistry Unit and Materials Rsch. Centre Indian Inst. Sci., Bangalore, 1977-84, dir., 1984-94; pres. Jawaharlal Nehru Ctr. for Advanced Sci. Rsch., Bangalore, 1990-99; Blackett lectr., 1991; mem. exec. bd. Internat. Coun. Unions; internat. sci. adv. bd. UNESCO; Linnett vis. prof. U. Cambridge. Author 34 books, 1000 rsch. publs.; mem. editorial bd. several jours. dealing with chemistry acad. materials. Pres. 3d World Acad. Sci. and Asia-Pacific Acad. Materials. Recipient Padma Vibhushan award Pres. India, 1985, G.M. Modi award, 1989, Hevrovsky Gold medal Czechoslovak Acad. Scis., 1989, Sahabdeen award Sri Lanka, TWAS medal lectr., Einstein Gold medal UNESCO, Golden Jubilee prize Coun. Sci. and Indsl. Rsch., 1991; hon. fellowship Cardiff U., Wales; centenary lectureship and medal Royal Soc. Chemistry. Fellow APS, Acad. Europaea (fgn.), Royal Soc. Chemistry, Japan Acad. (hon.), Third World Acad. Scis., Royal Soc., Brazilian Acad. Sci.; mem. Pontifical Acad. Scis., Polish, Czechoslovak, Serbian, Slovenian, Russian Acad. Scis., Royal Spanish Acad. Scis., French Acad. Scis. (fgn.), AAAS (hon. fgn.), NAS (fgn. assoc.). Avocations: gourmet cooking, gardening. Office: Jawaharlal Nehru Ctr Advanced Sci Rsch, Jakkur PO, Bangalore 560064, India

RAO, CHITALDROOG RAMACHANDRA, physician; b. Bangalore, Karnataka, India, Mar. 4, 1931; arrived in Eng., 1977; parents Santebennur Ranga and Rukmini Bai (Padaki) R.; m. Beryl James, Jan. 16, 1960; children: Anita, Brinda, Kiran. MB, BS, Mysore Med. Coll., Karnataka, India, 1955. Tng. grades Nat. Health Svc., Eng., 1955-61; univ. teaching appointments, cons. physician Karnataka U. Med. Colls., 1961-67; fellow in cardiology Nat. Health Svc., Can., 1967-68; cons. physician Nat. Health Svc., Eng., 1968-69; prof. medicine and cardiology, cons. physician, cardiologist Bangalore Med. Coll., India, 1969-77; cons. physician Welsh Regional Hosp. Bd., 1977-79; cons. physician, geriatrician Nat. Health Svc. S.E. Thames Regional Health Authority, Birchington, 1979—; chmn., examiner undergrad. and postgrad. exams. Bangalore U., Mysore U., 1966-75; hon. phys. to gov. of Karnataka. Mem. editorial bd. Indian Heart Jour., 1974-77; contbr. articles to med. jours. Organizer "Hypertension clinic for the Poor", Mahabodhi Soc., Bangalore, 1963-66, "Heart Disease Detection and Advice Campus for the Poor", Lyons Club, Bangalore, 1976-77. Named Citizen of yr. Lyons Internat., Bangalore, 1977. Fellow Indian Coll. Cardiology (founding), Royal Coll. Physicians (Edinburgh), Royal Coll. Tropical Medicine and Health; mem. Indian Assn. for the Advancement Med. Edn., Cardiological Soc. India, Assn. Physicians India, British Med. Assn., British Geriatric Soc., Rotary Club (chmn. community svcs. 1981-82), Masonic Lodge, Bangalore Club, North Foreland Golf Club. Home: 18 Daryngton Ave, Birchington CT7 9PS, England

RAO, D. S. PRAKASH, civil engineer, educator; b. Hyderabad, Andhra Pradesh, India, June 17, 1947; s. D. Yadgir and Bhujatha Devi Maramraju Rao; m. Roopa Latha Pulijala, June 11, 1973; 1 child, Deepa Rao. BE, Coll. of Engring., Hyderabad, India, 1968; ME in Structural Engring., IISc, 1970; PhD, U. Melbourne, Australia, 1988. Chartered profl. engr., India. Scientist B, 1971-75, scentist C, 1975-82, scientist E, 1982-84; tutor U. Melbourne, 1984-88, Royal Melbourne Inst. of Tech., Australia, 1984-88; prof. Biria Inst. of Tech. and Sci., Pilani, India, 1988-90; prof., head V. R. Siddhartha Engring. Coll., Vijayawada, India, 1991-92, Chaitanya Bharathi Inst. of Tech., Hyderabad, 1992-97; 5 U. Coll. of Engring., Hyderabad, 1997—. Author: Strength of Materials-A Practical Approach, Vol. I, 1999, Graphical Methods in Structural Analysis, 1997, Structural Analysis-A Unified Arrpaoch, 1996, Design Principles and Detailing of Concrete Structures, 1995, Design Tables for Concrete Bridge Deck Slabs, 1976, Durability of Concrete Structures, 1999; contbr. articles to profl. publs. Fellowship German Acad. Exch. Svc. (DADD), 1977-79; scholarship U. Melbourne, 1984-88; recipient Nagadi award Assn. of Cons. Civil Engrs., 1997, Bharat Ratna Sir Mokshagundam Visvesvaraya award Instn. of Engrs., 1998. Fellow Instn. of Engrs. (life), Indian Instn. of Bridge Engrs. (life); mem. Indian Concrete Inst. (life), Indian Soc. for Tech. Edn. (life), Eye Bank Assn. of India, Osmania Grads. Assn. (life). Office: Dept Civil Engring, Univ Coll Engring, Hyderabad 500 007, India

RAO, DESIRAJU LAKSHMI NARSIMHA, microbiologist; b. Pulletikurru, India, Nov. 26, 1954; s. Subrahmanyam and Manikyamba (Vakkalanka) D.; m. Surekha Palagummi, May 28, 1986; children: Arun Kumar, Naveen Kumar. BSc, U. Delhi, 1973; MSc, Indian Agrl. Rsch. Inst., New Delhi, 1975, PhD, 1979. Scientist Ctrl. Soil Salinity Rsch. Inst., Karnal, India, 1978-85; sr. scientist Ctrl. Soil Salinity Rsch. Inst., Karnal, 1986-98; project coord. All India Coord. Rsch. Project Biol. Nitrogen Indian Inst. Soil Sci., Bhopal, 1998—; prin. investigator Ctrl. Soil Salinity Rsch. Inst., Karnal, 1993-97; mem. exec. com. Dept. Biotech., Govt. India, Nat. Facility Rhizobium. Editor: Salinity Management for Sustainable Agriculture, 1994; contbr. over 70 articles to profl. jours. Vol. trainee Village Reconstruction Orgn., Guntur, India, 1979. Assn. Commonwealth Univs. London fellow, 1986-87, U. London fellow, 1995, U. Sussex fellow, 1995; grantee Dept. Biotech., Govt. India, 1993-97. Mem. Internat. Soc. Soil Sci. (life), Indian Soc. Soil Sci. (life), Assn. Microbiologists India (life). Hindu. Avocations: singing ghazals, travelling, games, reading. Home: H-01 Baba Apts, Chitragupta, Soc, E7 Arera Colony, Bhopal 462 016, India Office: Indian Inst Soil Sci, Nabi Bagh, Berasia Rd, Bhopal 462 038, India

RAO, DEVDAS, chemical executive; b. Anandapuram, Karnataka, India, Oct. 21, 1942; s. Vittal Gangalli Pai and Rukminiamma; m. Chhaya Devdas Prabhu Desai, May 18, 1976; two children. BSc, Ctrl. Coll., Bangalore, India, 1963; BL, SRCC, Bangalore, India, 1969; CALLB, AIIB, Mumbai, India, 1969; NCES, NPC, India. Exec. Syndicate Bank, Bangalore, 1964-89; ptnr. Pai & Pai Group Cos., Bangalore, 1989-92; dir. Pai & Pai Chems. (I) Pvt. Ltd., Bangalore, 1992—; project coord. Karnataka State Pollution Control Bd. Dir. Lions Club Internat., Bangalore, 1979-83. Mem. Century Club, Vijayanagar Club, Bowring Inst. Avocations: reading, traveling. Home: 29 II Blk Rajajinagar, Bangalore 560 010, India Office: Pai & Pai Chems Pvt Ltd, 438 1 I Blk Rajajinagar, Bangalore 560 010, India

RAO, GANTI PRASADA, engineering educator; b. Seethanagaram, India, Aug. 25, 1942; s. Venkatappadu and Rajeswaramma (Vedula) G.; m. Meenakshi Vedula, May 16, 1963; children: Nagalakshmi, Rajeswari, Venkata Lakshminarayana. BSEE with honors, Andhra U., 1963; MTech in Control Engring., Indian Inst. Tech., Kharagpur, 1965, PhD, 1969. Asst. prof. dept. elec. engring. PSG Coll. Tech., Coimbatore, India, 1969-71; asst. prof. dept. elec. engring. Indian Inst. Tech., Kharagpur, 1971-78, prof., 1978-97; tech. advisor Water and Electricity Dept., Govt. of Abu Dhabi, United Arab Emirates, 1992-96; advisor UNESCO-EOLSS Joint com., 1996—. Author: Piecewise Constant Orthogonal Functions and Their Applications to Systems & Control, 1983; co-author: Identification of Continuous Time Dynamical Systems—The PMF Approach, 1983, Identification of Continuous Systems, 1987, Generalized Hybrid Orhogonal Functions and Their Applications in Systems and Control, 1996; editor: Identification of Continuous Systems-Methodology & Computer Implementation, 1991; cons. editor Ency. of Desalination and Water Resources, Ency. of Life Support Systems; co-editor: Numerical Insights Book Series; mem. editl. bd. Internat. Jour. Modeling and Simulation, Control Theory and Advanced Technology, Sys. Sci., Sys. Analysis Modelling and Simulation, also others; contbr. over 150 rsch. articles to profl. jours. Patron PNK Parishad, India, 1994—. Recipient Best Tech. paper award Sys. Soc. India, 1989, Internat. Desalination Assn., 1995; postdoctoral fellow Commonwealth, U.K., 1975-76, AvH Found., Germany, 1982-83; Sys. and Info. Lab. named in his honor Indian Inst. Tech. (Kharagpur); hon. prof. East China U. Sci. & Tech., Shanghai, 1995. Fellow IEEE, Instn. Engrs. India (life), Inst. Electronics and Telecomm. Engrs. India, Indian Nat. Acad. Engring. Avocations: reading, writing, photography, videography, vegetarian cooking. Fax: 9712 6442565. E-mail: gantirao@emirates.net.ae. Office: PO Box 2623, Abu Dhabi United Arab Emirates

RAO, GOVIND P., plant pathologist; b. Murila, U.P., India, Jan. 15, 1960; s. Ravindra P. and Shail Bala (Singh) R.; m. Vineeta Singh, Nov. 24, 1988; children: Shambhavi, Shreya, Kaushiki. BSc in Biology, Gorakhpur (India) U., 1979, MSc in Botany, 1981, PhD in Plant Pathology, 1987. Sci. officer U.P. Coun. of Sugarcane Rsch., Gorakhpur, 1988-96, sr. sci. officer, 1996—, head divsn. plant pathology, 1993—. Editor: Current Trend in Sugarcane Pathology, 1994, Sugarcane Pathology, 1999; Author: Microbiology, 1994; editor Surgar Tech., 1999. Recipient Young Scientist award Dept. Sci. and Tech., Govt. of India, 1993, Boyscast award, 1996, Pres.'s award Soc. for Gen. Microbiology (U.K.), 1998. Fellow Indian Phytopathol. Soc., Sugarcane technologists Assn. of India; mem. Am. Phytopathol. Soc. Mem. Internat. Soc. for Krishna Consiousness. Avocations: writing, travel, inventing, research, social activities. Home: 81N Canal Rd Daudpur, 273001 Gorakhpur UP, India Office: Sugarcane Rsch Sta, Kunraghat, 273008 Gorakhpur UP, India

RAO, GUTTI MADANMOHAN, physiologist, educator, researcher; b. Jandrapet, India, Nov. 27, 1926; s. Gutti Lingaiah and Gutti Veeramma; m. Gutti Vimala Devi; 5 children. BS, Andhra Christian Coll., Guntur, India, 1948; BS with honors, Presidency Coll., Madras, India, 1950, MA, 1953; PhD, U. Toronto, Can., 1968. Lectr. in biology Andhra Med. Coll., India, 1950-51; lectr. in biology Sir Theagaraya Coll., Madras, 1951-57, prof., chmn., 1957-83, vice prin., 1968-72, prin., 1972-83; rschr. dept. medicine N.Y. Med. Coll., 1976-77; sr. rschr. Ctr. for Health and Drug Rsch., Tripoli, Libya, 1978-86; prof. physiology faculty medicine The Great Al-Fatah U. of Med. Scis., Tripoli, Libya, 1986-92; dir. Ctr. for Biomed. Rsch., Madras, 1994—; dir. Summer Inst. in Biology, 1970, 72, 74. Author: Pre-University Zoology, 1960-75, Essentials of Cell Biology, 1980; editor-in-chief Bull. Biology; mem. editl. bd. Indian Jour. Zoology; contbr. over 60 articles to profl. jours. Mng. trustee Dr. G. Madan Mohan Rao Edn1. and Charitable Trust, Madras. Recipient Caithness prize U. Madras, 1950, Bourne's prize Presidency Coll., 1950, Rsch. award Coun. Sci. Indsl. Rsch., New Delhi, 1969-72. Fellow Linnean Soc. London; mem. Soc. for Exptl. Biology and Medicine, N.Y. Acad. Scis. Home: 21 Second Main Rd, Ramakrishna Nagar, Madras 600 057, India Office: Biomed Rsch Ctr Ramakrishna Nagar, 21 Second Main Rd, Madras 600 057, India

RAO, IDUPULAPATI MADHUSUDANA, plant nutritionist, plant physiologist; b. Mandadam, Andhra Pradesh, India, July 1, 1951; s. Idupulapati Nageswara Rao and Rajya Lakshmi (Jammula) Idupulapati; m. Kusuma Kumari Yarlagadda, June 9, 1973; children: Madhuri, Subhashini. BS, Andhra U., Waltair, India, 1971; MS, Bhopal (India) U., 1973; PhD, Sri Venkateswara U., Tirupati, India, 1978. Rsch. assoc. U. Hyderabad, India, 1978-79; plant physiologist Internat. Crops Rsch. Inst. for Semi-Arid Tropics, Hyderabad, India, 1979-80; rsch. assoc. U. Ill., Chgo., 1981-82, Urbana, 1983-84; rsch. plant physiologist U. Calif., Berkeley, 1985-86, asst. specialist, 1987-88; plant nutritionist Internat. Ctr. for Tropical Agr., Cali, Colombia, 1989—; vis. sci. BTI at Cornell U., Ithaca, N.Y., 1982; assoc. editor Jour. Environ. Quality, 2000—. Assoc. editor Jour. Environ. Quality; contbr. articles to profl. jours. Rsch. grantee BMZ-GTZ, 1991. Mem. Am. Soc. Plant Physiology, Am. Soc. Agronomy, Crop Sci. Soc. Am., Soil Sci. Soc. Am., N.Y. Acad. Scis. Avocations: playing tennis, watching sports. Home: Mandadam P., Mangalagiri 522503, India Office: Internat Ctr for Tropical Agr, A.A. 6713, Cali Colombia

RAO, KAKARAPARTI VISWESWARA, statistician, researcher; b. Bhrugubanda, Andhra Pradesh, India, July 1, 1938; s. Kakaraparti Venkata Subbaiah and Nagaratnamma; m. Paluvayi Sita, May 15, 1957; children: Sarojini, Saraswati, Krishna, Suvarna. FA, Hindu Coll., Guntur, India, 1956, BA, 1960; MA, Delhi U., 1963; MS in Hygiene, Harvard U., 1972; PhD, Osmania U., Hyderabad, India, 1976. Biostatistics; researcher. Rsch. asst. Nat. Inst. Nutrition, Hyderabad, India, 1964-67, asst. rsch. officer, 1967-70, rsch. officer, 1970-74, sr. rsch. officer, 1974-84, asst. dir., 1984-92, dep. dir., 1992-96, dep. dir. sr. grade, 1997-98; cons. Biostatistics and Nutrition NIMS, Hyderabad, India, 1999-2000; vis. fellow Osmania U., Hyderabad, India; fellow WHO, Boston, 1971-72, cons. Manila, Philippines, KualaLumpur, Malaysia, 1983, 85. Author: Diet Atlas of India, 1969, 72; author, editor: Statistics in Health and Nutrition, 1990, Biostatistics-A Manual for Use in Health, Nutrition and Anthropology, 1996, Statistics in Brief, 2000; contbr. over 200 articles to scientific jours. Fellow Inst. Statisticians, Indian Soc. Med. Statistics (Prof. Rangacharis Gold Medal 1960, Prof. B.G. Prasad Gold Medal 1986, Prof. P.V. Sukhatme's Gold Medal, 1996, exec. 1983-92); mem. Nutrition Soc. India (exec. 1993—), Lions Club (Snehapuri pres. 1990-91, dist. chmn. dist. 324c2 1992, 93), Nutrition Soc. India (exec.). Avocations: writing, speaking, reading, discussing. E-mail: krishnak@logixit.com. Home: 9-79 Fourth St HMT Nagar, 500076 Hyderabad Andhra Pradesh, India Office: Nat Inst Nutrition ICMR, Jamai Osmania, 500007 Hyderabad Andhra Pradesh, India

RAO, KALYA JAGANNATHA, education educator; b. Kalya, Karnataka, India, Dec. 7, 1940; s. Kalya Bheemanna and Kalya Anantha Murthy Nagamma; m. Sudha Rao, June 3, 1973; children: Vijaya, Sarathy, Kalya-a. BSc with honors, Mysore U., India, 1960, MSc, 1961; PhD, Indian Inst. Tech., Kanapur, India, 1967; DSc, Indian Inst. Sci., Bangalore, India, 1988; DSc (hon.), U. Bordeaux, France, 1999. Lectr. Nat. Coll., Bangalore, 1961-64; fellow Indian Inst. Tech., Kanpur, 1964-68; rsch. assoc. Purdue U., West Lafayette, Ind., 1968-71, Case Western Res. U., Cleve., 1971-72; scientist Nat. Aerospace Lab., Bangalore, 1972-78; from asst. prof. to prof. Indian Inst. Sci., Bangalore, 1978—; rschr. in field. Fellow Indian Acad. Scis., Bangalore, 1982, Indian Nat. Sci. Acad., Delhi, 1985, Nat. Acad. Sci., Allahabad, India, 1994, Internat. Acad. Ceramics, Faenza, Italy, 1992; recipient Bhatnagar prize Coun. Sci. and Indsl. Rsch., India, 1984, Shanthi Ranjan Palit award Indian Assn. for Cultivation Sci., 1993, Materials Rsch. Soc. India medal, 1995, Indian Nat. Sci. acad. prize, 1999, Silver medal Chem. Rsch. Soc. India, 2000. Avocations: reading, classical music. Home: III Main I Cross NTI Layout, 560 094 Nagasettihalli India Office: Indian Inst Sci, Sci Inst PO, 560 012 Bangalore India

RAO, KATRAGADDA SARVESWARA, chemical and metallurgical engineer; b. Intur, Guntur, India, Mar. 15, 1950; s. Katragadda Lakshminarayana and Katragadda Lakshmiswaramma; m. Katragadda Lakshmi Bhavani Devi, May 8, 1970; children: Sarita Katragadda Manasi, Sarita Katragadda Chinmayee. B Tech., A.C. Coll. Tech., Madras, 1972, M Tech., 1974; PhD, Indian Inst. Tech., Kharagpur, India, 1990. Plant engr. Hanuman Vitamin Foods, Khamgaon, Maharashtra, India, 1975-77, Coromandel Agro Products & Oils, Chirala, India, 1977-78; rsch. scientist Regional Rsch. Lab. CSIR, Bhubaneswar, India, 1978—; on deputation German Agy. for Tech. Cooperation, Frankfurt, 1985, Uhde GmbH, Hagen, Germany, 1983. Assoc. editor: (book series) Engineering: Utilization of Natural Resources - Chemical Engineering Approach, 1994; contbr. articles to profl. jours. and publs. Mem. Indian Thermal Analysis Soc., Indian Inst. Mineral Engrs., Catalysis Soc. India, Indian Inst. Chem. Engrs. (life), Indian Inst. Metals (life, Best Paper award 1990, Neelamani Devi-Biswanath Das award 1999). Avocations: social work, reading.

RAO, MEKA RAMAMOHANA, agronomist, researcher; b. Avanigadda, India, July 1, 1947; s. Basavapurnaiah and Pushpa Leelavathi (Gadde) Meka; m. Malathi Kantamneni, May 31, 1974; children: Venkata, Vikas, Meka. BSc in Agr., Agrl. Coll., Bapatla, India, 1969; MSc in Agr., S.V. Agrl. Coll., Tirupathi, India, 1971; PhD, Indian Agrl. Rsch. Inst., New Delhi, 1975. Agronomist Internat. Crops Rsch. Inst. for Semi-Arid Tropics, Patancheri, India, 1975-81, 84-86; cropping sys. specialist EMBRAPA/IICA, Petrolina, Brazil, 1982-83; sorghum agronomist Internat. Inst. Tropical Agr., Maroua, Cameroon, 1986-88; exptl. agronomist ICRAF, Nairobi, Kenya, 1988-91; program coord. ICRAF, Nairobi, 1991—; assoc. prof. agroforestry U. Fla., Gainesville, 1994-99; presenter in field. Recipient Jenna Reddy Venkata Reddy Gold medal Farmers' Welfare Trust, Hyderabad, India, 1985. Hindu. Avocations: reading, gardening, spiritual discourses, social service. Home: 11 Akbar Rd, Secunderabad 500009, India Office: ICRAF, Box 30677, Nairobi Kenya

RAO, NAGARAJA BANGALORE, engineering educator; b. Bangalore, Karnataka, India, Mar. 23, 1934; s. Krishnamurthy R. and Laxmibayamma; m. Eng Eng Tsong, Dec. 20, 1975; children: Laxmi Ing, Aruna Ing. BS, Mysore U., Bangalore, India, 1955; DIISc, Indian Inst. Sci., Bangalore, 1963; MS, U. Southampton (Eng.), 1971; PhD, U. Birmingham (Eng.), 1978. European engr.; chartered engr. R&D mgr. Hairlok Co. Ltd., Eng., 1966-69; rsch. assoc. U. Coll. London, 1970-71; rsch. fellow U. Birmingham (Eng.), 1971-80; sr. lectr. Birmingham Poly., 1981-91; reader, prof. Southampton (Eng.) Inst., 1991-96; vis. prof. U. Sunderland, Eng., 1997—; tech. dir. Comadem Internat. Ltd., Eng., 1988-91; U.K. mem. Imeko, Budapest, Hungary, 1993—, Brit. Standards Instn., London, 1994—; mng. dir. Intelligent Info. Tech. Ltd., U.K., 1997—; hon. vis. prof. U. Exeter, 1997—; vis. prof. Glasgow Caledonian U., Scotland, 1998—; external prof. U. Glamorgan, Wales, 1998—; guest lectr. Vaxjo U., Sweden; external examiner U. Wolverhampton, U. Wales Inst. Cardiff and Robert Gordon U., 1999—. Author, editor: Handbook of Condition Monitoring, 1996; tech. editor: Jour. Condition Monitoring and Diagnostic Technology, 1989, (hon.) Brit. Inst. Nondestructive Testing, 1989-91; creator interdiscipline Comadem, 1987; editor-in-chief, pub. Internat. Jour. of COMADEM. Participant India's freedom movements, 1946-47; asst. Vietnamese boat people, 1979-80, poor students in India, 1980—, local jr. sch., 1986—; nominated gov. Turves Green Girls Sch. & Tech. Coll. Rsch. grantee Engring. and Phys. Sci. Rsch. Coun., 1992-95, product devel. grantee Econ. Devel. Unit, 1997. Mem. Inst. Measurement and Control, Inst. M.C. (editl. mem. 1987), Birmingham C. of C. and Industry. Avocations: broadcasting, cooking, publishing, gardening, photography. E-mail: rajbknrao@btinternet.com. Fax: 0121 472 2338. Home and Office: 307 Tiverton Rd Selly Oak, B29 6DA Birmingham England

RAO, NARAHARISETTY MURALIDHARA, retired microbiologist; b. Eluru, India, July 1, 1937; s. Naraharisetty Veera Raghavulu and Naraharisetty Lakshmi Kantamma; m. Naraharisetty Subhadra, June 13, 1963; children: Padmalatha, Narayana Rao. BSc, Sir C. R. Reddy Coll., Eluru, 1958; B of Vet. Sci., Vet. Coll., Tirupati, India, 1962, M of Vet. Sci., 1970; PhD in Microbiology, Madras U., India, 1979. Vet. surgeon Animal Husbandry Dept., Hyderabad, India, 1962-73; rsch. scientist Cen. Leather Rsch. Inst., Madras, 1973-94; FAO rsch. fellow Blacksburg, 1982; dep. dir. Cen. Leather Rsch. Inst., Madras, 1994-97; ret., 1997; nat. expert UNIDO, Vienna, Austria, 1997-98; cons. Textan Chems., Madras, 1998—; workshop coord. Commonwealth Sci. Coun., Madras, 1989, UN Devel. Program-Ctr. for Sci. and Tech. of Non-Aligned and other Developing Countries, Madras, 1994, UNIDO, Madras, 1995; coord. Leather Tech. Mission, Madras, 1996-97; hon. faculty mem. Anna U., Chennai, 1990-96. Contbr. articles to profl. jours. Achievements include development of economically viable technologies for processing and utilisation of animal wastes emanating from meat and leather industries into valuable end products. Avocations: reading science journals and books, writing scientific papers, cultural events. Home: OM Apts, 101/6 Medavakkamtank RD, Kellys Chennai 600010, India

RAO, NINGLING, research chemist, project leader; b. Zhenjiang, China, May 12, 1963; d. Jiayu Rao and Zhenluan Wang; m. Sun Weibin, May 7, 1993; 1 child. BS, U. Sci. & Technology China, 1985, MS, 1988; PhD, Delft Univ. Technology, 1991. Vis. scholar Risoe Nat. Labs., Roskilde, Denmark, 1989-90; rsch. fellow Delft Univ. Technology, The Netherlands, 1991-92; rsch. chemist Innovision A/S, Odense, Denmark, 1992-94; rsch. chemist Danionics A/S, Odense, 1994—, sr. scientist, project mgr., 1997—. Mem. Internat. Soc. Solid State Ionics, Electrochem. Soc., N.Y. Acad. Sci. Avoca-

tions: music, aerobics, badminton, cooking, gardening. Office: Danionics A/S, Hestehaven 21J, DK 5260 Odense Denmark

RAO, P. SYAMASUNDAR, pediatric cardiologist; b. Ullibhadra, India, Sept. 21, 1941; came to U.S., 1966; s. P.V.B. Krishna Rao and P. Savithramma; m. P. Hymavathi, Mar. 27, 1966; children: Vijay K. Patnana, Madhavi Patnana, Radhkika N. Patnana. Intermediate degree in Arts and Scis., Andhra U., Visakhapatnam, India, 1958; MBBS, Andhra Med. Coll., Visakhapatnam, 1964, diploma in child health, 1966. Diplomate Am. Bd. Pediats, Am. Bd. Pediat. Cardiology. Asst. prof. Med. Coll. Ga., Augusta, 1972-75, assoc. prof., 1975-79, prof. pediats., 1979-82, assoc. dir. pediat. cardiology, 1976-82; cons. pediat. cardiologist King Faisal Specialist Hosp., Riyadh, Saudi Arabia, 1982-87, chmn. pediats., 1986-87; prof., head pediat. cardiology U. Wis. Med. Sch., Madison, 1987-94; prof., dir. pediat. cardiology St. Louis U. Sch. Medicine, 1994-98, prof. pediats., 1998—; Author: Tricuspid Atresia, 1982, 2d edit., 1992, Transcatheter Therapy in Pediatric Cardiology, 1993; contbr. over 250 articles to profl. jours., 40 chpts. to books. Recipient award for outstanding contbn. to pediat. cardiology Telugu Assn. N.Am., John Lind's Lectr. award Swedish Pediat. Assn.,1 992, Meritorious Svc. award Wis.-Nicaragua Ptnr., 1993, Outstanding Scientist award Am. Assn. Cardiologists of Indian Origin, 1996. Fellow Am. Coll. Cardiology (councillor Mo. chpt. 1997), Am. Acad. Pediats., Soc. Cardiac Antiography (mem. pediat. cardiology com. 1996); mem. Am. Pediat. Soc., Soc. Pediat. Rsch., Am. Heart Assn. Avocations: tennis, movies. E-mail: rapos@slu.edu. Office: St Louis U Sch Medicine 1465 S Grand Blvd Saint Louis MO 63104-1003

RAO, RAJESH P.N., neuroscientist, computer scientist; b. Madras, India, July 2, 1970; came to the U.S., 1988; p. Anantha Padmanabha and Kamali Rao; m. Anupama Taranath, Jan. 23, 2000. BS in Computer Sci./Math summa cum laude, Angelo State U., 1992; MS in Computer Sci., U. Rochester, 1994, PhD in Computer Sci., 1998. Asst. adminstr. Microcomputer Lab. Angelo State U., 1989-92; rsch. asst. dept. computer sci. U. Rochester, 1993-97; rsch. assoc. Sloan Ctr. for Theoretical Neurobiology, Salk Inst., La Jolla, Calif., 1997-2000; asst. prof. U. Wash., Seattle, 2000—; presenter in field. Mem. editl. bd. Machine Learning Jour. and Autonomous Robots Jour., 1998; reviewer Neural Computation, Neural Networks, Network: Computation in Neural Systems, Nature Neurosci., Jour. Cognitive Neurosci., Cognitive Sci., Visual Cognition, Neuropharmacology, IEEE Trans. on Robotics and Automation, IEEE Pattern Analysis and Machine Intelligence, Human Computer Interaction, Phys. Rev. Letters, Info. Processing Letters, Theoretical Computer Sci., Videre: A Jour. of Computer Vision Rsch.; contbr. articles to profl. jours. Robert and Nona Carr acad. scholar Angelo State U., 1988-92; travel grantee Neural Info. Processing Sys. Conf., 1995, 97, 98, 99, 4th Internat. Conf. on Simulation of Adaptive Behavior, 1996, Workshop on Computational Neurosci. and Generative Models, 1998, Neural Info. and Coding Workshop, 1999. Mem. Am. Assn. for Artificial Intelligence (program com. annual conf. 1997, program com. computer vision and pattern recognition 2000), Assn. Computing Machiner (spl. interest group on algorithms and computation theory, spl. interest group on artificial intelligence), Soc. for Neurosci., N.Y. Acad. Scis., Alpha Chi, Epsilon Delta Pi, Pi Mu Epsilon. Avocations: ancient history, music, basketball, racquetball, table tennis. E-mail: rao@cs.washington.edu. Office: Dept Computer Sci and Engring Univ Washington Seattle WA 98195-0001

RAO, RAMA KRISHNA R., pharmaceutical company executive; b. Tanuku, Andhra P., India, Nov. 20, 1955; came to U.S., 1998; s. R.R. and Satyavani R. (Gudipati) R.; m. Kavitha Advikolanu, May 19, 1996. B in Tech., Indian Inst. Tech., Delhi, 1977; Postgrad. Diploma in Mgmt., Indian Inst. Mgmt., Calcutta, 1981; MBA, INSEAD, Fontainebleu, France, 1989. Asst. mgr. Metal Box India, Calcutta, 1977-84; exec. asst. to gen. mgr. Bank of Bahrain & Kuwait, Bahrain, 1985-88; fin. assoc. Eli Lilly, Geneva, credit and customer svc. mgr., 1993-94, fin. mgr. Africa, 1994-95; mgr. (global treasury) Gems Eli Lilly, Brussels, 1995-97; fin. advisor corp. fin. & investment banking Lilly Corp. Ctr., Indpls., 1998-99; finance mgr. PC/NS Lilly USA, Indpls., 1999—; alumni mem. panel for INSEAD interviews, Belgium, U.S., 1995-99. Contbr. journalist Students' Newsletter, IIT, Delhi, co-editor Students' Newsletter, I.I.M., Calcutta, INSEAD, Fontainebleu, France. Vol. Samaritans/Befrienders, Bahrain, 1987, 88; donor of blood Red Cross/Crescent, India, Belgium, U.S., Bahrain, 1974-97. Recipient First prize Nat. Young Mgrs. Competition, All India Mgmt. Assn., 1983. Mem. AMA, Assn. Investment Mgmt. and Rsch., Inst. Mgmt. Accts. Hindu. Avocations: travel, military history, foreign policy.

RAO, SRINATH JAYRAM, electronics professional; b. Mangalore, Karnataka, India, Aug. 18, 1948; s. Jayram Javali and Sita Jayram (Prabhu) R.; m. Mangala Kamath; children: Nishant, Mohnish. B Tech with honors, IIT, Bombay, 1970; Diploma in Mgmt., All India Mgmt. Assn., Delhi, 1984. Cert. in human rels. and mgmt. field. Mktg. engr. Blue Star, Ltd., Bombay, 1970-76; product mgr. Philips, Teheran, Iran, 1977-79; product sales mgr. Philips, Bombay, 1979-89; dir. Fountainhead Electronics, Pvt. Ltd., Bombay, 1989—; proprietor Fountainhead Solutions, San Antonio, 1997—. Founder, bd. dirs. Giants Group, Bombay, 1985-96, pres. 1986. Fellow Inst. Mktg. Mgmt., Inst. Electronics and Telecomms.; mem. Computer Soc. India, Instrument Soc. of India (life), Indian Cryogenics Coun. (life). Avocations: environ. issues, music, family activities, info. technology. E-mail address: sjrao@fountainheadsolutions.com.

RAO, TALASILA PRASADA, analytical chemist; b. Munipalle, India, June 2, 1955; s. Talasila Subba Rao and Talasila Sitaramamma; m. Talasila Sarada, Nov. 26, 1987; children: Sindhoor, Divya. BSc, Andhra U., Visakhapatnam, India, 1974, MSc, 1976; PhD, Indian Inst. Tech., Madras, India, 1981. Mgr. rsch. and devel. Purex Labs., Bangalore, India, 1981-82; scientist Regional Rsch. Lab., Hyderabad, India, 1983; scientist B Cecri, Karaikudi, India, 1983-86; scientist C Regional Rsch. Lab., Trivandrum, India, 1986-89, scientist EI, 1989-94, scientist EII, 1994-99, scientist F, 1999—; dep. dir. Regional Rsch. Lab., Trivandrum; lectr. Alagappa U., Karaikudi, India, 1985-86. Author (chpt. in book) Trace Determination of Lanthanides in High Purity Rare Earth Oxides, 1995; contbr. over 100 articles and 8 revs. to profl. jours.; author 3 patents. Recipient Prof. L. Ramachar award for best paper in electrochem. sci., 1987, medal Andhra U., 1994. Mem. Soc. Advancement of Electrochem. Sci. and Tech. Home: NP IX/846 Divyasadan, Kerala Trivandrum 695018, India Office: RRL, RRL Industrial Estate, Kerala Trivandrum 695019, India

RAO, TEKI NAGENDRA, soil chemist; b. Chilakalapalli, India, July 5, 1962; s. T.Y. Brahmam and T. Jaggayamma; m. T.V. Nagamani, May 17, 1989; children: Yashwanth Kumar, Om Swarup. BSc, A.P. Agrl. U., Bapatla, India, 1984, MSc, 1986; PhD, A.P. Agrl. U., Palampur, India, 1995. Tech. asst. Coun. Sci. and Indsl. Rsch. Complex, Palampur, 1986-90; rsch. scholar H.P. Agrl. U., Palampur, 1990-95; from agronomist to dep. dir. Potash and Phosphate Inst. Can. India Program, Gurgoan, Secunderabad, 1996—. Mem. Indian Soc. Soil Sci., Indian Sci. Congress Assn. Avocations: painting, landscape photography, numismatics. Home: 33 Ashok Colony, ViJaya High Sch, 500 062 Hyderabad India Office: Potash & Phosphate Inst Can, Sect 19 Delhi Gurgoan Rd, 122 001 Dundahera Haryana, India

RAO, TUMULA VENKATESHWAR, chemist, researcher; b. Nelapatla, Khammam, India, Feb. 5, 1965; s. Tumula Narayana Rao and Tumula Lakshmi; m. Tumula Lakshmi Kantha, Dec. 6, 1997; 1 child, Hema Sudha. MS in Chemistry, Osmania U., Hyderabad, India, 1988; MEd, Annamalai U., Annamalai Nagar, India, 1989; PhD in Chemistry, U. Roorkee (India), 1997. Jr. rsch. fellow Indian Inst. Petroleum, Dehradun, 1991-93, sr. rsch. fellow, 1993-96, scientist B, researcher, 1996—; scientist Coun. Sci. and Indsl. Rsch. Contbr. articles to profl. jours. Sci. sec. Sree Rama Bhaktavastaka Gantala Narayana Rao Govt. Coll., Khammam, India, 1985. Mem. Indian Soc. Analytical Scientists, Catalysis Soc. India, ACS, Roorkee U. Alumni. Avocations: sports, watching movies, social work. Office: Indian Inst Petroleum, Mohkampur, Dehradun 248005, India

RAO, VITHALA R., marketing educator; b. Pentapadu, India, July 3, 1936; came to U.S., 1967; s. Sitaramamurty and Kameswaramma (Kandarpa) V.; m. Saroj V. Rao, Oct. 15, 1964; children: Anil, Venkat. MS, U. Bombay, 1956; AM, U. Mich., 1962; PhD, U. Pa., 1970. Mktg. rschr. Tata Oil Mills, Bombay, 1959-64; exec. Delhi (India) Cloth Mills, 1965-66; asst. prof. Indian Inst. Mgmt., Calcutta, 1966-67; Malott prof. mktg. Cornell U., Ithaca, N.Y., 1970—; cons. GM, Detroit, 1988-90. Author: Applied MDS, 1972, Decision Criteria, 1991, New Science of Marketing, 1995, Analysis for Strategic Marketing, 1998. Mem. Am. Mktg. Assn., N.Am. Soc. for Mktg. Edn. in India (pres. Buffalo 1999—). Avocations: running, photography, bridge. E-mail: vrr2@cornell.edu. Home: 318 Blackstone Ave Ithaca NY 14850-1750 Office: Cornell U Sch Mgmt Ithaca NY 14853-0001

RAOOF, MOHAMMED, engineering educator; b. Tehran, Iran, Nov. 19, 1955; arrived in Britain, 1973; s. Ahmed and Maryam Banoo (Ashtari) R.; m. Shiva Radazari, July 13, 1981 (div. 1985); m. Mojgan Raoof, Mar. 23, 1995. BSc in Engring. with honors, Imperial Coll., London, 1978, MSc in Concrete Structures, 1979, PhD, 1983. Chartered engr., Eng. Rsch. asst. Imperial Coll., London, 1981-85; structural engr. Wimpey Offshore, London, 1985-86; from lectr. to Bridon prof. South Bank U., London, 1986-94; prof. structural engring. Loughborough (Eng.) U., U.K., 1994—; vis. prof. Czech Tech. U., Prague, Czech Republic, 1996—, Georgian Tech. U., Toilisi, Georgia, 1999—; cons. Bridon Ropes plc., Doncaster, 1989-95. Contbr. articles to profl. jours. Recipient T.K. Hsieh award Instn. Civil Engrs. in conjunction with Royal Soc., London, 1985, Henry Adams award Instn. Structural Engrs., 1992, 93, Trevithick Premium award Instn. of Civil Engrs., 1993, James Watt Gold medal, 1991, Ctrl. Electricity Generating Bd. prize Instn. Mech. Engrs. Mem. Instn. of Structural Engrs. London. Avocations: stamp collecting, classical music, Persian literature, collecting coins. Office: Loughborough Univ, Civil Bldg Engring Dept, Loughborough LE11 3TU, England

RAOULT, DIDIER ALAIN, medical educator; b. Dakar, Senegal, Mar. 13, 1952; arrived in France, 1957; s. Andre and Francine (Legendre) R.; m. Danielle Deroze, Dec. 13, 1976 (div. Dec. 1981); 1 child, Magali; m. Natacha Cain, Dec. 23, 1982; children: Sacha, Lola. MD, Sch. Medicine, Marseille, France, 1981; PhD in Biology, Sch. Medicine, Montpellier, France, 1985. Resident U. Hosp., Marseille, 1978-86, from asst. prof. to assoc. prof., 1986-89, prof., 1989—; pres. U. Aix Marseille, 1993—; chief Rickettsies unit WHO, 1988; chief microbiology dept. Hosp. Conception, Marseille, 1989—, Hosp. Timone, Marseille, 1989—; pres. sci. com. Sch. Medicine, Marseille, 1989; pres. Univ. Aix-Marseille, 1994—. Editor: Antimicrobial Agents and Intracellular Pathogens, 1993. Fellow Infectious Disease Soc. Am.; mem. Am. Soc. of Microbiology. Avocations: literature, philosophy. Office: Faculty of Medicine, Bd Jean Moulin, 13385 Marseille France

RAPACZ, MARCIN, plant physiologist, researcher, educator; b. Krakow, Poland, Dec. 12, 1968; s. Czeslaw and Elzbieta (Pankowska) R.; m. Dorota Kowalewska, Apr. 30, 1994; children: Michal, Dominik. MSc, Agrl. U. Krakow, 1992, PhD, 1996, DrEng of Agrl. Scis. Asst. Agrl. U., Krakow, 1992-96, sr. scientist, 1997—. Contbr. articles to profl. jours. Roman Catholic. Office: Agrl U Dept Plant Physiol, Podluzna 3, 30-239 Krakow Poland

RAPALLINO, MARIA VITTORIA, neurobiologist, researcher; b. Genoa, Italy, Oct. 5, 1942; d. Elio Fernando and Jone Maria (Tomaselli) R.; m. Renato Alessandro Frosini, Feb. 8, 1969; children: Nicola, Paolo. Degree in biol. scis., U. Genova, 1966. Asst. G. Gaslini Hosp., Genova, 1967-70; young rschr. U. Genova, 1970-73; rschr. Nat. Coun. Rsch., Genova, 1973—. Mem. N.Y. Acad. Scis. Roman Catholic. Avocations: archeology, diving, history, gardening. Office: CNR, Via de Toni 5, 16132 Genoa Liguria, Italy

RAPAPORT, RICHARD J., artist, researcher; b. N.Y.C., July 9, 1940; s. Stanley and Millicent R. BFA, Syracuse U., 1962; MFA, Yale U., 1965. Co-author: Crafts and Hobbies, 198; researcher, creator new local and global art movement To Cathc the Light of Peace-Let Freedom Ring. Honoree by N.Y.C., 1994, N.Y. State, 1994. Mem. AAAS, Nat. Space Soc., N.Y. Acad. Scis., Coast Guard Art Program, Planetary Soc. Republican. Jewish. Avocations: sports, music, reading. Office: To Catch the Light of Peace-Let Freedom Ring 215 E 68th St New York NY 10021-5718

RAPEANU, SEVASTIAN NICOLAE, physicist, researcher, educator, science administrator; b. Richitele, Romania, July 24, 1932; s. Nicolae Constantin and Ioana (Duminica) R.; m. Doina Nicolae Constantin, Apr. 30, 1958; children: Randus-Florin, Alecsandru-Ioan. MS, Bucharest Univ., Bucharest, 1957; specialization, Royal Inst. Tech., Stockholm, Sweden, 1963; PhD in physics, Inst. of Atomic Physics, Bucharest, 1969; docent in physics, Senate of Bucharest Univ., 1976. Rschr. Inst. of Atomic Physics, Bucharest, 1957-62, Royal Inst. of Tech., Stockholm, 1962-63, Inst. of Atomic Physics, Bucharest, 1964-77; sr. rschr. Inst. for Nuclear Power Reactors, Pitesti, Romania, 1977-83, Inst. for Phys. and Nuclear Engring., Bucharest, 1983—; prof. Coll., Bucharest, Pitesti, 1965-73, 78-81; head of lab. Coll., 1983-94; dir. gen. Min. Rsch. and Tech., 1994-97; sr. scientist NIR & DPHNE, Bucharest, 1997—; vis. scientist Inst. of Nuclear Rsch., Munich, 1969, Louvain U., Belgium, 1974, Helsinki, 1970, IAEA-Vienna, 1977, 96, Istanbul, Turkey, 1980, Rabat, Marocco, 1995, Tunis, 1996, Crete, Greece, 1996, Belgrade, 1996, 98, Buenos Aires, Cordoba, Argentina, 1996, Balatonfüured, Hungary, 1998, Islamabad, Pakistan, Inst. of Physics, Latvia, 1989, Royal Inst. for Tech., Stockholm, 1989-95; head lab., dep. dir. Inst. of Atomic Physics, 1969-70; special inspector NPP Div. Ministers Coun.; gen. insp. State Insp. for Control of Nuclear Activites, 1971-77; sci. dir. Inst. of Nuclear Power Reactors, 1977-83; bd. dirs. NISREE, 1997—. Contbr. numerous articles to profl. jours., chpts. to books. Mem. Senate of Iassy Univ., 1974-82; Romanian rep. IAEA-NDS, 1972-96; rep. Jt. Inst. of Nuclear Rsch., 1995-97. With Artillery, 1953-54. Recipient Physics award Romanian Acad., 1975, 1987. Mem. Romanian Scientists Acad., Romanian N.E. Assn., JINR, European Phys. Soc. Roman Orthodox. Avocations: dialogue, theatre, items for mass-media, politics, stamp collecting. Home: Sector 4, Terasei 8 bl R12A sc 2 ap54, 75582 Bucharest Romania Office: Inst Physics & Nuclear Engr, AtomistilorPOB Mg6 39, 79600 Bucharest Romania

RAPELA, CARLOS WASHINGTON, geochemistry educator, researcher; b. Santa Fe, Argentina, Jan. 22, 1944; s. Carlos Alberto and Celia Teresa (Rodriguez) R.; m. Carmen Beatriz de Jong, Aug. 13, 1971; children: Carlos Gonzalo, Melisa. Lic. in Geochemistry, U. La Plata (Argentina), 1970, PhD in Geochemistry, 1975. Fellow 1st stage CONICET, La Plata, Argentina, 1970-72; fellow 2nd stage CONICET, La Plata, 1972; demonstrator La Plata Nat. U., 1972-77, prof., 1986—; postdoct. fellow CONICET/McMaster U., Hamilton, Can., 1977-79; career investigator Nat. Rsch. Coun., Argentina, 1979—; leader IGCP 249 Internat. Union of Geol. Scis.-UNESCO, Paris, 1986-91, Internat. Geol. conelation Program 345, 1993-95, IGCP, 1995—. Author, editor: Geological Society of America, 1990, 91; contbr. articles to scientific jours. Fellow Am. Geophys. Union, Assn. Geologica Argentina (Storni award 1976), Geol. Soc. (Eng.). Home: 46 No 1543, 1900 La Plata Buenos Aires Argentina Office: Ctr Investigaciones Geologicas, 1 No 644, 1900 La Plata Buenos Aires Argentina

RAPER, CHARLES ALBERT, retired management consultant; b. Charleston, W.Va., Aug. 18, 1926; s. Kenneth B. and Louise (Williams) R.; m. Margaret Ann Weers, Dec. 26, 1947; children: Kathleen, Josephine, Charles. Student, Okla. State U., 1945; B.S., U. Ill., 1949. Sales mgr. Meyer Furnace Co., Peoria, Ill., 1949-54; v.p. mktg. Master Consol., Inc., Dayton, Ohio, 1954-61; mgmt. cons. McKinsey & Co., Inc., Chgo., 1961-67; v.p. mktg. Gen. Portland Inc., Dallas, 1967-69; pres., also dir. Gen. Portland Inc., 1969-75; v.p., gen. mgr. Scholl Inc., Chgo., 1975-81; pres. Oxford Group of Sara Lee, 1981-84; mgmt. cons. McKinsey & Co., 1984—. Vice chmn. devel. bd. U. Tex. at Dallas; exec. bd. Circle 10 council Boy Scouts Am.; Svc. Corp. of Ret. Execs. counselor. Served with USN, 1944-46. Mem. Dallas C. of C. (chmn. bd. dirs. 1974—), Sales Execs. Club, Cherokee Country Club, Chattooga Club, Atlanta Mallet Club (pres.), Phi Gamma Delta. Methodist. Home: 301 Townsend Pl NW Atlanta GA 30327-3035

RAPHAEL, ADAM ELIOT GEOFFREY, journalist; b. London, Apr. 22, 1938; s. Geoffrey George and Nancy May (Rose) R.; m. Caroline Rayner Ellis, May 29, 1970; children: Thomas, Anna. MA in History with honors, Oxford (Eng.) U., 1961. Washington corr. The Guardian, U.K., 1968-73, polit. corr., 1973-76; polit. corr. The Observer, U.K., 1976-81, polit. editor, 1981-87, exec. editor, 1988-93; presenter BBC Newsnight, U.K., 1987-88; writer The Economist, U.K., 1994—. Author: My Learned Friends, 1990, Grotesque Libels, 1993, Ultimate Risk, 1994. 2d lt. Royal Artillery, 1957-58. Named Journalist of Yr., Brit. Press Awards, 1973, Reporter of Yr., Granada TV, 1973. Mem. Hurlingham Club, RAC Club. Jewish. Avocations: tennis, skiing, fishing. Home: 50 Addison Ave, London W11 4EP, England Office: The Economist, 25 Saint James St, London SW1, England

RAPHAEL, DAVID DAICHES, academic philosopher, political theorist; b. Liverpool, Eng., Jan. 25, 1916; s. Jacob and Sarah Esther Raphael; m. Sylvia Daiches, Feb. 16, 1942 (dec. Oct. 1996); children: Sally, Anne. BA, Oxford (Eng.) U., 1938, DPhil, MA, 1940. Prof. philosophy Otago U., New Zealand, 1946-49; lectr. in moral philosophy Glasgow (Scotland) U., 1949-51, sr. lectr. in moral philosophy, 1951-60, Edward Caird prof. polit. and social philosophy, 1960-70; prof. philosophy Reading U., Eng., 1970-73, Imperial Coll., U. London, 1973-83; vis. prof. philosophy Hamilton Coll., Clinton, N.Y., 1959, U. So. Calif., 1959; vis. fellow All Souls Coll., Oxford, 1967-68; vis. prof. polit. sci. Johns Hopkins U., Balt., 1984. Author: The Moral Sense, 1947, Moral Judgement, 1955, The Paradox of Tragedy, 1960, Problems of Political Philosophy, 1970, 2d rev. edit., 1990, Hobbes, Morals and Politics, 1977, Justice and Liberty, 1980, Moral Philosophy, 1981, 2d rev. edit., 1994, Adam Smith, 1985; editor: Richard Price's Review of Morals, 1948; editor, contbr.: Political Theory and the Rights of Man, 1967; compiler, editor: British Moralists 1650-1800, 1969; joint editor: Adam Smith's Theory of Moral Sentiments, 1976, Adam Smith's Lectures on Jurisprudence, 1978, Adam Smith's Essays on Philosophical Subjects, 1980; joint translator: (by Henri Laboucheix) Richard Price as Moral Philosopher and Political Theorist, 1982; contbr. articles to profl. jours. Asst. prin. Ministry of Labour, London, 1941-44, prin., 1944-46; mem. various govt. coms., Edinburgh and London, 1961-84. Cpl. Brit. Army, 1940-41. Imperial Coll. fellow, London, 1987. Mem. Brit. Soc. for History of Philosophy, Aristotelian Soc. (pres. 1974-75), Internat. Assn. Philosophy of Law (v.p. 1971-87). Judaism. Avocations: music, theatre, walking, foreign travel. Office: Imperial Coll, Humanities Programme, London SW7 2BX, England

RAPHAEL, PAUL MICHEL, investment banker; b. Beirut, June 14, 1963; came to U.S., 1981; s. Michel and Nouhad (Breidi) R. BA, U. Md., 1983; MS, MIT, 1986. Analyst Banque Indosuez, Beirut, 1980-81; cons. First Investors Corp., Balt., 1983-84; assoc. Citibank/Citicorp, Miami, Fla., 1985; dir. Salomon Bros. Inc., N.Y.C., 1986-94; mng. dir. for Cen. and Ea. Europe, Mid. East, Africa Merrill Lynch Internat. Office: Merrill Lynch Internat, 25 Ropemaker St, London EC2 9L7, England

RAPIER, PASCAL MORAN, chemical engineer, physicist; b. Atlanta, Jan. 11, 1914; s. Paul Edward and Mary Clare (Moran) R.; m. Martha Elizabeth Doyle, May 19, 1945; children: Caroline Elizabeth, Paul Doyle, Mollie Clare, John Lawrence, James Andrew. BSChemE, Ga. Inst. Tech., 1939; MS in Theoretical Physics, U. Nev., 1959; postgrad., U. Calif., Berkeley, 1961. Registered profl. engr., Calif., N.J. Plant engr. Archer-Daniels-Midland, Pensacola, Fla., 1940-42; group supr. Dicalite div. Grefco, Los Angeles, 1943-54; process engr. Celatom div. Eagle Picher, Reno, Nev., 1955-57; project mgr., assoc. research engr. U. Calif. Field Sta., Richmond, 1959-62; project mgr. sea water conversion Bechtel Corp., San Francisco, 1962-66; sr. supervising chem. engr. Burns & Roe, Oradell, N.J., 1966-74; cons. engr. Kenite Corp., Scarsdale, N.Y., Rees Blowpipe, Berkeley, 1960-66; sr. cons. engr. Sanderson & Porter, N.Y.C., 1975-77; staff scientist III Lawrence Berkeley Lab., 1977-84; bd. dirs. Newtonian Sci. Found.; v.p. Calif. Rep. Assembly, 1964-65; discoverer phenomena faster than light, origin of cosmic rays and galactic red shifts. Contbr. articles to profl. jours.; patentee agts. to render non-polar solvents electrically conductive, direct-contact geothermal energy recovery devices; contbr. Marks' Standard Handbook for Mechanical Engineers, 10th edit., 1996. Mem. Am. Inst. Chem. Engrs., Gideons Internat., Lions Internat., Corvallis, Sigma Pi Sigma. Home: 8015 NW Ridgewood Dr Corvallis OR 97330-3026

RAPLEY, CHRISTOPHER GRAHAM, research institute director; b. West Bromwich, Eng., Apr. 8, 1947; s. Ronald and Barbara Helen (Stubbs) R.; m. Norma Kahn, June 13, 1970; children: Emma Jane, Charlotte Anne. BA in Physics with honors, Oxford (Eng.) U., 1969, MA in Physics, 1974; MSc in Radio Astronomy, U. Manchester, Eng., 1970; PhD in X-ray Astronomy, U. Coll. London, 1976. Head remote sensing group Mullard Space Sci. Lab. U. Coll. London, Dorking, Surrey, Eng., 1982-94, assoc. dir. Mullard Space Sci. Lab., 1990-94; prof. remote sensing sci. U. Coll. London, 1991-97; exec. dir. Internat. Geosphere-Biosphere Programme, Stockholm, 1994-97; prin. investigator European Space Agy., Paris, 1988-97, NASA, 1988—; vis. scientist NASA Jet Propulsion Lab., Pasadena, Calif., 1994; hon. prof. U. Coll. London, 1998—, U. East Anglia, 1999—; dir. British Antarctic Survey, 1998—; fellow St. Edmund's Coll., Cambridge, Eng., 1999—; chair U.K. Antarctic Com., 2000—; exec. European Polar Bd., 1999—; chair U.K. Nat. IGBP Com., 1998—. Contbr. over 120 articles to profl. jours. Mem. governing coun. European Sci. Found., 1998—. Fellow Royal Astron. Soc.; mem. Am. Geophys. Union, Internat. Coun. Sci. (v.p. scientific com. on Antarctic rsch. 2000—), Remote Sensing Soc., U.K. Royal Soc. (global environ. rsch. com. 1998—). Avocations: photography, jogging. E-mail: c.rapley@bas.ac.uk. Office: British Antarctic Survey, High Cross Madingley Rd, Cambridge CB3 OET, England

RAPOPORT, BERNARD, life insurance company executive; b. San Antonio, July 17, 1917; s. David and Riva (Feldman) R.; m. Audre Jean Newman, Feb. 15, 1942; 1 child, Ronald B. BA, U. Tex.-Austin, 1939. Chmn. bd., CEO Am. Income Life Ins. Co., Waco, Tex., 1951-99; cons. Am. Income Life, 1999—; pres., chmn. bd., CEO Southwestern Life Ins. Co., 2000—; chmn. bd. regents U. Tex., 1991; apptd. by pres. adv. com. for trade policy and negotiations, 1994—. Mem. Nat. Council on Crime and Delinquency, San Francisco, 1979—, Jerusalem Found., N.Y.C., 1979—, Hebrew Union Coll., Cin., 1980—, Union Am. Hebrew Congregations, 1981—; Nat. Hispanic Ctr. for Advanced Studies and Policy Analysis, Oakland, Calif., 1981—; assoc. mem. U. Cancer Found., Houston, 1976—, Jt. Ctr. Polit. and Econ. Studies, 1987—; appointed mem. Adv. Com. for Trade Policy and Negotiation; chmn. United Negro Coll. Fund, Waco, 1979-80, United Way of Waco, 1982-83; trustee Paul Quinn Coll., Waco, 1963-90, Boy's Club, Waco, 1982—; chmn. bd. regents U. Tex., 1991-97; bd. dirs. Libr. of Congress Trust Fund, Washington, 1998—. Recipient Horatio Alger award, 1999. Fellow City of Jerusalem., 1994. Democrat. Jewish. Club: Brazos. Avocations: tennis; politics; reading. Home: 2332 Wendy Ln Waco TX 76710-2011 Office: Am Income Life Ins Co PO Box 2608 Waco TX 76797-0001

RAPOPORT, EDUARDO HUGO, ecology educator, researcher; b. Buenos Aires, July 3, 1927; s. Nicolas and Sofia (Sulik) R.; m. Yolanda Aguirre, July 3, 1953 (dec. 1969); children: Guillermo, Andres, Osvaldo, Gabriel; m. Barbara Sofia Drausal, July 1, 1971; children: Manuel, Luz. Dr. Sci., U. Nac., La Plata, Argentina, 1956. Lectr. Faculty Nat. Sci. & Mus., La Plata, 1953-56; asst. prof. dept. geography U. Nac. Sur., Bahia Blanca, Argentina, 1956-58, prof. dept. agronomy, 1958-66; prof. faculty ciencias U. Central, Caracas, Venezuela, 1967-70; prof. Fundacion Bariloche, Argentina, 1971-79, Instituto De Ecologia, Mexico City, 1979-83, U. Nac. Comahue, Bariloche, 1984—; expert UNESCO, Caracas, 1973; vis. prof. U. London, 1976, Inst. Politecnico Nacional, Mexico City, 1982-83. Editor, author: Centre Nat. Recherche Scientifique, 1962-68, Soil Biology, 1966; author: Areography, 1982, Urban Ecology, 1983-88; contbr. over 100 articles to profl. jours. Fellow Linnean Soc. London; mem. Ecol. Soc. Am. (hon.), Third World Acad. Sci. (Ann. award 1990). Achievements include organization of French-Argentine expedition to Patagonia. E-mail: rapoport@cab.cnea.gov.ar. Office: Universidad Del Comahue, CRUB, 8400 Bariloche Argentina

RAPOPORT, LEV PAVLOVICH, physicist, educator; b. Usman, Lipetsk, USSR, Jan. 13, 1920; s. Pavel Lvovich and Pelageya Matveevna (Litvinova) R.; m. Mariya Pavlovna Kolpachova, Aug. 15, 1948 (div. May 1960); 1 child, Larisa Lvovna Rapoport Kukuyeva; m. Swetlana Minioryevna Yazykova, June 7, 1960; children: Georgy Lvovich, Swetlana Lvovna Rapoport Kirillova. Grad. physics and math., Voronezh (Russia) State U., 1948, Candidate of Physics and Math., 1951, D in Physics and Math., 1970. Technologist Moscow Aircraft Factory, 1941-45, engr., 1945-46; assoc. prof. phys. dept. Voronezh State U., 1951-57, head sub-faculty theoretical physics, 1957-93, full prof. sub-faculty theoretical physics, 1993—; creator Phys. Theoretical Sch., Voronezh State U. Author: Theory of Multiphoton Process in Atom, 1978; contbr. articles to profl. jours. Decorated medal for valiant

labour during Great Patriotic War, 1992; named Honoured Man of Sci. of Russia, Moscow, 1991; Soro's grantee, 1993, 95, grantee Russian Found. for Basic Rsch., 1994—, disting. scientist grantee Pres. Russia, 1994-96, 97—. Avocation: playing chess. Home: Apt 9, Fr Engels St 24a, 394000 Voronezh Russia Office: Voronezh State Univ, Universitetskaya pl 1, 394693 Voronezh Russia

RAPOPORT, ZALKIND TSALA, geophysicist; b. Drissa, Vitebsk, Belarus, Jan. 20, 1920; s. Tsala Zalka and Sophie Saul (Ioffe) R.; m. Lenina Miron Lisyansky, Apr. 22, 1954. Degree, Electrotech. Inst. Comm., Moscow, 1954; DSc in Physics and Math., Inst. Terrestrial Magnetism, Ionosphere and Radio Wave Propagation, Troitsk, 1990. Dep. dir. Polar Geophys. Inst., Murmansk, Russia, 1960-68; chief Ctrl. Ionospheric Obs., Inst. Terrestrial Magnetism, Ionosphere and Radio Wave Propagation, Troitsk, 1951-53; sr. sci. worker Murmansk br. Inst. Terrestrial Magnetism, Ionosphere and Radio Wave Propagation, 1953-60; sr. sci. worker Inst. Terrestrial Magnetism, Ionosphere and Radio Wave Propagation, Troitsk, 1968—. With USSR Army, 1939-40. Home: Tsentralnaya 30 Apt 266, 142092 Troitsk Moscow, Russia Office: Inst Terrestrial Magnetism, Ionosphere & Radio Wave Pro, 142092 Troitsk Moscow, Russia

RAPPAPORT, MARGARET M.W.E., psychologist, physician, author, pilot, consultant; b. Nov. 16, 1947; d. Leo J. and Marie L. (Rischle) Williams; m. Herbert Rappaport (div.); children: Amanda, Alexander. BA, U. Buffalo; MA, SUNY; PhD, MD, U. Colo. Prof., rschr. U. Dar es Salaam, Tanzania; with Rappaport Assocs., Phila., 1974-94; exec. dir. Inst. for Parent/Child Svcs., Phila., 1978-94; mem. adj. faculty Temple U., Phila., 1974-94; aviation safety counselor FAA; aviation cons.; nat./internat. spkr. Mem. AAUP, NOW, Airplane Owners and Pilots Assn., Nat. Aeronautical Assn., Fedn. Aeronautique Internat., Inter Seaplane Pilots Assn., Ninety-Nines Internt. Orgn. Women Pilots, Aero Club New Eng., Women in Aviation Internat., Exptl. Aircraft Assn., Cosmopolitan Club, Orleans Yacht Club. Home: PO Box 1845 Orleans MA 02653-1845

RAPPAPORT, RAPHAEL, medical educator; b. Leipsig, Germany, June 5, 1932; arrived in France, 1933; s. David and Helen (Rusniewsky) R.; m. Georgette Andrée Rathenau, June 19, 1959; children: Alain Thierry, Nathalie, Delphine. MD, U. Paris, 1959. Intern, resident Hosp. Enfants Malades, Paris, 1954-60; prof. pediat. U. Paris, 1970-83, prof. devel. biology, 1983—; dir. rsch. lab. Inserm, Paris, 1984-95; head pediatric endocrinology unit Hosp. Enfants Malades, Paris, 1970-98, chmn. pediat. dept., 1987-96, dir. rsch. inst., 1997-2000; cons., 1998—; vis. prof. Johns Hopkins U., Balt., 1973; advisor for edn. Ministry Univ., France, 1976-79, Inserm, 1986—. Editor: Pediatric Endocrinology, 1993. Rsch. fellow Johns Hopkins Hosp., Balt., 1960. Mem. European Soc. for Pediat. Endocrinology (sec.-elect 1976-86, pres. elect 1985, chmn. sci. program com. 1992-98, Andrea Prader prize 1990), Pediat. Endocrinology Soc., Endocrine Soc. USA. Avocations: mountain climbing, music, painting. E-mail: rappaport@necker.fr. Home: 17 Rue de L'Yvette, 75016 Paris France Office: Hosp Enfants Malades, 149 Rue de Sevres, 75015 Paris France

RAPPENEAU, JEAN-PAUL, film director, screenwriter; b. Auxerre, Yonne, France, Apr. 8, 1932; s. Jean and Anne-Marie (Bornhauser) R.; m. Claude-Lise Cornely, 1971; 2 children. Works include: (screenwriter) Signé Arsène Lupin, 1959, Le Mariage (in Française et l'Amour) 1959, Zazie dans le métro, 1960, Vie privée, 1961, Le Combat dans l'île, 1961, L'Homme de Rio, 1962; (dir.) La Maison sur la place, Chronique provinciale, 1958; (screenwriter, dir.) La Vie de château, 1966, (Prix Louis Delluc), Les Mariés de l'An Deux, 1970, Le Sauvage, 1975, Tout feu, tout flamme, 1982; (dir., adaptor) Cyrano de Bergerac, 1990 (Best Picture César award 1990, Best Dir. César award 1990, Best Fgn. Film Golden Globe award 1990, Best Fgn. Film U.S. Nat. Rev. Bd., 1990), Le Hussard Sur Le Toit, 1995. Decorated chevalier Legion of Honor, officier des Arts et des Lettres, officier Ordre Nat. du Mérite (France). Home: 24 rue Henri Barbusse, 75005 Paris France

RAPPOPORT, YURI MOISEVICH, research scientist; b. Moscow, June 6, 1953; s. Moisei Genrihovich Rappoport and Agnesa Bunimovna Zitlina. MA, Moscow State U., 1975; PhD, Moscow Phys. Tech. Inst., 1985. Spl. student rschr. Computer Ctr. RAS, Moscow, 1975-77, jr. scientific staff mem., 1977-86; jr. scientific staff mem. Inst. Scientific Progress/RAS, Moscow, 1986-88; scientific staff Computer Ctr. RAS, Moscow, 1988-94; sr. scientific staff Inst. Computer-Aided Design RAS, Moscow, 1994—; translator Scientific Info. Ctr., Moscow, 1978-80; reviewer Inst. of Scientific Info., Moscow, 1990-93. Author: (books) Tables of Modified Bessel Functions K1/2 ir(x), 1979, The Programs and Some Methods of the MacDonald's Function Computation, 1991. Dep. leader Soc. of Bookreaders, Computer Ctr. RAS, 1980-86. Fellow U. P. and M. Curie, Paris, 1992; grantee U.S. Civilian Rsch. and Devel. Found., Arlington, 1997; recipient medal Moscow Russian Govt., 1998. Mem. Moscow Math. Soc., Am. Math. Soc., N.Y. Acad. Scis. Avocations: computers, internet, sports, jogging, soccer. Office: Russian Acad Scis, Vlasov St Bldg 27 Apt 8, 117335 Moscow Russia

RAPTIS, NIKOS, civil engineer; b. Athens, Greece, June 29, 1930; s. Euthymios and Maria (Kostis) R.; m. Paraskevi Xiromeritou, Feb. 18, 1960. Diploma in Civil Engring., Nat. Tech. U. Athens, 1955; MSc, U. Ill., 1959. Engr. Pub. Works of Greece, Volos, 1955-56; soils engr. Air Force Pub. Wks. of Greece, Athens, 1960-63, Pub. Works of Greece, Athens, 1963-67; owner Geomechaniki, Athens, 1963-67, ptnr., 1967—; soils engr. Eupalinos, Athens, 1972-74. Author: Let's Discuss Earthquakes, Floods...and the Tram, 1981, The Nightmare of the Nukes, 1986; translator (into Greek) Year 501 by Noam Chomsky, 1994, Rethinking Camelot by Noam Chomsky, 1994. Mem. ASCE, ACI, Transp. Rsch. Bd. (assoc.). Avocations: sculpture, Baroque music.

RAR, ANDREI, research scientist; b. Novosibirsk, Russia, May 19, 1961; s. Aleksandr and Valentina (Okhrimenka) R.; m. Nadejda Furova; children: Rostislav, Ekaterina. M, Novosibirsk State U., 1983; PhD, U. Hokkaido, Sapporo, Japan, 1996. Rschr. Inst. for Catalysis, Novosibirsk, 1983-93; vis. rschr. Inst. for Applied Solid State Physics, Germany, 1996-97, Nat. Rsch. Inst. for Metals, Tsukuba, Japan, 1997-99; postdoctoral rschr. Materials for Info. Tech. U. Ala., Tuscaloosa, 1999—. Office: MINT U Ala PO Box 870209 Tuscaloosa AL 35487-0154

RAS, JUAN, engineer; b. Barcelona, Spain, July 28, 1948; s. Gregorio and Montserrat (Sirera) R.; m. Carolina Palleres, June 30, 1984; children: Guillermo, Inigo, Lucas, Gregorio. Engr., U. Politech., Barcelona, 1975. Mng. dir. Master S.D. Engr., Barcelona, Spain, 1975-84; mgr. internat. divsn., v.p. Corp. Agbar S.A., Barcelona, 1984—; chmn. Cespa S.A., Bilbao, Spain, Cespa GR S.A., Barcelona, Aquagest S.A., Madrid, Ansa S.A., Bilbao, Saur S.A., Barcelona, Sorea S.A., Barcelona; gen. mgr. Soc. Gen. Aguas Barcelona; lectr. World Bank Seminar, 1993-96; chmn. ECOMED. Treas. ACUDE, Barcelona, 1993-94; dep. chmn. Assn. Española de Abastecimento y Saweamiento, Madrid; chmn. environ. trade fair; chmn. Fundacion Forum Ambienal; bd. dirs. Western Water Co., San Diego, Calif. Mem. Internat. Water Supply Assn., Coll. of Engrs., Circulo del Liceo, Spanish Assn. Water Supply Co. (chmn.). Office: Sorea SA, Diputacion 353, 08009 Barcelona Spain

RÄSÄNEN, MIKA, information systems specialist; b. Espoo, Finland, Aug. 27, 1965; s. Erkki Olavi and Maija Inkeri (Karttunen) R.; m. Anu Sirkka-Liisa Kettunen, Aug. 10, 1993 (div. 1998); 1 child, Matias. MSc, Helsinki U. Technology, 1989, PhD, 1992, DSc, 1995. Engr. Rautaruukki Ltd., Raahe, Finland, 1985-86; rsch. asst., asst. prof. Helsinki U. Technology, Finland, 1988-93; rsch. asst. fellow Finnish Acad. Scis., Helsinki, 1993-95; info. sys. dir. Helsinki Energy, 1995-98; mgmt. cons. Cap Gemini, Espoo, Finland, 1998-99, Gemini Consulting, Helsinki, 1999—; cons. Fixedpoint Ltd., Espoo, Finland. Served in Finnish Air Force, 1985-86. Lutheran. Avocations: playing piano, triathlon, choir singing. Home: Kuunsdde 6 D 73, FIN02210 Espoo Finland Office: Gemini Consulting, Yrjonkato 13A 9, FIN-00120 Helsinki Finland

RASCH, DAVID GERARD, customer service representative; b. Pitts., Jan. 16, 1964; s. Gerard Frederick and Ruth (Blair) R. BS, Geneva Coll., Beaver Falls, Pa., 1987. Customer svc. rep. Liberty Mut. Group, Pitts., 1987-97, Wagner Agy., Inc., Pitts., 1997—. Mem. Dormont Lodge (master 1998). E-mail: raschdavid@wagneragency.com. Office: Wagner Agy Inc 5020 Centre Ave Pittsburgh PA 15213-1898

RASCHKA, CHRISTOPH JOSEF, sports physician, internist, anthropologist; b. Fulda, Hessen, Germany, Jan. 8, 1961; s. Herbert Helmut and Marga Rosa Elisabeth (Herget) R. MD cum laude, Justus-Liebig U., Giessen, Germany, 1987; PhD magna cum laude, Johannes-Gutenberg U., Mainz, 1988; DSc of Sports cum laude, Ruhr-U., Bochum, Germany, 1994. Cert. in sports medicine, acupuncture, chiropractic, homeopathy, tropotherapy. Asst. Inst. Anthropology, Mainz, 1987-88; resident Frankenklinik, Bad Neustadt/Saale, Germany, 1988-89, St. Markus-Krankenhaus, Frankfurt-Main, 1989, KVB-Klinik, Koenigstein/Taunus, 1989; resident in cardiology, gastroenterology, infectious disease Klinikum Fulda, 1990-98; asst. prof. Johann-Wolfgang Goethe U., Frankfurt-Main, 1998—; lectr. Acad. for Sch. Nurses, Fulda, 1992-93, U. Applied Scis. Fulda, 1999—; tchr. Sch. for Nurses of Klinikum Fulda, 1991—; lectr. anthropology Fulda, 1992-93; lectr. in field. Co-author: Ein Beitrag zur Medizinalgeschichte Fuldas unter spezieller Beruecksichtigung der Inneren Medizin; book reviewer Jour. Comparative Human Biology, 1995—, Jour. Naturarzt, 1995—; contbr. over 350 articles to profl. jours. Johannes-Gutenberg U. scholar, 1987. Mem. German Soc. Sports Physicians, German Soc. Physicians for Acupuncture, German Soc. Physicians for Naturheilverfahren, German Soc. Internal Medicine. Roman Catholic. Avocations: weight lifting, jogging, volleyball, cross-country skiing, aikido. Home: Edith-Stein-Strasse 34, 36100 Petersberg Hessen, Germany Office: Johann Wolfgang Goeth U, Dept Sports Medicine, 36043 Frankfurt Hessen, Germany

RASHID, ABDUL, drug delivery systems consultant; b. Karachi, Pakistan, June 15, 1947; arrived in Scotland, 1971; s. Haji Ghulam and Sugran (Begum) Rasool; m. Bilqees Akhtar, Aug. 30, 1974; children: Rifat, Rizwan, Azmat, Ihsan, Farhat, Faatima, Maryam, Somayah. BSc, U. Karachi, 1970, U. Strathclyde, Glasgow, Scotland, 1976; MSc, U. Strathclyde, Glasgow, Scotland, 1980, PhD, 1984, MBA, 1992. Rsch. asst. U. Strathclyde, Glasgow, 1980-84; project leader Polysystems Ltd., Glasgow, 1984-87, devel. mgr., 1987-90; mgr. product devel. Scherer DDS Ltd, Glasgow, 1990-92; tech. svcs. mgr. Scherer DDS Ltd,, Glasgow, 1992-93; freelance cons. drug delivery sys. Glasgow, 1993—. Patentee in field; inventor of Pulsincap tech. Mem. Royal Soc. Chemistry, Controlled Release Soc. Home: 25 Camphill Ave, Glasgow G41 3AU, Scotland Office: Pharma Innovations, 25 Camphill Ave, Glasgow G41 3AU, Scotland

RASHID, MAMUN UR, bank commission official; b. Noakhali, Bangladesh, Oct. 1, 1961; s. Mominul Hague and Sufia Momin Bhuiyan; m. Fahmida Akter Khatun, Mar. 11, 1988. BSc in Econs. with honors, Jahangir Nagar U., Dhaka, Bangladesh, 1983, MSc in Econs., 1984; MBA in Strategic Mgmt., Henley Mgmt. Coll., U.K., 1998. Cert. credit profl. Omega, London. Probationary officer Uttara Bank Ltd., Dhaka, 1984-86; trainee officer ANZ Grindlays Bank, Dhaka, 1986-87, country dealer, 1987-90, corp. account mgr., 1990-93; head treasury Std. Chartered Bank Bangladesh, Dhaka, 1993-94; head Treasury & Instnl. Banking, Dhaka, 1994-98; head special group Assel-Mgmt. and Instl. Banking, Dhaka, 1998—; assoc. faculty Bangladesh Inst. Bank Mgmt., Dhaka, 1989—; external reviewer Inst. Bus. Adminstrn., Dhaka U., 1997—. Author: Money Market in Bangladesh-Guide to Corporate Treasury, 1996, 98, Foreign Exchange and Funds Management, 1998; editor (mags.) Naibadda, 1980, Prattasha, 1983. Mem. Bangladesh Fgn. Exch. Dealers Assn. (mem. tech. com. 1999), Dhaka Club Ltd. (corp. mem.). Avocations: reading, traveling. Office: Std Chartered Bank, 18-20 Motijheel Comml Area, 1000 Dhaka Bangladesh

RASHID, MUHAMMED MOHSEN, lawyer; b. Dhaka, Bangladesh, Dec. 29, 1951; s. M. Abdul and Kurshid R.; m. Reshma Rashid, Nov. 26, 1977; children: Talha Mohsen, Hisham Mohsen, Zeesan Bin Mohsen. Law grad., U. Karachi, Pakistan, 1971, JD, 1976. Bar: Bangladesh Supreme Ct. Pvt. practice Business Law and Constitutional Law, Dhaka, Bangladesh, 1976—; legal adviser Banks, Corporates; vi. lectr. law clinic Dhaka U. Pres. Assn. for Dem. and Constitutional Adv. of Bangladesh, Dhaka, 1988; pres. AIDS Prevention Legal Aid. Mem. Dhaka Bar Assn., Supreme Ct. Bar Assn., SAARC Law Lawasia, Union Internatl. des Avocats, past pres. Rotary Club of Shebbogh, past pres., Al-Falah, pres. Friendship, Aventi, Ltd. Rotary (bd. dirs. Dhaka North 1986-89), Guishan Club (permanent). Home: 4/1 KM Das Ln Ticatuli, Dhaka Bangladesh Office: Moshen Assocs, 601 Stock, Exch Bldg 9F Motijheel CA, Dhaka Bangladesh

RASHID UBAYDI, AMIR RASHID MUHAMMAD AL-, Iraq minister of oil and industry; b. 1939; m.; 5 children. BSc, London U., 1961; PhD, Birmingham (Eng.) U., 1974. Dep. commdr. Iraq Air Force, 1978-83; head R&D Ministry of Defense Govt. of Iraq, Baghdad, 1984-88; undersec. ministry of industry Govt. of Iraq, Baghdad, 1988-91, dir. mil. industrialization commn., 1992-93, minister of Oil and Industry, 1994—. *

RASHKES, MOSHE, writer; b. Bialystok, Poland, June 16, 1928; s. Arieh Leib and Golda (Haas) R.; m. Rachel Haimowitch, Nov. 26, 1972; children: Arieh, Gideon. Grad., Montefiore Coll. Tech., Tel Aviv, 1951. Chmn. War Disabled Vets Orgn., 1950-58; Israel del. Gen. Assemblies of World Vets. Fedn., 1951-58; dir. Ilan Sport Centre for Physically Disabled, Ramat Gan, 1965—. Author: Days of Lead, 1962, Night Hunts Nights, 1966, Collapse, 1975, Doomed to Glory, 1995; founder, editor War Veteran, 1952; also plays. Served to lt. Israeli Def. Forces, 1948. Recipient Citation of Valour, 1948, Lifetime Achievement award Internat. Jewish Sports Hall of Fame, 1998. Mem. Internat. Writers Guild (cinema and TV sect., Israeli del. to founding assembly 1966, del. to Moscow 1969). Home: 1 Mizpe Yam St, Herzliyya 46590, Israel Office: 123 Rokach St, Ramat Gan Israel

RASIZADE, ARTUR, prime minister; b. Gyandja, Azerbaijan, Feb. 26, 1935; married; 1 child. Grad., Azerbaijan Inst. Industry. Engr., dep. dir. Azerbaijan Inst. of Oil Machine Construction, 1957-73, dir., 1973-78; chief engr. Trust Soyuzneftemash, 1973-77; dep. head Azerbaijan State Planning com., 1978-81; head of sect. Ctr. Com. of Azerbaijan CP, 1981-86; first dep. prime minister Azerbaijan, 1986-92, 96, asst. to pres. Aliyev, 1996, Prime Min., 1996—; adviser Found. of Econ. Reforms, 1992-96. *

RAŠKOVÁ, HELENA, pharmacologist; b. Zurich, Switzerland, Jan. 2, 1913; d. Robert and Esta (Sacrev) Heller; m. Karel Raška, Sept. 14, 1938 (dec. 1987); children: Karel Jr., Ivan. MD, Charles U., Prague, Czechoslovakia, 1937, DSc, 1957; MD (hon.), U. Lausanne, Switzerland. Internal medicine faculty U. Hosp., Prague, 1937-39; pharmacologist B. Fragner, Prague, 1942-45; asst. dept. pharmacology Charles U., Prague, 1945-48, lectr. pharmacology, 1948-56, chmn. pharmacology faculty of pediat. medicine, 1955-71, prof. pharmacology, 1957-70; dir. lab. Inst. Pharmacology, Chech Acad. Sci., 1963-70. Author: Practical Exercises in Pharmacology, 1956, Pharmacology for Medical Students, 1959, Textbook of Pharmacology, 1970; contbr. over 350 articles to profl. jours. V.p., sec. gen. Internat. Union Pharmacology, 1965-72. Recipient Golden medal Slovak Acad. Scis., 1993, Golden medal for merit in world pharmacology EPH AR I, Milan, 1995, Golden medal Faculty of Pharmacy, Comenius U., 1998. Mem. Assn. European Pharm. Socs., Czech Acad. Scis., Belgian Royal Acad. Medicine (hon.), Czech Pharm. Soc. (hon. pres. 1993—), European Soc. Toxicology (hon.), Italian Pharm. Soc. (hon.), French Physiol. Soc. (hon.), European Soc. for Study of Drug Toxicology (exec. bd. 1963-69), NIM (exec. com. 1987-93). Home: V Ondřejově 2, 14000 Prague Czech Republic

RASKOVIC, ALEXANDER, sports agent, yacht broker; b. Kraljevo, Serbia, Yugoslavia, July 1, 1956; arrived in Greece, 1990; s. Vukoje and Radmilla (Milanovic) R.; m. Daphne Helen Larounis; children: George, Philip. B Electronics, Air Force Tech., Yugoslavia, 1977; BEE, U. Belgrade, Yugoslavia, 1980, MEE, 1984. Prof. Air Force Acad., Yugoslavia, 1978-82; asst. prof. U. Belgrade, 1984-86; pres. North Star Yachting, Athens, 1992—; gen. mgr. Europe Falk Assocs. Mgmt. Enterprises, Athens, 1997—. Maj. Yugoslav Air Force, 1985-86. Mem. Royal Yacht Club of Greece, Polo Club of Paris. Orthodox Christian. Avocation: yachting.

RASMASON, FREDERICK CHARLES, III, emergency nurse; b. Evergreen Park, Ill., May 10, 1958; s. Frederick C. Jr. and Kathleen M. R.; m. Concepcion A. Rasmason, Nov. 14, 1981; children: F. Charlie IV, Randy. Diploma, Clin. Specialist Sch., 1977; BS in Nursing, Chgo. State U., 1988; MS in Human Svc. Adminstrn., Spertus Coll., 1997. RN, Ill.; CEN; cert. TNS, TNCC, ACLS, PALS, PHTLS, emergency dept. nursing. Staff nurse Holy Family Hosp., Des Plaines, Ill., Mt. Sinai Med. Ctr., Chgo., King Drew Med. Ctr., Calif.; emergency dept. staff Provident Hosp. Cook County, Chgo. Sgt. U.S. Army, 1976-82, 86-88. Named Nightingale Soc. Honors Mem.; recipient U.S. Achievement Acad. Scholastic All-Am. award, U.S. Achievement Acad. Nat. Collegiate Nursing award. Mem. Am. Assn. Critical Care Nurses, Emergency Nurses Assn., Ill. Nurses Assn., Calif. Nurses Assn. Home: 13260 Windward Trl Orland Park IL 60462-1860

RASMUS, JOHN CHARLES, trade association executive, lawyer; b. Rochester, N.Y., Dec. 27, 1941; s. Harold Charles and Myrtle Leota (Dybevik) R.; m. Elaine Green Reeves, Mar. 19, 1982; children: Kristin, Stuart, Karin. A.B., Cornell U., 1963; J.D., U. Va., 1966. Bar: Va. 1970, U.S. Supreme Ct. 1974. Spl. agt. Def. Dept., Washington, 1966-70; v.p., adminstrv. officer, legis. research counsel U.S. League Savs. Instns., Washington, 1970-83; asst. to exec. v.p. Nat. Assn. Fed. Credit Unions, 1983-84; sr. fed. adminstrv. counsel, mgr. regulatory and trust affairs Am. Bankers Assn., 1985—. Mem. ABA, Fed. Bar Assn. (disting. service award 1980, 82, past chmn. long range planning com., past chmn. council fin. instns. and economy), Univ. Club, Exchequer Club, Masons. Home: 303 Kentucky Ave Alexandria VA 22305-1739

RASMUSON, BRENT (JACOBSEN), photographer, graphic artist, lithographer; b. Logan, Utah, Nov. 28, 1950; s. Eleroy West and Fae (Jacobsen) R.; m. Tess Bullen, Sept. 30, 1981; children: John, Mark, Lisa. Grad. auto repair and painting sch., Utah State U. Pre-press supr. Herald Printing Co., Logan, 1969-79; profl. drummer, 1971-75; owner, builder auto racing engines Valley Automotive Specialties, 1971-76; exec. sec. Herald Printing Co., 1979-89; owner Brent Rasmuson Photography, Smithfield, Utah, 1986—, Temple Picture Classics, Smithfield, 1996—. Author photo prints of LDS temples: Logan, 1987, 95, 98, 2000, Manti, 1989, 2000, Jordan River, 1989, 96, 98, 2000, Provo, 1990, Mesa, Ariz., 1990, 96, Boise, Idaho, 1990, 96, 2000, Salt Lake LDS Temple, 1990, 96, Idaho Falls, 1991, 94, 2000, St. George, 1991, 93, 2000, Portland, Oreg., 1991, 96, 97, 2000, L.A., 1991, 96, 97, 2000, Las Vegas, Nev., 1991, Seattle, 1992, Oakland, Calif., 1993, 94, Ogden, 1992; author photo print: Statue of Angel Moroni, 1994; author photos used to make neckties and watch dials of LDS temples: Salt Lake, Manti, Logan, L.A., Oakland, Seattle, Las Vegas, Mesa, Portland, St. George, Jordan River, scenic tie Mammoth Hot Springs in Yellowstone Park, 1995; landscape scenic photographs featured in Best of Photography Ann., 1987, 88, 89, also in calendars and book covers; author photo print of Harris Rsch., Inc. Internat. Hdqrs. (recipient 1st prize nat. archtl. photo competition); designer several bus. logos. Mem. Internat. Platform Assn., Assoc. Photographers Internat., Internat. Freelance Photographers Orgn., Nat. Trust Hist. Preservation. Republican. Mem. LDS Ch. Avocations: landscape design, travel, reading, numismatics, philately. Home and Office: 40 N 200 E Smithfield UT 84335-1543

RASMUSON, ELMER EDWIN, banker, former mayor; b. Yakutat, Alaska, Feb. 15, 1909; s. Edward Anton and Jenny (Olson) R.; m. Lile Vivian Bernard, Oct. 27, 1939 (dec. 1960); children: Edward Bernard, Lile Muchmore (Mrs. John Gibbons, Jr.), Judy Ann; m. Col. Mary Louise Milligan, Nov. 4, 1961. BS magna cum laude, Harvard U., 1930, AM, 1935; student, U. Grenoble, 1930; LLD, U. Alaska, 1970, Alaska Pacific U., 1993. C.P.A., N.Y., Tex., Alaska. Chief accountant Nat. Investors Corp., N.Y.C., 1933-35; prin. Arthur Andersen & Co., N.Y.C., 1935-43; pres. Nat. Bank of Alaska, 1943-65, chmn. bd., 1966-74, chmn. exec. com., 1975-82, now chmn. emeritus; mayor City of Anchorage, 1964-67, dir., emeritus and cons., 1989; civilian aide from Alaska to sec. army, 1959-67; Swedish consul Alaska, 1955-77; Chmn. Rasmuson Found.; Rep. nominee U.S. Senate from Alaska, 1968; U.S. commr. Internat. N. Pacific Fisheries Commn., 1969-84; mem. Nat. Marine Fisheries Adv. Com., 1974-77, North Pacific Fishery Mgmt. Council, 1976-77, U.S. Arctic Research Commn., 1984-92. Mem. City Coun. Anchorage, 1945, chmn. city planning comm., 1950-53; pres. Alaska coun. Boy Scouts Am., 1953; regent U. Alaska, 1950-69; trustee King's Lake Camp, Inc., 1944—, Alaska Permanent Fund Corp., 1980-82; bd. dirs. Nat. Mus. Natural History Smithsonian Inst. 1994-97. Decorated knight first class Order of Vasa, comdr. Sweden; recipient silver Antelope award Boy Scouts Am., Japanese citation Order of the Sacred Treasure, Gold and Silver Star, 1988; outstanding civilian service medal U.S. Army; Alaskan of Year award, 1976. Mem. Pioneers Alaska, Alaska Bankers Assn. (past pres.), Defense Orientation Conf. Assn., NAACP, Alaska Native Brotherhood, Explorers Club, Phi Beta Kappa. Republican. Presbyn. Clubs: Masons, Elks, Anchorage Rotary (past pres.); Harvard (N.Y.C.; Boston); Wash. Athletic (Seattle), Seattle Yacht (Seattle), Rainier (Seattle); Thunderbird Country (Palm Desert, Calif.); Bohemian (San Francisco); Eldorado Country (Indian Wells, Calif.); Boone & Crockett. Home: PO Box 100600 Anchorage AK 99510-0600

RASMUSSEN, ANNE-METTE RIIS, librarian, writer; b. Lyngby, Denmark, Oct. 24, 1956; d. Poul Rasmussen and Kirsten Riis Lassen; children: Toke, Sine. Libr. grad., Royal Sch. Libr.-Info. Sci., Aalborg, Denmark, 1980; postgrad., Danish Acad. Creative Writing, Copenhagen, 1987-89. Libr. Nordjyllands Mus. Contemporary Art, Aalborg, 1981, Aalborg U. Libr., 1983-84, Aalborg U. Ctr., 1984-85, Frederiksberg (Denmark) Pub. Libr., 1987-88, 93-94, Danish Women's Soc., Copenhagen, 1990, Danish Broadcasting Corp., Gladsaxe, 1994—. Author: (novel) Mermaids Cannot Drown, 1987, (poems) The Mountain, 1989, (novel) Through the Sun's Eye, 1995. Grantee State Art Found., Denmark, 1991, 94. Home: Gunløgsgade 2, 4.TH, 2300 S Copenhagen Denmark Office: Danmarks Radio TV-ARC, TV-Byen, Blok A, 1.SAL, 2860 Søborg Denmark

RASMUSSEN, CLAUS, internist, rheumatologist; b. Koege, Denmark, Oct. 14, 1951; s. Poul and Karen (Sorensen) R.; m. Liv Damstedt, Mar. 31, 1979; children: Randi, Bjorn, Poul. MD, U. Copenhagen, 1979. Resident hosps., Frederikshaun, Hjorring, Denmark, 1979-86; gen. practice Taars, Denmark, 1987-88; sr. registrar in internal medicine Hjorring and Aalborg, Denmark, 1989-97; sr. registrar in rheumatology Hjorring Hosp., 1999—; cons. Danish Med. Assn., 1992—; project leader Danish Hosp. Evaluation Ctr. Contbr. articles to profl. jours. Initiator Social Emergency Ward, Aalborg, 1994-97. Lt. Royal Danish Air Force, 1980-81. Grantee Danish Med. Assn., 1994, Danish Arthritis Assn., 1996, 99. Mem. Back Rsch. Soc. No. Jutland, Danish Soc. Alcohol Rsch. Avocations: dendrology, garden architecture, Danish art 1798-1850, wine and beer. Office: Hjorring Hosp Dept Rheum, Bispensgade, DK-9800 Hjørring Denmark

RASMUSSEN, EBBE GERT, secondary education educator, researcher; b. Aakirkeby, Bornholm, Denmark, July 18, 1939; s. Gert Vagn Rasmussen and Aase Kiørboe; m. Ellen Margrethe Anker, Feb. 20, 1960 (div. July 1967); 1 child, Niels; m. Maria Gruber, Apr. 7, 1971 (div. Apr. 1985); children: Thomas Eske, Peter Esben. Cand mag, U. Copenhagen, 1967, Dr phil, 1985. Tchr. Rønne Statsskole, Rønne, Denmark, 1967-86, Ronne Handelsskole, 1967-82; asst. prof. Bornholms Amtsgymnasium, Rønne, 1986—. Author: Bornholm 1658, 1967, Pastor Lemvigs Betaenkning, 1968, Bornholm 1658-Kilder, 1972, Dette Gavebrev, 1982, Skuddet, 2000; editor Bornholmske Samlinger, 1974-82; contbr. articles to profl. jours., chpts. to books. Com. mem. Bornholms Mus., Rønne, 1971-95; com. mem. Bornholms Hist. Samfund, Rønne, 1975—, pres. corp., 1994—. With Danish Air Def., 1967-69. Recipient Bornholmer prize Bornholms Hist. Samfund, 1982, 19 Oct. Fonden award Town of Rønne, 1982. Mem. Danish Hist. Soc., Nat. Geog. Soc. Lutheran. Avocations: research, oil painting. Home: Østerled 43, 3700 Rønne Bornholm, Denmark Office: Bornholms Amtsgymnasium, Søborgstraede 2, 3700 Rønne Bornholm, Denmark

RASMUSSEN, GUNNAR, engineer; b. Esbjerg, Denmark, Nov. 23, 1925; s. Karl Sigurd and Frederikke Valentine (Gjerulff) R.; m. Hanna Hertz, June 27, 1973; children: Jan, Lise, Per, Thue. Student, Aarhus Teknikum, Denmark, 1950. Mgr. quality control Brüel and Kjaer, Nerum, Denmark, 1950-54, with devel. div., 1955-69, with product planning div., 1969-74, with innovation div., 1975-93; engr. GRAS Sound and Vibration, Vedbaek, Denmark, 1993—; lectr. Danish Tech. U., Copenhagen, 1974-79, Med. Air Force Acad., Jegersborg, Denmark, 1978-79; examiner Danish Engring. Acad., Copenhagen, 1972—, Chalmers Tech. U., Gothenburg, Sweden, 1984-85. Editor: Intensity Measurements, 1989; inventor measurement microphones, accelerometers; contbr. articles to profl. jours. Chairman

Audio Engring. Soc. Denmark, Cophenhagen, 1976. Recipient Danish Design prize for microphones, 1962, medal for contbn. to intensity techniques SETIM, 1990. Fellow Acoustical Soc. Am., Can. Acoustical Soc., Danish Medico Tech. Soc.; mem. Internat. Union Pure and Applied Physics (vice chmn. internat. commn. on accoustics), Danish Acoustical Soc. (bd. dirs.), Internat. Electronical Commn., Internat. Orgn. for Standarization. Home: Hojbjerggardsvej 15, 2840 Holte Denmark Office: GRAS Sound & Vibration, Skelstedet 10 B, DK-2950 Vedbaek Denmark

RASMUSSEN, JAN WILLIAM, librarian; b. Copenhagen, Aug. 12, 1936; s. William S. and Anna (Jensen) R.; m. Eva Margrete Behrend, Feb. 19, 1965; children: Mette, Dorte, Thomas. Grad., Danish Sch. Librarianship, Copenhagen, 1961. Libr. The Royal Libr., Copenhagen, 1958-96; inspector Døvehistorisk Selskab, Copenhagen, 1982—. Author: Dania Polyglotta, 1969-96, Døveundervisning i Danmark 1807-1982, 1983, Den Kongelige Døvstummeskole i Nyborg 1891-1991, 1992; editor Døvehistorisk Tidsskrift, 1983—. Recipient Castberg prize, 1999. Office: Døvehistorisk Selskab, Kastelsvej 58c, 2100 Copenhagen ø, Denmark

RASMUSSEN, JENS BØDTKER, zoologist researcher; b. Frederiksberg, Denmark, Apr. 16, 1947; s. Ludvig Hans Anders and Polly Edel Bødtker (Laustsen) R.; m. Heidi Aune, Sept. 25, 1982; 1 child, Kit. MSc, U. Copenhagen, 1975, PhD, 1977, DSc, 1994. Instr. Teacher's U., Copenhagen, 1975; asst. prof. Zool. Mus. U. Copenhagen, 1977-79, assoc. prof., 1979—; head of vertebrate divsn., mem. bd. dirs. Zool. Mus., U. Copenhagen, 1979-81, 88-89, 91-93, 99—; appt. examiner Geol. Ctrl. Inst., U. Copenhagen, 1983-93; mem. internat. herpetological com. World Congress of Herpetology, 1989-97; mem. African reptile and amphibian specialist group World Conservation Union, Switzerland, 1994-96. Contbr. articles to profl. publs. Recipient Rsch. grant Danish Nat. Rsch. Coun., 1991-93, 99—, Travel grant Conoco Congo Ltd., 1990. Mem. Soc. for Study of Amphibians and Reptiles, Soc. Europaea Herpetologica, Herpetological Assn. Africa. Avocations: crossword puzzles, brainteasers, crime novels, cooking. Office: Zool Museum, Universitetsparken 15, DK-2100 Copenhagen Ø, Denmark

RASMUSSEN, KJELD LEISGAARD, physician, consultant; b. Skovsborg, Jutland, Denmark, Apr. 2, 1957; s. Svend and Ella (Jensen) R.; m. Kirsten Overgaard Jensen. MD, Aarhus U., Denmark, 1984. Resident Herning Ctrl. Hosp., Denmark, 1984-85, Skive Hosp., Denmark, 1985-87, Randeri Hosp., Denmark, 1987-88, Alborg Hosp., Denmark, 1988-90; sr. resident Arhus U. Hosp., Denmark, 1990-93, Herning & Viborg, Denmark, 1993-96; cons. Herning Ctrl. Hosp., Denmark, 1996—; external lectr. U. Aarhus, 1997—; censor Danish Sch. Midwifery, 1998—. Contbr. articles to profl. jours. Mem. Danish Soc. Gyn. and Obstet. Avocations: football, handball, Danish history, public debate, archeology. Home: Glensovej 10, 8620 Kjellerup Denmark Office: Herning Ctrl Hosp, Dept Gyn and Obstet, 7400 Herning Denmark

RASMUSSEN, MICHAEL HOJBY, clinical research physician; b. Copenhagen, Denmark, Feb. 17, 1962; s. Aage Hojby and Gyda Lohmann (Thomsen) R.; m. Jeannette Haugaard Petersen, June 29, 1985; 1 child, Helena. MD, Univ. Copenhagen, 1990, PhD, 1995. Resident Hvidovre Univ. Hosp., Denmark, 1990-91; researcher Univ. Copenhagen, 1991-94; medical safety officer Novo Nordisk A/S, Denmark, 1994-95; internat. clinical devel. mgr. Novo Nordisk A/S, 1995-99, internat. clin. project mgr., 1999—; referee Internat. Medical Jours., 1994—. Contbr. articles to profl. jours. Recipient Young Investigator award Internat. Assn. Study of Obesity, 1994. Mem. Danish Assn. Study of Obesity (bd. dirs.). Home: Langs Hegnet 52B, 2800 Lyngby Denmark Office: Novo Nordisk A/S, Krogshojvej 53, 2880 Bagsvaerd Denmark

RASMUSSEN, MICHAEL SCHULTZ, geographer; b. Ringe, Denmark, Dec. 6, 1958; s. Mogens Laurits and Bodil (Zachariasen) R.; m. Anne Marie Sarauw Rasmussen, Aug. 3, 1985; children: Emil, Anna, Sophie. BA in Music, U. Copenhagen, 1989, MS in Geography, 1989, PhD in Sci., 1996. Expert UNDP, Dakar, Senegal, 1990-94; cons. Farum, 1995—; rsch. asst. U. Copenhagen, 1994-97, asst. prof., 1997-2000, assoc. prof., 2000—; dir. Geographic Resource Analysis and Sci. Ltd., 2000—. Mem. The Royal Danish Geograph. Soc., Am. Soc. Photogrammetry and Remote Sensing, Remote Sensing Soc. Office: Inst of Geography, Øster Voldgade 10, Copenhagen 1350 K, Denmark

RASMUSSEN, POUL NYRUP, prime minister of Denmark, economist; b. Esbjerg, Western Jutland, Denmark, June 15, 1943; s. Olof Nyrup and Vera Nyrup R.; married (div.); m. Lone Dybkjaer; 1 child (dec.). Grad., Esbjerg Statsskole, 1962; degree in Ecomomy, U. Copenhagen, 1971. Economist Danish Trade Union Coun., Brussels, 1971-80; chief economist Danish Trade Union Coun., 1980-86; mgn. dir. Employees Capital Pension Fund, 1986-88; dep. chair Social Democratic Party, 1987-92, chair of the parliamentary group, 1992—, chmn., 1992—; mem. Parliament, 1988, 1991—; prime minister Denmark, 1993—; chmn. Lalandia Invest, 1986-88; bd. mem. Euroventures Nordica, Dansk Erhvervsinvestering; chmn. Parliamentary Com. on Commerce, Industry and Shipping, 1988-92; mem. Parliamentary Labour Mkt. Com., 1991-92, Political Economic Committee, 1991-92, Standing Orders Com., 1992; v.p. Socialist Internat., 1992—. Office: Office Prime Minister, Prins Jorgens Gard II, 1218 Copenhagen Denmark*

RASMUSSEN, ROBERT, advertising executive; b. Aarhus, Jutland, Denmark, Jan. 14, 1951; s. Robert Herluf and Tove Helen (Andersen) R.; m. Anne Kruger Severinsen, Mar. 22, 1975; children: Cathrine, Anne Marie, Christian, Benedicte, Christopher. BS in Econs., Aarhus Sch. Bus., 1973, MS in Econs. and Bus. Adminstrn., 1975. Product mgr. A/S BlumÜller, Odense, Denmark, 1975-78; mktg. asst. Scan-Ad Advt. Agy., Odense, 1974-75, mktg. mgr., 1978-80, account dir., 1980-83, mng. dir., CEO, 1983—. Named Consul of The Netherlands, Embassy of The Netherlands, 1998. Office: Scan-Ad Reklamebureau A/S, Christiansgade 70, 5000 Odense C, Denmark

RASMUSSEN, ROBERT DEE, real estate appraiser; b. Lincoln, Kans., Dec. 24, 1936; s. Sam and Kristena (Andersen) R.; m. Beverly Bert Rowden, Mar. 22, 1959; children: Robert Denis, Kay Lynn. B Gen. Edn., U. Nebr., 1965; MA, Ariz. State U., 1970. Cert. gen. real estate appraiser, Fla. Commd. USAF, 1957, advanced through grades to col., 1978, fighter pilot various locations, 1956-75; comdr. 59th Tactical Fighter Squadron USAF, Eglin AFB, Fla., 1975-77; chief Europe/Nato Plans USAF, Washington, 1978-80; vice-comdr. 474th Tactical Fighter Wing USAF, Nellis AFB, Nev., 1980-81; chief of plans U.S. European Command Joint Chiefs of Staff, Stuttgart, Germany, 1981-84; dir. joint matters Hdqrs. Tactical Air Command USAF, Langley AFB, Va., 1984-86; ret. USAF, 1986; appraiser, cons. Appraisal House Inc., Ft. Walton Beach, Fla., 1987-94; gen. appraiser Niceville, Fla., 1994—; dir. U.S. Power Squadrons, Ft. Walton Beach, 1988-90. Decorated DFC, Legion of Merit. Mem. Ret. Officers Assn., Am. Assn. Ind. Investors, Fla. Assn. Realtors, NAR (gen. accredited appraiser, appraisal sect.), Am. Soc. Appraisers (sr. mem.), Appraisal Inst. (assoc.), Porsche Club Am. (v.p. Germany region 1983-84, pres. North Fla. region 1989, 97, dir. 1988-94), Mid-Bay Rotary Club (charter, dir. 1995-96). Avocations: boating, hunting, fishing, sports cars. Office: RD Rasmussen Gen Appraiser 2421 Duncan Dr Niceville FL 32578-2915

RASMUSSEN, THOMAS VAL, JR., lawyer, small business owner; b. Salt Lake City, Aug. 11, 1954; s. Thomas Val and Georgia (Smedley) R.; m. Donita Gubler, Aug. 15, 1978; children: James, Katherine, Kristin. BA magna cum laude, U. Utah, 1978, JD, 1981. Bar: Utah 1981, U.S. Dist. Ct. Utah 1981, U.S. Supreme Ct. 1985, U.S. Ct. Appeals (10th cir.) 1999. Atty. Salt Lake Legal Defender Assn., Salt Lake City, 1981-83, Utah Power and Light Co., Salt Lake City, 1983-89; of counsel Hatch, Morton & Skeen, Salt Lake City, 1989-90; ptnr. Morton, Skeen & Rasmussen, Salt Lake City, 1991-94, Skeen & Rasmussen, Salt Lake City, 1994-97; pvt. practice, Salt Lake City, 1997—; co-owner, developer Handi Self-Storage, Kaysville, Utah, 1984-93; instr. bus. law Brigham Young U., Salt Lake City, 1988-90. Adminstrv. editor Jour. Contemporary Law, 1980-81, Jour. Energy Law and Policy, 1980-81. Missionary Ch. of Jesus Christ of Latter-Day Sts., Brazil, 1973-75. Mem. Utah, Salt Lake County Bar Assn., Intermountain Miniature Horse Club (pres. 1989, 2d v.p. 1990), Phi Eta Sigma, Phi Kappa Phi, Beta Gamma Sigma. Avocations: tennis, scuba diving, showing horses, travel, collecting art. Home: 3094 Whitewater Dr Salt Lake City UT 84121-1561 Office: 4659 Highland Dr Salt Lake City UT 84117-5137

RASMUSSON, LARS GÖSTA, oral and maxillofacial surgeon, researcher; b. Tanum, Bohuslan, Sweden, May 28, 1962; s. Carl Gösta and Anna Lisa (Petersson) R.; m. Elisabeth Olin, June 27, 1992; children: Carl, Sofia, Sara. DMD, U. Göteborg, 1990, PhD in Medicine, 1998. Pvt. practice Göteborg, 1991-97; rschr. Biomaterial/Handicap Rsch., Göteborg, 1993—; asst. prof. dept. oral and maxillofacial surgery U. Göteborg, 1996—; clin. advisor Astra Tech AB, Mölndal, 1995—. Lt. Royal Swedish Navy Res. Office: U Göteborg Dept Oral Surgery, Box 450, SE-40530 Göteborg Sweden

RASPOPOV, IGOR MIKHAJLOVICH, hydrobotanist; b. Leningrad, USSR, July 30, 1927; s. Mikhail Petrovich Raspopov and Olga Yuljevna Felsner; m. Galina Vladimirovna Fomicheva, Dec. 10, 1955; 1 child, Vyacheslav. MSc, Leningrad State U., 1950, PhD, 1953; DSc in hydrobiology, Ukranian Acad. Sci., Kiev, USSR, 1986. Jr. rschr. Lab. of Limnology Acad. Sci. USSR, Leningrad, 1954-62, sr. rsch. scientist Lab. of Limnology, 1962-78, head of lab. hydrobiology, 1978-86; chief rsch. scientist Inst. Limnology Russian Acad. Sci., St. Petersburg, Russia, 1986—; mem. spl. sci. coun. acad. degrees Botanical Inst., St. Petersburg, 1993—. Author: Higher Aquatic Vegetation of the Great Lakes of USSR's North-Western, 1985; editor, co-author: Role of The Water Roughness in The Benthos Biocenoses Forming in The Great Lakes, 1990, editor, co-author: Land Water Ecotones of the Great Lakes, 1998; contbr. over 170 articles to profl. jours. Fellow Internat. Assn. Theoretical and Applied Limnology, Botanical Soc.; mem. Presidium Hydrobiol. Soc. Avocations: sporting tours, philately. Home: Vavilovich Str 7 3 124, 195257 Saint Petersburg Russia Office: Inst Limnology Russian Acad, Sevastyanov Str 9, 196105 Saint Petersburg Russia

RASSAM, SALWAN M. B., ophthalmologist; b. Aug. 6, 1961; s. Munir B. and Violet Y.S. (Albanna) R. MB BChir, Royal Coll. Surgeons, Dublin, Ireland, 1985, BA of Obstetrics, 1985; Diploma in Ophthalmology, Royal Coll. Surgeons, London, 1990; MD, Nat. U. Ireland, Dublin, 1994. House officer Richmond/St. James Hosps., Dublin, Ireland, 1985-86; med. officer Blood Transfusion Bd., Dublin, Ireland, 1986-87; ophthalmic sr. officer Kent and Canterbury Hosp., U.K., 1987-88, St. Thomas and Guys Hosp., London, 1988-89, Royal Free/UCH/Whittington Hosp., London, 1989-90; clin. rsch. registrar Hammersmith Hosp., London, 1990-92; ophthalmic registrar Charing Cross Hosp., London, 1992-93, Whipps Cross/Whittington Hosp., London, 1993-94; ophthalmic sr. registrar Western Eye Hosp., London, 1994-98; ophthalmic cons., dir. rsch. Worthing (West Sussex, U.K.) and Chichester Hosp., 1998—; sub-editor Current Opinion in Ophthalmology, London, 1994. Contbr. numerous articles to profl. jours and chpts. to books; designer of ophthalmic surg. instruments; inventor of surg. hardware. Collaborator Impact Found., West Sussex, U.K., 1988, Brighton U., Sussex, 1999. Fellow Royal Coll. Ophthalmologists; mem. Brit. Med. Assn., Royal Coll. Ophthalmologists. Avocations: flying, scuba diving, flute and saxaphone performances.

RASSEL, RICHARD EDWARD, lawyer; b. Toledo, Ohio, Jan. 10, 1942; s. Richard Edward and Madonna Mary (Tuohy) R.; m. Elizabeth Ann Frederick, Dec. 5, 1967 (dec. June 1977); children: Richard III, Elizabeth; m. Dawn Ann Lynch, Sept. 17, 1983; children: Lauren, Brian. BA, U. Notre Dame, 1964; JD, U. Mich., 1966; cert. judge advocate, USN Judge Advocate Sch., 1967. Law clk. Mich. Ct. Appeals, Detroit, 1966-70; shareholder, v.p. Butzel Long, Detroit, 1970-94, chmn., CEO, 1994—; bd. dirs. Robertson-Jamieson Corp., Birmingham, Mich., WTVS-Channel 56. Pres. Birmingham Cmty. House; bd. advisors U. Detroit Grad. Sch. Bus.; mem. steering com. Friends of Legal Aid; vice chmn. steering com. Libel Def. Resource Ctr.; bd. dirs. Lex Mundi, Detroit Legal News, Detroit Police Athletic League, Internat. Visitors Coun., Lourdes, Inc., Met. Affairs Coalition, Mich. Jobs Commn.; chair strategic planning com. Oakland U. Coll. Arts and Scis.; past pres., past bd. dirs. Rosa Parks Scholarship Found.; trustee Seed Found., William Beaumont Hosp. Lt. USNR, 1967-69. Named one of Best Lawyers in Am. Mem. ATLA, ABA (vice chmn. media and law com.), State Bar of Mich. (chmn. media and law com.), Birmingham Athletic Club, Detroit Athletic Club, Otsego Ski Club, Village Club. Home: 1601 Quarton Rd Birmingham MI 48009-1037 Office: Butzel Long 150 W Jefferson Ave Ste 900 Detroit MI 48226-4416

RASSIN, BARRY JONATHAN, health science facility administrator; b. London, June 28, 1947; arrived in Bahamas, 1947; s. Meyer and Rosetta (House) R.; children: Pascale, Michele, Anthony; m. Esther Knowles, Nov. 24, 1990. BBA, U. Miami, 1971; MBA, U. Fla., 1973. Adminstrv. intern Miami Heart Inst., Miami Beach, Fla., 1971; asst. dir. Mt. Sinai Med. Ctr., Miami Beach, Fla., 1973-77; adminstr.-at-large Am. Medicorp, Inc., Pompano Beach, Fla., 1977; adminstr. Doctors Hosp. of Hollywood, Fla., 1978; adminstr. Doctors Hosp. Health Sys., Nassau, Bahamas, 1979—, chmn., CEO, 1999—; founding pres. Nat. Health Edn. Coun., Nassau, 1980-82, 86; chmn. Bahamas Quality Coun., 1997-99; bd. dirs. Bahamas Supermarkets, Winn-Dixie; pres. Project Read Bahamas. Mem. Nat. Commn. for Physically Disabled, Nassau, 1981, adv. bd. St. Augustines, Nassau, 1983-88, Bahamas Employers Confedn., Nassau, 1987-88. Fellow Am. Coll. Healthcare Execs.; mem. Am. Hosp. Assn., Nassau C. of C. (com. chmn. 1980-82, bd. dirs. 1996-97), Rotary (pres. East Nassau 1987-88, dist. gov. 1991-92, Svc. Above Self Internat. award). Avocations: golf, boating. Office: Doctors Hosp, PO Box N972, Nassau Bahamas

RASSKAZOV, ALEXANDER OLEGOVICH, mechanics educator; b. Kiev, Ukraine, July 12, 1940; s. Oleg Alexandrovich and Katherine Georgievna (Bashkirova) R.; m. Nina Vladimirovna Kovalevska; children: Andrey, Nataly. Engr., Ukrainian Transport Univ., Kiev, 1962, cand. sci., 1970, DS, 1978. Asst., lectr. Ukrainian Transport Univ., 1962, prof., 1980-84, head of chair, 1984—, dean of mechanical faculty, 1985—. Author: Theory and Calculation of Layered Orthotropical Plates and Shells, 1986, Automatization of Calculations of Transport Construction Structures, 1989, Ultimate Equilibrium State of Shells, 1978, Carrying Capacity of Thin Wall Structures, 1990. Recipient Scientific award Acad. Sci. Ukraine, 1986, State Prize of Coun. of Min. Ukraine, 1994, Honored Activist Sci. & Tech., Ukraine, 1990. Fellow Inst. of Mechanics, Ukrainian Transport Univ. Home: Krasnoarmeiskaja str 120 Apt 21, 252006 Kiev Ukraine Office: Ukrainian Transport Univ, Suvorov str 1, 252010 Kiev Ukraine

RASSU, SERGIO GIANFANCO, physician, healthcare educator, editor; b. Sassari, Italy, June 26, 1953; s. Pietro and Vittoria (Muresu) R.; m. Giannina Nali, Sept. 8, 1979; children: Francesca, Pietro, Maria. M, Liceo Classico, Sassari, 1972; MD, U. Sassari, 1978. Asst. Hosp./U. Sassari, 1978-82, asst. emergency dept., 1982-91, dep. dir. emergency dept., 1991-99, dir. emergency dept., 2000—; prof. Inst. of Higher Edn. in Physics, U. Sassari, 1981-84, prof. Sch. of Hygiene, 1982-99; cons. Italian Soc. Emergency Medicine 1993-97. Editor Caleidoscopio, 1983, Jour. Preventive Medicine and Hygiene, 1991, Pandora, 1991, Jour. Clin. Ligand Assay, 1996. Mem. Italian Soc. Emergency Medicine. Avocations: educational videotapes, swimming, gardening. Home: Via P Nenni 6, 07100 Sassari Italy

RASTEGAR-DJAVAHERY, NADER E., private equities investor; b. Tehran, Iran, May 12, 1953; came to U.S., 1982; s. Morteza and Rabe'eh (Baghai-Kermani) R.; m. Soheila Gharai, Apr. 1979; children: Roya Z., Scheherazade B., Maryam A. BSc, U. Wis., 1976; MBA, Iran Ctr. Mgmt. Studies, 1979. Pres. Shahgard Indsl. Co., Tehran, 1977, Renafa, Inc., Atlanta, 1984—. Contbr. articles to various publs. Active various profl., historical, philatelical and environ. socs. and groups. Lt. Iranian Armed Forces, 1977-78. Avocations: historical research, social welfare, environmental issues, philatelics.

RASUL, MOHAMMAD GOLAM, engineer, researcher; b. Pabna, Rajshahi, Bangladesh, Oct. 30, 1963; arrived in Australia, 1991; s. Mohammad Abdul Kadir and Mosammat Rigia Bhanu Khatun; m. Ratna Islam, Feb. 4, 1993; children: Raqeeb, Rafeeqah. BSME, Bangladesh U. Engring. & Tech., Dhaka, 1987; M in Engring., Asian Inst. Tech., Bangkok, 1990; PhD, U. Queensland, Brisbane, Australia, 1996. Lectr. Bangladesh Inst. of Tech., Chittagong, 1987-88; rsch. assoc. Asian Inst. of Tech., Bangkok, 1990-91; tutor U. Queensland, Brisbane, 1992-95, rsch. fellow, 1996, rsch. officer, 1998—; lectr. U. Malaya, Kuala Lumpur, Malaysia, 1997-98. Contbr. articles to profl. jours. Grantee Australian Rsch. Coun., 1994, UNESCO, 1989. Mem. Inst. of Engrs. (Australia), Alumni Assn. of Asian Inst. Tech. Avocations: soccer, cricket, reading articles. Office: Univ Queensland, QLD Brisbane 4072, Australia

RASVAN, VLADIMIR B., mathematics educator, consultant; b. Bucharest, Romania, May 20, 1945; s. Berthold A. and Frederica I. (Avram) R.; m. Ecaterina R. Taralunga, Jan. 11, 1975. B degree, Nat. Coll., Bucharest, 1962; diploma in engring., Polytech. Inst., Bucharest, 1967, PhD in Engring., 1972. Jr. rschr. Power Inst. Romanian Acad., Bucharest, 1967-69, rsch. engr. Power Rsch. and Design Inst., 1972-75, sr. rschr., 1975-82; assoc. prof. Craiova (Romania) U., 1982-90, prof., faculty dean, 1990—; cons. Nat. Aerospace Isnt., Bucharest, 1993—. Author: Absolute Stability of Delay Control Systems, 1975, Stability Theory, 1987; co-author: Application of Liapunov Methods, 1993; contbr. more than 50 articles to profl. jours. Mem. IEEE (sr.). Avocations: philosophy and history of science and ideas, hiking. Office: Craiova U, A I Cuza St No 13, RO-1100 Craiova Romania

RATANASRI, TAWEESAK, military officer; b. Haadyai, Sonokhla, Thailand, Oct. 13, 1950; s. Jitt and Sawat (Dhammapandh) R.; m. Mukda Inta, Dec. 9, 1978; children: Chalermkiat, Chalermpon. BA in Anthropology, Silpakorn U., Bangkok, Thailand, 1974. Attache to sect. Supreme Command, Bangkok, 1978-95, asst. divsn. dir., group capt., 1995—. Home: 88/23212 Prachachuen St, Bangkok Thailand Office: Supreme Command Hdqrs, Chaengwattana St, Bangkok Thailand

RATCLIFF, MICHAEL, solitictor; b. Plymouth, Devon, U.K., Feb. 27, 1957; s. David John and Margaret Elizabeth (Daymond) R.; m. Catherine Jane Pannell, Sept. 3, 1988; children: Christopher James, Joanna Clare. BA, Oxford U., 1978, BCL, 1980. Solicitor of the Supreme Ct. Articled clk. Masons, London, 1980-82; solicitor Lovell, White & King, London, 1982-88; solicitor Denton Wilde Sapte, London, 1988-89, ptnr., 1989—. Author: (with others) Tolleys Insolvency Service, 1996; contbr. articles to profl. jours. Mem. Law Soc., Exeter West Group (sec.). Avocations: railway enthusiast, walking. Office: Wilde Sapte, 1 Fleet Pl, London EC4M 7WS, England

RATCLIFFE, FREDERICK WILLIAM, university librarian; b. May 28, 1927; s. Sydney and Dora Ratcliffe; m. Joyce Brierley, 1952; 3 children. MA, Manchester U., PhD; MA, Cambridge U. From asst. cataloguer to cataloguer Manchester U., 1954-62; sub-libr. Glasgow U., 1962-63; dep. libr. U. Newcastle upon Tyne, 1963-65; univ. libr. John Rylands U. Libr. Manchester U., 1965-80, dir., 1972-80; univ. libr. U. Cambridge, 1980-94, emeritus univ. libr., 1994—; Parker Librarian, Corpus Christi Coll. Cambridge U., 1995-2000; hon. lectr. hist. bibliography Manchester U., 1970-80; external prof. dept. libr. and info. studies Loughborough U., 1982-86; Sandars reader bibliography Cambridge U., 1988-89. Author: Preservation Policies and Conservation in British Libraries, 1984; contbr. articles to profl. jours. Justice of the peace, Stockport, 1972-80, Cambridge, 1981-97; chmn. adv. com. Nat. Preservation Office, 1984-94; chmn. libr. panel The Wellcome Trust, 1988-93; trustee St. Deiniol's Libr., Hawarden, 1975-98, Cambridge Found., 1989-93, Malaysian Commonwealth Studies Ctr., 1995-98. Decorated Comdr. of Brit. Empire, Encomienda de la Orden del Merito Civil (Spain); fellow Corpus Christi Coll., 1980—, Chpt. Woodard Schs., 1981-97; hon. student sch. of libr. and info. studies U. Coll. London U., 1987—; Grad. Rsch. scholar Manchester U., 1951-53. Fellow Libr. Assn. (hon.). Avocations: book collecting, hand printing, cricket. Office: Ridge House, Rickinghall Superior, Diss, Norfolk IP221DY, England

RATCLIFFE, KERMIT HERMAN, theology educator; b. Arlington, Ala., May 30, 1941; s. William Sr. and Lonia (Jackson) R.; m. Bertha L. Grayson, June 3, 1967; children: Andre' Kermit, Olivia Yvonne. BTh, Concordia Theol. Sem., Springfield, Ill., 1966; MDiv, Pitts. Theol. Sem., 1971; M Sacred Theology, Concordia Sem., St. Louis, 1980, D in Ministry, 1998. Ordained 1966. Pastor Prince of Peace Luth. Ch., Birmingham, Ala., 1966-69, Holy Cross Evang. Luth. Ch., Pitts., 1969-72, St. John-Unity Luth. Ch., East St. Louis, Ill., 1972-82, St. Paul Luth. Ch., Dallas, 1982-91; pastor assoc., chaplain St. Mary Hosp., East St. Louis, 1980-82; assoc. prof. theology Concordia U., Milw., 1991—; chaplain USAR hosp. Twenty First Gen. Hosp., St. Louis, 1974-76, 520th Maintenance USAR Battalion, St. Louis, 1976-83, USAR 493d Engr. Group, Dallas, 1983-91, HHC 4th Brigade 84th Divsn., Milw., 1991-93, divsn. chaplain, 1993—. Author: Which Way for Black Churches, Lutheran Witness, 1977; contbr. to Black Luth. Centennial, Luth. Women Quar., 1977, chpt. to book: African American, 1996. With USAR, 1974—. Mem. Res. Officer Assn., World Jewish Congress, Concordia Hist. Inst., Issues in Higher Edn. Office: Concordia U Wis 12800 N Lake Shore Dr Mequon WI 53097-2418

RATCLIFFE, SIMON TOBY, electronics executive; b. London, Eng., Sept. 26, 1953; s. John Montague Ratcliffe and Pauline Pavline (Atkinson) Scott; m. Hanan Edward Fahmi Yanny, Mar. 24, 1990; children: Julian Yanny, Amy Yanny. BArch, U. Witwatersrand, Johannesburg, S.A., 1981, BA with honors, 1983; MSc, U. Coll., London, 1989; MBA, Warwick Bus. Sch., Coventry, Eng., 1994. Coord. Media and Resource Svcs., Johannesburg, S.A., 1983-85, Planact, Johannesburg, S.A., 1986-88; arch. ARUP Assoc., London, 1988-89, U. Coll., London, 1988-89; urban affairs specialist UN Devel. Programme, Khartoum, Sudan, 1991-92; dir. Endeva Cons., Cape Town, S.A., 1993—. Treas. S.A. Vol. Svcs., Johannesburg, 1973-77, Johannesburg Dem. Action Com., 1984-85. Mem. The Strategic Planning Soc. Avocations: running, cycling, photography, computer graphics. Office: Commerce One S Africa Fl 4, Protea Pl Protea Rd Claremont, Cape Town 7708, South Africa

RATH, BISWANATH, physics educator; b. Puri, India, Mar. 3, 1955; s. Dasarathi and Dinamani (Sarangi) R.; m. Sabita Kar, May 19, 1983; children: Smruti, Sonali. BSc, Utkal U., 1975, MS, 1977, D of Philosophy, 1996; M of Philosophy, Ctrl. U., 1990. Lectr. in physics Engring. Coll., Warangal, India, 1981-84; lectr. in physics Govt. Coll. of Orissa, Keonjhar, India, 1984-87, Cuttack, India, 1987-92; sr. lectr. in physics Govt. Coll. of Orissa, Berhampur, 1992-95, Cuttack, 1995—. Contbr. articles to profl. jours. Fellowship Ctrl. U. Hyderabad, 1980; scholarship Govt. of Orissa, 1975. Mem. Orissa Phys. Soc. Avocations: reading short stories, visiting temples of worship. Home: At-Sriramnagar, PO Bhubaneswar, 751002 Khurda India Office: Ravenshaw Coll, 753003 Cuttack India

RATH, R. JOHN, historian, educator; b. St. Francis, Kans., Dec. 12, 1910; s. John and Barbara (Schauer) R.; m. Isabel Jones, June 26, 1937; children: Laurens John (dec.), Donald (dec.), Isabel Ferguson. A.B., U. Kans., 1932; A.M., U. Calif., Berkeley, 1934; Ph.D., Columbia U., 1941. Instr. history U. Ark., 1936-37, summer vis. prof., 1947; pre-doctoral field fellow Social Sci. Research Council in Austria and Italy, 1937-38; instr. history Coll. Puget Sound, Tacoma, Wash., 1938-39; head dept. history and polit. sci. Lindenwood Coll., St. Charles, Mo., 1939-41; assoc. prof. history Miss. State Coll. for Women, 1941-43; chief bur. documentary evidence UNRRA Bur. Documents and Tracing, U.S. Zone of Ger., 1945-46; asst. prof. history U. Ga., 1946-47; assoc. prof. history, assoc. editor Jour. Central European Affairs, U. Colo., 1947-51, vis. prof., summer 1958; prof. history U. Tex., Austin, 1951-63; prof. history, chmn. dept. history and polit. sci. Rice U., 1963-68, Mary Gibbs Jones prof., 1968-80, prof. emeritus, 1980—; prof. history U. Minn., Mpls., 1980-85; vis. prof. U. Wis., 1955, Duke U., 1963; Guggenheim fellow in Italy, 1956-57. Author: The Fall of the Napoleonic Kingdom of Italy, 1941, The Viennese Revolution 1948, 1957, L'amministrazione austriaca nel Lombardo Veneto, 1814-21, 1959, The Austrian Provisional Regime in Lombardy Venetia, 1969, The Deterioration of Democracy in Austria, 1927-1932, 1996, The Molding of Engelbert Dollfuss as an Agrarian Reformer, 1997; contbg. author: The Fate of East Central Europe (editor Stephen Kertesz), 1956, East Central Europe and the World (edited S. Kertesz), 1962; also Ency. Americana; founder, editor: Austrian History Newsletter, 1960-63, Austrian History Yearbook, 1965-82; contbr. Die Aufloesung des Habsburgerreiches, 1970, Native Fascism in the Successor States, 1971, Beitraege zur Zeitgeschichte, 1976, The Austrian Socialist Experiment, 1985, The Mirror of History, 1988, Austria, 1938-88, 1995. Recipient 1st class Austrian Cross of Honor in arts and scis., 1963. Mem. Am. Hist. Soc. (com. internat. activities 1960-66, exec. com. modern European history sect. 1963-66), So. Hist. Soc. (chmn. European sect. 1961-62, exec. coun. 1965-68), Soc. Italian Hist. Studies (Sr. Scholar Citation 1984), Conf. Ctrl. European History (nat. exec. bd. 1959-61, chmn. 1970, com. on Austrian history 1957-68, 70-81, exec. sec. 1957-68), Am. Assn.

Study of Hungarian History (chmn. 1978), Southwestern Social Sci. Assn. (pres. 1976-77), Austrian Acad. Sci. (corr.), Deputazione di Storia Patria par le Venezie (corr.), Phi Beta Kappa. Address: Woodside Manor 1050 Pilgrim Way Apt 209 Green Bay WI 54304-5879

RATHBONE, JULIAN, writer; b. London, Feb. 10, 1935. BA with honors, Magdalene Coll., Cambridge, Eng., 1958. Tchr. various schs. Turkey, 1959-62, Eng., 1962-73; lit. cons. Royal Berkshire Librs., 1984. Author: (novels) Diamonds Bid, 1966, Hand Out, 1968, With My Knives I Know I'm Good, 1969, Trip Trap, 1972, Kill Cure, 1975, Bloody Marvelous, 1975, King Fisher Lives, 1976 (Booker prize nomination 1976), Carnival!, 1976, A Raving Monarchist, 1977, (with Hugh Ross Williamson) The Princess, a Nun, 1978, Joseph: The Life of Joseph Bosham, Self-Styled 3d Viscount of Bosham, Covering the Years from 1790 to 1813, 1979 (Booker prize nomination 1979), The Euro-Killers, 1979, A Last Resort - For These Times, 1980, Base Case, 1981, A Spy of the Old School, 1982, Watching the Detectives, 1983, Nasty, Very: A Mock Epic in Six Parts, 1984, Lying in State, 1985, Greenfinger, 1987, Crystal Contract, 1988, ZDT, 1988 (Deutsche Krimi Preis 1989), The Pandora Option, 1990, Dangerous Games, 1991, Sand Blind, 1993, Intimacy, 1995, Accidents Will Happen, 1995, Blame Hitler, 1997, The Last English King, 1997, Brandenburg Concerto, 1998, Trajectories, 1998, Kings of Albion, 2000, (radio play) Albert and the Truth about Rats, 1990, Dangerous Games, 1994, (screenplay) for West Deutscher Rundfunk, President Mega (screenplay) for West Deutscher Rundfunk, The Last English King (screenplay) for Geoffrey Reeve Films; editor: Wellington's War: His Peninsular Dispatches, 1983; contbr. to Guardian, New Statesman, The Literary Rev., Independent on Sunday. Recipient So. Arts Bursary, 1978, CWA Silver Dagger for Best Short Story, 1993, Swanage Internat. Poetry prize, 1994. Office: Sea View, Sch Rd Thorney Hill Near Christchurch, Dorset BH23 8DS, England

RATHBURN, ROBERT CHARLES, retired educator; b. Chgo., Dec. 17, 1918; s. Harold Beecher and Lilian (Young) R.; m. Louise Evelyn Jones, Aug. 21, 1948. BA cum laude, Northwestern U., 1941, MA, 1942; PhD, U. Minn., 1956. Reporter Cedar Rapids (Iowa) Gazette, 1941; tchg. asst. Northwestern U., Evanston, Ill., 1941-42, U. Pa., Phila., 1945; YMCA sec. Northwestern U., Evanston, Ill., 1943; from instr. to assoc. prof. U. Minn., Mpls., 1946-69, prof., 1969-87, prof. emeritus, 1987—. Author: From Jane Austen to Joseph Conrad, 1958, 75 Prose Pieces, 1961. Bd. dirs. YMCA, U. Minn., 1950-59, bd. dirs., Mpls., 1964-69. Mem. MLA, AAUP, Soc. Profl. Journalists, Phi Beta Kappa. Avocation: reading. Home: 2360 Chilcombe Ave Saint Paul MN 55108-1626

RATHER, DAN, broadcast journalist; b. Wharton, Tex., Oct. 31, 1931; m. Jean Goebel; children: Dawn Robin, Dan M. B.A. in Journalism, Sam Houston State Tchrs. Coll., Huntsville, Tex., 1953; student, U. Houston, South Tex. Sch. Law. Instr. journalism Sam Houston State Coll., for 1 year; later worked for U.P.I. and Houston Chronicle; with CBS, 1962—; joined staff of radio Sta. KTRH (CBS affiliate), Houston; staying about 4 years as news writer, reporter, and later, as news dir.; became dir. news and pub. affairs with CBS Houston TV affiliate KHOU-TV, in the late 1950's; became White House corr., 1964; and then transferred to overseas burs., including chief of London bur., 1965-66, then worked in Vietnam, returned to White House position in fall of 1966; appearing nightly on segments of CBS Evening News; became anchorman-corr. for CBS Reports, 1974-75; co-editor 60 Minutes, CBS-TV, 1975-81; anchorman Dan Rather Reporting, CBS Radio Network, 1977—; anchorman, mng. editor CBS Evening News with Dan Rather, 1981—; co-editor show Who's Who, CBS-TV, 1977; anchor 48 Hours, 1986—; anchored numerous CBS News spl. programs. Author: (with Gary Gates) The Palace Guard, 1974, (with Mickey Herskowitz) The Camera Never Blinks, 1977, The Camera Never Blinks Twice: The Further Adventures of a Television Journalist, 1994, (with Peter Wyden) Memoirs, I Remember, 1991; editor Our Times, 1994. Recipient numerous Emmy awards; honors include dedication of Dan Rather Comm. Bldg., classroom facility Sam Houston State U., Huntsville, Tex. Office: CBS News 524 W 57th St New York NY 10019-2924

RATHIE, PUSHPA NARAYAN, statistician, mathematician; b. Nasirabad, Rajasthan, India, Nov. 16, 1941; s. Chaugan Mal and Sobhagyawati (Dodya) R.; m. Shanta Lakhotia, Nov. 19, 1965; children: Alok, Asha, Aman. BS, U. Rajasthan, 1961; MS, U. Jodhpur, India, 1963, PhD, 1965. Lectr. U. Jodhpur, 1963-66, Malaviya Regional Engring. Coll., Jaipur, 1966-73; asst. prof. Indian Inst. Tech., Bombay, 1973-75; prof. Universidade Estadual de Campinas, Brazil, 1975-91, Universidade Fed. de Minas Gerais, Belo Horizonte, Brazil, 1991-93, U. Brasilia, Brazil, 1993—; rsch. coord. Financiadora de Estudos e Projectos, Campinas, 1986-91; rsch. cons. Cooperativa de Desenvolvimento Tecnologico, Campinas, 1977-79; sci.-tech. advisor Fundacão de Amparo à Pesquisa do Estado de São Paulo, Brazil, 1975-91; sci. advisor Cooperaçãao de Aperfeiçomento de Pessoal de Nível Superior, Brasilia, 1994—. Author: (with A.M. Mathai) Some Basic Concepts in Information Theory, 1975, (with A.M. Mathai) Probability and Statistics, 1977, Probabilidade, 1996; mng. editor Internat. Jour. Math. and Statis. Scis., 1992—. Recipient Gold medal U. Rajasthan, 1961, Merit scholarship Govt. India, 1961-63, Gold medal U. Jodhpur, 1963. Mem. Am. Math. Soc., Internat. Jour. Math. and Statis. Scis. (founder, mng. editor 1992—), Indian Math. Soc. Avocations: tennis, chess, badminton, playing cards, reading. Home: Colina Bloco F Apt 604, 70910900 Brasília D.F., Brazil Office: EST/IED/UNB, Asa Norte, 70910900 Brasília D.F., Brazil

RATHKE, DALE LAWRENCE, community organizer and financial analyst; b. Rangely, Colo., Mar. 16, 1950; s. Edmann Jacob and Cornelia Ruth (Ratliff) R. BA, Yale U., 1971; MA, Princeton U., 1974, ABD, 1977. Dir. internal ops. Assn. of Cmty. Orgns. for Reform Now (ACORN), New Orleans, 1977—; CFO Citizens' Cons. Inc., New Orleans, 1979—; fin. dir. ACORN Housing Corp., New Orleans, 1984—, Affiliated Media Found. Movement, 1979—; sec.-treas. Broad St. Corp., New Orleans, 1986—, Elysian Fields Corp., New Orleans, 1986—, Greenwell Springs Corp., New Orleans, 1989—, ACORN Fund, Inc., New Orleans, 1991—, ACORN Beneficial Assn., Inc., New Orleans, 1991—, Houston Orgn. and Support Ctr., 1992—, St. Louis Orgn. and Support Ctr., 1992—. Pres. Assn. for Rights of Citizens, New Orleans, 1980—, ACORN Cultural Trust, Inc., 1988—; active Overture to Cultural Season, 1987—, treas., 1999—; active New Orleans Mus. Art, 1990—; dirs., assoc. treas. Raintree Svcs., Inc., 1998—, Santa Fe Opera Guild, 1995—, Metrolitan Opera Guild, 1998—. Mem. Yale Club of N.Y.C., Princeton Club of N.Y.C., Metairie County Club. Avocations: 18th century French furniture, English country homes. Office: ACORN 1024 Elysian Fields Ave New Orleans LA 70117-8454

RATHKOLB, OLIVER ROBERT, historian; b. Vienna, Austria, Nov. 3, 1955; s. Otto Aurelius and Margarete (Novy) R.; m. Lydia Rueckinger, Dec. 30, 1987; children: Victor Xaver Emanuel, Vincent Johannes Alexander. LLD, U. Vienna, 1978, PhD, 1982. Sci. researcher Inst. Contemporary History, Vienna, 1981-84; sci. asst. Ludwig Boltzmann Inst fuer Geschichte und Gesellschaft, Vienna, 1984—; dir. Ludwig Boltzmann Inst fuer Geschichte und Gesellschaft, 1994—; sci. dir. Bruno Kreisky Archives, Vienna, 1985—; rsch. coord. Bruno Kreisky Forum for Internat. Dialogue, 1992—. Author and editor: Gesellschaft und Politik in der Zweiten Republik, 1985, Es ist schwer jung zu sein. Jugend und Demokratie in Oesterreich 1918-1988, 1988, Fuehrertreu und Gottbegnadet. Kuenstlereliten im Dritten Reich, 1991, Insel Oesterreich Politische Geschichte 1945-2000, 2001; co-editor: Der Junge Kreisky 1931-1945, Verdraengte Schuld-Verfehlte Suehne. Entnazifizierung in Oesterreich 1945-55, 1986, Die veruntreute Wahrheit. Hitler's Propagandisten in Oesterreich, 1938, 1988, Oesterreich und Deutschlands Grösse. Ein schlampiges Verhältnis, 1990. Schumpeter fellow Harvard U., 2000—. Mem. Social Dem. Party. Roman Catholic. Office: Inst Zeitgeschichte, Spitalg 2 Hol 1, 1090 Vienna Austria also: Kreisky-Forum, Armbrustergasse 15, 1190 Vienna Austria

RATHMAYR, RENATE FELICITAS, Slavonic language educator; b. Graz, Styria, Austria, Apr. 28, 1947; d. Wilhelm and Ruth (Gropengiesser) Baierle; m. Bernhard Rathmayr, Jan. 3, 1973; children: Philipp, Michael. Magister, U. Graz, 1971; Doctorate, U. Innsbruck, Austria, 1975, Dozentin, 1985. Cert. translator Russian and French. Tchr. U. Innsbruck, 1971-89; guest prof. U. Hamburg, Germany, 1988-89; prof., head dept. Slavonic langs. Econ. U. Vienna, Austria, 1989—; cons. Russistik/Rusistika mag., Berlin, 1989—, Die russischen Partikel als Pragmalexeme, 1985. Author: Pragmatik der Entschuldigungen, 1996; co-author: Verhandeln mit Russen, 1992, Pons-Fachwörterbuch Marktwirtschaft, 1993, Verhandeln mit Tschechischen Wirtschaftspartnern, 1995. Mem. Internat. Pragmatic Assn. Avocations: skiing, mountain climbing, music, theatre, swimming. Office: Econ U Dept Slav Langs, Rossauer Laende 23/II, 1090 Vienna Austria

RATHORE, RUPAK, computer consultant; b. Rampur, India, Aug. 15; s. Krishna Chandra Pal and Veena Rathore. B of Chem. Engring., U. Roorkee, India, 1996. Asst. systems analyst Tata Consultancy Svcs., Delhi, India, 1996—. Founder, tech. cons. (news mag.) Watch Out, 1994. Nat. Sci. Talent Search scholar, 1990. Avocations: billiards, snooker, computer programming. Office e-mail: rupak@lucent.com. Fax: 31356875822. Home: Naarderstraat 28-B, 1211 AL Hilversum The Netherlands Office: Lucent Techs, Laarenseweg 50, 1221 CN Hilversum The Netherlands

RATHORE, UMA PANDEY, utilities executive; b. Mar. 5, 1950; d. O Nath and R Devi Pandey; m. Ram N.S. Rathore, Dec. 18, 1978; children: Dinesh, Rana. BS, Kanpur U., 1967, MS, 1969. Adviser Consul Gen. of Iceland to India, 1976-85; v.p. Nevaid Cons., 1974-82; with North Jersey Utilities, Mount Freedom, N.J., 1983—, pres.; sr. ptnr. Translantic Cons.; founder Maxim Imports, 1994—; ind. mgmt. cons.; bd. dirs. Revel Inc., N.Y. Mem. ethics bd. Randolph Twp., N.J., 1986-91, county and state rep. Shongum Sch. PTA, 1989—, mem. multicultural com., 1993-94; membership chmn. LWV, 1979-81, com. person Dem. dist. 3 Randolph Twp., 1992, 94, mem. ethics com., 1994, mem. com., 1995; mem. drug action com. Randolph Twp., 1994, 95, 96—; mem. Dem. task force N.J. Women's Polit. Caucus, 1994; county and state rep. Randolph Intermediate Sch. PTA, 1993-94, bd. edn. rep., 1996—; mem. PTA coun. Randolph Twp. Schs.; legis. chair Morris County Coun. PTA, 1997—, counselor Region I; mem. Morris Mus., Macculloch Hall, Frelinghuysen Arboretum; mem. Ctr. for Study of Presidency, 1997; mem. DBE, 1999. Mem. Internat. Platform Assn., Dau. Brit. Empire, Acad. Polit. Sci., Kiwanis Club Smithsonian, Libr. of Congress, Fgn. Policy Assn., N.Y. Acad. Scis., Nat. Trust Hist. Preservation, Nat. Wildlife Fedn. Democrat. Avocations: reading, jogging, hiking, mountaineering. Home and Office: 3 Hickory Pl Randolph NJ 07869-4528

RATISHVILI, IOSEB, physicist, researcher; b. Tbilissi, Republic of Georgia, Oct. 25, 1935; s. Gabriel and Ariadna (Comneno) R.; m. Natela Namoradze, Oct. 7, 1962. Grad., Tbilissi U., 1958, postgrad., 1960-64, PhD, 1968, Doctor of Phys.-Math. Scis., 1994. Rschr. Inst. Physics, Tbilissi, 1958-82, sr. rschr., 1982-94, leader/rschr., 1996—; maitre de recherche Ecole Polytech., Palaiseau, France, 1995. Contbr. articles to profl. jours. Mem. Phys. Soc. Georgia, N.Y. Acad. Sci. Avocations: playing the violin, home string quartet. Home: Ateni 20 Apt 10, 380079 Tbilissi Republic of Georgia Office: Inst of Physics, 6 Tamarashvili St, 380077 Tbilissi Republic of Georgia

RATIU, INDREI STEPHEN PILKINGTON, management consultant; b. London, July 12, 1946; s. Ion Augustin Nicolae and Elisabeth Blanche (Pilkington) R.; m. Ioana Georgescu, Sept. 28, 1974 (div. 1991); 1 child, Alexandru; m. Ana Maria da Silva Byrd, July 18, 1998. MA, Cambridge (Eng.) U., 1970; MBA, European Inst. Bus. Adminstrn., Fontainebleau, France, 1971. Scriptwriter BBC, London, 1967-69; coord. exec. devel. programs INSEAD, 1971-73, dir. ednl. tech., 1973-76; researcher cross-cultural learning London Bus. Sch., 1976-78; ind. mgmt. cons. personal devel. Paris, 1979-82; mng. ptnr. ICM, Paris, 1983-88; trustee Rainford Trust, Ratiu Family Found. Co-author: Leaders sans Frontieres, 1988; editor spl. issue on multicultural mgmt. devel. Jour. Mgmt. Devel., 1987. Avocations: healing, counseling. Home and Office: The Old Dye House, Spring Gardens, Frome, Somerset BA11 2NZ, England

RATIU, LIVIU GABRIEL, management consultant; b. Botosani, Romania, Nov. 25, 1953; s. Gavrila Ioan and Lidia R.; m. Maria Rascalachi, Aug. 20, 1977 (div.); children: Roxana, Raluca, Ioana; m. Iustina Luca, June 20, 1987; children: Razvan, Ruxandra, Raul. BBA, Railay Coll., Brasov, Romania, 1975; BA, Babes Bolyai U., Cluj, Romania, 1981; MBA, Pacific Western, Calif., 1994. With Pvt. Intelligence, Cluj, 1976-77; station master Romanian Railways, various cities, 1977-80; network mgr. Romanian Railways, Brasov, 1980-92; cons. Info Serv Mgmt. Ltd., Tagru Mures, Romania, 1994-96; chmn. bd. Info Serv Mgmt. Ltd., Tagru Mures, 1996—, gen. mgr.; cons. Romanian Railways. Avocations: amateur radio, martial arts, mountaineering. Office: Info Serv Mgmt Ltd, Liberstatii 109, Targu Mures MS, Romania 4300

RATKE, LORENZ, physicist, materials scientist, researcher; b. Brakel, Nordrhein, Germany, July 31, 1949; s. Ludger and Thea (Wagner) R.; m. Sylvia Arnim-Grimm, Jan. 23, 1979; 1 child, Sharon. Diploma, U. Muenster, Germany, 1975; D Rer Nat., U. Aachen, Germany, 1979, prof., 1997; D habil., U. Stuttgart, Germany, 1988. Rsch. prof. U. Clausthal, Germany, 1979-84; assoc. prof. Max Planck Inst., Stuttgart, Germany, 1984-89; rsch. group leader German Aerospace Ctr., Cologne, Germany, 1988—; head Inst. for Space Simulation German Aerospace Ctr., Cologne, 2000—. Editor: (books) Immiscible Liquid Metals, 1993, Materials and Fluids Under Low Gravity, 1995; contbr. over 100 sci. papers to internat. jours. Recipient Georg-Sachs award German Metal Soc., Oberursel, Germany, 1980, Outstanding Paper award Acta Materialia, Bethesda, Md., 1991. Mem. European Materials Rsch. Soc., German Soc. Crystal Growth, German Phys. Soc., German Materials Soc., Materials Rsch. Soc., N.Y. Acad. Scis. Office: German Aerospace Ctr, 51170 Cologne Germany

RATLEDGE, COLIN, microbial biochemistry educator, researcher; b. County Durham, Eng., Oct. 9, 1936; s. Fred and Freda Smith (Proudlock) R.; m. Janet Vivien Bottomley, Mar. 25, 1961; children: Alison, Stuart, Jane. BScTech, U. Manchester, Eng., 1957, PhD, 1962. Rsch. fellow Med. Rsch. Coun. Ireland, Dublin, 1960-64; rsch. scientist Unilever Ltd., Eng., 1964-67; univ. lectr. biochemistry U. Hull, Eng., 1967-73, sr. lectr., 1973-77, reader, 1977-83; personal prof. U. Hull, 1983—, prof. microbial biochemistry, 1988—, head dept. biochemistry, 1986; chmn. Brit. Coordinating Com. for Biotech., 1988-90; vis. lectr. Australian and New Zealand Socs. Microbiology, 1986; chmn. food rsch. grants Brit. Agrl. and Food Rsch. Coun., 1989-92, mem. food rsch. com., 1989-92; cons. Henkel, ICI, J&E Sturge, Enzymatix, Castrol, BNFL, Gist-brocades, Celsis; sec. Internat. Com. for Econ. and Applied Microbiology, 1991-94. Co-editor: The Biology of the Mycobacteria, Vol. 1, 1982, Vol. 2, 1983, Vol. 3, 1989, Microbial Lipids, Vol. 1, 1988, Vol. 2, 1989, Mycobacteria: Molecular Biology and Virulence, 1999; editor: Biochemistry of Microbial Degradation, 1993; editor-in-chief World Jour. Microbiology and Biotech., 1987—, Biotech. Techniques, 1987-99, Biotech. Letters, 1996—. Fellow Internat. Inst. Biotech., London, 1993. Fellow Royal Soc. Chemistry (chartered chemist), Inst. Biology (chartered biologist, chmn. indsl. biol. com. 1993—), Kathleen Barton-Wright Meml. lectr. 1994); mem. Soc. for Gen. Microbiology (coun. 1975-79, publ. officer 1980-85), Biochem. Soc., Am. Soc. Microbiology, Am. Oil Chemists Soc., Royal Soc. Arts, Soc. Chem. Industry (coun. 1991-93, v.p. 1993—). Avocations: hill walking, bonsai gardening, chess. Home: 49 Church Dr, Leven HU17 5LH, England Office: U Hull, Dept Biol Scis, Hull HU6 7RX, England

RATLIFF, CHARLES EDWARD, JR., economics educator; b. Morven, N.C., Oct. 13, 1926; s. Charles Edward and Mary Katherine (Liles) R.; m. Mary Virginia Heilig, Dec. 8, 1945; children: Alice Ann, Katherine Virginia, John Charles. BS, Davidson Coll., 1947; AM, Duke U., 1951, PhD, 1955; postgrad., U. N.C., Harvard, Columbia. Instr. econs. and bus. Davidson Coll., 1947-48, asst. prof., 1948-49; scholar econs. Duke, 1949-51; faculty Davidson (N.C.) Coll., 1951-60, prof., 1960—, chmn. dept. econs., 1966-83, Charles A. Dana prof., 1967-77, William R. Kenan prof., 1977-92, Kenan prof. emeritus, 1992—; prof. econs. Forman Christian Coll., Lahore, Pakistan, 1963-66, 69-70; summer vis. prof. U. N.C. at Charlotte, 1958, 60, Appalachian State U., 1962, Punjab U., Pakistan, 1963-64, Kinnaird Coll., Pakistan, 1965, Fin. Svcs. Acad., Pakistan, 1966, NDEA Inst. in Asian History, 1968; lectr. U.S. Cultural Affairs Office, East and West Pakistan, 1969-70. Author: Interstate Apportionment of Business Income for State Income Tax Purposes, 1962, A World Development Fund, 1987, Economics at Davidson: A Sesquicentennial History, 1987; co-author textbooks; contbg. author: Dictionary of the Social Sciences, 1964, Distinguished Teachers on Effective Teaching, 1986, Those Who Teach, 1988, Britain-USA: A Survey in Key Words, 1991; mem. editorial bd. Growth and Change: A Journal of Urban and Regional Policy, 1993-99; contbr. articles to profl. jours. Mem. Mayor's Com. on Affordable Housing, Davidson, 1996-97, Mayor's Com. Comty. Rels., Davidson, 1973-80, chmn., 1973-78; mem. Mecklenburg County Housing and Devel. Commn., 1975-81; mem. exec. com. Mecklenburg Dem. Com., 1967-69, precinct com., 1967-69, 72-74, 89-99, issues com., 1979-99, nat. bd. dirs. Rural Advancement Fund Nat. Sharecroppers Fund, Inc., 1978-94, exec. com., 1981-94, treas., 1981-94; mem. Mecklenburg County Comty. and Rural Devel. Exec. Com., 1981-99; bd. dirs. Bread for the World, Inc., 1983-84, Pines Retirement Comty., 1990-99, Crisis Assistance Ministry, 1992-96, Davidson Coll. Devel. Corp., 1992-95, Our Towns Habitat for Humanity, 1996-98, Davidson Coll. Alumni Assn., 1997-99, Davidson Affordable Housing Coalition, 1997-99; bd. advisors Mecklenburg Ministries, 1992-99, Drs. for Global Health, 1996—; mem. planning com. Fla. Presbyn. Homes, Inc., 2000—, spiritual life com., 2000—. With USN, 1944-46. Rsch. grant Ford Found., 1960-61, Fulbright-Hays grant, 1973; Rsch. fellow Inter-Univ. Com. Econ. Rsch. on South, 1960-61; recipient Thomas Jefferson award Davidson Coll., 1972, Gold medalist Prof. of Yr. award Coun. Advancement and Support of Edn., 1985, Tchg. Excellence and Campus Leadership award Sear Roebuck Found., 1991, Hunter-Hamilton Love of Tchr. award, 1992. Mem. AAUP, So. Econ. Assn. (exec. com. 1961-63, v.p. 1975-76, N.C. corr. So. Econ. Jour.), Am. Econ. Assn., So. Fin. Assn. (exec. com. 1966-68), Nat. Tax Assn. (chmn. interstate allocation and apportionment of bus. income com. 1972-74), Assn. Asian Studies, Fulbright Alumni Assn., Old Catawba Soc., Phi Beta Kappa, Omicron Delta Kappa (Teaching award 1991). Home: 29 Lake Hunter Dr Lakeland FL 33803-1288

RATLIFF, GERALD LEE, academic administrator/speech and theater educator; b. Middletown, Ohio, Oct. 23, 1944; s. Ray and Peggy (Donisi) R. BA magna cum laude, Georgetown (Ky.) Coll., 1967; MA, U. Cin., 1970; PhD, Bowling Green (Ohio) State U., 1975. Area head English theatre Glenville State Coll., 1970-72; prof., chair theatre Montclair State Coll., Upper Montclair, N.J., 1975-92; dean Sch. Fine and Performing Arts Ind.-Purdue U., Ft. Wayne, Ind., 1993-95; dean Coll. Arts and Architecture Mont. State U., Bozeman, Mont., 1995—; assoc. v.p. acad. affairs SUNY, Potsdam, 1997—; feature writer Lexington (Ky.) Herald-News, 1967-68. Author: Beginning Scene Study: Aristophanes to Albee, 1980, Speech and Drama Club Activities, 1982, Oedipus Trilogy, 1984, Combating Stagefright, 1985, Playscript Interpretation and Production, 1985, (Machiavelli's) The Prince, 1986, (with Suzanne Trauth) Introduction to Musical Theatre, 1986, Playing Scenes: A Sourcebook for Performance, 1993, Playing Contemporary Scenes: A Sourcebook for Performance, 1996; contbr. articles and revs. to profl. jours. Exec. coun. mem. Assn. for Commn. Adminstrn., 1995—; bd. dirs. Am. Conf. Acad. Deans. Fulbright scholar, 1989; recipient Nat. Medallion of Honor award Theta Alpha Phi, 1989; Alumni Assn. faculty rsch. grantee, 1980, 83, 86. Mem. Speech Comm. Assn. (legis. coun. 1987-88, chair theatre divsn. 1986-87), Am. Assn. Theatre in Secondary Edn. (nat. bd. dirs. 1986-87), Secondary Sch. Theatre Assn. (nat. bd. dirs. 1983-86), Internat. Arts Assn. (v.p. 1975-76), Ea. Comm. Assn. (exec. sec. 1986-89, 1st v.p. elect 1989, exec. com. 1986—, pres. 1991, Disting. Svc. award 1993, Disting. Svc. Tchg. award 1998), Theta Alpha Phi (nat. pres. 1984-87, nat. coun. 1979-82, 84-87). Avocations: writing, softball. Home: 2 Morningside Dr Potsdam NY 13676-3305

RATLIFF, WILLIAM D., III, lawyer; b. Ft. Worth, Aug. 25, 1949; s. William D. and Barbara (Warner) R.; m. Julie Martin, Oct. 4, 1980; children: William D., Emily Martin. B.B.A., U. Tex., 1971, J.D., 1974; LL.M., So. Meth. U., 1975. Law clk. U.S. Tax Ct., Washington, 1975-77; mem. Cantey, Hanger, Gooch, Munn & Collins, Ft. Worth, 1977-84, Haynes and Boone, Ft. Worth, 1984—. Fellow Am. Coll. Trust and Estate Counsel, Tex. Bd. Legal Specialization (cert.), Tex. Bar Found.; mem. ABA, State Bar Tex. Republican. Clubs: Ft. Worth, Rivercrest Country. Office: Haynes and Boone 901 Main St Ste 3100 Dallas TX 75202-3789*

RATNAYAKE, PARAKRAMA PAUL, health care scientist, physician; b. Kandy, Britain, Apr. 5, 1946; s. Wilson Richard and Rebecca Biso (Haluwana) R.; m. Chandani Wasantha Navaratne, May 8, 1976; 1 child, Rashika. Degree in Homeopathic Medicine, Internat. Coll. Nat. Health Sc, Lodnon, 1986, Degree Philosophy Naturopathic Medicine, 1988. Trainee, med. asst. Bexley Hosp., Kent, Eng., 1965-68; merchandising officer Internat. Tea Mkt. Expansion Bd., London, 1968-75; exec. mgr. Zamag Ltd., London, 1975-79; asst. to head solid dossage medicine Eblon Ltd., Allschwil, Switzerland, 1980-89; head solid dossage medicine Mepha Ltd., Aesch, Switzerland, 1989—; co-dir. Carat Cons., Aesch, 1997; pastoral counselor Holistic Health and Healing Min.; practitioner spiritual healing; chmn., dir. Belgrave Mgmt. Ltd.; dir. Merit award IBC, Cambridge, Eng., others. Minister, baron Universal Life Ch. Grantee Philosophy of Human Sci., U. Metaphysics, Calif., 1997, Holistic Philosophy, 1997; recipient Incorporating Outstanding award, Outstanding People of the 20th Century award, Cambridge, Eng. Mem. World Svc. Authority (registered), Assn. for Health and Human Scis. (founder, chmn. 1997—), Am. Metaphys. Drs. Assn. (registered mem.), Brit. Holistic Health Scis. Assn. Buddhist. Avocations: photography, video, travel, music, painting. Office: Mepha Ltd Pharms, Dornacherstrasse 114, CH-4147 Aesch Basel, Switzerland

RATNER, BUDDY DENNIS, bioengineer, educator; b. Bklyn., Jan. 19, 1947; s. Philip and Ruth Ratner; m. Cheryl Cromer; 1 child, Daniel Martin. BS in Chemistry, Bklyn. Coll., 1967; PhD in Polymer Chemistry, Polytech. Inst. Bklyn., 1972. Fellow U. Wash., Seattle, 1972-73, from rsch. assoc. to assoc. prof., 1973-86, prof., 1986—; dir. Nat. ESCA and Surface Analysis Ctr., Seattle, 1984-96; dir. U. Washington Engineered Biomaterials NSF Engring. Rsch. Ctr., 1996—. Editor: Surface Characterization of Biomaterials, 1989, Plasmas and Polymers, 1994-99, Biomaterials Science: An Introduction to Materials in Medicine, 1996, Characterization of Polymeric Biomaterials, 1997; mem. editl. bds. 9 jours. and book series; editor Jour. Undergrad. Rsch. in Bioengring., 1998—; contbr. over 300 articles to profl. jours. Recipient Faculty Achievement/Outstanding Rsch. award Burlington Resources Found., 1990, Perkin Elmer Phys. Electronics award for excellence in surface sci. Fellow Internat. Acad. Med. and Biol. Engring., Am. Inst. Med. Biol. Engring. (founder), Am. Vacuum Soc.; mem. AAAS, AIChE (C.M.A. Stine award 1998), Am. Chem. Soc., Internat. Soc. Contact Lens Rsch., Materials Rsch. Soc., Soc. for Biomaterials (pres. 1991-92, Clemson award 1989, fellow 1994), Biomed. Engring. Soc. Achievements include 10 patents in field. E-mail: ratner@uweb.engr.washington.edu. Office: U Wash Dept Bioengring PO Box 351720 Seattle WA 98195-1720

RATNER, PAMELA ANNE, nursing educator; b. Vancouver, B.C., Can., July 25, 1955; d. Michael Desmond and Nina Cecile (Morris) R.; m. Joy Louise Johnson, Feb. 25, 1984. BSc, U. Alta., Edmonton, Can., 1989, M Nursing, 1991, PhD, 1995. RN, B.C. Assoc. prof. Sch. Nursing, U. B.C., Vancouver, 1996—, asst. dir. Inst. Health Promotion Rsch., 1998—. Recipient Outstanding New Investigator award Can. Assn. for Nursing Rsch., 1998; health rsch. scholar Med. Rsch. Coun. Can., 1995-98, 2000-05. Mem. APHA, Can. Pub. Health Assn., Can. Nurses Assn., RN Assn. B.C. (award of excellence in nursing rsch. 1999). Jewish. Office: U BC Sch Nursing, 2211 Wesbrook Mall T201, Vancouver, BC Canada V6T 2B5

RATNIKOV, VIATCHESLAV YURIEVICH, paleontologist; b. Saratov, Russia, Nov. 13, 1957; s. Yury Vasilievich Ratnikov and Liudmila Alexandrovna Elovkova; m. Natalia Dmitrievna Nikolajeva, Oct. 25, 1983; 1 child, Alexander. Geologist, Geol. Faculty/Voronezh State U., Russia, 1980; DS, Saratov State U., Russia, 1991. Geologist Geol. Expedition, Orenburg, Russia, 1980-83; geologist Voronezh State U., 1983-87, tchr., 1988-92, sr. tchr., 1992-95, docent, 1995—; dean's asst. geol. faculty Voronezh State U., 1992—. Contbr. articles to profl. jours. Mem. Paleontol. Soc., Geological Soc., Herpetological Soc. Avocation: scientific rsch. Office: Voronezh State U/Geol Fac, University Sq 1, 394693 Voronezh Russia

RATO FIGAREDO, RODRIGO, Spanish government official; b. Madrid, Mar. 18, 1949; married; 2 daughters, 1 son. MBA, U. Calif., Berkeley. Mem. Nat. Exec. Com. of AP, 1979-86; co-founder Exec. Commn. of AP, 1979; spokesman for the econ., 1984-86; asst. gen. sec. AP, 1983-86; mem. Parliament for Cádiz in the 2d Legislature; v.p. of def. and security commn. NATO, 1987, 88, mem. spl. com. for strategy and control of armaments, 1988; asst. gen. sec. IXth Party Congress; nat. mem. Parliament for Madrid; spokesman for Grupo Parlamentario Popular Parliament in the IVth and Vth

Legislatures; mem. Parliament in the VIth Legislatures; vice gen. sec. of Partido Popular XIIth Nat. Congress, 1996—; 2d v.p. of govt., min. econ. Govt. for Econ. Affairs, 1996—. Office: Alcala n 11, 28071 Madrid Spain

RATSIRAKA, DIDIER, president of Madagascar; b. Vatomandry, Madagascar, Nov. 4, 1936. Student, Coll. St. Michel, Tananarive, Lycee Henri IV, Paris, Ecole Navale, Lanveoc-Poulimic, France, Ecole des Officiers Transmissions, Les Bormettes, Ecole Superieure de Guerre Navale, Paris. Holder several naval positions, 1963-70; now pres. Republic of Madagascar, Antananarivo; mil. attache Madagascar embassy, Paris, 1970-72; minister fgn. affairs, 1972-75; pres. Supreme Council Revolution, 1975—, prime minister and minister of def., 1975, pres. Democratic Republic Madagascar, 1976—. Sec.-gen. Arema; pres. Front Nat. pour la Def. de la Revolution, 1977—. Serves as adm. Navy. Office: Cabinet du President, Iavoloha Antananarivo Madagascar*

RATTAN, SURESH INDER SINGH, gerontologist, researcher, philosopher; b. Amritsar, Punjab, India, May 20, 1955; s. Mohinder Singh and Kamal Jit Rattan; m. Anita Doodani, July 23, 1979; 1 child, Anuresh Rishabh. BSc with honors, Guru Nanak Dev U., Amritsar, 1976, MSc with honors, 1977; MPh, Jawaharlal Nehru U., New Delhi, 1979; PhD, Nat. Inst. Med. Rsch., London, 1982; DSc, Aarhus U., Denmark, 1995. Pool officer Jawaharlal Nehru U., New Delhi, 1983-84; assoc. prof. Aarhus (Denmark) U., 1984—; cons. Senetek Biotech. Co., London, 1986—. Editor: (spl. issue) Mutation Research on Aging, 1991; mem. editl. bd. BioEssays Jour., 1985-90, Mutation Rsch.: DNAging, 1989-95, Jour. Bioscis., 1991-94; chief editor Biogerontology; inventor patent for certain anti-aging formulae of kinetin; originator of concept of virtual genes for aging called virtual gerontogenes and vitagenes; contbr. over 100 sci., psychol. and lit. articles to internat. jours., mags. and newspapers; book editor. Brit. Coun. fellow, 1979-82. Avocations: tabla drums, literary writing. Office: Aarhus U, Dept Molecular & Structural Biology, C Århus DK-8000, Denmark

RATTANSI, PYARALLY MOHAMEDALLY, history of science educator; b. Nyeri, Kenya, Oct. 15, 1930; arrived in Eng., 1951; s. Mohamedally and Maniben Rattansi; m. Zarin Charania, June 11, 1966; children: Afshin, Shihab. BSc in Econs., London Sch. Econs., 1956, PhD, 1961; MA, Cambridge (Eng.) U., 1967. Journalist Daily Chronicle, Nairobi, Kenya, 1947-51; rsch. fellow Leeds (Eng.) U., 1962-64, lectr., 1964-67; fellow King's Coll., Cambridge U., 1967-71; prof. history and philosophy of sci. U. London, 1971-96, head dept., 1971-96, emeritus prof., 1996—; vis. assoc. prof. U. Chgo., 1966; vis. lectr. Princeton (N.J.) U., 1969-70; mem. hist. div. Inst. for Advanced Study, Princeton, 1969; invited speaker numerous confs., 1974—; chmn. history of sci. sect. Brit. Assn. Advancement Sci., 1991-92; chmn., co-chmn. rsch. seminars. Author: Newton and Gravity, 1974; contbr. numerous articles to books and sci. jours. Mem. Brit. Soc. for History Sci. (v.p. 1974-77). Home: 6 Hillersdon Ave, Edgware HA8 7SQ, England Office: U London Univ Coll, Gower St, U Coll London, London WC1 6BT, England

RATTLEY, JESSIE MENIFIELD, former mayor, educator; b. Birmingham, Ala., May 4, 1929; d. Alonzo and Altona (Cochran) Menifield; m. Robert L. Rattley; children: Florence, Robin. BS in Bus. Edn.with hons., Hampton U., 1951; postgrad., Hampton Inst., 1962, IBM Data Processing Sch., 1960, LaSalle Extension U., 1955. Tchr. Huntington High Sch., Newport News, Va., 1951-52; owner, operator Peninsula Bus. Coll., Newport News, 1952-85; hosp. adminstr. Newport News Gen. Hosp., from 1986; fellow Inst. Politics John F. Kennedy Sch. Govt. Harvard U., 1990; sr. lectr. polit. sci. Hampton U.; elected mayor of Newport News, 1986-90. Mem. Nat. League Cities, bd. dirs., 1975, 2d v.p., 1977, 1st v.p., 1978, pres., 1979-90, active various coms. and task forces; active on adv. bds. and coms. State Dem. Party; mem. exec. com. Va. Black Elected Ofcls. Orgn., Va. Mcpl. League, 1974, 2d v.p., 1976, 1st v.p., 1977, pres., 1979; chair state adv. com. U.S. Civil Rights Commn.; apptd. trustee Va. Vet. Care Facility. Recipient Cert. of Merit Daus. of Isis, 2d annual Martin Luther King, Jr. Meml. award Old Dominion U., Sojourner Truth award Nat. Assn. of Negro Bus. and Profl. Women's Clubs, Cert. of Appreciation NAACP, Hampton Inst. Presdl. award for Outstanding Citizenship.

RÄTY, HANNU OLAVI, management consultant; b. Joensuu, Finland, May 17, 1955; s. Teemu and Taimi (Parviainen) R.; m. Anne Heikinnen, Dec. 31, 1999; children: Jani, Tuomas. MBA, Helsinki Sch. Econs., 1982; postgrad., Syracuse U., 1986. Product mgr. Enso Gutzeit Ltd., Helsinki, Finland, 1978-81; cons., sr. cons., project mgr. Mercuri Internat., Helsinki, 1981-88; mng. dir. Mktg. Mgmt. Concept Ltd., Espoo, Finland, 1988—. Avocations: tennis, sailing, downhill skiing, jogging. Office: MMC Ltd, Sinikallliontie 9, 02630 Espoo Finland

RATZINGER, JOSEPH ALOIS CARDINAL, prefect, former archbishop; b. Marktl, Germany, Mar. 16, 1927; s. Joseph and Maria (Peintner) R. Ed., U. Munich. Prof. theology U. Freising, 1951, U. Bonn, 1958, U. Munster, 1963, U. Tubingen, 1966, U. Regensburg, 1969; Ordained priest Roman Cath. Ch.; chaplain, 1951; archbishop, 1977; cardinal, 1977 former archbishop of Munich-Freising, chmn. Bavarian Bishops Conf., 1977-82; now Prefect Sacred Congregation for the Doctrine of Faith. Author books and articles. Office: 00120 Vatican City State Vatican City State*

RATZLAFF, DAVID EDWARD, minister; b. Kansas City, Mo., Mar. 12, 1938; s. John Henry and Amy May (Cathcart) R.; m. Shiela Paige Hickerson, June 9, 1958; children: Perry Dean, Kevin Lee, Kalista Kay. BA in Ministry, Nebr. Christian Coll., 1961; MDiv, Memphis Theol. Sem., 1991; DMin, Lake Charles Bible Coll., 1996. Ordained to ministry Christian Ch., 1962. Min. Christian Ch., Neligh, Nebr., 1959-67; owner, mgr. Kordsman Evangelistic Assn., Hiawatha, Kans., 1967-75; sr. min. Christian Ctr., Hiawatha, Kans., 1970-72; salesman Saladmaster Co., Springfield, Mo., 1975-76; ops. coord. Blackwood Bros. Quartet, Memphis, 1976-79, 85; mgr. sales and svc. Elliot Impression Products, Memphis, 1980-85; elder, tchr. Lindewood Christian Ch., 1985—; min. Bethany Christian Ch., Eads, Tenn., 1986-95; owner Soma Co., 1993-96; sales cons., fleet mgr., dealership coord. Midway Ford, Collierville, Tenn., 1996-99; customer rels. mgr. Landers Ford, 1999—; assoc. pastor Macon Christian Ch., Collierville, Tenn., 1997-99; program chmn. exec. commn. on ministry com. for Christian Chs. (Disciples of Christ), Tenn., 1988-95, ch. cons., 1996; western area moderator, mem. gen. and exec. bds. Region of Christian Ch. of Tenn., 1991-93; small bus. founder, 1993; mem. pastoral adv. bd. Genesis Cirsis Ctr., Memphis, 1994; cons. WYLT-FM Radio, Collierville, 1997—, WUVL-AM Radio, Mobile, Ala., 1997—. Co-author: (songbook) Kordsman Presents, 1966; recorded and produced 6 long play albums, 1966-74. Bd. dirs. Memphis Family Link, 1985-86; mem. United Cerebral Palsy, 1983-86; asst. police chief City of Neligh, 1962-67, coordinator, 1965-67. Mem. Nat. Arts and Recording Artists, Collierville Ministerial Assn., Christian Ch. Ministers Memphis. Republican. Mem. Disciples Christ. Avocations: fishing, weight lifting, basketball, coaching baseball and softball. Home: PO Box 1569 Collierville TN 38027-1569

RAU, BHIMANAKUNTE, surgeon, educator; b. Rajamundhry, India, Oct. 15, 1939; s. Sheshagiri and Sundari Sheshagiri Rau; m. Shylaja Krishna Rau; children: Sharon Krishna, Shilpa Krishna. MB BChir 1st rank, Madras (India) U., MS. Cert. specialist in gastrointestinal surgery, therapeutic gastrointestinal endoscopy, laser and laparoscopic surgery. Hon. asst. surgeon Govt. Gen. Hosp., Madras, 1965-73; hon. asst. prof. surgery Madras Med. Coll., 1965-73; hon. surgeon Govt. Royapettah Hosp., 1974-93; hon. prof. surgery Kilpauk Med. Coll., 1974-93; cons. surgeon, endoscopist Perambur Rlwy. Hosp.; prof., head dept. surgery, dir. gastroenterology Sri Ramachandra Med. Coll. and Rsch. Inst., Madras; hon. prof. Oncology Cancer Inst., Adyar, 1980-95; med. dir. Willingdon Hosp., Madras, 1967-97; faculty mem. ann. postgrad. course Internat. Gastrosurg. Club, Athens, Greece. Fellow Royal Coll. Surgeons (Eng.), Royal Coll. Surgeons (Edinburgh), Indian Acad. Med. Scis., Indian Med. Assn. (founder); mem. Assn. Surgeons India (hon. sec. 1989-91, hon. treas. 1992-95, pres. 1997), Assn. Surgeons S.E. Asia (founder mem.), Endoscopic and Laparoscopic Surgeons Asia (founder mem.), Asia Pacific Laser Application in Medicine and Surgery (coun. mem.), Soc. Gastrointestinal Endoscopy India (pres.), Indian Endoscopic Soc. (pres. 1995), Indian Assn. Surg. Gastroenterology (pres. 1995), Indian Soc. Gastroenterology (pres. 1996), Assn. Surgeons of India (col. Pandalai orator 1998), Gastro-Surg. Club (founder Indian chpt.), ACG, ICS. Fax: 0091 44 8594578. E-mail: krishnar@giasmd01.vsnl.net.in. Address: # 5 Chandra Bagh Ave, 2d St Mylapore, Chennai 600 004, India

RAU, JOHANNES, German politician; b. Wuppertal, Germany, Jan. 16, 1931; s. Ewald and Helene (Hartmann) Rau. Mem. North Rhine-Westphalian Diet, 1958—; minister-pres. North-Westphalian Land, 1978—; chmn. North Rhine-Westphalian Parliamentary Group, Social Deocratic Party, 1967-70, mem. exec. bd., 1968—, chmn. dist. bd., 1977—, mem. presidence, 1978—, dep. chmn., 1982—; pres. Bundesrat, 1982-83; lord mayor City of Wuppertal, 1969-70; minister of sci. and research North Rhine-Westphalia, 1970-78; pres. Fed. Republic Germany, 1999—. Author: Oberstufenreform und Gesamthochschule, 1970; Die Neue Fernuniversitat, 1974. Decorated grand cross Order of Merit (Fed. Republic Germany), numerous others. Office: Office of Fed Pres, Schlo B Bellevue Spreeweg 1, 10557 Berlin Federal Republic of Germany

RAU, ROLF, retired rheumatologist; b. Kolmar, Posen, Germany, Nov. 7, 1933; s. Paul and Hildegard (Guse) R. MD, Med. Clinic, Giessen, Germany, 1960, asst. prof. medicine, 1981, prof. medicine, 1989. Med. asst. Med. Clinic, Giessen, 1961-69, Rheumatism Clin. Kantonspital, Zürich, Switzerland, 1969-71; sr. physician Rheumatism Clin. Stadtspital Triemli, Zürich, 1971-78; head dept. rheumatology Evang. Fachkrankenhaus, Ratingen, Germany, 1978-98. Contbr. numerous articles to profl. jours. on rheumatism and its treatment, chpts. to texts on rheumatology. Fellow Am. Coll. Rheumatology, Swiss Assn. Rheumatology, Austrian Assn. Rheumatology, German Assn. Rheumatology, German Internal Medicine Assn.; mem. AAAS, N.Y. Acad. Sci. Avocations: hiking, tennis, piano. Home: Irisweg 5, D-40489 Düsseldorf Germany Office: Evangel Fachkrankenhaus, Dept Rheum Rosenstrasse 2, D-40882 Ratingen Germany

RAUB, DONALD WILMER, minister, author; b. Quakertown, Pa., Dec. 24, 1931; s. Harvey Wilmer and Estella Martha (Bleam) R.; m. Dolores Jean Kern, Oct. 20, 1951; children: Diane, Donald, Deborah, Devlyn. DRE, Evang. Bible Sem., Lake Worth, Fla., 1987, ThD, 1999. Ordained minister Evang. Ch. Alliance, 1951. Evangelist Evang. Ch. Alliance, Bradley, Ill., 1951-58; pastor Troy (Ohio) Gospel Tabernacle, 1959-60; writer and photographer Quakertown (Pa.) Free Press, 1963-73; pastor East Rockhill Chapel, 1965—; with Merck & Co., West Point, Pa., 1968-94; ret., 1994; advisor Lebanon (Pa.) Gospel Assn., 1992-94; lectr. in field. Author: I, Being of Sound Mind, 1988, 2d edit., 1989, Unusual Experiences and Special Moments, 1990, The Value of Christian Holiness, 1992; inventor fin. game: Independence, 1976; patentee in field; contbr. articles to profl. jours. Bd. dirs. Transylvania Bible Sch., Freeport, Pa., 1957—, North Penn Symphony Orch. Soc., Lansdale, Pa., 1980-90; v.p. Transylvania, Inc., 1994-97, chmn. bd. dirs., 1997—. Mem. Songwriters of N.Am. (founder). Republican. Avocation: horticulture. Address: PO Box 224 Tylersport PA 18971-0224

RAUCH, HELMUT, physicist, educator; b. Krems, Austria, Jan. 22, 1939; s. Hans and Hermine (Weidenauer) R.; m. Annemarie Krutzler; children: Peter, Astrid, Christoph. Diploma in physics, Tech. U., Vienna, 1962, D of Tech., 1965, dozent, 1970. Asst. prof. Atominstitut, Vienna, 1962-72, dir., 1972—; prof. physics Tech. U., Vienna, 1972—; 1985-90; v.p. Austrian Nat. Sci. Found., 1985-90, pres., 1991-94. Editor: Kerntechnik, 1977—, Neutron Interferometry, 2000; contbr. 250 articles on neutron physics to profl. jours. Recipient Erwin Schrödinger award Austrian Acad. Scis., 1977, Kardinal Innitzer award Innitzer Found., 1986. Mem. Austrian Phys. Soc., German Phys. Soc., Deutsche Naturforscher Leopoldina Halle. Roman Catholic. Avocations: tennis, swimming. Office: Atominstitut, Stadionallee 2, A-1020 Vienna Austria

RAUCH, WOLF DIETRICH, rector; b. Graz, Austria, Mar. 7, 1952; s. Dietrich Alfred and Anna Maria (Fattinger) R.; m. Reingard Wea Keller, Sept. 13, 1980; children: Carl, Ferdinand, Hermann. Dozent, U. Vienna, Austria, 1982, M, 1975, D, 1976. Rschr. Austrian Acad. Scis., Vienna, 1975-77; asst. prof. U. Vienna, Austria, 1977-81; dept. leader GID, Frankfurt, Germany, 1981-84; prof. U. Klagenfurt, Austria, 1984-87; prof. U. Graz, Austria, 1987—, dean econ. faculty, 1995-97, rector, 1997—; pres. Austrian Rectors Conf., 1999—. Author: Delphi-Prognose, 1978, Bueroinformationssysteme, 1982, Einfuehrung in die betriebliche Datenverarbeitung, 1986. Mem. Rotary (Paul Harris fellow 1994). Home: Waldheimatweg 33, A-8043 Graz Austria Office: U Graz, Universitaetsplatz 3, A-8010 Graz Austria

RAUCHSCHWALBE, RENAE, federal agency administrator; b. Cheverly, Md., Oct. 24, 1948; d. Otto and Lillian (Murray) R. MS, U. No. Colo., 1980. Statistician U.S. Consumer Product Safety Commn., Bethesda, Md., 1983-84, sr. compliance officer, 1985—. Contbr. articles to profl. jours. Democrat. Avocations: water color painting, photography. Home: 601 Apple Grove Rd Silver Spring MD 20904-2750 Office: US Consumer Product Safety Commn 4330 E West Hwy Bethesda MD 20814-4408

RAUDKIVI, ARVED JAAN, civil engineering educator; b. Tallinn, Estonia, Mar. 14, 1920; s. Jaan and Elvine Marie (Mannik) R.; m. Aino Jalg, Mar. 29, 1947; children: Peter Jaan, Pia Karen, Paavo Allan. B in Engring., Tech U. Braunschweig, Germany, 1949; PhD, U. Auckland, New Zealand, 1966; D of Engring. (hon.), U. Braunschweig, 1982. Sr. engr. Ministry of Works, New Zealand, 1950-55; lectr., sr. lectr. U. Auckland, New Zealand, 1956-64, prof., 1965-86; prof. Nanyang Tech. U., Singapore, 1987; coord. coastal engring. rsch. State of Schleswig-Holstein, Germany, 1988-94; scientific advisor Joint European Marine Sci. & Tech. Program, Germany, 1995-99. Author: Loose Boundary Hydraulics, 1967, 76, 90, 98, Advanced Fluid Mechanics, 1975, Analysis of Groundwater Flow, 1976, Hydrology, 1979, Grundlagen des Sedimenttransports, 1982, Scouring, 1991, Sedimentation, 1993; contbr. articles to profl. jours. Mem. senate U. Auckland, 1970-86. Recipient Hilgard Hydr. prize ASCE, 1992; Carnegie fellow, 1966, British Coun. fellow, 1973, Minna-James Heimeman fellow, Germany, 1977, 81. Fellow Inst. Civil Engrs. (London), Inst. Prof. Engrs. New Zealand; mem. Internat. Assn. Hydraulic Rsch. Home and Office: 7 Coates Rd Howick, Auckland 1705, New Zealand

RAUDYS, SARUNAS, computer science researcher; b. Kaunas, Lithuania, Feb. 24, 1941; s. Juozas and Antanina (Varkalaite) Baltrusis; m. Danute Gendrolyte, July 2, 1966 (div. 1982); children: Viltaras, Aistis; m. Lolita Aukse Mikalauskaite, Dec. 6, 1985 (div. May 1995); 1 child, Laimute. MS, Kaunas U. Tech., Lithuania, 1963; PhD, Inst. Math., Lithuania, 1969; DS, U. Moscow, 1979. Engr. Spl. Constrn. Bur., Lithuania, 1963-65; sr. rschr. Inst. Math. & Info., Lithuania, 1969, 1970-80, head dept., 1980—; cons. in field. Author: Small Sample Problems in Statistical Pattern Recognition, 1976; contbr. articles to profl. jours. Recipient prize Lithuanian Republic, Prime Min., 1978, Sic and Tech. award Lithuanian Republic Coun. Sci., 1987. Roman Catholic. Avocations: skiing, travel. Home: Ateities 3E-17, 2047 Vilnius Lithuania Office: Inst Math & Info, Akademijos 4, 2600 Vilnius Lithuania

RAUH, HELLGARD, psychologist, educator, researcher; b. Koenigs Wusterhausen, Teltow, Germany, Mar. 24, 1942; d. Kurt Ernst and Hildegard (Hartmann) R. Diploma in psychology, U. Bonn, 1965, PhD, 1971. Asst. U. Bonn, 1966-71; asst. prof. Tchrs. Coll., Landau, 1971-73; assoc. prof. U. Bielefeld, 1973-77; assoc. prof. Free U. Berlin, 1977-79, prof., 1979-95; prof. U. Potsdam, 1995—; spkr., dir. coord. com. for devel. psychology VW-Found., Germany, 1976-80, co-dir. postgrad. program in devel. psychology, 1983-89; guest prof. Queensland-U. Brisbane, Australia, 1985. Contbr. articles to profl. jours. Fellow German Acad. Exch. Svc., U. Chgo., 1965-66. Mem. APA, German Psychol. Assn. (pres. devel. psychology 1987-88), Soc. for Rsch. in Child Devel., Internat. Soc. for the Study Behavioral Devel., European Soc. Devel. Psychology. Office: U Potsdam, PO Box 60 15 53, D-14415 Potsdam Germany

RAUH, HIS EXCELLENCY HERMANN RUDOLF, materials scientist, educator; b. Metzingen, Germany, Mar. 8, 1946; s. Max and Katharina (Nagel) R.; m. Sigrid Ursula Löbker, July 25, 1980; children: Anne-Kathrin, Christine. Dipl.-Phys., U. Tübingen, Germany, 1971; Dr.rer.nat., U. Stuttgart, Germany, 1975; Dr.rer.nat.habil., U. Osnabrück, Germany, 1985; MA, U. Oxford, Eng., 1990. Rsch. assoc. Max Planck Inst. for Metals Rsch., Stuttgart, Germany, 1971-76; asst. prof. U. Osnabrück, Germany, 1976-86; vis. scientist Harwell Lab., Oxfordshire, Eng., 1980-83, Rsch. Ctr., Jülich, Germany, 1981; vis. fellow U. Oxford, 1986-87; vis. scientist Harwell Lab., Oxfordshire, 1987-88, Interuniversity Microelectronics Ctr. Leuven, Belgium, 1988; rsch. fellow Wolfson Coll., Oxford, 1988-94; prof. theoretical founds. of materials devel. Tech. U. Darmstadt, Germany, 1994—; mem. St. Edmund Hall, Oxford, 1986-87, governing body Wolfson Coll., Oxford, 1989-90, Congregation U. Oxford, 1990-94; cons. Harwell Lab., Oxfordshire, 1991-95. Co-editor: Materials Modelling: From Theory to Technology, 1992; contbr. numerous articles to profl. jours. Scholar Commn. European Cmtys., 1982, Sci. and Engring. Rsch. Coun., 1986. Fellow Inst. Physics (chartered), Inst. Materials; mem. Wolfson Coll., Oxford, German Physics Soc., European Physics Soc., Ernst Ludwig Soc., Oxford Soc., Order of Internatl. Ambs. (Medal Hon. 1999). Lutheran. Avocations: playing violin and piano, musical scholarship, languages and literature, walking. Office: Tech U Darmstadt, Petersenstrasse 23, D-64287 Darmstadt Germany

RAUH, JOHN DAVID, manufacturing company executive; b. Cin., May 28, 1932; s. Carl J. and Grace (Stix) R.; m. Elizabeth Gibbons, June 19, 1954; children: Carol Miller (dec. 1991), Daniel Gibbons.; m. Mary Stoner, Dec. 23, 1984; children: Brooks Tomb, Howard Tomb. AB, Harvard U., 1954, MBA, 1956. Gen. mgr. Rauh Shirt Co., Cin., 1959-61, Clopay Corp., Cin., 1961-85; pres. Clopay Corp., 1972-75, chmn., chief exec. officer, 1975-85, also chmn.; adj. faculty mktg. Colby-Sawyer Coll., New London, N.H., 1989-92; fellow Kennedy Sch., Harvard, 1989. Pres. Charter Com. Greater Cin., 1969-76; canidate U.S. Senate, N.H., 1990, 92, 96; trustee Franklin Pierce Coll., 1993—; chair Childrens Alliance N.H., 1997—; dir. Common Cause, 1998—. 1st lt. Finance Corps. AUS, 1956-59. Home: 11 Clearwater Dr # 729 Sunapee NH 03782-2608

RAULIC, PATRICK, gynecologist, consultant; b. Bron, France, Apr. 12, 1956; s. Paul and Odile (Guerin) R.; m. Florence Moniquet Raulic, June 16, 1990; children: Matthieu, Juliette. Diploma in Gynecology, C. Bernard U., Lyon, France, 1985; diploma in Colposcopy, R. Cartier Inst., Paris, 1987; diploma in Breast Diseases, L. Pasteur U., Strasbourg, France, 1989; cert. in Mammography, L. Tabar U., Falun, Sweden, 1986. Cons. in colposcopy Hop E. Herriot Pr. D. Dargent Dept., Lyon, France, 1986-95; cons. in breast diseases Hop E. Herriot Pav. L., Lyon, France, 1986—, Hop C. Rousse, Lyon, France, 1986-94; part time lectr. in colposcopy C. Bernard U., Lyon, France, 1986-92, part time lectr. in breast diseases, 1986—; cons. in colposcopy and breast diseases France, 1986—; in charge colposcopy lectr. C. Bernard U., Lyon, France, 1997; expert in gynecology French Govt. dealing with health ins. Contbr. papers in field. Mem. French Breast Diseases Soc., French Colposcopy Soc. (mem. sci. com.), Gynecology Assn. Rhone, Breast Cancer Screening Assn. Avocations: skiing, swimming, oenology. Home: 79 che de Fontanieres, 69350 La Mulatiere France Office: Hop E Herriot Pav L, Place d'Arsonval, 69437 Lyon France

RAUNEMAA, TAISTO MIKKO, environmental scientist; b. Loimaa, Finland, Dec. 13, 1939; s. Mikko and Hilma Raunemaa; m. Pirkko Marjetta, 1968; children: Ahti Pekka, Anni, Liisa. MS, U. Helsinki, 1965, PhD, 1975. Tchg. asst., lectr. U. Helsinki, 1966-83; assoc. prof., prof. U. Kuopio, Finland, 1983—; vis. rsch. prof. Clarkson U., Potsdam, N.Y., 1993-94, U. Minn., Mpls., 1994, U. Calif. Davis, 1995; vis. rschr. Lawrence Berkeley Lab., U. Calif., 1973-74; vis. lectr. U. Vienna, 1998, 99. Fellow Gesellschaft Fur Aerosolforschung, Am. Assn. Aerosol Rsch.; mem. Internat. Aerosol Rsch. Assn. (chmn., fellow awards com.), Finnish Assn. Aerosol Rsch. (pres.). Avocation: orienteering. Office: U Kuopio Dept Environ Scis, PO Box 1627, 70211 Kuopio Finland

RAUNEST, JUERGEN, surgeon, educator; b. Essen, Germany, June 23, 1959; s. Walter and Ursula (Senftner) R.; m. Julia L. Mameghani, 1999. MD, U. Essen, 1985. Surg. resident Ev. Krankenanstalten Duisburg-Nord, 1985-87; sr. surg. resident Dept. Gen. Surgery, Duesseldorf, 1988-91; rsch. fellow Inst. of Exptl. Surgery, U. Duesseldorf, 1989-90; cons. of traumatology U. Duesseldorf, 1992-2000, assoc. prof., docent in surgery/traumatology, 1993—, prof. surgery/traumatology, 1999—; chief surgeon, chmn. dept. traumatology Neuwerk Hosp., Moenchengladbach, 2000—. Editl. bd. Jour. Akt. Chir., 1987—; author: Arthroscopic Surgery of the Knee, 1987, Textbook of Arthroscopic Surgery, 1990, Laser Application in Joint Surgery, 1990; contbr. numerous articles to profl. jours. Mem. German Arthroscopic Assn. (scientific com. 1989—), German Surg. Soc., German Soc. of Traumatology, Westphalian Surg. Soc. Roman Catholic. Avocations: music (organ, piano), golf. Office: Dept Gen Surgery & Traumat, Neuwerk Hosp, 41066 Moenchengladbach Germany

RAURAMO, JAAKKO KAARLE MAUNO, media company executive; b. Helsinki, Finland, Nov. 27, 1941; s. Heikki and Maija (Massinen) R.; m. Eeva-Sofia Raustila, 1966; children: Markus, Juhana. MSc, Helsinki U. Tech., Espoo, Finland, 1966; postgrad., Finnish Inst. Mgmt., Helsinki, 1973-74, Stanford U., 1974-75. Engr. Sanomaprint subs. Sanoma Corp., Helsinki, 1966-67, prodn. mgr., 1967-71, gen. mgr., 1971-76; gen. mgr. newspaper div., exec. v.p. Sanoma Corp., Helsinki, 1976-84, pres., 1984-99, pres., CEO, 1999—; bd. dirs., chmn. bd. dirs. Rautakirja Oyj, 1988—; bd. dirs. Sanoma Corp. 1979—, chmn. 1999—; adv. bd. mem. Finnish Med. Found. 1993—, bd. vice chmn. 1996—; vice chmn. Helsinki Media Company Oyj, chmn. 1995—; bd. mem. European Publishers Coun., 1994—, Svenska Dagbladets AB, 1995—, Scandinavian Internat. Mgmt. Inst., 1995—, Metso Oyj, 1999—; adv. bd. mem. Helsinki Sch. Econs., 1995—; del. mem. Central C. of C. of Finland, 1998—, Helsinki C. of C., 1999—; chmn. Werner Söderström Osakeyhtiö, 1999—; trustee Reuters Founders Share Co. Ltd., 1999—. Contbr. articles to profl. publs. Decorated Knight 1 of Order of White Rose, Pres. of Republic of Finland, 1985. Office: SanomaWSOY Corp, PO Box 1229, FIN-00101 Helsinki Finland

RAUSCH, JOHN DAVID, JR., political science educator; b. W. Reading, Pa., Mar. 15, 1967; s. John David, Sr. and Barbara Ann R.; m. Mary Scanlon, May 25, 1991. BA in Polit. Sci., U. Alaska, 1989; MA in Polit. Sci., U. Okla., 1992, PhD in Polit. Sci., 1995. Asst. prof. polit. sci. Fairmont (W.Va.) State Coll., 1994-98, West Tex. A&M U., Canyon, Tex., 1998—. Sec./treas. North Cen. W.Va. Cmty. Action Assn., 1997-98. Mem. Am. Polit. Sci. Assn. Democrat. Lutheran. Avocations: writing, computer sci. E-mail: jrausch@mail.wtamu.edu. Office: W Tex A&M Univ PO Box 60807 Canyon TX 79016-0001

RAUSCHENBACH, BERND HANS, physicist, educator; b. Meissen, Saxonia, Germany, June 16, 1949; s. Hans Wilhelm and Marianne (Kirste) R.; m. Chrita Renate Riedel, June 4, 1970; children: Katrin, Stephan. Diplomphys., U. Halle, Germany, 1974; Dr.rer.nat., Acad. Sci., Dresden, Germany, 1981, Dr.habil., 1988; facultas docenti, U. Freiberg, Germany, 1989. Rschr. Acad. Sci., Dresden, 1974-89; prof. Tech. U. Hamburg, Germany, 1990-93, U. Augsburg, Germany, 1994-99, U. Leipzig, dir. Inst. for Surface Modification, 2000—. Recipient Gustav Hertz prize Phys. Soc. Germany, 1989. Office: Inst Surface Modivication, Permoserstr 15, D-0341 Leipzig Bavaria, Germany

RAUSCHMEIER, HANS, urologist; b. Vienna, Oct. 26, 1949; s. Johann and Hildegund (Mayerhofer) R.; m. Michaela Hönlinger, May 29, 1999; children: Eva, Peter, Alexandra, Andreas. MD, U. Vienna, 1975. Sr. registrar Clinic of Urology, Innsbruck, Austria, 1979-88; urologist Vienna, 1988—; expert in urology Ct. of Laws, Vienna, 1987. Contbr. articles to profl. jours. Health officer Vienna Police, 1990; works med. Dr. Assurance Co., Vienna, 1989. Capt. Austrian Army, 1985. Mem. AUA (corr. mem.), EAU. Roman Catholic. Avocations: tennis, riding, sailing. Home: Steinberg-Frankg 8, A-2380 Perchtoldsdorf Austria Office: Schweglerstr 24, A-1150 Vienna Austria

RAUST, JEAN VICTOR, health facility administrator, radiologist; b. Loches, Indre et Loire, France, Dec. 18, 1944; s. Jean and Fanny (D'Aleman) R.; m. Clotilde Haudos de Possesse, Sept. 20, 1971; children: Isabelle, Stéphanie, Pauline, Claire. D. Med. Sch., Paris, 1972. Specialist radiology. Extern Hosp., Paris, 1966-70, asst., 1975-78; intern Hosp., Caen, France, 1970-75; head dept. Hosp., St. Cloud, France, 1978—, chmn. med. commn., 1986—; v.p. exec. bd. Hosp., St. Cloud, 1990—; mem. regional com. health and social orgn., nat. commn. modernization of hosp. adminstrn. Exec. bd. Antoine Beclere Ctr. Med. officer French Navy res., 1972—. Mem. Inter Hosp. Union (bd. dirs.), French Nat. Hosp. Coun. (bd. dirs.), French Soc. Radiology, Rotary Club. Avocations: shooting. Home: 109

Blvd République, 92210 Saint Cloud Hauts de Seine, France Office: Saint-Cloud Hosp, 3 Place Silly, 92210 Saint Cloud France

RAUTALA, PEKKA JUHANI, cosmetics company executive; b. Cambridge, Mass., July 29, 1951; s. Pekka and Marita (Aaltio) R.; m. Anna-Maija Rautala, Mar. 30, 1974; children: Samuli, Taneli. BA in Econs., Helsinki Sch Econs., 1973, MA in Econs., 1981. Acctg. mgr. Orion-yhtymä Oy Noiro, Espoo, Finland, 1973—, assoc. dir., 1984—; fin. dir., v.p. Orion-Yhtymä Oy Noiro, Espoo, Finland, 1988—, sr. v.p., 1990-93, pres., 1993—. Home: Alakartanonkuja 1 A 3, SF-02360 Espoo Finland Office: Orion-yhtymä Oy Noiro, Lasihytti 9 Box 27, SF-02787 Espoo Finland

RAUTAVA, PÄIVI TUIRE, public health educator, pediatrician; b. Pori, Finland, July 13, 1956; d. Väinö and Sirkka (Nurmi) Wilén; m. Seppo Tapio Rautava, Aug. 6, 1977; children: Essi, Liisi, Nella, Kalle. BM, Turku (Finland) U. Med. Sch., 1977, MD, 1981, specialty in health care, 1989, specialty in pediat., 1991, specialty in adminstrv. competence, 1995. Dr.Med.Sci., 1989; docent health care, 1995; licensure, Finland, 1981. Gen. practitioner Pori Pub. Health Svc., Finland, 1981, 83; resident in pediat. Turku U. Hosp., 1982-85, 89-91; rschr. primary health care Dept. Pub. Health U. Turku, 1985-89; asst. prof., 1991-92; assoc. prof. U. Finland, Turku, 1992-98; prof. U. Turku, Finland, 1998—. Mem. Internat. Union Health Edn., European Assn. Perinatal Medicine, Finnish Med. Assn. Lutheran. Avocations: horseback riding, dressage, choral singing. Office: U Finland Dept Pub Health, Lemminkäisenkatu 1, 20520 Turku Finland

RAUTENBACH, ERNST ROBERT, chemical engineering educator; b. Wuppertal, N. Rhine, Germany, Aug. 23, 1931; s. Ernst and Marga (Luetticke) R.; m. Martha Christine Rinke, Oct. 26, 1957; 1 child, Jeannette. Diploma, U. Tech., Aachen, Germany, 1957, D in Engring., 1962. Rschr. U. Rochester, N.Y., 1962-63; plant designer Huels AG, Marl, Germany, 1963-67; prof., head dept. chemical engring. U. Aachen, Germany, 1967-96; cons. GNT mbH, Aachen, Germany, 1997-99; v.p. Internat. Desalination Assn., Topsfield, Mass., 1979-82; bd. dirs. Balcke Duerr Thermal, Philip Müller-Hager Elsasser. Author: Membranverfahren, 1981, Membrane Processes, 1989, Membranverfahren, Modul + Anglagenauslegung, 1997; also publs. on Desalination, Waste Water Treatment, Membrane Processes, Distillation Processes. Recipient Borchers medal U. Tech., Aachen, Germany, 1962, Willy Hager medal, Dechema, Frankfurt, Germany, 1996. Mem. Soc. Chemical Engrs. Avocations: biking, swimming. Office: Step Partnerschaft, Oppenhoffallee 49, 52066 Aachen Germany

RAUTENBERG, ROBERT FRANK, statistical advisor, stochastic process specialist; b. Milw., Sept. 14, 1943; s. Raymond Clarence and Anna Josephine (Winter) R.; m. Meredith Taylor, June 2, 1965 (div. Feb. 1975); 1 child, Matthew Carl. PhD in Bus. Adminstrn., Pacific Western U., 1983; postdoctorate, Sorbonne U., Paris. Pvt. practice in acctg. Kansas City, Mo., 1975-76; pres. Seven Diamond Enterprises, Inc., San Francisco, 1976-78; CEO Assurance Sys., San Francisco, 1984-96, Probability Investigations Mgmt. Models, Honolulu, 1997—. Author: The Analytical Management Handbook, 1985, Supplement to the Analytical Management Handbook, 1991, London edit., 1996, A Bayesian Approach to Management, 1996, A Lifetime of Achievement, Based Upon Prayer, Responsibility and Balance, 2000; contbr. articles to profl. jours. and conf. proceedings. Named Internat. Man of Yr., Internat. Biog. Ctr., Cambridge, Eng., 1998. Mem. Internat. Statis. Inst., Internat. Assn. Survey Statisticians. Episcopalian. Avocations: swimming, skiing, traveling, scuba diving (cert.), jungle hiking. E-mail: rautenbe@lava.net. Office: Prob Investig Mgmt Models 1164 Bishop St Ste 124 Honolulu HI 96813-2816

RAUTENSTRAUSS, BERND WALTER, molecular biologist; b. Ulm, Baden-W., Germany, Oct. 10, 1959; s. Walter Ludwig and Margarete (Osswald) R.; m. Karin Gudrun Michels, May 30, 1992. Diploma in Biology, Friedrich-Alexander U., Erlangen-Nürnberg, Germany, 1988, PhD in Biochemistry, 1992; postdoctoral studies, Neurogenetics Lab., Antwerpen, Belgium, 1996; doctor med. habil., 1998. Sci. asst. Inst. Biochemistry, Erlangen, Germany, 1988-92; asst. prof. Inst. Human Genetics, Erlangen, 1992—. Contbr. articles to profl. jours. including, Human Molecular Genetics, Jour. Neurosci. Rsch., Mammalian Genome, Acta Neuropathologica, Jour. Peripheral Nervous System, Trends in Genetics, Human Genetics. Recipient Sanofi-Winthrop award, 1999. Mem. German Soc. Human Genetics, Am. Soc. Human Genetics, Soc. Biol. Chemistry, Fedn. European Biochem Socs. Office: Inst Human Genetics, Schwabachanlage 10, 91054 Erlangen Bavaria, Germany

RAVAOARIMALALA, MARIE CLAIRE YVONNE, public health service officer; b. Ambohijanaka, Tananarive, Madagascar, Oct. 11, 1951; d. Thomas and Marcelline Razafindrakoto; m. Augustin Rafalimanana, May 3, 1976; children: Lovasoa, Hobiarisoa, Rivohery, Onimalala. Degree in medicine, U. Tananarive, Madagascar, 1982; degree in pub. health, ULB, Brussels, 1996, degree in epidemiology, 1995. Physician Childrens Hosp. Ministry Health, Tananarive, 1982-90, head of pharmacy, 1990-92; with dept. Schistosoma Ministry of Health, Tananarive, 1992, chief dept. STD and JIDA, 1995-97, with dept. health info., 1997-98, chief health protection at frontiers dept., 1999—. Home: Lot II M 35 R bis A, 101 Andrianalefy Madagascar Office: Svc de la Sante Aux Frontie, PO Box 460, 101 Antananarivo Madagascar

RAVAUX-KIRKPATRICK, FRANCOISE, language professional; b. Fes, Morocco, July 8, 1941; came to U.S., 1967; d. Gilbert Rondot and Simone (Martin) Amet; m. Jacques Ravaux, Oct. 15, 1960 (div. 1981); 1 child, Catherine; m. Peter Steven Kirkpatrick, June 16, 1990. MA in French, Mich. State U., East Lansing, 1969; PhD, 1973; DEA in Semiotics, U. Paris, 1981. Instr. French U. Richmond, Va., 1973-74; asst. prof., 1974-84, assoc. prof., 1984-91, prof., 1991—. Translator: The Pledge, 1990, The Dinner Party, 1993; editor (with A.J. Greimas): La Mode en 1830: Langage et Société, 2000. Named: Chevalier dans L'ordre des Palmes Académiques, Min. Nat. Edn., France, 1994, The Gaines Chair of Modern Fgn. Langs., U. Richmond, 1996. Mem. MLA, Semiotic Assn. Am., World Inst. Phenomenology. Avocations: acting, biking, flyfishing, travel. Home: 312 Rowland St Richmond VA 23220 Office: Dept Modern Language and Literature University of Richmond Richmond VA 23173

RAVELOJAONA, GASTON, bank executive. Gov. Banque Centrale de Madagascar, Antananarivo. Office: Banque Centrale, 101 Ave de France BP 550, 101 Antananarivo Madagascar*

RAVEN, JOHN, research psychologist, writer; b. London, July 21, 1936; s. John Carlyle and Mary Elizabeth Raven; m. Chynthia Jean Burton; children: John Arthur, Alexander Rex. BSc, Aberdeen (Scotland) U., 1959; postgrad. diploma in social psychology, London Sch. Econs., 1960; PhD, Trinity Coll., Dublin, Ireland, 1982. Chartered Psychologist, Assoc. Fellow Brit. Psychol. Soc. Scientific officer/sr. social svcs. officer Brit. Civil Svc., London, 1960-68; sr. rsch. officer Econ. & Social Rsch. Inst., Dublin, 1968-76; part-time project leader Scottish Coun. Rsch. on Edn., Edinburgh, 1976-82; freelance rschr., cons. Edinburgh, 1976—. Author over 20 books, including The New Wealth of Nations, 1995, The Tragic Illusion: Educational Testing, 1991 (Best Book of Yr., World Ednl. Fellowship 1992), Competence in Modern Society, 1984, others; co-author (10-vol. test manual) Manual for Raven's Progressive Matrices and Vocabulary Scales, numerous edits., 1972—; contbr. over 200 articles to profl. jours. Multiple grantee, 1974—. Home and Office: 30 Great King St, Edinburgh EH3 6QH, Scotland

RAVENSCROFT, PETER JAMES, anaesthesiologist, educator; b. London, May 14, 1951; s. Malcolm John and Patricia Lilian (Deadman) R.; m. Katharine Sophie Pracy, Nov. 9, 1974; children: James, Nicholas, Thomas. MBBS, St. Bartholomew's Hosp., 1974; D, Royal Coll. Ob-Gyn., 1978. Intern Whitby Hosp., Ont., Can., 1973; sr. house officer Musgrove Park, Taunton, Somerset, Eng., 1975-77; registrar dept. anesthesiology Sir Humphrey Davey, Bristol, Eng., 1977-79; underläkare Ctrl. Lasarettet, Västerås, Sweden, 1979-80; sr. registrar dept. anesthesiology Nuffield, Oxford, Eng., 1980-83; cons. Musgrove Park, Taunton, 1984—; clin. dir. Health Svc. Trust, Taunton, 1990-94; lectr. U. Plymouth, Eng., 1996—. Trustee Festival Med. Svcs., Eng., 1997—. Fellow Royal Coll. Anesthesists; mem. Internat. Anesthetic Rsch. Soc., Brit. Astron. Assn. Mem. Labour Party. Avocations: sailing, drumming, diving, skiing, computing. Home: 5 Elm Grove, Taunton Somerset TA1 1EG, England Office: Staplegrove Anesthetic Gr, Staplegrove Elm, Somerset Taunton England

RAVER, MIKI, recruiter, writer; b. N.Y.C., May 31, 1945; d. James Raver and Sophie Zimmerman; m. Martin Perlmutter, Feb. 17, 1980; 1 child, Sara Sasha. BS, Emerson Coll., 1968. Street worker Youth Svcs. Agy., N.Y.C., 1972-73; therapist Phoenix House, N.Y.C., 1973-76; dir. Women's Success Teams, San Francisco, 1976-78; prodr. Tele-Pros, N.Y.C., 1982-87; talent agt. Grimme & Mitchell Talent Mgmt., San Francisco, 1988-95; ptnr. Hookup!, San Francisco, 1995-98; dir. internat. editl. recruitment Look Smart, San Francisco, 1998-2000. Author: Listen to her Voice, 1998. Avocations: hiking, swimming. Home: 2866 Mckillop Rd Oakland CA 94602-1503

RAVETKAR, SATISH DAMODAR, microbiologist; b. Pune, India, July 14, 1951; s. Damodar Mohaniraj and Sulabha Damodar (Dwarka) R.; m. Anjali Satish Ravetkar, Feb. 5, 1979; children: Mansi, Prajakta. BS, Pune, India, 1971, MS, 1973, PhD, 1981, MDBA, 1984. Jr. scientific officer Serum Inst. India, Pune, 1973-85, mgr. vaccines, 1985-86, mgr. projects & materials, 1986-88, deputy dir. projects & materials, 1988-92, dir., 1992—. Contbr. articles to profl. jours. Mem. Indian Acad. Vaccinology & Immunobiology, All India Glass Mfrs. Fedn., Indo-German C. of C., Internat. Soc. Ayurvedic Medicine, Internat. Soc. Pharm. Engring., Pharm. Mfrs. Assn., Rotary. Avocations: reading, music, gardening, social service. Home: 4 Sadashanti Apts Ln #9A, Prabhat Rd, Pune 411 004, India Office: Serum Inst India Ltd, 212/2 Hadapsar, Pune 411 028, India

RAVI, GOVINDA PANICKER, urologist, consultant; b. Trivandrum, Kerala, India, Oct. 22, 1946; s. Sankara Panicker Govinda and Raman Addiamma Ponnamma; m. Mangalam Sumithra Devi, Nov. 12, 1972; children: Navin, Dhanya, Suvin. BSc, U. Coll., Trivandrum, Kerala, India, 1966; MB BS, Med. Coll., Trivandrum, Kerala, India, 1966; D in Urology, U. Coll., London, 1988. Tutor in surgery Med. Coll. Hosp., Calicut, India, 1973-74, tutor in microbiology, 1974; tutor in microbiology Med. Coll. Hosp., Trivandrum, India, 1974-75; tutor in paediats. SAT Hosp. Med. Ctr., Trivandrum, 1975; tutor in radiology Med. Coll. Hosp., Calicut, 1975-76, tutor in urology, 1976-78; physician in gen. surgery, accident and emergency surgery Downe Hosp., Down Patrick, No. Ireland, 1978-80; physician in surgery Ulster Hosp., Belfast, No. Ireland, 1980-81; registrar in surgery Regional Hosp., Limerick, Republic of Ireland, 1981, Caithness Gen. Hosp., Wick, Scotland, 1981-82; registrar in urology Ballochnyle Hosp., Ayrshire, Scotland, 1982-84; specialist in urology King Khalid Hosp., Najaran, Saudi Arabia, 1984-88, cons. in urology, 1988—; presenter in field. Contbr. articles to profl. jours. including Brit. Jour. Urology. Fellow Royal Coll. Physicians (Glasgow), Brit. Assn. Urologists, Brit. Assn. Paediat. Urologists. Avocations: photography, scientific research. Home: TC 17/36 Dhanusha, Sudarsan Nagar, Jagathy Trivandrum, Kerala 695014, India Office: King Khalid Hosp, PO Box 1120, Najran Saudi Arabia

RAVI, RAJAGOPALAN, surgery educator; b. Madras, Tamil Nadu, India, Mar. 12, 1949; came to U.S., 1977; s. Venkatraman and Alemelu (Ventkatraman) Rajagopalan; m. Vasanthi Vanchinathan, Sept. 8, 1978; children: Arun, Sunil, Sriram. Pre med., Delhi (India) U., 1967; MBBS, All India Inst. Med. Scis., New Delhi, 1973; Surgeon, N.J. Med. Sch., 1978; Vascular Surgery, Ariz. Heart Inst., 1979. Diplomate Am. Bd. Surgery. Instr. surgery N.J. Med. Sch., Newark, 1973-78; fellow Ariz. Heart Inst., Phoenix, 1978-79; active staff Casa Grande (Ariz.) Regional Med. Ctr., 1979-90, chief med. staff, 1986-87, mem. bd., 1986-89; cons. surgeon Tamilnad Hosp., Madras, India, 1991—; chmn. dept. surgery Tamilnad Hosp., Madras, 1993-96, chief med. staff, 1996-98; prof. surgery SRMC&RI, Madras, 1995—. Contbr. articles to med. jours. Bd. dirs. United Way Pinal County, Casa Grande, 1981, Am. Cancer Soc., Tanker, Madras, 1994-97. Fellow Am. Coll. Surgeons, Am. Coll. Angiology, Internat. Coll. Surgeons. Democrat. Hindu. Avocations: reading, golf, hiking, movies. Home: 1 First St, Kamraj Nagar, Thiruvanmiyur Chennai, India 600041 Office: SRMC&RI, Poror, 600116 Chennai India

RAVICHANDRAN, DURAISWAMY MAHESWARY, research scientist; b. Madras, Tamilnadu, India, June 19, 1964; came to the U.S., 1994; s. Natesan and Shantha Duraiswamy; m. Latha K. Mangavarme, Feb. 24, 1997; 1 child, Sandhiya. PhD, Madras U., 1994. Postdoctoral scholar Pa. State U., 1994-97; Nat. Rsch. Coun. fellow U.S. Army Rsch. Lab., Md., 1997-99; rsch. scientist Am. Rsch. Corp., Radford, Va., 1999—. Guest editor Jour. Displays, 1999; contbr. articles to profl. jours. Mem. Am. Ceramic Soc., Materials Rsch. Soc., Microelectronics and Packaging Soc., Soc. Info. Display. Achievements include 3 patents pending. Home: 1222 2d St Radford VA 24141

RAVICHANDRAN, MAHALINGAM, environmental engineer; b. Watrap, India; parents Mahalingam and Seeniammal M.; m. Grace, Aug. 7, 1991; children: Joshua, Joel. BSc, U. Madras, 1986; MS, Tex. A&M U., 1994; PhD, U. Colo., 1999. Geologist GWSSB, Surendranagar, India, 1990-91; rsch. assoc. NAS, Athens, Ga., 1999—. Mem. Am. Chem. Soc., Am. Geophys. Union.

RAVINDRAN, S.S., mathematician, educator; b. Sri Lanka, Jan. 28, 1963; d. M.S. and S. (Paramanayaki) S.; m. Tharan M., Aug. 5, 1995; 1 child, Maheswaralingam. BSc, U. Sri Lanka, Jaffna, 1987; MSc, U. (Vancouver) Brit. Columbia, 1991; PhD, Simon Fraser U., Vancouver, 1994. NRC rsch. fellow NASA Langley Rsch. Ctr., Hampton, Va., 1997-99; asst. prof. U. (Huntsville) Ala., 1999—; vis. asst. prof. N.C. State U., Raleigh, 1994-97; organizer mini-symposium for advances in optimal flow control parts I, II, III, IV SIAM Nat. Ann. Meeting, Rio grande, Puerto Rico, 2000, parts I, II, III, Atlanta, 1999. Contbr. articles to profl. jours. Nat. Rsch. Coun. award Nat. Acad. Scis., Washington, 1997. Mem. IEEE (conf. decision and control session chmn.), Soc. Indsl. and Applied Math. (session chmn. ann. meeting), SIAM activity group on control and sys. theory. Avocations: music, table tennis, movies, traveling. Fax: 256-890-6173. Home e-mail: tharanee@aol.com. Office e-mail: ravindra@ultra.math.uah.edu. Home: 108 Arabian Dr Madison AL 35758-6633 Office: U Ala Dept Math Scis Huntsville AL 35899-0001

RAVITZ, LEONARD J., JR., physician, scientist, consultant; b. Cuyahoga County, Ohio, Apr. 17; s. Leonard Robert and Esther Evelyn (Skerball) R. BS, Case Western Res. U., 1944; MD, Wayne State U., 1946; MS, Yale U., 1950. Diplomate Am. Bd. Psychiatry and Neurology, 1952, Am. Bd. Forensic Examiners, 1996, Am. Coll. Forensic Examiners; bd. cert. forensic examiner. Rsch. asst. EEG to A.J. Derbyshire, PhD Harper Hosp., Detroit, 1943-46; spl. trainee in hypnosis to Milton H. Erickson, MD Wayne County Gen. Hosp., Eloise, Mich., 1945-46, 46-80; rotating intern St. Elizabeth's Hosp., Washington, 1946-47; jr. asst. resident in psychiatry Yale-New Haven Hosp., 1947-48; asst. in psychiatry and mental hygiene Yale Med. Sch., 1947-48, assoc. in psychiatry and mental hygiene, 1948-49, rsch. fellow to Harold S. Burr, PhD, sect. neuro-anatomy, 1949-50, sr. resident in neuropsychiatry Richard S. Lyman svc., 1950-51; instr. Duke U. Med. Sch., Durham, 1950-51; assoc. to R. Burke Suitt, MD, Pvt. Diagnostic Clinic, Duke Hosp., Durham, 1951-53; assoc. Duke U. Med. Sch., 1951-53; vis. asst. prof. neuropsychiatry and asst. to vis. prof. Richard S. Lyman, MD, Meharry Med. Ctr., Nashville, 1953; asst. dir. profl. edn. in charge tng. U. Wyo. Nursing Sch. Affiliates; chief rsch. rehab. bldg. Downey VA Hosp. (now called VA Hosp.), N. Chicago, Ill., 1953-54; assoc. psychiatry Sch. Medicine and Hosp., U. Pa., Phila., 1955-58; electromagnetic field measurement project office dep. asst. sec. def. in charge health & med. E.H. Cushing MD Dept. Def., Pentagon, 1958; dir. tng. and rsch. Ea. State Hosp., Williamsburg, Va., 1958-60; pvt. practice neuropsychiatry specializing in hypnosis Norfolk, Va., 1961-69; psychiatrist, cons. Divsn. Alcohol Studies and Rehab. Va. Dept. Health (later Va. Dept. Mental Health and Mental Retardation), 1961-81; psychiatrist Greenpoint Clinic, Bklyn., 1983-87, 17th St. Clinic, N.Y.C., 1987-92, Downstate Mental Hygiene Assocs., Bklyn., 1983—; sec.-treas. Euclid-97th St. Clinic, Inc., Cleve., 1957-63, pres., 1963-69; spl. tng. in epistemology and methodologic foundations of sci. knowledge F.S.C. Northrop, PhD, 1973-92; electrodynamic field rschr. with Harold S. Burr, PhD, sect. neuro-anatomy Yale Med. Sch., 1948-73; cons. hypnosis with Milton H. Erickson, MD, 1945-80; clin. asst. prof. psychiatry SUNY Health Sci. Ctr. Med. Sch., 1983—; pvt. cons., Cleve., 1961-69, Upper Montclair, N.J., 1982-90; lectr. sociology Old Dominion U., Norfolk, 1961-62, cons. nutrition rsch. project Old Dominion U. Rsch. Found., 1978-90; spl. med. cons. Frederick Mil. Acad., Portsmouth, Va., 1963-71; cons. Tidewater Epilepsy Found., Chesapeake, Va., 1962-68, USPH Hosp. Alcohol Unit, Norfolk, 1980-81, Nat. Inst. Rehab. Therapy, Butler, N.J., 1982-83; participant 5th Internat. Congress for Hypnosis and Psychosomatic Medicine, Gutenburg U., Mainz, Germany, 1970; organizer symposia on hypnosis in psychiatry and medicine, field theory as an integrator of knowledge, hypnosis in gen. practice, history of certain forensic and psychotherapeutic aspects of the study of man, Eastern State Hosp., Coll. William and Mary, James City County Med. Soc., Va. Soc. Clin. Hypnosis, Williamsburg, Va., 1959-60. Asst. editor Jour. Am. Soc. Psychosomatic Dentistry and Medicine, 1980-83; mem. editorial bd. Internat. Jour. Psychosomatics, 1984—; contbr. sects. to books, articles, book revs., abstracts to profl. publs. Sr. v.p. Willoughby Civic League, 1971-75. ASTP AUS, 1946-48. Lyman Rsch. Fund grantee, 1950-53. Fellow AAAS, Am. Psychiat. Assn. (life), N.Y. Acad. Scis., Am. Soc. Clin. Hypnosis (charter, life, cons. cert. program), Royal Soc. Health (London); mem. Va. Soc. Clin. Hypnosis (founding pres. 1959-60), Norfolk Acad. Medicine, Soc. for Investigation of Recurring Events, Va. Med. Soc., Sigma Xi, Nu Sigma Nu. Achievements include discovery of electromagetic field correlates of hypnosis, emotions, psychiatric/medical disorders, aging, and electrocyclic phenomena in humans which parallel those of other life forms, earth and atmosphere underwriting beginning short- and long-range predictions preceding clinical changes, such seemingly disparate phenomena united under a single regulating principle defined in terms of measurable field intensity and polarity. Office: SUNY Health Sci Ctr Dept Psyc Box 1203 450 Clarkson Ave Brooklyn NY 11203-2056 also: PO Box 9409 Norfolk VA 23505-0409

RAVIV, ILANA, artist; b. Tel-Aviv, Nov. 29, 1945; d. Itzhak and Fanya (Albin) Oppenheim; m. Dov Raviv, Sept. 16, 1971; children: Anat, Boaz, Itzik. Student Delamonica, Dorfman, Martin, Art Student's League, New York, 1984. Artist in oil, acrylic, drawings, etchings, sculpting, more pvt. studio, Neve Tzedek/Tel Aviv, Jerusalem. Exhbns. include a mural for the largest Sukkah/Tabernacle event in the world, sponsored by the Jewish Comty. Rels. Coun., N.Y.C.; one-person shows include, Israelis Gallery, Tel-Aviv, 1971, 74, Cicchinnelli Galleries, N.Y.C., 1981, River Gallery, Irvington, N.Y., 1983, Bronx Mus. of Art, 1984, Dubelle Fine Art, N.Y., 1984, Lamontage Gallery, N.Y.C., 1989, Garret Stephens Gallery, E. Hampton, N.Y., 1990, Riverdale YM-YWHA Gallery, N.Y., 1990, Strauss Gallery, N.Y.C., 1990, Stavit Gallery, Paris, 1993, The Nat. Arts Club, N.Y.C., 2000; group exhibitions include ZOA House, Tel Aviv, 1972, Bergman Gallery, Tel Aviv, 1974, Cicchinelli Galleries, Ingberg Gallery, S. Morantz Gallery, N.Y.C., 1981, Riverton Gallery, Irvington, N.Y., Arras Gallery, N.Y.C., 24th Ann. Art Show Westfield Chpt. Hadassah N.J., Art Expo, N.Y., Jewish Comty. Ctr., Tenafly, N.J., S. Morantz Gallery, Cliffside Park, N.J., Guild Hall Mus. Art, East Hampton, N.Y., Fine Arts Mus. Long Island, N.Y., Bronx Mus. Art, N.Y., 599 Broadway, N.Y., 1982, C.D.S. Gallery, N.Y., Byer Mus. of Art, Painting, Succoth, N.Y., 1984, Dubelle Fine Art, N.Y., 1984, Peninsula Pub. Libr., Lawrence, N.Y., 1983, Lamontage Gallery, N.Y., 1989, Garret Stephens Gallery E. Hampton, N.Y., Riverdale YM-YWHA Gallery, N.Y., Strauss Gallery, N.Y., 1990, Stavit Gallery, Paris, 1993, Nat. Arts Club, N.Y., 1997, The Svan Pakkad Palace Mus., Bangkok, Thailand, 1999, Sylvia White Gallery, L.A., 2000, Touchstone Gallery, Washington, 2000; permanent collections include Holacaust Nat. Mus., Washington and numerous private collections. Mem. The Nat. Arts Club (N.Y.), N.Y. Artist Equity Assn., Painters and Sculptors Assn. Studio: Neveh Tzedeck, 12 Mahane Yoseph St, N Tzedek Tel Aviv 65153, Israel

RAVN, ANDERS PETER, computer science educator; b. Caracas, Venezuela, Oct. 29, 1947; arrived in Denmark, 1948; s. Niels and Henny (Sønder) R.; m. Annemette Lind, Aug. 31, 1973; children: Niels Søren, Mads Peter. MSc, U. Copenhagen, Denmark, 1973; D in Tech., Tech. U. Denmark, Lyngby, 1995. Systems programmer A/S Regnecentralen, Copenhagen, 1972-76; asst. prof. computer sci. U. Copenhagen, 1976-80, assoc. prof. computer sci., 1980-84; assoc. prof. computer sci. Tech. U. Denmark, Lyngby, 1984-90; reader Tech. U. Denmark, 1990-98; prof. Aalborg (Denmark) U., 1998—; vis. scientist IBM Rsch., N.Y.C., 1982-83; guest rschr. Oxford (Eng.) U., 1989-90; vis. prof. Kiel (Germany) U., 1994-95. Contbr. articles to internat. scientific jours. Mem. IEEE (Computer Soc.), Assn. Computing Machinery. Home: Snerlevej 4, DK-2800 Lyngby Denmark Office: Aalborg U, Fr Bajers vej 7E, DK-9220 Aalborg E, Denmark

RAVNSKOV, UFFE, retired internist, nephrologist and researcher; b. Copenhagen, Oct. 12, 1934; s. Knud Erik and Birgitte (Germer) R.; m. Kirsten Ravnskov, 1959; children: Søren, Pernille, Lars; m. Bodil Thordarson, June 6, 1992. MD, U. Copenhagen, 1962; PhD, U. Lund, Sweden, 1973. Intern dept. surgery Hosp. Hudiksvall, Sweden, 1962-63; intern dept. medicine Hosp. Skellefteå, Sweden, 1963-64; resident dept. medicine Hosp. Sandviken, Sweden, 1964-68; rsch. fellow dept. nephrology U. Hosp. Lund, Sweden, 1968-71, rsch. fellow dept. clin. chemistry, 1971-72, asst. prof. dept. nephrology, 1972-79; pvt. practitioner, ind. rschr. Lund, 1979-2000; ret., 2000. Author: The Cholesterol Myth, (Swedish edit.), 1991, (Finnish edit.), 1992, (Am. edit.), 2000; contbr. articles to profl. jours. Recipient Skrabanek award The Skrabanek Found. Trinity Coll., 1998. Mem. N.Y. Acad. Sci. Home: Magle Stora Kyrkogata 9, S-22350 Lund Sweden

RAWAT, ARUN SINGH, research scientist; b. Tharali, India, May 3, 1969; s. Prithavi Singh and Sulochama Devi (Negi) R.; m. Seema Bisht, Oct. 11, 1997; 1 child, Swapnil. BSc, G.P.G. Coll. Gopeshwar, Chamoli, India, 1987; MSc, Garhwal U., Srinagar, India, 1989; NET, CSIR, Panjab U., New Delhio, India, 1995-96. Lectr. Garhwal U., Tehri, India, 1991-92, H.N.B. Garhwal U., Pauri, India, 1993—; participant workshops, symposia in field. Contbr. articles to profl. jours. Avocations: friendships, travel, reading, photography. Home: Village Ajabpur, PO Tharali 246481, Tharali Chamoli India Office: HNB Garhwal U Pauri Garhwal, Dept Physics, Pauri Garhwal 246001, India

RAWDIN, GRANT, lawyer, financial planning company executive; b. N.Y.C., Nov. 17, 1959; s. Eugene and Nona (Neubauer) R.; m. Laura S. Schecter; children: Alexander, Jacob, Jesse, Aaron, Rachel. BA, Temple U., 1981, JD, 1987. Bar: Pa. 1987, N.J. 1987; CFP, Colo. Tax acct. Hepburn Willcox Hamilton & Putnam, Phila., 1978-81; mgr. tax acctg. dept. Duane Morris & Heckscher, Phila., 1981-86; dir. personal fin. planning Duane Morris & Heckscher, LLP, Phila., 1986-87; pres. Wescott Fin. Planning Group Inc. subs. Duane Morris & Heckscher, Phila., 1987—, also bd. dirs.; mem. adj. faculty Coll. for Fin. Planning, Denver, 1987-95; lectr. Inst. Tax and Fiduciary Mgmt., 1988-95. bd. dirs. Phila. Child Guidance Ctr., 1991-94; bd. dirs., pres. Am. Poetry Ctr., 1989-97, pres. People's Emergency Ctr., 1995—; pres. PEC Found., 1996—. Mem. ABA, Phila. Bar Assn., Internat. Assn. Fin. Planners (chmn.), Inst. CFP (bd. dirs. 1987-93). Home: 7615 Seminole Ave Elkins Park PA 19027-3506 Office: Wescott Fin Planning Group Inc 1 Liberty Pl Philadelphia PA 19103-7396 also: 249 Royal Palm Way Ste 403 Palm Beach FL 33480-4334

RAWL, ARTHUR JULIAN (LORD OF CURSONS), retail executive, accountant, consultant, author; b. Boston, July 6, 1942; s. Philip and Evelyn (Rosoff) R.; m. Karen Lee Werby, June 4, 1967; 1 child, Kristen Alexandra. BBA, Boston U., 1967, postgrad, 1972-74. CPA, Mass., N.Y., La. Audit mgr. Touche Ross & Co., Boston, 1967-77; audit mgr. Touche Ross & Co., N.Y.C., 1977-79, ptnr., 1979; ptnr. Touche Ross & Co., Newark, 1980-88, N.Y.C., 1988-89; ptnr. Deloite & Touche, N.Y.C., 1989-90; ret. Deloite & Touche, N.Y.C., N.J., 1990; exec. v.p., chief fin. officer Hanlin Group, Inc., Linden, N.J., 1990-94, United Auto Group, Inc., N.Y.C., 1994-97; pres., CEO Brazil Internat. Motors, Brazil Am. Auto Group, 1999—; also bd. dirs.; bd. dirs. BiakalInterPlast (USSR), Kuperwood Enterprises, Hanlin Group, Inc.; mem. adj. faculty Boston U., 1971-75. Contbr. articles to profl. journals, mags. and trade publs. Mem. Newton Upper Falls (Mass.) Hist. Commn., 1977; bd. dirs. Sherburne Scholarship Fund Boston U., 1977-80; mem. Englewood (N.J.) Planning Bd., 1981-83; trustee Englewood Bd. Edn., 1983-85, 89-93, pres., 1991-92; trustee, treas. exec. com. Englewood Econ. Devel. Corp., 1986-89; fin. and compensation com. Dwight Englewood Sch., 1985-90; mem. parent devel. com. Mt. Holyoke Coll., 1991-94. Served to 2d class petty officer USN, 1960-63. Fellow AICPA, Mass. Soc. CPAs, N.Y. Soc. CPAs; mem. VFW, Am. Legion, Navy League U.S., N.J. Hist. Soc. (bd. govs., exec. com., nominating com., treas. 1987-99), St. George's Soc. N.Y.

(treas. exec. com. 1998—), Univ. Club, Essex Club, Sloane Club (London). Home: 72 Booth Ave Englewood NJ 07631-1907 Office: Rua Paes Leme 215-Pinheiros, Sao Paulo 05424150, Brazil

RAWLING, ELEANOR MARION, geographical educator; b. Gloucester, Eng., May 11, 1949; s. Alfred James Hicks and Gladys (Sale) Hicks; m. John Rawling, Sept. 4, 1971; children: Helen, Richard. BA in Geography with honors, U. Oxford, 1970, MA, 1974. Cartographic editor Clarendon Press, Oxford, 1971; geography tchr. Oxfordshire County Coun., Oxfordshire, 1972-76; team mem., assoc. dir. geography 16-19 project Inst. of Edn., U. London, 1976-85; nat. coord. geography, schs., industry project U. Oxford, 1987-91; cons. in geog. edn., 1991—; profl. officer Sch. Curriculum and Assessment Authority, London, 1994-97; prin. subject officer geography Qualifications and Curriculum Authority, 1997—; Leverhume rsch. fellow U. Oxford, 1999-2000. Joint editor, author Geography 16-19 Student Materials, 1984-88; author: (with others) Geography 16-19: The Contribution of a Curriculum Project to 16-19 Education, 1987; joint editor, contbg. author: Geography into the Twenty First Century, 1996; contbr. articles to profl. jours. Named to Order of British Empire Her Majesty the Queen, 1995. Fellow Royal Geog. Soc. (coun. mem.); mem. Geog. Assn. (pres. 1991-92, coun. mem.), Coun. Brit. Geography (chair 1993-94), Geog. Edn. Commn. of Internat. Geographic Union. Avocations: mountain walking, running, literature, poetry. Office: Qualifications and Curricul Authority, 29 Bolton St, London W1Y 7PD, England

RAWLINGS, BOYNTON MOTT, lawyer; b. El Paso, Tex., Dec. 6, 1935; s. Junius Mott and Laura Bassett (Boynton) R.; m. Nancy Mary Peay, Aug. 24, 1962 (div. 1973); children: Laura Bassett, James Mott; m. Judith Reed, Dec. 10, 1977; 1 child, William Reed. AB, Princeton U., 1958; LLB, Stanford U., 1961; diploma, U. Strasbourg, France, 1963. Bar: Calif. 1962, D.C. 1980, Conseil Juridique Paris, 1973, Avocat Paris, 1992. Assoc. Broad, Busterud & Khourie, San Francisco, 1963-65, Homer G. Angelo, Brussels, 1966; assoc., ptnr. S.G. Archibald, Paris, 1967-74; ptnr. Boynton M. Rawlings, Paris, L.A., 1974-84, Kevorkian & Rawlings, Paris, 1984-90, Oppenheimer, Wolff and Donnelly, Paris, 1990-99, Rawlings & Giles LLP., Paris, 2000—. Contbr. articles to profl. jours. Mem. L.A. Bar Assn. (bd. dirs. sect. internat. law 1975-82), French Am. C. of C. L.A. (bd. dirs. 1985—). Republican. Episcopalian. Avocations: music, tennis, skiing, hiking. Office: Rawlings & Giles, 53 Ave Montaigne, 75008 Paris France also: The Farragut Bldg 500 17th St NW Ste 700 Washington DC 20006-4804

RAWLINGS, DOUGLAS ERIC, microbiology educator; b. East London, S. Africa, Nov. 11, 1950; s. Herbert Edward and Dorothy Grace (Immelman) R.; m. Janet Lesley Asbury, Dec. 15, 1973; children: Barry, Kim, Sarah-Jane. BS with hons., Rhodes U., S. Africa, 1972, PhD, 1976. Rsch. officer Leather Industries Rsch. Inst., Grahamstown, 1976-77; lectr. U. of the Witwatersrand, Johannesburg, 1978-81; sr. lectr. U. of Cape Town, 1982-87, prof., 1988-98; prof., chmn. dept. microbiology U. Stellenbosch (South Africa), 1998—; cons. Sasol, Secunda, 1979-81. Contbr. articles to profl. jours., books and publs. Capt. S. African Def. Force/Army, 1970-81. Fellow U. Cape Town, 1990; named A-Rated Scientist, Found. for Rsch. Devel., S. Africa, 1992, 96; recipient PanLabs award Soc. Indsl. Microbiology, 1997. Fellow Royal Soc. of S. Africa (gen. sec.); mem. S. Africa Acad. Scis., S. Africa Soc. for Microbiology (Silver medalist 1992). Assembly of God. Avocations: squash, cycling. Office: Dept Microbiology, Univ Stellenbosch, 7600 Stellenbosch South Africa

RAWLINGS, HUNTER RIPLEY, III, university president; b. Norfolk, Va., Dec. 14, 1944; married; 4 children. BA, Haverford Coll., 1966; PhD in Classics, Princeton U., 1970. Asst. prof. U. Colo., Boulder, 1970-75, assoc. prof., 1975-80, prof. classics, 1980-88, v.p. acad. affairs, rsch., dean System Grad. Sch., 1984-88; pres. U. Iowa, 1988-95; pres., prof. classics Cornell U., Ithaca, N.Y., 1995—; chair Iowa Commn. on Fgn. Lang. Studies and Internat. Edn., 1988-91; bd. dirs. Tompkins County Trust Co. Author: The Structure of Thucydides' History, 1981; editor-in-chief: Classical Jour., 1977-83; contbr. articles to jours. Bd. dirs. Norwest Bank Iowa, N.A., 1988-95. Jr. fellow Ctr. Hellenic Studies, 1975-76. Fellow Am. Acad. Arts and Scis.; mem. Assn. Am. Univs. (exec. com. 1990-92), Am. Coun. on Edn. (bd. dirs. 1994-97), Nat. Fgn. Lang. Ctr. (mem. nat. adv. bd. 1995—). Address: 511 Cayuga Heights Rd Ithaca NY 14850-1421

RAWLINGS, JERRY JOHN, president of Ghana; b. Accra, Ghana, June 22, 1947; s. Victoria Agbotui; m. Nana Konadu Agyeman; 4 children. Ed., Achimota Sch., Ghana Mil. Acad., Teshie. Commd. pilot officer Ghanaian Air Force, 1969, advanced through grades to flight-lt., 1978; arrested for leading mutiny of jr. officers, 1979; released from jail by popular uprising of mil. revolution which overthrew Govt. of Supreme Mil. Council, 1979; chmn. Armed Forces Revolutionary Coun. (head of state), 1979; ret. from armed forces, 1979; handed over to elected govt., 1979; leader mil. coup which overthrew Govt. of Dr. Hilla Limann, 1981; chmn. Provisional Nat. Def. Council, 1981-92; elected pres. 1992; inaugurated pres. under 4th Republican Constitution, 1993, re-elected, 1996; head of State, 1982—; comdr. in chief of Armed Forces, 1982—. Office: Office of the Pres, The Castle, PO Box 1627, Accra Ghana

RAWLINS, MARK IAN, surgeon; b. Montreal, Que., Can., Oct. 7, 1960; s. Timothy George and Pirkko Kaarina (Sairio) R.; m. Maija Johanna Joutsen, Aug. 22, 1982; children: Katarina, Pia, Nikolas. MD, Turku U., Finland, 1987. Resident Uusikaupunki Dist. Hosp., finland, 1987, Turku U Ctrl. Hosp., finland, 1988, Salo Dist. Hosp., finland, 1989-93, Turku U. Ctrl. Hosp., finland, 1994-96, Helsinki U. Hosp., 1997-98; cons., hand surgeon Tohtoritalo 41400, Turko, 1999—. Mem. Finnish Surg. Soc., Finnish Hand Surg. Soc., European Fedn. Hand Surgery. Avocations: computers, reading. Office: Tohtoritazo 41400, Yliopistonkatv 17-19, 20100 Turku Finland

RAWSON, JESSICA MARY, educator; b. London, Jan. 20, 1943; d. Roger Nathaniel and Paula (Webber) Quirk; m. John Graham Rawson. BA, Cambridge U., Eng., 1965, MA, 1967; BA, Sch. Oriental/African Studies, U.K., 1971; DLitt, Cambridge U., 1991; DLitt (hon.), U. London, 1997, U. London, 1998, Royal Holloway Coll., 1998, U. Sussex, 1998, U. Newcastle, 1999. Asst. prin. Ministry of Health, London, 1965-67; asst. keeper Brit. Mus., London, 1967-76, dep. keeper, 1976-87, keeper, 1987-94; warden Merton Coll., Oxford, Eng., 1994—, prof., 2000—; hon. fellow New Hall, Cambridge; vice-chair Govs. Sch. Oriental and African Studies, 1999—. Author: Animals in Art, 1977, Ancient China, Art and Archaeology, 1980, Chinese Ornament: the lotus and the dragon, 1984, Chinese Bronzes: art and ritual, 1987, The Bella and P.P. Chiu Collection of Ancient Chinese Bronzes, 1988, Western Zhou Ritual Bronzes from the Arthur M. Sackler Collection, 1990, Chinese Jade from the Neolithic to the Qing, 1995, Mysteries of Ancient China, 1996; (with John Ayers) Chinese Jade Throughout the Ages, 1975; (with Emma Bunker) Ancient Chinese and Ordos Bronzes, 1990; editor: The British Museum Book of Chinese Art, 1992. Decorated Comdr. of Brit. Empire, Queen of Eng., 1994. Fellow Brit. Acad.; mem. Oriental Ceramic Soc. (pres. 1993-97), Brit. Libr. Board. Office: Merton Coll, Warden's Lodgings, Oxford OX1 4JD, England

RAWSON, JIM CHARLES, accountant, executive; b. Houston, Apr. 20, 1947; s. Charles Manly and Georgie (Kearse) R.; m. Linda Eidman, Apr. 12, 1968; children: John Erich, Susan Margaret. BBA, Tex. Christian U., 1969. CPA, Tex. Acctg. clk. Tenneco, Inc., Houston, 1969-71; acctg. clk. Projects Am. Corp., Houston, 1971-74, office mgr., 1974-77, v.p., gen. mgr., 1977-82, pres., 1982—. Recipient Bronze award Am. Land Devel. Assn., 1985, Gold award, 1983, Silver award, 1983. Mem. Am. Inst. CPA's, Tex. Soc. CPA's (Houston chpt.), Sports Car Club of Am. Evangelical. Avocations: sports car racing, salt water fishing. Office: Projects Am Corp 6124 Beverlyhill St Houston TX 77057-6610

RAY, ANDRÉ PIERRE, orthopedic surgeon; b. Villefranche, Rhone, France, July 8, 1935; s. Paul Louis Ray and Marie Andrée Raphanel; m. Daniele Jeanne Gluntz; children: Sophie, Olivier, Lucie Dorothee. MD, U. Lyon, 1964. Specialist in orthopedic surgery. Chef clinique Hospices Civils de Lyon, Lyon, 1965-71, surgeon, 1971-85; surgeon Clinique du Parc, Lyon, 1977—; dir. Coll. Française des Chirurgiens Orthop., 1994. Mem. Soc. Française de Chirurgie Orthopedique et Traumatologique (hon.), Soc. Internat. de Chirurgie Orthopedique et Traumatologique (hon.). Home: 87 Blvd de Belges, 69006 Lyon France Office: Clinique Orthopedique du Parc, 86 Blvd de Belges, 69006 Lyon France

RAY, ASIM KUMAR, physics educator; b. Calcutta, India, Oct. 6, 1937; s. Barendra Nath and Prativamoyee (Basu) R.; m. Parul Basu, May 5, 1969; 1 child, Raka Dona. BSc with honors, U. Calcutta, 1956, MSc in Physics, 1958; PhD in Particle Physics, Carnegie Mellon U., 1969. Trainee Atomic Energy Establishment, Bombay, 1959-60; rsch. assoc. Tata Inst. Fundamental Rsch., Bombay, 1960-63; lectr. Visva-Bharati U., Santiniketan, India, 1969-76, reader, 1975-84, head dept. physics, 1981-87, prof., 1984, dean faculty sci., 1990-92, prof.-in-charge Computer Ctr., 1991-97, registrar, 1992-93; vis. scientist U. Wis., Madison, 1980, Stanford (Calif.) Linear Accelerator Ctr., 1980, 85, KEK Nat. Lab., Oho-machi, Japan, 1980, Yukawa Ctr. High Energy Physics, Kyoto, Japan, 1985, Internat. Ctr. Theoretical Physics, Italy, 1995; sr. assoc. Internat. U. Ctr. Astronomy and Astrophysics, Pune, 1994-97. Co-editor: Dirac and Feynmen, Pioneers in Quantum Mechanics, 1993; contbr. articles to profl. jours. Fulbright scholar, 1963. Mem. Indian Physics Assn. (life), Indian Phys. Soc. (life), Indian Assn. Cultivation Sci. (life), Indian Assn. Gen. Relativity and Cosmology. Hindu. Avocations: listening to music, singing, gardening, reading. Home: Flat E-5 Salt Lake Sect 3, Cluster IX Purbachal Housing, Calcutta 700097, India Office: Visva-Bharati U, Dept Physics, Santiniketan 731 235, India

RAY, BRADLEY STEPHEN, petroleum geologist; b. Ada, Okla., Feb. 15, 1957; s. Walter Lloyd and Betty Louise (McCurley) R. BS in Geology, Baylor U., 1980; MS in Geology, U. Tex., 1985. Cert. geologist. Asst. geologist Hunt Oil Co., Dallas, 1978, geologist, 1979-81; ind. oil and gas producer Dallas, 1981—; chmn. adv. bd. Geol. Info. Libr. Dallas, 1988—; bd. dirs. Global Mapping Internat. Trustee Dallas Bapt. U., 1988-94, Criswell Coll., 1990-92; chmn. The Habitats Project, 1993—; co-chmn. Peoples and Habitats Project, 1994—; mem. Peoples Info. Network. Mem. Am. Assn. Petroleum Geologists, Ind. Petroleum Assn. Am., Soc. Ind. Profl. Earth Scientists, Dallas Geol. Soc., Tex. Ind. Producers and Royalty Owners, Okla. Ind. Petroleum Assn., Geol. Soc. Am., Computer Oriented Geol. Soc., Nat. Stripper Well Assn., Energy Club, Oklahoma City Geol. Soc., Colbert-Tracht Club. Republican. Baptist. Home: 4925 Greenville Ave Ste 1348 Dallas TX 75206-4021 Office: 1348 One Energy Sq Dallas TX 75206

RAY, CHARLES DEAN, neurosurgeon, spine surgeon, bioengineer, inventor; b. Americus, Ga., Aug. 1, 1927; s. Oliver Tinsley and Katherine (Broadfield) R.; m. Nancy N. Melton, June 19, 1992; children: Bruce, Marlene, M. Scott, D. Blake, L. Elizabeth. AB, Emory U., 1950; MS, U. Miami, 1952; MD, Med. Coll. Ga., 1956. Diplomate Am. Bd. Neurol. Surgery, Am. Bd. Spine Surgery. Intern Bapt. Meml. Hosp., Memphis, 1956-57; resident, rsch. assoc. neurosurgery U. Tenn. Hosp., Memphis, 1957-62; fellow, rsch. asst. Mayo Clinic and Found., Rochester, Minn., 1962-64; asst. prof. neurosurgery, lectr. bioengring. Johns Hopkins U. Med. Sch., Balt., 1964-68; chief dept. engring. F. Hoffmann-LaRoche, Basel, Switzerland, 1968-73; practice medicine specializing in neurosurgery Norfolk, Williamsburg, Va., 1973—; lectr. U. Basel, 1968-73; dir. emeritus Inst. Low Back and Neck Care; med. dir. The Spine Program, Ea. Va. Med. Sch., Norfolk, Va.; pres. Am. Coll. Spine Surgery; mem. staff Sentara Hosps., Norfolk; clin. assoc. prof. medicine U. Minn., Mpls., 1973-73; v.p. med. rsch. Medtronic, Inc., Mpls., 1972-79; chmn. bd., pres. Cedar Devel. Corp., Cedar Surg., Inc., 1985—; bd. dirs. Herman Miller, Inc.; chmn. emeritus, med. dir. Raymedia, Inc., Mpls.; cons. in field. Author: Principles of Engineering Applied to Medicine, 1964, Medical Engineering, 1974, Lumbar Spine Surgery, 1988; contbr. over 320 articles to profl. publs. Chmn. com. materials and devices World Fedn. Neurosurg. Socs., 1977—, Cosmos Club, 1976—; vestry St. Martin's Episcopal Ch., Wayzata, Minn., 1976-79. With USN, 1945-49. Named Disting. Alumnus, Med. Coll. Ga., 1999; recipient Gold award for Best Med. Device Design of Yr. R&D 100, 2000. Fellow ACS, Am. Coll. Spine Surgery (pres.), Royal Soc. Health; mem. ASTM, IEEE (life sr.), AMA (sr.), Am. Assn. Neurol. Surgeons (sr.), Pan-Am. Med. Assn. (life), Congress Neurol. Surgeons, West Germany Armed Forces Med. Soc., Internat. Fedn. Med. Biol. Engring., Internat. Soc. Stereotaxic and Functional Neurosurgery, Internat. Orgn. Standardization, N.Am. Spine Soc. (past pres., chmn., Wilste award 1999), Lafayette Club, Sigma Xi, Others. Achievements include over 50 U.S. patents and over 100 foreign patents. Fax: 757-565-6262. E-mail: InveRay@aol.com. Home and Office: 125 Alexander Walker Williamsburg VA 23185-8919

RAY, CLAYTON EDWARD, paleontologist, curator; b. New Castle, Ind., Feb. 6, 1933; s. Lloyd Trevor and Ruth Virginia (Daggy) R.; m. Donna Ruth Johnson, Sept. 5, 1953; children: Rachel, Leah, Sarah, Carrie. BA, Harvard Coll., 1955; MA, Harvard U., 1958, PhD, 1962. Asst. prof., curator U. Fla., Gainseville, 1959-63; asst. curator, curator Nat. Mus. Natural History Smithsonion Inst., Washington, 1963-94, curator emeritus, 1994—; bd. trustees Va. Mus. Natural History, Martinsville, 1989-97; chair Com. Scientific Advisors, U.S. Marine Mammal Commn., 1976-78. Contbr. articles to profl. jours. Mem. Am. Soc. Mammalogists (life), Soc. Vertebrate Paleontology (chair devel. com. 1986-89, Gregory award 1993), Soc. Marine Mammalogy, N.C. Fossil Club (hon. mem.). Avocations: farming, animal husbandry. Home: 146 Hudson Rd Falmouth VA 22405-3563 Office: Nat Museum Natural History Smithsonian Inst Tenth And Constitution Washington DC 20560-0001

RAY, FRANK ALLEN, lawyer; b. Lafayette, Ind., Jan. 30, 1949; s. Dale Allen and Merry Ann (Fleming) R.; m. Carol Ann Olmutz, Oct. 1, 1982; children: Erica Fleming, Robert Allen. BA, Ohio State U., 1970, JD, 1973. Bar: Ohio 1973, U.S. Dist. Ct. (so. dist.) Ohio 1975, U.S. Supreme Ct. 1976, U.S. Tax Ct. 1977, U.S. Ct. Appeals (6th cir.) 1977, U.S. Dist. Ct. (no. dist.) Ohio 1980, Pa. 1983, U.S. Dist. Ct. (ea. dist.) Mich. 1983, U.S. Ct. Appeals (1st cir.) 1986; cert. civil trial adv. Nat. Bd. Trial Advocacy. Asst. pros. atty. Franklin County, Ohio, 1973-75; chief civil counsel Franklin County, 1976-78; dir. econ. crime project Nat. Dist. Attys. Assn., Washington, 1975-76; assoc. Brownfield, Kosydar, Bowen, Bally & Sturtz, Columbus, Ohio, 1978, Michael F. Colley Co., L.P.A., Columbus, 1979-83; pres. Frank A. Ray Co., L.P.A., Columbus, 1983-93, Ray & Todaro Co., LPA, Columbus, 1993-94, Ray, Todaro & Alton Co., L.P.A., Columbus, 1994-96, Ray, Todaro, Alton & Kirstein Co., L.P.A., Columbus, 1996, Columbus, Ray, Alton & Kirstein Co., L.P.A., 1996-98; sr. ptnr. Ray & Alton, L.L.P., 1998—; mem. seminar faculty Nat. Coll. Dist. Attys., Houston, 1975-77; mem. nat. conf. faculty Fed. Jud. Ctr., Washington, 1976-77; bd. editors Man. for Complex Litigation, Fed. Jud. Ctr., 1999—; bd. mem. bar examiners Ohio Supreme Ct., 1992-95, Rules Adv. Com., 1995-99. Editor: Economic Crime Digest, 1975-76; co-author: Personal Injury Litigation Practice in Ohio, 1988, 91. Mem. fin. com. Franklin County Rep. Orgn., Columbus, 1979-84; trustee Ohio State U. Coll. Humanities Alumni Soc., 1991-93, Nat. Coun. Ohio State U. Coll. Law Alumni Assn., 19985; mem. Legal Aid Soc. of Columbus Capital Campaign Fund Cabinet, 1998. 1st lt. inf. U.S. Army, 1973. Named to Ten Outstanding Young Citizens of Columbus, Columbus Jaycees, 1976; recipient Nat. award of Distinctive Svc., Nat. Dist. Attys. Assn., 1977. Fellow Am. Coll. Trial Lawyers, Internat. Soc. Barristers, Columbus Bar Found., Roscoe Pound Found., Ohio Acad. Trial Lawyers, Ohio State Bar Found.; mem. ABA, Am. Bd. Trial Advocates (sec. Ohio chpt. 19995), Columbus Bar Assn. (pres.-elect 1999—, Profl. award 1997), Million Dollar Advs. Forum, Ohio State Bar Assn. (com. negligence law 1990-97), Assn. Trial Lawyers Am. (state del. 1990-92), Ohio Acad. Trial Lawyers (pres. 1989-90, Pres.' award 1986), Franklin County Trial Lawyers Assn. (pres. 1987-88, Pres.'s award 1990), Inns of Ct. (pres. Judge Robert M. Duncan chpt. 1993-94). Presbyterian. Home: 2030 Tremont Rd Columbus OH 43221-4330 Office: 175 S 3rd St Ste 350 Columbus OH 43215-5188

RAY, JOHN WALKER, otolaryngologist, educator, broadcast commentator; b. Columbus, Ohio, Jan. 12, 1936; s. Kenneth Clark and Hope (Walker) R.; m. Susanne Gettings, July 15, 1961; children: Nancy Ann, Susan Christy. AB magna cum laude, Marietta Coll., 1956; MD cum laude, Ohio State U., 1960; postgrad., Temple U., 1964, Mt. Sinai Hosp., Columbia U., 1964, 66, Northwestern U., 1967, 71, U. Ill., 1968, U. Ind., 1969, Tulane U., 1969. Diplomate Am. Bd. Otolaryngology. Intern Ohio State U. Hosps., Columbus, 1960-61, clin. rsch. trainee NIH, 1963-65, resident dept. otolaryngology, 1963-65, 66-67, resident dept. surgery, 1965-66, instr. dept. otolaryngology, 1966-67, 70-75, clin. asst. prof., 1975-82, clin. assoc. prof., 1982-92, clin. prof., 1992-2000, clin. prof. emeritus, 2000—; hon. staff, past chief of staff Good Samaritan Hosp., also Bethesda Hosp., Zanesville, Ohio, 1967—; hon. active staff Meml. Hosp., Marietta, Ohio, 1992—; radio-TV health commentator, 1982—. Contbr. articles to sci. and med. jours.; collaborator with surg. motion picture: Laryngectomy and Neck Dissection, 1964. Past pres. Muskingum chpt. Am. Cancer Soc.; bd. dirs. Zanesville Art Ctr. Capt. USAF, 1961-63. Recipient Barraquer Meml. award, 1965; named to Order of Ky. Col., 1966, Muskingum County Country Music Hall of Fame. Fellow ACS, Am. Soc. Otolaryn. Allergy, Am. Acad. Otolaryngology-Head and Neck Surgery (gov.), Am. Acad. Facial Plastic and Reconstructive Surgery; mem. AMA, Nat. Assn. Physician Broadcasters, Muskingum County Acad. Medicine (past pres.), Ohio Med. Assn. (del.), Columbus Ophthalmol. and Otolaryn. Soc. (past pres.), Ohio Soc. Otolaryngology (past pres.), Pan-Am. Assn. Otolaryngology and Bronchoesophagology, Pan-Am. Allergy Soc., Am. Acad. Invitro Allergy, Am. Soc. Contemporary Medicine and Surgery, Acad. Radio and TV Health Commentators, Fraternal Order of Police Assocs., Phi Beta Kappa, Alpha Omega Alpha, Beta Beta Beta. Presbyterian. Office: 2945 Maple Ave Zanesville OH 43701-1753

RAY, KRISHNA, microbiologist, consultant; b. Bilaspur, India, Aug. 11, 1945; d. Niraj Mohan and Mira (Mitra) Basu; m. Ashish Chandra Ray, Apr. 27, 1970; children: Anshuman, Neelanjana. MBBS, Calcutta (India) Med. Coll., 1968; MD in Microbiology, All Indian Inst. Med. Scis., New Delhi, 1973. Cert. in parasitology, U. Queensland, in Hybridoma Technique, Nat. Inst. Immunology, New Delhi, in epidemiology, Emory U. Tutor in microbiology All Indian Inst. Med. Scis., 1973-75; asst. dir. dept. microbiology N.I.C.D., Delhi, 1975-87; microbiologist Safdarjang Hosp., New Delhi, 1987-88, sr. microbiologist, 1988-94, cons., head blood bank, 1995-96; head STD Ref. Lab. Safdanjang Hosp.; chairperson grievance redressal com. Safdarjung Hosp. Contbr. over 60 rsch. articles to nat. and internat. jours. Resource person Nat. AIDS Control Orgn., New Delhi. Fellow Indian Soc. Malaria and Other Communicable Diseases (life), Indian Assn. Med. Microbiologists. Avocations: reading, music, drama, cooking. Home: DII/59/1, Andrews Ganj, Delhi New Delhi 110049, India Office: Safdarjang Hosp, Delhi New Delhi 110029, India

RAY, KUMAR SANKAR, computer science educator, researcher; b. Burdwan, W Bengal, India, June 24, 1955; s. Anil Kumar and Sunity R.; m. Dhira Basu, Jan. 20, 1983; 1 child, Aratrika. B Engring., Bengal Engring. Coll., Howrah, India, 1978; MS, U. Bradford, Eng., 1980; PhD in Engring., U. Calcutta, 1987; postdoctoral tng., U. Tex., Austin, 1991. Cons. engr. Devel. Cons. Pvt. Ltd., Calcutta, 1980-82; computer engr. Indian Statis. Inst., Calcutta, 1983-87, assoc. prof. computer sci., 1988-92, prof. computer sci., 1993—; adjunct faculty computer sci. Bengal Engring. Coll., Howrah, 1986-90, 92—; cons. scientist Inst. Modern Mgmt., Calcutta, 1988-90; vis. scientist U. Calcutta, 1994—; mem. task force com. Govt. India Dept. Electronics, 1987. Author: Principle of Artificial Intelligence, 1993. Pres. Indian Statis. Inst. Workers' Orgn., Calcutta, 1987-89, 92-93. Merit scholar Bengal Engring. Coll., 1973-77, Rotary Club India scholar for study abroad, 1978, rsch. fellow for knowledge-based computing Govt. India Dept. Electronics and UN Devel. Program, India, 1990; recipient K.S. Krisnan Meml. award for best system-oriented paper in computer vision, Inst. Elec. and Telecomm. Engrs., 1993. Mem. Indian Soc. for Fuzzy Math. (founder), Indian Unit for Pattern Recognition and Artificial Intelligence. Mem. Janata Dal. Avocations: music, raj yoga, astrology. Home: 28/7 College Rd, Post Botanic Garden, W Bengal Howrah 711 103, India Office: Indian Statis Inst, 203 B T Road, W Bengal Calcutta 700 035, India

RAY, PRADEEP KUMAR, computing and information systeme educator; b. Calcutta, India, May 11, 1955; arrived in Australia, 1992; s. Sunil Kumar and Geeta (Sen) R.; m. Kumkum Sengupta, June 12, 1982; children: Supratik, Mililani. BTech. in Electronics Engring., Banaras Hindu U., India, 1976; MTech. in Elec. Engring., Indian Inst. Tech., Kanpur, 1978; PhD in Computer Sci., U. Tech., Sydney, Australia, 1997. Cert. in gen. mgmt. Indian Inst. Mgmt., Calcutta. Sr. project engr. Webel Bus. Machines, Calcutta, 1983-86; dep. mgr. EDP Webfil Ltd., Calcutta, 1986-87, mgr. digital sys., 1987-88, sr. mgr. digital sys., 1988-92; sr. rsch. scientist, rschr. Distributed Systems Tech. Ctr., Sydney, 1992-96; lectr. computing U. Western Sydney, 1996-99; sr. lectr. info. systems U. NSW, Australia, 1999—; program chmn. 8th Internat. Fedn. for Info. Processing-IEEE Conf., 1997, mem. internat. program com. ISEEE, IFIP Conf., 1997-99; vis. prof. Loria, France, 1999. Contbr. articles to sci. jours., including Jour. Network and Sys. Mgmt. Spl. grantee U. West Sydney, 1997—, grantee Australian Rsch. Coun., 1998, Internat. Industry Rsch. Partnership grantee, 1999. Mem. IEEE (sec. com. on networking 1998—, panels chmn. conf. Atlanta 1998, internat. liaison Oceania region 1999—, exec. com. on enterprise networking, 1998—), Assn. for Computing Machinery. Avocation: classical and light Indian music. Home: 11 Yengo Ct, Wattle Grove, Sydney NSW 2173, Australia Office: Univ NSW, Sch Info Systems, Sydney NSW 2052, Australia

RAY, PRASANTA KUMAR, science administrator; b. West Bengal, India, Sept. 29, 1941; s. Benode Behari Ray and Labanya Prava Das; m. Khana Basu; children: Partha Sarathi, Amartya Kumar. BSc, Calcutta (India) U., 1962, MSc, 1964, PhD, 1968, DSc, 1974. SSO BARC, Bombay, 1973-76; dir. CNCI, Calcutta, 1976-77, Bengal Immunity, Calcutta, 1977-78; dir. ADM Lab. Med. Coll. Pa. and Hosp., 1978-84; dir. ITRC, Lucknow, India, 1984-92, Bose Inst., Calcutta, 1992—. Author: Pollution and Health, 1992; editor Immunobiology, Transplantation, Cancer, Pregnancy, 1983; editor Advanced Immunity and Cancer Therapy, 1984, 85. Recipient Cancer Rsch. award Indian Coun. Med. Rsch., 1977, Ranbaxy Nat. award Ranbaxy Found., 1985. Fellow Inst. Biology (chartered biologist), Indian Nat. Acad. Scis., West Bengal Acad. Sci. Hindu. Avocations: listening to music, traveling, good food, watching television. Home: CD-246 1st Fl Sector I, Salt Lake City, Calcutta 700 064, India Office: Bose Inst, P-1/12 CIT SCHEME VIIM, Calcutta 700 053, India

RAY, ROBERT, educator, sculptor; b. Fort Wayne, Ind., Mar. 31, 1951; s. Robert Martin and Jewel J. R.; m. Dany Marie, Aug. 12, 1972; 1 child, Zackary Martin. AA, Miami Dade Jr. Coll., 1971; BS, Fla. State U., 1973; MS, Valdosta (Ga.) State Coll., 1985. Cert. early childhood tchr. Art tchr. Albany (Ga.) Jr. High Sch., 1975-77; children's libr. Roddenbery Meml. Libr., Cairo, Ga., 1977-78; kindergarten tchr. Beckbranch Kindergarten, Calvary, Ga., 1978-80, Whigham (Ga.) Pub. Sch., 1980-90, Northside Pub. Sch., Cairo, Ga., 1990—. Office: Northside Elementary School Cairo GA 31728 also: 2930 Hadley Ferry Rd Cairo GA 31728-7114

RAY, RONALD DUDLEY, lawyer; b. Hazard, Ky., Oct. 30, 1942. BA in Psychology and English, Centre Coll., 1964; JD magna cum laude, U. Louisville, 1971. Assoc. Greenebaum, Doll & McDonald, 1971-75, ptnr., 1975-84, 85-86; ptnr. Ray & Morris, Louisville, 1986-89; mng. ptnr. Ronald Ray Attys., Louisville, 1990—; dep. asst. sec. def. Pentagon, Washington, 1984-85; adj. prof. law U. Louisville Sch. Law, 1972-80; commr. Presdl. Commn. on Assigment of Women in Mil., 1992. Author: Military Necessity & Homosexuality, 1993; sr. legal editor: Personnel Policy Manual, Bank Supervisory Policies, The Bank Employee Handbook, 1985-86; mil. historian. State fin. chmn. Nat. Fin. Com. for George Bush for Pres.; chmn. Vietnam Vets. Leadership Program in Ky., 1982-85, Ky. Vietnam Vets. Meml. Fund, 1985-91; trustee Marine Corps Command and Staff Found., 1985-92; mem. exec. com. State Cen. Com., Ky. Rep. Party, 1986-90; mem. Am. Battle Monuments Commn., 1990-94; spokesman Coalition of Am. Vets., 1998—, chmn., 1999—. With USMC, 1964-69; col. USMCR (ret.). Decorated Silver Star medal with gold star, Bronze Star medal, Purple Heart, Vietnamese Cross of Gallantry, Vietnamese Honor Medal; recipient Nat. Eagle award Nat. Guard Assn., 1985. Mem. Naval Inst. (life), Marine Corps Res. Officers' Assn. Home: Halls Hill Farm 3317 Halls Hill Rd Crestwood KY 40014-9523

RAY, ROSABELL HARRIET See BATTIN, R(OSABELL) RAY

RAY, SIDDHARTHA SANKAR, former ambassador; b. Calcutta, India, Oct. 20, 1920; s. Sudhir Chandra and Shrimati Aparna Devi (Das) R.; m. Maya Battacharya, 1947. Grad., Presidential Coll., Calcutta. Bar: Inner Temple. Sr. advocate Supreme Ct.; former min. law Govt. West Bengal, India, leader opposition, 1969; mem. Lok Sabha, 1971-72, West Bengal Legis. Assembly, 1972-77; min. edn., culture and social welfare, min. in charge West Bengal Affairs Govt. of India, 1971-72, chief min. West Bengal

March, 1972-77; mem. Govt. of Pubjab, India, 1986-89; with adminstrn. of Chandigarh, 1986-89, amb. to U.S.A., 1992-96. Trustee Nehru Trust for Cambridge (U.K.) U.; mem. exec. com. Jawaharlal Nehru Meml. Fund; active Indian Nat. Trust Art and Cultural Heritage. Avocations: reading, sports. Home: 2 Beltala Rd, Calcutta 700026, India also: Indian Embassy 2107 Massachusetts Ave NW Washington DC 20008-2811*

RAY, STEPHEN ALAN, academic administrator, lawyer; b. Oklahoma City, Aug. 26, 1956; s. Thompson Eugene and Dorothea Hodges. BA summa cum laude, St. Thomas Sem., 1978; PhD, Harvard U., 1986; JD, U. Calif., Hastings, 1990. Bar: Calif. 1990, Mass. 1994. Assoc. Richards, Watson & Gershon, L.A., 1990-93; lectr. theology Boston Coll., Chestnut Hill, Mass., 1993-95; staff counsel Houghton Mifflin Co., Boston, 1995-96; asst. dean acad. affairs Harvard Law Sch., Cambridge, 1998—, dir. acad. affairs, 1996-98; vis. lectr. religion Harvard Divinity Sch., spring 1995; adv. bd. Harvard Native Am. Program, 1999—. Author: The Modern Soul, 1987. Vol. AIDS action com., Boston, 1994-96; atty. vol. AIDS Project L.A., 1991-93; Native Am. Adv. Com. on Repatriation, Peabody Mus., 1999—. Mem. ABA, Cherokee Nation Okla. E-mail: aray@law.harvard.edu. Office: Harvard Law Sch Griswold Hall 207 Cambridge MA 02138

RAY, SWAPAN KUMAR, molecular biologist; b. Chakdaha, W. Bengal, India, June 17, 1957; came to U.S., 1990; s. Somendra Chandra and Sefali Rani (Bhowmick) R. BS with hons., U. Calcutta, India, 1978, MS, 1980, PhD, 1989. Postdoctoral rsch. assoc. Brookhaven Nat. Lab., Upton, N.Y., 1990-92; postdoctoral fellow Med. U. S.C., Charelston, 1993, instr. medicine, 1994-95, rsch. scientist, 1997-98; instr. medicine Emory U., Atlanta, 1995-96; ast. prof. neurology Med. U. S.C., Charleston, S.C., 1998—. Contbr. over 100 articles to profl. jours. Recipient postdoctoral award NIH, 1990-92, 93, co-investigator award, 1997, co-investigator award, Am. Health Assistance Found., 1998. Mem. Soc. for Neurosci., N.Y. Acad. Sci., Am. Soc. for Biochemistry and Molecular Biology, Am. Assn. for Cancer Rsch., Am. Soc. Neurochem., Internat. Soc. Neurochem. Achievements include research revealing that chemotherapeutic drugs (Ara-C, Mitoxantrone and Taxol) cause internucleosomal DNA fragmentation in leukemic cells; Bcl-xS expression induces differentiation in CML K562 cells; retinoids downregulate telomerase activity in AML and glioblastoma cells; calpain is activated and involved in apoptosis in Alzheimer's disease, Parkinson's disease, spinal cord injury and EAE. Avocations: travel, writing, reading, photography and classical music. Office: Dept Neurology Med U of SC 96 Jonathan Lucas St Ste 309 Charleston SC 29425-8900

RAY, TERRILL WYLIE, physical scientist; b. Wichita, Kans., Nov. 29, 1967; s. Robert Gibson and Marvaline Joyce (Bannon) R. Student, Wichita State U., 1985-86; BS in Geophys. Enging., Colo. Sch. of Mines, 1990; MS in Planetary Sci., Calif. Inst. Tech., 1993, PhD in Planetary Sci. and Geophysics, 1995. Summer geophysicist Unocal, Midland, Tex., 1990; rsch./tchg. asst. Calif. Inst. Tech., Pasadena, 1990-95; phys. sci. officer U.S. Arms Control and Disarmament Agy., Washington, 1995-99, U.S. Dept. State, Washington, 1999—; mem. program com. Internat. Geosci. and Remote Sensing Symposium, Pasadena, 1994; mem. planning com. Global Environ. Monitoring Early in the Next Century, World Resources Inst./Calif. Inst. Tech., Washington and Pasadena, 1992-94. Judge Denver Met. Area Sci. Fair, 1987, Calif. State Sci. Fair, L.A., 1993-95. Recipient Meritorious Honor award U.S. Arms Control and Disarmament Agy., 1999; Grad. Rsch. fellow NASA, 1993-95, Planetary Geology and Geophysics Undergrad. Rsch. fellow, 1985. Mem. IEEE, Am. Geophys. Union, Soc. Exploration Geophysicists, Nat. Capital Area Skeptics. Avocations: softball, music, reading, writing, crocheting. Home: 3006 Furman Ln Apt 103 Alexandria VA 22306-1018

RAYA, AFRODITI CHR., nursing educator; b. Polygyros, Halkidiki, Greece, Mar. 23, 1928; d. Christos N. and Chryssoula Chr. (Kioroglou). Diploma, Higher Sch. Nursing Evangelism, Hosp, Athens, 1957; BSN magna cum laude, Boston U., 1965; MA, Columbia U., 1966, MEd, 1974, EdD, 1975. Staff nurse Evangelismos Hosp., Athens, 1957-61, tchr. Higher Sch. Nursing, 1961-66, dir. nursing studies, 1966-86; adj. assoc. and prof. dept. nursing, U. Athens, 1981-97, emeritus prof., 1997—; mem. ministry exam. com. Mental Health Nursing Specialty Cert., Athens, 1984—, Thessaloniki, Greece, 1992—, Ioannina, Greece, 1996. Author: (books) The Nurse: The Grandeur of Her Profession, 1972, Psychiatric Nursing: A Conceptual Approach, 1975, Psychiatric Nursing - Fundamental Principles, 1978, Basic Nursing, 1987, Mental Health and Psychiatric Nursing, 1993, 99, Basic Nursing - Theoretical and Deontological Principles, 1995, 98, 2000; co-editor: Collaborative Research in Nursing, 1981, Quality in Nursing-Realities and Visions, 1996; mem. editl. bd. Scandinavian Jour. Caring Scis., Nursing Ethics, Jour. Psychiat. and Mental Health Nursing. Recipient scholarship Greek State Scholarship Inst., Athens, 1963-66. Mem. Hellenic Nat. Grad. Nurses' Assn., Greek Soc. Nursing Studies, Greek Anti-Cancer Soc., Greek Gerontol. Soc. Greek Christian Orthodox. Avocations: reading, writing, travel. Home: Marousi, 12 Frangokklisias St, 151 25 Athens Greece

RAYBURN, WENDELL GILBERT, educational association executive; b. Detroit, May 20, 1929; s. Charles Jefferson and Grace Victoria (Winston) R.; m. Gloria Ann Myers, Aug. 19; children: Rhonda Renee, Wendell Gilbert; 1 stepson, Mark K. Williams. B.A., Eastern Mich. U., 1951; M.A., U. Mich., 1952; Ed.D., Wayne State U., Detroit, 1972. Tchr., adminstr. Detroit public schs., 1954-68; from asst. dir. to dir. spl. projects U. Detroit, 1968-72, assoc. dean acad. support programs, 1972-74; dean Univ. Coll., U. Louisville, 1974-80; pres. Savannah (Ga.) State Coll., 1980-88, Lincoln U., Jefferson City, Mo., 1988-97; v.p. fin. Am. Assn. State Colls. and Univs., Washington, 1997—; chmn. adv. com. Office for Advancement of Pub. Black Colls., 1989-97. Trustee Candler Gen. Hosp., 1982-85, Telfair Acad. Arts, 1980-87; bd. dirs. Candler Health Svcs., 1985-88, YMCA Blue Ridge Assembly, 1986-88, Internat. Food and Agrl. Devel. and Econ. Cooperation, 1988-94, Meml. Cmty. Hosp., Jefferson City, 1988-94, United Way Mo., 1989-97, Mo. Capital Punishment Resource Ctr., 1990-95, Stephens Coll., Columbia, Mo., 1993-97, Capital Regional Med. Ctr., 1994-97; campaign chmn. Jefferson City Area United Way, 1994-95. With AUS, 1952-59. Decorated Commendation medal with pendant; recipient Disting. Alumni award Wayne State U., 1993, Whitney M. Young Jr. award Lincoln Found., 1980, Disting. Citizens award City of Louisville, 1980. Mem. Mo. Bar Assn. (foresight com.), Am. Assn. Higher Edn., Am. Assn. State Colls. and Univs. (bd. dirs. 1988—, chmn. 1992-93), Nat. Assn. State Univs. and Land Grant Colls., Nat. Assn. for Equal Opportunity in Higher Edn., Coun. on Pub. Higher Edn. for Mo. (chmn. 1991-93), Coun. of 1890 Colls. and Univs., Jefferson City C. of C. (bd. dirs. 1988-97), Rotary (bd. dirs. Jefferson City 1989-96, pres. 1994-95), Kappa Alpha Psi, Sigma Pi Phi. Episcopalian. Office: Am Assn State Colls and Univs 1307 New York Ave NW Fl 5 Washington DC 20005-4704

RAYLESBERG, ALAN IRA, lawyer; b. N.Y.C., Dec. 6, 1950; s. Daniel David and Sally Doris (Mantell) R.; m. Caren Thea Coven, Nov. 20, 1983; children: Lisa Maris, Jason Todd. BA, NYU, 1972; JD cum laude, Boston U., 1975. Bar: N.Y. 1976, U.S. Dist. Ct. (so. dist.) N.Y. 1976, U.S. Dist. Ct. (ea. dist.) N.Y. 1978, U.S. Tax Ct. 1981, U.S. Ct. Appeals (2d and 5th cirs.) 1982, U.S. Ct. Appeals (1st cir.) 1986, U.S. Ct. Appeals (9th cir.) 1996. Assoc. Orans, Elsen & Polstein, N.Y.C., 1975-77; assoc. Guggenheimer & Untermyer, N.Y.C., 1977-83, ptnr., 1983-85; ptnr. Rosenman & Colin, N.Y.C., 1985—; co-chmn. litigation dept. Rosenman & Colin, 1998-99, chmn. litigation dept., 1999—; adj. instr. N.Y. Law Sch., 1980-83; instr. Nat. Inst. of Trial Advocacy; mem. adv. group comml. divsn., mem. mediation panel N.Y. State Supreme Ct.; mem. arbitration panel U.S. Dist. Ct. (ea. dist.) N.Y.; judge Nat. Moot Ct. Competition, 1980—. Bd. dirs. Fund for Modern Cts., 1994—. Mem. ABA, Fed. Bar Coun., Assn. Bar City N.Y., N.Y. County Lawyers Assn. (bd. dirs. 1995-98, 99—, fed. ct. com. 1988—, appellate ct. com. 1990—, co-chmn. appellate ct. com. 1992-93, chair appellate ct. com. 1993-96), N.Y. County Lawyers Assn. Found. (bd. dirs. 1998—), N.Y. State Bar Assn. (ho. delegates 1996—), Securities Industry Assn. (legal and compliance divsn) N.Y. Coun. Def. Lawyers, Town Club of Newcastle (mem. exec. com. 1987-91). Democrat. Jewish. Office: Rosenman & Colin 575 Madison Ave Fl 26 New York NY 10022-2585

RAYMAN, PAULA M., economics educator; b. N.Y.C., Feb. 27, 1947; d. Abraham Samuel and Rita (Relkin) R.; m. Robert Russell Read, Apr. 1, 1973; children: Alyssa, Lily. BA, Hunter Coll., 1970; PhD, Boston Coll., 1977. Postdoctoral fellow NIMH, Bethesda, 1982-84; assoc. prof. econs. Wellesley (Mass.) Coll., 1986-94, assoc. prof. sociology, 1990-94, dir. women's sci. program, 1991-94; exec. dir. Radcliff Pub. Policy Inst., Cambridge, Mass., 1994—; vis. prof. Harvard Med. Sch., Cambridge, 1983-85; mem. faculty Harvard Grad. Sch. Edn., 1995—; disting. vis. scholar Cambridge (Eng.) U., 1992. Editor Temple U. Press, 1983—. Mem. Mass. Jobs Coun., Boston, 1989-98; dir. work-family project Fleet Bank, Boston, 1996-98; bd. dirws. Baumann Found., Washington, 1996—, New England Bd. Higher Edn., 1997—; mem. adv. bd. Working Today, N.Y.C., 1996—. Bunting fellow Radcliffe Coll., 1985-86; grantee NSF, 1985-86; recipient Swedish Bicentennial award, 1990. Mem. Assn. Women Sci. (adv. bd. 1991—), Am. Sociol. Assn. (chair labor sect., Svc. award 1985), Boston Club. Jewish. Avocations: hiking, collage-making. Office: Radcliff Pub Policy Ctr 69 Brattle St Cambridge MA 02138-3442

RAYMOND, AZMAN ALI, neurologist, consultant; b. Penang, Malaysia, Apr. 28, 1960; s. Ali Jantan and Norene Goh; m. Fauziah Kassim, May 24, 1980. MBBS with honors, Monash U., Melbourne, Australia, 1984; MD in Neurology, Monash U., 1996; MMed in Internal Medicine, Nat. U. Singapore, 1989, Nat. U. Malaysia, Kuala Lumpur, 1991. Intern Alfred Hosp., Melbourne, Australia, 1985-86; resident med. officer Gen. Hosp., Kuala Lumpur, Malaysia, 1986-87; trainee lectr. and registrar Nat. U. Malaysia, Kuala Lumpur, 1987-91, lectr. and cons. neurologist, 1994-95, assoc. prof. neurology, 1995-98, cons. neurologist, 1995—, prof. neurology, 1999—; rsch. fellow, head deptt. medicine Nat. Hosp. Neurology and Neurosurgery, London, 1992-94. Contbr. articles to profl. jours., chpts. to books. Fellow Singapore Acad. Medicine, 1989, Internat. Fedn. Neurophysiology, 1993. Mem. Malaysian Soc. Epilepsy (life), Malaysian Neurosci. Soc., Headache Soc. Malaysia (v.p. 1996-98, pres. 1998—), SLE Soc. Malaysia (life), Acad. Medicine Malaysia, Islamic Med. Assn. Malaysia (treas. 1994-95, v.p. 1996-98), Asean Neurol. Assn. (Malaysian rep. epilepsy chpt. 1996—). Muslim. Avocations: reading, music, touring, table tennis, sketching portraits. Home: 44 Jalan PJS 9/28, Bandar Sunway, 46150 Petaling Jaya Selangor, Malaysia Office: Nat U Malaysia Dept Med, Jalan Yaaoob Lahf, 56000 Bandar Tun Razak Cheras, Kuala Lumpur, Malaysia

RAYMOND, LEE R., oil company executive; b. Watertown, S.D., Aug. 13, 1938; m. Charlene Raymond. BSChemE, U. Wis., 1960; PhDChemE, U. Minn., 1963. Various engring. positions Exxon Corp., Tulsa, Houston, N.Y.C. and Caracas, Venezuela, 1963-72; mgr. planning Internat. Co. divsn. Exxon Corp., N.Y.C., 1972-75, pres. Exxon Nuc. Co. divsn., 1979-81, exec. v.p. Exxon Enterprises Inc. divsn., 1981-83, sr. v.p., dir., 1984-86, pres., dir., 1987-93, chmn., CEO, 1993-99; v.p. Lago Oil, Netherlands Antilles, 1975-76, pres., dir., 1976-79; pres., dir. Esso Inter-Am. Inc., Coral Gables, Fla., 1983-84, sr. v.p., dir., 1984—; chmn., CEO & pres. Exxon Mobil Corp., Irving, TX, 1999—; bd. dirs. J.P. Morgan & Co., Inc., N.Y.C., Morgan Guaranty Trust Co. of N.Y., N.Y.C., Am. Petroleum Inst.; mem. nat. task force on minority high achievement in Coll. Bd. Bd. dirs. United Negro Coll. Fund, Project Shelter PRO-AM, 1991—, Dallas Citizens Coun., Jason Found. for Edn.; trustee Wis. Alumni Rsch. Found., 1987—, Bus. Coun. Internat. Understanding, Inc., 1988—; trustee So. Meth. U.; mem. Tri Lateral Commn., U. Wis. Found.; mem. emergency com. Am. trade; ptnr. emeritus N.Y.C. Partnership; active Am. Coun. on Germany, Dallas Com. Fgn. Rels., Dallas Wildcat Com., 1993. Mem. Am. Soc. Engring. (nat. adv. coun.), Am. Soc. Royal Bot. Garden (founder), Bus. coun., Bus. Roundtable, Nat. Petroleum Coun. (mem. product supply com.), Coun. Fgn. Rels., Singapore-U.S. Bus. Coun., Nat. Acad. Engring. (bd. dirs.), Am. Soc. Engring. Educators (nat. adv. coun. 1994), Occupl. Physicians Scholarship Fund (chmn. fundraising campaign 1995), Coll. Bd. (nat. task force on minority high achievement 1997).

RAYMOND, LLOYD WILSON, machinery company executive; b. Middleboro, Mass., Jan. 4, 1922; s. Millard Edgar and Ethel (Morrison) R.; m. Joyce Elaine Cox, Nov. 10, 1972. Student, N.Y.U., 1952; ThB, Christian Bible Coll., Rocky Mount, N.C., 1995, ThM, 1996, PhD in Religion, 1998; D Min., S.W. Bible Coll. and Sem., Sulphur, La., 1997; MBA, M. Photography, Internat. U., 1999. Clk. Pub. Housing Adminstrn., Washington, 1941-42; adminstrv. asst. devel. dept. Pub. Housing Adminstrn., Washington and N.Y.C., 1946-55; machinery data mgr., warehouse mgr. Nat. Machinery Exch., Inc., Newark, 1955-76; office mgr., machinery data mgr., sales exec. Nat. Machinery Exch., Inc., Pico Rivera, Calif., 1976—. Author: Titanic-What Went Wrong; composer (opera) Rag Doll, 1999; designer computerized info. mgmt. and quote generating sys., 1991, registered trademark Infodex. Founder, dir. Living Pictures Programs, 1965-95. Mem. Soc. Profl. Journalists, Investigative Reporters and Editors. Avocations: writing, photography. Fax: 909-949-6284. E-mail: lloyd-wraymond@cs.com.

RAYMOND, MARILYN PALMA, health care services executive; b. Niagara Falls, N.Y., Apr. 9, 1933; d. William Raymond and Grace (Crossley) Laffsa; children: Bryan, Matthieu. RN, St. Mary Hosp., Walla Walla, Wash., 1954; BSN, Hunter Coll., 1960; MA, NYU, 1962. Cert. RN; pub. health nurse supr. Drug counselor N.Y.C. Dept. Health, 1970-74; patient svc. mgr. Vis. Nurse Svc. N.Y., N.Y.C., 1974-80; dir. CHHA/LHHCP Montefiore Med. Ctr., Bronx, N.Y., 1980-85; corp. dir. N.Y.C. Health & Hosp. Corp., N.Y.C., 1986-88; adminstr. DPS VIP Health Svcs., Queens, N.Y., 1990-95; owner, chief cons. M-R Consultants, Yonkers, N.Y., 1984—; site visitor Nat. League Nursing, CHAP, 1995-98. Pub. Independent Community Health Nurse Project: A Changing Work Model, Hospitals Without Walls: Home Health Care can Reduce Costs and Hasten Recovery. Founder Soho 20 Women's Cooperative Art Gallery, N.Y.C., 1973. Fed. Nursing Edn. scholar, 1960-62. Mem. Home Care Assn. of N.Y. State, Rotary Club (West Yonkers), Sigma Theta Tau. Democrat. Avocations: music, jazz, classical and liturgical. Home: 120 Franklin Ave Yonkers NY 10705-2808

RAYMOND, NIGEL JOHN, consultant physician, educator; b. Timaru, New Zealand, Apr. 18, 1960; s. John Archdale Raymond and Mildred Pauline Holst; m. Maryse Karin Arnell; children: Camilla, Rebecka, Anton. MB, ChB, U. Otago, Dunedin, New Zealand, 1985. Registered in internal medicine, New Zealand. Registrar Christchurch (New Zealand) Hosp., 1987-88; med. registrar Waikato (New Zealand) Hosp., 1989-90, Auckland (New Zealand) Hosp., 1991; fellow in infectious diseases Emory U. Sch. Medicine, Atlanta, 1992-96; cons. physician Capital Coast Health Ltd., Wellington, New Zealand, 1996—; clin. sr. lectr. gen. medicine and infectious diseases U. Otago, 1996—; sr. med. examiner NZ REX, New Zealand Med. Coun. Contbr. articles on infectious diseases to med. jours., chpts. to books. Jr. scholar Govt. of New Zealand, 1977; travel grantee Am. Soc. for Microbiology, 1994, 95. Fellow Royal Australasian Coll. Physicians; mem. Australasian Soc. for Infectious Disease, Infectious Diseases Soc. Am. Avocations: hiking, skiing, kayaking. Office: Wellington Hosp Ward 17, Riddiford St, Wellington New Zealand

RAYMOND, ROBERT, banker; b. Paris, June 30, 1933; s. Henri and Andrée (Aubriere) R.; m. Monique Bremond, Apr. 30, 1970. M in Law and Econs., U. Paris Sorbonne, France, 1953; postgrad. in pvt. law and econs., U. Paris Sorbonne, 1954-55. Various profl. positions Bank of France, Paris, 1951-64, staff internat. dept., 1964-73, dir. internat. rels., 1973-75, dep. head of rsch., 1975-80, head of rsch., 1981-90, head of credit dept., 1990-93; dir. gen. European Monetary Inst., Franfurt, Germany, 1994-98; permanent rep., sr. spl. advisor to exec. bd. European Ctrl. Bank, Washington, 1999—; chmn. group monetary experts Com. of Govs. of European Economic Cmtys. Ctrl. Banks, Basle, Switzerland, 1981-91; dep. sec. gen. Nat. Coun. of Credit, Paris, 1975-81; assoc. prof. U. Paris Sorbonne, 1978-83; dir., prof. Ctr. for Advanced Study of Banking, Paris, 1978-89; advisor to exec. bd. European Ctrl. Bank, 1998; chmn. CPR, Paris. Author: La Monnaie, 1978, Les Institutions Monétaires en France 1991-95, L'unification Monétaire en Europe, 1993-96; co-author Les Relations Économiques et Monetaires Internationales, 3rd rev. edit., 1986. Decorated Officer Legion of Honor, France. Mem. AFEI (chmn.). Office: CPR, 30 rue St Georges, 75009 Paris France

RAYMONT, WARWICK DEANE, chemical engineer, environmental engineer; b. Jamestown, Australia, June 14, 1941; s. Keith Mostyn and Florence Brenda Dewhirst (Langdon-Parsons) Ring; m. Sandra Kay Sullivan, Oct. 23, 1989; children: Jason, Jared, Jenelle, Aleksei. BS, diploma edn., ASOPA/UNSW, 1962; PhD, U. San Moritz, 1970, Pa. State U., 1972; Dip.T.Sec, U. South Australia, 1977; DSc, City U. L.A., 1989. Lic. organic chemistry, chem. engring. Tchr. sci. Cath. and Ind. Colls., South Australia, 1963-65; chemist Dairy Analytical Labs., Tasmania, 1965-68, chief chemist, 1968-70, dir., 1970-72; tchr. sci. Edn. Dept., South Australia, 1972-77; postdoctoral fellow WHO/Columbia U., N.Y.C., 1977-79; pvt. practice rsch. cons. South Australia and N.S.W., 1979—; mgr. R&D Pharmalliance, Adelaide, Australia; del. WHO Codex Com., N.Y.C., 1970-71; mem. adv. com. Sr. Secondary Assessment Bd. South Australia, 1988-89; cons. South Australia Health Commn., 1989—. Leader Boy Scouts Assn., Australia, 1960—; chmn. Morella Community Assn., South Australia, 1985-87; exec. mem. South Australia Assn. State Sch. Orgns., 1973-78; chief instr. Air Tng. Corps, Royal Australian Air Force, South Australia, 1988—. Acting capt. Australian Army, 1961. Mem. Am. Chem. Soc., Australian Inst. Sci. Tech., Mentally Handicapped Children's Assn. (life), N.Y. Acad. Scis., ABI Rsch. Inst. (lifetime dep. gov.). Achievements include predictions of global warming, discovery of DDT in human breast milk, implication of cadmium in atherosclerosis. Fax: 618 8289 8289; e-mail: drraymont@pharma.com.au. Home: PO Box 346, Golden Grove SA 5125, Australia Office: Stolair Pty Ltd, PO Box 963, Kent Town SA 5071, Australia also: Pharmalliance Pty Ltd, 6 Chapel St, Norwood SA 5067, Australia

RAYMUNDO, PAULO MANSUR, petroleum engineer, consultant, explorer, researcher; b. Salvador, Bahia, Brazil, Feb. 11, 1956; s. Lutfalla and Hilda (Mansur) R. Degree in Electronic Enging., U. Fed. da Bahia, Salvador, 1978; degree in Elec. Enging., UFBA, Salvador, 1979. Various engring. positions Schlumberger, Aracaju, Sergipe, Brazil and Comodoro Rivadavia, Argentina, 1980; various engring., mgmt. positions Schlumberger Surenco, Bridgetown, Barbados, 1981, San Fernando, Trinidad and Tobago, 1981; rise dir., zero defect, log quality control chmn., various engring., mgmt., mktg. positions Schlumberger Middle East, Abu Dhabi, United Arab Emirates, 1982-84; various mgmt., recruiting positions Schlumberger, Europe, 1985-86; cons. engring., mgmt., recruiting oil svc. cos., Salvador, 1987—; satellite tv sys. cons., 1989—; founder Roaiche Observatory, 1996; lectr. univs. worldwide, 1983-86; expeditions to over 120 countries, 1980—; cons. in field. Author: LDT-CNL Application in BAB Field, 1983, The Response of Nuclear Tools in the Presence of Non-Damaging Fluid, 1984, Power, Intuition and the Harmonious Development of Man, Oriental Psychology Applied to Intercultural Management in the Corporate World, 1989; contbr. tech. papers to profl. jours.; holder 2 patents. Schlumberger fellow Heriott-Watt U., Scotland, 1983. Mem. AAAS, Am. Mgmt. Assn., Am. Astronomical Soc., Can. Soc. Petroleum Geologists, Norsk Petroleumsforening, Soc. Petroleum Engrs., Soc. Profl. Well Log Analysts, Am. Geophys. Union, World Future Soc., Planetary Soc., Mensa, Travelers' Century Club, The Explorers Club, Eta Kappa Nu. Roman Catholic. Avocations: world travel, running, astronomy, yoga, world paper money collecting. Office: 504 Golden Tower, Av Sete Setembro 2152, 40080-001 Salvador Bahia, Brazil

RAYNAL, JOSE ANGEL, hydrologist, educator; b. Chihuahua, Mex., June 30, 1951; s. Jose A. Raynal and Sara Villasenor; m. Maria Elena Gutierrez, July 9, 1977; children: Jose Angel, Maria Elena. Degree in civil engring., U. Autonoma Chihuahua, 1973; MSc, U. Nat. Autonoma Mex., Mexico City, 1976; PhD, Colo. State U., 1985. Office head Sec. Agr. and Water Resources, Mexico City, 1975-77, asst. head dept., 1977-78, head dept., 1978-80; prof. U. Nat. Autonoma Mex., Mexico City, 1983-90, U. Autonoma Chihuahua, 1989-94, U. de las America-Puebla, Cholula, Mex., 1995—; cons. Aqua Terra Cons., Chihuahua. Editor: Hydrology and Water Resources Education and Training; editor-in-chief: Environmental Engineering and Health Sciences, 2000; contbr. articles to profl. jours. State pres. partido Verde Ecologista de Mexico, Chihuahua, 1993, rep. candidate, 1991. Recipient excellence award Assn. Mex. Hidraulica, 1988. Fellow ASCE; mem. Acad. Nat. Ingenieria (treas. 1997-99), N.Y. Acad. Scis., Am. Inst. Hydrology (cert.). Mem. Green Party. Roman Catholic. Avocation: bowling. Fax: (52-2) 229-2258. E-mail: jraynal@mail.udlap.mx. Home: Casa D-6A, Cholula Puebla 72820, Mexico Office: U de las Americas-Puebla, Ex-Hacienda Sta Catarina Ma, Cholula Puebla 72820, Mexico

RAYNAUD, GUILLAUME ROGER, sales executive, marketing professional; b. Paris, France, May 13, 1968; s. Michel and Beatrix (Dogon) R. Degree in biology, Lycee Pasteur, Neuilly, France, 1988; degree in fin., E.S.D.E.-SUP, Paris, 1992; degree in Mandarin, T.L.I., Taipei, Taiwan, 1996. Salesperson, supr. Fairchief Coop., Taipei, 1994-97; sales coord. Linde Materials Handling, Singapore, 1997—. Dir. Singapore 99 Ultimate Disc Open Tourney, 1999. 1st class officer French mil., 1991-92. Avocations: ultimate disc, tennis, bowling, cycling, painting. Home: 6 rue Daubigny, F-75017 Paris France Office: Linde Material Handling, 5 Loyang Way, 508720 Singapore Singapore

RAYNER, COLIN ROBERT, plastic surgeon; b. London, Oct. 28, 1938; s. Charles Wilfred and Helen Patricia (Rollins) R.; m. Margaret Mary Salt, Jan. 1, 1966 (div.); children: Clare, Dominic, Suzannah; m. Ruth Louise Lester; 1 child: Matthew. MB, BS, London U., 1964, MS, 1980. House surgeon in traumatic and gen. surgery various hosps., Eng., 1965-71; sr. house officer in plastic surgery Queen Victoria Hosp., East Grinstead, Eng., 1971-72; plastic surgery registrar St. George's Hosp., London, 1972; sr. registrar dept. exptl. surgery Westminster Hosp., London, 1973, sr. registrar head and neck cancer surgery, 1974; sr. house officer plastic surgery Wexham Park Hosp., Slough, Eng., 1975; sr. registrar plastic surgery Withington Hosp., Manchester, Eng., 1975-77; pvt. practice Aberdeen, Scotland, 1977—; sr. cons. plastic surgeon Grampian Health Bd./U. Aberdeen, 1978-91; dir. clin. rsch., con. plastic surgeon Birmingham Accident Hosp., 1991—; founder Colin Rayner Enterprises, 1991—; clin. dir. plastic surgery & trauma unit Univ. of Birmingham Plastic Surgery Unit, Brimingham, England, 1992—; cons. plastic surgeon Selly Oak Hosp., Birmingham, 1991—; dir. jour. Wound Mgmt., 1990—; mem. staff Royal Aberdeen Children's Hosp., Aberdeen Royal Infirmary; editorial com. Brit. Jour. Plastic Surgery, 1974-76; reviewer for internat. abstracts Plastic and Reconstructive Surgery, 1981-85; mem. faculty U. Aberdeen, 1984-88; referee med. jours.; mem. Nat. Disaster Planning Group; mem. Brit. med. relief team Chelyabinsk train disaster USSR, 1989; presenter Integrity in Pub. Life seminar Balliol Coll., Oxford, 1995. Fellow Royal Soc. Medicine; mem. Brit. Assn. Plastic Surgeons (coun. mem. 1984-87), Brit. Soc. Surgery of the Hand, Brit. Burns Assn., Assn. Head and Neck Oncologists Gt. Britain, Brit. Assn. Aesthetic Plastic Surgeons. Fax: 0121 440 7708. Home: 64 Wellington Rd, Edgbaston, Birmingham B152ET, England Office: Bupa Parkway Hosp, Solihull, West Midlands B91 2PP, England also: Bupa Southbank Hosp, Worcester WR5 3YB, England

RAYNER, NANCY ALISON, zoologist, researcher; b. Masterton, New Zealand, Feb. 10, 1927; arrived in South Africa, 1949; d. James Patrick and Florence Letitia (Overman) Cooper; m. Arthur Asquith Rayner, July 8, 1949 (dec. July 1994); children: Alison Margaret, Colin Frederick, Brian Lindsay, Marion Patricia, John Philip. BS, Victoria U. Coll., New Zealand, 1947; BS with honors, U. Natal, South Africa, 1977, MS, 1982, PhD, 1991. Rsch. asst. animal ecology sect. Dept. Sci. and Indsl. Rsch., Wellington, New Zealand, 1947-49; lectr., tutor U. Natal, Pietermaritzburg, South Africa, 1977-94; lectr. U. Durban-Westville, South Africa, 1995, sr. rsch. assoc., 1996—; hon. rsch. fellow U. Natal, Durban, South Africa, 1996—; cons. freshwater invertebrates South Africa, 1977—; supervising and examining theses and rsch. projects U. Natal, 1991—; referee rsch. papers, 1991—. Author: Paradiaptominae Vol. 15 Zooplankton Guides, 1999; contbr. articles to profl. jours. Mem. Southern Africa Soc. Aquatic Scientists, Wildlife and Environ. Soc. South Africa, Zool. Soc. South Africa, Spider Club Southern Africa, World Assn. Copepodologists (founder), Crustacean Soc. Democrat. Mem. Ch. of Province South Africa. Avocations: reading, handwork (knitting and cross-stitch), Yoga, indigenous gardening, container gardening. Office: U Durban-Westville, Pvt Bay X54001 Sch Life Sci, Durban 4000, South Africa

RAYNOR, SUSANNE, chemical physics educator; b. Phila., May 18, 1948; d. William McLean and Susanne Louise (Chambers) R.; m. Louis H. Kipnis, Dec. 28, 1972 (div. Aug. 1999). BS, Duke U., 1970; PhD, Georgetown U., 1976. Grad. fellow Georgetown U., Washington, 1971-76; rsch. assoc. U. Toronto, Ont., Can., 1976-78, Harvard U., Cambridge, Mass., 1978-82; asst. prof. chem. physics Rutgers U., Newark, 1982-88, assoc. prof., 1988—;

collaborator Los Alamos (N.Mex.) Nat. Lab., 1984-90. Contbr. articles to profl. jours. Recipient Outstanding Tchr. award Rutgers U. Alumni Assn., 1986; grantee N.J. Dept. Higher Edn., 1985-88, Rsch. Corp., 1986-87. Mem. Am. Chem. Soc. (grantee Petroleum Rsch. Fund 1988-90), Am. Phys. Soc. Avocations: photography, southwestern cuisine, gardening. Office: Rutgers U Dept Chemistry Newark NJ 07102

RAYNOVICH, GEORGE, JR., lawyer; b. Pitts., Dec. 30, 1931; s. George Sr. and Zora (Mamula) R.; m. Mary Ann Senay, July 11, 1953; children: George III, Andrew. BS, U. Pitts., 1957; JD, Duquesne U., 1961. Bar: Pa. 1962, U.S. Dist. Ct. (we. dist.) Pa. 1962, U.S. Patent and Trademark Office 1962, U.S. Supreme Ct. 1966, U.S. Ct. Appeals (fed. cir.) 1986. Patent agt. Consolidation Coal Co., Library, Pa., 1959-62; ptnr. Stone & Raynovich, Pitts., 1962-75; atty. Wheeling-Pitts. Steel Corp., Pitts., 1975-77, gen. counsel, sec., 1978-85, v.p., 1980-85; sr. atty. Buchanan Ingersol P.C., Pitts., 1986-88, 89-96; ptnr. Price & Raynovich, Pitts., 1988-89; of counsel Gorr Moser Dell and Loughney, 1997—. Councilman Borough of Baldwin, Allegheny County, Pa., 1972-75, govt. study commr., 1973. 1st lt. USAF, 1952-56. Mem. Allegheny County Bar Assn., Pitts. Intellectual Property Law Assn., Acad. Trial Lawyers Allegheny County. Democrat. Mem. Serbian Orthodox Ch. Home: 335 Jean Dr Pittsburgh PA 15236-2511 Office: Gorr Moser Dell & Loughney 1300 Frick Bldg Pittsburgh PA 15219

RAYWARD-SMITH, VICTOR JOHN, computing educator; b. Kowloon, Hong Kong, Jan. 12, 1949; arrived in England, 1952; s. Stanley George and Winnifred (Rayward) S.; m. Mary Patricia Morris, July 12, 1976; children: Mark, William. MA, Hertford Coll., Oxford, England, 1970; PhD, Queen Mary Coll., London, 1973. Lectr., sr. lectr. U. East Anglia, Norwich, England, 1973-91, prof., 1991—; vis. prof. U. Colo., 1985, S.F.U. Burnaby, Can., 1989; tutor Open U., England, 1975-99. Author: A First Course in Formal Language Theory, 1983, A First Course in Computability, 1985; co-author: Mathematical Foundations in Computing, 1995; editor: Applications of Modern Meunstics, 1984; editor Intenrat. Jour. Math. Algorithms, 1998—. Fellow IMA, BCS. Mem. Ch. of England. Avocations: crosswords, walking. Office: U East Anglia, Sch Info Systems, Norwich NR4 7TJ, England

RAZ, JOSEPH, philosophy educator; b. Haifa, Israel, Mar. 21, 1939; arrived in Great Britain, 1970; M in Juris summa cum laude, Hebrew U., Jerusalem, 1963; PhD, Oxford (Eng.) U., 1967; Doctorate (hon.), Cath. U., Brussels, 1993. Lectr. then sr. lectr. depts. law and philosophy Hebrew U., Jerusalem, 1967-72; fellow, tutor in law Balliol Coll., Oxford, 1972-85; prof. philosophy of law Oxford U., 1985—; fellow Balliol Coll., 1985—; vis. prof. Law Sch., Columbia U., 1995—. Author: The Concept of a Legal System, 2nd edit., 1980, The Authority of Law, 1979, Practical Reason and Norms, 1975, 2nd edit., 1990, The Morality of Freedom, 1986, Ethics in the Public Domain, 1995, Engaging Reason, 2000; contbr. articles to profl. jours. Recipient The W.J.M. Mackenzie Book prize The Polit. Studies Assn. of the U.K., 1987, The Elaine and David Spitz Book prize The Conf. for the Study of Political Though, 1988. Fellow Brit. Acad.; mem. Am. Acad. Arts and Scis. (fgn. hon.). Office: Balliol Coll, Broad St, Oxford OX1 3BJ, England

RAZ, MOTI, electronics company executive; b. Botoshan, Romania, Aug. 8, 1947; s. Natan and Anita Rosenzweig; m. Miriam Ianko, Jan. 15, 1970; children: Sharon, Ganit, Shirley. BSc, Technion, Israel, 1973. Vice consul Consulate Gen. Israel, N.Y.C., 1979-83; mktg. mgr. Tadiran Electronic Sys. Ltd., Tel Aviv, 1986-90; dir. reconnaissance and surveillance sys. Tadiran Electronic Sys. Ltd., Holon, 1990-93, sr. v.p., 1994—. Lt. col. mil. intelligence Israeli Def. Forces, 1965-85. Fax: 972 3 5577539. E-mail: motiraz@tadsys.com. Office: Tadiran Electronic Sys Ltd, Hamerkava 29, 58101 Holon Israel

RAZA, AGHA ASAD, academic administrator; b. Lahore, Pakistan, July 26, 1948; s. Agha Anwar and Fahmida (Jabeen) R.; m. Tashina Zamir, June 15, 1980; children: Agha Mustapha, Agha Ali. BS, Kakul U., Abbottabad, Pakistan, 1971; B Civil Engring, Mil. Coll. of Engring., Risalpur, Pakistan, 1980; postgrad., Punjab U., Lahore, 1973. Site engr. Frontier Works Orgn., Karakaram Hwy., 1971-75; staff officer Govt. of Pakistan, 1976-77; project engr. Nat. Logistics Cell, Bahawalpur, Pakistan, 1981-82; work dir. Frontier Constabulary No. Areas, Gilgit Skardu, Pakistan, 1984-87; chief adminstrn. coord. Multan, Pakistan, 1988-91; porject dir. F.W.O., Zhob, Pakistan, 1992-96, dir. evaluation civil engring. projects, 1994-96; adminstr. St. Mary's Acad., Rawalpindi, Pakistan, 1997—. Col. Pakistan Army, 1971, 84-87. Recipient Sitara-e-Harb award Govt. of Pakistan, 1971, Tamgha-e-Difa award Govt. of Pakistan, 1987,. Mem. Pakistan Engring. Coun. (life), Alpine Club of Pakistan (cert. 1997). Avocations: mountaineering (first Paksitani to traverse the Siachen Glacier), tennis, outdoor activities, photography. Home: # 74A Lane 8, Askari VII Adiala Rd, Rawalpindi Punjab, Pakistan

RAZA, HILAL A., energy executive; b. Bahraich, India, Nov. 29, 1950; s. Mohammad Taqi and Mahparah (Alam) R.; m. Sarah Nasreen, Sept. 16, 1973; children: Mahparah, Alvina, Mohammad Ali. BSc, Panjab U., Lahore, Pakistan, 1967, MSc, 1968; diploma, MSc, Imperial Coll., London, 1979. Office: Hydrocarbon Devel Inst, PO Box 1308, Islamabad Pakistan

RAZA, MUHAMMAD RAZA, microbiologist, researcher; b. Sahiwal, Punjab, Pakistan, Apr. 1, 1956; s. Bashir and Saira Ali; m. Azra Bano Raza, Mar. 12, 1982; children: Hasan, Ali, Zeinab. BSc, Bahauddin Zakria U., Multan, Pakistan, 1977; MB, BChir, U. Punjab, Lahore, Pakistan, 1980; PhD, U. Edinburgh, 1992. Regimental med. officer Mil., Lahore, 1980-82; registrar Punjab Med. Coll. Hosp., Faisalabad, Pakistan, 1984-85; med. supt. WAPDA Hosp., Sahiwal, Pakistan, 1985-88; post-doctoral rsch. fellow U. Edinburgh Med. Sch., 1992-99; specialist registrar Postgrad. Sch. Medicine and Dentistry, Newcastle upon Tyne, U.K., 1999—; registrar medicine and acute care Punjab Med. Coll. Hosp., Faisalabad, Pakistan, 1984-85. Contbr. articles to profl. jours. Vice chmn. Lothian Interpretation and Translation Trust, Edinburgh, 1997. Capt. Army Med. Corps, 1980-82. Recipient Overseas Rsch. award U.K. Univs. Com. Vice Chancellors, 1990, 91. Mem. Overseas Doctors Assn. (sec. 1998-99). Avocation: reading. E-mail: newmraza@north.phls.nhs.uk. Fax: 191 201-0156. Office: Royal Victoria Infirmary, Queen Victoria Rd, Newcastle upon Tyne NE2 4HH, United Kingdom

RAZAFINDRATANDRA, ARMAND GAÉTAN, archbishop; b. Manjakandriana, Aug. 7, 1925. Attended, Inst. Catholique de Paris. Ordained priest, 1954. Various parochial and teaching assignments, consecrated bishop of Majunga, 1978; archbishop of Antananarivo Madagascar, 1994—; created and proclaimed cardinal, 1994; cardinal priest Basilica of St. Sylvester and St. Martin of the Hills, Rome, 1994. Office: Archeveche-Andohalo, 101 Antanarivo, BP 3030 Antananarivo 101, Madagascar

RAZIN, ALEXANDER VLADIMIROVICH, philosopher, educator; b. Moscow, Russia, Feb. 16, 1954; s. Vladimir Ivanovich and Dina Vasilievna (Denisova) R.; m. Olga Nikolaevna Marina, Sept. 27, 1983 (div. Dec. 21, 1993); 1 child, Polina; m. Vera Borisovna Evseeva, May 30, 1996; 1 child, Michail. Rschr. Inst. Philosophy, Moscow, 1979-84; docent Moscow Fin. Acad., 1985-90; prof. Moscow State U., 1991—. Contbr. articles to profl. jours. Vice dir. Russian Humanist Soc., Moscow, 1996—. Avocation: car modeling. E-mail: Razin@Log.philos.msu.ru. Home: 130, 50 let Oktiabria str, d 23 k 2, 119618 Moscow Russia Office: Moscow State Univ, Dept Ethics, 119899 Moscow Russia

RAZIN, ASSAF, economics educator; b. Afula, Israel, Feb. 28, 1941; s. Mordechai and Dora (Leibovitch) R.; m. Shula Hachlili, May 20, 1963; children: Ofer, Ronnie, Einat. PhD, U. Chgo., 1969. Prof. econs. Tel Aviv U., 1970—; vis. prof. econs. U. Calif., Berkeley, 1979, U. Stockholm, 1980, 81, 82, U. Pa., Phila., 1981, Princeton (N.J.) U., 1984, U. Chgo., 1986, 91, 93, 95, 97, Yale U., 1992, Harvard U., 1998, Stanford U., 1999—; chmn. Coun. Econ. Advice, State of Israel, Jerusalem, 1979; cons. World Bank, Washington, 1987—, Internat. Monetary Fund, 1988—; rsch. assoc. Nat. Bur. Econ. Rsch., Cambridge, Mass.; rsch. fellow Ctr. for Econ. Policy Rsch., London, 1990—. Co-author: International Trade Under Uncertainty, 1978, Household and Economy, 1987, Fiscal Policies and the World Economy, 1988, International Taxation in an Integrated World, 1991, The Israeli Economy: Malayse and Promise, 1992, Population Economics, 1995, Current Account Sustainability, 1996. E-mail: Razin@post.tau.acil. Home: 16 Pilichovsky St, Tel Aviv 69341, Israel Office: Dept Econs Tel Aviv U, Tel Aviv 69978, Israel

RAZOHARINORO, archivist, historian, researcher; b. Antsirabe, Madagasikara, Republic of Madagascar, Nov. 19, 1936; d. Rakotonjanahary and Razanamanana; m. Eugene Randriamboavonjy; children: Vonimbolanoro, Soalandy, Tianjanahary. Degree in Archives, Ecole Nat. des Chartes, Paris, 1964. Cert. archivist. Archivist Republic of Madagasikar Nat. Archives, Antananarivo, Madagasikara, 1964-69, chief, dir., 1969—; instr. history U. Antananarivo, 1973—. Editor Tantara, 1973-95; author articles and revs. Decorated Grand Officier Order Nat. Malagasy. Mem. Malagasy Acad. Lutheran. Office: Dir Archives Nat, BP 3384 Antananarivo 101, Madagascar

RAZPET, MARKO, mathematics educator and researcher; b. Planina, Cerkno, Slovenia, Mar. 22, 1949; s. Lovrenc Ivan and Marija (Planinc) R.; m. Nada Šmon, Aug. 10, 1974; children: Alenka, Andrej. BSc, U. Ljubljana, Slovenia, 1973, MSc, 1984, PhD, 1989. Asst. U. Ljubljana, Slovenia, 1973-89, asst. prof., 1989-95, assoc. prof., 1995—, dept. head Faculty of Edn.,, 1996-98. Author: Sit Down and Write by LATEX, 1991, An Application of Umbral Calculus to Combinatorial Counting, 1992, Planar Curves, 1998; also articles. Mem. Am. Math. Soc., Austrian Math. Assn., DMFA. Avocation: amateur radio. Office: U Ljubljana Faculty Edn, Kardeljeva Ploščad 16, SI-1000 Ljubljana Slovenia

RAZZALL, EDWARD TIMOTHY, lawyer; b. London, June 12, 1943; s. Leonard Humphrey and Muriel (Knowles) R.; m. Deirdre Taylor Smith, Sept. 30, 1982; children (by previous marriage): Katie, James. BA, Oxford (Eng.) U., 1965. Solicitor, 1969. Tchg. assoc. Northwestern U., Chgo., 1965-66; ptnr. Frere Cholmeley Bischoff, London, 1973-95, Argonaut Associates, London, 1995—; chmn. ABACO Investments, PLC, 1974-90, C&B Pub. PLC, 1997—; bd. dirs. Delance, Estates plc, 1999—. Councillor Richmond Coun., Eng., 1974-98, dep. leader, 1983-97; treas. Liberal Party, Eng., 1987, Liberal Dem. Party, England, 1988-2000; chmn. Gen. Elec. Campaign, 2000—. Decorated comdr. Order Brit. Empire; created life barony, 1997. Home: 110 Station Rd, London SW13 0NB, England

RAZZANO, FRANK CHARLES, lawyer; b. Bklyn., Feb. 25, 1948; s. Pasquale Anthony and Agnes Mary (Borgia) R.; m. Stephanie Anne Lucas, Jan. 10, 1970; children: Joseph, Francis, Catherine. BA, St. Louis U., 1969; JD, Georgetown U., 1972. Bar: N.Y. 1973, U.S. Dist. Ct. (so. dist.) N.Y. 1973, U.S. Dist. Ct. (es. dist.) N.Y. 1973, N.J. 1976, D.C. 1981, Va. 1984, U.S. Dist. Ct. N.J. 1976, U.S. Dist. Ct. Md. 1977, U.S. Dist. Ct. (no. dist.) Calif. 1981, U.S. Dist. Ct. D.C. 1982, U.S. Dist. Ct. (ea. dist.) Va. 1989, U.S. Dist. Ct. (we. dist.) Va. 1990, U.S. Ct. Appeals (2d cir.) 1973, U.S. Ct. Appeals (3d cir.) 1975, U.S. Ct. Appeals (D.C. and 5th cirs.) 1983, U.S. Ct. Appeals (4th cir.) 1984, U.S. Ct. Appeals (6th cir.) 1990, U.S. Supreme Ct. 1976. Assoc. Shea & Gould, N.Y.C., 1972-75; asst. U.S. atty. Dist. of N.J., Newark, 1975-78; asst. chief trial atty. SEC, Washington, 1978-82; ptnr. Shea & Gould, Washington, 1982-94, mng. ptnr., 1991-92; ptnr. Camhy Karlinsky Stein Razzano & Rubin, Washington, 1994-96, Dickstein, Shapiro, Morin & Oshinsky, Washington, 1996—; lectr. in field; adv. bd. Securities Litigation Reform Act Reporter, Securities Regulation Law Jour.; adj. prof. law U. Md. Sch. Law. Civil law editor Rico Law Reporter; mem. adv. bd. Corp. Confidentiality and Disclosure Letter; hon. adv. com. Jour. Internat. Law and Practice, Detroit Coll. Law; contbr. articles to legal jours. Scoutmaster Vienna coun. Boy Scouts Am., 1984. Recipient spl. achievement award Justice Dept., 1977, spl. commendation, 1978, Outstanding Achievement award Detroit Coll. of Law, 1993. Mem. ABA (chmn. criminal law com., sect. bus. law 1996—), Va. Bar, D.C. Bar (chmn. litigation sect. 1987-89, vice-chmn. coun. sects. 1988-89), Assn. Securities & Exch. Commn. Alumni (pres. 1993-95), Phi Beta Kappa, Eta Sigma Phi. Roman Catholic. Home: 1713 Paisley Blue Ct Vienna VA 22182-2326

RAZZANO, MICHAEL R., dental and healthcare industry consultant. BS in Chemistry and Psychology, U. Fla., 1962; DDS, U. Md., 1966. USPHS rotating dental intern, 1966-67; USPHS rsch. assoc., part-time instr. U. Pacific Sch. Dentistry, San Francisco, 1967-69; pvt. practice Ocala, Fla., 1969-85; dental dir. Cmty. Hosp., Ocala, Fla., 1973-76; pres. Razzano & Assocs., Inc., Marietta, Ga., Interactive Diagnostic Imaging, Inc., Marietta, Ga.; mng. dir. R & B Consulting Group, LLC, Falls City, Wash., Marietta; part-time rschr. U. Fla. Sch. Dentistry, 1969-73; founding mem. Bank of Belleview, Fla., 1971-74; pres., dir. Restorative Dental Study Club, Ocala, 1975-81; asst. prof. dept. reconstructive dentistry U. Louisville, 1989-92; adj. prof. divsn. radiology and imaging scis.; presenter in field; chmn. Spectrum HealthCare Group, Inc., Atlanta, 1990-91, pres. Trophy Radiology, Inc., Atlanta, 1990-95; bd. dirs. several corps. Editor Soft Tissue Care for GPs, 1990-92; contbr. articles to profl. jours., chpt. to book. Fellow Royal Soc. Health; mem. ADA, Acad. Dental Materials, Am. Assn. Dental Rsch., Am. Dental Trade Assn., Internat. Assn. Dental Rsch., Internat. Assn. Dento-Maxillo-Facial Radiology, Dental Mfrs. Am., Ga. Dental Assn., Omicron Kappa Upsilon. Fax: 770 591-1705. E-mail: mrrazzano@aol.com. Office: 3605 Sandy Plains Rd Marietta GA 30066-3068

RAZZANO, PASQUALE ANGELO, lawyer; b. Bklyn., Apr. 3, 1943; s. Pasquale Anthony and Agnes Mary (Borgia) R.; m. Maryann Walker, Jan. 29, 1966; children: Elizabeth, Pasquale, Susan, ChristyAnn. BSCE, Poly. Inst. Bklyn., 1964; student law, NYU, 1964-66; JD, Georgetown U., 1969. Bar: Va. 1969, N.Y. 1970, U.S. Ct. Appeals (2d, 3d, 7th, 9th and fed. cirs.), U.S. Supreme Ct., U.S. Dist. Ct. (so., ea. and western dists.) N.Y., U.S. Dist. Ct. (we. dist.) Tex., U.S. Dist. Ct. Hawaii, U.S. Dist. Ct. Conn. Examiner U.S. Patent Office, 1966-69; assoc. Curtis, Morris & Safford, P.C., 1969-71, ptnr., 1971-91; ptnr. Fitzpatrick, Cella, Harper & Scinto, 1991—; guest lectr. U.S. Trademark Assn., Am. Intellectual Property Law Assn., Practicing Law Inst., NYU Law Ctr., ABA, N.Y. Intellectual Property Law Assn. Mem. bd. editors Licensing Jour., 1986—; mem. bd. editors Trademark Reporter, 1987—, book rev. editor, 1989-91, pub. articles editor, 1991-94, domestic articles editor, 1992-93, 95, editor-in-chief 1996—. Rep. committeeman Rockland County. Recipient Robert Ridgeway award, 1964. Mem. ABA (guest lectr.), Fed. Bar Assn. (chmn. patent law com. 1999—), N.Y. Intellectual Property Law Assn. (bd. dirs. 1985—, sec. 1988-91, pres. 1994-95), Licensing Exec. Soc. (chmn. N.Y. chpt. 1996-99), Internat. Trademark Assn. (bd. dirs. 1996-99), Am. Intellectual Property Law Assn., N.Y. Bar Assn., N.Y. Coun. Bar Leaders (exec. coun. 1993-94), Va. Bar Assn., Italian Am. Bar Assn., Bar Assn. City N.Y., Columban Laws Assn., N.Y. Athletic Club, Minute Man Yacht Club, Shorehaven Golf Club. Republican. Roman Catholic. Address: 21 Covlee Dr Westport CT 06880-6407 also: 14 Deerwood Trl Lake Placid NY 12946-1834

REA, DESMOND, labor relations director, consultant; b. Belfast, Northern Ireland, Mar. 4, 1937; s. Samuel and Anne (Lemon) R.; m. Maeve Irene Williamson, Sept. 1, 1969; children: Catherine, Alison, Susanne, Jennifer. BSc in Econs., Queen's U., Belfast, 1962, MSc, 1969, PhD, 1972; MBA, U. Calif., Berkeley, 1967, OBE, 1996. Adminstr. Queen's U., Belfast, 1963-66, sr. lectr., 1969-75; prof., head dept. U. Ulster, No. Ireland, 1975-87; chmn. Labour Rels. Agy., Belfast, 1996—; non-exec. dir. Allied Irish Banks (U.K.) plc, 1996—, First Trust Bank's. Editor: Economic Outlook and Business Rev., 1985—. Non-exec. dir. Anglo-Irish Encounter, London and Dublin, 1983—; chmn. Currriculum Exams. and Assessment, Belfast, 1994-98. Royal Soc. of Arts fellow, 1998. Avocations: current affairs, reading, rugby, Northern Irish art, music. Office: Labour Rels Agy, 2-8 Gordon St, Belfast BT12LG, Northern Ireland

REA, DESMOND MAURICE VINCENT, plastic surgeon; b. Wellington, New Zealand, Nov. 1, 1925; arrived in Australia; s. John Patrick and Eustella Alice (Ryam) R.; m. Maime Fortune Lyle, Apr. 5, 1961 (dec. Nov. 1988); children: Jeremy, Elizabeth, Nicholas; m. Jacqueline Kay Arkley, Apr. 2, 1989; children: Alezzandra, Zachary. MBChB, Otago U., Dumedin, New Zealand, 1951; MD, U. NSW, 1981. Jr. ho. surgeon Wellington Hosp., 1951-52; surg. registrar Meml. Hosp., Hastings, New Zealand, 1954; locum resident surgeon Royal Victoria Hosp., Montreal, Can., 1954; surg. resident St. Marys Hosp., Rochester, N.Y., 1954-55; locum neuro-surg. registrar Old Ch. Hosp., Romfort, Eng., 1956; locum casualty sr. ho. officer Queen Mary's Hosp., Sidcup, Eng., 1956; sr. ho. officer S.W. Met. Regional Plastic Ctr. Queen Mary's Hosp., Roehampton, Eng., 1958-59; surg. registrar Mile End Hosp., London, 1956-57; sr. surg. registrar City Gen. Hosp., Sheffield, Eng., 1957-58, Waikato Hosp., Hamilton, New Zealand, 1960-61; tutor in physiology Med. Sch., Dunedin, 1946-47; hon. plastic surgeon Royal S. Sydney Hosp., 1964, Marrickville Hosp., 1970, Blacktown Dist. Hosp., 1971, Canterbury Hosp., 1985. Fellow Royal Coll. Surgeons, Royal Soc. Medicine; mem. Australian Soc. Plastic Surgeons, Brit. Assn. Plastic Surgeons (assoc.), Australian Hand Club, Soc. Surgery Hand (pres. 1981-82), Australian Soc. Aeshtetic Plastic Surgery. Avocations: tennis, reading, cycling, swimming. Home: 25 Stanley Ln, Sydney 2031, Australia Office: 49 View Ln, Sydney 2025, Australia

REA, STEPHEN, actor; b. Belfast, Ireland, 1949; m. Dolours Price, 1983; children: Oscar, Danny. Student, Queens Univ., Belfast. Formed (with Brian Friel) Field Day Theatre Co., 1980. Stage appearances include (London) The Shadow of a Gunman, The Cherry Orchard, Miss Julie, High Society; (Royal Court Theatre) Endgame, The Freedom of the City; (Field Day Theatre Co.) Translations, Communication Card, St. Oscar, Boesman and Lena, Hightime and Riot Act, Double Cross, Pentecost, Making History, Three Sisters (dir. only), The Cure at Troy (dir. only); (Broadway) Someone Who'll Watch Over Me, 1992 (Tony award nominee 1993), Uncle Vanya, 1995; (Double Tap Theatre) Ashes to Ashes, 1996; films include Angel, 1982, Danny Boy, 1984, Company of Wolves, 1985, The Doctor and the Devils, 1985, Loose Connections, 1988, Life Is Sweet, 1991, The Crying Game, 1992 (Acad. award nominee best actor 1993), Bad Behavior, 1993, Princess Caraboo, 1993, Angie, 1994, Interview with the Vampire, 1994, Ready to Wear (Prêt-à-Porter), 1994, All Men Are Mortal, 1994, Citizen X, 1994, The Devil and the Deep Blue Sea, 1994, Michael Collins, 1995, 96 Trojah Eddzie, 1995, Butcher Boy, 1995, 97, Crime of The Century, 1995, Troja Eddie, 1996, Lumiere et compagnie, 1995, Further Gesture, 1996, The Last of the High Kings, 1996, Hacks, 1997, Fever Pitch, 1997, Double Tap, 1997, This is My Father, 1998, Blue Vision, 1998, The Big Twist, 1998, Still Crazy, 1998, The Life Before This, 1999, Guinevere, 1999, In Dreams, 1999, The End of the Affair, 1999; TV appearances include Four Days in July, Lost Belongings, Scout, St. Oscar, Not with a Bang, Hedda Gabler, Shadow of a Gunman, 1995; TV guest appearances include The Professionals, 1977. Office: Peters Fraser & Dunlop Ltd, PFD Drury House 34-43 Russell St, Chelsea Harbor London WC2B 5HA, England

REACH, GÉRARD, endocrinologist, researcher; b. Nevilly, France, Apr. 22, 1950; s. Michel and Adéle (Schapira); m. Isabelle Couteaux, Jun 29, 1972; children: Anne, Claire, Pauline. DEA in Biochemistry, U. Paris, 1974, MD, 1977. Resident endocrinology Paris Hosps., 1973-77, chief resident, 1977-79; asst. prof. biochemistry U. Paris, 1973-77; Mayo endocrine rsch. fellow Internat. Fogarty Grant, Rochester, Minn., 1979-80; rsch. assoc. Inserm, Paris, 1981-85, rsch. dir., 1985-90, dir. U341 rsch. unit, 1991—; cons. Paris Hosps., 1981—; organizing sec. Artificial insjulin Delivery Systems, Pancreas and Islet Transplantation, 1995-98, pres.-elect). Editor-in-chief Diabetes and Metabolism, 1991-94; contbr. articles to profl. jours. Recipient Apollinaire Bouchardat award Internat. Com., Paris, 1987, Pierre Romancon award Found. Med. Rsch., Paris, 1996, ann. award Internat. Soc. Blood Purification, Paris, 1996, Jacques Mirouze award Nat. Acad. Medicine, Paris, 1997. Mem. European Assn. for Study of Diabetes, Am. Diabetes Assn. Avocations: music, philosophy. Home: 14 Rue Broca, 75005 Paris France Office: Svc de Diabetes Hotel Dieu, 1 Pl du Parvis Notre Dame, 75004 Paris France

READ, ADAM DAVID, research geographer; b. Kingston upon Thames, Eng., Jan. 15, 1974; s. Robert Charles Read and Jane Barbara Maybee. BA in Geography with honors, Exeter (Eng.) U., 1995. Recycling officer London Borough of Kensington & Chelsea, 1995-96; rsch. fellow Kingston (Eng.) U., 1996—; spkr. in field. Assoc. editor Internat. Jour. Solid Waste Tech. and Mgmt.; mem. editl. bd. Resources, Conservation and Recycling; contbr. articles to profl. jours. Fellow Royal Geog. Soc.; mem. Inst. Wastes Mgmt., Internat. Solid Waste Orgn. Avocations: soccer, table tennis, science fiction, walking, aerobics. Home: 11 Woodside Close, Surbiton KT5 9JU, England Office: Kingston U, Penrhyn Rd, Kingston KT1 2EE, England

READ, JAMES CARROLL, geneticist educator; b. Stephenville, Tex., Aug. 28, 1940; s. Edgar L. and LaRUe (Webber) R.; m. Patricia Ann Higgins, Mar. 24, 1969; children: Tambria L., Heather L., Pattillo H., Jeannette L. BS in agrl. edn., Tex. A&M Univ., 1966, MS plant breeding, 1969, PhD in genetics, 1971. Rsch. geneticist USDA ARS, Salinas, Calif., 1971-74; asst. prof. Tex. A&M Univ., Dallas, 1974-81, assoc. prof., 1981-99, prof., 1999—; higher pvt. edn. task force Dallas Ind. Sch. Dist., 1978-81; cons. B. Johnson, Inc.,Dallas, 1987. Contbr. articles to profl. jours. Pres. Plano Lions Club, 1984, election judge Collin County, Plano, 1995; bd. dirs. Tex. Forage & Grassland Coun., 1992-95. Recipient NDEA fellowhip U.S. Gov., 1969. Mem. Am. Soc. Agronomy, Crop Sci. Soc. Am., Soc. for Range Mgmt., Am. Forage and Grassland Coun. (merit award 1999), Tex. Forage Workers (pres. 1994-95), Alpha Zeta, Phi Kappa Phi, Gamm Sigma Delta. Republican. Presbyterian. Avocations: golf, hunting. Office: Tex A&M Univ 17360 Coit Rd Dallas TX 75252-6502

READ, SISTER JOEL, academic administrator. BS in Edn., Alverno Coll., 1948; MA in History, Fordham U., 1951; hon. degree, Lakeland Coll., 1972, Wittenburg U., 1976, Marymount Manhattan Coll., 1978, DePaul U., 1985, Northland Coll., 1986, SUNY, 1986, Lawrence U., 1997. Former prof., dept. chmn. history dept. Alverno Coll., Milw., pres., 1968—; pres. Am. Assn. for Higher Edn., 1976-77; mem. coun. NEH, 1977-84; bd. dirs. Ednl. Testing Svc., 1987-93, Neylan Commn., 1985-90; past pres. Wis. Assn. Ind. Colls. and Univs.; mem. Commn. on Status of Edn. for Women, 1971-76, Am. Assn. Colls., 1971-77; past mem. exec. com. Greater Milw. Com. GMC. Edn. Trust. Mem. exec. bd. Milw. YMCA, Greater Milw. Com. GMC. First recipient Anne Roe award Harvard U. Grad. Sch. Edn., 1980; recipient Jr. Achievement, Wis. Assn. of Independent Colls. and Univs.; recipient Morris T. Keaton award, Coun. for Adult and Experiential Learning, 1992; recipient Jean B. Harris award, Rotary; Paul Harris fellow, Rotary. Fellow Am. Acad. Arts and Scis., Wis. Acad. Arts and Scis.; mem. Wis. Found. of Ind. Colls. (past bd. dirs.), Women's Philanthropy Inst., Wis. Women in Higher Edn. Office: Alverno Coll Office of Pres PO Box 343922 Milwaukee WI 53234-3922

READ, KENNETH FRANCIS, JR., physics educator, researcher; b. Annapolis, Md., Apr. 24, 1959. BS, Stanford U., 1981; MS, Cornell U., 1984, PhD, 1987. Rsch. assoc. Princeton (N.J.) U., 1987-90, rsch. staff mem., 1990; rsch. staff mem. Oak Ridge (Tenn.) Nat. Lab., 1991—; asst. prof. U. Tenn., Knoxville, 1991-99, assoc. prof., 1999—; collaborating scientist Oak Ridge Nat. Lab. and U. Tenn. Knoxville, 1993—. Contbr. numerous articles to Physics Letters B. Recipient Andrew D. White fellowship, NSF Grad. fellowship, Cornell U., 1981; Nat. Merit scholar, 1977. Mem. Am. Phys. Soc., Sigma Xi, Phi Beta Kappa. Office: Oak Ridge Nat Lab Bldg 6003 MS 6372 PO Box 2008 Oak Ridge TN 37831-2008

READ, MARK EVERARD, art dealer; b. Johannesburg, South Africa; s. Everard Warwick and Patricia (Atkinson) R.; m. Christine Jane Renwick, Feb. 11, 1984; children: Lucy, Frances. BSc, BA, U. Cape Town, South Africa, 1979. With Everard Read Gallery, Johannesburg, 1980—, chmn. Trustee Palaeo Anthrop. Sci. Inst., Johannesburg, 1993—, John Voelker Fund, Cape Town, 1996—; exec. officer, trustee World Wildlife Fund, South Africa, 1995—; bd. dirs. Bus. and Arts South Africa, Johannesburg, 1995—. 2d lt. South African Def. Force, 1974-75. Avocations: botany, ornithology, archaeology, paleo anthropology. Home: Forestown, 14 Taltow Rd, Johannesburg South Africa Office: Everard Read Gallery, 6 Jellicoe Ave, Rosebank, Johannesburg South Africa

READ, MICHAEL OSCAR, editor, consultant; b. Amarillo, Tex., July 11, 1942; s. Harold Eugene and Madeline (Welch) R.; m. Jill Kay Vanderby, July 6, 1963 (div. Apr. 1967); 1 child, Rebecca Anne; m. Fawn Dale Barby, Apr. 10, 1977; 1 child, Nathan Michael. AA in Chemistry, Amarillo Coll., 1962; BA in Journalism, Tex. Tech. U., 1965. News editor Olton (Tex.) Enterprise, 1963-64; reporter, photographer Lubbock (Tex.) Avalanche-Jour., 1964-67, copy editor, 1967-70, city editor, 1970-72; copy editor Houston Post, 1972-74, systems editor, 1974-89, dir. news tech., 1989-95; electronic media content coord. Houston Chronicle, 1995—; supervisory com. Shell Employees Fed. Credit Union, Houston; tchr. Let's Compute!, Stafford, Tex., 1985—; cons. Newspaper Pub. Sys., Stafford, 1989—; mem. joint

Newspaper Assn. Am.-Internat. Press. Telecomm. Coun. Com. Wire Svc. Standards; mem. adv. bd. Found. for Am. Comms. FACSNET; strategic planning com. Sch. of Mass. Comm., Tex. Tech. U. Author weekly newspaper column, 1977—. Vol. United Way, Houston, 1973—; bd. dirs. Meadows (Tex.) Community Improvement Assn., 1985-95, Meadows Utility Dist., 1988-93, Meadows Econ. Devel. Corp., 1994-99. Eldon Durrett scholar, 1961-65. Mem. Am. MENSA, Am. Philatelic Soc., Am. 1st Day Cov. Soc. (life), U.S. Chess Fedn. (life), Soc. Profl. Journalists (conv. com. 1989-90), Press Club of Houston. Avocations: philately, photography, gardening. Office: Houston Chronicle 801 Texas St Houston TX 77002-2996 Home: 215 Lakeside Blvd Sugar Land TX 77478-3957

READ, PATRICIA ELLEN, administrator non-profit organization, editor; b. Indpls., Apr. 29, 1952; d. Horace Manson and Patricia (Downtain) R.; m. William A. Shunk, Jr., Dec. 29, 1995. BA in English cum laude, Rockford Coll., 1974; MS in Libr. Sci. with hons., Columbia U., 1978. Mng. editor Neal Schuman Publishers, N.Y.C., 1977-80; dir. publs. The Foundation Ctr., N.Y.C., 1980-84, v.p., sec., 1984-87; cons. N.Y.C., 1987-93; exec. dir. Am. Reading Coun., N.Y.C., 1988-91; cons., mktg. dir. The Feminist Press, N.Y.C., 1991-93; exec. dir. Colo. Assn. Nonprofit Orgns., Denver, 1993—. Contbr. articles in field. Mem. Comm. Network in Philanthropy, Washington, 1981-87, rsch. adv. group Independent Sector, Washington, 1982-87, membership com., 1983-85, adv. com. Giving USA, N.Y.C., 1984-87, adv. com. Nat. Ctr. for Charitable Stats., Washington, 1986-87, task force in classification of non-profit sector, 1984-86; bd. dirs. Support Ctr. of N.Y., 1990-93, Blue Hill Troupe (Gilbert and Sullivan Repertory Co.), N.Y.C., 1989-91, v.p. 1990-91; mem. Colo. Symphony Orch. Chorus, 1993-94; bd. dirs. Denver/Boulder Better Bus. Bur., 1998—; mem. philanthropic adv. stds. rev. panel Coun. Better Bus. Burs., 1999—. Finalist 1994 Women of Achievement, YWCA of Denver, 1994; named one of 50 most influential in the nonprofit sector Nonprofit Times', 1999. Mem. Nat. Coun. Non-profit Orgns. (bd. dirs., chair 1998—), Metro Vols., Denver (bd. dirs. 1993—, mem. transition team for merger with vol. ctr. 1993, co-chair nominating com. 1994, sec. 1998). Office: Colo Assn Nonprofit Orgns 22 E 16th Ave Ste 1060 Denver CO 80202-5109 Home: 630 High St Denver CO 80218-3638

READ, RICHARD EATON, newspaper reporter; b. St. Andrews, Scotland, Sept. 3, 1957; s. Arthur H. and Katharine (Eaton) R.; m. Kim R. Kunkle, July 26, 1986; 1 child, Nehalem Kunkle-Read. BA in English, Amherst Coll., 1980; postgrad., Harvard U., 1996-97. Press sec. Mass. Commn. on State and County Bldgs., 1980; staff writer The Oregonian, 1981-86; fellow The Henry Luce Found./The Nation, Bangkok, Thailand, 1986-87; freelance writer Tokyo, 1987-89; Asia bur. chief The Oregonian, Tokyo, 1989-94; sec. 1st dir., 1st v.p. Fgn. Corrs. Club of Japan, 1990-93; internat. bus. writer The Oregonian, Portland, 1994-99, sr. writer internat. affairs, 1999—. Recipient Pulitzer prize for explanatory reporting, 1999, Overseas Press Club award for bus. reporting from abroad, 1999, Scripps Howard Found. award for bus. reporting, 1999, Blethen award for enterprise reporting Pacific Northwest Newspaper Assn., 1999, Oreg. Gov.'s award for achievement in internat. bus., 2000; named Internat. Citizen of Yr. 1999 World Affairs Coun. Oreg.; Eisenhower Exch. fellow, Peru, 1997; Nieman fellow, 1996-97.

READE, JOHN BRIAN, mathematics educator; b. Wolverhampton, Eng., July 4, 1938; s. Thomas Brian and Evelyn Rosemary (Bashford) R.; m. Alison Mary Caunce, June 22, 1968 (div. Apr. 1980); children: Jane, Brian; m. Suzanne Mary Muddimer Bertinat, July 5, 1980; children: Amanda, John James, David Alan. BA, Cambridge (Eng.) U., 1962, PhD, 1965. Math. lectr. Birmingham (Eng.) U., 1965-67; schoolmaster Fairham Comprehensive Sch., Nottingham, 1968; math. lectr. Manchester (Eng.) U., 1969—; tutor Open U., 1974—. Author: Mathematical Analysis, 1986; contbr. articles to profl. jours. Cpl. Royal Signals, 1956-58. Mem. Cambridge Philos. Soc., London Math. Soc. Avocations: jazz piano, checkers. Home: 123 Andover Ave, Middleton M24 1JQ, England Office: Manchester U, Dept Math, Manchester M13 9PL, England

READER, JOHN GRANVILLE, family practitioner; b. Liverpool, Eng., Mar. 1, 1934; s. Walter John and Harriett Beatrice (Bolt) R.; m. Isabel Sanderson, March 7, 1959 (dec. Mar. 1983); children: Judith Rachel, Janet Elisabeth; m. Olive Alethea Coates, Mar. 1, 1986. MB ChB, Liverpool U., 1957. Sr. house officer Royal Infirmary, Liverpool, 1960-61; med. registrar Broadgreen Hosp., Liverpool, 1961-66; sr. ptnr. Stockport Rd. Med. Practice, Marple, Cheshire, Eng., 1966-94; gen. sec. Internat. Christian Med. and Dental Assn., London, 1994—. Fellow Royal Soc. Medicine; mem. Christian Med. Fellowship (chmn. 1991-92), Internat. Christian Med. and Dental Assn. (gen. sec. 1992). Mem. Ch. of England. Avocations: ornithology, music, gardening. Office: Internat Christian Med and Dental Assn, 157 Waterloo Rd, London SE1 8XN, England

READING, ALAN WILLIAM, marketing executive, graphic designer; b. London, Mar. 27, 1950; s. Henry William and Patricia June (Yetton) R.; m. Patricia Jane Blogg, Jan. 1, 1970 (div. Dec. 1974). BA in Art and Design, Maidstone Coll. of Art, 1970. Creative head Adverkit Internat. Ltd., Maidstone, 1974-79, 89-94, Multi-Ad Svcs., 1989-94; propr. Duo Internat., 1989—, CMR, 1994—; bd. dirs. VKR Enterprises Ltd. Judge for Newspaper Soc. Display Award, Classified Award, Creative Award. Mem. Mid-Kent C. of C. and Industry (jr. v.p. 1992-93, pres. 1994-96, 2000). Avocations: photography, peafowl, fish keeping, gardening, especially cacti and succulents. Home: Prospect House Hunton Rd, Marden TN12 9SL Kent, England

READING, MARTIN, translator; b. Bromsgrove, U.K., Feb. 17, 1953; s. Raymond Lincoln and Ruth M.T. (Senger) R.; m. Susan Elizabeth Cunningham, June 17, 1978; children: Eleanor, Arthur. BA, Cambridge U., 1974, MA, 1978. Translator Internat. Atomic Energy Agy., Vienna, 1975-84; reviser IAEA, Vienna, 1984-96, head English translation sect., 1997—. Mem. The Cambridge Soc., Vienna Internat. Ctr. Wine Club, Planetary Soc. Avocations: books, music, astronomy, wine, golf. Office: IAEA, Wagramerstrasse 5 Box 200, A-1400 Vienna Austria

READING, PHYLLIS ANN, social welfare administrator; b. Seattle, Apr. 21, 1954. ADN, Shoreline C.C., Seattle, 1975; BSN, Seattle U., 1979; M Nursing in Adminstrn., U. Wash., 1988. RN, Wash., Calif. Relief charge nurse CCU Group Health Hosp., Redmond, Wash., 1979-81; relief supr. pheresis unit Puget Sound Blood Ctr., Seattle, 1981-83; coord. critical care Snoqualmie (Wash.) Valley Hosp., 1983-85, asst. adminstr., 1985-89; staff devel. specialist U. Wash. Med. Ctr., Seattle, 1989-93; edn. specialist AACN, Aliso Viejo, Calif., 1993-94, program devel. and meeting svcs. dir., 1994-96, dir. profl. devel., 1996-97, exec. dir., 1997-2000, program dir. Ctr. for Leadership Excellence, 1994-96, exec. prodr. satellite video confs., 1994-96; exec. dir. Nat. Assistance League, L.A., 2000—; mem. nat. faculty tchg. improvement project sys. Kellogg Found., 1992. Mem. adv. bd. N.W. Emergency Physicians, Seattle, 1985-89; bd. dirs. Am. Cancer Soc., Kirkland, Wash., 1988-89. Mem. AACN, Am. Soc. Assn. Execs., Sigma Theta Tau. Avocation: tennis. Office: AACN 101 Columbia Aliso Viejo CA 92656-4109

REAGAN, LAWRENCE PAUL, JR., systems engineer; b. Honolulu, Nov. 5, 1957; s. Lawrence Paul Sr. and Laura Louise (Sears) R.; m. Ann Marie Decker, Apr. 15, 1989; children: Lawrence P. III, Andrew Scott, Kelly Rene, Ryan Joshua. BS in Mech. & Aerospace Engring., Ill. Inst. Tech., 1979; MS in Acquisition & Contract Mgmt., West Coast U., Santa Barbara, Calif., 1986. Product engr. R.G. Ray Corp., Schaumburg, Ill., 1978-80; launch integration mgr. USAF Hqrs. Space Divsn., L.A. AFB, 1980-84; chief Titan program mgmt. USAF Aerospace Test Group, Vandenberg AFB, Calif., 1984-89; chief joint comm. br. USAF Pentagon, Washington, 1989-91; sr. sys. engr. Dynamics Rsch. Corp., Arlington, Va., 1992-96; dir. Md. ops. Dynamics Rsch. Corp., California, Md., 1996-97; fed. programs mgr. Info. Builders, Inc., Arlington, 1997-98, dir. fed. programs, 1998—; CEO Jacob's Well, Inc., Lexington Park, Md., 1993—. Contbr. papers to profl. publs. Named Outstanding Young Engr., Air Force Assn. Mem. AIAA, Soc. Logistics Engring., Air Force Assn., Armed Forces Comms. Electronics Assn. Home: PO Box 22 Lusby MD 20657-0022 Office: Info Builders Inc 2300 Clarendon Blvd Ste 800 Arlington VA 22201-3382

REAGAN, LESTER FRANKLIN, securities executive; b. Upson County, Ga., Oct. 30, 1944; s. H.C. and Sallie Ruth (Fowler) R.; m. Patricia Ann Fayard, Apr. 28, 1967; children: Jennifer Leigh Hanna, Whitney Blaine Creech. Diploma, Jonesboro (Ga.) H.S., 1962. CFP; registered prin. NASD. Asst. v.p. We. Res. Life, Largo, Fla., 1973-77, v.p. agys., 1978-82; sr. v.p. mktg. Cons. Capital Cos., Emeryville, Calif., 1982-87; v.p. mktg., Fla. Pioneer Funds, Boston, 1987-88; exec. v.p. PW Securities/We. Res. Life, Largo, 1988-90; sr. v.p. Midland Equity Corp., Clearwater, Fla., 1991-93; regional mktg. v.p. Cronos Securities, San Francisco, 1993-95; regional v.p. Pacific Life, Newport Beach, Calif., 1996—. Mem. Internat. Assn. Fin. Planners (bd. mem.). Avocations: golf, fishing, grandchildren.

REAGAN, NANCY DAVIS (ANNE FRANCIS ROBBINS), volunteer, wife of former President of United States; b. N.Y.C., July 6, 1923; d. Kenneth and Edith (Luckett) Robbins; step dau. Loyal Davis; m. Ronald Reagan, Mar. 4, 1952; children: Patricia Ann, Ronald Prescott; stepchildren: Maureen, Michael. BA, Smith Coll.; LLD (hon.), Pepperdine U., 1983; LHD (hon.), Georgetown U., 1987. Contract actress, MGM, 1949-56; films include The Next Voice You Hear, 1950, Donovan's Brain, 1953, Hellcats of the Navy, 1957; Author: Nancy, 1980; formerly author syndicated column on prisoner-of-war and missing-in-action soldiers and their families; author: (with Jane Wilkie) To Love a Child, (with William Novak) My Turn: The Memoirs of Nancy Reagan, 1989. Civic worker, visited wounded Viet Nam vets., sr. citizens, hosps. and schs. for physically and emotionally handicapped children, active in furthering foster grandparents for handicapped children program; hon. nat. chmn. Aid to Adoption of Spl. Kids, 1977; spl. interest in fighting alcohol and drug abuse among youth: hosted first ladies from around the world for 2d Internat. Drug Conf., 1985; hon. chmn. Just Say No Found., Nat. Fedn. of Parents for Drug-Free Youth, Nat. Child Watch Campaign, President's Com. on the Arts and Humanities, Wolf Trap Found. bd. of trustees, Nat. Trust for Historic Preservation, Cystic Fibrosis Found., Nat. Republican Women's Club; hon. pres. Girl Scouts of Am. Named one of Ten Most Admired Am. Women, Good Housekeeping mag., ranking #1 in poll, 1984, 85, 86; Woman of Yr. Los Angeles Times, 1977; permanent mem. Hall of Fame of Ten Best Dressed Women in U.S.; recipient humanitarian awards from Am. Camping Assn., Nat. Council on Alcoholism, United Cerebral Palsy Assn., Internat. Ctr. for Disabled; Boys Town Father Flanagan award; 1986 Kiwanis World Service medal; Variety Clubs Internat. Lifeline award; numerous awards for her role in fight against drug abuse. Address: 2121 Avenue Of The Stars Fl 34 Los Angeles CA 90067-5062

REAGAN, RONALD WILSON, former President of United States; b. Tampico, Ill., Feb. 6, 1911; s. John Edward and Nelle (Wilson) R.; m. Jane Wyman, Jan. 25, 1940 (div. 1948); children: Maureen E., Michael E.; m. Nancy Davis, Mar. 4, 1952; children: Patricia, Ronald. AB, Eureka Coll., 1932, MA (hon.), 1957. Actor GE Theatre, 1954-62; host TV series Death Valley Days, 1962-66; gov. State of Calif., 1967-74; businessman, rancher, commentator on public policy, 1975-80, Pres. of U.S., 1981-89. Sports announcer, motion picture and TV actor, 1932-66. Author: Where's The Rest of Me?, Speaking My Mind: Selected Speeches, 1989, An American Life: The Autobiography, 1990. Mem. Calif. State Rep. Ctrl. Com., 1964-66; del. Rep. Nat. Conv., 1968, 72; chmn. Rep. Gov. Assn., 1968-73; mem. presdl. Commn. CIA Activities Within U.S., 1975; bd. dirs. Com. Present Danger, Washington, 1977—; cand. for Rep. nomination for Pres., 1976. Served as capt. USAAF, 1942-45. Recipient Great Am. of Decade award, Va. Young Am. for Freedom, Man of Yr. Free Enterprise award, San Fernando Valley Bus. & Profl. award, 1964, Am. Legion award, 1965, Horation Alger award, 1969, George Washington Honor medal, Freedoms Found. Valley Forge award, 1971, Disting. Am. award; inducted into Nat. Football Found. Hall of Fame, Am. Patriots Hall of Fame. Mem. SAG (pres. 1947-52, 59), Am. Fedn. Radio & TV Artists, Lions, Friars, Tau Kappa Epsilon. Republican. Address: 11000 Wilshire Blvd Fl 34 Los Angeles CA 90067

REAL, REINERIO AUGUSTO, English educator, consultant; b. Bilar, The Philippines, Aug. 4, 1942; s. Philip Ortiz and Crescentia Arguelles Real; m. Melinda Dolotina Concon, Jan. 4, 1969; children: Rhinehart Michelle, Renee Marjorie, Rochelle Margaret, Rein Michael. AA in Pre-Medicine, Southwestern U., Cebu City, The Philippines, 1960, BS, 1962; MA in English cum laude, U. Bohol, Tagbilaran City, The Philippines, 1970, postgrad. in English, 1980-81, 89-90. Field checker, liaison officer Emergency Employment Agy., Manila, 1962; confidential asst. R. Roces Publs., Inc., Manila, 1963-65; sales rep. St. Louise Realty Corp., Caloocan City, The Philippines, 1966, P.F. Colliers (Philippines), Inc., Manila, 1966; tchr. English Hoang Nguyen Sch., Saigon, South Vietnam, 1966-67; prof. English, speech U. Bohol, 1967—; sports coord. U. Bohol Alumni and Ext. Svcs., U. Bohol, 1986-88, editor-in-chief UB Update, 1990-94, head student affairs office, 1994—; spkr. in field. Author: Speech Communication Made Easy, 1991, rev. edit., 1997. Stage mgr. operetta Rafael Palma Coll., Tagbilaran City, 1968, dir. operetta, 1981; playing coach, team mgr. U. Bohol Faculty and Staff Basketball Team, 1970—; exec. v.p. ops., acting pres. Bohol Jaycees, 1973; regional chmn. Ctrl. Visayas, Youth Activities Commn., Philippine Jaycees, Inc., 1979-80; mem. JCP Spkrs.' Bur., 1974-83; advisdor Coll. Assurance Plan, Philippines, Inc. Tagbilaran City, 1981-85; pres. Holy Spirit Sch.'s Federated Parents-Tchrs. Assn., Inc., Tagbilaran City, 1981-82, 92-93; pres. Orgn. Bilanona in Tagbilaran, 1992—; ofcl. coach Bohol PRISAA Womens Basketball, Dumaguette City, 1993—, U. Bohol Women's Basketball, 1994; pres. Bohol Assoc. Jaycees, 1995—; chmn. steering com. Bohol Provincial Working Youth Ctr., 1966—; mem. Tagbilaran City Peace and Order Coun., 1997-98; actor/singer Teatro Bolanon, Tagbilaran City, 1997—; pres. Bohol Toastmasters Club, Tagbilaran City, 1998; singer Bohol Festival Chorus, 1998. Recipient numerous awards from Jaycees. Mem. Philippine Assn. Adminstrs. Student Affairs (nat. bd. dirs. 1998—), Bohol English Tchrs. Assn. (bd. dirs. 1973-75), Fedn. Bohol Employees (pres. 1973-74, 75-76), Miracle Mentors Ltd., Coll. English Tchrs. Assn., Alpha Bita Phi, Philippines Jaycees Inc., Bohol Assoc. Jaycees, Basketball Assn. of Philippines Referees Commn., Dagohoy Lions Club. Roman Catholic. Avocations: reading and writing, stamp and coin collecting. Home: Rizal St Cogon Dist, 6300 Tagbilaren City The Philippines Office: Univ Bohol, Dr C Putong St, 6300 Tagbilaran The Philippines

REAMAN, GREGORY HAROLD, pediatric hematologist, oncologist; b. Akron, Ohio, Sept. 9, 1947; s. Harold J. and Margaret U. (D'Alfonso) R.; m. Susan J. Pristo, Sept. 7, 1974; children: Emily Margaret, Sarah Elizabeth. BS in Biology, U. Detroit, 1969; MD, Loyola U., Chgo., 1973. Diplomate Nat. Bd. Med. Examiners, Am. Bd. Pediatrics. Pediatric intern Loyola U. Med. Ctr., 1973-74; resident in pediatrics Montreal Children's Hosp., McGill U., 1974-76; clin. assoc. pediatric oncology br. Nat. Cancer Inst., NIH, Bethesda, Md., 1976-78, investigator pediatric oncology br., 1978-79; assoc. dept. hematology/oncology, attending physician Children's Nat. Med. Ctr., Washington, 1979-87, chmn. dept. hematology/oncology, 1987—, dir. med. spl. svcs., 1997-99, exec. dir. Ctr. for Cancer and Blood Disorders, 1999—; asst. prof. pediatrics Sch. Medicine and Health Scis. George Washington U., 1979-82, assoc. prof. pediatrics, 1982-87, prof. pediats., 1987-97, prof., 1997—; mem. immunology devices panel FDA; assoc. chmn. Children's Cancer Group; bd. dirs., mem. med. affairs com., chmn., strategic planning com. Children's Oncology Svcs. of Met. Washington. Mem. editorial bd. Cancer Physicians Data Query, Nat. Cancer Inst.; reviewer Cancer Treatment Resports, Blood, Jour. Clin. Oncology; contbr. articles to profl. publs. Trustee Nat. Childhood Cancer Found., Arcadia, Calif.; bd. dirs. Am. Cancer Soc., Atlanta; trustee, chmn. patient care and profl. edn. coms. Leukemia Soc. Am. Lt. comdr. USPHS, 1976-79, Res., 1979—. Folger Summer scholar Am. Cancer Soc.; recipient Spl. Fellowship Rsch. award Leukemia Soc. Am., 1980-82; grantee DHHS, Nat. Cancer Inst., 1987—. Mem. Soc. Pediat. Rsch., Am. Soc. Hematology, Am. Pediat. Soc., Am. Fedn. Clin. Rsch., Am. Soc. Clin. Oncology, Am. Assn. Cancer Rsch., Am. Soc. Pediat. Hematology/Oncology, Children's Cancer Group, Washington Blood Club, Alpha Omega Alpha. Democrat. Roman Catholic. Home: 7306 Brennon Ln Chevy Chase MD 20815-4064 Office: Children's Nat Med Ctr 111 Michigan Ave NW Washington DC 20010-2916

REAMS, BERNARD DINSMORE, JR., lawyer, educator; b. Lynchburg, Va., Aug. 17, 1943; s. Bernard Dinsmore and Martha Eloise (Hickman) R.; m. Rosemarie Bridget Boyle, Oct. 26, 1968 (dec. Oct. 1996); children: Andrew Dennet, Adriane Bevin. BA, Lynchburg Coll., 1965; MS, Drexel U., 1966; JD, U. Kans., 1972; PhD, St. Louis U., 1983. Bar: Kans. 1973, Mo. 1986, N.Y. 1996. Instr., asst. librarian Rutgers U., 1966-69; asst. prof. law, librarian U. Kans., Lawrence, 1969-74; mem. faculty law sch. Washington U., St. Louis, 1974-95, prof. law, 1976-95, prof. tech. mgmt., 1990-95, librarian, 1974-76, acting dean univ. libraries, 1987-88; prof. law, assoc. dean, dir. Law Libr. St. John's U. Sch. Law, Jamaica, N.Y., 1995-97; assoc. dean acad. affairs St. John's U. Sch. Law, Jamaica, 1997-98; prof., dir. law libr. St. Mary's U., San Antonio, N.Y., 2000—; prof. law St. Mary's U., San Antonio, 2000—; vis. fellow Max-Planck Inst., Hamburg, 1995, 97, 98; vis. prof. law Seton Hall U., 1998-2000. Author: Law For The Businessman, 1974, Reader in Law Librarianship, 1976, Federal Price and Wage Control Programs 1917-1979: Legis. Histories and Laws, 1980, Education of the Handicapped: Laws, Legislative Histories, and Administrative Documents, 1982, Housing and Transportation of the Handicapped: Laws and Legislative Histories, 1983, Internal Revenue Acts of the United States: The Revenue Act of 1954 with Legislative Histories and Congressional Documents, 1983 Congress and the Courts: A Legislative History 1978-1984, 1984, University-Industry Research Partnerships: The Major Issues in Research and Development Agreements, 1986, Deficit Control and the Gramm-Rudman-Hollings Act, 1986, The Semiconductor Chip and the Law: A Legislative History of the Semiconductor Chip Protection Act of 1984, 1986, American International Law Cases, 2d series, 1986, Technology Transfer Law: The Export Administration Acts of the U.S., 1987, Insider Trading and the Law: A Legislative History of the Insider Trading Sanctions Act, 1989, Insider Trading and Securities Fraud, 1989, The Health Care Quality Improvement Act of 1989: A Legislative History of P.L. No. 99-660, 1990; The National Organ Transplant Act of 1984: A Legislative History of P.L. No. 98-507, 1990, A Legislative History of Individuals with Disabilities Education Act, 1994, Federal Legislative Histories: An Annotated Bibliography and Index to Officially Published Sources, 1994, Electronic Contracting Law, 1996, Health Care Reform, 1994, The American Experience: Clinton and Congress, 1997, The Omnibus Anti-Crime Act, 1997; co-author: Segregation and the Fourteenth Amendment in the States, 1975, Historic Preservation Law: An Annotated Bibliography, 1976, Congress and the Courts: A Legislative History 1787-1977, 1978, Federal Consumer Protection Laws, Rules and Regulations, 1979, A Guide and Analytical Index to the Internal Revenue Acts of the U.S., 1909-1950, 1979, The Numerical Lists and Schedule of Volumes of the U.S. Congressional Serial Set: 73d Congress through the 96th Congress, 1984, Human Experimentation: Federal Laws, Legislative Histories, Regulations and Related Documents, 1985, American Legal Literature: A Guide to Selected Legal Resources, 1985, The Constitution of the United States: A Guide and Bibliography, 1987, The Congressional Impeachment Process and the Judiciary, 1987, Tax Reform 1986: A Legislative History of the Tax Refrom Act of 1986, 1988, The Constitutions of the States: A State by State Guide and Bibliography, 1988, Executive and Professional Employment Contracts, 1988, The Legislative History of the Export Trading Company Act of 1982 Including the Foreign Trade Antitrust Improvements Act, 1989, Federal Deficit Control, 1989, The Legislative History of the Export Trading Company Act of 1982 Including the Foreign Trade Antitrust Improvements Act, 1989, United States-Canada Free Trade Act: A Legislative History, 1990, Trade Reform Legislation 1988: A Legislative History of the Omnibus Trade and Competitiveness Act of 1988, 1992, Disability Law in the United States, 1992, Bankruptcy Reform Amendments, 1992, The Law of Hospital and Health Care Administration: Case and Materials, 1993, The Civil Rights Act of 1991: A Legislative History, 1994, The North American Free Trade Agreement, 1994, Catalonia, Spain, Europe, and Latin America: Regional Legal Systems and their Literature, 1995, A Legislative History of the Prison Litigation Reform Act of 1996, 1997, Federal Backruptcy Law: A Legislative History of the Bankruptcy Reform Act of 1994, 1998, A Legislative History of the International Antitrust Enforcement Assistance Act of 1994, 1998. Bd. trustees Quincy Found. for Med. Rsch. Charitable Trust, San Francisco. Fellow Am. Bar Foun.; recipient Thornton award for excellence Lynchburg Coll., 1986, Joseph L. Andrews Bibliog. award, 1995; named to Hon. Order Ky. Cols., 1992. Mem. ABA, Am. Law Inst., ALA, Am. Soc. Law and Medicine, Nat. Health Lawyers Assn., Am. Assn. Higher Edn., Spl. Librs. Assn., Internat. Assn. Law Libr. Coll. and Univ. Attys., Order of Coif, Phi Beta Kappa, Sigma Xi, Beta Phi Mu, Phi Delta Phi, Phi Delta Epsilon, Kappa Delta Pi, Pi Lambda Theta. Office: St Marys U Sch Law One Camino Santa Maria San Antonio TX 78228

REARDON, ROBERT IGNATIUS, JR., lawyer; b. N.Y.C., Nov. 28, 1945; s. Robert I. and Mildred (Lomax) R.; m. Lise Hofffman; children: Colleen Brooke, Kelly Elizabeth. BS in Econs., Boston Coll., 1967; JD, Fordham U., 1970. Bar: Conn. 1970, U.S. Dist. Ct. Conn. 1974, U.S. Ct. Mil. Appeals 1971, U.S. Ct. Appeals (2d cir.) 1974, U.S. Supreme Ct. 1974, U.S. Ct. Claims 1986. Ptnr. Shapiro & Reardon, P.C., New London, Conn., 1973-83; pres. Reardon Law Firm P.C., New London, 1983—; state trial referee Conn. Superior Ct., 1985—. Chmn. Bd. Fin. Town of Waterford, Conn., 1974-79; mem. Bd. Edn. Town of East Lyme, Conn., 1981-84; trustee Eugene O'Neill Meml. Theater, Inc., 1978-84; active Conn. Commn. Pub. Trust, 1998—. Served as capt. USMC, 1970-73. Mem. ABA (award of achievement young lawyers sect. 1975), ATLA (bd. dirs. 1998—), Conn. Trial Lawyers Assn. (pres. 1997-98), Conn. Bar Assn. (bd. govs. 1979-81, ho. of dels. 1975-79), New London County Bar Assn. (mem. exec. com. 1975-79). Home: 95 Quarry Dock Rd Niantic CT 06357-1908 Office: 160 Hempstead St New London CT 06320-5638

REARDON, STEPHEN JAMES, JR., retired English speech educator; b. Butte, Mont., Nov. 6, 1929; s. Stephen James and Myrtle Agnes (MacKillican) R. PhB, Carroll Coll., 1952; MA in English, U. Wash., 1963. Tchr. English, speech Butte Jr. H.S., 1957-65; instr. English, speech Mont. State U., Bozeman, 1965-67; upward bound tchr. St. Michael's Coll., Colchester, Vt., summers 1968, 69; tchr. English West Jr. H.S., Butte, spring 1969, Butte H.S., Sch. Dist. No. 1, 1972-92; speech coach Butte H.S., Sch. Dist. No. 1, 1973-85. Mem. Am. Legion Post No. 1, Butte, 1976—. With U.S. Army, 1955-57. Named Class AA Mont. Speech Coach of Yr., Mont. Forensic Educators Assn., 1978-79, 83-84, named to Hall of Fame, 1997; recipient Gold Star Excellence Tchg award Rivendell Psychiat. Ctr. and Mont. Eagle Comm., 1990-91, Golden Apple Excellence in Edn. award Butte C. of C., 1992. Mem. U.S. Judo Assn. (5th degree black belt 1999), U.S. Judo, Inc. (5th degree black belt 1999), U.S. Tomiki Aikido Black Belt Fedn. (1st degree black belt 1998), Butte Tchrs. Union Local 332, Butte Judo Club (dir. 1972-80, 82—), Butte Karate Club N.W. Tae Kwon Do Assn. (hon. black belt 1989). Democrat. Roman Catholic. Avocations: martial arts, skiing, swimming, writing. Home: 616 W Gold St Butte MT 59701-2363

REASONER, BARRETT HODGES, lawyer; b. Houston, Apr. 16, 1964; s. Harry Max and Macey (Hodges) R.; m. Susan Hardig; children: Matthew Joseph, Caroline Macey, William Harry, Olivia Lucille. BA cum laude, Duke U., 1986; Grad. Dipl., London Sch. Econs., 1987; JD with honors, U. Tex., 1990. Bar: Tex. 1990, U.S. Dist. Ct. (so., we., and no. dists.) Tex. 1993, U.S. Ct. Appeals (5th cir.) 1993, U.S. Supreme Ct. 1997. Asst. dist. atty. Harris County Dist. Atty.'s Office, Houston, 1990-92; ptnr. Gibbs & Bruns, L.L.P., Houston, 1992—. Fellow Tex. Bar Found., Houston Bar Found.; mem. Am. Judicature Soc. (bd. dirs. 1994-99, exec. com. 1997-99), State Bar Tex. (jud. rels. com. 1998—), Houston Bar Assn. (bd. dirs. 2000—), Houston Young Lawyers Assn. (pub. schs. and pub. edn. com. 1994—, chmn. pub. schs. and pub. edn. com. 1997-99, outstanding com. chair 1999), Order of Barristers. Episcopalian. Office: Gibbs & Bruns LLP 1100 Louisiana St Ste 5300 Houston TX 77002-5215

REASONER, HARRY MAX, lawyer; b. San Marcos, Tex., July 15, 1939; s. Harry Edward and Joyce Majorie (Barrett) R.; m. Elizabeth Macey Hodges, Apr. 15, 1963; children: Barrett Hodges, Elizabeth Macey Reasoner Stokes. BA in Philosophy summa cum laude, Rice U., 1960; JD with highest honors, U. Tex., 1962; postgrad., U. London, 1962-63. Bar: Tex., D.C., N.Y. Law clk. U.S. Ct. Appeals (2d cir.), 1963-64; assoc. Vinson & Elkins, Houston, 1964-69, ptnr., 1970—, mng.ptnr., 1992—; vis. prof. U. Tex. Sch. Law, 1971, Rice U., 1976, U. Houston Sch. Law, 1977; chair adv. group U.S. Dist Ct (so. dist.) Tex.; mem. adv. com. Supreme Ct. Tex. Author: (with Charles Alan Wright) Procedure: The Handmaid of Justice, 1965. Trustee U. Tex. Law Sch. Found., Southwestern Legal Found., Rice U., Baylor Coll. Medicine; chair Tex. Higher Edn. Coordinating Bd., 1991; bd. dirs. Houston Music Hall Found. Bd., 1996—; mem. Houston Annenberg Challenge Child Centered Schs. Initiative Bd., 1997—. Rotary Found. fellow 1962-63; named Disting. Alumnus, U. Tex., 1997, U. Tex. Sch. Law, 1998. Fellow Am. Coll. Trial Lawyers, Internat. Acad. Trial Lawyers, Internat. Soc. Barristers, ABA Found., Tex. Bar Found.; mem. ABA (chmn. antitrust sect. 1989-90), Houston Bar Assn., Assn. Bar City N.Y., Am. Law Inst., Houston Com. Fgn. Rels., Houston Philos. Soc., Philos. Soc. Tex., Am. Bd. Trial Advocates, Century Assn. N.Y.C., Houston Country Club,

Eldorado Country Club (Calif.), Castle Pines Golf Club (Colo.), Cosmos Club (D.C.), Galveston Artillery Club, Chancellors, Barristers, Phi Beta Kappa, Phi Delta Phi. Office: Vinson & Elkins 2800 First City Tower 1001 Fannin St Houston TX 77002-6760

REAST, DEBORAH STANEK, executive assistant; b. Phila., Feb. 25, 1955; d. Chester Joseph and Thelma Sylvia (Hop) S. AS, Gwynedd Mercy Coll., 1975; Cert. Mgmt., Villanova U., 1987. Cert. med. mgr. Billing clk. Ophthalmic Assocs., Lansdale, Pa., 1971-75, exec. sec., 1975-80, ops. mgr., 1980-99; exec. asst. 24th Sen. Dist., State of Pa., Lansdale, 1999—; treas., bd. dirs. Montgomery County Chpt. Profl. Secs. Internat. Ch. organist Corpus Christi Parish, Gwynedd, 1970-86, Saint Marie Goretti Parish, Hatfield, 1986—, ch. organist, 1986-96. Mem. Pa. Assn. Notaries, The Wine Connection Bucks, 1st Sunday Soc. Republican. Roman Catholic. Avocations: writing, traveling, collecting. Office: Office Sen Ed Holl 24th Dist Office 427 W Main St Lansdale PA 19446-2007

REATH, GEORGE, JR., lawyer, mediator; b. Phila., Mar. 14, 1939; s. George and Isabel Duer (West) R.; children from a previous marriage: Eric (dec. 1995), Amanda; m. Ann B. Rowland, 1990. BA, Williams Coll., 1961; LLB, Harvard U., 1964. Bar: Pa. 1965, U.S. Dist. Ct. (ea. dist.) Pa. 1966, U.S. Ct. Appeals (3d cir.) 1996. Assoc. Dechert Price & Rhoads, Phila., 1964-70, Brussels, 1971-74; atty. Pennwalt Corp., Phila., 1974-78, mgr. legal dept., asst. sec., 1978-87, sr. v.p.-law, sec., 1987-89; sr. v.p., gen. counsel, sec. Elf Atochem N.Am., Inc. (formerly Pennwalt Corp.), Phila., 1990-92; sr. v.p., gen counsel, sec. Legal Triage Svcs., Inc., Phila., 1993-98; sr. v.p., gen. counsel, sec. Triage Mediation Svcs., Inc., Phila., 1999—; bd. dirs. Internat. Bus. Forum, Inc., 1978-91; arbitrator Am. Arbitration Assn. Trustee Children's Hosp., Phila., 1974—, sec., 1980-81, vice chmn., 1984-97; bd. mgrs. Phila. City Inst. Libr., 1974—, treas., 1981-88, pres., 1989-99; bd. dirs. Phila. Festival Theatre for New Plays, 1983-94, Ctrl. Phila. Devel. Corp., 1987-93; bd. dirs. Bach Festival Phila., 1990-98, v.p., 1992-93; bd. dirs. Crime Commn. Delaware Valley, 1st vice chmn., 1992-94, chmn., 1994-96; exec. com., 1996—; bd. coun. mem. Episcopal Cmty. Svcs. 1999—, treas., 2000—. Mem. ABA, Am. Arbitration Assn., Pa. Bar Assn., Phila. Bar Assn., Penllyn Club, Winter Harbor Yacht Club, Am. Corp. Counsel Assn., Penn Club, Soc. Profls. in Dispute Resolution (assoc.), Phi Beta Kappa.

REAUGH, O(RLAND) H., oil industry executive; b. Hanford, Wash., June 19, 1913; s. Harry Wallace Reaugh and Anna Charlotte Magnuson; m. Ruth Verne Davis, July 8, 1941 (dec. Sept. 1999); children: Dianne Reaugh Bauman, Harry Coleman. BSChemE, Wash. State U., 1933. Reg. profl. engr., Tex. Engr. Gulf Oil Corp., 1933-48; dist. supt. McElroy Ranch Co., Breckenridge, Tex., 1948-51; ptnr. Ibex Co., Breckenridge, 1951-54; v.p. Graridge Corp., Breckenridge, 1954-66; sr. v.p. Petroleum Corp. Tex., Breckenridge, 1966-83; sr. v.p. States Inc., Breckenridge, 1983—, co-chmn., 1998—. Mem. sch. bd. Breckenridge Ind. Sch. Dist.; trustee Breckenridge Libr. & Fine Arts Found., 1989—. Capt. USAF, 1942-46. Mem. West Central Tex. Oil and Gas Assn. (dir., v.p.), Breckenridge C. of C. (pres. 1978). Democrat. Methodist. Home: 304 N Harding St Breckenridge TX 76424-3219 Office: Breck Operating Corp PO Box 911 Breckenridge TX 76424-0911

REAVES, BOB H., pastor, counselor; b. Talladega, Ala., Oct. 22, 1941; s. Howard H. and Jewel I. (Storey) R.; m. Sharon L.; children: Timothy Mark, Jonathon Scott, Daniel Huston. BD, Luther Rice Seminary, 1978, MDiv, 1979, D in Ministry, 1981. Pastor First Baptist Ch., Marathon, Fla., 1971-75, Knights Baptist Ch., Plant City, Fla., 1975-79, North Kissimmee (Fla.) Baptist, 1979-89; staff counselor Osceola Sheriff's Office, Kissimmee, 1989—. Chaplain Kissimmee Police Dept., Fla. Highway Patrol. Avocations: western art, target shooting, collector of books on old west. Home: 2706 16th St # 701263 Saint Cloud FL 34769-4926 Office: Osceola Sheriffs Office 400 Simpson Rd Kissimmee FL 34744-4455

REAVES, CHARLES DURHAM, investment company executive; b. Florence, S.C., June 1, 1935; s. Howard Meacham and Kathleen (Durham) R.; m. Gretchen Wuerdeman, May 4, 1963; 1 son, Mark Charles. BA magna cum laude, Furman U., 1956; LLB, U. Ala., 1961; LLM, Georgetown U., 1966; MBA, Emory U., 1981. Bar: Ala. 1961, Mass. 1967, D.C. 1970. Legal adv. to chmn. FTC, Washington, 1963-67; sec., assoc. counsel Paul Revere Life Ins. Co., Worcester, Mass., 1967-70; v.p., sec., gen. counsel Saunders Leasing System, Inc., Washington, 1970-74, Birmingham, Ala., 1974-80; sr. v.p. fin., sec. Saunders Leasing System, Inc., 1981-86; pres. Southeastern Asset Mgmt. Funds Trust, Memphis, 1986-93; exec. v.p., gen. counsel, chief compliance officer Longleaf Ptnrs. Funds, 1993—; bd. dirs. ICI Mut. Ins. Co., Burlington, Vt. Bd. trustees Memphis Opera, 1993—. Capt. USAR, 1961-63. Decorated Army Commendation medal. Mem. ABA, FBA, Mass. Bar Assn., D.C. Bar Assn., Ala. Bar Assn., Ala. Assn. Corp. Counsel (pres. 1981-82), Fin. Execs. Inst. (dir. 1983-84), Rotary, The Club (Birmingham), Westwood Country Club (Vienna, Va.), Econ. Club of Memphis (dir. 1993-96), Crescent Club, Chickasaw Country Club. Office: Southeastern Asset Mgmt Inc 6410 Poplar Ave Ste 900 Memphis TN 38119-4841

REAVEY, WILLIAM ANTHONY, III, lawyer; b. Springfield, Mass., Dec. 27, 1944; s. William A. Jr. and Deborah M. (Clancy) R.; Jacqueline R. Beauvais, Sept. 2, 1967; children: Patrick, Kevin, Brian, Michael. BS, USAF Acad., 1966; MA, Yale U., 1968, JD, 1976. Bar: Calif. 1976. Assoc. Latham & Watkins, Newport Beach, Calif., 1976-81; ptnr. Aylward, Kintz & Stiska, San Diego, 1981-87, Lillick & McHose, San Diego, 1987-90, Pillsbury, Madison & Sutro, San Diego, 1991—, Hillyer & Irvin, San Diego, CA. Bd. dirs. Am. Liver Found., San Diego, 1991, Kind Found., San Diego, 1992, San Diego Comml. Indsl. Coun. Bldg. Industry Assn., 1992. Capt. USAF, 1966-73, Vietnam. Decorated Bronze Star. Mem. ABA. Roman Catholic. Avocations: fishing, back-packing, biking. Home: 10515 Livewood Way San Diego CA 92131-2203 Office: Hillyer & Irvin 550 W C St Fl 16 San Diego CA 92101-3540*

REAVIS, HUBERT GRAY, JR., metal products executive; b. Winston-Salem, N.C., May 4, 1945; s. Hubert Gray and Marie (Long) R.; m. Brenda Todd, Oct. 19, 1969; children: Anna Caroline, Jennifer Rebecca. BS in Engring., N.C. State U., 1967. Metall. engr. Alumninun Co. Am., Alcoa, Tenn., 1967-73; divisional metall. engr. Aluminum Co. Am., Newburgh, Ind., 1973-79; product metall. engr. Aluminum Co. Am., Pitts., 1979-86; quality assurance mgr. Alumninun Co. Am., Newburgh, Ind., 1986-88; tech. mgr. Aluminum Co. Am., Newburgh, Ind., 1988-96, mgr. materials devel. group, 1997—. Patentee in field. Mem. Alumninum Co. Am. Polit. Action, Pitts., 1979-86, Newburgh, 1986—. Recipient (3) Arthur Vining Davis awards. Mem. Am. Soc. for Metals, N.C. State Alumni Loyalty Fund, Phi Kappa Phi, Theta Tau, Alpha Sigma Mu, Tau Beta Pi. Office: Aluminum Co Am PO Box 10 Newburgh IN 47629-0010

REAVIS, SUSAN SCOTT, elementary educator; b. Tulare, Calif., Dec. 24, 1954; d. Eugene Ernest and Barbara Jane (Hyde) Scott; m. Robert Carl Reavis, June 14, 1987; stepchildren: Jaimie Rae, Peyton Ashley. BE, Northern Ariz. U., 1976; ME, U. Ariz., 1983. Cert. elem. tchr., Ariz. Tchr. Coolidge (Ariz.) Schs., 1976-78, Vail (Ariz.) Schs., 1978-85, Marana (Ariz.) Schs., 1985—. Active Red Cross Blood Program, Tucson, 1994—; mem. chancel choir Beautiful Savior Luth. Ch., Tucson, 1995—. Mem. Internat. Reading Assn., Nat. Council Tchrs. English, Marana Edn. Assn., Marana Schs. coms. Democrat. Home: 5117 W Malachite Pl Tucson AZ 85742-9402 Office: Quail Run Elem Sch 4600 W Cortaro Rd Tucson AZ 85742

REAY-YOUNG, PETER SHIRLEY, oncologist, consultant; b. Asansol, W. Bengal, India, Oct. 27, 1924; arrived in Australia, 1960; s. Percival and Adelaide Beatrice (Whaley) R.-Y.; m. Barbara Parton, Oct. 3, 1946 (div.); children: Susan, Nigel, Penelope, Sally; m. Jeanette Deirdre Cook, May 25, 1977; 1 child, Rebecca Sherwood. BA with hons., Cambridge U., 1949, MChir, 1959, MBBChir, 1952, MA, 1962; BA with hons., Sydney U., 1990. House surgeon St. Thomas Hosp., London, 1952-53, demonstrator anatomy, 1953-54, resident surg. registrar, 1956-57; cons. surgeon Port Moresby, Papua New Guinea, 1964-68; cons. radiation oncologist Papua New Guinea, Prince of Wales Hosp., Sydney, 1972-86; vol. health cons. Overseas Svcs. Bur. Australian vol. abroad Overseas Svc. Bur., Sydney, 1994-95. Sub-lt. Royal Navy, 1943-46. G.S. Caird scholar U. Sydney, 1989. Fellow Royal Coll. Surgeons; mem. Royal Australian Coll. Radiologists, Law Soc. New S. Wales (lay mem. ethics com. 1991), Mensa, Am. Soc. Therapeutic Radiologists (emeritus). Mem. Labour Party. Avocations: bird-watching. Home: 9/111 Arden St, 2034 Coogee Sydney NSW, Australia

REBAGLIATI, ROSS, snowboarder; b. Vancouver, Can., July 14, 1971. Snowboarder JW 4, 1987—, Can. Nat. Team, 1997—. Recipient Gold medal men's snowboard giant slalom, Olympic Games, Nagano, Japan, 1998. Avocations: surfing, golf, mountain biking, Nordic skiing. Office: Can Olympic Assn, Av Pierre Dupuy 2380, Montreal, PQ Canada H3C 3R4*

REBANE, KARL (KARLOVICH REBANE), physicist; b. Pärnu, Etonia, Apr. 11, 1926; s. Karl (Janovich) and Aleksandra (Tomberg) R.; m. Lyubov A. Shagalova; children: Inna K., Aleksander K. Degree, Tallinn (Estonia) Poly. Inst., 1949; Diploma in Physics, Leningrad State U., 1952, postgrad., 1952-55, D of Physics and Math., 1955, full doctor (Dr. habilit.), 1965. Researcher, educator, organizer of sci. Estonian Acad. Scis., Tartu U., Tallinn, 1955, pres., 1973-90; prof. physics Estonian Acad. Scis., Tartu U., 1966-94, 94—; prof. emeritus physics Tartu (Estonia) U., 1955-66, chmn. sub dept. of physics, 1976—. Author: Impurity Spectra of Solids, 1968, 70, Energy, Entropy, Environment, 1980, 84; patentee in field (12); editor several texts; contbr. over 200 articles to sci. jours. Mem. Parliament USSR, 1974-91. Served with Estonian Corps Soviet Army, 1943-46, ETO. Named Hero of Socialist Labor (for physics sci. and edn.); recipient 2 Lenin Orders, Order of Great Patriotic War (1st degree), Medal of Bravery, others. Mem. Russian Acad. Sci. (optics, P.N. Lebedev Golden medal), Estonian Acad. Sci (theor. phys.), European Acad., European Acad. of Sci. and Arts (A.V. Humboldt Sci. award, 2 Sci. prizes of Estonian Republic). Avocations: chess, fishing. Fax: 372-7-383033. E-mail: rebanek@fi.tartu. Office: Inst Physics Tartu U, 142 Riia Str, 51014 Tartu Estonia

REBEIZ, CONSTANTIN A., plant physiology educator, laboratory director; b. Beirut, July 11, 1936; came to U.S., 1969, naturalized, 1975; s. Anis C. and Valentine A. (Choueyri) R.; m. Carole Louise Conness, Aug. 18, 1962; children: Paul A., Natalie, Mark J. B.S., Am. U., Beirut, 1959; M.S., U. Calif. - Davis, 1960, Ph.D., 1965. Dir. dept. biol. scis. Agrl. Rsch. Inst., Beirut, 1965-69; research assoc. biology U. Calif. - Davis, 1969-71; assoc. prof. plant physiology U. Ill., Urbana-Champaign, 1972-76, prof., 1976—, dir. Lab. Plant Biochemistry and Photobiology, 1999—. Contbr. articles to sci. publs. plant physiology and biochemistry. Recipient Beckman rsch. awards, 1982, 85, Funk award, 1985, John P. Trebellas Rsch. Endowment, 1986, Sr. Rsch. award U. Ill., 1994, Presdl. Green Chemistry Challenge award, 1999; named One of 100 Outstanding Innovators, Sci. Digest, 1984-85. Mem. Am. Soc. Plant Physiologists, Comite Internat. de Photobiologie, Am. Soc. Photobiology, AAAS, Lebanese Assn. Advancement Scis. (exec. com. 1967-69), Sigma Xi. Achievements include research on pathway of chlorophyll biosynthesis, chloroplast devel., bioengring. of photosynthetic reactors; pioneered biosynthesis of chlorophyll in vitro; duplication of greening process of plants in test tube, demonstration of operation of multibranched chlorophyll biosynthetic pathway in nature; formulation and design of laser herbicides, insecticides and cancer chemotherapeutic agents. Home: 301 W Pennsylvania Ave Urbana IL 61801-4918 Office: U Ill 240A Pabl Urbana IL 61801

REBELLO, LEO, health facility administrator; b. Mumbai, Apr. 11, 1950. ND, PhD, U. London; MD, DSc, Colombo; DLitt, India; MBA, Malaysia. Dir. Natural Health Ctr., Mumbai, 1978—; pres. Indian Coun. Natural Medicine and Rsch., 1989—; faculty, adv. coun. mem. Ansted U., Malaysia; adv. Internat. Rsch. Inst. for Natural Medicine, Japan; Asian pres. World Orgn. Alternative Medicines, Spain; dean Open Internat. U. Complementary Medicine, Sri Lanka; lectr. in field. Editor: Nature Cure & Yoga Therapy, 3d edit., Iscador Therapy of Cancer, Life & Hereafter, Panacea for Pain, Miracles of Homoeopathy; co-author: Essays on Health Administration, Surya-Namaskar; editor Jour. Holistic Health Scis.; contbr. articles to profl. jours. Goodwill amb. St. Stanislas Order, Poland, 1997—; senator, minister Internat. Parliament for Safety and Peace, Italy, 1997—; v.p. Internat. League Drs. Against Vivisection, Switzerland; rep. for India, Internat. Assn. Educators for World Peace; prime minister Shadow Govt. of India. Decorated Grand Cross with Collar of St. Stanislas Chivalric Order; Acad. Diplomatique de la Paix fellow, Brussels, 1990; recipient Dag Hammarskjold Internat. award for excellence in alternative medicine, 1988, albert Schweitzer prize for humanism in medicine, 1994, Yellow Emperor prize for holistic healing, 1995. Fellow European Med. Assn., British Guild Drugless Practitioners, Indian Naturopathic Practitioners Assn., Medicine Alternative, British Inst. Drugless Therapy (adv.). Fax: (91-22)887-2741. E-mail: leorebello@vsnl.com. Home: Kandivli East, 28/552 Samata Nagar, 400101 Bombay India

REBELLO DA SILVA, LUIS A., glass company executive; b. Albergaria-A-Velha, Portugal, Sept. 20, 1931; s. Luis A. Rebello and Maria Jose (Roque) DaS.; m. Maria Teresa Bonneville Nesbitt, Dec. 22, 1958; children: Maria Margarida, Maria Teresa, Ana Filipa, Luis Augusto. Lic. mech. engring., U. Lisbon, 1955. With Sorefame, Vigola, Productora Lisbon, 1957-64; factory mgr. Produtora Garrafas, Marinha Grande, 1964-66; sr. exec. Co. Indsl. Vidreira, SA, Lisbon, 1967-70, chmn. bd. dirs., 1992-93; mng. dir. Barbosa & Almeida, Oporto, 1971-77; gen. mgr. J.M. Fonseca Internat., Vinhos, Azeito-Setubal, 1978-80; chmn. bd. dirs. Covina Co., Sta Iria de Azoia, Lisbon, 1980-88, Actividades Eléctricas Associadas, SA, Lisbon, 1988-91, Uniao de Transportadores para Importacao e Comercio, Lda, Lisbon, 1991-95, Complexo Cachão, SA, Mirandela, 1992-93, Interforma, SA, Oporto, 1993-95, Tratamento Mecanográfico da Informacao, SA, Lisbon, 1993-94, Soc. de Desenvolvimento da Industria Automovel, SA, Setubal, 1996-2000; lectr. Inst. Superior Tech., Lisbon, 1954-55, 56-57, 61-62; bd. dirs. SANEST, SA, Cascais. Chmn. Juventude Escola Catolica Portugal, 1952-56, Juventude Universitaria Catolica, 1954-55. Mem. Soc. Glass Tech., Ordem Dos Engenheiros, Sporting Club, Gremio Literario Club, Am. Club. Roman Catholic. Home: Cascais, Ave de Sintra, 267-r/c Esq, 2750 Lisbon Portugal Office: SANEST SA-Saneamento C Estr, Rue da Flor da Murta, 2780-742 Paco D'Arcos Portugal

REBELO, LUIS DE SOUSA, literary historian, researcher; b. Lisbon, Portugal, Mar. 4, 1922; s. Rebelo Luis De Sousa and Adelaide Augusta (Oliveira) R.; m. Maria Dolores Noriega De La Borbolla, July 17, 1965. MA, Lisbon U., 1946. Asst. lectr. U. Liverpool, 1948-54; lectr. Kings Coll., London, 1956-83, reader, 1983-87, emeritus reader, 1987, sr. fellow, 1987-92; vis. prof. Kings Coll., 1993—. Author: Shakespeare Para O Nosso Tempo, 1966, A Tradição Clássica Na Literatura Portuguesa, 1982, A Concepção Do Poder Em Fernão Lopes, 1983; editor: Camões E O Pensamento Filosófico Do Seu Tempo, 1979. Fellow Assn. Portuguese Writers; mem. Assn. Hispanists of Great Britain and Ireland, Order of St. James of the Sword (commander, pres.). Office: Kings Coll Dept Portuguese, Strand, WC2R2LS London England

REBER, CALVIN HENRY, theological studies educator, minister; b. Lebanon, Pa., Apr. 30, 1915; s. Calvin Henry Reber and Stella Elizabeth Meese; m. Audrie Eleanora Fox, June 6, 1939 (dec. Dec. 1987); children: Vera Blinn, James. BA, Lebanon Valley Coll., 1936, DD, 1959; MDiv, United Theol. Sem., Dayton, Ohio, 1939; PhD, Columbia U., 1958. Ordained to ministry Meth. Ch., 1939. Missionary to China, United Brethren Ch., Hong Kong, 1939-41; pastor Evang.-United Brethren Ch., Palmyra, Pa., 1942-46; Missionary to China, Evang.-United Brethren Ch., Canton, 1946-48; assoc. exec. sec. Kwangtung Synod Ch. of Christ, Canton, 1948-51; mission prof. United Theol. Sem., 1951-83, adj. faculty, 1983-88; vis. prof. Chung Chi Coll., Chinese U. Hong Kong, 1970-71. Author: Renewal Thru Mission, 1966; editor Telescore Messenger, 1990-94. Fellow Am. Assn. Theol. Schs., 1973. Mem. Assn. Profs. of Missions, Ea. Pa. Conf. of United Meth. Chs. Democrat. Avocations: photography, travel. Home: 248 Village Sq Chambersburg PA 17201-4000

REBER, MICHAEL F., English educator, consultant; b. St. Louis. BS in Econs., S.E. Mo. State U., 1991, MA in English, 1993. Tchr. English, Japan Exch. and Tchg. Program, Matto, Japan, 1994-97; prof. English, Kanazawa (Japan) Inst. Tech., 1997—; chmn. Cmty. Learning Ctr. Internat. Ad Hoc Com., Kanazawa, 1998—. Editor-in-chief: Holistic Student-Centered Language Learning for Teaching English in Japan, 1997. Mem. Japan Assn. for Lang. Tchg., Chubu Lang. Soc., Internat. Assn. Tchrs. English as Fgn. Lang. Republican. Avocations: tennis, travel. Office: Kanazawa Inst Tech, 7-1 Ohgigaoka, Ishikawa Nonoichi-machi 921-8501, Japan

REBERNIK, MIROSLAV, economist, researcher; b. Zgornji Razbor, Slovenia, July 31, 1952; s. Rudolf and Antonija (Jug) R.; m. Jana Černel, Apr. 28, 1984; children: Mik, Teja. BS, U. Maribor, Slovenia, 1978, MS, 1981, PhD, 1990. Analyst Slovenian Electro Sys., Maribor, 1978-81, exec., 1981-85; lectr. U. Maribor, 1985-91, asst. prof., 1991-95, assoc. prof., 1995—; head entrepreneurship studies U. Maribor, 1993—; mem. coun. Slovenian Intellectual Property Office, Ljubljana, 1994—; vis. prof. Portland (Oreg.) State U., 1991. Author: Economics of Innovative Firm, 1991, Economics of the Firm, 1995; contbr. articles to profl. jours. Recipient Hamilton/Fulbright Rsch. fellowship, 1995-96. Mem. Am. Econ. Assn., Internat. Soc. for Small Bus., N.Y. Acad. Scis. Avocations: music, skiing, travelling. Home: Uziska 12, 2000 Maribor Slovenia Office: Faculty Econs and Bus, Razlagova 14, 2000 Maribor Slovenia

REBHUN, MENAHEM E., environmental engineer, consultant; b. Tarnow, Poland, Mar. 12, 1929; arrived in Israel, 1950; s. Yehezkiel and Rachel (Blaser) R.; m. Stella Frankel Rebhun, Aug. 9. 1956; children: Varda-Rachel, Arie, Uzi. BS in Chem Engring., Technion, Haifa, Israel, 1953; MS in environ. Engring., U. Calif., Berkeley, 1958; DSc in Environ. Engring., Technion, Haifa, Israel, 1966. Process engr. Water Treatment Co., Haifa, Israel, 1955-57; lectr., assoc. prof., prof. Technion, Haifa, Israel, 1958-98; vis. prof. Numerous Am. and European Univs.; cons. Water Design and Planning Cos. Contbr. over 130 scientific papers in field. Sgt. Israel Army, 1954-56. Recipient Walter Haas Internat. award U. Calif., Berkeley, 1977, Willem Rudolfs medal Water Environ. Fedn., 1989. Mem. Am. Waterworks Assn., Water Environ. Fedn., Internat. Assn. Water Quality, Assn. Chem. Engrs. Jewish. Avocations: literature, history, judaica, social sciences. Home: 6 Asheer Str, Haifa 32297, Israel Office: Dept Civil Engring, Technion-Israel Inst Tech, Haifa 32000, Israel

REBMANN, NINA SOPHIE, research scientist; b. Huntington, N.Y., Oct. 2, 1964; d. Leonard Jerome and Erika Hermine (Busch) DiGiovanni; m. Wilhelm F.J. Rebmann, Sept. 30, 1990; 1 child, Andreas Wilhelm. BA in Biology, Douglass Coll., 1989. Cert. mobile intensive care paramedic, N.J. Cardiovascular pharmacologist Wyeth-Ayerst Rsch., Princeton, N.J., 1990-91; rsch. asst. dept. psychology Princeton U., 1991-97; scientist Novartis Pharm., Summit, N.J., 1997—. Contbr. articles to profl. jours. Vol. Watchung Rescue Squad, N.J., 1986-92; EMT Muhlenberg Regl. Med. Ctr., Plainfield, N.J., 1987-93. Mem. N.J. Assn. for Lab. Animal Sci. (editor, bd. trustee 1992—), Am. Acad. Scis., Soc. for Whole-Body Autoradiography, Am. Assn. for Lab. Animal Sci. Republican. Roman Catholic. Avocations: tennis, skiing, antiques, travel. Home: 2024 S Branch Rd Somerville NJ 08876-3918 Office: Novartis Pharm Corp 59 Rte 10 E East Hanover NJ 07936-1080

REBOLLEDO, GEMA, ophthalmologist; b. Vitoria, Alava, Spain, July 20, 1963; d. Alfredo Rebolledo and Carmen Fernandez; m. Francisco Muñoz-Negrete, Oct. 13, 1993. Med. Degree, Pais Vasco U., Vitoria, 1987; ophthalmologist, Ramon y Cajal HOsp., Madrid, 1992; MD, Alcala de Henares U., Madrid, 1997. Ophthalmologist Ramon y Cajal Hosp., Madrid, 1993—. Author: Contact Diode Laser Transcleral Cyclophotocoagulation for Glaucoma, 1997, Cyclodiode, 1998. Office: Ramon y Cajal Hosp, Carretera Colmenar Viejo 91, 28034 Madrid Spain

RECH, WOLF-HENNING, electrical engineering educator; b. Karlsruhe, Germany, July 1, 1960; s. Karl-Heinz and Gabriele S. (Uhrig) R. MS in Engring., U. Karlsruhe, 1985, PhD in Engring., 1991. Rsch. asst. U. Karlsruhe, 1985-91; mem. rsch. staff Robert Bosch GMBH, Darmstadt, Germany, 1991-94; mem. ctrl. corp. rsch. staff Robert Bosch GMBH, Stuttgart, Germany, 1994-97; prof. Fachhochschule, Pforzheim, Germany, 1997—. Editor Adacom mag., 1990—. Mem. German Red Cross, 1979-90. Recipient Rudolf-Horkheimer prize DARC, 1993. Mem. Tucson Amateur Packet Radio Corp. Avocations: amateur radio, reading, jogging. Office: Fachhochschule Pforzheim, Tiefenbronner Str 65, 75175 Pforzheim Germany

RECHENBERG, WOLFRAM JOACHIM FRIEDRICH, chemist, researcher; b. New Britain, Conn., Sept. 13, 1931; arrived in Germany, 1938; s. Friedrich Gustav and Hedwig Johanna (Freudel) R.; m. Elisabeth Schwarze, Aug. 28, 1966; children: Ailke, Folkert, Wolfram. Diploma in Chemistry, Tech. U., Brunswick, Germany, 1960; DEng, Tech. U., Hannover, Germany, 1965. Rschr. VDZ, Düsseldorf, Germany, 1967-92, sr. scientist, 1992—. Contbr. over 70 articles to profl. pubs. and conf. procs. Home: Am Höfel 1, D-40885 Ratingen Germany

RECHTIN, EBERHARDT, retired aerospace executive, retired educator; b. East Orange, N.J., Jan. 16, 1926; s. Eberhardt Carl and Ida H. (Pfarrer) R.; m. Dorothy Diane Denebrink, June 10, 1951; children: Andrea C., Nina, Julie Anne, Erica, Mark. B.S., Calif. Inst. Tech., 1946, Ph.D. cum laude, 1950. Dir. Deep Space Network, 1958-67; asst. dir. Calif. Inst. Tech. Jet Propulsion Lab., 1960-67; dir. Advanced Rsch. Projects Agy., Dept. Def., 1967-70, prin. dep. dir. def. rsch. and engring., 1970-71, asst. sec. def. for telecom., 1972-73; chief engr. Hewlett-Packard Co., Palo Alto, Calif., 1973-77; pres., CEO Aerospace Corp., El Segundo, Calif., 1977-87; pres.-emeritus Aerospace Corp., El Segundo, 1988; prof. U. So. Calif., 1988-94, emeritus prof., 1994—. Author: Systems Architecting, Creating & Building Complex Systems, 1991, The Art of Systems Architecture, 1997, Systems Architecting of Organizations, Why Eagles Can't Swim, 1999. Served to lt. USNR, 1943-56. Recipient maj. awards NASA, Dept. Def., USN, Disting. Alumni award Calif. Inst. Tech., 1984, NEC C&C prize, Japan, 1992. Fellow AAAS, AIAA (Robert H. Goddard Astronautics award 1991), IEEE (Alexander Graham Bell award 1977), Internat. Coun. Sys. Engring. (pioneer award 1999); mem. NEA, Tau Beta Pi. Home: 1665 Cataluna Pl Palos Verdes Peninsula CA 90274-2162

RECILE, GEORGE B., lawyer; b. New Orleans, Feb. 14, 1954; s. Sam J. Recile and Annie Mary Ciolino; m. Kathryn Nicole Morgan, July 1, 1995; children: Ashley, Bryan. BA, Tulane U., 1975; JD, Loyola U., 1978. Bar: La. 1978, U.S. Dist. Ct. (ea. dist.) La. 1979, U.S. Ct. Appeals (5th cir.) 1979, U.S. Dist. Ct. (we. and mid. dists.) 1989. Staff atty. La. State Atty. Gen., New Orleans, 1978-80; assoc. Tucker & Schonekas, New Orleans, 1980-82, Law Offices Charles McHale, New Orleans, 1982-83; atty. Recile & Gould, Metairie, La., 1983-87, George B. Recile & Assocs., New Orleans, 1987-95; ptnr. Chehardy, Sherman, Ellis, Breslin & Murray, Metairie, 1995—. Past mem. New Orleans Alcoholic Beverage Control Bd., La. State Bd. Pvt. Investigators. Mem. Am. Trial Lawyers Assn., La. Trial Lawyers Assn. (bd. govs.), Acad. New Orleans Trial Lawyers, La. State Bar Assn. (ho. of dels., 24th jud. dist.). Republican. Roman Catholic. Office: Chehardy Sherman Ellis Breslin & Murray 1 Galleria Blvd Ste 1100 Metairie LA 70001-2033

RECKERT, STEPHEN, researcher; b. Terre Haute, Ind., May 31, 1923; s. Frederick Carl and Aileen Templeton (Adams) R.; m. Olwen Roberts, Oct. 1, 1946 (dec. 1963); children: Nicholas, Victoria, Julian; m. Didia Marques, May 20, 1965. BA, Yale U., 1945, PhD, 1950; MLitt, Cambridge U., Eng., 1948. Asst. prof. Spanish Yale U., New Haven, 1950-58; prof., chmn. dept. Hispanic studies U. Wales, Cardiff, 1958-66; Camoens prof., chmn. dept. Portuguese and Brazilian studies U. London, 1967-82, prof. emeritus, 1982—; hon. research fellow Inst. for Study of Symbology, New U., Lisbon, Portugal, 1975—; vis. prof. U. Madrid, 1973, New U., Lisbon, 1975-78, U. Rome, 1985; hon. rsch. fellow romance studies U. London, 1995—. Author: Beyon Chrysanthemums, 1993, Do Cancioneiro de Amigo, 1980, 3d edit., 1996, Um Ramalhete Para Cesário, 1987. Recipient Oskar Nobiling medal Brazilian Soc. Lit., 1981. Fellow Brit. Acad., Acad. Das Ciências Lisbon (corresponding), Hispanic Soc. Am. (corresponding), Real Acad. Española (corresponding). Clubs: United Oxford Cambridge U. (London); Order So. Cross (Brazil) (comdr. 1981). Home: Ayot Weir, Weybridge Surrey KT13 8HR, England also: Janelas Verdes 17-4, 1200-690 Lisbon Portugal

RECORD, JENNIFER CATHERINE, community health nurse; b. Bushey, Eng., July 11, 1950; d. James Gerald and Mary Patricia (Cullen) Lynch; m. Adrian Richard Mohr (div. 1990); children: Simon, Matthew, Lucy; m. Anthony Record. Diploma in cmty. health, Christchurch Coll., U. Kent, Canterbury, Eng., 1993; BSc, Open U., 1995. Registered nurse (with honors). Nurse for student med. svcs. Christchurch Coll., Canterbury, 1989-90; sch. nurse South Kent Cmty. Healthcare Trust, Ashford, Eng., 1993-94; health visitor East Kent Cmty. Trust, Canterbury, Eng., 1994—. Chmn. PTO St. Augustines R.C.P. Sch., Hythe, Kent, Eng., 1985-87; Conservative

candidate Dover Coun., Kent, 1995, Kent Co. Coun., 1997; Conservative councillor for Dover Coun., 1997, 99. Decorated mem. Brit. Empire. Avocations: bridge, tennis, swimming, theater.

RECORDATI, ANDREA ALESSANDRO, chemical and pharmaceutical company executive; b. London, Nov. 6, 1971; s. Arrigo Silvio and Anna Maria (Fontana) R. BA in Medieval and Modern History, U. London, 1995. Asst. product mgr. Smithkline Beecham, London, 1995-96, pharm. terr. rep., 1996-97, project mgr., 1997-98; responsible pharm. bus. devel. Recordati S.p.A., Milan, 1998, also bd. dirs. Mem. Gruppo Giovani Industriali, Associazione Italiana Aziende Familiari, Annabel's Blue Bird Club, Yacht Club Costa Smeralda. Avocations: scuba diving, reading, art collecting, motor racing.

RECORDS, RAYMOND EDWIN, ophthalmologist, medical educator; b. Ft. Morgan, Colo., May 30, 1930; s. George Harvey and Sara Barbara (Louden) R.; 1 child, Lisa Rae. BS in Chemistry, U. Denver, 1956; MD, St. Louis U., 1961. Diplomate Am. Bd. Ophthalmology. Intern St. Louis U. Hosp. Group, 1961-62; resident in ophthalmology U. Colo. Med. Ctr., Denver, 1962-65; instr. ophthalmology, 1965-67, asst. prof., 1967-70; prof. ophthalmology U. Nebr. Coll. Medicine, Omaha, 1970-93, prof. emeritus, 1993, dept. chmn., 1970-89. Author: Physiology of Human Eye (Med. Writers award 1980), 1979. Author, editor: Biomedical Foundations of Ophthalmology, 1982. Med. dir. Nebr. Lions Eye Bank, 1970-81. Fellow Am. Acad. of Ophthalmology (outstanding contbn. award 1978, lifelong edn. award 1995); mem. AMA, Nev. Med. Assn., Clark County Med. Soc., Omaha Ophthal. Soc. (pres. 1981-82), Assn. Rsch. in Vision and Ophthalmology. Home: 21919 Riverside Cir Elkhorn NE 68022-1708 Office: 1640 Alta Dr Ste 1 Las Vegas NV 89106-4165

RECSKI, ANDRÁS, mathematician, educator; b. Budapest, Hungary, Apr. 21, 1948; s. György and Éva (Balás) R.; m. Judit Borsa, May 14, 1983; children: Julia, Gábor. MS in Math., L. Eötvös U., Budapest Hungary, 1971, PhD in Math., 1973; cand. Sci. Math., Hungarian Acad. Sci., Budapest Hungary, 1977, DSc in Math., 1984. Rschr. Rsch. Inst. Telecomm., Budapest, 1971-84; prof. L. Eötvös U., Budapest, 1984-90, Tech. U. of Budapest, 1990—; vis. rschr. U. Tokyo, 1978-79; vis. prof. Cornell U., Ithaca, N.Y., 1985, U. Bonn, 1987-89, Yale U., New Haven, Conn., 1994-95; John-von-Neumann prof. U. Bonn, 1998-99. Author: Matroid Theory and Its Applications, 1989; co-author: (text books) Discrete Mathematics, 1993, Combinatorial Optimization, 1995, (proceedings) Matroid Theory, 1985. Mem. IEEE (sr.), János Bolyai Math. Soc. (K. Rényi medal 1971, G. Grünwald medal 1975, G. Farkas medal 1977), Chinese Combinatorial Soc. (hon.). Avocations: classical music, skiing, sailing, oriental culture. Office: Budapest U Tech & Econs, Computer Sci Dept, H-1521 Budapest Hungary

RECUERO, ALFONSO, civil engineer, consultant; b. Barcelona, Spain, Jan. 23, 1944; s. Manuel and Maria (Fornies) R.; m. Esther De Los Santos Recuero, Mar. 6, 1967; children: Ma Luisa, Paloma, Raquel. M in Computer Sci., Informatics Faculty - Poly. U. Madrid, Madrid, 1972; PhDCE, Civil Engring. Faculty, 1973. Jr. rschr. Eduardo Torroja Inst. CSIC, Madrid, 1969-73; sr. rschr., 1973-89, rsch. prof., 1989—; head of computer divsn., 1978-90, head of rsch. Unid. of Structural Engring., 1980-94, head Dept. of Structural Mechanics, 1994—, Eduardo Torroja Inst. High Coun. Sci. Rsch. Author of 20 books, monographs and chpts., Use of Computers in Structural Analysis and Computers and the Blind, 1972-96; contbr. over 65 articles in profl. jours. Recipient Roberts Bequest, Instn. Civil Engrs., London, 1971-72, Eduardo Torroja award. Avocations: reading, music, stamp collecting, puzzles, mathematical activities. Office: Eduardo Torroja Inst CSIC, Serrano Galvache s/n, 28033 Madrid Spain

RECUPERO-FAIELLA, ANNA ANTONIETTA, poet; b. Boston, Nov. 22, 1966; d. Vittorio and Anna Maria Recupero; m. Mark Stephan James Faiella, May 30, 1998. Cert. early edn., Wheelock Coll. Tchr. N. Bennet St. Sch., Boston, 1981-87; clk. Post Office, Boston, 1988—; art coord. N. Bennett Sch., Boston, 1985-87; acting extra films and commls. Author: (poems) A View From the Edge, 1992, Dusting Off Dreams, 1994, Echoes From the Silence, 1995, Treasure the Moment, 1996, Whispers, 1996, Sensations, 1997; co-author: (poems) Distinguished Poets of Amercia, 1993, Outstanding Poets of 1994, 1994, Treasured Poems of America, 1995, Treasured Poems of America, 1996, Best Poems of the 90's, 1996, Best Poems of '97, 1997, Ten Years of Excellence, 1998. Recipient Editors Choice award Nat. Libr. Poetry, 1993, 94, 95, 96, 97, semifinalist, Discover G'Vanni's 500th Art Awd., 1992; scholar Mass. State Gen. Scholarship, 1985. Mem. Internat. Soc. Poets (disting. mem. adv. com. 1994), Nat. Mus. Women Arts, Point of Pines Assn. Democrat. Roman Catholic. Avocations: painting, writing poems, traveling, NASCAR racing, comedy. Home: 40 Bickford Ave Revere MA 02151-1723

REDA, JAMES FRANCIS, business consultant; b. Bklyn., Aug. 27, 1953; s. Ralph Charles and Evelyn Susan (Buchan) R.; m. Susan Rosemary Hisnay, June 10, 1982 (div. Oct. 1993); 1 child, Jennifer Beryl; m. Deborah Linda Grannis, July 4, 1994; children: Jennifer Rose, James Francis Jr., Linda Victoria. BS in Indsl. Engring., Columbia U., 1981; MS in Mgmt., MIT, 1983. 1st class FCC lic. Indsl. engr. IBM Corp., Bklyn., 1980, East Fishkill, N.Y., 1981; process engr. Hewlett-Packard Co., Andover, Mass., 1982; bus. mgr. Wang Labs., Inc., Lowell, Mass., 1983-85; sr. product mgr. Honeywell Fed. Systems, Inc., McLean, Va., 1985-87; assoc. cons. Touche Ross & Co., N.Y.C., 1987; v.p., cons. The Bachelder Group, N.Y.C., 1987-96; cons. Buck Cons., N.Y.C., 1996-97, Hewitt Assocs., Atlanta, 1997-99; sr. mgr. Arthur Andersen LLP, Atlanta, 1999—; bd. advisors Nat. Corp. Governance Ctr. Campaign advisor Friends of Vincent Gentile, Bklyn., 1994; exec. compensation adv. svcs., pres. Atlanta chpt. Nat. Assn. Corp. Dirs. With USN, 1971-77; lt. comdr. USCGR. Mem. Internat. Inst. Indsl. Engrs. (sr. mem., chpt. pres. 1979-81, Walter Rautenstrauch award 1981), Res. Officers Assn. (Top Grad. award 1983), Am. Compensation Assn., N.Y. Soc. Security Analysts (mem. com. shareholder rights and corp. governance, mem. com. improved corp. reporting), Assn. for Investment Mgmt. Rsch., Internat. Assn. Fin. Engring., U.S. Naval Inst., Armed Forces Comms. Assn., Ret. Officers Assn., Nat. Assn. Stock Plan Profls., Nat. Assn. Corp. Dirs. (pres. Atlanta chpt.), Nat. Ctr. Employee Ownership (bd. advisors, exec. compensation rsch. adv. svcs.), Naval War Coll. Found., Am. Legion, Tau Beta Pi, Alpha Pi Mu. Republican. Methodist. Avocations: spectator sports, exercise, travel, history, current events. Home: 4034 Willows Way Marietta GA 30062-5281 Office: Arthur Andersen LLP 225 Peachtree St NE Ste 1800 Atlanta GA 30303-1730

REDA, ROBERT SALVATORE, lawyer; b. Chgo., Feb. 23, 1962; s. Robert Charles and Elizabeth (Barrett) R.; m. Joyce Karen Bettinger, May 19, 1990. BA, Drake U., 1984; JD, John Marshall Law Sch., Chgo., 1988. Bar: Ill. 1989, U.S. Dist. Ct. (no. dist.) Ill. 1989, U.S. Dist. Ct. (no. dist. trial bar) Ill. 1991, U.S. Supreme Ct. 1993. Real estate broker Ill. Dept. Profl. Regulation, 1989; pvt. practice Chgo., 1989-91; pres. Reda & Assocs., P.C., Chgo., 1991—; producer Ill. Dept. Ins., 1999; arbitrator Cir. Ct. of Cook County, Ill., 1998-2000; bd. dirs. First 100 Group, Ltd., Chgo. 1989—; sec. Bibs Disposeables Corp., Chgo., 1998—; ptnr. Beatrice Assocs., Chgo., 1998—. Author: Battle the Expert and Win, 1995. Fellow Roscoe Pound Found.; mem. ATLA, Nat Inst. for Trial Advocacy, Ill. Bar Assn., Union League Club (mem. athletic com., trustee boys and girls club). Office: Reda & Assocs PC 53 W Jackson Blvd Ste 715 Chicago IL 60604-3668

REDDAWAY, RICHARD ALAN, insurance executive; b. London, May 5, 1952; s. Thomas and Jay (Horne) R.; m. Lynette Eu, Sept. 22, 1990; children: Mary-Anne, Alan. MA with honors, Oxford (Eng.) U., 1974; MBA, INSEAD, Fontainebleau, France, 1983. Grad. trainee Hogg Robinson, Manchester, Eng., 1974-77; internat. exec. Jardine Matheson, U.K., 1977-78, Hong Kong, 1978-80, The Philippines, 1980-82, Japan, 1983-86; group ins. mgr. Glaxo Wellcome, Greenford, Eng., 1987—; freeman Goldsmith's Co., 1973-2000, liveryman, 2000—; bd. dirs. Glaxo Wellcome Ins. (Bermuda) Ltd. Exec. tng. program scholar European Commn., 1983-85. Fellow Chartered Ins. Inst.; mem. Assn. Ins. and Risk Mgrs. (chair 1997-98), M200 (former policy bd. chair), Amwell Soc. (mem. com. 1990—), English Spkg. Union (life), Royal Soc. for Arts, Nat. Trust (life). Avocations: history, travel, conservation. Home: 27 Wharton St, London WC1X 9PJ, England Office: Glaxo Wellcome PLC, Berkeley Ave, Greenford UB6 0NN, England

REDDEL, CARL WALTER, educational administrator; b. Gurley, Neb., May 31, 1937; s. Walter Julius and Friedora Regina (Sorge) R.; m. Colette Marie Antoinette Mansuy, Oct. 26, 1963; children: Eric, Damien. BSED, Drake U., 1959; MA in Russian Studies, Syracuse U., 1962; PhD in Russian History, Ind. U., 1973, cert. Russian Studies, 1973. Lectr. U. Md., Toul-Rosieres, France, 1963-66; instr. U.S.A.F. Acad., Colorado Springs, Colo., 1967-68, 71-72, asst. prof., 1972-73, assoc. prof., 1973-80; prof., head dept. history, postdoctoral fellow U. Edinburgh, 1981-82; prof., head dept. history U.S. Air Force Acad., 1982-99; pres., CEO Eisenhower World Affairs Inst., 1999—; nat. coord., regional World History Assn., Phila., 1990-95; bd. editors, mem. Jour. Slavic Mil., London, 1988—; series editor Military Hist. Symposium Series, Colorado Springs, 1993—. Editor: Transformation in Russian and Soviet Military History, 1990; contbr. articles to profl. jours. Mem. Rotary Internat., 1994—. Served to brig. gen. U.S. Air Force, 1962-99. Recipient Young Faculty exch. Internat. Rsch. Exchs. Bd., Moscow State U., 1975; Woodrow Wilson fellow, 1959-60, Danforth Found. fellow, 1959-61. Mem. Am. Hist. Assn., Am. Assn. Advancement of Slavic Studies, World History Assn., Rocky Mountain World History Assn., Ctrl. Slavic Assn. Lutheran. Home: 420 7th St NW Apt 809 Washington DC 20004-2214 Office: Eisenhower World Affairs Inst 1620 Eye St NW Ste 703 Washington DC 20006-4005

REDDEN, ROBERT JOHN, plant breeder; b. Terowie, Australia, Jan. 23, 1943; s. Mathew John Redden and Mary Patricia Walsh; m. Virginia Luz Ramos, Sept. 1974; 1 child, Sean. B of Agrl. Sci., U. Adelaide, Australia, 1965, M of Agrl. Sci., 1969; PhD in Plant Breeding, Cornell U., 1972; MBA, U. So. Queensland, Australia, 1995. Wheat specialist Internat. Inst. Tropical Agrl., Nigeria, 1975-77, cowpea breeder, 1977-81; prin. plant breeder Dept. Primary Industries Queensland, Warwick, Australia, 1982—; wheat cons. in TCHAD, USDA, 1976; legume specialist, Ghana, 1978-80. Pres. State Pub. Svc. Fedn., Warwick, 1985-98. Mem. Australian Inst. Agrl. Sci. and Tech. (exec. mem.). Mem. Liberal Party. Home: MS 223, Nobby QLD 4360, Australia Office: Dept Primary Industries, PO Box 993, Dalby QLD 4405, Australia

REDDIHOUGH, DINAH SUSAN, pediatrician; b. Lincoln, Eng., June 2, 1947; m. Donald George Bryant, Dec. 23, 1982. BSc, U. Otago, N.Z., 1967, MB, BChir, 1971. Sr. house surgeon Dunedin (N.Z.) Hosp., 1973, pediat. registrar, 1974-75; supr. clin. studies dept. pediats. U. Melbourne/Royal Children's Hosp., 1977-79; sr. clin. med. officer Dudley Area Health authority, West Midlands, Eng., 1979-80; physician dept. developmental pediats. Royal Children's Hosp., Melbourne, 1982-86, dir. chield devel. and rehab., 1986—; bd. dirs. Yooralla Soc. Victoria, Melbourne, Wesley Ctrl. Mission, Melbourne; mem. Ministerial Rev. of Birthing Svcs. in Victoria, 1989-90, working party on conductive edn. Nat. Health and Med. Rsch. Coun., Australia, 1991-93. Contbr. over 39 articles to profl. jours.; contbr. to 4 books. Recipient 33 rsch. grants. Fellow Royal Australasian Coll. Physicians; mem. Australian Coll. Pediatrics, Am. Acad. Cerebral Palsy devel. Medicine, Early Intervention Assn. of Victoria. Mem. Uniting ch. of Australia. Office: Royal Childrens Hospital, Flemington Rd, Parkville VIC 3052, Australia

REDDISH, JOHN JOSEPH, management consulting company executive; b. Albany, N.Y., July 23, 1946; s. Leonard Frank and Marion Elizabeth (McElveney) R.; children: Jorin T., Adam Sledd, Lee Sledd; m. Susan Hartman-Brendel, 1996; 1 child, Nicholas Brendel. AB in Communication Arts, Fordham U., 1968; MSA, West Chester U., 1984. Cert. Inst. Mgmt. Cons. Pub. rels. asst. Civil Svc. Employees Assn., Albany, 1967-68; assoc. editor Edison Electric Inst., N.Y.C., 1968-69; dir. info. svcs. N.Y. State Nurses Assn., Guilderland, 1969-70; pres. RA Group, Inc., Advt. and Pub. Rels., Albany, 1970-77; v.p. The Presidents Assn. div. Am. Mgmt. Assocs., N.Y.C., 1977-78; pres. Advent Mgmt. Assocs. Ltd., Chadds Ford, Pa., 1978-92; pres., dir. Advent Mgmt. Internat., Ltd., Chadds Ford, 1992—; mem. adv. bd. PAC Strapping Products, Inc., 1995—; spkr. in field. Author: New Techniques For Motivation and Discipline; contbr. articles to profl. jours. Trustee N.Y. Theol. Sem., 1988-98; bd. dirs. Focus Chs. of Albany, 1973-76, Kennett Symphony Orch., 1991—; bd. deacons Emmanuel Bapt. Ch., 1974-77; chair Chester County Internat. Trade Coun., 1998-99. Mem. Am. Abritration Assn. (mem. panel of arbitrators 1990—), Nat. Spkrs. Assn., Liberty Bell Spkrs. Assn. (dir. 1999—). Office: Advent Mgmt Internat Ltd 411 Old Baltimore Pike Chadds Ford PA 19317-9444

REDDY, BENJARAM MAHIPAL, chemist, researcher; b. Andhra Pradesh, India, Mar. 1, 1957; s. Benjaram Raja and Saroja Reddy; m. Jayanthi Reddy, May 31, 1983; 1 child, Sindhuri. MSc, Kakatiya U., Warangel, India, 1981; PhD, Osmania U., Hyderabad, India, 1986. Scientist Indian Inst. Chem. Tech., Hyderabad, India, 1984—; rsch. assoc. SUNY, Buffalo, N.Y., 1993-95; vis. scientist Inst. Catalysis Novosibirsk, Russia, 1986-87, Inst. Phys. Chemistry, Munich, 1988-90, 98. Mem. Catalysis Soc. India (life; Young Scientist award 1993), Materials Rsch. Soc. India (life), Chem. Rsch. Soc. India. Avocations: reading, watching TV. Home: 1-216/210 Kartikeya Nagar, Hyderabad 500 076, India Office: Indian Inst Chem Tech, Uppal Rd, Hyderabad 500 007, India

REDDY, C. DEVENDRANATH, chemist, educator; b. Reddivaripalli, India, July 1, 1940; s. C. Chinnagi Reddy and C. Rangamma; m. A. Yellamma, 1967; children: C. Kaivalya, C. Eiswarya. BSc, Sri Venkateswara U., Tirupat, India, 1963, MSc, 1965, PhD, 1975. From lectr. to prof. Sri Venkateswara U., Tirupat, 1974-92, prof., 1992—. Contbr. over 70 articles to profl. jours. Mem. Indian Soc. Mass Spectrometry (life), Indian Coun. Chemists (life, bd. dirs.). Avocations: travel, music. Home: 3 65 A Vidyanagar, Tirupati 517502, India Office: Dept Chem, Sri Venkateswara U, Tirupati 517502, India

REDDY, CHILAKALA RAMAMUNI, business educator; b. Proddatur, India, May 16, 1953; s. Chilakala Chinna Gurivi Reddy and Chilakala Munemma; m. Chilakala Padmavathi; children: Ravali, Lahari. B in Commerce, Sri Venkateswara U., Tirupati, India, 1973, MPhil in Commerce, 1978, PhD of Commerce, 1980; M in Commerce, Jabalpur (India) U., 1976. Asst. prof. Sri Krishnadevaraya U., Anantapur, India, 1979-85; assoc. prof. Sri Krishnadevaraya U., Anantapur, 1985-90, prof., 1991—, dean commerce faculty, head commerce dept., chair BOS; coord. Refresher Course to Asst. Profs., 1993-97. Contbr. over 100 articles to profl. jours. Mem. All India Commerce Assn. (exec.). Home: Tapovanam Rd, 1-1-267 Vivekanandanager, Anantapur 515 004, India Office: Dept Commerce, Sri Krishnadevaraya Univ, Anantapur 515 003, India

REDDY, DANDU JAYAPRAKSHNARAYAN, English educator, researcher; b. Korisapadu, India, Aug. 8, 1946; s. Dandu Ramakrishna and Dandu Srilakshmi (Dodla) R.; m. Swarnalatha Devireddi, July 31, 1976; 1 child, Dandu Keerthi. BSc, Andhra U., Visakhapatnam, India, 1967, MA, 1970, PhD in Am. Lit., 1978. Lectr. Postgrad. Ctr. Andhra U., Kakinada, India, 1980-87, reader Postgrad. Ctr., 1987-94, prof. Grad. Ctr., 1994—, rsch. dir., 1984—, head dept. English, 1989-92, 99—, spl. officer, 1992-99. Editor: Literary Spectrum, 1994. Sec. E. Godavari Dist. Cricket Assn., Kakinada, 1981-85; v.p. E. Godavari Dist. Volleyball Assn., Kakinada, 1985-93. Recipient Dist. Janmabhoomi award Govt. Andhra Pradesh, 1997. Mem. Indo-Am. Ctr. Internat. Studies, All-India English Tchrs. Assn. Hindu. Avocations: reading, music, sports, socio-cultural activities. Home: Door No. 67-1-1/3A, Lalbahadurnagar, Kakinada 533003, India Office: Andhra U, MSN Postgrad Ctr, Thimmapuram 533005, Kakinada

REDDY, DOODIPALA SAMBA, pharmacologist, researcher; b. Warangal, India, June 15, 1969; s. Raji R. and Radha Doodipala; m. Mandala Savitha, June 18, 1995; 1 child, Sandesh. M in Pharmacy, Panjab U., Chandigarh, India, 1994, PhD in Pharmacology, 1998. Registered pharmacist. Jr. rsch. fellow Panjab U., Chandigarh, India, 1992-94, sr. rsch. fellow, 1994-96, lectr. pharmacology, 1997-98. Author: B. Pharm Entrance Guide: A Comprehensive Handbook of Pharmacy, 1992, Pharmacy Entrance, A Concise Guide for Pharmacy Board Exams, 1995, 98, Pharmacy Entrance, A Comprehensive Handbook for Pharmacy Professionals, 1996; referee Ind. Jour. Pharmacol., Ind. Jour. Exptl. Biology. Recipient 6 Gold medals Kakatiya U., 1992, G.P. Nair award Indian Drug Mfrs. Assn., 1994, Prof. Uvnas Rsch. award 1997, B.K. Anand prize in physiology, 1998, N.N. Dutta prize in pharmacology, 1999; NIH postdoctoral fellow, 1998—; NIH fellows award for rsch. excellence, 2000. Mem. AAAS, Indian Pharmacol. Soc., Indian Pharm. Assn., Assn. Physiologists and Pharmacologists India (C.L. Malhotra rsch. prize in pharmacology 1996, AVT Parvatidevi prize in Neuroendocrinology 1997, B.K. award rsch. prize in physiology 1998), Internat. Soc. Heart Rsch., Internat. Brain Rsch. Orgn. (travel grant 1997), Am. Soc. for Pharmacology and Exptl. Therapeutics, Am. Assn. Pharm. Scientists, Am. Epilepsy Soc., Soc. for Neurosci., N.Y. Acad. Scis. Office: Nat Inst Health Epilepsy Rsch Br 10 Center Dr Msc 1408 10 5 N 2 Bethesda MD 20892-0001

REDDY, ISKA GOPAL, electrical engineer, educator, administrator; b. Nellore, India, Dec. 20, 1936; s. Anjaneyulu Reddy and Eeswaramma (Ravooru) I.; m. Nirmala Gopal Reddy Ponnavolu, May 27, 1959; children: Maheswari, Anand. BE with honors, Govt. Coll. Engring., Anantapur, India, 1957; MTech, Indian Inst. Tech., Kharagpur, 1960; PhD, U. Liverpool, Eng., 1972. Lectr. Govt. Coll. Engring., Anantapur, 1957-58; asst. lectr. Indian Inst. Tech., Kharagpur, 1958-59; lectr. S.V.U. Coll. Engring., Tirupati, India, 1960-64; asst. prof Regional Engring. Coll., Warangal, India, 1964-73, prof. elec. engring., 1973-79; vice chancellor JNT U., Hyderabad, India, 1992-95; prin. NBKR Inst. Sci. and Tech., Vidyanagar, India, 1979-92, dir., 1995—. Contbr. articles to profl. jours.; author procs. Fellow Inst. of Engrs., A.P. Acad. Scis.; mem. IEEE. Avocations: gardening, television, bridge. Office: NBKR Inst Sci and Tech, Vidyanagar 524413, India

REDDY, KARNATI PRATHAP, science educator; b. Hyderabad, India, June 15, 1961; s. Karnati Mohan and Karnati Vimalamma Reddy; m. Karnati Madhavi Boommi, May 11, 1989; 1 child, Siddharth. BSc with honors, Osmania U., Hyderabad, 1981, MSc in Zoology, 1983, PhD in Neurobiology, 1988. Jr. rsch. fellow Coun. for Sci. and Indsl. Rsch., India, 1984-86, sr. rsch. fellow, 1986-89; asst. prof. Osmania U., Hyderabad, 1989—. Contbr. articles to rsch. jours. Recipient Parmars prize Indian Acad. Neurosci., 1987. Mem. Faculty Club Osmania U. (treas. 1993-94, joint sec. 1994-96). Avocations: gardening, horticulture, shuttle. Office phone: 009140-7018951. E-mail: pra zoo@yahoo.com.

REDDY, MOPURI NARASIMHA, microbiology educator; b. Madanapalle, Chittoor, India, Jan. 5, 1950; s. Mopuri Venkatramana Reddy and Mopuri Chennamma; m. Mopuri Naga Jyothy; children: Adithya Mopuri, Sadasiva. BSc in Gen. Scis., S.V. U., Tirupati, India, 1970, MSc, 1972, PhD in Microbiology, 1976'. Pool officer Nararjuna U., Guntur, India, 1976-79; quarantine officer India Ministry Agr., 1979; lectr. botany S.V. U., 1979-89, reader, 1989-93; prof. microbiology, head dept. Mahila U., Tirupati, 1993—; vis. scientist, Eng., Poland, Germany, Japan, The Netherlands, France, Czech Republic, Australia, Taiwan, 1987—. Author: Text Book of Microbiology, 1986, Principles of Plant Pathology, 1992; editor: Applied Microbiology. Acad. staff fellow Commonwealth Commn., London, 1989. Mem. Indian Phytopath. Soc., Assn. Microbiologists India, Soc. Mycology and Plant Pathology. Avocations: collecting stamps and coins. E-mail: mopuri nr@yahoo.com. Home: 5-69/4 Srikrishna Nagar, M R Palle, Tirupati 517502, India Office: SP Mahila U, Dept Applied Microbiology, Tirupati 517502, India

REDDY, MUCHELI VASUDEVA, geography educator; b. Tirupati, India, Apr. 10, 1952; s. Mucheli Sadasiva and Pullur Bangaramma; m. Vasudeva Mallika, Jan. 26, 1976; children M. Vasudev Niran, M.V. Suma. BA, Sri Venkateswara Arts U., Tirupati, 1972, MA, Tirupati, 1974, PhD, 1987; diploma, A.P. Productivity Coun., Hyderabad, India, 1988. Jr. rsch. fellow Sri Venkateswara Arts U., 1974-75, asst. prof. geography, 1975-87, assoc. prof., 1986-96; prof. geography Sri Venkateswara U., 1996—, chmn. bd. studies, 1994-97, head dept., 1987-90, head 2d term, 1999—; chmn. Tirupati Praja Sanitty, 1989—; gen. sec. Rayalaseema Geog. Soc., Tirupati, 1977—. Author: Agricultue and Agro-Based Industry, 1989; editor: Agriculture: Planning and Development, 1991; editor Geosphere, 1991; writer Geog. Soc. Lieg, Belgium, 1998; contbr. over 25 articles to profl. jours. Advisor Chandragiri Assn. for Rural Devel., Tirupati, 1991—, Bharat Ednl. and Cultural Trust, Tirupati, 1977—; chmn. Tirupati Praja Samithi, 1989—. With Nat. Health Corps, 1969-72. Life mem. Bharatiya Vidya Dhavan, Nat. Assn. for Geographers, Indian Geog. Soc., Deccan Geog. Soc., Tirupati Film Soc., Tirupati Cultural Acad., Inst. Landscape Ekistics and Environ. Studies, Varadrajanagar Devel. Soc., Inst. Indian Geographers. Avocations: social service, playing games, viewing TV. Home: 251 Varadaraya Nagar, KT Rd, Tirupati 517507, India Office: Sri Venkateswara U, Dept Geography, Tirupati 517502, India

REDDY, NAGESHWAR DUVVUR, gastroenterologist; b. Vishakapatnam, India, Mar. 18, 1956; s. Bhaskar Duvvur and Sharada Reddy; m. Carol Ann John, Aug. 23, 1983; 1 child, Sanjana. MBBS, Kurnool Med. Coll., India, 1979; MD, Madras (India) Med. Coll., 1982; M Gastroenterology, Postgrad. Inst. Med. Edn., Chandigarh, India, 1984. Asst. prof. gastroenterology Nizam Inst. Med. Scis., Hyderabad, India, 1984-85; prof. Guntur Med. Coll., India, 1989-90; chief gastroenterologist Medinova Diagnostic Svcs., Hyderabad, 1990-94; dir. Asian Inst. Gastroenterology, Hyderabad, 1994—; hon. cons. Nizam's Inst. Med. Scis., Hyderabad, 1997. Author: Manual of Therapeutic Endoscopy, 1993, 94; editor: International Manual of Therapeutic Endoscopy, 1998—; mem. internat. editl. bd. Glendsocopy/ASGE, 1997-99, Therapeutic Endoscopy of Japan, 1994-99. Recipient B.C. Roy award govt. India, 1995, award Assn. Surgeons India, 1993. Mem. Indian Soc. Gastroenterology (award 1992), Indian Med. Assn., Soc. Gastrointestinal Endoscopy of India, N.Y. Acad. Scis. Home: 27-A Journalists Colony, Jubilee Hills, Hyderabad 500033, India

REDDY, SASIRAGHA PRISCILLA, medical researcher, administrator; b. Durban, South Africa, Sept. 18, 1961; d. Soobiah Bungar and Sathiabama Kantha Reddy. BSc, U. Cape Town, 1986; MPH, U. Mass., 1992; PhD, Maastricht U., The Netherlands, 1999. Coord. sch. health svcs. South Africa, 1986-91; sr. rschr. Med. Rsch. Coun. South Africa, 1992-95, dir. Nat. Health Promotion Rsch. and Devel. Office, 1995—. Home: 29 Strubens Rd Mowbray, 7700 Cape Town South Africa

REDDY, SATTI SETHU-KUMAR, physician, educator; b. Tadepalligudem, India, Jan. 9, 1958; arrived in U.S., 1995; s. Satti Paddi and Satti Parvati Reddy; m. Lalitha Padala, Jan. 6, 1986; children: Pranav, Suparna, Vishal. MD, Meml. U. Newfoundland, 1980. Bd. cert. in internal medicine and endocrinology, metabolism, and diabetes. Intern in internal medicine Meml. U. Nfld., 1980-82, resident in internal medicine, 1982-83; clin. fellow endocrinology U. Toronto, Ont., Can., 1983-85; rsch. fellow Joslin Diabetes Ctr., Harvard Med. Sch., Boston, 1985-88; asst. prof. Dalhousie U., Halifax, N.S., 1988-93, assoc. prof., 1994—; full staff Cleve. Clinic, 1995—. Contbr. articles to profl. jours. Co-chair Mayfield Schs. Sci. Ctr., Mayfield Heights, Ohio, 1996-99, Sci. Bond Issue, Mayfield Heights, 1998. Fellow Royal Coll. Physicians and Surgeons Can., Am. Coll. Physicians, Am. Coll. Endocrinology. Avocations: reading, music, tennis. E-mail: reddys@ccf.org. Office: Cleve Clinic A30 9500 Euclid Ave Cleveland OH 44195-0001

REDDY, THIMMOJI KRISHNA RAMACHANDRA, retired microbiologist; b. Chittoor, India, June 15, 1929; p. T. Krishna and T. Narayanamma R.; m. G. Parvathi. BSc, Andhra U., Waltair, 1950; MSc, Banaras Hindu U., 1956; PhD, Madras U., 1960. Agrl. asst. dept. agrl. Madras (India) State, 1950-54, lectr. dept. botany, 1966-68; fellow NRC, Can., 1962-63; rsch. assoc. dept. bacteriology McGill U., Can., 1963-64; microbial geneticist dept. microbiology UCLA, 1964-66; sci. asst. U. Frankfurt (Germany) Inst. Therapeutic Biochemistry, 1968-70; prof. microbiology agrl. U. Bangalore, India, 1973-89; ret., 1989; cons. Global Barter Pvt. Ltd., Hyderabad, India; selection mem. Union Pub. Svc. Commn., New Delhi; acad. coun. U. Tirupati, India, Annamalai U., Tamil Nadu, India. Contbr. articles to profl. jours. Mem. Inst. for Social, Agrl. & Rural Devel. (life), Madabushi Anantha Sayanam Inst. Public Affairs (assoc.), Environ. Mutagen Soc. India (life), Assn. Microbiologist India (life). Hindu. Avocations: photography, biofuels, rural development. Home: 18 Nalandanagar, 517 502 Tirupati India

REDDY, VARDHAN JONNALA, surgeon; b. Kollipara, India, Nov. 26, 1960. MBBS, Guntur Med. Coll., Andhra U., 1985. Diplomate Am. Bd. Surgery. Internist Robert Packer Hosp., Sayre, Pa., 1990-91; res. L.I. Jewish Med. Ctr., New Hyde Park, N.Y., 1991-95; fellowship Tex. Heart Inst., Houston, 1995-96; staff surgeon Glades Gen. Hosp., Belle Glade, Fla., 1996-98, chief surgery, 1998—; v.p. Med. Staff Assocs. Glades Inc., 1998; pres.,

CEO Heartcom Inc., 1999; v.p. Med. Staff Assocs. of Glades Inc., 1998, pres., CEO Heartcom Inc., 1999. Mem. AMA, Internat. Coll. Angiology, Royal Coll. Surgeons Edinburgh (diplomate), Am. Coll. Angiology. Office: 1 Dogwood Hill Dr Jackson MS 39211-2201

REDFEARN, PAUL L., III, lawyer; b. Camp Cook, Calif., Oct. 1, 1951; s. Paul Leslie Jr. and Alice Ruby Redfearn; children: Ashley, Lauren; m. Denise Jean Davis, July 24, 1993. BS, S.W. Mo. State U., 1973; JD, Oklahoma City U., 1976. Bar: Mo. 1977, U.S. Dist. Ct. (we. and ea. dists.) Mo., U.S. Dist. Ct. Kans., U.S. Dist. Ct. N.D., U.S. Dist. Ct. Mont., U.S. Ct. Appeal (8th ant 11th cirs.); bd. cert. civil trial advocate. Assoc. Sheridan, Sanders & Simpson, P.C., 1977-79, William H. Pickett, P.C., 1979-84; ptnr. Redfearn & Brown, P.C., Kansas City, Mo., 1984—; lectr. and presenter in field. Contbr. chpts. to books. Bd. govs. S.W. Mo. State U., 1998—. Mem. ABA, ATLA, Mo. Bar Assn., Mo. Assn. Trial Attys. (bd. govs. 1986-94, exec. com. 1990—, pres. 1992), Am. Bd. Trial Advocates (charter, pres. chpt. 1996-97), Kansas City Met. Bar Assn., East Jackson County Bar Assn. Democrat. Christian. Avocation: tennis. Office: Redfearn & Brown PC 1125 Grand Blvd Ste 814 Kansas City MO 64106-2518

REDFORD, ROBERT (CHARLES ROBERT REDFORD), actor, director; b. Santa Monica, Calif., Aug. 18, 1937; m. Lola Van Wegenen (div.); children: Shauna, Jamie, Amy. Student, U. Colo., Pratt Inst. Design, Am. Acad. Dramatic Arts; LHD (hon.), U. Colo., 1987; D (hon.), U. Mass., 1990. Owner ski resort Sundance, Provo, Utah.; pres., founder The Sundance Inst., 1981—. Stage appearances include: Tall Story, The Highest Tree, Sunday in New York, Barefoot in the Park; Films include: (actor) War Hunt, 1961, Situation Hopeless But Not Serious, 1965, Inside Daisy Clover, 1965, The Chase, 1966, This Property Is Condemned, 1966, Barefoot in the Park, 1967, Butch Cassidy and the Sundance Kid, 1969, Tell Them Willie Boy is Here, 1969, Little Fauss and Big Halsey, 1970, The Hot Rock, 1972, Jeremiah Johnson, 1972, The Way We Were, 1973, The Sting, 1973 (Academy award nominee), The Great Gatsby, 1974, The Great Waldo Pepper, 1975, Three Days of the Condor, 1975, A Bridge Too Far, 1977, The Electric Horseman, 1979, Brubaker, 1980, The Natural, 1984, Out of Africa, 1985, Legal Eagles, 1986, Havana, 1990, Sneakers, 1992, Indecent Proposal, 1993, Up Close and Personal, 1996; (actor, exec. prodr.) Downhill Racer, 1969, The Candidate, 1972, All The President's Men, 1976; (exec. prodr.) Promised Land, 1988, Some Girls, 1988, The Dark Wind; (exec. prodr., narrator) Yosemite: The Fate of Heaven, 1989, Incident at Oglala, 1992, Anthem, 1997, Enredando sombras, 1998, (TV) Independent's Day, 1998, Horse Whisperer, The, 1998 (Audience award), Forever Hollywood, 1999; (dir.) Ordinary People, 1980 (Academy and Golden Globe Awards, Best Director); (dir., prodr.) The Milagro Beanfield War, 1988, (dir., prodr.) Quiz Show, 1994 (prodr.), Wild Bill: A Hollywood Maverick, 1995, Up Close and Personal, 1996, Air, 1997, The Horse Whisperer, 1998 (actor, prodr.); (dir., prodr., narrator) A River Runs Through It, 1993 (prodr.), A Civil Action, 1998 (prodr.), She's the One, 1998, exec. prodr.), The Legend of Bagger Vance, 1999 (dir., prodr., actor), How to Kill Your Neighbor's Dog (exec. prodr.), 2000. Recipient Audubon medal, 1989, Dartmouth Film Soc. award, 1990; Cecil B. Demille Golden Globe Award for Lifetime Achievement, 1994, Screen Actors Guild Awards for Life Achievement, 1996. Office: 1223 Wilshire Blvd # 412 Santa Monica CA 90403-5400 also: Creative Artists Agy c/o David O'Conner 9830 Wilshire Blvd Beverly Hills CA 90212-1804*

REDGRAVE, LYNN, actress; b. London, Mar. 8, 1943; d. Michael Scudemore and Rachel (Kempson) R.; m. John Clark, Apr. 2, 1967; children: Benjamin, Kelly, Annabel. Ed., Queensgate Sch., London, Central Sch. Speech and Drama, London. Stage debut as Helena in Midsummer Night's Dream, 1962; theatrical appearances include The Tulip Tree, Andorra, Hayfever, Much Ado About Nothing, Mother Courage, Love for Love, Zoo, Zoo, Widdershins Zoo, Edinburgh Festival, 1969, The Two of Us, London, 1970, Slag, London, 1971, A Better Place, Dublin, 1972, Born Yesterday, Greenwich, 1973, Hellzapoppin, N.Y., 1976, California Suite, 1977, Twelfth Night, Stratford Conn. Shakespeare Festival, 1978, The King and I, St. Louis, 1983, Les Liaisons Dangereuses, L.A., 1989, The Cherry Orchard, L.A., 1990, Three Sisters, London, 1990, Notebook of Trigorin, U.S., 1996; Broadway appearances include Black Comedy, 1967, My Fat Friend, 1974, Mrs. Warren's Profession (Tony award nomination), 1975, Knock, Knock, 1976, St. Joan, 1977, Sister Mary Ignatius Explains It All, 1985, Aren't We All?, 1985, Sweet Sue, 1987, A Little Hotel on the Side, 1992, The Masterbuilder, 1992, Shakespeare For My Father (Tony and Drama Desk nominations, Elliot Norton award 1993), 1993, also nat. tour, 1993, West End, 1993, Moon over Buffalo, 1996; film appearances include Tom Jones, Girl With Green Eyes, Georgy Girl (Recipient N.Y. Film Critics award, Golden Globe award, Oscar nomination for best actress 1967), The Deadly Affair, Smashing Time, The Virgin Soldiers, Last of the Mobile Hotshots, Don't Turn the Other Cheek, Every Little Crook and Nanny, Everything You Always Wanted to Know About Sex, The National Health, The Happy Hooker, The Big Bus, Sunday Lovers, Morgan Stuart's Coming Home, Getting It Right, Shine, 1996, Gods and Monsters, 1998 (Recipient Golden Globe award for best performance by an actress in a supporting role in a motion picture 1998), Strike, 1998, The Annihilation of Fish, 1999, The Simian Line, 2000, The Next Best Thing, 2000, How to Kill Your Neighbor's Dog, 2000; TV appearances include: The Turn of the Screw, Centennial, 1978, The Muppets, Gauguin the Savage, Beggarman Thief, The Seduction of Miss Leona, Rehearsal for Murder, 1982, Walking On Air, The Faintheart ed Feminist (BBC-TV), 1984, My Two Loves, 1986, The Old Reliable, 1988, Jury Duty 1989, Whatever Happened to Baby Jane, 1990, Fighting Back (BBC-TV), 1992, Calling the Shots (Masterpiece Theatre), 1993, Toothless, 1997, Indefensible: The Truth About Edward Brannigan, 1997, Different, 1999, White Lies, 1998, A Season for Miracles, 1999, AFI's 100 Years...100 Stars, 1999, Varian's War, 2000, Lion of Oz and the Badge of Courage (voice), 2000; guest appearances include Carol Burnett Show, Evening at the Improv and Steve Martin's Best show Ever, Circus of the Stars; co-host nat. TV syndication Not for Women Only, 1977—; nat., TV spokesperson Weightwatchers, 1984-92; TV series include House Calls, 1981, Teachers Only, 1982, Chicken Soup, 1989; Rude Awakening, 1998, albums: Make Mine Manhattan, 1978, Cole Porter Revisited, 1979; video: (for children) Meet Your Animal Friends, Off We Go, Off We Go Again: audio book readings include, Pride and Prejudice, The Shell Seekers, The Blue Bedroom, The Anastasia Syndrome, The Women in His Life, Snow In April, Gone With The Wind, 1994, The World of Philosophy, 1996; author: This is Living, 1990, Shakespeare For My Father, 1993. Named Runner-up Actress, All Am. Favorites, Box Office Barometer 1975; recipient Sarah Siddons award as Chgo.'s best stage actress of 1976, 94. Mem. The Players (pres. 1994). *

REDGRAVE, VANESSA, actress; b. London, Jan. 30, 1937; d. Michael and Rachel (Kempson) R.; m. Tony Richardson, Apr. 28, 1962 (div.); children: Natasha Jane, Joely Kim, Carlo. Student, Central Sch. Speech and Drama, London, 1955-57. First stage appearances include: Reluctant Debutante, Frincton Summer Theater, 1957, Come On Jeeves, Arts Theater, Cambridge, 1957, A Touch of the Sun, Saville Theater, London, 1958, Major Barbara, Royal Court, 1958, Mother Goose, Leatherhead, 1958,; Prin. theatrical roles include Helena in Midsummer Night's Dream, 1959, Stella in Tiger and the Horse, 1960, Katerina in The Taming of the Shrew, 1961, Rosalind in As You Like It, 1962, Imogene in Cymbeline, 1962, Nina in The Seagull, 1969, Miss Brodie in The Prime of Miss Jean Brodie, 1966; other plays include Cato Street, 1971, Threepenny Opera, 1972, Twelfth Night, 1972, Antony and Cleopatra, 1973, Design for Living, 1973, Macbeth, 1975, Lady from the Sea, 1976, 78, 79, (Best Actress award Evening Standard, 1979), The Aspern Papers, 1984, The Seagull, 1969, 85 (London Standard Drama award for Best Actress), Chekhov's Women, 1985, The Taming of the Shrew, Ghosts, 1986, Touch of the Poet, 1988, Orpheus Descending, 1989, A Madhouse in Goa, 1989, Chekov's Women, 1989, Three Sisters, 1990, When She Danced, 1991, Heartbreak House, 1991, Maybe, 1993, Brecht in Hollywood, 1994, Vita and Virginia, 1994; films include Behind The Mask, 1958, A Suitable Case for Treatment, 1965 (Best Actress award Cannes Film Festival 1966), Sailor from Gibraltar, 1965, La Musica, 1965, A Man For All Seasons, 1966, Red And Blue, 1966, Blow-Up, 1967, Camelot, 1967, Isadora Duncan, 1968 (Best Actress award Cannes Film Festival); other films include The Charge of the Light Brigade, 1968, The Seagull, 1968, A Quiet Place in the Country, 1968, Daniel Deronda, 1969, Dropout, 1969, The Trojan Women, 1970, The Devils, 1970, The Holiday, 1971, Mary, Queen of Scots, 1971, Murder on the Orient Express, 1974, Winter Rates, 1974, 7 per cent solution, 1975, Julia, 1977 (Academy award Best Supporting Actress, Golden Globe award), Agatha, 1978, Yanks, 1978, Bear Island, 1979, Playing for Time, 1980, My Body My Child, 1981, Wagner, 1981, The Bostonians, 1983 (Best Actress Nat. Film Critics, Best Actress New Delhi Internat. Film Festival), Wetherby, 1985, Steaming, 1985, Prick Up Your Ears, 1987, Comrades, 1987, Consuming Passions, 1988, Diceria dell'Untore, 1989, The Ballad of the Sad Café, 1990, Young Catherine, 1990, Howard's End, 1992, Crime and Punishment, 1993, The House of the Spirits, 1994, Mother's Boys, 1994, A Month by the Lake, 1995, Little Odessa, 1995, Mission Impossible, 1996, For The Love Of Tyler, 1996, Smilla's Sense of Snow, 1996, Deep Impact, 1998, Celebrity, 1998, Lulu on the Bridge, 1998, Uninvited, 1999, Toscano, 1999, A Rumor of Angels, 1999, Mirka, 1999, An Interesting State, 1999, If These Walls Could Talk 2, 1999, The Cradle Will Rock, 1999, Girl, Interrupted, 1999, A Rumor of Angels, 2000, Crime and Punishment, 2000; TV film and miniseries appearances include Snow White and the Seven Dwarfs, 1985, Three Sovereigns for Sarah, 1985, Peter the Great, 1986, Second Serve, 1986 (Emmy award, Golden Globe award), A Man for All Seasons, 1988, Young Catherine, 1990, Whatever Happened to Baby Jane, 1990, The Three Sisters, 1990, When She Danced, 1991, Playing for Time (Emmy award, TV Times award), The Wall, 1992, Heartbreak House, 1992, Great Moments In Aviation, 1993, Down Came A Blackbird, 1994, The Young Indiana Jones Chronicles, 1992; Author: Pussies and Tigers, 1964, (autobiography) Vanessa, 1991, Vanessa Redgrave: An Autobiography, 1994. Bd. govs. Central Sch. Speech and Drama, 1963—. Decorated comdr. Order Brit. Empire; recipient 4 times Drama award Evening Standard, 1961-91, Best Actress award Variety Club Gt. Brit., 1961, 66, Best Actress award Brit. Guild TV Producers and Dirs., 1966, Laurence Olivier award Best Actress for The Aspern Papers, 1984, London Standard Drama award Best Actress for The Seagull, 1985, New York Film Critics Circle award Best Supporting Actress for Prick Up Your Ears, 1988, Evening Standard award Best Actress for When She Danced, 1991, Ace award Best Supporting Actress movie/miniseries for Young Catherine, 1992, Variety Club of Great Britain award, 1992, Best Actress Nat. Film Critics (USA) New Delhi Internat. Film Festival for The Bostonians, Laurence Olivier award Actress of the Yr. in a Revival for A Touch of the Poet; fellow Brit. Film Inst., 1988, Emmy nomination for If These Walls Could Talk 2, TV. Office: ICM 8942 Wilshire Blvd Ste 219 Beverly Hills CA 90211*

REDHEAD, MICHAEL LOGAN GONNE, history and philosophy of science educator; b. London, Dec. 30, 1929; s. Robert Arthur and C. (Browning) R.; m. Jennifer Anne Hill, Oct. 3, 1964; children: Alexander, Julian, Roland. BS, Univ. Coll., U. London, 1950, PhD, 1970. Dir. Redhead Properties Ltd., London, 1962—; ptnr. Galveston Estates, London, 1970—; lectr. Chelsea Coll., London, 1981-83, sr. lectr., 1983-84, prof., 1984-85; prof. King's Coll., London, 1985-87, U. Cambridge, Eng., 1987-97; fellow Wolfson Coll., Cambridge, 1988—; v.p. Wolfson Coll., 1992-96; centennial prof. LSE, 1999—. Author: Incompleteness, Nonlocality and Realism, 1987; contbr. articles to profl. jours. Fellow Inst. Physic; mem. Brit Soc. Philosophy of Sci. Club: Hurlingham, commd. Queen's. Avocations: tennis, poetry, music. Home: 34 Coniger Rd, London SW6 3TA, England Office: Cambridge U Dept Hist Phil Sci, Free Sch Ln, Cambridge CB2 3RH, England

REDLICH, SHIMON, educator; b. Lvov, Poland, Apr. 2, 1935; s. Solomon and Chana (Bomze) R.; m. Judith Tamar Blumberg, Apr. 2, 1967; children: Shlomit Sharon, Efrat Sorelle. BA, Hebrew U., Israel, 1960; MA, Harvard U., 1964; PhD, NYU, 1968. Lectr. Ben Gurion U., Beer Sheva, Israel, 1972-79, sr. lectr., 1979-86, assoc. prof., 1986-96, prof., 1997—. Author: Propaganda and Nationalism in Wartime Russia, 1982, War, Holocaust and Stalinism, 1995; Editor: Jews and the Jewish People: Petitions, Letters and Appeals from Soviet Jews, 1968-1970, 1973; contbr. articles to profl. jours. Program Soviet Studies grantee Am. Coun. Learned Socs., 1976, Meml. Found. Jewish Culture grantee, 1992, Israel Acad. Scis. and Humanities grantee, Israel, 1992. Jewish. Avocations: jogging, biking. Home: 19 Sigalon St, 84965 Omer Israel Office: Ben Gurion U, 84105 Beer Sheva Israel

REDMAN, CHRISTOPHER WILLARD G., obstetric physician, educator; b. Pretoria, South Africa, Nov. 30, 1941; s. Roderick and Kathleen (Bancroft) R.; m. Corinna Susan Page, Aug. 8, 1964; children: Paul, Andrew, Sophie, George, Oliver. MA, Cambridge U., 1964, MBChB, 1967. Intern Johns Hopkins Hosp., Balt., 1967-68; resident Radcliffe Infirmary, Oxford, England, 1968-69, Children's Hosp., Jessop Hosp., Sheffield, England, 1969-70; from jr. lectr. to prof. Oxford U., England, 1970—. Author: Pre-eclampsia: The Facts, 1992; contbr. articles to profl. jours. Fellow Royal Coll. Obstetricians and Gynecologists, Royal Coll. Physicians (London), Lady Margaret Hall. Avocations: hiking. Office: Nuffield Dept Ob/Gyn, John Radcliffe Hosp, Oxford OX3 9DU, England

REDMAN, CINDA J., music educator; b. Lewiston, Idaho, May 21, 1945; d. Mackenzie Goold and Sara Kathryn Hamilton; m. Michael Redman, June 15, 1968; children: Jennifer Kathryn, Melissa Hope. MusB, U. So. Calif., 1968. Piano tchr. U. So. Calif. Prep. Sch., L.A., 1968-73; prodn. asst. Allen Ludden Prodn., Studio City, Calif., 1974, Dick Clark Prodn., Hollywood, Calif., 1975-77; pvt. practice, 1978-98. Author: Recipes for Remembrance, 1985; accompanist Wash. State Music Festivals, 1992—, Oreg. State Music Festivals, 1995—, Oreg. Baroque Festival, 1997—, Nat. Assn. Tchrs. Singing, 1997—, Coral Cross Ties, 1998—, Portland Symphonic Choir, 1999—; pianist Vancouver (Wash.) Symphony, 1995—. Mem. grant com. Children's Trust Aux., Vancouver, 1994—; bd. dirs. Vancouver Symphony, 2000—. Mem. Clark County Music Tchrs. Assn. (chmn. 1992-93, v.p. 2000—), Wauna Lake Club (social chmn. 1999—). Republican. Avocations: reading, fishing. Home and Office: 14711 SE 29th St Vancouver WA 98683-9261

REDMAN, DEBORAH A., scholar, writer, translator; b. Akron, Ohio, Oct. 9, 1957; d. James C. and Ruth M. (Slack) R. BA, Stephens Coll., Columbia, Mo., 1979; MA, Pa. State U., 1981; postgrad., Kiel (Germany) U., 1980-83, Mich. State U., 1983-85; PhD, Bielefeld (Germany) U., 1990; postgrad., Tubingen (Germany) U., 1990-94. Reader bus. and econs. dept. Tubingen U., 1990-94; profl. translator, 1982—; part-time prof. George Washington U. and Am. U., Washington, 1994—; dir. French and German tech. transl., 1995—. Author: Economic Methodology: A Bibliography with References to Works in the Philosophy of Science (1860-1988), 1989, Economics and the Philosophy of Science, 1991 (Outstanding Acad. Book award 1992), A Reader's Guide to Rational Expectations, 1992, Vade mecum to James Steuart's Principles of Political Economy (with others), Klassiker der Nationalökomomie series, 1993, The Rise of Political Economy as a Science: Methodology and the Classical Economists, 1997; contbr. to other works; author articles in jours. in English and German. Recipient Social Sci. award Stephens Coll., 1979; fellow Deutsche Forschungsgemeinschaft, 1993-95. Mem. History of Econs. Soc., Internat.

REDMAN, JOSHUA, jazz musician; s. Dewy Redman. Grad., Harvard U. Saxophonist; albums include Joshua Redman, 1993, Wish, 1993, Blues for Pat, 1994, Mood Swing, 1994, Spirit of the Moment: Live at the Village..., 1995, Freedom in the Groove, 1996, Introducing Joshua Redman, 1996; appearances include Stolen Moments: Red Hot and Cool, 1994, World Christmas, 1996, Eastwood After Hours: Live at Carnegie, Stretch Record Sampler, 1997, (with New York Stories) New York Stories, 1975, (with Elvin Jones) New York Stories, 1992, (with Mario Pavone) Toulon Days, 1991, (with Bob Thiele) Louis Satchmo, 1991, (with Kenny Drew Jr.) Look Inside, 1992, (with John Hicks) Friends Old and New, 1992, (with Elvin John) Youngblood, 1992, (with Paul Motian) Paul Motian & The Electric Bebop Band, 1992, (with Dewy Redman) Choices, 1992, African Venus, 1992, (with Eric Felton) T-Bop, 1993, (with Larry Goldings) Caminhos Cruzados, 1993, (with Jimmy Haslip) Arc, 1993, (with Joe Lovano) Tenor Legacy, 1993, (with Me'shell Ndege Ocello) Plantation Lullabies, 1993, Peace Beyond Passion, 1996, (with Red Baron Jazz Sampler) Red Baron Jazz Sampler, 1993, (with Mel Rhyne) Boss Organ, 1993, (with Dave Brubeck, Young Lions & Old Tigers, 1994, (with Lionel Hampton) For The Love of Music, 1994, (with Roy Hargrove) With the Tenors of Our Time, 1994, (with Milt Jackson) Prophet Speaks, 1994, (with Quincy Jones) Q's Jook Joint, 1994, (with Christian McBride) Gettin' to It, 1994, (with Marcus Miller) Tales, 1994, (with Dianne Reeves) Quiet After the Storm, 1994, (with Toots Thielemans) East Coast West Coast, 1994, (with McCoy Tyner) Prelude and Sonata, 1994, (with Micheal Franks) Abandoned Garden, 1995, (with Larry Goldings) Whatever it Takes, 1995, (with Milt Jackson) Burnin' in the Woodhouse, 1995, (with Chick Corea) Remembering Bud Powell, 1997, Timeless Tales, 1998, Beyond, 2000. Recipient 1st place prize Thelonious Monk competition, 1991. Office: care Warner Brother Records 3300 Warner Blvd Burbank CA 91505-4632*

REDMAN, ROBERT SHELTON, pathologist, dentist; b. Fargo, N.D., Aug. 1, 1935; s. Kenneth and Elizabeth Francis (McMillan) R.; m. Barbara Darlien Klug, Sept. 14, 1958; 1 child, Melissa Darlien Redman Johnson. Student, S.D. State U., 1953-55; BS, DDS, U. Minn., 1959, MSD, 1963; PhD, U. Wash., 1969. Cert. Am. Bd. Oral and Maxillofacial Pathology. Clin. asst. prof. sch. dentistry U. Minn., Mpls., 1963-64, assoc. prof., 1969-75; assoc. prof. sch. dentistry U. Colo., Denver, 1975-78; staff dentist, chief oral pathology rsch. lab. Dept. VA Med. Ctr., Denver, 1975-78, Washington, 1978—; clin. assoc. prof. Balt. Coll. Dental Surgery U. Md., 1989—; cons. Children's Orthop. Hosp., Seattle, 1966-69; program specialist in oral biology Dept. VA, Washington, 1982-86; adj. scientist Nat. Inst. Dental and Craniofacial Rsch., NIH, 1997—. Contbr. 14 chpts. to books, over 90 articles to profl. jours.; mem. editl. bd. Jour. Dental Rsch., 1995-98, Biotech. and histochemistry, 2000—. Mem. Biol. Stain Commn., 1999—. Capt. U.S. Army, 1959-61. Recipient Carl A. Schlack award Assn. Mil. Surgeons U.S., 1997. Fellow Am. Acad. Oral and Maxillofacial Pathology; mem. ADA, Am. Inst. Nutritional Scis., Internat. Assn. Dental Rsch. (program chmn. salivary rsch. group 1982-86, sec.-treas. 1995—), Soc. for In Vitro Biology, Omicron Kappa Upsilon. Presbyterian. Achievements include discovery and naming of an unique minor salivary gland in the rat; documentation of the relationship between weaning and maturation of salivary glands, of mitotic division of well-differentiated salivary gland cells of all types, including acinar, ductal and myoepithelial cells, of constant cell cycle length and very low rate of apoptosis in salivary glands during development and into maturity; determination of mode of inheritance of benign migratory glossitis, co-developer method to maintain salivary gland acinar cells in culture and several cell lines of these cells. Office: Dept VA Med Ctr (151-I) Oral Pathology Rsch Lab 50 Irving St NW Washington DC 20422-0001

REDMON, CYNTHIA ANN, poet, songwriter; b. Royal Oak, Mich., Feb. 10, 1951; d. Martin Lewis and Mary Elizabeth (Andrews) Hook; m. Robert Carl Nelson, Sept. 18, 1971 (div. Apr. 1983); children: Jennifer, Christina, David; m. Robert Marx Redmon, Mar. 23, 1985; 1 child, Karl. Grad., h.S., 1969. Contbr. poetry to 10 Best Poets of the 90s, Watermark Press, 10 Best Poets of the 90s, Nat. Library of Poetry, Poetic Voices of Am., 1998, The Best Poets, Nat. Library of Poets, 1991, others; pub. in numerous anthologies. Sgt. USAF, 1970-75. Recipient awards World of Poetry, 1991, 1997; named to Internat. Poetry Hall of Fame, 1997. Mem. Internat. Soc. Poets (life; bd. advisors), Charles F. Menninger Soc., Humane Soc. U.S. Christian. Avocations: cooking, reading, gardening, spirituality. Home: 4169 Old Brandon Rd Jackson MS 39208-3010

REDMOND, DONALD EUGENE, JR., neuroscientist, educator; b. San Antonio, June 17, 1939; s. Donald Eugene and Viola (Kellum) R.; m. Patricia Welder Robinson, Dec. 22, 1972; 1 child, Andy J. BA, So. Meth. U., 1961; MD, Baylor U., 1968; MAH, Yale U., 1987. Diplomate Am. Bd. Psychiatry and Neurology. With Lab. of Clin. Sci., NIMH, Bethesda, Md., 1973-74; assoc. chief clin. neurosci. unit Conn. Mental Health Ctr., New Haven, 1974-87; asst. prof. psychiatry Yale U., New Haven, 1974-77; assoc. prof. psychiatry Yale U., 1978-87, prof. psychiatry, dir. neurobehavior lab., 1987—, dir. neural transplant program for neurol. diseases, 1987—; pres. St. Kitts Biomed. Rsch. Found., St. Kitts, W.I., 1983—, Axion Rsch. Found., Hamden, Conn., 1985—; prof. neurosurgery, 1993—. Contbr. articles to profl. jours.; patentee in field. With USPHS, 1972-74. Recipient Rsch. Scientist award NIMH, 1980— Founds. Fund prize, 1981; grantee NIMH, 1974-91, Nat. Inst. Neurol. Diseases and Stroke, 1986—, others. Mem. Am. Psychiat. Assn., Am. Coll. Neuropsychopharmacology, Am. Soc. Neural Transplantation (coun. mem. 1994—), Internat. Med. Soc. Motor Disturbances. Office: Neurobehavior Lab PO Box 3333 New Haven CT 06510-0333

REDMOND, PAUL, law educator, university dean. Dean Faculty of Law U. N.S.W., Sydney, Australia. Office: U NSW Faculty of Law, Office of Dean, Sydney NSW 2052, Australia*

REDMONT, DENNIS FOSTER, journalist; b. Washington, Dec. 8, 1942; s. Bernard Sidney and Joan (Tokay) R.; m. Maria Manuela Paixao de Magalhaes, Apr. 16, 1968; children: Michael, Rodrigo. Baccalaureat cum laude, Paris, 1960; BA in Polit. Sci., Oberlin Coll., 1962; MS in Journalism cum laude, Columbia U., 1963. World svcs. editor AP, N.Y.C., 1963-65; corr. AP, Lisbon, Portugal, 1965-67, Rome, 1967-70; chief of bur. AP, Rio de Janeiro, 1970-75, Rome, 1975—; lectr., spkr. in field; guest lectr. Loyola U., Rome, 1980—, Trinity U., Rome, 1980—; guest lectr. St. George's English Sch., Rome, 1975—, also bd. govs.; appeared on numerous TV and radio broadcasts. Contbr. articles to profl. publs. and mags. Pres. Fgn. Press Assn., Rome, 1981-83, 84-87, Rio de Janeiro, 1973-75; mem. exec. com. Am. Club of Rome, 1983. Recipient Pulitzer prize nomination for coverage of Vatican and papacy, 1978, Carlo Casalegno award in Disting. Journalism, Italian Ministry of Culture, 1982, Solemare prize Italian Ministry of Culture, 1991. Mem. Vatican Corrs. Assn., Overseas Press Club, Internat. Ski Club of Journalists (pres. 1990-93), Circolo Giornalisti, Circolo Montecitorio, Aspen Inst. Italy. Avocations: tennis, skiing, reading. Office: AP, Piazza Grazioli 5, 00186 Rome Italy

REDNAM, KRISHNA RAO VENKATA, ophthalmologist; b. Visakhapatnam, India, Aug. 1, 1949. MD, Andhra Med. Coll., 1971. Diplomate Am. Bd. Ophthamology. Internist King George Hosp., Visakhapatnam, 1971-73, res. ophthamology, 1973-76; resident in surgery Jewish Hosp. and Med. Ctr., Bklyn., 1976-77; fellow in glaucoma Eye and Ear Infirmary, 1977-79; fellowship retina & citreous Ill. Eye and Ear Infirmary, Chgo., 1979-82; active staff St. Josephs Hosp., Kirkwood, Mo., 1983—; courtesy staff St. Lukes Hosp., Chesterfield, Mo., 1983—, Alexian Bros., St. Louis, Mo., 1984—, Lutheran Med. Ctr., St. Louis, Mo., 1985—; Courtesy staff St. Anthony Med. Ctr., St. Louis, 1985—; assoc. Depaul Med. Ctr., Bridgeton, Mo., 1985—; staff Out Patient Surg. Ctr., St. Louis, 1986—; assoc. St. Marys Eye Ctr., St. Louis, Mo., 1987—, St. Louis, 1988—; courtesy staff Christian Hosp., St. Louis, Mo., 1993—; provisional staff Mo. Bapt. Hosp., St. Louis, Mo., 1995—. Fellow ACS, Am. Acad. Ophthalmology, Internat. Coll. Surgeons; mem. AMA, Am. Assn. Opthamology. Office: St Louis Eye Clin 4530 Hampton Ave Saint Louis MO 63109-2238 also: St Louis Eye Clinic 135 W Adams Ave Kirkwood MO 63122-4043

REDNER, HARRY, social sciences educator, writer; b. Stanislaw, Galicia, Poland, Feb. 1, 1937; arrived in Australia 1947; s. Bernard and Elza (Fischer) R.; m. Jillian Mary Burge, Dec. 10, 1968; 1 child, Joachim Redner. BA with honors, Melbourne U., Australia, 1959, MA, 1962. Rsch. fellow Adelaide U., Australia, 1965-67; from lectr. to reader politics Monash U., Melbourne, Australia, 1967-96; hon. professorial fellow Monash U., 1997; prof. Haifa U., Israel, 1997, Technische U., Darmstadt, Germany, 1997-98, Ecole des Hautes Etudes en Scis. Sociales, Paris, 2000—. Author: In The Beginning Was The Deed, 1982, The Ends of Science, 1987, A New Science of Representation, 1994, Malign Masters, 1997, The Ends of Philosophy, 1986. Convenor Victorian Assn. of Peace Studies , Melbourne, Australia, 1980, Jewish Dem. Soc., 1981; cons. Senate Parliamentary Com., Canberra, Australia, 1983. Sr. Fulbright fellow Yale U., U. Calif., Berkeley, 1987-88. Jewish. Avocations: musical composition, piano, reading, art, traveling. Home: 20 Carnarvon Rd, North Caulfield VIC 3161, Australia Office: Monash Univ, Dept Politics, Clayton VIC 3168, Australia

REDO, DAVID LUCIEN, investment company executive; b. Lakewood, Ohio, Sept. 1, 1937; s. Joseph L. and Florence M. (Morse) R.; m. Judy L. Ijams, Aug. 4, 1962; children: Jenny, Mark. BSEE, U. Calif., Berkeley, 1961; MBA, U. Santa Clara, 1967. Registered investment advisor. Asst. engrng. mgr. AT&T, N.Y.C., 1968-71; pension fund mgr. Pacific Telephone, San Francisco, 1971-77; mng. dir. The Fremont Group (formerly Bechtel Investments Inc.), San Francisco, 1977—; chmn., CEO Fremont Investment Advisors, Inc., San Francisco, 1986—, Fremont Mutual Funds, San

Francisco, 1988—; bd. dirs. The Fremont Group (formerly Bechtel Investments, Inc.) San Francisco, Fremont Investors, Inc., Sequoia Ventures Inc., San Francisco, Fremont Investment Advisors, Sit/Kim Internat. Investments, Kern Capital Mgmt., LLC, chmn., CEO Fremont Mutual Funds. Bd. trustees U. Calif., Berkeley, 1988—; chmn. investment com. U. Calif. Found., 1988—. Mem. Sentinel Pension Inst. (bd. advisors), Internat. Assn. of Fin. Planners. Avocations: golf, traveling, reading, walking. Office: Fremont Investment Advisors 333 Market St Ste 2600 San Francisco CA 94105-2127

REDSTONE, SUMNER MURRAY, entertainment company executive, lawyer; b. Boston, May 27, 1923; s. Michael and Belle (Ostrovsky) R.; m. Phyllis Gloria Raphael, July 6, 1947; children: Brent Dale, Shari Ellin. BA, Harvard U., 1944, LLB, 1947; LLD (hon.), Boston U., 1994; LHD (hon.), N.Y. Inst. Tech., 1996. Bar: Mass. 1947, U.S. Ct. Appeals (1st cir.) 1948, U.S. Ct. Appeals (8th cir.) 1950, U.S. Ct. Appeals (9th cir.) 1948, D.C. 1951, U.S. Supreme Ct. 1952. Law sec. U.S. Ct. Appeals for 9th Circuit, San Francisco, 1947-48; instr. law and labor mgmt. U. San Francisco, 1947; spl. asst. to U.S. Atty. Gen., Washington, 1948-51; ptnr. Ford, Bergson, Adams, Borkland & Redstone, Washington, 1951-54; pres., CEO Nat. Amusements Inc., Dedham, Mass., 1967—, chmn. bd., 1986—; chmn. bd. Viacom, Inc., N.Y.C., 1987—; CEO Viacom, Inc., 1996; prof. Boston U. Law Sch., 1982, 85-86; bd. dirs. TV Acad. Arts and Scis. Found.; vis. prof. Brandeis U., Waltham, Mass.; lectr. Harvard Law Sch., Cambridge, Mass.; Judge on Kennedy Libr. Found., (sel. comm. John F. Kennedy Profile in Courage award). Chmn. met. divsn. NE Combined Jewish Philanthropies, Boston, 1963; mem. exec. bd. Combined Jewish Philanthropies of Greater Boston; mem. corp. New Eng. Med. Ctr., 1967—, Mass. Gen. Hosp. Corp.; trustee Children's Cancer Rsch. Found.; founding trustee Am. Cancer Soc.; chmn. Am. Cancer Crusade, State of Mass., 1984-86; Art Lending Libr.; sponsor Boston Mus. Sci.; chmn. Jimmy Fund Found., 1960; v.p., mem. exec. com. Will Rogers Meml. Fund; bd. dirs. Boston Arts Festival; bd. overseers Dana Farber Cancer Ctr., Boston Mus. Fine Arts; mem. presdl. adv. com. on arts John F. Kennedy Libr. Found., also judge ann. John F. Kennedy Profile in Courage Award com.; chmn. Corp. Commn. on Edn. Tech., 1996—, presdl. apptd. chmn., 1996. 1st lt. AUS, 1943-45. Decorated Army Commendation medal; named 1 of 10 Outstanding Young Men in New Eng., Boston Jr. C. of C., 1958; recipient William J. German Human Rels. award Am. Jewish Com. Entertainment/Comm. Divsn., 1977, Silver Shingle award Boston U. Law Sch., 1985, Variety New Eng. Humanitarian award, 1989, Golden Plate award Am. Acad. Achievement, 1993, 32d Ann. Salute to Excellence Program, 1993, Bus. Excellence award U. So. Calif. Sch. Bus. Adminstrn., 1994, The Stephen S. Wise award The Am. Jewish Congress, 1994, Man of Yr. award MIPCOM, the Internat. Film and Programme Market for TV, Video, Cable and Satellite, 1994, The Legends in Leadership award Emory U., 1995, Allan K. Jonas Lifetime Achievement award Am. Cancer Soc., 1995, Humanitarian award Variety Club Internat., 1995, Expeditioner's award N.Y.C. Outward Bound Ctr., 1996, Patron Arts award Songwriter's Hall Fame, 1996, Vision 21 award N.Y. Inst. Tech., 1996, Trustees award NATAS, 1997, Ripple of Hope award Robert F. Kennedy Meml., 1998, Humanitarian award Nat. Conf. Christians and Jews, 1998; named Communicator of Yr., B'nai B'rith Comm./Cinema Lodge, 1980, Man of Yr., Entertainment Industries Divsn. of UJA Fedn., 1988, Pioneer of Yr., Motion Picture Pioneers, 1991, Grad. of Yr., Boston Latin Sch., 1989, Honoree 7th ann. fundraiser Montefiore Med. Ctr., 1995, Hall of Fame award Broadcasting and Cable mag., 1995. Mem. ABA, Nat. Assn. Theatre Owners (chmn. bd. dirs. 1965-66, exec. comm. 1995—), Theatre Owners Am. (asst. pres. 1960-63, pres. 1964-65), Motion Picture Pioneers (bd. dirs.), Boston Bar Assn., Mass. Bar Assn., Harvard Law Sch. Assn., Am. Judicature Soc., Masons, Univ. Club, Harvard Club. Home: 98 Baldpate Hill Rd Newton MA 02459-2825 Office: Nat Amusements Inc PO Box 9126 Dedham MA 02027-9126

REDWOOD, JOHN ALAN, member British parliament; b. June 15, 1951; s. William Charles and Amy Emma (Champion) R.; m. Gail Felicity Chippington, 1974; 2 children. Student, Kent Coll., Canterbury, Eng.; MA, DPhil, Oxford U. Investment advisor Robert Fleming & Co., 1973-77; investment mgr. and dir. N. M. Rothschild & Sons, 1977-87; dir. Norcros, 1985-89, dep. chmn., 1986-87, non-exec. chmn., 1987-89; advisor Treasury and Civil Svc. Select Com., 1981; head policy unit PM, 1983-85; councillor Oxfordshire CC, 1973-77; parly under sec. state DTI, 1989-90, min. state, 1990-92; DoE, 1992-93, sec. state for Wales, 1993-95; shadow pres. The Bd. Trade, 1997-99; non-exec. chmn. Mabey Securities, 1999—; shadow sec. of state Environ., Transport and the Region, 1999-00; fellow All Souls Coll., 1972-87; gov. various schs., 1974-83; non-exec. dir. Murray Fin. PLC, 1998—. Author: Reason, Ridicule and Religion, 1976, Public Enterprise in Crisis, 1980, (with John Hatch) Value for Money Audits, 1981, (with John Hatch) Controlling Public Industries, 1982, Going for Broke, 1984, Equity for Everyman, 1986, Popular Capitalism, 1988, Our Currency Our Country, 1997, The Death of Britain?, 1999. Avocations: water sports, village cricket. Office: Mem Parliament, House of Commons, London SW1AOAA, England

REECE, DAVID BRYSON, information systems administrator; b. Phoenix, Aug. 5, 1953; s. Frank Williams and Margaret Leonora (Bryson) W.; div.; children: Ashley Cambridge, Christopher David. ADN, Phoenix C.C., 1974; Baccelaurette Sci. Wholistic Nursing, Westbrook U., 1991, Master Sci. Wholistic Nursing, 1992, PhD, 1993. V.p. Young Nursing Svc., Kingman, Ariz., 1987-89; CEO No. Ariz. Cons., Phoenix, 1987-92, Butterfield Health Systems, Phoenix, 1990-92; dean of nursing, co-founder Sch. Wholistic Nursing Westbrook U., Aztec, N.Mex., 1994-2000; co-founder Auditors Unlimited, Inc., Phoenix, 1997, bd. dirs., 1998-2000; prin. Reece & Assocs., 1999-2000; alternative health nurse practitioner; Human Rights, 1997. Author: Minerals, Metals and Gemstones of the Holy bible, 1998, Wholistic Nursing Theory, 1998, Homeopathy: Introduction to Healthcre Proffesional, Computer: Internet and Int-anet Site Development, Database Administration Fraud & Abuse Analysis, Software Development, 1% Solution-Ergonomic Designs for the Exceptionally Tall and Big, 2000. Mem. Ariz. Assn. Healthcare Agys. (bd. dirs. 1988-90). Avocations: scuba diving, aviation soaring, mining, treasure hunting, archeology.

REECE, GERALDINE MAXINE, elementary education educator; b. L.A., May 13, 1917; d. Charles Kenneth and Bertha (Austin) Ballou; m. Thomas Charles Bauman, Aug. 16, 1942 (div. Oct. 1971); children: Thomas Charles Bauman, Jr., Kathleen Marie Bauman Messenger, Stephen Kenneth Bauman; m. Wilbert Wallingford Reece, Nov. 3, 1973 (dec. 1988). AA, L.A. City Coll., 1942; BA, U. So. Calif., L.A., 1966. Specialist tchr. in reading, elem. edn. Tchr. Archdiocese of L.A., Altadena, Calif., 1962-66; master tchr. Alhambra (Calif.) City and H.S., 1966-79, writer multicultural component early childhood edn. program. Author poetry. Mem. San Gabriel Child Care Task Force, 1984-86; mem. steering com. West San Gabriel Valley Cmty. Awareness Forum, 1985-87; past pres. women's divsn., bd. dirs. San Gabriel C. of C., 1989-90, 98—, publicity chair, 1994-98, incoming pres. women's divsn., 1998—; mem. sch. site and facilities com. Sch. Dist. Unification, San Gabriel, 1992-93; mem. task force Episcopal Parish/Healing Our Cities, San Gabriel, 1992-93; docent San Gabriel Mus., 1989, 92-93; mem. Hearing Our Voice anti-violence com. Episcopal Parish. Recipient Exceptional Svc. awards Am. Heart Assn., West San Gabriel Valley, 1990, 91, 93, 94, 95, Dedicated Svc. award San Gabriel C. of C., 1989, Outstanding and Dedicated Cmty. Svc. award Fedn. Cmty. Coord. Couns., San Gabriel, 1986, 87, 97-98, others, Woman of Yr. award City of San Gabriel, 1994, Diamond Homer trophy Famous Poet Soc., 1995, 96; named Outstanding Older Am., City of San Gabriel, 1999; scholarship named in her honor Divsn. 1 Calif. Ret. Tchrs. Assn. Mem. AAUW (Money Talks sect. chairperson 1981-82, corr. sec.-treas. Alhambra-San Gabriel 1982-85), Calif. Ret. Tchrs. Assn. (pres. 1989-91, Outstanding Svc. plaque 1994, divsn. 1 scholarship named in her honor 1998, bd. dirs. 1999—), DAR (3rd vice regent 1994—, 1st Pl. Poetry award 1996, 3d Pl. Poetry award 1998), Pasadena Women's City Club, St. Francis Guild, San Gabriel Ret. Tchrs. (pres. 1985-89, cmty. rep. 1990-97), San Gabriel Hist. Assn., San Gabriel Cmty. Coord. Coun. (pres. 1986, 1st v.p. 1997-98). Democrat. Episcopalian. Avocations: reading, Bridge, writing poetry, stitchery.

REECE, JULIETTE M. STOLPER, community health and mental health nurse; b. Muskogee, Okla., Oct. 4, 1926; d. Joseph Harry and Marie (Duquesne) Stolper; m. Warren Crane, Apr. 12, 1947; children: Warren Crane, Judith Gayle Crane Cox Fitzpatrick, Janice M. Crane Sharp, Cathy L. Crane Hubble; m. Roy M. Reece Jr., July 16, 1970 (dec.). Diploma, Muskogee Gen. Hosp., 1947; BS in Psychology, Cameron Coll., Lawton, Okla., 1993, postgrad., 1993; student, U. Okla. Cert. pub. health nurse. ICU nurse Southwestern Hosp., Lawton, 1976-77; psychiat. nurse Taliaferro Community Mental Health Ctr., 1977-86; cons. nurse Cedar Crest Manor, Lawton, 1985-86, dir. nursing svc., 1986-87; asst. head nurse Reynolds Family Practice Clinic, Ft. Sill, Okla., 1987-91, head nurse, 1991-95, also diabetes educator, 1991-97; patient/staff edn. coord. dept. family practice Reynolds Army Cmty. Hosp., Ft. Sill, 1996-97; staff nurse Rapid-Temps., 1997-99; nurse cons., owner Jay Mar Assocs., Lawton, Okla., 1998—; sch. nurse Bishop Elem. Sch., Lawton, Okla., 1999—; vis. mem. Pub. Health Nursing Study Group, USSR, 1979. Vol. for Am. Cancer Soc., Am. Heart Assn., Am. Diabetes Assn., Am. Lung Assn., Am. Assn. Diabetes Educators, Assn. Western Okla. Diabetes Educators, ARC, Easter Seal Programs; tchr. classes for home health care aides, ARC; tchr. med. terminology to hosp. receptionists. Recipient nursing grants. Home: 1601 NW Pollard Ave Lawton OK 73507-2048

REECE, MONIQUE ELIZABETH, marketing, advertising and sales consultant; b. Eldora, Iowa, Jan. 12, 1960; d. Barry Lynne and Vera Marie (Powell) R.; m. Gordon Duane Myron, Mar. 14, 1992; children: Morgan Reece, Isabella Monique. BSBA, Regis U., 1991. Mgr. regional advt. Silo, Inc., Denver, 1979-86; dir. mktg. LaserLand Corp., U.S.A., Denver, 1986-87; advt. mgr. King Soopers, Denver, 1987-90; supr. brand devel. Garrison-Lontine Advt., Denver, 1991; pres. Monique Myron and Assocs., Denver and La Jolla, Calif., 1991-94, MarketSmarter, Denver and San Diego, 1994-99; v.p. corp. devel. mgmt. Tactical Mktg. Ventures, LLC, 1999—; chmn. bus. partnership com. Colo. Mktg. Tech. Advt. Com., Denver, 1987-91; spkr. in field. Co-author: Market Smarter Not Harder, 1996. Mem. publ. rels. com. Make-A-Wish Found., Denver, 1989. Recipient 1st Place Advt. award Nat. Frozen Food Assn., 1988, 89, 90, award Retail Advt. Coun., 1990. Mem. NAFE, ASTD, Nat. Assn. Women Bus. Owners (bd. dirs.), Colo. Women's C. of C., La Jolla C. of C. (bus. profl. com. 1992-93), Denver Met. C. of C. Avocations: skiing, running, hiking, diving, reading. Home and Office: 401 Monaco Pkwy Denver CO 80220-6015

REECE, RICHARD MARSDEN, retired archaeology educator; b. Cirencester, Eng., Mar. 25, 1939; s. Richard Marsden and Alice (Wedel) R. BSc in Biochemistry, U. Coll. London, 1961; DPhil, Wadham Coll., Oxford U., 1972, dip. edn., 1962. Chemistry tchr. St. Johns Sch., Leatherhead, Eng., 1962-65; head chemistry dept. St. Georges Sch., Harpenden, Eng., 1966-68; lectr. Inst. Archaeology U. London, 1970-84, sr. lectr., 1984-94, reader, 1994-99, reader emeritus, 1999—; cons. Roman coins to mus., Malta, Libya, Egypt, Algeria, Italy, France, others, 1968—. Author: Roman Coins, 1970, Excavations on Iona, 1981, My Roman Britain, 1987, Later Roman Empire, 1999; contbr. numerous articles to profl. jours. Pelham student U. Oxford, Rome, 1968. Fellow Soc. Antiquaries, Royal Numis. Soc. (coun. 1970-73). Mem. Ch. of Eng. Avocations: piano/organ playing, reading. Home: The Apple Loft, The Waterloo, Cirencester Glos GL7 2PU, England

REECE, RODNEY LEON, veterinarian; b. Sydney, Australia, Jan. 9, 1949; s. Travice and Alice Lena (Bullus) R.; m. Janette Gladys Mitchell, May 11, 1974; children: Natasha Anne, Michael David, Sally Jane. B of Vet. Sci., Sydney U., 1971; MS, James Cook U., 1975; Diploma Bibl. Studies, Vision Coll., 1987; PhD, Bristol U., 1995. Vet. Australian Devel. Assistance Bur., Honiara, Solomon Islands, 1974-77; avian pathologist Victorian Agrl., Parkville, Australia, 1977-87; vet. pathologist Inst. Animal Health, Houghton, England, 1987-92; pathology registrar Taronga Zoo, Mosman, Australia, 1992-94; avian pathologist NSW Agrl., Camden, Australia, 1995-97; vet. pathologist NSW Agrl., Camden, 1997—; registrar Nat. Registry Domestic Animal Pathology, Camden, 1992-97. Author: (with others) Poultry Diseases, 4th edit., 1995, Diseases of Poultry, 10th edit., 1996; editor: Color Atlas of Avian Histopathology, 1996; contbr. articles to profl. jours. Elder Macarthur Christian Life Ctr., Campbelltown. Fellow Australian Coll. Vet. Scientists in Avian Mgmt. and Diseases; mem. Australian Coll. Vet. Scientists (treas. pathobiology chpt. 1995-96, registered specialist in poultry medicine), Australian Soc. Vet. Pathologists, Australian Vet. Poultry Assn., World Poultry Sci. Assn. Avocations: canoeing, guitar, reading, swimming. Home: 257 Camden Valley Way, Narellan 2567, Australia Office: NSW Agrl, Agrl Inst PMB 8, Camden 2570, Australia

REECE, SYDNEY LORRAINE, English composition educator; b. L.A., June 14, 1965; d. Saul Leon Jr. and Dolores Antoinette Reece. BA in Clin. Psychology, UCLA, 1992, MA in Afro-Am. Studies, 1999. English trainer, instr. Orleans (France) C. of C., 1992-97; grad. student rschr. Diaspora project UCLA, 1997—, instr. women's studies, 1997-98, instr. English, 1998-99. Grad. Opportunity fellow UCLA, 1998. Avocations: yoga, reading. Office: Writing Program UCLA 271 Kinsey Hall 405 Hilgard Ave Los Angeles CA 90095-9000

REECH, CHRISTOPHE GILBERT DANIEL, financial executive; b. Nancy, France, July 29, 1966; s. Roland E. Josette R. (Valencas) R.; m. Brigitte Schweitzer, Aug. 20, 1994; 1 child, France. M of Math. and Physics, Nat. Inst. Applied Scis., Lyon, France, 1989. Cert. engring. and info. sys. and math. applications. Asst. engr. France Telecom, N.Y.C., 1988; project mgr. tech. dept. Banque Paribas, Paris, 1989; asst. v.p. Banque Paribas, Istanbul, Turkey, 1989-91; asst. v.p. custody dept. Banque Paribas, Paris, 1991-92; v.p. equity derivatives, head equity lending and borrowing Paribas Capital Markets, London, 1992-95; exec. dir. equity derivatives, head equity financing/arbitrage Commerz Fin. Products, Frankfurt, Germany, 1995-97; exec. dir. fin. products divsn., equity fin. global head Nikko Europe PLC, London, 1997-98, mng. dir. divsn. fin. products, 1997-98; chmn., CEO, Reech Capital PLC, London, 1999—. Avocations: sailing, tennis, scuba diving, opera. Home: 41 St Peters Sq, London W6 9NR, England Office: Reech Capital PLC, 107 Cannon St, London EC4N 5AF, England

REED, ALFRED DOUGLAS, university administrator; b. Bristol, Tenn., July 18, 1928; s. Roy Theodore and Elizabeth Brown (Tuft) R.; m. Emily Joyce Freeman, Mar. 18, 1950; children: Roy Frederick, Robert Douglas, David Clark, Timothy Wayne, Joseph William. AB, Erskine Coll., Due West, S.C., 1949. Reporter Citizen-Times, Asheville, N.C., 1949-51, city editor, 1953-60, mng. editor, 1962-63, assoc. editor, 1963-66, capital corr., 1959-66; asst. editor The Presbyn. Jour., Weaverville, N.C., 1951-52; assoc. editor Shelby (N.C.) Daily Star, 1961-62; dir. pub. info. Western Carolina U., Cullowhee, N.C., 1966-96, asst. to the chancellor, 1996—; cons. Devel. Office, East Carolina U., Greenville, 1980; bd. dirs. Wachovia Bank and Trust Co., Sylva, N.C., 1969—. Author: Prologue, 1968, Decade of Development, 1984; exec. editor: Western, The Mag. of Western Carolina University, 1991-96. Mem. Asheville City Bd. Edn., 1958-62; vice chmn. bd. dirs. Sta. WCQS FM, Western N.C. Pub. Radio Inc., Asheville, 1978-88; bd. dirs., mem. exec. com. Cherokee Hist. Assn., 1985—, Western N.C. Assn. Comtys., 1985—, Jackson County Fund of N.C. Comty. Found., 1991-93; mem. Hunter Libr. Adv. Bd., 1991-98, Pack Place Adv. Coun., Asheville, 1991-95. Recipient Paul A. Reid Disting. Svc. award Western Carolina U., 1980, Disting. Svc. award, 1996. Mem. Pub. Rels. Assn. Western N.C. (bd. dirs. 1988-98, treas. 1966-86), Coll. News Assn. Carolinas (bd. dirs. 1968-71, 80-82), Smoky Mountain Host Assn. (bd. dirs., 1st v.p. 1994-96, pres. 1996-98), Great Smoky Mountains Natural History Assn. (bd. mem. 1998—). Democrat. Presbyterian. Avocations: travel, stamps, gardening. Home: 931 University Heights Rd Cullowhee NC 28723-6953 Office: Western Carolina U Asst to Chancellor 408 Robinson Cullowhee NC 28723

REED, BERENICE ANNE, art historian, artist, government official; b. Memphis; d. Glenn Andrew and Berenice Marie (Kallaher) R. BFA, St. Mary-of-the-Woods Coll., Ind., 1955; MFA in Painting and Art History, Istituto Pio XII, Villa Schifanoia, Florence, Italy, 1964; ind. art history rsch., Ctr. for Advanced Study in the, Visual Arts, Nat. Gallery of Art, Washington, 1998—. Cert. art tchr., Tenn. Comml. artist Memphis Pub. Co., 1955-56; arts adminstr., educator pub. and pvt. instns., Washington, Memphis, 1957-70; arts adminstr. Nat. Park Svc., 1970-73; mem. staff U.S. Dept. of Energy, Washington, 1973-81, U.S. Dept. Commerce, Washington, 1983-84, Exec. Office of the Pres., Office of Mgmt. and Budget, Washington, 1985; with fin. mgmt. svc. U.S. Treasury Dept., Washington, 1985—; ind. art history rschr. Nat. Gallery of Art, Ctr. Advanced Study in Visual Arts, Washington, 1998—; cons. on art and architecture in recreation AIA, 1972-73; artist-in-residence St. Mary-of-the-Woods Coll., Ind., 1965; guest lectr. instr. Nat. Sch. Fine Arts, Tegucigalpa, Honduras, 1968; exec. com. Parks, Arts and Leisure Project, Washington, 1972-73; rschr. art projects, Washington, 1981-83. Developer (video) In Your Interest, 1992; TV interviewer Am. Fin. Skylink satellite programs, 1996-98. Bd. dirs. Am. Irish Bicentennial Com., 1974-76; advisor Royal Oak Found. Recipient various awards for painting; installed as Dame of Merit, Sacred Mil. Constantinian Order of St. George, 1997. Mem. Soc. Woman Geographers, Nat. Soc. Arts and Letters, Ctr. for Advanced Study in Visual Arts, Art Barn Assn. (bd. dirs. 1973-83), Patrons of the Arts in the Vatican Mus., Irish Georgian Soc. Roman Catholic. Avocations: photography, performing arts. Home: PO Box 34253 Bethesda MD 20827-0253 Office: Dept Treasury Fin Mgmt Svc 401 14th St SW Washington DC 20024-2106

REED, DAVID PATRICK, infosystems specialist; b. Portsmouth, Va., Jan. 30, 1952; s. Sherman Clark and Bernice Lois (Maul) R.; m. Lynn Susan Schwartz, June 10, 1973 (div. Mar. 1979); 1 child, Colin Alexander; m. Jessica Amy Kenn, Sept. 4, 1983; children: Katherine Anne, Carly Diana. BS, MIT, 1973, SM, 1975, Degree in Elec. Engring., 1976, PhD, 1978. Asst. prof. computer sci. and engring. MIT, Cambridge, 1978-84, lectr., 1984-86; chief scientist Software Arts, Wellesley, Mass., 1983-84, v.p. R&D, 1984-85; v.p. R&D, chief scientist Lotus Devel., Cmabridge, 1985-92; sr. scientist Interval Rsch. Corp., 1992-96; pvt. practice, 1996—; mem. adv. bd. Vanguard, 1991—; fellow Diamond Tech. Ptnrs. Exch. program, 1997—. Contbr. articles to profl. jours. Recipient Tchg. award MIT Elec. Engring. Dept., 1975. Mem. IEEE, Assn. Computing Machinery, Computer Soc., Sigma Xi. Democrat.

REED, EDDIE, pharmacologist; b. Hughes, Ark., Dec. 17, 1953; married; 1 child. BS magna cum laude, Philander Smith Coll., Little Rock, 1975; MD, Yale U., 1979. Diplomate Am. Bd. Internal Medicine, Nat. Bd. Med. Examiners. Commd. USPHS, 1978, advanced through grades to capt.; intern in internal medicine Stanford U. Hosp., Palo Alto, Calif., 1979-80, resident, 1980-81; clin. assoc. div. cancer treatment Nat. Cancer Inst., Bethesda, Md., 1981-83, investigator detailed to lab. cellular carcinogenesis, 1983-85, spl. asst. for pre-clin. sci. Office Dir., 1985-87, sr. investigator clin. pharmacology and med. br., 1987—, coord. ovarian cancer studies, 1988-91, head med. ovarian cancer sect. clin. oncology program, 1991—, chief clin. pharmacology br., 1993—, chief peritoneoscopy svc. med. br., 1987—, sr. attending physician clin. pharmacology and medicine brs., 1987—, sr. med. cons. medicine br., 1987—; participant numerous seminars in field, 1984—; chmn. ambulatory care com. NIH Clin. Ctr., 1989-93; mem. protocol com. Gynecologic Oncology Coop. Study Group, 1989—, mem. tumor biology and applied sci. com., 1990—; mem. com. on status of minorities in the intramural NIH, 1992—; mem. NIH Inter-Inst. Working Group on Breast and Gynecologic Tumors, 1993—; mem. sci. abd. bd. Nat. Ctr. for Toxicological Rsch., FDA, Jefferson, Ark., 1988—; reviewer Jour. Nat. Cancer Inst., Cancer Rsch., Jour. Clin. Oncology, Jour. Clin. Investigation, Jour. Biol. Chemistry, Gynecologic Oncology. Mem. editl. bd. Yale Jour. Biology and Medicine, 1976-79, Oncology Reports, 1993—, Jour. Nat. Med. Assn., 1994—; contbr. numerous articles to med. jours. Recipient commendation medal USPHS, 1993; EEO spl. achievement award NIH, 1993, tech. transfer award, 1995. Mem. AAAS, Am. Fedn. Clin. Rsch., Am. Assn. Cancer Rsch., Nat. Med. Assn. (sci. coun., head basic sci. subsect. 1994—), Assn. for Acad. Minority Physicians, Environ. Mutagen Soc., Internat. Assn. Environ. Mutagen Socs., Ark. Med., Dental and Pharm. Assn., Gynecologic Oncology Group, Soc. Gynecologic Oncology, Alpha Kappa Mu, Beta Kappa Chi. Home: 19302 Tattershall Dr Germantown MD 20874-6245 Office: Nat Cancer Inst Medicine Br Rm 12n226 Br Bldg 10 Bethesda MD 20892-0001

REED, ERBIE LOYD, dentist; b. Chesterfield, Tenn., Oct. 11, 1920; s. Erbie Lester and Mary Velt (Blankenship) R.; m. Marcille duke, Dec. 12, 1942; children: LInda Faye Reed McCalla, Mark Lloyd, Kevin Duke. Student, U. Tenn., Martin, 1937-38, U. Memphis, 1946; DDS, U. Tenn., Memphis, 1949. Mgr. Reed's Lumber Mill, Chesterfield, 1936, 38-41; postmaster, owner, operator Reed's Gen. Store, Chesterfield, 1941-42; pvt. practice dentistry U. Tenn., Memphis, 1949, Millington, Tenn., 1950-93. Mem., chmn. Com. Fluoridation of Water, Millington, Tenn., 1954—; mem. Millington Recreation Commn., 1951-58; mem., officer Millington Bd. Zoning Appeals, 1953—; chmn. Millington United Fund, 1964-75; chmn. Pub. Utilities Commn., Millington, 1959-60; deacon, trustee, Sunday sch. tchr., bldg. com., various other coms. First Bapt. Ch., Millington, 1949—. With USN, 1942-45. Mem. ADA, Tenn. Dental Assn., Pierre Fauchard Acad., Memphis Dental Soc. Avocations: swimming, yard work, bridge, reading, church visitation. Home: 4664 Cedar Rose Dr Millington TN 38053-3926 Office: 8020 Hwy 51 N Millington TN 38053

REED, FRANCES BOOGHER, writer, actress; b. Marion, Ky., May 29, 1938; d. Charles Boogher and Evelyn Shelby (Roberts) R.; m. José Joaquín Solis, June 1, 1957 (div. Sept. 1964); children: Julie, Michael Charles; m. Arnold Haslund, Jan. 30, 1965 (div. May 1967); 1 child, Elizabeth Evelyn Marie; 1 adopted child, Leni Ellis. BA in English and Spanish, U. Houston, 1960; MPH, U. P.R., 1970. Tchr. English as 2d lang. Author: A Dream With Storms, 1979, Thoughts, Feelings and Dreams, 1985, Black Mexican Necklace, 1990, TOEIC Test Guide, 1997, Miguel's Aztec Calendar, 1997, (with Koji Shimada) From Chocolate Bars to CEO, A MacArthur's Kid, 2000, (with Francisco Diaz Infante M.) Pockets and Jingles: Something for His Pockets, 2000; acctress (television shows) General Hospital, Rescue-911, others, also movies. Mem. Am. Pub. Health Assn., Screen Actors' Guild, Mensa, Phi Kappa Phi. Democrat. Methodist. Avocations: teaching, dancing, reading. Home: 239 Beach City Rd Apt 2113 Hilton Head Island SC 29926-4713 also: PO Box 23481 Hilton Head Island SC 29925-3481

REED, JAMES (RUDOLPH), foundation administrator; b. Mex., Mo., Nov. 9, 1938; s. Charles W. and Virginia (Cooper) R.; m. Katie Nowinski, Mar. 12, 1961; children: Philip R., Holly A. Mgmt. trainee Southwestern Bell Telephone, St. Louis, 1960-62; mgr. Southwestern Bell Telephone, Tulsa, Okla., 1962-64; dist. mgr. Southwestern Bell Telephone, Oklahoma City, 1964-69; coll. rels. dir. Southwestern Bell Telephone, St. Louis, 1969-72; comml. supr. Southwestern Bell Telephone, Kansas City, Mo., 1972-73; divsn. mgr. Southwestern Bell Telephone, San Antonio, 1973-92; exec. dir. Am. Heart Assn. So. Tex.Coun., San Antonio, 1992-98; pres. San Antonio Med. Found., 1999—; bd. dirs. Govt. Pers. Mut. Life Ins. Co., San Antonio; adv. bd. Tex. Golf Mag., 1990-91. Chmn. Target 90 Goals for San Antonio, 1988-89; chmn. adv. bd. Salvation Army, San Antonio, 1981-82; devel. bd. U. Tex., San Antonio, 1991—; vice-chmn. United Way, San Antonio, 1976; dist. chmn. Alamo Area Boy Scouts Am., 1977; crusade chmn. Am. Cancer Soc., San Antonio, 1979; pres. Rsch. and Planning Coun., San Antonio, 1974-75; tri-chair NCCJ, 1991. Recipient Alumni Achievement award Westminster Coll., 1991, Humanitarian award Nat. Jewish Ctr. for Immunology and Respiratory Medicine, 1991; named one of Outstanding Young Men of Am., 1976. Mem. World Affairs Coun. (exec. com. 1988-89), San Antonio Golf Assn. (vice chmn. 1988-89), Rotary (pres. 1983-84), Greater San Antonio C. of C. (chmn. 1990), Shriners, South Tex. C. of C. (vice-chmn. 1978-80), Oak Hills Country Club (pres. 1994), Tex. Club Assn. (pres. 2000). Presbyterian. Avocations: golf, travel. Home: 7317 Ashton Pl San Antonio TX 78229-4170

REED, JOYCE LASKY, foundation administrator, writer; b. N.Y.C., Sept. 5, 1934; m. Anatole Shub, (div. 1978); children: Adam Shub, Rachel A. Shub; m. Leonard Reed, Jan. 31, 1988. BA, Barnard U., 1952; MA, Georgetown U., 1981. Fgn. policy staff Ho. Fgn. Affairs Com., Washington, 1975-78, Senate Fgn. Rels. Com., Washington, 1978-81; dir. European program Am. Enterprise Inst., Washington, 1982-83; spl. advisor Dept. State, Washington, 1983-88; pres. Fabergé Arts Found., Washington, 1990—. Author: Moscow by Nightmare, 1974; editor: French Security Issues, 1982, Germany: Keystone to European Security, 1983; (with R. Carr) Spain Studies in Political Security. Scholar in residence Nat. Def. U., 1981. Jewish. Avocations: tennis, chess, swimming. Home: 4511 Dorset Ave Chevy Chase MD 20815-5449

REED, LOU, musician; b. Bklyn., Mar. 2, 1942; s. Sidney Joseph and Toby (Futterman) R. BA, Syracuse U., 1964. Songwriter Pickwick Records, N.Y.C., 1965; rec. artist Verve, MGM, Atlantic, Arista, RCA, Warner Bros., Reprise, ire Record Cos, N.Y.C., 1965—. Solo albums include Lou Reed, 1972, Transformer, 1972, Berlin, 1973, Rock 'N' Roll Animal, 1974, Sally

Can't Dance, 1974, Metal Machine Music, 1975, Lou Reed Live, 1975, Coney Island Baby, 1976, Rock and Roll Heart, 1976, Street Hassle, 1978, Live, Take No Prisoners, 1978, The Bells, 1979, Growing Up in Public, 1980, Blue Mask, 1982, Legendary Hearts, 1983, New Sensations, 1984, Mistrial, 1986, New York, 1989, Songs for Drella, 1990, Magic and Loss, 1992, Between Thought and Expression: The Lou Reed Anthology, 1992, Different Times: Lou Reed In The 70's, 1996, Set The Twilight Reeling, 1996, Perfect Night Live in London, 1998, Ecstasy, 2000; founding mem. (band) The Velvet Underground, 1966-70, touring with Andy Warhol's The Exploding Plastic Inevitable; albums include The Velvet Underground and Nico, 1967, White Light White Heat, 1968, The Velvet Underground, 1969, Loaded, 1970; albums after Velvet Underground include Live at Max's Kansas City, 1972, Velvet Underground Live MCM XCIII, 1993, VU, 1985, Another View, 1986; exhibited series of photographs Photographic Resource Ctr., 1997, Soho Triad Gallery, 1998, Le Printemps de Cahors, France, 1999, Closure, 1998; photos pub. in photographic mag. Blind Spot; author: Between Thought and Expression, 1991, Pass Thru Fire, 2000; actor in some film roles. Decorated chevalier comdr. Arts and Letters (France); recipient Best New Poet award Coun. on Small Lit. Mags., 1977, Heroes award N.Y. chpt. NARAS, 1997; inducted into Rock and Roll Hall of Fame as member of Velvet Underground, 1996; designated Am. Master, PBS Documentary Series, 1998. Mem. Musician's Union Local 802, Screen Actors Guild. Jewish. Office: Sister Ray Enterprises 584 Broadway Rm 609 New York NY 10012-3229

REED, MARK ARTHUR, educator, researcher; b. Suffern, N.Y., Jan. 4, 1955; s. Arthur Julius and Rita Margaret Reed; m. Elizabeth J. Schaffer; 1 child, Victor. BS in Physics with honors, Syracuse U., 1977, MS in Physics, 1979, PhD in Solid State Physics, 1983; MA (hon.), Yale U., 1990. Mem. tech. staff Ctrl. Rsch. Labs., Tex. Instruments, Dallas, 1983-88, sr. mem. tech. staff, 1988-90; prof. elec. engring. and applied physics Yale U., New Haven, 1990—, chmn. elec. engring. dept., 1995—, Harold Hodgkinson prof. engring. and applied sci., 1999—; chief tech. officer, dir. Molecular Electronics Corp., 1999—; chmn., organizer of numerous confs. Contbr. 100 articles to profl. jours., chpts. to books; author 3 books; speaker in field. Recipient Kilby Young Innovator award, 1994, Disting. Alumni award Syracuse U., 2000; named one of Fortune Mag.'s 12 most promising young Am. Scientists. Mem. IEEE (sr.), Am. Phys. Soc., Optical Soc. Am., Sigma Xi. Achievements include pioneered investigation of "Quantum Dots" and Quantum devices; invention of resonant tunneling transistor; 17 patents for novel quantum effect and heterojunction devices; pioneered research on molecular electronic systems. Avocations: scuba, chess. Office: Molecular Electronics Corp PO Box 208284 New Haven CT 06520-8284

REED, ROBERT PHILLIP, lawyer; b. Springfield, Ill., June 14, 1952; s. Robert Edward and Rita Ann (Kane) R.; m. Janice Leigh Kloppenburg, Oct. 8, 1976; children: Kevin Michael, Matthew Carl, Jennifer Leigh, Rebecca Ann. AB, St. Louis U., 1974; JD, U. Ill., 1977. Bar: Ill. 1977, U.S. Dist. Ct. (ctrl. dist.) Ill. 1979, U.S.Ct. Appeals (7th cir.) 1983, U.S. Dist. Ct. (so. dist.) Ill. 1992, Colo. 1993. Intern Ill. Legislature, Springfield, 1977-78; assoc. Traynor & Hendricks, Springfield, 1979-80; ptnr. Traynor, Hendricks & Reed, Springfield, 1981-88; pvt. practice Springfield, 1988—; pub. defender Sangamon County, Ill., Springfield, 1979-81; hearing examiner Ill. State Bd. Elections, Springfield, 1981-88; spl. asst. atty. gen. State of Ill., Springfield, 1983—; instr. Lincoln Land Community Coll., Springfield, 1988. Trustee Springfield Pk. Dist., 1985-89. Mem. Nat. Assn. Securities Dealers, Inc. (arbitrator 1996—), Comml. Law League Am., Ill. State Bar Assn., Colo. Bar Assn., Attys. Title Guaranty Fund, Inc., Phi Beta Kappa. Roman Catholic. Office: 1129 S 7th St Springfield IL 62703-2418

REED, ROLF KÅRE, physiology educator; b. Bergen, Norway, June 19, 1953; s. Arne and Oddny (Rygg) R.; m. Eva Skudal. MD, U. Bergen, Norway, 1979, U. Bergen, 1982. Assoc. prof. dept. physiology U. Bergen, 1979-90, prof. dept. physiology, 1991—, dep. dean med. faculty, 1993-98, dean med. faculty, 1999—; adj. prof. dept. chem. engring. U. B.C., Vancouver, Can., 1992—. Editor: Interstitium, Connective Tissue and Lymphatics, 1995, Connective Tissue Biology Integration and Reductionism, 1999; contbr. articles to profl. jours. Recipient Anders Jahre's award U. Oslo, 1993. Mem. Am. Physiol. Soc., Microcirculatory Soc., Scandinavian Physiol. Soc. Office: U Bergen Dept Physiology, Årstadveien 19, 5009 Bergen Norway

REED, RONALD KEITH, oceanographer, researcher; b. Mountain Top, Ark., May 6, 1932; s. Thomas Vernon and Bessie Thelma Reed; m. Annemarie Hills, Oct. 13, 1965 (div. May 1990); stepchildren: Christopher M. Hills, Mark S. Hills. BS, Ark. Poly. Coll., 1958; MS, Oreg. State U., 1973. Oceanographer Coast & Geodetic Survey, Washington, 1958-63, Seattle, 1963-70; oceanographer NOAA, Seattle, 1970—. Contbr. articles to profl. jours. With U.S. Army, 1954-56. Recipient Bronze medal U.S. Dept. Commerce, 1997. Mem. Am. Geophys. Union. Avocations: song writing, singing, photography. Home: 12417 NE 129th Ct # E14 Kirkland WA 98034-7437 Office: NOAA Pacific Marine Environ Lab 7600 Sand Point Way NE Seattle WA 98115-6349

REED, STANLEY FOSTER, editor, author, publisher, lecturer; b. Bogota, N.J., Sept. 28, 1917; s. Morton H. and Beryl (Turner) R.; m. Stella Swingle, Sept. 28, 1940 (div. 1978); children: Nancie, Beryl Ann, Alexandra; m. Shirley Weihman, Sept. 28, 1985 (dec. Feb. 1988); m. Catherine Case Commander, Dec. 16, 1989 (div. 1991). Student, George Washington U., 1939-40, Johns Hopkins, 1940-41; MBA, Loyola U., Md., 1981. Registered profl. engr., D.C. With Bethlehem Steel Corp., Balt., 1940-41; cons. engr., 1942-44; founder, pres. Reed Research, Inc., Washington, 1945-62; pres. Reed Research Inst. Creative Studies, from 1951; founder, chmn. LogEtronics, Inc., 1955; founder, pres., chmn. Tech. Audit Corp., 1962; assoc. Mgmt. Analysis Corp., 1978-81; sr. cons. Hay Assocs., Phila., 1980-83; entrepreneur-in-residence Coll. Charleston, S.C.; editor, CEO Merger Control.Com, Inc.; co-chmn. semi-ann. Merger Week Northwestern U.; lectr. numerous U.S. and fgn. groups and instns. including Union Theol. Sem., U. Pa., Pa. State U., U. Colo., Georgetown U., Rensselaer Poly. Inst., Am. U., Claremont Coll., So. Meth. U., Pace U., Wayne State U., U. Oreg., U. Conn., St. John's U., Pepperdine U., Loyola Coll. of Md., San Francisco State U., U. Pitts., U. R.I., Marquette U., Vanderbilt U., Boston U., U. Cin., Gustavus Adolphus Coll., U. Mo., Mich. State U., Lehigh U., Calif. Inst. Tech., Denver U., George Washington U., Elmhurst Coll.; vis. fellow Wilton Pk. Conf., Eng., 1968. Author: The Art of M&A: A Merger/Aquisition/Buyout Guide, 1989, 3d edit., 1999, The Toxic Executive, 1993; founder, editor, pub.: Mergers and Acqusitions mag., 1965—, Dirs. and Bds. mag., 1976—; founder, editor, pub.: Campaigns and Elections mag., 1980; founder, pub. Export Today mag., 1985; contbr. articles to leading jours., chpts. to books; patentee. Bd. dirs. Nat. Patent Coun., 1970—; founder, chmn. ann Merger Week, Washington, 1973-77, Northwestern U., 1977-87; entrepreneur-in-residence, mem. adv. bd. Tate Ctr. Entrepreneurship, Coll. Charleston, S.C.; CEO Merger Ctrl., Inc. Mem. Soc. Naval Architects and Marine Engrs. (life), Am. Econ. Assn., Dictionary Soc. of N.Am., La Confriedes Chevaliers du Tastevin (comdr., chef de protocol), N.Y. Yacht Club. E-mail: reeds@cofc.edu. Home: 330 Concord St Apt 18G Charleston SC 29401-1511

REED, TIMOTHY MICHAEL, conservationist; b. Boxmoor, Herts, U.K., Aug. 30, 1954; s. Frank E.E. and Barbara J. Reed; m. Felicity Jane Wright, Sept. 5, 1981; children: Naomi, William. BA, Cambridge U., 1977, MA, 1980; DPhil, Oxford U., 1981. Leader upland survey, res. strategy adviser NCC, Peterborough, U.K., 1981-91; head monitoring and stds. NCC, Peterborough, 1991-98; dir. EcoText Environ. Consultancy, 1999—; U.K. govt. rsch. fellow in N.Am., 1991. Co-author: (with D.A. Stroud, M.W. Pienkowsa, R. Lindsay) Birds, Bogs and Forestry, 1987, (with F.J. Wright) Site Management Plans for Nature Conservation, 1985, (with T. Lawson) Nature Reserves-Who Needs Them, 1996; contbr. articles to profl. jours. Mem. British Ornithologists Union. Avocations: antiques, watercolours, wood carving. E-mail: tim.reed@ukgateway.net. Home and Office: Highfield Fenstanton Rd, Hilton, Cambridgeshire PE18 9JA, United Kingdom

REED, WILLIAM GERALD, consulting firm executive; b. Abington Twp, Pa., Feb. 25, 1941; s. Frank Hibbs and Evelyn Hower; m. Joan Derby, Jul. 16, 1966; children: Kris, Michael. BSME, Pa. State Univ., 1963, MSME, 1964. Profl. engr. Supr. United Tech., Windsor Locks, Conn., 1964-70; gen. mgr. Gen. Elec. Co., Schenectady, N.Y., 1970-85; sr. v.p., gen. mgr. Impell Corp., Berkeley, Calif., 1985; pres. Reed Ventures, Inc., Danville, Calif., 1985—; dir. Barrier Systems, Inc., Carson City, Nev., 1986—; dir. Reed Ventures, Inc. Danville, Calif., 1985—, Thermal Technologies, Inc., Cambridge, Mass., 1986—. Inventor in field. Recipient Spl. CEO award Gen. Elec. Co., 1984. Avocations: basketball, gardening, photography. Office: Reed Ventures Inc 935 Blemer Rd Danville CA 94526-1501

REEDER, CLINTON BRUCE, economist, public policy consultant, farmer; b. Pendleton, Oreg., Apr. 22, 1939; s. Howard O. and Rachel B. (Porter) R.; m. Karen J. Durham, June 19, 1960; childre: Jeffrey T., Lori J., Paul D. BS, Oreg. State U., 1961, MS, 1963; PhD, Purdue U., 1966; postgrad., U. Oreg. Instr. agrl. econs. Purdue U., West Lafayette, 1963-66; contract mgmt. trainer Nat. Food Mfg. Corp., 1972-78; farmer Pendleton, Oreg., 1978—; mgmt. cons., 1968-80; mktg. economist, bus. mgmt. specialist Dept. Agrl., Econs. & Extension Svc, Oreg. State U., Corvallis, 1966-78; econ. & pub. policy cons. Clinton B. Reeder & Assocs., 1968—; dir. Northwest Wheat Policy Project, 1992—, WestFork Natural Resources Rsch. Ctr., 1995—. Recipient Disting. Svc. award Oreg. Wheat Growers League, 1998, County Points of Light award Nat. Assn. Counties, 1992, Voice of Industry award, 1989, OFS Unity award, 1988; inducted into Hall of Fame, Coll. Agr., Oreg. State U., 1998. Republican. Avocations: reading, public service, writing, research. Home and office: 47647 Reeder Rd Pendleton OR 97801-9226

REEDER, F. ROBERT, lawyer; b. Brigham City, Utah, Jan. 23, 1943; s. Frank O. and Helen H. (Heninger) R.; m. Joannie Anderson, May 4, 1974; children: David, Kristina, Adam. JD, U. Utah, 1967. Bar: Utah 1967, U.S. Ct. Appeals (1oth cir.) 1967, U.S. Ct. Appeals (D.C. and 5th cirs.) 1979, U.S. Ct. Mil. Appeals 1968, U.S. Supreme Ct. 1972. Shareholder Parsons, Behle & Latimer, Salt Lake City, 1968—. Bd. dirs. Holy Cross Found., 1981-90, chmn., 1987-90; bd. dirs. Holy Cross Hosp., 1990-93, treas., 1986-87, vice chmn., 1987-93; bd. dirs. Holy Cross Health Svcs. Utah, 1993-94, treas., 1993-94; bd. dirs. Sale Lake Regional Med. Ctr., 1995—, vice chmn., 1995-2000, chmn., 2000—; trustee Univ. Hosp. Found.; hon. col. Sale Lake City Police, Salt Lake County Sheriff. Served with USAF, 1967-73. Mem. ABA, Utah State Bar, Salt Lake County Bar (ethics adv. com. 1989-94), Cottonwood Country Club (bd. dirs. 1978-82, 83-86, pres. 1981-82), Rotary. Office: Parsons Behle & Latimer PO Box 45898 Salt Lake City UT 84145-0898

REEDER, MICHAEL S., consulting firm executive. BSBA, U. Fla., 1972; MBA, U. Tampa (Fla.), 1977. Mgr., employment svcs. Fla. Power Corp.; v.p. (exec. search div.) MSL Internat. Cons., Ltd., 1973-82; sr. ptnr. Lamalaie Amrop Internat., Atlanta, 1983-96; pres. Reeder & Assoc. Ltd., Roswell, 1996—. Mem. Assn. of Exec. Search Cons. Office: 1095 Old Roswell Rd Ste F Roswell GA 30076-1665

REEDY, HARRY LEE, financial services executive; b. Lebanon, Pa., Dec. 25, 1945; s. Harry Lee and Charlotte (Weedmark) R.; m. Linda Bartley, Nov. 7, 1970; children: Jennifer Beth, Sara Emily. BS in Indsl Engring., Pa. State U., 1967; MBA, U. Conn., 1977. Mgmt. asst. Bell Telephone Pa., Phila., 1967-70; field engring. rep. Travelers Cos., Hartford, Conn., 1971-72, ops. analyst, 1972-76, supervising ops. analyst, 1976-79, sr. mgmt. cons., 1979-83, adminstr. consumer affairs, 1983-85, asst. dir. consumer affairs, 1985-90; dir. corp. customer svc. John Hancock Fin. Svcs., Boston, 1990-91, dir. Ctr. for Quality, 1991-96; asst. v.p. quality State St. Corp., North Quincy, Mass., 1997-98; v.p., dir. quality State St. Corp., North Quincy, 1998—; mem. consumer affairs com. Ins. Info. Inst., N.Y.C., 1988-90. Contbr. articles to trade publs. Participant Leadership Greater Hartford, 1985; bd. dirs., treas. Woodland Manor Condominium Assn., Manchester, Conn., 1986-87; bd. examiners Malcolm Baldridge Nat. Quality award, 1995-2000, sr. examiner, 1997-2000; sr. examiner Mass. State Quality award, 1995-99, judge, 1999. With U.S. Army, 1968-70. Fellow Ins. Consumer Affairs Exch. (treas. 1985-87, v.p. 1987-88, pres. 1988-90), Soc. Consumer Affairs Profls. (v.p. New Eng. chpt. 1991-92); mem. Am. Coun. Life Ins. (consumer affairs com. 1987), Am. Soc. Quality Control, Am. productivity & Quality Ctr., Internat. Benchmarking Clearing House, Strategic Planning Inst., Mass. Coun. Quality (bd. dirs. 1998—, treas. exec. com. 1999—), Benchmarking Coun., Assn. Quality and Participation, Beta Gamma Sigma. Democrat. Avocations: photography, racquetball, swimming, reading. Home: 3 Auburn Ct # 2 Brookline MA 02446-6302

REEK, JAN VAN, epidemiologist, researcher; b. Oostvoorne, The Netherlands, July 10, 1945; s. Jacob and Inge (van der Meer) R. Drs., U. Leiden, 1969. Rschr. Maastricht U., The Netherlands, 1975-92, SORD, The Netherlands, 1992—. Author: The Ultramodern Endgame Study, 1989, Strategy in Chess, 1997; contbr. articles to profl. jours. Home: De Erk 8, 626g BY Margraten The Netherlands Office: SORD, PO Box 751, 6200 AT Maastricht The Netherlands

REEMS, ERNESTINE C., minister; b. Oklamugee, Okla., July 7; d. Elmer E. and Matilda Cleveland; m. Paul E. Reems, June 14; children: Brandon, Brian. Hon. degree, Trinity Coll. Founder, evangelist Ernestine Reems Ministries, Oakland, Calif.; founder, sr. pastor Ctr. of Hope Cmty. Ch., Oakland; founder Ernestine C. Reems Internat. Ministries, Oakland; CEO Lee Cleveland Manor, Hope Housing Devel., Oakland, Lee Reems Garden Hope Housing Devel., Oakland, Matilda Cleveland Hope Housing Devel. Transitional Housing, Oakland. Author: In the Storm, 1994; co-author: Fine Gold, 1999. Trustee Oral Roberts U., Tulsa. Named one of 15 Outstanding Women Preachers, Ebony mag., 1990's. Avocations: travel, reading, sports, cruises, social gatherings. Office: Ctr of Hope Cmty Ch 8411 Macarthur Blvd Oakland CA 94605-3553

REENPÄÄ, OLLI, graphic arts company executive; b. Helsinki, Mar. 25, 1934; s. Kari and Mertsi (von Freyman) R.; m. Märta Nordström; children: Antti, Anna, Eva, Elina. Grad., Helsinki U. Tech., 1960. Operating engr. Kustannusosakeyhtio Otava, Helsinki, 1962-64; dir. rotogravure and planographic plants Kustannusosalecyhtiö Otava, Helsinki, 1964-66; exec. v.p., bd. dirs. Kustannusosalecyhtiö Otava, Helsinki, 1966-79; exec. pres. Otava Pub. Co. Ltd., Helsinki, 1979-2000; pres., CEO Otava Books and Mags Group Ltd., 2000—; chmn. bd. dirs. United Mags. Mem. Cen. Assn. Graphic Arts Industries (chmn. 1973-93). Home: Hietalahdenranta 17 A 11, FIN00180 Helsinki Finland Office: Otava Books & Mags Group, Uudenmaankatu 8-12, FIN00120 Helsinki Finland

REENTS, LARRY G., secondary education educator; b. Peru, Ill., Nov. 7, 1948; s. Lawrence H. and Mildred M. BA, Bradley U., 1970, MA, 1973. Cert. tchr. lang. arts, secondary edn., Ill. Tchr. Peoria (Ill.) Pub. Schs., 1971—. Pres. Peoria Edn. Assn., 1974-80, exec. bd. 1974-80; bd. dirs. Universalist Unitarian Ch., Peoria. With U.S. Army, 1970-76. Democrat. Unitarian. Avocations: travel, art, antiques, literature, hist. restoration.

REES, ALUN ROCYN, crop physiologist, editor; b. Llangadog, Wales, Nov. 24, 1932; s. Joseph and Gwen (Davies) R.; m. Maureen Jill Foster, Dec. 29, 1954; children: David Rocyn, Sian Jill. BSc, U. Swansea, 1953; DSc, U. Wales, 1975. Plant physiologist West African Inst. for Oil Palm Rsch., Nigeria, 1955-62; flower bulb physiologist Glasshouse Crops Rsch. Inst., Eng., 1962-78, head hort. dept., 1978-80, head crop sci. divsn., 1980-87; editor Jour. Hort. Sci., Eng., 1987—; cons. OECD, European Union, 1970—; govt. cons. U.K. Ministries, 1970—; comml. cons., 1970—. Author: The Growth of Bulbs, 1972, Ornamental Bulbs, Corms and Tubers, 1992; editor: Crop Processes in Controlled Environments, 1972; contbr. more than 150 articles to profl. jours. Fellow Inst. Biology. Avocations: salmon fishing, gardening, writing. Home: Tithe Barn, 32 The Street Rustington, West Sussex BN16 3NX, England

REES, BRIAN, headmaster; b. Sydney, Australia, Aug. 20, 1929; s. Frederick Thomas and Anne (Keedy) R.; m. Julia Birley, Dec. 17, 1959 (dec. Dec. 1978); children: Robert, Jessica, Philip, Natalia, Camilla; m. Juliet Mary Akehurst, Jan. 3, 1987. BA, Trinity Coll., 1952, MA, 1958. Asst. master Eton Coll., Windsor, Eng., 1952-63, housemaster, 1963-65; headmaster Merchant Taylors' Sch., Northwood, Eng., 1965-73, Charterhouse, Surrey, Eng., 1973-81, Rugby, 1981-84. Author: (biography) A Musical Peacemaker, 1987, History and Idealism, 1990. Rsch. asst. House of Commons, Westminster, England, 1991, Camille Saint-Saens: A Life, 1999. Home: 52 Spring Lane Flore, Northampton NN7 4LS, England

REES, DAVID ANDREW SESSLER, mechanical engineer, educator; b. Carmarthen, Wales, Aug. 26, 1959; s. Dudley Sessle and Mary Elizabeth Margaret (John) R.; m. Sian Alison Maggs, Aug. 8, 1981; children: Matthew John Christopher, Aled Jonathan. Diploma, Trinity Coll. Music, London, 1977; BSc, Imperial Coll., London, 1980, Bristol (Eng.) U., 1985. Engr. British Aerospace, Filton, Bristol, 1980-82; rsch. asst. Bristol U., 1985-87; lectr. Exeter (Eng.) U., 1987-90, U. Bath, Eng., 1990—; asst. editor Jour. Porous Media, 1997—. Contbr. articles to profl. jours. Avocations: violin, cycling. Home: Whitefield House, 43/45 Stanley Rd, Warmley BS15 4NX, England Office: Dept Mech Engring U Bath, Claverton Down, Bath BA2 7AY, England

REES, DAVID ROY, aerospace company executive; b. Penclawdd, Wales, U.K., Oct. 13, 1933; arrived in Australia, 1967; s. John Norcliffe and Margaret Elveira (Jones) R.; m. Sandra Muriel Hansen, Feb. 10, 1968; children: Catharine Lynden, Samuel David Rothwell. BS, U. London, 1955, U. Cambridge, Eng., 1956. Tech. officer B.O.A.C. Airline, Eng., 1958-59; design engr. Hawker Aircraft Ltd., Eng., 1959-62; project design leader Hawker Siddeley Aviation Ltd., Eng., 1962-67; sr. aerodynamicist Commonwealth Aircraft Corp. Ltd., Australia, 1967-72, project mgr., 1972-75, mgr. planning and prodn. control, 1975-78, mktg. exec., 1978-88; planning exec. Ansett Airlines of Australia, Melbourne, 1988-98; engring. exec. Ansett Australia Airlines, 1998—, general mgr. engring. ops., 1998—. Co-author: The Future of Tactical Airspace in the Defense of Australia, 1976. With Royal Air Force, 1956-58. Royal MIT bus. adminstrn. fellow, Melbourne, 1976; MIT sr. fellow, Boston, 1983. Fellow Royal Aero. Soc. (pres. Australian div. 1985-87), Instn. Engrs. Australia; mem. AIAA, Metal Trades Industry Assn. (pres. export group 1981-86), Australian Air Transport Assn. (rep. 1990-99), Cambridge Soc. Anglican. Clubs: Naval and Mil. (Melbourne). Avocations: theatre, music, skiing, tennis. Home: 80 Cole St, Brighton VIC 3186, Australia Office: Ansett Australia Bldg 14, Melbourne Airport, Victoria 3045, Australia

REES, GARETH JOHN GLYN, oncologist; b. London, June 27, 1949. M.B., B.Ch., Welsh Nat. Sch. Medicine, Cardiff, Wales, 1972. Sr. registrar Weston Park Hosp., Sheffield, Eng., 1980-83; cons. Bristol Haematology & Oncology Centre, Eng., 1983—; clin. dir. Bristol Oncology Centre, Eng., 2000—. Contbr. articles on chemotherapy and radiotherapy of cancer to med jours. Fellow Royal Soc. Medicine, Royal Coll. Radiologists (mem. coun. 1998—), Royal Coll. Physicians. Home: 46 Clifton Park Rd., Bristol BS8 3 HN, England Office: Bristol Haematology & Oncology Centre, Horfield Rd, Bristol BS2 8ED, England

REES, GARETH MERVYN, cardiac surgeon consultant; b. Llangadog, Dyfed, Wales, Sept. 30, 1935; s. Joseph and Gwen (Davies) Rees; m. Lesley Howard Davis-Dawson, Dec. 21, 1968. MB BS, St. Mary's Hosp. Med. Sch., London, 1960; Master of Surgery, London U., 1973. Cons. in charge dept. cardiothoracic surgery St. Bartholomew's Hosp., London, 1984—, sr. surgeons, 1995—; cons. cardiac surgery Wellington Hosp., London, 1984—, The Heart Hosp., London, 1995—. Contbr. articles to profl. jours. Fellow Royal Coll. Surgeons Eng., Royal Coll. Physicians London; mem. Garrick Vlub (London). Avocations: skiing, fishing, rugby, football. Home: 50 Wimpole St, London W1M 7DG, England

REES, JOHN ELVAN, pharmaceutical consultant, researcher, educator; b. Cheltenham, Eng., Feb. 8, 1942; s. William Talvan and Elvie May (Davies) R.; m. Hannah Romary Forbes, June 24, 1967; children: William Tudor, Julia Bronwen. BPharm with honors, U. London, 1963, PhD, 1967. Head rsch. unit Merck Frosst Labs., Montreal, Que., Can., 1967-69; rsch. group leader Sandoz AG, Basle, Switzerland, 1969-73; sr. lectr. U. Aston, Birmingham, Eng., 1973-78; mgr. internat. devel. ctr. Abbott Labs., Queenborough, Eng., 1978-81; prof. pharmaceutics U. Bath, Eng., 1981-91, prof. pharmacy practice, 1991-97; head sch. pharmacy and pharmacology U. Bath, Eng., 1984-87; mem. chemistry, pharmacy and standards subcom. Com. on Safety of Medicines, 1990-93; mem. standing panel of experts in pharmaceutical engring. sci., U. London, 1984-93; cons. U.K. and overseas, 1973-78, 81—; external examiner higher edn., U.K., Kenya, Singapore, West Indies, The Netherlands, Sweden, Switzerland, Australia, 1975—. Contbr articles to sci. and profl. jours. Mem. Cmty. Supprt Group Bath Inst. Rheumatic Diseases, 1988-90, District Health Authority, Swindon, Eng., 1982-84; mem. Bathampton Scout Group exec. com., 1985—, chmn., 1997—. Recipient Thanks badge The Scout Assn., 1994, sci. award Brit. Pharm. Conf., 1975. Fellow Royal Pharmaceutical Soc. Gt. Britain; mem. Assn. Univ. Tchrs., Liveryman of Worshipful Soc. Apothecaries of London, Freeman of City of London. Avocations: music, photography, skiing, water sports, travel.

REES, PETER JOHN, medical educator, consultant; b. Cardiff, Wales, Mar. 2, 1949; s. Joseph Thomas and Doris Mary (Williams) R.; m. Helen Mary Heath, Mar. 31, 1973; children: Sarah Jane, Thomas William. MA, Cambridge U., U.K., 1973, MB BChir, 1973, MD, 1982. Lectr. Guys Hosp., U.K., 1979-83, cons. physician, 1983—; sr. lectr. medicine UMDS, London, 1983—, asst. clin. dean, 1993—; group clin. dir. Guys & St. Thomas Hosp., 1995—; non-exec. dir. Lewisham Hosp., London, 1995—, Mildmay Mission Hosp., London, 1992—. Author: (with D. Kanabar) ABC of Asthma, 4th edit., 1995, (with TJH Clark) Practical Management of Asthma, 4th edit., 1999, (with G.M. Cochrane, W. Jackson) Asthma: Current Perspectives, 1995; editor: (with D.G. Williams) Principles of Clinical Medicine, 1995. Fellow Royal Coll. Physicians. Avocations: theater, cricket, squash. Office: Guys Hosp, St Thomas St, London SE1 9RT, England

REES, PETRA, management consultant; b. Traben-Trarbach, Germany, Dec. 8, 1966; d. Heinz and Helga Rees; m. Thomas Schmitt; July 1, 1995. BA in Internat. Bus., Middlesex Bus. Sch., London, 1989; MBA, Harvard U., 1993. CPA. Mgmt. cons. Boston Consulting Group, Duesseldorf, Germany, 1989-91, McKinsey & Co., Atlanta, 1993-95; dir. investment rsch. Volume Investor, Atlanta, 1996-97; mgmt. cons. Fountainhead Consulting, Memphis, 1999—. Baker scholar Harvard Bus. Sch., 1993. Avocations: tennis, running. E-mail: prees1@midsouth.rr.com. Office: Fountainhead Consulting 2844 Waterleaf Dr Germantown TN 38138-7351

REESE, CLAUDIA, artist; b. Des Moines, May 1, 1949; d. William Lewis and Louise (Weeks) R.; m. Phil Martin, 1988; 1 child, Taylor. Student, SUNY, Albany, summer 1967, 68, RIT, summer 1969; BA, Conn. Coll., 1971; MFA, Ind. U., 1974. Vis. artist Iowa Wesleyan Coll., Mt. Plesant, 1974-75, U. No. Colo., Greeley, 1976-77, The Sch. of the Art Inst. of Chgo., 1980, Purdue U., West Lafayette, Ind., 1980-81, La. State U., Baton Rouge, 1981, Brookhaven Coll., Dallas, 1990, N.Mex. State U., Las Cruces, 1992; dir., designer Cera-Mix Studio, Austin, Tex., 1982—. Subject of various articles in profl.. jours.; one woman shows include Purdue U., West Lafayette, Ind., 1981, Objects Gallery, San Antonio, 1982, Willingheart Gallery, Austin, Tex., 1984, R.S. Levy Gallery, Austin, 1987, S.W. Craft Ctr., San Antonio, 1988, Everson Mus., Syracuse, N.Y., 1988, Tokyo, 1989, 90, 91, Lyons-Matrix Gallery, Austin, 1997; exhibited in group shows Edits Ltd., Indpls., 1981, Berkeley-Lainson Gallery, Denver, 1981, Renwick Gallery, Smithsonian Instn., Washington, 1981, Wichita Art Mus., Kans., 1981, St. Mary's Coll., South Bend, Ind., 1981, Herron Sch. Art, Indpls., 1981, Craftsman's Gallery, Scarsdale, N.Y., 1982, ACVAA Juried Show, Austin, 1982, Elements Gallery, N.Y.C., 1982, Greenwich, Conn., 1983, Mattingly Baker Gallery, Dallas, 1983, Adesso, Chgo., 1983, Coll. Mainland, Tex. City, 1983, S.W. Tex. State U., 1983, New Stone Age Gallery, 1984, Willingheart Gallery, 1984, Maple Hill Gallery, Portland, Maine, 1984, Tex. Christian U., Ft. Worth, 1984, Laguna Gloria Art Mus., Austin, 1985, Carol Hooberman Gallery, Birmingham, Mich., 1985, John Michael Kohler Arts Ctr., Sheboygan, Wis., Elizabeth Fortner Gallery, Santa Barbara, Calif., 1985, 86, Kimbell Art Mus., Ft. Worth, 1986, Contemporary Arts Ctr., New Orleans, 1986, Aeteilers D'Art, Paris, 1986, Mendocino (Calif.) Arts Ctr., 1986, Kimbell Art Mus., Ft. Worth, 1986, N.Mex. State U., Carlsbad, 1987, Aspen (Colo.) Art Mus., 1987, Longview (Tex.) Mus. Invitational, 1988, North Hampton, Mass., 1988, Huntington Gallery at U. Tex., Austin, 1989, S.W. Univ. in Georgetown, 1989, Nat. Mus. Women in the Arts, Washington, 1989, Nat. Mus. Ceramic Art, Balt., 1990, La. State U., Baton Rouge, 1990, Laguna Gloria Art Mus., Austin, 1990, 91, Twist Gallery, Portland, Oreg.,

1991, Virginia Breier gallery, San Francisco, 1991, Art Options, Santa Monica, Calif., 1991, Virginia Brier Gallery, San Francisco, 1991, Twist Gallery, Portland, Oreg., 1991, U. Tex., El Paso, 1992, Renwick Gallery, 1992, Mindscape Gallery, Evanston, Ill., 1992, Pittsburg Ctr. for the Arts, 1992, IO Gallery, New Orleans, 1993, Ruskin Place, Seaside, Fla., 1993, Martin Rathburn Gallery, San Antonio, 1995, Farmington Valley Art Ctr., Conn., 1996, Lyons-Matrix Gallery, 1997, Arlington Mus. Art, 1998, Irving Arts Ctr., Tex., 1998, U. Tex. San Antonio, 1999, San Antonio Mus. Art, 2000, numerous others; represented in permanent collections The Crescent Collection, Dallas, June Mattingly, Dallas, Bill Bostleman, Ft. Worth, Laurence Miller, Austin, Hadley Sleight, Austin, Marilyn Maxwell, Ft. Worth, Archer Huntington Mus. (now Blanton Mus. of Fine Art); commissioned work displayed at Austin Bergstrom Internat. Airport, S.E. Comm. Linr., Westbank Libr., St. Francis Hosp. for Chldrn., Los Angeles, Ch. of Conscious Harmony, Austin, Tex. Mem. Tex. Fine Arts Assn., Women and Their Work, Austin Visual Artists Assn. Democrat. Avocations: snow skiing, sailing, windsurfing, gardening. E-mail: ceramix@io.com. Fax: 512-263-5019. Office: Cera-Mix Studio 709 N Tumbleweed Trl Austin TX 78733-3240

REESE, COLIN BERNARD, chemistry educator; b. Plymouth, Eng., July 29, 1930; s. Joseph and Emily R.; m. Susanne Bird, June 29, 1968; children: Lucy, William Thomas. BA, Cambridge (Eng.) U., 1953, PhD, 1956, MA, 1957, ScD, 1972. Fellow Clare Coll., Cambridge, 1956-73; rsch. fellow Harvard U., Cambridge, Mass., 1957-58; demonstrator in chemistry Cambridge U., 1959-63, asst. dir. rsch., 1963-64, lectr., 1964-73; Daniell prof. chemistry King's Coll. London, 1973-98, prof. organic chemistry, 1999—. Contbr. articles to profl. jours. Fellow King's Coll., 1989. Fellow Royal Soc. (London), Royal Soc. Chemistry; mem. Am. Chem. Soc. Office: King's Coll London, London WC2R 2LS, England

REESE, DAVID JEN, stockbroker; b. Lahore, Pakistan, May 5, 1963; came to U.S., 1967; s. David Gene and Lydia Chuan (Wu) R.; m. Rochelle Anne Reed. BS in Math., Johns Hopkins U., 1988. Stockbroker F.N. Wolf & Co., Inc., Alexandria, Va., 1988-92, Prudential Securities, Inc., Vienna, Va., 1992-93, Consolidated Investments, Inc., Honolulu, 1994-95; v.p. Surf TV, Inc., Haleiwa, Hawaii, 1994-95; co-owner Tiare Internat., Inc., Sydney, Australia, 1994-95; fin. cons. Merrill Lynch, Honolulu, 1995-97, Merrill Lynch, Brisbane, Australia, 1997—. Home: 52 Brindisi Ave, Surfers Paradise QLD 4217, Australia Office: Merrill Lynch, 14/3482 Main Beach Parade, Main Beach QLD 4217, Australia

REESE, MARTHA GRACE, minister, lawyer; b. Newark, Ohio, Feb. 27, 1953; d. John Gilbert and Louella Catherine (Hodges) R.; 1 child, Elizabeth Lang Harman. BA with high distinction, DePauw U., 1975; JD magna cum laude, Ind. U., 1980; MDiv magna cum laude, Christian Theol. Sem., 1989. Bar: Ind. 1980, U.S. Dist. Ct. (so. dist.) Ind. 1980, U.S. Ct. Appeals (7th cir.) 1981; ordained to ministry Christian Ch. (Disciples of Christ), 1989. Law clk. U.S. Dist. Ct. (so. dist.) Ind., 1980-82; assoc. Baker & Daniels, Indpls., 1982-83; ptnr. Wilson, Hutchens & Reese, Greencastle, Ind., 1984-86; interim assoc. regional min. The Christian Ch. in Ind. (Disciples of Christ), 1988-89; sr. min. Carmel (Ind.) Christian Ch. (Disciples of Christ), 1989-96; dir. The Bethany Project of the Christian Chs., 1996—; cons. Lilly Endowment, Inc., 1989, 90. Steering com. Ind. Leadership Celebration, 1983-98; trustee Christian Theol. Sem., 1995-99. Mem. Phi Beta Kappa, Theta Phi. Home: 3942 N Delaware St Indianapolis IN 46205-2650

REESE, WILLIAM ALBERT, III, psychologist, clinical neuropsychologist; b. Tabor, Iowa, Nov. 23, 1932; s. William Albert and Mary-Evelyn Hope (Lundeen) R.; m. Barbara Diane Windermere, Dec. 22, 1954 (dec. Jan. 1995); children: Judy, Diane William IV, Sandra-Siobhan, Debra-Anne, Robert-Gregory, Barbara-Jaoanne; m. Ruth Alice Moller, Sept 12, 1996. BA, U. Washington Reed Coll., 1955; M.Ed., U. Ariz., 1964, PhD, 1981; postgrad., Fielding Inst. Clin. Neuropsyc, 1999. Diplomate Am. Bd. Christian Psychology, Am. Bd. Forensic Psychologists; cert. in clin. neuropsychology. Clin. psychology cons. Nogales Pub. Schs., Nogales-Tucson, Ariz., 1971-79; clin. psychologist Astra-Found., N.Y.C., 1979-86, chief psychology svc., neuropsychiatry, 1980-89; chief psychologist Family Support Ctr. Community-Family Exception Mem. Svcs., Sonoita, Ariz., 1986-89, Psychol. Svc. Ctr., Mount Tabor, Iowa, 1989-95, Calif. Ctr. Health and Wellness, 1995—; dir. religious Marriage and Family Life Wilderness Ctr., Berchtesgaden, W. Ger., lsummer, 1981-82; exec. sec. Astra Ednl. Found, 1975-79, bd. dirs, 1979—, EEO officer, 1978—. Author: Developing a Scale of Human Values for Adults of Diverse Cultural Backgrounds, 1981, rev. edit., 1988. Served with USAF, 1967-71, Vietnam. Decorated Bronze Star. Fellow in cons. psychology and holistic medicine Clin. Services Found., Ariz., 1979—. Fellow Am. Psychol. Soc., Am. Coll. Forensic Examiners, Clin. Neuropsychiatry and Neuropsychology, 1998; mem. APA, ACA, Internat. Neuropsychol. Assn., Calif. Psychol. Assn., Iowa Psychol. Assn., K.C., Los Padres Wilderness Ctr., Outdoor Club, Sierra Club, Skyline Estates Golf and Country Club (Tucson). Office: Astra WorldMedicine.com Integrated Med Ctr Wellness Box 969 Carmel Valley CA 93924

REEVE, JONATHAN, physician, researcher; b. Pembury, Eng., Jan. 5, 1943; s. Ernest Basil and Mary Sheila (Williams) R.; m. Stella Caroline Russell; children: Alex, Lucy, James, Josie, Katie. MA, BM, BCh, Oxford (Eng.) U., 1968, DM, 1976, DSc, 1984. Clin. scientist MRC Clin. Rsch. Ctr., Harrow, Eng., 1978-92; clin. scientist dept. medicine U. Cambridge (Eng.), 1993—; project leader prospective osteoporosis study European Union, 1993—. Editor: Vertebral Osteoporosis, 1994; contbr. articles to profl. jours. Recipient Prix André Lichtwitz INSERM, Paris, 1984; European Union concerted action grantee, 1993-96, Med. Rsch. Coun. program grantee, 1994—. Fellow Royal Coll. Physicians; mem. Assn. Physicians of Gt. Britain and Ireland, Bone & Tooth Soc. (hon. sec. 1991-95). Mem. Ch. of Eng. Avocations: family activities, antique automobiles, classical music, sailing. Office: Dept Medicine Box 157, Addenbrookes Hosp Hills Rd, Cambridge CB2 2QQ, England

REEVE, LAWRENCE JOHN, historian, educator; b. Melbourne, Victoria, Australia, Mar. 20, 1956; s. James Lawrence and Roma Yvette (Herm) R.; m. Barbara Hall Christen, July 25, 1981; 1 child, Edward. BA, U. Melbourne (Australia), 1978, MA, 1980; PhD, Cambridge (Eng.) U., 1984. Supr. in history Clare Coll., Cambridge, 1982-83; Rothmans rsch. fellow U. Melbourne, 1984-86; postdoctoral rsch. fellow U. Otago (New Zealand), 1986; rsch. fellow U. Tasmania (Australia), 1986-87, 88; lectr. in history Yale U., 1987-88, U. Hong Kong, 1988-93; lectr., sr. lectr. in history U. Sydney (Australia), 1993-97; sr. lectr., Osborne fellow naval history U. NSW Australian Def. Force Acad., Canberra, 1997—; vis. fellow Newberry Libr., Chgo., 1987; Fulbright postdoctoral fellow Yale U., 1987-88; vis. fellow Clare Hall Cambridge U., 1996; vis. rsch. fellow Inst. Hist. Rsch. U. London, 1996-99. Author: Charles I and the Road to Personal Rule, 1989; contbr. (book) The Oxford Illustrated History of Tudor and Stuart Britain, 1996; contbr. numerous articles to books and profl. jours. Australian Rsch. Coun. Instnl. grantee, 1995-96, Large grantee, 1996-99. Fellow Royal Hist. Soc.; mem. Internat. Inst. Strategic Studies, Australian and New Zealand Assn. for Medieval and Early Modern Studies, U.S. Naval Inst., Australian Naval Inst., Navy Records Soc., Soc. Nautical Rsch., Am. Hist. Assn., N.Am. Conf. on British Studies. Avocations: reading, music, cricket fan. Office: Sch History U Coll, Australian Def Force Acad, Canberra ACT 2600, Australia

REEVE, THOMAS GILMOUR, physical education educator; b. Memphis, Sept. 23, 1946; s. Paul Goodwin and Dorothy (Bourke) R.; m. Sandra Weidner, Mar. 26, 1992; children: Bourke, Spencer. BS in Phys. Edn., Tex. Tech. U., 1969, MEd, 1972; PhD, Tex. A&M U., 1976. Asst. prof. Auburn (Ala.) U., 1977-82, assoc. prof., 1982-87, prof., 1987-91, asst. v.p. for acad. affairs, 1992-93, alumni prof., 1991-95, prof. phys. edn., 1995-98, W.T. Smith Disting. prof., 1998-99; prof., chair Tex. Tech. U., 1999—; vis. asst. prof. Tex. A&M U., College Station, 1976-77. Co-editor: Stimulus-Response Compatibility, 1990; sect. editor Rsch. Quar. for Exercise and Sport, 1990-92, editor, 1999—; assoc. editor Jour. Sport Behavior, 1983—. Fellow AAHPERD, Rsch. Consortium, Am. Acad. Kinesiology and Phys. Edn.; mem. N.Am. Soc. Psychology of Sport and Phys. Activity (publ. dir. 1985-87, pres. 1991-92). Avocation: masters swimming. Office: Tex Tech U HPER PO Box 43011 Lubbock TX 79409-3011

REEVES, ALISON DAWN, geography educator; b. Bicester, Eng., July 10, 1963; arrived in Scotland, 1991; d. Garvin Trevor and Angela Mary (Belcher) R. BSc with honors, Plymouth (Eng.) U., 1984; PhD, Liverpool (Eng.) U., 1988. Postdoctoral rsch. asst. in hydrology Lancaster (Eng.) U., 1988-91; lectr. Dundee (Scotland) U., 1991—; sec. Women's Environ. Network, Dundee, 1994—, Women's Aquatic Network, 1998—. Office: Dundee U Dept Geography, Perth Rd, Dundee DD1 4HN, Scotland

REEVES, BARBARA, writer, educator; b. Wellington, Tex., Aug. 29, 1931; d. Edward Decatur Reeves and Ruth Caroline Rich; m. Stanley Kolaski, Jan. 15, 1956 (dec. Feb. 1987); children: Anne Marie, Linda Caroline, John Edward. Writing tchr. San Jacinto Coll. Sys., Houston, 1990—; curriculum cons. San Jacinto Coll. South, Houston, 1998-2000; literary cons. and mentor in field. Authro: Georgina's Campaign, 1991, The Dangerous Marquis, 1993, The Much Maligned Lord, 1995, My Buffalo Soldier, 2000. Mem. Romance Writers Am. (founder chpt. 30, chairperson, fundraiser for literacy), Bay Area Writer's League (founder, chairperson). Democrat. Roman Catholic. Avocations: social historian, interior design, family history. E-mail: bkwriter@swbell.net.

REEVES, BILLY DEAN, obstetrics and gynecology educator emeritus; b. Franklin Park, Ill., Jan. 17, 1927; s. Barney William and Martha Dorcus (Benbrook) R.; m. Phyllis Joan Faber, Aug. 25, 1951; children: Philip, Pamela, Tina, Brian, Timothy. BA, Elmhurst (Ill.) Coll., 1953; BS, U. Ill., Chgo., 1958, MD, 1960; post grad., UCLA, N.Mex. State U., 1953-54, 75-76. Diplomate Am. Bd. Ob-Gyn. Intern Evanston (Ill.) Hosp., 1960-61, resident ob-gyn., 1961-64; NIH fellow in reproductive endocrinology Karolinska Hosp. and Inst., Stockholm, 1968-69; pvt. practice Evanston, 1964-71, Las Cruces, N.Mex., 1972-77; from instr. to asst. prof. Dept. Ob-gyn. Northwestern U. Med. Sch., 1964-71; assoc. prof. Dept. Ob-gyn. Rush Med. Coll., Chgo., 1971-72; clin. assoc. in ob-gyn. U. N.Mex. Med. Sch., Albuquerque, 1972-77; clin. assoc. U. Ariz. Sch. Medicine, Tucson, 1975-78; from clin. prof. to prof. emeritus Tex. Tech. Med. Sch., El Paso, 1976-91; exec. dir. Mesilla Valley Hospice, 1997-98. Contbr. 70 articles and chpts. to med., profl. jours., 1958-93. Adv. bd. Associated Home Health Svcs., Inc., Las Cruces; adv. com. N.Mex. State U. Nursing Sch.; community adv. com. Meml. Gen. Hosp., Las Cruces; tech. advisor on health edn. N.Mex. Health Systems Agy.; mem. N.Mex. State U. Task Force 88; bd. dirs. Meml. Med. Ctr, Los Cruces, 1989-91, Parenthood Edn. Assn. of El Paso, Inc., Planned Parenthood of South Ctrl. N.Mex. (chmn. med. adv. com.). With USNR, 1945-46, 82-88, U.S. Army, 1946-47. Recipient Elmhurst Coll. Alumni Merit award, 1990, William W. Fry award for profl. excellence Tex. Tech. U. Sch. Medicine, 1979. Mem. AMA, ACS, AAAS, ACOG, Am. Coll. Physician Execs., Am. Assn. Advancement Humanities, Am. Fertility Soc., Assn. Profs. Ob-Gyn., North Am. Ob-Gyn. Soc., Ctrl. Assn. Ob-Gyn., Chgo. Gyn. Soc., Com. for Philosophy in Medicine, Dona Ana County Med. Soc. (assoc.), El Paso County Med. Soc., El Paso Surg. Soc., Endocrine Soc., Inst. Medicine in Chgo., Hasting Ctr., N.Mex. Med. Soc. (assoc.), N.Mex. Ob-Gyn. Soc., Soc. for Health and Human Values, Tex. Med. Assn., Tex. Assn. Ob-Gyn., U.S.-Mexico Border Health Assn. Home: 1620 Altura Ave Las Cruces NM 88001-1532

REEVES, RONALD VICTOR, construction engineering company executive; b. London, Nov. 18, 1952; s. Ronald Victor and Eileen Ethal (Newell) R.; m. Paula Denise Sharpless, Jan. 31, 1976 (div. July 1980); 1 child, Scott; m. Lynda Leigh Saunders, July 3, 1981; children: Adam Stuart, James Grant. BA, Open U., Eng., 1989; adv. mgmt. degree, Rice U., 1993; MBA, Brunel U., Eng., 1996. Comml. dir. Brown & Root Ltd., London, 1989-96, AMEC Process and Energy Ltd., London, 1996—. Fellow Royal Soc. Arts, Inst. Dirs.; mem. Assn. Cost Engrs., Brit. Inst. Mgmt. Avocations: golf, radio controlled modeling. Office: AMEC Process & Energy Ltd, Golden Ln, London EC14 ORR, England

REEVES, VAN KIRK, lawyer; b. N.Y.C., May 14, 1939; arrived in France, 1967; s. William Harvey and Caroline (Buck) R.; m. Ann Murchison, June 24, 1967; children: Daisy Fiona, Evander James. BA, Harvard U., 1961, JD, 1964. Ptnr. Coudert Frères, Paris, 1973-95, Coudert Bros., N.Y.C., 1973-95, Porter & Reeves, Paris, 1995—; mem. Ctr. du Droit de l'Art, Geneva, 1998—, Mona Bismark Found. Author: Confessions of an Art Lawyer, 1997, The Structure and Financing of Art Transactions, 1994; co-author: (with Dr. J. Boll) Auction Sales and Conditions, 1991. Bd. mem., v.p. Internat. Coun. Muss. Found., Paris, 1972-95; bd. suprs. Am. Tax Inst., London, 1978; bd. mem. Fabergé Arts Found., Washington, 1992. Mem. Inst. Internat. Bus. Law and Practice (assoc. mem.). Avocations: projects for the preservation of cultural heritage, hiking. Home: 8 Cité Nicolas Poussin, 240 Blvd Raspail, 75014 Paris France Office: Porter & Reeves, 5 Rue Cambon, 75001 Paris France

REFAAT, HOSSAM-ELDIN, AHMED ALY, engineering educator, researcher; b. Cairo, Abdeen, Egypt, Feb. 23, 1958; s. Ahmed Aly and Madiha Salaama (Hamza) R.; m. Maha Abdelghany Abou-Hassan, Oct. 10, 1985; children: Rana, Mohammed. BA in Sci., Cairo U., 1981, MA in Sci., 1985; PhD, Kyoto (Japan) U., 1990, rsch. fellow, 1991. Demonstrator engrng. Cairo U., 1981-85, asst. lectr., 1985-91, asst. prof. coastal and harbour engring., 1991-96, assoc. prof. coastal and harbour engrng., 1996—; design and consulting engr. Tech. Consultative Office, Cairo, 1981-85; gen. engring. dir. Integral Design System, Cairo, 1992-95, coastal and harbour expert Nile Cons., Maadi, Egypt, 1996-98; head harbour sect. Hamza Assocs., Giza, Egupt, 1998-99; cons. mgr. DRTPC Cairo U., 1999—. Served with Egyptian Mil., 1981-83. Grantee Japanese Govt., Kyoto U., 1985; nominated for Egyptian Govt. award 1996. Mem. Egyptian Engrng. Syndicate, Japanese Soc. Civil Engring. Avocations: sports, swimming, diving, reading. Home: 50 Abdeen Sq 1st Fl, PO 11111 Cairo Egypt Office: Cairo U Engring Faculty, Irrigation & Hydraulic Dept, Giza Egypt

REFINETTI, ROBERTO, biopsychologist; b. Sao Paulo, Brazil, Nov. 19, 1957; came to U.S., 1988; s. Renato and Maria Stella (Barroso) R.; m. Kathleen Diane Zylan, Mar. 5, 1988 (div. Aug. 1991); 1 child, Lauren Lynne; m. Theresa Kaye Tolleson, Aug. 11, 2000. BA in Philosophy, Pontifical Cath. U., Sao Paulo, 1981; BS in Psychology, U. Sao Paulo, 1981, MA in Psychology, 1983; PhD in Psychology, U. Calif., Santa Barbara, 1987. Asst. prof. U. Sao Paulo, 1986-88; fellow U. Calif., Santa Barbara, 1988-89, U. Ill., Champaign, 1989-90, U. Va., Charlottesville, 1990-92; asst. prof. Coll. William and Mary, Williamsburg, Va., 1992-97; mgr. profl. publs. Montage Media Corp., Mahwah, N.J., 1997-98; pvt. practice Birmingham, Ala., 1998-99; asst. prof. U. S.C., Salkehatchie, 1999—. Author: Ciradian Physiology, 1999; contbr. over 100 articles to profl. jours. Area grantee NIH, 1996; recipient Nat. Rsch. Svc. Individual award NIMH, 1991, Career award NSF, 1995. Mem. Am. Physiol. Soc., Am. Psychol. Soc., Soc. Neuroscience, Soc. Rsch. on Biol. Rhythms. Office: U SC Circadian Rythm Lab PO Box 617 Allendale SC 29810-0617

REGAN, PAUL JEROME, JR., manufacturing company executive, consultant; b. Ithaca, N.Y., Mar. 13, 1940; s. Paul Jerome and Mildred (Dempsey) R.; m. Barbara Ann Easton, Feb. 4, 1962 (dec. Nov. 1996); children: Paul J. III, Timothy Andrew, Allison Ann. BS, Cornell U., 1962, MBA, 1965. Pers. asst. Corning (N.Y.) Glass Works, 1963; pers. mgr. Corning (N.Y.) Glass Works, Corning and State College, 1964-68; dept. mgr. mfg. Corning (N.Y.) Glass Works, State College, 1968-70; personnel devel. cons. Corning (N.Y.) Glass Works, Corning, 1970-72; prodn. supt. Corning (N.Y.) Glass Works, Wilmington, N.C., 1972-74; devel. mgr. Corning (N.Y.) Glass Works, Corning, 1974-77, corp. dir., 1977-83, v.p. human resources, 1983-86; sr. v.p. Corning Inc., Corning, 1986-93; ret.; mem. adv. bd. Cornell U., Ithaca, N.Y., 1970-82, lectr., 1977—; founding mem. Human Resource Planning Soc., 1974-93; dir. Corning Can. Inc., Toronto, 1983-93. Contbr. articles to books and profl. jours. including Human Resource Planning Soc. jour.; expert comment on exec. compensation and succession including Wall St. Jour., N.Y. Times, Bus. Week, Forbes. Mem. exec. bd. Thousand Islands Assn., Gananoque, Ont., Can., 1988—, pres., 1999—; chmn. Blue Ribbon Fund, Corning Hosp., 1989-93; mem. Rep. Nat. Com., Washington, 1984—; dir. State College C. of C., 1967-73, Half Moon Bay Found., Friends of the 1000 Islands Mus., Inc., 2000—; chmn. Historic Thousand Islands Village Found., 1998—; pres. Friends Mus. St. Lawrence Run. Johnson Soc. fellow Cornell U., 1991; named Ky. Col., State of Ky., 1984, Adm. Thousand Islands Navy, 1999. Mem. Am. Compensation Assn. (regional chair 1978-81), Am. Acad. Polit. and Social Sci., Heron Soc. (life.), Cornell Club, Nat. Mus. Am. Indian (charter, membership com. 1991—), Antique Boat Mus., Save the River Com. (adv. 1982—), Menninger Found. (patron), Trust for Historic Preservation, chmn. 1000 Islands Heritage Village Found., Delta Phi (past pres.). Avocations: antique wooden boats, decoys, photographs, Inuit art, poetry.

REGAN, SUSAN GINSBERG, lawyer; b. N.Y.C., Oct. 20, 1947; d. Irwin Arthur and Sylvia (Rosen) Ginsberg; m. Neil A. Goldberg, Jan. 24, 1975 (div. May 1987); children: Jane Goldberg, Rafael Goldberg; m. Edward Van Buren Regan, Oct. 12, 1991. BA, U. Mich., 1969; JD, SUNY, Buffalo, 1974. Bar: N.Y. 1975. Asst. county atty. Erie County, Buffalo, N.Y., 1975-78; ptnr. Magavern, Magavern & Grimm LLP, Buffalo, N.Y., 1982-98; assoc. gen. counsel Vis. Nurse Svc. N.Y., N.Y.C., 1998—; mem., chair establishment com. N.Y. State Pub. Health Coun., 1996—; clin. asst. prof. SUNY Sch. Medicine and Biomed. Scis., Buffalo, 1997—. Mem. Nat. Health Lawyers Assn., N.Y. State Bar Assn. (health law com., com. on profl. ethics, N.Y.C., 1984-87). Avocation: skiing. Office: Vis Nurse Svc NY 107 E 70th St New York NY 10021-5006

REGAZZI, JOHN HENRY, retired electronic distributor executive; b. N.Y.C., Jan. 4, 1921; s. Caesar B. and Jennie (Moruzzi) R.; m. Doris Mary Litzau, Feb. 16, 1946; children: Mark, Dale. BBA, Pace Coll., 1951. CPA, N.Y. Mgr. Price Waterhouse, N.Y.C., 1946-62; comptroller ABC, N.Y.C., 1962-70; sr. v.p., CFO Avnet, Inc., N.Y.C., 1970-93; retired, 1993. Contbr. articles to profl. jours. Pres. bd. River Dell Regional High Sch., Oradell, N.J., 1962-65; trustee, treas. Oradell Pub. Library, 1970-79; councilman Borough of Oradell, 1979-88. Served as staff sgt. USAF, 1942-45. Mem. AICPA, Fin. Execs. Inst. Republican. Roman Catholic. Home: 8980 King John Ct Las Vegas NV 89149-3221

REGENBOOG, MAURITS ALEXANDER, banker; b. Leiden, The Netherlands, Nov. 10, 1957; m. Ina De Vries, June 22, 1985; four children. BS in Econs., Erasmus U., 1982, DSc in Econs., 1984. V.p. Abn-Amro Bank, The Netherlands, 1984-90; sr. v.p. Sanwa Bank, The Netherlands, 1990-94; mng. dir. BHF Bank, The Netherlands, 1994—.

REGENSBERG, CLAUDE, digestive and general surgeon; b. Paris, Nov. 13, 1937; s. Leon and Sonia (Basin) R.; m. Françoise Renée Konopny, June 25, 1967; children: Nathalie, Sandra. MD, U. Paris. Cert. in oncologic and coelio surgery, France. Extern hosps. of Paris, 1959, intern, 1972; asst. hosps of Paris; chief surg. clinic Med. Faculty Paris; cons., attache Hosp Paul Brousse, Villejuif, France, 1980—; pvt. practice, Paris, 1972—; mem. staff Clinique du Parc Monceau, Paris, Am. Hosp. Paris; mem. Commn. of Qualification in Gen. Surgery, 1994—; del. Union Regionale des Medecins Liberaux de l'Ile de France, 1994—; memb. bd. Comitee Regional Formation Medicale Continue, 1998—; gen. sec. United French Surgeons syndicate, Paris, 1998—. Chief editor Cahiers de Chirurgie. Lt. French Army Res., 1962-63. Recipient laureat, silver medal Faculty Medicine Paris, 1968. Fellow ACS, French Assn. Surgery. Avocations: movie,s theater, music. literature, skiing. Office: Internat Clin Parc Monceau, 21 Rue de Chazelles, 75017 Paris France

REGINALD, DANIEL, ophthalmic surgeon; b. London, Dec. 7, 1939; s. Reginald and Alice (Youell) D.;m. Carol Ann Bjorck, July 10, 1943; children: Lorne Piers, Claire Suzanne. MB, BS, Westminster Med. Sch., London, 1964. Cons. ophthalmic surgeon Guys Hosp., London, 1979—, St. Thomas Hosp., London, 1986—; ophthalmic surgeon London, 1979—; tchr. U. London. Contbr. articles to profl. jours. Freeman, City of London, 1981. Fellow Royal Coll. Surgeons, Coll. Ophthalmology; mem. Worshipful Co. Spectacle Makers (liveryman), City Livery Club. Avocations: golf, tennis, skiing. Home: 11 Stanmore Way, Loughton 1G1O 2SA, England Office: 152 Harley St, London W1M 1HH, England

REGINSTER, JEAN-YVES LUC, physician, researcher; b. Liège, Belgium, June 13, 1958; s. Paul Emile and Gilberte Marie (Haneuse) R.; m. Dominique M. de Ruyttere, Mar. 9, 1991; 1 child, Antoine. B Classical Humanities in Latin Sci., Coll. St. Servais, Liege, 1975; MD, U. Liege, 1982, specialist phys. medicine and rehab., 1987, specialist in public health, 1993, Agrégé prof. degree. Head bone and cartilege metabolism unit U. Liege, 1988—, prof. epidemiology and pub. health, 1996—; trustee Belgian Soc. Rheumatism, 1982—, Belgian Soc. Phys. Medicine, 1983—, exec. sec. 1991; trustee Belgian League Against Rheumatism, 1988—, v.p., 1991; lectr., adj. prof. Georgetown U. Med. Ctr., Washington, 1990—; sec. Belgian Group for Ednl. and Clin. Devel. Bone Diseases, Internat. Osteoprosis Found., 1998; dir. WHO Collaborating Ctr. Pub. Health Aspects Articular Disease, 1997—. Contbr. articles to profl. publs. Recipient Leo Young Investigator award Leo Foundn., Brussels, 1988, Florent Gommaerts prize Belgian Soc. Phys. Medicine, Brussels, 1990. Mem. Belgium Bone Club (pres. 1990-95), Gastronomic Club of Wallonie (pres.), Royal Golf Club Sart Tilman, Royal Tennis Club Liege. Roman Catholic. Home: 119 Rte du Condroz, 4031 Angleur Belgium Office: Bone Metabolism Unit ULG, 45 Ouai G Kurth, 4020 Liege Belgium

REGNELL, GERHARD, retired geology educator; b. Lund, Sweden, June 19, 1915; s. Otto G. and Agnes Charlotta (Påhlman) R.; m. Ulla V. Hadding, Dec. 15, 1945; children: Göran, Lave. DSc, Lund (Sweden) U., 1945. Demonstrator Dept. Geology, Lund, 1936-45; curator Swedish Mus. Natural History, Stockholm, 1946-54; prof. geology U. Lund, 1956-80, emeritus prof., 1980—; dean of faculty U. Lund, 1966-68, vice rector, 1968-70; mem. Swedish Natural Sci. Rsch. Coun., Stockholm, 1968-74. Contbr. monographs and papers to profl. jours. Named Comdr. of Order of Polar Star, His Majesty the King, 1974; recipient Silver Plaque, Swedish Soc. for Conservation of Nature, 1972. Mem. Royal Swedish Acad. Scis., Royal Danish Acad. Scis. and Letters, Royal Physiographical Soc. Lund (sec. 1970-80, chmn. 1981-82, Silver medal 1981), Internat. Commn. on History of Geol. Scis. (full mem. 1970-99). Home: Sölvegatan 3, S-223 62 Lund Sweden

REGNER, HERMANN, music educationalist, composer; b. Marktoberdorf, Germany, May 12, 1928; s. Alois and Maria (Ehrle) R. Dr.phil., U. Munich, 1958. Dozent Hochschule fur Musik, Trossingen, Germany, 1958-64; prof. U. Mozarteum, Salzburg, Austria, 1964-93; prof. emeritus Univ. Mozarteum, Salzburg, Austria, 1993—. Author books including Musik Lieben Lernen, 1988; composer music for orch., piano, choir, chamber music and brass. Mem. Carl Orff Found. (dir.), Orff Schulwerk Forum Salzburg.

REGN FRAHER, BONNIE, special education educator. BA, U. Calif., Santa Cruz, 1978; EdS, Rutgers U., 1982, MA, 1983. Cert. tchr. of the handicapped, cert. elem. tchr. Tchr. Search Day Program, Wanamassa, N.J., 1978-87; v.p. Fin-Addict Charters, Wall, N.J., 1987-93; v.p., dir. fin. William Cook Custom Homes, Wall, 1987-95; v.p. Archtl. Woodworking, 1993-95; tchr. Elmcrest Hosp., 1996; daycare owner Fraher Acad., West Hartford, Conn., 1996—. Mem. Autism Soc. Am., Long Branch Ski Club. Avocation: writing (short story pub.).

REGO, RICARDO AMARAL, psychotherapist, physician; b. São Paulo, Brazil, May 20, 1953; s. Germano Braga and Celina (Hummel) R.; m. Katia Regina Caputo, Dec. 20, 1997; 1 child, Ariel Velloso. MD, U. São Paulo, 1976, MS in Medicine, 1988; cert. psychotherapist, Inst. Body Psychotherapy IPE, 1987. Resident Papelok S.A., São Paulo, 1978-80; dir. State Govt. Health Ctr., São Paulo, 1979-80; dir. health svcs. Scopus S.A., São Paulo, 1980-83; rschr. State Health Inst., São Paulo, 1985-96; prof. postgrad. studies Sedes Sapientiae Inst., São Paulo, 1990-98; psychotherapist São Paulo, 1984—; dir. Brazilian Inst. for Biodynamic Psychology, São Paulo, 1992—, biodynamic -psychotherapy trainer, 1992—; body-psychotherapy trainer Agora, São Paulo, 1990-94. Editor Revista Reichiana, 1992-99; author: Grupos de Movimento, 1994; contbr. articles to profl. jours; composer recorded songs Big Keys Opens Big Doors, Sixth Sense, Sad Tropics. Coord. health policy Partido dos Trabalhadores, São Paulo, 1984-85; health issues adviser Sedes Sapientiae Inst., São Paulo, 1978-83. Avocation: music. Fax: 55 11 289 8394. E-mail: ric.rego@uol.com.br. Home: R dos Frances 427 Apt 51, 01329010 São Paulo Brazil Office: R Alm Marques Leao 785, 01330010 São Paulo Brazil

REGÖS, LÁSZLÓ, medical educator, cardiologist; b. Lábatlan, Hungary, Dec. 28, 1944; s. Ferenc and Ferencné (Borbála Gangl) R.; m. Ágnes Piros,

June 15, 1973 (div. 1984); children: László Péter, András Zoltán; m. Katalin Szabó. MD, Med. Univ. Budapest, Hungary, 1969; PhD, Hungarian Acad. Scis. Diplomate Bd. Internal Medicine, Bd. Cardiology. Physician Heart Hosp. Balatonfüred, Hungary, 1969-74; asst. lectr. Postgrad. Med. Sch., Budapest, 1975-83, jr. lectr., 1983-91, sr. lectr., 1991-98; mem. board Nat. Office Health & Recreation, Budapest, 1996—; head of cardiology, Károlyi Sándor Hosp., 1998—; sec. EKG Working Group, Budapest, 1989-94, pres. 1994—. Author: EKG Atlasz, 1992, Ambulatory Blood Pressure Monitoring, 1995; contbr. articles to profl. jours. Mem. Univ. Libr. Commn., Budapest, 1994—. Mem. Hungarian Heart Assn. (bd. dirs. 1995—), Hungarian Assn. Internal Medicine (bd. dirs. 1998—), European Heart Assn. Roman Catholic. Avocations: tennis, skiing.

REGUIGUI, NAFAA MOHAMED, science educator; b. Tunis, Tunisia, Dec. 2, 1963; s. Mohammed Metoui and Meriam M. (Bennour) R. BSc, Okla. State U., 1982, MSc, 1990, PhD, 1994. Lectr. Okla. State U., 1993-94, adj. assoc. prof., 1994-95; assoc. prof. CNSTN, Tunisia, 1996—; lectr. Esia, Tunisia, 1996—. Contbr. articles to profl. jours. Mem. Tunisian Scientific Consortium, African Student Orgn. (treas. 1992-94). Avocations: astronomy, soccer, cinema. Home: Rue 52 No 5, 1003 Tunis Tunisia Office: Centre Nat des Scis, Technologies Nucleaires, Tunis Tunisia

REGULA, RALPH, congressman, lawyer; b. Beach City, Ohio, Dec. 3, 1924; s. O.F. and Orpha (Walter) R.; m. Mary Rogusky, Aug. 5, 1950; children: Martha, David, Richard. BA, Mt. Union Coll., 1948, LLD, 1981; LLB, William McKinley Sch. Law, 1952; LLD, Malone Coll., 1976. Bar: Ohio 1952. Sch. adminstr. Stark County Bd. Edn., 1948-55; practiced law Navarre, 1952—; mem. Ohio Ho. of Reps., 1965-66, Ohio Senate, 1967-72, 93rd-106th Congresses from 16th Ohio dist., 1973—; chmn. appropriations subcom. on the interior; ptnr. Regula Bros.; Mem. Pres.'s Commn. on Fin. Structures and Regulation, 1970-71. Mem. Ohio Bd. Edn., 1960-64; hon. mem. adv. bd. Walsh Coll., Canton, Ohio; Trustee Mt. Union Coll., Alliance, Ohio, Stark County Hist. Soc., Stark County Wilderness Soc. With USNR, 1944-46. Recipient Community Service award Navarre Kiwanis Club, 1963; Meritorious Service in Conservation award Canton Audubon Soc., 1965; Ohio Conservation award Gov. James Rhodes, 1969; named Outstanding Young Man of Yr. Canton Jr. C. of C., 1957, Legis. Conservationist of Yr. Ohio League Sportsmen, 1969. Republican. Episcopalian. Office: US Ho of Reps 2309 Rayburn House Off Bldg Washington DC 20515-0001

REGULY, ZOLTÁN, retired electric power company executive; b. Budapest, Hungary, May 5, 1933; s. Zoltán and Éva (Kellner) R.; m. Kinga Andrássy, 1956; children: Zoltán, Krisztina. M in Elec. Power Engring., Poly. U., Budapest, 1956. Engr. Electricity Utility, Budapest, 1956-64; engr. Hungarian Electricity Bd. (now Hungarian Power Co. Ltd.), Budapest, 1963-67, dept. leader, 1967-86, head divsn., 1986-92, head divsn. intersys. cooperation, 1992-99, cons., 1999—; rschr. Elec. Energy Rsch. Inst., Budapest, 1958-62; pres. S. Danubian Distbn. Co., Pécs, Hungary, 1992-95, mem. supervisory bd., 1995—; asst. prof. elec. power networks Poly. U., 1963—; mem. CENTREL Coun., 1992-98. Author: (textbook) Electrical Networks, 1974; contbr. articles to sci. publs. Recipient Labor award Ministry of Industry, Budapest, 1988, Eötvös award, 1992, Renewal of Elec. Industry award Hungarian Power Co., Ltd., Budapest, 1992. Mem. IEEE, Hungarian Elec. Assn. (bd. dirs., Bláty award 1987). Avocations: classical music, windsurfing, activities with grandchildren.

REHA, ROSE KRIVISKY, retired business educator; b. N.Y.C., Dec. 17, 1920; d. Boris and Freda (Gerstein) Krivisky; m. Rudolph John Reha, Apr. 11, 1941; children: Irene Gale, Phyllis. BS in Bus. and Music Edn., Ind. State U., 1965; MA in Bus. and Psychology, U. Minn., 1967, PhD in Ednl. Psychology and Counseling, 1971. With U.S. and State Civil Svc., 1941-63; tchr. pub. schs., Minn., 1965-66; teaching assoc., instr. U. Minn., Mpls., 1966-68, 68-85; prof. coll. bus. St. Cloud (Minn.) State U., 1968-85, prof. emeritus, 1985—, chmn. bus. edn. & office adminstrn. dept., 1982-83; advisor Small Bus. Inst., 1972-85, SBA, 1972-85; ct. advocate for women in distress St. Cloud Women's Shelter, 1986-89; adj. prof. profl. and bus. comm. Fla. Atlantic U., Boca Raton, Fla., 1989-90; substitute tchr. Broward County, 1990—; tutor (reading) Lauderdale, Fla., 1990-92; moderator, counselor Posnack Jewish Cmty. Ctr., Davie, Fla.; lectr. in com. Soref Jewish Cmty. Ctr. Continuing Edn. for sr. groups, Sunrise, Fla., 1997—; cons., lectr. in field; small bus. cons. Small Bus. Inst. Coll. Bus. St. Cloud St. U. Minn. Reviewer of bus. comm. and consumer edn. textbooks. Contbr. articles to profl. jours. Camp dir. Girl Scouts U.S., 1960-62; active various cmty. fund drives; sec., mem. relicensure rev. Com. Minn. Bd. Teaching Continuing Edn., 1984-85. Recipient Achievement award St. Cloud State U., 1985, St. Cloud State U. Rsch. and Faculty Improvement grantee, 1973, 78, 83. Mem. Am. Vocat. Assn. (cert.), Am. Counseling Assn. (cert.), Am. Mental Health Counselors Assn. (cert.), Minn. Econ. Assn., Minn. Women of Higher Edn., NEA, Minn. Edn. Assn. (pres. women's caucus 1981-83, award 1983), St. Cloud U. Faculty Assembly (pres. 1975-76), St. Cloud State U. Grad. Coun. (chmn. 1983-85), Fifty-five-plus Sr. Group (moderator North Broward, Ft. Lauderdale chpts. 1994—), Pi Omega Pi (sponsor St. Cloud State U. chpt. 1982-85), Phi Chi Theta, Delta Pi Epsilon, Delta Kappa Gamma. Jewish. Home: # 465 3671 Environ Blvd Apt 465 Fort Lauderdale FL 33319-4221 Office: Coll Bus St Cloud State U Saint Cloud MN 56301

REHACEK, ZDENEK, microbiologist; b. Berehovo, Czechoslovakia, May 25, 1925; s. Josef and Josefa (Sukova) R.; m. Libuse Papikova, July 19, 1952; children: Zdenek, Pavel. MPharm, Charles U., Prague, Czechoslovakia, 1948, MD in Microbiology, 1952; PhD in Biology, Czechoslovak Acad. Sci., Prague, 1956, DSc in Biology, 1978. Pharmacy asst. drugstore, Prague, Czechoslovakia, 1945-47; tech. asst. Biol. Insts., Prague, 1952; scientific aspirant Inst. Microbiology, Czech Acad. Sci., Prague, 1952-56, scientific rschr., 1956-60, head lab. secondary metabolism of microorganisms, 1960-93; dir. internat. postgrad. courses UNESCO, 1965-93; sec. gen. UNESCO Assn. Sci. Tech., 1982-91. Recipient hon. recognition Govt. of Prague, 1979, State prize for sci., 1981, G.J. Mendel plaque for merit in biol. sci., 1985, prizes and awards Czech Acad. Sci., 1957-87. Mem. Czechoslovak Soc. Microbiology (hon.), World Acad. Art and Sci. Avocations: music, gardening. Home: Konevova 93, 13000 Prague Czech Republic

REHAK, JIRI, ophthalmologist; b. Hradec Kralove, Czech Republic, May 10, 1958; s. Svatopluk and Jirina (Svobodova) R.; m. Hana Berkova, Feb. 13, 1982; children: Jiri, Tereza. MD, Sch. of Medicine, 1983, PhD, 1991. Physician Univ. Hosp., Olomouc, Czech Republic, 1983-87; tchr. Sch. of Medicine, Palacki U., Olomouc, 1987-94; dep. head dept. ophthalmology Univ. Hosp., Olomouc, 1994-98; head dept. ophthalmology Univ. Hosp., Olomouc, Czech Republic, 1998—; assoc. prof. Charles U., Plzen, Czech Republic, 1996—. Mem. Am. Acad. Ophthalmology, N.Y. Acad. of Sci., Europian Glaucoma Soc. Avocation: skiing, karate. Home: Einsteinova 41, 779 00 Olomouc Czech Republic Office: Dept Ophthalmology Univ Hosp, I P Pavlova 6, 775 20 Olomouc Czech Republic

REHANY, URI, physician, ophthalmologist, lecturer; b. Baghdad, Iraq, Jan. 1, 1946; s. Abraham and Rina (Kalif) R.; m. Alice Blayer, Sept. 5, 1968 (div. Nov. 1993); children: Alon, Oren, Karen. MD, Hebrew U.-Hadassah, Jerusalem, Israel, 1969, postgrad., 1978. Diplomate Am. Bd. Ophthalmology; cert. specialist in ophthalmology, Israel. Rschr. corneal collagen Hebrew U./Hadassah Sch. Dental Medicine, 1979-80, 82-86, resident in ophthalmology, 1975-80; fellow in corneal diseases Beth Israel/Mt. Sinai Med. Ctr., N.Y.C., 1980-81; sr. ophthalmologist Hadassah Med. Ctr., Jerusalem, 1982-86, lectr. in ophthalmology, 1982—; dir. dept. ophthalmology Nahariya (Israel) Med. Ctr., 1986—, dir. corneal transplantation project and eye bank, 1986—; Contbr. numerous articles to profl. jours. Adviser, Non-Profit Environ. Group, Nahariya, 1996—; hon. bd. dirs. Assn. for Ednl. Advancement for Children of Lower-Income Families, 1986—; advisor Assn. for Soviet Union Immigrants, Jerusalem, 1986—. Lt. Israel Def. Forces Med. Corps, 1971-73; vol. organizer med. care for new emigrants from Ethiopia, 1992—. Recipient Outstanding Achievement award Nahariya Med. Ctr., 1992, 93, Outstanding Achievement and Pub. Health Care award Rotary Internat., 1993. Fellow ACS, Am. Acad. Ophthalmology, Internat. Soc. for Eye Rsch. Avocations: classical music, ballroom and Latino-American dancing, fishing. Home: 48 Hamaapilim, Nahariya 22387, Israel Office: Nahariya Med Ctr, PO Box 21, Nahariya 22100, Israel

REHMAN, ASIF BIN, pharmacologist, educator, researcher; b. Karachi, Pakistan, June 22, 1952; s. Rehman Abdul and Fatima (Begum) Syeda; m. Mahayrookh Asif, Oct. 8, 1992; children: Faisal Asif, Abdul Rehman Asif. BS, U. Karachi, 1970, MS, 1972, MPhil, 1978, postgrad. diploma in stats., 1981, cert. Spanish lang., 1993; MD, U. Eugenio Maria DeHostos, Santo Domingo, Dominican Republic, 1986; DSc (hon.), Internat. U., Sri Lanka, 1997. Registered med. practitioner Pakistan Med. and Dental Coun. Tchg. asst. U. Karachi, 1973-78, lectr., 1979-82, asst. prof. pharmacology, 1982-97, prof. pharmacology, 1997—, chmn. dept. pharmacology, 1997—; senate mem., mem. acad. coun. U. Karachi. Mem. editl. bd. Pakistan Jour. Pharmacology, Pakistan Jour. Pharmaceutical Sci.; contbr. articles to profl. jours. Fellow Royal Soc. Health, Interam. Coll. Physicians and Surgeons; mem. Pakistan Pharmacological Soc., Pakistan Med. Assn., Acad. Coun. U. Karachi. Avocations: reading newspapers, jogging, cricket, table tennis. Home: 8-1 Khayaban-E-Behria, Phase V Def Housing Author, Karachi Pakistan Office: U Karachi Dept Pharmacology, Faculty Pharmacy, Karachi Pakistan

REHNCRONA, STIG LENNART, neurosurgeon, researcher; b. Vadstena, Sweden, Feb. 20, 1943; s. Karl Georg and Thora Berta Rehncrona; m. Pia Marianne Valentin, July 27, 1968; children: Anna, Maria, Carl, Carin. MD, U. Lund, Sweden, 1970, PhD, 1980. Resident in neurosurgery Univ. Hosp., Lund, 1970-75, neurosurgeon, 1975-80; cons. neurosurgeon Univ. Hosp., 1980—, dir. functional neurosurgery, 1990—; assoc. prof. neurosurgery U. Lund, 1983—; cons. Harrison dept. surgery U. Pa., Phila., 1978, guest prof. Johnson Found., 1978, 79. Contbr. over 70 articles to profl. jours.; achievements include first to successfully perform brain cell transplantations in man. Recipient Frithiof Lennmalms sci. prize Swedish Med. Soc., 1981. E-mail: stig.rehncrona@neurokir.lu.se.

REHNQUIST, WILLIAM HUBBS, United States supreme court chief justice; b. Milw., Oct. 1, 1924; s. William Benjamin and Margery (Peck) R.; m. Natalie Cornell, Aug. 29, 1953; children: James, Janet, Nancy. BA, MA, Stanford U., 1948; MA, Harvard U., 1949; LLB, Stanford U., 1952. Bar: Ariz. Law clk. to former justice Robert H. Jackson, U.S. Supreme Ct., 1952-53; with Evans, Kitchel & Jenckes, Phoenix, 1953-55; mem. Ragan & Rehnquist, Phoenix, 1956-57; ptnr. Cunningham, Carson & Messenger, Phoenix, 1957-60, Powers & Rehnquist, Phoenix, 1960-69; asst. atty.-gen. office of legal counsel Dept. of Justice, Washington, 1969-71; assoc. justice U.S. Supreme Ct., 1971-1986, chief justice, 1986—; mem. Nat. Conf. Commrs. Uniform State Laws, 1963-69. Author: The Supreme Court: How It Was, How It Is, 1987, Grand Inquests: The Historic Impeachments of Justice Samuel Chase and President Andrew Johnson, 1992, All the Laws But One, 1999; contbr. articles to law jours., nat. mags. Served with USAAF, 1943-46, NATOUSA. Mem. Fed., Am. Maricopa (Ariz.) County bar assns., State Bar Ariz., Nat. Conf. Lawyers and Realtors, Phi Beta Kappa, Order of Coif, Phi Delta Phi. Lutheran. Office: Supreme Ct US 1 1st St NE Washington DC 20543-0001

REHNQVIST, NINA ANNA KRISTINA, physician; b. Teheran, Iran, Apr. 6, 1944; d. Lennart N. and Sonja BB. (Stönner) R.; m. Staffan P. Ahlberg, Apr. 4, 1970; children: Oskar, Lisa, Gunnar. MB, Karolinska Inst., Stockholm, 1965, MD, 1970, PhD, 1977. From resident to asst. prof. Karolinska Inst., Stockholm, 1981—; dep. gen. dir. Socialstyrelsen, Stockholm, 1995—; dept. head Karolinska Inst., 1993-95. Fellow Am. Coll. Cardiology., Royal Coll. Physician Educators, European Soc. Cardiology. Office: Nat Bd Health & Welfare, 10630 Stockholm Sweden

REHORN, LOIS M(ARIE), nursing administrator; b. Larned, Kans., Apr. 15, 1919; d. Charles and Ethel L. (Canaday) Williamson; m. C. Howard Smith, Feb. 15, 1946 (dec. Aug. 1980); 1 child, Cynthia A. Huddleston; m. Harlan W. Rehorn, Aug. 25, 1981. RN, Bethany Hosp. Sch. Nursing, Kansas City, Kans., 1943; BS, Ft. Hays Kans. State U., Hays, 1968, MS, 1970. RN, N.Mex.; lic. pvt. pilot. Office nurse, surg. asst. Dr. John H. Luke, Kansas City, Kans., 1943-47; supr. nursing unit Larned (Kans.) State Hosp., 1949-68, dir. nursing edn., 1968-71, dir. nursing, 1972-81, ret., 1981. Recipient Order of the Blue Key, 1942-43; named Nurse of Yr. DNA-4, 1986. Mem. Am. Nurses Assn., Kans. Nurses Assn. (dist. treas.), N.Mex. Nurses Assn. (dist. pres. 1982-86, dist. bd. dirs. 1986-88). Avocation: flying (pilot). Home: 1436 Brentwood Dr Clovis NM 88101-4602

ŘEHULKA, JIŘÍ, ichthyologist, ichthyopathologist; b. Olomouc, Czech Republic, July 5, 1941; s. Antonín and Vilemína (Fryčová) Ř; m. Ivana (Satková), Apr. 20, 1974. GCE, Tech. Sch. Agr., Opava, 1959; BSC, U. Agr. Brno, Czech Republic, 1967, PhD, 1982. Individual scientist Rsch. Inst. Fishery and Hydrobiology, Vodňany Ostrava Sta., 1970-92; leading scientist Rsch. Inst. Fishery and Hydrobiology, Opava, 1992-93; individual scientist Rsch. Inst. Fish Culture Hydrobiology U. South Bohemia, Vodňany Opava Sta., 1993—. Mem. Czech Parasitology Soc., N.Y. Acad. Scis. Home: Zacpalova 22, 746 01 Opava Czech Republic Office: U South Bohemia Vodňany, Rsch Inst Fish Culture, 746 01 Opava Czech Republic

ŘEHULKA, PAVEL, training company executive; b. Olomouc, Czech Republic, Sept. 16, 1971; arrived in Australia, 1986; s. Pavel and Alena Řehulka; m. Jana Vymětalova, June 29, 1996; 1 child, David. BComm, Murdoch U., Perth, Australia, 1992. Cert. mgmt. trainer, bus. valuer. Tax cons. H&R Block, Perth, 1990-92; mktg. mgr. Blade Skate Australia, Perth, 1992-93; spl. projects mgr. Czechinvest, Prague, Czech Republic, 1993; mng. dir. Czech Bus. Ctr., Olomouc, 1993-96; CEO Czech Tng. Ctr. Ltd, Olomouc, 1996—. Author: Successful Promotion, 1994, 3 Ways to Grow Your Business...Guaranteed, 1997, 100 Ways to Increase Your Sales, 1999. Mktg. mgr. Australian Jr. Chamber, Perth, 1990-92. Recipient Australian Inst. Mgmt prize, 1992. Mem. Czech Mktg. Assn., Czech Mgmt. Assn., Czech Trainer's Assn. (pres. 1999-2000). Avocations: squash, travel. Office: Czech Tng Ctr Ltd, Kosmonautu 6, 772 31 Olomouc Czech Republic

REIBLE, DANNY DAVID, environmental chemical engineer, educator; b. Rantoul, Ill., Dec. 21, 1954; s. George Anthony and Mavis Otilla (Prause) R.; m. Susanne Cecilia Schulte, Mar. 17, 1979; children: Kristin Nicole, Monica Lynn. BS, Lamar U., 1977; MS, Calif. Inst. Tech., 1979, PhD, 1982. Registered profl. engr., La. Asst. prof. La. State U., Baton Rouge, 1981-86, assoc. prof., 1986-92, prof. chem. engring., 1992—, Chevron prof. chem. engring., 1998—, dir. Hazardous Substance Rsch. Ctr., 1995—; Shell prof. environ. engring. U. Sydney, Australia, 1993-95; vis. rschr. U.S. Army Engr. Waterways Experiment Sta., Vicksburg, Miss., 1990; sr. visitor Cambridge (Eng.) U., 1992; cons. in field. Contbr. articles to profl. publs. Environ. Sci. and Engring. fellow AAAS, 1987. Mem. AIChE (exec. bd. 1990-95, mem. nat. programming com.), Am. Chem. Soc., Am. Geophys. Union, Am. Soc. Engring. Edn. (New Engring. Educator Excellence award 1985), Sigma Xi. Achievements include identification and evaluation of new mechanisms for contaminant release in the environment; further quantitative modeling of fate and transport contaminants in environmental systems. Avocations: sailing, computers, wines, jogging, diving. Home: 2112 Oakcliff Dr Baton Rouge LA 70810-1856 Office: La State U HSRC/S&SW 3418 Ceba Baton Rouge LA 70803-0001

REICH, AXEL MANFRED, mathematics educator, actuary; b. Leipzig, Germany, June 30, 1942; s. Erdmann Reich and Gerda (Dorn) Kranz; m. Gesine Knigge, May 24, 1969; children: Nils, Max. Diploma in math., U. Göttingen, Fed. Republic Germany, 1967, D. in Natural Scis., 1969, Habilitation, 1976, prof. degree, 1981. Asst. U. Göttingen, 1967-76, lectr., 1976; prof. math. U. Kiel (Germany), 1977-78, U. Göttingen, 1979-81; head rsch. dept. Cologne (Germany) Reinsurance Co., 1982—, apptd. actuary, 1996—; prof. U. Cologne, 1982—. Mem. editorial bd. ASTIN Bull.; contbr. articles to profl. jours. Mem. Deutsche Gesellschaft für Versicherungsmathematik, Swiss Assn. Actuaries, Deutsche Mathematiker-Vereinigung, Deutscher Aktuar Verein. E-mail: reicha@gcre. Office: Gen Cologne Re, Theodor Heuss Ring 11, D 50668 Cologne Germany

REICH, KARL HELMUT, religion educator, psychology educator; b. Krefeld, Rheinland, Germany, May 7, 1923; s. Fritz and Else (Pleines) R.; m. Ursula Elisabeth Pleines, Mar. 29, 1958; children: Sabrina, Bertrand. Diploma in engring., Tech. U., Braunschweig, Germany, 1951, DEng, 1954; PhD in Physics, U. Nottingham, Eng., 1955. Sr. physicist CERN (European Lab. Particle Physics), Geneva, 1955-83, from dep. divsn. leader to group leader, 1969-82; rsch. fellow U. Fribourg, Switzerland, 1984—; sr. prof. Sr. U. U.S. and Can., 1994—. Mem. APA (profl. assoc. divsn. psychology of religion, William James award 1997), Internat. Seminar Religious Edn. and Values. Avocation: reading. Home: 29 Rue de Bon-Port, CH 1820 Montreux Vaud, Switzerland Office: U Fribourg Dept Edn Sci, 2 Rue Faucigny, CH-1700 Fribourg Switzerland

REICH, OLEG, pediatric cardiologist, consultant; b. Prague, Czech Republic, July 14, 1954; s. Erich and Jaroslava (Bila) R.; m. Oldriska Prazska, Nov. 19, 1983; children: Stepan, Eva. MD, Charles U., Prague, 1979. Bd. cert. gen. pediat. and pediat. cardiology; license for invasive and interventional cardiology, Czech Republic. Pediat. resident Dist. Hosp., Karlovy Vary, Czech Republic, 1979-80; resident in pediat. and pediat. cardiology Kardiocentrum, U. Hosp. Motol, Prague, 1980-86, head nuc. cardiology divsn., 1986-91, cons. invasive and interventional cardiologist, 1993—; vis. scientist McGill U., Montreal, Can., 1992. Contbr. chpt. to book and articles to profl. jours. Mem. Assn. for European Pediat. Cardiology (prize for best poster at annual meeting 1996), Czech Soc. Cardiology (working group for pediat. cardiology 1993—, working group for interventional cardiology). Avocations: mountain biking, skiing, computers. E-mail: oleg.reich@lfmotol.cuni.cz. Fax: 420-2-24432920. Home: Belohorska 124, 169 00 Prague Czech Republic Office: Kardiocentrum U Hosp Motol, V uvalu 84, 150 06 Prague Czech Republic

REICH, ROBERT BERNARD, former federal official, political economics educator; b. Scranton, Pa., June 24, 1946; s. Edwin Saul and Mildred Dorf (Freshman) R.; m. Clare Dalton, July 7, 1973. BA, Dartmouth Coll., 1968, MA (hon.), 1988; MA, Oxford (Eng.) U., 1970; JD, Yale U., 1973. Asst. solicitor gen. U.S. Dept. Justice, Washington, 1974-76; dir. policy planning FTC, Washington, 1976-81; mem. faculty John F. Kennedy Sch. Govt. Harvard U., Cambridge, Mass., 1981-92; sec. Dept. of Labor, Washington, 1993-97; Maurice B. Hexter prof. econ. and social policy Brandeis U. Heller Grad. Sch., 1997—; chmn. biotech. sect. U.S. Office Tech. Assessment, Washington, 1990-91. Author: The Next American Frontier, 1983, Tales of a New America, 1987, The Work of Nations, 1991, Locked in the Cabinet, 1997; co-author: The Power of Public Ideas, 1987; contbg. editor The New Republic, Washington, 1982-93; chmn. editorial bd. The Am. Prospect, 1990—. Mem. governing bd. Common Cause, Washington, 1981-85; bd. dirs. Bus. Enterprise Trust, Palo Alto, Calif., 1989-93; trustee Dartmouth Coll., Hanover, N.H., 1989-93. Rhodes scholar, 1968; recipient Louis Brownlow award ASPA, 1983.

REICH, ROBERT CLAUDE, metallurgist, physicist; b. Paris, Nov. 2, 1929; s. Felix and Nelly (Belestin) R.; m. François Thiébault, June 10, 1972; m. Michéle Hélée Brand'Huy, Dec. 29, 1981. Engr., École Nat. Supèieure de Chimie Paris, U. Paris, 1954; Docteur ès Scis. Physiques, École Nat. Supèieure, U. Paris, 1965. Attachée de recherche Centre Nat. de La Recherche Sci., Centre d'Etudes de Chimie Mètallurgique, Vitry sur Seine, France, 1953-54, 58-65; chargé de recherche Lab. de Physique des Solides, Orsay, France, 1965-71, maître de recherche, 1971-83, directeur de recherche, 1984—. Mem. Soc. Française de Physique, Soc. Française de Métallurgie, European Phys. Soc., Electrochem. Soc. (U.S.), Internat. Soc. Electrochemistry (past sec. French sect.), Am. Soc. Metal Rsch. Achievements include research on purification of metals by zone-melting, elec. resistivity of metals versus purity (observed temperature squared term of ideal resistivity in non-magnetic metals), deviations from Matthiessen's rule, supraconducting transition in tin, determination of characteristic Debye temperatures, terminology studies in mercury, size-effect, ionic interactions in solutions, electrolyte glass transitions, anodic dissolution of metals, corrosion, superconducting oxides, metallurgy and structure of quasicrystals. Home: 7 Allée du Parc, 95600 Eaubonne France Office: U Paris XIII, Lab Prop Mech Therm Mater, F-93430 Villetaneuse Cedex, France also: U Paris-Sud Lab Phys Solide, Batiment 510, F-91405 Orsay Cedex, France

REICH, STEFAN, plastics engineer; b. Viena, Austria, Nov. 25, 1937; arrived in Mexico, 1970; s. Heinz and Hedi (Persikaner) R.; children from previous marriage: Nicole, Laura, Carola, Martin; m. Maria del Pilar Mercado, Jan. 23, 1976. B in Engring., U. Buenos Aires, 1963. Dir. sales Regie Renault, France, 1964-65; svc. mgr. Fasa-Renault, Spain, 1965-67; dir. sales IKA-Renault, Argentina, 1967-69; mgr. purchasing & exports Renault Mexicana, Mexico, 1970-74; mgr. Aconsa, Mexico, 1974-76; sales mgr. Sulzer Brothers, Mexico, 1976-82; mgr. Latin Am. JLG Industries, Mexico, 1982-83; pres. Recuperadora y Maquiladora de Plasticos, Mexico, 1983—. Mem. Soc. Plastics Engrs., Avandaro Golf Club. Avocations: bridge, golf, tennis. Office: Recuperadora y Maquiladora de Plasticos, Rio Totolica 31, 53470 Naucalpan Mexico

REICHEL, AARON ISRAEL, lawyer, rabbi, editor; b. N.Y.C., Jan. 30, 1950; s. Oscar Asher and Josephine Hannah (Goldstein) R. BA, Yeshiva U., 1971, MA, 1974; JD, Fordham U., 1976. Bar: N.J. 1977, N.Y. 1978; ordained rabbi, 1975. Atty. editor Securities Regulation Prentice-Hall, Englewood Cliffs, N.J., 1977-78; editor, founder govt. disclosure service Prentice-Hall, Paramus, N.J., 1978-82; atty. editor fed. taxation Prentice-Hall, Paramus, 1982-89; tech. editor Warren, Gorham & Lamont, Practical Acct., N.Y.C., 1989-90; assoc. Firm A. Edward Major, N.Y.C., 1990-91, Firm Allen L. Rothenberg, N.Y.C., 1991-93; pvt. practice N.Y.C., 1993—. Author: The Maverick Rabbi, 1984, 2d edit. 1986, Back to the Past for Inspiration for the Future—West Side Institutional Synagogue Jubilee 1937-87, 1987; co-author (manual) Style and Usage, 1984; contbr. The 1986 Jewish Directory and Almanac, 1986, The 1987-88 Jewish Almanac, 1988; contbg. editor Complete Guide to the Tax Reform Act of 1986, Prentice-Hall's Explanation of the Tax Reform Act of 1986, 1986, Prentice Hall's Complete Guide to the Tax Law of 1987, 1988, Prentice Hall's Explanation of the Technical & Miscellaneous Revenue Act of 1988, 1988, Guide to Equal Employment Practices, 1997; contbr. articles to profl. jours. bd. dirs. Union Orthodox Jewish Congregations Am., N.Y.C., 1973-74, Harry and Jane Fischel Found., N.Y.C., 1977—, West Side Instl. Synagogue, 1987-98, Amalgamated Dwellings, Inc., 1992-96; nat. pres. YAVNEH, N.Y.C., 1973-74; mem. youth commn. Am. Jewish Congress, N.Y.C., 1973-76. Mem. ABA, N.Y. State Bar Assn. (various coms.), N.Y. County Lawyers Assn. (various coms.), Am. Soc. Access Profls. (founder, 1st chmn. N.Y. chpt.), Nat. Jewish Commn. on Law and Pub. Affairs (family law com.), Yeshiva U. Alumni Assn. (exec. com. 1971-87, editor-in-chief Bull. 1974-78). Avocations: writing, baseball, tennis, compiling proverbs. Home: 83-28 Abingdon Rd Kew Gardens NY 11415-1714

REICHEL, MARTIN MANFRED, biomedical enginee., researcher, educator; b. Neunkirchen, Austria, Apr. 15, 1969; s. Gerhard and Inge Reichel; m. Gerhild Höllebrand, Mar. 20, 1998; 1 child, Felix. Dipl-Ing, Tech. U., Vienna, 1995, DrTechn, 1999. Ednl. trainer WIFI, Vienna, 1990-99; software developer Vienna, 1997—; asst. dept. biomed. engring. and physics Tech. U., Vienna, 1998—. Author: Artificial Organs, 1999. Avocations: windsurfing, snowboarding, skiing, tennis. E-mail: m.reichel@bmtp.akh-wien.ac.at. Office: Dept Biomed Engring/Physics, Waehringer Guertel 18-20, Vienna Austria A-1090

REICHEL, MICHAEL PHILIPP, parasitologist; b. Langenfeld, Germany, June 1, 1959; arrived in Australia, 1999; s. Josef and Annemarie (Kuhn) R.; m. Kristin Margarethe Wohlers, May 3, 1991; children: Robin Lucas, Tim Fabian. Vet. surgeon grad., Free U. Berlin, 1984, diploma vet. tropical sci., 1994; diploma Vet. Pub. Health, Massey U., Palmerston North, New Zealand, 1987, M Vet. Sci., 1992; DMV, U. Hannover, Germany, 1994. Vet. officer N.E. Ministry Agr. and Fisheries, Hastings, New Zealand, 1985-87; scientist Meat Rsch. Inst., Hamilton, New Zealand, 1988-89; supervising veterinarian N.E. Ministry Agr. and Fisheries, Paeroa, New Zealand, 1989-91; vet. officer Dept. Agr., Stanley, Falkland Islands, 1991-93; vis. rsch. fellow U. Melbourne, Australia, 1993; sect. leader Cahl-MAF, Upper Hutt, New Zealand, 1995-99; head parasitology Novartis Animal Health Australasia, Sydney, Australia, 1999—. Fellow Australian Coll. Vet. Scientists. Office: Novartis Animal Health, 245 Western Rd, Kemps Creek NSW 2171, Australia

REICHEL, ROBERT, ice hockey player; b. Litvinov, Czech Republic, June 25, 1971. Hockey player LITV/CZECH, 1987-90, CALG/NHL, 1990-95, 96-97, FRAN/GER, 1994-96, N.Y. Islanders/NHL, 1996-97, 97-99, Phoenix Coyotes/NHL, 1998-99; mem. Czech. Olympic team, 1997-98. Recipient Gold medal men's ice hockey, Olympic Games, Nagano, Japan,

1998. Avocation: travel. Office: Phoenix Coyotes Hockey Club Cellular One Ice Den 9375 E Bell Rd Scottsdale AZ 85260-1500*

REICHELT, RUDOLF, biophysics educator; b. Gallin, Germany, July 12, 1947; s. Rudolf and Marie (Schatzler) R.; m. Doris Lisa Frömke, July 26, 1979; 1 child, Hanna. Diploma in physics, Tech. U. Dresden, Germany, 1970, Dr.rer.nat., 1973. Postdoctoral fellow Ctrl. Inst. Molecular Biology, Berlin, 1973-81, U. Basel (Switzerland) Bioctr., 1982-90; prof. biophysics Inst. Med. Physics and Biophysics U. Münster, Germany, 1990—, head dept. electron microscopy and analysis, 1990—. Mem. editl. bd. Jour. Structural Biology, 1994—; contbr. articles to profl. jours. and book. Rsch. grantee Deutsch Froschungsgemeinschaft, 1992, 94, 96, 98-99, Interreg I-Program, 1994. Mem. German Soc. Electron Microscopy (v.p. 2000—), Swiss Soc. Optics and Microscopy. Avocations: photography, music. Office: U Munster Inst Med Physics, & Biophys Robert-Koch-St 31, D-48149 Münster Germany

REICHEN, JÜRG, hepatology and pharmacology educator; b. Aarau, Switzerland, Jan. 23, 1946; s. Hans A. and Susi (Aeberhard) R.; m. Suzi Graden, may 29, 1970; children: Hansjakob, Annemarie, Katharina. BA, Gymnasium City, Burgdorf, Switzerland, 1964; MD, U. Bern, Switzerland, 1971. Diplomate medicine. Fellow dept. exptl. medicine Hoffmann LaRoche, Basel, Switzerland, 1972; fellow dept. clin. pharmacology U. Bern, 1973-76, prof. medicine, clin. pharmacologist, 1986-94, dir. clin. pharmacology and clin. rsch. depts., 1994—; intern, resident Georgetown U. and V.A. Med. Ctr., Washington, 1978-79; fellow div. GI UCHSC, Denver, 1980; asst. prof. div. GI and Clin. Pharmacology USHSC, Denver, 1980-84, assoc. prof., 1984-85; guest scientist Liver Unit, NIH, Bethesda, Md., 1976-78; mem. rsch. com. AASLD, Chgo., 1984-85; sec. scientific com. EASL, 1988-91. Editl. bd. Hepatology, 1988-94, Jour. Hepatol, 1994—; assoc. editor Jour. Hepatology, 1989-94, Hepatology, 1994-96; contbr. articles to profl. jours., chpts. to books. Mem. Fed. Commn. for MDPhD, Bern, 1994; referee SNF, DFG, NIH, INSERM and others. Recipient Prize of Faculty award U. Bern, 1976, Faculty Devel. award Pharm. Mfg. Assn., 1981-83, Rsch. Career Devel. award NIH, 1983-88, Swiss Nat. Found. Sci. Rsch. award, 1986-91, prize Swiss Soc. for Internal Medicine, 1987, Cloëtta award Cloëtta Found., Zurich, 1995. Mem. European Assn. Study of the Liver, Am. Assn. Study of Liver Disease, Am. Gastroenterology Assn., Western Soc. Clin. Investigators, Internat. Assn. Study of the Liver (counselor 1992-94), United European Gastroenterologists Fedn. (counselor 1991-95), European Soc. Biochem. Pharms. Office: Univ Bern Dept Clin Pharmacology, Murtenstrasse 35, CH-3010 Bern Switzerland

REICHENBACH, JÜRGEN R., physicist; b. Freiburg, Germany, May 17, 1962; s. Heinz W. and Ingeburg S. (Rinderle) R. Diploma in physics, Tech. U. Karlsruhe, 1988, PhD, 1992. Postdoctoral study U. Montpellier, France, 1992-93; rschr. U. Dusseldorf, Germany, 1994; vis. rsch. assoc. Washington U., St. Louis, 1995-96; sr. scientist Friedrich-Schiller U., Jena, Germany, 1997—. Grantee Radiol. Soc. N.Am., 1997; recipient Marie Sklodowska Curie award German-Polish Radiol. Soc., 1998. Mem. German Phys. Soc., German Roentgen Soc., Internat. Soc. Magnetic Resonance in Medicine, European Congress Radiology. Office: Inst Diag & Intvl Radiology, Bachstr 18, D-07743 Jena Germany

REICHERT, LEO EDMUND, JR., biochemist, endocrinologist; b. N.Y.C., Jan. 9, 1932; s. Leo and Anne (Holsten) R.; m. Gerda Sihler, July 20, 1957; children: Leo, Christine, Linda, Andrew. B.S., Manhattan Coll., N.Y.C., 1955; Ph.D., Loyola U., Chgo., 1960. Asst. prof. biochemistry Emory U. Med. Sch., Atlanta, 1960-66; assoc. prof. Emory U. Med. Sch., 1966-72, prof., 1972-79; prof., chmn. dept. biochemistry Albany (N.Y.) Med. Coll., 1979-88, prof. biochemistry and molecular biology, 1988-99; dir. Tucker Endocrine Rsch. Inst., Atlanta, GA, 2000—; dir. human and animal hormone isolation and distbn. program (NIH), Emory U. Med. Sch., 1960-75; mem. med. adv. bd. Nat. Pituitary Agy., 1971-74; com. on glycoprotein hormones Nat. Hormone and Pituitary Program, 1968-86; mem. reproductive biology study sect. NIH, 1971-75; mem. adv. panel on cellular physiology NSF, 1983-86, div. of integrative and neuro biology, 1992; mem. WHO Expert Adv. Panel on Biol. Standardization, 1984—, Nat. Bd. Med. Examiners, Part I, 1989-91. Mem. editl. bd. Endocrinology, 1967-75, Molecular and Cellular Endocrinology, 1977-83, 90-94, Biology of Reproduction, 1968-70, 86-90, Andrology, 1983-86, Molecular Andrology, 1989-99; contbr. more than 275 articles to profl. jours.; patentee in field. Served with USMC, 1950-53. List among 75 endocrinologists, 1000 scientists most cited, 1965-78. Mem. AAAS, Am. Soc. Biol. Chemists, Endocrine Soc. (Ayerst award 1970), Andrology Soc. (coun. 1983-87), Soc. for Study of Reprodn. Home: 1974 Mountain Creek Dr Stone Mountain GA 30087-1018

REICHMANN, PÉTER IVÁN, mathematician; b. Budapest, Hungary, Feb. 10, 1942; came to U.S., 1959; s. Rezsö Rudolf and Margit (Grünberger) R. BSEE, Ill. Inst. Tech., 1967, MS in Math., 1973, PhD in Math., 1986. Elec. engr. Zenith Military and Motorola Comm. and Govt. divns., various cities, 1967-69; instr. math. and elec. engring. depts. Chgo. Tech. Coll., 1973-74; asst. prof. of math. Cath. U. Am., Washington, 1987-89. Grantee NASA, 1982. Achievements include research on the introduction of a novel geometry for individual cell for negative Poisson's ratio foam and computing its volume. Home: 1305 Coloma Way Roseville CA 95661-4604

REICIN, ERIC DAVID, lawyer; b. Chgo.; s. Ronald Ian and Alyta Reicin; m. Jodi Reicin, Sept. 3, 1994. Student, Regent Coll., England, 1990; AB in Econs. and Polit. Sci., U. Mich., 1991; JD cum laude, U. Ill., 1994. Bar: Ill. 1994, U.S. Dist. Ct. (no. dist.) Ill. 1994, D.C. 1995, U.S. Dist. Ct. D.C. 1995, U.S. Ct. Appeals (D.C. cir.) 1995, U.S. Dist. Ct. Md. 1997, U.S. Ct. Appeals (4th cir.) 1997, U.S. Supreme Ct. 1998. Intern U.S. Senator Robert W. Kasten, Washington, 1989; intern Office of Policy Devel. White House, Washington, 1990; intern U.S. Congressman Carl Pursell, Washington, 1991; law clk. State's Atty.-Champaign County, 1994; assoc. Laner Muchin Dombrow Becker Levin and Tominberg, Chgo., 1994-95, Birch Horton Bittner and Cherot, Washington, 1995-99; asst. gen. counsel Sallie Mae, Inc., Reston, Va., 1999—. Chpt. editor: Employment Discrimination Law, 3d edit., 1999, 2000. Harno scholar, 1993-94, Congrl. scholar, 1986; Pub. Interest Law Found. fellow. Mem. ABA (exec. lt. gov. 1993-94, EEO com. nat. co-chmn. regional liaison program 1997-98, nat. co-chmn. govt. liaison program 1998—, nat. co-chmn. ABA/EEOC joint tng. partnership 1997—), D.C. Bar Assn. (litigation, labor and employment sect.) Soc. for Human Resource Mgmt., Met. Washington Employment Lawyers Assn. (sec., bd. dirs. 1997-99), Washington Met. Area Corp. Counsel Assn. (labor and employment com. chair 1999—), Mortar Bd., Pi Sigma Alpha, Omicron Delta Epsilon, Sigma Iota Rho, Alpha Epsilon Pi (Arnold B. Hoffman award 1990). Republican. Office: Sallie Mae Inc 11600 Sallie Mae Dr Reston VA 20193-0001

REID, BENJAMIN FRANKLIN, bishop; b. Bklyn., Oct. 5, 1937; s. Noah W. Sr. and Viola Reid; m. Anna Pearl Batie, June 28, 1958; children: Benjamin Jr., Sylvia, Angela, Natalie. Student, U. Pitts., 1955-56, No. Bapt. Theol. Sem., 1956-58; DD, Am. Bible Inst., Kansas City, Mo., 1971; PhD, Calif. Western U., 1975; LittD (hon.), Calif. Grad. Sch. Theology, Glendale, 1981; DD (hon.), Anderson U., 1982, Pacific Christian Coll., Fullerton, Calif., 1996, Mid-Am. Bible Coll., Oklahoma City, 1997. Ordained to ministry Ch. of God (Anderson, Ind.), 1960; consecrated bishop, 1987. Pastor Adams St. Ch. of God, Springfield, Ill., 1958-59, 1st Ch. of God, Junction City, Kans., 1959-63; sr. pastor Southwestern Ch. of God, Detroit, 1963-71, 1st Ch. of God, L.A., 1971-96; presiding bishop 1st Ch. of God, Nigeria, 1981-95, Interstate Assoc. Ch. of God, Alaska, Ariz., Calif., Oreg., Wash., Nev., 1987—; pres. Nat. Assn. for the Ch. of God (U.S.A.), 1996—; pres. So. Calif. Sch. Ministry, L.A., 1985—; chmn. So. Calif. Mins.' Network, Inglewood, 1990. Author: Confessions of a Happy Preacher, 1971, Another Look at Other Tongues, 1974, rev. edit., 1981, Glory to the Spirit, 1990; contbg. editor Vital Christianity Mins. mag. Bd. dirs. L.A. Coun. Chs., 1974—, Inner City Found.-Excellence in Edn., L.A., 1987-95, Urban League, L.A., SCLC, L.A., Ecumenical Ctr.-Black Ch. Studies, L.A.; chaplain Inglewood (Calif.) Police Dept. Recipient Mayor's award City of L.A., 1981, 86, Community Svc. award U. So. Calif., 1982, Supr.'s Com. award County of L.A., 1986, Mayor's award City of Compton, Calif., 1987. Mem. NAACP (life mem. South Bay br.), Inter-Denominational Mins. Alliance (pres. 1974-76, Svc. award 1976), Concerned Clergy of L.A., Shepherd's Prayer Gathering, Fellowship Ind. Chs. (founder, pres. 1989—), L.A. Ecumenical Congress. Democrat. Office: First Ch of God 9550 Crenshaw Blvd Inglewood CA 90305-2912

REID, BRIAN HOLDEN, historian, educator; b. Dec. 4, 1952; s. Robert Holden and Doreen Joan (Kempton) R. BA in History, U. Hull, Eng., 1974; MA in Am. Studies, U. Sussex, Eng., 1975; PhD in War Studies, King's Coll., London, 1983; HCSC, Staff Coll., Camberley, 1988, psc, 1991. Lectr. in modern history Polytech. North London, London, 1978-80; lectr. in modern history dept. extra-mural studies U. London, 1981-87, rsch. assoc. dept. war studies, 1983-84, lectr. war studies, 1987-92, sr. lectr. war studies, 1992-2000; resident historian Brit. Army Staff Coll., Camberley, Surrey, Eng., 1987-97; tchg. fellow Inst. U.S. Studies U. London, 1988-96; prof. Am. history and mil. instns. King's Coll., U. London, 2000—; cons. Ministry Def., London, 1987—; co-chmn. mil. history rsch. seminar Inst. Hist. Rsch., London, 1987—; hon. vis. lect. dept. history George Washington (D.C.) U., 1995; resident historian Joint Svcs. Command and Staff Coll., Bracknell Berks, Eng., 1997-98. Author: J.F.C. Fuller: Military Thinker, 1987, The Origins of the American Civil War, 1996, Studies in British Military Thought: Debates with Fuller and Liddell Hart, 1998, The American Civil War and the Wars of the Industrial Revolution, 1999; editor: The Science of War, 1993, Military Power: Land Warfare in Theory and Practice, 1997; co-editor: The British Army and the Operational Level of War, 1989, New Technology and the Arms Race, 1989, Central Region Vs. Out-of-Area, 1990, American Studies: Essays in Honour of Marcus Cunliffe, 1991, Military Strategy in a Changing Europe: Towards the Twenty-First Century, 1991, The American Civil War: Explorations and Reconsiderations, 2000; editor Royal U.S. Inst. Jour., 1984-87; contbr. articles to profl. jours. Hon. friend Brit. Libr. Isodarco scholar, Verona, Italy, 1982. Fellow Royal Hist. Soc., Royal Geog. Soc., Royal U.S. Inst.; mem. U.S. Soc. Mil. History (awards com. 1996-99), Soc. Army Hist. Rsch. (coun. mem. 1992-98, chmn. 1998—), Army Records Soc. (coun. mem. 1995-98, 99—, pub. com. mem. 1996-99), Brit. Am. Nineteenth Century Historians (coun. mem. 1993-99 Reform Club, Cavalry and Guards. Avocation: country walks. Home: 22 Danesfield, Benfleet, Essex SS7 5EF, England Office: King's Coll Dept War Studies, Strand, London WC2R 2LS, England

REID, DANA MARIE, lawyer; b. Seattle, Mar. 16, 1966; d. Donald James and Linda Marie Reid. BA in History, Whitman Coll., Walla Walla, Wash., 1989; JD, Willamette U., Salem, Oreg., 1993; LLM in Taxation, U. Wash., 1997. Bar: Wash., U.S. Dist. Ct. (we. and ea. dist.) Wash. Asst. atty. gen. Wash. State Atty. Gen.'s Office, Olympia, 1994-96; assoc. Egger Betts Austin Ahrens & Treacy, Bellevue, Wash., 1997-98, Treacy Law Group, Bellevue, 1998-2000, Montgomery, Purdue, Blankinship & Austin PLLC, Seattle, 2000—. Bd. dirs. Overlake Svc. League, Bellevue, 1997-99; v.p. Wash. Women Lawyers Found., 1997-99; mem. Seattle Works, 1996—; mem. Nat. Com. on Planned Giving, 1997—, Wash. Planned Giving Coun., 1997—. Mem. ABA (taxation sect.), Wash. State Bar Assn. (taxation sect., real property, probate and trust section), Wash. Women Lawyers (exec. dir., bd. officer, Pres.'s award 1997, State Bd. Mem. of Yr. 1997). Avocations: tennis, skiing, running, cooking, the Arts. Office: Montgomery Purdue Blankinship & Austin PLLC 701 5th Ave Ste 5800 Seattle WA 98104-7096

REID, DAVID COREY, manufacturing executive; b. Boston, Dec. 27, 1945; s. Roland Eliot and Lucille Pauling R.; m. Cynthia Ann Wozniak, June 21, 1971; children: Lee M., Randy M., Kathie C. B.B.A., U. Mass., 1968. Sales rep. Procter & Gamble, Portsmouth, N.H., 1971-73, dist. field rep., Boston, 1973, unit mgr. Western New Eng., Springfield, Mass., 1973-76, mgr. new brands, Cin., 1976-78, dist. mgr., N.Y.C., 1978-81, Boston, 1981-85, mgr. new brand devel., Cin., 1985-86, mgr. Crush products div., Cin., 1986-89, mgr. sales reorganization and corp. environment, 1989-93, sales mgr. drug channel, 1993-99, retail pharm. sales mgr., 1999—. Served to 1st lt. Security Agy., U.S. Army, 1968-71. Republican. Unitarian. Home: 8405 Shawnee Run Rd Cincinnati OH 45243-3312 Office: Procter & Gamble One Procter & Gamble Pla Cincinnati OH 45201

REID, DAVID EARL, dentist, military officer; b. Gastonia, N.C., Nov. 11, 1950; s. Clawston Earl and Dorothy Jeanne (Lineberger) R.; m. Camilla Anne Brown, Aug. 16, 1975; children: David Griffin, Mary Deanna. BS, N.C. State U., 1972; DDS, U. N.C., 1976. Diplomate Am. Bd. Gen. Dentistry, Fed. Services Bd. Gen. Dentistry. Commd. 2d lt. U.S. Army, 1972, advanced through grades to col., 1993, dentist, 1976—; resident in comprehensive dentistry U.S. Army, Ft. Ord, Calif., 1981-83; dir. grad. edn. Ft. Gordon (Ga.) Dental Activity, 1994-96; chief operative dentistry Ft. Gordon (Ga.) Dental Activity, 1986 . Master Acad. Gen. Dentistry; fellow Internat. Coll. Dentists, Pierre Fauchard Acad.; mem. ADA. Baptist. Avocation: golf.

REID, DONNA JOYCE, small business owner; b. Springfield, Tenn., June 25, 1954; d. Leonard Earl Reid and Joyce (Robertson) Kirby; m. Kenneth Bruce Sadler, June 26, 1976 (div. Apr. 1980); m. John Christopher Moulton, Oct. 18, 1987 (div. Dec. 1992); m. Peter Leatherland, Apr. 3, 1993. Student, Austin Peay State U., Clarksville, Tenn., 1972-75. Show writer, producer WTVF-TV (CBS affiliate), Nashville, 1977-83, promotion producer, 1983-85, on-air promotion mgr., 1985-86; gen. mgr. Steadi-Film Corp., Nashville, 1986-90; co-owner Options Internat., Nashville, 1990—. Big sister Buddies of Nashville, 1981-87. Named to Honorable Order of Ky. Cols. John Y. Brown, Gov., 1980; recipient Significant Svc. award ARC, 1982, Clara Barton Communications award, 1983. Mem. NAFE, Nat. Assn. TV Arts and Scis., Nat. Film Inst., Nat. Assn. Broadcasters, Internat. Platform Assn., Am. Soc. Prevention of Cruelty to Animals, Humane Soc. U.S. Methodist. Avocations: reading, outdoor sports, travel. Office: Options Internat Inc 913 18th Ave S Nashville TN 37212-2102

REID, GAVIN CLYDESDALE, economics educator, researcher; b. Glasgow, Scotland, Aug. 25, 1946; s. Alexander Macfarlane and Sheila MacGregor (Jackson) R.; m. Margaret Morrice McGregor, Dec. 26, 1967 (div. Oct. 1983); 1 stepchild, Kevin John; 1 child, Neil Alexander; m. Maureen Johnson Bagnall, Aug. 5, 1986; 1 stepchild, Martin Johnson; children: Eilidh Ferguson, Annabel Macfarlane, Kenneth Clydesdale. MA with first class honors, Aberdeen U., 1969; MSc, Southampton U., 1971; PhD, Edinburgh U., 1975. Lectr. econs. U. Edinburgh (Scotland), 1971-84, sr. lectr., 1984-90, reader, 1990-91; dir. Ctr. for Rsch. into Industry, Enterprise, Fin. and the Firm, Scotland, 1991—; vis. assoc. prof. Queen's U., Ont., Can., 1981-82, U. Denver, 1984; vis. scholar Darwin Coll., Cambridge (Eng.) U., 1987-88; vis. prof. U. Nice, France, 1998; prof. econs. U. St. Andrews, Scotland, 1991—. Author: The Kinked Demand Curve Analysis of Oligopoly, 1981, Theories of Industrial Organization, 1987, Classical Economic Growth, 1989, Small Business Enterprise, 1993, Venture Capital Investment, 1998; co-author: The Small Entrepreneurial Firm, 1988, Profiles in Small Business, 1993, Information System Development in the Small Firm, 2000; rev. editor Scottish Jour. Polit. Economy, 1981-87, mem. editorial bd., 1986-98; editl. bd. Sm. Bus. Econs., 1997—, Venture Capital, 1997—. Coun. mem. Scottish Econ. Soc., 1990—. Rsch. fellow Leverhulme Trust, 1989-90, Nuffield Found., 1997-98. Mem. Royal Econ. Soc., Am. Econ. Assn., Scottish Econ. Soc. (pres. 1999—), European Assn. for Rsch. in Indsl. Econs., Nat. Trust for Scotland, Indsl. Orgn. Soc., St. Andrews Golf Club, Royal Overseas League, Network Indsl. Economists (chmn. 1997—). Presbyterian. Avocations: music, reading, running, badminton. Home: 23 South St, Saint Andrews Fife KY16 9QS, Scotland Office: St Andrews U Dept Econs, St Salvators Coll, Saint Andrews Fife KY16 9AL, Scotland

REID, JOYCE ELEANOR, musician, minister; b. Deckerville, Mich., June 14, 1936; d. William Elgin and Elizabeth Hazel (Dawson) Van Sickle; m. Harold Wesley Reid, Sept. 29, 1956; children: Bradley, Sharlene Lisa Thompson. Tchr.'s cert., Sherwood Music Conservatory, Chgo., 1973. Ordained min. Mins. for Christ, 1997. Composer various classical and religious solos, (musicales) History of Deckerville, Thumb Area History, Thumb Area Indian History, Light Houses of Michigan; author: The Thumb Area Indian History, 1990, Indian Recipe Book, 1996. Curator, treas., spkr., founder Deckerville (Mich.) Hist. Mus., 1988-00; dir. Deckerville Hymn Sing, 1989-93; vol. Autumnwood Nursing Home, Deckerville, 1997-00, Sanilac County Med. Ctr., Sandusky, 1983-00. Recipient award Autumnwood Med. Ctr., 1999, cert. Mich. Fedn. Music Clubs, 1999; grantee Saginaw Indian Group, 1998. Mem. Nat. Fedn. Music Tchrs., Pt. Huron Music Tchrs. Assn. (sec. 1975-85), Pt. Huron Musicale (cert. 1998), Mich. Music Tchrs. Assn., Mich. Arts Coun., Pt. Sanilac Mus., Gt. Lake Light Housekeepers Assn., Wolverine State Archaeology Soc., Cen. States Archaeol. Soc., White Rock Found. (treas. 1998-00), Young Musicians Club (pres. 1998-00). Republican. Avocations: antique collecting, gardening, traveling, reading. Home: 4028 Ruth Rd Deckerville MI 48427-9355

REID, MARY WALLACE, retired secondary education educator; b. Charlotte, N.C., Oct. 21, 1922; d. Isaac and Mamie Maude (Torrence) Wallace; m. James Samuel Reid, Feb. 13, 1946; 1 child, Virginia Anne. BA, Johnson C. Smith U., 1945; MEd, Temple U., 1970, Secondary Adminstrn. cert., 1982, EdD, 1983. Cert. English, secondary adminstr., French, reading, lang. arts tchr., Pa. Tchr. English, lang, arts, reading Sch. Dist. Phila.; ret., 1988; Title I reading coord., 1976-82; mem. pupil progress com.; past assn. student govt., mem. PFT Bldg. com. Mem. Internat. Reading Assn., Nat. Coun. Tchrs. of English. Home: 1704 Stenton Ave Philadelphia PA 19141-1433

REID, RICHARD ALFRED, manufacturers representative; b. Neuilly-Sur-Seine, France, June 7, 1918; came to U.S., 1918; s. William H. and F. Isabelle (Goodwin) R.; m. R. Crystelle Covington, Apr. 18, 1942 (dec. Mar. 1981); 1 child, Gary Watkins (dec.); m. Joan Elizabeth Crawford, May 23, 1985; children: Eric Edward, Kurt W., Mark H., Garth Robert. Student, Ohio U., Athens, 1936-38. Machinist Lima (Ohio) Locomotive Co., 1935-37, Ohio Steel Foundry Co., Lima, 1937-39; office mgr. U.S. War Assets Adminstrn., Phila., 1945-47; office mgr., divsn. mgr. James O. Welch Co., Pitts., 1947-57; ter. salesman eastern Pa. James O. Welch Co., 1957-76, Nabisco Candy Co., 1976-79; mfrs. rep. eastern Pa., 1980-97. Chmn. emeritus Svc. Corps. Ret. Execs. Assn., Lancaster, Pa., 1988-99. Capt. U.S. Army, 1939-45, ETO. Mem. Ctrl. Pa. Confectionery Salesmen's Club Inc. (pres. 1958-97). Avocations: reading, shopwork, travel. E-Mail: rareid1@juno.com.

REID, RICHARD DAWSON, chemist; b. Savannah, Ga., Dec. 15, 1959; s. Wade Hampton and Amanda Louise (Spear) R.; m. Catherine Ann Reed, May 29, 1982 (div. Nov. 1998); children: Margaret, Caitlin. BS in Chemistry and Math., Charleston So. U., North Charleston, S.C., 1982; PhD in Chemistry, Va. Inst. Tech., 1987. Postdoctoral rsch. assoc. Philip Morris, Blacksburg, Va., 1987; postdoctoral rsch. fellow NSF, Hampton, Va., 1987-88; chemist PN Svcs., Richland, Wash., 1993-94, mgr. chemistry R&D, 1994-97, dir. chemistry/health physics, 1997-99, v.p. chemistry/health physics, 1999—. Contbr. articles to profl. jours. Lt. U.S. Navy, 1988-92. Recipient R&D 100 award R&D Mag., 1998. Achievements include development of disposal protocol for chromium contaminated process wastes; assistance in the field deployment of a new chemical decontamination process; development and application of a non-hazardous chemical cleaning process for use in nuclear plants. Office: PN Svcs 10306 Baton Pl Ste 450 Fairfax VA 22030

REID, SIR ROBERT PAUL, rail transportation executive; b. May 1, 1934; m. Joan Mary Reid, 1958; 3 children. MA in Polit. Economics and Modern History, St. Andrews U., LLD (hon.), 1987; LLD (hon.), U. Aberdeen, U.K. Joined Shell, 1956, with Sarawak oilfields and Brunei, 1956-59; head of pers. Shell, Nigeria, 1959-67; with Africa and South Asia regional orgn. Shell, 1967-68; pers. asst. and planning advisor to chmn. Shell & Brit. Petroleum Svcs., Kenya, 1968-70; mng. dir. Shell & Brit. Petroleum Svcs., Nigeria, 1970-74, Thailand, 1974-78; v.p. internat. aviation and products tng. Shell & Brit. Petroleum Svcs., 1978-80; exec. dir. Downstream Oil Shell Co. of Australia, 1980-83; co-ord. for supply and mktg. Shell Co. of Australia, London, 1983; dir. Shell Internat. Petroleum Co., 1984-90; chmn., chief exec. Shell U.K., 1985-90; chmn. Brit. Railways Bd., London, 1990-95, London Electricity Plc, 1994-97, Sears Plc, 1995—, Rosyth 2000, 1995—; dep. gov. Bank of Eng., 1997; chmn. Brit.-Borneo Oil and Gas plc, $D; chmn. bd. dirs. Bank of Scotland; bd. dirs. London Electricity, Brit. Borneo Petroleum Syndicate plc; chmn. designate Shears plc. Chmn. Found. for Mgmt. Edn., 1986—; mem. coun. London Enterprise Agy., 1990—; trustee Sci. Mus., 1987-92; chancellor Robert Gordon U., 1993—. Mem. Royal and Ancient Golf Club, Royal Melbourne Club, Frilford Heath Golf Club, MCC. Avocations: golf, sailing. Office: Bowater House East Wing, 68 Knightsbridge 9th Fl, London SW1X 7BN, England*

REID, SUE TITUS, law educator; b. Bryan, Tex., Nov. 13, 1939; d. Andrew Jackson Jr. and Lorraine (Wylie) Titus. BS with honors, Tex. Woman's U., 1960; MA, U. Mo., 1962, PhD, 1965; JD, U. Iowa, 1972. Bar: Iowa 1972, U.S. Ct. Appeals (D.C. Cir.) 1978, U.S. Supreme Ct. 1978. From instr. to assoc. prof. sociology Cornell Coll., Mt. Vernon, Iowa, 1963-72; assoc. prof., chmn. dept. sociology Coe Coll., Cedar Rapids, Iowa, 1972-74; assoc. prof. law. U. Wash., Seattle, 1974-76; exec. assoc. Am. Sociol. Assn., Washington, 1976-77; prof. law U. Tulsa, 1978-88; dean, prof. Sch. Criminology, Fla. State U., Tallahassee, 1988-90; prof. pub. adminstrn. and policy Fla. State U., 1990—; acting chmn. dept. sociology Cornell Coll., 1965-66; vis. assoc. prof. sociology U. Nebr., Lincoln, 1970; vis. disting. prof. law and sociology U. Tulsa, 1977-78, assoc. dean 1979-81; vis. prof. law U. San Diego, 1981-82; mem. People-to-People Crime Prevention Del. to People's Republic of China, 1982; George Beto Vis. Prof. criminal justice Sam Houston U., Huntsville, Tex., 1984-85; lecture/study tour of Criminal Justice systems of 10 European countries, 1985; cons. Evaluation Policy Rsch. Assocs., Inc., Milw., 1976-77, Nat. Inst. Corrections, Idaho Dept. Corrections, 1984, Am. Correctional Inst., Price-Waterhouse. Author: (with others) Bibliographies on Role Methodology and Propositions Volume D - Studies in the Role of the Public School Teacher, 1962, The Correctional System: An Introduction, 1981, Crime and Criminology, 9th edit., 2000, Criminal Justice, 4th edit., 1998, Brown and Benchmark, 1996, 5th edit., 1999, Criminal Law, 5th edit., 2000; editor: (with David Lyon) Population Crisis: An Interdisciplinary Perspective, 1972; contbr. articles to profl. jours. Recipient Disting. Alumni award Tex. Woman's U., 1979; named One of Okla. Young Leaders of 80's Oklahoma Monthly, 1980. Mem. ABA, Am. Soc. Criminology, Acad. Criminal Justice Scis., Soc. Criminal Jus. Assn. Avocations: walking, swimming, reading, cooking, skiing. Office: Fla State Univ Dept Pub Adminstrn Tallahassee FL 32306

REID, VIRGINIA ANNE, school nurse; b. Phila., Sept. 14, 1950; d. James Samuel and Mary Virginia R. BA in History, Beaver Coll., 1973, MA in Edn., 1976; BSN, Thomas Jefferson U., 1986. RN; cert. tchr., Pa. Tchr. Sch. Dist. Phila., 1973-82; nurse VA Med. Ctr., Phila., 1986-87, Einstein Med. Ctr., Phila., 1987-90, Sch. Dist. Phila., 1989—. Active Girl Scouts Am., 1960; Sunday sch. tchr. House of Prayer Episcopal Ch., Phila. 1960. Mem. Nat. Assn. Sch. Nurses, Order Ea. Star, Phi Delta Kappa, Alpha Kappa Alpha. Avocations: travel, cooking, reading, concerts.

REIDENBERG, JOEL R., law educator. AB in Govt., Dartmouth, 1983; JD, Columbia U., 1986; Diplôme d'études approfondies dr.int.eco., U. Paris-Sorbonne, 1987. Bar: N.Y. 1986, D.C. 1988. Friedmann fellow PROMETHEE, Paris, 1986-87; assoc. Debevoise & Plimpton, Washington, 1987-90; prof. law, dir. grad. program Fordham U. Sch. Law, N.Y.C., 1990—; cons. FTC, Washington, 1997-99; expert advisor European Commn., Luxembourg, 1993-96, Brussels, 1997-98. Co-author: Data Privacy Law, 1996, Online Services and Data Protection and Privacy: Regulatory Responses, 1998; contbr. articles to profl. jours. Mem. Assn. Am. Law Schs. (chair sect. law and computers 1997, chair sect. defamation and privacy 1998). Fax: 212-636-6899.

REID SCOTT, DAVID ALEXANDER CARROLL, banker; b. Dublin, Ireland, June 5, 1947; m. Anne Clouet Des Pesruches, Apr. 22, 1972 (dec. Feb. 1988); children: Iona, Camilla, Serena; m. Elizabeth Albright Latshaw, July 7, 1990 (div.); m. Clare Straker, Sept. 25, 1997. BA in Modern History, Oxford U., 1969, MA, 1970. 1st v.p. White Weld & Co., 1969-78; sr. advisor to Saudi Arabian Monetary Agy., Merrill Lynch & Co. Inc., 1978-84; mng. dir. Phoenix Securities Ltd., London, 1984-97; vice chmn. Donaldson Lufkin & Jenrette Internat., London, 1997—. Mem. Turf Club, Kildare Street Club (Dublin), Royal St Georges GC. Mem. Conservative Party. Home: 33 Argyll Rd, London W87DA, England also: Ballynure Grange Con Co, Grange Co Wicklow Ireland Office: Donaldson Lufkin & Jenrette Internat, 99 Bishopsgate, London EC2M 3XD, England

REIDY, THOMAS MICHAEL, financial executive; b. Elmira, N.Y., Dec. 22, 1951; s. Bernard Thomas and Betty Pauline Reidy; m. Rosemarie Stella, June 12, 1982; 1 child, Carla. AS, Corning C.C., 1971; BA, St. John Fisher

Coll., 1973. Cert. fin. planner. Exec. br. dir. YMCA, Rochester, N.Y., 1975-84; fin. planner IDS/Am. Express, Rochester, 1984-86; pres., CEO TMR Adv. Group, Rochester, 1986-95; divsn. mgr. Waddall & Reed, Rochester, 1995-98; pres. Morgan & Alexander Ltd., Rochester, 1998—; pres. CPA/Bus. Forum, Rochester, 1988-80. Author: (tng. manual) The NOW Client System, 1996, The True Wealth Revolution, 1999, Quality Life Management System, 1999. Recipient Outstanding Young Man Am. Jaycees, 1979. Mem. Rotary Club, C. of C. Profl. Sales Soc. (bd. dirs. 1988-89). Home: 24 Columbine Cir Fairport NY 14450-9362

REIF, STEFAN CLIVE, Hebrew and Jewish studies educator, researcher; b. Edinburgh, Scotland, Jan. 21, 1944; s. Peter and Annie (Rapstoff) R.; m. Shulamit Stekel, Sept. 19, 1967; children: Tanya, Aryeh. BA, U. London, 1964, PhD, 1969; MA, Cambridge (Eng.) U., 1976. Lectr. in Hebrew and Semitic langs. U. Glasgow, Scotland, 1968-72; asst. prof. Hebrew lang. and lit. Dropsie Coll., Phila., 1972-73; dir. Genizah Rsch. Unit U. Cambridge, 19735; head, Oriental Divsn. U. Cambridge Library, 19835; prof. medieval Hebrew studies U. Cambridge, 1998—; vis. prof. Hebrew U. Jerusalem, 1989, 96-97; fellow St. John's Coll., Cambridge, 19985. Author: Shabbethai Sofer and His Prayer-Book, 1979, Published Material from the Cambridge Genizah Collections, 1988, Judaism and Hebrew Prayer, 1993, Hebrew Manuscripts at Cambridge University Library, 1997, A Jewish Archive From Old Cairo, 2000; editor: Interpreting the Hebrew Bible, 1982, Genizah Research After Ninety Years, 1992; contbr. 220 articles to profl. jours. Mem. standing adv. com. for religious edn., Cambridgeshire (Eng.) County Coun. Fellow Royal Asiatic Soc., Mekize Nirdamin Soc. Jerusalem (hon.); mem. Jewish Hist. Soc. Eng. (pres. 1991-92), Soc. Old Testament study (com. 1985-89), Brit. Assn. Jewish Studies (pres. 1992). Jewish. Avocations: squash, cricket, football. Office: Cambridge U Libr Genizah Rs. West Rd, Cambridge CB3 9DR, England

REIF, THOMAS HENRY, internist, health products company executive; b. Dayton, Ohio, Dec. 24, 1950; arrived in Brazil, 1995; s. Clifford Henry and Virginia Ann (Sewell) R.; m. Jeanne Brock, Apr. 20, 1985. BSME, Ohio State U., 1973, MS, 1974, PhD, 1977; MD, Chgo. Med. Sch., 1983. Registered profl. engr. Fla., Va.; diplomate Am. Bd. Internal Medicine. Intern internal medicine Jackson Meml. Hosp., Miami, Fla., 1983-84; resident internal medicine Wright State U., Dayton, Ohio, 1986-88; asst. prof. U.S. Naval Acad., Annapolis, Md., 1976-79; cons. Med. Inc., Mpls., 1973-84, dir. engring., 1984-86; locum tenens Internal Medicine, Miami, Fla., 1990-95; pres. Republic Med., Inc., Miami, 1986—, Tri Techs., Inc., Belo Horizante, Brazil, 1994—; cons. Carbomedics, Inc, Austin, Tex., 1986-89, Carbon Implants, Inc., Austin, 1989-90. Inventor mech. heart valves, pyrolytic carbon mfg. method, urinary catheter package design; contbr. articles to Jour. Biomechanics, Internat. Jour. Artificial Internal Organs, Jour. Biomech. Engring. Mem. ASME, AMA, Sigma Xi, Phi Kappa Phi. Avocations: scuba diving, running. Home: Alemeida Serra do May, 330 Nova Lima MG, Brazil Office: Tri Technologies, Rua Peperi 179, 30460560 Belo Horizonte MG, Brazil

REIJSWOUD, VICTOR EMIL VAN, information systems educator; b. Hengelo, Overijssel, Netherlands, May 16, 1963; s. Willem Van and Johanna Van Janssen Reijswoud; m. Liesbeth Steuten, June 28, 1996. BSc, Hogesch. Twente, The Netherlands, 1986; BPhil/MPhil, U. Maastricht, The Netherlands, 1991; PhD in Info. Systems, Delft U. of Tech., 1996. Rschr. Maastricht U., The Netherlands, 1988-94; sr. rschr. Delft U. of Tech., The Netherlands, 1994-95, asst. prof., 1996-99; vis. prof. U. Cape Town, South Africa, 1998-99; project advisor Essential Action Engrs., Rijswijk, 1996-99; mng. scientific officer Devote Inst. of Tech., The Netherlands, 1999—; chair Demo Found., Delft, 1997-99. Author: Demo Modelling Handbook, 1998, The Structure of Business Communication, 1996; contbr. articles to profl. jours. Chair Humanistic Found. South, Maastricht, 1995. Soldier Med. Troops, 1986-87. Humanist. Avocations: sailing, diving. Office: Devote Inst of Tech, PO Box 356, 3980 CB Bunnik The Netherlands

REIK, RITA ANN FITZPATRICK, pathologist; b. Cleve., Mar. 9, 1951; d. Charles Robert Sr. and Rita Mae (Wilke) Fitzpatrick; m. Curtis A. Reik, Oct. 19, 1974. BA in Chemistry, Fla. Internat. U., 1985; MD, U. Miami, 1989. Diplomate Am. Bd. Anatomic and Clinical Pathology, Am. Bd. Pathology in Transfusion Medicine. Resident in pathology Jackson Meml. Hosp., Miami, Fla., 1989-95; mem. faculty dept. pathology U. Miami Sch. Medicine, 1995-97; attending physician transfusion med. svcs. U. Miami/Jackson Meml. Hosp., 1996-97; dir. stem cell processing and graft engring. lab. U. Miami Sch. Medicine/Jackson Meml. Hosp., 1996-97; assoc. med. dir. Cmty. Blood Ctr., Dayton, Ohio, 1997-99; dir. sci. svc., med. dir. Cmty. Tissue Svc., Dayton, Ohio, 1997-99; faculty Wright State U., Dayton, Ohio, 1997-99; chief med. officer Pacific N.W. region ARC, Portland, Oreg., 1999—; dir. lab. svcs. Jackson U. Maternity Ctr., Miami; dir. lab. svcs. North Dade Amb. Care Ctr., 1996-97. Fellow Coll. Am. Pathologists; mem. AMA, NOW, U. Miami Med. Women (pres. 1988-89), Am. Soc. Clin. Pathologists, Alpha Omega Alpha, Phi Kappa Phi. Achievements include research in bone marrow and stem cell transplantation. Avocations: painting, raising Japanese Koi, gardening. Office: ARC Pacific NW Blood Svcs 3131 N Vancouver Ave Portland OR 97227-1560

REILEY, T. PHILLIP, consultant; b. Ft. Lewis, Wash., May 5, 1950; s. Thomas Phillip and Annie Marie (Russick) R. BSc in Biophysics, Pa. State U., 1973; postgrad. in Bus. Adminstrn., Rutgers U.; MBA, NYU, 1991. Cert. prodn. and inventory mgmt., cert. integrated resource mgmt. Inventory supr. Leland Tube Co., South Plainfield, N.J., 1973-76; prodn. inventory control supr. Bomar Crystal Co., Middlesex, N.J., 1976-79; prodn. control mgr. Codi Semicondr. Inc., Linden, N.J., 1979-81; mfg. systems analyst Western Union Info. Systems, Mahwah, N.J., 1981-85; bus. analyst Nabisco Brands Biscuit Div., Parsippany, N.J., 1985-91, sr. systems analyst, 1991-94, tech. advisor, 1994-97; applications cons. SAP America, Parsippany, N.J., 1997—. Mem. Am. Prodn. and Inventory Control Soc. (past chmn. ednl. com. Raritan Valley chpt.), N.Y. Acad. Scis., Mensa, Coun. Logistics Mgmt., Am. Inst. Mgmt. Accts. Republican. Home: 56 Carlton Club Dr Piscataway NJ 08854-3114 Office: SAP America 300 Interpace Pkwy Parsippany NJ 07054-1100

REILLY, EDWARD ARTHUR, lawyer; b. N.Y.C., Dec. 17, 1943; s. Edward Arthur and Anna Marguerite (Sautter) R.; children: M. Teresa, Edward A. A.B., Princeton U., 1965; J.D., Duke U., 1968. Bar: N.Y. 1969, N.C. 1971, Fla. 1979, Conn. 1983. Asst. dean law sch. Duke U., 1970-72; assoc. Shearman & Sterling, N.Y.C., 1972-80, ptnr., 1980-87; ptnr. Harlow, Reilly, Derr & Stark, Research Triangle Park, N.C., 1988-90; counsel Morris & McVeigh, N.Y.C., 1991-93, ptnr., 1993—. Pres. Am. Friends of Paris Opera and Ballet, Inc.; sec./treas. The Camille and Henry Dreyfus Found., Inc.; sec. The Owen Cheatham Found. Decorated Chevalier de l'Ordre des Arts et des Lettres, French Govt.-Ministry of Culture and Comm., 1992. Fellow Am. Coll. Trust & Estate Counsel; mem. N.Y. State Bar Assn., Fla. Bar Assn., Conn. Bar Assn. Episcopalian. Office: Morris & McVeigh 767 3rd Ave New York NY 10017-2023

REILLY, FRANK KELLY, business educator; b. Chgo., Dec. 30, 1935; s. Clarence Raymond and Mary Josephine (Ruckrigel) R.; m. Therese Adele Bourke, Aug. 2, 1958; children: Frank Kelly III, Clarence Raymond II, Therese B., Edgar B. BBA, U. Notre Dame, 1957; MBA, Northwestern U., 1961, U. Chgo., 1964; PhD, U. Chgo., 1968; LLD (hon.), St. Michael's Coll., 1991. CFA. Trader Goldman Sachs & Co., Chgo., 1958-59; security analyst Tech. Fund, Chgo., 1959-62; asst. prof. U. Kans., Lawrence, 1965-68, assoc. prof., 1968-72; prof. bus., assoc. dir. divsn. bus. and econ. rsch. U. Wyo., Laramie, 1972-75; prof. fin. U. Ill., Champaign-Urbana, 1975-81; Bernard J. Hank prof. U. Notre Dame, Ind., 1981—, dean Coll. Bus. Adminstrn., 1981-87; bd. dirs., chmn. Brinson Global Fund Inc., Assn. Investment Mgmt. and Rsch.; past chmn. Inst. Chartered Fin. Analysts; past chmn. bd. dirs. NIBCO Corp.; bd. dirs. Internat. Bd. CFPs, Greenwood Trust Corp., Ft. Dearborn Income Securities, Battery Park High Yield Fund., Morgan Stanley Dean Witter Trust Fed. Savs. Bank (FSB), Union Bank of Switzerland Funds. Author: Investment Analysis and Portfolio Management, 1979, 6th edit., 2000, Investments, 1982, 5th edit., 1999; co-editor: Ethics and the Investment Industry, 1989; editor: Readings and Issues in Investments, 1975, High Yield Bonds: Analysis and Risk Assessment, 1990; assoc. editor Fin. Mgmt., 1977-82, Quar. Rev. Econs. and Bus, 1979-87, Fin. Rev., 1979-87, 92—, Jour. Fin. Edn., 1981—, Jour. Applied Bus. Rsch., 1986—, Fin. Svcs. Rev., 1989-96, Internat. Rev. Econs. and Fin., 1992—, European Jour. Fin., 1994—. Arthur J. Schmidt Found. fellow, 1962-65; U. Chgo. fellow, 1963-65. Mem. Midwest Bus. Adminstrn. Assn. (pres. 1974-75), Am. Fin. Assn., Western Fin. Assn. (exec. com. 1973-75), Ea. Fin. Assn. (exec. com. 1979-84, pres. 1982-83), Midwest Fin. Assn. (pres. 1993-94), Fin. Analysts Fedn., Fin. Mgmt. Assn. (pres. 1983-84, chmn. 1985-91, bd. dirs.), Acad. Fin. Svcs. (pres. 1990-91), Inst. Chartered Fin. Analysts (coun. of examiners, rsch. and edn. com., edn. steering com., C. Stewart Sheppard award 1991), Internat. Assoc. Fin. Planners (ednl. resource com., bd. dirs.), Assn. of Investment Mgmt. and Rsch., Investments Analysts Soc. Chgo. (bd. dirs. 1988-89), Beta Gamma Sigma. Roman Catholic. Office: U Notre Dame Coll Bus Adminstrn Notre Dame IN 46556-0399

REILLY, JAMES FRANCIS, principal scientist; b. N.Y.C., Dec. 27, 1963; s. James and Margaret Reilly. MSEE, Cooper Union, 1987; DSc in Tech., Helsinki U. Tech., 1999. Engr. AT&T Bell Labs., N.J., 1985-89; rschr. Tech. Rsch. Ctr. Finland, Espoo, 1989-94; prin. scientist Nokia Rsch. Ctr., Helsinki, Finland, 1994—; lectr. Helsinki U. Tech., 1991-95. Contbr. articles to profl. jours. George Jaffin Fellow in Bioengring. Beth Israel Hosp. for Joint Diseases, N.Y.C., 1985. Mem. Esbo Segelforening. Avocations: sailing, carpentry, tennis.

REILLY, JOHN MARSDEN, English language educator; b. Pitts., Feb. 18, 1933; s. John Francis and Virginia (Marsden) R.; m. Joyce Jane Whisler, July 16, 1952; children: John David, Bridget Ann, Michael Timothy; m. Janet Louise Potter, June 17, 1995. BA with high honors, W.Va. U., 1954; MA, Washington U., 1963, PhD, 1967. Instr. Wash. U., St. Louis, 1960-61; asst. prof. U. P.R., Rio Piedras, 1961-63, SUNY, Albany, 1963-70; assoc. prof. SUNY, Albany, 1970-83, prof. dept. English, 1983-94; grad. prof., dir. grad. studies Howard U., Washington, 1994—; chief negotiator United Univ. Professions, 1981-94, pres., 1987-93 ; bd. advisors St. James Editorial, London, 1971-80, Melus, 1987-94, African Am. Rev., 1986—, Obsidian II, 1985—. Editor: Twentieth-Century Crime and Mystery Writers, 1980, 2d edit., 1985, Richard Wright: The Critical Reception, 1978, Tony Hillerman, 1996, Oxford Companion to Crime and Mystery Writing, 1999, Larry McMurtry, 2000; contbr. articles to profl. jours. Recipient Eugene V. Debs award Dem. Socialists of Am., 1983, George Dove award Popular Culture Assn., Johnetta Davis Svc. to Grad. Students award Howard U., 1999, Fund for Acad. Exellence awards, 1997, 99; Woodrow Wilson fellow, 1955, Humanist fellow NEH, 1970; Danforth Tchrs. grantee, 1966-67, disting. Contbns. to Ethnic Lit. Studies Melus, 1987. Mem. Soc. for Study of Multi-Ethnic Lit. U.S. (chmn. 1982-84), MLA, Am. Fedn. Tchrs., Coll. Lang. Assn., Soc. for Study of Narrative Lit., Mystery Writers Am. (Edgar Allan Poe award 1981), Phi Beta Kappa. Democrat. Avocations: hiking, cooking, travel writing. Home: 10 Overlook Dr Oneonta NY 13820-4635 Office: Howard U English Dept Washington DC 20059-0001

REILLY, PAUL ALEXANDER, rheumatologist, consultant; b. Glasgow, Scotland, July 13, 1957; s. Joseph Aloysius and Theresa Josephine (Coulter) R.; m. Beverly Parsons, Sept. 22, 1984; children: Cavan, Devin, Sorsha. MB ChB, U. Aberdeen, Scotland, 1980. Registrar in rheumatology Royal Nat. Hosp. for Rheumatic Diseases, Bath, Eng., 1985-87; sr. registrar East Dorset (Eng.) Hosps. Group, 1987-89; rsch. fellow in rheumatology Monash Med. Ctr., Melbourne, Australia, 1989-90; rheumatology cons. Frimley Park NHS Trust Hosp., Camberley, Eng., 1991—; environ. control assessor Dept. Health, Surrey, Eng., 1991-94; invited lectr. Internat. League Against Rheumatism, Barcelona, 1993, Rheumatology Action for Eastern Europe, Moscow, 1993, Phys. Medicine Rsch. Found., Vancouver, Can., 1994, European League Against Rheumatism Meeting, Glasgow, 1999. Contbr. articles to profl. jours. including Med. Jour. Australia, Annals of the Rheumatic Diseases, and Jour. Rheumatology. Fellow Royal Coll. Physicians Edinburgh, Royal Coll. Physicians London, Royal Coll. Physicians Glasgow, Brit. Soc. for Rheumatology. Avocations: golf, skiing, badminton, tennis. Home: Brackenwood Hollybush Ride, Finchampstead, Berkshire RG40 3QP, England Office: Frimley Park NHS Trust Hosp, Portsmouth Rd, Camberley, Surrey GU16 5UJ, England

REILLY, ROBERT FREDERICK, valuation consultant; b. N.Y.C., Oct. 3, 1953; s. James J. and Marie (Griebel) K.; m. Janet H. Steiner, Apr. 16, 1975; children: Ashley Lauren, Brandon Christopher, Cameron Courtney. BA in Econs., Columbia U., 1975, MBA in Fin., 1976. CPA, Ohio, Ill.; cert. mgmt. acct., CFA; cert. real estate appraiser; cert. review appraiser; cert. gen. appraiser Ill., Va., Utah, Oreg., N.Y.; cert. bus. appraiser; accredited bus. valuator. Sr. cons. Booz, Allen & Hamilton, Cin., 1975-76; dir. corp. planning Huffy Corp., Dayton, Ohio, 1976-81; v.p. Arthur D. Little Valuation, Inc., Chgo., 1981-85; ptnr., nat. dir. of valution svcs. Deloitte & Touche, Chgo., 1985-91; mng. dir. Willamette Mgmt. Assocs., Chgo., 1991—; adj. prof. accounting U. Dayton Grad. Sch. Bus., 1977-81; adj. prof. fin. econs., Elmhurst (Ill.) Coll., 1982-87; adj. prof. fin. Ill. Inst. Tech. Grad. Sch. Bus., Chgo., 1985-91; adj. prof. taxation U. Chgo. Grad. Sch. Bus., 1985-87. Co-author: Valuing Small Businesses and Professional Practices, 1993, 4th edit., 2000, Business Valuation Video Course, 1993, Valuing a Business, 1995, 4th edit., 2000, Valuing Accounting Practices, 1997, Valuing Professional Practices--A Practitioner's Approach, 1997, Valuing Intangible Assets, 1998, Handbook of Advanced Business Valuation, 1999; editor, columnist Small Bus. Taxation, 1989-90, Bus. Valuation Rev., 1989-90, Jour. of Real Estate Acctg. and Taxation, 1991-93, Ohio CPA Jour., 1984-86, 91—, Jour. Property Taxation Mgmt., 1993—, Jour. Am. Bankruptcy Inst., 1993—; co-editor: Financial Valuation-Valuation of Business and Business Interests, 1997; contbr. more than 200 articles to profl. jours. Mem. AICPA, Am. Soc. Appraisers (mem. bd. examiners 1985-89), Nat. Assn. Real Estate Appraisers, Inst. Cert. Mgmt. Accts. (chpt. dir. 1976—), Inst. Property Taxation, Ill. Soc. CPAs, Ohio Soc. CPAs (chpt. dir. 1978-81), Accreditation Coun. Accountancy (accredited in fed. income taxation), Bus. Valuation Assn., Chgo. Soc. Investment Analysts, Inst. CFAs, Am. Bamkruptcy Inst., Am. Econ. Assn., Nat. Assn. Bus. Economists, Appraisal Inst. Home: 310 Algonquin Rd Barrington IL 60010-6109 Office: 8600 W Bryn Mawr Ave Chicago IL 60631-3579

REILLY, WILLIAM KANE, former government official, educator, lawyer, conservationist; b. Decatur, Ill., Jan. 26, 1940; s. George P. and Margaret (Kane) M.; m. Elizabeth Buxton; children: Katherine, Megan. B.A. in History, Yale U., 1962; J.D., Harvard U., 1965; M.S. in Urban Planning, Columbia U., 1971. Bar: Ill., Mass. 1965. Atty. firm Ross & Hardies, Chgo., 1965; assoc. dir. Urban Policy Center, Urban Am., Inc., also Nat. Urban Coalition, Washington, 1969-70; sr. staff mem. Pres.'s Council Environ. Quality, 1970-72; exec. dir. Task Force Land Use and Urban Growth, 1972-73; pres. Conservation Found., Washington, 1973-89, World Wildlife Fund, Washington, 1985-89; adminstr. U.S. EPA, Washington, 1989-93; Payne vis. prof. Stanford U., 1993-94, vis. prof., 1994-97; CEO Aqua Internat. Ptnrs., Tex. Pacific Group, San Francisco, 1997—; chmn. Natural Resources Coun. Am., 1982-83; head U.S. del. Earth Summit, 1992; head U.S. del. to negotiate Amendments to Montreal Protocol on the Ozone Layer, 1990, 92; ; chmn. bd. dirs. Am. Farmland Trust; bd. dirs. E.I. DuPont de Nemours and Co., Evergreen Holdings, Inc., Nat. Geog. Soc., World Wildlife Fund, Yale U., Presidio Trust; mem. internat. adv. bd., Lafarge; bd. dir. Goldman Sch. Pub. Policy U. Calif. at Berkeley. Editor: The Use of Land, 1973, Environment Strategy America, 1994-96; author articles in field, chpts. in books. Served to capt., CIC U.S. Army, 1966-67. Clubs: University (Washington), Univ. (N.Y.C.). Office: Aqua Internat Ptnrs 345 California St Ste 3300 San Francisco CA 94104-2606

REIMER, CHARLES WILSON, curator; b. Indpls., May 14, 1923; s. Charles Louis Reimer and Cora Morton-May Wilson; m. Reba Marjorie Fines, Jan. 2, 1944 (div. June 1976); children: Bruce W., Kurt L.; m. Jacquelyn Gayle White, Nov. 13, 1976; children: Laura E., Emilie G. BA, Butler U., 1946, MA, 1948; PhD, Mich. State U., 1952. Instr. Butler U., Indpls., 1946-48, DePauw U., Greencastle, Ind., 1950-51, Mich. State U., East Lansing, 1951-52; from asst. curator to curator Acad. Nat. Scis., Phila., 1952-91, curator proprius, 1991—; adj. prof. Drexel U., Phila., 1965-72; vis. prof. Iowa Lakeside Lab., Milford, Iowa, 1966-90, Jinan U., Guangzhow, China, 1983, U. Concepcion, Chile, 1984. Co-author: Diatoms of the U.S. vol. I, 1966, vol. II, 1975. With U.S. Army, 1942-45. Decorated Purple Heart; recipient Spl. Recognition award Biennial N.Am. Diatom Symposium, 1993. Mem. Phycol. Soc. Am., Ind. Acad. Sci., Sigma Xi. Avocations: fishing, chess. Home: 458 Woodcrest Ln Media PA 19063-4835 Office: Acad Natural Scis 19th & The Parkway Philadelphia PA 19103

REIMERS, JEFFREY ROBERT, chemist; b. Sydney, Australia, Nov. 15, 1956; s. Robert Timothy and Frances May (Wheeler) R.; m. Susan Horton, Dec. 5, 1987; children: Robert, Andrew, Matthew. BSc with honors, Australian Nat. U., Canberra, 1979, PhD, 1983. Fellow U. Calif., San Diego, 1983-85; rsch. fellow U. Sydney, 1985—. Contbr. articles to profl. jours. Fellow Royal Australian Chem. Inst. Anglican. Office: Univ Sydney, Sch of Chemistry, 2006 Sydney Australia

REIMERS, ROBERT STOLLT, III, health sciences educator, consultant; b. June 9, 1943. BA, Cornell Coll., 1966; MA, U. Tex., 1968; PhD, Vanderbilt U., 1973. Rsch. scientist process tech. sect. Battelle Columbus Labs., Columbus, Ohio, 1973-75; prof. Sch. Pub. Health & Tropical Medicine Tulane U., New Orleans, 1975—. Fax: 504-584-1726. E-mail: rreimers@mailhost.tcs.tulane.edu. Home: 4705 Clearview Pkwy Metairie LA 70006-2311 Office: Tulane U Med Ctr Sch Pub Health/Tropical Med 1501 Canal St New Orleans LA 70112-2817

REIMOSER, FRIEDRICH, wildlife ecologist, researcher; b. Weiz, Austria, Oct. 13, 1952; s. Fritz and Rosa Reimoser; m. Susanne Wagner; children: Linda, Elena, Juliana, Sonja, Elias. Diploma in Engring., U. Bodenkultur, Vienna, Austria, 1979, D of Engring., 1985, Habilitation, 1995. Univ. asst. Inst. of Silviculture U. Bodenkultur, 1979-82, assoc. prof., 1995—; leading asst. Wildlife Inst. Vienna Vet. U., 1982-94; assoc. prof. Veterinary U., Vienna, 1995—; wildlife and silviculture specialist Austrian State Forests, 1989-90. Author: Interactions Between Forest Structure, Roe Deer Distribution and Roe Deer Huntability as Dependence on the Silvicultural System, 1986, Target Definition for Forest Rehabilitation, 1998; editor Boku-Reports on Wildlife Rsch. and Game Mgmt., 1990—. Mem. N.Y. Acad. Scis. Avocations: climbing, skiing. Office: Vienna Vet U Rsch Inst, Wildlife Eco Savoyenstr 1, A 1160 Vienna Austria

REINA-ESOJO, DAVID, veterinary educator, parasitology researcher; b. Puente Genil, Córdoba, Spain, July 8, 1960; s. José Reina and Vicenta Esojo; m. Maria del Carmen Illanes, Aug. 18, 1989; children: Alvaro, Mario. Lower bachelor's cert., Manuel Reina Secondary Sch., Puente Genil, Spain, 1974, higher bachelor's cert., 1977; lic. in vet. sci., Vet. Faculty, Córdoba, 1982; PhD in Vet. Sci., Vet. Faculty, Cáceres, Spain, 1987. Free collaborator Vet. Faculty, Córdoba, 1983-84; asst. lectr. Vet. Faculty, Cáceres, Spain, 1984-89, prof., 1989—; mem. staff senate U. Extremadura, Caceres-Badajoz, Spain, 1987-93; mem. exec. bd. Vet. Faculty, 1988-89, 95—. Author: Programa de Acciones Contra la Trichinellosis, 1991, Guia Práctica de Parasitologia y Enfermedades Parasitarias, 1998; contbr. articles to profl. p ubls. Soldier Branch of Chivalry, 1982-83. Recipient 2d Pl. for investigation in pets Purina Ltd., 1985, regional prize Coca Cola Espana, S.A., Badajoz, Spain, 1989. Mem. Spanish Parasitologist Assn., World Assn. Advancement Vet. Parasitology, Entomol. Soc. of Am. Roman Catholic. Avocations: folk and pop music, bricolage, traveling, popular traditions. Home: San Jorge 3, 10004 Cáceres Spain Office: Vet Faculty U Extremadura, Avenida de la Universidad, 10071 Caceres Spain

REINALDA, BOB, political scientist; b. Haarlem, The Netherlands, Nov. 11, 1947; s. Leo Reinalda and Frida Lina Bortoli. D of Polit. Sci., U. Amsterdam, The Netherlands, 1973; PhD in Social Sci., U. Groningen, The Netherlands, 1981; grad. summer inst. Am. polit. sys., Am. U., Washington, 1994. Asst. prof. U. Nymegen, The Netherlands, 1973—; lectr. history and polit. sci. in trade union courses, 1976—. Author: The International Transportworkers Federation 1914-1945, 1997, (with B. Verbeek) Autonomous Policy Making by International Organizations, 1998, others; contbr. articles to profl. jours.; editor Biographical Dictionary of Socialism and Labor in the Netherlands. Mem. Internat. Studies Assn., Am. Polit. Sci. Assn., Nederlandse Kring voor Wetenschap der Politiek, Dutch Polit. Sci. Assn. (sec.). Avocation: long distance walking. E-mail: B.Reinalda@bw.kun.nl. Home: Achterloseweg 45, NL6615AG Leur The Netherlands Office: U Nymegen, PB 9108, NL6500HK Nymegen The Netherlands

REINALDA, DAVID ANTHONY, elementary education educator; b. Lynwood, Calif., May 17, 1966; s. Robert Aarlen and Marie Antoinette (Presicci) R. AA, Riverside (Calif.) City Coll., 1989; BA, Calif. State U., San Bernardino, 1992; cert. elem. tchr., U. Calif., Riverside, 1994. Instrnl. aide Jurupa Unified Sch. Dist., Riverside, 1985, 89-93; substitute tchr. Jurupa Unified Sch. Dist., 1993—; day care worker Our Lady of Perpetual Help, 1988-89; substitute tchr. Riverside Unified Sch. Dist., 1996—; adult edn. tchr. Jurupa Unified Sch. Dist., 1999—; vol. aide Jurupa Unified Sch. Dist., 1989-91; home tutor, 1987-89. Author: ABC, What's at School for Me, 1997; author children's stories Stone Soup, 1981. Little League coach, Riverside, 1980-82, scorekeeper, 1982-84; Sunday sch. tchr., supr. Hope Cmty. Ch., Riverside, 1988-98. Winner 1st pl. Lions Club speech contest, 1984; named Christian Youth of Yr. Kiwanis Club, 1985, Outstanding Young Man Am., 1992, 96. Mem. Phi Lambda Omega. Democrat. Mem. Christian Reformed Ch. Avocations: bowling, dancing, writing, acting.

REINBOLT, DONNA MCNULTY, lawyer; b. N.Y.C., Apr. 16, 1961; d. Robert Joseph and Hannah Theresa McNulty; m. Paul Christian Reinbolt; children: Robert, Jake. BA, SUNY, Albany, 1983; JD, Western New Eng. U., 1986. Bar: Conn. 1987, N.Y. 1988, Pa. 1993. Assoc. Gallagher and Gallagher, Garden City, N.Y., 1986-87, Bachner Tally, N.Y.C., 1987-88, Wagner Davis and Gold, N.Y.C., 1988-92; assoc. legal counsel Zamagias Properties, Pitts., 1992-95, dir. ops., legal counsel, 1995-98; bd. dirs. County Fair Air Conditioning Corp., Westbury, N.Y., 1986—, 360 E 72d St. Owners Corp., 1990-92. Mem. Allegheny County Bar Assn. (coun. mem. real estate sect. 1993-97, treas. 1997-98), Am. Women Lawyers of London. Avocations: travel, skiing, reading, golf. Home: 206 Edelweiss Dr Wexford PA 15090-9441

REINECKE, LEOPOLD, radiation oncologist; b. Johannesburg, South Africa, Dec. 12, 1943; s. Leopold Dirk and Marth Maria (Van Niekerk) R.; m. Laraine Margaret Tatham, Jan. 6, 1972; children: Dirk, John, Karl. MB, BCh, U. Witwatersrand, Johannesburg, 1969. Registered speciast therapeutic radiologist, South Africa, Malawi. Intern in medicine Johannesburg Hosp., 1970; intern in surgery Baragwanath Hosp., Soweto, South Africa, 1970; gen. practitioner, Midrand, South Africa, 1971-74, 75-83; sr. med. officer in medicine Thembisa (South Africa) Hosp., 1974-75; med. officer, registrar in oncology Nat. Hosp. Bloemfontein, South Africa, 1983-85; registrar in radiation oncology Johannesburg, 1985-92, pvt. practice radiation oncology, 1992—. Contbr. articles to med. jours., including Brit. Jour. Clin. Practice, Cancer, Brit. Jour. Radiology, Jour. Nat. Cancer Inst. Lt. South African Def. Force, 1984-89. Recipient Hannah Freed Meml. prize Witwatersrand U., Cluver prize South African Int. Med. Rsch., 1967. Fellow Royal Soc. Medicine; mem. Royal Johannesburg and Kensington Golf Club. Avocations: golf, fishing, studying history. Home: 54 8th St, Houghton Johannesburg 2198, South Africa Office: Box 46119, Orange Grove 2119, South Africa

REINECKE, MARTIN, neurologist, psychiatrist; b. Ehra-Lessien, Lower Saxony, Germany, Mar. 12, 1948; s. Gerhard and Margarete (Ruhland) R.; m. Elisabeth Möller, Mar. 31, 1970 (div. Dec. 1984); m. Bettina Ordu, Mar. 1, 1990; children: Emanuel, Raphael, Rebecca. Student, U. Goettingen, Germany, 1970-75, MD, 1982. Cert. Ednl. Commn. for Fgn. Med. Grads. Intern U. Goettingen, 1976; capt. MC German Army, 1977-78; clin. rsch. fellow dept. neurology, dept. clin. neurophysiology, dept. psychiatry U. Goettingen, 1978-84; sr. physician dept. neurology and clin. neurophysiology Staedtische Kliniken, Fulda, Germany, 1984-89; pvt. practice Frankfurt, Germany, 1990—. Contbr. articles to profl. jours. Mem. German Migraine and Headache Soc. Lutheran. Avocations: reading, collecting. Office: Zeil 77, 60313 Frankfurt Germany

REINEKER, PETER, physics educator, researcher; b. Freudenstadt, Germany, Jan. 17, 1940; s. Paul and Hilde (Weiss) R.; m. Hilda Jacobi; children: Katja, Martina. Diploma in physics, U. Stuttgart, Fed. Republic Germany, 1966, PhD, 1971; Habilitation, U. Ulm, Fed. Republic Germany, 1974. Asst. U. Stuttgart, 1966-72; asst. U. Ulm, Fed. Republic Germany, 1972-75, sci. advisor, 1975-78, prof. physics, 1978—; chmn. conf. dept.

physics German. Univs., 1993-97. Author: Exciton Dynamics, 1981, Molecular Aggregates, 1983; contbr. numerous articles to profl. jours. Mem. Am. Phys. Soc., European Phys. Soc. (exec. com. 1999—), German Phys. Soc. (chmn. div. molecular physics 1990-92, div. chem. physics 1992-93, coun. 1990-93, bd. dirs. 1993-97). Office: U Ulm, Albert-Einstein-Allee 11, D-89081 Ulm Germany

REINEMUND, JOHN ADAM, geologist, geoscience consultant; b. Muscatine, Iowa, Jan. 14, 1919; s. Julius Adam and Eve Elizabeth (Nelson) R.; m. Ruth Ramona Rees, Nov. 29, 1943. BA, Augustana Coll., 1940; postgrad studies, U. Chgo., 1940-42, 50; LHD (hon.), Augustana Coll., 1952. Jr. geologist U.S. Geol. Survey, Washington, 1942-44, geologist eastern coal investigations, 1946-53; regional supr. fuels br. U.S. Geol. Survey, Denver, 1953-56; chief aid project U.S. Geol. Survey, Quetta, Pakistan, 1956-63; chief office of Int. Geology U.S. Geol. Survey, Reston, Va., 1964-84; scientist emeritus U.S. Geol. Survey, Reston, 1984—; exec. dir. Circum-Pacific Coun. Energy & Mineral Resources, Houston, 1984—; treas. Internat. Union of Geol. Scis., Ottawa, Can., 1980-84; mem. internat. geol. correlation program Bd. Internat. Union Geol. Scis. and UNESCO, Paris, 1974-80. Author: (books) Geology of the Deep River Coal Field, 1949, Geologic Controls of Lead and Zinc Deposits, Goodsprings Nev., 1952, Geology of the Macha-ri Coal Fields, Korea, 1957. With U.S. Army, 1945, 46. Avocations: gardening, cycling. Home: 945 Oakwood Ln Myrtle Beach SC 29572-5749

REINER, JOHN, cartoonist; b. N.Y.C., Nov. 9, 1956; s. Allen and Mildred Reiner. BA, SUNY, Stony Brook, 1978. Freelance illustrator Joe Simon, Editor, Stony Brook, 1974-80, Marvel Comics Group, N.Y.C., 1978-84, Mort Drucker, Woodbury, N.Y., 1984-87, Bill Hoest/Wm. Hoest Enterprises, Lloyd Neck, N.Y., 1985—; freelance illustrator for various mags., newspaper, advt. agys., also others, 1978—. Cartoonist syndicated daily comic strips Lockhorns, 1986—, Agatha Crumm, 1986-96, What A Guy!, 1986-96; cartoons appear in Parade mag., 1986—. Mem. Nat. Cartoonists Soc. (nat. rep. 1985-87, Best Gag Cartoonist awad 1994), Graphic Artists Guild. Avocation: bibliophile. E-mail: wmhoest@aol.com. Office: Wm Hoest Enterprises 27 Watch Way Lloyd Harbor NY 11743-9707

REINER, MARGOT ELLEN, political scientist, educator; b. N.Y.C., Aug. 16, 1944; d. Elkan and Grace (Leed) R. Student, May O'Donnell-Gertrude Schurr Sch. of Dance, 1955-59; AB in Polit. Sci., Rutgers U., 1965; student, Fgn. Svc. Inst., Washington, Ateneo Sch. Law, Manila, Philippines, 1972-74. Cert. adult educator, Calif. Rsch. aide Woodrow Wilson Sch. Internat. Studies, Princeton U., 1965; staff U.S. Ho. of Reps., 1965-66; joined Fgn. Svc., Dept. State, 1966; adminstrv., immigrant visa officer Buenos Aires, 1966-67; consular officer Am. Svcs., Lima, Peru, 1967-69; personnel officer Saigon, Vietnam, 1969-70; consular, personnel officer Manila, Philippines, 1970-75; country desk officer, edn. officer Bur. Cultural, Ednl. Affairs, Washington, 1975-76; mem. staff U.S. delegation U.N., N.Y.C., 1976; adminstrv. officer, spl. asst. to dir. nat. commn. Internat. Women's Yr., Washington, 1977-78; analyst info., computer syss. Washington, 1978-79, examiner, aide spl. com., 1979-81; liaison with Ednl. Testing Svc., 1980-81; country personnel officer Brasilia, Brazil, 1981-82; lectr., cons. Unified Sch. Dist., Beverly Hills, Calif., 1984—; lectr. Emeritus Coll. Santa Monica, Calif., 1988—. Creator, publ. (poster) Dear Mr. President, 1985; group shows include Greenwich Village Art Show, N.Y.C., Malibu (Calif.) Arts Festival, 1983. Named Outstanding Educator Kiwanis Club, 1989. Mem. Hadassah (hon.), Pi Sigma Alpha. Avocations: photography, writing, research of current events, swimming, bicycling. Office: Beverly Hills Unified Sch Dist Adult Edn 255 S Lasky Dr Beverly Hills CA 90212-3644

REINERT, KARL-ERNST WILHELM, physicist, researcher; b. Gräfenhain, Germany, Feb. 12, 1929; s. Alfred Martin and Emma Bertha (Schaller) R.; m. Gertrud Friedericke Wotzel, June 10, 1955; 1 child, Hans-Martin. Diploma in Physics, F. Schiller U., Jena, Germany, 1955, Dr.rer.nat., 1961; Dr.sc.nat., Acad. Scis., Berlin, 1984. Sci. asst. F. Schiller U., 1955-60; sci. oberasst. Acad. Scis., Jena, 1961-64, head lab., 1964-91; rsch. scientist F. Schiller U., 1992-94; ret., 1994; lectr. F. Schiller U., 1969-90. Contbr. articles to profl. jours. Recipient Leibniz medal German Acad. Scis., 1971, Van't Hoff medal Acad. Scis. Germany, 1985. Mem. AAAS (invited), N.Y. Acad. Scis. (invited), Phys. Soc. Germany, Biophys. Soc. Germany, Soc. German Rschrs. and Physicians. Avocations: classical music, literature. Home: Leo Sachsestr 34, D-07749 Jena Germany Office: Univ Inst Molecular Biology, PO Box 100873, D-07708 Jena Germany

REINHARDT, BIRGIT HEDWIG ELFRIEDE, chemist; b. Frankfurt, Germany, Sept. 4, 1962; d. Edwin Alfred and Gisela Maria Caecilia (Goeddertz) Reinhardt; m. Burghard Roger Hartmann, Sept. 11, 1992; children: Marcus Sebastian, Julian Marcel. BS in Chemistry, U. Hannover, Germany, 1987, PhD summa cum laude, 1991. Mgr. analytical lab. Akzo Faser AG, Wuppertal, Germany, 1991-93; mgr. biochem. lab. Akzo Nobel Faser AG, Wuppertal, 1993-99; mgr. scientific and clin. affairs Membrana GmbH, 1999—. Co-author: Analytische Methoden in der Biotechnologie, 1991; contbr. articles to profl. jours. Roman Catholic. Avocations: music (playing musical instruments), photography. Home: An der Herkertminhle 10, 63820 Elsenfeld Germany Office: Akzo Nobel Faser AG Acordis Rsch GmbH, Oehder Str 28, 63784 Obernburg Germany

REINHARDT, HUGO, physicist, educator; b. Martinfeld, Germany, July 16, 1949; s. Nikolaus and Erna (Mootz) R.; m. Pia Preissiger, Feb. 28, 1976; children: Claudia, Friderike, Constanze. Degree in physics, Tech. U., Dresden, Germany, 1972, Dr.sc.nat., 1981; Dr.rer.nat., Acad. Sci., Dresden, 1976. Rschr. Acad. of Sci., Dresden, 1972-75, Ctrl. Inst. for Nuclear Rsch., Rossendorf, Germany, 1975-76, Joint Inst. for Nuc. Rsch., Dubna, USSR, 1976-79, Ctrl. Inst. for Nuclear Rsch., Rossendorf, Germany, 1976-90; prof. U. Tübingen, Germany, 1990—. Author: Chiral Quark Dynamics, 1995; mem. editl. bd. Jour. Physics G, 1992-94; contbr. articles to profl. jours. Roman Catholic. Avocations: volleyball, tennis, tango Argentino. Home: Philosphenweg 63, D-72076 Tübingen Germany Office: U Tübingen, Auf der Morganstelle 14, D-72076 Tübingen Germany

REINHARDT, KURT, retired radiologist and nuclear physician; b. Limbach, Saar, Feb. 18, 1920; s. Friedrich and Elisabeth (Hock) R.; m. Maria Lefeber, Dec. 29, 1951. Student, U. Berlin, 1939-40, U. Heidelberg, 1940-45; med. diploma, Ul Innsbruck, 1945. Resident dept. radiology U. Homburg, 1951-58; head physician dept. radiol. nuclear medicine Kreiskrankenhaus, Volklingen, 1958—; habilitation, 1958, prof., 1964—, now ret. Mem. Deutsche Roentgengesellschaft, Internat. Skeletal Soc. Author 10 monographs and med. books including Krankhafte Haltungsänderungen Skoliosen und Kyphosen, and hist. books Gedanken über Erinnerungen an den RuBlandkrieg, 1991, Quellen der Geschichte des deutschen Nobobs von Sardhana, 1994, Ein Justizverbrechen, 1995, Mr. Dyce Sombres Refutation, 1995, Aufgewachsen zur Zeit Hitlers, 1998, Reisebider, 1999; contbr. 220 articles to med. jours. Achievements include the discovery of the first mesomelic dysplasya, which was later named Reinhardt-Pfeiffer Syndrome. Decorated Cross of Merit 1st class Fed. Republic Germany. Mem. Deutsche Roentgengesellschaft, Internat. Skeletal Soc. Home: 32 am Kirschenwaldchen, 66333 Volklingen Germany

REINHARDT, LINDA KAY, minister; b. Glen Ridge, N.J., Apr. 4, 1950; d. Irving Raymond and Margaret Louise (Mills) Vanderberg; m. Robert Richard Reinhardt, Feb. 16, 1969. B of Liberal Studies summa cum laude, St. Edward's U., 1991; MDiv, Austin Presbyn. Theol. Sem., 1996. Cert. spiritual counselor; ordained to Presbyn. Ch. 1996; commd. Stephen's min. Payroll tax specialist Great So. Life, Houston, 1980-82; comptr. Cayman Constrn., Houston, 1981-83; owner, acct. Reinhardt Acctg. Firm, 1984-93; pastor, dir. The Jeremiah Project, Canyon Lake, Tex., 1994—; restoring creation enabler Mission Presbytery, PC (USA), 1998—; resource cons. Mission Presbytery, Tex., 1994—; workshop facilitator environtl. theology, 1996—. Editor (newsletter) I Am Jeremiah, 1994—; contbr. articles to profl. publs. Bd. dirs. Tri-Living Cmty. Austin, 1989-91, The Dispossessed Project, 1998—; vol. in parks Fort Davis Nat. Hist. Site, 1986-87; vol. Children's Ctr. for Austin, 1989-91; spokesperson, advocate rights of disabled people, 1969—; worship leader RBJ Retirement Ctr., Austin, 1992-93; worship organizer Brown Schs., Austin, 1991-93. Recipient The Spragens award in Christian Edn., 1996. Mem. Assn. of Civil Litigants (advisor-com. on status of women 1996—), Presbyn. Clergywomen, Friends of the Fort (life), Presbyn. Health, Edn. and Welfare Assn., Christian Environ. Assn., Evangel. Environ. Network, Soc. of the Green Cross. Avocations: environmental concerns, writing, reading, cross stiching. Home and Office: The Jeremiah Project 222 Soft Wind Canyon Lake TX 78133-2414

REINHARDT, MAX, publisher; b. Istanbul, Nov. 30, 1915; s. Ernest and Frieda (Darr) R.; m. Joan MacDonald, 1957; 2 daus. Student, English H.S. for Boys, Istanbul, Ecole des Hautes Etudes Commerciales, Paris, London Sch. Econs. Chmn. HFL (Pulishers) Ltd. (now Reinhardt Books Ltd.), London, 1948, Max Reinhardt Ltd., London, 1948-87, Nonesuch Press, Ltd., 1985—; bd. dirs. The Bodley Head , chmn. 1982-87. Mem. coun. Royal Acad. Dramatic Art, 1965-96, Pilgrim, 1965. Mem. Publishers Assn. (mem. coun. 1963-69), Royal Soc. Arts. Address: 43 Onslow Sq Flat 2, London SW7 3LR, England

REINHARDT-RUTLAND, ANTHONY HOPE, psychology educator, researcher; b. Reading, Berkshire, Eng., Oct. 13, 1950; s. Patrick Hope and Elise Visinia (Prada) R.; m. Frances Hanvey, July 19, 1980. BSc, Edinburgh U., Scotland, 1973; MSc, Bristol U., Eng., 1977; D.Phil., U. Ulster, Northern Ireland, 1988. Cert. in psychology. Lectr. Ulster Polytechnic, 1977-84, U. Ulster, 1984—; vis. scientist Inst. F. Arbeitsphysiologie, U. Dortmund, Germany, 1995. Contbr. many articles to profl. jours. and chpts. in books. Fellow Brit. Psychol. Soc. (assoc., chartered psychologist); mem. Psychol. Soc. Ireland (grad. mem.), Internat. Assn. applied Psychology. Avocations: cycling, music, bird watching, railways. Office: Univ Ulster Dept Psychology, Shore Road, Newtownabbey BT37 OQB, Northern Ireland

REINIG, GASTON, NATO official; b. Diekirch, Luxembourg, Nov. 17, 1956; m. Marianne Schaack, 1995. Grad., Royal Mil. Acad., Brussels, 1980, French Infantry Sch., Montpellier, France, 1982. Early assignments include rifle platoon leader, dep. comdr. Armed Forces of Luxembourg, advanced through grades to lt. col.; comdg. officer Luxembourg contingent Allied Command Europe Mobile Force, 1984-87; dep. head of command, control and comm. divsn. Armed Forces of Luxembourg, 1997; perm. mil. rep. to NATO Mil. Com. Brussls, 1998—; mem. subsidiary coms. finance, logistics and adminstrv. com. of NATO Maintenance and Supply Orgn., Capellen, Luxembourg. Decorated Chevalier, l'Ordre du Mérite, Cross of honor, Officier, l"ordre de la Couronne de chêne. Office: NATO Hdqrs, Blvd Leopold III, 1110 Brussels Belgium*

REINIKE, IRMA, writer, fine artist, poet; b. White Harbor, Long Beach, Miss., Oct. 20, 1927; d. Chester Henry and Edna Claire (Latille) R.; children: Harvey Franklin Shows Jr., George David Shows, Thelma Jewell Shows Hoffman. Student, St. Mary's Dominican Coll.; grad., North Light Art Sch., Cin., 1996, 97, 99. Freelance writer, student Famous Writer's Sch., Westport, Conn.; freelance writer New Orleans, Long Beach, Miss. Author: Mystery, 1941, My Beach, 1990, Thelma, 1996, (poetry) My Lady of Medjugorje, 1990; columnist Round the Town, Long Beach, Miss., 1963-66, radio-TV paper The Illustrated Press, Irma Reinike's Personality Parade, New Orleans, 1950's; composer songs, poet; stage play Ethel Chichester, Peg O' My Heart, Kaye Hamilton, Stage Door, 1949, Song, Dance Dixieland Minstrel and Variety Artists, 1950-51, Charity Performer, New Orleans and Donaldsonville, La., Le Petit Theatre de Vieux Carre' Sunday, 1996, Destruction by Hurricane Camille, St. Thomas Ch., Long Beach, Miss., Times Picayune, New Orleans; Introduction Camille Book-Hurricane; exhbited artworks books, St. Thomas, 1992. Mem. Nat. Rep. Senatorial Com., 1997; mem. La. Libr. Found., 1999, New Orleans Friends of Pub. Libr., 1998. Honored Author, La. Libr. Assn., 1994, 96, La. State Librarian, 1995, Friends Fest New Orleans Pub. Libr., 1994-96. Mem. Long Beach Hist. Soc., Miss. Hist. Soc. Republican. Roman Catholic. Avocations: fine arts, songwriting, poetry.

REINISCH, AUGUST ALEXANDER, lawyer, educator; b. Vienna, Jan. 29, 1965; s. August and Herta (Lenninger) R.; m. Elisabeth Feitzinger, July 3, 1993; children: Johanna, August. LLM, NYU, 1989; JD, U. Vienna, 1991; diploma, Acad. Internat. Law, The Hague, The Netherlands, 1994. Bar: N.Y. 1990, Conn. 1990. Law clk. fed. cts. Vienna, 1990-91; univ. asst. Inst. Internat. Law, Vienna, 1991-92, lectr., 1993-98; prof. pub. internat. and European law U. Vienna Sch. Law, 1998—; cons. Legal Advisor's Office/Fgn. Ministry, Vienna, 1992-93; vis. scholar Sch. Advanced Internat. Studies Johns Hopkins U., Washington, 1995-96, adj. prof., 1996; lectr. Austrian Diplomatic Acad., Vienna, 1993—; professorial lectr. Sch. Advanced Internat. Studies, Johns Hopkins U., Bologna, 1999—; univ. prof. pub. internat. law and European law U. Vienna Sch. of Law. Author: US-Exportkontrollrecht in Österreich, 1991 (Vienna Juridical Soc. award 1992), State Responsibility for Debts, 1995, International Organizations Before National Courts, 2000; co-author: Staatensukzession und Schuldenübernahme, 1995; contbr. articles to profl. jours. including Austrian Jour. Pub. and Internat. Law, Nordic Jour. Internat. Law, Am. Jour. Internat. Law, and European Jour. Internat. Law. Recipient scholarship Fulbright Commn., 1988. Mem. ABA, Am. Soc. Internat. Law, Internat. Law Assn. Avocations: tennis, skiing, opera, medieval music. Office: Inst Internat Law, Universitatsstr 2, A-1090 Vienna Austria

REINKE, WILLIAM JOHN, lawyer; b. South Bend, Ind., Aug. 7, 1930; s. William August and Eva Marie (Hein) R.; m. Sue Carol Colvin, 1951 (div. 1988); children: Sally Sue Taelman, William A., Andrew J.; m. Elizabeth Beck Lockwood, 1991. AB cum laude, Wabash Coll., 1952; JD, U. Chgo., 1955. Bar: Ind. 1955. Assoc. Barnes & Thornburg and predecessors, South Bend, Ind., 1957-61; ptnr. Barnes & Thornburg and predecessors, 1961-96, of counsel, 1996—; former chmn. compensation com., former mem. mgmt. com. Trustee Stanley Clark Sch., 1969-80, pres., 1977-80; mem. adv. bd. Salvation Army, 1973—, pres., 1990-92; bd. dirs. NABE Mich. chpt., 1990-94, pres. 1993-94, Isaac Walton League, 1970-81, United Way, 1979-81; pres. South Bend Round Table, 1963-65; trustee First Meth. Ch., 1976-70. Served with U.S. Army, 1955-57. Recipient Outstanding Local Pres. award Ind. Jaycees, 1960-61, Boss of Yr. award, 1979, South Bend Outstanding Young Man award, 1961. Mem. ABA, Ind. State Bar Assn., St. Joseph County Bar Assn., Ind. Bar Found. (patron fellow), Am. Judicature Soc., Ind. Soc. Chgo., Summit Club (past gov., founders com.), Rotary (bd. dirs. 1970-73, 94-97). Home: 51795 Waterton Square Cir Granger IN 46530-8317 Office: Barnes & Thornburg 1st Source Bank Ctr 100 N Michigan St Ste 600 South Bend IN 46601-1632

REINKEN, GÜNTER HELMUT, agricultural scientist, educator, administrator; b. Offenbach, Germany, Aug. 18, 1927; s. Heinrich and Klara (Stüber) R.; m. Erika Poetsch, July 30, 1958; 3 children. Diploma in agr., U. Bonn., Germany, 1952, D in Agr., 1956. Asst. in agr. U. Bonn, 1956-61; head dept. Land Wirtschaft n Kammer, Bonn, 1960-89, vice dir., 1989-91. Patentee growth receptacle for trees. Recipient Gold medal Fruit Growers Assn., Bonn, 1991, Chamber of Agr., Bonn, 1991. Mem. European Deer Farmers Assn. (pres. fedn. 1994-97), German Fed. Deer Farmers Assn. (advisor 1978—). Roman Catholic. Home: Höhlenweg 10, 53125 Bonn Germany

REINL, HARRY CHARLES, economist; b. Muttersdorf, Suden, Germany, Nov. 13, 1932; came to US, 1946; s. Carl and Angela (Plass) R. BS, Fordham U., 1953; MA, George Washington U., 1968; Cert. Career English, USDA Grad. Sch., Washington, 1966; D of Humanistics, London Inst. Applied Rsch., 1992; PhD, Brownell U., 1993. Head market rsch. Timex Mfg., Waterbury, Conn., 1955-58; jr. observer Sperry-Rand Corp., N.Y.C., 1958-62; labor economist manpower adminstrn. U.S. Dept. Labor, Washington, 1962-68; labor economist Office Personnel Mgmt. U.S. Civil Svc. Commn., Washington, 1968—; mgr. N.Y. br. Willmark Svc., N.Y.C., 1971; prof. rsch. Haute Ecole Rsch. Alliance Universelle pour la Paix par la Connaissance, Paris, 1992; rsch. bd. advs. Am. Biograph. Inst., Raleigh, N.C., 1991; mem. adv. coun. Internat. Biograph. Ctr., Cambridge, Eng., 1992. Author: (on microfilm) The Story of My Life, 1984;. With neurology testing VA Med. Ctr., Washington, 1989—; mem. choir Internat. Biograph Ctr., 1981, 82; life mem. Rep. Nat. Com., Washington, 1979—; mem. Rep. Nat. Senatorial Com., Washington, 1990. Fellow AA, 1988—; recipient John Edgar Hoover Meml. award Police Assn., 1983, HIR Citation of Leadership Rep. Nat. Conv., 1996, Medal of Freedom Rep. Nat. Senatorial Inner Cir., 1999; decorated knight templar Bur. Internat., 1993. Mem. N.Y. Acad. Scis., Family Immigration History Ctr. Ellis Island, Collegiate Network, Inc. (hon. sponsor), George Mason U. Mercatus Ctr. (contbr.). Republican. Mem. LDS Ch. Home: 2425 Mount Vernon Ave Alexandria VA 22301-1347

REINOEHL, RICHARD LOUIS, artist, scholar, martial artist; b. Omaha, Oct. 11, 1944; s. Louis Lawrence and Frances Margaret (Robinson) R.; m. Linda Dale Iroff, Feb. 28, 1982; 1 child, Joy Margaret Iroff-Reinoehl. BS in Sociology, Portland State U., 1970; MSW, U. Minn., Duluth, 1977; postgrad., Cornell U., 1984-88. Acting dir. Vanguard Group Homes, Virginia, Minn., 1976-77; dir. Minn. Chippewa Tribe Group Home, Duluth, 1978, Human Devel. Consortium, Minn., N.Y., Ohio, 1978—; faculty Social Work Program U. Wis., Superior, 1981-84; adv. bd. Computers in Social Svcs. Network, 1982-85; mem. com. on Internat. Social Welfare Edn., 1982-86, Am. Evaluation Assn., 1986-89; affiliate scholar Oberlin Coll., 1991—. Editor: Computer Literacy in Human Services Education, 1990, Computer Literacy in Human Services, 1990, Men of Achievement, 16th edit., 1993; mem. editorial bd. Computers in Human Svcs., 1983-96, 99, Jour. Technology in Human Scis., 1999—; assoc. editor book rev., 1996-99; contbr. numerous articles to profl. jours. Mem. Legis. Task Force Regional Alcoholism Bd., 1972-73, Assn. Drug Abuse, Prevention and Treatment, 1973-74, Minn. Pub. Health Assn., 1976-78, Minn. Social Svc. Assn., 1976-83, Wis. Coun. Social Work Edn., 1983-84, N.Y. State Coun. Family Rels., 1986-89, Nat. Coun. Family Rels., 1986-89; exec. bd. Duluth Community Action Program, 1982-83; Dem. precinct chair, Portland, Oreg., 1972-74; precinct vice-chair Dem. Farmer-Labor Party, Duluth, 1979-81, chair, 1981-83, 2d vice-chair exec. bd., 1981-83; mem. Zoning Appeals Bd., New Russia Twp., Ohio, 1996—; mem. art edn. com. Fireland Assn. Visual Arts, 1996-99; mem. land use planning com. New Russia Twp., Ohio, 1998—; chair Lorain County Comprehensive Plan Growth Mgmt. Com., 1999—; mem. Smart Devel. Coalition of Lorain County, 1998—. Mem. NASW (exec. com., chair program com. Arrowhead Region Minn. chpt., 1980-81, co-chair task force on computers in social work, 1981-82), Acad. Cert. Social Workers, Cornell U. Sailing Club (pres. 1990). Avocations: canoeing, sailing, wilderness hiking. Office: Human Devel Consortium Inc 46180 Butternut Ridge Rd Oberlin OH 44074-9778

REINOSO, LUIS ALBERTO, retired physician; b. Arequipa, Peru; s. Victor Manuel Reinoso and Cristina Carretero; m. Maria Cristina Maradieque, Apr. 16, 1966; children: Luis Enrique, Victor Andreés, Francisco José, Ricardo Antonio, Juan Pablo. MD, U. San Marcos, Lima, 1957. Intern, resident Bon Secours Hosp./Johns Hopkins U., Balt., 1959-61; staff psychiatrist Western State Hosp., Hopkinsville, Ky., 1961-66, Ea. State Hosp., Vinita, Okla. 1966-68; staff physician Hansome Med. Ctr., Tulsa, 1968-94, Enid (Okla.) Ctr., 1994-97; ret., 1997; consul of Peru, 1972—; asst. clin. prof. ORU, Tulsa, 1976-80, Osteo. Med. Sch., Tulsa, 1972-76. Bd. dirs. Sch. of St. Mary's, Tulsa, 1975-79, Arthritis Found., Tulsa, 1990-92, Cmty. Svc. Coun., Tulsa, 1997—; exec. bd. Boy Scouts Am., Tulsa, 1997—; mem. Greater Tulsa Hispanic Commn., Tulsa; chmn. Hispanic Am. Found., Tulsa, 2000—. Mem. Rotary Internat. (mem. med. bd. 1999). Roman Catholic. Avocations: stamps, classical Hispanic music, gardening, soccer. E-mail: tulsaPeru@aol.com.

REINSDORF, JERRY MICHAEL, professional sports teams executive, real estate executive, lawyer, accountant; b. Bklyn., Feb. 25, 1936; s. Max and Marion (Smith) R.; m. Martyl F. Rifkin, Dec. 29, 1956; children: David Jason, Susan Janeen, Michael Andrew, Jonathan Milton. BA, George Washington U., 1957; JD, Northwestern U., 1960. Bar: D.C., Ill. 1960; CPA, Ill.; cert. specialist real estate securities, rev. appraiser; registered mortgage underwriter. Atty. staff regional counsel IRS, Chgo., 1960-64; assoc. law firm Chapman & Cutler, 1964-68; ptnr. Altman, Kurlander & Weiss, 1968-74; of counsel firm Katten, Muchin, Gitles, Zavis, Pearl & Galler, 1974-79; gen. ptnr. Carlyle Real Estate Ltd. Partnerships, 1971, 72; chmn. bd. Balcor Co., 1973-87; mng. ptnr. TBC Films, 1975-83; chmn. Chgo. White Sox, 1981—, Chgo. Bulls Basketball Team, 1985—; ptnr. Bojer Fin., 1987—; lectr. John Marshall Law Sch., 1966-68; former bd. dirs. Shearson Lehman Bros., Inc., Project Academus of DePaul U., Chgo., Sports Immortals Mus., 1987-89, Com. Commemorate U.S. Constn., 1987; bd. dirs. La Salle Nat. Bank, La Salle Nat. Corp.; bd. overseers Inst. for Civil Justice, 1996-98; lectr. in real estate, sports and taxation. Author: (with L. Herbert Schneider) Uses of Life Insurance in Qualified Employee Benefit Plans, 1970. Co-chmn. Ill. Profls. for Senator Ralph Smith, 1970; mem. Chgo. region bd. Anti-Defamation League, 1986—; mem., trustee Ill. Inst. Tech., 1991-96; mem. Ill. Commn. on African-Am. Males, 1992—; bd. dirs. Chgo. Youth Success Found., 1992—, Corp. for Supportive Housing, 1995—; nat. trustee Northwestern U., 1993—; bd. govs. Hugh O'Brian Youth Found.; mem. internat. adv. bd. Barrow Neurol. Found., 1996-97; Chgo. Baseball Cancer Charities, 1994, 98; bd. trustees Equity Office Properties, 1997—. Recipient Hallmark award Chgo. Baseball Cancer Charities, 1986, Corp. Superstar award Ill. chpt. Cystic Fibrosis Found., 1988, Sportsman of Yr. award, 1994, Chicagoan of Yr. award Chgo. Park Dist., 1990, Kellogg Excellence award, 1991, Cmty. Hero award Interfaith Organizing Project, 1991, Operation Push Bridgebuilder award, 1992, Alumni Merit award Northwestern U., 1992, Ellis Island Medal of Honor award Nat. Ethnic Coalition of Orgns., 1993, Lifetime Achievement award March of Dimes, 1994, Hallmark Hall of Fame Civic award Ind. Sports Charities, 1994, Am. Spirit award USAF, 1995, Alpha Epsilon Pi Arthur and Simiteich Outstanding Alumnus award, 1995, Order of Lincoln, 1997, Mayor's medal Hon., 1997, Bklyn. Businessman of Yr., 1997; inductee B'nai B'rith Nat. Jewish Am. Sports Hall of Fame, 1994, Chgo. Sports Hall of Fame, 1997, Guardian of Children award Jewsih Coun. for Youth Svc., 1998. Mem. ABA, FBA, Ill. Bar Assn., Chgo. Bar Assn., Nat. Sports Lawyers Assn., Nat. Assn. Rev. Appraisers and Mortgage Underwriters, Northwestern U. Law Sch. Alumni Assn. (bd. dirs.), Comml. Club Chgo., Order of Coif, Omega Tau Rho. Office: Chgo White Sox 333 W 35th St Chicago IL 60616-3651

REINSMA, HAROLD LAWRENCE, design consultant, engineer; b. Slayton, Minn., Sept. 6, 1928; s. Frank and Ida M. (Zabel) R.; m. Julia A. Tusek, Oct. 18, 1958; children: Frank, Michael, Diane. Student, Macalester Coll., 1948-50; BCE, U. Minn., 1953. Registered profl. engr., Ill. Cons. engr. GM Orr Engring. Co., Mpls., 1953-54; rsch. test engr. Caterpillar Tractor Co., Peoria, Ill., 1955-58, rsch. design engr., 1958-71, rsch. project engr., 1971-73, rsch. supervising engr., 1973-76, rsch. staff engr., 1976-91; design cons. Dunlap, Ill., 1991—. Achievements include 44 patents including 1st viable sealed and lubricated track, fundamental to success of a new generation of large high performance elevated sprocket tractors, also sealed maintenance-free linkage and large diameter high speed pressure balanced oil cooled brake wheel seals for mining trucks, all used in abrasive environments. Avocations: skiing, cycling, hiking, gardening. Home and Office: 13600 Lucerne Dr Dunlap IL 61525-9619

REINTZEL, WARREN ANDREW, trust company executive; b. Phila., Jan. 4, 1945; s. Warren H. and Lorna (Geibel) R.; m. Susan Rodgers, Dec. 20, 1969; children: Lisa S., Kurt W. BA with high honors, U. Del., 1967; MA in History, Rutgers U., 1968; JD, U. Pa., 1971. Trust adminstrn. trainee First Pa. Bank, Phila., 1971, trust adminstr., 1972-73, trust officer, 1973-79, sr. trust officer, 1979-81; v.p. Provident Nat. Bank, Phila., 1981-86; v.p., head trust adminstrn. dept. Glenmede Trust Co., Phila., 1986—, sr. v.p., 1994—. Trustee Wanamaker Inst., Phila., 1986—, 1st v.p., 1995—; trustee Meml. Fund, Luth. Ch. of our Saviour, Haddonfield, N.J., 1989—, Haddonfield Hist. Soc., 1997—. Mem. Phila. Bar Assn., Phila. Fin. Assn. (treas. bd. trustees 1987-89), Phila. Estate Planning Coun. (trustee 1991, sec. 1994-95, treas. 1995-96, v.p. 1996-97, pres. 1997-98), Corp. Fiduciaries Assn. Phila. (mem. personal trust com. 1986-89, pres. 1996-98), Phi Beta Kappa. Republican. Office: Glenmede Trust Co 1650 Market St Ste 1200 Philadelphia PA 19103-7391

REIS, ERNANE D., surgeon, researcher; b. Campo Grande, Brazil, Mar. 16, 1961; came to the U.S., 1988; s. Daniel and Thereza Reis; m. Katharina Jeker, 1994. MD, U. Fed. do Rio de Janeiro, 1984. Resident Hosp. Clementino Fraga Filno, Rio de Janeiro, 1985-87; cons. Ambulatory Surgery Ctr. Hosp. Israelita Albert Sabin, Rio de Janeiro, 1986-87; rsch. fellow Mt. Sinai Med. Ctr., N.Y.C., 1988-90; intern, resident, chief resident dept. surgery Mt. Sinai Sch. Medicine, N.Y.C., 1990-95; asst. prof. Mount Sinai Sch. Medicine, N.Y.C., 1997—; staff physician, rschr. Lausanne (Switzerland) U. Med. Sch., 1995-97; dir. Vascular Microsurgery Lab. Mount Sinai Sch. Medicine, N.Y.C., 1998—. Named Young Investigator award Merck & Co., Inc., 1999. Fellow ACS (assoc.); mem. Swiss Surg. Soc., N.Y. Acad. Scis., Alpha Omega Alpha. Office: Mount Sinai Sch Medicine Box 1259 1 Gustave L Levy Pl New York NY 10029-6500

REIS, HARRY TED, psychologist, educator; b. N.Y.C., Mar. 28, 1949; s. Gustav and Margot Pauline Reis; m. Carolyn New, June 14, 1970 (div. June 1975); m. Ellen Nakhnikian, June 2, 1985; 1 child, Lianna Jean. BS, CUNY, 1970; MA, NYU, 1972, PhD, 1975. Prof. U. Rochester, N.Y., 1974—; vis. prof. U. Denver, 1981-82, Rijksuniversiteit Limburg, Maastricht, The Netherlands, 1991, U. Calif., Santa Barbara, 1998. Author: Interpersonal Influence, 1981, Handbook of Research Methods in Social Psychology, 2000; editor Jour. Personality Social Psychology, 1980-85. Fulbright Sr. scholar, 1991. Mem. Soc. Personality Social Psychology (exec. officer 1995—). Office: U Rochester Dept Psychology Rochester NY 14627

REIS, JEAN STEVENSON, administrative secretary; b. Wilburton, Okla., Nov. 30, 1914; d. Robert Emory and Ada (Ross) Stevenson; m. George William Reis, June 24, 1939 (dec. 1980). BA, U. Tex., El Paso, 1934; MA, So. Meth. U., 1935; postgrad., U. Chgo., 1937-38, U. Wash., 1948-49. Tchr. El Paso H.S., 1935-39; safety engr., trainer Safety and Security Divsn., Office of Chief Ordnance, Chgo., 1942-45; tchr. Lovenberg Jr. H.S., Galveston, Tex., 1946; parish sec. Trinity Parish Episcopal Ch., Seattle, 1950-65; adminstrv. sec., asst. Office Resident Bishop, United Meth. Ch., Seattle, 1965-94; observer Africa U. installation, Mutare, Zimbabwe, 1994; com. on legislation for 1996 gen. conf. Hist. Soc. of United Meth. Ch. Recipient Bishop's award, 1980. Mem. AAUW, Beta Beta Beta. Home: 9310 42nd Ave NE Seattle WA 98115-3814

REIS, LUIS ROCHA DOS, marketing professional; b. Lisbon, Portugal, Feb. 11, 1966; s. Fernando and Maria Helena (Franchi Rocha) R. Economist, Cath. U., Lisbon, 1990, MBA in Mktg., 1994. Product mgr. Companhia Portuguesa Radio Marconi-Marconi, Lisbon, 1989-91; team leader Banco Comercial Portugues, Lisbon, 1991-93; mktg. dir. UNIFINA, Lisbon, 1993-95; mktg. mgr. Barclays Bank, Lisbon, 1995-99, info. tech. and ops. mgr., 1999-2000; CEO, Economica Digital, 2000—. Avocations: traveling, squash, skiing, scuba diving.

REISCH, FRIGYES, nuclear engineer; b. Budapest, Hungary, Oct. 14, 1932; arrived in Sweden, 1957; s. Marton and Elisabet (Schwarcz) R.; m. Susanna Herczog, Apr. 4, 1958; children: Ann-Britt, Anders, Charlotte. MScEE, Budapest Tech. U., 1956; PhD in Physics, Stockholm Royal Inst. Tech., Sweden, 1965. Design engr. ABB, Vasteras, Sweden, 1957-61; rsch. scientist Studsvik, Nykoping, Sweden, 1961-68; chief engr. Swedish Nuc. Power Inspectorate, Stockholm, 1969-97; assoc. prof. Royal Inst. of Tech., Stockholm, 1998—; team leader Internat. Atomic Energy Agy., Vienna, 1993, Internat. Electrotech. Commn., Geneva, 1985—; chmn. nuclear com. TK 45 Swedish Electrotech. Kommission, Stockholm, 1982—; presenter profl. confs.; lectr. in field. Contbr. articles to sci. publs. Mem. N.Y. Acad. Sci., Soc. Parliamentarians and Rschrs., Assn. Swedish Engrs., European Nuc. Soc., Royal Swedish Yacht Soc., Environmentalists for Nuclear Power (chmn. Stockholm sect.), Swedish Nuclear Soc., Assn. of Swedish Elec. Engrs. Avocations: boating, skiing, hiking, opera, concerts. Home: Fatburs Brunnsgata 11, SE-11828 Stockholm Sweden Office: KTH Royal Inst of Tech, Nuclear Reactor Enging, SE-10044 Stockholm Sweden

REISE, KARSTEN, marine ecology educator; b. Kiel, Germany, Nov. 11, 1946. Diploma in biology, U. Göttingen, 1972, PhD, 1976, Habilitation, 1982. Prof. marine ecology U. Göttingen, 1987-91, U. Hamburg, Germany, 1991—; head dept. Biology Inst., Helgoland, Germany, 1991-98, Alfred Wegener Inst. Found. for Polar and Marine Rsch., List, Germany, 1998—. Author: Tidal Flat Ecology, 1985; editor Ökosystem Wattenmeer, 1998. Office: Wegener Inst Found Polar-MR, D-25992 List Sylt, Germany

REISINGER, KARL, manufacturing executive; b. Steyr, Austria, Sept. 13, 1964; s. Karl and Hannelore (Leitner) R. Diploma, U. Linz, Austria, 1988. System mgr. BMW Motoren Gesmbh, Steyr, 1986-89; univ. lectr. U. Linz, 1988-90, system mgr., 1989-90; system mgr. Kone Sowitsch AG, Scheibbs, Austria, 1990-93; network & telecomm. mgr. tech. and Infrastructure Kone Elevators, Brussels, 1993-97; devel. mgr. Nokia Oy, Helsinki, 1998-99; area mgr. Austria, Germany, Switzerland Nokia GmbH, Düsseldorf, Germany, 1999—. Author: Storage and Production Optimization in an Engineering Factory, 1987.

REISNER, LORIN L., lawyer; b. Bklyn., Dec. 30, 1961; s. Ira Aaron and Roberta Goldglit. AB in Politics, Brandeis U., 1983; JD, Harvard U., 1986. Bar: N.Y. 1987, U.S. Dist. Ct. (so. dist.) N.Y. 1987, U.S. Ct. Appeals (2d cir.) 1991. Law clk. to judge U.S. Dist. Ct. (so. dist.) N.Y., N.Y.C., 1986-87; assoc. Debevoise & Plimpton, N.Y.C., 1987-90; asst. U.S. atty. for so dist. N.Y. U.S. Atty.'s Office, N.Y.C., 1990—. Author: (with Bruce P. Keller) Tademark Related Causes of Action and Defenses, 1989. Mem. alumni admissions coun. Brandeis U., 1987—. Mem. ABA, Assn. of Bar of City of N.Y. Democrat. Jewish. Office: US Atty's Office One St Andrews Pla New York NY 10007

REISS, HANS SIEGBERT, German language educator; b. Mannheim, Germany, Aug. 19, 1922; s. Berthold and Maria (Petri) R.; m. Linda Wahter, Aug. 3, 1963; children: Thomas Herbert, Richard Stephen. BA, U. Dublin, Ireland, 1943, PhD, 1945, MA, 1965; diploma in econs., U. Dublin, 1944; diploma in history of arts, 1945. Asst. U. Dublin, 1943-46; asst. lectr. London Sch. Econs., 1946-49, lectr., 1949-53; lectr. Queen Mary Coll., London, 1953-58; prof. McGill U., Montreal, 1958-65; prof. German U. Bristol, London, 1965-88; prof. emeritus U. Bristol, 1988—, sr. rsch. fellow, 1995—; vis. prof. McGill U., Montreal, Can., 1957-58, 68-69, 73, Middlebury (Vt.) Coll., 1967, U. Munich, 1970-71, 78-79, 2000, U. Heidelberg, 1997-98, 99. Author: Franz Kafka, 1952, 56, Goethes Romane, 1963, Emanuel Geibels Briefe an Henriette Nolting, 1963, Das Politische Denken in der deutschen Romantik, 1966, Goethe's Novels, 1969, Goethe's Die Wahlverwandtschaften, 1971, The Writer's Task, 1978; editor: Political Thought of the German Romantics 1793-1815, 1955, Kant: Political Writings, 1970, 91, Formgestaltung und Politik Goethe Studien, 1993. Recipient Officer's Cross, German Order of Merit, 1988, Goethe Gesellschaft Gold medal, 1997. Mem. English Goethe Soc., Modern Humanities Research Assn., Am. Goethe Soc., German History Soc., Brit. Soc. for 18th Century Studies, Goethe Gesellschaft, Deutsch e Schillergesellschaft, Internationale Vereubugung der Germanisten. Home: 198 Stoke Ln, Bristol BS9 3RU, England Office: U Bristol Dept German, 21 Woodland Rd, Bristol BS8 1TE, England

REISS, MITCHELL B., lawyer; b. Dayton, Ohio, June 12, 1957; s. Martin H. and Rhea E. (Cohen) R.; m. Elisabeth M. Reiss, Oct. 25, 1986; children: Mathew A., Michael E. BA, Williams Coll., 1979; postgrad., Fletcher Sch., 1982; PhD, Oxford U., Eng., 1985; JD, Columbia U., 1988. Bar: D.C. Spl. asst. Nat. Security Coun., Washington, 1988-89; assoc. Covington & Burling, Washington, 1989—; guest scholar Woodrow Wilson Ctr., 1992-95; asst. exec. dir. KEDO, 1995-99; dean internat. affairs Coll. William & Mary, 1999—. Contbr. articles to profl. jours. Presdl. Commn. on White House fellows, 1988. Avocations: tennis, squash. Home: 108 John Fowler Williamsburg VA 23185-6540

REISSIG, HANS-ULRICH, chemist, educator; b. Helmbrechts, Bavaria, Germany, May 9, 1949; s. Helmut and Gertraud (Meister) R.; m. Elke Seidel. Diploma in chemistry, U. Munich, 1975, D of Natural Scis., 1978; D of Natural Scis. Habilitation, U. Würzburg, Germany, 1984. Privatdozent U. Würzburg, 1984-86; prof. Technische Hochschule, Darmstadt, Germany, 1986-93, Technische U., Dresden, Germany, 1993-99, Freie U. Berlin, Germany, 1999—. Editor: Liebigs Annalen, 1995-97, European Jour. Organic Chemistry, 1998—. Office: Freie U Berlin Inst Chem, Takustr 3, D-14195 Berlin Germany

REISSMAN, PETACHIA, physician, general surgeon, researcher; b. Suchava, Romania, Apr. 14, 1955; arrived in Israel, 1959; s. Joseph and Marietta (Freir) R.; m. Aviva Ravivo, May 27, 1986; children: Einav, Tom, Nitzan, Noah. MD, Hebrew U., Jerusalem, Israel, 1985. Diplomate in gen. surgery; lic. physician, Fla., Israel. Dir. undersea and hyperbaric divsn. Israeli Naval Hyperbaric Inst., Haifa, 1988-89; resident in gen. surgery Mt. Sinai Med. Ctr., N.Y.C., 1989-90; chief resident in surgery Hadassah U. Hosp., Jerusalem, Israel, 1991-92, staff surgeon, 1992-93; fellow dept. colorectal surgery Cleveland Clinic Fla., Ft. Lauderdale, 1993-95; staff surgeon Hadassah U. Hosp., Jerusalem, 1995—; sr. lectr. in surgery Hebrew U. Med. Sch., Jerusalem, 1995—. Mem. editl. bd., reviewer So. Med. Jour., 1994—; contbr. chpt. to book, articles to profl. jours. Recipient Rsch. award Soc. Surgery Alimentary Tract, 1995, Internat. Rsch. award Am. Soc. Colon and Rectal Surgery, 1995; Hebrew U. grantee, 1991. Fellow ACS (assoc.); mem. Am. Coll. Gastroenterology, Soc. Am. Gastrointestinal Endoscopic Surgeons. Avocations: deep sea diving, teaching diving. Home: 50 Kubovy St, 96757 Jerusalem Israel Office: Hadassah U Hosp, Ein-Kerem, PO Box 12000, 91120 Jerusalem Israel

REISSMAN, ROSE CHERIE, elementary education educator; b. N.Y.C., Nov. 4, 1951; d. Seymour Frank and Sidonia (Blank) R.; m. Steven Feld. Cert. tchr., N.Y. Classroom tchr. various schs., N.Y.C., from 1972; now tchr. specialist for curriculum design Sch. Dist. 25, N.Y.C.; founder, mgr. Writing Inst. Peer Teaching, Forum, and Oral History, 1983—; grant writer, curriculum writer N.Y.C. Bd. Edn.; adj. prof. edn. Manhattanville (N.Y.) Coll., Fordham U., N.Y.C.; mem. tchr. network Cradle Ctr. for Law-Related Edn., Writing Notebook; mem. adv. bd. Giraffe Educator, N.Y. Newsday; v.p. edn. Wedgewood Brandeis Community Group; mem. tchr. adv. coun. Impact II; presenter workshops on grant writing; ednl. liaison project for social and emotional learning, 1998; dir. curriculum Literacy and Learning Project, 1998; rsch. devel. and standards alignment coord. Futurekids Tech. Literacy Ctr., 1998, ednl. cons. Mus. of City N.Y., 1999—, Milennium Mus. City N.Y., 1999—. Author: Newday's 1988 Elections, 1989, Mayoral Curriculum, 1990, Gubernatorial Presidentes Curriculum, 1987, N.Y. Board of Education Infusing Critical Thinking in the Middle Schools with World Processing Software and Picture Disc, 1994, Entrepreneurial Empowerment 6-12 Curriculum Workbook, Rights and Responsibilities, 1992, Mayoral Campaign, 1993, The Evolving Multicultural Classroom, 1995, The Sun's On - It's Your Turn, 1997, Rhythm & Dues, 1997, Anthony Ant and the Grasshopper, Newsday Governor Curriculum, 1999, Newsday Character Education Curriculum, 1999; field editor Learning Mag., 1991—; editor Learning and Leading through Technology Lang. Arts, 1999—. Christa McAuliffe fellow, 1988; grantee Dupont Found., Am. Cancer Heart Assn., 1992; recipient Judy Blume Ctr. award, 1988, Valley Forge Bill of Rights medal, 1992, Newspaper in Edn. Curriculum award, 1996, Md. English Coun. Multicultural award, 1996, Edn. award Mus. of the City of N.Y., 2000; named NYSEC Tchr. of Excellence, 1993; recipient numerous other awards and grants. Mem. Nat. Coun. Tchrs. English (dir. funding), N.Y.C. Assn. Tchrs. English (v.p. 1993, pres. 1994), Nat. Found. Teaching Entrepreneurships (cons., bd. dirs.), Assn. Computers in Edn. (pres.). E-mail: sjm887@yahoo.com. Office: Writing Inst 110 Seaman Ave Apt 5C New York NY 10034-2808

REISTAD, RAGNHILD, biochemist; b. Oslo, Aug. 7, 1930; parents Ole Imerslun and Bergljot (Huseby) R.; m. Tore Olsen, Dec. 27, 1956. MSc, U. Oslo, 1962, PhD, 1978. Rsch. asst. U. Oslo, 1963, asst. prof., 1970-71; rsch. asst. U. Tex. S.W. Med. Sch., Dallas, 1964; chemist Nat. Inst. Public Health, Oslo, 1965-66; fellow Norwegian Rsch. Coun. for Sci. and the Humanities, 1967-70; sr. scientist Nat. Inst. for Consumer Rsch., Lysaker, Norway, 1979—. Home: Monolitveien 34, Oslo N-0375, Norway Office: Nat Inst for Consumer Rsch, PO Box 173, Lysaker N-1325, Norway

REITAN, HAROLD THEODORE, management consultant; b. Max, N.D., Nov. 3, 1928; s. Walter Rudolph and Anna Helga (Glesne) R.; m. Margaret Lucille Bonsac, Dec. 29, 1954 (div.); children: Eric, Karen, Chris, Jon. BA, St. Olaf Coll., 1950; MA in Social Psychology, U. Fla., 1962, PhD, 1967. Commd. officer USAF, 1951, advanced through grades to col., 1971; comdr. USAF Spl. Treatment Ctr., Lackland, Tex., 1971-74, USAF Corrections and Rehab. Group, Lowry, Colo., 1974-76, USAF Tech. Tng. Wing, 1976-78; ret., 1978; mgr. health svcs. Coors Industries, Golden, Colo., 1978-84, mgr. tng. and orgnl. devel., 1984-89, cons. mgmt. assessment, tng. and devel., 1989—. Contbr. articles to profl. jours. Decorated D.F.C. with oak leaf cluster, Bronze Star, Legion of Merit with oak leaf cluster, Air medal with 5 oak leaf clusters. Mem. APA, Phi Kappa Phi. Republican. Lutheran.

REITER, MICHAEL D., family therapist, educator; b. Brooklyn, Fla., June 28, 1969; s. Harold J. Reiter and Sondra Horowitz. BS, U. Fla., 1990, EdS, 1994; PhD, Nova Southeastern U., 1999. Lic. marriage and family therapist, Fla. Therapist Nova Southeastern U., Ft. Lauderdale, Fla., 1998-2000; prof. Nova Southeastern U., Ft. Lauderdale, 1998—; therapist Atrium Family Ctr., Davie, Fla., 1998—. Contbr. articles to profl. jours. Recipeint 1st and 3rd place student paper awards Fla. Assn. Marriage and Family Therapy, 1996, 2nd place student paper award Fla. Assn. Marriage and Family Therapy, 1999. Avocation: fiction writing. E-mail: mdreiter@nsu.acast.nova.edu. Office: Atrium Family Ctr 4801 S University Dr Ste 2040 Davie FL 33328-3843

REITER, WILLIAM MARTIN, chemical engineer; b. Phila., Sept. 23, 1925; s. William Henry and Marie Catherine (Farrell) R.; m. Helen C. Fuchs, May 31, 1947; children: William L., Ann C. B.Sc. in Chem. Engring., Drexel U., 1949. Chem. engr. Allied Chem. Co., Claymont, Del., 1949-52; process design engr. Catalytic Constrn. Co., Phila., 1952-53; engring. group leader Allied Chem. Co., Phila., 1953-65; mgr. research and devel., vinyl products Allied Chem. Co., Painesville, Ohio, 1965-72, asst. corp. dir. air and water pollution control, Morristown, N.J., 1972-77, corp. dir. pollution control, 1977-86; pres. Cape Environ. Assocs., Ocean City, N.J., 1986-91; ind. cons. chem. engr., 1991—; mem. nat. air pollution control techniques adv. com. EPA, 1979-82, 85-89; mem. N.J. Hazardous Waste Adv. Commn., 1980-81; commr., chmn. Ocean City Utility Commn., 1990-92; mem. Cape May County Indsl. Pollution Control Fin. Authority, 1992-93; adj. asst. prof. chem. engring. Drexel U., Phila., 1960-65; pres. Springview Farms (Pa.), 1963-65. Contbr. articles to profl. jours. Served with AUS, 1943-46. Registered profl. engr., Pa., N.J. Mem. Am. Inst. Chem. Engrs., Water Pollution Control Fedn., Air Pollution Control Assn. (dir. sect. 1962-65, dir. Mid-Atlantic States sect.), Tau Beta Pi, Phi Kappa Phi. Home: 6 Coral Ln Ocean City NJ 08226-2638

REITER, WOLFGANG LEO, national government official; b. Bad Ischl, Austria, May 25, 1946; s. Leo and Fanny (Stoegner) R.; m. Bettina Schmitt, Oct. 31, 1990; 1 child, Fanny Vera Judith. PhD, U. Vienna, 1974. Rsch. asst. Inst. fuer Radiumforschung und Kernphysik, Vienna, Austria, 1974-80; rsch. asst. PSI (formerly Swiss Inst. for Nuclear Rsch.), Villigen, Switzerland, 1974-80; dir. Ministry Sci. and Transport, Vienna, 1980—, head unit natural scis.; lectr. U. Vienna, 1988—; v.p. OECD Megsci. Forum, Paris, 1992-96, Internat. Erwin Schroedinger Inst. Math. Physics, 1992—, OECD Global Sci. Forum, Paris, 1999—. Editor Series in the History Sci., 1992—; contbr. articles to profl. jours. Co-founder Republikanischer Club-Neues Oesterreich, Vienna, 1987. Mem. Austrian Phys. Soc. Office: Fed Min Edn Sci, Rosengasse 4 A-1014 Wien Austria

REITH, PETER, administrator; b. Melbourne, Australia, July 15, 1950; married; 4 children. BA in Econs., Monash U., 1972, BA in Law, 1974. Mwm. Ho. of Reps., Australia, 1982; shadow min. Dept. Housing & Constrn., Australia, 1987, Dept. Sport, Recreation & Tourism, Australia, 1987, Dept. Indsl. Rels., Australia, 1988-89, 95-96, Dept. Edn., Australia, 1989-90, Dept. Defense, Australia, 1994; shadow min. Dept. Fgn. Affairs, Australia, 1994-95, shadow atty. gen., 1987-88, shadow treas., 1990-93; deputy leader opposition Australian Senate, 1990-93; leader Ho. of Reps., 1996-97, 98—; min. Dept. Workplace Rels. & Small Bus., 1997-98, Dept. Employment, Workplace Rels. & Small Bus., 1998—. Office: Dept Workplace Rels, Parliament House Ste MF43, Canberra ACT 2600, Australia

REIVER, JULIUS, mechanical engineer; b. Wilmington, Del., Sept. 25, 1916; s. Hyman and Ethel R.; m. Iona Peterson, June, 11, 1941; children: Daniel (dec.), Alan Theodore, Joanna, Betsy. BME, Univ. Del., 1938. Engr. E.I. DuPont Co., Wilmington, Del., 1939-42; pres. Hyman Reiver & Co., Wilmington, Del., 1946-78; ret. Author: U.S. Large Cents 1843-1857, 1981, U.S. Half-Dimes 1794-1837, 1984, U.S. Half-Dollars 1836-1839, 1988, U.S. Quarter Dollars, 1987, The U.S. Early Silver Dollar 1793-1803, 1999 (Nat. Literary Guild award of Extraordinary merit 1999). Lt. Col. U.S. Army, 1942-45. Decorated Bronze Star U.S. Army, 1944, Cert. of Merit, 1944. Mem. Optimist Club (Man of Yr. 1986), Citizens Commemorative Coin Adv. Com., Floor Covering Assn. of Greater Phila. (pres. 1975), Nat. Floor Covering Assn. (v.p. 1976). Avocations: coin collecting, classic & antique automobiles, cameras, photography. Home: 1802 Forrest Rd Wilmington DE 19810-4319

REJZEK, MARTIN, organic chemist, entomologist, researcher; b. Prague, Czech Republic, 1965; s. Přemysl and Hana (Jablonská) R.; m. Lenka Kozlová, Oct. 15, 1994 (div. 1998). MSc, Charles U., Prague, 1988; PhD, Inst. Organic Chemistry and Biochemistry, Prague, 1994. Vis. scientist SUNY, Stony Brook, 1995; Humboldt Found. scholar U. Dortmund, Germany, 1996-97; ind. rschr. Inst. Organic Chemistry and Biochemistry, Prague, 1997—. Contbr. articles to profl. jours. With Army of Czech Republic, 1988-89. Recipient award Josef, Marie and Zdenka Hlávek Found., 1995. Mem. Czech Chem. Soc., Czech Entomol. Soc. Avocations: coleoptera, cerambycidae of West Palearctic region. Home: Jetelová 2857/3, Záběhlice, 10600 Prague 10, Czech Republic Office: Inst Organic Chemistry and Biochemistry, Flemingovo Nam 2, 16610 Prague Czech Republic

RELE, PRADYUMNAKUMAR KESARINATH, lawyer; b. Mumbai, India, June 13, 1936; s. Kesarinath Shamrao and Pirojbai Kesarinath Rele; m. Jayashree Pradymnakumar; children: Rajesh P., Vandana P. BSc, U. Mumbai, India, 1956, LLB, 1961. Sr. lawyer Supreme Ct. India; exec. com. mem. Employers Fedn. of India, 1988—, mem. human rels. com. Indian Merchants Chamber, India, 1986. Mem. Bombay Corp. Law Soc., Bar Coun. of India. Home: 64 Sea Lord B Cuffe Parade, 400 005 Mumbai India Office: 817 Maker Chamber V, Nariman Point, 400 021 Mumbai India

RELLO, JORDI, epidemiologist, intensivist, researcher; b. Barcelona, Spain, June 2, 1961; s. Jordi Rello and Enriqueta Condomines; m. Maite Ricart. MD, U. Barcelona, 1985, PhD, 1990. Intern Hosp. Clinic, Barcelona, 1985-86; resident Hosp. Santa Creu i Sant Pau, Barcelona, 1986-90; assoc. physician Hosp. Clinic, Barcelona, 1991-92, Hosp. de Sabadell, Spain, 1992-99; chief critical care dept. Hosp. Univ. de Tarragona, 1999—; prof. critical care Sch. Medicine, U. Rovira & Virgili; cons. Servei Catala de Salut, Barcelona, 1993-97, Decision Resources, Mass., 1993-97; dir. doctoral course, Autonomous U. Barcelona, 1995-99; cons. Sociedad Española Medicina Intensiva y Unidades/Sociedad Española Infecciones y Microbiologia Clinica, Madrid, 1996-97. Assoc. editor monograph issues on severe infections and pneumonia, 1997—; editor-in-chief Perspectives on Critical Care Infectious Diseases, 1999. Recipient Young Investigator awards Am. Coll. Chest Physicians, New Orleans, 1994, N.Y.C., 1995. Mem. Spanish and European Intensive Care Soc., Infectious Diseases and Clin. Microbiology Soc. Avocations: chess, skiing, reading. Home: Corcega 454, E-08025 Barcelona Spain Office: Hosp U de Tarragona Joan XXIII, Carrer Dr Mallafre Guasch 4, 43007 Tarragona Spain

RELTIEN, PHILIPPE LOUIS, journalist; b. Thionville, France; s. Paul and Josette Reltien; m. Marie Pierre Reltien, June 6, 1989; children: Pierre, Camille, Valentine. Lic. in journalism, Ctr U Enseignement Jour., Strasbourg, France, 1976. Corr. Radio France, Washington, 1990—. E-mail: radiofranc@aol.com. Home: PO Box 30370 Bethesda MD 20824-0370

RELYEA, CARL MILLER, hydrologist; b. Claverack, N.Y., Dec. 29, 1912; s. Charles Miller Croswell and Edna (Pulver) R.; m. Harriet Watson, Sept. 6, 1946 (dec. Nov. 1982); children: Richard, Deborah, Cornelia. AB, Columbia Coll., 1935; MA, Columbia U., 1938; postgrad., MIT, 1943. Organist, choirmaster Morrow Meml. Ch., Maplewood, N.J., 1937-41; meteorologist Air Corps, Pan Am., Weather Bur., Bermuda, 1946-48, Weather Bur., JFK Internat. Airport, N.Y., 1948-50; hydrologist Ohio River Forecast Ctr., Cin., 1950-65, hydrologist-in-charge, 1965-77; ret., 1977; dep. dir. Hamilton County Emergency Mgmt. Agy., Cin., 1979—. Contbr. articles to profl. jours. Organist Highland United Meth. Ch., Fort Thomas, Ky., 1962-99, now organist emeritus; clk. of vestry Grace Episcopal Ch., Cin. Capt. U.S. Army Air Corps, 1943-46. Recipient Pub. Svc. cert. Hamilton County Disaster Coun., Cin., 1990. Mem. Ret. Engrs. and Scientists Cin. (chmn. 1984-86), N.Y. Acad. Scis., Columbia U. Club N.Y., Downtown Kiwanis Club. Republican. Avocations: travel, music, organist, home maintenance. Home: 1346 Teakwood Ave Cincinnati OH 45224-2126 Office: Hamilton County Emergency Mgmt Agy 2377 Civic Center Dr Cincinnati OH 45231-1305

REMBA, GIDON DANIEL, political scientist; b. N.Y.C., Sept. 24, 1953; s. Oded Isaac Remba and Claire Chaya Angstreich; m. Carole Elyse Wasserman, Sept. 17, 1995. Student, Clark U., 1972-74; BA magna cum laude, Hebrew U., 1978; postgrad., U. Chgo., 1978-84, U. Chgo., 1998—. Fgn. press translator Israel Prime Minister's Office and the Knesset, Jerusalem, 1977-78; rsch. asst., acad. translator dept. philosophy Hebrew U., Jerusalem, 1977-78; nat. network mktg. mgr. Satellite Bus. Sys./IBM, Chgo., 1984-86; nat. account mgr. Sprint, Chgo., 1986-92; mgr. Healthcare/Enhanced Bus. Svcs., Ameritech, Chgo., 1993-95; mgr., Internet/Data-Voice Network cons. MCI WorldCom, Chgo., 1995—; spkr. Israel Consulate of the Midwest, Chgo., 1997—. Translator: Kant and the Renewal of Metaphysics, 1978; contbr. articles and essays to publs. Mem. Am. Philos. Assn., Assn. for Jewish Studies, Ams. for Peace Now, New Israel Fund. Jewish. Avocations: guitar, choral singing. E-mail: doni.remba@wcom.com. Fax: 312-470-4702. Home: 1335 Laurel Ave Deerfield IL 60015-4756 Office: MCI WorldCom 205 N Michigan Ave Ste 2900 Chicago IL 60601-5924

REMBUSCH, JOSEPH JOHN, psychologist, management consulting company executive; b. Joliet, Ill., June 29, 1939; s. Joseph Earl and Agnes Cecilia (Heinen) R. AA, Joliet Jr. Coll., 1959; BS in Psychology, U. Ill., 1962; MA in Teaching, Rockford (Ill.) Coll., 1970; postgrad., No. Ill. U., 1961-66, 70-73, Western Colo. U., 1973-75. Registered psychologist, Ill. Sci. tchr. Crete-Monee Sch. Dist., Crete, Ill., 1963-64; clin. caseworker Ill. State Sch. Boys, St. Charles, 1964-65; dir. guidance Hiawatha Unit Dist. #426, Kirkland, Ill., 1966-69; registrar Kishwaukee Community Coll., Malta, Ill., 1969-81; spl. rep., dist. mgr., regional mgr. George S. May Internat., Park Ridge, Ill., 1982-86, 89—, divisional sales mgr., 1986-89; pvt. practice psychology DeKalb, Ill., 1971-80; cons. psychologist Ill. Div. Vocat. Rehab., DeKalb, 1971-79. Mem. Illini Great Dane Club, Delta Upsilon, Phi Delta Kappa. Republican. Roman Catholic. Home: 3499 Regent Dr Palatine IL 60067-4744

REMENGESAU, THOMAS, JR., Palauan government official; b. Koror, Palau, Feb. 28, 1956; married; 4 children. BS in Criminology, Grand Valley State U., 1979; postgrad., Mich. State U., 1979-81. Legal rschr. Fed. Dist. Ct., Saipan, No. Mariana Islands, 1981; health planner, adminstrn. officer Govt. of Palau, 1982; pub. info. officer Palau Nat. Congress, 1983; senator Second & Third Olbiil Era Kelulau, 1984-92; chmn. ways and means com.; v.p., min. adminstrn. rep. Rep. of Palau Nat. Govt., 1992—; chmn. Palau/Micronesia Olympic Games Com., 1990, Compact of Free Assn. Transition Commn., 1994; mem. Presdl. Task Force on Polit. Status Negotiations with USA Govt., 1991; chmn. Palau Sports Commn., 1994—, chmn. disaster plan task force, 1996—; Palau rep. Internat. Monetary Fund, 1998—. Office: Office of Vp PO Box 100 Palau PW 96940-0100*

REMICK, FORREST JEROME, JR., former university official; b. Lock Haven, Pa., Mar. 16, 1931; s. Forrest Jerome Sr. and Ruth Betsy (Saiers) R.; m. Grace Louise Grove, June 7, 1953; children: Beth Ann Remick Gillio, Eric Forrest. BSME, Pa. State U., 1955, MSME, 1958, PhD in ME, 1963; diploma, Oak Ridge (Tenn.) Sch. Reactor Tech., 1956. Engr. Bell Telephone Labs., Whippany, N.J., 1955-56; dir. nuclear reactor facility Pa. State U., University Park, 1959-65, dir. Inst. Sci. Engring., 1967-79, acting dir. Ctr. Air Environ. Studies, 1976-78, dir. intercoll. research programs, 1979-85, asst. v.p. research, grad. studies, 1979-84, assoc. v.p. research, 1985-89; dir. Curtiss Wright Nuclear Research Lab., Quehanna, Pa., 1960-65; chief tng. sect. dept. tech. assistance IAEA, Vienna, Austria, 1965-67; mem. Nat. Nuclear Accrediting Bd., Inst. Nuclear Power Ops., Atlanta, mem. adv. coun., 1995—; mem. Sci. Adv. Com. Idaho Nat. Enging. Lab., Idaho Falls, 1984-89, Reactor Safety Adv. Com., Savannah River Lab., Aiken, S.C., 1986-89, chmn., 1989; mem. Adv. Com. on Reactor Safeguards, Washington, 1982, vice chmn., 1987-88, chmn., 1989; commr. U.S. Nuclear Regulatory Commn., 1989-94, cons., 1994—; bd. dirs. Pub. Svc. Enterprise Group, Pub. Svc. Electric and Gas; mem. adv. bd. Applied Rsch. Lab., Pa. State U., 1994—. Served to sgt. U.S. Army, 1951-52. Named Outstanding Engring. Alumnus, Pa. State U., 1993; recipient Thomas P. Hamrick award for contbns. to tng. of nuclear facility pers., 1995. Fellow Am. Nuclear Soc. (bd. dirs. 1995—, meml. lectr. award 1971, disting. speaker award 1983); mem. ASME, Am. Soc. Engring. Edn., Nuclear Accrediting Bd. Republican. Lutheran. Home and Office: 305 E Hamilton Ave State College PA 16801-5413

REMINE, WILLIAM HERVEY, JR., surgeon; b. Richmond, Va., Oct. 11, 1918; s. William Hervey and Mabel Inez (Walthall) ReM.; m. Doris Irene Grumbacher, June 9, 1943; children: William H., Stephen Gordon, Walter James, Gary Craig. B.S. in Biology, U. Richmond, 1940, D.Sc. (hon.), 1965; M.D., Med. Coll. Va., Richmond, 1943; M.S. in Surgery, U. Minn., Mpls., 1952. Diplomate Am. Bd. Surgery. Intern Doctor's Hosp., Washington, 1944; fellow in surgery Mayo Clinic, Rochester, Minn., 1944-45, 47-52; instr. surgery Mayo Grad. Sch. Medicine, Rochester, Minn., 1954-59, asst. prof. surgery, 1959-65, assoc. prof. surgery, 1965-70, prof. surgery, 1970-83, prof. surgery emeritus, 1983—; surg. cons. to surgeon gen. U.S. Army, 1965-75; surg. lectr., USSR, 1987, 89, Japan, 1988, 90, Egypt, 1990; lectr. Soviet-Am. seminars, USSR, 1987, 89. Sr. author: Cancer of the Stomach, 1964, Manual of Upper Gastro-intestinal Surgery, 1985; editor: Problems in General Surgery, Surgery of the Biliary Tract, 1986; mem. editorial bd. Rev. Surgery, 1965-75, Jour. Lancet, 1968-77; contbr. 200 articles to profl. jours. Served to capt. U.S. Army, 1945-47. Recipient St. Francis surg. award St. Francis Hosp., Pitts., 1976, Disting. Svc. award Alumni Council, U. Richmond, 1976, Dist. Alumnus award Mayo Found., 2000. Mem. ACS, AAAS, Am. Assn. History of Medicine, AMA, Am. Med. Writers Assn., Am. Soc. Colon and Rectal Surgeons, Soc. Surgery Alimentary Tract (v.p. 1983-84), Am. Surg. Assn., Assn. Mil. Surgeons U.S., Internat. Soc. Surgery, Digestive Disease Found., Priestley Soc. (pres. 1968-69), Central Assn. Physicians and Dentists (pres. 1972-73), Central Surg. Assn., Soc. Med. Cons. Armed Forces, Mayo Clinic Surg. Soc. (chmn. 1964-66), Soc. Head and Neck Surgeons, Soc. Surg. Oncology, So. Surg. Assn., Western Surg. Assn. (pres. 1979-80), Minn. State Med. Assn., Minn. Surg. Soc. (pres. 1966-67), Zumbro Valley Med. Soc., Sigma Xi; hon. mem. Colombian Coll. Surgeons, St. Paul Surg. Soc., Flint Surg. Soc., Venezuelan Surg. Soc., Colombian Soc. Gastroenterology, Dallas So. Clin. Soc., Ga. Surg. Soc., Soc. Postgrad. Surgeons Los Angeles County, Japanese Surg. Soc., Argentine Surg. Digestive Soc., Bassanese Surg. Assn. (Italy), Tex. Surg. Soc., Omicron Delta Kappa, Alpha Omega Alpha, Beta Beta Beta, Kappa Sigma. Methodist. Avocations: hunting, fishing, golf, photography, boating, music. Home: Sawgrass Players Club 8212 Seven Mile Dr Ponte Vedra Beach FL 32082-3129

REMINGER, RICHARD THOMAS, lawyer, artist; b. Cleve., Apr. 3, 1931; s. Edwin Carl and Theresa Henrietta (Bookmyer) R.; m. Billie Carmen Greer, June 26, 1954; children: Susan Greer, Patricia Allison, Richard Thomas. AB, Case-Western Res. U., 1953; JD, Cleve. State U., 1957. Bar: Ohio 1957, Pa. 1978, U.S. Supreme Ct. 1961. Pers. and safety dir. Motor Express, Inc., Cleve., 1954-58; mng. ptnr. Reminger & Reminger Co., L.P.A., Cleve., 1958-90; mem. nat. claims couns. adv. bd. Comml. Union Assurance Co., 1980-90; lectr. transp. law Fenn Coll., 1960-62; lectr. bus. law Case Western Res. U., 1962-64; lectr. products liability U. Wirtschaft at Schloss Gracht, Erfstadt-Liblar, Germany, 1990-91, Bar Assn. City of Hamburg, Germany, 1990; mem. faculty Nat. Inst. for Trial Advocacy, 1992. Mem. joint com. Cleve. Acad. Medicine-Greater Cleve. Bar Assn.; trustee Cleve. Zool. Soc., mem. exec. com., 1984-89, v.p., 1987-89; trustee Andrew Sch., 1984-96; Meridia Huron Hosp., Cleve., Cleve. Sch. for Blind, 1987-88, Cerebral Palsy Assn., 1984-87; trustee Intracoastal Health Sys., Palm Beach, Fla., 1992-2000. With AC, USNR, 1950-58. Mem. ABA (com. on law and medicine, profl. responsibility com. 1977-90), FBA, ATLA, Fedn. Ins. and Corp. Counsel, Internat. Bar Assn., Ohio Bar Assn. (coun. dels. 1987-90, internat. law com. 1990-91), Pa. Bar Assn., Cleve. Bar Assn. (chmn. med.-legal com. 1978-79, prof. liability com. 1977-90), Transp. Lawyers Assn., Cleve. Assn. Civil Trial Attys., Am. Soc. Hosp. Attys., Soc. Ohio Hosp. Attys., Ohio Assn. Civil Trial Attys., Am. Judicature Soc., Def. Rsch. Inst., Maritime Law Assn. U.S., Am. Coll. Law and Medicine, 8th Jud. Bar Assn. (life Ohio dist.), Internat. Ins. Law Soc., Palm Beach County Bar Assn., Oil Painters Am., Soc. Four Arts, Internat. Soc. Marine Painters (profl. mem., v.p.), Mayfield Country Club (pres. 1980-82), Union Club, Hermit Club (pres. 1973-75), Lost Tree Club (bd. govs. 1991-94), Everglades Club (Fla.), Kirtland Country Club (Cleve.), Rolling Rock Club (Pa.), The Bohemian Club (Calif.), Salmagundi Club (N.Y.C.), Case Res. Athletic Club (life), The Old Guard Soc. Palm Beach.

REMKO, MILAN, chemist, educator; b. Jasenova, Slovakia, Oct. 29, 1948; s. Matej and Zofia (Malikova) R.; m. Anna Okrucka, Apr. 26, 1997; children: Martina, Zuzana. Chemist, Slovak Tech. U., Bratislava, Slovakia, 1971, PhD, 1977, DSc, 1994; Habil, Comenius U., Bratislava, 1991. Chartered chemist, U.K. Rsch. worker Inst. of Polymers, Bratislava, 1972-74, Pulp and Paper Rsch. Inst., Bratislava, 1974-78; assoc. prof. Comenius U., Bratislava, 1992-98, dep. head dept. pharm. chemistry, 1996—, prof., 1998—; vis. rschr. U. Groningen, Holland, 1981, 96, U. Innsbruck, Austria, 1991-2000; vis. prof. So. Ill. U., Carbondale, 1987, U. Oxford, Eng., 1999; mem. sci. coun. Faculty of Pharmacy, Comenius U., Bratislava, 1990-94, 96—, senator, 1993-94; vis. scientist U. Erlangen, Germany, 1994; vis. fellow U. Cambridge, Eng., 1995. Author: Methods of Drug Design and Development, 1999, Molecular Modelling, Principles and Applications, 2000; contbg. author QSAR in Design of Bioactive Compounds, 1992; contbr. over 140 articles to sci. chem. and pharm. jours. Author: (textbook) Molecular Basis for Drug Action, 1997. Sr. Fulbright scholar, 1987; DAAD scholar, Germany, 1994. Fellow Royal Soc. Chemistry (U.K.); mem. Internat. Soc. for Theoretical Chem. Physics, World Assn. Theoretically Oriented Chemists, Slovak Chem. Soc. (chmn. divsn. 1991—), Slovak Pharm. Soc.. Lutheran. Avocations: geography, hiking, football.

REMNIOV, ANATOLIY MICHAILOVITCH, engineering educator; b. Vladivostok, Russia, Feb. 16, 1947; s. Mikhail Egorovitch and Anna Ivanovna (Dgidkova) R.; m. Valentina Georgievna Maximova, July 13, 1951; children: Natalia, Mikhail. Degree in engring., Tech. U. Moscow Power Inst., 1971, PhD, 1985. Engr. Smolensk br. Tech. U. Moscow Power Inst., 1971-73, asst., 1973-78, 1981-90, prof., 1990. Author: Circuit Engineering of Device on MOSFET, 1994; contbr. articles to profl. jours. Avocation: photography. Home: Kirova 25 6 14, 214004 Smolensk Russia Office: Tech U Moscow Power Inst, Energetskil 1, 214013 Smolensk Russia

REMO, JOHN LUCIEN, physicist, business executive; b. Bklyn., Dec. 13, 1941; s. John G. and Mary (DiVitis) R.; m. Claudia Jill Kyser (div. Feb. 2000); children: John Christopher, Allison Mary.; BS, Manhattan Coll., 1963; MS, SUNY, Stony Brook, 1971, Poly. Inst. N.Y., 1973; PhD, Polytech. Inst. N.Y., 1979. Pres. ERG Cons., St. James, N.Y., 1981-2000; prof. Ctr. Energy Policy and Research N.Y. Inst. Tech., Old Westbury, 1983-87; pres. ERG Systems Inc., St. James, N.Y., 1984—, Quantametrics, Inc., St. James, 1987—; rsch. scientist Harvard U. dept. astronomy, Cambridge, Mass., 1997—; vis. scientist Harvard Smithsonian Ctr. Astrophysics, Cambridge, Mass., 1997—; pres. Quantum Resonance, Inc., St. James, 2000—; organizer and chmn. UN Conf. on Near-Earth Objects, N.Y., 1995; contbr. to UNISPACE III UN Space benefits for Humanity in the Twenty-First Century, Vienna, 1999; rsch. cons. various cos. Contbr. articles to profl. publs. Recipient Nininger Meteorite award Ariz. State U., 1973-74, Chancellor's Excellence in Teaching award State U. N.Y., 1976, rsch. award on displacement sensors NASA, 1996, Minor Planet Remo 2114T-2 award Internat. Astron. Union, 1999. Fellow Explorers Club; mem. Optical Soc. Am., Soc. for Optical Engring., N.Y. Acad. Scis., Sigma Xi, Sigma Pi Sigma. Achievements include developing patents in laser design, instrumentaion (electro-optics) and materials processing. Home: 1 Brackenwoods Path Saint James NY 11780-1121 Office: Quantum Resonance Inc Brackenwood Path Head of Harbor Saint James NY 11780

REN, JIAN-FANG, echocardiologist, medical educator; b. Shanghai, Feb. 27, 1937; came to U.S., 1982; s. Dao-Yuan and De-Xin (Sun) R.; m. He Tong, Jan. 13, 1963; 1 child, Kenna. MD, Zhe-Jiang Med. U., Hangzhou, China, 1960. Cert. Am. Registry Diagnostic Cardiac Sonographer. Rsch. dr. Inst. Ocupl. Hygiene, Beijing, 1963-72; attending dr. Beijing Rlwy. Gen. Hosp., 1972-81; sr. investigator Likoff Cardiovasc. Inst. Hahnemann U., Phila., 1982-84; chief physician, dir. diagnostic ultrasound divsn. Beijing Rlwy. Gen. Hosp., 1984-88; prof. medicine Shanghai Rlwy. Med. Coll., 1985-88; prof., faculty cardiology fellow Third Tchg. Hosp., Beijing Med. U., 1988; rsch. prof. medicine Likoff Cardiovasc. Inst. Hahnemann U., Phila., 1988-92; dir. ultrasound rsch., adj. prof. medicine Phila. Heart Inst., Presbyn. Med. Ctr., U. Pa., 1993-95; rsch. prof. medicine Hahnemann divsn. Allegheny U. Hosps., Phila., 1996-98; rsch. assoc. exptl. and clin. electrophysiology labs. Hosp. U. Pa., 1999—; adv. prof. medicine Nanjing (China) Rlwy. Med. Coll., 1985-88. Author: (book chpts.) Practical Cardiology, 1993, Doppler Echocardiography, 1993; contbr. articles to profl. jours. including Chinese Jour. Cardiology, Am. Heart Jour., Jour. Am. Coll. Cardiology, Am. Jour. Cardiology, Circulation, Echocardiography, PACE, Ultrasound in Medicine and Biology. Recipient Pioneer award World Fedn. Ultrasound in Medicine and Biology and Am. Inst. Ultrasound in Medicine, 1988. Fellow Am. Coll. Cardiology; Internat. Cardiac Doppler Soc. (bd. dirs. 1986-91), Soc. Ultrasound in Medicine of Chinese Med. Assn. (pres. 1986-91), Asian Fedn. Socs. for Ultrasound in Medicine and Biology (councillor, v.p., pres. 1985-93). Achievements include advanced research on diagnostic ultrasound cardiovascular diseases; recent contributions to development of intracardiac catheter echocardiography. Office: Cardiac Electrophysiology Rsch Lab Divsn Cardio Med MSRL Bldg Presbyn Med Ctr 39th & Market Sts Philadelphia PA 19104

REN, JIYU, library director; b. Pingyuan County, Shandong, China, Apr. 15, 1916; s. Zijiu and Guofang (Song) R.; m. Zhong Yun Feng, Sept. 15, 1946; children: Ren Yuan, Ren Zhong. Student, Beijing U., 1934-37; BA, Southwest Union U., Kun Ming, China, 1938; MA, Southwest Union U., 1939-42. Lectr. philosophy dept. Southwest Union U., 1946-49; assoc. prof. philosophy dept. Beijing U., 1949-56, prof. philosophy dept., 1956-64; dir. Inst. for World Religion Study Chinese Acad. Social Scis., Beijing, 1964-87; dir. Nat. Libr. of China, Beijing, 1987—. Author: Re-Explanation of Philosophy, 1981; editor: History of Chinese Philosophy, vols. 1-4, 1963-79 (Nat. Excellent Textbook spl. prize 1987), Chinese History of Buddhism, Vols. 1-3, 1984, The Complete Collections of Buddhism, Vols. 106 (Zhung Hwa Da Zangjing), 1984-93, History of Chinese Taoism, 1990, Religion Dictionary, 1981, (100 books) The Historical Knowledge of Chinese Culture Series, 1998; co-editor: Abstracts of Classical Works of Daoism, 1991, Selected Essays of Ren Jiyu, 1991, Ren Jiyu's Essays on Philosophy and Religion, 1996, Relations Between God and Man, 1998, Great Religion Dictionary, 1998; mem. editl. bd. Chinese Ency., philosophy vol., 1987. Rep. Nat. People's Congress 1980, 84, 88, 92. Mem. Chinese Religion Soc. (dir.), Chinese Soc. Philosophy History (pres.), Chinese Libr. Soc. (dir.), Chinese Inst. of Tibetan Buddhists. Mem. Communist Party of China. Home: Sanlihe Rd, 100045 Beijing China Office: Nat Libr of China, 39 Baishiqiao Rd, 100081 Beijing China

REN, LEI-MING, pharmacology educator, dean; b. Zhangjiakou, Hebei, China, June 28, 1956; s. Huan-Xing Ren and Gang Li; m. Jing-Min Wu, July 7, 1984; 1 child, Xue-Jiao. Master's degree, Shandong Med. U., Jinan, China, 1984; PhD, Shinshu U., Matsumoto, Japan, 1993. Lectr. Hebei Med. U. Pharmacy Sch., Shijiazhuang, 1985-88; asst. prof. Shinshu U. Med. Sch., Matsumoto, Japan, 1993-94, lectr., 1994; rsch. fellow Univ. Coll. London, 1994-96; prof. Hebei Med. U. Pharmacy Sch., Shijiazhuang, 1996-98, prof., dean, 1998—; overseas vis. fellow Brit. Heart Found., London, 1994-96; cons. Drug Adminstrn. Bur. of State, Beijing, 1999—. Standing mem. editl. bd. Chinese Pharmacol. Comm., 1997—; referee Acta Pharmacol. Sinica, 1997—; contbr. 60 articles to sci. jours. Recipient fgn. studentship Ministry of Edn., 1988-93. Mem. Chinese Physiol. Soc., Chinese Pharmacol. Soc. (bd. dirs. 1997-02), Hebei Pharmacol. Soc. (v.p. 1999—). Avocations: sports, reading, fishing. Office: Hebei Med U Pharmacy Sch, Zhongshan E Rd 361, 050017 Shijiazhuang Hebei, China

REN, SHOU JU, engineering educator; b. Nanjing, Jiangsu, China, Dec. 30, 1936; parents Guang Yu and Su Zhen (Huang) R.; m. Xin Xin Chen, May 19, 1967; children: Qiang, Tian. BS, Tsinghua U., Beijing, 1959. Lectr. Tsinghua U., Beijing, 1959-81; vis. scholar Stanford U., Palo Alto, Calif., 1981-84; dir. R&D group Tsinghua U., Beijing, 1984-87; chmn. China Nat. Computer Integrated Mfg. Sys. Expert Com., Beijing, 1987-92; prof. Tsinghua U., Beijing, 1989—; vis. prof. Fraunhofer Inst. Arbeitswirschaft Orgn., Stuttgart, Germany, 1991, City U. Hong Kong, 1994-95; dir. State 863/CIMS/Madis Lab., Beijing, 1988-97; panelist Nat. Natural Sci. Found. China, Beijing, 1991-97. Author: High Technical Encyclopedia, 1994, Analysis and Design for Advanced Manufacturing Systems, 1999; contbr. rsch. articles to profl. publs. Recipient Sci. and Tech. Progress award Nat. Edn. Com., 1995, Tsinghua Friendship award Motorola Inc., 1991. Mem. Chinese Mech. Engring. Soc. (governing coun. 1990-96), Chinese Nat. Natural Sci. Found. Avocations: sports, travel. Home: Tsinghua U 505 Apt 16, Beijing China Office: Tsinghua U, Dept Automation, 100084 Beijing China

REN, TIANSHAN, health educator; b. Jiyuan, China, Aug. 31, 1936; s. Zhenghua and Luishi (Liu) R.; m. Shunying Liu, Jan. 4, 1964; children: Xiaoyang, Xiaoming. Diploma, Nankai U., Tainjing, China, 1962, Zhongshan U., Guangzhou, China, 1979. Engr. Beijing Radiation Protection Inst., 1962-81; prof. MOH Lab. Indsl. Hygiene, Beijing, 1984-89, 90-96, 1996—; vis. prof. Australian Radiation Lab., Melbourne, 1989-90; guest prof. Chongqing U., China, 1994—, Nagoya U., Japan, 1996; cons. China Health & Quarantine Bur., Beijing, 1992-97. Author: Measurements of Radionuclides in Environmental & Food at Nuclear Emergency, 1992, Tritium Activity Concentrations in Water and Foodstuff of China, 1999; inventor in field. Recipient NAt. Sci. & Tech. Progress award, Min. Sci. & Tech., Beijing, 1988, Guangdong Province Govt., 1992, Outstanding Youth Scientist award Beijing City Govt., 1982; vis. scholar Environ. Measurement Lab., N.Y.C., 1981-83. Mem. China Radiation Protectin Soc. (dir. 1983—), China Nuclear Instrument Assn. (dir. 1986—), N.Y. Acad. Scis. Avocations: music, walking, table tennis. Office: Lab Indsl Hygiene, 2 Xinkang St, Deshengmenwai, Beijing 100088, China

REN, XIAOBING, materials scientist, researcher, applied physicist; b. Baotou, Neimongol, China, Feb. 16, 1966; s. Jinshen and Cuizen (Wang) R.; m. Xiaofei Lü, Jan. 24, 1990; 1 child, He. BS, Xi'an Jiaotong U., China, 1986, PhD, 1994; overseas student, Osaka (Japan) U., 1990-92. Postdoctoral fellow Nanjing (China) U., 1994-96; Japan Soc. Promotion of Scis. postdoctoral fellow U. Tsukuba, Japan, 1996-97, rsch. assoc., 1997-2000; sr. staff scientist Nat. Rsch. Inst. for Metals, Tsukuba, Japan, 2000—. Founder origin of martensite aging effect; formulated unified theory of point defects in B2 intermetallic compounds; contbr. articles to profl. jours. Mem. AAAS, China Youth Materials Rsch. Soc. (bd. dirs. 1994-96), Japan Inst. Metals (award for disting. young scientist 1998), Materials Rsch. Soc. Avocations: photography, badminton, volleyball. Home: Azuma 4-103-304, Tsukuba, Ibaraki 305-0031, Japan Office: Nat Rsch Inst for Metals, Sengen 1-2-1, Tsukuba 305-0047, Japan

RENATO DE SOUZA, PAULO, government official; b. Rio Grande do Sul, Brazil, 1946; married; 3 children. Degree in econs., Fed. U. Rio Grande do Sul, Brazil. Edn. sec. Sao Paulo State, Brazil, 1982-86; head Nat. Bank Econ. & Social Devel.; coord. Cardoso's Electroal Platform, 1994; min. Ministry Edn. & Recreation, Brasilia, Brazil, 1994—; cons. in field. Office: Ministry Edn & Recreation, Bloco L 8 andar, 70047900 Brasilia DF Brazil*

RENAUD, PETER FRANCIS, mathematician, educator; b. Villefranche, France, July 18, 1942; s. Jean Charles and Marie Louise (Lamoureux) R.; children: Helen, Michelle, Nicole, André. BS with honors, U. New England, Australia, 1964; MS, Nonash U., Australia, 1968; PhD, U. Canterbury, New Zealand, 1972, LLB, 1984. Sr. tutor Monash U., Melbourne, Australia, 1964-68; lectr. then sr. lectr. Canterbury U., Christchurch, New Zealand, 1968—. Mem. New Zealand Math. Soc. (hon. legal advisor 1985—), Am. Math. Soc. Avocations: wine, music. Office: U Canterbury, Dept Math & Statis, Christchurch New Zealand

RENCKENS, CEES N.M., gynecologist, consultant; b. Hoorn, The Netherlands, May 29, 1946; s. Reinier A. Renckens and Divera G.M. Ursem; m. Fokelien Y. Stenneberg, Feb., 1970; children: Rosemarijn, Jesse. MD, U. Gronigen, The Netherlands, 1971; gynecologist, U. Amsterdam, The Netherlands, 1980. Jr. doctor St. Josef Hosp., The Netherlands, 1971-72, gen. practitioner, 1972-73; registrar Ndola Ctr. Hosp., Zambia, 1973-75, U. Amsterdam, 1975-80; cons. gynecologist Westfries Gasthuis, Hoorn, 1980—; chmn. Union Against Quackery, 1988—, Hoorn. Author: Contemporary Quackery, 1992. Avocations: poetry, tennis, cinema. Office: Westfries Gasthuis, Postbux 600, 1620 AR Hoorn The Netherlands

RENDA, THOMAS ANTHONY, judge; b. Des Moines, Sept. 19, 1937; s. Anthony Thomas and Helen Louise (Reid) R.; m. Shirley Ann Murphy, June 13, 1959 (div. Apr. 1977); children: Anthony T., Tamara Ann, John Andrew, Tracy Suzanne; m. Connie Jean Wood, June 1, 1977 (div. June 1986); m. Dixie J. Brown, Sept. 10, 1988. BA, Loras Coll., 1959; JD, Drake U., 1962. Bar: Iowa 1963, U.S. Dist. Ct. (so. dist.) Iowa 1963. Sole practice Des Moines, 1963-71, dist. assoc. chief judge, 1973—; faculty rep. Iowa Ct. Adminstr., Continuing Legal Edn., Des Moines, 1973—. Mem. Iowa Ho. of Reps., 1965-71. Mem. Polk County Bar Assn., Iowa Bar Assn., Iowa Judges Assn. Ltd. Jurisdiction (bd. dirs. 1982-84), Stemma D'Italia, Italian Ams. Des Moines (pres. 1975-78), Italian Cultural Bd. Des Moines. Home: 3601 SW 14th St Des Moines IA 50315-2113 Office: Polk County Courthouse Room 110 5th and Mulberry Sts Des Moines IA 50309

RENDIC, DUBRAVKO, nuclear physicist; b. Zagreb, Croatia, Nov. 27, 1937; s. Sime and Anna Rendic; m. Nada Dokic, Dec. 28, 1963; children: Zoran-Sime, Dubravko. BSc, U. Zagreb, 1961, MSc, 1964, PhD, 1967. Rsch. asst. Rudjer Boscovic Inst., Zagreb, 1964-67, asst. prof., 1971-77, assoc. prof., 1977-92, prof. physics, 1992—, accelerator group leader, 1967-68, 71-77, head dept., 1987-97; rsch. assoc., lectr. Rice U., Houston, 1968-71. Editor Internat. X-ray Emission Spectroscopy, 1979-84. Mem. Internat. Radiation Physics Soc., Am. Phys. Soc., Croatian Phys. Soc., Croatian Vacuum Soc. Roman Catholic. Avocation: amateur radio. E-mail: rendic@rudjer.irb.hr. Fax: 385-1-4680-239. Home: V Varicaka 10, 10010 Zagreb Croatia Office: Rudjer Boskovic Inst, Bijenicka 54, 10000 Zagreb Croatia

RENDIC, SLOBODAN PETAR, biochemistry and chemistry educator; b. Maribor, Slovenia, Mar. 14, 1941; s. Milivoj and Marija Veronika Rendic; m. Vjekoslava Milic; children: Borut, Petra. Diploma in engring. biotechnology, U. Zagreb, Croatia, 1964; MSc, U. Zagreb, 1970, PhD, 1974. Cert. pharmacy and medicinal chemistry. Rsch. asst. Rsch. Inst., Pharm. and Chem. Works KRKA, Novo Mesto, Slovenia, 1966-68; head biotechnology dept. Rsch. Inst., Serum Zavod Kalinovica, Zagreb, 1968-70; rschr. Pharm. and Chem. Works, PLIVA, Zagreb, 1970; rsch. asst. faculty biotechnology, chair biochemistry U. Zagreb, Croatia, 1970-77; head biochemistry dept. Compagnia di Ricerca Chimica, Udine, Italy, 1978-80; higher rschr. Rsch. Inst. Podravka, Zagreb, 1980-83; head rsch. dept. Inst. for the Control of Drugs, Zagreb, 1983-87; prof. Faculty Pharmacy and Biochemistry, Zagreb, 1987—; dir. Doping Control Lab., Inst. for the Control of Drugs, Zagreb, 1984-87; guest prof. U. Konstanz, Germany, 1991, 98; cons. in field. Contbr. articles to profl. jours. Mem. Med. Commn. and Subcommn. for Doping, Nat. Olympic Com. for Croatia, Zagreb, 1993-98. Lt. Chem. and Biol. Def., 1974-75. Alexander von Humboldt fellow Alexander von Humboldt Found., Bonn, Germany, 1975, 78, 83, 85, 88, 94, 96, 99; Rsch. fellow U. Konstanz, 1984, 87, 95, 98, UCLA, 1991. Mem. Internat. Assn. Athletes Against Drugs (bd. dirs. 1998-99), Internat. Soc. for Study Xenobiotics (award com. 1994-99), Internat. Union Pure and Applied Chemistry (assoc. mem. commn. on toxicology 1987-91), Internat. Fedn. Clin. Chemistry (mem. com. lab. assessment on drugs of abuse 1989-91), European Soc. for Biochem. Pharmacology. Roman Catholic. Avocations: swimming, sailing, nature. E-mail: rens@nana.pharma.hr. Fax: 385 1 4856201. Home: Haulikova 6, 10000 Zagreb Croatia Office: Faculty Pharmacy & Biochem, A Kovacica 1, 10000 Zagreb Croatia

RENDIC-MIOCEVIC, ANTE, archaeologist, museum director; b. Split, Croatia, Dec. 31, 1943; s. Duje and Marjana (Cambj) R-M.; m. Marija Čemer, July 7, 1973; 1 child, Nikola. Degree, U. Zagreb, Croatia, 1969. Curator Archaeol. Mus., Split-Zagreb, Croatia, 1970-79; sr. curator Archaeol. Mus., Zagreb, 1979-86, mus. councillor, 1986—, mus. dir., 1984—. Editor Vjesnik Arheol. muzeja u Zagrebu, 1984—. Mem. Croatian Archaeol. Soc. (v.p. 1990-93, pres. 1993—). Roman Catholic. Avocations: photography, gardening. Home: Poljicka ulica 29A, 10000 Zagreb Croatia Office: Arheol Muz, Trg N Subica Zrinskog 19, 10000 Zagreb Croatia

RENDL-MARCUS, MILDRED, artist, economist; b. May 30, 1928; d. Julius and Agnes (Hokr) Rendl; m. Edward Marcus, Aug. 10, 1956. BS, NYU, 1948, MBA, 1950; PhD, Radcliffe Coll., 1954. Economist GE, 1953-56, Bigelow-Sanford Carpet Co., Inc., 1956-58; instr. econs. Hunter Coll. CUNY, 1959-60; instr. econs. Columbia U., 1960-61, rschr., 1961-63; sr. economist Nat. Indsl. Conf. Bd., 1963-66; asst. prof. Pace Coll., 1964-66; assoc. prof. Borough of Manhattan C. of C. CUNY, 1966-71, prof., 1972-85; lectr. econs. CCNY, 1953-58; vis. prof. Fla. Internat. U., 1986; bd. dirs. N.Y.C. Coun. on Econ. Edn.; cons. in field. Exhibited group shows at in New Canaan Art Show, 1982-85, Am. Soc. Bus. and Behavioral Scis., 1996, New Cannan Soc. for Arts Ann., 1983, 85, New Canaan Arts, 1985, Silvermine Galleries, 1986, Stamford Art Assn., 1987, Phoenix Gallery, 1988, N.Y.C., Parkview Point Gallery, 1982-89, Miami Beach, Fla., 1982-89, Art Complex, New Canaan, Miami Beach, 1985—, Lever House, N.Y.C., 1990, Cork Gallery, Lincoln Ctr., N.Y.C., 1990, Women's Caucus for Art, San Antonio, 1990, Artist's Equity, Broome St. Gallery, N.Y.C., 1991, Greater Hartford Architecture Conservancy, 1991, N.H. Arts Ctr., 1997, Just Originals Art Web, Albuquerque, 1999, Ward-Nasse Gallery, N.Y.C., 2000; author (with E. Marcus) Investment and Development of Tropical Africa, 1959, International Trade and Finance, 1965, Monetary and Banking Theory, 1965, Economics, 1969, Economic Progress and the Developing World, 1970, Economics, 1978, Fine Art with Many Equilibrium Prices, 1995; editor Women in the Arts Found. Newsletter, 1986-92; contbr. articles to profl. jours. Founder Rendl Fund for Slavic Art, Mus. of Modern Art, N.Y.C., 1999—, Harvard U. Art Mus., Cambridge, Mass., 2000—. Recipient Disting. Svc. award CUNY, 1985, Merit award Manhattan Arts Internat., 1998, Excellence award 1998, Artist Showcase award Manhattan Arts Internat., 1999; Dean Bernice Brown Cronkhite fellow Radcliffe Coll., 1950-51, Anne Radcliffe Econ. Rsch. Sub-Sahara Africa fellow, 1958-59; fellow Gerontol. Assn. Mem. AAUW, Internat. Schumpeter Econs. Soc. (founding), Comm. Internat. Am. (vice chmn. ann. meeting 1973), Met. Econ. Assns. (sec. 1954-56), Indsl. Rels. Rsch. Assn. (vice chmn. conv. 1973, artist Boston nat. conv. 1994), Women's Econ. Roundtable (program planning com.), N.Y.C. Women in Arts, Allied Social Sci. Assn. (artist 1994), Women's Econ. Roundtable, Art Commn. Internat. (Phila. chpt.), Greater Hartford Architecture Conservancy, NYU Grad. Sch. Bus. Adminstrn. Alumni (sec. 1956-58), Radcliffe Club, Women's City Club (art and landmarks com.). Office: Art Complex PO Box 814 New Canaan CT 06840-0814 also: 7441 Wayne Ave Miami Beach FL 33141-2534

RENE, FRANCE ALBERT, president of Seychelles; b. Seychelles, Nov. 16, 1935; s. Price and Louisa (Morgan) R.; m. Karen Handley, 1956; 1 child; m. Geva Adam, 1975; m. Sarah Zarquani, 1992; 1 child. Ed., St. Louis Coll., Seychelles, St. Louis Coll., St. Moritz, Switzerland, St. Mary's Coll., Southampton, Eng., King's Coll., U. London, London Sch. Econs. and Polit. Sci. Called to bar, 1957. Pvt. practice law, 1958-75; founder, leader Seychelles People's United Party, 1964—; mem. Legis. Coun., 1965—, Governing Coun., 1967, Legis. Assembly, 1970, 74; min. of works and land devel., 1975-77; prime min., 1976-77; pres. of Seychelles, 1977—, former min. for adminstrn., min. for industry; pres. Seychelles People's Progressive Front, 1978-84, sec.-gen., 1984-94, pres., 1994—. Address: Office of Pres State House, PO Box 655, Victoria Mahé, Seychelles*

RENFREW, ANDREW COLIN (LORD RENFREW OF KAIMSTHORN), archaeologist, academic administrator; b. July 25, 1937; s. Archibald and Helena Douglas (Savage) R.; m. Jane Margaret Ewbank, Apr. 21, 1965; children: Helena Margaret, Alban Robert, Magnus Archibald. BA, St. John's Coll., Cambridge U., 1962, MA, 1964, PhD, 1965, ScD, 1976. Lectr. archaeology U. Sheffield, 1965-72; prof. U. Southampton, 1972-81; Disney prof. archaeology Cambridge U., 1981—; vis. lectr. UCLA, 1967; fellow St. John's Coll., 1981-86; master Jesus Coll., Cambridge, 1986-97, fellow, 1997—; George Grant McCurdy lectr. Harvard U., 1977; Patten lectr. Ind. U., 1982; field excavations in Saliagos, 1961-64, Sitagroi, 1968-70, Quanterness, Orkney, 1972-74, Phylakopi, Melos, 1974-76. Author: (with J. D. Evans) Excavations at Saliagos Near Antiparos, 1968 in Orkney, 1979, Problems in European Prehistory, 1979, (with J. M. Wagstaff) An Island Polity, 1982, Approaches to Social Archaeology, 1984, The Prehistory of Orkney, 1985, The Archaeology of Cult, 1985, Archaeology and Language, 1987, (with G. Daniel) The Idea of Prehistory, 1988, The Cycladic Spirit, 1991, (with P. Bahn) Archaeology, 1991; editor: The Explanation of Culture Change, 1973, British Prehistory, 1974, Transformations: Mathematical Approaches to Culture Change, 1979, Theory and Explanation in Archaeology, 1982; presenter: (TV films) The Tree That Put the Clock Back, 1970, Islands Out of Time, 1973, Orkney Underground, 1974, Aphrodite's Other Island, 1977, Bronze Age Blast Off, 1978, Lost Kings of the Desert, 1980, The Emperor's Immortal Army, 1981, City of the Dead, 1982, Who Built Stonehenge, 1986. Trustee Brit. Mus. With RAF, 1956-58.

Recipient Rivers Meml. medal Royal Anthrop. Inst., 1979, Huxley Meml. medal, 1991; named Fgn. Assoc. NAS, 1996; elevated to peerage, 1991. Fellow Brit. Acad., Soc. Antiquaries London; mem. Ancient Monuments Bd. (adv. com.), Athenaeum. Office: Dept Archaeology, Downing St, Cambridge CB2 3DZ, England also: House of Lords, London SW1A 0PW, England

RENGANATHAN, RADHAKRISHNAN, physician; b. Chandigarh, Punjab, India, Nov. 21, 1969; s. Radhakrishnan and Thangam; m. Priscilla Elizabeth Janet, Aug. 28, 1998. M.B.B.S., U. Madras, 1990; Diploma in Acupuncture, Open Internat. U., 1996. Diplomate Nat. Bd. in Phys. Medicine and Rehab. Sr. house officer dept. medicine Christian Med. Coll. Hosp., Vellore, India, 1992-93, registrar dept. of phys. med./rehab., 1993-96; head dept. phys. med./rehab. Santosh Hosp., Madras, 1996-97; sr. house officer dept. medicine St. Luke's Gen. Hosp., Kilkenny, Ireland, 1998-99; sr. house officer dept. phys./rehab. medicine Nat. Rehab. Hosp., Dublin, Ireland, 1999—. Contbr. articles to profl. jours. Mem. Indian Assn. Phys. Medicine and Rehab., Internat. Med. Soc. of Paraplegia, Inst. of Complementary Medicine (life), Irish Med. Coun. Avocations: cricket, football, swimming, karate (yellow belt), amateur radio. Home: 16 8th Cross St, Shastrinagar Adyar 600 020, India

RENGEL-AVILES, LUIS ENRIQUE, geography educator; b. Quito, Ecuador, June 10, 1951; arrived in Venezuela, 1951; s. Luis T. and Martha V. (Aviles) Rengel. BS in Geography, Los Andes U., Merida, Venezuela, 1978; MA, Ball State U., Muncie, Ind., 1986. Cert. geographer. Cartography asst. Los Andes U., Merida, 1976-78, geography lectr., 1978-79; lectr. geomorphology East Zamora U., Guanare, Venezuela, 1979-83, prof., 1986—; geography rsch. asst. Ball State U., Munice, Ind., 1984-86; tech. asst. Ministry Natural Resources, Merida, 1978-79, Ministry Agr., Guanare, 1986-88; cons. Home Regulations Guanare Municipality, 1995—. Author: Orinoco River Geography, 1996. Founder Young's Advancement Assn., Guanare, 1996; coord. Natural Disasters Workshop, Guanare, 1991. Mem. Internat. Soc. Soil Sci. (life), Conf. Latin Americanist Geographers (life). Roman Catholic. Avocations: field journeys, treks. Office: U Ezequiel Zamora, Unellez Carr 3, 3310 Guanare Venezuela

RENI (ARLENE PATRICIA THERESA BROWN), artist; b. Jan. 3, 1953; d. William J. and Adelaide Elizabeth Brown. Student, Union Coll., 1971; BA Visual Comm., BA Occupl. Therapy, Kean Coll., 1980; student, Union Coll., $D71. Cert. personal trainer, health fitness instr. Am. Coll. Sports Medicine, water safety instr./swim instr., Red Cross. Owner, pres. Reni Co., Roselle Park, N.J., 1979—; profl. faux surface finishes artist residential and comml.; pvt. tchr. art, Glass and Mirror Abrasive Etching, comml. carved glass designs and creation, air brush artist designer, pinstripper metal and wood, crystal engraving and carving, Roselle Park, 1979—; owner Twinks Trademark and Associated Characters; performance nutrition specialist Internat. Sports Sci. Assn. Exhibited in The Children's Mus., Ind.; patentee in field. Recipient 3d Pl. award Custom Car and Van Show, Meadowlands, N.J., 1981, 2d Pl. award Custom Car and Van Show, Asbury Park, N.J., 1982. Mem. Graphic Artists Guild, Artists' Equity Assn., Summit Art Assn., Princeton Art Assn., Am. Women's Econ. Devel. Assn., Found. Christian Living, Positive Thinkers Club, N.J. Art Dirs. Club, Morris County C. of C., N.J. Jewelers Assn., Internat. Jet Sports Boating Assn. (standup womans' ski pts. champion 1996), Assn. Jensen Owners, Westfield Art Assn., Alumni Assn. Kean Coll. E-mail: R777eni@aol.com. Address: 475 E Westfield Ave Roselle Park NJ 07204-2431

RENKAR-JANDA, JARRI J., retired paint manufacturing executive; b. Chicago Heights, Ill., Feb. 26, 1951; d. Eugene N. and RoseMarie (Morgenson) Zar; m. Leonard F. Renkar (div.); 1 child, Sandra R.; m. James E. Janda. Student, Northeastern Ill. U., 1978, Harper Jr. Coll., 1978, Mundelein Coll., 1979-80. Acctg. clk. Wittek Mfg., Chgo., 1970-73; credit clk. McKesson Chem., Chgo., 1973, purchasing agt., 1973-75; product supply mgr. Gen. Paint and Chem., Cary, Ill., 1975-78; purchasing mgr. Glidden Coatings and Resins, Chgo., 1978-80, Columbus and Oakwood, Ga., 1980-84; purchasing mgr. paint div. Ace Hardware Corp., Matteson, Ill., 1984-87, materials mgr. paint div., 1987-96; software cons. Sys. Software Assocs., Inc., Chgo., 1996-97; ret., 1997; software cons. Sys. Software Assocs., Inc., Chgo., 1996. Counselor Shelter for Battered Women, Gainesville, Ga., 1982; chairperson Ill. Paint Coun., 1996—. Mem. Chgo. Paint and Coatings Assn. (buyers com. 1985-87, bd. dirs. 1990—, chmn. com. Chgo. legis. affairs, mem. legis. and reg. com. 1991—, pres. 1994-95, chmn. bd. dirs. 1995-96), Chgo. Soc. Coatings (mfg. com. 1986-87).

RENKENS, JACK H., seminar speaker; b. Green Bay, Wis., Nov. 10, 1948; s. Jack Leo and Leona Lena Renkens; m. Kathleen Mae R., Nov. 21, 1970; 1 child, Brooke Courtney. BS, U. Wis., River Falls, 1974; MS in Edn., U.S. Sports Academy, 1985. Math. instr., coach Winslow (Ariz.) H.S., 1975-79, Woodstock (Ill.) H.S., 1979-81; head basketball coach Colby (Kans.) Jr. Coll., 1981-85; assoc. athletic dir., coach Assumption Coll., Worcester, Mass., 1985-95; CEO Recruiting Realities Inc., Scottsdale, Ariz., 1995—. Author: Recruiting Realities, 1996. Bd. advisors Coll. Bound Alliance, Cedarburg, Wis., 1997—; cons. Athletes Against Drugs, Chgo., 1998—. Recipient Key to City, Winslow, 1979, Worcester, 1992; recipient 7 Coach of Yr. awards, including Ariz. Coach of Yr., 1979. Avocations: golf, basketball, travel. Office: Recruiting Realities Ste 2052 6400 E Thomas Rd Apt 2052 Scottsdale AZ 85251-6080

RENKIN, EUGENE MARSHALL, retired physiology educator; b. Boston, Oct. 21, 1926; s. Harry Benjamin and Mary Chernaik Renkin; m. Barbara Zaun, 1955 (div. 1966); children: Miriam Lohr, Hadley Zaun, Joshua Nathan; m. Elizabeth Russell, 1967; 1 child, Daniel Russell. BS in Biology, Tufts U., 1948; PhD in Med. Sci., Harvard U., 1951. Assoc. scientist Brookhaven Nat. Lab., Upton, N.Y., 1951-55; sr. asst. scientist USPHS Nat. Heart Inst., Bethesda, Md., 1955-57; from asst. to assoc. prof. physiology George Washington U., Washington, 1957-61, prof. chmn. physiology, 1961-63; prof. pharmacology Duke U. Med. Ctr., Durham, N.C., 1963-69; prof. physiology Duke U. Med. Ctr., Durham, 1969-74; prof., chmn. human physiology U. Calif., Davis, 1974-91, prof. human physiology, 1991-94, prof. emeritus, 1994—. Contbr. chpts. to books and articles to profl. jours. Lt. jr. grade USPHS, 1955-57. Recipient Wellcome Visiting professorship Med. Coll. N.J., 1978. Mem. AAUP, Internat. Union Physiol. Scis. (microcirculatory coun. 1978-86), Am. Physiol. Soc. (several coms., H.P. Bowditch lectr. 1963, C.J. Wiggers award circulation group 1985), Am. Heart Assn., Microcirculatory Soc. (pres. 1974, E.M. Landis award 1977, B.W. Zweifach award 1984), Brit. Microcirculatory Soc. (hon.); grantee NIH and NSF, 1958-94. Jewish. Avocations: music appreciation, hiking, birdwatching. Office: Dept Human Physiology Univ Calif Davis Davis CA 95616

RENN, ORTWIN, sociologist; b. Schmidtheim, Germany, Dec. 26, 1951; s. Heinrich and Paula (Krumpen) R.; m. Regina Kozikowski, May, 1974; children: Silvia, Marius, Fabian. MS, U. Cologne, Germany, 1977, PhD, 1980. Rschr. Rsch. Ctr., Julich, Germany, 1976-86; assoc. prof. Clark U., Worcester, Mass., 1986-92; prof. Swiss Inst. Tech., 1992-93; dir. Ctr. Tech. Assessment, Stuttgart, Germany, 1993—; prof. Stuttgart U., 1994—; mem. adv. bd. Global Environ. Change Govt. of Germany, Future Commn. state Govt. Author: (with R. Keeney, D. von Winterfeldt, U. Kotte) Die Wertbaumanalyse Entscheidungshilfe für die Politik, 1984, Risikowahrnehmung der Kernenergie, 1984, Verheissung und Illusion: Chancen und Grenzen einer Alternativen Gesellschaft, 1984, (with G. Albrecht, U. Kotte, H.P. Peters, H.U. Stegelmann) Sozialverträgliche Energiepolitik-Ein Gutachten für die Bundersregierung, 1985, Umweltstandards-Fakten und Bewertungsprobleme am Beispiel des Strahlenrisikos, 1992, (with H.S. Brown, P. Derr, A.L. White) Corporate Environmentalism in a Global Economy-Societal Values in International Technology Transfer, 1993, (T. Webler and P. Wiedemann) Fairness and Competence in Citizen Participation-Evaluating New Models for Environmental Discourse, 1995, (with M. Berg, G. Erdmann, A. Leist, P. Schaber, M. Scheringer, H. Seiler, R. Wiedemann) Risikobewertung im Energiebereich, 1995; editor: Risk Management in Europe: New Challenges for the Industrial World, 1997, Risk Perception and Communication in Europe, 1997, (with J.L. Mumpower, L.D. Phillips, V.R.R. Uppuluri) Expert Judgment and Expert Systems, 1987, (with K. Pinkau) Environmental Standards-Scientific Foundations and Rational Procedures of Regulation with Emphasis on Radiological Risk Management, 1998, (with A. Klinke, J.-P. Lehners) Ethnic Conflicts and Civil Society, Proposals for a New Era in Eastern Europe, 1998; co-editor: GAIA, book series on risk; contbr. articles to profl. jours. Active environ. adv. bd. Protestant Ch. Mem. Soc. for Risk Analysis (pres.), N.Y. Acad. Scis. Roman Catholic. Office: Ctr Tech Assessment, Industriestr 5, 70565 Stuttgart Germany

RENN, STEPHEN DONALD, religious studies educator; b. Sydney, NSW, Australia, Oct. 28, 1950; s. Ernest Norman and Marjorie May (Stephenson) R.; m. Helen Lorrain Morante, May 8, 1976; children: Joshua, Chantelle. BA with hons., Sydney (Australia) U., 1972, diploma in Edn., 1973, MA, 1991; MDiv., Westminster Theol. Sem., Phila., 1979. Modern lang. tchr. Sydney (Australia) H.S., 1974-76; pastoral minister Bapt. Ch., Dapto, Australia, 1979-83; studies dir. Enchiridion Co., Bowral, Australia, 1984-85; lectr. in old testament Sydney Missionary and Bible Coll., 1986—, dean of studies, 1990—. Author: (Bible Study Booklet) The Song of Songs, 1989. Mem. Soc. Biblical Lit., Jour. for Study of the Old Testament. Avocations: classical music, golf, history, cricket. Home: 47 Badminton Rd, Croydon NSW 2132, Australia Office: Missionary & Bible Coll, 43 Badminton Rd, Croydon NSW 2132, Australia

RENNER, CURTIS SHOTWELL, lawyer; b. Paris, France, June 24, 1958. Grad., Phillips Acad., Andover, Mass., 1981; BA, Wesleyan U., Middletown, Conn., 1981; JD cum laude, Harvard U., 1988. Bar: Mass. 1988, D.C. 1995. Assoc. Crowell & Moring, Washington, 1988-95; founding ptnr. Watson & Renner, Washington, 1995—. Contbr. articles to profl. jours. Mem. ABA, ATLA, D.C. Bar Assn., Phi Beta Kappa. Office: Watson & Renner 2000 M St NW Ste 330 Washington DC 20036-3366

RENNIE, JANET MARY, neonatal physician; b. Bromborough, U.K., Dec. 2, 1954; d. Arthur and Marjorie (Jones) Ball; m. Ian Rennie, Aug. 28, 1976 (div. June 1986); m. Ian Roscoe Watts, Aug. 28, 1992. MBBChB, U. Sheffield, U.K., 1976, MD, 1985. Rsch. fellow U. Liverpool, U.K., 1981-85; house physician Sheffield Children's Hosp., 1982-83; cons. Cambridge U., 1988-95; neonatal physician Kings Coll. Hosp., London; lectr. U. Cambridge, U.K., 1985-88. Sep. editor Archives Disease Childhood; author: Neonatal Cranial Ultrasound, 1997, Manual of Neonatal Intensive Care, 4th edit.; editor: Textbook of Neonatology, 3d edit.; contbr. articles to profl. jours. Fellow Royal Coll. Physicians; mem. Neonatal Soc. (ex-sec.), Brit. Assn. Perinatal Medicine (exec. com.). Office: 4th Flr New Ward Block, NICU/Kings Coll Hosp-Denmark Hill, London SE5 9RS, England

RENNIE, MORAG LILIAN, retired psychiatrist; b. Lennox Town, Scotland, Nov. 26, 1943; d. Thomas James Davis and Lily Frew Smith; m. Gordon Grant Rennie, Apr. 3, 1967. MB, BChir, Glasgow (Scotland) U., 1968; DPM, Royal Coll. Physicians, London, 1973. Jr. ho. officer medicine/surgery So. Gen. Hosp., Glasgow, 1968-69, sr. ho. officer psychiatry, 1969-70; jr. registrar psychiatry Leverndale Hosp., Glasgow, 1970-73; sr. registrar psychiatry Glasgow Rotation Scheme, 1973-74; sr. registrar, locum cons., psychiatrist Hartwood Hosp., Lanarkshire, Scotland, 1974-75; cons. psychiatrist Hartwood Hosp., Lanarkshire, 1975-81, Birkwood Hosp., Lanarkshire, 1981-90, Law Hosp., Carcuke, Scotland, 1990-99; ret., 1999; founding mem. Alzheimer Scotland/Action on Dementia Motherwell Project, Lanarkshire, 1985. Contbr. articles to profl. jours. Fellow RSPB, Royal Coll. Psychiatrists; mem. Med. Women's Fedn., Soroptimist Internat. (pres.-elect 1999-2000, Motherwell and Wishaw pres. 2000—). Home: Blairmont, 48 Station Rd, Carluke ML8 5AD, Scotland

RENNINGS, KLAUS PETER, economist; b. Kevelaer, Westphalia, Germany, Mar. 21, 1963; s. Heinrich and Anna (Smitmans) R.; m. Dorothea Katharina Kempkens, Aug. 5, 1996; children: Mats, Michel. MS, U. Muenster, Germany, 1990, PhD, 1994. Scientific asst. Coun. Environ. Advisers, Wiesbaden, Germany, 1992-94; sr. rschr. Ctr. for European Econ. Rsch., Mannheim, Germany, 1994-2000; expert evaluator European Commn., Brussels, 1997-98; cons. Ministry of Environ., Bonn, 1994-98. Editor: (books) Man-made Climate Change, 1998, Social Costs and Sustainability, 1996, Innovation-oriented Environmental Regulation, 2000, Social Costs and Sustainable Mobility, 2000; contbr. articles to profl. jours. Mem. Scientific Coun., Friends of the Earth, Bonn, 1997-98, Joint Scientific Com. European Commn., DGVII, Brussels, 1996-98. Mem. Internat. Soc. for Ecol. Econs., European Soc. for Ecol. Econs./Paris, Verein fuer Socialpolitik/Munich. Home: Dreikreuzweg 35, 69151 Neckargemuend/Baden Germany Office: Ctr European Econ Rsch L7 1, PO Box 103443, D-68034 Mannheim/Baden Germany

RENO, JANET, attorney general; b. Miami, Fla., July 21, 1938; d. Henry and Jane (Wood) R. A.B. in Chemistry, Cornell U., 1960; LL.B., Harvard U., 1963. Bar: Fla. 1963. Assoc. Brigham & Brigham, 1963-67; ptnr. Lewis & Reno, 1967-71; staff dir. judiciary com. Fla. Ho. of Reps., Tallahassee, 1971-72; cons. Fla. Senate Criminal Justice Com. for Revision Fla.'s Criminal Code, spring 1973; adminstrv. asst. state atty. 11th Jud. Circuit Fla., Miami, 1973-76, state atty., 1978-93; ptnr. Steel Hector and Davis, Miami, 1976-78; atty. gen. Dept. Justice, Washington, 1993—; mem. jud. nominating commn. 11th Jud. Circuit Fla., 1976-78; chmn. Fla. Gov.'s Council for Prosecution Organized Crime, 1979-80. Recipient Women First award YWCA, 1993. National Women's Hall of Fame, 2000. Mem. ABA (Inst. Jud. Adminstrn. Juvenile Justice Standards Commn. 1973-76), Am. Law Inst., Am. Judicature Soc. (Herbert Harley award 1981), Dade County Bar Assn., Fla. Pros. Atty.'s Assn. (pres. 1984-86). Democrat. Office: Office of the Attorney General Rm 10-130 950 Pennsylvania Ave NW Dept Justice Washington DC 20530-0001

RENO, JOSEPH HARRY, retired orthopedic surgeon; b. Allentown, Pa., Mar. 5, 1915; s. Harvey Luther and Olive May (Wilson) R.; m. Maude Olivia Mutchler, June 27, 1942; children: Joseph David, Sally Jo, Diana Jane, Deborah Marion. Student, Temple U., 1934-37, MD, 1941. Intern. Chester (Pa.) Hosp., 1941-42; residency Tex. Scottish Rite Hosp. for Crippled Children, Dallas, 1942-43, 44-45, Robert Packer Hosp., Sayre, Pa., 1943-44; assoc. Homer Stryker, M.D., Kalamazoo, 1945-46; pvt. practice Bethlehem, Pa., 1946-71, Flagstaff, Ariz., 1971-93; team physician Lehigh U., Bethlehem, 1946-70, No. Ariz. U., Flagstaff, 1971-77, Ariz. State U., Tempe, 1977-84; chief surg. staff Flagstaff Hosp., 1975. Contbr. articles to profl. jours.; prodr. surg. films for Am. Acad. Ortho. Surgeons and others, 1952-70. Pres. Coconino County Easter Seal Soc., 1973; bd. dirs., med. advisor Ariz. Easter Seal Soc., 1974-84. Recipient Pioneer award Ariz. Med. Assn., 1981, Cert. of Appreciation, Pa. Dept. Health Crippled Children's Div., 1971; Dr. Joseph Reno Sports Medicine award named in honor, No. Ariz. State U. and Blue Cross Blue Shield, 1986. Fellow Am. Acad. Ortho. Surgeons, Am. Assn. for Surgery of Trauma, Am. Coll. Sports Med., Am. Coll. Surgeons (chmn. Lehigh Valley subcom. on trauma 1954-66, Ea. Pa. chpt. pres. 1969); mem. NRA, Am. Bd. Ortho. Surgery (cert., diplomate 1948), Coconino County Med. Soc. (pres. 1976), Western Ortho. Assn., Babcock Surg. Soc., Mason, Phi Chi, Alpha Tau Omega. Home: 475 Jacks Canyon Rd Apt 219 Sedona AZ 86351-9222

RENO, OTTIE WAYNE, former judge; b. Pike County, Ohio, Apr. 7, 1929; s. Eli Enos and Arbannah Belle (Jones) R.; A in Bus. Adminstrn., Franklin U., 1949; LLB, Franklin Law Sch., 1953; JD, Capital U., 1966; grad. Coll. Juvenile Justice, U. Nev., 1973; m. Janet Gay McCann, May 22, 1947; children: Ottie Wayne II, Jennifer Lynn, Lorna Victoria. Admitted to Ohio bar, 1953; practiced in Pike County; recorder Pike County, 1957-73; common pleas judge Probate and Juvenile divs. Pike County, 1973-79. Mem. adv. bd. Ohio Youth Services, 1972-74. Mem. Dem. Central Com. Camp Creek precinct, 1956-72, 83-90; sec. Pike County Central Com., 1960-70, 83-87; chmn. Pike County Dem. Exec. Com., 1971-72, 1988-90; del. Dem. Nat. Conv., 1972, 96; mem. Ohio Dem. Central Com., 1969-70; Dem. candidate 6th Ohio dist. U.S. Ho. of Reps., 1966, 88th Dist. Ohio Ho. of Reps., 1992; pres. Scioto Valley Local Sch. Dist., 1962-66. Recipient Distinguished Service award Ohio Youth Commn., 1974; 6 Outstanding Jud. Service awards Ohio Supreme Ct.; 15 times Ala. horseshoe pitching champion; named to Nat. Horseshoe Pitchers Hall of Fame, 1978; mem. internat. sports exchange, U.S. and Republic South Africa, 1972, 80, 82. Mem. Ohio, Pike County (pres. 1964) Bar Assns., Nat. Council Juvenile Ct. Judges, Am. Legion. Mem. Ch. of Christ in Christian Union. Author: Story of Horseshoes, 1963; Pitching Championship Horseshoes, 1971, 2d rev. edit., 1975; The American Directory of Horseshoe Pitching, 1983, Ohio vs. Smith, Murder, 1990, Reno and Apsaalooka Survive Custer, 1996. Home: 148 Reno Rd Lucasville OH 45648-9580

RENO, ROBERT MARIUS, newspaper columnist; b. Miami, Fla., Dec. 11, 1939; s. Henry O. and Jane Wallace Wood Reno; 1 child, Janet Meliha. BA, Tulane U., 1960. Reporter Miami Herald, 1960-68, Newsday, L.I., N.Y., 1969-74; columnist Newsday, L.I., 1974—, L.A. Times-Washington Post Wire Svc., 1974—. With U.S. Army, 1963-65. Home: 12 Dean Rd Napanoch NY 12458-2231 Office: Newsday 2 Park Ave Rm 601 New York NY 10016-5679

RENOUF, EDDA, artist; b. Mexico City, June 17, 1943; d. Edward and Catharine (Smith) R.; m. Alain Middleton, Sept. 20, 1977; 1 child, Mélisande. B.A., Sarah Lawrence Coll., 1965; M.F.A., Columbia U., 1971. One-woman exhbns. include Yvon Lambert Gallery, Paris, 1972, 74, 76, 78, 80, 82, 84, 93, Konrad Fischer Gallery, Düsseldorf, Fed. Republic Germany, 1974, 79, Blum-Helman Gallery, N.Y.C., 1978, 80, 82, 85, 87, 89, U. Mich. Mus. Art, 1995, Elisabeth Kaufmann Gallery, Basel Switzerland, 1994, 96, Galerie Sollertis, Toulouse, France, 1994, 96, 98, Staatliche Kunsthalle Karlsruhe, Germany, 1997, Galerie Hubert Winter, Vienna, Austria, 1998; group exhbns. include 8th Paris Biennale, 1973, Mus. Modern Art, N.Y.C., 1973, 90, 98, Stedelijk Mus., Amsterdam, 1974, Whitney Mus. Am. Art, N.Y.C., 1979, 85, Centre Georges Pompidou, Paris, 1979, Met. Mus. Art, N.Y.C., 1982, 87, Serpentine Gallery, 1984, Galerie Denise René, Paris, 1985, The Tel Aviv Mus., 1986, 98, Mus. Fridericianum, Kassel, Fed. Republic of Germany, 1988, Mus. d'Art Moderne de Lille, France, 1992, Bibliothèque Nationale, Paris, 1992, Nat. Gallery Art, Washington, 1993, 94, Harvard U. Straus Gallery, 1996, Yokohama (Japan) Mus. Art, 1998, Yale U. Art Gallery, 1998, The Tel Aviv Mus. Art, 1998, Mus. Art, N.Y.C., 1998, Cabinet des Estampes et des Dessins. Liege, Belgium, 1999, British Mus. Dept. Prints and Drawings, 2000; represented in permanent collections, Mus. Modern Art, Whitney Mus. Am. Art, Met. Mus. Art, Centre Georges Pompidou, Chgo. Art Inst., Museum of Contemporary Art, Chgo., Phila. Art Mus., Yale U. Art Gallery, Met. Mus. Art, Neuberger Mus., Australian Nat. Gallery, Cin. Mus. Art, St. Louis Art Mus., Tel Aviv Mus., La. Mus., Denmark, Walker Art Ctr., Nat. Gallery Art, Washington, Biblioteque Nationale Paris, British Mus., London, Bklyn. Mus. Am. Art, Dallas Mus. Fine Art, Detroit Mus. Art, Mus. Contemporary Art, L.A., High Mus., Atlanta, others; subject of articles in art publs. Nat. Endowment Arts grantee, 1976-77, Pollock-Krasner Found. Inc. grantee, 1990-91, Ctr. Nat. Arts Plastiques grantee, 1996. Address: 37 Rue Volta, 75003 Paris France also: 26 Juniper Meadow Rd Washington Depot CT 06794-1214

RENOUX, ANDRÉ, physicist, educator; b. Courbevoie, France, Oct. 27, 1937; s. Robert and Jeanne (Noël) R.; divorced; children: Vincent, Nathalie. Lic. Sci., Faculty Scis. Paris, 1958, Dr 3rd cycle, 1961, Drs, 1965. Asst. Faculty Scis., Paris, 1959-61, master asst., 1961-66; prof. Faculty Scis., Tunis, 1966-69; prof. Faculty Scis. U. Brest (France), France, 1969-80; prof. U. Paris, 1980—, dir. lab. phys. aèrosols et transfert des contaminations, 1980—, dir. DESS (3d cycle) sci. des aerosols-génie de l'Aéroncontamination, 1983—; gen. conf. chmn. European Aerosol Conf., Blois, France, 1994; del. Internat. Coun. for Engring. and Tech., UNESCO, 2000—. Author: (with D. Boulaud and E. Lavoisier) Les Aérosols, Physique et Tétrologie, 1998; editl. bd. Idojaras, 1979—, Pollution Atmospherique, 1979—, Aerosol Sci. & Tech., 1992-2000; contbr. over 300 articles to sci. publs. Gen. sec. Syndicat d'initiative, Brest, 1973-77; mem. Cons. Com. Univs., France, 1973-77. Mem. AAAS, N.Y. Acad. Scis., Com. Regional Anti-Pollution Brest (pres. 1973-80), Soc. France for Nuclear Energy idFNE (pres. 1987-91), Am. Assn. Aerosol Rsch., Gesellschaft Aerosolforschung, Hungarian Meteorol. soc. (hon.), French Aerosol. Rsch. Assn. (pres. 1983-2000), European Aerosol Assembly (co-founder, pres. 1998-2000), Office Professionnel de qualification des Entreprises de l'Ultrapropreté (pres. 1995—). Avocations: tennis, opera, photography. Home: 11 Sq de L'eau Vive, 94000 Creteil France Office: U Paris XII, Lab Phys Aerosols, 94000 Creteil Cedex, France

RENSHAW, AMANDA FRANCES, retired physicist, nuclear engineer; b. Wheelwright, Ky., Dec. 10, 1934; d. Taft and Mamie Nell (Russell) Wilson; divorced; children: Linda, Michael, Billy. BS in Physics, Antioch Coll., 1972; MS in Physics, U. Tenn., 1982, MS in Nuclear Engring., 1991. Rsch. asst. U. Mich., Ann Arbor, 1970-71; teaching asst. Antioch Coll., Yellow Springs, Ohio, 1971-72; physicist GE, Schenectady, N.Y., 1972-74, Union Carbide Corp., Oak Ridge, Tenn., 1974-79; rsch. assoc. Oak Ridge Nat. Lab., 1979-91, mgr. strategic planning, 1991-92, liaison for environ. scis., 1993-96; ret., 1996; asst. to counselor for sci. and tech. Am. Embassy, Moscow, 1990; asst. to dir. nat. acid precipitation assessment program Office of Pres. U.S., 1993-94. Contbr. articles to profl. jours. Mem. AAUW, Am. Women in Sci., Am. Nuclear Soc. (Oak Ridge chpt.), Soc. Black Physicists. Avocations: reading, travelling. Home: 1850 Cherokee Bluff Dr Knoxville TN 37920-2215

RENSHAW, PATRICK RICHARD GEORGE, history educator, writer; b. West Ham, London, Eng., Feb. 26, 1936; s. George Albert and Winifred Norah (Thorpe) R.; m. Mary Davies, Aug. 29, 1959; children: Donovan, Caradoc, Rebecca, Richard (dec.). BA, Oxford (Eng.) U., 1959, MA, 1963; postgrad., Northwestern U., 1960-61. Journalist Oxford Mail, 1961-68; lectr. Am. history Sheffield (Eng.) U., 1968-76, sr. lectr., reader, 1976—; examiner A-level Cambridge (Eng.) U. Bd., 1968-96; Ph.D., examiner Oxford, Kent, London, Glasgow and Sheffield univs., 1977—. Author: The Wobblies, 1967, 2d edit., 1999 (transl. into Italian 1970, Jpanese 1973), The General Strike, 1975, Nine Days in May, 1976, American Labor and Consensus Capitalism, 1935-1990, 1991, American in the Era of the Two World Wars 1910-1945, 1996; editor: Alexis de Tocqueville's American Democracy, 1998; contbr. numerous articles to various publs. Br. treas. Nat. Union Journalists, Oxford, 1965-67. Sr. aircraftsman RAF, 1954-56. Rockefeller fellow, 1960-61, Fulbright fellow, Syracuse, N.Y., 1971-72, Am. Coun. Learned Socs. fellow, Binghamton, N.Y., 1981-82, Kaiser fellow Walter P. Reuther Libr., Detroit, 1989, 93; Nuffield Coll. grantee U.S. librs., 1966. Fellow Royal Hist. Soc.; mem. Brit. Assn. Am. Studies, Orgn. Am. Historians, Oxford Union. Mem. Labour Party. Avocations: swimming, tennis, walking, politics, bridge. Office: Sheffield U, Dept History, Sheffield S10 2TN, England

RENSHAW, PETER, music educator; b. London, Apr. 3, 1936; s. Edward Summers and Hilda May (Cox) R.; m. Virginia Helen Nagelschmidt, July 27, 1962 (div. Jan. 1985); children: Sophie, Ben; m. Milena Anna Staehelin, Aug. 3, 1985. BA, Cambridge U., 1957, MA, 1960; MPhil, London U., 1970; FGSM (hon.), Guildhall Sch. Music & Drama, 1987. Tchr. Eltham Green Sch., London, 1961-64; lectr. history Coll. All Saints, London, 1964-67; lect. edn. Wall Hall Coll., Herts, Eng., 1967-69, Leeds (Eng.) U., 1970-75; prin. Yehudi Menuhin Sch., Cobham, Eng., 1975-84; head dept. performance and comm. skills Guildhall Sch. Music and Drama, London, 1984-96, head rsch. and devel., 1996—; prof. music Gresham Coll., London, 1986-94; cons. London Philharm., 1986-95, City of London Sinfonia, 1986-95, Royal Philharm., London, 1993-95; cons. Irish Govt., 1999—, Brit. Coun., Tanzania, 1998—. Author: (booklet) The Management of Creativity, 1993; contbr. articles to profl. jours. 2d lt. Royal Corps of Signals, 1958-59. Named Freeman, City of London, 1989. Fellow Royal Soc. Arts; mem. Inc. Soc. Musicians. Avocations: travel, climbing, reading, music. Home: 107 Barnsbury St, London N1 1EP, England Office: Guildhall Sch Music & Drama, Barbican, London EC2Y 8DT, England

RENSON, MARCEL GILLES (KNIGHT RENSON), psychosociologist, international lecturer and consultant; b. Liege, Belgium; s. Gilles and Marie (Berry) R.; m. Christine Paulette Hansen-Soulie, Feb. 2, 1986; 5 children. Grad. in Adm. Sc., State U., Liege, 1947, grad. psychosociology, 1949; grad. Gestalt Therapy, Cleve.; grad. in musicology, State Conservatory, Liege, 1979. First asst. UNESCO, Paris, 1949; promotion mgr. P.C.B., Brussels, 1949; gen. mgr. Internat. Union Advertisers, Brussels, 1958; rsch. counsellor U. Louvain, 1958; lectr. U. Ghent, 1958; gen. mgr. Renson Internat. Mktg. Co., Brussels, 1968; seminar exec. State U., Liege, 1976-94, dean Inst. Strategy of Change, 1992—; pres. exec. programs EPI Ctr., Brussels, 1976; chmn. III European Congress Distbn., Brussels, 1958; internat. reporter VI European Congress for Humanistic Psychology, Paris, 1986. Author: Dare the Revolution-The General Pedagogy of Change, European Youth, Future Leadership; contbr. articles on social work and mktg. mgmt. to profl. jours. Bd. dirs. Assn. for cultural Devel., Wallonie, 1975, North Atlantic Inst., 1975; gen. sec. Liege Inst. Musicology, 1975; bd. dirs. Les Voies de la Connaissance, Vichy, 1997; founder Colloquie Thomas More, 1999. 2d lt. 14th Inf. Regt., Belgium Army, 1945. Decorated knight

Equestrian Order Holy Sepulcre Jerusalem, Arm Resistance, WW 40-45 and Recognition medals. Mem. French Soc. Gestalt (bd. dirs. 1981), Univ. Group Study Biol. Fields (assoc.), NATO Belgian Assn. (bd. dirs 1975), European Assn. Belgium, Internat. C. of C. (internat. reporter 1958). Mem. Secular Order of St. Benedict. Avocations: horseback riding, mountain climbing, organ music. Home and Office: H Le Chene, F-03150 Montaigu-le-Blin France

RENTCHNICK, PIERRE, retired physician; b. Geneva, July 17, 1923; s. Jacques and Blanche (Spiegel) R.; m. Paule Adam, Dec. 23, 1948; 1 child, Philippe. Physician, Sch. Medicine, Geneva, 1950; MD, U. Geneva Sch. Medicine, Switzerland, 1954. Med. diplomate. Author: Esculape au Pays des Soviets, 1955, Esculape Chez Mao-Tse Tung, 1974, Ces Malades Qui Nous Gouvernent, 1976, Les Orphelins Mènent-Ils Le Monde?, 1978, Ces Nouveaux Malades Qui Nous Gouverment, 1988, 96; contbr. articles on antibiotics, infectious diseases, and medical ethics to profl. jours. editor-in-chief (hon.) Medicine and Hygiene. Fellow Med. Soc. Prague, N.Y. Acad. Scis.; mem. Swiss Soc. Internal Medicine, Geneva Med. Soc., Kiwanis Club (pres. 1976-77). Home: chemin Bouchattet 8, 1291 Commugny Vaud, Switzerland

RENTON, RIGHT HON. LORD (DAVID LOCKHART-MURE), retired lawyer; b. Dartford, Kent, Eng., Aug. 12, 1908; s. Maurice Waugh and Eszma Olivia (Borman) R.; m. Claire Cicely Duncan, July 17, 1947 (dec. Apr. 24, 1986); children: Caroline, Clare, Davina. MA BCL, Univ. Coll., Oxford (Eng.) U., 1930, 33. Barrister-at-law, 1933—; Queen's Counsel, 1954. Practicing barrister, 1933-39, 45-55, 62-74; M.P. for Huntingdon Eng., 1945-79; Parliamentary sec. Ministry of Power, 1955-58; under sec. of state Home Office, 1958-61; minister of state, 1961-62, life peer, 1979—; dep. speaker House of Lords, London, 1982-88; vice chmn. Coun. of Legal Edn., Eng. and Wales, 1973-77; mem. Bar Coun., Eng. and Wales, 1938-39, 68-79; treas. Lincoln's Inn, 1979. Mem. Royal Commn. on Constn., 1972-74; chmn. Royal Soc. for Mentally Handicapped Children, 1978-82; apptd. Privy Coun., 1962; joint pres. All Party Arts and Heritage Group. Decorated Knight Brit. Empire, Territorial Efficiency Decoration; hon. fellow Univ. Coll., Oxford, 1990—. Conservative. Anglican. Avocations: tennis, shooting, gardening. Office: House of Lords, London SW1A 0PW, England

RENTZEPERIS, PANAYIOTIS IOANNIS, physicist; b. Thessaloniki, Macedonia, Greece, Jan. 31, 1928; s. Ioannis Panayiotis and Anna Ioannis (Missailidou) R.; m. Chrysula Panayiotis Markosi, Jan. 1, 1958; children: Ioannis, Anna-Maria. BSc in Physics, Aristotle U., Thessaloniki, Greece, 1951, DSc in Physics, 1956, Habilitation, 1964. Sci. asst. Aristotle U., 1951-63, chief asst., 1963-67, lectr., 1964-67, assoc. prof. to prof., 1967-96, prof.emeritus, 1996—, dean faculty of physics and math., 1977-78; dir. Selme, Thessaloniki, 1980-82; chmn. Dikatsa, Athens, Greece, 1981-82; bd.dirs. Kysats, Nicosia, Cyprus. Author: Introduction to Crystal Structure Analysis and x-ray Physics, 1985, Introduction to Fourier Analysis, 1985, Special Topics of Applied Physics, 1986; contbr. over 100 rsch. papers to sci. jours. Chmn. State Conservatory, Thessaloniki, 1991-94. 2d lt. Greek Army, 1951-54. Alexander von Humboldt Stiftung scholar, U. Frankfurt, 1958-59; Fulbright Found. fellow, M.I.T., 1962-63. Mem. N.Y. Acad. of Sci., Greek Phys. Soc., Tech. Mus. Thessaloniki, Am. Crystallographic Assn. Greek Orthodox. Avocations: archaeology, music, photography, stamps. Home: 13 M Alexandrou Ave, GR-54640 Thessaloniki Greece Office: Aristotle U, University St, GR-54006 Thessaloniki Greece

RENTZMANN, WILLIAM, legal agency administrator; b. Frederiksberg, Denmark, June 9, 1941; s. Alfred William Due and Rigmor Margrethe (Henriksen) R.; m. Charlotte Thaning; children: Christian, Tobias, Joakim, Nikolaj, Cecilie. LLM, Copenhagen U., 1970. Prin. Dept. Prisons and Probation Ministry Justice, Copenhagen, 1970-80, head divsn. Dept. Prisons and Probation, 1980-87, dep. dir. gen. Dept. Prisons and Probation, 1987-96, dir. gen. Directorate Pvt. Law, 1996-98; dir. gen. Ministry Justice Dept. Prisons and Probation, Copenhagen, 1998—; appted examiner Copenhagen and Århus Law Faculties; pres. Coun. Penol. Affairs, Strasbourg, France, 1991-94; gen. adv. Con. Europe, Estonia, 1994-96; bd. reps. Laan & Spar Bank, pres., 1997—. Author: Community Service Orders and Other Community Sanctions and Measures, 1994, (with Ed. Jack Kamerman) Negotiating Responsibility in the Criminal Justice System, 1996; contbr. articles to profl. jours. Decorated knight and. comdr. of Dannebrog (Denmark), Medaille Penitentiaire Republique Française; recipient Disting. Svc. Order, Estonian Prison Bd., 1999. Mem. Assn. Danish Lawyers and Economists (pres. 1997-98), Danish Assn. Criminology (pres. 1998—), Danish Soc. Criminal Law (pres. 1998—), Greenland Penal Reform Commn., Standing Com. Penal Law Reform. Home: Lemchesvej 22, DK-2900 Hellerup Denmark Office: Min Justice Dept Prisons and Probation, 1 Klareboderne, DK 1115 Copenhagen Denmark

RENWICK, ANDREW GORDON, pharmacology educator; b. London, Sept. 24, 1943; s. Adolphus Henry and Alice Vera Renwick; m. Janet Mary Halliday, Oct. 2, 1965; children: Anthony Brian, Amanda Claire. BSc 1st class, U. London, 1967, PhD, 1971, DSc, 1991. Analytical chemist Merck, Sharp & Dohme, Eng., 1962-67; lectr. biochemistry St. Mary's Hosp., London, 1969-76; sr. lectr. clin. pharmacology U. Southampton, Eng., 1976-86; reader clin. pharmacology U. Southampton, 1986-97, prof. biochem. pharmacology, 1997—; cons. Internat. Sweeteners Assn., Brussels, Belgium, 1987—; mem. com. toxicity U.K., 1988—, com. on carcinogenicity, 1991—; mem. Medicines Commn., U.K., 1992-99. Author: Principles of Medical Pharmacology, 1994; contbr. numerous articles to profl. jours., chpts. to books. Decorated Officer of the Order of Brit. Empire, 2000. Mem. Avocation: classical music. Office: U Southampton Biomed Scis, Basset Crescent East, SO16 7PX Southampton Hants, England

RENWICK, EDWARD S., lawyer; b. L.A., May 10, 1934. AB, Stanford U., 1956, LLB, 1958. Bar: Calif. 1959, U.S. Dist. Ct. (cen. dist.) Calif. 1959, U.S. Ct. Appeals (9th cir.) 1963, U.S. Dist. Ct. (so. dist.) Calif. 1973, U.S. Dist. Ct. (no. dist.) Calif. 1977, U.S. Dist. Ct. (ea. dist.) Calif. 1981, U.S. Supreme Ct. 1985. Ptnr. Hanna and Morton LLP, L.A.; mem., bd. vis. Stanford Law Sch., 1967-69; mem. environ. and natural resources adv. bd. Stanford Law Sch. Bd. dirs. Calif. Supreme Ct. Hist. Soc. Fellow Am. Coll. Trial Lawyers, Am. Bar Found.; mem. ABA (mem. sect. on litigation, antitrust law, bus. law, chmn. sect. of nat. resources, energy and environ. law 1987-88, mem. at large coord. group energy law 1989-92, sect. rep. coord. group energy law 1995-97, Calif. del. legal com., interstate oil compact com.), Calif. Arboretum Assn. (trustee 1986-92), L.A. County Bar Assn. (chmn. natural resources law sect. 1974-75), The State Bar of Calif., Chancery Club (pres. 1992-93), Phi Delta Phi. Office: Hanna and Morton LLP 444 S Flower St Ste 2050 Los Angeles CA 90071-2922

RENWICK OF CLIFTON, LORD ROBIN WILLIAM, former diplomat, banker; b. Dec. 13, 1937; s. Richard Renwick and Clarice Henderson; m. Annie Colette Giudicelli, 1965; 2 children. Student, U. Paris, Cambridge U.; LLD (hon.), Witwatersrand, 1991, Am. U., London, 1993; DLitt (hon.), Coll. William and Mary, 1993, Oglethorpe U., 1995. With Fgn. Svc., Dakar, Senegal, 1963-64, New Delhi, 1966-69; FO Fgn. Svc., 1964-66, FCO,, 1970-72; with Fgn. Svc., Paris, 1972-76; counsellor Cabinet office Fgn. Svc., 1976-78, FCO Rhodesia dept., 1978-80; polit. advisor Gov. of Rhodesia, 1980; vis. fellow Ctr. Internat. Affairs Harvard U., 1980-81; head Chancery, Washington, 1981-84; asst. under sec. of state, FCO, 1984-87, Brit. amb. to South Africa, 1987-91, Brit. amb. to Washington, 1991-95; bd. dirs. Brit. Airways, Compagnie Financière Richemont AG, Billiton, Canal Plus, Fluor Corp., Liberty Internat., South African Breweries, Harmony Gold; chmn. Robert Fleming Inc., Fluor Daniel U.K.; dep. chmn. Robert Fleming Holdings Ltd. Author: Economic Sanctions, 1981, Fighting with Allies, 1996, Unconventional Diplomacy, 1997. With Brit. Army, 1956-58. Decorated knight comdr. Order St. Michael and St. George; hon. fellow Cambridge Jesus Coll., 1992. Mem. Brook's Club, Hurlingham Club, Travellers' Club. Avocations: tennis, trout fishing. Office: care Robert Fleming, 25 Copthall Ave, London EC2R 7DR, England

RENYI, JUDITH A., foundation administrator; b. Phila., July 31, 1947; d. Eric and Liselotte Feyertag; children: Jessica, Quentin, Hodgson. AB, U. Pa., 1968, PhD, 1973; MA, Warwick U., 1972. Sponsored programs assoc. N.Y. U., N.Y.C., 1979-80, asst. dean, 1980-83, fellow humanities coun., 1983-84; exec. dir. Phila. Partnership Edn., 1984-89, Collaboratives Humanities and Arts Tchg., Phila., 1989-94, Nat. Found. Improvement Edn., Washington, 1994—; bd. dirs. Atwater Kent Mus., Phila., 1980's, Phila. Cultural Alliance, Phila, 1980's, Grantmakers for Edn., 1990—, and numerous other adv. bds. and commns. Author: Going Public, 1993; contbr. articles to profl. jours. Bd. dirs., founder Richard H. DeLone Meml. Scholarship, Phila., 1991, A.H. Scounten Meml. Book Fund, Phila., 1997. Recipient of numerous grants from founds. and pub. agencies. Mem. Nat. Ctr. Nonprofit Bds., Coun. on Founds., Washington Regional Assn. Grantmakers, Univ. Club. Avocations: avid amateur cellist, chamber music.

RENZ, ALFONS, scientist; b. Schwaebisch Hall, Germany, June 16, 1949. Diplombiologe, U. Tübingen, 1976, Dr.rer.nat., 1985. Sci. employee U. Tübingen, 1975-92, U. Hohenheim, Germany, 1992—; cons. WHO, Africa, 1982-83. Author studies on human and animal filaria parasites in Africa. Recipient Preis fuer Tropenmedizin, Germany, 1991. Mem. SOVE, DTG, DPG, others. Home: Friedhofstrasse 73, 72074 Tübingen Germany

RENZULLI, ATTILIO, cardiothoracic surgeon; b. Naples, Italy, May 18, 1955; s. Fransesco and Crescenzina (Corbo) R.; m. Gemma Laudati; children: Francesco and Maria Vittoria (twins). MD, 1979. Resident U. Naples, 1979-84; asst. prof. V. Monaldi Hosp., Naples, 1984-86, staff surgeon, 1989-96, 98—; registrar Freeman Hosp., Newcastle Upon Tyne, U.K., 1986-89; cons. surgeon Hamad Med. Corp. Hosp., 1996-98; bd. dirs. Surgical Rsch., Naples; prof. cardiac surgery Postgrad. Sch., Naples, 1998—. Author: First Aid, 1978; co-editor: Anticoagulation Protocols, 1995; contbr. articles to profl. jours. Vol. Red Cross, Naples, 1978. Fellow Italian Soc. Cardiology, European Cardiothoracic Surgeons. Democrat. Avocations: sports, classical music, fishing, books. Home: via Aquila 144, 80143 Naples Italy Office: Univ Monaldi Hosp, Dept Cardiac Surgery, Naples Italy

REPA, PETR, physicist, researcher, educator; b. Praha, Bohemia, Czech Republic, Nov. 2, 1941; s. Antonin and Ela (Hartmanova) R.; m. Jana Mrtkova, May 15, 1945. PhD, Charles U., Praha, 1976; MS, Charles U., 1964. Lectr. Charles U., Praha, Czech Republic, 1965-68, sr. lectr., 1968-89, docent, 1990—; head of vacuum sci. group, Charles U., Praha, 1990—; head of lab. for vacuum metrology, Charles U., 1996—; expert in modern techs. Contbr. articles to profl. jours. Meritorious award Union of Czech Mathematics and Physics, 1988. Fellow Czech Vacuum Soc. (v.p. 1994—), Union of Czech Matematics and Physics; mem. Internat. Union for Vacuum Sci., Technique and Application. Avocations: sports, graphic arts. Office: Faculty Math and Physics, V Holesovickach 2, 180 00 Praha Czech Republic

REPASSY, DENES LASZLO, urologist; b. Budapest, Hungary, Oct. 30, 1947; s. Denes and Adel (Wesselowsky) R.; m. Helga Ida Schmidt, May 24, 1975; children: Balazs, Helga. Univ. diploma medicine, Pote, Pecs, Hungary, 1974; postgrad. in pathology, U. Sote, Budapest, 1978, PG in Urology, 1981; PhD in Med. sci., Hungarian Acad. Sci., Budapest, 1988; habilitation, U. Med. Szeged, Hungary, 2000. Pathologist Ul Pest Hosp., Budapest, 1974; asst. prof. pathology Postgrad. Sch. Medicine, Budapest, 1974-78; pr. prof. urology U. Sote, Budapest, 1978-86, asst. prof. urology, 1986-91, asst. prof., 1991-96; head dept. urology St. Stephen Hosp., Budapest, 1996—; bd. dirs. Assn. Cancer Rsch., Budapest. Author: (books) Minimally Invasive Surgery, 1997, Reconstructive Urol. Surgery, 1997; inventor in field. Mem. Chor Franz Liszt, 1975, City Cultural Heritage Assn., Budapest, 1981, Fishing Assn. Hungary, 1983. Mem. Hungarian Cancer Rsch. Soc. (bd. dirs. 1997), EAU, CEAU (bd. dirs. 2000), Urol. Cancer Found. (pres. 1998). Avocations: philosophy, singing, music, tennis, fishing. Home: Rakoczi 4, 1072 Budapest Pest, Hungary Office: St Stephen Hosp Dept Urol, Nagyvarad T 1, 1083 Budapest Pest, Hungary

REPLOGLE, MICHAEL A., civil engineer, urban planner, environmentalist; b. Gt. Lakes, Ill., Dec. 28, 1953; s. Fred W. and Wilma E. (Furhman) R.; m. Linda Frazee Baker, June 6, 1986. BA in Sociology cum laude, U. Pa., 1978, BSE in Civil & Urban Engring. cum laude, 1978, MSE in Civil & Urban Engring., 1978. USPHS officer U.S. Indian Health Svc., Kayenta, Ariz., 1978; rsch. assoc. Pub. Tech. Inc., Washington, 1979-82; transp. coord. for Montgomery County Nat. Capital Park and Planning Commn., Silver Spring, Md., 1983-92; transp. dir. Environ. Def., Washington, 1992—; cons. World Bank, U.S. Fed. Hwy. Adminstrn., 1990-92. Author: Bicycles and Public Transportation, 1983, Transportation Conformity and Demand Management, 1993; contbr. articles to profl. jours. Nat. coord., founder, Bikes Not Bombs Campaign, Washington, 1984-89; steering com. Campaign for New Transp. Priorities, Washington, 1989-92; bd. dirs. Transportation 2000, Boulder, Colo., 1992-95; bd. dirs., cofounder Clean Air and Transp., Inc., 2000—. Mem. Inst. for Transp. Devel. Policy (founder, pres. 1985-92, bd. dirs. 1992—). Office: Environ Def 1875 Connecticut Ave NW Washington DC 20009-5728

REPS, DAVID NATHAN, finance educator; b. N.Y.C., July 30, 1926; s. Samuel and Fannie (Ginsberg) R.; m. Helene Shifrin, Aug. 10, 1958; children: Tamara, Aaron, Steven, Jennifer. BSEE, Columbia U., 1948; MSEE, U. Pitts., 1953, PhD, 1966. Elec. utility systems engr. Westinghouse Elec. Corp., Pitts., 1950-63, corp. planner, 1963-67; prin. mgmt. svcs. Ernst & Young, N.Y.C., 1967-75; prof., chmn. bus. econs., fin., pub. policy L.I. Univ., N.Y.C., 1975-78; prof. fin. Pace U., Pleasantville, N.Y., 1978—; v.p. Video Frame Store, Inc., N.Y.C., 1983—, The Photoboard Group, N.Y.C., 1989-92; v.p. and treas. Digital Video Photo Imaging, Inc., N.Y.C., 1992—; bd. dirs. The Storyboard Group, Inc., N.Y.C.; exec. v.p. Video Frame Imaging, Inc., N.Y.C., 1994—. Contbr. articles to profl. jours. With USN, 1944-46. Home: 98 Soundview Ave White Plains NY 10606-3617 Office: Pace U Bedford Rd Pleasantville NY 10570

REPŠE, EINARS, banker; b. Jelgava, Latvia, Dec. 9, 1961; s. Aivars-Rihards and Aldona (Krašauska) R.; children: Gunars, Gustavs, Madara. BS in Physics, Latvian U., Riga, 1986. Computer systems designer Spl. Designers Bur. Sci. Instrumentation/Latvian Acad. Scis., Riga, 1986-90; mem. econs. commn. Supreme Coun. of the Republic of Latvia, Riga, 1990-91; gov. Bank of Latvia, Riga, 1991—; alt. gov. IMF, Riga, 1991—. Mem. Parliament of the Republic of Latvia, 1990-91. Office: Bank of Latvia, 2a Kr Valdemara St, LV-1050 Riga Latvia

REQUEJO, FERRAN, political science educator; b. Barcelona, Spain, Nov. 14, 1951; s. Eutimio Requejo and Isabel Coll; m. Teresa Colomer; children: Xavier, Laura. MA in Philosophy, U. Barcelona, 1976, MA in Modern history, 1978, PhD in Philosophy, 1986; MA in Indsl. Engring., U. Politecnica de Catalunya, Spain, 1979. Asst. U. Barcelona, 1979-86, rschr., 1986-87, assoc. prof. econs., 1987-91; assoc. prof. polit. scis. U. Pompeu Fabra, Spain, 1991-93; prof. polit. sci. U. Pompeu Fabra, 1993—; dir. rschr. Generalitat de Catalunya, 1995—. Author: Federalisme, per a què?, 1998, European Citizenship, Multiculturalism and the State, 1998, Asimetría Federal y Estado Plurinacional, 1999; contbr. articles to profl. jours. Advisor Polit. Parties, Barceloan, 1994—. 2nd lt. Spanish Artillery, 1978. Recipient Pérez Serrano prize, Madrid, 1987, Rudolf Wildenmann prize, Oslo, 1997. Mem. ECPR (ofcl. rep. 1997—), IPSA, AECPA. Avocations: tennis, cinema, jazz music. Office: Univ Pompen Fabra, Ramon Trias Fargas 25-27, 08005 Barcelona Spain

RERON, ELZBIETA, otolaryngologist, researcher; b. Zakopane, Poland, Oct. 4, 1939; d. Andrzej and Józefa (Podmokly) Pietrzak; m. Alfred Reron, Feb. 1, 1964; 1 child, Małgorzata. MD, Jagellonian U., Cracow, Poland, 1965, PhD, 1977. Asst. otolaryngol. dept. Jagiellonian U., 1967-77, lectr., 1977-90, assoc. prof., 1990-99, prof., 1999—, dep. head otolaryngol. dept., 1990—. Contbr. articles to profl. jours. Recipient award for best sci. presentation First World Congress Pediat. Otolaryngology, 1977. Mem. Brit. Soc. Audiology, Politzer Soc., Polish Soc. Otorhinolaryngologists (chair bd. dirs. Cracow br.). Office: Klinika Otolaryngologiczna, ul Śniadeckich 2, 31-501 Cracow Poland

RESENDE, MARCELO, economist, educator; b. Rio de Janeiro, Aug. 26, 1963; s. Eduardo de Mendonça e Silva and Edna Vieira de Resende. BA in Econs., State U. Rio de Janeiro, 1985, BS in Psychology, 1990; MSc in Econs., Pontifical Cath. U., Rio de Janeiro, 1989; MA in Econs., U. Pa., 1993; DPhil in Econs., Oxford (Eng.) U., 1997. Lectr. Pontifical Cath. U. Rio de Janeiro, 1987-89; asst. prof. econs. State U. Rio de Janeiro, 1990; asst. prof. econs. Fed. U. Rio de Janeiro, 1990-98, assoc. prof., 1998—. Contbr. articles to profl. jours., including Oxford Econ. Papers, Bull. Econs. Rsch., Oxford Bull. Econs. and Stats., Rev. Indsl. Orgns., Info. Econs. and Policy. Scholar Brazilian Ministry Sci. and Tech., 1986-88, Brazilian Ministry Edn., 1991-95; rsch. grantee Brazilian Ministry Planning, 1988. Mem. Brazilian Econometric Soc. Avocations: music concerts, movies, sports practice (soccer), Theatre. E-mail: mresende@ism.com.br; or mresende@ie.ufrj.br. Office: Fed U Rio de Janeiro Inst Econs, Av Pasteur 250, 22290-240 Rio de Janeiro Brazil

RESER, ELIZABETH MAY (BETTY RESER), bookkeeper; b. Le Roy, Kans., Sept. 4, 1939; d. William David II and Vera Hazel (Dreyer) Meats; m. William Joseph Reser, Sept. 26, 1958; children: Dee Anna Reser, Donna Sue Reser Larson. Diploma in computer programming, Control Data Inst., St. Louis, 1980; student, Washburn U., 1991. Cert. computer programmer, Mo. Computer programmer Regional Justice Info. Sys., St. Louis, 1980; sec. Shawnee Heights H.S., Tecumseh, Kans., 1973-78, bookkeeper, 1984-90. Treas. Secs. Assn. Shawnee Heights Unified Sch. Dist. 450, 1975-76, 86-87; vol. March of Dimes, Topeka, 1995-00; mem. bd. trustees Susanna Wesley United Meth. Ch., Topeka, 1992-94, mem. prayer chain, 1993-94. Republican. Avocations: computers, quilting, shopping, crocheting, family activities. Home: 2849 SW Dukeries Rd Topeka KS 66614-4726

RESHETNIKOV, MICHAEL EVGENIEVITCH, company executive; b. Moscow, Nov. 27, 1955; s. Evgeny Mikhailovitch and Antonina Davydovna (Bushueva) R.; m. Olga Fedorovna Yaksanova, Mar. 14, 1979; children: Michael, Cyrill. Magister, Moscow State U., 1979, PhD, 1987. Scientist Moscow State U., 1979-89; dep. dir. Soviet-Swiss Joint Venture, Russia, 1989—; gen. dir. Zoolex Ltd., Russia, 1991—; comml. dir. Falcon Ltd., Russia, 1994—. Contbr. articles to profl. jours. Office: Zoolex, Baltiyskaya St 8, 125315 Moscow Russia

RESHETOV, VLADIMIR ALEXANDROVICH, physics educator; b. Poltava, Ukraine, Nov. 7, 1957; s. Alexander Ivanovich and Galina Ippolitovna (Khudyakova) R.; m. Marina Yurievna Abramova, May 4, 1992; 1 child, Andrey. MS, Engring. Physics Inst., Moscow, 1984. Lectr. Aviation Inst., Samara, USSR, 1985-90; assoc. prof. Pedagogical Inst., Tolyatti, Russia, 1990—. Contbr. articles to profl. jours. Named Soros assoc. prof. ISSEP, Moscow, 1997. Home: Tatisceva 3-33, 445031 Tolyatti Samara, Russia Office: Pedagogical Inst, Korolyova 13, 445859 Tolyatti Samara, Russia

RESIDORI, STEFANIA, physicist, researcher; b. Verona, Veneto, Italy, Jan. 23, 1964; d. Valentino and Edda (Zampini) R. BS, U. Verona, Italy, 1984; M in Physics, U. Florence, Italy, 1989, PhD in Optics, 1993. Rschr. Nat. Inst. Ottica, Florence, 1992—; sci. cons. Inst. Enciclopedia Italiana Fondata Giovanni Treccani, 1994. Office: Inst Nat Ottica, Largo Enrico Fermi 6, 50129 Florence Italy and: Inst Non-Lineaire de Nice, 1361 Rte des Lucioles, F-06560 Valbonne France

RESKE, STEVEN DAVID, lawyer, writer; b. Mpls., May 31, 1962; s. Albert Edgar Reske and Florence Mae Altland. BA with distinction, St. Olaf Coll., Northfield, Minn., 1985; JD cum laude, Boston U., 1988. Bar: Ill. 1988, Minn. 1989, D.C. 1998, U.S. Dist. Ct. Minn. 1991, U.S. Ct. Appeals (5th cir.) 1989, (7th and 8th cir.) 1992, (D.C. circuit) 1998, U.S. Supreme Ct. 1993. Intern U.S. Senator Durenberger, Washington, 1981-82, Citizens for Ednl. Freedom, Washington, D.C., 1981-82, Abbott-Northwestern Hosp., Mpls., 1984, U.S. Dist. Ct. Judge Magnuson, St. Paul, 1986; summer assoc. Faegre & Benson, Mpls., 1987; assoc. Sidley & Austin, Chgo., 1988; law clk. to Hon. Judge Politz U.S. Ct. Appeals 5th cir., Shreveport, La., 1988-89; pvt. practice, 1989—, writer, 1989—. Contbr. CD Rev., 1993-95, JAZZIZ, 1996—, Skyway News, 1997—, City Pages, 2000—; contbr. articles to profl. jours.; mem. Am. Jour. Law and Medicine, 1986-87, editor, 1987-88; legal editor-at-large Law and Politics, 1998—; columnist Twin Cities Revue, 1998—. Recipient Minn. Super Lawyer award, 1998, Am. Jurisprudence award, 1988; Edward F. Hennessey scholar, 1988, G. Joseph Tauro scholar, 1986. Mem. ABA (antitrust divsn.), Minn. State Bar Assn., Hennepin County Bar Assn., Am. Econ. Assn., Am. Philos. Assn. Office: 3422 Douglas Dr N Crystal MN 55422-2414

RESNICK, HENRY ROY, pharmacist; b. N.Y.C., Dec. 12, 1952; s. Samuel and Miriam (Jacobson) R.; m. Mary Lee Monroe. Sept. 13, 1981; children: Jacob Monroe, Aaron Leo. BS in Pharmacy, L.I. U., 1975, MS in Drug Info. & Comm., 1978; PharmD, U. Fla., 2000. Pharmacist Sagamore Childrens Ctr., Melville, N.Y., 1976-77; staff pharmacist Montefiore Hosp. and Med. Ctr., N.Y.C., 1977-80; mgr. clin. pharmacy svcs. Beth Israel Med. Ctr., N.Y.C., 1980-82, from asst. dir. pharmacy to sr. assoc. dir., 1982-90; dir. pharmacy New Rochelle (N.Y.) Hosp. Med. Ctr., 1990-94; asst. dir. pharmacy Allied Pharmacy Mgmt. Inc., Lantana, Fla., 1994-95; pharmacy supr. Delray Cmty. Hosp., Delray Beach, Fla., 1995-97; dir. pharmacy Leader Health Care Ctr., Inc., Boca Raton, Fla., 1997-98; pres., founder Resnick Profl. Holdings, P.A., 1998—; dir. pharmacy Hospice By The Sea Inc., Boca Raton, 2000—; adj. clin. instr. Arnold and Marie Schwartz Coll. Pharmacy Health Scis., N.Y.C., 1980-82. Mem. Am. Soc. Hosp. Pharmacists, Am. Soc. Pharmacy Law, Fla. Soc. Hosp. Pharmacists, N.Y. State Coun. Hosp. Pharmacists (monitoring com. on legislation 1989-90, joint com. with industry 1989-90, govt. affairs com. 1991-94), Westchester Soc. Hosp. Pharmacists (chmn. legis., constn. and bylaws com. 1991-94, exec. com. 1991-94, pres.-elect 1992-93, pres. 1993-94, del. N.Y. State coun. hosp. pharmacists 1992-94). Avocations: fishing, photography. Office: Hospice By The Sea Inc 1531 W Palmetto Park Rd Boca Raton FL 33486-3395

RESNICK, KENNETH, photography director; b. N.Y.C., May 11, 1934; s. Reuben and Helen (Edelson) R.; m. Marijke Koch, Aug. 1960 (div. Aug. 1974); children: Sonya, Paul, Karen; m. Karen louise Matthesius, July 23, 1977; children: Margaret Rose, Charles Andrew. Student, Trinity Coll., 1952-56. Dir. photography Ga. Ctr., U. Ga., Athens, 1960-61; cameraman, editor Milner and Fenwick, Inc., Balt., 1961-63; film maker U.S. Info. Agy., Washington, 1963-66; producer Nat. Ednl. TV, N.Y.C., 1965; cameraman, asst. cameraman NBC-TV, Washington, 1967-68; chief photographer Md. Ctr. for Pub. Broadcasting Sta. WMPB-TV, Owings Mills, 1968-69; cameraman, asst. dir. BF&J Prodns., Balt., 1969-72; news film cameraman Sta. WTTG-TV, Metromedia Prodns., Washington, 1972-78; producer, videographer Cable News Network, Atlanta, 1981-82; video producer Wang Labs., Inc., Lowell, Mass., 1986-90; freelance dir. of photography; instr. Md. Inst. Coll. of Art, Balt., 1968-73; guest lectr. Goucher Coll, Towsen, Md., 1969-70, Caselton (Vt.) State Coll., 1985; conf. participant Arts and Soc., Morgan State Coll, Balt., 1966. Co-produced, co-directed, cinematographer Sunday on the River, 1962 (Bronze medal, Silver Gondola award humanitarian idealism in film Venice Internat. Documentary Film Festival 1962, An Outstanding Film of Yr. Brit. Film Inst. and London Film Festival 1962, Golden Eagle award Council Internat. Nontheatrical Events 1962, 63, work inducted in the Mus. Modern Art Film Archives 1991); produced, directed, photographed Men, Marble and Machines, 1984 (Bronze medal Internat. Film and TV Festival of N.Y.C. 1984, Golden Eagle award, 1984 Chris plaque Columbus Film Festival 1985, Emmy award 1987); photographed Now and in the Future (Silver Plaque INTERCOM 1988); producer, dir., photographer A Celebration of Architecture (Gold Camera award, 3 Silver Screen awards, U.S. Indsl. Film and Video Festival 1989, Gold CINDY award, Rose Layos Green Meml. award 1989, Chris award Columbus Film Festival 1989, Silver Plaque INTERCOM, 1989, 2 Silver Medals Internat. Film & TV Festival N.Y. 1990, Golden Eagle award 1990). Mem. World Wildlife Found., Wilderness Soc., Nature Conservancy. Recipient First Prize Gen. News Class award, 1973, Spot News Class award, 1976, 78, White House News Photographer's Assn., First Place Spot News award Nat. Press Photographer's Assn., 1978, Emmy news film photography Washington Chpt. Nat. Acad. TV Arts and Scis., Inc., 1978. Mem. Internat. Photographers of Motion Picture and TV Industries (local 644), sierra Club. Democrat. Unitarian Universalist. Home: 73 Washington St Concord NH 03301-4172

RESNICK, PAUL R., research chemist; b. N.Y.C., Apr. 7, 1934; married, 1966; 1 child. BA, Swarthmore Coll., 1955; PhD in Organic Chemistry, Cornell U., 1961. Fellow U. Calif., Berkeley, 1960-62; from chemist to sr. rsch. chemist E.I. DuPont De Nemours & Co., Inc., 1962-74, rsch. assoc., 1974-85, rsch. fellow, 1985-88, sr. rsch. fellow, 1988-91, DuPont fellow,

1991—. Recipient Dupont Lavoisier medal for tech. achievement, 1996. Mem. Am. Chem. Soc. (Award for Creative Work in Fluorine Chemistry 1995). Office: DuPont Fluoroproducts 22828 NC Highway 87 W Fayetteville NC 28306-7332

RESNIK, DAVID BENJAMIN, medical humanities educator, researcher; b. Boston, Nov. 30, 1962; s. Michael David and Janet Depping Resnik; m. Susan Preston, Aug. 6, 1988; children: Peter Benjamin, Michael Thomas. BA, Davidson Coll., 1985; MA, U. N.C., 1987, PhD, 1990. Asst. prof. U. Wyo., Laramie, 1990-95, assoc. prof., dir. Ctr. for Advancement Ethics, 1995-98; assoc. prof. dept. med. humanities East Carolina U. Brody Sch. Medicine, Greenville, N.C., 1998—; assoc. dir. Bioethics Ctr., Univ. Health Sys., Greenville, 1998—. Author: The Ethics of Science, 1998, Germline Gene Therapy, 1999; contbr. articles to profl. jours., including Bioethics, Jour. Med. Ethics. Vol. Univ. Health Sys. Hospice, Greenville, 1998—, Beverly Health Care, Greenville, 1998—. Grantee Gen. Elec., 1991, NSF, 1996. Mem. AAAS, Am. Philos. Assn., Philosophy of Sci. Assn. Baptist. Avocations: music, creative writing, running, swimming, biking. E-mail: dresnik@brody.med.ecu.edu. Office: East Carolina U Brody Sch Medicine 25-17 Brody Bldg Greenville NC 27858

RESNIK, HARVEY LEWIS PAUL, psychiatrist; b. Buffalo, Apr. 6, 1930; s. Samuel andCelia (Greenberg) R.; m. Audrey Ruth Frey, Aug. 30, 1964 (dec. 1993); children: Rebecca Gabrielle, Henry Seth Maccabee, Jessica Ruth. B.A. magna cum laude, U. Buffalo, 1951; M.D., Columbia, 1955; grad., Phila. Psychoanalytic Inst., 1967. Diplomate: Am. Bd. Psychiatry and Neurology. Intern Phila. Gen. Hosp., 1955-56, resident in surgery, 1956-57; resident in psychiatry Jackson Meml. Hosp., Miami, Fla., 1959-61; fellow U. Pa. Hosp., 1961-62, mem. staff, 1962-67; instr; Sch. Medicine, U. Pa., 1962-66; instr. med. hypnosis Sch. Medicine, U. Pa. (Grad. Sch. Medicine), 1963-65; clin. dir. psychiatry E. J. Meyer Meml. Hosp., Buffalo, 1967; dir. psychiatry E. J. Meyer Meml. Hosp., 1968; assoc. prof. psychiatry Sch. Medicine, SUNY at Buffalo, Buffalo, 1967, prof., 1968-70, dep. chmn. dept. psychiatry, 1968-69; chief Nat. Center for Studies of Suicide Prevention, NIMH, 1969-74, chief mental health emergencies sect., 1974-76; with Reproductive Biology Research Found., St. Louis, 1971; clin. prof. psychiatry Sch. Medicine, George Washington U., 1969—; dir. Human Behavior Found., 1975—; lectr. Sch. Medicine, Johns Hopkins, Balt., 1969-74; adj. lectr. Johns Hopkins U. Sch. Pub. Health, Balt., 1981-82; prof. cmty. health Fed. City Coll., 1971-75; med. dir. Johns Hopkins U. Compulsive Gambling Ctr., 1981-83; med. dir. alcohol and substance abuse program U. Md., College Park, 1986-2000; vis. prof. Katholieke U., Leuven, Belgium, 1986-93; cons. to Sec.-Gen. Ministry of Health, Belgium, 1986-95, NATO fellow, 1986-87; cons. various hosps. and orgns., Medicare, Pa. Blue Shield, 1984-96, Trailblazer Health, 1996-99, Blue Cross/Blue Shield S.C., 1999. Author: Suicidal Behaviors: Diagnosis and Management, 1968, 2d edit., 1994, (with M. E. Wolfgang) Treatment of the Sexual Offender, 1971, Sexual Behaviors: Social, Clinical and Legal Aspects, 1972, (with B. Hathorne) Suicide Prevention in the Seventies, 1973, (with H.L. Ruben) Emergency Psychiatric Care, 1974, (with others) The Prediction of Suicide, 1974, Emergency and Disaster Management, 1976; (with J.T. Mitchell) Emergency Response to Crisis, 1981; Editor: Bull. Suicidology, 1969-74; Contbr. (with others) articles on hypnosis, sexual offenders, marriage and sexual dysfunction treatment, suicide, death and dying, emergency psychiatric care. Mem. Addictions Adv. Bd. Prince Georges County, 1980-85. Served to capt. USAF, 1957-59, ETO-Middle East; capt. USNR; ret. Decorated officer in the Order King Leopold, Belgium, 1990. Fellow Am. Coll. Mental Health Adminstrs. (life), Am. Coll. Psychiatrists (life), Am. Psychiat. Assn. (life); mem. Med-Chi of Md., Prince Georges County Med. Assn. (co-chair joint com. with Bar Assn. 1996—), Am. Acad. Psychiatry and Law (suicidology com. 1998-2000), Phila. Psychoanalytic Soc., NIH Alumni Assn., Columbia U. Med. Alumni Assn. (bd. dirs. 1993-95), Phi Beta Kappa, Beta Sigma Rho (grand vice warden 1963), Cosmos Club (Washington). Jewish. Office: Univ Profl Ctr 4700 Berwyn House Rd Ste 202 College Park MD 20740-4717

RESPONDEK-LIBERSKA, MARIA, physician; b. Lodz, Poland, Feb. 15, 1955; d. Barbara Lipinska. MD, Med. Acad. Lodz, 1979, PhD, 1984. From asst. pediat. cardiology to sr. asst. nuclear medicine Med. Acad. Lodz, 1979-90; from asst. prof. to assoc. prof. perinatal malformations Polish Mother's Meml. Hosp., Lodz, 1990—. Author: Fetal Echocardiography and Fetal Cardiology (in Polish); contbr. chpts. to numerous textbooks and profl. jours. Mem. Internat. Soc. Ultrasound Ob-Gyn., Am. Inst. Ultrasound in Medicine, Assn. European Pediat. Cardiology (fetal working group), Am. Echocardiography Soc. Avocations: skiing, music, internet surfing, books. E-mail: majkares@krysia.mni.lodz.pl. Office: Polish Mothers Meml Hosp, Rzgowska 281/289, 93-345 Lodz Poland

RESS, CHARLES WILLIAM, management consultant; b. Columbus, Ohio, Aug. 6, 1933; s. George Leonard and Martha (Lake) R.; m. Virginia M. Beck, Aug. 28, 1954; children: Beverly Beck, Suzanne E., Charles W. Jr., Linda Perrins, Jennifer Laurel. BS, Miami U., 1955; MA in Psychology, Rutgers U., 1969. Buyer The Higbee Co., Cleve., 1956-59; asst. to gen. mdse. mgr. The Halle Bros. Co., Cleve., 1959-64; research dir. The Associated Mdse. Corp., N.Y.C., 1964-73; v.p. Mgmt. Horizons, Columbus, 1973-76; founder, chmn. bd. C.W. Ress & Assoc., Inc., Columbus, 1976-90; gen. mgr. Levi Strauss & Co., Columbus, 1990-94, mgmt. cons., 1994—; lectr. in field. Author: Future Trends in Retailing, 1983, Trans National Retailing, 1988, Retailing 2000, 1991; contbr. articles to profl. jours. Republican. Avocations: cooking, wine tasting. Office: 3860 Lyon Dr Columbus OH 43220-4907

RESSETAR, NANCY, foreign language educator; b. Paterson, N.J., Dec. 19, 1947; d. Marino Angelo and Florence Mae (Patterson) DeMattia; m. Michael Ressetar, Jr., Aug. 15, 1981; 1 child, Tatyana Marina. BA, Montclair State U., 1970. Cert. tchr., N.J. Model various agencies, 1953-84; tchr. Spanish Clifton (N.J.) Sch. Sys., 1970—. Sponsor Spanish Club, Clifton, 1981—, Student Leadership, Clifton, 1988—, Travel to Spain, Clifton, 1982-96; campaign worker Dem. Party, Clifton, 1968-72. Recipient Gov.'s award for excellence in tchg. State of N.J., 1996. Mem. NEA, N.J. Edn. Assn., Passaic County Edn. Assn., Clifton Tchrs. Assn. (sec. 1973-75), Fgn. Lang. Tchrs. N.J., Am. Assn. Tchrs. Spanish and Portuguese. Democrat. Lutheran. Avocations: travel, theatre, doll collecting, classic Hollywood, tutoring. Home: 20 Robin Hood Rd Clifton NJ 07013-3112

REST, FRANCO HANS OTTO, sociophilosophy educator; b. Ferrara, Italy, Aug. 20, 1942; arrived in Germany, 1945; s. Walter and Mariette (Sieben) R.; m. Gisela Hartjes, Aug. 1, 1968; children: Esther-Maria, Pascal Amos. D of Pedagogy, U. Münster, Germany, 1980. Asst. prof. Sch. for Social Work, Dortmund, Germany, 1970-82; prof. Poly., Dortmund, 1982—; chmn. Rsch. Group Orthothanasy, Dortmund, 1978-79; com. mem. Action More Humanity, Düsseldorf, 1980-88, Hospice Movement, Northrhine-Westfalia, 1992-97; founder Omega, Hann.Muenden, 1985. Author: Care for the Dying, 1981, Waldorf (Rudolf Steiner) Pedagogie, 1992, Damaskus Experiences, 1990, Care for the Dying Instead of Assisted Suicide, 1997, Dying at Home, 1997, Who are you, Christians?, 2000. Mem. Bensberger Kreis, Bonn, 1969—. Mem. Com. of Social Gerontology. Roman Catholic. Avocations: music, archaeology. Home: Storstweg 41a, 44227 Dortmund Germany Office: Poly/Social Work, Emil Figge Str 44, 44227 Dortmund Germany

RESTAINO, GIOVANNI FRANCO, philosophy educator; b. Alghero, Italy, Mar. 1, 1938; s. Angelo and Remigia (Manunta) R.; m. Teresa Isetta, Aug. 4, 1937; children: Alessandra, Gabriella. Laurea, Facoltá Lettere e Filosofia, Cagliari, Italy, 1961. Asst. prof. Facoltá Lettere e Filosofia, Cagliari, 1962-69, prof. in charge, 1969-75, prof., 1975-94; pres., 1986-93; prof. U. Tor Vergata, Rome, 1994—. Author: (monograph) J.S. Mill e La Cultura Filosofica Britannica, 1968, Storia dell'Estetica, 1991, Le Filosofie Femministe, 1999, Storia della Filosofia, 6 Vols., 1999. Home: Via Tortona 16, 00183 Roma Lazio, Italia Office: Dipartimento Ricerche Filos, Via A Cavaglieri 6, 00173 Rome Italy

RESTIAN, ADRIAN GRATIAÖ, physician, researcher; b. Zizih, Brasov, Romania, Aug. 21, 1936; s. Gratian Vasile and Ana Gheorghe Restian; m. Aurelia Nicoleta Cristea; children: Serban, Adrian. MD, Med. U., 1961; PhD, Inst. of Anthropology, 1990. Physician Hosp. Ceahlau, Romania, 1961-65, Hosp. Tractoral Brasov, 1966-85; med. officer Health Ministry, Bucharest, 1986-90; expert Postgrad. Tng. Inst., Bucharest, 1990-95; sr. rschr. Inst. of Pub. Health, Bucharest, 1995—; dir. Postgrad. Tng. Inst., Bucharest, 1990-95; assoc. prof. Med. U. Bucharest, 1998—. Author: Information Pathology, 1977, Homocibereticus, 1981, Cybermetic Medicine, 1984, Medical Diagnosis, Integronics, 1990, Basis of Family Medicine, 1999; contbr. articles to profl. publs. Recipient Romanian Acad. award, 1977, 84. Mem. Romanian Med. Academy, European Acad. of Tchr. in Family Medicine, Internat. Assn. of Cybernetics, Internat. Brain Rsch. Orgn., Internat. Coll. of Psychosomatic Medicine. Mem. Orthodox Ch. Avocations: music, reading, walking. Home: Aviator Sanatescu Nr 43, 71324 Bucharest Romania Office: Inst of Pub Health, Bucharest Romania

RESTORI, GABRIELE, emergency medicine physician; b. Parma, Italy, Apr. 23, 1956; s. Maria Teresa Dall'Asta; m. Sandra Mari, May 24, 1992; children: Eleonora, Angelica. MD, U. Parma, 1980; student, Chieti U., Italy, 1994-2000. Physician, psychiatrist Reggio Emilia (Italy) Hosp., Reggio Emilia, Italy, 1987-88; med. asst. Blood Transfusion Hematology, Reggio Emilia, 1988-92; physician in internal medicine Reggio Emilia, 1992-94; emeregency medicine physician Hosp. U. Parma, 1994—; contract prof. medicine Chieti U., Italy, 1987—; expert natural medicine and holistic therapies, 1998—. Author 10 medical books; contbr. over 300 articles to scientific publs. Mem. Italian Emergency Medicine Soc. Avocations: running, furniture restoration, judo, swimming, painting. Home: Via Bianconese 60, 43010 Bianconese Parma, Italy Office: Emergency Med, Az Osp Di PR Via Gransci 12, 43010 Parma Italy

RESTREPO, DANIEL ESTEBAN, engineering executive, engineering educator; b. Medellin, Antioquia, Colombia, Dec. 10, 1962; s. Pedro Restrepo and Bertha Posada; m. Lina Maria Bayter. BS in Mech. Engring., U. Pontificia Bolivariana, Medellin, 1988. Maintenance engr. Aerolineas Centrales de Colombia, Medellin, 1986-89, dir. engring., 1989-99; v.p. engring. and tech. svcs. Aerodinamica S.A., 1999—; prof. faculty U. Pontificia Bolivariana; prof. Acad. Antioquena de Aviacio, Medellin, 1989-94, Esc. de Aviacion lo Halcones, Medellin, 1994-99. Home: Cr 32B #10-99, AA 75659 Medellin Colombia Office: Aerodinamica SA, CLL 10 Sur # 50FF 28, Medellin Colombia

RETEY, JANOS, biochemistry educator; b. Szeged, Hungary, Feb. 4, 1934; s. Imre and Klara (Hammesz0 R.; m. Elisabeth Witzig, May 18, 1966; children: Barbara, Albert, Julia. Dipl.Ing. Chem., ETH, Zurich, 1960, DS, 1963. Oberassistent ETH, Zurich, 1968-72; prof. biochem. U. Karlsruhe, Germany, 1972—. Author: (with J.A. Robinson) Stereospecificity in Organic Chemistry and Enzymology, 1982; contbr. articles to profl. jours.; mem. editl. adv. bd. European Jour. Biochem., 1980—, Bioorganic Chemistry, 1984—, Archives Biochemistry and Biophys., 1994—, Biofactors, 1988—, Current Opinion in Chem. Biology, 1997—. Recipient Alfred Werner prize Swiss Chem. Soc., 1971; postdoctoral fellow Max Planck Inst., Munich, Germany, 1963-65, ETH, Zurich, 1965-68. Mem. New Swiss Chem. Soc., Soc. German Chemists, Soc. Biochem. & Molecular Biology, Royal Soc. Chemistry. Home: Erikaweg 6, D-76149 Karlsruhe Germany Office: Chair of Biochemistry U, Kaiserstr 12, D-76128 Karlsruhe Germany

RETHMAN, NORMAN FREDERICK GEORGE, agriculturist, educator; b. Harding, Natal, South Africa, July 21, 1940; s. William George Field and Elizabeth Mary (Broomhead) R.; m. Angela Mary Page, Apr. 11, 1964; children: Vivienne Jean, Michael Field, Nicola Clare. BSc in Agr., U. Natal, 1962, MSc in Agr., 1965, PhD, 1990. Rschr. Dept. Agr., Mpumulanga, South Africa, 1963-67, 69-85; field officer Kynoch-Capex Fertilizer, Natal, South Africa, 1968; prof. U. Pretoria, Gauteng, South Africa, 1986—. Recipient Silver medal Fertilizer Soc. South Africa, 1985. Mem. Internat. Erosion Ctrl. Assn. (So. African chpt.), Internat. Assn. Land Reclaimationists, Am. Soc. Surface Mining and Reclamation, Soc. Range Mgmt., Grassland Soc. Southern Africa, Tropical Grassland Soc. Australia, South Africa Soc. Crop Prodn. Episcopalian. Avocations: sailing, hiking, travel, gardening, wildlife. Office: Univ Pretoria, Lynnwood Rd, Gauteng Pretoria 0002, South Africa

RETHORÉ, MARIE-GDILE, medical genetics educator; b. Neuilly sur Seine, France, July 11, 1929; d. Charles and Marie Thérèse (de Maussé) R. MD, Paris, 1957. Stagiaire rsch. Nat. Inst. Health and Med. Rsch., Paris, 1955, attachée rschr., 1957, chargée rsch., 1960, maître rsch., 1965, dir. rsch., 1975, 82-97; assoc. prof. Ctr. Med. Jérôme Lejeune, Paris, 1982—, dir. med., 1997. Office: Ctr Med Jerome Lejeune, 66 rue des Plantes, 75014 Paris France

RETIEF, FRANÇOIS PIETER, retired university administrator; b. Nkhoma, Malawi, Dec. 16, 1932; arrived in South Africa, 1943; s. Renaldo Leopold and Andrisina Hermansina (Müller) R.; m. Maria Catherina Crous, Feb. 10, 1962; children: Pierre Renaldo, Jacques Johan, Françis Pieter. MBChB, U. Cape Town, South Africa, 1955; DPhil, Oxford (Eng.) U., 1959; MD, U. Stellenbosch, Bellville, South Africa, 1965; MD (hon.), U. Orange Free State, Bloemfontein, South Africa, 1986; PhD (hon.), U. Stellenbosch, 1997. Mem. Royal Coll. Physicians, Edinburgh, 1959, Fellow, 1976. Lectr., cons. U. Stellenbosch, 1960-69; dean of medicine U. Orange Free State, 1970-78; rector/vice-chancellor Med. U. Southern Africa, Pretoria, South Africa, 1978-82; dir.-gen. Dept. Health Govt. Republic of South Africa, 1983-87; rector/vice-chancellor U. Orange Free State, 1988-97; ret., 1997; mem. Premier's Scientific Coun., South Africa, 1972-76, 80-84; chmn. Med. Rsch. Coun., South Africa, 1989-94; chmn. Akademie Wetenskap en Kuns, South Africa, 1995-97; dir. Med. Leasing Svcs. Bank, Johannesburg, 1988—; chmn. Free State Bd. ABSA Bank, Bloemfontein, 1994—. Contbr. over 85 articles and 25 rsch. abstracts to internat. scientific jours. Hon. pres. Free State Rugby Union, Bloemfontein, 1990-97; past hon. v.p. Christian Med. Fellowship, South Africa; sponsor Odeion String Quartet, Bloemfontein, 1993—. Rhodes scholar U. Oxford, 1956-59, USPHS Rsch. fellow Mt. Sinai Hosp., N.Y.C., 1965, South African Med. Rsch. Coun. grantee 1963-78; recipient Hamilton Maynard medal for best article in South African Med. Jour., 1982, Alumnus of Yr. award U. Orange Free State, 1997; named Boemfonteiner of Yr., 1991. Mem. South African Bot. Assn., South African Ornithol. Soc., South African Huegenot Soc. Mem. National Party. Mem. Dutch Reformed Church. Avocations: nature conservation, animal photography, indigeous gardening, classical music, medical history. Home: PO Box 29521, Danhof 9310, Bloemfontein Free St, South Africa

RETIK, ARKADY, civil engineering educator, researcher, consultant; b. Minsk, USSR, Nov. 3, 1956; arrived in Israel, 1978; m. Nora Retik, Apr. 9, 1981; children: Arik, Mathan. BSc, Israel Inst. Tech., Haifa, 1981, MSc, 1987, DSc, 1990. Chartered engr., Israel. Designer, engr. Eidelman & Sons Co., Haifa, 1980-81; lt. engr. IDF, Israel, 1981-85; rschr., engr. Technion, Israel, 1985-90; rsch. fellow Salford, Eng., 1990-91; lectr. Strathclyde U., Glasgow, Scotland, 1992-95, sr. lectr., 1995-2000; prof. Caledonian Univ., Glasgow, 2000—; cons. Marine Engring., Tel Aviv, 1987-89, Eyal Mgmt., Tel-Aviv, 1988-89. Author: (with D. Langford) Computer Integrated Planning & Design for Construction, 2000; co-author: Information Sources in Engineering, 1996; co-editor: Management of Construction, 3 vols., 1996, Representation & Delivery, 1996. Lt. Israeli Def. Forces, 1981-85. Carnegie Trust grantee, Glasgow, 1994, rsch. grantee EPSRC, U.K., 1996; recipient Gutwirth Prize Dist., Haifa, 1990. Mem. ASCE, Assn. Project Mgmt., Virtual Reality Soc., Brit.-Technion Soc. (Scottish rep. 1993—). Jewish. Avocations: jazz, sport, travelling. Office: Glasgow Caledonian Univ, Cowcaddeus Rd, Glasgow G-4 OBA, Scotland

RETSAS, ANDREW PHILIP, nursing educator, consultant; b. Ceduna, Australia, Sept. 1, 1954; s. Yalitopolous Jean and Mina Dorothy (Victor) R.; m. Heather Crabbe; 1 child: Tracey Crabbe. Diploma in nursing edn., Armidale Coll. Advanced Edn., Australia, 1982; B Applied Sci., Phillip Inst., Australia, 1983; BA in Social Sci., La Trobe U., Australia, 1989, PhD in Edn., 1994. Lectr. La Trobe Univ., Australia, 1986-87, sr. lectr., 1987-91; sr. lectr. Griffith U., Australia, 1992-97; prof. RMIT U., Bundoora, Australia, 1998—. Contbr. articles to profl. jours.

RETSAS, SPYROS, oncologist; b. Thessaloniki, Greece, Dec. 4, 1942; arrived in U.K., 1969; s. Stylianos and Panaghiota (Alexandri) R.; m. Diana Gillian Rees, July 8, 1972; 1 child, Philip-Alexander. MD, Aristotle U., Thessaloniki, 1967, U. Athens, 1978. Accredited specialist. Sr. house officer Royal Marsden Hosp., Surrey, Eng., 1971-72; registrar in medicine Whipps Cross Hosp., London, 1973-75; sr. lectr. Westminster Hosp., London, 1978-85; cons. med. oncologist Chelsea & Westminster Hosp., Charing Cross Hosp., London, Imperial Coll. of Sci., Tech. and Medicine, London, 1985—; tchr. U. London, 1979—; chmn. adv. com. on cancer svcs. Riverside Health Authority, 1990; vis. prof. U. Ioannina (Greece) Med. Sch., 1991-92; lectr. cancer med. instns. in Europe, N.Am. S.Am. and China; chmn. 1st Internat. Conf. on Adjuvant Treatment of Malignant Melanoma, London, 1995, 2d, 1997, 3d, 1999. Editor: Palaeooncology-The Antiquity of Cancer, 1986, Hunterian Soc.; mem. editl. bd. Melanoma Rsch., Seminars in Oncology; contbr. articles to profl. jours. Founder, pres. Hellenic Med. Soc. Gt. Britain, 1987. 2d lt. M.C. Greek Army, 1967-69. Fellow RCP (London), Royal Soc. Medicine, Hunterian Soc. (mem. coun.); mem. Royal Coll. Physicians (U.K.), British Assn. Cancer Physicians, British Assn. Cancer Rsch., European Soc. Med. Oncology, Am. Soc. Clin. Oncology. Avocations: skiing, horseback riding, travel, history of medicine. Home: Parnassus Park Hill, Essex Loughton 1G10 4ES, England Office: Med Oncology Unit, Charing Cross Hosp, London W6 8RF, England

RETTEDAL, ARNE, engineering educator; b. Oslo, Norway, Apr. 11, 1949; s. Sverre and Liv (Bjerklie) R.; m. Tove Karin Haugland, July 7, 1973; children: Silje, Bjarte, Mari. BSc, U. Oslo, 1972, MSc, 1975. Rsch. asst. Ctrl. Inst. Indsl. Rsch., Oslo, 1975-77; sci. tchr. Stavanger (Norway) Engring. Coll., 1978-92, assoc. prof., 1992—; NK-62 Norwegian electrotech. com. Internat. Electrotech. Commn. and CENELEC, Oslo, 1985—; tech. assessor Norwegian Metrology and Accreditation Svc., Oslo, 1993—; bd. dirs. Found. for Rheumatism, Stavanger, Norwegian Conf. Med. Safety. Contbr. articles to profl. jours. Com. mem. Norwegian Luth. Ch., Stavanger, 1978—. Mem. Norwegian Soc. for Biomed. Engring. (chmn. 1995-2000), European Soc. for Computing and Tech. in Anesthesia and Intensive Care, Soc. in Europe for Simulation in Applied Medicine, Internat. Soc. Biotelemetry. Avocations: amateur radio, magic, outdoor life, sea kayaking. Home: KS Jonasensgt 7, 4019 Stavanger Norway Office: Stavanger Coll, Ullandhaug, 4004 Stavanger Norway

RETTERSTOL, KJETIL, physician; b. Oslo, Norway, Sept. 20, 1962; s. Nils and Kirsten (Christensen) R.; m. Annechen Bahr Bugge; children: Nils Herman, Eilif. MD, U. Copenhagen, 1990; PhD, U. Oslo, 2000. Jr. surgeon, then jr. physician Buskerud Ctrl. Hosp., Drammen, Norway, 1990-93; gen. practitioner Oslo, 1993; med. researcher lipid clinic Nat. Hosp., Norway, 1993-94; med. researcher Inst. Clin. Biochemistry U. Oslo, 1993—; physician dept. nuclear medicine Nat. Hosp. of Norway, 2000—. Lt. Norwegian Army, 1990. Avocations: soccer, aeroplanes. Office: U Oslo Rikshosp, Inst Clin Biochem, N-0027 Oslo Norway

RETTICH, THOMAS, electrical engineer; b. Essen, Germany, Apr. 4, 1962; s. Hans and Hildegard Rettich; m. Anke Rettich; 1 child, Juliane. Diploma in Elec. Engring., RWTH Aachen, Germany, 1988, PhD in Elec. Engring., 1992. Rsch. engr. Fraunhofer Inst. for Lasertechnik, Aachen, 1988-93; mgr. R&D Huettinger Electronic GmbH, Freiburg, Germany, 1994-95, tech. dir., 1996—. Author: Elektrodenlose Pumplichtquellen für Festkörperlaser, 1993; patentee in field; contbr. articles to profl. jours. Avocations: sailing, snowboarding. E-mail: rettich@huettinger.com. Home: Zum Litzfürst 2, 79194 Gundelfingen Germany Office: Huettinger Elektronik GmbH, Elsasser Str 8, 79110 Freiburg Germany

RETTIG, TERRY, veterinarian, wildlife consultant; b. Houston, Jan. 30, 1947; s. William E. and Rose (Munves) R.; m. Helen Rettig, Mar. 12, 1996; 1 child, Bill; children from previous marriage: Michael Thomas, Jennifer Suzanne. BS in Zoology, Duke U., 1969, MAT in Sci., 1970; DVM, U. Ga., 1975. Resident veterinarian, mgr. animal health The Wildlife Preserve, Largo, Md., 1975-76; wildlife veterinarian dept. environ. conservation State of N.Y., Delmar, 1976-77; owner Atlanta Animal Hosp., 1976—, Atlanta Svcs., P.C. Quality Home Builders, 1976—; sec., dir. Atlanta Pet Supply, Inc., 1983-89; cons. Six Flags Over Ga., Yellow River Game Ranch, Stone Mountain Park Animal Forest, Atlanta Zoo. Author: (with Murray Fowler) Zoo and Wild Animal Medicine (Aardvark award 1978), 1978, 2d edit., 1986 (Order of Kukukifuku award 1986); contbr. articles to profl. jours. Del. Dekalb County Republican Conv., 1983; mem. Roswell United Meth. Ch., Boy Scouts Am., 1954—, mem. troop coun., asst. scoutmaster, scout master, Philmont expedition leader, 1988, 89. Spl. scholar Cambridge U. Coll. Vet. Medicine, 1973-74, Honor Medal with Crossed Palms, 1995. Mem. AVMA, Ga. Vet. Med. Assn., Greater Atlanta Vet. Med. Assn., Dekalb Vet. Soc., Acad. Vet. Medicine, Am. Assn. Zoo Veterinarians, Am. Assn. Zool. Parks and Aquaria, Nat. Wildlife Health Found., Nat. Wildlife Assn., Atlanta Zool. Soc., Am. Fedn. Aviculturists, Cousteau Soc., Am. Assn. Avian Veterinarians, Am. Animal Hosp. Assn., Internat. Wildlife Assn., Soc. Aquatic Veterinary Medicine, Am. Buffalo Assn. Methodist. Home and Office: Atlanta Animal Hosp 5035 Kimball Bridge Rd Alpharetta GA 30005-5649

RETTORI, CARLOS, physics educator; b. Parana, Entre Rios, Argentina, Aug. 8, 1941; s. Santiago and Julda (Mangold) R.; m. Susana Beatriz Pratico, Dec. 23, 1944; 1 child, Daniel. M Physics, U. Buenos Aires, 1967, PhD in Physics, 1971; postgrad., UCLA, 1971-72. Asst. prof. U. Buenos Aires, 1967-71, UCLA, 1972-74; asoc. prof. physics U. Campinas, Sao Paulo, Brazil, 1974-80, prof., 1980—. Contbr. articles to sci. jours., including Phys. Rev. Letters, Solid Sate Comm., Synthetic Metals, Physics Letters A. Rsch. grantee Found. Amparo a Pesquisa, 1974—, Conselho Nat. Pesquisa, 1974-97, NSF, 1997—. E-mail: rettori@ifi.unicamp.br. Office: U Campinas Inst Physics, Unicamp, University City, 13083970 Campinas (SP), Brazil

RETZER, MARY ELIZABETH HELM, retired librarian; b. Balt.; d. Francis Leslie C. and Edna (Smith) Helm; m. William Raymond Retzer, June 28, 1945; children: Lesley Elizabeth, April Christine. BA, Western Md. Coll., 1940; MA, Columbia U., 1946; postgrad., George Washington U., 1941, Ind. U., 1952, U. Ill., 1958-59, Ill. State U., 1964-66, Bradley U.; PhD, Western Colo. U., 1972. Mem. faculty Rockville (Md.) Bd. Edn., 1940-47, elem. supr., 1945-47; mem. staff Peoria Pub. Libr., 1957-63, homebound libr., 1961-63; cons., organizer libr. Bergan High Sch., 1964-67; condr. libr. sci. course in reference Bradley U., 1966-83; libr. Hines Elem. Sch., 1963-66, Roosevelt Jr. High Sch., 1966-69; head media ctr. Manual High Sch., Peoria, Ill., 1969-83. Instr. water safety courses ARC, 1938-93; pres. Entre Nous, 1949-51; pres. women's bd. Salvation Army, 1952-54; pres. Peoria Nursery Sch. Assn., 1953-54; mem. legis. action com. Ill. Congress PTA, 1955-56; mem. Crippled Children's Adv. Com., Peoria, 1957-60; active various community drives; mem. women's adv. bd. Peoria Jr. Star, 1970-73. Mem. AAUW (life), NEA, ALA (life), Ill. Edn. Assn., Peoria Edn. Assn., Ill. Libr. Assn., Ill. Valley Librs. Assn. (pres. 1971-72), Ill. Assn. Media in Edn. (cert. com. 1973-80), Ill. Audiovisual Assn., Internat. Platform Assn., Order Ea. Star, Ill. State U. Adminstrs. Club, Willowknolls Country Club, Sarasota Yacht Club, Ladies Oriental Shrine. Republican. Presbyterian. Home: 435 S Gulfstream Ave Apt 308 Sarasota FL 34236-6705

REUBEN, BRYAN GODEL, chemical technology educator, consultant; b. Bradford, Yorkshire, Eng., Jan. 12, 1934; s. Jacob Victor and Rachel (Cohen) R.; m. Catherine Ann Katzenstein; children: David Gabriel, Deborah Louise, Anthony Jacob. BA, Queen's Coll., Oxford, Eng., 1955, MSc, 1957, DPhil, 1958, MA, 1960. Postdoctoral fellow Brookhaven Nat. Lab., Upton, L.I., N.Y., 1958-60; phys. chemist Distillers Co. Ltd., Epsom, Surrey, Eng., 1960-61; sales devel. exec. Distillers Co. Ltd., London, 1961-63; lectr. in phys. and indsl. chemistry U. Surrey, Guildford, Eng., 1963-77; prin. lectr. in chem. engring. South Bank Poly., London, 1977-83, faculty reader in chem. tech., 1983-91; prof. chem. tech. South Bank U., London, 1991-97, prof. emeritus, 1997—; cons. ptnr. Remit Cons., London, 1990-97; cons. Economists Adv. Group, London, 1987-90; now cons. in field. Co-author: (with M.L. Burstall) The Chemical Economy, 1973, The Cost of "Non-Europe" in the Pharmaceutical Industry, 1988, (with H.A. Wittcoff) Pharmaceutical Chemicals in Perspective, 1989, Industrial Organic Chemicals, 1996. Fellow Royal Soc. Chemistry (treas. com. mktg. group 1977—); mem. Soc. Chem. Industry. Jewish. Avocations: magazine design and production, skiing, journalism. Home: 7 Clarence Ave, London SW4 8LA, England Office: South Bank U, 109 Borough Rd, London SE1 0AA, England

REUBEN, DON HAROLD, lawyer; b. Chgo., Sept. 13, 1928; s. Michael B. and Sally (Chapman) R.; m. Evelyn Long, Aug. 27, 1948 (div.); children: Hope Reuben Boland, Michael Barrett, Timothy Don, Jeffrey Long, Howard

Ellis; m. Jeannette Hurley Haywood, Dec. 13, 1971; stepchildren: Harris Hurley Haywood, Edward Gregory Haywood. BS, Northwestern U., 1949, JD, 1952. Bar: Ill. 1952, Calif. 1996. With firm Kirkland & Ellis, Chgo., 1952-78, sr. ptnr., until 1978; sr. ptnr. Reuben & Proctor, Chgo., 1978-86, Isham, Lincoln & Beale, Chgo., 1986-88; sr. counsel Winston & Strawn, 1988-94; of counsel Altheimer & Gray, Chgo., 1994—; spl. asst. atty. gen. State of Ill., 1963-64, 69, 84; gen. coun. Tribune Co., 1965-88, Chgo. Bears Football Club, 1965-88, Cath. Archdiocese of Chgo., 1975-88; coun. spl. session Ill. Ho. of Reps., 1964, for Ill. treas. for congl., state legis. and jud. reapportionment, 1963; spl. fed. ct. master, 1968-70; dir. Lake Shore Nat. Bank, 1973-93; dir. Heitman Fin., 1993-98; mem. citizens adv. bd. to sheriff County of Cook, 1962-66, mem. jury instrn. com., 1963-68; rules com. Ill. Supreme Ct., 1963-73; mem. pub. rels. com. Nat. Conf. State Trial Judges; mem. com. study caseflow mgmt. in law div. Cook County Cir. Ct., 1979-88; mem. adv. implementation com. U.S. Dist. Ct. for No. Dist. Ill., 1981-82; mem. Chgo. Better Schs. Com., 1968-69, Chgo. Crime Commn., 1970-80; mem. supervisory panel Fed. Defender Program; gen. counsel Palm Springs Air Mus., 1996—; dir. News-Gazette, Champaign, Ill., 1997-99; lectr. on libel, slander, privacy and freedom of press. Bd. dirs. Lincoln Park Zool. Soc., 1972-84 ; trustee Northwestern U., 1977—; mem. vis. com. U. Chgo. Law Sch., 1976-79; bd. dirs. Blood Bank of the Desert, 1999—; sec. Palm Springs Air Mus., 2000—. Mem. Ill. Bar Assn., Chgo. Bar Assn. (chmn. subcom. on propriety and regulation of contingent fees com. devel. law 1966-69, subcom. on media liaison 1980-82, mem. com. on profl. info. 1980-82), ABA (standing com. on fed. judiciary 1973-79, standing com. on jud. selection, tenure and compensation 1982-85), Am. Law Inst., Am. Judicature Soc., Fellows Am. Bar Found., Am. Coll. Trial Lawyers (Rule 23 com. 1975-82, judiciary com. 1987-91), Am. Arbitration Assn. (nat. panel arbitrators), Calif. Bar Assn., Desert Bar Assn., Internat. Acad. Trial Lawyers, Union League Club (Chgo.), Tavern Club, Mid-Am. Club, Lawyers Club Chgo., Casino Club, The Springs Club, Desert Riders of Palm Springs, The Chgo. Club, Phi Eta Sigma, Beta Alpha Psi, Beta Gamma Sigma, Order of Coif. Home: 20 Jill Ter Rancho Mirage CA 92270-2635

REULAND, PETER, nuclear medicine physician, researcher; b. Gürzenich, Nordrhein-Westfalen, Germany, Oct. 3, 1953; s. Heinz Jakob and Hanni (Müller) R.; m. Marietta Antonia Anspach, Sept. 29, 1977; children: Anna-Kristina, Milena, Irina. MD, Tech. H.S., Aachen, Ger., 1984; PhD, Eberhard-Karls U., Tübingen, Ger., 1991. Physicist Inst. Theor. Physics Tech. H.S., Aachen, Ger., 1977-79, physiologist Inst. Cardiac Physiology, 1979-84; fellow dept. nuclear medicine Eberhard-Karls U., Tübingen, Ger., 1985-89, resident dept. nuclear medicine, 1989-91; tech. dir. Inst. Nuclear Medicine, Freiburg, Ger., 1992—; dir. Euro-PET Ctr., Freiburg, 1995—; assoc. prof. U. Tübingen, 1992—, Eberhard-Karls U., 1991; head PET Group. Author: Skeletal Scintigraphy, 1989; contbr. articles to profl. jours. Mem. So. W. Ger. Soc. Nuclear Medicine (v.p. 1993—), Soc. Nuclear Medicine, Soc. European Nuclear Medicine, Assn. German Nuclear Physicians (head 1995—). Avocations: fine arts, classical music, swimming, ethnology. Office: Schwabentorplatz 6, 79098 Freiburg Baden-Württemberg, Germany

REUS, WERNER ALOIS, physician; b. Darmstadt, Germany, Oct. 14, 1951; s. Luitpold A. and Gertrud K. (Jarisch) R.; m. Maria E. Nagler, Oct. 31, 1980. MD, Heidelberg U., Germany, 1978. Asst. physician U. Heidelberg, 1978-79, Frauenklinik Stuttgart, Germany, 1979-81, U. Tübingen, Germany, 1981-87; cons. Frauenklinik Ingolstadt, Germany, 1987-88, U. Zürich, Switzerland, 1988-89, Free Univ., Berlin, 1990-93, Panorama Health Ctr., Scheidegg im Allgäu, Germany, 1996-98; pvt. practice ob-gyn., psychotherapy, and couple therapy Tübingen, 1999—. Mem. Internat. Soc. Ultrasound in Ob-Gyn. (founding mem.), N.Y. Acad. Scis., World Coun. Psychotherapy, Sigmud Freud Soc., Milton Erickson Soc., German Assn. Ultrasound in Medicine, Brit. Med. Ultrasound Soc., German Assn. Perinatal Medicine. Roman Catholic. Avocations: ancient medicine, history, archeology.

REUSCH, ROSETTA NATOLI, biochemistry educator, researcher; b. N.Y.C., Mar. 23, 1937; d. Joseph Natoli and Eugenia Zennaro; m. William Henry Reusch; children: Kathryn Linda, Christophr Robert, David William. AB, CCNY, 1951; MS, Columbia U., 1952, PhD, 1955. Rsch. chemist Am. Cyanamid Co., Stamford, Conn., 1955-57; instr. Albion (Mich.) Coll., 1958-59; rsch. assoc. Mich. State U., East Lansing, 1972-83, rsch. asst. prof., 1983-89, rsch. assoc. prof., 1989-94, assoc. prof., 1994-98, prof., 1998—; cons. Metabolix Corp., Cambridge, Mass., 1995—. Author: (with P. Carnell) Molecular Equilibrium, 1963; contbg. author: Spores VI, 1975, Microbiology, 1981, Progress in Molecular and Subcellular Biology: Inorganic Polyphosphates, 1999, Advances in Supramolecular Chemistry, 2000; contbr. articles to sci. jours., including Jour. Organic Chemistry, Jour. Bacteriology, Nature, Chem. Phys. Lipids, Can. Jour. Microbiology, Procs. NAS USA, Soc. Exptl. Biol. Medicine, Biochim. Biophys. Acta, FEMS Microbiol. Revs., European Jour. Biochemistry, Jour. Biol. Chemistry, Biophys. Jour., Mirobiology, Jour. Membrane Biology, Macromolecules, Biochemistry. Mem. Am. Chem. Soc., Am. Soc. for Biochemistry and Molecular Biology, Biophys. Soc. Achievements include patents for banched polyhydroxyalkanoate polymer salt compositions and method of preparation, for polyhydroxybutyrate and polyphosphate: membranes with channels, analytical method for detection of artherosclerotic risk, antibodies for olyhydroxybutyrate. E-mail: rnreusch@msu.edu.

REUTER, GERHARD, veterinary medicine educator; b. Suhl, Thuringia, Germany. DVM, Free U. Berlin, 1957, PhD, 1958; PhD honoris causa, Ludwig Maximilians U., Munich, Germany, 1997. Mem. staff Free U. Berlin, 1958-59, asst. prof., 1960-69, assoc. prof., 1969-72, prof. vet. medicine, 1972-97, prof. emeritus, 1997—; dir. Inst. Food Hygiene/Meat Hygiene, 1972-97; dean Vet. Faculty, West Berlin, 1987-89. Contbr. 250 articles to profl. jours.; author monographs in field. Mem. Am. Soc. Microbiology, Soc. Intestinal Microbial Ecology and Disease, Internat. Union Microbiol. Socs. (mem. taxonomic subcom. lactobacilli and bifidobacteria 1962—), German Vet. Med. Soc. (hon.). Office: Free U, Bruemmer Str 10, 14195 Berlin Germany

REUTERSWÄRD, PATRIK ANDERS ADOLF, curator, educator; b. London, Nov. 10, 1922; Swedish citizen; s. Patrik and Karin (Herdin) R.; m. Michaela Topelius, Oct. 15, 1948; 1 child, Nadine. Licentiat, U. Stockholm, 1954, PhD, 1960. Curator Nat. Mus., Stockholm, 1958-62, 69-72; asst. prof. U. Göteborg, Sweden, 1962-69; prof. Stockholm U., 1973-88; vis. assoc. prof. Columbia U., N.Y.C., 1968, U. Va., Charlottesville, 1979. Author: Studien zur Polychromie der Plastik, 1960, The Two Churches of the Hôtel des Invalides, 1965, Hieronymus Bosch, 1970, The Forgotten Symbols of God, 1986, The Visible and Invisible in Art, 1991; editor Konsthistorisk Tidskrift, 1981-90. Avocations: piano, translation of poetry. Home: Lilla Bergshamra, S 170 73 Solna Sweden

REUTHER, DAVID LOUIS, children's book publisher, writer; b. Detroit, Nov. 2, 1946; s. Roy Louis and Fania (Sonkin) R.; m. Margaret Alexander Miller, July 21, 1973; children: Katherine Anna, Jacob Alexander. BA with honors, U. Mich., 1968. Tchr. Lewis-Wadhams Sch., Westport, N.Y., 1969-71; asst. dir. Children's Book Council, N.Y.C., 1971-73; editor children's books Macmillan Publishing Co., N.Y.C., 1973-76; sr. editor Four Winds Press-Scholastic Inc., N.Y.C., 1976-82; sr. v.p., pub. Morrow Jr. Books, N.Y.C., 1982-98; co-founder Baseball Ink, Inc., 1986-90; pub. Lothrop Lee & Shepard, N.Y.C., 1996-98, Beech Tree Books, N.Y.C., 1997-98; pres., pub. North-South Books, N.Y.C., 1999—; mem. Nat. Sci. Tchrs. Assn.-Children's Book Coun. Joint Com., 1982-85; mem. Am. Bookseller Assn., 1990-93, Children's Book Coun.joint.com. Author: with Roy Doty) Fun To Go, A Take-Along Activity Book, 1982, Save-the-Animals Activity Book, 1982, (with John Thorn and Pete Palmer) The Hidden Game of Baseball, 1984, Total Baseball, 1989, The Whole Baseball Catalog, 1990, Total Baseball II, 1991; editor: (with John Thorn) The Armchair Quarterback, 1982, The Armchair Aviator, 1983, The Armchair Mountaineer, 1984, The Armchair Book of Baseball, 1985, The Armchair Angler, 1986, The Armchair Book of Basesball II, 1987, The Armchair Traveler, 1988. Mem. ALA, Authors Guild, Soc. Children's Book Writers. Home: 271 Central Park W New York NY 10024-3020

REUTHINGER, GEORGEANNE, special education educator; b. Laredo, Tex., Mar. 10, 1952; d. George and Maria Josefina (Elizondo) Ramon; m. David Lawrence Reuthinger, Apr. 5, 1952; 1 child, David L. Jr. AA in Music and Drama, Laredo Jr. Coll., 1972; BS in Speech and Drama Edn., Tex. A&I U., 1974, MS in Edn., 1978; postgrad., Tes. A&M Internat. U. Lic. speech therapist, Tex.; cert. speech therapist, ednl. diagnostician, profl. supervision. Speech and drama tchr. Laredo ISD Martin High Sch., 1974; supr., diagnostician spl. edn. program Laredo ISD Martin H.S., 1992-96, Cigarra H.S., Nixon H.S., 1998—; speech therapist Laredo ISD, 1974-78, ednl. diagnostician, 1978-92; sales assoc. Country Wide Real Estate, Laredo, 1997—; cons. in spl. edn. United Ind. and Laredo Ind. Sch. Dists., 1997-98. Founding mem., lead actress in bilingual theatrical touring co. Tex. A&I U., 1974. Active in fundraising for charities Women's City Club, Boy Scouts Am.; judge UIL Acad. & Fine Arts events, Spl. Olympics. Scholar Art League, 1970, Tex. A&I Alumni, 1972-74; recipient awards U.S. Army, 1973, USO Shows, 1973-74. Mem. Tex. Speech and Hearing Assn. (legis. network 1992-97), Coun. for Exceptional Children (lobbyist 1995, sec. Laredo chpt. 1975), Valley Coun. Adminstrs. and Suprs. in Spl. Edn., ASCD, Tex. Coun. Adminstrs. and Suprs. in Spl. Edn., Delta Kappa Gamma (sec. Alpha Nu chpt. 1977-78). Avocations: directing and acting in theatrical productions, singing in community choirs, Special Olympics volunteering and judging. Home: 206 Granada Dr Laredo TX 78041-2615 Office: Country Wide Real Estate 1303 Calle Del Norte Ste 6 Laredo TX 78041-6041 also: Laredo Ind Sch Dist 1702 Houston St Laredo TX 78040-4906

REUTSCHLER, CARL THOMAS, real estate executive, consultant; s. Franklin K. Reutschler and Della Diana Bucks; m. Madelynne Layden, Aug. 8, 1946; children: Patricia, Laron, Deborah. BS in Indsl. Edn., Pa. State U., 1942. Mem. Alaska Territorial Legis., Juneau, 1952; active in organization of First Fed. Savings and Loan, Anchorage, 1955, Anchorage Real Estate Multiple Listing Svc., 1955, Alaska Mutual Savings Bank, Anchorage, 1960. Capt. Army Air Corps, 1944-47. Republican. Baptist. Avocations: golfing, traveling, hunting, fishing. E-mail: madcarl2@alaska.net. Home: 2901 Mccollie Ave Anchorage AK 99517-1223 Office: Reutschler Ins Agy 440 Eagle St Anchorage AK 99501-2631

RÉVAI, TAMÁS, nephrologist; b. Budapest, Hungary, Oct. 13, 1962; s. István and Istvánné (König Éva) R.; m. Andrea Földes, July 13, 1986; 1 child, Peter. MD, Med. U., Budapest, 1988; med. diploma in internal diseases, 1994. Physician Hosp. Ujpest, Budapest, 1988-93; dialysis physician Hosp. SZT László, Budapest, 1993; head outpatient dept. nephrology Hosp. SZT János, Budapest, 1996—; cons. nephrologist Hosp. SZT Imre, Budapest, 1996—; cons. nephrologist, dir. nephrol. dept. Hosp. of Police Force, Budapest, 1997—; lectr. in field. Mem. European Dialysis and Transplant Assn.-European Renal Assn., Hungarian Soc. for Hypertension. Avocations: golf, swimming, excursions, collecting books and stamps. Home: Jókai u 26, 1066 Budapest Hungary Office: SZT János Hosp, Diósárok u 1, 1125 Budapest Hungary

REVANKAR, CHANDRAKANT RAMCHANDRA, health facility administrator, consultant; b. Hanehalli, Karnatak, India, July 31, 1950; s. Ramchandra Shantyya and Sulochana (Ramchandra) R.; m. Anamika Chandrakant, Nov. 4, 1980; children: Manasi, Nikhil. MBBS, Karnatak (India) Med. Coll., Hubli, 1974; diploma in pub. health, T.N. Med. Coll., Bombay, 1978; MD in Preventive and Social Medicine, Topiwala Nat. Med. Coll., 1981. Asst. rsch. officer Indian Coun. Med. Rsch., India, 1974-75; asst. med. officer AL Hosp., Bombay, 1975-78; med. officer Bombay Leprosy Project, 1978-83, asst. dir., 1983-86, dep. dir., 1989—; program officer Danida, New Delhi, 1986-89; short term cons. WHO, Afghanistan, 1991, Malaysia, 1993, F.S. Micronesia, 1995, 96, Indonesia, 1996, 97. Contbr. more than 100 articles to profl. jours., chpts. to books. Mem. Indian Assn. Leprologists (hon. treas. ctrl. br. 1981-83, hon. sec. Maharashtra br. 1996-99, hon. v.p. 1999-2000), Rsch., Rehab. and Edn. in Leprosy Soc. (mem. com. 1989—). Avocation: photography. Home: 3-15-14 Bhavani Nagar Marol, Andheri-East, 400059 Bombay Maharashtra, India Office: Bombay Leprosy Project II, VN Purav Marg Chunabhatti, 400022 Mumbai Maharashtra, India

REVEAL, ARLENE HADFIELD, retired librarian, consultant; b. Riverside, Utah, May 21, 1916; d. Job Oliver and Mabel Olive (Smith) Hadfield; children: James L., Jon A. BS with honors, Utah State U.; grad. in Librarianship, San Diego State U., 1968; M in Libr. and Info. Sci., Brigham Young U., 1976. Social case worker Boxelder County Welfare, Brigham City, Utah, 1938-40; office mgr. Dodge Ridge Ski Corp., Long Barn, Calif., 1948-65, Strawberry (Calif.) Inn, 1950-65, Pinecrest Permittees Assn., 1955-65; adminstrv. asst. Mono County Office of Edn., Bridgeport, Calif., 1961-67; catalog libr. La Mesa (Calif.)-Spring VAlley Sch. Dist., 1968-71; libr. Mono County Libr., Bridgeport, 1971-96; cmty. grandmother, 1996—; chair Mountain Valley Libr. Sys., 1987-89. Author: Mono Country Courthouse, 1980. Mem. Devel. Disabilities Area Bd. 12, 1974-96, chair, 1990-92. Recipient John Cotton Dana award H.W. Wilson Co., 1974; named Bridgeport Citizen of Yr., 1993, Wild Iris Woman of Yr., Mono County, 1996. Mem. Rebekah (treas. 1973-90), Delta Kappa Gamma (pres. chpt. 1984-88), Beta Sigma Phi (treas. chpt. 1981, 83-85, 91-96, pres. 1982, 85, 89), Beta Phi Mu. Home: PO Box 156 15425 N 5250 W Riverside UT 84334

REVEILHAC DE MAULMONT, ANNE-LAURE, lawyer; b. Neuilly sur Seine, France, Feb. 17, 1955; d. Paul-Emmanuel Reveilhac and Monique Argod de Maulmont. Bachelors degree, Ho. Edn. of Legion of Hon., 1973; M in Pvt. Law, U. Nanterre, 1977. Bar: Paris 1979. Corr., sr. assoc. dept. litigation Baker & McKenzie, Paris, 1980-95; nat. com. coord. Sponsorship-cultural heritage, 1985; gen. sec. Study Com. for Devel. Exchs. with Croatia. Mem. DACEM (pres. 1991), Am. C. of C. in France, Archeol. Hist. Soc. Limousin, Vaudreuil Golf Club. Office: 44 Ave d'Iena, 75116 Paris France

REVENGA, JORGE EDUARDO, aquaculture researcher; b. Córdoba, Argentina, Dec. 6, 1956; s. Eduardo and Vilma Antonia (Di-Rienzo) R.; m. Beatriz Teresa Davila, Dec. 22, 1983; children: Agustina, Sofía. Bachiller, Manuel Belgrano U. Cordoba, Argentina, 1975; Aquaculture Technologist, U. Comahue, Bariloche, Argentina, 1987. Rschr. U. Comahue, Bariloche, Argentina, 1986—, aquaculture tchr., 1988-89, 1992—. Contbr. articles to profl. jours. Recipient Rsch. award U. Comahue, Bariloche, 1987-92,. Mem. N.Y. Acad. Scis. Avocations: garden, philosophic books, music. Office: Quintral 1250, 8400 Bariloche Argentina

REVERTE, MARIA, pharmacologist; b. Caracas, Venezuela, May 24, 1953; arrived in Spain, 1972; d. Isidoro Reverte and Maria Bernal; m. Juan Antonio Garcia Iglesias; children: Juan Antonio, Rosa Maria, Carmen. MD, U. Salamanca, Spain; PhD in Medicine, U. Salamanca, 1989. Cooperator in edn. U. Complutense, Madrid, 1980-81; mem. med. dept. Glaxo Lab., Madrid, 1982-83; clin. trials monitor Hoechst Iberia, Barcelona, Spain, 1983-84; lectr. pharmacology U. Salamanco, 1985-92, assoc. prof. pharmacology, 1992—; colaborator Inst. Reins Sofia Investigation Nefrologia, Salamanca, 1994—. Contbr. articles to books and profl. jours. Recipient Travel award Am. Soc. for Biochemistry and Molecular Biology, 2000. Mem. Assn. Española de Méchias de la Industria Farmnientio, French Soc. Pharmacology and Spanish Soc. Pharmacology, N.Y. Acad. Sci. Roman Catholic. Office: U Salamanca Sch Medicine, Av Campo Charro s/n, 37007 Salamanca Spain

REVESZ, PAL, retired mathematics educator; b. Budapest, Hungary, June 6, 1934; s. Mark and Olga (Deutschlander) R.; m. Klara Földesi, May 25, 1963; children: Agnes, Zsuzsanna. PhD, U. Budapest, 1958. Asst. prof. of math. U. Budapest, 1956-63; research fellow Math. Inst., Budapest, 1963-85; prof. Technische U., Wien, Austria, 1985-97, Tech. U. Budapest; ret., 1998. Author: Strong Approximation in Probability and Statistics, 1981, Random Walk in Random and Non-Random Environments, 1990, Randon Walks of Infinitely Many Particles, 1994. Fellow Inst. Math. Statistics; mem. Bernoulli Soc. (pres. 1981-83), Hungarian Acad. Sci., Academia Europaea. Home: Herbert Rauchgasse 1-i, 2361 Laxenburg Austria

REVILLON, ANDRÉ, chemistry researcher, educator; b. Lyon, France, Sept. 9, 1935; s. Louis and Jeanne (Corlier) R.; m. Anne Court, 1967; children: Hélène, Agnès, Vincent. Bachelor, Lycée du Parc, Lyon, 1954, lic. in phys. sci., 1960; degree in chem. engring., ESCIL, Lyon, 1960, DSc, 1967. Rschr. attaché Nat. Ctr. Sci. Rsch., Lyon, 1963-67, rschr. chargé, 1968-76, rschr. maître, 1977-85, dir. rsch., 1986—; prof. U. Lyon, 1968-83, 87-89. Contbr. over 180 articles to profl. jours. and books; editor 12 conf. procs.; editor 14 books on edn.; patentee in field. Pres. Assoc. String Quartet, 1989—, Hist. Villeurbanne, 1986—; vice pres., Saint Exupery, Lyon, 1982—; adminstr. H. Berlioz, 1992—. Sgt. French Army, 1960-62. Mem. Groupe français des polymères (vice pres. 1980-83), Assn. for Tech. pentures Vernis adhesifs (adminstr. 1992—), UATCM (adminstr. 1997—). Roman Catholic. Avocations: music, reading, arts. Home: 200 Ave Felix Faure, 69003 Lyon RhoneAlp, France Office: CNRS, PO Box 24, 69390 Vernaison RhneAlps, France

REVIN, BENGT, financial executive; b. Helsingborg, Skane, Sweden, Apr. 13, 1940; s. Axel and Evy (Jonsson) R.; m. Ingrid Gullberg, 1964 (div. 1982); children: Anders, Par; m. Lotta Thuvesson, 1982. High bus. economist, U. Lund, Sweden, 1966. Acct. Lindells Revisions Byra AB, Helsingborg, 1967-73; v.p. fin. and adminstrn. Bokförlaget Braböcker, Höganäs, Sweden, 1973-79; pres. Bokförlaget Braböcker, Höganäs, 1979-93; cons. in adminstrn. & publishing, 1993—; pres. Blechert & Johansson Direct Mktg., Stockholm, 1994-97; bd. dirs. N.S. Frakt ek.for.and Begab AB, Helsingborg, Sweden, 1997—. Home: Slettvagen 10, Skane, S-260 41 Viken Sweden

REVIN, VALERY PETROVICH, government official; b. Alma-ata, Republic of Kasachstan, Apr. 20, 1943; d. Peter Ivanovich and Valentina Afanasyevna (Kalitina) R.; m. Ludmila Alexandrovna Zhdanova; 2 children. 1st degree, Law Coll., Omsk, 1972; higher degree, Acad. Police Mgmt., Moscow, 1978; Candidate, Coun. Mins. USSA, Moscow, 1982; D, Highes Examining Com. RF, Moscow, 1994. Rschr. Acad. Min. of Interior of USSR, Moscow, 1978-80, dep. head dept., 1981-94; head dept. Acad. Min. of Interior of Russia, Moscow, 1994—; asst. prof. Acad. Min. of Interior of USSR, Moscow, 1985-87; prof. Acad. Min. Interior Russia, Moscow, 1994—; hon. prof. European U., 1997-99. Author: Chernobyl Victims: Children Suffered from the Chernobyl Catastrophe, 1992, Criminal-Code eans of Drug Addiction Control, 1994, Financial Crime, 1997, Criminal Law in Russia, 1997, Conceptual Problems iof Struggle with Terrorism, 2000. Expert Fed. Duma, Moscow; cons. Security Coun., Moscow, Gen. Dept. Law. Col. Moscow mil., 1986—. Recipient medal for revival of sci. Internat. Acad. Nature and Soc., Moscow, 1995, medal of sci. discovery Acad. Natural Sci., Moscow, 1996. Mem. Internat. Acad. Info. Sci. Avocations: music, sports. Home: 5 Novopodmoscovny pereulok, 125130 Moscow Russia Office: Acad Police Mgmt of Min, Kosmodemyansky 8, 125171 Moscow Russia

REVINA, SVETLANA VASILIEVNA, mathematician, educator; b. Sizran, Russia, Aug. 26, 1964; d. Vasilii and Zoia (Kholodkova) Nikonov; m. Mikhail Revin, Aug. 28, 1993. Grad., Rostov State U., 1986, MSc, 1993. Asst. prof. Rostov State U., Russia, 1988—. Avocation: swimming. Office: Mech-Math Dept Rostov U, Zorge 5, Rostov-na-Donu Russia 344090

REVOL, JEAN-PIERRE CHARLES, physicist; b. Neuville-les-Dames, Ain, France, Aug. 15, 1948; came to U.S., 1974; s. Joseph and Andrée (Ruet) R.; m. Sophia Reith, June 8, 1991; children: Rebecca, Emilie. Degree in engring., ENSAM, Paris, 1972; lic. de math., Paris VI U., 1973; PhD, MIT, 1981. Fellow CERN, Geneva, Switzerland, 1982-84, mem. sr. staff, 1989—; asst. prof. MIT, Cambridge, Mass., 1984-89, assoc. prof., 1989-92; advisor to dir. gen. CERN, Switzerland, 1991-93; sr. rsch. physicist CERN, Switzerland, 1994—. Sgt. French Army, 1975-76. Mem. Am. Phys. Soc., European Phys. Soc., Sigma Xi. Office: CERN, EP Divsn, 1211 Geneva 23, Switzerland

REVUELTA, MARIA DOLORES, library director, methodology educator; b. Logroño, Rioja, Spain, Feb. 11, 1956; d. Laureano Revuelta and Ana Maria Saez; m. Fernando Gómez-Bezares, July 6, 1979; children: Fernando, Ana-Maria. MA in History, U. Deusto, Bilbao, Spain, 1978, PhD in History, 1986. Prof. linguistics Valvanera Sch., Logroño, 1979; libr. dir. U. Deusto, 1982—, prof. methodology, 1988—. Author: Partidos Politicos en Rioja, 1988, La Universidad Comercial de Deusto, 1992, La Asociacion de Licenciados de la Universidad Comercial de Deusto, 1998; contbr. articles to profl. jours. Mem. Colegio Letras Bilbao, Hipica Club (Logroño), Cantabria Club (Logroño). Roman Catholic. Office: U Comercial de Deusto, Hnos Aguirre 2 Ap 20044, 48080 Bilbao Spain

REW, WILLIAM EDMUND, civil engineer; b. Corning, N.Y., Nov. 24, 1923; s. Robert James and Clara (Neal) R.; m. Jean Ella Ohls, Aug. 16, 1947 (dec.); children: Virginia Ann, Robert James, John Edward. BE, Yale U., 1954, M in Engring., 1955. Registered profl. engr., N.Y., Fla., Calif., Ill. Project engr. Texaco & Affiliate, USA and Saudi Arabia, 1955-62; sr. engr. Martin-Marietta Corp., Cape Kennedy, Fla., 1962-63, Chrysler Corp, Cape Kennedy, 1963-65, The Boeing Co., Cape Kennedy, 1965-70; project mgr. Brevard Engring. Co., Cape Canaveral, Fla., 1970-74; city engr. City of Vero Beach (Fla.), 1974-77; resident engr. Post, Buckley, Schuh & Jernigan, Miami, Fla., 1977-85; mgr. Keith & Schnars, P.A., West Palm Beach, Fla., 1985-90; pvt. practice consulting Lake Placid, Fla., 1990—. Active Dem. Party of Brevard County. 1st lt. U.S. Army, 1942-46, ATO. Scholar of 2d rank Yale U., 1953, grad. scholar, 1955. Fellow ASCE (chmn. Fla. ann conv. 1971, Engr. of Yr. 1974); mem. NSPE, Soc. Am. Mil. Engrs. (bd. dirs. 1982-83), Fla. Engring Soc. (chpt. pres. 1976), Yale Club, Browning Assn. Club. Episcopalian. Avocations: woodworking, reading. Home: 1425 S Washington Blvd NW Lake Placid FL 33852-4031

REWERSKI, WOJCIECH, pharmacologist; b. Warszawa, Poland, Mar. 17, 1936; s. Czeslaw and Zeonna (Karczewska) R.; m. Grazyna Kalinska, 1974 (div. 1986); children; Agata, Bartosz. MD, Medical Univ. Warsaw, 1960, D in philosophy, 1965. Fellowship Pharmacological Inst. Mario Negrl, Milano, Italy, 1965-67; fellowship dept. of clinical pharmacology UCHMS, London, 1974-75; tutorial dept. experimental & clinical pharmacology Warsaw, 1961—. Author: The Thermoregulation, 1972 (Warsaw Univ. award 1972), The Pharmocotherayp of Pain, The Natural Medicine, 1994 (Warsaw Univ. award 1994), The Doping, 1995 (Min. of Health award 1995). Recipient Award of Min. of Health for Ednl. Activities, 1995, Award of Medical Univ. of Poznan, 1996. Mem. Polish Pharmacological Soc., Polish Clinical and Pharmacological Soc., German Clinical Pharmacological Soc. Roman Catholic. Avocations: theater, tourism, boxing. Home: Niska 8 m 13, 00 176 Warsaw Poland Office: Dept Pharmacology, Krakowskie Predmiescie 2628, 00927 Warsaw Poland

REX, CHRISTOPHER DAVIS, classical musician; b. Orlando, Fla., Feb. 1, 1951; s. Charles Gordon Rex and Betty Helen (MacCauslin) Soubricas; m. Martha Anne Wilkins, Nov. 30, 1985; children: Caroline Bethea, Christopher Austell. MusB, Curtis Inst. of Music, Phila., 1972; postgrad., The Juilliard Sch., 1972-73, Atlanta Coll. Art, 1997—. Cellist Lyric Opera and Grand Opera, Phila., 1970-75, Phila. Orchestra, 1972-79, Georgian Chamber Players, Atlanta, 1984—; cello tchr. Gettsburg (Pa.) Coll., 1972-73, New Sch. of Music, Phila., 1969-74, Ga. State U., 1980-83; cellist, tchr. Eastern Music Festival, Greensboro, N.C., 1969-74; prin. cello Atlanta Symphony Orchestra, 1979—; concert soloist Hillyer Internat. Inc., N.Y.C., 1984—; bd. dirs. Ga. Cello Soc., Inc., Atlanta, Georgian Chamber Players, Atlanta; acting prin. during Europe Tour Cello of N.Y. Philharm., 1988; premiered Double Concerto for Violin, Cello, and Orch. N.Y. Philharm., 1994. Recordings include The Muse and the Poet (with Boheslaw Martina Philharm. Orch.), 1998; editor: (mus. transcription) Pictures at an Exhibition (Moussorgsky), 1987. Recipient First prize Young Artist Competition Am. Fedn. of Music Clubs, 1979. Mem. Phila. Musical Soc., Atlanta Fedn. of Music. Presbyterian. Avocations: art, watercolor painting. Home: 3602 Hadden Hall Rd NW Atlanta GA 30327-2628 Office: Atlanta Symphony Orch Woodruff Arts Ctr Atlanta GA 30309

REX, JOHN ARDERNE, educator; b. Port Elizabeth, South Africa, Mar. 3, 1925; s. Frederick Edward George and Winifred Natalie Rex; m. Pamela Margaret Rutherford, July 7, 1949 (div. Aug. 1964); children: Catherine Ann, Helen Joan; m. Margaret Ellen Biggs, June 6, 1965; children: Frederick John, David Malcolm. BA, Rhodes U., South Africa, 1948, BA with honors, 1949; PhD, Leeds (Eng.) U., 1956; DSc (hon.), Plymouth U., Eng., 1993. Lectr. Leeds U., 1949-62, Birmingham (Eng.) U., 1962-64; prof. Durham (Eng.) U., 1964-70; prof. Warwick U., Coventry, Eng., 1970-79, prof. emeritus, 1990—; dir. Rsch. Unit on Ethnic Rels., Eng., 1979-84; rsch. prof. Ctr. for Rsch. in Ethnic Rels., Eng., 1984-90; mem. experts com. on racism and race UNESCO, 1967; pres. rsch. com. on racial rels. Internat. Sociol. Assn., 1964-72. Author: Key Problems of Sociological Theory, 1961,

Race Relations on Sociological Theory, 1983, Race and Ethnicity, 1986, Gunic Minorities in the Modern Nation State, 1996; co-author: Race Community and Conflict, 1967. Parliamentary candidate Labour Party, 1959. With Royal, 1943-45. Avocations: football, music. E-mail: j.a.rex@warwick.ac.uk. Home: 33 ARlington Ave, Leamington Spa LU32 5OD, England Office: U Warwick, Ctr Rsch Ethnic Rels, Coventry CV4 7AL, England

REX, LONNIE ROYCE, religious organization administrator; b. Caddo, Okla., May 11, 1928; s. Robert Lavern and Lennie Cordy (Gilcrease) R.; m. Betty Louise Sorrells, Apr. 8, 1949; children: Royce DeWayne, Patricia Louise, Debra Kaye. MusB, Oklahoma City U., 1950; DD (hon.), Am. Bible Inst., 1970; LLD (hon.), Wesley Synod, N.Y.C., 1999, Meth. Wesley Synod, Toledo, 1999; LittD, Wesley Synod, 2000. Advt. mgr. Oral Roberts Evang. Assn., Tulsa, 1955-57; bus. mgr. T.L. Osborn Found., Tulsa, 1957-69; gen. mgr. Christian Crusade, Tulsa, 1969-80; sec.-treas. David Livingstone Missionary Found., Tulsa, 1970-80, pres., 1980—; dep. dir. gen. Internat. Biog. Assn.; bd. dirs. Intra-Ch. Pension Fund, Bethany, Okla.; spkr. internat. confs. Eng., Hungary, Korea, Singapore, Spain, N.Y.C., Congress of Arts and Comms., Oxford U., 1997; invited Pyongyang, North Korea to meet as an NGO with Peace Com. and med. aid, 1996, 97; participant peace conf. Carter Ctr. between North Korea and South Korea, 1997. Author: Never a Child, 1989. Mem. Internat. PHC Loan Fund; bd. dirs. Armand Hammer United World Coll. of Am. West, 1993—; bd. mem. Internat. Humanitarian Centre Russia, Moscow, 2000. Recipient Merit award Korea, 1975, Moran medal Republic of Korea, Humanitarian award Senator Hugh Scott, 1983, Svc. to Mankind award Internat. Biog. Congress, Spain, 1987, Internat. Lions Club award, UN award, medal Gen. Ground Forces USSR, 1990, World Humanitarian Leadership award by M. Susan Savage Mayor of Tulsa, 1998, Roseland Cook Bronze award David Livingstone Found., 1998; knighted in Moscow, 1993; Lonnie Royce Rex Day named in his honor by Gov. Keating of Okla., Jan. 24, 1998. Mem. Knights of Malta (Sword of Svc. 1996), Phi Beta Kappa. Home: 2437 E 73d Pl Tulsa OK 74136-5520 Office: St Matthews Pub Tulsa OK 74136-1010

REXED, BROR ANDERS, educator emeritus; b. Gunnarskog, Sweden, June 19, 1914; s. Daniel and Agda (Andersson) R.; m. Ursula Schalling, Nov. 10, 1941 (div. 1970); children: Magnus, Knut, Inga, Anders, Gerd; m. Anja-Riitta Ketokoski, July 8, 1977. Medicine Licentiate, Karolinska Inst., Stockholm, 1943, MD, 1945; MD (hon.), U. Helsinki, 1966, U. Oslo, 1969, U. Poznan, 1974. Assoc. prof. Karolinska Inst., Stockholm, 1945-53; prof. U. Uppsala, Sweden, 1953-67; dir. gen. Nat. Bd. Health and Welfare, Stockholm, 1967-78; exec. dir. UN Fund for Drug Abuse Control, Geneva and Vienna, 1978-82; mem. Internat. Narcotics Control Bd., Vienna, 1982-87; cons. WHO, Geneva, 1987-97; mem. com. on med. edn. Swedish Govt., Stockholm, 1946-63; sec., mem. Nat. Bd. Sci. Policy, Stockholm, 1962-67; chief Swedish del. WHO Assembly and UN Commn. on Narcotics, 1967-78. Author: Post Natal Development of Spinal Cord, 1944, Guidelines for Control of Narcotic and Psychotropic Substances, 1984, Cytoarchitectonic Organization of Spinal Cord, 1953; author articles. Instr., hon. chmn. Varmland Student Nation, Uppsala, 1956-68; chmn. Vol. Assn. Aging is Growing, Stockholm, 1988-93, Forum 50, 1993-95. Recipient prix Leon Bernard, WHO, 1979. Fgn fellow Royal Coll. Surgeons (London); mem. Engring. Acad. Scis. Avocation: collecting old maps. Home: Meritullink 20 A 10, 00170 Helsinki Finland

REXINE, JOHN EFSTRATIOS, JR., museum registrar, artist; b. Hamilton, N.Y., Oct. 3, 1960; s. John Efstratios and Elaine Lavrakas R. BA, Colgate U., 1983. Chief registrar Everson Mus. Art, Syracuse, N.Y., 1985-92; mus. registrar Rose Art Mus. Brandeis U., Waltham, Mass., 1993-2000; registrar List Visual Arts Ctr. MIT, Cambridge, Mass., 2000—. Core fellow Glassell Sch. Art Mus. Fine Arts, Houston, 1992-93. Mem. Am. Assn. Mus. (registrar's com. 1985—), Archaeological Inst. Mem. Greek Orthodox Ch. Avocations: contemporary art, Aegean bronze age archaeology. E-mail: rexine@mit.edu. Home: 118 Myrtle St Fl 2 Waltham MA 02453-0517 Office: MIT List Visual Arts Ctr Cambridge MA 02139

REX-TAYLOR, DAVID, publishing executive; b. Birmingham, England, Jan. 25, 1947; s. William Walter and Annie (Jones) Taylor. Student, Birkbeck Coll., London. Asst. mgr. Russia BEA, London, 1969-71; regional organizer Nat. Fund Rsch. into Crippling Diseases, London, 1971-72; founder Bibliagora Pubs. & Internat. Book Mail Order Co., England, 1973—. Exec. editor Internat. Bridge Press Assn., 1982—. Founder British Nat. Youth Suffrage Group. Fellow Inst. Sales Mktg. and Mgmt. Avocations: snooker, contract bridge. Fax: 44 20 8844 1777. Office: PO Box 77, Feltham TW14 8JF, England

REY, ALIX CHARLES, psychiatrist; b. Port-Au-Prince, Haiti, Nov. 4, 1940; came to U.S., 1965; s. Stenon and Luce (St. Gerard) Rey; m. Phyllis Ann Harris, Oct. 24, 1969; children: David Alix, Marc Christopher. Baccalaureate, St Louis De Gonzague, Port-Au-Prince, 1960; physician and surgeon, Facultad De Medicina, Mex. City, 1968. Resident in psychiatry Med. Coll. Ohio, 1973-75; clin. rsch. assoc. NIMH, Bethesda, Md., 1975-78; sr. rsch. assoc. Hispano Health Ctr. Md. Psychiat. Rsch. Ctr., 1976-78; asst. prof. psychiatry Psychiat. Rsch. Ctr., 1978-81; clin. dir. psychiat. svc. Howard County Gen. Hosp., 1979-85, chmn. dept. psychiatry, 1985-91, 99—, pres. med. staff, 1989—, vice chmn. dept. psychiatry, 1991—; med. dir. Howard Emergency Psychiat. Svc., 1991—. Lt. comdr. USPHS, 1975-81. Fellow Am. Psychiat. Assn.; mem. AMA, Med. and Chirurgical Facility Md., Md. Psychiat. Soc., Soc. Biol. Psychiatry, Black Psychiatrists Am. Roman Catholic. Avocations: swimming, fishing. Office: 10808 Hickory Ridge Rd Columbia MD 21044-3622

REY, BOLESLAW LUDWIK, mechanical engineer; b. Warsaw, Poland, Jan. 11, 1953; s. Antoni and Maria (Podhorska) R.; m. Ewa Milobedzka Rey, Feb. 9, 1974; children: Andrzej, Anna. BS, Warsaw (Poland) Tech. U., 1975. Specialist Car Factory Rsch., Warsaw, Poland, 1975-77; head of divsn. Mazoniau Regional Gas Co., Warsaw, Poland, 1977-91; deputy dir. Polish Oil and Gas Co., Warsaw, Poland, 1991, dir., 1992—; expert Ct. of Warsaw, Poland, 1980-91, Automobile Club of Poland, Warsaw, Poland, 1987—, chmn. working party on gas UN/ECE, 1999—; vice chmn. working transit group Energy Ctr., 1998—; mem. exec. coun. Internat. Gas Union, 2000—. Avocations: cars, swimming. Home phone: 48226217118. Office phone: 48225835561. Office: Polish Oil and Gas Co, 6/14 Kruccza St, 00-537 Warsaw Poland

REY, JAN MICHAL, financial consultant; b. Warsaw, Dec. 1, 1951; s. Antoni Kazimierz and Maria (Podhorska) R.; m. Maria Małgorzata Szwykowska, Oct. 28, 1973; children: Katarzyna, Piotr, Przemysław. MS, BS in Engr., Tech. U., Warsaw, 1974. Asst., sr. asst. Tech. U., Warsaw, 1974-85; IT splst., cons. INAR Co., Warsaw, 1988-90; mng. dir., ptnr. Taylor Assoc., Warsaw, 1990-92; adv. to the minister Ministry for Environ. Protection, Warsaw, 1992; v.p. Nat. Fund Environment Protection and Water Mgmt., Warsaw, 1992-93; oracle fins. applications mgr. Oracle Pl, Warsaw, 1993-95; project mgr. SAP (Poland), Warsaw, 1995—; external advisor to mgr. Police Chem. Works, Poland, 1992. Contbr. articles to profl. jours.; patentee in field. Regional coun. mem. Union of Freedom, Warsaw, 1996-97. Avocations: sailing, windsurfing, mountain climbing. E-mail: jan.rey@w.pl. Home: Symfonii 3/11, 02-787 Warsaw Poland Office: SAP Polska Co Ltd, Domaniewska 41, 02-672 Warsaw Poland

REY, LOUIS PHILIBERT, scientific adviser; b. La Tronche, France, Aug. 21, 1931; s. Louis A. and Louise A. (Feugier) R.; m. Monique Dhaussy, Sept. 20, 1954; children: Jean-Louis, Pascal. Elève ENS, Ecole Normale Supérieure, Paris, 1950; Prof. Agrégé, Sorbonne, Paris, 1954, PhD, 1958. Rsch. assoc. Ctr. Nat. Recherche Sci., Paris, 1958-62; assoc. prof. Faculty of Scis., Dijon, France, 1962-64, prof., 1964; exec. corp. head R&D Nestle, Vevey, Switzerland, 1964-80; vis. prof. U. Alaska, Fairbanks, 1983-86, UCLA, 1984; adj. prof. U. Savoy, Chambéry, France, 1992-97; scientific advisor Lausanne, Switzerland, 1980—; instr. and cons. in field. Contbr. article on freeze-drying/lyophilization of pharmaceutical and biological products; author of other numerous books on Freeze-Drying, Arctic Rsch. and Environment. Recipient Underwood Prescott award MIT, 1979. Mem. Sovereign Order of Malta. Fax: 00 41 21 652 09 67. Home and office: Verdonnet 2, CH 1010 Lausanne Switzerland

REY, PATRICIA FATIMA, lawyer; b. Principality of Monaco, Aug. 21, 1966; d. Henry and Susan (Zanganeh) R. Maitrise de droit, U. Droit, Nice, France, 1989; LLM, Georgetown U., Washington, 1990. Bar: Principality of Monaco. Paralegal O'Connor & Hannan, Washington, 1990; Soc. Civil Profl. Piasezzi, Cardix, Carlotti, Nice, 1991; paralegal Gide, Loyrette & Nouel, Brussels, 1992; rschr. Price Waterhouse, Brussels, 1992; paralegal EEC Commn., Brussels, 1992; pvt. practice Principality of Monaco, 1996—. Mem. Dem. Nat. Union. Avocations: golf, painting. Office: Avocat 19 Bvd des Moulins, MC 98000 Monaco Principality of Monaco

REY, PETE F., city official; b. Torrijos, Marinduque, The Philippines, May 31, 1937; s. Jose M. and Apolonia Fajora Rey; m. Patricia G. Catabona, Feb. 21, 1964; children: Melissa, Daniel. AS in Bus. Mgmt. and Adminstrn., Solano C.C., Suisun, Calif., 1988. Enlisted man USN, 1958, advanced through grades to E-9, master chief storekeeper in U.S., ships and overseas, 1958-82; ret., 1982; dir. tech. support dept. Fleet Integrated Logistics Overhaul Team-Mare Island, Vallejo, Calif., 1983-94; head integrated logistics support br. Mil. Sealift Command Pacific/Naval Fleet Aux. Force-West, Oakland, Calif., 1994-98; coord. reutilized materials program Info. Network Sys./Maritime Adminstrn., Alameda, Calif., 1998-99; chief procedures, analysis and quality assurance sect. 60th Supply Squadron, Air Mobility Wing, Travis AFB, Calif., 1999; ret., 1999; vice mayor City of Vallejo, 1999—. mem. Vallejo City Coun., 1997—; bd. dirs. Fighting Back Program, Vallejo, 1989-97; bd. dirs. Filipino-Am. Social Svcs. Solano County, Inc., 1991-93; mem. Vallejo Planning Commn., 1996-97, Vallejo Human Rels. Commn., 1993-97. Recipient cert. of appreciation Filipino-Am. Social Svcs. Solano County, Inc., 1995, Vallejo Planning Commn., 1997, Vallejo Human Rels. Commn., 1997. Mem. Filipino-Am. Ret. U.S. Armed Forces Assn. (life:, pres. Vallejo 1987-91). Democrat. Roman Catholic. Avocations: travel, camping, listening to country and western music, Tagalog, Portuguese and Spanish languages. Fax: 707-554-4756. E-mail: skcmretca@aol.com. Office: City of Vallejo 555 Santa Clara St Vallejo CA 94590-5939

REY-BELLET, JEAN JULIEN, physician; b. St Maurice, Switzerland, Jan. 15, 1925; s. Oscar and Louise Jeanne (Mottiez) Rey-B.; m. Monique Chantal Muller, July 21, 1962; children: Denis, Philippe, Luc. Diploma in medicine, U. Geneva, 1950, MD, 1952. Resident Psychiat. Hosp., Geneva, 1951, Rsch. Inst., Davos, Switzerland, 1952; fellow in neurology Mayo Clinic, 1953-54; rsch. fellow Children's Hosp., Boston, 1955-56; chief resident Bellevue Hosp., N.Y.C., 1954-58; resident Med. Policlin, Geneva, 1958-59; chief resident Psychiat Hosp., Geneva, 1959-62, Child Psychiatry, Geneva, 1962-64; dir. Psychiat. Hosp., Monthey, Switzerland, 1965-90, Child Psychiatry., Monthey, Switzerland, 1965-81; retired. Contbr. articles to profl. jours. Com. mem. Parents of Handicapped Children, 1966-70, Pro Infirmis, Zurich, 1967-72, Enfants de Monde, Geneva, 1968-71; med. del. Internat. Com. Red Cross, Geneva, 1991O. 1st lt. Med. Svc. Swiss Army, 1946-75. Mem. Swiss Psychiat. Assn., Swiss Neurol. Assn., Swiss Child Psychiat. Assn., Swiss Neurophysiological Assn., Swiss Epidemiology Psychiat. Assn., Swiss Psychoanalytic Assn., Am. Acad. Neurology, Soc. Medicale Valais, Dedn. Medicine. Swiss, N.Y. Acad. Scis. Roman Catholic. Avocations: history, genealogy, skiing. Home: Rte de Martoret 29, 1870 Monthey Switzerland

REY-COQUAIS, JEAN-PAUL, ancient history educator; b. Lyons, France, Oct. 27, 1928; s. Georges and Germaine (Thevenot) R.-C.; m. May Juvin, Dec. 21, 1961; children: Cyrille, Monique, Odile. BA in Classical Langs. and Lit., Sorbonne, Paris, 1951; diploma, Ecole Pratique des Hautes Études, Paris, 1968; PhD, Sorbonne, 1973. Tchr. Coll. of Jesuits, Lyons, France, 1955-58, 59-60, Avignon, France, 1958-59; tchr. Lycée d'État Claude Fauriel, St-Étienne, France, 1960-61, Lycée Nat. du Parc, Lyons, France, 1961-62; researcher Nat. Ctr. Scientific Rsch., Lyons, France, 1962-68; prof. ancient history U. Burgundy, Dijon, France, 1968-94; emeritus prof., 1995—; researcher Inst. Fernand-Courby, Lyons, 1959—. Author: Inscriptions Grecques et Latines de la Syrie VI, 1968, VII, 1970, Arados et sa Pérée, 1974, Inscriptions Grecques et Latines de la Nécropole de Tyr, 1977; editor: Géographie Historique au Proche Orient, 1988, La Syrie de Byzance à l'Islam, 1992. Laurent-Vibert Found. fellow, 1965, Inst. for Advanced Study fellow, 1989-90. Mem. Internat. Assn. and French Com. Save Tyre, German Archaeological Inst. (corrs. mem.). Avocation: photography. Home: 33 E Blvd Chevremorte, 21240 Talant France Office: Inst Fernand-Courby, Maison de l'Orient 7 rue Raulin, 69007 Lyon France

REYERS, FRED, clinical pathologist, veterinary educator; b. Ermelo, Gerderland, Holland, June 1, 1947; s. Robert Henry and Wilhemina (Eijckenduijn) Reyers; m. Lynn Anderson, Apr. 8, 1972; children: Belinda, Michelle. BVSc, U. Pretoria, South Africa, 1971, BVSc with honors, 1981, MMedVet, 1990, tertiary edn. diploma, 1980. Govt. vet. officer Rhodesian Govt., Sinoia, 1971-73; vet. rsch. officer Vet. Rsch. Lab., Salisbury, Rhodesia, 1973-76, sr. vet. rsch. officer, 1976-78; sr. lectr. Faculty of Vet. Sci., Pretoria, 1978-84, assoc. prof., 1984-90, prof., 1990-97, head of dept., chmn., 1997-99; cons. Biocon Rsch., Pretoria, 1997—. Contbr. articles to profl. publs. Civic and ratepayer rep. Greater Pretoria Met. Negotiating Forum, 1993-94. Capt. Grey Scouts Rhodesia Def. Force, 1975-78. Corecipient Clin. medal South African Vet. Assn., 1995. Mem. South African Vet. Assn. Avocations: marathon and long distance running, birdwatching. Office: Dept Companion Animal Med, Pbag X04 Onderstepoort, Pretoria 0110, South Africa

REYES, ANNA MARIA, broadcast executive; b. Phoenix, Aug. 21, 1957; d. Perfecto C. and Esperanza (Del Castillo) R. BA in Fin., Ariz. State U., 1983. Radio-Tel. operators permit FCC; notary public, Ariz. Traffic/continuity dir. First Media Corp./KOPA AM and FM, Scottsdale, Ariz., 1978-81; music dir., air talent First Media Corp./KOPA AM and FM, Scottsdale, 1981-83; bus. mgr., asst. sta. mgr. Cook Inlet Radio Ptnr. KSLX-FM and KOPA-AM, 1983-92; sta. contr., asst. gen. mgr. Jacor/Citicasters KSLX AM/FM, Phoenix, 1992-96; gen. mgr. Jacor Comm. KSLX AM/FM, Phoenix, 1997—; interviewer KSLX FM/KOPA AM, Scottsdale, 1990. Coauthor: INXS Newsletter, 1994. spokeswoman campaign against radio for men format KSLX FM/KOPA AM, Scottsdale, 1988. Recipient Cert. for Announcing, City of Phoenix-Hello Phoenix, 1985, Bus. Mgr. award Corp. Chain Contest, Phoenix, 1990-92. Mem. AAUW, Am. Women in Radio and TV, Broadcast Cable Fin. Mgmt., Univ. Women London. Democrat. Roman Catholic. Avocations: European travel, ballet, reading, music. Home: 12340 W Elwood St Avondale AZ 85323-9618 Office: KSLX Radio FM/AM 4343 E Camelback Rd Ste 200 Phoenix AZ 85018-8306

REYES, CARLITO ABAD, chemical engineer; b. Manila, The Philippines, Nov. 5, 1963; s. Manuel and Aurora (Abad) R.; m. Elizabeth Mauricio, Dec. 30, 1995. BSChE, Mapua Inst. Tech., Manila, 1985; M in Indsl. Engring. and Mgmt., Poly. U. The Philippines, Manila, 1992; postgrad., Poly. U. The Philippines, 1998-2000. Registered chem. engr., The Philippines. Quality assurance technician Pure Foods Corp., Marikina, Metro Manila, The Philippines, 1986, quality assurance specialist, 1986-87; trade and industry devel. rschr. dept. trade and industry Bur. Patents, Trademarks and Tech. Transfer, Makati City, The Philippines, 1988-89, trade and industry devel. analyst dept. trade and industry, 1989, trade/industry devel. specialist dept. trade and industry, 1989-93, 93-97; sr. trade and industry devel. specialist Dept. Trade and Industry, Makati City, 1993-97, sr. specialist intellectual property office, 1998—. Mem. AIChE, Am. Chem. Soc., Philippine Inst. Chem. Engrs. Baptist. Avocations: reading hist. biographies, science and technology subjects, collecting stamps, tennis, swimming. Office: Dept Trade/Intell Prop Ofc, 351 Sen Gil J Puyat Ave, Makati City 1200, The Philippines

REYES, PERLA FANDINO, hotel management educator; b. Manila, Philippines, July 15, 1941; d. Juan and Emeteria (Banzuela) Fandino; m. Romeo Reyes, Apr. 26, 1969; children: Jason, Gerard, Macee. BS in Home Econs., Coll. Holy Spirit, Manila, Philippines, 1963, BS in Foods and Nutrition, 1964, BS in Edn., 1965. Home econs. tchr. Capitol City Coll., Manila, 1963-65; religion tchr. Ramon Avancena H.S., Manila, 1964-65; chair art dept. Manuel L. Quezon U., 1967-95; pres. Nutrideleco Food House, Manila, 1964-94; chair home econs. dept. Manuel L. Quezon U., 1969-95; faculty Coll. Holy Spirit, 1966-96; chair Coun. Deans & Heads of Home Econs. of Philippines, 1989-90, 91-92; curriculum planner Commn. Higher Edn. Philippines, 1987-89. Recipient Silver Humanitarian Svc. Cross award Red Cross, 1977; UNICEF-WHO scholar U. Philippines, 1966-67. Roman Catholic. Avocations: flower arranging, handicrafts, needlecrafts, cooking, baking. Home: 1945 Anonas St NDC Compound, Manila 1016, Philippines

REYES, RAUL GREGORIO, surgeon; b. Tegucigalpa, Morazan, Honduras, June 18, 1928; came to U.S., 1939; s. Julio Gregorio and Mercedes Ofelia (Mazzoni) Reyes-Zelaya; m. Mildred Dane Smith, 1951 (dec. May 1990); children: Tyra, Kimberly; stepchildren: Javier, Christian; m. Blanca Lidia Milla, Apr. 2, 1993. BS, Georgetown U., 1945; MD, George Washington U., 1950. Diplomate Nat. Bd. Med. Examiners, Am. Bd. Surgery. Intern Charity Hosp., New Orleans, 1950-51; resident Emergency Hosp./George Washington U., Washington, 1951, Charity Hosp., New Orleans, 1952-55; chief thoracic surgery San Felipe Hosp., Tegucigalpa, 1955-56; assoc. to ptnr. Browne-McHardy Clinic, New Orleans, 1955-60, 60-73; med. dir. New Orleans Indsl. Clinic, 1956-58; chief of surgery and orthopedics Lallie Kemp Regional Hosp., Independence, La., 1987-89, med. dirs., 1988-89; owner, pres. Raul G. Reyes, A Med. Corp., New Orleans, 1973—; owner, pres. Internat. Maritime Med. Svcs., New Orleans, 1978—, Catracho Enterprises, New Orleans, 1975—, Phys. Therapy Svcs. of New Orleans, 1975—; faculty La. State Univ. Sch. Medicine, 1953—, others. Inventor in field; contbr. articles to profl. jours. Chmn. Rep. Hispanic Assembly, New Orleans, 1983; pre-cand. Nat. Party, Honduras, 1985; founder Literacy Ctrs. of Honduras, 1991; presdl. candidate Christian Dem. Party of Honduras, 1994. Named to Hon. Consul of Honduras, Hon. Citizen, City of New Orleans. Mem. Am. Coll. Surgeons, AMA, So. Med. Assn., La. State Med. Soc., Orleans Parish Med. Soc., Colegio Medico de Honduras. Roman Catholic. Avocations: tennis, reading, writing, social progs. Office: PO Box 15379 New Orleans LA 70175-5379

REYES, SALOMON FRANCISCO, lawyer; b. Manila, Jan. 29, 1933; s. Luis F. and Adriana R. Reyes. AA with honors, U. of the Philippines, 1951, BA cum laude, 1955, LLB, 1955. Bar: The Philippines 1956. Assoc. atty. Ozaeta, Lichauco & Picazo Law Offices, Manila, 1956-57; ptnr. Lichauco, Picazo & Agcaoili Law Offices, Manila, 1957-71, Picazo, Agcaoili, Santayana, Reyes & Tayao Law Offices, Makati City, The Philippines, 1971-75, Picazo, Santayana, Reyes & Tayao Law Offices, Makati City, 1975-79; sr. ptnr. Reyes, Santayana, Tayao & Picazo Law Offices, Makati City, 1979-82, Reyes, Santayana, Tayao & Molo Law Offices, Makati City, 1982-90, Reyes, Santayana, Tayao, Molo & Alegre Law Offices, Makati City, 1990—; corp. sec. Warner-Lambert Philippines, Inc., 1957—, dir., 1961—; dir., corp. sec. CBI (Philippines) Inc., 1962—; dir. W D. Scott & Co., Inc., The Philippines, 1963—, pres., 1978-93; dir. Ace/Saatchi & Saatchi Advt., Inc., The Philippines, 1971—. Mem. Philippine Bar Assn. (dir. 1980-82, v.p. 1981-82), Integrated Bar of the Philippines, Rotary Club Makati-Guadalupe (founder, charter, v.p. 1981—), Met. Club, Inc. (proprietary mem.), Dasmarinas Village Assn., Inc. (proprietary mem.), Phi Kappa Phi (life), Pi Gamma Mu (life), Upsilon Sigma Phi. Avocations: music, travels, sports, Humanitarian work, reading. Home: 1556 Mahogany Rd, Dasmarinas Village, Makati City Metro Manila, The Philippines Office: Reyes Santayana Tayao et al, 102 Gamboa St Legaspi Vill, Makati City Metro Manila, The Philippines

REYES HEROLES, JESUS, Mexican government official; b. Tuxpan, Veracruz, Mex., Apr. 3, 1921; s. Jesus Reyes Martinez and Juana Heroles Lombera; m. Gloria Gonzalez Garza, May 8, 1951; children: Jesus, Federico. LL.B. with special honors, Nat. Autonomous U. Mex., 1944; postgrad., U. Buenos Aires and La Plata, Colegio Libre de Estudios Superiores de Buenos Aires, 1945; honoris causa doctorate, Alcalá de Henares U., Madrid, 1981. Assessor Dept. Labor and Social Planning, Mexico City, 1944; substitute pres. special group no. 1 Fedl. Bd. Reconciliation and Arbitration, Mexico City, 1946; sec. gen. Mexican Book Inst., 1949-53; assessor Office of Pres., Mexico City, 1952-58; chief economic studies Mexican Nat. Railroads, Mexico City, 1953-58; tech. subdir. gen. Mexican Inst. Social Security, Mexico City, 1958-64; dir. gen. Petroleos Mexicanos, Mexico City, 1964-70, Diesel Nacional (S.A.), Constructora Nacional de Carros de Ferrocarril (S.A.), Siderurgica Nacional (S.A.), Mexico City, 1970-72, Mexican Inst. Social Security, 1975-76; Sec. Interior (Fed. Govt.) Mexico City, 1976-79; full-time investigator Nat. Autonomous U., Mexico City, 1979-82; Sec. Edn. Mex. Govt., Mexico City, 1982-96, min. energy, 1996-97; amb. to Am. Mexican Government, Washinton, DC, 1997—; various professorial positions, colls. in, Mex., 1944-67; pres. Interamerican Center for Studies in Social Security; bd. dirs. Fondo para la Historia de las Ideas Revolucionarias de Mex.; Various positions in the Partido Revolucionario Institucional (PRI), 1939-60; rep. XLV legis. Congreso de la Union; pres. Nat. Exec. Com. PRI. Author: various studies in politics, economics, including El Liberalismo Mexicano (3 volumes), 1957, 58, 61. Hon. mem. Spanish Royal Acad. Hist.; mem. Mex. Acad. Hist., Mex. Soc. Geography and Statistics, College Lawyers.; Partido Revolucionario Institucional. Office: Embassy of Mexico 1911 Pennsylvannia Ave NW Washington DC 20006*

REYES-NOYLA, JOSE GODOY, pediatrician, endocrinologist; b. Comayaguela, Honduras, June 25, 1945; s. Ricardo and Mary (Essley) R.; m. Ann Mary, Feb. 24, 1979; children: Gabriela Maria, Ana Felicidad. MD, U. Honduras, 1972. Diplomate Am. Bd. Pediatrics. Intern U. Honduras, 1970-71; physician Health Ministry, Honduras, 1972; pediatric resident Children's Hosp., Honduras, 1972-73, U. Miss., Jackson, 1973-76; fellow in pediatric endocrinology U. Miami, Fla., 1976-; attending and chief pediatrics Children's Hosp., 1978—, chief med. ward, 1987—, chief pediatric endocrinology divsn., 1978—, cons. in pediatric endocrinology, 1978—; vis. prof. Children's Hosp., 1978—. Contbr. articles to profl. jours. Fellow Am. Acad. Pediatrics; mem. Endocrine Soc., Lawson Wilkins Pediatric Endocrinology Soc. Avocations: reading, exercise, family. Office: PO Box 113, Comayaguela Honduras

REYES-TREJO, BENITO, chemist, researcher; b. Mexicali, Baja, Mex., Mar. 21, 1957; s. Anselmo and Juana (Trejo-Moreno) Reyes-Taizán; m. Jovita garcía, Dec. 23, 1983; children: Ibsán Leonel, Dalia Tonantzin, Eliel Rodolfo, Neftalí Sebastián. B.Chemistry, U. Nac. Autonoma de Mex., Mexico City, 1981; MS, Fac. of Chemistry/Indsl. Sci., Cuernavaca, Mex., 1988; ScD, Centro Investigacion Estudios, Mexico City, 1999. Faculty of chemistry U. Autónoma Chapingo, Texcoco, Mex., 1982—; lab. prof. U. Nacional Autónoma de Mex., Mexico City, 1982—; dir. Lab. de Productos Naturales, U. Autónoma Chapingo, Texcoco, 1985—. Contbr. articles to profl. jours. Cand. to nat. investigator Sistema Nacional de Investigadores, Mex., 1990-93, 93-94. Mem. Pharm. Assn. Mex., Sociedad Quimica de Mex., Internat. Soc. Annonaceas (founding mem.). Avocations: music, playing guitar, reading, travel. Home: Margaritas #4, Fraccionamiento Tolimpa, 56230 Texcoco Mexico Office: Km 38.5 carretera Mex-Texco, Ap 74 Oficina de Correos Ch, 56230 Texcoco Mexico

REYMOND, JEAN CHARLES, surgeon; b. St. Etienne, France, June 3, 1918; s. Charles and Evelyne (Trolet) R.; m. Vinsot Jacqueline, Sept. 1943 (div. 1959); children: Helene, Elisabeth, Anne, France-Marie; m. Commenay Any, Dec. 4, 1961; children: Charles, Philippe. MD, Paris, 1945. Resident Hosp., Paris, 1944; rschr. Lab. Physiology, Paris, 1944-49; surgeon, prof. Grenoble, 1949-89, surgical & clin. rsch., 1950-90. Author: Praticien et l'Urgence ca Chirurgicale, 1960, 4th edit., 1973; contbr. articles to profl. jours. Capt. French Mil., 1939-60; 1st lt. U.S. Army, 1945. Roman Catholic. Avocations: writing, tennis, table tennis. Home and Office: L'Hermitage, 19 Ave Des Sept Laux, F 38240 Meylan France

REYN, ALEX, Belgian ambassador. Permanent rep. Belgium UN, N.Y.C.; now Belgian amb. to U.S., Belgium Embassy, Washington, 1998—. Office: Belgian Embassy 3330 Garfield St NW Washington DC 20008-3515*

REYNIER, CLAUDE, mathematician, engineer; b. Neuilly-sur-Seine, France, Apr. 5, 1935; s. Maurice and Suzanne (Lapraye) R. Ing., Polytechnique, Paris, 1957, Mines de Paris, 1960. Officer Engr. Corps, France, 1959-67; engr. Aerospatiale, France, 1967-95. Mem. AAAS, Société Mathematique de France, N.Y. Acad. Scis. Avocations: math, history, the universe. Home: Grand Rue, 52300 Vaux sur Saint-Urbain France

REYNOLDS, ALBERT MARTIN, Irish government official; b. Rooskey, Co. Roscommon, Ireland, 1932; m. Kathleen Coen, 1962; 2 sons, 5 daus. Educated, Summerhill Coll., Sligo. Min. for posts and telegraphs, and for transport Republic of Ireland, Dublin, 1979-81, min. for industry & energy, 1982, Opposition spokesperson for industry and employment, 1983-85, Opposition spokesperson for energy, 1985-87, min. for industry & com-

merce, 1987-88, min. for finance, 1988-92; prime min. Republic of Ireland, 1992-94; dir. Jefferson Smurfit Group, Dublin, 1996—; chmn. A.P.R. Group P.L.C., Singapore, Adm McDonagh Boland Ltd., P.L.C. Mem. Oireachtas Joint Com. on Comml. State-Sponsored bodies, 1983-87; pres. Longford C. of C., 1974-78. *

REYNOLDS, CLARK WINTON, economist, educator; b. Chgo., Mar. 13, 1934; m. Nydia O'Connor Viales; children: Rebecca, C. Winton III, Matthew, Camila. AB, Claremont (Calif.) Men's Coll., 1956; student, MIT, 1956-57, 58; student divinity sch., Harvard U., 1957-58; MA, U. Calif., Berkeley, 1961, PhD in Econs., 1962. Asst. prof. Occidental Coll., L.A., 1961-62; from asst. to assoc. prof. dept. edn. and econ. growth Yale U., New Haven, 1962-67; sr. fellow The Brookings Inst., Washington, 1975-76; prof. econs., prin. investigator, founding dir. Ams. program Stanford (Calif.) U., sr. fellow Inst. Internat. Studies, 1996—, prof. emeritus econs., 1996—; vis. prof. Nat. U. Mex., Chapingo, 1966, El Colegio de Mex., Mexico City, 1964, 65, 79, Hopkins-Nanjing Ctr. for Chinese and Am. Studies, Nanjing, China, 1999—; vis. lectr. in econs. Stockholm U. Econs., 1968; fellow St. Antony's Coll., Oxford, 1975; vis. rsch. scholar Internat. Inst. for Applied Systems Analysis, Laxenburg, Austria, 1978. Author: The Mexican Economy, 1970; co-author: Essays on the Chilean Economy, 1965, (with C. Tello) U.S.-Mexican Relations: Economic and Social Aspects, Las Relaciones Mexico Estados Unidos, 1983, Dynamics of North American Trade, 1991, North American Labor Market Interdependence, 1992, Open Regionalism in the Andes, 1996. Dir. Monticello West Found., 1980—. Woodrow Wilson Found. fellow, 1956-57, Rockefeller Found. fellow, 1957-58, Doherty Found. fellow, 1960-61, Inst. Internat. Studies fellow Stanford U., 1990—; grantee Social Sci. Rsch. Coun., Ford Found., Hewlett Found., Rockefeller Found., Mellon Found., MacArthur Found., Tinker Found. Mem. Am. Econ. Assn., Cosmos Club (Washington). Office: Stanford U Inst Internat Studies Encina Hall W Rm 305 306 Stanford CA 94305-6084

REYNOLDS, EDWARD OSMUND ROYLE, neonatal pediatrician; b. Brighton, Sussex, Eng., Feb. 3, 1933; s. Edward Royle and Edna (Jones) R.; m. Margaret Lindsay Ballard, July 14, 1956; children: Edward Mark Royle, Matthew Osmund Royle. MB, BS, U. London, 1958, MD, 1965. House physician, registrar St. Thomas' Hosp., London, 1959-63; rsch. fellow in pediatrics Harvard U., Yale U., 1963-64; rsch. asst., lectr., sr. lectr. Univ. Coll. Hosp. Med. Sch., London, 1964-76; head dept. pediatrics Univ. Coll. and Middlesex Sch. Medicine, 1987-92; William Julius Mickle fellow U. London, 1976-77; cons. pediatrician Univ. Coll. Hosp., London, 1969-94; prof. neonatal pediatrics Univ. Coll. London Med. Sch., 1976-96, emeritus, 1996—; pres. Baby Life Support Systems, 1982-97; hon. prof. pediatrics Inst. Child Health, London, 1993. Contbr. chpts. to books, articles to profl. jours. Specialist adviser Ho. of Commons Social Svcs. and Health Select Coms., 1978-92. Decorated comdr. Brit. Empire; recipient James Spence medal Brit. Paediatric Assn., 1994, Harding award ActionRsch., 1995, Dawson Williams Meml. prize Brit. Med. Assn., 1992. Fellow Royal Soc. (London), Royal Coll. Physicians (Eng.), Royal Coll. Ob-Gyn. (Eng.) (ad eundem), Inst. Child Health (hon.), Royal Coll. Pediat. and Child Health (hon.), Acad. Med. Sci. (founder), Univ. Coll. London Hosps. Found., Royal Soc. Medicine (hon.); mem. Neonatal Soc. (pres. 1991-94), European Assn. Perinatal Medicine (sci. com. 1972-73, Maternité prize 1994), European Soc. Pediat. Rsch. (coun. 1978-81). Avocations: music, photography, travel, sport. Home: 72 Barrowgate Rd, London W4 4QU, England also: 4 Ginge, Oxon OX12 8QR, England

REYNOLDS, ERNEST EUGENE, III, lawyer; b. Aug. 5, 1949; s. Ernest Eugene Jr. and Marianne Reba Reynolds; m. Barbara Ann Lovas, Dec. 27, 1973; children: Colleen, Sarah, Katherine. BA in Polit. Sci. with honors, U. Tex. El Paso, El Paso, 1972, MA, 1974; JD with honors, U. Tex., Austin, 1977. Bar: Tex., U.S. Dist. Ct. (ea. dist.) Tex. 1978, U.S. Dist. Ct. (no. dist.) Tex. 1984, U.S. Dist. Ct. (we. dist.) Tex. 1983, U.S. Ct. Appeals (5th cir.) 1987; diplomate Taft Seminar of Govt. Former ptnr. Cantey & Hanger, L.L.P., Ft. Worth, Tex.; ptnr. Reynolds & Pennington, L.L.P., Ft. Worth, 1995—; course dir. Profl. Liability--A Performance Enhancement Course (sponsored by State Bar of Tex.), 1986; mem. Tex. Disciplinary Rules of Profl. Conduct Com., State Bar Tex. Contbr. articles to profl. jours.; editor-in-chief Am. Jour. Criminal Law, 1976-77; former mem. legal rsch. bd. U. Tex. Sch. Law. Bd. dirs. Tex. Girls' Choir; co-course dir. The Ultimate Trial Notebook: Masters of Trial, State Bar of Tex., 1993. Recipient Pres.'s award Tex. Young Lawyers Assn., 1983-84. Fellow (charter) Tarrant County Bar Found.; mem. Am. Health Lawyers Assn., Tex. Assn. Def. Counsel (former bd. dirs., chmn. continuing legal edn. com. 1987-88, punitive damages legis. team 1993-94, chmn. trial acad. 1994), Tarrant County Civil Trial Lawyers Assn. (past pres.), Def. Rsch. Inst., State Bar of Tex. (former vice chmn. continuing legal edn. com., past mem. com. on ct. rules, past mem. adminis-trn. justice com., past mem. citizens adn law focused edn. com., task force on practice skills 1987, chmn. continuing legal edn. planning com. 1999, annual meeting mem. annual meeting com. 1998-99), Ft. Worth C. of C. (aviation com.), Tarrant County Bar Assn. (Pres.'s cert. of outstanding achievement 1999, co-chair law and tech./web page com. 1998-99, past chmn. CLE com.), Fort Worth Club. Episcopalian. Avocations: reading, travel, art. Office: Reynolds & Pennington LLP 500 Throckmorton St # 2900 PO Box 44105 Fort Worth TX 76102

REYNOLDS, EVA MARY BARBARA, foreign language educator; b. Bristol, Eng., June 13, 1914; d. Alfred Charles and Barbara (Florac) R.; m. Lewis Thorpe, Sept. 5, 1939 (dec. Oct. 1977); children: Adrian, Kerstin. BA in French with honors, U. London, Eng., 1935, BA in Italian with honors, 1936, PhD in Italian, 1949; MA in Italian, U. Cambridge, Eng., 1940; DLitt (hon.), Wheaton Coll., 1979, Hope Coll., 1982, Durham U., Eng., 1995. Asst. lectr. in Italian London (Eng.) Sch. Econs., 1937-40; lectr. in Italian Cambridge (Eng.) U., 1940-62; reader in Italian Nottingham (Eng.) U., 1963-78; hon. reader Warwick (Eng.) U., 1975-80; mng. editor Seven: An Anglo-Am. Literary Rev., 1980-88, 93—; vis. prof. U. Calif., Berkeley, 1974-75, Wheaton (Ill.) Coll., 1977-78, Hope Coll., Holland, Mich., 1982. Author: The Linguistic Writings of Alessandro Manzoni, 1952, The Passionate Intellect: Dorothy L. Sayers' Encounter with Dante, 1989, Dorothy L. Sayers: Her Life and Soul, 1993, The Letters of Dorothy L. Sayers: 1899-1936, The Making of a Detective Novelist, 1995, From Novelist to Playwright, 1997, A Noble Daring, 1998, In the Midst of Life, 2000; translator Orlando Furioso, 2 vols., 1975, 77; gen. editor: The Cambridge Italian Dictionary, 2 vols., 1962, 81. Decorated Cavaliere Ufficiale al Merito Della Repubblica Italiana, Italian Govt., 1978. Mem. Univ. Women's Club (chmn. 1988-90), R.A.F. Club. Anglican. Avocations: family life, friendships. Home: 220 Milton Rd, Cambridge CB4 1LQ, England

REYNOLDS, GAVIN PAUL, research scientist; b. Feb. 2, 1952. BA in Chemistry, U. York, Eng., 1973; PhD in Biochemistry, U. London, 1977. Rsch. asst. U. London, 1973-76; Schizophrenia Rsch. Fund fellow Queen Charlotte's Hosp., London, 1976-81; vis. rsch. scientist L. Boltzmann Inst., Vienna, Austria, 1979-81; scientist med. Rsch. Coun., Cambridge, Eng., 1982-84; lectr. U. Nottingham, Eng., 1985-89; sr. lectr. U. Sheffield, Eng., 1990-92; reader U. Sheffield, 1992-95, prof., 1995—. Mem. adv. bd. Jour. Neural Transmission; contbr. some 200 articles to profl. jours. Chair med. adv. bd. Huntington's Disease Assn., London; mem. adv. bd. Med. Rsch. Coun. Grantee Med. Rsch. Coun., Wellcome Trust. Mem. Brit. Pharmacol. Soc., Brit. Assn. Psychopharmacology (mem. coun.), Brit. Neurosci. Assn., Internat. Soc. Neurochemistry. Office: U Sheffield, Dept Biomed Sci, Sheffield S10 2TN, England

REYNOLDS, GLENN G., rehabilitation medicine physician; b. Najibabad, India, Nov. 28, 1925; naturalized U.S. citizen; s. Earl Robert and Maude Evelyn (Lower) R.; m. Lois R. Mills, Aug. 1948 (div. 1965); children: Shirley, Valerie, Mary; m. Margaret Ann Lee, Jan. 31, 1969. BA, La Sierra Coll., 1948; MD, Loma Linda U., 1954. Diplomate Am. Bd. Electrodiagnostic Medicine. Med. dir. rehab. unit Washington Adventist Hosp., Takoma Park, Md., 1959-65; assoc. med. dir. rehab. unit Georgetown U. Hosp., Washington, 1965-70; med. dir. rehab. ctr. Santa Clara Valley Med. Ctr., San Jose, Calif., 1970-79, Emanuel Hosp., Portland, Oreg., 1982-86, St. Joesph Hosp., Tacoma, Wash., 1986-93; med. dir. Rehab. Hosp. of Pacific, Honolulu, 1981-82; ret.; asst. prof. Howard U., Washington, 1960-64; asst. prof., then assoc. prof. Georgetown U., 1965-71; asst. prof., then assoc. clin. prof. Stanford U., Palo Alto, Calif., 1970-81; vis. prof. U. Western Australia, Perty, 1979-81; sr. cons. rehab. medicine Royal Perth Hosp., 1979-81; prof. U. Hawaii, Honolulu, 1981-82. Patentee gasoline powered motorized wheelchair; contbr. articles to profl. jours., chpt. to book. Chmn. Oreg. State Commn. for Handicapped, 1982-86; chmn. sports medicine and sci. com. U.s. Wheelchair Athletic Com., 1985-90; mem. rehab. adv. com. Sec. U.S. Dept. Vets. Affairs, 1991-93. Sgt. U.S. Army, 1944-46. Named Physician of Yr. Jour. AMA, 1981; recipient Cert./Plaque for med. health sys. leadership Calif. State Senate, 1979. Fellow Am. Acad. Phys. Medicine and Rehab. (emeritus); mem. Wash. State Med. Soc., Am. Congress Rehab. Medicine (emeritus), Am. Spinal Injury Assn. (emeritus), Am. Paraplegia Soc. Avocations: rehabilitation engineering and assistive technology, woodworking, history, genealogy. Home: 34 Doran Rd, 3815 Bunyip Victoria Australia Office: 10519 NE 198th St Battle Ground WA 98604

REYNOLDS, HERBERT YOUNG, physician, internist; b. Richmond, Va., Aug. 20, 1939; s. George Audney and Pearle Maupin (Young) R.; m. Anne Browning Leavell, July 11, 1964; children: Nancy, George, William Stuart. BA in English, U. Va., 1961, MD, 1965; MA (hon.), Yale U., 1979. Diplomate Am. Bd. Internal Medicine, Am. Bd. Allergy and Immunology. Intern The N.Y. Hosp., Cornell Med. Ctr., N.Y.C., 1965-66, asst. physician, fellow in medicine, 1966-67; clin. assoc., lab. clin. investigation Nat. Inst. Allergy and Infectious Diseases, NIH, Bethesda, Md., 1967-70, chief clin. assoc. lab. clin. investigation, 1968-69; sr. investigator lab. of clin. investigation Nat. Inst. Allergy and Infectious Diseases, NIH, 1971-76; chief resident, instr. medicine U. Hosp. U. Wash., Seattle, 1970-71; assoc. prof. internal medicine, head pulmonary div. Sch. Medicine Yale U., New Haven, 1976-79, prof., 1979-88; J. Lloyd Huck prof. medicine, chmn. dept. Pa. State U.-Milton S. Hershey Med. Ctr., 1988—; assoc. chmn. divsn. medicine Pa. State Geisinger Health Sys., 1997-2000, chief medicine ops. Hershey Med. Ctr. Region, 1997-2000; exec. com. Coll. Medicine Pa. State U.-Hershey Med. Ctr., 1988—, exec. bd. U. Hosp., 1988—, fin. bd. acad. enrichment fun, 1988-95, dean's adv. com., 1988-97, mem. diversity task force, 1995—, Univ. Physicians Faculty Practice Plan Exec. Com. 1996-97; departmental chair rep. Milton S. Hershey Med. Ctr. Bd., 2000—; cons. in infectious diseases Nat. Naval Med. Ctr. NIH, Bethesda, 1971-76, clin. rsch. com., 1971-76, chmn., 1974-76, med. bd., 1974-76, pulmonary disease adv. com. divsn. of lung diseases Nat. Heart, Lung and Blood Inst., 1978-82, sci. counselors bd., 1984-88, data and safety monitoring bd. registry of patients with deficiency of Alpha-1 Antitrypsin, 1989-96. Assoc. editor, mem. editl. bd. Lung, 1978—, Am. Jour. Medicine, 1979-89, Jour. Clin. Investigation, 1980-86, Am. Rev. Respiratory Disease, 1980-87, Jour. Applied Physiology, 1981-89, Resident Physician, 1981-95; contbr. over 275 articles to profl. jours. Parent com. Troop 1 Boy Scouts Am., Madison, 1979-82; bd. dirs. Neighborhood Music Sch., Guilford, Conn., 1978-87, Music at Gretna, 1994—; bd. dirs. Harrisburg Symphony, 1996—; active All Saints Episc. Ch., Hershey; pulmonary infections com. Cystic Fibrosis Found., Bethesda, 1980-86; mem. coun. sci. advisors Parker B. Francis Found., Kansas City, Kans., 1983-87; internat. com. World Orgn. for Sarcoidosis and other Granulomatous Disorders, 1987-95; bd. dirs., mem. coun. Am. Lung Assn., 1989-93, bd. govs. 1990-93, com. mem., 1990—; coach Guilford Soccer League, 1985-88. Surgeon USPHS, 1967-70. John Edward Nobel fellow, 1961-65; named Outstanding Med. Specialist in USA, Town and Country Mag., 1989, 97, The Best Med. Specialists, Town & Country mag., 1995, One of 400 Best Doctors in U.S. Good Housekeeping Mag., 1991, named in The Best Doctors in Am., 1st edit. 1992-93, 2d edit. 1994-95, 3rd edit. 1997-98, The Best Doctors in Am., N.E., 1st edit., 1996-97. Fellow ACP (coun. subsplty. socs. 1989-00, gov.-elect Pa. eastern region I 1999, gov. Pa. 2000—), Am. Coll. Chest Physicians (program com. 1978-84), Infectious Disease Soc. Am., Coll. Physicians Phila.; mem. Am. Thoracic Soc. (sec.-treas. 1987-88, bd. dirs. 1989-93, v.p. 1988-89, pres. 1992-93), Am. Soc. Clin. Investigation, Assn. Am. Physicians, Am. Assn. Immunologists, Am. Fedn. Clin. Rsch., Am. Clin. and Climatological Soc., Interurban Clin. Club (emeritus 1989), Assn. Profs. Medicine, Country Club of Hershey, Farmington Country Club, Raven Soc., Phi Beta Kappa, Alpha Omega Alpha, Omicron Delta Kappa. Republican. Avocations: tennis, violin. Home: 226 E Caracas Ave Hershey PA 17033-1309 Office: Pa State U Milton S Hershey Med Ctr 850 University Dr Hershey PA 17033

REYNOLDS, MARSHALL TRUMAN, printing company executive; b. Logan, W.Va., Feb. 21, 1937; s. Douglas Vernon and Dorothy Lee (Dingess) R.; m. Shirley Ann Earwood, Mar. 24, 1968; children: Jack Marine, Douglas Vernon. Student, Marshall U., 1956-58. Sales mgr. Chapman Printing Co., Huntington, W.Va., 1960-61, gen. mgr., 1961-64; pres., gen. mgr. Chapman Printing Co., Huntington, Parkersburg and Charleston, W.Va., Lexington, Ky., 1964—; chmn. bd. McCorkle Machine & Engring., Huntington, KY-OWVA Corrugated Container, Huntington, Stationers, Inc., Huntington, Charleston, Radisson Hotel, Huntington, Huntington Indsl. Corp., Champion Industries Inc., Am. Babbit Bearing Inc.; bd. dirs. Guyan Machinery, Huntington, United Huntington Industries, Persinger Supply Co., Prichard, W.Va., First Guaranty Bank, Hammond, La., Banc One WV Corp., Charleston, W.Va. Bd. dirs. W.Va. Roundtable, Huntington, 1989—, W. Va. Bus. Found., Huntington, 1989—, Boys and Girls Club, Huntington, 1989—, Huntington United Way, 1989—; mem. Gov.'s Task Force on Children, Youth and Families, 1989—; guest lectr. various high schs. on free enterprise. Named Outstanding Small Businessman of Yr., Huntington Jaycees, 1983, Business Man of Yr. Jaycess, 1988. Mem. Huntington C. of C., Western Star Lodge (Guyandotte, W.Va.). Republican. Baptist. Avocation: raising cattle. Home: 1130 13th St Huntington WV 25701-3632 Office: Chapman Printing Co 2450 1st Ave Huntington WV 25703-1218

REYNOLDS, NANCY BRADFORD DUPONT (MRS. WILLIAM GLASGOW REYNOLDS), sculptor; b. Greenville, Del., Dec. 28, 1919; d. Eugene Eleuthere and Catherine Dulcinea (Moxham) duPont; m. William Glasgow Reynolds, May 18, 1940; children: Kathrine Glasgow Reynolds, William Bradford, Mary Parminter Reynolds Savage, Cynthia duPont Reynolds Farris. Student, Goldey-Beacom Coll., Wilmington, Del., 1938. One-woman shows include Caldwell Inc., 1975, Nat. Museum of Women in Arts, 1998; exhibited in group shows at Corcoran Gallery, Washington, 1943, Soc. Fine Arts, Wilmington, 1937-38, 40-41, 48, 50, 62, 65, Rehoboth (Del.) Art League, 1963, NAD, N.Y.C., 1964, Pa. Mil. Coll., Chester, 1966, Del. Art Ctr., 1967, Del. Art Mus., Wilmington, Wilmington Art Mus., 1976, Met. Mus. Art, N.Y.C., 1977, Lever House, N.Y.C., 1979, Nat. Mus. Women in the Arts, Washington, 1998; represented in permanent collections Wilmington Trust Co., E.I. duPont de Nemours & Co., Children's Home, Inc., Claymont, Del., Children's Bur., Wilmington, Stephenson Sci. Ctr., Vanderbilt U., Nashville, Lutheran Towers Bldg., Travelers Aid and Family Soc. Bldg., Wilmington, bronze fountain head Longwood Gardens, Kennett Square, Pa., bronze statue Brookgreen Gardens, Murrells Inlet, S.C., bronze sculpture "Veiled Lady" , Nat. Mus. Women in Arts, Washington, 1998; contbr. articles to profl. jours. Organizer vol. svc. Del. chpt. ARC, 1938-39; chmn. Com. for Revision Del. Child Adoption Law, 1950-52; pres., bd. dirs. Children Bur. Del.; pres., trustee Children's Home, Inc.; del., past regent Gunston Hall Plantation, Lorton, Va.; mem. adv. com. Longwood Gardens, Kennett Sq., Pa.; garden and grounds com. Winterthur (Del.) Mus.; mem. rsch. staff Henry Francis DuPont Winterthur Mus., 1955-63; mem. archtl. com. U. Del., Newark. Recipient Confrerie des Chevaliers du Tastevin Clos de Vougeot-Bourgogne France, 1960; Hort. award Garden Club Am., 1964, medal of Merit, 1976, Dorothy Platt award Garden Club of Phila., 1980, Alumni medal of merit Westover Sch., Middlebury, Conn., Medal of Distinction, U. Del., 1999. Mem. Pa. Hort. Soc., Wilmington Soc. Fine Arts, Mayflower Descs., Del. Hist. Soc., Colonial Dames, League Am. Pen Women, Nat. Trust Hist. Preservation. Garden Club of Wilmington (past pres.), Garden Club of Am. (past asst. zone 4 chmn.), Vicmead Hunt Club, Greenville Country Club, Chevy Chase Club (Washington), Colony Club (N.Y.C.). Episcopalian. Address: PO Box 3919 Greenville DE 19807-0919

REYNOLDS, RAYMOND JULIAN ARTHUR (JULIAN JINGLES), writer, producer, media and marketing consultant; b. Kingston, Jamaica, July 28, 1949; came to U.S., 1972; s. Edmund A. Roy and Agatha (Lewinson) R.; m. Charmaine Jasmin Golding, Oct. 12, 1972; children: Asheba, Shaka, Kamu. Student, Kingston Coll., 1961-66. Reporter, columnist Gleaner Co., Kingston, 1967—; freelance writer, editor Everybody's mag., Bklyn., 1977-93, The Answer newsletter, Queens, N.Y., 1994-95, Jet mag., Chgo., 1994; freelance reporter The Amsterdam News, N.Y.C., 1987—; pres. Fiwi Prodns., N.Y.C., 1987—; media rels. cons. several businesses, N.Y., 1987—; prodn. mgr. serveral video prodns., 1988—; media and mktg. cons. Nat. Minority Bus. Coun., N.Y.C., 1987—; bd. dirs. 843 Studio Gallery, Bklyn., 1989-95. Author: A Reason for Living, 1996; writer, prodr. (documentary) It All Started with the Drums, 1989; writer, prodr., dir.: (documentaries) A Jamaican Gun Court, 1974, It All Started With the Drums, 1989, Jammin in Jamaica, 1996; poet: (anthology book) Voices from the Caribbean, 1996. Mem. Smithsonian, Nat. Writers Union. Episcopalian. Avocations: reading, walking, reasoning. Home: 1502 E 222nd St Bronx NY 10469-2619

REYNOLDS, ROBERT JOEL, economist, consultant; b. Indpls., May 13, 1944; s. Joel Burr and Betty (Schimpf) R.; m. Lucinda Margaret Lewis, May 27, 1979; children: Joel, Sarah. BSBA in Fin., Northwestern U., 1965, PhD in Econs., 1970. Asst. prof. econs. U. Idaho, Moscow, 1969-73, assoc. prof., 1973-75; asst. dir, sr. economist econ. policy office Dept. Justice, Washington, 1973-81; sr. economist, v.p. ICF Inc., Washington, 1981-87, sr. v.p., 1987-91; exec. v.p., prin. Econsult Corp., Washington, 1991-96; chmn., exec. v.p. Econsult of D.C., Inc., Washington, 1997, Competition Econs., Inc., Washington, 1997—; vis. assoc. prof. U. Calif., Berkeley, 1976-77, Cornell U., Ithaca, N.Y., 1981; chmn. Competition Econs., Inc., Washington, 1997—. Reviewer: NSF, Rand Jour. of Econs., Internat. Econ. Rev., Internat. Jour. Indsl. Orgn., Jour. Indsl. Econs., Am. Econ. Rev.; mem. editorial bd. Managerial and Decision Econs.; contbr. numerous papers to profl. jours. Recipient Dow Jones award Wall St. Jour., 1965; AT&T grantee, 1971-72, Brookings Instl. grantee, 1968-69; NDEA fellow, 1965-69. Mem. AAAS, IEEE (computer sect.), SIAM, Am. Math. Assn., Am. Econ. Assn., Econometric Soc., Royal Econ. Soc., Am. Statis. Assn., European Assn. for Rsch. in Indsl. Econs., Soc. for the Promotion of Econ. Theory, Math. Assn. Am. Congregationalist. Home: PO Box 59712 Potomac MD 20859-9712 Office: Econsult Corp 901 15th St NW Ste 370 Washington DC 20005-2327

REYNOLDS, RONALD DAVISON, family physician; b. Boston, July 31, 1958; s. Orland Bruce and Moira (Davison) R.; m. Diana May Prieur; children: Brittany, Andrew, Avery, Isabelle. BS in Biochemistry, No. Mich. U., 1980; MD, U. Mich., 1984. Bd. cert. family practice. Resident family practice Flower Meml. Hosp., Sylvania, Ohio, 1984-87; family physician New Richmond (Ohio) Family Practice, 1987—; instr. family medicine U. Cin. Coll. Medicine, 1988-98, asst. prof., 1996-98, assoc. prof., 1999—; ctr. dir. New Richmond Family Practice, 1993—; mem. quality assurance com. So. Ohio Health Svcs. Network, Cin., 1993—; mem. Tri Health steering com. for computerized med. records, 1996-97; faculty Nat. Procedures Inst., Midland, Mich., 1996-98; beta tester Logician Internet, Med. Logic Corp., 1999—; mem. logician internet clin. adv. team Bur. of Primary Healthcare, 2000—; presenter in field. Reviewer Am. Family Physician, Jour. Family Practice, Mosby-Year Book Publishers; contbr. chpts. to books and articles to profl. jours. Fellow Am. Acad. Family Physicians; mem. Ohio Acad. Family Physicians, Southwestern Ohio Soc. Family Physicians, Assn. for Voluntary Surg. Contraception. Achievements include; development of Modified U. technique of Norplant removal; trainer in No-scalpel vasectomy; coined Limbic Dysfunction to describe depressive illness; discovered way to reverse antidepressant-induced sexual dysfunction; authority on Mogen technique of circumcision; discovered danger in using common slaine solution for breathing treatments. Office: New Richmond Family Practice 1050 Old US 52 New Richmond OH 45157-9773

REYNOLDS, ROY ERNEST, artist, sculptor; b. Idaho Falls, Idaho; s. Von Jefferson and Wanda Louise (Helm) R.; m. Monnette Louise Ashton, Aug. 6, 1976; children: Christopher, Cassidy, Zachary. Student, U. Idaho, 1959-60, Art Ctr. Sch., L.A., 1962-63. Artist, designer Magpie Studios, Idaho Falls, 1975—; artist EG&G Idaho, Idaho Falls, 1978-95, Lockheed Martin, Idaho Falls, 1995-99, Bechtel Corp., Idaho Falls, 1999—; artist, art dir. Carole King, Hollywood, Calif., 1975-78. Artist/art dir. (album design) Simple Things, 1977; artist (sculptures/mural) Bank of Idaho, 1996, (political cartoons) The Post Register, 1997-98. Active Nat. Alliance for the Mentally Ill, Idaho Falls, 1999. Recipient Best of Show awards Ea. Idaho State Fair, Blackfoot, 1979, Internat. Graphics Instn., Balt., 1979, awards of excellence Soc. Tech. Comm., Salt Lake City, 1980—. Mem. Eagle Rock Art Guild (v.p. 1997-98). Democrat. Avocations: cowboy, bonsai, goldfish, antique autos. Home: 3040 Gustafson Cir Idaho Falls ID 83402-4639

REYNOLDS, RUTH CARMEN, school administrator, secondary school educator; b. Dec. 30; d. Jim and Beulah Eliza (Woods) R. BS in Math., Chgo. State U., 1973, BS in Acctg., 1983, MS in Edn., 1986; MA in Math. Edn., DePaul U., 1991. Cert. tchr., high sch. math., gen. adminstrv. Tchr. Chgo. Pub. Schs., 1973—; adminstrv. asst. South Shore Cmty. Acad., Chgo., 1995-96, registrar, 1995-96, dir. scheduling, grade coord., 1995-96; dir. scheduling, registrar Phillips H.S. Acad., Chgo., 1996-97; adminstrv. asst. Harper H.S., Chgo., 1997—; adj. prof. Columbia Coll., Chgo., 1988-89; program officer Lindblom Tech. H.S., Chgo., 1985-95; mem. symposium com. Chgo. Pub. Schs. Student Sci. Fair, Inc.; mem. Ill. Jr. Sci. Fair, Inc. Contbr. articles to profl. jours. Treas. Chgo. Chpt. NAAF, 1988, nat. phone contact. Frye Found. Math. fellow U. Chgo., 1991. Mem. ASCD, Nat. Coun. Tchrs. Math., Ill. Coun. Tchrs. Math. (del. to Japan 1988), Nat. Coun. Suprs. Math., Notaries Assn. Ill., Benjamin Banneker Assn., Andover-Dartmouth Urban Tchr. Inst., Exeter Math. Inst., Nat. Afro-Am. Hist. and Geneal. Soc., Patricia Liddell Rschrs., Afro-Am. Geneal. and Hist. Soc. Chgo. (bd. dirs.), Afro-Am. Hist. & Geneal. Soc. Washington, Nat. Coun. Negro Women, Met. Math. Club Chgo., Daus. of Union Vets. of the Civil War 1861-1865 (mem. Sarah M.W. Sterling Tent # 3), U.S. Colored Troops Inst. for Local History and Family Rsch., Internat. Soc. of Sons and Daus. of Slave Ancestry, Phi Delta Kappa. Avocations: reading mystery novels, travel, genealogy. Home: 2901 S King Dr Apt 1802 Chicago IL 60616-3315 Office: Harper High Sch 6520 S Wood St Chicago IL 60636-3098

REYNTJENS, FILIP LODEWIJK, law and politics educator; b. Antwerp, Belgium, June 14, 1952; s. André J. and Christiane M. (Poucet) R. LLB, U. Antwerp, 1972, LLM, 1975, PhD, 1983; LLM, U. London, 1979. Lectr. law U. Rwanda, 1976-78; lectr. law U. Antwerp, 1978-90, prof. law, 1991—; prof. law U. Leuven, Belgium, 1986—; lectr. law U. Brussels, 1992—; chmn. Belgian Assn. Africanists, 1984-88; v.p. Internat. Third World Legal Studies Assn., N.Y.C., 1989—;. Author: Pouvoir et Droit au Rwanda, 1985, Burundi 1972-1988. Continuitè et changement, 1989, L'Afrique des grands lacs en crise, 1994, Rwanda. Trois jours qui ont fait basculer l'histoire, 1996, La guerre des grands lacs, 1999. Mem. Royal Acad. Overseas Scis. (Belgium). Home: Keizerstraat 84, 2000 Antwerp Belgium Office: Inst Devel Polity & Mgmt, Middelheimlaan 1, 2020 Antwerp Belgium

REZA, ALI, mechanical engineer, consultant; b. Bombay, Mar. 23, 1964; came to U.S., 1982; s. Amir and Naushina (Sajanlal) A.; m. Fawzia Reza, Jan. 8, 1989; children: Tania Fatima, Sonia Fatima. BSME, Princeton U., 1986; MSME, Stanford U., 1988. Registered profl. mech. engr. Calif., Ariz. From engr. to sr. mng. engr. Failure Analysis Assocs., Menlo Park, Calif., 1988-98, prin. engr., 1999—; cons. to over fifty Fortune 500 companies; rsch. assoc. Stanford U., 1987-88. Princeton U. scholar, 1982-86, Aga Khan scholar, 1987-88. Mem. ASME. Intl. Soc. Explosives Engrs., Nat. Fire Protection Assoc., Combustion Inst., Mensa, Sigma Xi. Achievements include more than 100 technical reports to clients with investigations on fires and explosions product design, engineering failure; appearances on NBC, CBS, and ABC television; expert witness in large loss fire and explosion cases, co-authored report to Congress Ammonium nitrate and detonability and effect of additives. Home: 539 Castlebrook Ct Sunnyvale CA 94087 Office: Exponent Failure Analysis Assoc 149 Commonwealth Dr Menlo Park CA 94025-1133

REZAIAN, MOHAMAD ALI, scientist; b. Fassa, Fars, Iran, July 29, 1945; arrived in Australia, 1983; s. Bozorg Rezaian and Iran Shariati; m. Mitra Iraji, Aug. 3, 1978; children: Pouria, Nimah. BSc, Tehran (Iran) U., 1968, MSc, 1970; PhD, U. Adelaide, Australia, 1975. Asst. prof. Shiraz (Iran) U., 1975-80, chmn. dept. biology, 1978-79, assoc. prof., 1980-83; rsch. fellow U. Adelaide, 1983-85; sr. prin. scientist CSIRO, Adelaide, 1985—; vis. asst. prof. Purdue U., West Lafayette, Ind., 1979-80. Contbr. articles to profl. jours. Mgr. rural cmty.-assisted water supply project Nat. Devel. Scheme, Shiraz, 1976. Recipient Disting. Student award Ministry of Sci., Iran, 1970. Mem. AAAS, Internat. Soc. for Plant Molecular Biology, Iranian Assn. South Australia (co-founder). Avocations: hiking, woodcraft, community work. Home: 14 Sitters Memorial Dr, Burnside SA 5066, Australia Office: CSIRO Divsn Plant Industry, GPO Box 350, Adelaide SA 5001, Australia

REZCHIKOV, VICTOR GRIGORIEVICH, physicist, researcher; b. Gorky, Russia, Nov. 8, 1938; s. Gregory Ivanovich and Agaphiya Antonovna R.; m. Vera Vasiligevna Kulikova Rezchikov, Apr. 30, 1980; 1 child, Nadezhda Victorovna. D of Tech. Scis., Moscow, Russia, 1988. Student Gorky (Russia) U., 1961-66, tchr., 1966-71; engr. Enterprise Salyt, Gorky, Russia, 1971-85; chief rschr. Salyt, North Novgorod, Russia, 1985—; prof. physics Afrl. Acad., North Novgorod, Russia, 1989—. Inventor: Journal of Applied Stereoscopyigz; contbr. articles to profl. jours. Capt. Navy, 1957-61, Russia. Home: 16 Zhukovstr Flat 118, 603137 Nizhny Novgorod Russia Office: NPP Salut, Larinat, 603600 Nizhny Novgorod Russia

REZEK, FRANCISCO, judge International Court of Justice, former supreme court justice, educator; b. Cristina, Brazil, Jan. 18, 1944; s. Elias and Baget Rezek; m. Myreia de Palma Castro, Jan. 14, 1971; children: Adriana, Veronica, Francisco, João Paulo. LLB., U. Minas Gerais, Belo Horizonte, 1966; LLD, U. Paris, 1970; diploma in law, Oxford (Eng.) U., 1979. Atty. Rep. of Brazil, 1972-79, dep. atty. gen., 1979-83, justice Supreme Ct., 1983-90, 92-98; fgn. min. Dept. State, Brasilia, 1990-92; dean faculty of law U. Brasilia, 1978-79; judge Intl. Ct. of Justice (the Hague), Brussels, Netherlands, 1998—; chief justice at the High Electoral Ct., Brasilia, 1989. Author: Law of Treaties, 1984, International Law, 1989, 4th edit., 1994. Recipient Grand Cross Orders of Brazil, Argentina, Chile, Colombia, Lebanon, Tunisia, Korea, Portugal, Spain, and Italy, 1986-92. Roman Catholic. Office: Supremo Tribunal Fed, 70175 Brasilia Brazil*

REZIN, ANDREW ANTHONY, academic administrator, educator; b. Cleve., May 25, 1950; s. Andrew Frank and Josephine (Rozinka) R.; m. Michele Elizabeth Rezin, Mar. 31, 1973; children: Jennifer, Jonathan, Jessica, Jordan. BA in Mktg., Kent State U., 1972; MA in Vocat. Edn., Ohio State U., 1993, PhD in Edn., 1998. Dist. mgr. Chrysler Corp., Centerline, Mich., 1976-81; svc. dir. Bob Caldwell Chrysler-Plymouth, Columbus, Ohio, 1981-86; ops. mgr. Spitzer Columbus, 1986-87; svc. dir. David Hobbs BMW, Columbus, 1987-88; svc. mgr. Dennis Pontiac, Columbus, 1988-93; dept. chair automotive tech. Columbus State C.C., 1993-99, adminstr. automotive and applied tech., 1999—; Adv. bd. Paul C. Hayes Tech. H.S., Grove City, Ohio, 1997—, Northwest Career Ctr., Dublin, Ohio, 1997—; mem. nat. ASSET steering com. Ford Motor Co., Dearborn, Mich., 1996—. Contbr. articles to profl. jours. Chmn. Westerville Baha'i Assembly, Westerville, Ohio, 1995—. Mem. Ohio Coop. Edn. Assn. (bd. dirs.), Phi Kappa Phi, Omicron Tau Theta (bd. dirs., past pres.). Office: Columbus State Cmty Coll 550 E Spring St Columbus OH 43215-1722

REZIN, JOYCE JUNE, pediatric nurse practitioner; b. Kalamazoo, Apr. 29, 1936; d. Stephen Palc and Alexandra Kwiatkowski Salerno; m. Joseph Gerald Rezin, Feb. 15, 1958; children: Michael, William, Valerie. BSN, San Diego State U., 1971; MS, U. LaVerne, 1991. Cert. pediatric nurse practitioner; RN, Calif. Staff nurse med./surg. St. Vincent's Hosp., L.A., 1957-58; staff nurse surgery City of Hope Med. Ctr., Duarte, Calif., 1958-59; sch. nurse Sweetwater Union H.S. Dist., Chula Vista, Calif., 1973-84, San Diego Unified Sch. Dist., 1984—; guest lectr. San Diego State U. Sch. Pub. Health, 1994, 95, 96, 97. Vol. nurse Otay Cmty. Clinic, Chula Vista, 1978-79; CPR instr., ARC, Chula Vista, 1977-81, 95, 96, 97, 98, 99, 2000; sch. nurse governance team mem. San Diego Unified Sch. Dist., 1991-94, 98-2000; bd. dirs. Adult Protective Svcs., Inc., San Diego, 1995-96, 97, 98, 99, 2000; mem. outdoor phys. activities com. San Diego Unified Sch. Dist., 1998-2000; NAPNAP liaison to AAP com. on early childhood and dependent care, 1998-2000. Named Woman of Achievement, Southland Bus. and Profl. Woman's Club, 1987. Fellow Nat. Assn. Pediatric Nurse Assocs. and Practitioners (bd. dirs. San Diego chpt. 1984-85, 95—, vol. liaison to Healthy Child Care Am. Campaign 1996-97, 98, 99, 2000, vol. adv. task force Healthy Child Care Calif. 1997, liaison com. on early childhood, adoption and dependent care 1998-2000, co-chair child care spl. interest group 1998-2000); mem. Calif. Sch. Nurse Orgn. (bd. dirs. San Diego/Imperial counties chpt. 1981-86, pres. elect 2000—), Nat. Assn. Sch. Nurses. Roman Catholic. Avocations: travel, reading. Home: 10747 Viacha Dr San Diego CA 92124-3418 Office: San Diego City Schs Early Childhood Edn Program 2441 Cardinal Ln IMC San Diego CA 92123

REZNIK, LEONID CARLOVICH, engineering and information technology educator, researcher; b. St. Petersburg, Russia, Oct. 18, 1955; arrived in Australia, 1992; s. Carl and Ninel (Kaganovich) R.; m. Olga Kuftova, Dec. 6, 1982; 1 child, Dmitry. Diploma in Elec. Engring., St. Petersburg Aircraft Acad., 1978; PhD, St. Petersburg U. Tech., 1983. Engr., programmer, prin. scientist, sr. scientist Rsch. Inst. Electromeasuring Instruments, St. Petersburg, 1978-87; leading scientist Rsch. Inst. Shipbldg. Tech., St. Petersburg, 1987-88, Interguadro, Moscow, 1988-91; sr. lectr., lectr. Victoria U., Melbourne, Australia, 1992—; sr. rschr./lectr. High Certifying Commn., Russia, 1986. Author: Fuzzy Controllers, 1997; editor: Fuzzy System Design, 1998. Mem. IEEE, N.Y. Acad. Sci. and Tech. Avocations: detective stories, swimming. Office: Victoria U MCMC, PO Box 14428, Melbourne 8001 VIC, Australia

REZVANI, MOHIADDIN, radiobiologist, medical herbalist; b. Tabriz, Iran, Nov. 6, 1947; arrived in Gt. Britain, 1979; s. Abolfazl and Fatima (Sheikholeslami) R.; m. Zakieh Nadjari-Asl, Sept. 6, 1972; children: Arzu, Ida. BS, U. Tabriz, 1971; MS, U. Dundee, 1980, PhD, 1983; MA (status), U. Oxford, 1994. Radiobiologist U. Oxford (England), 1984—. Author: Fundamentals of Nuclear Medicine, 1991. Mem. British Inst. Radiology, Assn. Radiation Rsch., Nat. Inst. Med. Herbalists. Office: U Oxford Rsch Inst, Churchill Hosp, Oxford OX3 7LJ, England

RHEE, DAE-YEON, manufacturing executive; b. Seoul, Sept. 28, 1950; s. Yong-Cheol Rhee and Nang-ho Shin; m. Sang-Eun Chung, Nov. 22, 1992; children: Jung-Hoon, Jung-Min, Sun-Min. BE, Seoul Nat. U., 1976. Mgr. Kukje Machinery Co., Ltd., Ok Chun, Korea, 1981-84; mgr. product devel. Daedong Indsl. Co. Ltd., Jinju, Korea, 1976-81; gen. mgr. Daedong Indsl. Co. Ltd., Seoul, 1984-87; dir. GE Plastics Korea Mktg., Seoul, 1987-95; mng. dir. constrn. bus. divsn. EHWA Diamond Ind. Co., Ltd., O'san, Korea, 1995—. Patentee in field. Cpl. intelligence, 1971-74, Korea. Avocations: golf, photography, travel. Office: EHWA Diamond Ind Co Ltd, 520-2 Won-Dong, 447-060 Osan City/Kyungki-do Korea

RHEE, DONG-KWON, microbiology educator, researcher, pharmacist; b. Poo Yeo, Chung Nam, Korea, Mar. 28, 1953; s. Man-Seok and Mok-Ja (Do) R.; m. Myoung Ran Park, Mar. 28, 1982; children: Eun-Jung, Kyoung-Min, June-Hyeok. BS, Sung Kyun Kwan U., Seoul, Korea, 1977; MS, Korea Adv. Inst. Sci. & Tech., Seoul, Korea, 1979; PhD, U. Ill., Chgo., 1987. Cert. pharmacist, Korea. Rsch. scientist Korea Ginseng and Tobacco Rsch. Inst., Seoul, 1979-82; rsch. asst. U. Ill., Chgo., 1982-87, rsch. fellow, 1987-88; from asst. to prof. Sung Kyun Kwan U., Su Won, Korea, 1988—; acting chmn. dept. pharmacy Sung Kyun Kwan U., Su-Won, Korea, 1989-92; advisor Nat. Inst. Safety Rsch., Seoul, 1990-92; mem. Ministry Pub. Health Drug Safety Review Bd., Seoul, 1991—; fellow Yale U., Dept. Pharmacology, New Haven, Conn., 1993-94. Recipient fellowship Sung Kyun Kwan U., Seoul, 1973-75, Korean Govt., Korea Advanced Inst. Sci. and Tech., Seoul, 1977-79, U. Ill., Chgo., 1987-88. Mem. Biochem Soc. of Korea (coun. 1992-98), Pharm. Soc. Korea (sec.-gen., 1997-98, Pharmicist Assn. Seoul (chmn. bd. sci. com. 1992), Pharmicist Assn. Korea (bd. dirs. sci. com. 1992). Buddhist. Fax: 82-331-292-8800. Office: Sung Kyun Kwan U Coll Pharm, 300 Chunchun-dong, 440-746 Su-Won Kyongido, Korea

RHEE, HAE-IK, science educator; b. Chunchon, Kangwondo, South Korea, Nov. 20, 1953; s. Kwang-ryong Rhee and Ssi Kim; m. Kyeong-soon Park, Dec. 24, 1978; children: Do-young, So-young. B of Agr., Kangwon Nat. U., Chunchon, 1977, M of Agr., 1979; D of Agr., Kyoto (Japan) U., 1988. Rsch. chemist Shiga U., Otsu, Japan, 1982-83, USDA-ARS, Bozeman, Mont., 1992-93; prof. Kangwon Nat. U., Chunchon, 1989—, vice dean, 1998-00; advisor Forestry Rsch. Inst., Seoul, 1997-99. Author: Understanding of Agriculture, 1996, (with A. Kimura) Enzyme Technology, 1988; inventor in field. Sgt. Korean Army, 1979-82. Mem. Korean Soc. Applied Microbiology, Biochem. Soc. Republic of Korea, Korean Soc. Biotech. and Bioengring. Fax: 82 33 254 3835. E-mail: rheehae@kangwon.ac.kr. Office: Kangwon Nat U, Hyojadong, Chunchon Kangwondo 200-701, South Korea

RHEE, JONG-CHAN, political science educator; b. Seoul, Republic of Korea, Jan. 2, 1957; s. Hyung-Sung and Keum (Huh) R.; m. Young-Mee Lym, May 30, 1983; 1 child, Jae-June. BA, Seoul Nat. U., 1982, MA, 1984; PhD, U. Pa., 1991. First chief rsch. fellow Hanhwa Rsch. Ctr., Seoul, 1994-96; prof. Kookmin U., Seoul, 1996—; Am. adv. mem. Ministry Fin. and Economy. Grantee Asia Found., Seoul, 1987. Mem. Am. Polit. Sci. Assn., Internat. Polit. Sci. Assn., Korean Polit. Sci. Assn. Avocation: tennis. Home: 2-506 Sunkyung Apt, Daechi Dong Gangnam Gu, Seoul Republic of Korea Office: Kookmin U, Sungbook Gu, Seoul Republic of Korea

RHEE, SANG-KI, microbiologist, educator; b. Taegu, Republic of Korea, June 5, 1951; s. Byong-shik Rhee and In-Soon Cha; m. Young-Mee Yun, Oct. 7, 1989; children: Jung-Woo, Ji-Yoon, Jae-Woo. BS, Seoul (Republic of Korea) Nat. U., 1975; MS, Korea Advanced Inst. Sci. and Tech., Seoul, 1977, PhD, 1980. Postdoctoral rschr. U. NSW, Sydney, Australia, 1980-82; sr. scientist Korea Inst. Sci. and Tech., Seoul, 1982-87; lab. chief Genetic Engring. Rsch. Inst. Korea Inst. Sci. and Tech., Taejon, 1988-93, group leader, 1987-88; vis. assoc. scientist NIH, Bethesda, Md., 1987-88; dir. Korea Rsch. Inst. Biosci. and Biotech., Taejon, 1996-98, dir. Bioinfo. Ctr., 1997-99, v.p., 1999—, chief, microbial and bioprocess engring. lab., 2000—; CEO Bioholdings Co., Inc., Taejon, 1997—; adj. prof. Chungham Nat. U., Taejon, 1993—, Korea U., 1993-96, KAIST, 1996—. Contbr. articles to profl. jours. Nat. fellow KAIST, 1975-80; recipient Best Publ. award KRIBB, 1991. Mem. KIBB (chmn. internat. cooperation 1994-97, v.p. 1998-99), Korean Soc. for Applied Microbiology (editor 1994—), Microbiol. Soc. Korea (sec. gen. 1993-94). Avocations: music, video, skiing, travel, working out. Office: Korean Rsch Inst Biosci & Biotech, PO Box 115 Yusong, Taejon 305-600, Korea

RHEE, SUH-BONG, chemist; b. Seoul, Korea, Aug. 3, 1937; s. Suh-Gil and Young-Sook (Kwon) R.; m. Jane Jungkang Lee, Aug. 15, 1975; children: Susan Edith, Yonghee. BS, Seoul Nat. U., Korea, 1962; PhD, U. Cin., 1971. Rschr. Korea Nat. Indsl. Rsch. Inst., Seoul, 1962-64; rsch. & devel. supr. Bldg. Products Can., Rexdale, 1973-75; lab. head Korean Rsch. Inst. Chem. Tech., Taejon, 1978-95, pres., 1996—. Contbr. articles to profl. jours.; patentee in field. With Korean Army, 1958-60. Mem. Am. chem. Soc., Polymer Soc. Korea, Korea Chem. Soc. Avocations: golf, Scrabble, crossword puzzles. Home: 109-402 Hana Apt, Sinsung dong, Yusungku Taejon 305-345, Korea Office: Korea Rsch Inst Chem Tech, 100 Jang dong, Taejon 305-600, Korea

RHEE, SUNG KYU, steel company executive; b. Masan, Kyungnam, Korea, Nov. 18, 1939; s. S.T. Rhee and S.S. Lee; m. Bong Ja Jung, Jan. 16, 1969; children: Hak Jun, Hak Sung, Hak Young. BS in Engring. and Metallurgy, Seoul (South Korea) Nat. U., 1964. Rsch. engr. Korea Inst. Sci. Tech., Seoul, 1967-72; asst. gen. mgr. Sammi Steel Co., Changwon, South Korea, 1973—, sr. mng. dir., 1983, exec. v.p., 1988; pres. Sammi Steel Co., Seoul, 1992-95, Samwon Precision Metals Co., Seoul, 1996—, Sammi Metal Product Co., Changwon, 1984; exec. v.p. Sammi Corp., Seoul, 1985-87; pres. Sammi Precision Ind. Co., Seoul, 1989-91. Decorated Order of Civil Merit (Korea); recipient medal of indsl. achievement Pres of Korea, 1978, citation Korean Miin. Commerce and Industry, 1991. Avocation: mountain hiking. Home: Apt Apkujung-Dong, 24-1004 Hyundai, Kangnam-ku Seoul 135-110, Republic of Korea Office: Samwon Precision Metals Co, 1688-1 Seocho-dong Tuksu Bldg, 137-070 Seocho-Ku Seoul Republic of Korea

RHEE, YOUNG, engineering educator; b. Seoul, Republic of Korea, Mar. 14, 1958; s. Bongsoo Rhee and Hyosook Shim; m. Kyeongsook Lee, May 9, 1987; 1 child, Paul. MS, Korea U., 1985, U. Okla., 1990; PhD, N.C. State U., 1995. Sr. mgr. Samsung SDS, Seoul, 1995-98; prof. Keimyung U., Taegu, Republic of Korea, 1998—. Fax: 82-53-583-3092. Home: 1332 moojige apt. 102-308, Egok-dong Dalseo-gu, Taege 704-140, Republic of Korea Office: Keimyung U, 1000 Shindang-dong Dalseo-gu, Taegu 704-701, Republic of Korea

RHEINBERG, FALKO, psychologist; b. Parchim, Germany, May 14, 1945; s. Otto and Berta (Tegeler) R.; m. Antje Schulte, Dec. 18, 1970. Diploma in psychology, Ruhr U., Bochum, Germany, 1973, PhD, 1977, Dr.habil., 1983. Cons. psychologist Friedrich Krupp GmbH, Essen, Germany, 1973; rschr. U. Bochum, Germany, 1973-83; prof. U. Heidelberg, Germany, 1983-95, U. Potsdam, Germany, 1995—. Author: Achievementevaluation and Motivation to Learn, 1980, Purpose and Action, 1989, Enhancing Motivation in Schools, 1993, 2d edit., 1999, Motivation, 1995, 3d edit., 2000; editor German Jour. Ednl. Psychology, 1987-93; contbr. articles to profl. jours. Lt. German Mil., 1965-67. Fellow Deutsche Gesellschaft Psychologie, Arbeitsgruppe empirisch-padagogischer Forschung. Avocations: windsurfing, snowboarding. Home: Bulser Str 21, 45964 Gladbeck Germany Office: Inst Psychology U Potsdam, Am Neuen Palais 10, 14415 Potsdam Germany

RHEINBERGER, HANS JOERG, scientist, historian of science; b. Grabs, Switzerland, Jan. 12, 1946; s. Rudolf and Brigitte (Ludwig) R.; m. Ineke Phaf, July 27, 1979. MA in Philosophy, Free U., Berlin, 1973, diploma biology, 1979, Dr.rer.nat., 1982. Rsch. scientist Max Planck Inst. for Molecular Genetics, Berlin, 1982-90; asst. prof. U. Luebeck, Germany, 1990-94; assoc. prof. U. Salzburg, Austria, 1994-97; scientist, historian of sci. Max Planck Inst. for the History of Sci., Berlin, 1997—. Author: Toward a History of Epistemic Things, 1997. Fellowship Inst. for Advanced Study, 1993-94, Collegium Helveticum, 2000. Mem. Berlin-Brandenburg Acad. of Sci. Office: Max Planck Inst Hist Sci, Wilhelmstr 44, D-10117 Berlin Germany

RHEINHEIMER, MARTIN, historian, educator; b. Reinbek, Germany, Oct. 31, 1960; s. Gerhard Wilhelm and Ellen Herta Liddie (Remer) R. Student, Christian Albrechts U., Kiel, Germany, 1980-84, 85-89, Aristoteles U., Thessaloniki, Greece, 1984-85; PhD, Christian Albrechts U., 1989; Cert. in Tchg., Christian-Albrechts U., Kiel, 1998. Rschr. Schleswig-Holsteinische Landesbibliothek, Kiel, 1993-95; lectr., rschr. Christian Albrechts U., 1995-99; assoc. prof. U. So. Denmark, Esbjerg, 1999—. Author: The Crusaders' Principality of Galilee, 1990, Carnevale passato, 1991, Bibliography of the Economic and Social History of Schleswig-Holstein, 1997, The Village By-laws in the Duchy of Schleswig, 1999, Poar, Beggaro and Vaprants, 2000; editor: Subjective Worlds, 1998, The Passage Through the World, 2000; editor Newsletter of the Study Group of Economic and Social History of Schleswig-Holstein, 1993—; co-editor Psychohist. Rsch., 1999—, The Psychohistory of Experience, 2000; contbr. over 30 articles to profl. jours. Univ. tchg. qualification scholar Deutsche Forschungsgemeinschaft, 1995-98. Mem. Arbeitskreis für Wirtschafts-und Sozialgeschichte Schleswig-Holsteins (sec. 1992—), German Assn. Psychohist. Rsch. (vice-chmn. 1999—). Avocation: poetry. Home: Ulvevej 8, DK-6715 Esbjerg N Denmark Office: U So Denmark, Niels Bohrs Vej 9, DK 6700 Esbjerg Denmark

RHEINISH, ROBERT KENT, university administrator; b. Mt. Vernon, N.Y., Oct. 27, 1934; s. Walter Washington and Doris Elizabeth (Standard) R.; m. Dorothy Ellen Steadman, May 3, 1957 (div. 1976); children: Robert Scott, Joel Nelson; m. Shirley Marie Suter, Aug. 1, 1976. BA, U. South Fla., 1963; MS, Ind. U., 1969, EdD, 1971. Staff engr. Armed Forces Radio & TV Svc., Anchorage, 1960-61; trainee Nat. Park Svc. Tng. Ctr., Grand Canyon, Ariz., 1965; historian Home of F.D.R., Nat. Historic Site, Hyde Park, N.Y., 1964-65, Sagamore Hill Nat. Hist. Site, Oyster Bay, N.Y., 1965-66; asst. coord. nat. environ. edn. devel. program Dept. of Interior, Washington, 1968; supervisory historian Lincoln Boyhood Nat. Meml., Lincoln City, Ind., 1966-68; dir. learning resources ctr. Whittier (Calif.) Coll., 1971-73; dir. media and learning resources Calif. State U., Long Beach, 1973-88; chmn. media dirs. The Calif. State Univs., Long Beach, 1975-76; radio announcer Sta. WTCX-FM, St. Petersburg, Fla., 1961-63; co-host with David Horowitz (2 broadcasts) On Campus, Sta. KNBC-TV, L.A., 1972-73; guest lectr. 6th Army Intelligence Sch., Los Alamitos Armed Forces Res. Ctr., 1987; founder Rheino Ltd., 1997. Coord. multi-media program: In Search of Yourself, 1975 (Silver award Internat. Film and TV Festival of N.Y.), The House that Memory Built, 1981 (Cindy award Info. Film Producers of Am.), The Indochinese and Their Cultures, 1985 (Silver award Internat. Film & TV Festival of N.Y.); holder 2 patents. With RCAF, 1954-55, USAF, 1957-61. U.S. Office of Edn. grad. fellow, 1969-71; recipient Learning Resources Ctr. Devel. Fund award Pepsico, Sears, Prentice-Hall, et al, 1973; Nat. Def. Edn. Act grantee, 1974-76. Mem. NRA, Am. Legion. Republican. Avocations: collecting militaria, boating, political writing. Home: 380 Long Br W Prescott AZ 86303-5306

RHEINSTEIN, PETER HOWARD, health care company executive, consultant, physician, lawyer; b. Cleve., Sept. 7, 1943; s. Franz Joseph Rheinstein and Hede Henrietta (Neheimer) Rheinstein Lerner; m. Miriam Ruth Weissman, Feb. 22, 1969; 1 child, Jason Edward. BA with high honors, Mich. State U., 1963, MS, 1964; MD, Johns Hopkins U., 1967; JD, U. Md., 1973. Bar: Md., D.C.; diplomate Am. Bd. Family Practice; cert. added qualifications in geriatric medicine. Intern USPHS Hosp., San Francisco, 1967-68; resident in internal medicine USPHS Hosp., Balt., 1968-70; practice medicine specializing in internal medicine, Balt., 1970—; instr. medicine U. Md., Balt., 1970-73; med. dir. extended care facilities CHC Corp., Balt., 1972-74; dir. drug advt. and labeling div. FDA, Rockville, Md., 1974-82, acting dep. dir. Office Drugs, 1982-83, acting dir. Office Drugs, 1983-84, dir. Office Drug Standards, 1984-90, dir. medicine staff Office Health Affairs, 1990-99; sr. v.p. for med. and clin. affairs Cell Works, Inc., Balt., 1999—; chmn. Com. on Advanced Sci. Edn., 1978-86, Rsch. in Human Subjects Com., 1990-92; adj. prof. forensic medicine George Washington U., 1974-76; WHO cons. on drug regulation Nat. Inst. for Control Pharm. and Biol. Products, China, 1981-90; advisor on essential drugs WHO, 1985-90; FDA del. to U.S. Pharmacopeial Conv., 1985-90, coord. com. for assessment and transfer of tech. NIH, 1990-99, mem. health care fin. adminstrn. tech. adv. com., 1990-98, Nat. Adv. Coun. on Healthcare Policy, Rsch. and Evaluation, 1990-99, Healthy People 2000/2010 Steering Com., 1990-99, CDC and Prevention Task Force on Cmty. Preventive Svcs., 1996-99, Nat. Task Force on Industry/Provider CME Collaboration, 1992—; cons. in legal medicine and regulatory affairs, 1999—. Co-author: (with others) Human Organ Transplantation, 1987; spl. editorial advisor Good Housekeeping Guide to Medicine and Drugs, 1977-80; mem. editorial bd. Legal Aspects Med. Practice, 1981-89, Drug Info. Jour., 1982-86, 91-95; contbr. articles to profl. jours. Recipient Commendable Svc. award FDA, 1981, Group award of merit, 1983, 88, Group Commendable Svc. award 1989, 92, 93, 95, 99, Commr.'s Spl. citation, 1993. Fellow Am. Coll. Legal Medicine (bd. govs. 1983-93, treas., chmn. fin. com. 1985-88, 90-91, chmn. publs. com. 1988-93, jud. com. 1993-95; Pres.'s awards 1985, 86, 89, 90, 91, 93), Am. Acad. Family Physicians; mem. Am. Acad. Pharm. Phys. (bd. trustees 1999—, v.p. AMA rels. 1999—), AMA, ABA, Drug Info. Assn. (bd. dirs. 1982-90, pres. 1984-85, 88-89, v.p. 1986-87, chmn. ann. meeting 1991, 94, steering com. Ams. 1991—, Outstanding Svc. award 1990), Fed. Bar Assn. (chmn. food and drug com. 1976-79, Disting Svc. award 1977), Med. and Chirurgical Faculty Md., Balt. City Med. Soc., Johns Hopkins Med. and Surg. Assn., APHA, Md. Bar Assn., Math. Assn. Am., Soc. Indsl. and Applied Math., Mensa (life), U. Md. Alumni Assn. (life), Fed. Exec. Inst. Alumni Assn. (life), Johns Hopkins U. Alumni Assn., Mich. State U. Alumni Assn. (life), Mich. State U. Honors Coll. Alumni Assn. (bd. dirs. 1998—, pres. 2000—), Chartwell Golf and Country Club, Annapolis Yacht Club, Johns Hopkins Club, Delta Theta Phi (life). Avocations: boating, electronics, physical fitness, real estate investments. Home: 621 Holly Ridge Rd Severna Park MD 21146-3520 Office: Cell Works Inc U Md Balt County TEC I Bldg 5202 Westland Blvd Baltimore MD 21227-2349

RHEINTGEN, LAURA DALE, research center official; b. Takoma Park, Md., July 13, 1962; d. Robert William and Ethel Frances (Snyder) Schiedel. BA in Internat. Studies and German, W.Va. U., 1984; MA in Internat. Affairs, Am. U., 1988. Rsch. asst. Brookings Instn., Washington, 1986; staff cons. Birch & Davis Assocs., Inc., Silver Spring, Md., 1988-89; devel. analyst Ctr. for Strategic and Internat. Studies, Washington, 1989-92, mgr. devel. rsch. and records, 1992-93; asst. dir. devel. Ctr. for Strategic and Internat. Studies, 1994-95, dir. found. rels., 1995-97; assoc. dir. devel. Aspen Inst., Washington, 1997-98; devel. assoc. Nat. Acad. Scis., Washington, 1998-99, devel. officer, 1999; devel. dir. Am. Inst. Contemporary German Studies, Johns Hopkins U., Washington, 1999—. Mem. Women in Internat. Security Studies, German Lang. Soc. Office: Am Inst Contemporary German Studies Johns Hopkins U 1400 16th St NW Ste 420 Washington DC 20036-2216

RHEINWALD, GOETZ, curator; b. Landsberg, Poland, Apr. 29, 1936; s. Hans and Edith (Bieneck) R.; m. Ingrid Wahl; children: Frank, Bärbel. Grad. tchr., Tech. U., Stuttgart, Germany, 1964; PhD, U. Hamburg, Germany, 1967. Sci. asst. Max-Planck Assn., Radolfzell, Germany, 1966-70; curator Zool. Rsch. Inst. and Mus. A. Koenig, Bonn, Germany, 1970—; head German sect. Internat. Coun. Bird Preservation, Radolfzell, 1981-90; chief atlas working group European Bird Census Coun., 1993-96. Author: Brutvogelatlas der Bundesrepublik Deutschland, 1982, Atlas der Verbreitung und Haufigkeit der Brutvögel Deutschlands, 1993, Menschsein-biologische Aspekte einsichtigen Handelns, Ginster-Verlag, 1999. Recipient Golden Hon. Needle, Naturschutzbund Deutschland, Hannover, Germany, 1997. Mem. Am. Ornithology Union, British Ornithology Union, Deutsche Ornithology Assn. (coun. mem. 1973-75). Avocations: bee-keeper, gardening. E-mail: g.rheinwald.zfmk@uni-bonn.de.

RHI, SANG-KYU, lawyer, educator; b. Namwon, Cheon-buk, Republic Korea, July 1, 1933; s. Byong-Choon and Pil-Soon (Huh) R.; m. Hyo-Sook Kim, June 4, 1956; children: Eun-Sook, Jihn-u, Eun-Yong, Jihn-Soo. LLB, Chongchy Coll., 1955; LLM, So. Meth. U., 1961; postgrad., Nottingham (Eng.) U., 1966-67; LLD (hon.), Harding U., 1992, Taegoo U., 1999. Legislating officer Office Legislation, Republic Korea, 1961-67; pres. Korea Environ. Law Assn., Seoul, 1977-83; vice min. Ministry Edn., Republic Korea, 1980; lawyer Rhi Law Offices, Seoul, 1981—; prof. Coll. Law Korea U., Seoul, 1982-94; rep. Korea Legal Ctr., Seoul, 1989-93. Author: American Administrative Law, 1962, Administrative Law, 1965, Law of Administrative Remedy, 1985, State Liability and Compensation, 1995. 1st Lt. Republic Korea army, 1957-58. Recipient Presdl. commendation Govt. Korea, 1963, Red-Stripe Keunjeong medal, 1971. Mem. Seoul Bar Assn. (chmn. legis. com. 1989-91, Commendation Merit 1990), Korea Bar Assn. (exec. dir. 1991-93, bd. dirs. 1994—, pres. Tng. Inst. for Lawyers 1997—), Inter-Pacific Bar Assn. (mem. coun. 1995—), Internat. Bar Assn., Lawasia (mem. coun. 1995-97). Avocations: golf, classical music. Fax: 82 2 753 3029. E-mail: rhilaw@netsgo.com. Home: 2-201 Asia Athletes Apt, 86 Jamshil 7-dong Songpa-ku, Seoul 138-227, Republic of Korea Office: Rhi Law Offices Ste 1153, KCCI BLDG 45 Namdaemunro 4ka, Seoul 100-743, Republic of Korea

RHIEW, FRANCIS CHANGNAM, physician; b. Korea, Dec. 3, 1938; came to U.S., 1967, naturalized, 1977; s. Byung Kyun and In Sil (Lee) R.; m. Kay Kyungja Chang, June 11, 1967; children: Richard C., Elizabeth. BS, Seoul Nat. U., 1960, MD, 1964. Cert. Am. Bd. Nuclear Medicine. Intern St. Mary's Hosp., Waterbury, Conn., 1967-68; resident in radiology and nuclear medicine L.I.U.-Queens Hosp. Ctr., N.Y., 1968-71; instr. radiology W. Va. U. Sch. Medicine, Morgantown, 1971-73; mem. staff Mercy Hosp. and Moses Taylor Hosp. Scranton, Pa., 1973—; also dir. nuclear medicine; clin. instr. Temple U., 1987—; pres. Radiol. Consultants, Inc., 1984—, F.C.R. Co. Chmn., CEO Francis and Kay Rhiew Charitable Found. With M.C., Korean Army, 1964-67. Recipient Minister of Health and Welfare award, 1963. Mem. AMA, Soc. Nuclear Medicine, Radiol. Soc. N.Am., Am. Coll. Nuclear Medicine, Am. Coll. Radiology, Am. Inst. Ultra Sound, Country Club Scranton, Pres.'s Club U. Scranton, Elks. Home: 14 Lakeside Dr Clarks Summit PA 18411-9419 Office: 746 Jefferson Ave Scranton PA 18510-1624

RHIM, JOHNG SIK, physician, educator, medical researcher; b. Kwang Ju, Korea, July 24, 1930; came to U.S., 1958; s. Hac Woon and Moo Duc (Choi) R.; m. Mary Margaret Lytle, Aug. 24, 1930; children: Jonathan, Christopher, Peter, Andrew, Michael, Kathleen. MD, Seoul (Korea) Nat. U., 1957. Intern Seoul Nat. U. Hosp., 1958; rsch. fellow Children's Hosp. Rsch. Found., Cin., 1958-60, Baylor U. Coll. Medicine, Houston, 1961; rsch. assoc. Grad. Sch. Pub. Health, U. Pitts., 1962, La. State U. Acad. Medicine, New Orleans, 1962-64; vis. scientist Nat. Inst. Allergy and Infectious Diseases, NIH, Bethesda, Md., 1964-66; project dir. cancer rsch. Microbiol. Assocs., Bethesda, Md., 1966-78; sr. investigator Nat. Cancer Inst., NIH, Bethesda, 1978-98; assoc. dir. Ctr. for Prostate Disease Rsch., Dept. of Def., Bethesda, 1999—; adj. prof. Georgetown U. Med. Ctr., Washington, 1988—. Editor: Neoplastic Transformation in Human Cell Culture, 1991, 94, 99; mem. editl. bd. Internat. Jour. Oncology; contbr. articles to profl. jours., chpts. to books; patentee in field. Mem. AAAS, AMA, Am. Assn. Cancer Rsch., Am. Soc. Virology, Soc. Exptl. Biology and Medicine, Internat. Assn. Leukemia Rsch. Home: 11455 S Glen Rd Potomac MD 20854-1851 Office: CPDR ancer Inst Uniformed Svcs Univ Health 4301 Jones Bridge Rd Bethesda MD 20814-4712

RHIMES, RICHARD DAVID, civil engineer; b. Dromana, Victoria, Australia, June 2, 1947; s. Ernest Howard and Betty Grace (Hill) R.; m. Heather Marie Harcourt, Oct. 16, 1971; children: Timothy Harcourt, Andrew David, Anthony Jon. Diploma in Civil Engring., Caulfield Inst. Tech., 1969; B in Engring., U. Tasmania, Australia, 1980; Diploma in Indsl. mgmt., Swinburne Coll. Tech., Burwood, Australia, 1974. Cert. profl. engr., 1975, mcpl. engr., 1980, mcpl. bldg. surveyor, 1979, cert. safety profl., 1992. With Mobil Oil Australia, 1973-99; environ. health and safety advisor Mobil Oil Corp., Fairfax, Va., 1990-91; risk assessment advisor Mobil Oil Corp., Princeton, N.J., 1991-93; consulting risk engr. Mobil OilAustralia, Melbourne, 1993-95; mgr. risk assesment Mobil Oil Australia, Altona, Australia, 1995-98, mgr. EHS projects and customer svc., 1998-99; with ExxonMobil, 2000—; regional risk coord. Melbourne Asia Pacific Region, 2000—; mem. telecommunications com. Inst. Traffic Engrs., U.S., 1975; chmn. safety com. Australia Inst. Petroleum, Australia, 1989, chmn. security com. 1989. Recipient Safety Auditor award Internat. Loss Control Inst., 1988. Fellow Australian Inst. Mgmt. (assoc.); mem. Am. Soc. Civil Engrs., Australian Inst. Risk Mgrs., Australian Inst. Engrs. Office: Mobil Oil Australia, Corner Millers & Kororoit Creek Rds, Altona 3018, Australia

RHINE, KELLY ANNE, secondary education educator; b. Ft. Ord, Calif., June 9, 1966; d. Edward V. and Sandra J. (Berthiaume) R.; m. Carmine J. Pellicone (div. Dec. 1990). BS in Elem. Edn. and Spl. Edn., St. Thomas Aquinas Coll., Sparkill, N.Y., 1989; MS in Spl. Edn., SUNY, New Paltz, 1995. Part-time tchr. Spanish and French St. Peter's Elem. Sch., Haverstraw, N.Y., 1987-88; part-time resource rm. tchr. Warwick (N.Y.) Valley Schs., 1989; tchr. multiply handicapped Assn. for the Help of Retarded Children Presch., Middletown, N.Y., 1989; resource rm. tchr. Beacon (N.Y.) City Schs., 1989-90; spl. educator Fallsburg (N.Y.) Ctrl. Schs., 1990-92, West Park (N.Y.) Union Free Sch. Dist., 1993-94; presch. home worker, classroom tchr. Western Orange Cty. Head Start, Middletown, 1994-96; spl. educator rehabilitating teens DAYTOP Village Secondary Sch., Millbrook, N.Y., 1996-98; spl. educator grades 6, 7, 8 Valley Ctrl. Schs., Montgomery, N.C., 1998—; spl. educator incarcerated youth N.Y. State Divsn. Youth, 1993, 95, 96, 99; Adkins life skills educator DAYTOP, Millbrook, 1997—. Vol. tchr., writer curriculum Latino Coalition of Middletown, 1994-96. Recipient cert. of appreciation Blythdale Children's Hosp., Valhalla, N.Y., 1988, outstanding tchr. award N.Y. State Divsn. Youth, 1996. Mem. ASCD, Nat. Head Start Assn., N.Y. State Spl. Educators, N.Y. State Reading Coun., N.Y. State Unified Tchrs., The Nature Conservancy, Audubon Soc. Am. (theater devel. fund vol.), Ulster County Reading Coun., Smithsonian Inst., Museum of Natural History, ANYSEED, Assn. of N.Y. Spl. Educators of the Emotionally Disturbed. Democrat. Roman Catholic. Home: 25 Sheldon Rd Wallkill NY 12589-3324

RHO, MANNQUE, theoretical physicist, researcher; b. Hamyang, Kyung Nam, Korea, Dec. 14, 1936; s. Byung-Serk and Nam-Soon (Baick) R.; m. Helga Rosalinde Heldeis, June 14, 1965; 1 child, Oliver. AB, Clark U., 1960; PhD, U. Calif., Berkeley, 1964. Prof. Commissariatà l'Energie Atomique Saclay, Gif-sur-Yvette, France, 1965—; vis. prof. CERN, 1969-70, SUNY, Stony Brook, 1973-74, 78-79, 82-83, 88-89, U. Nagoya, Japan, 1988, Seoul Nat. U., Korea, 1990; Humboldt award prof. GSI, Darmstadt, Germany, 1995, Korea Inst. for Advanced Study, 1998-2000, Tech. U. Munich, 1996. Author: Chiral Nuclear Dynamics, 1996; editor: Mesons in Nuclei, 1979; contbr. more than 200 articles to profl. jours. Decorated Nat. Order of Merit (Republic of Korea); recipient Paul Langerin prize, 1985, Alexander von Humboldt prize Humboldt Found., 1995, Nat. Acad. Scis. of Korea prize, 1999. Mem. French Phys. Soc., N.Y. Acad. Sci., Korean Acad. Scis. and Tech. Avocations: skiing, hiking. Home: 27 Ave Auguste Renoir, 78160 Marly-le-Roi France Office: Svc de Physique Theorique, CEA Saclay, 91191 Gif-sur-Yvette France

RHOADS, GEORGE GRANT, medical epidemiologist; b. Phila., Feb. 11, 1940; s. Jonathan Evans and Teresa (Folin) R.; m. Frances Ann Secker, June 5, 1965; children: Thomas C., James E. MD, Harvard U., 1965; MPH, U. Hawaii, 1970. Intern Hosp. of U. Pa., Phila., 1965-66, resident in internal medicine, 1966-68; resident in preventive medicine U. Hawaii Sch. Pub. Health, 1968-71; epidemiologist Japan-Hawaii Cancer Study, Honolulu, 1974-75; assoc. prof. U. Hawaii, Honolulu, 1974-79, chair dept. pub. health sci., 1978-81, dir. gen. preventive medicine, 1978-81, prof. pub. health, 1979-82; chief epidemiology br. Nat. Inst. Child Health and Human Devel./NIH, Bethesda, Md., 1982-89; prof., dir. grad program in pub. health U. Medicine and Dentistry N.J.-Robert Wood Johnson Med. Sch., Piscataway, 1989—. Contbr. more than 160 articles on the epidemiology of non-infectious diseases to profl. jours. Recipient Dirs. award NIH, 1987, EEO award NICHD, 1984. Fellow Am. Coll. Physicians; mem. Am. Epidemiol. Soc. Mem. Soc. of Friends. Achievements include research on the protective effect of high density Lipoprotein in the blood against development of heart attacks. Office: Environ and Occupl Health Scis Inst 170 Freinghuysen Rd Piscataway NJ 08854

RHOADS, JONATHAN EVANS, surgeon; b. Phila., May 9, 1907; s. Edward G. and Margaret (Ely Paxson) R.; m. Teresa Folin, July 4, 1936 (dec. 1987); children: Margaret Rhoads Kendon, Jonathan Evans Jr., George Grant, Edward Otto Folin, Philip Garrett, Charles James; m. Katharine Evans Goddard, Oct. 13, 1990. BA, Haverford Coll., 1928, DSc (hon.), 1962; MD, Johns Hopkins U., 1932; D. Med. Sci., U. Pa., 1940, LLD (hon.), 1960; DSc (hon.), Swarthmore Coll., 1969, Hahnemann Med. Coll., 1978, Duke U., 1979, Med. Coll. Ohio, 1985; DSc (Med.) (hon.), Med. Coll. Pa., 1974, Georgetown U., 1981, Yale U., 1990; LittD (hon.), Thomas Jefferson U., 1979. Diplomate Am. Bd. Surgery (mem. 1963-69, sr. mem. 1969—). Intern Hosp. of U. Pa., 1932-34, fellow, instr. surgery, 1934-39; assoc. surgery, surg. research U. Pa. Med. Sch., Grad. Sch. Medicine, 1939-47, asst. prof. surg. research, 1944-47, asst. prof. surgery, 1946-47, assoc. prof., 1947-49; J. William White prof. surg. research U. Pa., 1949-51; prof. surgery Grad. Sch. Medicine, U. Pa., 1950; prof. surgery and surg. research U. Pa. Sch. Med., 1951-57, prof. surgery, 1957-59; chmn. faculty senate U. Pa., 1954-55, provost, 1956-59, provost emeritus, 1977—, John Rhea Barton prof. surgery, chmn. dept. surgery, 1959-72, prof. surgery, 1972—, acting dir. Harrison dept. surg. research, 1944-46, asst. dir., 1946-59, dir., 1959-72; chief surgery Hosp. U. Pa., 1959-72, chmn. med. bd., 1959-61; dir. surgery Pa. Hosp., 1972-74; surg. cons. Pa. Hosp., Germantown (Pa.); mem. staff Hosp. of U. Pa.; mem. bd. pub. edn., City of Phila., 1965-69; co-chmn. Phila. Mayor's Commn. on Health Aspects of Trash to Steam Plant, 1986, mem. chief justice Pa. Com. on Phila. Traffic Ct.; former mem. bd. mgrs. Haverford Coll., chmn., 1963-72, pres. corp., 1963-78, emeritus bd. mgrs. 1989—; bd. mgrs. Friends Hosp. of Phila., 1952-99, emeritus, 1999—; trustee Coriell Inst. Med. Rsch., 1957-90, v.p. sci. affairs, 1964-76, life trustee, 1990—; trustee GM Cancer Rsch. Found.. 1978-98; chmn. bd. trustees Measey Found.; trustee Bryn Mawr, 1960-79; emeritus trustee, 1979—; mem. com. in charge Westtown Sch., 1962-94, emeritus, 1994; treas. Germantown Friends Sch.; cons. Bur. State Services, VA, 1963; cons. to divsn. med. scis. NIH, 1962-63; nat. adv. gen. medical scis. council USPHS, 1963; adv. council Life Ins. Med. Research Found., 1961-66, pres. Phila. div., 1955-56; chmn. adv. commn. on research on pathogenesis of cancer Am. Cancer Soc., 1956-57, del., 1956-61, dir. at large, 1965—, pres., 1969-70, past officer dir., 1970-77, hon. life mem., 1977—; chmn. surgery adv. com. Food and Drug Adminstrn., 1972-74; chmn. Nat. Cancer Adv. Bd., 1972-79; bd. dirs. Fairview Products Corp. Author, co-editor: Surgery: Principles and Practice, 1957, 61, 65, 70; author: (with J.M. Howard) The Chemistry of Trauma; mem. editl. bd. Jour. Surg. Rsch., 1960-71, Oncology Times, 1979—; co-editor: Accomplishments in Cancer research, 1979-94; editor Jour. Cancer, 1972-91, editor emeritus, 1991—, Festschrift Dedicated in Cancer, 1997; editl. bd. Annals of Surgery, 1947-77, emeritus, 1977-95, sr. 1995—, chmn. 1971-73; editl. adv. bd. Guthrie Bull., 1986—; contbr. articles to med. jours., chpts. to books; subject of biography by John Rombeau and Donna Muldoon, 1997. Trustee John Rhea Barton Surg. Found. Recipient Roswell Park medal, 1973, Papanicolaou award, 1977, Phila. award, 1976, Swanberg award, 1987, Benjamin Franklin medal Am. Philos. Soc., Medal of the Surgeon Gen. of U.S., Disting. Alumnus award U. Pa., 1993, Russell W. Richie award Friends Hosp. Phila., 1994, Presdl. award Nat. Assn. Psychiat. Health Systems, 1994, Internat. Assn. Surgical Metabolism and Nutrition award for humanism and academic excellence transmitted in surgical and nutritional edn. Internat. Assn. Surg. Metabolism and Nutrition, Mex., 1997, C.W. Hanson, Jr., MD award U. Pa. Med. Ctr., 1997; Patient Care Pavilion at Hosp. U. Pa. named in honor of Jonathan Evans Rhoads, 1994, Clarence E. Shaffrey S.J. medal 1996. Fellow AAAS (sec. med. sci. sect. 1980-86), Am. Med. Writers Assn., Am. Surg. Assn., Am. Philos. Soc. (sec. 1963-66, pres. 1976-84, Jonathan E. Rhoads lectr. endowed, 1997—), ACS (regent, chmn. bd. regents 1967-69, pres. 1971-72), Royal Coll. Surgeons (Eng.) (hon.), Royal Coll. Surgeons Edinburgh (hon.), Deutsches Gesellschaft für Chirurgie (corr.), Assn. Surgeons India (hon.), Royal Coll. Physicians and Surgeons Can. (hon.), Coll. Medicine South Africa (hon.), Polish Assn. Surgeons (hon.), Royal Coll. Surgeons in Ireland (hon.), Benjamin Franklin Fellow Royal Soc. Arts; mem. Hollandsche Maatschappij der Wetenschappen (fgn.), Am. Public Health Assn., Assn. Am. Med. Colls. (chmn. council acad. socs. 1968-69, disting. service mem. 1974—), Fedn. Am. Socs. Exptl. Biology, Am. Assn. Surgery Trauma (Fitts lectr., 1995), Am. Soc. Clin. Nutrition, Am. Trauma Soc. (founding mem., chmn. bd. dirs. 1986-94, Curtis Artz award 1996), AMA (co-recipient Goldberger award 1970, Dr. Rodman and Thomas G. Sheen award 1980), Pa. Med. Soc. (mem. jud. coun. 1991-94, vice chmn. 1994-96, chmn. 1996, Disting. Svc. award 1975), Phila. County Med. Soc. (pres. 1970, Strittmater award 1968), Coll. Physicians Phila. (v.p. 1954-57, pres. 1958-60, Disting. Svc. award 1987), Phila. Acad. Surgery (pres. 1964-66, Ann. Oration named for Jonathan E. Rhoads 1985), Phila. Physiol. Soc. (v.p. 1945-46), Am. Surg. Assn. (pres. 1972-73, Disting. Service medal, trustee found., vice chmn. 1992-96, chmn. 1997, co-recipient Flance/Karl award 1997), Pan Pacific Surg. Assn. (v.p. 1975-77), So. Surg. Assn., The Internat. Surg. Group (pres. 1958), Internat. Fedn. Surg. Colls. (v.p. 1972-78, pres. 1978-81, hon. pres. 1987—), Fellows of Am. Studies, Soc. of U. Surgeons, Soc. Clin. Surgery (pres. 1966-68), Am. Assn. for Cancer Research, Am. Chem. Soc., Am. Physiol. Soc., Coun. Biology Editors, Internat. Soc. Surgery (hon.) N.Y. Acad. Scis., Surg. Infection Soc. (pres. 1984-85), Surgeons Travel Club (pres. 1976, hon. mem.), Am. Inst. Nutrition, World Med. Assn., Am. Acad. Arts and Scis. (mem. coun. 1977-81), Inst. of Medicine (sr.), Soc. for Surgery Alimentary Tract (pres. 1967-68), Southeastern Surg. Congress, Soc. Surg. Chmn. (pres. 1966-68), Buckingham Mountain Found. (sec., treas., pres., 1996—), James IV Soc. (hon.), Halsted Soc. (hon.), Phi Beta Kappa, Alpha Omega Alpha, Sigma Xi. Clubs: Union League, Phila. (Phila.); Cosmos (Washington, award 1997); Penn (N.Y.C.). Achievements include demonstration that protein malnutrition could retard callus formation in experimental fractures and that positive nitrogen balance could be induced by intravenous feeding in protein deficient patients who could not take things by mouth. Office: 3400 Spruce St Philadelphia PA 19104-4206

RHOAN, CHESTER D., adult education educator; b. L.A., Jan. 19, 1938; s. Chester D. Rhoan and Emilie Le Barge; m. Julene Smith, Sept. 2, 1978; children: Brendan, Teresa, Nancy, Donna. BA, San Francisco State U., 1962, MA, 1966; D, Golden State U., 1984-88. Instr. Chabot Coll., Hayward, Calif., 1968—; pres. faculty senate Chabot Coll., Hayward, 1986-87. V.p. Diamond Heights Neighborhood Assn., San Francisco, 1971-72, pres., 1972-73; pres. Excelsior Dem. Club, 1992-93. Avocations: skiing, swimming, tennis. Home: 170 Trumbull St San Francisco CA 94112-1653 Office: Chabot Coll 245555 Hesperian Blvd Hayward CA 94545

RHODD, ALICE JANE MONICA, producer, script writer, educator, broadcaster; b. Montego Bay, Jamaica, Sept. 4, 1922; d. James Arthur and Johanna Matilda (Clarke) R. BSc in Early Childhood Edn., Columbia U., 1956, MA in Higher Edn., 1957; postgrad. in TV, Inner London Ednl. Authority, 1969-70. Co-prodr. Sta. WWRL, N.Y.C., 1957-59; sch. broadcast officer, edn. officer Sch. Broadcasting Svcs. Radio and TV, Jamaica, 1960-64; attachment BBC RAdio & TV Program Prodn., 1959-60, BBC Caribbean Mag. program, 1959-60; mem. TV rsch. and tng. unit U. London, 1969-70; founder, dir. Studio Workshop 4922 Inst., Montego Bay, 1986—. Author: Neither 7 Nor 11 Dyslexia: A Reading Remediation Teachers' Guidebook, 1983, ed. edit., 1994, Broadcasting Guidelines, 1990. Recipient Independence fellowship for TV to Jamaica, BBC, 1966-67, Edn. award Montego Bay C. of C., 1994, Journalism award Press Assn. of Jamaica, 1993. Mem. Jamaica Tchrs. Assn., Ret. Tchrs. Assn. Mailing: 37 St James St, Montego Bay Jamaica

RHODE, KIM, Olympic athlete; b. El Monte, CA, July 16. Recipient Bronze medal in women's skeet 1994 USASNC, bronze medal women's double trap 1995 Seoul World Cup, team Gold medal skeet, team Bronze medal double trap 1995 World Shotgun Championships, Gold medal women's double trap 1995 U.S. Olympic Festival, Gold medal women's double trap Olympic Games, Atlanta, 1996; winner Doubletrap Champion USA Shooting Nat. Championships, 1997.Spokewoman for WPRO 7 Guncleaner & Snake Oil. Mem. Safari Club Internat., Women's Sports Shooting Found. Avocations: skiing, hunting. Office: care USA Shooting One Olympic Plz Colorado Springs CO 80909

RHODES, ALICE GRAHAM, lawyer; b. Phila., June 15, 1941; d. Peter Graham III and Fannie Isadora (Bennett) Graham; m. Charles Milton Rhodes, Oct. 14, 1971 (div. Apr. 21, 1997); children: Helen, Carla, Shauna. BS, East Stroudsburg U. Pa., 1962; MS, U. Pa., 1966, LLB, 1969, JD, 1970. Bar: N.Y. 1970, U.S. Dist. Ct. (so. and ea. dists.) N.Y. 1971, U.S. Ct. Appeals (2d cir.) 1971, Ky. 1983, U.S. Dist. Ct. (ea. dist.) Ky. 1985. Staff atty. Harlem Assertion Rights, Mobilization of Youth Office Econ. Opportunity, N.Y.C., 1969-70, coord. Cmty. Action Legal Svcs., 1970-72; assoc. dir. in charge of civil representation HUD Model Cities Cmty. Law Offices, N.Y.C., 1972-73; resource assoc. Commn. on Women, N.C. Dept. Adminstrn., Raleigh, 1975-76; mgr. policies and procedures Div. for Youth, N.C. Dept. Human Resources, Raleigh, 1976; petroleum atty. Ashland (Ky.), Inc. (formerly Ashland Oil, Inc.), 1980-82; corp. atty. Ashland (Ky.), Inc., 1985-87, 88-91, Ashland City Commn. Human Rights, 1993-99; bd. regents Ea. Ky. U., 1994—; mem. exec. bd., chmn. internal affairs com., academic affairs, 1997-98; asst. county atty. Jefferson County, Louisville, 1999-2000; pvt. practice Arlington, Va.; cons. Pub. Mems. Fgn. Svc., 2000—; mem. task force on sex discrimination ins. N.C. Dept. Ins., 1976; mem. Property Valuation Appeals Commn., 1994; pub. mem. selection and performance stds. review bd. Fgn. Svc., U.S. Dept. State, 1995, Fgn. Agrl. Svc. USDA, 1997; prison program planner, cons. N.Y. City Dept. Corrections, 1971; lectr. N.Y.C. Correction Acad., Riker Island, 1971; lectr. juvenile justice N.C. Law Enforcement Acad., Salemburg, 1976. Mem. usher bd. New Hope Bapt. Ch., Ashland, 1980-94; bd. dirs. YWCA Ashland, 1983-84, Ashland Heritage Pk. Commn., 1983-85; bd. dirs., budget com. United Way, Greenup County, Ashland, 1988-92; driver Meals on Wheels, Ashland, 1983-91; vol. Am. Heart Assn., 1982-91; bd. dirs. Our Lady of Bellefonte Hosp. Found. (Franciscan Sisters of the Poor), 1996-99, Ky. Coun. of Trustees, Ky. Health System, 1996-99, Carter G. Woodson Found. 1997-97, Study Afro-Am. Life and History; mem. adv. com. task force post secondary edn. Gov. of Ky.; bd. dirs. exec. com. Boyd County Dem. Women, 1996—; mem. presdl. search com. Ea. Ky. U., 1997-98; participant Ky. Gov.'s Conf. on Postsecondady Edn., 1999. Recipient Cmty. Svc. award Queens Community Corp., N.Y.C., 1972, Ashland C.C., 1986, Cmty. Svc. award NAACP, Ky.; NSF fellow, 1964, 65, ; faculty friends of Pa. scholar U. Pa., 1966-69, Reginald Heber Smith postgrad. fellow cmty. law, 1969-71; named to Hon. Order of Ky. Cols., 1989. Fellow Ky. Bar Found.; mem. AAUW (bd. dirs. Phila. chpt. 1963-65), Nat. Bar Assn., N.Y. Bar, Ky. Bar Assn. (mem. edn. law, corp. house counsel, family law, and workers compensation law sects.), Boyd County Bar Assn., Ky. Assn. Black Pub. Adminstrs., Nat. Forum Black Pub. Adminstrs., Ky. Blacks in Higher Edn., Pilot Club (exec. bd. Ashland 1983), Links, Inc., Paramount Women's Assn., Penn Club (charter mem. N.Y. chpt.), Aux. Our Lady of Bellefonte Hosp., Pub. Mems. Assn. of Fgn. Svc., Ky. Assn. Blacks in Higher Edn., Assn. Gov. Bds. Colls. and Univs. Democrat. Avocations: interior decorating, sports, dancing, gourmet cooking, gardening. Home and Office: 5300 Columbia Pike Apt 101 Arlington VA 22204-3118

RHODES, ANN FRANCES BLOODWORTH, artist, art history lecturer; b. Gadsden, Ala., Jan. 30, 1940; d. Frederick Allen and Mildred (Chunn) Bloodworth; m. Thomas Willard Rhodes, May 31, 1975; children: Mildred Ruth, Andrew James Howard. BA, Queens Coll., Charlotte, N.C., 1962; MA, Ga. State U., 1972. Computer programmer 1st Nat. Bank, Atlanta, 1962-63; child welfare aide Fulton County Dept. Family and Children Svcs., Atlanta, 1963; tchr. Brandon Hall, Atlanta, 1964-66; lectr. art history Atlanta Coll. Art, 1973-77, mem. adj. faculty, 1987-90; lectr. art history DeKalb C.C., Atlanta, 1975; vis. prof. Ga. State U., Atlanta, 1985; lectr. DAR, Atlanta, 1997. One-woman show Vines Bot. Garden, Loganville, Ga., 1998; exhibited in group shows Art South, Avondale Estates, Ga., 1995, Level II Gallery, Atlanta, 1996, Creative Arts Guild, Dalton, Ga., 1996, 97, Atelier, Atlanta, 1996 (award of merit), Atlanta Bot. Garden, 1996, Art Sta., Stone Mountain, Ga., 1996, 98, Chateau Elan, Ga., 1997, Quinlan Art Ctr., Gainesville, Ga., 1997, Opus One Gallery, Atlantz, 1997, Madison (Ga.)-Morgan Cultural Ctr., 1998 (award of merit), Roswell (Ga.) Visual Arts Ctr., 1998; represented in collections: Frameworks Gallery, Lynne Farris Gallery, Vermilion Gallery, Atlanta, Gallery One, St. Simon's Island, Ga. Chmn. St. Helena chpt. of women All Saints Ch., Atlanta, 1980, 81, 83, 98, lectr. art history, 1991—, participant numerous on-going outreach programs; chmn. Twigs svc. club Egleston Children's Hosp., Atlanta, 1985; chmn. Party with Purpose, Am. Cancer Soc., Atlanta, 1987. Recipient numerous awards for paintings. Mem. Fine Art Folio, Ansley Park Garden Club (sec. 1993-95, parliamentarian 1995-97). Democrat. Episcopalian. Avocations: reading, swimming, photography, walking, gardening. Studio: Tula K-1 75 Bennett St NW Atlanta GA 30309-5206

RHODES, BETTY FLEMING, rehabilitation services professional, nurse; b. Franklin, Pa., Nov. 28, 1920; d. John and Twyla Odella (Callen) Fleming; m. Donald Muir Cain, Dec. 31, 1952 (div.); m. Lee Chester Rhodes, June 23, 1962 (dec. Apr. 1997). RN, Allegheny Gen. Hosp., Pitts., 1942. Lic. phys. therapist, Pa. Phys. therapist Ky. Soc. for Crippled Children, Louisville, 1947-51, St. Anthony Hosp., Louisville, 1953-78. Nurse U.S. Army, 1943-45; capt. Army Nurse Corps, 1951-52. Decorated Bronze Star. Mem. Am. Phys Therapy Assn. (pres. Ky. chpt.). Roman Catholic. Home: 5 Woodland Rd Jeffersonville IN 47130-6815

RHODES, DAISY CHUN, writer, researcher, oral historian; b. Kahuku, Hawaii, Nov. 16, 1933; d. Pyung Chan Chun and Shin Ai Park; children: Joseph, Carmella, Thomas Francese. BA in Creative Writing, Eckerd Coll., 1995. Info. specialist Reconstrn. Devel. Corp., Washington, 1970; specialist indigent funding George Washington U. Hosp., Washington, 1971-74; mgr. hosp. assistance Alexandria (Va.) Hosp., 1975-79; asst. editor Employee Futures Rsch., Luray, Va., 1980-84; editor Inside Negotiations, Rochester, N.Y., 1985-87, Educators Negotiating Svc., New Port Richey, Fla., 1987-89; novelist, writer New Port Richey, 1989-95; rschr., oral historian Honolulu, 1994; writer Colorado Springs, 1995—; rschr., cons. Donna Ladd, Writer, Colorado Springs, 1996; presenter Asian Studies Conf., Honolulu (scholarly and abstract) Korean Picture Brides, Western Asian Studies Conf., Boulder, Colo., 1997; lectr. Ctr. for Korean Studies, U. Hawaii, 1998. Author: (nonfiction) Forever Long-Never End, 1990, Wahiawa Red Dirt, 1991, At Crossroads of Inspiration, 1993, Shirley Temple Feet, 1993, Remembering the Fallen, 1994, Passages to Paradise: Early Korean Immigrant Narratives from Hawaii, 1998; (play) I Know About Olympus, 1993; (novel) Eye of the Dragon (finalist Hemingway 1st Novel Competition), 1994, (scholarly and abstract) How Oral History of the First Koreans in America Advances Archival Research, 1996. Pres. Colo. Springs Friends of Aquatics, 1997—; bd. dirs. All Souls Unitarian Ch., 1998—. Recipient Work Study award for profls. Rotary Internat. Found., South Korea, 1998-99. Mem. Assn. for Asian Studies, Korea Soc., Korean Am. Women's Soc. Greater Washington (pres. 1983-84, bd. dirs. 1984—, Commendation), West Pasco Kiwanis (pres. 1990-92). Home: 1994 Copper Creek Dr Colorado Springs CO 80910-1867

RHODES, EDDIE, JR., medical technologist, phlebotomy technician, educator; b. Memphis, Apr. 14, 1955; s. Eddie Sr. and Mabel (Payne) R. AS, Shelby State C.C., Memphis, 1979; BS, Memphis State U., 1981. Cert. med. technologist. Rsch. technologist St. Jude's Children Rsch. Hosp., Memphis, 1980-81; med. lab. asst. Roche Biomedical Lab., Tucker, Ga., 1991-92; med. technologist Damon / MetPath Clin. Lab., Smyrna, Ga., 1992-93, ARC, Norcross, Ga., 1993-95, Ga. Bapt. Med. Ctr., Atlanta, 1994—; instr. microbiology Atlanta Area Tech., 1995-96; adv. bd. mem. Atlanta Area Tech., Atlanta, 1995—; blood donor specialist Civitan Regl. Blood Sys., Atlanta, 1996—; med. lab./phlebotomy program coord. W. Ga. Tech., LaGrange, 1996—. Named one of the Outstanding Young Men of Am., Atlanta, 1989. Mem. Am. Soc. Microbiology, Am. Soc. of Phlebotomy Technicians. Avocations: cycling, basketball, chess. Home: 410 Park Pl Lagrange GA 30240-1747 Office: West Ga Technical 303 Fort Dr Lagrange GA 30240-5901

RHODES, EDWARD JOSEPH, national security specialist, political scientist; b. Elmhurst, Ill., Oct. 1, 1959; s. Charles Harker Jr. and Mae Ellen (Svoboda) R.; m. Anne Catherine Case, Oct. 18, 1986 (div. June 1996). AB, Harvard U., 1980; MPA, Princeton U., 1982, PhD, 1985. Fellow Princeton (N.J.) U., 1980-84; peace studies fellow Cornell U., Ithaca, N.Y., 1984; arms control fellow Stanford U., 1984-85; Hubert H. Humphrey fellow U.S. Arms Control and Disarmament Agy., 1984-85; Paul-Henri Spaak fellow, fellow Ford program Harvard U., Cambridge, Mass., 1985-86; fellow Rutgers U., New Brunswick, N.J., 1986-88, asst. prof. polit. sci., 1986-92; assoc. prof. polit. sci. Rutgers U., New Brunswick, 1992—, dir. Ctr. Global Security and Democracy, 1997—; assoc. Ctr. Internat. Affairs Harvard U., Cambridge, Mass., 1988-89, vis. scholar Charles Warren Ctr. Studies in Am. History, 1989-90; fellow office chief naval opers. USN, Washington, 1996-97. Author: Power and Madness: The Logic of Nuclear Coercion, 1989; editor: Intenational Relations, 1992, 98; co-editor: The Politics of Strategic Adjustment: Ideas, Institutions, and Interests, 1999, Global Politics in a Changing World, 2000; mem. editl. bd. Internat. Studies Quarterly, 1999—, Defense Analysis, 2000—; contbr. articles to profl. jours. Pew fellow, 1990, Fulbright fellow U. Latvia, 2000—. Mem. Internat. Studies Assn., Internat. Studies Assn., U.S. Naval Inst., Internat. Inst. Strategic Studies. Avocation: travel, outdoor sports. Office: Rutgers U Ctr Global Security and Dem 89 George St New Brunswick NJ 08901-1411

RHODES, JAMES RICHARD, economics educator; b. Omaha, Nov. 28, 1945; s. Jack Richard and Mary Elizabeth (Doherty) R.; m. Kimie Hyoto, Dec. 27, 1980; children: John Makoto, Emi Alicia. BA, U. Wash., Seattle, 1969, MA, 1973, PhD, 1981. Tchg. asst. U. Wash., Seattle, 1974-75, tchr. assoc., 1975-76, 77-79; asst. prof. Western Wash. U., Bellingham, 1976-77, Wash. State U., Pullman, 1979-80, Kans. State U., Manhattan, 1980-88; vis. prof. Internat. U. Japan, Urasa, Niigata, Japan, 1987-88, lectr., 1988-96; assoc. prof. econs. Grad. Sch. Policy Sci., Saitama U., Urawa, Japan, 1988-91, prof., 1991—; prof. Nat. Grad. Inst. for Policy Studies, Tokyo, 1997—; lectr. Rikkyo U., Tokyo, 1992—, Japan-IMF Scholarship Program for Asia, 1993—; mem. selection com. in econs. Japan-U.S. Edn. Fulbright Commn., 1993-96. Reviewer Wall St. Rev. Books, South Salem, N.Y., 1982-87, profl. jours., 1984—; regional editor (Japan) Bus. Libr. Rev., N.Y.C., 1990—; contbr. articles to profl. jours., news media. 1st lt U.S. Army, 1969-71, Vietnam; col. USAR, 1997—, dep. chief of staff host nation activities U.S. Army Japan, 1996—. Decorated Bronze Star with two oak leaf clusters, Meritorious Svc. medal, Army commendation medal with one oak leaf cluster; Inst. Humane Studies F. Leroy Hill fellow, 1984; Internat. Edn. Found. grantee, 1988, Kellogg Found. grantee, 1984. Mem. Am. Econ. Assn., Western Econ. Assn. Internat., Civil Affairs Assn. (life), Res. Officers Assn. (life, membership chmn., sec.-treas. Far East dept. 1990-93, treas. 1993-95, pres. 1995—), 196th Light Inf. Brigade Assn. (life), Americal Divsn. Vets. Assn. (life), Assn. Asia Studies, Nat. Eagle Scout Assn. (life), U. Wash. Alumni Assn.-Japan (bd. dirs. 1995—), Am. Legion (life), Fgn. Area Officers Assn. (founding, life mem.). Avocations: swimming, jogging, lit., history, languages. E-mail: rhodes@grips.ac.jp. Home: 7-24-14 Kamikizaki, Urawa Saitama 338-0804, Japan Office: Nat Grad Ins Policy Studies, 2-2 Wakamatsu-cho, Tokyo Shinjuku-ku 162-8677, Japan

RHODES, JESSE THOMAS, III, lawyer; b. Memphis, Jan. 1, 1955; s. J. Thomas Sr. and Carolyn (Ross) R.; m. Joye Beth, May 28, 1983; children: Jessica Elizabeth, Robert Thomas. BA magna cum laude, Southwest Tex. State U., 1977, JD, 1980. Bar: Tex. 1980, U.S. Dist. Ct. (so. dist.) Tex. 1984; diplomate Am. Bd. Profl. Liability Attys.; bd. cert. in personal injury trial law. Assoc. Southers & Lyons, San Antonio, 1980-94; ptnr. Lyons & Rhodes, San Antonio, 1994—; mem. adv. coun. Nat. Jud. Coll. Fellow Tex. Bar Found. (life), Coll. State Bar; mem. ATLA (sustaining), Tex. Trial Lawyers Assn. (exec. com. 2000), San Antonio Bar Assn., San Antonio Trial Lawyers Assn. (pres. 1994). Office: Lyons & Rhodes 126 Villita St San Antonio TX 78205-2735

RHODES, JOHN GUY, lawyer; b. Kent, U.K., Feb. 16, 1945; s. Cecil and Gladys Amy (Farlie) R.; m. Christine J. Batt, June 11, 1977; children: Alexander Luke, Nicholas Hugh. MA, Jesus Coll., Cambridge, Eng., 1967. Bar: U.K. Supreme Ct. 1970. Assoc. MacFarlanes, London, 1968-75, ptnr., 1975—. Avocations: woodlands, tennis, skiing. Office: MacFarlanes, 10 Norwich St, London EC4A 1BD, England

RHODES, JONATHAN MICHAEL, physician; b. Newcastle-Upon-Tyne, Apr. 21, 1949; s. Wilfred Harry and Ellen Linda (Wreford) R.; m. Elizabeth Geraldine Morris, July 29, 1978; children: Meriel, Jennifer, Freya. BA, Cambridge Univ., 1970, MA, 1973, MD, 1981. MRCP, FRCP. Sr. lectr. in medicine Liverpool (U.K.) Univ., 1985-91, reader in medicine, 1991-94, prof. medicine in gastroenterology, 1995—. Mem. editorial bd. Gut mag., Clin. Sci., Aliment Pharm. Therapeutics. Grantee Med. Rsch. Coun., 1991—, British Digestive Found., Nat. Assn. Colitis and Crohn's Disease. Mem. Internat. Orgn. Inflammatory Bowel Diseases, British Soc. Gastroenterology, Assn. Physicians Great Britain and Ireland, Med. Rsch. Soc. (sec. 1991—), Biochem. Soc., Hawks Club, Leander Club. Avocations: classical guitar, squash. Office: U Liverpool, Dept Medicine PO Box 147, Liverpool L69 3BX, England

RHODES, KARREN, public information officer; b. Calif., Aug. 6, 1947; d. Jack and Ruth; married: two children. Diploma in Journalism, U. Utah, 1984. Journalist Salt Lake City, 1983-85, UPI, Cheyenne, Wyo., 1985-86; journalist, editor Green River (Wyo.) Star, 1986-88; pub. info. officer Nev. Dept. Employment Security, Carson City, 1989-94, Nev. Dept. Employment, Tng. and Rehab., Carson City, 1994—; trustee Carson Access TV Found., 1996-2000; e-commerce entrepreneur NuEworld.com. Photograph (recipient Best of Nat. Collegiate Photography award 1984). Vol. of Yr. award State of Utah Gov.'s Office, Salt Lake City, 1984. Mem. Soc. Profl. Journalists. Avocations: graphic design, reading, writing, travel, web site design.

RHODES, LAWRENCE, artistic director; b. Mt. Hope, W.Va., Nov. 24, 1939. Studied with Violette Armand. Joined Ballet Russe de Monte Carlo, 1958-60; from dancer to prin. dancer Joffrey Ballet, N.Y.C., 1960-64; prin. dancer Harkness Ballet, 1964-68, dir., prin. dancer, 1968-70; tchr. dance dept. NYU, 1978—, prin. ballet tchr., 1981—, chmn. dance dept., 1981-91; prin. dancer, ballet master, choreographer, tchr., artistic dir. Les Grands Ballets Canadiens, Montreal, 1989-99; guest artist Het Nationale Ballet, Amsterdam, 1970-71, Pa. Ballet, 1971-76, Feld Ballet, N.Y.C., 1973-75. Danced with Makarova, Hayden and Fracci; danced for Butler, Joffrey, Ailey, Lubovitch, Harkarvy, Nault, Van Dantzig and Mac Donald; featured dancer in film A Dancer's Vocabulary, PBS's Dance Am. series, CBS's Camera Three. Office: Les Grands Ballets Canadien, 4816 rue Rivard, Montreal, PQ Canada H2J 2N6

RHODES, LESLEY ELIZABETH, dermatologist, educator; b. Barry, South Glamorgan, Apr. 2, 1958; d. Harold Victor Rhodes and Mair Gwenllian (Rees) Dibble. BSc with 1st class honors, U. Coll., London, 1979; MB BS, Kings Coll., London, 1982; MD, U. Liverpool, 1995; MRCP, London, 1985, FRCP, 1999. Registrar in hematology Leeds Gen. Infirmary, 1986-88; sr. registrar in hematology Royal Liverpool U. Hosp., 1988-91, registrar in dermatology, 1991-93, sr. registrar in dermatology, 1993-95, cons. dermatologist, 1995—; vis. rsch. fellow Wellman Labs. of Photomedicine, Boston, 1995; hon. sr. lectr. in medicine Liverpool U. Hosp. Contbr. articles to profl. jours. including Jour. Investigative Dermatology and Brit. Jour. Dermatology. Grantee ROC European award in Photodermatology, 1995, World Cancer Rsch. Fund, 1996, Ministry of Agr. Fisheries and Food, 1996, European Commn., 1998—. Mem. Royal Coll. Physicians, European Soc. Photobiology, European Soc. for Dermatol. Rsch., Am. Soc. for Photobiology. Avocations: physical anthropology, scuba diving. Home: 316 The Colonnades, Albert Dock, Formby Liverpool L3 4AB, England Office: U Liverpool Dermatol Unit, Univ Clin Dept Duncan Bldg, Liverpool L69 3GA, England

RHODES, THOMAS WILLARD, lawyer; b. Lynchburg, Va., Mar. 9, 1946; s. Howard W. and Ruth R.; m. Ann Bloodworth, May 31, 1975; children: Mildred Claiborne, Andrew. AB, Davidson (N.C.) Coll., 1968; JD, U. Va., 1971. Bar: Ga. 1971. Assoc. Smith, Gambrell & Russell and predecessor firms, Atlanta, 1971-76, ptnr., 1976—; dir., pres. Atlanta Vol. Lawyers Found., 1984-89, Fed. Defender Program, Atlanta, 1989-94. Contbr. articles to profl. jours. Capt. USAR, 1971-72. Recipient Heiner award, Atlanta Vol. Lawyers Found., 1989. Fellow Am. Law Inst.; mem. Ga. Bar Assn. (past chmn. antitrust law sect.), ABA. Office: Smith Gambrell & Russell Promenade II 1230 Peachtree St NE Ste 3100 Atlanta GA 30309-3592

RHODES, WILLIAM REGINALD, banker; b. N.Y.C., Aug. 15, 1935; s. Edward R. and Elsie Rhodes; divorced; 1 child, Elizabeth. BA in History, Brown U., 1957. Sr. officer internat. banking group-Latin Am. and Caribbean Citibank, N.A., N.Y.C., 1977-80, sr. corp. officer Latin Am. and Caribbean, 1980-84, chmn. restructuring com., 1984-90, group exec., 1986-90, also chmn. bank adv. coms. for Brazil, Argentina, Peru, and Uruguay, 1982-90, co-chmn. bank adv. com. for Mexico, 1982-90, sr. exec.-internat., 1990-91, vice chmn., 1991—; vice chmn. Citigroup, 1999—; vice chmn. Inst. Internat. Fin., Met. Mus. Bus. Com.; mem. exec. com. Bretton Woods Com., U.S.-Russia Bus. Coun.; past chmn. adv. com. Export-Import Bank of U.S.; past chmn., U.S. Sect., Venezuela-U.S. Bus. Coun.; founding mem. U.S. Nat. Adv. Coun. to the Internat. Mgmt. Ctr., Budapest; active U.S.-Egyptian Pres. Coun.; bd. dirs. Conoco, Inc., Pvt. Export Funding Corp., Coun. Econ. Devel., ChipCo. Chmn. Northfield-Mt. Hermon Sch.; bd. dirs. N.Y. and Presbyn. Hosp., N.Y.C. Partnership; bd. overseers of Watson Inst. for Internat. Studies; active Lincoln Ctr. Corporate Leadership Com.; bd. dirs. Africa-Am. Inst. Decorated comdr. and grand officer Nat. Order of the Southern Cross, Brazil, chevalier Legion of Honor, France, Orden de Mayo, Argentina, officer Order Francisco Miranda 1st and 3rd classes, Order Merito en el Trabajo 1st class, Venezuela, Order of Diplomatic Service, Heung-In medal, Korea, Americas award, 1997; recipient African Bus. Devel. award African Am. Inst., 1998, Banker's Lifetime Achievment award Arab Bankers Assn. N.Am., 1999, Stephen P. Duggan award for Internat. Understanding, Inst. for Internat. Edn., 1999, William I. Spencer award N.Y. Blood Ctr., 1999. Mem. Americas Soc. (chmn. bd. dirs.), Coun. of Ams. (chmn. bd. dirs.), EastWest Inst. (bd. dirs.), Bankers Assn. for Fgn. Trade (past pres.), Coun. Fgn. Rels., Venezuelan-Am. C. of C. (past pres.), Fgn. Policy Assn. (bd. dirs.). Avocations: reading history, jogging, swimming, archeaology. Office: Citigroup Inc 399 Park Ave New York NY 10043-0001

RHOTEN, KENNETH D., writer; b. Hammond, Ind., Dec. 28, 1950; s. James Edward and Helen Louise (Wasson) R.; m. Virginia Haynie (div.); m. Linda Robin Damron (div.); m. Josephine Meese (dec.). Grad. H.S., New Carlisle, Ind. Draftsman Hahn, Inc., Evansville, Ind., 1973-75; laborer Inland Steel Works, Ind., 1975; draftsman N.W. Ind. Regional Planning Com., Highland, 1975-76; draftsman, artist graphic sys. divsn. Rockwell Internat., Cicero, Ill., 1977-78; designer Roper Outdoor Products (in cooperation with Espo Engring.), Bradley, Ill., 1978-79; draftsman Fedders Corp., Effingham, Ill., 1982-83. Author, editor: Dark Twist of Fate, 1995, Dark Twist of Fate and Other Works, 1999; author: A Voice From Beyond, 1999, The Complete Works of Kenneth D. Rhoten, 1999; composer pub. songs; patentee automatic brewing apparatus, 1984. Candidate state rep. State of Ill.-Rep. Party, 1986. Achievements include successful redevelopment of the Edison storage cell, and development of new secondary cell. Avocations: classical music, nature study. Home: PO Box 225 Stoy IL 62464-0225

RHYNE, CHARLES SYLVANUS, lawyer; b. Charlotte, N.C., June 23, 1912; s. Sydneyham S. and Mary (Wilson) R.; m. Sue Cotton, Sept. 16, 1932 (dec. Mar. 1974); children: Mary Margaret, William Sylvanus; m. Sarah P. Hendon, Oct. 2, 1976; children: Sarah Wilson, Elizabeth Parkhill. BA, Duke U., 1934, LLD, 1958; JD, George Washington U., 1937, DCL, 1958; LLD, Loyola U., Calif., 1958, Dickinson Law Sch., 1959, Ohio No. U., 1966, De Paul U., 1968, Centre, 1969, U. Richmond, 1970, Howard U., 1975, Belmont Abbey, 1982. Bar: D.C. 1937. Pvt. practice Washington; sr. ptnr. Rhyne & Rhyne; gen. counsel Nat. Inst. Mcpl. Law Officers, 1937-88, of counsel; prof. govt. and aviation law George Washington U., 1948-53; prof. govt. Am. U., 1939-44; gen. counsel Fed. Commn. Jud. and Congl. Salaries, 1953-54; spl. cons. Pres. Eisenhower, 1957-60; Dir. Nat. Savs. & Trust Co., 1941-76, ACCIA Life Ins. Co., 1966-84; Mem. Internat Commn. Rules Judicial Procedures, 1959-61, Pres.'s Commn. on UN, 1969-71; spl. ambassador, personal rep. of Pres. U.S. to UN High Commr. for Refugees, 1971-73. Author: Civil Aeronautics Act, Annotated, 1939, Airports and the Courts, 1944, Aviation Accident Law, 1947, Airport Lease and Concession Agreements, 1948, Cases on Aviation Law, 1950, The Law of Municipal Contracts, 1952, Municipal Law, 1957, International Law, 1971, Renowned Law Givers and Great Law Documents of Humankind, 1975, International Refugee Law, 1976, Law and Judicial Systems of Nations, 1978, Law of Local Government Operations, 1980, (autobiography) Working for Justice in America and Justice in the World, 1996; editor Mcpl. Atty., 1937-88; contbr. articles to profl. jours. Trustee George Washington U., 1957-67, Duke U., 1961-85, now trustee emeritus. Recipient Freedoms Found. award for creation Law Day-U.S.A., 1959; Alumni Achievement award George Washington U., 1960; Nat. Bar Assn. Stradford award, 1962; 1st Whitney M. Young award, 1972; Harris award Rotary, 1974; U.S. Dept. State appreciation award, 1976; Nansen Ring for refugee work, 1976, 1st Peacemaker award Rotary Internat., 1988. Mem. ABA (life mem. ho. dels., pres. 1957-58, chmn. ho. dels. 1956-58, chmn. commn. world peace through law 1958-66, chmn. com. aero. law 1946-48, 51-54, chmn. internat. and comparative law sect. 1948-49, chmn. UN com., chmn. commn. on nat. inst. justice 1972-76, nat. chmn. Jr. Bar Conf. 1944-45, ABA Gold Medal 1966, Advocacy award state and local govt. sect. 1999), D.C. Bar Assn. (pres. 1955-56, Grotius Peace award 1958, Disting. Svc. award, 1975, Heroes in Law award 1999), Inter-Am. Bar Assn. (v.p. 1957-59), Am. Bar Found. (pres. 1957-58, chmn. fellows 1958-59), Internat. Bar (founder patron 1947, v.p. 1957-58), Am. Judicature Soc. (dir. life), Am. Law Inst. (life), Am. Soc. Internat. Law (life), World Peace Through Law Ctr. (pres. 1963-89), World Jurist Assn. (pres. 1989-91, hon. life pres.), Nat. Aero. Assn. (bd. dirs. 1945-47), Washington Bd. Trade, Duke U. Alumni Assn. (chmn. nat. coun. 1955-56, pres. 1959-60), Barristers, Met. Club Washington (life), Nat. Press Club, Congl. Country Club (life), Nat. Lawyers Club (life), Univ. Club, Order of Coif (life), Scribes, Delta Theta Phi (life), Omicron Delta Kappa. Home and Office: 1404 Langley Pl Mc Lean VA 22101-3010

RHYNE, SIDNEY WHITE, lawyer; b. Charlotte, N.C., Apr. 2, 1931; s. Sidney White and Ruth (Dry) R.; m. Rosemarie Kennedy, July 11, 1959; children: Patricia Ruth, Kendall Sidney, Randall Sylvanus. AB, Roanoke Coll., 1952; LLB, U. Pa., 1955; LLM, Georgetown U., 1961. Bar: Pa. 1955, D.C. 1957, U.S. Supreme Ct. 1959, Md. 1987. Assoc. Rhyne, Mullin, Connor and Rhyne, Washington, 1957-60; mem. Mullin, Rhyne, Emmons and Topel, Washington, 1961-97; individual practice law Washington, 1997—; lectr. law ctr. Georgetown U., Washington, 1964-70. Pres. Legal Aid Soc. of D.C., 1976-78, trustee, 1968-80, pres. coun., 1991—; trustee Luth. Theol. Sem. at Phila., 1988-93, pres. coun., 1993—. With U.S. Army, 1955-57. Prettyman fellow Georgetown U., 1960-61. Fellow Am. Bar Found. (life); mem. ABA (mem. house delegates 1972-73, 75, 76-78, 98-2000), Bar Assn. D.C. (bd. dirs. 1969-73, 92-94, 98-2001, trustee Found., v.p. 1990-91, presidential award 2000), Fed. Comm. Bar Assn. (mem. exec. com. 1988-96, treas. 1991-92, Disting. Svc. award 1992, pres. 1994-95). Republican. Lutheran. Office: 3250 Arcadia Pl NW Washington DC 20015-2330

RHYNE, THERESA-MARIE, computer graphics and university executive; b. Denver, Sept. 20, 1954; d. Jimmie Lee and Marie Baker (Britt) R. BSCE, Stanford U., 1976, MS, 1977; MS, Stanford U., 1981. Engr. Stanford (Calif.) U., 1979, systems analyst Ctr. for Info. Tech., 1981-82, long range planner, 1982-83, budget and planning officer, 1983-85; fine artist, cons. Stanford, 1986—; sr. systems requirements analyst Unisys Corp., Research Triangle Park, N.C., 1987-90, tech. leader U.S. EPA sci. visualization lab., 1990-92; lead-sci. visualization rschr. USA EPA Sci. Vis. Lab. Lockheed Martin Svcs. Group, Research Triangle Park, N.C., 1993—; teaching fellow English for fgn. students Stanford (Calif.) U., summers 1977-81; artist-in-residence Wake County Arts Coun., N.C., 1987-89; lectr. Meredith Coll., 1990; instr. N.C. Mus. of Art, 1992; keynote spkr. Eurographics, 1994; invited spkr. Interface, 1995, Assn. Computing Machinery Siggraph Panels chair, 1996; Siggraph exec. com., dir.-at-large, 1996—; lead co-chair IEEE Visualization 98. One woman shows include Old Uncle Gaylord's Expresso and Ice Cream Parlor, Palo Alto, Calif., 1981, numerous others U.S. and abroad; author video procs. ACM/SIGGRAPH, IEEE Visualization, 1993; mem. editl. bd. IEEE Computer Graphics and Applications Mag., 1998—. Mem. Accessibility Cons. Team for Physically Handicapped, Stanford, 1978-80; coord. Celebration '85 Palo Alto Celebrates the Arts, 1985. Mem. AAAS, NAFE, Coun. Arts of Palo Alto (membership chmn. bd. dirs. 1985-86, pres. 1986-87), Assn. for Computing Machinery (chair SIGGRAPH panel visualizing environ. data sets 1993, SIGGRAPH panels com. 1995, SIGGRAPH panels chair 1996, SIGGRAPH conf. adv. group 1999—, SIGGRAPH Ednl. Resource grantee 1986, keynote spkr. Eurographics '94), Western Art Dirs. Club, Am. Craft Coun., Nat. Art Edn. Assn., Nat. Mus. Women in Arts (charter), Pacific Art League, Menlo Art League, San Jose Art League, USEPA/RTP Macintosh Users' Group (founder-leader 1987—), Am. Math. Assn., IEEE Computer Soc. (organizer visualization tutorial process visualizing environ. scis. data 1993, chair IEEE/Visualization panel on visualization and beyond 1993, co-chair demonstrations IEEE/Visualization 1993, co-chair publicity 1994, co-chair panels 1995, IEEE/Visualization, 1996, chair panels, 1996, program co-chair, 1997, past co-chair 1999—, IEEE/Visualization program com. 2000, IEEE tech. com. on Visualization and Graphics, 1997—, conf. dir. internat. environ. scis. visualization symposium 1993, 94, 95, Internat. Cartographic Assn.'s Commn. on Visualization, organizer supercomputing tutorial on visualizing and examining large sci. data sets Assn. Computing Machinery/IEEE Super Computing '95), Air and Waste Mgmt. Assn., Artspace (Raleigh, N.C.), Durham Art Guild, Internat. Application Visualization Sys. Users' Group (chair earth scis. track 2d ann. internat. conf. 1993, 94, 95). Avocations: mountain and rock climbing, jazz music, fashion design. Office: Lockheed Martin Svcs Group US EPA Sci Vis Lab US EPA Md-34C Durham NC 27713

RHYNEDANCE, HAROLD DEXTER, JR., lawyer, consultant; b. New Haven, Conn., Feb. 13, 1922; s. Harold Dexter and Gladys (Evans) R.; m. Barbara Ann Hall (dec.); 1 child, Harold Dexter III; m. Ruth Cosline Hakanson. BA, Cornell U., 1943, JD, 1949; grad., U.S. Army Command and Gen. Staff Coll., 1961, U.S. Army War Coll., 1970. Bar: N.Y. 1949, D.C. 1956, U.S. Tax Ct. 1950, U.S. Ct. Mil. Appeals 1954, U.S. Supreme Ct. 1954, U.S. Ct. Appeals (D.C. cir.) 1956, (2d cir.) 1963, (3rd cir.) 1965, (4th cir.) 1973, (5th cir.) 1968, (7th cir.) 1973, (9th cir.) 1964, U.S. Temporary Emergency Ct. Appeals 1975, U.S. Dist. Ct. D.C. 1956, U.S. Dist. Ct. (so. and ea. dist.) N.Y. 1963. Pvt. practice Buffalo, Eggertsville, N.Y., 1949-50; examiner/gen. atty. ICC, Washington, 1950-51; atty.-advisor Subversive Activities Control Bd., Washington, 1951-52; trial atty., spl. asst. to atty. gen., asst. U.S. atty. U.S. Dept. Justice, Washington, 1953-62; sr. trial atty., asst. gen. counsel, gen. counsel FTC, Washington, 1962-73; counsel Howrey & Simon, Washington, 1973-76; mng. atty., asst. gen. counsel, corp. counsel Washington Gas Light Co., 1977-87; counsel Conner & Wetterhahn, 1987-90; cons. Fairview, N.C., 1990—; exec. sec. adv. coun. on rules of practice and procedures FTC; mem. Jud. Conf. (D.C. Cir.), 1967—; chmn. legal and regulatory subcom. Solar Energy Com., Am. Gas Assn., Washington, 1978-84; lectr. George Washington U. Law Ctr., 1974; faculty moderator Def. Strategy Seminar Nat. War Coll., 1973; participant spl. programs Indsl. Coll. of Armed Forces, 1962, 69, Armed Forces Staff Coll., 1964. V.p. bd. dirs. Peninsula Symphony Assn., Palos Verdes Peninsula, Calif., 1989-94; bd. dirs. Help-The-Homeless-Help-Themselves, Inc., Palos Verdes Peninsula, 1991-93. 1st lt. U.S. Army, 1943-46, PTO; col. AUS, 1982—. Mem. ABA, Fed. Bar Assn., D.C. Bar Assn., Bar Assn. of D.C., Washington Met. Area Corp. Counsel Assn. (bd. dirs. 1981-84), Cornell Lawyers Club D.C. (pres. 1959-61), The Selden Soc. (London), Biltmore Forest Country Club (Asheville, N.C.), Montreat (N.C.) Scottish Soc., Ret. Officers Assn., Res. Officers Assn. (life), Mil. Order Carabao, U.S. Army War Coll. Alumni Assn. (life), Leadership Asheville Forum, Downtown Club Asheville (bd. dirs. 1998—), Cornell Alumni Assn., Am. Legion (life), Sigma Chi, Phi Delta Phi. Republican. Episcopalian. Home and Office: Eagles View 286 Sugar Hollow Rd Fairview NC 28730-9559

RIACH, PETER ANDREW, economist; b. Melbourne, Victoria, Australia, May 15, 1937; arrived in Eng., 1989; s. Andrew Brown and Doris Hope (Stanley) R.; m. Lorraine Margaret Trew, Jan. 16, 1960; 1 child, Emma Simone. B of Commerce, Melbourne U., 1958; PhD in Econs., London U., 1965. Asst. lectr. Melbourne U., 1960-61; lectr., reader Monash U., Australia, 1965-88; prof. econs. De Montfort U., 1989—. Editor: A "Second Edition" of the General Theory, 1997; contbr. articles to profl. jours. Office: De Montfort U, The Gateway, Leicester LE1 9BH, England

RIAD, BAHIA YEHIA, organic chemistry educator; b. Cairo, May 2, 1947; d. Yehia Riad and Fatma Ahmed (Tewfik) Sallam; m. Assem Abdulla El-Alaily; 1 child, Yehia Assam. BS, U. Cairo, 1969; MS, U. Bath, Eng., 1972; PhD, U. Cairo, 1976. Teaching asst. Cairo U., 1969-72, asst. lectr., 1972-76, lectr., 1976-83, asst. prof., 1983-89, prof., 1989—; hon. fellow Drexel U., 1982; v.p. Micro Analytical Ctr., Cairo, 1981-85. Contbr. articles to profl. jours. Avocations: gardening, music. Home: 32 Shagarat Eldor St, Cairo Egypt Office: Cairo U, Chemistry Dept, Cairo Egypt

RIANTAWAN, PRATHEEP, physician; b. Bangkok, May 5, 1962; s. Sonthi and Sanguan (Jairuen) R. MD, Chulalongkorn U., Bangkok, 1986; degree, Royal Coll. Physician, 1992; MSc in Med. Sci., U. Glasgow, Scotland, 1996. Cert. Bd. Respiratory Medicine. Hon. registrar dept. respiratory medicine West Norwich (Eng.) Hosp., 1990-92; registrar dept. respiratory medicine Royal Infirmary, Glasgow, 1993; clin. rsch. asst. U. Glasgow, 1994; cons. physician dept. medicine Ctrl. Chest Hosp., Bangkok, 1995—, chief pulmonary function lab., 1995—; chief acad. divsn. dept. communicable disease control Ctrl. Chest Hosp./Min. Pub. Health, 1995—. Contbr. articles to profl. jours. Mem. Thoracic Soc. Thailand (com. on mgmt. of asthma), European Respiratory Soc. Avocation: playing guitar. Home: 42 SOI 109 Ladprao Rd, 10240 Bangkok Thailand Office: Central Chest Hosp, 39 Tiwanon Rd, 11000 Nonthaburi Thailand

RIAZ, MAHNAZIR, psychology educator, researcher; b. Mansehra, Pakistan, Dec. 2, 1943; d. Mohammad Yaqub and Shala (Jan) R.; m. Ahmad Jahangiri, Aug. 14, 1966; children: Faisal, Hassan, Fawad. BEd, U. Peshawar, Pakistan, 1964, MA in Psychology, 1968, PhD, 1979. Psychology lectr. U. Peshawar, 1966-78, asst. prof. psychology, 1978-83, assoc. prof. psychology, 1983-96, prof. psychology, 1996—, chairperson dept. psychology, 1988-92, 95-98; prof. Nat. Inst. Psychology, Centre of Excellence, Islamabad, Pakistan, 1999—, bd. govs., 1997-99, mem. acad. com., 1999—. Author: Growth and Maturation, 1989, Individual and Society in the Quranic Concepts; contbr. articles to profl. jours. Gen. sec. Peshawar Mental Health Assn., 1988—; pres. Jahangiri Women, 1981—. Recipient gold medal U. Peshawar, 1966, Pres. of Pakistan award, 1966. Mem. APA, All Pakistan Psychol. Assn. (treas. 1994-98), Internat. Coun. Psychologists, Lioness Club (pres. 1989-91). Muslim. E-mail: mrriaz@isb.comsats.net.pk. Office: Nat Inst Psychol, Quaid-E-Azam U, Islamabad Pakistan

RIBACK, ESTELLE POSNER, independent art historian; b. Bklyn., June 8, 1934; d. Max Jacob and Rose (Rosen) Posner; m. Arnold O. Riback, June 17, 1956; children: Phillip Scott, Stephen Craig, Debra Lyn. BS in Psychology, Tufts U., 1956; MS in Elem. Edn., Hofstra U., 1964; MA in Art History, Inst. Fine Art, NYU, 1981; cert. art appraiser, NYU, 1993. Cert. elem. tchr., N.Y. Tchr. reading improvement Glen Cove (N.Y.) Pub. Schs., from 1964; ptnr., v.p. Artlego, N.Y.C., 1980-83; devel. officer East Harlem Tutorial Program, N.Y.C., 1985-86; asst. to dir. devel. Ams. Soc., N.Y.C., 1986-89; pres., ptnr. Manley-Riback, Inc., N.Y.C., 1989-96; pres. Estelle Riback Fine Arts Inc., N.Y.C., 1996-98; curator Am. Barbizon Art. Author: (monograph) Henry Ward Ranger, 2000. Pres., bd. dirs. Azizz Theatre, Inc., Bklyn., 1993-95, chmn. benefit com., 1993-94, chmn. fundraising, 1993-95; former mem. bd. Hebrew Sch. of Congregation Tifereth Israel Bd. Edn., Glen Cove; former chmn. major gifts Suffolk region Hadassah Med. Orgn., former v.p. for fundraising Huntington chpt. Mem. Coll. Art Assn., Assn. Historians of Nineteenth Century Art, Westhampton Yacht Squadron, Psi Chi, Alpha Xi Delta, West End Synagogue. Democrat. Avocations: tennis, sailing, bridge, travel, collecting art and artifacts. Home and Office: 201 E 79th St Apt 19D New York NY 10021-0844

RIBARI, OTTO, audiologist, physician; b. Budapest, Feb. 26, 1932; s. Ferenc and Ferencne (Bukor Maria) R.; m. Judit Reok, Dec. 19, 1960; children: Laszlo, Agnes. MD, U. Budapest, 1956; PhD, Semmelweis U., 1965, Hungarian Acad. Scis., 1986. Physician Semmelweis U., Budapest, 1956-67, assoc. prof., 1967-77, prof., dir., 1985-97; prof., dir. U. Szeged, Budapest, 1977-85; dir. Nat. Inst. ORL, Budapest, 1990—; fellow WHO, 1966-85. Author: Otorhinolaryngology, 1977, 3d rev. edition 1986, Otorhinolaryngology Head and Neck Surgery, 1997; editor: Otorhinolaryngology, 1990; contbr. articles to sci. and prof. jours. Recipient Ludwig Turck award Austrian Soc. ORL, 1990, Tato-claussen award Internat. Neuro-otol. Soc. Bad-Kissingen, 1998; named Excellent Med. Dr. Hungarian Ministerium of Welfare, 1980. Mem. Hungarian Assn. Otorhinolaryngol. Socs. (pres. 1995-96), Hungarian Assn. Otorhinolaryngologists (pres. 1985-93), European Assn. Otorhinolaryngol. Socs. (v.p. 1996—), Hungarian Med. Assn., Interdisciplinary Med. Soc. (pres. 1998—), Collegium Otorhinolaryngol. Sacrum, Rotary (pres. 1997-98). Avocations: tennis, music. Office: Nat Inst Oto-Rhino-Laryngology, Szigony 36 PO Box 109, 1431 Budapest Hungary

RIBAS-XIRGO, LLUÍS, computer science educator, researcher; b. Cassà de la Selva, Girona, Spain, Sept. 3, 1966; s. Enric Ribas-Torrent and Lourdes Xirgo-Llach. Grad., U. Autònoma, Bellaterra, Spain, 1984-89, MSc, 1991, PhD, 1996; postgrad., Nat. Microelectronics Ctr., Bellaterra, Spain, 1989-95. Asst. lectr. U. Autònoma de Barcelona, Bellaterra, 1989-91, lectr., 1991-95, full lectr., 1995-2000, assoc. prof., 2000—; lectr. Poly. U. Catalonia, 1997-98, 98-99; presenter in field. Author: Programming in C for Mathematicians, 1999, Practical Exercises of Computer Fundamentals, 2000; contbr. articles to profl. jours. Mem. IEEE, Cineclub 8 1/2 (co-founder). Avocation: cinema. Office: Univ Autònoma, Campus UAB, 08193 Cerdanyola Spain

RIBBLE, RONALD GEORGE, psychologist, educator, writer; b. West Reading, Pa., May 7, 1937; s. Jeremiah George and Mildred Sarah (Folk) R.; m. Catalina Valenzuela (Torres), Sept. 30, 1961; children: Christina, Timothy, Kenneth. BSEE cum laude, U. Mo., 1968, MSEE, 1969, MA, 1985, PhD, 1986. Diplomate Am. Bd. Psychol. Specialties. Enlisted man USAF, 1956-60, advance through grades to lt. col., 1976; rsch. dir. Coping Resources, Inc., Columbia, Mo., 1986; pres., co-owner Towers and Rushing Ltd. (Pubs., Troubadour 1997—), San Antonio, 1986—; referral devel. Laughlin Pavilion Psychiat. Hosp., Kirksville, Mo., 1987; program dir. Psychiat. Insts. of Am., Iowa Falls, Iowa, 1987-88; lead psychotherapist Gasconade County Counseling Ctr., Hermann, Mo., 1988; lectr. U. Tex., San Antonio, 1989—, Trinity U., San Antonio, 1995-96; assessment clinician Afton Oaks Psychiat. Hosp., San Antonio, 1989-91; faculty cons. Edn. Testing Svc., 1997; psychologist Olmos Psychol. Svcs., Inc., San Antonio, 1991-93; vol. assessor Holmgreen Children's Shelter, San Antonio, 1992-93; founder Ruth Bohn Weissman Scholarship in Creative Writing, U. Tex., San Antonio, 1994; condr. seminars, revs. for maj. publs. Author: Apples, Weeds, and Doggie Poo, 1995, Don't Eat the Snake!, 1999, Pushcart Nominee, 1999; contbr. essays to psychol. reference books and poetry to anthologies periodicals, lyrics to popular music; interviewer celebrities in performing and lit. arts, 1995—; columnist Feelings, 1993-97; public access TV appearances, 1991—. Del. Boone County (Mo.) Dem. Conv., 1984; vol. announcer pub. radio sta., Columbia, 1993; contbg. mem. Dem. Nat. Com., 1983—, Presdl. Congl. Task Force, 1994; vol. counselor Cath. Family and Children's Svc., San Antonio, 1989-91; chpt. advisor Rational Recovery Program for Alcoholics, San Antonio, 1991-92; mem. Pres. Leadership Cir., 1994-99. Recipient Roberts Meml. Prize in Poetry, 1995; Pushcart nominee, 1999. Fellow Am. Coll. Forensic Examiners; mem. APA, AAUP, NEA, ACLU, Internat. Platform Assn. (Poetry award 1995), Bexar County Psychol. Assn., Air Force Assn., Ret. Officers Assn., Interfaith Alliance, Soc. Profl. Journalists, Poetry Soc. Am., Acad. Am. Poets, Physicians for Social Responsibility. Roman Catholic. Avocations: running and fitness, poetry, singing, pub. speaking. Home: 14023 N Hills Village Dr San Antonio TX 78249-2534 Office: U Tex Divsn Behavioral and Cultural Scis San Antonio TX 78249 also: Towers and Rushing Ltd San Antonio TX 78249

RIBEIRO, FRANK HENRY, banker, energy consultant; b. Kowloon, Hong Kong, July 1, 1949; came to U.S., 1955; s. Henry Augusto and Agatha Marie (Rodriques) R.; m. Margaret Ann Mitchell, July 23, 1988. BA, Calif. State U, Northridge, 1973; M in Pub. and Internat. Affairs, Princeton U., 1976. Cons. Omega Rsch. Assocs., Northridge, 1973; economist Fed. Power Commn., San Francisco, 1974; economist dept. state U.S. Embassy, London, 1975; fin. analyst Exxon Corp., N.Y.C., 1976-81; mgr. swaps Marine Midland Bank, N.Y.C., 1982-83; v.p., dir. Bank of Am., N.Y.C., 1983-89; v.p., mgr. corp. fin. ABN-AMRO Bank N.V. (formerly Algemene Bank Nederlands, N.V.), N.Y.C., 1989-92; cons., trainer Fin. Dirs., Inc., N.Y.C., 1993-96; mng. dir. Paradigm Strategy Group, 1996—; cons. UN, N.Y.C., Malaysia and Thailand, 1984-85; bd. dirs. Mark Degarmo Dance Co. Contbr. articles to profl. publs.; contbr. chpt. to Handbook of Internat. Corp. Fin., 1988. Mem. Internat. Swap Dealers Assn., N.Y.C. Folk Dance Found. (program coordinator 1982-86). Office: care DEM 4582E Kingwood Dr Kingwood TX 77345-2600

RIBEIRO, ISABELA QUILELLI CORREA ROCHA, infectious disease physician, internist; b. Rio de Janeiro, Aug. 7, 1965; d. Roberto Alexandre and Celmy de Alencar Araripe Quilelli Correa; m. Rogerio Rocha Ribeiro, July 6, 1989; children: Rodrigo, Guilherme. MD, U. Fed. do Rio de Janeiro, 1989; postgrad., Ohio State U., 1994, 1996. Diplomate Am. Bd. Internal Medicine; diploma Ednl. Commn. for Fgn. Med. Grads. and Fed. Licensure Examination; cert. Conselho Regional de Medicina do Rio de Janeiro. Med. rsch. asst. Farmitalia Carlo Erba (now Pharmacia & Upjohn), Milan, 1990-91; intern internal medicine Beth Israel Med. Ctr., N.Y.C., 1991-92; resident internal medicine Ohio State U., Columbus, 1992-94, fellow infectious diseases, 1994-96; hon. clin. rsch. fellow divsn. infectious diseases St. George's Hosp. Med. Sch., London, 1997-98; pvt. practice infectious diseases and internal medicine Rio de Janeiro, 1998—; cons. Artesunate Task Force, WHO, Geneva, 1996—. Contbr. chpts. to books, articles to profl. jours. Field supr. Census of Favela da Mare, U. Fed. do Rio de Janeiro, 1988. Mem. ACP-ACIM, Am. Soc. Microbiology, Infectious Diseases Soc. Am. Avocations: family, friends, arts, sports. Office: Rua Gal Garzon 22 sala 508, CEP22460 Rio de Janeiro Brazil

RIBEIRO, JOAQUIM ALEXANDRE, medical researcher, educator; b. Vila Fernando, Guarda, Portugal, Aug. 9, 1941; s. Antonio Alexandre and Joaquina (Purificacao) Ribeiro; m. Isabel Maria Perdigao, Dec. 28, 1962 (div. Feb. 1992); children: Patricia, Filipa, Tiago; m. Ana Sousa Sebastiao, June 21, 1993; children: Francisco, Joaquim. MD, U. Lisbon, Portugal, 1966; PhD, U. Edinburgh, Scotland, 1982. Asst. Gulbenkian Inst. Sci., Oeiras, Portugal, 1970-74, asst. investigator, 1974-82, investigator, 1982-88, sr. investigator, 1988-97; dir. Lab. Neuroscis., Faculty Medicine U. Lisbon, 1997—; prof. U. Lisbon, Portugal. Contbr. articles to profl. jours. Tenent Health Corps, Mozambique, 1967-70. Mem. Brit. Pharm. Soc., Internat. Soc. Neurochemistry. E-mail: jaribeiro@neurociencias.pt. Office: Lab Neuroscis Fac Medicine, U Lisbon Ave Prof Egas Moniz, 1649-028 Lisbon Portugal

RIBEIRO, LUIS CANDIDO, banker. Gov. Ctrl. Bank Guinea-Bissau. Office: Banco Central da Guinee-Bissau, Avenida Amilcar Cabral, CP38 Bissau Guinea-Bissau*

RIBEIRO, RENATO JANINE, political philosophy educator; b. Aracatuba, Sao Paulo, Brazil, Dec. 9, 1949; s. Benedicto and Maria-Therezinha Janine Ribeiro; 1 child, Rafael Schritzmeyer Ribeiro. PhB, U. Sao Paulo, 1971; MPhilosophy, U. Sorbonne, Paris, 1973; PhD, U. Sao Paulo, 1984. Cert. journalist. Asst. in polit. philosophy U. Sao Paulo, 1975-91, assoc. prof., 1991-93, prof., 1993—, chmn. internat. coop. com., 1991-94; mem. coun. CNPQ, Brasilia, Brazil, 1993-97; freelance op-ed writer for maj. Brazilian newspapers, 1989—. Author: Ao Leitor Sem Medo, 1984, A Ultima Razao dos Reis, 1993, A Etiqueta No Antigo Regime, 1983, A Sociedade contra o Social, 2000. Mem. Brazilian Assn. for Advancement of Sci. (mem. coun. 1995-97, 99—, mem. bd. dirs. 1997-99). Office: U Sao Paulo, Rua do Lago 707, 05508900 São Paulo Brazil

RIBEIRO DE PAIVA, SYLENO, lawyer; b. Natal, Brasil, Apr. 2, 1934; s. Francisco and Taurina (Navarro) R.; m. Christina Maria de Barros Guimarães, Dec. 24, 1957; children: Bruno, Genaro, Christina, Luciana. Advocacy, Law Sch. Fed. U., 1957; postgrad., Law Sch. of Paris, 1962. Atty. Previdence Inst. of Pernambuco, 1957-61; prof. Pernambuco Sch. of the Fed. U., 1958-89; advocate Law Office, Recife-Pe, 1958—; atty. Fed. U. of Pernambuco, 1961-85; prof. comml. law recite-pe U. of Adminstrn. of the State of Pernambuco, 1970-78; cons. Brazilian Industry from the N.E. and South of Brazil, 1970-78. Named Citizen from Pernambuco, 1993; recipient Ednl. Merit of Pernambuco, Order of the Merit of Guararapes, Order of the Mil. Merit, Aeronautical Merit, Nat. Order of the Ednl. Merit, Order of Rio Branco. Avocations: reading, music. Office: Advocate Office, Rua Marcelino Lisboa 77, 52060040 Recife Brazil

RIBES, JEAN-CLAUDE HENRI, astronomer, writer; b. Lyon, France, Aug. 11, 1940; s. Jean Joseph and Julie Marie (Chenevaz) R.; m. Elizabeth Marie Nesme, July 2, 1966 (div. 1980); m. Catherine Colette Dibot, Dec. 28, 1982. Engr., Ecole Poly., Paris, 1962; DSc, U. Paris, 1969. Cert. astronomer. Scientist Obs. Paris, 1963-69, 72-75, Commonwealth Sci. and Indsl. Rsch., Sydney, Australia, 1970-71; sci. attache Nat. Inst. Astronomy Astrophysics, Paris, 1976-82; assoc. dir. Nat. Inst. Astronomy Astrophysics/Sci. of Universe, Paris, 1983-85; scientist Obs. Lyon, France, 1986-87, dir., 1987-94, scientist, 1995-2000; ret., 2000. Co-author: (books) Le Dossier des Civilisations Extraterrestres, 1970, Le Dossier de L'Intelligence Artificielle, 1975, Les Cometes, Mythes et Realites, 1985, La Vie Extraterrestre, 1990. Vice-mayor Coun., Montagny-sur-Grosne, 1995—. Lt. French Army, 1960-63. Mem. French Astronomy Soc., N.Y. Acad. Scis. Home: Le Breuil, 71520 Montagny-sur-Grosne France

RICARD, JACQUES LOUIS, microbiologist; b. Neuilly, Seine, France, May 23, 1926; arrived in Sweden, 1968; s. Joseph Honoré and Suzanne (Chalon) R.; m. Odette Cadart, 1948 (div. 1970); children: Suzanne, Michele; m. Suoma Kanerva Leinonen, June 19, 1971; 1 child, Thomas. Diploma, Institut Agricole, Fribourg, Switzerland, 1945; AB with honors, U. Calif., Davis, 1955, MA, 1961; PhD, Oreg. State U., 1966. Cert. secondary tchr., Calif. Bacteriologist Campbell Soup Co., Sacramento, 1948-60; rsch. asst. U. Calif., Davis, 1960-61; instr. Sacramento City Coll., 1961-63; rsch. asst. Oreg. State U., Corvallis, 1963-66, asst. prof., 1966-68; vis. scientist Skogshögskolan, Stockholm, 1968-69; mgr. IC Lab., Incentive AB, Stockholm, 1969-72; pres. BINAB Bio-Innovation AB, Älgarås, Sweden, 1972-98, tech. adviser, 1998—. Patentee biofungicides. With French infantry, 1944-45. Roman Catholic. Avocation: aquaculture. Office: BINAB Bio-Innovation AB, Box 56, S-545 02 Älgarås Sweden

RICARD, JEAN-HENRY GEORGES, electromechanical and electronics engineer; b. Le Havre, France, Nov. 25, 1937; s. Jean-Paul and Lucie (Montagne) R.; m. Giannina Lanata de las Casas, July 25, 1947; children: Xavier, Jacques, Sophie. Ingenieur civil, de l'aeronautique et de l'espace, Ensae-Paris, 1962; D of Physics, U. Toulouse, France, 1967; MBA, CPA, Paris, 1975. Project mgr. guidance and control systems Soc. d' Etudes et Realisation pour Engins Balistiques, Paris, 1964-65; advanced rsch. mgr. defense CAE, Paris, 1966-68; head computer systems SNECMA, Paris, 1969-73, program dir. Concorde aircraft, 1974-77; pres. Auxitrol, Paris, 1978-80; v.p., dir. CISI Engring. Group, Paris, 1981-84; pres. CRIS, Paris, 1985-89; cons., dir. Defense & Security Govtl. Orgns., Paris, 1990—; Author: Cybernetique Notions for Systems, 1975, Les Nouveaux Jacobins, 1994; contbr. articles to profl. jours. Mayor, Town of Croissy. Mem. IEEE, CEH, CEPS, Ctr. Evaluationet Prospective Strategique. Roman Catholic. Achievements include research on linear control digital theory for non linear unstable process and it's applications to missiles, aircrafts and engines in French defense programs; advanced contributions to development of interactives design and information computerized systems. Office: Town Hall, Rue Maurice Bertaux, 78290 Croissy France

RICARD, PHILIPPE OLIVIER, cardiologist, electrophysiologist; b. Marseilles, France, Nov. 30, 1962; s. Jacques Robert and Catharina Maria (Reigers) R.; m. Roselyne Josee Abaziou, June 6, 1992; children: Camille, Guillaume. M in Molecular Pharm., U. Nice, France, 1990. Asst. prof. medicine & cardiology U. Marseilles, France, 1993-97, assoc. prof. medicine & cardiology, 1999—. Contbr. articles to profl. jours. Lt. French Navy, 1989. French Fedn. Cardiology grantee, Paris, 1995; cardiology fellow U. Marseilles, 1988-93, fellow pharm. Columbia U., N.Y.C., 1995-96. Mem. French Soc. Cardiology, European Soc. Cardiology. Home: Rolland, 122 Rue du Commandant, 13008 Marseilles France Office: CHU NORD Svc Cardiology, Bvd Pierre Dramard, 13015 Marseilles France

RICARD, THOMAS ARMAND, electrical engineer; b. Waterbury, Conn., Sept. 10, 1954; s. Armand Andrew and Mary Jean (Clark) R.; m. Gina Marie Harris, Sept. 10, 1983; children: Bernadette Allison, Amanda Valentine. BSEE, U. Hartford, 1988; MSEE, Syracuse U., 1991. Edison engr. GE, Syracuse, N.Y., 1988-92; radio frequency/microwave engr. EZ Form Cable Corp., New Haven, Conn., 1992—; mem. Electronic Industry Assn. Working Group on Cable and Connectors, New Haven, 1995—. Mem. Am. Radio Relay League, Tau Beta Pi, Eta Kappa Nu. Avocations: amateur radio, amateur musician. Home: 186 Peck Ln Cheshire CT 06410-2000 Office: EZ Form Cable Corporation 275 - 285 Welton St Hamden CT 06517

RICCA, RENZO LUIGI, mathematician, researcher; b. Casale Monferrato, Italy, Jan. 24, 1960; arrived in Eng., 1989, naturalised, 1996; s. Simone and Luciana Teresa (Penna) R. Laurea with honors, Poly. of Turin, Italy, 1988; PhD, Cambridge (Eng.) U., 1994. Sr. rsch. fellow applied math. Univ. Coll., London, 1992—; vis. prof. U. Geneva; sci. cons. Assn. Sviluppo Sci. e Tech. Piemonte, Turin, 1990-93; projects reviewer NSF, Washington, 1993—; articles referee JFM, Procs. of Royal Soc., Phys. Letters, others. Contbr. articles to Phys. Rev., Physics Fluids, JFM, Jour. Physics, others. Recipient J.T. Knight prize in math. Cambridge U., 1991; rsch. fellow Assn. Sviluppo Sci. e Tech. Piemonte, 1989-92; hon. rsch. fellow Poly Turin, 1992-94. Fellow Cambridge Philos. Soc.; mem. European Math. Soc., Am. Math. Soc., N.Y. Acad. Scis. Avocations: mountaineering, skiing. Office: U Coll London Dept Math, Gower St, London WC1E 6BT, England

RICCARDO, BENNY, day trader, stock broker; b. Bethpage, N.Y., Sept. 19, 1974; s. Patsy Riccardo and RoseAnne Isasi. Degree in carpentry, Levittown Mem. Edn. Ctr. Owner, pres. Bugg Clothing Co., Massepequa, N.Y., 1992-99; stock broker, day trader Babylon Village, N.Y., 1999—. E-mail: mixman812@aol.com. Home: 246 Park Ave Babylon NY 11702-1623

RICCI, FRANCO MARIA, publisher, designer; b. Parma, Italy, Dec. 2, 1937; s. Angelo and Carolina (Vitali) R. Grad. in geology, U. Parma, 1958. Publs. include: facsimile edit. of Ency. by Diderot and d'Alembert, 1979, FMR art mag.(founder), various series of art books and limited edits.; pub. over 300 books. Recipient Les insignes de Chevalier dans l'ordre des Arts et des Lettres, France, 1980. Mem. Grolier Club (N.Y.C.). Office: Via Montecuccoli 32, 20147 Milan Italy

RICCI, GIOVANNI MARIO, finance company executive, government consultant; b. Barga, Lucca, Italy, Aug. 7, 1929; s. Ettore and Jolanda (Bardoni) R.; m. Lia Cheli, Feb. 14, 1949 (div. 1970); children: Ettore, Franco, Cristiana; m. Angela Carbognin, Oct. 21, 1973; children: Mariangela, Rebecca. Ed. Italian schs.; D. honoris causa in Theology, 1983. Fin. advisor Seychelles Republic, 1974—; journalist, corr. ANSA (Italian News Agy.), 1980—; chmn., CEO sales, restructuring, mergers and indsl. mgmt. GMR Group; founder, hon. chmn. Fondazione Ricci, Barga, Italy, 1990—. Office: Arbobyl Ltd GMR Group, Via Canonica 14, CH-6900 Lugano Switzerland

RICCI, GRACIELA NILBET, linguist; b. Rosario, Argentina, Feb. 1, 1944; arrived in Italy, 1976; d. Ferdinando and Olga (Pardini) R.; m. Federico Ernesto Della Grisa, Nov. 19, 1977; 1 child, Giorgia. LitD, U. Rosario, 1970. Asst. prof. Catholic U., Rosario, 1972-74; assoc. prof. U. Rosario, 1976; prof. U. Macerata, Italy, 1977—; dir. Fng. Langs. Inst., Macerata, 1986-90, dir. dept. linguistics, 1994—; master didathicus in comm., trainer in neurolinguistic programmation. Author: Los circuitos interiores, 1974, Realismo Magico y Conciencia mitica en America Latina, 1985; editor: Normativita e trasgressione, 1988, Discorso fizionale e realta storica, 1992, I Linguaggi: Spazi immaginari, contestuali e didattici, 1993, La lingua, Le lingue: Le frontiere della devianza, 1996, Homenaje a J.L. Borges, 1999; contbr. articles to profl. publs. Mem. Italian Hispanic Assn., Italian Semiotic Assn., Internat. Semiotic Assn. Roman Catholic. Avocations: music, arts. Home: Viale di Pta Vercellina 9, 20123 Milan Italy Office: U Macerata, Via Crescimbeni 14, 62100 Macerata Italy

RICCI, MICHAEL ANTHONY, surgeon; b. Utica, N.Y., July 8, 1956; s. Charles Carmen and Antoinette Ricci; 1 child, Justin. BA, Hamilton Coll., 1978; MD, SUNY Upstate Med. Coll., Syracuse, 1982. Diplomate Am. Bd. Gen. Surgery, Am. Bd. Vascular Surgery, Am. Bd. Critical Care. Asst. prof. U. Vt., Burlington, 1989-94, assoc. prof., 1994-99, prof., 2000—. Mem. Soc. Vascular Surgery, Internat. Soc. Cardiovascular Surgeons, New eng. Soc. Vascular Surgery, Am. Telemedicine Assn. E-mail: michael.ricci@vtmednet.org. Office: Fletcher Allen Healthcare 1 S Prospect St Burlington VT 05401-3456

RICCIARDI, CHRISTINE SECOLA, international trade consultant; b. New Haven, Apr. 19, 1963; d. Carl Albert and Marie Rose (Pupello) Secola; m. Carmine C. Ricciardi, Nov. 24, 1990. BA, Fairfield (Conn.) U., 1985. Editl. asst. Conn. Woman Mag., Fairfield, 1984-85; corr. internat. money transfer divsn. Chase Manhattan Bank, N.Y.C., 1985-86; editor employee comm. Port Authority of N.Y. & N.J., N.Y.C., 1986-88; internat. trade assn. adminstr. World Trade Ctrs. Assn., Inc., N.Y.C., 1988-95, dir. mem. svcs., 1990-95; ind. cons., 1995—. Editor, contbg. author Corporate Comm., 1986-95; contbg. writer newspaper and mag. articles and trade publs., 1988—. Vol. mem. Conn. Spl. Olympics Com., 1981-82; big sister Conn. Big Sister Program, Bridgeport, 1984-85. Recipient Good Citizenship award City of Hamden, Conn., 1981. Mem. Am. Soc. Assn. Execs., Internat. Assn. Bus. Communicators, Alpha Mu Gamma, Nat. Lang. Honor Soc. Avocations: art, theater, skiing, foreign languages.

RICE, ANNE, writer; b. New Orleans, Oct. 14, 1941; d. Howard and Katherine (Allen) O'Brien; m. Stan Rice, Oct. 14, 1961; children: Michele (dec.), Christopher. Student, Tex. Woman's U., 1959-60; BA, San Francisco State Coll., 1964, MA, 1971. Author: Interview with the Vampire, 1976, The Feast of all Saints, 1980, Cry to Heaven, 1982, The Vampire Lestat, 1985, The Queen of the Damned, 1988, The Mummy or Ramses the Damned, 1989, The Witching Hour, 1990, Tale of the Body Thief, 1992, Lasher, 1993, Taltos, 1994, Memnoch the Devil, 1995, Servant of the Bones, 1996, Violin, 1998, The Vampire Armand, 1998, Pandora: New Tales of the Vampires, 1998, Vittorio the Vampire, 1999; (as A.N. Roquelaure) The Claiming of Sleeping Beauty, 1983, Beauty's Punishment, 1984, Beauty's Release: The Continued Erotic Adventures of Sleeping Beauty, 1985 (as Anne Rampling) Exit to Eden, 1985, Belinda, 1986 ; screenwriter: Interview with a Vampire, 1994. Office: care Alfred A Knopf Inc 201 E 50th St New York NY 10022-7703

RICE, DAVID PRESTON, minister, educator; b. Parkersburg, W.Va., July 7, 1953; s. Ernest Granville Rice and Mary Alice Lee; m. Dorothy Lee Tehas, Sept. 18, 1976; 1 child, Nathan Granville. BS, U. Tex., San Antonio, 1978; M of Divinity, Christian Bible Coll. and Sem., 1993, D of Divinity, 1996. Cert. trainer Evangelist Explosion, Tex. Pastor, ch. planter Benjamin Ave. Bapt. Ch., Grand Rapids, Mich., 1986-88; assoc. pastor Columbia Ave. Bapt. Ch., Pontiac, Mich., 1988-90, Bell Shoals Bapt. Ch., Brandon, Fla., 1990-93; sr. pastor Belmont Bapt. Ch., Tampa, Fla., 1993-97; assoc. dir. Sunday sch. dept. Fla. Bapt. Conv., Jacksonville, 1997-99; sr. pastor Ancient City Bapt. Ch., Augustine, Fla., 1999—; nat. ch. growth cons. So. Bapt. Conv., Nashville, 1991—. Author: (implementation strategy) FAITH Sunday School Evangelism Strategy, 1998. Sgt. 1st class U.S. Army, 1972-85, Vietnam. Mem. So. Bapt. Religious Educators Assn., Fla. Bapt. Religious Educators. Southern Baptist Convention. Avocations: golf, horticulture, collecting miniature lighthouses. Office: Ancient City Bapt Ch 27 Sevilla St Saint Augustine FL 32084-3550

RICE, DELBERT, retired missionary, anthropologist; b. Corvallis, Oreg., Jan. 24, 1928; s. Arthur Delbert and Linnie Opal (Shipley) R.; m. Esther Rhoda Bernham, June 13, 1950; children: Harold, Alfred, Eugene, Timothy, Flora Joy. BSEE, Oreg. State U., 1950; MDiv, We. Evang. Seminary, Oreg., 1955; MA in Anthropology, Silliman U., Philippines, 1972. Pastor E.U.B. Ch., Oreg., 1952-55; dist. missionary UCCP, Philippines, 1956-65, dir. Kalahan mission, 1965-80; exec. officer Kalahan Edn. Found., 1973-99; dir. of rsch. Kalahan Edn. Found., Oreg., 1999—; trustee Assn. of Founds., Philippines, 1989-93, 94-98; ednl. coord. Kalahan E.F., 1990—. Author: (books) Pattern for Development, 1972, Ecology Manual for Upland Farmers, 1993, Quiest Ones Speak, 1999; contbr. articles to profl. jours. With USCG, 1945-46. Named Outstanding Alumnus We. Evang. Sem., 1992, Silliman U., 1975; recipient Likas Yaman award Philippine Govt., 1989, Svc. to Minorities award, 1975. Mem. Philippine Assn. Intercultural Devel. (treas. 1990—), Upland NGO Asst. Cmty. Avocations: ecology, gardening.

RICE, DENIS TIMLIN, lawyer; b. Milw., July 11, 1932; s. Cyrus Francis and Kathleen (Timlin) R.; children: James Connelly, Tracy Ellen. A.B., Princeton U., 1954; J.D., U. Mich., 1959. Bar: Calif. 1960. Practiced in San Francisco, 1959—; assoc. firm Pillsbury, Madison & Sutro, 1959-61, Howard & Prim, 1961-63; prin. firm Howard, Rice, Nemerovski, Canady, Falk & Rabkin, 1964—; bd. dirs. Gensler & Assocs., Inc., Vanguard Airlines; chmn., mng. com. San Francisco Inst. Fin. Svcs., 1983-92. Councilman, City of Tiburon, Calif., 1968-72, mayor, 1970-72; dir. Marin County Transit Dist., 1970-72, 77-81, chmn., 1979-81; supr. Marin County, 1977-81, chmn., 1979-80; commr. Marin Housing Authority, 1977-81; mem. San Francisco Bay Conservation and Devel. Commn., 1977-83; bd. dirs. Planning and Conservation League, 1981—, Marin Symphony, 1984-92, Marin Theatre Co., 1987-97, Marin Conservation League, 1995—, Digital Village Found., 1995—, pres., 1997—; mem. Met. Transp. Commn., 1980-83; mem. bd. visitors U. Mich. Law Sch. 1st lt. AUS, 1955-57. Recipient Freedom Found. medal, 1956. Fellow Am. Bar Found.; mem. ABA (fed. regulation of securities com., chair Asia-Pacific Bus. Law Com.), State Bar Calif. (editor 1978-80, vice chair sect. bus. law 1978-80, chair com. adminstrn. justice 1997-98, chair com. cyberspace law 1997—), San Francisco Bar Assn., Am. Judicature Soc., Bankers Club, Tiburon Peninsula Club, Pacific Union Club, Olympic Club, Order of Coif, Phi Beta Kappa, Phi Delta Phi. Office: 3 Embarcadero Ctr Ste 700 San Francisco CA 94111-4003

RICE, FIONA CATHERINE-MARY, lawyer; b. Hythe, Hampshire, Eng., Jan. 1, 1962; d. Edward John and Sheelagh Teresa (O'Toole) R.; m. Jonathan Stanley Tolson Mellor, Dec. 9, 1989; children: Charlotte, Lucy, Olivia, James. BA, Oxford (Eng.) U., 1983, MA, 1986. Ptnr. Linklaters & Alliance, London. Office: Linklaters & Alliance, One Silk St, London EC2Y 8HQ, England

RICE, JOSEPH ALBERT, banker; b. Cranford, N.J., Oct. 11, 1924; s. Louis A. and Elizabeth J. (Michael) R.; m. Katharine Wolfe, Sept. 11, 1948; children: Walter, Carol, Philip, Alan. B in Aero. Engring., Rensselear Poly. Inst., 1948; M in Indsl. Engring., NYU, 1952, MA, 1968. With Grumman Aircraft Engring. Corp., 1948-53; with IBM, N.Y.C., 1953-65, mgr. ops., real estate, constrn. divsns., 1963-65; dep. group exec. N.Am. comml. telecommunications group, pres. telecommunications div. ITT, N.Y.C., 1965-67; sr. v.p. Irving Trust Co., N.Y.C., 1967-69, exec. v.p., 1969-72, sr. exec. v.p., 1972-73, vice chmn., 1973-74, pres., 1974-83, chmn., 1984-88; exec. v.p. Irving Bank Corp., 1971-74, vice chmn., 1974-75, pres., 1975-83, chmn. bd., CEO, 1984-88; bd. dirs. Apache Corp. Chmn., trustee John Simon Guggenheim Meml. Found.; trustee Blanton-Peale Inst., vice chmn., trustee Hist. Hudson Valley. Mem. Coun. Fgn. Rels., N.Y. Acad. Scis., Univ. Club, Links, Sky Club.

RICE, PAUL JACKSON, lawyer, educator; b. East St. Louis, Ill., July 15, 1938; s. Ray Jackson and Mary Margaret (Campbell) R.; m. Carole Jeanne Valentine, June 6, 1959; children: Rebecca Jeanne Ross, Melissa Ann Hansen, Paul Jackson Jr. BA, U. Mo., 1960, JD, 1962; LLM, Northwestern U., 1970; student, Command and Gen. Staff Coll., 1974-75, Army War Coll., 1982-83. Bar: Mo. 1962, Ill. 1969, U.S. Dist. Ct. (no. dist.) Ill. 1970, U.S. Supreme Ct. 1972, U.S. Ct. Appeals (D.C. cir.) 1991, D.C. 1993, U.S. Dist. Ct. (D.C.) 2000. Commd. 1st lt. U.S. Army, 1962, advanced through grades to col., 1980; asst. judge advocate 4th Armored Div., Goeppingen, Fed. Republic Germany, 1966-69; dep. staff judge advocate 1st Cavalry Div., Republic Vietnam, 1970-71; inst., prof. The Judge Adv. Gen. Sch., Charlottesville, Va., 1971-74, commdt., dean, 1985-88; br. chief Gen. Law Br., Pentagon, 1975-78; chief adminstrv. law div. Office Judge Adv. Gen., Pentagon, Washington, 1978-79; staff judge adv. 1st Inf. Div., Ft. Riley, Kans., 1979-82, V Corps U.S. Army, Frankfurt, Fed. Republic Germany, 1983-85, USACAC, Ft. Leavenworth, Kans., 1989-90; faculty Indsl. Coll. Armed Forces, 1988-89; chief counsel Nat. Hwy. Traffic Safety Adminstrn., Washington, 1990-93; ptnr. Arent Fox Kintner Plotkin & Kahn, Washington, 1993—. Contbr. articles to profl. jours. Granted Legal Svc. award State of Hessen, Weisbaden, Fed. Republic Germany, 1985, Cert. Merit U. Mo. Alumni Assn., 1987. Mem. ABA, Mo. Bar Assn., Ctr. For Law and Nat. Security, U. Va. Sch. Law (1985-89), Lion Tamers, Phi Delta Phi. Methodist. Avocations: writing, reading, sports. Home: 7835 Vervain Ct Springfield VA 22152-3107 Office: Arent Fox Kintner Plotkin & Kahn 150 Connecticut Ave NW Washington DC 20036-5339

RICE, STANLEY ARTHUR, biology educator; b. Cushing, Okla., May 30, 1957; s. Arthur John and Nina Irene (Hicks) R.; m. Althea Lisette Clarkston, June 9, 1984; 1 child, Anita. BA, U. Calif., Santa Barbara, 1979; PhD, U. Ill., 1987. Vis. teaching specialist Univ. Ill., Urbana, 1986-87; asst. prof. The King's Coll., Briarcliff Manor, N.Y., 1987-90; vis. faculty Sarah Lawrence Coll., Bronxville, N.Y., 1989-90; asst. prof. Huntington (Ind.) Coll., 1990-93, S.W. State U., Marshall, Minn., 1993-98, S.E. Okla. State U., Durant, Okla., 1998—; vis. faculty mem. Wheaton (Ill.) Coll. Sci. Sta., 1993—, Taylor U., Upland, Ind., 1993. Contbr. articles to Am. Biol. Tchr., Oecologia, Perspectives on Sci. and Christian Faith, Creation/Evolution. Predoctoral fellowship NSF, Univ. Ill., 1980. Mem. Ecol. Soc. Am., British Ecol. Soc., Bot. Soc. Am., Am. Sci. Affiliation, Am. Biol. Tchrs. Office: Dept Biol Sci SE Okla State Univ Durant OK 74701

RICE, VICTOR ALBERT, manufacturing executive, heavy; b. Hitchin, Hertfordshire, Eng., Mar. 7, 1941. With Ford Motor Co., U.K., 1957-64, Cummins Engines, U.K., 1964-67, Chrysler Corp., U.K., 1968-70; comptroller N. European ops. Perkins Engines Group Ltd., Peterborough, U.K., subsequently Group's dir. fin., Group dir. sales, and dep. mng. dir. ops., 1970-75; comptroller world-wide Varity Corp. (formerly Massey-Ferguson Ltd.), Toronto, Ont., Can., 1975-77; v.p. staff ops. Varity Corp., Toronto, Ont., Can., 1977-78, pres., chief operating officer, 1978-80; chmn., chief exec. officer LucasVarity, Inc., Buffalo, N.Y., 1980-96, CEO, 1996—. Mem. Chief Execs. Orgns., World Pres. Orgns., philanthropic and arts orgns.

RICE, WINSTON EDWARD, lawyer; b. Shreveport, La., Feb. 22, 1946; s. Winston Churchill and Margaret (Coughlin) R.; m. Barbara Reily Gay, Apr. 16, 1977; 1 child, Andrew Hynes; children by previous marriage: Winston Hobson, Christian MacTaggart. Student, Centenary Coll. La., 1967; JD, La. State U., 1971. Bar: La. 1971, Colo. 1990, Tex. 1992. Cons. geologist Gulfport, Miss., 1968-70; ptnr. Phelps, Dunbar, New Orleans, 1971-88; sr. ptnr. Rice, Fowler, New Orleans, Houston, Miami, Fla., London and Bogota, 1988—; instr. law La. State U., Baton Rouge, 1970-71. Assoc. editor La. Law Rev., 1970-71. Mem. La. Bar Assn., Colo. State Bar Assn., Tex. State Bar, New Orleans Bar Assn., Canadian Transp. Lawyers Assn., New Orleans Assn. Def. Counsel, La. Assn. Def. Counsel, Fedn. Ins. and Corporate Counsel, Com. Maritime Internat. (titulary mem.), Maritime Law Assn. U.S. (chmn. subcom. on offshore exploration and devel. 1985-88, vice chmn. com. internat. law of the sea 1988-91, chmn. 1991-95, mem. sec. 1998—), Assn. Average Adjusters U.S., Assn. Average Adjusters (U.K.), Soc. Ins. Trainers and Educators, Ctr. Transp. Law and Policy, Trucking Ind. Defense Assn., Mariners Club (treas. 1974-75, 78-79, sec. 1975-76, v.p. 1976-77, pres. 1977-78), Boston Club, Stratford Club, New Orleans Country Club, Coral Beach and Tennis Club, Order of Coif, Phi Delta Phi, Phi Kappa Phi, Kappa Alpha. Republican. Episcopalian. Office: 201 Saint Charles Ave Ste 3600 New Orleans LA 70170-3600

RICH, ALAN JOHN, medical educator, surgeon; b. Newcastle Upon Tyne, Eng., Oct. 2, 1942; s. John Albert and Margaret (Monaghan) R.; m. Joy Jackson, Sept. 10, 1971; children: Harriet, Tamsin. B Medicine B Surgery, U. Newcastle Upon Tyne, 1968, MD, 1982. Registrar No. Region Tng. Scheme, Newcastle Upon Tyne, 1968-76; sr. rsch. assoc. U. Newcastle Upon Tyne, 1976-79, lectr. in surgery, 1980-90, assoc. postgrad. dean, 1996—; mem. faculty dept. surgery Med. Coll. Va., Richmond, 1980-81; cons. surgeon City Hosps., Sunderland, Eng., 1991—; surveyor Kings Fund Orgnl. Audit, London. Contbr. chpt. to book: Venous Access for Parenteral Nutrition, 1995. Travelling fellow Coun. Europe, 1979, Nat. Assn. Clin. Tutors, 1993. Fellow Royal Coll. Surgeons Eng. (Arris and Gale lectr. 1978); mem. Brit. Soc. Gastroenterology. Office: Postgrad Inst Medicine, 10-12 Framlington Pl, Newcastle upon Tyne NE2 4AB, England

RICH, ALBERT CLARK, solar energy manufacturing executive; b. Wolfeboro, N.H., Feb. 8, 1950; s. Nelson Barnard and Alberta Louise (Pigon) R.; m. Patricia Ann Murphy, July 16, 1973 (div. Aug. 1975); m. Susan Maura McGee, Jan. 26, 1985; children: Ashley, Katherine, Clark, Thomas. BA in Polit. Sci. and Research Processes, Principia Coll., 1979; cert., Solar Energy Research Inst., Golden, Colo., 1981. Owner Antique Classic Auto Restoration, Ft. Lauderdale, Fla., 1975-77, AC-Rich & Sun, Herndon, Va., 1979—; pres., CEO AnuPower Corp.; founder., pres. Am. Solar Network Ltd., 1989—; pres. Suncorps Inc., Watertown, Mass., 1980-82, Cambridge Alt. Power Co., 1982-83; dist. mgr. Sears/Am. Solar King,

Herndon, 1983-85; bd dirs. Monegon Solar, Washington br., 1984; cons. NEEIC, Boston, 1982; chmn. Sec. Energy, Boston, 1983; speaker New Eng. Solar Energy Assn. MIT, Cambridge and Boston, 1983; chmn. solar thermal div. New Eng. Solar Energy Assn., Bay chpt., Boston, 1982-83; contractor White House Pagent of Peace Exhibit. Developer heat cell, heliophase, solar storage tank; inventor, patentee Solar "Skylite" water heater, "Fireball 2001", "Megamatt." Organizer Earth Day, Boston, 1982-83, Sec. of Energy, Boston, 1983, founder ACR Solar Internat., 1997, SolarRoof.com, 1998. Mem. Sacramento Solar Energy Industries Assn. (DOE energy innovation award 1992, DOE energy related inventions program grantee 1994). Avocations: automobile restoration, squash, woodcraft. Four patents granted, including Modular Firebar 2001 solar system, Megamat solar system, 1999. Home and Office: ACR Solar Internat 5840 Gibbons Dr Carmichael CA 95608-6903

RICH, CHARLES ANTHONY, hydrogeologist, consultant; b. London, Nov. 5, 1951; came to U.S., 1955; s. Eric Hebert and Ilse (Renard) R.; m. Linda Christine Johnson, June 23, 1984; 1 child, Oliver Sandor. BS in Geology, Utica Coll. of Syracuse U., 1973; MA in Geology, Queens Coll., CUNY, 1975. Cert. in dispute resolution; cert. profl. geologist. Hydrologic technician U.S. Geol. Survey, Mineola, N.Y., 1973-75; hydrogeologist H2M Corp., P.C., Melville, N.Y., 1975-76, Geraghty & Miller, Inc., Port Washington, N.Y., 1976-79; prin.-in-charge Dames and Moore, Cranford, N.J., 1979-82; pres. C.A. Rich Cons., Inc., Plainview, N.Y., 1982—; cons. to various indsl. and govtl. orgns., mcpls., law firms, comml. developers, 1975—; expert witness Nat. Forensic Ctr., 1989; spkr. Innovative Remedial Techs., 1992, water summit forum, 1993; spkr. Govt. Inst., N.Y. State Conf. on Environ. Due Diligence, 1998, 99, 2000, SUNY-Stonybrook Environ. Compliance for Comml. and Indsl. Properties, 1999. Mem. ASTM (standards com., environ. audits for real property transfer com., environ. monitoring com.), Am. Inst. Profl. Geologists (pres. N.E. sect. 1981-92, nat. govt. affairs com. 1983—, chair N.E. U.S. membership screening bd.), Am. Water Resources Assn., Am. Water Works Assn., Nat. Water Well Assn. (cons. com.), N.Y. Water Pollution Control Assn., Am. Geol. Inst./Geol. Soc. Am., Nat. Forensic Ctr. (expert writer) Cons. Bus. and Industry Assn., Conn. Ground Water Assn., N.Y. State Coun. Profl. Geologists (dir. 2000), Long Island Assn., Expert Witness Assn. E-mail: carcons@rcn.com. Home: 168 Baldwin Ave Locust Valley NY 11560-1920 Office: CA Rich Cons 17 Dupont St Plainview NY 11803-1602

RICH, DAVID BARRY, financial executive, accountant, entertainer; b. Bronx, N.Y., July 3, 1952; s. Steven and Gizella (Kornfeld) R.; m. Biverly Hayag, Dec. 6, 1995; 1 child, Suzanne Stephanie. BS in Health Adminstrn., Ithaca Coll., 1976; postgrad. in acctg., Bryant and Stratton Coll., Buffalo, 1977. Office mgr. Rubin Gorewitz, CPA, N.Y.C., 1977-78; auditor State of Ariz., Phoenix, 1979-83; internal auditor City of Phoenix, 1983-84; sales use tax auditor City of Mesa (Ariz.), 1984-98; pres. Clovis Acctg. Inc., Mesa, 1980-94; rep. H.D. Vest Investment Inc., Irving, Tex., 1984-94; owner D.B. Rich Enterprises Import/Export, Mesa, 1992—; stage name Barry Rich, Stand-up Comedy, 1994—. Treas., bd. dirs. Missing Mutts Inc., Tempe, Ariz., 1986-88. With USAF, 1971-76. Fellow Nat. Assn. Tax Preparers; mem. Toastmasters (treas. Mesa 1986-87), Phi Beta Kappa.

RICH, GEORG, economist, bank executive; b. Schaffhausen, Switzerland, Nov. 11, 1939; s. Arthur Georg Rich and Elisabeth Schneider; m. Ruth Beatrice Bischhausen, 1980; children: Daphne, Clemens. Lic.oec.publ., U. Zurich, Switzerland, 1962; PhD in Econs., Brown U., 1969. Asst. prof., then assoc. prof. Carleton U., Ottawa, Ont., Can., 1967-78, chmn. dept. econs., 1972-74; postdoctoral fellow Yale U., New Haven, 1974; economist, head rsch. Swiss Nat. Bank, Zurich, 1977-85, chief economist, 1985—; vis. prof. Grad. Inst. Internat. Studies, Geneva, 1975; vis. scholar Grad. Sch. Indsl. Adminstrn., Carnegie Mellon U., Pitts., 1989; lectr. U. Zurich, 1978-95, U. Bern, Switzerland, 1980-81. Author monograph: The Cross of Gold. Money and the Canadian Business Cycle, 1867-1913, 1988; contbr. articles to profl. jours. Mem. Swiss Soc. for Stats. and Econs. (pres. 1999—), Am. Econs. Assn., Can. Econs. Assn., German Econs. Soc. Avocation: hiking. Fax: 41-1-6313910. E-mail: rich.georg@snb.ch. Home: Parkweg 7, CH 5000 Aarau Switzerland Office: Swiss Nat Bank, Boersenstrasse 15, CH 8022 Zurich Switzerland

RICH, PAUL JOHN, educator, political consultant; b. Buffalo, Dec. 10, 1938. BA with honors, Harvard U., 1959, EDM, 1963; PhD, U. Western Australia, Perth, 1989. Cons. Ministry Higher Edn., Saudi Arabia, 1979-81; faculty King Saud U., Saudi Arabia, 1979-81; adviser Govt. Qatar, 1981-90; rsch. fellow U. Western Australia, Perth, 1990-93, mem. univ. coun., 1991-93; prof. Univ. de las Americas, Puebla, Mex., 1993—; rsch. coun. of Can. fellow, 1996-97; mem. Govt. House Found., Royal Soc. Western Australia; bd. dirs. Nat. Intelligence Study Ctr., Digest of Mid. East Studies, Acad. Coun. UN Sys., Coun. European Studies, U.S. Commn. Mil. History; gov. Harris Manchester Coll., Oxford Univ.; rsch. assoc. Fed. Res. Bank Dallas, 1995—; Huntington lectr. U.S. Cong., 2000, Library of Cong., 2000. Author: Elixir of Empire, 1989, Invasions of the Gulf, 1991, Chains of Empire, 1991, Tenure and the Demise of Academic Accountability, 1995, America Secret Societies, 2000; editor: A Soldier in Kurdistan, 1992; co-author: Benefits Bestowed?, 1988, Secret Texts, 1995, Promise Keepers, 2000; editor series Allborough Middle East Classics; prodr. (film) The Night of Death, 1995. Vis. fellow Hoover Instn., Stanford U., 1992—; recipient Cameron medal for Rsch., James award for Rsch., Grand Lodge of Tex. Fellow Royal Asiatic Soc. (London-Malaysian, Hong Kong brs.), Royal Anthrop. Inst., Royal Geog. Soc., Royal Soc. Antiquaries, Royal Meteorol. Soc., Royal Microscopical Soc. (hist. sect.), Royal Numis. Soc., Royal Soc. Arts, Coll. Preceptors, Geog. Soc. India, Brit. Soc. Middle East Studies; mem. AAAS, ALA, KP, Am. Hist. Assn. (life), Archeol. Inst., Am. (life), Assn. Geographers (life), Popular Culture Assn., Am. Culture Assn. (chmn. endowment com.), Co. Mil. Historians (life), Nat. Coun. Geographic Edn. (life), Calif. Inst. Internat. Studies (v.p. 1994—), Inst. Advanced Philos. Rsch. (life), Masons, Bostonian Soc. (life), Pilgrim Soc. (life), Knight Templar, Knight of Malta, Shriners, Grange, Stanford Faculty Club, Challoner Club London, Authors Club London, Explorers Club Lima, Royal Soc. Lit., Sutton Ho Soc. (life), Tangier Am. Legation Soc., Delta Phi Epsilon, Phi Beta Delta, Pi Lambda Theta. Democrat. Unitarian. Avocations: water lily propagation, speleology, croquet. E-mail: rich@hoover.stanford.edu. Office: Univ de las Americas, Cholula, 72820 Puebla Mexico also: Stanford U Hoover Instn Stanford CA 94305

RICH, PHILIP DEWEY, publishing executive; b. Nashua, N.H., Feb. 1, 1940; s. John Parker and Olive Frances (Hussey) R.; m. Leslie Ann Burke, June 14, 1974 (div. 1982). AB magna cum laude, Harvard U., 1961; MA, NYU, 1962; postgrad., Princeton U., 1962. Editor Houghton Mifflin Co., Boston, 1964-73; asst. mng. editor UpCountry Mag. Berkshire Eagle, Pittsfield, Mass., 1976-77; editor Book Creations Inc., Canaan, N.Y., 1977-80, editor-in-chief, 1980-91, v.p., exec. editor, 1991-92; cons. editor Berkshire Ho. Publs., Lee, Mass., 1992-93, mng. editor, 1993-96, mng. editor and prodn. editor, 1996-99, editl. dir., prodn. dir., 1999—. Office: Berkshire House Pubs 480 Pleasant St Ste 5 Lee MA 01238-9265

RICH, ROBERT F., law and political science educator; married; 3 children. BA in Govt. with honors, Oberlin Coll., 1971; student, Free U. of Berlin, 1971-72; MA in Polit. Scis., U. Chgo., 1973, PhD in Polit. Scis., 1975. Project dir., asst. rsch. scientist Ctr. for Rsch. on Utilization Sci. Knowledge, Inst. Social Rsch., U. Mich., lectr. dept. polit. sci., 1975-76; asst. prof. politics and pub. affairs Princeton U., 1976-82, coord. domestic and urban policy field Woodrow Wilson Sch., 1976-82; assoc. prof. polit. sci., pub. policy and mgmt. Sch. Urban and Pub. Affairs, Carnegie-Mellon U., 1982-86; prof. polit. sci. law, health resources mgmt., medical humanities and social svcs., community health, prof. Inst. Environ. Studies U. Ill., Urbana, 1986—, dir. Inst. Govt. and Publ. Affairs, 1986-97; acting head med. humanities and social scis. program U. Ill., Urbana-Champaign, 1988-90; prof. law and polit. sci., health resources mgmt. U. Ill., 1996—; prof. law U. Ill., Urbana-Champaign; fellow Johns Hopkins U. Ctr. for Study of Am. Govt., Washington, 1993-95; cons. U.S. Dept. Health and Human Svcs., Carnegie-Mellon U., 1986—, MacArthur Found., NIMH, 1988-89, Food, Drug and Law Inst., HHS, 1989, Am. Career Soc., 1996-97; disting. lectr. German Marshall Fund, Hamburg, Germany, 1997. Author: Social Science Information and Public Policy Making: The Interaction Between Bureaucratic Politics and the Use of Survey Data, 1981; co-author: Government Information Management: A Counter-Report of the Commission on Federal Paperwork, 1980; editor: Translating Evaluation into Policy, 1979, The Knowledge Cycle, 1981, Knowledge, Creation, Diffusion, Utilization, 1979-88, 88-91; co-editor: Competitive Approaches to Health Policy Reform, 1993, Health Policy, Federalism and the Role of the American States, 1996; assoc. editor Society, 1984-88, Evaluation Rev., 1985-89; mem. editl. bd. Policy Studies Rev. Series, 1980-83, Evaluation and Change, 1979-82, Law and Human Behavior, 1983-87; contbr. articles to profl. jours., book chpts. Recipient Emil Limbach Teaching award Carnegie-Mellon U., Sch. Urban and Pub. Affairs, 1985; fellow German Acad. Exch. Program, Fed. Republic Germany, 1971-72, Nat. Opinion Rsch. Ctr. fellow, 1972-73, German Govt. fellow, 1974, Russel Sage Found. Rsch. fellow, 1974-75; vis. scholar Hastings Ctr. for Society, Ethics and Life Scis., 1982. Mem. APA (task force on victims of crime and violence 1982-84), Soc. for Traumatic Stress Studies (bd. dirs. 1980—), World Fedn. for Mental Health (chmn. com. on mental health needs of victims 1985—, vice chmn. 1981-83, Robert F. Rich rsch. ann. award established in his honor, sci. com. on mental health needs of victims 1983), Howard R. Davis Soc. for Knowledge Utilization and Planned Change (pres. 1986-89), Polit. Sci. 400, Policy Studies Assn. (Aaron Wildausky award 1994), Phi Beta Kappa, Sigma Xi, Phi Kappa Phi. Office: U Ill Inst Govt & Pub Affairs 1007 W Nevada St # 204 Urbana IL 61801-3812 also: 815 W Van Buren St Chicago IL 60607-3506

RICHARD, ALAIN, French government official; b. Paris, Aug. 29, 1945; married; three children. Diploma in pub. law, Inst. Polit. Studies, Paris, diploma in lit. Mayor St.-Quen l'Aumone, France, from 1977; now min. defense Ministry Def., Paris; PS dep. Nat. Assembly, Val d'Oise, 1978-93; mem. PS steering com. Nat. Coun., 1981—; v.p. Nat. Assembly, 1987-88; judge Haut Cour de Justice, 1978-93; chmn. Cergy-Pontoise New Town Assn., 1989—; dir. French Inst. for Internat. Rels., 1991—; mem. Conseil d'Etat, 1993-95; senator Val d'Oise, 1995; min. of def., 1997—. Socialist. Office: Ministry of Defense, 14 rue St Dominique, 75007 Paris Cedex 01, France*

RICHARD, GERALD LAWRENCE, soil scientist; b. Brush, Colo., Oct. 26, 1931; s. Donald Lehman and Gladys Lucile (Eikenbary) R.; m. Phyllis Darlene Hansen, Dec. 28, 1952; children: Donald Lawrence, Dale Kendall, Lori Ann Fosmire, Julie Lynn Young. BS in Agronomy, Colo. State U., 1956. Soil scientist Soil Conservation Svc., Wheatland, Wyo., 1957, Torrington and Cheyenne, Wyo., 1959-65; work unit conservationist Soil Conservation Svc., Laramie, Wyo., 1965; area soil scientist Soil Conservation Svc., Bellefonte, Pa., 1965-71; asst. state soil scientist Soil Conservation Svc., Spokane, Wash., 1971-78; sr. soil scientist Soil Conservation Svc./U.S. Agy. for Internat. Devel., Lashkar Gah, Afghanistan, 1978-79; soil scientist/land use interpreter Soil Conservation Svc./U.S. Agy. for Internat. Devel., Kathmandu, Nepal, 1979-80; dep. co-mgr./soil scientist Soil Conservation Svc./Western Carolina U., Kathmandu, 1980-82, team leader resource conservation project, 1982-85; state soil scientist Soil Conservation Svc., Boise, Idaho, 1985-89; cons. soil scientist Spokane, 1989—; Contbr. articles to profl. publs. 1st lt. U.S. Army, 1957-59. Mem. Am. Soc. of Agronomy, Soil Sci. Soc. Am., Soil and Water Conservation Soc. (pres. keystone chpt. Pa. 1971), Washington Soc. of Profl. Soil Scientists. Methodist. Avocations: woodworking, fishing, travel. Home: 2709 S Post St Spokane WA 99203-1877

RICHARD, GISBERT, educational director; b. Emssteck, Germany, May 10, 1949; s. Kurt and Adelheid Richard; m. Claudia Richard. Dr. med., Univ. Münster, Germany, 1974; priv. doz., Univ. Tübingen, Germany, 1984. Fellow Univ. Münster, 1973-78, chief resident, 1978-80; chief resident Univ. Tübingen, 1980-85; prof. Univ. Mainz, 1985-95; chmn. dir. Univ. Hamburg, 1995—. Author: Fluorescein Angiography, 1990, 93, Ophthalmologischer Untersuchungskurs, 1991, Choroidal Circulation, 1992, Flouroresceiriand SCG-Angiography, 1998; contbr. articles to profl. jours. Office: Univ Eye Clinic, Martinistrabe 52, 20246 Hamburg Germany

RICHARD, KARL EDUARD, neurosurgeon, educator; b. Duesseldorf, NRW, Germany, Feb. 8, 1935; s. Marcel Armand and Katharina (Preckel) R.; m. Gabriele Eleonore Heinen, Jan. 23, 1957; children: Felix, Matthias, Robert, Ruth, Stephan, Anton, Martin, Kathrin. Diploma, U. Muenchen, Germany, 1961; MD, München, Germany, 1962; Habilitation Neurosurgery, U. Cologne, Germany, 1977; hon. degree, U. Cologne, 1980. Asst. U. Cologne, 1964-76, Oberarzt neurosurigical dept., 1977-80, prof. neurosurgery, 1981-92; prof. neurosurgery Heinrich-Heine U. Duesseldorf, Germany, 1993-2000. Author: Pathophysiologische Grundlagen der Chirurgie, 1975, Advances in Neurotraumatology, 1991. Patentee in field. Mem. European Soc. Pediatric Neurosurgery, German Assoc. Neurosurgery. Avocations: music, history, literature, classic philology, mountain climbing. Office: Heinrich-Heine U., Moorenstrasse 5, D40225 Duesseldorf Germany

RICHARD, PATRICE, food and cosmetic company executive; b. Paris, Sept. 23, 1946; s. René Richard and Eliane Dedieu; m. Christiane Velasco, Dec. 22, 1969; children: Romain, Raphaël, Elsa. Sales dir. Schmoller et Bompard, 1980-85; mng. dir. Warwick France, Paris, 1985-99; pres. Fontarome, St. Ouen L'Aumône, France, 1999—. Mem. French Soc. Cosmetology (bd. dirs. 1989-99). Avocation: tennis. Office: Fontarome, 66 Rue du Chateau, 95310 Saint Ouen L'Aumône France

RICHARDS, DARRIE HEWITT, investment company executive; b. Washington, May 31, 1921; s. George Jacob and Esmee (MacMahon) R.; m. Patricia Louise Moses, Jan. 1, 1947; children: Hilary Wade, Craig Hewitt, Lynn Cotter. Student, Brown U., 1937-39; BS, U.S. Mil. Acad., 1943; MS, Princeton U., 1949. Commd. 2d lt. U.S. Army, 1943, advanced through grades to maj. gen., 1970; mem. Army Gen. Staff Logistics, 1962-66; brigade comdr., logistics staff officer Europe, 1966-68; comdr. Qui Nhon (Vietnam) Support Command, 1968-69, Western Area Mil. Traffic Mgmt. Command, 1969-70; asst. dep. chief staff for logistics Dept. Army, 1970-73; dep. dir. Def. Logistics Agy., 1973-74, ret., 1974; v.p. Capital Resources Inc., Washington, 1974-75; asso. Devel. Resources, Inc., Alexandria, Va., 1975-79; pres. the Montgomery Corp., Alexandria, 1976-84; mng. gen. ptnr. Craighill Co., Alexandria, 1980—; pres., chmn. Montgomery Group, Inc., 1987—. Author publs. on devel allied strategy in World War II, also nat. transp. policy. Decorated D.S.M. with oak leaf cluster, Legion of Merit with 3 oak leaf clusters, Bronze Star, Air medal with 3 oak leaf clusters; Order Chung Mu (Republic of Korea); Disting. Svc. Order; Honor medal 1st class (Vietnam). Mem. Def. Mgmt. Assn. (v.p. 1973-74), Am. Def. Preparedness Assn. (nat. council 1974-76), Assn. U.S. Army (pres. Heidelburg chpt. 1967-68), alumni assns. U.S Mil Acad., Princeton U., Brown U. Episcopalian. Home: Apt 709 1250 S Washington St Alexandria VA 22314-4455 Office: 300 Montgomery St # 200 Alexandria VA 22314-1516

RICHARDS, DAVID GORDON, financial executive; b. London, Aug. 25, 1928; s. Gordon Charles and Vera Amy (Barrow) R.; m. Catherine Stephanie Woodward, June 18, 1960; children: Victoria Stephanie Amy Brocklebank-Fowler, Edwin David Charles, Katharine Alice Ann Greenwood. Cert., Highgate Sch., London, 1944. Fellow Inst. Chartered Accts. Articled clk. Harmood Banner & Co., London, 1945-55, ptnr., 1955-74; ptnr. Deloitte & Co., London, 1974-84; chmn. Walker Greenbank Plc., 1989-99; Master Chartered Accts. Livery Co., 1987-88. Contbr. articles to profl. jours. Chmn. Highgate Sch., 1983-98; gov. Assoc. Bd. Royal Schs. of Music, Royal Acad. of Music. With Royal Tank Regiment, Brit. Mil., 1947-49, Eng. Decorated Commdr. of Brit. Empire, 1990; hon. fellowship Royal Acad. of Music, 1994. Fellow ICAEW; mem. Inst. Chartered Accts. (pres. 1979-80), British Psychol. Soc. (hon.). Conservative. Ch. of England. Avocations: tennis, golf, shooting, music, silviculture. Home: Eastleach House, Eastleach GL7 3NW Gloucester England

RICHARDS, EDWARD GRAHAM, retired physics educator; b. Congleton, Cheshire, Eng., Mar. 2, 1932; s. Edward Horase and Joan (Kew) R.; m. Dallas Mary Swallow, Aug. 22, 1970. BA, Cambridge (Eng.) U., 1953, PhD, 1960. Rsch. assoc. Princeton (N.J.) U., 1960-63; sci. officer Med. Rsch. Coun., London, 1964-70; lectr. King's Coll., London, 1970-72, sr. lectr., 1972-82, ret., 1982. Author: The Physical Properties of Large Molecules in Solution, Mapping Time: The Calendar and Its History, 1980; contbr. articles to profl. jours. Pilot officer Royal Air Force, 1954-56. Democrat. Avocation: cooking. Home: 2 Peckarmans Wood, London SE26 6RX, England

RICHARDS, GERALD THOMAS, lawyer, consultant, educator; b. Monrovia, Calif., Mar. 17, 1933; s. Louis Jacquelyn Richards and Inez Vivian (Richardson) Hall; children: Patricia M. Richards Grauf, Laura J., Dag Hammarskjold; m. Mary Lou Richards, Dec. 27, 1986. BS magna cum laude, Lafayette Coll., 1957; MS, Purdue U., 1963; JD, Golden Gate U., 1976. Bar: Calif. 1976, U.S. Dist. Ct. (no. dist.) Calif. 1977, U.S. Patent Office 1981, U.S. Ct. Appeals (9th cir.) 1984, U.S. Supreme Ct. 1984. Computational physicist Lawrence Livermore (Calif.) Nat. Lab., 1967-73, planning staff lawyer, 1979, mgr. tch. transfer office, 1980-83; sole practice Lawrence Livermore (Calif.) Nat. Lab., Livermore, 1976-78, Oceanside, Calif., 1994-97; emeritus atty. pro bono participant Calif. State Bar, Concord, Calif., 1998—; emeritus atty. pro bono participant Contra Costa Sr. Legal Svcs., Concord, 1998—, 1998—; constrn. law instr. Contrs. State License Schs., Van Nuys, Calif., 1998; mem. exec. com., policy advisor Fed. Lab. Consortium for Tech. Transfer, 1980-88; panelist, del. White House Conf. on Productivity, Washington, 1983; del. Nat. Conf. on Tech. and Aging, Wingspread, Wis., 1981. Commr. Housing Authority, City of Livermore, 1977, vice chairperson, 1978, chairperson, 1979; pres. Housing Choices, Inc., Livermore, 1980-84; bd. dirs. Valley Vol. Ctr., Pleasanton, Calif., 1983, pres., 1984-86. Served to maj. U.S. Army, 1959-67. Recipient Engrng. award GE, 1956. Mem. ABA, Calif. State Bar (conv. alt. del. 1990-92), Alameda County Bar Assn., Contra Costa County Bar Assn., Ea. Alameda County Bar Assn. (sec. 1978, bd. dirs. 1991-92, chair lawyers referral com. 1992-93), Santa Barbara County Bar Assn., San Diego County Bar Assn., Bar Assn. No. San Diego County, San Francisco Bar Assn., Phi Beta Kappa, Tau Beta Pi, Sigma Pi Sigma. Home: 2505 Whitetail Dr Antioch CA 94509-7744

RICHARDS, JAMES CARLTON, microbiologist, business executive; b. Storm Lake, Iowa, Aug. 19, 1947; s. Jack M. and June G. Richards; m. Lois Ruth Rebbe, July 22, 1974 (div. Sept. 1986); 1 child, Kimberly Ann; m. Susan M. Wos, Aug. 27, 1988; children: Derek Anthony, Kristin Marie. BS in Microbiology, U. Ill., 1970; PhD in Microbiology, So. Ill. U., 1977. Postdoctoral fellow Pa. State U. Med. Ctr., Hershey, Pa., 1977-79; sr. scientist E.I. duPont de Nemours, Wilmington, Del., 1979-85; program mgr. Amoco, Naperville, Ill., 1985-86; dir. bus. Gene-Trak Systems, Framingham, Mass., 1986-90; mng. dir. Carlton BioVenture Ptnrs., Sudbury, Mass., 1990—; pres., CEO, bd. dirs. Symbollon Corp., Framingham, Mass., 1991-95; pres., CEO, bd. dirs. IntelliGene, Ltd., Sudbury, Mass., 1995-2000, Jerusalem, Israel, 1995-2000; pres., CEO, chmn. bd. dirs. Edgelight Bioscis., Inc., Sudbury, Mass., 2000—; invited lectr. on genetic analysis and advances in gene amplification and detection 4th ann. Advances in Gene Amplification and Selection Conf. Cambridge Healthtech Inst., McLean, Va., 1996. Contbr. chpt. to books, articles to sci. jours.; patentee in field. Deacon, chair capitol fund dr. United Ch. of Christ, Framingham, 1988—. Mem. AAAS, Am. Soc. for Microbiology, Am. Chem. Soc., Inst. Food Technologists, N.Y. Acad. Scis., Clin. Ligand Soc., Ill. Alumni Assn., Sigma Xi, Theta Xi. Avocations: golf, travel, jogging, gardening, skiing. E-mail: intelli@tiac.net; also jim@edgeLightbiosciences.com. Home and Office: 44 Codman Dr Sudbury MA 01776-1745

RICHARDS, JAY CLAUDE, commercial photographer, news service executive, historian; b. Glen Ridge, N.J., Apr. 6, 1954; s. Jacob Tilghman and Joan Louise (Walsh) R. Student, Tenn. Wesleyan Coll., Athens, 1972-73. Various positions armed security work, 1973-75; reporter, photographer Press Publs.: The News, Belvidere, N.J., 1977-98; pres. J.C. Richards Assocs., Harmony Twp., N.J., 1980—; owner Poor Richards' Brit. Gun Shop, Harmony Twp., 1976—; reporter The Knowlton News, 1998—; photography judge Warren County 4-H, Belvidere, 1990—; press officer Warren County Office Emergency Mgmt., Belvidere, 1989-98. Author: Penn, Patriots and the Pequest: The History of Pre-Victorian Belvidere, 1716-1845, 1995, Flames Along the Delaware, 1996 (N.J. Frontier Guard's Book award 1997), Bugles, Battles and Belvidere: Warren County, N.J. in the Civil War, 1997, Officers and Men of Warren County, N.J. in the Civil War, 1998, More Bugles, Battles and Belvidere: Warren County, N.J. Civil War Letters to Home, 1999, Following the Hand of Franklin: Warren County, N.J. and the Search for the North Pole, 2000. Mem. Hazardous Materials Adv. Coun., Warren County, N.J., Joint Emergency Mgmt. coun., Belvidere/White Twp., N.J., Warren County Arts Adv. Coun., Warren County War Meml. Com., 1997-98; trustee Warren County War Meml. Corp. 1999—; cons. Harmony N.J. Hist. Preservation Commn., 2000—. Named Hon. Mem. Boy Scout Troop 141, Belvidere, 1993; recipient Outstanding Cmty. Svc. award Am. Legion Post 131, 1994. Mem. Nat. Press Photographers Assn., Soc. Profl. Journalists, Res. Officers Assn. U.S., Sr. Army Res. Comdrs. Assn., U.S. Naval Inst, Oxford N.J. Hist. Soc. Episcopalian. Avocations: militaria collecting, gourmet cooking, gardening, herbal medicine. Home and Office: 3110 Belvidere Rd Phillipsburg NJ 08865-9515

RICHARDS, KEITH, musician; b. Dartford, Kent, Eng., Dec. 18, 1943; s. Bert and Doris Richards; m. Anita Pallenberg; children: Marlon, Angela; m. Patti Hansen, Dec. 18, 1983; children: Theodora, Alexandra. Student, Sidcup Art Sch. Recording artist on label Mindless Records. Lead & rhythm guitarist, vocalist, Rolling Stones, 1962—; films include: Sympathy for the Devil, 1970, Gimme Shelter, 1970, Ladies and Gentlemen, the Rolling Stones, 1974, Let's Spend the Night Together, 1983, The Magic Years, Vol. 1, 1989, 25X5: The Continuing Adventures of the Rolling Stones, 1989, At the Max, 1991, Rolling Stones: Voodoo Lounge, 1994, The History of Rock 'N' Roll, Vol. 7, 1995, The Rolling Stones Rock 'N' Roll Circus, 1996, Can't You Hear the Wind Howl? The Life & Music of Robert Johnson, 1997, Rolling Stones: Bridges to Babylon Tour '97-98; film mus. dir. (with Chuck Berry, Eric Clapton and friends) Hail! Hail! Rock & Roll, 1987; composer (with Mick Jagger) numerous songs and ablums, 1964—, including (albums) The Rolling Stones, Now!, 1964, Aftermath, 1966, Flowers, 1967, Beggars Banquet, 1968, Let It Bleed, 1969, Sticky Fingers, 1971, Hot Rocks, 1972, Exile on Main Street, 1972, Goat's Head Soup, 1973, It's Only Rock and Roll, 1974, Metamorphosis, 1975, Black and Blue, 1976, Some Girls, Emotional Rescue, 1980, Tattoo You, 1981, Still Life, 1982, Under Cover, 1983, Dirty Work, 1986, Steel Wheels, 1989, Flashpoint, 1991, Voodoo Lounge, 1994 (Grammy award Best Rock Album), Stripped, 1995, Bridges to Babylon, 1997, No Security, 1999; (songs) Wild Horses, Angie, Start Me Up, Honky Tonk Woman, Jumpin' Jack Flash, (I Can't Get No) Satisfaction, Before They Make Me Run, Miss You, Happy, Shattered, Paint It Black, Waiting On a Friend, Ruby Tuesday, You Can't Always Get What You Want, Brown Sugar, Tumbling Dice, Faraway Eyes, Mixed Emotions, Rock and a Hard Place, Highwire, Love is Strong, Anybody Seen My Baby; prodr.: Wingless Angels, 1997, (soundtrack album) Hail! Hail! Rock 'N Roll, 1987; solo albums: Talk Is Cheap, 1988, Keith Richards & The X-Pensive Winos Live At The Hollywood Palladium, Dec. 15, 1988, 1991, Main Offender, 1992. Recipient Living Legend award Internat. Rock; inducted into Rock and Roll Hall of Fame, 1989. Address: care Raindrop Svcs 1776 Broadway New York NY 10019-2002*

RICHARDS, KENNETH ROLAND, drama and theater studies educator; b. London, Feb. 21, 1934; s. Harold Gordon and Hilda Jane (Everett) R.; m. Laura Anna Trotta, July 14, 1962; children: Francesca, Rebecca. BA, Oxford (U.K.) U., 1959, MA (hon.), 1963; MA (hon.), Manchester (U.K.) U., 1981; student, Royal Acad. Dramatic Art, 1952-53. Lectr. Ljabljana U., Slovenia, 1960-63, Trondheim (Norway) U., 1963-64; reader Uppsala (Sweden) U., 1964-66; vis. lectr. Oslo U., 1967; lectr., sr. lectr., reader Manchester U., 1968-78, prof. drama, head dept., dir. Univ. Theatre, 1978-00, prof. emeritus, 1999—; vis. prof. U. Rome, U. Milan, Italy, U. Genoa, Italy, U. Catania, Italy. Co-author: Comedy, 1976, Revels History of Drama, Vol. VI, 1978, The Commedia Dell'Arte: A Documentary History, 1990, Shakespeare Nas Telas: Cinema e Video, 1995; co-editor: Nineteenth Century British Theatre, 1971, 18th Century English Stage, 1973, Western Popular Theatre, 1978; contbr. to Oxford Companion to the Theatre, Cambridge Guide to World Theatre, International Dictionary of Theatre, Blackwell Companion to Enlightenment; co-editor Theatre Rsch. Internat., 1972-78; gen. editor Drama and Theatre Studies, 1971-85, Stage and Screen Studies, 2000—. Mem. coun. Contact Theatre Co., Manchester, 1975-98, European Inst. for Media, 1982-94; dir. Internat. Shakespeare Globe Ctr., London, 1987-90, Courtyard Theatre Co., Manchester, 1977-80; mem. mgmt. bd. Oldham Coliseum Theatre Co., 1979-82; mem. City of Manchester Cultural Com., 1978-84, City of Manchester Art Galleries Com., 1984-88. Recipient various rsch. award from Leverhulme, Brit. Acad.; rsch. fellow Folger Shakespeare Libr., Washington, 1973, Huntington Libr., Pasadena, Calif., Jean Monnet fellow European U. Inst., Florence, Italy, 1988-89. Mem. Soc. for Theatre Rsch., Internat. Fedn. for Theatre Rsch. Avocations: music, gardening. Home: Calgarth 48 Barlow Moor Rd, Didsbury

Manchester M20 2GJ, England Office: Manchester U Dept Drama, Oxford Rd, Manchester M13, England

RICHARDS, LACLAIRE LISSETTA JONES (MRS. GEORGE A. RICHARDS), social worker; b. Pine Bluff, Ark.; d. Artie William and Geraldine (Adams) Jones; m. George Alvarez Richards, July 26, 1958; children: Leslie Rosario, Lia Mercedes, Jorge Edward Ferguson. BA, Nat. Coll. Christian Workers, 1953; MSW, U. Kans., 1956; postgrad, Columbia U., 1960. Diplomate Clin. Social Work, Am. Bd. of Examiners in Clin. Social Work, Nat. Assn. Social Workers; cert. gerontologist. Psychiat., supr., tchg., cmty. orgn., adminstrv., cons. Hastings Regional Ctr., Ingleside, Nebr., 1956-60; supr., cons., adminstrv. VA Hosp., Knoxville, Iowa, 1960-74; field instr. for grad. students U. Mo., 1969-74, 78-90, com. chmn., 1969-70; sr. social worker Mental Health Inst., Cherokee, Iowa, 1974-77; adj. asst. prof. dept. social behavior U. S.D., Cherokee, Iowa, 1974-77; instr. dept. psychiat. U. S.D., 1988-96, Augustina Coll., 1981-86; outpatient social worker VA Med. and Regional Office Ctr., Sioux Falls, S.D., 1978-96, med., surg. and intensive care social worker, 1992-96, 1990-92, sur. and intermediate care social worker, 1992-96, EEO counselor; EEO counselor. Mem. Knoxville Juvenile adv. com., 1963-65, 68-70, sec., 1965-66, chmn., 1966-68; sec. Urban Renewal Citizens' adv. com., Knoxville, 1966-68; mem. United Meth. Ch. task force Expt. Styles Ministry and Leadership, 1973-74, mem. adult choir, mem. ch. and society com.; counselor Knoxville Youth Line program; sec. exec. com. Vis. Nurse Assn., 1979-80; canvasser cmty. fund drs., Knoxville; mem. Cherokee Civil Rights Commn.; bd. dirs., pub. rels., mem. devel. and program devel. cons. YWCA, 1983-85; bd. dirs. Family Svc. Agy., 1989-90, Food Svcs. Ctr., Inc., 1992-96, mem. S.D. Symphonic Choir, 1991—; mem. Youth-At-Risk Task Force and Multicultural Ctr. Advocate; deaconness 1st Evang. Free Ch., 1999—. Named S.D. Social Worker of Yr., 1983. Mem. NAACP (chmn. edn. com. 1983-85), AAUW (sec. Hastings chpt. 1958-60), Nat. Assn. Social Workers (co-chmn. Nebr. chpt. profl. standards com. 1958-59), Acad. Cert. Social Workers, S.D. Assn. Social Workers (chmn. minority affairs com., v.p. S.E. region 1980, pres. 1980-82, exec. com. 1985-84, mem. social policy and action com.), Nebr. Assn. Social Workers (chmn. 1958-59), Seventh Dist. S.D. Med. Soc. Aux., Coalition on Aging., Nat. Assn. Social Workers (qualified clin. social worker 1991—), Methodist (Sunday Sch. tchr. adult divsn.; mem. commn. on edn.; mem. Core com. for adult edn.; mem. Adult Choir; mem. Social Concerns Work Area). Mem. 1st Evangelical Free Ch. (deaconness 1999—). Home: 1701 E Ponderosa Dr Sioux Falls SD 57103-5019

RICHARDS, LEONARD MARTIN, investment executive, consultant; b. Phila., June 4, 1935; s. Leonard Martin and Marion Clara (Lang) R.; m. Phyllis Janelle Mowrey, Aug. 26, 1961 (div. Aug. 1978); children: Lisa, David Reed. BS, Pa. State U., 1957; MBA, U. Pa., 1963; MTh, Universal Theol. Sem., 1996, ThD, 2000. Asst. to sr. ptnr. Van Cleef, Jordan & Wood, N.Y.C., 1963-68; v.p., portfolio mgr. Bernstein-Macaulay, Inc., N.Y.C., 1968-72; ptnr. G. H. Walker, Laird Co., N.Y.C., 1972-74; v.p., trust officer, mgr. instnl. funds group Republic Bank N.A., Dallas, 1974-77; v.p., sr. investment officer, mem. exec. com. Variable Annuity Life Ins. Co., Houston, 1977-88; v.p., sr. investment officer Am. Gen. Series Portfolio Co., 1985-88; bd. dirs., pres. L.M. Richards & Co., Houston, 1982—, Capital Instnl. Svcs., Inc., Dallas, 1990-99, Trinity Life Ctr., Houston, 1996—. Pres., bd. dirs. Sand Dollar, Inc., Houston, 1985-96; bd. dirs. Houston Chorale, 1988-90; trustee Post Oak Sch., Houston, 1997-99, Universal Theol. Sem., 1997—. Capt. U.S. Army, 1957-65. Mem. Assn. Investment Mgmt. and Rsch., Houston Soc. Fin. Analysts. Republican. Avocations: skiing, travel, scuba. Home: 9023 Briar Forest Dr Houston TX 77024-7220 Office: LM Richards & Co 4600 Post Oak Place Dr Ste 301 Houston TX 77027-9727

RICHARDS, MARTIN GOMM, transportation planner; b. Dorridge, Eng., July 15, 1939; s. Sidney Edward and Phyllis (Gomm) R.; m. Jennifer Margaret Round; children: Mark Sidney, Matthew John, Sarah Jennifer. BSc in Engring., U. Coll., London, 1960; MSc, Birmingham (Eng.) U., 1962, diploma in planning, 1965. Assoc. TPA, Birmingham, 1965-69; dir. Buro Goudappel en Coffeng Deventer, The Netherlands, 1969-75, Alan M. Voorhees & Assocs. Ltd., London, 1975-76; dir. Martin and Vorhees Assocs., London, 1976-78, mng. dir., 1978-83; chmn. The MVA Group, Woking, 1983-2000. Gov. Reigate Grammar Sch., 1988—. Decorated officer Brit. Empire. Fellow U.K. Coun. Chartered Inst. Transport. Avocations: walking, wine, food. Home: The Old Sch House, Coldharbour, Dorking Surrey RH5 6HF, England Office: The MVA Group MVA House, Victoria Way, Woking Surrey GU21 1DD, England

RICHARDS, MARTIN PAUL M., social scientist; b. Cambridge, England, Jan. 26, 1940; s. Paul Westmacott and Sarah Anne (Hotham) R.; children: Laura, Casey. BA, Cambridge U., 1962, MA, 1965, PhD, 1965, ScD, 2000. Research fellow Trinity Coll., Cambridge, 1965-69, Mental Health Res. Fund, Cambridge, 1970; lectr. Cambridge U., 1970-89, reader in human devel., 1989-97, prof. family rsch., 1997—; advisor Penguin Books, London, 1976-87. Author: Infancy, 1980; co-author: Divorce Matters, 1987, Sexual Arrangments, 1993; editor: Children of Social Worlds, 1986, The Toubled Helix, 1996, others. Mem. coun. Tavistock Inst., London, 1986-99; trustee Bardsey Island Trust, Wales, 1980-2000; mem. Human Genetics Commn., 2000—. mem. Soc. Research Child Devel., Soc. Reproductive and Infant Psychology (editorial bd. 1985—). Labour Party. Avocations: gardening and bird watching. Office: Ctr for Family Rsch, Free School Ln, Cambridge CB2 3RF, England

RICHARDS, PATRICIA JONES, artist, poet; b. Pomona, Calif., Nov. 20; d. Earle Feurte Jones and Florence Frable Slawson; m. Addison Whitaker Richards, May 1, 1950 (dec. Mar. 1964). BA, Pomona Coll., 1944; cert. nursery sch. tchr., Scripps Coll., 1944. Acquistions libr. Calif. State Polytechnic U., Pomona, 1979-85. Author: Self-Expression, Poems and Watercolors, 1996, "Old Friends" Through Sun and Shower, 1997, Pensative Poems and Watercolors (Golden Leaves award 1996-97, 99-2000), 2000. Author: Poems and Self-Expression and Watercolors, 1996, Through Sun and Shower, 1997.

RICHARDS, RANDAL WILLIAM, chemist, educator; b. Wednesbury, U.K., Aug. 30, 1948; s. William James and Anne Florence (Fletcher) R.; m. Patricia Margaret Magee, Sept. 7, 1972; children: Robert James, Gregory Peter. BS, U. Salford, 1971, PhD, 1974, DSc, 1994. Rsch. fellow Deutsches Kunststoff Ins., Darmstadt, Germany, 1974-75; rsch. assoc. Imperial Coll., London, 1975-77; lectr., sr. lectr. U. Strathclyde, Glasgow, Scotland, 1977-89; reader U. Durham, U.K., 1990-95, prof., 1995—; chmn. Neutron Beam Rsch. Com., U.K., 1991-94; mem. sci. bd. Sci. and Engring. Rsch. Coun., U.K., 1991-93. Editor: Polymer; contbr. over 100 articles to profl. jours. Fellow Royal Soc. Chemistry (Macromolecules and Polymers prize 1990), Am. Chem. Soc. Home: 25 Telford Close, High Shincliffe DH1 2YJ, England Office: U Durham, Dept Chemistry, Durham DH1 3LE, England

RICHARDS, SIR REX EDWARD, scientist, university administrator, educator; b. Colyton, Devon, Oct. 28, 1922; s. H.W. and E.N. Richards; m. Eva Edith Vago, 1948; 2 children. BA, Oxford U., 1945. Prof. chemistry Oxford U., 1964-69; warden Merton Coll. Oxford U., 1969-84, vice chancellor, 1977-81; chmn. Oxford Enzyme Group, 1969-83; chmn. Br. Postgrad. Med. Fedn., 1986-93; pres. Royal Soc. Chemistry, 1990-92; commr. Royal Commn. Exhbn. 1851, 1984-97; chancellor U. Exeter, 1982-98; dir. The Leverhulme Trust, 1984-94. Trustee Ciba Found., 1978-97, Nat. Heritage Meml. Fund, 1980-84, Tate Gallery, 1982-88, 91-93, Nat. Gallery, 1982-88, 89-93, Nat. Gallery Trust, 1997—, Henry Moore Found., 1989—. Address: 13 Woodstock Close, Oxford OX2 8DB, England

RICHARDS, RUTH, psychiatrist, educational psychologist; b. Lincoln, Nebr.; d. Dexter N. and Ruth (Fulton) R. BS with honors, Stanford U., 1965; MA, U. Calif., Berkeley, 1969, PhD, 1971; MD, Harvard Med. Sch., Boston, 1980. Diplomate Am. Bd. Psychiatry and Neurology; lic. psychologist, Mass.; cert. secondary edn. educator in physics, math, art, Calif. Asst. prof. ednl. psychology Boston U. Sch. Edn., 1971-75; lectr. in psychology dept. psychiatry Harvard Med. Sch., Boston, 1978—, fellow, instr., asst. clin. prof. psychiatry, 1981-94; assoc. attending psychiatrist, various appointments McLean Hosp., Belmont, Mass., 1978—, rsch. affiliate; assoc. clin. prof. U. Calif., San Francisco, 1994—; prof. psychology Saybrook Grad. Sch., San Francisco, 1995—, faculty co-chair, 1996-98; chair Consciousness and Spirituality, 1999-2000; exec. adv. bd. Ency. of Creativity, 1996—; adv. bd. Manic-Depressive Illness Found., 1989—. Mem. editl. bd. Creativity Rsch. Jour., 1992—, Jour. Humanistic Psychology, 1996—; co-editor: Eminent Creativity, Everyday Creativity and Health, 1997; contbr. numerous articles to profl. jours. and chpts. to books. Adv. panel biol. application program, Office of Technol. Assessment, U.S. Congress, 1987-88; dir. women's leadership project in adult edn., Boston U., 1974-75, others. Sr. asst. surgeon USPHS, 1980-81. Mem. Am. Psychol. Assn., Soc. Chaos Theory in Psychology and the Life Scis. Avocations: visual art, creative writing, photography, physics.

RICHARDS, SIMON PAUL, diplomat. BA, U. West Indies, Mona, Jamaica, 1963; postgrad., CUNY, 1968; LLB, U. London, 1974. Bar: Eng. and Eales 1975, N.Y. 1977, U.S. Dist. Ct. (so. and ea. dists.) N.Y. 1978, Commonwealth of Dominica, West Indies 1980. Clerical officer Treasury Dept., Dominica, 1957-58; asst. master Dominica Grammar Sch., 1958-60, sr. asst. master, 1963-66; supr. Govt. Statis. Dept., Dominica, 1966-67; caseworker City of N.Y. Dept. Social Svcs., 1967-74; assoc. Silver & Brooks, 1977, Mary Ann Jennings, 1977—; perm. rep. of Dominica to UN N.Y.C., 1995—. Office: Perm Mission of Dominica to UN 800 2d Ave Ste 400 H New York NY 10017-4504

RICHARDS, STEVEN THOMAS, psychotherapist, educator, consultant, author; b. Liverpool, England, Mar. 22, 1957; s. Thomas Maxwell and Joan (Dickman) R.; m. Pauline Anne Elcock, Sept. 19, 1981; children: Gareth Patrick, Rhiannon. Police officer Liverpool, Eng., 1974-87; dir. Systems Therapy Ltd., Liverpool, England, 1989-92; dir., lectr. Ctr. Psycho-Sustems Therapy, Liverpool, England, 1990-92; psychotherapist Claughton Med. Ctr., Birkenhead, England, 1991-92, Grove Med. Ctr., Wallasey, England, 1992-93; psychotherapist, respiratory psychophysiologist Neston Med. Ctr., Cheshire, England, 1991-93; clin. dir., lectr. Inst. Psycho-Systems Analysis, Liverpool, 1993—; psychotherapist, respiratory psychophysiologist Homlands Med. Ctr., Birkenhead, 1994-2000, Seabank Med. Ctr., Wallasey, 1997-99; founder Psycho-Systems Analysis Model of Psychotherapy, 1989, Dialectical Syncretic Sch. of Philosophy, 1990; cons. Brit. Coun. for Complementary Medicine, 1996; dir. Renaissance Acad. for Analytical Psychotherapy, 2000, Renaissance Books Ltd., 2000. U.K. rep. Bamboo Tmeple Chinese Benevolent Assn., 1999. Fellow Soc. Martial Arts (prin. N.W. U.K. br. 1998-99); mem. European Assn. Counseling (prof. issues working group 1993-94), British Assn. Counseling (cons. coun. 1992—, mem. media team 1993—), British Assn. Holistic-Med. Psychotherapists (chair 1999), Internat. Soc. Advancement Respiratory Psychophysiology, Amateur Martial Assn. (U.K., black belt 6th degree 1997), Chin Woo Athletic Assn. of Hong Kong (life). Avocations: astronomy, history, archaeology, anthropology, Chinses martial arts. Office: Mayer Hall, The Village, Bebington CH63 7PL, England

RICHARDS, SUZANNE V., lawyer; b. Columbia, S.C., Sept. 7, 1927; d. Raymond E. and Elise C. (Gray) R. AB, George Washington U., 1948, JD with distinction, 1957, LLM, 1959. Bar: D.C. 1958. Sole practice Washington, 1974—; lectr. in family and probate law. Bd. dirs. Coun. for Ct. Excellence. Recipient John Bell Larner award George Washington U., 1958; named Woman Lawyer of Yr., Women's Bar Assn. D.C., 1977. Mem. Bar Assn. D.C. (pres. 1989-90), Women's Bar Assn. (pres. 1977-78), Trial Lawyers Assn. of D.C. (bd. govs. 1978-82, 85—, treas. 1982-85), D.C. Bar, Fed. Bar Assn., ABA (ho. dels. 1988-90), D.C. Jud. Conf. Home: 530 N St SW Washington DC 20024-4546 Office: PO Box 65466 Washington DC 20035-5466

RICHARDS, WESLEY JON, newscaster, writer, producer; b. N.Y.C., Apr. 9, 1942; s. Mark and Pearl R. Richards; m. Carole A. Louis, June 8, 1962; children: Wesley, Julie, Lynn, Charles. Student, Hofstra U., 1959-62; MA, Antioch U., 1990. Radio personality Sta. WFYI, Mineola, N.Y., 1965, Sta. WGBB, Freeport, N.Y., 1966-70; editor AP, N.Y.C., 1971-74; radio personality Sta. WHLI, Hempstead, N.Y., 1974-76, Sta. WRFM, N.Y.C., 1976-86; broadcaster NBC Radio Network, N.Y.C., 1987-89; newscaster Sta. WYNY, N.Y.C., 1989-90, Sta. WOR, N.Y.C., 1990-92; writer, prodr. NBC News, 1992—, 1992—; freelance entertainer, 1955—; correspondent ABC Radio Network, N.Y.C., 1975, 90. Writer numerous essays, poems and songs, 1960—. Mem. AFTRA, Writers Guild Am., Broadcast Pioneers, Nat. Assn. Broadcast Employees and Technicians.

RICHARDSON, ANTHONY JAMES, marine biologist, researcher; b. Penrith, NSW, Australia, Feb. 15, 1970; s. Graham Arthur and Lynette (Morris) R. BSc, U. Queensland, Australia, 1991, BSc with 1st class honours, 1992; PhD, U. Cape Town, South Africa, 1998. Part-time lectr. U. Western Cape, Bellville, South Africa, 1996-99; sr. rsch. scientist U. Cape Town, 1999—. iology. articles to sci. jours., including Limnology and Oceanography, Jour. Plankton Rsch., South African Jour. Marine Sci., Jour. Fish Biology, Fisheries Oceanography, ICES Jour. Marine Sci., NAGA. Scholar U. Cape Town, 1993-97; fellow Found. for R & D, South Africa, 1998-99. Mem. Am. Soc. Limnology and Oceanography. Avocations: bird watching, squash, racquetball, wine collecting. Office: U Cape Town Ocean Dept, Rondebosch, Cape Town 7701, South Africa

RICHARDSON, ARLINE ANNETTE, accountant, comptroller; b. N.Y.C., Aug. 20, 1939; d. Charles Sidney and Kathleen Gertrude (Sinclair) Hunt; m. David Edward Richardson, Sept. 13, 1958; children: Valerie-Jayne, LaVerne. AA, Bronx (N.Y.) C.C., 1976; BBA, CUNY, 1979, MPA, 1984. Mgr. patient accounts Jewish Home and Hosp. for Aged, N.Y.C., 1960-80; chief bookkeeper Edwin Gould Svcs. for Children, N.Y.C., 1980-81; staff acct. N.Y. Hosp., N.Y.C., 1981-84; mgr. Met. Transp. Authority, N.Y.C., 1984-92; compt. The Computer Lab., Morrisville, N.C., 1993—; substitute tchr. Vance County Schs., 1998-2000; instr. Vance-Granville C.C., 1999—. Vol. cmty. tax aide, N.Y.C., 1979-83; tutor Henderson (N.C.) Mid. Sch., 1993-95; vol. Maria Parham Hosp., 1993-99, mem. ethics com., 1996—; mem. Henderson-Vance County Human Rels. Commn., 1996—; mem. Henderson Zoning Bd. Adjustment, 1996—; active Leadership Vance, 1996. Recipient Mitchell-Titus award, 1979. Mem. Am. Assn. Ret. Persons (assoc. dist. coord., instr. tax-aide program North Ctrl. N.C. 1993-99, dist. coord.), Henderson Bus. and Profl. Women's Club, (v.p.), Beta Gamma Sigma, Phi Theta Kappa (Mitchell-Titus award 1979). Home: 1614 Peace St Henderson NC 27536-3549 Office: The Computer Lab 2700 Gateway Centre Blvd Morrisville NC 27560-9137

RICHARDSON, A(RTHUR) LESLIE, former medical group consultant; b. Feb. 21, 1910; came to U.S., 1930, naturalized, 1937; s. John William and Emily Lilian (Wilkins) R.; m. B. Kathleen Sargent, Oct. 15, 1937. Student spl. courses, U. So. Calif., 1933-35. Mgr. Tower Theater, L.A., 1931-33; acct. Felix-Krueper Co., L.A., 1933-35; indsl. engr. Pettengill, Inc., L.A., 1935-57; purchasing agt. Gen. Petroleum Corp., L.A., 1937-46; adminstr. Beaver Med. Clinic, Redlands, Calif., 1946-72, exec. cons., 1972-75, 85; sec.-treas. Fern Properties, Inc., Redlands, 1955-75, Redelco, Inc., Redlands, 1960-67; pres. Buinco, Inc., Redlands, 1956-65; vice-chmn. Redlands adv. bd. Bank of Am., 1973-80; exec. cons. Med. Adminstrs. Calif., 1975-83. Pres. Redlands Area Cmty. Chest, 1953; vol. exec. Internat. Exec. Svc. Corps, Jakarta, 1977, Singapore, 1979; mem. San Bernardino County (Calif.) Grand Jury, 1952-53; bd. dirs. Beaver Med. Clinic Found., Redlands, 1961-2000, sec.-treas., 1961-74, pres., 1974-75, chmn. bd. dirs., 1992-2000. Lt. Med. Adminstrv. Corps, AUS, 1942-45. Recipient Redlands Civic award Elks, 1953. Fellow Am. Coll. Med. Practice Execs. (life, disting. fellow 1980, pres. 1965-66, dir.); mem. Med. Group Mgmt. Assn. (hon. life; mem. nat. long range planning com. 1963-68, pres. western sect. 1960), Kiwanis (pres. 1951), Masons. Episcopalian. Home: 1 Verlie Dr Redlands CA 92373-6943

RICHARDSON, DANA ROLAND, video producer; b. Mason City, Iowa, Jan. 11, 1945; s. Dana Roland Richardson and Louise Marion (Duke) Sarles; m. Sandra Anderson, June 12, 1966; children: Patricia Nan, Dana Roland, Jr. BS, UCLA, 1966, MBA, 1967. CPA, Calif., N.Y. Staff acct. Arthur Young, L.A., 1967-72, mgr., 1972-76; prin. Arthur Young, N.Y.C., 1976-78; ptnr. Ernst & Young, N.Y.C., 1978-94, Dream Street Prodns., New Canaan, Conn., 1994—. Author: A Manager's Guide to Computer Timesharing, 1975, Audit and Control of Information Systems, 1987. Staff sgt. Reserves USANG, 1967-73. Recipient Nat. Videographer award, 1998, 99, Telly award, 1999; named one of Techology 100 Top 100 Achievers in Technology in Am., Technology Mag., 1982. Mem. AICPA, Calif. Soc. CPA's. Republican. Episcopalian. Avocations: boating, fishing, music, videography, multimedia. Office: Dream St Prodns PO Box 73 New Canaan CT 06840-0073

RICHARDSON, DOREEN GLADYS, retired medical administrator; b. Ilford, Essex, Eng., Jan. 2, 1926; d. Wilfrid John and Gladys Lily (Shaw) R. Cert., Herts and Essex H.S., 1942. Stage mgr. various Broadway shows, N.Y.C., 1959-69; adminstr. cmty. medicine Mt. Sinai Med. Ctr., N.Y.C., 1969-90; ret., 1990. Mem. WRNS, 1943-45. Pres. outreach programs Holy Trinity Ch., N.Y.C., 1982-90; area chmn. Children's Hospice for Ea. Region, Cambridge, 1991—; vice chmn. Co. at Christmas; vol. Whitechapel Mission for the Homeless; local fund raiser Mercy Ships Hosp. Outreach Program, 1998—; com. mem. Cancer Soc., 2000—. Mem. BSNADFAS. Democrat. Episcopalian. Home: Balfour, 6 Foxley Dr, Bishop's Stortford Herts CM23 2EB, England

RICHARDSON, ELIZABETH HALL, ecologist; b. Waltham, Mass., June 5, 1937; d. Livingston and Elizabeth (Blodgett) Hall; m. (div.); children: Elisabeth F. Richardson, Anne K. Richardson. AB, Radcliffe Coll., 1959; MPA, U. So. Calif., 1975; MBA, U. Denver, 1986. Asst. biology tchr. Presbyn. Ladies Coll., Pymble, NSW, Australia, 1959; tchr. drama Middlesex Sch., Concord, Mass., 1961-62; adminstrv. asst. Gov. Richard D. Lamm, Denver, 1975-76; coord. govt. affairs Rocky Mountain Energy Co., Lakewood, Colo., 1977-79; exec. dir. Thorne Ecol. Inst., Boulder, Colo., 1981-82; rsch. asst. Boettcher & Co., Denver, 1988-89; land protection specialist Colo. Open Lands, Lakewood, 1991—; sec. Colo. Coalition of Land Trusts, Golden, 1992—. Sec. Simon's Rock Coll. of Bard, 1989—. Mem. ASPA, Rocky Mountain Women's Inst. (chair 1982-97). Democrat. Home: 2400 S Jackson St Denver CO 80210-5637

RICHARDSON, EVERETT VERN, hydraulic engineer, educator, administrator, consultant; b. Scottsbluff, Nebr., Jan. 5, 1924; s. Thomas Otis and Jean Marie (Everett) R.; m. Billie Ann Kleckner, June 23, 1948; children—Gail Lee, Thomas Everett, Jerry Ray. B.S., Colo. State U., 1949, M.S., 1960, Ph.D., 1965. Registered profl. engr., Colo. Hydraulic engr. U.S. Geol. Survey, Wyo., 1949-52; hydraulic engr. U.S. Geol. Survey, Iowa, 1953-56; rsch. hydraulic engr. U.S. Geol. Survey, Ft. Collins, Colo., 1956-63, project chief, 1963-68; prof. civil engring., adminstr. engring. rsch. ctr. Colo. State U., Ft. Collins, 1968-82, prof. in charge of hydraulic program, 1982-88, prof. civil engring., 1988-94, prof. emeritus, 1994—, dir. hydraulic lab. engring. rsch. ctr., 1982-88, dir. Egypt water use project, 1977-84, dir. Egypt irrigation improvement project, 1985-90; dir. Egypt Water Rsch. Ctr. Egypt Water Rsch. Ctr. Project, Ft. Collins, 1988-89; sr. assoc. Ayers Assocs. Inc. (formerly Resource Cons./Engrs., Inc.), Ft. Collins, Colo., 1989-93, Ayres Assocs., Ft. Collins, Colo., 1994—; dir. Consortium for Internat. Devel., Tucson, Ariz., 1972-87; developer, instr. stream stability and scour at hwy. bridges course for State Dept. Transps. for NHI, FHWA; cons. in field. Sr. author: Highways in the River Environment, Fed. Hwy. Adminstrn., 1975, 90, 2000, Evaluating Scour at Bridges, Fed. Hwy. Adminstrn., 1991, 93, 95, 2000, contbr. to Engring. and Civil Engring. Handbook, 1995, Handbook of Fluid Dynamics and Fluid Machinery, 1996, Water Resources-Environmental Planning, Management, and Development, 1996; contbr. articles to profl. jours., chpts. in books. Mem. Ft. Collins Water Bd., 1969-84; mem. N.Y. State Bridge Safety Assurance Task Force, 1988-91. Decorated Bronze Star, Purple Heart; Combat Infantry Badge, U.S. Govt. fellow MIT, 1962-63. Fellow ASCE (J.S. Stevens award 1961, chair task com., bridge scour rsch. 1990-96, hydraulics divsn. task com. excellence award, 1993, Hans Albert Einstein award 1996, editor Compendium of Stream Stability and Scour Papers, 1991-98); mem. Internat. Congress for Irrigation and Drainage (bd. dirs.), Sigma Xi, Chi Epsilon, Sigma Tau. Home: 824 Gregory Rd Fort Collins CO 80524-1504 Office: Ayres Assocs PO Box 270460 Fort Collins CO 80527-0460

RICHARDSON, GARY B., lawyer; b. Windsor, Vt., Oct. 16, 1944; s. Dwight Bailey and Lucy B. Richardson; m. Katrina Copeland, Oct. 8, 1966; children: Justin C., Sarah B. BA, Middlwbury Coll., 1967; JD, Boston Coll. Law Sch., 1970. Atty. Upton, Sanders & Smith, Concord, N.H., 1970-75, ptnr., 1976—. Chair N.H. Ballot Law Com., Concord, 1991—, Hopkinton (N.H.) Zoning Bd., Hopkinton Planning Bd.; bd. dirs. Biddeford Pool Improvement Assn., 1999—, New Vision Teen Ctr., 1999—. Mem. N.H. Trial Lawyers Assn. (pres. 1990-91), Am. Bd. Trial Advs. Avocations: golf, tennis, sailing, skiing. E-mail: Grichardson@Upton-Sanders.com. Office: Upton Sanders and Smith 10 Centre St Concord NH 03301-6302

RICHARDSON, IAN WILLIAM, actor; b. Edinburgh, Scotland, Apr. 7, 1934; s. John and Margaret R.; m. Maroussia Frank, Feb. 2, 1961; children: Jeremy, Miles. Diploma in Acting and Teaching, Royal Scottish Acad. Music and Drama; D in Drama, 1999. Actor Royal Shakespeare Co., Stratford on Avon and London, 1960-75, Shaw Festival Theatre, Niagara, Ont., Can., 1977. Appeared in plays including My Fair Lady, Broadway, 1976-77, The Miser, 1995, The Magistrate, 1997-98, The Seven Ages of Man, 1999; films and TV plays include Tinker, Tailor, Soldier, Spy, Private Shulz, The Sign of Four, The Hound of the Baskervilles, Phantom of the Opera, 1990, The Gravy Train, 1990, House of Cards, 1991, The Gravy Train Goes East, 1991, To Play the King, 1993, Foreign Affairs Remember, Savage Play, 1994, The Final Cut, 1995; films include Brazil, Whoops!, Apocalypse, The Fourth Protocol, Cry Freedom, The Fifth Province, 1996, Dark City, 1998; TV programs includes Star Quality, Porterhouse Blue, The Winslow Boy, 1989, An Ungentlemanly Act, 1992, Catherine the Great (miniseries), 1994, Gormenghast, 1999, (miniseries) Magician's House, 1999, Murder Rooms, 1999; author prefaces to Shakespearean works. Recipient CBE award, 1989, BAFTA award, 1991, award Royal TV Soc., 1991. Fellow Royal Scottish Acad. Music and Drama; mem. Brit. Actors Equity, Actors Equity, Screen Actors Guild, Garrick Club (London), Players Club (N.Y.C.). Office: care London Mgmt, 2-4 Noel St, London W14 3RB, England

RICHARDSON, JASPER EDGAR, nuclear physicist; b. Memphis, Nov. 8, 1922; s. Jasper Edgar and Katherine Cecil (Copp) R.; m. Nellie Carolyn Harwell, May 30, 1947; children: Ann Helen, Janet Katherine, Susan Carolyn, Patricia Lynn, Ellen Claire. BS in Physics, Yale U., 1944; MA in Physics, Rice U., 1948, PhD in Physics, 1950. Instr. physics U. Miss., Oxford, 1946-47; asst. prof. Auburn (Ala.) U., 1950-51; AEC fellow Oak Ridge (Tenn.) Inst. Nuc. Studies, 1951-53; physicist U. Tex. M. D. Anderson Hosp., Houston, 1953-55; rsch. physicist Shell Bellaire Rsch. Ctr., Houston, 1955-69; sr. engr. Shell Oil Co., Midland, Tex., 1969-74; staff engr. Shell Oil Co., Houston, 1974-86; ret. Patentee in electronics, oil discovery, measurement; contbr. articles to profl. jours. With USN, 1944-46, Guam. Mem. Am. Phys. Soc., Soc. Petroleum Engrs. Episcopalian.

RICHARDSON, JOHN, retired international relations executive; b. Boston, Feb. 4, 1921; s. John and Hope (Hemenway) R.; m. Thelma Ingram, Jan. 19, 1945; children: Eva Teleki, Teren de Cossy, Hope Gravelly, Catherine Munch, Hetty L. AB, Harvard U., 1943, JD, 1949. Bar: N.Y. 1949. Assoc. Sullivan & Cromwell, N.Y.C., 1949-55; with Paine, Webber, Jackson & Curtis, N.Y.C., 1955-69, gen. ptnr., 1958-61, ltd. ptnr., 1961-69; pres., chief exec. officer Free Europe, Inc. (Radio Free Europe), 1961-68; asst. sec. for ednl. and cultural affairs Dept. State, 1969-77, also acting asst. sec. state for pub. affairs, 1971-73; exec. dir. for social policy Ctr. for Strategic and Internat. Studies; research prof. internat. communication Sch. Fgn. Service, Georgetown U., Washington, 1977-78; pres., chief exec. officer Youth for Understanding, Inc., 1978-86, bd. dirs., 1986-98; counselor U.S. Inst. of Peace, 1987-90; spl. advisor Aspen Inst. Humanistic Studies, 1977-80. Mem. Coun. Fgn. Rels., 1957—, Citizens Commn. on S.E. Asian Refugees, 1978-85; founder Polish Med. Aid Project, 1957-61; co-founder, chmn. bd. Am. Com. to Aid Poland, 1989-95; pres. Internat. Rescue Com., 1960-61, bd. dirs., 1958-61, 78—; chmn. N.Y.C. Met. Mission United Ch. of Christ, 1966-69, Am. Coun. for UN U., 1977-87, Consortium for Internat. Citizens Exch., 1980-84, Delphi Internat., 1995-99, bd. dirs. 1991—; chmn. Nat. Endowment for Democracy, 1984-88, 91-92, bd. dirs., 1984-92, chmn. emeritus, 1992—; bd. dirs. Freedom House, 1963-69, pres., 1977-84; Kennedy Ctr. for Performing Arts, 1970-77, Inter-Am. Found., 1970-77, East-West Ctr., 1975-77, Fgn. Policy Assn., 1958-68, 77-86, Japan-U.S. Friendship Commn., 1976-77, Am. Forum for Global Edn., 1977—, Social Sci. Found., U. Denver, 1992—, Meridian House Internat., 1978-83, Atlantic Coun. U.S., 1982-84, Fgn. Student Svc. Coun., 1978-82, Coun. for Advancement of Citizenship, 1991-96, Coun. for Cmty. of Democracies, 1996—. With U.S. Army, World War II. Decorated Bronze Star with v device, Japan Order of the Sacred

Treasure, Gold and Silver Star; Germany Order of Merit, Commdr.'s Cross, Poland Order of Merit, Knight Cross. Home: 9707 Old Georgetown Rd Apt 1104 Bethesda MD 20814-1746

RICHARDSON, JONATHAN, anesthesiologist, consultant; b. Leeds, Yorkshire, England, Mar. 28, 1954; s. Guy Stanley and Ruth (Beck) R.; m. Mary Christine O'Brien; children: Alison Clare, Sean Stanley, Hannah Louise. MB, ChB, Liverpool (England) Med. Sch., 1977, MD, 1994. Mem. Royal Coll. Physicians (MRCP), 1982. Sr. house officer Liverpool Hosps., 1978-80, registrar in medicine, 1980-84, registrar in anesthetics, 1984-86; sr. registrar Leeds (England) Hosps., 1986-88; cons. anesthetist Bradford (England) Hosps., 1989—; Gordon McDowall prof. anaesthetics Bradford Royal Infirmary, 1996—; vis. prof. Oreg. Health Scis. U., Portland, 1988-89; co-exec. dir. Micro-Endoscopy Tng. & Rsch. Ctr., Bradford; specialist in spinal endoscopy. Co-inventor rib punch for use in minimally invasive thoracic surgery. Recipient Fight Against Cancer Trust prize Soc. Cardio-Thoracic Surgeons, 1995. Fellow Royal Coll. of Physicians; mem. Internat. Paravertebral Soc. (founder; treas. 1996—), Pain Soc. Great Britain and Ireland. Office: Bradford Royal Infirmary, Dept Anesthetics, Bradford BD9 6RJ, England

RICHARDSON, MELVIN ORDE WINGATE, engineering educator; b. Sept. 26, 1944. BTech with honors, Brunel U., 1968, PhD, 1972. Chartered chemist. Engr. Ault & Wiborg Ltd., 1968-69, GLC Sci. Br., 1972-74; sr. lectr. Inst. Polymer Tech. and Materials Engring. Loughborough U., Eng., 1974—; vis. prof. Sichuan U. (formerly Chengdu U. Sci. and Tech.), China; chmn. FINATURA/CHINAFIM Consortium. Editor: Polymer Engineering Composites, 1977; contbr. over 190 articles to profl. jours. Chmn. Care and Share Found., 1991—. Decorated Mem. Most Excellent Order of Brit. Empire. Fellow Royal Soc. Chemistry, Inst. of Materials, Royal Soc. Arts. Fax: 44-1509-223-161. E-mail: m.o.richardson@lboro.ac.uk. Office: IPTME, Loughborough U, Leics Loughborough LE11 3TU, England

RICHARDSON, MERVYN LEWIS, chemist, biologist, toxicologist; b. Birmingham, Eng., Aug. 28, 1934; s. Lewis Harry and Hilda Laura (Burke) R.; m. Beryl Rosemary Hill, Jan. 12, 1963. BS, U. Aston Birmingham, 1957. Chartered biologist, chemist, European chemist. Analytical chemist John & E. Sturge Ltd., Birmingham, Eng., 1958-67; chief chemist Croda Internat. Ltd., Oldham, Eng., 1967-72; tech. mgr. Ch. Goldrei Fouchard Ltd., Liverpool, Eng., 1972-75; scientist catchment quality control Thames Water Authority, London, 1975-89, Nat. Rivers Authority, Reading, Eng., 1989-90; prin. Birch Assessment Svcs. for Info. on Chems., Poole, Eng., 1990—; cons. to UN Agys., 1993—; acting sci. pubs. sec. Internat. Union Pure and Applied Chemistry, 1997; mem. Brit. Dept. Trade and Industry World Aid Sect. Users Forum; mem. organizing com. Internat. Symposium on Air Quality Mgmt., Istanbul, 1997, 1st Internat. Conf. on Environ. Restoration, Ljubjana, Slovenia, 1997; expert/contbr. to Environ. Performance Rev., Croatia. Author, editor: The Effects of the War on the Environment: Croatia, 1995; editor: The Dictionary of Substances and Their Effects, 1993-95, Risk Reduction: Chemicals and Energy into the Twenty First Century, 1996, Environmental Xenobiotics, 1996; author: UNESCO's Ency. of Life Support Systems; contbr. articles to profl. jours. Recipient Environ. award, Zagreb, Croatia, 1996; The Royal Soc. London travelling fellow Ukraine, 1994, Croatia, 1996, Slovenia, 1997. Mem. Coun. of the Royal Soc. of Chemistry. Avocation: travel. Home and Office: Birch Assessment Svcs Info on Chemicals, Flt 15/Melton Ct 37 Lindsay, Poole BH13 6BH, England

RICHARDSON, MILDRED TOURTILLOTT, retired psychologist; b. North Hampton, N.H., May 8, 1907; d. Herbert Shaw and Sarah Louise Tourtillott; m. Harold Wellington Richardson, June 25, 1932; children: Elizabeth Fern Ruben, Constance Joy Van Valer, Carol Louise Dennis. AB, Bates Coll., 1930; MA, U. Mich., 1948; EdS, Butler U., 1961; PhD, U. Ind., 1965. Diplomate Am. Bd. Profl. Psychology (examiner of candidates Mid-West region 1978-95, emeritus 1995), Nat. Register Health Svc. Providers in Psychology, hosp. staff mem. 1994; cert. clin. and sch. psychologist, Ind. Tchr. math. and sci. Norwich (Conn.) Free Acad., 1930-32, Port Huron (Mich.) High Sch., 1943-45; dir. intermediate girls Interlochen Nat. Music Camp, Mich., 1953, asst. dean univ. women, 1954; tchr., guidance counselor Community Sch. Corp., Franklin, Ind., 1956-64; supr. tng. Devereux Found., Devon, Pa., 1965-78, cons. clin. tng. in sch. and clin. psychology, 1975-78; tchr. psychology of spl. edn. Pa. State U.ext., King of Prussia, 1966-68; sch. psychologist Johnson County (Ind.) Spl. Svcs., 1979-82; head clin. psychology Community Psychiat. Ctrs. Valle Vista Hosp., Greenwood, Ind., 1983-88; pvt. practice psychol. health svc. Greenwood, 1985-95; clin. psychologist St. Francis Hosp., Indpls., 1988-95; ret., 1995; part-time clin. assoc. prof. Hahnemann Med. Coll., Phila., 1973-78; part-time dir. psychodiagnostics seminar; assoc. prof. sch. psychology, condr. grad. seminar, practicum Ind. U., Bloomington, 1982, lectr., 1987; cons. Valle Vista Guidance Ctr., 1991-94; assoc. prof. psychology Ind. U., 1992-93, U. Indpls., 1992-94; cons. clin. psychologist Am. Stress Ctr., Inc., 1993-95; pvt. practice, Pa., 1970-78. Contbr. articles to profl. jours. Active Johnson County Commn. on Child Abuse, 1988-89, Gov.'s Drug-Free Ind. Coun. on Alcoholism; bd. dirs. Greater Johnson County Cmty. Found., 1990-95. Recipient Headliner award Theta Sigma Phi, 1964, Disting. Svc. award Bates Coll. Alumni Assn., 1990. Fellow Am. Acad. Sch. Psychology; mem. APA, Inst. Clin. Tng. Devereux Found. (hon.), Internat. Coun. Psychologists, Franklin Coll. Alumnae (hon., assoc. 1988), Ben Franklin Soc., Phi Kappa Phi. Republican. Baptist. Avocations: travel, symphony concerts, spectator sports, community volunteering. Address: Marquette Manor Apt 5302 8140 Township Line Rd Indianapolis IN 46260-5832

RICHARDSON, MILES EDWARD, anthropology educator; b. Palestine, Tex., Jan. 22, 1932; s. Mark Carl and Florence (Adams) R.; m. Valerie Thorn Woodger, Dec. 19, 1959; children: Victoria, Penn, Stanley. BS, Stephen F. Austin U., 1957; PhD, Tulane U., 1965. From asst. to assoc. prof. Ind. U. of Pa., 1963-65; asst. prof. anthropology La. State U., Baton Rouge, 1965-69, assoc. prof., 1969-72, prof., 1972—, chmn. dept., 1970-72, 86-87, Fred B. Kniffen prof., 1992-97, Doris Z. Stone prof., 1997—. Author: San Pedro, Colombia, 1974, Cry Lonesome, 1990; editor: Anthropology and Humanism Quar., 1984-90. Nixon fellow Whittier Coll., 1989. Democrat. Office: La State U Dept Geography Anthrop Baton Rouge LA 70803-0001

RICHARDSON, MIRANDA, actress; b. Lancashire, Eng., Mar. 3, 1958. Studied, Drama Program Bristol. Stage performances include: Moving, All My Sons, Who's Afraid of Virginia Woolf, The Life of Einstein, A Lie of the Mind, Edmond, Insignificance, Aunt Dan & Lemon, The Changling, Mountain Language; TV appearances: The Hard Word, Sorrel and Son, A Woman of Substance, Underworld, Death of the Heart, The Scold's Bridle, 1998, Merlin, 1998, Alice, 1999, (series) Black Adder II & III, Sweet as You Are, (miniseries) Die Kinder, The James Bond Story, 1999, (voice) The Miracle Maker, 2000; films: Dance with a Stranger, 1985, The Innocent, 1986, Empire of the Sun, 1987, Eat the Rich, 1987, Twisted Obsession, 1990, The Bachelor, 1991, Enchanted April, 1992 (Golden Globe award), Damage, 1992 (B.A.F.T.A. award for Best Supporting Actress), The Crying Game, 1992 (B.A.F.T.A. award for best supporting actress), Fatherland, HBO, 1994 (Golden Globe award), Tom & Viv, 1994 (Acad. award nominee for best actress 1995), La Nuit et Le Moment, 1994, Kansas City, 1996, The Evening Star, 1996, Swann, 1996, Saint-Ex, 1997, The Apostle, 1997, The Designated Mourner, 1997, All for Love, 1998, Jacob Two Two and the Hooded Fang, 1998, Sleepy Hollow, 1999, Blackadder Back and Forth, 1999, Get Carter, 2000, (voice) Chicken Run, 2000, The Man Who Killed Don Quixote, 2000. Address: c/o Harriet Robinson, 76 Oxford St, London W1D 1BS, England*

RICHARDSON, PAUL JOSEPH, pastor; b. Houston, Jan. 4, 1936; s. Joseph GIlman and Ruth Laura R.; m. Faye Richardson, Aug. 21, 1930; children: Melody, Paul Joe, Jason Neal. B in Biblical Studies, Internat. Sem., Plymoth,Fla., 1979; M, North Gate Gard Sch., Edmons, Wash., 1979; D of theology, Internat. Sem., 1980; Hon. Dr. of E. Ed, Tabernacle of Light Inst., Stafford, Va., 1999. Host/speaker Pastor's Panel TV Program, 1986-93; pastor Christ Worship Ctr., Richmond, Va., 1993—; chancellor Spirit of Truth Inst., Richmond, 1972—; founder Full Gospel of Christ Fellowship, Inc., 1972—; exec. pres. World Wide Accrediting Commission, 1993—; speaker at Bible Schs.; marriage/family counsellor , 1985-99. Editor: Christian Communicator 1974-84; contbr. numerous articles to profl. jours. Charter mem. Christian Chamber of Commerce, Inc., Richmond, 1995; chmn. Greater Richmond Christian Coun., 1988-92. Recipient Cert. of Recognition Triangle Christian Coun., 1983, Prison Fellowship Ministries, 1988. Republican. E-mail: drpaulrich@juno.com.

RICHARDSON, PETER JOHN, software engineering consultant; b. Sydney, Australia, July 4, 1962; s. Alan Thomas and Mary Elizabeth (Fischer) R.; m. Pauline Branley, Jan. 13, 1996. B in Engring. (hons.), Monash U., Melbourne, Australia, 1983, M in Engring. Sci., 1986. Engr. Telecom Australia, Melbourne, 1984-86, sr. engr., 1986-88, prin. engr., 1988-95; prin. cons. Object Oriented, Melbourne, 1993%; program com. mem. Telecomms. Info. Networking Arch., 1995, 97, 99, Tools Pacific, 1993, Object World, 1993, 94, 95, 96, 98, 2000, Internat. Conf. on Open Distributed Processing, 1995, 97. Contbr. numerous articles to profl. jours. Mem. IEEE. Avocations: sailing, squash. E-mail: p.richardson@oopl.com.au. Office: Object Oriented P/L, 11/484 St Kilda Rd, Melbourne 3004, Australia

RICHARDSON, PETER JOHN, cardiologist, consultant; b. Farnham, Surrey, Eng., Aug. 28, 1939; s. John Dixon and Edith Mary (Cleasby) R.; m. Brenda Jane Pettifer, Sept. 12, 1970; children: Christopher, Emma, James. MB, Kings Coll. Hosp., London, 1963, BS, 1963; MRCP, Royal Coll. Physicians, London, 1969; MD, London U., 1984; FRCP, Royal Coll. Physicians, 1985. House physician Kings Coll. Hosp., London, 1963, sr. registrar, sr. lectr., 1971-79, cons. cardiologist, 1979—; med. registrar Royal Free Hosp., London, 1966-69; cons. cardiologist, dir. cardiology Cromwell Hosp., London, 1982—. Contbr. over 150 articles in field of cardiology to profl. jours. Mem. Brit. Cardiac Soc., Internat. Soc. and Fedn. Cardiology (coun. sect. cardiomyopathy), Am. Heart Assn. (fellow Coun. Clin. Cardiology), Internat. Med. Club (pres. 1994-99). Avocations: shooting, fishing. Office: Kings Coll Hosp Cardiac Dept, Denmark Hill, London SE 5 9RS, England

RICHARDSON, RALPH HERMAN, lawyer; b. Detroit, Oct. 12, 1935; s. Ralph Onazime and Lucinda Ollie (Fluence) R.; m. Arvie Y., June 1, 1956 (div. 1961); children: Cassandra, Tanya, Arvie Lynn; m. Julia A., Sept. 16, 1962 (div. 1982); children: Traci, Theron. BA, Wayne State U., 1964, JD, 1970. Bar: Mich., U.S. Ct. Appeals (6th cir.), Supreme Ct. U.S., 1970. Postal transp. clk. U.S. P. O., Detroit, 1954-56; clk. pub. aid worker City Detroit, 1956-65; sr. labor relations rep. Ford Motor Co., Ypsilanti, Mich., 1965-70, wage admins., 1966, labor relations rep., 1967; atty. Brown Grier, Richardson P.C., Detroit, 1970-71; atty Richardson, Grier P.C., Detroit, 1971-73; ptnr. Stone, Richardson P.C., Detroit, 1973—; bd. dirs. Legal Aid, Defender Assn. Detroit, 1985-86; apptd. hon. spl. agt. Office of Investigations, Office Inspector gen., U.S. Printing Office, 1997. Mem. bd. dirs. YMCA Fisher Branch; Boy Scouts Am.; apptd. to Bd. Appeals for Hosp. Bed Reduction by Gov. State of Mich., 1982, apptd. Spl. Asst. Atty. Gen., by Frank J. Kelley, Atty Gen. for the State Mich., May 23, 1984, apptd. to Task Oriented Com. to review the issue in-home child care by Detroit City Council Mem., Maryann Mahaffey. With U.S. Army, 1964. Mem. NAACP (life), Am. Arbitration Assn., Legal Aid Defender Assn., Mich. State Bar Fellows, Optimists, Masons, Shriners (imperial legal advisor, gen. counsel 1994-97, Right Eminent Grand Comdr. of the Knights Templar, State of Mich. 1997—), Phi Alpha Delta, Kappa Alpha Psi. Democrat. Fax: 313-393-6701. E-mail: aretwo@msn.com. Office: Stone Richardson PC 2910 E Jefferson Ave Detroit MI 48207-4208

RICHARDSON, ROBERT COLEMAN, physics educator, researcher; b. Washington, June 26, 1937; s. Robert Franklin and Lois (Price) R.; m. Betty Marilyn McCarthy, Sept. 2, 1962; children: Jennifer, Pamela. BS in Physics, Va. Poly. Inst. and State U., 1958, MS, 1960; PhD in Physics, Duke U., 1966. Research assoc. Cornell U., Ithaca, N.Y., 1966-67, asst. prof., 1968-71, assoc. prof., 1972-74, prof., 1975—; chmn. Internat. Union Pure and Applied Physics Commn. (C-5), 1981-84; mem. bd. assessment Nat. Bur. Standards, 1983—. Mem. editorial bd. Jour. of Low Temperature Physics, 1984—. Served to 2d lt. U.S. Army, 1959-60. Guggenheim fellow 1975, 83; recipient Simon Meml. prize Brit. Phys. Soc., 1976; co-recipient Nobel prize in physics, 1996. Fellow AAAS, Am. Phys. Soc. (Oliver E. Buckley prize 1981); mem. Nat. Acad. Scis. Avocations: photography, gardening. Office: Cornell Univ Dept Physics Clark Hall Ithaca NY 14853

RICHARDSON, ROGER CHARLES, history educator, author; b. Middleton, Lancashire, Eng., Aug. 31, 1944; s. Clifford and Doris (Taylor) R. BA, U. Leicester, Eng., 1965; PhD, U. Manchester, Eng., 1969. From lectr. to sr. lectr. Thames Poly., London, 1968-77; head of history King Alfred's U. Coll., Winchester, Eng., 1977-98; head rsch. Grad. CTr. King Alfred's U. Coll., Winchester, 1998—; vis. prof. U. So. Maine, Portland, 1988, So. Oreg. U., Ashland, 1993, 95, 96, 97. Author: Puritanism in North West England, 1972, Debate on the English Revolution, 1977, 3d edit., 1998; editor: The Urban Experience, English, Scottish, and Welsh Towns, 1450-1700, 1983, Freedom and the English Revolution, 1986, The Study of History, 1988, Town and Countryside in the English Revolution, 1992, Images of Oliver Cromwell, 1993, The English Civil Wars. Local Aspects, 1997, Rhetoric Revolution and Restoration, 1998; co-editor Lit. and History, 1975—. Fellow Royal Hist. Soc. Avocations: reading, travel, theatre, music. Office: King Alfred's U Coll, Sparkford Rd, Winchester SO22 4NR, England

RICHARDSON, STEPHEN GILES, biotechnology company executive; b. Mpls., Sept. 17, 1951; s. Richard Giles and Constance Bernice (Krieg) R. BA cum laude, Wartburg Coll., 1972; MS, U. Iowa, 1974, PhD, 1981; postdoctoral, Duke U., 1982-84. Ter. mgr. Wyeth Labs., Phila., 1974-76; rsch. asst. U. Iowa, Iowa City, 1976-82; rsch. assoc. Duke, Durham, N.C., 1982-84; scientist Becton Dickinson Rsch. Ctr., Research Triangle Park, N.C., 1984-86; devel. group leader Dade Diagnostics divsn. Baxter Healthcare, Miami, Fla., 1986; rsch. group leader Organon Teknika Corp divsn., Akzo Nobel N.V, Durham, N.C., 1987-89, R & D sect. head, internat. R & D area mgr., 1989-90, program mgr., 1990-94, assoc. dir., head product devel., 1994-96, project mgmt. dir., microbiology bus. area R & D, 1997—. Contbr. articles to profl. jours.; patentee in field; bd. readers IVD Technology Mag. Co-founder Libertarian Party Minn., Mpls., 1972, del. nat. conv., 1998; exec. sec. Iowa Coun. to Repeal Conscription, Waterloo, 1971. Mem. Am. Soc. for Microbiology, Am. Chem. Soc., Am. Assn. for Clin. Chemistry, Royal Soc. Chemistry (U.K.), N.Y. Acad. Scis., Electronic Frontier Found., Sigma Xi. Achievements include discovery of transient neutral heteroaryl radicals as viable organic synthetic intermediates, such as, to halopurine nucleosides; MDA-180 hemostasis analyzer system, BacT/ALERT 3D blood culture system. E-mail: srichardson@orgtek.com. Home: PO Box 17284 Chapel Hill NC 27516-7284 Office: Organon Teknika Corp Divsn Akzo Nobel NV 100 Akzo Ave Durham NC 27712-9402

RICHARDSON, TIMOTHY VICTOR, poet, writer; b. Edmounton, Alberta, Can., Sept. 7, 1948; came to U.S., 1950; s. Allyn St. Clair and Nancy May Richardson; m. Toni Marie Seger, June 30, 1972. BS, Boston U, 1973, MEd, 1975. Cert. psycologist, Mass.; cert. spl. edn. tchr., Mass. Asst. tchr. Melrose (Mass.) Pub. Schs., 1971-72; mental health worker McLean Hosp., Belmont, Mass., 1973-74; rehab. counselor Washingtonian Inst. Drug & Alcohol Abuse, Jamaica Placa, Mass., 1974-75; program coord. EdCo, Brookline, Mass., 1975-77; art dealer Met. Art Assocs., N.Y.C., 1977-91; co-owner ProseWorks Assocs., Lovell, Maine, 1991—; prodr. multimedia poetry Deertrees Theatre & Cultural Ctr., 1998. Editor: Taking Your Business Global, 1997. Author: (poems) Frost in Spring, 1989, Celebrating T.S. Eliot, 1988, Edgen Allen Poe: Poetic Mystery in Celebration, 1990, Partisan Review, 1994. Mem. Jefferson Group, Androscoggin County C. of C. (ProseWorks). Avocations: playing jazz drums, drawing, painting, writing. E-mail: PWORKS@NXI.COM. Office: ProseWorks Assocs RR 2 Box 560 Lovell ME 04051-9712

RICHARDSON, WILLIAM BLAINE, federal official; b. Pasadena, Calif., Nov. 15, 1947; m. Barbara Flavin, 1972. BA, Tufts U., Medford, Mass., 1970; MA, Fletcher Sch. Law and Diplomacy, 1971. Mem. staff U.S. Ho. of Reps., 1971-72, Dept. State, 1973-75; mem. staff fgn. relations com. U.S. Senate, 1975-78; exec. dir. N. Mex. State Democratic Com., 1978, Bernalillo County Democratic Com., 1978; businessman Santa Fe, N. Mex., 1978-82; mem. 98th-103rd Congresses from 3rd N.Mex. dist., Washington, 1982-96; democratic chief dep. majority whip 103d Congress; U.S. amb. U.S. Mission to UN, 1997-98; sec. U.S. Dept. Energy, Washington, 1998—; ranking minority mem. Resources Com. on Nat. Pks., Forests and Lands; mem. Select Com. on intelligence, Helsinki Commn. Vice chair Dem. Nat. Com.; active Big Bros.-Big Sisters, Santa Fe. Mem. Santa Fe Hispanic C. of C., Santa Fe C. of C., Council Fgn. Relations, NATO 2000 Bd., Congl. Hispanic Caucus, Am. G.I. Forum. Office: US Dept Energy 1000 Independence Ave SW Washington DC 20585-0001

RICHARDSON, WILLIAM RUSSELL, foundation executive; b. Bluefield, W.Va., Feb. 27, 1958; s. Ralph Jackson and Anna J. (Wallace) R.; m. Kathryn Lucas Richardson, July 30, 1983; children: Kathryn Anne, Thomas Russell. BS, U. Tampa, 1980. Cert. assn. exec. Chpt. cons. Phi Delta Theta Fraternity, Oxford, Ohio, 1980-82, dir. alumni svcs., 1982-91, dir. bus. affairs, 1992-95; v.p. Phi Delta Theta Ednl. Found., Oxford, 1994-96, COO, 1995-96, pres., 1997—. Bd. zoning appeals chmn. City of Oxford, 1995-98; trustee, treas. Greater Cin. Planned Giving Coun., 1999—. Mem. Cin. Soc. of Assn. Execs., Fraternity Execs. Assn. (found. sect. chmn. 2000), Nat. Soc. of Fund Raising Execs., Phi Delta Theta. Republican. Methodist. Avocations: fishing, squash, raquetball. Fax: 513-523-9200. E-mail: rusty@phideltatheta.org. Home: 625 French Dr Oxford OH 45056-2023 Office: Phi Delta Theta Ednl Found 2 S Campus Ave Oxford OH 45056-1801

RICHBURG, W. EDWARD, nurse educator; b. New Orleans, Jan. 18, 1948; m. Kathryn S. Richburg, June 24, 1972; children: Bill, Kate. BA, U. Miss., 1970; BSN, U. Miss., Jackson, 1973; MEd, Memphis State U., 1977; MSN, Med. U. of S.C., 1991. RN, Fla., S.C.; cert. nursing adminstrn. advance, continuing edn. and staff devel. Commd. ensign USN, 1971, advanced through grades to comdr.; instr. hosp. corps Naval Sch. of Health Sci., San Diego, 1978-81; head nurse U.S. Naval Hosp.; dir. nursing svcs. Branch Med. Clinic, Mayport, Fla., 1983-87; head staff edn. and tng. U.S. Naval Hosp., Charleston, S.C., 1987-92; asst. dir. nursing U.S. Naval Hosp., Yokosuka, Japan, 1992-95; head Command Edn. Dept., 1995—; head command edn. dept. U.S. Naval Hosp., Yokosuka, Japan, 1995-96; performance improvement coord. U.S. Naval Hosp., Charleston, S.C., 1996-98; instr. nursing Trident Tech. Coll., Charleston, 1998—. Recipient Excellence in Nursing Education award Trident Nurses' Assn., 1991, S. C. Nurses' Assn., 1992. Mem. ANA (cert.), S.C. Nurses Assn. (pres. 1999—, chair continuing edn. com., treas. dist. chpt., pres. 1999—, Excellence in Nursing Edn. award 1992), Navy Nurse Corps Assn. (treas. Palmetto chpt. 1998—), Trident Nurses Assn. (pres.-elect 1997-98, pres. 1998—, Excellence in Nursing Edn. award 1991), Continuing Edn. Coun. (chair), Sigma Theta Tau.

RICHE, WENDY, television producer; b. N.Y.C., Jan. 8, 1945; d. Elliot and Janice (Fantel) Fields; m. Alan Riche, Dec. 4, 1966; children: Tim, Peter. Student, Syracuse U. Sec. ABC, 1973, program coord. Late Night Programs, 1974, assoc. prodr. In Concert series and specials, 1974; developer, prodr. Levenback/Riche and Wittman/Riche Prodn. Co., 1975-78; prodr. Universal TV, 1978-86; exec. prodr. ABC Entertainment, 1986-89; sr. v.p. prodr. Fox Broadcast Co., 1989-91; exec. prodr. Gen. Hosp. ABC-TV, 1992—, exec. prodr. Port Charles, 1997-99. Prodr. (movies of the week) Who Will Love My Children? (8 Emmy award nominations), Madame X, I Saw What You Did, Friendships, Secrets, and Lies, Deadly Care; exec. prodr. (ABC pilot) Never Again, (movies for TV, dir. programming ABC Entertainment) God Bless the Child, David (Emmy award nomination), My Name is Bill W (Emmy award winner), Women of Brewster Place, Unspeakable Acts, Our Sons, Fight for Life, (exec. producer daytime drama) General Hosp. (Emmy award for outstanding drama series 1994/95, 95/96, 96/97, 98/99, 99/2000 (after school spl.) Positive: A Journey Into Aids (3 Emmy award nominations). Recipient Soap Opera Update Editors award, 1993, Pub. Svc. award Nat. Kidney Found., 1994, Soap Opera Hall of Fame, 1994, 96, Nancy Susan Reynolds award, 1994, 95, 96, Chair's award Am. Cancer Soc., 1994/95, 15th Media Access award, 1995, Imagen award, 1996, Komen award, 1996, Ryan White Youth Svc. award, 1996, Daytime TV Mag. Readers Poll award for best show, 1996/97, Soap Opera Digest award for Gen. Hosp. favorite show, 1997, 98, 99, Media Access Michael Landon award, 1997. Office: Gen Hosp/Port Charles ABC 4151 Prospect Ave Los Angeles CA 90027-4524

RICHENS, MURIEL WHITTAKER, marriage and family therapist, educator; b. Prineville, Oreg.; d. John Reginald and Victoria Cecilia (Pascale) Whittaker; children: Karen, John, Candice, Stephanie, Rebecca. BS, Oreg. State U.; MA, San Francisco State U., 1962; postgrad., U. Calif., Berkeley, 1967-69, U. Birmingham, Eng., 1973, U. Soria, Spain, 1981. Lic. sch. adminstr., tchr. 7-12, pupil pers. specialist, Calif.; lic. marriage and family therapist, Calif. Tchr. Springfield (Oreg.) High Sch.; instr. San Francisco State U.; instr., counselor Coll. San Mateo, Calif., San Mateo High Sch. Dist., 1963-86; therapist AIDS Health Project U. Calif., San Francisco, 1988—; marriage and family therapist, pvt. practice San Mateo; guest West German-European Acad. seminar, Berlin, 1975. Lifeguard, ARC. postgrad. student Ctr. for Human Communications, Los Gatos, Calif., 1974, U. P.R., 1977, U. Guadalajara (Mex.), 1978, U. Durango (Mex.), 1980, U. Guanajuato (Mex.) 1982. Mem. U. Calif. Berkeley Alumni Assn., Am. Contract Bridge League (Diamond Life Master, cert. instr., cert. dir.), Women in Comm., Computer-Using Educators, Commonwealth Club, Pi Lambda Theta, Delta Pi Epsilon. Republican. Roman Catholic. Home and Office: 847 N Humboldt St Apt 309 San Mateo CA 94401-1451

RICHERT, HARVEY MILLER, II, ophthalmologist; b. Weatherford, Okla., Aug. 25, 1948; s. Harvey Miller and Catherine Cornelia (Ryan) R.; m. Diana Dee Sisney, Nov. 23, 1966; children: Ronald Lance, Rachelle Lea. BS, Southwestern Okla. State U., 1970; MD, U. Okla., Oklahoma City, 1974. Intern St. Anthony Hosp., Oklahoma City, 1974-75; resident in ophthalmology Tulane U., New Orleans, 1975-78; physician Tucker & Walker Ophthalmology Assocs., Abilene, Tex., 1978-80; ptnr. Tucker, Walker & Richert, Abilene, 1980-86; pvt. practice Abilene, 1986—; med. dir. Lions Eye Bank, Abilene, 1979—; head opthalmology sect. Humana Hosp., 1984-90, Hendrick Med. Ctr., 1984-92. V.p. Chisholm Trail coun. Boy Scouts Am., 1984-89, 92-96, dist. chmn., 1990-92, asst. scoutmaster, 1982-85, scoutmaster, 1985-88, nat. coun. rep., 1997—. Recipient Scoutmaster of Merit award, Silver Beaver award, Dist. award of Merit, Boy Scouts Am., 1988. Fellow Am. Acad. Ophthalmology, Castroviejo Soc. (assoc.); mem. AMA, Tex. Ophthal. Assn., Tex. Med. Assn., Lions (founders club), Abilene C. of C. Republican. Baptist. Avocations: backpacking, snow skiing, tennis, camping. Home: 15 Glen Abbey St Abilene TX 79606-5023 Office: 1750 Pine St Abilene TX 79601-3044

RICHERT, ROBERT A., artist; b. Oak Park, Ill., Mar. 6, 1947; s. Joseph and Anne (Bodish) R. AA, Long Beach (Calif.) City Coll., 1968; BA, Calif. State U., Long Beach, 1999. Group shows include Leigh, Yawkey, Woodson Art Museum, Wausau, Wis.,, 1984, 86, L.A. County Mus. Natural History, 1992; one-man shows include Showcase Gallery, Greenwood, Ind., 1996, Art World Gallery, El Cajon, Calif., 1998; prin. works include Anhauser-Busch; contbr. articles to profl. jours. With U.S. Army, 1968-70. Decorated Army Commendation medal with V-Device; winner Calif. Duck Stamp Competition, 1982; named Sponsor Artist of the Yr., Nat. Waterfowl Alliance, 1989, Artist of the Yr., Calif. Ducks Unltd., 1992. Mem. Toastmasters (area gov. 1990, pres. 1995, mentor). Democrat. Avocations: interpretive naturalist, bird-watching. Office: Richert Art Studio 11110 Los Alamitos Blvd Ste 201 Los Alamitos CA 90720-3602

RICHESON, HUGH ANTHONY, JR., lawyer; b. Aberdeen, Md., Apr. 22, 1947; s. Hugh Anthony Sr. and Mary Evelyn (Burford) R.; m. Melissa Anne Baum, Apr. 4, 1970; children: Hugh Anthony III, Heidi E., Holly K., Hagin G., Herald Joshua. BBA, U. Richmond, 1969; JD, U. Fla., 1973; student, St. Catherine's Coll., Oxford U., Eng., summer 1973. Bar: Fla. 1974, U.S. Dist. Ct. (mid. dist.) Fla. 1975, U.S. Supreme Ct. 1992. Assoc. Bryant, Dickens, Rumph, Franson & Miller, Jacksonville, Fla., 1974-76, ptnr., 1977; sole practice Orange Park, Fla., 1977-82; ptnr. Smith, Hallowes & Richeson, Orange Park, 1982-83; sole practice Palm Harbor, Fla., 1984-98; of counsel Carey & Hilbert, Clearwater, Fla., 1998—. Pres. Full Gospel Bus. Men's Fellowship Internat., Orange Park, 1983-84, Palm Harbor, 1985-92, field rep., 1987—. Mem. ATLA, Fla. Coun. Bar Assn. Pres. (life), Christian Legal Soc., Gideons Internat., Countryside Country Club, Phi Delta Phi. Republican. Methodist.

RICHEY, MARVIN E(LDEN), electrical engineer, administrator; b. Wichita, Kans., Nov. 21, 1946; s. Marvin Elden Sr. and Barbara Jean (Carterette) R.; m. Linda Louise Wheeler, Oct. 15, 1966 (div. Sept. 1977); m. Janice Ellen Doyle, Nov. 21, 1990; children: Brittany, Sean, Amy, Rachel. BBA, Nat. U., San Diego, 1991, MBA, 1992. Registered profl. elec. engr., Nev., Ariz. Elec. project mgr. Intercontinental Engring., Riverside, Mo., 1971-78; engr. IV Princeton (N.J.) U., 1980-89; engr. specialist I EG&G, Morgantown, W.Va., 1978-80; sr. engr. EG&G, Las Vegas, Nev., 1989-94; dir. elec. engring. Design Engring. Assocs., Las Vegas, 1994-96; pres. Argus Engring., 1995—; dir. R & D U-Products, Internat., Las Vegas, 1989—. Cons. Aid for Aids Nev., Las Vegas, 1990-92. Recipient Nuclear Weapons award for Excellence, U.S. Dept. Energy and U.S. Dept. Def., Las Vegas, 1991, 94. Mem. Assn. Energy Engrs. (sr.). Achievements include patents for coin-operated games. Avocations: restoring classic cars, woodworking. Home: 5309 Sly Fox Ct Las Vegas NV 89130-7001

RICHIE, ROBERT DOUGLAS, foundation executive; b. Washington, Sept. 25, 1962; s. David Arthur and Catherine Richie; m. Cynthia R. Terrell, Apr. 6, 1964; children: Savanna, Lucas, Rebecca. BA, Haverford Coll., 1987. Media rels. profl. Christic Inst., Washington, 1987-89; rschr. Jolene Unsoeld for Congress, Olympia, Wash., 1990-92; exec. dir. Ctr. for Voting and Democracy, Washington & Takoma Park, Md., 1992—; mem. adv. bd. Democracy 2000, N.Y.C., 1999—; coord., newsletter editor S.P.E.E.C.H., Olympia, Wash., 1990-91. Co-author: (book) Reflecting All of Us, 1999; contbr. articles to profl. jours.; mem. editl. adv. bd. Representation, 1997—. E-mail: fairvote@compuserve.com. Office: Ctr for Voting and Democracy 6930 Carroll Ave Ste 901 Takoma Park MD 20912-4466

RICHIE, RODNEY CHARLES, critical care and pulmonary medicine physician; b. Big Springs, Tex., Aug. 17, 1946; s. Howard Mouzon and Gloria (Hollingshead) R.; m. Sara Lee Dilley, July 13, 1968; children: Megan Kathryn, Paul Nathan. BA in Chemistry, So. Meth. U., 1968; MD cum laude, Baylor Coll., 1972. Diplomate in Internal Medicine, Pulmonary, Crit. Care and Ins. Medicine. Resident in medicine Baylor Affiliated Hosps., Houston, 1973-75, chief med. resident, 1975, fellow in pulmonary medicine, 1976-77; pvt. practice, pres. Waco (Tex.) Lung Assocs., 1977—; v.p. IMS, Houston, 1995—; med. dir. Tex. Life Ins., Waco, 1985—, Cmty. Hospice of Waco, 1996—, PMSI, Waco, Tex., 1997—. Chmn. med. staff Hillcrest Bapt. Med. Ctr., Waco, 1993; chmn. bd. dirs. GH Pape Found., Waco, 1993. Fellow Am. Coll. Chest Physicians; mem. ACP, AMA, Am. Thoracic Soc., Tex. Club Internists. Episcopalian. Avocations: snow skiing, writing, reading. Home: 3509 Lake Heights Dr Waco TX 76708-1005 Office: Waco Med Group 2911 Herring Ave Ste 212 Waco TX 76708-3244

RICHLER, MORDECAI, writer; b. Montreal, Que., Can., Jan. 27, 1931; s. Moses Isaac and Lily (Rosenberg) R.; m. Florence Wood, July 27, 1959; children: Daniel, Noah, Emma, Martha, Jacob. Student, Sir George Williams U., 1948-50. vis. prof. Carleton U., Ottawa, Ont., 1972-74; assoc. judge for Can., Book-of-the-Month Club, 1974-88, mem. editl. bd., N.Y. Author: (novels) The Acrobats, 1954, Son of a Smaller Hero, 1955, A Choice of Enemies, 1957, The Apprenticeship of Duddy Kravitz, 1959, Stick Your Neck Out, 1963, Cocksure, 1967, St. Urbain's Horseman, 1971, Joshua Then and Now, 1980, Solomon Gursky Was Here, 1990, Barney's Version, 1997, Belling the Cat, 1998; (essays) Notes on an Endangered Species, 1974, Home Sweet Home, 1984, Oh Canada!, Oh Quebec! A Lament for a Divided Nation, 1992, Knopf, Canada, 1998; (stories) The Street, 1975; (nonfiction) Oh Canada! Oh Quebec! Requiem for a Divided Country, 1992, This Year in Jerusalem, a memoir, 1994; children books Jacob Two-Two Meets The Hooded Fang, 1975, Jacob Two-Two and the Dinosaur, 1987; film The Apprenticeship of Duddy Kravitz, 1974 (Acad. award nomination 1974, Writers Guild of Am. award 1974), Joshua, Then and Now, 1985, Jacob Two-Two's First Spy Case, 1995; editor: The Best of Modern Humor, 1983, Writers on World War II, 1991; contbr. articles to profl. jours. Recipient Gov.-Gen.'s award for lit., 1968, 71, Paris Rev. Humour prize, 1968, Commonwealth Writer's prize, 1990, Giller Fiction prize Giller Found., Can., 1997, Leacock Humor award Leacock Found., Ont., 1998; Guggenheim fellow, 1961; various Can. Coun. fellowships. Fellow Royal Soc. Lit., Royal Soc. Literatese (London); mem. Montreal Press Club. Home: Apt 80 C, 1321 Sherbrooke St W, Montreal, PQ Canada H3G 1J4

RICHLING, BERND, neurosurgeon; b. Vienna, Austria, Nov. 19, 1946; s. Werner and ERika (Dirtl) R.; m. Annegret Wagner, Apr. 25, 1972; children: Nina, Florian. MD, U. Graz, Austria, 1972. Resident in neurosurgery U. Salzburg, Austria, 1973-79; assoc. prof. neurosurgery U. Vienna, 1980-89, prof. neurosurgery, vice chmn. dept. neurosurgery, 1989-98; head dept. neurosurgery Christian Doppler Med. Ctr., Salzburg, Austria, 1998—. Co-editor: Processes of the Cranial Midline, 1991, Stereotactic Neuro-Radio-Surgery, 1993; contbr. to Cerebral Vascular Microsurgery, 1994; patentee in field. Mem. World Fedn. (gen. sec.), Interventional and Therapeutic Neuroradiology, Austrian Soc. Neurosurgery, Soc. Neurosurgery Lang. French, German Soc. Neuroradiology, Austrian Soc. Neurol. and Neurosurg. Intensive Care Medicine (pres.). Lutheran. Office: Dept Neurosurgery, Christian Doppler Med Ctr, A-5020 Salzburg Austria

RICHMAN, JOEL ESER, lawyer, mediator, arbitrator; b. Brockton, Mass., Feb. 17, 1947; s. Nathan and Ruth Miriam (Bick) R.; m. Elaine R. Thompson, Aug. 21, 1987; children: Shawn Jonah, Jesse Ray, Eva Rose. BA in Psychology, Grinnell Coll., 1969; JD, Boston U., 1975. Bar: Mass. 1975, U.S. Dist. Ct. Mass. 1977, U.S. Supreme Ct. 1980, U.S. Ct. Appeals (1st cir.) 1982, Hawaii 1985, U.S. Dist. Ct. Hawaii 1987. Law clk. Richman & Perenyi, Brockton, Mass., 1973-75, atty., 1975-77; atty. pvt. practice, Provincetown, Mass., 1977-82, Paia, Hawaii, 1985—; arbitrator Am. Arbitration Assn., Paia, 1992—, mediator, 1994—. Pres. Jewish Congregation Maui (Hawaii), 1989-97, bd. dirs., 1984-89; bd. dirs. Pacific Primate Ctr., 1991 , pres., 1994 . Mem. Haiku Cmty. Assn. (dir. 1998). Avocations: windsurfing, youth soccer, T'ai Chi. Office: PO Box 46 Paia HI 96779-0046

RICHMOND, DAVID ERIC, geriatrician, consultant; b. Auckland, New Zealand, Jan. 1, 1938; s. Louis Eric and Dinah Wilhelmina (Green) R.; m. Pauline Reynolds, Jan. 15, 1966; children: Anthony John, Mary Elizabeth-Anne. MBChB, U. Otago, Dunedin, New Zealand, 1962, MD, 1977; MPHEd, U. New South Wales, Sydney, Australia, 1982; BD, Melbourne (Australia) Coll. Divinity, 1995. Diplomate Am. Bd. Internal Medicine, Am. Bd. Nephrology. Chief resident in medicine Georgetown U., Washington, 1969-70; sr. lectr. in medicine U. Auckland (New Zealand), 1970-78, Masonic prof. geriatric medicine, 1986-94, asst. dean, 1994-97; med. dir. Ciba-Geigy, Auckland, 1984-86; cons. delivery med. svcs. to South Vietnam, Govt. of New Zealand, 1972-73; vis. cons. in medicine U. Papua, New Guinea, 1975-76, vis. cons. in nephrology Queen Mary Hosp., Hong Kong, 1978; con. med. edn. WHO, Singapore, 1979, New Delhi, India, 1990, Manila, 1991. Contbr. articles to profl. jours., chpts. to books. chair New Zealand Coun. Asia Pacific Christian Mission, Auckland, 1978-97; active Bapt. Edn., Svc. & Tng. Bd., Auckland, 1992-94; chair bd. trustees Auckland Found. Tng. Rsch. & Edn. in the Health of Older People, 1993—; active bd. mgmt. Carey Bapt. Theol. Coll., Auckland, 1994-98. Grantee in field. Fellow Royal Australian Coll. Physicians (dir. continuing med. edn. 1979-84), Royal Coll. Physicians (London); mem. New Zealand Geriatrics Soc. (pres. 1995-96), New Zealand Assn. Gerontology, Australia/New Zealand Assn. Med. Edn. Baptist. Avocations: windsurfing, running, playing piano, writing poetry, horticulture. Office: Health Svcs for the Elderly, Pvt Bag 92024, Auckland New Zealand

RICHMOND, DAVID WALKER, lawyer; b. Silver Hill, W.Va., Apr. 20, 1914; s. David Walker and Louise (Finlaw) R.; m. Gladys Evelyn Mallard, Dec. 19, 1936; children: David Walker, Nancy L. LL.B., George Washington U., 1937. Bar: D.C. 1936, Ill. 1946, Md. 1950. Partner firm Miller & Chevalier, Washington; lectr. fed. taxation. Contbr. to profl. jours. Served from ensign to lt. comdr. USNR, 1942-46. Decorated Bronze Star; recipient Disting. Alumni Achievement award George Washington U., 1976. Fellow Am. Bar Found., Am. Coll. Trial Lawyers, Am. Coll. Tax Counsel; mem. ABA (chmn. taxation sect. 1955-57, ho. of dels. 1958-60), Am. Law Inst., Lawyers' Club of Washington, Union League (Chgo.), Masons. Republican. Methodist. Home: 7979 S Tamiami Trl Apt 359 Sarasota FL 34231-6819 Office: 655 15th St NW Washington DC 20005-5701

RICHMOND, GILLIAN, playwright; b. Kuala Lumpur, Malaya, Jan. 27, 1954; 2 children. BA honors Econs./Politics, St. Aidan's Coll., U. Durham, England, 1975; postgrad. cert. edn., Westminster Coll., Oxford, England, 1976. Freelance actress, teacher, artist, theatre adminstr., 1976-84; playwright-in-residence Soho Poly Theatre, London, 1988; script-writer TV and radio series including The Archers, 1986-92, Eastenders 1986—, Eldorado, 1993, Casualty, 1994-98, Silent Witness, 1997, Maisie Raine, 1998, Heartbeat, 1999-2000. Author: (plays) In the Groove, 1984, Ellen, 1985, The Last Waltz, 1986, Sitting Duck, 1989, The Legacy, 1990, Within the Fortress, 1991, The Snatch, 1991. Mem. Writers' Guild Great Britain. Office: Casarotto Ramsay Ltd, 60-66 Wardour St, London WIV 3HP, England

RICHMOND, MARISA JEANNE, columnist; b. Nashville, Oct. 3, 1958. AB, Harvard U., 1980; MA, U. Calif., Berkeley, 1985; PhD, George Washington U., 1992. Columnist Tenn. Vals, Nashville, 1994—; also bd. dirs.; columnist Transgender Cmty. News, 1999—. Contbr. articles to Transgender Tapestry, Chrysalis. Bd. dirs. Gender Polit. Action Com., Washington, 1996-99; com. mem. Ctr. for Gay, Lesbian, Bi and Transgendered Life, Nashville; co-founder Magnolia Transgender Alliance, Ashville, N.C., 1994—. Mem. Am. Hist. Assn., Soc. History of Tech., Orgn. Am. Historians, Tenn. Hist. Soc., Phi Kappa Phi. E-mail: marisaval@aol.com. Office: Tenn Vals PO Box 92335 Nashville TN 37209-8335

RICHON, DOMINIQUE JEAN-FRANCOIS, thermodynamicist; b. Clermont-Ferrand, France, June 24, 1949; d. Paul Jean-Marie and Andree Georgette-Marie (Geneix) R.; m. Inocencia Delgado-Martin, July 9, 1972; children: Thierry, Nathalie, Gregory, Jonathan. MS, U. Clermont-Ferrand, 1972; PhD, McGill U., Can., 1977; DSc, U. Clermont-Ferrand, 1979. Rsch. engr. Ecole Nat. Superieure des Mines de Paris, 1976-79; rsch. dir., head thermodynamic lab. Ecole des Mines de Paris, 1979—; prof. Ecole Nat. Superieure de Techniques Avancees, Paris, 1980—; cons. in field; designer equipments for high-pressure high-temperature phase equilibria measurements. Patentee in field; contbr. over 120 articles to profl. jours.; mem. adv. bd. (jour.) Indsl. & Engring. Chemistry Rsch., Jour. Chem. Engring. Data, and Internat., Electronic Jour. Physico-Chem. Data. Mem. AIChE, AAAS, Am. Chem. Soc. Home: 17 rue de Montmelian, 77210 Samoreau France Office: Ecole Nat Superieure Mines Paris, 35 Rue St Honore, 77305 Fontainebleau France

RICHTER, ANTHONY JOHN, artificial intelligence company executive; b. Yankalilla, S.A., Australia, Dec. 5, 1942; s. Percy William and Jessie Thelma (Howard) R. Student, Beaconsfield Primary W.A., 1964, Western Australia Inst. Tech., Perth Coll., U. Western Australia. Various profl. certs. Officer advt. and promotion Lewis Berger & Sons; mgr. pers. and tng. ALCO; owner, mgr. Richter Resource Group, Singopore; prin. cons. Richter Resource Group, 1981; founder Formulab Internat., 1982; founder, exec. chmn. Formulab Neuronetics Corp. Ltd., 1992; bd. dirs. Formulab Hong Kong, Formulab Tech. Australia, Neuronetics Corp. Inc., U.S.; state chmn. Australian Sci. Industry Assn., 1984-87; mem. bd. tchg. and learning West Australia Coll. Advanced Edn., 1986; chmn. neuronetics tech. com., founding chmn. Australian Inst. Applied Neuronetics Sci., 1995—; lectr. orgnl. theory Western Australian Inst. Tech., 1986. Co-author: Richters Laws. Past dir. commerce Boy Scout Assn., 1973; co-founder West Australia Opera Co., 1976. Fellow Australian Inst. Co. Dirs.; mem. AAAS, Australian Inst. Tng. and Devel., Sales Execs. Soc. Australia, Inst. Pers. Mgmt. Australia, N.Y. Acad. Scis. Achievements include patents for design of brain-based computing paradigm 'A Cognitive System;' inventor science and technology of neuronetics, principles of relational connectivity, also Neuronetic, Richter's Paradigm parallel computer. Avocations: archaeology, anthropology, sailing, under-water exploration. Home and Office: 35-B Pagoda St, Singapore 059194, Singapore

RICHTER, BRANKO BRANIMIR, retired parasitologist; b. Zagreb, Croatia, Jan. 10, 1920; s. Franjo and Vjera (Marakovic) R.; m. Željka Vodopija, Jan. 10, 1953; children: Jasna, Darko, Davor. MD, U. Zagreb, 1943, PhD, 1978. Diplomate Bd. Tropical Medicine. Epidemiologist Antimalaria Unit, Yugoslav Nat. Army, 1947-49; coord. animalaria campaign Fed. Com. Health, Belgrade, Yugoslavia, 1949-50; parasitologist Pub. Health Inst. Croatia, Zagreb, 1950-60; head dept. microbiology, parisitology U. Zagreb, 1960-86, prof. microbiology, 1965-86; vice dean Zagreb med. Sch., 1981-85; ret., 1986; malaria experts panel WHO, Geneva, 1955-95. Author: Medicinska Parasitologija, 5th edit., 1991; contbr. articles to profl. jours. Mem. Croatian Med. Assn., Croatian Acad. med. Sci. (v.p. 1993-2000, Laudatio 1995), German Soc. Tropical Medicine. Avocations: casting and collecting tin soldiers. Home: 36 Gajeva ul, HR 10000 Zagreb Croatia

RICHTER, BURTON, physicist, educator; b. N.Y.C., Mar. 22, 1931; s. Abraham and Fanny (Pollack) R.; m. Laurose Becker, July 1, 1960; children: Elizabeth, Matthew. B.S., MIT, 1952, Ph.D., 1956. Research assoc. Stanford U., 1956-60, asst. prof. physics, 1960-63, assoc. prof., 1963-67, prof., 1967—, Paul Pigott prof. phys. sci., 1980—, tech. dir. Linear Accelerator Ctr., 1982-84, dir. Linear Accelerator Ctr., 1984-99; dir. emeritus, 1999—; cons. NSF, SAEB; bd. dirs. Varian Med. Systems, Litel Instruments; Loeb lectr. Harvard U., 1974; DeShalit lectr. Weizmann Inst., 1975; pres. designate Internat. Union of Pure and Applied Physics, 1997. Contbr. over 300 articles to profl. publs. Recipient E.O. Lawrence medal Dept. Energy, 1975; Nobel prize in physics, 1976. Fellow Am. Phys. Soc. (pres. 1994), AAAS; mem. NAS, Am. Acad. Arts and Scis. Achievements include research in elementary particle physics. Office: Stanford Linear Accel Ctr PO Box 20450 Stanford CA 94309-0450

RICHTER, HANS PETER, neurosurgeon, educator; b. Wesermuende (Bremerhaven), Germany, May 17, 1943; s. Walther and Gerda (Sticht) R.; m. Ingrid Berenbold, June 20, 1975; children: Christine, Friederike, Johannes, Peter H. MD, Freiburg (Germany) U., 1968; prof. of Neurosurgery, Ulm (Germany) U., 1984. Head dept. of neurosurgery City Hosp., Fulda, Germany, 1984-89; prof. and chmn. dept. neurosurgery Ulm U., 1989—. Co-author: (book) Kompressions Syndrome, Peripherer Nerven, 1989; sr. editor: (book) Schiefhals- Behandlungskonzepte des Tortico llis Spasmodicus, 1993. Physician German Vol. Svc. Benin, W. Africa, 1970-72. Decorated Officer de l'Ordre de Merite, Rep. of Benin, West Africa, 1972, commandant, 1998. Mem. German Soc. Neurosurgery (pres. annual nat. congress 1995, sec. 1998—). Roman Catholic. Avocations: history, third world problems, foreign cultures, travel, hiking. Office: U Ulm Dept Neurosurgery, L Heilmeyer Strasse 2, 89312 Günzburg Germany

RICHTER, INGO KARL ALBERT, director youth institute, law educator; b. Pollnow, Germany, Jan. 27, 1938; s. Friedrich and Irmgard (Kolmsee) R.; m. Sabine U. Ellermann, Sept. 30, 1967; children: Konstantin, Franziska. Grad. 1st Legal State Exam., U. Hamburg, Germany, 1961, LLD, 1965; LLD, U. Paris, 1966; grad. 2d Legal State Exam., U. Berlin, 1967. Lawyer German Ednl. Counsel, Bonn, 1963-65; head dept. Max-Planck-Inst. for Edn., Berlin, 1967-79; prof. law U. Berlin, 1975-80, U. Hamburg, 1980-93; dir. German Youth Inst., Munich, 1993—; mem. numerous adv. bds. German Youth Inst. Co-author: Administrative Law Casebook, 2d edit., 1995, Constitutional Law Casebook, 3d edit., 1997; co-author, editor: Comparative School-Law, 1992; co-editor Ednl. Law jour. Avocations: music, hiking, literature, writing, tennis. Office: Deutsches Jugendinstitut, Nockherstrasse 2, 81541 Munich Germany

RICHTER, JAY ALAN, physician, educator; b. Boulder, Colo., Sept. 26, 1955; s. Henry John and Dorothy Madelyn Richter; m. Elissa Mary Ball, May 21, 1983; 1 children: Chesney Kirstin. BA, Middlebury Coll., 1977; MD, U. Colo., Denver, 1983. Diplomate Am. Bd. Internal Medicine. Sr. instr. dept. psychiatry U. Colo., 1986-94; chief of medicine Colo. Mental Health Inst. Pueblo, 1987-94; ptnr. Internal Medicine Assocs. Pueblo, 1994—; cons. Colo. Dept. Corrections, Canon City, 1989—; vol. faculty St. Mary Corwin Family Medicine Program, Pueblo, 1994—. Bd. dirs. Montessori Assn. Pueblo, 1996-98. Mem. ACP, AMA, Physicians for Social Responsibility, Colo. Med. Soc. Office: Internal Medicine Assn 1600 N Grand Ave Ste 350 Pueblo CO 81003-2729

RICHTER, PETER ROLF, botanist, researcher; b. Nuremberg, Bavaria, Germany, Feb. 13, 1965; s. Adolf Gustav and Gertraude Anna (Steinmann) R.; m. Ursula Ute Jahreis, Aug. 7, 1999. BS, U. Erlangen, Germany, 1990, MS, 1993, PhD, 2000. Compounder Psychiat. Hosp., Erlangen, 1991-92; scientist Inst. Fishery, Hochstadt, Germany, 1992-95, Inst. Botany I, Erlangen, 1995—; cons. Inst. Botany, Bonn, Germany, 1999. Contbr. articles to sci. jours., including Jour. Plant Physiology, Planta, Advanced Space Rsch., Image Analysis Methods and Applications. Active German Red Cross, 1988. With German Army, 1985-86. Mem. European Soc. Photobiology. Avocations: sightseeing, electronics, computer science. Home: Philipp Kittler Strasse 22, 90480 Nuremberg Bavaria, Germany Office: Inst Botany I, Staudtstrasse 5, 90158 Erlangen Bavaria, Germany

RICHTEROVÁ, VĚRA, chemical and oil industry journalist, consultant; b. Prague, Czech Republic, Mar. 31, 1935; d. Otto and Jolana (Weiszová) R.; m. Stephan Dulá, Jan. 19, 1996. MSc, Tech. U. Chem. Tech., Prague, 1958, PhD, 1970; grad., Inter U. Ctr., Dubrovnik, Yugoslavia, 1991. Rschr. State Rsch. Inst. Machinery, Prague, 1958-66, Rsch. Inst. Sci.-Tech. Devel., Prague, 1985-91, Ctr. Fgn. Econ. Rels., Prague, 1992-93; rschr. gen. mgmt. divsn. R&D Chemopetrol, Prague, 1967-84; journalist Tech. Weekly, Prague, 1994-99; ret., 1999. Contbr. articles to profl. jours. Mem. polling com., Prague, 1992, 96; tour guide Sport-Turist, Prague, 1979-89. Mem. Czechoslovak Sci. Tech. Soc. (hon. acknowledgement 1986), Energy Soc., Czech Chem. Soc., World Future Study Fedn. (pres. 1991—). Czech Social Democratic Party. Avocations: cooking, suit making, gardening, travel, swimming. Home: Mladeze 5, 169 00 Prague 6, Czech Republic

RICKARDS, RICHARD BARRIE, palaeontologist, educator, curator; b. Leeds, Eng., June 12, 1938; s. Robert and Eva (Sudborough) R.; m. Christine Townsley (div. 1991); 1 child, Jeremy. BSc, Hull (Eng.) U., 1960, PhD, 1963; ScD, Cambridge (Eng.) U., 1977; DSc, Hull U., 1990. Chartered geologist. Curator Univ. Coll. London, 1963-64; rsch. asst. U. Cambridge, 1964-67; sr. scientific officer Brit. Mus. Natural History, London, 1967; lectr. in geology Trinity Coll., Dublin, Ireland, 1967-69; univ. lectr., curator Sedgwick Mu. U. Cambridge, 1969-90, univ. reader, curator, 1990—; fellow and ofcl. lectr. Emmanuel Coll., U. Cambridge, 1978—, cur. mus., 1994-99, admissions tutor in scis., 1983-87; univ. proctor U. Cambridge, 1983-85. Author: (with R. Webb) Fishing for Big Pike, 1971, Big Pike, 3d edit., 1986, Perch, 1974, (with R. Webb) Fishing for Big Tench, 1976, 2d edit., 1986, Pike, 1976, (with K. Whitehead) Plugs and Plug Fishing, 1976, Spinners, Spoons and Wobbled Baits, 1977, A Textbook of Spinning, 1987, (with N. Fickling) Zander, 1979, 3d edit., 1990, (with K. Whitehead) Fishing Tackle, 1981, (with K. Whitehead) A Fishery of Your Own, 1984, Angling: Fundamental Principles, 1986, (with M. Gay) A Technical Manual of Pike Fishing, 1986, (with M. Gay) Pike, 1989, (with M. Bannister) The Ten Greatest Pike Anglers, 1991, Success with Pike, 1992, Success with the Lure, 1993; co-author: Encyclopaedia of Fishing, 1991; editor: River Piking, 1987, Best of Pikelines, 1988; contbr. over 500 articles on angling to newspapers and mags.; author: Graptolites: Writing in the Rocks, 1991; editor: (with D.C. Palmer) H.B. Whittington, Trilobites, 1992; contbr. over 200 scientific articles and monographs, mostly on fossils and evolution, to profl. jours. Fellow Geol. Soc. U.K. (coun. 1960—, Murchison Fundaward 1982, Lyell medal 1997); mem. Palaeontol. Assn. (coun. 1987-95), Yorkshire Geol. Soc. (John Phillips medal 1988). Avocations: marathon running, angling, fisheries management, environment agency work, writing. Office: Emmanuel Coll, Regent St, Cambridge CB2 3AP, England

RICKAYZEN, GERALD, physics educator; b. London, Oct. 16, 1929; s. Solomon and Jane (Culank) R.; m. Gillian Thelma Lewin, Dec. 20, 1953; children: Alan Michael, Sonia Ruth, Martin Asher, Benjamin David. BSc, Queen Mary Coll., London, 1951; PhD, Christ's Coll., Cambridge, Eng., 1954. Chartered physicist. Rsch. fellow Admiralty, Baldock, Eng., 1954-57; rsch. assoc. U. Ill., Urbana, 1957-59; lectr. U. Liverpool (Eng.), 1959-65; reader U. Kent, Canterbury, Eng., 1965-66, prof., 1966—, dean faculty of natural scis., 1977-81, pro-vice-chancellor, 1981-90, dep. vice-chancellor, 1984-90; chmn. governing body Simon Langton Girls Sch., 1985-93. Author: Theory of Superconductivity, 1965, Green's Functions, 1980, 84; contbr. articles to profl. jours. Chmn. Harbledown Parish Coun., 1998-2000. Fellow Inst. Physics London; mem. Am. Inst. Physics. Office: U Kent Physics Lab, Canterbury CT2 7NR, England

RICKELS, KARL, psychiatrist, physician, educator; b. Wilhelmshaven, Germany, Aug. 17, 1924; came to U.S., 1954, naturalized, 1960; s. Karl E. and Stephanie (Roehrhoff) R.; m. Rosalind Wilson, June 27, 1964; children: Laurence Arthur, Stephen W., Michael R. M.D., U. Muenster, 1951. Intern Dortmund (Germany) Hosp., 1951-52; postgrad. tng. U. Erlangen, U. Frankfurt, City Hosp. Kassel, 1952-54; resident in psychiatry Mental Health Inst., Cherokee, Iowa, 1954-55, Hosp. U. Pa., Phila., 1955-57; from instr. to assoc. prof. U. Pa., Phila., 1957-69; prof. psychiatry U. Pa., 1969—, prof. pharmacology, 1976—, Stuart and Emily B.H. Mudd prof. human behavior, 1977—, chief mood and anxiety disorders program, 1964—; chmn. com. on studies involving human beings U. Pa., Phila., 1985-98; chief psychiatry Phila. Gen. Hosp., 1975-77. Editor, author 7 books; contbr. over 500 articles to profl. publs. Fellow Am. Coll. Neuropsychopharmacology (charter), Am. Coll. Clin. Pharmacology, Am. Psychiat. Assn., Coll. Physicians Phila., Collegium Internat. Neuro-Psychopharmacologicum; mem. Arbeits Gemeinschaft Neuro-Psychopharmacology, Psychiat. Rsch. Soc., European Coll. Neuropsychopharmacology (corr.). Home: 1324 Youngsford Rd Gladwyne PA 19035-1231 Office: U Pa Dept Psychiatry 803 Sci Ctr 3600 Market St Philadelphia PA 19104-2641

RICKENBACH, MARK ALAN, physician; b. Chemlsford, England, May 25, 1959; s. Alan Gustav and Veronica Christine (Short) R. MBBS, London Hosp. Med. Coll., 1984. House officer NHS, London, 1984-85; sr. house officer NHS, Portsmouth, 1985-90; gen. practitioner Denmead, England, 1991-92; lectr. U. Portsmouth, England, 1992—; ptnr. Practice Family Medicine, England, 1993—; chmn. Wessex Rsch. Club, 1973—. Contbr. articles to profl. jours. Fellow Royal Coll. Gen. Practitioners; mem. Royal Coll. Physicians, Brit. Med. Assn., Royal Coll. Ob-gyn. (mem. faculty family planning). Avocations: sailing, badminton, swimming. Office: Park Surgery, Hursley Rd, Chandlers Ford SO53 22H, England

RICKERS, CARSTEN, physician; b. Lingen, Germany, Oct. 6, 1964; s. Erich and Helga (Hampel) R.; m. Hedwig Silies, July 12, 1996; children: Eva Sophia, Karla Maria. MD, Munster, Germany, 1993. Med. trainee U. Hosp. Eppendorf, Hamburg, Germany, 1993-94, 94-95, resident, 1995-96, 96—. Contbr. articles to profl. jours. Rsch. grantee German Rsch. Soc., 2000—; Cardiovascular Rsch. fellow U. Minn., Mpls., 2000—. Mem. Germen Soc. Cardiology, German Soc. Pediatric Cardiology. Roman Catholic. Avocations: skiing, swimming, soccer. Home: Lehmweg 31 A, 20251 Hamburg Germany Office: U Minn Ctr MRS-Rsch 385 E River Rd Minneapolis MN 55455-0367

RICKERSHAUSER, PAUL E., benefits compensation director; b. Newark, Nov. 14, 1957; s. Carl Rickershauser and Edna Wright; m. Anita M. Essig, Sept. 24, 1983; children: Lisa, Katie. BA, Rutgers U., 1980, MS, 1985. Cert. SPHR, SHRM. Human rels. mgr. RH Macy, N.Y.C., 1980-86, Rexham Corp., Charlotte, N.C., 1986-88; dir. benefits, compensation and employee rels. United Stationers, DesPlaines, Ill., 1988—. Avocations: sailing, traveling. E-mail: perickershauser@hotmail.com and prickershauser@ussco.com. Office: United Stationers 2200 E Golf Rd Des Plaines IL 60016-1257

RICKERT, EDWARD JOSEPH, psychologist, consultant, researcher; b. Houston, July 24, 1936; s. Edward Joseph and Beatrice (Pierros) R.; m. Barbara Moutray, Dec. 19, 1974 (div.); children: Stephen, Stuart, Michael, Bruce; m. Donna Lee, May 26, 1975; children: Adrian, Jeff. BA, U. N.Mex., 1960, MS, 1963; PhD, 1968; MPH, U. Ala., 1986. Lic. psychologist, Ala. Teaching asst. U. N.Mex., Albuquerque, 1960-61, rsch. asst., 1963-66, univ. fellow, 1966-67; program writer, supr. Teaching Machines, Inc., Albuquerque, 1961-63; asst. prof. Calif. State U., Sacramento, 1967-71; assoc. prof. U. Ala., Birmingham, 1971-99; cons. NASA, Huntsville, Ala., 1984-88, U.S. Army, Huntsville, 1986-88, North Sacramento Sch. Dist., 1969-71, legal firms, Birmingham and Huntsville, 1989—; sec./treas. Sigma Assn., Inc., Birmingham, 1988—; lectr. psychology, adj. prof. dept. epidemiology and biostatistics U. S.C., 1999—. Co-author: Psychology of Learning and Memory, 1979; contbr. articles in books and jours. Univ. fellow U. N.Mex., 1966. Mem. AAAS, APA, Internat. Soc. Polit. Psychology, Am. Psychol.

Soc., Am. Statis. Assoc., Rocky Mountain Psychol. Assn., Sigma Xi, Phi Kappa Phi. Democrat. Avocations: fly fishing, philosophy, coaching little league baseball. Office: U SC Dept of Psychology Barnwell Hall 414 Columbia SC 29208-0001

RICKERT, ROBERT RICHARD, pathologist, educator; b. Harrisburg, Pa., Oct. 19, 1936; s. Alton G. and Henrietta (Gey) R.; m. Sonja Murray Hansen, Aug. 26, 1961; children: Kristin, Robin, Anne. AB, U. Mich., 1958; MD, John Hopkins U., 1962. Diplomat Am. Bd. of Pathology. Intern Yale-New Haven (Conn.) Med. Ctr., 1962-63, resident in internal medicine, 1963-64, 66-67; rsch. assoc. Atomic Bomb Casulty Commn., Hiroshima, Japan, 1964-66; asst. prof. pathology Yale U. Sch. Med., New Haven, 1968-70; attending pathologist Yale New Haven Med. Ctr., 1968-70; dir. surg. pathology U. Med. and Dentistry N.J.-N.J. Med. Sch., Newark, 1970-73, assoc. prof. pathology, 1970-73; clin. prof. pathology U. of Med. and Dentistry N.J.-N.J. Med. Sch., Newark, 1985—; co-chmn. dept. pathology St. Barnabas Med. Ctr., Livingston, N.J., 1973-2000; chmn. dept. pathology St. Barnabas Med. Ctr., Livingston, 2000—; adj. assoc. prof. pathology Columbia U. Coll. Physicians & Surgeons, N.Y.C., 1974-89. Contbr. chpts. to med. textbooks and articles to profl. jours. Chmn. med. com. Am. Cancer Soc., N.J., 1989-91, v.p. 1991-93, pres. elect 1993-94, pres. 1995-97 (Physician of Yr., N.J. Divsn., 1998), chief med. spokesperson Ea. divsn., 1998—. Fellow Coll. Am. Pathologists (vice-chmn., overseas regional commr. commn. on lab. accreditation), Am. Soc. Clin. Pathologists, U.S.-Can. Acad. Pathology; mem. AMA, N.J. Soc. Pathologists (pres. 1980-82), Gastrointestinal Pathology Soc. (pres. 1988-89), Med. Soc. N.J., Acad. Medicine N.J. (trustee 1988—, treas. 1994-95, v.p. 1995-97, pres. 1998), Am. Soc. Cytopathology, Short Hills Club, Phi Beta Kappa, Alpha Omega Alpha. Republican. Congregational. Avocations: antiques, wine collecting, art. Office: St Barnabas Med Ctr Dept Pathology Livingston NJ 07039

RICKETT, CAROLYN KAYE MASTER, artist, criminologist; b. Ft. Worth, Apr. 24, 1941; d. Lester Buford and Dorothy Minerva (Whittington) Master; m. David Franklin Rickett, May 3, 1981; 1 child, Julia Beth Allen. BFA, Tex. Christian U., 1993; MFA, Tex. Woman's U., 1997; M in Criminology, U. Tex., Arlington, 1998—. Artist, owner StarMaster Graphic Design and Fine Art, Ft. Worth, 1988—; presenter in field. One-woman shows Jasper (Alta. Can.) Mus., 1994, Downstairs Gallery, Jasper, 1994, Del Bello Gallery, Toronto, Ont., Can., 1996; exhibited in group shows Tex. Christian U., Ft. Worth, 1991, Greater Denton (Tex.) Coun. for Arts, 1994-96, Tex. Christian U., 1995, 97, UN 4th Conf. for Women, Beijing, 1995, Bass Mus., Miami Broward C.C., Davie, Fla., 1996, San Jacinto Coll., Houston, 1996, Aisling Studio, Durango, Colo., 1996, U. Tex., Arlington, 1998, World Trade Ctr., Dallas, 1998, Beijing and Beyond traveling show, N.Y., 1998-00, also others; represented in permanent collections Jasper Mus., Nat. Women's Caucus for Arts Archives, also pvt. collections; represented by Kincannon Fine Arts Gallery, Dallas, Downstairs Gallery. Grantee Tex. Christian U., 1990-93, scholar, 1991-93, Ray and Bertha Lakey Meml. scholar, 1994-96. Mem. Am. Criminal Justice Criminology, Am. Soc. Criminology, Mus. of Women in Arts, Alpha Phi Sigma, Lambda Sigma Khi Chpt. Nat. Criminal Justice Honor Soc. Home: 5816 Broadway Ave Fort Worth TX 76117-3305

RICKETTS, HERBERT A., retired business owner; b. Arequipa, Peru, Aug. 17, 1924; s. Jose A. Ricketts and Teresa M. Olivares; m. Angela M. Bustamante, Nov. 17, 1957; children: Herbert, Veronica, Sandra, Lottie, Andres, Ursula. BA, Rollins Coll., 1947; MBA, Harvard U., 1949. From asst. mgr. to bus. mgr. Ricketts & Co., Arequipa, 1950-88; bd. dirs. Inca Tops S.A., Arequipa; pres. bd. dirs. SUR Motors S.A., Arequipa; past pres. Cámara de Comercio e Industrias de Arequipa, Club Arequipa, Decano del Cuerpo Consular de Aquipa, hon. consul of Netherlands. Avocations: golf, tennis, hiking, traveling, reading. Home: Avenida Parra #218, PO Box #1, Arequipa Peru

RICKETTS, VIRGINIA LEE, historian, researcher; b. Jamestown, Kans., Jan. 12, 1925; d. Roy Earl Eastman and Alma Anna Hunter; m. Clair Keith Ricketts, June 3, 1944; children: Keith Alan, Dennis Lee, Donald Gene. G-rad. H.S., Filer, Idaho. Clk. dist. ct., auditor, recorder Jerome County, Idaho, 1972-79; pvt. practice historian, rschr. Jerome, 1979—; mem. Idaho State Hist. Records Adv. Bd., Boise, 1976-2002; pres. Idaho Assn. Recorders and Clks., 1977-78; cons. Idaho State Supreme Ct., Boise, 1979-81; tour dir., instr. Coll. So. Idaho, Twin Falls, 1984-97; mem. Bur. Land Mgmt. Adv. Bd., Shoshone, Idaho, 1989-95, Upper Snake River Ecosystem Adv. Bd., Idaho, 1995-98; lectr. in field. Authro: The History of the North Side-The First 75 Years, 1982, Greater Twin Falls Historical Guide, 1988, A History of the Middle Snake River, 1996, Then and Now in Southern Idaho, 1998. Organizer Friends St. Stricker Ranch, Inc., Twin Falls, 1984. Recipient Cert. of Commendation, Am. Assn. for State and Local History, 1984, Cert. of Resolution of Appreciation, Idaho State Bd. Edn., 1998; named Idaho Disting. Citizen, Idaho Statesmen, 1988, Centennial Citizen, Citizens of Jerome County Idaho, 1990. Mem. Idaho State Hist. Soc. (trustee 1987-99, chairperson bd. trustees 1991-98), Oreg. Calif. Trails Assn. (organizer Idaho chpt. 1984, treas. Idaho chpt. 1985-99), Jerome County Hist. Soc., Inc. (co-organizer 1984, former pres., curator 1985-2000), PEO (chpt. E Idaho, historian 1987-98). Republican. Presbyterian. Avocations: needlework, gardening, sports, family activities. Home: 516 E 300 S Jerome ID 83338-6747

RICKMAN, HANS PETER, philosopher, educator, writer; b. Prague, Czechoslavakia, Nov. 11, 1918; came to Eng., 1938.; s. Ernst and Grete (Wollin) Weisskopf. BA, U. London, 1941; D Philosophy, Oxford U., 1943, MA, 1948. Freelance lectr. adult edn., London, 1947-49; staff tutor U. Hull, Eng., 1949-61; sr. lectr. City U. London, reader, 1962-82, vis. prof. philosophy, 1982—. Author: The Adventure of Reason, 1983, Understanding and the Human Studies, 1967; Dilthey Today, 1988, Philosophy in Literature, 1996, In Defense of Philosophy, 2000; contbr. articles to profl. jours. Served with Brit. mil., 1943-47. Mem. Soc. Authors, PEN, CRUSE, Assn. U. Tchrs. Conservative. Avocations: chess, bridge, swimming. Home: 12 Fitzroy Ct, 57 Shepherds Hill, London N6 5RD, England Office: The City U Northampton Sq, London ECIV OHB, England

RICKS, DAVID TRULOCK, cultural affairs administrator; b. London, June 28, 1936; s. Percival Trulock and Annetta Helen (Hood) R.; m. Nicole Estelle Chupeau, Aug. 1, 1960; children: Ralph, Quentin. MA, Merton Coll./Oxford U., 1958; Lic.-es-Lettres, Lille U., France, 1967; MA, Essex U., U.K., 1971. Dir. of studies The Brit. Coun., Morocco, 1967-70, State Inst. of Langs., Rajasthan, India, 1971-74; dept. dir. The Brit. Coun., Tanzania, 1974-76; cultural attache The Brit. Embassy, Tehran, 1976-80; asst. controller personnel The Brit. Coun., U.K., 1980-85; cultural counsellor The Brit. Embassy, Rome, 1985-90, Paris, 1990-96; founder/mem. Entente Cordiale Scholarships, U.K.-France, 1996. Joint editor: (book) The Penguin French Reader, 1967, The New Penguin French Reader, 1992. Decorated Officer of the Order of the Brit. Empire, HM The Queen, U.K., 1981, Companion of the Order of St. Michael and St. George, 1997. Mem. United Oxford and Cambridge Univ. Club. Avocations: piano, music, skiing. Home: Saint Jean, Bvd Raoul Dufy, 04300 Forcalquier France

RICKS, N(ORMAN) RICHARD, JR., engineering executive; b. Portsmouth, Ohio, Sept. 28, 1961; s. Norman R. Sr. and La Vonda M. Ricks; m. Denna M. Flanagan, Oct. 21, 1991. BS in Chem. Engring., Ohio State U., 1983; postgrad., U. Findlay. Chartered indsl. gas cons.; cert. energy mgr. Tech. svcs. engr. Goodyear Atomic Corp., Piketon, Ohio, 1984-85; indsl. engr. I Columbia Gas Ohio, Cambridge, 1985-89, indsl. engr. II, 1989-94, indsl. sales and svcs. engr., 1994-96, mgr. key accounts, 1996—]. Mem. Assn. Chem. Engrs. (sr.), Assn. Energy Engrs., Assn. Iron and Steel Engrs., Iron and Steel Soc. Republican. Avocations: backpacking, cycling, hunting, fishing, traveling. Home: 113 Grand Ave Senecaville OH 43780 Office: Columbia Gas Ohio Inc 216 Highland Ave Cambridge OH 43725-2528

RICNY, VACLAV, TV technology engineer, educator; b. Brno, Czech Republic, July 19, 1937; s. Frantisek and Anna (Sedlackova) R.; m. Alena Mikulcova, Sept. 30, 1961; children: Michal, Martin. MSc in Elec. Engring., Tech. U. Brno, 1961, Phd, 1972. Cert. in radioelectronics engring. Lectr. Tech. U. Brno, 1961-77, assoc. prof., 1977-91, prof., 1991—, vice chmn. dept. radioelectronics, 1990—, vice dean Faculty of Elec. Engring., 1992—; mem. sci. bd. Tech. U. Brno, 1990—, mem. pedagogical bd., 1990—; mem. sci. bd. Czech Tech. U., Prague, 1993—. Author: (textbook) Television Technology, 1984 (Rector's TU Brno award 1985); contbr. more than 200 sci. articles to profl. jours., 20 textbooks. Grantee Tech. U. Brno, 1993, Ministry of Edn. of Czech Republic, 1994, Grand Agy. Czech Republic, 1995-96, 2000-2002. Fellow IEEE; mem. N.Y. Acad. Scis., Czech Soc. Sci. (mem. regional bd. 1980-87), Czech Soc. Radioengring. Roman Catholic. Achievements include 7 patents. Office: Tech U Brno Dept Radioelectronics, Purkynova 118, 612 00 Brno Czech Republic

RICO CLAROS, JULIO ALBERTO, orthopaedic surgeon, educator; b. Tegucigalpa, Honduras, Nov. 9, 1954; s. Jose Ismael and Victoria Asuncion (Claros) R.; m. Karla Estela Schwarzbauer Pinel de Rico, Oct. 10, 1993. Diplomate Teology Great Commn. Internat. Instr. morphologic sci. medicine faculty Nat. U., 1977, asst. prof. neuroanatomy, 1978; intern Hosp. Escuela, Tegucigalpa, 1979-80, resident in orthopaedics, 1982-85; med. social svc. Hosp. Gabriela Alvarado, Danli, Paraiso, 1980-81; resident in pediat. Hosp. Materno-Infantil, Tegucigalpa, 1981-82; orthopedic resident exchange tng. program Mayo Clinic and Tulane Med. Ctr., 1984; orthopaedic surgeon Hosp. Materno-Infantil, Tegucigalpa, 1985—, Hosp. Viera, Tegucigalpa, 1985—; cons. orthopaedics Panamerican Found. for Devel./Am. States Orgn., Tegucigalpa, 1988-90; ad-hon. tchr. orthopaedics Nat. U., 1988—; assoc. mem. Hosp. Viera, 1985; pres. Symposium Med. Christian, 4th Med. Christian Congress, 1996. Named Best Resident in Orthopaedics by Honduras Med. Assn., 1984; recipient Acad. Excellence award Great Commn. Internat., 1994. Mem. Orthopaedic Assn. (sec. 1988-90), Christian Med. Science Assn. (pres. 1995), Nat. Ctr. Continuing Med. Edn. Avocations: photography, handcrafting, writing, design, fishing. Office: Hosp y Clinicas Viera, 224 Tegucigalpa Honduras

RICORDI, CAMILLO, surgeon, transplant and diabetes researcher; b. N.Y.C., Apr. 1, 1957; m. Valerie A. Grace, Aug. 8, 1986; children: M. Caterina, Eliana G., Carlo A. MD, U. Milan (Italy) Sch. Medicine, 1982. Trainee in gen. surgery San Raffaele Inst., Milan, 1982-85; NIH trainee Washington U. Sch. Medicine, St. Louis, 1985-88; attending surgeon San Raffaele Inst., Milan, 1988-89; asst. prof. to assoc. prof. surgery U. Pitts., Pa., 1989-93; prof. surgery and medicine, pathology, microbiology and immunology, chief divsn. cellular transpl. Diabetes Rsch. Inst., U. Miami, Fla., 1993—, sci. dir., chief acad. officer, 1996—; Stacy Joy Goodman chair in Diabetes Rsch. Diabetes Rsch. Inst., U. Miami, 1998—; reviewer of applications for grants Can. and Am. Diabetes Assns., Juvenile Diabetes Found., NIH; chmn. First and Third Internat. Congresses of Cell Transplant Soc., Pitts., 1992, Miami, 1996, 5th Internat. Congress on Pancreas and Islet Transplantation, Miami, 1995, others; mem. editl. bd. Transplantation, Cell Transplantation, Transplantation Procs., Jour. Tissue Engring. Editor: Pancreatic Islet Cell Transplantation, 1992, Methods in Cell Transplantaion, 1995; co-editor-in-chief Cell Transplantation, Graft; contbr. numerous chpts. to books and articles to jours. including Immunology Today, Jour. Clin. Investigation, New Eng. Jour. Medicine, Hepatology, Diabetes, Transplantation, Endocrinology, Procs. NAS, USA, Am. Jour. Physiology, Surgery, Nature, Nature Genetics, Lancet. Grantee Juvenile Diabetes Found. Internat., 1988—, NIH, 1993—; recipient NIH traineee award, 1986-88. Mem. AAAS, Cell Transplant Soc. (founder, pres. 1992-94), Am. Soc. Transplant Surgeons, Internat. Pancreas and Islet Transplant Assn. (v.p. 1979-99, pres. 1999—), The Transplantation Soc., Am. Diabetes Assn. (Rsch. award 1996), Am. Fedn. Clin. Rsch., Nat. Diabetes Coalition (co-founder 1994—, chmn. 1997—). Achievements include patent for Automated Method for Cell Separation. Office: U Miami Diabetes Rsch Inst 1450 NW 10th Ave Miami FL 33136-1011

RICUPERO, RUBENS, Brazilian government official; b. Sao Paulo, Mar. 1, 1937. Min. of fin. Govt. of Republic of Brazil, Brasilia, until 1994; sec. gen. UN Conf. on Trade and Devel., Geneva, 1995—. Office: Esplanada dos Ministerios, Bloco P 5 piso, 70048 Brasilia DF, Brazil also: Office of the Sec-Gen, Palais des Nations, 1211 Geneva 10, Switzerland*

RIDD, JOHN HOWARD, chemistry educator; b. London, Oct. 7, 1927; s. Herbert William and Emma Roadley (Elmes) R.; m. Freda Marie Williams, Dec. 31, 1955; children: David Howard, Margaret Anne. BS, U. Coll., London, 1948, PhD, 1951, DS, 1965. Rsch. fellow Harvard U., 1951-52; asst. lectr. U. Coll., London, 1952-55, lectr., 1955-65, reader, 1965-71, prof., 1971-93, emeritus prof., 1993—; chmn. Bd. Studies in Chemistry, U. London, 1983-85. Author: (with P.B.D. DeLa Mare) Aromatic Substitution, 1959; editor: (book) Studies of Chemical Structure and Reactivity, 1966. Fellow Univ. Coll. London, 1996. Fellow Royal Soc. Chemistry (Organic Reaction Mechanisms award 1984). Avocation: photography. Office: Chem Dept/Univ Coll London, 20 Gordon St, WCIH OAJ London England

RIDDICK, WINSTON WADE, SR., lawyer; b. Crowley, La., Feb. 11, 1941; s. Hebert Hobson and Elizabeth (Wade) R.; m. Patricia Ann Turner, Dec. 25, 1961;1 child, Winston Wade. BA, U. Southwestern La., 1962; MA, U. N.C., 1963; PhD, Columbia U., 1965; JD, La. State U., 1973. Bar: La. 1974, U.S. Dist. Ct. (so., mid. and we. dists.) La., U.S. Ct. Appeals (5th cir.), U.S. Supreme Court. Asst. prof. gov., dir. Inst. Gov. Research, La. State U., Baton Rouge, 1966-67; dir. La. Higher Edn. Facilities Commn., Baton Rouge, 1967-72; exec. asst. state supt. La. Dept. Edn., Baton Rouge, 1972-73; law ptnr. Riddick & Riddick, Baton Rouge, 1973—; asst. commnr., gen. counsel La. Dept. Agr., Baton Rouge, 1981-82; cons. Riddick & Assoc., Baton Rouge, 1973—; part-time law faculty mem. So. Univ. Law Ctr., Baton Rouge, 1974-95; assoc. prof., 1995-99, prof. law, 1999—, exec. asst. atty. gen. State of La., 1987-91. Spl. asst. to Gov. John J. McKeithen on Nat. Ctr. for Edn. in Politics Fellowship, 1966-67; state campaign mgr. Gillis W. Long for Gov., Baton Rouge, 1971; mem. East Baton Rouge Parish Dem. Exec. Com., 1981-84. Mem. La. Trial Lawyers Assn. (bd. govs. 1978-80), real estate investor and property mgr., 1975—. Presbyterian. Office: Riddick & Riddick 1563 Oakley Dr Baton Rouge LA 70806-8622

RIDDLE, MICHAEL LEE, lawyer; b. Oct. 7, 1946; s. Joy Lee and Francis Irene (Brandes) R.; m. Suzan Ellen Shaw, May 25, 1969 (div.); m. Carol Jackson, Aug. 13, 1977; 1 child, Robert Andrew. BA, Tex. Tech U., 1969, JD with honors, 1972. Bar: Tex. 1972, U.S. Dist. Ct. (no. dist.) Tex. 1972, U.S. Ct. Appeals (5th cir.) Tex. 1972. Assoc. Geary Brice Barron & Stahl, Dallas, 1972-75; ptnr. Baker Glast Riddle Tuttle & Elliott, Dallas, 1975-80; ptnr., mng. ptnr. Middleburg, Riddle & Gianna, 1980—; chmn., CEO MRG Document Techs., 2000—; bd. dirs. Dallas Opera. bd. dirs. U.S.A. Film Festival, pres., 1984-86, North Tex. Pub. Broadcasting, 1992-97; chmn., bd. dirs. Provident Bancorp Tex., 1987-90. Mem. ABA, Tex. Bar Assn., Dallas Bar Assn., Coll. of State Bar of Tex., Lakewood Country Club, Crescent Club. Democrat. Lutheran. Office: 4004 Belt Line Rd Ste 200 Addison TX 75001-5844

RIDDLE, WESLEY ALLEN, army officer, writer; b. Houston, Apr. 19, 1961; s. Walter Abige Riddle and Gloria Texane (Longnecker) Riddle-Roe; m. Maria Aida Albesa, Dec. 21, 1985; stepchildren: Catalina Louise Oates, Danilo Albesa Calabia. BS cum laud, U.S. Mil. Acad., 1983; MPhil in Modern History with distinction, Oxford (Eng.) U., 1993. Commd. U.S. Army, 1983, advanced through grades to lt. col., 2000; platoon leader, battery exec. officer 1-62 ADA (C/V) U.S. Army, Schofield Barracks, Hawaii, 1984-87; asst. S-3 Plans, S-4 and Battery Comdr. 2-43 ADA (Patriot) Hanau, Germany, 1988-91; battery comdr. B/2-43 ADA Gulf War SWA, 1991; asst. prof. history U.S. Mil. Acad., West Point, N.Y., 1993-96; Theater Missile Def. evaluation officer Air Def. Directorate Operational Test and Evaluation Command, Alexandria, Va., 1996-98; exec. officer 2-6 ADA, Ft. Bliss, Tex., 1998-99; chief AD br., requirements divsn. DCD, Ft. Bliss, 1999-2000; air def. readiness br. chief (OMC-K) USASATMO, Ft. Bragg, N.C., 2000—; chmn. Am. Civility Project, 1996-99. Mem. adv. bd. The Social Critic mag., 1996-99; U.S. corr. Fragments Mag., 1998—; contbr. chpts. to books; columnist Belton Jour., 2000—. Founder, pres. Northbrook Teenage Reps., Houston, 1975-79; youth advisor State of Tex. to Citizens for the Republic, 1978-79; page, Rep. Nat. Conv., Kansas City, Mo., 1976. Decorated Bronze Star; Salvatori fellow Heritage Found., Washington, 1996-99; Nat. Humanities Inst. fellow, 1997—. Mem. VFW, Am. Legion, Mil. Order of Saint Barbara, Phi Kappa Phi, Phi Alpha Theta. Republican. Christian Scientist. Avocations: music, poetry, weightlifting, running, water sports.

RIDEN, MICHAEL DAVID, nuclear engineer; b. Maryville, Tenn., July 2, 1947; s. William Walter and Grace Ella (Elrod) R.; m. Perry Dene Thyberg, Mar. 28, 1970; children: Chad Michael, Kirk David, Eric Wesley. Cert. nuclear weapons specialist, Lowry Tng. Ctr., Denver, 1968; cert. nuclear weapons technician, Gen. Electric Co. Tng. Program, King of Prussia, Pa., 1969; BS, U. Tenn., Knoxville, 1974. Asst. engr. Duke Power Co. Oconee Nuclear Sta., Seneca, S.C., 1974-78; reactor insp. Nuclear Regulatory Commn., Glen Ellyn, Ill., 1978-79; gen. mgr. Chgo. Barra Corp. Am., Inc., Wheaton, Ill., 1979-82; reg. mgr. Watpro, Inc., Orland Park, Ill., 1982-83; pres. ETs, Glen Ellyn, 1983-87; engring. assurance engr. TVA Watts Bar Nuclear Plant, Spring City, Tenn., 1987-88, Sequoyah Nuclear Plant, Soddy-Daisy, Tenn., 1988-89; supervising engr. United Energy Svcs. Corp., Palo Verde Nuclear Power Plant, Wintersburg, Ariz., 1989-90; nuclear engr. Sigma Sci. Browns Ferry Nuclear Plant, Athens, Ala., 1990-93; lead auditor SECORE Svcs. Inc., Trans-Alaska Pipeline, Anchorage, 1994; plant ops. and betterment I&C cons. engr. Raytheon Engrs. and Constructors Inc. TVA Watts Bar Nuclear, Spring City, Tenn., 1994-95; cons. nuclear engr. Sci. Applications Internat. Corp. TVA Sequoyah Nuclear Plant, Soddy-Daisy, Tenn., 1995-96; sports staff mem. Atlanta com. Olympic Games, Cherokee Nat. Forest, Tenn., 1996; cons. nuclear engring. environ. qualification Cooper Nuclear Station, Brownville, Nebr., 1996-97; sys. engring. mentor Duke Engring. & Svc. Resources, Inc., Two Rivers, Wis., 1997-98; maintenance commitment project mgr. Cook Nuclear Plant Duke Engring. & Svc. Resources, Inc., Sun Technical Svcs., Inc. and S&L, Bridgman, Mich., 1998—; re-entry system evaluation team mem. minuteman III missile USAF, Minot, N.D., 1969-71. Deacon Presbyn. Ch. U.S., Seneca, 1976-77. Served to sgt. USAF, 1967-71. Mem. Am. Nuclear Soc. Republican. Home: 172CR759 Riden Rd Riceville TN 37370-5207

RIDEOUT, EDNA BAKER, artist; b. Billings, Mont., Sept. 29, 1918; d. Frederick Hubbard and Edna Beers (Baker) Ballou; m. Horton Burbank Rideout, May 26, 1951; children: Douglas Burbank Rideout, Nancy Penelope Rideout, Thomas Ballou Rideout. BA, U. Wash., 1940, MA, 1949. Cert. secondary tchr., Wash. Art editor Croftonian Crofton House Sch., Vancouver, B.C., Can., 1935-36; art tchr. Neah Bay (Wash.) High Sch., 1940-41, Winlock (Wash.) High Sch., 1942-44, Seattle Pub. Schs., 1945-47, 49-51, Fish and Wildlife Svc. Pribilof Islands, St. George Island, Alaska, 1951-53; dir. Visual Art Sch., Edmonds, Wash., 1972-74; sec. Gallery North, Edmonds, 1974-76; artist, 1953—. Watercolors included in nat. juried exhbns., 8 juried mem. and regional exhbns., 36 nat. juried shows in 7 yrs., invitational exhbns. sponsored by Bellevue, Wash. Art Mus., North West Water Color Soc., Arts Olympia; works included in In Harmony with Nature, 1990, Seattle Asian Art Mus. Kado Shows, 1998, 99; 2 ink drawings used as cover designs for Alaska Timber Econ. Studies texts. Recipient Masterfield award Fla. Soc. Exptl. Artists, 2 purchase awards Watercolor U.S.A., Ajomari/Arches/Rives award Watermedia Mont., 1st pl. award Artstravaganza Nat., 3rd pl. award Navarro Coun. of Arts, Judge's Spl. award North Coast Collage Soc. Mem. Nat. Collage Soc. (sec. 1994), Women Painters of Wash. (program dir. 1992-93), North West Watercolor Soc. (asst. program dir. 1989-91), Soc. Exptl. Artists Fla., Pa. Watercolor Soc., North West Collage Soc. (sec. 1995—), East Side Assn. Fine Arts, Gallery North (hon.), Planetary Soc. Avocations: photography, hiking, observing nature, studying outer space. Home: 18616 92nd Ave NE Bothell WA 98011-2207

RIDER, FAE B., freelance writer; b. Summit Point, Utah, Mar. 1, 1932; d. Lee Collingwood and Jessie (Hammond) Blackett; m. David N. Rider, Jan. 26, 1952; children: David Lee, Lawrence Eugene. BS, No. Ariz. U., 1971, MA, 1974; postgrad., U. Nev., Las Vegas, 1985-88. Lic. tchr. in elem., reading, spl. edn. Learning specialist Las Vegas, summers 1974-76; tchr. kindergarten Indian Springs (Nev.) Pub. Schs., 1971-76; reading tchr. Las Vegas Pub. Schs., 1976-80; curriculum coord. Indian Springs Pub. Schs., 1980-91; tchr. 1st grade Las Vegas Pub. Schs., 1991-92, reading specialist, 1992-93; pvt. edn./reading cons. Las Vegas, 1993—. Author booklet: Door to Learning - A Non-Graded Approach, 1978. Bd. dirs. Jade Park, Las Vegas, 1988. Recipient Excellence in Edn. award, 1988, Outstanding Sch.and Cmty. Svc. award, 1990. Mem. Internat. Reading Assn., Ret. Tchrs. Assn., Am. Legion Aux., A.R.E study group, Delta Kappa Gamma (pres., Rose of Recognition), Kappa Delta Phi. Avocations: reading, writing, travel.

RIDER, ROBIN, secondary education educator; b. Millinocket, Maine, Sept. 23, 1963; cons. Pitt County Schs. Ctr. Sci, Math. and Tech. Edn., Greenville, 1994—; d. Richard William Angotti and Ruth Frances Jewell; m. Charles Dinh Rider, Aug. 15, 1987; children: Patrick Michael, Jessica Lyn. BS in Math., East Carolina U., 1988, MA in Math., 1990. Lectr. math. East Carolina U., Greenville, N.C., 1990-92; tchr. West Craven H.S., Vanceboro, N.C., 1992-94, D.H. Conley H.S., Greenville, N.C., 1994—. Mem. Tchrs. for Ednl. Policy Awareness and Change (founding mem.), N.C. Coun. Tchrs. of Math., Delta Kappa Gamma. Democrat. Roman Catholic. E-mail: rlarider@hotmail.com. Office: DH Conley High Sch 2006 Worthington Rd Greenville NC 27858-8377

RIDGEWAY, SHARON MARILYN, psychologist, mental health services professional; b. Bromley, Kent, Eng., Aug. 27, 1957; d. Lawrence Donald and Greta (Polchar) R.; m. Noel Thomas Traynor. Student, Solihull Tech. Coll., Eng., 1976-77; BA in Psychology/Sociology with honors, Sunderland U., Eng., 1983; MSc in Applied Social Sci., U. London, 1987; D in Psychology, Mental Health and Deafness, U. Manchester, Eng., 1992-98, PhD in Psychology, 1998. Chartered psychologist; cert. qualification in social work, psychodynamic approaches to practice. Social work asst. with deaf people Cumbria Deaf Assn., 1983-85; team leader social svc. London Borough of Barnet, 1988-90; rsch. psychologist, head counseling svcs. Nat. Ctr. Mental Health and Deafness, Manchester, Eng., 1990—; dir., designer tutor counseling skills, personal growth courses, U. Manchester, 1983—, dir. bd. studies counseling skills deaf people, 1992-96, designer, coord. nat. cert. course in mental health and deafness, 1994; mem. adv. group deaf issues and social work diploma Open U., mem. diploma social work course team, 1989-91; tng. com. Alliance Deaf Svc. Users and Providers, 1989-92; mem. working group Keep Deaf Children Safe, 1989-92; mgmt. com. exec. Manchester Disability Group, 1991-93; designer media programme for mental health awareness, deaf cmty. programme; presenter in field. Author: The Deaf Alliance (Counselling and Deaf People), 1994; editor: (newsletter) Spl. Interest Group Psychologists in Deafness, 1992-94, Progress Through Equality, 1995; contbr. articles to profl. jours. Mgmt. com. exec. Manchester Disability Group, 1991-93; gov. local edn. authority Newbrook Sch., W. Didsbury, Manchester, 1993—; trustee Deafway, Preston, Lancashire, 1998—. Hon. fellow U. Manchester; recipient Leo Baeck award Leo Baeck Coll., 1984, 85. Mem. Deaf Profls. in Mental Health Care (founder, sec. 1991-96, chair 1998—), European Deaf Profls. in Mental Health Care (pres. 1994-96, Brit. Deaf Assn. rep. 1994—), Brit. Soc. Mental Health and Deafness (rep. Brit Deaf Assn. 1993—, v.p. 1996, chmn. 2000—), Brit. Assn. Social Workers, Brit. Assn. Psychologists, European Soc. Mental Health and Deafness Coun. Socialist. Jewish. Avocations: debates on deaf issues, reading, oil painting. Home: 11 Aitken St, Irwell Vale, Ramsbottom Bury BL0 0QG, England Office: Nat Ctr Mental Health & Deafness, MH Svc Salford Bury New Rd, Prestwich M25 3BL, England

RIDGWAY, ALAN EDWARD, ophthalmic surgery consultant; b. Stanmore, Middlesex, Eng., Mar. 15, 1940; s. A.E. George and Helene Genevieve (Jansanne) R.; m. Susan Elisabeth Wilkinson, 1963; children: A.E. Graham, Paul E.R., Marianne E. BA, Cambridge U., 1961, MB BCh, 1964, MA, 1966. House surgeon Oxford Eye Hosp., 1966-68; ophthalmic registrar Cardiff Royal Infirmary, Wales, 1968-70; ophthalmic sr. registrar Birmingham & Midland Eye Hosp., Eng., 1970-74; cons. ophthalmic surgeon Manchester Royal Eye Hosp., Eng.; examiner Royal Coll. Surgeons of Eng., 1981-87; chmn. examiners U.K., British Orthoptic Council, 1983. Contbr. numerous articles to profl. jours. Fellow Royal Soc. Medicine (coun. mem. 1983—), Royal Coll. of Surgeons of Eng.; mem. Internat. Intraocular Implant Club (sec.-treas. 1977-83, treas. 1977—). Roman Catholic. Home: 10 Framingham Rd, Sale, Cheshire M33 3SH, England Office: 24A Saint John St, Manchester M3 4DU., Russell House, Russell Rd, Manchester M16 8AR, England

RIDGWAY, JAMES MASTIN, government official; b. Sedalia, Mo., Mar. 14, 1917; s. Amelius Biddle and Maude Anna (Brandt) R.; m. Lillian Belle

Shaneyfelt, May 25, 1941; children: Duressa, Richard (dec.), Cheryl. BSBA, U. Mo., 1939, MA, 1940; PhD, U. Chgo., 1953. Tchr. High Schs., Mo., Kans., 1940-44; prin. High Schs., Butler, Mo., 1944-45; instr. Southwest & Ctrl. Mo. State U., Springfield, Warrensburg, Mo., 1945-47; chmn. dept. edn. Carroll Coll., Waukesha, Wis., 1949-55; instr. dept. head Nat. Civil Def. Coll., Battle Creek, Mich., 1955-62, dir., 1958-62; deputy asst. dir. tng. & edn. Office Civil Def., Def. Civil Preparedness Agy., Washington, 1963-73; edn. advisor OCPA/DOD and FEMA, Washington, 1973-80; cons. in field. Contbr. articles to profl. jours. Mem. Am. Civil Def. Assn., Am. Strategic Def. Assn., Internat. Assn. Emergency Mgrs. Avocation: stamp collecting.

RIDGWAY, JOHN WILLIAM THOMAS, engineering executive; b. Newcastle, Australia, May 20, 1946; s. Thomas Henry and Isabel (Black) R.; m. Ruth Arlene Hartman, Jan. 15, 1983; children: Ranjini, Raja. BSc with honors, U. NSW, 1966, PhD in Physics, 1970. Adminstr. Navigators, Colorado Springs, Colo., 1973-74; lectr. U. N.S.W., Sydney, 1975-76; exec. MVE Inc., Bangalore, 1980-94, Oracle Engring. Pty. Ltd., Singapore, 1995—; cons. Sciencon, Bangalore, 1980-94, Barlow Jonker Pty. Ltd., Malaysia, 1997-98, Comm. Mgmt. Inc., Malaysia, 1996—. Pvt. tutor Crown Prince of Thailand, 1971-72. Lt. Australian Army, 1971-72. Mem. Australian Inst. of Physics, Vacuum Soc. of India, Malaysian Australian Bus. Coun. Mem. Anglican Ch. of Australia. Avocations: hockey, squash, swimming, tennis, bowling. Home: 46 Taman Hillview, Ulu Kelang, Ampang Selangor 68000, Malaysia Office: 24A Jalan Watan 4, Taman Sri Watan, Ampang 68000, Malaysia

RIDIGUER, ALEXEI MIKHAILOVICH See ALEXY, PATRIARCH II

RIDLER, ANN MARGARET, retired registrar; b. Southampton, England, Jan. 29, 1935; d. John Frederick and Edith Maud (Cummins) M.; m. William Henry Ridler, Aug. 5, 1959 (dec. 1980). BA, St. Hugh's Coll., Oxford, Eng., 1956; PhD, Counsel for Nat. Academic Awards, London, 1983. Cert. in edn., 1957. Tchr. St. Austell County Grammar Sch. for Girls, Cornwall, Eng., 1957-59, Faringdon County Grammar Sch. for Girls, Berkshire, Eng., 1959-61; course supr. Wolsey Hall Correspondence Coll., Oxford, Eng., 1961-69; adminstrv. asst. Council for Nat. Academic Awards, London, 1969-70, asst. registrar, 1970-73, registrar for Arts and Humanities, 1973-84, registrar for spl. academic devels., 1984-99; ret., 1999. Mem. St. Hugh's Coll. Assn. (sr. mem., editor Chronicle, 1982—), Henry Sweet Soc. for History of Linguistic Ideas. Avocations: reading, writing, music, gardening. Home: St Marys Cottage, 61 Thame Rd, Warborough Oxon OX9 8EA, England

RIDLEY, SIR ADAM NICHOLAS, economist; b. Hitchin, Herts., Eng., May 14, 1942; s. Jasper Maurice Alexander and Helen Cressida (Bonham) R.; m. Katharine Asquith, June 1971 (div. 1976); m. Margaret Ann Passmore, Aug. 27, 1987; children: Jasper, Luke, Joseph. Deg. Econs. 1st class hons., U. Oxford (Eng.), 1965. Econ. asst. Dept. Econ. Affairs, London, 1965-68; fellow U. Calif., Berkeley, 1968-70; econ. advisor Treasury, London, 1970-71, Cen. Policy Rev. Staff, London, 1971-74; asst. dir. rsch. dept., econ. advisor to leader Conservative Party and Shadow Cabinet, London, 1974-79; spl. advisor Chancellor of the Exchequor, Her Majesty's Treasury, London, 1979-84; spl. advisor to Lord Gowrie Chancellor of Duchy Lancaster, Minister for Arts/Civil Svc., 1985; exec. dir. Bd. Hambros Bank and Hambros PLC, 1985-97; Mem., dept. chmn. bd. Nat. Lottery Charities, 1994-2000; chmn. names settlement com., Lloyds of London, 1996-96, mem. coun., 1997-2000; chmn. bd. trustees Equitas Group Cos., 1996-2000; dir. gen. London Investment Banking Assn., 2000—. Contbr. articles to profl. jours. Conservative Party. Office: London Investment Banking, 6 Fredericks Pl, London EC2R 8BT, England

RIDLEY, ANDREW JEAN, small business owner; b. Tifton, Ga., Apr. 27, 1943; d. Andrew Ridley and Idella (James) Rivers; m. John Columbus Neeley, July 7, 1958 (dec. Jan. 1969); children: Brenda Denise, Sonja Lucille, Cassandra, Jeffery. AA, Wayne County C.C., Detroit, 1976; cert., Madonna Coll., Livonia, Mich., 1976; BA, Wayne State U., 1984; student, Meharry Allied Health Ctr., Detroit, 1988. Cert. real esate broker. Spl. svc. worker State of Mich. Social Svc., Detroit, 1976-78; med. surg. asst. Allied Med. Ctr., Detroit, 1980-84; supr. U.S. Maintenance, Oak Park, Mich., 1985-86; dept. head med. records Detroit Med. Group, 1988-90; office mgr., receptionist Family Med. Clinic, Detroit, 1990-93; CEO Andrea's & Vernell Inc., Detroit, 1996—; mem. adv. bd., pers. dir. Jefferson & Chalmers, Detroit, 1978-80; mem. adv. bd. cmty. rels. Detroit Pub. Schs., 1980-84; sec. adv. bd. Detroit Bd. Edn. Truency, 1980-84; dir. parents and cmty. coun. Detroit Bd. Edn., 1977-85. Contbr. articles to profl. jours. Asst. sec., resolution vice chair 13th Congl. Dem. Dist., Detroit, 1977-82, co-founder, chairperson cmty. grievence com. Jefferson & Chalmers, Detroit, 1982-84; sec. precinct coun. 13th Congl. Dem. Dist., Detroit, 1984-86; coord. mother's enrichment program City of Detroit, 1982-86; hon. mem. Am. Biog. Rsch. Bd. Advisors, 1996—. Recipient Outstanding Achievement award Jefferson & Chalmers Citizen Dist. Coun. Detroit, 1977, Outstanding Cmty. Svc. award N.E. Guidance Ctr. Mental Health, Detoirt, 1978, Outstanding Svc. award 13th Congl. Dm. Dist., Detroit, 1987-88; named Detroit Afro-Am. Leader Detroit Pub. Sch./Outstanding Volumteerism, 1981-84. Avocations: golf, dancing, cooking, travel, recreation. Office: Andrea's & Vernell Inc 3929 Field St Detroit MI 48214-1065

RIDLEY, ANNE JAQUELINE, cell biologist; b. Oxford, England, Apr. 3, 1963; d. Kenneth Fred and Jane (Baldry) R.; m. Edward James Kay, Dec. 29, 1990; children: Emily Jane, Rachel Mary. BA, Cambridge U., 1985; PhD, U. London, 1989. Postdoctoral fellow Whitehead Inst., Cambridge, Mass., 1989-90, Inst. Cancer Rsch., London, 1990-93; lab. head Ludwig Inst., London, 1993—. Mem. Br. Soc. Cell Biology. Office: Ludwig Cancer Rsch, 91 Riding House St, London W1W 7B5, England

RIDLEY, BETTY ANN, religous educator, church worker; b. St. Louis, Oct. 19, 1926; d. Rupert Alexis and Virginia Regina (Weikel) Steber; m. Fred A. Ridley, Jr., Sept. 8, 1948; children: Linda Drue, Clay Kent. BA, Scripps Coll., Claremont, Calif., 1948. Christian Sci. practitioner Oklahoma City, 1973—; tchr. Christian Sci., 1983—; mem. Christian Sci. Bd. Lectureship, 1980-85. Trustee Daystar Found.; mem. The First Ch. of Christ Scientist, Boston, Fifth Ch. of Christ Scientist, Oklahoma City. Mem. Jr. League Am. Home: 2933 Lansdowne Ln Oklahoma City OK 73120-4343 Office: Suite 100-G 3000 United Founders Blvd Oklahoma City OK 73112

RIDLEY, BRIAN KIDD, physicist, educator; b. Newcastle Upon Tyne, England, Mar. 2, 1931; s. Oliver Archbold and Lillian Beatrice (Dunn) R.; m. Sylvia Jean Nicholls, May 16, 1959; children: Aaron, Melissa. BSc, Durham U., 1953, PhD, 1957. Rsch. physicist Mullards, Redhill, Surrey, UK, 1956-64; from lectr. to rsch. prof. U. Essex, Colchester, 1967—; vis. prof. Cornell U., 1967, 76, 90—, Stanford U., 1967, Danish Tech. U., 1969, Princeton (N.J.) U., 1973, U. Lund, 1977, U. Calif. Santa Barbara, 1981, U. Oreg., 1981, Eindhoven Tech. U., 1983. Author: Time, Space & Things, 1976, 84, 94, The Physical Environment, 1979, Quantum Processes in Semiconductors, 1982, 88, 93, 99, Electrons and Phonons in Semiconductor Multilayers, 1997. Fellow Royal Soc., Inst. Physics; mem. Am. Phys. Soc. Avocations: piano, tennis. Office: U Essex, Colchester CO4 3SQ, England

RIDLEY, COLIN CHARLES SHERIDAN, psychiatrist; b. London, Sept. 17, 1954; s. Cyril Frank and Brenda Hilary (Malady) R.; m. Huan Rainbow Tan, Aug. 2, 1976; children: Khy Sien Jeremy Christopher, Faith Erng Whey, Houw Tchuwang Peter, Tchi Hung Joy Revival. MB, BS, St. Georges Hosp. Med. Sch., London, 1978; Assoc., Kings Coll., London, 1980; diploma in social learning theory & practice in applied settings, Leicester (Eng.) U., 1988; diploma in psychoanalytic observational studies, U. East London, 1995. Registrar in psychiatry St. Crispin Hosp., Northampton, Eng., 1979-85; clin. asst. adolescent psychiatry Hollymoor Hosp., Birmingham, Eng., 1985-93; staff grade physician in adolescent psychiatry Park View Clinic, Birmingham, Eng., 1993—. Contbr. articles to profl. jours. Elder Jesus Fellowship, Jesus Army, Birmingham, 1979—. Mem. Royal Coll. Psychiatrists (affiliate), Assn. Family Therapy, Assn. Psychiatric Study of Adolescents. Baptist. Avocation: making music. Home: Cornerstone Cofton Ch Lane, Cofton Hacket, Birmingham B45 8BB, England Office: ParkView Clinic Irwin Unit, 60 Queenbridge Rd, Moseley Birmingham B13 8QE, England

RIDLEY, DENNIS, computer scientist, educator, consultant; b. St. Andrew, Jamaica, June 23, 1948; came to U.S., 1979; s. Astley Dennis and Ruby Maud Ridley; m. Pamela Ridley, Oct. 6, 1975; children: Andrew, Jon. PhD, Clemson U., 1982. Mgr. Jamaica Pub. Svc. Co., Kingston, 1970-79; prof. George Mason U., Fairfax, Va., 1982-84, Howard U., Washington, 1984-87; faculty assoc. Supercomputer Computations Rsch. Inst., Tallahassee, 1994—; prof. Fla. A&M U., Tallahassee, 1987—; spkr. confs. presentations, 1977-99. Contbr. articles to profl. jours. Fellow OAS, 1980, IAEA, 1977; named Vol. of Yr. Tallahassee Dem., 1996. Mem. Econ. Club Fla., Golden Eagle Country Club. Avocations: golf, tennis, chess, mathematical statistics, reading. Office: Fla State U Supercomputer Computations Rsch Inst Tallahassee FL 32306

RIDLEY, KEITH ALEXANDER, IV, funeral director; b. Petersburg, Va., Jan. 7, 1968; s. Janice Ridley Harkins. BA, U. D.C., 1987; MBA, Am. U., 1992. Funeral svc. asst. James M. Wilkerson Funeral Establishment, Va., 1977-89; pres., gen. mgr. Ridley Funeral Establishment, Washingtno, 1991—. Bd. dirs. Kate B. Moorefield Scholarship, 1993—, Moorefield Found., 1993—, Greater S.W. Hosp., Washington, 1995—; vice chmn. Dem. Bus. Coun. Mem. NAACP, Alpha Phi Alpha, Pi Sigma Eta. Democrat. Baptist. Avocations: reading, travel, classical studies, history, writing. Office: Ridley Funeral Establishment Inc 131 Mississippi Ave SE Washington DC 20032-6162

RIDLEY, STANLEY EUGENE, clinical psychologist, consultant; b. Atlanta, Aug. 9, 1950; s. Young Walter and Bessie M. (Jones) R.; children: Mark B., Jason. BA in French and Human Rels., Domincan Coll., 1972; MS in Clin.-Cmty. Psychology, Howard U., 1975, PhD in Clin. Psychology, 1981. Lic. psychologist. Clin. instr. child devel. and psychiatry George Washington U. Med. Sch., Washington, 1981-89; dir. clin. psychology grad. program Howard U., Washington, 1984-90; clin. psychologist, cons. Ridley and Assocs., Washington and Lanham, Md., 1983—; grad. assoc. prof. psychology Howard U., Washington, 1987-91; rsch. cons. Hogan and Hartson Attys. at Law, Washington, 1988-90; assessment, tng. and rsch. cons. Carter Goble Assocs. Inc., Washington, 1988-92; dir. mental health unit Correctional Med. Svcs., Arlington, Va., 1994-97; sr. assoc. tng. and orgn. Resolution Dynamics Inc., Washington, 1994—; vis. assoc. prof. George Mason U., Fairfax, Va., 1992-94; cons. St. Luke Inst., Suitland, Md., 1991-94; cons., trainer Nuclear Regulatory Commn., Rockville, Md., 1995—, IRS, Washington, 1995—; distbr. Carlson Learning Co., Mpls., 1996—. Author (book chpt.) Ethnic Minority, 1991; contbr. articles to profl. jours. Bus. champion Archbishop Carroll H.S., Washington, 1996-99; mem. mental health adv. bd. D.C. Pub. Schs. Head Start, 1997—. Mem. APA, ASTD, Am. Coll. Forensic Examiners, Orgn. Devel. Network, Am. Bd. Psychol. Spltys., Soc. Indsl. and Orgnl. Psychology, Beta Kappa Chi, Alpha Mu Gamma. Avocations: roller skating, tennis, bowling, golf, developing quotable sayings. Home and Office: Ridley & Assocs 4360 Varnum Pl NE Washington DC 20017-2101

RIDSDALE, LEONE LORNA, physician, educator; b. London, Sept. 7, 1947; arrived in Can., 1980; d. Philip and Lorna Ridsdale; children: Serife, Ozge. BA, Kent U., Eng., 1969; MSc, London Sch. Econs., 1970; MD, McMaster U., Eng., 1974; PhD, London U., 1994. Lectr. Manchester U., Eng., 1970-71; resident McGill, Royal Victoria Hosp., Montreal, Can., 1974-76, 77-80; registrar Nat. Hosp., London, 1977-78; trainee gen. practice surgery Surrey, Eng., 1980-81; gen. practitioner Surrey, 1981-97; sr. lectr. London U., 1985-96, reader, 1996—; cons. Neurologist, 1999—. Author: Evidence-Based General Practice, 1995. Grantee Welcome Trust, London, 1993, various rsch. funders, U.K., 1993-95. Fellow Royal Coll. Gen. Practitioners London; mem. Am. Acad. Neurology, Hurlingham Club. Office: UMDS Guys & St Thomas Hosp, 5 Lambeth Walk, London SE11 6SP, England

RIEBER, ALFRED JOSEPH, historian, educator, researcher; b. Mt. Vernon, N.Y., Oct. 1, 1931; s. John J. and Albertina (George) R.; m. Edith Martha Finton, Oct. 16, 1954 (div. Nov. 1995). BA, Colgate U., 1953; MA, Columbia U., 1954, PhD, 1959. Vis. asst. prof. Colo. State U., Ft. Collins, 1956-57; asst. prof. Northwestern U., Evanston, Ill., 1957-58, 59-62, assoc. prof., 1962-65; prof. U. Pa., Phila., 1966-97, chair history dept., 1967-72, 83-88, assoc. dean, 1975-77, Alfred L. Cass prof., 1993-97; prof. Ctrl. European U., Budapest, Hungary, 1995—, chair history dept., 1995-99; trustee Nat. Coun. for Soviet and East European Rsch., Washington, 1989-95, chmn. bd., 1991-95; co-founder, co-dir. Internat. Commn. for Joint Projects in Russian History, Moscow and N.Y., 1992-95; sec., co-founder Nat. Seminar in History of Russian Soc. in Twentieth Century, Phila., 1980-84; mem. selection com. Fulbright Fellowships, 1972, NEH, 1973-74, Interuniv. Com. on Travel Grants, 1962, 81-82; trustee history dept. European U., St. Petersburg, Russia, 1995—; sr. rsch. fellow St. Anthony's Coll., Oxford, Eng., 2000. Author: Stalin and the French Communist Party, 1963, Merchants and Entrepreneurs in Imperial Russia, 1983; author, editor: The Politics of Autocracy, 1966; editor, contbr.: Perestroika at the Crossroads, 1991, Forced Migration in Central and Eastern Europe, 2000; contbr. articles to profl. publs. Trustee Inst. of Record, Budapest, 1996—. Fellow Guggenheim Found., 1965, NEH, 1973, 81, Woodrow Wilson Ctr., 1992-93; Am. Coun. Learned Socs. grantee, 1985-86; recipient E. Harris Harbison award for Disting. Tchg., Danforth Found., 1968, Henry Allan Moe prize Am. Philos. Soc. Mem. Am. Hist. Assn. (chair nominating com. 1983), Am. Assn. for Advancement of Slavic Studies (chair edn. com. 1994-98). Avocations: classical music, swimming. Office: Ctrl European U History Dpt, 9 Nador Ut, H-1051 Budapest Hungary

RIECKE, JÖRG, educator; b. Bielefeld, Germany, June 30, 1960; s. Otto and Gertrud (Specht) R.; m. Svetlana Schernus, Oct. 26, 1989. MA, U. Regensburg, 1988, PhD, 1992. Asst. prof. U. Regensburg, Germany, 1989-92; prof. U. Brno, Czech Republic, 1993-94; asst. prof. hist. linguistics U. Giessen, Germany, 1995—; dir. exch. program U. Giessen, 1996—. Author: (books) Die schwachen jan-Verben des Althochdeutschen, 1996 (with Klaus Matzel) Spätmittelalterlicher deutscher Wortschatz, 1989; contbr. articles to profl. jours. Scholar Studienstiftung des deutschen Volkes, 1987-92. Avocations: Tibetan medicine and philosophy. Home: Ring str 28, 35112 Oberwalgern Germany Office: Justus-Liebig U Giessen, Otto-Behaghel-Str 10, 35394 Giessen Germany

RIECKEN, ERNST-OTTO, gastroenterologist, physician, educator; b. Kiel, Germany, May 23, 1932; s. Ernst and Käthe (Johannsen) R.; m. Brigitte Lang, Oct. 7, 1966; children: Bettina, Philipp-Asmus. MD, Kiel, Freiburg Germany, 1959. Registrar Hamburg-Eppendorf Med. Ctr. Hamburg U., Germany, 1960-61, U. Besançon (France) Hosp. Ctr., 1960-61; rsch. asst. dept. medicine U. Hamburg, 1961; rsch. asst. dept. pathology U. Tübingen, 1963-64; rsch. asst. dept. cytochemistry Postgrad. Med. Sch., London, 1964-65; rsch. asst. dept. medicine U. Marburg, Germany, 1965, dozent, cons. dept. medicine, 1969; head dept. medicine Mcpl. Hosp., Bremen, Germany, 1976; head dept. gastroenterology Klinikum Steglitz, Free U. Berlin, 1978—, chmn., prof. medicine, 1980-83, 93—, dean med. sch., 1985-87, med. dir., 1998—. Editor, author: Intestinal and Pancreatic Adaptation, 1990; coeditor: Basic Mechanisms in Mucosal Immunology, 1991, Molecular and Cell Biological Aspects of Gastroenteropancreatic Neuroendocrine Tumor Disease, 1994; co-editor, author: Intestinal Adaptation, 1974, Entero-pancreatic Adaptation, 1987; editor: Malignancy and Chronic Inflammation in the Gastrointestinal Tract—New Concepts, 1994, Intestinal Plasticity in Health and Disease, 1998, Mucosal Immunity in HIV-infection, 1998. Brit. Coun. scholar, London, 1964, Adolf Schmidtmann-Stiftung scholar, London, 1965. Fellow Royal Coll. Physicians (London); mem. deutsche Gesellschaft fuer Innere Medizin, Deutsche Gesellschaft für Verdauungs-u. Stoffwechselkrankheiten, Deutsche Gesellschaft fuer Histochemie, Am. Assn. Gastroenterology, Medizinische Gesellschaft Berlin, Deutsche Forschungsgemeinschaft (mem. Leibniz price com. Bonn, chmn. Aronson price com. Berlin), N.Y. Acad. Scis. Avocations: painting (still lifes), chamber music. E-mail: riecken@ukbf.fu-berlin.de. Office: Klinikum Steglitz, Hindenburgdamm 30, 12200 Berlin Germany

RIED, WALTER GEORG, chemistry educator, researcher; b. Frankfurt/main, Germany, Mar. 5, 1920; s. Karl Christian and Amalie (Leger) R.; m. Hildegard Maria Moos, Mar. 30, 1953; children: Matthias, Sibylle, Walter-Antonius. Diploma in chemistry, U. Frankfurt/Main, 1942, DPhil, 1942, habilitation, 1952, prof., 1955; MD (hon.), Med. Acad. Łodz, Poland, 1989. Asst. prof. chemistry U. Frankfurt, 1941-46, sr. asst., 1946-52, docent, 1952-55, assoc. prof. chemistry, 1955-73, prof. chemistry, 1973-90, prof. emeritus, 1990—, hon. freeman; cons. chem. industries, Germany, 1957-90. Contbr. over 600 articles to internat. chemistry jours. Mem. German Chemistry Soc., Soc. German Med. and Natural Sci. Rehab. Maurus Acad., New Soc. Swiss Chemists, Physikal Verein (hon.). Avocations: travel, arts, genealogy, literature, opera. Home: Arndt-str 27, D-60325 Frankfurt am Main, Germany Office: U Frankfort Organic Chem, Marie-Curie-Str 11, D-60439 Frankfurt am Main, Germany

RIEDEL, GERHARDT FREDERICK, oceanographer; b. Santa Monica, Calif., July 8, 1951; s. Gerhardt Walter and Elizabeth Susanne (Ray) R.; m. Georgia Susanne Massei, Aug. 19, 1973; children: Corwin, Alexander. BS in Oceanography, Humboldt State U., 1974, BA in Biology, 1974; PhD in Oceanography, Oreg. State U., 1983. Postdoctoral fellow Harbor Br. Found., Ft. Pierce, Fla., 1983-85; postdoctoral investigator, sr. scientist Acad. Nat. Scis. Benedict (Md.) Estuarine Rsch. Lab., 1985-93; asst. curator Acad. Nat. Scis. Estuarine Rsch. Ctr., St. Leonard, Md., 1993-99, assoc. curator, 1999—. Avocations: guitar, fishing. Office: Acad Natural Scis Estuarine Rsch Ctr 10545 Mackall Rd Saint Leonard MD 20685-2433

RIEDI, RUDOLF HERMANN, mathematics researcher; b. St. Gallen, Switzerland, June 18, 1961; s. Hermann Albiez and Martha Zellweger. MSc, Swiss Fed. Inst. Tech., Zurich, 1986, MEd, 1987, DSc in Math., 1993. Rsch. asst. ETH Zurich, 1987-93; postdoctoral assoc. Yale U., New Haven, 1993-95, Nat. Rsch. Inst. France, Le Chesnay, 1995-97; faculty fellow Rice U., Houston, 1997—. Contbr. articles to profl. jours. Rsch. grantee Ctr. Internat. Etudiants & Stagiares, 1996, Nat. Found. Sci., Switzerland, 1993. Mem. Swiss Math. Assn., Am. Math. Soc. Avocations: skiing, basketball, photography. Office: Rice U Dept ECE 380 6100 Main St Dept Ece380 Houston TX 77005-1892

RIEDRICH, THOMAS, mathematician, researcher; b. Dresden, Saxony, Germany, Dec. 22, 1934; s. Max Kurt and Ruth Hanna (Tradel) R. Diploma in math., Technische Hochschüle, Dresden, 1958. Sci. asst. Technische Hochschule, Dresden, 1958-63; sci. supr. asst. Tech. U. Dresden, 1963-67, docent, 1967-69, full prof., 1969-92, prof. new law, 1992—, dean Inst. for Analysis, 1979-94. Author: Vorlesungen über nichtlineare Operatorengleichungen, 1976; co-author: Differentialrechnung für Funktionen mit mehreren Variablen, 8th edit., 1993, Funktionalanalysis, 4th edit., 1994. Office: Tech U Dresden, Mommsenstr 13, D-01069 Dresden Saxony, Germany

RIEDWEG, CHRISTOPH ANTON, classics educator; b. Zug, Switzerland, Dec. 26, 1957; s. Xaver and Ida (Müller) R.; m. Anna Regula Broger, July 5, 1997. Lic., U. Zurich, Switzerland, 1982, diploma for higher edn., 1984, PhD, 1987, Habilitation, 1992. Organ tchr. diploma. Prof. classics Johannes Gutenberg U., Mainz, Germany, 1993-96; asst. classics dept. Zurich U., 1983-88, 91-93, prof., 1996—. Author: Mysterienterminologie bei Platon, Philon und Klemens von Alexandrien, 1987, Jüdisch-hellenistische Imitation eines orphischen Hieros Logos, 1993, Ps.-Justin (Markell von Ankyra?), Ad Graecos de vera religione, Introduction and Commentary, 1994; editor: Antike und Abendland, 1997, Zeitschrift fur antikes Christentum, 1997, Museum Helveticum, 1997, Hypomnemata, 1997, Ashgate Studies in Philosophy and Theology in Late Antiquity, 2000; also articles. Swiss Nat. Found. scholar, Oxford, Eng., Louvain, Belgium, Munich, Germany, 1988-91. Avocations: jogging, hiking, playing the organ. Home: Kluseggstrasse 18, CH-8032 Zurich Switzerland Office: U Zurich Klass-Phil Sem, Rämistrasse 68, CH-8001 Zurich Switzerland

RIEDY, PATRICIA ANN, international development specialist; b. Casco, Wis., May 28, 1961; d. Patrick Robert and Rose Ann (Kugel) R. BA in Cultural Anthropology, Cmty. Edn., Evergreen State Coll., 1983; MA in Internat. Adminstrn., Sch. for Internat. Tng., 1991. Founder, dir. Southeast Asian/Am. Cultural Exch. Program, Olympia, Wash., 1981-83; co-dir. Latchkey Sch. Aged Daycare Collective, Olympia, 1984; acting dir. Internat. Student Office St. Martin's Coll., Lacey, Wash., 1985; participant affairs coord. U. Conn. Inst. for Pub. Svc. Internat., West Hartford, 1987; dist. supr. JobStart Program Office of Mayor, Divsn. Jobs and Cmty. Svcs., Boston, 1988-89; electoral supr. Transitional Authority in Cambodia UN, Kampong Chnang, Cambodia, 1992-93; Observer Mission in South Africa UN, Northern Cape Province, South Africa, 1994; liaison officer Volunteer Programme UN, Geneva, 1996-99; spl. fellow program in peacemaking and preventive diplomacy UN Inst. for Tng. and Rsch., Geneva, 1999—; cons. in conflict resolution, Milw., 1994-96; ind. researher fgn. policy and conflict resolution, Washington, N.Y.C., Cambridge, Mass., 1989-91; speaker in field. Contbr. articles to profl. jours. Vol. Re-election Campaign for Senator Kerry, Boston, 1990, Planned Parenthood, Olympia, 1982-83, Am. Friends Svc. Com., Seattle, 1982-83; fundraiser Common Cause, 1985. Mem. Soc. for Internat. Devel., Inst. for Multi-Track Diplomacy. Avocations: hiking, playing guitar, learning languages, Tai Chi. Home: 3748 S 55th St Milwaukee WI 53220-2043 Office: UN Vol Programme Humanitari, Palais des Nations, CH 1211 Geneva Switzerland

RIEF, WINFRIED JOSEF, health facility administrator, educator; b. Ellwangen, Germany, May 12, 1959; s. Kaspar and Berta (Steinacker) R.; m. Sabine Brobeil, May 27, 1983; 1 child, Maximilian. Diploma in psychology, U. Trier, Germany, 1984; PhD, U. Konstanz, Germany, 1987; Habilitation, U. Salzburg, Austria, 1994. Rsch. asst. U. Konstanz, 1984-85; psychotherapist Psychiatric Hosp., Rottweil, Germany, 1986-87; head psychology Ctr. Behavioral Medicine, Prien, Germany, 1987—; lectr. U. Salzburg, 1991—; psychotherapist Psychiat. Psychosomatic Hosp., Rottweil, Prien, Germany, 1986—. Author: Somatoform Disorders, 1992, Biofeedback, 2000; contbr. articles to profl. jours. Grantee German Rsch. Found., 1993, 96. Mem. German Soc. Psychology (sec. clin. psychology 1996), German Assn. Behavioral Medicine. Roman Catholic. Avocations: skiing, jogging, swimming, music. Home: Luft 14, D 83236 Uebersee Germany Office: Ctr Behavioral Medicine, Clin Roseneck Am Roseneck 6, D 83209 Prien Germany

RIEGE, HANS KARL, physicist; b. Berlin, Mar. 16, 1938; s. Paul and Erna (Schiller) R.; m. Astrid Brigitte Jansen, Dec. 19, 1938; children: Daniela Rabany, Christian. Physics diploma, U. Munich, 1963; PhD, Tech. U., 1967. Scientific asst. Tech. U., Munich, 1963-68; R&D engr. Man-Turbo, Munich, 1968; physicist CERN, Geneva, 1968-75, sr. physicist, 1975—. Contbr. articles to profl. publs.; patentee in field. Patentee in field of electron beam generation. Avocations: music (piano playing), sports. Home: 80 La Ravoire SUD, F-01280 Prevessin-Moens France Office: CERN, EP-Division, CH-1211 Geneva 23 Switzerland

RIEGEL, BYRON WILLIAM, ophthalmologist; b. Evanston, Ill., Jan. 19, 1938; s. Byron and Belle Mae (Huot) R.; m. Marilyn Jills, May 18, 1968; children: Marc William, Ryan Marie, Andrea Elizabeth. BS, Stanford U., 1960; MD, Cornell U., 1964. Diplomate Am. Bd. Ophthalmology, Nat. Bd. Med. Examiners. Intern King County Hosp., Seattle, 1964-65; asst. resident in surgery U. Wash., Seattle, 1965; resident in ophthalmology U. Fla., Visalia, Calif., 1968-71; pvt. practice medicine specializing in ophthalmology Sierra Eye Med. Group, Inc., Visalia, Calif., 1972—; mem. staff Kaweah Delta Dist. Hosp., chief of staff, 1978-79. bd. dirs., asst. sec., 1983-90. Served as flight surgeon USN, 1966-68. Co-recipeint Fight-for-Sight citation for rsch. in rentinal dystrophy, 1970. Fellow ACS, Am. Acad. Ophthalmology; mem. Calif. Med. Assn. (del. 1978-79), Tulare County Med. Assns., Calif. Assn. Ophthalmology (v.p. 3d party liaison 1994-96, dir. 1996-98), Am. Soc. Cataract and Refractive Surgery, Internat. Soc. Refractive Surgery, Internat. Phacoemulsification and Cataract Methodology, Phacoemulsification and Cataract Methodology Soc., Rotary (Visalia). Roman Catholic. Home: 3027 W Keogh Ct Visalia CA 93291-4228 Office: 2830 W Main St Visalia CA 93291-4331

RIEGER, GEBHARD, physician, researcher, medical educator; b. Vienna, Austria, Mar. 10, 1940; s. Herwigh and Marianne (Kerschbaum) R.; m. Irmgard Strasser, June 18, 1966; children: Reingard, Herwig, Wolfgang, Bernhard. Med. dr. Med. Sch. U., Vienna, 1966; asst. I. U. Eye Clinic, Vienna, 1966-72, eye specialist, 1972; lectr. U. Eye Clinic, Innsbruck, Austria, 1998; head dept. ophthalmology Paracelsus Inst., Bad Hall, Austria, 1972. Helene ADAM grantee Dr. Heinz U., Frankfurt, 1990. Mem. Austrian Opthal. Soc., Vienna Opthal. Soc., German Opthal. Soc., N.Y. Acad.

Scis., Soc. Free Radical Rsch., Austrian Soc. Balneology and Med. Climatology, Assn. Austrian Cure Physicians, Paracelsus Soc. Balneology and Iodine Rsch., Med. Soc. Upper Austria, Van Swieten Soc. Vienna. Fax: 0049 7258 2193. Avocations: mountaineering, hiking, editing of a cultural review. Home: Eduardshoehe 19, A-4540 Bad Hall Upper Austria, Austria Office: Paracelsus Inst Eye Dept, Dr Karl Renner Strabe 6, A-4540 Bad Hall Upper Austria, Austria

RIEGNELL, GÖRAN ALVAR, information consultant; b. St. Lundby, Sweden, Feb. 2, 1949; s. Alvar and Ingrid (Elmlund) R.; m. Marie Silfverstolpe, May 11, 1988; 1 child, Anne. MBA, U. Gothenburg, Sweden, 1974. Bus. cons. Marknadskollegium AB, Gothenburg, 1974-76; corp. contr. Stena Metall AB, Gothenburg, 1976-78, treas., 1978-80; comml. dir. Stena Metal Ltd., London, 1980-82; mem. Swedish Parliament, 1982-85; info. cons. Kreab AB, Stockholm, 1986—; privatisation advisor Swedish Govt., Stockholm, 1992, 94; IPO advisor Stadshypotek AB, Stockholm, 1994, Scania AB, Södertälje, Sweden, 1995-96. City councellor, Gothenburg, 1979-80, Lidingö, Sweden, 1993-98; chmn. Urban Planning Bd, Lidingö, 1992—. Conservative. Lutheran. Avocations: sailing, food, wine. Home: Yxvägen 17, 18147 Lidingö Sweden Office: Kreab AB, Floragatan 13, SE-11475 Stockholm Sweden

RIEHL, JANE ELLEN, education educator; b. New Albany, Ind., Oct. 17, 1942; d. Henry Gabbart Jr. and Mary Elizabeth (McGraw) Willham; m. Richard Emil Riehl, June 15, 1968; 1 child, Mary Ellen. BA in Elem. Edn., U. Evansville, 1964; MS, Ind. U., Bloomington, 1966; postgrad., Spalding U., 1979, Ind. U. S.E., New Albany, 1991-93. Cert. 1-8 and kindergarten tchr., Ind.; lic. profl. kindergarten tchr., Ind. Elem. tchr. Clarksville (Ind.) Cmty. Sch., 1964-68, 70-75, 81-82, tchr. kindergarten, 1975-81; elem. tchr. Chapelwood Sch. Wayne Twp., Indpls., 1968-70; lectr. edn. Ind. U. S.E., 1988-97, dir. tchg. and rsch. project, 1990-91, 92-93; dir. field and career placement, cert./lic. advisor Ind. U. S.E., New Albany, 1998, coord. elem./spl. edn. field & career placement & license advisor, 1998—; cons. Riehl Assocs., Jeffersonville, Ind., 1995—. Co-author: An Integrated Language Arts Teacher Education Program, 1990, The Reading Professor, 1992, Multimedia: HyperStudio and Language Education, 1996, Technology: Hypermedia and Communications, 1997, others; author procs. Parent vol. Girl Scouts U.S.A., Jeffersonville, 1988-95; mem. adminstrtv. bd. Wall Street United Meth. Ch., Jeffersonville, 1993-95; mem. women's health adv. coun. Clark Meml. Hosp., Jeffersonville, 1995—; bd. dirs. Clark Meml. Hosp. Found., vice chair, 1999, chair 2000; team mem. People to People Citizen Amb. Program, 1993, 95, 96. Named Young Career Woman of Yr. Bus. and Profl. Women New Albany and Dist. 13 Ind., 1966; tchg. and rsch. grantee Ind. U. S.E., 1990, 94, 95, 96, 97, 2000; recipient Disting. Tchg. award Ind. U. S.E., 1997, Tchg. Excellence Recognition award, 1997. Mem. Nat. Coun. Tchrs. English, Profs. Reading Tchr. Edn., Ind. State Med. Assn. Alliance (v.p. so. area 1999—), Clark County Med. Soc. Alliance (pres.-elect 1997-98, pres. 1998-99), Altrusa Internat. Inc. (internat. bd. 1993-95, dist. gov. 1993-95, svc. award 1995), Phi Delta Kappa (v.p. 1991-92, pres. 1997—, svc. award 1991), Kappa Kappa Kappa (pres. Jeffersonville 1975-76, 90-91, Outstanding Mem. award 1987). Avocations: travel, reading, crafts, decorating. Home: 1610 Fox Run Trl Jeffersonville IN 47130-8204 Office: Ind U SE 4201 Grant Line Rd New Albany IN 47150-2158

RIEHM, SARAH LAWRENCE, writer, arts administrator; b. Iowa City, Sept. 8, 1952; d. Stuart Parker and Elizabeth Jane (Munson) Lawrence; m. Charles Curtis Riehm, May 18, 1974; children: Andrew, Amanda, Jennie Frances. BGS, U. Iowa, 1974; MA in Internat. Fin., U. Tex., 1981. Mgr., adminstr. IBM, Cedar Rapids, Iowa, 1974-75; program mgr. Rockwell Internat., Dallas, 1975-80; mgr. internat. tax Peat, Marwick, Mitchell, Hong Kong, 1981-82; writer, playwright, 1981—; exec. dir. Playwright's Project, Dallas, 1992-94, Tex. Composers Forum, Dallas, 1995-96; faculty mem. U. Tex., Dallas, 1996-97; co-founder, mng. ptnr. Azimuth, 1997—; bd. dirs. Radio for Peace Internat.; lectr. So. Meth. U., 1999—. Playwright: Liberty-A Drama in Two Acts, 1994 (So. Playwrights award 1994), The King & Me, 1994, The Chute, 2000; author: Entrepreneurship: Building the American Dream, 1993, 50 Great Businesses for Teens, 1997. Founder Playwrights Project; chair Dallas 10,000, 1995; commr. Richardson Arts Commn., 1998—. Mem. NOW, Handgun Control, Amnesty Internat. Democrat. Presbyterian. Avocations: pipe organ, composer, racquetball, skiing, travel.

RIEIRO-MARIN, IGNACIO, mathematics educator; b. Madrid, Jan. 21, 1954; s. Antonio Rieiro-Blanco and Asuncion Marin-Bartolome; m. Carmen Diaz-Martin, July 28, 1975; children: Rodrigo, Amaya. Lic. in Phys. Scis., U. Complutense, Madrid, 1978, M in Math. Stats., 1992, D in Phys. Scis., 1997; grad. nuc. engring., Inst. Estudios Nucleares, Madrid, 1979. Bellboy Cia Ins. Agy. Alianza, Madrid, 1970-71; adminstrv. Ministry of Industry, Madrid, 1971-76; prof. asst. faculty phys. scis. U. Complutense, Madrid, 1979-81, prof. stats. Sch. Stats., 1998—; prof. secondary edn. Ministry Edn. and Scis., Spain, 1984—; rsch. assoc. Centro Investigaciones Energeticas Medio Ambientales y Tecnologicas, Madrid, 1990-91; collaborating rschr. Consejo Superior Investigaciones Cientificas-Centro Nacional Investigaciones Metalurgicas, Madrid, 1993—; head edn. stats. Autonomic Adminstrn. Castile-La Mancha, Toledo, Spain, 1997-98. Author: History of the Informatics, 1980, Numerical Methods and Their Programation, 1981, The Information and Their Representation, 1982, The Magnitude and the Measurement, 1992. Ofcl. Artilleria, 1976-78. Socialist. Roman Catholic. Avocation: research. E-mail: rieima@ctv.es. Home: Travesia Salvador Dali 11, 45200 Illescas Toledo, Spain Office: Escuela Univ Estadistica, Univ Complutense, Madrid Spain

RIEKE, FORREST NEILL, lawyer; b. Portland, Oreg., May 26, 1942; s. Forrest Eugene and Mary Neill (Whitelaw) R.; m. Madonna Bernardi, Apr. 2, 1966; children: Mary Jane, Forrest Ermelindo. AB in Polit. Sci., Stanford U., 1968; JD, Willamette U., 1971. Bar: Oreg. 1971, U.S. Dist. Ct. Oreg. 1974, U.S. Ct. Appeals (9th cir.) 1975, U.S. Supreme Ct. 1977. Sr. dep. dist. atty. Multnomah County, Portland, 1971-76; ptnr. Rieke & Savage P.C., Portland, 1977—; instr. Oreg. State Police Acad., Ft. Rilea, 1979—. Contbr. editor Williamette U. Law Rev., 1971. Pres., bd. dirs. Council Great City Schs., Washington, 1985-93; trustee Emanuel Hosp. Found., 1987-93; bd. dirs. Portland Pub. Schs., 1978-93, Columbia Willamette United Way, Portland, 1983-94; organizer Oreg. Conservation and Devel. Found., Portland, 1986-90. Mem. ABA, Oreg. Bar Assn. (indigent accused def. com., chmn. law related edn. com. 1985, bd. dirs. criminal law sect. 1979-84, mem. pub. info. com. 1987-90, ho. dels. 1995—), Nat. Criminal Def. Lawyers Assn., Multnomah County Bar Assn., Oreg. Criminal Def. Lawyers Assn., Multnomah Athletic, Rotary. Presbyterian. Avocations: skiing, reading, coaching youth sports. Home: 820 SW 2nd Ave Apt 6 Portland OR 97204-3086 Office: Rieke & Savage PC 140 SW Yamhili St Portland OR 97204-3007

RIEKE, RONALD ALFRED, computer company executive; b. Rugby, N.D., Aug. 16, 1951; s. Lawrence Allen Rieke and Emma Marie (Lord) Cooper; m. Madelyn E. Owens, May 2, 1987; children: Ronald Alexander, Sara Emma, Reu William. AS, N.D. State U., 1971; BS, U. N.D., 1973; MA, Webster U., St. Louis, 1976. Operator Lystads, Inc., Kansas City, Kans., 1972-74; sales rep. Parke-Davis Co., St. Louis, 1974-76; with bio-med. engring. and sales Gen. Electric Corp., Tulsa, 1976-78; mgr., sales engr. Digital Equipment Corp., Houston, 1978-85; pres. R.A.R.E. Systems, Inc., Houston, 1985—; bd. dirs. TechSmith Corp., Dallas, Cam-Eng, Inc., Houston, Title Techs., Houston. Mem. Houston Fine Arts Council, 1988. Mem. Am. Mgmt. Assn., Digital Dealer Assn., Digital Equipment Soc. Republican. Mem. Christian Ch. (Ch. of Christ). Avocation: karate, computer technology. Office: RARE Systems Inc 1500 W Sam Houston Pkwy N Houston TX 77043-3113

RIEKELS, LYNDA MARIE, materials engineer; b. Detroit, Oct. 4, 1949; d. Carl Herman and Shirley Jean (Page) Piethe; m. Bruce Warren Riekels, Mar. 27, 1971; children: Ryan, Robyn. BS in Geology cum laude, Mich. Tech. U., 1971; MS in Geology, U. Ill. Chgo., 1973; PhD of Materials and Sci. Engring., Northwestern U., 1979. Engr., rsch. engr.,s r. rsch. engr. Inland Steel Co., East Chicago, Ind., 1973-82; pres. Geomet Tech., Longview, Tex., 1982-84; dir. R&D, v.p. tech. ops., v.p. quality and tech. Lone Star (Tex.) Steel, 1984-89; from sr. rsch. engr. to engring. cons. Mobil R&D Co., Dallas, 1989-95; group mgr. materials and corrosion Mobil Tech. Co., Dallas, 1995-98; tech. mgr. Mobil de Venezuela, Caracas, 1998-99; sr. engr. cons. Mobil Tech. Co., 2000—; mem. adv. bd. North Tex. Rsch. Inst., Dallas, 1993-96. Patentee in field; contbr. articles to profl. jours. Mem. Am. Soc. Metals, Nat. Assn. Corrosion Engrs., Am. Soc. Quality Control, Soc. Petroleum Engrs., The Metals Soc., Am. Assn. Iron and Steel Engrs., Phi Kappa Phi, Tau Beta Pi (hon.), Alpha Sigma Mu (hon.). Avocations: painting, drawing, rock collecting, sailing, gardening. Home: 3403 Raintree Dr Flower Mound TX 75022-6314

RIEMENSCHNEIDER, OSWALD WILHELM, mathematician, educator; b. Kassel, Hessen, Germany, Nov. 22, 1941; s. August and Margarete (Häfer) R.; m. Christina Sydow (div. 1991); children: Stephanie, Nadja; m. Kyoko Honda, Sept. 29, 1995. Diploma, U. Göttingen (Germany), 1966, Dr.rer.nat., 1966, Habilitation, 1971. Asst. U. Göttingen, 1968-72, assoc. prof., 1972-74; prof. U. Hamburg, Germany, 1974—; vis. asst. prof. Rice U., Houston, 1972. Contbr. articles to profl. jours. Mem. Joachim Jungius Assn. Scis. Avocations: flute. Office: Math Sem U Hamburg, Bundesstrasse 55, D 20146 Hamburg Germany

RIEMSMA, ROBERT PAUL, psychologist, researcher; b. Hilversum, Netherlands, Jan. 23, 1960; s. Hendrik and Pieterke (Zorge) R.; m. Wendy Burke, Aug. 25, 1998. MPA, U. Twente, Enschede, Netherlands, 1988, PhD, 1998. Rsch. fellow dept. psychology U. Twente, 1987-99; rsch. fellow NHS-Ctr. for Revs. and Dissemination, U. York, Eng., 1999—. Contbr. articles to profl. jours.

RIENDEAU, THERESA FRANCES, rehabilitation nurse; b. Revere, Mass., June 12, 1953; d. Samuel and Eleanor M. (Rizzo) Spinazzola; m. Armand D. Riendeau, Dec. 31, 1994; children: James, Richard, Mark Russo. Diploma, New Eng. Bapt. Hosp. Sch., Boston, 1975. Reiki practioner. Charge nurse VA Med. Ctr., West Roxbury, Mass., 1975-80; asst. nurse mgr. Braintree (Mass.) Hosp., 1981-90; supr. nursing Randolph (Mass.) Crossings Nursing Ctr., 1990-93; utilization rev. coord., home health aide/homemaker educator Alternative Care Med. Svcs., Salem, N.H., 1990-98; rehab. nurse Vis. Nurse Assocs. Inc., Dedham, Mass., 1993-94, VNA Homecare, Andover, Mass., 1994-95; unit mgr., restorative coord., staff developer Greenery Extended Care Ctr., North Andover, 1998—; Reiki practitioner. Mem. Assn. Rehab. Nurses. Home: 35 Wheeler St Dracut MA 01826-4219 Office: Greenery Extended Care Ctr 75 Park St North Andover MA 01845-2820

RIEPE, DALE MAURICE, philosopher, writer, illustrator, educator, Asian art dealer; b. Tacoma, June 22, 1918; s. Rol and Martha (Johnson) R.; m. Charleine Williams, 1948; children: Kathrine Leigh Riepe Herschlag, Dorothy Lorraine. BA, U. Wash., 1944; MA, U. Mich., 1946, PhD, 1954; postgrad. (Rockefeller-Watamull-McInerny fellow), U. Hawaii, Banaras and Madras, India, Tokyo and Waseda, Japan, 1949; diploma, Universidad de la Habana, 1997. Instr. philosophy Carleton Coll., 1948-51; asst. prof. U. S.D., 1952-54; assoc. prof. U. N.D., 1954-59, prof., 1959-62, chmn. dept., 1954-62; prof., chmn. C.W. Post Coll., 1962-63; prof. philosophy SUNY, Buffalo, 1963—; chmn. dept. social scis., assoc. dean SUNY Grad. Sch., 1964—; instr. marine electricity Naval Tng. Program, Seattle, 1943-45; mem. nat. screening bd. South Asia, Fulbright Selection, 1968-70, Asia, 1970-72; chmn. Fulbright Selection Com. for Asia, 1972, 82; vis. Fulbright lectr. Tokyo U., 1957-58; vis. lectr. Western Wash. U., 1961, Delhi U., 1967; exchange lectr. U. Man., 1955, Moscow State U., 1979, Beijing Higher Edn. Inst., 1984; docent Albright-Knox Art Gallery; cons. Ctr. for Sci., Tech. and Devel., Council of Sci. adn Indsl. Rsch., Govt. India, 1978—, Inst. Fang Studies, 1987—; del. Cuban-N.Am. Philosophy Conf., Cuban Inst. Social Sci., 1982, Fang Centennial, Taiwan Nat. U., Taipeh, 1987, Hungarian-Am. Philos. Conf., Budapest, 1988; sports columnist The Town Crier; vis. scholar Andhra U., 1996; lectr. NSF, 1960. Author: The Naturalistic Tradition in Indian Thought, 1961, The Philosophy of India and its Impact on American Thought, 1970, Indian Philosophy Since Independence, 1979, The Owl Flies by Day, 1979, Asian Philosophy Today, 1981, Objectivity and Subjectivism in the Philosophy of Science, 1985, Philosophy and Revolutionary Theory, 1986, also articles in field.; editor: Phenomenology and Natural Existence, 1973, Philosophy and Political Economy; co-editor: The Structure of Philosophy, 1966, Contributions of American Sankritists in the Spread of Indian Philosophy in the United States, 1967, Radical Currents in Contemporary Philosophy, 1970, Reflections on Revolution, 1971, Philosophy at the Barricade, 1971, Contemporary East European Philosophy, 1971, Essays in East-West Dialogue, 1973, Explorations in Philosophy and Society, 1978; illustrator The Quick and the Dead, 1948; editorial com. Chinese Studies in History, 1970—, Chinese Studies in Philosophy, 1970—; publs. bd. Conf. for Asian Affairs; Editor various series.; editl. bd. Philos. Currents and Revolutionary World, 1972-86, Soviet Studies in Philosophy, 1979-87, Marxist Dimensions, 1987—,. Active ACLU; mem. com. overseers Chung-an U., Korea; bd. dirs. Evergreen Coll. Cmty. Orgn., 1988—; bd. dirs. Friends of Evergreen Coll. Libr., 1992—; active Henry Gallery, Frye Gallery, Palm Springs Desert Mus., Seattle Art Mus., Phila. Mus. Art; mem. Capital Mus. and Art Soc., Wash. State Hist. Soc.; mem. libr. bd. Evergreen Coll.; founder Ars Asiatica. Fulbright scholar India, 1951-52; Fulbright lectr. U. Tokyo, 1957-58; U. Mich. fellow, 1945-48, Carnegie Corp. fellow Asian Studies, 1960-61, Am. Inst. Indian Studies Rsch. fellow, 1966-67; grantee 4th East-West Philosophers Conf., 1964, Penrose fund Am. Philos. Soc., 1963; SUNY Research Found., 1965-67, 69, 72-73, Bulgarian Acad. Sci., 1975, London Sch. Oriental and African Studies, 1971. Fellow Royal Asiatic Soc., Far Eastern Inst. (Tokyo); mem. AAAS, Internat. Hegel-Vereinigung, Conf. Asian Affairs (sec. 1995), Am. Oriental Soc., Am. Philos. Soc., Indian Inst. Psychology, Philosophy and Psychical Rsch. (hon. adviser), Soc. for Am. Philosophy (chmn. 1960), Am. Inst. Indian Studies (trustee 1965-66), Soc. for Creative Ethics (sec.), Am. Archaeol. Soc., Am. Assn. Asian Studies, Am. Math. Soc., Am. Aesthetics Soc., Internat. Soc. Aesthetics, Am. Soc. Comparative and Asian Philosophy, N.Y. Acad. Scis., Asiatic Soc. (Calcutta), Soc. for Philos. Study Dialectical Materialism (founding sec.-treas. 1962—), Soc. for Philos. Study Marxism (publs. sec. 1973-86), Union Am. and Japanese Profls. Against Nuclear Omnicide (treas. U.S. sec. 1978—), Internat. House of Japan, Internat. Philosophers for Prevention Nuclear Omnicide, United Univ. Profs. of SUNY-Buffalo (v.p.), Kokusai Bunka Shinkokai, N.Y. Acad. Scis., Union Concerned Scientists, Olympia Philosophy Club (co-founder 1988—), Alpha Pi Zeta. Office: SUNY 605 Baldy Hall Buffalo NY 14260-1000

RIEPER, HANS OLAF, government studies researcher; b. Hellerup, Copenhagen, Feb. 26, 1945; s. Olaf Rieper and Aase Rønholt Hansen; m. Laila Launsø; children: Jonas, Adam, Sune. MA in Sociology, U. Copenhagen, 1974; PhD, Copenhagen Bus. Sch., 1984. Asst. prof., rsch. fellow Copenhagen Bus. Sch., 1971-74; rsch. fellow U. Copenhagen, 1975-77; rsch. cons. Inst. Tech., Denmark, 1978-82; sr. lectr. Copenhagen Bus. Sch., Denmark, 1983-96; sr. rsch. assoc. AKF Inst. Local Govt. Studies, Copenhagen, 1985-94, assoc. prof., 1994—; vis. assoc. prof. Sch. Social Work, U. Mich., 1988; expert Ctr. for European Evaluation Expertise, Lyon, France, 1995-96; mem. eval. com. U. Copenhagen, 1993-97, U. Trondheim, Norway, 1993, 95; mem. IIAS Working Group on Policy and Program Evaluation, 1991—. Co-editor: Politics and Practices of Inter Governmental Evaluation, 1997. Mem. Danish Evaluation Soc. (pres. 2000—). Avocations: cross-country skiing, sailing, hiking. Home: Buskevej 3, 4330 Hvalsø Denmark Office: AKF Inst Local Govt Studies, Nyropsgade 37, 1602 Copenhagen Denmark

RIERSON, ROBERT LEAK, retired broadcasting executive, television writer; b. Walnut Cove, N.C., Sept. 5, 1927; s. Sanders C. and Anna (Cox) R.; m. Barbara Eugenia McLeod, Sept. 23, 1950 (dec. Feb. 1988); children: Barbara Elaine, Richard Troy; m. Rosemary L. McCampbell, Apr. 20, 1997. Student, Duke U., 1945-46, Davidson Coll., 1946-47; BS in Speech cum laude, Northwestern U., 1948. Program dir., program ops. mgr. WBT Radio and WBTV, Charlotte, N.C., 1948-66; program mgr. WJBK-TV, Detroit, 1966-69, WTOP-TV, Washington, 1969-71; dir. broadcasting WCBS-TV, N.Y.C., 1971-73; pres. Rierson Broadcast Consultants, N.Y.C., 1973-75; program exec. Grey Advt., N.Y.C., 1975-77; v.p., dir. programming Dancer-Fitzgerald-Sample, N.Y.C., 1977-80; exec. producer Corinthian Prodns., N.Y.C., 1980-82; dir. news programming CNN TV, Atlanta, 1982-96; ret., 1996. Producer-creator TV show ABCs of Democracy, 1965; producer, writer TV show George Washington's Mt. Vernon, 1970; creator, writer TV series 24 Days of Christmas, 1978, 21 Days of America, 1979. Bd. dirs. Mich. Coun. Chs., Detroit, 1968-69, ARC, Charlotte, 1960-62; 1st v.p. Charlotte Oratorio Singers, 1960-66. Lt. USNR, 1952-54. Recipient Edn. award Charlotte Jr. Woman's Club, 1961, George Washington Honor medal Freedoms Found., 1970; named Young Man of Yr., 1960. Mem. Nat. Assn. Radio-TV Program Execs. (charter mem., bd. dirs. 1964—), Radio-TV News Dirs. Assn., Order of Long Leaf Pine (hon. N.C. award). Republican. Mem. Moravian Episcopal Ch. Avocations: reading, travel, movies. Home: 31 S Cherrywood Ln Pisgah Forest NC 28768-9543

RIES, BARBARA ELLEN, alcohol and drug abuse services professional; b. Chgo., Oct. 27, 1952; d. Laurence B. and Genieveve (Wasiek) R. AAS in Human Svcs., Coll. of DuPage, Glen Ellyn, Ill., 1973; BA in Social Work, Sangamon State U., Springfield, Ill., 1978; postgrad., U. Mo., 1987-88, U. Tex., Arlington, 1991—. Cert. social therapist, criminal justice counselor-master addiction counselor; nat., internat. cert. alcohol and drug counselor; lic. social worker, Ohio. Counselor Ray Graham Assn. for Handicapped, Addison, Ill., 1975-76; child abuse counselor Ill. Dept. Children and Family Svcs., Springfield, 1977-78; alcoholism counselor non-med. detoxification program S.H.A.R.E., Villa Park, Ill., 1978-80; outpatient therapist Ingalls Meml. Hosp., Harvey, Ill., 1980-83; dir. aftercare Lifeline Program, Chgo., 1984-85; case mgr. Lifecenter Program, Kansas City, Mo., 1985-87; counselor, acting clin. coord. Lakeside Hosp., Kansas City, 1988-89; program mgr., dir. chem. recovery programs Two Rivers Psychiat. Hosp., Kansas City, 1989-90; dir. day program and chem. dependency program SW Hosp./Citadel, Dallas, 1990—; dir. Flexcare program Dallas Meml. Hosp., 1990-91; pvt. practice Columbus, Ohio, 1991—; program coord. Advanced Clin. Svcs., Federal Way, 1992-94; recovery svc. adminstr. Orient Correctional Insts., 1996—; spkr. in field. Recipient commendation Ingalls Hosp., 1983. Mem. APA, ACA, nat. Assn. Forensic Counselors (cert. criminal justice specialist), Am. Correctional Assn., Nat. Assn. Drug and Alcohol Counselors (cert., NCAC II, Ohio alcohol and drug cert. III-E, master addiction counselor), Nat. Assn. for Advanced Relapse Prevention Counselors. Avocations: exercise, reading, listening to music, writing.

RIES, EDWARD RICHARD, petroleum geologist, consultant; b. Freeman, S.D., Sept. 18, 1918; s. August and Mary F. (Graber) R.; m. Amelia D. Capshaw, Jan. 24, 1949 (div. Oct. 1956); children: Rosemary Melinda, Victoria Elise; m. Maria Wipfler, June 12m 1964. AB magna cum laude, U. S.D., 1941; MS, U. Okla., 1943, PhD, 1951; postgrad., Harvard U., 1946-47, Harvard, 1946-47. Asst. geologist Geol. Survey S.D., White River area, 1941; geophys. interpreter Robert Ray Inc., Western Okla., Okla., 1942; jr. geologist Carter Oil Co., Mont., Wyo, 1943-44; geologist Standard Vacuum Oil Co., Mont., Wyo., Colo., India, 1944-49; sr. geologist Standard Vacuum Oil Co., Asam, Tripura, Bangladesh, India, 1951-53; sr. regional geologist N.Y. Standard Vacuum Petroleum, Maatschappij, N.Y., Indonesia, 1953-59; geol. advisor Far East and Africa N.Y. Standard Vacuum Petroleum, White Plains, N.Y., 1959-62, Oceania, Mobile Petroleum Co., N.Y.C., 1962-65; geol. advisor Europe, Far East Mobil Oil Corp., N.Y.C., 1965-71, sr. regional explorationist Far East, Australia, New Zealand, 1971-73, sr. regional explorationist Asia-Pacific, Dallas, 1973-76, sr. geol. advisor Rsch. Geology, 1976-79; assoc. geol. advisor Geology-Geophysics, Dallas, 1979-82; sr. geol. cons., 1982-83; ind. internat. petroleum geol. cons. Europe, Africa, Sino-Soviet and S.E. Asia, 1986—; grad. asst., teaching fellow U. Okla., 1941-43, Harvard, 1946-47. Contbr. numerous domestic and internat. proprietary and pub. hydrocarbon generation and reserve evaluations, reports and profl. papers. With AUS, 1944-46. Warden-Humble fellow, U. Okla., 1951. Mem. AAAS, Am. Inst. Econ. Rsch., Am. Assn. Petroleum Geologists (assoc. editor 1978-83, 50 Yr. Mem. Svc. award 1993), Geol. Soc. Am., Am. Geol. Inst., Nat. Wildlife Fedn., Nat. Audubon Soc., N.Y. Acad. Sci., Soc. Exploration Geophysicists, Wilderness Soc., Am. Legion, Harvard Club (Dallas), Phi Beta Kappa, Sigma Xi, Sigma Gamma Epsilon. Republican. Mennonite. Home and Office: 6009 Royal Crest Dr Dallas TX 75230-3434

RIES, PETER, judge, educator; b. Munich, Mar. 29, 1961; s. Henrich Ries and Annemarie (Preissler) Shaw; m. Verena Glaser, Dec. 3, 1993; children: Anna, Marie, Jakob. Student, London Sch. Econs. & Polit., 1985; LLB, Munich U., 1989, PhD in Law, 1989. Bar: Munich 1990, Berlin 1994. Fgn. assoc. McGuire, Woods, Battle & Boothe, Washington, 1990; atty. Droste, Munich, 1990-95; judge Dist. Ct., Berlin, 1996—; prof. corp. law Fachhoschule für Verwaltung und Rechtspflege, Berlin, 2000—. Author: Bauverträge im römischen Recht, 1990; co-author: CCH Business Law Guide to Germany; contbr. articles to law jours. Lt. 1st class German mil., 1980-82. Mem. Judge Assn., Munich Bar Assn.

RIESER, JOHN PAUL, lawyer; b. Homestead, PA, Sept. 24, 1956. BA with distinction, Northwestern U., 1978; cert., Pushkin Inst., Moscow, 1978; JD cum laude, Harvard U., 1981. Bar: Ohio 1981, Fla. 1998, U.S. Dist. Ct. (so. dist.) Ohio 1981, U.S. Ct. Appeals (6th cir.) 1982, U.S. Tax Ct. 1991, U.S. Dist. Ct. (so. dist.) Fla. 2000. Assoc. Estabrook, Finn & McKee, Dayton, Ohio, 1981-83; sole practice Dayton, 1983-85; ptnr. Rieser & Marx, Ohio, 1985—, Fla., 1998—; lectr. bus. law Sinclair Community Coll., Dayton, 1984—, other orgns.; mem. rules com. for so. dist. Ohio, U.S. Bankruptcy Ct. Editor Harvard Internat. Law Jour., 1979-81; contbr. articles to newspapers and profl. jours. Arbitrator Montgomery County (Ohio) Arbitration Panels, 1983—; trustee Chpt. 7 Bankruptcy, 1989—; participant Vol. Lawyer Project. Mem. ABA, ATLA, Am. Bankruptcy Law Forum (trustee), Nat. Assn. Bankruptcy Trustees, Ohio Bar Assn., Fla. Bar, Palm Beach County Bar Assn., Dayton Bar Assn., Harvard U. Alumni Assn. E-mail: jprieser@aol.com. Office: Rieser & Marx 130 W 2d St Ste 1520 Dayton OH 45402

RIESS, FRIEDRICH-CHRISTIAN EDGAR, surgeon, researcher; b. Reinbek, Germany, Aug. 24, 1955; s. Edgar Christof and Hildegard Maria (Popp) R.; m. Annette Eberhardt, May 9, 1986; children: Henrik, Timon, Janika, Juliane. MD, U. Hamburg (Germany), 1982. Intern dept. thoracic and cardiovascular surgery U. Hamburg (Germany), 1982-86; intern Albertinen-Krankenhaus Divsn. Gen. Surgery, Hamburg, 1986-88; cons. cardiac surgeon, 1991—; cons. cardiac surgeon Kerckhoff-Klinik Max-Planck-Inst. divsn. thoracic and cardiovascular surgery, Bad Nauheim, Germany, 1988-91; assoc. prof. cardiac surgery U. Giessen, Germany. Contbr. articles to profl. jours., chpt. to book. Avocations: music, painting, photography. Home: Langer Kamp 75, 22850 Norderstedt Germany Office: Albertinen-Krankenhaus, Suentelstr 11A, 22457 Hamburg Germany

RIESTER, WALTER, government official. Former vice-chmn. trade union IG Metall; now labor min. Govt. of Germany. Office: Fed Ministry Labor/Social, Affairs Jägerstrasse 9, 10117 Berlin Germany*

RIETBROCK, NORBERT, clinical pharmacology educator; b. Borken, Germany, June 9, 1931; m. Ingrid Kreiss, Mar. 1960 (dec. July 1988); children: Stephan, Andreas; m. Regina Zahlmann, Dec. 1994. MD, U. Hamburg, Germany, 1960. Sci. asst. U. Hamburg, 1960-66, U. Würzburg, Germany, 1966-69; prof. Free U., Berlin, 1969-77; head prof. Inst. of Clin. Pharmacology, Frankfurt/Main, Germany, 1977-98; mem. A. Commn. BGA, Berlin, 1982—; mem. Narcotic Drug Commn., Ministry of Health, Bonn, 1986—. Author: Klinische Pharmakologie, 1990, Methods in Clinical Pharmacology; editor Internat. Jour. Clin. Pharmacology and Therapy, 1993-2000; mem. editl. bd. Jour. Cardiovascular Pharmacology. Mem. German Soc. Clin. Pharmacology and Therapy (founder, chmn. 1990-98), European Assn. Clin. Pharmacology and Therapeutics (founder 1994, hon. pres.). Christian Democrat. Roman Catholic. Avocations: travel, music, restoring a 17th Century House. Office: Klinikum der Johann, Wolfgang Goethe U, Theodor-Stern-Kai 7, D-60590 Frankfurt Germany

RIETH-WINTERHERBST, GABRIELE, editor-in-chief; b. Karlsruhe, Germany, Mar. 10, 1953; d. Kurt and Emma (Hurst) Rieth; m. Pablo Erich Winterherbst, Nov. 7, 1990. MA, U. Munich, 1981. Asst. editor TR-Verlagsunion, Munich, 1981-82, editor, 1983-87, chief editor, 1987—. Author: English Grammar for Telekolleg, 1992; editor: Film & Television - a Handbook, 1984 (4th edit. 1997), Film Editing Handbook, 1993 (3rd edit. 1999), Filmproduction Volume 1: The Producer, 1997, 2d edit., 2000, Filmproduction Vol. 3: Budgeting of Movie and TV-Productions, 1998. Avocations: cinema, classical music, literature, foreign languages. Office: TR Verlagsunion GmbH, Thierschstrasse 11, 80538 Munich Germany

RIETSCHEL, ROBERT LOUIS, dermatologist; b. New Orleans, Oct. 9, 1946; s. Frederick Arnt and Estelle Marie (Fleckinger) R.; m. Connie Joanne Dent, Sept. 3, 1966; children: Eric, Penny. BA, North Tex. State U., 1968;

MD, U. Tex., Galveston, 1972. Diplomate Am. Bd. Dermatology. Med. intern Letterman Army Med. Ctr., San Francisco, 1972-73, dermatology researcher, 1973-74; resident in dermatology Brooke Army Med. Ctr., San Antonio, 1974-77, staff dermatologist, 1977-79; assoc. prof. dermatology Emory U. Sch. Medicine, Atlanta, 1981-85, acting chmn. dept. dermatology, 1984-85; assoc. chmn. dept. dermatology Ochsner Clinic, New Orleans, 1985-88; chmn. dept. dermatology, 1988—. Contbr. articles to profl jours. Cubmaster, Boy Scouts Am., Decatur, Ga., 1983-84. Served to maj. U.S. Army, 1971-79. NIOSH grantee, 1981-84. Fellow Am. Acad. Dermatology, Soc. for Investigative Dermatology; mem. Am. Dermatol. Assn., N.Am. Contact Dermatitis Group (sec. 1985-93), Am. Contact Dermatitis Soc. (sec. 1989-93, pres. 1993-95). Republican. Lutheran. Avocation: sailing. Office: Ochsner Clinic 2005 Veterans Blvd Metairie LA 70005

RIFAI, GHASSAN MOUTIEH, urologist, consultant; b. Homs, Syria, Sept. 15, 1939; came to U.S., 1966; became U.S. citizen, 1976; s. Mouti M. Rifai and Zuhniya Khateeb. MD, Damascus (Syria) U., 1962. Diplomate Am. Bd. Urology. Surg. res. N.Y. Polyclinic Med. Sch., N.Y.C., 1966-68; res. in urology William Beaumont Hosp., Royal Oak, Mich., 1968-71; staff urologist Seaway Hosp., Trenton, Mich., 1971-82, chief surgery, 1980-82; chief urology Al Hada Mil. Hosp., Taif, Saudi Arabia, 1982-85, Security Forces Hosp., Riyadh, Saudi Arabia, 1985—. Contbr. articles to med. jours. Med. officer, Syrian Army, 1963-65. Fellow Internat. Coll. Surgeons (urology Am. sect.); mem. Arab Am. Med. Assn. (pres. 1981-82), Am. Urol. Assn., Internat. Urol. Soc., Soc. Study of Impotence, Syrian Urol. Soc. (hon.). Avocations: travel, international politics, movies, theater, swimming. Office: Security Forces Hosp, PO Box 3643, Riyadh Saudi Arabia

RIFAI, HISHAM K., political scientist, consultant; b. Aleppo, Syria, Aug. 11, 1931; came to U.S., 1955; s. Omar Besim and Samira Hibatulla (Ghori) R.; m. Branka Koljensic, June 1, 1968; 1 child, Maja. JD, Damascus U., Syria, 1952; postgrad., Columbia U., 1956-58. Translator UN, N.Y.C., 1955-57, polit. officer, 1957-68, sect. chief, 1968-78, dir., 1978-84; exec. sec. UN, Vienna, 1984-88; sr. fellow UN Inst. for Tng. and Rsch., N.Y.C., 1989-94; vis. prof. Ga. State U., Atlanta, 1992-93; sr. cons. Inter-Univ. Assocs., N.Y.C., 1994—; lectr., prof. L.I. U., N.Y.C., 1995-96. Vice pres. Francophone Cultural Assn., N.Y.C., 1994—; mem. Problems of Peace Seminars, CColumbia U., 1994—, Ralph Bunche Inst., CUNY, 19956. Avocation: violin playing. Office: 11 Robinhood Rd White Plains NY 10605-3540

RIFBJERG, KLAUS THORVALD, writer; b. Copenhagen, Dec. 15, 1931; s. Thorvald Frants and Lilly (Nielsen) R.; m. Inge M.G. Andersen, May 28, 1955; children—Lise Beate, Synne Marie, Frands Carl. Ed., U. Copenhagen, Princeton U.; Dr.Phil. (hon.), Lund U., 1992. Freelance writer, poet and dramatist; lit. critic Info., 1955-57, Politiken, from 1959; lit. dir. Gyldendal Pubs., 1984-92; hon. prof. Danish Tchrs. Coll., 1987. Author (novels) Den Kroniske Uskyld, 1958, Til Spanien, 1971, Brevet til Gerda, 1972, Det sorte hul, 1980, numerous others, (short stories) Og Andre Historier, 1964, Sommer, 1974, (plays) Gris Pa Gaflen, 1962, Udviklinger, 1965, numerous other books of short stories, plays, also criticism. Recipient award Danish Acad., 1967, Nordic Council prize, 1970, Holberg medal, 1979, Nordic prize The Swedish Acad., 1999, others. Mem. Danish Acad. Arts and Letters, Princeton Colonial Club (hon.). Office: care Gyldendal Pubs, 3 Klareboderne, 1001 Copenhagen Denmark

RIFKIND, MALCOLM (LESLIE), British government official; b. Scotland, June 21, 1946; s. E. Rifkind; m. Edith Amalia Steinberg, 1970; 1 son, 1 dau. LLB, Edinburgh U., MSc. Bar: Scotland, 1970. Lectr. U. Rhodesia, 1967-68; opposition front bench spokesman on Scottish affairs Parliament, London, 1975-76, under sec. of state, Scottish Office, 1979-82, under sec. of state Fgn. & Commonwealth Office, 1982-83, minister of state Fgn. & Commonwealth Office, 1983-86, sec. of state for Scotland, 1986, sec. of state for transport, 1990-92, sec. of state for def., 1992-95, sec. of state for fgn. affairs, 1995-97; mem. Queen's Bodyguard for Scotland, Royal Co. of Archers, London; mem. Edinburgh Town Coun., 1970-74; joint sec. Conservative Fgn. and Commonwealth Affairs Com., 1978; mem.Select Com. on European Secondary Legis., 1975-76; Select Com. on Overseas Devel., 1978-79. Office: Pentlands Conservatives, Splyaw St, Edinburgh Scotland

RIGALI, JUSTIN F., archbishop; b. L.A., Apr. 19, 1935; s. Henry Alphonsus and Frances Irene (White) R. B in Sacred Theology, Cath. U. Am., 1961; Lic. in Canon Law, Gregorian U., Rome, 1963, D in Canon Law, 1964; LHD (hon.), St. Louis U., 1995. Ordained priest Apr. 25, 1961. Titular archbishop of Bolsena, 1985-94; sec. Congregation for Bishops Holy See, Vatican City, 1989-94, sec. Coll. of Cardinals, 1990-94; archbishop Archdiocese of St. Louis, 1994—; pres. Pontifical Ecclesiastical Acad., 1985-89. Office: Archdiocese of St Louis 4445 Lindell Blvd Saint Louis MO 63108-2403

RIGAMONTI, ALESSANDRO, pharmacist, pharmaceutical association executive; b. Cunardo, Varese, Italy, July 24, 1928; s. Ettore and Rita (Taglioretti) R.; m. Teresacarla Merli, Sept. 20, 1954. Degree in pharmacy, U. Pavia, Italy, 1951; PhD, U. Turin, Italy, 1968. Rschr. Farmitalia, Milan, 1952-58, head lab., 1958-65; top exec. Pharma Devel., Milan, 1965-83; prof. pharmaceutical sci. U. Turin, 1970-85; cons. in field, 1985—; owner Cmty. Pharmacy Varese, Italy, 1980—; bd. dirs. Pharm. Practice Sect., Varese, 1991—. Co-author: Good Manufacturing Practice, Impianti Industria Farmaceutica; co-patentee formulation for anti-tumoral agt. Mem. Italian Indsl. Pharmacy Assn. (pres.), Cmty. Pharmacy Assn. (bd. dirs. 1990—), CRS, FIP, SISF. Roman Catholic. Avocations: skiing, bicycling, skating. E-mail: avtf@libero.it. Fax: 39-332-830101. Office: Ordine Dei Farmacisti, Piazza Marsala n.4, 21100 Varese Italy

RIGANTI DI SERRES, MARIO, reliability engineer; b. Turin, Italy, Jan. 2, 1930; s. Enrico and Angelina (Gruppi) Riganti. Projector Fiat Auto, Turin, 1948-65, Fiat Rsch., Turin, 1965-70, Fiat Nuclear, Turin, 1965-85; coord. modern and particle physics Ancient's U., Turin, 1995—; adviser Assn. Ex-Allievi Fiat, Turin, 1957; magister emeritus in sci. Pro Deo U. of N.J., 1997-99; mem. h.c. nuclear physic Acad. Europeau U. Moscow. Contbr. articles to profl. jours. Judge Corte Assise d'Appello, Turin, 1971. Mem. Ancients Group Fiat, Soc. Italian Orgn. Internat., Ctr. Internat. Study Sturziani. Roman Catholic. Avocations: study of astrophysics and relativity, finance, economic policy. Home: Via San Donato 76, 10144 Turin Italy

RIGBY, MICHAEL JOHN, health policy analyst, educator; b. Okehampton, England, June 29, 1946; s. Robert Alfred and Margaret Annie (Boulton) R. BA, Keele U., England, 1968. Rsch. officer Cheshire County Coun., England, 1968-74; head rsch. & svc. planning Cheshire Area Health Authority, England, 1975-80, planning officer, 1980-83; regional svc. planning officer Mersey Regional Health Authority, Liverpool, England, 1983-88; lectr. health planning mgmt. Keele U., England, 1988—. Co-author: (with McBride, Shiels) Computers in Medical Audit, 1992; co-editor: (with Ross, Begg) Management for Child Health Services, 1998, (with Draper) Electronic Reviews: Ethical Guidance-A Framework, 2000, (with Roberts, Thick) Taking Health Telematics into the 21st Century; series editor: Harnesing Health Information, 1999. Mem. Internat. Med. Informatics Assn. (chair mental health informatics working group 2000—). Avocations: walking, travel, cultural activities. Office: Ctr Health Planning Mgmt, Darwin Bldg Keele Univ, Keele ST5 5BG, England

RIGBY, PAUL CRISPIN, artist, cartoonist; b. Melbourne, Australia, Oct. 25, 1924; came to U.S., 1977; s. James Samuel and Violet Irene (Wood) R.; m. Marlene Anne Cockburn, Nov. 16, 1956; children: Nicole, Pia, Peter, Paul, Danielle. Student, Brighton Tech. Sch., Australia, Art Schs., Victoria, Victoria Nat. Gallery, Australia. Free lance artist, 1940-42; illustrator West Australian News, Ltd., 1948-52; editorial cartoonist Daily News Australia, 1952-69; daily cartoonist London Sun and News of the World, 1969-74; editorial cartoonist New York Post, 1977-84, 93—, New York Daily News, 1984-93. Illustrator numerous books; represented in exhbns. of painting in, Australia, Europe and U.S.A.; Contbr. work to numerous publs., U.S., Europe, Asia. With Royal Australian Air Force, 1942-46. Decorated Order of Australia, knight comdr. Order of St. John, Knights of Malta; recipient Walkley award Australia, 1960, 61, 63, 66, 69; N.Y. Press Club award for art, 1981, 83, Page One award for excellence in journalism Newspaper Guild, 1982, 83, 84, 85. Mem. Ch. of Eng. Clubs: Rolls Royce Owners, Royal Freshwater Bay Yacht; Friars, Players (N.Y.C.). Home: 180 E End Ave Apt 2B New York NY 10128-7778

RIGBY, PERRY GARDNER, medical center administrator, educator, former university dean, physician; b. East Liverpool, Ohio, July 1, 1932; s. Perry Lawrence and Lucille Ellen (Orin) R.; m. Joan E. Worthington, June 16, 1957; children: Martha, Peter, Thomas, Matthew. B.S. summa cum laude, Mt. Union Coll., 1953, D.Sc. hon., 1976; M.D., Western Res. U., 1957. Diplomate: Am. Bd. Internal Medicine. Intern in medicine U. Va. Hosp., Charlottesville, 1957-58, asst. resident in medicine, 1958-60; research fellow in hematology Mass. Meml. Hosp., Boston, 1960-62; clin. asst. in medicine Boston City Hosp., 1961-62; research assoc. in medicine Mass. Meml. Hosp., Boston U. Med. Ctr., 1961-62; asst. prof. internal medicine and anatomy U. Nebr., Omaha, 1964-66, assoc. prof. internal medicine and anatomy, 1966-69, prof. internal medicine, 1969-78, prof. anatomy, 1969-74, prof. med. edn., 1973-74, head sect. hematology Eugene C. Eppley Inst. for Research in Cancer and Allied Diseases, 1964-68, dir. hematology div., 1968-74, asst. dean for curriculum Coll. Medicine, 1971-72, assoc. dean for acad. affairs, 1972-74, dir. office ednl. services, 1972-74, acting assoc. dean for allied health professions, 1973-74, vice chmn. dept. med. and ednl. adminstrn., 1974, dean, 1974-78, chmn. dept. med. and ednl. adminstrn., 1974; prof. internal medicine La. State U., Shreveport, 1978—, assoc. dean acad. affairs Sch. Medicine, 1978-81, acting dean, 1981-82, dean, 1982-85; chancellor La. State U., 1985-94; dir. Health Care Systems La. State U., New Orleans, 1994—; mem. clin. bd. Univ. Hosp. La. State U., 1978-94, chmn. clin. bd., 1981-85, program dir. biomed. research support grant program, 1980-81; chmn. dean's com. VA Hosp., 1978-85; mem. courtesy staff Immanuel Med. Ctr.; bd. dirs. Health Planning Council of Midlands, Omaha, 1976-78; cons. WHO, Kabul, Afghanistan, 1976. Bd. dirs. Fontenelle Forest, Omaha, 1976-78; bd. dirs. River Cities High Tech. Group, Shreveport, 1982-85. Served as capt. M.C. U.S. Army, 1962-64. Markle scholar, 1965. Fellow ACP; mem. Am. Fedn. Clin. Research (councillor 1971), AMA (del.), Am. Soc. Hematology, N.Y. Acad. Scis., Am. Assn. Med. Colls. (council of deans of Midwest-Gt. Plains 1974-78, chmn. Midwest-Gt. Plains 1976), Am. Assn. Cancer Research, AAAS, Am. Heart Assn., Central Soc. Clin. Research, Internat. Soc. Hematology, Health Edn. Media Assn., Am. Assn. Physicians' Assts., So. Soc. Clin. Investigation, Shreveport C. of C. (dir. 1982-85), Sigma Xi, Alpha Omega Alpha, Phi Rho Sigma. Office: La State U Med Ctr Resource Ctr 433 Bolivar St New Orleans LA 70112-2223

RIGG, CHARLES ANDREW, pediatrician; b. Hamilton, Vic., Australia, Oct. 18, 1926; came to U.S., 1963; s. Arthur Oscar and Mary Eileen (Wingrove) R. B in Medicine, Surgery with honors, Sydney U., 1951. Registrar, professorial unit Children's Hosp., Sydney, Australia, 1954-56; registrar pediat. unit St. Mary's Hosp. Med. Sch., London, 1956, 58; from sr. resident to chief resident Children's Hosp., Boston, 1957, fellow in adolescent medicine, 1963-64, staff adolescent medicine, 1964-65; chief dept. adolescent medicine Children's Hosp., Washington, 1967-80; asst. prof. pediat. Georgetown U. Med. Sch., 1965-67; from asst. prof. to assoc. prof. child health George Washington U. Med. Sch., 1967-80; chief dept. adolescent medicine Boston City Hosp., 1981-83; assoc. prof. pediatrics Sch. Medicine Boston U., 1981-83; med. dir. Outer Cape Health, Provincetown, Mass., 1983-88; pediatrician, med. dir. Medicenter Five, Harwich, Mass., 1988-95, pediatrician, 1995-97; pediatrician May Ctr. Child Devel., Chatham, Mass., 1990—, Harwich Town Pub. Sch. System, 1997—; cons. Nat. Naval Med. Ctr., Bethesda, Md., 1973-80, Walter Reed Army Med. Ctr., Washington, 1973-80; courtesy staff medicine Children's Hosp., Boston, 1983—; vis. prof. Philippine Pediat. Soc., 1978, 9th Congress of the Brazilian Med. Assn., 1979, 16th Internat. Congress of Pediat., Barcelona, 1980. Editor: Adolescent Medicine Present and Future Concepts, 1980; contbr. articles to profl. jours. Mem. Mus. Fine Arts, Boston, Folger Shakespeare Libr., Washington, Nat. Trust for Hist. Preservation, Nat. Trust Australia, Tasmania, Royal Oak Soc. Maj. M.C. Royal Australian Army, 1951-60; lt. col. USAR, 1985-91. Model Tng. Program in Adolescent Medicine grant Maternal and Child Health Svcs.-U.S. Govt., 1967-80, Comprehensive Health Svcs. Adolescent Ctr. grant Mass. Dept. Pub. Health, 1981-83. Fellow Am. Acad. Pediatrics (life), Am. Headache Soc., Royal Australasian Coll. Physicians, Soc. Adolescent Medicine (charter, treas., chmn., legis. com.); mem. Royal Sydney Golf Club, City Tavern Club Washington, D.C. Episcopalian. Avocations: historic preservation, gardening, theater, music, walking. Office: Pediatrics/Adol Medicine PO Box 401 940 Main St South Harwich MA 02661

RIGG, DAME DIANA, actress; b. Doncaster, Yorkshire, Eng., July 20, 1938; d. Louis and Beryl (Helliwell) R.; m. Menahem Gueffen, July 6, 1973 (div. Sept. 1976); m. Archibald Hugh Stirling, Mar. 25, 1981 (div. Apr. 1993); 1 child, Rachael Atlanta. Grad., Fulneck Girls' Sch., Pudsey, Yorkshire; student, Royal Acad. Dramatic Art, London; D (hon.), Stirling U., Eng., 1988, Leeds U., Eng., 1992, Southbank U., Eng., 1996. Stage debut as Natella Abashwilli in The Caucasian Chalk Circle, Theatre Royal, York, Eng., 1957; joined Royal Shakespeare Co., Stratford-on-Avon, 1959, debut as Andromache in Troilus and Cressida, 1960; London debut as Philippe Trincant in The Devils, London, 1961; numerous repertory appearances; joined Nat. Theatre, 1972; appeared in Jumpers, Macbeth, 1972, The Misanthrope, 1973, Pygmalion, 1974, Phaedra Britannica, 1975, Night and Day, 1978, Colette, 1982, Heartbreak House, 1983, Little Eyolf, 1985, Antony and Cleopatra, 1985, Wildlife, 1986, Follies, 1987, Love Letters, 1990, All for Love, 1991, Putting It Together, 1992, Berlin Bertie, 1992, Medea, 1992 (Tony award, Broadway prod., 1994, Eve. Standard award, Variety Club award), Mother Courage and Her Children, 1995, Who's Afraid of Virginia Wolf, 1996; film appearances include A Midsummer Night's Dream, The Assassination Bureau, On Her Majesty's Secret Service, Julius Caesar, The Hospital, Theatre of Blood, A Little Night Music, The Great Muppet Caper, Evil Under the Sun, A Good Man in Africa, Parting Shots, 1998; co-starred as Emma Peel in Brit. TV series The Avengers, 1965-67; star TV series Diana, 1973-74; numerous TV movies including This House of Brede, 1975, Hedda Gabler, 1981, Little Eyolf, 1982, Witness for the Prosecution, 1982, King Lear, 1983, Bleak House, 1984, A Hazard of Hearts, 1987, Worst Witch, 1987, Unexplained Laughter, 1989, Mother Love (Broadcasting Guild Award, BAFTA), 1989, Genghis Cohn, 1994, Zoya, 1995, The Haunting of Helen Walker, 1995, Moll Flanders, 1996, Samson and Delilah, 1996, Rebecca, 1997; host PBS series Mystery, 1989—, Mrs. Bradley Mysteries, 1999—; author: No Turn Unstoned, 1982, U.S. edit., 1983, So To The Land, 1994. Decorated comdr. Brit. Empire; created dame, 1994; recipient Tony award nomination as best actress in Abelard and Heloise and The Misanthrope; Plays and Players award for Phaedra Britannica and Night and Day; Variety Club Gt. Britain award for best actress for Evil Under the Sun; Brit. Acad. Film and TV Arts award for best TV actress in Mother Love, 1989. Mem. United Brit. Artists (co-founder, dir. 1982—). Address: c/o Lionel Larner Ltd 119 W 57th St New York NY 10019-2303

RIGGIN, LEH-DAW ALICE, analytical chemist; b. Da Pu, Kwangtung, China, Nov. 14, 1948; arrived in Hong Kong, 1949, Taiwan, 1952; came to U.S., 1973; d. Sha-Ou and Ju-Ing (Lee) Rau; m. Ralph Meridith Riggin, May 24, 1975; children: Esther Tonia, Daniel Evan. BS in Chemistry, Nat. Taiwan Normal U., Taipei, 1971; MS in Organic Chemistry, Mich. State U., 1976; PhD in Analytical Chemistry, Purdue U., 1991. Tchg. asst. chemistry dept. Mich. State U., East Lansing, 1973-76; rsch. assoc. Coll. Pharmacy Ohio State U., Columbus, 1976-78; rsch. chemist Adria Labs., Dublin, Ohio, 1978-82; environ. analytical chemist Stilson Labs., Columbus, 1982-83; rsch. scientist Battelle Columbus Labs., Columbus, 1983-85; pharm. chemist dept. pharm. rsch. Eli Lilly, Indpls., 1985-88; rsch. asst. dept. chemistry Purdue U., West Lafayette, Ind., 1988-91; sr. analytical chemist Eli Lilly and Co., Indpls., 1991—. Assoc. editor: Current Pharm. Biotech.; contbr. articles to profl. jours. including Biopharm., Jour. Chromatography, Analytical Chemistry. Mem. AAAS, Am. Chem. Soc., Protein Soc., Assn. Chinese Ams. (treas., coun. mem. 1988-91). Achievements include new technologies for residual DNA analysis, immunochromatographic analysis, protein characterization. Avocations: Chinese music instrument, Chinese painting, photography, gardening, travel. Home: 708 Suffolk Ln Carmel IN 46032-8661 Office: Eli Lilly and Co 307 E Mccarty St Indianapolis IN 46285-0002

RIGGLE, MARY LOU, missionary educator, academic adminstrator; b. New Castle, Ind., Apr. 26, 1938; d. Glen and Jennie Christena (Souther) R. BSc in Edn., Olivet Nazarene U., 1960; MSc in Edn., Ind. U., 1964; MDiv in Theology, Nazarene Theol. Sem., Kansas City, Mo., 1981, DMin in Spiritual Formation, 1989. Cert. tchr., Ind.; ordained to ministry Ch. of Nazarene. Elem. tchr. Richmond (Ind.) Cmty. Schs., 1960-65; tchr., supr. Nazarene Schs., Belize, 1965-67; prin. Nazarene H.S., Belize City, Belize, 1968-69; dir., tchr. theol. edn. Ch. of Nazarene, Belize, 1970-77; acad. dean Seminario Teológico Nazareno, Guatemala City, Guatemala, 1977-84; prof. theology Seminario Nazareno, Guatemala City, Guatemala, 1978-87, coord. extension edn., 1987; dir. Seminario Teológico Nazareno, Guatemala City, Guatemala, 1985-86; acad. vice rector Universidad Nazarena, San José, Costa Rica, 1987-93, prof. theology and spiritual formation, 1987-96, campus pastor, 1994-95; acad. v.p. Seminario Nazareno de las Americas, San José, Costa Rica, 1996-2000; pastor Nazareno Mozotal Ch., San José, 1998-2000; dist. supt. central dist. Ch. of the Nazarene, San José, 1998—; prof. theology Universidad Mariano Galvez, Guatemala City, 1983-87. Author: Prologómeno de Teología, 1970, La Teología Wesleyana en Perspectiva..., 1988; contbr. articles to profl. jours. Bd. govs. Belize Tchrs. Coll., 1966-72, Belize Tech. Coll., 1967-70, Belize Comprehensive Sch., Belmopan, 1971-72. Recipient Disting. Svc. award Ch. of Nazarene, Northwest Ohio Dist., 1995. Mem. Am. Soc. Missionology, Wesleyan Theol. Soc., Assn. Evangelica de Educacion Teologica en America Latina (bd. dirs., vocal, 1992-95, team leader accrediting commn. 1995—). Church of the Nazarene. Avocations: gardening, stamp collecting. Home and Office: Apartado 126-2110, San José Costa Rica

RIGGS, BYRON LAWRENCE, JR., physician, educator; b. Hot Springs, Ark., Mar. 24, 1931; s. Byron Lawrence and Elizabeth Ann (Patching) R.; m. Janet Templeton Brewer, June 24, 1955; children: Byron Kent, Ann Templeton. B.S., U. Ark., 1953, B.S. in Medicine, 1955, M.D., 1955; M.S. in Medicine, U. Minn., 1962. Diplomate: Am. Bd. Internal Medicine. Intern Letterman Army Hosp., San Francisco, 1955-56; resident in internal medicine Mayo Grad. Sch. Medicine Hosp., Rochester, Minn., 1958-61; asst. to staff Mayo Clinic and Found., Rochester, 1961, mem. staff internal medicine and metabolism, 1962—; mem. faculty U. Minn. Med. Sch., Rochester, 1962—, assoc. prof., 1970-72, prof., 1972—; Purvis and Roberta Tabor prof. med. rsch. Mayo Clinic and Med. Sch., Rochester, 1974—, chmn. divsn. endocrinology and metabolism, 1974-84; mem. gen. medicine B study sect. NIH, 1979-82; nat. adv. bd. NIAMS/NIH, 1987-91, disting. investigator Mayo Found., 1991—. Contbr. articles to med. jours. Dist. investigator Mayo Found., 1991—. Served with M.C. AUS, 1956-58. Recipient Mayo Found. postgrad. travel award, 1961, Kappa Delta award Am. Acad. Orthopedic Surgery, 1972, Disting. Alumni award U. Ark., 1998; traveling fellow Royal Soc. Medicine, 1973. Fellow ACP; mem. AMA, AAAS, Assn. Am. Physicians, Am. Soc. Clin. Investigation, Endocrine Soc. (Rorer Clin. Investigator award 1989), Am. Fedn. Clin. Rsch. (councillor Midwest sect. 1969-71), Am. Soc. for Bone and Mineral Rsch. (pres. 1985-86, Bartter Clin. Investigation award 1990, Career Recognition award, 9th Workshop on Vitamin D rsch.), Ctrl. Soc. Clin. Rsch. (councillor). Home: 432 10th Ave SW Rochester MN 55902-2911 Office: Mayo Clinic 200 1st St SW Rochester MN 55905-0002

RIGGS, DONALD EUGENE, librarian, university official; b. Middlebourne, W.Va., May 11, 1942; m. Jane Vasbinder, Sept. 25, 1964; children: Janna Jennifer, Krista Dyonis. BA, Glenville State Coll., 1964; MA, W.Va. U., 1966; MLS, U. Pitts., 1968; EdD, Va. Poly. Inst. and State U., 1975. Head librarian, tchr. sci. Warwood (W.Va.) High Sch., 1964-65; head librarian, audiovisual dir. Wheeling (W.Va.) High Sch., 1965-67; sci. and econs. librarian California State Coll. of Pa., 1968-70; dir. library and learning center Bluefield State Coll., 1970-72; dir. libraries and media services Bluefield State Coll., Concord Coll., Greenbrier Community Coll., and So. campus W.Va. Coll. of Grad. Studies, 1972-76; dir. libraries U. Colo., Denver, Met. State Coll., and Community Col. of Denver—Auraria Campus, 1976-79; univ. librarian Ariz. State U., 1979-88, dean univ. libraries, 1988-90; prof. info. and libr. sci., dean univ. libr. U. Mich., Ann Arbor, 1991-97; prof., v.p. for info. svcs., univ. libr. Nova Southeastern U., Ft. Lauderdale, Fla., 1997—; adj. prof. Calif. State Coll., 1968-70, W.Va. U., 1970-72, U. Colo., 1977-79, U. Ariz., 1985, Emporia State U., 1996—, U. South Fla., 1997—; fed. rels. coord. Am. and W.Va. Libr. Assns., 1970-75; chmn. bd. dirs. Ctrl. Colo. Libr. Sys., 1976-79; chmn. Colo. Coun. Acad. Librs., 1977-78; mem. exec. bd. Colo. Alliance Rsch. Librs., 1978-79; cons. to librs.; fgn. assignments in Xi'an, China, 1988, Guadalajara, Mex., 1990, Budapest, Hungary, 1991, 95, Hong Kong, 1992, 94, San Juan, P.R., 1993, Melbourne, Australia, 1994, Eupatory, Republic Crimea, Ukraine, 1995, London, 1996, Prague, Czech Republic, 1996, Beijing, China, 1996, 98, Pretoria, South Africa, 1996, others; del. Users Coun. Online Computer Libr. Ctr., Dublin, Ohio, 1987-91, pres.-elect, 1990-91, chair artificial intelligence and expert systems nat. group, 1987-88; bd. govs. Rsch. Librs. Group, Inc., Mountain View, Calif., 1991-92; vice chmn. mgmt. com. William L. Clements Libr., 1991-97. Editor: W.Va. Librs., 1973-75, Libr. Hi Tech, 1993-96, Coll. & Rsch. Librs., 1996— ; founding editor: Libr. Adminstrn. and Mgmt., 1987-89; assoc. editor: Southeastern Libr., 1973-75; contbg. editor: Libraries in the Political Process, 1980, Options for the 80's, 1982, Library and Information Technology: At the Crossroads, 1984; contbg. author, editor: Library Leadership: Visualizing the Future, 1982; author: Strategic Planning for Library Managers, 1984, (with Helen Gothberg) Time Management in Academic Libraries, 1986, (with Gordon Sabine) Libraries in the 90's: What the Leaders Expect, 1988, Creativity, Innovation and Entrepreneurship in Libraries, 1989, Library Communication: The Language of Leadership, 1991, (with Rao Aluri) Expert Systems in Libraries, 1990, Cultural Diversity in Libraries, 1994; editl. bd. Am. Librs., 1987-89, Jour. Libr. Adminstrn., 1987-97, Coll. and Rsch. Librs. News, 1990-96. Trustee Mesa (Ariz.) Pub. Library, 1980-86, chmn., 1985-86; mem. Ariz. State Library Adv. Council, 1981-84; bd. dirs. Documentation Abstracts, Inc., 1986-90. Recipient Alumnus of Yr. award Glenville State Coll., 1992; named Outstanding Young Educator, Ohio County Schs., 1966; Coun. on Libr. Resources grantee, 1985; sr. fellow UCLA, 1989. Mem. ALA (councilor-at-large 1982-86, 89-93, chmn. coun.'s resolutions com. 1985-86, pub. com. 1988-92, Hugh Atkinson award 1991), Ariz. Libr. Assn. (pres. coll. and univ. divsn. 1981-82, pres. 1983-84, Spl. Svc. award 1986, Disting. Svc. award 1990), Colo. Libr. Assn. (pres. 1978-79), W.Va. Libr. Assn. (pres. 1975-76), Assn. Coll. and Rsch. Librs. (pres. Tri-State chpt. 1972-74, pres. Ariz. chpt. 1981-82), So. Libr. Assn. (chmn. coll. and univ. sect. 1982-83), Assn. Rsch. Librs. (100th meeting planning com. 1982, mgmt. of rsch. libr. resources com. 1990-93, rsch. collections com. 1993-96), AMIGOS Bibliograph Coun. (trustee 1986-90, chmn. bd. trustees 1988-89), Libr. Adminstrn. and Mgmt. Assn. (bd. dirs. 1987-89, pres.-elect 1993-94, pres. 1994-95), Libr. Info. and Tech. Assn. (bd. dirs. 1989-93), Ctr. for Rsch. Librs. (councilor 1979-97), Mountain Plains Libr. Assn. (bd. dirs. 1987-90, pres.-elect 1990-91), S.E. Fla. Libr. Info. Network (exec. com., bd. dirs. 1997—, pres. 1998-99), Beta Phi Mu, Chi Beta Phi, Phi Delta Kappa, Phi Kappa Phi. Office: Nova Southeastern U Einstein Libr 3301 College Ave Fort Lauderdale FL 33314-7721

RIGGS, RORY, pharmaceutical executive; b. Orange, N.J., May 5, 1953; d. Thomas Jeffries and Virginia (Griggs) R. BA, Middlebury Coll.; MBA, Columbia U. Mng. dir. PaineWebber, Inc.; CEO RF&P Corp.; mng. dir. Pharma Ptnrs. LLC; bd. dirs. Biomatrix, Inc. 1990—, pres. 1995—; bd. mem. Fibrogen Corp., Spartan Corp., Pharma Ptnrs, LLC. Mem. Young Pres. Orgn. Office: Biomatrix Inc 65 Railroad Ave Ste 3 Ridgefield NJ 07657-2176*

RIGGS-HALL, CARLA LYNN, entertainer-performing arts educator, restaurateur; b. Louisville, Jan. 13, 1953; d. Carleton Lee and Eva Inelle (Chapman) Riggs; m. Timothy Earl Hall, Jan. 11, 1972 (div. Mar. 1973); 1 child, Carmen Lynette; m. Bruce Allen Caldera, Mar. 17, 1992. Student, U. Louisville, 1971-72, Elizabethtown Community Coll., 1974-77; cert., Vogue Models, Louisville, 1982. Pvt. instr. Radcliff, Ky., 1973—; music tchr. Comprehensive Care, Elizabethtown, Ky., 1974-75; owner Carla Riggs-Hall Entertainment, Elizabethtown, 1975—, Studio C, Elizabethtown, 1991—, MediaMax, Elizabethtown, 1997—; co-owner retro dance theatre, Elizabethtown, 2000—, Cafe Caldera, Elizabethtown, 2000—, Backstage Cafe, Elizabethtown, 2000—; rec. artist Alpha Records, Elizabethtown, 1981—; promotions dir. Carnival Shoes, Elizabethtown, 1988; exec. asst. Joe Evans for Sec. of State, Bardstown, Ky., 1990-91; promotion dir. Hardin County Playhouse, Radcliff; coord. News-Enterprise Bridal Fair, Elizabethtown, 1992; guest artist Ky. Gov.'s Sch. for Arts, 1999, 2000; co-founder The Way Too Much Caffeine Players. Composer piano music Caldera Compilation, 1980, Maidens in a Row; singer One More Try, 1983 (Country Music Showcase Single of 1983); lyricist Rumours and Lies, 1997,

It's Your Crime, Two Lovers, Two Friends; lyricist, composer Take a Real Close Look, I Don't Want To Do That. Pres. Hardin County Young Dems., Elizabethtown, 1976; adminstrv. bd. Longview Meth. Ch., Elizabethtown, 1979—; entertainment dir. Red Cross Cooking for Life, Hardin County, Ky., 1989—; campaign dir. Goodman/Magistrate, Hardin County, 1989; precinct chair McCloy for Dist. Judge, Hardin County, 1991. Named Hon. State Treas., State of Ky., 1979, Ky. Col., State of Ky., 1983, Outstanding Young Woman of Am., 1983, Carla Riggs-Hall Day, Hardin County, 1984, Disaster Svc. 10 Yr. award of Svc., ARC, 1995, 96, 97, Drivers's Svc. award MADD, 1995. Mem. Country Music Assn., Hardin County Playhouse (dir. 1975—), Heartland Songwriters Assn. Ky. (sec.). Democrat. Avocations: roller skating, writing, swimming. Office: 202 Master St Elizabethtown KY 42701

RIGGULSFORD, MICHAEL JAMES, public relations consultant; b. Swansea, Wales, Mar. 10, 1956; s. Peter Henry and Shirley Alison (Burford) R.; m. Jennifer Mary Kimber, Oct. 31, 1992. Student, Exeter (Eng.) U., 1974-78, Stirling U., Scotland, 1992-97. Radio broadcaster ILR Plymouth Sound, Automobile Assn., Exeter, 1978-80, pub. rels. asst., 1980-84; head pub. rels. U.K. Transplant Svc., Bristol, Eng., 1984-91; dir. Rsch. for Health Charities Group, Somerset, Eng., 1991-94, Transplant Info. Bur., Somerset, Eng., 1991—; mng. dir., pub. rels. cons. The Walnut Bur., 1991—; freelance journalist, gossip columnist, mag. editor, Eng., 1980-86; freelance pub. rels. officer, Bristol, 1980-88. Author numerous satirical and medical articles to various publs. Hon. pub. rels. officer TIME, 1990-93, Transplant Sports Assn. Gt. Britain, 1987-93, hon. sec., 1989-93. Mem. Inst. Journalists, Inst. Pub. Rels., Brit. Assn. of Tissue Banks, Brit. Transplantation Soc., MENSA, Brit. Assn. for Advancement of Sci. Home and Office: The Walnut Bur, Dadland High Bickington, Pilton Umberleigh Devon EX37 9BS, England

RIGHTER, ROSEMARY, writer, journalist; b. Chesterfield, Derbyshire, Eng., Apr. 2, 1943; d. Archibald Andrew Henry Douglas and Marjorie Gordon (Brown) Beaumont; m. William Righter, Mar. 30, 1968. BA in English Lit. with honors, U. Cambridge, 1964, MA, 1967. Pub. relations officer Thos Nelson Publs., London, 1964-65; reader Chatto and Windus Publs., London, 1965-66; research asst. London, 1966-69; asst. editor Far Eastern Econ. Rev., Hong Kong, 1970-72; reporter Newsweek, Hong Kong, 1972-73; devel. corr. Sunday Times, London, 1973-85, diplomatic corr.; project dir. 20th Century Fund, N.Y.C., 1985-88; editl. writer Times, London, 1988-89, chief eidtl. writer, 1989—, asst. editor, 1992—. Author: (with Peter Wilsher) The Exploding Cities, 1974, The Undivided Word, 1976, Whose News? Politics, the Press and the Third World, 1978, (with editor Richard Hoggart) Liberty and Legislation, 1988, Utopia Lost: The United Nations and World Order, 1995; contbr. articles to newpapers and jours. Mem. coun. Overseas Devel. Inst., London, 1981-90. Mem. Internat. Press Inst., Royal Inst. for Internat. Affairs. Home: 10 Quick St, London N1 8HL, England Office: The Times, 1 Pennington St, London E1 9XN, England

RIGOR, BRADLEY GLENN, lawyer; b. Cheyenne Wells, Colo., Aug. 9, 1955; s. Glenn E. and Lelia (Teed) R.; m. Twyla G. Helweg, Sept. 4, 1983; children: Camille, Brent, Tiffany, Lauren. BS in Mktg., Ft. Hays State U., 1977; JD, Washburn U., 1980. Bar: Kans. 1980, U.S. Dist. Kans., 1980, U.S. Tax Ct. 1981, U.S. Ct. Appeals (10th cir.) 1982, U.S. Supreme Ct. 1986, Colo. 1990, Tex. 1991, U.S. Dist. Ct. Colo. 1991, Mo. 1993, Fla. 1998; cert. trust and fin. advisor Inst. Cert. Bankers; cert. fin. planner. Ptnr. Zuspann & Rigor, Goodland, Kans., 1980-82; city atty. Goodland, 1981-82; asst. county atty. Wallace County, Sharon Springs, Kans., 1982-84, county atty., 1984; city atty. Sharon Springs, 1983-84; judge Mcpl. Ct., Goodland, 1988-93; ptnr. Fairbanks, Rigor & Irvin, P.A., Goodland, 1982-93; v.p., mgr. personal trusts Merc. Bank, St. Joseph, Mo., 1993-96; sr. v.p., mgr., personal trust adminstr. SunTrust Bank, Naples, Fla., 1996-98, Bond Schoeneck & King P.A., Naples, Fla., 1998—; mem. Estate Planning Coun., Naples. Mem. Kans. Bar Assn., Tex. Bar Assn., Mo. Bar Assn., Colo. Bar Assn., Fla. Bar Assn., Collier County Bar Assn. (trust and estates sect.). Republican. Baptist. Office: Bond Schoeneck & King PA 4001 Tamiami Trl N Ste 404 Naples FL 34103-3555

RIGOS, GEORGE, judge; b. Athens, Greece; s. Constantine and Helen (Rorri) R.; m. (div.); 1 child, Constantine. Law degree, Athens, 1961. Lawyer Athens, 1964-66; judge of 1st instance Athens, Xanthi, Nafplia, 1966-78; pres. of 1st instance Edessa, 1978-81; appellate judge Corfu, Patras, Athens, 1981-93; pres. ct. appeals Piraeus, 1993-97; judge supreme ct. Athens, 1997—. Author: Liberty and Language, 1995; editor: (periodical) Greek Justice-Organ of the Greek Judges Union; contbr. articles to profl. jours. Mem. Union of Greek Judges, Assn. of Greek Constitutionalists, Soc. Judicial Studies. Avocations: reading, travel, movies, theater, concerts. Home: 37 Gouda St, 11476 Athens Greece

RIGSBY, LINDA FLORY, lawyer; b. Topeka, Kans., Dec. 16, 1946; d. Alden E. and Lolita M. Flory; m. Michael L. Rigsby, Aug. 14, 1963; children: Michael L. Jr., Elisabeth A. MusB, Va. Commonwealth U., 1969; JD, U. Richmond, 1981. Bar: Va. 1981, D.C. 1988. Assoc. McGuire, Woods, Battle & Boothe, Richmond, Va., 1981-85; dep. gen. counsel and corp. sec. Crestar Fin. Corp., Richmond, 1985-99, gen. counsel, 1999-2000; mng. atty. Sun Trust Banks Inc., 2000—. Recipient Disting. Svc. award U. Richmond, 1987; named Vol. of Yr. U. Richmond, 1986, Woman of Achievement, Met. Richmond Women's Bar, 1995. Mem. Va. Bar Assn. (exec. com. 1993-96), Richmond Bar Assn. (bd. dirs. 1992-95), Va. Bankers Assn. (chair legal affairs 1992-95), U. Richmond Estate Planning Coun. (chmn. 1990-92). Roman Catholic. Avocations: music, gardening. Home: 163 W Square Pl Richmond VA 23233-6157 Office: SunTrust Bank 919 E Main St Richmond VA 23219-4625

ŘÍHA, JAN, agriculturist; b. Litomyšl, Czech Republic, Mar. 16, 1949; s. Josef and Ružena (Kabrhelová) Ř.; m. Milena Večeřová, June 29, 1974; children: Lenka, Jan. Engring. degree, Agrl. Coll., Brno, Czech Republic, 1972; DSc, Agrl. Coll., Prague, 1991; Doctorate, Faculty of Agr., Č. Budějovice, Czech Republic, 1994. Rschr. Rsch. Inst. Cattle Breeding Ltd., Rapotin, Czech Republic, 1973—; bd. dirs. Agrl. Acad., Czech Republic. Author 5 books; contbr. over 150 articles to profl. jours. Office: Rsch Inst Cattle Breeding, 788 13 Rapotín Czech Republic

RIHA, KAREL, information systems educator; b. Prague, Czechoslovakia, July 25, 1949; arrived in U.K., 1968; s. Karel Riha and Helena (Buricova) Rihova; m. Jana Travnickova, Aug. 5, 1972; children: Anna, Robert. BA, Oxford (Eng.) U., 1972, PGCE, 1973; MSc, Kingston (Eng.) Poly., 1980, PhD, 1988. Cert. engr. Asst. master Kingston Grammar Sch., 1973-80; researcher Kingston Poly., 1980-83, lectr., 1983—; cons. Data Dictionary Sys., U.K., 1988, Property Svcs. Agy., U.K., 1988, Nat. Centre for Postgrad. Pharmacy Edn., U.K., 1991, Inst. for Mcpl. Informatics, Prague, 1991, SQA Ltd., 1993. Author: (with others) Automating System Development, 1988. Mem. Brit. Computer Soc. Avocations: squash, tennis, chess. Home: 17 Pembroke Ave, Surbiton KT5 8HN, England Office: Kingston Univ, Penrhyn Rd, Kingston KT12EE, England

RIHMER, ZOLTAN, psychiatrist, neurologist; b. Pécs, Baranya, Hungary, Mar. 25, 1947; s. Zoltán Rihmer and Erzsébet Csizmadia; m. Lidia Harmati, Aug. 23, 1969; children: Zoltán, Annamária. MD, Med. U. of Pécs, 1971; cert. in psychiatry, Postgrad. Med. Sch., Budapest, Hungary, 1975, cert. in neurology, 1979. Psychiat. intern Psychiat. Inst. Pomáz, Hungary, 1971-73; psychiat. intern Nat. Inst. for Nervous and Mental Diseases, Budapest, 1973-75, neurology intern, 1976-79, chief psychiat. dept., sec. sci. com., 1982—; assoc. prof. psychiatry Semmelweis Med. Sch., Budapest, 1984; lectr. in psychiatry Postgrad. Med. Sch., 1980—. Editor: (with I. Bitter) Practical Psychopharmacology, 1st edit., 1986, 2d edit., 1989; mem. editl. bd. Jour. Affective Disorders, Neuropsychobiology, Internat. Jour. Psychiatry in Clin. Practice, Assn. European Psychiatrists; contbr. more than 170 articles to sci. publs.. Mem. Assn. Hungarian Neurologists and Psychiatrists Assn. (sec. 1975-89), European Coll. Neuropsychopharmacology, Hungarian Psychiat. Assn. (dep. sec. gen. 1988—), Nat. Inst. Nervous and Mental Diseases (pres. sci. com. 1988—). Avocation: classical music. Home: Magyar Jakobinusok Tere 6, 1122 Budapest Hungary Office: Nat Inst Nervous Diseases, 16 Hüvösvölgyi, 1281 Budapest Hungary

ŘÍHOVÁ, BLANKA JIŘINA, immunologist, researcher; b. Prague, Czech Republic, Oct. 21, 1942; d. Václav and Vlasta (Suchánková) Vokoun; m. Jaroslav Škára, Dec. 14, 1963 (div. 1967); m. Ivan Říha, Jan. 23, 1970; children: Helena, Martina. RNDr, Charles U., Prague, 1964; PhD, Inst. Microbiology, Prague, 1969. Postdoctoral rsch. assoc., sr. rsch. fellow Inst. Microbiology, Czech Acad. Sci., Prague, 1969-90, head lab. of humoral immunity, 1990—, head sci. bd., 1992—; head joint immunology dept. Acad. Sci. and Charles U., Prague, 1996—; sr. acad. visitor Okla. Med. Rsch. Found., Oklahoma City, 1987-88; vis. assoc. prof. U. Utah, Salt Lake City, 1990-96; vis. prof. Paris-North U., 1993; mem. com. on inter-polymer liv. sys. IUPAC, Paris, 1982—; dir. regional office East Europe Soc. for Leukocyte Biology, Washington, 1993—; mem. Coun. Acad. Sci. Czech Republic Acad. Sci., 1994—. Contbr. articles to profl. jours.; patentee in field. Recipient Acad. Prize for Sci., Czech Acad. Sci., 1975, J.E. Purkyně medal, 1987. Mem. Czech Immunol. Soc. (mem. com.), N.Y. Acad. Sci., Controlled Rel. Soc., Sigma Xi. Avocations: music, theatre, hiking, skiing. Home: Pod Terebkou 11/1136, 140 00 Prague 4, Czech Republic Office: Inst of Microbiology, Vídeňská 1083, 142 20 Prague 4, Czech Republic

RIIHENTAUS, LEO JUHANI, mathematics educator; b. Helsinki, Finland, Mar. 4, 1942; s. Leo and Leeni Lemmikki (Saarnilahti) R.; m. Leena Anneli Laurio, Nov. 6, 1965; children: Jyrki Juhani, Aila Marjaana. PhD in Math., U. Helsinki, 1976. Asst. U. Jyvaskyla, 1966-68; asst. Helsinki Tech. U., 1968-70, temp. assoc. prof., 1970-71; temp. assoc. prof. Lappeenranta Tech. U., 1971-72; lectr. U. Joensuu, 1972-77; sr. lectr. Oulu Coll. Tech., 1977-94, South Carelia Polytech., 1994—; docent U. Joensuu, Finland, 1980—, temp. assoc. prof., 1994; docent U. Oulu, Finland, 1983—. Contbr. articles to profl. jours. Lt. Mil. Svc., 1961-62. Mem. Finnish Math. Soc., Am. Math. Soc., Math. Assn. Am. Evangelican Lutheran. Home: Kirjaajankatu 5B2, 53300 Lappeenranta Finland Office: South Carelia Polytech, PO Box 99, 53101 Lappeenranta Finland

RIIKONEN, RAILI SYLVIA, child neurologist; b. Kuopio, Finland, Nov. 23, 1941; d. Vaino Johannes and Selma Sofia (Vartiainen) Jaaskelainen; m. Antti Juhani Riikonen, Dec. 27, 1969; children: Esa, Simo. MD, U. Helsinki, 1981, Professorship Child Neurology, 1990; Assoc. Professorship, U. Kuopio, 1990; Professorship Child Neurology, U. Turku, Finland, 1990. Specialist in pediatrics, child neurology, health adminstrn. Gen. officer, hosp. physician Ctrl. Hosp. of Porvoo, 1971-82; asst. and sr. physician Ctrl. Hosp./U. Helsinki, 1982-86; assoc. prof. U. Turku and Helsinki, 1986-89, head dept. child neurology, 1986-90; rschr. Rinnekoti Found., Helsinki, 1983-84; head dept. child neurology Ctrl. Hosp. Kotka, Finland, 1993-96, Ctrl. Hosp. U. Kuopio, 1997—; chief physician, Cen. Hosp./U. Turku, 1986-90, U. Helsinki, 1990-91. Contbg. author: (books) Epilepsies in Infancy and Childhood, 1991, West Syndrome, 1994, Epilepsy in Children, 1996. Mem. Internat. Assn. Child Neurology. Avocations: rsch., lit. Home: Kajavatie 7, 06100 Porvoo Finland Office: Ctrl Hosp, U Kuopio, FIN70211 Kuopio Finland

RIJAL, KIRAN PRASAD, orthopedic surgeon; b. Biratnager, Nepal; s. Shambhu Prasad and Mitra Kumari (Acharya) R.; m. Nisha Parajuli, June 5, 1987; children: Nishchal, Rika. MBBS, Calcutta U., 1982; cert. in sports medicine, Indian Assn. Sports Medicine, 1985; MD, PhD, Tohoku U., 1994. Intern R.G. Kar Med. Coll., Calcutta, India, 1983-84, residential house surgeon, jr. and sr., 1984-85; residential med. officer Bir Hosp., Kathmandu, 1985—; resident in master of surgery Rehab. Inst. and Hosps., Dhaka, Bangladesh, 1987-88; postdoctoral trainee Tohoku U. Hosp., Sendai, Japan, 1988-94; sr. registrar Bir Hosp., Kathmandu, Nepal, 1994—; residential med. officer Bir Hosp., Kathmandu, 1995-85; intern R.G. Kar Med. Coll., Calcutta, India, 1983-84, residential house surgeon, jr. and sr., 1984-85; cons. HM Hosps. and Rsch. Ctr. Ltd., Kathmandu, 1995—, Hargangs Nursing Home Ltd., Kathmandu, 1995—, Curex Poli Clinic, Kathmandu, 1995—, Hosp. and Rehab. Ctr. for Disabled Children, Kathmandu, 1995—. Contbr. articles to profl. jours. Treas. Tohoku U. Fgn. Students Assn., Sendai, Japan, 1990. Mem. Nepal Orthopaedic Assn. (life), Indian Orthopaedic Assn. (life), Nepal Med. Assn. (life). Avocations: table tennis, camping, music, reading, driving. Office: Bir Hosp, PO Box 10109, Kathmandu Nepal

RIJKENBERG, FRITS HERMANUS, plant pathology and rural development educator; b. Wormerveer, The Netherlands, Nov. 21, 1940; s. Hermanus Petrus and Elizabeth Maria (Vet) R.; m. Merle Carmel Akal, Jan. 15, 1966; children: Marc Herman, Paul Anthony, Lisa Celeste. BS Agr., U. Natal, Scottsville, South Africa, 1965, MS Agr., 1969, PhD, 1974. Lectr. U. Natal, 1967-75, sr. lectr., 1975-78, assoc. prof., 1978-88, prof., 1988—, head dept., 1988-94, dean Faculty Agr., 1994-99, dir. Ctr. Rural Devel. Systems, 1999—, prof., chmn. rural devel., 2000—; chmn. com. South African Deans of Agr., 1998-99. Contbr. articles to profl. jours. Recipient fellowship Natal U., Pietermaritzburg, 1994. Fellow South African Soc. for Plant-Pathology (past v.p., fellowship 1993); mem. Fedn. Brit. Plant Pathologists. Roman Catholic. Achievements include publication of the first electron microscope studies of the pycnial and aecial stages of a rust fungus. Home: 15 Fuller Rd, Pietermaritzburg 3201, South Africa Office: U Natal, Pvt Bag X01, Scottsville 3209, South Africa

RIKMANIS, MĀRIS INTS, engineering educator; b. Valka, Latvia, Feb. 28, 1940; s. Arnolds Julijs and Vanda Jadviga (Marcinkjane) R.; m. Sarma Sudmale, Oct. 27, 1962; 1 child, Indra. Degree in chem. engring., Poly. Inst. Riga, Latvia, 1965; Candidate in Engring. Sci., Technol. Inst. Leningrad, USSR, 1990; D in Biology, U. Latvia, 1992, Habilitation, 1993. Sr. technologist, head dept. Dzintars, Riga, 1965-74; tchr. 69 Secondary Sch. Riga, 1974-75; sr. engr., sr. rschr., head lab. Kirchenstein Inst. Microbiology, Latvian Acad. Sci., 1975-92, dep. dir., 1993; sr. sec., prof., head lab. Inst. Microbiology and Biotech., U. Latvia, 1994-96, dep. dir., 1997—; experts com. Latvian Coun. Sci., Riga, 1993-96. Patentee in field. Vice chmn. Latvian Peoples Front, Riga, 1990-92; mem. com. Union Latvian Intellectuals, 1996-98. Mem. N.Am. Mixing Forum, Latvian Assn. Scientists (mem. coun. 1991—), European Fedn. Biotechnology Working Party Measurement Control. Fax: 3712-428039. Home: Dammes 22-11, LV 1069 Riga Latvia Office: Inst Microbiol U Latvia, Rātsupites 1, LV 1067 Riga Latvia

RIKON, MICHAEL, lawyer; b. Bklyn., Feb. 2, 1945; s. Charles and Ruth (Shapiro) R.; m. Leslie Sharon Rein, Feb. 11, 1968; children: Carrie Rachel, Joshua Howard. BS, N.Y. Inst. Tech., 1966; JD, Bklyn. Law Sch., 1969; LLM, NYU, 1974. Bar: N.Y. 1970, U.S. Dist. Ct. (so. and ea. dists.) N.Y. 1971, U.S. Ct. Appeals (2d cir.) 1972, U.S. Supreme Ct. 1973, U.S. Ct. Appeals (5th and 11th cirs.) 1981. Asst. corp. counsel City of N.Y., 1969-73; law clk. N.Y. State Ct. Claims, 1973-80; ptnr. Rudick and Rikon, P.C., N.Y.C., 1980-88; pvt. practice, N.Y.C., 1988-94; ptnr. Goldstein, Goldstein and Rikon, P.C., N.Y.C., 1994—. Contbr. articles to profl. jours. Pres. Village Greens Residents Assn., 1978-79; chmn. bd. Arden Heights Jewish Ctr., Staten Island, N.Y., 1976-77; pres. North Shore Republican Club, 1977; mem. community bd. Staten Island Borough Pres., 1977. Fellow Am. Bar Found.; mem. ABA (chair com. Condemnation), ATLA, TLPJ Found., N.Y. State Bar Assn. (spl. com. of condemnation law), Suffolk County Bar Assn., N.Y. County Lawyers Assn. (chair Condemnation com.), Republican. Jewish. Avocations: collecting stamps, photography, collecting miniature soldiers. Home: 133 Avondale Rd Ridgewood NJ 07450-1301 Office: 80 Pine St New York NY 10005-1702

RIKOSKI, RICHARD ANTHONY, engineering executive, electrical engineer; b. Kingston, Pa., Aug. 13, 1941; s. Stanley George and Nellie (Gober) R.; m. Giannina Batchelor Petrullo, Dec. 18, 1971 (div. 1979); children: Richard James, Jennifer Anne. BEE, U. Detroit, 1964; MSEE, Carnegie Inst. Tech., 1965; PhD, Carnegie-Mellon U., 1968; postdoctoral fellow, Case-Western Res. U./NASA, 1971. Registered profl. engr., Ill., Mass., Pa. Engr. 1st communication satellite systems Internat. Tel. & Tel., Nutley, N.J., 1961-64; engr. Titan II ICBM program Gen. Motors, Milw., 1964; trainee NASA, 1964-67; instr. Carnegie-Mellon U., Pitts., 1966-68; asst. prof. U. Pa., Phila., 1968-74; assoc. prof., dir. hybrid microelectronics lab., chmn. ednl. TV com. IIT, Chgo., 1974-80, chmn. ednl. TV com., 1974-80; rsch. engr. nuclear effects IIT Rsch. Inst., Chgo., 1974-75; pres. Tech. Analysis Corp., Chgo., 1980—; engr. color TV colorimetry Hazeltine Rsch., Chgo., 1969; engr. Metroliner rail car/roadbed ride quality dynamics analysis U.S. Dept. Transp., ENSCO, Inc., Springfield, Va., 1970; pres. Tech. Analysis Corp., Chgo., 1978-91; contractor analysis of color TV receiver safety hazards U.S. Consumer Product Safety Comm., 1977, analysis heating effect in aluminum wire Beverly Hills Supper Club Fire, Covington, Ky., 1978; engr. GFCI patent infringement study 3M Corp., St. Paul, 1979-81; elec. systems analyst Coca-Cola Corp., Atlanta, 1983-91; fire investigator McDonald's Corp., Oak Brook, Ill., 1987-90; engring. analyst telephone switching ctrs. ATT, Chgo., 1990-91; expert witness numerous other govtl. and corp. procs. Author: Hybrid Microelectronic Circuits, 1973; editor: Hybrid Microelectronic Technology, 1973; contbr. articles to profl. jours. Officer Planning Commn., Beverly Shores, Ind., 1987-93, trustee town coun., 1992—, police liason 1993-96, dir. emergency mgmt., 1998, coun. pres., 1999—; mem. Chgo. Coun. Fgn. Rels., USAF SAC Comdrs. Disting.is. Program; adv. coun. Nat. Park Svc. Ind. Dunes Nat. Lake Shore, 1993—. NASA fellow, 1964-67, 70. Mem. IEEE (sr. ednl. activities bd. N.Y.C. 1970-74, USAB career devel. com. 1972-74, editor Soundings 1973-75, Cassette Colloquia 1973-74, del. Popov Soc. Tech. Exch. USSR, mgr. Dial Access Tech. Edn. program 1972), Assn. for Media Based Continuing Engring. Edn. (bd. dirs.), Nat. Fire Protection Assn., Sigma Xi, Tau Beta Pi, Eta Kappa Nu. Republican. Avocations: sailing, travel. Home: One E Lakefront Dr Beverly Shores IN 46301-0444 Office: Tech Analysis Corp 1032 W Diversey Pkwy Chicago IL 60614-1317

RIKVOLD, PER ARNE, physics researcher and educator; b. Hadsel, Norway, Oct. 4, 1948; came to U.S., 1980; s. Per and Inger-Johanne (Corneliussen) R.; m. Paulette Alice Bond, Apr. 10, 1993. BS, U. Oslo, 1971, MS in Physics, 1976; cert. Japanese lang., Osaka (Japan) U. Fgn. Studies, 1977; PhD in Physics, Temple U., 1983. Rsch. assoc. dept. physics U. Oslo, 1978-81; rsch. assoc. dept. mech. engring. SUNY, Stony Brook, N.Y., 1983-85; sr. rsch. chemist ARCO Chem. Co., Newtown Square, Pa., 1985-87; assoc. prof. physics Fla. State U., Tallahassee, 1987-92, prof. physics, 1992—; vis. scientist Kyushu U., Fukuoka, Japan, 1979, U. Geneva, Switzerland, 1981-82, Inst. Solid State Physics, Jülich, Germany, 1982; vis. rschr. IBM, Bergen, Norway, 1987, 88, U. Colo., Boulder, 1997, U. Tex., Austin, 1999; cons. Pony Industries, Malvern, Pa., 1987; vis. scholar Temple U., Phila., 1986-87, Tohwa Inst. Sci., Japan, 1991, Kyushu (Japan) U., 1991, Kyoto (Japan) U., 1993, 96, 98, McGill U., Montreal, Que., Can., 1995. Contbr. numerous articles to profl. jours. and books. Rsch. grantee Petroleum Rsch. Fund, 1988-91, NSF, 1991—; grad. rsch. fellow Japanese Ministry Edn., 1976-78, Norwegian Rsch. coun., 1981-83, Japan Found., Ctr. for Global Partnership Sci. fellow, 1996. Mem. AAAS, Am. Phys. Soc., Materials Rsch. Soc., Electrochem. Soc., Norwegian Phys. Soc., European Phys. Soc., Sigma Xi. Democrat. Achievements include theoretical and computational research in statistical and condensed-matter physics and complex-systems theory, with applications to materials science, electrochemistry and engineering. Office: Fla State U Physics Dept Tallahassee FL 32306

RILEY, DANIEL JOSEPH, lawyer, educator; b. Amarillo, Tex., Jan. 14, 1947; s. Roy Weldon and Joette Aline (Winger) R.; m. Glenda Joy Hoel, Apr. 15, 1947; children: Carla Annette, Ragan Patrick. BA cum laude, U. Tex., 1969, JD summa cum laude, 1971. Bar: Tex. 1971, U.S. Ct. Fed. Claims 1974, U.S. Supreme Ct. 1979, U.S. Ct. Appeals (fed. cir.) 1982, D.C. 1999. Ptnr. Baker Bolts LLP, Washington, 1993—; adj. prof. grad. sch. U. Dallas, 1983-94. Assoc. editor U. Tex. Law Rev., 1970. Mem. constitution rev. com. State of Tex., Austin, 1978. Mem. ABA (uniform state procurement code com. 1980), Nat. Contract Mgmt. Assn. (bd. advisors), Tex. Bar Found., Tex. Bar Assn., Dallas Bar Assn., Order of Coif, Phi Beta Kappa. Republican. Home: 712 W Braddock Rd Alexandria VA 22302-3601 Office: Baker Bolts LLP 1299 Pennsylvania Ave NW Washington DC 20004-2400

RILEY, DIANA MARGARET, psychiatrist; b. London, Oct. 25, 1929; d. Frederick and Elizabeth (Hudson) Dean; m. Colin Riley, Sept. 18, 1954; children: Teresa, Clare, Christopher, Josephine, Lucy, Elizabeth. MB BChir, Univ. Coll., London, 1953; Diploma in Psychol. Medicine, U. London, 1974. Cons. Nat. Health Svc., U.K., 1981-95; pvt. practice, 1981—. Author: (book) Perinatal Mental Health, 1994; editor: (book) Child Sexual Abuse, 1992; contbr. numerous papers to profl. jours. Trustee Bucks Assn. Mental Health, 1997—; treas. Marcé Soc., 1991-96. Fellow Royal Coll. Psychiatrists; mem. Internat. Soc. for Psychosomatic Ob-Gyn., Royal Coll. Coll. Surgeons, Royal Coll. Physicians (licentiate), Royal Soc. Medicine. Avocation: silversmithing. Home: The Red House, Wendover HP22 6JQ, England

RILEY, JACK, actor, writer; b. Cleve., Dec. 30, 1935; s. John A. and Agnes C. (Corrigan) R.; m. Ginger Lawrence, May 18, 1975; children: Jamie, Bryan. BS in English, John Carroll U., 1961. Mem.: Rolling Along of 1960, Dept. Army Travelling Show; co-host: Baxter & Riley, Sta.-WERE, Cleve., 1961-65; numerous TV appearances, including: as Mr. Carlin on Bob Newhart Show, CBS-TV, 1972-78; Occasional Wife, 1966, Mary Tyler Moore, 1972, Barney Miller, 1979, Diff'rent Strokes, 1979, Hart to Hart, 1980, Love Boat, 1984, Night Court, 1985-91, St. Elsewhere, 1986, Evening Shade, 1992, Family Matters, 1993, Married with Children, 1994, Coach, 1996, The Drew Carey Show, 1996, Seinfeld, 1997, Working, 1998, numerous appearances on Tonight Show with Jay Leno, 1997-99; appeared in feature films including Catch-22, 1969, McCabe and Mrs. Miller, 1970, Long Goodbye, 1972, Calif. Split, 1974, World's Greatest Lover, 1978, High Anxiety, 1978, Butch and Sundance: The Early Years, 1979, History of the World, Part I, 1981, Frances, 1983, To Be or Not To Be, 1983, Finders Keepers, 1984, Spaceballs, 1987, Rented Lips, 1987, Gleaming the Cube, 1988, C.H.U.D. II, 1988, The Player, 1992, T-Rex, 1995, (voice) The Rugrat's Movie, 1998, Boogie Nights, 1997; plays West Coast premier of Small Craft Warnings, 1975, Los Angeles revival of 12 Angry Men, 1985, Zeitgeist, 1990, House of Blue Leaves, at Cleve. Playhouse and tour Ea. Europe, 1993, The Odd Couple, Beck Ctr., Cleve., 1999; TV writer: Don Rickles Show, 1968, Mort Sahl Show, 19667; writer commls. for, Blore & Richman Inc., Los Angeles, 1966-84; numerous radio commls. and TV voice-overs, Rugrats (cartoon series), 1993. Served with U.S. Army, 1958-61. Mem. Screen Actors Guild, Actor's Equity, AFTRA, Writers Guild Am., Acad. Motion Picture Arts and Scis., Acad. TV Arts and Scis. Office: c/o Ho Reps 400 S Beverly Dr Beverly Hills CA 90212-4424

RILEY, JAMES JOSEPH, retired union executive; b. Cleve., Nov. 12, 1919; s. Frank James and Mary Jane (Connor) R.; m. Ruth Marie Pearce, Apr. 10, 1939; children—Janet M., Nancy C., Catherine A., James F., Thomas M., Dennis J., Ruth E., Mary H., John R. B.S., Western Res. U., 1940. Mem. Cleve. Motion Picture Operators Union, Local 160, 1941—; partner Electric Speed Indicator Co. (weather instrument maker), Cleve., 1965-67; bus. agt. Internat. Alliance of Theatrical Stage Employees and Moving Picture Operators of U.S. and Can., Cleve., 1967-78, internat. gen.-sec. treas., 1978-93, internat. trustee, 1969-78; v.p. Union Label and Service Trades dept. AFL-CIO, 1979-93. Editor: Bull., Internat. Alliance Quar, 1978-93. Served to lt. USNR, 1943-46, PTO. Roman Catholic. Home: 17134 Amber Dr Cleveland OH 44111-2901

RILEY, JIM L., political science educator; b. Harrisburg, Ill., Sept. 13, 1940; s. Lee Ward Riley and Helen Louise Potts; m. Stella Marie Onik (div.); m. Mary Jane Hampton, Nov. 18, 1998; children: Lee, Scott. BA, So. Ill. U., 1962, MA, 1964, PhD, 1971. Grad. asst. U. Kans., Lawrence, 1964-65; grad. asst. So. Ill. U., Carbondale, 1965-68, preceptor, 1968-71; asst. prof. polit. sci. U. Nebr., Omaha, 1970-76; prof. polit. sci. Regis U., Denver, 1976—; mem. com. on pub. edn. Colo. Supreme Ct., Denver. Contbr. articles to profl. jours. Chmn. PreLaw Advisor's Nat. Coun., 1994-96. Mem. AAUP (pres. Regis Coll. chpt. 1986-88), Western Assn. Prelaw Advisors (founder, pres. 1979-95). Republican. Avocations: skiing, web page design. Fax: (303) 964-3647. E-mail: jriley@regis.edu. Office: Regis U 3333 Regis Blvd Denver CO 80221-1099

RILEY, NORMAN, applied mathematics educator; b. Halifax, Eng., Dec. 3, 1934; s. Willie and Minnie (Parker) R.; m. Mary Ann Mansfield, Sept. 5, 1959; children: Stephen Mansfield, Susan Jane. BS, Manchester (Eng.) U., 1956, PhD, 1959. Asst. lectr. Manchester U., 1959-60; lectr. Durham (Eng.) U., 1960-64; sr. lectr. U. East Anglia, Norwich, Eng., 1964-66, reader, 1966-71, prof. applied math., 1971-99, prof. emeritus, 1999—; cons. Royal Aircraft Establishment, Farnborough, Eng., 1977-92. Contbr. rsch. papers on fluid mechanics, aerodynamics, combustion and crystal growth to profl. jours., including Jour. Fluid Mechanics, Quarterly Jour. Mechanics and Applied Math., Jour. Engring. Math., Aeronautical Jour., Jour. Crystal Growth, Combustion and Flame, others. Fellow Inst. Applied Math. (chartered). Avocations: music, photography, travel. Office: U East Anglia, Sch of Math, Norwich NR4 7TJ, England

RILEY, PATRICK ANTHONY, pathologist; b. Paris, Mar. 22, 1935; s. Bertram Hurrell and Olive (Stephenson) R.; m. Christine Elizabeth Morris, July 5, 1958; children—Sian Isobel, Caroline Anthea, Benjamin Patrick Hurrell. M.B., B.S., U. Coll., London, 1960, Ph.D., 1965, D.Sc., 1990. Research fellow Med. Research Council, London, 1969-71, Beit Meml. Univ. Coll., London, 1971-74; lectr. chem. pathology dept. Univ. Coll. London, 1974-76, reader biochem. pathology dept., 1976-84, prof. cell pathology, 1984—. Editor: Hydroxyanisole, 1984, Melanoma Rsch., 1990—. Contbr. articles to sci. publs. Fellow Royal Coll. Pathologists, Linnean Soc., (mem. council 1980-84), Inst. Biology; mem. Biol. Council of Gt. Britain (mgmt. com. 1982—), Royal Instn., Nat. Conf. Univ. Profs. (council mem., treas. 1990-93), Athenaeum Club. Avocations: reading; walking; skiing; 3-D photography. Office: UCL Med Sch, London W1P 6DB, England

RILEY, PATRICK JAMES, professional basketball coach; b. Rome, N.Y., Mar. 20, 1945; s. Leon R.; m. Chris Riley; children: James Patrick, Elisabeth. Grad., U. Ky., 1967. Guard San Diego Rockets, 1967-70; guard L.A. Lakers, 1970-75, asst. coach, 1979-81, head coach, 1981-90; head coach N.Y. Knicks, 1991-95; guard Phoenix Suns, 1975-76; broadcaster L.A. Lakers games Sta. KLAC and Sta. KHJ-TV, 1977-79, NBC Sports, 1990-91; player NBA Championship Team, 1972, coach, 1982, 85, 87, 88; head coach Miami (Fla.) Heat, 1995—. Author: The Winner Within: A Life Plan for Team Players, 1993. Named NBA Coach of Yr., 1990, 93, 97. Achievements include being a holder of NBA record most playoff wins (137). Office: Miami Heat SunTrust Int'l Ctr One SE 3rd Ave Ste 2300 Miami FL 33131-4102

RILEY, PATRICK JOHN, judge; b. Fond du Lac, Wis., Dec. 9, 1930; s. Remington Brainard and Marcella (Walsh) R.; m. Roberta L. Riley, Mar. 2, 1957; children: Kathleen Riley Stille, Michael Joseph. BA, U. Notre Dame, 1953; JD, U. Calif., Berkeley, 1956. Bar: Calif. 1956, U.S. Ct. Appeals (9th cir.) 1956, U.S. Supreme Ct. Assoc. Beverly & Weidman, Placerville, Calif., 1958-61, ptnr., 1961-62; ptnr. Beverly & Riley, Placerville, 1962-65, Riley & Peterson, Placerville, 1965-75, Riley, Peterson & Combelladi, Placerville, 1975-85, Riley, Combelladi & Drake, Placerville, 1985-89; judge El Dorodo City Superior Ctr., Placerville, 1989—; adj. prof. McGeorge Sch. of Law, U. Pacific, Sacramento, 1977-80. Trustee Placerville Union Sch. Dist., 1963-73, El Dorado Union High Sch., 1967-71; bd. dirs. Marshall Hosp., 1968-79; pub. mem. Bd. of Accountancy, State of Calif. Roman Catholic. Office: Superior Ct Dept 1 495 Main St Placerville CA 95667-5628

RILEY, PAUL RICHARD, molecular geneticist; b. Shipley, Yorkshire, Eng., Sept. 7, 1968; s. Peter Malcolm and Patricia (Walton) R. BS in Zoology with honors, Leeds U., 1990; PhD, Univ. Coll., London, 1996. Embryologist London Fertility Ctr., 1990-92; postdoctoral fellow dept. physiology R.F.H.S.M., London, 1995-96; postdoctoral rsch. fellow M.S.H.R.I., Toronto, Can., 1996-99; non-clin. lectr. Inst. Child Health, London, 1999—; reproductive biol. tng. fellowship Wellcome Trust, Can., 1997. Contbr. articles to profl. jours. Fellow Zool. Soc. London. Mem. Labour Party. Avocations: football, swimming, outdoor pursuits, attending popular and classical concerts. Office: Inst Child Health, 30 Guilford St, London WC1N 1EH, England

RILEY, RICHARD WILSON, federal official; b. Greenville, S.C., Jan. 2, 1933; s. Edward Patterson and Martha Elizabeth (Dixon) R.; m. Ann Osteen Yarborough, Aug. 23, 1957; children: Richard Wilson, Anne Y., Hubert D., Theodore D. B.A., Furman U., 1954; J.D., U. S.C., 1959. Bar: S.C. 1960. Ptnr. Riley & Riley, Greenville, 1959-78, Nelson, Mullins, Riley & Scarborough, Greenville and Columbia, S.C., 1987-93; gov. State of S.C., 1979-87; sec. U.S. Dept. Edn., Washington, 1993—; spl. asst. to subcom. U.S. Senate Jud. Com., 1960; mem. S.C. Ho. of Reps., 1963-66, S.C. Senate senate from Greenville-Laurens Dist., 1966-76. Lt. (j.g.) USNR, 1954-56. Recipient Dist. Svc. award Coun. Chief State Sch. Officers, 1994, James Bryant Conant Award, Edn. Comm. of the States, 1995, T.H. Bell award for Outstanding Edn. Advocacy Com. for Edn. Funding, 1996, Dist. Svc. award Am. Coun. on Edn., 1998. Mem. S.C., Greenville bar assns., Furman U. Alumni Assn. (pres. 1968-69), Phi Beta Kappa. Rotarian. Office: US Dept Edn 400 Maryland Ave SW Washington DC 20202-0001

RILEY, RONALD JIM, industrial engineer, consultant; b. Flint, Mich., June 10, 1950; s. Jack Robert and Rose Alice (Millard) R.; m. Laura Jean Gill, June 23, 1979; children: Meghan Kathleen, Caitlin Rose. Student, C.S. Mott C.C., Flint, 1969-70. Asst. mgr., salesman Howat Electronics, Flint, 1968-70; proprietor Customtronics, Flint, 1970-74; engr. med. equipment Werby Labs., Flint, 1974-76; plant engr. Cara Corp., Detroit, 1976-78; indsl. controls engr. Atlas Techs., Fenton, Mich., 1978-84; engr., mgr. J.N. Fauver Co. subs. Sun Oil, Madison Heights, Mich., 1984-90; inventor Riley & Assocs. Inc., Grand Blanc, Mich., 1990—; founder, exec. dir. InventorEd, Inc., 1996-2000. Contbr. articles to profl. jours.; patentee in field. Mem. ACLU, Union of Concerned Scientists, Action on Smoking and Health, Pub. Citizen, Profl. Inventors Alliance (pres. 1996-2000), Alliance for Am. Innovation Inc. (pres. adv. bd. 1996-2000), Intellectual Property Creators (adv. bd. 1995-99), Student Coalition for Handling Intellectual Property. Avocations: horticulture, carpentry, solar and renewable energy, learning. E-mail: rjriley@rjriley.com. Office: Riley & Assocs 1323 W Cook Rd Grand Blanc MI 48439-9364

RILEY, SCOTT C., lawyer; b. Bklyn., Oct. 5, 1959; s. William A. and Kathleen (Howe) R.; m. Kathleen D. O'Connor, Oct. 6, 1984; children: Matthew, Brendan. BA, Seton Hall U., South Orange, N.J., 1981; JD, Seton Hall U., Newark, 1984. Bar: N.J. 1985, U.S. Dist. Ct. N.J. 1985. Assoc. Dwyer, Connell & Lisbona, Montclair, N.J., 1985-87; assoc. gen. counsel, v.p. Consolidated Ins. Group, Wilmington, Del., 1987-91; counsel Cigna Ins. Group, Phila., 1991-94; assoc. gen. counsel KWELM Cos., N.Y.C., 1994-98, head U.S. legal ops., 1998—; head U.S. ops. Bevis Ins. Svcs. Ltd., 1998—. Mem. ABA (com. on environ. ins. coverage), Fedn. of Ins. and Corp. Counsel, Excess and Surplus Lines Claims Assn., N.J. State Bar Assn., Profl. Liability Underwriting Soc. Office: KWELM Companies 599 Lexington Ave New York NY 10022-6030

RILEY, THOMAS JOSEPH, anthropologist, educational administrator; b. Portland, Maine, Nov. 2, 1943; s. Joseph Gerard and Virginia C. (Cunningham) R.; m. Karma Jean Ibsen, July 10, 1967 (div. 1985); children: Kirsten, Katharine, Erin; m. Carol Ann, Nov. 21, 1989; 1 child, Julia Wade. BA, Boston Coll., 1965; MA, U. Hawaii, 1970, PhD, 1973. Asst. prof. NYU, 1972-74; from asst. prof. to prof. anthropology U. Ill., Urbana, 1974-96, assoc. dean Grad. Coll., 1983-86, head dept. anthropology, 1986-93, chmn. univ. senate coun., 1995-96; dean Coll. Arts, Humanities/Social Scis., prof. anthropology N.D. State U., Fargo, 1996—; dir. N.D. Inst. for Regional Studies, 1996—; acad. adv. bd. SALT Ctr., Portland, 1980-96. Co-author: Prehistoric Agriculture, 1972; mem. editl. bd. Ency. of World Cultures, 1993-96, Ency. of Cultural Anthropology, 1994-95; bd. dirs. Prairie Pub. Broadcasting, 1999—, Plains Art Mus., Fargo, 1999—; contbr. over 100 articles to profl. jours. Chmn. bd. Devel. Svcs. Ctr., Champaign, 1986-89, Human Rels. Area Files at Yale U., 1995-96, v.p. 1996; sec. bd. C-U Independence, Champaign, 1987-96; bd. dirs. Disabled Citizens Found., Champaign, 1988-96, Ill. Assn. Retarded Citizens, Chgo., 1988-94, Champaign County Mental Health Bd., 1993-96, Ill. State Hist. Sites Adv. Coun., 1986-89. NSF fellow, 1978-79; NSF grant, 1978-99. Mem. AAAS, Am. Assn. State and Local History, Am. Anthropology Assn., Ill. Archeol. Survey, Soc. Am. Archaeology, Soc. Archeol. Scis. (treas. 1982-83), Sigma Xi (chpt. v.p. 1987-88, chpt. pres. 1988-91). Roman Catholic. E-mail: thomas riley@ndsu.nodak.edu. Home: 1108 42nd Ave N Fargo ND 58102-5318 also: 155 Beach Ave Kennebunk ME 04043-7625 Office: ND State U 221 Minard Hall Fargo ND 58105

RILEY, WILLIAM, corporate executive, writer; b. Indpls., June 30, 1931; s. Leo Michael and Edna (Wilhelm) R.; m. Laura Etz, Apr. 20, 1957. AB, U. Notre Dame, 1952; LLB, Yale U., 1955. V.p., dir., chmn. Ivy Corp., Atlanta, 1960-80; CEO, chmn. Moore-Handley, Inc., Birmingham, Ala., 1981—; bd. dirs. Tru-Die, Inc., Franklin Pk., Ill., Fabco-Air, Inc., Gainesville, Fla. Author: (with Laura Riley) Guide to the National Wildlife Refuges, 1979 (Pulitzer prize nominee), 2d edit., 1993, Lifetime Conservation award Nat. Audubon Soc., 2000. Trustee The Raptor Trust, Basking Ridge, N.J., 1980—; bd. dirs. Nat. Wildlife Refuge Assn., Potomac, Md., 1985-94, Hawk Mountain Sanctuary Assn., Kempton, Pa., 1989-98, Nat. Audubon Soc., N.Y.C., 1990-94; Everglades Fdn., 1997—. With U.S. Army, 1957-58. Mem. Met. Club of N.Y.C. Office: 590 Madison Ave New York NY 10022-2524

RILEY-SMITH, JONATHAN SIMON CHRISTOPHER, history educator; b. Harrogate, U.K., June 27, 1938; s. William Henry Douglas and Elspeth Agnes Mary (Henderson) Riley-S.; m. Marie-Louise Jeannetta Field, July 27, 1968; children: Tobias Augustine William, Tamsin Elspeth Hermione, Hippolyta Clemency Magdalen. BA, Trinity Coll., Cambridge, U.K., 1960, MA, 1964, PhD, 1964. Asst. lectr. U. St. Andrews, Scotland, 1964-65, lectr., 1966-72; asst. lectr. U. Cambridge, Eng., 1972-75, lectr., 1975-78, Dixie prof. ecclesiastical history, 1994—; prof. history Royal Holloway Coll. U. London, 1978-94; fellow Queen's Coll., Cambridge, 1972-78, Emmanuel Coll., Cambridge, 1994—. Author: The Knights of St. John in Jerusalem and Cyprus, 1967, The Feudal Nobility and the Kingdom of Jerusalem, 1973, What Were the Crusades?, 1977, 2d edit., 1991, The First Crusade and the Idea of Crusading, 1986 (prix Schlumberger 1988), The Crusades, 1987, The First Crusaders, 1997, Hospitallers, 1999. Librarian Priory Scotland Most Venerable Order St. John, 1966-78, Grand Priory Most Venerable Order St. John, London, 1982—. Named Knight of Justice Most Venerable Order St. John, 1969, Knight Magistral Grace Sovreign Mil. Order Malta, 1971. Fellow Royal Hist. Soc.; mem. Soc. Study Crusades & Latin East (pres. 1987-95). Roman Catholic. Office: Emmanuel Coll, Cambridge CB2 3AP, United Kingdom

RILL, JAMES FRANKLIN, lawyer; b. Evanston, Ill., Mar. 4, 1933; s. John Columbus and Frances Eleanor (Hill) R.; m. Mary Elizabeth Laws, June 14, 1957; children: James Franklin, Roderick M. AB cum laude, Dartmouth Coll., 1954; LLB, Harvard, 1959. Bar: D.C. bar 1959. Legis. asst. Congressman James P. S. Devereux, Washington, 1952; pvt. practice Washington, 1959-89; assoc. Steadman, Collier & Shannon, 1959-63; ptnr. Collier, Shannon & Rill, 1963-69, Collier, Shannon, Rill & Scott, 1969-89; asst. atty. gen., antitrust div. U.S. Dept. Justice, Washington, 1989-92; ptnr. Collier, Shannon, Rill & Scott, Washington, 1992-2000; co-chair internat. competition policy adv. com. U.S. Dept. Justice, 1997-2000; ptnr. Howrey Simon Arnold & White, Washington, 2000—; pub. mem. Adminstrv. Conf. of U.S., 1992-94; coun. prin. Coun. for Excellence in Govt.; mem., advisor panel Office of Tech. Assessment of Multinat. Firms and U.S. Tech. Base. Contbr. articles to profl. jours. Trustee emeritus Bullis Sch., Potomac, Md. Served to 1st lt. arty. AUS, 1954-56. Fellow Am. Bar Found.; mem. ABA (antitrust law sect., past chmn.), D.C. Bar Assn., Phi Delta Theta, Met. Club, Loudon Valley Club. Home: 7305 Masters Dr Potomac MD 20854-3850 Office: Howrey Simon Arnold and White Rm 621 1299 Pennsylvania Ave NW Washington DC 20004-2400

RILLER, ULRICH PETER, geologist; b. Biberach/Riss, Germany, Feb. 11, 1965; s. Johannes Arthur and Ruth (Adler) R. Diplomgeologe, U. Tübingen (Germany), 1992; PhD, U. Toronto, 1996. Asst. prof. U. Giessen (Germany), 1997-98, Geoforschungszentrum, Potsdam, Germany, 1998—. Contbr. articles to scientific jours. Served with Music Corps, 1984-85. Scholar German Sci. Found., 1998. Mem. Am. Geophys. Union, Geol. Soc. Am. Home: Steinstr 13, 14482 Potsdam Germany Office: Geoforschungszentrum, Potsdam Telegrafenberg, 14473 Potsdam Germany

RILLING, DAVID CARL, surgeon; b. Phila., Oct. 10, 1940; s. Carl Adam and Elizabeth Barbara (Young) R.; m. Karina Sturman, Mar. 25, 1972; children: Jonathan David, Alexander Valentine, Claudia Carla. BS with honors in Biology, Dickinson Coll., Carlisle, pa., 1962; MD, Hahnemann U., 1966. Diplomate Am. Bd. Surgery. Intern Hosp. of U. Pa., Phila., 1966-67; resident Abington (Pa.) Meml. Hosp., 1967-68, 70-73; surgeon Pennridge Surg Assocs., Sellersville, Pa., 1973—; active staff Grand View Hosp., Sellersville, Pa., chmn. dept. surgery, 1985-89, pres. med. staff, 1995. Lt. col. U.S. Army, 1968-70, Vietnam, USARMC. Decorated Bronze Star medal, Nat. Def. Svc. medal, Vietnam Svc. medal. Fellow Am. Coll. Surgeons; mem. AMA, Soc. Clin. Vascular Surgery, Pa. Med. Soc., Bucks County Med. Soc., Vietnam Vascular Registry. Avocations: paleontology, tennis, skiing. Office: Pennridge Surg Assocs 670 Lawn Ave Sellersville PA 18960-1571

ŘÍMAN, JOSEF, biology educator; b. Horní Suchá, Karviná, Czechoslovakia, Jan. 30, 1925; s. Alois and Hilda (Glaserová)Ř.; m. Věra Tomková, July 16, 1950. MD, Charles U., Prague, Czechoslovakia, 1950; PhD, Czechoslovak Acad Sci., Prague, 1955, DSc in Chemistry, 1966; DSc in Biology (hon.), J.E. Purkyně U., Brno, Czechoslovakia, 1987. Rsch. physician 1st Clinic Pediatrics Charles U., Prague, 1950-51, prof. med. faculty, 1967-72; sr. scientist Inst. Organic Chemistry Czechoslovak Acad. Sci., Prague, 1951-74, founder, dir. Inst. Molecular Genetics, 1976—, sci. sec., 1978-81, v.p., 1981-86, pres., 1986-90; acad. rep. UNESCO, 1980-86; Czechoslovak nat. rep. Internat. Coun. Scientific Unions, 1982-84; dep. Ho. Nations Fed. Assembly, Prague, 1986-89; chmn. commn. INTERKOSMOS, 1986-90; founder Czechoslovak Biochemistry of Retroviruses, Inst. Molecular Genetics, Prague; participant UNESCO Symposium, Vancouver, Can., 1989. Mem. editorial bd. Neoplasma Slovak Acad. Scis., 1967, Acta Virologica, 1970, Biologica, 1982, Cancer Biochemistry and Biophysics, 1985; chmn., chief editor Czechoslovak Encyclopaedia, 1986-90; contbr. articles to profl. jours. Recipient State Prizes Govt. of Czechoslovakia, 1968, 78, J.E. Purkyne medal Govt. of Czechoslovakia, 1979, Order of Labor Govt. of Czechoslovakia, 1983, Gold medal Slovak Acad. Sci., 1989, State Prize of USSR, 1979, J. Dimitrov medal Govt. of Bulgaria, 1986, Gold Einstein-Russel Pugwash medal Pugwash Conf., 1987, Hippocrates medal Kyoto U. Med. Sch., 1988, J.E. Fogarty medal NIH, 1988, Gold medal Nagoya U. Med. Sch., 1990, Kunio Yagi Gold Meml. medal, 1990. Fellow Indian Nat. Sci. Acad. (fgn.); mem. Russian Acad. Sci. (fgn., M.L. Lomonosov Gold medal 1987), Czech Acad. Sci. (chief editor Folia Biologica 1975, G.J. Mendel Gold plaque 1975, numerous others, Medal of Honor), German Acad. Scis. (fgn.), Hungarian Acad. Sci. (hon.), Slovak Soc. Biochemistry (hon.), Czechoslovak Soc. Immunology (hon.), Bulgarian Acad. Sci. (fgn.), German Soc. Biol. Chemistry (fgn.), G.W. Leibniz Soc. (fgn.), Ctrl. European Acad. Sci. and Art., Academician. Avocation: history of science. Office: Czech Acad Sci & Inst Mol Genetics, Flemingovo n2, 166 37 Prague Czech Republic

RIMAR, STEPHEN, pediatric anesthesiologist; b. Mar. 28, 1955. BS, Yale U., 1977; MD, George Washington U., 1982; MBA, U. New Haven, 1997. Diplomate Am. Bd. Pediats., Am. Bd. Anesthesiology. Resident in pediatrics and anesthesiology Yale-New Haven Hosp.; chief pediat. anesthesiology Yale U. Sch. Medicine, New Haven, Conn., 1992-96, vice chmn. anesthesiology, 1996—, med. dir., 1999—, dir. mgmt. program for physicians, 1999—. Office: Yale Faculty Practice PO Box 9805 New Haven CT 06536-0805

RIMBOTTI, FRANCESCO MAURO, management consultant; b. Genoa, Italy, July 9, 1936; s. Luigi and Maria (Bertelli) R.; m. Maria Luisa Iannantuono, Dec. 12, 1962; 1 child, Riccardo. DBA, Inst. V. Emanuele II, Genoa. Account mgr. Edison Group, Milan, 1956-61; acctg. head ESSO (Exxon Group), Genoa, 1961-67; orgn. mgr. Rumianca, Turin, 1967-69, Fiat, Turin, 1969-70; gen. mgr. Sir Group, Milan, 1970-77; profl. mgmt. cons. Milan, 1977—; mgmt. tchr., Milan, 1982-84. Contbr. articles to profl. jours. Recipient Gold Coin award Rotary Club, 1983. Mem. Internat. Mgmt. Assn. N.Y., The Inst. of Internal Auditors, Press Club, Propellers Club. Home and Office: Viale Stelvio 43, 20159 Milan Italy

RIME, FINN, lawyer; b. Kråkstad, Norway, Jan. 2, 1926; s. Thorleif and Berit Rime; m. Randi Brun, Dec. 29, 1951; children: Karen Margrethe, Dagfinn. LLB, U. Oslo, 1952. Lawyer before Supreme Ct. of Norway. Assisting judge Alesund, Norway, 1955-57; lawyer Oslo, 1957-64, prin. firm, 1964—; lectr. seminars for Norwegian trade and industry leaders. Mem. ABA, Norwegian Bar Assn. (chmn. bankruptcy com. 1975-86),European Insolvency Practitioners Assn. (Eng.), Am. Club (Oslo). Mem. Conservative Party. Christian. Avocations: classical music, antiques, literature, art. Office: Øvre Slottsgt 12 B, 0157 Oslo Norway

RIMM, HALLIKI, psychotherapist, educator; b. Tartu, Estonia, Mar. 21, 1960; d. Aulin and Eha-Ruth (Hints) H.; step-daughter, Diana. MD, U. Tartu, 1984, applied psychologist, 1992, MSc, 1993, postgrad., 1993-98. Orthopaedist, traumatologist Maarjamõisa Hosp., U. Tartu, 1984-92, psychologist, 1992-93, physician, psychotherapist, 1993-95; psychotherapist Outpatient Clinic, U. Tartu, 1996—; lectr. U. Tartu, 1992-98, trainer, supr. faculty postgrad. med. tng., 1994—. Contbr. articles to profl. jours. Mem. gymnastics team, U. Tartu, 1980-91; participant Olympic Games, 1980, Good Will Games, Moscow, 1985, Gymnaestrada, Amsterdam, 1991. Erasmus U. scholar, 1994, Cornell Med. Ctr. scholar, 1995, 99; grantee Limburg's U., 1995, Estonian Sci. Found., 1995-97. Avocations: alternative medicine. Fax: 37 07 319136. E-mail: halliki.rimm@kliinikum.ee. Home: Tartu Postimaja PO Box 249, EE 50002 Tartu Estonia Office: Outpatient Clinic U Tartu, Puusepa 1a Str, EE 50406 Tartu Estonia

RIMOLDI, REYNOLD LOUIS, orthopedic surgeon; b. Grosse Point, Mich., June 17, 1956; s. Reynold Frank and Dorothy Ann R.; m. Kirsten Houby, Sept. 10, 1994; children: Alexandra Ann, Christian Jens. BA, Calif. State U., 1979; MD, Med. Coll. Wis., 1984. Gen. ptnr. Southwestern Ortho, Thousand Oaks, Calif., 1991-93, Western Orthopedics, Las Vegas, Nev., 1993-95, Advanced Ortho Care Assocs., Las Vegas, Nev., 1995—. Author: (with others) Hightston Sports Medical Text, 1994, Management Spine Trauma, 1996, Orthopedic Spina Trauma, 1996. Fellow ACS, Am. Acad. Ortho Surgury; mem. Am. Bd. Spine Surgery, Am. Bd. Ortho Surgery. Roman Cath. Avocations: golf, travel, wine collecting. E-mail: krimoldi@aol.com. Office: Advanced Orthopedic Care Assocs 600 South Ranchero Las Vegas NV 89103

RIMÓN, RANAN HILEL, psychiatry educator; b. Turku, Finland, Apr. 3, 1938; s. Salomon and Polja (Kagan) Portnoj; m. Anni Helena Laakso, June 16, 1967; children: Iris Bracha, Markus Mikael, Arje Salomon, Sonja Ilana. Lic. Medicine, U. Turku, 1963, MD, 1969. Commd. lt. Finnish Med. Corps, 1960, advanced through grades to col., 1973, resigned, 1974; asst. clin. chief physician U. Turku, 1967-70, asst. prof. psychiatry, 1969-72; asst. clin. prof. U. Calif., San Diego, 1971; prof., chmn. psychiatry U. Kuopio, Finland, 1974-75; vis. prof., sr. scientist Hebrew U., Israel, 1975-79; asst. prof. U. Helsinki, Finland, 1971-74, prof., 1980—. Contbr. articles to profl. jours. Mem. Finnish Med. Assn., Finnish Psychiat. Assn., Israel Med. Assn. Assn. Mil. Surgeons Finland, Assn. Scandinavian Mil. Surgeons, Scandinavian Assn. Psychopharmacologists. Home: Italahdenkatu 1A, SF-00210 Helsinki Finland Office: U Helsinki Dept Psychiatry, Lapinlahdentie, FIN00180 Helsinki Finland

RINAKER, SAMUEL MAYO, JR., retired utilities executive; b. Chgo., Sept. 29, 1922; s. Samuel Mayo and Marjorie (Horton) R.; m. Alice Benthey, Dec. 17, 1949 (div. 1974); children: Elizabeth Cherry, Samuel M. III, Laura Frazier, Mary Clark. Student, UCLA, 1941-42. Farmer Nebr. and Ill., 1946-49; exec. sec. to atty. gen. Olympia, Wash., 1949-52; news dir. Sta. KTNT-TV, Tacoma, Wash., 1952-57, Sta. KIRO-TV, Seattle, 1957-60; assoc. news dir., news anchor Sta. KGTV, San Diego, 1960-75; dir. pub. policy San Diego Gas & Electric Co., 1976-84; bd. dirs. 1st Nat. Bank, Beatrice, Neb., 1976-93. Maj. U.S. Army Air Corps, 1942-46, ETO. Mem. Rotary (bd. dirs. 1965-67), La Jolla Beach Tennis Club. Republican. Presbyterian. Avocations: golf. Home: 5935 Rutgers Rd La Jolla CA 92037-7834

RINCK, PETER A., radiologist, research scientist; b. Plochingen, Germany, Dec. 7, 1953. MD, Free U. Berlin, 1979, PhD, 1980; MD, U. Mons-Hainaut, Belgium, 1986, U. Trondheim, Norway, 1987. Resident radiology, nuclear medicine, radiation therapy Charlottenburg U. Hosp. dept. radiology, radiation therapy and nuclear medicine Free U. Berlin, 1979-82; sr. rsch. assoc. dept. chemistry and exptl. radiology SUNY, Stony Brook, 1982-83; physician in charge Deutsche Klinik Diagnostik Nuclear Magnetic Resonance Group, Wiesbaden, Ger., 1983-84; resident conventional, interventional, computed radiology dept. radiology Wiesbaden Gen. Hosp., 1984-85; sr. lectr. med. faculty Nuc. Magnetic Resonance Lab. U. Mons-Hainaut (Belgium), Mons, 1986-87, vis. prof. Med. Faculty, 1994—; head med. sect. Magnetic Resonance Ctr., prof. radiology and magnetic resonance U. Trondheim (Norway), 1987-94; scientific adv. Found. Scientific and Indsl. Rsch. Norwegian Inst. Tech., Trondheim, 1990-91; lectr. Johann Gutenberg U., Mainz, Ger., 1983-85; vis. prof. Neurol. Inst. Colombia, Bogotá, 1986, radiology Humboldt U., Berlin, 1991-92; sr. lectr. State U. Mons, Belgium, 1985—; vis. physician Loyola Med. Ctr. dept. nuclear medicine, Chgo., 1980; dir. IV internat. course med. physics, Bogotá, 1990; expert Commn. European Cmties. concerted rsch. project, 1994, 99; cons. magnetic resonance imaging techniques U.N. Indsl. Devel. Orgn., 1990, Norwegian Medicine Control Auth., 1993; chmn. nominating com. European Magnetic Resonance award; mem. scientific com. Lucien Appel prize for neuroradiology; presenter in field. Author, editor: 7 books; asst. editor: Jour. Magnetic Resonance Imaging; mem. editl. bd.: Diagnostic Imaging Europe; contbr. 100 articles to profl. jours. Chmn. bd. European Magnetic Resonance Forum Found., 1991—. Max-Kade rsch. fellow Max Kade Found., 1981; rsch. grantee Deutsche Forschungsgemeinschaft, 1985, 86; collaborative rsch. program grantee NATO scientific affairs divsn., 1989; recipient Feodor-Lynen award Alexander von Humboldt Found., 1981, award BIOMED rsch. program Commn. European Cmties., 1992, 94, awards Fonds Nat. Recherche Scientifique Belgique, 1993, 94. Mem. European Workshop on Magnetic Resonance in Medicine (lectr. 1982—, mem. exec. com. 1982—, pres. annual meetings 1984, 89, mem. steering com. European Congresses of Magnetic Resonance in Medicine and Biology, 1987-92), Internat. Soc. Magnetic Resonance in Medicine, European Soc. Magnetic Resonance, Radiol. Soc. N.Am. (corr.), German Roentgen Soc., Egyptian Soc. Radiology and Nuclear Medicine (hon.). Office: EMRF Found, PO Box 1235, CH-6648 Minusio Switzerland

RINCON, FREDDY, professional soccer player; b. Buenaventura, Colombia, Aug. 14, 1966. Midfielder Napoli Football Club, Italy, 1994-95, Real Madrid Football Club, Spain, 1995-96, Corinthians Football Club, Brazil, Colombian Nat. Team, 1998, Santos; winner Colombian League Title (with Am. Cali), 1990, 92, Brazilian Championship (with Palmeiras), 1993. Office: care Brazil Football, Rue de Alfandega 70, 20070001 Rio de Janeiro Brazil*

RINDEL, JENS HOLGER, acoustical engineer, educator, researcher; b. Copenhagen, Denmark, May 28, 1947; s. Sofus and Rigmor (Skipper) R.; m. Anne Kirstine Fabricius, Oct. 31, 1970 (div. 1994); children: Christine, Bodil, Louise. MS, Tech. U. Denmark, 1971, PhD, 1977. Lectr. Tech. U. Denmark, Lyngby, 1975-77, sr. lectr., 1977-90, assoc. prof., 1990—; acoustical expert Nat. Bd. Testing, Denmark, 1982-86, Danish Broadcasting Corp., 1986-89; vis. prof. U. Sydney, Australia, 1991; guest rschr. PTB, Braunschweig, Germany, 1993; rschr. Norwegian Bldg. Rsch. Inst., Oslo, 1998-99. Author, editor: Indoor Climate - Sound, 1979; author: Building Acoustics, 1989; contbr. articles to profl. publs. Recipient award Radio Parts Foundation, Copenhagen, 1990; San Cataldo grantee, Italy, 1993. Fellow Inst. Acoustics (U.K.); mem. Acoustical Soc. Am., Australian Acoustical Soc., Acoustical Soc. Scandinavia (pres. 1992-98). Avocation: playing flute. Office: Tech U Denmark, Bldg 352, DK-2800 Lyngby Denmark

RINDERMANN, HEINER, psychologist, researcher; b. Cologne, Germany, Mar. 12, 1966; s. Wigbert and Karin (Handel) R. Dr. and Diploma in Psychology, Wilhelmi-Gymnasium, Sinsheim, Germany, 1985; PhD, Heidelberg U., 1995. Asst. prof./rschr. in psychology U. Munich, 1994-99; asst. prof., rschr. in psychology U. Magdeburg, 1999—. Contbr. articles to profl. jours.; author of books. Mem. Germany Soc. Psychology, German Soc. Herpetology. Avocations: photography, nature, graffity. Office: Inst Psych Otto-von, Guericke-U Postfach 4120, 39016 Magdeburg Germany

RINDONE, JOSEPH PATRICK, clinical pharmacist, educator; b. Santa Fe, Oct. 4, 1954; s. Guido Salvatore and Elizabeth Ann (Murphy) R.; m. Diane Marie Rollins, June 11, 1991; children: Jacqueline, Alexandra. BS, U. Nebr., 1977; PharmD, Creighton U., 1978. Lic. pharmacist, Nebr., Calif. Staff pharmacist Bergan Mercy Hosp., Omaha, 1978; staff pharmacist Phoenix (Ariz.) VA Med. Ctr., 1978-81, clin. resident, 1981; clin. pharmacist Tucson VA Med. Ctr., 1982-93; assoc. prof. U. Ariz., Tucson, 1982—; clin. pharmacist Prescott (Ariz.) VA Med. Ctr., 1993—, rsch. coord., 1994—. Author: Therapeutic Monitoring of Antibiotics, 1991; contbr. articles to Arch. Internal Medicine, Pharmacotherapy, Clin. Therapeutics, Am. Jour. Cardiology, Am. Jour. Therapeutics, Chest, West Jour. Medicine, Am. Jour. Health Sys. Pharm., Jour. AMA. Regents scholar U. Nebr., 1976. Mem. Ariz. Soc. Hosp. Pharmacists. Avocations: sports, photography, bridge, astronomy.

RINEHART, JAMES FORREST, educator; b. Kansas City, Mo., Dec. 1, 1950; s. Kenneth Perry and Eleanor Louise (Lane) R.; m. Betty Keller, Feb. 3, 1973; children: Erica Christine, Andrew James. BA, U. Fla., 1972; M of Social Sci., Syracuse U., 1991, PhD, 1993. Vis. prof. internat. rels. U. Tenn., Chattanooga, 1993-95; dir., prof. grad. program in internat. rels. U.S. Army John F. Kennedy Spl. Warfare Sch. Troy State U., 1995—, lectr. regional studies program, 1996—. Author: Revolution and the Millennium: China, Mexico and Iran, 1997; contbr. articles to profl. jours. Mem. Coun. on Peace Rsch. in History, 1992-94; founding mem. Mediation Svcs. Task Force for Chattanooga, 1991-95; active Program on Analysis and Resolution of Conflict, Syracuse U., 1991-93; bd. dirs. Ulster Project Chattanooga, 1993-94. Capt. USAR, 1972-80. Recipient Cert. of Achievement U.S. Army JFK Spl. Warfare Ctr. and Sch., 1996. Mem. Am. Polit. Sci. Assn., Internat. Studies Assn, Soc. for Scientific Study of Religion, Internat. Soc. Polit. Psychology, Am. Radio Relay League, Pinewild Country Club, Phi Gamma Delta, Fla. Blue Key Soc. Democrat. Presbyterian. Home: 16 Tayport Ct Pinehurst NC 28374-9752 Office: US Army JFK Spl Warfare Sch Attn AOJK-GP-C Fort Bragg NC 28307

RINER, RONALD NATHAN, cardiologist, business consultant; b. Mar. 7, 1949. AB, Princeton U., 1970; MD, Cornell U., N.Y.C., 1974. Diplomate Am. Bd. Internal Medicine, Am. Bd. Cardiovasc. Disease. Resident in internal medicine N.Y. Hosp., Meml. Sloan-Kettering, Hosp. for Spl. Surgery, 1974-76; resident in cardiology Mayo Grad. Sch. Medicine, Rochester, Minn., 1976-79; chmn. dept. internal medicine St. Mary's Health Ctr., St. Louis, 1980-82, program dir. internal medicine, 1979-82; pvt. practice St. Louis, 1979-95; asst. prof. medicine, Washington U. Med. Ctr., 1985-88, pres. Riner Group, Inc., 1980—, Riner Heart Group, Inc., 1980-95; sr. sci. advisor pharm. divsn. BioMed Sys., St. Louis, 1984-95; prof. St. Louis U.; corp. dir. quality affairs SSM Health Care Sys. 1989-91; chmn. Mo. State Med. Assn. Commn. on Med. Econs., 3rd Party Medicine and Govt. Rels., 1990-92; v.p. clin. svcs. Daus. Charity Nat. Health Sys., 1991-95; bd. dirs. Alleghany Health Sys., Tampa, Fla., 1991-96, chmn. bd. dirs., 1994-96; bd. dirs. Horizon/CMS Healthcare, 1996-98, Seton Inst. for Internat. Devel., San Francisco, 1995-97. Bd. dirs. Seton Inst. for Internat. Devel., San Francisco, 1995-97; bd. dirs. Liferate Sys., Inc., 1997-99; bd. dirs. Assn. for Corp. Growth, 1998—, Mathew Dickey Acad., St. Louis, Mo., 1998—. Editor practice mgmt. and econs. sect. Jour. Invasive Cardiology, 1996—. Fellow Inst. for Advanced Study in Internat. Bus., Washington U., 1991. Fellow ACP, Am. Coll. Cardiology, Am. Acad. Med. Dirs.; mem. AAAS, N.Y. Acad. Scis. (life), Mo. Soc. Internal Medicine (coun.), Gov. Rel. Com., Am. Acad. Physician Execs., Mayo Alumni Assns., Am. Cons. League, Am. Mgmt. Assn., Cornell U. Alumni Assn., Princeton Alumni Assn., Princeton U. Club. Office: The Riner Group Inc 1034 S Brentwood Blvd Ste 1640 Saint Louis MO 63117-1216

RING, CLARE CHARLOTTE, information systems specialist; b. Bristol, Eng., Sept. 26, 1950; d. Gerald William and Margaret Hetty (Guthrie) R.; m. Stacey Philip Bernard (div. 1985). BSc with honors, Leeds (Eng.) U., 1973; MBA, South Bank U., London, 1999. Dept. head Manchester (Eng.) Edn. Com., 1974-79; sales mgr. CLAAS, Bury St. Edmunds, Eng., 1979-85; software mgr. Micro Bus. Sys. plc, Eton, Eng., 1985-88; bus. analyst Constrn. Industry Tng. Bd., Kings, Eng., 1988-95; sr. mgr. info. sys. Braintree (Eng.) Coll., 1995—; cons. in field. Mem. Ch. of Eng. Avocations: golf, internet, reading. Office: Braintree Coll, Church Ln, Braintree CM7 5SN, England

RING, LEONARD M., lawyer; b. Taurage, Lithuania, May 11, 1923; came to U.S., 1930, naturalized, 1930; s. Abe and Rose (Kahn) R.; m. Donna R. Cecrle, June 29, 1959; children—Robert Steven, Susan Ruth. Student, N.Mex. Sch. Mines, 1943-44; LLB, DePaul U., 1949, JD; LLD (hon.), Suffolk U., 1990. Bar Ill. 1949. Spl. asst. atty. gen. State Ill., Chgo., 1967-72; spl. atty. Ill. Dept. Ins., Chgo., 1967-73; spl. trial atty. Met. San. Dist. Greater Chgo., 1967-77; lectr. civil trial, appellate practice, tort law Nat. Coll. Advocacy, San Francisco, 1971, 72; chmn. and spl. atty. com. jury instrns. Ill. Supreme Ct., 1967—; nat. chmn. Attys. Congl. Campaign Trust, Washington, 1975-79. Author: (with Harold A. Baker) Jury Instructions and Forms of Verdict, 1972. Editorial bd. Belli Law Jour., 1983—; adv. bd. So. Ill. U. Law Jour., 1983—. Contbr. chpts. to books including Callaghan's Illinois Practice Guide, Personal Injury, 1988 and chpt. 6 (Jury Selection and Persuasion) for Masters of Trial Practice, also numerous articles to profl. jours. Trustee, Roscoe Pound-Am. Trial Lawyers Found., Washington, 1978-80; chmn. bd. trustees Avery Coonley Sch., Downers Grove, Ill., 1974-75. Served with U.S. Army, 1943-46. Decorated Purple Heart. Fellow Am. Coll. Trial Lawyers, Internat. Acad. Trial Lawyers, Internat. Soc. Barristers, Inner Circle Advs.; mem. Soc. Trial Lawyers, Am. Judicature Soc., Appellate Lawyers Assn. (pres. 1974-75), Assn. Trial Lawyers Assn. (nat. pres. 1973-74), Ill. Trial Lawyers Assn. (pres. 1966-68), Trial Lawyers for Pub. Justice (founder, pres. 1990-91), Chgo. Bar Assn. (bd. mgrs. 1971-73, 2d v.p. 1993), ABA (coun. 1983—, chair tort and ins. sect. 1989—, fed. jud. standing com. 7th cir. 1991—), Ill. Bar Assn., Kans. Bar Assn. (hon., life), Lex Legion Bar Assn. (pres. 1976-78), Met. Club, Plaza Club, Meadow Club, River Club, Monroe Club. Home: Ginger Creek 6 Royal Vale Dr Oak Brook IL 60523-1648 Office: Ill Supreme Ct PO Box 4987 Oak Brook IL 60522-4987

RING, LUCILE WILEY, lawyer; b. Kearney, Nebr., Jan. 2, 1920; d. Myrtie Mercer and Alice (Cowell) W.; m. John Robert Ring, Mar. 28, 1948; children: John Raymond, James Wiley, Thomas Eric. AB, U. Nebr., Kearney, 1944; JD, Washington U., 1946. Bar: Mo. 1946, U.S. Dist. Ct. (ea. dist.) Mo. 1947, U.S. Ct. Appeals (8th cir.) 1972. Atty.-adviser, chief legal group adjudications br. Army Fin. Ctr., St. Louis, 1946-52; exec. dir. lawyer referral svcs. St. Louis Bar, 1960-70; pvt. practice St. Louis, 1960-2000; staff law clk. U.S. Ct. Appeals (8th cir.), St. Louis, 1970-72; exec. dir. St. Louis Com. on Cts., 1972-85; legal advisor Mo. State Anat. Bd., 1965-95; adj. prof. adminstrv. law Webster Coll., Webster Groves, Mo., 1977-78; mem. Mo. Profl. Liability Rev. Bd., State of Mo., 1977-79. Author, editor: Guide to Community Services - Who Do I Talk To, 1974, 75, 76-79, St. Louis Court Directories, 1972, 73, 74, 75, Felony Procedures in St. Louis Courts, 1975; author: Breaking Barriers: The St. Louis Legacy of Women in Law 1869-1969, 1996; author (series): Women Lawyers in St. Louis History, 1996, Women Breaking Barriers, 1998; contbr. articles to profl. jours. Mem. Mo. Mental Health Authority, 1964-65; bd. dirs., v.p. Drug and Substance Abuse Coun., met. St. Louis, 1976-83; mem. adv. coun. St. Louis Agy. on Tng. and Employment, 1976-83; mem. Mayor's Jud. Reform Subcom., St. Louis, 1974-76. Washington U. Sch. Law scholar, 1944-46; 1st Mo. woman nominated for St. Louis Ct. Appeals, Mo. Appellate Commn., 1972; 1st woman nominated judgeship Mo. Non-Partisan Ct. Plan, 1972; recipient letter of commendation Office of Chief of Fin., U.S. Army, 1952, Outstanding Alumni award U. Nebr., Kearney, 1994. Mem. Bar Assn. Met. St. Louis (v.p. 1975-76), Legal Svcs. Ea. Mo., Inc. (v.p. 1978-79, dir.), Legal Aid Soc. St. Louis City and County (bd. dirs. 1977-78), HUD Women and Housing Commn. (commr. 1975), Women's Bar Assn. (treas. St. Louis chpt. 1949-50), Mo. Assn. Women Lawyers (treas. 1959-60, pres. 1960-61), Pi Kappa Delta, Sigma Tau Delta, Xi Phi, Washington U. Dental Faculty Wives (pres. 1972-74). Methodist. Home and Office: 2041 Reservoir Loop Rd Selah WA 98942-9616

RINGELSTEIN, ERICH BERND, neurology educator; b. Boppard on the Rhine, Germany, Jan. 9, 1948; s. Anton and Katharina (Muders) R.; m. Hannelore Wirz, Oct. 19, 1974; children: Adrian, Marius. MD, Johannes-Gutenberg U., Mainz, Germany, 1973. Diplomate Bd. Psychiatry and Neurology, Germany. Intern various hosps., Mainz, Wiesbaden, Germany, 1973-75; rsch. fellow dept. neuropathology U. Hosp. Mainz, 1976-77; fellow State of Hessia Psychiat. Hosp., Hadamar, Germany, 1977-79; fellow dept. neurology U. Hosp. Aachen (Germany), 1980-82, fellow dept. neuroradiology, 1982-83, attending physician neurology, 1983-86, vice chmn., sr. attending neurologist, assoc. prof. neurology, 1986-92; prof., chmn. dept. neurology U. Hosp. WWU, Muenster, Germany, 1992—; with dept. neurology, dept. hematology Scripps Clinic and Rsch. Found., La Jolla, Calif., 1986, 87, dept. neurology U. N.C., Winston-Salem, 1986, dept. epileptology U. Hosp. Bonn, Germany, 1988-89; cons., reviewer of jours. in field. Editor: New Trends in Diagnosis and Management of Stroke, 1987; editor New Trend in Cerebral Neurodynamics and Neurosonology, 1997; mem. editl. bd. Stroke. Bd. dirs. Stiftung Schlaganfall-Hilfe, Guetersloh, 1994—. Capt. German Army, 1975-76. Recipient Hugo Spatz prize German Neurol. Soc., 1992; named Educator of Yr., 1993. Fellow World Fedn. Neurology (bd. dirs. Rsch. Group Neurosonology), Am. Heart Assn. (stroke coun.); mem. European Neurol. Soc., German Soc. Neurology, German Soc. Neuroradiology, German Soc. of Clin. Neurophysiology, German Angiological Soc. (bd. dirs. 1992-96), German Soc. Ultrasound in Medicine, German Soc. Neurol. Rehab. Roman Catholic. Avocations: aerobics, sailing, travelling, restaurants, wines. Office: U Hosp WWU Dept Neurology, Albert Schweitzer Str 33, 48129 Münster Germany

RINGER, DARRELL WAYNE (DAN), lawyer; b. Elizabeth, N.J., Apr. 14, 1948; s. Darrell Wayne and Elva (Brown) R.; m. Rebecca Ruth Bonner, Feb. 23, 1979; children: Daniel Benjamin, Darren Wayne. BS in Physics, W.Va. U., 1971; MBA, U. N.D., 1975; JD, W.Va. U., 1978. Bar: W.Va. 1978, U.S. Dist. Ct. (no. and so. dists.) W.Va. 1978. Assoc. Jones, Williams, West & Jones, Clarksburg, W.Va., 1978-80, Moreland & Ringer, Morgantown, W.Va., 1980-83, Reeder, Shuman, Ringer & Wiley, Morgantown, 1983-91, Ringer Law Offices, Morgantown, 1991—; 1st asst. prosecutor Monongalia County, W.Va., 1985-87; host W.Va. Pub. TV, PBS Pub. Affairs Programming, 1991—. Bd. dirs. Monongalia County (W.Va.) Mental Health Assn., Morgantown, 1981-83; mem. W.Va. U. Animal Care and Use Com., 1985—. Capt. USAF, 1971-75. Named W.Va. Bar Found. Lawyer Citizen of Yr., 1996. Mem. ABA (named Sole Practitioner of Yr., 2000), ATLA, W.Va. State Bar (pres. 1999-2000), Monongalia County Bar Assn. (sec. 1980-92), W.Va. Trial Lawyers Assn. (bd. govs. 1982-91). Democrat. Avocation: amateur radio. Home: 18 W Front St Morgantown WV 26501-4507 Office: 68 Donley St Morgantown WV 26501-5907

RINGERTZ, HANS GÖSTA, radiology educator; m. Brittmarie Ringertz, 1963; three children. MB, Karolinka Inst., Stockholm, 1960, MD, 1964, PhD in Biophysics magna cum laude, 1969. Swedish med. lic.; cert. specialist family practice and diagnostic radiology. Intern dept. internal medicine Karolinska Hosp., Stockholm, 1962-63, intern dept. radiology, 1964; asst. dept. med. physics Karolinska Inst., Stockholm, 1962, 1st asst. dept. med. physics, 1963, rsch. asst. dept. physiology and med. physics, 1964-69, prof., chmn., 1984—; resident dept. diagnostic radiology Karolinska Hosp., Stockholm, 1969-73, asst. head dept. pediat. radiology, 1973-77; chmn. dept. radiology Sach's Pediat. Hosp., Stockholm, 1978-84; assoc. prof. biophysics Karolinska Inst., Stockholm, 1969-73, assoc. prof. radiology, 1973-84; vis. fellow dept. radiology U. Calif., San Francisco, 1975, vis. prof. dept. radiology, 1983-84; asst. adminstrv. head All Diagnostic Svcs. So. Sector, Stockholm, 1980-82, 86-87, adminstrv. head, 1982-84; lectr. dept. machinery engring. Royal Inst. Tech., Stockholm, 1980-82; chmn. dept. radiology Huddinge U. Hosp., Stockholm, 1984-87; mem. coording and monitoring com. Merrell Dow Rsch. Inst., Cin., 1985-93; chmn. dept. radiology Karolinska Hosp., Stockholm, 1987-94; expert radiol. scis. Swedish Govt. Nat. Bd. Health and Welfare, 1987—; expert The Swedish Coun. on Tech. Assessment in Health Care, 1989-95; med. advisor, local chmn. Swedish Nat. Inst. Radiation Protection, Stockholm County Coun., Swedish Nat. Bd. Health and Welfare, 1989-95; mem. Internat. Commn. on Radiation Protection Com. 3, Protection in Medicine, 1993—. Ad hoc referee Acta Crystalographica, 1969-71, Acta Radiologica Diagnosis, 1975—, Acta Pediatrica Scandinavica, 1980—, Clin. Physiology, 1988—, European Jour. Radiology, 1988—, Jour. Internal Medicine, 1991—, Quality Assurance in Health Care, 1992—, Pediat. Rsch., 1996—, Pediat. Radiology, 1997—; mem. editl. bd. Current Opinion in Radiology, 1988—, Investigative Radiology, 1989-94, European Radiology, 1990—, Radiologia Diagnostica, 1990—, Acad. Radiology, 1994-97, assoc. editor, 1997—; mem. editl. bd. Asian Oceanian Jour. Radiology, 1996—. Mem. Internat. Assn. Radiology (Swedish del. 1977—, commn. on standardization in PACS 1991—, others), European Assn. Radiology (commn. jr. mem. 1977-84, Swedish del. in the assembly 1979-97, auditor 1991-95, v.p. 1995-97, pres. 1997-99, others), European Soc. Pediat. Radiology (hon.), European Congress Radiology Found. (founder), European Congress Radiology Assn. (founder), Swedish Acad. Med. Scis. (voting del. for diagnostic radiology in the assembly of the acad 1974—, exec. bd. 1980-85, nominating com. 1987-90, asst. auditor 1992-98, others), Swedish Soc. Pediat. Radiology, Swedish Soc. Radiation Physics, Swedish Soc. Med. Radiology (hon., newsletter editor 1974-79, sec. gen. 1974-79, exec. bd. 1980-90, v.p. 1994-95, acting pres. 1995, pres. 1996-98, others), Scandinavian Soc. Med. Radiology (hon., Swedish del. exec. bd. 1976-79, treas. 1980-96, others), Radiol. Soc. N.Am. (hon., mem. com. on internat. radiology edn. 1996—), Danish Soc. Diagnostic Radiology (corr.), Finnish Soc. Med. Radiology (corr.), Norwegian Soc. Med. Radiology (corr.), Am. Roentgen Ray Soc., Assn. Univ. Radiologists (com. on internat. affairs 1993—, meml. award com. 1996). Avocations: carpentry, painting, sailing, tennis, golf. E-mail: hari@adr.ks.se. Fax: 468 5177 6000. Office: Dept Radiology, Karolinska Hosp, SE-17176 Stockholm Sweden

RINGGOLD, FAITH, artist; b. N.Y.C., Oct. 8, 1930. BS, CCNY, 1955, MA, 1959; DFA (hon.), Moore Coll. Art, Phila., 1986, Coll. Wooster, Ohio, 1987, Mass. Coll. Art, Boston, 1991, CCNY of CUNY, 1991, Russell Sage Coll., Troy, N.Y., 1996, Parsons Sch. Design, 1996; DSc (hon.), Brockport (N.Y.) State U., 1992, Calif. Coll. Arts and Crafts, Oakland, 1993; DHL (hon.), Malloy Coll., 1997. Art tchr. N.Y. Pub. Schs., 1955-73; lectr. Bank St. Coll. Grad. Sch., N.Y.C., 1970-80; prof. art U. Calif., San Diego, 1984—. Solo exhbns. include Spectrum Gallery, N.Y.C., 1967, 70 10 year retrospective, Studio Mus. in Harlem, N.Y.C., 1984, Bernice Steinbaum Galleryn N.Y.C., 1987-88, Balt. Mus., Deland (Fla.) Mus., Faith Ringgold 25 Yr. Survey Fine Arts Mus. L.I., Hempstead, 1990-93, Textile Mus., Washington, 1993, Children's Mus. of Manhattan, N.Y.C., 1993-95, Hewlett-Woodmere Pub. Libr., Hewlett, N.Y., 1993-94, St. Louis Art Mus., 1994, Athenaeum, La Jolla, Calif., 1995, A.C.A. Gallery, N.Y.C., 1995, 98, Ind. U. of Pa., 1995, Bowling Green State U., Ind., 1996, New Mus. Contemporary Art, N.Y.C., 1998; exhibited in group shows at Harlem Cultural Coun., N.Y.C., 1996, Meml. Exhibit for MLK, Mus. Modern Art N.Y.C., 1968, Chase Manhattan Bank Collection, Martha Jackson Gallery, N.Y.C., 1970, Am. Women Artists, Gedok, Kunstalle, Hamburg, Ger., 1972, Jubliee, Boston Mus. Fine Arts, 1975, Major Contemporary Women Artists, Suzanne Gross Gallery, Phila., 1984, Committed to Print Mus. Modern Art, N.Y.C., 1988, The Art of Black Am. in Japan, Terada Warehouse, Tokyo, Made in the USA, Art in the 50s and 60s U. Calif. Berkeley Art Mus., Craft Today Poetry of the Physical, Am. Craft Mus., N.Y.C., Portraits and Homage to Mothers Hecksher Mus. Huntington, 1987, N.J. State Mus., Trenton, 1992-94, Fukui Fine Art Mus., Fuki, Japan, 1992, Takushima Modern Art Mus., Japan, 1993, Otani Meml. Art Mus., Japan, 1993, Salina Art Ctr., Kans., 1993, Bruce Watkins Ctr. Kansas City, Mo., 1993, Barton County C.C., Great Bend, Kans., 1993, Del. State Coll. Arts Ctr. Gallery, Dover, 1993-94, Roswell Mus. and Art Ctr., N.Mex., 1994, Aknaton Gallery, Cairo, Alexandria, Egypt, Exit Art, N.Y.C., 1994, New Mus. Contemporary Art, N.Y.C., 1996, Spellman Coll. Mus., Atlanta, 1996, Whitney Mus., N.Y.C., 1996, Centre Georges Pompidou, Paris, 1997, Mus. Art, Ft. Lauderdale, Fla., 1997, N.J. Ctr. Arts, Summit, N.J., 1997, Trout Gallery Dickenson Coll., Carlisle, Pa., numerous others; represented in collections at Chase Manhattan Bank, N.Y.C., Philip Morris Collection, N.Y.C., Children's Mus., Bklyn., Newark Mus., The Women's House of Detention, Rikers Island, N.Y., The Studio Mus., N.Y.C., High Mus., Atlanta, Guggenheim Mus., Met. Mus. Art, Boston Mus. Fine Arts, MOMA, AARP, Washington, Am. Craft Mus., N.Y.C., Clark Mus., Williamstown, Mass., ARCO Chem., Phila., Coca-Cola, Atlanta, Ft. Wayne Mus. Fine Art, Ind., Harold Washington Libr. Ctr., Chgo., Lang Comm. Corp., Coll., Phila. Mus. Art, Pub. Art Pub. Schs., P.S. 22, Bklyn., Spenser Mus. Lawr., Kans., St. Louis Mus. Art, Balt. Mus., Nat. Mus., Washington, Woman's Mus., Washington, Eugenio Maria de Hostos C.C., N.Y.C., MTA 125th St. IRT subway sta. installation, N.Y.C., numerous others; author: Tar Beach, 1991, Aunt Harriet's Underground Railroad in the Sky, 1992 (Picture Book award 1993, Best Children's Book of Yr. 1993), Dinner at Aunt Connie's House, 1993 (Reading Magic award 1993), We Flew Over the Bridge: Memoirs of Faith Ringgold, 1995, Talking to Faith Ringgold, 1995, Bonjour Lonnie, 1996, My Dream of Martin Luther King, Jr., 1996; contbr. articles to profl. jours. Recipient AAUW travel award to Africa, 1976; John Simon Guggenheim Meml. Found. Fellowship (painting), 1987, N.Y. Found. for Arts award (painting), 1988, Nat. Endowment Arts award (sculpture), 1978, (painting) 1989, La Napoule Found. award (painting in So. of France), 1990, Video and Software award Calif. children's book, 1991, Parent's Choice Gold award, 1991, Artist award Studio Mus., Harlem, 1991, Artist of Yr. award Sch. Art League N.Y., 1991, Coretta Scott King award for illustration, 1992, Dist. Artist award Nat. Coun. Art Adminstrs., 1992, award, 1993, Arts Internat. award (travel to Morocco), 1992, Honors award for outstanding achievement in the visual arts Woman's Caucus Arts, N.Y., 1994, Towsend Harris medal City Coll. Alumni Assn., 1995, N.J. Artist of Yr. award N.J. Ctr. Visual Arts, 1997, 31st NAACP Image award, 1999. Home: PO Box 429 Englewood NJ 07631-0429 Office: ACA Gallery 529 W 20th St Fl 5 New York NY 10011-2800

RINGHOLM, BOSSE, federal official; b. Malmo, Jan. 11, 1950; married, 2 children. BA in Law, Lund U., 1975. Mem. Malmo City Coun., 1973-79; prin. adminstrv. officer Malmo, 1976-79; chmn. Malmo SDP, 1983; vice chmn. Parlimentary Com. on Justice, 1986-88; mem. SDP Exec., 1987; chmn. Com. on Swedish Security Svc., 1989-90, Govt. Offices Econ. Crimes Inquiry, 1994-98, Com. of Inquiry into Police Command Orgn., 1997-98; min. of fin. Ministry of Fin., Stockholm, 1998—. Mem. Social Dem. Party. Office: Ministry of Fin, Rödbodgatan 6, S-10333 Stockholm Sweden*

RINGLER, JEROME LAWRENCE, lawyer; b. Detroit, Dec. 26, 1948. BA, Mich. State U., 1970; JD, U. San Francisco, 1974. Bar: Calif. 1974, U.S. Ct. Appeals (9th cir.) 1974, U.S. Dist. Ct. (no. dist.) Calif. 1974, U.S. Dist. Ct. (ctrl. dist.) Calif. 1975, U.S. Dist. Ct. (so. dist.) Calif. 1981. Assoc. Parker, Stansbury et al, L.A., 1974-76; assoc. Fogel, Feldman, Ostrov, Ringler & Klevens, Santa Monica, Calif., 1976-80, ptnr., 1980—; arbitrator L.A. Superior Ct. Arbitration Program, 1980-85. Named Verdictum Juris Trial Lawyer of Yr., 1996. Mem. ATLA, ABA, State Bar Calif., L.A. County Bar Assn. (litigation sect., exec. com. 1994—), L.A. Trial Lawyers Assn. (bd. govs. 1981—, treas. 1988, sec. 1989, v.p. 1990, pres.-elect 1991, pres. 1992, Trial Lawyer of the Yr. 1987), Calif. Trial Lawyers Assn., Am. Bd. Trial Advs. (assoc. 1988, adv. 1991), Inns of Ct. (master). Avocations: skiing, tennis. Office: Fogel Feldman Ostrov Ringler & Klevens 1620 26th St # 100S Santa Monica CA 90404-4013

RINGOIR, SEVERIN MARIA GHISLENUS, medical educator, physician; b. Aalst, Belgium, June 17, 1931; s. Benoni and Mariette (Vlasschaert) R.; children: Marc, Yves. MD, U. Gent, Belgium, 1956, PhD, 1967. Resident Med. Clinic U. Gent, 1958-61, instr., 1961-71, assoc. prof., 1971-75, prof. nephrology, 1975-96, chief renal divsn., 1971-96, chmn. medicine, 1981-84; chmn. biomed engring. program U. Gent, 1991-94; pres. Inst. Biomed. Tech. Ghent U., 1995-97; chmn. 1st Internat. Symposium Single Cannula Hemodialysis, Tampa, Fla., 1984; co-founder Internat. Faculty Artificial Organs. Inventor pressure-pressure single cannula hemodialysis; contbr. sci. articles to profl. jours. Maj. Mil. Health Svc., 1956-58, Res., 1958-89. Decorated comdr. Order of Leopold, Grand officer Order of Crown (Belgium); recipient J. Lemaire prize, 1970, Internat. Disting. medal Nat. Kidney Found. U.S.A., 1991. European Dialysis and Transplant Assn. (coun. 1981-84, pres. 1985 Congress), European Soc. for Artificial Organs (gov. 1988-92, pres. Congress 1989), Internat. Soc. Artificial Organs (v.p. 1981-85, gen. sec. 1984-90). Home: Vaderlandstraat 44, B9000 Ghent Belgium

RINGSTAD, VIDAR JOHAN, research scientist, writer; b. Ulstein, Sunnmøre, Norway, Jan. 23, 1939; s. Vilhelm and Johanne (Osnes) R.; m. Anne Rollem, Dec. 19, 1969; children: Gry, Tron, Vegard. Cand. oecon., U. Oslo, 1965, PhD, 1971. Rsch. fellow U. Oslo, 1965-71; rschr. Statistics Norway, Oslo, 1971-73; prof. Telemark Coll., Bø, Norway, 1973-89; rschr. Telemark Rsch. Inst., Bø, 1989—; freelance author econs. textbooks, 1983—. Author: (with Zvi Griliches) Economies of Scale and the Form of the Production Function, 1971, Samfunnsøkonomi, vols. 1-3, 4th edit., 1997-99, Innføring i Samfunnsøkonomi, 3d edit., 2000; contbr. articles to profl. jours. Mem. Am. Econ. Assn. Home: Hesteskoen 21, 3800 Bø Norway Office: Telemark Rsch Inst, 3800 Bø Norway

RINK, THOMAS, nuclear medicine physician; b. Hanau, Hessen, Germany, May 20, 1963; s. Karl-Heinz and Gisela (Goebel) R. MD, U. Frankfurt, 1989. Physician in-tng. Nuclear Medicine Mcpl. Hosp., Hanau, 1989-90, asst. physician, 1991-93; asst. physician surgery Hanau, 1993-94; asst. physician U. Frankfurt, 1995-96; chief dept. nuclear medicine Mcpl. Hosp., Hanau, 1996—. Contbr. articles to profl. jours. Mem. Soc. of Nuc. Medicine, European Assn. of Nuc. Medicine, Rotary Internat. Fax: 49 6181 23368. E-mail: rink@em.uni-frankfurt.de. Home: Röntgenstr 36, 63454 Hanau Germany Office: Mcpl Hosp Dept Nuclear Med, Leimenstr 20, D-63450 Hanau Germany

RINKER, RUBY STEWART, foundation administrator; b. Dayton, Ohio, June 11, 1936; d. Encle Stewart and Addie (Hamilton) Stewart-Smith; children: William Bertram Klawonn, Elizabeth Lynn Dennis, William Stewart-Bradley Klawonn. Human relations counselor Palm Beach County Sch. System, West Palm Beach, Fla., 1974-84; adminstrv. asst. Bohmfalk Estate, Palm Beach, Fla., N.Y.C, Newport, R.I., 1984—; pres., CEO Ruby S. Rinker Co., Inc., Palm Beach; hon. counselor U.S. Naval Acad., U.S. Air Force Acad.; mem. exec. bd. Intercoastal Health Care Sys. Trustee Bohmfalk Charitable Found., Crystal Cathedral Ministries; bd. dirs. Crystal Cathedral Ministries Internat. Bd., Vatican Mus.; mem. adv. bd. Drug Free Am. Mem. Phi Delta Kappa. Home: 561 Island Dr Palm Beach FL 33480-4746 Office: 225 Peruvian Ave Palm Beach FL 33480-4672

RINKEVICH, ANATOLY BRONISLAVOVICH, physicist, educator; b. Volsk, Russia, Nov. 26, 1950; s. Bronislav Ivanovich and Appolinariya Nikolajevna (Filippova) R.; m. Olga Semenovna Shadrina; 1 child, Evgeny Anatoljevich. Diploma with distinction, Saratov (Russia) State U., 1973; PhD, Inst. Metal Physics, Ekaterinburg, Russia, 1984, DSc, 1997. Worker State Bearing Plant No. 3, Saratov, 1967-70, engr., 1970-73; scientific worker Inst. Metal Physics, 1976-88, sr. scientific worker, 1988-97, head of lab., 1998—; lectr. Engr. Ctr., Ekaterinburg, 1993—; mem. Sci. Coun. on Physics of Condensed Matter, Ekaterinburg, 1997—. Contbr. articles to profl. jours., chpt. to book. Mem. N.Y. Acad. Scis., Russian Acoustical Soc. Avocation: chess (1st Russian category). Home: 137 Amundsen Str Ap 113, 620016 Ekaterinburg Russia Office: Inst Metal Physicas RAS, 18 S Kovalevskaya Str, 620219 Ekaterinburg Russia

RINSKI, WOLF LÔBO, psychologist, educator, consultant; b. São Paulo, Brazil, Oct. 24, 1928; s. Jospeh Nathan and Margan Golda (Waiman) R. Student, Staford Coll., São Paulo, Cath. U., Rio de Janeiro. With Fedn. Acad., Rio de Janeiro, also bd. dirs.; psychologist Pinnel Hosp., Rio de Janeiro, 1972-75; journalist Correio da Manhã/Singra Editores, Rio de Janeiro; mem. faculty Acad. of Letters, Rio de Janeiro, also bd. dirs. Editor books and jours. Mem. AAAS, Am. Soc. Rio de Janeiro, British and Commonwealth Soc. of Rio de Janeiro, N.Y. Acad. Scis. Office: Assn Brazil Imprensa, Rua Araujo Porto Alegre 71, Castelo Rio de Janeiro 20030010, Brazil

RINSKY, JOEL CHARLES, lawyer; b. Bklyn., Jan. 29, 1938; s. Irving C. and Elsie (Millman) R.; m. Judith L. Lynn, Jan. 26, 1963; children: Heidi M., Heather S., Jason W. BS, Rutgers U., 1961, LLB, 1962, JD, 1968. Bar: N.J. 1963, U.S. Dist. Ct. N.J. 1963, U.S. Supreme Ct. 1967, U.S. Ct. Appeals (3d cir.) 1986; cert. civil trial atty., N.J. Pvt. practice, Livingston, N.J., 1964-97; sr. ptnr. Rinsky & Marley L.L.C., Livingston, 1997-98; of counsel Gonzalez and Weichert P.C., Livingston, 1999—. Committeeman Millburn-Short Hills (N.J.) Dem. Com., 1982-97, vice chmn., 1983-87; trustee Student Loan Fund, Millburn, 1983-91. Fellow Am. Acad. Matrimonial Lawyers; mem. N.J. Bar Assn., Essex County Bar Assn. (exec. com. sect. family law). Jewish. Avocations: tennis, chess, golf, piano. Home: 87 Sullivan Dr West Orange NJ 07052-2262 Office: 127 E Mount Pleasant Ave Livingston NJ 07039-3005

RINSLER, NORMA SYBIL, French educator; b. London, Oct. 5, 1927; d. Julian and Frances (Marks) Lee; m. Michael Gerald Rinsler, Mar. 23, 1948; children: Stephen, Susan, Miriam. BA, U. London, 1951, PhD, 1961. Asst. lectr. King's Coll., London, 1962-65, lectr., 1965-76, reader, 1976-83, prof. French, 1983—, vice-prin., 1987-92; dean faculty arts U. London, 1988-92; mem. coun. Univs. Funding Coun., U.K., 1991-93. Author: Gérard de Nerval, 1973, Nerval: Les Chimères, 1973; contbr. articles to profl. jours., chpts. to books. Named Officier dans l'Ordre des Palmes Académiques, French Govt., 1989. Jewish. Avocations: music, theatre. Office: Kings Coll London, Strand, London WC2R2LS, England

RIO, MARIA ESTHER, nutrition educator; b. Buenos Aires, Apr. 5, 1936; d. Demetrio Rio and Maria Garcia Barrera; m. Fermin Gomez (dec. July 1993); childen: Maria Manuela, Gabiela. Degree in pharmacy, U. Buenos Aires, 1960, U. Buenos Aires, 1962; PhD Pharmacy and Biochemistry, U.

Buenos Aires, 1969, degree in biochemistry (hon.), 1962. Head lab. Lab. Andromaco, Buenos Aires, 1960-66; asst. prof. U. Buenos Aires, 1966-81, assoc. prof., 1981-85, prof. nutrition, 1985-93, full prof. nutrition, 1993—; career investigator Nat. Rsch. Coun., Buenos Aires, 1970-9, ind. investigator, 1989-98, prin. investigator, 1998—; dir. project UNICEF, Buenos, 1997, Sancor-Conicet-Cerela, Buenos Aires, 1990-92; mem. com. on nutritional requirements Internat. Union for Nutrition Scis., 1981-93. Author, editor: Biochemistry and National Assessment, 1997; contbr. articles to profl. jours., chpts. tob ooks. Grantee Internat. Devel. Rsch. Ctr., Can., 1987-91, OMNI Project, Cairo, 1997. Mem. Internat. Soc. Nutrition Scis., Am. Soc. Clin. Nutrition, Soc. L.Am. Nutrition (gen. sec. 1980-82, pres. Argencine br. 1976-78. Roman Catholic. Avocations: science-fiction, travel, painting, fine arts. Fax: 54 11 4964 8243. E-mail: merio@ffyb.uba.ar. Office: Sch Pharmacy & Biochem, Junin 956 p2, 1113 Buenos Aires Argentina

RIORDAN, DEBORAH TRUBY, lawyer; b. Georgetown, S.C., May 29, 1968; d. David Charles and Vickie (Turner) Truby; m. Gary Ray Riordan, Aug. 26, 1995; children: Katherine Spencer, Neely McAdams. BA, U. Ark., 1990; JD, Vanderbilt U., 1993. Bar: Ark. 1993, U.S. Dist. Ct. (ea. and we. dists.) Ark. 1993. Law clk. various law firms, Little Rock, 1991-92; assoc. Shults & Ray LLP, Little Rock, 1993-99; dir. Hill, Gilstrap, Perkins, Trotter & Warner, Little Rock, 1999—. Staff writer Interaction mag., 1997-98. Vol. Ctrl. Ark. Legal Svcs., Little Rock, 1993-97; vol. coord. Ark. Arts Ctr., Little Rock, 1993-95; tng. com., sec., yearbook editor Jr. League, Little Rock, 1996—; pastor parish rev. com. Trinity United Methodist Ch., Little Rock, 1998—. Mem. ABA, Arkansas County Bar Assn., Pulaski County Bar Assn. Avocations: tennis, walking, reading, Arkansas Razorbacks football, spending time with daughters. Home: 8 Auriel Dr Little Rock AR 72223-9111 Office: Hill Gilstrap Perkins Trotter & Warner 1 Information Way Ste 200 Little Rock AR 72202-2290

RIORDAN, JAMES CORNELL, cultural association administrator; b. Hastings, Nebr., Mar. 4, 1945; arrived in Brazil, 1966; s. Charles Aeneas and Genevieve (Wride) R.; m. Sonia Regina Silva, Dec. 20, 1974; 1 child, Karen Silva. BA in L.Am. Studies, U. Nebr., 1970; postgrad., Sch. for Internat. Tng., 1990. Vol. Peace Corps., Feira de Santana, Brazil, 1966-68, trainer, 1968; cons. Portugese lang. St. John's U., N.Y.C., 1969-70; acad. dir. Your English Sch., Salvador, Bahia, Brazil, 1971-72, Brasilian Am. Cultural Assn., Salvador, 1973—; lectr. Brazilian Assn. Binat. Ctr., 1980—; resident dir. Brown U. in Brazil, Salvador, 1984-89; book reviewer pubs. ESL text books, 1975—. Hon. pres. Pan Am. Sch., Salvador, 1994-97; mem. adv. coun. Angolan Capoeira Group, Salvador, 1993—; mem. Ptnrs. of the Ams., Salvador, 1980—, People to People, Salvador, 1978—. Mem. BRAZ-TESOL (adv. coun. 1994-96). Office: Associacão Cultural Brasil Estados Unidos, Av Magalhaes Netto 1520, 41820140 Salvador Bahia, Brazil

RIORDAN, SHEILAGH MARGARET, literature and language educator; b. Long Beach, Calif., Dec. 24, 1964; d. Michael John and Carolyn Antoinette (Boydstun) R.; m. Keith Eric Jakee, May 9, 1992. AB, Occidental Coll., 1988; MA, U. Mich., 1990; PhD, U. Md., 1996. French instr. U. Md., College Park, 1990-93; EFL, French instr. North Mon Lang. Inst., Cork, Ireland, 1993-95; lectr. English dept. Uppsala U., Sweden, 1996; Fulbright rsch. fellow Fulbright-Roth Founds./Uppsala U., 1995-96; sessional lectr. in French U. Melbourne, Australia, 1997—; mgr. of study abroad U. Melbourne, 1997—. Author: (jours.) Cahiers staeliens, 1997, Moderna Sprak, 1996. Recipient Fulbright-Roth Rsch. fellowship Sweden, 1995-96, rsch. fellowship U. Md., 1994-95, rsch. scholarship Occidental Coll., France, 1985. Mem. N. Am. Fgn. Study Assn., Soc. des etudes staeliennes, Women in French. Avocations: playing jazz and blues flute, writing children's stories.

RIOS, MARCELLO, tennis player; b. Santiago, Chile, Dec. 26, 1975. Profl. tennis player, 1994. Recipient 16 singles titles and 2 doubles titles. Office: c/o ATP Tour Internat Hdqr 201 Atp Tour Blvd Ponte Vedra Beach FL 32082*

RIOUX, PATRICE, medical facility administrator; b. Neuilly, France, Feb. 17, 1951. MD, Paris U., 1976, PhD, 1978. Rschr. French Nat. Inst. Health and Med. Rsch., France, 1975-95; assoc. med. dir. Biogen, France, 1995-98; dir. clin. pharm.-genetics Variagenics, Inc., Cambridge, Mass., 1998-99; dir. clin. affairs Arrow Internat., Walpole, Mass., 1999—; med. dir. Group for Pharmacol. Rsch., France, 1990-95. Author (med. software) Expert Sys. Mem. Faculty Pharm. Medicine, Royal Coll. Physicians (London), Internat. Assn. for Study of Pain, French Pharmacol. Soc. Avocation: rowing club. Office: Arrow Internat 1600 Providence Hwy Walpole MA 02081-2553

RIOUX, PIERRE AUGUST, psychiatrist; b. Hartford, Conn., Sept. 2, 1953; s. Berchmans and Mary (Sauter) R. BA, Concordia Coll., 1975; MD, U. N.D., 1981. Diplomate Am. Bd. Psychiatry and Neurology. Intern U. Mich., 1981-82, resident, 1982-85; asst. prof. dept. psychiatry Emory U., Atlanta, 1985-86; attending physician VA Med. Ctr., Atlanta, 1985-86; staff physician UniMed Med. Ctr., Minot, N.D., 1986-87; med. dir. adult partial hospitalization program UniMed Med. Ctr., Minot, 1988-98, dir. behavioral health svcs., 1990—; med. dir. North Ctrl. Human Svc. Ctr., Minot, 1987-98; cons. North Ctrl. Human Svc. Ctr., 1986—, chem. dependency unit UniMed Med. Ctr., 1986—; clin. asst. prof. neurosci. U. N.D. Sch. Medicine, 1986-96; mem. U. N.D. family practice residency adv. bd. com., 1987-95; physician advisor N.D. Health Care Rev., Inc., 1987—; dir. psychiat. svcs. Dakota Boys Ranch, Minot, 1990-94; adv. bd. UniMed Med. Ctr., 1998—; med. dir. Rural Mental Health Consortium, 1999—. Recipient Nat. Alliance for the Mentally Ill Exemplary Psychiatrist award, 1993. Fellow Am. Coll. Forensic Examiners (life); mem. AMA, Am. Psychiat. Assn. (pres. N.D. dist. br. 1993-96, dep. rep. area IV coun. 1993—, bd. mem. psychiat. svcs. achievement awards bd. 1996-97, chmn. 1998, fellowship award 1996), Assn. Am. Physicians and Surgeons, Am. Soc. Clin. Psychopharmacology, N.D. Psychiat. Assn. (dist. br. exec. coun. 1997—), N.D. Med. Assn. (mem. commn. on socio-economic affairs), Internat. Soc. for Philos. Enquiry (diplomate), The Nat. Assn. of Established Families in Am. (adv. coun. 2000). Avocation: art. Office: UniMed Med Ctr Fifth Ave Med Bldg 307 5th Ave SE Ste 300 Minot ND 58701-4781

RIPANDELLI, GUIDO ALBERTO, ophthalmologist, researcher; b. Rome, Feb. 2, 1964; s. Francesco and Annamaria (Stirpe) R. MD, U. Rome, 1990. Resident in ophthalmology U. Rome, 1990-94, Pa. State U., Hershey, 1993; clin. surg. retina specialist, asst. Found. G.B. Bietti Oftalmologia, Rome, 1994—; assoc. prof. ophthalmology U. Rome. Guest editor, mem. editl. bd. Seminars in Ophthalmology, 1998. Found. G.B. Bietti Oftalmologia fellow, 1994-95. Mem. Am. Acad. Ophthalmology (internat.), Italian Soc. Ophthalmology, Vitreous Soc. Avocations: sports, music. Office: Found GB Bietti Oftalmol, Piazza Sassari # 5, 00161 Rome Italy

RIPKA, OTTO, internal medicine educator; b. Pardubice, Czechoslovakia, Sept. 16, 1917; s. Josef and Olga (Pacovska) R.; m. Zdenka Cervinkova, Dec. 20, 1950 (div. June 1956); 1 child, Blanka; m. Helena Kostkova, Dec. 7, 1956; 1 child, Pavel. MD, Charles U., Praha, Czechoslovakia, 1948, candidate of scis., 1955, DSc, 1966. Staff physician Internal Clinic, Pardubice, 1948-50, 2nd Med. Dept., Praha, 1951-54; asst. prof. internal medicine Charles U., 1954-59, assoc. prof., 1959-67, prof., 1967—; chief med. dept., Faculty of Medicine Charles U., Praha, 1968-86; dir. Cardiologic Inst., Praha, 1968-86. Author: Therapy of Hypertension, 1964, Epidemiological Study of Blood Pressure, 1967, Hypertensive Disease, 1968. Mem. Am. Soc. Hypertension, European Soc. Hypertension, Internat. Soc. Hypertension, N.Y. Acad. Scis. Roman Catholic. Home: Vrazska 340, 25228 Cernosice Czech Republic Office: 2nd Med Dept, U Nemocnice 2, 12000 Praha 2, Czech Republic

RIPMA, BARBARA JEAN STIERLE, realtor; b. Ann Arbor, Mich., July 20, 1927; d. Carl Joseph and Helen Esther (Koch) Stierle; m. Gale George Ripma, Oct. 27, 1945; children: David Carl, Mark Gale. Student, Mich. State U., 1950-51, U. Minn., 1968, Coe Coll., 1990-91. Lic. real estate salesperson, Iowa. Realtor Skogman Real Estate, Cedar Rapids, Iowa, 1985—. Rd. to Recovery driver Am. Cancer Soc., Cedar Rapids, 1971—. Mem. Toastmasters Internat. (Cedar Rapids pres. 1986). Republican. Avocations: art, creative writing, reading, walking, travel. Home: 341 Indiandale Rd SE Cedar Rapids IA 52403-2005

RIPOSAN, IULIAN, engineering educator; b. Petren, Hunedoara, Romania, Feb. 17, 1948; s. Gheorghe and Maria (Dincan) R.; m. Ligia Iacobescu, May 9, 1970; children: Alexandru, Adina Ilinca. BS in Engring., Poly. Inst., Bucharest, Romania, 1970, PhD, 1978. Cert. metall. engr. Instr. Poly. Inst., Bucharest, 1970-76, asst. prof., 1976-90, assoc. prof., 1990-93, prof., head cast metals dept., 1993—; dir. Romanian Foundry Plants, 1993; cons. Romanian Foundry Cos., 1980, Rsch. and Tech. Ministry, Romania, 1993, Nat. Coun. Univ. Rsch. Romania, 1995. Author 5 books; contbr. some 160 articles to profl. jours.; patentee in field. Recipient Aurel Vlaicu Romanian Sci. Acad., Bucharest, 1985, 8 awards Romanian Nat. Patent Exhbns., 1986-89, nat. awards for sci. creativity, 1987, 88; Fulbright grantee, Washington, 1991. Mem. Romanian Foundry Tech. Assn. (chmn. 1995), Am. Soc. Metals Internat., Romanian Inventors Assn. (hon. diploma 1988), Romanian Soc. Metallurgy. Mem. Orthodox Ch. Avocations: reading, travel, history, metallurgical antiquary. Home: N Titulescu 155, 21-A-2, 78163 Bucharest Romania Office: Politehnica U Bucharest, 313 Splaiul Independentei, 77206 Bucharest Romania

RIPPERE, VICTORIA, retired psychologist, retired psychology educator; b. N.Y.C., Aug. 20, 1943; arrived in Eng., 1966, citizen, 1988; d. Ralph Elliott and Fanny (Spector) R. BA, Columbia U., 1965; MA, Harvard U., 1966; PhD, U. London, 1972; BSc with honors, Birkbeck Coll., London, 1972; MPhil, Inst. Psychiatry, London, 1974. Rsch. asst. Tchrs. Coll. Columbia U., N.Y.C., summers 1965-66; rsch. asst. Univ. Coll., London, 1966-72, lectr. psychology, 1974-76; lectr. psychology Inst. Psychiatry, 1976-90, ret., 1990. Author: Schiller and Alienation, 1981, The Allergy Problem, 1983, Wounded Healers, 1985, Diet-Related Diseases, 1985. Woodrow Wilson Found. fellow Harvard U., 1965-66. Fellow Brit. Psychol. Soc., Royal Soc. Medicine. Avocations: writing, photography, cats, handicrafts. Home: 61 Queen Alexandra Mansions, Hastings St, London WC1H 9DR, England

RIPPLINGER, GEORGE RAYMOND, JR., lawyer; b. East St. Louis, Ill., Apr. 19, 1945; s. George Raymond and Virginia Lee (Toupnot) R. AB, U. Ill., 1967, JD, 1970. Bar: Ill. 1970, U.S. Dist. Ct. (so. dist.) Ill. 1970, U.S. Ct. Appeals (7th cir.) 1970, U.S. Dist. Ct. (cen. dist.) Ill. 1972, U.S. Tax Ct. 1971, U.S. Claims Ct. 1973, U.S. Ct. Mil. Appeals 1985, U.S. Supreme Ct. 1973, U.S. Ct. Internat. Trade 1973, U.S. Dist. Ct. (ea. dist.) Mo. 1977, U.S. Ct. Appeals (8th cir.) 1977. Assoc. Meyer & Meyer, Belleville and Greenville, Ill., 1970-72; assoc. Meyer & Kaucher, Belleville and Highland, Ill., 1972-73; sole practice Belleville, 1974; ptnr. Ripplinger & Walsh, Clayton, Mo., 1974-76, Ripplinger, Dixon & Johnston, Belleville, Ill., St. Louis, Scott AFB, and Bellvue, Neb., 1976-94; prin. George Ripplinger & Assoc., Belleville, Ill., 1994—. Bd. visitors Coll. of Law U. Ill., 1979-86, pres., 1983-84; chmn. Southwestern Ill. chpt. ACLU, 1971-74, 76-80; mem. exec. com. Sierra Club, 1981-85. Lt. col. USAR, 1970—. Fellow Am. Bar Found., Ill. Bar Found. (bd. dirs. 1994—, treas. 1998—); mem. ABA (ho. of dels. 1989-93, 95-99, chmn. workers compensation com. 1985-88, divsn. dir. 1988-89, 95-99, mem. coun. 1989-93, 99—, sec. 1999-2000, chair-elect 2000—, gen. practice/solo and small firm sect.), ATLA, Lawyers Trust Fund Ill. (bd. dirs. 1988-94), Ill. Bar Assn. (bd. govs. 1981-83, 87-93, sec. 1991-92), St. Clair County Bar Assn., Met. St. Louis Bar Assn., Mo. Bar Assn., Ill. Trial Lawyers Assn. (bd. advs. 1993—), Land of Lincoln Legal Assistance Found. (bd. dirs. 1982-88, vice chmn. 1987-88), Res. Officers Assn. Democrat. E-mail: ripplinger@prodigy.net. Office: George Ripplinger & Assoc 2215 W Main St Belleville IL 62226-6668

RIPPY, FRANCES MARGUERITE MAYHEW, English language educator; b. Ft. Worth, Sept. 16, 1929; d. Henry Grady and Marguerite Christine (O'Neill) Mayhew; m. Noble Merrill Rippy, Aug. 29, 1955 (dec. Sept. 1980); children: Felix O'Neill, Conrad Mayhew, Marguerite Hailey. BA, Tex. Christian U., 1949; MA, Vanderbilt U., 1951, PhD, 1957; postgrad., U. London, 1952-53. Instr. Tex. Christian U., 1953-55; instr. to asst. prof. Lamar State U., 1955-59; asst. prof. English Ball State U., Muncie, Ind., 1959-64; assoc. prof. English, Ball State U., 1964-68, prof., 1968—, dir. grad. studies in English, 1966-87; editor Ball State U. Forum, 1960-89; vis. asst. prof. Sam Houston State U., 1957; vis. lectr., prof. U. P.R., summers 1959, 60, 61; exch. prof. Westminster Coll., Oxford, Eng., 1988; cons.-evaluator North Cen. Assn. Colls. and Schs., 1973—, commn.-at-large, 1987-91; cons.-evaluator New Eng. Assn. Schs. and Colls., 1983. Author: Matthew Prior, 1986; contbr. articles to profl. jours., encys., ref. guides, chpts. to anthology; contbr. to Dictionary of Literary Biography. Recipient McClintock award, 1966; Danforth grantee, 1964, Ball State U. Rsch. grantee, 1960, 62, 70, 73, 76, 87, 88, 89, 90, 92, 93, 95, 96, 98, Lilly Libr. Rsch., 1978; Fulbright scholar U. London, 1952-53; recipient Outstanding Faculty award Ball State U., 1992, Ind. Coll. Tchr./Scholar of 1994, Ind. Coll. English Assn., 1994. Mem. MLA, AAUP, Coll. English Assn. Nat. Coun. Tchrs. English, Am. Soc. 18th Century Studies, Am. Fedn. Tchrs., Ind. Coll. English Assn. (pres. 1984-85) Johnson Soc. Midwest (sec. 1961-62). Home: 4709 W Jackson St Muncie IN 47304-3514

RISI, LOUIS JAMES, JR., business executive; b. Highland Park, Ill., July 2, 1937; s. Louis J. and Ann E. R.; m. Mary Jean Anson, Jan. 15, 1957; children: Steven, Janet, Andrew. B.S., Bradley U., 1958; MBA, U. Chgo. Pres., bd. dirs., mem. exec. com. Norin Corp., Miami, Fla., 1969-81; exec. com. dir. Maple Leaf Mills Ltd., Toronto, Can., 1970-81, Corp. Foods, Inc., 1970-81; chmn. bd. dirs. Louis Sherry, Inc., 1976-81; chmn. bd., chief exec. officer Nat. Investors Fire & Casualty Co., 1975-77; exec. com. dir. Investors Equity Life Ins. Co. of Hawaii, 1970-75; pres., dir. The Abbey, Lake Geneva, 1970-75; exec. com., dir. Upper Lakes Shipping, Ltd., Toronto, Can., 1970-76; pres., dir. The Pioneer, Lake Oshkosh, 1971-76; exec. com., dir. Port Weller and St. Lawrence Dry Dock, Ltd., St. Catharines, Can., 1971-76; pres., dir. Homosassa Springs, Fla., 1971-78, Ivan Tors Films Inc., Culver City, Calif., 1971-78; exec. v.p., dir. Ivan Tors Studios Inc., Miami, Fla., 1976-80; exec. com. dir. Midland Nat. Bank, 1976-80; pres., dir. Norris Grain Co., 1980-82; chmn. bd., CEO CTC Corp., 1981-83; exec. com., dir. Nat. Investors Life Ins. Co., 1970-77; chmn. bd., CEO EngineNuity.com, Inc.; chmn. bd., pres. Victory Industries, Inc.; chmn. bd. dirs. Red Wing Co., Oklawaha Farms, Inc., Assured Security Co.; dir. Breckinridge Group; exec. v.p., bd. dirs. Detroit Red Wings Hockey Club, Inc., 1976-82; bd. govs. Nat. Hockey League, 1976-82; bd. dirs. Chgo. Rock Island and Pacific R.R., dir. exec. com., Bankmgrs. Corp.; exec. com., bd. dirs. Afriair Corp., 1972-79; exec. com., bd. dirs. Peter Bowden Drilling Ltd.; U.S. rep. Grain negotiations with USSR; U.S. rep. Feedstuffs negotiations with China; mem. adv. coun. Am. Stock Exch.; mem. Agrl. Processors Liaison com. FTC; mem. adv. bd. Nat. Millers Assn.; exec. v.p., bd. dirs. Adirondack Red Wings Hockey Club, Inc., 1976-82, Ft. Worth Red Wings Hockey Club, Inc., 1975-78; bd. govs. Internat. Hockey League, 1978-82, Am. Hockey League, 1975-79; dir. TBA Entertainment, Inc.; pres., chmn. bd. dirs. Kinnard Body Works, Inc., 1970-73; exec. com., bd. dirs. Southeastern Airlines, Inc., 1972-78. Trustee Fairchild Tropical Garden, Miami, Fla. Lt. comdr. USN, 1959-66. Mem. Ocean Reef Yacht Club (Key Largo, Fla.), Santa Rosa (Calif.) Country Club, Riviera Country Club (Coral Gables, Fla.), Coral Reef Yacht Club (Miami, Fla.), Anabelle's Club (London), St. James Club (London). Home: 10915 Lakeside Dr Coral Gables FL 33156-4209 Office: 9200 S Dadeland Blvd Ste 705 Miami FL 33156-2715 also: 4535 E Elwood St Phoenix AZ 85040-1981

RISIN, JACK See BUTCHER, JACK ROBERT

RISK, THOMAS NEILSON, retired banker; b. Glasgow, Scotland, Sept. 13, 1922; s. Ralph and Margaret Nelson (Robertson) R.; m. Suzanne Eiloart, Sept. 10, 1949; 4 sons, 1 dec. BL, Glasgow U., 1949, LLD (hon.), 1985. Ptnr. Maclay Murray & Spens, Solicitors, Glasgow, 1950-81; chmn. Standard Life Assurance Co., 1969-77; dep. gov. Bank of Scotland, Edinburgh, 1977-81; gov. Bank of Scotland, 1981-91. Flight lt. RAF, 1941-46. Fellow Royal Soc. Edinburgh; mem. New Club (Edinburgh), RAF Club (London), Royal and Ancient Golf Club (St. Andrews). Avocations: art, opera, theater, golf. Home: 10 Belford Pl, Edinburgh EH4 3DH, Scotland

RISKO, KATHERINE JEAN, constituent services coordinator; b. Sept. 23, 1974. BA in Polit Sci. and History, U. Pitts., 1996. Constituent svcs. coord. Senator Arlen Specter, Pitts., 1997—. Office: 1000 Liberty Ave Ste 2031 Pittsburgh PA 15222-4101

RISKOWSKI, GERALD L., engineering educator; b. Loup City, Nebr., Feb. 26, 1952; s. Stanley George and Rose Marie (Eurek) R.; m. Janet Ann Riskowski, June 19, 1976; 1 child, Ryan Lee. BS in Agrl. Engring., U. Nebr., 1974, MS in Agrl. Engring., 1976; PhD in Agrl. Engring., Iowa State U., 1986. Registered profl. engr., Ill., Iowa, Wis. Design engr. Lesters Bldgs., Lester Prairie, Minn., 1976-77; product engr. Wick Bldg. Systems, Mazomanie, Wis., 1977-80; instr. Iowa State U., Ames, 1980-86; prof. dept. agrl. engring. U. Ill., Urbana, 1986—; swine facilities cons. Am. Tech. Products, Savoy, Ill., 1997—; pres. Internat. Air Technologies, Savoy, 1994—. Author: Designing Facilities for Pesticide and Fertilizer Containment, 1991 (Am. Soc. Agrl. Engrs. Blue Ribbon 1992); editor: Swine Housing and Equipment Handbook, 1983 (Am. Soc. Agrl. Engrs. Blue Ribbon 1984), Livestock Waste Facilities, 1985, Farm Buildings Wiring Handbook, 1986 (Am. Soc. Agrl. Engrs. Blue Ribbon 1987). Named to Rural Builders Hall of Fame, 1998. Mem. ASHRAE (TC.2 Handbook chair 1993—), Am. Soc. Agrl. Engrs. (S&E program chair, stds. chair), Am. Assn. for Lab. Animal Sci. Office: Univ of Illinois 1304 W Pennsylvania Ave Urbana IL 61801-4713

RISLEY, ALLYN WAYNE, oil company executive; b. Great Bend, Kans., Sept. 22, 1950; s. Albert Louis Risley and Hazel Mae Hull; m. Maria Paula Gimre, Sept. 18, 1977 (div.); children: Jessica, Michael; m. Tonya Jill Bogan, July 18, 1998; stepchildren: Erica, Natalie. BS in Petroleum Engring., U. Kans., 1972. Registered profl. engr., Kans. Engring. staff Phillips Petroleum, various locations, 1973-75, Stavanger, Norway, 1975-77, Jakarta, Indonesia, 1977-81; engring. staff div. Phillips Petroleum, Singapore, 1981-84; various middle mgmt. positions Phillips Petroleum, London, 1984-87, drilling prodn. mgr., 1987-89; mgr. sales Phillips Petroleum, Bartlesville, Okla., 1989-91; corp. planning mgr. Phillips Petroleum, Bartlesville, 1992, v.p. drilling and prodn., 1992-94; md ppco U.K. Phillips Petroleum, Woking, Eng., 1994-97; v.p. lng gas and coal Phillips Petroleum, Bartlesville, 1998—. Dist. chmn. Osage Dist. Boy Scouts Am., Bartlesville, 1992-94; bd. mem. Bartlesville Symphony, 1999—. Fellow Inst. Petroleum; mem. Soc. Petroleum Engrs. (chmn. Singapore sect. 1983-84). Avocations: tennis, golf, travel. E-mail: awrisle@ppco.com. Home: PO Box 2531 Bartlesville OK 74005-2531

RISLEY, GREGORY BYRON, furniture company executive, interior designer; b. Vincennes, Ind., Feb. 2, 1949; s. Jack Byron and Elizabeth Louise (Rockwell) R.; children: Christopher Byron, Timothy Neal. BS, Oakland City (Ind.) Coll., 1973; postgrad., Butler U., 1973-74, Oxford Worcester Coll. Pres. Risley Furniture & Design, Bicknell, Ind., 1974—, Risley Enterprises Inc., Bicknell, Ind., 1979—. Co-author: Preview IV The Home Furnishings Store. Pres. Better Bicknell Club, 1971; coach Pee Wee League, Bicknell, 1975-77; leader cub pack Boy Scouts Am., Bicknell, 1977; chmn. Queen Pageant, Bicknell, 1978-85. Mem. Nat. Home Furnishings Assn. (chmn. nat. execs. 1978-80), Am. Contract Bridge League (life master, unit sec. 1986-88, v.p. 1989, pres. 1991-92, bd. dirs. unit 193, 1993-95), Bicknell Mchts. Assn., Interior Design Soc. (outstanding rm. design award 1980), Knox County Assn. Retarded Citizens, French Club, Masons, Scottish Rite, Old Town Players (charter), Elks (past exalted ruler Bicknell 1976-77). Avocations: bridge, golf, reading. Office: 114 S Main St Bicknell IN 47512-2626

RISSANEN, KARI TAPANI, organic chemistry educator; b. Iisalmi, Kuopio, Finland, Nov. 29, 1959; s. Tarmo Veli and Pirkko Kyllikki (Julkunen) R.; m. Jaana Irmeli Vilpponen, Mar. 8, 1984; children: Ilona, Olli, Ilari, Ilkka. BS, U. Jyväskylä, Finland, 1984, MS, 1985, PhD, 1990. Chemistry asst. U. Jyväskylä, 1985-89, asst. prof., 1989-93; docent U. Jyväskylä, Jyväskylä, 1991-95, prof., 1995—; rsch. fellow Acad. Finland, Jyväskylä, Finland, 1988-91; sr. rsch. fellow Acad. Finland, Jyväskylä, 1991-93; assoc. prof. U. Joensuu, Finland, 1993-95. Contbr. articles to profl. jours. Recipient grant Emil Aaltonen Found., 1986, 91, grant Wihuri Found., Finland, 1989, award Finnish Sci. Acad., 1991. Mem. European Coop. in Sci. and Tech. Rsch. (mgmt. com. 1992—), Assn. Finnish Chem. Socs. (div. synthetic chemistry, vice-chmn. 2000), German Chem. Soc. Avocations: cooking, reading, sports. Office: Univ Jyväskylä, Survontie 9 PO Box 35, FIN40351 Jyväskylä Finland 80101

RISTIC, RAMIR DAROSLAV, physics educator; b. Zagreb, Croatia, Mar. 20, 1953; s. Daroslav Jovan and Anka Kata (Delija) R.; m. Ljerka Dobaj, June 7, 1980; children: Davor, Vedran. BS, Faculty of Sci., Zagreb, Croatia, 1975, MD, 1987, PhD, 1992. Prof. Grammar Sch., Osijek, Croatia, 1975-77; asst. prof. Faculty Edn., Osijek, Croatia, 1978—. Contbr. articles to profl. jours. Mem. County Assembly, Osijek, 1993-97, 97—. Home: Sjenjak 101, HR-31000 Osijek Croatia Office: Faculty Edn, Lorenza Jagera 9, HR-31000 Osijek Croatia

RISTICH, MIODRAG, psychiatrist; b. Belgrade, Yugoslavia, July 19, 1938; came to U.S., 1967; s. Teodosije and Gordana (Isailovic) Ristic; m. Yvonne Muriel Cunliffe, May 6, 1967; children: Katharine Alexandra, Elizabeth Victoria. MD, U. Belgrade, 1962. Diplomate Am. Bd. Psychiatry and Neurology. Resident in psychiatry Manhattan Psychiat. Ctr., NYU, 1980-83; med. dir. Cambridge (Minn.) State Hosp., 1967-72; dir. Willowbrook State Sch., Staten Island, N.Y., 1972-74; med. dir. DeWitt Rehab. and Nursing Ctr., N.Y.C., 1976—; clin. asst. prof. psychiatry NYU Med. Sch., 1996—; pvt. practice psychiatry, N.Y.C., 1973—. Mem. AMA, Am. Psychiat. Assn., Am. Assn. for Geriatric Psychiatry, Royal Coll. Psychiatrists. Republican. Avocation: tennis. Home: 37 Sunrise Ln Upper Saddle River NJ 07458-1631 Office: 201 E 79th St Apt 7J New York NY 10021-0833

RISTOW, BRUNNO, plastic surgeon; b. Brusque, Brazil, Oct. 18, 1940; came to U.S., 1967, naturalized, 1981; s. Arno and Ally Odette (von Buettner) R.; student Col. Sinodal, Brazil, 1956-57, Coll. Julio de Castilhos, Brazil, 1957-58; M.D. magna cum laude, U. Brazil, 1966; m. Urannia Carrasquilla Gutierrez, Nov. 10, 1979; children by previous marriage: Christian Kilian, Trevor Roland. Intern in surgery Hosp. dos Estrangeiros, Rio de Janeiro, Brazil, 1965, Hospital Estadual Miguel Couto, Brazil, 1965-66, Instituto Aposentadoria Pensão Comerciarios Hosp. for Gen. Surgery, 1966; resident in plastic and reconstructive surgery, Dr. Ivo Pitanguy Hosp. Santa Casa de Misericordia, Rio de Janeiro, 1967; fellow Inst. of Reconstructive Plastic Surgery, N.Y. U. Med. Center, N.Y.C., 1967-68, jr. resident, 1971-72, sr. and chief resident, 1972-73; practice medicine specializing in plastic surgery, Rio de Janeiro, 1967, N.Y.C., 1968-73, San Francisco, 1973—; asst. surgeon N.Y. Hosp., Cornell Med. Center, N.Y.C., 1968-71; clin. instr. surgery N.Y. U. Sch. of Medicine, 1972-73; chmn. plastic and reconstructive surgery div. Presbyn. Hosp., Pacific Med. Center, San Francisco, 1974-92, chmn. emeritus, 1992—. Served with M.C., Brazilian Army Res., 1959-60. Decorated knight Venerable Order of St. Hubertus; Knight Order St. John of Jerusalem; fellow in surgery Cornell Med. Sch., 1968-71; diplomate Am. Bd. Plastic and Reconstructive Surgery. Fellow A.C.S., Internat. Coll. Surgeons; mem. Am. Soc. Aesthetic Plastic Surgery (chmn. edn.), Am. Soc. Plastic and Reconstructive Surgeons, Internat. Soc. Aesthetic Plastic Surgeons, Calif. Soc. Plastic Surgeons, AMA (Physician's Recognition award 1971-83), Calif. Med. Assn., San Francisco Med. Assn. Republican. Mem. Evang. Lutheran Ch. Club: San Francisco Olympic. Contbg. author: Cancer of the Hand, 1975, Current Therapy in Plastic and Reconstructive Surgery, 1988, Male Aesthetic Surgery, 1989, How They Do It: Procedures in Plastic and Reconstructive Surgery, 1990, Middle Crus: The Missing Link in Alar Cartilage Anatomy, 1991, Surgical Technology International, 1992, Aesthetic Plastic Surgery, 1993, Mastery of Surgery: Plastic and Reconstructive Surgery, 1993; Reoperative Aesthetic Plastic Surgery of the Face and Breast, 1994, 95; contbr. articles on plastic surgery to profl. publs. Office: Calif Pacific Med Ctr 2100 Webster St San Francisco CA 94115-2373

RISTOW, GAIL ROSS, art educator, paralegal, children's rights advocate; b. Carmel, Calif., Oct. 18, 1949; d. Kenneth E. and Lula Mae (Craft) Ross; m. Steven Craig Ristow, Sept. 15, 1971. BS in Biochemistry, Calif. Polytech State U., San Luis Obispo, 1972; MEd, Ariz. State U., 1980. Cert. tchr., Calif. Asst. instr. Calif. State Polytech U., Pomona, 1972; grad. asst. Calif. Polytech State U., Pomona, 1973-74; tchr. Mt. Carmel High Sch., L.A., 1974-76, Cartwright Sch. Dist., Phoenix, 1976-80; pres., owner Handmade With Love, Bay City, Tex., 1984-88; tchr. art Aiken, S.C., 1989-96; tchr. Community Edn., Bay City, 1986-88, Palacios, Tex., 1987. Sec. Chukker Creek Homeowners, Aiken, S.C., 1989-96; mem. S.C. Foster Care Rev. Bd.,

1991-96; vol. tchr. elem. schs., Korea. Mem. AAUW, Am. Chem. Soc., Nat. Soc. Tole and Decorative Painters, Aiken Newcomer's Club (sec. 1989-91), Aiken Lioness Club (pres. 1991-94), Alpha Delta Kappa (v.p. 1986-87). Avocations: painting, woodworking, sewing, reading, children's rights advocacy. Home: Apt 1096-24 650 S Town Center Dr Las Vegas NV 89144

RITACCO, PATSY RICHARD, sales executive; b. Newark, Aug. 27, 1956; s. Michael Patsy and Adelaide (Caruso) R.; m. Linda La Falce, Nov. 5, 1978; children: Michael A., Patsy Richard Jr. B of History, William Paterson Coll., 1978. Notary pub., N.J., 1990—. Tchr. Belleville (N.J.) High Sch., 1978-82; bd. pneumatics Robert Tool, Saddle Brook, N.J., 1983-94; dist. sales mgr. Standard Abrasives, Simi Valley, Calif., 1994—; concert promotion dir. for edn. groups of 50s and 60s, Brooklyn Bridge, Coasters, 1980—; guest lectr. in field. Contbr. poetry to anthologies. Fellow Christ Ch. Sch. Bd., bldgs. & grounds publ rels., 1985-88; assoc. mem. Mus. Natural History; scholar bd. Unico Nat., Nutley, N.J., 1995—, treas., 1998-99. Recipient Editor's Choice award "Riddle of the Rose" Internat. Libr. of poetry; inclusion in Greatest Poets and Poems of the 20th Century., 1999. Mem. Soc. Engrs. (contbg.), Platers Assn. (contbg.), Am. Softball Assn. (assoc.), Internat. Soc. Poets. Roman Catholic. Avocations: reading, cooking, music, sports. Home: 45 Edgar Pl Nutley NJ 07110-1747 Office: Standard Abrasives 4201 Guardian St Simi Valley CA 93063-3372

RITCHEY, HAROLD W., retired chemical engineer; b. Kokomo, Ind., Oct. 5, 1912; s. Glen Robert and Mabel Ann (Wilson) R.; m. Helen Hively, Aug. 29, 1941; children: Stephen, David. BSChemE, Purdue U., 1934, MS in Chemistry, 1936, PhD in Chemistry, 1938; MSChemE, Cornell U., 1945. Rsch. chemist Union Oil Corp., Calif., 1938-41, 46-47; nuclear reactor engr. GE Co., Richland, Wash., 1947-49; tech. dir. rocket divsn. Thiokol Corp., Huntsville, Ala., 1949-60; v.p. rocket divsn. Thiokol Corp., Ogden, Utah, 1960-64; pres. Thiokol Corp., Bristol, Pa., 1964-70; CEO, chmn. bd. dir. Thiokol Corp., Newtown, Pa., 1970-77. Patentee in rocketry, astronautics, and petroleum and nuclear energy fields. Mem. Rotary Club, Ogden, 1974-96. Lt. comdr. USN, 1941-46. Named Outstanding Chem. Engr., Purdue U., 1994. Mem. AIAA, ADPA, AUSA, AIA, AFA, Purdue Rsch. Found., Am. Rocket Soc. (bd. dirs. 1956-60, v.p. 1960, pres. 1961, C.N. Hickman award 1954), Sigma Xi, Phi Lambda Upsilon. Home: 1756 Doxey St Ogden UT 84403-0524

RITCHEY, KENNETH WILLIAM, administrator; b. Washington, June 7, 1947; s. Conrad Monroe and Katherine Costance (Sheris) R.; m. Nancy Jayne Kirk, Aug. 22, 1970; children: Kirk Damon, Erin Kathryn (dec. Apr. 1988). BS in Edn., Shippensburg U., 1969; MEd in Spl. Edn., U. Va., 1972; MS in Ednl. Adminstrn., U. Dayton, 1980; grad. sr. execs. in state & local govt. program, Harvard U., 1992. Spl. edn. tchr. Shippensburg (Pa.) Area Sch. Dist., 1969-71; head cross country and track coach Shippensburg U., 1970-74; master tchr., coord. work experience program Lincoln Intermediate Unit, New Oxford, Pa., 1971-76; adult edn. tchr. Franklin County Prison, Chambersburg, Pa., 1972-76; asst. supt. mgmt. svcs. Montgomery County Bd. Mental Retardation & Devel. Disabilities, Dayton, Ohio, 1977-83; supt. bd. Montgomery County Bd. Mental Retardation & Devel. Disabilities, Dayton, 1983-99; dir. Ohio Dept. Mental Retardation and Devel. Disabilities, Columbus, 1999—; mem. part-time faculty edn. dept. U. Dayton, 1983-97; mem., vice-chair cmty. and mil. adv. com. ARC, 1986-99, needs and priorities com. Human Svcs. Levy Coun., 1982-84, 87-99; bd. trustees Ohio Polit. Action Com., Brighter Tomorrow Found., 1990-99, County Corp., 1992-98. Former editor statewide newsletter for tchrs. and profls. in Work Experience. Vol. mem. Cmty. and Agys. Resources Coun., United Way, 1986-98; bd. dirs., past pres. Ohio Pub. Images, Inc.; v.p., pres. HelpLink Bd. Mem. Am. Assn. Mental Retardation, Ohio Supts. County Bds. Mental Retardation (v.p., pres.), Supts. Assn. (exec. com.), Phi Delta Kappa. Democrat. Methodist. Home: 7660 Turtle Creek Dr Dayton OH 45414-1756 Office: Ohio Dept MRDD 1810 Sullivant Ave Columbus OH 43222-1055

RITCHIE, ALEXANDER BUCHAN, lawyer; b. Detroit, Apr. 19, 1923; s. Alexander Stevenson and Margaret (May) R.; m. Sheila Spellacy, June 1998; 1 child, Barbara Ritchie Drolshagen. BA, Wayne State U., 1947, JD, 1949. Bar: Mich. 1949. Pvt. practice Detroit, 1949-52, 84—; asst. gen. counsel, asst. v.p. Maccabees Mutual Life Ins. Co., Detroit, 1952-65; v.p., sec., gen. counsel Maccabees Mutual Life Ins. Co., Southfield, Mich., 1977-84; sec., house counsel Wayne Nat. Life Ins. Co., Detroit, 1966-67; ptnr. Fenton, Nederlander, Dodge & Ritchie, Detroit, 1967-77; spl. asst. atty. gen. State Mich., 1974-77. Bd. mem. Detroit Bd. Edn., 1971-77, Detroit Ctrl. Bd. Edn., 1971-73; bd. Police Commrs., Detroit, 1974-77; bd. dirs. Doctor's Hosp., Detroit, 1974-89. With U.S. Army, 1943-46. Recipient Key to the City of Detroit, Mayor Coleman Young, 1977. Mem. Mich. State Bar Assn. Avocations: reading, golf, theatre, gourmet. Home: 29255 Laurel Woods Dr Apt 201 Southfield MI 48034-4647

RITCHIE, ANNE, educational administrator; b. Grants Pass, Oreg., July 1, 1944; d. William Riley Jr. and Allie Brown (Clark) R.; m. Charles James Cooper, Sept. 4, 1968 (div. 1985); children: Holly Anne, Wendy Nicole. BA in Edn. with honors, Calif. State U., Sacramento, 1981. Cert. elem. tchr., Calif. CEO El Rancho Schs., Inc., Carmichael, Calif., 1981—; citizen amb. del. People to People Internat., Russia, Lithuania, Hungary, 1993, China, 1994. Active Crocker Art Mus.; mem. Rep. Senatorial Inner Circle, Washington, 1999. Mem. AAUW, Nat. Assn. Edn. for Young Children, Profl. Assn. Childhood Educators, Nat. Child Care Assn. Episcopalian. Avocations: traveling, skiing, reading.

RITCHIE, CEDRIC ELMER, banker; b. Upper Kent, N.B., Can., Aug. 22, 1927; s. E. Thomas and Marion (Henderson) R.; m. Barbara Binnington, Apr. 20, 1956. Student pub. schs., Bath, N.B. With The Bank of N.S., Bath, 1945—; chief gen. mgr. The Bank of N.S., Toronto, Ont., Can., 1970-72, pres., 1972-93, chief exec. officer, 1972-93, chmn. bd. dirs., 1974-95; mem. adv. coun. for Can. Exec. Svc. Orgn.; dir. Can. Life Assurance Co., Can. Nat. Rlwys., Concord Pacific Group Inc., Mercedes-Benz Can., Inc., Pacific Basin Econ. Coun. Can. Com., Can. Hunter Exploration Ltd., CCR Techs. Ltd. Mem. hon. com. Can. Orgn. for Devel. Through Edn.; internat. adv. coun. Ctr. for Inter-Am. Rels.; chmns. coun. Ams. Soc.; dir.-at-large Jr. Achievement Can.; gov. Asian Inst. Mgmt.; chmn. Can.-Philippines Coun., Can. Bus. Com. on Jamaica; mem. adv. coun. Can. Exec. Svc. Orgn.; hon. dir. Save Our N.W. Atlantic Resources; hon. consul-gen. Republic of Singapore. Decorated Officer Order of Can., 1981; recipient Sikatuna award Can. Fedn. for Humanities, 1993; named Bus. Man of Yr., Harvard Bus. Sch. Club, 1993, Bus. Leader of Yr., Western Bus. Sch. Club Toronto, 1993; inducted into New Brunswick Bus. Hall of Fame, 1999, Can. Bus. Hall of Fame, 2000. Mem. Am. Soc. Edn. (mem. hon. com.). Clubs: Canadian, Donalda, Mt. Royal, National, Toronto, York, Lyford Cay. Office: Scotia Plz 44 King Street W, Toronto, ON Canada M5H 1H1

RITCHIE, RAYMOND JAMES, science educator; b. Sydney, Australia, June 30, 1954; s. Albert Reginald and Lottie (Hoadley) R. BSc with honors, U. Sydney, 1977, PhD, 1984. Postdoctoral rschr. U. Stirling, Scotland, 1982-83; sci. officer State Pollution Control, NSW, Australia, 1984; part-time lectr. TCAE, Tasmania, Australia, 1984; postdoctoral fellow Cornell U., N.Y., 1985-87, U. B.C., Vancouver, Can., 1988-89, Washington State U., 1989-91; rsch. assoc. U. Sydney, 1991-92, Australian rsch. fellow postdoctoral, 1993-97; lectr. U. Western Sydney, 1999—. Contbr. numerous articles to profl. jours. Rsch. grantee Australian Rsch. Coun., 1996-98. Mem. Am. Soc. Plant Physiologists, Australian Soc. Plant Physiologists, Australian Soc. Biophysics, Japanese Soc. Plant Physiologists. Avocations: fishing, bush walking. Office: U Western Sydney, Richmond NSW, Australia

RITCHIE, STAFFORD DUFF, II, lawyer; b. Buffalo, June 13, 1948; s. Stafford Duff Ritchie and A. Elizabeth Smith Cavage; m. Rebecca P. Thompson, June 27, 1975; children: Stafford D. III, Thompson C., Glynis A. Student, Rensselaer Poly. Inst., Troy, N.Y., 1966-68; BS in Econs., U. Pa., 1970, JD, 1974. Bar: N.Y. 1975. Atty., advisor, asst. gen. counsel, spl. asst. gen. counsel Adminstrv. Office of U.S. Cts., Washington, 1974-82, assoc. gen. counsel, to 1982; gen. counsel Cavages, Inc., Buffalo, 1982-94; pvt. practice Buffalo, 1994—; counsel Coms. of Jud. Conf. of U.S., Jud. Conf. Com., Jud. Conf. of 9th Cir. of U.S.; spl. counsel for major procurement Supreme Ct. of U.S. Trustee Calasanctius Sch., Buffalo, 1990-92; dir. Suicide Prevention and Crisis Svc. Inc., Buffalo, 1997—, sec., 2000—. Sgt. USMCR, 1970-76. Mem. ABA, ATLA, N.Y. State Bar Assn. Avocation: computers. Office: 438 Main St Ste 200 Buffalo NY 14202-3207

RITSILÄ, VEIJO ANTTI, surgeon, researcher, consultant, educator; b. Sortavala, Finland, Apr. 27, 1930; s. Frans Sten and Helmi Lydia (Siitonen) R.; m. Irja Aira Peltonen, aug. 17, 1958. MD, Helsinki U., 1956. Med. diplomate; cert. in gen. surgery, plastic and reconstructive surgery, orthop. surgery. Resident in gen. surgery Univ. Ctrl. Hosp., Helsinki, 1956-63; resident in orthop. surgery Orthop. Hosp. of Invalid Found., Helsinki, 1964-66; resident in plastic and reconstructive surgery Univ. Ctrl. Hosp., Helsinki, 1966-69; sr. plastic surgery Univ. Ctrl. Hosp. and Finnish Red Cross Hosp., Helsinki, 1969-78; assoc. chief surgeon Orthop. Hosp. of Invalid Found., Helsinki, 1978-93; assoc. prof. plastic surgery Helsinki U., 1979—; cons. plastic surgeon Hosp. Orton of Invalid Found., Helsinki, 1993—; head Rsch. Unit of Hosp. Orton, 1988-93; coun. mem. Prosthesis Found. in Helsinki, 1983-93; cons. plastic surgeon Derm Clin. Helsinki U., 1967-75, Käpylä rehab. Ctr., Helsinki, 1969-93; pvt. practice Hakaniemi Med. Ctr., 1966—, Diacor Med. Ctr., 1976-98; orthopedic cons. Patient Indemnity Soc., 1988—; cons. surgeon Eira Hosp., 1966-78, Mehiläinen Hosp., 1978—; chmn. continued specialist edn. course Finnish Orthop. Assn., 1982, 84, 86; instr. and lectr. numerous internat. profl. courses and congresses; mem. IBC adv. coun. 1999—; bd. advisors ABI Rsch. 1999—. Chmn. of Contd. Specialist Edu. Course of Finnish Orthop. Assn., 1982, 84, 86, Instr. and lectr. in numerous internatl. profl. courses and congresssis; Editl. bd. European Jour. Exptl. Musculo-skeletal Rsch.; referee Acta orthopaedica Scandinavica, Scandinavian Jour. Plastic and Reconstructive Surgery, European Jour. Exptl. Musculoskeletal Rsch., Jour. Orthop. Rheumatology, Duodecim (Jour. of Finnish Med. Soc. Duodecim), Jour. of Finnish Med. Soc.; contbr. more than 160 articles to profl. jours. Recipient award Paulo Found. 1969, recipient awd. Finnish Phys. Soc. Duodecim 1970, recipient awd. Sigrid Juselius Found., 1972-89, Finnish Orthop. and Traumatologic Rsch. Found., 1974, Anders Langenskiöld medal, 1994, award Paulo Found., 1969, Duodecim award Finnish Physicians Soc., 1970, award Sigrid Juselius Found., 1972-89; Tord Skoog Soc. grantee, 1973-74. Mem. AAAS, N.Y. Acad. Scis., Joint Arthroplasty Survey Group, Internat. Confedn. for Plastic and Reconstructive Surgery, Internat. Soc. Orthop. Surgery and Traumatology, Scandanavian Assn. Plastic Surgery, European Assn. Plastic Surgeons (coun. mem. 1992—), Paasikivi Soc., Finnish-Arabic Soc., Finnish-Africa Soc., Finnish Red Cross Soc., Finnish Med. Assn., Finnish Red Cross Soc., Helsinki Med. Assn., Finnish Surg. Soc., Finnish Orthopedic Soc., Finnish Soc. Hand Surgeons, Finnish Soc. Pediatric Orthopedics, Chirugi Plastici Fenniae, Finnish Physicians Soc. Duodecim, Helsinki U. Docents' Soc., Nordic Surg. Assn., Nordic Orthopedic Assn., Scandanavian Assn. Hand Surgery, Nordic Scoliosis Study Assn., Internat. Coll. Surgeons, Tord Skoog Soc., Spinal Deformity Soc., Scoliosis Rsch. Soc., European Sect. Internat. Fedn. for Plastic and Reconstructive Surgery. Lutheran. Avocations: music, fine arts, gardening, motorboating, travel. Office: Hosp Orton of Invalid Found, Tenholantie 10, 00280 Helsinki Finland

RITSMA, RINTJE, speed skater; b. Lemmer, The Netherlands, Apr. 13, 1970. Speed skater, 1983—. Recipient Bronze medal men's speed skating 1500 meters, Olympic Games, Nagano, Japan, 1998, men's speed skating 10000 meters, 1998, Silver medal men's speed skating 5000 meters, 1998. Avocation: wind surfing. Office: Dutch Olympic Com, PO Box 302, 6800 AH Arnhem The Netherlands*

RITSON, SCOTT CAMPBELL, real estate management and development consultant; b. New London, Conn., July 20, 1945; s. Ian Douglas and Ann Breyer (Maxwell) R.; m. Diane Kischitz, May 16, 1966 (div. Oct. 1977); children: Mark Douglas (dec.), Carrie Stewart; m. Donna Diane Nietschmann, Feb. 25, 1978; 1 child, Evan Ray-Bernard. Student, U. Vt., 1963-65. Field engrs. asst. Gilbane Bldg. Co., Providence, 1966-67; project control engr. Olin Corp., Stamford, Conn., 1967-73; v.p. Reed Corp., Roxbury, Conn., 1973-76; pres. Ritson & Assocs., Lake Forest, Ill., 1976—; sr. project engr. Abbott Labs., North Chicago, Ill., 1990-95; pres., treas. Axeman Island, Ltd., Gananoque, Ont., Can., 1990—, v.p., 1979-90, dir., 1981-90; pres. Ritson, Ryan Inc., Gurnee, Ill., 1983-86. Charter mem. Congrl. Adv. Com., Washington, 1982. Can. nat. sailfish champion, 1961. Mem. Internat. Assn. Profl. Planners and Schedulers (charter mem.), Chgo. Yacht Club, Lake Forest Yacht Club. Home: 1084 Old Colony Rd Lake Forest IL 60045-3898 Office: 14048 W Petronella Dr Ste 101 Libertyville IL 60048-9699

RITT, ROGER MERRILL, lawyer; b. N.Y.C., Mar. 26, 1950; m. Mimi Santini, Aug. 25, 1974; children: Evan Samuel, David Martin. BA, U. Pa., 1972; JD, Boston U., 1975, LLM, 1976. Bar: Mass. 1977, Pa. 1975, U.S. Tax Ct. Sr. ptnr. Hale and Dorr, Boston, 1984—; adj. prof. grad. tax program Boston U., 1979-92; panelist Am. Law Inst., Mass. Continuing Legal Edn., World Trade Inst., NYU Inst. on Fed. Taxation; mem. exec. com. Fed. Tax Inst. New Eng. Treas. Found. for Tax Edn. Mem. ABA (tax sect.), Boston Bar Assn. Office: Hale and Dorr 60 State St Boston MA 02109-1816

RITTENHOUSE, NANCY CAROL, elementary education educator; b. Humeston, Iowa, May 26, 1941; d. Myrl Matthews and Opal L. (McCartney) Hixson; m. J. Kent Rittenhouse, Dec. 18, 1960 (div. Mar. 1984); children: Brenda L. Carroll, J. Aaron, Timothy K. Grad., Kirksville State Tchrs. Coll., 1960; student, St. Mary of the Plains Coll., 1984-87; degree in elem. edn., Ft. Hays State Coll., 1989. Cert. tchr., Kans. Reading instr. Sacred Heart Sch., Dodge City, Kans., 1984; elem. tchr. Miller Sch., Dodge City, Kans., 1985-86, Washington Sch., Hays, 1987; city-county recreation dir. Sherman County, Goodland, 1988; elem. tchr. Northside Sch., Larned, 1989-90; with Great Bend (Kans.) Tribune. Artist numerous paintings; author poetry. Mem. Menninger Found., Topeka, 1984—; hon. mem. Boy Scouts Am., 1978; camp instr. Spl. Olympics Blind Found., Junction City, Kans., 1985-90, Dodge City, 1984; leader Girl Scouts USA, 1975-77. Recipient Hon. award Spl. Olympics, 1984, 1st pl. poetry award, 1990, watercolor award, 1990, oils award, 1988, pen and ink award, 1984. Mem. AAAS, Nat. Trust for Hist. Preservation, Nat. Geog. Soc., Planetary Soc., Smithsonian Assn., MIT. Republican. Avocations: painting, drawing, walking, swimming, writing prose. Home: PO Box 1872 Great Bend KS 67530-1872 Office: Great Bend Tribune 2012 Forest Ave Great Bend KS 67530-4014

RITTER, ELISE DAWN, therapist, clinical social worker, writer; b. Balt., Aug. 14, 1952; d. Nelson Fred and Marjorie Jean (Corke) Ritter; m. Philip Anthony Gibson, Apr. 7, 1979 (div. Feb. 1990); 1 child, Christopher Ritter Gibson; m. Victor Wayne Clough, Jr., Mar. 3, 1990; stepchildren: Wesley T., Lindsay, Sharon. Student, Austro-Am. Inst., Vienna, Austria, 1973; BS, U. Kans., 1974; M Psychiatric Social Work, Va. Commonwealth U., 1998. Rschr. impeachment inquiry staff U.S. Ho. of Reps., Washington, 1974; rschr. APA, Washington, 1975; editor prodn. The New Republic Mag., Washington, 1976-77; copy editor Time-Life Books, Alexandria, Va., 1977-79, assoc. editor, 1979-83, adminstrv. editor, 1983-87, asst. dir. editorial resources, 1988-90; dir. editorial resources Time Warner, Time-Life Books, Alexandria, 1990-94. With Arlingtonians Ministering to Emergency Needs-AMEN, 1995; vol. Mental Health Program, Visiting Nurse Assn., 1996, Women's Ctr., Vienna, Va., 1997—, PsychologyNetwork.com, 2000—.

RITTER, GERHARD ALBERT, historian, educator; b. Berlin, Mar. 29, 1929; s. Wilhelm Erich Albert and Martha Ida (Wietasch) R.; m. Gisela Ritter, June 18, 1955; children: Michael, Clemens. PhD, Free U., Berlin, 1952; BLitt, U. Oxford, Eng., 1959; habilitation, U. Berlin, 1961; PhD (hon.), U. Bielefeld, 1994, Humboldt U., Berlin, 1999. Rschr. St. Antony's Coll., Oxford, 1952-54; asst. Free U., Berlin, 1954-61, prof. polit. sci., 1962-65; prof. modern history U. Munster, Germany, 1965-74; prof. modern history U. Munich, 1974-94, prof. emeritus, 1994—; vis. prof. St. Antony's Coll., Oxford, 1965-66, 72, Washington U., St. Louis, 1965, U. Calif., Berkeley, 1971-72, U. Tel Aviv, 1973. Author: Die Arbeiterbewegung im Wilhelminischen Reich, 2d edit., 1963, Parlament und Demokratie in Grobritannien, 1972, Arbeiterbewegung, Parteien und Parlamentarismus, 1976, Die II Internationale 1918-1919, 1980, Staat, Arbeiterschaft und Arbeiterbewegung in Deutschland, 1980, Sozialversicherung in Deutschland und England, 1983, Die deutschen Parteien 1830-1914, 1985, Social Welfare in Germany and Britain: Origins and Development, 1986, Der Sozialstaat. Entstehung und Entwicklung im internationalen Vergleich, 2d edit., 1991, The New Social History in the Federal Republic of Germany, 1991, Das Deutsche Kaiserreich 1871-1914. 5th edit., 1992, Grossforschung und Staat in Deutschland, 1992, Der Umbruch von 1889/91 und die Geschichtswissenschaft, 1995, Arbeiter, Arbeiterbewegung und soziale Ideen, 1996, Soziale Frage und Sozialpolitik in Deutschland Geschichte, 1998, über Deutschland, Die Bundersrepublik in der deutschen Geschichte, 1998; co-author: (with J. Kocka) Deutsche Sozialgeschichte 1870-1914, 3rd edit., 1982, (with M. Niehuss) Wahlen in Deutschland 1946-91, 1991, Wahlen in Deutschland, 1990-94, 1995, (with K. Tenfelde) Arbeiter im Deutschen Kaiserreich 1871 bis 1914, 1992; editor: Handbuch der Geschichte des deutschen Parlamentarismus, 6 vols., Geschichte der Arbeiter und der Arbeiterbewegung in Deutschland seit seit dem Ende des 18th Jahrhunderts, 7 vols. Mem. Senate, main com. German Rsch. Assn., 1973-76; chmn. Assn. Historians Germany, 1976-80; mem. Bavarian Acad. Sci. Internat. Commn. for the History of Parliamentary and Representative Instns. Named hon. fellow St. Antony's Coll., Oxford. Mem. Historische Kommission zu Berlin, Historische Kommission bei Bayer, Akademie der Wissenschaften, Kommission für Geschichte des Parlamentarismus und der politischen Parteien, Beirat Inst. für Zeitgeschichte Munich (hon. mem.). Home: Bismarckweg 3, D-82335 Berg Starnberger See Germany Office: U Munich Hist Seminar, geschwister scholl Platz 1, D-80539 Munich Germany

RITTER, GUNTER, mathematician, researcher, educator; b. Chemnitz, Germany, Dec. 8, 1940. Diploma, Ohm-Polytechnikum, Nuremberg, Germany, 1962, U. Erlangen-Nuremberg, 1970; Dr.rer.nat., U. Erlangen-Nuremberg, 1974, Dr.rer.nat.habil., 1978. Assoc. prof. U. Bochum, Germany, 1978-79, U. Eichstätt, Germany, 1979-80, U. Erlangen-Nuremberg, 1980-83; prof. math. U. Passau, Germany, 1983—; head dept. math. and computer sci. U. Passau, 1990-92. Contbr. articles to profl. publs. Recipient prize of the Faculty of Sci. of U. Erlangen for outstanding doctoral dissertation, 1974. Mem. Deutsche Mathematiker-Vereinigung, Gesellschaft für Klassifikation.

RITTER, HENNING, consultant in obstetrics and gynecology; b. Braunschweig, Germany, June 6, 1948; s. Helmuth H. and Ingeborg A. (Leichtweiss) R.; m. Dagmar A. Traulsen, Apr. 17, 1973; children: Inga, Ole, Maximilian, Linus. MD, Georg Augusta U., Göttingen, Germany, 1976, PhD, 1978. Cert. specialist in ob-gyn.; cert. in ultrasound. Med. officer Georg Augusta U., 1976-77, BL Hosp., Ramotswa, Botswana, 1979-82; sr. med. officer Stadt. Krankenhaus, Salzgitter, Germany, 1982-86; cons. gynecologist DRM Hosp., Mochudi, Botswana, 1987-92, Frauenklinik Ibbenbüren, Germany, 1992—; chmn. workshop com. Assn. Med. Mission in Botswana; lectr. U. Gaborone, Botswana, U. Munster, Germany, U. Heidelberg, Germany, U. Belgorod, Russia. Contbr. articles to profl. jours. Active CARE, German Red Cross. Served with German Army, 1977-78. Recipient honors from German Red Cross for refugee work in Tanzania. Mem. Assn. Christian Med. Drs., Assn. Gynecol. Endoscopy, Tropical Gynecology Soc. (exec. bd.), Internat. Assn. for Maternal and Neonatal Health. Lutheran. Avocations: photography, computer, skiing, diving. Home: Dornroeschenweg 40, D-49477 Ibbenbüren Germany Office: OKG Frauenklinik, Grosse Strasse 41, D-49477 Ibbenbüren Germany

RITTER, SANDRA HELEN, psychotherapist, counselor; b. Kingston, Pa., Dec. 31, 1947; d. Earl Jean and Lois Mae (Hartley) R.; stepfather Harry R. Smith; m. Billy Lee Ferguson, May 23, 1995; children: Christopher Andrew Hawkins, Alexander Cameron Hawkins (dec.); stepchildren: William Lee Ferguson, Ann Ferguson Bishop. BSME, Villanova U., 1969; MBA, Ctrl. Mich. U., 1981; MEd in Counseling, U. N.C., Greensboro, 1994, PhD in Counseling, 2000. Nat. cert. counselor; lic. profl. counselor, N.C. Engr. Automation Industries, Silver Spring, Md., 1974-83; sr. engr. Naval Sea Sys. Command, Alexandria, Va., 1983-85; ptnr. Clemmons (N.C.) Primary Care, 1987-91; owner, proprietor Serendipity Resource Ctr., Clemmons, 1985-91; mental health asst. Charter Hosp., Greensboro, N.C., 1992-94; pvt. practice Greensboro, 1994—. Co-author: Assessment in Counseling and Therapy, 1995; sr. author: Leadership Development on a Shoestring, 1995; mem. edtl. bd. Jour. Addictions and Offenders Counselors, 1995-97. Vol. hospice, Winston-Salem, N.C., 1990-92; vol. counselor The Listening Post, Greensboro, 1993-94; vol. Southeastern Regional Vision for Edn., 1999—; mem. worship com. Unitarian Universalist Fellowship, Greensboro, 1993-95, svc. leader coord., 1994-95. Mem. ACA (mem. adv. coun. 1996-98), Assn. for Adult Devel. and Aging (Midlife chair 1996-97), Internat. Assn. Addictions and Offenders Counselors (chair addictions com. 1993-96, mem. accreditation com. 1995-96, pres. 1997-99), Am. Mental Health Counselors Assn., Assn. for Counseling Edn. and Supervision (Outstanding Doctoral Student 1995), C.G. Jung Soc., N.C. Assn. for Adult Devel. and Aging (pres. 1995-96), N.C. Assn. for Specialists in Group Work (pres. 1996-97), N.C. Counseling Assn. (co-chair spl. task force 1995-96, treas. 1995-96, exec. coun. 1994—, chair strategic planning com. 1996-97, pres.-elect 1997-98, pres. 1998-99), Chi Sigma Iota (fellow, mem. Upsilon Nu Chi chpt., treas. 1993-94, awards chair 1993-96, pres.-elect 1994-95, pres. 1995-96, Internat. Outstanding Master's Student 1994). Avocations: reading, volunteer work, duplicate bridge, travel, breeding Persian cats. Office: 5000 Edinborough Rd Greensboro NC 27406-9328

RITTERHOFF, C(HARLES) WILLIAM, retired steel company executive; b. Balt., Nov. 1, 1921; s. Ernest F. and Anna M. (Luerssen) R.; m. Margery A. McKenney, June 24, 1944 (dec. May 1987); children: Leslie, William, James; m. Marita C. Halsey, Feb. 20, 1988. B.S. in Mech. Engring, Mass. Inst. Tech., 1947; grad., Advanced Mgmt. Program, Harvard, 1973. Asst. engr. mech. dept., then various supervisory positions Bethlehem Steel Co., Sparrows Point, Md., 1948-57; asst. supt. Sparrows Point plate mills, 1957-60, asst. chief engr. plant engring. dept., 1960-63; asst. chief engr. Burns Harbor project, 1963, asst. gen. mgr., 1963-67; gen. mgr. Burns Harbor plant, 1967-70; v.p. manufactured products and West Coast steel plants, 1970-71, v.p. steel operations-prodn., 1971-74, dir., 1974-82, exec. v.p., 1974-77, vice chmn., 1977-80, exec. v.p. steel ops., 1980-82. Served to 1st lt. U.S. Army, 1943-46. Mem. NAM (past bd. dirs.), Am. Iron and Steel Inst., Assn. Iron and Steel Engrs., Hwy. Users Fedn. (past bd. dirs.), Moorings Club, Bridgehampton Club (N.Y.). Home: 150 Anchor Dr Vero Beach FL 32963-2957

RITTICH, BOHUSLAV, chemistry educator, researcher; b. Brno, Czech Republic, July 24, 1946; s. Bohuslav and Marie (Mihovská) R.; m. Maria Kotiková, Oct. 19, 1974; 1 child, Aleš. MSc, Tech. U. Praha, Czech Republic, 1969; PhD, Masaryk U., Brno, 1976. Rschr. Acad. Scis., Praha, 1969-70; sr. rschr. Rsch. Inst., Pohořelice, Czech Republic, 1971-87, Acad. Scis., Brno, 1987-92, Vet. U., Brno, 1992-94; assoc. prof. Tech. U., Brno, 1994-97, Masaryk U., Brno, 1997—. Contbr. articles to profl. jours. Mem. Czech Chem. Soc. Avocations: ancient and modern history, philately. Home: Modřická 106, 619 00 Brno Czech Republic Office: Masaryk U, Kotlářská 2, 611 37 Brno Czech Republic

RITTNER, LEONA PHYLLIS, comparative literature scholar; b. Peekskill, N.Y., Sept. 2, 1948; d. Edmund Sydney and Marcella (Wiener) R. Student, Syracuse U., 1967-68, NYU, 1968-70; BA in French, CCNY, 1973, MA equivalent in French, 1982, postgrad., 1982—; student, U. Valencia, Spain, 1973. Permanent cert. tchr. bilingual (French) common brs., N.Y.C. Substitute tchr. combination of bilingual (French) common brs. and H.S. French & social studies N.Y.C. Bd. Edn., 1977-89; scholarly rschr., presenter in field, translator, artist. Author abstracts, adminstrv. proposals, articles and book reviews (French and Eng.), Contrbr. of color photos to archives of W.B. Yeats Soc. (Ireland) and Prof. Gerald Meyer's History Archive of Italian East Harlem. Baruch scholar (twice), CCNY, 1972, George D. McDonald scholar, CCNY, 1985; grad. assistantship CCNY, 1973; Women's Caucus for Modern Langs. Convention grantee, 1990, N.E. MLA grantee, 1993. Mem. AAUW, AAUP, MLA (S. Atlantic, N.E. and Rocky Mountain regions), Women's Caucus for Modern Langs., Women in French (exec. com. 1988-90), Soc. Phenomenology and Existential Philosophy, Am. Assn. French-Lang. Philosophy, Soc. for Critical Exch., Internat. Assn. for Philosophy and Lit., Sartre Soc. N.Am., Internat. Simone de Beauvoir Soc., Assn. French and Francophone Tchrs. Am., Nat. Coalition Ind. Scholars, Romance Lit. Rels. (exec. com. 1987-91), Am.-Italy Soc., W.B. Yeats Soc. (N.Y.C.), G. Bernard Shaw Soc., Alliance Française (N.Y.C.), Friends NYU Bobst Libr., Fieri Manhattan, Bklyn. Coll. Alumni Assn., Bklyn. Mus., Theatre Devel. Fund, Assocs. Rare Book and Manuscript Libr. Columbia U., Harvard U. English Inst., CUNY Francophone Assn. Democrat. Avo-

cations: swimming, collecting art posters and gallery cards, viewing art exhibitions and art history slide lectures, letter writing, theatre. Home: 120 Kenilworth Pl Apt 1J Brooklyn NY 11210-2407

RITTNER, LUKE PHILIP HARDWICK, arts administrator, marketing/communications executive; b. Bath, Avon, Eng., May 24, 1947; s. Stephen Hardwick and Joane Madeleine (Thunder) R.; m. Corinna Frances Edholm, Aug. 29, 1974; 1 child, Emily. Asst. adminstr. Bath (Eng.) Internat. Festival, 1967-72, joint adminstr., 1972-74, adminstrv. dir., 1974-76; founder, dir. Assn. for Bus. Sponsorship of the Arts, London, 1976-83; sec. gen. Arts Coun. of Gt. Britain, London, 1983-90; cultural dir. U.K. Pavilion Expo '92, Seville, Spain, 1990-92; dir. corp. affairs Sothebys, London, 1992-99; chief exec. Royal Acad. Dancing, 1999—; chmn. London (Eng.) Acad. Music and Dramatic Art, 1994—. Councillor City Coun., Bath, 1975-76; mem. Olivier Awards Panel, 1991-93; bd. dirs. City of London Ballet, 1996-99, New London Orch., 1996—; mem. coun. Almeida Theatre, London. Mem. London Choral Soc. (chmn. 1994—), Garrick Club, The Actors Ctr. (mem. bd. 2000—). Roman Catholic. Home: 29 Kelso Pl, London W8 5QG, England

RITZ, STEPHEN MARK, financial advisor, lawyer; b. Midland, Mich., Aug. 23, 1962; s. Alvin H. and Patricia M. (Padway) R. BA, Northwestern U., 1985; JD, Ind. U., 1989. Bar: Ill. 1990, U.S. Dist. Ct. (no. dist.) Ill. 1990, Ind. 1996. Atty. Chapman & Cutler, Chgo., 1990-93; pres., CEO S.M. Ritz and Co., Inc., Indpls., 1994-97; CEO Newport Pension Mgmt. LLC, 1997—; dir. Indsl. Logistics, Inc., Indpls., 1994-96. Mem. ABA, Inst. CFPs, Registry CFPs, Internat. Assn. Fin. Planners. Office: Newport Pension Mgmt 9465 Counselors Row Ste 108 Indianapolis IN 46240-3816

RIUTTALA, TIMO PEKKA, lawyer; b. Helsinki, Finland, Sept. 23, 1953; s. Niilo A. and Anna-Liisa (Viiliäinen) R.; m. Arja Irmeli Kataja, 1977; children: Lotta Elina, Laura Johanna. LLM, U. Helsinki, 1984. Lawyer Postipankki Ltd., Helsinki, 1984-88; gen. counsel Oy Sisu Ab, Espoo, Finland, 1988-97, NK Cables Oy, Helsinki, 1997—. Lt. Finnish Army, 1975-76.

RIVA, ALESSANDRO LODOVICO, anatomy educator, scientist; b. Milan, Aug. 25, 1939; s. Giuseppe and Carolina (Ajmar) R.; m. Francesca Testa, Oct. 10, 1969; children: Laura, Giulia, Margherita. MD, U. Pavia, Italy, 1964. Prof. anatomy U. Cagliari, Italy, 1969-75, dep. chmn. Inst. Anatomy, 1971-75, prof. anatomy, 1975—, dir. dept. cytomorphology, 1987-92, prof. history of medicine, 1989—; dir. doctorate morphological scis. U. Cagliari, 1987—; curator Mus. Anatomical Waxes, U. Cagliari, 1991—, dean Sch. of Nursing, 1998—. Editor: (with P. M. Motta) Ultrastructure of Extraparietal Glands of the Digestive Tract, 1990, (with L. Cattaneo) The Anatomical Waxes of Clemente Susini of the University of Cagliari, 1993, (with P. M. Motta and F. Testa-Riva) Ultrastructure of Male Urogenital Glands, 1994; editor European Jour. Morphology, 1999—, Clemente Susinis Wax Anatomical Models of the University of Cagliari, 1999 Italian-English edit., 2000 Italian-Japanese edit.; contbr. articles to profl. jours. Olzai freeman, 1994; bd. govs. U. Cagliari, 1980-96. Mem. Anat. Soc. Gt. Britain and Ireland, Histochem. Soc., Am. Assn. Anatomists, Am. Assn. Andrology, Am. Fertility Soc., Am. Assn. Dental Rsch., Italian Assn. Anatomists (bd. dirs. 1993—), Italian Histochem. Soc. (mem. bd. 1989-93), Italian Soc. Electron Microscopy, Italian Coll. Anatomists (v.p. 1997—), Federative Com. on Anatomical Terminology. Home: Via Stampa 15, I 09131 Cagliari Sardinia, Italy Office: U Cagliari Dept Cytomorphol, Cittadella Universitaria, I 09042 Monserrato Sardinia, Italy

RIVA, AMADEO, general contractor, airline executive and owner; b. Buenos Aires, July 19, 1937; s. Amadeo Angel and Pilgrim (Gosende) R.; m. Martha Weber (dec.); children: Caroline, Amadeo, Santiago; m. L. Susana Agulnik; children: Sophie, Adriana, Peter. Civil engr. degree, Buenos Aires U., 1959. Project engr. Buck Seifert & Jost, N.Y.C., 1960-62; gen. mgr. Gllardon Cordoba y Riva, Buenos Aires, 1963-70; chmn., pres. Riva SA, Buenos Aires, 1968—; pres. Austral Lineas Aereas, Buenos Aires, 1988-91, Aerolineas Argentinas, Buenos Aires, 1990-94; dir. Aeropuertos 2000, Buenos Aires, 1997—; v.p. Camara Argentina Construccion, 1990-94. Mem. ASCE, Bolsa de Comercio de Buenos Aires, Centro Argentino de Ingenieros (bd. dirs. 1990-95), Soc. Rural Argentina, Ocean Club, Wings Club (N.Y.). Roman Catholic. Office: Riva SA, Suipacha 1067, 1008 Buenos Aires Argentina

RIVADENEYRA, MARIAN, science educator; b. Fuente Uaqueros, Granada, Spain, July 12, 1953; d. Jose Rivadeneyra and Ana Ruiz; m. Jose Torres, Mar. 18, 1984 (div. 1990); 1 child, Torres Rivadeneyra Almudena. Master's degree, Pharmacy Faculty, Granada, 1976, PhD, 1982. Asst. prof. pharmacy faculty Granada U., 1977-83, prof. colaborador, 1983-85, prof. titular, 1985—. Contbr. sci. papers to profl. jours. Avocations: reading, traveling, psychology. Office: Granada U, Pharmacy Faculty, 18071 Granada Spain

RIVAS, SILVIA, artist, educator; b. Buenos Aires, Apr. 23, 1957; d. Manuel Rivas and Olga Blanco; m. Mariano Edo (div. May 1990); 1 child, Julia; m. Chrystian Colombo, July 2, 1993; 1 child, Alan. B of Lit., Mater Misericordia, Buenos Aires, 1974; Hautes Etudes Français, Alliance Français, Buenos Aires, 1975. Cert. prof. design and sculpture. Prof. sculpture, prof. design Nat. Sch. Fine Arts P. Pueyrredón, Buenos Aires, 1980; prof. visual arts Inst. Lenguas Vivas, Buenos Aires, 1983-85; prof. design Kenneth Kemble Atelier, Buenos Aires, 1986-89; prof. art Silvia Rivas Pvt. Atelier, Buenos Aires, 1987—. One-person shows include Galería de Benedictis, Buenos Aires, 1984, 85, Galería TEMA, Buenos Aires, 1988, 89, 90, 91, 93, 94, Casa de la Parra, Santiago de Compostela, Spain, 1993, Der Brücke Gallery, Buenos Aires, 1995, 98, Joan Prats Gallery, N.Y., 1996, Museo Nacional de Bellas Artes, 1998; exhibited in group shows Taller de Kenneth Kemble, Buenos Aires, 1985, Premio Manliba, Centro Cultural Malvinas, Buenos Aires, 1987, Salón Manuel Belgrano, Museo de Artes Plásticas Eduardo Sívori, Buenos Aires, 1988, Premio Manliba, Centro Cultural Ciudad de Buenos Aires, 1989, Museo de Arte Moderno, Mex., 1990, San Diego Mus. Art, 1991, Harrod's en el Arte, Buenos Aires, 1992, Premio Günther de Pintura IV, Buenos Aires, 1993, Espace Eiffel-Branly, Paris, 1994, Premio Banco Mayorista del Plata, Museo Nacional de Bellas Artes, Buenos Aires, 1995, Art Chgo. '96, Galería Der Brücke, Chgo., 1996, Premios de Pintura Unilever, 1997, Galería Der Brücke, N.Y. 1998. Recipient 1st prize Argentine Critica Asociation, 1996, 1st prize Siemens, Estandartes por la Paz, 1997; grantee Mexico City, 1991. Avocation: photography. E-Mail: silrivas@arnet.com.ar. Home: Mosconi 2769, 1642 San Isidro Argentina Office: Atelier, Costa Rica 4165, 1176 Buenos Aires Argentina

RIVAS DEL FRESNO, MANUEL, urologist, consultant; b. Mexico City, Apr. 29, 1962; s. Manuel Rivas Alonso and Maria Teresa del Fresno; m. Maria Paz Perez, Sept. 27, 1991; children: Guillermo Rivas Perez, Jorge Rivas Perez. BS, Alfonso II Inst., Oviedo, Spain, 1981; MD, U. Oviedo, 1987. Resident in urology Hosp. Ctrl. De Asturias, Oviedo, 1989-93; cons. urologist Hosp. Cabuenes, Gijon, Spain, 1994—. Contbr. articles to profl. jours. Recipient A. Puigvert 1st prize award in investigative urology Am. Conf. of Urology, 1996. Mem. Spanish Urol. Assn. (Madrid), Spanish Andrological Assn. (Barcelona). Home: Arquitecto Reguera 3-6A, 33004 Oviedo Spain Office: Hosp de Cabuenes, Cabuenes s/n, 33394 Gijon Spain

RIVERA, ALEJANDRO FLORES, surgeon, medical researcher; b. Pachuca, Hidalgo, Mexico, Feb. 24, 1958; s. Roque Flores Romero and Consuelo Rivera Vazquez; m. Aida Araceli Gomez Bravo, Sept. 21, 1997; 1 child, Alejandro Leonel. Surgeon physician, UAEH, Pachuca, Mexico, 1981; gen. surgeon, UNAM, Mexico City, 1987, M in Medicine, 1990. Cons. IMSS, Pachuca, 1987-89, dir., 1990-92, gen. surgeon, 1987—; med. rschr. 5, Pachuca, 1995—. Author: Human Anatomy, 1988, Clinic Anatomy, 1990, Designing Clinical Research, 1991, Clinical Epidemiologic, 1993. Named counsellor Assn. Mexican Cirugia Gen., 1988. Mem. AAAS, Internat. Coll. Surgeon, N.Y. Acad. Scis., Consejo Mexican Cirugia Gen., Assn. Mexico Gastroenterologia. Avocations: football, basketball, natation, baseball, lecture. Home: Abasolo 1104-2, 42000 Pachuca Hidalgo, Mexico Office: Inst Mex Seguro Social, Av Madero 405, 42000 Pachuca Hidalgo, Mexico

RIVERA, ROBERT LEROY, university administrator, educator; b. San Diego, Calif., Feb. 13, 1921; s. Reynaldo Jose and Maude (LaMain) R.; m. Barbara Ann Clark, June 23, 1963; children: Randall, Marla Baker, Caryl Blue, Clark. AB, U. So. Calif., 1945, MA in Speech Comm., 1947. Cert. gen. secondary tchr. (life), Calif., community coll. supervisory credential, Calif. Head history dept. Adolph Leutzinger H.S., Lawndale, Calif., 1947; dir. dramatics Bonita Union H.S., LaVerne, Calif., 1947, 48, San Pedro (Calif.) H.S., 1948-53, Eagle Rock (Calif.) H.S., 1953-56; chmn. theatre arts L.A. Valley Coll., Van Nuys, Calif., 1956-70; dist. coord. instructional TV L.A. Community Coll. Dist., 1970-78; dir. forensics U. LaVerne, Calif., 1978—; cons., sales trainer Don Baxter Co., Glendale, Calif., 1957-59; speech cons. City Nat. Bank, Beverly Hills, Calif., 1960-70. Contbr. articles to profl. publs. With USMC, 1943-45. Fellow Toastmasters Internat. (gov. greater L.A. dist., 1982-83), Univ. club of Claremont Calif. (membership chmn.). Republican. Avocations: professional speaking, tennis. Home: 2319 Chapman Rd La Crescenta CA 91214-3014 Office: Univ LaVerne 1950 3rd St La Verne CA 91750-4401

RIVERA, WINDELL LABERINTO, molecular microbiologist, researcher; b. Quezon City, The Philippines, Nov. 18, 1968; s. Nicolas Dilan Rivera and Iluminada Castaneda Laberinto. BS in Biology, U. Philippines, 1989, MS in Microbiology, 1995; PhD in Cellular/Molecular Microbiology, Nagasaki (Japan) U., 1999. Univ. rsch. assoc. U. Philippines, Marine Sci. Inst., 1989-90, U. Philippines, Natural Scis. Rsch. Inst., 1990-92; sci. rsch. specialist U. Philippines, Molecular Biology and Biotech. Program, 1992-94; rsch. fellow Tokai U. Sch. Medicine, Japan, 1999—. Contbr. articles to sci. and profl. jours. Fellow Australasian Coll. Tropical Medicine; mem. Am. Soc. Tropical Medicine and Hygiene, N.Y. Acad. Scis., Japanese Soc. Tropical Medicine, Japanese Soc. Parasitology, Phil. Acad. of Microbiology, Phil. Soc. Microbiology.

RIVERA CARRERA, NORBERTO CARDINAL, archbishop. Archbishop primate Mexico City, 1995—. Office: Apartado Postal 24-433, 06700 Mexico DF Mexico

RIVERA-LA SCALA, GLADYS MARY, Romance languages educator, researcher; b. Livorno, Tuscany, Italy, July 15, 1947; came to U.S., 1961; d. Robert Yescas and Giovanna AnnaMaria (Ciucci) Rivera; m. Frank James La Scala, July 14, 1973; 1 child, Annamaria Norma Rivera. B.A., Manhattanville Coll., 1969; M.A., Middlebury Coll., 1971; Ph.D., U. Pa., 1977. Instr. U. Pa., Phila., 1974-75; lectr. Dept. Agr., Washington, 1977-79, No. Va. Community Coll., Alexandria, 1977-79, George Mason U., Fairfax, Va., 1979-80; asst. prof. Romance langs. U.S. Naval Acad., Annapolis, Md., 1980-84, assoc. prof., 1984-90, prof., 1990—; dir. Annapolis Interactive Video Project, 1986-87; chmn. Lang. Studies Dept. U.S. Naval Acad., 1989-93; reader-evaluator NEH, Washington, 1980. Author: Coplas de los Siete Pecados Mortales: A Critical Edition and Study, Vol. I, 1982. Music scholar Loyola U., New Orleans, 1965; U. Pa. fellow, 1971-74; research grantee U.S. Naval Acad., 1981-82, publ. grantee U.S. Naval Acad., 1982, 84. Mem. MLA (chmn. Spanish medieval lit. sect. N.E. sect. 1983-84), Am. Council on Teaching Fgn. Langs., Internat. Assn. Hispanists, Middle States Assn. Fgn. Lang. Tchrs. (sec.-treas. 1980—). Avocations: music; swimming; drawing; painting. Office: US Naval Acad Lang Studies Dept Annapolis MD 21402

RIVERA PORTILLO, MIGUEL ANGEL, judge. Pres. Supreme Ct. of Justice, Tegucigalpa, Honduras. Office: Centro CÍvico Gubernamental, Colonia miraflores Supreme Ct, Tegucigalpa Honduras*

RIVERS, JULIE A., wildlife biologist; b. Oak Park, Ill., Nov. 20, 1967; d. John D. Rivers and Elizabeth C. Molnar. BS, Beloit Coll., 1989. Marine mammal biologist Nat. Marine Fisheries Svc., La Jolla, Calif., 1993-95; fish and wildlife biologist Wash. Dept. Fish and Wildlife, Olympia, 1995-98; forestry and wildlife biologist Dept. Land and Natural Resources, Honolulu, 1999—. Contbr. articles to profl. jours. Advocate domestic violence Womencare Shelter, Bellingham, Wash., 1994-98. E-mail: jrivers@lava.net.

RIVERSO, EMANUELE, philosophy educator, researcher; b. Naples, Italy, Dec. 23, 1928; s. Gennaro and Filomena (Sorace) R.; m. Mariagrazia Mancassola, Aug. 24, 1968; children: Nicla, Tecla. Degree in philosophy, U. Naples, 1956. Privatdozent U. Naples, 1959-63, lectr., 1973-82, assoc. prof., 1982-87; privatdozent U. Rome, 1964-66; lectr. U. Salerne, 1961-79, prof., 1987—; cons. editor, Rome, 1969-84; sci. journalist, Naples, 1985-96. Author: The Thought of B. Russell, 1958, 3d edit., 1972, The Thought of L. Wittgenstein, 1964, 2d edit., 1970, Philosophy of Language, 1990, Intercultural Translation, 1993. Mem. Academia Tiberina, Internat. Inst. für Kunstwissenschaften, Acad. of 500 (hon.), N.Y. Acad. Scis., The Planetary Soc. Avocations: journeys, intercultural contacts, painting, gardening, humanist. Home: Viale Delle Mimose 12, 80131 Naples Italy Office: U Salerne, Dept Philosophy, 84084 Fisciano Salerne, Italy

RIVES, STANLEY GENE, university president emeritus; b. Decatur, Ill., Sept. 27, 1930; s. James A. and Frances (Bunker) R.; m. Sandra Lou Belt, Dec. 28, 1957; children: Jacqueline Ann, Joseph Alan. B.S., Ill. State U., 1952, M.S., 1955; Ph.D., Northwestern U., 1963; EdD (hon.), Lincoln Coll., 1998. Instr. W.Va. U., 1955-56, Northwestern U., 1956-58; prof. Ill. State U., Normal, 1958-80, Am. Council on Edn. Fellows Program, 1969-70, assoc. dean faculties, 1970-72, dean undergrad. instrn., 1972-80, assoc. provost, 1976-80, acting provost, 1979-80; provost, v.p. acad. affairs, prof. Eastern Ill. U., Charleston, 1981-83, pres., 1983-92, pres. emeritus, 1992—; vis. prof. U. Hawaii, 1963-64. Author: (with Donald Klopf) Individual Speaking Contests: Preparation for Participation, 1967, (with Gene Budig) Academic Quicksand. Trends and Issues in Higher Education, 1973, (with others) Academic Innovation: Faculty and Instructional Development at Illinois State University, 1979, The Fundamentals of Oral Interpretation, 1981; contbr. articles to profl. jours. Bd. dirs. Ill. State Univs. Retirement System, 1992—, treas., 1995—, Ea. Ill. Univ. Found., 1993-98, also pres., 1996-98, East Ctrl. Ill. Devel. Corp., 1983-92, Charleston Area Econ. Devel. Found., 1986-92, Coles Together, 1988-92; mem. pres. commn. NCAA, 1986-91; trustee Nat. Debate Tournament, 1967-75. With U.S. Army, 1952-54. Recipient Alumni Achievement award Ill. State U., 1998. Mem. Am. Assn. State Colls. and Univs., Ill. State C. of C. (bd. dirs. 1990-92), Charleston C. of C. (bd. dirs. 1985-88), Theta Alpha Phi, Phi Kappa Delta, Pu Gamma Mu. Home: 2231 Andover Pl Charleston IL 61920-3807

RIVIERE, FREDERIC, business executive; b. Lyon, France, Apr. 24, 1964; s. Daniel André Riviere and Arlette Henriette Manzoni; m. Arlette Riviere, Feb. 11, 1963 (div. Feb. 1989); 1 child, Frederic. With Le Patio RDC, Lyon. Home: 20 rue de Belfort RDC, 69004 Lyon France

RIVIN, ROBERTA, art gallery director; b. N.Y.C., Dec. 20, 1937; arrived in France, 1972; d. Henry and Roslyn B. (Rivin) Schuldenfrei; m. Melvin J. Grossgold (div. 1977); children: Melissa, Céleste. Student, U. Calif., 1955-59. Asst. Jean Renoir/U. Calif., Berkeley, 1959; writer, rschr. Westinghouse Ind. Prodn., San Francisco, 1960-62, CBS Ind. Prodn., N.Y.C., 1962-67; tchr. Internat. Sch., Prague, 1967-69; adminstr. Peace Corps., Brazil, 1973—; dir. Galerie Uruhamba, Paris, 1973—. Contbr. articles to profl. jours. Avocations: travel, reading. E-mail: urubamba.galerie6@fnac.net. Office: Galerie Urubamba, 4 Rue de la Bucherie, Paris 75005, France

RIVNER, MICHAEL HARVEY, neurologist; b. Bklyn., Sept. 26, 1950; s. Norman and Carol (Simson) R.; m. Roberta Fran Gottlieb, Aug. 13, 1978; children: Asher, Joshua, Peter, Harold. BA, Duke U., 1972; MD, Emory U., 1978. Diplomate Am. Bd. Psychiatry and Neurology, added qualifications in clin. neurophysiology; diplomate Am. Bd. Electrodiagnostic Medicine. Intern, resident in neurology Med. Coll. Ga., Augusta, 1978-82; from fellow to assoc. prof. neurology Med. Coll. Ga., 1982—; cons. neurology Eisenhower Med. Hosp., Ft. Gordon, Ga., 1982—, VA Med. Ctr., Augusta, 1982—. V.p., campaign chmn. Augusta Jewish Found., 1994, pres., 1995-97; treas. CSRA Swim League, Augusta, 1993-97; treas. Augusta Jewish C.C. Fellow Am. Acad. Neurology; mem. Am. Assn. Electrodiagnostic Medicine (equipment com. 1984-87, tng. program com. 1989-92, edn. com. 1992-97, chmn. edn. com. 1994-97), Southeastern Neuromuscular Group (pres. 1996—). Avocations: computer programming, bicycling. Office: Med Coll Ga EMG Lab Augusta GA 30912

RIVOLI, LOUIS JOHN, economic development consultant; b. Bklyn., Feb. 22, 1933; s. Gaetano Tom and Liboria Florence Rivoli; children: Denise, Louis J. Jr. Student, St. Johns U., Bklyn., 1955-57, Hofstra U., East Meadow, L.I., N.Y., 1959-61. Sales rep. Bklyn. Union Gas, 1950-69, area devel. coord., 1969-94; econ. devel. cons. Queens (N.Y.) C. of C., 1994—, chair bus. industry com., 1990-94. Dir. Queens Overall Econ. Devel. Corp., 1969-90, Boy Scouts Am., 1992-94. Seaman USN, 1951-53. Recipient awards East N.Y. Devel. Corp., 1972, Brighton Neighbors Assn., Brighton Beach, N.Y., 1974, proclamation N.Y. State Assembly, 1994. Mem. Kiwanis Internat. (life, pres. 1991-92). Avocation: swimming. E-Mail: lou41955@aol.com. Home: 67 Pell Ter Garden City NY 11530-1928 Office: Queens C of C 75-20 Astoria Blvd Ste 140 Jackson Heights NY 11370-1131

RIVONKER, CHANDRASHEKHER UMANATH, science educator; b. Karwar, Karnataka, India, Mar. 18, 1962; s. Umanath Voikunt and Girijabai Umanath (Anvekar) R.; m. Annapurna Chandrashekher Raikar, Feb. 9, 1992; 1 child, Shraddha C. B of Fishery Scis., Coll. Fisheries, Mangalore, India, 1984, M of Fishery Scis., 1987; PhD, Goa (India) U., 1992. Rsch. fellow Nat. Inst. Oceanography, Goa, 1987-92; rsch. assoc. Goa U., 1992-94, lectr., 1994—; cons. Goa U., 1997. Inventor in field. Mem. Goa U. Tchrs. Assn., 1996-97, Jaycees, Goa, 1999. Mem. Assn. Microbiology India (life). Avocations: writing scientific articles, reading, sharing information, swimming, outdoor sports. Office: Goa U, Taleigao Plateau, 403 206 Bambolim Goa, India

RIVOSH, VICTOR, philologist, translator; b. Riga, Latvia, Apr. 20, 1949; s. Isidor and Galina (Glinternik) R. MA, U. Riga, 1974. Cert. philologist, English tchr. Tchr. Secondary Sch., Riga, 1974-81; reviewer Pub. House Raduga, Moscow, 1984-90; translator Pub. House Progress, Moscow, 1983-96; freelance writer, 1996—. Translator: Problems in Middle and High School Teaching, 1983, Happy Children a Challenge to Parents, 1986, Identity Youth and Crisis, 1996. Mem. Nat. Geographic Soc., N.Y. Acad. Scis. Avocations: painting, photography, music, oriental arts.

RIX, GERALD, public relations consultant, archeologist; b. Barnet, Htfdshire, Eng., Nov. 19, 1934; arrived in France, 1993; s. Frederick Thomas and Olive Louisa (Sharp) R.; m. Patricia Evelyn Dyer, Nov. 8, 1957 (div. June, 1973); children: Charlotte, Jonathan, Matthew; m. Jessie Isla MacLauchlan, Dec. 16, 1975. Diploma in Comms., Advt. and Mktg. Found., 1972; MA, U. Dundee, Scotland, 1993. Exec. Shell Internat., London, 1955-61; dir. Welbeck Pub. Rels., London, 1961-84; mng. dir. Carl Byoir, London, 1984-86; dep. chmn., group mng. dir. Hill & Knowlton, London, 1986-87; dir. Hallmark Comm., Winchester, Eng., 1986-91; CEO Minerva Comm., Scotland, 1986-90; freelance polit. cons. France, 1993—; chief examiner Comm. Adv. and Mktg. Found., London, 1974-79, vis. lectr. Athens, 1976. Contbr. articles to jours. in Pub. Rels., Mktg. and Polit. Rels.; articles on Scottish 19th Century History and The Roman Landscape History of Scotland. Bd. dirs. Assn. for Bus. Sponsorship of the Arts, 1983-85. Maj. Brit Territorial Army, 1959-85. Recipient Geography and History awards Abertay Soc., Dundee, 1993, History award, 1993. Mem. Royal Scottish Geographical Soc., Spl. Forces Club. Avocations: fly fishing, game shooting, hill walking. Home and Office: Minerva, Montchanin, 71250 Bergesserin France

RIZA, IQBAL, United Nations agency administrator; b. India, May 20, 1934; s. Sharif Alijan; m. 1959. Student, Pakistan, U.S. With Pakistan Fgn. Svc., Spain, Germany, Sudan, U.K., U.S., 1958-77; dir. Fgn. Svc. Acad. Lahore, 1968-71; dep. chief of mission Washington, 1972-76; chargé d'Affaires Paris, 1977; joined UN, 1978, assigned to negotiations in Iran-Iraq war, 1981-87, dir. gen. asst., 1988; chief electoral mission UN, Nicaragua, 1988-90; spl. rep. UN sec. gen. UN, El Salvador, 1991-93; asst. sec. gen. for peace-keeping ops. UN, 1993-97, under sec.- gen., 1997—, chief cabinet to the sec.-gen. Avocations: reading, music, riding. Office: Exec Sec Gen UN Plz New York NY 10017*

RIZK, ASSAAD TOUFIC, surgeon, urology educator; b. Beirut, Lebanon, July 23, 1931; s. Toufic I. and Olga A. (Toubia) R.; m. Colette M.T. Le Breton, Dec. 26, 1959; children: Toufic, Fady, Sami. MD, Paris U., 1960, teaching qualification, 1963. From intern to resident Paris Hosp., 1950-59; prof. urology St. Joseph U., Beirut, 1969—; bd. dirs. Dr. Rizk Clin., 1981-86; pres. 1st Bd. High Relief com. Lebanese Govt., 1977-79, pres. bd. Com. for the South of Lebanon, 1977-79, pres. Bd. Office Social Devel., 1977-79. Author: Treatment of Imperforated Anus with Vulvar Fistulae, 1959, Physiology in Micturition, 1960; contbr. articles to med. jours. Min. Nat. Edn. and Arts, Lebanese Govt., 1976-79, Min. Labor and Social Affairs, 1979, Min. Agriculture, 1976-77, Min. Industry and Petroleum, 1978-79, 92-95. Recipient Officer of the Order of Merit award, Italy, 1970, Chevalier of the Legion of Honor award, France, 1980. Fellow ACS; mem. Am. Urological Assn., Internat. Assn. Urology. Home: PO Box 11-3288, Beirut Lebanon Office: U St Joseph Sch Medicine, Rue de Damas BP 293, Beirut Lebanon

RIZK, LAILA GALAL, English lecturer; b. Cairo, Sept. 6, 1961; s. Galal El-Deen Aly and Safaa Hosny El-Karamany. BA in English Lang. and Lit., Faculty of Modern Langs., 1982; MA in Brit. Drama, Ain Shams U., 1986, PhD in Contemporary Brit. Drama, 1993. Translator, interpreter Tng. Team Hospitex/Ain Shams Specialised Hosp., Cairo, 1984-85; cons. Am. Telemedia, Cairo, 1987-88; rsch. asst. Centre for Developing English Lang. Teaching, Cairo, 1988-89; asst. editor Nat. Symposium on English Lang. Teaching, Cairo, 1988—; jr. cons. Am. Fulbright, San Francisco U., summer 1989. Exec. editor: Teaching English in Egypt, 1989—. Home: 175 Gisr El Suez St., Heliopolis Egypt Office: Ain Shams Univ, Faculty Modern Langs, Abbassia Egypt

RIZK, MAHER FARID SAMI, university official, research consultant; b. Itay Barood, Bihera, Egypt, July 1, 1940; s. Farid Sami Rizk and Izabel Farag Rofael; m. Sonia George Michel, Aug. 27, 1978. BSME, Ain Shams U, Cairo, 1111969. Cert. cons. engr. Head engring. sect. tech. affairs Pub. Transport Orgn., Cairo, 1969-75, chief engr. tech. affairs for north region, 1970-75; asst. svc. mgr. Gen. Contracting Co., Khobar, Saudi Arabia, 1975-79; head transp. sect. Rsch. Inst. King Fahd U. Petroleum and Minerals, Dhahran, Saudi Arabia, 1979-81, head maintenance fabrication engring. sect., 1981-82, head maintenance and operation, 1982-86, supr. shop and maintenance, 1986-90, mgr. fabrication and maintenance, 1990—, head maintenance, engring., field support, constrn. project handling, and fabrication sect. Rsch. Inst., 1979-86, rsch. support, design cons. Rsch. Inst., 1986-90, tech. cons. Rsch. Inst., 1990—. Designer, inventor device for laying down comm. wire cable wire for Egyptian army; designer new method of gear reconditioning, new lighter chassis for heavy duty busses; inventor method of increasing cooling efficiency of air-cooled engine. Recipient Best Engr. award Gov. of Cairo, 1973, Disting. Rsch. Ministry Higher Edn., 1997; grantee Ministry Transport, Helwan, Egypt, 1975. Mem. ASME, Saudi Computer Soc., Cairo Syndicate Engrs. Avocations: fishing, cycling, basketball, volleyball, hunting. Office: King Fahd U Petrol-Minerals, Rsch Inst 1525, Dhahran 31261, Saudi Arabia

RIZK, TAREQ ABDUL KAREEM, investment company executive; b. Alexandria, Egypt, May 1, 1958; s. Abdul Kareem Helal and Fatma Ahmad R.; m. Nahla Aly Mamdouh Abulazm, July 28, 1983; children: Judy, Mohammad. BSc in Computer Sci., Automatic Control, Faculty Engring., Alexandria, 1980. Cons. Saudi Arabia, 1983-95; pres. Internat. Maritime Svc. & Process Control, Alexandria, 1994—; mng. dir., dept. chmn. Papyrus Securities, Cairo, 1996-98, chmn., 1998—. Author: Easy Stock Picking, 1994; editor Daily Favorite Stocks, 1998. Mem. Alexandria Sporting Club. Avocations: music, reading. Home: 678 Hurreia St-Laurent, Alexandria 21411, Egypt Office: Papyrus Securities, 1 Jawad Hosni St Bab Ellouq, Cairo Egypt

RIZKALLAH, MARIE-THERESE YOUSSEF, pediatrician; b. Cairo, Egypt, Sept. 6, 1952; d. Youssef Rizkallah and Chanchette Wassef; m. Tewfik Zarif Said, Feb. 1, 1991. MB BCh, Cairo U., 1978, MS in Pediats., 1982, MD, 1992. Intern Cairo U. Hosp., Ministry Pub. Health Hosp., 1978-79; resident Nat. Rsch. Ctr., Dokki, 1979-83; cons. pediat. New Pediat. Hosp., Cairo U., 1983-91, Anglo-Am. Hosp., Cairo, 1983—; cons. pvt. clinic Cairo, 1983—; product mgr. Internat. Trade Ctr. Med. and Marine Divsn., Cairo, 1992—; Francexpo '99 organizer French Embassy, Cairo, 1999, internat. fair exhbn. organizer, 1979-99. Editor: (booklet in Arabic) Enteral Nutrition Oral Feeding, 1998. Recipient Hon. award Egyptian Med. Syndicate, 1986. Mem. Egyptian Pediat. Assn. (congress organizer 1984-2000, hon. award 1986), Cairo Rotary Club (first lady 1996). Avocations: painting, collecting antiques, arts, decoration, reading. Office: Internat Trade Ctr, 36 Ministry Agriculture St, Dokki Cairo, Egypt

RIZOPOULOS, ANDREAS C(HRISTOS), public relations consultant, journalist; b. Patras, Greece, July 3, 1941; s. Christos A. and Anna S. (Economopoulos) R.; children: Anna Christina, Paul Christos. M.A. in Polit. Sci., Panteios U., Athens, 1973. Owner, C&A Communications, Athens, 1967-98. Author 3 books; translator 4 books; contbr. numerous articles to profl. jours. Active Boy Scouts Greece, Athens, 1953-98. With Greek Army, 1962-64. Fellow Inst. Pub. Rels. U.K., Periodical Press Journalists Union, Faith and Friendship, Internet Lodge, Albion, Southwark. Home: 5 Miltiadou St, 155 62 Holargos Athens Greece

RIZOVA, ELENA, dermatologist, consultant; b. Sofia, Bulgaria, Dec. 19, 1959; arrived in France, 1990; d. Rizo and Ivanka Gueorguiev; m. Marin Dimitrov; 1 child, Ivona Dimitrova. MD, Acad. Medicine, Bulgaria, 1983, degree in dermatology, 1991; PhD, U. Paris, 1998. Med. diplomate. Gen. practitioner Hosp. Blagovgrad, Bulgaria, 1984-86; dermatologist Med. U. Sofia, 1986-90, Hosp. E. Herriot, Lyon, France, 1990-92, Hosp. St. Louis, Paris, 1992-94; internat. med. advisor Galderma, Sophia Antipolis, France, 1994—, dir. clin. rsch., 2000—. Recipient 1st pl. for rsch. Bd. European Acad. Dermatology and Venerology, Denmark, 1993, best article of yr. award Japanese Soc. Investigative Dermatology, Japan, 1995. Office: Galderma, 635 route des Lucioles, 06902 Sophia Antipolis France

RIZOWY, CARLOS GUILLERMO, lawyer, educator, political analyst; b. Sarandi Grande, Uruguay, Mar. 5, 1949; came to U.S., 1973, naturalized, 1981; s. Gerszon and Eva (Visnia) R.; m. Charlotte Gordon, Mar. 14, 1976; children: Brian Isaac, Yael Deborah, Michal Evie. BA, Hebrew U., Jerusalem, 1971; MA, U. Chgo., 1975, PhD, 1981; JD, Chgo. Kent Coll. Law, Ill. Inst. Tech., 1983. Bar: Ill. 1983, U.S. Dist. Ct. (no. dist.) Ill. 1983, U.S. Ct. Appeals (7th cir.) 1983. Asst. prof. polit. sci. Roosevelt U., Chgo., 1982-89, chmn. dept. polit. sci., 1983-86, dir. internat. studies program, 1986-89; mng. ptnr. Ray, Rizowy & Fleischer, Chgo., 1983-90; ptnr. corp. law dept. Gottlieb and Schwartz, 1990-92; ptnr. Levenfeld, Eisenberg, Janger, Glassberg, Samotny & Halper, 1993-94; of counsel Sonnenschein, Nath & Rosenthal, 1994—; dir. Midwest Am. Friends of Hebrew U., 1997—; hon. consul of Uruguay, Chgo., 1994—; adj. assoc. prof. Spertus Coll. Judaica, Chgo., 1984—; weekly polit. analyst on Middle East, internat. law and fgn. policy, resource specialist Sta. WBEZ Pub. Radio and BBC Latin Am.; mem. panel of arbitrators of Mediation and Arbitration Ctr., Internat. Arbitration Ct. for Mercosur Bolsa de Comercio, Uruguay, 1999—. Author: Avoiding Premises Liability Suits by Improving Security, 1991, Middle East Security: Five Areas to Watch, 1997. V.p., resource specialist to exec. com. Orgn. Children of Holocaust Survivors, Chgo., 1982; pres. Assn. Children Holocaust Survivors, 1986-91; pres. bd. dirs. Soviet Jewry Legal Advocacy Ctr., 1986-88; rsch. com. Nat. Strategy Forum, bd. dirs. UN Assn. U.S., 1985-89; mem. cmty. rels. com. Jewish Fedn. Met. Chgo., 1983-84; mem. adv. bd., chmn. internat. affairs commn. Am. Jewish Congress, Chgo., 1983-85, chmn. subcom. for Israel, 1986-88; mem. Nat. Spkrs. Bur. United Jewish Appeal, Nat. Spkrs. Bur. Devel. Corp. for Israel; mem. adv. bd. Chgo. Action for Soviet Jewry, 1983-85; bd. dirs. Am. Friends of Hebrew U., Chgo., 1984-86, Florence Heller Jewish Cmty. Ctr., 1986-88, Soviet Jewry Legal Advocacy Ctr., 1986-88; mem. human rights com. Anti-Defamation League, 1986, bd. dirs., 1989—; bd. dirs. Bd. Jewish Edn., 1989-91, Hispanic Coalition for Jobs, 1991-94; chmn. univ. educators divsn. Jewish United Fund, 1988-90; mem. consular corp. adv. bd. Internat. Vis. Ctr. Chgo., 1995—, com. fgn. affairs Chgo. Coun. Fgn. Rels., 1994—. Scholar Hebrew U., 1967-72, U. Chgo., 1972-78, Hillman Found., 1978, Peter Volid Found., 1980; recipient Globalist award Heritage Internat. Trade Assn., 1997. Mem. ATLA, ABA (chmn. bus. com. 1993-95), Assn. Ibero-Am. Consuls of Chgo., Ill. State Bar Assn., Chgo. Bar Assn. (internat. trade com.), Latin Am. Bar Assn., Nat. Hispanic Bar Assn., Am. Immigration Lawyers Assn., Am. Polit. Sci. Assn., Am. Judicature Soc., Exec. Club Chgo., Internat. Platform Assn., Wexner Heritage Found., Am. Forum, Latin Am. C. of C. (bd. dirs. 1991—, gen. counsel 1992—), Anshe Emet Congregation, Masons. Office: Sonnenschein Nath & Rosenthal 8000 Sears Tower Chicago IL 60606

RIZVI, MOHAMMAD SADIQ, chemistry educator; b. Barabanki, India, Jan. 16, 1939; s. Mohammad T. Tahir Rizvi and Gohar Gebum; m. Sohela Nazvi; 1 child, Mohammad Shahid. BSc, U. Lucknow, India, 1958, MSc in Phys. Chemistry, 1960; PhD, U. Birmingham, Eng., 1967. Lectr. phys. chemistry Jamia Millia Coll., Malir Karachi, Pakistan, 1960-61; asst. lectr. chemistry U. Karachi, 1961-67, lectr. chemistry, 1967-70, asst. prof. chemistry, 1970-72, asst. prof. applied chemistry, 1972-90, chmn. dept. applied chemistry, 1972-76, 80-81, assoc. prof. applied chemistry, 1990-99, adj. prof., 1999—; rschr. in field. Contbr. articles to profl. jours. Pres. Soc. Applied Chemistry, U. Karachi, 1974-76, 80-81. Mem. N.Y. Acad. Scis., Soc. Plastics Engrs., Royal Soc. Chemistry (Eng.). Home: A-34 Roofi Homes, Gulzari-Hijri, Scheme33 Karachi 32, Pakistan

RIZZA, CHARLES ROCCO, hematologist; b. Dundee, Scotland, Mar. 26, 1930; s. Domenico and Rosa (Iannetta) R.; m. Sheena Gilroy Henderson, July 4, 1956; children: Philip, Paul, Jane, Christopher. MB, ChB, St. Andrews U., Scotland, 1955, M.D., 1962; M.R.C.P., Edinburgh, 1964, F.R.C.P., 1972. House physician Dundee (Scotland) Hosp., 1955-56; clin. rsch. fellow Med. Rsch. Coun., Eng., 1958-61; lectr. in therapeutics St. Andrews U., Scotland, 1965-66; cons. physician Oxfordshire Health Authority, Eng., 1966-93, dir. Oxford Haemophilia Ctr., 1977-93; chmn. Haemophilia Ctr. Dirs. Orgn., Eng., 1987-90; med. advisor to Haemophilia Soc., 1970-93. Contbr. articles to profl. jours. Mem. British Soc. Haematology, Internat. Soc. for Thrombosis and Haemostasis. Avocations: painting, walking, reading. Office: Oxford Haemophilia Ctr, Old Rd, Oxford England

RIZZO, RONALD STEPHEN, lawyer; b. Kenosha, Wis., July 15, 1941; s. Frank Emmanuel and Rosalie (Lo Cicero); children: Ronald Stephen Jr., Michael Robert. BA, St. Norbert Coll., 1963; JD, Georgetown U., 1965, LLM in Taxation, 1966. Bar: Wis. 1965, Calif. 1967, Ill. 1999. Assoc. Kindel & Anderson, L.A., 1966-71, ptnr., 1971-86; ptnr. Jones, Day, Reavis & Pogue, L.A., 1986-93, Chgo., 1993—; bd. dirs. Guy LoCicero & Son Inc., Kenosha, Wis. Contbg. editor ERISA Litigation Reporter; mem. internat. adv. editl. bd. Jour. Pensions Mgmt. and Mktg. Schulte zur Hausen fellow Inst. Internat. and Fgn. Trade Law, Georgetown U., 1966. Fellow Am. Coll. Tax Counsel, Am. Coll. Employee Benefits Counsel (charter); mem. ABA (chmn. com. on employee benefits sect. on taxation 1988-89, vice chair com. on govt. submissions 1995-99), Los Angeles County Bar Assn. (chmn. com. on employee benefits sect. on taxation 1977-79, exec. com. 1977-78, 90-92), State Bar Calif. (co-chmn. com. on employee benefits sect. on taxation 1980), West Pension Conf. (steering com. L.A. chpt. 1980-83). Avocations: reading, golf, travel. Home: 1040 N Lake Shore Dr Apt 19C Chicago IL 60611-6164 Office: Jones Day Reavis & Pogue 77 W Wacker Dr Ste 3500 Chicago IL 60601-1692

RIZZO, STEFANO, journalist, writer; b. Turin, Piedmont, Italy, Feb. 5, 1946; s. Giuseppe and Paola (Giannattasio) R.;m. Lilli Mazzitelli, Sept. 11, 1971; children: Michela, Tommaso. AA, Westchester C.C., White Plains, N.Y., 1965; BA, CCNY, 1967; PhD, U. Rome, 1972. Editor Ency. Britannica, Chgo., 1970; translator, copy editor for various publs., 1969; asst. Am. Lit. U. Rome, 1972; sr. exec. Camera dei Deputati, Rome, 1977—, dir. parliamentary publs., 1985—, dir. info. svcs., 1997—; Italian cons. U. Chgo. Press, 1969. Author: (short story collection) Variazioni Rubbettimo, 1998; contbr. articles to profl. publs. Mem. Phi Beta Kappa. Mem. Dem. Party of the Left. Avocations: gardening, labyrinths, mazes, writing fiction. E-mail: rizzo s@camera.it. Office: Camera dei Deputati, Palazzo Montecitorio, 00186 Rome Italy

RIZZO, VITO, physician, researcher in cardiovascular diseases; b. Rome, Italy, July 5, 1961; s. Vincenzo and Giuseppina (Sciascia) R. MD, La Sapienza U., Rome, 1994; postgrad. in geriatric medicine, La Sapienza U. Cons. Aurelia Hosp., Rome, 1998—, I Clinica Medica, La Sapienza U., Rome, 1998—, S.S. Aritmologia, Rome, 1990—. Contbr. over 170 articles to profl. jours. SIGG-Florence grantee, 1995. Fellow Italian Soc. Geriatric Medicine (grantee 1995), Italian Soc. Internal Medicine, Italian Soc. Cardiology.

RO, DUSIK, oriental medicine physician; b. Inchon, Korea, Aug. 22, 1948; s. Hakyoung and Kyuwhan (Kim) R.; m. Minhae Kang, Feb. 5, 1973; children: Seungjo, Boyeon. B of Oriental Medicine, Kyunghee U., Seoul, Korea, 1974, M of Acupuncture, 1976, DPhil, 1982. Dir. Youngje Oriental Med. Clinic, Inchon, Korea, 1976—; prof. Kyungsan U., Korea, 1989-91; expert mgr. Rsch. Inst. Oriental Med. Sci. & Tech., Seoul, Korea, 1997—; v.p. supporter's assn. Inchon Nat. Tchrs. Coll., 1996—. Author: Medical Plants of Korea, 1981, Love Drawn with Crayon, 1984, Songs of Barite, 1986, On the Naked Branches, 1996, Interesting Oriental Medicine, 1990, Breed Me Healthy and Good, Mom, 1994, Oriental Medicine for Everyday, 1996. Recipient Ministry Health & Welfares Korea award, 1997. Mem. Internat. Acupuncture Soc. (dir. rsch. 1977-79), Korean Oriental Med. Assn. (pres. 1996—), Korean Lit. Writer's Assn., Assn. Hyundai Poets, Lions (pres. 1987-91). Avocations: golf, skiing, shooting. Office: Youngje Oriental Med Clinic, 147 Sungui-Dong Nam-Ku, Inchon 402-011, Korea

RO, YONG MAN, electrical educator; b. Seoul, Sept. 4, 1962; s. Sung-Lin and Sun-Oak (Kim) R.; m. Jae-Ran Ryu, Jan. 9, 1968; children: Eugene, Eusung. BS, Yonsei U., Seoul, South Korea, 1985; MS, Korean Advanced Inst. Sci., Seoul, 1987, PhD, 1992. Staff assoc. Columbia U., N.Y.C., 1987-88; rschr. Korea Advanced Inst. Sci. and Tech., 1992-95; prof. Taejon (Korea) U., 1992-96; rsch. fellow U. Calif., Berkeley, 1996-97; prof. Info. and Commn. U., Taejon, 1997—; vis. rschr. U. Calif., Irvine, 1993-95. Inventor MPEG-7 Texture Descriptor (Young Investigator Finalist 1992). Mem. IEEE (sr.), SPIE, ISMRM. Avocations: skiing, mountain climbing, golf, music. Office: ICU Multimedia Comm Group, Yusong-Gu PO Box 77, 305-600 Taejon Korea

ROACH, DAVID GILES, information technology administrator; b. Wisner, La., Oct. 26, 1948; s. David and Annie Laura (Hanks) R.; m. Vivian Viola Curry, July 23, 1967. BS in Math., U. La., 1970; MSc in Math. and Geology, U. Miss., 1975. Grad. teaching asst. computer ctr. U. La., Monroe, 1970-72; grad. asst. computer ctr. U. Miss., University, 1972, user svcs. mgr., 1973-74, asst. dir. user svcs., 1974-78; assoc. dir. computer ctr. Office Computing & Info. Systems, University, 1978-88; dep. dir. Office of Info. Tech., University, 1988-98; dir. Miss. Ctr. for Supercomputing Rsch., 1998—; apptd. mem. Miss. Info. Tech. Svcs. Bd., 1994-00, chmn. 1997-98, 99-00; chmn. Miss. Higher Edn. Rsch. Network Policy and Planning Com., 1992-94; chmn. bd. dirs. DEC Computer User Soc. S.E. U.S., 1977-78; voting rep. IBM Share, 1981—, CDC Users Group, 1987-90, Amdahl Users Group, 1986-98, Cray Users Group, 1991—. Contbr. article to profl. jour. Planning com. mem. Oxford (Miss.)/Lafayette County Sequicentennial, 1987; bd. dirs. Oxford/Lafayette County United Way, 1987-90; sustaining mem. Yocona Area Coun. Boy Scouts Am., 1981—. Mem. Assn. Computing Machinery, Spl. Interest Group on Univ. and Coll. Computing Svcs., Miss. Hist. Soc., Oxford Lions (pres. 1986-87, Lion of Yr. 1986-87, Svc. award 1992-93). Methodist. Avocations: college football, fishing, Miss./La. history, genealogy.. E-mail: ccdavid@olemiss.edu. Home: PO Box 2241 University MS 38677-2241 Office: Office Info Tech Miss Ctr Supercomputing Rsc 303 Powers Hall University MS 38677-1848

ROACH, DONALD ARTHUR, manufacturing company executive; b. Cleve., July 27, 1930; s. Cecil C. and Mildred L. (Guin) R.; m. Nancy G. Gifford, Jan. 15, 1955; children: Deborah, Cynthia, Donald, Douglas. B.S. in M.E., Purdue U., 1952; M.B.A., Harvard U., 1957; HDR Engring., Purdue U., 1995. Vice-pres., gen. mgr. Brown & Sharpe, Manchester, Mich., 1965-69; pres. Double A/B & S, Manchester, 1969-71; exec. v.p. Brown & Sharpe Mfg. Co., North Kingstown, R.I., 1971-76, pres., 1976—, chief operating officer, 1976-80, chief exec. officer, 1980—; dir. New Eng. Telephone & Telegraph Co. Boston, R.I. Hosp. Trust Nat. Bank, B.A. Ballou & Co. Inc., Providence, Kilburn Glass Industries, Norton Mass. Founder, pres. Greenhills Sch., Ann Arbor, 1967-71; chmn. R.I. Bus. Group on Health, 1983-90; trustee R.I. Sch. Design, 1976—; chmn. Pres.'s Coun., Purdue U. Served with USN, 1952-55. Recipient Iron Key award Purdue U., 1952, Disting. Alumnus award Sch. Engring. Purdue U., 1973, Disting. Mech. Engr., 1991, Disting. Indsl. Engr., 1997, Chester Kirk Disting. Engr. award U. R.I., 1989. Mem. Nat. Machine Tool Bldrs. Assn. (dir. 1980-83), Purdue Rsch. Found. Republican. Clubs: Agawam Hunt; Hope (Providence); Lakota (Woodstock, Vt.). Office: Kilburn Isotronics 111 S Worcester St Chartley MA 02712

ROACH, JOHN MICHAEL, gastroenterologist; b. Walla Walla, Wash., Feb. 28, 1947; s. John Francis and Johanna Patricia (Sullivan) R.; m. Nancy Marie Mudd, Mar. 31, 1973; children: Shannon, John, Luke, Patrick, William, Bartholomew, Michelle. BS, Seattle U., 1969; MD, U. Wash., 1973. Diplomate Am. Bd. Internal Medicine. Intern straight medicine Maricopa County Gen. Hosp., Phoenix, 1974, resident internal medicine, 1975-76, gastroenterology fellow, 1976-78; pvt. practice gastroenterology Kennewick, Wash., 1978—; pres. med. staff Kennewick Gen. Hosp., 1985. Contbr. articles to Gastrointestinal Endoscopy, Surgical Laparoscopy & Endoscopy, Gastroenterology. Mem. Tri-City Renaissance Com., Pasco, Wash., 1987-91. Mem. ACP, Am. Soc. Gastrointestinal Endoscopy, Am. Gastroent. Assn., Am. Coll. Gastroenterology, Benton-Franklin County Med. Soc. (chmn. continuing med. edn. 1987-88, pres. 1989), Wash. State Med. Assn., Pacific NW Endoscopy Soc. Republican. Roman Catholic. Avocations: camping, photography, electronics, elk hunting, moose hunting. E-mail: jmroach@bossig.com. Fax: 509-586-7092. Office: 811 S Auburn St Kennewick WA 99336-5661

ROACH, ROBERT MICHAEL, JR., lawyer; b. Bronxville, N.Y., May 27, 1955; s. Robert M. and Mary Dee R.; m. Elizabeth Preston Roach, Sept. 22, 2000. BA, Georgetown U., 1977; JD, U. Tex., 1981. Bar: Tex. 1981, U.S. Dist. Ct. (so. dist.) Tex. 1982, U.S. Ct. Appeals (5th cir.) 1982, U.S. Dist. Ct. (we. dist.) Tex. 1984, U.S. Supreme Ct. 1986, U.S. Dist. Ct. (ea. dist.) 1986, U.S. Dist. Ct. (no. dist.) Tex. 1988. Assoc. Vinson & Elkins, Houston, 1981-83, Ryan & Marshall, Houston, 1983, Mayor, Day & Caldwell, Houston, 1983-88; ptnr. Mayor, Day, Caldwell & Keeton, Houston, 1989-93; founding ptnr. Cook, Roach & Lawless, L.L.P. (former name Cook & Roach LLP), Houston, 1993—; dir. appellate advocacy U. Houston Law Ctr., 1994—; adj. prof. law U. Houston, 1990; lectr. continuing legal edn. U. Houston Law Ctr., 1989—; lectr. continuing legal edn. State Bar Tex., U. Tex., South Tex. Coll. Law, So. Meth. U., ABA; rschr., editor U.S. Senate Com. on Nutrition, 1975, 76, 77; rschr. U.S Supreme Ct., Washington, 1977; mem. Tex. Law Rev., 1979-81. Editor Def. Counsel Jour., 1990-93. Active U.S. Supreme Ct. Hist. Soc. Mem. Internat. Assn. Def. Counsel, Fedn. Ins. and Corp. Counsel, Def. Rsch. Inst. (grievance com.), Tex. Assn. Def. Counsel, State Bar Tex. (appellate sect. coun. officer 1989—), Houston Bar Assn. (officer, appellate sect.), Houston Club, Houston Met. Racquet Club, Houston Ctr. Club. Avocations: music, travel, oenology, tennis. Office: Cook & Roach LLP Texaco Heritage Plz 1111 Bagby St Ste 2650 Houston TX 77002-2543

ROACH, VICTOR RANDOLPH, government official; b. Bridgetown, Barbados, Nov. 18, 1937; s. John Richard Taylor and Rosalie Albertha Roach; m. June Eureka Linton, Feb. 7, 1959 (div. Mar. 1975); m. Penelope Hynam, Mar. 27, 1993. Diploma in Data Processing/Computer Prog, Barbados Inst. Mgmt., 1988. Jr. office clk. Knight's Ltd., 1953-65; sr. warehouse clk. DaCosta & Co. Ltd., 1956-61; asst. mgr. stacking area Port Contrs. (Barbados) Ltd., 1961-63, ships report mgr., 1963-73, office mgr./asst. acct., 1973-79; office mgr./asst. acct. Barbados Port Authority, Bridgetown, 1979-81, internal auditor, 1981-86, sec. - bd. dirs. (Ag.), 1986-92, sec. bd. dirs., 1993—, dep. gen. mgr., 1994—; Chmn. nat. adv. com. on continuing edn. programme in agrl. tech. U. W.I. Coun. mem. Barbados Nat. Trust; past sec. Barbados Full Gospel Bus.. Men's Fellowship. Mem. Inst. Profl. Mgmt., Inst. Internat. Auditors, Inst. Fin. Accts., Am. Mgmt. Assn., Inst. Internat. Trade Assn., Am. Assn. Port Authorities (bd. dirs., chmn. Caribbean delegation), Bridgetown Jaycess (past v.p. and sec.), Barbados Rugby Football Club (past pres. and sec.), Barbados Hort. Soc. (past pres. and sec., pres.), Rotary Club West (sec.), Am. Assn. of Port Authorities (bd. dirs.). Home: Costain Dr, Pine Gardens St Michael, Bridgetown Barbados

ROACH, WILLIAM RUSSELL, training and education executive; b. Bedford, Ind., 1940; s. George H. and Beatrice M. (Schoenlaub) R.; m. Margaret R. Balogh, 1961 (div. 1994); children: Kathleen L., Keith W. BS in Fin. and Acctg., UCLA, 1961. CPA, Calif. Internal auditor Hughes Aircraft Corp., L.A., 1962; sr. acct. Haskins & Sells, L.A., 1962-66; asst. to group v.p., asst. corp. contr. Lear Siegler, Inc., Santa Monica, Calif., 1966-71; exec. v.p., corp. sec., dir. Optimum Sys. Inc., Santa Clara, Calif., 1972-79; pres., dir. Banking Sys. Inc. subs. Optimum Sys. Inc., Dallas, 1976-79, BancSystems, Inc., Santa Clara, 1976-79, DMA/Optimum Honolulu, 1978-79; v.p. URS Corp., San Mateo, Calif., 1979-81; pres. URS Internat., Inc., 1980-81; pres., CEO, dir. Advanced Sys., Inc., 1981—; pres., CEO, dir. Applied Learning Internat., Inc. (formed from merger of Advanced Systems, Inc. and Deltak Training Corp.), Naperville, Ill., 1981-88; sr. v.p., bd. dirs. Nat. Edn. Corp. (parent co. Applied Learning Internat.), Irvine, Calif., 1988-89; chmn. bd., CEO Plato Learning Inc. (former known as TRO Learning Inc. (acquisition and edn. group Control Data Corp.), Hoffman Estates, Ill., 1989—; guest speaker numerous industry related funtions including Rep. Platform Com., 1988. Mem. AICPA, Calif. Soc. CPAs, Theta Delta Chi. Office: Plato Learning Inc 3150 W Higgins Rd Ste 155 Hoffman Estates IL 60195

ROACH-REEVES, CATHARYN PETITT, librarian, educator; b. Houston, Sept. 25, 1950; d. Robert Duane and Nelma Belle Petitt; m. Paul Alton Roach, Aug. 21, 1971 (div. Aug. 1982); m. Gary L. Reeves, Nov. 27, 1991. BS in Elem. Edn., Dallas Bapt. Coll., 1974; MLS, North Tex. State U., 1976; PhD in Libr. Sci., U. North Tex., 1989. Cert. elem. tchr., Tex.; cert. libr., Tex. Tchr., libr. White Hall Sch., Cedar Hill, Tex., 1976-78; libr. Patton Elem. Sch., Dallas, 1978-83, Macmillan Elem. Sch., Dallas, 1981-82, George Washington Carver Elem. Sch., Dallas, 1982-86, Arlington Pk. Elem. Sch., Dallas, 1982-86, W.L. Cabell Elem. Sch., Dallas, 1986-90, Dan D. Rogers Elem. Sch., Dallas, 1990—; presenter various workshops; cons. (video) In Search of a Libr. Adventure, 1995. Author: Teaching Library Skills in Grades K-6, 1993; co-editor Libr. Media Program Handbook, 1991. Troop leader Girl Scouts AM., 1982-88, coun. trainer, 1987-88; instr. Dallas Mus. Natural History, Summer Ednl. Program, 1984-87; hon. life mem. PTA, 1990, 93. Recipient Green Angel award Girl Scouts USA, 1985. Mem. Tex. Libr. Assn., Tex. Assn. Sch. Librs., Dallas Assn. Sch. Librs. (v.p., pres. elect. 1991-92, pres. 1992-93, Elem. Libr. of Yr. 1992-93, Positive Parents of Dallas Libr. Apple award 1992-93), Delta Kappa Gamma, Alpha Chi, Lambda Sigma Alpha, Phi Lambda Theta. Republican. Avocations: rubber stamp art, doll collecting, cake/cookie decorating, needlework, collecting Beatrix Potter and Laura Ingalls Wilder books and memorabilia. Home: 10106 Deermont Trl Dallas TX 75243-2523 Office: Dan D Rogers Elem Sch 5314 Abrams Rd Dallas TX 75214-2001

ROADARMEL, STANLEY BRUCE, civilian military employee; b. Albion, N.Y., May 5, 1937; s. Kenneth A. and Catherine Louise (Bobel) R.; m. Carole Ann Hayes, Nov. 26, 1959; children: Karen Marie, Oscar Pacific, Ann Catherine, William Hayes. Student, Purdue U., 1956-58; BA, Syracuse U., 1962; postgrad., Golden Gate U., 1976-78; grad., Squadron Officer Sch., 1965, Air Command Staff Coll., 1974-76, Indsl. Coll. Armed Forces, 1976. Commd. 2d lt. USAF, 1962, advanced through grades to maj.; adminstrv., security and recruiting ops. officer Air Tng. Command, Tex. and W.Va., 1962-69; chief field maintenance Titan II ICBM Strategic Air Command, Davis Monthan AFB, Ariz., 1969-71; chief 3901st Titan II maintenance evaluation team Strategic Air Command, Vandenberg AFB, Calif., 1971-74, logistics staff officer, 1974-77, contract specialist, 1977-82; contract specialist U.S. Air Forces Europe, Adana, Turkey, 1980-81; ret. USAF, 1982; launch complex constrn. contract negotiator, adminstr. NASA/USAF Space Shuttle Program, Lompoc, Calif., 1983-89, USAF Titan IV Space Booster, Vandenberg AFB, 1991-92; constrn. and maj. svcs. contract negotiator, adminstr. 30th Contracting Squadron USAF Space Command, Vandenberg AFB, 1992—; pres. Ctrl. Coast Profls., Mut. Profl. Counseling/Placement, Santa Maria, Calif., 1990-91. Author manual: Man Lifting Crane Operations, 1976 (Air Force Commendation award 1977); revision officer Air Force Manual 66-1 Maintenance Management, 1976 (Air Force Commendation award 1977); contbr. Strategic Air Command Manual 66-12 ICBM Maintenance Mgmt. Spkr. World Orgn. Ovulation Method, Calif., 1987—; pro life advocate, activist Am. Life League, Nat. Right to Life, 1980—; vol. Rep. Party, 1992—; marriage preparation instr. Cath. Archdiocese of L.A., Santa Maria, Calif., 1995—. Mem. NRA, Nat. Contract Mgmt. Assn., Air Force Assn. (life), Ret. Officers Assn. (life), Assn. Air Force Missileers (life), Am. Legion, Couple to Couple League. Avocations: aviation, music, marksmanship, travel, literature. Home: 4532 Glines Ave Santa Maria CA 93455-4313

ROADS, CURTIS, music educator, composer; b. Cleve., May 9, 1951. BA summa cum laude, U. Calif., San Diego, 1977; PhD, U. Paris, 1999. Editor, assoc. editor Computer Music Jour., MIT Press, Cambridge, Mass., 1978-2000; rsch. assoc. MIT, Cambridge, 1980-87; lectr. Harvard U., Cambridge, 1989, U. Paris 8, 1994-95; dir. pedagogy Les Ateliers UPIC, Paris, 1993-96; prof. U. Calif., Santa Barbara, 1996—; vis. prof. Oberlin (Ohio) Conservatory, 1991. Author: Foundations of Computer Music, 1985, The Music Machine, 1987, The Computer Music Tutorial, 1996, Field electronic music, 1981, Clang-Tint, 1994, Half-life, 1999; inventor Creatovox Synthesizer. Office: U Calif Dept Music Santa Barbara CA 93106

ROALD, CURT, banknote and securities designer, retired; b. Vardø, Finnmark, Norway, Apr. 6, 1926; s. Conrad and Maja (Axelsson) R.; m. Hjørdis Sigrid Skarland, Aug. 22, 1970 (dec. Feb. 1995). Student, State Arts and Crafts Sch., Oslo, 1945-49. Cert. comml. layout designer, securities layout designer. Designer/engraver Ctrl. Bank Norway Printing Works, Oslo, 1949-58; designer Jeffries Banknote Co. (now U.S. Banknote Co.), L.A., 1959-91; ret., 1991; cons. Jeffries Banknote Co., L.A., 1991-94. Design/artwork/Guillosche for banknotes for Norway; design Norwegian Passport; Guillosche designs for Danish banknotes; design/artwork for stock certificates, bonds, checks, bank ID cards, travelers checks for Bank of Am. (3 currencies), travelers checks for VISA (15 currencies); banknote design/artwork for D'Haiti, Estonia, Malaysia, Venezuela; computer-aided Guillosche patterns, Thomas de la Rue Giori, Lausanne, Switzerland. Avocations: drawing, lettering, painting and sculpting, stamps, reading. Home: Vetlandsveien 54A-1116, N 0685 Oslo Norway

ROAN, FORREST CALVIN, JR., lawyer; b. Waco, Tex., Dec. 18, 1944; s. Forrest Calvin and Lucille Elizabeth (McKinney) R.; m. Vickie Joan Howard, Feb. 15, 1969 (div. Dec. 1983); children: Amy Katherine, Jennifer Louise; m. Leslie D. Hampton Roan, Jan. 2, 1999. BBA, U. Tex., Austin, 1973, JD, 1976. Bar: Tex. 1976, U.S. Dist. Ct. (we. dist.) Tex. 1977, U.S. Dist. Ct. (so. dist.) Tex. 1998, U.S. Ct. Appeals (5th cir.) 1977, U.S. Supreme Ct. 1979, U.S. Ct. Appeals (11th cir.) 1981, U.S. Ct. Appeals (fed. cir.) 1998, U.S. Ct. Internat. Trade, 1998. Prin. Roan & Assocs., Austin, 1969-71; counsel, com. dir. Tex. Ho. of Reps., 1972-75; assoc. Heath, Davis & McCalla, Austin, 1975-78; prin. Roan & Gullahorn, P.C., Austin, 1978-85, Roan & Autrey (formerly Roan & Simpson), P.C., 1986-99; sr. ptnr. Cantey, Hanger, Roan & Autrey, 1999—. Bd. dirs. Lawyers Credit Union, chmn., 1982-83; bd. dirs. pub. law sect. State Bar Tex., 1980-84; dir. Am. Bankers Gen. Agy.; mem. chancellor's coun. U. Tex. With Tex. Army N.G., 1966-74. Fellow Tex. Bar Found.; mem. ABA, Tex. Assn. Def. Counsel, Tex. Assn. Bank Counsel, Def. Rsch. Inst., Travis County Bar Assn., Tex.-Mexico Bar Assn., Knights of the Symphony (vice chancellor 1997—), Tex. Lyceum Assn. (v.p., bd. dirs. 1980-87), Austin C. of C., Met. Club, Austin Club, Headliners Club, Masons, Shriners (Parsons Masonic master 1976-77). Methodist. Office: Cantey Hanger Roan & Autrey 200 Wells Fargo Bank Tower 400 W 15th St Austin TX 78701-1600

ROARK, ROBERT CAMERON, insurance broker; b. San Diego, Jan. 11, 1931; s. Alfred T. and Virginia J. Roark; m. Lois J. Maynard, July 19, 1952; children: Cynthia, Susan, Kellie, Robert. BA, San Diego State U., 1954. Life underwriter Mass. Mut. Life, San Diego, 1955-57; supr. John Hancock Mut., San Diego, 1957-59; gen. agt., mgr. Am. Mut. Life Ins., San Diego, 1959-65; regional v.p. Northwestern Life Ins., Seattle, 1965-68; broker, owner Roark Ins., San Juan Capistrano, Calif., 1968—. Author: Good News Letter, 1991—. Divsn. capt. USCG Aux., 1990, flotilla comdr., 1987, vice capt., 1989, publs. officer, 1997. Mem. Mission Hills Homeowners Assn. (pres. 1970-73, bd. mem. 1991-92), Lions Internat. (zone chmn. 1972, club pres. 1971)

ROAZZI, VINCENT MICHAEL, marketing professional; b. June 6, 1949; E-mail: C1028@bellatlantic.net.; s. John Michael and Rose Mary Roazzi; m. Marlene Sciame, Oct. 20, 1973; children: Daria, Jessica, Vincent, Dana, Victoria. BA in Econs., Bklyn. Coll., 1972. Various positions various Wall St. firms, N.Y.C., 1969-73; bus. investor, buyer, 1973-89; area mktg. dir. Cornerstone Mktg., Dallas, 1989-97; exec. dir. mktg., devel. Alliance for Affordable Svcs., Washington, 1997—. Author: The Spirituality of Success,

1999; contbr. Wealth mag. Pres. Red Fox Farm Homeowners Assn., Solebury, Pa., 1998. With USMC, 1969-71. Recipient national acknowledgement award Nat. Assn. Bus. Leaders, 1999. Mem. Inst. of Noetic Scis., Rosicrucians. Roman Catholic. Avocations: reading, writing, public speaking, coin collecting, intellectual challenges. E-mail: c1028@bellatlantic.net. Home and Office: 21 Red Fox Dr New Hope PA 18938-9664 Office: PO Box 292 Lahaska PA 18931-0292

ROBAKIS, NIKOLAOS K., medical educator; b. Finikounda, Messinia, Greece, Dec. 4, 1945; came to U.S., 1974; s. Konstantinos G. and Efstathia A. (Koutris) R.; m. Davida Ellen Scharf, June 4, 1974; children: Thalia, Daphne, Efstathia. Diploma, U. Thessaloniki, Greece, 1971; MA, NYU, N.Y.C., 1976, PhD, 1979. Tchg. fellow NYU, N.Y.C., 1974-79; postdoctoral fellow Roche Inst. Molecular Biology, Nutley, N.J., 1979-82; rsch. fellow Hoffman-LaRoche, Inc., Nutley, 1982-83; sr. rsch. mem. N.Y. Inst. Basic Rsch., S.I., 1983-87; assoc. prof. Mt. Sinai Sch. Medicine, NYU, N.Y.C., 1987-93, prof. dept. psychiatry and neurobiology, 1993—; rsch. advisor Merck Sharp and Dohme, 1992-93, Bristol-Myers Squibb Co., Wallingford, Conn., 1991-93; advisor Am. Fedn. on Aging, N.Y.C., 1999, Internat. Symposium on Alzheimer's Disease, 1994—. Contbr. numerous sci. articles to profl. publs. Pres. Greek Dem. Assn., N.Y.C.-Boston, 1985. Recipient McKnight Neurosci. award McKnight Neurosci. Inc., 1988, Zenith award Alzheimer's Assn., 1994, Disting. Scientist award Hellenic Med. Assn., 1997; named Endowed Prof., Mt. Sinai Sch. Medicine, NYU, 1994. Office: Mount Sinai Sch of Medicine One Gustave Levy Pl New York NY 10029

ROBARDS, JASON NELSON, JR., actor; b. Chgo., July 26, 1922; s. Jason Nelson and Hope (Glanville) R.; m. Eleanore Pitman, May 7, 1948; children: Jason III, Sarah Louise, David; m. Lauren Bacall, July 4, 1961 (div.); 1 son, Sam; m. Lois O'Connor, 1970; children: Shannon, Jake. Student, Am. Acad. Dramatic Arts, 1946; DHL, Fairfield U., 1982; DFA, Williams Coll., 1983. Bd. dirs. Am. Acad. Dramatic Arts, 1957—. Broadway plays include Stalag 17, 1951-53, The Chase, 1952, The Iceman Cometh, 1956, Long Day's Journey Into Night, 1956-58, 76, 88, The Disenchanted, 1958, 1958-59, Toys in the Attic, 1960, Big Fish, Little Fish, 1961, A Thousand Clowns, 1962, After the Fall, 1964, But for Whom, Charlie, 1964, Hughie, 1964, The Devils, 1965, We Bombed in New Haven, 1968, The Country Girl, 1972, A Moon for the Misbegotten, 1973, A Touch of the Poet, 1977-78, A Month of Sundays, 1987, No Man's Land, 1993; other plays include Henry IV, Part I, Stratford (Ont., Can.), 1958, Macbeth, Cambridge, Mass., You Can't Take It With You, 1983, Iceman Cometh, 1985, Love Letters, 1989, A Month of Sunday, 1990, Ah Wilderness, 1988, Park Your Car in Harvard Yard, 1991, No Man's Land, 1995, Molly Sweeny, 1996, Moonlight, 1997; motion picture appearances include The Journey, 1959, No Mans Land, 1993, By Love Possessed, 1961, Long Day's Journey into Night (Cannes Internat. Film Festival, Best Actor Award, 1962), A Thousand Clowns, Big Hand for the Little Lady, 1966, Any Wednesday, 1966, St. Valentine's Day Massacre, 1967, Night They Raided Minsky's, 1968, Hour of the Gun, 1967, Loves of Isadora, 1969, Once Upon a Time in the West, 1969, Ballad of Cable Hogue, 1970, Julius Caesar, 1970, Tora, Tora, Tora, 1970, Fools, 1970, Johnny Got His Gun, 1971, Murders in the Rue Morgue, 1971, The War Between Men and Women, 1972, Pat Garrett and Billy the Kid, 1973, Mr Sycamore, 1975, A Boy and His Dog, 1975, All the President's Men, 1976, Julia, 1977, Comes a Horseman, 1978, Hurricane, 1979, Raise The Titanic, 1990, Melvin and Howard, 1979, Something Wicked This Way Comes, 1983, Max Dugan Returns, 1983, Square Dance, 1987, The Good Mother, 1988, Parenthood, 1989, Quick Change, 1990, Storyville, 1992, The Trial, 1993, The Adventures of Huck Finn, 1993, Philadelphia, 1993, Little Big League, 1994, The Paper, 1994, Crimson Tide, 1995, Thousand Acres, 1997, Enemy of the State, 1998, Beloved, 1998, Heartwood, 1998, Magnolia, 1999, Going Home, 2000, voice over (documentary) The Irish in America: The Long Journey Home, 1999; TV appearance Roberto in For Whom the Bell Tolls, CBS, 1959; starred in TV films including: The Iceman Cometh, 1961, One Day in the Life of Ivan Denisovitch, 1963, Washington Behind Closed Doors, 1977, F.D.R.: The Last Year, 1980, The Day After, 1983, Sakharov, 1984, Johnny Bull, 1986, Inherit the Wind, 1988 (Emmy award, 1988), The Christmas Wife, 1988, Chernobyl: The Final Warning, 1991; appeared in TV miniseries Haywire, 1980, The Atlanta Child Murders, 1985. Served with USN, 1939-46. Recipient ANTA award for outstanding contbn. to living theater, 1959, Antoinette Perry award as best actor, 1959, Obie award, 1956, Tony award for best dramatic actor, 1959, Acad. awards for best supporting actor, 1976-77, N.Y. Film Critics Circle award for best supporting actor, 1976, Emmy as best actor, 1988, Nat. Arts Medal, 1992. Mem. Players Club, Century Club, N.Y. Athletic Club. Office: William Morris Agy care Ames Cushing 131 S El Camino Dr Beverly Hills CA 90212-2704

ROBB, DEAN ALLEN, SR., lawyer, farmer; b. Feb. 26, 1924; s. Zenas Allan and Mary Dorothy (Cunningham) R.; m. Barbara Gulley, Aug. 24, 1947 (div.); children: Laura, Dean Allen Jr., Blair M.; m. Cindy Mathias, 1983; 1 child, Matthew Zenas, 1 stepson, Ben. BS, U. Ill., 1946; JD, Wayne State U., 1949. Bar: Mich. 1949, U.S. Dist. Ct. (ea. dist.) Mich. 1950, U.S. Dist. Ct. (we. dist.) Mich. 1960, U.S. Dist Ct. Appeals (6th cir.) 1960, U.S. Dist. Ct. (no. dist.) Ind. 1962, U.S. Dist. Ct. (no. dist.) Ohio 1968, U.S. Supreme Ct. Sr. ptnr. Goodman, Crockett, Eden & Robb, Detroit, 1950-71; sole practice, owner Dean A. Robb, P.C., Traverse City, Mich., 1971-76; pres. Robb, Dettmer & Phillips, Traverse City, 1976-81, Robb, Dettmer, Messing & Thompson, P.C., Traverse City, 1983-86, Robb, Messing, Palmer & Dignan PC, Traverse City, 1986-96; pres. Dean Robb Law Firm, Traverse City, 1997-99, Suttons Bay, Mich., 1999—; lectr. various nat., state and local bar assns.; guest lectr. Detroit Coll. Law, Thomas Colley Law Sch., U. Detroit Law Sch., U. Mich., U. Miss.; mem. faculty Nat. Coll. Advocacy Assn. Trial Lawyers Am., Practicing Law Inst., N.Y.C., Inst. Continuing Legal Edn., Ann Arbor, Mich.; apptd. to jud. selection com. we. dist. U.S. Dist. Ct. Mich., 1986-93; designated counsel for Brotherhood of Locomotive Engrs., 1989-92; bd. dirs. NW Mich. br. ACLU, Rehab. Inst. Detroit ; vol. atty. Penrickton Nursery Sch. for Visually Handicapped Children, Taylor, Mich.;. Co-author: Lawyers Desk Reference, 1964-75; co-editor Rights of Railroad Workers, 1973; contbr. articles to legal publs. Mem. Traverse City and Leelanau Players; exec. sec. Met. Detroit Fair Employment Practices Coun., Dodge Cmty. House; pres. Grand Traverse Hist. Soc., 1987-91; contbr., bd. trustees Traverse City Civic Players, 1973-78; active supporter Traverse Area Found.; active supporter 3d level Crisis Invention Ctr., bd. dirs., 1996; Dem. nominee Mich. Supreme Ct., 1986; intern Presbyn. Ch., 1946-47; exec. bd. dirs. Boys & Girls Club, Grand Traverse. Served with USN, 1942-44. Recipient Lawyer of Yr. award Wayne State U., 1975-76, Outstanding Lawyers Alum award, 1975; Champion of Justice award State Bar of Mich., 1994. Fellow Am. Coll. Trial Lawyers; mem. ABA, DAV, NOW, NAACP (life), Trial Lawyers for Pub. Justice (nat. pres.), Assn. Trial Lawyers Am. (past nat. co-chmn. nat. com. on civil rights, past chmn. R.R. law sect.), Mich. Trial Lawyers Assn. (past pres., Champion of Justice award 1998), Nat. Lawyers Guild (mem.-at-large), Grand-Traverse-Leelanau-Antrim County Bar Assn., Mich. Bar Assn., Nat. Assn. Ciminal Def. Lawyers, Actors Equity, Wayne State U. Alumni Assn. (exec. bd.), Sierra Club, Friends of the Earth, Amnesty Internat., Grand Traverse Area C. of C., U. Ill. Alumni Assn. Fax: 231-271-6555. Office: Dean Robb Law Firm PO Box 879 416 St Joseph St Suttons Bay MI 49682

ROBB, JOHN WESLEY, religion educator; b. Los Angeles, Dec. 1, 1919; s. Edgar Milton and Alta (Boger) R.; m. Ethel Edna Tosh, June 13, 1942; children: Lydia Joan Robb Durbin, Judith Nadine Robb Eggerman. A.B., Greenville Coll., 1941; Th.M., U. So. Calif., 1945, Ph.D., 1952; L.H.D., Hebrew Union Coll.-Jewish Inst. Religion, 1977. Asst. prof. philosophy and religion Dickinson Coll., Pa., 1948-51; fellow Fund for Advancement Edn., 1951-52; asso. prof. U. So. Calif., L.A., 1954-62, chmn. dept. religion, 1954-67, assoc. dean humanities Coll. Letters, Arts and Scis.,, 1963-68, Leonard K. Firestone prof., 1974-75, prof., 1962-87, prof. emeritus, 1987—; prof. Sch. Medicine U. So. Calif., 1981-87; coun. mem. Inst. of Lab. Animal Resources Nat. Acad. Scis. Nat. Rsch. Coun., 1986-93; vis. disting. prof. USAF Med. Ctr., Wilford Hall, Tex., 1985; mem. rev. com. NIH Guide for the Care and Use of Lab. Animals, NRC, NAS, 1993-96; advisor/tutor Med. Quality Assurance Commn., Dept. Health, State of Wash., 1994—; mem. ethics com. Swedish Med. Ctr., N.W. Hosp., Seattle, Highline Hosp., Burien; adj. prof. bioethics Sch. Medicine, U. So. Calif., 1989-91, adj. prof. emeritus, 1991—. Author: Inquiry Into Faith, 1960; co-editor: Readings in Religious Philosophy; The Reverent Skeptic, 1979. Served as lt. (j.g.) USNR, 1945-47; to lt. 1952-54. Recipient award for excellence in tchg. U. So. Calif., 1960, 74, Dart award for acad. innovation, 1970, Raubenheimer Disting. Faculty award divsn. humanities, 1980, Outstanding Faculty award Student Senate, 1981, Disting. Emeritus award, 1995; Robert Fenton Craig award Blue Key, 1980. Fellow Soc. for Values in Higher Edn.; mem. Am. Acad. Religion (v.p. 1966, pres. 1967), Am. Philos. Assn., AAUP (v.p. Calif. Conf. 1977, pres. 1978-79), Phi Beta Kappa (hon.), Phi Kappa Phi, Phi Chi Phi. United Methodist. Home: 8001 Sand Point Way NE Apt C35 Seattle WA 98115-6356

ROBB, THOMAS LINDSEY WYATT, theatre producer, set and costume designer; b. Hamilton, Victoria, Australia, Apr. 7, 1947; s. Lindsey Wyatt and Olive Albina (Rackham) R. Prodr. Australian Internat. Entertainment, Perth, 1969—. Prodns. include International Fantasy, 1972-75, High Society Follies, 1976-78, Braziliana, 1979-81, Viva Australia, 1982-86, Broadway Follies, 1985, Show Girls/Queens, 1995-97, Aladdin on Ice, 1999, Sinbad on Ice, 2000. Asst. sec. Latin Am. Cultural Assn., Perth, 1998-99.. Avocations: world history, Egyptology, travel, languages, health issues.

ROBBE-GRILLET, ALAIN, author, filmmaker; b. Brest, France, Aug. 18, 1922; s. Gaston and Yvonne (Canu) R.; m. Catherine Rstakian, 1957. Ed., Lycee Buffon, Lycee St. Louis, Inst. Nat. Agronomique, Paris. Charge de mission Inst. Nat. de la Statistique, 1945-48; engr. Inst. des Fruits Tropicaux (French Guina, Morocco, Martinique and Guadeloupe), 1949-51; lit. adviser Editions de Minuit, 1955-84; dir. Ctr. Sociology of Lit., U. Brussels, 1980-87; Disting. prof. NYU and Wash. U. Author: (novels) Les Gommes, 1953 (pub. as The Erasers, 1964; Prix Fénéon 1954), Le Voyeur, 1955 (pub. as The Voyeur, 1958; Prix des Critiques 1955), La Jalousie, 1957 (pub. as Jealousy, 1959), Dans le Labyrinthe, 1959 (pub. as In the Labyrinth, 1960), L'Année dernière à Marienbad, 1961 (pub. as Last Year at Marienbad, 1962), Instantanés, 1962 (pub. as Snapshots, 1965), L'Immortelle, 1963 (pub. as The Immortal One, 1971; Prix Louis Delluc 1963), La Maison de rendez-vous, 1965 (pub. as The House of Assignation, 1970), Projet pour une révolution à New York, 1970 (pub. as Project for a Revolution in New York, 1972), Glissements progressifs du plaisir, 1974, Topologie d'une cité fantôme, 1976 (pub. as Topology of a Phantom City, 1977), Un Régicide, 1978, Souvenirs du triangle d'or, 1978 (pub. as Recollections of the Golden Triangle, 1984), Djinn, 1981 (Premio Internazionale Mondello 1982); (screenplays) L'Année dernière à Marienbad, 1961; (screenplay and direction) L'Immortelle, 1963, Trans-Europ-Express, 1967, L'Homme qui ment, 1968 (Best Screenplay Berlin Festival 1969), L'Eden et après, 1970, Glissements progressifs du plaisir, 1973, Le Jeu avec le feu, 1975, La Belle Captive, 1983, Un Bruit que rend Fou, 1995; (other writings) Pour un Nouveau Roman, 1963 (pub. as Towards a New Novel, 1965), Rêves de jeunes Filles, 1971 (pub. as Dreams of a Young Girl, 1971), Les Demoiselles d'Hamilton, 1972 (pub. as Sisters, 1973), Construction d'un temple en ruines à la déesse Vanadé, 1975, La Belle Captive, 1976, Temple aux miroirs, 1977, Le Miroir qui revient, 1985 (pub. as Ghosts in the Mirror, 1988), Angélique ou l'Enchantement, 1987, George Segal, invasion blanche, 1990, Les Derniers Jours de Corinthe, 1994. Decorated chevalier Legion d'Honneur; officier Ordre nat. du merit; recipient Prix Louis Delluc, 1963.

ROBBEN, MARY MARGARET, portrait artist, painter; b. Bethesda, Md., Oct. 30, 1948; d. John Otto and Mary Margaret (McConnaughy) R. Student, Ohio U., 1967-71; B of Visual Art, Ga. State U., 1984. Visual merchandising staff Macy's Dept. Store, Union City, Ga., 1985-86; embroidery designer So. Promotions, Peachtree City, Ga., 1987-90; portrait artist Personal Touch Portraits, Peachtree City, Ga., 1991-95, Margy's Portraiture, Peachtree City, 1996-98, Margy's Studios, 1999—. Mem. Internat. Platform Assn., Ga. State U. Alumni Assn., Golden Key, Nat. Mus. of Women in the Arts, Nat. Trust for Hist. Preservation, Am. Craft Coun. Avocations: cooking, gardening, reading. Home and Office: 207 Battery Way Peachtree City GA 30269-2126

ROBBERSTAD, MAGNUS KNUTSON, neurology consultant; b. Oslo, May 20, 1932; s. Knut and Eldrid (Fjalestad) R.; m. Aslaug Goderstad, Sept. 29, 1956; children: Eldrid Gro, Tonje Solveig, Ingunn Kristin. MD, U. Oslo, 1956; examinee, Govt. Health Adminstrn. Sch., Oslo, 1964; specialist in phys. medicine and rehab., U. Oslo, 1975, specialist in neurology, 1978, specialist in soc. adminstrn., 1983. Intern Porsgrunn Hosp. Group, 1957-58; staff mem. Oslo Mcpl. Hosp. Group, 1969-73, Oslo Univ. Hosp. Group, 1973-80; staff Tromsoe Univ. Hosp., 1981; med. cons. in neurology Nat. Ins. Adminstrn., Oslo, 1982-84, chief med. cons., 1984—; fed. health officer, Nord-Odal, 1959-61, Leirfjord, 1961-69. Co-author: (encyclopedia) Norsk Allkunnebok, 1958-64, (textbooks) Medisinsk journalskriving, 1979, rev., 1987, Nevrologi fra barn til voksen, 1997, (nonfiction) Målreising, 1967; author: (textbook) Rettleiing i journalskriving, 1956. Mem. County Parliament, Leirfjord, 1963-69, Nesodden, 1971-75; chmn. Ednl. Bd., Leirfjord, 1963-69; mem., vice-chmn. Bd. Energy, Nesodden County, 1988—. 1st lt. Royal Norwegian Air Force, 1958-59. Storebrand grantee Storebrand Ins. Co., 1972. Mem. Norwegian Soc. Neurology, Norwegian Soc. Phys. Medicine, Acad. Norwegian Lang. (bd. dirs., pres. 1979—), Medisinsk Mållag (direction bd., pres. 1954—). Lutheran. Avocations: developing and conserving Norwegian language, outdoor living, local politics. Home: Bjornemyr terrasse 12, N-1453 Bjornemyr Norway Office: Nat Ins Adminstrn, Drammensvegen 60, N-0241 Oslo Norway

ROBBINS, ANNE FRANCIS See **REAGAN, NANCY DAVIS**

ROBBINS, CORNELIUS (VAN VORSE), educational administration educator; b. Wilmington, Del., Nov. 2, 1931; s. Cornelius V. and Irene (Tatman) R.; m. Janet Porter, Aug. 1953; children: Eva Robbins Burke, Susan Robbins, Laurel Robbins, Melissa Robbins Beegle. BA in Polit. Sci, U. Del., 1953, MEd in Social Scis, 1961; EdD in Ednl. Adminstrn, U. Pa., 1964. Asst. mgr. Robbins & Clark Hardware, 1953-57; mem. faculty U. Del., 1957-58; tchr. Marshallton (Del.) Sch. Dist., 1958-60, Mt. Pleasant (Del.) Sch. Dist., 1960-62; asst. to dir. sch. study councils U. Pa., 1962-64; dean instrn. Ocean County Coll., 1965-67; dean of coll. C/C. of Delaware County, Pa., 1967-69; sr. assoc., coll. div. dir. McManis Assocs., Washington, 1969-70; pres. Genesee C.C., 1970-75; assoc. chancellor for community colls. SUNY, 1975-85; acting pres. Potsdam State Coll. (N.Y.), 1982-83; pres. Cobleskill (N.Y.) Coll. Agr. & Tech., 1985-92; prof. edn. adminstrn. SUNY, Albany, N.Y., 1992—; cons. Middle States Assn. Colls.; area liaison officer U.S. Mil. Acad., 1971-75; chmn. SUNY West Pres.'s Council and mem. Chancellor's Council, 1973-91. Contbr. articles to profl. pubs. Served with U.S. Army, 1954-56; maj. USAR ret. Recipient Outstanding Educator's award N.Y. State Assn. Jr. Colls., 1975, Disting. Svc. award Faculty Coun. Community Colls., 1988. Mem. Am. Assn. Higher Edn., State Dirs. of Community Colls. Assn., Phi Delta Kappa. Office: SUNY Albany Ed 329 Albany NY 12222-0001

ROBBINS, ELDORA KING, retired secondary education educator; b. Asheboro, N.C., Dec. 19, 1927; d. Clyde Augusta King and Lucy Dale Chriscoe; m. Jame Bryce Robbins, Dec. 31, 1950; 1 child, James Bryce II. A. Pfeiffer Coll., 1947; AB, High Point U., 1957; MEd, U. N.C., Greensboro, 1967. Tchr. N.C., 1947-91; mem. legis. bd. N.C. Edn. Assn., 1947-87. Treas., bd. dirs. Guardian Ad Litem Assn., Asheboro, 1990-99. Named Randolph County Woman of Yr., Family Crisis Ctr., Asheboro, 1995; recipient Gov.'s Vol. award, N.C., 1999. Democrat. Methodist. Avocations: reading, travel, dolls, plates. Home: 1237 Arrowwood Rd Asheboro NC 27203-7009

ROBBINS, FREDERICK CHAPMAN, retired physician, medical school dean emeritus; b. Auburn, Ala., Aug. 25, 1916; s. William J. and Christine (Chapman) R.; m. Alice Havemeyer Northrop, June 19, 1948; children: Alice, Louise. AB, U. Mo., 1936, BS, 1938; MD, Harvard U., 1940; DSc (hon.), John Carroll U., 1955, U. Mo., 1958, U. N.C., 1979, Tufts U., 1983, Med. Coll. Ohio, 1983; LLD, U. N.Mex., 1968. Diplomate Am. Bd. Pediatrics. Intern Children's Hosp., Boston, 1941-42, resident, 1940-41, resident pediatrician, 1946-48; sr. fellow virus disease Nat. Rsch. Coun., 1948-50; staff rsch. div. infectious diseases Children's Hosp., Boston, 1948-50, assoc. physician, assoc. dir. isolation svc., assoc. rsch. div. infectious diseases, 1950-52; instr., assoc. in pediatrics Harvard Med. Sch., 1950-52; dir. dept. pediatrics and contagious diseases Cleve. Met. Gen. Hosp., 1952-66; prof. pediatrics Case Western Res. U., 1950-80, dean Sch. Medicine, 1966-80, dean emeritus, 1980—, univ. prof. emeritus, 1987—, now dir. Ctr. Adolescent Health Sch. Medicine; pres. Inst. Medicine, NAS, 1980-85; vis. scientist Donner Lab., U. Calif., 1963-64. Served as maj. AUS, 1942-46; chief virus and rickettsial disease sect. 15th Med. Gen. Lab. investigations infectious hepatitis, typhus fever and Q fever. Decorated Bronze Star, 1945; recipient 1st Mead Johnson prize application tissue culture methods to study of viral infections, 1953; co-recipient Nobel prize in physiology and medicine, 1954; Med. Mut. Honor Award for, 1969; Ohio Gov.'s award, 1971. Mem. Assn. Am. Med. Colls. (Abraham Flexner award 1987), Nat. Acad. Scis., Am. Acad. Arts and Scis., Am. Soc. Clin. Investigation (emeritus mem.), Am. Acad. Pediatrics, Soc. Pediatric Research (pres. 1961-62, emeritus mem.), Am. Pediatric Soc., Am. Philos. Soc., Phi Beta Kappa, Sigma Xi, Phi Gamma Delta. Office: Case Western Res U Sch Med 10900 Euclid Ave Cleveland OH 44106-1712

ROBBINS, IAN JOHN, molecular genetics educator, researcher; b. Redhill, Surrey, Eng., Jan. 9, 1957; arrived in France, 1984; s. Ralph Peter and Joyce Barbara (Fleetwood) R.; m. Françoise Hélène Flouret, July 12, 1979; children: Chloë, Ailsa, Glenn. BSc, U. Liverpool, U.K., 1978; PhD, U. Glasgow, U.K., 1982. Temporary lectr. U. Caen, France, 1984-90; lectr. U. Montpellier 2, France, 1990-96, sr. lectr., 1996—; dir. Aqualex Multimedia Consortium, Dublin, 1997—. Co-author: Aqualex, 1997; editl. bd. Internat. Jour. of Bioscis. and the Law, 1996—. Avocation: painting. Office: Inst Genetique Moleculaire, 1919 Route de Mende, F 34293 Montpellier France

ROBBINS, JEANETTE LEE, sales and manufacturing executive; b. Portland, Oreg., July 21, 1956; d. Robert Lee and Norma Yvonne (Smith) Rassi; m. Michael Keith Robbins, May 22, 1981. A in Gen. Sci., Portland C.C., 1982. Cert. engring. aide, Oreg. With prodn. thrift Salvation Army, Portland, 1979, Goodwill Industries, Denver, 1983-87, St. Vincent De Paul, Portland, 1987-88; owner Job Devel. Rsch. Ctr., Portland, 1985—, Eye-Dea Devel. Sales & Mfg., Portland, 1988—; detective scientist, 1980—; reviewer publs. and forms IRS, 1997—, U.S. Govt., Washington, 1997—, local bus map rev., 1998. Author: (textbook) Prime Factor Pattern, 1991, Prime Pattern of (Square) Root Ends, 1994; contbr. articles and book revs. to profl. publs. and books; artist, author: (visual aid) Artrithmetic, 1982, Patricia Mae, U.S. White House, 1996, Artrithmetic-Reference, 1997, Combination, 1998, Large Combination Deluxe, 1999. Corr., adviser, World Gov., Nat. Gov., State Gov., Local Gov., Private Citizen, Bus. Owners, 1978—, Dem. Nat. Com., Washington D.C., 1993—. With USAF, 1977. Mem. Pub. Libr. Sys. (rschr. 1978—), Nat. Geographic Soc. (corr. 1993—). Avocations: alpinist, photography, languages. Office: Eye Dea Devel Sales & Mfg PO Box 66221 Portland OR 97290-6221

ROBBINS, KEITH GILBERT, academic administrator; b. Bristol, Eng., Apr. 9, 1940; s. Gilbert Henry and Edith Mary Robbins; m. Janet Carey Thomson, Aug. 24, 1963; children: Paul, Daniel, Lucy, Adam. Lectr. U. York, Eng., 1963-71; prof. U. Wales, Bangor, 1971-79, U. Glasgow, Scotland, 1980-91; vice-chancellor U. Wales, Lampeter, 1992—; pres. Hist. Assn., U.K., 1988-91. Author: Munich 1938, 1968, Sir Edward Grey, 1971, The Eclipse of a Great Power: Modern Britain 1870-1992, 1994, Great Britain: Identities Institutions and the Idea of Britishness, 1997, The World Since 1945: A Concise History, 1998. Winston Churchill Traveling fellow, Europe, 1990. Fellow Royal Hist. Soc., Royal Soc. Edinburgh. Avocations: walking, music, gardening. Home: Rhydyfran Cribyn Lampeter, Ceredigion SA48 7NH, Wales

ROBBINS, KELLY, professional golfer; b. Mt. Pleasant, Mich., Sept. 29, 1969; d. Steve and Margie R. BA, U. Tulsa. Mem. Ladies Pro Golf Assn., 1991—. Winner LPGA Corning Classic, 1993, jamie Farr Toledo Classic, 1994, McDonald's LPGA Championship, 1995, Twelve Bridges LPGA Classic, 1996, Diet Dr. Pepper Nat., 1997, Jamie Farr Kroger Pro-Am. Classic, 1997, Health South Inaugural, 1998, 99, Lifetime's AFLAC Tournament of Champions, 1998. Avocations: fishing, tennis, swimming, basketball. Office: c/o Ladies Pro Golf Assn 100 International Golf Dr Daytona Beach FL 32124-1082

ROBBINS, NANCY LOUISE See **MANN, NANCY LOUISE**

ROBBINS, NORMAN NELSON, lawyer; b. Detroit, Sept. 27, 1919; s. Charles and Eva (Gold) R.; m. Pamela Anne Eldred, April 22, 1946; children: Susan, Aimee. LLB, JD, Wayne State U., 1943. Bar: Mich. 1943. Pvt. practice Birmingham, Mich., 1943—; chmn. Mich. Bd. for Marriage Counselors, 1971-75; lectr. Inst. Continuing Legal Edn. Editor Mich. Family Law Jour., 1974—; mem. editorial bd. Am. Jour. Family Law; co-editor: Michigan Family Law, 2 vols., 1988; contbr. 600 articles to legal publs. Chmn. Wayne County unit Am. Cancer Soc., Detroit, 1971-76, Mich. Dept. Vets. Trust Fund, 1977-8. Capt. USMCR, 1943-46, PTO. Recipient Gov.'s award State of Mich., Cert. of Appreciation, Gov. of Mich., Cert. of Recognition, Detroit Common Coun. award Mich. Assn. Marriage Counselors, Lifetime Achievement award Mich. Family Law Sect. Mem. ABA (mem. family law coun. 1993-95, sr. editor ABA Family Adv. 1991—), Mich. Bar Assn. (chmn. family law sect. 1974-75), Oakland County Bar Assn., Am. Acad. Matrimonial Lawyers (pres. Mich. chpt. 1982), Am. Legion (judge adv. Mich. dept. 1968-69, comdr. Detroit chpt. 1970-71). Home and Office: 5543 Tadworth Pl West Bloomfield MI 48322-4016

ROBBINS, PAT SWEENEY, political organization executive; b. Akron, Ohio, July 12, 1940; d. Martin J. Sweeney and Winifred M. Bailey; divorced; children: Cheryl, Wendy Perez, Colleen Little. Adminstrv. asst. U.S. Senator John Tower, Austin, Tex., 1972-75; founder, assoc. dir. Associated Reps. of Tex., Austin, 1976—. Vol., bd. dirs. March of Dimes, Austin; vol., pres. Brackenridge Hosp. Aux., Austin. Recipient Appreciation award March of Dimes, Austin, Brackenridge Hosp., Austin, Bluebonnet Pachyderm Club, Austin. Mem. Epsilon Sigma Alpha (dist. pres.). Avocations: travel, photography. Office: Associated Reps of Tex 807 Brazos St Ste 601 Austin TX 78701-2526

ROBBINS, PETER ALISTAIR, physiologist, educator; b. Bristol, Eng., Aug. 28, 1957; s. Michael John Robbins and Shirley Dean (Swift) Daynes; m. Helen Sian Kilner, July 13, 1985. BA in Physiology, Oxford (Eng.) U., 1978, DPhil in Physiology, 1981; B.M.,B.Ch. in Medicine, U. Oxford, 1984; BA in Math., Open U., Eng., 1993. Registered med. practitioner, U.K. House surgeon Gloucester (Eng.) Royal Hosp., 1984; house physician John Radcliffe Hosp., Oxford, 1985; lectr. physiology Oxford U., 1985-96, reader in physiology, 1996-98, fellow and med. tutor Queens Coll., 1985—, prof. physiology, 1998—; mem. physiology and pharmacology panel The Wellcome Trust, London, 1993-98. Contbr. articles to profl. jours. including Jour. of Physiology, Jour. of Applied Physiology, Respiration Physiology, Exptl. Physiology, Respiration, Brit. Jour. Anesthesia, Circulation, Am. Jour. Cardiology; mem. editl. bd. Am. Physiol. Soc., 1996-99; mem. internat. adv. com. Jour. Applied Physiology, 1999—. Rsch. grantee Wellcome Trust. Mem. Am. Physiol. Soc., Physiol. Soc. Achievements include research on respiratory control. Avocations: walking, fishing, piano, bridge, sailing. Office: Univ Laboratory Physiology, Parks Rd, Oxford OX1 3PT, England

ROBBINS, RAY CHARLES, manufacturing company executive; b. Syracuse, N.Y., Sept. 15, 1920; s. Frederick and Mary Elizabeth (Field) R.; children: Sandra Robbins Jannetta, Ray Charles Jr., Eric L. With Lennox Internat. Inc. (formerly Lennox Furnace Co.), 1940-48; asst sales mgr. Lennox Industries Inc. (formerly Lennox Furnace Co.), Syracuse, 1948-52; gen. mgr. new factory and sales office, Lennox Industries, Inc. (formerly Lennox Furnace Co.), Toronto, Ont., Can., 1952-67; dir. Lennox Can. and Timeplan Fin. Co. Ltd., 1953-65; pres. Lennox Can., 1965-69; exec. v.p. Lennox-Worldwide, 1969-70, pres., CEO, 1970-77; chmn. bd. Lennox Can., 1976-92; chmn. bd., chief exec. officer Lennox Industries Inc., 1977-80, chmn. bd., 1980-91, chmn. emeritus, 1991—; bd. dirs. Lennox Internat., Inc., Des Moines, Ia., Hawkeye Security Ins. Co., Des Moines, Fin. First Interstate of Iowa, Inc., Des Moines, Q-Dot, Garland, Tex.; pres., founder, bd. Security Group, Inc., Dallas, 1983—; bd. advisor Internat. Exec. Svc. Corp., dirs. Exec. Inst., Inc., Dallas, 1983—; bd. advisor Internat. Exec. Svc. Corp., 1993—. Bd. dirs. Metro Toronto Big Bros., 1964-69, Queensway Gen. Hosp., 1957-69, Texx Found., 1979-81, Bus. Industry Polit. Action Com.; bd. govs., mem. exec. com. Iowa Coll. Found., 1975-78; v.p., mem. exec. bd. Mid-Iowa County Boy Scouts Am., 1972-78; mem. Pres.' Phys. Fitness Council, from 1979; exec. bd. Circle 10 council Boy Scouts Am., from 1979; mem. Dallas Citizens Council; bd. of govs. Nat. Women's Econ. Alliance Found.; bd. dirs. North Tex. Commn. Served with AUS, 1942-45, PTO. Mem. ASHRAE (life), Am. Refrigeration Inst. (bd. dirs. 1973-74, 78, life from 1979, v.p. 1975-76, chmn. 1977), NAM (bd. dirs. 1974-75, dir. at large

1976, dir. State of Iowa 1977-78, dir. State of Tex. 1979-92), Nat. Mgmt. Assn. (exec. adv. com. 1979-92), Gas Appliance Mfrs. Assn. (past bd. dirs.), Can. Gas Assn. (pres.), Can. Mfg. Assn. (chmn. Toronto dist.), U.S. C. of C. (Can.-U.S. sect.), Bus.-Industry Polit. Action Com. (bd. dirs. 1991). Clubs: Park Cen., Landmark Athletic, Aerobics Activity Ctr. (Dallas); Canyon Creek Country (Richardson, Tex.).

ROBBINS, STEPHEN J. M., lawyer; b. Seattle, Apr. 13, 1942; s. Robert Mads and Aneita Elberta (West) R.; m. Nina Winifred Tanner, Aug. 11, 1967; children: Sarah E.T., Alicia S.T. AB, UCLA, 1964; JD, Yale U., 1971. Bar: D.C. 1973, U.S. Dist. Ct. D.C. 1973, U.S. Ct. Appeals (D.C. cir.) 1973, U.S. Ct. Appeals (3d cir.) 1973, U.S. Dist. Ct. (ea. and no. dists.) Calif. 1982, U.S. Dist. Ct. (cen. dist.) Calif. 1983, Supreme Ct. of Republic of Palau, 1994. Pres. U.S. Nat. Student Assn., Washington, 1964-65; dir. scheduling McGovern for Pres., Washington, 1971-72; assoc. Steptoe & Johnson, Washington, 1972-75; chief counsel spl. inquiry on food prices, com. on nutrition and human needs U.S. Senate, Washington, 1975; v.p., gen. counsel Straight Arrow Pubs., San Francisco, 1975-77; dep. dist. atty. City and County of San Francisco, 1977-78; regional counsel U.S. SBA, San Francisco, 1978-80; spl. counsel Warner-Amex Cable Communications, Sacramento, 1981-82; ptnr. McDonough, Holland and Allen, Sacramento, 1982-84; v.p. Straight Arrow Pubs., N.Y.C., 1984-86; gen. legal counsel Govt. State of Koror, Rep. of Palau, Western Caroline Islands, 1994-95; pvt. practice law, 1986—; adj. prof. govt. Calif. State U., Sacramento, 1999—. Staff sgt. U.S. Army, 1966-68. Mem. ABA (sect. urban, state and local govt. sect. real property, probate and trust law, sect. natural resources energy, environ. law, forum com. on affordable housing and cmty. devel.), D.C. Bar, State Bar of Calif., Urban Land Inst., Am. Hist. Assn., Supreme Ct. Hist. Soc., Acad. Polit. Sci., Chamber Music Soc. of Sacramento, Oreg. Shakespeare Festival, Shaw Island Hist. Soc. Democrat. Unitarian. Avocations: theatre, art, hiking. Office: 2150 3rd Ave Sacramento CA 95818-3102

ROBBINS, SUSAN PAULA, social work educator; b. Bklyn., Aug. 15, 1948; d. Harold Jess and Rose (Bernstein) R. AA, Manhattan C.C., 1972; BA summa cum laude, Hamline U., 1974; MSW, U. Minn., 1976; PhD, Tulane U., 1979. Adj. instr. dept. sociology and social work Augsburg Coll., Mpls., 1975-76; part-time instr. women's studies program U. Minn., Mpls., 1976; rsch. and grant cons. Seminole Tribe of Fla., Hollywood, 1978-79, child and adolescent caseworker, program planning cons., 1979-80; coord. criminal justice/corrections program St. Mary's Dominican Coll., New Orleans, 1979-80; asst. prof. social work New Orleans Consortium, 1978-80; asst. prof. social work U. Houston, 1980-86, assoc. prof., 1986—, assoc. dean acad. affairs, 1998-2000; cons. ABA Multi Door Program, Houston, Cmty. Svc. Option Program, Houston; mediator Dispute Resolution Ctrs., Houston, 1982—; trainer Tex. Dept. Protective Svcs. Tng. Inst., 1995—. Contbg. author: Encyclopedia of Social Work; author numerous articles on Native Am. delinquency, cults, and recovered memories of abuse. Women's Club of Mpls. fellow, 1975, Nat. Inst. of Mental Health fellow, 1976-78; recipient Nat. Faculty Excellence award Univ. Continuing Edn. Assn., 1998. Mem. NASW, Coun. on Social Work Edn., Social Welfare Action Alliance, Assn. for Cmty. Orgn. and Social Adminstrn., So. Sociol. Soc., Phi Kappa Phi (sec. Houston chpt. 1984—). Democrat. Jewish. Office: Univ Houston 4800 Calhoun Rd Houston TX 77204-0001

ROBBINS, THOMAS LANDAU, humanities researcher; b. N.Y.C., Oct. 13, 1943; s. Manuel Lee and Elly (Landau) R. AB, Harvard U., 1965; MA, U. N.C., 1968, PhD in Sociology, 1973. Instr., asst. prof. Queens Coll., 1971-78; instr. Cen. Mich. U., 1982-83; NIMH postdoctoral trainee in sociology Yale U., New Haven, 1979-81; sr. rsch. assoc. Santa Barbara (Calif.) Ctr. for Humanistic Studies, 1990—. Author: Cults, Converts and Charisma, 1988; co-editor: In Gods We Trust, 1981, 2d edit., 1990, Cults, Culture and the Law, 1985, Church-State Relations, 1987, Millennium, Messiahs and Mayhem, 1997; assoc. editor Sociol. Analysis, 1984-90; editl. cons. Nova Religio, 1997—; contbr. articles to various publs.; edtl. cons. Nova Religio. Mem. Soc. for the Sci. Study of Religion (exec. coun. 1988-91), Assn. for the Sociology Religion, (exec. coun. 1985-87), Am. Sociol. Assn., Soc. for the Study of Social Problems. Meher Baba. Home and Office: 427 4th St SW Apt 8A Rochester MN 55902-3226

ROBBINS, TIMOTHY (FRANCIS), director, actor; b. N.Y.C., Oct. 16, 1958. BA, UCLA, 1981. Founder, artistic dir. The Actor's Gang, 1981—. Actor: (films) No Small Affairs, 1984, Toy Soldiers, 1984, Fraternity Vacation, 1985, The Sure Thing, 1985, Howard the Duck, 1986, Top Gun, 1986, Five Corners, 1987, Bill Durham, 1988, Tapeheads, 1989, Eric The Viking, 1989, Twister, 1989, Miss Firecracker, 1989, Cadillac Man, 1990, Jacob's Ladder, 1990, Jungle Fever, 1991, The Player, 1992 (Best Actor award Cannes Film Festival 1992), Short Cuts, 1993, The Hudsucker Proxy, 1994, The Shawshank Redemption, 1994, Ready to Wear (Prêt-à-Porter), 1994, I.Q., 1994. The Typewriter, the Rifle, and the Movie Camera, 1994, Nothing to Lose, 1997, Austin Powers: The Spy Who Shagged Me, 1999, Mission to Mars, 2000, High Fidelity, 2000; dir., writer, actor: Bob Roberts, 1992; dir., writer: Dead Man Walking, 1995 (Golden Globe award nominee for best dir. of film 1996, Acad. award nominee for best dir. 1996), The Moviegoer, 1998, Arlington Road, 1998, The Cradle Will Rock, 1999 ; (TV movies) Quarterback Princess, 1983, Malice in Wonderland, 1985; dir., actor: (play) Ubu Roi (L.A. Weekly Dir. award); dir. (plays) A Midsummer's Night Dream, Methusalem, the Eternal Bourgeois, The Good Woman of Setzuan (L.A. Drama Critics Circle nominee); co-writer: Alagazam, After the Dog Wars, Violence: The Misadventures of Spike Spangle, Farmer, Carnage, A Comedy. Office: Care ICM c/o Elaine Goldsmith Thomas 40 W 57th St New York NY 10019*

ROBBINS-WILF, MARCIA, educational consultant; b. Newark, Mar. 22, 1949; d. Saul and Ruth (Fern) Robbins; 1 child, Orin. Student, Emerson Coll., 1967-69, Seton Hall U., 1969, Fairleigh Dickinson U., 1970; BA, George Washington U., 1971; MA, NYU, 1975; postgrad., St. Peter's Coll., Jersey City, 1979, Fordham U., 1980; MS, Yeshiva U., 1981, EdD, 1986; postgrad., Monmouth Coll., 1986. Cert. elem. tchr., N.Y., N.J., reading specialist, N.J., prin., supr., N.J., adminstr., supr., N.Y. Tchr. Sleepy Hollow Elem. Sch., Falls Church, Va., 1971-72, Yeshiva Konvitz, N.Y.C., 1972-73; intern Wee Folk Nursery Sch., Short Hills, N.J., 1978-81, dir. day camp, 1980-81, tchr., dir., owner, 1980-81; adj. prof. reading Seton Hall U., South Orange, N.J., 1987, Middlesex County Coll., Edison, N.J., 1987-88; asst. adj. prof. L.I. U., Bklyn., 1988, Pace U., N.Y.C., 1988—; ednl. cons. Cranford High Sch., 1988; presenter numerous workshops; founding bd. dirs. Stern Coll. Women Yeshiva U., N.Y.C., 1987; adj. vis. lectr. Rutgers U., New Brunswick, N.J., 1988. Chairperson Jewish Book Festival, YM-YWHA, West Orange, N.J., 1986-87, mem. early childhood com., 1986—, bd. dirs., 1986—; vice chairperson dinner com. Nat. Leadership Conf. Christians and Jews, 1986; mem. Hadassah, Valerie Children's Fund, Women's League Conservative Judaism, City of Hope; assoc. bd. bus. and women's profl. divsn. United Jewish Appeal, 1979; vol. reader Goddard Riverside Day Care Ctr., N.Y.C., 1973; friend N.Y.C. Pub. Libr., 1980—; life friend Millburn (N.J.) Pub. Libr.; pres. Seton-Essex Reading Coun., 1991-94. Co-recipient Am. Heritage award, Essex County, 1985; recipient Award Appreciation City of Hope, 1984, Profl. Improvement awards Seton-Essex Reading Council, 1984-86, Cert. Attendance award Seton-Essex Reading Council, 1987. Mem. N.Y. Acad. Scis. (life), N.J. Council Tchrs. English, Nat. Council Tchrs. English, Am. Ednl. Research Assn., Coll. Reading Assn. (life), Assn. Supervision and Curriculun Devel., N.Y. State Reading Assn. (council Manhattan), N.J. Reading Assn. (council Seton-Essex), Internat. Reading Assn., Nat. Assn. for Edn. of Young Children (life N.J. chpt., Kenyon group), Nat. Council Jewish Women (vice chairperson membership com. evening br. N.Y. sect. 1974-75), George Washington U. Alumni Club, Emerson Coll. Alumni Club, NYU Alumni Club, Phi Delta Kappa (life), Kappa Gamma Chi (historian). Club: Greenbrook Country (Caldwell, N.J.); George Washington Univ. Avocations: reading, theatre. Home: 242 Hartshorn Dr Short Hills NJ 07078-1914

ROBERSON, MARK ALLEN, physicist, educator; b. Lufkin, Tex., Nov. 12, 1961; s. Roy and Thelma (Weist) R. AAS, Angelina County Jr. Coll., 1982; BSEE, Tex. A&M U., 1984; MS, Stephen F. Austin State U., 1989; PhD, Tex. Tech. U., 1994. From rsch. asst. to instr. Tex. Tech. U., Lubbock, 1990-95; instr. Vernon (Tex.) Regional Jr. Coll., 1995—. Robert A. Welch Found. fellow, 1991-94. Mem. AAAS, Am. Phys. Soc., Sigma Pi Sigma. Avocation: books. Office: Vernon Regl Jr Coll Vernon TX 76384-4092

ROBERSON, ROBERT S., investment company executive; b. Mt. Kisco, N.Y., 1942; m. Barbara Drane, 1967; children: Elizabeth de V., Merritt B., Barbara D. BS, NYU, 1964; MBA, Coll. William and Mary, 1973. Various positions in fin. and bldg. industries, 1964-67; mem. N.Y. Produce Exchange, 1965-66; with Weaver Bros., Inc., Newport News, Va., 1967—, now pres., dir.; bd. dirs. First Peninsula Bank & Trust Co., Hampton, Va., 1977-78. Past dir. Peninsula Unit Am. Cancer Soc., Newport News; past dir. Heritage Coun. Girl Scouts U.S.A., Hampton; former trustee Newport News Pub. Libr., Va. Living Mus., Am. Assn. Mus., Newport News; former trustee Hampton Roads Acad., Newport News; former mem. bd. visitors to George Washington's Mt. Vernon Nat. Shrine; hon. dep. chief N.Y.C. Fire Dept.; pres., chief curator Golf Mus., Newport News; mem. bd. visitors Coll. William and Mary, Williamsburg, Va., Richard Bland Coll., Petersburg, Va. Decorated officer Order of St. John (England). Mem. Newcomen Soc. of the U.S., Hon. Fire Officers Assn., Gen. Soc. Colonial Wars, St. Nicholas Soc. of the City N.Y., Colonial Order Acorn, Sovereign Mil. Order of the Temple of Jerusalem (comdr.), Squadron A Assn., Pilgrims of the U.S., Union Club, Church Club (N.Y.C.), Southampton Club (N.Y.), James River Country Club, Hampton Roads German Club, The Hundred Club (Newport News, Va.), N.Y. Yacht Club, Fishers Island Yacht Club (N.Y.), Rotary Internat. (Paul Harris fellow), Blue Key, Delta Sigma Pi. Republican. Episcopalian. Home: PO Box 3 Williamsburg VA 23187-0003

ROBERT, VINCENT MARIE, chemicals executive; b. Limoges, France; s. Jacques and Elisabeth (Bizalion) R.; m. Sylviane des Brest, July 10, 1982; children: Etienne, Charlotte, Thibault, Tanguy. Mgr. sales merchandising, mgr. south dist. Lab, France, 1986-92; mgr. sales Procter & Gamble, Gulf Country, France, 1992-94, Scandnavia, 1994-96, France, 1996-99; v.p. global sales water divsn. Danone, Paris, 2000—. Lt. French Cavalry, 1978-79. Avocations: golf, tennis, skiing. Home: 9 Bis Clos Toutain, 92420 Vaucresson France

ROBERT CARTERET, JEAN-YVES, lawyer; b. Paris, Feb. 20, 1948; s. Yves and Monique Robert Carteret; m. Valérie Constant, Oct. 1, 1977; children: Gwendoline, Tiffany, Soazic. Lic. in law, U. Paris, 1972; diploma, Sch. Oriental Langs., Paris, 1972; hon. degree, Inst. Higher Studies Nat. Def., Paris, 1983. Bar: Paris 1973. Pvt. practice, Paris, 1973-77, Versailles, France, 1978—; def. counsellor adviser to prefect of Paris, 1993-94; judge Cons. Prud'hommes, 1992—. Served with French Navy, 1974. Mem. Internat. Union Lawyers, Internat. Bar Assn., Amnesty Internat., Racing Club France, Yacht Club France, Wig and Pen Club (London). Roman Catholic. Avocations: golf, hunting, skiing, yachting. Home: 7 bd de la Reine, 78000 Versailles France Office: 3 rue de Marly, 78000 Versailles France

ROBERTS, (EDWARD) ADAM, international relations educator; b. Penrith, Cumbria, Eng., Aug. 29, 1940; s. Michael and Janet Buchanan (Adam-Smith) R.; m. Frances Primrose Dunn, Sept. 16, 1966; children: Hannah Theresa, Bayard Adam. BA in Modern History, Oxford (Eng.) U., 1962. Asst. editor Peace News, London, 1962-65; lectr. internat. rels. London Sch. Econs. Polit. Sci., 1968-81; Alastair Buchan reader internat. rels. Oxford U., 1981-86, Montague Burton prof. internat. rels., 1986—; Mem. Bd. of War Studies, London U., 1979-90; mem. Principles and Law Panel, Brit. Red Cross Soc., London, 1985—; mem. Ditchley (Eng.) Found. Programme Com., 1992—. Author: Nations in Arms, 2d edit., 1986, Documents on the Laws of War, 3d edit., 2000, United Nations, Divided World, 2d edit., 1993, Humanitarian Action in War, 1996. Chmn. govs. William Tyndale Sch., London, 1976-80. Hon. fellow London Sch. Econs. Polit. Sci., 1997, Leverhulme major rsch. fellow, 2000—. Fellow Brit. Acad.; mem. Royal Inst. Internat. Affairs (coun. mem. 1985-91), Internat. Inst. for Strategic Studies, Alpine Club. Avocations: rock climbing, mountaineering. Office: Balliol Coll, Oxford OX1 3BJ, England

ROBERTS, ALBERT DEE, internist; b. Ft. Worth, Mar. 7, 1930; s. Albert D. and Irene Burnett (Lewis) R.; m. Diane Truett, Dec. 22, 1952; children: Truett, Hillary. BS, So. Meth. U., 1951; MD, U. Tex. Southwestern, Dallas, 1954. Diplomate Am. Bd. Internal Medicine, Am. Bd. Nephrology. Pvt. practice Dallas, 1960-75, 88-91; assoc. dean, prof. medicine U. Tex. Southwestern, 1975-88, prof. medicine, 1991—, Hartman prof. medicine, 1995—. Mem. ACP (master, gov. 1977-81, regent 1981-87, vice chair 1986-87), AMA, Am. Soc. Nephrology, Internat. Soc. Nephrology, Tex. Med Assn., Dallas County Med. Assn. Avocations: reading, music, tennis, travel.

ROBERTS, BERNARD, applied mathematician, solar physicist; b. Cork, Ireland, Feb. 19, 1946; s. John William and Annie Margaret (Leahy) R.; m. Margaret Patricia Cartlidge, Oct. 2, 1971; children: Alastair, James, Michael, Richard. BSc, U. Hull, Eng., 1967; PhD, U. Sheffield, Eng., 1971. Jr. rsch. fellow U. Sheffield, 1967-71; lectr. U. St. Andrews, Scotland, 1971-87, reader, 1987-94, prof., 1994—; rsch. fellow U. Chgo., 1974-75; NASA vis. scientist U. N.H., Durham, 1980-81; NASA innovative rsch. program scientist, U. Iowa, 1985-86; cons. Open U., Milton Keynes, Eng., 1987—. Co-author: Solar System Magnetic Fields, 1985, Solar and Planetary Plasma Physics, 1990, Advances in Solar System Magnetohydrodynamics, 1991; contbr. articles to profl. jours. Fellow Royal Astron. Soc., Royal Soc. Edinburgh (Saltire award for disting. contbn. to phys. sci. 1998). Avocations: hill walking, squash, five-a-side football. Office: Sch Math & Stats, U St Andrews, Saint Andrews KY169SS, Scotland

ROBERTS, BERT C., JR., telecommunications company executive; b. 1942; married. BS, Johns Hopkins U., 1965. Project dir., mgr. Westinghouse Electric Corp., 1960-69; dir. Leasco Response Inc., 1969-72; with MCI Communications Corp., Washington, 1972—, v.p., 1974-76, sr. v.p., 1976-83, pres., 1983-85; chief operating officer MCI Telecommunications Corp., Washington, 1985-91, chief exec. officer, 1991-94; chmn. World Comm. Inc., Washington, 1992—. Office: World Comm Inc 1801 Pennsylvania Ave NW Washington DC 20006-3606

ROBERTS, CARYL, artist; b. N.Y.C., June 2, 1933; d. Robert Bernard and Miriam Francis Roberts; m. Martin Herbert Kahn, Oct. 31, 1954; children: David, Randy, Steven. Student, Pratt Inst., 1951, Sorbonne, 1952; BFA, Columbia U., 1956. Instr. East Ramapo Sch. Dist. # 1, Spring Valley, N.Y., 1969-90; freelance artist N.Y.C. and White Plains, N.Y., 1970—. One-woman shows include Family Ct. New City, N.Y., 1977, Arts Coun. of Rockland, 1995, Armory Arts Ctr., West Palm Beach, Fla.; exhibited in group shows Ward-Nasse, N.Y.C., 1995—, Renaissance, Blauvelt, N.Y., PaintingsDirect.com. Mem. Commn. on Gun Control, N.Y.C., 1960's, Correctional Assn., N.Y.C., 1960's; chair tree cert. Temple Beth Scholom, New City, 1970—. Mem. Nat. Mus. Women in the Arts, Rockland Ctr. for the Arts, Hopper Ho., Armory Arts Ctr., Arts Fedn. N.Y. Avocations: gardening, travel. Office: 89 Robinhood Ln New City NY 10956-6636

ROBERTS, COLIN, microbiologist, consultant; b. Rhosymedre, Wales, Jan. 25, 1937; s. Theophilus and Daisy Roberts; m. Marjorie Frances Conway, July 8, 1961; children: David Colin, Philip John. BSc, U. Liverpool, Eng., 1960, MB, ChB, 1963, MD, 1968; diploma in Bacteriology, U. Manchester, Eng., 1972. Lic. med. microbiology. House physician, surgeon Sefton Gen. Hosp., Liverpool, 1963-64, registrar pathology, 1964-66; asst. microbiologist Pub. Health Lab. Svc., Liverpool, 1970-73, sr. microbiologist, 1973-75, cons. med. microbiologist, 1975-84, cons. med. microbiologist, dept. dir., 1984-87, cons. med. microbiologist, dep. dir. svc., 1987-93, cond. med. microbiologist, med. and sci. postgrad. dean, 1993—; lectr. in pathology U. Liverpool, 1966-69, lectr. in medical microbiology, 1969-70; vis. prof. Strathclyde U., Scotland, 1993—, London Sch. Hygiene & Tropical Medicine, 1997—; founder fellow Acad. Med. Scis., London, 1998. Editor Procs. of Seminar on Tb: Old Adversary-New Problems, 1996, Procs. of Seminar on Helicobacter pylori: Update, 1996, Procs. of Seminar on Clin. Waste Mgmt., 1997; co-editor: Quality Control: Principles and Practice in the Microbiology Laboratory, 1999. Fellow Royal Soc. Medicine, Royal Coll. Pathologists (registrar 1992-96, v.p. 1996-99), Royal Coll. Pediatrics and Child Health (hon.); mem. Faculty of Pub. Health Med., Royal Coll. Physicians, Naval and Mil. Club, Assn. Med. Microbiologists (pres. 1994-95), Cen. Star Club (chmn. 1992-96), Savage Club, Atheneum Club, Ctrl. Sterlizing Club (chmn. 1992-96). Avocations: theatre, music, art, sports. Office: Pub Health Lab Svc, 61 Colindale Ave, London NW9 5DF, England

ROBERTS, DAVID ALUN, construction industry consultant, expert witness, arbitrator; b. London, July 3, 1947; s. Cyril Alun R. and Dorothy (Porter) Nash; m. Hazel Margaret Swift, July 21, 1973; children: Alick Alun, Andrew James, Ruth Isobel. Chief surveyor Alfairuz, Oman, 1978; sr. surveyor Kuk Dong, Saudi Arabia, 1978-79; co. surveyor SLP Fabricating Engrs. Ltd., Lowestoft, 1979-82; with BKI, Mid. East, 1983; contracts adminstr. John Brown/Brit. Gas, London, 1983-85; marine contracts adminstr. Marathon, London, 1985; sr. contaracts engr. Shell Expro, Lowestoft, England, 1985-89; lead cost engr. BP Chems., London, 1989; contracts engr. Amoco, London, 1989-96; contracts mgr. EMC/Salpem, China, 1995-96; sr. cons. TCSL, London, 1995—; cons. contracts and comml. claims U.K., Europe, Mid. and Far East, China; cons. constrn., mining and engring., petrochem. and marine concerns for internat. contractors, other orgns.; expert witness in constrn.-related matters. Fellow Faculty of Bldg., Chartered Inst. Arbitrators (assoc.); mem. Assn. Chartered Inst. Builders, Assn. Cost Engrs., Archs. and Surveyors Inst., Inst. Petroleum, Grad. Inst. Quantity Surveyors. Avocations: target shooting, swimming, Tai Chi, reading, law. Home: 47 Arcadia Ct, 45 Old Castle St, London E1 7NY, England

ROBERTS, DAVID GLEN, prospector, investor; b. Plainview, Tex., Feb. 8, 1952; s. Doris Glen and Anna Grace (Mathis) R. Student, Tex. A&M U., 1970-71, Dallas Bapt. Coll., 1971-75; BA in Comm., U. Tex. Permian Basin, 1987. Lic. minister Bapt. Ch.; cert. profl. landman. Profl. stuntman, actor, 1972-76; mgr. Channel 100, Midland, Tex., 1976-78; owner D.G. Roberts Land Mgmt., Midland, Tex., 1978—, Diamond Developers Fire and Enviro-Safety Co.; regional mktg. dir. Nochar Inc.-Region 11, Midland, Tex., 1990-96; pub., owner Basin Voice newspaper; cons. EPA, Indpls., 1991—. Appeared in film Giovanni & Ben, 1974, Drive In, 1976; theatre appearance at Globe Theatre, Odessa, Tex., 1975, Shakespeare in the Park, Dallas, 1976. Past chair Midland County Libertarian Party; past mem. exec. com. Dist. 31 Tex. Libertarian Party; organizer Sons of Liberty, Midland, 1990—. Mem. Am. Assn. Petroleum-Landmen, Five Aces, NRA, Tex. State Rifle Assn., Permian Basin Landman's Assn., N.O.R.M.L. Libertarian. Avocations: golf, motorcycling, hiking, shooting, photography. Office: Diamond Developers 3105 Barkley Ave Midland TX 79701-6215

ROBERTS, DAVID LOWELL, journalist; b. Lusk, Wyo., Jan. 12, 1954; s. Leslie James and LaVerne Elizabeth (Johns) R. BA, U. Ariz., 1979; MA, U. Nebr., 1997. Founder, editor, publisher Medicine Bow (Wyo.) Post, 1977-88; journalism instr. U. Wyo., Laramie, 1987-92; adviser U. Wyo. Student Publs., Laramie, 1987-92; gen. mgr. Student Media Corp U No. Colo., Greeley, 1995-98; founder, publisher Hanna Herald, Wyo., 1979-80; exch. reporter The Washington Post, 1982; freelance reporter Casper (Wyo.) Star-Tribune, 1978-83, various publs.; freelancer, 1977—. Co-author: (book) The Wyoming Almanac, 1988, 90, 94, 96; author: (book) Sage Street, 1991; columnist Sage Street, 1989-92. Chmn. Medicine Bow Film Commn., 1984; treas. Friends of the Medicine Bow Mus., 1984-88; pres. Medicine Bow Area C. of C., 1984; dir. Habitat for Humanity of Albany County, Laramie, 1991-92. Recipient Nat. Newspaper Assn. awards, over 40 Wyo. Press. Assn. awards, Five Editorial awards U. Wyo., Citizen of Yr. award People of Medicine Bow, 1986, Student Publs. awards U. Wyo., 1990, 92. Mem. Friends of Medicine Bow Mus. Mem. Green Party. Methodist. Avocations: writing, golf, visiting museums, photography. Home: PO Box 278 Eastlake CO 80614-0278

ROBERTS, DELMAR LEE, editor; b. Raleigh, N.C., Apr. 9, 1933; s. James Delmer and Nellie Brockelbank (Tyson) R. BS in Textile Mgmt., N.C. State U., 1956; MA in Journalism, U. S.C., 1974. Product devel. engr. U.S. Rubber Co. (Uniroyal), Winnsboro, S.C., 1959-64; process improvement engr. Allied Chem. Co., Irmo, S.C., 1965-67; assoc. editor S.C. History Illustrated Mag., Columbia, 1970; editor-in-chief, editl. v.p. Sandlapper-The Mag. of S.C., Columbia, 1968-74; mng. editor, art dir. Legal Econs. mag. of the ABA, Chgo., 1975-89; mng. editor, art dir. Law Practice Mgmt. mag. of the ABA, Chgo., 1990-2000, editor emeritus, 2000—. Editor: The Best of Legal Economics, 1979; freelance editor and/or designer of over 35 books. Active World Affairs Coun. Columbia, 1997—; 1st v.p. English-Speaking Union, 1996-97, pres. 1997—. With U.S. Army, 1956-58. Hon. fellow Coll. of Law Practice Mgmt., Golden, Colo., 1995—. Mem. Soc. Profl. Journalists, Capital City Club (Columbia), Phi Kappa Tau, Kappa Tau Alpha. Avocations: European travel, Turkish carpet/Kilim collecting, antique collecting.

ROBERTS, SIR DENYS (TUDOR EMIL), chief justice; b. London, Jan. 19, 1923; s. William David and Dorothy Elizabeth (Morrison) R.; m. Brenda Marsh, Jan. 1, 1949 (div. July 1973); children: Nigel Charles Emil, Amanda Karen Patricia; m. Fiona Alexander, Feb. 20, 1985; 1 child, Henry David Alexander. MA, Oxford U., 1948, BCL, 1949. Bar: London, 1950. Crown counsel Nyasaland, 1953-59; atty. gen. Gibraltar, 1960-62; solicitor gen. Hong Kong, 1962-66, atty. gen., 1966-73, chief sec., 1973-78, chief justice, 1979-88; chief justice Brunei, 1988—; pres. Court of Appeals Bermuda, 1989-94; mem. exec. and legis. councils, Gibraltar, 1960-62, Hong Kong, 1966-78. Author of 8 books. Served to capt. Royal Arty., 1942-46. Decorated knight Order of Brit. Empire; SPMB (Sultan of Brunei); hon. fellow Wadham Coll., Oxford U.; hon. bencher Lincoln's Inn, Lonodn, pres. MCC, 1989-90. Mem. Garrick Club (Hong Kong), Royal Commonwealth Soc. (London). Avocations: walking, tennis, cricket, music, writing. Home: Leithen Lodge, Innerleithen Peeblesshire EH44 6NW, Scotland Office: The Supreme Court, Bandar Seri Begawan Darussalam, Brunei

ROBERTS, DONALD WILSON, pathologist, consultant; b. Phoenix, Jan. 20, 1933; s. Alpha Wilson and Rubye Clotilde (Finklea) R.; m. Mae Astrid Strand, June 17, 1959; children: Marc Donald, Sara Judith Roberts Roundy. BS, Brigham Young U., 1957; MS, Iowa State U., 1959; PhD, U. Calif., Berkeley, 1964. Postdoctoral Swiss Fed. Inst. Tech., Zurich, 1964-65; insect pathologist Boyce Thompson Inst. for Plant Rsch., Ithaca, N.Y., 1965-96; insect pathologist, res. prof. dept. biology Utah State U., Logan, 1997—; cons. WHO, Kaduna, Nigeria, 1974, 76, Empresa Brasileira de Pesquisa Agropecuaria, Brasilia, Brazil, 1978, 79, 80, 94, 96; mem. sci. adv. bd. EcoSci. Corp., Worcester, Mass., 1990-95; project reviewer UN Devel. Program, Africa and South Am., 1993-96, USAID Africa, 1991-96; adj. prof. dept. entomology Cornell U., Ithaca, N.Y., 1993—, adj. prof. dept. plant pathology, 1994-99. Editor: (3 books) Diseases of Medically Important Arthropods, 1977, 80, 83, Invasion Processes of Fungi, 1983, Biotechnology in Pest Control, 1989; contbr. over 200 articles to profl. jours. Recipient Fulbright Sr. Rsch. scholarship Fulbright Found., Australia, 1985; named Family of Yr., Utah State U. Internat. Students, 1999. Mem. Soc. for Invertebrate Pathology (hon. 1998, founding mem., pres. 1988-90, Founder's Lectr. 1996), Entomol. Soc. Am. (Ea. br., Ciba-Geigy Recognition award 1985, 86, L.O. Howard Disting. Achievement award 1989), Am. Soc. Microbiology, Mycol. Soc. Am., Brazilian Entomol. Soc. (hon., recognition award 1996). Avocations: ballroom and swing dance. Fax: 435-797-1575. E-mail: dwroberts@biology.usu.edu. Office: Utah State U Dept Biology Logan UT 84322-0001

ROBERTS, DORIS EMMA, epidemiologist, consultant, nurse; b. Toledo, Dec. 28, 1915; d. Frederic Constable and Emma Selina (Reader) R. Diploma, Peter Bent Brigham Sch. Nursing, Boston, 1938; BS, Geneva Coll., Beaver Falls, Pa., 1944; MPH, U. Minn., 1958; PhD, U. N.C., 1967. RN, Mass. Staff nurse Vis. Nurse Assn., New Haven, 1938-40; sr. nurse Neighborhood House, Millburn, N.J., 1942-45; supr. Tb Baltimore County Dept. Health, Towson, Md., 1945-46; Tb cons. Md. State Dept. Health, Balt., 1946-50; cons., chief nurse Tb program USPHS, Washington, 1950-57; cons. divsn. nursing USPHS, 1958-63; chief nursing practice br. Health Resources Adminstrn., HEW, Bethesda, Md., 1966-75; adj. prof. U. N.C. Sch. Pub. Health, 1975-92; cons. WHO, 1961-82. Contbr. articles to profl. jours. With USPHS, 1945-75. Recipient Disting. Alumna award Geneva Coll., 1971, Disting. Svc. award USPHS, 1971, Outstanding Achievement award U. Minn., 1983. Fellow APHA (v.p. 1978-79, Disting. Svc. award Pub. Health Nursing sect. 1975, Sedgwick Meml. medal 1979), Am. Acad. Nursing (hon.); mem. Inst. Medicine of NAS, Soc. Nursing, Delta Omega, Sigma Theta Tau. Democrat. Episcopalian. Avocations: reading, needlepoint, gardening. Home: 9707 Old Georgetown Rd Apt 1112 Bethesda MD 20814-1746

ROBERTS, DWIGHT LOREN, engineering consultant, writer; b. San Diego, June 3, 1949; s. James Albert and Cleva Lorraine (Conn) R.; B.A., U. San Diego, 1976, M.A., 1979; m. Phyllis Ann Adair, Mar. 29, 1969; children: Aimee Renee, Michael Loren, Daniel Alexandr. Engring. aide Benton Engring. Inc., San Diego, 1968-73; pres. Robert's Tech. Research Co., also subs. Marine Technique Ltd., San Diego, 1973-76; pres. Research Technique Internat., 1978—; freelance writer, 1979—; owner Agrl. Analysis, 1985-88; constrn. mgr. Homestead Land Devel. Corp., 1988-92; sr. engr. cons. Morrison Knudson, 1992-95; sr. soils analyst Geotechnics, Inc., 1995-98; offsite field supt. coastal divsn. Kaufman and Broad, 1998—. Served with U.S. Army, 1969-71. Mem. ASTM, AAAS, Nat. Inst. Sci., N.Y. Acad. Scis., Nat. Inst. Cert. in Engring. Techs., Soil and Found. Engr. Assn., Phi Alpha Theta. Baptist. Author: Geological Exploration of Alaska, 1898-1924, Alfred Hulse Brooks, Alaskan Trailblazer, Papaveraceae of the World, Demarchism, Arid Regions Gardening, Visions of Dame Kind: Dreams, Imagination and Reality, Antal's Theory of the Solar System, Science Fair-A Teacher's Manual, Common Ground: Similarities of the World Religions, Black Sheep-Scientific Discoveries From the Fringe, After Manhattan, The Christofilos Effect; and others; contbr. articles to profl. jours. Office: 3111 E Victoria Dr Alpine CA 91901-3679

ROBERTS, ELEANOR STERETT (RUTH ELEANOR STERETT ROBERTS), osteopathic physician; b. Chgo., July 6, 1921; d. Dwight and Edith (Maine) Sterett; m. Edward Morse Roberts, Oct. 9, 1948 (dec. June 1999); children: Alfred D., Marjorie R. Carpenter, James R. BA, Allegheny Coll., 1943; cert. meteorology, MIT, 1944; DO, Kirksville Coll. Osteo. Med., 1950. Physician pvt. practice Queen City, Mo., 1950—; mem. bd. N.E. Mo. Home Health Agy., Kirksville, Mo., 1974-87. Bd. dirs. N.E. Mo. Libr. Svcs. Kahoka, 1974-82, pres.; pres. Queen City Sr. Housing Bd., 1968-76. Lt. W (A), USNR, 1943-46. Named Woman of Yr. Schuyler Bus. and Profl. Women, Lancaster, Mo., 1972. Mem. Am. Osteo. Assn. (life), Mo. Assn. Osteo. Physicians and Surgeons (life), N.E. Mo. Osteo. Assn. (life parliamentarian 1988, 97), Order Eastern Star (worthy matron 1961, 83-87, treas. 1990-2000), Delta Omega (nat. pres. 1961-63, nat. sec. 1984-89). Avocations: painting, collecting stamps, genealogy.

ROBERTS, ERIC HYWEL, retired agriculture educator; b. Welshpool, U.K., Jan. 27, 1930; s. John Hywel and Elizabeth Mildred (Ryle) R.; m. Dorothy Laura Mollart; children: Peter John Hywel, Ian James Hywel. BSc, U. Manchester, Eng., 1951, PhD, 1954, DSc, 1965; DSc (hon.), U. Reading, Eng., 1999. Sr. scientific officer West African Rice Rsch. Sta., Rokupr, Sierra Leone, 1955-63; lectr. U. Manchester, 1963-68; prof. crop prodn. U. Reading, Eng., 1968-95, emeritus prof. crop prodn., 1996—; dean faculty agr. and food, U. Reading, 1977-80, 89-92; pro-vice-chancellor U. Reading, 1982-86; chmn. bd. trustees Internat. Crops Rsch. Inst. for the Semi-Arid Tropics, India, 1993-96; apptd. OBE, 2000; dir. rsch. Internat. Corp. Rsch. Inst. for Semi-and Tropics, India, 1997. Contbr. numerous publs. in crop physiology and genetic conservation. OBE, 2000. Fellow Inst. Biology. Avocation: sailing. Home: Abbots Loft Upton Slip, Church St, Falmouth TR11 3DQ, England

ROBERTS, ESTHER LOIS, piano educator, composer, writer; b. Rockwood, Tenn.; d. Reva Gretchen (Crowder) H. BA in Biology, U. Tenn., Knoxville, BA in Botany, BM in Piano Lit./Pedagogy, MM in Piano Lit./Pedagogy. Pvt. piano instr. Knoxville; law clk. Baker, McReynolds, Byrne, O'Kane, Shea & Townsend. Composer (youth choir cantata) Children of Love, (soprano solo) Corn Husk Moon; author: (children's book series) Sam the Horse, Sam Gets Ready for School, others, 1996; contbr. to Tenn. Law Review. Mem. Am. Musicians Coll., Am. Indian Horse Registry, Great Smoky Mountain Indian Horse Club (pres.), Crossroads Dressage Soc., Nat. Soc. DAR, Scottish Clan Donnachaidh. Christian Scientist. Home and Office: Starlight Farm PO Box 32663 Knoxville TN 37930-2663

ROBERTS, JONATHAN MICHAEL, research scientist; b. Whitehaven, Eng., Dec. 18, 1969; s. Christopher Alan and Pamela Roberts; m. Kelly Jane Greenop. BEng in Aerospace Engring., U. Southampton, Eng., 1991, PhD in Computer Vision, 1994. Rsch. scientist CSIRO, Brisbane, Australia, 1995—. E-mail: jmr@cat.csiro.au. Office: CSIRO, 2643 Moggill Rd, Pinjarra Hills 4069, Australia

ROBERTS, KATHLEEN JOY DOTY, secondary education educator; b. Jamaica, N.Y., Apr. 19, 1951; d. Alfred Arthur and Helen Caroline (Sohl) Doty; m. Robert Louis Roberts, Nov. 24, 1974; children: Robert Louis, Michael Sean, Kathleen Meagan. BA in Edn., CUNY, 1972, MS in Spl. Edn., 1974; cert. advanced study in ednl. adminstrn., Hofstra U., 1982. Cert. sch. adminstrn., tchr. math., N.Y.; cert. N.Y. Dept. Mental Hygiene; lic. spl. edn. supr., ednl. dminstr., N.Y. Tchr. health conservation Woodside (N.Y.) Jr. H.S., 1973-77; coord. spl. edn. dept. Ridgewood (N.Y.) Jr. H.S., 1977-81; adminstrv. asst., health, compliance and mainstream coord. Grover Cleveland H.S., Ridgewood, 1981—, also coord. transition linkage, resource tchr. mentor, 1981—. Author: Closed Circuit Televion and Other Devices for the Partially Sighted, 1971, National Society Colonial Daughters of the Seventeenth Century Lineage Book (Centennial Remembrance Edit.), 1999; grant writer. Legis. chmn. Fairfield Jr. and Sr. H.S. PTA and Massapequa coun., 1987-92. Mem. NEA, AAUW, DAR, N.Y. State Tchrs. Assn., Coun. for Exceptional Children, Soc. Mayflower Descs., Colonial Daus. 17th Century (pres. 1985-91, 2000—, registrar, historian Founders chpt. 1991-94, nat. chmn. hist. activities com. 1988-91, nat. councillor, publicity chmn. 1991-94, centennial com. 1994-96, historian gen. nat. soc. 1994-97, registrar gen. nat. soc. 1997-2000), Pilgrim Edward Doty Soc. Republican. Home: 52 Hicksville Rd Massapequa NY 11758-5843 Office: Grover Cleveland HS 2127 Himrod St Flushing NY 11385-1299

ROBERTS, KENNETH, sociology educator, researcher; b. Stockport, Eng., Sept. 24, 1940; s. Ernest William and Nancy (Williams) R.; m. Patricia Newton, Aug. 9, 1964; children: Gavin Paul, Susan Alexis, Vanessa Jane. BSc in Sociology, London Sch. Econs., 1961, MSc in Econs., 1966. From asst. lectr. to prof., head sociology Liverpool (Eng.) U., 1966—. Author: Contemporary Society and The Growth of Leisure, 1977, Youth and Leisure, 1983, School-leavers and their Prospects, 1984, The Changing Structure of Youth Labor Markets, 1987, Leisure and Lifestyle, 1989, Youth and Employment in Modern Britain, 1995, Poland's First Post-Communist Generation, 1995, Leisure in Contemporary Society, 1999, Surviving Post-Communism: Young People in the Former Soviet Union, 2000. Home: 2 County Rd, Ormkirk L39 1QQ England Office: Liverpool U Dept Sociology, PO Box 147, Liverpool L69 3BX, England

ROBERTS, LYNNE JEANINE, physician; b. St. Louis, Apr. 19, 1952; d. H. Clarke and Dorothy June (Cockrum) R.; m. Richard Allen Beadle Jr., July 18, 1981; children: Richard Andrew, Erica Roberts. BA with distinction, Ind. U., 1974, MD, 1978. Diplomate Am. Bd. Dermatology, Am. Bd. Pediatrics, Am. Bd. Laser Surgery. Intern in pediats. Children's Med. Ctr., Dallas, 1978-79, resident in pediats., 1979-80; resident in dermatology U. Tex. Southwestern Med. Ctr., Dallas, 1980-83, chief resident in dermatology, 1982-83, asst. instr. dermatology and pediatrics, 1983-84, asst. prof., 1984-90, assoc. prof., 1990-99; prof., 1999—; physician Cons. Dermatol. Specialists, Dallas, 1990-93; pres. Lynne J. Roberts, MD, PA, Dallas, 1993—; dir. dermatology Children's Med. Ctr., Dallas, 1986—; dermatology sect. chief Med. City Dallas Hosp., 1994-95, 95-97. Contbr. articles to profl. jours., chpts. to books. Recipient Scholastic Achievement Citation Am. Med. Women's Assn., 1978. Fellow Am. Acad. Dermatology, Am. Soc. Laser Medicine and Surgery (bd. dirs. 1994-97); mem. Soc. Pediatric Dermatology, Am. Soc. Dermatologic Surgery, Tex. Med. Assn., Dallas Zool. Soc., Dallas Arboretum, Kappa Alpha Theta, Alpha Omega Alpha. Avocations: horseback riding, reading, fishing, swimming, camping. Office: 7777 Forest Ln Ste B314 Dallas TX 75230-2540

ROBERTS, MARK (ROBERT ELLIS SCOTT), actor, writer; b. Denver, June 9, 1921; s. Ward Ellis and Daisy (Hobson) Scott; m. Audrey von Clemm (dec.); children: Ward Ellis II, Margot, Jeffrey Frazier. Student, U. Kans., 1940-41; BA, U. Ariz., 1943. Cert. tchr. life, Calif. Ind. TV, stage, film actor, 1944—; co-founder Kairos Theater, Los Angeles, 1964; dir. Theater Arts Program of Los Angeles, 1975-79. Novelist: The Only Man in Hollywood, 1980; playwright Summer's Welcome, 1954; film actor: (as Robert Scott) Girl in the Case, The Black Arrow (serial), One Mysterious Night, 1944, Ten Cents A Dance, 1945, Prison Ship, 1945, Gilda, 1946, The Unknown, 1946, Shadowed, 1946, Dead Reckoning, 1946, (as Mark Roberts) Taxi, 1950, Onionhead, 1955, The Money Jungle, 1957, Once is Not Enough, 1975, Posse, 1976, For the Boys, 1991, Intersection, 1993; actor: (TV series lead roles) The Front Page, 1950, Miss Susan, 1951, Three Steps to Heaven, 1953, Date With Life, 1955, The Brothers Brannigan, 1959-60, (TV episodes) Kraft Theatre, Philco Playhouse, Studio One, Suspense, Playhouse 90, FBI, Dan August, Perry Mason, Cannon, Highway to Heaven, Who's the Boss, Murder She Wrote, L.A. Law, Murphy Brown, (Broadway prodns.) Stalag 17, 1951, The Sacred Flame, 1952, (Chgo. prodn.) Dial 'M' For Murder, 1953 (Los Angeles prodn.), Garden Distict, 1958-59, Mornings at Seven, 1986, Summer and Smoke, 1991. Mem. Acad. Motion Picture Arts and Scis., Actors Equity Assn., Screen Actors Guild, AFTRA, Writers Guild Am. West, ASCAP, Phi Delta Theta (pres. U. Ariz. chpt. 1942). Democrat. Presbyterian. Avocation: collecting American and early California art, songwriting.

ROBERTS, MEL (MELVIN RICHARD KELLS), retired film editor; b. Toledo, Aug. 26, 1923; s. Paul Mickle and Letha Ellen (Mize) Kells. BA, U. So. Calif., 1950, postgrad., 1951. Film editor Graphic Films, Hollywood, Calif., 1951-52; music editor Salt of the Earth, Ind. Film Co., Hollywood, 1952-53; film editor Ford Found., Columbia Pictures, Hollywood, 1953-62; cinematographer and film editor Wexler Films, Hollywood, 1956-62; still photographer L.A., 1962-81, video prodr., dir., 1993-97. Photographer, pub. 14 books, including Mel Roberts Male, Rex, and others; photographs featured in 2 bound vols. from Foto Factory Press: Uniforms, Male Bonding 2, 1998; film editor Paul Coates Confidential File, Tim McCoy Show, Rudy Vallee Prodns., documentary City That Disappears, Graphic Films; video prodr., dir. Classic Males Videos, 5 vols., 1993-97, 2000; editor (TV documentary) Segregation and the South, 1957; exhibited photographs in group show Male Bonding 2 at David Aden Gallery, Venice, Calif., 1998. Sgt. USAF, 1943-45, PTO. Avocations: collecting classic films and film publications, music. Office: 1335 N La Brea Ave Apt 2102 Hollywood CA 90028-7526 also: care Lilo Korenjak, Fremersbergstrasse 16 A, 76530 Baden Baden Germany

ROBERTS, MICHAEL, computer consultant; b. Reading, Berks, Eng., Apr. 10, 1952. BA, Downing Coll., Cambridge, Eng., 1973. Project mgr. Toltec Computer Ltd., Cambridge, Eng., 1977-84; prin. cons. Logica Comm. Ltd., London, 1984-91; sys. analyst AEG Mobile Comm. GmbH, Ulm, Germany, 1991-98, Nokia Mobile Phones, Ulm, Germany, 1998—. Avocations: science fiction, astronomy, classical music, cinema, badminton. Home: Postfach 3331, 89023 Ulm Germany

ROBERTS, MICHAEL JOSEPH, journalist; b. Canton, Ohio, Nov. 22, 1954; s. Francis Joseph and Flora Louise (Taylor) R.; m. Lynn Ellen Lantry Streetman, 1973 (div. 1984); children: Amy Kathleen, Jennifer Anne. BS in Speech and Telecomms., Kent State U., 1979. Cert. master wildlife conservationist, Fla. News dir. WNYN Radio, Canton, 1979-80, WTAL Radio, Tallahassee, Fla., 1980-82; broadcast journalist WCTV TV, Tallahassee, 1982-90; mng. editor WCTV News (CBS), Tallahassee, 1990-95; journalist, cons. Spl. Projects Group, Tallahassee, 1995—; assignment editor Sta. WTXL News, Tallahassee, 1999—; spl. projects cons. Freestyle Prodns., Fla., 1989-90; mem. tng. cadre manhunt exercise U.S. Army Spl. Forces/Blue Ridge Tech. Coll., Hendersonville, N.C., 1989-94. Author screenplay: Diamondback, 1989; prodr. TV documentaries: Common Ground: A Citizen Summit, 1989, Vietnam: Beyond the Battles, 1991; editor, pub. newsletter Threat Level; co-creator spl. ops. Basic Sniper course. Bd. dirs. Big Bend chpt. ARC, Tallahassee, 1990; mem. Tallahassee-Krasnodar Sister City Program; master wildlife conservationist U. Fla.-IFAS, Gainesville. Recipient Nat. Broadcast award UPI, 1989, Outstanding Documentary award UPI, 1989, Best Documentary award AP, 1991, Best Overall Coverage award AP, 1991, 93, 94, Best Newscast award AP, 1991, 92, 94. Mem. Am. Soc. Law Enforcement Trainers, Vietnam Vets. Am. (POW/MIA award 1993), Fla. Swat Assn., Sigma Delta Chi. Avocations: collecting firearms, shooting sports, cooking. Office: Spl Projects Group PO Box 37205 Tallahassee FL 32315-7205

ROBERTS, MONTY A., Saint Vincentian government official; b. May 7, 1945. Min. state Office of the Prime Minister; min. finance Govt. Saint Vincent and the Grenadines, Kingstown, 1994—, min. housing, local govt., youth, sports and cmty. devel. Office: Govt Bldgs, Kingstown Saint Vincent and the Grenadines*

ROBERTS, NANCY MIZE, retired librarian, composer, pianist; b. Corsicana, Tex., Apr. 19, 1931; d. Edward Harvey and Llora Inez (Huffman) Mize; m. Sam Butler Roberts, July 26, 1952 (dec.); children: Sam Butler Roberts Jr., John Daniel Roberts (dec.). Attended, Corsicana H.S. Cert. county librarian. Inventory clk. Oil City Iron Works, Corsicana, 1949-51; programmer KAND Radio, Corsicana, 1959-60; libr. Corsicana Pub. Libr., 1966-69, 70-73; owner dress shop Hang-Up, Corsicana, 1969-70; women's editor Corsicana Daily Sun, 1973-75; libr. Corsicana Pub. Libr., 1975-96; staff libr. Corsicana H.S., 1999—. Composer: (church anthems) Clap Your Hands, Two Commandments, God Moves in A Mysterious Way, I Must Tell Jesus. Bd. dirs. Warehouse Living Arts, Women's Clubhouse Assn., 1996-99, Consicana Pub. Libr. Bd., 1997—. Recipient Lifetime Achievement award Northeast Tex. Library Assn., 1996. Mem. Women's Clubhouse Orgn. Democrat. Methodist. Avocations: playing piano, arranging music, writing reviews, directing plays, singing. Home: 1443 W 3rd Ave Corsicana TX 75110-4409

ROBERTS, PETER JOHAN, surgical oncologist, surgery educator; b. Helsinki, Finland, Oct. 19, 1948; s. Rafael and Else (Simons) R.; m. Christel Holmsten, 1971; children: Pamela, Ted, Tom, Richard. MD, U. Helsinki, 1974, PhD, 1977. House officer Meltola Hosp., Helsinki U. Ctr. Hosp., Maria City Hosp., Helsinki, 1972-75; asst. dept. pathology U. Helsinki, 1975-77; gen. practitioner Hanko and Kerava Mcpl. Health Ctrs., 1974-75; lectr. in surgery U. Helsinki, 1982-88, cons., 1989-97; assoc. prof. U. Turku, 1997—, prof. surgery, 1998—. Assoc. editor Annales Chirurgiae et Gynaecologiae, 1979-98, editor-in-chief, 1998—; co-editor European Jour. Surg. Oncology, 1988-98. Rsch. grantee Finnish Med. Soc., 1993. Mem. Finnish Surg. Soc., European Soc. Surg. Oncology (exec. com. 1988-94). Office: Dept Surgery, U Turku, 20520 Turku Finland

ROBERTS, PRISCILLA MARY, history educator; b. Aldershot, England, July 6, 1955; d. Donald and Barbara May (Baumber) R. BA, King's Coll., Cambridge, England, 1976, MA, 1980, PhD, 1981. Lectr. U. Hong Kong, 1984—, dir. Ctr. Am. Studies, 1995—. Author: The Cold War, 2000; editor: Sino American Relations Since 1900, 1991, (with Spencer C. Tucker, et al) Encyclopedia of the Korean War, 2000. Pres. Am. Studies Assn. Hong Kong, 1986-87. Tom L. Evans rsch. grantee Harry S. Truman Libr. Inst.; Fulbright fellow, Washington, 1992. Mem. Am. Hist. Assn. (J. Franklin Jameson fellow 1981-82), Orgn. Am. Historians, Soc. Historians Am. Fgn. Rels. Avocations: reading, theatre, travel. E-mail: proberts@hkucc.hku.hk. Office: U Hong Kong Dept History, Pokfulam Rd, Hong Kong China

ROBERTS, RICHARD DEAN, psychologist, researcher, educator; b. Pembroke, Bermuda, Mar. 25, 1962; arrived in Australia, 1972; s. James Arthur and Patricia Anne (Benevides) R.; m. Emma-Louise Todey Jordon, Feb. 10, 1984 (div. Feb. 1989); 1 child, Matthew Dean. BA with honors, U. Sydney, Australia, 1985, PhD, 1996. Tutor U. Sydney, 1983-95, lectr., 1993-96, lectr., scientist, 1998—; rsch. scientist USAF, San Antonio, 1996-98; NRC fellow NAS, Washington, 1996-98; assoc. dir. Unit of Individual Differences and Assessment, Sydney, 1999—. Editor: Learning and Individual Differences: Process, Trait and Content Determinants, 1999; contbr. articles to profl. jours.; patentee psychol. test Lark-Owl Chronotype Indicator. Rsch. grantee U. Sydney, 1996, 99. Mem. APA, Am. Psychol. Soc., Internat. Soc. for Study of Individual Differences. Avocations: website development, cricket, Australian football, fine wine and cuisine, travel. Office: U Sydney, Dept Psychology, Sydney NSW 2006, Australia

ROBERTS, RICHARD JOHN, molecular biologist, consultant, research director; b. Derby, Eng., Sept. 6, 1943; came to U.S., 1969; s. John Walter and Edna Wilhelmina (Allsop) R.; m. Elizabeth Dyson, Aug. 21, 1965 (dec.); children: Alison, Andrew; m. Jean E. Tagliabue, Feb. 14, 1986; children: Christopher, Amanda. BS, Sheffield (Eng.) U., 1965, PhD, 1968. Rsch. fellow Harvard U., Cambridge, Mass., 1969-70, rsch. assoc., 1971-72; sr. staff investigator Cold Spring Harbor Lab., N.Y., 1972-87, asst. dir., 1987-92; rsch. dir. New England Biolabs, 1992—, cons. New Eng. Biolabs, Beverly, Mass., 1974-92; sci. adv. bd. Genex, Rockville, Md., 1977-85, Molecular Tool, Balt., 1994—. Contbr. articles to profl. jours. Recipient Nobel prize in Physiology and Medicine, Nobel Foundation, 1993. John Simon Guggenheim Found. fellow, 1979. Fellow Royal Soc.; mem. Am. Soc. Microbiology, Am. Soc. Biol. Chemists. Office: New Eng Biolabs 32 Tozer Rd Beverly MA 01915-5599

ROBERTS, RICKY ELIAS, linguist, educator; b. Oct. 20, 1961. PhD in Old Testament and New Testament, Christian Bible Coll., 1991; ThD in Greek, Hebrew, Latin and Aramaic. Founder, pres. True Light Ministries, Inc., Jacksonville, Fla., 1997—. Home: 10507 Villanova Rd Jacksonville FL 32218-5124

ROBERTS, STANLEY DWAYNE, physician, medical educator; b. Edmonton, Alta., Can., Sept. 17, 1959; came to U.S., 1994; s. Stan and Margaret Rosslyn (Rye) R.; m. Debra Elizabeth Bell, Aug. 20, 1981; children: Matthew, Brent, Michelle, Jared, Bradley. BSc with honors, U. Alta., Edmonton, 1980, BSc in Psychology with distinction, 1981, MD, 1985; grad., IHC Inst., 1999. Diplomate in family practice and sports medicine Am. Bd. Family Practice; cert. Family Medicine and Emergency Medicine, Coll. Family Physicians of Can. Resident in family medicine U. Alta., 1985-87; resident in physical rehab. and sports medicine McMaster U., Hamilton, Ont., Can., 1987-88, resident in emergency medicine, 1988-89, asst. prof. family and emergency medicine, 1989-94; med. dir., internat. med. cons. Med. Emergency, Inc., Toronto, Ont., Can., 1990-94; chief emergency svcs. Queensway Gen. Hosp., Toronto, Ont., Can., 1992-94; employee health physician, family physician Norman (Okla.) Regional Hosp., 1994-95; family physician Bigstone Creek Indian Reserve, Alberta, 1995, 96; pvt. family practice Provo, Utah, 1996-97; faculty physician Utah Valley Family Practice Residency, Provo, Utah, 1997—; emergency physician Utah Valley Regional Med. Ctr., Provo, 1997—; assoc. team physician Brigham Young U., 1999—; med. dir. Redcliff Ascent Wilderness Behavioral Reclamatin Program Youth, 2000—; moderator, planner Telemedicine Can./USA Broadcasts, 1990-98; team doctor World Cup Speed Skating, Oct., 1999; dir. Utah Valley Sports Medicine Fellowship, 1999—; cons. Global Emergency Medicine Support; developer internat. tng. program for physicians, Nepal, 2000; lectr. in field. Contbr. articles to profl. jours.; guest radio talk shows; developer internat. tng. program in emergency medicine: Art in EM = Advanced Resuscitation Training in Emergency Medicine. Chmn. coms. life support Heart and Stroke Found. (Can.) Ont., 1991-93; scoutmaster Boy Scouts Am., Kaysville, Utah, 1995, Orem, Utah, 1998—. Recipient Achievement award for internat. distinction in music Govt. Alberta, 1976, Disting. Lectr. award Thailand and Asia Coll. Surgeons, 1993. Mem. AMA, Am. Acad. Family Physicians, Utah Med. Assn., Coll. Family Physicians (Can.), Am. Med. Soc. for Sports Medicine, Am. Coll. Sports Medicine. Mormon. Avocations: mountain biking, photography, family enrichment. Office: Utah Valley Sports Medicine Fellowship 1134 N 500 W Ste 102 Provo UT 84604-6101

ROBERTS, SUZANNE CATHERINE, freelance reporter, artist; b. San Antonio, Oct. 27, 1953; d. Thomas Simons and Marceline Margaret (Conrady) Garrett; m. Ted Blake Roberts, May 22, 1976; 1 child, Elizabeth. BS in Radio-TV-Film, U. Tex., 1975, B of Journalism, 1977; MA in Interdisciplinary Studies, Corpus Christi State U., 1982, MS in Gen. Counseling, 1989; MA in Polit. Sci., S.W. Tex. State U., 1995. News announcer Sta. KIXL Radio, Austin, Tex., 1976, Sta. KSIX Radio, Corpus Christi, Tex., 1977-78; news anchor Sta. KZTV-TV, Corpus Christi, 1979, news reporter, 1977-80, news announcer, reporter Sta. KRYS-AM-FM, Corpus Christi, 1983-87; freelance reporter United Press Internat., Austin, 1989-94, Tex. State Network, Austin, 1995-97; freelance reporter Des Moines, Iowa, 1997—, artist, 1998—.

ROBERTS, THOMAS ANDREW, II, urban development executive; b. Jersey City, Sept. 5, 1949; s. Thomas Andrew and Muriel Cecelia (Burt) R.; m. Myrtle Beatrice Mumford, Sept. 15, 1971 (div. May 1991); children: Chantey P., Thomas Andrew III; m. Yvonne Coleta Belefanti, Apr. 3, 1994; children: Andrew Belefanti, Oliver Basilio. BA, Rutgers U., 1973; JD, Seton Hall U., 1977. Bar: N.J. 1984. Cmty. specialist City of Newark, 1970-73; area coord. project Jersey City Redevel. Agy., 1973-75; dir. housing Urban League Essex County, Newark, 1976; dist. supr. Nat. Neighborhood Reinvestment Corp., Washington, 1977-85; lawyer East Orange, N.J., 1985-88; exec. dir. Camden (N.J.) Redevel. Agy., 1988—; bd. dirs. A Better Camden Corp. Pres. Camden Coun. on Alcohol Abuse, 1990-2000; trustee, vice chmn. CamCare Health Corp., Camden, 1990-2000; trustee South Jersey Mus. Art, Lawnside, 1996-99, Camden Empowerment Zone Corp., 1996-2000; advisor Explorer Post 2044, Camden, 1995-97; fellow Leadership N.J., 1999. Mem. Fencing Acad. South Jersey (instr. 1997—). Presbyterian. Avocation: fencing. Home: 1380 Whitman Ave Camden NJ 08104-1264 Office: Camden Redevel Agy Ste 1300 City Hall Camden NJ 08102

ROBERTS, THOMAS GEORGE, retired physicist; b. Ft. Smith, Ark., Apr. 27, 1929; s. Thomas Lawrence and Emma Lee (Stanley) R.; m. Alice Anne Harbin, Nov. 14, 1958 (dec. 1994); children: Lawrence Dewey, Regina Anne; foster child, Marcia Roberts Dale; m. Betty Howard McElyea, July 28, 1995. AA, Armstrong Coll., 1953; BS, U. Ga., 1956, MS, 1957; PhD, N.C. State U., 1967. Research physicist U.S. Army Missile Command, Huntsville, Ala., 1958-85; cons. industry and govt. agys., 1970—, SAIC, Huntsville, Ala., 1997—; owner Technoco, Huntsville. Contbr. articles to profl. jours. Patentee in field. Served to sgt. USAF, 1948-52. Fellow Am. Optical Soc.; mem. Am. Phys. Soc., IEEE, Huntsville Optical Soc. Am. (pres. 1980, 92). Episcopalian. Club: Toastmaster Internat. (pres. 1963). Current work: Laser physics, optics, particle beams and instrumentation; diagnostic devices and techniques development. Subspecialties: Laser physics; Plasma physics. Office: Technoco 1780 Joe Quick Rd New Market AL 35761-9636

ROBERTS, WILLIAM LEWIS, clinical pathologist; b. Columbus, Ohio, July 23, 1960; s. William Warren and Kathryn (Butler) R.; m. Wendy Lee Higginson, Aug. 5, 1989. BS in Chemistry, Ohio State U., 1982; PhD in Pharmacology, Case Western Res. U., Cleve., 1988, MD, 1990. Resident Yale-New Haven Hosp., 1990-92; postdoctoral fellow Yale U., New Haven, 1992-95; asst. prof. U. Miss. Med. Ctr., Jackson, 1995-98, U. Utah, Salt Lake City, 1998—. Contbr. articles to profl. jours. Fellow Coll. Am. Pathologists; mem. Am. Soc. Clin. Pathology, Am. Assn. Clin. Chemistry, Acad. Clin. Lab. Physicians and Scientists, Phi Beta Kappa, Phi Kappa Phi, Alpha Omega Alpha. Republican. Pentecostal Ch. Achievements include development of high temperature polymeric liquid crystals; characterization of the glycolipid membrane anchor of erythrocyte acetylcholinesterase; characterization of membrane-binding domain of brain acetylcholinesterase; research on the mechanism of action of antileishmanial antimony compounds. Home: 8574 Snowville Dr Sandy UT 84093-1009 Office: ARUP Labs Dept Pathology 500 Chipeta Way Salt Lake City UT 84108-1221

ROBERTS, WILLIAM RICHARD, III, record company executive, fire fighter; b. Denver, Nov. 8, 1969; s. William Richard Roberts and Dorothea (Pryor) Glover. BS, U. Colo., 1993; Cert., Red Rocks C.C., 1994, 95. Project engr. Bur. Reclamation, Denver, 1989-90, Empire Constrn. Svc., Denver, 1993—; owner No Coast Entertainment, Denver, 1998—; fire fighter City and County of Denver, 1998—. Pres. Jr. NAACP Colo., Denver, 1986-87, Machebeuf Sophomore Class, Denver, 1986-87, U. Colo. Student Union, Boulder, 1991-92/. Recipient Points of Light award U.S. Govt., 1990. Mem. ASCAP, Internat. Assn. Fire Fighters, Colo. Profl. Black Firefighters, 100 Black Men (fin. com. 1995-97). Democrat. E-mail: Nocoast@uswest.net. Home: PO Box 390533 Denver CO 80239-1533 Office: No Coast Entertainment 3904 Niagara St Denver CO 80207-1424

ROBERTS, WINIFRED LAURA, psychiatric social worker, consultant; b. Dublin, Ireland, June 16, 1920; d. Robert Edward and Dorothea (Goodchild) R. Diploma in Social Scis., London U., 1954, Mental Health Cert., 1959. Tchr., Dept. Edn., London, 1947-52; social worker Univ. Settlement, Bristol, Eng., 1952-58; psychiat. social worker West Middlesex Hosp., 1958-65, Woodberry Down Clinic, 1965-77, Marlborough Hosp., 1977-81; staff cons. Social Services Depts., London, 1981—. Contbr. articles to profl. jours., chpts. to books. Mem. Group Analytic Soc., Inst. Family Therapy (tchr. therapist 1974—), Group for Advancement Psychotherapy in Social

Work. Quaker. Avocations: tapestry weaving; gardening. Home: 59 Normanby Rd, Dollis Hill, London NW10 1BU, England

ROBERTSHAW, JOHN DESMOND, company executive. MS. Cert. chartered acct. Non-exec. dir. United Sci. Holdings, London, 1967—, chmn., 1968-81, dep. chmn., 1981-89, chmn. exec. bd., 1989—; chmn. bd. Alvis Plc, London, vice chmn. Office: Alvis Plc, 34 Grosvenor Gardens, London SW1W 0AL, England*

ROBERTSON, ABEL L., JR., pathologist; b. St. Andrews, Argentina, July 21, 1926; came to U.S., 1952, naturalized, 1957; s. Abel Alfred Lazzarini and Margaret Theresa (Anderson) R.; m. Irene Kirmayr Mauch, Dec. 26, 1958; children: Margaret Anne, Abel Martin, Andrew Duncan, Malcolm Alexander. BS, Coll. D.F. Sarmiento, Buenos Aires, Argentina, 1946; MD suma cum laude, U. Buenos Aires, 1951; PhD, Cornell U., 1959. Fellow tissue culture div. Inst. Histology and Embryology, Sch. Medicine Inst. Histology and Embryology, 1947-49; surg. intern Hosp. Ramos Mejia, Buenos Aires, 1948-50; fellow in tissue culture research Ministry of Health, Buenos Aires, 1950-51; resident Hosp. Nacional de Clinicas, Buenos Aires, 1950-51; head blood vessel bank and organ transplants Research Ctr. Ministry of Health, Buenos Aires, 1951-53; fellow dept. surgery and pathology Sch. Medicine Cornell U., N.Y.C., 1953-55; asst. vis. surgery U. Hosp. N.Y., N.Y.C., 1955-60; asst. prof. research surgery Postgrad. Med. Sch. NYU, N.Y.C., 1955-56; asst. vis. surgeon Bellevue Hosp., N.Y.C., 1955-60; assoc. prof. research surgery NYU, 1956-60, assoc. prof. pathology Sch. Medicine and Postgrad Med. Sch., 1960-63; staff mem. div. research Cleve. Clinic Found., 1963-73, prof. research, 1972-73; assoc. clin. prof. pathology Case Western Res. U. Sch. Medicine, Cleve., 1968-72, prof. pathology, 1973-82, dir. interdisciplinary cardiovascular research, 1975-82; exec. head dept. pathology Coll. Medicine, U. Ill., Chgo., 1982-88; prof. pathology Coll. Medicine U. Ill., 1982-93, prof. emeritus, 1993—; vis. prof. emeritus in cardiovascular medicine Stanford U. Coll. Medicine, 1995—; rsch. fellow N.Y. Soc. Cardiovasc. Surgery, 1957-58; mem. rsch. study subcom. of heart com. N.E. Ohio Regional Med. Program, 1969—. Mem. internat. editorial bd.: Atherosclerosis, Jour. Exptl. and Molecular Pathology, 1964—, Lab. Investigation, 1989—, Acta Pathologica Japonica, 1991—; contbr. articles to profl. jours. Recipient Research Devel. award NIH, 1961-63. Fellow AAAS, Am. Coll. Cardiology, Am. Coll. Clin. Pharmacology, Am. Heart Assn. (established investigator 1956-61, nominating com. council on arteriosclerosis 1972), Royal Microscopical Soc., Royal Soc. Promotion Health (Gt. Britain), Am. Geriatrics Soc., N.Y. Acad. Scis., Cleve. Med. Library Assn.; mem. AMA, AAUP, Am. Soc. for Investigative Pathology, Am. Inst. Biol. Scis., Am. Judicature Soc., Am. Soc. Cell Biology, Am. Soc. Pathologists, Am. Soc. Nephrology, Assn. Am. Physucabs and Surgeons, Assn. Computing Machinery, Electron Microscopy Soc. Am., Assn. Pathology Chmn., Internat. Acad. Pathology, Soc. Cardiovascular Pathology, Internat. Cardiovascular Soc., Internat. Soc. Cardiology (sci. council on arteriosclerosis and ischemic heart disease), Internat. Fed. on Genetic Engring. and Biotechnology, Internat. Soc. for Heart Rsch., Internat. Soc. Nephrology, Internat. Soc. Stereology, Pan Am. Med. Assn. (life, councillor in angiology 1966), Ill. Registry Anatomical Pathology (treas. 1985-87), Chgo. Pathology Soc., Reticuloendothelial Soc. Leucocyte Biology, Soc. Cryobiology, Tissue Culture Assn., Ohio Soc. Pathologists, Electron Microscopy Soc. Northeastern Ohio (pres., trustee 11966-68), Heart Assn. Northeastern Ohio, N.Y. Soc. Cardiovascular Surgery, N.Y. Soc. Electron Microscopists, Cuyahoga County Med. Soc., Cleve. Soc. Pathologists, The Oxygen Soc., Sigma Xi. Fax: 650-712-0357. E-mail: alrrob@pol.net. Home: PO Box 3125 340 5th Ave Half Moon Bay CA 94019-5123

ROBERTSON, ANDREW GEOFFREY, public health physician, naval officer; b. Gundagai, NSW, Australia, May 24, 1959; s. Geoffrey John and Margaret Jean (Fletcher) R.; m. Laura Joan Klassen, July 31, 1982; children: Katherine, David. MB, BS, U. Sydney, Australia, 1981; grad. diploma in occupl. health-safety, Curtin U. Tech., Perth, Australia, 1988, MPH, 1990, M in Health Svc. Mgmt., 1998. Commd. officer Royal Australian Navy, 1979, commd. comdr., 1997; resident med. officer Royal Prince Alfred Hosp., Sydney, 1982-83; med. officer Royal Australian Navy, Sydney, 1984-85, Perth, 1985-92; staff officer Naval Health, Canberra, Australia, 1992-93; staff officer Office Surgeon Gen., Australian Def. Force, Canberra, 1993-96; chief insp. UN Spl. Commn., Iraq, 1996; sr. med. officer Her Majesty's Australian Ship Stirling, Perth, 1996-98, Area Health Svc. Western Australia, 1998; staff officer Def. Health Svc. Br., 1999—. Contbr. articles to med. jours., including Mil. Medicine, Jour. Royal Naval Med. Svc., Australian Mil. Medicine. Recipient Broken Hill Proprietary-Utah award, 1989, Alumni award Curtin U. Tech., 1990, Conspicuous Svc. Cross, 1999. Fellow Royal Australasian Coll. Med. Adminstrs., Australasian Faculty Pub. Health Medicine (sec. Australian Capital Ter. chpt. 1995-96, sec. WA chpt. 1997-98, pres. WA chpt. 1998), Australasian Coll. Health Svc. Execs. (assoc.); mem. Australian Mil. Medicine Assn. (councillor 1994-97, asst. editor 1994-99, treas. 1998-99, editor 1999—), Australian Radiation Protection Soc. Baptist. Avocations: military medical history, tennis, volleyball, cinema, literature. Office: Defence Health Svc Br, Campbell Park ACT 2600, Australia

ROBERTSON, CHARLES MORVEN, electronics company executive; b. Cambridge, Eng., Aug. 1, 1954; s. Charles speirs an Nora Beatrice (Kearle) R.; m. Martha Elizabeth Sadlick, Apr. 23, 1988; 1 child, Marion Elizabeth. MA, Cambridge U., 1975, PhD, 1979. Account mgr. Tex. Instruments Ltd., Bedford, 1980; sales and mktg. mgr. Edinburgh (Scotland) Instruments Ltd., 1980-82; dir. Speirs Robertson and Co. Ltd., Bedford, 1982—. Office: Speirs Robertson and Co Ltd, Bromham, Bedford MK43 8HY, England

ROBERTSON, DONNA VIRGINIA, architect, educator, dean; b. Richmond, Va., Feb. 26, 1952; d. Charles Henry and Florence (Givens) R.; m. Robert M. McAnulty, May 24, 1986; 1 child, Robertson. Cert. theater arts studies, Webster Coll., St. Louis, 1972; BA, Stanford U., 1974; MArch, U. Va., 1978. Registered arch., N.Y. Asst. prof. Harvard U., Cambridge, Mass., 1983-84; asst. prof. Barnard Coll. Columbia U., N.Y.C., 1984-92; dean Sch. Arch. Tulane U., New Orleans, 1992-96; dean Coll. Arch. Ill. Inst. Tech., Chgo., 1996—; ptnr. Robertson McAnulty Archs., Chgo., 1986—; owner Donna V. Robertson Archs., N.Y.C., 1982-86; sr. designer Kohn Pedersen Fox Archs., N.Y.C., 1980-82, Mitchell Giurgola Archs., N.Y.C., 1979-80; adj. asst. prof. Barnard Coll., Columbia U., N.Y., 1982-83, dir. arch. program, fall 1985-92; vis. critic in design Harvard U., Cambridge, fall 1990, U. Va., Charlottesville, fall 1991; organizer, panelist Arch. and Lit. Symposium, N.Y.C., 1985; jury chair Am. Collegiate Schs. Arch., Boston, 1996. Prin. arch. Fishback residence, New Orleans, Sunkel residence, New Orleans, Pisar residence, N.Y.C., Dachs residence, N.Y.C. Mem. AIA (juror annual design hons. awards 1996, educators and practitioners network), Chgo. Network-Internat. Women's Forum, Raven Soc., Arts Club (Chgo.). Office: Ill Inst Tech 3360 S State St Chicago IL 60616

ROBERTSON, DOUGLAS STUART, lawyer; b. Portland, Oreg., Jan. 9, 1947; s. Stuart Neil and Mary Katherine (Gates) R.; m. Nan Reinhorn, Dec. 27, 1970; 1 child, Lauren Amanda. BS, Oreg. State U., 1969, MA in Bus. Adminstrn., 1970; JD U. Denver, 1973. Bar: Oreg. 1973, U.S. Dist. Ct. Oreg. 1974, U.S. Ct. Appeal (9th cir.) 1977, U.S. Supreme Ct. 1977. Staff atty. Multnomah County Bar Assn. Legal Aid, Portland, 1973-75; ptnr. Bouneff, Chally & Marshall, Portland, 1975-80; asst. gen. counsel Orbanco Fin. Services, Portland, 1980-83; v.p., gen. counsel Hyster Credit Corp., Portland, 1983-86; v.p., gen. counsel PacifiCorp Credit Inc., 1986-90; ptnr. Lane, Powell, Spears Lubersky, Portland, 1990-91; v.p., gen. counsel, sec., In Focus Systems, Inc., Wilsonville, Oreg., 1991-96, bd. dirs. Lightware, Inc., 1996—; chmn. bd., CEO Deschutes River Preserve, Inc., Portland, 1982—. Mem. editl. bd. Denver Jour. of Internat. Law and Policy, 1971. Served with U.S. Army 1968-70. Mem. ABA, Comml. Law League, Multnomah County Bar Assn., Am. Assn. of Equipment (lessor's law forum), Am. Corp. Counsel Assn. (bd. dirs., treas. N.W. chpt.). Republican. Club: Flyfisher's of Oreg., Oreg. Trout. Home: 29 Hillshire Dr Lake Oswego OR 97034-7375 Office: Lightware Inc 9875 SW Sunshine Ct Ste 200 Beaverton OR 97005-4190

ROBERTSON, EDWIN DAVID, lawyer; b. Roanoke, Va., July 5, 1946; s. Edwin Traylor and Norma Burns (Bowles) R.; m. Anne Littelle Ferratt, Sept. 7, 1968, 1 child, Thomas Therit. BA with honors, U. Va., 1968, LLB, 1971. Bar: N.Y. 1972, U.S. Ct. Appeals (2d cir.) 1972, U.S. Dist. Ct. (ea. and so. dists.) N.Y. 1973, U.S. Supreme Ct. 1975, U.S. Dist. Ct. (ea. dist.) Mich. 1986. Assoc. Cadwalader, Wickersham & Taft, N.Y.C., 1972-80, ptnr., 1980—. Bd. dirs. Early Music Found. N.Y.C., 1983-99, chmn., 1993-99; bd. dirs. Oratorio Soc. of N.Y.C., 1988—, sec., 1991—. 1st lt. USAF, 1971-72. Echols scholar. Mem. ABA, Fed. Bar Coun., N.Y. County Lawyers Assn. (chmn. bankruptcy com. 1983-87, chmn. fin. com., bd. dirs. 1985-88, 95-99, 2000—, investment com. 1992—, exec. com. 1996-99, 2000—), Assn. Bar City N.Y., Soc. Colonial Wars, Down Town Assn., Jefferson Soc., Echols Scholar, Order of Coif, Phi Beta Kappa, Phi Kappa Psi. Republican. Episcopalian. Home: 315 E 72nd St New York NY 10021-4625 Office: Cadwalader Wickersham & Taft 100 Maiden Ln New York NY 10038-4818

ROBERTSON, EDWIN OSCAR, banker; b. Speedwell, Tenn., May 28, 1923; s. John M. and Etta (Mayes) R.; m. Althea Maxine Moyers, June 3, 1948 (dec. Nov. 1970); children: Edwin Glenn, Craig Eric; m. Sarah Alice Parkman, Nov. 16, 1974. BS in Agr., U. Tenn., 1950; LLD (hon.), Lincoln Meml. U., 1984. Supr. vets. farm tng. County of Claiborne, Tazewell, Tenn., 1950-52; agr. rep. Citizens Bank, New Tazewell, Tenn., 1952; v.p., agr. rep. Nat. Bank, Middlesboro, Ky., 1953-57; chmn. bd., chief exec. officer Comml. Bancgroup, Inc., Harrogate, Tenn., 1976—; pres., chief exec. officer Comml. Bank, Middlesboro, 1958—; chmn., CEO Comml. Bank, Harrogate, 1988—; chmn. bd. Comml. Bank, Harrogate, 1976—; mem. Govt. Task Force on Banking, Ky., 1983; trustee Lincoln Meml. U., Harrogate, 1974—; bd. dirs. Cumberland Devel. Corp., Middlesboro. Gov. Ruritan Nat. Tenn. Dist., 1954-55; bd. dirs. Middlesboro Indsl. Commn., 1962—, Ky. C. of C., 1983-84. With USAF, 1943-45. Mem. Rotary. Republican. Baptist. Avocations: farming, horseback riding. Home: PO Box 100 Harrogate TN 37752-0100

ROBERTSON, GEORGE, international organization official; b. Apr. 12, 1946; married; three children. MA, U. Argyll, Scotland; MA in Econ. with honors, U. Dundee, 1968. Rsch. asst. Tayside Study Econs. Group, 1968-69; gov. Scottish Police Coll., 1974-78; bd. mem. Scottish Devel. Agy., 1976-78; M.P. for Hamilton, 1978-99; parliamentary pvt. sect. to Sec. of State for Social Svcs., 1979; opposition front bench spokesman on Scotland, 1979-80, opposition front bench spokesman on def., 1980-81, opposition front bench spokesman on fgn. and commonwealth, 1981-93, European and cmty. affairs, 1985-93, shadow sec. of state for Scotland, 1993-97; sec. state for def. U.K., 1997-99; sec. gen. NATO, 1999—. Recipient Order of the Star, 2000. Mem. Labour Party. Office: NATO HQ Office Sec Gen, Blvd Leopold 3, B-1110 Brussels Belgium

ROBERTSON, GRAEME LANCE, mining executive, energy executive; b. Sydney, Australia, May 10, 1950; arrived in Indonesia, 1971; s. Frank Albert and Bernice Joy (Beattie) R.; m. Fena Anne Yeannette Suhirman, May 19, 1979 (div. 1994); children: Mark, Natalie, David. BA, U. New South Wales, Sydney, 1972. Lectr. U. Indonesia, Jakarta, 1972-74; cons. Jakarta, 1974-80; dep. gen. mgr. New Hope Collieries PL, Brisbane, Australia, 1980-83, dir., CEO, 1983-87; mng. dir. New Hope Corp., Ltd., Brisbane, Australia, 1987—; chmn., CEO Swabara Group, Jakarta, 1984—, Kalimaya Group, Jakarta, 1995—; bd. dirs. P.T. Multi Harapan Utama, Jakarta, P.T. Adaro Indonesia, Jakarta, P.T. Indonesia Bulk Terminal, Jakarta, Australian Internat. Sch., Jakarta; dir. Washington Soul Pattinson & Co. Ltd., Sydney. Recipient Asean Devel. award Asean Program Cons., Jakarta, 1996. Fellow Australian Inst. of Co. Dirs.; mem. Australian Inst. of Energy, Young Presidents Orgn., Indonesian Coal Mining Assn. (v.p. 1989—), World Coal Inst. (bd. dirs.). Avocations: tennis, running, swimming, martial arts. Office: Swabara Group 7th Fl WTC, Jl Jend Sudirman 31, 12920 Jakarta Indonesia

ROBERTSON, IAN WILLIAM, Church of Scotland parish minister; b. Glasgow, Scotland, Dec. 18, 1925; s. William Henderson and Isabella (Malcolm) R.; m. Irene Finlayson, Feb. 16, 1957; children: David William, John Malcolm Baillie, Moray John, Graham Andrew, Alastair Malcolm. MA, Glasgow U., 1949; B of Divinity, Edinburgh (Scotland) U., 1952. Ordained min. Ch. of Scotland, 1956. Min. Galston (Scotland) New Parish Ch., 1956-65, Queen's Park High Parish Ch., Glasgow, 1965-74, Colvend, Southwick & Kirkbean Parish Ch., Scotland, 1974-95; ret., 1995; asst. presbytery clk., Dumfries, Scotland, 1974-83. Translator: Anselm-Fides Quaerens Intellelctum, Karl Barth, 1958. Sgt., Brit. Army, 1944-47, Western Europe. Home: 10 Marjoriebanks, Lochmaben DG11 1QH, Scotland

ROBERTSON, JAMES IAN, medical educator, researcher; b. Welbeck, Eng., Mar. 5, 1928; s. James Charles and Violet Sybil (Summers) R.; m. Maureen Patricia Doherty, Sept. 10, 1955; children: Fiona Elizabeth, James Andrew, Kirstin Alexandra. BSc, St. Mary's Hosp., London, 1949, MB BChir, 1952; MD, Free U., Brussels, 1986. Lectr. in medicine St. Mary's Hosp., London, 1956-64, sr. lectr. in therapeutics, 1964-67; physician MRC Blood Pressure Unit, Glasgow, Scotland, 1967-87; sr. cons. in cardiovasc. medicine Janssen Rsch. Found., Beerse, Belgium, 1987-94; sci. advisor Janssen Internat. Rsch. Coun., Beerse, 1988-94; vis. prof. medicine Prince of Wales Hosp., Hong Kong, 1988-93; cons. in cardiovasc. disease WHO, 1975-85; Hall lectr. Cardiac Soc. Australia/New Zealand, 1976; Corcoran lectr. Am. Heart Assn., 1978. Author: (with S. G. Ball) Hypertension for the Clinician, 1994; editor: Clinical Hypertension, 1992, (with M. G. Nicholls) The Renin-Angiotensin System, 1993; contbr. numerous papers to profl. jours. Bd. dirs. Scottish Opera, 1999—. Fellow Royal Coll. Physicians London, Royal Coll. Physicians Glasgow, Royal Soc. Edinburgh; mem. Internat. Soc. Hypertension (pres. 1976-78, Gross Meml. lectr. 1980), Brit. Hypertension Soc. (found. pres. 1982-84), European Soc. Cardiology (chmn. working group on hypertension and heart 1988-90). Avocations: music, opera, sports, cricket, history, travel. Home: Elmbank House Manse Rd, Bowling Glasgow G60 5AA, Scotland

ROBERTSON, JOHN MAXWELL, service company executive; b. Dunedin, Otago, N.Z., Aug. 20, 1943; s. James Norman and Christina (Hamilton) R.; m. Allison Ayre Melville, Dec. 18, 1965; children: Janine Marie, Susanne Gael, Gavin David. BSc with honors, Otago U., 1965, PhD in Chemistry, 1969; Dip BA in Bus. Adminstrn., Canterbury U., 1992. Chartered chemist. Sect. leader water analysis DSIR, Auckland, N.Z., 1969-82, sect. leader food and water, 1971-82, dep. govt. analyst, 1972-82; govt. analyst DSIR, Christchurch, N.Z., 1982-92; campus chmn. DSIR, Ilam, Christchurch, 1989-92; quality sys. cons. Grayson Group, Auckland, 1992-95, quality mgr., 1992-95; gen. mgr. accreditation Internat. Accreditation N.Z., Auckland, 1995—. Editor/co-author: New Zealand Standard Code of Practice for the Operation of Swimming Pools, 1985; contbr. articles to profl. jours. Chmn. Owairaka Sch. Pool Com., Auckland, 1980-81, Riccarton H.S. PTA, Christchurch, 1984-85; mem. boys h.s. com. Owairaka, Wesley, Riccarton, Christchurch, 1975-88; youth group leader various orgns., 1967-93; elder Presbyn. Ch., various locations, 1971—; mem. food stds. com. Ministry of Health, 1988-93, mem. drinking water stds. com., 1990-2000; lab. accreditation mgmt. com. TELARC, N.Z., 1982-92. Fellow N.Z. Inst. Chemistry; mem. Royal Soc. Chemistry U.K., Inst. Food Sci. and Tech. N.Z., Australasian Forensic Sci. Soc., Lions (pres.). Avocations: electronics, home maintenance, walking/hiking, square dancing. Office: Internat Accreditation NZ, Private Bag 2 8 908, Auckland 1136, New Zealand

ROBERTSON, JOSEPH EDMOND, grain processing company executive; b. Brownstown, Ind., Feb. 16, 1918; s. Roscoe Melvin and Edith Penina (Shields) R.; m. Virginia Faye Baxter, Nov. 23, 1941; 1 son, Joseph Edmond, Jr. BS, Kans. State U., 1940, postgrad., 1940. Cereal chemist Ewing Mill Co., 1940-43, flour milling engr., 1946-50, feed nutritionist, 1951-59; v.p., sec. Robertson Corp., Brownstown, Ind., 1960-80, pres., 1980-97, CEO, 1997—; forest products tech. writer Forest Products Jour., 1973-78. Author: On Kilroy's Trail, 1998. Mem. Kans. State U. Varsity Basketball Team, 1937-40; pres. Jackson County (Ind.) Welfare Bd., 1948-52; mem. Ind. Port Commn., 1986-91; mem. Ind. Gov.'s Coun. of Sagamores of the Wabash. Served with USAAF, 1943-45. Named to Hon. Order Ky. Cols. Mem. Hardwood Plywood Mfrs. Assn. (v.p. affiliate div. 1971-73, 87-88, internat. lectr. forest products industry 1973-97), Am. Assn. Cereal Chemists, Assn. Operative Millers, Am. Legion, Brownstown C. of C. (dir. All Am. city program 1955), Kans. State U. Alumni Assn. (life), Blue Key, Phi Delta Theta, Phi Kappa Phi, Alpha Mu. Clubs: Harrison Lakes Country Club, Internat. Travelers Century (L.A.), Circumnavigators Club (N.Y.C.), Elks. Presbyterian. Home: Lake and Forest Club 1268 E Lake Shore Dr PO Box A Brownstown IN 47220 Office: 200 N Front St Brownstown IN 47220-1040

ROBERTSON, LORNA DOOLING, artist, real estate developer; b. N.Y.C., Aug. 29, 1929; d. Francis Joseph and Evelyn Julia (Adle) Dooling; m. James Gregory Robertson (div. 1977); children: Bonnie, Kim, Sue, James. BS, Purdue U., 1951; dietetic intern, Cornell Med. Sch. Hosp., N.Y.C., 1951-52. Cert. dietician Am. Dietetic Assn. Real estate developer, 1963—. Artist: one woman exhibitions include: Gallery Seghier, Vienna, Austria, 1992, Willow Gallery, SoHo, Manhattan, N.Y., Gelabert Gallery, N.Y.C., 1993, Art Addiction Gallery, Stockholm, Sweden, 1995; group exhibitions include Art 54 Gallery, SoHo Manhattan, N.Y., 1991, 92, Die Treppe Gallery, Stuttgart, Germany, 1991, 92, 94, Lever House Gallery, N.Y.C., 1992, Gallery Herouet, Paris, 1994, Osaka Internat. Art Festival, Japan, 1994 (prix d' honneur), Salon Internat. de l'Art, Aix en Provence, France, 1994, Arles Art Intr, Avignon, France, 1994 (Bronze medal), Magdelen Coll., Oxford U., Eng., Luneville, Chateau Stanislas Nimes, France, 1994, 1st Internat. Female Artists' Exhbn., Stockholm, 1994 (Gold medal), Alliance Francaise, Miami, Fla., 1994, Palais de Congres, Marseilles, France, 1994, 4th Internat. Exhbn. Minature Art, Art Addiction Internat. Gallery, Stockholm, 1996. Pres. Young Patroneses of Opera, Miami, Fla., 1968-69; bd. dirs. Opera Guild, Miami, 1966-69; founding mem. Vt. Studio Ctr., Johnson, 1984. Home: 13656 Lake Mary Jane Rd Orlando FL 32832-6532 also: 752 Kaupakalua Rd Haiku HI 96708-5350

ROBERTSON, PAUL DOUGLAS, Jamaican government official; b. July 7, 1946. BA, Jamaica Coll.; MSc in Government, U. West Indies; PhD, U. Mich. Tchr. Oberlin High Sch., 1965, 68; lectr. Dept. Govt., U. West Indies, 1968-69, 73-74; rsch. assoc. Inst. Urban Affairs of Polit. Scis., Howard U.; asst. prof. Dept. Govt.; chmn. JAMAL Found., 1978; spl. asst. Prime Min. Manley, 1978, 80; dep. gen. sec. adminstrn. People's Nat. Party, 1978-80; asst. Mr. Manley, 1981-82; gen. sec. People's Nat. Party, 1983-91; spl. asst. Min. Justice; senator Jamaican Senate, dep. leader of the govt. bus.; min. Dept. Info. and Culture, Govt. Jamaica, 1989-91; now min. Fgn. Affairs and Fgn. Trade, Govt. Jamaica, 1993-95; min. industry, investments & commerce, 1995—, now min. industry & investment. Contb. to profl. jours. and publs. Office: Min Industry Investments & Commerce, Petrojam Bldg, 36 Trafalgar Rd, Box 76, Kingston 10, Jamaica*

ROBERTSON, PAUL JOSEPH, lawyer, educator; b. Chgo., Dec. 31, 1963; s. Mary Ellen (Statom) R. BSBA in Mktg., Georgetown U., Washington, 1985; BA in Sociology, St. Leo (Fla.) Coll., 1988; MBA, U. Ill., 1992, JD, 1992. Bar: Ill. 1992, U.S. Dist. Ct. (ea. dist.) Ill. 1992, U.S. Ct. Appeals (7th cir.) 1992. Counsel Region V U.S. Dept. Health and Human Svcs., Chgo., 1992-93, staff atty. Social Security Adminstrn., 1993-94; sr. atty. Office Gen. Counsel U.S. Dept. Health and Human Svcs., Bethesda, Md., 1994—; lectr. NIH, Found. for Advanced Edn. in Scis., Bethesda, 1995—; mem. black employees fed. adv. com. NIH, 1994-97. Campaign aide, FEC compliance, com. to elect Carol Moseley-Braun for U.S. Senate, Chgo., 1992. 1st lt. USAF, 1985-88. Decorated Air Force Meritorious Medal; recipient Joseph W. Rickert Award for Cmty. Svc., Faculty of Law, U. Ill., 1992. Mem. ABA, Nat. Bar Assn., Chgo. Bar Assn., Am. Legion, Masons. AME Ch. Avocations: Lacrosse, basketball, travel, reading, wine tasting. Office: NIH Bldg 31 -50 Rm 2B Bethesda MD 20892-0001

ROBERTSON, RUTH ANN, systems analyst, engineer; b. Oak Ridge, Tenn., Nov. 20, 1959; d. Arnold Powell and Beatrice (Lazaroff) Litman. BME, Ga. Inst. Tech., 1982; postgrad., U. Redlands, Calif., 1991. Engring. intern IBM, Gaithersburg, Md., 1980-81; packaging engr. Hughes Aircraft Co., El Segundo, Calif., 1982-85; field engr. Spectrum Control, Inc., Valencia, Calif., 1985-86; pres. Precision Jaunt, El Segundo, 1986-87; sr. systems analyst Marquardt Co., Van Nuys, Calif., 1987-91, Axcom Computer Cons., Springfield, Mo., 1991-92; open systems product mgr. Data-Trade, Inc., Springfield, 1992-96; mgr.product realization Dayco Products, Inc., Springfield, 1996-99; MIS mgr. S.W. Mo. State U., Springfield, 1999—. Mem. Whitehead Leadership Soc., Tau Beta Pi, Phi Tau Sigma. Office: SW Mo State U Computer Svcs 901 S National Ave Springfield MO 65804-0088

ROBERTSON, SIR RUTHERFORD NESS, chemical biologist; b. Melbourne, Australia, Sept. 29, 1913; s. Joshua and Josephine (Hogan) R.; m. Mary Helen Bruce Rogerson, Sept. 9, 1937; 1 child, Robert James. BSc, U. Sydney, Australia, 1934, DSc, 1961; PhD, U. Cambridge, Eng., 1939, ScD (hon.), 1970; DSc (hon.), U. Tasmania, Australia, 1965, Monash U., 1971, Australian Nat. U., 1979. Linnean Macleay fellow Sydney U., 1935-36, lectr., sr. lectr., 1939-46, hon. visitor Sch. Biol. Scis., 1978-87, asst. lectr., then lectr. botany, 1939-46; rsch. officer, then chief rsch. officer Commonwealth Sci. and Indsl. Rsch. Orgn., 1946-59, mem. exec. bd., 1959-62; prof. botany Adelaide Australian Nat. U., Canberra, 1962-69, master Univ. House, 1969-72, dir. Rsch. Sch. Biol. Scis., 1973-78, pro-chancellor, 1984-86; vis. prof. UCLA, 1958-59; Kearney lectr. U. Calif., Berkeley, 1959; found. chmn. Australian Rsch. Grants Com., 1965-69; dep. chmn. Australian Sci. and Tech. Coun., 1977-81; active Australia-China Coun., 1979-81; Australian com. Cambridge Commonwealth Trust, 1986-91, patron, 1993-97; pres. 13th Internat. Bot. Congress, 1981; honor roll faculty sci. Sydney U., 1997. Author: (with G.E. Briggs and A.B. Hope) Electrolytes in Plant Cells, 1961, Protons, Electrons, Phosphorylation and Active Transport, 1968, The Lively Menbranes, 1983; contbr. numerous articles to sci. jours. Decorated companion Order of St. Michael and St. George; knight bachelor; companion Order of Australia; recipient Clarke Meml. medal Royal Soc. NSW, 1954, Farrar Meml. medal, 1963, Australian and New Zealand Assn. Advancement of Sci. medal, 1968, Mueller medal, 1970, Burnet medal, 1975. Fellow Australian Acad. Sci. (pres. 1970-74), Royal Soc. London, St. John's Coll. Cambridge (hon.), Royal Soc. Edinburgh (hon.); mem. U.S. Nat. Acad. Scis. (fgn. assoc.), Am. Philos. Soc. (fgn.), Am. Soc. Plant Physiologists (corr.), Royal Soc. N.Z. (hon.), Am. Acad. Arts and Scis. (hon. fgn.), Union Club. Home: Unit 12 Linton Retirement Village, Yass NSW 2582, Australia

ROBERTSON, SARA STEWART, private investor, entrepreneur; b. N.Y.C., Feb. 4, 1940; d. John Elliott and Mary Terry (Schlamp) Stewart; m. James Young Robertson, Nov. 29, 1975 (dec. Mar. 1988). BA, Conn. Coll., 1961; MBA, Am. U., 1969. From trainee to officer First Nat. Bank/First Chgo. Corp., 1969-75, v.p., 1975-92; prin. Royall Enterprises, Chgo., 1992—; prin., dir. Zeppelin Press, Inc., Miami, Fla., 1995—; bd. dirs. Youth Guidance, Chgo., 1982-85, 92-95, chair individuals fundraising, mem. exec. com., 1993-95. Bd. dirs. Harbor House Condominium Assn. Chgo., 1990-92; trustee Sherwood Conservatory Music, 1993—, chair bd. devel., 1993-95, 97-99; mem. allocations com. and family priority grants com. United Way-Chgo., 1992-95; co-founder, sec./treas ASKK (Animal Support Kindness and Kinship, Inc.), 1999—. Mem. Club 13 Palm Beach (pres. 1996-98). Home and Office: 339 Westminster Pl West Palm Beach FL 33405-1652

ROBERTSON, WYNDHAM GAY, university official; b. Salisbury, N.C., Sept. 25, 1937; d. Julian Hart and Blanche Williamson (Spencer) R. AB in Econs., Hollins Coll., Roanoke, Va., 1958. Rsch. asst. Standard Oil Co., N.Y.C., 1958-61; rschr. Fortune Mag., N.Y.C., 1961-67, assoc. editor, 1968-74, bd. of editors, 1974-81, asst. mng. editor, 1981-86; bus. editor Time Mag., N.Y.C., 1982-83; v.p. comm. U. N.C., Chapel Hill, 1986-96; bd. dirs. Media Gen. Inc. Contbr. numerous articles to Fortune Mag. Trustee Thomas S. Kenan Inst. for the Arts, Nat. Humanities Ctr., Hollins U., chair. Recipient Gerald M. Loeb Achievement award, U. of Conn., 1972. Mem. Phi Beta Kappa. Episcopalian.

ROBERTS-PARAST, ANN TALBOT, English, foreign language educator; b. Roanoke, Va.; d. David Charles and Audrey Louise (Cassell) Roberts; m. Rudy M. Parast, Feb. 22, 1980; 1 child, Layla Ann. BA in French, Tulane U.; BA in Fgn. Lang. Edn., U. New Orleans; degree in translating and interpreting, U. Paris, profl. diploma; M English, U. Paris VIII; MA in French, U. Wash., ABD in Comparative Lit. Freelance translator, interpreter, English instr. Paris, 1968-72; French/English instr. pub. and pvt. schs., New Orleans, 1972-78; translator, adminstrv. asst. Ivory Coast Embassy, Washington, 1974-75; tchg. asst. in French U. Wash., Seattle, 1978-83; French tchr. Marine Mil. Acad., Harlingen, Tex., 1983-84, Harlingen H.S., 1984-89; English instr. Tex. State Tech. Coll., 1989—; freelance translator, interpreter, New Orleans and Seattle, 1975—; French/English interpreter, 1994—; placement of fgn. exch. students, 1990—; mgr., writer Profl. Resume and Writing Svc., Harlingen, 1989—. Contbr. articles

to profl. publs. Former bd. dirs. Jr. Peacemaker Club, Harlingen; former bd. dirs. Tex. French Symposium. French Govt. scholar, Vichy, France, 1983. Mem. DAR (chair good citizens com. 1997—), Tex. C.C. Tchrs. Assn., Alliance Française of Lower Rio Grande, Nat. Coun. Tchrs. English. Mem. Baha'i Faith. E-mail: eroberts@tstu.edu. Home: 2402 E Adams Ave Harlingen TX 78550-2723 Office: Tex State Tech Coll Dept English Harlingen TX 78550

ROBERTS-THOMSON, IAN CHARLES, physician, gastroenterologist; b. Burnie, Tasmania, Australia, Aug. 9, 1946; s. Eric and Kathleen Grace (Brownscombe) R.-T.; m. Kaye Frances Williams, Dec. 10, 1969; children: Kurt, Simon, Laura, Clark, Ross. MB BS, Melbourne U., 1969, MD, 1975. Melbourne-Cleve. fellow Univ. Hosps. of Cleve., 1974-76; asst. gastroenterologist Royal Melbourne Hosp., 1976-84, asst. physician, clin. rsch. unit, 1981-84; dir. dept. gastroenterology Queen Elizabeth Hosp., Adelaide, Australia, 1985—; assoc. prof. U. Adelaide, 1988-99, clin. prof., 1999—, assoc. dean faculty of health scis., 1991—; pres. Australian bd. Vellore Christian Med. Coll. and Hosp., 1999—. Contbr. articles to profl. jours. Pres. Friends of Vellore, Adelaide, 1997—. Recipient Elton Hoyt II Meml. award Case Western Res. U., 1976; Macquarie Bank fellow, 1994. Fellow Royal Australasian Coll. Physicians; mem. Gastroenterol. Soc. Australia, Am. Gastroenterol. Assn., Australian Soc. for Med. Rsch., Digestive Health Found. (v.p. 1997—). Mem. Uniting Ch. Australia. Avocations: gardening, golf. Office: Queen Elizabeth Hosp, Woodville Rd, 5011 Woodville Australia

ROBEY, SHERIE GAY SOUTHALL GORDON, secondary education educator, consultant; b. Washington, July 7, 1954; d. James Edward and Gene Elizabeth (Gray) Southall; children: m. Robert Jean Claude Robey; children: Michael Aaron Gordon, Robert Eugene Robey, Jamie Lea Robey. BS, U. Md., 1976; MA in Edn. and Human Devel., George Washington U., 1988. Tchr. Esperanza Mid. Sch., Hollywood, Md., 1980-84, Chopticon High Sch., Morganza, Md., 1984—; coach Odyssey of the Mind, 1985-95; sponsor Future Tchrs. Am., Morganza, 1990—, S.H.O.P/S.A.D.D., Morganza, 1990—; cons. Ednl. Cosn., Waldorf, 1980—; pres. BNA Swim Team, 1992—; driver edn. classroom and lab instr. Choptican High Sch., 1996. Mem. Ednl. Rep. Assn. St. Mary's County, Lighthouse Hist. Soc. Methodist. Avocations: swimming, writing, visiting lighthouses, collection miniature lighthouses. E-mail: rrobey@olg.com. Home and Office: 11181 Carroll Dr Waldorf MD 20601-2656

ROBILLARD, EDMOND, priest; b. LeGardeur, Que., Can., Dec. 20, 1917; s. William and Marie (Lachapelle) R. B Arts and Scis., Coll. de l'Assomption, 1936; postgrad., Couvent Dominicain d'Ottawa, 1938-41; Licentiate in Theology, Cath. U. Am., 1943; ThD, U. Montreal, Can., 1944-45. Joined Dominican Order, Roman Cath. Ch., ordained priest, 1941. Prof. theology Coll. Dominicain, Ottawa, Ont., Can., 1943-50; prof. U. Montreal, 1955-83, prof. titulaire, 1970—; pres. Soc. des Ecrivains canadiens, 1973-77; sec. Soc. Letters of Que., 1977-83. Author: De l'analogie et du concept d'etre, 1963, John Henry Newman: L'idee d'universite, 1968, John Henry Newman: Conferences sur la Doctrine de la justification, 1980, Reincarnation: Illusion or Reality, 1982, Quebec Blues, 1983, Nos Racines chrétiennes, 1985, La messe catholique de tous les dimanches de l'année sur des chorals de J. S. Bach, Itinéraire 1986, Tout ce qu'il vous dira, Faites-le, 1987, S. Justin: philosophique, 1989, Qui aime connaît Dieu, 1989, La sagesse et les 1050 sentences du mime syrien Publilius Lochius, 1991, Jeux d'hiver et d'enfer, 1995, Le Discours poétique, 1996, Blaise Pascal: Le pari sur l'incertain, 1996, L'Expérience De La Trinité Dans Les Ames Saintes D'AprÈs Saint Thomas D'Aquin, 1997, Du temps que le goglu chantait. (poems) 2000, La Rédemption: une amoureuse Folie de Dieu, 1998, Les Saintes et Saints de la Liturgie Canadienne, 1998, Le Christ Jesus, 2000, Du Temps Que Le Gogly Changait, 2000; mem. editorial bd. jour. Carrefour Chretien, 1984—; contbr. articles to profl. jours. Mem. Soc. Can. Theologie, Assn. Can. Francaise L'avancement Scis., Quebec Writers Assn. (gen. pres., regional pres.), Académie des Lettres du Québec. Fax: 514-731-0676. Address: Les Péres Dominicians, Montreal, PQ Canada H3T 1B6 Office: 271 Chemin St Catherine, Montreal, PQ Canada

ROBILLARD, LUCIENNE, federal official; b. Montreal, Canada. BA, Coll. Basile-Moreau, 1965; MA in Social Work, U. Montreal, 1967; Diploma in Adminstrn., École des hautes études commerciales, Montreal, 1983, MBA, 1986. Social worker, clin. practitioner Maisonneuve-Rosemont Hosp.; appt. min. of labour and fed. campaigns Que., 1995-96; sr. adminstr. Centre de svcs. sociaux Richelieu; youth leader in a kibbutz Israel, 1969-72; apptd. pub. curator City of Quebec, Canada, 1986-89; elected mem. Quebec Nat. Assembly for Chambly, 1989; apptd. min. cultural affairs, 1989-90, apptd. min. higher edn. and science, 1990-92, apptd. min. of edn., 1992-93, min. edn. and science, 1993-94, min. health and social svcs., 1994-95, minister of labor, minister responsible for fed. campaign, 1995; elected mem. parliament Saint-Henri-Westmount, 1995—; min. citizenship and immigration, 1996-99; re-elected to parliament Westmount-Ville-Marie, 1997—; pres. Treas. Bd., 1999—; min. infrastructure., 1999—; mem. Corp. professionelle des travailleurs sociaux de Québec, 1967—; mem. editl. com. (book) Le travail social et la santé au Québec, 1984-86, departmental study com. psychiatric svcs., Montreal region, 1984-85; pres. Commn. adminstrv. des svcs. de santé mentale de the Conseil régional de la Montérégie, 1983-86, Association des praticiens de service social en milieu de santé du Québec, 1984-86; cons. mental health dossier Rochon Commn., 1986. Office: 140 O'Connor St, East Tower, Ottawa, ON Canada K1A OR5

ROBIN, DONALD P., business educator; b. New Orleans, Dec. 8, 1939; s. Donald F. and Anna P. Robin; m. Eleanor F. Robin, May 8, 1963 (div. July 1997); children: Donald F., Dianna P., Danielle S. BSME, La. State U., 1963, MBA, 1966, D Bus. Adminstrn., 1969. Asst. prof. U. Ga., Athens, 1969-71; assoc. prof. Miss. State U., Starkville, 1971-75, prof., 1975-87; prof. La. Technol. U., Ruston, 1987-89, U. So. Miss., Hattiesburg, 1989-97; J. Tylee Wilson prof. bus. ethics Wake Forest U., Winston-Salem, N.C., 1997—; mem. editl. rev. bd. ann. edits. Bus. Ethics, 1991-99; ad hoc reviewer Jour. Acad. Mktg. Sci., 1995-00. Author: Questions and Answers about Business Ethics, 2000, also others; co-author, co-editor: Theoretical Foundations in Marekting Ethics, 1999; contbr. over 40 articles to profl. jours. Rschr. Winston-Salem Symphony, 1998; vol. ARC, Winston-Salem, 1999. Fellow Soc. for Mktg. Advances (found. pres. 1998-00); mem. Soc. for Bus. Ethics (editl. rev. bd. Bus. Ethics Quar. 1995-00). Avocations: golf, wine appreciation. E-mail: robind@wfu.edu. Home: 1019 Paschal Dr Winston Salem NC 27106-4150 Office: Wake Forest U PO Box 7285 Reynolda St Winston Salem NC 27109

ROBIN, JEAN-PAUL GUY, science educator, researcher; b. Nantes, France, Nov. 12, 1958; s. René Léon Robin and Roxane Ginette Olivier. Masters, U. de Rennes, France, 1983; PhD, U. Brest, France, 1992. Temporary asst. U. Caen, France, 1992-93, lectr., 1993—; membership working group on cephalopod life-history I.C.E.S., Copenhagen, 1993—. Trade union del. SGEN-CFDT, Caen, 1995—. Mem. Fisheries Assessment Soc. Office: U Caen Lab Biology, Biotech Marines, 14032 Caen Cedex, France

ROBIN, THEODORE TYDINGS, JR., lawyer, engineer, consultant; b. New Orleans, Aug. 29, 1939; s. T.eodore Tydings and Hazel (Corbin) R.; m. Helen Jones, June 8, 1963; children: Corbin, Curry, Ted, Phil. BME, Ga. Inst. Tech., 1961, MS in N.E., 1963, PhD, 1967; LLB, Blackstone Sch. Law, 1979. Bar: Calif. 1980, U.S. Patent and Trademark Office 1982; registered profl. engr., Ala., Calif. Rsch. engr. Oak Ridge (Tenn.) Nat. Lab., 1967; asst. prof. radiology and physics Emory U., Atlanta, 1968-69; project engr. Atomic Internat. divsn. N.Am. Rockwell, Canoga park, Calif., 1970-72; engr. mgmt. engring. divsn. So. Co. Svcs., Birmingham, Ala., 1972-83, mgr. nuclear support and quality assurance, 1989-90, mgr. quality assurance and resources, 1991-92; mgr. Hatch Design Configuration, 1993-94; program mgr. pooled inventory mgmt. program So. Electric Internat., Birmingham, 1984-88, bd. dirs. polit. action com., 1985-87; dir. nuclear stds., radiation safety officer, sr. patent counsel, prin. nuclear engring Theragenics Corp., Atlanta, 1996—. Mem. ABA, ASME (mem. nuclear quality assurance subcom. on stds. coordinating and radioactive waste 1991-99), Am. Assn. Physicists Medicine, Am. Nuclear Soc. (chmn. Birmingham sect. 1987-88, nuclear power plant stds. com. 1989-94), Ga. Tech. Alumni Assn. (trustee 1997-00), Rotary (pres. Shades Valley club 1987-88, chmn. dist. 6860 internat. youth exch. com. 1989-90, R.I. dist. gov. 6860 1994-95), Sigma Xi. Achievements include research on power plant performance and reliability and effect of coal quality, space radiation effects on human cells, boiling heat transfer, nuclear reactor safety, multi-utility contracting, reliability economics, benchmarking and total quality management; patent law. Home and Office: 4524 Pine Mountain Rd Birmingham AL 35213-1828

ROBINS, BETTY DASHEW, antiques and arts dealer; b. N.Y.C., Feb. 14, 1923; d. Leon and Esther (Turits) Dashew; m. Arthur Joseph Robins, Sept. 26, 1948; children: Lisa Dale, Michael Lee. BA, NYU, 1952. Field staff Pearl Buck Open Door, N.Y.C., 1944-45; dir. MacArthur House, San Francisco, 1945-47, Georgetown House, Washington, 1948-50; asst. curator S. Asian Collection Mus. of Art and Archaeology, U. Mo., Columbia, 1967-68; owner BDR Assocs. Arts and Antiques, Columbia, 1976—; founding mem., 1st pres. Columbia Art League, 1959-61; gen. chmn. 1st Tenn. Artist Craftsman Fair, Nashville, 1971-72; bd. mem. Mus. Assocs., Mus. Art and Archaeology, U. Mo., 1975-85, mem. S. Asian studies com., 1976-85; coord. Festival of India, 1985-86, Festival of China, 1986-87, Peace Through the Arts, 1987-88, yr.-long programs commemorating 50th anniversary India independence, Columbia, 1997; mem. profl. visual arts adv. com. Mo. Arts Coun., 1980-82; cons. Denver Art Mus., 1991-92; advisor India Arts exhibit U. Mo. Mus. Art and Archaeology, 1997; organizer gallery exhibits, such as carved coconut Scrapers of Malaysia, India, Indonesia, Nat. Inst. of Pub. Adminstrn., Kuala Lumpur, 1989, Traditional Arts of India and U.S.A., U. Mo., 1989, Healing Imagery of Malaysia and U.S.A., U. Mo., 1991, Decorative Arts India, Stephens Coll., 1998, Storytelling through the Everyday Art of Mo. and India, Boone County Hist. Mus., 1998. Co-author: Everyday Art of India, 1968; contbr. articles to profl. jours. Bd. dirs. PAST (hist. preservation of Mo.), 1978-79. Named Woman of the Yr., Women in Comms., 1977-78, Vol. of Yr., Vol. Action Coun., 1983; recipient Quiet Hero award Columbia Pub. Schs., 1998. Home: 2316 Woodridge Rd Columbia MO 65203-1550

ROBINS, MITCHELL JAMES, management consultant; b. Detroit, May 23, 1956; s. Melvin M. Robins and Judith (Bell) Martin; m. Amy Elizabeth Green, July 2, 1978; children: Alexander Philip, Sean Lewis, Emily Dinah. BBA, U. Mich., 1977; postgrad., U. Detroit, Oakland U. CPA, Mich., Fla., Ind., Nev., Calif. Exec. mgr. GM; founder, mng. ptnr., CEO Robins-Assocs., CPAs and Cons., Southfield, Mich., 1981—; founder, mng. ptnr. Robins-Assocs., CPAs and Cons., La Jolla, Calif., 1980—; founder, mgr., ptnr. Lumedics, Ltd., La Jolla, Calif., Paris; bd. dirs. Campus Distbn., Inc., Ann Arbor, Mich., Internat. Med.-Dental Hypnotherapy Assn., LumeDics Ltd., San Diego; mem. Restaurant Bus. Research Adv. Panel, N.Y.C. Mem. steering com. Rep. 300 Com. of Mich., Oakland County, zoning bd. appeals City of Farmington Hills, Rep. Senatorial Inner Circle; mem. Carmel Valley Planning Bd., 1997. Named Nat. Rep. Congl. Com. Businessman of the Yr., 1999. Mem. AICPA, ABA, Mich. Assn. CPA's, Mich. Soc. Planning Ofcls., Assn. MBA Execs., U. Mich. Alumni Assn., Internat. Platform Assn. Republican. Clubs: Economic (Detroit), Detroit Athletic, Heritage Hills Country, Skyline. Avocations: golf, tennis, history, politics, travel. Fax: 858-551-1215; email: mrobinsooo@usa.net. Home: 12885 Ralston Cir San Diego CA 92130-2447

ROBINS, SIR RALPH, manufacturing executive; b. June 16, 1932; s. Leonard Haddon and Maud Lillian R.; m. Patricia Maureen Grimes, 1962; 2 children. Student, Imperial Coll.; BS, U. London; DL (hon.), U. Derby (Eng.), 1992; DSc (hon.), U. Cranfield, 1990; DBA (hon.), U. Strathclyde, 1996. Devel. engr. Rolls-Royce, Derby, Eng., 1955-66; exec. v.p. Rolls-Royce Inc., 1971-73; mng. dir. RR Indsl. & Marine Divsn., 1973-78; comml. dir. RR Ltd., 1978-83; chmn. Internat. Aero Engines AG, 1983-84; mng. dir. Rolls-Royce plc, 1984-89, dep. chmn., 1989-92, ceo, 1990-92, chmn., 1992—; non-exec. chmn. Cable and Wireless plc; non-exec. dir. Schroders plc, Standard Chartered Plc, Coopers Industries Inc., Marks and Spencer plc; chmn. Def. Industries Coun., 1986—; pres. SBAC, 1986-87. Decorated comdr.'s cross Order of Merit (Germany), 1996. Fellow Instn. Mech. Engrs. (hon.), Fellowship of Engring., Royal Aeronaut. Soc., City and Guild Inst.; mem. Coun. Sci. and Tech. Avocations: tennis, golf, music, classic cars. Office: Rolls-Royce plc, 65 Buckingham Gate, London SW1E 6AT, England*

ROBINS, REED W., music recording executive; b. Richmond, Va., June 4, 1957. BA in Music Composition, Va. Commonwealth, 1981; cert., Rec. Inst. Am., 1984. Owner Synergy Prodns., Richmond, 1984, N.Y.C., 1984-95; owner Macintyre Music Rec., N.Y.C., 1995—; pres. Changing Tones Records, N.Y.C., 1995—; owner Tactus Music Pub., N.Y.C., 1995—. Composer (film score): The Painter, 1993; prodr. music recs. including Songs of Jimi Hendrix for Solo Jazz Piano, 1995, My Happiness, 1995. Mem. ASCAP, Am. Music Ctr. E-mail: reed@changingtones.com. Office: Macintyre Music 874 Broadway New York NY 10003-1222

ROBINS, RICHARD WHITNEY, psychologist, educator; b. Washington, June 2, 1966; s. Alexander and Betty Robins; m. Kristina Elizabeth Whitney, July 29, 1989 (div. Sept. 1997). BA, U. Calif., Berkeley, 1988, PhD, 1995. Rsch. psychologist U. Calif., Berkeley, 1995—; prof. psychology U. Calif., Davis, 1996—; vis. rsch. psychologist U. London, 1998-00; mem. grant rev. panel NIMH, Bethesda, Md., 1999—; cons. editor Jour. Personality and Social Psychology, 1999—, Personality and Social Psychology Bull., 1999—. Contbg. author: Handbook of Personality, 1999; contbr. articles to profl. jours., including Psychol. Sci., Am. Scientist, Am. Psychologist. Rsch. fellow NSF, 1989-92; grantee NIMH, 1999-03. Mem. APA, Am. Psychol. Soc. Democrat. Jewish. E-mail: rwrobins@ucdavis.edu. Office: U Calif One Shields Ave Davis CA 95616

ROBINSON, ALICE HELENE, English language educator, administrative assistant; b. Cleve., Oct. 16, 1946; d. Alford B. and Willie Helena (Knuckles) R. BA, Cleve. State U., 1968, MA, 1992; postgrad., John Carroll U. Cert. tchr., Ohio. English language educator Cleve. Bd. Edn., Ohio; presenter 1st Celtic Conf. Cleve. State U., 1993. Cleve. Edn. Fund scholar, 1991. Mem. Cleve. Mus. Art, Cleve. Ballet. Episcopalian. Avocations: collecting stamps, plates, and artifacts, word puzzles, logic problems. Home: 3344 E 142nd St Cleveland OH 44120-4009 Office: Cleve Bd Edn 1380 E 6th St Cleveland OH 44114-1606

ROBINSON, ALICE JEAN MCDONNELL, retired drama and speech educator; b. St. Joseph, Mo., Nov. 17, 1922; d. John Francis and Della M. (Mavity) McDonnell; m. James Eugene Robinson, Apr. 21, 1956 (dec. 1983). BA, U. Kans., 1944, MA, 1947; PhD, Stanford U., 1965. Tchr. Garden City (Kans.) High Sch., 1944-46; asst. prof. Emporia (Kans.) State U., 1947-52; dir. live programs Sta. KTVH-TV, Hutchinson-Wichita, Kans., 1953-55; assoc. prof. drama and speech U. Md. Baltimore County, Balt., 1966-99, rsch. theatre history. Author: The American Theatre: A History in Slides, 1992, Betty Comden and Adolph Green: A Bio-Bibliography, 1993; co-editor: Notable Women in the American Theatre, 1989; appeared in plays, including Landscape, 1983, Tartuffe, 1985, Rockaby, 1990. Mem. Am. Soc. Theatre Rsch., Assn. Theatre Higher Edn., Phi Beta Kappa. Republican. Avocations: travel, reading, acting, directing. Home: 111 N Main St Caldwell KS 67022-1535

ROBINSON, ARTHUR NAPOLEON RAYMOND, president; b. Trinidad and Tobago, Dec. 16, 1926; s. James and Isabella R.; married; 2 children. Student, Castara Meth. Sch., 1931-38, Bishop's High Sch., 1938-45; LLB, London U., 1949; honors, St. John's Coll., Oxford, U.K., 1955. Acting 2d class clk. Magistracy, Tobago, Trinidad, 1946, St. George West, Trinidad, 1946; 2d class clk. Social Services Dept., 1947; registrar Gen. Dept., 1951; with Sir Courtenay Hannays, barrister, Port of Spain, Scarborough, Trinidad and Tobago, 1955; treas. Peoples Nat. Movement, Trinidad, 1956-1959; mem. Fed. Parliament Trinidad, 1958-61; 1st minister of fin. Trinidad and Tobago, 1961-67; dep. polit. leader People's Nat. Movement, Trinidad and Tobago, 1966, minister of external affairs, 1967-70; leader Action Group of Dedicated Citizens (later Action Com. of Dedicated Citizens and Dem. Action Congress), Trinidad and Tobago, 1970—; mem. of opposition Parliament, Trinidad and Tobago, 1971-85; chmn. Tobago House of Assembly, Trinidad and Tobago, 1980-86; polit. leader Nat. Alliance for Reconstruction, Trinidad and Tobago, 1985-97; prime minister Port of Spain, Trinidad and Tobago, 1986-91, min. economy, 1986-88; President Trinidad and Tobago, 1997; cons. to UN on Internat. criminal law and human rights. Author: The Mechanics of Independence, 1971, Carribean Man, 1986; contbr. articles to profl. jours. and article on Trinidad and Tobago to Encyclopedia Brittanica, 1971 edit. Address: La Fantaisie Rd, The President's House, St Ann's Port of Spain Trinidad and Tobago

ROBINSON, BARBARA ELLEN, film production executive; b. Urbana, Ill., June 4, 1960; d. Benjamin Earl and Martha June (Dodson) R. BS in Biology, Bradley U., 1984. V.p. prodn. and licensing Era Internat., Taipei, Taiwan, 1989-96; v.p. programming Encore Internat., Denver, 1996-98; mng. dir. Columbia Pictures Film Prodn. Asia, Hong Kong, 1998—; exec. cons. Taiwan Golden House Film Festival, 1995; coord. Sundance from Festival in Beijing, 1995; jury mem. San Sebastian Film Festival, Spain, 1997. Assoc. prodr. (film) To Live, 1994; prodn. exec. (film) Raise the Red Lantern, 1991, Not One Less, 1999; co-prodr. (documentary) Music in the Movies, 1996, Zhang Yimou Directs Turandot in the Forbidden City, 1998. Avocations: snow skiing, horseback riding, singing, reading. Office: Columbia Pictures Film Prod, 32F Bank China 1 Garden Rd, Hong Kong Hong Kong

ROBINSON, CHARLES GRAHAM FRANCIS, radiologist, consultant; b. Birmingham, Warks, U.K., Aug. 25, 1947; s. Bernard Harry Daly and Sibyl Elizabeth (Weeks) R.; m. Lesley Margaret Carter, July 15, 1971; children—Jane Courage, Rory Grahme Louis. Grad., King's Sch., Kent, Eng., 1966, London Hosp., 1971. House officer in medicine Jersey Health Service, Jersey Channel Islands, 1972, house officer in surgery, 1973; sr. house officer in medicine Southeast Kent Area Health Authority, Kent, Eng., 1973-74; registrar in radiology Nottinghamshire Area Health Authority, 1974-77; sr. in radiology Longstershire Area Health Authority, 1977-79; cons. radiologist Pembrokeshire Dist. Health Authority, 1979—. Mem. Royal Coll. Radiologists. Avocation: goat keeping. Home: Y Bodau O'R Cathod Llanfallteg, Whitland Carmarthenshire Dyfed SA 34 OUJ, England Offices: Withybush Hosp, Fishguard Rd, West Pembs Haverford Dyfed SA 61 2JZ, England

ROBINSON, DAVID, academic administrator. Vice-chancellor Monash U., Victoria, Australia. Office: Monash U Vice Chancellor, Wellington Rd, Clayton 3168, Australia*

ROBINSON, DAVID MAURICE, professional basketball player; b. Key West, Fla., Aug. 6, 1965. Grad., U.S. Naval Acad., 1987. Commd. ensign USN, 1987; with San Antonio Spurs, 1989—; mem. U.S. Olympic Basketball Team, 1988, 92, 96. Recipient Naismith award, 1987, Wooden award, 1987, IBM award, 1990, 91, 94, Schick Pivotal Player award, 1990, 91; named to Sporting News All-Am. First Team, 1986, 87, Sporting News Coll. Player of Yr., 1987, NBA Rookie of Yr., 1990, All-NBA First Team, 1991, 92, All-Star team, 1990-94; named NBA Defensive Player of Yr., 1992, MVP, 1994-95, season MVP, 1995. Mem. NBA Champions, 1999, San Antonio Spurs. Achievements include being a holder of NCAA Divsn. 1 single season record most block shots per game (5.91), most blocked shots in 1 game (14), 1986, NBA career record most blocked shots per game (3.65). Office: care San Antonio Spurs 100 Montana St San Antonio TX 78203-1033

ROBINSON, DEREK, author; b. Bristol, Eng., Apr. 12, 1932; s. Alexander Smith and Margaret Low (MacAskill) R.; m. Sheila Collins, Apr. 29, 1968. BA in History, Cambridge (Eng.) U., 1956, MA, 1958. Copywriter McCann-Erickson Advt. Ltd., London, 1956-60, B.B.D.O. Inc., N.Y.C., 1960-66; freelance writer, 1966—. Author numerous books, including Goshawk Squadron, 1971, Piece of Cake, 1983 (made into TV series shown on Masterpiece Theater), A Good Clean Fight, 1993, Hornet's Sting, 1999. Served with RAF, 1951-53. Various novels selected for Book-of-Month Club and Lit. Guild selections. Avocations: squash, fishing. Home: Shapland House, Somerset St, BS2 8LZ Bristol England Office: David Higham Assocs Ltd, 5/8 Lower John St Golden Sq, London W1R 4HA, England

ROBINSON, DEREK, medical editor; b. Manchester, Eng., May 25, 1928; came to U.S., 1957.; MBChB, Manchester U., 1952, MD, 1961; diploma in child health, London U., 1958, diploma in pub. health, 1959. Diplomate Am. Bd. Preventive Medicine. Assoc. editor Med. Jour. Australia, 1955-57; resident in pub. health Va. State Health Dept., 1957-58; dir. child health Hampshire, Eng., 1959-61; fellow Toronto Sch. Pub. Health, Can., 1961-62; instr. Harvard Sch. Pub. Health, 1962-66; assoc. pediatrics Boston Childrens Hosp., 1963-68; dep. state health commr. Mass., 1966-75; sr. clin. lectr. Liverpool Sch. Tropical Medicine, Eng., 1975-85; dir. pub. health, exec. dir. Shropshire Health Authority, 1985-93; pvt. practice med. writer, infectious disease epidemiologist. Editor, contbr.: Epidemiology and the Community Control of Disease in Warm Climate Countries, 1985; editor pub. health New Eng. Jour. Medicine and Mass. Physician; contbr. articles to profl. jours. Mem. Mass. Med. Soc. Home and Office: Axland Assocs, 15 Claremont Hill, Shrewsbury SY1 1RD, England

ROBINSON, EARL JAMES, academic administrator, information systems and statistics educator, consultant; b. Wilmington, Del., Apr. 15, 1949; s. Harry and Minerva Ruth (James) R.; m. Karen Frances Smith, July 5, 1980; children: Ruth Frances, Sarah Rebecca. AB, Davidson Coll., 1971; MS, Bucknell U., 1973; PhD, U. Ga., 1977. Asst. prof. U. Ga., Athens, 1977-78; asst. prof. St. Mary's U., Halifax, N.S., Can., 1978-81, assoc. prof., 1981-84, chmn. dept., 1981-84; assoc. prof., chmn. St. Joseph's U., Phila., 1984-91; dean, prof. Coll. Bus. Minot (N.D.) State U., 1991-94; exec. v.p. acad. affairs, dean faculty, prof. Briar Cliff Coll., Sioux City, Iowa, 1994-98; pres., prof. Lees-McRae Coll., Banner Elk, N.C., 1998—; cons. Mgmt. Rsch. Assocs., Halifax, 1978-84; pres., cons. Robinson & Assocs., Phila., 1984-91, Minot, N.D., 1991-94, Sioux City, Iowa, 1991-98, Banner Elk, 1998—. Contbr. numerous articles to profl. jours. Recipient Golden M award St. Mary's U., 1981; grantee St. Joseph's U., 1985, St. Mary's U., 1982, Ashland Oil Corp., 1973, FAA, 1977, NSF, 1978. Mem. AAUP, Am. Assn. Higher Edn., Soc. for Sigma Xi, Sigma Phi Epsilon (social chmn. 1969-70, chpt. counselor 1988-91, nat. coms. 1996), Psi Chi. Presbyterian. Avocations: choral music, flying. Home: PO Box 1856 Banner Elk NC 28604-1856 Office: Lees-McRae Coll PO Box 128 Banner Elk NC 28604-0128

ROBINSON, ELIZABETH ANGELA, hematologist, consultant; b. Chester, U.K., Dec. 27, 1942; d. Harold and Phyllis Eleanor (Field) Jeffs; m. Philip Joseph Robinson, July 3, 1965; children; Amy Miranda, Robert Alexander, Isobel Mary. MB BS LRCP MRCS, St. Mary's Hosp. Med. Sch., 1967. Houseman St. Mary's Hosp., London, 1967-68; sr. houseman Leeds Gen. Infirmary, 1968-70; registrar in hematology Infirmary and Bradford St. Luke's Hosp., 1970-71; sr. registrar in clin. hematology and blood transfusion Yorks Rotational Tng. Scheme, Leeds, 1976; cons. hematologist and hon. cons. Regional Blood Transfusion, Leeds, 1976-88; dir. Yorks Regional Blood Transfusion Ctr., 1988-94; nat. med. dir. Nat. Blood Authority, Watford, Eng., 1994—; mem. Nat. Adv. Com. Plasma Supply for Self Sufficiency, 1981-83; sec. Nat. Working Party Code of Practice for Automated Plasmaphereses of Volunteer Donors, 1981-85; mem. Sci. Com. European Soc., 1984—; examiner Royal Coll., Pathologists, 1984-94; mem. Ministerial Adv. Com. on Blood and Tissue Safety, 1994—; expert Coun. Europe, European Union, 1994—. Contbr. articles to profl. jours. Fellow Royal Coll. Pathologists; mem. Brit. Soc. Hematology, Brit. Blood Transfusion Soc. (founder), European Soc. Hemapheresis (founder), Internat. Soc. Blood Transfusion, Am. Assn. Blood Banking. Avocations: chamber choir, horse riding, flautist. Office: Nat Blood Authority, Oak House Reeds Crescent, Watford WD1 1QH, England

ROBINSON, FRANCIS JOHN GIBSON, publishing executive, bibliographer, historian; b. Newcastle, Eng., Oct. 26, 1938; s. George and Elizabeth (Gibson) R.; m. Jennifer Margaret Bews; children: Charlotte Elizabeth, Francis John, Xanthe Louise. BA, Oxford (Eng.) U., 1960, MA, 1965; PhD, Newcastle U., 1973. Diploma in edn., 1963. Sr. rsch. assoc. U. Newcastle, 1970-80; mng. dir. Avero Publs., Newcastle, 1980—; cons. dir. Waterloo (Can.) Periodicals & Series, 1993—, Eighteenth Century Legal Lit., Canterbury, Kent, Eng., 1979-85, Nineteen Century Legal Lit., Sheffield, Eng., 1990-97, Project for Hist. Bibliography, Newcastle, 1969-84. Author: (retrospective bibliography, book and CD-ROM and website) Nineteen Century Short Title Catalogue, 1801-1870, 66 vols., 1983-96, (CD-ROM database) Biography Database 1680-1830, 1993—, (bibliography) Book Subscription Lists: A Guide, 1975, Eighteenth Century Legal Literature, 1983, (CD-ROM and website) Nineteenth Century Short Title Catalogue, 1871-1919, 1996—. Avocations: chess, bridge. Home: 3 Otterburn Villas South,

Newcastle NE2 3AQ, England Office: Avero Publs Ltd, 20 Great North Rd, Newcastle NE2 4PS, England

ROBINSON, GERRARD JUDE, television company executive; b. Donegal, Ireland, Oct. 23, 1948; s. Anthony and Elizabeth Ann (Stuart) R.; m. Maria Ann Borg, 1969 (div. 1990); children: Samantha Erica, Richard Steven; m. Heather Peta Leaman, 1990; children: April Heather, Timothy Gerrard. Student, St. Mary's Coll. Works acct. Lesney Products, London, 1965-74; fin. contr. Lex Indsl. Distbn. & Hire, London, 1974-80; fin. dir. Coca Cola, London, 1980-81, sales and mktg. dir., 1981-83, mng. dir., 1983-84; mng. dir. Grand Met. Contract Svcs., London, 1984-87; chief exec. Compass Group PLC, London, 1987-91; CEO Granada Group PLC, London, 1991-96, chmn., 1996—; chmn. now Granada Compass PLC; chmn. Brit. Sky Broadcasting PLC, 1995-98, Ind. TV News, 1995-97; chair Arts Coun. England, 1998—. Office: Stornoway House, 13 Cleveland Row, London SW1A 1GG, England

ROBINSON, GLENDA CAROLE, pharmacist; b. Johnson City, Tenn.; d. Harry and Jackie Evelyn Bowers; m. Richard Haynes Robinson, 1967 (div. 1985); children: Rachel Corianne, Fredrick David. BS in Pharmacy, U. Tenn., 1967. Pharmacist supr. Sommers Drug Stores, San Antonio, 1968-69; staff pharmacist Crawford Long Hosp., Atlanta, 1971-72, Rich's Pharmacy, Atlanta, 1973-74; relief staff pharmacist Atchley Drug Ctr., Greeneville, Tenn., 1977-86; staff pharmacist Takoma Hosp. Pharmacy, Greeneville, 1983-86; staff pharmacist Greene Valley Developmental Ctr., Greeneville, 1987-91, dir. pharmacy, 1991—. Mem. First Dist. Pharmacy Assn. East Tenn., Greeneville Jr. Women's Club (sec., internat. affairs chair), Greeneville Morning Rotary Club (pres., Polio Plus chair, Outstanding Rotarian 1996-97, Found. Dist. Svc. award 1998-99), Soc. Cicero.

ROBINSON, GUY MARTIN, geography educator; b. Stourbridge, Eng., Sept. 29, 1951; s. Roy Malcolm and Eileen Lois (Martin) R.; m. Susan Rebecca Carbone, Aug. 26, 1989. BSc with honors, U. London, Eng., 1973; PhD, U. Oxford, Eng., 1978. Part-time lectr. in geography Lady Spencer-Churchill Coll., Oxford, 1974-76; Radcliffe Meteor. observer U. Oxford, Eng., 1977-78; lectr./sr. lectr. geography U. Edinburgh, 1979-94; prof. geography Kingston U., Surrey, Eng., 1994—; vis. lectr. geography U. Regina, Can., 1979, U. Canterbury, New Zealand, 1984; vis. fellow U. Melbourne, Australia, 1987, U. Queensland, Australia, 1990, U. Newcastle, NSW, Australia, 1993, U. Otago, New Zealand, 1997. Author: Agricultural Change, 1988, Conflict and Change in the Countryside, 1990, Methods and Techniques in Human Geography, 1998, Australia and New Zealand: Economy, Society and Environment, 2000; editor, author: A Social Geography of Canada, 1991; editor (periodical) Brit. Rev. of New Zealand Studies, 1988—. Mem. Inst. Brit. Geographers, Royal Scottish Geog. Soc. (Pres.'s award 1993), Geog. Assn., Brit. Australian Studies Assn. (pres. 2000—). Anglican. Avocations: golf, travel, gardening. Home: 34 Epsom Ln North, Epsom KT18 5PY, England Office: Sch Geography Kingston Univ, Penrhyn Rd, Kingston-upon-Thames KT1 2EE, England

ROBINSON, HELENE SUSAN, pharmacist, manager; b. Cleve., July 10, 1956; d. Martin Stanley and Elaine (Steinhardt) Grumbach; children: Marie, Michelle, Michael. BS in Pharm. Scis., U. Cin., 1979; cert. Women in Mgmt., Ursuline Coll., Pepper Pike, Ohio, 1983. Asst. mgr. Cunningham Drugs, Cleve., 1979-80; staff pharmacist St. Luke's Hosp., Cleve., 1980-84, oncology pharmacist, 1984-85; dir. of pharmacy Care Plus-Cleve., Beachwood, Ohio, 1985-87; staff pharmacist Kaiser Permanente, 1987-88; pharmacist HMSS, Cleve., 1988-94, Coram, Cleve., 1995-97; asst. dir. pharmacy Mt. Sinai Med. Ctr., Richmond Heights, Ohio, 1998; dir. pharmacy Mt. Sinai East Med. Ctr., 1999-2000; pharmacist Marc's Pharmacy, Solon, Ohio, 2000—. Mem. Cleve. Soc. Hosp. Pharmacists (chmn. oncology 1984-85), Ohio Soc. Hosp. Pharmacists, Am. Soc. Hosp. Pharmacists, Kappa Epsilon. Baptist. Avocations: needlepoint, reading, sewing. Office: Marc's Pharmacy 6239 Som Center Rd Solon OH 44139

ROBINSON, IDA LAFOSSE, minister, broadcaster; b. Phila., July 27, 1934; d. Charles and Alma Elizabeth (Johnson) B.; m. Benjamin H. LaFosse; children: Andre, Marcel, Benita, Tania. DD, Trinity Hall Coll. & Sem., Denver, 1985. Ordained to ministry Pentacostal Ch., 1963. Min. Ch. of God in Christ, Phila., 1959-63; evangelist Ch. of the Open Door, Phila., 1963-66; pastor Miracle Tabernacle, Camden, N.J., 1966-67, Salvation Tabernacle, Phila., 1967—; broadcaster Move of God Inc., Phila., 1967-73, overseer, 1985—; pastor Move of God Cathedral, N.Y.C., 1968—, broadcaster, 1985—; pres. Move of God Crusade Team and Radio Prayer Line. Editor Amb. mag., 1973. Avocation: youth counselor. Office: Move of God Cathedral 501503 W 152nd St New York NY 10031-1435

ROBINSON, IRWIN JAY, lawyer; b. Bay City, Mich., Oct. 8, 1928; s. Robert R. and Anne (Kaplan) R.; m. Janet Binder, July 7, 1957; children: Elizabeth Binder Schubiner, Jonathan Meyer, Eve Kimberly Wiener. AB, U. Mich., 1950; JD, Columbia U., 1953. Bar: N.Y. 1956. Assoc. Breed Abbott & Morgan, N.Y.C., 1955-58; asst. to ptnrs. Dreyfus & Co., N.Y.C., 1958-59; assoc. Greenbaum Wolff & Ernst, N.Y.C., 1959-65; ptnr. Greenbaum Wolff & Ernst, 1966-76; sr. ptnr. Rosenman & Colin, N.Y.C., 1976-90; of counsel Pryor, Cashman, Sherman & Flynn, 1990-92; sr. ptnr. Phillips, Nizer, Benjamin, Krim & Ballon, N.Y.C., 1992-99; treas. Saarsteel, Inc., Whitestone, N.Y., 1970—. Bd. dirs. Henry St. Settlement, N.Y.C., 1960-85, Jewish Cmty. Ctr. Assn. N.Am., 1967-94, mem. adv. bd., 1998—; bd. dirs. Heart Rsch. Found., 1989-94, pres., 1991-93. Mem. ABA, N.Y. State Bar Assn., Assn. Bar City of N.Y., Internat. Bar Assn., Thai-Am. C. of C. (founder, bd. dirs. 1992-95, pres. 1992-95), Vietnam-Am. C. of C. (founder, bd. dirs. 1992-95, pres. 1992-95), Philippine-Am. C. of C. (bd. dirs. 1960-98), Sunningdale Country Club, The Desert Mountain Club. Jewish. Home: 4622 Grosvenor Ave Riverdale NY 10471-3305 Office: c/o Kramer Levin Naftalis & Frankel 40th Flr 919 3rd Ave Fl 29 New York NY 10022-3902

ROBINSON, JACK FAY, clergyman; b. Wilmington, Mass., Mar. 7, 1914; s. Thomas P. and Ethel Lincoln (Fay) R.; m. Eleanor Jean Smith, Sept. 1, 1937 (dec. 1966); 1 child, Alice Virginia Dungey; m. Lois Henze, July 16, 1968. AB, Mont. State U., 1936; BD, Crozer Theol. Sem., 1939; AM, U. Chgo., 1949, postgrad., 1950-52. Ordained to ministry Bapt. Ch., 1939; Min. Bethany Ch., American Falls, Idaho, 1939-41, 1st Ch., Council Grove, Kans., 1944-49; ordained (transfer) to ministry Congl. Ch., 1945; min. United Ch., Chebanse, Ill., 1949-52, 1st Ch., Argo, Ill., 1954-58, Congl. Ch., St. Charles, Ill., 1958-64; assoc. min. Plymouth Congl. Ch., Lansing, Mich., 1964-66; tchr. Chgo. Pub. Schs., 1966-68; min. Waveland Ave. Congl. Ch., Chgo., 1967-79; interim pastor Chgo. Met. Assn., 1979—; interim pastor United Ch. of Christ, 1973, First Congl. Ch., Des Plaines, Ill., 1979, Bethany United Ch., Chgo., 1980, Eden United Ch. of Christ, Chgo., 1983-84, St. Nicolai Ch., Chgo., 1984, Grace United Ch. of Christ, Chgo., 1985-86, Christ Ch. of Chgo., 1987, First Congl., Evanston, Ill., 1987-88, First Congl. Ch., Brookfield, Ill., 1988-89, Steger, Ill., 1990-91, Berwyn, Ill., 1992, Immanual United Ch. of Christ, Streamwood, Ill., 1993, Immanuel United Ch. of Christ, Bartlett, 1994; assoc. pastor, calling min. of visitation People's Ch., Chgo., 1990-93; hist. cons. Bell & Howell Co., Chgo., 1981-82; coord. Inst. Cont. Learning Roosevelt U., 1998—. Author: The Growth of the Bible, 1969, From A Mission to a Church, 1976, Bell & Howell Company: A 75 Year History, 1982; co-author: Harza: 65 Years, 1986, History of the Illinois Conference, United Church of Christ, 1990. Assoc. Hyde Park dept. Chgo. YMCA, 1942-44, U. Chgo. Libr., 1952-54; chmn. com. evangelism Kans. Congl. Christian Conf., 1947-48; city chmn. Layman's Missionary Movement, 1946-49; trustee Congl. and Christian Conf. Ill., v.p., 1963-64; mem. exec. coun. Chgo. Met. Assn. United Ch. of Christ, 1968-70, sec. ch. and ministry com., 1982-88; mem. gen. bd. Ch. Fedn. Greater Chgo., 1969-71; mem. Libr. Bd. Coun. Grove, 1945-49; dean Northside Mission Coun. United Ch. of Christ, 1975-77, sec. pers. com. Ill. Conf. United Ch. of Christ, 1986-88; bd. dirs. Tri-Village United Way, 1996—; coord. Inst. Continued Learning Roosevelt U., Schaumburg, Ill., 1998—. Mem. Chgo. Coun. Fgn. Rels. Recipient Pres.' award Congl. Christian Hist. Soc. Home: 321 E Morse Ave Bartlett IL 60103-4168

ROBINSON, JAMES LAWRENCE, biochemistry educator, researcher; b. Boston, Feb. 23, 1942; s. Lawrence Hanny and Carolyn Ruth (Conklin) R.; m. Janet Lynn Thorpe, Feb. 23, 1963; children: Mark, Marjorie, Glen. BS in Chemistry, U. Redlands, 1964; PhD in Biochemistry, UCLA, 1968. Postdoctoral rschr. Inst. Cancer Rsch., Phila., 1968-70; asst. prof. U. Ill., Urbana, 1970-76, assoc. prof., 1976-85, prof., 1985—; vis. scientist Inst. Nat. Recherche Agrom, Jouy-en Josas, France, 1978-79; vis. scientist dept. biochemistry U. Nijmegen, The Netherlands, 1986-87, MaCarthur Agrl. Inst., Camden, NSW, Australia, 1993-94. Mem. Am. Soc. Biochem. Molecular Biology, Am. Dairy Sci. Assn., Am. Soc. Nutritional Sci. Democrat. Methodist. Avocations: camping, hiking, bicycling, gardening. Home: 902 E Mumford Dr Urbana IL 61801-6327 Office: U Ill Dept Animal Sci 1207 W Gregory Dr Urbana IL 61801-4733

ROBINSON, JAMES M., religious studies educator; b. Gettysburg, Pa., June 30, 1924; s. William Childs and Mary McConkey Robinson; m. Gesine Robinson; children: Francoise Mary Anne, James Claude, Joy Odile, Rosemary Kathleen, Gesa Schenke, Genia Schenke. AB summa cum laude, Davidson Coll., 1945, ThD (hon.), 1987; BD magna cum laude, Columbia Theol. Sem., 1946; postgrad., U. Zürich, Switzerland, summer 1947, U. Heidelberg, Germany, summer 1947, U. Basel, 1947-48, 49-50, U. Marburg, Germany, 1950-51, U. Strasbourg, 1951, École des Hautes Études, Paris, 1952; ThD summa cum laude, U. Basel, Switzerland, 1952, Princeton Theol. Sem., 1955; postgrad., U. Heidelberg, 1960; HHD (hon.), Miami U., 1993. Asst. prof. Greek and Bible Davidson Coll., N.C., 1946-47; instr. Candler Sch. Theology, Emory U., Atlanta, 1952-53, asst. prof., 1953-56, assoc. prof. bibl. theology, 1956-58; faculty inst. Liberal Arts, Grad. Sch. Emory U., Atlanta, 1953-58; assoc. prof. Claremont Sch. Theology, 1958-61, prof. theology and New Testament, 1961-64, affiliate prof., 1964—, vis. prof., summer 1971, 79, affiliate mem. faculty, 1959-64, Arthur Letts Jr. prof. religion, 1964-99, assoc. dir., 1967-68, dir. Inst. for Antiquity and Christianity, 1968-99, chair faculty religion, 1990-93; vis. prof. Columbia Theol. Sem., 1955-58, U. Göttingen, Germany, 1959, U. Zürich, 1960, 62, U. Calif., Berkeley, 1972, Scripps Coll., 1978, State U. San Bernardino, 1981, U. Calif., Santa Barbara, 1981, Occidental Coll., 1981, Calif. State U., Long Beach, 1981-82, Inst. für ökumenische Forschung, U. Tübingen, Germany, 1986, U. Geneva, 1992, U. Bamberg, Germany, 1997; ann. prof. Am. Sch. Oriental Rsch., Jerusalem, 1965-66; Fulbright prof. U. Strasbourg, France, 1970-71; founder, chair, mem. New Testament Colloquium, 1960-77; founder, mem. New Testament bd. Hermeneia-A Critical and Hist. Commentary on the Bible, 1960—. Founder, mem. editl. bd. Jour. for Theology and the Church, 1965-70; contbr. articles to profl. jours. Fulbright scholar; Am. Coun. Learned Socs. fellow, Am. Assn. Theol. Schs. fellow. Mem. Am. Acad. Arts and Scis., Soc. Archéologie Copte, Internat. Assn. for Coptic Studies, Assn. Francophone de Coptologie, Internat. Assn. Manichaean Studies, Soc. Bibl. Lit. (assoc. in coun. 1962-64, rsch. com. 1964-65, western sect. v.p. 1962, pres. 1963, alt. del. to Am. Schs. Oriental Rsch. 1968-69, del. to founding meeting coun. on the study of religion 1969, nominating com. 1969, chmn. com. on the 1972 internat. congress of learned socs. in the field of religion 1968-72, chair com. on rsch. and publs. 1969-72, com. on hon. mems. 1978-80, pres. elect 1979-80, pres. 1980-81, chair consultation on the study of Q 1983-84, chair seminar on the study of Q 1985-89, co-chair internat. Q project 1989, mem. con. on access to ancient materials 1993-94), Soc. for New Testament Studies, Pacific Coast Theol. Group, Phi Beta Kappa, Omicron Delta Kappa. Democrat. Presbyterian. E-mail: James.Robinson@cgu.edu. Home: 548 W 8th St Claremont CA 91711-4210

ROBINSON, JANE JENIFER ANN, nurse researcher, educator; b. Birmingham, Eng., Nov. 6, 1935; d. Reginald Milton and Florence (Troop) London; m. Anthony David Robinson, Feb. 6, 1959; children: Ann Louise Robinson Sutcliffe, Felicity Jane Robinson Wood, Kathryn Mary Robinson Roodner. MA, U. Keele, Eng., 1980, PhD, 1986. Theatre sister Winford Orthopaedic Hosp., 1957-58; staff nurse Bristol (Eng.) Homeopathic Hosp., 1959, North Staffs Royal Infirmary, 1968-69; health visitor Staffs. County Coun., 1970-74; nursing officer Mid-Staffs. Health Authority, 1974-77, health visitor, 1977-79; lectr. Wolverhampton Poly., 1980-81, 83-84; rsch. officer Sandwell Health Authority, 1981-83; dir. nursing policy studies ctr. U. Warwick, 1985-89; prof., head dept. U. Nottingham, Eng., 1989—, emeritus prof., 1997—; advisor Internat. Coun. Nurses, 1999. Author: The NHS Under New Management, 1990, Nurses Manage, 1995, Health Needs Assessment: Theory and Practice, 1996, Interdisciplinary Perspectives on Health Policy and Practice, 1999; editor Jour. Advanced Nursing, 1997—; contbg. author conf. procs. Advisor PTO, 1985—. Fulbright sr. rsch. scholar, 1996-97. Fellow Royal Coll. Nursing (mem. health and social policy com. 1991-92, chair women's issues subcom. 1995-99, mem. rsch. com. 1997-99, rep. workgroup European Nurse Rschrs. 1998—); mem. Chartered Inst. Pers. and Devel., Social Policy Assn. (mem. women's nat. commn. 1995-98), Univ. Women's Club. Avocations: family, travel. Office: U Nottingham Blackwell Sci, Osney Mead, Oxford OX2 0EL, England

ROBINSON, JOE SAM, neurosurgeon; b. Atlanta, Ga., July 21, 1945; s. Joe Sam and Nell (Mixon) R.; m. Elizabeth Ann Moate, Apr. 3, 1982; children: Joe Sam III, Edward Richard, Thomas McRae. AB cum laude, Harvard Coll., 1967; MD, U. Va., 1971; MS, Northwestern U., 1975. Surg. intern Emory U., 1971-72, resident in surgery, 1972-73; resident in neurosurgery Northwestern U., 1973-78; instr. U. Ill., 1978-79, Yale U., 1979-81; pres. Neurol. Inst. Ctrl. Ga., Macon, 1981—; prof., chief neurosurgery Mercer U. Sch. Medicine, Macon, 1986; chief surgery Med. Ctr. Ctrl. Ga., Macon, 1989—, vice chmn. surgery, 1991-97, chmn. dept. surgery, 1996—; vis. neurosurgeon China, 1992, Konaus Acad. Neurosurgery Inst., Lithuania, 1992. Lt. col. USANG, 1972-95. Fellow Internat. Coll. Surgeons (vice regent 1983-93); mem. Am. Assn. Neurol. Surgeons, Congress Neurol. Surgeons, AAAS, Ga. Neurosurg. Soc., Alpha Omega Alpha. Republican. Methodist. Office: Neurol Inst 840 Pine St Ste 880 Macon GA 31201-7525

ROBINSON, JOHN RICHARD, retired psychiatrist; b. Cheltenham, Eng., Oct. 17, 1927; s. William Joseph and Gladys Margaret (Botterill) R.; m. Catherine Josephine Ledwith, Sept. 16, 1961; children: Margaret, Shaun, Timothy, Nicola. MB, St. Thomas' Hosp., London, 1954; MA, Oxford (Eng.) U., 1979; diploma in psychol. medicine, Cojoint Bd., London, 1964. House surgeon, physician St. Helier Hosp., Carshalton, Eng., 1954-56, Amersham (Eng.) Hosp., 1954-56; house physician dept. psychol. medicine St. Thomas Hosp., London; med. registrar Gulson Hosp., Coventry, Eng., 1956-58; gen. practitioner Rugby, Warwickshire, Eng., 1958-62; registrar Ctrl. Hosp., Warwick, Eng., 1962-65; Nuffield rsch. fellow Littlemore Hosp., Oxford, Eng., 1965-68, sr. registrar, 1968-73; cons. psychiatrist Dept. Psychiatry of Old Age, Oxford, 1973-93; joint mgr. Oxford Project to Investigate Memory and Ageing, 1991-95; exec. chmn. Oxford Project for Peace Studies, 1985-95, trustee, 1989-95; exec. chmn. U.K.-USSR Med. Exch. Programme, London, 1984-89. Contbr. articles to med. jours. Hon. cons. Cath. Marriage Adv. Coun., Oxford. Fellow Royal Coll. Psychiatrists, Royal Soc. Medicine; mem. Brit. Geriatrics Soc., Brit. Med. Assn., Soc. Genealogists. Roman Catholic. Avocations: reading, history, theology, violin, walking. Home: 480 Banbury Rd, Oxford OX2 8EN, England

ROBINSON, JOHN VICTOR, lawyer; b. Harare, Zimbabwe, July 9, 1958; s. Denis Antony Beck and Elizabeth Jill R. BA, Rhodes U., Grahamstown, South Africa, 1983; MA, Oxford (Eng.) U., 1985; JD, U. Richmond (Va.), 1986. Bar: Va. Assoc. atty. Hunton & Williams, Richmond, Va., 1986-89, McSweeney, Burtch & Crump, Richmond, 1989-93, Cantor, Arkema & Edmonds, P.C., Richmond, 1993-97; pvt. practice Richmond, 1997—; past mem. regional com. Nat. Trial Competition, Richmond; apptd. adminstrv. hearing officer Va. Supreme Ct.; adj. asst. prof. Law U. Richmond Sch. Law. Rhodes scholar Oxford U., 1983-85. Mem. ABA, Va. Bar Assn., Bar Assn. City of Richmond. Office: Koger Ctr Randolph Bldg 1500 Forest Ave Ste 222 Richmond VA 23229-5104

ROBINSON, KENNETH CHARLES, business educator; b. Macon, Ga.; s. Charles William Robinson and Joyce R. Sorrow. BBA, U. Ga., 1984, MBA, 1991, PhD, 1995. Gen. mgr., CFO Shoe Shack, Inc., Macon, 1984-90, controller, buyer, 1990-91, mgmt. advisor, 1991-94; grad. tchg. asst. U. Ga., Athens, 1991-95; lectr. U. Wollongong, NSW, Australia, 1995-96; asst. prof. strategy & entrepreneurship Kennesaw (Ga.) State U., 1996—. Mem. rels. com. Greater Macon C. of C., 1988-90, vice chmn. small bus. coun., 1989-90. Kauffman Ctr. Entrepreneurial Leadership fellow, 1994, Comer fellow U. Ga., 1994; recipient Heizer Best Doctoral Dissertation award Entrepreneurship Divsn. Acad. Mgmt., 1996, Mescon/Coles Best Empirical Paper award, 1999. Mem. Acad. Mgmt. (mem. exec. com. entrepreneurship divsn. 1996—, chair awards com. 1998—), U.S. Assn. Small Bus. and Entrepreneurship (Runner-Up award 1999), Strategic Mgmt. Soc. Presbyterian. Avocations: traveling, skiing, scuba diving, hiking. Fax: 770-423-6606. Home: 55 Pharr Rd NW Unit E101 Atlanta GA 30305-2145 Office: Kennesaw State U Coles Coll Bus 1000 Chastain Rd NW Kennesaw GA 30144-5591

ROBINSON, KENNETH ROGER, art educator; b. Auckland, New Zealand, Nov. 24, 1940; s. Ebenezer Isaasac and Mary (Johnson) R.; m. Eve Kaye De Castro, July 2, 1980; 1 child, Cyprian. Diploma in fine art, St. Martins Sch. Art, London, 1965. Lectr. Middlesborough Coll. Art, England, 1967-68; tchr. Westlake Coll., Auckland, New Zealand, 1971; lectr. Auckland Soc. Arts, 1970-71; lectr. Auckland Inst. Tech., 1972-93, sr. lectr., 1993—. One-man shows include Soc. Arts, Auckland, 1970—, 4th Fl. Auckland Bldg. Soc., 1975—, Petar/James Gallery, Auckland, 1982, 85, Studio Gallery, Hamilton, New Zealand, 1982—, C.S.A. Gallery, Christchurch, New Zealand, 1988—, Louise Beale Gallery, Wellington, New Zealand, 1990—, R.K.S. Gallery, Auckland, 1991—, Hawke's Bay Mus., Napier, New Zealand, 1993—, Warwick Brown Gallery, Auckland, 1995—, Drawing Gallery, Auckland, 1996—, Del Bello Gallery, Toronto, 1997, Monserrat Gallery, N.Y.C., 1997, Portfolio Gallery, Auckland, 1998, others; group shows include St. Martins Gallery, London, 1964—, Mcpl. Gallery, Middlesborough, 1967—, Hastings Gallery, New Zealand, 1977—, C.S.A. Gallery, Christchurch, 1978—, Backroom Gallery, Dunedin, New Zealand, 1984—, Petar/James Gallery, 1984—, Louise Beale Gallery, 1986—, Stanley St. Art Ctr., Auckland, 1992—, Exhbn. in Miniature Art, Stockholm, 1994, C.S.A. Gallery, Christchurch, New Zealand, 1994, Pump House Gallery, Auckland, 1996, Art Sale 96, Titirangi Auckland, 1996, The Autumn Annual Exhbn., Venice, Italy, 1998, Te Wa-The Space, 1999, others; contbr. articles to profl. jours. Mem. New Zealand Soc. Sculptors-Painters (sec. 1985-86, pres. 1988), Grammar Old Boys Club. Avocations: gardening, trout fishing, Flamenco guitar, travel. Home: 31 Fancourt St, Auckland 5, New Zealand Office: Auckland Inst Tech, Wellesley St, Auckland New Zealand

ROBINSON, KIM STANLEY, science fiction author; b. Calif., 1952; m. Lisa Howell; 2 children. BS, U. Calif., San Diego, PhD in English and Am. Lit., 1982; MS, Boston U. Author: (book series) Mars (Red Mars 1992, Green Mars 1994, Blue Mars 1996), Orange County (The Wild Shore 1984, The Gold Coast 1988, Pacific Edge 1990), (novels) Icehenge, 1984, The Memory of Whiteness, 1985, Escape from Kathmandu, 1989, A Short, Sharp Shock, 1990, Antarctica, 1997, (collections) The Planet on the Table, 1986, Escape From Kathmandu, 1990, Remaking History, 1991, The Martians, 1999, (anthologies) Future Primitive: The New Ecotopias, 1994, (non-fiction series) Studies in Speculative Fiction, 1984; author numerous short fiction, essays and articles. Recipient World Fantasy award, 1984, John W. Campbell Meml. award, 1991, Nebula award, 1987, 93, Locus Poll award, 1985, 91, 94, 97, Hugo award, 1994, 97, SF Chronicle award, 1984, 92, Brit. Sci. Fiction award, 1993. Avocations: mountain trekking, swimming. Office: c/o Random House Inc Bantam Books 1540 Broadway New York NY 10036-4039

ROBINSON, LEONARD HARRISON, JR., international government consultant, business executive; b. Winston-Salem, N.C., Apr. 21, 1943; s. Leonard Harrison and Winnie Cornelia (Thomas) R.; children: Kimberly Michelle, Rani Craft. NSF cert., Bennett Coll., Greensboro, N.C., 1959; BA, Ohio State U., 1964; postgrad., SUNY, Binghamton, 1966-67, Am. U., 1982-89, Harvard U., 1991; LLD (hon.), Shaw U., Raleigh, N.C., 1983; LHD (hon.), Huston-Tillotson Coll., 1991. Vol. Peace Corps., Bihar, India, 1964-66; assoc. dir. for India Peace Corps, Madras, 1967-70; dir. recruitment Peace Corps., Washington, 1970-71; dir. inner-city programs EPA, Washington, 1971-72; dir. mgmt. Family Planning Internat. Assistance, N.Y.C., 1972-74; Africa dir. Family Planning Internat. Assistance, Accra, Ghana and Nairobi, Kenya, 1974-77; task force dir. U.S. Ho. Reps., Washington, 1977-78; dir. population Africa AID, Washington, 1978-79; dir. Internat. Devel. Ctr. Battelle Inst., Washington, 1979-83; dep. asst. sec., sr. exec. svc. Dept. State, Washington, 1983-85; pres. African Devel. Found., Washington, 1985-90; dep. asst. sec. state, sr. exec. svc. Dept. State, Washington, 1990-93; vice chmn., COO Washington Strategic Consulting Group, Inc., Washington, 1993-97; founder, pres. LHR Internat. Group, Inc., Washington, 1997—; exec. v.p., then pres. and CEO Nat. Summit on Africa Secretariat, Washington, 1997—; cons. area studies U. Mo. Peace Corps, summer 1966; mgmt. analyst ATAC, Washington, 1971; mem. U.S. presdl. del. to Dakar, Senegal, 1987, to Malawi, Mozambique, and Uganda, Sept. 1988, to Mali, Uganda, and Kenya, Dec. 1988, v.p.'s visit to Africa, 1991; hon. consul Govt. Sao Tome and Principe, 1996—. Author: monographs Assessment and Analysis of Population Attitudes in Tanzania, 1981, Analyze African Official Attitudes Concerning U.S. Population Assistance in Lesotho, Tanzania, Senegal and Togo, 1981. Adviser Population Resource Ctr., N.Y.C., 1978-82; adviser internat. program for health and tng., U. N.C., Chapel Hill, 1980-84; vice-chmn. New Directions Task Force Rep. Party, Montgomery County (Md.), 1982-83; adv. coun. Nat. Coun. Returned Peace Corps Vols., 1987—; bd. dirs. Washington Ballet, 1982-85, 86-91, v.p. bd. dirs. 1988-90; bd. dirs. Friends of Smithsonian Mus. African Art, Washington, 1982-84, Coalition for Equitable Representation in Govt., Montgomery County, Montgomery County Bd. Soc. Svcs., 1986-89, Joint Agrl. Consultative Corp., 1985-86, Alan Gutmacher Inst., 1992-96, Friends of the U. of Natal, South Africa, 1995—. Decorated commandeur de l'Ordre National du Niger, 1989; recipient Africare Disting. Svc. award, 1990, Key to the City of Greensboro, N.C., 1991, Christian D. Maxwell Disting. Svc. award Liberian Com. for Relief, Resettlement and Reconstruction, 1993; hon. counsel for the Govt. of Sao Tome and Principe, Ctrl. Africa; sr. fellow U. Mass. John W. McCormack Inst. Mem. Soc. Internat. Devel. (dir. 1982), Am. Pub. Health Assn. (sec. population sect. 1979-81), Coun. on Fgn. Rels., C. of C. of D.C. (dir. 1979-82), Metro Club Washington, Kappa Alpha Psi, Sigma Pi Phi. Office: Nat Summit on Africa Secretariat Enos Cosby Internat House 1218 16th St NW Washington DC 20036-3202

ROBINSON, LYNDA HICKOX, artist; b. Bakersfield, Calif., June 26, 1932; d. George Philip and Naida (Hathaway) Hickox; m. Arthur C. Robinson; children: Jill, Scott. BA, U. Calif., Berkeley, 1953; MA, Mills Coll., 1957. 1st v.p. San Francisco Women Artists, 1985-86, pres., 1986-87; chair exhbns. com. East Bay Women Artists, Montclair, Calif., 1994—; invited artist Glasgow Scotland City of Culture Exhbn., 1990. Dancer, tchr. dance, 1957-82; photographer, 1982-89, painter, 1990—; exhbns. include San Francisco Women Artists Gallery, 1992, 93, 94, Kaiser Cmty. Gallery, 1992, 93, 94, 95, 97, Alta Bates Cmty. Gallery, 1994, 95, 96, 97, 98, 99, Valley Art Ctr. Gallery, 1992, 93, 94, 95, 96, 97, 98, 99, 2000, Royal Ground Gallery, 1994, 95, 96, 97, 98, 99, 2000; represented in permanent collections Fuji Vending, Dr. Louise Annand MacFarquar, Prof. and Mrs. Fred Casmir; contbr. artworks to jours. and mags. Recipient Tchg. fellowship Mills Coll., 1954, Francis Coen cash award, 1993. Mem. Phi Beta Kappa.

ROBINSON, MARK LEIGHTON, oil company executive, petroleum geologist, horse farm owner; b. San Bernardino, Calif., Aug. 4, 1927; s. Ernest Guy and Florence Iola)Lemmon) R.; m. Jean Marie Ries, Feb. 8, 1954; children; Francis Willis, Mark Ries, Paul Leighton. AB cum laude in Geology, Princeton U., 1950; postgrad., Stanford U., 1950-51. Geologist Shell Oil Co., Billings, Mont., Rapid City, S.D., Denver, Midland, Tex.; geologist Shell Oil Co., Roswell, N.Mex., 1957-60, divsn. mgr., 1961-63; divsn. mgr. Shell Oil Co., Jackson, Miss., 1964-65, Bakersfield, Calif., 1967-68; mgr. exploration econs. Shell Oil Co., N.Y.C., 1969; ctrl. office staff BIPM (Royal Dutch Shell Oil Co.), The Hague, The Netherlands, 1966; pres., chmn. bd. dirs. Robinson Resource Devel. Co., Inc., Roswell, 1970—; chmn., pres. Como Petroleum Corp., Roswell, 1994—. Campaign chmn. Chaves County Rep. Com., Roswell, 1962; mem. alumni schs. com. Princeton U., 1980—; vestry St. Andrew's Episcopal Ch., Roswell, N.Mex., 1999—. With USNR, 1945-46. Mem. Assn. Petroleum Geologists, Stanford U. Earth Scientists Assn., Yellowstone Bighorn Rsch. Assn., Am. Horse Show Assn., SAR, Sigma Xi. Episcopalian. Achievements include discovery of Como oil field, Miss., 1971, McNeal oil field, Miss., 1973, North Deer Creek gas field, Mont., 1983, Bloomfield East oil field, Mont., 1986, West Cat Claw Draw gas field, N.Mex., 1997. Home: 2003 Southridge Rd Roswell NM 88203-9346 Office: Robinson Resource Devel Co Inc PO Box 1227 Roswell NM 88202-1227

ROBINSON, MARY, high commissioner for human rights; b. Ballina, County Mayo, Ireland, May 21, 1944; d. Aubrey Bourke and Tessa O'Donnell; m. Nicholas Robinson; children: Tessa, William, Aubrey. MA, Dublin U., Trinity Coll., Ireland, 1967; Barrister, King's Inns, Ireland, 1967, Mid.

Temple, 1973; LLM, Harvard U., 1968; LLD, Oxford U.; doctorate (hon.), Brown U., Cambridge U., Columbia U., Coventry U., Yale U., Fordham U., Harvard U.; LLD (hon.), Liverpool U., London U., Melbourne U., Montpellier U., Nat. U. Ireland, Nat. U. Wales, Poznan U.; Dr. Sci. Humans (hon.), Queen's U., Belfast; doctorate (hon.), St. Andrew's U.; D.Phil (hon.), Dublin City U., Toronto U.; doctorate (hon.), Essex U., Kyung Hee U., Northeastern U., Renne U. Reid prof. constitutional and criminal law Trinity Coll., Dublin, Ireland, 1969-75; lectr. in European Cmty. law Trinty Coll., Dublin, Ireland, 1975-90; senator Irish Parliament, 1969-89; pres. Ireland, 1990-97; high commr. for human rights UN, 1997—; mem. Dublin City Coun., 1979-83; chancellor Dublin U., 1998—. Mem. Editorial Bd. Irish Current Law Statutes Annotated, 1984-90; adv. bd. Common Market Law Rev., 1976-90. Pres. Cherish, 1973-90; mem. Internatl. Commn. Jurists, 1987-90. Recipient Marisa Bellisario prize, Italy, Spl. Humanitarian award CARE, Internat. Human Rights award Internat. League of Human Rights, N.Y., Liberal Internat. prize for freedom, New Zealand Suffrage Centennial medal, Berkeley medal U. Calif., Medal of Honour, U. Coimbra, Portugal, Ordem dos Advogados, Portugal, Gold Medal of Honour, U. Salamanca, Spain, U. Chile, Global Leadership award UN Assn., Freedom prize Max Schmidheiny Found., Switzerland, UNIFEM award Noel Found., U.S., Collar of Hussein Bin Ali, Hashemite Kingdom of Jordan, North South prize Coun. of Europe, 1997, F.D. Roosevelt Four Freedoms medal, 1998, Dag Hammerskjold Medal, 1998, Erasmus prize, Govt. The Netherlands, 1999, Fulbright Found. prize, 1999; named to Internat. Hall of Fame, Internat. Women's Forum, USA. Fellow Instn. Engrs. of Ireland (hon.), Royal Coll. Physicians Ireland (hon.), Royal Coll. Psychiatrists London (hon.), Royal Coll. Surgeons, Ireland (hon.), Royal Coll. Obstetricians and Gynecologists London; mem. Royal Irish Acad., Am. Philos. Soc. Office: UNOG-OHCHR, UNOG-AHCHR, 1211 Geneva 10, Switzerland

ROBINSON, MAUREEN LORETTA, retired secondary school educator; b. N.Y.C., May 17, 1945; d. Arthur Vincent and Paula (Dillon) R.; m. Derish Michael Wolff, Feb. 13, 1992. BA in English, Wagner Coll., 1967; MS, CUNY, 1970. Cert. tchr. secondary sch. English, K-12 reading, N.Y. Tchr. English Curtis H.S., S.I., N.Y., 1968-95, coord. student activities, 1985-94; vis. lectr. Coll. of S.I., 1982; guest lectr. NYU, 1991, Pace U., N.Y.C., 1993; dir. Soc. de Management de Projets Internat., Paris, 1996—. Mem. Somerset Hills Bd. Edn., Bernardsville, N.J., 1997—; v.p. Somerset County Ednl. Svcs. Commn., Raritan, N.J., 1997—; bd. dirs. Bernardsville Garden Club, pres., 1997-99, pub. chair 1995-97, sec. 1999—; bd. dirs. Friends of the Bernardsville Libr., pub. chair, 1996-2000, Friends of the Shelter, pub. chair 1997-98; trustee Somerset Hills Edn. Found., 1996-97; class agt. Wagner Coll., 1995—, trustee, 1998—. Staff sgt. USAR, 1979-85. Recipient Human Rels. award Greater N.Y. Region of NCCJ, 1994, Army Achievement medal Dept. of the Army, 1983. Mem. AAUW, Wagner Coll. Nat. Alumni Assn. (1st v.p. 1999—). Avocations: reading, gardening, skiing, cooking, travel. Home: 160 Jockey Hollow Rd Bernardsville NJ 07924-1312

ROBINSON, MICHAEL FINLAY, musicologist, educator; b. Gloucester, Great Britain, Mar. 3, 1933; s. Alexander George and Monica (Finlay) R.; m. Ann James, Dec. 28, 1961; children: Andrew, Paul. BA in Music with honors, Oxford U., 1956, BMus, 1957, MA, 1960, PhD, 1963. Lectr. in music U. Durham, Great Britain, 1961-65; asst. prof. music McGill U., Montreal, Can., 1965-67, assoc. prof. music, 1967-70; lectr. in music U. Wales, Cardiff, Great Britain, 1970-75, sr. lectr. in music, 1975-91, prof. music, 1991-94. Author: Opera Before Mozart, 1966, Naples and Neapolitan Opera, 1972, A Thematic Catalogue of the Works of Giovanni Paisiello, 1991, 93; contbr. articles to profl. jours. Lt. British Army, 1951-53. Fellowship Can. Coun. Ottawa, 1967; grantee Leverhulme Found., 1975, many others. Mem. Royal Musical Assn., Am. Musicol. Soc., Internat. Musicol. Soc. Home: Northridge House Usk Rd, Shirenewton, Chepstow Great Britain

ROBINSON, MICHAEL FRANCIS, private art dealer and appraiser; b. London, Oct. 6, 1954; came to U.S., 1978; s. Canon Joseph and Anne (Antrobus) R. Student, The King's Sch., Canterbury, Eng., 1968-72; LLB, King's Coll., London U., London, 1976; postgrad., The Coll. Law, London, 1976-77, Centre Study European Law, London & Luxembourg. Head rare books Brentano's, Inc., N.Y.C., 1978-81; head rare books Phillips Auctioneers, N.Y.C., 1981-85, auctioneer fine arts, 1982-85; pres. M.F. Robinson & Assocs., N.Y.C., 1985—; cons. to mus. and pvt. collectors, IRS, 1989—, Presbyn. Ch. (USA), 1999—; Prforzheimer lectr. N.Y. Pub. Libr., N.Y.C., 1989; chmn. writers panel San Francisco Internat. Antique Fair, 1989, 90. Author articles Archtl. Digest, Connosieur, Art and Auction, Manuscripts and other mags.; contbg. editor The Am. Book Collector, 1985-89, Art and Auction, 1989-96; assoc. editor Jour. Guild of Bookworkers; editor Treasures of Eton College, The Pierpont Morgan Library, 1990; joinr editor, co-author: In August Co. The Collections of the Pierpont Morgan Library, 1991-92, Mark Twain: An American Voice to the World, 1996. Chmn. The Bach Ensemble, N.Y., 1984-99; cons. to dept. of history, Presbyn. Ch. U.S.A., 1999—. Mem. The Hon. Soc. Inner Temple (Duke of Edinburgh Scholar 1974), The Manuscript Soc., The Hardwick Soc. Episcopalian. Club: The Worshipful Co. of Wax Chandlers (London), Westside (Georgetown). Lodge: Masons (curator 1984—). Avocation: music before 1800. Office: PO Box 1947 Middleburg VA 20118-1947

ROBINSON, MICHAEL R., aeronautical engineer. Dir. bus. devel. The Boeing Co. (formerly Rockwell Internat. Corp.), Long Beach, Calif.; co-originator and first program manager of the X-31 enhanced maneuverability fighter demonstrator and originator of the international team to conduct the program. Recipient DGLR Team award in recognition of exceptional achievements in the field of Aeronautics, 1996. Fellow Am. Inst. Aeronautics & Astronautics (aircraft design award 1994). Office: The Boeing Co Mail Stop C078-0600 2401 E Wardlow Rd Long Beach CA 90807-5309

ROBINSON, NICHOLAS ADAMS, lawyer, educator; b. N.Y.C., Jan. 20, 1945; s. Albert Lewis and Agnes Claflin (Adams) R.; m. Shelley Miner, Jan. 5, 1969; children: Cynthia M., Lucy A. BA cum laude, Brown U., 1967; JD cum laude, Columbia U., 1970. Bar: N.Y. 1971, U.S. Dist. Ct. (so. and ea. dists.) N.Y. 1972, U.S. Supreme Ct. 1974, U.S. Ct. Appeals (2d and 7th cirs.) 1972. Law clk. to U.S. dist. judge So. Dist. Ct., N.Y., 1970-72; assoc. Marshall, Bratter, Greene, Allison & Tucker, N.Y.C., 1972-78, counsel, 1978-82; assoc. prof. Pace U. Sch. Law, White Plains, N.Y., 1978-81, prof., 1981-99, Gilbert and Sarah Kerlin Disting. prof. environ. law, 1999—; counsel Winer, Neuburger & Sive, N.Y.C., 1982-83; dep. commr., gen. counsel N.Y. State Dept. Environ. Conservation, Albany, 1983-85; counsel Sive, Paget & Reisel, 1985-92, Sidley & Austin, N.Y., London, 1992-96; legal adv. Internat. Union Conservation of Nature and Natural Resources, 1996—; dir. Ctr. for Environ. Legal Studies, 1982—; del. U.S.A. environ. law meetings with USSR, 1974-92; chmn. Environ. Adv. Bd. to Gov. Mario Cuomo, 1985-94. Cons. editor Environ. Law, 1996—; contbr. articles to profl. jours. Nat. bd. dirs. UN Assn. U.S.A., 1966-76, 79-84, U.S. Com. for UNICEF, 1970-80, World Environment Ctr., 1981—, chmn., 1993-96; bd. dirs. Westchester County Soil and Water Conservation Dist., 1976-83; chmn. N.Y. State Freshwater Wetlands Appeals Bd., 1976-83; chmn. planning bd. Village of Sleepy Hollow, N.Y., 1999—; bd. edn. Union Free Sch. Dist., Tarrytown, 1981-83, 85. Recipient N.Y. State Gov.'s Citation for Hist. Preservation, 1983, Eliz Haub prize in environ. law Free U., Brussels, 1992. Fellow Am. Bar Found.; mem. Internat. Coun. Environ. Law (gov. 1993—), Internat. Union Conservation of Nature and Natural Resources, Commn. Environ. Law (chmn. 1996—), Am. Soc. Internat. Law, ABA, ALI, N.Y. State Bar Assn. (chmn. environ. law sect. 1979-80, Environ. Law award 1981), Assn. Bar City N.Y. (chmn. environ. law com. 1977-78, internat. law com. 1985-88, internat. environ. law com. 1990-92, Russian law com. 1992-95), Westchester County Bar Assn., Sierra Club (nat. bd. dirs. 1979-83), Phi Beta Kappa. Democrat. Unitarian. Home: 258 Kelbourne Ave Sleepy Hollow NY 10591-1322 Office: Pace U Sch Law 78 N Broadway White Plains NY 10603-3710

ROBINSON, RICHARD M., technical communication specialist; b. Bklyn., Nov. 28, 1934; s. Allen and Syd (Bell) R.; m. Rochelle Wolf, Dec. 25, 1967; children: Michelle P., Steven E. BS in Physics, Rensselaer Poly. Inst., Troy, N.Y., 1956, MS in Tech. Comm., 1959. Assoc. engr. Convair-Astronautics, San Diego, 1956-57; tech. writer Raytheon, Andover, Mass., 1957-58; pubs. engr. Hazeltine Electronics, Little Neck, N.Y., 1959-61; sr. pubs. engr. Sperry Gyroscope, Great Neck, N.Y., 1961-68; mgr. editl. svcs. Grumman Corp., Bethpage, N.Y., 1968-94; tech. comm. specialist/cons. Setauket, N.Y., 1995—; adj. faculty Suffolk County C.C. Contbr. articles to profl. jours.; referee papers IEEE Trans. on Profl. Comm. Mem. IEEE (life sr., conf. chmn. 1989, tech. activities bd. 1992-93, Profl. Com. Soc. adminstrv. com. 1977-97, Profl. Com. Soc. pres. 1992-93, Alfred N. Goldsmith award 1983, 3d Millennium medal 2000), Soc. Tech. Comms. (sr. mem.), Miramar Ski Club (pres. 1966-67), Amateur Ski Instrs. Assn. (cert. instr.). Home and Office: 10 Penelope Dr Setauket NY 11733-2010

ROBINSON, ROBERT EARL, chemical company executive; b. Covington, Ky., Aug. 3, 1927; s. Adolph Earl and Frances Elizabeth (Rouse) R.; m. Myrtle Caroline Tonne, June 10, 1951; children: Linda Ann, Carol Eileen Robinson Cranford, Timothy John. AB, Berea Coll., 1949; MS, Purdue U., 1951, PhD, 1953; postgrad., U. Cin., 1962-64. Project leader U.S. Indsl. Chems., Cin., 1953-64; group leader Stauffer Chem. Co., Weston, Mich., 1964-65; rsch. dir. Cardinal Chem. Co., Columbia, S.C., 1965-66; exec. v.p. Lindau Chems. Inc., Columbia, 1966-86, pres., 1986—; dir. Richland Land Devel. Co., Columbia. Contbr. articles to profl. jours. and encys.; 25 patents in field. Fundraiser Am. Cancer Soc., Columbia, 1991; mem. bd. dirs. S.C. Philharmonic Orch., 1993-99, 2000—. With U.S. Army, 1946-47. Fellow Am. Inst. Chemists; mem. AAAS, Am. Chem. Soc. (chair divsn. small chem. bus. 1993, 98), N.Y. Acad. Scis., Baker St. Irregulars, Sherlock Holmes Soc. London, Mensa. Avocations: Sherlock Holmes, computer science, serious music. Home: 6117 Lakeshore Dr Columbia SC 29206-4331 Office: Lindau Chems Inc 731 Rosewood Dr Columbia SC 29201-4633

ROBINSON, ROBIN WICKS, lawyer; b. Roanoke Rapids, N.C., June 5, 1961; d. Wallace Wayne and Rozelle Royall Wicks; m. James Hendry Robinson, Jr., Nov. 7, 1992; children: James Hendry Robinson III, Wallace Katherine McLean Robinson. BA in Politics (hon.), Converse Coll., Spartanburg, S.C., 1982; JD, U. N.C., Chapel Hill, 1985. Bar: N.C. 1986; 5th Jud. Dist. 1986, U.S. Dist. Ct. (ea. dist.) 1987; U.S. Dist. Ct. (we. dist.) 1997, 5th Jud. Dist. Arbitrator 1993, Superior Ct. Cert. Mediator, N.C., Dispute Resolution Commn, 1996; family fin. cert. mediator N.C. Dispute Resolution Commn., 1999. Assoc. atty. Ryals, Jackson & Mills, Wilmington, N.C., 1986-90; ptnr. Pennington & Wicks, Wilmington, N.C., 1990-93; pres, profl. corp. Ryals, Robinson & Saffo P.C., Wilmington, N.C., 1993—; ethics com. N.C. State Bar, Raleigh, N.C., 1990-93; exec. com. New Hanover County Bar Assn., Wilmington, 1994-97. Bd. mem. Cape Fear Mus. Assocs., Inc., Wilmington, N.C., 1991-2000, v.p. 1994-97, pres. 1997-2000; bd. mem., counsel Wilmington Symphony Orchestra, Inc., Wilmington, N.C., 1991-99; comm. mem. USS N.C. Battleship Commn., Wilmington, N.C., 1989-93; memn. Bd. Deacons First Presbyn. Ch., Wilmington, N.C., 1996-99, Chancel Choir, 1988—. Recipient Women of Achievement New Hanover Commn. for Women, Wilmington, N.C., 1997, Trustee Merit Scholarship Converse Coll., Spartanburg, S.C., 1978-82; named Mortar Bd. Converse Coll., Spartanburg, S.C., 1981—, Crescent Converse Coll., Spartanburg, S.C., 1979-80, Pro bono publico award Legal Svcs. of the Lower Cape Fear, 1997. Mem. Am. Bar Assn., N.C. Bar Assn., N.C. Acad. Trial Lawyers, New Hanover County Bar Assn., Phi Delta Phi, Phi Sigma Iota, Pi Gamma Mu. Republican. Presbyterian. Avocations: travel, piano, choral, swimming, tennis, sailing. Home: 1940 Hawthorne Rd Wilmington NC 28403-5329 Office: Ryals Robinson & Saffo PC 701 Market St Wilmington NC 28401-4646

ROBINSON, ROXANA BARRY, writer, art historian; b. Pine Mountain, Ky., Nov. 30, 1946. Student, Bennington Coll., 1964-66; BA, U. Mich., 1969. Art cataloguer Sotheby's, N.Y.C., 1970-74; exhbn. dir. Terry Dintenfass Gallery, N.Y.C., 1974-76; freelance writer, 1976—. Author: (novel) Summer Light, 1988 (Washington Irving award Westchester Libr. Assn.), This Is My Daughter, 1998 (Notable Book Yr. award N.Y. Times 1998, Washington Irving award Westchester Libr. Assn.), (biography) Georgia O'Keeffe: A Life, 1989 (Notable Book Yr. award N.Y. Times 1989, Washington Irving award Westchester Libr. Assn.), (short stories) A Glimpse of Scarlet, 1991 (Notable Book Yr. award N.Y. Times 1991), Asking For Love, 1995 (Washington Irving award Westchester Libr. Assn.). Bd. trustees Katonah Mus. Art, 1980—, Eugene Lang Coll., N.Y., Nat. Humanities Ctr., N.C., 1995—, PEN Am. Ctr., N.Y., 1998—. Recipient Lit. Lion award N.Y. Pub. Libr., 1991; fellow Nat. Endowment Arts, 1987, MacDowell Colony, 1999, John S. Guggenheim Found. fellow, 2000.

ROBINSON, SAMIRA E. WATSON, marketing executive, writer; b. Chgo., Feb. 24, 1965; d. Christine Watson. BA with honors, Columbia Coll., Chgo., 1989, postgrad., 1996—. Rsch. asst. Columbia Coll./CBMR, Chgo., 1986-89; account exec. asst. ketchum Pub. Rels., Chgo., 1989; mktg. coord. Muntu Dance Co., Chgo., 1990; program asst. Cath. Charities, Chgo., 1991-96; youth care worker/advocate Mercy Home for Boys and Girls, Chgo., 1995-97; program dir. Cath. Charities, Chgo., 1996—; cons. in field; founder, min. Circle of Life Universal Family Ministries, 1999. Author: A Tribute to the Youth of Mercy Home, 1997; poet contbr. (anthology) Kaliedioscope, Ink, Women at Work, 1993; editor Forever Free News, 1992-96; contbr. articles to profl. jours. Host Dem. Nat. Conv., Chgo., 1996; proposal screener CBS-TV Network, Channel 2, Chgo., 1995; Telethon on-air asst. The Coll. Fund./UNCF, Chgo., 1997; mem. Cath. Charities Generation Coun., Chgo., 1993-95. Recipient Cert. of Appreciation, Christian Women's Network, Apostolic Ch. of God, 1992, Act of Kindness award Mayor's Light Up Chgo. Vol. Program, Chgo., 1997. Mem. Columbia Coll. Alumni Assn. (treas., exec. bd.), Apostolic Ch. of God Ministerial Alliance, Chgo. Assn. Black Journalists (affiliate), Phi Beta Sigma (silhouette mem., little sister 1984-85, life). Avocations: creative writing, reading, motivational speaker, youth advocacy, church ministry. Office: Catholic Charities 721 N Lasalle St Chicago IL 60610-3751

ROBINSON, SPENCER CADE, publishing company executive, author, editor; b. London, Nov. 4, 1961; arrived in Hong Kong, 1984; s. Lionel and Alma Robinson; m. Georgina Wong Chit-Yu, July 31, 1999. Sports reporter Watford (Eng.) Observer, 1979-84; soccer corr. South China Morning Post, Hong Kong, 1984-86, golf corr., 1986-95, dep. sports editor, 1987-90; mng. editor Asian Golfer, Hong Kong, 1990-97; publs. mgr. Asia Sport Group, Kowloon, Hong Kong, 1998—; commentator, presenter Asia TV, Hong Kong, 1986—; commentator Star TV, Hong Kong, 1994—. Author: Festina Lente, 1989, A History: Hong Kong Cricket Club, 1989. Named Sports Journalist of Yr., 1987. Mem. Royal Hong Kong Golf Club, Fgn. Corr. Club Hong Kong, Chung Shan Hot Spring Golf Club. Avocations: golf, soccer, travel, theatre, reading. Office: 15th Fl One Harbour Front, 18 Tak Fung St, Hunghom, Kowloon Hong Kong

ROBINSON, SPENCER MICHAEL, research scientist, writer, educator; arrived in New Zealand, 1998; BA in Psychology, U. South Fla., 1965; postgrad. in Psychometry, Stetson U., 1970; postgrad. in Anthropology, Union Inst., Cin., 1995—. Founder, pres. Microelectronics Design Lab, Tokyo and Boston, 1984-97; lectr. info. tech. Otago Poly., Dunedin, New Zealand, 1999; rschr., lectr. various, 2000—; rsch. scientist, writer, educator in computer sci. and info. systems, microelectronics, social implications of sci. and tech., sci. and tech. in prehistory, philosophy of sci., anthropology, archaeology, and humanistic studies. Contbr. papers to profl. publs. Mem. AAAS, IEEE, IEEE Computer Soc., IEEE Soc. Profl. Comm., IEEE Soc. for the Social Implications of Tech., IEEE Comm. Soc., Soc. Tech. Comm., Archaeol. Inst. Am., Archaeol. Inst. Am. We. Mass. Soc., Am. Schs. Oriental Rsch., Bibl. Archaeology Soc., N.Y. Acad. Scis., Com. Scientific Investigation of Claims of the Paranormal. Achievements include major contributions to the design and devel. of a number of leading-edge microprocessors, including the devel. of the user specifications for the Hitachi H32/200 32-Bit Microprocessor, the Hitachi H32 Floating-Point Processing Unit (FPU), the Hitachi H32/500 64-Bit Superscalar Microprocessor, the Hitachi PA-50L and PA50M 32-Bit Precision Architecture RISC Microprocessors, and the Hitachi SH-3 and SH-4 32-Bit RISC Microprocessors. Other achievements include the devel. of a front-end blueprint for an autocompiled horizontal sales-control sys. for Olivetti Corp. of Am., the front-end codifying the input parameters and the matrix of interconnections and formulas converting the input parameters into an integrated set of software modules compiled from an extensive module database to define a rigorously tailored sales-control system. Recipient award of achievement in the 1992 Soc. for Tech. Comm. (STC) Publ. Competition for Hitachi H32 Floating-Point Processing Unit User's Manual (Release 1.0), 1993 (Release 2.0), Hitachi H32/200 32-Bit Microprocessor User's Manual, Hitachi H32/500 64-Bit Superscalar Microprocessor User's Manual (Release 1.0), Hitachi H32/500 64-Bit Superscalar Microprocessor Tech. Summary, and Hitachi PA/50L 32-Bit Precision Architecture Microprocessor Tech. Summary, 1996 APEX Ann. Awards for Publ. Excellence for Hitachi H32/500 64-Bit Superscalar Microprocessor User's Manual (Release 2.0). Melding computer sci. and information tech. with studies in anthropology and archaeology, current rsch. is directed toward the isolation of time-transgressive phenomena and the devel. of an ethology of formal variation by the spatial/temporal investigation of material culture patterns and the reassessment of the role of sci. and tech. in soc. in ancient and modern times. Doctoral dissertation (in progress) centers on the design and devel. of a tightly integrated, modular, platform-independent, data collection/information mgmt./online publ. sys. prototype that includes each major step of an archaeological rsch. project, from on-site field recording to analysis (including visualization and statistical analysis), and final report generation with on-demand report distribution and publishing. Fax: 011-64-3-481-4830. E-mail: artefact@world-net.co.nz.

ROBINSON, TIMOTHY STEPHEN, lawyer; b. Kilgore, Tex., Dec. 31, 1958; s. Eddie Max and Mittie Cleo Robinson; m. Anisa Jane Laurence, May 20, 1978; children: Aaron Caleb, Alexandra Grace. BA in Econs., Austin Coll., Sherman, Tex., 1984; JD, Baylor U., 1987. Bar: Tex. 1987, Okla. 1997; cert. in personal injury Tex. Bd. Legal Specialization. Atty., litigation assocs. Ramey & Flock, Tyler, Tex., 1987-88, Fulbright & Jaworski, Dallas, 1988-91; ptnr. Robinson Carmody, Dallas, 1991-94, Robinson & Schwab, Plano, Tex., 1994—. Mem. ATLA, Tex. Bar Assn., Okla. Bar Assn. Office: Robinson & Schwab LLP 101 E Park Blvd Ste 769 Plano TX 75074-8820

ROBINSON, WILLIAM DAVID, priest; b. Blackburn, Lancashire, Eng., Mar. 15, 1931; s. William and Margaret (Bolton) R.; m. Carol Averil Roma Hamm, July 30, 1955; children: Christopher, Catherine. BA, Durham U., Eng., 1954, Diploma in Theology, 1958; MA, Durham U., 1962. Curate Ch. of Eng., Standish, 1958-61; sr. curate Ch. of Eng., Lancaster, 1961-63; vicar of St. James Ch. of Eng., Blackburn, 1963-73; priest, Shireshead Ch. of Eng., Lancashire, 1973-86, stewardship adviser, 1973-86; archdeacon Blackburn Ch. of Eng., Blackburn, 1986-96. Pilot officer Royal Air Force, 1949-51, Eng. Avocations: family, fell walking, bridge. Home: 21 Westbourne Rd Warton, Carnforth Lancashire, England

ROBINSON, WILLIAM HENRY, industrial engineer; b. Auckland, New Zealand, Oct. 2, 1938; s. Leonard and Anne (Pointer) R.; m. Barbara Jennifer Miller, Dec. 16, 1961; children: Riki, Michael, Sian. B in Engring., U. Auckland, 1960, M in Engring., 1961; PhD, U. Ill., 1965; DSc, Victoria U., 1995. Mech. engr. Mason Brothers, Auckland, 1961; rsch. fellow U. Sussex, England, 1966-67; scientist Physics & Engring. Lab., Wgn, New Zealand, 1967-91; CEO Robinson Seismic Ltd., Wgn, 1995—; bd. dirs. Antarctic Rsch. Com., New Zealand, 1979-89. Fellow Royal Soc. New Zealand, New Zealand Soc. Earthquake Engrs., New Zealand Inst. Physics. Avocations: reading, walking, home maintainence. Office: Robinson Seismic Ltd, PO Box 33-093, Petone New Zealand

ROBINSON, WILLIAM P., academic administrator, consultant, speaker; b. Elmhurst, Ill., Sept. 30, 1949; s. Paul Frederick and Lillian (Horton) R.; m. Bonnie Van Laan, Aug. 10, 1974; children: Brenna Kay, Benjamin Paul, Bailley Kay. Student, Moody Bible Inst., Chgo., 1967-70; AB, U. No. Iowa, 1972; postgrad., Princeton (N.J.) Theol. Sem., 1972-73; MA, Wheaton Coll., 1975; PhD, U. Pitts., 1979. Assoc. minister First Presbyn. Ch., Pitts., 1975-77; instr. U. Pitts., 1977-79; asst. prof. sch. continuing studies Nat. Coll. Edn., Evanston, Ill., 1979-80, dean sch. continuing studies, 1980-84, sr. v.p., 1984-86; pres. Manchester Coll., North Manchester, Ind., 1986-93, Whitworth Coll., Spokane, Wash., 1993—; bd. dirs. Coun. Indep. Colls., Ind. Colls. Wash., Whitworth Coll.; cons., speaker for U.S. corps. and svc. orgns. Bd. dirs. Wash. Friends of Higher Edn., Spokane Symphony; vol. various orgns., especially prion work and hunger projects. Recipient various acad. awards. Mem. Nat. Assn. Ind. Colls. and Univs., Coun. Ind. Colls., Spokane Country Club, Spokane Club. Presyterian. Avocation: sports. Office: Whitworth Coll Office of Pres 300 W Hawthorne Rd Spokane WA 99218-2515

ROBINSON, WILLIAM PETER, psychology professor; b. Chichester, Sussex, Eng., May 8, 1933; s. John and Winifred (Napper) R.; m. Elizabeth Joan Peill, May 16, 1947 (div. 1987); children: Katherine, Clare. BA, Oxford U., 1957, MA, 1958, PhD, 1961. Chartered psychologist. Lectr. U. Hull, Eng., 1961-65; sr. rsch. fellow U. London, 1965-66; reader in psychology U. Southampton, Eng., 1967-74; prof. edn. MacQuarie U., Sydney, Australia, 1974-77, U. Bristol, Eng., 1977-88; prof. social psychology U. Bristol, 1988—. Author: Language and Social Behavior, 1972, A Question of Answers, 1972, Language Management, 1978; editor: (with H. Giles) Handbook of Language and Social Psychology, 1991, Deceit, Delusion and Detection, 1996. Trustee Bristol Mcpl. Charities, 1992—, The Red Maids' Sch., Bristol, 1982—, Cheltenham Coll. Higher Edn., 1977-88. Recipient Smyth medal U. Melbourne (Australia), 1976, Japanese Soc. for Promotion of Sci. fellowship, 1991; named hon. prof. Inst. Superior Psychol. Applications, Portugal, 1981—. Fellow Brit. Psychol. Soc., Australian Psychol. Soc. Avocations: gardening, squash. Office: U Bristol-Dept Psychology, 8 Woodland Rd, Bristol BS8ITN, England

ROBINSON, ZELIG, lawyer; b. Balt., July 7, 1934; s. Morton Matthew and Mary (Ackerman) R.; m. Karen Ann Bergstrom (div. Oct. 1987); children: John, Christopher, Kristin; m. Linda Portner Strangmann, Dec. 23, 1987. BA, Johns Hopkins U., 1954; LLB, Harvard U., 1957. Bar: Md. 1958. Legis. analyst Md. House of Dels., Annapolis, 1958; tech. asst. IRS, Washington, 1958-60; pvt. practice Balt., 1960-62; assoc. gen. counsel commerce com. U.S. Ho. of Reps., Washington, 1962-64; assoc. Weinberg & Green, Balt., 1964-66; special legal cons. commerce com. U.S. Ho. of Reps., Washington, 1966-68; pvt. practice Balt., 1966-72; mem. Gordon, Feinblatt, Rothman, Hoffberger & Hollander, LLC, 1972—; bd. dirs. Durapak Mfg. Co., Balt., Vac Pac, Inc., Balt., Universal Die Casting Co., Inc., Saline, Mich.; chmn. Balt. City Minimum Wage Commn., 1974-82, Md. Pub. Broadcasting, 1991-95; mem. Gov.'s Commn. to revise Md. Code, Annapolis, 1968-89. Contbr. articles to profl. jours. Bd. dirs., v.p./sec. Gov.'s Mansion Found., Annapolis, Md.; v.p. bd. dirs. Md. Cmtys. and Citizens Fund, Chestertown, Md.; sec. bd. dirs. William Donald Schaefer Civic Fund; bd. dirs. Md. Arts Pl., Balt., Balt. Coalition of Homeowners, 1989—; mem. Found. for Md. Pub. Broadcasting; bd. dirs., pres. Celebrate 2000, Inc., 1998—, bd. dirs., Baltimore Efficiency and Econ. Found., 1999—. With U.S. Army, 1958. Mem. ABA, Md. State Bar Assn. (laws com., internat. law com.). Democrat. Office: Gordon Feinblatt Rothman Hoffberger & Hollander LLC 233 E Redwood St Baltimore MD 21202-3332

ROBISON, JOHN JEFFREY, university official; b. Cleve., Dec. 12, 1946; s. C. Richard and Patricia (Zovack) R.; children: Rebecca Terese, Matthew Charles, Kathryn Ann. BS, Ohio U., 1970, MEd, 1971. Asst. registrar Marshall U., Huntington, W.Va., 1971-73; asst. dir. records Ohio State U., Columbus, 1973-78, devel. officer, 1978-79, dir. ann. giving, 1979-80; dir. corp. and fin. rels. U. Fla., Gainesville, 1980-85, assoc. dir. univ. devel., 1985-88; assoc. v.p. Ohio U., Athens, 1988-92, assoc. v.p., campaign mgr., 1992-94, instr., 1993-94; pres. Fla. State U. Found., 1994—; speaker in field. Coach Gainesville Recreation League, 1984-88; chair fin. com. parish coun. St. Augustine Cath. Ch., 1986-87; vol. Christ the King Ch., 1988-94, Co Cathedral of St. Thomas More, 1999-2000; mem. Wash. chpt. Coun. Advancement and Support of Edn., Wash. chpt. Assn. for Governing Bds. Roman Catholic. Avocations: physical fitness, WWII history, reading. Office: Fla State U Found Univ Ctr 225 Bldg C Rm 3100 Tallahassee FL 32306

ROBISON, KENNETH GERALD, former naval officer, national security consultant, historian; b. Great Falls, Mont., Sept. 30, 1938; s. Perry Russell and Ruth Elsie Helen (Johnson) R.; m. Mary Margaret Michele Crovitz, Mar. 6, 1964; children: Karin Michele, Mark Charles. Student, U. Wash., 1958; BA, U. Mont., 1960, postgrad., 1965; MA, George Mason U., 1994. Commd. ensign USN, 1960, advanced through grades to capt., 1980, intelligence officer, 1960; asst. naval attache U.S. Embassy, Stockholm, 1975-78; asst. chief of staff intelligence U.S. Naval Forces Europe, London, 1980-84; dir. plans, policy and requirements Office Naval Intelligence, Washington, 1984-88; ret., 1988; sr. cons. Booz, Allen & Hamilton, Vienna, Va., 1988—.

Author: Prisoner of War Debrief--Capt. James Bond Stockdale, 1973; contbr. articles to hist. and genealogical jours. Decorated comdr. Order No. Star (Sweden), Legion of Merit, Meritorious Svc. medal with oak leaf cluster, Navy Commendation medal, Presdl. Unit Commendation medal. Mem. Orgn. Am. Historians, Mont. Hist. Soc., Va. Hist. Soc., U.S. Naval Inst., Navy League, Am. Legion, VFW, Phi Alpha Theta, Delta Sigma Phi. Republican. Presbyterian. Avocations: western Americana, genealogy, hist. rsch. and writing, squash, tennis. Home: 315 Lamplighter Ln Great Falls MT 59405-4168

ROBITAILLE, LUC, professional hockey player; b. Montreal, P.Q., Can., Feb. 17, 1966. With Hull Olympiques Major Jr. Hockey League, Que., 1983-84, L.A. Kings, 1984-94, Pitts. Penguins, 1994-95, N.Y. Rangers, 1995-97, L.A. Kings, 1997—; scored winning goal for nat. team of Can. at 1994 World Hockey Championship. Recipient Guy LaFleur trophy, 1985-86, Can. Hockey Player of Yr. award, 1985-86, Calder Meml. trophy, NHL Rookie of Yr., 1986-87; named to NHL All-Star team, 1987, 88, 90-91, 92-93. Office: Los Angeles Kings 1111 S Figueroa St Los Angeles CA 90015-1300

ROBLE OLHAYE OUDINE, ambassador; b. Republic of Djibouti, Apr. 24, 1944; married; 5 children. Grad., Comml. Sch. of Addis Ababa, Ethiopia, 1964, Inst. Fin. Accts., London, 1966. Cert. gen. acct., Ethiopia. Various sr. positions in auditing, acctg. and taxation Addis-Ababa, Ethiopia, 1964-73; regional chief acct. TAW Internat. Leasing Corp., Nairobi, Kenya, 1973-75, fin. contr. Africa, 1975-80; ind. cons., 1980—; founder Banque de Djibouti et du Moyen Orient S.A., Djibouti, 1982—, Djibouti Embassy, Nairobi, Kenya, 1985; permanent rep. to UNEP, UNCHS Nairobi, 1986-87; permanent rep. of Djibouti to UN N.Y.C., 1987—; amb. to U.S.A., 1987—, amb. to Can. (non-resident), 1989—; del. World Conf. to Rev. and Appraise Achievements of UN Decade for Women, 1985, Non-Aligned Summit, Harare, Zimbabwe, 1986, UN Environ. Programme, Nairobi, 1986, UN Human Ctr. for Habitat, 1987; head del. UN Disarmament Conf., N.Y.C., 1988, Ad Hoc Com. of Whole UN Gen. Assembly Rev. and Appraisal UN Programme of Action for African Econ. Recovery and Devel., 1986-90; vice chmn. Djibouti del. to UN Gen. Assembly, 1988, 89, 91, 92, 93, chmn., 1989, numerous other confs. and meetings with UN; chief rep Djibouti UN Security Coun., 1993, chmn. sanction com. on Haiti, 1993, pres. 1994; del. Orgn. African Unity, Dakkar, Senegal, 1992. Fellow Assn. Internat. Accts. (London); mem. Brit. Inst. Mgmt. Office: Permanent Mission of Djibouti UN 866 U N Plz Rm 4011 New York NY 10017-1822*

ROBLES, ALFREDO, neurologist; b. Astorga, León, Spain, Aug. 25, 1957; s. Alfredo Robles and Sinaita Bayón; m. Azucena Castrillo, Dec. 27, 1985. B Medicine and Surgery, U. Barcelona, Spain, 1980; D Medicine and Surgery, U. Santiago, Spain, 1985. Gen. practitioner Nat. Health Inst., León, 1981; asst. physician neuropsychiatry Mil. Hosp. Valladolid, Spain, 1981; house physician neurology Gen. Hosp. Galacia-Santiago de Compostela, Spain; specialist in neurology U. Clin. Med. Ctr. Santiago, 1985; staff neurologist Hosp. Nuestra Señora de las Nieves, Santa Cruz de la Palma, Spain, 1987-89, U. Clin. Med. Ctr. Santiago, 1990—; pvt. practice Santa Cruz de la Palma, 1989-90; head dementia unit U. Clin. Med. Ctr., Santiago, 1992—, clin. tutor, 1997—; clin. coord. on Creutzfeld-Jakob disease Health Sect. Galacian Autonomous Govt., Spain, 1997—. Meml. editl. bd. Revista de Neurologia, 1998—; contbr. articles to profl. jours. Founder, 1st pres. Galacian Assn. to help patients with Alzheimer's disease and other dementias, 1994-96. 2d lt. Spanish Health Svc., 1981. Mem. Galician Soc. Neurology (sec. 1995-99), Royal Acad. Medicine and Surgery of Galacia (corr., Antonio Usero prize 1984, Barrié de la Maza-Conde de Fenosa prize 1998), Spanish Soc. Neurology (mem. exec. com. group on behavior and dementia 1997—, vice-sec. 1999—). Office: U Clin Med Ctr Divsn Neurol, La Choupana s/n, 15706 Santiago Compostela Spain

ROBLES, ELIODORO GONZALES, consulting company executive, educator; b. Paniqui, Tarlac, The Philippines, July 3, 1923; s. Mariano Abraham and Lucia (Gonzales) R.; m. Rosario Palaganas Lavitoria, Oct. 30, 1964; children: Michael, Elmer, Eliodoro Jr., Marilou, Jonathan, Jay. BS in Polit. Sci., Far Eastern U., 1953; MA in Internat. Rels., Cornell U., 1954; MA in Polit. Economy, Harvard U., 1955, PhD in Polit. Economy, 1959. Cert. tchr., Calif.; cert. C.C. instr., Calif. C.C.; cert. C.C. supr., Calif. C.C. Instr. Far Eastern U., Manila, 1952-53; tech. cons., staff asst. Embassy of the Rep. of Indonesia in the Philippines, 1950-53; spl. asst. on fgn. econ. policies Program Implementation Office of the Pres. of the Philippines, 1962-64; prof. econs. and polit. sci., dean Grad. Sch. Far Eastern U., Manila, 1959-64; econ. officer, dep. dir. for econ., cultural, social affairs S.E. Asia Treaty Orgn. (SEATO), Bangkok, 1964-74; project dir. San Francisco Unified Sch. Dist., 1975-79; sr. assoc. Devel. Assocs., Inc., Walnut Creek, Calif., 1979—; evaluation specialist including polit. economist USAID, various locations, Calif., 1984-85; ednl. adminstrn. specialist USAID, Manila and Islamabad, Phillipines and Pakistan, 1987; tng. specialist, Asia Narcotics Edn. Program USAID, 1988-89, polit. economist, 1992—; presenter, attendee numerous confs., seminars and workshops including Nat. Conf. on Sch. Sys. and Bilingual Edn., San Jose, Calif., 1975, Conf. on Bilingual Edn.: Asian Am. Bilingual Materials Devel. Ctr., Berkeley, Calif., 1975, Ctr. for Ednl. Devel., San Francisco, Calif., 1975, among others. Author: Economic Analysis, 1966, The Philippine in the Nineteenth Century, 1969. Lt. col. Philippine Army, 1941-46; 1st lt. inf. U.S. Army, 1946-49. Recipient scholarship Fulbright Assn., 1954; Telluride fellow Cornell U., 1954, Fletcher fellow Harvard U., 1954-55, Newberry fellow Newberry Libr., 1957-58. Mem. Fulbright Assn., Filipino Am. Tchrs. Assn., Far Eastern U. Alumni Assn. (bd. dirs., adviser 1991—), Harvard Club San Francisco. Democrat. Methodist. Avocations: general gardening, orchid growing, stamp and coin collecting. Home: 1335 Greenway Dr Richmond CA 94803-1204 Office: Devel Assocs Inc 1475 N Broadway Walnut Creek CA 94596-4649

ROBLES-AUSTRIACO, LILIA SINOGBA, information specialist; b. Calabanga, The Philippines, Dec. 28, 1940; d. Panfilo Cantanduanes and Maria Agravante (Sinogba) Robles; m. Nicanor Camacho Austriaco, June 24, 1967; children: Nicanor Victor Jr., Neil Vincent, Maria Lilibelle. BS in Civil Engring. cum laude, Mapua Inst. Tech., Manila, 1962; M of Engring., Asian Inst. Tech., Bangkok, 1965; diploma in Bus. English, Bus. Tng. Ltd., Manchester, Eng., 1982, advanced diploma in Bus. English, 1983; PhD in Comm., LaSalle U., 1997. Registered civil engr., The Philippines. Civil engr. Bur. Pub. Works, Manila, 1962-63; assoc. prof. Mapua Inst. Tech., Manila, 1965-73; info. scientist I Asian Inst. of Tech., Bangkok, 1973-75; lectr. U. Sains Malaysia, Penang, 1975-79; sr. info. scientist, assoc. editor Asian Inst. Tech., Bangkok, 1980-85, sr. info. scientist, editor, 1985-92, mgr., editor, 1992—; course dir. Internat. Ferrocement Info. Ctr., Bangkok, 1980—, lectr., 1983—; prin. investigator for projects Asian Inst. Tech., Bangkok, 1980—; internat. coord. Ferrocement Internat. Network, IFIC Ref. Ctrs. Network, IFIC Cons. Network, Bangkok, 1985—; cons. Internat. Ref. Ctr. for Cmty. Water Supply and Sanitation, 1987. Author: Ferrocement Primer, 1992, Managing Training, 1992; co-author: Women in the Thai Construction Industry, 1993, Thai Women Construction Worker, 1993; author various audio/visual slide presentations; co-author: (manuals) Ferrocement Biogas Digester, 1985, Ferrocement Canal Lining, 1988, Ferrocement Pour-Flush Latrine, 1988, Ferrocement Footbridge, 1991, Production of Rice Husk Ash Ferrocement Incinerator, 1992; editor: Ferrocement Thesaurus, 1990; compiler Ferrocement directories, 1985; contbr. more than 100 articles to profl. jours. Mem. Thai Nat. Red Cross, 1974—; mem. Internat. Women's Group, Thailand, 1980—, Filipino Cmty. of Thailand, 1980—; couple leader Christian Family Movement, Thailand, 1989-99. Southeast Asia Treaty Orgn. scholar, 1963-65; recipient Presdl. Gold medal for acad. excellence Mapua Inst. of Tech., 1962. Fellow Internat. Ferrocement Soc.; mem. Inst. Info. Scientists, Philippine Inst. Civil Engrs. Office: Asian Inst Tech, PO Box 4 Klong Luang, Pathum Thani 12120, Thailand

ROBLETO, RANDY E., pharmaceutical company director; b. Valencia, Carabobo, Venezuela, Oct. 29, 1953; arrived in Panama, 1995; s. Gastón J. Robleto and Carmen M. López; m. Batista Costante, Jan. 24, 1976; children: Tindy V., Leonardo E. B of Chemistry, U. Cen. Venezuela, Caracas, 1978. New products launch mktg. coord. Eli Lilly & Co., Indpls., 1989; mktg. mgr. Searle-Venezuela, Guarenas, 1990-92, Glaxo-Venezuela, Caracas, 1992-95, Bristol Myers Squibb, Panama, 1995; country mgr. Bristol Myers Squibb, San Jose, Costa Rica, 1996; mktg. dir. Bristol Myers Squibb, Panama, 1997-98; gen. dir. Cen. Am. Laboratorios Leti, Panama, 1998-2000. Roman Catholic. Avocations: soccer, bowling. E-mail: lttr@sinfo.net. Home: Ste 26 3000042 4405 NW 73d Ave Miami FL 33166-6488

ROBOCK, ALAN, meteorology educator; b. Boston, Sept. 7, 1949; s. Stefan Hyman Robock and Shirley Ruth (Bernstein) Fox; m. Sherri Lynne Carpini West, May 12, 1990; children: Brian, Daniel. BA, U. Wis., 1970; SM, MIT, 1974, PhD, 1977. Vol. Peace Corps, The Philippines, 1970-72; rsch. scientist Lawrence Livermore (Calif.) Lab., 1973; asst. prof. dept. meteorology U. Md., College Park, 1977-82, assoc. prof., 1982-96, prof., 1996-97; prof. dept. environ. scis. Rutgers U., New Brunswick, N.J., 1998—; snow forecaster Montgomery County (Md.) Pub. Schs., 1980-81; state climatologist State of Md., 1991-97; vis. rsch. scientist Princeton U., NOAA/Geophys. Fluid Dynamics Lab., 1994-95. Editor Jour. Climate and Applied Meteorology, 1985-87, Jour. Geophys. Research-Atmospheres, 2000—; assoc. editor Revs. Geophysics, 1994-2000, Jour. Geophys. Rsch.-Atmospheres, 1998-2000; contbr. articles to profl. publs., chpts. to books. Fellow Am. Meteorol. Soc.; mem. AAAS (Congressional sci. fellow 1986-87), Am. Geophys. Union. Avocations: tennis, Bob Dylan music, travel, politics. E-mail: robock@envsci.rutgers.edu. Office: Rutgers-State Univ NJ Dept Environ Scis 14 College Farm Rd New Brunswick NJ 08901-8551

ROBSON, BARRY, biopharmaceutical and computer company executive, biochemist; b. Sunderland, Eng., Mar. 14, 1947; s. Douglas and Evelyn Dorothy (Fisher) R.; m. Margaret Elizabeth Hodgson, July 13, 1968; children: Tanith, Adam. BSc with honours in Physiology and, U. Newcastle Upon Tyne, U.K., 1968, PhD in Biochemistry, 1971; DSc in Biochemistry, Manchester (Eng.) U., 1984. Postdoctoral rschr. Weizmann Inst., Rehovot, Israel, 1971-74, U. Newcastle Upon Tyne, Eng., 1971-74; lectr. biochemistry U. Manchester, 1974-85, reader, 1985-97; founder, sci. dir. Proteus Biotechnology, Proteus Molecular Design Ltd., Macclesfield, U.K., 1987-95; sci. dir. Proteus Internat. Plc. (now Protherics Plc), Macclesfield, 1987-95; CEO, chmn. Dirac Found., U. London, 1994—; sci. dir., chief sci. officer Gryphon Scis., San Francisco, 1995-96; prin. scientist MDL INfo. Sys. Inc., San Leandro, 1996-98; IBM strategic advisor, exec., IBM disting. engr. IBM Rsch. Hdqrs., Yorktown Heights, N.Y., 1998—; hon. chmn. Tech. U. Denmark, 1990—; vis. prof. U. Paris-Sud, 1978-84, vis. hon. prof. II, 1980-84; vis. prof. Stanford U., 1996-98; founder, dir. Epsitron Rsch. Lab., Manchester U., 1984—. Author: (with J. Garnier) Introduction to Proteins and Protein Engineering, 1986, 2d edit., 1988; contbr. over 180 articles and revs. to sci. jours. Adv. bd. mem. EC Commn., Brussels, 1990—, Danish Rsch. Coun., Copenhagen, 1993; adv. bd. mem. lobbying powers Biotech Indsl. Assn., London, 1994. Recipient Biotech. Action Program award European Commn., U.K., 1985-89; grantee Sci. Rsch. Coun., U.K., 1974—. Mem. AAAS, Biochem. Soc. U.K., N.Y. Acad. Scis., Assn. Univ. Tchrs. Achievements include IBM Disting Engr. award, successful pharmaceutical agents; co-inventor of the successful diagnostics for Mad Cow Disease.

ROBSON, BRIAN EWART, retired British government official, historian; b. Dartford, Kent, Eng., July 25, 1926; s. Walter Ewart and Lily May (Drain) R.; m. Cynthia Margaret Scott, Mar. 17, 1962 (dec. 1997); children: Suzanne Alexandra, Vanessa Jane. BA with honours, Oxford (Eng.) U., 1950. Prin. Air Ministry, London, 1955-66; head div. Ministry Def., London, 1966-76, asst. under sec. of state, 1976-82, dep. under sec. of state, 1982-86, head army dept., 1982-84, mem. army bd., 1982-84; commr. Royal Hosp., Chelsea, 1982-84; ret., 1986; cons. Price Waterhouse, London, 1986-89. Author: Swords of the British Army, 1975, The Road to Kabul: the Second Afghan War 1878-1881, 1986, Fuzzy Wuzzy: the campaigns in the Eastern Sudan 1884-85, 1993; editor: Roberts in India: the military correspondence of Lord Roberts, 1993, Sir Hugh Rose and the Campaign in Central India 1858, 2000. Mem. ctrl. bd. fin. Ch. of Eng., London, 1987-95; gov. Roehampton Inst. Higher Edn., London, 1988-95. Lt. Brit. Army, 1944-48, CBI, ETO. Decorated companion of Bath. Fellow Royal Hist. Soc., Soc. Antiquaries; mem. Soc. Army Hist. Rsch. (chmn. 1993—), Army Records Soc. (coun. 1986—). Avocations: military history, cricket, travel, book collecting. Home: 17 Woodlands, Hove BN3 6TJ, England

ROBSON, GEOFFREY DAVID, microbiologist, researcher; b. Doncaster, Eng., Sept. 6, 1962; s. Thomas Joseph and Hazel Mary (Bolton) R.; m. Amanda Jane Williams, Mar. 26, 1988; 1 child, James. BSc, U. Salford, Eng., 1984; PhD, U. Manchester, Eng., 1987. Rsch. assoc. U. Manchester, Eng., 1987-91, lectr., 1991—. Inventor, patentee in field; contbr. to books in field. Mem. Brit. Mycol. Soc. (sec. 1987—, Berkely award 1994), Soc. Gen. Microbiology, Internat. Soc. Human Animal Mycology. Avocations: walking, photography. Office: U Manchester Sch Biol Sci, 1.800 Stopford Bldg, Manchester M13 9PT, England

ROBSON, GEOFFREY ROBERT, geologist, seismologist, consultant; b. Stockton on Tees, Eng., Jan. 24, 1929; s. Robert and Mary (Darbyshire) R.; m. Dorothy Elizabeth Jewitt, Aug. 26, 1953; children: James Alexander, Charles Robert. BSc, U. Durham (Eng.), 1949, PhD, 1956. Registered geologist, mining engr. Sci. officer Brit. Ea. Caribbean area Colonial Rsch. Svc., 1952-60; head seismic rsch. U. W.I., Trinidad, 1960-68; econ. affairs officer energy resources br. UN Secretariat, N.Y.C., 1968-74, chief mineral resources br., 1974-86; hon. fellow dept. geol. scis. U. Durham, 1987—; cons. UN, N.Y.C., 1986—, Fgn. and Commonwealth Office, Eng., 1995—. Editor: Economics of Mineral Engineering, 1976, The Development Potential of Precambrian Mineral Deposits, 1982, Legal and Institutional Arrangements in Minerals Development, 1982, Mineral Processing in Developing Countries, 1982, Jour. Volcanology and Geothermal Rsch., 1970-92, Natural Resources Forum, 1988-91; author: Catalogue of Eastern Caribbean Earthquakes, 1964, Catalogue of Active Volcanoes of the West Indies, 1966; contbr. articles on earthquakes, volcanic activity and mineral resources to profl. jours. Fellow Geol. Soc. London, Instn. Mining and Metallurgy; mem. AIME, Royal Commonwealth Soc. Anglican. Avocation: gardening. Home: Little Leake, Nether Silton, Thirsk Y07 4BL, England Office: U Durham Dept Geol Scis, South Rd, Durham DH1 3LE, England

ROBSON, MARTIN CECIL, surgery educator, plastic surgeon; b. Lancaster, Ohio, Mar. 8, 1939; children: Karen Iredell, Douglas Spears, Martin Cecil III. Student, Northwestern U., 1957-59; B.A., Johns Hopkins U., 1961, M.D., 1964. Diplomate Am. Bd. Surgery, Am. Bd. Plastic Surgery (chmn. 1996-97; pres. 196-97). Intern U. Chgo. Hosps. and Clinics, 1964-65; resident in surgery Balt. City Hosp., 1965-67, Brooke Gen. Hosp., Ft. Sam Houston, Tex., 1967-69; resident in plastic surgery Yale-New Haven Hosp., 1971-73; instr. dept. surgery Yale U. Sch. Medicine, New Haven, 1973-74, asst. prof. plastic surgery, 1973-74, assoc. prof., 1974; assoc. prof., chief plastic surgery U. Chgo., 1974-77, prof. and chief plastic surgery, 1977-83, dir. Burn Center, 1976-83; prof., chmn. divsn. plastic and reconstructive surgery Wayne State U., Detroit, 1983-88; dir. Detroit Med. Ctr. Burn Ctr., 1983-88; Truman Blocker Disting. prof., chief divsn. plastic surgery U. Tex. Med. Br., 1988-93; dir. surg. svcs. Shriners' Burn Inst., Galveston, Tex., 1988-93; prof. surgery U. South Fla., Tampa, 1993—, chair divsn. surgery rsch., 1993-97; chair surg. svc. Bay Pines (Fla.) VA Med. Ctr., 1993-97. Mem. editl. cons. bd.: Jour. Trauma. Served to maj. M.C. U.S. Army, 1967-71; col. USAR Med. Corps, 1991-97. Fellow ACS, Royal Australasian Coll. Surgeons (hon.); mem. Plastic Surgery Rsch. Coun. (chmn. 1983-84), Am. Burn Assn. (pres. 1985-86, Disting. Svc. award), Am. Surg. Assn., Wound Healing Soc. (pres. 1995-96, Lifetime Sci. Achievement award 1998), Am. Assn. Plastic Surgery, Am. Bd. Med. Specialties (chmn. Am. Bd. Plastic Surgery, 1996-97), Nu Sigma Nu, Phi Delta Theta, Alpha Omega Alpha.

ROBSON, MAUREEN ANNE, museum conservation consultant; b. Portsmouth, Eng., Feb. 16, 1947; d. Robert Kirkley and Muriel Evelyn (Nash) R. Diploma in ceramics, Birmingham (Eng.) Sch. Art, 1969; diploma in conservation, U. London, 1975; cert. in design mgmt., Chartered Soc. of Designers, 1984. Asst. conservation officer The Brit. Mus., London, 1969-74, The Victoria and Albert Mus., London, 1974-76; conservation officer Ancient Monuments Lab., English, London, 1976-79, Birmingham Mus. and Art Gallery, 1979-97, Hardman Stained Glass Studio, Birmingham, 1997—; cons. conservator West Midlands Area Mus. Svc., Birmingham, 1980-90; exec. mgr. cons. conservator, 1985—; lectr. U. Birmingham, Malvern Hills Coll., U. Warwick. Contbr. chpts. to books. Mem. com. Alliance Residents Assn., Multi-Nat. Inner City of Hockley, Birmingham, 1984—. Travel grantee Brit. Coun., Slovakia, 1990. Mem. United Kingdom Inst. for Conservation of Hist. and Artistic Works (assoc.), Internat. Inst. for Conservation of Hist. and Artistic Works (assoc.), Chartered Soc. Designs (assoc.). Mem. Labour Party. Anglican. Achievements include micro-excavation of early dovetail joints on a wooden chest of Roman date. Home and Studio: 29 Park Ave, Hockley Birmingham B18 5ND, England

ROBSON, PETER WILLIAM GREENWELL, law educator; b. Birmingham, England, Mar. 28, 1947; s. John Leslie and Florence (Greenwell) R.; m. Andrina Ann Marie Smith, Mar. 3, 1946. LLB, U. St. Andrews, Scotland, 1967, PhD, 1980. Apprentice solicitor pvt. firm, Edinburgh, Scotland, 1967-69, solicitor, 1969-70; lectr. U. Strathclyde, Glasgow, Scotland, 1970-82, sr. lectr., 1982-89, reader, 1989-92, prof., 1992—; chair Shelter, Scotland, 1984—; vice chair Shelter, Eng., 1991-99, chair, 1999—; chair SSAT & CSAT, Scotland, 1993—; dir. WESLO Housing Mgmt., Bathgate, Scotland, 1992—. Author: Justice, Lord Denning and The Constitution, 1981, Homelessness and the Law, 1983, 3d edit., 1996, Residential Tenancies, 1994, 2d edit., 1998, Property Law, 2d edit., 1998; editor: Welfare Law, 1992. Chair East End Advice Ctr., Glasgow, 1990—. Avocations: football, golf, cinema, country music, in-line skating. Office: U Strathclyde, 173 Cathedral St, Glasgow G4 0RQ, Scotland

ROBSON, ROBERT HOWARD, pharmacologist; b. Rossendale, Eng., Nov. 20, 1944; s. Dorothy Beryl R.; m. Phyllis Mary Heath, Sept. 8, 1973; 1 child, Simon Howard. M.A., M.B., Trinity Coll., Cambridge U., 1969, B.Chir., 1970. Sr. house officer Walton Hosp., Liverpool, Eng., 1970-71, med. registrar, 1971-72; research registrar Central Middlesex Hosp., London, 1972-75; sr. registrar Edinburgh Royal Infirmary/U. Edinburgh, Scotland, 1975-80; cons. physician Cumberland Infirmary, Carlisle, Eng., 1980—. Author: (with Connechan and Shanley) Pharmacology for Nurses, 1983; also articles. Fellow Royal Soc. Medicine, Royal Coll. Physicians-Edinburgh; men. Brit. Cardiac Soc., Brit. Pharmacology Soc., Med. Research Soc., Brit. Med. Assn. (div. pres. 1984-86). Avocations: outdoor activities, music. Home: Glencairn House, Heads Nook, Carlisle CA4 9AA, England Office: Cumberland Infirmary, Newtown Rd, Carlisle CA2 7HY, England

ROBSON, ROSS MCKENZIE, barrister, Queen's Counsel; b. Hamilton, July 20, 1946; s. Stanley George and Bessie Winifred (McKenzie) R.; m. Kathyrn Mary Symes, Jan. 14, 1974 (div. 1990); children: David Ninian Morgan McKenzie, Jessie Kathryn Frances McKenzie; m. Maureen Patricia Stockdale, Jan. 15, 1994; children: Victoria Isabella McKenzie, Antonia Jane McKenzie. Ed., Hamilton Coll., The Geelong Coll., Ormond Coll., London U., U. Melbourne. Articles Mallesons, 1971; barrister, solicitor Supreme Ct. of Victoria, 1973—; assoc. to justice of the High Ct. Australia, 1972; pupil master Mr. J.D. Merralls Order of Australia, QC, 1988—; pres. MUFS, 1969; tutor in fin. acctg. U. Melbourne, 1971, tutor in property law RMIT, 1971; auditor Ormond Coll. Students Coun., 1971-72; chmn. Barfund Pty. Ltd., 1997—; bd. dirs. So. Ind. Liquor Groups Australia Ltd. Contbr. articles to profl. jours. Mem. Melbourne Film Festival Com., 1969-71; treas. UNIFED Film Found., 1970-73; trustee Victorian Bar Superannuation Fund, 1980-94; dir. Barristers' Chmbers Ltd., 1994, chmn., 1998—. Mem. Order of Australia, Melbourne Club, Australian Club, Hamilton Club, Essoign, Melbourne U. Boat Club, Melbourne Cricket Club, Victorian Racing Club. Avocations: reading, film, rowing. Office: Owen Dixon Chambers West, 205 William St, Melbourne 3000, Australia Home: 74 Gipps St, East Melbourne VIC 3002, Australia

ROBULE, VESMA HERBERTA, neurologist; b. Ledurga, Latvia, Jan. 9, 1945; d. Herberts and Herta (Terina) Robulis. Grad., Med. Sch. for Nurses, Cesis, Latvia, 1962; MD, Med. Inst., Riga, Latvia, 1980, PhD, 1987. Lic. neurologist, sonographer. Nurse Dist. Hosp., Cesis, Latvia, 1963-65; with Riga Med. Inst. P. Stradins Republic Hosp., Latvia, 1965-71, Riga Med. Inst. P. Stradins Pub. Hosp., Latvia; neurologist Dist. Hosp., Cesis, Latvia, 1972-74, The 7th and 1st Riga City Hosps., Riga, 1975-86; researcher, sr. researcher Riga Med. Inst., 1974-80; chief researcher Med. Acad. Latvia, Riga, 1981-93; neurologist outpatients' clinic Riga Rwy., 1993—; cons. The Baltic and Nordic Stroke Project, Latvia, 1993—; lectr. Med. Acad. Latvia, Assn. Neurology Latvia, Riga, 1980-93; participant symposia World Congress Ultrasound in Medicine, Copenhagen, 1991, European Congress Ultrasound in Medicine, Vienna, 1993, 3rd World Stroke Congress, 5th European Stroke Conf., Munich, 1996. Author: Echopulsography of Cerebral Arteries, 1982 (Latvian Prize in Sci. 1980), 1st European Congress of Neurology, 1988, 4th Interantional Conference on Headache, 1989 (Silver Prize Trade Exhbn. of USSR 1989). Mem. Assn. Neurologists Latvia, Soc. Psychosomatology Latvia, Internat. Headache Soc., World Fedn. Neurology, Internat. Soc. Environ. Epidemiology. Lutheran. Avocations: travel, music, reading, photography, gardening. Home: PO Box 168, LV 1082 Riga Latvia

ROBY, B. ANDREW, music educator; b. Harlan, Ky., July 23, 1959; s. Billy E. and Bobbie Z. (Gatewood) R.; m. Mary D. Martin, June 23, 1982; children: Rachel Karis, David Andrew. MusB, Union U., 1981; M in Ch. Music, So. Bapt. Theol. Sem., 1985, D in Musical Arts., 1991. Mem. faculty Asbury Coll., Wilmore, Ky., 1987-90, Shorter Coll., Rome, Ga., 1990-93, Union U., Jackson, Tenn., 1993—; chair dept. music Union U., Jackson, 1994—. Conductor chorus, vocal soloist recitals. Interim min. music 1st Baptist Ch., Savannah, Tenn., 1993-94, Paris, Tenn., 1994-96, Ripley, Tenn., 1998-99, Jackson, 1999—, Meridian Bapt. Ch., Jackson, 1996-98, 1st Bapt. Ch., Jackson, 1999—; v.p. Andrew Jackson Sch. PTO, Jackson, 1996-97. Mem. Nat. Assn. Tchrs. Singing (state chair auditions 1989-90, state gov. 1997—) Am. Choral Dirs. Assn. (editor newsletter 1993-98), Rotary. Democrat. Avocations: racquetball, bicycling, traveling. Home: 201 Laurie Cir Jackson TN 38305-3046 Office: Union U 1050 Union U Dr Jackson TN 38305

ROBY, JOE LINDELL, investment banker; b. Metropolis, Ill., May 22, 1939; s. Gerald C. and Inez (DeLaine) R.; m. Elizabeth Shute, June 17, 1967 (dec. Oct. 1980); m. Hilppa Pirila, June 15, 1984. BA cum laude, Vanderbilt U., 1961; MBA with distinction, Harvard U., 1967. Asst. v.p. Kidder, Peabody & Co., N.Y.C., 1967-72; v.p. Donaldson, Lufkin & Jenrette, N.Y.C., 1972-75, sr. v.p., 1976-83, mng. dir. investment banking, 1984-89, chair. banking grp., 1989-95, coo, 1995-99, pres., 1996-99, ceo, pres., 1999-; bd. dirs. Sybron, Inc., Muskland Group, Inc. Served to lt. USN, 1961-65. Mem. Down Town Assn., Bond Club of N.Y. Club: Down Town Assn. (N.Y.C.). Office: Donaldson Lufkin & Jenrette, Inc 277 Park Ave Fl 7 New York NY 10172-3400

ROBY, PAMELA ANN, sociology educator; b. Milw., Nov. 17, 1942; d. Clark Dearborn and Marianna (Gilman) R.; m. James Peter Mulherin, July 15, 1977 (div. 1987). BA, U. Denver, 1963; MA, Syracuse U., 1966; PhD, NYU, 1971. Instrn. ednl. sociology NYU, 1966; asst. prof. George Washington U., Washington, 1970-71; asst. prof. sociology and social welfare Brandeis U., Waltham, Mass., 1971-73; chair cmty. studies bd. U. Calif., Santa Cruz, 1974-76, 79, assoc. prof., 1973-77, prof. sociology and women's studies, 1977—, dir. sociology grad. program, 1988-91, chair sociology dept., 1998—; vis. scholar U. Wash., Seattle, 1991-92; mem. anthropology, linguistics and sociology panel NSF, Washington, 1993; mem. sociology doctoral program com. Northeastern U., Boston, 1990; assessor Social Scis. and Humanities Rsch. Coun. Can., Toronto, 1993; cons. James Irvine Found., San Francisco, 1986; vice chair Nat. Commn. on Working Women, Washington, 1977-80; mem. social sci. rsch. rev. com. NIMH, Washington, 1976-78; re-evaluation counselor (coll. and U. faculty reference person), 1980—. Author: Women in the Workplace, 1981; editor: The Poverty Establishment, 1974, Child Care: Who Cares? Foreign and Domestic Infant and Early Childhood Development Policies, 1973-75; co-author: The Future of Inequality, 1970; adv. editor: Sociol. Quar., 1990-93, Gender and Society, 1986-89. Andrew W. Mellon sr. scholar Wellesley Coll., 1978-79; vis. fellow Indian Coun. Social Sci. Rsch., 1979. Mem. Soc. for Study Social Problems (pres. 1996-97), Sociologists for Women in Soc. (pres. 1978-80), Am. Sociol. Assn. (chair sect. on sex and gender 1974-78, exec. coun. mem.-at-large 1975-78), Internat. Sociol. Assn. (rsch. coun. mem.-at-large 1978-82), Pacific Sociol. Assn. (v.p. (1996-97), Ea. Sociol. Assn. (exec. coun. mem.-at-large 1973-74), Re-evaluation Counseling (internat. ref. person for coll. and univ. faculty), Phi Beta Kappa, Alpha Kappa Delta. Avocations: camping, hiking, painting, swimming, pen and ink drawing. Office: U Calif Dept Sociology C8 Santa Cruz CA 95064

ROCARD, MICHEL LOUIS LÉON, French politician; b. Courbevoie, France, Aug. 23, 1930; s. Yves Rocard and Renée Favre; m. Michèle Legendre, 1972; children: Sylvie, Francis, Olivier, Loïc. Ed., U. Paris, Ecole

Nat. Adminstrn. Nat. sec. Parti Socialiste Unifié, 1967-73; dep. to Nat. Assembly, Paris, 1969-73, 78-81; mem. Parti Socialiste, 1974, mem. exec. bur., 1975-81, nat. sec. in charge of pub. sector, 1975-79; mayor Conflans-Sainte-Honorine, 1977-94; minister state, minister planning and regional devel. France, Paris, 1981-83, minister agr., 1983-85, prime minister, 1988-91; 1st sec. Parti Socialiste, Paris, 1994—; mem. European Parliament, 1994—, senator, 1995-97. Address: 266 Blvd St Germain, 75007 Paris France*

ROCCA, MARIO AGOSTINO, physics educator; b. Genoa, Italy, June 27, 1956; s. Luigi Piero Rocca and Angela Gennaro; m. Franca Debandi, Dec. 18, 1987; children: Ilaria, Martino. Laurea in fisica, U. Genoa, 1981; PhD in Physics, Tech. Hochschule, Aachen, Germany, 1985. Ricercatore Dept. di fisica, Genoa, 1984-92, assoc. prof., 1992—; cons. Surface Sci. Divsn. Italian Inst. Physics of Matter, 1991—. Sec. Union of Scientists for Disarmament, Genoa, 1990—. Recipient award of sci. productivity Soc. Italian di Fisica, 1988. Avocations: ski alpinism, mountaineering. Address: CNR Ctr Fis Superf & Basse, Via Dodecaneso 33, 16146 Genoa Italy

ROCCHI, MARC CHRISTIAN, engineering educator; b. Paris, July 14, 1948; s. Ottavio and Geneviève (Guimard) R.; m. Margriet Van der Plaats, Nov. 29, 1974; children: Alice, Mathieu, Camille. Degree in Elec. Engring., Ecole Sup. d'Electricité, Paris, 1942; Diploma in Physics and Materials, U. Paris, 1972. Rsch. engr. Philips Rsch. France, 1976-82, GaAs IC group leader, 1982-88; rsch. group leader Philips Rsch. Netherlands, 1988-90; gen. mgr. Philips Microwave, Limeil, France, 1990—; prof. Inst. Sup. d'Electronique de Paris, 1974-76, 80-88, Ecole Sup. d'informatique et d'electronique, France, 1992-95; tchr. electromagnetic field theory Algiers U., 1972-74. Author, editor: High Speed Digital IC Technology, 1990; contbr. articles to profl. jours.; patentee in field. Mem. IEEE (sr.), SEE (sr.). Avocations: astronomy, golf, foreign languages, wine tasting. Office: Labs d'Electronique Philips, 22 Ave Descartes, 94453 Limeil Brevannes France

ROČEK, ZBYNĚK J., paleontologist, researcher; b. Litomyšl, Bohemia, Czech Republic, Aug. 16, 1945; s. Josef and Karolina (Minaříková) R.; m. Jana Berná, July 3, 1970; 1 child, Hana. Grad. in biology, Charles U., Prague, Czech Republic, 1968, rerum naturalium doctor, 1972, PhD, 1981, DSc, 1991. Curator Regional Mus., Rychnov N.K., Czech Republic, 1969-75; asst. prof. Charles U., 1975-87, assoc. prof., 1981-91; sr. rschr. Acad. Scis., Prague, 1997—; dir. World Congress of Herpetology, Prague, 1994-98. Co-author: Život, 1986 (Book of Yr. award 1987). Grantee Swedish House, 1989, Conseil Régional Rhone-Alpes, 1992, Deutsche Akademische Austauschdienst, 1994. Mem. Soc. European Herpetology (chmn. organizing com. 1983-85), Czech Herpetological Soc. (v.p. 1992—). Avocation: horse racing. Home: Nad Vavrouskou 17/696, 181 00 Prague Czech Republic Office: Acad Scis, Vinicna 7, 128440 Prague Czech Republic

ROCES, ALEJANDRO REYES, journalist, educator; b. Manila, Philippines, July 13, 1924; s. Rafael Gonzlez and Inocencia Batista (Reyes) R.; m. Irene Viola, June 25, 1950; 1 child, Elizabeth. BFA, U. Az.; MA, Far Eastern U., Philippines; PhD (hon.), Tokyo U.; DHL, Ateneo de Manila. Dean inst. arts & scis. Far Eastern U., Manila, 1955-61; chmn. bd. regents U. Philippines, Manila, 1962-66; sec. edn. Republic Philippines, Manila, 1962-66; chmn. Colegio de San Agustin, Makati, Philippines, 1966—, St. Louis U., Baguio, Philippines, 1966—; pres. Bulletin Pub. Corp., Manila; chmn./pres. CAP Coll., Manila, U. City Manila; dir. CAP Philippines, CAP Pension. Author: (books) Cocks and Kites, Something to Crow About, 1997. Founder Lakas Ng Bayan, Manila, 1986. Recipient SEA Writing awardee, HRH Crown Prince Vajiralongkorn, Thialand, 1997, Conde de Foxa award, Bilbao, Spain. Founder Internat. PEN. Avocations: reading, writing, walking, weight-lifting. Office: CAP Bldg, 126 Amorsolo St Legaspi, Makati Philippines

ROCH, LEWIS MARSHALL, II, ophthalmic surgeon, medical entrepreneur; b. Mineola, Tex., Aug. 13, 1934; s. Lewis Marshall and Gladys Irene (Hoover) R.; m. Lois Afton Price; children: Lewis Marshall Roch III, Katrina Ann Seitz. BA, U. Tex., Austin, 1955; MD, U. Tex. Southwestern, 1959. Diplomate Am. Bd. Ophthalmology. Intern USPHS Hosp., Boston, 1959-60; resident in ophthalmology USPHS Hosp., New Orleans, 1960-63, dep. chief ophthalmology, 1963-64; chief opthalmology USPHS Hosp., Seattle, Wash., 1964-67; attending ophthalmic surgeon Ball Meml. Hosp., Muncie, Ind., 1967—; chmn. dept. surgery Ball Meml. Hosp., Muncie, chmn. clin. staff, 1975, chmn. exec. com., 1980-93; founder, CEO, med. dir. The Eye Ctr. Group, Muncie, 1985—, 1985—; founder, CEO, med. dir. The Surgi Ctr. Group, Muncie, 1985—; ho. of dels. Ind. State Med. Assn., 1975-87; exec. com. Ind. Acad. Ophthalmology, 1978-82; bd. dirs. Ball Meml. U., Muncie, 1984-90; clin. asst. prof. Ind. U. Sch. Medicine, 1978—; bd. dirs. Primary Care Delivery Corp. Chmn. Muncie-Delaware Devel., 2000—; mem. Ball State U. Bus. Forecasting Roundtalbe, 2000—. Comdr. USPHS, 1959-67. Fellow ACS, Am. Acad. Ophthalmology; mem. AMA, Ind. State Med. Assn., Muncie Acad. Medicine (pres. 1981-82), Am. Soc. Cataract and Refractive Surgeons, Am. Coll. Physicians Execs., Muncie-Delaware C. of C. (bd. dirs. 1999—). Republican. Achievements include pioneering work in outpatient ambulatory surgery; innovation in intraocular lens implantation in cataract surgery; integration of physician's practices with hospital health care delivery systems. Avocations: treaking, gardening, woodworking. Home: 2006 E Robinwood Dr Muncie IN 47304-2857 Office: The Eye Ctr Group LLC 200 N Tillotson Ave Muncie IN 47304-3988

ROCH, PHILIPPE GERARD, developmental immunologist, researcher; b. St. Pierre d'Irube, France, Aug. 11, 1949; children: Florence, Anne-Catherine. M, U. Bordeaux, France, 1971; DSc, U. Bordeaux, 1980. Asst. prof. Med. U., Bordeaux, 1973; asst. prof. Nat. Ctr. Sci. Rsch. (CNRS), Bordeaux, 1974-80; asst. prof. Nat. Ctr. Sci. Rsch. (CNRS), 1983-90, rsch. dir., 1991-92; postdoctoral fellow UCLA, 1981-82; lab. dir. Inst. French Rsch. Expl. Mer-CNRS, Montpellier, France, 1993—; coord. Erasmus program European Union, 1985-92, European Union expert, 1995-96; cons. Univ. Nat. Coun., Paris, 1986-91. Author: Invertebrate Models: Cell Receptors, 1987, Defense Mechanisms and Disease Prevention in Aquacultural Invertebrates; co-author, editor: Collection de Biologie Evolutive, 1993; co-author: Immunology of Annelids, 1994, Modulators of Immune Responses, 1996; contbr. over 100 articles to profl. jours.; inventor of antibiotic peptides in mollusks. Founding pres. Socio-Cultural Soc., Bordeaux, 1976-81. Postdoctoral fellow NATO, 1981-82. Mem. Internat. Soc. Devel. and Comparative Immunology, Am. Soc. Zoologists, French Soc. Immunology, French Soc. Zoologists. E-mail: proch@ifremer.fr. Office: U Montpellier 2, CC 080 Pl Eugene Bataillon, 34095 Montpellier France

ROCHA, CARLOS SERGIO, marine chemistry researcher; b. Lourenço Marques, Mozambique, Oct. 7, 1969; arrived in Portugal, 1980; s. Ilidio José and Rosa Borges de Carvalho Rocha; m. Raquel Coelho Lavado, Oct. 4, 1998. BSc, U. Lisbon, Portugal, 1988, MSc, 1991, PhD in Marine Scis., 1997. Jr. rschr. Faculty Pharmacy, Lisbon, 1991-92; jr. rschr., technician Inst. Potuguese Investigation Marinha, Lisbon, 1991-93; tchr. Secondary Sch., Lisbon, 1995-97; postdoctoral rsch. asst. U. Algarve, Faro, Portugal, 1997—; sci. ctr. Ctr. for Marine and Environ. Rsch., Faro, 1999—. Contbr. articles to profl. jours. Recipient Sci. prize Gulbenkian Found., Portugal, 1998, Luiz Saldanha Sci. prize IMAR, Portugal, 1999; PhD grantee FCT Found. for Sci. and Tech., Lisbon, 1993, postdoctoral grantee FCT-Found. for Sci. and Tech., Faro, 1997. Mem. Am. Soc. Limnology and Oceanography, N.Y. Acad. Sci. Avocations: fishing, painting, writing, martial arts. Home: Casa Genoveva Apt 187, 8000 Santa Barbara Nexe Faro, Portugal Office: Univ Algarve, Campus de Gambelas, 8000-062 Faro Portugal

ROCHA, DARRELL DEAN, dean; b. Corpus Christi, Tex., Aug. 9, 1956; s. Louis and Nickie R.; m. Mary A.; 1 child, Grace D. BA in Govt., U. Tex., Austin, 1981. Adminstrv. clk. coll. comm. U. Tex., Austin, 1981-83, degree plannng evaluator II, 1983-92, asst. dean minority affairs, 1992-96, asst. dean student affairs, 1996—. Mem. Nat. Assn. Hispanic Journalists, Nat. Acad. Advising Assn., U. Tex. Hispanic Faculty.Staff Assn. (chair 1995), Hispanic C. of C. Roman Catholic. Avocations: painting, tennis, classical music. Home: 1406 Romeria Dr Austin TX 78757-3320 Office: U Tex Coll Comm CMA 4.140 Student Affairs Austin TX 78712

ROCHA, PAULO ROBERTO, hemodynamicist, cardiologist; b. Rio de Janeiro, Nov. 1, 1936; arrived in France, 1966; s. Ulysses and Sylvia (Lopes) R. MD, Med. Sch., Rio de Janeiro, 1961; cardiologist, Heart Inst., Rio de Janeiro, 1963; MD, cardiologist, Paris V, 1976, physiologist, 1983. Chef de travaux des univ. U. Paris V, 1983-90, maitre de confs. des univ., 1990—. Contbr. chpts. to books and articles to profl. jours. Home: 10 Imp du Mont Tonnerre, 75015 Paris France Office: Hosp Ambroise Pare, 9 av Charles du Gaulle, 92104 Boulgne Billancourt France

ROCHAT, JEAN-PAUL, translator, business owner; b. Oran, Algeria, North Africa, Feb. 22, 1943; s. Lucien Henri and Manuela (Luis) R.; m. Alice Staeheli, Apr. 26, 1965; children: Janine Alice, Marcel Jean-Paul. Swiss and French Nat. Lycée Francais, Sch. Interpreters, Zurich, 1966; PhD, Sussex Coll. Tech., Eng., 1972; D honoris causa, Thomas Jefferson U., 1984; D (hon.) en Ciencias Linguisticas, U. El Salvador, 1985; D honoris causa en Ciencias Sociales, U. Politècnica El Salvador, 1986; PhD in Linguistics, World U.; Dr. honoris causa en filosofia, U. Poly. de el Salvador, 1988, U. Prague, 1989; LittD (hon.), Pacific So. U., 1989; PhD (hon.), Meridian U., 1991. Interpreter, translator Wild Heerbrugg AG, 1961-63; translator Pro Jurentute, Zurich, 1964, F. Hoffman-La Roche & Co., S.A., Basle, Switzerland, 1965; translator, asst. mgr. Doetsch, Grether & Co. AG, Basle, 1966; translator, sales mgr. Agence Economique et Financiere, Zurich, 1967; owner Rochat Translation Agy., 1961—; adj. prof. Meridian U., 1991—. Author: La Traduction en Suisse, 1972. Nominated non. consul Burkina Faso, Cameroon in Switzerland, Swaziland. Named a hon. col. a.d.c. Ala. State Militia, 1985, Chevalier de l'Ordre Impèrial Byzantin de Constantin le Grand, Chevalier World Parliament Confedn. Chivalry. Mem. Swiss Assn. Translator and Interpreter (founder), Swiss Assn. Translation Agys. (pres. 1983), Société Française des Traducteurs, Verband der Uebersetzungsbüros e.V. Home: Seestrasse 231, 8700 Kusnacht Zurich Switzerland

ROCHE, BERNARD PIERRE, nuclear engineer; b. Grenople, Isere, France, Jan. 21, 1948; s. François Jean and Georgette Marie (Bechier) R.; m. Daniele Lucienne Patyn, Sept. 5, 1970; 1 child, Anne-Bernadette. Student, Sch. Mines Paris, 1967-71, 73. Cert. profl. eng. Branch head Ministry of Industry, Lyon, France, 1973-81; reg. dir. Ministry of Industry, Nantes, France, 1981-88; dep. dir. Electricite De France-Dist., Le Mans, France, 1988-89; reg. dir. Electricite De France-Dist., Dijon, France, 1989-93; gen. mgr. Electricite de France Septen, Lyon, 1993-99; v.p. engring. divsn. Electricite de France, Paris, 1999—; nuclear safety inspector Govt., Paris, 1974-88; chmn. Reactor Safety Working Group European Cmty., 1996-98; chmn. Safety Commn. Internat. Nuclear Socs. Coun., 1997—; chmn. European Utilities Requirement Steering Com., 1997—. Author: La Societe De Partenariat, 1988. Lt. Artillery, 1971-72, Paris. Recipient Medal of Merit French Govt., 1987. Mem. Am. Nuclear Soc. Roman Catholic. Avocations: geology, electric guitar. Home: 4 Rue de SFax, 75116 Paris France Office: Engring Divsn CAP AMPERE, 1 Pl Pleyel, 93282 Saint Denis Cedex, France

ROCHE, GERARD RAYMOND, management consultant; b. Scranton, Pa., July 27, 1931; s. Joseph Arthur and Amelia Jane (Garcia) R.; m. Marie Terotta, Apr. 27, 1957; children: Mary Margaret, Anne Elizabeth, Paul Joseph. B.S. in Acctg., U. Scranton, 1953; M.B.A., NYU, 1958. Mgmt. trainee AT&T, Phila., 1955-56; account exec. ABC-TV, N.Y.C., 1956-58; sales and mktg. positions Kordite Corp. subs. Mobil Oil Co., Macedon, N.Y., 1959-63; assoc. Heidrick & Struggles, Inc., N.Y.C., 1964-68, ptnr., 1968—, mgr. N.Y., 1968-73, mgr. East, 1973-77; pres., chief exec. officer Heidrick & Struggles, Inc., N.Y.C., 1978-81; chmn. Heidrick & Struggles, Inc., N.Y.C., 1981-2000; sr. chmn. Heidrick & Struggles, Inc., 2000—; bd. dirs. Value Am. Corp. Former trustee Cath. U. Am., U. Scranton; bd. dirs. Covenant House, N.Y.C. Served to lt. USN, 1953-55. Mem. Univ. Club, Sky Club, Yale Club, Sleepy Hollow Country Club (bd. govs.), Blind Brook Club, The Golf Club of Purchase, Loblolly Pines C. C., Knights of Malta, Alpha Sigma Nu (past treas.), Community Anti-Drug Coalitions of America (bd. dirs.). Roman Catholic. Office: Heidrick & Struggles Inc 245 Park Ave Fl 43 New York NY 10167-0152

ROCHE, GILLES, pharmaceutical company executive; b. Grenoble, France, Dec. 25, 1949; s. Marcel François and Janine (Fossenagne) R.; m. Anne-Marie Gatel, June 23, 1973; children: Caroline, Julien, Benjamine. MS in Biostatistics, 1973, MS in Pharmacology, 1981, MS in Microbiology, 1981, MD, 1974. Resident Nancy U. Hosp., 1973-79, asst. des Kapikaux and chief of clinic, 1979-83; rsch. mgr. Sanofi, France, 1983-87; med. dir. Pharmuka (RP), France, 1987-92; sr. dir. Rhône Poulenc Rorer, Antony, 1992-97, v.p., 1997—, dir., 1987—. Contbr. over 120 articles to profl. jours.; patentee in field. Mem. Am. Soc. Microbiology, French Internal Medicine Soc. Avocations: sports, reading, philately. Home: 246 rue de Charenton, 75012 Paris France Office: Rhône-Poulenc Rorer, 20 Ave Raymond Aron, 92165 Antony France

ROCHE, JOAN I., artist; b. Hamilton, Ont., Can., Jan. 21, 1935; came to U.S., 1964; d. Thomas Dick and Florence (Eaves) Bowman; m. E. Michael Roche, Jan. 23, 1954; 1 child, Wayne P. Grad., Can. Bus. Coll., 1952, Coll. of Marin, 1968, Irvine Valley Coll., 1986. Various secretarial and adminstrv. positions, 1952-70. Exhibited in numerous shows, including Irvine Valley Coll., 1986, Pa. Watercolor Soc. (award of merit 1990), Catharine Lorrilard Art Club, N.Y., Niagara Frontier Watercolor Soc., N.Y., Rocky Mountain Nat. Watermedia Exhibit, Colo., Costa Mesa (Calif.) Fine Arts Competition (People's Choice award), Irvine Art Ctr., 1991, 92, Newport Beach Salute to Arts, Arts on the Green, Costa Mesa, Ariz. Aqueous VIII, Irvine Creative Arts Show (Best of Show), Irvine Fine Art League (1st Pl. award), Watercolor Art Soc., Tex., Art Show at the Dog Show, Kans., Brush With Nature, Newport Beach (Best of Show award), Am. Watercolor Soc., N.Y., Watercolor West, Nat. Watercolor Soc., 1995 (Watercolor West award), Nat. Watercolor Soc. Signature Mem. Show, 1996, Fallbrook Art Assn. Fall All Media Show (Best of Show), Fallbrook Art Assn. (Spring All Media Show (Best of Show), Adirondacks Nat. Exhbn., 1997, Am. Watercolor Soc. (Winsor and Newton award 1998), Am. Watercolor Soc., 2000; contbr. to books: Places in Watercolor, Painting Shapes and Edges, How To Capture Movement in Your Painting, Ency. of Flower Painting Techniques, Watercolor Planning & Painting, Splash 6. Mem. Nat. Watercolor Soc. (Signature, 2d v.p. bd. dirs., travel show chair 1996, 97, Am. Watercolor (signature),Fallbrook Art Assn., San Diego Watercolor Soc., Laguna Niguel Art Assn. Avocation: reading, gardening. Home: 1149 McDonald Rd Fallbrook CA 92028-3548

ROCHE, KEVIN (EAMONN ROCHE), architect; b. Dublin, Ireland, June 14, 1922; came to U.S., 1948, naturalized, 1964; s. Eamon and Alice (Harding) R.; m. Jane Tuohy, June 10, 1963; children: Eamon, Paud, Denis, Anne, Alice. B.Arch., Nat. U. Ireland, 1945; D.Sc. (hon.), Nat. U. Ireland, 1977; postgrad., Ill. Inst. Tech., 1948; D.F.A. (hon.), Wesleyan U., 1981; Yale U., 1995. With Eero Saarinen and Assocs., Hamden, Conn., 1950-66; partner Kevin Roche John Dinkeloo and Assocs., Hamden, from 1966. Prin. works include Ford Found. Hdqs., 1967, Oakland (Calif.) Mus, 1968, Met. Mus. Art, N.Y.C., Creative Arts Ctr., Wesleyan U., Middletown, Conn., 1971, Fine Arts Ctr., U. Mass., 1971, Union Carbide Corp. World Hdqs., Conn., Gen. Foods Corp. Hdqs., Rye, N.Y., 1977, 1978, Conoco Inc. Hdqs., Houston, 1979, Central Pk. Zoo, N.Y.C., 1980, DeWitt Wallace Mus. Fine Arts, Williamsburg, Va., 1980, Bouygues World Hdqs., Paris, 1983, J.P. Morgan and Co. Hdqs., N.Y.C., 1983, UNICEF Hdqrs., N.Y.C., 1984, Leo Burnett Co. Hdqs., Chgo., 1985, Corning (N.Y.) Inc. Hdqs., 1986, Merck & Co. Headquarters, N.J., 1987, Dai Ichi Hdqs./Norinchukin Bank Hdqrs., Tokyo, 1989, Nations Bank Hdqs., Atlanta, 1989, Pontiac Marina Pvt. Ltd., Singapore, 1990, Metropolitano, Madrid, 1990, Borland Internat. Headquarters, Scotts Valley, Calif., 1990, Tanjong & Binariang/Ampang Tower, Kuala Lumpur, Malaysia, 1993, Mus. of Jewish Heritage Holocaust Meml., N.Y.C., 1993, Tata Cummins Pvt. Ltd., Jamshedpur, India, 1994, Vis. Ctr., Columbus, Ind., 1994, Cummins Engine Co. APEX Mfg. Facility, 1994, Lucent Techs. Hdqs., Murray Hill, N.J., 1996, Wuxi Newage Cummins, Wuxi, China, 1996, Total Sys. Svcs. Corp. Headquarters, Columbus, Ga., 1997. Mem. Fine Arts Commn., Washington; trustee Am. Acad. in Rome, 1968-71, Woodrow Wilson Center for Scholars in Smithsonian Instn. Recipient Creative Arts award Brandeis U., 1967; A.S. Bard award City Club N.Y., 1968, 77, 79; award Gov. of Calif., 1968; N.Y. State award Citizens Union N.Y., 1968; total design award Am. Soc. Interior Design; Pritzker Archtl. prize, 1982; Albert S. Bard award, 1990. Fellow AIA (medal of honor N.Y. chpt. 1968, Gold Medal award 1993, 25-yr. award 1995), AAAS; mem. NAD (academician), AAAL (pres. 1994-97), Am. Acad. Arts and Letters (Brunner award 1965, Gold medal 1990), Académie d'Architecture (Grand Gold medal 1977), Mcpl. Art Soc. N.Y. (Brendan Gill prize 1989), Acad. di San Luca. Office: Kevin Roche John Dinkeloo & Assoc PO Box 6127 20 Davis St Hamden CT 06517-3501

ROCHELLE, LUGENIA, academic administrator; b. Maple Hill, N.C., July 14, 1943; d. John Edward and Ruby Lee (Holmes) R. BA, St. Augustine's Coll., 1965; MS, N.C. A & T State U., 1969; D of Pedagogy, Barbar-Scotia Coll., 1993. Cert. tchr., N.C. Tchr. French, English Butler High Sch., Barnwell, S.C., 1965-67; instr. English N.C. A & T State U., Greensboro, 1970-77; instr. English St. Augustine's Coll., Raleigh, N.C., 1977-86, dir. freshman studies program, 1986-91, dean lower coll., 1991-95, asst. to v.p. acad. affairs, 1991-92; dir. gen. studies, asst. prof. English Voorhees Coll., Denmark, S.C., 1996-98, spl. asst. to pres. external affairs, 1999—, dir. Hons. Coll., 1999—; dir. Mellon program St. Augustine's Coll., Raleigh, 1980-83; adv. bd. cooperating Raleigh Colls., 1986—, Off to Coll., Montgomery, Ala., 1993—; mem. profl. practices commn. N.C. Dept. Pub. Instrn., 1994—; coord. Title III, coord. Bd. Trustees Rels.; dir. Ctr. Excellence in Humanities. Author: English Manual of Writing, 1980, (with others) Off to College, 1997, 98, reprint 1999 edit.; editor: Can't Nobody Do You Like Jesus, 1998. Judge oratorical contests, Optimist Club, Raleigh, 1985-93; chair pro tem Raleigh Bicentennial Hist. Com., Raleigh, 1991-92; initiated, effected chartering of Phi Eta Sigma St. Augustine's Coll., 1995; bd. dirs. Garner Rd. YMCA, Raleigh, 1994—; coord. Honda Campus All-Star Challenge, 1996—; lay min., sec. vestry St. Philip's Episcopal Ch., 1997—; instnl. rep. S.C. Women in Higher Edn., Voorhees Coll., 1998—. Nat. teaching fellow N.C. A & T State U., Greensboro, 1968-70. NCTE. Fellow Nat. Coun. Tchrs. English; mem. ASCD (assoc.), Profl. Practices Commn. N.C. State Dept. Pub. Instrn., Cardinal Club. Avocations: reading, collecting antique birds, traveling.

ROCHETTE, BRUNO ROBERT JEAN ARMAND GHISLAIN, classicist, researcher, educator; b. Namur, Belgium, June 27, 1965; s. Robert Rochette and Amabile Cambruzzi. Lic. in Classic Philology, 1987, D in Philosophy and Letters, 1994. Sci. collaborator dept. philosophy of antiquity and moral philosophy U. Liège, Belgium, 1991-93; candidate dept. Latin langs. and lit. Nat. Found. Sci. Rsch., U. Liè, 1993-95, head rsch. dept. Latin langs. and lit., 1995-97; in charge course Nat. Found. Sci. Rsch., U. Liege, 1997—; rschr. Hardt Found. for the Study of Antiquity, Geneva, 1993, 95, Acad. Belgica Rome, 1994, 95, 97, 98, 99, City U., Paris, 1994; lectr. U. Fribourg, Switzerland, 1996, Acad. Belgica Rome (commemoration of Franz Cumont), 1997; presenter in field. Author: Le Latin dans le Monde Grec: Recherches sur la Diffusion de la Langue et des Lettres Latines dans les Provinces Hellénophones de l'Empire Romain,1997; collaborator, mentor: Guide Bibliographique de la Religion Grecque Antique, 1992, 98; contbr. over 50 articles to profl. jours. Recipient Lauréat du Concours des Bourses de Voyage, 1988, Prix Gantrelle Acad. Royal Belgique, 1996-97. Mem. Belgian Soc. Byzantine Studies, Ctr. Internat. Study of Greek Antique Religion. Home: 7 Rue Lonhienne, B-4000 Liege Belgium Office: U Liè Class Langs-Lits, 32 Place du XX-Août, B-4000 Liege Belgium

ROCHETTE, JEAN-FRANÇOIS, bank executive; b. Paris, Mar. 15, 1939; s. Gilbert Gustave and Aileen (Duvillard) R.; m. Veronique Turettini, Apr. 15, 1967; children: Coraline, Sylvie, Gabriel. Comml. Maturite, Ecole Superieure Commerce, Geneva, 1960; lic. in econ. sci., U. Geneva, 1964, lic. in polit. sci., 1966; cert. of fin., N.Y. Inst. of Fin., N.Y.C., 1970. Cert. economist, banker. Exec. trainee First Nat. City Bank, Geneva, N.Y.C., 1967-69; v.p. Lombard Odier Cie, Geneva, 1970-81; sr. v.p. Cramer Cie, Geneva, 1980-83; dep. pres. United Overseas Bank, Geneva, 1983-93; owner, investment counselor J.Fr. Rochette Assocs., Geneva, 1993—; bd. dirs. Banque Patrimoines Prives Geneve, Banque Commerciale et de Placement S.A., Geneve, Media Passage, Inc. USA, Quantum Biotechnologies, Inc. (Can.), S.C.C. at Lloyd's (U.K.); mem. adv. bd. Revi Suisse Price Waterhouse. Contbr. econ. articles to newspapers; temp. corr. Jour. Geneva à New York, 1969. Gen. treas. World Alliance of Reformed Chs., Geneva, 1976-96; v.p. Bur. of Families, Geneva, 1975—; mem. ctrl. bur. Parti Liberal, Geneva, 1981-89; hon. pres. Amis de Pugwash, Geneva, 1978—; mem. exec. com. John Knox Orgn., Geneva, 1975-96. Col. gen. staff Swiss mil., comdr. Geneva regiment, 1960—. Recipient Prix Lyon's 1965 Geneva, Lyon's Club, 1965; named hon. pres. Assn. Liberale Champel, Geneva, 1979, Entente Liberale Bellevue. Mem. Soc. Militaire Geneva (gen. sec.), Golf Club Geneva, Yacht Club Geneva. Avocations: football, skiing, ice hockey, tennis. Fax: 022 312 30 24. E-mail: rochette.assoc@span.ch. Home: La Lézardière, 290 B route Lausanne, 1293 Geneva Switzerland Office: 10 b Vieux College, 1204 Geneva Switzerland

ROCHETTE, PIERRE EUGENE, geophysicist, educator; b. Ambilly, France, Dec. 20, 1960; s. Marceau Rochette and Claudie Perret; m. Nathalie Berlon, Mar. 22, 1997; children: Camille, Lucas, Etienne. MSD, Institut de Physique du Globe, Paris, 1981; PhD, U. Grenoble, France, 1988. Rschr. CNRS, Grenoble, 1985-91; prof. geophysics U. Marseille, France, 1991—. Co-author: Magnetisme, 1999; contbr. articles to profl. jours. With French armed forces, 1983-85. Named Jr. Mem. Inst. Universitaire de France, 1995. Mem. European Union Geoscis. (Outstanding Young Scientist award 1991), Am. Union Geoscis. Office: Cerege Europole l'Arbois, BP 80, 13545 Aix-En-Provence Cedex 4, France

ROCHEV, VLADIMIR EFIMOVICH, physicist, educator; b. Troitsko-Pechorsk, Russia, Aug. 20, 1947; s. Efim Efimovich and Ekaterina Stepanovna (Bessonova) R.; m. Natalia Vladimirovna Krasnokutskaya, Nov. 22, 1969; 1 child, Vladimir. PhD, Inst. High Energy Physics, Moscow, 1977, D Phys. and Math. Scis. Jr. scientist Inst. High Energy Physics, Protvino, Moscow Region, Russia, 1974-84, sr. scientist, 1984-93, head scientist, 1993-95, prin. scientist, 1995—; sr. lectr. Moscow State U., 1988—. Contbr. articles to Jour. of Physics, Nuovo Cimento, Yadernaya Fizika, others. Recipient prize for Jr. Scientists of Moscow Region, 1978, State scholarship for Scientists of Russia, 1993; Internat. Sci. Found. and Russian Founds. for Basic Rsch. grantee. Home: 14 Lenin str app 28, Protvino 142284, Russia Office: Inst High Energy Physics, Protvino Moscow region Russia 142284

ROCHFORD, CHRISTOPHER ERIC, computer consultant, educator; b. Sydney, Australia, Feb. 22, 1952; s. Violet Prentice (Hudson) R.; m. Belinda Ann Johnston, Feb. 17, 1990; children: Nicholas Eric, David Laurie, Alexandrea Violet, Ewan Nathaniel. B in Bus., Queensland U. Tech., Brisbane, Australia, 1982; MA, U. Lancaster, U.K., 1986. Mgmt. svcs. officer Dept. of Works, Brisbane, 1974-85; cons. Scott Grant Mgmt. Svcs., London, 1986-88; sr. bus. cons. State Bank of New South Wales, Sydney, Australia, 1988-91; prin. cons. Windana Cons., Sydney, 1991-97; sr. bus. analyst U. Tech., Sydney, 1997-99, Compaq, Sydney, 1999—; cons. IBM (U.K.) Ltd., North Harbor, 1986, South-East Thames Regional Health Authority, Tunbridge Wells, U.K., 1986-87, Royal Borough of Kensington and Chelsea, London, 1987-88, Philips Industries, Sydney, 1992, Australian Fed. Police, 1994, NSW Fisheries, Sydney, 1995, QANTAS, Sydney, 1995-96, We. Sydney Area Health Svc., 1996, U. Tech., Sydney, 1996-97. Mem. Assn. MBAs, Royal Agrl. Soc. NSW, Australian Computer Soc., Mosman Rowing Club. Avocations: rugby, athletics, skiing, family. Home: 7/19 Cairo St, Cammeray Sydney NSW 2062, Australia Office: Compaq, 50 Miller St, North Sydney NSW 2060, Australia

ROCHFORD, PATRICIA ANNE, executive search organization executive; b. Sydney, NSW, Australia; d. Joseph and Marie Josephine (Bishop) R.; divorced, 1977. Assoc. in Music, Sydney Conservatorium of Music, 1963; BA, U. Sydney, 1969, MA, 1977. Tchr., psychologist, counselor Dept. Edn., Sydney, 1970-77; with exec. devel. dept. IBM Australia, Sydney, 1978-80, mktg. assoc., 1979-80; mgmt. cons. Touche Ross, Sydney, 1980-82; dir. Rochford William Internat., Sydney, 1982-85, chmn., 1985-97; chmn. Rochford Internat., Sydney, 1997—; bd. dirs. found. bd. U. NSW, Sydney, Sydney Tourism Bd. Trustee Com. for Econ. Devel. Australia, 1982-91, 95-98; bd. dirs. Sydney Symphony Orch., 1992-93; mem. coun. U. New South Wales, 1993-98. Mem. Australian Psychol. Soc., Chief Exec. Women, Am. Club, U. and Schs. Club. Avocations: classical music, theater, dance, opera, reading. Office: Rochford Internat Level 28, Chifley Tower 2 Chifley Sq, Sydney NSW 2000, Australia

ROCHMAN-HALPERIN, ARIEH PINHAS, archivist; b. Haifa, Israel, Mar. 1, 1952; s. David and Ester Lea Rochman; m. Irit Halperin, Aug. 26, 1990; children: Sivan, Elior. Cert. of Laboratoria, Secondary Vocat. Sch., Haifa, 1970; 1st Degree, Ben Gurion U., Be'er Sheva', Israel, 1979. Lab. Shemen Oil Industry, Haifa, 1973, Technion-Inst. of Technology, Haifa, 1974-76, Dor Chemicals, Haifa, 1976; asst. of antiquities inspector, antiques and mus. dept. Ministry of Edn. and Culture, Jerusalem, 1979, archivist, 1981-90; head of archive br. Israel Antiquities Authority, Jerusalem, 1990—; area supr. Refa'im Excavations, Jerusalem, 1987-90, 92; asst. to area supr. Tel žArad (Israel) Excavations, 1977; area supr. David Tower Excavations, Jerusalem, 1980; supr. of excavations žEmeq Hefer Expedition, Mikhmoret-Mevo'ot Yam, Israel, 1982, excavation's dir. Horvat Ruma Excavations, Israel, 1983; excavations dep. dir. Givžat Yasaf, Israel, 1984, 85; exec. dir. Botanical Gardens, Jerusalem, 1986. Contbr. articles to profl. publs. Apprentice and guide Hashomer Hazair Youth Movement, Haifa, 1965-70. Sgt. Israeli Army, 1970-73. Recipient scholarship Zahal Invalids Orgn., 1981. Mem. House of Fighters/Jerusalem. Avocations: collecting stamps, coins and medals, bird watching, swimming. Office: Israel Antiquities Authority, PO Box 586, 91004 Jerusalem Israel

ROCK, ALLAN MICHAEL, Canadian government official; b. Ottawa, Ont., Can., Aug. 30, 1947; s. James Thomas and Anne (Torley) R.; m. Deborah Kathleen, June 24, 1983; children: Jason, Lauren, Andrew, Stephen. BA, U. Ottawa, 1968, LLB, 1971. Certified specialist in civil litigation. Sr part Fasken Campbell & Godfrey, Ottawa; min. of justice, atty. gen. Govt. of Can., 1993-97, min. of health, 1997—; treas. Law Soc. Upper Can., 1992-93; bencher Law Soc., 1983, 87, 91; former chmn. discipline and legal edn. coms.; past chmn. litigation dept. Fasken Campbell Godfrey. Fellow Am. Coll. Trial Lawyers. Office: Brooke Claxton Bldg, Tunney's Pasture 0916A, Ottawa, ON Canada K1A 0K9

ROCK, PAUL ELLIOT, sociologist, educator; b. London, Aug. 4, 1943; s. Ashley Rock and Charlotte Carnegie Dickson; m. Barbara Ravid, Sept. 25, 1965 (dec. 1998); children: Matthew, Oliver. BSc in Sociology, London Sch. Econs., 1964; DPhil, U. Oxford, Eng., 1970. Asst. lectr. London Sch. Econs. and Polit. Sci., 1967-70, lectr., 1970-76, sr. lectr., 1976-83, reader, 1983-85, prof. sociology, 1985-95, prof. social instns., 1995—; vis. prof. Princeton U., 1974-75; vis. scholar Ministry of Solicitor Gen., Ottawa, Can., 1981-83; cons. BBC. Author: A View from the Shadows, 1986, Helping Victims of Crime, 1990, The Social World of an English Crown Court, 1993, Reconstructing A Women's Prison, 1996, After Homicide, 1998. Fellow Ctr. for Advanced Study of The Behavioral Scis., Stanford, Calif., 1996; social sci. fellow Nuffield Found., 1985, 96. Fellow Royal Soc. Arts, Brit. Acad. Office: London Sch Econs Polit Sci, Houghton St, London WC2A 2AE, England

ROCK, PETER ALFRED, chemistry educator, researcher, consultant, dean; b. New Haven, Sept. 29, 1939; s. Alfred Milton and Mabel (Neider) R.; m. M. Elaine Rousseau, Dec. 5, 1959; children: Michael, Deborah, Lisa. AB summa cum laude, Boston U., 1961; PhD in Chemistry, U. Calif., Berkeley, 1964. Prof. chemistry U. Calif., Davis, 1964—, chmn. dept., 1980-85, dean divsn. math. and phys. scis., 1995—; cons. World Book Ency., N.Y.C., 1985—, Dorland Med. Dictionary, Phila., 1978-82; expert witness in the energy field and product liability for numerous law firms, Calif., 1979—. Author: Chemical Thermodynamics, 1983, General Chemistry, 1986, 3d edit., 1991, Descriptive Chemistry, 1986; editor: Isotopes and Chemical Principles, 1975, Special Topics in Electrochemistry, 1977; contbr.: World Book Encyclopedia, 1990—, Encyclopedia of Geochemistry, 1994—, McGraw-Hill Encyclopedia of Science and Technology, 1999—, Encyclopedia of Geochemistry, 1998—, Encyclopedia Britannica, 2000—; over 60 research papers. Named to Collegium Disting. Alumni, Boston U., 1974; Chemistry Achievement award Chem. Mfrs. Assn., 1961. Mem. AAAS, Am. Chem. Soc. (program chmn. 1974-76), Nat. Fire Protection Assn., N.Y. Acad. Scis., Sigma Xi, Phi Beta Kappa. Avocations: writing. Home: 608 Georgetown Pl Davis CA 95616-1822 Office: Letters and Sci Dean's Office One Shields Ave Davis CA 95616

ROCK, ROSALIND, international business consultant, educator; b. N.Y.C., Dec. 14, 1937; d. Samuel and Beatrice (Schildhaus) R.; m. Michael C. Young, Feb. 1, 1967; children: Tracy Beth, Todd Alden. BA, CUNY, 1959, MS in Edn., 1963; MBA, NYU, 1985. Tchr. elem. schs., N.Y.C., 1961-67; creator, implementor pilot project Boggle in the Classroom, Parker Bros., 1968; coord. group sales Pepsico's Summerfare Arts Festival, 1980; ednl. cons. Northside Devel. Ctr., 1981; mktg. dir. real estate investments Saxon Capital, N.Y.C., 1986-88; pres. Rock Internat. Investments, bus. cons. represents companies, govt. agencies, and devel. zones in China, India, and Eastern Europe, seeking strategic partners, N.Y.C., 1989—. Author: (children's rec.) Let's Create, 1972, (syndicated children's page for TV data) Channel Marker, 1974-79. Mem. Fin. Women's Assn., Women's Econ. Round Table. E-mail: rockintl@aol.com. Office: Rock Internat Investments 1065 Park Ave New York NY 10128-1001

ROCKART, JOHN FRALICK, information systems researcher; b. N.Y.C., June 20, 1931; s. John Rachac and Janet (Ross) R.; m. Elise Jean Feldmann, Sept. 16, 1961; children: Elise B. Liesl, Scott F. AB, Princeton U., 1953; MBA, Harvard U., 1958; PhD, MIT, 1968. Sales rep. IBM, 1958-61, dist. med. rep., 1961-62, fellow in Africa, 1962-64; instr. MIT, Cambridge, Mass., 1966-67; asst. prof. IBM, Cambridge, Mass., 1967-70, assoc. prof., 1970-74, sr. lectr., 1974—; dir. MIT, Cambridge, 1976—; bd. dirs. Keane, Inc., Boston, Comshare, Inc., Ann Arbor, Mich., Lifespan Inc., Providence, New Eng. Medicare Ctr., Boston. Co-author: Computers & Learning Process, 1974, Rise of Managerial Computing, 1986, Executive Support Systems, 1988 (Computer Press Assn. 1989); contbr. articles to profl. jours. Trustee New Eng. Med. Ctr., Boston. Lt. USN, 1953-56. Mem. Assn. for Computing Machinery, Inst. for Mgmt. Sci., Ops. Rsch. Soc. Am., Soc. for Info. Mgmt. (bd. dirs. mem. at large 1989-94), Weston (Mass.) Golf Club, Lake Sunapee Country Club (New London, N.H.). Republican. Unitarian. Home: 150 Cherry Brook Rd Weston MA 02493-1308 Office: CISR MIT Sloan Sch Mgmt 77 Massachusetts Ave # E40-187 Cambridge MA 02139-4301

ROCKEFELLER, DAVID, banker; b. N.Y.C., June 12, 1915; s. John Davison Jr. and Abby Greene (Aldrich) R.; m. Margaret McGrath, Sept. 7, 1940 (dec. Mar. 1996); children: David, Abby A., Neva, Margaret D., Richard G., Eileen M. BS, Harvard Coll., 1936; student, London Sch. Econs.; PhD, U. Chgo., 1940; LLD (hon.), Columbia U., 1954, Bowdoin Coll., 1958, Jewish Theol. Sem., 1958, Williams Coll., 1966, Wagner Coll., 1967, Harvard U., 1969, Pace Coll., 1970, St. John's U., 1971, Middlebury, 1974, U. Liberia, 1979, Rockefeller U., 1980, Am. U., 1987, U. Miami, 1988; DEng (hon.), Colo. Sch. Mines, 1974, U. Notre Dame, 1987. Sec. to Mayor Fiorello H. La Guardia, 1940-41; asst. regional dir. Office Def., Health and Welfare Services, 1941-42; asst. mgr. for. dept. Chase Nat. Bank, N.Y.C., 1946-47, asst. cashier, 1947-48, 2d v.p., 1948-49; v.p. Chase Nat. Bank, 1949-51, sr. v.p., 1951-55; exec. v.p. Chase Manhattan Bank (Chase Nat. Bank merged with Bank of Manhattan), 1955-57; vice chmn. bd. Chase Manhattan Bank, 1957-61, pres., chmn. exec. com., 1961-69, chmn., 1969-81, CEO, 1969-80; chmn. Chase Internat. Adv. Com., 1981-99, Rockefeller Group, Inc., 1981-95, N.Y. Clearing House, 1971-78, Ctr. for Inter-Am. Rels., 1966-70, Overseas Devel. Coun., U.S.-USSR Trade and Econ. Coun. Inc.; chmn. Internat. Exec. Svc. Corps., 1964-68; chmn. Rockfeller Ctr. Properties Trust, Inc., 1996—. Author: Unused Resources and Economic Waste, 1940, Creative Management in Banking, 1964. Active Urban Devel. Corp., N.Y. State Bus. Adv. Coun., 1968-72, U.S. Adv. Com. on Reform on Internat. Monetary System, 1973-77, U.S. exec. com. Dartmouth Conf. Bd. Inst. Internat. Econs., Am. Friends of LSE, U.S. Hon. Fellows LSE, Bus. Com. for Arts; founding mem. Commn. on White House Fellows, hon. mem., 1964-65; exec. com., chmn. Downtown Lower Manhattan Assn., 1958-75; trustee Rockefeller U., 1940-95, Carnegie Endowment Internat. Peace, Hist. Hudson Valley, 1981—; chmn. Rockefeller Bros. Fund, 1981-87, vice-chmn., 1968-80; hon. trustee Rockefeller Family Fund; life trustee U. Chgo.; trustee, chmn. bd., exec. com. Mus. Modern Art, 1962-72, 87-93; bd. overseers Harvard Coll., 1954-60, 62-68; co-founder Trilateral Commn., 1973-91, N.Am. chmn. 1981-92, hon. chmn., 1992; hon. chmn. Internat. House, 1940—, dir., 1940-63; pres. Morningside Heights, Inc., 1947-57, chmn., 1957-65; chmn. Am. Soc., 1981-92, hon. chmn., 1992—, N.Y.C. Partnership, 1979-88. Capt. AUS, 1942-45, NATOUSA, ETO. Decorated Legion of Honor France; Order of Merit, Italy, Order of Southern Cross, Brazil, Order of the White Elephant and Order of Crown, Thailand, Order of the Cedars, Lebanon, Order of the Sun, Peru, Order of the Humane African Redemption, Liberia, Order of the Crown, Belgium, Nat. Order of Ivory Coast, Grand Cordon Order of Sacred Treasure, Japan, Order Bernardo O'Higgins, Chile; recipient Merit award N.Y. chpt. AIA, 1965, Gold medal Nat. Inst. Social Scis., 1967, AIA medal of Honor for City Planning N.Y.C., 1968, Charles Evans Hughes award NCCJ, 1974, World Brotherhood award Jewish Theol. Sem, 1953, C. Walter Nichols award NYU, 1970, Regional Planning Assn. award, 1971; Hadrian award, World Monuments Fund, 1994, U.S. Presdl. Medal of Freedom, 1998. Mem. Council Fgn. Relations (dir. 1949-51, v.p. 1951-70, chmn. 1970-85), Japan Soc. (hon. chmn.), Internat. House (hon. chmn.), Bilderberg Conf., Harvard Club, Univ. Club, Century Club, The Links, The Knickerbocker. Avocation: sailing. Address: 30 Rockefeller Plz Rm 5600 New York NY 10112-0002

ROCKEFELLER, LAURANCE S., philanthropist; b. N.Y.C., May 26, 1910; s. John Davison, Jr. and Abby Greene (Aldrich) R.; m. Mary French, Aug. 15, 1934; children—Laura Rockefeller Chasin, Marion French Rockefeller Weber, Lucy Rockefeller Waletzky, Laurance. BA, Princeton U., 1932; LLD (hon.), SUNY Sch. Forestry at Syracuse U., 1961, U. Vt., 1968; D.Pub. Svc. (hon.), George Washington U., 1964; LHD (hon.), Tex. Tech. Coll., 1966, Duke U., 1981, Marymount Coll., 1983; HHD (hon.), Princeton U., 1987. Chmn. Rockefeller Center, Inc., 1953-56, 58-66, dir., 1936-78; founding trustee, pres., chmn. Rockefeller Bros. Fund, 1958-80, vice chmn., 1980-82, adv. trustee, 1982-85; dir. Ea. Airlines, 1938-60, 77-81, adv. dir., 1981-87; chmn. Woodstock Resort Corp.; bd. dirs. Readers Digest Assn., 1973-93. Mem. Nat. Cancer Adv. Bd., 1972-79; hon. chmn. N.Y. Zool. Soc., 1975; life trustee Wildlife Conservation Soc.; Meml. Sloan-Kettering Cancer Ctr., 1947-60, chmn. 1960-82, hon. chmn. 1982—; chmn. Citizens Adv. Coun. on Environ. Quality, 1969-73, Jackson Hole Preserve, Inc., pres., 1940-87, chmn. and trustee, 1987-96, chmn. emeritus and trustee, 1997—; commr. Palisades Interstate Pk. Commn., 1939-78, pres., 1970-77, commr. emeritus, 1978—; chmn. Outdoor Recreation Resources Rev. Commn., 1958-65, N.Y. State Coun. of Pks., 1963-73, White House Conf. on Natural Beauty, 1965; life mem. corp. MIT; trustee emeritus Princeton U.; hon. trustee Nat. Geog. Soc.; trustee Alfred P. Sloan Found., 1950-82, Greenacre Found., Nat. Pk. Found., 1968-76, Sleepy Hollow Restorations, 1975-87, chmn., 1981-85; trustee Hist. Hudson Valley, 1987—, chmn. emeritus, 1997—; chmn. Woodstock Found., 1968-97, chmn. emeritus, 1997—; hon. dir. Nat. Wildflower Ctr., 1988—. Decorated commandeur de Ordre Royal du Lion, Belgium, 1950; comdr. most excellent Order Brit. Empire, 1971; recipient Conservation Service award U.S. Dept. Interior, 1956, 62, Horace Marden Albright Scenic Preservation medal, 1957, Disting. Service medal Theodore Roosevelt Assn., 1963, Audubon medal, 1964, Nat. Inst. Social Scis. award, 1959, 67, Alfred P. Sloan, Jr. Meml. award Am. Cancer Soc., 1969, Medal of Freedom, 1969, Cert. of Award, Am. Assn. for Cancer Research, 1980, James Ewing Layman's award Soc. Surg. Oncology, 1980, Congl. gold medal, 1990, McAneny Hist. Pres. medal, 1993, Chmn.'s award Nat. Geograph. Soc., 1995, Theodore Roosevelt Nat. Park medal of honor, 1995, Lady Bird Johnson Conservation award Lifetime Achievement, 1997, Gov.'s Parks & Preservation award, N.Y., 1997. Mem. Am. Conservation Assn. (pres. 1958-80, chmn. 1980-85, hon. chmn. 1985—), Princeton Club, University Club, Brook Club, Capitol Hill Club, Cosmos Club, Boone and Crockett Club, Knickerbocker Club, Lotos Club (N.Y.C.), Sleepy Hollow Club (Tarrytown). Office: 30 Rockefeller Plz Rm 5600 New York NY 10112-0002

ROCKEMANN, DAVID DOUGLAS, health services administrator; b. Jefferson City, Mo., Mar. 9, 1954; s. Raymond William and Irene Pauline (Strobel) R.; m. Margaret Ann Perkinson, June 20, 1986. BA in Sociology, U. Mo., 1976, MS in Community Devel., 1978. State health planner State Health Planning Devel. Agy., Jefferson City, 1978; health cons., research assoc. Syncaredian Health Assn., Walnut Creek, Calif., 1978-79; asst. dir. day care Jewish Home for the Aged, San Francisco, 1979; adminstr. St. Regis Retirement Ctr., Hayward, Calif., 1979-82; dir. aging services Community and Econ. Devel. Assn., Chgo., 1982-86; exec. dir., chief exec. officer Community Nutrition Network, Chgo., 1986-87; dir. of bus. devel. Health Services div. John Knox Village, Lee's Summit, Mo., 1987-89; adminstr. Ctr. on Rural Elderly, U. Mo., Kansas City, 1989-90; dir. program devel. geriatric svcs. Chestnut Hill Hosp. Healthcare, Phila., Pa., 1991-92; adminstr. Twining Village Continuing Care Retirement Ctr., South Hampton, Pa., 1992-95, Riddle Village Continuing Care Retirement Cmty., Media, Pa., 1995-96; v.p. Plexus Group, Quakertown, Pa., 1996-98; reg. dir. Cathedral Rock, St. Louis, 1998—; cons. Wade West Inc., San Francisco, 1979; rschr. Calif. Dept. Health Svcs., San Francisco, 1978-79; rsch. asst. Ctr. for Rsch. in Social Behavior, Columbia, Mo., 1977-79; gerontology rsch. cons. Ctr. for Aging, U. Mo., Kansas City, 1987-90; cons. Diversified Health Svcs., Plymouth Meeting, Pa., 1990-91. Author: Outreach to the Elderly, 1983; (with others) Health Care Trends, 1978, Consumer's Guide to Nursing Homes, 1978. Mem. adv. coun. Suburban Cook County Area Agy. on Aging, Chgo., 1983-84; legis. adv. State of Ill. Spl. Com. on Aging, Chgo., 1985; presenter XIV meeting Internat. Assn. Gerontology, Acapulco, Mex., 1989, presenter XV meeting, Budapest, Hungary, 1993, XVI meeting, Adelaide, Australia, 1997; coord., moderator Mid-Am. Congress on Aging, Kansas City, Mo., 1985; mem. planning com. Mid-Am. Congress on Aging, Chgo., 1986; bd. mem. Elder Abuse Coun., Kansas City, Mo. Adminstrn. on Aging scholar U. Mo., 1977-78; Older Americans Act grantee, 1982-87. Mem. Gerontol. Soc. Am. (presenter ann. sci. meeting 1992, 93, 94, 95, 97, 98, 99), Am. Soc. on Aging (presenter ann. meeting 1989, 90, 94, 98), Am. Coll. Health Care Adminstrs. Lutheran. Office: Cathedral Rock 415 Ft Worth Club Bldg 306 W 7th St Fort Worth TX 76102

ROCKENBAUER, ANTAL ISTVÁN, physicist, researcher; b. Budapest, Hungary, July 6, 1938; s. István and Malvin (Márton) R.; m. Edit Fülöp, July 10, 1965 (div. 1989); children: Anna, Eszter; m. Margit Tolnay, Mar. 19, 1994. Diploma in physics, Roland Eotvos U., Budapest, 1962, PhD, 1965; cand. scis., Hungarian Acad. Scis., 1974, DSc, 1987. Rsch. fellow Cen. Rsch. Inst. Chemistry, Budapest, 1962-74, sr. rschr., 1974-87, sci. advisor, 1987—; dir. lab. Tech. U., Budapest, 1995—; vis. prof. Osaka (Japan) U., 1994, U. Provence, Marseille, France, 1995—. Co-author: Molekulaspektroszkopia, 1987, Electron Spin Resonance, Vol. 11A, 1988; editor: Polymer Spectroscopy, 1988; mem. editl. bd.: Models in Chemistry, Acta Chimica Hungarica, 1992-99; co-editor: Molecular Physics Reports. Mem. presidency Hungarian-Japan Friendship Soc., 1988—. Mem. AMPERE Group (mem. com. 1996), N.Y. Acad. Sci. Avocation: Japanese culture. Office: Chem Rsch Ctr Inst Chemistr, PO Box 17 Pusztaszeri ut 59/67, H-1525 Budapest Hungary

ROCKS, BERNARD FRANCIS, clinical chemist; b. Belfast, Ireland, Oct. 29, 1946; s. Michael Francis and Anna May (O'Connel) R.; m. Tanya Christine Thurgate, June 17, 1985; children: Brendan, Anna May. MSc, Loughborough U. of Technol., Eng., 1971, PhD, 1974. Exptl. officer Richardson's Fertilisers, Belfast, Ireland, 1968-69; rsch. student, lectr. Loughborough U., 1969-74; rsch. fellow Sussex U., Brighton, Eng., 1974-75; basic grade biochemist Brighton Health Authority, 1975-76, sr. grade biochemist, 1976-82, prin. biochemist, 1982-86, top grade biochemist, 1986—; hon. cons. Dist. Health Authority, Brighton, 1986—; tutor Regional Health Authority, South East Eng., 1988—; rsch. fellow Sussex U., 1975—. Contbr. more than 60 sci. articles to profl. publs. Fellow Royal Soc. of Medicine, Royal Soc. Chemistry; mem. Inst. of Biology, Assn. Clin. Biochemists, Royal Coll. Pathologists. Office: Biochemistry Lab, Royal Sussex Hosp, Brighton BN2 5BE, England

ROCKSTROH, SYBILLE ANGELICA, psychologist, researcher; b. Wiesbaden, Germany, Sept. 20, 1958; d. Achim and Christel R.; m. Karl Andreas Schweizer, March 29, 1994; 1 child, Christoph. Vordiplom, Albert-Ludwigs U., Freiburg, Germany, 1981, diploma in psychology, 1984, PhD, 1987. Rsch. fellow Univ., Freiburg, 1981-82, tutor in Statistics, 1982-83, rsch. assoc., 1984-87, 88-89; rsch. assoc. Univ., Tübingen, Germany, 1987-88, Sandoz Pharm. Ltd., Basel, Switzerland, 1990-95; pvt. practice Freiburg, Germany, 1997—; cons. and lectr. in field. Contbr. articles to profl. jours. Mem. Bund Deutscher Psychologen, Assn. Neuropsychologie.

ROCKSWOLD, GAYLAN LEE, neurosurgeon; b. Valley City, N.D., Dec. 11, 1940; s. E. Palmer and Myrna Christine R.; m. Mary Helen Garnass, June 27, 1964; children: Sarah Beth, Payl Gaylan, Nathan Kristopher. BA, St. Olaf Coll., 1962; MD, U. Minn., 1966, PhD, 1976. Diplomate Am. Bd. Neurol. Surgery. Intern Hennepin County Gen. Hosp., Mpls., 1966-67; gen. surgery resident USPHS Hosp., Balt., 1967-68; med. assoc. sect. neurosurgery Nat. Cancer Inst., Balt., 1969; med. fellow dept. surgery U. Minn., Mpls., 1969; med. assoc. Nat. Cancer Inst., Balt., 1969; from instr. to prof. U. Minn., Mpls., 1974-92, prof., 1992—; chief neurosurgery divsn. Hennepin County Med. Ctr., Mpls., 1977—; pres. Neurosurgical Assocs., Ltd., Mpls., 1997—; adv. bd. Mpls. Neurosci. Inst.,1992—, v.p. 1998—; presenter in field. Author: (with others) 11 chpts. in books; contbr. over 45 articles in profl. jours. Adv. THINK First Head and Spinal Cord Injury Prevention Program, Mpls., 1990-91; mentor Mentor Connection Program for High Sch. Students, Mpls., 1995-96. Recipient Recognition award Minn. Head Injury Assn., Mpls., 1993; Smith-Kline-French Foreign fellow Malawi, East Africa, 1965. Mem. ACS (Minn. chpt. com. on trauma), AMA. (Minn. state chpt.), Am. Assn. Surgery of Trauma, Neurosurg. Soc. Am., Am. Assn. Neurological Surgeons, Congress Neurological Surgeons, Minn. Neurosurg. Soc. (sec., treas., v.p., pres. 1989-95), Hennepin County Med. Soc., Hitchcock Surg. Soc., The Wilderness Soc., Phi Beta Kappa, Alpha Omega Phi. Lutheran. Avocations: sailing, backpacking, reading history and biographies, canoeing, fishing. E-mail: rocks001@maroon.tc.umn.edu. Office: Hennepin County Medical Ctr 701 Park Ave Minneapolis MN 55415-1623

ROCKWELL, DON ARTHUR, psychiatrist; b. Wheatland, Wyo., Apr. 24, 1938; s. Orson Arthur and Kathleen Emily Rockwell; m. Frances Pepitone-Arreola, Dec. 23, 1965; children: Grant, Chad. BA, Wash. U., 1959; MD, U. Okla., 1963; MA in Sociology, U. Calif., Berkeley, 1967. Diplomate Am. Bd. Psychiatry and Neurology. Intern in surgery San Francisco Gen. Hosp., 1963-64; resident in psychiatry Langley-Porter Neuropsychiatric Inst. U. Calif. Med. Ctr., San Francisco, 1964-67; instr. dept. psychiatry U. Calif. Sch. Medicine, Davis, 1969-70, asst. prof., 1970-74, assoc. prof., 1974-80, acting. assoc., dean curricular affiars, 1979-80, acting assoc. dean student affairs, 1980, assoc. dean student affairs, 1980-82, prof., 1980-84; career tchr. NIMH, 1970-72; assoc. psychiatrist Sacramento Med. Ctr.; med. dir. U. Calif. Med. Ctr., Davis, 1982-84; prof., vice chmn. dept. psychiatry and biobehavioral scis. UCLA, 1984-96; dir. UCLA Neuropsychiat. Hosp., 1984-95; chief profl. staff Neuropsychiat. Inst., UCLA, 1984-85, also dir. outpatient svcs.; chmn. U. Calif. Hosp. Dirs. Council, 1988-89; cons. Nat. Commn. on Marijuana, Washington, 1971-73. Co-author: Psychiatric Disorders, 1982; contbr. chpts. to books; articles to profl. jours. Bd. dirs. Bereavement Outreach, Sacramento, 1974-84, Suicide Prevention, Yolo County, 1969-84; bd. visitors U. Okla. Sch. Medicine; chmn. hosp. dirs. coun. U. Calif. Hosp.; governing coun. AHA Psychiat. Hosp. Fellow Am. Psychiat. Assn., Am. Coll. Psychiatrists, Am. Coll. Mental Health Adminstrs.; mem. AMA (gov. coun. psych. hosp.), Am. Sociologic Assn., Calif. Med. Assn. (med. staff survey com.), Cen. Calif. Psychiat. Assn. (sec.-pres. 1977-78), U. Okla. Alumni Assn. (trustee 1981-86), Alpha Omega Alpha. Home: 1816 E Las Tunas Rd Santa Barbara CA 93103-1744

ROCKWELL, ELIZABETH DENNIS, retirement specialist, financial planner; b. Houston; d. Robert Richard and Nezzell Alderton (Christie) Dennis. Student Rice U., 1939-40, U. Houston, 1938-39, 40-42. Purchasing agt. Standard Oil Co., Houston, 1942-66; v.p. mktg. Heights Savs. Assn., Houston, 1967-82; exec. dir. Investments CIBC Oppenheimer Corp., Houston, 1982—; 2d v.p. Desk and Derrick Club Am., 1960-61. Contbr. articles on retirement planning, tax planning and tax options, monthly article 50 Plus sect. for Houston Chronicle newspaper. Bd. dirs. ARC, 1985-91, Houston Heights Assn., 1973-77; named sr. v.p. Oppenheimer, 1986—; mem. Coll. Bus. U. found. bd. Houston, 1990, mem. million dollar roundtable, 1991—, mem. ct. of the table, 1991—, Top of Table, 1996—, mem. U. Houston Sys. Planned Giving Coun., exec. prof. U. Houston Coll. of Bus., 1992—, mem. coll. bus. adv. bd., 1992—, mem. alumni bd., 1987-95; appointed trustee U. Houston Sys. Found., Inc., 1992; bd. gov. The Houston Forum; active Tex. Leader's Round Table, 1994; pres. U. Houston Coll. Bus. Adminstrn. Found.; mem. Houston C.C. Adv. Bd. for Ednl. TV. Named Disting. Alumnae Coll. Bus. Alumn. Assn. U. Houston, 1992, Disting. Alumna U. Houston Alumni Orgn., 1996; named YWCA Outstanding Woman of Yr., 1978. Mem. Am. Savs. and Loan League (state dir. 1973-76, chpt. pres. 1971-72; pres. S.W. regional conf. 1972-73; Leaders award 1972), Savs. Inst. Mktg. Soc. Am. (Key Person award 1974), Inst. Fin. Edn., Fin. Mgrs., Soc. Savs. Instns., U.S. Savs. and Loan League (com. on deposit acquisitions and adminstrn.), Houston Heights Assn. (charter, dir. 1973-77), Friends of Bayou Bend, Harris County Heritage Soc., U. Houston Alumni Orgn. (life), Rice U. Bus. and Profl. Women, River Oaks Bus. Womens Exchange Club, U. Houston Bus. Womens Assn. (pres. 1985), Forum Club, Greater Houston Women's Found. (charter). Office: CIBC Oppenheimer Corp Houston TX 77002-7347

ROCKWELL, R(ONALD) JAMES, JR., laser and electro-optics consultant; b. Cin., May 7, 1937; s. Ronald James and Mary Cornelius (Thornton) R.; m. Diane Lundin, Feb. 3, 1968; children: James Gregory, Christopher Derrick. BS, U. Cin., 1960, MS, 1964. Directing physicist, assoc. prof. laser scis., laser research labs. Med. Center, U. Cin., 1963-76; dir. continuing edn. services Electro-Optical Systems Design Jour., Cin., 1976-77; v.p. laser/electro-optics Control Dynamics, Inc., Cin., 1977-79; pres. Rockwell Assocs., Inc. (cons. lasers, optics and electro-optics), Cin., 1979-89; pres., chief exec. officer Rockwell Laser Industries (cons. lasers, optics and electro-optics), Cin., 1989—; exec. com. safe use lasers com. Am. Nat. Standards Inst., 1971—; exec. sec. Laser Inst. Am., 1976-77, dir., 1972-92, pres., 1974; mem. adv. com. Laser History Project, 1983-89; dir. Laserworks, Inc., Rockwell Devel. Co.; cons. WHO, Internat. Electrotechnical Commn., founder Consortium of Laser and Tech. Cons., 1988; mem. tech. com. Laser Fire Protection of the Nat. Fire Protection Assn., 1991—. Co-author: Lasers in Medicine, 1971; author: Laser Safety Training Manual, 1982, Laser Safety in Surgery and Medicine, 1985, Laser Safety: Concepts, Analysis and Controls, 1992, Laser Safety: Modularized Training Package, 1994, Users Guide for Laser Safety, 1997, Multi-Lingual Laser Safety Training Program, 1998, Laser Accidents, a 30 Year Review, 2000, Medical User's Guide for Laser Safety, 2000; created software program: Laser Hazard Analysis, 1987, LAZAN for Windows, 1995, SKYZAN for Windows, 1996; co-developer: LASERNET page on the World-Wide Web (Internet), 1996; contbr. chpts. to books and articles to profl. jours.; editor jours. in field; mem. editl. bd. Jour. Laser Applications, 1994—. Co-chmn. Internat. Laser Safety Conf., 1990, 92, mem. planning com., keynote spkr., 1997. Recipient Pres.' award Laser Inst. Am., 1985. Mem. IEEE, N.Y. Acad. Scis., Am. Soc. Laser Medicine and Surgery, Midwest Bio-Laser Inst., Internat. Laser Display Assn., Newcomen Soc., Sigma Xi (nat. lectr. 1971-75), Delta Tau Delta (D.S.C. award 1985, dir. acad. affairs, nat. bd. dirs. 1975-83). Methodist. Achievements include designer, builder portable laser entertainment system in laser light artistic shows; patentee in field. Home: 6282 Coachlite Way Cincinnati OH 45243-2920 Office: PO Box 43010 7754 Camargo Rd Cincinnati OH 45243-2661

RODÁ DE LLANZA, ISABEL, archeology educator; b. Barcelona, Spain, Sept. 25, 1948; d. Tomas and Margarita (De Llanza) R.; m. Marc Mayer Olive; children: Lavinia, Claudia. PhD, U. Autonoma de Barcelona. Aux. curator Mus. History, Barcelona, 1968-76, curator, 1976-80; asst. U. Autonoma de Barcelona, 1970-72, assoc. prof., 1972-85, adj. prof., 1985-93, prof., 1993—; co-dir. Excavation of Pompey's Trophy, La Jonquera, Spain, 1989-93; rsch. assoc. U. Calif., Berkeley, summer 1991; mem. Internat. Rsch. Ctr. for Archaeology, Medulin, Croatia, 1994—. Author: Cataleg de L'Epigrafia i L'Escultura Classiques del Museu Episcopal de Vic, 1989; co-author: Inscriptions Romaines de Catalogne I-IV, 1984, 85, 91, 97, Corpus Inscriptionum Naronitanarum I, 1999; editor: Ciencias, Metodologias y Tecnicas Aplicadas a la Arqueologia, 1992; mem. editl. bd. Jour. Roman Archaeology, 1994—, Histria Antiqua, 1995—; contbr. articles to profl. jours. Office: U Autonoma de Barcelona, Edifici B, 08193 Barcelona Spain

RODARIE, DENIS, financial company executive; b. Chalon Sur Saone, France, Dec. 30, 1956; s. Marc and Madeleine (Bertholon) R.; m. Veronique Repellin, Aug. 31, 1980; children: Benedicte, Thibault, Baudine, Aude, Alix. Grad., EM Lyon, France, 1979. Auditor Arthur Andersen, Lyon, France, 1980-83; mng. dir. Siparex, Lyon, France, co. sec., sr. mng. dir. Mem. AURA. Home: 25 rue Vaubeour, 69002 Lyon France Office: Siparex, 139 rue Vendome, 69006 Lyon France

RODDAM, FRANC, film director; b. Stockton, Eng., Apr. 29, 1946. Dir.: (film) Mini, 1975, Dummy, 1977, Quadrophenia, 1979, The Lords of Dis-

cipline, 1983, The Bride, 1985, Aria, 1987, War Party, 1988, K2, 1992, Moby Dick, 1997, (mini-series) Cleopatra, 1999. Office: Writers & Artists Agy c/o Joan Scott 8383 Wilshire Blvd Ste 550 Hollywood CA 90211 also: Union Pictures, 36 Marshall St, London W1, England*

RODDAM, PETER LEOPOLD BABER, communications executive, accountant; b. Blyth, Northumberland, Eng., Aug. 30, 1932; s. John and Irene (Andrews) R.; married; 1 child, Louis Daniel. BA (hon.), Durham. Programmer Ferranti Computers Ltd., London, 1960-63; cons. Coopers & Lybrand, London, 1963-66; sr. analyst Internat. Pub. Corp., London, 1966-68; mgr. computer bur. Blue Circle Industries, London, 1969-84; mgr. govt. sales Mannesman (U.K.) Ltd., Slough, Berkshire, Eng., 1984-86; mgr. major accts. Brit. Telecom, London, 1986-92. Contbr. articles to profl. jours. Served as navigator RAF, 1951-53. Mem. ACA, Brit. Computer Soc., Chartered Inst. Secs. (assoc.). Mem. Ch. of Eng. Club: RAF (London). Avocations: tennis, house renovation. Home: 42 Gloucester Rd, Kew Gardens, Richmond, Surrey TW9 3BU, England

RODDEN, APPLETREE FRANK, neuroscientist; b. San Angelo, Tex., Sept. 16, 1937; s. Archie Aaron and Lucile Lila R.; m. Annegret Kathrin Pieper, Aug. 10, 1994; children: Laura Pastor, Diana Olson. BS, Southwestern U., Georgetown, Tex., 1964; PhD, U. Iowa, 1969; MD, U. Marburg Med. Sch., Marburg, Germany, 1983. Postdoctoral fellow, Dept. Psychiatry Stanford U. Med. Sch., Stanford, Calif., 1969-73; ballet dancer corps de ballet Staatstheater Ballet, Kassel, Germany, 1973-75; ballet dancer soloist Israel Nat. Opera Ballet, Tel-Aviv, 1975-76; neurochemist Dept. Genetics U. Marburg, 1976-78; neurosurgeon U. Marburg Med. Sch., 1984-92; village physician German Devel. Svc., Kiembara, West Africa, 1993-94; neurorehab. physician Ctr. for Severe Brain Injuries, Hamburg, Germany, 1996-98; neuroscientist, Dept. Neuroradiology U. Tuebingen, Tuebingen, Germany, 1999—; cons. San Angelo Acad. Ballet, 1989—. Author: (essay in book) How Smaller Refrigerators Can Save the Human Race, 1975; translator: (book) Hysteoscopy Text and Atlas, 1994; contbr. articles to profl. jours. Democrat. Prebyterian. Avocations: ballet, piano, singing, guitar. Home E-mail: annetree@aol.com. Office E-mail: fkrodden@med.uni-tuebingen. Home: Hamburger Str 3, Hamburg D-22083, Germany Office: U Tuebingen Med Sch, Hoppe-Seyler Str 3, Tuebingen D-72076, Germany

RODDICK, DAVID BRUCE, construction company executive; b. Oakland, Calif., Oct. 31, 1948; s. Bruce Ergo and Hortensia Cabo (Castedo) R.; m. Sharon Ann Belan, May 25, 1975; children: Heather Marie, Christina Dee-Ann. BSCE, U. Calif., Davis, 1971. Engr. Bechtel Corp., San Francisco, 1971-77, contract specialist, 1977-78; subcontract adminstr. Boecon Corp., Richland, Wash., 1978-79; constrn. mgr. BE&C Engrs., Inc., Vancouver, Wash., 1979-81; contracts mgr. Boecon Corp., Tukwila, Wash., 1981-83; sr. constrn. mgr. BE&C Engrs., Inc., Wichita, Kans., 1983-84; project mgr., v.p. ops. Carl Holvick Co., Sunnyvale, Calif., 1984-88, also corp. sec. bd. dirs.; v.p., gen. mgr. Brookman Co. div. B.T. Mancini Co., Inc., Milpitas, Calif., 1988-92; v.p., sec., CFO B.T. Mancini Co., Inc., 1992-98, sr. v.p. ops., CFO, corp. sec., 1998-2000, exec. v.p., CFO, corp. sec., 2000—. Mem. devel. com. San Jose (Calif.) Mus. Assn., 1993-95; mem., dir. Contstrn. Fin. Mgmt. Assn., 1995—, pres. Silicon Valley chpt., 1999-00; pres. Reed Sch. PTA, San Jose, 1986-88, San Jose Coun. PTA's, 1988-89; trustee Heart of Valley Bapt. Ch.; bd. dirs. Vinehill Homeowners Assn., 1975-77. Lt. col. USAR Corps Engrs., 1969-99. Decorated Army Achievement medal, 1988, Commendation medal, 1991, 96, 98, meritorious svc. medal, 1998, 99; recipient Calif. State PTA Hon. Svc. award, 1988, Bronze de Fleury medal Army Engr. Assn., 1998. Mem. Am. Soc. Civil Engrs., Res. Officers Assn., Am. Arbitration Assn. (mem. panel arbitrators), Am. Subcontractors Assn., Engr. Regimental Assn., Calif. Aggie Alumni Assn., Ill. State Geneal. Soc., Floor Covering Installation Contractors Assn., Oreg. Calif. Trails Assn., Santa Maria Valley Geneal. Archtl. Engring. Inst. (founding mem.), Soc., Army Engr. Assn. (de Fleury medal 1998), U. Calif.-Davis Century Club, Sigma Nu. Republican. Office: B T Mancini Co Inc 876 S Milpitas Blvd Milpitas CA 95035-6311

RODDICK, NICK, writer, publisher, editor; b. Heswall, Cheshire, Eng., July 27, 1945; s. George and Peggy (Large) R.; m. Jo Hayes; children: Sam, Luke, Chloë, Saskia. BA in Modern Langs., Oxford (Eng.) U., 1966; MA, U. Bristol, Eng., 1968, PhD, 1976. Translator Agence Europe, Brussels, 1966-67; lectr. French, Trinity Coll., Dublin, Ireland, 1970-74; lectr. drama Manchester (Eng.) U., 1974-80; vis. prof. Calif. State U., Long Beach, 1980-81; editor Cinema Papers, Melbourne, Australia, 1985-86, Screen Internat., London, 1986-88, Moving Pictures Internat., London, 1990-92, Preview, London, 1992—; mem. prodn. bd. Brit. Film Inst., London, 1988-92; dir. Split Screen Rsch. Consultancy, 1992—. Author: A New Deal in Entertainment, 1983, Encyclopedia of Great Movies, 1985; co-author: A Night at the Pictures, 1985; co-editor: British Cinema Now, 1985. Home and Office: 15 Carden Ave, Brighton BN1 8NA, England

RODDIE, IAN CAMPBELL, physiologist, educator, consultant; b. Portadown, No. Ireland, Dec. 1, 1928; s. John Richard Wesley and Mary Hill (Wilson) R.; m. Elizabeth Ann Gillon Honeyman, Mar. 14, 1957 (dec. 1974); children: Mary, Catherine, Sarah, Patrick; m. Katherine Anne O'Hara, Nov. 29, 1974 (div. 1983); children: Claire, David; m. Janet Doreen Saville, Nov. 14, 1987. BSc with 1st honors, Queen's U., 1950, MBBCh, BAO, 1953, MD, 1957, DSc, 1962. Intern, resident med. officer Royal Victoria Hosp., Belfast, No. Ireland, 1953-54; asst. lectr. Queen's U., Belfast, 1954-57, lectr. in physiology, 1954-60, sr. lectr., 1961-62, reader in physiology, 1962-64, Dunville prof., 1964-87; Harkness fellow U. Wash., Seattle, 1960-61; dean of medicine Queen's U., 1976-81, pro vice chancellor, 1984-87; vis. prof. Chinese U. Hong Kong, 1987-90; dep. med. dir., head med. edn. Nat. Guard King Khalid Hosp., Jeddah, Saudi Arabia, 1990-94; cons. Internat. Fin. Corp./ World Bank, 1994—. Author: Physiology for Practitioners, 1971, 2d edit., 1975; co-author: The Physiology of Disease, 1975, Multiple Choice Questions in Human Physiology, 1971, 5th edit., 1996, Textbook of Physiology and Biochemistry, 4th edit., 1988. Chief regional scientific advisor for civil def. No. Ireland Office, Belfast, 1977-88; mem. Gen. Med. Coun., London, 1979-81; bd. dirs. Med. Rsch. Coun., London, 1974-76; mem. Home Def. Scientific Adv. Com., London, 1977-88. Major RAMC, 1955-67. Decorated Comdr. of Order of Brit. Empire, 1987. Mem. Physiol. Soc. (chmn. com. 1986-88, hon.), Royal Acad. Medicine in Ireland (pres. 1985-87), Royal Soc. Medicine, Royal Irish Acad. Methodist. Avocations: writing, travel, cooking. Email: icroddie@mercuryin.es. Home: Lomas Club Pueblo, Calle San Bernabe 3, 29600 Marbella Spain

RODDIE, ROBERT KENNETH, otolaryngologist, educator; b. Portadown, No. Ireland, Aug. 30, 1928; s. John Richard Wesley and Mary Hill (Wilson) R.; m. Anne Templeton Mathews, Oct. 5, 1957; children: Alison Mary Sherwood, Richard Kenneth Templeton, Angus Gregg Wilson. Student, Meth. Coll., Belfast, No. Ireland; MB BCh, BAO, Queen's U., Belfast, 1947; DLO, London U., 1952. Registrar Royal Victoria Hosp., Belfast, 1948-57; sr. registrar Inst. Laryngology and Otology, Royal Nat. Throat Nose and Ear Hosp., London, 1957-60; cons. ear, nose and throat surgeon, dept. otolaryngology Bristol (Eng.) U., 1960—; head dept. otolaryngology, lectr., dir. Hearing and Speech Centre; cons. to civil service commrs. Contbr. articles to profl. jours. Fellow Royal Coll. Surgeons (Eng.), Royal Soc. Medicine; mem. Brit. Assn. Otolaryngologists, Brit. Med. Assn., Joseph Soc., Irish Otolaryngol. Soc., Southwestern Laryngol. Assn. (pres. 1978), Bristol and Clinton Golf Club, Clifton Club (Bristol), Lansdowne Club (London), Masons. Conservative. Methodist. Avocations: golf, gardening, oil painting, travel, photography. Home: 1 Briercliffe Rd, Bristol Avon BS9 2DB, England Office: Cons Rooms, 7 Percival Rd, Bristol BS8 3CE, England

RODDIE, THOMAS WILSON, retired obstetrician-gynecologist; b. Belfast, No. Ireland, Aug. 19, 1921; s. John Richard and Mary Hill (Wilson) Roddie; m. Alix Pauline Mary Hurst, Apr. 21, 1949; children—Elisabeth Margaret Anne, Alexandra Frances Mary. M.B., B.Ch., Queen's U., Belfast, 1944. House surgeon, physician Royal Victoria and Royal Maternity Hosps., Belfast, 1944-46, prin. registrar, tutor, 1949-54; obstet. officer Princess Mary Maternity Hosp., Newcastle-on-Tyne, Eng., 1947; sr. house officer Jessop Hosp. for Women, Sheffield, Eng., 1948; cons. obstetrician-gynecologist, sr. lectr. ob-gyn U. Malaya, Singapore, 1955-59; cons. obstetrician-gynecologist Easter Health and Social Services Bd., Belfast, 1959-86; examiner Royal Coll. Midwives, London, 1960—; civilian cons. ob-gyn U.K. Land Forces, No. Ireland, 1969—. Contbr. papers to profl. lit. Served to surgeon lt. comdr. Royal Naval Vol. Res., 1950-69. Fellow Royal Coll. Obstetricians-Gynecologists, Ulster Med. Soc.; mem. Ulster Ob-Gyn Soc., Brit. Med. Assn., No. Eng. Ob-Gyn Soc. Mem. Ch. of England/Ireland. Club: Royal Naval Res. (London). Avocation: travelling. Home: Lodge Farm,, Kirkby Fleetham,, Northallerton,, North Yorkshire, England

RODE, BERND MICHAEL, theoretical chemistry educator; b. Innsbruck, Tyrol, Austria, July 14, 1946; s. Hans Wolf and Gabriele (Toggler) R.; m. Evelin Veronika Roedlach, June 14, 1975. PhD, U. Innsbruck, 1973; PhD (hon.), Chulalongkorn U., Bangkok, Thailand, 1995, King Mogkut Inst. Tech., Bangkok, Thailand, 1998, Gadjah Mada U., Yogyakarta, Indonesia, 2000. Asst. prof. U. Innsbruck, 1973-76, assoc. prof., 1976-79, prof. inorganic and theoretical chemistry, 1979—, senator, 1997—; rep. East Asia, Austrian Rectors Conf., 1985—, chmn. Devel. Coop. Commn., 1991—; chmn. PhD Commn., U. Innsbruck, 1988—; vis. prof. numerous orgns., Japan, Greece, Thailand, 1980—. Contbr. articles to sci. jours. Rep. of Austria, UN Commn., UNCSTD, 1991—, v.p. 1999—; counselor Devel. Coop., Austrian Govt., 1987—. Recipient Sandoz rsch. award, 1976. Avocations: languages, motorbiking, shooting. Office: Inst Allgemeine U Innsbruck, Anorgan u Theoret Chemie, 6020 Innsbruck Innrain 52 a, Austria

RODECK, CHARLES HENRY, obstetrician and gynecologist, educator; b. Jablonec, Czechoslovakia, Aug. 23, 1944; s. Heinz Walter and Charlotte Emma Berta (Remus) R.; m. Elisabeth Kate Rampton, Jan. 29, 1971; children: Daniel, Elsa. BSc, U. Coll., London, 1966, MB, BS, 1969; DSc in Medicine, U. London, 1991. Tng. residency Univ. Coll. Hosp., London, 1970-73, Queen Charlotte's and Chelsea Hosps., London, 1974-75, King's Coll. Hosp., London, 1976-78; sr. lectr., cons. King's Coll. Hosp. Med. Sch., London, 1978-86, dir. Harris-Birthright Rsch. Ctr. for Fetal Medicine, 1983-86; prof. Inst. Ob-Gyn. Royal Postgrad. Med. Sch., Queen Charlotte's Hosp., London, 1986-90, U. Coll. London Med. Sch., 1990—; pres. Internat. Fetal Medcine and Surgery Soc., 1985-86. Co-editor: Prenatal Diagnosis and Screening, 1992, Fetal Medicine: Basic Science and Clinical Practice; assoc. editor Prenatal Diagnosis; contbr. over 500 articles to profl. med. jours. Fellow Royal Coll. Ob-Gyn., Royal Soc. Medicine (coun. sect. 1986-87, 91-92), Royal Coll. Pathologists; mem. Acad. of Med. Scis., Am. Inst. Ultrasound Medicine (hon.), Italian Soc. Perinatal Medicine, South African Soc. Ob-Gun. Avocations: music, literature, history, gastronomy, stroking the cat. Office: UCL Med Sch Dept Ob-Gyn, 86-96 Chenies Mews, London WC1E 6HX, England

RODECK, HEINRICH F.J., pediatrician, educator; b. Gladbeck, Nov. 1, 1920; s. Franz and Ottilie (Hahne) R.; m. Kathe Dreses, Apr. 25, 1952; children: Wolfgang, Burkhard, Ulrich, Ortwin, Egbert, Ute. Student, Univs. Halle, Munster Wurzberg; state exam, U. Munster, 1946; MD, U. Munich, 1946. Sci. asst. Children's Clinic U. Dusseldorf, Germany, 1950—, mem. med. faculty, 1956—; asst. prof. pediatrics; vis. asst. U. Kiel, Germany, 1955; vis. lectr. U. Montreal, Que., Can., Harvard U., Albert Einstein Coll. Medicine, N.Y.C., NIG, Bethesda, Md., 1959; dir. Children's Hosp., Datteln, Germany, 1960-86. Author: Neurosekretion und Wasserhaushalt bei Neugeborenen und Sauglingen, 1958, Untersuchungen uber den Einfluss der Dehydration auf die postnatale Entwicklung der Regulationszentren des Wasserhaushaltes, 1962, Physiology and Pathology of the Hypothalamo-neurohypophyseal System, 1967, Was erwartet der Kinderarzt von der Ausbildung der Kinderkrankenschwester, 1969, Hypothalamus-Neuropophyse, 1971, Epiphysis cerebri, 1971, Das Krankenhaus in der sozialen Umwelt, 1976, Standort und Perspektiven der Klinischen Medizin in der heutigen Industriegesellschaft, 1976, Zur derzeitigen Situation der Klinischen Pädiatrie, 1977, Kind-Familie-Gesellschaft, 1980; also numerous articles. Mem. German Soc. Pediatrics (Moro prize 1959), Rhenish-Westphalian Assn. Pediatrics, Med. Soc. Dusseldorf, German Soc. Perinatal Medicine, Austrian Soc. Pediatrics (corr.). Home: 17 am Rosengarten,, Recklinghausen, Federal Republic of Germany Office: 5 Lloydstrasse, Datteln, Federal Republic of, 5 Lloydstrasse, Datteln Germany

RODEN, JOHN STEPHEN, biology educator; b. Syracuse, N.Y., Oct. 8, 1959; s. Robert Charles and Gloria Ann R.; m. Lin Da Pfaff, Nov. 10, 1990; children: Alison, Audrey. BS, U. Wash., 1987; MS, U. Calif., Davis, 1990, PhD, 1992. Rsch. tech. Weyerhauser, Centralia, Wash., 1980-85; rsch. asst. U. Wash., Seattle, 1986-87; grad. asst. U. Calif., Davis, 1987-92; post doctoral fellow Australian Nat. U., Canberra, 1992-95; rsch. assoc., rsch. asst. prof. U. Utah, Salt Lake City, 1995-99; asst. prof. So. Oreg. U., Ashland, 1999—. Contbr. articles to profl. jours.; presenter paper at internat. meetings. Earle C. Anthony Grad. fellow U. Calif., Davis, 1988; Jastro-Shields scholar U. Calif., Davis, 1990, Foresters scholar U. Wash., 1987, C.D. Carlisle scholar U. Wash., 1986. Mem. Ecol. Soc. Am., Am. Soc. Plant Physiologists, Golden Key Honor Soc., Xi Sigma Pi. Avocations: sailing, hiking, skiing, kayaking. Office: So Oreg U Dept Biology 1250 Siskiyou Blvd Ashland OR 97520-5010

RODENBAUGH, MARCIA LOUISE, elementary school educator; b. Pitts., Nov. 11, 1942; d. F. Thomas and Lucy Indiana (Fry) Wimer; m. John Anthony Lee, Mar. 21, 1964 (div. Nov. 1971); m. Richard Allan Rodenbaugh, Aug. 3, 1975 (div. Dec. 1989); stepchildren: Ken, Tiffany, Tricia. BA in Edn., Westminster Coll., New Wimington, Pa., 1964, MEd in Remedial Reading, 1966. Tchr. North Hills Sch. Dist., Pitts., 1964-69, Ctrl. Bucks Schs., Doylestown, Pa., 1969-92; sabatical Ctrl. Bucks Schs., Doylestown, 1993—; fellow Pa. Writing Project, West Chester U., 1990; presenter in field. Author children's books: Marci Books (set of 6), 1983-99. Pres. Maple Leaf Day Care Ctr. Bd., Warminster, Pa., 1971; pres. Wesley Coll. Parents Assn., Dover, Del., 1985-86. Mem. NEA, AAUW, Pa. Edn. Assn., Ctrl. Bucks Edn. Assn. Republican. Presbyterian. Avocations: skiing, sailing, writing, piano, church choir. Home: 7-16 Aspen Way Doylestown PA 18901-2756 Office: Ctrl Bucks Sch Dist 315 W State St Doylestown PA 18901-3525

RODENBURG, CLIFTON GLENN, lawyer; b. Jamestown, N.D., Apr. 5, 1949; s. Clarence and Dorothy Irene (Peterman) R.; m. Donna Michele Stockman, Mar. 1, 1980. BS, N.D. State U., 1971; JD, U. N.D., 1974; M.L.I.R., Mich. State U., 1976. Bar: N.D. 1974, U.S. Dist. Ct. N.D. 1974, U.S. Ct. Appeals (8th cir.) 1974, Minn. 1980, U.S. Supreme Ct. 1980, S.D. 1983, Nebr. 1984, U.S. Dist. Ct. Minn. 1984, U.S. Dist. Ct. Nebr. 1984, Wis. 1985, U.S. Dist. Ct. Wis. 1985, Mont. 1986, U.S. Dist. Ct. Mont. 1986. Ptnr. Johnson, Rodenburg & Lauinger, Fargo, N.D., 1976—; pres., gen. counsel Rodenburg Group, Inc., Fargo, 1980—. Contbg. editor: The Developing Labor Law, 1976-80; drafter N.D. garnishment statutes, 1982. Mem. Acad. Comml. and Bankruptcy Law Specialists.

RÖDER, GERHARD, lawyer; b. Biberach, Germany, May 15, 1952; s. Karl and Maria (Gnannt) R.; m. Susanne Stiewing, May 14, 1982; children: Eva, Julia. 1st exam., Freiburg (Germany) U., 1976, 2d exam., 1980, JD, 1983. Ptnr. Gleiss Lutz Hootz Hirsch, Stuttgart, Germany, 1984—; prof. law Freiburg U., 1995. Co-author: Sickness in Labor Law, 1987, Taschenbuch zur Kündigung, 1995, ed edit., 2000, Interessenausgleich and Sozialplan, 2d edit., 1996, Kündigungsfibel, 3d edit., 1997. Mem. Internat. Bar Assn., German Bar Assn. (labor law com.), Comp. Pension Shedy Group, European Employment Lawyers Assn. Fax: 49-711-855095. E-mail: gerhard.roeder@gleiss-law.com. Office: Gleiss Lutz Hootz Hirsch, Maybachstrasse 6, 70469 Stuttgart Germany

RODERO, JOSEPH SANTIAGO, electronics executive; b. San Sebastian, Spain, Dec. 16, 1941; came to U.S., 1951; s. Santiago and Flora (Barainca) R.; m. Carole Ann Elkin, Aug. 16, 1969; 1 child, Elisa Marie. BEE, Manhattan Coll., 1964; MS, U. So. Calif., 1970; postgrad., Nat. War Coll., Washington, 1981-82. Commd. 2d lt. USAF, 1964, advanced through grades to col.; vice comdr. 56th Tactical Tng. Wing, McDill AFB, Fla., 1984; asst. chief of staff plans and programs USAF Europe, Ramstein, Federal Republic of Germany, 1984-85; vice comdr. 316th Air Divsn., Ramstein, 1985-86; comdr. 86th Tactical Fighter Wing, Ramstein, 1986-87; asst. chief of staff ops. Allied Air Forces Ctrl. Europe, Ramstein, 1987-90; retired USAF, 1990; prin. scientist SHAPE Tech. Ctr., The Hague, The Netherlands, 1990-91; sr. prin. scientist, head Air C2 br. SHAPE Tech. Ctr., The Hague, 1991-96, NATO Cons. Command and Control Agy., The Hague, 1996—; chmn. Innovative Studies Group USAF, Washington, 1982-83; chmn. NATO Rsch. Study Group 16, Brussels, 1992—. Chmn. U.S. German Community Bd., Ramstein, 1985-86. Decorated D.F.C., Legion of Merit; recipient Def. Superior Svc. medal, 1990. Mem. IEEE (sr.), Armed Forces Comm. and Electronics Assn., Order of Daedalians, Air Force Assn., MENSA. Avocations: painting, reading, writing, computers.

RODGERS, BILLY RUSSELL, chemical engineer, research scientist; b. Fitzgerald, Ga., Sept. 5, 1936; s. Jimmie R. and Ruby Doris (Morris) R.; divorced; children: Cheryl, Donna, Angie, Rusty. AA, U. Fla., 1956, BSChemE with high honors, 1966, MS in Engring., 1967; PhD, U. Tenn., 1980. Project leader Shell Devel. Co., 1968-72; group leader Keene Corp. Fluid Handling, Cookeville, Tenn., 1972-74, Oak Ridge (Tenn.) Nat. Lab., 1974-92; sr. engr. Walk Haydel & Assocs., New Orleans, 1992-94; pres. Rodgers USA Enterprises, Orange Park, Fla., 1992—, Intelligent Cons., Orange Park, 1993—; qualifying agt./mgr. Rodgers Constrn. Co., 1996—. Author 3 books in field; contbr. articles to profl. publs. Fellow AIChE (bd. dirs. 1993-97, chmn. fuels and petrochem. divsn. 1992-95, chmn. program com. fuels and petrochem. divsn. 1990-92). Republican. Achievements include 1 patent in field. Avocation: computers. Office: Rodgers USA Enterprises 794 Foxridge Center Dr Orange Park FL 32065-8716

RODGERS, GRACE ANNE, university official; b. South Bend, Ind., Apr. 19, 1936; d. Morris and Barbara Mae (Hamm) Morrow; m. Eugene M. Rodgers, July 7, 1956; children: Craig Eugene, Kimberly Sue. BS, Ind. State U., 1981; pub. mgmt. cert., Ind. U., South Bend, 1991, MPA, 1993. Dir. spl. programs Ivy Tech. State Coll., South Bend, 1990-94, mktg. cons., 1994; mem. assoc. faculty dept. pub. affairs--non-profit marketing and environ. Ind. U., 1994—, dir. internships-student svcs. Sch. Pub.-Environ. Affairs, 1994—, dir. cmty. links, 1997—. Author: (manuals) Resume and Beyond, 1990, Strategic Marketing Plan, 1994. mem. Youth Svcs. Bur., South Bend. Recipient Indiana U. South Bend Student Gov. Lifetime Achievement award. Mem. Ind. U. Sch. Pub. end Environ. Affairs Alumni Assn. (adv. coun. 1993—), Ind. U.-South Bend Alumni Assn., Ind. State U. Alumni Assn., Phi Theta Kappa (hon., award for outstanding svc. 1993), Pi Alpha Alpha (sec. 1996—). Republican. Methodist. Avocations: travel, reading, classical music. E-mail: profgrac@aol.com. Home: 17120 Killarney Ct Granger IN 46530-9771 Office: Ind U 1800 Mishawaka Ave South Bend IN 46615-1621

RODGERS, ROBERT AUBREY, physicist; b. Huntsville, Ala., May 10, 1967; s. Aubrey and Peggy Joyce (Hairald) R.; m. Rocio Palacios, Oct. 25, 1997. BS, U. Ala., Huntsville, 1990, MS, 1992; MS in Health Physics, Ga. Inst. Tech., 1993. Cert. Am. Bd. Radiology Med. Nucl. Physics, Am. Bd. Sci. Nucl. Medicine, Nucl. Medicine Physics and Instrn. Grad. student physics rschr. Polarization and Lens Design Lab., U. Ala., Huntsville, 1991-92; grad. student med. physics rschr. Emory U.-Ga. Inst. Tech., Atlanta, 1992-94; staff med. health physicist, officer USAF, Lackland AFB, Tex., 1996-97; diagnostic med. physics fellow USAF, Lackland AFB, 1997-98, chief diagnostic med. physics element, 1998-2000; assoc. chief med. physics Keesler AFB, 2000—. U. Ala.-Huntsville Honor scholar, 1988-89, scholar, 1986-87. Mem. Am. Assn. Physicists in Medicine, Health Physics Soc., Air Force Assn., Soc. Photo-Optical Instrumentation Engrs., Soc. Nuclear Medicine. Baptist. Achievements include research on development of scattering polarimeter and measurement/analysis of diffraction grating polarization and efficiency properties, validation of compton scatter and attenuation correction methods for cardiac SPECT imaging.

RODGERS, STEPHEN JOHN, lawyer, physician, consultant; b. Phila., July 10, 1943; s. Harry Edward Rodgers and Antoinette Julia (Battaglini) Muckenfuss; m. Roberta Elaine Rhine, Sept. 21, 1974; children: Abigail Elizabeth, Rebecca Elizabeth. MD, Hahnemann U., 1969; JD, Widener U., 1989. Bar: Pa. 1990, N.J. 1990; med. lic., Pa., Del., N.J. Pvt. practice in family practice and emergency medicine Del. Pain Clinic, Wilmington, 1975-89, asst. dir., 1989-92; pvt. practice as medicolegal cons. Wilmington, 1992—; mem. Med. Assistance and Health Svcs. Adv. Bd., N.J., 1996-98; chair Task Force on Ind. Med. Exam., Dept. Labor and Industry, Commonwealth of Pa., 1996-98. Comdr. USN, 1968-75; capt. USNR, 1975—. Fellow Am. Acad. Family Physicians, Am. Acad. Disability Evaluating Physicians, Am. Acad. Emergency Medicine, Am. Coll. Legal Medicine; mem. Aerospace Med. Assn., Pa. Bar Assn. (health care com. 1991—), Del. Acad. Medicine, N.J. Acad. Family Physicians (ho. of dels. 1989, 90, 91), Vietnam Vets. of Am. Republican. Roman Catholic. Avocations: equestrian, pro bono veterans and disability advocate. Home: PO Box 54 Alloway NJ 08001-0054 Office: Ste 30 1701 Augustine Wilmington DE 19803

RODGERS, STEVEN EDWARD, tax practitioner, educator; b. Pierre, S.D., Feb. 8, 1947; s. Thomas Edward and Dorothy Zoe (Barker) R.; m. Donna Lynn Joyner, June 10, 1984; 1 child, Michelle Ann. Student, State U. S.D., 1964-65, U. Calif., Berkeley, 1968-72; cert., Coll. for Fin. Planning, 1986-87; fellow, Nat. Tax Practice Inst., 1988-89. CFP, Enrolled Agent. Collection mgr. Cenval Leasing-Ctrl. Bank, Long Beach, Calif., 1972-77; tax preparer Rodgers Tax Svc., Las Vegas, 1977-78; CEO Rainbow Tax Svc. Inc., Las Vegas, 1978—; pres. Rainbow Tax Svc., Inc., Las Vegas, 1978-90. Author: Marketing To Build Your Tax Practice, 1994. Active Amnesty Internat., Mensa; chmn. Best in the West Edn. Found., Las Vegas, 1994—, Nat. Assn. Enrolled Agents Edn. Found., 1995-96. With U.S. Army, 1965-68, Vietnam. Mem. Nat. Assn. Enrolled Agts. (nat. sec. 1989-90, nat. treas. 1991-92, nat. edn. chair 1994-95, named Tax Educator of the Yr., 1995), Nat. Assn. Enrolled Agents Edn. Found. (chair 1995-96), Nev. Soc. Enrolled Agts. (charter pres. 1985-86, fellow edn. found.), So. Nev. Assn. Tax Cons. (pres. 1981-82), Nat. Soc. Pub. Accts., Vietnam Vets. Am. Home: 1101 Cahill Ave Las Vegas NV 89128-3335 Office: Rainbow Tax Svc Inc 6129 Clarice Ave Las Vegas NV 89107-1401

RODGERS, SUE ANN, academic counselor; b. Tulsa, Okla., Aug. 20, 1943; d. Harold Sanford and Ann Louise (Landry) R.; m. James R., July 2, 1966; children: Mark Allen, Christopher. BS in Bus. Edn., U. Okla., 1965; MEd, Northwestern Okla. State U., 1994. Tchr. Garland (Tex.) H.S., 1966-68; bus. tchr. Blackwell (Okla.) H.S., 1968-69, guidance counselor, 1991-96; counselor, dir. internship program No. Okla. Coll., Tonkawa, 1996—. Bd. dirs. Edwin Fair Mental Health Found., Ponca City, Okla., 1994-2000, Blackwell Pub. Sch. Found., 1999—; com. mem. Child Care Advocacy Bd., Ponca City, 1999—. Mem. Tonkawa C. of C., Am. Counseling Assn., Okla. Counseling Assn., Okla. Acad. Advising Assn. Methodist. Avocations: travel, needlework. Office: No Okla Coll 1220 E Grand Ave Tonkawa OK 74653-4022

RODHE, HENNING, atmospheric science educator; b. Uppsala, Sweden, Feb. 15, 1941; s. Knut and Anna (Edling) R.; m. Karin Belfrage, June 12, 1964; children: Håkan, Jonas, Amina, Rasmus. Fil Kand, Lund (Sweden) U., 1964; PhD, Stockholm U., 1972. Sr. lectr. U. Nairobi, Kenya, 1972-75; rsch. asst. Stockholm U., 1965-69, sr. lectr. chem. meteorology, 1969-72, assoc. prof., 1975-79, prof., 1980—, chmn. dept. meteorology, 1979-81, 88-90, dean Faculty Scis., 1990-96, 20—; pres. Internat. Commn. on Atmospheric Chemistry and Global Pollution, 1990-98; mem. sci. com. Internat. Geosphere-Biosphere Program, 1997-99. Editor, author: Acidification in Tropical Countries, 1988, The Legacy of Svante Arrhenius, Understanding the Greenhouse Effect, 1998, Earth Systems Sciences, From Biogeochemical Cycles to Global Change, 2000. Mem. Royal Swedish Acad. Scis. (chmn. environ. com. 1997—). Avocations: bird watching, cross-country skiing. Office: Stockholm U, Dept Meteorology, S-10691 Stockholm Sweden

RODIN, PETER RODIONOVICH, manufacturing engineer, educator, researcher; b. Kruki, Russia, June 17, 1922; s. Rodion Marckovich Rodin and Anastasy Michaylovna (Osokina) Rodina; m. Lidia Michaylovna Shilkina, Aug. 2, 1948; children: Tatiyana, Rodion. MS in Engring., Aviation Inst., Moscow, 1945, PhD, 1949; DSc in Engring., Polytechnic Inst., Kyiv, Ukraine, 1961. Registered profl. manufacturing engr. From sr. lectr. to faculty dean Polytechnic Inst., Odessa, Ukraine, 1950-57, faculty dean, 1957-60, dept. head, prof., 1969—; dept. chief Ministry of Edn., Kyiv, Ukraine, 1963-78. Author: Design and Production of Cutting Tools, 1968, The Basis of Design of Cutting Tools, 1977, Metal Cutting Tools, 1986, The Basis of Design of Cutting Tools, 1990 (KPJ award 1992). Recipient Honorary Scientist of Ukraine award The Pres., 1972, State Prize of Ukraine award The Pres., Kyiv, 1979, 91, Pres. of Ukraine award The Pres., Kyiv, 1998. Mem. USSR Soc. of Sci. and Tech. (bd. mem. 1985-91), Soc. Machine Builders (chmn. 1985-91). Home: Brest-Litovsky prov 6/10, apt 106, 01055 Kyiv Ukraine Office: Kyiv Polytechnic Inst, Pr Peremohy 37, 01056 Kyiv Ukraine

RODIN, VICTOR VASILIEVICH, physicist; b. Glasov, Udmurtiya, Russia, July 1, 1954; s. Vasilii Ivanovich and Ekaterina Yakovlevna (Sorokina) R.; m. Vera Il'inichna Gaitan, May 6, 1988; children: Pavel, Natasha, Il'ya. Diploma, Moscow Physics-Tech. Inst., 1977; PhD, Inst. Biophysics, Pushchino, Russia, 1986; DS in Chemistry, Moscow State U., 1997; postgrad., U. Calif., Santa Barbara, 1991; doctorant, Moscow State U., 1993-96. Engr. Inst. Chem. Physics, Chernogolovka, Russia, 1977-78; rschr. Inst. Applied Microbiology, Obolensk, Russia, 1978-87; sr. rschr. Inst. for Biotech., Moscow, 1987-93, Inst. Phys. Chemistry, Moscow, 1996-97; prof. Moscow Avia-Technol. U., 1997—; docent Spl. Rsch. Ednl. Ctr. Moscow State U., 1995—; presenter in field; postdoctoral fellow U. Calif.-Santa Barbara, 1991, Moscow State U., 1993-96. Contbr. articles to profl. jours. Grantee Internat. Sci. Found., 1994, 96, European Soc. Magnetic Resonance in Medicine and Biology, Berlin, 1992, Italy, 1994, Prague, 1996, Geneva, 1998. Mem. Internat. Soc. for Magnetic Resonance in Medicine. Avocations: sports, painting, writing. E-mail: vrodin@aesc.msu.ru., vvrodin@mail.ru. Home: Lenin Str 3-a Apt 62, 142283 Serpukhov Russia Office: SLRC at Moscow State U, Kremenchugskaya str 11, Moscow 121357, Russia

RODINKOV, OLEG VASILIY, chemist, researcher; b. Korsakov, Russia, July 17, 1958; s. Vasiliy Alexey and Zinaida Vasiliy (Nikolaeva) R.; m. Ludmila Victor Udina, Jul. 4, 1981; children: Nina, Nadezhda. M, Univ., St. Petersburg, Russia, 1980, D, 1992. Engr. Rsch. Inst., SosnovyBor, Russia, 1980-86, researcher, 1986-93; researcher State Univ., St. Petersburg, 1993—. Inventor in field; contbr. articles to profl. jours. Recipient Badge USSR Inventor, 1986. Avocation: chess. E-mail: rodinkov@pobox.spbu.ru. Office: State Univ Chem Rsch Inst, Universitetskki prospekt 2, 198904 Saint Petersburg Russia

RODIONOV, ALEXANDR VIKENTIEVICH, geneticist, researcher; b. Murmansk, Russia, July 15, 1952; s. Vikentii Alexandrovich Rodionov and Alexandra Alexeevna Rodionova-Barabkina; m. Maria Sergeevna Rautian, Mar. 19, 1976; children: Anastasiya, Sonia. Biologist, animal geneticist, Leningrad State U., 1977, PhD, 1985. Tchr. 280th Leningrad H.S., 1977-78; mem. rsch. staff Nat. Rsch. Inst. Animal Breeding and Genetics, Leningrad-Pushkin, Russia, 1978-86; sr. mem. rsch. staff Biol. Inst. St. Petersburg State U., 1986—. Contbr. articles to sci. jours. Named Soros Assoc. Prof., Internat. Sci. Found., 1998, 2000. Fellow Vavilov Genetic Soc., Russian Bot. Soc., mem. Russian Geneal. Soc. (advisor adv. bd. 1997—, mem. cen. coun. 1997—, v.p. 2000—). Avocation: genealogy. Fax: 812-427-7310. E-mail: ark@ar1062.spb.edu. Home: Pionerskaya 47a, Stary Peterhof, Saint Petersburg 198904, Russia Office: St Petersburg State U, Oranienbaumskoye shosse 2, 198504 Saint Petersburg Russia

RODIONOV, IVAN MIKHAILOVICH, physiologist, researcher; b. Moscow, Oct. 13, 1928; s. Mikhail Semenovich and Elisaveta Fladimizovna (Giazintova) R.; m. Natalia Arsenievna Jankelevich, Feb. 10, 1952; children: Vladimir, Elena. Grad., U. Moscow, 1952, candidate, 1958, Doctor, 1968. Technician U. Moscow, 1952-58, sr. sci. worker, 1967-69, prof., 1969—; minor sci. worker Inst. Therapy, Moscow, 1958-62; sr. sci. worker Inst. Biophysics, Moscow, 1962-67; mem. sci. coun. U. Moscow, 1970—, U. Twer, Russia, 1994—. Author: Chemical and Immunological Sympathectomy, 1988; contbr. articles to profl. jours. Lt. res. Russian Army, 1954. Mem. Physiol. Soc. Avocation: hunting. Home: Apt 315, Home 4 Dm Ulianov Str, 117333 Moscow Russia Office: Moscow U, Vorobiov Hills, Moscow Russia

RODLEY, NIGEL SIMON, lawyer, educator; b. Leeds, Yorkshire, Eng., Dec. 1, 1941; s. John Peter and Rachel (Kantorowitz) R.; m. Lyn Bates, May 26, 1967. LLB, U. Leeds, 1963; LLM, Columbia U., 1965, NYU, 1970; PhD, U. Essex, Eng., 1992. Asst. prof. law Dalhousie U., Halifax, N.S., Can., 1965-68; assoc. econ. affairs officer UN Secretariat, N.Y.C., 1968-69; rsch. fellow NYU Ctr. for Internat. Studies, N.Y.C., 1970-72; legal adviser, head of legal office Amnesty Internat., London, 1973-90; part-time lectr. in law London Sch. Econs., 1973-90, rsch. fellow, 1983; reader in law U. Essex, 1990-94, prof. law, 1994—; spl. rapporteur on torture UN, Geneva, 1993—. Author: The Treatment of Prisoners Under International Law, 1987, 2d edit., 1999; co-author: Enhancing Global Human Rights, 1979; co-editor, contbr.: International Law in the Western Hemisphere, 1974; editor, contbr. To Loose the Bands of Wickedness--International Intervention in Defence of Human Rights, 1992. Mem. exec. com. David Davies Meml. Inst. Internat. Studies, London. Decorated knight Brit. Empire, 1998. Avocations: theatre, cinema, music, reading, walking. Home: 1 Meyrick Crescent, Colchester CO2 7QX, England Office: U Essex Dept Law, Wivenhoe Park, Colchester Essex CO4 3SQ, England

RODMAN, ALPINE C., arts and crafts company executive; b. Roswell, N.Mex., June 23, 1952; s. Robert Elsworth and Verna Mae (Means) R.; m. Sue Arlene Lawson, Dec. 13, 1970; 1 child, Connie Lynn. Student, Colo. State U., 1970-71, U. No. Colo. Ptnr. Pinel Silver Shop, Loveland, Colo., 1965-68, salesman, 1968-71; real estate salesman Loveland, 1971-73; mgr. Traveling Traders, Phoenix, 1974-75; co-owner Deer Track Traders, Loveland, 1975-85; pres. Deer Track Traders, Ltd., 1985—. Author: The Vanishing Indian: Fact or Fiction?, 1985. Mem. Civil Air Patrol, 1965-72, 87-92, dep. comdr. for cadets, 1988-90; cadet comdr. Ft. Collins, Colo., 1968, 70, Colo. rep. to youth tng. program, 1969, U.S. youth rep. to Japan, 1970. Mem. Bur. Wholesale Sales Reps., Western and English Salesmen's Assn. (bd. dirs. 1990), Internat. Platform Assn., Indian Arts and Crafts Assn. (bd. dirs. 1988-94, exec. com. 1989-92, v.p. 1990, pres. 1991, market chmn. 1992), Crazy Horse Grass Roots Club. Republican. Office: Deer Track Traders Ltd PO Box 448 Loveland CO 80539-0448

RODMAN, RAYMOND G., insurance company executive; b. Topeka, Kans., Aug. 2, 1946; s. John T. and Wilma D. (Cox-Betts) R.; m. Sherri L. Shughart, Aug. 31, 1968; children: Eric, Erin, Tara, Charisse. BS in Math., Emporia State U., 1970; MBA, Ill. State U., 1980. CLU, ChFC, CPCU, cert. data processing profl. Programmer State Farm Ins., Bloomington, Ill., 1970-72, analyst, 1973-75, team leader, 1975-77, project leader, 1977-80, supt., 1980-86, mgr., 1986-90, IS mgr., 1990—. Chmn. economy subcom., steering com. 2020 Planning Com., Normal, Ill., 1995-96; mem. McLean County Bd., 1990—. Mem. CPCU Soc., CLU Soc. Republican. Baptist. Home: 719 N School St Normal IL 61761-1620 Office: State Farm Insurance 3 State Farm Plz # K2 Bloomington IL 61791-0002

RODMAN, SUE A., wholesale company executive, artist, writer; b. Ft. Collins, Colo., Oct. 1, 1951; d. Marvin F. Lawson and Barbara I. (Miller) Lawson Shue; m. Alpine C. Rodman, Dec. 13, 1970; 1 child, Connie, Lynn. Student, Colo. State U., 1970-73. Silversmith Pinel Silver Shop, Loveland, Colo., 1970-71; asst. mgr. Traveling Traders, Phoenix, 1974-75; co-owner, co-mgr. Deer Track Traders, Loveland, 1975-85; v.p. Deer Track Traders, Ltd., Loveland, 1985—. Author: The Book of Contemporary Indian Arts and Crafts, 1985. Mem. U.S. Senatorial Club, 1982-87, Rep. Presdl. Task Force, 1984-90; mem. CAP, 1969-73, 87-90, pers. officer, 1988-90. Mem. Internat. Platform Assn., Indian Arts and Crafts Assn., Western and English Sales Assn., Crazy Horse Grass Roots Club. Mem. Am. Baptist Ch. Avocations: museums, piano, recreation research, fashion design. Office: Deer Track Traders Ltd PO Box 448 Loveland CO 80539-0448

RODNEY, MARILYN ANN, community health educator, consultant; b. Allentown, Pa., Oct. 8, 1947; d. Howard Oscar and Estella Genetta (Ferguson) Fegely; m. Ronald Lee Rodney, Sept. 6, 1969; children: Lisa Marie Saylor, Christopher Lee, Jeffery Scott. Diploma in nursing, Phila. Gen. Hosp., 1969; BSN, Wright State U., 1989, MS in Nursing Edn. and Adminstrn., 1991. RN, Ohio. Relief supr. St. Joseph Hosp., Asheville, N.C., 1982-86; relief charge nurse Greene Meml. Hosp., Xenia, Ohio, 1986-89; primary nurse Miami Valley Hosp., Dayton, Ohio, 1989-92; adj. faculty Miami U., Middletown, Ohio, 1991-92, Sinclair C.C., Dayton, 1992—; dir. divsn. cmty. health advocacy Ctr. for Healthy Communities, Dayton, 1992—; cons. Wis. Med. Coll., Madison, 1998-99, chair adv. bd. Injury Prevention Ctr., Dayton, 1997-98. Trustee Spicer Hts. Neighborhood Assn., Beavercreek, Ohio, 1993-95. Named Innovator of Yr., League for Innovators Sinclair, Dayton, 1996. Mem. APHA, Ohio Nurses Assn., Sigma Theta Tau (v.p. Zeta Phi chpt. 1997—). Avocations: hiking, swimming, photography, gourmet cooking. E-mail: mrodney@sinclair.edu. Office: Ctr Healthy Cmty 140 E Monument Ave Dayton OH 45402-1211

RODNUNSKY, SIDNEY, lawyer, educator; b. Edmonton, Alta., Can., Feb. 3, 1946; s. B. and I. Rodnunsky; m. Teresita Asuncion; children: Naomi, Shawna, Rachel, Tevie, Claire, Donna, Sidney Jr. BEd, U. Alberta, 1966, LLB, 1973; MEd, U. Calgary, 1969, grad. diploma, 1990; BS, U. of State of N.Y., 1988; MBA, Greenwich U., 1990. Served as regional counsel to Her Majesty the Queen in Right of the Dominion of Can.; former gov. Grande Prairie Regional Coll.; now prin. legal counsel Can.; nat. exec., Alta. coord. for gifted children, SIG coord. Mensa Can.; past pres. Grande Prairie and Dist. Bar Assn., Alta. Tchrs. Assn., Aspenview. Author: Breathalyzer Casebook; editor: The Children Speak. Decorated knight Grand Cross Sovereign and Royal Order of Piast, knight Grand Cross Order of St. John the Baptist; knight Hospitaller Order St. John of Jerusalem; Prince of Kiev, Prince of Trabzon, Prince and Duke of Rodari, Duke of Chernigov, Count of Riga, Count of St. John of Alexandria; named to Honorable Order of Ky. Colonels; named adm. State of Tex.; recipient Presdl. Legion of Merit. Mem. Law Soc. Alta., Law Soc. Sask., Can. Bar Assn., Inst. Can. Mgmt., Phi Delta Kappa. E-mail: dubai7@hotmail.com. Address: PO Box 106, Chilanko Forks, BC Canada V0L 1H0

RODOCANACHI, EMMANUEL A., government official; b. Toulon, Provence, France; s. André P. and Nada R. (Diplarakos) R.; m. Elizabeth J. Demargne, July 2, 1968; children: Ariane, Andre, Jean. Diploma, Inst. Etudes Politiques, Paris, 1962; diploma d'etudes superieures de droit, Ecole Nat. d'Adminstrn., Paris, 1968. Officer Ministry of Fin., Paris, 1968-78; sr. adviser Presidency of the Republic, Paris, 1978-81; asst. mgr. Ministry of Fin., Paris, 1981-85, dep. dir., 1985-86; chief adviser econs. Prime Min., Paris, 1986-88; CEO Hottinguer Bank, Paris, 1988-94; chmn., CEO Natexis Banque, Paris, 1994-99; sr. adviser Ministry of Fin., Paris, 1999—. Dep. mayor Town Coun., Vaison and la Romaine, France, 1983-89, mem. 1989-95. Decorated Ordre Nat. du Merite, Legion d'Honneur, Prime Min., 1993. Mem. Polo de Paris (1975—), Acad. des Sports, C. of C. France-Can (pres. 1995-99). Avocations: tennis, skiing, opera. Office: Ministry of Fin, 139 rue de Bercy, 75012 Paris France

RODOLFF, DALE WARD, sales executive, consultant; b. Casa Grande, Ariz., Aug. 5, 1938; s. Norval Ward and Mary Louise (Grasty) Rodolff; m. Kathleen Pennington, Sept. 3, 1960 (div. July 1983); children: David Ward (dec.), Julia Ann. BS in Mining Engring., U. Ariz.; PMD, U. Cape Town; postgrad., Denver Sem. Registered profl. engr., Republic of South Africa. Supt. smelting and fabricating Inspiration Consol. Copper Co., Claypool, Ariz., 1960-72; smelter and refinery supt. Palabora Mining Co, Phalaborwa, Republic of South Africa, 1972-74; asst. mgr. Empress Nickel Mining Co., Gatooma, Zimbabwe, 1974-77; smelter supt. Magma Copper Co., San Manuel, Ariz., 1977-81; v.p., gen. mgr. Sentinel Mgmt. Corp., Tucson, 1981-82; dir., mgr. metallurgy Outokumpu Engring. Inc., Denver, 1982-86, mgr. N.Am., 1986-96, also bd. dirs.; supt. flash smelting and flash converting Kennecott Utah Copper, 1996-97; cons., pres. D.W. Rodolff Cons. Corp., 1986—; pres. Bus. Performance Svcs., Inc., 1986-90; dir. Grace Ministries, 1995-99. Contbr. articles to tech. jours.; inventor scrap rod feed system, 1970. Pres. Y Men's Club, Miami, Ariz., 1969. Kennecott scholar U. Ariz., 1959. Mem. AIME (metall. soc., soc. mining engrs., chmn. smelter div. 1970, 71, pyro metall. com. 1973-77), Mining and Metall. Soc. Am. Avocations: flying, skiing, Christian endeavors. Home and Office: 6527 S Jungfrau Way Evergreen CO 80439-5308

RODOTÀ, ANTONIO, executive; b. Cosenza, Italy, Dec. 24, 1935. Degree in electronics engring., Rome U., 1959. With Selenia, 1966-80; head Compagnia Nazionale Satelliti, Italy, 1980-83; with Alenia-Spazio, 1983-97, chief exec., 1995-97; dir.-gen. European Space Agy., Paris, 1997—; italian del. NATO, Paris, 1965-66; mem. staff SISPE S.p.A., Italy, 1959-80; dir. gen. Compagnia Nazionale Satelliti SpA, 1980-83; joint mng. dir. Selenia Spazio SpA, 1983-95, mng. dir., 1995-96; head space divsn. Finmeccanica, 1996-97; chmn., mng. dir. Quadrics Supercomputer world Ltd.; dir. gen. Coun. European Space Agy., 1997—; mem. high-performance computer group Italian Ministry Rsch. Mem. Italian Nat. Assn. Elect. Industries (vice chmn.), Italian Aerospace Assn. (mng. com.). Office: European Space Agency, 8-10 rue Mario Nikis, 75738 Paris France

RODOWICK, DAVID NORMAN, media educator; b. Youngstown, Ohio, Aug. 27, 1952; s. Rudolph Judson and Betty Jane (Madden) R.; m. Dominique Eliane Bluher, May 28, 1997; 1 child, Sarah Louise Dominique. BA, U. Tex., 1976, MA, 1979; PhD, U. Iowa, 1983. Assoc. prof. Yale U., New Haven, 1983-91; prof. English & Visual and Cultural Studies U. Rochester, N.Y., 1991-2000; chmn. in film King's Coll., U. London, 2000—; dir. film studies program Yale U., 1986-91, U. Rochester, 1993-97; adv. bd. Camera Obscura, Santa Barbara, Calif., 1995—. Author: The Crisis of Political Modernism, 1988, The Difficulty of Difference, 1991, Gilles Deleuze's Time Machine, 1997; editl. bd. PMLA, N.Y.C., 1997-2000. Mem. MLA.

RODRIGO, RAMÓN SALINAS, pathophysiology educator, researcher; b. Santiago, Chile, Oct. 10, 1944; s. Ramón Rodrigo and Clara Salinas. BS, U. Chile, Santiago, 1963, Degree in Chemistry, 1968, Magister (hon.), 1989. Cert. pharm. chemist. Instr. Faculty Medicine U. Chile, Santiago, 1970-75, asst. prof. Faculty Medicine, 1975-87, assoc. prof. Faculty Medicine, 1987—. Author rsch. articles, reviews. Grantee Comision Nacional de Investigacion Cientifica y Tecnologica, Chile, 1975, 91, 99, U. Chile, 1978, 90. Mem. Sociedad de Farmacologia de Chile. Opus Dei. Avocations: classic lit., baroque music. E-mail: rrodrigo@machi.med.uchile.cl. Home: Las Condes, Reyes Lavalle 3415 Apt 71, Santiago Chile Office: Univ Chile Med Sch, Independencia 1027, 75008 Casilla Santiago, Chile

RODRIGUES, ADRIANO DUARTE, communication educator; b. Lisbon, Portugal, Apr. 4, 1942; s. José Rodrigues and Silvina Duarte de Candida Rodrigues. B.Theology, U. Strasbourg, France, 1968, B.Sociology, 1970; PhD in Comm., U. Louvain, Belgium, 1977. Lectr. U. Louvain, 1971-77; assoc. prof. New U. Lisbon, 1977-80, prof. comm., 1980—, dean Coll. Social and Human Scis., 1988-93. Author: Communication Strategies, 1989, Introduction to Semiotics, 1992, Communication and Culture, 1994, Pragmatic Dimensions in Communication, 1995, Pragmatic Dimensions of Sense, 1996, Communication and Information Techniques, 1999. Mem. Portuguese Assn. Sociology, Internat. Assn. Semiotics, Assn. Internat. Sociologues de Langue Francaise. E-mail: adrodrigues@mail.telepac.pt. Office: U Lisbon Dept Ling Studies, Ave de Berna 26-C, 1050 Lisbon Portugal

RODRIGUES, ALLAN, chemicals executive; b. Mangalore, Karnataka, India, June 3, 1956; s. Michael Joseph and Aureen Rita (Sequeira) R.; m. Romula Fluorina Pereira, Oct. 17, 1983; children: Aditya Padival, Anuj Padival. BSChemE, Manipal (India) Inst. Tech., 1980. Trainee Mysore Lamp Works, Bangalore, 1980-81; asst. engr. Tata Consulting Engrs., Mumbai, 1981-84; mng. dir. Pragati Glyoxal (Pvt.) Ltd., Mysore, 1984—; ptnr. Pragati Biotech., Mysore, 1984—, Pragati Foods & Beverages, Mysore, 1996—, Pragati Mekem, Mysore, 1995; propr. Eliza Coffee Estate, Pollibetta, 1975—. Mem. Bangalore Club, Sri Kanteeravanarashimaraja Sports Club, Karnataka Golf Assn., Rotary (cmty. svc. dir. Mysore West chpt. 1996-97). Roman Catholic. Avocations: reading, rock music, golf, television. Office: Pragati Glyoxal Pvt Ltd, 162 (P) Belagola Indsl Area, Mysore Karnataka 570016, India

RODRIGUES, AUGUSTO SILVEIRA, educator; b. Porto, Portugal, Jan. 4, 1966; s. Augusto Maria and Olinda Silveira (Noia) R. MS, U. Ariz., 1994, PhD, 1996. Lab. asst. U. Porto, Portugal, 1986-87, asst. jr. league, 1987-90, jr. lectr., 1990-96, asst. prof., 1996—. Contbr. articles to profl. jours. Grantee JNICT, 1991-93, 94; fund. Gomes Teixeira fellow, 1990. Avocations: running, skiing, reading, scuba diving. Home: RS Bento Das Peras 119, 4435-432 Rio Tinto Portugal Office: U Porto Physics Dept, R Campo Alegre 687, 4169-007 Porto Portugal

RODRIGUES, CAROL MARIA, secondary school educator; b. Manchester, N.H., Dec. 17, 1947; d. Carlos and Anna (Andersen) R. BA, Notre Dame Coll., Manchester, 1970, MEd, 1980, Cert., 1982. Asst. to registrar Notre Dame Coll., Manchester, 1966-70; bus. tchr. West High Sch., Manchester, 1970-76; work experience coord., tchr. Meml. High Sch., Manchester, 1976—; instr. Notre Dame Coll., 1987; tchr. externship Am. Express Fin. Advisors, Bedford, N.H., summer 1998, Citizens Bank, Manchester, N.H., summer 1999. Mem. adv. coun. Manchester School-to-Careers Partnership, 1999. Recipient Meritorious Svc. Prin.'s award, Meml. H.S., 1996, For Manchester award, 1997, Oustanding Educator of Yr. award for School-to-Work Initiative, 1997, Gold Circle award N.H. Ptnrs. in Edn., 1998. Mem. NEA, Manchester Edn. Assn. Avocations: gardening, crafts, outdoor sports, travel. Home: 199 Barrett St Manchester NH 03104-2884

RODRIGUES, JOSÉ DIONÍSIO, advertising executive; b. Travanca do Mondego, Coimbra, Portugal, Mar. 19, 1947; arrived in Brazil, 1957; s. Alexandre and Maria (Asunção) R.; m. Marilia Helena Hauro, Oct. 19, 1970; children: Rodrigo, José Henrique, Camila. Bachelor, U. Fed. Paraná, Curitiba, Brazil, 1970; postgrad., FAE-Paraná, Curitiba, Brazil, 1975, ESPM, Curitiba, Brazil, 1991. Cert. journalist, advertising, publicitary. Reporter Ed. Gazeta do Povo, Curitiba, 1968-72, copy writer, 1972-75; dir. Opus Propaganda, Curitiba, 1974-86, Opus & Multipla Propaganda, Curitiba, 1986—. pres. Sinapro, Curitiba, 1998—. Named Publicitary of the Yr., Colunistas, Curitiba, 1983, Publicitary of Decade, Colunistas, Curitiba, 1985. Roman Catholic. Avocations: music, reading, movies, golf, traveling. Office: Opus & Multipla Propaganda, Itupava 362, 80060250 Curitiba Parana, Brazil

RODRIGUES, MANUEL AUGUSTO, educator, archive administrator; b. Penela, Portugal, June 10, 1930; s. Augusto and Maria Lucinda Rodrigues; m. Alice Correia Rodrigues, 1979; 1 child, Sara Miriam. Lic., Pontificia U., Rome, 1960, Pontificia Inst. Biblico, Rome, 1962; Master, Sch. Archeology, Jerusalem, 1963; Doctor, U. Coimbra, Portugal, 1975. Prof. philosophy U. Coimbra, 1963—, dir. archives, 1980—. Contbr. articles to publs. in field. Mem. Acad. Portuguese Historians, others. Home: Rua Luis De Camoes, 3000-252 Coimbra Portugal Office: Arquivo Univ Coimbra, 3000 Coimbra Portugal

RODRIGUES, WALDYR ALVES, JR., mathematical physics educator; b. Araraquara, S.P., Brazil, Mar. 14, 1946; s. Waldyr Alves and Alayde (De Almedia) R.; m. Dulce Madalena Autran von Pfuhl, Jan. 31, 1968 (div. Oct. 1979); children: Adriano, Renata; m. Maria De Fátima Grangeiro, Aug. 10, 1985; children: Fabio, Maria Paula, Maria Larissa. BS in Physics, U. São Paulo, Brazil, 1968; DSc in Physics, U. Torino, Italy, 1971; Prof. Math. Physics, U. Campinas, Brazil, 1986. Asst. prof. physics U. São Paulo, 1969; assoc. prof. physics U. Campinas, 1971-86, prof. math., physics, 1986—, dir. Inst. Maths., 1994-98; vis. prof. U. Trento, Italy, 1987-88; vis. scientist MIT, Cambridge, Mass., 1976-78; cons. Brazil Rsch. Coun., 1980—, São Paulo State Rsch. Coun., 1995—; v.p. Found. Devel. U. Campinas, 1997—. Editor: (with P. Letelier) Gravitation. The Spacetime Structure, 1994, (with B.N. Apanasov, S.B. Bradlow, and K.K. Uhlenbeck) Geometry Topology and Physics, 1997, (with A.A. Grib and W.R. Rodrigues Jr.) Nonlocality in Quantum Physics, 1999; contbr. articles to profl. jours.; mem. editl. bd. Advances in Applied Clifford Algebras, 1986—, Random Operators and Stochastic Equations, 1997—, Boletim Sociedade Paranaense de Matematice, 1996—. Fellow Brazilian Math. Soc., Brazilian Phys. Soc.; mem. AAAS, Am. Math. Soc. Office: IMECC-UNICAMP, Inst Maths CP PO Box 605, 13081970 Campinas SP, Brazil

RODRIGUES FILHO, ARLINDO, electrical engineer; b. Barra do Pirai, Brazil, Dec. 1, 1962; s. Arlindo Rodrigues and Neusa Rodrigues; m. Yara Adami, Jan. 6, 1996. EE, Fed. U. Rio de Janeiro, 1986, MSEE, 1998. Cert. in equipment engring. Equipment mgr., maintenance supr. exploration-prodn. segment PETROBRAS, Macae, Brazil, 1986-94; rsch. engr., rschr. R & C Ctr., PETROBRAS, Rio de Janeiro, 1994-96, equipment engr., automation and control project engr., 1996-98, project supr. Engring. Office, 1998—. Contbr. numerous articles to profl. jours. Mem. IEEE (sr.), Instrument Soc. Am. (sr.). Roman Catholic. Fax: 55-21-8765529. E-mail: arlindor.@petrobas.com.br. Home: Cond Uba Pendotiba, Rua 3/401-JD, Uba 24350370, Brazil Office: PETROBRAS Engring Office, Rua Gen Canabarro 500 9 Fl, 20271900 Rio de Janeiro Brazil

RODRIGUES-RADISCHAT, MARGARIDA POCINHO, physician, researcher; b. Coimbra, Portugal, June 16, 1958; arrived in Austria, 1993; d. Alfredo and Maria de Jesus (Pocinho) Rodrigues; m. Bernd Guenter Radischat, Dec. 24, 1993; children: Rafael and Lara (twins). MD, Faculty of Medicine, Lisbon, Portugal, 1982; Gen. Physician, U. Hosp., Lisbon, 1985; Specialist Nuclear Medicine, Oncology, Oncology Hosp., Lisbon, 1990. Asst. faculty of medicine Lisbon, 1982-90; head and prof. of anatomy and physiology Sch. Physical Rehab., Estoril, Portugal, 1982-85; gen. physician U. Hosp., Lisbon, 1982-85; nuclear medicine physician Oncology Hosp., Lisbon, 1985-93; nuclear medicine rschr. physician U. Hosp., Vienna, Austria, 1993—; rschr. Faculty of Medicine, Lisbon, 1977-90. Contbr. chpts. to books, articles to profl. jours. Vol. Portuguese Red Cross, Lisbon, 1975-76; collaborator in social orgns. helping or taking care of children in risk, South of Portugal, 1990—, Vienna, Austria, 1998—. Recipient award Portuguese Soc. of Orthopaedics and Traumatology, 1987, Portuguese Ciba Geigy award of rheumatology, 1991, Med. Pro Free Paper award, 1994. Mem. Ordem dos Médicos Portuguesa, Soc. Portuguesa de Medicina Nuclear, Soc. Portuguesa de Radiologia Medicina Nuclear, European Assn. of Nuclear Medicine, Soc. Española de Medicina Nuclear, Grupo de Estudos de Cardiologia Nuclear da Soc. Portuguesa de Medicina Nuclear, Grupo de Estudos de Cardiologia Nuclear da Soc. Española de Medicina Nuclear, Internat. Soc. of Radiolabelled Blood Elements (bd. dirs. 1996-97, treas. 1997—), Soc. of Med. Scis. of Lisbon, Soc. Portuguesa de Cardiologia, European Soc. of Cardiology, Soc. Portuguesa de Anatomia, European Assn. of Anatomy, Group of Biotherapy of the Portuguese Assn. of Investigation in Oncology, Österreichische Ärztekammer, Österreichische Gesellschaft für Prostaglandinforschung, Danubian League Against Thrombosis and Hemorrhagic Disorders, Gesellschaft der Ärzte in Wien, Wilhelm-Auerswald-Atherosklerose Forschungsgruppe (Vienna), Austrian Assn. for Morphol. and Functional Rsch. in Atherosclerosis (treas. 1998—). Roman Catholic. Avocation: swimming. E-mail: margarida.rodrigues@akh-wien.ac.at. Home: Bruennerstrasse 221/2/16, 1210 Vienna Austria Office: Dept Nuclear Medicine-U Hosp, Waehringer Guertel 18-20, 1090 Vienna Austria

RODRIGUEZ, ANTONIO JOSE, lawyer; b. New Orleans, Dec. 7, 1944; s. Anthony Joseph and Josephine Olga (Cox) R.; m. Virginia Anne Soignet, Aug. 23, 1969; children: Henry Jacob, Stephen Anthony. BS, U.S. Naval Acad., 1966; JD cum laude, Loyola U. of the South, New Orleans, 1973. Bar: La. 1973, U.S. Dist. Ct. (ea. dist.) La. 1973, U.S. Ct. Appeals (5th cir.) 1973, U.S. Dist. Ct. (mid. dist.) La. 1975, U.S. Dist. Ct. (we. dist.) La. 1977, U.S. Ct. Appeals (11th cir.) 1981, U.S. Supreme Ct. 1987, U.S. Dist. Ct. (so. dist.) Miss. 1991, U.S. Ct. Appeals (4th cir.) 1991, U.S. Ct. Appeals (1st cir.) 1997, U.S. Ct. Internat. Trade, 1991. Assoc. Phelps, Dunbar, Marks, Claverie & Sims, New Orleans, 1973-77; ptnr. Phelps Dunbar, New Orleans, 1977-92, Rice Fowler Rodriguez Kingsmill & Flint, LLP, New Orleans, 1992—; prof. law Tulane U., New Orleans, 1981—; mem. nat. rules of the road adv. coun. U.S. Dept. Transp., Washington, 1987-90, chmn. nat. navigation safety adv. coun., 1990-94; spkr. on admiralty and environ. Co-author: Admiralty-Limitation of Liability, 1981—, Admiralty-Law of Collision, 1990—; author: (chpt.) Benedict on Admiralty, 1995—; assoc. editor Loyola Law Rev., 1971-73; contbr. articles to profl. maritime and environ. jours. Bd. dirs. Greater New Orleans Coun. Navy League, 1988—, Propeller Club of New Orleans, 1997—. Lt. USN, 1966-70; capt. USNR, 1970-95. Decorated Navy Commendation medal; recipient Disting. Pub. Svc. award U.S. Dept. Transp., 1993. Fellow La. Bar Found.; mem. ABA, La. Bar Assn., La. State Law Inst., Maritime Law Assn. U.S. (proctor 1975—), New Orleans Bar Assn., Southeastern Admiralty Law Inst., Assn. Average Adjusters U.S., Assn. Average Adjusters U.K., Naval Res. Assn. (chpt. pres. 1982-84), U.S. Naval Acad. Alumni Assn. (chpt. pres. 1981-83), Bienville club, Phi Alpha Delta, Alpha Sigma Nu. Republican. Roman Catholic. Home: 4029 Mouton St Metairie LA 70002-1303 Office: Rice Fowler Rodriguez Kingsmill & Flint LLP 201 Saint Charles Ave Fl 36 New Orleans LA 70170-1000

RODRIGUEZ, BEATRIZ LORENZA, epidemiologist; b. Monterrey, Mexico, Aug. 10, 1962; d. Antonio L. and Diana R.; m. J. David Curb. MD, Inst. Tech. de Monterrey, Monterrey, Mex., 1985; MPH, Univ. Tex., 1986, PhD, 1990. Fellow Univ. Tex., Houston, 1991; asst. prof. Univ Hawaii, Honolulu, 1991-96, assoc. prof., 1996-2000, prof., 2000—. Contbr. articles to profl. jours. Fellow Am. Heart Assn. (coun. on epidemiology and prevention 1994—, nat. bd. dirs. 1998), Am. Heart Assn. Hawaii (pres. 1996). E-mail: beatriz@phri.hawaii-health.com.

RODRIGUEZ, CARLOS ALBERTO, pathologist; b. San Miguel de Tucuman, Argentina, Apr. 27, 1948; s. Belarmino and Blanca Rosa (Gallo) R.; m. Elena Teresa Conejos, Nov. 30, 1974; children: Sebastian A., C. Gonzalo, Santiago M. BS, Colegio Nacional Bartolome Mitre, Tucuman, 1965; MD, Faculty of Medicine, Tucuman, 1974. Diplomate Am. Bd. Pathology. Resident and chief resident dept. pathology Montefiore Hosp., N.Y.C., 1975-79; fellow orthopedic pathology Presbyn. Hosp., N.Y.C., 1978; fellow dept. pathology Meml. Sloan-Kettering Cancer Ctr., N.Y.C., 1979-80; chief dept. pathology Hosp. Avellaneda, Tucuman, 1980-90, Hosp. Maternidad, Tucuman, 1990—; prof. pathology Faculty of Medicine, Tucuman, 1990—, councillor, 1989; dir. pvt. practice Departamento de Patologia, Tucuman, 1980-98; dir. pvt. practice Instituto de Patologia, Tucuman, 1998—. Contbr. articles to profl. jours., chpts. to books. Recipient 1st prize Best Paper on Poster, Argentine Congress of Senology, Argentine Soc. Senology, 1987, 1st prize Best Paper on Poster, Argentine Congress of Cytology, Argentine Soc. Cytology, 1992, prize Prof. Eugenio Borello, Facultad de Odontologia, U. Rosario, Argentina, 1997. Mem. Internat. Acad. Cytology, Internat. Acad. Pathology, Argentine Soc. Pathology, Argentine Soc. Cytology. Office: Instituto de Patologia, Rivadavia 353-PB, 4000 San Miguel Tucuman Argentina

RODRIGUEZ, ENRIQUE MARCELO, biologist, educator; b. Buenos Aires, Mar. 6, 1960; s. Edgardo Roberto and Amelia Ramona (Miralles) R. Licenciado, U. Buenos Aires, 1984, PhD in Biol. Sci., 1991. Rsch. fellow U. Buenos Aires, 1986-90, sr. asst., 1990-92, asst. prof., 1992—; rsch. project dir. U. Buenos Aires, 1991—, and other insts., rsch. of Argentine Sci. Rsch. Coun., 1995—; participation in various projects, 1992—. Contbr. articles to profl. jours. Officer Argentine Navy, 1974-78. Mem. AAAS, N.Y. Acad. Scis., Argentine Toxicol. Assn., The Crustacean Soc. Avocations: playing the sax and guitar, photography, tango dancer. Home: Oro 2462 1C, 1425 Buenos Aires Argentina Office: Dept Biol Scis FCEyN UBA, PAB II Ciudad Univ, 1428 Buenos Aires Argentina

RODRIGUEZ, GUILLERMO, physicist, secondary education educator; b. Santa Cruz de la Palma, Canary Isl, Spain, Oct. 19, 1939; s. Ramón and Lina R.; m. Maria Dolores Quintana, Dec. 13, 1970; children: Victoria, Iballa, Pedro, Guillermo. Bachelor, U. Complutense, Madrid, 1966; MSc in Astrophysics, U. Talence, Bordeaux, France, 1969. Rschr. Astron. Observatory Teide, Spain, 1967-70; tchr. high sch., 1970—. Author, editor: Indirect Influences of the Moon, 1980; inventor in field. Mem. Mcpl. Coun., Garafia, Spain, 1973-75. With Spanish mil., 1965. Recipient award in field Kunglica Svenska Vetenskapsakademien, 1985. Mem. Am. Geophys. Union. Roman Catholic. Achievements include: finding a new theory over the influence of chinois in the world 5000 years ago. Avocations: photography, archaeology, cosmology, theology, travel. Home: calle Mayor 103-1C, 28922 Alcorcon Madrid, Spain

RODRIGUEZ, GUILLERMO GERARDO, physician, surgeon; b. San Jose, Costa Rica, Jan. 25, 1949; s. Mariano and Margo (Gomez) R.; m. Lena Monge, Aug. 3, 1996. MD, U. Costa Rica, 1975. Intern U. Costa Rica Med. Sch., 1975; resident in internal medicine México Hosp., San Jose, 1977-79; clin. fellow in critical care medicine Baylor Coll. Medicine, Houston, 1979-81; attending physician critical care dept. Hosp. México, San Jose, 1981-88, chief respiratory therapy unit, 1986-98, med. dir. MICU, 1988-98; prof. medicine U. Costa Rica, San Jose, 1982—, dir. residency program in emergency medicine, 1993-95, acad. dir. respiratory therapy program, divsn. med. tech., 1985-98; Robert F. Kennedy vis. prof. L.Am. studies Harvard U., 1999; exec. dir. Nat. Emergency Program, San Jose, 1987-93; adj. prof. medicine Baylor Coll. Medicine, Houston, 1988—; pres., founder Costa Rican Inst. for Clin. Rsch., San Jose, 1992—; med. dir. Project HOPE, Costa Rica, 1985—; asst. dir. Cath Clinic Hosp., San Jose, 1985-87. Co-author: Manual de diabetes mellitus, 1982, Manual de Emergencies Médicas, 1984, Manual de procedimientos medico-quiruigicos, 1988, Manual de soporte avanzado de trauma, 1992, Guia de diagnóstico y terapéutica de emergencies más frecuentes, 1980, Manual de emergencias en cirugia, 1988; author clin. rsch. manual, 1999; contbr. articles to profl. jours. Commr. Nat. Emergency Commn., San Jose, 1986-94. Recipient Premio A La Superacion, Pres. of Costa Rica, 1991, Recognition of Profl. Excellence, Costa Rican Congress, 1992; fellowship Am. Coll. of Critical Care Medicine, 1999. Mem. ACP, Soc. Critical Care Medicine, Am. Soc. Microbiology, Am. Assn. Respiratory Care, Costa Rican Soc. Critical Care Medicine, Costa Rican Coll. Physicians (Disting. Physician award 1990, 94), Costa Rican Acad. Medicine. Roman Catholic. Office: Costa Rican Inst Clin Rsch, PO Box 250-1000, San José Costa Rica

RODRIGUEZ, JOSE ERNESTO, environmental manager; b. Buenos Aires, June 16, 1947; s. Jose Antonio Rodriguez and Elena Eiroa; m. Adriana Leonor Napoli, Jan. 24, 1972; children: Barbara, Guadalupe. Navy Engrng. diploma, U. Tech. Nat., Buenos Aires. Devel. mgr. Indsl. Metall. Pescarmona Soc. Anonima/Limpieza Urbana Soc. Anonima, Buenos Aires, 1992—. Mem. Jr. Chambers Internat. (The Best V.P. award 1974; former pres., devel. dir.). Roman Catholic. Avocations: tennis soccer, canoeing, golf, gymnastics. Home: Alcaraz 4442 PB 1, 1407 Buenos Aires Argentina Office: Indsl Metall Pescarmona Soc Anonima/Limpieza Urbana Soc Anon, Ave Eduardo Madero 940 Piso 19, 1106 Buenos Aires Argentina

RODRIGUEZ, JUAN FRANCISCO, chemical engineering educator; b. Ciudad Real, Spain, Aug. 11, 1967; s. Juan Rodriguez and Cira Romero; m. Carmen Velasco, Aug. 31, 1991; children: Maria Teresa, Juan Francisco, Antonio. MSc, Complutense, Madrid, 1989; PhD in Chem. Engring., U. Castilla-La Mancha, Ciudad Real, 1993. Assoc. U. Castilla-La Mancha, Ciudad Real, 1989-92, doctoral assoc., 1992-94, lectr., 1994—; rschr. REPSOL, Puertollano, Spain, 1987; acad. visitor Imperial Coll., London, 1994; scientific visitor Faculty Engrng., Porto, 1996, 97, mem. faculty bd. U. Castilla-La Mancha, Ciudad Real, 1990-94, mem. univ. claustro, 1994, dep. head dept., 1999—; rsch. in field. Patentee in field. Grantee U. Castilla la Mancha, 1994, 97, Brit. Coun., London, 1994, E.U., Brussels, 1996, 97. Mem. Spanish Royal Soc. of Chemistry. Roman Catholic. Avocations: traveling, football, sports. Office: U Castilla La Mancha Fac, Chem, Campus Universitario, 13004 Ciudad Real Spain

RODRIGUEZ, MARIA CARMELA, physician; b. Caracas, Venezuela, June 1, 1953; d. Oscar Henrique Rodriguez and Maria Carmen Yárnoz; m. Michel Antoun Otayek, Sept. 17, 1976 (div. 1987); children: Michel Enrique, Daniel Antonio. MD, Ctrl. U., Caracas, 1984. Intern Hosp. Policlinico los Teques, Venezuela, 1984-86; surg. resident Hosp. Perez Carrento, Caracas, 1986-89; pvt. practice Grupo Medico Hatillo, Caracas, 1989—, Clinica Santa Sofia, Caracas, 1989—. Mem. Colegio Medico de Miranda, Colegio Medico Distrito Fed. Home: Ave Principal La Trahona, Caracas Miranda Venezuela Office: Grup Medico El Hatillo, Calle Comercio el Hatillo, 1083-A Caracas Venequela

RODRIGUEZ, MARINO, management assistant; b. Carbayin Alto, Spain, Feb. 9, 1969; s. Eloy R. and Concepcion Montes. D of Chem. Engrng., U. Oviedo, Spain, 1996. Rsch. asst. U. Oviedo, Spain, 1992-96; rschr. UTMA, Oviedo, Spain, 1997, mgmt. asst., 1997—. Author: Removal of Carboxile Acids - From Aqueous Streams By Membrane Assisted Extraction, 1998; contbr. articles to profl. jours. Avocations: theatre, sports, bricolage, nature. Home: La Cabanona 14, 33936 Carbayon Alto Spain Office: Lignotech Iberica SA, Ganzo S/N, 39300 Torrelanega Spain

RODRIGUEZ, PLACIDO, bishop; b. Celaya, Mex., Oct. 11, 1940; came to U.S., 1953; s. Eutimio and Maria Concepcion (Rosiles) R. STB, STL, Cath. U., Washington, 1968; MA, Loyola U., 1971. Ordained priest Roman Cath. Ch., 1968, ordained to bishop, 1983. Pastor Our Lady Guadalupe Ch., Chgo., 1972-75, Our Lady of Fatima Ch., Perth Amboy, N.J., 1981-83; vocat. dir. Claretians, Chgo., 1975-81; bishop aux. Archdiocese of Chgo., 1983-94; bishop Diocese of Lubbock, Tex., 1994—. Office: The Catholic Ctr PO Box 98700 Lubbock TX 79499-8700

RODRIGUEZ, RICARDO VÉLEZ, philosopher educator; b. Bogotá, Colombia, Nov. 15, 1943; s. Alfonso Vélez Martinez and Victoria Rodriguez; m. Gleci Nascimento, Sept. 25, 1971 (div. Oct. 1987); 1 child, Maria Vitória; m. Maria Lúcia Marques Viana, May 1, 1989. BA, Inst. Tihamer Toth, Bogotá, Colombia, 1960; Licentiate in Philosophy, U. Javeriana, Bogotá, Colombia, 1964; MPhil, Cath. U., Rio de Janeiro, 1974; PhD, Gama Filho U., Rio de Janeiro, 1982. Register U. Bolivariana, Medellin, Colombia, 1968-72; postgrad. studies dir. U. Medellin, Colombia, 1975-79; sr. register State Univ. of Londrina, Brazil, 1981-83; cons. State Univ. of Rio de Janeiro, 1985-89, Fed. Univ. of Juiz de Fora, Brazil, 1985—; prof. Gama Filho U., Rio de Janeiro, 1983—; bd. dirs. Documentation Ctr. of Brazilian Thought, Salvador, Brazil, Brazilian Confederation of Commerce, Rio de Janeiro; lectr. Brazilian Army State Maior Coll., Rio de Janeiro, 1988—; expert War Coll., Rio de Janeiro, 1994—. Author: (book) Liberalism and Conservatism in Latin America, 1978, Castilhism, a Philosophy of Republic, 1980, The Brazilian Republican Propaganda, 1994, The Positivist Dictatorship in Brazil, 1994. Bd. dirs. Boy Scouts Colombian Coun., Medellin, 1971; lectr. Soc. Culture Convivio, São Paulo, Brazil, 1979-80; mem. Tocqueville Soc., 1986, Inst. of Humanities, São Paulo, 1988. Recipient fellowship OAS, 1973, 74, Konrad Adenauer Found., Perú, 1972, medal Honored Collaborator of Brazilian Army, 1986. Mem. Brazilian Acad. of Philosophy, Inst. of Luso-Brazilian Philosophy, The Planetary Soc. Liberal. Roman Catholic. Avocations: lyric singing, cyclism, swimming. Home: Santos 11 Apt 502, Praça Jarbas de Lery, 36016390 Juiz de Fora Brazil Office: Univ Federal Juiz de Fora, Ave Rio Branco 3539 Bloco B#1006, 36021630 Juiz de Fora Brazil

RODRIGUEZ, TIMOTHY ALLEN, language educator; b. Fond Du Lac, Wis., July 11, 1958; s. Donald William and Margaret Ann Rodriguez; m. Kathryn Marie Hébert, July 9, 1988; children: William Joseph, Kathryn Ann, Bryan Allen. BS, Western Ill. U., 1982, MS, 1984; PhD, U. Iowa, 1995. Tchr. bilingual edn. Danville (Ill.) Sch. Dist. 118, 1982-83, Houston Ind. Sch. Dist., 1984-86; ESL tchr. Palm Beach (Fla.) County Sch. Dist., 1986-88, 95-97, Martin County Sch. Dist., Stuart, Fla., 1988-91, 98-99; asst. prof. Western Ill. U., Macomb, 1993-95; adj. prof. Nova Southeastern U., Ft. Lauderdale, Fla., 1996-2000; vis. prof. Fla. Atlantic U., 2000-01, Port St. Lucie; validator Nat. Bd. for Profl. Tchg. Stds. Contbr. articles to profl. jours.; presenter Internat. TESOL Conf., 1996. Mem. Internat. TESOL, Internat. Reading Assn., Nat. Assn. Bilingual Edn., Sunshine State TESOL (bd. dirs. 1998—).

RODRIGUEZ, VIVIAN N., lawyer, accountant; b. Riverdale, N.Y., Dec. 16, 1969; d. Felix and Maria Rodriguez. AA in Bus., Miami Dade C.C., Miami, Fla., 1989; B of Acctg., Fla. Internat. U., Miami, 1991, M of Acctg., 1992; JD, U. Miami, 1995. Bar: Fla.; CPA, Fla. Acct. Norman A. Eliot & Co., Miami, 1991-96; atty., acct. Managed Recovery Svcs. Corp., Miami, 1996-97; sole practitioner Miami, 1997—. Mem. ABA, AICPA, ATLA, Am. Assn. Atty.-CPAs, Fla. Assn. Atty.-CPAs, Fla. Inst. CPAs, Dade County Bar Assn., Fla. Bar. Republican. Roman Catholic. Avocation: science fiction.

RODRIGUEZ, WILLIAM JULIO, physician; b. Ponce, P.R., June 18, 1941. BS, MD, Georgetown U., Washington, 1967; PhD, Georgetown U., 1975. Intern and resident Univ. Hosp., San Juan, P.R., 1967-72; fellow Children's Hosp., Washington, 1972-75; attending in infectious disease Children's Hosp. Nat. Med. Ctr., Washington, 1975—; assoc. chief infectious disease and microbiology rsch. Children's Hosp. Med. Ctr., 1979-80, chief infectious disease and microbiology, 1980-83, chmn. infectious disease dept., 1983—; cons. staff Hosp. for Sick Children, Washington, 1985—; cons. staff Shady Grove Adventist Hosp., Rockville, Md., 1988—, Holy Cross Hosp., Silver Spring, Md., 1988—, Columbia Hosp. for Women, 1990—. contbr. articles to profl. jours. MARC fellow, XIII, 1973-76. Fellow Infectious Disease Soc.; mem. AAAS, Am. Fedn. Clin. Rsch., Am. Soc. Microbiology, Assn. of Puerto Ricans in Sci. & Engrng. Office: Childrens Nat Med Ctr 111 Michigan Ave NW Washington DC 20010-2916

RODRIGUEZ, XOSE-PEDRO, archaeologist, researcher; b. Fradelo, Spain, Oct. 30, 1965; s. Teolindo Rodriguez and Luz Alvarez. MA, U. Barcelona, 1991; PhD, U. Rovira i Virgili, Tarragona, Spain, 1997. Lab. technician U. Rovira i Virgili, Tarragona, 1995-99, rschr., tchr., 1999—; cons. Fundacio la Caixa, Barcelona, 1999—. Contbr. articles to profl. jours. Recipient ciencias sociales y humanidades Junta de Castilla Y Leon, 1998. Mem. Am. Anthropology Assn., Societat Catalna D'Arqueologia. Home: Doctor Ferran no 32 20 10, 43202 Reus Spain Office: U Rovira i Virgilo, Placa Imperial Tarraco 1, 43005 Tarragona Spain Address: Dr Ferran, 32 2 La, 43202 Revs Spain

RODRIGUEZ-AMAT, JORDI, artist, educator, architect; b. Barcelona, Spain, Nov. 2, 1944; s. Francesco and Enriqueta (Amat) R. Grad., Fine Art Sch., Barcelona, 1964; Ba, U. Barcelona, 1970; degree in tech. arch., Polytechnic U. Catalonia, 1972. Prof. U. Barcelona, 1977-86, Polytechnic U. Catalonia, 1990-94; pres. Rodriguez-Amat Found., 1994—. Artist, sculptor, photographer.

RODRÍGUEZ AVILA, EDUARDO RENÉ, information systems analyst; b. Xalapa, Ver., Mexico, Apr. 26, 1967; s. Juan Silvino Rodriguez Burgos and Blanca Celia Avila Blancas. BS, Inst. Politecnico Nat., Mexico, 1993, MS, 1994. Analyst Tesoreria de la Federacion, Mexico, 1988-90, Grupo ICA, Mexico, 1990-91, Sears, Mexico, 1991-92; data base adminstrn. Cia Mexicana De Aviacion, Mexico, 1992-94, Cablevision, Mexico, 1995-97; mgr. Banco Nacional de Mexico, Mexico City, 1997—; prof. asst. Inst. Politecnico Nal., Mexico, 1994—. Recipient Reward to Excellence Inst. Politecnico Nal., 1993, Award to Distinction, 1993. Mem. IEEE, The Planetary Soc., N.Y. Acad. Scis., Internat. Assn. Calculator Collectors. Avocations: calculator collectionist, music, recreational mathematics, reading. Home: Valle de Corzos 5, Valle de Aragon, 57100 Netzahualcoyotl Mexico Office: Inst Politecnico Nacional, Av the 950 Granjas, 08400 Mexico City Mexico

RODRIGUEZ BURGOS, ANTONIO, biologist, educator; b. Porcuna, Spain, June 13, 1934; s. Manuel Rodriguez Aguilera and Trinidad Burgos Corpas. B, Portacoeli, Sevilla, Spain, 1951; MD, U. Medicine, Barcelona, Spain, 1957; PhD, U. Medicine, Granada, Spain, 1961. Asst. tchr. Faculty Medicine, Granada, Spain, 1959-62; asst. lectr. Faculty Medicine, Pamplona, Spain, 1963-75, Cordoba, Spain, 1975-77; asst. prof. Faculty Vet., Madrid, 1977-81; prof. of microbiology Faculty Biology, Cordoba, 1981—. Author: Gran Enciclopedia Rialp, 1975; contbr. articles to profl. jours. Mem. Soc. Spanish Parasitologists, Spanish Soc. Microbiology, Internat. Soc. Devel. Biology. Roman Catholic. Avocation: jogging. E-mail: a.r.burgos@uco.es. Office: U Cordoba, Campus Rabanales Edific C-6, 14074 Cordoba Spain

RODRÍGUEZ-CAMPS, SALVADOR, plastic surgeon; b. Buñol, Valencia, Spain, Nov. 9, 1952; s. Jose Rodriguez Blasco and Remedios Camps Devís; m. Concepcion Bolumar Navarro, Mar. 10, 1979; children: Salvador, Alexandra. PhD, U. Valencia, Spain, 1977. Med. diplomate. Emergency physician Pub. Health Svc., Valencia, 1978-87; plastic surgeon Gen. U. Hosp., Valencia, 1977-82, Mil. Hosp., Valencia, 1982-86, Oncology Hosp., Valencia, 1994-96, Casa de Salud Hosp., Valencia, 1980—; guest prof. emergency medicine Health Ministry, Valencia, 1984, 87; guest prof. Swiss Plastic and Aesthetic Soc., Lausanne, 1998; guest prof. aesthetic medicine, U. Balearic Islands, Mallorca, Spain, 1997-99; cons. Spanish Aesthetic Surgery Soc., Valencia, 1991-95. Contbr. articles to med. jours., including Aesthetic Plastic Surgery Jour., Ibero-Latinam. Jour. Plastic Surgery, others. V.p. Adoption of Children in Ea. Europe, Valencia, 1995-98. Fellow Lijublyana Hosp., Yugoslavia, 1974; grantee Valencian Govt., 1998. Mem. Spanish Plastic, Reconstructive and Aesthetic Soc., Internat. Soc. Plastic and Aesthetic Surgery, N.Y. Acad. Scis. Avocations: golf, soccer, music. Home: Paseo Porta Coeli, 4 Urb Los Monas, 46530 Puzol Valencia, Spain Office: Hosp Casa de Salud, M Candela 41 Planta 3A 3-3, 46021 Valencia Valencia, Spain

RODRIGUEZ GARCIA, JOSE LUIS, Cuban government official; b. Havana, Cuba, Mar. 18, 1946. Student, Inst. Adminstrn. and Commerce, 1963; BA in Econ., U. Havana, Cuba, 1969; PhD in Econ., Latin Am. Inst. USSR Acad. Scis., Moscow, 1978. Acct. Cuban Fishing Inst., 1962-67; planning dir. Nat. Fishing Authority, 1967; prof. econ. U. Havana, 1967-80; dep. dir. econ. policy dept. Rsch. Ctr. Internat. Economy, dir. postgrad. studies; dep. dir. Rsch. Ctr. World Economy, 1982-93; min.-pres. state com. for fin., 1993-94; min. of finances and prices Rep. of Cuba, 1994-95, min. economy & planning, v.p. coun. mins., 1995—; mem. Nat. Assembly Popular Power Coun. of State, 1998. Contbr. articles to profl. jours.; author of more than 7 books including An Strategy for Economic Development in Cuba, 1990, Economic Development in Cuba 1959-1988, 1990. Mem. Nat. Acad. Scis. of Cuba (sr.). Office: Min Econ & Planning, 20 de Mayo y Territorial, Plaza de la Revolución Havana Cuba

RODRIGUEZ GIAVARINI, ADALBERTO, minister of foreign relations. Grad., U. Buenos Aires, 1971. Chief economist Nat. Atomic Energy Commn., 1971-74, chief coord. tech. team, 1975; dir. mgmt. control Gen. Assn. Pub. Enterprises, 1975-82; budget under-sec. Ministry Economy, 1983-85; planning sec. Ministry of Def., 1986-89; nat. dep. Radical Civic Union, 1995; sec. economy and fin. City of Buenos Aires, 1996-98, rep. internat. credit agys. and instns., 1998; min. fgn. affairs, internat. trade and religion Argentina; cons. dept. economy Arthur Andersen; tchr., presenter at confs., seminars in field. Contbr. articles to profl. jours.; guest columnist nat. and fgn. publs. Mem. Argentine Indsl. Union (mem. acad. coun.), Argentine Coun. Fgn. Affairs. Office: Min Fgn Affairs, Reconquista 1088, 1003 Buenos Aires Argentina*

RODRIGUEZ IGLESIAS, GIL CARLOS, judge; b. Gijón, Spain, May 26, 1946; m. Teresa Diez Gutiérrez, 1972; 2 children. Student, Oviedo U., Madrid; D (hon.), U. Turin, 1996, U. Babes-Bolyai, Cluj-Napoca, Romania, 1996, U. Saarbrücken, 1997. Hon. bencher, Gray's Inn, London, 1995, King's Inn, Dublin, 1997. Asst. U. Oviedo, Freiburg, Germany, 1969-77, U. Autónoma, U. Complutense, Madrid, 1969-77; lectr. U. Complutense, Madrid, 1977-82, prof., 1982-83; prof. U. Granada, Spain, 1983—, dir. dept. internat. law, 1983-86; now judge, ct. justice European Cmtys., Luxembourg, 1986—; pres. of the court European Union, Luxembourg, 1994—. Writings include: El régimen jurídico de los monopolios de Estado en la Comunidad Económica Europea, 1976; contbr. articles to profl. jours. Decorated Order Isabel la Católica, Order San Raimundo de Peñafort. Office: Ct of Justice European Cmty, Blvd Konrad Adenauer, Kirchberg L-2925, Luxembourg*

RODRIGUEZ-LEON, JOSE ANGEL, chemical engineer; b. Havana, Cuba, Oct. 2, 1943; s. Jose Luis Rodriguez-Dominguez and Ana Leon Montes de Oca; m. Isabel Fernandez-Sainz; children: Daniel, Ana Isabel. Degree in chem. engrng., Havana U., 1968; MS, Centro Nacional de Investigaciones Cientificas, 1977; PhD, Cuban Acad. Sci., 1984. Lectr. asst. Havana U., 1968-70; jr. rschr. Nat. Ctr. Sci. Rsch., Cuba, 1971-72; dept. head Inst. Chem Exptl. Biology, Cuba, 1973-86; sr. rschr. Inst. Cubano de Investigación de los Derivados de la Cana de Azucar, Cuba, 1987—, project mgr., 1996—; lectr. on solid state fermentation, U. Pontificia de Parana, Brazil, 1994, U. Autonoma Metropolitana (IZTAPALAPA), Mexico City, 1995. Patentee in field. Mem. Nat. Acad. Scis. (corres. mem., expert com. on biotech. 1992-95, expert com. on biol. control, 1994-97, Outstanding Work award 1986). Avocations: movies, reading, art museums, baseball, swimming. Home: Calle 58-B 4118 Playa, Havana Cuba Office: Inst Cubano Investigaciones Derivados Cana Azucar, Via Blanca y Carr Ctr 804, 11000 Havana Cuba

RODRIGUEZ-MARIATEGUI CANNY, LUIS, lawyer, journalist; b. San Isidro, Lima, Peru, Sept. 25, 1962; s. Luis and Maria (Canny) R.; children: Cristina, Luis José. LLB, Cath. U. Lima, 1989. With Rodriguez-Mariategui & Vidal, Lima, 1989-95, ptnr., 1996—; dir. Minera Austria Du Vaz S.A., Minera Lizandro Proaño, Lima, Compañia Minera Huarón, Samex S.A. Lima. Author/editor bullfighting sect.: Diario Expreso, 1991-94; prodr. (bullfighting TV show) Afición, 1992-97; host bullfighting TV show A Capa y Espada, 1999. Dir. Nat. Soc. Mining Petroleum, Lima, 1991—; pres. Instituto Nacional de Derecho de Mineria Petroleo, 1998-2000. Mem. Inst. de Estudios Energético Mineros (pres. 1999—), Assn. Peruana de Derecho Marítimo (dir. 1996—). Office: Rodriguez Mariategui & Vidal, Miguel Aljovín 530, Lima 18, Peru

RODRIGUEZ MORALES, JULIO, cardiologist; b. Cumanacoa, Venezuela, Nov. 25, 1962; s. Juan Rodriguez and Aurora Morales; m. Natalia Vokhmianina (dec. Oct. 1989); children: Julio Aldjandro, Marco Stefan. MD, Med. inst. Rostov, Rostov on Don, Russia, 1981-88, postgrad., 1993. Gen. physician Ctrl. Hosp., Curiana, Venezuela, 1988-89, Rural Ambulatory Hosp., San Vicente, Venezuela, 1988-89; cardiologist Clinica Figuera, Cumana, Venezuela, 1993-96, Policlinica J.G. Hernandez, Punta de Mata, Venezuela, 1996-97, Centro Profl. E. Zamora, Punta de Mata, 1997—; chief cardiology svc. Centro Clinico Monagas, Tejero, Venezuela, 1996-97, Clinica Virgen del Valle, Punta de Mata, 1997—. Mem. Am. Heart Assn., Am. Soc. Echocardiography, N.Y. Acad. Scis., Heart Failure Soc. Am. Avocations: tennis, swimming, travel. Home: Calle 4 Ota Koshka, Urr Raul Leoni, 6217 Punta de Mata Venezuela Office: Ctr Profl Ezequiel Zamora, Av Bolivar, 6217 Punta de Mata Venezuela

RODRIGUEZ PARRILLA, BRUNO, diplomat. Amb. from Cuba UN, N.Y.C. Office: Permanent Mission of Cuba to UN 315 Lexington Ave # 38th St New York NY 10016-2606*

RODRÍGUEZ-PASQUÉS, RAFAEL HÉCTOR, chemist, educator; b. Buenos Aires, May 9, 1922; s. Rafael Aurelio and Nélida Mariana (Pasqués) Rodríguez; m. Petrona Mignon Dominguez, Apr. 27, 1962. D in Chemistry, U. Buenos Aires, 1950; cert., U. Concepción, Chile, 1956, Oak Ridge (Tenn.) Inst. Nuclear Studies, 1959. Chemist Navy Lab., Buenos Aires, 1946-47; with chemistry dept. Armour Co., Avellaneda, Argentina, 1947-53, head dept., 1951-53; radiochemist Nat. Bur. Standards, Gaithersburg, Md., 1964-69, asst. sect. chief, 1967-69; rschr. Nat. Commn. Atomic Energy, Buenos Aires, 1953-64, 69-89, dept. head, 1985-89; part-time prof. chemistry Buenos Aires U., 1956-64, 70-87, prof., 1987—; mem. subcom. U.S. Nat. Acad. Scis., Washington, 1964-68, ASTM, 1966-69; mem. adv. commn. Nat. Bd. Sci. and Tech. Rsch., Buenos Aires, 1980-82; mem. Internat. Com. for Radionuclide Metrology, 1974—, v.p. bd. dirs., 1986-89. Author: Introduction to Nuclear Technology, 1978, Scintillation Cameras, 1980, Radioactivity, X Rays, and Other Ionizing Radiations, 1994. French Fellowships Sorbonne Arcueil Lab, Centre d'Études Nucléaires de Saclay; U.S. Fellowships Oak Ridge Inst. of Nuclear Studies, Oak Ridge Nat. Lab., Nat. Bur. of Standards. Mem. Am. Chem. Soc. (nuclear sci. divsn.), Argentine Chem. Assn. (mem. directive bd. 1958-60), Argentine Assn. Nuclear Tech. (treas. 1974-77), N.Y. Acad. Scis. Roman Catholic. Avocation: astronomy. Home: 16-D, Ave Coronel Diaz 2089, 1425 Buenos Aires Argentina

RODRIGUEZ-SEIJO, JOSÉ MANUEL, mathematician, educator; b. A Coruña, Spain, Apr. 16, 1967; s. José Rodriguez-Barreiro and Manuela Seijo-Viñal; m. Carmen Coronado-Carvajal, Aug. 29, 1997; 1 child, Carmen Rodriguez-Coronado. Lic. in math. scis., U. Santiago de Compostela, Spain, 1990, PhD of Math. Scis., 1994; Diplome d'Etudes Approfondies d'Analyse Numérique, U. Pierre et Marie Curie, Paris, 1991, PhD in Math., 1997. Assoc. prof. U. Coruña, Spain, 1993-94, titular prof. univ. interino, 1994-95, titular prof., 1995—. Contbr. articles to profl. jours. Mem. Soc. Española of Math. Applications. Office: U Coruña ETS Arch, Campus Zapateira, 15071 A Coruña Spain

RODRIGUEZ VALERO, FRANCISCO JOSE, management consultant, accountant, international travelling consultant; b. Cali, Valle, Colombia, July 24, 1945; s. Rafael Antonio and Elvira (Valero) Rodriguez Franco; children: Diego Andres, Clara Ines. Student U. Valle, Cali, 1963-64. Adminstrv. mgr. Envases Industriales, Barranquilla, 1975-77; plant exec. Graficas Claveria, Barranquilla, 1977-78; asst. mgr. Coomarico Ltd., Barranquilla, 1978-79; asst. controller Can Cun Sheraton, Mexico, 1979; supt. Plasticesta, Barranquilla, 1979-80; gen. mgr. Granco Lombiana de Ventas-Granventas, Cali, 1981—; cost acct. IMP South Am., Palmira, Valle, 1972, I&D Products Plastics; cons. Montero and Leon, Cali, 1973, Cimet de Colombia, Cali, 1974, S. Calderon and Sandoval, Cali, 1975. Inventor of technologies of process for the food industry, (1999 awarded in the 27th annual Internat Fair of Inventions, Geneve, Switzerland). Avocations: cycling, mountain climbing. E-mail: pachocali@yahoo.com. Address: PO Box 18342, Cali Colombia

RODRIGUEZ-VIVAS, ROGER IVAN, veterinarian; b. Yucatan, Mexico, June 22, 1966; s. Carlos and Josefina Rodriguez-Vivas; m. Lizette Rossana, Apr. 9, 1995; children: Lizette, Ivan. BS, CBTA #14, SEP-DEGTA, Tizimin, Yucatan, 1984; veterinarian, U. Autonoma de Yucatan, Merida, Mexico, 1989; M in Veterinary Sci., Liverpool Sch. Tropical Med., England. Cert. veterinarian. Rsch. asst. Yucatan U., Merida, Mexico, 1993; prof. Yucatan U., Merida, 1993-2000; coord. master course tropical animal health, Yucatan U., Mexico. Author: (book) Veterinary Laboratory, 1994; contbr. articles to profl. jours. Recipient Pfizer Class prize, Pfizer Co., Liverpool, 1992; grantee Internat. Found. Sci., Stockholm, 1997. Roman Catholic. Avocation: animals. E-mail: rvivas@tunku.uady.mx. Office: Yucatan U Vet Fac, KM 15 Carretera Merida, Merida 9700, Mexico

RODRIGUEZ Y BAENA, RUGGERO, oral surgeon, educator; b. Milan, Jan. 8, 1957; s. Ferdinando and Velia (Vergano) R. y B.; m. Cinzia Codebó, Feb. 29, 1992; children: Alessandra, Arianna. MD, DDS, U. Pavia, Italy, 1981, specialist in dentistry and oral surgery, 1985. Pvt. practice oral surgery Pavia, 1982—; asst. prof. oral pathology U. Pavia, 2000. Author: Implant Prostheses, 1996, Minor Pre-Prosthetic Surgery, 1998, (CD-Rom) Implant Dentistry, 1998. With Italian Air Force, 1978-79. Mem. Am. Acad. Osseointegration, Italian Soc. Osseointegration (treas. 1999). Avocations: gymnastics, tennis, flying, computers. Home: Viale Battisti 12, 27100 Pavia Italy Office: Via Colombo 1, 27100 Pavia Italy

RODRIQUEZ, MIGUEL ANGEL, federal official. Pres. Govt. of Costa Rica. Office: Office Pres Casa Presl, Apartado 520-2010 Zapote, 1000 San Jóse Costa Rica*

ROE, FRANCIS J. CALDWELL, pathologist, consultant; b. London, Aug. 16, 1924; s. Stanley Bernard and Ivy Olive (Caldwell) R.; m. Brenda Joan Beckett, Aug. 28, 1948; children: Sarah Jane, Jonathan Caldwell, Catherine Elizabeth, Julian James. B.M. B.Ch., Oxford U., 1948, M.A., 1950, D.M., 1957; D.Sc., London U., 1965. House physician, surgeon London Hosp., 1948-49; graded pathologist Royal Army Med. Corps., 1949-51; lectr. in cancer research London Med. Coll., 1951-61; reader in exptl. pathology Chester Beatty Research Inst., Inst. Cancer Research, London, 1961-71; research coordinator Tobacco Research Council, London, 1971-73; ind. cons. exptl. pathology and toxicology London, 1973—; mem. WHO expert adv. panel on food additives, 1970—; mem. food safety com. Nuffield Found., 1962-70; mem. exec. com. Marie Curie Found., 1983—. Editor, contbr.: The Biology of Cancer, 1966; The Prevention of Cancer, 1967; editor: The Pathology of Laboratory Rats and Mice, 1967; Metabolic Aspects of Food Safety, 1970. Contbr. numerous articles to med., sci. jours. Served to capt. Brit. Army, 1949-51. Price U. scholar, 1945, Lord Kitchener scholar, 1945; recipient Ver Heyden de Lancey prize for Medicine and Art, Royal Soc. Medicine, 1980. Fellow Royal Coll. Pathologists, Acad. Toxicological Scis.; mem. Brit. Assn. Cancer Research, Brit. Toxicol. Soc., Brit. Occupational Hygiene Soc., Soc. Toxicology, Royal Soc. Medicine, Brit. Med. Assn., Med. Art Soc. (past pres.). Mem. Ch. of England. Address: 11B Raymond Rd, Wimbledon, London SW19 4AD, England

ROE, NICHOLAS HUGH, English educator; b. Fareham, Hampshire, Eng., Dec. 14, 1955; s. Dennis and Stella Mary (Bennett-Powell) R.; m. Susan Jane Stabler. BA, Oxford U., 1978, PhD, 1985. Lectr. in English Queen's U., Belfast, No. Ireland, 1982-85; lectr. English, St. Andrew's U., Scotland, 1985-94, reader, 1994-96, prof., 1996—; acad. dir. Coleridge Summer Conf., 1994—. Author: (books) Wordsworth and Coleridge: The Radical Years, 1988, The Politics of Nature: Wordsworth and Some Contemporaries, 1992, John Keats and the Culture of Dissent, 1997; editor: Keats and History, 1995. Rsch. fellow Leverhulme Trust, 1994-95. Mem. Keats-Shelley Meml. Assn. (trustee 1998—). Avocations: cooking, walking, wine, France. Office: Sch of English, Univ of St Andrews, KY16 9AL Saint Andrews Scotland

ROE, ROGER ROLLAND, JR., lawyer; b. Mpls., Dec. 31, 1947; s. Roger Rolland Roe Jr.; m. Paula Speltz, 1974; children: Elena, Madeline. BA, Grinnell Coll., 1970; JD, U. Minn., 1973. Bar: Minn. 1973, U.S. Dist. Ct. Minn. 1974, U.S. Ct. Appeals (8th cir.) 1977, U.S. Supreme Ct. 1978, Wis. 1988, U.S. Dist. Ct. Nebr. 1995, U.S. Dist. Ct. (ea. and we. dists.) Wis. Law clk. to Hon. Judge Amdahl Hennepin County Dist. Ct., Mpls., 1973-74; from assoc. to ptnr. Rider, Bennett, Egan & Arundel, Mpls., 1974-91; mng. ptnr. Yaeger, Jungbauer, Barczak, Roe & Vucinovich, PLC, Mpls., 1992—; mem. nat. panel arbitrators Am. Arbitration Assn.; judge trial practice class and moot ct. competitions law sch. U. Minn.; guest lectr. Minn. Continuing Legal Edn. courses. Fellow Internat. Soc. Barristers; mem. ATLA (guest lectr.), Am. Bd. Trial Advs. (diplomat, Minn. chpt. pres. 1996-97), Minn. Trial Lawyers Assn., Million Dollar Round Table, Mich. Trial Lawyers Assn. Avocations: golfing, downhill skiing. Office: Yaeger Jungbauer Barczak Roe & Vucinovich PLC 701 4th Ave S Ste 1400 Minneapolis MN 55415-1816

ROEDDER, WILLIAM CHAPMAN, JR., lawyer; b. St. Louis, June 21, 1946; s. William Chapman and Dorothy (Reifeiss) R.; m. Gwendolyn Arnold, Sept. 13, 1968; children: William Chapman, Barcley Shane. BS, U. Ala., 1968; JD cum laude, Cumberland U., 1972. Bar: Ala. Law clk. to chief justice Ala. Supreme Ct., Montgomery, 1972; ptnr. McDowell Knight Roedder & Sledge, L.L.C., Mobile, Ala., 1997—. Comments editor Cumberland-Samford Law Rev.; contbr. articles to legal publs. Mem. ABA (vice chair com. trial tactics, torts and ins. practice 1995-96), Ala. State Bar Assn., Mobile County Bar Assn. (past sec., past chmn. ethics com. 1988-90, grievance com. 1994-96), Fed. Ins. and Corp. Counsel (chmn. products liability sect. 1990-93, regional v.p. 1994-96, bd. dirs. 1993-2000, exec. com. 1997—, sec.-treas. 1999-2000, pres.-elect 2000-2001), Ala. Def. Lawyers Assn., Curia Honoris, Order of Barristers, Def. Rsch. Inst., Phi Alpha Delta (pres. 1971-72). Home: 211 Levert Ave Mobile AL 36607-3219 Office: McDowell Knight Roedder & Sledge LLC PO Box 350 Mobile AL 36601-0350

ROEFS, HANS FRANS ALBERT, electrical engineer; b. Utrecht, The Netherlands, May 15, 1946; s. Frans A. and Maria C. (Wesselink) R.; m. Cisca E. Bezemer, Sept. 3, 1971; children: Menno, Arno. Grad., Delft U. Tech., The Netherlands, 1970; PhD, U. Ill., 1977. Rsch. asst. Delft U. Tech., 1970-74, U. Ill., Urbana, 1974-77; rsch. engr. TNO-FEL, The Hague, The Netherlands, 1977-79; sr. rsch. engr. NLR, Amsterdam, The Netherlands, 1979-84, head systems dept. space divsn., 1984—; rsch. asst. Inst. Teknologi Bandung, Indonesia, 1971-74. Contbr. articles to profl. jours. Chmn. VVD polit. party, Coun. of Noordoostpolder, 1994—; v.p. VVD-Kamercentrale, Flevoland, 1991-94. Mem. Lions (pres. 1997s), Phi Kappa Phi. Avocations: politics, classical music (Mozart), sailing. Home: Schokkerhaven 49, 8308 PX Nagele, Flevoland The Netherlands Office: NLR Nat Aerospace Lab, PO Box 153, 8300 AD Emmeloord, Flevoland The Netherlands

ROEG, NICOLAS JACK, film director; b. London, Aug. 15, 1928; s. Jack Nicolas and Mabel Getrude (Silk) R.; m. Susan Rennie Stephen, May 12, 1957; children: Joscelin Nicolas, Nicolas Jack, Lucien John, Sholto Jules; m. Theresa Russell, 1985; children: Maximilian Nicolas Sextus, Statten Jack. Student Brit. schs.; LittD honoris causa, Hull (Eng.) U., 1995. Cinematographer films The Caretaker, 1963, Masque of Red Death, 1964, Fahrenheit 451, 1966, A Funny Thing Happened on the Way to the Forum, 1966, Far from the Madding Crowd, 1967, Petulia, 1968; co-dir. film Performance, 1970; dir. films Walkabout, 1970, Don't Look Now, 1973, Glastonbury Fayre, 1973, The Man Who Fell to Earth, 1976, Bad Timing, 1980, Eureka, 1982, Insignificance, 1985, Castaway, 1986, 89, Track 29, 1987, Aria, 1987, The Witches, 1988-89, Cold Heaven, 1990, Heart of Darkness, 1994, Two Deaths, 1994, Hotel Paradise, 1995, Full Body Massage, 1995, Samson & Delilah, 1996; dir. TV films: Sweet Bird of Youth, 1989, Heart of Darkness, 1994; exec. producer Without You I'm Nothing, 1989, Young Indy, 1991, The Sound of Claudia Schiffer, 1999—. Decorated comdr. Brit. Empire. Fellow Brit. Film Inst.; mem. Dirs. Guild Am., Dir. Guild Gt. Britain, Acad. Motion Picture Arts and Scis., Assn. Cinematograph, TV and Allied Technicians.

ROEHL, JERRALD J., lawyer; b. Austin, Tex., Dec. 6, 1945; s. Joseph E. and Jeanne Foster (Scott) R.; m. Nancy J. Meyers, Jan. 15, 1977; children: Daniel J., Katherine C., J. Ryan, J. Taylor. BA, U. N.Mex., 1968; JD, Washington and Lee U., 1971. Bar: N.Mex. 1972, U.S. Ct. Appeals (10th cir.) 1972, U.S. Supreme Ct. 1977. Practice of Law, Albuquerque, 1972—; pres. Roehl Law Firm P.C. and predecessors, Albuquerque, 1976—; lectr. to profl. groups; real estate developer, Albuquerque. Bd. dirs. Rehab. Ctr. of Albuquerque, 1974-78; mem. assocs. Presbyn. Hosp. Ctr., Albuquerque, 1974-82; incorporator, then treas. exec. com. Ctr. City Coun., 1991—. Recipient award of recognition State Bar N.Mex., 1975, 76, 77. Mem. ABA (award of achievement Young Lawyers div. 1975, council econs. of law practice sect. 1978-80, exec. council Young Lawyers div. 1979-81, fellow div. 1984—, council tort and ins. practice sect. 1981-83), N.Mex. Bar Assn. (pres. young lawyers sect. 1975-76), Albuquerque Bar Assn. (bd. dirs. 1976-79), N.Mex. Def. Lawyers Assn. (pres. 1983-84), Sigma Alpha Epsilon, Sigma Delta Chi, Phi Delta Phi. Roman Catholic. Clubs: Albuquerque Country, Albuquerque Petroleum. Bd. advs. ABA Jour., 1981-83; bd. editors Washington and Lee Law Rev., 1970-71. Home: 4411 Constitution Ave NE Albuquerque NM 87110-5721 Office: Roehl Law Firm PC 300 Central Ave SW Albuquerque NM 87102-3298

ROEHLE, INGO, aerospace scientist; b. Bonn, Germany, Mar. 23, 1968; s. Roehle Gerhard and Lore (Lewald) R. Physics Diploma, U. Bonn, 1993; PhD, U. Bochum, 1999. Scientist German Aerospace Ctr., Cologne, 1, 1993—; rschr. Nat. Office Aerospatial Rsch., Paris, 1997; lectr. Von Karmann Inst., NATO Sci. Orgn. Contbr. articles to profl. jours.; patentee in field. Mem. German Phys. Soc. Avocations: climing, sailing, contemporary art, cat. Home: Karlvotrat-Kreiten-Str 3, 53113 Bonn Germany Office: DLR Enat, Linderhoehe, 51140 Cologne Germany

ROEHR, MAX, biochemist; b. Kufstein, Tyrol, Austria, Mar. 11, 1931; s. Maximilian and Maria Theresia (Kofler) R.; m. Susanna Terez Kovarcz, Jul. 3, 1957; children: Peter Andreas. Geologist, U. Innsbruck, 1949-50; diploma, Tech. U., Wien, 1957, dr. tech, 1962, u. dozent, 1969. Teaching asst. Tech. U., Wien, Austria, 1955-57, asst. prof., 1957-69, sr. lecturer, 1969-73, full prof., 1973—; cons. in field, 1962—, chmn. Inst. Biochemical Tech. and Microbiology, Wien, Austria, 1973-86, 94-99. Contbr. articles to profl. jours. Recipient Silver medal, Rep. of Austria, 1968. Mem. Austrian Soc. Microbiology, Austrian Soc. Biotech. Roman Catholic. Avocations: classical and modern music, modern art, european political history, science history. Home: Franz Asenbauergasse 32, A1230 Vienna Austria Office: Tech U Vienna, Getreidemarkt 9, A 1060 Vienna Austria

ROEL, JOSÉ ENRIQUE, physician; b. Buenos Aires, Oct. 25, 1955; s. Juan Alfredo and Marcela Emilia (Olive) R.; m. Adriana Miriam Aiman, Nov. 18, 1988; children: Camila, Francisco. MD, U. Buenos Aires, 1979. Resident in internal medicine Sanatorio Güemes, Buenos Aires, 1982-84, chief resident, 1985, ward chief, 1986-92; ward chief CIM (HMO), Buenos Aires, 1993-96; jefe Servicio de Internacion de la Clinica Suizo, Argentina, 1996-99. Author: Cardiologia Actual, 1992. Home: Malabia 2277, Buenos Aires 1425, Argentina Office: TM de Anchorena, 1407 9D, Buenos Aires 1425, Argentina

ROELANTS, ANDRE, banking executive; b. Schaerbeek, Belgium, Nov. 25, 1943; arrived in Luxembourg, 1988; m. Anne Finet, Nov. 10, 1986; three children. BSc, Cath. U. DeMons, 1966. V.p. Chase Banque Commerce, Brussels, Belgium, 1985-86; gen. mgr. Chase Manhattan Bank, Copenhagen, 1986-88; v.p., mng. dir. Bank of Am., Luxembourg, 1988-90; mng. dir. Cregem Internat. Bank, Luxembourg, 1990-91; from vice-chmn. to chmn. exec. bd. Banque Internat. Luxembourg, 1991—. Mem. Brit. C. of C. (chmn.), Cercle Royal Gaulois, Rotary. Office: 69 Route d'Esch, 2953 Luxembourg Luxembourg

ROELS, HARRY A., educator; b. Lede, Flanders, Belgium, Aug. 14, 1941; s. Remi Roels and Aline Lievens; m. Erna Carion, July 1, 1966; children: Peter, Bart, Wim. MSc, Cath. U. Leuven, Belgium, 1963, PhD, 1966. Asst. prof. Cath. U. Leuven, 1966-72; assoc. prof. U. Cath. de Louvain, Brussels, 1972-99, prof., 1999—; H. Hooker disting. vis. prof. McMaster U., Hamilton, Ont., Can., 1999-2000. Mem. editl. bd. Occupl. Environ. Medicine, 1996—; internat. adv. bd. mem. Scan. Jour. Work, Environ. and Health, 1990—; contbr. articles to profl. jours. Recipient Belgian Environ. Hygiene award, Brussels, 1978, Health and Enterprise award European Club Health, Brussels, 1989. Mem. Internat. Commn. on Occupl. Health. Avocations: classical music, Alpinism. Office: U Catholique de Louvain, Chapelle Aux Champs 30 54, B-1200 Brussels Belgium

ROEMER, RONALD, educator, educational administrator; b. Teaneck, N.J.; s. Ronald Raymond and Dolores Lorraine Roemer. BA, Fairleigh Dickinson U., 1975, MA, 1981. Cert. social studies tchr. K-12; cert. in distance learning-coll. level. Sr. lectr. Fairleigh Dickinson U., Teaneck, N.J., 1981—, acad. adminstr., 1990—; adj. instr. Union County Coll., Cranford, N.J., 1997—; spkr. in field. Asst. field coord., asst. coord. reception com. 4th Am. Ethnic Parade, Internet Immigrants Found., N.Y.C., 1989. Named to Outstanding Young Men of Am., 1985. Mem. Phi Alpha Theta. Avocations: horseback riding, swimming, computer simulation games, reading. E-mail: roemerr@hotmail.com. Office: Fairleigh Dickinson U/New Coll 150 Kotte Pl Hackensack NJ 07601-6112

ROENGSUMRAN, SOPHON, chemist, educator, researcher; b. Klongluang, Patoomthan, Thailand, May 17, 1944; s. Plai and Hant (Hongsachai) R.; m. Supattra Rachataromeya, Aug. 12, 1973; children: Arisara, Kamolwan, Araya. BSc, Chulalongkorn U., Bangkok, 1970, MSc, 1973; PhD, U. Tex., 1979. Lectr. chemistry Chulalongkorn U., Bangkok, 1971-79, asst. prof., 1979-82, assoc. prof., 1983—, dep. dir. Metallurgy and Materials Sci. Rsch. Inst., 1989-96; cons. Bangkok Wood Products, 1979-91, K.M. Internat. Lab., Bangkok, 1991-93, Petroleum Authority of Thailand, 1994-97. Author: Chemistry for Nursing Students, 1982, 2d edit., 1985, General Chemistry for the Life Science Science and Nursing, 1985, 3d edit., 1996, Organic Chemistry I, 1983, 6th edit., 1996, Organic Chemistry II, 1996. Mem. AAAS, N.Y. Acad. Sci., Sci. Soc. Thailand. Home: 179 Charansanitwong 4, Bangkok 10600, Thailand Office: Chulalongkorn Univ, Dept Chemistry, Bangkok 10330, Thailand

ROENNINGEN, OTTAR NYHUS, retired electronics engineer; b. Trysil, Hedmark, Norway, May 8, 1926; s. Ole Olausen and Margit (Nyhus) R.; m. Gulla Wenche Hagen, Apr. 14, 1954; children: Mona, Staale. Student, Eidsvoll (Norway) Coll., 1943, 45-46, Norwegian Coll., Upsala, Sweden, 1944, Oslo Sailors Sch., 1947, Gothenburg (Sweden) Tech. Inst, 1952-53. Avionics engr. Scandinavian Airlines Sys., Oslo, 1954-57; avionics devel. engr. Scandinavian Alirlines Sys., Stockholm, 1960-91; mem. staff electronic lab. Internat. Atomic Rsch. Inst., Halden, Norway, 1958-59; ret., 1991. Sgt. Norwegian Arty., 1944-45. Mem. Amnesty Internat. Avocations: working with youth. Home: Oxenstiernasväg 5, S-13440 Gustavsberg Sweden

ROESKY, HERBERT WALTER, chemistry educator; b. Laukischken, Germany, Nov. 6, 1935; s. Otto and Lina (Hublitz) R.; m. Christel Glemser, July 24, 1964; children: Rainer, Peter. Diploma, U. Göttingen, Fed. Republic Germany, 1961, PhD, 1963; prof. (hon.), Nankai U., Teinjin, China, 1990; PhD (hon.), U. Bielefeld, Germany, 1992, U. Brno, Czechoslovakia, 1994, U. Bucharest, Romania. Postdoctoral fellow DuPont Co., Wilmington, Del., 1965-66; docent U. Göttingen, 1968-71, dir. Inst. Inorganic Chemistry, 1980—; prof. inorganic chemistry U. Frankfurt, Fed. Republic Germany, 1971-80; vis. prof. Tokyo Inst. Tech., 1987, Kyoto U. Elsevier: Rings, Clusters and Polymers of Main Group and Transition Elements, 1990, Verlagsgesellschaft: Chemische kabinettstuecke, 1994, Chemie en miniature, 1998; contbr. over 750 articles to profl. publs. Recipient Dozenten prize Fonds der Chemischen Industrie Frankfurt, 1970, Alfred-Stock-Gedächtnis prize Gesellschaft Deutscher Chemiker, 1990, Grand Prix de la Fondation de la Maison de la Chimie, 1998, ACS Fluorine award, 1999, Wilkinson prize. Fellow Nat. Indian Acad. (hon.); mem. Acad. Scis., Akademie der Naturforscher Leopoldina, Austrian Acad. Scis. (corr.), Berlin Brandenburgische Akademie (corr.), Russian Acad. Scis. Achievements include 12 patents in field. Home: Emil-Nolde-Weg 23, 37085 Göttingen Germany Office: Inst Anorganische Chemie, Tammannstrasse 4, 37077 Göttingen Germany

ROESSLER, JOCHEN, physicist, researcher; b. Welzheim, Kreis Waiblingen, Germany, June 27, 1949; s. Heinz and Gerlinde (Blumtritt) R. MSc in Physics, U. Stuttgart, Germany, 1977; PhD in Meteorology, U. Edmonton, Can., 1984; PhD in Physics, U. Hobart, Australia, 1991. Cert. theoretical physics, atmospheric physics. Killam postdoctoral fellow Dalhousie U., Halifax, Can., 1986-88; rschr. U. Tübingen, Germany, 1991-95, U. Frankfurt, Germany, 1995—; visitor U. Delaware, Newark, 1985, Kent State U., 1987-88; rschr. U. Karlsruhe, Germany, 1988. Contbr. physics articles to prof. jours. Cpl. German Army, 1968-70, Degerndorf. Rsch. grantee German Rsch. Found., 1995, 96. E-mail: j.roessler@em.uni-frankfurt.de. Office: Inst für Geologie, Senckenberganlage 32-34, Hesse Frankfurt D-60054, Germany

ROFF, ALAN LEE, lawyer, consultant; b. Winfield, Kans., July 2, 1936; s. Roy Darlis and Mildred Marie (Goodaile) R.; m. Sonyia Ruth Anderson, Feb. 8, 1954; 1 child, Cynthia Lee Roff Edwards; m. Molly Gek Neo Tan, July 21, 1980. BA with honors and distinction, U. Kans., 1964, JD with distinction, 1966. Bar: Okla. 1967. Staff atty. Phillips Petroleum Co., Bartlesville, Okla., 1966-75, sr. atty., 1976-85, sr. counsel, 1986-94; cons. in Asia, 1995—. Mem. editl. bd. Kans. Law Rev., 1965-66. Precinct com. man Rep. Party, Lawrence, Kans., 1963-64; assoc. justice Kans. U. Chancery Club; mem. Kans. U. Young Reps. Elizabeth Reeder scholar U. Kans., 1965-66, Eldon Wallingford award, 1964-66. Mem. ABA, Okla. Bar Assn., Washington County Bar Assn., Phoenix Club (Bartlesville) (bd. dirs. 1985-86, gen. counsel 1986-91), Order of the Coif, Masons, Hon. Order Ky. Cols., Phi Alpha Delta, Pi Sigma Alpha. Mem. First Christian Ch. Avocation: travel. Home and Office: 2247 Mountain Dr Bartlesville OK 74003-6954

ROGACHKO, STANISLAV IVANOVICH, marine laboratory administrator; b. Odessa, Ukraine, USSR, June 16, 1945; s. Ivan Grigorievich Polamarchuk and Vera Dmitrievna (Rogachko) Bubelich; m. Svetlana Azimovna Islamova, Aug. 1, 1968; children: Dmitry, Marina. Diploma, Naval Coll. Tech. Fleet, Odessa, Ukraine, USSR, 1965; Higher Diploma, Civil Engring. Inst., Moscow, 1971, PhD, 1977. Foreman Novorossiyskmorstroy Trust, Novorossiysk, USSR, 1965-67; rschr. Civil Engring. Inst., Moscow, 1972-74, sr. researcher, 1979-82; chief dept. Civil Engring. Inst., 1983-94; sr. engr. Transport Engring. Rsch. Inst., Moscow, 1975-79; chief rsch. lab. Moscow State U. Civil Engring., 1994—; participant Internat. Assn. Promotion of Cooperation with Scientists from Independent States of former Soviet Union, Finland, 1995-97; predictor K.R. Croasdale Assocs., Calgary, Can., 1996; project expert Sakhalin Nauchno-Issledovatelsky Proektry Inst. Morneft Okha, Russia, 1993; team leader INTAS project Reliability of Engineering Facilities in the Artic Seas, 1998—. Contbr. numerous articles to profl. jours.; inventor in field. Recipient Govt. Medal Govt. of Russia, 1997. Achievements include development of codes for offshore structures design. Avocations: fishing, hunting. Home: Apt 57 27/1 Yubileynay St, 141021 Mytishchy Moscow, Russia Office: Moscow State U Civil Engr, Yaroslavskoe shosse 26, 129337 Moscow Russia

ROGALSKI, ANTONI, physicist; b. Wojdal, Poland, June 12, 1946; s. Franciszek and Joanna (Wisniewska) R.; m. Teresa Miron, Feb. 10, 73; children: Marta, Alicja. MSc, Mil. U. Tech., Warsaw, 1972, DSc, 1976. From asst. to tutor Mil. U. Tech., 1972-83; from vice chief to head Inst. Applied Physics, Warsaw, 1984—; vis. prof. Northwestern U., Evanston, 1995; program bd. Opto-Electronics Rev., 1992—, Jour. Tech. Physics, 1995—, Jour. Infrared & Millimeter Waves, 1998—; dep. editor-in-chief Opto-Electronics, Rev., 1997—; Polish Optoelectronics Com., 1991—, v.p., 1998—; guest editor Optical Engring., 1994; chmn. of over 10 conf. sessions, 1991—. Author: Semiconductor Infrared Detectors, 1992, New Ternary Alloy Systems for Infrared Detectors, 1994, Infrared Detectors, 2000; editor: Infrared Photon Detectors, 1995; contbr. articles to profl. jours. Recipient Found. for Polish Sci. Rsch. and Devel. award, 1997. Fellow Intenat. Soc. Optical Engring.; mem. IEEE. Avocations: mountain climbing, cycling, cinema. Home: Piastow Slaskich 37/16, 01-494 Warsaw Poland Office: Mil U Tech Inst Applied Phys, Kaliskiego 2, 00-908 Warsaw Poland

ROGALSKI, MIRCEA SERBAN, physics researcher; b. Bucharest, Romania, Aug. 11, 1949; s. Valerian and Elena (Marin) R.; m. Ileana Mihaela Busuioc, Apr. 21, 1972 (div. 1979); 1 child, Ion Victor; m. Eugenia Nastasoiu, June 5, 1980. MSc, U. Bucharest, 1972; PhD in Solid State Physics, Inst. Atomic Physics, Bucharest, 1981. Sr. rsch. scientist Inst. Atomic Physics, Bucharest, 1981-93, assoc. rsch. prof., 1993-96, rsch. prof., 1996—; lectr. Tech. U., Bucharest, 1981-90, sr. lectr., 1990-93; vis. rsch. fellow U. Warwick, Eng., 1993-94, vis. fellow Royal Soc., 1995; vis. prof. PRAXIS, U. Porto, Portugal, 1996-97; referee Inst. Physics, Eng., 1993—; invited prof. U. Algarve, Portugal, 1997—. Author: Advanced University Physics, 1996, Quantum Physics, 1999, Solid State Physics, 2000; editor Magnetism of Rare-Earth and Actinides, 1983; contbr. articles to profl. jours. Lt. Romanian Army, 1973. Mem. European Phys. Soc. Eastern Orthodox. Avocation: cats. Home: 25 Calea Victoriei apt 22, 70707 Bucharest Romania Office: UCEH Univ do Algarve, Gambelas, 8000 Faro Portugal

ROGER, JERRY LEE, school system administrator; b. Chase, Kans., Mar. 11, 1945; s. LeRoy J. and Lottie E. (Maphet) R.; m. Tucky Saint Smith, 1995. BS, U. Tulsa, 1966, MA, 1969, EdD, 1975. Cert. tchr., supt., Okla. Math. tchr. Kansas City (Mo.) Pub. Schs., 1966-67, Shawnee Mission (Kans.) Pub. Schs., 1967-71; rsch. asst. Tulsa Pub. Schs., 1972-73, rsch. coord., 1973-81, adminstrv. asst., 1981-90, rsch. dir., 1990-95, dir. planning and assessment, 1995-2000; chmn. U. Pheonix Sch. Gen. Studies, Tulsa, 2000—; adj. instr. Tulsa Jr. Coll., 1975-88; adj. asst. prof. U. Tulsa, 1980-85; sr. faculty U. Phoenix, Tulsa campus, 1998-2000. Contbr. book revs. to Tulsa Sunday World, 1990-92. Paul Harris fellow; Rotary benefactor. Mem. NEA, Am. Ednl. Res. Assn., Nat. Book Critics Cir., Nature Conservancy, Nat. Conf. for Cmty. and Justice, Phi Delta Kappa. Home: 3538 S Winston Ave Tulsa OK 74135-2045

ROGER FRANCE, FRANCIS HENRI, medical educator; b. Etterbeek, Brussels, Belgium, July 24, 1941; s. Charles Oscar and Yvonne Hélène (France) Roger; m. Anne-Marie Roger France-Wouters, July 12, 1967; children: Emmanuel, Jean-Francois, Marie-Isabelle. MD, U. Louvain, Belgium, 1967, internal medicine, 1972, PhD, 1982; MS in Biometry, U. Minn., Mpls., 1972. Lic. in internal medicine, Ministry Pub. Health, Brussels, 1972. Rsch. fellow U. Minn., Mpls., 1970-72; head med. record dept. Clin. U. St. Luc, Brussels, 1976, assoc. chief of svc., 1988; clin. prof. U. Louvain, Louvain-la-Neuve, Belgium, 1989; extraordinary prof. U. Louvain, Louvain en Woluwe, Belgium, 1991, dir. med. informatics unit, 1994—, pres. Sch. Pub. Health; cons. European Union DGXIII, Brussels, 1973—, Coun. Europe, Strasbourg, France, 1976-78, WHO European Office, Copenhagen, 1992—; sci. expert Ministry Pub. Health, Brussels, 1984—, Inst. Nat. Maladie et Invalidite, Brussels, 1989-92. Active Commn. Relief in Belgium, Belgian Am. Ednl. Found. CRB fellow BAEF, Brussels and N.Y., 1970. Fellow European Fed. Med. Informatics (hon. fellow, past pres. 1984-89); mem. INternat. Med. Info. Assn. (past v.p. 1989-91), Alumni de la Fond. Univ. (v.p. 1994-96). Office: Ctr for Med Info UCL, 10 ave Hippocrate, 1200 Brussels Belgium

ROGERS, ALICE LOUISE, retired bank executive, writer, researcher; b. McLoud, Okla., Feb. 18, 1929; d. John Edmond and Katy McNora (Williams) Stanka; m. Jesse Ray Rogers, Apr. 18, 1948; children: Jimmy Allen Rogers, Bonnie Kay Calhoun. Student, Am. Inst. Banking, 1967-69. Clk. typist loan dept. Security Pacific Nat. Bank, L.A., 1960-64; office mgr., adminstrv. asst. to v.p. loan adminstn. divsn. City Nat. Bank, Beverly Hills, 1964-75, credit mgr. Pershing Square branch, 1975-77. Author, editor: Dance Bands and Big Bands Reference Book and Price Guide, 1986, Dance Bands, Big Bands and Swing Reference Book and Price Guide, 1993; contbr. articles to DISCoveries mag., Internat. Assn. of Jazz Record Collectors Jour., Joslin's Jazz Jour., Dancing USA mag. Mem. Internat. Assn. Jazz Record Collectors, Big Band Acad. Am., Libr. Congress Assocs. (founding nat. mem.), Smithsonian Instn. (nat. assoc. mem.). Republican. Avocations: phonograph record collection, researching jazz and dance information, postcard collection. Home: 700 Clark St Apt 108 Deming NM 88030-4589

ROGERS, ANNA MARGARET, solicitor; b. London, May 15, 1961. BA in Jurisprudence, Oxford (Eng.) U., 1982. Trainee Nabarro Nathanson, London, 1983-85, solicitor, 1985-87; solicitor Rowe & Maw, London, 1987-89, ptnr., 1989—. Assoc., coun. mem. Pensions Mgmt. Inst., Assn. Pension Lawyers. Mem. Pensions Mgmt. Inst. (assoc.), Assn. Pension Lawyers (mem. main com. 1990—). Avocations: cinema, reading. Office: Rowe & Maw, Rowe & Maw, 20 Black Friars Ln, London EC4V 6HD, England

ROGERS, BARRIE, psychologist, educator; b. Hawarden, Clwyd, Wales, Mar. 6, 1939; s. Albert and Beatrice Alice (Thomas) R. BA in Natural Sci., Trinity Coll., Dublin, Ireland, 1962, MA, 1965; MEd, U. Birmingham, Eng., 1967; MLitt in Ednl. Psychology, U. Aberdeen, Scotland, 1979. Chartered psychologist; chartered biologist; accredited hypnotherapist, counselor. Head biology Ondo (Nigeria) High Sch., 1963-65; researcher Race Rels. Unit, Eng., 1965-66; lectr. then sr. lectr., head div. ednl. scis. Northumberland (Eng.) Coll. of Higher Edn., 1966-78; pvt. practice Eng., 1979—; subject leader Bath Coll. Higher Edn., 1979-93; cons. psychologist in various pvt. schs., Eng., 1980—; hypno therapist, 1990—. Author: (book) Human Personality: Towards a Unified Theory, 1971; contbr. articles to profl. publs. Various offices Morpeth Liberal Party, Eng., 1973-79; cand. for parliament

Liberty Party, Eng., 1974; regional exec. Liberal Party, N. of Eng., 1975-81; mem. nat. coun. Liberal Party, 1976-78; constituency exec. Bath Liberal Party, 1980-84; vice chair Wansbeck Liberal Dem. Party, 1995-99. Fellow Hypnotherapy Soc., Hypnotherapy Rsch. Soc.; mem. Inst. of Biology (charter), Psychology and Psychotherapy Assn., Psychology and Psychotherapy Assn. (chair 1999-2000), Brit. Psychol. Soc. (charter, Scottish divsn. edn. psychology, counselling divsn.), Counseling and Psychotherapy Soc. Democrat. Episcopalian. Avocations: football, science fiction. Office: 6 Alder Close, Morpeth Northumberland NE61 1XH, England

ROGERS, BENJAMIN TALBOT, consulting engineer, solar energy consultant; b. Cleve., Oct. 4, 1920; s. Benjamin Talbot and Marie Aline (Miller) R.; m. Dale Hays, Sept. 11, 1961 (dec. Nov. 1975); children: Leslie, Phyllis. BS in Mech. Engring., U. Wis., 1944. Registered profl. engr., N.Mex., Colo., Ariz., Tex. Mech. engr. Black & Veatch, Kansas City, Mo., 1946-49; staff mem. U. Calif., Los Alamos, N.Mex., 1949-76; cons. engring. Los Alamos, N.Mex., 1949-76, Embudo, N.Mex., 1976-80, 81—; vis. prof. Ariz. State U., 1980-81, 84; v.p. Barkmann & Rogers Cons. Engrs., Santa Fe, N.Mex., 1964-70. One-man shows include Millicent Rogers Mus., Taos, N.Mex., 1994, Roller Mill Mus., Cleveland, N.Mex., 1995, Ariz. State U. Coll. Architecture, Tempe, 1996, First State Bank Taos, 1997 (Artist of Month 1997), Johnson Gallery, Madrid, N.Mex., 1998-99; contbr. articles to tech. and profl. jours.; 6 patents in field of optics, high speed photography and explosive tech. Commr. Rinconada Cmty. Acequia, Embudo, 1961-70; v.p. adv. bd. Embudo Presbyn. Hosp., 1972; pres. Embudo Valley Health Found., 1974. 1st lt. C.E., 1942-46. Recipient Solar Design award HUD, Dept. of Energy, Solar Energy Rsch. Inst., 1978, Peter van Dresser award N.Mex. Solar Energy Assn., 1983, Maharishi award Maharishi Found., 1984; grantee Graham Found. for Advanced Studies in Fine Arts, 1992, 95. Fellow ASHRAE; mem. ASME (life), NSPE (life), Am. Soc. Materials (life). Republican. Home and Office: PO Box 2 Embudo NM 87531-0002

ROGERS, BERNARD WILLIAM, military officer; b. Fairview, Kans., July 16, 1921; s. William Henry and Lora (Haynes) R.; m. Ann Ellen Jones, Dec. 28, 1944; children: Michael W., Diane E., Susan A. Student, Kans. State Coll., 1939-40; BS, U.S. Mil. Acad., 1943; BA (Rhodes scholar), Oxford (Eng.) U., 1950, MA, 1954, DCL (hon.), 1983; grad., Command and Gen. Staff Coll., 1954-55, Army War Coll., 1959-60; LLD, Akron U., 1978, Boston U., 1981. Commd. lt. U.S. Army, 1943, advanced through grades to gen., 1974; aide to supt. U.S. Mil. Acad., 1945-46, comdt. cadets, 1967-69; aide to high commr. Austria Gen. Mark W. Clark, 1946-47; bn. comdr. Korea, 1952; exec. to comdr.-in-chief Far East Command, 1953-54; mil. asst. to Chief Staff U.S. Army, 1956-59; exec. to chmn. (Joint Chiefs of Staff), 1962-66; asst. div. comdr. (1st Inf. Div.), Vietnam, 1966-67; comdg. gen. (5th Inf. Div.), Ft. Carson, Colo., 1969-70; chief legis. liaison Dept. Army, 1971-72, dep. chief of staff for personnel, 1972-74; comdg. gen. U.S. Army Forces Command, 1974-76; chief of staff U.S. Army, 1976-79; supreme allied comdr. Europe; comdr. in chief (U.S. European Command), 1979-87; ret. U.S. Army, 1987; former bd. dirs. Atlantic Coun. U.S., George C. Marshall Found., Gen. Dynamics Co., Kemper Nat. Ins. Co., Thomas Industries; former sr. cons. The Coca-Cola Co.; chmn. USO World Bd. of Govs., 1988-94. Decorated DSC, Def. DSM, DSM of Army, Navy and Air Force, Silver Star, Legion of Merit with 3 oak leaf clusters, D.F.C. with 2 oak leaf clusters, Bronze Star medal with V device; hon. fellow Univ. Coll., Oxford U.; recipient Disting. Svc. Citation U. Kans., 1984, Disting. Grad. award U.S. Mil. Acad., 1995, Assn. U.S. Army George C. Marshall medal, 1999. Mem. VFW, Assn. U.S. Army (bd. dirs.), Assn. Am. Rhodes Scholars, Soc. 1st Inf. Divsn., Am. Soc. French Legion of Honor, Ret. Officers Assn., Mil. Order of World Wars, The Pilgrims, Army-Navy Country Club, Army and Navy Club, Alfalfa, Phi Delta Theta.

ROGERS, BRENDA GAYLE, educational administrator, educator, consultant; b. Atlanta, July 27, 1949; d. Claude Thomas and Louise (Williams) Todd; m. Emanuel Julius Jones Jr., Dec. 17, 1978; children: Lavelle, Brandon, Albre Jede, Briana Adanne. BA, Spelman Coll., 1970; MA, Atlanta U., 1971, EdS, 1972; PhD, Ohio State U., 1975; postgrad., Howard U., 1980, Emory U., 1986. Program devel. specialist HEW, Atlanta, 1972; rsch. assoc. Ohio State U., Columbus, 1973-75; asst. prof. spl. edn. Atlanta U., 1975-78, program adminstr., 1978—, CIT project dir., 1977-91, exec. dir. Impact project, 1992—; tech. cons. Dept. Edn., Washington, 1978-93, 96, 97-98, cons. Head Start, 1990-91; cons. Princeton Testing Svcs., 1996—; due process regional hearing officer Ga. State Dept. Edn., Atlanta, 1978-84, adv. bd., 1980-84; regional cons. Access project, 1995—; mem. parent adv. coun. APS, 1988—; cons. program devel. Ga. Respite Care, Inc., 1988-89; mem. exec. bd., pres. PTA Stone Mountain elem. Sch., 1989-92; mem. test verification panel Edn. Testing Svcs., Princeton, N.J., 1995-96; cons. So. Assn. Colls. & Univs., 1998. Mem. Ga. Assessment Project com. Atlanta Pub. Schs. Adv. Coun., 1986—; bd. dirs. Mountain Pines Civic Assn., 1988—; mem. Grady Meml. Hosp. Cmty. Action Network, Atlanta, 1982-83; exec. bd. PTA Shadow Rock Elem. Sch., 1992-94. Recipient disting. svc. award Atlanta Bur. Pub. Safety, 1982, Mountain Sch. PTA, 1995, award Atlanta Pub. Sch. Sys., 1980, 82, 83, 89-90, Disting. Svc. award CAU, 1998; fellow Ohio State U., 1972-74, Howard U., 1980. Mem. NAFE, Assn. for Retarded Citizens, Coun. for Exceptional Children, So. Assn. Colls. and Univs. (cons. com. 1998—), Nat. Assn. Learning Disabilites, Phi Delta Kappa, Phi Lambda Theta. Democrat. Roman Catholic. Avocation: gourmet cooking. E-mail: dr.brenda.rogers@worldnet.att.net. Office: Clark Atlanta U James P Brawley Atlanta GA 30314-3913

ROGERS, CHARLES MYERS, lawyer; b. Monticello, Utah, Nov. 21, 1947; s. Milton David and Wanda (Myers) R.; m. Jean Evelyn Rankin, Dec. 12, 1970 (div. June, 1983); m. Christine Theresa Sill, Apr. 14, 1984; children: Christopher Thales, Fiona Eleanor. BA in Philosophy, U. Mo., Kansas City, 1973, JD, 1976. Bar: Mo. 1976, U.S. Dist. Ct. (we. dist.) Mo. 1976, U.S. Supreme Ct. 1994, U.S. Ct. Appeals (8th cir.) 1997, U.S. Ct. Appeals (9th cir.) 1999. From asst. pub. defender to 1st asst. pub. defender Jackson County Pub. Defender's Office, Kansas City, Mo., 1976-89; regional defender Mo. State Pub. Defender Sys., Kansas City, 1989-94; staff atty. Mo. Capital Punishment Resource Ctr., Kansas City, 1994-95; shareholder Wyrsch Hobbs Mirakian & Lee, Kansas City, 1995—; sole practice law, Kansas City, 1982-86. Served in U.S. Army, 1968-70. Mem. ABA, Nat. Assn. Criminal Def. Lawyers, Mo. Bar Assn., Mo. Assn. Criminal Def. Lawyers (bd. dirs. 1988—, 1st. v.p. 1999-00), Kans. City Metro Bar Assn. (co-chair criminal law com.). Democrat. Avocations: cycling, oenology. Home: 7434 Madison Ave Kansas City MO 64114-1506 Office: Wyrsch Hobbs et al 1101 Walnut St Ste 1300 Kansas City MO 64106-2180

ROGERS, DAVID FREEMAN, aerospace engineering educator; b. Theresa, N.Y., Sept. 3, 1937; s. Lewis Freeman and Gladys Marion Zoller; m. Nancy Ann Nuttall, Sept. 5, 1959; children: Stephen David, Karen Nanci, Ransom Robert. B in Aero. Engring., Rensselaer Poly. Inst., 1959, MS in Aero. Engring., 1960, PhD, 1967. Asst. prof. U.S. Naval Acad., Annapolis, Md., 1964-67, assoc. prof., 1967-74, prof., 1974—; Fujitsu rsch. prof. Royal Melbourne Inst. Tech.; hon. rsch. scholar U. Coll. London, 1977-78. Author: Mathematical Elements for Computer Graphics, 1976, 2d edit. 1990; Procedural Elements for Computer Graphics, 1985, 2d edit., 1997, Laminar Flow Analysis, 1992; mem. editl. bd. Visual Computer, CAD, the Computer Aided Design Jour.; contbr. articles to profl. jours. David F. Rogers Chair in Aerospace Engineering name in his honor, 2000. Avocations: flying, photography, sailing. Fax: 410-293-2591. Office: US Naval Acad Aerospace Engring Dept Annapolis MD 21402

ROGERS, DAVID WILLIAM, solicitor, academic administrator; b. Sydney, NSW, Australia, Mar. 21, 1926; s. John David and Irene Myrtle (Lowe) R.; m. Janette Leslie Christian, Sept. 8, 1952; children: John William, Janet Amanda Rogers Yencken, James Christian, David Allan. LLB, U. Melbourne, Australia, 1949; LLD honoris causa, Monash U., Australia, 1999. Ptnr. Hedderwick Fookes & Alston, 1956-84; sr. ptnr. Arthur Robinson & Hedderwicks, 1984-93, cons., 1993—; chmn. bd. dirs. Woodside Petroleum Ltd., 1985-99, Denso (Australia) Pty. Ltd. Chancellor Monash U., 1992-99. Served Intelligence Corps AIF, 1944-45. Mem. Australian Club (Melbourne), Melbourne Club, Met. Golf Club, Royal South Yarra Tennis Club. Avocations: tennis, golf, fishing, music. Home: 38 Grandview Grove, East Prahran 3181, Australia

ROGERS, ERIC WILLIAM EVAN, aeronautical research consultant; b. London, Apr. 12, 1925; s. William Percy and Margaret (Evans) R.; m. Dorothy Joyce Loveless, Apr. 1, 1950; children: Christopher, Margaret, Andrew. BSME with honors, Imperial Coll., London, 1944, MS in Aero. Engring., 1952, DSc in Aero. Engring., 1964, postgrad. in Aero. Engring., 1945. Chartered engr. Rsch. on high-speed aerodynamics Nat. Phys. Lab., Teddington, Eng., 1945-61, head hypersonic aerodynamics, 1961-70; head project assessment Royal Aircraft Establishment, Farnborough, Eng., 1970-71, head aerodynamics dept., 1972-74, group head, airframe depts., 1974-78, dep. dir., 1978-85, aircraft rsch. cons., 1985—; U.K. govt. rep. in internat. rsch. collaboration with NATO, NASA and European Orgns. Contbr. articles to profl. jours. Fellow Royal Aero. Soc. London (Silver medal 1983), City and Guilds Inst. Avocations: music, history, English literature. Home and Office: 64 Thetford Rd, New Malden KT3 5DT, England

ROGERS, EVA, artist, poet; b. Poughkeepsie, N.Y., May 27, 1958; d. Clyde Benjamin Van Leuven and Gloria Alice (Stanton) Myers and Wilton E. Myers; m. Bruce L. Rogers. Exhbns. include one-woman shows, Adorondack Ctr. for the Arts, Blue Mt. Lake, N.Y., Tinker Street Cafe; group shows include Woodstock Artists Assn., 1994, 95, Springfield Art League 75th Ann. Nat. Exhibit, Small Works '94/Catskill Art Soc., The Tonawanda Ann. Nat. Juried Show/Carnegie Art Ctr., N.Y., Art WYO'94/West Wind Gallery, Casper, Wyo., Baystreet Galleria Nat. Open, Balboa Island, Calif., Nat. Soc. of Artists, '95, Santa Fe, others; prodr. Woodstock pub. access TV. Recipient Fire and Rose award Artspirit Internat., Marlbourgoh, Mass., 1996, Spl. Recognition award Baystreet, Balboa Island, Calif., 1994, awards profl. divsn. Nat. Soc. of Artists, Santa Fe, Tex., numerous others. Mem. Woodstock Artists Assn., Catskill Art Soc.

ROGERS, FERGUS JOHN, medical association administrator; b. Loughton, Essex, Eng., June 4, 1938; s. Benjamin and Dorothy (Pearce) Rogers; m. Magdalene Rogers (div. 1985) ; 1 child, Phipps. Mgmt. trainee Eastwoods Ltd., Lowrin, 1956-59; chartered acct. trainee Buxton & Beresford, London, 1960-65; mgr. Wells Direct Mail Ltd., London, 1965-68; dir. Account Control Ltd., London, 1968-80, Nat. Ankylosing Spondylitis Soc., London, 1980—; pres. Ankylosing Spondylitis Internat. Fedn., London, 1988—. Sect. editor Jour. Med. Biography, 1995—; editor AS News, 1980—; contbr. articles to profl. jours. Recipient NASS/FRINK award NASS, 1996. Avocations: mountain walking, painting. Home: Waterfalls, Lake St, East Sussex TN20 6PS, England Office: Nat Ankylosing Spondylitis, PO Box 179, East Sussex TN20 6ZL, England

ROGERS, FRANK ANDREW, restaurant, hotel executive; b. Indpls., May 9, 1931; s. Andrew Jackson and Jane (Safford) R.; m. Beulah Frances White, Sept. 28, 1971; children: Jane, Debra, Anne, Gina, Andrea. BA in Bus., Ind. U., 1967. Chmn., pres., CEO Brown County Fed. Savs. and Loan, NAshville, Ind., 1963-80, Bloomington (Ind.) Nat. Bank, 1980-88; chmn., CEO Lake Shore Bank, Michigan City, Ind., 1984-88; pres. Nashville Hillside Corp., 1966—, Ordinary Corp., Nashville, 1974—, Brown County Inn, Inc., Nashville, 1992—; mgr. AbeMartin Lodge, Nashville, 1962-66, 89—; pres. Nashville House, Inc., 1959—; bd. dirs., chmn. First Bank Greenwood, Ind., Ind. Emergency Mgmt. Found. Mem., pres. Nashville Town Bd., 1959-62, Brown County Sch. Bd., Nashville, 1972-75, Monroe County Conv. and Visitors Bur., Bloomington, Ind.; bd. dirs. Bloomington Hosp., Citizens Bank of Cen. Ind., 1988-90; bd. dirs., pres. Brown County Conv. and Visitors Commn. Served with USN, 1950-54. Mem. VFW, Lions, Am. Legion, Ind. U. Alumni Assn. Home and Office: Nashville House PO Box 187 Nashville IN 47448-0187

ROGERS, GRAHAM ALLAN JOHN, philosophy educator; b. Murree, Pakistan, June 11, 1938; s. Allan Leslie and Muriel Vera (Turner) R.; m. Jo-Ann Kipke Eastman, Apr. 9, 1969; children: Sara Jo, Rachel Ann. BA, Nottingham U., 1960; postgrad., Oxford U., 1960-62; PhD, Keele U., 1971. Lectr. Keele U., Eng., 1962-72; sr. lectr. Keele U., 1972-87, head dept. philosophy, 1985—, prof. history of philosophy, 1995—; vis. fellow UCLA, 1981, 85. Founder-editor Brit. Jour. for the History of Philosophy, 1983—; author, editor more than 12 books; contbr. over 120 articles and revs. to profl. jours. Mem. Mind Assn., Brit. Soc. for History of Philosophy (steering com.), Rotary. Clubs: Alsager Tennis, Alsager Cricket. Avocations: photography, walking, talking, golf. Home: 87 Pikemere Rd, Alsager, Cheshire ST7 2SN, England Office: U Keele, Dept Philosophy, Keele ST5 5BG, England

ROGERS, HON PAULLETTO, researcher, writer; b. Washington, Mich., Aug. 22, 1961; s. Paulleto Rogers I and Dorothy L.R. Rogers; children: Alexis R. Roycia July, Ambre L. Majasticaa, Ericka J. Student, Wayne County C.C.; cert. computer ops., Mother Waddles Sch. Cert. paralegal; notary pub. Pres. C.C.OA, L.A., 1983; gen. operator CBOU, 1983—; regent agent Security MGN, 1984; collector Nat. Credit Corp., L.A., 1985; craftman Vinyl Indsl. Products, Chgo., 1986; field insp. Mortgage Svcs. Assoc., Inc., 1995; sales cons. Swepo, 1996; legal tech. Probone Legal Svcs., 1997; directorate Prousa Internat. Projects 2001, 1998; substaining member Rep. Platform Commn., 1986; substaining sponsor Ronald Reagan Presdl. Found., Libr., and Ctr. Pub. Affairs, Ventura County, Calif., 1988; sponsor Statue of Liberty Ellis Island Centennial Commn., 1985, Ronald Reagan Congressional-Vicotry Fund, 1987; advisorate Senate Adv. Coun., 1997. Creator, founder The Collectionals Survey. At-large-del. Rep. Presdl. Task Force, 1992—, lobbyist, 1994—; activist U.S. Def. Com., 1985; lobbyist Prousa Legal Corpsusa, 1999; del. Wayne County Clk. Office; Mich. state advisor Rep. Senatorial Com.; mem. Jaycees, 1981, GOPAC, congl. VIP, 1984; GOP Victory Fund sponsor NRCC, 1984; supporter KIDSFIRST YESMI, 2000. Decorated Rogers Coat of Arms, Medieval Knight, Chevron, 2000; recipient Cert. Recognition, NRCC, 1990, Cert. Appreciation, Presdl. Commn. A.A., 1990, Presdl. award Rep. Presdl. Legion of Merit. Avocations: copyrights, activism, lobbying, community investing. Home: PO Box 27473 Detroit MI 48227-0473

ROGERS, IAN MUNRO, surgeon, researcher; b. Glasgow, Scotland, Mar. 1, 1944; s. John and Jean Norris (Munro) R.; m. Katherine Judith Sanders, Oct. 24, 1970; children: Lucy, Emily, Caroline, Alastair. MB, ChB, Glasgow U., 1967. Pre-registration houseman Western Infirmary, Glasgow, 1967-68, So. Gen. Hosp., Glasgow, 1967-68; lectr. anatomy Glasgow U., 1968-69; sr. house officer surgery Westminster Hosp., London, 1969-71; registrar surgery Glasgow Royal Infirmary, 1971-74, sr. registar surgery, 1974-78; cons. surgeon Ingham Infirmary, South Shields, Eng., 1978—; hon. lectr. surgery Newcastle U., 1988—; hon. examiner surgery Royal Coll. Physicians and Surgeons Glasgow, 1990—, v.p. North England Surgical Soc., pres., 2000—. Author: Robert Ingham and His Friends, 1996; contr. articles to profl. jours. Fellow Royal Coll. Surgeons Edinburgh, Royal Coll. Physicians Glasgow, Royal Coll. Physicians and Surgeons Glasgow; mem. South Shields Rotary Club (pres. 2000—). Methodist. Avocations: golf, tennis, singing. Home: 46 Whitburn Rd, Cleadon Tyne and Wear SR6 7QS, England Office: c/o South Tyneside, Health Care Trust, Tyne and Wear NE34 OPL, England

ROGERS, JAMES EDWIN, geology and hydrology consultant; b. Waco, Tex., Feb. 24, 1929; s. Charles Watson and Jimmie (Harp) R.; m. Margaret Anna Louise Bruchmann, Oct. 10, 1957; 1 child, James Fredrick. Student, Rice U., 1947-49, Baylor U., 1953; BS, U. Tex., 1955, MA, 1961. Geologist U.S. Geol. Survey, St. Paul, 1956-59; geologist U.S. Geol. Survey, Alexandria, La., 1959-63, supervisory hydrologist, 1963-85; ind. cons. Alexandria, 1985—; cons. geol. survey for map State of La., Baton Rouge, 1982-85, mapping com., 1997—, mem. adv. bd. La. geol. survey, 1998—. Author: Water Resources of Kisatchie Well-Field Area Near Alexandria, Louisiana, 1981, Preconstruction and Simulated Postconstruction Ground-Water Levels at Urban Centers in the Red River Navigation Project Area, Louisiana, 1983, Red River Waterway Project - Summary of Ground-Water Studies by the U.S. Geological Survey, 1962-85, 1988; co-author: Water Resources of Vernon Parish, Louisiana, 1965, Water Resources of Ouachita Parish, Louisana, 1972, Water Resources of the Little River Basin, Louisana, 1973. Scoutmaster Boy Scouts Am., Alexandria, 1971, 72. Sgt. U.S. Army, 1950-52, Japan. Fellow Geol. Soc. Am.; mem. Gem Mineral and Lapidary Soc. Ctrl. La. (pres. 1972, 86-87, 94-96), Baton Rouge Geol. Soc., Phi Beta Kappa. Presbyterian. Avocations: numismatics, minerals, genealogy, travel, history. Home and Office: 4008 Innis Dr Alexandria LA 71303-4738

ROGERS, JAMES GARDINER, accountant, educator; b. St. Louis, May 6, 1952; s. Gardiner and Virginia Joy (Goodbar) R.; m. Barbara May Baird, Feb. 14, 1976; children Andrew Baird, Benjamin Baird, Samuel Baird. BA, Washington and Lee U., 1973; MBA, Am. U., 1975. CPA, Pa. Credit officer loan workout div. Phila. Nat. Bank, Phila., 1975-78; mgr. cash and banking Gen. Waterworks Corp., Phila., 1978-81, asst. treas., 1981-85; v.p. fin., treas. Phila. Presbyn. Homes, Inc., Phila., 1985-88; exec. dir. devel. Eastern Coll., St. Davids, Pa., 1988—; ptnr., bd. dirs. PC Mgmt. Enterprises, Inc., Bryn Mawr, Pa.. Treas. Lower Merion Bapt. Ch., Bryn Mawr, 1978-85; v.p. Lupus Foundn. of Am., Inc., Washington, 1985-87, asst. v.p., 1982-85, bd. dirs., 1977—; pres., bd. dirs. Pa. Lupus Foundn., Wayne, 1973—, bd. dirs.; elder Proclamation Presbyn. Ch., 1996—. Mem. Mensa. Republican. Club: Merion Cricket (Haverford, Pa.). Avocations: reading, microcomputers, tennis, skiing. Home: 308 Chamounix Rd Wayne PA 19087-3612 Office: Eastern Coll Saint Davids PA 19087

ROGERS, JAMES STEVEN, lawyer; b. Seattle, Sept. 18, 1947; s. Fred and Frances Ruth (Teitelbaum) R.; m. Theresa M. Rosellini; children: Zoey, Sabina. BS, U. Wash., 1969; JD, U. Ariz., 1972. Bar: Wash. 1973; cert. civil trial advocate. With Law Office of Lembhard G. Howell, Seattle, 1974-75, Wolfstone Panchot & Bloch, Seattle, 1975-78, Franco, Asia, Bensussen Coe & Finegold, Seattle, 1978-81, Crane, Stamper, Dunham, Drury & Rogers, Seattle, 1981-86, Law Offices of James S. Rogers, Seattle, 1987-98. Fellow Internat. Acad. Trial Lawyers; mem. ATLA (bd. govs. 1993—), Am. Bd. Trial Advocates, Wash. State Trial Lawyers Assn. (pres. 1991-92, Lawyer of Yr.), Attys.Info. Exch. Group (bd. dirs. 1991—), Western Trial Lawyers Assn. (pres. 1999-2000). Office: 705 2nd Ave Ste 1601 Seattle WA 98104-1711

ROGERS, JON MARTIN, financial consultant, financial company executive; b. Piedmont, S.C., June 4, 1942; s. James Robert and Eunice (Ashley) R.; m. E. Jeanette Owen, June 16, 1962; children: E. Elaine, Jonette Marie, Melissa Anne. BS, Clemson U., 1964, MS, 1966; PhD in Fin. Mgmt., LaSalle U., 1994. CLU, Chartered Fin. Cons. Sales rep. Met. Life, Greenville, S.C., 1969-71; dist. sales mgr. Met. Life, Atlanta, 1972-74; regional sales mgr. Met. Life, Milw., 1975-81, Liberty Corp., Greenville, 1982-88; chmn. bd., chief exec. officer Rogers Fin. Group, Greenville, 1989-2000; CEO Rogers Fin. Group LLC, Greenville, 2000—; ptnr. J&J Enterprises, Piedmont, S.C., 1975—; registered securities rep. Royal Alliance Assocs., Inc., N.Y.C., 1986—; adj. prof. Webster U. Mem. C. of C., Greenville, 1985-86; pres. Rep. Party precinct, Piedmont, 1988; bd. dirs. Optomist Club, Greenville, 1985; deacon, chmn. Washington Ch., Pelzer, S.C., 1985-87, 93-94. Capt. U.S. Army, 1967-69, Vietnam. Decorated Bronze Star. Mem. Nat. Assn. Life Underwriters (v.p. 1972-73, recipient awards), Internat. Assn. Fin. Planners, Nat. Assn. Securities Dealers, Million Dollar Round Table, Gideons Internat. Club (S.C. pres. 1985-87), Child Evangelism Fellowship (bd. dirs. 1988-89), Rotary Internat. (bd. dirs., pres. 1996-97). Baptist. Avocations: photography, golf, walking. Home: 21 Fairway Dr Piedmont SC 29673-9167 Office: Rogers Fin Group Inc 1 Whitsett St Greenville SC 29601-3136

ROGERS, KATE ELLEN, interior design educator; b. Nashville, Dec. 13, 1920; d. Raymond Lewis and Louise (Gruver) R.; diploma Ward-Belmont Jr. Coll., 1940; BA in Fine Arts, George Peabody Coll., 1946, MA in Fine Arts, 1947; EdD in Fine Arts and Fine Arts Edn., Columbia U., 1956. Instr., Tex. Tech. Coll., Lubbock, 1947-53; co-owner, v.p. Design Today, Inc., Lubbock, 1951-54; student asst. Am. House, N.Y.C., 1953-54; asst. prof. housing and interior design U. Mo., Columbia, 1954-56, assoc. prof., 1956-66, prof., 1966-85, emeritus, 1985—, chmn. dept. housing and interior design, 1973-85; mem. accreditation com. Found. for Interior Design Edn. Rsch., 1975-76, chmn. stds. com., 1976-82, chmn. rsch., 1982-85. Mem. 1st Bapt. Ch., Columbia, Mo.; bd. dirs. Meals on Wheels, 1989-91. Nat. Endowment for Arts rsch. grantee, 1981-82. Fellow Interior Design Educators Coun. (pres. 1971-73, chmn. bd. 1974-76, chmn. rsch. com. 1977-78); mem. Am. Soc. Interior Designers, (hon., medal of honor 1975), Am. Home Econs. Assn., Columbia Art League (adv. bd. 1988-93), Pi Lambda Theta, Kappa Delta Pi, Phi Kappa Phi (hon.), Gamma Sigma Delta, Delta Delta Delta (Phi Eta chpt.), Phi Upsilon Omicron, Omicron Nu (hon.). Democrat. Author: The Modern House, USA, 1962; editor Jour. Interior Design Edn. and Research, 1975-78.

ROGERS, LEONARD JOHN, business executive; b. Croydon, Surrey, Eng., Oct. 30, 1931; s. Leonard Samuel and Amy Mary (Martlew) R.; m. Avery Janet Morgan, July 16, 1955; children: Paul, Nicholas, Jonathan, Crispin. BA, Cambridge U., 1955, MA, 1959. Contracts adminstr. Bristol Aircraft Ltd., Eng., 1958-60; asst. sec. Bristol Aeroplane Plastics Ltd., Eng., 1960-62; asst. comml. mgr. Brit. Aircraft Corp., London, 1962-66; mgr. civil export contracts Brit. Aircraft Corp., Weybridge, Eng., 1973-76, bus. dir., 1976-77; mktg. dir. Brit. Aerospace, Weybridge, Eng., 1978-79; cons. in aerospace Roconsult A.G., Zug, Switzerland, 1980-84; dir. AIM Group PLC, Southampton, Eng., 1984—, non-exec. dir., 1995—; mng. dir. AIM Aviation (Henshalls) Ltd., Byfleet, Eng., 1984-93, aviation advisor, 1994-97. Mem. fin. and gen. purposes com. London Vol. Service Council, 1980-84, chmn. adv. com. on sociol. research into the self-help economy, 1981-82. Served to lt. Intelligence Corps, Brit. Army, 1950-52. Decorated officer Order Brit. Empire. Fellow Inst. Dirs.; mem. Royal Aero Soc. (assoc.), Soc. Brit. Aerospace Cos. (assoc. mems. com. 1994-2000), Old Whitgiftian Assn. Methodist. Avocations: roses, opera, European languages, family history. Home: Willow Pool, Effingham, Surrey KT24 5JG, England Office: AIM Group Plc, 16 Carlton Crescednt, Southampton SO15 2ES, England

ROGERS, MAL DAVID, JR., chemical engineer; b. July 26, 1922. BSChemE, U. Okla., 1948, M of Chem. Engring., 1949; cert. in nuc. engring., Pa. State U. and Argonne Nat. Lab., 1957. Chem. engr. Pure Oil, Wyo., 1949-51, Shell Chem., Deer Park, Tex., 1951-56; sr. chem., nuclear engr. Gen. Dynamics, Ft. Worth, 1956-59; sr. chem. engr., tech. staff Tex. Instruments, Dallas, 1959-90. Lt. USAF, 1942-45. Decorated DFC, Purple Heart; recipient Air medals with 2 oak leaf clusters USAF. Mem. N.Y. Acad. Scis. Home: 1240 Derby Dr Richardson TX 75080-5834

ROGERS, MIKE J. WARRINGTON, writer; b. London, Apr. 10, 1926; s. James F. Warrington and Dorothy M. Warrington (Rooff) R.; m. Rachel Brittain; children: Lee, John, Marcus. Aircraft engring. cert., DeHavilland Aircraft Tech Sch., Hatfield, Eng., 1949. Devel., flight test engr. De Havilland Propellers Ltd., Hatfield, 1950-53; plastics applications engr. De Havilland Propellers Ltd., Stevenage, U.K., 1953-59; from staff tng. officer to mktg. engr. electron beam welding Hawker Siddeley Dynamics, Hatfield, 1960-70; asst. mgr. mgmt. devel. Hawker Siddeley Aviation, Hatfield, 1970-73; sales and mgmt. tng. mgr., x-ray CT diagnostic scanners EMI Med. Ltd., Windsor, U.K., 1973-79; tng. coord. Thorn EMI Def. Electronics, Hayes, U.K., 1980—; freelance writer, author Berkhamsted, Eng., 1980—; motoring corr. Disabled Jour., 1980—. Contbr. articles on aerospace, motorsport and mgmt. to popular mags.; road test reporter on new car models, 1980—. Recipient Ratcliffe Mobility award U.K. Sec. State for Transport, 1990. Mem. De Havilland Aero. Tech. Sch. Assn. (com. mem. 1952—), British Inst. Mgmt., Inst. Tng. and Devel., Inst. Advanced Motorists, Planetary Soc. Avocations: driving race cars, flying zero gravity. Home and Office: Drumnessie, Ivy House Ln, Berkhamsted HP4 2PP, England

ROGERS, PATRICK R., management educator; b. Munich, Jan. 3, 1959; (parents Am. citizens); s. James Harvey and Margaret Ann R.; m. Rachel Rutherford Rogres, June 6, 1981; children: Lauren, Jordan, Salem, Mollie. BSBA, Western Carolina U., 1982, MBA, 1987; PhD, U. Tenn., 1994. Food and beverage dir. Fairfield Corp., Sapphire Valley, N.C., 1982-85; loan officer 1st Citizens Bank, Franklin, N.C., 1986-90; prof. Western Carolina U., Cullowhee, N.C., 1990-91, U. Tenn., Knoxville, 1992-95, N.C. Agrl. and Tech. U., Greensboro, N.C., 1995—; cons. Sea Ray Boats, Knoxville, 1994. Contbr. articles to profl. jours., including Strategic Mgmt. Jour., Jour. Bus. Strategies, Jour. Bus. Rsch., others. Coach Jamestown (N.C.) Youth League, 1995-98, Piedmont Soccer Alliance, High Point, N.C., 1997-98. Mem. Acad. Mgmt., Soc. Advancement of Mgmt. (faculty advisor 1998-99), So. Mgmt. Assn., Ea. Acad. Mgmt. Avocations: learning, reading, movies. E-mail: rogersp@ncat.edu. Home: 914 New Hampshire Dr Jamestown NC 27282-9038 Office: NC Agrl & Tech U Dept Bus and Econ 315 Merrick Hl Greensboro NC 27411-0001

ROGERS, RICHARD LEE, educator; b. N.Y.C., Sept. 17, 1949; s. Leonard J. and Beverly (Simon) R.; m. Susan Jane Thornton, Aug. 14, 1976; children: Caroline, Meredith. BA, Yale U., 1971, MA in Religion, 1973; postgrad., U. Chgo., 1977-80; MS in Edn., Bank St. Coll. Edn., N.Y.C., 1989. Tchr. Foote Sch., New Haven, 1974-77; devel. assoc. U. Chgo., 1980-81, spl. asst. to v.p. planning, 1981-82; spl. asst. to pres. New Sch. Social Rsch., N.Y.C., 1982-83, sec. of corp., then v.p., sec., 1983-94; pres. Ctr. for Creative Studies, Detroit, 1994—. Office: Ctr Creative Studies 201 E Kirby St Detroit MI 48202-4048

ROGERS, RUBY ELIZABETH, artist; b. New Kensington, Pa., June 24, 1952; d. Claude Ray and Dora Jean (Remaley) Downing; m. Kenneth Michael Rogers, June 26, 1970; children: Aaron Nathan, Jason Edward. Student, Fed. Tax and Bus. Sch., Chgo., 1990, NRI Sch. Computer Programming, Washington, 1990-93, ICS Sch. Med. Tng., Scranton, Pa., 1996—. Owner Kenneth M. Rogers Gen. Contractor, Claysville, Pa., 1975-90, Art by R. Rogers, Claysville, 1991—; mem. staff Home and Cmty. Based Svcs., Inc. United Cerebal Palsy of Southwestern Pa., 1998—. Exhibited in group show at Calif. State Coll., 1969 (cert. of merit Washington County Fedn. Women's Clubs). Occupl. therapy vol. Washington (Pa.) Hosp., 1994-96, United Cerebal Palsy of Southwestern, Inc., Washington, 1994—; ptnr. Spl. Olympics, 1996098; mem. The Shepherd's Guide, Christian Advertisers Orgn., 1995-99; mem. WQED Pitts. Pub. Broadcasting, 1990—. Mem. AAUW, Nat. Mus. Women in Arts. Republican. Lutheran. Avocations: reading, walking, gardening. Home and Office: 1285 Templeton Run Rd Claysville PA 15323-1147

ROGERS, SCOTT DENNIS, lawyer; b. L.A., Mar. 12, 1956; s. Jeffrey R. and Renee R. Rogers; m. Margaret Kerr, Sept. 24, 1983; children: Jamie, Katie, Lauren. BA, U. Calif., Irvine, 1978; MBA, JD, UCLA, 1982. Bar: Calif. 1982. Assoc. Rutan & Tucker, Costa Mesa, Calif., 1982-84; ptnr. Landels Ripley & Diamond LLP, San Francisco, 1985—. Office: Landels Ripley & Diamond LLP Ste 208 60 E Sir Francis Drake Blvd Larkspur CA 94939-1713

ROGERS, SEAN JOSEPH, lawyer, arbitrator; b. New Orleans, July 24, 1947; s. Warren Joseph and Hilda Kenny R.; m. Maureen Lisa Ruddy, Aug. 17, 1971 (div. Nov. 1985); m. Laureen Karen Manning, July 18, 1992. BS, Georgetown U., 1970, JD, 1977; MS, Am. U., 1976. Bar: D.C. 1978, M.D. 1986. Police officer Met. Police, Washington, 1970-74; asst. gen. counsel Nat. Assn. Govt. Employees, Washington, 1974-78; nat. counsel Nat. Treasury Employees Union, Washington, 1978-86; dir. labor rels. Montgomery County Govt., Rockville, Md., 1986-96, IRS, Washington, 1995-98; sr. hearing officer Nat. Mediation Bd., Washington, 1998—; labor arbitrator Am. Arbitration Assn., Fed. Mediation and Counciliation Svc. Avocations: motorcycling, antique car collecting. E-mail: rogers@nmb.gov. Office: Nat Mediation Bd 1301 K St NW Ste 250E Washington DC 20572-0001

ROGERS, STEPHEN HITCHCOCK, former ambassador; b. Flushing, N.Y., June 21, 1930; s. Francis Walker and Julia (Wheeler) R.; m. Kent Brain, June 23, 1956; children: Kryston R. Fischer, F. Halsey, Julia L., John H. BA, Princeton U., 1952; MA, Columbia U., 1956; MPA, Harvard U., 1962. Fgn. svc. officer Dept. of State, 1956-93; econ. counselor Am. Embassy, London, 1970-72; counselor U.S. Mission to OECD, Paris, 1972-75; office dir. Bur. Inter.-Am. Affairs Dept. of State, Washington, 1975-78; econ. counselor Am. Embassy, Mexico City, 1978-82; prof. Nat. Def. U., Washington, 1982-85; econ. counselor Am. Embassy, Pretoria, South Africa, 1986-90; amb. Am. Embassy, Mbabane, Swaziland, 1990-93. Bd. dirs. Cen. Atlantic Conf., United Ch. of Christ, 2000—. Lt. (jg) USN, 1952-55. Recipient Outstanding Civilian Svc. award Dept. of Army, 1985. Mem. Am. Fgn. Svc. Assn., Nassau Club (Princeton, N.J.). Mem. United Ch. of Christ. Home: 3803 Ivydale Dr Annandale VA 22003-2006

ROGERS, THEODORE COURTNEY, investment company executive; b. Lorain, Ohio, Aug. 25, 1934; s. William Theodore and Leona Ruth (Gerhart) R.; m. Elizabeth B. Barlow, June 28, 1984; children by previous marriage: Pamela Anne Rogers Harmon, Theodore Courtney Jr. BS in Social Sci., Miami U., Oxford, Ohio, 1956; postgrad., Johns Hopkins U., 1957; MBA summa cum laude, Marquette U., 1968. With Armco Inc., 1958-80; pres. Olympic Fastening Systems, 1970-74; with Bathey Mfg. Co. subs., 1970, group v.p. indsl. products, 1971-74; exec. v.p. Nat. Supply Co. subs., Houston, 1974-76, pres., 1976-80, v.p. parent co., 1976-79, group v.p. parent co., 1979-80; pres., COO NL Industries, Inc., N.Y.C., 1980-82, pres., CEO, 1982-83, chmn., pres., CEO, 1983-87; ptnr. Am. Indsl. Ptnrs., N.Y.C., N.Y., 1987—; bd. dirs. Sweetheart Cup, Gt. Lakes Carbon Corp. (chmn.), Bucyrus Internat., Stanadyne Automotive Corp., Steel Heddle Mfg. Co.; chmn. bd. RBX Corp. Bd. dirs. United Cerebral Palsy Rsch. and Ednl. Found., Inc., Lincoln Ctr. for Performing Arts, City Ctr. for Music and Drama, Nat. Ocean Industries Assn.; chmn. bd. Theatre for New Audience; former chmn. Ctr. Cmty. Interests, emeritus chmn. N.Y.C. Ballet; bd. dirs., trustee Ballet Rev. Quar.; nat. coun. Theatre Communications Group. Lt. USN, 1956-58. Mem. Petroleum Equipment Suppliers Assn. (bd. dirs.), N.Y. Soc. Libr. (trustee), World Pres. Orgn., Century Assn. (N.Y.), Bus. Roundtable, Poets and Writers (bd. dirs.), Achilles Track Club (founder, bd. dirs.), Ramada Club, Houston Country Club, Links Club, Sky Club, Econ. Club (N.Y.), Met. Club (Washington), The Union Club (Cleve.), Univ. Club (Milw.), Century Assn., Beta Gamma Sigma (bd. dirs.). Office: Am Indsl Ptnr 551 5th Ave Ste 3800 New York NY 10176-0001

ROGERS, THEODORE OTTO, JR., lawyer; b. West Chester, Pa., Nov. 17, 1953; s. Theodore Otto and Gladys (Bond) R.; m. Hope Tyler Scott, Nov. 7, 1981; children: Helen Elliot, Theodore Scott, Robert Montgomery Bond. AB magna cum laude, Harvard U., 1976, JD cum laude, 1979. Bar: N.Y. 1980, U.S Ct. Appeals (2nd cir.) 1984, U.S. Dist. Ct. (so. and ea. dists.) N.Y. 1980, D.C. 1981, U.S. Ct. Claims, 1982, U.S. Supreme Ct. 1983, U.S. Ct. Appeals (6th and 10th cirs.) 1983, U.S. Ct. Appeals (1st cir.) 1984, U.S. Ct. Appeals (fed. cir.) 1986. From assoc. to ptnr. Sullivan & Cromwell, N.Y.C., 1979—. Co-author: Employment Litigation in New York, 1996. Mem. U.S. Presdl. Transition Team, 1980. Mem. N.Y. State Bar Assn. (co-chair individual rights and responsibilities com. labor and employment law sect.), Assn. of Bar of City of N.Y. (labor and employment law). Republican. Home: 535 E 86th St New York NY 10028-7533 Office: Sullivan & Cromwell 125 Broad St Fl 28 New York NY 10004-2489

ROGIERS, XAVIER, surgeon; b. Ieper, Belgium, Nov. 1, 1956; s. Frans and Francine (Gruwez) R.; m. Anita Elisabeth Rogiers-Delsupehe, Aug. 25, 1989; children: Matthias, Nicolas, Pierre. MD, Catholic U. of Leuven, 1982; surgeon, 1989. Cert. surgeon, 1989. Attending surgeon Dept. Abdominal Surgery U. Hosps. Leuven, Belgium, 1990-92; Oberarzt Dept. Surgery UkEppendorf, Hamburg, Germany, 1992-98, dir. dept. hepatobiology and transplant surgery, 1998—; assoc. dir. Hamburg Liver and Pancreas Transplantation Programs, 1992—. Inventor: In-Situ Technique for splitting livers before transplantation. Med. Res. Lt. 1st Belgian Paratrooper BN. Recipient The Dressers prize, St. Thomas' Hosp., London, 1982. Office: UkEppendorf Dept Surgery, Martinistrasse 52, 20246 Hamburg Germany

ROGILLIO, KATHY JUNE, musician, piano rebuilder, educator; b. Baton Rouge, La., Nov. 4, 1950; d. David Hunter and Thelma Ruth (Tucker) R. MusB, La. State U., 1972, MusM, 1974. Organist Plains Presbyn. Ch., Zachary, La., 1963-73; teacher's aid Gifted/Talented East Baton Rouge Parish, Baton Rouge, La., 1974-75; staff accompanist La. State U., Baton Rouge, 1975-76; music enrichment tchr. Episcopal H.S., Baton Rouge, 1976-77; organist, choirmaster Grace Episcopal Ch., St. Francisville, La., 1977-82; piano-technician So. U., Baton Rouge, La., 1977-84; apprentice in piano rebuilding and concert tuning, 1978-81; music tchr., organist, choirmaster St. Patrick's Episcopal Day Sch. and Ch., Zachary, La., 1985-86; vis. organist, dir. Numerous Chs., La. and Miss., 1982—; piano rebuilder pvt. practice, Zachary, La., 1986—; ind. contract work Santi Falcone, Falcone Piano Co., Haverhill, Mass., 1987-88, part time organist/choirmaster St. Patrick's Episcopal Ch., Zachary, La., 1999-2000; pvt. piano tchr. La. Sch. for Visually Impaired, 2000—; recitalist, vis. organist. Arranger: Piano-Trio Arrangement Brahms Intermezzo Opus 118, #2, 1986 (2d pl. Composer's Guild Farmington, Utah, 1986). Treas. Beulah Plains Cemetery Assn., Zachary, La., 1987; mem. Landowners for Equitable Flood Control, Zachary, La., 1994—. Mem. Am. Guild Organists, Baton Rouge Musicians' Assn. (exec bd. 1990-92, v.p. 1992-94. pres. 1994-96), La. Endowment for the Humanities, La. Pub. Broadcasting, Pi Kappa Lambda (profl. mus. hons. frat.). Democrat. Episcopalian. Avocations: needlework, cooking, animals. Home and Office: Artist Pianos 18153 Barnett Rd Zachary LA 70791-8114

ROGISTER, JOHN MARIE JULIEN, history professor; b. Solihull, West Midlands, Eng., Mar. 26, 1941; s. J.J.A. and A.A.F. (Smal) R.; m. Margaret K. Jury, Sept. 7, 1972. Student, Oxford U., Eng., 1959-60, PhD, 1972; BA with honours, U. Birmingham, Eng., 1964. Lectr. in history U. Durham, Eng., 1967-82, sr. lectr., 1982—; assoc. prof. U. Paris Extension, Nanterre, France, 1982-84; guest prof. Coll. France, Paris, 1987, 1999; assoc. dir. of studies, Ec. pratique des Hautes Etudes, Sorbonne, Paris, 1988—. Editor Durham U. Jour., 1975-81; founder, editor Parliaments, Estates and Representation, 1981—; contbg. author: (book) Louis XV and the Parliament of Paris, 1995; contbr. articles to profl. jours. Recipient Officier dans L'Ordre des Palmes Academiques, Govt. France, 1988. Fellow Royal Hist. Soc., Soc. of Antiquaries of London; mem. Soc. Histoire de France, Brit. Soc. 18th Century Studies (sec. 1979-83), Internat. Commn. History of Representative and Parliamentary Instns. (v.p. 1985-90, pres. 1990-99, hon. pres. 1999—). Clubs: United Oxford and Cambridge (London), Found. Univ. (Brussels). Avocations: music, travel. Office: U Durham Dept History, 43-46 N Bailey, Durham DH1 3EX, England

ROGNONI, PAULINA AMELIA, cardiologist; b. Panama City, Panama, Mar. 21, 1947; d. Mario Carlos-Enrique and Isabel Maria (Rodriguez) R.; B.S. in Chemistry (Tulane scholar), Tulane U., New Orleans, 1969, M.D., 1973. Rotating intern Gorgas Hosp., C.Z., Panama, 1973-74; intern internal medicine Touro Infirmary, New Orleans, 1974-75; resident in internal medicine Charity Hosp., New Orleans, 1975-77; fellow in cardiology Charity Hosp., 1977-79, VA Hosp., New Orleans, 1979-80; compulsory rural intern Panamanian Govt., Hosp. Amador Guerrero, Panam, 1980-81; cardiology cons. Clinica San Fernando. Mem. ACP, Med. Assn. Panama Canal Area, Am. Coll. Cardiology (asso.), Am. Med. Women's Assn., Am. Heart Assn., Mussor-Burch Soc., AMA. Assn. Mil. Surgeons U.S., Sociedad Panamena de Cardiologia, Sociedad Panamena de Mecidina Interna, Soc. Critical Care Medicine (internat. mem.), Chi Beta, Beta Beta Beta. Alpha Epsilon Delta. Roman Catholic. Club: Panama Soroptomists. Home: PO Box 914 Zona 1, Panama Panama City

ROGO, KATHLEEN, safety engineer; b. Carrollton, Ohio, Sept. 28, 1952; d. Silvio and Mary (Siragusano) R. Grad. high sch., Carrollton; PhD in Med. Sci. (hon.), Ohio Valley Pathologists, Inc., 1992. Cert. histotechnologist, emergency med. technologist, safety engr. Rsch. pathology trainee Aultman Hosp., Canton, Ohio, 1970-75, supr. anatomic pathology, 1974-75; lab. mgr. W. Morgan Lab., Canton, 1973-74; supr. anatomic pathology Dr.'s Hosp., Massillon, Ohio, 1975-78; emergency med. technician Canton Fire Dept., 1976-81; safety engr. Ashland Oil Co., Canton, 1980-82; rsch. pathologist assoc., med. cons, v.p. Ohio Valley Pathologists, Inc., Wheeling, W.Va., 1990—. Mem. Am. Soc. Clin. Pathology (cert. histotechnician), Am. Soc. Safety Engrs. (cert.), Am. Soc. Emergency Med. Technicians (cert.), Ohio State Med. Soc., Internat. Platform Assn. Democrat. Roman Catholic. Avocations: professional model, dancer and musician.

ROGOWSKI, RALF, educator; b. Wilster, Germany, July 2, 1953; s. Bruno Werner and Ingeborg (Nagel) R. LLM, U. Wis., 1981; PhD, European U. Inst., Italy, 1992; Ass. inr, Berlin, 1993. Lectr. law U. Lancaster, England, 1989-92; sr. lectr. law U. Warwick, Coventry, England, 1992-99, reader law, 1999—. Author: Reflexive Labour Law, 1994, Civil Law, 1996, Challenges to European Legal Scholarship, 1996, Labour Market Efficiency in the European Union, 1998, Constitutional Courts in Comparison, 2000; editor (book series): Studies in Modern Law and Policy. Vis. fellow U. Wis., Madison. Home: 8 Bertie Terr Warwick Pl, Leamington Spa CV32 5BL, England Office: U Warwick, Sch Law, Coventry CV4 7AL, England

ROGOZKIN, VICTOR ALEXEEVITCH, biochemist, researcher; b. Leningrad, Russia, Feb. 23, 1928; s. Alexis Michailovitch Rogozkin and AnastasiaGeorgievna Berezina; m. Antonina Ivanovna Komkova, Dec. 19, 1960. AB, Mil. Inst. Phys. Culture, Leningrad, 1953, State U. Leningrad, 1958; BD (hon.), State U. Leningrad, 1960; DSc, Inst. of Physiology, Leningrad, 1966. Researcher Rsch. Inst. Phys. Culture, Leningrad, 1959-65, prof. biochemistry, 1966-70, dir., 1970—; mem. med. com. Inter-Olympic Com., Lausanne, Switzerland, 1975-81. Co-editor: Nutrition, Physical Fitness and Health, 1978, Current Research in Sport Science, 1996; author: Physical Activity in Disease Prevention and Treatment, 1985, Metabolism of Anabolic Androgenic Steroids, 1991. Lt. Baltic Fleet, 1944-49. Recipient medal U.S. Sports Acad., 1992. Mem. Am. coll. Sports Medicine, Isostar Sport Nutrition Found., Rsch. Group on Biochemistry Exercise. Avocations: music, theater, walking, jogging, chess. Office: Rsch Inst Phys Culture, Dynamo Ave 2, 197110 Saint Petersburg Russia

ROGSTAD, ODDVIN MOERCH, physician; b. Flekkefjord, Norway, July 28, 1947; s. Odd Moerch and Kari (Moerch) Rogstad. MD, U. Vienna, 1973, U. Oslo, 1973. Resident ASA, Arendal, Norway, 1974-75, AKH, Vienna, 1975; dist. med. officer Randaberg, Norway, 1976-92; pvt. practice pvt. practice, Randaberh-Stavanger, Norway, 1992—. Mem. City Coun., Randaberg, 1977-93, mayor, 1984-92. Maj. Norwegian Royal Air Force. Mem. Masons, Rotary. Roman Catholic. Avocations: music, reading, travel. Home: St Olavs gate 13, 4005 Stavanger Norway Office: Randaberg Legesenter, Jon Torbergsonsvei 7, 4070 Randaberg Norway

ROGUEDA, PHILIPPE GUY AUGUSTE, physical chemist; b. Bordeaux, Gironde, France, Oct. 29, 1970; s. Francis and Janine (Vignau) R. Diploma in Engring., U. Bordeaux, 1993; MSc in Chemistry, U. Bristol, Eng., 1993, PhD, 1996. Sr. pharm. scientist Astra Zeneca, Loughborough, Eng., 1997—. Contbr. articles on colloids and surfaces to sci. jours. With French Air Force, 1996-97. Mem. Royal Soc. Chemistry, Soc. Chem. Industry, Soc. Chemistry and Industry London (colloid com. 1997—). Avocations: singing, flute, skiing, hiking, theology. Home: 31 Rue Félix Faure, 33600 Pessac France also: 93 Park Rd, Loughborough LE11 2HD, England

ROGUL, JUNE AUDREY, fundraising executive, government relations specialist; b. N.Y.C., Dec. 30, 1942; d. Caroll Mitchell and Gail (Arkin) Silver; m. Marvin Rogul, Mar. 17, 1974; children: Jonathan, Daniel. BA, Tufts U., 1964; MS, Columbia U., 1966. Cmty. orgn. specialist D.C. Redevel. Land Agy., Washington, 1966-70; asst. to the dir. Prime Minister's Commn. on Disadvantaged Children & Youth, Jerusalem, Israel, 1971-72; rep. Nat. Conf. Soviet Jewry, Washington, 1973-75; lobbyist Am. Israel Pub. Affairs Com., Washington, 1975-77; dir. JWB, Washington, 1980-82, GNK Assocs., Washington, 1982-83; dir. Washington region Am. Com. for Weizmann Inst. Sci., Washington, 1983-98, dir. govt. rels., 1992-98; dir. nat. outreach New Israel Fund, Washington, 1998—; assoc. The Kahn Pub. Policy Report, Washington, 1982-83; cons., rep. Na'Amat U.S.A., Washington, 1982-89; cons. in field. Del. Allied Civic Group, Silver Spring, Md., 1978-79; chmn. Linden Civic Assn., Silver Spring, 1978-79; appointee Montgomery County Housing Policy Implementation Com., Rockville, Md., 1979; mem. Joint Action Com. for Polit. Affairs, Washington, 1982—, co-chmn., 1992. Mem. Nat. Soc. Fund Raising Execs., Nat. Jewish Dem. Coun., Washington Reps. Nat. Jewish Orgns. Democrat. Avocations: travel, foreign languages, jogging, skiing. Home: 6132 Roseland Dr North Bethesda MD 20852

ROGULŚKI, WITOLD, biochemist; b. Wypychy, Warsaw, Poland, Sept. 10, 1938; s. Anthony and Cecilia (Chmiel) R. Msc in Biology, Warsaw U., 1969; Dr in Agrl. Sci., Warsaw Agrl. U., 1982. Asst., acad. tchr. biochemistry Warsaw U., 1969-70; sr. asst., acad. tchr. animal nutrition and feed sci. Warsaw Agrl. U., 1971-82, adj. acad. tchr. animal nutrition and feed sci., 1982-86, sr. specialist in biochemistry, feed sci., feed analysis, 1987—; tchr., cons. feed analysis, Africa, 1982, Asia, 1993, Beloruss, 1999. Co-author: The Animal Nutrition and Feed Science, 1994; contbr. articles to profl. jours. Scout Polish Scouting Union, 1949. Common soldier Polish Army, 1958-60. Mem. Polish Animal Sci. Soc., Tecator Users Club. Roman Catholic. Avocations: volleyball, bicycling, fishing, movies, sports. Home: Krochmalna 2/517, 00-864 Warsaw Poland Office: Warsaw Agrl U, Rakowiecka 26-30, 02-528 Warsaw Poland

ROHACK, JOHN JAMES, cardiologist; b. Rochester, N.Y., Aug. 22, 1954; s. John Joseph and Margaret Elizabeth (McLaughlin) R.; m. Charlotte McCown, Dec. 7, 1980; 1 child, Elisha Monique Feigle. BS, U. Tex., El Paso, 1976; MD, U. Tex., Galveston, 1980. Diplomate Am. Bd. Internal Medicine. Intern internal medicine U. Tex. Med. Br. Hosps., Galveston, 1980-81, resident internal medicine, 1981-83, chief resident internal medicine, 1983-84, fellow cardiology, 1984-86; instr. medicine U. Tex. Med. Br., Galveston, 1983-86; asst. prof. medicine Tex. A&M Coll. Medicine, College Station, 1986-95, assoc. prof., 1995—, sect. chief cardiology, 1989-97; assoc. med. dir. Scott and White Health Plan Bryan Coll. Sta., 1995-97; assoc. med. dir. for med. ops. Scott and White Health Plan and Clinic, 1997-2000, med. dir. Health Plan, 2000—; bd. dirs. Health for All Clinic, v.p., 1994-96; mem. Accreditation Coun. on Continuing Med. Edn., 1995-99, Liaison Com. on Med. Edn., 1999—; med. dir. Fitlife Ctr. Tex. A&M U., College Station, 1990-97. Bd. dirs. Am. Heart Assn., Brazos Valley College Station, 1987-97, Tex. affiliate Austin, 1991-98, 1st v.p., 1994-95, pres.-elect, 1995-96, pres., 1996-97. Fellow ACP, Am. Coll. Cardiology (bd. dirs. Tex. chpt. 1992-97); mem. AMA (alt del. ho. of dels. 1984-93, del. 1993—, coun. on med. edn. 1995—, chair elect 1996-97, chair 1997-98), Tex. Med. Assn. (exec. coun. med. student sect. 1981-82, ho. of dels. 1982—, trustee 1994—, pres.-elect 1999-2000, pres. 2000—. Avocations: golf, gardening, reading, ranching. Office: Scott and White Clinic 2401 S 31st St Temple TX 76508-0001

ROHAN, BRIAN PATRICK, lawyer; b. Bklyn., July 1, 1964; s. John Eamon and Janet Dee (Trebian) R.; m. Lori Lanahan, Aug. 18, 1990; children: Connor James, Taylor Kathleen. BS, SUNY, Plattsburgh, 1986; MBA, Union Coll., 1990; JD, Union U., 1990. Bar: N.Y. 1991, Mass. 1991, U.S. Dist. Ct. (no. dist.) N.Y. 1991. Atty. Waite & Assocs., P.C., Albany, N.Y., 1990-96; pvt. practice Brian P. Rohan Law Offices, Albany, 1996-99; atty. Dreyer Boyajian LLP, Albany, 1999—. Bd. dirs. Catholic Family & Cmty. Svcs., Albany, 1991-94. Mem. ATLA, N.Y. State Bar Assn., Albany County Bar Assn. Office: Dreyer Boyajian LLP 75 Columbia St Albany NY 12210-2708

ROHATSCHEK, HANS BRUNO, physicist; b. Krems, Austria, May 18, 1926; s. Johann and Hilda (Lerche) R.; m. Hertha Grammer, Aug. 9, 1958; children: Peter, Sonja. Dr.phil., U. Vienna, 1952. Devel. engr. Reichert Optical Works, Vienna, 1955, Austrian Nitrogen Works, Linz, Austria, 1956-70; univ. asst. U. Linz, 1971-91; exec. dept. for physics didactics U. Linz, 1985-91. Contbr. articles to profl. jours., Encyclopaedic Dictionary of Physics. Soldier German Air Force, 1944-45. Fellow Austrian Phys. Soc. Achievements include research in photophoresis. Home: Lueftenegger Strasse 15, A-4020 Linz Austria

ROHATYN, FELIX GEORGE, ambassador; b. Vienna, Austria, May 29, 1928; came to U.S., 1942, naturalized, 1950; s. Alexander and Edith (Knoll) R.; m. Jeannette Streit, June 9, 1956; children: Pierre, Nicolas, Michael; m. Elizabeth Fly, May 31, 1979. BS, Middlebury (Vt.) Coll., 1948; LLD (hon.), Adelphi U., Bard Coll., Hofstra U., 1981, L.I. U., 1981, Middlebury Coll., 1982, Fordham U., 1983; LLB (hon.), NYU, 1979, Brandeis U., 1987. With Lazard Freres & Co., LLC, N.Y.C., 1948—, mng. dir., 1960—; amb. to France Paris, 1997—; bd. dirs. Pfizer Co., Gen. Instrument, Crown, Cork & Seal Corp. mem bd. govs. NYSE, 1968-72. Served with AUS, 1951-53, Korea. Office: Lazard Freres & Co 30 Rockefeller Plz Fl 59 New York NY 10112-5900 Address: Am Embassay, 2 Avenue Gabriel, Paris Cedex08 75382, France

ROHDE, CLAUS JOHANNES GERD, lawyer, accountant; b. Leipzig, Sachsen, Germany, Feb. 13, 1948; s. Guenther and Christa (Goetz) R.; m. Angela Grundmann, Aug. 7, 1970 (div.); children: Stephan, Dorothea; m. Elke Guenther, Dec. 31, 1987; children: Anke, Tina. Staatsexamen, Bayer Julius-Matimilaius-U., Wurzburg, Bavaria, 1971; JD, Bayer J.M. Univ., Wurzburg, Bavaria, 1974. Bar: Landgericht Leipzig, Oberlandesgericht Dresden. Pvt. practice Leipzig, Federal Republic of Germany, 1974—; dir. R&R Pelzwirtschaftsberatungsgesellschaft mbH, Frankfurt, 1983—, R&R Steuerberatungsges. OHG, Frankfurt, 1986—, OAS Overseas Adv. Svcs. Ltd., London, 1982—. Author: The Impossibility of Performance with regard to "Inderminate Obligations, Die Unmöglichkeit der Leistung bei Gattungsschulden. County chmn. Freie Demokratische Partei (Liberal Dem. Party), Wurzburg, 1978, dist. chmn., 1980; county councillor Regional Com., Wurzburg, 1978; judge on the high ct. for barristers. Fellow ODD; mem. Internat. Bar Assn., Lions. Avocations: private pilot, trap shooting, classic car racing. Home and Office: Nikolaistrabe 12/14, 04109 Leipzig Saxonia Germany Office: Rechtsanwaltskanzlei, Kaiserstrasse 13, 8700 Wurzburg Germany

ROHDE, JAMES VINCENT, software systems company executive; b. O'Neill, Nebr., Jan. 25, 1939; s. Ambrose Vincent and Loretta Cecilia R.; m. Tatiana Rohde; children: Maria, Sonja, Daniele, Olga. B of Comml. Sci., Seattle U., 1962. Chmn. bd. dirs., pres. Applied Telephone Tech., Oakland, Calif., 1974; v.p. sales and mktg. Automation Electronics Corp., Oakland, 1975-82; pres., CEO, founder Am. Telecorp, Inc., Redwood City, Calif., 1982-99; founder, vice-chmn. Ceon Corp., Redwood City, 1999—; also bd. dirs.; chmn. exec. com., chmn. emeritus Pres.'s Coun. Heritage Coll., Toppenish, Wash., 1985—; chmn. bd. dirs. Calif. chpt. Coun. of Growing Cos., 1990-93. Bd. dirs. Ind. Colls. No. Calif., 1991-93. Named U.S. Dept. Commerce Export Exec. Yr. No. Calif., 1993. Mem. Am. Electronics Assn. (bd. dirs. 1992-94, vice-chmn. No. Calif. coun. 1992-93, chmn. 1993-94). Republican. Roman Catholic. Office: Ceon Corp 720 Bay Rd Redwood City CA 94063-2469

ROHEE, CLEMENT, Guyanese government official; b. Georgetown, Mar. 16, 1950. Gen. cert. edn., Nat. Evening Coll., Guyana; student, Inst. Social Sci., Moscow, Accabre Coll. Social Scis., Guyana. Sr. min. fgn. affairs Govt. Guyana, Georgetown; newspaper columnist; permanent rep. editl. bd. Problems of Peace and Progress, Prague, 1979-83; mem. ctrl. com., exec. com. People's Progressive Party, 1979—, sec. ctrl. com. internat. affairs, 1979—, exec. sec., 1990-92. Office: Min Fgn Affairs Takuba Lodge, 254 New Garden St and South Rd, Georgetown Guyana*

RÖHL, HARDY FRODE, surgeon, consultant; b. Copenhagen, Nov. 10, 1944; s. Hans Willy and Edit Natali Renda (Hansen) Röhl-Larsen; m. Renate Kückelhahn, Apr. 5, 1969 (div. 1992); children: Katja, Christina; m. Lis Andersen, Aug. 20, 1994; children: Christopher, Malthe. Physician, U. Copenhagen, 1974; specialist in surgery and urology, 1982. Surgeon Hosp., Sweden, 1974-82, Kolding, Denmark, 1981-82, Sönderborg, Denmark, 1982-83; surgeon U. Hosp., Odense, Denmark, 1983-87; surgeon Hosp., Ålborg, Denmark, 1987-88, Vejle, Denmark, 1988-89; cons. in urology and surgery, Aabenraa, Denmark, 1990—; clin. lectr. U. Hosp., Odense, 1983-87. Mem. Danish Urol. Soc., Danish Surg. Soc., Danish Gastroenterol. Soc. Home: Gl Bjert 47, 6091 Bjert Denmark Office: Borgmester Finksgade 4A, 6200 Åbenrå Denmark

RÖHL, JOHN CHARLES GERALD, educator, historian; b. London, May 31, 1938; s. Hans Gerhard and Freda Kingsford (Woulfe-Brenan) R.; m. Rosemarie Elfriede von Berg, Sept. 18, 1964; children: Stephanie Angela, Christoph Andreas and Nicholas John (twins). BA, Corpus Christi Coll., Cambridge, Eng., 1961, PhD, 1965. Lectr. in history U. Sussex, Brighton, U.K., 1964-72, reader in history, 1972-79, prof. history, 1979-99—, dean sch. European studies, 1982-85; prof. history Hamburg (Germany) U., 1974, Freiburg (Germany) U., 1977-78; mem. Inst. Advanced Study, Princeton, 1994. With Royal Air Force, 1956-58. Co-recipient Wolfson History prize, 1994; fellow Historisches Kolleg, Munich, 1986-87, Woodrow Wilson fellow, 1989-90; Nat. Humanities Ctr. fellow, 1997-98. Avocations: walking, bird watching, jazz. Home: 11 Monckton Way, Kingston-Near-Lewes, Sussex BN7 3LD, England

ROHLENA, KAREL, physicist; b. Prague, Czech Republic, July 27, 1941; s. Karel and Marie (Andelova) R.; m. Ivana Raskova, May 25, 1972; children: Jakub, Anna. Grad. Physicist, Charles U., Prague, 1963, RNDr, 1972; PhD, Czechoslovakia Acad. of Scis., Prague, 1972. Rsch. asst. Inst. of Physics/Czechoslovak Acad. of Scis., 1963-72, rschr., 1972-86, sr. rschr., 1986, head of dept., 1990. Contbr. articles to profl. jours. Mem. selection panel Czech Literary Fund, 1991-97. Cpl. Czechoslovakian Signals, 1963-64. Mem. Union of Czech Mathematicians and Physicists. Roman Catholic. Avoca-

tions: hiking, cross-country skiing. Office: Inst of Physics, NA Slovance 2, 182 21 Prague 8, Czech Republic

ROHLENA, ROBERT CHARLES, retired, real estate manager; b. Cedar Rapids, Iowa, Aug. 22, 1932; s. Charles and Tillie Sadie (Varva) R.; m. Sylvia Blaha, Dec. 9, 1967; children: John, Janelle, Charles. BS, U. Iowa, 1959, MS in Sociology, 1970. Tax preparer H&R Block, Cedar Rapids, Iowa, 1959-64; farmer Cedar Rapids, 1959-97; bank mgr. First Trust and Savs. Bank, Ely, Iowa, 1972-76; landowner, mgr. Cedar Rapids, 1976-98; ret., 1998. With U.S. Army, 1952-54. Mem. Ind. Order of Odd Fellows (Noble Grand 1961), Am. Legion (comdr. 1975-76), Czech Heritage Soc. Avocation: travel. Home: 3105 76th Avenue Dr SW Cedar Rapids IA 52404-9004

ROHLF, F. JAMES, biometrician, educator; b. Blythe, Calif., Oct. 24, 1936. BS, San Diego State Coll., 1958; PhD in Entomology, U. Kans., 1962. Asst. prof. biology U. Calif., Santa Barbara, 1962-65; assoc. prof. statis. biology U. Kans., 1965-69; assoc. prof. biology SUNY, Stony Brook, 1969-72, prof., 1972—, chmn. dept. ecology and evolution, 1975-80, 90-91; statis. cons. N.Y. Pub. Svc. Commn., 1975-78, IBM, 1977-81, U.S. EPA, 1978-80; vis. scientist IBM, Yorktown Heights, N.Y., 1976-77, 80-81; vis. prof. U. Rome, 1997, 99. Mem. Biometric Soc., Soc. Systematic Biologists, Classification Soc. Achievements include research and development of statistical methods and software for geometric morphometrics and applications of multivariate analysis to systematics and population biology. Office: SUNY at Stony Brook Dept Ecology And Evolution Stony Brook NY 11794-0001

ROHLWINK, ANTHONY, bank executive; b. Hannover, Germany, Dec. 26, 1954; s. Bertrum William and Ruth Rohlwink; m. Annaick Marie-Jeanne Autret, Sept. 19, 1987; children: Charlotte, Juliette. MA in Math., Oxford (Eng.) U., 1978; MSc in Bus., Imperial Coll., London, 1979; MSc in Econs., London Sch. Econs., 1982. Cons. Arthur D. Little, London, 1979-81, sr. cons., 1983-87; ptnr. Spicer & Oppenheim, London, 1988-91; dir. Booz Allen & Hamilton, Munich, 1991-92; head strategic planning Westdeutsche Landesbank, Düsseldorf, 1992—. Author: Strategic Positioning for Financial Institutions, 1991; contbr. articles to profl. jours. including Euromoney, The Banker, and Mgmt. Today. With German Army, 1974-75. Mem. Free Dem. Party. Home: Wendersstr. 20, 40472 Düsseldorf Germany Office: Westdeutsche Landesbank, Herzogstr 15, 40217 Düsseldorf Germany

ROHN, JIRI, mathematician, researcher, educator; b. Prague, Czech Republic, June 19, 1947; s. Robert and Nina (Bagnjuk) R.; m. Helena Havajová, Aug. 17, 1974; children: Zuzana, Martin, Julie. MS with hons., Charles U., Prague, 1970, PhD, 1977, DrSc, 1992. Lectr. Charles U., Prague, 1970-77, asst. prof., 1977-91, assoc. prof. math., 1991—; rschr. Rsch. Inst. for Agr., Prague, 1974-79, Acad. Scis., Prague, 1994—; cons. Rsch. Inst. for Bldg. Industry, Prague, 1974-87. Contbr. articles to profl. jours. Mem. Am. Math. Soc., Internat. Linear Algebra Soc., Gesellschaft für Angewandte Mathematik und Mechanik, Mathematische Gesellschaft in Hamburg. Roman Catholic. Office: Charles U Fac Math and Physics, Malostranské nám 25, 118 00 Prague Czech Republic

ROHRBAUGH, WAYNE JOSEPH, chemical company executive; b. York, Pa., Aug. 13, 1948; s. Clair Joseph and Mary Elizabeth Rohrbaugh; m. Phyllis Theresa Leonard, June 19, 1971; children: Stephanie Elaine, Michael Wayne, Daniel Philip, Christine Marie. BS in Chemistry with honors, Drexel U., 1971; PhD in Phys. Chemistry, Iowa State U., 1977. Rsch. asst. Ames Lab./U.S. Dept. Energy, Ames, Iowa, 1971-76; assoc. prof. chemistry Wesley Coll., Dover, Del., 1976-78; group leader material structure rsch. Mobil R&D Corp., Paulsboro, N.J., 1978-90; mgr. analytical sect. ICI Americas, Inc., Wilmington, Del., 1990-94; rsch. mgr. corp. R&D dept. Ashland Chem. Co., Columbus, Ohio, 1994-96, dir. corp. R&D dept. 1996—; adj. prof. chemistry Rowan Coll., Glassboro, N.J., 1980-88; guest scientist Brookhaven (N.Y.) Nat. Lab., 1985-88. Contbr. articles to profl. jours. Mem. council Ames Cmty. Coun. on Drugs, 1973, All-Univ. Cmty. Coun., Ames, 1975, Wesley Coll. Coun., Dover, 1977, 78. Recipient Outstanding Young Men of Am. citation U.S. Jaycees, 1978. Mem. Am. Chem. Soc. (undergrad. award in analytical chemistry 1970, South Jersey sect. chmn. 1987-88, sec. Carothers Award com. 1991-92), Indsl. Rsch. Inst., Dirs. Indsl. Rsch., Analytical Lab. Mgrs. Assn. (pres.), Coun. for Chem. Rsch., Sigma Xi, Phi Lambda Upsilon, Pi Lambda Phi. Republican. Roman Catholic. Achievements include zeolite structure research; led group that solved the framework molecular structures of ten zeolite compositions, one of which, ZSM-18, represents the only known aluminosilicate structure containing rings of three (Si,Al)-O species. Office: Ashland Chemical Co PO Box 2219 Columbus OH 43216-2219

ROHRER, HEINRICH, physicist; b. Buchs, Switzerland, June 6, 1933. Diploma in physics, Swiss Inst. Tech., Zurich, 1955, PhD in Physics, 1960; D. Sci. (hon.), Rutgers U., 1987, Marseille (France) U., 1988, Madrid U., 1988, Tsukuba (Japan) U., 1994, Frankfurt (Germany) U., 1996, Tohoku (Japan) U., 2000. Rsch. asst. Swiss Inst. Tech., Zurich, 1960-61; post-doc. Rutgers U., New Brunswick, N.J., 1961-63; with IBM Rsch. Lab., Zurich, 1963-97; rschr. CSIC, Madrid, 1997—, RIKEN, Waco, Japan, 1997—, Tohoku U., Sendai, Japan, 1997—; vis. scholar U. Calif., Santa Barbara, 1974-75. Co-recipient King Faisal Internat. prize for sci., 1984, Hewlett Packard Europhysics prize, 1984, Nobel prize for Physics, 1986, Cresson medal Franklin Inst., Phila., 1987; IBM fellow, 1986; named to Nat. Inventors Hall of Fame, 1994. Fellow Royal Microscopical Soc. (hon. 1988); mem. NAS (fgn. assoc.), Swiss Acad. Tech. Scis., Swiss Phys. Soc. (hon. 1990), Swiss Assn. Engring. and Architecture (hon. 1991), Zurich Phys. Soc. (hon. 1992). Office: Rebbergstr 9d, CH 8832 Wollerau Switzerland

ROHRER, RICHARD JEFFREY, surgeon, educator; b. Columbus, Mar. 14, 1950; s. James William and Nancy Lenore (Acheson) R.; m. Jill Ellen Stein, Nov. 29, 1981; children: Benjamin, Noah. BS, Yale U., 1973; MD, Columbia U., 1977. Surgeon New England Deaconess and Harvard Med. Sch., Boston, 1984-87; surgeon, chief transplantation New Eng. Med. Ctr., Boston, 1988—; assoc. prof. surgery Tufts Sch. Medicine, Boston, 1988—. Trustee New Eng. Organ Bank, Boston, 1988—, chmn. bd. dirs., 1999—; councillor United Network for Organ Sharing, 1996—, sec., 2000—. Fellow ACS; mem. Am. Soc. Transplant Surgeons, Transplantation Soc., Physicians for Social Responsibility, Assn. for Acad. Surgery, Assn. for Surg. Edn., Soc. Critical Care Medicine. Office: New England Med Ctr Box 40 750 Washington St Boston MA 02111-1526

ROHRMANN, DOROTHEA, urologist; b. Langerwehe, Germany, Oct. 9, 1959; d. Matthias Josef and Klara (Spoelgen) Glasmacher; m. Gert Stephan Rohrmann, Oct. 30, 1984 (div. May 1991); 1 child, Christian Matthias. MD, RWTH Aachen, 1984, Dr.med., 1991; privatdozent, 1998. Resident RWTH Aachen, Karlsruhe, Germany, 1984-87, resident in pediatric surgery, 1988-89, resident, gen. registrar in urology, 1989-94, sr. registrar, 1996—; fellow in urology/pediatric urology CHOP, Phila., 1994-96. Author: Pediatric Urology, 1997; contbr. articles to profl. jours.; inventor in field. Rsch. grant DFG, 1997. Mem. AUA, German Urology Assn., European Assn. of Urology. Roman Catholic. Office: Univ RWTH, Pauwelsstrasse 30, 52057 Aachen Germany

ROHRMOSER, DIAMANTINA CELIA CLEGHORN DE, public health nurse, educator; b. Panama City, Apr. 20, 1948; came to the U.S., 1987; d. Donald Oswald and Dorothy (Else) Spencer de Cleghorn; m. Roberto Felix Rohrmoser, May 15, 1976. BSN, U. Panama, 1975; MPH, Hebrew U., 1982; PhD, U. Del., 1992. Cert. RN, Panama, prof. U. Panama, 1978. Nurse Social Security Hosp., Panama City, 1972-76; asst. prof. U. Panama, 1976-84, adj. prof., 1984-89, prof., 1989—; cons. Social Security Occupational Health Program Met. Hosp., Panama, 1984-87. Mem. Assn. Nacional de Enfermeras Panama, Assn. de Profs. de U. Panama, Internat. Commn. Occupational Health, Shalom Assn. Panama, Am. Pub. Health Assn., Nat. Coun. Family Rels., Kappa Omicron Nu Honor Soc. Roman Catholic. Home: PO Box 55-2603, Estafeta de Paitilla, Panama Republic of Panama Office: Facultad de Enfermeria, U Panama, Panama Republic of Panama

ROHWER, KLAUS, aerospace researcher; b. Wismar, Germany, July 23, 1941; s. Theodor Claus and Elisabeth (Dibbern) R.; m. Ute Beyrau, Sept. 10, 1971. Diploma in engring., U. Braunschweig, Germany, 1968, D Engring., 1974; D Engring. Habil., U. Magdeburg, Germany, 1996. Cons. engr. U. Braunschweig, 1968-69; rsch. scientist German Aerospace Rsch. Establishment, Braunschweig, 1969-92; sr. scientist German Aerospace Rsch. Establishment, 1992—; dep. inst. dir. German Aerospace Rsch. Establishment, Braunschweig, 1994-98; vis. assoc. Calif. Inst. Tech., Pasadena, 1976-77. Contbr. over 30 articles to profl. publs. Mem. AIAA (affiliate), Gesellschaft für Angewandte Math. und Mechanik. Home: Rosenstr 12, D38533 Vordorf Germany Office: DLR Inst Structural Mech, PO Box 3267, D38022 Braunschweig Germany

ROIF, HENRY IRVING, flight test engineer, electronic engineer; b. Lima, Peru, Dec. 15, 1955; came to U.S., 1991; s. Israel Meyer and Raquel (Rotstain) R. BSEE, U. Nat. de Ingenieria, Lima, 1984; MS in Agrl. Engring., Israel Inst. Tech., Haifa, 1989; comml. pilot, Escuela de Aviacion Civil Peru, Lima, 1981. Flight test engr. Quiet Tech. Venture, Miami, Fla., 1996—. Mem. IEEE, AIAA, Aerospace and Electronics Systems Soc. Jewish. Avocations: hang gliding, scuba diving, outdoors, music; achievements include 18 patents including aircraft landing taxing system, special project for the recovery of the ozone layer; patent pending on automobile automatic steering and cruise guidance control, airport surface movement detection system. Office: Quiet Tech Venture 8000 NW 56th St Miami FL 33166-4015

ROILIDES, EMMANUEL JOHN, pediatrician; b. Chalkis, Euboea, Greece, Oct. 12, 1955; s. John and Polymnia (Mpouli) R.; m. Maria Karanintziou, May 30, 1982; children: Polixeni, Dimitrios, John, Nectarios, Anna, Glyceria, Kyriaki, Filothei. MD, U. Athens, 1979, PhD, 1988. Med. diplomate. Rsch. asst. Saint Sophia Children's Hosp., Athens, 1982-83; pediatric resident Gen. Hosp., Alexandroupoli, Greece, 1983-86; vis. fellow Nat. Inst. Child Health and Human Devel., Bethesda, Md., 1986-88; vis. fellow Nat. Cancer Inst., Bethesda, Md., 1989-90, vis. scientist, 1990-92; instr. pediatrics U. Thessaloniki, Greece, 1993-97, asst. prof., 1997—. Contbr. articles to profl. jours. Recipient Scholarship Onasis Inst., Athens, 1982. Mem. Infectious Disease Soc. Am., Am. Assn. Immunologists, Immunocompromised Host Soc. Home: Ionias 23, GR-57019 Perea Thessal Greece Office: Hippokration Hosp-3d Dept Peds, Konstantinoupoleos 49, GR-54642 Thessaloniki Greece

ROISLER, GLENN HARVEY, quality assurance professional; b. Milw., Apr. 6, 1952; s. George Harvey and Mayme Elvin (Salo) R.; m. Jacqueline Bout, July 27, 1971; 1 child, Renee Jenette. Student electronics tech., DeVry Inst. Tech., Chgo., 1976; student computer engring. tech., Capitol Radio Engring. Inst., Washington, 1980; BA in Econs., N.C. State U., 1992. Instr. scuba Pirate's Cove, Inc., Milw., 1969-70; sr. electronics technician Bendix Field Engring. Corp., Columbia, Md., 1977-79; field engr. Technicare, Inc., Solon, Ohio, 1979; supr. electronics Troxler Labs., Inc., Research Triangle Park, N.C., 1979-81; mgr. prodn. Matrix Corp., Raleigh, N.C., 1981; vendor surveillance specialist Carolina Power and Light Co., Raleigh, N.C., 1981-84, sr. quality assurance specialist, 1984-91, sr. systems analyst, 1991—. Contbr. articles to profl. publs. Served with USN, 1971-77. Mem. Am. Soc. Quality Control (crt. quality engr., reliability engr.), Gamma Beta Phi, Sigma Pi Sigma, Omicron Delta Epsilon. Methodist. Avocations: scuba diving, ice hockey. Office: Carolina Power & Light Co PO Box 1551 Raleigh NC 27602-1551

ROISMAN, HANNA MASLOVSKI, classics educator; b. Wroclaw, Poland; d. Leon and Eugenia (Shlager-Katz) Maslovski; m. Joseph Roisman, Aug. 5, 1971; children: Elad L., Shalev G. BA in Classics, MA in Classics, Tel Aviv U., Ramat Aviv, Israel, 1977; PhD in Classics, U. Wash., 1981. Lectr. classics Tel Aviv U., 1981-87, sr. lectr. classics, 1987-90; assoc. prof. classics Colby Coll., Waterville, Maine, 1990-94, prof., 1994—; jr. fellow Ctr. Hellenic Studies, Washington, 1985-86; vis. scholar U. Wash. Seattle, 1983, Cornell U., Ithaca, N.Y., 1989, 1995-96; sec. Israel Soc. for Promotion of Classical Studies, 1987-89; vis. assoc. prof. Cornell U., 1986-94, vis. prof., 1995-97, 2000. Author: Loyalty in Early Greek Epic and Tragedy, 1984, Nothing is as it Seems: The Tragedy of the Implicit in Euripides' Hippolytus, 1999; co-author: The Odyssey Re-Formed, 1996; co-editor: Essays on Homeric Epic, 1993, Studies in Roman Epic, 1994, Essays on the Drama of Euripides, 1997; editor Text and Presentation, Jour. Comparative Drama Conf., 1999-2000; contbr. articles to profl. jours. AAUW fellow, 1980-81. Office: Colby Coll Mayflower Hill Waterville ME 04901

ROITSCH, PAUL ALBERT, pilot; b. Hermosa Beach, Calif., Oct. 15, 1926; s. George Arthur and Margaret (Pattillo) R.; m. Phyllis T.A. McCoy, Aug. 26, 1955; children—Sharon Elise, Alison Carol, Paul Eric. BA, U. So. Calif., 1952; postgrad. U.S. Navy Test Pilot Sch., 1965. Copilot, navigator Pan Am. Airways, San Francisco, 1952-53, pilot, 1955-64, asst. chief pilot tech., Jamaica, N.Y., 1965-69, chief pilot tech., 1969-73, line pilot, 1973-86, pres. Paul Roitsch Assocs., Internat. Aviation Cons., Greenwich, Conn., 1986—, pilot Civil Air Transport, 1954-55; bd. dirs. Pan Am Hist. Found., 1993—, v.p., 1994—, exec. v.p., 1995—. With USN, 1944-49, 53-54. Mem. AIAA, Soc. Automotive Engrs. (airplane handling qualities and flight deck design com., recipient cert. of appreciation 1981), Internat. Soc. Air Safety Investigators. Home: 39 John St Greenwich CT 06831-2608 Office: PO Box 786 Greenwich CT 06836-0786

ROJANY, LISA ADRIENNE, publishing company executive, writer; b. L.A., Feb. 14, 1964; d. Aviezer Rojany and Mary Marks. B of Comms. magna cum laude, UCLA, 1986; cert. in translation, Sorbonne U., Paris, 1987; M English and Am. Lit., Brown U., 1990. Newspaper journalist UCLA Daily Bruin, Together Newsmag., L.A., 1985-86; English tutor Paris, 1986-87; writer, reviewer TV Guide, L.A., 1987-88; freelance editor, writer Creative Ideaz, 19885; sr. editor Intervisual Books, Santa Monica, Calif., 1991-93; editl. dir. Price Stern Sloan divsn. Penguin/Putnam Pub., L.A., 1993-97, Gateway Learning Corp., 1997; west coast publ. dir. Golden Books Family Entertainment, L.A., 1998-2000; editl. dir. bus. devel. MyPotential.com, 2000—; proofreader MIT U. Press, Cambridge, Mass., 1990, Fidelity, Inc., Boston, 1990, Heinle & Heinle Pubs., Inc., Boston, 1990; correlator, proofreader Houghton Mifflin Co., Boston, 1990; spkr. in field. Author: (children's books) The Hands-on Book of Big Machines, 1992, Exploring the Human Body, 1992, King Arthur's Camelot, 1993, The Story of Hanukkah, 1993, Where's That Pig?, 1993, Santa's New Suit, 1993, Jake and Jenny on the Town, 1993, ,96, Andrews & McMeel Mini Pop-Up Quote Books, 1993, Alice in Wonderland, 1994, Token of Love and Spring Gardens, 1994, Mickey Mouse: Where's the Picnic, 1994, Winnie the Pooh: The Suprise Party, 1994, Make Your Own Valentines, 1994, 3d edit., 1996 (Pub.'s Weekly Bestseller list 1994, 95), Melvin Martian, Dumbo's Circus Train, 1995, Cinderella's Coach, 1995, The Magic Feather, 1995, Pandora's Box (CD ROM), 1995, Over in the Meadow (CD ROM), 1995, Tell Me About When I Was a Baby, 1996, Gold Diggers: The Novelization, 1996, Hanukkah Candles, 1995, Dragonheart: The Jr. Novelization, 1996, Giant Animal Fold-Outs: Big Trucks & Bigger Diggers, 1996, Giant Giants & Magic Mermaids, 1996, Hippo & Pals, 1996, Kangaroo & Company, 1996, Dena Dinosaur, Morty Monster, Wanda Witch, 1996, Code Blue: In the Emergency Room, 1996, Code Blue: Making the Grade, 1996, Leave It to Beaver: The Novelization, 1997; I Love You Because...Love, Barbie, 1999, Make Your Own Valentine Cards, 2000; ghostwriter children's books: Dinotopia Pop-Up Book, 1993, Sliding Surprise Books, 1993-97, The Facts of Life, 1994, All Mixed Up, 1994, Little Merlin's Book of Magic Pets, 1994, Claverie Fairytale Theater, 1994. Vol. kids activity days Dutton's Books, Brentwood, Calif., 1996; spkr. UCLA Extension, 1993-98. Recipient one of 10 Best New Parenting Books award Child Mag., 1993. Mem. PEN Ctr. U.S.A. West (editor-in-chief 1992-95), Soc. Children's Book Writers and Illustrators (manuscript reviewer 19955), Internat. Women's Writing Guild, Author's Guild, Brown Alumni Assn. (interviewer 1995-98), UCLA Alumni Assn., Phi Beta Kappa. Avocations: reading, hosting discussion salon, rollerblading, walking, mentoring. Office: MyPotential.com 2821 Main St Fl 2 Santa Monica CA 90405-4009

ROJAS, GONZALO, historian; b. Santiago, Chile, Aug. 26, 1953; s. Ignacio and Ines (Sanchez) R. LLM, U. Catolica, Santiago, Chile, 1976; PhD, U. De Navarra, Pamplona, Spain, 1980. Lectr. Law Sch. P.U.C., Santiago, Chile, 1980-93; tenured prof. Law Sch. Puc, Santiago, Chile, 1993-98; dir. Coll. MIS and Letters U.A.I., 1998—. Author: Assembly and Association Political Rights in Spain, 1981, The University: Passion and Vocation, 1997; editor: Fundamental Texts on the University, 1988, Fundamental Texts for a Free Society, 1989. Recipient Fulbright Fellowship, 1992. Office: Law Sch P Univ Catolica, Alameda 340, Santiago Chile

ROJAS, LEONARDO GARCIA, integration technology administrator; b. Puautitlan, Mex., Nov. 6, 1968; s. Mateo Garcia Lugardo and Carmen Rojas Reyes. BS, Nat. Poly. Inst., Mexico City, 1992. Sr. analyst PMI Comercio Internat., Mexico City, 1992-95; tech. mgr. Banco Nat. Mex., Mexico City, 1995-97; strategical projects mgr. Multix, Mexico City, 1997—; technologist Pemex Gas and Petroquimica, Mexico City, 1997-99; online transactions cons. Hypercone Internat., Phoenix, 1997-98; econ. cons. Prosa, Mexico City, 1998-99. Contbr. articles to profl. jours. Avocations: lecturing, jogging, rafting. Home: Cda 21 de Marzo 10, Cuautitlan 54879, Mexico Office: Maltix, Av Revoluccor 2042 P6, Mexico City 01090, Mexico

ROJAS-FERNANDEZ, CARLOS H., geriatric medicine and pharmacology educator; b. La Serena, Chile, June 21, 1967; arrived in U.S., 1998; s. Carlos P. Rojas and Maria Fernandez-Lathrop; m. Kellee Ann Howard, Aug. 9, 1996. BSc in Pharmacy, Dalhousie U., Halifax, N.S., Can., 1990; PharmD, Wayne State U., 1996. Pharmacist Shoppers Drug Mart, Lower Sackville, N.S., Can., 1990-91, Lawton's Drugs, Halifax, 1991-93, Victoria Gen. Hosp., Halifax, 1993-94; rsch. assoc. in geriat. medicine Queen Elizabeth II Health Sci. Ctr., Halifax, 1996-98; asst. prof., dir. geriat. residency program Tex. Tech U. Health Sci. Ctr. Sch. Pharmacy, Amarillo, Tex., 1998—. Contbr. articles to profl. jours. Mem. Am. Coll. Clin. Pharmacy, Am. Soc. Clin. Pharmacology and Therapeutics, Am. Geriat. Soc., Gerontol. Soc. Am. Avocations: skiing, kickboxing, hockey. Office: Tex Tech U HSC Sch Pharmacy 1300 Coulter Dr Amarillo TX 79106-1712

ROJEK, CHRIS, sociology educator; b. Reading, Berkshire, Eng., Aug. 22, 1954; s. Joe and Elizabeth (O'Flynn) R. BA in Sociology with honors, Leicester (Eng.) U., 1976, MPhil in Sociology, 1979; PhD in Sociology, Glasgow (Scotland) U., 1991. Lectr. in sociology Coll. of St. Mark and St. John, Plymouth, Eng., 1981-82, Glasgow Queen's Coll., 1982-86; sr. editor Routledge Pubs., London, 1986-94; prof. sociology, head dept. Staffordshire (Eng.) U., 1994-96; prof. sociology and culture Nottingham (Eng.) Trent U., 1996—. Author: Social Work and Received Ideas, 1988, Capitalism and Leisure Therapy, 1995, Ways of Escape, 1993, Decentring Leisure, 1995, Leisure and Culture, 2000. Avocations: music, films, photography, literature. E-mail: rojek@ntu.ac.uk. Home: 4 Thurlow Park Rd, London SE21 8JB, England Office: Nottingham Trent Univ, Fac Media and English Clifton Ln, Nottingham NG11 8NS, England

ROJO DUQUE, LUIS ANGEL, banker; b. Madrid, May 6, 1934; m. Concepcion de Castro; 3 children. Degree in law, U. Madrid, D in Econs.; postgrad., London Sch. Econs.; D honoris causa, U. Alcala de Henares, Madrid, 1995. Accredited economist Spanish Gov., 1957. Economist, 1958; prof. econ. theory Complutense U., Madrid, 1966; gen. dir. rsch. dept. Bank of Spain, Madrid, 1971-88, dep. gov., 1988-92, gov., 1992—; v.p. European Monetary Inst., 1994-98. Contbr. articles to profl. jours. Mem. Royal Acad. Moral and Polit. Scis. Office: Banco de España, Alcala 50, E-28014 Madrid Spain

ROKHMANOV, NICKOLAI YAKOVLEVICH, physicist, researcher; b. Kotelva, Ukraine, Dec. 23, 1956; s. Yakov Iosifovich Rokhmanov and Ekaterina Ivanovna Tschernjavskaja; m. Ludmila Fedorovna Omelaenko, May 7, 1989; children: Tatjana, Dmitrii. Diploma, Kharkov (Ukraine) State U., 1980, PhD in Physics and Math., 1991. Sr. lab. asst. Kharkov State U., 1980-87, scientist, 1991-92, sr. rschr., 1992—. Contbr. numerous articles on internal friction of ferromagnetics, and elasticity, anelasticity and high damping state of metals and alloys to profl. jours. Avocations: family, sports, philosophy, classical music. E-mail: n.ya.rokhmanov@univer.kharkov.ua. Office: Kharkov Nat U Dept Physic, Svobody Sq 4, 61077 Kharkov Ukraine

ROKHVARGER, ANATOLY EFIM, materials science and ceramic technology scientist; b. Moscow, July 24, 1937; came to U.S., 1991; s. Efin Laser and Avgustina Naum (Leschiner) R.; m. Zina Gregory Mikhelson, Feb. 17, 1965; 1 child, Avgustina. MS, Mendeleev Chem.-Tech. U., Moscow, 1959, PhD, 1967; cert., Moscow U., 1965; DS, Tech. U., Leningrad, USSR, 1986. Engr. Electronic Industry Design Inst., Moscow, 1959-63; rschr. Bldg. Materials Inst., Moscow, 1964-68; project leader, head dept. Ceramic Industry Analytical Ctr., Moscow, 1969-91; rsch. prof. Poly. U., Bklyn., 1992—; v.p. R&D Nucon Sys., Inc., N.Y.C., N.Y., 1996-2000; vis. scientist Rutgers U. Ctr. Ceramic Rsch., Piscataway, N.J., 1998-99. Author 3 books, 1 textbook in field; contbr. over 175 articles to profl. jours. Named One of the Greatest Innovators of 20th Century Am. Ceramic Soc. Achievements include development of nine advanced technological systems and six ceramic products; research in application of system analysis, quality assurance methods in ceramic engineering; inventor of cost-effective technology of gas impenetrable and thick-walled ceramics; ultimate safe and durable ceramic containers for nuclear and hazardous waste, including techniques for their mass production and seamless covering using microwave, and industrial processing of high temperature superconductor continuous wire and other shaped products, using Y-Ba-Cu-O powder, silicone compound and silver. E-mail: aerokhv@aol.com. Office: Polytechnic U 6 Metrotech Ctr Brooklyn NY 11201-3840

ROKICKA-MILEWSKA, ROMA, pediatrician, hematologist, oncologist; b. Grudziadz, Poland, June 6, 1932; d. Eustachy and Wanda (Popławska) Rokicki; m. Bohdan Milewski, Aug. 12, 1955; 1 child, Alina. MD, Med. Sch. Warsaw, 1955, PhD, 1974. Asst. dept. pediats. Med. Sch. Warsaw, 1956-68, asst. prof. dept. pediats., 1969-73, assoc. prof., 1974-89, prof., 1990—, head hematol. ward, 1970-83, head dept. pediat. hematology/oncology, 1984—; gen. cons. in pediats. Ctrl. Poland, Warsaw, 1994—; mem. nat. com. Min. of Health for Hemofilic Patients Rehab., 1997—; mem. Rector Com. for Fin. Affairs, Warsaw, 1994—. Editor, co-author: Hemophilia in Children, 1992; co-author: Correction of genetic Diseases by Transplantation III, 1996, Clinical Use of Cytokines, 1997, Pediatric Hematology, 1982; editor, co-author: Pediatrics for dentistry, 1986, 4th edit., 1995; editl. bd. Internat. Jour. Pediat. Hematology/Oncology, 1994—. Pres. Found. for Support of Children with Blood Cancer, Warsaw, 1989—. Recipient award Rector of Med. Sch. Warsaw, 1990, 91, 94, 98, 99, Min. of Health, 1987, 89, 92-93, Pres. of Warsaw, 1989, awd. of Com. of Natl. Edn., 1999. Mem. N.Y. Acad. Sci., European Haematology Assn., Internat. Soc. Pediat. Oncology, Am. Soc. Pediat. Hematology/Oncology. Roman Catholic. Avocations: fine arts, theatre, architecture. Home: Marszalkowska 27/35 m 20, 00-639 Warsaw Poland Office: Dept Pediat Hematology/Onc, Marszałkowska 24, 00-579 Warsaw Poland

ROKICKI, WLADYSLAW STANISLAW, pediatrician; b. Stebnik, Poland, Mar. 17, 1942; s. Stanislaw Szczesny and Helena (Romanowska) R.; m. Anna Wanda Oredarz, Jan. 5, 1947; children: Joanna, Ewa, Anna. Diploma, U. Medicine, Cracow, Poland, 1965, MD, 1967. Asst. U. Medicine, Cracow, 1966-75; fellow Columbia U., N.Y.C., 1972, U. Pa., Phila., 1972-73; sr. asst., head divsn. neonatology Silesian Med. U., Katowice, Poland, 1975-86; rschr. I.N.S.E.R.M-U.34, Lyon, France, 1977-78; assoc. prof. pediatrics Silesian Med. U., Katowice, 1986-91, head dept. pediatric cardiology, 1986—, prof. pediatrics, 1991—; mem. sci. coun. Mother and Child Inst., Warsaw, 1991-95; regional cons. pediatric cardiology, 1995—. 2d lt. Mil. Health Svc., 1965. Mem. Polish Pediatric Assn. (v.p. Silesian br. 1992—), Internat. Perinatal Assn., Polish Cardiol. Soc. Roman Catholic. Avocation: poetry. Home: Ul Kepowa 22p, 40 583 Katowice Poland Office: Dept Pediatric Cardiology, ul Ziolowa 47, 40 635 Katowice Poland

ROKITA, HANNA KASPERCZYK, biochemist; b. Zawiercie, Katowice, Poland, June 22, 1952; d. Alojzy and Maria (Symczak) K.; m. Eugeniusz Rokita, June 24, 1984. MSc, Jagiellonian U., Cracow, Poland, 1976, PhD, 1983, Habilitation, 1994. Rsch. asst. Med. Coll., Cracow, 1977-78; rsch. asst. Jagiellonian U., 1978-85, asst. prof., 1985-94, assoc. prof., 1994—; vis. rschr. Boston U., 1986-87, 91; coord. ednl. program European Union Jagiellonian U., 1994—. Rsch. grantee Polish Sci. Com. Jagiellonian U., 1994—. Mem. Polish Biochem. Soc. Office: Jagiellonian U, Mickiewicza Av 3, 31-120 Cracow Poland

ROKITA, PRZEMYSLAW STEFAN, computer scientist, researcher; b. Warsaw, Poland, Apr. 1, 1962; s. Zbigniew and Zdzislawa (Cieslik) R.; m. Waleria Przelaskowska, Dec. 26, 1994; 1 child, Michal Jan. MSc, Warsaw U. Tech., 1985, PhD, 1993. Software designer CGL, Grasse, France, 1983, LDW, San Jose, Calif., 1989-91; rsch., tchg. asst. Warsaw U. Tech., 1984-93, asst. prof., 1993—; acad. vis. Imperial Coll., London, 1995; vis. scientist Hiroshima Prefectural U., 1995-96; cons. CERP, Rouen, France, 1991; reviewer IEEE, 1996—. Co-author: Computer Graphics: Methods and Tools, 1994; contbr. articles to profl. jours. Recipient award Polish Computer Sci. Soc., 1986, Polish Min. Edn., 1995. Mem. SPIE. Avocation: music. Home: Laserowa 15, 01-490 Warsaw Poland Office: Warsaw U Tech, Nowowiejska 15/19, 00-665 Warsaw Poland

ROKSTAD, KIRSTEN SKINLO, physician, educator; b. Aalesund, Norway, Mar. 3, 1956; d. Kolbjørn and Margreth (Sunde) S.; m. Knut Rokstad, Nov. 8, 1982; 1 child, Ingrid. MD, U. Bergen, Norway, 1982, PhD, 1997; M of Epidemiology and Stats., U. London, 1992. Internist U. Bergen, 1982-83, physician in gen. practice, 1983-88, psychiatrist, 1988-90, rsch. fellow, 1990-97, prof. medicine, 1997; med. dir. LexMed, Bergen, 1997—. Co-author Aschohoug's Med. Encyklopedia, 1996; contbr. articles to profl. jours. Mem. Norwegian Med. Assn. (chair Hordaland divsn.; mem. rsch. group). Avocations: golf, tennis, salmon fishing, downhill skiing, cross-country skiing. Office: Lexmed Asa, C Sundts Gate 51, 5004 Bergen Norway

ROKUSHIMA, KATSU, optical science and engineering educator; b. Osaka, Japan, Oct. 10, 1926; s. Isaburou and Hiro Rokushima; m. Yoriko Ono, Dec. 1, 1954; 1 child, Kijima Rokushima Atsuko. BE, Osaka U., 1950, PhD, 1971. Rsch. assoc. U. Osaka Prefecture, Sakai, Japan, 1950-61, asst. prof., 1961-63, assoc. prof., 1963-73, prof., 1973-90, prof. emeritus, 1990—; prof. Osaka Sangyo U., Daito, Japan, 1990-98; ret. Osaka Sangyo U., 1998. author: Selected Papers on Diffraction Gratings, 1993; contbr. articles to profl. jours. Paul Harris fellow, 1991. Mem. IEEE (life), IEE of Japan, IEICE, Electromagnetics Acad., Rotary (pres. Tondabayashi-Minami club 1991-92, mem. found. dist. com. 1994-96, dist. chmn. internat. svc. subcom. 1996-97). Avocations: tennis, reading, photography. Home: 2 4 15 Teraikedai, Osaka P Tondabayashi 584-0073, Japan

ROKYTA, RICHARD, physiologist, educator; b. Užhorod, Czech republic, Jan. 19, 1938; s. Richard and Ružena (Laštuvková) R.; m. Věra Vinklářová, July 8, 1961; children: Richard, Pavel. MD, Charles U., Plzeň, Czech Republic, 1961, CSc, 1969, DrSc, DSc, 1991. Sr. lectr. dept. pathophysiology med. faculty Charles U., Plzeň, 1961-82; asst. prof. dept. physiology/pathophysiology Charles U., Prague, 1982-91, prof., 1991—, vice dean 3d med. faculty, 1990-97. Editor/author: Lecture Notes on Physiology and Pathophysiology, 1969, 81, 87, 93, 95, 96; translator textbook: Memorix, 1993, Textbook of Physiology, 1995, Douleur (pain), 1998; contbr. over 375 articles to profl. jours., chpts. to books. Recipient Gold medal City of Grenoble, 1988, Bronze and gold medals of 3d Med. Faculty, Charles U., 1988-98. Fellow Physiol. Soc. U.K.; mem. Czech Physiol. Soc. (v.p. 1982—), The Physiological Soc., N.Y. Acad. Sci., Internat. Union Physiological Suences, Internat. Brain Rsch. Orgn., Fedn. European Physiological Socs., Collegium Internat. Activitatis Nervosae Superioris, Czech Med. Assn. (hon.), Czech Physiol. Soc. (hon.), Football Club Slavia (pres. 1961—), Tennis Sport Club Slavia (pres. 1971-75), Czech Med. Soc. (hon., Laufberger medal 1993), Soc. Physiologie (sci. sec. 1980—). Avocations: football, tennis, skiing, literature. Fax: 420 2 299528; e-mail: richard.rokyta lf3.cuni.cz. Home: Polní 50, 307 07 Plzeň Czech Republic Office: 3d Med Fac Dept Physiology, Ke Karlovu 4, 120 00 Prague 2, Czech Republic

ROLAND, CATHERINE DIXON, entrepreneur; b. Andalusia, Ala., Mar. 9, 1939; d. Charles and Thelma (Chapman) Dixon; m. Henry F. Roland, Dec. 16, 1966 (div. Nov., 1976); 1 child, Charles H.; stepchild, Vickie Roland Little. Student, Huntingdon Coll., 1954-56; BS, Auburn U., 1956-59; MA in History, U. Ala., Tuscaloosa, 1965-66. Sec. Dixon Lumber Co., Inc., Andalusia, 1969-74, v.p., 1974-78; land and timber owner, mgr. Catherine D. Roland & Co., Andalusia, 1978—; owner Sta. WCTA, andalusia, 1947-75, bd. dirs., 1972-75; owner, bd. dirs. D & G Property Ltd., Perth, Australia, 1967—, Covington County Bank, 1979—, So. Nat. Corp., 1985—. Chmn. Thelma Dixon Found., Andalusia, 1981—; mem. Rep. Senatorial Inner Cir., Washington, 1980—, 2d Congl. Com., Montgomery, Ala., 1980—, Andalusia Pub. Libr. Friends, Inc., 1981—; mem. adv. coun. Mises Inst. Auburn (Ala.) U., Auburn and Washington, 1983-85, Coll. Bus. Auburn U., 1987—; mem. Com. of 100, Huntington Coll., 1978, trustee, 1978—, vice chmn. bd. trustees 1985-93; bd. dirs. Women Health, Birmingham, Ala., 1978-82, Health Svcs. Found., 1982—, Andalusia Hosp., 1980-82. Named countess Huntingdon Coll., Montgomery, 1978, named to Hall of Honor, 1980; recipient commendation for Outstanding Svc. and Leadership, 1980, Loyalty award, 1988. Mem. DAR, Nat. Soc. Colonial Dames XVII Century, Ams. of Royal Descent, Dames of Magna Charter, Forest Landowners Assn., Ala. Landowners Assns., Ala. Wildlife Fedn., Andalusia Area C. of C., Auburn Alumni Assn., Huntingdon Coll. Alumni Assn. (chmn. Andalusia area chpt. 1983—), Am. Legion, Study Club. Methodist. Avocations: numismatics, reading, horses, tennis.

ROLAND, GERARD, economics educator; b. Jemappes, Belgium, Oct. 3, 1954; s. Yves and Marie Thérèse (Leclercq) R.; m. Heddy Riss, Nov. 18, 1980; children: Elsa, Florence, Juliette. PhD in Econs., U. Libre Brussels, 1988. Asst. U. Libre Brussels, 1983-88, maitre de conf., 1988-91; prof. U. Libre Brussels, Brussels, 1991—; program dir. on transition econs. Ctr. for Econ. Policy Rsch., London, 1995—; vis. prof. U. Cath. Louvain, 1989, Ecole des Hautes Etudes en Scis. Sociales, Paris, 1990, U. Calif., Davis, 1991, London Sch. Econs., 1993, Collegium Budapest, 1993, Stanford U., 1994, 95, Inst. for Internat. Econ. Studies, Stockholm, 1995; William Davidson Inst. vis. chair Mich. Bus. Sch., 1997. Contbr. articles to profl. jours. Soldier Belgian Air Force, 1974. Fellow Ctr. Advanced Studies Behavioral Scis., Stanford U., 1998-99. Office: U Libre, 50 Roosebelt Ave CP 114, B-1050 Brussels Belgium

ROLAND, GRETE, language educator; b. Chgo., Sept. 15, 1937; d. Sverre Roland and Ingrid Jacobeane Schöning; m. Vikan Salman, Mar. 17, 1963 (div. Dec. 1979); 1 child, Attila Roland Salman. BS in Speech-Theatre, Northwestern U., 1958; MS in Linguistics, Ill. Inst. Tech., Chgo., 1971; MA in Multicultural Edn., Loyola U., 1978, PhD in Comparative & Internat. Edn., 1988; cert. of German, Goethe Inst., U. Munich, 1963; cert. of Turkish, Cihangir Derscunesi, Turkey, 1974; cert. of Norwegian, U. Oslo, Norway, 1987. Sec., transl. Mil. Assistance Adv. Group, Oslo, 1959-61; tchr. English Cambridge Inst., Munich, 1962-63; tchr. English, entertainment dir. Am. Lisan ve. dersanesi, Istanbul, Turkey, 1963-64; ESL tchr. Cen. YMCA C.C., Chgo., 1965-82; assoc. prof. Nat.-Louis U., Evanston, Ill., 1989—. Author: (book) Communicative American English, 1990. Dir., actor Players' Workshop Play Readers, San Miguel de Allende, Mex., 1999-00; diversity leader antiracism Saka Gakkai Internat., Chgo., 1997-99. Mem. TESOL (presenter), Am. Anthropology Assn. (presenter 1994-99), Ill. TESOL and Bilingual Edn. (job coord. 1995-98, bd. dirs.), GREDOR-Multicultural Tchg. (co-founder, co-pres. 1993-99), Actors' Equity. Democrat. Buddhist. Avocations: yoga, swimming, writing, skiing, dancing.

ROLAND, JAN PATRICK, nuclear medicine physician; b. Antwerp, Belgium, Sept. 5, 1955; s. Max Roland and Marie-Rose Camerlinckx; m. Anne Antoinette Chapelle; children: Gill, Yasmin. MD, U. Brussels, 1980. Cert. specialist radiotherapy and nuc. medicine, Belgium. Fellow radiotherapy Middelheim Gen. Hosp., Antwerpen, Belgium, 1980-84; fellow nuc. medicine Middelheim Gen. Hosp./U. Hosp. Brussel, Antwerpen, Brussel, 1984-86; resident nuc. medicine Middelheim Gen. Hosp., Antwerpen, 1987-92, staff mem. dept. nuc. medicine, 1993—; trainee Inst. Curie, Paris, 1982; trainee dept. nuc. medicine UCLA Sch. Medicine, Harbor Gen. Hosp., 1987; trainee Pet and SPECT Imaging in Oncology, Johns Hopkins Med. U., Balt., 1994; active Iocoregional Quality Controle, Antwerpen, 1997—. Contbr. articles to profl. jours. Lt. Belgium Med. Svc., 1987-88. Recipient award Acad. Soc. Antwerp, 1986; grantee Nat. Fund Scientific Rsch., 1985. Mem. European Assn. Nuc. Medicine, European Soc. Therapeutic Radiology and Oncology, Soc. Nuc. Medicine, Belgisch Genootschap voor Nucleaire Geneeskunde. E-mail: agfa03@pophost.eunet.be. Fax: 32-3-280 40 04. Office: Dept Nuc Med AZ Middleheim, Lindendreef 1, B-2020 Antwerpen Belgium

ROLAND, MELISSA MONTGOMERY, accountant; b. Houston, Mar. 6, 1961; d. John Edgar and Mariann (Guggino) Montgomery; m. Larry Dean Roland, Sept. 20, 1984. BBA, Tex. A&M U., 1983. CPA, Tex., cert. fraud examiner, Tex. Audit sr. Arthur Andersen & Co., Houston, 1983-87; cons. mgr.-performance improvement group Ernst & Young, San Antonio, 1988-91; COO Roy Smith Shoes, Inc. d/b/a Accenté, Houston, 1991-96; v.p., COO 3d Coast Mgmt., Inc., Jacksonville, Fla., 1996—. Bd. dirs., treas. Grandparents Outreach, San Antonio, 1989—. Mem. AICPA, Tex. Accts. and Lawyers for the Arts (adv. bd.), Tex. Soc. CPAs, Young Reps., Jr. League Jacksonville, S.W. Found. Forum. Presbyterian. Avocations: running, scuba diving, weight lifting, bicycling. Office: 515 Rutile Dr Ponte Vedra Beach FL 32082-2319

ROLAND, RAYMOND WILLIAM, lawyer, mediator, arbitrator; b. Ocala, Fla., Jan. 3, 1947; s. Raymond W. and Hazel (Dunn) R.; m. Jane Allen, Dec. 28, 1968; children: John Allen, Jason William. BA, Fla. State U., 1969, JD, 1972. Bar: Fla. 1972, U.S. Dist. Ct. (no. dist.) Fla. 1973, U.S. Dist. Ct. (mid. dist.) Fla. 1985, U.S. Ct. Appeals (5th cir.) 1974, U.S. Ct. Appeals (11th cir.) 1983, U.S. Supreme Ct. 1985; cert. civil trial lawyer; cert. cir. ct. mediator. Assoc. Keen, O'Kelley & Spitz, Tallahassee, 1972-74, ptnr., 1974-77; ptnr., v.p. McConnaughhay, Roland, Maida & Cherr, P.A., Tallahassee, 1978-97; owner, mediator Roland Mediation Svcs.; diplomate mem. Fla. Acad. of Profl. Mediators, Inc. Diplomate mem., bd. dirs. So. Scholarship Found., Tallahassee, 1985-89, 98-99, v.p. 1989; bd. visitors Bapt. Coll. Fla. Mem. Internat. Assn. Def. Coun., Def. Rsch. Inst., Fla. Bar, Tallahassee Bar Assn. (treas. 1979), Kiwanis (life, lt. gov. 1984- 85), Capital City Kiwanis Club (Kiwanian of Yr. 1978, pres. 1979), Fla. Kiwanis Found. (life fellow). Republican. Baptist. Avocations: reading, hiking, camping, golf. Home: 1179 Ox Bottom Rd Tallahassee FL 32312-3519

ROLATER, FREDERICK STRICKLAND, history educator, consultant; b. McKinney, Tex., July 22, 1938; s. Frederick Gladstone and Vern (Strickland) R.; m. Jeannette Baker, Aug. 5, 1960. BA, Wake Forest U., 1960; MA, U. So. Calif., 1963, PhD, 1970. Assoc. prof. history Blue Mountain (Miss.) Coll., 1963-64; chmn. dept. social studies Grand Canyon Coll., Phoenix, 1964-67; Fulbright prof. history U. Kyushu and Seinan Gakuin U., Fukuoka, Japan, 1987-88; prof. history, dir. grad. studies dept. history Middle Tenn. State U., Murfreesboro, 1967—. Author: Japanese Americans, 1991; contbr. articles to profl. jours. Mem. exec. bd. So. Bapt. Hist. Commn., Nashville, 1984-92; chmn. history com. Tenn. Bapt. Conv., Brentwood, Tenn., 1984-85, 98—; mem. hist. com. Bapt. World Alliance, Seoul, Korea, 1990; mem. Rutherford County Hist. Com., Murfreesboro, 1980-83. Recipient Meritorious Svc. award Tenn. Bapt. Conv., 1991; Nat. Merit scholar, 1956-60. Mem. Tenn. Bapt. Hist. Soc. (pres.), Gideons Internat., Concord Bapt. Assn. (moderator 1998-2000), Phi Beta Kappa. E-mail: frolater@mtsu.edu. Office: Middle Tenn State U Dept History PO Box 336 Murfreesboro TN 37132-0001

ROLDAN-MORÉ, ALFONSO, physician, educator, dean; b. San Sebastian, Spain, June 27, 1958; s. Alfonso and Maria Luisa (Moré) R.; m. Beatriz Estebanez; children: Edgar, Denis. MD, U. Valladolid, Spain, 1981; MS, U. Alcala, 1995; PhD, Pacific Western U., 1997, Am. U.; PhD (hon.), Inst. Psychoanalysis, Santa Maria, Brazil, 1999, Adam Smith U., 1996. Journalist El Diario Vaslo, San Sebastian, 1986-90; physician Nat. Health Svc., San Sebastian, 1983-93; pres. Safe Work, Madrid, 1995-96; dir. dept. Suffolk U., Madrid, 1996—; pres. Albert Schweitzer U., Geneva, 1999; chair occupational health Inst. Ciences Solud, Buenos Aires, 2000; del. Eureka-Brussels, 1999; cons. Annual Collective, UNESCO, Paris, 1998, mem. UNESCO Inst. for Edn., Hambourg, 1998. Author: Proteccion o Prevencion, 1999; contbr. more than 100 articles to profl. jours. Pres. Internat. Commn. on Distance Edn., Zurich, 1996, Spanish Occupl. Health, 1995; del. UN, Bangledesh, 2000; vice chmn. Internat. World Human Rights Svc. Coun., N.Y., 2000; pres. London Diplomatic Acad., 2000. Recipient hon. medal ACOEM, European Parliament, 1997; named hon. citizen Prefectura, Santa Maria, Brazil, 1999, consul gen. First Embassy Medjhasi, 1998. Mem. World Acad. Medicine (gold medal 1998), N.Y. Acad. Scis. Avocations: handball, turf. Office: Suffolk U, l/Londres 17 bajo, 28028 Madrid Spain

ROLEK, FERENC, bank executive, human resources professional; b. Budapest, Hungary, Sept. 29, 1953; s. Ferenc and Mária (Farkas) R.; m. Judit Marcsinák, July 10, 1982; children: Tamás, Anna. MA, Budapest U. Econs., 1978, PhD, 1984. Rschr. Nat. Planning Inst., Budapest, 1978-81; head dept. Nat. Planning Office, Budapest, 1981-90; dep. state sec. Ministry of Labor, Budapest, 1990-91, state sec., 1991-92; human resources dir. GE Lighting Tungsram, Budapest, 1992-95; European affairs and compensation mgr. GE Lighting Europe, Budapest, 1995-98; dep. CEO human resources GE Capital Budapest Bank, 1998—; mem. GE Lighting Tungsram Supervisory Bd., Budapest, 1994-95, Adv. Com. to the Min. Labor, Budapest, 1996-98, Adv. Com. to the Prime Min., Budapest, 1998—, Budapest Bank Bd. Dirs., 1999—. Bd. mem. Hungarian Assn. Internat. Cos., 1994-98. Recipient award for the Hungarian Labor, Min. of Labor, 1998. Mem. Nat. Assn. Employers and Mfrs. (v.p. 1996—), Hungarian Internat. Labour Orgn. Coun. (v.p. 1999—). Avocations: sports, music. Office: Budapest Bank, Alkotmány U 5, H-1054 Budapest Hungary

ROLFES, LEONARD JOSEPH, pediatrician; b. New Orleans, Apr. 23, 1923; s. Frederick John and Catherine (Cunningham) R.; m. Elizabeth Browder, June 19, 1954; children: Frederick, James, Katherine, Elizabeth, Leonard, Jr., Anne. BS, Tulane U., 1949, MD, 1951. Diplomate Am. Bd. Pediatrics. Resident in pediatrics Charity Hosp., New Orleans, 1954-55, U. Chgo., 1955-57; pediatrician Hamilton Med. Group, Lafayette, La., 1957-92; cons. pediatrician Charter-Cypress Hosp., Lafayette, 1992-2000; clin. faculty Tulane Med. Sch., New Orleans, 1959-92. Lt. comdr. USN, 1943-65. Fellow Am. Acad. Pediatrics. Roman Catholic. Avocations: computers, golf. Home: 408 Beverly Dr Lafayette LA 70503-3112

ROLIN, JEAN GASTON, lawyer, financial consultant; b. Nancy, Lorraine, France, Mar. 21, 1937; s. Roger Abel and Marie-Louise (Emilie) Thietry) R.; m. Marie-Louise Lucie Hamant, July 1, 1961 (div. Mar. 1972); 1 child, Jean-Christophe. Gen. Math. Degree, Sci. Faculty, Paris, 1959; Degree in Law, Faculty of Law, Paris, 1963, JD, 1964. Bar: France. Atty. Fiduciaire de France, Paris, 1965-75; pvt. practice Rolin Enterprise, Paris, 1976—; fin./fiscal cons. Rolin Enterprise, Evry, France, 1976—. Contbr. articles to profl. jours. Hon. mem. Union of Police Retirees, Paris, 1992. Named Hon. Lawyer, Bar of Essonne, Paris-Evry, 1995. Mem. Am. Express Travel Club, L'Esprit Diners Club of France. Roman Catholic. Avocation: long-distance swimming. Home: 9 Rue Chateau D'Eau, 91130 Ris-Orangis France

ROLL, LORD ERIC (LORD ROLL OF IPSDEN), merchant banker; b. Nova Sulita, Austria, Dec. 1, 1907; arrived in Gt. Britain, 1925; s. Mathias and Fany (Frendel) R.; m. Winifred Taylor, Sept. 22, 1934 (dec. 1998); children: Joanna, Elizabeth. B of Comm., U. Birmingham, 1928, PhD, 1930, D of Social Sci. (hon.), 1967; DSc (hon.), Hull U., 1967; LLD (hon.), Southampton, 1974. Prof. econ. and commerce U. Coll Hull, 1935-46; dep. head British Food Mission to N. Am., 1941-46; dep. mem., CEO Combined Food Bd., Washington, 1946; asst. sec. Ministry of Food, 1946-47; under sec., ctrl. econ. planning staff HM Treasury, 1948; min. U.K. Delegation to OEEC, 1949; dep. head U.K. Del. to North Atlantic Treaty Orgn., Paris, 1952; under sec. Min. Agriculture, Fisheries and Food, 1953-57, dep. sec., 1959-61; exec. dir. Internat. Sugar Coun., 1957-59; dep. leader U.K. Del. for Negotiations with the European Econ. Cmty., 1961-63; econ. min., head U.K. Treas. Delegation, Washington, 1963-64; exec. dir. U.K. Internat. Monetary Fund, Internat. Bank of Reconstruction and Devel.; permanent under-sec. state Dept. Econ. Affairs, 1964-66; chancellor U. Southampton, 1974-84; dir. Bank of England, 1968-77; dep. chmn. S.G. Warburg & Co., Ltd., 1967-74, chmn., 1974-84, joint chmn., 1984-87; pres. S.G. Warburg Group Plc., 1987-95; sr. advisor SBC Warburg, 1995—; chmn. UN Sugar Conf., 1958; dir. Times Newspapers Ltd., 1967-80, Times Newspapers Holdings Ltd., 1980-83; pres. Mercury Internat. Group, 1985-87, Mercury Securities Ltd., 1985-87, chmn. 1974-84. Author: An Early Experiment in Industrial Organization, 1930, Spotlight on Germany, 1933, About Money, 1934, Elements of Economic Theory, 1935, A History of Economic Thought, 1954, 5th edit., 1992, Where Are We Going?, 2000, The Combined Food Board, 1957, The World After Keynes, 1968, The Uses and Abuses of Economics, 1978, Crowded Hours, 1985, Where Did We Go Wrong, 1995; editor: The Mixed Economy, 1982; co-author: Organized Labour, 1938, The British Commonwealth at War, 1943; contbr. articles to profl. jours. Comdr. 1st Class Danish mil., 1981. U. Rsch. scholar, 1929; Special Rockefeller Found. fellow, 1939-41; named Companion Order of the Bath, 1956, Knight Comdr. Order of St. Michael and St. George, 1962, Grand Cordon of the Order of the Sacred Treasure, Japan, 1994, Officier Legion d'Honneur, France, 1984; recipient Gladstone Meml. prize, 1928, Grosses Goldenes Ehrenzeichen award, Austria, 1979, Grand Cross of the Order of Merit Republic of Italy, 2000. Mem. Brooks Club. Avocation: reading. Home: D2 Albany Piccadilly, London W1J 0AP, England Office: UBS Warburg, 2 Finsbury Ave, London EC2M 2PA, England

ROLLAIN, RICHARD ANDRE, airline company administrator; b. El Paso, May 7, 1957; s. Richard St. Charles and Gertrude Pope Rollain; m. Yang Chun Choi, Nov. 30, 1977 (div. Oct. 1988); 1 child, Michael St. Charles; m. Sandra Smith Rollain, Oct. 28, 1988; 1 child, Amanda Lee. Degree in criminal justice, Columbia Coll., Redstone Arsenal, Ala., 1984; AA in Specialized Bus. Computer Sci., Harcourt Learning Direct, Scranton, Pa., 1999. A cert. svc. technician, Computing Tech. Industry Assn. Ops. sgt. U.S. Army, Atlanta, 1975-97; coord. Delta Air Lines, Inc., Atlanta, 1998—; freelance technician, Atlanta, 1997. Recipient Commendation medals U.S. Army, 1993, 96, Achievement medals, 1975-96, Meritorious Svc. medal, 1997. Mem. VFW, Am. Legion. Republican. Presbyterian. Avocations: computers, camping, fishing, web design.

ROLLASON, CHRISTOPHER RICHARD, European Parliament official; b. Amersham, Eng., Dec. 8, 1954; s. Ormond Robert and Jean (Woodford) R.; m. Ileana Farcasiu, Apr. 2, 1994. BA with 1st class honors, Trinity Coll., Cambridge, Eng., 1975, MA, 1980; PhD, U. York, Eng., 1988. Lectr. in English U. Coimbra, Portugal, 1980-87; offcl European Parliament, Luxembourg, 1987—. Translator: Leibniz and the Problem of a Universal Language, 1987.; contbr. articles to profl. publs. Trinity Coll. scholar, 1971. Avocations: literature, music, fine arts, travel, internet.

ROLLASON, PETER VINCENT, pharmacist, consultant; b. Loughborough, Eng., May 16, 1929; arrived in Zimbabwe, 1947; s. Frank Arthur and Jessie Marguerite (Vincent) R. Chemist, Druggist, Witwatersand Tech. Coll., Johannesburg, South Africa, 1951. Qualified pharmacist, South Africa; registered pharmacist, Zimbabwe, South Africa, U.K. Apprentice Boots Ltd., Blackpool, U.K., 1945-47, Med. Hall Ltd., Bulawayo, Zimbabwe, 1947; mgr. Queens Pharmacy, Bulawayo, 1951-52; owner, proprietor, mng. dir. Hillside Pharmacy (Pvt.) Ltd., Bulawayo, 1953—; founder shareholder, mem. Chemists Emergency Svc. Ltd., Bulawayo, 1958—; mem. Drugs Control Coun., Zimbabwe, 1980-91, chmn., 1986-91; mem. Health Professions Coun., 1958-96, mem. exec. com., pharm. chemist edn. and liaison com., disciplinary com., chmn. profl. conduct rev. com.; radio presenter spl. features and reports. Prodr., presenter Wildlife Forum, radio program, 1969—, Music for Pleasure, radio program, 1975—, The Carpet and the Clock, dance music program, 1989-90, It's in the Air, classical music program, 1982-90; compiler, prodr., presenter Young Rhodesia Scrapbook, 1953-81; resident commentator Matabeleland Turf Club, 1952-90; TV sports editor, presenter Sports Round-up, 1961-68; prodr., presenter med. programs Lifeline, 1969, Medicus, 1971, You and Your health, 1980-84; news reporter, interviewer, 1952—; commentator current events and state occasions; writer, prodr. features and drama; prodr., presenter programs on drug abuse, 1988; co-prodr., presenter feature program on AIDS, 1989; contbr. articles to profl. jours. Hon. life v.p. Bulawayo Agrl. Soc., 1990; trustee, steward Matabeleland Turf Club, Bulawayo, 1990. Lt. comdr. Zimbabwe Sea Cadet Corps, 1987—; maj. Zimbabwe Corps Signals, 1952-83, M.C., 1984—. Recipient travelling scholarship for malaria rsch. F.I.P. Edn. Found., 1994-95, civic honors City Coun. Bulawayo, 1988. Mem. Chipangali Wildlife Orphanage Trust (chmn.), Wildlife Soc. Zimbabwe, Pharm. Soc. Zimbabwe (hon. life), Royal Pharm. Soc. Gt. Britain, Coll. Pharmacy Practice (U.K.), Coll. Pharmacy Practice Zimbabwe, Commonwealth Pharm. Assn., Internat. Pharm. Fedn. (assoc., mem. gen. practice and mil. sects., liaison officer, pharmacist cons., inititator Madrid rsch. group), Diabetic Assn. (hon., cons. Matabeleland br.), Assn. Mil. Surgeons U.S., Bulawayo South Rotary Club, Belmont Rotary Club (pres., fellowship 1992). Avocations: wildlife safaris, music, Sea Cadet Corps., electronics. Home: PO Box 9002, Hillside, Bulawayo Zimbabwe

ROLLE, ROSA SONYA, food biotechnologist; b. Roseau, Dominica, Sept. 26, 1960; d. James Patrick and Edith Florence (Butler) R. HND, Grimsby (Eng.) Coll. Tech., 1981; MSc, Ohio State U., 1983, PhD, 1987. Postdoctoral fellow U. Fla., Gainesville, 1987-90, postdoctoral assoc., 1990-94; agrl. industries officer FAO of UN, Rome, 1995—; organizer Internat. Symposium Small Scale Fermentations in Developing Countries, 1999. Editor tech. bull. series: Fermented Foods: A Global Perspective, 1998-99; contbr. articles to profl. jours. Ohio State U. Grad. Student Alumni Rsch. award, 1986. Mem. Caribbean Lit. Group (v.p. 1999), Phi Tau Sigma, Gamma Sigma Delta. Avocations: gardening, sightseeing. Office: FAO of UN, Viale Delle Terme di Caraca, 00100 Rome Italy

ROLLER, MARION, sculptor. Student, Vesper George Sch. Art, Boston, Art Students League, N.Y.C.; BA in Art, Queens Coll., 1980. instr. Fashion Inst. Tech., N.Y.C., Sculpture Ctr.; head design dept. Traphagen Sch. of Fashion. Exhbns. include The Newark Mus., 1995-96, Nat. Acad. Design, N.Y., 1994, Nat. Sculpture Soc., N.Y., 1996-97, Scottsdale, Ariz., Serravezza, Italy, 1994, Transco Mus., Phila., U.S. Mint, San Francisco, Denver, Albany (N.Y.) Inst. History and Art, Pittsfield (Mass.) Mus., Fedn. Internat. de la Medaille, Helsinki, Finland, Budapest, Hungary, 1993, Price Waterhouse Galleries, N.Y.C., 1997, Janus Gallery, Santa Fe, Chesterwood, Stockbridge, Mass., 1997, Hillsdale (Mich.) Coll., 1997, Nat. Sculpture Soc., 2000, UN, N.Y.C., 1995, Cannon House Rotunda, Washington, others; commns. include Nassau Ctr. for Emotionally Disturbed Children, St. Mary's Children and Families Found., Traphagen Sch. Fashion, Rosemary Harris Meml., Brookgreen Gardens, medal Nat. Acad. Design, others; contbr. articles, book reviews to Sculpture Review. Recipient Helen Gapen Oehler Meml. award Allied Artists, 1991, Samuel Cashwan Meml. award Audubon Artists, 1992, Audubon Artists award, 1994, Pen & Brush award for Watercolor, 1997, Nat. Sulpture Soc. Annual Exhibit award, 1998, Lou Magnani award Salmagundi Club, 1998, Gold medal of Honor 56th Annual Audubon Artists Exhibit, 1998, medal Internat. Exhibit of Medallic Art Museium Beelden ann Vee, 1998, award for Medallic Sculpture Pen & Brush, 1999. Fellow Nat. Sculpture Soc. (sec., Kalos Kagathos Found. prize, C. Percival Dietsch Sculpture prize, Tallix Foundry prize, Edith H. & Richman Proskauer prize, Joel Meisner Foundry award); mem. Nat. Acad. Design (academician), Audubon Artists (treas., past pres., Gold medal of honor, Art Students League award, 1999), The Pen & Brush (chmn. sculpture sect., Pen and Brush award for watercolor, 1997, Bronze medal for sculpture, Chaim Gross Found. award, 1996, Samuel Cashwan meml. award, 1992, Margaret Sussman award 2000, Charlotte Dunwiddie award for medallic art 2000), Allied Artists Am. (past pres., Silver medal honor, Sybil and Bob Porton award, Helen Gapen Oehler Meml. award, 1991), Am. Medallic Sculpture Assn., Fine Arts Fedn. (bd. mem.). Address: 30 W 60th St New York NY 10023-7902

ROLLIN, HENRY RAPOPORT, psychiatrist; b. Glasgow, Scotland, Nov. 17, 1911; s. Aaron R. and Rebecca (Sorkin) R.; m. Anna-Maria Tihanyi, July 28, 1973; children: Aron, Rebecca. MB, BChir, Leeds U., 1935, MD, 1948. Cons. psychiatrist Horton Hosp., Epsom, Surrey, Eng., 1948-77; emeritus Horton Hosp., Epsom, 1977—; cons. psychiatrist Home Office, London, 1977—; mem. U.K. Parole Bd., 1970-73. Author: Mentally Abnormal Offenders and the Law, 1969; editor: Coping with Schizophrenia, 1980; contbr. articles to profl. jours. Served with RAF, 1941-47. Fulbright fellow, 1953; Nuffield Coll., Oxford fellow, 1963. Fellow Royal Coll. Psychiatrists (hon. libr.), Royal Soc. Medicine. Avocations: music, literature, gardening. Home: 101 College Rd, Epsom Surrey KT17 4HY, England

ROLLINS, ALBERT WILLIAMSON, civil engineer, consultant; b. Dallas, July 31, 1930; s. Andrew Peach and Mary (Williamson) R.; B.S. in Civil Engring., Tex. A. and M. U., 1951, M.S. in Civil Engring., 1956; m. Martha Ann James, Dec. 28, 1954; children—Elizabeth Ann, Mark Martin. Engring. asst. Tex. Hwy. Dept., Dallas, 1953-55; dir. pub. works City of Arlington (Tex.), 1956-63, city mgr., 1963-67; partner Schrickel, Rollins & Assos., land planners-engrs., Arlington, 1967—. Mem. Gov.'s Energy Adv. Council; chmn. Tex. Mass Transp. Commn.; bd. dirs. Tex. Turnpike Authority.

Served as 1st lt. AUS, 1951-53. Registered profl. engr., Tex., La., Okla. Mem. Internat. City Mgmt. Assn., Nat. Soc. Profl. Engrs., ASCE, Am. Water Works Assn., Water Pollution Control Fedn., Sigma Xi, Phi Eta Sigma, Tau Beta Pi, Phi Kappa Phi, Chi Epsilon. Contbr. articles to profl. jours. Home: 3004 Yellowstone Dr Arlington TX 76013-1166 Office: Suite 200 1161 Corporate Dr W Ste 200 Arlington TX 76006-6819

ROLLINS, JAMES GREGORY, air force officer; b. Vandenberg AFB, Calif., Apr. 6, 1963; s. Clarence Leslie and Mary Ethel (Brooks) R. BS in Bus. Adminstrn., San Jose State U., 1985; MSA in Gen. Adminstrn., Ctrl. Mich. U., 1992; MBA in Aviation Mgmt., Embry-Riddle Aero. U., 1992. Commd. 2d lt. USAF, 1985, advanced through grades to maj., 1997; minuteman intercontinental ballistic missile dep. crew comdr. USAF, Grand Forks AFB, N.D., 1985-86, minuteman intercontinental ballistic missile instr. dep. crew comdr., 1986-87, minuteman intercontinental ballistic missile evaluator dep. crew comdr., 1987-88, strategic air command missile combat competition instr., 1987-88, intercontinental ballistic missile crew comdr., 1988-89, scheduling br. chief ops., 1989-90, order tng. officer emergecy war, 1990-91, intercontinental ballistic missile ops. plans officer, 1991-92; acquisition info. mgr. USAF, L.A. AFB, 1992-93, dep. dir. program control divsn., 1993-94, chief plans and analysis divsn., 1994-96; dep. chief Peace Shield Deployment USAF, Hanscom AFB, Mass., 1996, chief Peace Shield Sustainment, 1996-99, chief strategic planning, 1999—. Editor (newsletters) Families First, 1991, Vol. Network, 1990-91. Asst. project officer Project Sandbox fundraiser, 1986; founder Above and Beyond Vol. Tutoring, 1988, cons., 1988—; vol. staff Youth Ctr., Grand Forks AFB, 1988-91, Rebuild L.A. Edn. and Job Tng. Task Force; base project officer Rob's Coats for Kids, 1990, 91; vol. Grand Forks United Way Cmty. Svcs., 1990-91; mem. Points of Light Found., 1991—, Minn. Office Vol. Svcs., 1991-95, Commdrs. Cmty. Ptnrs. Program, 1994-96; project coord. L.A. Works, 1995-96; bd. dirs., vol. Habitat for Humanity, 1994-99, People Making a Difference, 1996-99; vol. Boston Cares, 1996—, Greater DC Cares, 1999—. Decorated Air Force Achievement medal, 1990, Air Force Commendation medal, 1992; Meritorious Svc. medal, 1999, named Vol. of Yr., 321st Strategic Missile Wing, 42d Air Divsn., 8th Air Force, Strategic Air Command, 1990; recipient Presdl. award for volunteerism, 1991, Outstanding Vol. Svc. medal Mil., 1996. Mem. Air Force Assn., Air Force Cadet Officer Mentor Action Program, Performance Mgmt. Assn., Soc. Cost Estimating & Analysis, Tuskegee Airmen, Inc., Assn. of Air Force Missileers, Points of Light Found., Ctr. Corp. Cmty. Rels. Home: 2408 S Culpeper St Arlington VA 22206-1029 Office: USAF AF/REX 1150 Air Force Pentagon Washington DC 20330-1150

ROLLITT, IAN WILLIAM, project manager; b. Nottingham, U.K., Sept. 24, 1957; s. James William and Avis May (Walker) R.; m. Jacqueline Anne Pratt, June 30, 1979 (div. 1994); children: Christopher David William, Harriet Ruth; m. Penelope Jane Gooding, Feb. 25, 1995; children: Katrina Dawn Rose, Samuel Joshua James, Luke Charles William. BSc, Trent U., 1983. Chartered surveyor, chartered builder, profl. engr. Sr. surveyor Henry Boot & Sons Plc, Birmingham, U.K., 1984-86; project mgr. LC Wakeman & Ptnrs., Birmingham, 1986-87; devel. dir. Pemberton Resorts, Barbados, 1988-92; sr. projects mgr. Nehaul Constrn. Co. Ltd., Barbados and Guyana, 1993-95; dir. Rotherley Constrn. Inc., Barbados, 1996-98; project mgr. CD Consult, Barbados, 1989—; comml. dir. Crane Constrn. Inc., Barbados, 1998—; mem. steering com. for extending CIOB Code of Estimating Practice; cons. Inston Design Internat., London, 1996—. Author: Extending the Code of Estimating Practice, 1980-83. Life mem. Barbados Nat. Trust, 1992—, Internat. Tree Found., 1996. Fellow RICS, CIOB; mem. BAQS (pres. 1997—). Avocations: architecture, landscaping, reading, swimming. Office: CD Consult, PO Box 1118, Bridgetown West Indies

ROLLO-KOSTER, JOËLLE, history educator; b. Ollioules, France, July 2, 1956; came to U.S., 1980; d. Jean Antoine and Rosette Barton Rollo; m. Randall Harmon Koster, Mar. 25, 1977; children: Auriane, Laudine. MA, U. Nice, France, 1982; PhD, SUNY, 1992. Mem. adj. faculty Castleton (Vt.) State Coll., 1987-96; asst. prof. history U. R.I., 1996—. Contbr. articles to profl. publs. Mem. Soc. for French History, Soc. for Confrat. Studies (mem. editl. bd. 1999), Medieval Acad. Am., Western Soc. for French History (mem. coun. 1999), Soc. Medieval Studies Que. Avocations: jogging, tennis, cross-country skiing, travel, baking. E-mail: joelle@uri.edu. Office: Univ RI Dept History Washburn Hall Kingston RI 02881

ROLNICK, ARNON, psychologist; b. Tel Aviv, June 7, 1951; s. Shmariahu and Devorah (Greenhouse) R.; m. Ziporah Jamous, Oct. 5, 1976; children: Itai, Hallelli. BA with honors, Tel Aviv U., 1978, MA with honors, 1981, PhD, 1984. Cert. clin. psychologist, biofeedback therapist and supr. Sr. psychologist Israeli Army, 1978-91; vis. rschr. Brandeis U., Waltham, Mass., 1982-84; lectr. Tel Aviv U., 1984-87; head human performance lab. Meir Hosp., Israel, 1984-87; head rsch. unit Nat. Rehab. Ctr., 1991-94; cons. psychophysiology unit Sheaba Med. Ctr., 1994—; cons. psychologist Ultramind Ltd., London, 1994—; founder, supr. biofeedback unit Child Mental Health Clinic, Ministry of Health, Israel, 1995—; founder, moderator Clin. Psycholphysiology Internet Discussion Forum, 1994—. Contbr. articles to profl. publs., chpt. to book. Youth guide Hashomer Hatzair, Israel, 1969-70; mem. Ein Shemer Kibootz, Israel, 1970-74; vol. Israeli Forum for Helping New Immigrants, 1990—. Lt. comdr. Israeli Def. Force, 1971-91. Rothschild Found fellow, 1981, Lewis fellow Ministry of Health, Eng., 1985; Israel-Holland Cultural grantee Dutch Govt., 1987. Mem. Israel Psychol. Assn. (bd. dirs. 1995-97), Am. Assn. Applied Psychophysiology and Biofeedback (bd. dirs., mem. internat. com.). Avocations: computers, sports, politics. Home: 244 Bney Efraim St, 69107 Tel Aviv Israel

ROLNIK, ZACHARY JACOB, publishing company executive; b. Bayonne, N.J., Oct. 2, 1961; s. Joseph and Katie (Simon) R. BA, U. Rochester, 1982; M. in Pub. Policy, Harvard U., 1984. Ops. analyst, presdl. mgmt. intern U.S. Dept. Treasury, Washington, 1984-85; sr. editor, pub. Kluwer Acad. Pubs., Norwell, Mass., 1985-95, v.p., dir., 1996—. Home: 146 Pleasant St Hanover MA 02339-1844 Office: Kluwer Acad Pubs 101 Philip Dr Norwell MA 02061-1677

ROLOFF, HANS-GERT, educator; b. Hohenstein, East Prussia, Sept. 11, 1932; s. Johannes and Anna-Elisabeth (Abramowski) R.; m. Anke Schulz-Schneidemühl. Staatsexamen, Free U., Berlin, 1958, PhD, 1965, habilitation, 1970; Dr. honoris causa, U. Wroclaw, Poland, 1991, Bundesverdienst-Kreüz, 1993. Tchr. Free U., Berlin, 1957-66; asst. prof. Technische U. Berlin, 1966-70, prof., 1970-84; leader Inst. for Researching Middle German Lit., Free U. Berlin, 1984; guest prof. U. Melbourne, 1981, The Sorbonne, Paris, 1987, Kansas U., Lawrence, 1995, U. Wroclaw, 1996, U. Wien, 1999. Chief editor: Die Deutsche Literatur, 1979, Ausgaben Deutscher Literatur, 1967, Germanistische Lehrbuchsammlung, 1980, Jahrbuch für Intern. Germanistik, 1969, Daphnis Zeitschrift für Mittlere Deutsche Literatur, 1972, Mittlere Deutsche Literatur in Neu-u. Nachdrucken, 1980, Bibliotheca Neolatina, 1989, Berliner Ausgaben, 1990, Berliner Beiträge zur Editions-Wissenschaft, 1997, Bibliothek seltener Texte, 1997, Arbeiten und Editionen zur Mittleren Deutschen Literatur, 1997, Memoria, 1998, Studium Litterarum, 2000; contbr. numerous articles to profl. publs., 1962—. Avocations: reading, golf, theatre, travelling. Home: Marthastrabe 4a, D 12205 Berlin-Lichterfelde-West Germany Office: Free U Berlin, Habelschwerdter Allee 45, Dahlem Berlin D-14195, Germany

ROLSTON, HOLMES, III, theologian, educator, philosopher; b. Staunton, Va., Nov. 19, 1932; s. Holmes and Mary Winifred (Long) R.; m. Jane Irving Wilson, June 1, 1956; children: Shonny Hunter, Giles Campbell. BS, Davidson Coll., 1953; BD, Union Theol. Sem., Richmond, Va., 1956; MA in Philosophy of Sci., U. Pitts., 1968; PhD in Theology, U. Edinburgh, Scotland, 1958. Ordained to ministry Presbyn. Ch. (USA), 1956. Asst. prof. philosophy Colo. State U., Ft. Collins, 1968-71, assoc. prof., 1971-76, prof., 1976—; vis. scholar Ctr. Study of World Religions, Harvard U., 1974-75; official observer UNCED, Rio de Janiero, 1992. Author: Religious Inquiry: Participation and Detachment, 1985, Philosophy Gone Wild, 1986, Science and Religion: A Critical Survey, 1987, Environmental Ethics, 1988, Conserving Natural Value, 1994, Genes, Genesis and God, 1999; assoc. editor Environ. Ethics, 1979—; mem. editorial bd. Oxford Series in Environ. Philosophy and Pub. Policy, Zygon: Jour. of Religion and Sci.; contbr. chpts. to books, articles to profl. jours. Recipient Oliver P. Penock Disting. Svc. award Colo. State U., 1983, Coll. award for Excellence, 1991, Univ. Disting. Prof., 1992; Disting. Russell fellow Grad. Theol. Union, 1991, Disting. Lectr., Chinese Acad. of Social Scis., 1991, Disting. Lectr., Nobel Conf. XXVII, Gifford Lectr., U. Edinburgh, 1997. Mem. AAAS, Am. Acad. Religion, Soc. Bibl. Lit. (pres. Rocky Mountain-Gt. Plains region), Am. Philos. Assn., Internat. Soc. for Environ. Ethics (pres. 1989-94), Phi Beta Kappa. Avocation: bryology. Home: 1712 Concord Dr Fort Collins CO 80526-1602 Office: Colo State U Dept Philosophy Fort Collins CO 80523-0001

ROM, (MELVIN) MARTIN, investor; b. Detroit, Mar. 2, 1946; s. Jack and Thelma (Meyer) R.; m. Barbara Miller, July 12, 1970. BA magna cum laude, U. Mich., 1967. Founder MultiVest, Inc., Southfield, Mich., 1969; pres. MultiVest, Inc., Southfield, 1969-73; chmn. bd., chief exec. officer MultiVest, Inc., 1973-75; pres. Real Estate Securities and Syndication Inst., Nat. Assn. Realtors, Washington, 1975-76; dir., bd. govs. Real Estate Securities and Syndication Inst., Nat. Assn. Realtors, 1972-77; pres. Martin Rom Co., Inc., 1976—; vice chmn. Sports Illus. Ct. Clubs, Inc., 1977-79; bd. dirs. Mocatta Corp., 1979-80; founder, dir. Real Age, Inc., 1994—; mem. joint com. Nat. Assn. Securities Dealers-Nat. Assn. Realtors, 1975-76; mem. adv. com. on market instruments Commodity Futures Trading Commn., 1975-76; mem. Com. on Gold Regulations, 1974-75. Author: Nothing Can Replace the U.S. Dollar . . . and It Almost Has, 1975; Adv. bd.: Housing and Devel. Reporter, Washington. Trustee U. Chgo. Found. Mem. Phi Beta Kappa. Home and Office: 60 Quarton Ln Bloomfield Hills MI 48304-3456

ROMAIN, PIERRE R., commercial and television production executive, producer; b. Nyack, N.Y., Sept. 24, 1967. Grad. h.s., Nyack. Dir. mktg. Harolds Evergreen Restaurant, East Orange, N.J., 1990-91; v.p. and prodr. Giraldi Entertainment, North Haledon, N.J., 1991-93; chmn., CEO, prodr. Pierre Romain, Inc., N.Y.C., 1994—; chmn., CEO Workout Ptnrs., N.Y., Fla., 1994—. Dir. TV and film prodn. St. Jude's Champions for Charity Found., Newcity, N.Y., 1996—. Mem. CFO Svcs. Network Group. Avocations: weight training, music, drawing. Office: Pierre Romain Inc 208 W 29th St Rm 203 New York NY 10001-5206

ROMAN, ANDREW MICHAEL, lawyer, educator; b. Pitts., Aug. 19, 1951; s. James Andrew and Lois Roman; m. Heather Lynne Harms; children: Rebecca Lynne, Carolyn Elizabeth. BA, Bucknell U., 1973; JD, Duquesne U., 1976. Bar: Pa. 1976. Law clk. U.S. Dist. Ct. (we. dist.) Pa., Pitts., 1976-77; assoc. Eckert Seamans Cherin & Mellott, Pitts., 1977-84, ptnr., 1985-91; dir. Cohen & Grigsby, P.C., Pitts., 1991—, v.p. tech., 1998—; adj. prof. law Duquesne U. Sch. Law, Pitts., 1993—; arbitrator Fed. Ct. Arbitration Panel, Pitts., 1991—; faculty mem. seminar on bad faith litigation in Pa. Nat. Bus. Inst., 1995, 99, 2000. Editor-in-chief Duquesne Law Rev., 1976, A New Look at the Broad Form Nuclear Exclusion, Risk Management, 1995. Bd. dirs. Codes Rev. Bd., Mt. Lebanon, Pa., 1991—, The Extended Court House, Inc., 1997—; mem. vestry St. Paul's Episcopal Ch., Mt. Lebanon, 1995-98. Recipient Am. Jurisprudence awards Lawyers Coop. Pub. Co., 1974; T. Robert Brennan scholar Duquesne U. Sch. Law, 1974, Duquesne U. Sch. Law scholar, 1975. Mem. ABA, Am. Arbitration Assn. (mem. panel 1991—), Pa. Bar Assn., Allegheny County Bar Assn., Duquesne U. Law Alumni Assn. (treas. 1985-86, bd. dirs. 1988-90, pres. 1992-93). Office: Cohen & Grigsby PC 11 Stanwix St Ste 15 Pittsburgh PA 15222-1312

ROMAN, GREGG WILLIAM, geneticist, researcher; b. Passaic, N.J., May 25, 1964; s. William Edward and Anna Elizabeth R.; m. Beth Carole, Oct. 18, 1987; children: Jacob, Maxwell. BS, U. N.H., Durham, 1986, MS, 1989; PhD, U. Pa., Phila., 1995. Postdoc. fellow Baylor Coll. Medicine, Houston, 1995-2000, instr., 2000—. Inventor Plant genes for sensitivity to ethylene and pathogens, 1996; contbr. articles to profl. jours.; patentee in field. Phillip O'Bryan Montgomery fellow Damon Runyun-Walter Winchell Cancer Rsch. Fund, 1995-98. Mem. AAAS. Office: Dept Cell Biology Baylor College of Medicine Houston TX 77030

ROMAN, MARCO ANTONIO, educator; b. Mexico City, Mex.; s. Juan and Josefina (Jimenez) R.; m. Guillermina Sanchez, Dec. 30, 1969; children: Monica, Ligia, Xochitl, Marco Antonio, Guillermo. B of Philosophy, Montezuma Coll., 1960; B of Theology, Pontificia U., Rome, 1964; M of Edn., Centro Interdisciplinario de Investigacion y Docencia en Educacion Tecnica, Mex., 1977; MLS, Ind. U., 1980, PhD, 1983. Indsl. security asst. Frisco Mines Co., Chihuahua, Mex., 1972-75; prof. Tech. Parral, Chihuahua, Mex., 1975-77; ednl. rsch. Centro Interdisciplinario de Investigacion y Docencia en Educacion Tecnica, Queretaro, Mex., 1978, 85-89; prof., rschr. Tecnol. Parrel, Chihuahua, Mex., 1983-85; prof. Inst. Tech. Estudios Superiores de Monterrey, Queretaro, Mex., 1990—; rschr. in field. Contbr. articles to profl. jours. rschr. in field. Mem. NAHLS, AMEI, ACA, ALA, SNI. Roman Catholic. Home: E F Kino N 40, Cimatario Queretaro 76030 QRO, Mexico

ROMAN, PATRICIA ANN, sculptor; b. Dallas, Feb. 16, 1933; d. Solon Augustus and Thelma Mae (Macon) Tubbs; m. John Robert Hoyt, Mar. 26, 1951 (div. May 1982); children: John Robert Jr., Jerry Lynn; m. Evan Roman, June 8, 1996. BA, So. Meth. U., 1965; student, Baylor U., 1949-50. Piano tchr. Dallas, 1956-79, jewelry designer, 1968-85; designer tennis clothes for women Longmont, Colo., 1989—. Past pres. and life mem. Lake Highlands PTA. Mem. Nat. guild of Piano Tchrs. Hall of Fame. Mem. Dallas Music Tchrs. Assn. (v.p. 1978-79), Jr. Pianist Guild (founding 1976-79), Lake Highlands Women's League (founder), Dallas Artists and Craftsmen, Lake Highlands Book Club (founder), Lake Highlands Garden Club (founder). Methodist. Home: 7322 Debbe Dr Dallas TX 75252-6324

ROMANELLI, ANNA MARIA, epidemiologist, researcher; b. Trebisacce, Italy, Apr. 18, 1954; d. Guiseppe Romanelli and Giuseppina Adriani; m. Raffaele Cortese, June 25, 1983; 1 child, Matteo Carlos. BSc, U. Pisa, Italy, 1979, postgrad. in computer calculation, 1983, postgrad. in officinals plants, 1990. Rschr. 1st Clin. Physiology/CNR, Pisa, 1981—; prof. stats. Postgrad. Med. Sch., U. Pisa, 1991-95, Paramed. Sch., 1996-98. Fellow Nat. Assn. Biologists; mem. Italian Epidemiol. Assn. Office: 1st Fisiol Coin, Via Trieste 41, 56126 Pisa Italy

ROMANENKO, ANATOLY SIDOROVITCH, plant physiologist, educator, administrator; b. Karaganda, Kazakh, USSR, Feb. 20, 1938; s. Sidor Gordeevitch and Dora Phylippovna (Beloded) R.; m. Zinaida Legryevna Mamaladze, 1980; 1 child. Student, Siberian Technol. Inst., Krasnoyarsk, 1958-63; postgrad., Siberian Inst. Plant Physiology, Irkutsk, 1967-70, candidate in biol. sci., 1971, D in Biol. Sci., 1990. Engr. Forest Tapping Exptl. Sta., Tulun, USSR, 1963-67; head rsch. team Inst. Biology and Pedol., Vladivostok, Russia, 1974-85, sr. rschr., 1980; rschr. Siberian Inst. Plant Physiology, 1971-74, head rsch. team, 1985-93, head of labor, 1993—. Author: Endocytosis, 1979, Endocytosis in Plants, 1991; also over 60 articles. Mem. Russian Plant Physiology Soc. Office: Siberian Inst Plant Physiol, PO Box 1243, 664033 Irkutsk Russia

ROMANIV, OLEH, materials scientist, educator; b. Sokal, Ukraine, Mar. 21, 1928; s. Mykola and Maria (Hrushecka) R.; m. Alla Havryshko, Aug. 12, 1989. Engr., Poly. Inst. Lviv, Ukraine, 1950, CandTechSc, 1957, DTech, 1971. Engr., sr. engr. Elec. Power Sta. Installation Svc., Lviv, 1950-53; sr. rschr. Acad. Sci. of Ukraine, Lviv, 1956-61, head sci. dept., 1961-76; dep. dir. Physico-Mech. Inst. Lviv, 1977-90, head sci. dept., 1991—; sec.-gen. World Coun. Shevchenko Sci. Socs., 1992—. Contbr. over 400 articles to profl. jours.; patentee in field. Recipient State award of Ukraine in Technol. Sci., 1976, 96. Mem. Nat. Acad. Sci. of Ukraine (corr.), N.Y. Acad. Sci., Shevchenko Sci. Soc. (pres. 1989—, Hrushevsky award 1998). Mem. Ukrainian Greek Cath. Ch. Avocations: skiing, travel. Home: Konovaltsa Str 28/6, 290013 Lviv Ukraine Office: Shevchenko Sci Soc, 21 Gen Chyprynka Str, 290013 Lviv Ukraine

ROMANO, ENNIO, oncologist, medical educator; b. Assoro, Enna, Italy, Jan. 1, 1925; s. Marcello and Giuseppina (Fasanaro) R.; m. Giuseppina Di Grazia, Oct. 25, 1952; children: Marcello, Anita, Maria. MD, U. Rome, 1951; degree in fine arts, UCLA, 1983. Diplomate in gen. surgery, gen. pathology and oncology. Gen. surgeon Hosp., Catania, Italy, 1952-54, head gen. surgeon, 1955-80; cancer rschr. City of Hope, Duarte, Calif., 1981-91; pres. Calif. Acad., L.A., 1983-93, prof. anatomy, 1988-93; prof. anatomy U. Rome, 1994—; head surgery cons. Italian Navy, 1964-81, USN, 1981-91; chancellor Galilei U., L.A., 1988-93. Author: Tumors of the Thoracic Skeleton, 1981, Intestinal Obstructions, 1982, Gastrointestinal Tumors, 1984. Decorate commendatore Ordine Rep. Italiana. Mem. Am. Cancer Soc., NY Acad. Scis., Italian Am. Med. Assn., Internat. Burckhardt Acad. (Switzerland), Am. Legion (life), Masons. Republican. Roman Catholic. Avocations: painting, philately. Fax: 06-7004469. E-mail: enniorom@tiscalinet.it. Office: Via Gallia 214, 00183 Rome Italy

ROMANO-MAGNER, PATRICIA R., English studies educator, researcher; b. N.Y.C., Mar. 22, 1928; d. Al and Nicole (Siriani) Romano; m. Ralpha M. Magner, Dec. 24, 1954. AA, L.A. City Coll., BA; MA, Calif. State U., L.A.; D (hon.), Stanford U., Cambridge (Eng.) U., Queens Coll. Master tchr. Burbank (Calif.) Unified Sch. Dist., L.A. City Schs., Stanford (Calif.) U. Sch. for the Gifted; prof. Calif. State U., L.A. Mem. AAUP (award 2000). Republican. Avocation: horseback riding. Home: 5975 N Odell Ave Chicago IL 60631-2358

ROMANOV, IGOR GRIGOR'EVICH, engineering researcher, consultant; b. Gorky, USSR, Mar. 15, 1955; s. Grigoriy Georgevich Romanov and Maria Petrovna Denisova; m. Galina Mihailovna Belonuchkina, June 9, 1981; 1 child, Nadia. DS in Electron Technics Enging., Gorky State U., 1975; postgrad., U. Gorky, 1982-85. Engr. U. Gorky, 1977-82; sr. sci. worker br. Inst. Machine Sci. Russian Acad. Scis., Nizhny Novgorod, USSR, 1985-89, head lab., 1989-99, leading sci. worker, 1999—; assoc. prof. U. Novgorod, 1990-97; cons. Enterprise Sci. and Prodn., Novgorod, 1997—. Contbr. articles to profl. jours. State Sci. scholar Russian Acad., 1997-2000. Mem. Volgo-Viatskogo sect. tech. Russian Acad. Sci. Avocations: tennis, football, fishing. Home: Vaneeva str. 1A-8, 603006 Nizhny Novgorod Russia Office: Russian Acad Sci, Belinskiy, 85, 603024 Nizhny Novgorod Russia

ROMANOV, VITALY ALEXANDROVICH, science educator; b. Ussurlysk, Russia, Aug. 1, 1941; s. Alexandr Gerasimovich and Vera Semyonovna (Tsarenkova) R.; m. Galina Ivanovna Galachova, June 30, 1972; 1 child, Nadejda. MD, Voronezh (Russia) Med. Inst., 1964, postgrad., 1967; PhD, Inst. Exptl. Medicine, St. Petersburg, Russia, 1987. Asst. prof. microbiology Yaroslavl Med. Acad., Russia, 1967-75, head dept. microbiology, 1975—; dir. Immunology Lab., Yaroslavl, 1975—. Author, editor: Study of Humoral and Cell Immunity in Healthy and Ill, 1980, Hyperbaric Oxygenation and Sepsis, 1978; contbr. articles to profl. jours. Fellow Acad. of Natural Scis., Epidemiological, Microbiological and Parasitological Soc., Immunological Scientific Soc. Avocations: photography, classical music, travel, computers, automobiles. Office: Yaroslavl Med Acad, Revolutionnaya 5, Yaroslavl Russia

ROMANOV, VLADIMIR ALEXANDROVICH, computer engineering; b. Kiev, Ukraine, Dec. 8, 1944; s. Alexander Timofeevich and Irina Mihaylovna (Shurjan) R.; m. Ljudmila Leonidovna Koval, July 28, 1974; 1 child, Olga Vladimirovna. Enging. degree, Tech. U., Kiev, Ukraine, 1967; PhD, Inst. Cybernetics, Kiev, Ukraine, 1973, DS, 1994. Engr. Inst. cybernetics, Kiev, Ukraine, 1967-69, rschr., 1972-86, head dept., 1986—; asst. prof. Tech. U., Kiev, 1988-94, prof., 1994—. Co-author: Professional Personal computers, 1990. Mem. IEEE. Avocations: music, theatre, swimming. Home: Saksaganskogo str 30 f 21, 01033 Kiev Ukraine Office: Inst Cybernetics, Prospect Acad Glushkov 40, 03680 Kiev Ukraine

ROMANOV, VOLODYMYR ALEXEEVICH, computer science educator, researcher; b. Kamynino, Kursk, Russia, Jan. 23, 1960; s. Alexey Filippovich and Olga Sergeevna Romanov; m. Svitlana Egorivna Chistova, Oct. 16, 1981; children: Olga Volodymyrivna, Volodymyr Volodymyrovych. MD, State U., Kharkov, Ukraine, 1983, PhD, 1987. Cert. computer scis. and nuc. physics. Rschr. Nuc. Phys. Lab., Kharkiv, Ukraine, 1983-88; prof. State Tech. Univ. Agr., Kharkiv, 1988-96; head Info. Tech. Ctr., Kharkiv, 1996-2000; vice-head Coun. Young Rschrs., Kharkiv, 1984-91; editor Regional TV, Kharkiv, 185-87; prof. State Tech Univ. Agr., Kharkiv, 1996-2000. Author: (with S. Troubnikov) Nuclear Forces, 1992; contbr. articles to profl. jours. Mem. Can. Info. Processing Soc. Russian Orthodox. Avocations: Russian literature, history, music. E-mail: volodymyr romanov@yahoo.com. Home: Apt 81, 4645 Bourret, Quebec, Canada H3W 1K9 Office: Kharkiov State Tech U Agr, 44 Artema St, 61024 Kharkiv Ukraine

ROMANOVA, LIYA, physicist; b. Moscow, Aug. 14, 1929; d. Martinian and Mariya (Ivanova) R. Student, U. Moscow, 1946-51, 55-58; CandScis, Acad. Scis. USSR, Moscow, 1963, DSc in Physics and Math., 1974. Lab. asst., lectr. U. Moscow, 1952-54; jr. rsch. worker Inst. Atmospheric Physics, Acad. Scis. USSR, Moscow, 1958-67, sr. rsch. worker, 1967-86, sr. rsch. worker, cons., 1986-94, leading rsch. worker, 1995—. Contbr. articles to profl. jours. Avocations: study of Latin, music, reading classical Russian literature. Office: Acad Scis/Atmos Physics, Pyzhevskii per 3, 109017 Moscow Russia

ROMANOVICH, NELLY ALEXANDROVNA, sociologist, design engineer; b. Voronezh, Russia, Jan. 20, 1960; d. Alexander Maximovich Gorobtsov and Nina Stepanovna Gorobtsova; m. Alexander Leonidovich Romanovich, Oct. 17, 1981, 1 child, Oksana. Diploma in civil engring., Inst. Civil Enging., Voronezh, 1982; postgrad., Russian Acad. Sci., 1990-97; PhD, St. Petersburg U., 1997. Design engr. State Design & Tech. Inst., Voronezh, 1982-88; sociologist Rosagroprom, Voronezh, 1988-92; dir. regional br. VCIOM, Voronezh, 1992-96; dir. Russian Inst. Pub. Opinion, Voronezh, 1992—, Inst. Pub. Opinion Qualitas, Voronezh, 1996—. Author: Foundation of Market Economy in Agribusiness, 1992, (almanac) Recircling Processes in Nature and Socium, 1994; contbr. articles to profl. jours. Mem. ESOMAR, Russian Mktg. Assn. Avocation: poetry. E-mail: nelli@riom.voronezh.su, qualitas@comch.ru. Home: Pushkinskaya str 4 r43, Voronezh 394000, Russia Office: Inst Pub Opinion Qualitas, Revolution Ave 44 kv14, Voronezh 394000, Russia

ROMANOVSKI, MIKHAIL REM, mathematician; b. Samara, Russia, June 22, 1952; s. Rem Vladimir and Lubov Mikhail (Volgina) R.; m. Elena Vladimir Kurtashina, Aug. 27, 1983; children: Victoria, Valeria. MS, Moscow Tech. U., 1975; PhD, Inst. Termophysics, Kiev, Ukraine, 1982. Rschr. Chelomey Constrn. Bur., Moscow, 1975-78; head dept. math. Kriogenmash, Balashikha, Russia, 1978-93; head dept. CAD/CAM Point Ltd., Moscow, 1993—; tchr. math. modeling Chem. Industry Inst., Moscow, 1982-93. Contbr. articles to profl. jours. Mem. N.Y. Acad. Sci. Avocations: sports, skiing. Home: Schelkovskoe Ave 79-1-334, 107497 Moscow Russia Office: Point Ltd, Prospekt Andropova 22/30, Moscow Russia

ROMAS, EVANGELOS, physician, health services administrator; b. Melbourne, Australia, July 24, 1962; s. Lazaros Romas and Valerie Sirillas; m. Mary Kiratzis, May 16, 1987; children: Jeremy, Jesse. MB, BS, U. Melbourne, 1986, PhD, 1999. Sr. lectr. U. Melbourne, 1998—; dep. dir. Arthritis Ctr. St. Vincent's Hosp., Melbourne, 1998—; cons. rheumatologist St. Vincent's Hosp., Melbourne, 1994—. Recipient Young Investigator award Am. Soc. Bone and Mineral Rsch. Ann. Meeting, 1995. Office: Erin St Med Ctr, 2 Erin St, Melbourne VIC 3121, Australia

ROMBACH, LOUIS HERMAN, lawyer, chemist; b. Cin., Apr. 4, 1926; s. Charles and Mathilda Elizabeth (Lauck) R.; m. Ann Marie O'Brien, June 9, 1951; children: Louis J., Linda M., Stephen E., Charles M., Thomas A. BS in Chemistry, Xavier U., 1948, MS in Chemistry, 1949; PhD in Chemistry, U. Cin., 1953; JD, Temple U., 1964. Bar: Del. 1965, U.S. Dist. Ct. D.C. 1965, U.S. Ct. Appeals (D.C. cir.) 1965, U.S. Claims Ct. 1966, U.S. Ct. Appeals (D.C. cir.) 1982. Rsch. chemist Du Pont Co., Wilmington, Del., 1953-64; sr. counsel Dupont Co., Wilmington, Del., 1965-91; ret., 1991. Patentee in polymer chemistry; contbr. articles to profl. jours. Pres. Pembrey Civic Assn., 1993-95. Ensign USN, 1944-46. Cancer rsch. fellow NIH, 1951-53. Mem. Am. Chem. Soc., Am. Inst. Chemists, Royal Soc. Chemistry, Del. Bar Assn., D.C. Bar Assn., Sci. Rsch. Soc. Am., Xavier U. Nat. Alumni Assn. (founder, first pres. Del. Valley chpt. 1993-95), Phi Alpha Delta, Phi Lambda Upsilon. Avocations: running, tennis, computers, travel.

ROMBOUT, LUC ERNA THEO, management consultant; b. Zele, Oost Vlaanderen, Belgium, Nov. 8, 1966; s. Maurits and Christiane (De Kegel) R. M in Econs., U. Ghent (Belgium), 1988; MBA, De Vlerick Sch. Voor

Mgmt., Ghent, Belgium, 1989; postgrad. in fire prevention, ANPI-NVBB, Louvain-La-Neuve, Belgium, 1995, postgrad. in risk analysis, 1997, postgrad. in crisis mgmt., 1998, postgrad. in arson, 1999. Cert. fire and explosion safety cons. Researcher De Vlerick Sch. voor Mgmt., Ghent, 1989-94; mgmt. cons., 1994—; cons. U. Ghent, 1997—, sr. adviser, Emergency Planning & Ops., dir. Crisis and Emergency Mgmt. Ctr., 2000—. Co-author: Boekhoudrecht En Informatica, 1996, Conceptenrapport Voor integrale Bibliotheek Ontwikkeling, 1998. Air force res. officer Belgian Air Force, 1990—. Mem. Armed Forces Comms. and Electronics Assn. (Belgian chpt.), Ctr. Recherche Archéologique Fluviale. Roman Catholic. Avocations: scuba diving, horseback riding, reading, gardening, photography. Home: Lokerenbaan 38, B-9240 Zele Oost-Vlaanderen, Belgium Office: U Ghent, Stalhof 6, B-9000 Gent Belgium

ROMBURGH, ALAN DESMOND MICHAEL, hotel executive; b. Johannesburg, South Africa, June 1, 1952; s. Desmond Theodore and Loretta Manuella (Taranto) R.; m. Diana Victoria Giovanna Griffiths, Apr. 28, 1979; children: Daniel, Victoria. Nat. diploma hotel sch. mgmt., Technikon Witwatersrand, Johannesburg, 1976, part-time student, 1980-87; cert. exec. mgmt. program, Grad. Sch. Bus., Cape Town, South Africa, 1988. Trainee George Hotel, Manzini, Swaziland, 1973; mgmt. trainee Carlton Hotel, Johannesburg, 1976, Elangeni Hotel, Durban, South Africa, 1976; night auditor Millpark Hotel, Johannesburg, 1977; asst. food and beverage mgr. Royal Swazi Hotel and Spa, Durban, 1977-78, food and beverage mgr., 1978-79; gen. mgr. Nhlangano Casino Hotel, Durban, 1979-84, Protea Hotels, Gauteng, Cape Town, South Africa, 1984-88; dir. Romlor Hospitality Cons., Cape Town, 1988-93, Romlor Hospitality T/A Relais Hotels, Cape Town, 1993—; chmn. mktg. com. Western Cape Tourism Bd., Cape Town, 1995—. Mem. Cape Overberg Tourism Assn. (bd. dirs. 1993-96). Fax: 0027-21-4231439. E-mail: arrelais@satis.co.sa. Home: Romcor Hospitality, 21 Bronmersvlei Rd, Constantia 7800, South Africa Office: T/A Relais Hotels S Africa, 47 Strand St, Cape Town 8001, South Africa

ROMEO, MARIO FRANCESCO, physics researcher; b. Fiumefreddo, Catania, Italy, Aug. 15, 1955; s. Francesco G. Romeo and Maria Cavallaro. D physics, U. Catania, 1979. Substitute temp. tchr. State Sch., 1979-80; assoc. rschr. Nat. Italian Nuclear Physics Inst., 1979-80; physicist French Comissariat Atomic Energy, 1980; R & D rschr. ST Microelectroelectronics, Catania, 1982—, patent officer, info. tech. expert, 1988—; sci. tech. rsch. expert in analytical techniques and metrology. Contbr. articles to sci. jours., including Italian Jour. Anatomy and Embryology. Patent trade secret grantee, 1996. Mem. IEEE. Roman Catholic. Avocations: playing chess and guitar, ecological trips, speleology. Office: ST Microelectronics, Strad Primosole 50, 95121 Catania Italy

RÖMER, FRANZ JOSEF, philologist, educator; b. Vienna, July 19, 1943; s. Franz and Anna (Haider) R.; m. Ottilie Rott, Aug. 2, 1969; children: Franz, Andrea. PhD, U. Vienna, 1968, U. Dozent, 1975. Asst. prof. Latin philology U. Vienna, 1968-78, prof., 1978—. Author: Manuscripts of the Works of Saint Augustine, 2 vols., 1972 '73, Tacitus Annals 15-16, 1976, Progress Reports: Plinius Minor, Plinius Major, Tacitus; contbr. 30 articles to profl. jours. Mem. Eranos Vindobonensis, Wiener Humanistische Gesellschaft, Internat. Soc. for the Classical Tradition, Internat. Assn. for Neo-Latin Studies. Home: Sommarugagasse 8/6, Vienna Austria A-1180 Office: U Vienna, Dr Karl Lueger-Ring 1, Vienna Austria A-1010

ROMERO, ALEJANDRO FRANCISCO, academic administrator; b. Tucapel, Chile, Mar. 9, 1946; s. Alejandro Segundo Romero and Ines Raquel Mella; m. Gloria Maria Muñoz, Mar. 23, 1973; children: Claudia, Rodrigo, Carlos, Paulina. Lic. in biochemistry, U. Chile, Santiago, 1970; PhD in Chemistry, Tex. A&M U., 1978. Rschr. U. Chile, 1971-72, asst. prof., 1972-77; assoc. prof. U. Austral de Chile, Valdivia, 1979-84, prof., 1984—, dir. Dairy Tech. Ctr., 1983-84, dir. Food Engring. Sch., 1988-90, dir. Food Sci. and Tech. Inst., 1990-92, 93-96, dir. grad. studies, 1996—; mem. editl. com. Revista Alimentos, 1990—; editor procs. seminar on quality assurance, 1984; contbr. articles to profl. jours. Fondecyt rsch. grantee CONICYT, 1990-94, 95-98; fellow Spain Ministry of Edn. and Sci., 1985, 92. Mem. Food Tech. Soc. Avocations: tennis, camping, dancing, reading. Home: Turin 202, Valdivia Chile Office: U Austral Chile, Independencia 647, Valdivia Chile

ROMERO, EDWARD L., diplomat, environmental engineering executive; b. Albuquerque, Jan. 2, 1934; m. Cayetana Garcia; 4 children. Student, L.A. State Coll., 1955-59, Citrus Coll. Founder, chmn., CEO, Advanced Scis., Inc. (merged with Commodore Applied Techs.), Albuquerque, 1976-98; amb. to Spain, Am. Embassy, Madrid, 1998—; former mem. U.S. Trade Rep.'s Svcs. Policy Adv. Com., leader numerous U.S. dels. to Mex.; former mem. fed. adv. com. for trade negotiations; former mem. U.S. del. to Helsinki Accords. Active numerous civic and charitable orgns.; former mem. President's Hispanic Adv. Com.; bd. dirs. Congl. Hispanic Caucus Inst. With U.S. Army, Korea. Recipient numerous awards from various orgns., including Nat. Kidney Found., N.Mex. Anti-Defamation League, Nat. Hispanic Scholarship Found., Multiple Sclerosis Soc.; named Nat. Hispanic Businessman of Yr., Hispanic C. of C., 1989. Mem. Albuquerque Hispanic C. of C. (founder). Office: Am Embassy Madrid Spain PS6 61 Box 43 APO AE 09642

ROMERO, JOAQUIM JOSÉ BARBOSA, engineering educator; b. Lisbon, Portugal, Jan. 11, 1928; s. Joaquim Gonçalves and Adosinda Encarnação (Barbosa) R.; m. Magda Otília Ricardo Cabrita, July 27, 1953; children: Joaquim Filipe, Manuel José, Fernando Carlos, Luís Miguel. Lic., Inst. Superior Ténico, Lisbon, Portugal, 1951; MSc, U. Birmingham, U.K., 1961, PhD, 1967; agregado, U. Lourenco Marques, Moçambique, Portugal, 1972. Mem. steering com. U. Minho, Braga, Portugal, 1974-81, dep. vice chancellor, 1978-81, dean Sch. Engring., 1984-89; dir. Inst. Indsl. Tech. INETI, Lisbon, 1981-84; mgr. subprogram higher edn. PRODEP, Lisbon, 1990-94; pres. Sch. Tech. and Mgmt. Poly. Viana do Castelo, Portugal, 1991-97; cons. Lab. Normal Pharm., Lisbon, 1952-65, Portuguese Atomic Authority, Lisbon, 1956-65; advisor to dir. Nat. Inst. for Indsl. Rsch., Lisbon, 1965; dir. Prodn. Orfina (Fine Chems.), Lisbon, 1965-67; head Ctr. Engring. and Sys. of Prodn. and Ctr. of Rsch. in Energy and Prodn. Tech., U. Minho, 1994-98; coord. extended evaluation com. degree programmes Portuguese Univs. Indsl. Engring., 1998-2000. Contbr. sci. articles to profl. jours. Recipient Merit Gold medal Cath. U., 1994, Great Cross Portuguese Pub. Edn. Order, 1998, Silver medal U. Minho, 1999. Fellow Ordem dos Engenheiros; mem. IEEE, Soc. Portuguesa de Química, Inst. Chem. Engrs. Avocations: literature, music. Home: R do Caires 278-8 E, 4700-207 Braga Portugal Office: Univ Do Minho Sch Engring, Dept Prodn and Sys, Azurem 4800 Guimarães, Portugal

ROMERO, JORGE ENRIQUE, laboratory administrator, microbiology researcher; b. Lima, Peru, Mar. 14, 1967; s. Victor Manuel Romero and Alicia Juana Alvarez; m. Luz Elvira Palacios, Sept. 7, 1996; children: Andrea, Daniela. BS, Cayetano Heredia U., Lima, 1990; MSc, U. Chile, Santiago, 1994. Chief microbiology La. Cantella, Lima, 1990-92; microbiologist Cantella-Colichon Inst., Lima, 1994-96; mgr. quality assurance CERSA, Lima, 1995-96; supr. microbiology Medlab, Lima, 1996-97, adminstr., 1997—. Avocations: soccer, basketball, collecting pens, movies, weekends with his family. Home: Coop 27 Abril, Calle Chincheros 175, Lima 03, Peru Office: Medlab, Av Santa Cruz 367, Miraflor Lima 18, Peru

ROMERO, JOSEFINO TABERNILLA, nurse anesthetist; b. Tayabas, Quezon, The Philippines; came to U.S., 1963; s. Melanio Merca and Teodorica (Tabernilla) R. Diploma, Quezon Meml. Hosp., 1961; cert. nurse anesthetist, Mt. Carmel Hosp., Detroit, 1968; D in Art, U. Found., Malta, 1986. RN, Mich. Psychiat. nurse Nat. Mental Hosp., Manila, 1961-63; operating room nurse St. Vincent Hosp., Worcester, Mass., 1963-64, Michael Reese Hosp., Chgo., 1964-65, Sarnia (Canada) Gen. Hosp., 1965-66; operating room nurse, nurse anesthetist Quezon Meml. Hosp., 1971-72; nurse anesthetist Mt. Carmel Hosp., 1973-74, Brent Hosp., Detroit, 1974-86, Straith Hosp., Southfield, Mich., 1986—. Exhibited paintings in numerous one-man shows including Beijing Internat. Conv. Ctr., 1991, Pontiac Art Ctr., 1989, Troy Libr. and Gallery, 1989, Scarab Club Detroit, 1989, Lawrence St. Gallery, Pontiac, Mich., 1989, Acad. Art Gallery, Paris, 1988, Gallert in the Grove, Canada, 1987, Southfield Civic Ctr., 1986, Electric Fantasy Gallery, 1986, Philippine Orgn. and Filipino Artists, Chgo., 1978, others; exhibited in several group shows including Detroit Press Club, 1989, Mich. Design Ctr., 1988, Philippine Cultural Ctr., Ayala Mus., Casa de Communidad de Tayabas, 1997, Seattle Asian Art Mus., 1997, Gov.'s Mansion-The Philippine, 1998, Galleria Romero, The Philippines, 1998. Named one of Outstanding Men. Mich., City of Detroit, 1976, Outstanding Alumnus quezon Meml. Hosp. Sch. Nursing, 1994; recipient Albert Einstein award Internat. Acad. Found., 1991, Merit award Mich. Ann. Art Festival, 1975, Cert. of Appreciation Gov. of Mich., 1986, Quezon medal honor (The Philippines), 1997. Mem. Am. Assn. Nurse Anesthetists, Mich. Assn. Nurse Anesthetists, Filipino Nurse Assn., Beijing Watercolor Soc., Scarab Club Detroit (bd. dirs. 1988—), Knights of Rizal, Internat. Assn. Educators for World Peace. Roman Catholic. Avocations: photography, travel, tennis. Home: 2230 S Shore Ct Rochester Hls MI 48307-4359

ROMERO, MURILO ARAUJO, educator; b. Rio de Janeiro, Brazil, Mar. 23, 1965; s. Dagoberto Romero and Maria Helena (Araujo) R. BSc, Catholic Univ. Rio de Janeiro, 1988, MSc, 1991; PhD, Drexel Univ., 1995. Rsch. asst. Catholic Univ., Rio de Janeiro, Brazil, 1987-91, Drexel Univ., Phila., 1991-95, Univ. Sao Paulo, Sao Carlos, Brazil, 1995-96; asst. prof. Univ. Sao Paulo, Sao Carlos, 1996—. Contbr. articles to profl. jours. Recipient Telexpo award Brazilian Min. of Communications, 1997, scholarship Brazilian Min. of Sci. & Tech., 1989, 91. Mem. SBMO, IEEE. Office: Univ Sao Paulo, Carlos Botelho 1465, 13560250 Séo Carlos Brazil

ROMERO, REGHIS M., II, port city and real estate developer. Prin. R-II Builders Inc., Quezon City, The Philippines. Mem. Philippine C. of C. and Industry, Philippine Constrn. Assn., Chamber of Real Estate & Builders Assn., Order of Knights of Rizal (3d degree comdr.). Avocations: yachting, snorkeling, jet skiing, motorbiking. Office: R-II Builders Inc, 136 Malakas St Diliman, Quezon City The Philippines

ROMERO-ROJAS, JAIRO ALBERTO, civil engineering educator; b. Garagoa, Colombia, Nov. 12, 1942; s. Juan B. and Helena (Rojas) Romero; m. Bertha Mora, June 26, 1965; children: Jairo A., Claudia H. Bachelor, San Bartolome la Merced, Bogota, 1959; degree civil engr., U. Nacional Colombia, 1965; M in Engring., Rensselaer Poly. Inst., 1968; diploma, Hebrew U. Jerusalen, 1971. Asst. instr. Fac. de Ing. Univ. Nal. de Col., Bogota, 1966-67, assoc. instr., 1967-68, asst. prof., 1968-72, dean, 1973-74; assoc. prof. Univ. Nacional de Colombia, Bogota, 1972—; prof. Escuela Col. de Engenieria, Bogota, 1975—; cons. Gomez Cajiao y Asociados, Bogota, 1982—; cons. in field. Author: Acuitratamiento Por Lags. de Estab., 1994, Acuiquimica, 1996, Acuipurificacion, 1997, Tratamiento de Aguas Residuales, 2000; translator Acuianalisis, 1989. Lt. engring., 1977. Fellow ASCE; mem. Am. Water Works Assn. (life), Water Environment Fedn., Internat. Assn. Water Quality, Club de Profs. Univ. Nacional. Avocations: basketball, traveling. Home: Ap 501, CRA 25B No 153-81 Int 7, Bogota Colombia Office: Escuela Colombiana, Ingenieria, AA 14520 Bogota Colombia

ROMICS, IMRE, urology educator; b. Erd, Hungary, May 16, 1947; s. Istvan and Katalin (Berenyi) R.; m. Eva Gorbe, May 1, 1953; children: Katalin, Miklos. MD, Semmelweis Med. U., 1971, PhD, 1985; DSc, Hungarian Acad. Scis., 1995. Asst. prof. Semmelweis Med. U., Budapest, Hungary, 1971-86; asst. urology dept. St. Agnes Hosp. U., Bocholt, Germany, 1986-88; sr. lectr. Semmelweis Med. U., Budapest, 1988-92, assoc. prof., 1992-95; prof. dept. head Nat. Inst. Rheumatology, Budapest, 1995-97; prof., chmn. dept. urology Semmelweiss U. Medicine, Budapest, 1997—. Contbr. to books and articles to profl. jours. Mem. Hungarian Urology Soc. (sec. 1988—, exec. com. 1990—), German Urology Soc., Am. Urology Assn. (pres. bd.), N.Y. Acad. Scis. Avocations: 20th century history, languages. Office: Semmelweiss Med U Urol Dept, Semmelweiss Med U, Urology Dept, Ulloi ut 78B, 1082 Budapest Hungary

ROMI-LEVIN, RIVKA, information center head, librarian; b. Vilnius, Lithuania, Nov. 12, 1946; p. Ya'acov and Roza (Toker) Levin; div.; children: Mordechai, Eliyahu. Diploma, Technikum for Libr. Studies, Vilnius, 1967. Libr. Mcpl. Archive, Vilnius, 1965-67, Israel Shipping Rsch. Inst., Haifa, Israel, 1970-87; head info. ctr. Wydra Inst. Shipping and Aviation Rsch., U. Haifa, 1987—. Editor Shipping Bibliographic Series. Mem. Maritime Info. Assn., Shipping Rsch. Soc. Israel. Fax: 972-8-348908. E-mail: rromi@research.haifa.ac.il. Home: Einstein 67a, 34602 Haifa Israel Office: Wydra Inst Shipping Rsch, Univ Haifa, 31905 Haifa Israel

ROMINGER, RICHARD, federal agency administrator; b. Woodland, Calif., July 1, 1927; M. Evelyne Rowe; children: Richard S., Charles A., Ruth E., Bruce J. BS in Plant Sci. summa cum laude, U. Calif., Davis, 1949. Farmer Calif.; dir. Dept. Food and Agriculture, Calif., 1977-82; dep. sec. USDA, 1993—. Recipient Disting. Svc. award Calif. Farm Bur. Fedn., 1991; named Agriculturalist of Yr. Calif. State Fair, 1992; numerous others. Office: US Dept of Agriculture Office of the Deputy Secy 1400 Independence Ave SW Washington DC 20250-0002

ROMÎNU, MIHAI, dentist; b. Arad, Romania, Mar. 24, 1969; s. Pavel and Mona (Poenaru) R. Degree in dentistry, U. Medicine and Pharmacy, Timisoara, Romania, 1993. Asst. prof. U. Medicine and Pharmacy, Timisoara, 1994-98, chef de travaux, 1998—. Co-author: The Human Permanent Teeth, 1991, 2d edit., 1997, The Veneer Crown, 1992, 2d edit., 1998, Dental Materials, Vols. 1, 2, 3, 1994 (prize Romanian Acad. 1995), The Implant Supported Bridge, 1996; author: The Stomatognathic System, 1997 (prize Helicon Ediutl. House 1997). Avocations: motorcycling, travel, music. Office: U Medicine and Pharmacy, Spl Tudor Vladimirescu 14, 1900 Timisoara Romania

RÖMLING, UTE MARIA, molecular microbiologist, researcher; b. Bamberg, Bavaria, Germany, Apr. 11, 1964; d. Herbert and Dorothea (Brehm) R. MSc, U. Hannover, Germany, 1989, PhD, 1993. Postdoctoral fellow Med. Sch. Hannover, 1993-95, Karolinska Inst., Stockholm, 1995-98; postdoctoral fellow dept. cell biology and immunology GBF, Braunschweig, 1998—. Avocations: sports, culture, cooking. Office: GBF Dept Cell Bio and Immun, Mascheroder Weg 1, 38124 Braunschweig Germany

ROMM, FREDDY ALEXANDRE, chemist, researcher; b. Moscow, Nov. 11, 1960; arrived in Israel, 1991; s. Alexandre Pavel and Tamara Hema (Slavkin) R. MSc, U. Moscow, 1982; DSc in Chem. Engring., Technion, Haifa, Israel, 1996. Engr. Inst. Energy, Moscow, 1982-84, sr. engr., 1984-85, jr. sci. rschr., 1985-89, sr. rschr., 1989-91; tchr. asst., rschr. Technion, 1993-96, rschr., 1997—; rschr. U. St. Etienne, France, 1996. Author: Philosophy of Dialectical Dualism, 1995, Thermodynamics of Microporous Material Formation, 1999; contbr. articles to profl. publs; patentee in field. Mem. Memorial, Moscow, 1989-91, Dem. Party of Russia, 1990-91; v.p. Movement of Singles of Haifa, 1996-97. 2d lt. Soviet Army, 1989. Chataubriand fellow Govt. of France, 1996. Avocations: literature, music, video. E-mail: cercafr@techunix.technion.ac.il. Home: PO Box 4405, Haifa Israel Office: AMSIL Ltd Co, PO Box 73, 10550 Migdal Emek Israel

ROMME, GIANNI PETRUS CORNELIS, speed skater; b. Made, The Netherlands, Feb. 12, 1973. Swimming instr.; speed skater Dutch Nat. Team, 1995—; with Spaar Select. Recipieng Gold medal men's speed skating 5000 meters, Olympic Games, Nagano, Japan, 1998, men's speed skating 10000 meters, 1998. Avocations: swimming, golf, cars. Office: Dutch Olympic Com, PO Box 302, 6800 AH Arnhem The Netherlands also: Madese Fan Club, Valkenhof 37, 4921 WD Made The Netherlands*

ROMMELAERE, CARLO LEOPOLD, land surveyor; b. Likasi, Shaba, Zaire, Aug. 14, 1954; arrived in South Africa, 1965; s. Albert Boudewyn and Godelieve (Ruytinx) R.; m. Linda Klopper, Apr. 7, 1980 (div.). BSc in Land Survey with honors, U. Cape Town, 1976, MSc in Engring., 1990. Registered profl. land surveyor, cadastral, engring.; sect. title cons. precise surveys, deformation surveys, property law. Articled surveyor Rollo Hemsley Myrdal, South Africa, 1976-77, Elzinga & Sandler, South Africa, 1976-77, L. Saacks, South Africa, 1976; land surveyor P.E. Blignaut, Parow, South Africa, 1978-80; land surveyor, ptnr. Blignaut Rommelaere, South Africa, 1980-90; land surveyor, ptnr. Blignaut Rommelaere & Chapman, South Africa, 1990-96, ptnr., 1990—; land law lectr. U. Cape Town, 1990—; external examiner Cape Technikon, 1994—; mem. coun. Inst. Land Surveyor Western Cape, 1988-90. Exec. mem. Penhill Ratepayers Assn., 1988-89; chmn. Lower Gardens Ratepayers Assn., Cape Town, 1994-96. Mem. Inst. Land Surveyors (past coun. mem.), Inst. Dirs., Hydrographic Soc. South Africa, Photogrammetry Soc. South Africa. Avocations: photography, electronics, reading. E-mail: brcsurvy@iafrica.com. Fax: 021 930 2308. Office: Blignaut Rommelaere Chapman, PO Box 334 12 Picton St, Parow 7500, South Africa

RONA, PETER ARNOLD, oceanographer, researcher, educator; b. Trenton, N.J., Aug. 17, 1934; s. Gustav G. and Elizabeth Rona; m. Donna Cook, Aug. 16, 1974; 1 child, Jessica. AB, Brown U., 1956; MS, Yale U., 1957, PhD, 1967. Exploration geologist Standard Oil Co., N.J., 1957-59; rsch. assocs. Hudson Labs, Columbia U., Dobbs Ferry, N.Y., 1960-69; sr. rsch. geophysicist NOAA, Miami, Fla., 1969-94; prof. marine geology and geophysics Inst. Marine and Coastal Scis., Rutgers U., New Brunswick, N.J., 1994—; cons. on seafloor resources UN, N.Y.C., 1970—; trustee, advisor Internat. Oceanographic Found., Miami, 1981-95; cruise lectr. Royal Caribbean Line, 1991; organizer Atlantic Deep Sea Rsch. Ctr., 1994—, Ocean Sys. Engring. Ctr.; Geraldine R. Dodge lectr. Liberty Sci. Ctr., 1999. Author: The Central North Atlantic, 1980; editor: Seafloor Spreading Centers, 1981, Hydrothermal Processes at Seafloor Spreading Centers, 1983; contbr. over 250 articles to profl. jours. Trustee Mus. Sci., Miami, 1974—, also past chmn.; officer Dade County Cultural Affairs Coun., Miami, 1979-84. Recipient Shepard medal Soc. Econ. Paleontologists and Mineralogists, 1986, gold medal U.S. Dept. Commerce, 1987, outstanding sci. paper award NOAA, 1989, Hans Pettersson Bronze medal of the Royal Swedish Acad. of Scis., 1999. Fellow Geol. Soc. Am. (assoc. editor 1975-82), AAAS, Explorers Club; mem. Am. Geophys. Union (assoc. editor 1988-92), Am. Assn. Petroleum Geologists, Soc. Econ. Geologists, Brown U. Club, Sigma Xi. E-mail: rona@imcs.rutgers.edu. Office: Rutgers U Inst Marine & Coastal Scis 71 Dudley Rd New Brunswick NJ 08901-8521

RÓNAI, FERENC, forest engineer, educator; b. Nagyigmánd, Hungary, Sept. 21, 1926; s. Ferenc and Veronika (Nagy) R.; m. Magdolna Kulacsy, Dec. 8, 1951; children: R. Ferenc, R. Eniko. Forest Engr., U. Forestry and Wood Tech., Sopron, Hungary, 1950, D Tech., 1961; Candidate Sci., Sci. Acad., Budapest, Hungary, 1968, DSc, 1990; D (hon.), U. Sopron, 1999. Cert. engr. Forest engr. Praxis, Kaposvár, Hungary, 1950-52; asst. Dept. Transport, Sopron, 1952-62; docent Dept. Mechanics, Sopron, 1962-73; prof. dept. mechanics U. Sopron, 1973-96, prof. emeritus, 1996—, head dept. mechanics, 1962-91, vice-rector, 1981-87, dean faculty wood tech., 1972-78. Author: Fatartószerkezetek, 1982 (level prize 1982). Recipient Eötvös Loránd prize, State Sec. for Agr., Budapest, 1991. Mem. Qualification of Sci. Acad. (mem. com. 1981—), Mechanics of Sci. Acad. (mem. com. 1991-96), Com. PhD of Univ., 1990—. Roman Catholic. Fax: (36) (99) 311-103. E-mail: mmechadm@efe.hu. Office: U Sopron, Bajcsy zs u 4, H-9400 Sopron Hungary

RÓNAI, ZOLTÁN, allergist, immunologist, researcher; b. Kaposvár, Hungary, Aug. 22, 1964; s. Zoltán and Márta (Györfi) R.; m. Anikó Pesti, Apr. 15, 1989; 1 child, Peter. MD, Univ. Med. Sch., Pecs, Hungary, 1988. Med. diplomate; specialist in pediats., allergology and clin. immunology. Resident Dept. Pathology, Kaposvár, 1988-89; resident Dept. Pediat. Pulmonology, Mosdós, Hungary, 1989-93, pediatrician, 1993-96, allergologist, 1996; pvt. practice leader Pvt. Health Care Ctr., Pecs, 1996—. Translator: Childhood Asthma, 1992; founder, editor-in-chief Amega; contbr. articles to profl. jours. Lt. Hungarian Mil. Health Care, 1989-90. Fellow U. Toronto, Ont., Can., 1987, U. Innsbruck, Austria, 1986. Mem. Hungarian Assn. Asthma Patients (adv. bd. 1994, v.p. 1995—), Hungarian Assn. Asthma Nurses, Hungarian Med. Chamber, Hungarian Respiratory Soc. (Best Young Pulmonologist 1993, 94, 95). Roman Catholic. Avocations: skiing, playing chess. Office: Asthma & Allergy Ctr, Citrom u # 10, H-7621 Pécs Hungary

RONALD, ADHAMI, financial expert and planner, advisor; b. Hadadine, Lebanon, Nov. 5, 1971; arrived in France, 1987; Walid Adhami and Madeleine Awwad. Diplôme d'Etudes Prop. Complubles et Fin, Conservitoire Nat. Arts Metiers, France, 1993; Diploma d'Etudes Comptables et Fin., Inst. Nat. Tech. Econ. et Comptabilitie, Paris, 1994; Diplôme d'Etudes Sup. Comptables et fin. (MBA acctg. fin.), INTEL, Paris, 1996. Cert. fin. expert. Francais comptabe Lab. Prothodent, Paris, 1991-93; comptabe Hotel Aletti Palace, Vichy, France, 1993-97; fin. advisor Hotel Aletti Palace, Vichy, 1993-97; chef comptable Axione SA, Paris, 1993-97, Gestion-Investissement-Tourrisme, Paris, 1993-97; assoc. consulting Soc. d'Expertise Financiere et CompiableSEFCO, Paris, 1997-98; fin. planner Euro-Trade and Svcs. Corp., Miami, Fla., 1998—. Active Rassemblement Pour la Republique Paris, 1995. Mem. Holiday In. Avocations: windsurfing, water sports, cigars. Home: 25 Rue Pierre Nicole, 75005 Paris France Office: SEFCO Sarl, 76-78 Ave Champs Elysees, 75008 Paris France

RONALD, THOMAS IAIN, retired financial services executive; b. Glasgow, Scotland, Feb. 16, 1933; s. Newton Armitage and Elizabeth (Crawford) R.; m. Cristina de Yturralde, Aug. 30, 1962; children: Christopher, Isobel. B in Law, Glasgow U., 1956; MBA, Harvard U., 1963. Chartered acct. Pres., CEO Zellers, Inc., Montreal, Que., Can., 1982-85; exec. v.p., dir. Hudson's Bay Co., Toronto, Ont., Can., 1985-87; pres. Mgmt. Svcs. Group CIBC, Toronto, 1987-88, Adminstrv. Bank CIBC, 1988-92; vice chmn. CIBC, Toronto, 1992-95 (ret.), ret., 1995; dir. The North West Co. Inc., Loblaw Co. Ltd., Leon's Furniture Ltd., Holt Renfrew & Co., Can. Life Assurance Co., PC Fin. Trust; chmn. Transalta Power Ltd. Dir. Toronto Symphony Found., Sunnybrook Found. Lt. Royal Navy, 1956-58. Fellow Inst. Chartered Accts. Ont.; mem. Inst. Chartered Accts. Scotland. Presbyterian. Club: Granite (Toronto). Avocations: music, squash, tennis. Office: 1 Chedington Pl Ste 6C, Toronto, ON Canada M4N 3R4

RONALDO (RONALDO LUIZ NAZÁRIO DA LIMA), professional soccer player; b. Bento Ribeiro, Brazil, Sept. 22. Forward Social Ramos Club, 1990-91, São Cristóvão Club, Brazil, 1991-93, Cruzeiro Football Club, Belo Horizonte, Brazil, 1993-94, PSV Eindhoven Football Club, Holland, 1994-96, FC Barcelona Football Club, Spain, 1996-97, Inter Milan Football Club, Italy, 1997—; with Brazilian Nat. Team; winner World Cup, 1994, runner-up, 1998; runner-up Copa Am., 1995; winner Dutch Cup (with PSV Eindhoven), 1996, Cup Winner's Cup (with Barcelona), 1997, Spanish Cup (with Barcelona), 1997, Copa Am. (with Brazil), 1997;. Named Dutch Topscorer, 1995, Player of Yr., FIFA, 1996, 97, Spanish Topscorer, 1997; recipient Bronze medal Olympic Games, 1996, Golden Ball, Europe, 1997. Office: FC Inter Milan, Via Durini 24, 20122 Milan Italy also: care Nike Inc Soccer Div 1 SW Bowerman Dr Beaverton OR 97005-0979*

RONAN, WILLIAM JOHN, management consultant; b. Buffalo, Nov. 8, 1912; s. William and Charlotte (Ramp) R.; m. Elena Vinadé, May 29, 1939; children: Monica, Diana Quasha. AB, Syracuse U., 1934; PhD, NYU, 1940, LLD, 1969; certificate, Geneva Sch. Internat. Studies, 1933. Mus. asst. Buffalo Mus. Sci., 1928-30; with Niagara-Hudson Power Co., 1931; transfer dept. N.Y.C.R.R., 1932; Penfield fellow internat. law, diplomacy and belles lettres, 1935, Univ. fellow, 1936; editor Fed. Bank Service, Prentice-Hall, Inc., 1937; instr. govt. N.Y. U., 1938, exec. sec. grad. div. for tng. in pub. services, 1938, asst. dir., 1940, asst. prof. govt., dir. grad. div. for tng. pub. service, 1940, assoc. prof. govt., 1946-47, prof., 1947, dean, grad. sch. pub. adminstrn. and social service, 1953-58; Cons. N.Y.C. Civil Service Commn., 1938; prin. rev. officer, negotiations officer U.S. Civil Service Commn., 1942; prin. div. asst. U.S. Dept. State, 1943; cons. Dept. State, 1948, Dept. Def., 1954; dir. studies N.Y. State Coordination Commn., 1951-58; project mgr. N.Y. U.-U. Ankara project, 1954-59; cons. ICA, 1955, N.Y. State Welfare Conf.; adminstrv. co-dir. Albany Grad. Program in Pub. Adminstrn.; 1st dep. city adminstr. N.Y.C., 1956-57; exec. dir. N.Y. State Temporary Commn. Constl. Conv., 1956-58; sec. to Gov. N.Y., 1959-66; chmn. interdept. com. traffic safety, commr. Port Authority N.Y. and N.J., 1967-90, vice chmn., 1972-74, chmn., 1974-77; with UTDC Corp., West Palm Beach, Fla.; trustee Crosslands Savs. Bank; chmn. bd. L.I. R.R., 1966-74; chmn. Tri-State Transp. Com., N.Y., N.J., Conn., 1961-67; chmn. interstate com. New Haven R.R., 1960-63; chmn. N.Y. Com. on L.I. R.R., 1964-65; mem. N.Y. State Commn. Internstate Coop., 1961, N.Y. State Com. Fgn. Ofcl. Visitors, 1961, N.Y. State Coordination Commn., 1960; mem. N.Y. Civil Svc. Commn., Temporary State Commn. on Constl. Conv., 1966-67; chmn. N.Y. State Met. Commuter Transp. Authority, 1965-68, Met. Transp. Authority, 1968-74, Tri-Borough Bridge and Tunnel Authority, 1968-74, N.Y.C. Transit Authority, 1968-74, Manhattan and Bronx Surface Transit

Operating Authority, 1968-74; chmn. bd., pres. 3d Century Corp., 1974-94; mem. Commn. Critical Choices for Am., 1973—, acting chmn., 1975—; mem. urban transp. adv. com. U.S. Dept. Transp.; sr. adviser Rockefeller family, 1974-80; pres. Nelson Rockefeller Collection, Inc., 1977-80; trustee Power Authority of State of N.Y., 1974-77; cons. to trustees Penn Ctrl. Transp. Co.; vice chmn. bd. CCX, Inc.; sec.-treas. Sarabam Corp. N.V.; chmn., dir. UTDC (U.S.A.) Inc., 1987-88; chmn. UTDC Corp., 1989-94, Transit Svcs. Corp., 1989-94; cons. Herzog Transit Svcs., 1995-99, Dime Savs. Bank, Metal Powder Products Inc., Flomet Inc., 1997—, Internat. Mining and Metals Inc., Quadrant Mgmt. Inc., 1990—, Ohio Highspeed Rail Authority, 1991-93; chmn. N.Y. and N.J. Inland Rail Rate Com.; dir. Nat. Mgmt. Coun., 1951. Author: Money Power of States in International Law, 1940, The Board of Regents and the Commissioner, 1948, Our War Economy, 1943, (with others), articles in profl. jours.; adviser: Jour. Inst. Socio-Econ. Studies. Mem. U.S. FOA, Am. Public Health Assn.; staff relations officer N.Y.C. Bd. Edn.; Mem. Nat. Conf. Social Work, Nat. Conf. on Met. Areas, Citizens Com. on Corrections, Council on Social Work Edn.; bd. dirs. World Trade Club; adv. bd. World Trade Inst.; mem. 42d St. Redevel. Corp., chmn., 1980-94; mem. Assn. for a Better N.Y.; bd. advisers Inst. for Socioecon. Studies, 1977—; dir. Nat. Health Council, 1980-86; dep. dir. policy Nelson Rockefeller campaign for Republican presdl. nomination, 1964; mem. N.Y. State Gov.'s Com. on Shoreham Nuclear Plant, 1983-85, Nassau County Indsl. Devel. Authority, 1982-90, U.S. Dept. Transp. Com. on Washington and Capital Dist. Airports, 1985-86; bd. dirs. Ctr. Study Presidency, 1986-90, Alcoholism Council of N.Y., 1986—; trustee N.Y. Coll. Osteopathic Medicine, 1986-91; v.p. Am. Cancer Soc., Palm Beach. Served as lt. USNR, 1943-46. Mem. ASPA, NEA, Am. Polit. Sci. Assn., Am. Acad. Pub. Adminstrn., Civil Svc. Assembly of U.S. and Can., Internat. Assn. Met. Rsch. and Devel., Nat. Mcpl. League, Mcpl. Pers. Soc., Citizens Union of N.Y., Nat. Civil Svc. League, Am. Acad. Polit. and Social Sci., L.I. Assn. Commerce and Industry (dir.), Internat. Inst. Adminstrv. Scis., Am. Fgn. Law Assn., Internat. Union Pub. Transport (mgmt. com., v.p.), Am. Pub. Transit Assn. (chmn. 1974-76), Nat. Def. Transp. Assn. (v.p. for Mass transit), English Speaking Union (bd. dirs. Palm Beach), Met. Opera Club, Maidstone Club, Devon Yacht Club, Knickerbocker Club, Hemisphere Club, Harvard Club, Creek Club, Wings Club, Traffic Club, Univ. Club, Am. Club Riviera, Beach Club (Palm Beach), Everglades Club. Home: 525 S Flagler Dr West Palm Beach FL 33401-5922 also: Villa La Pointe Du Cap, Ave de La Corniche, 06230 Saint Jean Cap Ferrat France

RONC, MICHAEL JOSEPH, company executive; b. Chambery, France, June 23, 1944; came to U.S., 1987; s. Albert and Renée (Jeantet) R.; m. Marie Rose E. Lux, Mar. 25, 1967; children: Valerie, Joelle, Cecile. License es Sciences, U. Toulouse, France, 1967; diplome d'ingénieur, Institut Genie Chimique, Toulouse, 1968; PhD in Chem. Engring., McGill U., 1973; grad. advanced mgmt. program, Harvard U., 1987. Head R & D project Elf-France, Solaize, 1973-79; head energy mgmt. R & D div. Societe Nationale Elf Aquitaine, Paris, 1979-83, dir. innovation, 1984-87; dir. rsch. NEU, Lille, France, 1982-84; pres., dir. gen. Inovelf, Paris, 1985-92; pres., CEO Elf Techs., Inc., Stamford, Conn., 1984-92; dir. new bus. devel. Europe, refining and mktg. Elf Aquitaine, Paris, 1991-93, dir. devel. Germany, 1993-94, dir. devel. & mktg., refining Germany, 1994-97; v.p. Internat. Bus. Devel., Elf Antarga, 1997-2000; mng. dir. Mittel Deutsche Erdöl Rafinerie; chmn. Elene, Paris, 1983-86, Societe Oric, Paris, 1984-87; chmn. Elf Gas So. Africa, Elf Gas El Salvador, Elf Gas Honduras, Venado Gas (Argentina). Contbr. articles to profl. publs. Chevalier de l'Ordre du Mérite National. Address: Elf Antargaz, 3 place de Saverne, 92901 Paris La Defense Paris FRANCE

RONCARATI, CHRISTINA, publisher; b. Sao Paulo, Brazil, June 3, 1955; d. Nelson and Nilza (Corrêa) R.; m. Avelino Luz Pessoa Souza; children: Nelson, Pedro. Grad., Oswaldo Cruz Coll., Sao Paulo, 1976. With Editora Manuais Tecnicos de Seguros, Sao Paulo, 1989-91, dir., 1992-93, pres., 1993—. Mem. Soc. Brasileira de Ciências do Seguro (dir. 1994-95), Inst. Brasileiro dos Executivos de Financas, Acad. Nat. Suguros & Previdencia, Inst. Brasileiro de Direito do Seguro. Avocations: music, reading, travel. Office: Editora Manuais Tecnicos Seguros, Rua Dr Neto de Araujo 212, 04111000 São Paulo 01244, Brazil

RONCHI, ALFREDO MICHELE, engineering educator; b. Milan, Italy, Jan. 31, 1956; s. Enrico and Francesca (D'Amato) R.; m. Marisa Maria Paganini, Sept. 12, 1979 (div. 1988); 1 child, Andrea Enrico; m. Ileana Elisabetta Baronio; 1 child, Francesca Alba Beatrice. BEE, Politecnico, Milano, 1981, D, 1981. Rschr. Politecnico, Milan, 1983; lectr. in CAD, algorythms and data structure Multimedia publishing Resp. Virtual Group, Milan, 1989—; resp. ICT for Cultural Heritage Unit, gen. sec. European Commn. MEDICI Framework; coord. EC TEN Telecom project MOSAIC, UNESCO OCCAM, resp. EMWAC program, resp. and coord. Euro Sino Ednl. Network project De Architectura Project, Italy; cons. IBM, Lugano, 1982-83, Thorn/GE Lighting, Vicenza, 1989-94, GE Medical Systems, Milano, 1990-93, BolognaFiere, 1994-95, expert evaluator, European Commn.; mem. UNESCO OCCAm. Author: Introduction to Computer Aided Architectural Design, 1990; contbr. articles to profl. jours. Mem. Ente Nazionale Unificazione Italiana, 1993-94. Mem. Assn. Computer Machinery, Spl. Interest Group Computer Graphics of Assn. Computer Machinery, IES, Eurographics. Avocations: sailing, cross country skiing, photography, music. Office: Politecnico di Milano, Via Bonardi 15, 20133 Milan MI, Italy

RONCHI, AMÉRICO ROBERTO, education educator; b. Maria Grande, Entre Rios, Argentina, Dec. 10, 1939; s. José Américo and Florinda (Saccani) R.; m. Maria Magdalena Bier, Sept. 9, 1940; 1 child, Mauro Roberto. Lic., prof. in scis. of edn., U. Nacional del Litoral, Paraná, Argentina, 1967. Instr. U. Litoral, Paraná, 1968-75; chief tech. edn. Paraná, 1970-84; cons. Edn. Tech. B/D, La Paz, Bolivia, 1981-82; dir. Coun. Edn., Paraná, 1982-83; head distance edn. divsn. Luján, Argentina, 1984-86; dir. media ctr. Oro Verde, Argentina, 1987—; prof. distance edn. U. Cuyo, Mendoza, Argentina, 1990-94; with U. Entre Rios, Argentina, 1975—, acad. sec. Coll. Engring., 1988-89, head distance edn. Faculty Humanities, 1990—; edn. coord. audiovisual divsn. A.E. Editors. Co-author: Módulos de Fisica (I), 1995, (II), 1996; editor Guide Tecnologia Educativa, 1975-80. Recipient Cybernetics and Soc. award U. Nat. Córdoba, 1970. Mem. Argentine Assn. Distance Edn. (pres. 1992-98). Avocations: photography, video. E-mail: rronchi@gamma.com.ar. Home: Las Golondrinas 354, Oro Verde, ER, 3100 Entre Rios Argentina Office: Univ Entre Rios Fac Engring, Ruta 11, Km 10, Oro Verde, 3100 Entre Rios Argentina

RONCHINO, PEDRO LUIS, bishop; b. Rosario, Santa Fe, Argentina, June 14, 1928; s. Antonio Luis and Rosa (Scapini) R. Student, Inst. José Clemente Villada y Cabrera, Córdoba; PhD, U. Pontifica Salesiana, Turin, Italy. Dir. Inst. Ntra. Sra. del Rosario, Colonia Vignaud, 1960-65, Inst. José Clemente Villada y Cabrera, 1966-67; dir. philos. studies U. Pontifica Salesiana, Rome, 1968-70; vicar Inspectoria San fco. Solano, Córdoba, 1971-75; vicar gen. Obispado, Comodoro Rivadavia, 1975-92, obispo diocesano, 1993—. Author: Rene Le Senne. Fisonomia de su Pensamiento, 1959. Office: Obispado CC 30, Rivadavia 750 Comodoro, 9000 Rivadavia Chubut, Argentina*

RONDE, JOHN HERMAN, author, translator; b. Lonneker, Overyssel, The Netherlands, July 12, 1929; s. Johannes Maria Ronde and Lamberdina Hulsschreuder. BA in Econs., Columbia U., 1973, MA in Social Studies, 1974, MPhil in Geography, 1983. Substitute tchr. N.Y.C. H.S., 1985-86, 92-93; asst. geographer U.S. Census Bur., N.Y.C., 1988-91. Author: Migration, Social Infrastructure and Urban Development in Selected German Cities, and Housing Policy and Supply in the Federal German Republic (1970-85), 1996, Urban Development and Migration in Kiel with Reference to City Center and Fringe Area Development Initiatives, 1971-84, Philosophical Interpretations of Modern Science, The Developing New World View of Man and His Activities for The Fulfillment of His Needs, An Introduction To and A Discussion of A Model of The Location of Man and His Activities, or: Geography as a Theory of Man. Mem. N.Y. Acad. Scis., Fgn. Policy Assn. (assoc.). Democrat. Avocations: collecting and playing music, collecting books on history and philosophy of science. Home: 75 E 3d St New York NY 10003-9015

RONDEAU, DORIS JEAN, entrepreneur, consultant; b. Winston-Salem, N.C., Nov. 25, 1941; d. John Delbert and Eldora Virginia (Klutz) Robinson; m. Robert Breen Corrente, Sept. 4, 1965 (div. 1970); m. Wilfrid Dolor Rondeau, June 3, 1972. Student Syracuse U., 1959-62, Fullerton Jr. Coll., 1974-75; BA in Philosophy, Calif. State U.-Fullerton, 1976, postgrad., 1976-80. Ordained to ministry The Spirit of Divine Love, 1974. Trust real estate clk. Security First Nat. Bank, Riverside, Calif., 1965-68; entertainer Talent, Inc., Hollywood, Calif., 1969-72; co-founder, dir. Spirit of Divine Love, Huntington Beach, Calif., 1974—; pub., co-founder Passing Through, Inc., Huntington Beach, 1983—; instr. Learning Activity, Anaheim, Calif., 1984—; chmn. bd., prin. D.J. Rondeau, Entrepreneur, Inc., Huntington Beach, 1984—; co-founder, dir. Spiritual Positive Attitude, Inc., Moon In Pisces, Inc., Vibrations By Rondeau, Inc., Divine Consciousness, Expressed, Inc., Huntington Beach, Doris Wilfrid Rondeau, Inc., Huntington Beach, Calif. Author, editor: A Short Introduction To The Spirit of Divine Love, 1984; writer, producer, dir. performer spiritual vignettes for NBS Radio Network, KWVE-FM, 1982-84; author: Spiritual Meditations to Uplift the Soul, 1988. Served with USAF, 1963-65. Recipient Pop Vocalist First Place award USAF Talent Show, 1964, Sigma chpt. Epsilon Delta Chi, 1985, others. Mem. Hamel Bus. Grads., Smithsonian Assocs., Am. Mgmt. Assn., Nat. Assn. Female Execs. Fax: (714) 841-3286. Avocations: long-distance running, body fitness, arts and crafts, snorkeling, musical composition.

RONELL, STANLEY L., sales executive; b. Cracow, Poland, June 7, 1934; came to U.S., 1951; s. Edward and Pauline Ronell; m. Eileen Ronell, Mar. 25, 1961; children: Paul, Lisa. BME, CCNY, 1958, MBA, 1962. Internat. sales mgr. S&S Corrugated Paper Machinery Co., Bklyn., 1958-85; dir. sales Interfic, Inc., Dallas, 1992—; pvt. practice sales/mktg. cons. Marktech Internat., Port Washington, N.Y., 1985-91. Reporter Port Washington Sentinel, 1996—. Pres. Brotherhood, Cmty. Synagogue, Port Washington, 1982-84, bd. dirs., 1982-86; pres. CCNY chpt. ASME, 1956-58. Avocations: bicycling, tennis, woodworking, classical music, Civil War history. E-mail: sronell@aol.com. Home: 6 Dock Ln Port Washington NY 11050-1732

RONELLENFISCH, MICHAEL HERMANN, law educator; b. Mannheim, Germany, Sept. 21, 1945; s. Gunther Ferdinand and Gertrud Elisabeth (Moll) R.; m. Renate Rensch, Nov. 20, 1947; 1 child, Lisa. LLM, U. Heidelberg, 1970, U. Heidelberg, Germany, 1972. Bar: Germany 1970. Prof. U. Bonn, Germany, 1982-88, U. Berlin, Germany, 1988-92; prof. U. Tuebingen, Germany, 1992—, dean faculty of law, 1996-98. Author: Assessorexamen, 1977, 10th edit., 1999, Atomrechtl Genehmigungsuerfahren, 1982, Srasse und Energienuersortung, 1996. Adviser Senate of Berlin, 1990—, City of Mannheim, Germany, German Rwy. Bd., 1995. Mem. Internat. Nuclear Law Assn. Avocation: rock and roll. Office: U Tuerbingen, Wilhelmstr 7, 72074 Tuebingen Germany

RONEY, JOHN HARVEY, lawyer, consultant; b. L.A., June 12, 1932; s. Harvey and Mildred Puckett (Cargill) R.; m. Joan Ruth Allen, Dec. 27, 1954; children: Pam Roney Peterson, J. Harvey, Karen Louise Hanke, Cynthia Allen Harmon. Student, Pomona Coll., 1950-51; BA, Occidental Coll., 1954; LLB, UCLA, 1959. Bar: Calif. 1960, D.C. 1976. Assoc. O'Melveny & Myers, L.A., 1959-67, ptnr., 1967-94, of counsel, 1994—; gen. counsel Pa. Co., 1970-78, Baldwin United Corp., 1983-84; dir. Coldwell Banker & Co., 1969-81, Brentwood Savs. & Loan Assn., 1968-80; spl. advisor Rehab. of Mut. Benefit Life Ins. Co., 1991-94; cons., advisor to Rehab. of Confederation Life Ins. Co., 1994-95; mem. policy adv. bd. Calif. Ins. Commn., 1991-95. Served to 1st lt. USMCR, 1954-56. Mem. ABA, Calif. Bar Assn. (ins. law com. 1991-95, chmn. 1993-94), L.A. County Bar Assn., D.C. Bar Assn., N.Y. Coun. Fgn. Rels., Pacific Coun. on Internat. Policy, Conf. Ins. Counsel, Calif. Club, Sky Club (N.Y.), Gainey Ranch Golf Club (Scottsdale), L.A. Country Club. Republican. Home: The Strand Hermosa Beach CA 90254 Office: 400 S Hope St Ste 1600 Los Angeles CA 90071-2801

RONG, YIMING, manufacturing engineering educator; b. Harbin, China, Sept. 3, 1958; came to U.S., 1985; s. Yanmo Rong and Kunyi Shen; m. Jiaoshi Dong, June 12, 1986; 1 child, Zhixin (Blake). BS in Mech. Engring., Harbin U. Sci. & Tech., 1981; MS in Mfg. Engring., Tsinghua U., Beijing, 1984; MS in Indsl. Engring., U. Wis., 1987; PhD in Mech. Engring., U. Ky., 1989. Instr. Tsinghua U., 1984-85; postdoctoral rsch. assoc. U. Ky., Lexington, 1990; asst. prof. mfg. systems So. Ill. U., Carbondale, 1990-96, assoc. prof. mfg. sys., 1996-98; assoc. prof. mfg. engr. Worcester (Mass.) Poly. Inst., 1998—; faculty rsch. assoc. Wright-Patterson AFB, Dayton, Ohio, 1995; vis. assoc. prof. U. Ill., Urbana, 1996; adj. prof. Huazhong U. Sci. & Tech., Wuhan, China, 1998—, Harbin U. Sci. & Tech., 1996—. Author: Computer-aided Fixture Design, 1999; editor, organizer Procs. Symposium Mfg. Engring./Computer-aided Tooling, 1995, Procs. Symposium Mfg. Engring./Concurrent Design of Product & Mfg. Processes, 1998, Procs. Symposium Mfg. Engring./Decision Machining in Design and Mfg., 1999. Pres. Chinese Friendship Assn., Lexington, 1988-89. Recipient Rsch. Initiation award NSF, 1993-96; rsch. grantee USAF Office Scientific Rsch., 1995-96, NSF, 1997-98, 98—, Pratt & Whitney Rsch. Ctr., East Hartford, Conn., 1996-97, Caterpillar, Peoria, Ill., 1998—, Ford, Dearborn, Mich., 1999—, Delphi Automotive Sys., 1999—, numerous others. Mem. ASME, Soc. Mfg. Engrs., Am. Soc. Engring. Edn., Chinese Mech. Engring. Soc. Achievements include development of first comprehensive computer-automated modular and dedicated fixture design techniques and systems, development of tolerance analysis method for manufacturing processes with multiple setups, development of an automated setup and fixture planning technique and system, development of fixture design analysis and verification technique, and exploration of new area of flexible fixturing with phase-change materials. Fax: 508-831-5680. E-mail: rong@wpi.edu. Office: Worcester Poly Inst Mech Engring Dept 100 Institute Rd Worcester MA 01609-2247

RONISH, ROBERT RAY, retired civil service administrator; b. Cheyenne, Wyo., Sept. 10, 1934; s. Theodore Roosevelt and Beulah Irene (Logan) R.; m. Lois Irene Dallas, Sept. 5, 1954; children: Renee Ellen, Shane Theodore, Clayton Robert. BA, U. Wyo., 1957; MA, U. No. Colo., 1974. Hdqr. commdt., co. comdr. USASTRATCOM, Ft. Huachuca, Ariz., 1967-69; subsystems mgr. SAFCA, Ft. Huachuca, 1969-73; chief morale and welfare, mgmt. analyst USACC, Ft. Huachuca, 1973-82; resource mgmt. chief USACOMISA, Ft. Huachuca, 1982-84; support div. chief USAISCA, Ft. Huachuca, 1984-86; records mgmt. chief USAISCA, 1986-89. Contbr. articles to profl. jours. Pres. Mountain Ranch Estates Home Owners Assn., Bisbee, Ariz.,1984-86. Capt. U. S. Army, 1958-68, col. Res. ret. Recipient Grand Cross of Color Internat. Order of Rainbow for Girls, Tucson, 1975. Mem. Res. Officers Assn. (pres. 1985-87), VFW. Republican. Baptist. Avocations: weight lifting, Bible study, teaching, swimming. Home: 5629 Spruce Ave Castle Rock CO 80104-2184

RÖNNBERG, STEN O., social work educator emeritus, consultant; b. Kalix, Sweden, Apr. 7, 1931; s. Oskar E. and Justina L. (Wennstrom) R.; m. AnnaLisa Olofsson, 1959 (div. 1966); m. Brit E. Rönnback, Sept. 2, 1972 (div. 2000); children: Ida, Oskar. Psychologist, Uppsala U., 1965; PhD, Stockholm U., 1978. Cert. psychologist, 1966. Asst. in instrn. Uppsala U., 1961-64; lectr. Preschool Tchr. Coll., Solna, Sweden, 1967-68; lectr., dir. dept. edn. Stockholm U., 1969-70, rsch. assoc. dept. edn., 1971-78, sr. lectr. dept. edn., 1978-89, prof. dept. social work, 1989-96. Author: Introduction to Behavior Therapy, 1969, Guidelines for Behavior Analysis, 1978; editor-in-chief Scandinavian Jour. Behaviour Therapy, 1993-96; contbr. articles to profl. jours. Cpl. Swedish Mil., 1951-52. Mem. Swedish Behaviour Therapy Assn. (pres. 1971), Swedish Soc. for Alcohol and Drug Rschrs. (pres. 1985-88). Avocations: gardening, research, literature, hiking. Home: Jarvstigen 12, S-17071 Solna Sweden

RØNNE, MOGENS, retired cytogeneticist, researcher; b. Rønne, Denmark, Nov. 6, 1941; s. Harry and Manna (Rønne) Pedersen; m. Elisabeth Andersen; Feb. 26, 1965; children: Annette My, Mark. BS in Biology, U. Copenhagen, 1968, MS in Biology, 1971, PhD in Genetics, 1973, DSc, 1998. Postdoctoral Copenhagen U., 1973-75; asst. prof. Odense (Denmark) U., 1975-77, sr. rsch. scientist, 1977-85, assoc. prof., 1985-91; sci. cons. Odense Rsch. Park, 1992-93; sr. rsch. scientist Aarhus (Denmark) U., 1993-94; sabbatical, 1994-95; environ. mgr. Nordisk Tekstil A/S, 1996-2000, retired, 2000; vis. prof. Notre Dame U., South Bend, Ind., 1985, Purdue U., Lafayette, Ind., 1987, Hokkaido (Japan) U., 1988, M.D. Anderson Cancer Ctr., Houston, 1989; mem. various chromosome standardization coms. Mem. editl. bd. In Vivo, 1989—; referee Hereditas, 1990—, Anticancer Rsch., 1987—, Genet. Sel. Evol., 1988—, Cytogenetic Cell Genetics, 1997, Biotechnology, 1998; contbr. over 100 articles to profl. jours. Served to sgt. Denmark Infantry, 1960-62. Recipient Rsch. grant Odense U., 1977-83, grant Danish Med. Rsch. Coun., 1983-85, grant Danish Cancer Soc., 1986-91, grant Sasakava Found., Japan, 1988. Mem. Danish Soc. Med. Genetics. Home: Skovvej 20, DK-5462 Morud Denmark

RÖNNESTAD, MICHAEL HELGE, psychology educator, psychologist; b. Syvde, Norway, Aug. 21, 1944. Laererpröva, Sagene Laererskole, Oslo, 1967; MA, No. Ariz. U., 1969; PhD, U. Mo., 1973. Lic. psychologist; specialist in clin. psychology. Psychologist State Ctr. for Child and Adolescent Psychiatry, 1977-78; rsch. fellow Ctr. for Rsch. in Clin. Psychology, Oslo, 1981-84; from asst. prof. to assoc. prof. U. Oslo, 1973-92, prof., 1993—; co-coord. Collaborative Rsch. Network/SPR, Chgo., 1997—; sr. cons. Karolinska Inst., Stockholm, 1995—; Ida Beam prof. U. Iowa, 1994. Author: (with T. Skovholt) The Evolving Professional Self, 1995, (with P. A. Stolanowski) Profesjonell Utvikling i Psykososialt Arbeid, 1997, (with S. Reichelt) Psykoterapiveiledning, 1999, (with A. Holte, G.H. Nielsen) Psykoterapi og Veiledning, 2000; contbr. articles to profl. jours. Recipient Rsch. award Assn. Counselor Edn. Supr., 1994. Mem. APA, Norwegian Psychol. Assn. (Prof. Bjorn Christiansen's Meml. award 1991), Norwegian Soc. Hypnosis. Office: U Oslo Dept Psychology, Box 1039 Blindern, Oslo Norway

RØNNINGEN, KJERSTI SKJOLD, physician; b. Bergen, Norway, Jan. 3, 1959; parents Gunnar and Astrid (Skjold) R.; m. Trond Sundby Halstensen, June 30, 1984 (div. 2000); children: Victoria Skjold, Christian Fredrik Skjold, Carl Henrik Skjold, Rasmus Oscar Skjold. MD, U. Oslo, 1984, PhD, 1991. Authorized Norwegian med. doctor. Resident gen. practice Haugenstua Health Ctr., Oslo, 1986; rsch. fellow Norwegian Rsch. Coun., Inst. Transplantation Immunology, Oslo, 1987-90, postdoctoral rsch. fellow, 1991-92, 94, sr. scientist, head diabetes rsch. group, 1994-96; project leader, sr. physician Nat. Inst. Pub. Health, Oslo, 1996—; sr. physician, sr. scientist, project leader Norwegian Bio-Bank, Type 1 Diabetes Study; vis. scientist U. Alta., Edmonton, Can., 1993; mem. adv. coun. Eurodiab Tiger, 1994—; mem. adv. group European Nicotinamide Diabetes Interrvention Trial, 1994—. Contbr. articles to profl. jours., chpts. to books. Recipient gold medal for best disease study Internat. Histocompatibility Workshop and Conf., Yokohama, Japan, 1991, Young Investigators award Scandinavian Soc. for Study of Diabetes, Geilo, 1992. Mem. Norwegian Diabetes Assn. (mem. med. coun. 1995—, Herta Bjerkedals award 1993). Home: Jegervn 42, N-0777 Oslo Norway Office: Nat Inst Pub Health, PO Box 4404 Torshov, N-0403 Oslo Norway

RONOLD, KNUT OLAV, geotechnical engineer, researcher; b. Oslo, Jan. 14, 1956; s. Olav Anker and Turid (Nygård) R. MS, Norwegian Inst. Tech., Trondheim, 1978, Stanford (Calif.) U., 1991; PhD, Stanford (Calif.) U., 1993. Rsch. engr. Det Norske Veritas, Høvik, 1979-84, sr. rsch. engr., 1984-90; prin. rsch. engr. Det Norske Veritas, Copenhagen, 1993-94, 99—, Høvik, 1994—; Fulbright fellow Stanford U., 1990-91, rsch. fellow, 1991-93. Contbr. articles to profl. jours.; editl. bd. Jour. Applied Ocean Rsch. Fulbright fellow U.S. Ednl. Found. in Norway, 1990, Rsch. fellow Royal Norwegian Coun. for Sci. and Indsl. Rsch., 1991, Det Norske Veritas, 1991. Mem. Norwegian Soc. Chartered Engrs. Avocations: genealogical research, publication of family histories. Home: Skogstuveien 45, N-1363 Høvik Norway Office: Det Norske Veritas, PO Box 300 Veritasveien 1, N-1322 Høvik Norway

RONSE, CHRISTIAN, information science educator; b. Ankara, Turkey, June 9, 1954; s. Léon Ronse and Monique Debels; m. Leloir, May 11, 1985; children: Raphael, Henri. Lic., Free U. Brussels, 1976; MSc, Oxford (Eng.) U., 1977, DPhil, 1979; habilitation, Bordeaux (France) U., 1992. Prof. info. sci. Strasbourg (France) U., 1992—, head computer sci. dept., 1994-96; program com. Internat. Symposium Math. Morphology, 1998. Author: Feedback Shift Registers, 1984; co-author: (with P. Devijver) Connected Components in Binary Images, 1984; contbr. articles to profl. jours. Mem. Force Ouvrière, Strasbourg, 1992—. Avocation: study of Charles Fourier. Office: U Strasbourg Dept Informat, Blvd Sébastien Brant, F-67400 Illkirch France

RONTO, MIKLÓS, mathematician, educator, researcher; b. Beregszász, Bereg, Hungary, Mar. 31, 1943; s. Jozsef and Julianna (Kiss) R.; m. Valentyina Kozlova, June 8, 1968; 1 child, Andrei. Diploma in math., Uzhgorod (Ukraine) U., 1964; Candidate of Sci., Ukrainian Acad. Sci., Kiev, 1971, D Physics-Math. Sci., 1986, D Math. Sci., 1994. Rschr. Inst. Cybernetics, Kiev, 1965-71; sr. rschr. Inst. Modelling, Kiev, 1971-88; leading rschr. Inst. Math., Kiev, 1988-92; prof. Kiev U., 1987-90; prof. U. Miskolc, Hungary, 1992—, head dept., 1997—. Co-author: Numerical-Analytic Methods of Investigating Periodic Solutions, 1979, Numerical-Analytic Methods in the Theory of Boundary Value Problems, 1992 (in Russian); contbr. articles to profl. jours.; editor-in-chief Publ. U. Miskolc-Math., 1995—. Recipient State award Pres. of Ukraine, 1996; named Széchenyi prof. Hungarian Ministry of Edn., 1997. Office: U Miskolc, Egyetemváros, 3515 Miskolc Borsod, Hungary

RONTOYANNIS, GEORGE PANAYOTE, sports medicine, researcher; b. Tsoukalades, Greece, Jan. 15, 1946; s. Panayote George and Alice Asterios (Papatoliou) R.; m. Aspasia Nikolas Vezyryannis, Jul. 29, 1976; children: Panayote, Victoria. B in medicine, Athens U., Athens, 1969; diploma in sports medicine, Rome U., 1976; diploma in cardiology, Athens U., 1982, D, 1978. Dir. Sanitary Ctr., Ithaca, Greece, 1974; vis. rsch. assoc. Pa. State U., 1979-80; tutor Ergospir Lab Laikon Gen. Hosp., Athens, 1980-84; asst. prof. sports medicine phys. edn. dept. U. Thessaloniki, Greece, 1984-89; head of sports medicine dept. Hellenic Sports Rsch. Inst., Athens, 1989—; prof. sports medicine, phys. edn. dept. U. Thessalia, Tricala, 1997—; sec. of sci. com. 25th World Cong. Sport Medicine, Athens, 1991-94, Mediterranean Sports Medicine Congress, 1990-91, treas. 2nd Internat. Nutrition Fitness Conf., 1990-92, mem. orgn. com. 3rd Internat. Congress Physiology & Exercise Biochemistry, 1984-86, 5th Internat. Congress Sport Biomechanics, 1985-87, 3rd European Seminar Sport in Elderly, 1984-85, 3rd Internat. Congress Sports Medicine Applied in Football, 1983-85; prof. sports medicine dept. physical edn. U. Thessalia, Tricala, Greece, 1997—. Author: Current Topics in Sport Medicine, 1989; contbr. articles to profl. jours. Recipient grant for specialization in sports medicine Sec. of Sport & Youth, 1972-73. Mem. Hellenic Sports Med. Assn. (spl. sec. 1994—), Hellenic Diabetologic Assn., N.Y. Acad. Scis., Grand Lodge of Greece, Filothei Track-Field Club of Athens, Bridge Club of Scientists. Avocations: road cycling, tournament bridge, nat. level athlete of decathlon. Home: 5 Faneromenis St, Cholargos 15561 Greece Office: Hellenic Sports Rsch Inst, 37 Kifissias Ave, Athens 15123, Greece

ROOF, MICHAEL KITCHING, demographer, researcher; b. Lexington County, S.C., Dec. 18, 1921; s. Michael Lowman and Eunice Ernestine (Kitching) R.; m. July 24, 1949 (div. Sept. 1970); children: Michael Kitching Jr., Melanie June Roof Brown, Brian Eugene; m. Kristina Marietta Medrano, Dec. 18, 1976. Student, Am. U., 1954-57; BA, George Washington U., 1956; postgrad., U.S. Dept. Agr. Grad. Sch., 1979-83. Manpower splst. Office of Prodn. Mgmt. and War Prodn. Bd., Washington, 1941-46; labor editor Bur. Nat. Affairs, Inc., Washington, 1947-48; demographer rsch. divsn. ref. svc. The Libr. of Congress, Washington, 1949-64; sr. demographer fgn. manpower rsch. office U.S. Bur. Census, Suitland, Md., 1958-59; expert demographic cons. fgn. manpower rsch. office U.S. Bur. Census, Suitland, 1960-61; demographer, statistician Ctr. Internat. Studies U.S. Bur. Census, Washington, 1977-89; ret., 1989; cons. to the demography as UN adviser various orgns., So. Calif., 1965-76; cons. Author: (mongraph) Angelenos on the Move: 1960-74, 1975, (mongraph) Detailed Statistics on the Population of Israel, 1950-84, with Projections to 2010, 1984, (monograph) Jordan Population and Manpower Estimates and Projections: 1979 to 2010, 1987; co-author: (monograph) Detailed Statistics on the Population of Turkey, 1950-82, with Projections to 2000, 1982, (monograph) Palestinian Population: 1950-84, 1985, The Roof (Rueff, Ruff) Family and Kinfolk of Central South Carolina: 1748-1999, 1999; contbr. numerous articles to profl. jours., chpts. to books. Mem. Population Assn. Am., Internat. Union Scientific Study of Population. Democrat. Lutheran. Avocations: geneaolgy, aerobic activities, swimming, softball. Home: 306 E Custis Ave Alexandria VA 22301-1202

ROOKE, STEPHEN, bureau executive; b. London, Aug. 3, 1944; s. Monarch and Kate (Langton) R.; m. Lynne Rooke, Dec. 25, 1967; 1 child, Kathleen. BA, Open U., Eng., 1978. Mng. dir. Stephen Friendship Bur., Witham, Essex, Eng., 1981—. With English mil., 1962-64. Anglican. Avocations: weightlifting, horticulture, hi-fi model aeronautical engineering, photography. Home and Office: Stephen Friendship Bur, 19 Stourton Rd, Witham CM8 2EZ, England

ROOMI, RIAD, cosmetic surgeon, physician; b. Najaf, Iraq, Mar. 21, 1951; arrived in U.K., 1978, naturalized Brit. citizen, 1984; s. Kadhim Jawad and Raheema (Sha'aban) R.; m. Yasmine Madani, June 23, 1983; children: Hasan, Husain. MB, ChB, Coll. of Medicine, Baghdad, Iraq, 1977. House officer Nat. Health Svc., Medway, U.K., 1979-80; sr. house officer Nat. Health Svc., Leicester, U.K., 1980-82, rschr., 1982-83; acting registrar in plastic surgery Nat. Health Svc., Rochdale, U.K., 1983-84; pvt. practice cosmetic surgery London, 1989—; dir. The New You Clinic for Lasear and Cosmetic Surgery, London, 1984—. Inventor ready-stitch. Recipient Small Firm Merit award for rsch. and tech. Dept. of Trade and Industry, 1988, 1st prize Toshiba Yr. of Invention, Toshiba and Design Coun., 1989. Fellow Internat. Coll. Surgeons, Inst. Patentees and Inventors (Richardson Gold medal 1989); mem. Brit. Med. Assn., Am. Acad. of Cosmetic Surgery, Internat. Soc. Aesthetic Surgery. Avocations: inventing, writing. Fax: 44-171-381-8180. Office: The New You Clinic, 591 Fulham Rd, London SW6 5UA, England

ROONEY, MARIA DEWING, photographer; b. N.Y.C., July 25; d. Madeleine L'Engle (Camp) Franklin; m. John Bryon Rooney, Jan. 21, 1984; children: Bryson, Alexander. BFA, Phila. Coll. Art. Tchr. photography Bishop Bright Grammar Sch., Leamington Spa, Eng., Mid-Warwickshire Sch. of Further Edn., Leamington Spa, 1976-80; photographer, owner The Studios, Shipston-on-Stour, Eng., 1977-80; photographer Gary Studios & Comini Studios, Dallas, 1980-83; owner, photographer studio, Essex, Conn., 1990—. Exhbns. include Warwick (Eng.) Gallery, Derby (Eng.) Coll. Art Gallery, Bath (Eng.) Place Cmty. Ctr., Midland Group Gallery, Nottingham, Eng., Wimbledon Sch. Art, London, Warwich U. Arts Ctr., Birmingham, Eng., Essex Art Assn., 1998, R.J. Julla, Madison, Conn., 1998, State Capitol Hartford, Conn., 1999; photographer (book) Anytime Prayers, 1994, (book) Mothers and Daughters, 1997, (book) Mothers and Sons, 1999 (with Madeleine L. Engle); photographs published in Co-Optic Publs., London, 1976-80; prodr. series greeting cards with personal photography. Mem. Child and Family Svcs. Mem. AAUW, Essex Art Assn. (Photography award 1997). Avocation: sailing, writing. Home and Office: PO Box 658 Old Lyme CT 06371-0658

ROOP, JOSEPH MCLEOD, economist; b. Montgomery, Ala., Sept. 29, 1941; s. Joseph Ezra and Mae Elizabeth (McLeod) R.; m. Betty Jane Reed, Sept. 4, 1965; 1 dau., Elizabeth Rachael. BS, Ctrl. Mo. State U., Warrensburg, 1963; PhD, Wash. State U., Pullman, 1973. Economist Econ. Rsch. Svc., U.S. Dept. Agr., Washington, 1975-79; sr. economist Evans Econs., Inc., Washington, 1979-81; staff scientist Battelle Pacific N.W. Nat. Lab., Richland, Wash., 1981—; adj. prof. dept. econs. Wash. State U., 1999—; with Internat. Energy Agy., Paris, 1990-91. Contbr. tech. articles to profl. jours. Served with U.S. Army, 1966-68. Dept. Agr. Coop. State Rsch. Svc. rsch. grantee, 1971-73. Mem. Am. Econ. Assn., Econometric Soc., Internat. Assn. Energy Econs., Am. Statis. Assn. Home: 715 S Taft St Kennewick WA 99336-9587 Office: PO Box 999 MSIN K8-17 Richland WA 99352-0999

ROOS, ANNA MARIE, history educator; b. Denver, Mar. 5, 1967; d. Gordon J. and Norma Ann Roos; m. Steven Craig Eisenberg, May 29, 1992. BA, U. Colo., Boulder, 1987; M in Humanities, U. Colo., Denver, 1991; PhD in History, U. Colo., Boulder, 1997. Asst. dir., vis. asst. prof. Bellavance honors program Salisbury (Md.) State U., 1996-99; asst. prof. history U. Minn., Duluth, Minn., 1999—; Rhodes campus rep., Marshall scholarship campus rep. Salisbury State U., 1997-99; active Nat. Collegiate Honors Coun. Author: Luminaries of the Natural World: Perceptions of the Sun and Moon in England, 2000. Bd. dirs., chair grant com. ExceL Sci. Mus. for Children, Salisbury, 1998-99; mezzo soprano Colo. Symphony Orch. Choir, Denver, 1990-91. Newberry Libr. Consortium grantee, Chgo., 1996. Mem. Am. Hist. Assn., Western Assn. for Women Historians, Mensa, Phi Eta Sigma (Salisbury State U. chpt.). Democrat. Avocations: piano, choral singing, drawing and painting. E-mail: aroos@d.umn.edu.

ROOS, FRANK EVERT, lawyer; b. Schiedam, Netherlands, Mar. 30, 1957; s. Frans and helena (Bruinse) R.; m. Johanna Wesselina Hesselink; Apr. 6, 1991; children: Leontien M.H., Michiel W.F., Evianne F. Law Degree, R.U. Utrecht, 1982, Notarial Law Degree, 1982. Lawyer Houthoff/Van Heycop ten Ham, Rotterdam, 1984-87; lawyer, notarial candidate Nauta Dutilh, Rotterdam, 1987-91; lawyer, notarial candidate Trenité Van Doorne, Rotterdam, 1992-93, civil-law notary, 1993—; dir., vice chair Jonge Balie, Rotterdam, 1985-87. Bd. dirs., sec. S.V. Victoria, Rotterdam, 1988-94; bd. dirs. J.C. Rotterdam-Haven, 1988-90. Capt. Netherlands Army, 1982-84. Salzburg Seminar fellow, 1990. Mem. KNB, Vereniging Handeslrecht. Avocations: golf, archeology, national trust, sailing. Home: Charlois Vijverlaan 30, 3062 HK Rotterdam The Netherlands Office: Trenité Van Doorne, Weena 666, 3012 CN Rotterdam The Netherlands

ROOSENDAAL, GORIS, physician, researcher; b. Westbroek, Utrecht, The Netherlands, Feb. 18, 1956; s. Goris Roosendaal and Adriana VandenBroek; m. Leonie Louise Gabeler; 1 child, Maarten Ronald. MD, U. Utrecht, 1986, PhD, 1998. Physician Gen. Hosp., Woerden, The Netherlands, 1986-88; rschr. Lab. of Virology Nat. Inst. Pub. Health and Environ. Protection, Bilthoven, The Netherlands, 1988-89; physician Van Creveld Clinic U. Med. Ctr. Utrecht, 1989—, rschr. lab. dept. rheumatology and clin. immunology, 1992—. Author, editor: Blood Induced Cartilage Damage in Hemophilia, 1998; author: Recent Advances in Rehabilitation in Haemophilia, Sirot 99; contbr. articles to profl. jours. 1st lt. Dutch Army, 1977-78. Mem. Dutch Soc. Physicians Treating Hemophilia Patients, World Fedn. Haemophilia (mem. musculoskeletal com. 1991). Avocations: athletics, marathons, sailing, gardening. Office: U Med Ctr Utrecht, Heidelberglaan 100, 3584 CX Utrecht The Netherlands

ROOT, LAURA LEE, personal care industry executive; b. Oxnard, Calif., Mar. 8, 1953; d. Robert James Dodge and Barbara Louise (Forest) Mickle; m. Thomas Mayfield Root, Aug. 8, 1989; children: Virginia Anne, Robert William, Sara Michelle. Grad., Internat. Esthetic/Cosmetology, Vancouver, 1997. Diplomate Internat. Com. Aesthetics. Paralegal Hughes Hubbard & Reed, L.A., 1987-89; owner, esthetician Face to Face, McMinnville, Oreg., 1994-96, Body & Soul Esthetic Retreat, McMinnville, 1997-98; owner Body & Soul Esthetic Retreat, Phoenix, 1999—. Author: (book) The Complete Guide to Microdermabrasion: Treatment, Technique & Technology, 1999, (booklet) Professional Salon Services, 1995, (leaflet) Hip & Cellulite Reduction, 1997; contbr. articles to profl. jours.; editl. bd. PCI Jour. Mem. Aestheticians Internat. Assn., Am. Acad. Med. Esthetics, Am. Soc. Esthetic Medicine, Am. Acad. Anti-Aging Medicine, Soc. Permanent Cosmetic Profls. Republican. Avocations: Russian Classic ballet, private pilot, motorcycles. Office: Body & Soul Esthetic Retreat 8535 E Hartford Dr Ste 100 Scottsdale AZ 85255-5443

ROOT, TAMMY MARIE, zoo keeper; b. Jan. 21, 1971. B of Wildlife Sci., Purdue U., 1993. Animal keeper Ft. Wayne (Ind.) Zoo, 1988-93, Topeka Zoo, 1994-97, Indpls. Zoo, 1997—. Author: Animals From A to Z, 1997, Edzoocational Insights for Teachers, 1999. Mem. Am. assn. Zoo Keepers. Office: 416 Walnut St Greenfield IN 46140-2048

ROOTES, CHRISTOPHER ALAN, political science educator; b. Blackpool, Lancashire, Eng., Jan. 12, 1948; s. Peter James Rootes and Jean Margaret Robertson. BA with honors, U. Queensland, Australia, 1970; postgrad., Yale U., 1970-71; BPhil, Oxford (Eng.) U., 1973. Lectr. sociology U. NSW, Sydney, Australia, 1975; lectr. polit. sci. U. Melbourne, Australia, 1986-88; lectr. sociology U. Kant at Canterbury, Eng., 1973-86; dir. Ctr. for Study Socßial and Polit. Movements U. Kent at Canterbury, Eng., 1992—, reader polit. sociology and environ. politics, 1999—; chmn. European Consortium for Polit. Rsch. Green Politics Standing Group, 1997—. Editor Environ. Polotics. Mem. Polit. Studies Assn., Am. Polit. Sci. Assn.

ROOTS, KEITH DYLAND, academic administrator; b. Richmond, Va., Oct. 2, 1965; s. Samuel and Willia Tina (Perkins) R.; m. Keena Lea Ose, July 11, 1998. BA in Govt., U. Va., 1986; MEd, U. Tex., 1991. Dist. exec. Stonewall Jackson Area Coun. Boy Scouts Am., Wanesboro, Va., 1986-89; asst. to pres. Longwood Coll., Farmville, Va., 1991-95; ast. to provost U. Va., Charlottesville. Recipient Eagle Scout award Boy Scouts Am., 1980; Am. Assn. State Colls. & Univs. fellow, 1993. Mem. Am. Assn. Higher Edn., Rotary, Alpha Phi Omega (disting. svc. key 1997, 98). Avocations: sports, coin collecting, Scouting memorabilia. Office: U Va PO Box 400308 Charlottesville VA 22904-4308

ROOZEN, JACQUES PETRUS, food chemist, educator; b. Oud-Gastel, Netherlands, Feb. 28, 1943; s. Adrianus M. Roozen and Hendrica A. De Nys; m. Joanna M.A. Verweij, Nov. 25, 1967; children: Arjan, Hans. DR, Agr. U., Netherlands, 1972. Cert. food chemist. Lectr. Agr. U., Wageningen, Netherlands, 1971-77, 1977-85, sr. lectr., 1986—; Fulbright fellow Cornell U., Geneva, N.Y., 1977; sabbatical USDA, SRRC, New Orleans, 1985-86, U. Calif., Davis, 1992-93; Erasmus coord. European Cultural Found., Brussels, 1987—, Tempus coord., 1992-94. Editor: Food Chemistry jour., 1992—. Mem. Koninklijke Nederlandse Chemische Vereniging, Nederlandse Vereniging Voeding Levensmiddelen-Technologie, Inst. Food Tech. Avocations: tennis, golf. Office: Wageningen U, Bomenweg 2, Wageningen 6703 HD, The Netherlands

ROPAC, DARKO IVAN, epidemiologist, educator; b. Varaždin, Zagorje, Croatia, Jan. 22, 1947; s. Ivan Petar and Ljerka Milan (Zuber) R.; m. Alenka Zlata Dolenčič, July 3, 1970; children: Hrvoje, Martina. MD, Sch. Medicine, Zagreb, Croatia, 1970; MS, U. Zagreb, 1976, epidemiologist, 1978, DSc, 1984; prof., Sch. Medicine, Zagreb, 1995, Sch. Medicine, Split, Croatia, 1997. Cert. specialist in epidemiology. Med. dr. primary care Osijek, Croatia, 1971-75; epidemiologist mil. hosp. Zagreb, 1975-91; chief med. corps hdqs. Osijek, Croatia, 1991-92; chief med. hdqs. Republic of Croatia, Zagreb, 1992-93; epidemiologist Clin. Hosp., Zagreb, 1993-95; dir. Naval Med. Inst., Split, 1995—. Editor: (book) Lyme Borreliosis in Yugoslavia, 1989; co-author: (book) Military Epidemiology, 1989; mem. editl. bd.: Acta Med. Croatica, 1996. Brigadier Naval Med. Inst., Split, 1995. Decorated Spomenica Domovinskag rata, 1990-92, 1994, Orden Hrvatskog trolista, 1996, Orden Hrvatskog pletera, 1996. Mem. Acad. Med. Sci., Croatian, Croatian Soc. Anthropology, Croatian Soc. Epidemiology, Croatian Soc. Infection, Croatian Soc. Naval Medicine. Office: Naval Med Inst, Šoltanska 1, 21000 Split Croatia

ROPER, HARRY JOSEPH, lawyer; b. Bridgeport, Conn., Apr. 15, 1940; s. Harold Joseph and Madeline (Sullivan) R.; m. Helen L. Marlborough, Oct. 1, 1976; children—Kendall, Timothy, Melissa, Elizabeth. B.E.E., Rensselaer Poly. Inst., 1962; LL.B., NYU, 1966. Bar: Ill. 1966, U.S. Dist. Ct. (no. dist.) Ill. 1966, U.S. Ct. Appeals (7th cir.) 1966, U.S. Ct. Appeals (fed. cir.) 1982. Assoc., Neuman, Williams, Anderson & Olson, Chgo., 1966-70, ptnr., 1970-90, Roper & Quigg, 1990—. Mem. ABA (chmn. intellectual properties com. litigation sect. 1982-85), Chgo. Bar Assn., Bar Assn. 7th Fed. Cir., Patent Law Assn. Chgo., Am. Patent Law Assn., Chgo. Council Lawyers. Club: Union League (Chgo.). Home: 611 W Fullerton Pky Chicago IL 60614-2613 Office: Roper & Quigg 200 S Michigan Ave Chicago IL 60604-2402

ROPER, MICHAEL, retired governmental official; b. Halifax, Yorkshire, Eng., Aug. 19, 1932; s. Jack and Mona (Nettleton) R.; m. Joan Barbara Earnshaw, Sept. 7, 1957; children: Karen Lesley Phillips, Nigel David. BA, Manchester (Eng.) U., 1956, MA, 1958; DLitt, Bradford (Eng.) U., 1991. Registered archivist. Asst. keeper Pub. Record Office, London, 1959-70, prin. asst. keeper, 1970-82, records adminstrn. officer, 1982-85, dep. keeper pub. records, 1985-88, keeper pub. records, 1988-92; ret., 1992; part-time lectr. Univ. Coll., London, 1972-87, hon. rsch. fellow, 1988; external examiner Nat. U. Dublin, Ireland, 1982-86, Liverpool U., 1986-89; cons. UNESCO; disting. vis. U. B.C., Vancouver, 1994; vis. prof. Surugadai (Japan) U., 1999. Author: Yorkshire Fines 1300-1314, 1965, Records of the Foreign Office, 1969, Guidelines on the Preservation of Microforms, 1986, Planning an Archives Preservation Service, 1989, Records of the War Office, 1998; contbr. articles on profl. and tech. aspects of records and archives mgmt. to profl. publs. Fellow Royal Hist. Soc. (hon. treas. 1974-80, v.p. 1989-93); mem. Soc. Archivists (chmn. 1985-86, pres. 1989-92, v.p. 1992—), Internat. Coun. on Archives (sec. gen. 1988-92). Avocations: reading, music, gardening. Home: 157 B Fairfax Rd, Teddington England TW11 9BU

ROPERS-HUILMAN, BECKY, educator; b. Boscobel, Wis., Sept. 30, 1970; d. Raymond Gale and Rosa Marie Ropers; m. Brian David Ropers-Huilman, Aug. 21, 1992. BA, U. Wis., Eau Claire, 1991; MS, U. Wis., Madison, 1993, PhD, 1996. Asst. prof. La. State U., Baton Rouge, 1996—. Author: Feminist Teaching in Theory and Practice, 1998. Mem. Am. Ednl. Rsch. Assn., Assn. for Study of Higher Edn., Nat. Women's Studies Assn. Avocations: reading, singing, health and fitness activities. Home: 2313 Ebony Ave Baton Rouge LA 70808-2152 Office: La State U 121C Peabody Hl Baton Rouge LA 70803-0001

ROQUE, FATIMA MOURA, economist, educator; b. Luanda, Angola, Feb. 28, 1951; arrived in Portugal, 1985; d. Ezequiel Augusto and Engrácia Augusta Freitas; m. Horacio da Silva Roque, Nov. 11, 1967 (div.); children: Teresa, Cristina. BA in Econs., U. Luanda, 1975; MS in Econometrics, U. South Africa, Johannesburg, 1982; PhD in Internat. Econs., U. of Witwatersrand, South Africa, 1985. Tchr. math. and history Luanda, 1969-71, jr. lectr., 1973-75, dir. internal trade, 1974-75; economist Bank of Lisbon, South Africa, 1978-80; lectr. U. Witwatersrand, Johannesburg, 1981-84; prof. econs. U. Lisbon, 1985-93; dir. Ctr. for African Studies, 1997, prof. econ. devel. of Africa, 2000—. Author: Economia de Angola, 1991, Angola: Em Nome da Esperanca, 1993, Building the Future in Angola, 1997, Building Peace in Angola: A Political and Economic Vision, 2000; contbr. articles to profl. jours., newspapers, and mags. Active Polit. Commn. UNITA, 1989-96, Angolan Parliament, 1992-97, Conflict Resolution Com. in Angola, 1992; founder-mem. Forum for Peace in Angola; active Pro Dignitate Found., 1988-93, 95-96, numerous instns. related to human rights and democracy in Africa; coord. campaign to reduce poverty in Angola, 1995-96. Roman Catholic. Avocations: reading, travel, movies, safaris. Home: Av Conde de Barcelona 4, 2765 Estoril Portugal Office: U Lusofona, Faculdade de Economia, Campo Grande Portugal

RORABACK, ERIK SHERMAN, English educator; b. Seattle, June 24, 1966; s. Steven Roger and Teresa Lynn (Jensen) R. BA, Pomona Coll., 1989; postgrad., U. Western Australia, Perth, 1993, Oxford/École Normale Supérieur Exchange, Paris, 1995; PhD, U. Oxford, Eng., 1997. Asst. prof. U.S. lit./lit. theory Charles U., Prague, Czech Republic, 1997—. Grantee Ctr. Rsch. James Joyce, Paris, 1999; Rotary Found. Grad. Ambassadorial scholar Rotary Internat., 1993; recipient Overseas Rsch. Student award Govt. U.K., 1992, 94, 95. Mem. MLA, Internat. James Joyce Found., Henry James Soc. Avocations: tennis, classical music, jazz music, world architecture, world cinema. Office: Charles U English & Am Stud, Jana Palacha 2, 116 38 Prague 1, Czech Republic

RORIE, NANCY KATHERYN, elementary and secondary school educator; b. Union County, N.C., May 31, 1940; d. Carl Van and Mary Mildred (Pressley) R. BA, Woman's Coll. U. N.C., 1962; MEd, U. N.C., 1967; EdD, Duke U., 1977. Cert. curriculum and instrnl. specialist, social studies tchr. for middle and secondary levels, English tchr., N.C. Social studies and English tchr. Guilford County Schs., Greensboro, N.C., 1962-67; social studies instr. Lees-McRae Coll., Banner Elk, N.C., 1967-76; social studies tchr. Monroe (N.C.) City Schs., 1977-93; curriculum instrnl. specialist, social studies tchr. Union County Schs., Monroe, N.C., 1993—. Mem. Prof. Educators N.C., Phi Alpha Theta, Kappa Delta Pi. Democrat. Baptist. Home: 2401 Old Pageland Monroe Rd Monroe NC 28112-8163

RORKE, WILLIAM BUCKLAND (PADDY RORKE), accountant, consultant; b. Witbank, Transvaal, South Africa, Feb. 22, 1915; s. Claude Oriel and Kathleen Elizabeth Josephine (Röcher) R.; m. Gertrude Ethel Dreyer, Jan. 25, 1945 (div. 1970); 1 child, Shane O.; m. Yvonne Mary Collinnette, Aug. 25, 1970. BCom, U. Pretoria, South Africa, 1933. Chartered acct. Articled clk. Price Waterhouse Peat, Pretoria, 1932-37; sec. Beckett Murray (Pty) Ltd., Pretoria, 1937-38; pvt. practice as acct. and auditor, 1938—; lectr. U. Pretoria, 1938-65; chmn. Trek Airways, Johannesburg, South Africa, 1953-83; dir. various cos. Writer accountancy course for Univ. Correspondence Coll., 1939. Mem. Pub. Accts Bd. Avocations: sports (cricket, hockey, rugby), playing bowls. Office: WB Rorke, 534 Jacqueline Dr, Garsfontein Pretoria South AFrica

RÖRSCH, ARTHUR, biotechnology executive; b. Rotterdam, The Netherlands, Feb. 2, 1933. Grad. in Chem. Engring., U. Tech. Delft, The Netherlands, 1957; PhD cum laude, Leiden U., The Netherlands, 1962. Scientist TNO Med. Biol. Lab., Rijswijk, The Netherlands, 1957-73; assoc. prof. molecular genetics, med. faculty Leiden U., 1966-96, prof. biochemistry, faculty sci., 1973-80; bd. mgmt. Netherlands Orgn. for Applied Sci. Rsch., TNO, 1980-94, v.p., 1990; pres. Netherlands Agr. Rsch. Coun., 1994-99; bd. dirs. biotech. Gist-Brocades, Delft, The Netherlands, State Mus. on History of Sci. Cecaelia Found.; vis. prof. Sishuan Normal U., China, 1995. Assoc. editor Mutation Rsch. jour., 1964-80; contbr. over 70 articles to profl. jours. Decorated Knight, Order of Dutch Lion, 1994. Office: Leiden U, Rapenburg 73 PO Box 9516, 2300 RA Leiden The Netherlands

ROSA, BOBBIE CAROL, music educator; b. Moline, Ill., July 27, 1971; d. Adrian Wayne and Carol Ann (Morgan) R. MusB, Palm Beach Atlantic Coll., 1995; MA in Music, Fla. Atlantic U., 2000. Instr. piano private, home, studio, Hobe Sound, Fla., 1989-95, The Stuart Sch. Music, Stuart, Fla., 1995—; pianist, choir accompanist First Baptist Ch. Tequesta, Fla., 1994-96; dir. mus. Northlake Ch. of Nazarene, Palm Beach Gardens, Fla., 1996—. Vol. counselor Care Net Pregnancy Svcs., Port St. Lucie, Fla., 1996—. Mem. Am. Coll. Musicians, Music Tchrs. Nat. Assn., Fla. State Mus. Tchrs. Assn., Palm Beach County Music Tchrs. Assn., Fla. Fedn. Music Clubs. Republican. Office: The Stuart Sch Music 1608 S Kanner Hwy Stuart FL 34994-7152

ROSA, JOAO WILLY CORRCA, physicist; b. Belem, Brazil, June 26, 1959; s. Wilson Pagel and Maria Lourdes (Correa) R.; m. Luciana Ansoneli Naves, Feb. 14, 1998; 1 child, Isabella. BS in geology, Universidade de Brasilia, Brazil, 1981; PhD in geophysics, MIT, Cambridge, Mass., 1986. Prof. geophysics U. de Brasilia, Brasilia, Brazil, 1987—. E-mail: jwilly@unb.br. Fax: (305561) 368-4361. Home: SHIN QI 15, Conjunto 2 Casa 10, 71535220 Brasilia Brazil Office: Instituto de Geociencias, Universidade de Brasilia, 70910900 Brasilia Brazil

ROSA, NICOLA, ophthalmologist; b. Napoli, Italy, Nov. 16, 1957; s. Donato and Angela (Brosca) R.; m. Silvana Canonico, Dec. 16, 1991; children: Donato, Gianmarco. MD, U. Naples, 1983, Ophthalmologist, 1987. Med. diplomate. Resident in ophthalmology U. Naples, 1983-87; fellow ophthalmic echography U. Iowa, Iowa City, 1987-88; assoc. prof. U. Naples, 1999—. Author: Color Doppler Gvascolarizzazione Strutture Orbitarie, 1995; editor: Procs. XV Siduo Congress, 1996; contbr. articles to profl. jours. Recipient awards Soc. Italiana Oftalmologia. Mem. Am. Acad. Ophthalmology, Soc. Internat. pro Diagnostica Ultrasonica in Ophthalmologia (sec.), Soc. Italian and Ergoftalmologia e Traumatologia Ocular (bd. dirs.). Avocations: tennis, guitar. Home: Via Vincenzo Padula 2, 80123 Napoli Italy

ROSADO, ALVARO JAIME, university administrator; b. Santa Elena, Belize, Feb. 19, 1947; s. Cresencio and Anita (McField) R.; m. Dorla Elaine Humphreys, Nov. 15, 1980; children: Albert, Lysette, Alya, Ian, Ariel. Student, U. Southampton, Eng., 1973; BEd, U. Calgary, Alta., Can., 1978; MEd, BostonColl., 1983, PhD, 1990. Prin. elem. sch., Belize, 1964-66; tchr. Wesley Coll., Belize, 1967-68, Lynam Agrl. Coll., Belize, 1968-69, EPY Jr. H.S., Belize, 1969-78; lectr. Belize Tchrs. Coll., 1978-90, asst. dean, 1983-86; v.p. Univ. Coll. of Belize, 1990—, acting pres., 1990-91; adj. prof. U. North Fla., 1996-98; rsch. fellow Fulbright Found., 1994-95. Recipient awards for acad. excellence Belize Tchrs. Coll., 1968, Boston Coll., 1989. Home: 967 Mayflower Garden, Mile 3 No Hwy, Belize City Belize Office: Univ Coll of Belize, West Landivar, Belize City Belize

ROSADO, RODOLFO JOSE, psychologist, educator; b. N.Y.C., Jan. 9, 1959; s. Rodolfo Jose and Maria (Gonzalez) R.; m. Ruth Laura Morrison, June 11, 1982; children: Emily Hope, Adam Philip. BS in Psychology, Fordham U., Bronx, N.Y., 1979, MA in Clin. Psychology, 1986, PhD in Clin. Psychology, 1992. Diplomate in clin. psychology and child psychology Am. Bd. Psychol. Specialties; lic. psychologist, N.Y., Conn. Psychology tng. fellow N.Y. Med. Coll., Valhalla, 1979-81; clin. psychology intern Hall-Brooke Hosp., Westport, Conn., 1982-83; therapist Child Guidance Ctr., Bridgeport, Conn., 1983-85, office coord., 1985-90, program dir., 1990-93; asst. prof. Fairfield (Conn.) U., 1993-97, program dir. coll. access, 1995-96; pvt. practice specializing in psychol. evaluations Norwalk, Conn., 1993—; Initial Rev. Group profl. reviewer USPHS, Rockville, Md., 1990-95; regional adv. com. Dept. Children & Families, Bridgeport, 1995—; oversight collaborative Bridgeport Futures, 1994-95; faculty co-sponsor SALSA Hispanic Students Assn., Fairfield U., 1995-97; bd. dirs., clin. cons. R.E.A.C.H. Program, Riverside, Conn. Author, moderator TV show Conversation in Edn., 1994; co-author proposal Empowerment Zone Grant, 1994; author proposal Comprehensive Child & Adolescent Svc., 1993. Mem. Youth Svc. Bur., City of Bridgeport, 1991-93; family preservation initiative Conn. Dept. Children & Families, Bridgeport, 1995—; coach Little League Baseball. Recipient N.Y. Regents scholarship, 1975-79, scholarship Fordham U., Bronx, 1975-79, Appreciation award for collaborative support State of Conn. Dept. Children & Families, 1995, Outstanding Contbns. to Latino Cmty. Recognition award Puerto Rican/Latino employees of Human Resources Adminstrn. and Affiliated Agys., Dept. Homeless Svcs. and Adminstrn. for Children's Svcs., 1999. Mem. APA, Am. Coll. Forensic Examiners, Hispanic Assn. Mental Health and Allied Professions (exec. com., treas. 1988-92), Conn. Coalition for Children of Alcoholics (steering com. 1986-87), Sigma Xi. Avocations: skiing, racketball, hiking. Office: 5 Elmcrest Ter Norwalk CT 06850-3938

ROSALES, CARLOS, immunology educator, researcher; b. Mexico City, Oct. 8, 1957; s. Carlos Rosales-Salinas and Clara Ledezma. BS in Chemistry, U. Mex., Mexico City, 1981, MSc in Chemistry, 1984; PhD in Immunology, Washington U., St. Louis, 1993. Rsch. asst. Wistar Inst., Phila., 1984-87; postdoctoral fellow Washington U., 1993, U. N.C., Chapel Hill, 1993-95; instr. chemistry U. Mex., 1980-84, assoc. prof. immunology, 1995—; cons. Cryopharma, Mexico City, 1998. Contbr. articles to sci. jours., including Jour. Biol. Chemistry, Jour. Leukocyte Biology, Cancer Rsch. Scholar Rotary Found., Phila., 1984; Spencer T. and Ann W. Oliva fellow Washington U., 1991; rsch. grantee CONACyT, Mexico City, 1996. 010Mem. Am. Soc. for Cell Biology, Mexican Immunology Soc. Avocations: photography, swimming, scuba diving, cooking. Office: UNAM Inst Inv Biomémicas, Apto Postal 70228 Univ City, 04510 Mexico City Mexico

ROSALES, SUZANNE MARIE, hospital coordinator; b. Merced, Calif., July 23, 1946; d. Walter Marshall and Ellen Marie (Earl) Potter; children: Anita Carol, Michelle Suzanne. AA, City Coll., San Francisco, 1966. Diplomate Am. Coll. Utilization Review Physicians. Utilization review coord. San Francisco Gen. Hosp., 1967-74; mgr. utilization review/discharge planning UCLA Hosp. and Clinics, 1974-79; nurse III Hawaii State Hosp., Kaneohe, 1979-80; review coord. Pacific Profl. Std. Review Orgn., Honolulu, 1980-81; coord. admission and utilization reviewq The Rehab. Hosp. of the Pacific, Honolulu, 1981-85; coord. Pacific Med. Referral Project, Honolulu, 1985-87; dir. profl. svcs. The Queen's Healthcare Plan, Honolulu, 1987-88; utilization mgmt. coord. Vista Psychiat. Physician Assocs., San Diego, 1989; admission coord. utilization review San Francisco Gen. Hosp., 1989-91, quality improvement coordinator, 1991—; cons. Am. Med. Records Assn. Contbr. articles to profl. jours. Mem. Nat. Assn. Utilization Review Profls. Home: 138 Alta Vista Way Daly City CA 94014-1402 Office: San Francisco Gen Hosp 1001 Potrero Ave San Francisco CA 94110-3594

ROSALSKY, BARBARA ELLEN, artist, home health aide; b. N.Y.C., Nov. 16, 1948; d. Ellis M. Rosalsky and Claire (Schwartz) Rosalsky Shapiro; m. Dennis Robinson. BA, SUNY, Plattsburgh, 1970. Sales girl Cambridge (Mass.) Artist mag., 1970-71; artist Pillar of Fire mag., Zarephath, N.J., 1977; home health aide CMR, Bound Brook, N.J., 1978—; designer New Brunswick (N.J.) Tomorrow, 1980-87; art therapist Middlesex Hosp., New Brunswick, 1981-83. Solo exhibitions include The Bird and Me, 1980; group exhibitions include Other Artists Other Art, 1983. Mem. Cultural Arts Commn., Piscataway, N.J., 1993—. SUNY Plattsburgh scholar, 1970.

Mem. Women's Caucus Art, Marriott Swim Club. Democrat. Avocations: piano, swimming, dancing, hiking, print making. Home: 114 Woodland Rd Piscataway NJ 08854-4222

ROSANDER, REINE, physicist, science educator; b. Vetlanda, Sweden, Dec. 1, 1940; s. Stig Reinhold and Margit (Johansson) R.; m. Anita Rosemarie Gustafsson, Nov. 16, 1963; children: Marie Charlotte, Per Marcus. MSc, Lund (Sweden) U., 1963, PhD, 1972; cert. proficiency English, U. Cambridge, Eng., 1990. Tchg. diploma Sch. Edn., Sweden, 1965. Asst. lectr. The Coll. for Boys, Helsingborg, Sweden, 1963-66; rsch. asst. dept. physics Lund U., 1966-73; lectr. Joenkoeping (Sweden) U. Sch. Health Scis., 1973-82, assoc. prof., 1982—, dir. studies dept. sci., 1992—, dep. dean dept. sci., 1997—, v.p. appointments bd., 1999—; tech. cons. Gambro Med., Lund, 1973. Author: (with H. Alfvén) Energy to Death?, 1973, (with Alfvén) Atomic Power, 1974, From Growth to Balance, 1977; chief editor R&D Report Series, 1986-99; mem. editl. bd. Environment and Future, 1979-86; contbr. articles to profl. jours. Assoc. mem. Coun. of Europe Working Party on Space Biophysics, 1973-83; mem. rsch. adv. bd. The Swedish Parliament, 1984-91; head Radiation Protection Unit, Civilian Def. Office, 1986—. Rsch. grantee USAF, U.S. Office Naval Rsch., Swedish Atomic Rsch. Coun., Swedish Natural Sci. Rsch. Coun. Mem. European Phys. Soc., Swedish Phys. Soc., Swedish Assn. Univ. Tchrs., N.Y. Acad. Sci. Lutheran. Avocations: hunting, fishing, jazz music. E-mail: rosander@sverige.nu. Home: Vapplingstigen 143, SE-56241 Taberg Sweden Office: U Coll Health Sci, PO Box 1038, 551 11 Joenkoeping Sweden

ROSANDIĆ, MARIJA, gastroenterologist, researcher; b. Zagreb, Croatia, Oct. 5, 1943; d. Ivan and Katica (Sorić) R.; m. Vladimir Pilaš; 1 child, Ivan. MD, U. Zagreb, 1967, MSc, 1984, PhD, 1988. Cert. specialist in internal medicine and gastroenterology. Physician Gen. Hosp., Požega, Croatia, 1967-71; resident U. Hosp., Ljubljana, Slovenia, 1971-78; internist U. Hosp., Zagreb, 1978—, prof., 1994—. Author, editor: Interventional Gastroenterology, 1993; contbr. articles to profl. jours. Mem. Internat. Gastrosurgical Club, Croatian Med. Assn., Croatian Gastroent. Assn. Roman Catholic. Avocations: poetry, gardening, mountaineering.

ROSANOV, NIKOLAY NIKOLAEVICH, optical engineering educator, researcher; b. St. Petersburg, Russia, Dec. 26, 1940; s. Nikolay Semenovich and Marianna Vladimirovna (Makarova) R.; m. Galina Evgenievna Bereznitskaya, July 26, 1966; children: Alexey, Marianna. MS, St. Petersburg State U., 1963; PhD, Vavilov State Optical Inst., St. Petersburg, 1970, degree in habilitation, 1983. Engr. Vavilov State Optical Inst., St. Petersburg, 1963-65, rschr., 1965-73, head of lab., 1973—; prof. Inst. Fine Mechs. and Optics, St. Petersburg, 1988—. Author: Optical Bistability and Hysteresis in Distributed Nonlinear Systems, 1997; dep. editor: Jour. Optics and Spectroscopy, 1987—, Inst. Laser Phys., St. Petersburg, head of dept., 1996—; contbr. articles to profl. jours.; patentee in field. Mem. SPIE, Russian Acad. Engring. Scis. (corr.), Optical Soc. Russia, Optical Soc. Am., Phys. Soc. Russia (prize 1993). Avocations: gardening, literature, chess. Home: Naberezhnaya Karpovki 21-8, 197022 Saint Petersburg Russia Office: Vavilov State Optical Inst Inst Laser Physics, Birzhevaya Liniya 12, 199034 Saint Petersburg Russia

ROSAR, VIRGINIA WILEY, librarian; b. Cleve., Nov. 22, 1926; d. John Egbert and Kathryn Coe (Snyder) Wiley; m. Michael Thorpe Rosar, April 8, 1950 (div. Feb. 1968); children: Bruce Wiley, Keith Michael, James Wilfred. Attended, Oberlin Coll., 1944-46; BA, U. Puget Sound, 1948; MS, C.W. Post Coll., L.I.U., Greenvale, N.Y., 1971. Cert. elem. and music tchr., N.Y.; cert. sch. library media specialist, N.Y. Music programmer Station WFAS, White Plains, N.Y., 1948; prodn. asst. NBC-TV, N.Y.C., 1948-50; tchr. Portledge Sch., Locust Valley, N.Y., 1967-70; librarian Syosset (N.Y.) Schs., 1970-71, Smithtown (N.Y.) Schs., 1971-92; ret., 1992; pres. World of Realia, Woodbury, N.Y., 1969-86; founder Cygnus Pub., Woodbury, 1985-87. Active local chpt. ARC, 1960-63, Community Concert Assn., 1960-66, Leukemia Soc. Am., 1978—. Mem. AAAS, N.Y. Acad. Scis., L.I. Alumnae Club of Pi Beta Phi (pres. 1964-66). Republican. Presbyterian. Avocations: music, sewing, gardening, writing. Home: 10 Warrenton Ct Huntington NY 11743-3750

ROSARIO, LUIS BRAS, cardiologist; b. Lisbon, Portugal, Nov. 21, 1964; s. Antonio and Maria (Bras) R. MD, Lisbon U., 1988. Cert. cardiologist Health Ministry and Med. Order; cert. Am. Soc. Echocardiography, Am. Soc. Nuclear Cardiology. Intern Hosp. Santa Maria, Lisbon, 1989-91; resident Hosp. Santa Marta, Lisbon, 1991-92, fellow, 1992—; monitor Lisbon U. Med. Sch., 1986-91; fellow Univ. Coll., London, 1995, Harvard Med. Sch., Boston, 1995-96; cardiologist Hosp. Santa Marta, Lisbon, Portugal; head heart failure unit Hosp. Garcia Orta, Lisbon. Recipient Rsch. award Portuguese Health Ministry, 1996. Avocations: music, painting, tennis, mountain biking. Home: R Quinta Grande 8 r/c, 2780 Oeiras Portugal Office: Hosp Garcia de Orta, Servico Cardiologa, 2806 Pragal Almada, Portugal

ROSARIO, MANUEL TAINHA RIBEIRO, physician; b. Lisbon, Portugal, July 7, 1951; s. Manuel Ribeiro Antony and Maria Lurdes Mendes (Tainha) R.; m. Alice Minnie Freudenthal. Diploma, Faculdade De Medicina Lisboa, Lisbon, 1976; lic. physician, Hosp. Setubal, Portugal, 1974. Diplomate Am. Bd. Internal Medicine. Resident Bronx V.A. Med. Ctr., N.Y.C., 1981-84; fellow Harlem Hosp., N.Y.C., 1984-86; dir. GI Dept. St. Francisco Xavier Hosp., Lisbon, 1987-96. Contbr. numerous articles to med. jours. Lt. Portuguese Army, Lisbon, 1980. Fellow Am. Coll. Physicians; mem. Am. Gastroenterological Assn., Am. Coll. Gastroenterology. Avocations: motorcycling, photography. Home: Soares De Passos 10 5th, 1300 Lisbon Portugal Office: Icil, S Sebastiao Da Pedreira 82, 1000 Lisbon Portugal

ROSCA, RADU GHEORGHE, mechanical engineer educator; b. Iasi, Romania, Mar. 5, 1960; s. Dumitru and Eugenia (Zgura) R.; m. Olga Guguiman, Dec. 14, 1985. Grad., Tech. U., 1985. Engr. Bearings Factory, Birlad, Romania, 1985-87; rsch. engr. Automobiles Rsch. Inst., Pitesti, Romania, 1987-88; rsch. engr. U. Agronomy, Iasi, 1988-90, from assoc. asst. to lectr., 1989-2000; lectr. Tech U., Iasi, 1998-2000, asst. prof., 2000—; head transp. forge dept. Bearings Fact., Birlad, 1985-87; assoc. asst. U. Agronomy, 1989-90. Co-author: Tractors, 1995, Agriculture's Energetical Basis, 1996, Vehicle Body and Structure, 1998, 2d edit., 1999; contbr. articles to profl. jours. Mem. Internat. Soil and Tillage Rsch. Orgn., Soc. Automotive Engrs. Avocations: electronics, computers. Home: Dumbrava Rosie 21, 6600 Iasi Romania

ROSCHER, WOLFGANG, composer, music educator, musicologist; b. Komotau, Bohemia, Czechoslovakia, May 29, 1927; s. Franz and Martha (Gröschel) R.; m. Eva Nagel Roscher, Nov. 11, 1950; 1 child, Angela Margaretha. PhD, U. Erlangen, Fed. Republic Germany, 1951. Organist Tepl Abbey, Bohemia, 1945-46; music tchr. U. Bamberg, Fed. Republic Germany, 1946-48; music tchr. U. Erlangen, Fed. Republic Germany, 1948-51, choir dir., 1949-54; music tchr. Ettal Abbey, Bavaria, 1957-60; prof. music pedagogics Alfeld Coll., Lower Saxony, 1960-71, Hildesheim U., Lower Saxony, 1971-81, Mozarteum Salzburg, Austria, 1981—; head Inst. Integrative Music pedagogics/polyaesthetic edn. Hochschule Mozarteum, Salzburg, Austria, 1982-2000; rector univ. music and dramatic arts Hochschule Mozarteum, 1991-95; guest lectr. Acad. Fine Arts, Istanbul, Turkey, 1979, also courses in Finland, Germany, Hungary, Poland, Portugal, Switzerland; guest lectr. U. Haifa, Israel, 1981; dir. Ensembles for Music Theatre Improvisation, modern and early music, 1960—. Editor Polyaisthesis Multiperceptional Consciousness, 1986-92; editor: A Selection of 5 Years' Contributions, 1991, Jahrbücher Polyaisthesis 1-7, Wien bzw. München, 1994-2000; author: Daniel-Musictheater-Production, 1991, Musiktheater im Unterricht, 1989, Erfahren and Darstellen, 1984, Integrative Musikpädagogik, 1983, 84, Polyästhetische Erziehung, 1976, Musik, Kunst, Kultur als Abenteuer, Kassel 1997 Sinn und Klang, Philosophisch-theologische Streiflichter auf, aisthesis und poiesis in Musik, Kultur, Bildung, Salzburg, 1997, Klangszenen zum Weltfrieden: Golem-Babel-Hoheslied, München, 2000; films: Zeichen, 1979, Doktor Faust, 1978, Wechselspiele, 1975; composer and conductor. Mem. Internat. Soc. for Polyaesthetic Edn. (pres.), European Acad. Scis. and Arts (dean). Roman Catholic. Office: Hochschule Mozarteum, Univ Mozarteum Salzburg, Alpenstr 48, 5020 Salzburg Austria 5020

ROSE, CHARLES ROBERT, internet communications company executive; b. Columbus, Ohio, Feb. 5, 1958; s. John Oakley and Mary Jacqueline (Newbern) R.; m. Barbara Jean Skeith, Aug. 25, 1983 (div. Mar. 1989); 1 child, Hillary Beth; m. Darlene Marie Peshoff, Aug. 27, 1994; 1 child, Robert Jesse. Student, U. Md., Germany, 1979-80, Pikes Peak C.C., Colorado Springs, Colo., 1980-82, U. Houston, 1992-93. Mgr. Grandy's Restaurants, Housto, 1983-84; v.p. ops. Popco, Inc., Colorado Springs, 1984-86; regional tng. mgr. A. Copeland Enterprises, Irvine, Calif., 1986; dir. ops. Kansas City (Mo.) Resturant Assn., 1986-91, Frontier Foods, Denver, 1991-92; owner, mgr. Republic Mgmt. & Trade, Houston, 1992-95; pres. WorldNet Comm., Inc., Leesville, La., 1995—. Mem. Open-Net Coalition, New Orleans, 1999—. With U.S. Army, 1977-83. Republican. Methodist. Avocations: bicycling, music, landscaping. E-mail: robertrose@wnonline.net. Home: 211 Tower St Leesville LA 71446-3625 Office: WorldNet Comm Inc 116 S 3d St Leesville LA 71446

ROSE, DANIEL, real estate company executive, consultant; b. N.Y.C., Oct. 31, 1929; s. Samuel B. and Belle (Bernstein) R.; m. Joanna Semel, Sept. 16, 1956; children: David Semel, Joseph Benedict, Emily, Gideon Gregory. Student, Yale U., 1947-50; cert. of proficiency in Russian lang., U.S. Air Force Program, 1951; BA, Syracuse U., 1952; postgrad., U. Paris. With Dwelling Mgrs., Inc., N.Y.C., 1954—, pres., 1960—, vice-chmn., sec.-treas. Baltic-Am. Enterprise Fund, 1994—; dir. Dreyfus Tax Exempt Bond Fund Inc., 1976-82, Dreyfus Money Market Fund, Inc., 1980-82; pres., CEO Rose Assocs., Inc., N.Y.C., 1980-99, chmn., 1999—; chmn. 22 Dreyfus Funds, 1992—; assoc. fellow Pierson Coll. Yale U., 1974—; bd. govs., hon. life mem. Technion-Israel Inst. Tech.; bd. dirs., grants com. Realty Found. N.Y.; vice-chmn. Lionel Trilling seminars Columbia U., 1977—; bd. dirs. Ventures in Edn.; trustee, mem. exec. and compensation and benefits coms. U.S. Trust Co. of N.Y., 1982-92; trustee, vice-chmn. mixed use devel. coun. Urban Land Inst., 1986-93; exec. com. Urban Land Found., 1989—, gov., Urban Land Inst., 1993—; designated Cert. Property Mgr. Inst. for Real Estate Mgmt. Expert adv. to sec. HUD, 1972; expert/cons. to commr. edn. HEW, 1974; cons. HUD panel on urban devel., 1984-86; dir. N.Y. Coun. Humanities, 1980-86, N.Y. Conv. Ctr. Devel. Corp., 1980-90, Get Ahead Found., 1989-98, Fifth Ave. Assn., 1989-98; mem. Governor's Task Force on Housing, 1975, Task Force on Taxation, Mcpl. Assistance Corp., 1976-77, Planning Commn. Theatre Adv. Group, coun. of fellows, vis. com. to grad. faculty, bd. overseers Ctr. for Study of N.Y.C. affairs New Sch. for Social Rsch.; overseers com. to visit Ctr. Internat. Affairs Harvard U., 1992-98; mem. adv. bd. CUNY-TV channel A, 1986—, Mcpl. Broadcasting System, 1977-78, MIT Ctr. for Real Estate Devel.; donor Daniel Rose chair urban econs., trustee NYU N.Y. Inst. for Humanistic Studies, Mus. of City of N.Y., 1984-90; chmn. bd. trustees, Horace Mann-Barnard Sch., 1971-74, trustee, 1962-89, hon. trustee, 1989— ; v.p., assoc. treas., bd. dirs. Police Athletic League of N.Y., vice chmn. Cen. Harlem Facility; pres. Harlem Ednl. Activities Fund Inc., YM & YWHA of the Bronx, 1963-67; v.p. N.Y. Landmarks Conservancy, bd. dirs. 1977-90; bd. dirs. Jewish Cmty. Ctrs. Assn., 1970—, pres. 1974-78, hon. pres. 1978—; v.p. World Confedn. of Jewish Cmty. Ctrs., 1977-83; former trustee and exec. com. mem. Fedn. of Jewish Philanthropies of N.Y., chmn. standing functional com. on cmty. ctrs., 1969-73; ptnr. N.Y.C. Partnership, 1990—; treas., bd. dirs. Citizens Housing and Planning Coun. of N.Y., 1972—; chmn. Dem. platform adv. com., 1984 Nat. Conv.; bd. advisors Dem. Leadership Coun., 1992—, Progressive Policy Inst.; trustee Dem. Nat. Com., 1988; chmn. Del. Svcs. Host Com., N.Y.C.; bd. trustees MBA of N.Y. Scholarship Found., Inc., 1996—. Served with USAF, 1951-54. Mem. Internat. Inst. Strategic Studies (dir. Am. com. for IISS 1987—), Coun. on Fgn. Rels., Fgn. Policy Assn. (bd. dirs. 1971—, chmn. fgn. policy assocs. 1972-75), Inst. for East-West Security Studies (bd. dirs. 1982—, treas. 1988—, co-chmn. fin. com. 1990—), Am. Soc. Real Estate Counselors (mem. publs.-rsch. com.), Real Estate Bd. of N.Y. Inc. (chmn. housing com. 1975—, mem. bd. govs. 1977-80, 90—, mem. REBNY Found.), Assn. of Yale Alumni (del.-at-large 1978-81, class of 1951 del. 1986-89), Century Assn. (N.Y.C.), Coffee House, Yale, Union League Club, Cosmos (Washington), Quaker Ridge Country Club, Noyac Country Club, Econ. Club N.Y. E-mail: drose@rosenyc.com. Office: Rose Associates Inc 200 Madison Ave Fl 5 New York NY 10016-3912

ROSE, DAVID L., lawyer; b. Ft. Monmouth, N.J., Feb. 18, 1955; s. Llewellyn Paterson and Bebe (Faulk) R.; m. Laura Marie Jarvis, Sept. 3, 1989; children: Allison Michelle, Jessica Morgan, Ashley Elizabeth. BA in Comm., U. Colo., 1980; JD, Ariz. State U., 1991. Bar: Ariz. 1991, U.S. Dist. Ct. Ariz. 1991, U.S. Ct. Appeals (9th cir.) 1993, U.S. Supreme Ct. 1997. Law clk. Bonn & Anderson, Phoenix, 1988-91, Maricopa County Superior Ct., Phoenix, 1990-91; lawyer Anderson, Brody, Levinson, Weiser & Horwitz, Phoenix, 1991-92, Brandes, Lane & Joffe, Phoenix, 1992-93; pvt. practice Phoenix, 1993—; lawyer Rose & Hildebrand, P.C., 1997—; pvt. practice Phoenix, 1993—. Editor: Missive, 1992. Bd. dirs. Maricopa County Family Support Adv. Com., Phoenix; adv. coun. Washington Sch. Dist., Phoenix; mem. Ariz. State Legis., Domestic Rels. Reform Com., Phoenix. Mem. Maricopa County Bar Assn. (adv. family law com.), ABA (adv. family law sect.), Nat. Congress for Men (pres.), Father's for Equal Rights of Colo. (pres.). Avocations: aviation, computer systems. Office: 1440 E Washington St Phoenix AZ 85034-1109

ROSE, DAVID SEMEL, internet executive, entrepreneur; b. N.Y.C., June 12, 1957; s. Daniel and Joanna (Semel) R.; m. Gail R. Gremse, Dec. 26, 1982. BA, Yale U., 1979; MBA, Columbia U., 1983. Spl. asst. urban affairs U.S. Senator Daniel P. Moynihan, N.Y.C., 1979-80, dep. regional dir., 1980-81; assoc. Rose Assocs. Inc., N.Y.C., 1981-83, v.p., 1983-90; chmn. Computer Classroom, N.Y.C., 1983-86; founder, CEO Ex Machina, Inc., N.Y.C., 1988-97; founder, chmn. AirMedia.com, N.Y.C., 1998—; guest lectr. Columbia U., N.Y.C., 1985—; mem. tech. adv. bd. Indsl. Tech. Assistance Corp., N.Y.C., 1998—. Author: Fontographer Historical Bibliography of Typography, 1993. Bd. dirs., co-founder Millennium Soc., Washington, 1980—; bd. dirs. 92d St. YM-YWHA, N.Y.C., 1986—; bd. dirs. People Am. Way Found., Washington, 1987—, mem. exec. com., 1991—, vice chmn., 1999—; mem. adv. coun. Save Am.'s Treasures, Washington, 1998—. Named A Patriarch of Silicon Alley Red Herring Mag., 1996, Top Dogs in Tech. Crain's N.Y. Bus., 1996; Robert Bates fellow Yale U., 1978. Mem. Personal Comm. Industry Assn. (editor 1992-96), Associated Builders and Owners (bd. dirs. 1986-91, Outstanding Builder award 1990), N.Y. New Media Assn. (co-leader 2000—), Grolier Club N.Y.C., Yale Club N.Y.C., Coffe Ho. Club N.Y.C. Democrat. Avocations: book collecting, printing, Japanese culture. Fax: 212-447-9712. Office: AirMedia.com 11 E 26th St Fl 16 New York NY 10010-1402

ROSE, DEBORAH, epidemiologist; b. N.Y.C., Mar. 14, 1950; d. Frederick Phineas and Sandra (Priest) R.; m. Jan A.J. Stolwijk, Sept. 16, 1990; 1 child, Sarah Leia. BA, Yale U., 1972; SM, Harvard U., 1975; MPH, Yale U., 1977, PhD, 1989. Epidemiologist Nat. Inst. Occupl. Safety and Health, Rockville, Md., 1978-79; assoc. in rsch. II dept. epidemiology and pub. health Yale U., New Haven, Conn., 1986-88, lectr. Sch. Nursing,, 1986-88; epidemiologist Nat. Ctr. Health Stats., Hyattsville, Md., 1989—; cons. to the Min. of Health, Hungary, 1999—. Mem. adv. bd. Dwight Hall at Yale, New Haven, 1982—. Recipient Elm-Ivy award Yale U., 1987, Alumni award Assn. Yale Alumni, 1997, Mary E. Ives award New Haven Free Pub. Libr., 1999. Mem. APHA, Soc. Epidemiologic Rsch., Harvard Sch. Pub. Health Alumni Coun., Sigma Xi. Avocations: computer consultant, Nat. Bonsai and Penjing Museum. Home: 4414 Harbour Town Dr Beltsville MD 20705-1081 Office: Nat Ctr Health Stats 6525 Belcrest Rd Rm 870 Hyattsville MD 20782-2003

ROSE, DONALD MCGREGOR, retired lawyer; b. Cin., Feb. 6, 1933; s. John Kreimer and Helen (Morris) R.; m. Constance Ruth Lanner, Nov. 29, 1958; children: Barbara Rose Mead, Ann Rose Weston. AB in Econs., U. Cin., 1955; JD, Harvard U., 1958. Bar: Ohio 1958, U.S. Supreme Ct. 1962. Asst. legal officer USNR, Subic Bay, The Philippines, 1959-62; with Office of JAG USNR, The Pentagon, Va., 1962-63; assoc. Frost & Jacobs, LLP, Cin., 1963-70, ptnr., 1970-93, sr. ptnr., 1993-97, ret. ptnr., 1997; co-chmn. 6th Cir. Appellate Practice Inst., Cin., 1983, 90, mem. 6th Cir. adv. com., 1990-98, chmn. subcom. on rules, 1990-94, chmn., 1994-96. Trustee Friends of Cin. Pks., Inc., 1980-89, 93-98, pres. 1980-86; trustee Am. Music Scholarship Assn., Cin., 1985-88; pres. Social Health Assn. Greater Cin. Area Inc., 1969-72; co-chmn. Harvard Law Sch. Fund for So. Ohio, Cin., 1985-87; pres. Meth. Union, Cin., 1983-85; chmn. trustees Hyde Pk. Cmty. United Meth. Ch., Cin., 1974-76, chmn. coun. on ministries, 1979-81, chmn. adminstrv. bd., 1982-84, chmn. mem. canvass, 1985, chmn. staff parish rels. com., 1988-90, chmn. commn. missions, 1993-95; trustee Meth. Theol. Sch. Ohio, vice chmn. devel. com., 1990-94, sec. 1992-94, chmn. devel. com., 1994-98, vice chmn., 1998, chmn., 1999—; loaned exec. United Way, Cin., 1999. Lt. USNR, 1959-63. Mem. Cin. Bar Assn., Univ. Club (Cin.), Cin. Country Club. Republican. Avocations: sailing, golf. Home: 8 Walsh Ln Cincinnati OH 45208-3435 also: 11 Blackstone Rd Boothbay Harbor ME 04538-1943

ROSE, GEORGE ANDREW, software developer, information systems specialist; b. Mt. Clemens, Mich., Dec. 17, 1950; s. George Hubert and Geraldine Marie (Benoit) R. BA, BSW in Psychology and Biology, Ea. Mich. U., 1975; MBA in Internat. Fin., George Washington U., 1987. Inpatient substance abuse therapist St. Joseph's Hosp., Mt. Clemens, Mich., 1974-77; dep. twp. clk. Twp. of Clinton (Mich.), 1977-79; social worker Bur. Rehab, Washington, 1979-84; sr. social worker Comprehensive Alcohol and Drug Abuse Ctr., Washington, 1984-88; contract mgmt. UMWA Health and Retirement Funds, Washington, 1988-91; dir. software devel., info. svcs. United Seniors Health Coop., Washington, 1993-98; pres., CEO The Portsmouth Group, Inc., Washington, 1997—. E-mail: georgerose@portsmouth-group.net. Home: 2929 Connecticut Ave NW Ste 306 Washington DC 20008-1435 Office: The Portsmouth Group Inc PO Box 11735 Washington DC 20008-0935

ROSE, HUGH, management consultant; b. Evanston, Ill., Sept. 10, 1926; s. Howard Gray and Catherine (Wilcox) R.; m. Mary Moore Austin, Oct. 25, 1952; children: Susan, Nancy, Gregory, Matthew, Mary. BS in Physics, U. Mich., 1951, MS in Geophysics, 1952; MBA with highest distinction, Pepperdine U., 1982. Mgr. Caterpillar, Inc., Peoria, Ill., 1952-66; v.p., mktg. mgr. Cummins Engine Co., Columbus, Ind., 1966-69; pres., CEO Cummins Northeastern, Inc., Boston, 1969-77; pres. Power Systems Assocs., L.A., 1980-83, C.D. High Tech., Inc., Austin, Tex., 1984-87; mgmt. cons. Rose and Assocs., Tucson, 1984, 87—. Contbr. articles to profl. jours. Bd. dirs. Raymond Alf Mus., Claremont, Calif., 1975—, Comstock Found., Tucson, 1988, Environ. Edn. Exch., 1991, Heart Ctr. U. Ariz., Tucson, 1992. With USAAF, WWII. Fellow AAAS; mem. Acacia, Soc. Vertebrate Paleontology, Beacon Soc. Boston (pres. 1979-80), Algonquin Club Boston (v.p., bd. dirs. 1974-80), Duxbury Yacht Club, Longwood Cricket Club, Skyline Country Club, Phi Beta Kappa, Delta Mu Delta, Sigma Gamma Epsilon, Sigma Pi Sigma, Beta Beta Beta, Cum Laude Soc. Republican. Presbyterian. Office: Rose & Assocs 5320 N Camino Sumo Tucson AZ 85718-5132

ROSE, JOANNA SEMEL, cultural activist; b. Orange, N.J., Nov. 22, 1930; d. Philip Ephraim and Lillian (Mindlin) Semel; m. Daniel Rose, Sept. 16, 1956; children: David S., Joseph B., Emily, Gideon G. Cert., Shakespeare Inst., U.K., 1951; BA summa cum laude, Bryn Mawr Coll., 1952; postgrad., St. Hilda's Coll., Oxford U., 1953. Chmn. adv. bd. Partisan Rev., N.Y.C.; mem. exec. com. Am. Friends of St. Hilda's Coll., former chmn.; former pres. bd. dirs., current bd. dirs. Paper Bag Players, N.Y.C.; former bd. dirs., current mem. adv. coun. Poets and Writers, Inc., N.Y.C., Nat. Dance Inst., N.Y.C.; bd. dirs. Bay Street Theatre, Sag Harbor, Eldridge St. Project, N.Y.C., Am. Friends Jewish Mus. Greece; former bd. dirs. N.Y. Pub. Libr., Guild Hall East Hampton, Musical Theatre Works, N.Y.C., Brit. Inst., N.Y.C., Ctr. for Visual History, N.Y.C.; assoc. fellow Berkeley Coll. Yale Univ. Mem. Cosmopolitan Club, Bryn Mawr Club of N.Y., LVIS East Hampton. Home: 895 Park Ave New York NY 10021-0327 also: 1 Lily Pond Ln East Hampton NY 11937

ROSE, JONATHAN CHAPMAN, lawyer; b. Cleve., June 8, 1941; s. Horace Chapman and Katherine Virginia (Cast) R.; m. Susan Anne Porter, Jan. 26, 1980; 1 son, Benjamin Chapman. A.B., Yale U., 1963; LL.B. cum laude, Harvard U., 1967. Bar: Mass. 1968, D.C. 1972, U.S. Supreme Ct. 1976, Circuit Ct. Appeals 1977, Ohio 1978. Law clk. Justice R. Ammi Cutter, Mass. Supreme Jud. Ct., 1967-68; spl. asst. to U.S. pres., 1971-73; gen. counsel Council on Internat. Econ. Policy, 1973-74; assoc. dept. atty. gen. U.S. Dept. Justice, 1974-75; dept. asst. atty. gen. U.S. Dept. Justice (Antitrust Div.), 1975-77; asst. atty. gen. Office of Legal Policy, 1981-84; ptnr. firm Jones, Day, Reavis & Pogue, Washington, 1977-81, 84—. Prin. Ctr. for Excellence in Govt.; pres. Yale Daily News Found.; bd. govs. Yale Alumni Assn., 1996-99. 1st lt. U.S. Army, 1969-71. Mem. ABA, D.C. Bar Assn., Mass. Bar Assn., Ohio Bar Assn., Fed. Bar Assn., Am. Law Inst. Republican. Episcopalian. Clubs: Met, Chevy Chase, Union, Yale, Harvard. Office: Jones Day Reavis & Pogue 51 Louisiana Ave NW Washington DC 20001-2113

ROSE, KEITH, biochemist, researcher; b. Stamford, U.K., Oct. 20, 1951; arrived in Switzerland, 1981; s. Victor and Rose Pamela (Rudkin) R.; m. Christine Montel, July 27, 1974; children: Philippe, Christophe. BA, Oxford U., Eng., 1974, MA, 1975, PhD, 1979. Rsch. asst. U. Oxford, 1979-80; rsch. asst. U. Geneva, 1981-83, sr. rsch. asst., 1983-86, assoc. prof. biochemistry, 1986-2000, prof. med. biochemistry, 2000—; co-founder Gryphon Scis., South San Francisco, 1993—, Geneva Proteomics Inc., 2000; cons. and lectr. in field. Editorial advisor Biochem. Jour., London, 1985-99; editorial bd. Bioconjugate Chemistry, 1994—; contbr. articles to profl. jours.; patentee in field. Swiss Sci. Found. grantee, 1981—, others. Mem. Royal Soc. Chemistry, Am. Chem. Soc., Am. Peptide Soc., N.Y. Acad. Scis., European Peptide Soc., Swiss Soc. for Mass Spectrometry, Swiss Soc. for Edn. in Medicine, Swiss Soc. Biochemistry. Avocations: mountain walking, cross-country skiing. Office: CMU Dept Med Biochemistry, 1 rue Michel Servet, 1211 Geneva 4, Switzerland

ROSE, KIM MATTHEW, lawyer, educator; b. Gallipolis, Ohio, Mar. 21, 1956; s. Dave and Lois Ann R.; m. Pamela Carol Sims, Aug. 11, 1990. Student, USMA, 1974-76; BBA, Ohio U., 1977; JD, Capital U. Law, 1981; MBA, Ashland Coll., 1988. Bar: Ohio 1981, U.S. Dist. Ct. (so. dist.) Ohio 1981, U.S. Ct. Appeals (6th cir.) 1987, U.S. Supreme Ct. 1988. Asst. prosecutor Knox County Prosecutor, Mt. Vernon, Ohio, 1982-90; with Critchfield, Critchfield & Johnston, Mt. Vernon, 1982—; adj. prof. Mt. Vernon Nazarene Coll., 1982—. Mem. Met. Housing Authority, Knox County, 1990—; mem. adv. bd. Salvation Army, Mt. Vernon, 1991—; mem. Boys Village Corp. Bd., Smithville, Ohio, 1991—; mem. Knox Cmty. Hosp. Bd., Mt. Vernon, Ohio, 2000. Maj. USAR, 1974-95. Mem. Ohio State Bar Assn. (mem. substance abuse lawyer's assistance com.), Knox County Bar Assn. (past pres.), Mt. Vernon Nazarene Coll. Found. (rec. sec. bd. 1995—), Mt. Vernon-Knox County C. of C., Masons. Avocations: flying, skiing, fishing, golfing, biking. Home: 1413 Greenbrier Dr Mount Vernon OH 43050-9101 Office: Critchfield Critchfield & Johnsotn 118 E Gambier St Mount Vernon OH 43050-3546

ROSE, LIVINGSTONE MURRAY, chemical engineer; b. Kingston upon Hull, England, Aug. 22, 1935; s. Livingstone Lund and Mary (Buddy) R.; m. Jane Winifred Lovegrove, Apr. 12, 1958; children: Nicola Margaret, Benita Jane, Duncan Murray. BS in Chemistry, Birmingham (England) U., 1957, PhD in Chem. Engring., 1960. Process engr. ICI, Runcorn, England, 1960-68; sr. process engr. Exxon, Florham Park, 1968-71; lectr. ETH, Zurich, 1971-86; dir. Chemeng Software, Beaminster, England, 1987-2000; chmn. Eurecha, Europe, 1995-97; series editor Elsevier, Holland, 1981-97. Author: Application of Modelling, Reactor Design, Distillation Design, The Art of Process Design, Engineering Investment Decisions, 1972-97. Gov. Beaminster Sch., 1993—. Avocation: old building restoration. Home and Office: The Old Vicarage, Beaminster DT8 3BU, England

ROSE, MALCOLM EDWARD, novelist, chemist; b. Coventry, Eng., Jan. 31, 1953; s. Reginald and Mary Kathleen (Robinson) R.; m. Barbara Anne Warner, Aug. 2, 1975; 1 child, Colin Mark. BA, U. York, Eng., 1974, DPhil in Chemistry, 1978. Chartered chemist. Postdoctoral fellow U. Liverpool, Eng., 1977-81, sr. exptl. officer, 1981-83; lectr. in chemistry Sheffield (Eng.) City Poly., 1983-86, sr. lectr. in analytical chemistry, 1986-87; lectr. in chemistry The Open U., Milton Keynes, Eng., 1988-96; freelance writer Milton Keynes, 1996—. Author: Mass Spectrometry for Chemists and Biochemists, 1982, 2d edit., 1996, (novels for young people) The Highest Form of Killing, 1992, Formula for Murder, 1994, Tunnel Vision, 1996 (Angus Book award 1997), others; editor Specialist Periodical Reports in mass spectrometry, 1984-89. Recipient numerous grants for chemistry rsch. Fellow Royal Soc. Chemistry. Avocations: philately, hill-walking, cycling, daydreaming.

ROSE, MERRILL, public relations counselor; b. Beaufort, N.C., Apr. 20, 1955; d. Robert Lloyd Rose and Betty Lou (Merrill) Ellis. Student, U. N.C., 1977. Reporter, editor Consumer News, Washington, 1978-79; v.p. Fraser/Assocs., Washington, 1979-82; sr. assoc. Porter/Novelli, Washington, 1982-85, v.p., 1985-87; sr. v.p., food practice leader Porter/Novelli, N.Y.C., 1989-91, exec. v.p., 1990—; gen. mgr. Chgo. Porter/Novelli, 1991-96; dir. Europe Porter Novelli Internat., Brussels, 1996-98; exec. v.p. Porter Novelli, N.Y.C., 1998-2000; ind. cons., 2000—. Bd. dirs. CARE, 1991-98; bd. visitors U. N.C. Sch. Journalism, Chapel Hill, 1992—; bd. dirs. Friends of Prentice affiliate Northwestern Meml. Hosp., 1993-2000; mem. accrediting com. Accrediting Coun. for Edn. in Journalism and Comm., 1994-2000. Mem. Am. Inst. of Wine and Food, Pub. Rels. Soc. Am. Office: 43 5th Ave Apt 1N New York NY 10003-4368

ROSE, MICHAEL ROBERTSON, evolutionary biology educator, consultant; b. Iserlohn, Germany; s. James Barry and Charlotte Julia Rose; children: Darius, Caitlin, Liam, Muireann. BS, Queen's U., Kingston, Ont., Can., 1975, MS, 1976; PhD, U. Sussex, Eng., 1979. NATO sci. fellow U. Wis., Madison, 1979-81; asst. prof. Dalhousie U., Halifax, N.S., Can., 1981-85, assoc. prof., 1985-87; assoc. prof. evolutionary biology U. Calif., Irvine, 1987-90, prof., 1990—. Author: Evolutionary Biology of Aging, 1991, Adaptation, 1996, Darwin's Spectre, 1998. Recipient President's prize Am. Soc. Naturalists, 1992, Busse award World Congress Gerontology, Adelaide, Australia, 1997. Mem. Soc. for Study Evolution. Avocation: music. E-mail: mrrose@uci.edu.

ROSE, NOEL RICHARD, immunologist, microbiologist, educator; b. Stamford, Conn., Dec. 3, 1927; s. Samuel Allison and Helen (Richard) R.; m. Deborah S. Harber, June 14, 1951; children: Alison, David, Bethany, Jonathan. BS, Yale U., 1948; MA, U. Pa., 1949, PhD, 1951; MD, SUNY, Buffalo, 1964; MD (hon.), U. Cagliari, Italy, 1990; ScD (hon.), U. Sassari, Italy, 1992; Order of the First Class (hon.), Ctrl. U. Venezuela, 1997. From instr. to prof. microbiology SUNY Sch. Medicine, Buffalo, 1951-73; dir. Center for Immunology SUNY Sch. Medicine, 1970-73, dir. Erie County Labs., 1964-70; dir. WHO Collaborating Center for Autoimmune Disorders, 1968—; prof. immunology and microbiology, chmn. dept. immunology and microbiology Wayne State U. Sch. Medicine, 1973—82; prof., chmn. dept. immunology and infectious diseases Johns Hopkins U. Sch. Hygiene and Pub. Health, Balt., 1982-93, prof. medicine and environ. health scis., 1982—, prof. molecular microbiology and immunology, 1993—; prof. pathology Johns Hopkins U. Sch. Medicine, 1994—; cons. in field. Editor: (with others) International Convocation on Immunology, 1969, Methods in Immunodiagnosis, 1973, 3d rev. edit., 1986, The Autoimmune Diseases, 1986, 2d edit., 1992, 3d edit., 1998, Microbiology, Basic Principles and Clinical Applications, 1983 Principles of Immunology, 1973, 2d rev. edit., 1979, Specific Receptors of Antibodies, Antigens and Cells, 1973, Manual of Clinical Laboratory Immunology, 1976, 2d rev. edit., 1980, 4d edit. 1992, 5th edit., 1997, Genetic Control of Autoimmune Disease, 1978, Recent Advances in Clinical Immunology, 1983, Clinical Immunotoxicology, 1992, Manual of Human Immunology, 1997; editor in chief Clin. Immunology and Immunopathology, 1988-98; contbr. articles to profl. jours. Recipient award Sigma Xi, 1952, award Alpha Omega Alpha, 1976, Lamp award, 1975, Faculty Recognition award Wayne State U. Bd. Govs., 1979, Pres.'s award for excellence in teaching, 1979, Disting. Service award Wayne State U. Sch. Medicine, 1982, U. Pisa medal, 1986, U. Venezuela medal, 1998; named to Acad. Scholars Wayne State U., 1981; Josiah Macy fellow, 1979. Fellow AAAS, APHA, Am. Acad. Allergy and Immunology, Am. Acad. Microbiology, Assn. Med. Lab Immunologists; mem. Acad. Clin. Lab. Physicians and Scientists, Am. Assn. Immunologists, Am. Soc. Investigative Pathology, Am. Soc. Clin. Pathologists, Am. Soc. Microbiology (hon.; Abbott Lab. Clin. and Diagnostic Immunology award 1993), Brit. Soc. Immunology, Coll. Am. Pathologists, Société Française d'Immunologie, Can. Soc. Immunology, Soc. Exptl. Biology and Medicine Coun., Clin. Immunology Soc. (sec., treas., pres. 1993), Austrian Immunology Soc. (hon. mem.), Sigma Xi (pres. Johns Hopkins U. chpt. 1988), Alpha Omega Alpha, Delta Omega. Office: Johns Hopkins U 615 N Wolfe St Baltimore MD 21205-2103

ROSE, NORMAN ANTHONY, history educator; b. London, Dec. 29, 1934; arrived in Israel, 1953; s. Simon and Minnie (Sloam) R.; m. Tslilla Kuper, Feb. 19, 1959; 1 child, Inbal. BS in Econ., London Sch. Econ., 1965, PhD, 1968. Sr. rsch. editor Weizmann Letters, Israel, 1968-71; lectr. The Hebrew U., Jerusalem, 1971-74, sr. lectr., 1974-78, assoc. prof., 1978-82, Chaim Weizmann prof. internat. rels., 1982—. Author: The Gentile Zionists, 1973, Baffy, The Diaries of Blanche Dugdate, 1973, Vansittart. Study of a Diplomat, 1978, Lewis Namier and Zionism, 1980, Chaim Weizmann. A Biography, 1986, Churchill. An Unruly Life, 1994, From Palmerston to Balfour, 1996, The Cliveden Set, 2000; contbr. articles to profl. publs. Fellow Royal Hist. Soc., Inst. Hist. Rsch., Leonard Daws Inst. Internat. Rels. Avocations: walking, movies, theatre, music, reading. Office: Hebrew Univ, Mt Scopus, 91905 Jerusalem Israel

ROSE, PAUL LAWRENCE, history educator; b. Glasgow, Scotland, Feb. 26, 1944; m. Susan Ellen Kaplow, June 3, 1969; children: Alexander, Olivia, Zoe, Ariel. BA, MA, Oxford U., Eng., 1968; D in History, U. Paris, 1973. Vis. lectr. UCLA, 1968-69; research assoc. Toronto U., 1969-70; instr. St. John's U., N.Y., 1970-71; APS research fellow Cambridge (Eng.) U., 1974-75; from lectr. to sr. lectr. to reader/research prof. James Cook U., Australia, 1974-84; prof. history Newcasle U., Australia, 1984-85; prof. history Haifa (Israel) U., 1985-92, Reuben Hecht prof. Zionist history, 1987-92. Author: The Italian Renaissance of Mathematics, 1975, Bodin and the Great God of Nature, 1980, German Question/Jewish Question, 1990, Wagner-Race and Revolution, 1992, Heisenberg and the Nazi Atomic Bomb Project, 1998. Recipient various research awards; Am. Philos. Soc. grantee, Am. Coun. Learned Socs. grantee, Australian Rsch. Commn. grantee. Fellow Royal Hist. Soc.; mem. Am. Hist. Assn., Inst. for Advanced Study. Avocations: music, chess, billiards. Office: Pa State U Inst Arts and Humanistic Studies Ihlseng Cottage E University Park PA 16802

ROSE, ROBERT BARRIE, historical writer, educator; b. Bebington, Cheshire, Eng., July 10, 1929; arrived in Australia, 1960; s. Charles William and Elsie (Brown) R.; m. Madeline Mary Hebden, Oct. 16, 1954; children: Alison, Michael. BA in History with honors, Manchester (Eng.) U., 1950, MA in History, 1953, LittD, 2000. Asst. archivist Liverpool (Eng.) Record Office, 1954-56; pilgrim trust rsch. asst. to editor Victoria County Histories, London; lectr., sr. lectr., reader U. Sydney, Australia, 1960-71; prof. history U. Tasmania, Australia, 1971-90; dean of arts U. Tasmania, 1976-77, emeritus prof., 1991—; assoc. editor Hist. Records of Australia, 1991—; hon. rsch. assoc. dept. history U. Tasmania, 1991—; vis. scholar Woodrow Wilson Ctr., Washington, 1985. Author: The Enragés, Socialists of the French Revolution, 1965, 68, The Russian Revolution of 1917, 1970, 78, Gracchus Babeuf, 1760-1797, 1978, The Making of the Sans Culottes, 1982, Tribunes and Amazons, 1998; contbr. articles to hist. periodicals. Sgt. Royal Army Edn. Corps., 1952-54. Fellow Australian Acad. Humanities, Royal Hist. Soc.; mem. Royal Yacht Club Tasmania. Avocations: listening to music, sailing. Home: 11 Woolton Pl, 7005 Sandy Bay Tasmania, Australia

ROSE, ROBERT JOHN, bishop; b. Grand Rapids, Mich., Feb. 28, 1930; s. Urban H. and Maida A. (Glerum) R. Student, St. Joseph Sem., 1944-50; B.A., Seminaire de Philosophie, Montreal, Que., Can., 1952; S.T.L., Pontifical Urban U., Rome, 1956; M.A., U. Mich., 1962. Ordained priest Roman Catholic Ch., 1955; dean St. Joseph Sem., Grand Rapids, 1966-69; dir. Christopher House, Grand Rapids, 1969-71; rector St. John's Sem., Plymouth, Mich., 1971-77; pastor Sacred Heart Parish, Muskegon Heights, Mich., 1977-81; bishop Diocese of Gaylord, Mich., 1981-89, Diocese of Grand Rapids, Mich., 1989—. Mem. Nat. Conf. Cath. Bishops.

ROSE, ROBERT NEAL, brokerage house executive; b. Chgo., Feb. 27, 1951; s. James Allan Rose and Hazel (Gordon) Kaufman; m. Anna Yvette Trujillo, Aug. 23, 1981; children: David James, Michelle Elizabeth, Daniel Jonathan. BS, Georgetown U., 1973; MPA, Harvard U., 1995. Trader Salomon Bros., N.Y.C., 1974-75; regional coord. Latin Am. Merrill Lynch Govt. Securities, N.Y.C., 1975-76; dir. fed. govt. affairs Pub. Service of N.Mex., Albuquerque, 1977-78; exec. dir. Gov. Jerry Apodaca, Washington, 1979-80; expert cons. U.S. Dept. Commerce, Washington, 1980-81; asst. treas. Am. Express Internat. Bank, N.Y.C., 1981-82; sr. v.p. Refco, Inc., N.Y.C., 1982-84; v.p., mgr. Thomson McKinnon Securities, N.Y.C., 1984-88; sr. v.p. Lehman Bros., N.Y.C., 1988-92; mng. dir. Credit Agricole Futures Inc., N.Y.C., 1992-95; sr. mng. dir. Bear Stearns, N.Y.C., 1995-99; cons. BDM Corp., McLean, Va., 1981-88; Presdl. appointee J. William Fulbright Fgn. Scholarship Bd., 1993-97. Mem. Dem. conv. site selection com., 1989-90; mem. arrangements com. Dem. Conv., San Francisco, 1984; fin. chmn. Conn. Dem. State Ctrl. Com., 1993; chmn. nat. fin. coun. Dem. Nat. Com., 1998-99; mem. rules com. Dem. Conv., L.A., 2000; trustee Conservative Synagogue of Westport, 2000—; mem. exec. com. Conn. Yankee Boy Scouts Coun., 2000—; mem. rules com. Dem. Century, L.A., 2000. Wexner Heritage Found. fellow, 1992-94. Jewish. Avocations: skiing, tennis. Home: 326 Bayberry Ln Westport CT 06880-1315 Office: 245 Park Ave New York NY 10167-0002

ROSE, STEPHEN JOHN, pediatrician, consultant; b. London, Mar. 20, 1951; s. Bernard and Grace Alberta (Hefford) R.; m. Beatriz Alessandra Miranda, Jan. 29, 1983; children: Sybilla, Eilidh. BA, Cambridge (Eng.) U., 1972, MB Chir, 1975, MA, 1976; MD, Aberdeen U., 1983. Sr. house officer Guy's Hosp., London, 1975-76, 76-77, Northwick Park Hosp., London, 1976; registrar Wonford Hosp., Exeter, 1977-78, Westminster Hosp., London, 1978-79; lectr. U. London, 1979-83, U. Aberdeen, 1983-87; dir. Hopkins & Netherwood Ltd., 1990—; cons. U. Birmingham, 1987—, Birmingham Heartlands Hosp. Dept. Paediatrics. Author: Case Histories in Paediatrics, 1981, 2d edit., 1993, Textbook of Medicine, 1985, Recognition of Child Abuse, 1982. Chmn. Regional Negotiations, Birmingham, 1994. Recipient Rsch. award Brit. Med. Assn., 1984, Travel award WHO, 1987, Rsch. award Action Aid, 1991. Fellow Royal Coll. Pediats. & Child Health, Royal Coll. Physicians (London); mem. Brit. Paediat. Assn. (convenor 1993). Mem. Labour Party. Avocations: car restoration, flute playing, philately. E-mail: sjrosefrcpch@hotmail.com. Office: Birmingham Heartlands Hosp, 45 Bordesley Green E, Birmingham B9 5SS, England

ROSEANNE (ROSEANNE BARR), actress, comedienne, producer, writer; b. Salt Lake City, Nov. 3, 1952; d. Jerry and Helen Barr; m. Bill Pentland, 1974 (div. 1989); children: Jessica, Jennifer, Brandi, Buck, Jake; m. Tom Arnold, 1990 (div. 1994); m. Ben Thomas, 1994. Former window dresser, cocktail waitress; prin. Full Moon & High Tide Prodns., Inc. As comic, worked in bars, church coffeehouse, Denver; produced showcase for women performers Take Back the Mike, U. Boulder (Colo.); performer The Comedy Store, L.A.; showcased on TV special Funny, 1986, also The Tonight Show; featured in HBO-TV spl. On Location: The Roseanne Barr Show, 1987 (Am. comedy award Funniest Female Performer in TV spl., 1987, Ace award Funniest Female in Comedy, 1987, Ace award Best Comedy Spl. 1987); star of TV series Roseanne ABC, 1988-97 (U.S. Mag. 2nd Ann. Readers Poll Best Actress in Comedy Series, 1989, Golden Globe nomination Outstanding Lead Actress in Comedy Series 1988, Emmy award Outstanding Lead Actress in Comedy Series, 1993); actress: (motion pictures) She-Devil, 1989, Look Who's Talking Too (voice), 1990, Freddy's Dead, 1991, Even Cowgirls Get the Blues, 1994, Blue in the Face, 1995, Unzipped, 1995, Meet Wally Sparks, 1997; TV movies: Backfield in Motion, The Woman Who Loved Elvis, 1993; appeared in TV spl. Sinatra: 80 Years My Way, 1995; exec. prodr. Saturday Night Spl., Fox-TV; author: Roseanne: My Life as a Woman, 1989, My Lives, 1994; (host) Roseanne Show, 1998—, I am Your Child, 1997 (TV), Get Bruce, 1999. Active various child advocate orgns. Recipient Peabody award, People's Choice award (4), Golden Globe award (2), Am. Comedy award, Humanitas award, Nickelodeon Kids Choice award, 1990, Eleanor Roosevelt award for Outstanding Am. Women, Emmy award, 1993.

ROSEBERG, CARL ANDERSSON, sculptor, educator; b. Vinton, Iowa, Sept. 26, 1916; s. Swan Bernard and Selma (Olson) R.; m. Virginia M. Gorman, Aug. 23, 1942. B.F.A., U. Iowa, 1939, postgrad., 1939-41, M.F.A., 1947; postgrad., Cranbrook Acad. Art, summers 1947-48, U. Hawaii, 1950-51, U. Va., summer 1964, Mysore (India) U., summer 1965, Tyler Sch. Art, Temple U., summer 1967. Faculty Coll. William and Mary, Williamsburg, Va., 1947—; prof. fine arts Coll. William and Mary, 1966-82, prof. emeritus, 1982—, William and Mary Heritage fellow, 1968-82; founding bd. mem. 20th Century Gallery, Williamsburg.; active judge various art groups. Exhibited one man shows at Radford Coll., 1962, Roanoke Fine Art Gallery, 1962-63, Norfolk Mus., 1963, Asheville (N.C.) Gallery Art, 1963, Longwood Coll., 1966, Phi Beta Kappa Hall, William and Mary Coll., 1970; 35 yr. retrospective William and Mary Coll., 1982; retrospective Twentieth Century Gallery, 1983; exhibited in numerous group shows; represented in permanent collections at U. Iowa, Springfield (Mo.) Mus., Va. Mus. Fine Arts, Colonial Williamsburg, Chrysler Mus. Norfolk, Rockingham County Citizens Com., Longwood Coll., Farmville, Va., Thalhimer Bros., Inc., Swem Libr., Coll. William and Mary, Patriot's Colony '98, others; designer, creator bronze meml. plaque honoring Donald W. Davis for, Millington Hall, Coll. William and Mary, 1970, bronze plaque honoring William G. Guy, Rogers Hall, 1975; I.L. Jones, Jr., Bruton Parish Ch., 1985. designer: James City County Bicentennial Medallion, 1976; designer, creator Carter O. Lowance Bronze Medallion Marshall-Wythe Sch. Law Coll. William and Mary, 1989, Bronze Medallion honoring 300th Ann. Coll. William and Mary, 1991, Bronze Medallion honoring L. I'Anson Marshall-Wythe Sch. Law, 1991. Served to comdr. USNR, 1941-45, 50-52; ret. Res. Recipient Thomas Jefferson award, 1971, numerous art awards, Cheek award William & Mary, 1993. Fellow Internat. Inst. Arts and Letters; mem. Am. Audubon Artists, Fulbright Assn., Res. Officers Assn. Am., Va. Watercolor Soc., Navy League U.S., Williamsburg German Club, Mid. Plantation Club. Masons, Lambda Chi Alpha. Presbyterian. Home: PO Box 1468 Williamsburg VA 23187-1468

ROSEGARTEN, RORY, talent manager, television and theater producer; b. N.Y.C., Feb. 12, 1962; s. Robert Joel and Rita Honey (Mandel) R.; m. Wendy Jill Korn, May 4, 1991; children: Danielle Sydney, Ryan Harris. Student, Ariz. State U., 1980-81. Pres. The Conversation Co., Ltd., Great Neck, N.Y., 1983—. Prodr.: (Broadway musical) Late Nite Comic, 1987; exec. prodr.: (audio CD) Robert Klein: Let's Not Make Love, 1990, (TV sitcom CBS) Everybody Loves Raymond, 1996—, (TV spl. HBO) Robert Klein: It All Started Here, 1996, (audio CD) Brian Regan: Live, 1997, (tv spl. Showtime) Something's Wrong with the Regan Boy, 1992, (tv. spl. Showtime) A Pair of Jokers: Brian Regan and Dennis Regan, 1991. Bd. govs. Comic Relief, 1999—; assoc. bd. dirs. Parker Jewish Geriat. Inst., New Hyde Park, N.Y., 1995-98. Mem. NATAS, League N.Y. Theatres and Producers, Friars Club. Avocations: autograph and memorabilia collecting, ice hockey, water skiing. Office: The Conversation Co Ltd 697 Middle Neck Rd Great Neck NY 11023-1216

ROSEINGRAVE, JANICE ANNE, accountant; b. Masterton, New Zealand, Sept. 3, 1965; d. Patrick Ian and Beryl Anne (Thomas) Wood; m. Matthew Joseph Roseingrave, Mar. 19, 1988. B Bus. Studies, Massey U., New Zealand, 1981, diploma in bus. studies, 1981. Revenue acct. Hutt City Coun., Lower Hutt, New Zealand, 1989-91; sr. auditor Ministry of Def., Wellington, New Zealand, 1990-91; taxation acct. Deloitte & Touche Tohmatsu, Wellington, 1991-93; sr. acct. Land Corp. Ltd., Wellington, 1993-95; sr. mgr. Hutt Valley Health Corp., Wellington, 1995-97; acct. MC Holdings Ltd., Wellington, 1997—; bd. dirs. Auckland Med. Info. Svcs. Ltd. Mem. Katherine Mansfield Birthplace Soc., Inc., Wellington, 1991; bd. dirs. Assoc. New Zealand Myalgic Encephalomyelitis Socs. for sufferos of M.E. of Chronic Fatigue Syndrome. Mem. Inst. Chartered Accts., Inst. Mgmt., Inst. Corp. Mgmt. (assoc.), All New Zealand Inst. Corp. Treas., N.Y. Acad. Scis. Avocations: gardening, medical research, walking, dogs. Office: Med Info Svcs Ltd, PO Box 54-201, Bucklands Beach Auckland, New Zealand

ROSELLE, PAUL LUCAS, material scientist; b. Balt., Mar. 9, 1960; s. William Charles and Marsha (Lucas) R.; m. Dori Lynn Knoff, June 1, 1985; children: Anna Kristen, Lucas Vernon. BS in Chemistry, U. Wis., Milw., 1982, MS in Material Sci., 1985. Cert. haz-mat first responder OSHA, 1987-95. Rsch. scientist Kodak Rsch. Labs. (Microelectronics Tech. Divsn.), Rochester, N.Y., 1985-94; R&D project mgr. Planar Sys., Lake Mills, Wis., 1994-99, active matrix liquid crystal display (AMLCD) process mgr., 1999-2000; diode laser process mgr. Alphalight, Inc., Madison, Wis., 2000—; mfg. process evaluation team Semiconductor Rsch. Corp., 1991-94; monodispersed advanced colorant system RFP team mem. U.S. Display Consortium, patterned glass inspection RFP team mem. Contbr. articles to profl. jours. AFS student, Austria, 1977. Named Eagle Scout Boy Scouts Am., 1977. Mem. NRA (cert. firearms instr. 1993—), Soc. for Info. Display (sec. exec. program com. 1997-98). Achievements include patents for low temperature insitu image reversal process for microelectronic fabrication, method of making a two phase charge coupled device, plasma etching indium tin oxide using a deposited silicon nitride mask, plasma etching indium tin oxide, forming planar ITO gate electrode array structures, etching indium tin oxide, gaseous cleaning method for silicon devices, process to eliminate the reentrant profile in double polysilicon gate structures. Office: Alphalight Inc 505 S Rosa Rd Madison WI 53719-1262

ROSELLE, WILLIAM CHARLES, librarian; b. Vandergrift, Pa., June 30, 1936; s. William John and Suzanne Esther (Clever) R.; m. Marsha Louise Lucas, Aug. 2, 1959; 1 child, Paul Lucas. BA, Thiel Coll., 1958; MLS, U. Pitts., 1963. Lic. profl. guide State of Mont., 1978. Mem. faculty Milton Hershey (Pa.) Sch., 1960-62; trainee Pa. State Library, 1962-63; asst. catalog librarian Pa. State U., 1963-65; engring., math. librarian U. Iowa, 1965-66, library adminstrv. asst., 1966-69, asst. dir. libraries, 1969-71; prof., dir. library U. Wis.-Milw., 1971-89; dir. univ. library system U. Pitts., 1989-90; pvt. cons. Thiensville, Wis., 1991—; chmn. Morris Fromkin Meml. Lectr. Com., 1972-89; chmn. planning task force on computing U. Wis. System, 1973-74, mem. library planning study com., 1978-79, co-chmn. library automation task force, 1983-85; chmn. computing mgmt. rev. team U. Wis.-Stout, 1976; chmn. Council for U. Wis. Libraries, 1981-82; library cons. Grambling (La.) State U., Viterbo Coll., LaCrosse, Wis., N.C. A&T U., Greensboro, Mt. Mary Coll., Milw., U. Ill. at Chgo., Milw. Sch. Engring., Bklyn. Coll., U. South Ala., Concordia Coll., Milw., Metrics Rsch. Corp., Cardinal Stritch Coll., Milw., N.Y. Inst. Tech., Indiana U. of Pa., Med. Coll. Wis., Wis. Luth. Coll., Milw.; participant Library Adminstrs. Devel. Program, U. Md., 1973, micrographics seminar Nat. Microfilm Assn., 1973, Mgmt. Skills Inst., Assn. Rsch. Libraries, Kansas City, Mo., 1977, Meadowbrook Symposium Midwest Library Network, 1976; mem. sect. geography and map libraries Internat. Fedn. Library Assns. and Instns., 1978-83; mem. bldg. com. Ctr. for Rsch. Libraries, 1980-82. Editorial cons. The Quest for Social Justice, 1983, Current Geographical Publications, 1978-89; contbr. articles to profl. jours. Pres. Thiensville (Wis.) Village Bd., 1987; bd. dirs. Charles Allis Art Mus., 1979-84. Served with AUS, 1958-60. Named Disting. Alumnus, Thiel Coll., 1985. Hon. fellow Am. Geog. Soc.; mem. Spl. Libraries Assn. (spl. citation 1979), ALA (life), Iowa Library Assn. (chmn. audit com. 1968-70, chmn. intellectual freedom com. 1969-70), Wis. Library Assn., Midwest Acad. Librarians Conf. (chmn. 1969-71), AAUP (treas. U. Iowa chpt. 1969-70), Coun. Wis. Libraries (chmn. 1973-74), Soc. Tympanuchus Cupido Pinnatus, Milw. Civil War Round Table, Ozaukee Corvette Club, Beta Beta Beta, Beta Phi Mu, Phi Alpha Theta, Phi Kappa Phi, Phi Delta Kappa. Lutheran. Home: 324 Sunny Ln Thiensville WI 53092-1334

ROSELLI, RICHARD JOSEPH, lawyer; b. Chgo., Mar. 2, 1954; s. H. Joseph and Dolores Roselli; m. Lisa McNelis; children: Nicholas Joseph, Christiana Elise, Alexandra Grace, Michaela Luciana, Anthony Santino. BA, Tulane U., 1976, JD, 1980. Bar: Fla. 1981, U.S. Dist. Ct. (so. dist.) Fla. 1981, U.S. Ct. Appeals (5th and 11th cirs.); bd. cert. civil trial lawyer. Assoc. Krupnick & Campbell, Ft. Lauderdale, Fla., 1981-84; ptnr. Krupnick, Campbell, Malone, Roselli, Ft. Lauderdale, 1984-91, Krupnick Campbell Malone Roselli Buser Slama & Hancock P.A., Ft. Lauderdale, 1999—, Krupnick Campbell Malone Roselli Buser Slama Hancock McNelis Liberman & McKee P.A., Ft. Lauderdale, 1999—. Trustee Fla. Dem. Party, 1992-95. Mem. ATLA (pres.' coun. 1996-97), Am. Bd. Trial Advocates, Am. Soc. Law and Medicine, So. Trial Lawyers Assn. (founder), Acad. Fla. Trial Lawyers (bd. dirs. 1987—, exec. com. 1990-97, sec. 1993, treas. 1994, pres. elect. 1995, pres. 1996, chmn. Fla. lawyers action group-PAC 1996, Golden Eagle award, 1989, 1996, 98, Silver Eagle award, 1990, Crystal Eagle award 1995), Broward County Trial Lawyers (bd. dirs.), Trial Lawyers for Pub. Justice, Lawyer Pilots Bar Assn., St. Jude Catholic Ch. Office: 700 SE 3rd Ave Fort Lauderdale FL 33316-1154

ROSEMANN, PHILIPP WOLFRAM, philosopher, educator; b. Frankfort/Main, Hesse, Germany, Feb. 24, 1964; s. Herwart Heinrich and Helga Gertrud (Steinbuechel) R. Candidate Philosophy, U. Hamburg, Germany, 1986; MA in Medieval Philosophy, Queen's U., Belfast, No. Ireland, 1989; Lic. Philosophy, Cath. U. Louvain, Belgium, 1991, D Philosophy, 1995. Warburg scholar Warburg Inst. U. London, 1987-88; tchg. fellow Queen's U., Belfast, 1988-90; rschr. Cath. U. Louvain, 1990-93, lectr., 1995-96; lectr. Uganda Martyrs U., Nkozi, 1996-97; prof. U. Dallas, 1997—. Co-author: (with Werner Welte) Alltagssprachliche Metakommunikation in English and German, 1990; author: Omne ens est aliquid: Introduction à la lecture du "système" philosophique de saint Thomas d'Aquin, 1996, Omne agens agit sibi simile: A "Repetition" of Scholastic Metaphysics, 1996, Understanding Scholastic Thought with Foucault, 1999; editor: Robert Grosseteste, Tabula, 1995, Dallas Library of Medieval Latin Texts- Translations; co-editor: (with M. Lejeune) Business Ethics in the African Context Today, 1996; (with S.G. Lofts) Éditer, traduire, interpréter: Essais de méthodologie philosophique, 1997; assoc. editor Am. Cath. Philos. Quar.; contbr. articles to newspapers. Mem. Soc. Internat. pour l'Étude de la Philosopie Médiévale, Martin-Heidegger-Gesellschaft, AAUP, Am. Philos. Assn., Am. Cath. Philos. Assn., Soc. Promotion Eriugenian Studies, Uganda Soc., Tex. Medieval Assn. Roman Catholic. Avocations: running, weight lifting. Home: 709 W Rochelle Rd Apt 2114 Irving TX 75062-7916 Office: U Dallas Dept Philosophy 1845 E Northgate Dr Irving TX 75062-4736

ROSEN, ARTHUR DAVID, neurology educator; b. Bklyn., Sept. 19, 1935; s. Elihu and Gertrude (Simonson) R.; m. Patricia Dailey, Dec. 24, 1997. BA, Columbia U., 1956; MD, SUNY, Bklyn., 1960. Diplomate Am. Bd. Psychiatry and Neurology. Intern Bklyn. Jewish Hosp., 1960-61; fellow in neurophysiology SUNY, Bklyn., 1961-62; resident in neurology Kings County Hosp., Bklyn., 1962-64; asst. prof. medicine SUNY, Bklyn., 1966-73; assoc. prof. neurology SUNY, Stony Brook, 1973-80, prof. neurology, 1980-98, prof. neurology emeritus, 1998—; prof. biol. scis. Purdue U., West Lafayette, Ind., 1998—; clin. prof. neurology Ind. U. Sch. of Medicine, 1998—; NIH/NRSA fellow in neurobiology, 1993-94. Contbr. articles to Jour. Neurophys., Exptl. Neurology, Jour. Neurol. Sci., Am. Jour. Physiology, 1974-94. Lt. comdr. USNR, 1964-66. Grantee NINDB, 1971, NIH, 1973, VA, 1974, 77, Haemoneties Inst., 1985, KROC Found., 1985. Fellow Am. Acad. Neurology; mem. Am. Neurol. Assn., Soc. for Neuroscience, Biophys. Soc., Sigma Xi. Achievements include research on demonstration of antidromic activity in the CNS and demonstration of effect of magnetic fields on several biological systems. Address: Purdue U Dept Biol Scis Lilly Hall Lafayette IN 47907

ROSEN, FREDERICK, political science educator; b. N.Y.C., Sept. 13, 1938; s. David and Rae (Reich) R.; m. Maria Rosaline Barron, May 25, 1968; children: Gregory, Alexander. BA, Colgate U., 1960; MA, Syracuse U., 1963; PhD, U. London, 1965. Asst. prof. Franklin and Marshall Coll., 1966-68; lectr. City U. London, 1968-70; from lectr. to sr. lectr. London Sch. Econs., 1970-86; rsch. asst. U. Coll. London, 1965-66, reader in history of polit. thought, prof., 1986—, dir. Ctr. Politics Law & Soc., 1996—; dir. Bentham project Univ. Coll., 1986—. Author: Jeremy Bentham and Representative Democracy, 1983, Progress and Democracy: William Godwin's Contribution to Political Philosophy, 1986, Bentham, Byron and Greece, 1992; gen. editor: The Collected Works of Jeremy Bentham, 1983—; editor The Jeremy Bentham Newsletter, 1984-86, Utilitas: A Journal of Utilitarian Studies, 1989-96; co-editor: Bentham's Constitutional Code, Vol. 1, 1983, Lives, Liberties and the Public Good, 1987, Introduction to J. Bentham, An. Introduction to the Principles of Morals and Legislation, 1996. Avocations: reading, walking. Office: Univ Coll London, Gower St, London WC1, England

ROSEN, HARALD REINIER, physician, researcher; b. Vienna, Austria, May 28, 1960; s. Siegmund and Ruth (Frankfurter) Rosen; m. Elisabeth Danzer, May 14, 1994; children: Rebecca, David. MD, U. Vienna, 1984. Bd. cert. surgeon. Resident in surgery Hanusch Med. Ctr., Vienna, 198-491; staff surgeon Danube Hosp., Vienna, 1992—; vice chair Ludwig Boltzmann Rsch. Inst., 1993—; cons. Medtronic, Maastricht, Netherlands, 1997—, Merck, Darmstadt, Germany, 1997—. Contbr. articles to profl. jours. Mem. Am. Soc. Clin. Oncology, Brit. Assn. for Coloproctology, Austrian Soc. Surgery (award). Avocations: golf, skiing. Office: Danube Hosp, Langobardenstr 122, A-1220 Vienna Austria

ROSEN, JON HOWARD, lawyer; b. Bklyn., May 20, 1943; s. Eli and Vera (Horowitz) R.; m. Georgeanne Evans, 1993; children from previous marriage, Jason Marc, Hope Terry. BA, Hobart Coll., 1965; JD, St. John's U., 1968; postgrad., CCNY, 1969-71. Bar: N.Y. 1969, Calif. 1975, Wash. 1977. Atty. FAA, N.Y.C., 1968-71; regional atty., contract adminstr. Air Line Pilots Assn., N.Y.C., Chgo., L.A., San Francisco, 1971-77; pvt. practice Seattle, 1977-80; ptnr. Frank and Rosen, Seattle, 1981-98, Frank Rosen Freed Roberts LLP, Seattle, 1999—; instr. labor studies Shoreline C.C., 1978-90. Trustee Temple DeHirsch Sinai, 1992-98, v.p., 1998-00, pres.-elect 2000—. Fellow Coll. Labor and Employment Lawyers; mem. ABA (union co-chmn. com. on employee rights and responsibilities 1992-96, union co-chmn. regional programs sub com. 1998-2000, co-regional EEOC liaison), King County Bar Assn. (past chmn. aviation and space law sect., past chmn. Pacific Coast Labor and Employment Law Conf., past chmn. labor law sect.), Nat. Employment Lawyers Assn. (founding state chair, state steering com. 1990-95), Wash. State Trial Lawyers Assn. (past chair employment law com.). Office: Frank Rosen Freed Roberts LLP 705 2nd Ave Ste 1200 Seattle WA 98104-1729

ROSEN, JOSEPH, technical researcher, lecturer; b. Haifa, Israel, Jan. 5, 1958; s. Israel and Dalia (Trifon) R.; m. Rona Baitner, Sept. 14, 1983; children: Oryan, Omer. BSc, Technion-Israel Inst. Tech., Haifa, 1984, MSc, 1987, DSc, 1992. Sr. lectr. Ben-Gurion U. of the Negev, Beer-Sheva, Israel, 1996—; Contbr. articles to profl. jours. E-mail: rosen@bgumail.bgu.ac.il. Office: Ben- Gurion U of the Negev, Dept Elec/Comp Engr/POB 653, Beer-Sheva Israel 84105

ROSEN, MICHEL, retired prosthodontist; b. Mulhouse, France, Jan. 25, 1936; came to U.S., 1970; s. Jean-James and Suzanne (Mulstein) R.; m. Naomi Schultz, May 20, 1965; 1 child, Robert. DDS, U. Louis Pasteur, Stasbourg, France, 1962; MSc in Dentistry, Boston U., 1973, DSc in Biology, 1974. Lic. dentist, Mass. Hosp. prin. French Air Force, Dakar, Senegal, 1963-64; pvt. practice Belfort and Antibes, France, 1964-70, various, Mass., 1974-91, Switzerland, 1991-92; ret., 1992; consul gen. Senegal, West Africa, Boston, Mass., 1994—; asst. clin. prof., asst. dir. overseas affairs Boston U., 1971-74; asst. clin. prof. Tufts U., Boston, 1980-81; instr. Harvard U., Boston, 1990-91; internat. cons. West Africa. Contbr. articles to profl. jours. Lt. French Air Force, 1985-94; maj. Mass. Mil. Res. Recipient Gold medal City of Nice, France, 1981, Bronze Eagle award City of Nice, France, 1982, Officier de l'ordre du merite award Rep. of Senegal, 1998, Comdr. de l'ordre du Lion Senegal, 2000. Mem. Assn. Mil. Surgeons of U.S., Rabboni Lodge AF and AM, Nat. Sojourners, Assn. of First Corps. of Cadets, Ancient and Hon. Artillery Co. Avocations: diplomacy, travel, reading. Fax: 617 566-3333. E-mail: MRosewDr@aol.com. Home and Office: Consulate Gen of Senegal 381 Dudley Rd Newton MA 02459-2808

ROSEN, MOISHE, religious organization founder; b. Kansas City, Mo., Apr. 12, 1932; s. Ben and Rose (Baker) R.; m. Ceil Starr, Aug. 18, 1950; children: Lyn Rosen Bond, Ruth. Diploma, Northeastern Bible Coll., 1957; DD, Western Conservative Bapt. Sem., 1986. Ordained to ministry Bapt. Ch., 1957. Missionary Am. Bd. Missions to the Jews, N.Y.C., 1956; minister in charge Beth Sar Shalom Am. Bd. Missions to the Jews, Los Angeles, 1957-67; dir. recruiting and tng. Am. Bd. Missions to the Jews, N.Y.C., 1967-70; leader Jews for Jesus Movement, San Francisco, 1970-73, exec. dir., 1973-96, founder, 1973—; speaker in field. Author: Saying of Chairman Moishe, 1972, Jews for Jesus, 1974, Share the New Life with a Jew, 1976, Christ in the Passover, 1977, Y'shua, The Jewish Way to Say Jesus, 1982, Overture to Armageddon, 1991, The Universe is Broken: Who on Earth Can Fix It?, 1991, Demystifying Personal Evangelism, 1992, Witnessing to Jews, 1998. Trustee Western Conservative Bapt. Sem., Portland, Oreg., 1979-85, 86-91, Bibl. Internat. Coun. on Bibl. Inerrancy, Oakland, Calif., 1979-89; bd. dirs. Christian Advs. Serving Evangelism, 1987-91. Named Hero of the Faith, Conservative Bapt. Assn. Am., 1997. Office: Jews for Jesus 90 Miraloma Dr San Francisco CA 94127-1641

ROSEN, MURRAY HILARY, lawyer; b. London, Aug. 26, 1953; s. Joseph and Mercia (Herman) R.; m. Lesley Samuels, Dec. 9, 1975; 4 children. MA with honors, Cambridge U., 1975; postgrad., Brussels Free U., 1976. Called to Bar, Eng. 1976; apptd. Queen's Counsel 1993. Pvt. practice London, 1976—; recorder, 2000—; chmn. Bar Sports Law Group, 1997—. Fellow Chartered Inst. Arbitrators. Avocations: music, sports, books. Office: 11 Stone Bldgs, Lincolns Inn, London WC2A 3TG, England

ROSEN, PAUL PETER, pathologist; b. Bklyn., Aug. 16, 1938; s. George and Beate (Caspari) R.; m. Mary Sue, Aug. 7, 1994; children: Susan Deborah, Jonathan Daniel. BS, Swarthmore Coll., 1960; MD, Columbia U., 1964. Asst. attending pathologist Meml. Hosp., N.Y.C., 1970-73; asst. prof. pathology Cornell U. Med. Sch., N.Y.C., 1972-78; assoc. attending pathologist Meml. Hosp., N.Y.C., 1973-78, attending pathologist, 1978-98; assoc. prof. pathology Cornell U. Med. Sch., N.Y.C., 1978-84, prof. pathology, 1984—; assoc. mem. Sloan Kettering Inst., N.Y.C., 1980-84, mem. tenure title, 1984-98; mem. tenure title Meml. Sloan-Kettering Cancer Ctr., N.Y.C., 1984-98; sr. cons. pathologist Dickstein Cancer Treatment Ctr., White Plains, N.Y., 1998-99; attending pathologist N.Y. Presbyn. Hosp., N.Y.C., 1999—; adj. prof. pathology N.Y. Med. Coll., Valhalla, N.Y., 1996-99. Author: Rosen's Breast Pathology, 1996, Breast Pathology: Diagnosis by Needle Core Biopsy, 1999; co-author: Tumors of the Mammary Gland, 1993; co-editor Pathology Annual, 1977-95, Revs. Pathology, 1996-98; contbr. more than 270 articles on diseases of breast to profl. jours. Mem. Internat. Acad. Pathology, Am. Soc. Clin. Pathologists, Soc. Surg. Pathologists, N.Y. Acad. Medicine. Fax: 212-746-6484.

ROSEN, RICHARD DAVID, lawyer; b. Pitts., June 24, 1940; s. Benjamin H. and Bertha B. (Broff) R.; m. Ellaine H. Heller, June 23, 1963; children: Deborah H. Fidel, Jaime M. Cohen. BA, Yale U., 1962; JD, Harvard U., 1965. Bar: Pa. 1966, Fla. 1979. Mgr. Bachrach, Sanderbeck & Co., Pitts., 1965-70; mng. ptnr. Grant Thornton, Pitts., 1970-76; chmn. tax dept. Baskin & Sears, Pitts., 1977-78; pres. Gas Transmission, Inc., Pitts., 1979—; dir., shareholder Cohen & Grigsby, Pitts., 1989—; bd. dirs., pres. R & R Oil Corp., Pitts.; bd. dirs., sec. Comml. Data Svcs., Sim Computer Leasing Corp., Pitts., Direct Mail Svc., Inc. Contbr. articles to profl. jours. Mem. investment com., trustee Jewish Healthcare Found., 1995—. Fellow Am. Coll. Trust and Estate Counsel; mem. ABA, Pa. Bar Assn. (mem. estate planning com. 1996—, chmn. 1998-2000), United Jewish Fedn. Greater Pitts. (chmn. profl. adv. com. 1997—), Concordia Club (dir. 1998-2000), Green Oaks Country Club (dir. 1997—). Avocations: golf, tennis. Home: 1198 Beechwood Ct Pittsburgh PA 15206-4522 Office: Cohen & Grigsby PC 11 Stanwix St 15 Fl Pittsburgh PA 15222-1312

ROSEN, SANFORD JAY, lawyer; b. N.Y.C., Dec. 19, 1937; s. Alexander Charles and Viola S. (Grad) R.; m. Catherine Picard, June 22, 1958; children: Caren E. Andrews, R. Durelle Schacter, Ian D., Melissa S. AB, Cornell U., 1959; LLB, Yale U., 1962. Bar: Conn. 1962, U.S. Supreme Ct. 1966, Calif. 1974. Law clk. to Hon. Simon E. Sobeloff U.S. Ct. Appeals, Balt., 1962-63; prof. sch. law U. Md., Balt., 1963-71; assoc. dir. Coun. on Legal Edn. Opportunity, Atlanta, 1969-70; vis. prof. law U. Tex., Austin, 1970-71; asst. legal dir. Nat. ACLU, N.Y.C., 1971-73; legal dir. Mex.-Am. Legal Def. Fund, San Francisco, 1973-75; ptnr. Rosen, Remcho & Henderson, San Francisco, 1976-80, Rosen & Remcho, San Francisco, 1980-82; prin. Law Offices of Sanford Jay Rosen, San Francisco, 1982-86; sr. ptnr. Rosen & Phillips, San Francisco, 1986-89; prin. Rosen & Assocs., San Francisco, 1990; sr. ptnr. Rosen, Bien & Asaro, San Francisco, 1991—; mem. Balt. Cmty. Rels. Commn., 1966-69; mem. com. Patuxent Instn., Md., 1967-69; ad hoc adminstrv. law judge Calif. Agrl. Labor Rels. Bd., San Francisco, 1975-80; interim monitor U.S. Dist. Ct. for no. dist. Calif., San Francisco, 1989, early neutral evaluator, 1987—, mediator, 1993—; judge pro tem San Francisco Superior Ct., 1991—; perm. atty. del. Jud. Conf. U.S. Ct. Appeal for 4th Cir.; atty. del. Jud. Conf. U.S. Ct. Appeals 9th cir., 1996-98. Contbr. articles to profl. jours. Mem. Com. on Adminstrn. of Criminal Justice, Balt., 1968; mem. adv. com. HEW, Washington, 1974-75. Mem. ABA, Assn. Trial Lawyers Am. (chair civil rights sect. 1993-94), D.C. Bar Assn., Calif. Bar Assn., Bar Assn. San Francisco. Avocations: reading, travel, movies. Office: Rosen Bien & Asaro 155 Montgomery St Fl 8 San Francisco CA 94104-4113

ROSEN, SERGEI (SERGEI TER-KAZARIAN), bacteriologist; b. St. Petersburg, Russia, Apr. 5, 1930; arrived in Israel, 1994; s. Shmavon Ter-Kazarian and Elka Rosina; m. Helena Nudelstein, July 20, 1956; children: Michael, Ariadna. Ed., St. Petersburg State U., 1948-53; CandBiolScis, St. Petersburg Vet. Inst., 1960; D Biol. Scis., Nat. Acad. Scis. Armenia, 1994. Cert. sr. sci. worker, prof. Sr. sci. worker, then head biochem. dept. All-Union Rsch. Inst. Breeding and Genetics of Farm Animals, St. Petersburg, 1958-62; head dept. microbiology, lab. dairy tech. Yerevan Zootech. and Vet. Inst., 1963-94; prof. ad hoc Yerevan State Inst. for Tng. of Physicians, 1986-94; head Bactaxon Ctr. on Continuous Post Register Tng. Bacteriologists of USSR in taxonomy, Nomenclature and Identification of Bacteria, Yerevan, 1980-92, Bactaxon Ctr. on Nat. Names and Regional Florae of Armenia, 1988-92, Bactaxon Ctr., Yerevan, 1992-94, Eilat, Israel, 1994—. Translator, compiler, part-publisher 10 vol. series on popularization of results of Intl. nomenclatural reform in bacteriology, 1974-90; contbr. articles to profl. jours. Recipient award in Memory of 250th Anniversary of Leningrad. Mem. Commn. D of Nat. Com. USSR in dairying, Com. taxonomy and nomenclature of pathogenic bacteria, protozoa and fungi of USSR, Ctrl. Coun. Acad. Scis. USSR in combined problem Microbilogy, Internat. Informatization Acad. (pres. Eilat chpt.). Home: PO Box 2314, Eilat 88122, Israel

ROSEN, SIDNEY WALTER, gastroenterologist; b. Lynn, Mass., July 26, 1918; s. Lewis Harold Rosen and Augusta Gorden; m. Lorraine A.; 1 child, Melanie Jane. BS, U. Mass., 1940; MD, U. Middlesex, 1943; MPH, Harvard U., 1999. Diplomate Am. Bd. Internal Medicine. Commd. USN, 1944, advanced through grades to comdr., 1944, comdr., 1944-58; intern Cumberland Hosp., Bklyn., 1943-44; resident in internal medicine U.S. Naval Hosp., Chelsea, Mass., 1956-58; fellow in gastroenterology Lahey Clinic, Boston, 1958-60; dir. utilization revues Charlton Hosp., Fall River, Mass., 1965-86, med. dir., 1983-86; cons. Blue Cross, Boston, 1968-85, U.S. Dept. Pub. Health, Washington, 1970-72, Physician Rev. Orgn., Eastern Mass., 1975-85; pres. Health Review Specialists, Boston, 1999—, Health Benefit Rev. LLC, Fall River, Mass. Fellow ACP, Am. Coll. Gastroenterology (gov. 1980-86), Mass. Med. Soc.; mem. Harvard Club., Ledgemont Country Club. Avocations: golf, sailing, horseback riding, travel. E-mail: call-sid@aoh.com. Home: 229 Highcrest Rd Fall River MA 02720-6619

ROSEN, WENDY WORKMAN, marketing professional; b. Miami, Sept. 17, 1954; d. Robert L. and Mildred E. (Duck) Workman; m. Steven David Rosen, June 22, 1972, children: Rebecca, Jeffrey. AS, Santa Fe Coll., 1974; BS, U. Fla., 1976. Cert. exhbn. mgr. Advt. exec. Balt. News Am., 1978-80, Balt. Mag, 1980-82; pres. The Rosen Group, Inc., Balt., 1982—; cons. Times Pub. Group, Balt., 1982; gen. ptnr. Mill Ctr. Artists Studios, Balt.; pres. Am. Craft Showroom; founder The Buyers Markets of American Crafts, founder Craft Bus. Inst. Author: Crafting as a Business, Cash For Your Crafts; pub.: Niche mag., Am. Style mag., Market Insider. Bd. mem. Craft Emergency Relief Fund. Mem. Natl. Assn. Exposition Mgrs., Glass Art Soc., James Renwick Alliance. Democrat. Jewish. Avocation: gardening. Office: The Rosen Agy 3000 Chestnut Ave Ste 300 Baltimore MD 21211-2769

ROSENBACH, LEOPOLD, engineer, consultant; b. Walbrzych, Poland, Jan. 10, 1947; came to the U.S., 1969; s. Samuel and Halina (Kormicz) R.; m. Pola Knott, Dec. 23, 1969; 1 child, Coleene Rosenbach. MSEE, Polytechnic, Wroclaw, Poland, 1968. Cert. mfg. engr. Mfg. mgr. Leviton Mfg. Co., Bklyn., 1973-77; mfg. engr. Eagle Electric, Long Island City, N.Y., 1977-78; electric mfg. engr. Standard Motor Products, Long Island City, 1979-83, product devel. mgr., 1984-87, design mgr., 1988-90, engring. mgr., 1991-93, dir. materials, 1994-96, dir. ops., 1996—. Contbr. numerous articles to sci. jours. Mem. IEEE, Am. Soc. Metals, Am. Purchasing Soc., Internat. Soc. for Hybrid Microelectronics (met. chpt. treas. 1988-89, sec. 89-90, pres. 90-91), Soc. Mfg. Engrs. Avocations: music, astronomy. Home: 10262 Cove Lake Dr Orlando FL 32836-3756 Office: Standard Motor Electronics 170 Sunport Ln Orlando FL 32809-7892

ROSENBACH, THOMAS GEORG, dermatologist; b. Bochum, Germany, June 3, 1959; s. Klaus and Wiltrud (Schaefer) R.; m. Bettina Hedwig Eberitsch, Nov. 28, 1980; 1 child, Alexandra. BA, Graf, Osnabrueck, Germany, 1977; MD, U. Muenster, 1986. Postdoctoral fellow dept. biochemistry U. Konstanz, Germany, 1986-87, CIIT, Rsch. Triangle Park, N.C., 1987-89; resident in dermatology U. Mainz, Germany, 1989-90; sr. staff scientist dept. dermatology U. Berlin, 1990-97; free practice dermatology Osnabrueck, Germany, 1997—. Editor: Dermatology and Venereology, 1998; contbr. articles to profl. jours.

ROSENBAUM, BELLE SARA, appraiser, interior designer, museum director, educator; b. N.Y.C., Apr. 1, 1922; d. Harry and Hinda (Sits) Heimowitz; m. Jacob H. Rosenbaum, Mar. 12, 1939; children: Linda Zelinger, Simmi Brodie, Martin, Arlene Levene. Cert., N.Y. Sch. Interior Design, 1945; MA in Judaic Art, U. B.C., 1997, PhD, 1997. Sr. mem. Am. Soc. Appraisers, Washington, 1979—; tchr. Judaica Yeshiva U., 1984—; dir. Mus. Contemporary Judaica; pres. Jarvis Designs, Inc., Union City, N.J., 1955-75, Design Assocs., BLS, Monsey, N.Y., 1970-78; v.p. Lord & Lady Inc., Union City, 1955-70, Cardio-Bionic Scanning, Inc., Spring Valley, N.Y., 1975-78; v.p., treas. Rapitech Sys., inc., 1985; exec. bd. State of Israel Bonds Orgn., 1992—. Author short stories, 1947-48, Chronicle of Jewish Traditions, 1992, Upon Thy Doorposts, 1996; contbr. articles on interior design to profl. jours. Bd. dirs. Midgal Ohr Schs., 1971—, Shaare Zedek Hosp., Jerusalem, 1998—, Jewish Fedn. Rockland County, 1999—, Riverdale (N.Y.) Jewish Mus., 1999—, Am. Guild Judaic Art, 1999—; chmn. bd. artifacts Rockland Holocaust Ctr., 1991—; trustee Rockland Ctr. Holocaust Studies, 1994; pres. Ednl. Ctr. Jewish Values Jerusalem Gt. Synagogue, Israel, 1998—; co-chair Nat. Jewish Art Week, 2000.

ROSENBAUM, DIETER, exercise scientist; b. Muenster, Germany, Dec. 27, 1957; s. Ferdinand and Margarete (Bungert) R.; m. Nikola Wolf, Dec. 6, 1988; two children. BA, U. Muenster, 1984; MA, U. Iowa, 1988; PhD, U. Konstanz, 1992. Rsch. asst. U. Essen, Germany, 1987-91, U. Muenster, Germany, 1991-92; rsch. fellow U. Ulm, Germany, 1992-97; rsch. fellow U. Muenster, 1997—, head Movement Analysis Lab., 1998—. Mem. Internat. Soc. Biomechs., European Orthopedic Rsch. Soc., European Soc. Foot & Ankle Surgeons. Office: U Muenster Dept Orthopedics, Domagkstr 3 Movement Anal, D-48129 Münster Germany

ROSENBAUM, ERNEST HAROLD, internist, oncologist, educator; b. Cleve., Jan. 5, 1929; s. Lionel Clarence Rosenbaum and Dora Beatrice Heldman; m. Isadora Ray, May 5, 1949; children: Eileen, Alexandra, Diane, Steven. BA, U. N.Mex., 1951; MD, U. Colo., 1956. Diplomate Am. Bd. Internal Medicine, Am. Bd. Oncology. Intern San Francisco Gen. Hosp., 1956-57, resident, 1957-58; resident Mt. Zion Hosp., San Francisco, 1958-59; resident New England Ctr. Hosp., 1961-63, fellow, 1961-63; mem. staff U. Calif. San Francisco/Mt. Zion Hosp. Med. Ctr.; clin. prof. medicine U. Calif. San Francisco; med. dir. Better Health Found., San Francisco, 1987-98; bd. dirs. Susan B. Komen Found., San Francisco, 1989-98; program dir. Cancer Supportive Care Program, Complementary Medicine Clinic, Stanford U. Sch. Medicine, 1999—. Med. advisor San Francisco Opera, 1988-97. Fellow ACP; mem. Calif. Med. Assn., San Francisco Med. Soc., Am. Soc. Oncologists. Jewish. Office: U Calif/Mt Zion Cancer Ctr 2356 Sutter St Fl 7 San Francisco CA 94115-3006

ROSENBAUM, GREG ALAN, merchant banker, consultant; b. Toledo, Aug. 7, 1952; s. Marvin and Ida Edith (Millman) R.; m. Martha Jane Radlo, Sept. 3, 1978; children: Eli Samuel, Eve Hannah, Elliott Jacob. AB, Harvard U., 1974, M in Pub. Policy, 1978, JD, 1978. Bar: Ohio 1978, Ill. 1980. Summer assoc. Jones, Day, Reavis & Pogue, Cleve., 1977; tchg. fellow in govt. and social scis. Harvard U., Cambridge, Mass., 1976-78; cons. Boston Consulting Group, Boston and Chgo., 1978-82; v.p. Dyson-Kissner-Moran Corp., N.Y.C., 1982-87; mng. dir. Carlyle Group, Washington, 1987-88; pres. Palisades Assocs., Inc., Bethesda, Md., 1988—; debating coach Harvard U., 1976-79; dir. Varlen Corp., Naperville, Ill., 1985-99, Richey Electronics, Inc., Garden Grove, Calif., 1993-99, McLaren/Hart Inc., Rancho Cordova, Calif., 1995-2000, Expressions Furniture, Inc., Anaheim, Calif., 1992-97, AMCO Corp., Chgo., 1993-97, The Whaler on Kaanapali Beach, 1999—, PlayCore Holdings, Inc., 2000—. Co-author: The Crime of Poverty, 1973, Beyond Politics, 1974, World Without Plenty, 1975. Dir. Lifeline, A Mental Retardation Partnership, Washington, 1993-98; baseball coach Potomac (Md.) Boys' Club, 1992-96; co-chair Harvard Debate Centennial, 1991—; mem. Harvard Law Sch. 20th Reunion gift com., 1997-98, 25th Reunion gift com., 1998-99. Winner Ames Moot Ct. competition Harvard Law Sch., 1976. Mem. ABA, Am. Forensic Assn. (nat. intercollegiate debate champion 1974, coach nat. intercollegiate debate champion 1979), Am. Acad. Polit. and Social Scis., Ctr. for Study of Presidency, Toledo Bar Assn., Chgo. Bar Assn., Phi Beta Kappa. Democrat. Jewish. Avocations: major league baseball, golf, computers, sports memorabilia. Office: Palisades Assocs Inc 9140 Vendome Dr Bethesda MD 20817-4021

ROSENBAUM, TOMAS PEDRO, surgeon; b. Buenos Aires, Aug. 15, 1947; arrived in Eng., 1975; s. Joseph Rosenbaum and Elizabeth Wilhermsdorfer; 1 child, Leah Alexandra. MD, U. Buenos Aires, 1973. LRCP/MRCS, London, FRCS/Edinburgh, FRCS Intercollegiate Bd. in Urology, U.K., FEBU/European Bd. Urology; medical diplomate in Argentina, U.K.; cert. urol. surgeon U.K. and Europe. Clin. lectr. in urology Inst. Urology, London, 1989-91; registrar in urology St. Peter's Hosp., London, 1992; sr. registrar in urology Hammersmith Hosp., Eng., 1992-93, St. Helier Hosp., Eng., 1994, Royal Marsden Hosp., Eng., 1995; cons. urol. surgeon Ealing Hosp., Eng., 1996—; sec. Assn. of Argentinian Doctors, Inc., U.K., 1990—; clin. lectr. Inst. Urology, London, 1989-91; anatomy demonstrator Oxford U., 1979; pharmacology demonstrator Faculty of Medicine, U. Buenos Aires, 1971-72. Patentee in field; contbr. articles to profl. jours. Mem. Royal Soc. Medicine, Brit. Assn. Urol. Surgeons, Internat. Continence Soc. Avocations: travel, social critic, teacher, family. Office: Ealing Hosp, Uxbridge Rd, UB1 3HW Southall Middlesex, England

ROSENBERG, ALEX JACOB, art dealer, curator, fine arts appraiser, educator; b. N.Y.C., May 25, 1919; s. Israel and Lena (Zar) R. Student, Albright Coll., 1935-37, Sch. Phila. Mus. Art, 1937-40; BS, Phila. Coll. Textiles and Sci., 1948; DHL (hon.), Hofstra U., 1989. completed Personal Property courses, levels I, II, III and IV, Am. Soc. of Appraisers, Uniform Standards of Profl. Appraisal Practice, 1994. Pres. Anserphone, 1959-66; sec., dir. Gen. Cablevision Tex., 1968-72; v.p., dir. Communicable, Inc., Fla., 1967-71, Gen. Cablevision Palatka, Fla., 1967-71, Beacon Cable Corp., 1966-71; pres., dir. Modern Cable Corp., 1966-71, B.F.C.-C.A.T.V. Corp., 1966-71; v.p., dir. Starfax Corp. Real Estate, 1968-70; gen. ptnr. Lakewood Plaza Assocs., N.J., 1973-92, Rostin Assocs., Austin, Tex., 1970-83; pres. Transworld Art Inc., 1973-92, Alex Rosenberg Gallery and Alba Edits., N.Y.C., 1968-89, Rostin Mgmt. Corp., 1986-89, The Abbot Group, 1987-89, Ardmore Affiliates Ltd., Alex Rosenberg Fine Art, 1985—, Neikrug-Rosenberg Assocs., 1989-97; lectr. Parsons Sch. Design, N.Y.C., 1979-88; instr. appraising modern art NYU, 1992-95, adj. prof. appraising NYU, 1995—; vis. prof. fine art Advanced Inst. Arts, Havana, Cuba, 1993—; organizer Henry Moore exhbn. Mus. Budapest, Bratislava and Prague, 1993, Havana, 1997. Contbr. articles to profl. jours.; co-curator Romare Bearden as Printmaker, 1992-97; assoc. editor exhbn. catalogue; curator An american Portrait, 1976-78, Mus. Fine Art, Havana, 1992-93; co-curator Henry Moore Mother and Child Exhbn., 1987-88. Trustee Alice Baber Art Fund, 1991-93, Phila. Coll. Textiles and Sci., 1992-95, Tel Aviv Mus. Art (mem. internat. bd. dirs.), 1999—; Bd. dirs. Artists' Rights Today, 1974-80; mus. adv. bd. Hofstra Mus., Hempstead, N.Y., 1987-92; mem. collection and exhbn. com. Parrish Art Mus., Southhampton, N.Y., 1989-95; mem. adv. com. Pollock-Krasner House and Study Ctr., 2000—; mem. bd. Ludwig Found of Cuba, 1998—; trustee Guttman Inst., 1979-92; mem. exec. bd. Nat. Emergency Civil Liberties Com., 1970-98, treas., 1981—; trustee Nat. Emergency Civil Liberties Found., 1984-98, chmn., 1992—; nat. bd. dirs. and bd. dirs. local coun. SANE, 1974-83, bd. dirs. Ctr. for Constitutional Rights, 1998—; trustee, treas. New Lincoln Sch., 1968-71; trustee Givat Haviva Ednl. Found., N.Y.C., 1969—, chmn. exec. com., 1992-99; trustee Givat Haviva Inst., Hadera, Israel, 1993—, Stephen Wise Free synagogue, 1967-70, 73-76, 99, Mus. Borough Bklyn., 1986-89; del. 28th World Zionist Congress, Jerusalem, 1972; mem. Cmty. Planning Bd. # 7, 1965-67, 70-72; mem. Lower West Side Anti-Poverty Bd., 1965-66, Lincoln Ctr. Cmty. Coun., 1968-74, Com. for Ind. Civilian Police Rev. Bd., 1967; mem. steering com. Com. Pub. Edn. and Religious Liberty; chmn. Am. Israel Civil Liberties Coalition, 1988-89; Dem. dist. leader, 1964-74, state committeeman, 1970-73, mem. county exec. com., 1964-74; del. Dem. Nat. Conf., 1968, 72; bd. dirs. Raoul Wallenberg Commn. of U.S., 1986-90, chmn., 1990-92; mem. print and drawing coun. Israel Mus., 1980-85; assoc. dir. Snug Harbor Cultural Ctr., S.I., 1982-88; mem., AAA del., Pres. Coun. of Appraisal Orgns., 1995-96; bd. mem. Ludwig Found. of Cuba, 1995—, Cuban-American Cultural Grp., 1995—; mem. Assn. Governing Bds. of Univs. and Colls., 1994-96, Nat. Registry of Forensic Examiners, 1994-96. Recipient Spl. prize Grenschen Triennial, Switzerland, 1976, Israel prize, 1974, Cuban Order of Culture, 1995, Cert. of Commendation, Am. Soc. Appraisers, 1993, Cert. for Disting. Svc., Appraisers Assn. of Am., 1993, Graham J. Littlewood III award for profl. excellence Phila. Coll. of Textiles and Sci., 1996, Alex and Carole Rosenberg Collection, Savannah Coll. of Art and Design, 1999. Mem. Am. Soc. Appraisers (sr., bd. examiners 1987—, personal property com. 1987-89), Appraisers Assn. Am. (cert. mem., bd. dirs. 1990-96, v.p. 1992-94, 1st v.p. 1994, pres. 1994-96), Fine Art Pubs. Assn. (v.p., bd. dirs. 1981-83, pres. 1983-86, treas. 1986-89), Nat. Arts Club. Home and Office: 3 E 69th St New York NY 10021-4943

ROSENBERG, CAROLE, art dealer, real estate broker; b. Bklyn., Nov. 16, 1936; d. Hugo and Mildred (Wilinsky) Clemente; m. Melvyn S. Sponder; m. Jerome A. Hasband; children: Michael S. Halsband, Kenneth L. Halsband; m. Alex J. Rosenberg, May 15, 1977. Student, Hunter Coll., 1954-56; BA, Bklyn. Coll., 1958; postgrad., NYU, 1961-62, 64-65. Tchr. N.Y.C. Sch. System, 1958-59, 61-63, Fla. Sch. System, Miami Beach, 1959-61; gallery owner and dir. Original Graphics/Carole Halsband Gallery, N.Y.C., 1971-76; assoc. editor Transworld Art Inc., N.Y.C., 1974-78; exec. dir., curator Alex Rosenberg Gallery/Transworld Art Inc., N.Y.C., 1978-87; exec. dir., v.p. Ardmore Affiliates Ltd., N.Y.C., 1987—; real estate salesperson N.Y.C., 1986-91; real estate broker Carole Rosenberg Properties Internat. Ltd., 1992—; treas. 3/69 Owners Corp., N.Y.C.1984-87, pres., 1987-91, v.p., 1991-93; chmn. bd. dirs. Friends of the Hofstra U. Arboretum, Hempstead, N.Y., 1991-94. Editor: (art catalogs) Henry Moore, Howard Kanovitz, Mark Tobey, Lila Katzen, 1975; assoc. editor (portfolio) An American Portrait, 1976. Com. mem. Friends of Upper East Side Hist. Dist., N.Y.C., 1983-96—; mem. adv. bd. Women/Beyond Borders, 1995—, Ludwig Found. Cuba, 1995—; mem. Watermill Ctr. Cmty. Bd., 1999—; internat. bd. mem. Tel Aviv Mus. Art, 1999—; pres. Am. Friends of the Ludwig Found. of Cuba, 2000—; bd. dirs. Am. Friends of the Tel Aviv Mus., 2000—; bd. mem. Lotos Found., 2000—. Recipient Lotos medal of merit, 1995, Mgmt. Achievement Award for Innovation, N.Y. Habitat Mag., N.Y.C., 1989. Mem. Real Estate Bd. N.Y.C., Parrish Art Mus. (patron garden com.), Met. Mus. Art, Mus. Modern Art, Guggenheim Mus., Nat. Arts Club, Hort. Soc. N.Y., Lotos Club (mem. art com. 1989—, chmn. art com. 1992-98, dir. 1993-99), City Gardens Club, Women's City Club Am. Hort. Soc., N.Y. Hort. Soc., (Longhouse Res. garden comm. 1995—), Hort. Alliance of the Hamptons, Guggenheim Mus. Democrat. Jewish. Avocation: gardening.

ROSENBERG, GÖRAN J., editor; b. Södertalje, Sweden, Oct. 11, 1948; s. David and Hala (Staw) R.; m. Annikka Isaksson, May 30, 1972 (div. 1974) 1 child, Vanna; m. Ann Charlotte Hedberg, May 31, 1985; children: Elin, Agnes. BA, U. Stockholm, 1968; degree in journalism, Stockholm Sch. Journalism, 1970; PhD (hon.), U. Gothenburg, 2000. Reporter A-pressens Redaktionstjanst, Stockholm, 1970-72, Swedish Broadcasting Corp., Stockholm, 1972-75, Swedish TV News, 1975-77, 79-81; producer, moderator Swedish TV Current Affairs, 1981-85; writer, reporter Aftonbladet Weekly mag., 1977-79; corr. Swedish TV, Washington, 1985-89; editor-in-chief Moderna Tider, Stockholm, 1990-99; freelance writer, 1999—. Author: Friare kan ingen vara, 1991, Medborgaren som forsvann, om politikens kris och möjligheter, 1993, Dacapo a Fine och andra efterkloka berättelser, 1994, Det förlorade landet, en personlig historia, 1996, Das Verlorene Land, Suhrkamp, 1998.

ROSENBERG, HERB, sculptor, educator; b. N.Y.C., Feb. 4, 1942; s. David and Eve Rosenberg; m. Jean Rosenberg, Nov. 14, 1976 (div. Nov. 1998); 1 child, Andrew. BA, SUNY, Binghamton, 1964; MFA, Pratt Inst., 1967. Cert. art therapist. Dir. art therapy studies N.J. City U., Jersey City, 1971—. Exhibited in group shows at World's Fair, Brisbane, Australia, 1988, UNESCO, Paris, 1992, Grand Palais, Paris, 1994. Bd. dirs. Hurley Found., N.Y.c., 1994—, Ctr. Bros d'Or Cultural Ctr., N.S., Can., 1996—, C.A.S.E. Mus., Jersey City, 1995—. Grantee Jersey City State Coll., 1979, 81, 84, 88; recipient Juror's award Hong Kong Mus. Art, 1992; named

Sculptor of Yr., Hudson County Cultural Ctr., 1984. Mem. Internat. Arts Therapy Assn. (chair 1984-86), Internat. Sculpture Soc., Am. Art Therapy Assn., Australian Sculpture Soc., Kans. Sculpture Soc. E-mail: pneuonce@aol.com. Office: NJ City U 5930 Kennedy Blvd Jersey City NJ 07300

ROSENBERG, JILL, realtor, civic leader; b. Shreveport, La., Feb. 17, 1940; d. Morris H. and Sallye (Abramson) Schuster; m. Lewis Rosenberg, Dec. 23, 1962; children: Craig, Paige. BA in Philosophy, Tulane U., 1961, MSW, 1965; grad., Realtor Inst., 1994. Cert. residential specialist Residential Sales Coun.; grad. Realtor Inst. 1993. Social worker La. Dept. Pub. Welfare, 1961-62, 63-64; genetics counselor Sinai Hosp., Balt., 1967-69; ptnr. Parties Extraordinaire, cons., 1973-77; realtor assoc. Robert Weil Assocs., Long Beach, Calif., 1982—. Pres. we. region Brandeis U. Nat. Women's Com., 1972-73; bd. dirs. Long Beach Symphony Assn., 1984-85; v.p. Jewish Cmty. Fedn. Long Beach and West Orange County, 1983-86, bd. dirs., 1982-86; pres. Long Beach Cancer League, 1987-88, exec. bd. dirs., 1984-96; pres. Long Beach Jewish Cmty. Sr. Housing Corp., 1989-91; v.p. fundraising S.E. unit Long Beach Harbor chpt. Am. Cancer Soc., 1989-90; bd. dirs. Westerly Sch. Assoc., 1991—; bd. trustees St. Mary Med. Ctr. Found., 1991—; fund chair St. Mary Med. Ctr., 1992-94; pres. nat. conf. NCCJ, 1994-96, bd. dirs. 1989—; pres. Leadership Long Beach, 1994-95; bd. dirs. Phoenix Long Beach Mus. Art, 1992-98, Am. Diabetes Assn., Long Beach, Calif., 1997-99. Recipient Young Leadership award Jewish Community Fedn. Long Beach and West Orange County, 1981, Jerusalem award State of Israel, 1989, Hannah G. Solomon award Nat. Coun. Jewish Women, 1992, Alumnus of Yr. award Leadership Long Beach, 1995, Humanitarian award The Nat. Conf., 1997, Leadership award Calif. Assn. Leadership Programs, 2000; named Rick Racker Woman of Yr., 1999; scholar La. Dept. Pub. Welfare, 1962, NIMH, 1964. Mem. Rotary Club of Long Beach (bd. dirs. 2000—). Office: Robert Weil Assocs 5220 E Los Altos Plz Long Beach CA 90815-4251

ROSENBERG, JONATHAN MICAH, mathematics educator; b. Chgo., Dec. 30, 1951; s. Jerome L. and Shoshana (Gabriel) R.; m. Jeanne Marie Sauber, May 20, 1990; children: Arieh Joseph, Liora Miriam. AB summa cum laude, Harvard U., 1972; diploma, U. Cambridge, Eng., 1973; PhD, U. Calif., Berkeley, 1976. Instr. math. U. Pa., Phila., 1976-77, asst. prof. math., 1977-81; assoc. prof. math. U. Md., College Park, 1981-85, prof. math., 1985—. Author: Alegraic K-Theory and its Applications, 1994; contbr. articles to profl. jours. Recipient Frank Knox Meml. fellowship, Harvard U., 1972-73, NSF grad. fellowship, 1973-76, rsch. fellowship, Alfred P. Sloan Found., 1980-84. Mem. Am. Math. Soc. (editor Proceedings, 1988-91, assoc. editor jour. 2000—, mem.-at-large coun. 2000—), Math. Assn. Am. Avocation: piano playing. Office: U Md Dept Math College Park MD 20742-0001

ROSENBERG, PIERRE MAX, museum director; b. Paris, Apr. 13, 1936; s. Charles and Gertrude (Nassauer) R.; m. Béatrice de Rothschild, July 29, 1981. Baccalauréat, Lycée Charlemagne, Paris; Licence, Law Faculty, Paris; Diplome, Louvre Sch., Paris. Chief curator dept. paintings Musée du Louvre, Paris, 1982-94, pres., dir., 1994—. Author: Chardin, 1963, 99, Peyron, 1983, (catalogue) La peinture francaise du XVIIe siècle dans les coll. américaines, 1981, (catalogue) Watteau, 1984, 96, Fragonard, 1987, Frères Le Nain, 1993, Poussin, 1994, G. de la Tour, 1997, D. Vivant Denon, 1999. Mem. Soc. Histoire Art Francais (pres. 1982-84), Com. Francais Histoire Art (pres. 1984-96), Acad. Francaise. Home: 35 rue de Vaugirard, 75006 Paris France Office: Musée du Louvre, 34 quai du Louvre, 75058 Paris France

ROSENBERG, RAYMOND DAVID, secondary education educator, consultant; b. Jersey City, Apr. 25, 1951; s. Fabulous Sam and Arlene (White) R.; m. JoAnn Gabriella Simchera, June 10, 1984; 1 child, Anna Teresa. BA, Boston U., 1974; MEd, William Paterson Coll., 1978, MEd in Sch. Adminstrn., 1994. Cert. tchr., N.J. Child care worker Bergen Residential Ctr., Rockleigh, N.J., 1975; substitute tchr. aide South Cliff Elem. Sch., Ft. Lee, N.J., 1975-76; mgr. Betty Gercek Residence, N.Y.C., 1977-78; tchr. Lodi (N.J.) Boy's and Girl's Club Preschool, 1979-80; tchr. reading Passaic County Tech. Vocat. High Sch., Wayne, N.J., 1980-82; specialist learning disabilities North Jersey Devel. Ctr., Totowa, 1983-84, adaptive switch tchr., 1986-87; ednl. specialist Div. Devel. Disabilities, Springfield, N.J., 1984-85, tchr. profoundly retarded students, 1987-89, tchr. medically frail, 1990-91; tchr. mildly retarded, emotionally disturbed students North Jersey Devel. Ctr., Totowa, 1992-93; learning disabilities tchr. Office of Edn., N.J., 1993-96; cons. youth consultation svcs. George Washington Sch. Annex, Hackensack, N.J., 1993-96; learning cons. child study team North Bergen (N.J.) H.S., 1996-98; GED tchr. Bergen C.C. Computer Learning Ctr., Paramus, 1998—; learning disabilities tchr., cons., 1995-2000, cons. Juvenile Justice Commn., 1995—; pres. Ednl. Assessment Svcs., Inc.; sales assoc. Radio Shack, 2000—. Editor: Common Sense Newsletter, 1972, Jour. Learning Cons., 1996. Asst. scoutmaster Boy Scouts Am., Teaneck, N.J., 1980-83; mem. St. James Episcopal Ch., Sexton. Recipient Eagle Scout award Boy Scouts Am., Ridgefield, N.J., 1968. Mem. Nat. Eagle Scout Assn., Pi Lambda Theta (Beta Chi chpt.). Episcopal. Lodge: Order of Arrow. Avocations: applied behavior analysis, behavior modification, behavior therapy.

ROSENBERG, RICHARD MARK, orchestral conductor, artistic director; b. Bronx, N.Y., Aug. 31, 1954; s. Abraham and Ethel Pearl (Fox) R.; m. Laura Julianne Schnayer, Dec. 31, 1983. BA, Queens Coll., 1975; MusM, Yale U., 1977. Music dir. Resonance, N.Y.C., 1975-87, Pa. Ballet, Phila., 1990-95, Tex. Chamber Symphony, Austin, 1991—; asst. prof. U. Mich., Ann Arbor, 1987-90; music. assoc. London Classical Players, 1988-91; artistic dir. Hot Springs (Ark.) Music Festival, 1995—; apprentice condr. Baverian State Opera, Munich, 1985; guest condr. Rochester (N.Y.) Philharm., 1988, Classical Band, Schleswig-Holstein, Germany, 1990-91, Miami City Ballet/Naples (Fla.) Philharm. Orch., 1994—. Condr. recording: (CD) Works for Viola and Orchestra, 1988, Music of Gottschalk, 1999, Music of Lambert, 1999, Music of Dédé, 1999; editor string sextet (Schönberg) Transfigured Night, 1989. Advisor Clinton Cultural Campus, Hot Springs, 1994—, Hot Springs Civic Ctr., 1995—, Greenway Project, Hot Springs, 1995—; adjudicator Stella Boyle Competition, Little Rock, 1997. Calhoun fellow Yale U., 1976, Rackham fellow U. Mich., 1988; recipient Music award USMC, 1971. Mem. Nat. Symphony Orch. League, Sigma Alpha Iota. Avocations: sculpture, woodworking, horticulture, travel, photography. Office: Hot Springs Music Festival 634 Prospect Ave Hot Springs National Park AR 71901-3918

ROSENBERG, RICHARD MORRIS, banker; b. Fall River, Mass., Apr. 21, 1930; s. Charles and Betty (Peck) R.; m. Barbara K. Cohen, Oct. 21, 1956; children: Michael, Peter. BS, Suffolk U., 1952; MBA, Golden Gate U., 1962; LLB, Golden Gate Coll., 1966. Publicity asst. Crocker-Anglo Bank, San Francisco, 1959-62; banking services officer Wells Fargo Bank, N.A., San Francisco, 1962-65; asst. v.p. Wells Fargo Bank, N.A., 1965-68, v.p. mktg. dept., 1968, v.p., dir. mktg., 1969, sr. v.p. mktg. and advt. div., 1970-75, exec. v.p., from 1975, vice chmn., 1980-83; vice chmn. Crocker Nat. Corp., 1983-85; pres., chief operating officer Seafirst Corp., 1986-87, also dir.; pres., chief operating officer Seattle First Nat. Bank, 1985-87; vice chmn. bd. BankAm. Corp., San Francisco, 1987-90, chmn., CEO, 1990-96; bd. dirs. Airborne Express, Northrop Cor., Pacific Mut.; past chmn. Mastercard Internat.; past pres. Fed. Res. Adv. Coun. Bd. dirs. San Francisco Symphony, United Way; trustee Calif. Inst. Tech.; bd. dirs. Am. Ctr. for Wine, Food and the Arts. Jewish. Office: BankAm Corp Dept 3001-B PO Box 37000 San Francisco CA 94137-0001

ROSENBERG, RUDY, chemical company executive; b. Feb. 26, 1930; came to U.S., 1949, naturalized, 1954; s. Hilaire and Frieda Rosenberg; m. Rose H. Wauters, Nov. 7, 1953; 1 child, Rudy. Student in classical studies, Atheneum Leon Lepage, Brussels, 1946. Buyer Lever Bros., Brussels, 1946-49; head biochem. divsn. Mann Rsch. Labs., N.Y.C., 1954-61, Gallard-Schlesinger, Carle Place, N.Y., 1961-75; pres. Accurate Chem. & Sci. Corp., Westbury, N.Y., 1975—; prin., v.p., Leeches U.S.A. Ltd. Served with U.S. Army, 1951-53. Mem. Reticuloendothelial Soc. Internat. Clubs: Antique Automobile, Rolls Royce, Puppetry Guild Greater N.Y. Democrat.

ROSENBERG, THEODORE ROY, financial executive; b. Nyack, N.Y., Aug. 6, 1933; s. Rebecca Sheer R.; m. Eleanor Schmalsteig, Feb. 19, 1956 (div); children: Bradley Scott, Martha Ann; m. Mary Frances McVay, Sept. 21, 1991. BS, U. Conn., 1955; MBA, U. Pa., 1964. Commd. 2nd lt. U.S. Army, 1955, advanced through grades to col., 1976, retired, 1982; portfolio mgr. The Burney Co., Falls Church, Va., 1979—, v.p. mktg., 1982-94, v.p., 1994-95; pres., 1995—. Bd. dirs. Army Transp. Mus., U. Conn. Found., 1995—. Decorated Legion of Merit, Bronze Star; recipient Vietnam Medal of Honor, Govt. of Vietnam, 1966; inducted into Alumni Hall of Fame, U. Conn. Sch. Bus. Adminstrn., 1994. Mem. U. Pa. Mid-Atlantic Regional Adv. Bd., Wharton Club of Washington (Man of Yr. 1995). Avocations: scuba diving, snorkeling, golf. Office: The Burney Co 121 Rowell Ct Falls Church VA 22046-3174

ROSENBERGER, GERHARD, mathematics educator; b. Wentorf, Germany, Dec. 8, 1944; s. Horst and Jutta (Bless) R.; m. Katariina Kangas, July 24, 1976; children: Anja, Aila. Grad. U. Hamburg, Fed. Republic Germany, 1973, Inauguration, 1974. Asst., U. Hamburg, 1972-76; professorial chair rep. U. Bielefeld, Fed. Republic Germany, 1976-77; prof. math. U. Dortmund, Fed. Republic Germany, 1977—. Contbr. rsch. articles to math. jours., 2 math. books. Mem. Hamburger Math. Gesellschaft, Deutsche Mathematikervereinigung, Am. Math. Soc., Suomen Matemaattinen Yhdistys, Hochschulverband, Deutsch-Finnische Gesellschaft, London Math. Soc. Lutheran. Office: U Dortmund, Fachbereich Mathematik, 44221 Dortmund Germany

ROSENBERGER, JEAN ALEXANDRE, radiologist; b. Paris, Sept. 24, 1934; s. Jean Jacques Rosenberger and Marie Celestine Tousch; m. Josette Nicole DeBiesse, Dec. 20, 1956; children: Corinne, Gilles, Celine. BS, U. Paris, 1952, cert. in scis., 1953, MD, 1959. Extern Hosp. Paris, 1957; intern Hosp. Region, Paris, 1961-65, asst., 1965-72; attache Ctr. Hosp. U., Paris, 1963; radiologist Liberal Ctr. Radiology, Choisy Le Roi, France, 1968—; charge d'enseignnement CHU Clinic Créteil, 1971-72. Syndicate radiologist Tresorier, 1973—; medecin honoraire Marine Nationale, 1961-63. Recipient Temoignage de Satisfaction, Marine Nat., 1968. Avocations: botany, books. Home: 57 Ave du Mesnil, 94210 La Varenne France Office: Ctr Radiology, 2 Av Anatole France, 94600 Choisy le Roi France

ROSENBLAD, ELSA FRITZE SUSANNE, technology educator, researcher; b. Stockholm, Aug. 21, 1943; d. Gösta and Märta (Wendels) R.; m. Peter Wallin, Oct. 30, 1964 (div. 1991); 1 child, Jens; m. Ebbe Björkquist, June 24, 1993. MSc, U. Goteborg, 1967; PhD, Chalmers U. of Tech., 1983. Rsch. engr. Swedish Textile Rsch. Inst., Goteborg, 1968-72; rsch. engr. Nat. Swedish Bd. for Tech. Devel., Goteborg, 1972-79, Stockholm, 1979-81; rsch. engr. Nat. Swedish Def. Material Adminstrn., Stockholm, 1981-87; rsch. leader Swedish Furniture Inst., Stockholm, 1987-89; prof. Chalmers U. of Tech., Göteborg, 1989—; mem. bd. Swedish Transport and Comms. Rsch. Bd. Avocation: golf, bridge. Office: Chalmers U of Tech, Dept Human Centered Tech, SE-41296 Göteborg Sweden

ROSENBLATT, DAVID, mathematical statistician, research consultant; b. N.Y.C., Sept. 5, 1919; s. Hyman and Esther M. (Goldberg) R.; m. Joan Eliot Raup, June 10, 1950. BS in Biology with honors in math. logic, CCNY, 1940. Assoc. statistician Office Price Adminstrn., Washington, 1941-44; sr. economist div. statis. standards U.S. Bur. Budget, Washington, 1944-49, statis. cons., 1949-53; asst. prof. econs. Carnegie Inst. Tech., Pitts., 1949-51; assoc. prof. stats. Am. U., Washington, 1953-55; prin. investigator Office Naval Rsch., Washington, 1953-57; math. cons. info. tech. div. Nat. Bur. Standards, Washington, 1961-63, mathematician, mem. editorial rev. bd., 1963-67; rsch. cons. to industry, univs., fed. sci. agys., Washington, 1951-53, 55-61, 68—; adj. prof. math. and stats. Am. U., 1959-61. Contbr. articles to profl. jours. Littauer fellow Harvard U., 1947-48. Fellow AAAS, Am. Statis. Assn., Royal Statis. Soc. (London), Washington Acad. Scis.; mem. Inst. Math. Stats., Am. Math. Soc., Philos. Soc. Washington, Phi Beta Kappa, Sigma Xi. Achievements include research in applied stochastic processes, invention of probabilistic group testing, in automata and networks, theory of graphs and theory of relations, matrix theories, mathematical theory of organizations and complex systems, logic and design of large-scale information systems, boolean and relation-algebraic methods, history of mathematical and symbolic methods in resource and social sciences, and biological structures and relations. Home and Office: 2939 Van Ness St NW Apt 702 Washington DC 20008-4628

ROSENBLATT, JULIA CARLSON, journalist, psychology educator; b. Orange, N.J., Dec. 26, 1940; d. Harold S. and Anabel (Alberts) Carlson; m. Albert M. Rosenblatt, Aug. 23, 1970; 1 child, Betsy L. BA, Upsala Coll., East Orange, N.J., 1962; MA, U. Iowa, 1964, PhD, 1965. Postdoctoral fellow Ednl. Testing Svc., Princeton, N.J., 1965-67; asst. prof. psychology Vassar Coll., Poughkeepsie, N.Y., 1967-73; freelance journalist Pleasant Valley, N.Y., 1973—; instr. Mohawk Mountain Ski Sch., Cornwall, Conn., 1983-93; bd. dirs. Poughkeepsie Savs. Bank, 1979-88; vis. asst. prof. Victorian studies Vassar Coll., 1993. Co-author: Dining with Sherlock Holmes, 1976, rev., 1990; also articles. Bd. dirs. Dutchess County Assn. Sr. Citizens, Poughkeepsie, 1980-86, Mid-Hudson Civic Ctr., Poughkeepsie, 1982-91, Dorothy Albertson Fund for Little People, Pleasant Valley, 1984-92, Luth. Housing Devel. Corp., 1995—; treas. Ret. Sr. Vol. Program, Poughkeepsie, 1980-81; mem. adv. bd. Wartburg Luth. Svcs., 1993—; bd. dirs. Luth. Housing Devel. Fund, 1996—. USPHS fellow, 1962-65. Mem. APA, N.Am. Ski Journalists Assn., Profl. Ski Instrs. Am., Ea. Ski Writers Assn. Avocations: photography, skiing. Home and Office: 300 Freedom Rd Pleasant Valley NY 12569-5431

ROSENBLATT, MICHAEL, medical researcher, educator; b. Lund, Sweden, Nov. 27, 1947; s. Arthur Rosenblatt and Jean (Strosberg) Bialer; m. Patricia Ellen Regenbogen, Aug. 23, 1969; children: Anna Miriam, Adam Richard. AB summa cum laude, Columbia U., 1969; MD magna cum laude, Harvard U., 1973. Diplomate Am. Bd. Internal Medicine. Intern then resident Mass. Gen. Hosp., Boston, 1973-75, clin. rsch. fellow in endocrinology and metabolism, 1975-77, chief endocrine unit, 1981-84; instr. in medicine Harvard U., Boston, 1976-78, asst. prof. medicine, 1978-82, assoc. prof. medicine, 1982-85; v.p. for biol. rsch. Merck Sharp & Dohme Rsch. Labs., 1984-87, v.p. for biol. rsch. and molecular biology, 1987-89; sr. v.p. rsch. Merck Sharp & Dohme Rsch. Labs., West Point, Pa., 1989-92; dir. divsn. health sci. and tech. Harvard-MIT, 1992-98; Ebert prof. molecular medicine Harvard Med. Sch., Boston, 1992-98; chief divsn. bone and mineral metabolism Beth Israel Hosp., Boston, 1992—; faculty dean acad. programs Beth Israel Deaconess Med. Ctr., Harvard Med., 1996-2000, George R. Minot prof. med., 1998-2000; sr. v.p. acad. affairs Beth Israel Deaconess Med. Ctr., 1996—; exec. dir. Carl J. Shapiro Inst. for Edn. and Rsch. at Harvard Med. Sch. and Beth Israel Deaconess Med. Ctr., 1996-2000, pres., 1999—. Editor: Atrial Natriuretic Factor Endocrinology and Metabolism Clinics of N.Am., 1987; contbr. numerous sci. articles on parathyroid hormone and calcium metabolism to leading sci. jours. Recipient Vincent du Vigneaud award Gordon Confs., Kingston, R.I., 1986, Fuller Albright award Am. Soc. for Bone and Mineral Rsch., 1986, citation Japan Endocrine Soc., Tokyo, Taiwanese Osteoporosis Soc., Tainan. Fellow AAAS; mem. The Endocrine Soc., Am. Soc. for Biochemistry and Molecular Biology, Am. Soc. for Clin. Investigation, Am. Soc. Bone and Mineral Rsch. (pres. 1997-98), Assn. Am. Physicians, Inter-Urban Clin. Club (pres. 1997-98). Home: 130 Lake Ave Newton MA 02459-2108 Office: Beth Israel Deaconess Med Ctr 330 Brookline Ave # FD-230 Boston MA 02215-5400

ROSENBLITH, WALTER ALTER, scientist, educator; b. Vienna, Austria, Sept. 21, 1913; came to U.S., 1939, naturalized, 1946; s. David A. and Gabriele (Roth) R.; m. Judy Olcott Francis, Sept. 27, 1941; children: Sandra Yvonne, Ronald Francis. Ingenieur Radiotelegraphiste, U. Bordeaux, 1936; Ing. Radioelectricien, Ecole Supérieure d'Electricité, Paris, 1937; ScD (hon.), U. Pa., 1976, S.D. Sch. Mines, 1980, Brandeis U., 1988, U. Miami, Fla., 1992; PhD (hon.), Fed. U. of Rio de Janeiro, 1976. Research engr. France, 1937-39; research asst. N.Y. U., 1939-40; grad. fellow, teaching fellow physics U. Calif. at Los Angeles, 1940-43; asst. prof., asso. prof., acting head dept. physics S.D. Sch. Mines and Tech., 1943-47; research fellow Psycho-Acoustic Lab., Harvard U., 1947-51; lectr. otology and laryngology Harvard Med. Sch., 1969—; assoc. prof. comm. biophysics MIT, Cambridge, Mass., 1951-57, prof., 1957-84, inst. prof., 1975-84; inst. prof. emeritus MIT, Cambridge, 1984—; staff Research Lab. Electronics, 1951-69, chmn. faculty, 1967-69, assoc. provost, 1969-71, provost, 1971-80; dir. Kaiser Industries, 1968-76; chmn. com. electronic computers in life scis. Nat. Acad. Scis.-NRC, 1960-64, mem. brain scis. com., 1965-68, chmn., 1966-67; mem. cen. coun. Internat. Brain Rsch. Orgn., 1960-68, mem. exec. com., 1960-68, hon. treas., 1962-67; cons. life scis. panel Pres.'s Sci. Adv. Com., 1961-66; mem. coun. Internat. Union Pure and Applied Biophysics, 1961-69; inaugural lectr. Tata Inst. Fundamental Rsch., Bombay, 1962; Weizmann lectr. Weizmann Inst. Sci., Rehovoth, Israel, 1962; U.S. Nat. Commn. on Pure and Applied Biophysics, 1964-69; mem. Pres.'s Com. Urban Housing, 1967-68; cons. communications scis. WHO, 1964-65; mem. bd. medicine NAS, 1967-70; charter mem. Inst. Medicine, 1970—, mem. coun., 1970-76; mem. adv. com. to dir. NIH, 1970-74; mem. governing bd. NRC, 1974-76; mem. adv. com. med. sci. AMA, 1972-74; mem. selection com. Tyler Prize for Environ. Achievement, 1973—; chmn. sci. adv. coun. Callier Ctr. for Communication Disorders, 1968-85; chmn. rsch. com of the Health Effects Inst., 1981-89, bd. dirs., 1989—; chmn. internat. adv. panel of Chinese U. Devel. Project, 1986-91; mem. gov. coun. Internat. Centre Insect Physiology and Ecology, Kenya, 1987-90; mem. Am. and internat. panels on UNESCO (UN Assn. U.S. Am.), 1988-89; mem. Com. on Scholarly Communication with People's Republic of China, 1977-86, Coun. on Fgn. Rels., 1983-92. Bd. Fgn. Scholarships, 1978-81, chmn., 1980-81; co-chmn. NRC-IOM com. for study of saccharin and food safety policy, 1978-79; cons. Carnegie Corp. N.Y., 1986—, Carnegie Commn. on Sci., Tech. and Govt., 1988—; hon. consulting prof. U. of Electronic Sci. and Tech. of China, 1988. Editor: Sensory Communication, 1961; contbr. articles, chpts. to profl. publs. Bd. govs. Weizmann Inst. Sci., 1973-86; chmn. com. on rehab. of physically handicapped NRC, 1975-77; trustee Brandeis U., 1979—. Decorated croix du chevalier Legion d'Honneur (France); recipient Alexander von Humboldt medal, 1989; Rosenblith lectr. created in his honor NAS, 1992, Rosenblith chair of neurosci. named in his honor MIT, 1995. Fellow Acoustical Soc. Am., World Acad. Art and Sci., Am. Acad. Arts and Scis. (exec. bd. 1970-77), AAAS, IEEE; mem. Internat. Council Sci. Unions (v.p. 1984-88), Biophys. Soc. (council 1957-61, 69-72, exec. bd. 1957-61), NAE, NAS (fgn. sec. 1982-86), Soc. Exptl. Psychologists, Engrng. Acad. of Japan (fgn. assoc., Okawa prize 1999). Office: MIT 77 Massachussetts Ave Cambridge MA 02139

ROSENBLOOM, MINDY SHARON, psychiatrist; b. N.Y.C., May 16, 1960; d. Donald T. and Belle L. Rosenbloom; m. Stuart T. Schwartz. BA summa cum laude, Barnard Coll., 1981; MD, U. Medicine/Dentistry of N.J., 1985. Diplomate Am. Bd. Psychiatry and Neurology, Am. Bd. Geriatric Psychiatry. Intern Brown U., Providence, 1985-86, resident in psychiatry, 1986-89; med. dir. East Bay Mental Health Ctr., Barrington, R.I., 1989—; adjunct prof. URI Sch. Nursing; clin. asst. prof. dept. psychiatry and human behavior Brown U., Providence; spkr. in field. Mem. APA, AAGP, Cmty. Psychiatrists of R.I. (chair), Phi Beta Kappa. Office: East Bay Mental Health Ctr 2 Old County Rd Barrington RI 02806-1602

ROSENBLUM, EDWARD G., lawyer; b. Union City, N.J., Aug. 2, 1944; s. Milton and Frances (Nardi) R.; m. Charis Ann Schlatter, Dec. 1, 1971; children: Deborah, Michelle. BA, Rutgers U., 1966, JD, 1969. Bar: N.J. 1969. Ptnr. Rosenblum & Rosenblum, P.A., Jersey City, 1971-79, Secaucus, N.J., 1979-93; ptnr. Rosenblum Wolf & Lloyd, P.A., Secaucus, 1994—, Teaneck, 1998—; lectr. in field. Author: N.J. Lawyer, 1980, N.J. Municipalities, 1987. Active Hudson County chpt. Am. Cancer Soc., Hoboken, N.J., 1987—. Mem. N.J. State Bar Assn. (vice chmn. tax ct. rules com. taxation sect. 1984—, chmn. real property tax com. 1984—, vice chmn. taxation sect. 1987—, chmn.-elect 1987, chmn. 1988-89, Supreme Ct. com. on tax ct. 1982-92). Office: 300 Frank Burr Blvd Teaneck NJ 07666

ROSENBLUM, LISA LYNN, molecular evolutionist, researcher; b. Steubenville, Ohio, Mar. 1, 1967; d. Lee Allen and Rosalind Barbara (Miller) R.; m. Saar Banin, Jan. 15, 1995; 1 child, Alexandra. BA, Northwestern U., 1989; MA, Columbia U., 1991, MPhil, 1993, PhD, 1996. Rsch. assoc. Northwestern Med. Sch., Chgo., 1988-90; post-doctoral scientist Imperial Coll., London, 1996—. Contbr. abstracts and articles to profl. jours. Rsch. grantee Louis B. Leakey Found., 1994, U.S. NSF, 1996. Mem. AAAS, Soc. Systematic Biologists, N.Y. Acad. Sci., Sigma Xi. Achievements include research on population genetics and evolutionary history of leaf monkey species on a molecular level. Avocations: horse riding, skiing. Home: 119 Barkston Gardens, London SW5 0EX, England Office: St Marys 2nd Fl Jefferiss Wing, Praed St, London W2 1NY, England

ROSENBLUM, SCOTT S., lawyer; b. N.Y.C., Oct. 4, 1949; s. Harold Lewis and Greta Blossom (Lesher) R.; m. Barbara Anne Campbell, Oct. 29, 1977; children: Harold, Emma, Casey. AB summa cum laude, Dartmouth Coll., 1971; JD, U. Pa., 1974. Bar. U.S. Dist. Ct. (so. dist.) N.Y. 1975. From assoc. to ptnr. Stroock & Stroock & Lavan, N.Y.C., 1974-91; ptnr. Kramer, Levin, Naftalis & Frankel, N.Y.C., 1991-93, mng. ptnr., 1994—; N.Y. adv. bd. Mid. East Quarterly, Phila., 1994—; bd. dirs. Dovenmuehle Mortgage, Inc., Schaumburg, Ill, Greg Manning Auctions, Inc., West Caldwell, N.J., Temco Svc. Industries, Inc., N.Y.C., I.T. Internat. Theatres Ltd., Herzlia, Israel. Co-author: Public Limited Partnerships and Roll-Ups, Securities Law Techniques, The Practitioner's Guide to Transactions and Litigation, 1995. Trustee Village of Saltaire, N.Y., 1993—. Mem. ABA (high tech. com. 1983-84), Assn. Bar City N.Y. (corps. com. 1991-94), Phi Beta Kappa. Avocation: sailing. Home: 19 Wildwood Cir Larchmont NY 10538-3426 Office: Kramer Levin Naftalis & Frankel 919 3rd Ave New York NY 10022-3902

ROSENBLUM GREVÉY, ESTELLE, retired dean, nursing educator; b. Davenport, Iowa, Feb. 8, 1933; d. Dan and Cecil (Spiewak) Masters; m. Sidney Rosenblum, Aug. 30, 1953 (dec. 1988); children: Jay Douglas, Gail Rae, Paul Mitchell; m. Jack Grevey, Mar. 31, 1996; stepdaughter: Eileen Grevey Hillson. Student, U. Iowa, 1950-53; BSN, Wayne State U., Detroit, 1956; MSN, U. Tex., El Paso, 1981; PhD, U. N.Mex., 1979, MA in Audiology, 1971. Head nurse Northville (Mich.) State Hosp., 1956; head nurse, supr. Sister Kenny Polio/Rehab. Hosp., 1957-60; pub. health nurse Englewood County Health Dept., 1961-62; nursing supr. Bernalillo County Indian Hosp., Albuquerque, 1962-63; asst. dir. nursing Bernalillo County Indian Hosp., 1963-64; clin. tchr. U. N.Mex. Coll. Nursing, Albuquerque, 1964-65, inst. to prof., 1972-86; dean and prof. nursing U. N.Mex. Coll. Nursing, 1986-93, dean and prof. emerita, 1993—; sch. nurse West Mesa High Sch., Albuquerque, 1967-69; internat. nursing cons.; dir. ANA Approved CE program, Profl. Seminar Cons., 1979-89; spkr. Hong Kong Nurse Educators Soc., 1985; founder convenio U. N.Mex. and U. Mex., 1990, first nurse midwifery grad. program, U. N.Mex., 1989, first nurse practitioner program at grad. level, 1987. Author: Fundamentals of Hearing for Health Professionals, 1981; contbr. articles to profl. jours., chpts. to book. Bd. dirs. U. N.Mex. Found., 1996—; docent City of Albuquerque, 1996—; chair recognition com. Jewish Cmty. Ctr., 1998—. USPHS grantee, 1989; recipient Centennial Disting. Alumni award, U. N.Mex., 1989, Helene Fuld award to Coll. Nursing, U. N.Mex., 1987, Sigma Delta Tau Nat. Disting. Alumni award, 1988, State N.Mex. Gov.'s Disting. Svc. award, 1993, Estelle H. Rosenblum Thesis award U. N.Mex. Coll. Nursing, 1995. Fellow Am. Acad. Nursing; mem. Am. Assn. Colls. of Nursing (emeritus, exec. devel. series 1988-92), Am. Colls. Nursing (bd. dirs. 1990-92), N.Mex. Nurses Assn. (pres. 1975), N.Mex. Health Resources (bd. dirs. 1986-88), The Rotary Club of Albuquerque (Harvest ball fundraiser 1994—), Sigma Theta Tau (founder, pres. Gamma Sigma chpt. 1974-76, Mentor award), Phi Kappa Phi.

ROSENBLUTH, FRANCES MCCALL, political scientist, educator; b. Osaka, Japan, Oct. 22, 1954; d. Robert Donnell McCall and Virginia Lancaster Montgomery; m. James Edward Rosenbluth, Oct. 5, 1985; children: Benjamin Lee, John Gabriel, William Lancaster. BA, U. Va., 1980; MIA, Colubia U., 1983, PhD, 1988. Asst. prof. U. Va., Charlottesville, 1988-89, U. Calif., San Diego, 1989-92; asst. prof. UCLA, 1992, prof., 1993; prof. Yale U., New Haven, 1994—; mem. editl. bd. Am. Polit. Sci. Rev., Washington, 1996—, Internat. Orgn., MIT Press, 1996—. Author: Financial Policies in Japan, 1989; co-author: Japan's Political Marketplace, 1993, The Politics of Oligarchy, 1995 (Luebbert award 1997). Fellow Fulbright Found., 1985-86, Social Sci. Rsch. Coun., 1987-88, Coun. on Fgn. Rels., 1999—; NSF rschr., 1991. Mem. Am. Polit. Sci. Assn. Avocations: reading, hiking. E-mail: frances.rosenbluth@yale.edu. Office: Yale U Dept Polit Sci New Haven CT 06520-8301

ROSENBUSCH, JÜRG PETER, molecular biologist; b. Zürich, Switzerland, May 24, 1938; s. Hans Julius and Elsbeth Sophie (Weil) R.; m. Brigitte Magdalena Silberschmidt, Dec. 11, 1964; children: Andrea Elisabeth, Ivan Felix. MD, U. Zürich, 1963, MA, 1968; PhD, Harvard U., 1971. MD resident Hosp. Richterswil, Zürich, 1964; rsch. fellow Harvard Med. Sch.,

Boston; postdoctoral fellow biol. labs. Harvard U., Cambridge, Mass., 1971-72; asst. prof. Biozentrum, U. Basel, Basel, Switzerland, 1972-78; assoc. prof. Biozentrum, U. Basel, 1978-82; sr. scientist European Molecular Biology Lab., Heidelberg, Fed. Republic Germany, 1982-85; Forschungsgruppenleiter Biozentrum, U. Basel, 1985—. Author: (with others) Solubilization of Lipoprotein Complexes, 1977, Transport of Macromolecules in Cellular Systems, 1978, Electron Microscopy at Molecular Dimensions, 1980, Protides of the Biological Fluids, 1982, Physical Chemistry of Transmembrane Ion Motions, 1983, Structure and Function of Membrane Proteins, 1983, Reverse Micelles, 1984, Bacterial Outer Membranes as Model Systems, 1986, Methods Enzymology 172, 1987, Bacterial Protein Toxins, 1987, Ion Pumps: Structure, Function, and Regulation, 1988, Transport Through Membranes, 1988, Phosphate in Microorganisms Cellular and Molecular Biology, 1994, Transport Processes in Eukaryotic and Prokaryotic Organisms, 1996; editor Molecular Membrane Biology, 1993—, Assoc. editor Annales de l'Institut Pasteur, Paris, 1985—; 150 references in profl. jours. Recipient Fried. Miescher award, Switzerland, 1976; grantee NIH, Am. Cancer Assn., Am.-Swiss Found. for Sci. Exchange, rsch. grantee Swiss Nat. Sci. Found., 1980—, European Biomed. and Biotech. Mem. AAAS, European Molecular Biology Orgn., Swiss Biochem. Soc., Swiss Soc. Cell Biology, N.Y. Acad. Scis. Avocations: lit. Home: Rheinsprung 17, CH 4051 Basel Switzerland Office: U Basel Biozentrum, Klingelbergstr 70, CH 4056 Basel Switzerland

ROSENDAL, TAGE, anesthesiologist, consultant; b. Sindbjerg, Denmark, Oct. 9, 1937; s. Knud and Jensine (Olesen) R. MB BS, U. Arhus, Denmark, 1963; Diploma in Anesthesiology, U. Copenhagen, 1967. Cert. specialist in anesthesia; registered with Danish Nat. Health Bd. Intern Nyborg Hosp., Denmark, 1963-64; jr. med. officer Roskilde Hosp., Denmark, 1964-66; resident in anesthesia Bispebjerg Hosp., Denmark, 1966-69, sr. registrar dept. anesthesia, 1970-72; fellow in anesthesia Northwestern U., Chgo., 1969-70; sr. registrar dept. anesthesia Gentofte Hosp., Denmark, 1972-74; cons. in anesthesia Odense U. Hosp., Denmark, 1974-90; chmn. anesthesia King Fahd Hosp., Saudi Arabia, 1981-83; cons. King Faisal Hosp., Riyadh, Saudi Arabia, 1990-92; chmn. anesthesia Aabenraa Hosp., Denmark, 1992-99; cons. anesthesia Fredericia Hosp., Denmark, 2000—; Mem. Com. for Specialists' Tng., 1976-79. Co-author: (textbook) Anaestesi, 1991. Lt. Danish Air Force, 1966-67. Mem. Danish Soc. Anesthesiology (mem. com. for postgrad. edn. 1975-78, mem. exec. com. 1978-79. Lutheran. Avocations: languages (especially Arabic), tennis, travel, bridge. Office: Frederica Hosp Dept Anes, Dronningensgade 97, DK-7000 Fredericia Denmark

ROSENFELD, DAVID, defense research and development executive; b. Mexico City, Dec. 4, 1957; s. Idel and Ilana Lana (Kener) R.; m. Ayala Eisner, Sept. 6, 1981; children: Nir, Liron, Shiri, Nuphar. BSc, Technion, Haifa, Israel, 1983, MSc, 1985, DSc, 1989. Rsch. assoc. Technion, 1989-91, sr. rsch. assoc., 1993-95; vis. scientist NASA, Cleve., 1991-93; head optronic tech. dept. IMOD-MAFAT, Tel Aviv, 1995—. Sgt. Israel Def. Forces, 1976-79. Recipient award NRC, 1991, 92. Avocations: science fiction, reading, collecting books. Office: IMOD-MAFAT, 32 Kaplan St, Tel Aviv 61909, Israel

ROSENFELD, DAVID, psychoanalyst, psychiatrist; b. Buenos Aires, June 23, 1935; s. Jacob and Margarita (Burstyn) R.; m. Estela Mordo; children: Karin, Deborah, Daniel. MD, Buenos Aires U., 1959, degree in psychiatry, 1962. Psychiatrist Moyano Psychiat. Hosp., Buenos Aires, 1958-62, Rawson Gen. Hosp., Buenos Aires, 1961-62; pvt. practive psychoanalysis Buenos Aires, 1961—; prof. psychoanalysis Buenos Aires Psychoanalytic Soc., 1975—; prof. psychiatry Buenos Aires U., 1992—; lectr. in field. Author: Psychoanalysis and Groups: History and Dialectics, 1988, The Psychotic Aspects of the Personality, 1992, (play) Imaginary Dialogue, 1991; contbr. chpts. to books. cons. psychotherapist to victims of bombing of Jewish Cmty. Ctr. at U. Hosp., San Martin, 1994-95; human rights activist. French Govt. grantee in social psychology Sorbonne, 1962-63; recipient Outstanding Internat. Psychoanalyst award U. Va. Sch. Medicine, 1993. Mem. Buenos Aires Psychianalytic Soc. (tng. analyst), Internat. Psychoanalytic Assn. (assoc. editor, publs. standing com. on psychosis 1993—, v.p. 1989-93, mem. editl. bd. Internat. Jour. Psychoanalysis, 1993—, co-chmn. internat. com. rsch. on psychosis 1998). Avocations: Middle Ages history, Shakespeare. Home: Billinghurst 1451, 1425 Buenos Aires Argentina Office: Pacheco de Melo, 2864 Buenos Aires 1425, Argentina

ROSENFELD, EDWARD, travel company executive; b. Phila.. Cert. Travel Agt., Inst. Cert. Travel Agents, Wellesly, Mass., 1978. Cert. Inst. Cert. Travel Agts., 1978. V.p. Cefra Travel, Scottsdale, Ariz., 1973—; pres. Learco Travel Enterprises, Phoenix, 1985—; cons. Am. Soc. Travel Agts., 1980-85, Indian Nation, Ariz., 1999. Author: Outside Sales, A Travel Book, 1990. Mem. ICTA. E-mail: learco@uswest.net. Office: Learco Travel Enterprises 4317 E Osborn Rd Phoenix AZ 85018-5923

ROSENFELD, MARTIN JEROME, executive recruiter, educator; b. Flint, Mich., Oct. 3, 1944; s. Israel Edward and Lillian Edith (Natchez) R.; m. Marcy Tucker Colman; 1 child, Joshua; stepchildren: Jessica Colman, Zachary Colman. BA, Mich. State U., 1968, MHA, 1978; MBA with high honors, Ind. No. U., 1979. Adminstr. Care Corp., Grand Rapids, Mich., 1969-70, Chandler Convalescent Ctr., Detroit, 1970-71, Grand Community Hosp., Detroit, 1971-73; exec. v.p., chief exec. officer Msgr. Clement Kern Hosp. Spl. Surgery, Warren, Mich., 1973-84; pres. M.J. Rosenfeld Assocs., 1984-85; COO Dickenson, Wright, Moon, Van Dusen & Freeman, 1985-88; chmn. Rosenfeld Assocs., 1989-91; pres. Sanford Rose Assocs., Detroit, 1991-97; acting COO New Ctr. Hosp., Detroit, 1995-96; pres., CEO, chmn. Rosenfeld & Co., Inc., 1998-99; CEO, chmn. Brookside Consulting Group, LLC, Farmington, Mich., 1999—; instr. Marygrove Coll., 1975-80; assoc. prof. Mercy Coll., Detroit, 1978-80; mem. faculty Inst. on Continuing Legal Edn., Ann Arbor, Mich., Inst. Law Firm Mgmt., Ann Arbor; instr. Legal Tech '87, Chgo. Author papers in field. Mem. editl. bd. The Human-Size Hosp.; mem. panel of experts The Health Care News. V.p. Detroit chpt. Jewish Nat. Fund, 1978—; pres. Cranbrook Village Homeowners Assn., 1977; chmn. Community Hosps. of Southeastern Mich., 1981-84; mem. tech. work group Comprehensive Health Planning Coun. of Southeastern Mich., 1981-84; mem. fin. mgmt. com., mem. hosp. affairs bd. Greater Detroit Area Hosp. Coun., 1981-84; bd. dirs., com. chmn. Detroit Symphony Orch., 1984-90; bd. dirs., mem. fund raising com. Detroit Met. Orch., 1984-87. Mem. ABA, Assn. Legal Adminstrs., Am. Assn. Health Care Cons., Royal Soc. Health, Am. Podiatry Assn. (com. hosps. 1981-84), Warren C. of C. (com. chmn. 1975), Nat. Assn. Legal Search Cons., Nat. Assn. Pers. Svcs., Mich. Assn. Pers. Svcs., Sanford Rose Assocs. Dirs. Assn. (pres. 1993-95, treas. 1995-97). Office: Brookside Consulting Group LLC 27600 Farmington Rd Ste 104 Farmingtn Hls MI 48334-3364

ROSENFELD, SARENA MARGARET, artist; b. Elmira, N.Y., Oct. 17, 1940; d. Thomas Edward and Rosalie Ereny (Fedor) Rooney; m. Robert Steven Bach, June 1958 (div. 1963); children: Robert Steven, Daniel Thomas; m. Samson Rosenfeld III, June 5, 1976. Student, Otis/Parson Art Inst., L.A., 1994—, Idyllwild Sch. Music and Arts, 1994—. One-woman shows and group exhbns. include Robert Dana Gallery, San Francisco, Gordon Gallery, Santa Monica, Calif., Hespe Gallery, San Francisco, Gallery 444, San Francisco, Art Expressions, San Diego, Ergane Gallery, N.Y.C., Orlando Gallery, Sherman Oaks, Calif., L.A., La Jolla, Calif., Aspen, Colo., New Orleans, Soho, N.Y.C., Santa Barbara, Calif., Tanglewood, Mass., Honolulu, Johannesburg, South Africa, La Sierra U., Riverside, Calif., U. Enklinik, Bochum, Germany, Ruhr U., Germany. Mem., vol., animal handler Wildlife Waysta., Angeles Nat. Forest, Calif.; vol. animal keeper L.A. Zoo. Recipient Best of Show award Glendale Regional Arts Coun., 1984-85, 1st pl. awards Santa Monica Art Festival, 1982, 83, 84, 85, 86, Sweepstakes award and 1st pl., 1986, Purchase prize awards L.A. West C. of C., 1986-87, Tapestry in Talent Invitational San Jose Arts Coun., 1986, 1st pl. awards Studio City and Century City Arts Couns., 1976-84, 1st award Pacific Palisades Art Affair XII, 1997, Sherman Oaks Fall Arts Festival, 1997. Mem. Nat. Mus. of Women in the Arts. Republican. Home: 6570 Kelvin Ave Canoga Park CA 91306-4021

ROSENFELD, STEVEN IRA, artistic director, music publisher; b. Bklyn., May 24, 1949; s. Harry Allen and Rosina (DeStefano) R. BA, Southampton Coll., 1971; MFA, St. Francis Coll., Bklyn., 1975. V.p. mktg. JVC, Inc., Maspath, N.Y., 1972-74; dir. Yamaha Internat. Corp., Buena Park, Calif., 1974-75; v.p., gen. mgr. Audio Mktg. Cons., Yorktown, N.Y., 1976-88; pres. World Wide Mgmt., Yorktown, 1970—; dir. Parsec Electronics, Wilmington, Del., 1986-88; mng. dir. Westchester Shakespeare Festival, N.Y.C., 1987-90; dir. The Roger Hendricks Simon Studio, N.Y.C., 1987—; v.p. Barnett Labs., Houston, 1992-93; CEO Apple Pie Products, 1996—; pres., CEO The F.C. Sturtevant Co., 1998—; dir. The Neworld Order Recording Co., 1998—. Editor (newspaper) The Windmill, 1968-69. Mem. Internat. Platform Assn., Audio Engrng. Soc. (cert.), Soc. Audio Cons. (cert.), Nat. Trust, Nat. Acad. Rec. Arts and Scis. Jewish.

ROSENGART, TODD KENNETH, cardiothoracic surgeon, researcher; b. Bklyn., Jan. 24, 1960; s. Martin Rosengart and Barbara Kodish; m. Debra Helen Rosengart, June 15, 1989; children: Michael, Eric. BS with distinction, Northwestern U., Evanston, Ill., 1981; MD with distinction, Northwestern U., Chgo., 1983. Diplomate Am. Bd. Surgery, Am. Bd. Thoracic Surgery. Intern in gen. surgery NYU Med. Ctr., N.Y.C., 1983-84, resident in gen. surgery, 1984-85, resident and chief resident in gen. surgery, 1987-89; med. staff fellow NIH, Bethesda, Md., 1985-87; asst. thoracic surgeon N.Y. Hosp., 1989-90, thoracic surgeon, 1990-91; instr. Cornell U. Med. Coll., N.Y.C., 1989-90, asst. prof. surgery, 1991-93, asst. prof. cardiothoracic surgery, 1993-97, assoc. prof. cardiothoracic surgery, 1997—; assoc. prof. cardiothoracic surgery Weill Med. Coll. Cornell U., N.Y.C., 1998—; assoc. attending cardiothoracic surgeon N.Y. Presbyn. Hosp., N.Y.C., 1997-99; chief cardiothoracic surg. Evanston (Ill.) Hosp., 1999—; assoc. prof. surgery Northwestern U. Med. Sch., 1999—; sr. registrar Hosp. for Sick Children, London, 1991; asst. Harley St. Clinic, London, 1991; tchg. asst. NYU Med. Ctr., 1988-89; asst. attending surgeon Jamaica Hosp., 1993-96; United Hosp. Med. Ctr., 1994—; attending physician N.Y. Hosp. Med. Ctr. of Queens, 1995—; mem. Ctr. for Vascular Biology, 1996—; assoc. attending cardiothoracic surgeon N.Y. Hosp., 1997, N.Y. Presbyn. Hosp., 1998—; vis. assoc. prof. surgery Columbia U., 1997—; vis. assoc. attending surgeon Presbyn. Hosp., 1997—; manuscript reviewer, presenter, cons. in field. Editl. bd. Cardiac and Vascular Regeneration: Angiogenesis and Myogenesis, Basic th Therapeutic, 1999—; contbr. numerous articles to profl. publs., chpts. to books; patentee gene transfer therapy delivery devide and method, perfusion and occlusion device and method. Nat. Merit scholar, 1977; recipient rsch. award A.G. Morrow Soc., 1987, 97; grantee miles Labs., 1992—, N.Y. Heart Assn., 1994-97, Datascope Corp., 1995—, AccuLase, Inc., 1995—, St. Jude Med., 1996—, Picower Found., 1996—, U.S. Surg. Corp., 1996—, Thoracic Surgery Found. Rsch. and Edn. 1997-99, OrthoBiotech, 1997—, Baxter Healthcare Corp., 1998—, NIH, 1998—. Fellow ACS, Am. Coll. Cardiology, Am. Coll. Chest Physicians; mem. AAAS, Am. Fedn. Clin. Rsch., Am. Heart Assn. (sci. coun. on cardiothoracic and vascular surgery), Nat. Assn. for Bloodless Medicine and Surgery (bd. dirs. 1997—), Andrew Morrow Soc. Cardiac Surgeons, N.Y. Soc. Thoracic Surgery (membership com. 1994-97, chmn. membership com. 1998—, program com. 1994—, chmn. program com. 1997—), Soc. Thoracic Surgeons, Soc. Univ. Surgeons, N.Y. Acad. Scis., 21st Century Cardiac Surg. Soc. (pres., membership chmn. 1995-96, v.p. 1996-98), Spencer Soc. Surgeons, Alpha Omega Alpha, Phi Rho Sigma. Office: Evanston Northwestern Healthcare 2650 Ridge Ave Burch 100 Evanston IL 60201

ROSENGREN, BJÖRN, Swedish government official. Minister industry and commerce Govt. of Sweden, Stockholm, 1998—. Mem. Social Democratic Party. Office: Ministry Industry/Commerce, S-103 33 Stockholm Sweden*

ROSENGREN, ULF CARL GÖSTA, equestrian series director; b. Lund, Sweden, Mar. 8, 1945; s. Gösta and Calla J. M. (Sjölin) Rosengren; m. Margareta I. Thorsén, Oct. 19, 1970; children: Caroline, Max. B of Law, Uppsala U., Sweden, 1972, postgrad., 1973. Trainee County Govt. Bd. Malmö, Sweden, 1973-75; asst. sec. gen., lawyer Swedish Riding Assn., Stockholm, 1976-81; sec. gen. Swedish Equestrian Fedn., Stockholm, 1982-92; sec. gen., pres. exec. com. World Equestrian Games, Stockholm, 1986-90; sec. gen. SW Equestrian Fedn., 1992-97; dir. Samsund Nations Cup Series worldwide, 1997—. Author: Horses and the Law, 1978. Capt. Swedish Cavalry Res. Recipient Gold Medal of Honors Swedish Equestrian Fedn., 1997. Mem. Stockholm Internat. Horseshow (pres. organizing com. 1993—). Avocations: family, horses. Office: Samsung, Box 713, 19427 Uppland Väsby, Sweden

ROSENHEIM, ELCHANAN SHIMSHON, property consultants company executive; b. Haifa, Israel, Dec. 11, 1944; s. Emil Eliakim and Hella Ruth (Bamberger) R.; m. Shari R. Pollack Eshet, May 30, 1976 (div. 1981); 1 child, Asaf; m. Rivka Seinfeld, Aug. 29, 1991; children: Shiri, Tal. Grad. in auditing and accountancy, U. Haifa, 1969; BA in Social Scis., Tel Aviv U., 1970; MBA, L.I. U., 1973. CPA, Israel. Supervising auditor M. Peleg, CPA, Haifa, 1965-70; comptroller Hamashbir-Lazarchan, Jerusalem, 1970-72; chief acct. Israel Ministry of Def., N.Y.C., 1972-73; gen. mgr. Haft Cons., N.Y.C., 1973-79; mng. dir. Bamberger-Rosenheim Ltd., Tel Aviv, 1979—; dir. AES Systems, Inc., 1990-93, dir. mktg. Omnitech-Echut, Israel, 1993-95; cons. to govt. and multinat. corps., 1977—; lectr. Israel Def. Forces, 1989-00; guest lectr. univs. and acad. instns., 1998—. Contbr. articles to profl. jours. Founder, mgr. Elizur K'rayot, Israel, 1960-63. Master sgt. Israel Def. Forces, 1962-65. Mem. Inst. CPAs in Israel. Avocation: skiing. Home: 11 Achi-Dakar St, Raanana 43259, Israel

ROSENHOUSE, MICHAEL ALLAN, lawyer; b. Chgo., Nov. 8, 1946; s. Seymour Samuel and Jeanne Mozette (Rosenthal) R. BA, Yale U., 1968; JD, U. Chgo., 1974. Bar: Ill. 1974, N.Y. 1982. Atty. in pvt. practice, Rochester, N.Y. Mng. editor Am. Jurisprudence, 2d edit., 1991-93, Am. Law Reports, 1991-93; editor: Bank Human Resources: Question & Answer Book, 1998; editor Bank Employment Law Report newsletter, 1998-99. Mem. Monroe County Bar Assn. (co-chair Disability Labor and Employment law Commn. 1998-99), U. Chgo. Law Sch. Alumni Assn. (bd. dirs. 1977-80), Yale Alumni Assn. (schs. com. 1997—), N.Y. State Bar Assn., Rochester Squash Racquets Assn. (bd. dirs. 1998-99), U. Chgo. Club of Rochester (bd. dirs. 1999-2000). Avocation: squash, tennis, golf. Office: 36 Wined Mill Rd Pittsford NY 14534

ROSENKNOP, JOHN, mathematician; b. Dec. 28, 1929; divorced. MSc, Moscow U., 1952; DSc, Kazan's U., 1962. Lectr. Moscow Regional Pedagogical Inst., 1953-77; scientific assoc. Zentralblatt Math., 1980-99; ind. editor, 1998—; participant Internat. Math. Congrs., 1966, 86, 90, 94, 98, others. Recipient Groebner bases co-inventor spl. award RISC, Linz, Austria, 1998. Avocations: tourism. Address: Box 15 11 21, 10673 Berlin Germany

ROSENLUND, HANS LENNART, architect; b. Mjällby, Sweden, Mar. 29, 1953. MS in Arch., Lund U., Sweden, 1980, PhD in Arch., 1995. Rschr., lectr. Lund U., 1981—; cons. Habitat AB, Lund, 1983-90. Mem. Swedish Assn. for Devel. of Low-Cost Housing (bd. dirs.). E-mail: hans.rosenlund@hdm.lth.se. Office: Housing Devel & Mgmt, Box 118, SE-22100 Lund Sweden

ROSENN, HAROLD, lawyer; b. Plains, Pa., Nov. 4, 1917; s. Joseph and Jennie (Wohl) R.; m. Sallyanne Frank, Sept. 19, 1948; 1 child, Frank Scott. BA, U. Mich., 1939, JD, 1941; LLD (hon.), Coll. Misericordia, 1991. Bar: Pa. 1942, U.S. Supreme Ct. 1957. Ptnr. Rosenn & Rosenn, Wilkes Barre, Pa., 1948-54; ptnr. Rosenn, Jenkins & Greenwald, Wilkes Barre, 1954-87, of counsel, 1988—; mem. Pa. State Bd. Law Examiners, 1983-93, Pa. Gov.'s Justice Commn., 1968-73, Pa. Crime Commn., 1968-73, Fed. Jud. Nominating Com., Pa., 1977-79, Appellate Ct. Nominating Com., Pa., 1979-81; asst. dist. atty. Luzerne County, Pa., 1952-54. Chmn. ARC, Wilkes-Barre, 1958-60, life mem. bd.; pres. Pa. Coun. on Crime and Delinquency, Harrisburg, 1969-71; bd. dirs. Coll. Misericordia, Dallas, Pa., 1976-86, emeritus, 1986—, Hoyt Libr., Kingston, Pa., 1971-78, Nat. Coun. on Crime and Delinquency, N.Y.C., 1969-71; chmn. United Way Campaign of Wyoming Valley, 1975, chmn. of bd., 78-80; pres. Temple Israel of Wilkes Barre, 1972-74, chmn. bd. 1974-84, life mem. bd.; comdr. post 395 Am. Legion, Kingston, 1948; bd. dirs. Keystone State Games, 1982—, Jewish Fedn. Bd. of Greater Wilks-Barre, 1994—, St. Vincent de Paul Soup Kitchen, 1987—. Capt. USAAF, 1942-45, ETO. Recipient Erasmus medal Dutch Govt., Disting. Svc. award in Trusteeship, Assn. Governing Bds. Univs. and Colls., 1990, Disting. Cmty. Svc. award Greater Wilkes-Barre Soc. Fellows Anti-Defamation League, 1991, Clara Barton honor award Wyoming Valley chpt. ARC, 1992, Lifetime Achievement award United Way of Wyoming Valley, 1992, Outstanding Vol. Fundraiser award Greater Pocono chpt. Nat. Soc. of Fundraising Execs. 1995; honoree Wyoming Valley Interfaith Coun., 1986; named Golden Key Vol. of Yr., United Way of Pa., 1989; inductee Jr. Achievement Hall of Fame for N.E. Pa., 1997. Mem. ABA, Pa. Bar Assn., Am. Judicature Soc., The Pa. Soc., B'nai B'rith (pres. Wilkes Barre 1952-53, Cmty. Svc. award 1976), U. Mich. Club N.E. Pa. (pres. 1946-76), Westmoreland Club (Wilkes-Barre), Huntsville Golf Club (Lehman, Pa.). Republican. Jewish.

ROSENSAFT, LESTER JAY, management consultant, lawyer, business executive; b. Leominster, Mass., Jan. 11, 1958; s. Melvin and Beatrice (Golombek) R.; m. Elisabeth Amanda Lahti, July 29, 1992, 1 child, Mia Elisabeth. BS in Econs., Wharton Sch., U. Pa., 1978; JD, Case Western Res. U., 1981, MBA, 1981; LLM in Corp. Law, NYU, 1983. Bar: Ohio 1981, U.S. Dist. Ct. (no. dist.) Ohio 1982, U.S. Dist. Ct. (all dists.) N.Y. 1982, Mass. 1992. Practice corp. and comml. law Ohio, 1981—; reorgn. law fed. cts. Ohio, N.Y., 1982—; mem. firm. Hall, Rosensafi & Yen, Cleve. and Singapore, 1961-90; with Cons. to Mgmt., Inc., Clve., N.Y.C., Boston, Hong Kong, 1977—, v.p., 1977-80, pres., CEO, 1980-83, chmn., 1983-85; pres., CEO Eljay Devel. Corp., 1985-86; chmn., CEO Logistix Ltd., 1987-90; ptnr. Sanctuary Assocs., Boston, 1988-89; exec. v.p., CFO The Union Meat Co., East Hartford, Conn., 1989-90, also bd. dirs.; pres. Golub Enterprises II, Inc., 1989-90; also bd. dirs.; COO The CCC Fin. Orgn., Cleve., 1992-95, also bd. dirs.; pres., CEO, bd. dirs. ASA Investment Commn., Inc., N.Y.C., 1995—; pres., CEO ASA Adminstrn., Inc., Chgo., Greensboro, N.C., 1999—, also mem. bd. dirs; bd. dirs. ASA Acquisition Corp., 1998—, fin. and strategic planning com.; mem. ASA Mgmt. and Exec. Com., 1995—, ASA Investment Com., 1996-98; chmn. Chatham Fin., Cleve., N.Y.C., 1995-96; vice chmn. bd. dirs. Paramount Sys. Design Group, Inc., N.Y.C., 1982-89, v.p. corp. devel.; bd. dirs. Ameritech Corp., N.Y.C., 1983-85; v.p., CFO, bd. dirs. Chipurnoi Inc., L.I. City, N.Y.; v.p., CFO Kannerton Industries, N.Y.C., London, 1983-85; vice chmn., gen. counsel, bd. dirs. GIOIA Couture, Inc., Akron, Ohio, 1984-86; dir. Honeybee Robotics Ltd., Taiwan and N.Y.C., Pelletier Brothers, Inc., 1986-88, Advanced Radiator Techs., Inc., Fitchburg, Mass., 1987-88. Co-author: Industrial Development Survey for City of Leominster, 1978; contbr. articles to profl. jours. Ednl. cons., advisor indsl. devel. and strategic urbanism; cons. federally funded biomed. rsch. projects; active Combined Jewish Philanthropies; participant 40th Anniversary II Pres.'s Mission, 1987; chmn. Region V Outreach Mission, 1988; vice chmn. Regional Campaign Leadership Nission, 1991; mem. Russian Resettlement Com., 1988-91, Major Gifts Gala Com., 1989; assoc. alumni trustee U. Pa., 1991-95; active U. Penn. Seondary Com. Ctrl. Mass., U. Penn. Bd. Govs., Cleve., 1992-95; exec. adv. coun. Keene State Coll., 1984-88. Recipient APEX Grand award 1999, ESMA best of show award, 1999, numerous ACE awards, silver and gold Quill awards, 1996-99. Mem. ABA, Assn. Crop. Growth Turnaround Mgmt. Assn., Greater Cleve. Bar Assn., Ohio State Bar Assn., Assn. Bar City N.Y., Bankruptcy Lawers Bar Assn., N.Y.C. Reorgn. Roundtable, Internat. Soc. Strategic Planning Cons., Soc. Profl. Mgmt. Cons., Inst. Mgmt. Cons. (cert.), Coun. Cons. Orgns., Coll. Firm Prins., North Ctrl. Mass. C. of C. (dinsl. devel. com. 1984-86), Phi Alpha Delta (vice justice), Boca Pointe Golf and Racquet Club. Address: 9 Whispering Ivy Way Mendham NJ 07945-1241 Office: 750 Lexington Ave New York NY 10022-1200

ROSENSTEIN, MARY ELISABETH MALLORY, retired clinical social worker; b. Los Gatos, Calif., Feb. 25, 1916; d. Merton Shannon and Mabel Beatrice (Penny) Mallory; m. Albert Rosenstein, Sept. 20, 1947; children: Nathan Stewart, Thomas Mallory. AB, U. Calif., Berkeley, 1937; MA in Social Work, U. Chgo., 1950. Licn. clin. social worker, marriage, family and child counselor, Calif. Caseworker Calif. Relief Adminstrn., San Francisco, 1938-40, San Francisco Children's Agy., 1940-42; caseworker foster home placement Oakland (Calif.) Family Svc., 1942-44; psychiat. social worker ARC Hosp. Svc., Oakland and Long Beach, Calif., 1946-51, Calif. Dept. Mental Health, L.A., Long Beach, Santa Ana, Calif., 1950-51; dist. supr. Calif. Dept. Mental Health, L.A., 1951-53; caseworker, acting dir. Family Svc. Assn. Rio Hondo Area, Whittier, Calif., 1954-81; pvt. practice, 1981-91, ret.., 1991; chmn. mental health study LWV, Whittier, 1974-76; workshop leader Montebello (Calif.) Child Study Workshop; chmn. liaison com. San Gabriel Valley Regional County Mental Health, Pasadena, Calif., 1976-81; cons. dist. teen mothers Montebello Unified Sch. Dist. Mem. Whittier Area Coordinating Coun., 1960—; pres. Birney Elem. Sch. PTA, Pico Rivera, Calif., 1957; cellist Rio Hondo Symphony Assn. Orch., Whittier, 1970-97; v.p., membership chmn. UN Assn., Whittier, 1968-97. Recipient commendation Calif. Legislature, 1981, U.S. Ho. of Reps., 1981, County of L.A., 1981, spl. citation UN Assn. U.S.A., 1996. Fellow Soc. for Clin. Social Workers; mem. NASW (diplomate in clin. social work), Acad. Cert. Social Workers, AAUW (Las Distinguitas award 1979), LWV. Democrat. Unitarian Universalist. Avocations: music, gardening, swimming, river rafting, live theater.

ROSENSTEIN, PETER D., educational association administrator; b. N.Y.C., Jan. 23, 1947; s. Heinz and Dorrit Rosenstein. BA, CCNY, 1969; MPA, Baruch U., 1978. Coord. local govt. Mayor's Office, N.Y.C., 1974-77; exec. dir. implementation unit White House Conf. on Handicapped Individuals, Washington, 1978-80, Am. Acad. Physician Assts., Alexandria, Va., 1981-84; exec. dir. Accts. for Pub. Interest, Washington, 1985-89; exec. dir. individual implementation unit Nat. Assn. for Gifted Children, Washington, 1989—; trustee U. D.C., Washington. Issues coord. Williams for Mayor, Washington, 1998. Mem. Profl. Conv. Mgmt. Assn. (bd. dirs. Capital chpt. 1995—), Arts in Action (pres. 1995—), Masons. Democrat. Jewish. Avocations: travel, theater. Office: Nat Assn for Gifted Children 1707 L St NW Ste 550 Washington DC 20036-4212

ROSENSTEIN, ROBERT BRYCE, lawyer, financial advisor; b. Santa Monica, Calif., Feb. 26, 1954; s. Franklin Lee and Queen Esther (Shall) R.; children: Shaun Franklin, Jessica Laney, Madeline Frances. BA, Calif. State U., Northridge, 1976; JD, Southwestern U., 1979. Bar: Calif. 1979, U.S. Dist. Ct. (cen. and no. dists.) Calif. 1980, U.S. Tax Ct. 1981; registered environ. assessor. Service rep. Social Security Adminstrn., Los Angeles, 1974-77; tax cons. Am. Tax Assocs., Los Angeles, 1970-78, ptnr., 1978; prin., pres. Robert B. Rosenstein, PC, Los Angeles, 1979-84; ptnr. Rosenstein and Werlin, Los Angeles, 1984-87; pres. Robert Bryce Rosenstein Ltd., Temelula, 1987-99; chief fin. officer BSE Mgmt. Inc., Los Angeles, 1987-90, corp. counsel, 1987-92, sr. v.p. corp. devel., acquisitions, 1990-92; pres. Robert Bryce Rosenstein, a Profl. Law Corp., 1999—; bd. dirs. BSE Mgmt. Inc, Sirius Computer Corp., Spartan Computer, Unicomp, Inc., Diagnostic Engrng. Inc.; pres. Will Find Inc., 1986-87; judge pro tem Three Lakes Jud. Dist., 1997—. Judge pro tem Riverside County, Calif., 1996—. Recipient Am. Jurisprudence award Bancroft Whitney; Order of Cheviler. Mem. ABA (taxation and environ. coms., vice chmn. gen. bus. sect. 1995), Assn. Trial Lawyers Am., L.A. Bar Assn. Republican. Jewish. Lodges: Masons, Ionic, Composite. Avocations: sports, reading, golf. Office: 41877 Enterprise Cir N Ste 200 Temecula CA 92590-5628

ROSENSTOCK, WOLFGANG HANS, physicist; b. Bonn, Germany, May 11, 1949; s. Hans and Marianne (Hansen) R.; m. Astrid Eleonore Meyer, Oct. 18, 1985; 1 child, Sabrina. Diploma in Physics, F. Wilhelms U., Bonn, Germany, 1974; Dr.rer.nat., Inst. Strahlenphysik, Bonn, Germany, 1978. Technician U. Köln, Cologne, Germany, 1972-73; teaching asst. Physikalisches Inst., Bonn, Germany, 1973-74; rschr. Inst. Strahlenphysik, 1974-78; sci. asst. F. Wilhelms U., 1978-79; applied scientist, radiation protection officer Fraunhofer Int, Euskirchen, Germany, 1980—, group leader nuclear detection, 1993—. Contbr. articles to profl. jours. Mem. Fachverband Strahlenschutz, Inst. Nuclear Material Mgmt. Office: Fraunhofer INT, PO Box 1491, D 53864 Euskirchen Germany

ROSENTHAL, GERT, economist; b. Amsterdam, The Netherlands, Sept. 11, 1935; arrived in Guatemala, 1937; s. Ludwig and Florence (Koenigsberger) R.; m. Margit Uhlmann, Oct. 18, 1959; children: Caroline, Deborah, Jacqueline, Susan. BA, U. Calif., Berkeley, 1957, MA, 1958. Economist Nat. Planning Office, Guatemala, 1960-65; sr. ofcl. Ministry of Fin., Guatemala, 1966-67; sr. economist Secretariat of Cen. Am. Common Market, Guatemala, 1967-68; min. of planning Nat. Planning Office, Guatemala, 1969-70, 73-74; fellow Adlai Stevenson Inst. for Internat. Affairs, Chgo., 1971; coord. UN Tech. Assistance Project UN Conf. of Trade and Devel., Geneva, 1972; dir. Mex. office Econ. Commn. for Latin Am., Mexico City,

1975-85; dep. exec. sec. Econ. Commn. for Latin Am., Santiago, Chile, 1986-89; exec. sec. Econ. Commn. for Latin Am., Santiago, 1990-97; rep. of Guatemala to the United Nations, 1999—. Author: Direct Foreign Investment in Central America, 1973; contbr. articles to profl. jours. Home: 6 Avenida 12-35 Zona 10, Guatemala Guatemala Office: Permanent Mission of Guatemala to UN 57 Park Ave New York NY 10016-3006

ROSENTHAL, HARALD KARL, fishery biologist, educator; b. Berlin, June 9, 1937; m. Ingrid Busse, Jan. 4, 1969; children: Birgit, Karin. BEd (h.s. tchr.), Free Univ., Berlin, 1965; D in Natural Scis., U. Hamburg, Germany, 1968; DSc (hon.), Heriot Watt U., Edinburgh, Scotland, 1985; D in Environ. Sci. (hon.), U. Moncton, New Brunswick, Can., 1996. Sr. scientist Biologische Anstalt, Helgoland, Germany, 1968-89; prof. Univ. Kiel Inst. Marine Sci., 1989—; disting. vis. scientist Nat. Rsch. Coun., Can., 1985-86; chmn. mariculture com. Internat. Coun. for Exploration of Sea, 1987-90. Editor-in-chief Jour. Applied Ichthyology, 1988—; assoc editor Aquatic Living Resources, 1991—; mem. editl. bd. Marine Biology, 1967-88, Marine Ecology (Progress Series), 1981-89; editor or co-editor 10 internat. conf. proceedings. Fellow Japanese Soc. Promotion Sci.; mem. European Aquaculture Soc. (pres. Belgium 1981-83), World Aquaculture Soc. (v.p. 1985-86). Office: U Kiel Inst Meereskunde, Düsternbrooker Weg 20, 24105 Kiel Germany

ROSENTHAL, IRVING, journalism educator; b. N.Y.C., July 31, 1912; s. Max and Rose Rosenthal; m. Ruth M. Rosenthal, May 22, 1943; children: David, Robert, Risa. BSS, CCNY, 1933, MS, 1934. Reporter N.Y. Times, N.Y.C., 1933; fellow to full prof. dept. English CCNY, 1933-77, chmn. comms. and mass media, 1946-77; asst. to pres. CCNY, N.Y.C., 1933-43; coord. broadcasting courses Sta. WCBS-TV, N.Y.C., 1969-90, emeritus prof., 1977—; adj. prof. C.W. Post Coll., Brookville, N.Y., 1967-70; editl. cons. Dance mag., 1983-87, Med. Soc. State of N.Y. Editl. adv. bd. Hadassah mag., 1978-96; co-author: Modern Journalism, 1962, A Contemporary Reader, 1961, Art of Writing Made Simple, 1958, Business English Made Simple, 1955. Mem. Silurians, awards chmn. 1989-91. 1st lt. U.S. Army, 1943-45. Mem. Alpha Phi Gamma, Phi Delta Sigma, Phi Delta Kappa. Home and Office: 62 Hampshire Rd Great Neck NY 11023-1537

ROSENTHAL, ISADORE IRVING, chemist; b. N.Y.C., June 10, 1925; s. Charles Rosenthal and Ruth Obernowitz; m. Judith Kamen, Feb. 27, 1999; children: Cynthia, Richard, Leslie, Seth. BA, NYU, 1947; BS, Purdue U., Lafayette, Ind., 1949; PhD, Penn State, 1952. Sr. rsch. chemist Rohm & Haas, Phila., 1953-55, rsch. lab head, 1955-60, rsch. supr., 1960-65, tech. dir. fibers divsn., 1965-74, dir. health and safety, 1974-90; sr. fellow Wharton Sch. U. Pa., Phila., 1990-98; bd. dirs. U.S. Chem. & Hazard Investigation, Washington, 1998—; postdoctoral fellow chemistry dept. Pa. State U., State Coll., 1952-53. Co-author: Basics of Chromotography, 1953, Communicating Major Hazards, 1990. Sgt. U.S. Army, 1943-46. Home: 54 Rain Lily Rd Levittown PA 19056-2302 Office: U Pa Wharton Sch Philadelphia PA 19104

ROSENTHAL, KENNETH W., lawyer; b. Frankfurt, Fed. Republic Germany, Nov. 2, 1929; came to U.S., 1944; s. Ludwig and Florence (Koenigsberger) R.; m. Joan Finkelstein, Apr. 10, 1960; children: Jeffrey, David. BA, Syracuse U., 1951; LLB, U. Calif., San Francisco, 1958. Bar: Calif. 1959, U.S. Dist. Ct. (no. dist.) Calif. 1959, U.S. Ct. Appeals (9th cir.) 1959, U.S. Supreme Ct. 1972. Assoc. Jay A. Darwin, San Francisco, 1959-61; ptnr. Darwin, Rosenthal & Leff, San Francisco, 1961-69; pres. Rosenthal & Leff Inc., San Francisco, 1969-89; of counsel Molligan, Cox & Moyer, San Francisco, 1989-98, Cox & Moyer, San Francisco, 1998—; del. 9th Cir. Jud. Conf., 1986-89. Contbr. numerous articles to profl. jours. Mem. Nat. Bd. Trial Advocacy (cert.), Am. Bd. Trial Advs. (cert.), Calif. Bar. Assn. (legal specialization sect., civic trial advocacy com., mediator, arbitrator 1993—), San Francisco Bar Assn., San Francisco Trial Lawyers Assn. (bd. dirs. 1976-84, pres. 1984). Democrat. Jewish. Avocations: photography, walking. Office: Cox & Moyer 703 Market St San Francisco CA 94103-2102

ROSENTHAL, LYOVA HASKELL See GRANT, LEE

ROSENTHAL, MILTON FREDERICK, minerals and chemical company executive; b. N.Y.C., Nov. 24, 1913; s. Jacob C. and Louise (Berger) R.; m. Frieda Bojar, Feb. 28, 1943; 1 child, Anne Rosenthal Mitro. BA, CCNY, 1932; LLB, Columbia U., 1935. Bar: N.Y. 1935. Rsch. asst. N.Y. State Law Revision Commn., 1935-37; law sec. Fed. Judge William Bondy, 1937-40; assoc. atty. Leve, Hecht & Hadfield, 1940-42; sec., treas. Hugo Stinnes Corp., 1946-48, exec. v.p., treas., CEO, 1948-49, pres., dir., CEO, 1949-64; pres., dir., CEO Minerals and Chems. Philipp Corp., N.Y.C., 1964-67; pres., dir., COO Engelhard Minerals & Chem. Corp., N.Y.C., 1967-71; chmn., pres., CEO, dir. Engelhard Minerals & Chems. Corp., N.Y.C., 1971-81; dir. Salomon, Inc., N.Y.C., 1981-88, dir. emeritus, 1988-98; chmn. Engelhard Corp., N.J., 1981-86; ret. dir. US-USSR Trade and Econ. Coun., 1974-82, Nat. Coun. US-China Trade, 1977-82; chmn., dir. Romanian-Am. Econ. Coun., 1974-89; dir. Fgn. Policy Assn., 1971-91. Trustee Mt. Sinai Med. Ctr. and Mt. Sinai Hosp.; bd. dirs. United Cerebral Palsy Rsch. and Ednl. Found., Inc.; ret. trustee Am. Fedn. Arts, Manhattanville Coll., Purchase Coll. Found. 1st lt. JAG dept. U.S. Army, 1942-45. Mem. Assn. of Bar of City of N.Y., Chgo. Bar Assn., Columbia Law Sch. Alumni Assn., Judge Adv. Assn., Phi Beta Kappa. Home: 450 Woodlands Rd Harrison NY 10528-1220 also: 1602 Quartz Valley Dr Carefree AZ 85377 Office: 450 Park Ave Ste 2701 New York NY 10022-2605

ROSENTHAL, RAFAIL LEON, surgeon; b. Riga, Latvia, Sept. 27, 1937; s. Leon Solomon and Maria Nicolai (Liebermann) Rosenthal; m. Inna Abraham Aronova, Dec. 6, 1937; 2 children. MD, Riga Med. Inst., Latvia, 1960. Surgeon Dist. Hosp., Dagda, Latvia, 1960-62; rsch. fellow Med. Inst. Riga, Children's Hosp., 1965-67; rsch. surgeon Surg. Enptl. Lab. Med. Inst., Riga, Latvia, 1967-74, head lab., 1974-76; head transplant dept. Latvia Acad. Medicine, Riga, 1976—; cons. in field. Author: Treatment of Chronic Renal Failure, 1984; co-author: Immunological Experience of Kidney Transplant, 1984, Donors Problems in Organ Transplant, 1987, Kidney Transplant Pathology, 1990. Pres. Latvian Kidney Found., Riga, 1989—, Dem. Religious M. Dubina Found., Riga, 1993—. Mem. ESOT, EDTA, Latvian Assn. Transplantology (pres. 1992—), Internat. Transplant Soc., Latvian Acad. Sci. Avocations: chess, swimming. Home: Zolitudes str 38 2 apt 64, LV-1029 Riga Latvia Office: Latvian Acad Medicine, Dzierciema 16, LV 1007 Riga Latvia

ROSENTHAL, RANDALL MARC, artist; b. N.Y.C., Nov. 3, 1947; s. Harold Maxwell Rosenthal and Lila Joy Nelson; m. Caren S. R., July 15, 1979; 1 child, Jesse. BFA, Carnegie-Mellon U., 1969. Self-employed artist, 1969-86; designer-artist with Norman Jaffe, 1986-93; pres. Bonac Design, Inc., East Hampton, N.Y., 1996—. Multiple juried commns. include East Hampton Airport, St. James Cathedral, Seattle; subject numerous publs. and TV documentary. Recipient 2 religious art awards Am. Inst. Architects, 1998, 1st place Excellence in Craftsmanship award Am. Woodworker, 1996, Fed. Bank purchase award, Guild Hall Mus., 1988, Excellence in Design award N.Y. State Assn. Architects, 1988. Avocations: surfing, snowboarding, softball. Office: Bonac Design Inc 37 Fort Pond Blvd East Hampton NY 11937-4220

ROSENTHAL, STEVEN SIEGMUND, lawyer; b. Cleve., May 22, 1949; s. Fred Siegel and Natalie Josephine Rosenthal; m. Ilene Edwina Goldstein, Oct. 1, 1983; children: Alexandra M., Eliana D. AB, Dartmouth Coll., 1971; JD, Harvard U., 1974. Bar: Fla. 1974, D.C. 1975, U.S. Supreme Ct. 1978, Calif. 1983. Law clk. judge Malcolm R. Wilkey U.S. Ct. Appeals (D.C. cir.), 1974-75; assoc. Covington & Burling, Washington, 1975-80; assoc. Morrison & Foerster, Washington, 1980-81, ptnr., 1981-97; ptnr. Cooper, Carvin & Rosenthal, PLLC, Washington, 1998—; lawyer rep. Jud. Conf. D.C. Cir., 1981-83. Pres. Family and Child Services Washington, 1986-88, trustee, 1978—. Mem. ABA, Am. Law Inst., Phi Beta Kappa. Republican. Office: Cooper Carvin & Rosenthal PLLC 1500 K St NW Ste 200 Washington DC 20005-1264

ROSENZWEIG, CHARLES LEONARD, lawyer; b. N.Y.C., Apr. 12, 1952; s. William and Frieda (Dechner) R.; m. Rya R. Mehler, June 14, 1975; children: Jessica Sara, Erica Danielle. AB cum laude, Princeton U., 1974; JD, NYU, 1977. Bar: N.Y. 1978, U.S. Dist. Ct. (ea. and so. dists.) N.Y. 1978, U.S. Ct. Appeals (7th cir.) 1980, U.S. Ct. Internat. Trade 1981, U.S. Ct. Appeals (2d cir.) 1985. Assoc. Graubard, Moskovitz et al, N.Y.C., 1977-85; ptnr. Rand, Rosenzweig, Smith, Radley, Gordon & Burstein LLP, N.Y.C., 1987—; mem. panel of neutrals comml. divsn. Supreme Ct. State N.Y. Editor NYU Jour. Internat. Law. and Politics. Chmn. of bd. Jewish Cmty. Ctr., Harrison. Mem. ABA (internat. law sect.), N.Y. State Bar Assn. (co-chair internat. litigation com. 1995-98, mem. exec. com. comml. and fed. litigation sect.), Am. Arbitration Assn., NYU Alumni Assn. (chmn. jour. internat. law and politics alumni 1985-87), Assn. of Commercial Fin. Attys. Avocations: skiing, cycling, tennis, scuba diving. Home: 37 Franklin Rd Scarsdale NY 10583-7563 Office: Rand Rosenzweig et al 605 3rd Ave New York NY 10158-0180

ROSENZWEIG, HERBERT STEPHEN, stockbroker; b. Phila., Aug. 5, 1943; s. Morton and Helen (Katzen) R.; m. Myra Pauline Saltzburg, June 7, 1964; children: Helene, Michael, Elisa, Jeffrey. BS in Fin., Temple U., 1965. CFP. Stockbroker Walston & Co., Phila., 1967-73, Reynolds Securities, Phila., 1974, Merrill Lynch, Riverside, Calif., 1974—. Vol. Spl. Olympics, 1980-96; chmn. Pomona Valley Coun. Chs. Hunger Walk, 1995-97; pres. Upland Youth Accountability Bd., 1995-97. Mem. Kiwanis (past pres., lt. gov. Divsn. 15 1992-93, Club Kiwanian of Yr., Divsn. Kiwanian of Yr. 1992). Republican. Jewish. Office: Merrill Lynch 4141 Inland Empire Blvd Ste 150 Ontario CA 91764-5001

ROSHONG, DEE ANN DANIELS, dean, educator; b. Kansas City, Mo., Nov. 22, 1936; d. Vernon Edmund and Doradell (Kellogg) Daniels; m. Richard Lee Roshong, Aug. 27, 1960 (div.). BMusEd., U. Kans., 1958; MA in Counseling and Guidance, Stanford U., 1960; postgrad., Fresno State U., U. Calif.; EdD, U. San Francisco, 1980. Counselor, psychometrist Fresno City Coll., 1961-65; counselor, instr. psychology Chabot Coll., Hayward, Calif., 1965-75; coord. counseling svcs. Chabot Coll., Livermore, Calif., 1975-81, asst. dir. student pers. svcs., 1981-89; asst. dir. student pers. svcs. Las Positas Coll., Livermore, Calif., 1989-91, assoc. dean student svcs., 1991-94, dean student svcs., 1994—; life coach Las Positas Coll., Livermore, 2000—; writer, coord. I, A Woman Symposium, 1974, Feeling Free to Be You and Me symposium, 1975, All for the Family Symposium, 1976, I Celebrate Myself Symposium, 1978, Person to Person in Love and Work Symposium, 1978, The Healty Person in Mind and Spirit Symposium, 1980, Change Symposium, 1981, Sources of Strength Symposium, 1982, Love and Friendship Symposium, 1983, Self Esteem Symposium, 1984, Trust Symposium, 1985, Prime Time: Making the Most of This Time in Your Life Symposium, 1986, Symposium in Healing, 1987, How to Live in the World and Still Be Happy Symposium, 1988, Student Success is a Team Effort, Sound Mind, Sound Body Symposium, 1989, Creating Life's Best Symposium, 1990, Choices Symposium, 1991, Minding the Body, Mending the Mind Symposium, 1992, Healing through Love and Laughter Symposium, 1993, Healing Ourselves Changing the World Symposium, 1994, Finding Your Path Symposium, 1995, Build the Life You Want Symposium, 1996, Making Peace With Yourself and Your Relationships Symposium, 1997, Everyday Sacred Symposium, 1998, Wisdom of the Heart Symposium, 1999, Inner Wisdom Symposium, 2000, Second Half of Life Symposium, 2000; mem. cast TV prodns. Eve and Co., Best of Our Times, Cowboy; chmn. Calif. C.C. Chancellor's Task Force on Counseling, Statewide Regional Counseling Facilitators, 1993-95, Statewide Conf. Emotionally Disturbed Students in Calif. C.C.s, 1982—, Conf. on the Upper Represented Student in Calif. C.C.s, 1986, Conf. on High Risk Students, 1989. Author: Counseling Needs of Comunity College Students, 1980. Bd. dirs. Teleios Sinetar Ctr., Ctr. for Cmty. Dispute Resolution, 1998—, Pleasanton Youth Collaborative Bd., 1997—, Pleasanton Youth Master Plan Bd., 1998—; choir dir., 1996-99; pres. Tri-Valley Unity Ch. bd., 1998; title III activity dir. Las Positas Coll., 1995-99, dir. pace program, 1999—, dir. quest program, 2000—. Mem. Assn. Humanistic Psychologists, Western Psychol. Assn., Nat. Assn. Women Deans and Counselors, Assn. Counseling and Devel., Calif. Assn. C.C. (chmn. commn. on student svcs. 1979-84), Calif. C.C. Counselors Assn. (svc. award 1986, 87, award for Outstanding and Disting. Svc. 1986, 87, Spl. Svc. award for outstanding svc. Calif. advocated for reentry edn. 1991), Alpha Phi. Home: 1856 Harvest Rd Pleasanton CA 94566-5456 Office: 3033 Collier Canyon Rd Livermore CA 94550-9797

ROSICH, RONALD STEVEN, water and environmental scientist, researcher, consultant, educator; b. Perth, Australia, Nov. 20, 1939; s. Joseph Kresimir and May (Turkich) R.; m. Maureen Elizabeth Fletcher, Oct. 13, 1962; children: Michael John, Gregory Paul, Bradley Mark. BSc with honors, U. Western Australia, Perth, 1960; PhD, U. Western Australia, 1964. Postdoctoral fellow Nat. Rsch. Coun. Can., Ottawa, 1964-66; rsch. fellow Calif. Inst. Tech., Pasadena, 1966-67; postdoctoral fellow UCLA, 1967-68; Merck, Sharp and Dohme rsch. fellow Monash U., Melbourne, Australia, 1968-70; lectr. in chemistry Canberra (Australia) U., 1970-73, sr. lectr. in natural resources, 1973-83; mgr. water supply lab. Water Corp. of Western Australia, Perth, 1983-88, mgr. consulting sect., sci. svcs. br., 1988-95, prin. scientist, cons., 1996-98; pvt. cons., 1998-99; prin. environ. scientist Atech Group, 1999—; acting mgr. sci. svcs. br. Water Corp. Western Australia, 1990-95; mem. acad. bd., bd. studies Sch. Applied Sci., various coms. Canberra U., 1970-83; vis. prof. Swiss Fed. Inst. Water Resources and Water Pollution Control, Zürich, 1976; vis. rsch. scientist Environ. Rsch. Lab. EPA, Duluth, Minn., 1976; plenary spkr. UNESCO, Havana, 1988; spkr., cons. referee in field. Author: (reports) Resource Recovery in Solid Waste Management, Procs. Australian Waste Mgmt. and Control Conf., 1974, Wetlands of the Swan Coastal Plain, Vol. 6, 1993, Perth Coastal Waters Study, 1994, Research in Water and Wastewater Quality Issues, 6 vols., 1998; contbr. over 60 articles to jours. in field. Del. Energy and Resource Devel. Projects People to People Citizen Amb. Program, China, 1995. Postgrad. and undergrad. scholar Commonwealth Dept. Edn., Australia, 1957-64. Mem. Soc. Internat. Limnology (editl. bd. 1980), Internat. Water Assn., Australian Water Assn. (chmn. various state brs.), Am. Water Works Assn., Water Environ. Fedn. Avocations: photography, electronics, personal computers. E-mail: rsr@bigpond.com. Office: 15 Kalyba Pl, Duncraig WA 6023, Australia

ROSICKY, BOHUMIR, parasitologist, educator; b. Brno, Apr. 18, 1922; Dr.rer.nat., Dr.Sc., Charles U., Prague, Czechoslovakia. Mem. staff Rovnost (Brno daily paper), 1945-46; chem. research worker, lab. head, chem. industry, 1947-50; specialist Central Biol. Inst., Prague, 1950-53; head dept. parasitology Biol. Inst., Czechoslovak Acad. Scis., Prague, 1954-61; dir. Inst. Parasitology, Prague, 1962-80, Inst. Hygiene and Epidemiology, 1980-90; prof. natural scis. Comenius U., Bratislava, 1965—; dep. Czech Nat. Council, 1969-91, mem. presidium, from 1969; WHO cons., India, 1964-65; mem. Joint WHO/FAO UN Panel of Zoonoses. Author: Czechoslovak Fauna-Aphaniptera, 1957; co-author: Modern Insecticides, 1951, Parasitologische Arbeitsmethoden, 1965, Med. Entomology and Environ., 1989, Probleme der Stadthygiene-Tierische Umwelt, 1992, Salmonelloses, 1994; author numerous papers on ecology, taxonomy, entomology, med. zoology and parasitology. Decorated Order Cyril and Method (Bulgaria), Krzyz Oficerski (Poland), Order Labor; recipient State prize, 1954, G. Mendel Gold medal, 1970; co-recipient Klement Gottwald State prize, 1956, 72. Mem. Czechoslovak Acad. Scis. (academician 1970-92, v.p. 1970-77, Silver plaque 1972, Gold 1987), Bulgarian Acad. Scis., Polish Acad. Scis. (corr., pres. 3d and 8th Cong. of Acarology). Office: Moravanu 19, 16900 Prague 6, Czech Republic

ROSIER, FREDERICK DAVID STEWART, securities company executive; b. Halton, Bucks, Eng., Apr. 10, 1951; s. Frederick Ernest and Hettie Denise (Blackwell) R.; m. Julia Elizabeth Gomme, Sept. 27, 1975; 1 child, Charles Frederick James. MA in Jurisprudence, Oxford U. Dir. S.G. Warburg and Co. Ltd, London, 1984-87; dir. Mercury Asset Mgmt. Group, London, 1987-98, dep. chmn., 1991-98; also bd. chmn. Mercury Fund Mgrs. Ltd., London; mnging. dir. Merrill Lynch Investment Mgrs., 1998—; chmn. Mercury Life Assurance Co. Ltd.; mnging. dir. Channel Islands Ltd. Capt. The Brit. Army, 1973-78. Avocations: golf, skiing, shooting. Home: 99 Thurleigh Rd, London SW128TY, England Office: 33 King William St, London EC4R 9AS, England

ROSIN, ARNOLD JACK, physician, educator; b. Glasgow, Scotland, Oct. 5, 1930; arrived in Israel, 1969; s. Isaac and Ethel (Levine) R.; m. Marta Weinstock, Nov. 8, 1960; children: Joanna, Jonathan, Simon, Ariel. MBChB, U. Glasgow, 1953. Intern in orthops. Victoria Infirmary, Glasgow, 1953; intern in internal medicine Jewish Hosp., London, 1954; registrar Royal Alexandra Infirmary, Paisley, Scotland, 1958, U. Coll. Hosp. and Whittington Hosp., London, 1961-64; registrar, sr. registrar, cons. geriatrics/internal medicine Guy's Hosp., London, 1964-69; dir. Harzfeld Hosp. for Geriatric and Chronic Diseases, Gedera, Israel, 1969-77; chief dept. geriatrics Shaare Zedek Med. Ctr., Jerusalem, 1977-96, dir., 1982-84; chmn. pub. com. Internat. Yr. of Older Person, 1999; assoc. prof. medicine and geriatrics Hebrew U., Hadassah Med. Sch., 1978-85; prof., 1985—. Author, editor: Special Edition of Gerontology on Degenerative Brain Disorders in the Aged; contbr. articles to profl. jours. Chmn. Nat. Com. Svc. Devel. of Nursing Ins. Law, Israel, 1986-97; dir. Melabev, Jerusalem. Flight lt. RAF, 1955-56. Grantee Wolfson Family Trust, 1988-93. Fellow Royal Coll. Physicians; mem. Brit. Geriatric Soc., Israel Soc. Geriatric Medicine. Jewish. Avocations: Jewish studies, English literature, running. Home: 17 Mehalkey Hamayim St, 93222 Jerusalem Israel Office: Shaare Zedek Med Ctr, PO Box 3235, 91000 Jerusalem Israel

ROSIN, RICHARD DAVID, consultant surgeon; b. Harare, Zimbabwe, Apr. 29, 1942; arrived in Eng., 1960; s. Isadore Rowland and Muriel Ena (Wolfe) R.; m. Michele Shirley Moreton, June 3, 1971; children: Natasha Jane, Alexei John, Katya Sarah. MB BS, London U., 1966. Rsch. sr. registrar Westminster Hosp., London, 1974-75, sr. registrar, 1977-78, 79; sr. registrar Kingston Hosp., 1975-77; vis. lectr. U. Hong Kong, 1979; cons. surgeon St. Mary's Hosp., Imperial Coll. Medicine, London, 1980—. Joint editor: Cancer of the Bile Duct and Pancreas, 1989, Head and Neck Oncology for The General Surgeon, 1991, Diagnosis and Management of Melanoma in Clinical Practice, 1992; editor: Minimal Access Medicine and Surgery—Principles and Practice, 1993, Minimal Access General Surgery, 1994; co-editor: Minimal Access Surgical Oncology, 1995, Minimal Access Thoracic Surgery, 1998; contbr. chpts. to books, articles to profl. jours. Fellow Royal Coll. Surgeons Edinburgh, Royal Coll. Surgeons Eng. (mem. coun., Arris and Gale lectr., Hunterian prof., Arnott demonstrator), Royal Soc. Medicine (prev. pres. and sec. surgery and clin. sect.); mem. Brit. Assn. Surg. Oncologists (prev. hon. sec., v.p. 2000—), Assn. Endoscopic Surgeons Gt. Britain and Ireland (mem. coun.), Melanoma Study Group (v.p., prev. hon. sec. and pres.), Surg. Rsch. Soc., 1979—, fell. Assn. Surgeons of Gt. Britain and Ireland, 1975—, fell. Assn. Upper Gastro Intestinal of Gt. Britain and Ireland, 1997—, mem. British Soc. Gastroenterology, 1980, Roehampton Club, Garrick Club, Middlesex Cricket Club, New Zealand Golf Club, Livery Cos., Worshipful Co. of Apothecaries, Worshipful Co. of Barber-Surgeons. Avocations: golf, opera, theatre, chess, travel. Home: 2 St Simon's Ave, London SW15 6DU, England Office: Cons Rooms, 80 Harley St, London W1G 7HL, England

ROSINSKI, ANDRZEJ ZDZISLAW, poultry scientist, researcher, educator; b. Poznań, Poland, Aug. 28, 1955; s. Gwidon Andrzej and Zofia Janina (Borowiecka) R.; m. Anna Maria Witkowska, July 29, 1978; 1 child, Monika Agnieszka. MS, Agrl. U. Poznan, 1979, diploma in poultry breeding, 1984, diploma in edn., 1990; D of Agrl. Scis., Inst. Animal Husbandry, 1990. Sr. specialist Comml. Poultry Farm, Nekla, Poland, 1979-82; sr. rschr. Exptl. Sta. Inst. Animal Husbandry, Koluda Wielka, Poland, 1982—; lectr. poultry sciu. dept. Agrl. U. Poznan, Poland, 1989—; leader Polish-French rsch. project Polish Com. Sci., 1991-95, head rsch. projects, Cracow, 1992-94, 94-98; expert in geese breeding Food and Agr. Orgn. UN, Rome, 1993—; mem. Polish standardization com. Poultry Products Sect., Poznan, 1996—; arbiter/expert Copenhagen Arbitration, 1996-98. Contbr. articles to profl. jours. Recipient Award Ministry Agr. and Food, 1996. Mem. Polish Soc. Animal Prodn. (sec. Poznan br. 1980—), World's Poultry Sci. Assn. (Polish br. and waterfowl group), Leading Tech. Orgn. Bydgoszcz (Silver award 1990). Roman Catholic. Avocations: travel, geography, history of art, swimming. Home: Os Stefana Batorego 20E/41, 60-687 Poznań Poland Office: Agrl Univ Poultry Sci, Wolynska 33, 60-637 Poznań Poland also: Inst Animal Husbandry, Koluda Wielka Exptl Sta, 88-160 Janikowo Poland

ROŠKO, PETER KAROL, mechanics educator; b. Bratislava, Czechoslovakia, June 17, 1956; s. Karol and Izabela (Hüttner) R.; m. Eva Kačániová, Oct. 6, 1984; children: Peter, Beata. MS, Slovak Tech. U., Bratislava, 1980, PhD, 1987. Lectr. Slovak Tech. U., Bratislava, 1980-93, assoc. prof., 1999—; rschr. Czech Tech. U., Prague, 1983, Aalborg (Denmark) U., 1993; lectr. Tech. U. Vienna, 1993-97; cons. Design Automation, Vienna, 1990-93; dir. Statik, Bratislava, 1990-93. Author: Structural Models in Statics and Dynamics, 1997; contbr. numerous articles to profl. jours. Mem. Gesellschaft für Angewandte Mathematik und Mechanik, N.Y. Acad. Sci. Avocations: architecture, traveling, swimming. Office: Slovak Tech U, Radlinskeho 11, SK-81368 Bratislava Slovakia

RÖSLER, NORBERT FELIX, neurologist, neuroscientist; b. Lörrach, Germany, Mar. 19, 1962. MD, Freiburg U., Germany, 1989. Sci. asst. dept. neurology Marburg U., Germany, 1989-94; sci. asst. dept. psychiatry Freiburg U., Germany, 1995-97; neuroscientist Ludwig Boltzmann Inst. Clin. Neurobiology, Vienna, Austria, 1994-95, 98—; asst. med. dir. dept. neurorehabilitation Hosp. Rodach, Coburg, Germany, 1997-98. Contbr. articles to profl. jours. and books. Mem. German Socs. Neurology Clin. Neurophysiology, Psychiatry and Psychotherapy, World Fedn. Neurology, European Soc. Clin. Neuropharmacology, N.Y. Acad. Scis. Office: Ludwig Boltzmann Inst Clin Neurobiol, Pav. XI Wolkersbergenstr 1, A-1130 Vienna Austria

ROSLOW, SYDNEY, marketing educator; b. N.Y.C., July 29, 1910; s. Joseph and Anna (Lipman) R.; m. Irma Sternberg, Oct. 21, 1932; children: Richard Jay, Susan Jane, Peter Dirk. BS, NYU, 1931, MA, 1932, PhD, 1935. Rsch. asst. in market, indsl and pers. rsch. Psychol. Corp., 1931-41; sch. psychologist, mem. Bd. Edn., Hastings on Hudson, N.Y., 1937-48; pub. opinion rsch. program surveys divsn. U.S. Dept. Agr., 1939-43; founder Pulse, Inc., market and audience rsch. in radio, TV, advt., N.Y.C., 1941-78; assoc. prof. Baruch Coll., CUNY, 1967-75; assoc. prof. dept. mktg. Fla. Internat. U., 1976-83, prof. mktg., assoc. dean Coll. Bus. Adminstrn., 1983-90, prof. emeritus, 1990—, acting assoc. dean, 1996; rschr. in mktg. Contbr. chpts. to books, more than 90 articles to profl. jours. Fellow APA; mem. Am. Mktg. Assn. (pres. Miami chpt. 1980-82), Market Rsch. Coun. (inducted into Hall of Fame, N.Y. 1992), Radio-TV Rsch. Coun. (past pres.), Radio and TV Execs. Soc., Phi Beta Kappa. Home: 1035 NE 202nd Ter Miami FL 33179-2548 Office: Fla Internat U North Miami Campus North Miami FL 33181

ROSMUNDSSON, OLAFUR INGÌ, internal auditor; b. Reykjavik, Iceland, Dec. 27, 1941; s. Tomasson Rosmundur and Olafsdottir Berga; m. Karitas Haraldsdottir, Dec. 14, 1963; children: Alda Ros, Olafur Mar, Maria Erla. Student, Reykjavik, 1961; Diploma in Econs., U. Iceland, 1966. Cashier Nat. Bank Iceland, Reykjavik, 1962-66, EDP programmer, 1966-74; EDP chief analyst Reiknistofa Bankanna, Reykjavik, 1974-78, systems devel. exec., 1978-88, internal auditor, 1988—. Mem. Ind. Order Odd Fellows. Lutheran. Home: Brekkuseli 21, 109 Reykjavik Iceland Office: Reiknistofa Bankanna, Kalkofnsvegi 1, 150 Reykjavik Iceland

ROSMUS, ANNA ELISABETH, writer; b. Passau, Germany, Mar. 29, 1960; d. Georg Rudolf and Anna Johanna (Friedberger) R.; divorced; children: Dolores Nadine, Beatrice Salome Kassandra. M. U. Passau, 1994; PhD (hon.), U. S.C., 2000. speaker and organizer in field. Author: Resistance and Persecution, 1983 (Geschwister Scholl Preis 1984), Exodus In The Shadow of Mercy, 1988, Robert Klein A German Jew Looks Back, 1991, Wintergreen Suppressed Murders, 1993 (Conscience in Media award 1994), Pocking End and Renewal, 1995, What I Think, 1995, Out of Passau, 1999; guest talk shows including Documentaries and Features in Germany, Austria, Great Britain, Denmark, Holland, France, Italy, Sweden, Poland, Can., U.S., South Am., Australia, 1983—. Fundraiser Anne Frank Found., Jewish Cmty. Ctrs., Holocaust Ctrs., others, 1992—. Recipient Immigrant Achievement award Am. Immigration Lawyers Assn., 1998; named Best German Writer, European essay Competition, 1980; Sarnat award Anti Defamation League, 1994; Anna Rosmus Day, City of Santa Cruz, 1994. Mem. PEN Internat., NAFE. Avocations: environment protection, multicultural projects, minority programs.

ROSNER, MENACHEM, sociology educator; b. Cernauti, Romania, Oct. 16, 1922; arrived in Israel, 1941; s. Bernhard and Yetti (Schmidt) R.; m.

Rina Lenobel, July 7, 1943; children: Ely (dec.), Noga, Orna. BA in Sociology, Hebrew U., Jerusalem, 1962, MA in Sociology, 1967, PhD in Sociology, 1972. Dir. Kibbutz Rsch. Ctr., Givat Haviva, Israel, 1966-76, Kibbutz Rsch. Inst., Haifa (Israel) U., 1976—; sr. lectr. Haifa U., 1976-80, assoc. prof., 1980-87, prof., 1987-92, prof. emeritus, 1992—; vis. scholar Harvard U., Cambridge, Mass.; vis. prof. Inst. Sci. Politique, Paris, Free U., Berlin; pres. Israeli Sociol. Soc., 1988-91. Author: (book) The Second Generation, 1990; co-author: (books) Hierarchy in Organization, 1974, Alienation, Community, Work, 1991, The Changing Kibbutz, 1996. Mem. Internat. Sociology Assn. (v.p. RC36 1992), Israeli Sociology Soc. (pres. 1988-91). Meretz. Jewish. Home: Kibbutz Reshafim, 10905 Post Habika Israel Office: Haifa U, Inst for Rsch on Kibbutz, Haifa Israel

RÖSNER, PETER, chemist; b. Köthen, Germany, July 31, 1944; s. Helmut and Ilse (Baumgardt) R.; m. Eva Bartsch, July 18, 1969. Diploma in chemistry, U. Kiel, Germany, 1978, dr.rer.nat., 1981. Head sect. of toxicology Landeskrimalamt, Kiel, 1981—. Author: Structural Data of Compounds under Control, 1999. Home: Posener Strasse, 24161 Altenholz Stift Germany Office: Landeskriminalamt Schleswig-Holstein, Mühlenweg 166, 24116 Kiel Germany

ROSNOW, RALPH LEON, psychology researcher and educator; b. Balt., Jan. 10, 1936; s. Irvin and Rebecca (Faber) R.; m. Mimi Quin Medinger, Aug. 12, 1963. BS, U. Md., 1957; MA, George Washington U., 1958; PhD, Am. U., 1962. Asst. prof. Boston U., 1963-67; assoc. prof. Temple U., Phila., 1967-70, full prof., 1970—; vis. prof. London Sch. Econs., 1973, Harvard U., Cambridge, Mass., 1978, 1988-89; Thaddeus Bolton prof. Temple U., 1982—, dir. social and orgnl. psychology dept. psychology, 1988-2000; cons. editor jours. and encys. in psychology and comm.; cons. on rsch. methods and data analysis, 1976—. Author: Paradigms in Transition, 1981, (with Robert Rosenthal) The Volunteer Subject, 1975, Essentials of Behavioral Research, 1984, 2d edit., 1991, Contrast Analysis, 1985, Beginning Behavioral Research, 1993, 2d edit., 1996, 3d edit., 1999, People Studying People, 1997, Contrasts and Effect Sizes in Behavioral Research, 2000; (with Gary Fine) Rumor and Gossip, 1976, (with Mimi Rosnow) Writing Papers in Psychology, 1986, others; editor: (with Robert Rosenthal) Artifact in Behavioral Research, 1969, (with Marianthi Georgoudi) Contextualism and Understanding in Behavioral Science. Recipient George A. Miller award Soc. Gen. Psychology, 1999. Fellow AAAS, APA, Am. Pschol. Soc.; mem. Soc. Exptl. Social Psychology. Avocations: reading, walking, window shopping, cable surfing. Office: Temple U Psychology Dept 517 Weiss Hall Philadelphia PA 19122

ROSOCHACKI, STANISLAW JÓZEF, scientist, biochemist; b. Holowienki, Poland, May 29, 1946; s. Józef and Janina (Mazurczak) R.; m. Halina Bialenska, Sept. 30, 1972 (dec. Aug. 1996); 1 child, Marcin. MS, U. Warsaw, Poland, 1970; PhD, Inst. Genetics/Animal Breeding, Jastrzebiec, Poland, 1976; DSc, Agrl. Acad. Kracow, Poland, 1993. PhD fellow Inst. Genetics & Animal Breeding, 1970-73, rsch. asst., 1974, sr. rsch. asst., 1975-76, rsch. assoc., 1977-85, dep. head growth & devel. dept., 1981-83, head growth & devel. unit Dept. Animal Nutrition, 1983-85, rsch. fellow, 1985-93, sr. rsch. fellow, 1993—. Mem. Polish Genetic Soc. (treas. 1975-78, 81-85). Roman Catholic. Avocations: opera, theatre, sightseeing. Home: Wlasna 2, 05090 Raszyn Poland Office: Inst Genetics & Animal, Breeding, 05551 Mrokow Poland

ROSOFF, WILLIAM A., lawyer, executive; b. Phila., June 21, 1943; s. Herbert and Estelle (Finkel) R.; m. Beverly Rae Rifkin, Feb. 7, 1970; children: Catherine D., Andrew M. BS with honors, Temple U., 1964; LLB magna cum laude, U. Pa., 1967. Bar: Pa. 1968, U.S. Dist. Ct. (ea. dist.) Pa. 1968. Law clk. U.S. Ct. Appeals (3d cir.), 1967-68; instr. U. Pa. Law Sch., Phila., 1968-69; assoc. Wolf, Block, Schorr & Solis-Cohen, Phila., 1969-75, ptnr., 1975-96, chmn. exec. com., 1987-88; also vice chmn. bd. dirs. Advanta Corp., Spring House, Pa., 1996—, pres., 1999—; trustee RPS Realty Trust, 1990-96, Atlantic Realty Trust, 1996—; guest lectr. confs. and seminars on tax law; mem. tax adv. bd. Commerce Clearing House, 1983-94; mem. legal activities policy bd. Tax Analysts, 1978—; mem. Little, Brown Tax Adv. Bd., 1994-96; chmn. bd. dirs. RMH Telesvcs., Inc., 1997—. Editor U. Pa. Law Rev., 1965-67; mem. bd. contbg. editors and advisors Jour. Partnership Taxation, 1983—; author reports and papers on tax law. Bd. dirs., mem. com. on law and social action Phila. coun. Am. Jewish Congress. Fellow Am. Coll. Tax Counsel; mem. Am. Law Inst. (cons. taxation of partnerships 1976-78, assoc. reporter taxation of partnerships, 1978-82, mem. adv. group on fed. income tax project 1982—, cons. taxation of pass-through entities 1995—), Locust Club (dir.), Order of Coif, Beta Gamma Sigma, Beta Alpha Psi. Office: Advanta Corp Welsh and McKean Rd Spring House PA 19477

ROSOLINO, MASSIMILIANO, olympic athlete; b. Naples, Italy, July 11, 1978; s. Salvatore and Caroline R. Degree in Hotel Mgmt., Naples, 1998. Mem. swim team Italy; sixth pl. in 200 and 400 meter freestyle Olympics, Atlanta, 1996, sixth pl. in 4x200 meter freestyle relay, 1996; winner gold in 200 meter individual medley Olympics, Sydney, Australia, 2000, winner silver in 400 meter freestyle, 2000, winner bronze in 200 meter freestyle, 2000; winner silver in 200 and 400 meter freestyle European Championship, 1997, third pl. in 200 meter freestyle, 1999, winner 200 meter freestyle and 200 meter individual medley, 2000; second pl. in 200 meter freestyle World Championship, 1998. Office: Fedn Italiana Nuoto, Stadio Olimpico-Curva Nord, 00194 Rome Italy*

ROSS, BEATRICE BROOK, artist; b. N.Y.C., Mar. 31, 1927; d. Alexander and Ray (Tennenbaum) Brook; m. Alexander Ross, Dec. 23, 1945; children: Robert Alan, Kenneth Jay, Stefani Lynn. Student, Hunter Coll., 1943, CCNY, 1944, Bklyn. Mus. Art Sch., 1959-60, 64-65; pupil of Ruben Tam, Wang Chi Yuan, Leo Manso; scholar, Sch. Chinese Brush Work, 1973. Owner, operator Jean Rosenthal Bea Ross Gallery, Jericho, 1961-64; represented by Gillary Gallery, Jericho, N.Y., Patrician Gallery, West Palm Beach, Fla.; founder Birchwood Art League, 1958-63; lectr. bd. edn., Ont., Can., 1972; mem. ad hoc com. with Lucy Lippard Women in Art, 1970-74. Exhbns. include Women in Art, Huntington, N.Y., 1972, C.W. Post Coll., 1972, 73-76, Guild Hall Mus., East Hampton, 1969-72, Lever House, Inc., 1969-72, J. Walter Thompson Loan Show, 1970, Whitehouse Gallery, 1970, Park Ave. Synagogue, 1970, Locust Valley Ann., 1970, Nat. Arts Club, 1970, Loeb Student Ctr., NYU, 1969, Suffolk Mus., Stony Brook, N.Y., 1969, Lynn U., Boca Raton, 1992, Suffolk Mus., Stony Brook, N.Y., 1971, NAD, 1968, Audubon Artists, 1968, 70, Silvermine Guild, 1968, 71, Port Washington (N.Y.) Library, 1968, 70, 76, Profl. Artists Guild L.I., 1968, Bklyn. Coll., 1968, Huntington Twp. Art League, Cold Spring Harbor, N.Y., 1967, Gillary Gallery, Jericho, N.Y., 1966, 68, 70, 72, 79, 83, Hecksher Mus., 1960, 63, 70, Ho. of Reps., 1965, Library of Congress, 1965, Merrick (N.Y.) Gallery, 1963, N. Shore Community Art Ctr. ann., Roslyn, N.Y., 1959, 62, Birchwood Art League, Jericho, N.Y., 1958, 61-62, Hofstra U., 1960, City Ctr., N.Y.C., 1960, Emily Lowe Gallery, 1960, Nassau Democratic County Com. ann., 1958, R.A.A. Gallery, N.Y.C., 1969-70, 77, Roosevelt Field Art Gallery, Garden City, N.Y., 1958, Boca Raton (Fla.) City Hall, 1991, Bryant Library, Roslyn, N.Y., 1973, Women's Interart Ctr., N.Y.C., 1974, Wantagh (N.Y.) Library, 1975, Port Washington Library, 1976, LIU, 1976, N.Y. Tech., 1974, C.W. Post Coll. Schwartz Library, 1976, St. Johns U., 1976, Union Carbide, N.Y.C., 1977, Harley U. Ctr. Gallery, Adelphi U., 1976, 82, Lincoln Ctr., N.Y.C., 1978, 82, Gallery 84, N.Y.C., 1981, Jericho Libr., 1984Donell Libr., N.Y.C., 1991, Am. Properties Inc., Boca Raton, Fla., 1996; represented in pvt. collections, traveling shows in France, Italy and Japan; mus. curated show No. Trust Bank, Boca Mus., Fla., 1992, Nations Bank, Boca Raton Mus., Fla., 1995; contbr. poetry to Nat. Libr. Poetry, anthology Montage of Life. Recipient 1st prize oil Birchwood Art League, 1958; certificate award outstanding contbn. Mid Island Plaza Art League, Hicksville, N.Y., 1961, 2d prize oil, 1962; hon. mention oil Operation Democracy, Inc. ann., Locust Valley, 1967, 1st prize oil, 1970; Benjamin Altman landscape prize N.A.D., 1968; 2d prize Heckscher Mus., Huntington, N.Y., 1970; hon. mention Port Washington Ann., 1971, Benjamin Altman Landscape prize, Nat. award Nat. Acad. Design, N.Y.C., 1969, RAA Gallery, 1967-78, Harbor Gallery, Glen Cove, N.Y., 1983-85, Gillary Gallery Jericho, N.Y., 1984, Judge's Recognition award Boca Raton Mus., 1989, others; named to Nat. Women's Hall of Fame; MacDowell fellow, 1975, 80; selected for Unique and Universal South Fla. Artists Slide and Lctr., 1997. Mem. Profl. Artists Guild L.I. (v.p. admissions 1971-74, exec. v.p. 1975-77, 2d prize for group show 1990), Profl. Artists Guild Fla., Boca Raton Mus. Artist Guild, Easthampton Guild-Women in Arts, N.Y. Artists Equity, Nat. Mus. Women in Arts (charter), Gallery 84 (N.Y. 1979-85). Home and Studio: 5253 Bolero Cir Delray Beach FL 33484-1302

ROSS, BERNARD, engineering consultant, educator. BME, Cornell U., 1957; MSc in Aero. Engring., Stanford U., 1959, PhD in Aero. and Aerospace Engring., 1965; Diploma, Ecole Nat. Superieure L'Aero., France, 1960; cert., U. Edinburgh, Scotland, 1961. Registered profl. engr., Calif. Structural test engr. Gen. Dynamics Corp., Montreal, Quebec, Can., 1956; servomechanism and control sys. design engr. Marquardt Corp., Van Nuys, Calif., 1957; stress analyst Douglas Aircraft Co., Santa Monica, Calif., 1959; vibration and dynamics engr. ONERA, Paris, 1960; rsch. asst. Stanford U., 1961-63, rsch. assoc., 1963-65; sr. rsch. engr., program mgr. Stanford Rsch. Inst., Menlo Park, Calif., 1965-70; founder, chmn. emeritus Failure Analysis Assocs., San Francisco, 1967—; vis. prof. U. Santa Clara, Calif., 1970-79; adv. coun. Stanford U., 1991—, cons. prof., 1992—; pres. internat. adv. bd. structural failure, product liability and tech. ins. confs. U. Vienna, 1986—; mem. univ. coun. Cornell U., 1995; speaker and lectr. in field. Contbr. articles to Exptl. Mechanics, AIAA Jour., Israel Jour. Tech., Profl. Safety, others. Cons. U.S. Consumer Product Safety Commn., Washington. NATO scholar, 1960. Mem. ASME, NSPE, AIAA, AAAS, Am. Soc. Safety Engrs., Am. Soc. Agrl. Engrs., Calif. Soc. Profl. Engrs., Soc. Automotive Engrs., Soc. Exptl. Mechanics, Internat. Soc. for Law, Technology and Ins. Achievements include research in analysis of structural collapse, mechanics of impact and penetration, accident reconstruction, safety warning design for heavy equipment, mechanical failure of machine parts, transportation system design. Office: Failure Analysis Assocs PO Box 3015 149 Commonwealth Dr Menlo Park CA 94025-1133

ROSS, CARL ADRIAN, science educator; b. Burnham, Eng., Feb. 16, 1945; s. Harold Fredrik and Grace Margery (Swadling) R.; m. Pamela Anne Goodey, 1964 (wid. 1968); 1 child, Clarie Elise (dec.); m. Kristina (Ulla) Sundman, Feb. 27, 1971; children: Miriam, Alexander. Fil.Kand., Uppsala U., Sweden, 1974; Sociology Diploma, Uppsala U., 1975; MA in Social Sci., Durham U., Eng., 1975; Swedish Diploma, U. Goteborg, 1981. Draughtsman, designer, illustrator Eng., 1961-70; vocat. tchr. in English Sweden, 1975-80; supply tchr. State schs., Sweden, 1982-87; sci. tchr. Ystad, Sweden, 1987—; head bilingual tchg. Sci. in English, Ystad, 1995—; active environmentalist, 1972-87. Avocations: astronomy, art, history of ideas and thinking. E-mail: carl.ross@ebox.tninet.se. Office: Museigatan 4, S-27232 Simrishamn Sweden

ROSS, CARLISLE THOMAS, mechanical engineer, educator, consultant; b. Kharagpur, Bengal, India, Oct. 3, 1935; parents Brit. citizens; s. Thomas Vincent and Phyllis Helen (Beale) R.; m. Millicent Anne Bell, Jan. 16, 1960; children: Nicolette Anne Ross Dryden, Jonathan Carl Thomas. BSc in Naval Architecture with honors, U. Durham, Eng., 1959; PhD in Civil Engring., U. Manchester, Eng., 1963; DSc in Mech. Engring., Coun. Nat. Acad. Awards, London, 1992. Shipwright apprentice H.M. Dockyard, Chatham, Eng., 1951-56; design asst. Vickers, Barrow, Eng., 1959-62, dep. chief, 1962-64; lectr. Constantine Coll. Tech., Middlesbro, Eng., 1964-66; sr. lectr., reader U. Portsmouth, Eng., 1966-93, prof., 1993—; cons. structural analyst; cons. U. Portsmouth, 1964—. Author: Pressure Vessels under External Pressure, 1990, Mechanics of Solids, 1996, Finite Element Programs in Structural Engineering and Continuum Mechanics, 1996, Finite Element Techniques in Structural Mechanics, 1996. Elgar-Martell scholar, 1956-59. Fellow Royal Instn. Naval Architects; mem. Soc. Naval Architects and Marine Engrs. Roman Catholic. Avocation: long distance walking. Inventor of the bean can submarine pressure hull and the submarine dome cup ends; co-inventor of the tube-stiffened pressure hull and the perforated car deck for safer car ferries. Fax: (44) 02392791129. E-mail: carl@t-fross.freeserve.co.uk. Office: U Portsmouth, Anglesea Rd, Portsmouth PO1 3DJ, England

ROSS, CURTIS BENNETT, lawyer; b. Carbondale, Ill., June 7, 1955; s. Bernard Harris and Marian Frager Ross. BS in Acctg., U. Ill., 1977, JD, 1980. Bar: Ill., 1984. Tax staff Arthur Andersen & Co., Chgo., 1980-82; lawyer Jerome H. Torshen, Ltd., Chgo., 1983, Curtis Bennett Ross, Chgo., 1984—. attorney We Are Concerned, Chgo., 1995-99. Mem. Chgo. Bar Assn., CBA Matrimonial Com., Decalogue Soc. Office: 135 S Lasalle Fl 36 Chicago IL 60603-4159

ROSS, DANIEL MANUEL, insurance agent; b. N.Y.C., May 19, 1918; s. Max and Tillie (Klein) Rosenbaum; m. Norma Mandelbaum Ross, Nov. 24, 1949; children: Joan Carol, Paul. BS, Mich. State U., 1941. CLU. Life underwriter D.M. Ross, Inc., 1941—; speaker Life Underwriters, 1950—, Top of the Table, Las Vegas, 1984, Mich. State U. Bus. Sch., 1989; tchr. life ins., 1960—. Fund raiser Am. Cancer Soc., N.Y.C., YMCA, Weizman, Inst. of Israel, ARC, 1950—, Am. Coll., Bryn Mawr, Pa., 1977-79; bd. overseers Hebrew Union Coll., N.Y.C., 1986—; bd. trustees Pritikin Rsch. Found., Santa Monica, Calif., 1987—; bd. dirs. Stamford (Conn.) Symphony, 1988—; mem. Vanderbilt YMCA; coll. advisor. Mem. Life Underwriters of N.Y. (v.p. 1950), Life Underwriters Conn., Million Dollar Roundtable (charter mem. 1977—, Top of Table award, various coms. 1955—), Estate Planning Coun. N.Y. (co-founder), Estate Planning Coun. Conn. (bd. dirs.), Soc. CLUs (fund raiser 1977-79), Top of the Table (speaker 1990), Boca Lago Country Club (Fla.), Masons. Avocations: charity work. Office: 21720 Arriba Real Boca Raton FL 33433-3148

ROSS, DARIUS ALEXANDER, merger and acquisition specialist; b. Laurel, Miss., July 16, 1965; s. Malachi and Alice Audrey (Rodgers) R.; m. Rose Mary Mitchell, Feb. 17, 1995 (div. Dec. 1996); children: Tomika, Alexander, T'mia; m. Linda Johnson, Sept. 17, 1998 (div. Dec. 1999). Student, Chicago State U., 1983-86, Wright Coll., 1984, Internat. Acad. Design, 1985, Lake Forest Coll., 1986, AMA Inst., 1992, World Trade Inst. of N.Y., 1992, U. Pa. Dirs. Inst., 1996-97, Harvard U. Dirs. Inst., 1997, Northwestern U., Evanston, Ill., 1997—, Kennesaw State U., U. Chgo., NYU, Columbia U., N.Y. Inst. Fin., Oxford-Templeton Inst., MIT; cert. divinity & ministry, Abaak Acad., 1999, cert. futurist studies, 1999. Cert. bus. broker, merger and acquisition intermediary cons., corp. valuation cons.; lic. real estate comml. broker and appraiser. Pres. Darius Ross Interest Ltd., 1989—, BG III MDW Holdings, 1989—, BG III Ohio Holding, 1989—, BG III Wis., 1989—, BG III Mich., 1989—; bd. dirs. Rossfinaco, Darfin Holdings, Cacig Group, Creamie Inc., Tamco Holdings, Daril Holdings, Darmac Interest., Ross & Ross Assocs., Altimia Holdings, Tamco Industries, Cacicg Group, Tadar Investments, Rossco Equities, Macross Trading, Ross To Ross Assoc., Daalta Devels., Nelgui Holdings, Katdad Investments, Soumislau Holdings, The 79th St. Entertainment Group, Albaltal Internat., LLC, Macalicon Multi State Holdings, The Ross 7AM Agrl. Co., Dam 7AM Ross Co. Holdings Group LLC. Bd. dirs. Tilman Cmty. Health Clinic, 1997, N.Y.C. H.S. of Econs. and Fin. Benefit Bd./Bus. Adv. Bd., Chgo. Acad. of Performing Arts Benefit Bd.; active Jobs for Youths, 1991-96, George W. Ross African Am. Studies Award and Found., Target 79th St. Redevel. Group, Kennedy King Coll. Computer Info. Sys. Adv. Bd.; mem. Consolidated Corp. Fund of Lincoln Ctr., N.Y. Trust, Chgo. Symphony Orch. Assn., Rep. Senatorial Trust; bd. dirs. DA 7AM Ross Co. Found., Malalic Inst., NWO-3 Charity Trust, D. Alexamder Ross Ptnrs. Internat. LLC, Alexisal Internat. Edn. Charities. Recipient award Chgo. Directory of Apparel Mfrs., 1989; named Young Leader, S.W. Herald, 1989, N.Y. Times Heir Column, 1989, YEO/The Bridge Wealthy 100, 1990, Ace Young Entrepreneur of Yr., 1989, 90, YEO Entrepreneur Data Directory, 1993. Mem. ABA (assoc. mem.), U.S. Postal Adv. Bd., Chgo. Postal Adv. Bd., Auburn Pk. Postal Adv. Bd., Hyde Pk. Postal Adv. Bd., Urban Bankers Assn., Turnabout Mgmt. Assn., Internat. Assn. Fin. Engrs., Treasury Mgmt. Assn., Chgo. Coun. Fgn. Rels., Nat. Assn. Female Execs., Am. Bus. Women's Assn. Nat. Assn. Women in Edn., Bus. Brokers Assn., Future Industry Assn., World Trade Assn., Nat. Cmty. Econ. Devel. Assn., Nat. Assn. Corp. Dirs. (sec. Chgo. chpt. 1997), N.Y. Stock Exch. Luncheon Club, Mid-Day Club (Chgo.), Met. Club (Chgo.), Chgo. Mercantile Exch. Club, Midam. Club of Chgo., Profl. Security Internat., World Super Projects Fedn., Execs. Club (Chgo.), Mpls. Athletic Club, Univ. Club of Mich. State U., Assn. for Corp. Growth, Nat. Assn. Corp. Treasurers, Coun. Instl. Investors, Nat. Black MBA Assn., Alliance of Bus. Brokers and Intermediaries, Assn. Midwest Bus. Brokers, East Manhattan C. of C., Midwest Assn. Family Bus. Owners, Am. Soc. Corp. Secs., Comml. Fin. Assn., Young Execs. Club, Forest Akers Golf Club, Ohio State U. Faculty Club, Chgo. Athletic Assn., Chgo. Symphony Orch. Assocs., U. R.I. Club, Wellesley Coll. Club, Nat. Bar Assn. Women Lawyers Divsn., Am. Bar Assn., Hispanic Nat. Bar Assn., U. Wash. Faculty Club, World Future Soc., Hispanic Nat. Bar Assoc., Women's Bar Assn., Women's Bar Assn. of DC, Nat. Assn. Women Lawyers, Nat. Assn. Women Execs., Chgo. Social Sports Club, Brown U. Faculty Club, Columbia Faculty HSE Club, Harvard Club, Canebrake Golf Club. Republican. Roman Catholic. Avocations: tennis, soccer, golf, international travel, shooting. Home and Office: D Alexander Ross Ptnrs Internat Ltd PO Box 201040 Chicago IL 60620-7040

ROSS, EDWARD, cardiologist; b. Fairfield, Ala., Oct. 10, 1937; s. Horace and Carrie Lee (Griggs) R.; m. Catherine I. Webster, Jan. 19, 1974; children: Edward, Ronald, Cheryl, Anthony. BS, Clark Coll., 1959; MD, Ind. U., 1963. Diplomate Am. Bd. Internal Medicine; cert. specialist in clin. hypertension Am. Soc. Hypertension. Intern Marion County Gen. Hosp., Indpls., 1963; resident in internal medicine Ind. U., 1964-66, 68, cardiology rsch. fellow, 1968-70, clin. asst. prof. medicine, 1970; cardiologist Capitol Med. Assn., Indpls., 1970-74; pvt. practice medicine, specializing in cardiology Indpls., 1974—; staff cardiologist Winona Meml. Hosp., Indpls., chief cardiovascular disease, 2000—, med. dir. cardiovascular svcs., 2000—, med. dir. cardiac cath lab, 2000—, chief interventional cardiology, 2000—; staff Meth. Hosp., Indpls., chmn. cardiovasc. sect., 1989-96; chmn. cardiovasc. sect., dir. cardiovasc. ctr. Meth. Hosp., 1990-92; bd. dirs. Meth. Hosp. Heart-Lung Ctr., 1990—, mem. dir. cardiovasc. svcs., 1991-98. Assoc. editor Angiology, Jour. Vascular Disease; sr. editor Jour. Vascular Medicine, 1983—. Mem. Ctrl. Ind. Health Planning Coun., 1972-73; bd. dirs. Ind. chpt. Am. Heart Assn., 1973-74, multiphasic screening East Side Clinic, Flanner Ho. of Indpls., 1968-71; med. dir. Nat. Ctr. for Health Svc. R&D, HEW, 1970; consumer rep. radiologic device panel health FDA, 1988-92; dir. hypertensive screening State of Ind., 1974; J.B. Johnson Cardiovasc. lectr. Nat. Med. Assn., 1991. Capt. MC, USAF, 1966-68. Woodrow Wilson fellow, 1959; Nat. Found. Health scholar, 1955, Gorgas Found. scholar, 1955. Fellow Royal Soc. Promotion of Health (Eng.), Am. Coll. Angiology (v.p. fgn. affairs, sec. 1993—), Internat. Coll. Angiology, Am. Coll. Cardiology, Assn. Black Cardiologists (mem. bd. dirs. 1990-94); mem. NAACP, AMA, Am. Soc. Contemporary Medicine and Surgery, Nat. Med. Assn. (coun. sci. assembly 1985-89), Ind. Med. Soc., Marion County Med. Soc., Am. Soc. Internal Medicine, Am. Heart Assn., Ind. Soc. Internal Medicine (pres. 1987-89), Ind. State Med. Assn. (chmn. internal medicine sect. 1987-89), Ind. Med. Soc., Aesculapean Med. Soc., Hoosier State Med. Assn. (pres. 1980-84, 90-95), Urban League, Alpha Omega Alpha, Alpha Kappa Mu, Beta Kappa Chi, Omega Psi Phi. Baptist. Office: 3231 N Meridian St Ste 700 Indianapolis IN 46208-4668

ROSS, EDWIN WILLIAM, rubber company executive; b. Phila., May 28, 1938; s. Edwin Morrison and Frances Louise (Ort) R.; m. Dorothy Anne Reilly, Sept. 24, 1966; children: E. William Jr., Catherine Ross Conlin, James David. BS, Lehigh U., 1960. Chmn. bd., CEO, Key Chems., Inc., Phila., 1965-87, Ross Enterprises, Inc., Villanova, Pa., 1987—; pres., CEO Pelmor Labs., Inc., Newtown, Pa., 1989—; chmn. Pelseal Techs., LLC, Newtown, Pa., 1998—; mem. adv. bd. Prime Bank, Ft. Washington, Pa., 1995-98; bd. dirs. Baker Industries. Deacon Bryn Mawr (Pa.) Presbyn. Ch., 1977-81, elder, 1985-91, trustee, 1997—; bd. dirs. Main Line Adult Day Care Ctr., 1999. Recipient Alumni award Lehigh U. Alumni Assn., 1985. Mem. SAR, MidAtlantic Employers Assn. (chmn. 1995-96), Metal Finishing Suppliers Assn. (pres. 1986-88, 89-90, Munning award 1992), N.E. Phila. C. of C. (chmn. 1983), Lehigh U. Alumni Assn. (bd. dirs. 1997—), Swedish Colonial Soc., Sons. of the Revolution Soc., St. Andrew's Soc., Colonial Soc., Exch. Club (pres. Frankford-Phila. 1972), Phila. Country Club (pres. 1986-89). Republican. Avocations: downhill skiing, hunting, travel, golf. Home: 1514 Willowbrook Ln Villanova PA 19085-1912 Office: Pelmor Labs Inc 401 Lafayette St Newtown PA 18940-2167

ROSS, HELEN ELIZABETH, psychology researcher; b. London, Dec. 2, 1935; d. John MacDonald and Helen Margaret (Wallace) R. BA, U. Oxford, Eng., 1959; PhD, U. Cambridge, Eng., 1966. Chartered psychologist, 1988. Rsch. asst. in psychology U. Cambridge, Eng., 1961-63; lectr. in psychology U. Hull, Eng., 1965-68; lectr. in psychology U. Stirling, Scotland, 1969-72, sr. lectr. psychology, 1972-83, reader in psychology, 1983-94, hon. sr. rsch. fellow, 1994-97, hon. reader, 1997—; vis. rschr. U. Cambridge, 1974; vis. fellow DFVLR, Bonn, Germany, 1979, Royal Soc. rsch. fellow, 1980-81; Leverhulme fellow U. Stirling, Scotland, 1983-84. Author: (book) Behaviour and Perception in Strange Environments, 1974; co-author: Weber on The Sense of Touch, 1978, Weber on The Tactile Senses, 1996. Mem. Underwater Assn. com. for revision of govt. diving regulations, 1978, Microgravity expert panel for UK study of Columbus Space Sta., 1985-86, S.E. Regional Bd., Nature Conservancy Coun. for Scotland, 1991-92. Grantee for parabolic flight experiments Med. Rsch. Coun., 1987-88; grantee for psychophysics conf., USAF, 1988; grantee to visit co-author Leverhulme Trust, 1994. Fellow Brit. Psychol. Soc., Royal Soc. of Edinburgh (convenor of Women in Sci. com. 1994-97, fellowship sec. 1994-97). Home: Bridge of Allan, 16 Allanwater Apts, Stirling FK9 4D2, Scotland Office: Univ of Stirling, Dept of Psychology, Stirling FK9 4LA, Scotland

ROSS, IAN NORMAN, research physicist; b. Woodbridge, England, June 16, 1943; m. Angela Christine Bishop; three children. BA, U. Oxford, 1965, MA; PhD, U. London, 1972. Physicist Nat. Physical Lab., London, 1966-73, UK Atomic Energy Auth., 1973-75, Rutherford Lab., Didcot, England, 1975—. Mem. Inst. Physics. Achievements include patents in field. Home: 13 Manor Rd South Hinksey, Oxford OX15AS, England Office: Rutherford Appleton Lab, Chilton, Didcot OX110QX, England

ROSS, JAMES H., telecommunciations executive; b. London, Sept. 13, 1938; s. T. Desmond and Lettice Ferrier (Hood) R.; m. Sara Blanche Vivian Purcell, Aug. 8, 1964; children: Emma, Tom, Sophie. BA, Oxford U., 1962; diploma advanced studies in bus. mgmt., Manchester Bus. Sch., 1967. With BP, 1962-63, BP France, Paris, 1964-66; with mktg. dept. BP, London, 1967-69; gen. mgr. BP Zaire, Burundi and Rwanda, 1969-72; mgr. corp. planning function BP, London, 1972-76; asst. gen. mgr. comml. BP Tanker Co., 1976-77; dep. chmn. Stolt Tankers and Terminals, 1977-79; regional coord. Western hemisphere London, 1979-81, gen. mgr. corp. planning dept., 1981-85; chief exec. officer, mng. dir. BP Oil Internat. Ltd., 1986-88; pres., chief exec. officer BP Am. Inc., Cleve., 1988-91, former chmn., chief exec. officer; former mng. dir. The British Petroleum Co., PLC, London; chief exec. Cable and Wireless Plc, London, 1992-96; chmn. bd. Littlewoods Orgn., Liverpool, 1996—; bd. dirs. Nat. City Corp., McGraw-Hill, Inc., Am. Petroleum Inst. Trustee Oberlin Coll., Cleve. Inst. Music, Cleve. Orch., Univ. Circle Inc., Com. for Econ. Devel., Coun. Community-Based Devel.; chmn. bd. Neighborhood Progress, Inc., Manchester Bus. Sch., 1993—; bd. dirs. Cleve. Tomorrow. Sub. lt. Brit. Royal Navy, 1957-59. Avocations: music, gardening. Office: Littlewoods Orgn Sir John Moores Bldg, 100 Old Hall St, Liverpool L70 1DX, England*

ROSS, K. SCOTT, utility company executive; b. Monongahela, Pa., Aug. 30, 1949; s. John James and Shirley (Scott) R.; m. Mary Donna Ross, June 2, 1979; children: Justin, Scotty, Gina. BS in Mech. Engring., U. Pitts., 1972. Engring. mgmt. trainee U.S. Steel, Clairton, Pa., 1972-74; buyer Wheeling-Pitts. Steel, 1974-77; mech. engr. Westinghouse Electric, Pitts., 1978-79, buyer, 1989-96; procurement specialist Westinghouse Electric, Cheswick, Pa., 1998-99; sr. contract svcs. buyer Duquesne Light Co., Pitts., 1996-98, 99—. V.p. Scott Twp. Athletic Assn., Pitts., 1996, 98, 2000, baseball mgr., coach, 1996—. Mem. Purchasing Mgmt. Assn. Pitts. Avocations: golf, jogging, coaching baseball. E-Mail: Scott.Ross@dlc.dge.com. Home: 25 Crosswinds Dr Pittsburgh PA 15220-1501 Office: Duquesne Light Co 2101 Beaver Ave Pittsburgh PA 15233-1199

ROSS, MARY ANN, principal; b. Chgo., Aug. 1, 1946; d. Louis and Mary (Zappa) Sirianni; m. Gregory T. Ross, June 27, 1970 (div. 1985). BA, U. Ill., Chgo., 1968; MA, DePaul U., Chgo., 1970, Northeastern U., Chgo., 1975; PhD, Loyola U., Chgo., 1989. Cert. Engish secondary tchr., guidance and counseling, Type 75 adminstrn., supt. 6th grade tchr. Nettelhorst Elem., Chgo., 1968-69; tchr. English Orr H.S., Chgo., 1969-70; tchr. English, guidance counselor, adminstr. Steinmetz H.S., Chgo., 1970-85; adminstrv. intern Rhodes Elem., River Grove, Ill., 1985-86; prin. Sandburg Jr. H.S., Elmhurst, Ill., 1986-91, Palatine, Ill., 1991—; trainer Ill. Adminstrn. Acad.,

Ednl. Svc. Ctr., DuPage, 1997; ednl. cons. Colonial Bank, Chgo., 1978; ednl. advisor in Japan, Japanese C. of C., 1996; Lincoln examiner quality Lincoln Found., Chgo., 1999. James scholar U. Ill., 1964, state scholar for women in adminstrn. State of Ill., 1985; recipient Those Who Excel award Ill. State Bd. Edn., 1993. Mem. ASCD, Nat. Mid. Sch. Assn., Nat. Assn. Secondary Prins., Internat. Reading Assn., Palatine Kiwanis (pres., sec., bd. dirs. 1991—, Kiwanian of Yr. 1991), Phi Delta Kappa. Roman Catholic. Avocations: boating, dancing. E-Mail: rossm@wrs.ccsd15.k12.il.us. Office: Walter Sundling Jr HS 1100 N Smith St Palatine IL 60067-2606

ROSS, MATTHEW ALAN, real estate company executive. AB, Harvard U., 1984, JD, MBA, 1989. Ptnr. Hall Properties, Inc., Boston, 1989-98; pres. ValueRealty, Inc., Cambridge, 1998—. Office: PO Box 381707 Cambridge MA 02238-1707

ROSS, MICHAEL WALLIS, public health educator; b. Palmerston North, New Zealand, Nov. 17, 1951; came to U.S., 1993; s. Wallis Malcolm and Lois Verrell (Stewart) R. BA with honors, Massey U., New Zealand, 1974; BS in Med. Sociology, SUNY, 1976; MA in Social-Clin. Psychology, Victoria U. Wellington, New Zealand, 1975; diploma in Tertiary Edn., U. New England, Australia, 1984; PhD, U. Melbourne, Australia, 1980; MPH, U. Adelaide, Australia, 1989; M Health Personnel Edn., U. NSW, Australia, 1991; diploma in STDs, Prince of Songkla U., Thailand, 1992. Postdoctoral fellow U. Helsinki, 1975-79; sr. demonstrator psychiatry Flinders U., Adelaide, Australia, 1979-85; dir. STD/HIV Epidemiology and Rsch. South Australian Health Commn., Adelaide, 1985-89; assoc. prof. Sch. Cmty. Medicine U. NSW, Sydney, 1989-93; prof. Sch. Pub. Health, U. Tex., Houston, 1993—; bd. mem. Kolbe House, Houston, 1994—. Author: The Married Homosexual Man: A Psychological Study, 1983, Psychovenereology: Personality and Lifestyle Factors in Sexually Transmitted Diseases in Homosexual Men, 1986; (with L.C. Channon-Little) Discussing Sexuality: A Guide for Health Practitioners, 1991; (with L.A. Lewis) A Select Body: The Gay Dance Party Subculture and the HIV/AIDS Pandemic, 1995; (with L. Nilsson Schönnesson) Coping With HIV Infection: Psychological and Existential Responses in Gay Men, 1999; (with L.C. Channon-Little and B.R.S. Rosser) Sexual Health Concerns: Interviewing and History Taking for Health Practitioners, 1999; editor: Homosexuality and Social Sex Roles, 1983, Homosexuality, Masculinity and Femininity, 1985, The Treatment of Homosexuals with Mental Health Disorders, 1988, Psychopathology and Psychotherapy in Homosexuality, HIV/AIDS and Sexuality, 1995; (with W.A.W. Walters) Transsexualism and Sex Reassignment, 1986; (with L. Bennett and D. Miller) Health Workers and AIDS: Research, Intervention and Current Issues in Burnout and Response, 1995; contbr. articles to profl. jours. Fellow APA, Brit. Psychol. Soc., Royal Soc. Health, Royal Inst. Pub. Health and Hygiene, Royal Soc. Arts, New Zealand Psychol. Soc. Roman Catholic. Avocations: aerobatic flying, reading. Home: 401 Anita St Apt 34 Houston TX 77006-3434 Office: Sch Pub Health U Tex PO Box 20186 Houston TX 77225-0186

ROSS, MOLLY OWINGS, gold and silversmith, jewelry designer, small business owner; b. Ft. Worth, Feb. 5, 1954; d. James Robertson and Lucy (Owings) R. BFA, Colo. State U., 1976; postgrad., U. Denver, 1978-79. Graphic designer Amber Sky Illustrators and Sta. KCNC TV-Channel 4, Denver, 1977-79; art dir. Mercy Med. Ctr., Denver, 1979-83, Molly Ross Design, Denver, 1983-84; co-owner Deltex Royalty Co., Inc., Colorado Springs, Colo., 1981—, LMA Royalties, Ltd., Colorado Springs, 1993—; art dir., account mgr. Schwing/Walsh Advt., Mktg. and Pub. Rels., Denver, 1984-87, prodn. mgr., 1987-88; jewelry designer Molly O. Ross, Gold and Silversmith, Denver, 1988—. Pres. Four Mile Hist. Park Vol. Bd., Denver, 1985-87; bd. dirs. Four Mile Hist. Park Assn., 1985-86, Hist. Denver, Inc., 1986-87, Denver Emergency Housing Coalition, 1989-90; coun. mem. feminization of poverty critical needs area coun. Jr. League Denver, 1989-90, chmn. children in crisis/edn. critical needs area, 1990-91, chmn. project devel., 1991-92, co-chmn. Done in a Day Cmty. Project 75th Anniversary Celebration, 1991-93; mem. bd. dirs., 1993-94, v.p. comty. projects, 1993-94; co-chmn. Project IMPACT, 1994-95; exec. v.p. external affairs Jr. League of Denver, 1995-96; co-chmn. Cmty. Coalitions Com., 1996-98; co-founder, bd. dirs. Ctr. for Ethics and Social Responsibility/PREP, 1994—, pres. bd. dirs., 1997-99, treas. bd dirs., 1999—; mem. steering com. Denver Urban Resources Partnership, 1995—, chmn. steering com., 1997-98; pres.-elect Jr. League of Denver, 1998-99, pres. 1999-00; bd. dirs. Jr. League Denver Found. 1998-2000. Named Vol. of Month (March), Jr. League Denver, 1990, Vol. of Yr., Four Mile Hist. Pk., 1988; recipient Gold Peak Mktg. award-team design Am. Mktg. Assn., 1986, Silver Peak Mktg. award-team design Am. Mktg. Assn., 1986, Gold Pick award-art dir. Pub. Rels. Soc. Am., 1980-81, cert. Appreciation USDA, 1999. Mem. Natural Resources Def. Coun., Physicians for Social Responsibility, Am. Farmland Trust, Nat. Trust for Hist. Preservation, Environ. Def. Fund. Avocations: horseback riding, bicycling, hiking, backpacking, pastel drawing.

ROSS, PHILIP ROWLAND, retired library director; b. Indiana, Pa., Apr. 7, 1940; s. David Biddle and Miriam Elizabeth (Hill) R.; m. Elaine Lucille George, July 17, 1965; children: Mary Elizabeth, David Bruce. BA, Pa. State U., 1962; MSLS, U. Md., 1969. Postal fin. officer USAF, Tachikawa AFB Tokyo, 1963-65; chief data control and quality control Hdqrs. Air Force Systems Command, Andrews AFB, Md., 1965-68; asst. libr. acquisitions West Liberty (W.Va.) State Coll., 1969-86; dist. mgr. Wheeling (W.Va.) office First Investors Corp., 1986-89; divs. mgr. State of Ark. First Investors Corp., Little Rock, 1989-92; dir. Lonoke (Ark.) Prairie County Regional Libr. System, 1992-2000; ret., 2000; founder, treas.-mgr. West Liberty (W.Va.) State Coll. Fed. Credit Union, 1977-82, chmn. bd., 1984-85; mem. Ark. On Line Network Adv. Com., Little Rock, 1993-96, Libr. Devel. Dist. State Coun., Little Rock, 1993-2000, vice chmn., 1996. Maj. USAF, 1962-68; maj. Res., 1968-84, ret. Decorated various USAF medals and decorations. Mem. ALA, Assn. Ark. Pub. Librs. (treas.-sec. 1993, 94, v.p. pres.-elect 1995, pres. 1996), Ark. Libr. Assn. (com. mem. 1994-95, conv. com. 1996, 97), S.E. Libr. Assn., Lonoke, Ark. C. of C., Am. Legion, Lions. Republican. Methodist. Avocations: reading, gardening, refinishing antique furniture. Home: 691 Wayne Elmore Rd Lonoke AR 72086-9126 Office: Lonoke/Prairie County Regional Libr Sys 204 E 2nd St Lonoke AR 72086-2804

ROSS, ROGER SCOTT, lawyer; b. Columbus, Ohio, Oct. 25, 1946; s. Donald William and Iris Louise (Smith) R.; m. Lynn Louise Patton, July 29, 1967; 1 child, Anastacia Lynn. Student, Ohio State U., 1964-66; BS in Laws, Western State U., Fullerton, Calif., 1983; JD, Western State U., 1985. Bar: Calif. 1985, U.S. Dist. Ct. (cen. dist.) Calif. 1985. Office mgr. Dial Fin. Co., Buena Park, Calif., 1970-78; asst. br. mgr., loan officer Calif. 1st Bank, Rolling Hills Estates, 1978-79; asst. v.p., loan officer Lloyds Bank, Monterey Park, Calif., 1979-85; pvt. practice law Tustin, Calif., 1985-86; ptnr. Anderson & Ross, El Toro, Calif., 1986-87; pvt. practice Orange, Calif., 1987-90, Bellflower, Calif., 1990-94, Anaheim, Calif., 1994—; atty., coach Constnl. Rights Found. of Orange County, 1987—. Mem. AAONMS, ABA, Calif. Bar Assn., L.A. County Bar Assn., Assn. Trial Lawyers Am., Orange County Trial Lawyers Assn., Calif. F&AM, Nat. Forensic Club, Rotary. Republican. Avocations: golf, sailing, tennis. Office: 421 N Brookhurst St Ste 126 Anaheim CA 92801-5618

ROSS, STANFORD G., lawyer, former government official; b. St. Louis, Oct. 9, 1931; m. Dorothy Rabin, June 9, 1958; children: John, Ellen. AB with honors, Washington U., 1953; JD magna cum laude, Harvard U., 1956. Bar: D.C. 1969, Calif. 1956, N.Y. 1959. Assoc. firm Irell & Manella, Los Angeles, 1956-57; teaching fellow, research asst. Harvard Law Sch., 1957-58; assoc. firm Dewey, Ballantine, Bushby, Palmer & Wood, N.Y.C., 1958-61; asst. tax legis. counsel U.S. Dept. Treasury, 1961-63; prof. law N.Y. U., 1963-67; White House staff asst. to Pres. Johnson, 1967-68; gen. counsel U.S. Dept. Transp., 1968-69; ptnr. Caplin & Drysdale, Washington, 1969-78; commr. Social Security Adminstrn., Washington, 1978-79; ptnr. Califano, Ross & Heineman, Washington, 1980-82, Arnold & Porter, Washington, 1983—; pub. trustee Social Security Trust Funds, Washington, 1990-95; chair Social Security Adv. Bd., 1997—. Editor: Harvard Law Rev, 1954-56. Mem. ABA, Fed. Bar Assn., Internat. Fiscal Assn., Nat. Acad. Social Ins. Office: Arnold & Porter 555 12th St NW Washington DC 20004-1206

ROSS, STEVEN CHARLES, business administration educator, consultant; b. Salem, Oreg., Jan. 14, 1947; s. Charles Reed and Edythe Marie (Calvin) R.; m. Meredith Lynn Buholts, June 15, 1969; children: Kelly Lynn, Shannon Marie. BS, Oreg. State U., 1969; MS, U. Utah, 1976, PhD, 1980. Cons. IRS Tng. Staff, Ogden, Utah, 1977-80; asst. prof. Marquette U., Milw., 1980-88; assoc. prof. Mont. State U., Bozeman, 1988-89; assoc. prof. bus. adminstrn. Western Wash. U., Bellingham, 1989—; govt. and industry cons.; cons. editor microcomputing series West Pub. Co. Author 30 books and several articles in computer systems field. Mem. adv. com. Milwaukee County Mgmt., 1981-85, Port of Bellingham, 1990-2000; chmn. 1998 U.S. Sailing Jr. Championships. Capt. U.S. Army, 1969-75. Rsch. fellow U. Utah, 1977-79, Marquette U., 1981-84, Western Wash. U., 1998. Mem. Acad. Mgmt., Decision Scis. Inst., Inst. Mgmt. Scis., Assn. for Computing Machinery, Assn. Computer Educators, Bellingham Yacht Club (trustee 1992-93, sec. 1993-94, rear commodore, 1994-95, vice commodore 1995-96, commodore 1996-97). Office: Western Wash U Coll Bus and Econs Bellingham WA 98225

ROSS, TERENCE WILLIAM, architect; b. Saginaw, Mich., Sept. 27, 1935; s. Oran Lewis and Drucilla (Chadman) R.; m. Patricia Ann Marshall, Sept. 27, 1974; children by previous marriage: Deborah, David. BArch, U. Mich., 1958. Designer Roger W. Peters Constrn. Co., Fond du Lac, Wis., 1958-62; draftsman Kenneth Clark, Arch., Santa Fe, N.Mex., 1962-63, Holien & Buckley, Archs., Santa Fe, 1963-64; office mgr. Philippe Register, Architect, Santa Fe, 1964-68; prin. Register, Ross & Brunets archts./engrs., Santa Fe, 1968-71, Luna-Ross & Assocs., 1971-77; staff CNWC Archs., Tucson, until 1981, ADP Archs., 1981-89; sr. arch. U. Calif., 1989-95; arch. ADP Flour Daniel Archs./Engrs., 1995-97, Ross Assocs. Architects, 1997-2000; ret., 2000. Author: Track of the Cats. vice chmn. N.Mex. R.R. Authority, 1969-74, sec., 1970-72; bd. dirs. colo., N.Mex. Soc. Preservation of Narrow Gauge; v.p. El Dorado Western Narrow Gauge Railway Found. Recipient award for hist. preservation N.Mex. Arts Commn., 1971, award for outstanding svcs. to cmty. Santa Fe Press Club, 1972; named col. aide-de-camp State of N.Mex., 1968, hon. mem. staff atty. gen. Mem. AIA (chpt. pres. 1970, dir.), Constrn. Specifications Inst., N.Mex. Soc. Architects (dir. 1972), Ariz. Soc. Archs., N.Mex. R.R. Authorities (chmn. joint exec. com. 1970-74), Sacto. Valley Garden Ry. Soc. (pres. 1993, dir. 1994-99), San Gabriel Hist. Soc. (hon.), Alpha Rho Chi, Sashay Rounders Sq. Dance Club (pres. 1974), Diamond Squares Sq. Dance Club, Railroad Club (pres. N.Mex. 1969, 70, dir.). E-mail: terry ross@msn.com. Home and Office: 2813 57th St Sacramento CA 95817-2403

ROSS, THOMAS MCCALLUM, professional society administrator; b. Hamilton, Ont., Can., May 5, 1931; s. Laverne Robinson and Della Louise (McCallum) R.; m. Marguerite Hilda Ross, Aug. 14, 1954; children: Thomas Wayne, Gregory (dec.), Karyn. Mgr. Sutherland Pharmacy, Hamilton, 1955-60; assoc. sec. Can. Pharm. Assn., Toronto, Ont., 1960-63; mem. research staff Royal Commn. Health Services Govt. Can., Ottawa, Ont., 1963-64; exec. dir. Can. Retail Hardware Assn., Toronto, 1964-98; retired. Bd. dirs. People for Sunday Assn., pres. 1987-88. Founding fellow Hardware Mgmt. Inst.; mem. Internat. Fedn. Ironmongers Assn. (coun. 1970-98), Can. Soc. Assn. Execs. (chmn. edn. com. 1986-88, bd. dirs. 1990-92, Pinnacle award 1989), Am. Soc. Assn. Execs., Can. C. of C. Home: 59 Walby Dr, Oakville, ON Canada

ROSS, WILBUR LOUIS, JR., investment banker; b. Weehawken, N.J., Nov. 28, 1937; s. Wilbur Louis and Agnes (O'Neill) R.; m. Judith Nodine, May 26, 1961 (div. 1995); children: Jessica, Amanda. AB, Yale U., 1959; MBA with distinction, Harvard U., 1961. Assoc. Wood, Struthers and Winthrop, N.Y.C., 1963-64; pres. Faulkner, Dawkins and Sullivan Securities Corp., N.Y.C., 1964-76; sr. mng. dir. Rothschild, Inc., N.Y.C., 1976-2000; CEO News Comms., Inc., N.Y.C., 1996-98; chmn., chief investment officer Rothschild Recovery Fund, N.Y.C., 1997-2000; chmn. Seoul Debt Restructuring Fund, 1998-99; chmn., CEO WL Ross & Co. LLC, N.Y.C., 2000—; bd. dirs. Aileen Inc., N.Y.C., Geo Internat. Corp., Stamford, Conn., Biocraft labs Inc., Rutherford, N.J., FurVault Inc., N.Y.C., Investors Ins. Co., Lawrence Harbor, N.J., Revere Copper and Brass Co., Stamford, Syms Corp., Secaucus, N.J., Am. Bankruptcy Inst., Washington, Allis Chalmers Corp., Milw., Mego Corp., Las Vegas, Nev., KTI Inc., RH Cement Co., Seoul, Korea; fin. advisor equity holders com. Texaco Co., A.H. Robins Co., Pub. Service N.H.; hon. econ. amb. from Korea to APEC Investment, Mont., 1999; chmn. Asia Recovery Fund L.P., WL Recovery Fund LP, Asia Co. Investment Ptnrs. L.P. Treas. N.Y. State Dem. Com., 1980-83, Am. Fedn. Arts, 1993—, The New Mus., 1993—; vice chmn. Bklyn. Mus., 1981—; chmn. univ. coun. com. on art Yale U., 1983-88; chmn. NAD, N.Y.C., 1985—, Am. Art Forum, Smithsonian Instn., 1987—; trustee, vice chmn. Nat. Mus. Am. Art, Washington, 1986-91, chmn., 1991—; trustee Sarah Lawrence Coll., 1986—, chmn. art gallery, 1984—; pres. Parrish Art Mus., 1991-95; chmn. N.Y. Hist. Soc., 1993-94; bd. dirs. Smithsonian Inst. Nat. Bd., 1994—, chmn. bd. 1995; nat. chmn. Smithsonian Bicentennial Celebration, 1996. With U.S. Army, 1961-63. Fellow Jonathan Edward Coll. of Yale U., Met. Mus. Art; mem. Fin. Analysts Fedn. (chartered), Century Assn., Southampton Bath and Tennis Club (chmn. bd. dirs.), Harvard Bus. Sch. Club N.Y. (bd. dirs.). Avocation: collecting art. Office: WL Ross & Co LLC Ste 4400 1251 Avenue Of The Americas New York NY 10020-1104

ROSSBACH, VOLKER WILHELM, textile and polymer chemistry educator; b. Erfurt, Germany, Jan. 27, 1943; s. George and Elizabeth (Schnitger) R.; m. Marie-Rose Chantal Magnien, Aug. 6, 1976; 1 child, Christine. MSc in Biochemistry, U. Tübingen, Germany, 1970; PhD in Chemistry, U. Tech., Aachen, Germany, 1972, habil. textile and polymer chemistry, 1978. Lectr., team leader German Wool Rsch. Inst., U. Tech., Aachen, 1970-83; prof. textile tech. U. Hamburg, Germany, 1983-93; prof. textile chemistry and textile finishing U. Tech., Dresden, Germany, 1993—; cons. in field. Contbr. articles to profl. jours.; patentee in field. Office: Dresden U Tech, Inst Macromol & Textile Chemistry, D-01062 Dresden Germany

ROSSDALE, PHILIP SAMUEL ANTHONY, barrister; b. London, Jan. 1, 1924; s. Frank Archibald and Viola Zillah (Beddington) R.; m. Doreen Réva Zimbler, May 27, 1952. Student, Clifton Coll., Bristol, Eng., 1937-42; MA, Magdalene Coll., Cambridge, Eng., 1943, LLM, 1947. Barrister London, 1948-00. Author: Probate and the Administration of Estates, A Practical Guide, 1991, 2d edit., 1996; co-author: Maaser Kesafim: On Giving a Tenth to Charity, 1992. Mem. Chancery Bar Assn., United Oxford and Cambridge Club. Conservative. Jewish. Avocations: attending operas, riding, gardening.

ROSSDEUTSCHER, REINHARD KURT PAUL, JR., radiologist, educator, nuclear medicine physician; b. Wiesbaden, Germany, June 25, 1953; s. Reinhard Kurt Alfred and Ingeburg (Liese) R. MD, Free U., Berlin, 1979. Cert. radiologist and nuc. med. physician. Resident in radiology Klinikum Charlottenburg, Free U., Berlin, 1979-86; mem. staff dept. radiology Heckeshorn Chest Hosp., Berlin, 1986-2000, vice dir. dept. radiology, 1987; dir. head dept. radiology and nuc. medicine Johanniter Hospital im Flaeming, Treuenbrietzen and Jueterbog, 2000—; instr. Roentgen Diagnostic Postgrad. Course, Neuss, Germany, 1994—. Author: Leitfaden Radiologie Manual of Radiology, 1996, (with others) Memorix Innere Medizin, 1996; contbr. chpts. articles to profl. pubs. Recipient Film Quiz 2d Place award Internat. Diagnostic Course Davos, 1989, 1st Place award, 1991, 95. Fellow Berlin Roentgen Soc., German Roentgen Soc. (Film Quiz 2nd Place award 1991, 92, 1st Place award 1997); mem. Radiol. Soc. N.Am. (corr., Grand winner 1997), Am. Roentgen Ray Soc., Berlin-Brandenburg Soc. Nuclear Medicine. Avocations: music, literature, theatre, cinema/history of cinema. Home: Tuebinger Str 4, D-10715 Berlin Germany Office: Johanniter-Krankenhaus, Dept Radiol Suedstr 20-28, D-14929 Treuenbrietzen Germany

ROSSE, THERESE MARIE, reading and special education educator, curriculum, school improvement and instruction consultant; b. Orleans, Nebr., Dec. 23, 1936; d. Ford Huston and Bertha Therese (Flamming) McCoy; m. John A. Rosse, Apr. 19, 1958 (div. 1979); children: Michelle, John, Robert, David. BS, Coll. St. Mary, Omaha, 1972; MS, U. Nebr., Omaha, 1973; PhD, U. Nebr., Lincoln, 1994. Cert. tchr. reading, spo. edn., history, elem. Tchr., reading clinician Omaha Pub. and Parochial Schs., 1958-72; grad. asst. U. Nebr., Omaha, 1972-73; reading cons. Ralston (Nebr.) Pub. Schs., 1973-75; reading and spl. edn. cons. Area Edn. Agy. 13, Council Bluffs, Iowa, 1975—; adj. prof. Buena Vista Coll., Storm Lake, Iowa, 1976-79, U. Nebr. Omaha, 1978-79, Marycrest Coll., Danveport, Iowa, 1985—, N.W. Mo. State U., Maryville, 1985—, Met. Cmty. Coll., Omaha, 1990—; tester Ednl. Testing Svcs., Princeton, N.J., 1972-73; cons. Creative Cons., Muncie, Ind., 1973-75, Midlands Ednl. Cons., Omaha, 1974-75; rschr. Iowa Dept. Pub. Instrn., Dept. Edn., Des Moines, 1980-82, advisor, 1987-89; text reviewer Scott Foresman, Glenview, Ill., 1980-82, Zepher Press, Tucson, Ariz.; evaluation team North Ctrl. Accreditation Assn., 1980-82. Author: Viewing Reading Comprehension as a Problem Solving Skill: Approaches to Developing Comprehensive Strategies, 1982, Breaking the Language Barrier of Mathematical Thought Problems, 1982, A Grounded Theory of An Organizaed Learner; A Balanced Ecological System, 1994. Advisor Mayor's Commn. on Status of Women Edn. Divsn., Omaha, 1973-75; trustee Links-for-the-Future. Mem. ASCD, Internat. Reading Assn. (state bd. sec. 1973-75, v.p. local chpt., state co-chairperson, reading chairperson), Am. Ednl. Rsch. Assn. (sec.), The Brain and Edn., Coun. Exceptional Children, Phi Delta Kappa, Phi Delta Gamma (pres. local chpt. 1979-80, mem. nat. bd. 1980-82), Phi Alpha Theta. Avocations: travel, reading, classical music and art, writing/research, tennis. Home: 817 N 131st Plz Omaha NE 68154-4037

ROSSEEL-JONES, MARY LOUISE, lawyer; b. Detroit, Apr. 19, 1951; d. Rene Octave and Marie Ann (Metcko) Rosseel; m. Mark Christopher Jones, Mar. 16, 1984; 1 child, Kathleen Marie. BA in French with honors, U. Mich., 1973, MA in French, 1976; JD, U. Detroit, 1981. Bar: Mich. 1982, U.S. Ct. Appeals (6th cir.) 1982, U.S. Dist Ct. (ea. dist.) Mich. 1982, U.S. Dist. Ct. (we. dist.) Mich. 1983. Teaching asst. French U. Mich., Ann Arbor, 1974-76; law clk. Johnson, Auld & Valentine, Detroit, 1979-80; assoc. Monaghan, Campbell et al, Bloomfield Hills, Mich., 1981-82; lectr. law U. Clermont, Clermont-Ferrand, France, 1981-82; staff atty. Mich. Nat. Corp., Bloomfield Hills, 1983-85; litigation atty. Am. Motors Corp., Southfield, Mich., 1985-87; staff counsel Chrysler Corp., Auburn Hills, Mich., 1987-98; freelance designer, pvt. lang. and piano tutor, eitor, writer; solo law practice, 1998—. Editor: sequel One Life to Give. Recipient Mich. Competitive scholarship, 1969-70, Julia Emanuel scholarship, 1974-75, Henderson House scholarship, 1973, Wayne State Univ. fellow, 1973-74, Univ. Mich., 1974-76. Republican. Roman Catholic. Avocations: classical pianist, interior design.

ROSSEINSKY, DAVID REUBEN, chemist, educator; b. Queenstown, South Africa, July 25, 1933; arrived in England, 1961; s. Reuben Norris and Valda Webster (Simpson) R.; m. Angela Joyce Oliver, June 30, 1961; children: Matthew Jonathan, Nicholas Martin, James Patrick. BS with honors, Rhodes U., South Africa, 1953, MS, 1957; PhD, U. Manchester, England, 1959, DSc, 1979. Jr. lectr. Rhodes U., 1954-55; rsch. fellow U. Pa., Phila., 1959; lectr. chemistry U. Witwaterstand, Johannesburg, South Africa, 1960-61; Leverhulme and ICI rsch. fellow U. Exeter, England, 1961-64, lectr. chemistry, 1964-78, reader in phys. chemistry, 1979-98, hon. rsch. fellow, 1998—; sci. advisor Gestetner Mfg. Ltd., London, 1987-90; cons. Raychem Ltd., Swindon, England, 1990; sr. rsch. fellow Nanyang Technol. U., Singapore, 2000—. Co-author: Electrochromism-Fundamentals and Applications, 1995. Fellow Royal Soc. of Chemistry (chmn. Applied Solid State Chemistry Group 1995—). Nominal Methodist. Avocations: gym work, scuba, music. Office: The Univ, Sch Chem, Exeter Devon EX4 4QD, England

ROSSEL, SVEN HAKON, literature educator; b. Bangkok, Oct. 25, 1943; came to U.S., 1974; s. Leo Hancke and Maria Katharina (Muller) R.; m. Dominika Jagiella; children: Eva Maria Katharina, Pia Elisabeth, Sven Dominik. PhD, U. Copenhagen, 1968. Asst. prof. U. Hamburg, Fed. Republic of Germany, 1968-69, U. Kiel, Fed. Republic of Germany, 1969-71; rsch. fellow U. Copenhagen, Denmark, 1971-74; assoc. prof. U. Wash., Seattle, 1974-80, prof., 1980-96, chmn. Scandinavian dept., 1981-90; chmn. Scandinavian dept. U. of Vienna, 1996—; affiliate prof. U. Wash., 1996—; rsch. prof. U. Wash., 1989, Carlsberg Found., 1993. Editor: A History of Danish Literature, 1992, Ludvig Holberg: A European Writer, 1994, Hans Christian Andersen: Danish Writer, 1996, Johannes V. Jensen: Madame D'Ora-Hjulet, 1977; author: Den litteraere vise, 1971, A History of Scandinavian Literature, 1982, Scandinavian Ballads, 1982, Johannes V. Jensen, 1984, Hans Christian Andersen und seine Märchen, 1996; co-editor: Danmarks gamle Folkeviser, 1976, H.C. Andersen's Tales, 1980, Scandinavian Literature in a Transcultural Context, 1986, The Diaries of Hans Christian Andersen, 1990, Ludvig Holberg: Jeppe of the Hill and Other Comedies, 1990, Christmas in Scandinavia, 1996, Documentary Literature in Scandinavia, 1997, Images of America in Scandinavia, 1998, New Approaches to August Strindberg, 1999, Authority and Anthropology in Søren Kierkegaard, 2000, others; contbr. articles, revs. and translations to profl. jours. Decorated Knighthood of the Order of Dannebrog; recipient Honor award Denmark-Am. Found., Copenhagen, 1980, State of Wash. Spl. award 1981, Am. Scandinavian Found. award, 1985; Grundtvig-Olrik grantee 1976, 80, 83, 85, 88. Mem. Soc. for Advancement of Scandinavian Studies, Internat. Assn. Scandinavian Studies, Danish Club (Seattle, v.p. 1975-76, 89—), Royal Danish Acad. of Sci. and Letters. Roman Catholic. Home: Waldheimstrasse 60, A-3004 Ollern-Waldheim Austria

ROSSELL, JOHN BARRY, chemist; b. Nottingham, England, Aug. 23, 1938; s. Francis Lawrence and Florence Gwendoline (Wittering) R.; m. Linda Margaret Wiltshire, Nov. 1, 1969; children: Michael Christopher, Jennifer Margaret. BSc, Imperial Coll., 1960; DPhil, U. Oxford, 1962. Scientist Margarine Union GmbH, Hamburg, Germany, 1962-63, Unilever Rsch., Welwyn, England, 1963-68; tech. officer Unilever Patents, London, 1968-69; product devel. mgr. Loders & Nucoline, London, 1969-80; mgr. oils & fats Leatherhead Food R.A., England, 1980—; tech. cons. FOSFA, London, 1980—; cons. Internat. Olive Oil Coun., Madrid, 1990—. Editor: Analysis of Oils & Fats, 1986, Analysis of Oilseeds, Fats & Fatty Foods, 1991; patentee in field. Membership sec. Royal Soc. Protection Birds, 1986-94. Mem. Soc. Chem. & Industry (oils & fats com. 1985—). Mem. Ch. England. Avocations: cycling, ornithology, horseback riding, walking, old buildings. Office: Leatherhead Food Rsch Assn, Randalls Rd, Leatherhead Surrey, England KT227RY

ROSSELLINI, ISABELLA, actress, model; b. Rome, June 18, 1952; d. Roberto Rossellini and Ingrid Bergman; m. Martin Scorsese, Sept. 1979 (div. Nov. 1982); m. Jonathan Wiedemann (div.); 1 child, Elettra Ingrid. Student, Finch Coll., 1972, New Sch. for Social Research, N.Y.C. Became model for Lancôme, 1982. Appeared in films A Matter of Time, 1976, Il Pap'occhio, 1980, The Meadow, 1982, White Nights, 1985, Blue Velvet, 1986, Siesta, 1987, Red Riding Hood, 1987, Tough Guys Don't Dance, 1987, Zelly and Me, 1988, Cousins, 1989, Wild at Heart, 1990, Les Dames Galantes, 1990, Death Becomes Her, 1992, The Pickle, 1992, Fearless, 1993, Wyatt Earp, 1994, Immortal Beloved, 1994, The Innocent, 1995, The Funeral, Crime of the Century, 1996, Big Night, 1996, The Real Blonde, 1998; TV films: The Last Elephant, 1990, Lies of the Twins, 1991; TV miniseries: The Odyssey, 1997, Merlin, 1998, The Impostors, 1998, Left Luggage, 1998. Office: William Morris Agy attn Pakseghian Planco 1350 Avenue Of The Americas New York NY 10019-4702

ROSSELLO, PEDRO, governor; b. San Juan, P.R., Apr. 5, 1944; m. Maga Nevares, Aug. 9, 1969; children: Juan Oscar, Luis Roberto, Ricardo Antonio. BS, U. Notre Dame, 1966; MD, Yale U., 1970; MPH, U. P.R., 1981; LLD (hon.), U. Notre Dame, 1995, U. Mass., 1995. Intern straight surgery Beth Israel Hosp., Boston, 1970-71, resident gen. surgery, 1971-74; resident cardiac and burns Mass. Gen. Hosp., Boston, 1972; resident trauma San Francisco Gen. Hosp., 1973; sr. resident pediat. surgery Children's Hosp., Boston, 1974-75, chief resident, pediat. surgery-urology, 1975-76; instr. surgery Harvard Med. Sch., 1975-76; pvt. practice San Juan, 1976-92; asst. prof. surgery U. P.R., 1978-82, assoc. prof. surgery, 1982-92; dir. Dept. Health City of San Juan, 1985-87; chief surgery San Jorge Hosp., San Juan, 1989-92, med. dir., 1990; gov. Puerto Rico, 1993—; lead gov. So. Regional Project Infant Mortality, 1993-95; chair So. States Energy Bd., 1995-96; chmn. So. Growth Policies Bd., 1999-2000; chair So. Tech. Coun., 1998-99, So. Internat. Trade Coun., 1998-99; mem. intergovtl. policy adv. com. U.S. Trade Rep.; pres. Coun. State Govts., 1998; mem. adv. coun. Welfare to Work Partnership; mem. Dem. Nat. Com.; bd. dirs. U.S.-Spain Coun.; mem. nat. adv. bd. Initiative and Referendum Inst. Contbr. articles to profl. jours. Mem. P.R. Olympic Com., 1982-84, 87-88; v.p. New Progressive Party, 1988-91, pres., 1991-99; mem. exec. com. Edn. Commn. States; bd. visitors emeritus Georgetown U. Law Ctr., Washington; del. Dm. Nat. Conv., Chgo., 1996, 2000. Capt. USNG, 1970-76. Recipient Pres.'s award U.S. Hispanic

C. of C., 1996, Pres.'s award League of United Latin Am. Citizens, 1998, Rolex Achievement award, 1999. Mem. Nat. Govs. Assn. (host 1996 ann. meeting), So. Govs. Assn. (chair 1997-98), Dem. Govs. Assn. (chair 1998), P.R. Tennis Assn. (pres. 1982-84), Caribbean Tennis Assn. (pres. 1983-84), Alpha Omega Alpha. Avocations: jogging, tennis, ocean kayaking.

ROSSER, RHONDA LANAE, psychotherapist; b. Champaign, Ill., Aug. 29, 1953; d. Neill Albert and Grace Lee (Byers) R.; (div. June 1, 1993); children: Anthony Neill Williams, Joseph Neill Jackson Hogan. BS in Psychology, Guilford Coll., 1975; MEd in Edn., U. N.C., Greensboro, 1979, PhD in Counseling, 1991. Instr. U. N.C., Greensboro, 1985-88; dir. Montagnard Program Luth. Family Svcs., Greensboro, 1985-88; pvt. practice pvt. practice, Greensboro, 1989—. Contbr. articles to profl. jours. Active Shalom Cmty. Christian Ch. Disciples of Christ, Greensboro. Recipient Presdl. citation U.S. Govt., 1987. Mem. Am. Counseling Assn. (Outstanding Rsch. award 1991), Chi Sigma Iota. Democrat. Mem. Disciples of Christ. Avocations: hiking, bible study, bird watching, writing, prayer. Home and Office: 2318 W Cornwallis Dr Greensboro NC 27408-6802

ROSSETER, THOMAS ARTHUR, insurance company executive; b. St. Petersburg, Fla., Dec. 22, 1935; s. John Creagan and Margaret (Morrow) R.; m. Sandra Gail McCall, Feb. 20, 1965; children: Julie Anna, Amanda Leigh. AB, Stetson U., 1958; JD, John Marshall, 1961. Agt. Equitable Life, Atlanta, 1971-72, dist. mgr., 1972-76, dir. agt. & mgmt. tng., 1976-91; v.p. mktg. Equitable Life, Chgo., 1991-92; v.p. mgmt. devel. and industry rels. Equitable Life, N.Y.C., 1992-94; ret., 1994; pres. V. Vision Group, 1995-96, Rosseter & Assocs., 1996—. Pres. Atlanta Symphony Youth Orch. Comdr. USCGR, 1963-83. Mem. Am. Soc. CLU's and ChFC's, Res. Officers Assn., Gen. Agts. and Mgrs. Assn. Republican. Methodist. Home and Office: 205 N Madison Ave Eatonton GA 31024-1005

ROSSI, GIOVANNI ARTURO, pneumatologist; b. Legnano, Italy, June 28, 1947; s. Geremia and Maria Luisa (Donelli) R.; m. Guendalina Bosio; children: Umberto, Filippo, Giulia, Giorgia, Giordana. MD, U. Genoa, 1972. Diplomate Italian Bd. Med. Examiners. Med. asst. Hosp. San Martino, Genoa, Italy, 1973-79; vis. assoc. NIH, Bethesda, Md., 1979-81; from med. asst. to assoc. in pneumology Hosp. San Martino, 1981-90; chief dept. pneumolgy G. Gaslini Inst., Genoa, 1990—; adj. prof. respiratory physiology U. Genoa, 1989—, adj. prof. pediat. pulmonology, 1992—. Editl. bd. Pediat. Pulmonology, 1992—, Mondaldi Archives Chest Diseases, 1992—; assoc. editor Bulletin Europeen de Physiopathologiae Respiratoire, 1985-87; cons. editor European Jour. Respiratory Diseases, 1985-87. Mem. Am. Thoracic Soc., Associazione Italiana Pneumologi Ospedalieri, European Respiratory Soc., Italian Soc. Paediatric Respiratory Disorders (exec. com. 1995-98). Office: Giannina Gaslini, Largo G Gaslini 5, 16148 Genoa Italy

ROSSI, GUIDO A(NTONIO), mathematics educator, researcher; b. Moretta, Cuneo, Italy, Jan. 17, 1944; s. Giulio Cesare and Anna Maria (Ferraris di Celle) R.; m. Maria Emilia Zucchi, Mar. 27, 1978. Dr. in Math., U. Torino, Italy, 1967. Asst. U. Torino, 1969-82, asst. prof. Facoltá di Economia e Commercio, 1969-82, assoc. prof. math., 1982-86, Prof. math. social scis. and econs., 1986; full prof. 1986—, prof. math. for fin., 1996, dir. Istituto di Matematica Finanziaria, 1974-81, 83-85, 1992-94, dir. dept. stats. and applied math. human scis., 1995—. coord. rsch. projects, 1986—; prof. Scuola di Applicazione Italian Army, 1992—; mem. sci. bd. 3d A.F.I.R. Colloquium, 1993; bd. tchrs. doctorate program in math. for fin. markets joint Univs. Brescia, Milan, Torino, Udine, 1991—. Contbr. articles to profl. and sci. jours. Served to lt. Italian Army, 1967-68, diplomated Sommelier, 1986. Decorated cavaliere dell'Ordine al Merito Civile di Savoia, 1990, comdr., 1996. Mem. Unione Matematica Italiana, Assn. per la Matematica Applicata alle Scienze Economiche Sociali (auditor 1977-89, adminstr. 1990—), Assn. Italiana di Ricerca Operativa (auditor 1990—), Assn. Italiana Sommeliers, Assn. Museo Ferroviario Piemontese (pres. 1986—), Am. Mathematical Soc., European Math. Soc., Inst. Vienna Cir., Istituto Italiano dei Castelli-Internat. Burgen Institut, Fondo per l'Ambiente Italiano. Roman Catholic. Club: I Neoteri (pres. 1990-92). Achievements include contributions to the foundations of probability, decision theory and financial decisions. Avocations: skiing, sailing, modelling, wine tasting. Office: Dept Statistica & Matematica Applicata, Piazza Arbarello 8, I-10122 Turin Italy

ROSSI, MARIE-LOUISE ELIZABETH, insurance company association executive; b. London, Feb. 18, 1956; d. Sir Hugh Alexis Louis and Lady Philomena Elizabeth Rossi. BA with hons., St. Anne's Coll., Oxford, U.K., 1979, MA, 1982. Registered ins. broker, U.K. Grad. trainee to asst. dir. Hogg Group Plc., London, 1979-87; asst. dir. Sedgwick Group Plc., London, 1987-90; cons. Tillinghast (Towers Perrin), London, 1990-93; sr. cons. De Lisle Jessup Scott, London, 1993; chief exec. London Internat. Ins. and Reins. Mkt. Assn., 1993-98, Internat. Underwriting Assn. London, 1998—; expert witness in ins. regulation European Union Econ. and Social Com., Brussels, 1990-91; ins. advisor Hungarian Ministry of Fin., Budapest, 1993. Co-author pamphlet: Single Market in Insurance, 1990. Councillor Westminster City Coun., London, 1986-94, chmn. edn., 1988-92; chmn. The Bow Group, London, 1988-89; trustee Found. for Young Musicians, 1990—, Montessori St. Nicholas Ctr., London, 1992-96; mem. Women's Transport Svc./First Aid Nursing Yeomanry, U.K., 1981—; chmn. Fgn. Affairs Forum Conservative Party, 1993-96. Fellow Royal Soc. for Encouragement of Arts, Mfrs. Commerce, 21st Century Trust, Brit. Am. Project; mem. Brit. Invisibles Stats. Com., Brit. Insurers Internat. Com., Royal Inst. Internat. Affairs, Soc. of Bus. Econs. (chmn. environ. working party 1990-94), Inst. of Export, Am. Soc. Assn. Execs., Carlton Club, Spl. Forces Club. Conservative. Roman Catholic. Avocations: skiing, sailing, gardening. Office: Internat Underwriting Assn, 3 Minster Ct, London EC3R 7DD, England

ROSSI, PIERRE MARIE, consultancy company executive; b. Alessandria, Italy, Dec. 30, 1949; s. Vincent Nello and Daisy Desiree (Montmorency) R.; m. Susan Caroline Ellis, Feb. 20, 1990; 1 child, David. BSc, Royal Malta U., 1971; MBA, IMEDE, Lausanne, Switzerland, 1974. Cons. Arthur D. Little, Boston, 1975-76; contr. ITT, Brussels; exec. C.G.E.R., Brussels, 1976-79; dir., ptnr. Deville Petersen & Assocs., Brussels, 1979-88; exec. I.M.R., Manchester, Eng.; v.p. devel. I.M.R., Milan, Italy, 1988-91; v.p. Alexander Proudfoot Productivity Mgmt. Co., Brussels, 1992-95; mng. ptnr. European Inst. Mgmt., London, 1995—; bd. dirs. P.M.R. Cons. Ltd., London; cons. SAFT (U.K.), SAFT (France) Alcatel Group, Paris, 1990-92; mng. ptnr. European Inst. Mgmt., London, Brussels and Geneva, 1995—. Author: Une nuit a Pise, 1976, Basic Elements of Europe Accounting, 1991, Total Vision Management, 1995; contbr. articles to profl. publs. Mem. European Acctg. Inst., Inst. Dirs. (London). Avocations: competitive sailing, historic cars, opera, collecting contemporary art. Home: Prince Consort Rd, 60 Albert Ct, London SW7 2BH, England Office: EIM, 113 Bud Louis Schmidt, 1040 Brussels Belgium also: EIM (Suisse) S.A., 16 Chemin des Aulx, Plans Les Quakes, 1228 Geneva Switzerland

ROSSIER, WILLIAM, world trade organization; b. 1942. Degree in econs., U. lausanne, 1970. Head diplomatic secretariat Conf. on Security and Cooperation in Europe, 1972-73; dep. head divsn. gen. fgn. econ. questions Swiss Diplomatic Svc., 1973-76; counsellor Swiss Mission to Europeqn Cmty. Swiss Diplomatic Svc., Brussels, 1976-80; head divsn. in charge of rels. Fed. Office for External Econ. Affairs, Switzerland, 1981-88; chmn. trade and devel. bd. UN Conf. on Trade and Devel., Geneva, 1988—; plenipotentiary ambassador of Switzerland UN, Geneva; chair UN/ECE Com. for Devel. of Trade, OECD Working Party on East West Trade; head divsn. in charge of relations with Western Europe; chmn. gen. coun. World Trade Assn., chmn. working party on accession of Russia; chmn. EFTA Coun., Econ. Commn. ofr Europe. Mem. European Free Trade Assn., Econ. Commn. for Europe. Office: 154 Rue Lausanne, CH-1211 Geneva 21 Switzerland*

ROSSIGNOLI, JOSE LUIS, educator; b. Zaragoza, Spain, Nov. 17, 1948; s. JoseLuis and Teresa (Susin) R.; m. Maria de Los Angeles Palomeque, July 11, 1981; children: Alvaro, Laura, Angela, Teresa. Grad., Complutense U., Madrid, 1972, 75, MD, 1980. Asst. tchr. Complutense U., Madrid, 1974-75; asst. prof. Navarra U., Pamplona, Spain, 1976-77; asst. prof. Complutense U., 1978-88, interim prof., 1989-91, prof., 1992—; cons. in field. Author: Instructional Psychology, 1996; contbr. articles to profl. jours. Asst. Schs. of Parents, Madrid, 1994—. With Spanish Mil., 1968-70. Mem. Assn. Psychology. Avocations: classical music, mountaineering, cross-country skiing, reading, theatre. Office: Complutense U, Paseo de Las Moreras S/N, 28040 Madrid Spain

ROSSINI, JOSEPH, contracting and development corporate executive; b. New Rochelle, N.Y., Nov. 25, 1939; m. Antonia Rossini; children: Katherine, Anthony, Andrew. Student, Fordham U., 1965-66, Iona Coll., 1972. Pres. Rossini Contracting Corp., Mt. Vernon, N.Y., 1963—; prin. Rossini Devel. Co., Monticello, N.Y., 1965—; bd. dirs. Circuit Realty Corp., New Rochelle, 1970-71. Mem. planning bd. City of New Rochelle, 1986-92, mem. bldg. dept. adv. com., 1985; vol. instr. N.Y. State Dept. Environ. Conservation, Albany, 1968-95; vice chmn. New Rochelle Conservative Party, 1984—; county committeeman Westchester County Conservative Party; pres., bd. trustees Beechwoods Cemetery, New Rochelle; dir. New Rochelle Neighborhood Revitalization Corp., 1993-96. With USN, 1959-61. Mem. NRA (endowment mem.), Gen. Contractors Assn. N.Y., Constrn. Industry Coun. Westchester and Hudson Valley, Bldg. Trades Employers Assn., Soc. Explosives Engrs., Deep Founds. Inst., Young Ams. for Freedom, Am. Lauretana Assn., Mensa, Assoc. Gen. Contractors Am., Caths. in Constrn., Tin Can Sailors, Westchester County Firearm Owners Assn., N.Y. State Rifle and Pistol Assn. Roman Catholic. Office: Rossini Contracting Corp 113 Edison Ave Mount Vernon NY 10550-5005

ROSSIT, CARLOS ADOLFO, civil engineer, educator; b. Bahia Blanca, Argentina, Oct. 28, 1956; s. Jorge Eugenio and Nelly (Romanelli) R.; m. Diana Virginia Bambill, Dec. 9, 1982; children: José Alberto, Daniel Alejandro, Diego Gabriel. Degree in civil engring., Nat. U. South, Bahia Blanca, 1980, MEng, 1995; D in Engring., Nat. U. South, 2000. Asst. prof. Nat. U. Patagonia, Comodoro Rivadavia, Argentina, 1983-86, assoc. prof., 1986-87; asst. prof. Nat. Tech. U., Bahia Blanca, 1986-89, prof., 1989—; asst. prof. Nat. U. South, 1987-96, assoc. prof., 1997—; sci. rschr., dir. Applied Inst. Mechanics, CONICET. Contbr. articles to profl. jours. Mem. Am. Acad. Mechanics, Argentina Assn. Mech. Engring. Roman Catholic. Office: Nat U South, Avenida Alem 1253, 8000 Bahia Blanca Argentina

ROSSITTI, SANDRO L., physician, researcher; b. Tiete, Sao Paulo, Brazil, Apr. 16, 1962; arrived in Sweden, 1990; s. Humberto Heitor and Lizete (Demartini) R.; m. Eva Maria Olovsson, May 7, 1994; children: Hugo, Bruno. MD, Pontifical Cath. U., Campinas, Brazil, 1986; PhD, Göteborg U., Sweden, 1995. Tchg. asst. Faculty Medicine PUCCAMP, Campinas, 1984-86, resident Univ. Hosp., 1987-90; tchg. asst. Göteborg U., 1993; physician Sahlgrenska U. Hosp., Sweden, 1991-93, 95, Uppsala Univ. Hosp., Sweden, 1996—; assoc. prof. neurosurgery Göteborg U. Hosp., 1996. Contbr. articles to profl. jours. Grantee Göteborg U., 1994-95. Mem. Svenska Läkarsällskapet. Roman Catholic. Achievements include expertise in cerebral hemodynamics. Office: Univ Hosp, Dept Diagnostic Radiology, S-751 85 Uppsala Sweden

ROSS-LANGLEY, RICHARD S., software engineer, consultant, researcher; b. Bournemouth, U.K., Apr. 29, 1946; children: Martin Alexander, Benjamin Thomas, Amy Alexander. MA in Natural Sci., Cambridge U., 1967. Rsch. scientist Eng. Electric Computers, London, 1967-68; tech. programmer Midland Bank, London, 1968-73; software cons. SPL Internat., London, 1973-74; internat. software support cons. Burroughs Co., Mexico and Europe, 1975-77; micro programmer Data 100, Hemel Hempstead, U.K., 1978; mng. dir. Mine of Info. Ltd., St. Albans, Eng., 1979—; bd. dirs. Games of Skill Ltd., St. Albans. Editor, contbg. author: Spectrum Machine Code Reference Guide, 1983; contbg. author: What to Read in Microcomputing, 1982. Mem. City and Guilds Instn. (external examiner 1970-92), Brit. Computer Soc. (chartered engr. 1990), Mensa. Avocations: artificial intelligence, psychology, motorcycling. Office: Mine Info Ltd, PO Box 1000, Saint Albans Hertfordshire AL3 5NY, England

ROSSLER, WILLIS KENNETH, JR., petroleum company executive; b. Houston, Nov. 17, 1946; BS in Indsl. Engring., Tex. Tech. U., 1969; postgrad. Stanford U.; s. Willis Kenneth and Fay Lee (Olle) R.; m. Jennifer Hill West; children: Nancy Rossler Ewing, Deborah Anne, Ryan Konrad, Eric George; 1 stepson, Jason Hill Yelverton. Dist. mgr. Tex.-La. ops. Continental Pipe Line Co., Lake Charles, La., 1974-75, mgr. engring., Houston, 1976-77; asst. mgr. corp. planning and devel. Conoco, Inc., Houston, 1977-78; v.p. project devel. PetroUnited, Inc., Houston, 1978-80, pres., 1981-86, also dir. Pres., Village Pl. Cmty. Assn., Houston, 1978, also partnership com. Antwerp Gas Terminal, V.G.N., 1982-85, v.p., gen. mgr., Pilko and Assoc., Inc., Houston, 1986-90; pres., CEO Houston Fuel Oil Terminal Co., 1990—; bd. dirs. Pilko and Assocs., Naylor Industries, Inc., Clean Channel Assn. (chmn.), Greater Houston Port Bur., Grace Presbyn. Sch. Mem. Am. Inst. Indsl. Engrs., Am. Petroleum Inst., Houston Mgmt. Council, Intensive Mgmt. Devel. Inst. (adv. dir. 1983-84), Ind. Liquid Terminals Assn. (vice chmn. 1986, chmn.-elect 1987), Am. Mgmt. Assn., Tex. Tech Acad. Indsl. Engrs., Planning Forum (pres. chpt. 1985), Petroleum Club of Houston, Lakeside Country Club. Office: Houston Fuel Oil Terminal Co 16642 Jacintoport Blvd Houston TX 77015-6541

ROSSMAN, ROBERT HARRIS, management consultant; b. Phila., Jan. 27, 1932; s. Benjamin Bernard and Vivian (Silnutzer) R.; m. Wanda Ward, Aug. 9, 1980; 1 child, Victoria Anne; children from previous marriage: Rodger Samuel, Robbi Jennifer, Ronni Esther. BS, U.S. Merchant Marine Acad., 1953; MSME with honors, U.S. Naval Postgrad. Sch., 1963; cert. advanced naval architecture, MIT, 1973. Cert. mgr. human resources; cert. value specialist. Commd. ensign USN, 1953, advanced through grades to comdr., 1967, shipboard engr., 1953-55, maintenance and repair officer Reserve Fleet, 1955-57; served as ship supt. Norfolk Naval Shipyard, Portsmouth, Va., 1957-60; maintenance and logistics planning officer Amphibious Squadron Twelve, Little Creek, Va., 1963-65; planning and estimating supt. U.S. Naval Ship Repair Facility, Yokosuka, Japan, 1965-67; design and planning advisor USN, Saigon, Republic Viet Nam, 1967-68; chief prodn. engring. Def. Contract Adminstrn. Svcs., Alexandria, Va., 1968-70; dir. cost reduction Naval Ship Systems Command, Washington, 1970-73; dep. program mgr. new ship class Naval Ship Engring. Ctr., Hyattsville, Md., 1973; ret. USN, 1973; ptnr. Kempter-Rossman Internat., Washington, 1974-91; owner Rossman Assocs. Internat., 1991—; cons. in cost and time reduction, mgmt. improvement, productivity and competition enhancement. Author: (textbook) Function Based Analysis, 1983, Total Cycle Time Reduction, 1992; editor mag. Performance, 1970-73; contbr. articles to profl. jours. Pres. PTA, Fairfax County, Va., 1969-70, Community Civic Assn., Fairfax County, 1970-71; chmn. Boy Scouts Am. and Weblos troops, 1969-71, del. at large 1st Congl. Dist. Rep. Com., N.C., 1989-90; chmn. Chowan County (N.C.) Rep. Com., 1990-92. Decorated USN Commendation medals, Honor medal-1st Class (Republic of Vietnam Armed Forces), Combat Action medal. Fellow Soc. Am. Value Engrs. (v.p. 1970-73, Disting. Svc. award 1976); mem. U.S. Merchant Marine Acad. Alumni Assn., Am. Legion, Sigma Xi. Jewish. Avocations: gardening, home remodeling, restoration, writing. Office: Rossman Assocs Internat Speight House 110 Old Hertford Rd Edenton NC 27932-9608

ROSSMANN, ANTONIO, lawyer, educator; b. San Francisco, Apr. 25, 1941; s. Herbert Edward and Yolanda (Sonsini) R.; m. Kathryn A. Burns, Oct. 6, 1991; children: Alice Sonsini, Maria McHale. Grad. Harvard U., 1963; JD, 1971. Bar: Calif. 1972, D.C. 1979, U.S. Supreme Ct. 1979, N.Y. 1980. Law clk., Calif. Supreme Ct., 1971-72; assoc. Tuttle & Taylor, Los Angeles, 1972-75; pub. advisor Calif. Energy Commn., 1975-76; sole practice, San Francisco, 1976-82, 85—; exec. dir. Nat. Center for Preservation Law, 1979-80; mem. McCutchen, Doyle, Brown & Enersen, San Francisco, 1982-85; adj. prof. law Hastings Coll. Law, 1981-84; vis. prof. UCLA Sch. Law, 1985-88; adj. prof. Stanford Law Sch., 1989-90, U. Calif. Sch. Law, 1991—. Bd. dirs. Planning and Conservation League, 1984—, Calif. Water Protection Council, 1982-83, San Francisco Marathon, 1982-90; pres. Western State Endurance Run, 1986-96, counselor, 1996—; pres., bd. dirs. Toward Utility Rate Normalization, 1976-79. Served to lt. comdr. USN, 1963-68. Fulbright lectr., U. Tokyo, 1987-88. Mem. Calif. State Bar (chmn. com. on environment 1978-82), Assn. Bar City of N.Y., U.S. Rowing Assn., U.S. Soccer Fed. (state referee), L.A. Athletic Club, Harvard Club (San Francisco, N.Y.C.), Harvard Law Sch. Assn. of No. Calif. (pres. 1997—). Contbr. articles to legal jours.; editor Harvard U. Law Rev., 1969-71. Office: 380 Hayes St San Francisco CA 94102-4421

ROSSMANN, PAVEL, pathologist; b. Bratislava, Czechoslovakia, Jan. 4, 1933; s. Zdenek and Marie (Dolezelova) R.; m. Svetluse Valentova, July 18, 1968; children: Michael, Zdenek. MD, Charles U., Prague, Czechoslovakia, 1957; CSc, Charles U., Hradec, Kralove, 1965; DSc, Charles U., Prague, 1986. Mem. staff med. faculty Inst. Pathology, Charles U., Hradec Kralove, Czechoslovakia, 1957-60, Prague, 1960-62; researcher Inst. Clin. and Exptl. Medicine, Prague, 1962-79, cons. pathologist Transplant Ctr., 1979-97; stagiaire etranger Clin. Nephrologique Hopital Necker, Paris, 1965-66; sr. rschr. dept. immunology Inst. Microbiology, Acad. Scis. Czech. Republic, 1979—. Author: Rejection Nephropathy (Sci. prize Czech. Republic Ministry Health 1980), 1979, Renal Allograft Biopsy, 1997; contbr. articles to profl. jours. Recipient Sci. award Lit. Fund, Prague, 1980. Mem. Czech. Republic Med. Assn. (Sci. prizes 1970, 73, 76, 88, 98), Czech. Republic Immunol. Assn. Club: Czech. Republic Alpine (Prague) (tng. officer 1963—). Avocations: climbing, trekking, travel. E-mail: rossmann@biomed.cas.cz. Office: Acad Scis Czech Republic, Inst Microbiology Dept 152, 142 20 Prague 4, Czech Republic

RÖSSNER, STEPHAN, health facility administrator, medical researcher; b. Norrköping, Sweden, Apr. 3, 1942; s. Nils and Susanne (Rössner) Eriksson; m. Kerstin Jarvenius; children: Charlotte, Carolina; m. Britta Hylander, Aug. 16, 1974; children: Sophia, Gustaf. Docent of medicine, Karolinska Inst., Stockholm, 1974. Dir. obesity unit Karolinska Hosp., 1982; prof. health behavior rsch. Huddinge (Sweden) U., 1990—. Editor Swedish Soc. Medicine, 1980—; author 20 books; contbr. 400 articles to scientific jours., 600 lay articles to mags. Recipient Leopold II medal Kingdom of Belgium, 1993, Golden Pen award Swedish Gastronomic Acad., 1996. Mem. Internat. Assn. Study of Obesity (pres. 1998—), Swedish Gastronomic Acad. Office: Obesity Unit, Huddinge Univ Hosp, SE 14186 Huddinge Sweden

ROSSOF, ARTHUR HAROLD, internal medicine educator; b. Chgo., Dec. 12, 1943; s. Jack and Libby (Gordon) R.; m. Rebecca Ann, Aug. 11, 1967 (div. 1983); children: Jacob Earl, Lizabeth Eva; m. Kristine Ann, Feb. 14, 1985. Student, Bradley U., 1961-64; MD, U. Ill., 1968. Diplomate Nat. Bd. Med. Examiners, Am. Bd. Internal Medicine, Am. Bd. Oncology, Am. Bd. Hematology. Fellow sect. neurobiology dept. neurology Presbyn.-St. Luke's Hosp., Chgo., 1965-68, intern straight medicine, 1968-69, resident dept. medicine, 1969-71, Eastern Coop. Oncology Group fellow sect. oncology, dept. medicine, 1971-72, asst. attending physician dept. internal medicine, 1976-80, assoc. attending physician, dept. internal medicine, 1980-82, sr. attending physician dept. internal medicine, 1982-90; med. dir. MacNeal Cancer Ctr., Berwyn, Ill., 1985-99; asst. medicine U. Ill. Coll. Medicine, 1969-71; clin. asst. prof. medicine U. Tex. health Sci. Ctr., San Antonio, 1973-76; instr. medicine Rush Med. Coll., 1971-72, asst. prof. medicine, 1976-81, assoc. prof. medicine, 1981-90; assoc. prof. medicine Loyola U. Med. Ctr., Chgo., 1990-91, attending physician, 1990-97, prof., 1991-97; mem. resident selection com. Rush-Presbyn.-St. Luke's Med. Ctr., 1976-88, mem. ethics conf. planning group, 1981-90, tumor com., 1981-90; chmn. med. edn. com., continuing med. edn. subcom., 1982-90; mem. pharmacy and therapeutics com., chmn. instnl. rev. bd., chmn. cancer com. MacNeal Hosp.. chmn. med. edn. com., continuing med. edn. subcom., 1993-97; cons. Cancer Info. Svcv., Ill. Cancer Coun., mem. clin. trials com. 1978-92, credentials rev. com.; mem. adv. com. Lincoln Park Zoo, 1978—; med. advisor Y-ME sci. adv. bd. Chgo. chpt. Israel Cancer Rsch. Found. Author: Lithium Effects on Granulopoiesis and Immune Function, 1980; contbr. articles in field to profl. jours.; patentee in field. Mem. exec. com. prevention com. Cancer Incidence and End Results com. Am. Cancer Soc.; mem. profl. adv. bd. Wellness House, Y-ME, Israel Cancer Rsch. Found. Fellow ACP; mem. AAAS, Internat. Soc. Exptl. Hematology, Am. Soc. Clin. Oncology, Am. Assn. Cancer Research, Am. Soc. Hematology, N.Y. Acad. Scis., Soc. Air Force Physicians, Soc. Med. History Chgo., Chgo. Soc. Internal Medicine, Assn. Community Cancer Ctrs., Sigma Xi, Phi Eta Sigma, Alpha Omega Alpha. Republican. Jewish. Avocation: tennis. Fax: 708-484-8426. Office: Hematology/Oncology Assocs Ill 3245 Grove Ave Berwyn IL 60402-3474

ROSSON, DENNIS MCKINLEY, manufacturing company executive; b. Cushing, Okla., Nov. 26, 1938; s. Vivian McKinley and Ethyl Juanita (Harris) R.; m. Sharon Martin, June 5, 1960 (div. July 1965); children: Velisa Dawn, Lance Elliot; m. Linda Kay Gant, June 23, 1972; 1 child, Kari Cheree; stepchildren: Kimberly Gaye, Billie Jean. AS in Diesel Engring., Okla. State U., 1960, BS, 1969. Diesel mechanic instr. Tulsavo Tech., Tulsa, 1969-70, Ctrl. Area Vo-Tech., Drumright, Okla., 1970-73, Del Mar Coll., Corpus Christi, Tex., 1973-75; mfg. rep. Outdoor Recreational Dist., Springfield, Mo., 1975-79; tech. sales engr. Cato Oil and Grease Co., Oklahoma City, Okla., 1979-81; tech. svc. mgr. S.W. Petro-Chem., Olathe, Kans., 1981-84, Dryden Oil Co., Balt., 1984-89; OEM rep. BP Oil Co., Clevel., Ohio, 1989-92; tech. dir. BG Products Inc., Wichita, Kans., 1992—. With U.S. NG, 1957. Fellow Nat. Lubricating Grease Inst.; mem. Soc. Automotive Engrs. Avocation: fishing. Home: 6301 E 8th St N Wichita KS 67208-3611 Office: BG Products Inc 701 S Wichita St Wichita KS 67213-5496

ROSSOR, MARTIN NEIL, neurologist; b. London, Apr. 24, 1950; s. Bruce Eileen (Curry) R.; m. Eve Lipstein, July 7, 1973; children: Alexander, Thomas, Charlotte. MB BChir MA, Jesus Coll., Cambridge and Kings Coll. Hosp. Med. Sch., London, 1974; MD, U. Cambridge, Eng., 1976. Clin. scientist neurochem. pharmacology unit Med. Rsch. Coun., Cambridge, 1978-82; registrar Nat. Hosp. for Nervous Diseases & King's Coll. Hosp., London, 1982-83, sr. registrar, 1983-86; cons. neurologist Nat. Hosp. Neurology and Neurosurgery and St. Mary's Hosp., London, 1986—; clin. dir. Nat. Hosp. for Neurology and Neurosurgery, London, 1994-98, prof. clin. neurology, 1998. Author, editor: Unusual Dementias, 1992; European editor Alzheimer Disease and Associated Disorders, 1992—; editor: (with Growdon) Dementia, 1998; contbr. articles to profl. jours. Recipient Ralph Horton Smith prize U. Cambridge, 1986. Fellow RCP, Royal Soc. Medicine; mem. Assn. Brit. Neurologists (mem. coun. 1992-96), World Fedn. Neurology Rsch. Group on Dementia (exec. com. 1993—), Ct. of Assts., Soc. Apothecaries London, Athenaeum. Avocations: English literature, Equestrian sports, sailing. Office: Nat Hosp Neurology, Queen Sq, London WC1N 3BG, England

ROSS-PETERSEN, JAKOB, company executive; b. Copenhagen, Sept. 27, 1967; s. Karl Jakob and Bodil (Riemann) R.-P. Grad., U. Copenhagen, 1992, M in Nat. Econs., 1994. Fin. mgr. Burmeister & Wain, Copenhagen, 1994-96; CEO TAG Copenhagen, 1996—; dir. KJ Ross Petersen A/S, Horsholm, Denmark, 1992—, TAG Copenhagen, 1996—, TAGC Aps, Copenhagen, 1996—. Avocation: former profl. windsurfer. Home: Vasehøjvej, 2920 Charlottenlund Denmark Office: TAG Copenhagen A/S, Fruebjergvej 3, 2100 Copenhagen Denmark

ROSS-SERAKOS, VONIA P., insurance agent, small business owner; b. Taylorville, Ill., Dec. 4, 1942; d. Alvin Clyde and Lois Eva (Weller) Brown; children: Craig Allen Ross, Cayle Allen Ross; m. Leo A. Serakos, May 13, 2000. Student, So. Ill. U., 1962-64, Palomar Coll., 1986-88, San Diego State U., 1988-90. Real estate agt. Joe Foster Agy., Collinsville, Ill., 1964-69; office mgr. real estate Bank of St. Louis, 1969-73; real estate agt. Palmer-Stelman, San Diego, 1986-89; office mgr. real estate McMillin Realty, San Diego, 1989-90; mgr., ins. agt. Calif. Plus Ins., San Diego, 1990-93; prin. Vonia Ross Ins. Agy., 1993—; owner, pres. Bernardo Flooring, San Diego, 1993—; mem. Calif. Assn. Real Estate, Sacramento, 1986—, San Diego Bd. Realtors, 1986—, Health Underwriters, 1991—. Mem. adv. com. Rancho Bernardo Libr. Campaign, 1994—; active NOW, San Diego, 1988; mem. activist Barbara Boxer Campaign, San Diego, 1992, Susan Golding Campaign, San Diego, 1992, Barbara Warden Campaign for San Diego City Councilwoman, Barbara Warden Campaign for Mayor of San Diego, 1999—. Scholar Ill. Assembly, 1962; named Philanthropy Coun. Vol. of the Year, 1996; named Hon. Mayor of Rancho Bernardo, Calif., 1999—. Mem. Rancho Bernardo C. of C. (v.p., bd. dirs. 1993—, pres.-elect 1996-97, pres. 1997-98), Soroptimists (pres. Rancho Bernardo 1993-94, 95-96), City of San Diego Status of Women Commn. Avocations: walking, reading, golf. Home: 18284 Fernando Way San Diego CA 92128-1213

ROSS STANTON, RONALD, publisher, retired; b. London, Jan. 27, 1927; s. Louis Eva (Kinsler) R.; m. Shirley Rosanne Berg, Apr. 29, 1965; children: Louis David, Michelle Deborah. Area sales mgr. World Book Ency., Germany, 1955-57; sales mgr. Caxton Pub. Co. Ltd., Australia, 1958-60;

European sales mgr. Std. Educators Inc., Lichtenstein, 1961-70; CEO Ednl. Rsch. Inst. Am., 1971-80; mng. dir. Janus Pub. Co., London, 1991-98. Mem. Pubs. Assn. Avocations: travel, theatre, fine dining. Office: Janus Pub Co Ltd, Edinburgh Ho, 19 Nassau St, London W1N 7RE, England

ROSTAD, LEE B., rancher, writer; b. Roundup, Mont., Oct. 28, 1929; d. Edward and Emma Gail (Haddock) Birkett; m. O. Phillip Rostad, June 29, 1952; children: Phillip, Carl Eric. BA with honors, U. Mont., 1951; LLD (hon.), Rocky Mountain Coll., Billings, Mont., 1995. Rancher Rostad and Rostad, Martinsdale, Mont., 1952—; tchr. Pub. Sch., Great Falls, Mont., 1953-54, White Sulphur Springs, Mont., 1967-68, Helena, Mont., 1968-72; chmn., bd. dirs. C.M. Bair Family Trust, Billings, 1993—; bd. dirs., fundraiser Mountainview Med. Ctr., White Sulphur Spings, 1990-2000. Author: Honey Wine and Hunger Root, 1985, Fourteen Cents and Seven Green Apples, 1992, Mountains of Gold, Hills of Grass, 1994; illustrator, author: Meagher County Sketchbook; newspaper columnist, 1992—. Bd. dirs. Mont. Com. for Humanities, 1989-96; trustee Mont. State Hist. Soc., 1997—; sec.-treas. Mont. chpt. Nat. Mus. Women in the Arts, 1992—; mem. County Study Commn., Meagher County, 1975. Fulbright scholar, 1952. Mem. Mont. Watercolor Soc., Meagher County Hist. Assn. (fundraiser 1960—), Meagher County Archives Assn. (charter). Republican. Avocations: pottery, art, writing. Home and Office: Rostad and Rostad HC 83 Box 550 Martinsdale MT 59053-9709

ROSTAIN, JEAN-CLAUDE, research scientist, neurobiologist; b. Alger, Algerie, July 8, 1942; s. Jean Joseph and Odette Therese (Merckel) R.; m. Charlette Elisabeth Fasano, July 9, 1944; children: Arnaud, Frederic. MSc, U. Provence, Marseille, France, 1968, PhD, 1973, DSc, 1980. From rschr. to rschr. in charge Ctr. Nat. Rsch. Sci., Marseille, 1968-88, rsch. dir., 1988—. Contbr. articles to profl. jours. Recipient Internat. Oceaneering award Undersea Med. Soc., 1976, Zetterstrom Meml. medal Zetterstrom Soc. and Swedish Soc. History of Diving, 1995, Ajaccio Town medal, 1995, Medsubhyp medal, 1999. Mem. Undersea and Hyperbaric Med. Soc. (award 1976), Société de Physiologie et de Médecine Subaquatiques et hyperbores de langue francaise (pres.), Neurosci., Internat. Union Physiol. Scis., Assn. Physiologists. Avocations: movies, mountain climbing, photography. Office: Univ Mediterranee, Bd Drammard Faculy Medicine, 13015 Marseille France

ROSTAING, LIONEL PAUL-EMILE, transplant physician; b. Vinay, France, Jan. 24, 1959; s. Lucien Albert and Suzanne Juillette (Rousset) R.; m. Véronique Pierrette Bourg, May 19, 1989; children: Jean-Baptiste, Marie Anais, Mathilde. MS, Paul Sabatier U., Toulouse, France, 1988, degree in nephrology, 1988, PhD, 2000. Intern Toulouse U. Hosp., France, 1985-88, asst. medicine, 1990-94, cons. nephrology/transplantation, 1995—. Grantee INSERM, Bristol, England, 1989. Mem. French Soc. Nephrology, French Transplant Soc., Am. Soc. Transplantation, Am. Soc. Nephrology, Internat. Soc. Nephrology, European Soc. Organ Transplantation, European Soc. Nephrology, Dialysis and Transplantation. Roman Catholic. Achievements include research in chronic hepatitis B and C in dialysis and renal transplant patients; cytokines dialysis and renal transplant patients. Home: 6 Chemin Pouciquot, 31520 Ramonville St Agne France Office: UTO Chu Rangueil, Ave Jean Poulhes, 31054 Toulouse France

ROSTOKER, GUY PASCAL FRANCIS, nephrologist; b. Neuilly, France, June 11, 1956; s. Wolf Lucien Rostoker and Jeanne-Marie Balestrieri; m. Catherine Elisabeth Lerault; children: Pauline, Thomas. MD, St. Louis-Lariboisière, Paris, 1986; degree in biochemistry, U. Paris VII, 1986; PhD in Immunology, Paris VII Inst Jacques Monod, 1992; M. in Immunology, U. Paris XII, Créteil, France, 1987. Intern, hosp. specialist Internat de Rouen (France), 1982-83; intern Internat. de Paris (Assistance Publique), 1983-87; chief resident Henri Mondor Hosp., Créteil, 1987-91, assoc. prof. nephrology, 1991-96; med. dir. divsn. nephrology Pvt. Hosp. Claude Galien, Quincy Sous Senart, France, 1997—. Mem. French Soc. for Electrophoresis, French Soc. Nephrology, IgA Nephrophaty Club, Soc. for Mucosal Immunology, European Soc. for Clin. Investigation, Internat. Soc. Nephrology. Fax: 0165 39 9184. Office: Svc de Nephrologie, Hosp Prive Claude Galien, 91480 Quincy Sous Senart France

ROSTOW, ELSPETH DAVIES, political science educator; b. N.Y.C.; d. Milton Judson and Harriet Elspeth (Vaughan) Davies; m. Walt Whitman Rostow, June 26, 1947; children: Peter Vaughan, Ann Larner. AB, Barnard Coll., 1938; AM, Radcliffe Coll., 1939; MA, Cambridge (Eng.) U., 1949; LHD (hon.), Lebanon Valley Coll.; LLD (hon.), Austin Coll., 1982, Southwestern U., 1988. Mem. faculty various instns. Barnard Coll., N.Y.C. and MIT, Cambridge, 1939-69; mem. faculty U. Tex., Austin, 1969—, dean div. gen. and comparative studies, 1975-77, prof. govt., 1976—, dean Lyndon B. Johnson Sch. Pub. Affairs, 1977-83, Stiles prof. Am. studies, 1985-88, Stiles prof. emerita, 1988—; mem. Pres.'s Adv. Com. for Trade Negotiations, 1978-82, Pres.'s Commn. for a Nat. Agenda for the Eighties, 1979-81; rsch. assoc. OSS, Washington, 1943-45; Geneva corr. London Economist, 1947-49; lectr. Air War Coll., 1963-81, Army War Coll., 1965, 68, 69, 78, 79, 81, Nat. War Coll., 1962, 68, 74, 75, Indsl. Coll. Armed Forces, 1961-65, Naval War Coll., 1971, Fgn. Svc. Inst., 1974-77, Dept. of State, Europe, 1973; bd. dirs. U.S. Inst. of Peace, vice chmn., 1991, chmn. 1991-92; co-founder The Austin Project, 1991; mem. Gov.'s Task Force on Revenue, Tex., 1991. Author: Europe's Economy After the War, 1948, (with others) American Now, 1968, The Coattailless Landslide, 1974; editor (with Barbara Jordan) The Great Society: A Twenty-Year Critique, 1986; columnist Austin Am. Statesman, 1985-92; contbr. articles to revs., poems to scholarly jours., newspapers, and mags. Trustee Sarah Lawrence Coll., 1952-59, Nat. Acad. Pub. Adminstrn., 1989-95, So. Ctr. for Internat. Studies, 1990—; bd. visitors and govs. St. John's Coll., 1986-89; bd. dirs. Barnard Coll., 1962-66, Lyndon Baines Johnson Found., 1977-83, Salzburg Seminar, 1981-89, co-chair sr. fellows, 1997—; vis. scholar Phi Beta Kappa, 1984-85; mem. bd. adv. to pres. Naval War Coll., Newport, R.I., 1995-99; mem. nat. adv. Commn. on Deliberative Polling, 1999—. Recipient award Air U., Top Hand award U. Tex. Ex-Students Assn., 1996, Presdl. citation U. Tex., 1998, Disting. Alumna award Barnard Coll., 1998; Fulbright lectr., USIA participant, 1983-84, 90. Mem. Tex. Philos. Soc. (trustee 1989-95, 97—), Headliners Found. (vice-chmn. 1996—), Phi Beta Kappa, Phi Nu Epsilon (hon.), Mortar Bd. (hon.), Omicron Delta Kappa. Home: 1 Wildwind Pt Austin TX 78746-2434 Office: U Tex PO Box Y University Station Austin TX 78713

ROSTRON, CHAD KENNETH, ophthalmologist; b. St. Ives, England, May 6, 1951; s. Kenneth William Briggs and Rosemary (Arkwright) R.; m. Josephine Rose; 1 child. MB BS, U. Newcastle-upon-Tyne, 1975; DO, U. London. Hon. sr. lectr. ophthalmology U. London, 1988—; cons. ophthalmologist St. George's Hosp., London, 1988—; dir. Keratec Eye Bank, London, 1989—. Fellow Royal Coll. Surgeons, Royal Coll. Ophthalmologists. Office: 10 Harley St, London W1N 1AA, England

ROSTROPOVICH, MSTISLAV LEOPOLDOVICH, musician; b. Baku, USSR, Mar. 27, 1927; s. Leopold and Sofia (Fedotova) R.; m. Galina Pavlovna Vishnevskaya; children: Olga, Elena. Grad., Moscow Conservatory 1948; numerous hon. doctorate degrees. Faculty mem. Moscow Conservatory, 1953, prof., 1960; head cello and double-bass dept., formerly prof. Leningrad Conservatory; music dir., conductor Nat. Symphony Orch., Washington, 1977-94; hon. prof. Cuban Nat. Conservatory, 1960-78; pres. Evian Internat. Music Festival. Debut as violoncellist, 1940; performer world concert tours, Moscow Philharm. Orch.; recordings include (with various artists) Mstislav Rostropovich Melodiya Recordings, 1949-56, 48-59, The Young Rostropovich: Rare Recordings for the 1950-52 Years, Schnittke's Cello Concerto No. 2, In Memorium, Return to Russia. Decorated Hon. Knight of the Brit. Empire, 1987; Commdr. French Legion of Honor, 1987; Officer's Cross of Merit, Fed. Republic Germany, 1987; recipient Stalin prize, 1951, 53, Lenin prize, 1963, Life in Music prize, 1984, Albert Schweitzer Music award, 1985, Grammy awards, 1970, 77, 80, 84, Presdl. Medal Freedom, 1987, Ditson Condr.'s award, Columbia U., 1990, Four Freedoms award Franklin and Eleanor Roosevelt Inst., 1992; named Musician of Yr., Mus. Am., 1987. Mem. Am. Acad. Arts and Scis., Union Soviet Composers, Brit. Royal Acad. Music (hon.), Acad. Arts of French Inst.-Forty Immortals. Address: c o CAMI 165 W 57th St New York NY 10019-2201 also: Gazetny per 13 Apt 79, 103009 Moscow Russia

ROSVALL, JAN CHRISTER, conservation scholar scientist, educator; b. Malmö, Sweden, Aug. 4, 1941; s. Johan A.K. and Eva (Eriksson) R.; m. Nanne E.M. Engelbrektsson, July 21, 1984; 1 child, J. Torulf E. BA with honors, Göteborg (Sweden) U., 1966, PhD in Art History, 1975; diploma in Typographic Arts & Tech., Göteborg Coll. Applied Arts, 1968. Rsch. fellow in art history Göteborg U., 1973-75, sr. rsch. fellow, 1976-81, asst. prof. art history, 1979—, assoc. prof. dept. conservation, 1982—, dir. Inst. Conservation, 1985-95, head of rsch., 1997—, acting prof., head discipline, 1998-2000; vis. prof. conservation of Göteborg U., Swedish Inst., Rome, 1996-97; bd. dirs. Advanced Rsch. Sch. in Enterprising of Environ. and Conservation Materials, 1999—; founding pres. Eurocare Eureka, Europe, 1986-90, bd. dirs., 1991—; bd. dirs. Swedish Inst. Classical Studies, 1977-93, Kiruna Ctr. of Conservation, Stockholm, 1986-97; evaluation cons. Baylor U., Waco, Tex., 1995-97. Author, editor, conf. organizer: Air Pollution and Conservation of Our Architectural Heritage, 1986-88 (Volvo Corp grant 1985); contbr. articles to profl. publs.; editor Göteborg Studies in Conservation, 1988—. Pres. Elna Bengtsson Rsch. Found., Stockholm, 1981—; v.p. exptl. theater FEM, Göteborg, 1965-68; Swedish govtl. del. CSCE, Cracow, Poland, 1991; expert advisor City Coun. of Göteborg, 1986-91. 1st sgt. Swedish Army, 1962-88. Recipient Dr. Albert Wallin award Royal Acad. Letters, 1987. Mem. ICOM (bd. dirs.), ICOMOS, IIC, Internat. Com. for Tng. of Personnel, Com. Internat. de Formation (pres.), Save Göteborg Historic Center Found. Home: Hagtornsstigen 1, SE-41321 Göteborg Sweden Office: Göteborg U Inst Conservn, Bastionsplatsen 2 Box 130, SE-40530 Göteborg Sweden

ROSZKOWSKA, ANNA MARIA, ophthalmologist; b. Cracow, Poland, Dec. 25, 1963; arrived in Italy, 1988; d. Janusz Ryszard and Zofia (Szydek) R.; m. Andrea Laquidara, Sept. 28, 1991. MD, Jagiellonian U., Cracow, 1988; specialization in ophthalmology, U. Messina Inst. Ophthalmology, Italy, 1990-94; PhD, U. Padua, Italy, 1998. Diplomate European Bd. Ophthalmology. Ophthalmologist Inst. Ophthalmology, Polyclin. U., Messina. Mem. Am. Acad. Ophthalmology, ARVO, SOI. Roman Catholic. Office: Inst Ophthalmology, Via Consolare Valeria, 98125 Messina Italy

ROTA, EMILIA, zoologist; b. Rome, Latium, Italy, June 24, 1958; d. Antonio and Eleonora (Piva) R. Laurea cum laude, U. La Sapienza, Rome, 1982; PhD in Sci., Nat. U. Ireland, Dublin, 1994. Profl. biologist, Italy, 1984. Trainee U. La Sapienza, 1982-84; guest rschr. U. La Sapienza and Tor Vergata, Rome, 1985-88; contract tchr. U. Milan, Italy, 1995, 97; rschr. U. Siena, Italy, 1993—; vis. sci. Swedish Mus. Natural History, Stockholm, 1994-98. Contbr. over 40 articles to profl. jours. such as Jour. Natural History, Hydrobiologia, Italian Jour. Zoology, others. Fellow Soc. Italiana di Biogeografia, Unione Zoologica Italiana; mem. Ordine Nazionale dei Biologi. E-mail: rota@unisi.it. Office: U Siena Dept Biologia Evolu, Via Mattioli 4, 53100 Siena Italy

ROTA, MASSIMO TOMMASO, oral surgeon; b. Turin, Italy, Sept. 21, 1967; s. Renzo Rota and Anna Sabatino. Doctor dental medicine, U. Pavia, Italy, 1994, M in Statistics, 1997. Pvt. practice Alessandria, Italy, 1994—; rschr. dept. exptl. medicine Faculty of Medicine, U. Pavia, 1996—, rschr. anatomy-embryology dept. anatomy, 1997—; cons. web-site, 1997—; spkr. in field. Contbr. articles to profl. jours. Recipient award Italian Soc. Periodontology, Henry M. Goldman prize XI Nat. Congress Italian Soc. of Periodontology, 2000. Mem. N.Y. Acad. Scis., Italian Coll. of Applied Molecular Medicine, Rotaract City of Pavia. Home: Via Don Canestri 67, 15100 Alessandria Italy Office: Via dei Martiri 39, 15100 Alessandria Italy

ROTAR, TOMAZ, stock exchange executive. COO, exec. v.p. Ljubljana Stock Exch., Slovenia. Office: Ljubljana Stock Exch, Slovenska 56, 1000 Lulbljana Slovenia*

ROTARU, ALEXANDRU ISIDOR, maxillofacial surgeon, educator; b. Diviciorii Mari, Cluj, Romania, May 4, 1938; s. Isidor T. and Maria V. Rotaru; m. Maria I. Sirb, May 27, 1967; children: Ovidiu, Horatiu. DDS, Dental Sch., Cluj, 1968; PhD, U. Medicine and Pharmacy, Cluj, 1980. Med. diplomate; sr. specialist in oral and maxillofacial surgery. Intern U. Medicine and Pharmacy, Cluj, 1967-68, asst. prof., 1968-74, lectr., 1974-90, sr. lectr., 1990-91, prof., 1991—; prof., head surgery Dept. Oral and Maxillofacial Surgery, Cluj, 1991—; cons. Romanian Soc. Oral and Maxillofacial Surgery, Cluj, 1991—. Author: Emergency, Risks and Difficulties of the Stomatological Practice, 1992; co-author: Oral and Maxillofacial Surgery, vol. 1, 1994, vol II, 1999; patentee in field. Capt. Mil. Engring., 1958-60. Recipient Bilascu award U. Medicine and Pharmacy, 1993. Mem. Internat. Assn. Oral and Maxillofacial Surgeons, European Assn. of Cranio-Maxillofacial Surgery, Union Medicale Balcanique. Avocations: travel, music. Home: Tarnita nr 1 ap 13, 3400 Cluj-Napoca Romania Office: Clinic Maxillofac Surgery, Str Motilor nr 33, 3400 Cluj-Napoca Romania

ROTBERG, IRIS COMENS, social scientist; b. Phila., Dec. 16, 1932; d. Samuel Nathaniel and Golda (Shuman) Comens; m. Eugene H. Rotberg, Aug. 29, 1954; children: Diana Golda, Pamela Lynn. BA, U. Pa., 1954, MA, 1955; PhD, Johns Hopkins U., Balt., 1958. Research psychologist Pres.'s Commn. on Income Maintenance Programs, Washington, 1968-69, Office Planning, Research and Evaluation, Office Econ. Opportunity, Washington, 1970-73; dep. dir. compensatory edn. study Nat. Inst. Edn., Washington, 1974-77, dir. Office Planning and Program Devel., 1978-82; program dir. NSF, Arlington, Va., 1985-87, 89-91, 1993-96; tech. policy fellow Com. on Sci., Space and Tech., U.S. Ho. of Reps., Washington, 1987-89; sr. social scientist RAND, Washington, 1991-93; rsch. prof. edn. policy Grad. Sch. Edn. and Human Devel. George Washington U., Washington, 1996—. NSF fellow, 1956-58. Home: 7211 Brickyard Rd Potomac MD 20854-4808

ROTBLAT, SIR JOSEPH, physicist, educator; b. Warsaw, Nov. 4, 1908; s. Z. Rotblat. MA, DPhys, U. Warsaw; PhD, U. Liverpool; DSc, U. London; DSc (hon.), U. Bradford, 1973, Liverpool U., 1989, City U., 1996, Acadia U., 1998; Richmond U., 1998; D (honoris causa), U. Moscow, 1988. Rsch. fellow radiol. lab. Scientific Soc. Warsaw, 1933-39; asst. dir. atomic physics Inst. of Free Univ. of Poland, 1937-39; Oliver Lodge fellow U. Liverpool, Eng., 1939-40; lectr., sr. lectr. dept. of physics U. London, 1940-49, dir. rsch. in nuclear physics, 1945-49, prof. physics St. Bartholomew's Hosp. Med. Coll., 1950-76, prof. emeritus, 1976—; pres. Pugwash Confs. on Sci. and World Affairs, 1988-97; mem. mgmt. group WHO. Author: Nuclear Strategy and World Security, 1985, World Peace and the Developing Countries, 1986, Strategic Defense and The Future of the Arms Race, 1987, Coexistence, Cooperation and Common Security, 1989, Nuclear Proliferation: Technical and Economic Aspects, 1990, Building Global Security Through Cooperation, 1990, Towards a Secure World in the 21st Century, 1991, Striving for Peace, Security and Development in the World, 1992, A Nuclear-Weapon-Free World: Desirable? Feasible?, 1993, A World at the Crossroads, 1994, World Citizenship: Allegiance to Humanity, 1997, Nuclear Weapons: the Road to Zeno, 1998, also numerous others. Decorated Order of Merit (Poland), Knight Comdr. Order of Merit (Germany), Knight Comdr. of St. Michael and St. George (Eng.); recipient Bertrand Russell Soc. award, 1983, Albert Einstein Peace prize, 1992, Nobel Peace prize, 1995, Bajej Found. award, 1999, Toda Peace Rsch. prize, 2000; hon. fellow U. Manchester Inst. Sci. and Tech.; hon. freeman London Borough of Camden, 1997. Fellow Royal Soc.; mem. AAAS, Am. Acad. Scis. (fgn. hon.), Royal Soc. Edinburgh, Edn. Physics in Medicine and Biology, Hosp. Physicists' Assn. (pres.), Brit. Inst. Radiology (pres.), Internat. Youth Sci. Forum (pres.), Polish Acad. Scis., Czechoslovak Acad. Scis. (fgn.). Avocations: travel, music. Address: 8 Asmara Rd, West Hampstead NW2 3ST, England

ROTE, NELLE FAIRCHILD HEFTY, business consultant; b. Watsontown, Pa., May 23, 1930; d. Edwin Dunkel and Phebe Hill (Fisher) Fairchild; m. John Austin Hefty, Mar. 20, 1948 (div. June 1970); children: Harry E. Hefty, John B. Hefty, Susan E. Hefty DeBartolo; m. Keith Maynard Rote, Dec. 16, 1983 (dec. Aug. 1985). Student, Bucknell U., 1961, Williamsport Sch. of Commerce, 1968-69, Pa. State U., 1971-72, 83, Susquehanna U., 1986. Typesetter, page designer Colonial Printing House, Inc., Lewisburg, Pa., 1970-76; account exec. Sta. WTGC Radio, Lewisburg, 1976-78; co-owner Colonial Printing Co., Lewisburg, 1978-83; temp. HATS-Temps, Lewisburg, 1986-89; artist, editor Create-A-Book, Inc., Milton, Fla., 1980-92; census crew leader, spl. svc. Dept. Commerce, Washington, 1990; cons. Create-A-Book, Inc., Div. John B. Hefty Pub., Gulf Breeze, Fla., 1991-99. Author: McGruff and Me, 1999, My Christmas Wish 1999, School Fun Book, 1999, My Fishing Adventure, 1999; contbg. author: American Nursing: A Biographical Dictionary, 2000; artist: Children's Playmate Mag., 1942; contbr. articles to profl. jours. 1997 proofreader Lewisburg Bicentennial Commn., 1976; editor-poet Holiday Newspaper Bus. Assn., Lewisburg, 1987; charter mem. Women's Art Mus., Washington; charter sponsor and field rep. Women in Mil. Svc. Meml., Arlington, Va., 1991; founder, donor Nelle Fairchild Rote Book Fund, Union County Libr. Recipient Humanitarian recognition Tri-County Fedn. Women's Clubs, Pa., 1965, Grand Prize in Cooking, Milton Std., 1966, Most Profl. Photo award, Lewisburg Festival of Arts, 1980, Hon. Mention Award Women in Arts, Harrisburg, Pa., 1981, Photo Contest award Congressman Allen Ertel, Washington, 1981, Photo awards 2d and 3d place Union County Fair, Laurelton, Pa., 1981, Hon. Mention Photo award Susquehanna Art Soc., Selinsgrove, Pa., 1981, Silver award for poetry World of Poetry, 1990. Mem. DAR (nat. def. reporter Shikelimo chpt. 1989-95, sec. 1992-95, regent 1995—, vice chmn. Pa. State Soc. DAR women vets. com., Prize for safety poster 1942), Western Front Assn., Civic Club Lewisburg (v.p. 1994-97), Orgn. United Environ., Marine Corps League Aux. (life), Warrior Run Heritage Soc. Home: 1015 St Paul St Lewisburg PA 17837-1213

ROTELLA, FRÉDÉRIC, engineering educator; b. Paris, Aug. 30, 1957; children: Didier, Hélène, Yann. Diploma in engring., Indsl. Inst. of the North, Villeneuve D'Ascq, France, 1981; DEng, U. Sci. and Tech. of Lille, Villeneuve D'Ascq, 1983, D of Phys. Scis., 1987. Asst. Ctr. Sch. of Lille, Villeneuve D'Ascq, 1984-89, instr., 1989-94; prof. automatic control Nat. Sch. Engring., Tarbes, France, 1994—. Co-author books; contbr. articles to profl. publs. Mem. IEEE, EEA. Office: ENI-Lab Genie Prod, 47 Ave Azereix, 65016 Tarbes France

ROTEM, YAACOV, editor, pediatrician; b. Turka, Poland, Nov. 25, 1912; s. Israel and Helena (Wilder) Deutsch; m. Frieda Rotenstreich, Nov. 25, 1938; children: Yael, Anat. MD, U. Bratislava, Czechoslovakia, 1938. Sr. lectr. Hadassah U., Jerusalem, Israel; prof. pediatrics Tel Aviv U.; chief of dept. Hosp. Pardess Katz, Bnei Braque, 1952-53, Sheba Hosp., Ramat Gan, Israel, 1953-88; editor-in-chief Harefuah, Ramat Gan, 1984—; vis. guest prof. Albert Einstein Coll. Medicine, NYU Coll. Medicine, Boston U. Author: Rearing of Children, The Book of the Mother, (booklet) Feed Your Child Properly; co-author: The Road to Life; editor Family Medical Encyclopedia, columns in newspapers; contbr. med. articles and papers to encys. Capt. Israeli Army. Recipient awards Municipality of Tel-Aviv including Prize Sold, 1975, Prize Einhorn, 1983, Title of Hon. Citizen of Tel-Aviv-Yaffo Municipality, 1999. Mem. Internat. Coll. Pediatrics. Home: 19 Bartenura Str, 62-282 Tel Aviv Israel Office: Israeli Med Assn, Jabotinsky Str 35, 52136 Ramat Gan Israel

ROTENBERG, VADIM SEMIONOVICH, psychiatrist, educator; b. Kirov, Russia, Aug. 5, 1941; arrived in Israel, 1990; s. Semion I. and Anna B. (Rogover) R.; m. Nataly Samarovich, Apr. 5, 1995; children: Simona, Anna. MD, 1st Moscow Med. Inst., 1964, PhD, 1970, DSc, 1979. Lic. physician. Unior doctor City Hosp., Moscow, 1964-66; unior scientist 1st Moscow Med. Inst., 1969-78, sr. scientist, 1978-88, head lab., 1988-90; head lab. Abarbanel Mental Health Ctr., Bat-Yam, Israel, 1992—; sr. lectr. Tel-Aviv U., 1995—; vis. prof. Wuppertal U., 1989, 90, Bar-Ilan U., 1993-94, U. Toronto, 1998; head psychology project Zionistic Forum, Israel, 1996—; chair various symposia. Author: The Adaptive Function of Sleep, 1982 (best ann. sci.. publ. 1st Med. Inst. 1984); (with V.V. Arshavsky) Search Activity and Adaptation, 1984 (best ann. sci. publ. 1st Med. Inst. 1985); (with S.M. Bondarenko) Brain, Education, Health, 1989; Poems of 60th, 1996; contbr. numerous articles to profl. jours. Recipient Wolfson grant Tel-Aviv U., 1992; named Internt. Man of Yr., Internat. Biog. Cambridge, 1993-94. Mem. European Soc. Sleep Rsch., N.Y. Acad. Sci. Achievements include development of the search activity concept which integrates behavior, body resistance, REM sleep functions, brain monamines activity and brain laterality. Office: Abarbanel Mental Health Ctr, Keren Kayemet 15, Bat Yam Israel

ROTFELD, ADAM DANIEL, research institute director; b. Przemyslany, Lwow, Poland, Mar. 4, 1938; arrived in Sweden, 1989; s. Leon and Berta Rothfeld; m. Barbara Sikorska, Jan. 15, 1970; 1 child, Alicja. Degree in law and diplomacy, Warsaw U., 1960, postgrad., 1962; PhD in Internat. Law, Jagiellonian U., 1969; habilitation, Inst. Internat. Affairs, Warsaw, 1990. Mem. staff Polish Inst. Internat. Affairs, 1961-89, dep. editor-in-chief monthly, 1963-68, sr. rschr., 1969-77, head European Security Dept., 1978-89; fellow Inst. East-West Security Studies, N.Y., 1984-85; project leader European security Stockholm Internat. Peace Rsch. Inst., 1989-90, dir., leader security project, 1991—; negotiator Helsinki Final Act of Conf. for Security and Coop. in Europe, Geneva, 1973-75, Belgrade, 1977-78, Madrid, 1980-83, Vienna, 1986-88; personal rep. chmn.-in-office Trans-Dniester Conflict Region of the Republic of Moldova, 1992-93; mem. numerous internat. coms.; editor, pub. SIPRI Yearbook on Armaments, Disarmament and Internat. Security, 1992—; mem. adv. bd. UNESCO Studies on Peace and Conflict, European Fellowship Programme, Ctr. for European Securities Studies; co-chmn. ind. working group Future Security Agenda for Europe, 1994-96, Stockholm Agenda for Arms Control, 1999. Author: European Security System In Statu Nascendi, 1990; co-editor: (with Walther Stützle) Germany and Europe in Transition, 1991, (with Armand Clesse) Sources and Areas of Future Possible Crisis in Europe, 1995; editor: Military Security and Confidence Building Measures, 1991, Human Rights-International Obligations of Poland, 1989, Building Security in Europe: CBMs and CSCE, 1986; contbr. articles to profl. jours. Pres. Polish UN Student Assn., 1962-64; sec. gen. Polish UN Assn., 1975-80. Recipient award Polish Acad. Scis., 1988, Polish Inst. Internat. Affairs, 1990. Mem. Internat. Inst. Strategic Studies, Swedish Royal Acad. of War Studies, Sci. Coun. of the Inst. for Peace Rsch. and Security Studies (Hamburg, Germany). Avocations: films, reading, walking. Office: Stockholm Peace Rsch Inst, Signalistgatan 9, S-169 70 Solna Sweden

ROTH, ANDREW, journalist; b. N.Y.C., Apr. 23, 1919; s. Emil and Bertha (Rosenberg) R.; m. Mathilda Anna Friederich, June 12, 1949 (div. 1984); children: Bradley Neil, Susan Teresa Roberta. BSS, CCNY, 1939; MA, Columbia U., 1940; cert. in Japanese, Harvard U., 1941; D (hon.), Open U., Exeter, U.K., 1992. Reader in history CCNY, N.Y.C., 1939-40; rsch. assoc. Inst. Pacific Rels., N.Y.C., 1940; editl. writer The Nation, N.Y.C., 1945-46; fgn. corr. The Nation and other publs., 1946-50; London corr. France Observateur, Paris, 1950-60, Singapore Standard, Singapore, Sekai, Tokyo, 1950-60; polit. corr. Manchester (Eng.) Evening News, 1972-84, New Statesman, London, 1984-96; obituarist The Guardian, 1996—; dir. Parliamentary Profiles, London, 1955—. Author: Dilemma in Japan, 1945, Enoch Powell, 1970, Heath and Heathmen, 1972, Sir Harold Wilson, 1977, Parliamentary Profiles, 1984-87, 88-91, 94—. Lt. (s.g.) USN, 1941-45. Avocations: sketching, jazz dancing. Home and Office: 34 Somali Rd, London NW2 3RL, England

ROTH, EUGENE, lawyer; b. Wilkes-Barre, Pa., June 28, 1935; s. Max and Rae (Klein) R.; m. Constance D. Smulyan, June 16, 1957; children: Joan Roth Kleinman, Steven P., Jeffrey H., Lawrence W. BS, Wilkes U., 1957; LLB, Pa. State U., 1960. Bar: Pa. 1960, U.S. Dist. Ct. (mid. dist.) Pa. 1961. Assoc. Rosenn, Jenkins & Greenwald LLP, Walkes-Barre, 1960-64, ptnr., 1964—; mem. Northeastern Pa. Regional bd. 1st Union Bank; bd. dirs. RCN Corp., Commonwealth Telephone Enterprises, Inc.; chmn. Greater Wilkes-Barre Partnership, Inc., 1991-93. Trustee Wilkes U., 1979—, chmn. 1993-98; chmn. United Way of Wyoming Valley, 1983; chmn. annual campaign Osterhout Free Libr. Campaign, 1999; Northeastern Pa. regional bd. dirs. Geiseinger-Wyoming Valley Hosp. Recipient Disting. Pennsylvanian award Phila. C. of C., 1980, Disting. Citizen award N.E. Pa. Boy Scouts Am., 1998; named Outstanding Vol. Fund Raiser Nat. Soc. Fund Raising Exec., 1993; Cmty. Svc. award B'nai B'rith, 1994. Mem. ABA, Pa. Bar Assn., Luzerne County Law and Libr. Assn., Wilkes-Barre C. of C. (chmn. 1980, vice com. for econ. growth), Wyo. Valley United Jewish Campaign (chmn. 1978 and 1993), B'nai B'rith. Republican. Jewish. Avocations: reading, community svc. Office: Rosenn Jenkins & Greenwald 15 S Franklin St Wilkes Barre PA 18711-0076

ROTH, GARY NEAL, accountant; b. Santa Monica, Calif., Nov. 30, 1961; s. Lewis David and Beverly Sue (Steel) R.; m. Tiffany Anne Lachtman, Aug. 8, 1998. BS in Bus. Adminstrn., Calif. State U., Northridge, 1983. CPA, Calif.; cert. tax profl. Clk., field rep. Equifax Svcs., Inc., Santa Monica, Calif., 1979-86; acctg. mgr., contr. OneCard Systems Corp., L.A., 1983-88;

sr. tax acct., auditor Pannell Kerr Forster, CPAs, L.A., 1989-91; sr. acct., auditor Getz, Krycler & Jakubovits, CPAs, Sherman Oaks, Calif., 1992-96; sr. acct. London & Co, CPAs, L.A., 1996—; cons. U.S. Resolution Trust Corp., Denver, 1991. Auditor Stop Cancer, L.A., 1992-96; acct. Fair-Taste of L.A., Santa Monica, Calif., 1989-90; venue acct. L.A. Summer Olympics, 1984; tax preparer Vol. Income Tax Assn., L.A., 1983. Mem. AICPA, Calif. Soc. CPAs, Nat. Soc. Tax Profls., Zeta Beta Tau. Avocations: exercise enthusiast, musician, international traveler. Home: 19728 Lull St Winnetka CA 91306-2675 Office: London & Co CPAs 11601 Wilshire Blvd Ste 2040 Los Angeles CA 90025-1756

ROTH, GEORG FRANZ, pharmaceutical company executive; b. Linz, Austria, Oct. 24, 1949; s. Franz Anton and Renate Maria Anna Berta (Neuhauser) R.; m. Gertraud Ederer, May 29, 1973; children: Rupert, Florian Michael, Matthias David, Sebastian. JD, Kepler U., Linz, 1975. Examination for wholesale trade with pharms. and venoms. Product mgr. AESCA, Traiskirchen, Austria, 1979-93; mktg. mgr. AESCA, Traiskirchen, 1984-89; internat. mktg. mgr. Essex Chemie, Luzern, Switzerland, 1983-84; mgr. mktg. and distbn. Schering, Vienna, Austria, 1989-90; gen. mgr. Serono Austria, Vienna, 1990-98; CEO, mng. dir. Roth Pharma, Hinterbruhl, Austria, 1998—. Office: Roth Pharma, Wagnerstr 29, A2371 Hinterbruhl Austria

ROTH, HANS RUDOLF, commercial and industrial ventures executive, consultant; b. Aarau, Switzerland, May 25, 1927; Jules Oswald and Lena (Haessig) R.; m. Mercy Knadua Kwafo, Jan. 5, 1957; children: Henry Frederik, Peter Jules, William Arthur, Marie-Louise. Diploma of commerce, Comml. Coll., Schoenenwerd, Switzerland, 1946. Clk. Ernst Z. Schneeberg, Winterthur, Switzerland, 1947-48; comml. asst. Swiss African Trading Co. Ltd., Kumasi, Ghana, 1948-52, br. mgr., 1952-56; gen. mgr. Swiss African Trading Co. Ltd., Kumasi, Accra, Ghana, 1957-66; mng. dir. Devag Group of Cos., Accra, Ghana, 1966-84, chmn., 1985—; chmn. bd. Ghana Pioneer Alumnium Factory Ltd., Tema, 1980-99, Indsl. Containers Ltd., Tema, 1981—; dir. Aluworks Ltd., Tema. Hon. Consul-Gen. Pres. Republic of Finland, 1978-98; dean Consular Corps, Ghana, 1983-98. Fellow Inst. Dirs. (London), Ghana Inst. Mgmt. (nat. coun. 1979); mem. Ghana Nat. C. of C. (ctrl. exec. 1965-70, v.p. 1965-70). Presbyterian. Avocations: hunting, fishing, travel. Home: Ho Pampaso, Onyaase-Kitase, Akuapem Ghana Office: Devag Ltd,, PO Box m 262,, Ministry Post Office,, Accra, Ghana

ROTH, HAROLD, architect; b. St. Louis, June 30, 1934; s. Samuel and Dorothy (Yawitz) R.; m. Dvora Feigon, Dec. 6, 1959; children: Elizabeth, David. AB, Washington U., 1956; MArch, Yale U., 1957. Designer Warner Burns Toan & Lunde, N.Y.C., 1957; sr. designer Eero Saarinen & Assocs., Roche Dinkeloo & Assocs., Hamden, Conn., 1959-65; ptnr. Harold Roth - Edward Saad, Hamden, Conn., 1965-72; sr. ptnr. Roth & Moore Architects, New Haven, 1973—; critic archtl. design Yale U. Sch. Architecture, New Haven, 1964-98; profl. advisor Western European Arch. Found.; pres., trustee Perspecta, Yale Archtl. Jour. Trustee Long Wharf Theatre, New Haven, 1972-98, Conn. Trust for Hist. Preservation, 1983-90; pres. bd. trustees Conn. Architecture Found., 1990-93; bd. govs. Bldg. Stone Inst., 1999—; bd. regents Am. Arch. Found., 1999—; profl. advisor Western European Architecture Found., 2000—. Officer U.S. Army, 1957-59, Korea. Recipient Design award Nat. Coun. Religious Arch., 1970, 96, Design award New Haven Preservation Trust, 1978, 88, Tucker award Bldg. Stone Inst., 1983, 88, Honor award Concrete Reinforcing Steel Inst., 1983, Design award Portland Cement Assn., 1984, Design award Archtl. Record, 1970, 80, Design award AIA/ALA, 1983, Faculty Design award Assn. Collegiate Schs. of Arch., 1988, Healthcare Facilities Design award Boston Soc. Archs., 1992; fellow Pierson Coll., Yale U., 1978—. Fellow AIA (chmn. nat. com. on design 1990, bd. dirs. 1992-94, sec. Coll. of Fellows 1998-99, vice-chancellor 2000, Design award Conn. 1974, 78, 83, 86, 88, 90, 93, 97, 98, New Eng., 1968, 84, 92, Design award of merit 2000). Home: 37 Autumn St New Haven CT 06511-2220 Office: Roth & Moore Architects 65 Audubon St New Haven CT 06510-1205

ROTH, HERMANN JOSEF, secondary school administrator; b. Montabaur, Germany, Jan. 2, 1938; s. Heinrich and Gertrud Appolonia (Ebert) R. Grad., Theol. Inst., Heiligenkreuz, Austria, 1963; M in Natural Sci., U. Cologne, Germany, 1970; PhD in Natural Sci., U. Nijmegen, The Netherlands, 1990. Clergyman Cistercian-Abbey, Marienstatt, Germany, 1963-70; chaplain Archbishopric, Cologne, 1970—; master Fed. State Nordrhein-Westfalen, Cologne, 1971—, vice-headmaster, 1995—; coord. postgrad. studies, govtl. dist., Cologne, 1991; mem. adv. bd. Düsseldorf land govt., 1993-99. Editor Cistercienser-Chronik, 1973-96, Natur-und Landschaftskunde, 1995; author books. Recipient Albert Steeger stipendium, Rheinland, 1979, Umweltschutzmedaille, Germany, 1985, Bruno H. Schubert prize, Frankfurt, 1988, Rheinlandtaler, Cologne, 1999. Mem. Landesgemeinschaft Naturschutz und Umwelt Nordrhein-Westfalen (chmn. 1993-2000), Dt. Gesellschaft Geschichte Theorie Biologie, Ökoglobal (cofounder 1992). Avocations: photography, art history. Home: Postfach 420606, 50900 Cologne NRhnWfln, Germany Office: Städtisches Gymnasium, Kantstr 3, 51103 Cologne NRhnWfln, Germany

ROTH, JOHN ANDREW, internet communications executive; b. Calgary, Alta., Can., Oct. 6, 1942; s. Henry and Sophia (Brix) R.; m. Margaret Anne Roth, 1968. BE, McGill U., 1964, M Engring, 1966. Exec. v.p. prodn. line mgmt. No. Telecom Ltd., Mississaugai, Ont., Can.; ceo Nortel Networks; mem. Nat. Adv. Bd. Sci. and Tech. Mem. Assn. Profl. Engrs. Ont. Office: Nortel Networks Corp, 8200 Dixie Rd Ste 100, Brampton, ON Canada L6T 5P6

ROTH, J(OHN) REECE, electrical engineer, educator, researcher-inventor; b. Washington, Pa., Sept. 19, 1937; s. John Meyer and Ruth Evangeline (Iams) R.; m. Helen Marie DeCrane, Jan. 14, 1972; children: Nancy Ann, John Alexander. S.B. in Physics, MIT, 1959; Ph.D., Cornell U., 1963. Engrng. aide Aerojet-Gen. Corp., Azusa, Calif., 1957, 58; aerospace engr. N.Am. Aviation, Canoga Park, Calif., 1959; prin. investigator NASA Lewis Research Ctr., Cleve., 1963-78; prof. elec. engring. U. Tenn., Knoxville, 1978-99, Weston Fulton prof. elec. engring., 1999—; hon. prof. U. Electronic Sci. and Tech. of China, Chengdu, 1992—; prin. investigator Office Naval Rsch., Washington, 1980-89, Air Force Office Sci. Rsch., Washington, 1981-95, Army Rsch. Office, 1988-93, NASA Langley Rsch. Ctr., Hampton, Va., 1995-98, March Instruments, Inc., Concord, Calif., 1996-98; cons. TVA, Chattanooga, 1982-84, BDM Corp., 1987-88, Tenn. Eastman, 1989-90, March Instruments, 1995-98; Procter & Gamble, 1996; Internat. Eco Scis., 1997-98; Environ. Elements Corp., 1997-2000, Tetra Pak Suisse, 1998—; mem. NAS-NRC Com. on Aneutronic Fusion, 1986-87; spkr. at profl. meetings. Author: Industrial Plasma Engineering, Introduction to Fusion Energy; contbr. articles to profl. jours; 7 patents since 1991. Sloan scholar, 1955-59; Ford fellow, 1961-62; recipient B. Otto and Katherine Wheeley award for Excellence in Tech. Transfer, 1999. Fellow IEEE, AIAA (assoc.); mem. Am. Phys. Soc., Am. Nuclear Soc. (exec. com. No. Ohio sect. 1975-78), Nuclear and Plasma Scis. Soc., Am. Soc. Engring. Edn., Knoxville Art Gallery, East Tenn. Soc. of Archaeol. Inst. Am., Sigma Xi (pres. U. Tenn. Knoxville chpt. 1985-86). Club: U. Tenn. U. Club (Knoxville). Home: 12359 N Fox Den Dr Knoxville TN 37922-3755 Office: U Tenn Dept Elec Engring 409 Ferris Hall Knoxville TN 37996-0001

ROTH, KENNETH, human rights advocate; b. Elmhurst, Ill., Sept. 23, 1955; s. Walter and Muriel (Teitell) R.; m. Nina Brodsky, May 29, 1983; children: Lisa, Emma. BA magna cum laude, Brown U., 1977; JD, Yale U., 1980. Bar: N.Y. 1981. Law clk. to Judge Edward Weinfeld U.S. Dist. Ct. for So. Dist. N.Y., N.Y.C., 1980-81; assoc. Paul, Weiss, Rifkind, Wharton & Garrison, N.Y.C., 1981-83; from asst. U.S. atty. to chief appellate atty. criminal div. U.S. Atty.'s Office for So. Dist. N.Y., N.Y.C., 1983-87; assoc. counsel Office Ind. Counsel for Iran/Contra, Washington, 1987; dep. dir. Human Rights Watch, N.Y.C., 1987-93, exec. dir., 1993—. Editor, author numerous reports on human rights worldwide; contbr. articles to newspapers and mags. Mem. Assn. Bar City N.Y., Coun. Fgn. Rels. Office: Human Rights Watch 350 5th Ave Fl 34 New York NY 10118-3499

ROTH, LANE, communications educator; b. N.Y.C., Apr. 10, 1943. BA, NYU, 1964; MA, Fla. State U., 1974, PhD Mass Comm., 1976. Camera operator Sta. WFSU-TV, Tallahassee, 1973-74; broadcast engr., producer-creator, writer, performer Sta. WFSU-FM, Tallahassee, 1974-76; co-host Sta. WNIN-TV, Evansville, Ind., 1976-77; asst. prof. radio-TV-film U. Evansville, 1976-78; asst. prof. comm. Lamar U., Beaumont, Tex., 1978-82, assoc. prof., 1982—; Bd. dirs. Mental Health Assn. of Jefferson County, pres., 1997, 98; writer, performer fund-raising promos, Sta. KVLU-FM, Beaumont, 1995—. Author: Film Semiotics, Metz, and Leone's Trilogy, 1983; contbr. articles to profl. mags., jours.; contbr. to acad. books. Bd. dirs. Mental Health Assoc. of Jefferson Co., 1993—. Recipient Regents Merit award for excellence in tchg., 1980, Mental Health Assn. award for dedicated leadership, 1999. Mem. Internat. Assn. for the Fantastic in the Arts, World Comm. Assn., Lehmann-Grossbahn Club of Am. Roman Catholic. Avocations: Jungian psychology, analysis of popular film and TV, singer-impressionist-songwriter. Office: Lamar U Dept Communications Beaumont TX 77710

ROTH, OLIVER RALPH, radiologist; b. Cumberland, Md., Nov. 30, 1921; s. DeCoursey Andrew and Mabel (Lathrum) R.; BS, Frostburg (Md.) State Coll., 1942, DSc (hon.), 1980; MD, U. Md., 1950; m. Virginia McBride, June 2, 1943; 1 child, Tiija. Diplomate Am. Bd. Radiology. Resident, Johns Hopkins Hosp., Balt., 1954-57; cancer research fellow Middlesex Hosp., London, 1957-58; founder dept. radiation oncology Presbyn. Hosp., Charlotte, N.C., 1958-62; attending radiologist King's Daus. Hosp., Ashland, Ky., 1962-80; radiologist Our Lady of Bellefonte Hosp., 1981-86; mem. faculty Sch. of Allied Health Shawnee State U., Portsmouth, Ohio, 1986-90; prof. radiology Sch. Medicine Marshall U., Huntington, W.Va., 1990—; mem. adv. com. Ky. Cancer Commn., 1978; bd. dirs. Boyd County chpt. Am. Cancer Soc., 1978. With USN, 1942-45. Commanded to Buckingham Palace, June 17, 1958; recipient Disting. Alumni award Frostburg State U., 1979. Mem. AMA, Am. Coll. Radiology, Radiol. Soc. N.Am., Am. Radium Soc., Royal Faculty Radiology, Brit. Inst. Radiology. Democrat. Lutheran. Club: Shriners (Cumberland, Md.). Book reviewer Radiology, 1954-55. Home: 2912 Cogan St Ashland KY 41102-5230

ROTH, RICHARD HARRISON, petrochemical inspection company executive; b. Washington, July 8, 1955; s. Donald Davis and June Martha (Pleacher) R.; m. Julia Ann Hamel, Dec. 16, 1978 (div. Oct. 1990); 1 child, Martha Marie; m. Holly Lee Hilbrink, May 18, 1991 (div. June 1997); 1 child, Carina Michelle; m. Paula Ann Toepfer, Aug. 22, 1998; 1 step-child, Jenna Michelle. BS in Biology, U. N.C., 1977. Cert. grade II wastewater treatment plant operator, N.C. Chemist, supr. SGS Control Svcs. Inc., Wilmington, N.C., 1981-85; br., lab. mgr. SGS Control Svcs. Inc., Savannah, Ga., 1990—; chemist, wastewater plant operator Republic Refining, Wilmington, 1985-86; chemist Oxford Lab., Wilmington, 1986-88, 89-90; rsch. asst. Hazleton Labs. Am., Inc., Vienna, Va., 1988-89. Author: Manual of Operations for ATC Petroleum Refinery, 1979, Crude Assay Handbook, 1979. Mem. Propeller Club of U.S., Savannah Kennel Club (pres. 1994-98). Republican. Lutheran. Achievements include implementation of ISO 9002 quality program laboratory. Office: SGS Control Svcs Inc PO Box 1504 Savannah GA 31402-1504

ROTH, SOL, rabbi; b. Rzeszow, Poland, Mar. 8, 1927; came to U.S., 1934, naturalized, 1939; s. Joseph and Miriam (Lamm) R.; m. Debra H. Stitskin, Nov. 26, 1957; children: Steven, Michael (dec.), Sharon. B.A., Yeshiva U., 1948, D.D. (hon.), 1977; M.A., Columbia U., 1953, Ph.D., 1966; Rabbi, Yeshiva U. Theol. Sem., 1950; D in Divinity (hon.), Yeshiva U., 1977. Ordained rabbi Orthodox Jewish Congregations, 1950; pres. Rabbinical Council Am., 1980-82, N.Y. Bd. Rabbis, 1976-79; chmn. Israel Commn. Rabbinical Council Am., 1976-78; dean Chaplaincy Sch., N.Y. Bd. Rabbis, 1976-79; Samson R. Hirsch prof. dept. philosophy Yeshiva U., N.Y.C.; rabbi Jewish Ctr. Atlantic Beach, N.Y., 1956-86; Fifth Ave Synagogue, 1986—; pres. Religious Zionists Am., 1991-94. Author: Science and Religion, 1967, The Jewish Idea of Community, 1977, Halakhah and Politics: The Jewish Idea of a State, 1988 (Samuel Belkin Meml. Lit. award 1989), The Jewish Idea of Culture, 1997; editor: Morasha. Recipient award Synagogue Adv. Council United Jewish Appeal, 1975; named Rabbi Dr. Sol Roth Chair in Talmud and Contemporary Halakha established at Yeshiva U., 1989. Home: 30 E 62nd St New York NY 10021-8026 Office: Yeshiva U Dept Philosophy 500 W 185th St Dept New York NY 10033-3299

ROTH, TOBY, former congressman, political consultant; b. Strasburg, N.D., Oct. 10, 1938; s. Kasper and Julia (Roehrich) R.; m. Barbara Fischer, Nov. 28, 1964; children: Toby Jr., Vicky, Barbie. BA, Marquette U., 1961. Mem. 96th-104th Congresses from 8th Wis. dist., Washington, D.C., 1979-97; ptnr. Flippo, Roth & Assocs., Washington, D.C., 1997—; pres. Roth Group, Washington, 1997—; mem. banking, fin., urban affairs com., subcoms. fin. instns. and consumer credit, internat. rels. com., chmn. econ. policy, trade coms., Africa. 1st lt. USAR, 1962-69. Named Wis. Legislator of Yr. Wis. Towns Assn., 1978. Mem. VFW (hon.), Optimists (hon.), Kiwanis (hon.). Republican. *

ROTHBARD, SHMUEL, geneticist; b. Krakow, Poland, Sept. 1, 1933; arrived in Israel, 1947; s. Moshe and Chava (Zucker) R.; m. Frida Studen, July 16, 1954; children: Zahara, Hamutal, Avi-Moshe. BEd, Dranim Coll., 1958; MSc, Tel Aviv U., 1982, PhD, 1990. Mgr. Fish Breeding Ctr., Gan Shmuel, Israel, 1970-74; trainee SISFFA, Tamano, Japan, 1974-76; rsch. scientist Inst. Agrl. Rsch. Orgn., Dor, Israel, 1976-81, 87-89; mgr. Fish Breeding Ctr., Gan Shmuel, 1981-87; dir. YAFIT (R&D) Lab., Gan Shmuel, 1989—; cons. Fish Devel. Corp., South Africa, 1978, G.T.Z., Costa Rica, 1988; bd. dirs. Yozmoth Granot Complex; fellow Aquaculture Steering Com., Negev, Israel, 1990-94. Co-author: Broodstock Management and Egg and Larval Quality, 1995, The Completely Illustrated Guide to KOI, 1996, KOI Breeding, 1997; contbr. articles to profl. jours. Sgt. maj. Israel Def. Army, 1951-53. Recipient Prize for Agrl. Achievement Menashe Mcpl., 1973; Ramy Levin grant Tel Aviv U., 1982, David Benn Gorion grant Fedn. of Labor, 1988. Mem. Israel Aquaculture Soc., Network of Tropical Aquaculture Scientists, Israel Zool. Soc. Avocations: music, readings, gardening, travel. Office: YAFIT R&D Lab, Fish Breeding Ctr, 38810 Gan Shmuel Israel

ROTHBERG, GLENDA FAY MORRIS, lawyer; b. Rome, Ga., Aug. 7, 1946; d. Glenn Howell and Fay (Givens) Morris; m. Gerald Rothberg, June 18, 1970 (div. Jan. 1989); children: Laura, Abigail. AB, Randolph-Macon Woman's Coll., 1968; JD, Benjamin Cardozo Law Sch., 1985. Bar: N.Y. 1986, U.S. Dist. Ct. (so. and ea. dists.) N.Y. 1987, U.S. Supreme Ct. 1990. Law guardian juvenile rights divsn. Legal Aid Soc., N.Y.C., 1988-91; pvt. practice N.Y.C., 1992—; faculty dir. Inst. for not-for-profit Mgmt. Columbia Bus. Sch., N.Y.C., 1994-98. Vol. Manhattan Mediation Ctr., N.Y.C., 1996-99. Fellow Am. Bar Found.; mem. ABA, Assn. of Bar of City of N.Y. (com. chair 1996-99, mem. coun. on children 1999—). Office: 271 Madison Ave New York NY 10016-1001

ROTHCHILD, DONALD SYLVESTER, political science educator; b. N.Y.C., Aug. 11, 1928; s. Sylvester Edward and Alice Levy Rothchild; m. Edith White, Apr. 23, 1954; children: Derek Edward, Maynard White. BA with high honors, Kenyon Coll., 1949; MA, U. Calif., Berkeley, 1954; PhD, Johns Hopkins U., 1958. From instr. to assoc. prof. Colby Coll., Waterville, Maine, 1957-65; prof. U. Calif., Davis, 1965—, faculty rsch. lectr., 1996-97; vis. Fulbright lectr. Makerere U., Kampala, Uganda, 1962-64; sr. lectr. U. Nairobi, Kenya, 1966-67; vis. Ford prof. U. Zambia, Lusaka, 1970-71; vis. prof. U. Ghana, Legon, 1975-77, 85; professorial lectr. Johns Hopkins U., Washington, 1993, 95; internat. adv. bd. mem. Internat. Negotiation, 1995—; vis. scholar Brookings Instn., 1992-93, Ctr. for Internat. Security and Cooperation, Stanford U., 1998-99. Author: Racial Bargaining in Independent Kenya, 1973, Managing Ethnic Conflict in Africa, 1997; coauthor: Sovereignty as Responsibility, 1996; co-editor: The International Spread of Ethnic Conflict, 1998; editor Jour. Nationalism and Ethnic Politics, 1994—; contbr. articles to profl. jours. Internat. observer mission Carter Ctr., Ghana, 1992; rapporteur Friedrich Ebert Found., Kampala, Uganda, 1993; Hubert H. Humphrey spkr. Alumni Assn. Conf., Accra, Ghana, 1994. Sgt. U.S. Army, 1950-52. Disting. Am. Specialist grantee USIA, Thika, Kenya, 1993; Peace fellow U.S. Inst. Peace, Washington, 1994-95. Mem. Internat. Polit. Sci. Assn. (pres. rsch. com. 1988-94), Am. Polit. Sci. Assn., African Studies Assn. Democrat. Avocations: opera, theatre, ballet. E-mail: dsrothchild@ucdavis.edu. Home: 208 W 8th St Davis CA 95616-3637 Office: Univ Calif Dept Polit Sci 1 Shields Ave Davis CA 95616-5271

ROTHENBERG, ELLIOT CALVIN, lawyer, writer; b. Mpls., Nov. 12, 1939; s. Sam S. and Claire Sylvia (Feller) R.; m. Sally Smalying; children: Sarah, Rebecca, Sam. BA summa cum laude, U. Minn., 1961; JD, Harvard U. (Fulbright fellow), 1964. Bar: Minn. 1966, U.S. Dist. Ct. Minn. 1966, D.C. 1968, U.S. Supreme Ct. 1972, N.Y. 1974, U.S. Ct. Appeals (2d cir.) 1974, U.S. Ct. Appeals (8th cir.) 1975. Assoc. project dir. Brookings Inst., Washington, 1966-67; fgn. svc. officer, legal advisor U.S. Dept. State, Washington, 1968-73; Am. Embassy, Saigon; U.S. Mission to the UN; nat. law dir. Anti-Defamation League, N.Y.C., 1973-74; legal dir. Minn. Pub. Interest Rsch. Group, Mpls., 1974-77; pvt. practice law Mpls., 1977—; adj. prof. William Mitchell Coll. Law, St. Paul, 1983—; faculty mem. several nat. comm. law and First Amendment seminars. Author: (with Zelman Cowen) Sir John Latham and Other Papers, 1965, The Taming of the Press: Cohen v. Cowles Media Co., 1999, The Taming of the Press, 1999; contbr. articles to profl. and scholarly jours. and books, newspapers, popular mags. State bd. dirs. YMCA Youth in Govt. Program, 1981-84; v.p. Twin Cities chpt. Am. Jewish Com., 1980-84; mem. Minn. Ho. of Reps., 1978-82, asst. floor leader (whip), 1981-82; pres., dir. North Star Legal Found., 1983—; legal affairs editor Pub. Rsch. Syndicated, 1986—; briefs and oral arguments published in full Landmark Briefs and Arguments of the Supreme Ct. of the U.S., Vol. 200, 1992; mem. citizens adv. com. Voyageurs Nat. Pk., 1979-81. Recipient Legis. Evaluation Assembly Legis. Excellence award, 1980, Vietnam Civilian Svc. medal U.S. Dept. State, 1970, North Star award U. Minn., 1961; Fulbright fellow, 1964-65. Mem. ABA, Minn. Bar Assn., Harvard Law Sch. Assn., Am. Legion, Mensa, Phi Beta Kappa. Jewish. Home and Office: 3901 W 25th St Saint Louis Park MN 55416-3803

ROTHENBERGER, ARIBERT, psychiatrist; b. Woerrstadt, Germany, Nov. 21, 1944; s. Karl and Margarethe (Dechent) R.; m. Lilo Werner, June 2, 1978; children: Lillian Geza, Liane Tessa. MD, U. Mainz, 1972. Med. diplomate in neurology, psychiatry, child and adolescent psychiatry, psychotherapy. Asst. U. Ulm, Germany, 1973-80, U. Essen, Germany, 1980-83, Ctr. Inst. Mental Health, Mannheim, Germany, 1983-85; privatdozent Ctr. Inst. Mental Health, Mannheim, 1985-87, prof., 1987-94; prof., chair child and adolescent psychiatry U. Göttingen, 1994—, dir. dept., 1994—; del. European Union of Med. Specialists, Brussels, 1993—. Author/editor: Brain and Behavior in Child Psychiatry, 1990; author: Children Developing Tics, 1991, EEG and Evoked Potentials, 1987, translated Japanese, 1990; coauthor: Child Psychiatry, 2000, On the Traces of Autism, 2000, Frontal Lobesand Course of Psychiatric Disorders, 2000, My Child Has Not Only Tics and Compulsions, 2000; editor: Event-Related Potentials in Children, 1982, Affective Psychoses, 1992, Autism, 2000, Child Psychiatry, 2000, Frontal Lobes and Course of Psychiatric Disturbances, 2000; co-editor: Obsessive-Compulsive Disorders, 2000; adv./editl. bd. various jours. Cofounder Tourette Assn., Germany, 1993, OCD Assn., Germany, 1995, pres., 1999—. Recipient Hermann Emminghaus prize Tropon, Cologne, Germany, 1986. Achievements include research in TS, ADHD, OCD, biological psychiatry. Avocations: music, sports, literature, art, history. Office: Univ Gottingen, Von Siebold Str 5, 37075 Göttingen Germany

ROTHENBERGER, JACK RENNINGER, clergyman; b. Boyertown, Pa., Oct. 4, 1930; s. Stuart Henry and Beulah (Renninger) R.; m. Jean Delores Schultz, Sept. 8, 1951; children: Susan Marie, Bruce Wayne. BS, Juniata Coll., 1952; MDiv, Hartford Theol. Sem., 1955; STM, Temple U., 1962; D Ministry, Lancaster Theol. Sem., 1977. Ordained to ministry Schwenkfelder Ch., 1955. Pastor Palm and Lansdale (Pa.) Schwenkfelder Ch., 1955-63, 65-66; stated supply, interim pastor Pa. United Ch. of Christ, 1963-69; chaplain, tchr., coach, dir. admissions Perkiomen Sch., Pennsburg, Pa., 1955-56, 62-67, asst. headmaster, headmaster, coach football backfield, basketball, 1967-69; min. Christian edn. Cen. Schwenkfelder Ch., Worcester, Pa., 1969-74, sr. min., 1974-95; ret., 1995; interim supply worker Wentz United Ch. of Christ, Worcester, Pa., 1997-99, interim pastor, 1997-99; pres. World Christian Endeavor, 1994—, Internat. Christian Endeavor, Columbus, Ohio, 1983-87; v.p. World Christian Endeavor, 1990-94; mem. cabinet and bd. Pa. Coun. Chs., 1957—, sec., 1993-97; mem. Pa. Conf. Interch. Coop.; mem. Schwenckfelder Mission Bd., 1957—, Schwenckfelder Bd. Pubs., 1957—, Schwenckfelder Libr. Bd., 1957—, Schwenckfeldian in Exile Soc., 1955—; chmn. expansion com. Schwenckfelder Libr., also others. Author: Casper Schwenckfeld and the Ecumenical Ideal, 1962; editor The Schwenkfeldian mag., 1964-87; contbr. articles to profl. jours. First v.p. Schwenckfeld Manor, Lansdale, 1973-97, pres., 1997—; v.p. Meadowood Total Care Retirement Community, Worcester, Pa., 1983-98. Mem. No. Pa. Assn. United Ch. of Christ Ministerium, No. Pa. Ministerium, Methacton Area Ministerium, Montgomery County Sunday Sch. Assn. (past pres.), also others. Republican. Home: Spruce Run # 73 Meadowood at Worcester Lansdale PA 19446

ROTHENHAUSLER, HANS-BERND MATTHAUS, psychiatrist; b. Wangen, Germany, Mar. 2, 1967; s. Franz X. and Hilda A. (Karrer) R. MD, U. Ulm, Germany, 1991, Tech. U. Munchen, Germany, 1995. Resident Burger Hosp., Stuttgart, Germany, 1995, Ludwig-Maximilians u., Munchen, Germany, 1995—; cons. in field. Contbr. articles to profl. jours. 1st lt. German Mil., 1986-88. Mem. AGNP, DGNP. Office: Psychiat Cons-Liaison Svc, Konsiliardienst Grosshadern, D-80336 Munchen Germany

ROTHERMEL, DOROTHY G. NOAK, retired secondary education educator; b. Carmine, Tex., Dec. 20, 1929; d. Herbert Paul and Clara M. (Keng) Noak; m. Thomas Hugh Rothermel, Dec. 28, 1947; children: Connie R. Bird, Pamela R. Guthrie. Student, Blinn Jr. Coll., Brenham, Tex., 1947, Southwest Tex. State U., 1949, 50; BS, U. Houston, 1960. Cert. tchr. vocat. home econs., Tex. 6th grade tchr. Pearland (Tex.) Ind. Sch. Dist., 1961-63; home econs. h.s. tchr. Pasadena (Tex.) Ind. Sch. Dist., 1963-87, chmn. vocat. homemaking dept., 1963-87; ret., 1987; supr. student tchrs., Univ. Houston. Contbr. genealogy articles to German-Texan Heritage Soc. Jour., 1980—. Sec. ch. coun., Martin Luther Luth. Ch., 1994-97; nom. com., Louise Giddings Ret. Rchrs., 1999-00, history book com., area coord., rschr., photographer Fayette Co., Fayette County Tex. Heritage History books, 2 vols. Mem. VFW Aux. (pres. LaGrange, Tex., chpt., 1959), Washington County Geneaol. Soc., Tex. Wendish Heritage Soc. Avocations: geneal. rsch., sewing, computers. Home: 2504 Brookbend Dr Brenham TX 77833-9245

ROTHERMEL, JOAN ASHLEY, artist; b. Winchester, Mass., Mar. 10, 1930; d. Mark Braden Ashley and Anne Jorgenson; m. Harold Christian Rothermel, Dec. 30, 1950; children: Lynn Schoenfield, Lawrence. BFA, Miami U., Oxford, Ohio, 1951, MEd in Art, 1970. Art tchr. Middletown (Ohio) Fine Arts Ctr., 1971-77; sole juror nat. and state watercolor exhbns., including Ohio Watercolor Soc., Cen. Ohio Watercolor Soc., Capital U., Columbus, Beaufort (S.C.) Art Assn., S.C. Watercolor Soc., Toledo Artists Club, 1982-99; instr. watercolor workshops nat. and state exhbns., including Firelands Area Art League, Norwalk, Ohio, Hilton Head Island Workshops, S.C., Wyoming Valley Art League, Wilkes-Barre, Pa., Idaho Watercolor Soc., Boise, St. Louis Artists' Guild, Hawaii Watercolor Soc., Honolulu, 1982—. One-person shows include Middletown, Sandusky, Boston Mills Art Festivals, Peninsula, Ohio; exhibited in group shows Am. Watercolor Soc., Nat. Watercolor Soc., Allied Artists of Am., Nat. Acad. Design, Rocky Mountain Nat. Watermedia Exhbn., Knickerbocker Artists, Nat. Arts Club, Ohio Watercolor Soc., San Diego Watercolor Soc., Ga. Watercolor Soc.; represented in corp. collections and galleries Owens-Ill. Corp., Toledo, Soc. Bank, Sandusky, Oglesby-Barnitz Bank, Middletown, 1st Nat. Bank, Middletown, Cen. Bank, Cleve., Livingstine Taylor Gallery, Sandusky; works featured in books Painting the Spirit of Nature, 1984, Exploring Color, 1985, The Creative Artist, 1990, others, also mags., including Am. Artist, The Artist's Mag. Mem. Am. Watercolor So. (treas. 1986—, Dolphin fellow, Gold medal honor, Bronze medal, 8 other awards 1983-99), Nat. Watercolor Soc., Allied Artists of Am., Midwest Watercolor Soc., Ohio Watercolor Soc., Knickerbocker Artists, Salmagundi Club. E-mail: johal@kellnet.com. Home: 221 46th St Sandusky OH 44870-4894

ROTH-MAIER, DORA, animal nutrition science educator, researcher; b. Stuttgart, Germany, Aug. 8, 1940; d. Martin and Dora (Zerrweck) Maier; m. Franz X. Roth, Dec. 23, 1969; 1 child, Barbara. Diploma in agrl. engring., Tech. U. Munich, 1963, PhD in Agr., 1966. Asst. Inst. Nutrition Physiology, Munich, 1963-73, lectr., 1963-73; prof. animal nutrition and feed sci. Tech. U. Munich, 1978—. Mem. editl. bd. Jour. Animal Physiology and Animal Nutrition, 1996, Annales de Zootechnie, 1996. Recipient Hen-

neberg-Lehmann-Forder prize, U. Göttingen, Germany, 1976, Internat. Roche Rsch. prize for animal nutrition, Swiss Fed. Inst. Tech., Zürich, 1994. Mem. Assn. Nutrition Physiology. Office: Tech U MunichInst of Nutritional Scis, Hochfeldweg 6 Divsn Animal Nutrition, D-85350 Freising Germany

ROTHMAN, ADAM ALAN, financial consultant; b. Bklyn., Apr. 5, 1960; s. Bernard and Barbara (Schaeffer) R.; children: Seth Daniel, Joshua David. BBA, Am. U., 1982. Acct. exec. Invention Mktg. Co., Washington, 1982-84; sales assoc. Michael Franblau Assoc., Hartsdale, N.Y., 1984-89; exec. v.p. Adam A. Rothman and Assocs., New Rochelle, N.Y., 1989-96; ptnr. Singer Nelson Charlmens, 1996—. Author: Wealth Accumulation Strategy for Educators, 1987, Estate Planning for the 21st Century, 1999, How Does the IRA Get Inherited?, 2000, How Does the Defective Insurance Trust Work, 2000; contbg. editor: The Realtor. Chmn. devel. com. The Guidance Ctr. Mem. Interstate Alliance Fin. Planners (founding mem.). Democrat. Jewish. Office: 1086 Teaneck Rd Teaneck NJ 07666-4838

ROTHMAN, BERNARD, lawyer; b. N.Y.C., Aug. 11, 1932; s. Harry and Rebecca (Fritz) R.; m. Barbara Joan Schaeffer, Aug. 1953; children: Brian, Adam, Helene. BA cum laude, CCNY, 1953; JD, NYU, 1959. Bar: N.Y. 1959, U.S. Dist. Ct. (ea. and so. dists.) N.Y. 1962, U.S. Ct. Appeals (2d cir.) 1965, U.S. Supreme Ct. 1966, U.S. Tax Ct. 1971. Assoc. Held, Telchin & Held, 1961-62; asst. U.S. atty. Dept. Justice, 1962-66; assoc. Edward Gettinger & Peter Gettinger, 1966-68; ptnr. Schwartz, Rothman & Abrams, P.C., 1968-78, Ferster, Bruckman, Wohl, Most & Rothman, LLP, N.Y.C., 1978-98, Law Offices of Bernard Rothman, N.Y.C., 1999—; acting judge Village of Larchmont, 1982-88, dep. Village atty., 1974-81, former arbitrator Civil Ct., N.Y.C., family disputes panel Am. Arbitration Assn.; guest lectr. domestic rels. and family law on radio and TV, also numerous legal and mental health orgns. Author: Loving and Leaving-Winning at the Business of Divorce, 1991; co-author: Family Law Syracuse Law Rev. of N.Y. Law, 1992, Leaving Home, Family Law Review, 1987; contbr. articles to profl. jours. Mem. exec. bd., past v.p. Westcherster Putnam coun. Boy Scouts Am., 1975—; past mem. nat. coun., 1977-81; mem. adv. com. N.Y. State PEACE, 1994—; pres. Congregation B'nai Israel, 1961-63, B'nai Brith, Larchmont chpt., 1981-83. Recipient Silver Beaver award Boy Scouts Am., Wood Badge award. Fellow Am. Acad. Matrimonial Lawyers (bd. govs. N.Y. chpt. 1986-87, 91-93), Interdisciplinary Forum on Mental Health and Family Law (co-chair 1986-97); mem. ABA (family law sect.), N.Y. State Bar Assn. (exec. com. family law sect. 1982—, co-chmn. com. on mediation and arbitration 1982-88, 93—, com. on legis. 1978-88, com. on child custody 1985-88, com. alt. dispute resolution), Assn. of Bar of City of N.Y. (women in the cts. com. 1996-99), N.Y. State Magistrate Assn., Westchester Magistrate Assn., N.Y. Rd. Runners Club, Limousine & Track Club. Democrat. Address: Law Offices of Bernard Rothman 750 3rd Ave Fl 29 New York NY 10017-2703

ROTHMAN, JOEL HARRY, medical educator, research scientist; b. Walnut Creek, Calif., July 21, 1956; s. Albert and Jeannette Rothman; m. Molly Catherine Baird, June 15, 1980. BS, U. Calif., Davis, 1978; PhD, U. Oreg., 1988; postdoctoral fellow, Med. Rsch. Coun., Cambridge, 1988-91. Asst. prof. U. Calif., Santa Barbara, 1996-97, U. Wis., Madison, 1991-96; grad. rschr. U. Oreg., Eugene, 1983-88; winemaker and prodn. dir. Buena Vista Winery, Sonoma, Calif., 1981-83; chemist Souverain Cellars, Geyserville, Calif., 1979-81; grad. rschr. U. Calif., San Francisco, 1978-79; assoc. prof. U. Calif., Santa Barbara, 1997—; vis. scientist Med. Rsch. Coun. Lab. of Molecular Biology, Cambridge, U.K., 1988-91; organizer, instr. Woods Hole Marine Biol. Lab., Mass., 1993—. Editl. bd.: Apoptosis jour., 1995—; contbr. articles to profl. jours. Recipient Searle scholars award Searle Found./Chgo. Cmty. Trust, 1992-96, Shaw Scientists award Milw. Found., 1993-96; rsch. grantee NIH, 1992—, March of Dimes Birth Defects Found., 1995—. Mem. AAAS, Genetics Soc. Am. Avocations: writing, hiking, photography, travel. E-mail: rothman@lifesci.ucsb.edu.

ROTHMAN, MOSES, library administrator; b. Montreal, Que., Can., Jan. 14, 1919; s. Myer and Molly (Schechtman) Rotman; m. Yoke Wah Loh, Dec. 31, 1947 (div. Sept. 1957); 1 child, Keith; m. Johanna Rucker, Oct. 4, 1957 (div. June 1976); children: Nicole, Monique; m. Lyn Doreen Serrell-Watts, Nov. 11, 1976; stepchildren: Sebastian Serrell-Watts, Arabella Serrell-Watts. Grad., Baron Bing H.S., Montreal, 1935. Trainee mgr. Universal Pictures, Bombay, India, 1946-48; mgr. Paramount Pictures, Caracas, Venezuela, 1948-50; worldwide rep. Edward Small Prodns., Munich, 1950-59; European sales mgr. United Artists, Paris, 1952-59; worldwide sales mgr. United Artists, N.Y.C., 1968-70; European sales mgr. Columbia Pictures, Paris, 1959-68; distbr. Chaplin Libr., London, 1970—. Cpl. Royal Can. Air Force, 1939-45. Named Commendatore of Order of Merit, Italian Govt., 1982. Mem. Acad. Motion Picture Arts and Scis., Royal Automobile Club. Avocations: art history, skiing, tennis.

ROTHMAN, STEPHEN SUTTON, physiology educator, researcher; b. N.Y.C., July 10, 1935; s. Abraham and Bertha (Band) R.; m. Doreen Lenore Zinn, Sept. 1, 1957; children: Peter Lorin, Jennifer Elise. AB, U. Pa., 1956, DDS, 1961, PhD, 1964. Instr. physiology U. Pa., Phila., 1959-64; assoc. prof. Harvard U., Cambridge, Mass., 1964-71; prof. U. Calif., San Francisco, 1971—; mem. faculty Sch. Engring., U. Calif., Berkeley, 1988—, project coord. advanced life source Life Scis. Ctr., 1988-90, founding chmn. group in biophysics and med. physics U. Calif., San Francisco, 1983-86, sr. faculty scientist Lawrence Berkeley Lab., 1987-96; founding pres., CEO, chmn. bd. Genteric Corp., Alameda, Calif., 1996-99. Author: Protein Secretion, 1985, Membrane Protein Transport, (Vols. 1, 2 & 3), 1995; editor: Nonvesicular Transport, 1985; mem. editl. bd. Am. Jour. Physiology, 1970-80; contbr. numerous articles to profl. jours. Mem. governing bd. joint program in medicine U. Calif. Berkeley and San Francisco, 1976-79, mem. joint program in bioengring., 1978—, mem. exec. com. joint program in biophysics, 1981-83; mem. U. Calif. San Francisco program in biophysics, 1972-97. NIH grantee, NSF grantee. Mem. AAAS, AAUP, Am. Soc. Zoologists, Am. Physiol. Soc., Biophys. Soc., Soc. Gen. Physiologists, Sigma Xi. Jewish. Avocations: painting, drawing, piano. Home: 98 Acacia Ave Berkeley CA 94708-1202 Office: U Calif 3d and Parnassus Sts San Francisco CA 94143-0001

ROTHMAN, STEVE ANDREW, advertising executive; b. L.A., Nov. 22, 1961; s. Nathan Paul and Dona Lyn Rothman. BS in Bus. Adminstrn., U. Calif., Berkeley, 1983; MBA, Columbia U., 1989. Asst. buyer Macy's Calif., San Francisco, 1984-87; account mgr. GGK iNternat., Paris, 1989-94; sr. account mgr. DDB Needham, Paris, 1995; internat. account dir. Saatchi & Saatchi, Paris, 1996—, also bd. dirs. Fax: 33142218809. Home: 29 Rue du Pont Neuf, 75001 Paris France Office: Saatchi & Saatchi, 30 Blvd Vital Bouhot, 92200 Neuilly sur Siene France

ROTHMAN, ULF SVEN ERIK, plastic surgery educator, inventor; b. Arboga, Sweden, May 19, 1942; s. Carl-Erik and Ingrid Albertina (Nordstrøm) R.; m. Gunnvôr Rothman, Dec. 16, 1967 (div. Dec. 1982); m. Waltraud Brigitte Schütze, June 20, 1983; children: Magnus, Jonas, Katarina, Niclas. MD, U. Uppsala, Sweden, 1966. V.p. R & D Pharmacia AB, Uppsala, 1975-78; resident dept. plastic surgery Malmö (Sweden) U., 1970-75; 1st asst. dept. exptl. medicine Malmö (Sweden) U., $D, 1980-85; sr. lectr. Inst. Medicine, Gen. Surgery and Orthopaedics Malmö (Sweden) U., 1985-95; asst. prof. plastic surgery U. Lund, Sweden, 1980-95; ret., 1995. Patentee wound cleansing agt., ethical anti-cancer drug, ethical anti-influenza agt., world's 1st rechargeable lithium battery, tire deflator-active air-lock immobilizer, Edulin-anti-microbial precipatation system, guernsin ripupcin plant peptide antibiotics for industrial food preservation. Recipient French Gold medal for inventions Salon Internat. de l'Invention de Paris, 1998. Home: PO Box 212 Hadsley House, Lefebvre St St Peter Port, Guernsey Channel Islands GY1 4JE

ROTHSCHILD, DONALD PHILLIP, lawyer, arbitrator; b. Dayton, Ohio, Mar. 31, 1927; s. Leo and Anne (Office) R.; m. Ruth Eckstein, July 7, 1950; children: Nancy Lee, Judy Lynn Hoffman, James Alex. AB, U. Mich., 1950; JD summa cum laude, U. Toledo, 1965; LLM, Harvard U., 1966. Bar: Ohio 1966, D.C. 1970, U.S. Supreme Ct. 1975, R.I. 1989. Teaching fellow Harvard U. Law Sch., Cambridge, Mass., 1965-66; instr. solicitor's office U.S. Dept. Labor, Washington, 1966-67; vis. prof. U. Mich. Law Sch., Ann Arbor, 1976; prof. law George Washington U. Nat. Law Ctr., Washington, 1966-89, emeritus, 1989; prof. law N.Y. Law Sch., 1989-96; dir. Consumer Protection Ctr., 1971—; dir. Inst. Law and Aging, Washington, 1973-89, Ctr. for Community Justice, Washington, 1974-88, Nat. Consumers League, Washington, 1981-87; v.p. Regulatory Alternatives Devel. Corp., Washington, 1982—; cons. Washington Met. Council Govt., 1979-82; mayoral appointee Adv. Com. on Consumer Protection, Washington, 1979-80; chmn. bd. dirs. D.C. Citizens Complaint Ctr., Washington, 1980; counsel Tillinghast, Collins & Graham, Providence, 1989-95, chair human resource group. Co-author: Consumer Protection Text and Materials, 1973; Collective Bargaining and Labor Arbitration, 1979; Fundamentals of Administrative Practice and Procedure, 1981. Contbr. numerous articles to profl. publs. Mem. Fed. Trade Commn. Adv. Council, Washington, 1970. Recipient Community Service award Television Acad., Washington, 1981. Mem. ABA, Nat. Assn. Coll. and Univ. Attys. (Brown U.), Nat. Acad. Arbitrators, Fed. Mediation and Conciliation Service, Am. Arbitration Assn., D.C. Bar Assn., Phi Kappa Phi. Jewish. Office: Shadow Farm Way Unit 4 Wakefield RI 02879-3631

ROTHSCHILD, JENNIFER ANN, artist, educator; b. Mesa, Ariz., Aug. 16, 1948; d. Joe Dean and Frances Ann (McFarland) Johnston; m. Harry Ronald Rothschild, Feb. 14, 1981. Diploma, El Camino Jr. Coll., 1968; BA in Art Edn., Calif. State U., 1970. Cert. secondary sch. tchr., Calif. Arts and crafts specialist City of Hawthorne (Calif.) Parks and Recreation, 1966-67; portrait artist Disneyland, Anaheim, Calif., 1970-74; secondary sch. art tchr. Orange (Calif.) Unified Schs., 1972-80; freelance custom apparel designer Honolulu, 1982-94, sculptor, artist, 1994—. One woman show at Art Centre Gallery, Honolulu, 1997; corp. artist Arts of Paradise Gallery, Honolulu, 1997—; exhibited in show at City of Manhattan Beach, Calif., 1966, Assn. of Hawaii Artists, 1996—, in book Encyclopedia of Living Artists, 10th edit., 1997. Bd. dirs. Hawaii Tennis Patrons, Honolulu, 1996—. Recipient scholarship Chouinard Sch. Art Inst., 1965-66, 1st Place Stamp Design award Easter Seals, 1995-96, Hokele Artists award Hawaiian Airlines, 1996, Most Unique Art award Assn. of Hawaii Artists Aloha Show, 1997. Fellow Nat. Mus. Women in Arts; mem. AAUW, Honolulu Art Acad., Hawaii Watercolor Soc., Assn. Hawaii Artists (v.p. 1996-97, pres. 1999-2000), Hawaiian Pacific Tennis Assn. (rules chmn. 1997), Alpha Omicron Pi. Republican. Presbyterian. Avocations: tennis, reading, writing, painting, sculpting.

ROTHSCHILD, MIRIAM LOUISA, entomologist, writer; b. Eng., Aug. 5, 1908; d. Nathaniel Charles and Rozsika (De Wertheimstein) R.; m. George Lane, 1943 (div. 1957); 4 children. DSc (hon.), Oxford (Eng.) U., 1968, Gothenburg (Sweden) U., 1983, Hull (Eng.) U., 1984, Northwestern U., 1986, Leicester (Eng.) U., 1987, Open U., Eng., 1988, Essex (Eng.) U., 1988, Cambridge (Eng.) U., 1999. vis. prof. biology Royal Free Hosp., London; Romanes lectr. Oxford U., 1985, hon. fellow St. Hugh's Coll. Author: Catalogue Rothschild Collection of Fleas, Vol. I, 1953, Vol. II, 1956, Vol. III, 1962, Vol. IV, 1966, Vol. V, 1971, Vol. VI, 1983, (with Theresa Clay) Fleas, Flukes and Cuckoos, 1952, (with Clive Farrell) The Butterfly Gardener, 1983, Dear Lord Rothschild, 1983, (with Schlein and Ito) Atlas of Insect Tissue, 1985, Animals and Man, 1986, (with Lionel de Rothschild) The Rothschild Gardens, 1996; editor Novitates Zoologica, 1938-41; contbr. over 300 articles to sci. jours. Trustee Brit. Mus. Natural History, 1967-75. Decorated dame comdr. Brit. Empire; decorated Def. medal, R.H.S. Victoria Medal of Honour, 1991; recipient Floral medal Lynn Soc., 1968 Royal Entomol. Soc. Wigglesworth gold medal, 1982, medal Soc. Chem. Ecology, 1989. Fellow Royal Soc.; mem. Zool. and Entomol. Rsch. Coun., Marine Biol. Assn., Royal Entomol. Soc., Systematics Assn., Soc. for Promotion Nature Res., Zool. Soc. Fgn. Office (publs. com. 1940-42), Am. Acad. Arts and Scis., Queens Club (London), Entomol. Club (London). Home: Ashton Wold, Peterborough PE8 5LZ, England

ROTHSCHILD, ROBERT, economics educator; b. Cape Town, Cape Province, South Africa, June 3, 1945; arrived in Eng., 1970; s. Kurt and Erna (Erdman) R.; m. Sandra Jacqueline Sarembock, Dec. 7, 1969; children: Daniel, Peter. MA cum laude, U. Cape Town, 1968. Statistician Philips GmbH, Berlin, 1965-66; economist Steel Co. of Wales, London, 1966-67; lectr. econs. U. Cape Town, 1968-70, U. Lancaster (Eng.), 1974-89; prof. econs. Case Western Res. U., Cleve., 1978-79; fellow Australian Grad. Sch. of Mgmt., Sydney, 1983; sr. lectr. econs. U. Lancaster, 1989-99, reader, 1999—. Contbr. articles to profl. jours. Field Marshall Smuts scholar Field Marshall Smuts Fund, Cambridge U., 1970-73. Fellow Royal Econs. Soc.; mem. Am. Econs. Assn. Jewish. Avocation: cycling. Home: 10 Sandown Rd, Lancaster LA1 4LN, England Office: U Lancaster, Bailrigg, Lancaster LA1 4YX, England

ROTHWELL, ELAINE B., artist; b. Mpls., May 8, 1926; d. Frederick Roscoe and Stella Frances (LaVallee) Bartholomew; m. William Stanley Rothwell, May 10, 1946; children: Suzanne, Amy (Mrs. Donald Verrett), Wendy, Bart. BA in Fine Art, San Jose State U., 1966; pvt. study, Woodbury Graphic Studio, Los Altos, Calif., 1975-76, Amaranth Intaglio Workshop, Los Altos, 1985. One woman shows at Triton Mus. Art, Santa Clara, Calif., 1976, Palo Alto (Calif.) Civic Ctr., 1977, Stanford (Calif.) Art Spaces, Stanford U., 1985, 88, 89, West Valley Art Mus., Surprise, Ariz., 1996; exhibited in group shows at Carnegie Art Ctr., North Tonawanda, N.Y., 1995, 96, N.J. Ctr. for Visual Arts Internat., Summit, N.J., 1997, 98, Brand Libr. and Art Ctr., Glendale, Calif., 1996, Internat. Exhbn. Art League of Manatee County, Fla., 1996 (Merit award), Nat. Soc. Artists, 1997 (Philip J. Paratore Meml. award), Am. Color Print Soc. (Hugh Hutton Meml. award for Intaglio 1997), Grand Exhbn. Nat. Competition, Akron, Ohio, 1998, Printwork'98, Barrett House, Poughkeepsie, N.Y., 1998, 73d Ann. Internat. Print Competition/The Print Ctr., Phila., 1999, Manhattan Arts Internat., 1999, Chautauqua Nat. Exhbn. of Am. Art, 1999, No. Colo. Ann. Nat. Exhbns., 1999, 2000, The Stage Gallery, Merrick, N.Y., 2000, others; represented in permanent collections at Newberry Libr., Chgo., Triton Mu. Art, Santa Clara, Calif., West Valley Art Mus., Brand Libr. Art Ctr., Glendale, Calif. Mem. Triton Mus. Art, Nat. Mus. Women in Arts (charter), Am. Color Print Soc., Gallery 9 (Los Altos, Calif., treas. 1973-93), Gallery II (Nevada City, Calif.). Home: 3030 Eagles Nest Auburn CA 95603-5918 Office: Rothwell Graphic Studio PO Box 488 Auburn CA 95604-0488

ROTIM, KREŠIMIR, neurosurgeon; b. Vukovar, Croatia, Apr. 23, 1967; s. Milienko and Zorka (Jurišić) R. MD, U. Zagreb, Croatia, 1991, MS in Neurobiology, 1996. Lic. neurosurgeon. Chief resident Univ. Hosp. Ctr., Zagreb, 1997-98, resident, 1993-98. Mem. World Fedn. Neurol. Surgeons. Office: Univ Hosp Ctr, Dept Neurosurgery, 10600 Zagreb Croatia

ROTOLO, VILMA STOLFI, immunology researcher; b. Villa Diego, Argentina, Jan. 27, 1930; d. Eduardo and Manuela (Gallego) Stolfi; m. Jose Jaime Rotolo, Dec. 6, 1957; children: Gloria Claudia, Alejandro Claudio. Degree in pharmacology, U. Litoral Med. Sch., Rosario, Argentina, 1953, Lic. in Biochem. Sci., 1956, PhD in Biochem. Sci., 1966. Asst. dir., rsch. mem. oncology lab. Oncology Inst., Nat. Ministry Pub. Health, Rosario, 1956-67; rsch. mem. dept. pathology-tissue culture div. U. Rosario Med. Sch., 1967-72, chief Exptl. Immunopathology Inst., 1972-89, dir. immunotoxicology program, 1989-91; sr. rsch. scientist Prodinar Co., Rosario, 1991—; pres. internat. symposium Assn. Allergy and Immunopathology, Argentina, 1981; rapporteur internat. seminar Commn. European Communities and IPCS, WHO, ILO, UNEP, EPA, NIEHS, Luxembourg, 1984; cons. Fed. Justice, Argentina, 1989. Guest editor: African Jour. Clin. and Exptl. Immunology, 1982; contbr. paper to Triduo Sci. Ann. (hon. diploma award 1965). Active For the Life Found., Neuquén, Argentina, 1987-90; pres. Found. Nature and Sci., 1990—. Recipient rsch. visitor travel award WHO, 1983, expert immunotoxicology travel award Commn. European Communities and UNEP, ILO, IPCS, WHO, EPA, NIEHS, Luxembourg, 1984; WHO travel award fellow, 1973, 78; Nat. Coun. Sci. Investigation grantee, 1974-77, 79-81, 82-83. Mem. Internat. Soc. Immunopharmacology (mem. internat. coun.), Argentine Assn. Immunopharmacology and Immunotoxicology (pres. 1987), Argentine Environ. Protection Assn., Latin Am. Assn. Immunology, Argentine Soc. Ecology, Sigma Delta Epsilon. Avocations: drawing, painting, horticulture. Home: Mendoza 2435, Santa Fe, 2000 Rosario Argentina

ROTT, NATALIA NIKOLAEVNA, embryologist, researcher; b. Tula, USSR, Aug. 4, 1930; d. Nikolai Alexandrovich and Lydia Vasilievna (Delieva) R.; m. Yuri Alexeevich Lapkin, June 16, 1958 (div. 1973). Diploma, Moscow Lomonosov U., 1953; PhD, USSR Acad. Scis., Moscow, 1957, DSc, 1985. Cert. embryologist. Jr. rsch. worker USSR Acad. Scis., Moscow, 1957-66, sr. rsch. worker, 1966-93, leading rsch. worker, 1993—; head Cryobank of Genoms Commn., Moscow; coun. mem. fish genetics and selection, Moscow; mem. Cell Culture Assn., St. Petersbourgh, Russia. Author: Physical General Biology, 1997; contbr. articles to profl. jours. Recipient diploma Internat. Sci. Found., 1992-93; grantee Russian Found. Basic Investment, Moscow, 1993-98, Russian Acad. Sci., Moscow, 1993-97. Mem. World Conservation Union (Switzerland), Russian Acad. Natural Sci. Russian Ortodox. Avocations: traveling, cats. Home: Univ Prospect 6-161, 117333 Moscow Russia

ROTTER, HANS, theology educator; b. Hemhof, Germany, Oct. 6, 1932; s. Georg and Zäzilia (Daxenberger) R. Student, Philos. Coll. Munich, 1956-59, U. Innsbruck, Austria, 1961-65; ThD, U. Innsbruck, 1967, D Moral Theology, 1969. Lectr. moral theology U. Innsbruck, 1969-70, prof., head dept. moral theology, 1970, dean Faculty of Theology, 1974-75; rector Internat. Theol. Sem., Innsbruck, 1979-86, Inst. Moraltheologie, Innsbruck, 1986-98. Author books; contbr. numerous articles to religious jours.; co-editor: Innsbrucker Theologische Studien. Home: Sillgasse 6 Jesuitenkolleg, A 6020 Innsbruck Austria Office: Inst Systematische Theology, Karl Rahner Platz 1, A 6020 Innsbruck Austria

ROTTER, MANFRED LUDWIG, medical microbiologist, educator; b. Vienna, Austria, June 6, 1940; s. Hans and Herta (Kornherr) R. MD, U. Vienna, 1965; diploma in bacteriology, U. London, 1971. Asst. physician Hygiene Inst., U. Vienna, 1965-76, sr. lectr., 1976-79, assoc. prof., 1979-95, prof., 1995—, head dept. med. microbiology, 1972-91, deputy dir., head dept. clin. microbiology Hygiene Inst., 1991-95, dir. Hygiene Inst., 1995—; head dept. clin. microbiology Gen. Hosp., Vienna, 1991—. Author: Hygiene of Textile Floor Coverings, 1975; contbr. numerous articles on disinfection, med. microbiology and hosp. hygiene to sci. jours. Recipient Unilever award, 1974, Austrian Hygiene award, 1976, R. Schülke award, 1982, Düsseldorfer Hygiene award, 1984. Roman Catholic. Office: Hygiene-Inst of U, Kinderspitalgasse 15, A-1095 Vienna Austria

ROTTER, PAUL TALBOTT, retired insurance executive; b. Parsons, Kans., Feb. 21, 1918; s. J. and LaNora (Talbott) R.; m. Virginia Sutherlin Barksdale, July 17, 1943; children—Carolyn Sutherlin, Diane Talbott. BS summa cum laude, Harvard U., 1937. Asst. mathematician Prudential Ins. Co. of Am., Newark, 1938-46; with Mut. Benefit Life Ins. Co., Newark, 1946—; successively asst. mathematician, asso. mathematician, mathematician Mut. Benefit Life Ins. Co., 1946-59, from v.p. to exec. v.p., 1959-80, ret., 1980. Mem. Madison Bd. Edn., 1958-64, pres., 1959-64; Trustee, mem. budget com. United Campaign of Madison, 1951-55; mem. bd., chmn. advancement com. Robert Treat council Boy Scouts Am., 1959-64. Fellow Soc. Actuaries (bd. govs. 1965-68, gen. chmn. edn. and exam. com. 1963-66, chmn. adv. com. edn. and exam. 1969-72); mem. Brit. Inst. Actuaries (asso.), Am. Acad. Actuaries (v.p. 1968-70, bd. dirs., chmn. edn. and exam. com. 1965-66, chmn. rev. and evaluation com. 1968-74), Asso. Harvard Alumni (regional dir. 1965-69), Actuaries Club N.Y. (pres. 1967-68), Harvard Alumni Assn. (v.p. 1964-66),Am. Lawn Bowls Assn. (pres. SW div.), Phi Beta Kappa Assos., Phi Beta Kappa. Clubs: Harvard N.J. (pres. 1956-57); Harvard (N.Y.C.); Morris County Golf (Convent, N.J.); Joslyn-Lake Hodges Lawn Bowling (pres. 1989-90). Home: 18278 Canfield Pl San Diego CA 92128-1002

ROTUNDA, DONALD THEODORE, public relations consultant; b. Blue Island, Ill., Feb. 14, 1945; s. Nicholas and Frances (Manna) R. B.A., Georgetown U., 1967; M.A., London Sch. Econs., 1968, Ph.D., 1972. Analyst NASA, Washington, 1972; lectr. in econs. U. D.C., 1973; legis. asst. Ho. of Reps., Washington, 1974-76, economist budget com., 1977; mgmt. analyst Office Mgmt. and Budget, Washington, 1977-81; cons., 1981-82; mgr. editorial svcs. United Technologies Corp., Hartford, Conn., 1982-87, Pepsico, Inc., Purchase, N.Y., 1987-89, Union Carbide Corp., Danbury, Conn., 1989-90; dir. editorial svcs. Martin Marietta, Bethesda, Md., 1990-92; cons. pub. rels., 1992—. Contbr. numerous articles to Washington Post, New Republic, Saturday Rev. Roman Catholic. Home: 4431 Klingle St NW Washington DC 20016-3578

ROUAYHEB, GEORGE MICHAEL, scientific research council advisor; b. Kobba, Batroun, Lebanon, Sept. 7, 1933; came to U.S., 1952; s. Michael George and Naimeh (Fattouh) R.; m. Leila Isaac Koussa, July 5, 1964; children: Michel, Marwan. BS, La. State U., 1956, MS, 1958; postgrad., Okla. State U., 1961. Rsch. scientist Conoco R&D, Ponca City, Okla., 1958-61; process engr. Medreco Refinery, Sidon, Lebanon, 1962-65; prodn. mgr. Esso Fertilizer Co., Beirut, 1965-70; dir. tech. div. Idcas Arab League, Cairo, 1970-73; dir. applied scis. div. Nat. Coun. Sci. Rsch., Beirut, 1973—; profl cons. ECWA UN, Beirut, 1978; regional advisor UNIDO, Vienna, Austria, 1982-83. Mem. Order of Engrs. Lebanon. Greek Orthodox. Achievements include patent on the use of tritium in gas chromatography ionization detector. Home: Kobba, Batroun Lebanon Office: Nat Coun Sci Rsch, PO Box 11-8281, Beirut Lebanon

ROUBÍČEK, TOMÁŠ, mathematician; b. Prague, Apr. 23, 1956; s. Hanuš and Jarmila (Meisnerová) R.; m. Eva Kalvasová, Feb. 21, 1986 (div.); children: Michal, Martin. MS, Czech. Tech. U., Prague, 1980; PhD, Czechoslovak Acad. Scis., Prague, 1987; DrSc., Acad. Scis. Czech Republic, Prague, 1995. With Czech Tech. U., Prague, 1981-82; sr. rsch. fellow Acad. Scis. Czech Republic, Prague, 1982—; rsch. fellow Charles U., Prague, 1995—. Author: (monograph) Relaxation in Optimization Theory and Variational Calculus, 1997; contbr. over 50 articles to jours. in field. Rsch. fellow Alexander von Humboldt Found., Germany, 1991-92; rsch. grantee École Normale Supérieure Lyon Région Rhône-Alpes, France, 1992-93, prize Min. of Edn. Czech Republic for Rsch., 1999. Mem. Union Czech Mathematicians and Physicists, Soc. Indsl. and Applied Math., Am. Math. Soc. Office: Mathematical Inst Charles U, Sokolovská 83, CZ186 75 Prague Czech Republic

ROUCO VARELA, ANTONIO MA, archbishop; b. Villalba, Lugo, Spain, Aug. 20, 1936; s. Vicente Rouco and Ma Eugenia Varela. Degree in Theologia, U. Salamanca, 1958; D in Canon Law, U. München, 1964. Ordained sacerdotal, Mar. 28, 1959. Prof. Seminario Mondoñedo, Lugo, 1964-66, U. München, 1966-69, U. Salamanca, 1969-76; bishop aux. Santiago de Compostela, 1976, archbishop, 1984; archbishop Madrid, 1994—; elevated to Cardinal, 1988. Office: Arzobispado Madrid, Bailen 8, 28071 Madrid Spain

ROUDE, JEAN-CLAUDE MAURICE, road construction company executive; b. Nice, France, May 24, 1940; s. Raymond Fèlix and Andrèe Lina (Lochon) R.; m. Colette Marcelle Lecuyer, Apr. 10, 1965; children: Bertrand, Françoise (dec.), Cèdric, Pauline. Engr., Ecole Poly., Paris, 1963, Ecole Ponts et Chaussées, Paris, 1966. Civil engr. French Civil Svc., 1966-69; v.p. Tunnel under Mont Blanc, Chamonix, France, 1969-76; dep. CEO, Underground Rys., Lyon, France, 1976-79; v.p. Jean Lefebvre Co., Neuilly, France, 1979-88, CEO, 1988—, chmn., 1992—; bd. dirs. Hubbard Construction Co., Orlando, Fla., 1988—. Lt. engrs. French Army, 1964. Mem. Road Contractors Assn. (vice chmn. 1993—), Gen. Contractors Assn. (bd. dirs. 1989—), Rotary. Avocation: golf. Office: Jean Lefebvre Co, 11 blvd Jean Mermoz, 92200 Neuilly-sur-Seine France

ROUDNICKY, DUNJA SOLDO, physicist, researcher; b. Krizevci, Croatia, Feb. 6, 1950; m. Edgard Roudnicky, Oct. 24, 1981; 1 child, Filip. B, U. Zagreb, Croatia, 1973; MSc, U. Zagreb, 1976. Rschr. Rudjer Boskovic Inst., Zagreb, 1976—; rschr. atomic physics Rudjer Boskovic Inst., Zagreb, 1973-89, rschr. optics, 1990-99. Avocations: horticulture, skiing. E-mail: dsoldo@rudjer.irb.hr. Office: Rudjer Boskovic Inst, Bijenicka 54, Zagreb Croatia

ROUECHE, JOHN EDWARD, II, education educator, leadership program director; b. Sept. 3, 1938; s. John Edward and Mary (Harris) R.; m. Suanne Davis; 1 stepchild, Robin Sue Maca; children by previous marriage: Michelle Renee, John Edward III. BA, Lenoir Rhyne Coll., Hickory, N.C., 1960; MA, Appalachian Coll., Boone, N.C., 1961; PhD, Fla. State U., 1964. Dean Gaston Coll., Gastonia, N.C., 1964-67; assoc. rsch. educator UCLA, 1967-69; dir. jr. coll. divsn. Nat. Lab. Higher Edn., 1968-71; assoc. prof. edn. Duke U.; prof. edn., dir. c.c. leadership program U. Tex., Austin, 1971—,

Sid W. Richardson regents chair, 1987—; mem. chancellor's coun. U. Tex. Sys., 1990—, U. Tex. Littlefield Soc., 1992—; lectr. Earl Pullias lectr. U. So. Calif., 1992, Coll. Bd. Disting. Lectr. N.Y.C., 1993, Frances Crain Cook Disting. Lectr. U. Tex., 1994; chmn. nat. ednl. adv. bd. Gt. Am. Res. Ins. Co., 1988-94; co-chair Nat. Adv. Bd. for C.C.s, Invest Learning Corp., 1993-96; chair nat. adv. com. Kaplan Ednl. Partnerships, 1995-98; La Platica Disting. lectr. Ariz. State U., 1999. C.C. editor Jossey-Bass Publs., 1971-82; editor Creative Teaching Series, Media Systems Corp., 1980-85; mem. editl. bd. C.C. Times, C.C. Jour., 1990-94, others; author 34 books, including Profiles of Excellence in America's Schools, 1986, Access with Excellence, 1987, Shared Vision, 1989, Teaching as Leading, 1990, Under-representation: A Question of Diversity, 1991, Between a Rock and a Hard Place, 1993, The Company We Keep, 1995, Strangers in Their Own Land: Part Time Faculty, 1995, Embracing the Tiger: The Effectiveness Debate and the Community College, 1997, High Stakes, High Performance: Making Remedial Education Work, 1999; contbr. numerous articles and monographs. Pres. Doss Sch. PTA, 1974-75; chmn. bd. N.W. Hills United Meth. Ch., 1973-76. Recipient Disting. Svc. award Nat. Coun. Univs. and Colls., 1990, 93, 95, Disting. Rsch. Publ. award, 1990, Outstanding Alumnus award Appalachian State U., 1979, Disting. Grad. award Fla. State U., 1981, Tchg. Excellence award U. Tex., 1982, Outstanding Rschr. award, 1985, Excellence award for outstanding learned article U.S. Edn. Press Assn., 1983, Disting. Rsch. award Nat. Assn. Devel. Edn., 1984-86, Disting. Rsch. Publ. award Nat. Coun. Student Devel., 1987, Disting. Rsch. award Nat. Coun. Staff, Program, and Orgn. Devel., B. Lamar Johnson Nat. Leadership award, 1988, Disting. Svc. 1942; d. Raymond Louis and Edna Sue (Leatherwood) Davis; m. Benjamin Frank Maca, June 12, 1964 (div. Feb. 1975); 1 child, Robin Sue; m. John Edward Roueche, May 22, 1976; children: Michelle, John III. BA in English, North Tex. State U., 1964, MA in English, 1967; PhD, U. Tex., 1976. Tchr. English Sam Houston H.S., Arlington, Tex., 1964-65, MacArthur H.S., Irving, Tex., 1966-67; instr. El Centro Coll., Dallas, 1967-74; dir. cmty. coll. internship program U. Tex., Austin, 1976-82, dir. Nat. Inst. for Staff and Orgnl. Devel., 1982—; cons. in field. Co-author: Between a Rock and a Hard Place, 1993 (Disting. Rsch. award 1993-94), Strangers in Their Own Land, 1995 (Dist. Rsch. award 1995-96), Embracing the Tiger, 1997, The Company We Keep, 1995, High Stakes, High Performance: Making Remedial Education Work, 1998. Mem. Wildlife Rescue, Austin, 1981—. Named Ky. Col., Ky. State Legis. and Gov., 1979; recipient Disting. Leadership award Fla. State Legis., 1989, Leadership award Am. Assn. Cmty. Colls., 1997. Mem. Am. Assn. C.C. (coun. of univs. and colls., Leadership award 1997), Delta Gamma (pres. alumnae 1979-81). Avocations: needlepoint, reading, gardening. Office: Nat Inst Staff/Orgnl Devel MLK/Speedway SZB 348 Austin TX 78712

ROUGEOT, HENRI MAX, medical imaging engineer, physicist; b. Paris, Nov. 22, 1934; arrived in U.S., 1989; s. Henri Felix and Yvette Therese (Ferreira) R.; m. Fanny Astrid Brebion, July 11, 1960; children: Claire, Anne, Pierre, Helene. BSc, Acad. Paris, 1954; degree in math., physics and chemistry, U. Sorbonne, Paris, 1957, M in Physics, 1962; degree in physics of accelerators, Orsay (France) U., 1968. Rsch. engr. Nat. Ctr. Scientific Rsch., Strasbourg, France, 1962-64, Corp. Rsch. Lab., Orsay, 1964-69; project mgr. Thomson-CSF Electron Tube, Grenoble, France, 1969-74; engring. mgr. x-ray II Thomson CSF, Grenoble, 1974-85, tech. dir., 1985-89; program mgr. G.E. Corp. Rsch. & Devel., Schenectady, N.Y., 1989-96; dir. med. detectors Noranda Advanced Materials, 1996; chmn. bd. FTNI, 1997—; dir. med. detectors NORANDA Advanced Material, Que., Can., 1996—; chmn. bd. dirs. FTNI; pres., chief tech. officer ANRAD Corp., 1999—. Author: Negative Election Affinity, Digital Imaging in Medicine, 1993. With Artillery, 1959-62, Algeria. Recipient grant Nat. Cancer Inst., 1993. Mem. Am. Assn. Physicists in Medicine. Roman Catholic. Achievements include development and promotion of fifth generation high resolution image intensifiers at Thomson-CSF standard in medical industry since 1989; initiation of concept and launching of panel digital radiography image detector at Thomson-CSF and development of a full field digital Mammography system at GE, flat panel detectors for digital radiography and foproasofig wring direct corrosion methods. Home: 79 Celtic Dr, Beaconsfield, PQ Canada H9W 3M6 Office: 4950 Levy, Saint Laurent, PQ Canada H4R 2P1

ROULET, GEORGES-EDDY, linguistics educator; b. Nyon, Switzerland, Apr. 28, 1939; s. Roger Roulet and Luzia Arpagaus. MA, U. Nevchatel, Switzerland, 1962, PhD, 1969. Prof. U. Nevchatel, 1971-77; prof. U. Geneva, 1977—, vice rector, 1991-95; mem. Nat. Found. Sci. Rsch., Berne, Switzerland, 1996—. Author: Linguistic Theory, Linguistic Description and Language Teaching, 1975, The Articulation of Discourse in Contemporary French, 1985, The Description of the Organization of Discourse: From Dialogue to Text, 1999. Home: Chemin de la Ruelle 4, CH 1224 Chene-Bougeries Switzerland Office: U Geneva, Dept Linguistics, CH 1211 Geneva 4, Switzerland

ROULHAC, NELLIE GORDON, retired special education administrator; b. Washington, June 5; d. Levi Preston and Agnes Pauline (Lee) Gordon; m. Christopher Maxwell Roulhac, Jr., Aug. 1, 1942; children: Christopher Maxwell III, Yvonne Agnes Roulhac Horton. BS, Cheyney (Pa.) State U., 1944; MA, Columbia U., 1946; EdD, U. Sarasota, Fla., 1978; postgrad., Temple U., U. Pa. Cert. spl. edn. tchr., Pa. Instr. Albany (Ga.) State Coll., 1947-51; tchr. Coatesville (Pa.) sch. sys., 1944-46; special class tchr. Phila. sch. sys., 1957-71, supr. special classes, 1971-84. Author: (books) Seventeen Days of Jimmie, 1981, Work, Play and Commitment: The First Fifty Years Jack and Jill of America, Incorporated, 1989, Jumping Over the Moon, 1994; (booklet) ABC's of Fundraising, 1984. Del. to White House Conf. on Children and Youth, 1955; nat. pres. Jack and Jill of Am., Inc., 1954-58; pres. Jack and Jill of Am. Found., 1975-78, bd. dirs., 1975-78; bd. commns. Mayors Comm. for Women, Phila., 1983-91; trustee Combs Coll. of Music, Phila., 1976-77, Free Libr. Phila., 1986-96; pres., bd. trustees Pennhurst State Sch. and Hosp., Spring City, Pa., 1979-82; trustee United Cerebral Palsy Assn., 1970-74; vol. ARC, Phila.; attendee Centennial World Congress of YMCA, Paris, 1955. Recipient award Nat. Found. for Infantile Paralysis, 1956, Leadership in Fundraising award, Svc. to Youth award Century Club award YMCA, Memphis, 1953-54, Phila., 1965-69, 1st prize Best Student Tchg. award Cheyney State U., Meritorious Svc. award ARC, Phila., 1954, Continuing Svc. award Jack and Jill of Am., 1974, 78, 88, Cert. of award Phila. Assn. for Retarded Children, 1967, Outstanding Contribution award Pennhurst Ctr., Spring City, 1973-87, Main Line Comm. Phila. Grand Opera Co., Humanitarian Svc. award Liberian Children Rehab. Network, 1995, award for contbn. in field of spl. edn. Phila. Assn. Sch. Adminstrs, citation City of Phila., 1994, Award for Pioneering in Field of Spl. Edn. Phila. Assn. for Retarded Citizens, 1987. Mem. Thirty Clusters (founder), The Links Inc., Karma Club, Nat. Assn. Parliamentarians (N.L. Carter unit), Delta Sigma Theta (Phila. alumnae chpt., nat. sec. 1954-60, chairperson nat. pers. com. 1960-64, Sadie T.M. Alexander award 1988). Avocations: writing, decoupage, crafts, collecting foreign dolls and autographs, travel.

ROULIDIS, ZESES CHRIS, physician, medical educator; b. Corning, N.Y., Sept. 10, 1960; s. Chris and Potoula R.; m. Maria Eugenia Hallas, May 24, 1987. BA with distinction, U. Va., 1982, MD, 1986. Diplomate Am. Bd. Internal Medicine. Resident U. Calif., San Francisco, 1988-91; assoc. Yater Med. Group, Washington, 1991-92; asst. clin. prof. Georgetown U., Washington, 1993-95; assoc. Duke U. Affiliated Physicians, Durham, N.C., 1995-96; asst. clin. prof. Duke U. Dept. Medicine, Durham, N.C., 1996—. Gen. Internal Medicine fellow Georgetown U., 1992-93. Fellow Am. Coll. Physicians; mem. AMA, N.C. Med. Soc. Avocations: music, piano, flute, bonsai, golf. Office: Duke U Med Ctr PO Box 3228 Durham NC 27715-3228

ROUMAN, JOHN CHRIST, classics educator; b. Tomahawk, Wis., May 1, 1926; s. Christ and Soteria (Dedes) R. BA in Greek, Carleton Coll., 1950; MA in Greek, Columbia U., 1951; student, Rutgers U., 1951-53, U. Kiel, Germany, 1956-57, U. Minn., Mpls., 1959-60; PhD in Classics, U. Wis., 1965. German tchr. Seton Hall Preparatory Sch., South Orange, N.J., 1954-56; ancient history tchr. Malverne (N.Y.) High Sch., 1957-59; tchg. asst. in ancient history U. Wis., Madison, 1960-61, rsch. asst. in ancient history, 1961-65; rsch. asst. in Greek epigraphy Inst. Advanced Study, Princeton, N.J., 1962-63; asst. prof. Classics U. N.H., Durham, 1965-71, assoc. prof., 1971-91, prof., 1991—, prof. classics emeritus, 1999, co-chmn. Spanish and Classics depts., mem. adv. bd. Prof. John C. Rouman classical lectr. series, 1997—; examiner N.H. State Bd. Edn. in Latin and Greek, 1979-80; judge Warren H. Held Jr. Exam-Contests in Latin and Mythology, 1988—; cons. Nat. Classical Greek Examination, 1980; presenter, lectr. in field. Active Colovos Rd. Com., 1981-82. With USN, 1944-46. Fulbright scholar U. Kiel, 1956-57; recipient Disting. Tchg. award U. N.H. Alumni Assn., 1985, Pericles award Am. Hellenic Ednl. Progressive Assn. and Daus. of Penelope, 1993, Profile of Svc. award U. N.H. Aumni Assn., 2000; Prof. John C. Rouman Classical Lecture Series named in his honor. Mem. Am. Classical League (rep. to TCNE at ann. meeting 1978, mem. fin. com. 1981-82, treas. 1982-83), Am. Philol. Assn. (Nat. Excellence in Teaching Classics award, 1991), Archaeol. Inst. Am., Classical Assn. Can., Classical Assn. New Eng. (mem. exec. com. at-large 1981-84, mem. nominating com. 1983-84, 86-87, pres. 1987-88, Barlow-Beach award 1991, mem. ad hoc com. on elections and appointments), Medieval Acad. Am., Modern Greek Studies Assn., Nat. Assn. Advisors for Health Professions, N.H. Classical Assn. (mem. exec. com. 1965—, chair nominating com. 1986—), Strafford County Greco-Roman Found. (pres. 1978—), Vergilian Soc. Am., Carleton Coll. Alumni Assn. (Alumni award for Dist. Achievement 2000), Phi Kappa Theta (faculty advisor, 1982—, chmn. nat. bd., 1993-94, nat. found. mem. 1993—, Man of Achievement award 2000).

ROUND, ALICE FAYE BRUCE, school psychologist; b. Ironton, Ohio, July 19, 1934; d. Wade Hamilton and Martha Matilda (Toops) Bruce; children: Leonard Bruce, Christopher Frederick. BA, Asbury Coll., 1956; MS in Sch. Psychology, Miami U., Oxford, Ohio, 1975. Cert. tchr., sch. psychologist, supr., Ohio; cert. tchr., Calif. Tchr. Madison County (Ohio) Schs., 1956-58, Columbus (Ohio) Pub. Schs., 1958, San Diego Pub. Schs., 1958-60, Poway (Calif.) Unified Sch. Dist., 1960-64; substitute tchr. Princeton City Schs., Cin., 1969-75; sch. psychologist, intern Greenhills/Forest Park City Schs., Cin., 1975-76; sch. psychologist Fulton County Schs., Wauseon, Ohio, 1976-77, Sandusky (Ohio) pub. and Cath. schs., 1977-96, Eric County Ednl. Svc. Ctr., 1996-98; pre-sch. psychologist Huron County Bd. Edn., Norwalk, Ohio, 1998—; tchr. art cmty. group and pvt. lessons, Sandusky, 1962, Springdale, Ohio, 1962-69; mem. Youth Svcs. Bd., Sandusky, 1978-88; bd. dirs., cons. Sandusky Sch. Practical Nursing, 1983-91; presenter suicide prevention seminars for mental health orgns.; speaker at ch., civic and youth orgns., local radio and TV programs; cons. on teen pregnancy to various schs., health depts. Mem. Huron (Ohio) Boosters Club, 1978-92, Vols. in Action, Sandusky, 1987—. Mem. NAACP, NEA, Nat. Sch. Psychologist Assn., Ohio Sch. Psychologist Assn., Maumee Valley Sch. Psychologist Assn., Ohio Edn. Assn., Sandusky Edn. Assn., Phi Delta Kappa (historian 1984-88, Most Innovative Preservation of History award 1988). Home: 821 Seneca Ave Huron OH 44839-1842 Office: Huron City Schs Cleveland Ave Huron OH 44839

ROUND, TONY, independent financial adviser; b. Birmingham, West Midlands, Eng., Nov. 2, 1949; s. Wilfred and Joyce Elsie (Mew) R.; m. Lynne Rosemary Smith; children: Gemma Louise, Alexander Anthony. Owner Alexander Anthony Investments, Wolverhampten, Eng., 1974—; bd. dirs. Adhesive Tape Mfg. Co. Ltd., Darlaston, Eng., Delta Plastics Ltd., Willenhall, Eng.; owner Alexander Anthony Investments Plc., Alexander Anthony Assett Mgmt. Plc. Fellow Life Ins. Assn.; mem. Enville Golf Club. Anglican. Avocations: football, golf, rugby. Home: Brandelhowe Springhill Ln, Lower Penn, Wolverhampton, West Midlands WV4 4TW, England Office: Alexander Anthony Investmen, 30 Waterloo Rd, Wolverhampton WV1 4BL, England

ROUNTREE, PATRICIA ANN, youth organization administrator; b. Rochester, N.Y., Apr. 2, 1942; d. Robert James and Myrtle Margaret (Cuthbertson) R. AA, Cazenovia Coll., 1961; BA, Parsons Coll., 1965. Gen. clk. Eastman Kodak, Rochester, 1961-63; 6th grade tchr. Wayland (N.Y.) Ctrl. Sch., 1965-67; field dir. Seven Lakes Coun. Girl Scouts U.S.A., Phelps, N.Y., 1967-73; program dir. Palm Glades Coun. Girl Scouts U.S.A., Lake Worth, Fla., 1973-76; asst. exec. dir. Seven Lakes Coun. Girl Scouts U.S.A., 1976-86; exec. dir. Mich. Trails Coun. Girl Scouts U.S.A., Grand Rapids, 1986-89; exec. dir. Ctrl. N.Y. Coun. Girl Scouts U.S.A., Syracuse, 1989—. Pres., bd. dirs. Planned Parenthood of Fingerlakes, Geneva, N.Y., 1982-86. Mem. Rotary Syracuse. Presbyn. Avocations: needlework, reading, travel. Home: 4 Robinson Dr Baldwinsville NY 13027-2807 Office: Ctrl NY Girl Scout Coun 6724 Thompson Rd # 482 Syracuse NY 13211-2122

ROUOT, JACQUES, retired physician, educator; b. Paris, July 17, 1922; s. Leon and Therese (Begis) Rouot; m. Monique Liagre, July 7, 1952; 1 child, Nathalie. MD, Faculte of Medecine, Paris, 1948; DDS, Northwestern U., 1951. Prof., chmn. advanced prosthodontics Paris VI U., Paris, 1958-87; various internat. tchg. missions. Author: Prothese Dentaire Squelettique, 1960, protesi Denturia Scheletrata, 1967. Home: 8 Rue de Longpont, Neuilly 92200, France

ROUPAKIAS, DEMETRIOS GEORGE, genetics educator; b. Doxara, Greece, Dec. 15, 1948; arrived in Can., 1973; s. George and Eythemia (Kravare) R.; m. Alexandra Maria Muscat, Oct. 1, 1978; children: Eythemia-Lydia, Georgia. BSc, Agriculture U., Greece, 1971; PhD, Agriculture U., Winnipeg, Can., 1978. Post doctoral rsch. assoc. dept. genetics N. C. State U., Raleigh, 1977-79; spl. scientist A.U. Thessaloniki, Greece, 1980-81, asst. prof., 1982-83, assoc. prof., 1984-87, prof., 1987—. With M.P., Greece, 1971-73. Recipient Assistanship award Nat. Found., Greece, 1967-71, fellowship U. Manitoba, 1975, N.R.C. of Can., 1976-78. Mem. Genetics Soc. of Can., Pl. Br. Soc. of Greece (pres. 1987-88, v.p. 1988-90). Greek Orthodox. Home: Plagiari, PO Box 317, GR-57500 Epanome Greece Office: Sch Agrilculture, Dept Genetics & Plant Breeding, GR-54006 Thessaloniki Greece

ROUSE, JOHN WILSON, JR., technology consultant; b. Kansas City, Mo., Dec. 7, 1937; s. John Wilson and Gail Agnes (Palmer) R.; m. Susan Jane Davis, May 3, 1981; 1 son, Jeffrey Scott. A.S., Kansas City Jr. Coll., 1957; B.S., Purdue U., 1959; M.S., U. Kans., 1965, Ph.D., 1968. Registered profl. engr., Mo., Tex. Engr. Bendix Corp., Kansas City, Mo., 1959-64; rsch. coord. Ctr. for Rsch., U. Kans., Lawrence, 1964-68; prof. elec. engring., dir. remote sensing ctr. Tex. A&M U., College Station, 1968-78; Logan prof. engr., chmn. elec. engring. U. Mo., Columbia, 1978-81; dean engring. U. Tex., Arlington, 1981-87; pres. So. Rsch. Inst., Birmingham, Ala., 1987-97, The Rouse Group, Hoover, Ala., 1997—; mgr. microwave program NASA Hdqrs., Washington, 1975-77. Contbr. articles to profl. jours. Recipient Outstanding Tchr. award Tex. A&M U., 1971; Outstanding Prof. award U. Mo., 1980; Engr. of Yr. Tex. Soc. Profl. Engrs., 1983. Mem. IEEE, Nat. Soc. Profl. Engrs., Am. Soc. Engring. Edn., Internat. Bus. Fellows, Internat. Union Radio Sci., Sigma Xi, Eta Kappa Nu., Tau Beta Pi. Home: 11 The Oaks Cir Birmingham AL 35244-1455 Office: The Rouse Group LLC PO Box 361921 Birmingham AL 35236-1921

ROUSE, PRUDENCE ALISON, security services executive; b. Epsom, Surrey, England, Aug. 8, 1944; arrived in Fiji Islands, 1969; d. Cecil Maxwell Cade and Margaret Jeanne (Polden) Mossom; m. Grahame Thomas Rouse, Oct. 28, 1967 (dec. Feb. 1998); children: Jason Douglas, Daniel Maxwell. Hons. degree in Spanish, Inst. of Linguists, London, 1987. Airline stewardess BOAC London, 1965-67; sec. to mgr. PA BOAC Bermuda, 1967-69; sec., personal asst. BOAC Fiji, 1969-70; dir. Sentinel Ltd., Fiji, 1977-82; exec. dir. Sigma Security Ltd., Fiji, 1990-98, SIGMA Security Svcs., 1998; translator, interpretor Spanish Meet and Greet Svc., Fiji. Trustee Reddy Ernest Vision Trust, Fiji, 1998; mem. Western Constituency Coun. of Gen. Electors Party, 1997-98, Western Crimestoppers Com.; chmn. Vuda Neighborhood Work Com. Mem. Inst. of Linguists (U.K.), Women in Politics - Fiji, Pacific-Asia Travel Assn. (Fiji chpt.), Fiji Hotel Assn. (assoc.), Women in Bus. (v.p. 2000—), Fiji Islands (v.p., 1999), Western Comm. (comm. mem. elect), Royal Commonwealth Soc., Fiji Islands (mem. com. 2000—), BOAC (British Overseas Airways Corp.), MIL (Mem. Inst. of Linguists), London, Royal Overseas League. Avocations: classical music, literature, theatre, travel, cultural activities. Observer, Unifem-Funded Post-General Election 1999 Conf., 1999, March 2000 Conf. Office: PO Box 10051, Nadi Airport Fiji

ROUSH, CHARLES DOW, lawyer; b. Phoenix, Nov. 18, 1937; s. Dow Ben and Mary Elizabeth (Spalding) R.; m. Carol Ann Carrigan, Aug. 18, 1962 (div. Aug. 1984); m. Cecilia Helen Roush, Dec. 18, 1984; children: Charles 1959; s. Roushdi Sobhi and Sofie (Morcos) R.; 1 child, Taymour Karim. BS in Internat Bus. Adminstrn., Am. U. Switzerland, 1980; MA in Mgmt., Webster U., 1981. Bank exec. Allied Arab Bank Ltd., London, 1981-85; dir., shareholder Angio Care Ltd., London, 1985-89, Kenetech Internat. Ltd., London, 1985-89, Televideo Overseas Prodns. Ltd., London, 1985-89, Lara Food Ltd., Cairo, 1989—, Lara Internat., Cairo, 1989—, Prestige Cosmetics, Cairo, 1989—, Egyptian Co. Supplies, Cairo, 1989—, Hapi Travel & Tourism, Cairo, 1989—; dir., investor Dhabi Trading Co., Abu Dhabi, United Arab Emirates, 1992—. Avocations: swimming, skiing, squash, stamp colecting, reading. Office: Dhabi Trading Co, PO Box 586, Abu Dhabi United Arab Emirates also: 8 Rostom St Garden City, Cairo Egypt

ROUSSEAU, PIETER GERHARDUS, engineering educator; b. Pretoria, Gauteng, South Africa, Nov. 28, 1963; s. Pieter Gerhardus Rousseau and Johanna Gertruida (Vermeulen) Maartens; m. Amanda Jordaan, July 1, 1989; children: Nicol, Michelle. BMechE, U. Pretoria, 1987, MMechE, 1990, PhD, 1994. Engr. Lab. Advanced Engring. Pty. Ltd., Pretoria, 1988-89; from lectr. to assoc. prof. U. Pretoria, 1989-95; prof. Potchefstroom (South Africa) U., 1995-98, dir. Sch. for Mech. and Materials Engring., 1998—; cons. LGI Pty. Ltd., Pretoria, 1989-91; bd. dirs. M-Tech Cons., Potchefstroom, Enerflow Tech., Potchefstroom, EPS South Africa, Potchefstroom. Contbr. articles to profl. jours. Served with South African Artillery Corps., 1982-83. Found. for R & D Y-rated Rschr. grant, 1995. Mem. ASHRAE, South African Inst. Mech. Engrs., South African Inst. Refrigeration and Air Conditioning Engrs. Avocations: cycling, golf. Office: Potchefstroom U Sch Mechanical and Mater, PO Box X6001, 2520 Potchefstroom South Africa

ROUSSELY, FRANCOIS, electric power industry executive. CEO Electricite De France, Paris. Office: Electricite De France, 2 Rue Louis Marat, 75384 Paris France*

ROUSSET, MICHEL RENÉ, legal educator; b. Chambéry, France, Dec. 27, 1933; s. Pierre Rousset and Suzanne Hérault; m. Yvonne Thérese Cousseau, Apr. 2, 1963; children: Olivier, Jean-François, Anne-Frédérique. Degree in law, U. Grenoble, 1955, degree in polit. sci., 1955, LLD, 1959. Fellow in law and polit. sci. U. Paris, 1962; tchr. U. Rabat, Morocco, 1962-66, Sch. of Adminstrn., Rabat, 1968-72; tchr. Univ. Social Scis., Grenoble, 1972-96, dir. Faculty of Law, 1975-79, pres., 1979-87. Author: The Idea of Public Power in Administrative Law, 1960, Morroco Administrtive Law, 1970, 5th revised edition, 1992, Administrative Law Vols. 1 and 2, 1994, Morrocan Administration, Law and Justice, 1995, The International Action of Local Organizations, 1998. Home: Allée des Contamines, 38240 Meylan France Office: U Social Scis Faculty Law, B P 47-X, 38040 Grenoble France

ROUTLEDGE, EDWIN JOHN, biologist, researcher; b. Ashton-U-Line, Lancashire, Eng., Nov. 1, 1970; s. Timothy William and Catherine (McGivern) R.; m. Priya Mande, Aug. 21, 1999. BSc in Applied Biology with hons., Brunel U., London, 1993, PhD, 1997. Postdoctoral rsch. fellow Brunel U., London, 1993—. Contbr. articles to profl. jours. Avocations: camping, hill walking, guitar, squash. Office: Brunel Univ, Cleveland Rd, Uxbridge UB8 3PH, England

ROUTRAY, JAYANT KUMAR, science educator; b. Govindpur, India, Nov. 11, 1956; s. Nilamani and Uma Devi (Pradhan) R.; m. Manjurani Patnaik, June 20, 1981; children: Sambit, Sumansudha. BS with honors, Utkal U., Bhubaneswar, India, 1974, MS in Geography, 1976, PhD in Geography, 1987; MRP in Regional Planning, Indian Inst. of Tech., Kharagapur, 1979. Asst. dir. Nat. Inst. of Rural Devel., Hyderabad, India, 1979-80; lectr. in geography Utkal U., Bhubaneswar, 1980-88, reader in geography, 1990; asst. prof. Asian Inst. of Tech., Bangkok, 1988-93, assoc. prof. regional and rural devel. planning, 1993—; cons. UNDP, Kathmandu, Nepal, 1997. Fellow Royal Geograph. Soc./Londong, Inst. of Town Planners/India. Hinduism. Avocations: info. collecting on devel. and environ., stamp collecting, cooking. Office: Asian Inst Tech, PO Box 4/Klong Luang Pathum Thani, 12120 Bangkok Thailand

ROUTSON, CLELL DENNIS, manufacturing company executive; b. Elkhart, Ind., Oct. 8, 1946; s. Clell Dean and Olene Maize (Replogle) R.; m. Paula Leone McLallin, Sept. 2, 1967 (div. June 1988); children: Clell Dustin, Courtney Trevor; m. Suzann Kay Bron, 1995. BSBA, Ball State U., Muncie, Ind., 1971. With Proctor & Gamble, Cin., 1971-74; nat. sales mgr. Palmer Instruments, Inc., Cin., 1974-76; with Nordson Corp., Amherst, Ohio, 1976-81, MCC Powers, Cleve., Chgo., Singapore, 1981-86; sales mgr., v.p., pres. Burgess, Inc., Freeport, Ill., 1986-89; mgr. mktg. and sales, v.p. sales and mktg. Kloppenberg & Co., Englewood, Colo., 1990-92; v.p. ops., gen. mgr. T.E.I. Engineered Products, Englewood, 1992-96; pres. (one-yr. contract) Bailco Svc. Corp., Englewood, 1996-97; pres. Composite Tek, Boulder, Colo., 2000—; mng. dir. Resource Dynamics, Singapore, Chgo., and Denver, 1985-86, 96-99. Contbr. articles to profl. jours. Mem. Met. Club (Denver). Republican. Baptist. E-mail: croutson@compositetek.com. Office: Compositetek Mfg Co 6101 Lookout Rd Ste B Boulder CO 80301-3359

ROUTTI, RISTO ILKKA, advocate; b. Jyvaskyla, Finland, Jan. 25, 1937. Stockman Western Auto, Wichita, Kans., 1959-60; mng. dir. Sisa-Suomen Moottori Oy, Jyvaskyla, Finland, 1960-63; zone mgr. Oy Ford Ab, Helsinki, Finland, 1963-66; bus. mgmt. rep. GM, Helsinki, Finland, 1966-68; trainee Pontiac (Mich.) Motor Divsn., 1968-70; mktg. GM, 1970-81; human rights activist, 1982—. Mem. Equality of Justice Orgn., Finland, 1988-89, Acad. Polit. Sci., N.Y.C., 1997—, Ctr. for Study of the Presidency, Washington, 1998—. Baptist. Avocations: biking, photography, chess.

ROUVEIX, BERNARD JEAN, pharmacology educator; b. Paris, Mar. 16, 1946; s. Jacques and Monique (Dupin) Rouveix; m. Agnes Grenier; children: Charlotte, Marion, Mathieu. MD, diploma cellular pharmacology, U. Paris, 1975, M in Human Biology, 1976, diploma of study/rsch. in human biology, 1978; PhD, U. London, 1981. Resident Pasteur Inst. Hosp., Paris, 1971-74;

sr. registrar and head clin. pharmacology dept. Claude Bernard Hosp., Paris, 1979-90; assoc. prof. clin. pharmacology Bichat Cochin, Paris, 1997; expert in clin. pharmacology Health Ministry; expert Paris law cts.; lectr. in field. Author 10 sci. books; contbr. numerous publs. to internat. med. jours. Recipient Laureat French Med. Acad., Wellcome Found. Trust. Mem. Internat. Soc. Immunopharmacology, Internat. Union Pharmacology, Am. Soc. Clin. Pharmacology and Therapeutic, Am. Soc. Microbiology, French Soc. Pharmacology, Soc. de Pharmaco-Toxicologie Cellulaire, Soc. de Pathologie infectieuse de Langue Française. Office: Hosp Cochin, 27 rue Faubourg St Jacques, 75679 Paris Cedex 14, France

ROUVINEZ, CHRISTOPHE, risk manager; b. Sion, Valais, Switzerland, June 8, 1965. BSc in Physics, ETH, Zurich, 1990, PhD in Physics, 1995. Cert. fin. risk mgr. Rschr. EPFL, Lausanne, Switzerland, 1990-95; quantitative analyst Credit Suisse First Boston, Zurich, 1995-97; risk mgr. Credit Suisse First Boston, London, 1997-98, Zurich, 1998—. Contbr. articles to profl. jours.

ROUX, DIDIER CHARLES, chemist; b. Neuilly, France, May 16, 1955; s. Raymond and Nicole (Fontanille) R.; m. Denise Bordet, July 15, 1976 (div. 1985); children: Aurelien, Guillaume; m. Marie-Lise Bonnet, July 26, 1997; children: Manon, Julia. Diploma in physics, U. Paris, 1979; DSc, U. Orsay, 1990. Prof. Edn. Dept., France, 1975-80; from rschr. to dir. rsch. CNRS, Bordeaux, France, 1980—. Office: CNRS, Ave Schweitzer, 33600 Pessac France

ROUX, MICHEL ANDRE, restaurateur; b. Charolles, Saone Loire, France, Apr. 19, 1941; s. Henri and Germaine (Triger) R.; m. m. Francoise Becquet, Feb. 1963 (Jan. 1979); children: Christine, Francine, Alain; m. Robyn Margaret Joyce, May 1984. Apprentice, Patisserie Loyal, Paris, 1955-58. Commis patissier-cuisinier/Ambassador to Gt. Britain Paris, 1958-59; commis de cuisine Melle Cecile de Rothschild, Paris, 1960, chef, 1963-67; cons. Brit. Airways, Celebrity Cruises Ships. Co-star (with Albert Roux) on BBC2/thirteen week cookery program; appearances on This is Your Life, Terry Wogan, Jim'll Fix It, Inat the Deep End, This Morning, TV AM, Open Air, That's Life, Masterchefs in England, also nat. TV and radio shows in France, U.S.A., Australia and S. Africa; contbr. articles to profl. jours./newspapers; author: New Classic Cuisine, 1983—, Roux Brothers on Patisserie, 1986—, At Home with the Roux Brothers, 1988, French Country Cooking, 1989, Cooking For Two, 1991, Desserts - "A Lifelong Passion" 1994, Sauces, 1996, (autobiography) Life is a Menu, 2000, others. Recipient Silver medal des Cuisiniers Francais, Paris, 1963, Ville de Paris, 1966, finalist Prosper Montagne, Paris, 1967, Silver medal Sucre Tire et Souffle, London, 1970, second prize, Prix Internat. Taittinger, Paris, 1971, Gold medal Cuisiniers Francais, Paris, 1972, Meilleur Ouvrier de France en Patisserie, Paris, 1976; laureat Krug Prize of Excellence, 1979, Restaurant of Yr. award, London, 1981, numerous to Man of Yr., Royal Assn. Disability/Rehab., London, 1989, Third Egon Ronay Star, 89. Mem. Acad. Culinaire de France, Assn. Relais et Desserts/France (v.p.), Assn. Relais et Chateaux (1st v.p.), Benedicts Club, others. Avocations: shooting, walking, skiing. Office: The Waterside Inn Ferry Rd, Bray on Thames, Berkshire SL6 2AT, England

ROUZAUD, PETER BAPTISTE, toxicologist, educator; b. Auch, France, June 4, 1943; s. Peter Leonard and Juliette (Dulong) R.; m. Liliana Simon, Sept. 15, 1978; 1 child, John Baptiste Charles. DS in Physics, U. Toulouse, France, 1966, D Pharmacy, 1971, MD, 1975; postgrad., U. Paris, 1976, 81. Mem. staff Atomic Energy Commn., Limeil, France, 1967; asst. Sch. Pharmacy U. Toulouse, 1968, tchr. Sch. Pharmacy, 1985—; practitioner Hosp. Purpan, Toulouse, 1975—; pvt. gen. practice medicine Toulouse, 1975—; physician specialist in work medicine Air France, Toulouse, 1978-88; expert Ct. d'Appel, Toulouse, 1989—; physician cons. World Bank, Washington, 1989, Air France, 1978-88. Journalist Panorama du medecin, Paris, 1976-86; contbr. articles to profl. publs. Col. med. corps French armed forces, 1970-71. Avocations: skiing, music, water skiing, bicycling. Home: 30 Ave Victor Segoffin, 31400 Toulouse France Office: Hosp Purpan, Pl Baylac, 31059 Toulouse Cedex, France

ROVELL, MICHAEL JAY, lawyer; b. Chgo., Mar. 30, 1949; s. Bernard and Charlotte (Schaefer) R.; m. Laurie Strauss, Sept. 2, 1979; children: Brandon, Kendall, Ryan. BA with honors, U. Ill., Chgo., 1969; JD with honors, U. Ill., 1972. Bar: Ill. 1972, U.S. Dist. Ct. (no. and so. dists.) Ill. 1972, U.S. Ct. Appeals (7th cir.) 1973, U.S. Ct. Appeals (8th cir.) 1981, U.S. Supreme Ct. 1983, U.S. Ct. Appeals (5th cir.) 1986, U.S. Ct. Appeals (1st cir.) 1990, U.S. Dist. Ct. P.R. 1992, U.S. Ct. Appeals (10th cir.) 1992, U.S. Ct. Appeals (3rd cir.) 1993, U.S. Ct. Appeals (2nd cir.) 1996, U.S. Ct. Appeals (9th cir.), 1997, Belgium 1997. Assoc. Jenner & Block, Chgo., 1972-78, ptnr., 1979-90; prin. Law Offices of Michael J. Rovell, Chgo., 1990—; dir. Cook County Spl. Bail Project, 1972-74; chief exec. officer, bd. dirs. Sunbelt Communications, Colorado Springs, Colo., 1976-78; of counsel Wampler, Buchanan & Breen, Miami, Troncoso & Becker, San Juan, P.R., Law Offices of Robert Bright, Oklahoma City and affiliate offices London, Paris, Brussels; bd. editors U. Ill. Law Forum, 1971-72. Bd. dirs. Steppenwolf Theatre, Chgo., 1979-81. Mem. ABA (coord. litigation seminar on electronic surveillance), Ill. Bar Assn., Hillcrest Country Club (Long Grove, Ill.). Avocations: golf, tennis, bowling. Home: 1516 Christina Ln Lake Forest IL 60045-3848 Office: 20 N Clark St Ste 2450 Chicago IL 60602-5002

ROVERA, GIOVANNI DANIELE, electrical engineer; b. Paesana, Italy, Feb. 22, 1950; s. Alberto and Caterina (Martino) R.; m. Fulvia Rey, Nov. 19, 1996; 1 child, Martina. Grad. in engring., Poly. U. Torino, 1981. Rschr. IEN, Torino, Italy, 1982-84; cons. in field, 1984-89; rschr. BNM-LPTF, Paris, 1989—. Mem. IEEE. Avocation: hang gliding. Office: BNM-LPTF Obs Paris, 61 avde l'Observatoire, 75014 Paris France

ROVERSI-MONACO, FABIO, academic administrator; b. Addis Ababa, Ethiopia, Dec. 18, 1938. Degree in law, U. Bologna (Italy), 1962, doctorate, 1967; hon. degree, Brown U., Complutensian U. Madrid, Pantheon-Sorbonne U., Johns Hopkins U., Soka U., U. Externado de Colombia, St. Petersburg U., U. Barcelona, U. Cordoba, Pontifica U. Cattolica de Minas Gerais in Belo Horizonte, U. Salta (Argentina), U. Montreal, Victoria U., U. Denver, U. Catolica de Uruguay. Lectr. Instns. Pub. Law, Faculty Polit. Sci. U. Bologna, 1969-72, prof. adminstrv. law, 1971, prof. Instns. Pub. Law, Faculty Polit. Sci., 1972-74, prof. Constnl. Law, Faculty of Law, 1974-77, chair Adminstrv. Law, Faculty of Law, 1977—, mem. bd. adminstrn., 1973-78, dir. Sch. Adminstrv. Sci. (now Postgrad. Sch. Adminstrv. Law and Sci. of Adminstrn.), 1978—, rector, 1985-2000; vice chmn. Cassa di Risparmio, Bologna, Spain, 1995; now v.p. Cassa di Risparmio; dir. energy project Nat. Rsch. Coun.; chair legal com. Italian Assn. Urban Heating; vis. prof. U. La Plata. Author: Gli enti de gestion-struttura-funzioni-limiti, 1967, La delegazione amministrativa nel quadro dell'ordinamento regionale, 1970, Profili giuridici del decentramento nell'organizzazione amministrativa, 1970, Commento alla Statuto della Regione Emilia-Romagna, 1972, Le partecipazioni statali. Un'analisi critica, 1977; editor jour. and monographic series Sanita pubblica, monographic series Energia e Ambiente; assoc. editor various pub. law jours.; contbr. articles, studies, revs. to profl. jours. Decorated Commendatore Republic of Italy, Ordem de Sant'Iago de Espada Republic of Portugal, Legion d'Honneur Pres. French Republic, Cross of Grand Officer Maltese Order of Merit, Gran Cruz de Alfonso X El Sabio of the King of Spain. Italian Acad. Advanced Studies in Am. (bd. gurantors), European Secretariat Sci. Publs. (pres.), Internat. Inst. Adminstrv. Sci. (pres. Italian br.). Office: U Bologna, Via Zambani 33, 40126 Bologna Italy

ROVINE, ARTHUR WILLIAM, lawyer; b. Phila., Apr. 29, 1937; s. George Isaac and Rosanna (Lipsitz) R.; m. Phyllis Ellen Hamburger, Apr. 7, 1963; children: Joshua, Deborah. AB, U. Pa., 1958; LLB, Harvard U., 1961; PhD, Columbia U., 1966. Bar: D.C. 1964, N.Y. 1984. Assoc. Curtis, Mallet-Prevost, Colt & Mosle, N.Y.C., 1964-66; asst. prof. Cornell U., Ithaca, N.Y., 1966-72; editor Digest of U.S. Practice in International Law U.S. Dept. State, Washington, 1972-75, asst. legal adviser, 1975-81; agt of U.S. Govt. to Iran-U.S. Claims Tribunal U.S. Dept. State, The Hague, Netherlands, 1981-83; of counsel Baker & McKenzie, N.Y.C., 1983-85, ptnr., then sr. ptnr., 1985—; adj. prof. law Georgetown U., Washington, 1977-81; vis. lectr. law Yale U., 1998. Author: The First Fifty Years: The Secretary-General in World Politics, 1920-1970, 1970; editor: Digest of U.S. Practice in International Law, 1973, 74; co-editor: The Case Law of the International Court of Justice, 1968, 1972, 1974, 1976; bd. editors Am. Jour. Internat. Law, 1977-87; also articles on internat. law. Mem. panel on settlement of transnat. bus. disputes, N.Y. panel Ctr. for Pub. Resources; chmn. law subcom. of internat. adv. coun. on profl. edn. Coun. on Internat. Ednl. Exch.; mem. Coun. on Fgn. Rels. Mem. ABA (chmn. internat. law sect. 1985-86, del. to Ho. of Dels. 1988-90), Am. Soc. Internat. Law (cert. of merit 1974, exec. coun. 1975-77, v.p. 1998-99, pres. 2000—), U.S. Coun. for Internat. Bus. (arbitration com.), Am. Arbitration Assn. (panel of arbitrators), Assn. Bar City N.Y. (coun. on internat. affairs). Home: 150 E 61st St New York NY 10021-8529 Office: Baker & McKenzie 805 3rd Ave New York NY 10022-7513

ROVINELLI, JUDITH FRANCES, financial advisor; b. Bklyn., Nov. 6, 1959; d. Frank Henry and Cecilia Josephine Czajkowski; m. Robert Thomas Rovinelli, July 22, 1989. AA, Sacred Heart U., Fairfield, Conn., 1988, BS, 1992, MBA, 1998. Reg. rep. Conn., N.Y. State Ins. and Securities Commr.; lic. Nat. Assn. Securities Dealers. Product mgr., acct. mgr. Anthem Blue Cross/Blue Shield, North Haven, Conn., 1981-98; project mgr. Empire Blue Cross/Blue Shield, Middletown, N.Y., 1998-99; personal fin. advisor Am. Express Fin. Advisors, Woodbridge, Conn., 1999—; cions. Consortium Health Plans, Columbia, Md., 1998; mem. adv. bd. Marine Mktg. to Women, Winter Park, Fla., 1996-98. Sec. Gov.'s Ridge Condominium Assn., Trumbull, Conn., 1993-95. Mem. Alpha Sigma Lambda. Avocations: fishing, boating, interior design. Home: 23 Old Coach Ln Trumbull CT 06611-1613 Office: Am Express Fin Advisor 4 Armstrong Park Rd Shelton CT 06484

ROVINSKY, LEV ABRAM, food engineer; b. Moscow, Nov. 30, 1940; s. Abram Evsey Rovinsky and Adelheid July Szwirbljansky; m. Elen Nikolai Piskareva, Nov. 6, 1950; children: Michail Lev, Marina Lev. MS, Moscow State Acad. Food Techs., 1968; PhD, All-Russian Inst. Food Biotech, 1980. Lab. mgr. Inst. Food Biotechnology, Moscow, 1968-83; sr. rschr. Sci.-Indsl. Corp. of Food Equipment, Moscow, 1985-94, State Food Inst., Moscow, 1996—. Author: Mathematical modeling and optimization of microbiological processes, 1978, (textbook) Automation of Food Manufactures, 1977, 85, Handbook for Alcohol Production; contbr. articles to profl. jours.; patentee in field. Mem. Russian Microbiology Soc., N.Y. Acad. Scis. Home: 19-1-284 Krasny kazanetz Ul, 111395 Moscow Russia

ROVIRA, ALFREDO L., lawyer; b. La Rioja, Argentina, Feb. 7, 1945; s. Lauro and Virginia H. (Santirso) R.; m. Monica E. Escalante; 5 children. Grad. law, U. Buenos Aires. Pvt. practice law Buenos Aires, 1967-71; sr. ptnr. Brons & Salas, Buenos Aires, 1971—; chmn. bd. dirs. Monsanto Argentina S.A. Buenos Aires. Mem. U.S. C. of C. in Argentina (chmn. legal and tax com. 1988—, bd. dirs. 1991). Roman Catholic. Office: Brons & Salas, Marcelo T de Alvear 624, 1058 Buenos Aires Argentina

ROVIRA, ANTONI, academic administrator; b. Barcelona, Spain, Jan. 5, 1948; s. Ramón Rovira and Maria Benet; m. Rosa Maria Coll, Oct. 28, 1977; children: Beatriz, Isabel. Grad. in Econs., Barcelona U., 1970. Export mgr. Electrolisis del Cobre, S.A., Spain, 1971-86; dir. COPCA, Spain, 1987-92, Escuela Superior de Comercio Internat., Spain, 1992—. Pres. Young Chamber Barcelona, 1975, Import/Export Fedn. Spain, 1981. Avocations: sailing, tennis, skiing. Office: ESCI, Po Pujades 1, 08003 Barcelona Spain

ROVIROSA, ANGELES, radiotherapist; b. Barcelona, Spain, Aug. 9, 1960; d. Jose and Rosario (Casino) R.; m. Jose Maria Oliva, Apr. 22, 1989. Degree in medicine & surgery, U. Barcelona, Spain, 1985. Cons. Hosp. Clinic, Barcelona, Spain, 1993—. Contbr. articles to profl. jours. Radiation Oncology fellow Hosp. Vall Hebron, Barcelona, 1989-92. Mem. Soc. Therapeutic Radiology & Oncology, Assn. Espanola Radiotherapy.Oncology, Soc. Catalano-Balear Oncology. Avocations: classical music, opera, museums, travel, cooking. Office: Hosp Clin U Barcelona, C/Villarroel No 170, 08036 Barcelona Spain

ROVISON, JOHN MICHAEL, JR., chemical engineer; b. North Tonawanda, N.Y., June 15, 1959; s. John Michael and Veronica Marie (Donat) R.; m. Beverly Jean Farinet, Sept. 6, 1986 (div. Oct. 1989); m. Janet Marie Konieczny, Apr. 27, 1991; 1 child, Kevin Michael (dec.). BA in Biology, BSChemE, Washington U., 1982; MS in Cancer Biology, Niagara U., 1986. Physics tchr. North Tonawanda High Sch., 1985; assoc. process engr. Ag Chem. Group FMC Corp., Middleport, N.Y., 1982-83, process engr. Ag Chem. Group, 1983-84, sr. process engr. Ag Chem. Group, 1986-90; sr. process engr. divsn. peroxygen chem. FMC Corp., Buffalo, 1990-91, process group leader divsn. peroxygen chem., 1992-93, prod. area supr. divsn. peroxygen chem., 1993-94, prodn. mgr. PXD, 1994-96, tech. mgr. AOD, 1996—; mem. new products evaluation bd. Chem. Engring. McGraw Hill, 1983-84; tech. cons. Ag Chem. Group FMC Corp., Middleport, 1985. Mem. Resolve through Sharing Parents Group, Williamsville, N.Y., 1992. Mem. Am. Inst. Chem. Engrs., Am. Chem. Soc. Roman Catholic. Achievements include redesigning Furadan Milling Plant to reduce N2 usage, persulfate caking issues and development of mineral peroxides; design and installation of process ventilation system for phosplant; originated mathematical system to study S1 endonuclease activity on plasmids in alcohol environments using hyperchromic shifts; helped lead effort for plant ISO 9002 certification, implemented first self-directed union workforce in FMC; converted potential waste stream into environmental end use product; principle author of FMC corporate standard for storage and handling of ammonia; co-chmn. behavior-based safety and implementation team, 1997-99; co-author: Preoxygen product quality and safety optimization using systematic and innovative tools, understanding and controlling peroxygen product safety and quality in the critical drying step; prin. author paper detailing the use of risk benefit evaluations to minimize off-site hazard consequences with anhydrous ammonia storage systems. Home: 6066 Ward Rd Sanborn NY 14132-9366 Office: FMC Corp Sawyer Ave And River Rd Tonawanda NY 14150

ROWAN, CHAD See AKEBONO, TARO

ROWAN-ROBINSON, JEREMY, law educator; b. Edinburgh, Scotland, Mar. 29, 1944; s. John Christopher and Audrey Christine (Wynne) Rowan-Robinson; m. Yvonne Joan Lee, Apr. 23, 1978; children: Timothy, Matthew. MA, U. Kent, Canterbury, Eng., 1971; LLM, U. Aberdeen, Scotland, 1982. Solicitor Supreme Ct. Eng. and Wales. Sr. asst. solicitor Hillingdon London Borough Coun., 1968-70; solicitor, dep. clk. Westmorland County Coun., Kendal, Eng., 1971-75; solicitor Lake Dist. Spl. Planning Bd., Kendal, 1975-78; lectr., sr. lectr. dept. land econs. Aberdeen U., 1978-89, prof. planning and environ. law, 1989—, head dept. land economy, 1994-97, dir. Ctr. for Environ. Law, 1994-99; cons. in planning and environ. law Paull & Williamsons Solicitors, Aberdeen, 1992—. Author: Scottish Planning Law and Procedure, 1985, Land Development and the Intrastructure Lottery, 1988, Planning by Agreement in Scotland, 1989, Planning Law and Procedure, 1989, Compulsory Purchase and Compensation: The Law in Scotland, 1990, Crime and Regulation, 1990, Public Access to the Scottish Countryside: A Guide to Law Practice and Procedure, 1993, Compulsory Purchase and Compensation, 1995. Mem. Royal Town Planning Inst. (legal assoc.), Soc. Pub. Tchrs. Law, U.K. Environ. Law Assn., Scottish Nat. Heritage (bd. dirs.). Avocations: hill walking, sailing. Office: Aberdeen U Dept Law, Taylor Bldg Kings Coll, Old Aberdeen AB24 3UB, Scotland

ROWDEN, MARCUS AUBREY, lawyer, former government official; b. Detroit, Mar. 13, 1928; s. Louis and Gertrude (Lifsitz) Rosenzweig; m. Justine Leslie Bessman, July 21, 1950; children: Gwen, Stephanie. B.A. in Econs, U. Mich., Ann Arbor, 1950, J.D. with distinction, 1953. Bar: Mich. 1953, D.C. 1978. Trial atty. Dept. Justice, 1953-58; legal advisor U.S. Mission to European Communities, 1959-62; solicitor, assoc. gen. counsel, gen. counsel AEC, 1965-74; commr., chmn. U.S. NRC, Washington, 1975-77; 2tnr. Fried, Frank, Harris, Shriver and Jacobson, Washington, 1977—. Served with AUS, 1946-47. Decorated officer Order Legion of Honor Republic of France; Recipient Disting. Service award AEC, 1972. Mem. Am., Fed., Mich., D.C. bar assns., Internat. Nuclear Law Assn., Order of Coif. Home: 7937 Deepwell Dr Bethesda MD 20817-1927 Office: Fried Frank Harris Shriver and Jacobson 1001 Pennsylvania Ave NW Washington DC 20004-2505

ROWE, BONNIE GORDON, music company executive; b. Buford, Ga., May 3, 1922; s. Bonnie Gordon and Alma (Poole) R.; m. Mary Wilburta Shidler; 1 child, Sharon Lynn; m. Gloria Lucille Fairfax, Feb. 17, 1962 (div.); 1 child, Susan Rebecca. Student, Ga. Evening Coll., 1939-41, U. Wichita, 1948-49, Ga. State Coll., 1949-52. Traffic mgr. Bonanza Air Lines, Las Vegas, 1946-48, music tchr., 1948-52; owner Rowe Accordion Distbg. Co., Rowe Accordion Ctr., Atlanta, 1952-56, Atlanta Music Pub. Co., 1956—, B. Rowe Music Co., Atlanta, 1957—; pres.-treas. B. Rowe Enterprises, Inc., 1973—. Composer: Accordionique, 1953, Vivolet, 1956, More and More and More, 1964, Dedication, 1964, All I Really See is You, 1965, I Love Only You, 1965, Festival March, 1965, Perdudio Reminisci, 1969. Bd. dirs. Sandtown Found., Atlanta. Lt. col. USAAF, World War II, ETO. Decorated Air medals with three oak leaf clusters. Mem. 781st Bomb Squadron Assn. (465th bomb group WWII), Southeastern Accordion Assn. (past pres.), Nat. Assn. Music Mchts., Atlanta Fedn. Musicians (life), Travelers Protective Assn., Atlanta C. of C., Res. Officers Assn., Ret. Officers Assn., Air Force Assn., Internat. Platform Assn., Am. Legion, Sandtown Civitan Club (past pres., lt. gov., past pres. Met. Atlanta Coun.), Elks (exalted ruler 1976, 88, 89, past pres. past exalted rulers assn., trustee Union City, state organist Ga. Elks Assn.), Dobbins AFB Officers Club, The Mil. Order of the World Wars (jr. vice commdr.), Gamma Delta Phi. Home: 5085 Erin Rd SW Atlanta GA 30331-7810 Office: 6102 Mableton Pkwy Mableton GA 30126-4302

ROWE, HARRISON EDWARD, electrical engineer; b. Chgo., Jan. 29, 1927; s. Edward and Joan (Golden) R.; m. Alicia Jane Steeves, Feb. 10, 1951; children—Amy Rogers, Elizabeth Joanne, Edward Steeves, Alison Pickard. B.S. in Elec. Engring, Mass. Inst. Tech., 1948, M.S., 1950, Sc.D., 1952; M of Engring. (hon.), Stevens Inst. Tech., 1988. Mem. tech. staff Radio Research Lab., Bell Labs., Holmdel, N.J., 1952-84; Anson Wood Burchard prof. elec. engring. Stevens Inst. Tech., Hoboken, N.J., 1984-93, prof. emeritus, 1993—; vis. lectr. U. Calif., Berkeley, 1963, Imperial Coll., U. London, 1968; mem. Def. Sci. Bd. Task Force, 1972-74. Author: Signals and Noise in Communication Systems, 1965, Electromagnetic Propagation in Multi-Mode Random Media, 1999; assoc. editor: IEEE Trans. on Communication, 1974-76; contbr. articles to profl. jours.; patentee in field. Served with USN, 1945-46. Co-recipient Microwave prize, 1972, David Sarnoff award, 1977. Fellow IEEE; mem. Internat. Union Radio Sci., Monmouth Symphony Soc., Navesink Country Club, Sigma Xi, Tau Beta Pi, Eta Kappa Nu. Unitarian. Clubs: Shrewsbury Sailing and Yacht, Appalachian Mountain. Home: 9 Buttonwood Ln Rumson NJ 07760-1045

ROWE, MICHAEL DUANE, artist; b. Lykens, Pa., Nov. 5, 1947; m. Kathryn Jean Branoff. Student, Art Inst. Pitts., 1971-72. Exhibited in shows at Art Assn. Harrisburg, Pa., 1985, 86, 87, State Mus. Pa., 1986, 87, Doshi Gallery, Harrisburg, 1987, Cheltenham (Pa.) Art Ctr., 1989, 92, Delaplaine Art Ctr., Frederick, Md., 1989 (1st prize 1989), 90, 91, Immaculata (Pa.) Coll., 1990, U. of the Arts, Phil., 1990, Butler Inst. of Am. Art, Youngstown, Ohio, 1990, 92, Phila. Art Alliance, 1990, Altenative Mus., N.Y.C., 1990, 91, 95, Spaces, Cleve., 1991, Alexandria (La.) Art Mus., 1991, Pa. State U., 1992, Allentown (Pa.) Mus. Art, 1992, Muhlenberg Coll., Allentown, 1992 (award 1992), Michael Stone Gallery, Washington, 1992, Ea. N.Mex. U., 1992, Del. Ctr. for Contemporary Arts, Wilmington, 1993, Laguna Gloria Art Mus., Austin, Tex., 1993, Silvermine Art Guild Exhibit, New Cannan, Conn., 1993, Pa. State U., Univ. Park, 1993, East Tenn. U., Johnson City, 1994, Chrysler Mus., Norfolk, Va., 1994, Davidson (N.C.) Coll. Visual Arts Ctr., 1995, Southern Alleghenies Mus. of Art, 1995, Loretto, Pa., 1996, 97, 99, Susquehanna Art Mus., Harrisburg, Pa., 1998, Whitaker Ctr., Harrisburg, 1999; represented in permanent collection So. Alleghenies Mus., Loretto, Pa. Grantee Art Matters, Inc., 1988; Pa. Coun. of the Arts fellow, 1993. Episcopalian. Avocations: running, travelling, reading. Home: 814 Meadow Ln Camp Hill PA 17011-1545

ROWE, PETER NOEL, chemical engineering educator; b. Lancaster, Eng., Dec. 25, 1919; s. Charles H. and Kate W. (Storry) R.; m. Pauline Garmirian, Dec. 20, 1952; children: Andrew Francis, Timothy David. BSc in Tech., U. Manchester Inst Sci & Tech., Eng., 1949; PhD, Imperial Coll., London, 1954; DSc in Engring., London U., 1965; DSc (hon.), U. Brussels, 1978. Chartered engr., U.K. Prin. sci. officer U.K. Atomic Energy Authority, 1958-65; Ramsay Meml. prof. Univ. Coll., London, 1965-85, prof., 1985—. Editor Chem. Engring. Sci., 1966-86; contbr. numerous articles to profl. jours. With Royal Air Force, 1940-46. Liveryman, Co. of Engrs., London, 1984. Fellow Inst. Chem. Engrs. (pres. 1981-82, mem. coun. 1984, Moulton medal 1973), Royal Acad. Engring. (hon. sec. 1982-85). Office: Univ Coll Dept Chem Engring, Gower St, London WC1E 6BT, England

ROWE, SUNG MAN, university executive, educator; b. Kwangju, Korea, Apr. 26, 1939; parents Chun Eun Rowe and Kwang Sin Cha; m. Jo Ja Han, Mar. 20, 1968; children: Hye Gyung, Hye Won, Hey Eun, Young Hak. BSc, Chonnam Nat. U., Kwangju, 1964, MSc, 1967, PhD, 1974. Cert. Bd. Orthopedic Surgery, Bd. Rehab. From instr. to asst. prof. to assoc. prof. Chonnam Nat. U., Kwangju, 1973-85, prof., 1985—; supt. Chonnam Univ. Hosp., Chonnam Nat. U., Kwangju, 1993-96; pres. Chonnam Nat. U., Kwangju, 1996—. Inventor in field; contbr. articles to profl. jours. V.p. YMCA Bd. Com., Kwangju, 1996, Korean Hosp. Assn., Seoul; mem. Com. New Ednl. Comty., 1998; permanent mem. Adv. Com. of Dem. and Peaceful Unification, 1998; vice chmn. Korean Coun. of Pres. of Nat. and Public U., 1998-2000; v.p. Social Service Assn. of Korean U., 1999-2000. Maj. Korean Army, 1969-72. Decorated Order of Mil. Merit, Govt. Korea, 1972; named Best Citizen of Kwangju, Kwangju City, 1987; recipient Acad. Award of Mudung prize, 1992. Fellow SIROT, SICOT, Western Pacific Orthopaedic Assn.; mem. Korean Pediat. Orthopedic Soc. (pres. 1991-92), Korean Orthopaedic Sports Medicine (pres. 1992-94), Korean Hip Soc. (pres. 1995-96), Korean Fracture Soc. (pres. 1995-96), Assn. for Orthopaedic Rsch. (bd.). E-mail: smrowe@chonnam.chonnam.ac.kr. Home: 101-501 Hyundae Apt 270, Hak-dong Dong-gu, Kwangju Korea Office: Chonnam Nat U Hosp, 8 Hak-Dong Dong-Gu Dept Ortho, 501-757 Kwangju Korea

ROWE, WILLIAM BRIAN, university director, mechanical engineering educator; b. Plymouth, Devon, U.K., June 17, 1939; s. Herbert Tyack and Daisy Ella Bertram (Whitehead) R.; m. Margaret Ruth Gemmell, Apr. 1, 1961; children: Ivor James, Ella Christine. BSc in Prodn. Engring., Aston U., Birmingham, Eng., 1961; PhD in Machine Tools, Manchester (Eng.) U., 1964, DSc, 1975. Engring. apprentice Austin Motor Co., Birmingham, 1955-61; sponsored researcher Wickman Machine Tool Co., Coventry, Eng., 1961-64, sr. project engr., 1964-67; sr. lectr. Lanchester Poly., Coventry, 1967-68, prin. lectr., 1968-73; head mech. engring. dept. Liverpool (Eng.) Poly., 1973-88, assoc. rector, 1988-90, asst. rector, 1990-92; dir. AMTREL Liverpool John Moores U., 1992—; chmn. HEFCE Gen. Engring. Rsch. Assessment Exercise, 1991, 96; mem. programme adv. group for engring. Polys. and Colls. Funding Coun., London, 1989-92; mem. advanced mfg. tech. com. Dept. Trade and Industry/Sci. and Engring. Rsch. Coun., London, 1989-93; mem. Lickley Report Engring. Design W.P., Sci. and Engring. Rsch. Coun., London, 1982-83, chair edn. and tng. panel of advanced mfg. tech. com., 1990-93; Theodore Krengel vis. prof. Technion Inst., 1978; mem. parliamentary and sci. com. House of Commons, 1990-97. Author: Design Procedures for Externally Pressurized Bearings, 1971, Hydrostatic and Hybrid Bearing Design, 1983; patentee in field; contbr. numerous articles to profl. jours. Goldsmiths Co. fellow, 1972; Sci. and Engring. Rsch. Coun. grantee, 1968—, Brit. Coun. grantee, 1980; recipient Joseph Whitworth award, 1971, 91. Fellow Instn. Mech. Engrs. (tribology group com. London chpt. 1988—, trustee, recipient Donald Julius Groen prize 1988, recipient A.M. Strickland prize, 1997); Instn. Prodn. Engrs.; mem. Internat. Coll. Prodn. Rsch. (U.K.) Ltd. (chair 1994-98), Coll. Internat. Rsch. Prodn., Mensa. Avocations: books, gardening, bridge. Home: Formentor Dibbinsdale Rd, Bromborough CH63 0HJ, England Office: Liverpool John Moores U, Byrom St, Liverpool L3 3AF, England

ROWELL, BARBARA CABALLERO, academic administrator; b. New Orleans, Sept. 5, 1922; d. Albert Henry Wischnewske (stepfather) and Antoinette (Angelo) Caballero; m. J.C. Rowell, Dec. 17, 1941; children: Jerrie Carlene, Kerry Gene, Ricky Ray. AA in Bus. Adminstrn., Okaloosa Walton Jr. Coll., Niceville, Fla., 1973; BA in Social Scis., U. West Fla., 1987. Exec. sec. Bishop Enterprises, Ft. Walton Beach; office mgr. and real estate property mgr. Fred Cooke Real Estate, Ft. Walton Beach, Fla., adminstrv. sec. to v.p. Okaloosa Walton Jr. Coll., Niceville. Leader brownie scouts Girl Scouts U.S., 1954-56, cub scouts Boy Scouts Am., 1957-59; bd. dirs. U. West Fla., Sr. Ctr. for Life Long Learning, 1993-98, chair univ svc. com., 1993-94,

97-98, pres. 1995, began Writing Lab, 1997; pres. 1995; originator, implementor U. West Fla. Tutor Program, 1993, 94, 97, 98, Career Fair, 1994, started scholarship program, 1995, Proctor Program, 1995, Writing Lab., 1997; presenter S.E. Conf. Insts. of Learning in Retirement, Charleston, S.C., 1995; gov.'s campaign vol.; state legislature campaign vol. Mem. AAUW, DAV Aux., Order of Ea. Star (past matron). Democrat. Roman Catholic. Avocations: education, travel, reading, gardening, dancing, volunteering.

ROWELL, EDWARD MORGAN, retired foreign service officer, lecturer; b. Oakland, Calif., Oct. 13, 1931; s. Edward Joseph and Mary Helen (Mohler) R.; m. Lenora Mary Wood, Aug. 23, 1957; children: Edward Oliver, Karen Elizabeth Schuler, Christopher Douglas. B.A. in Internat. Relations, Yale U., 1953; postgrad., Stanford U., 1964-65, Stanford Bus. Sch., 1970-71. Fgn. service insp. U.S. Dept. State, Washington, 1971-74; dep. dir., econ. officer Office Iberian Affairs, Washington, 1974-75; dep. dir. Office West European Affairs, Washington, 1975-76, dir., 1977-78; minister-counselor U.S. Embassy, Lisbon, Portugal, 1978-83; dep. asst. sec. Bur. Consular Affairs, Washington, 1983-85; U.S. amb. to Bolivia La Paz, 1985-88; U.S. amb. to Portugal Lisbon, 1988-90; U.S. amb. to Luxemburg, 1990-94; sr. assoc. Global Bus. Access, Ltd., 1994—; bd. dirs. F.Y.I. Inc., Dallas, 1996—. Treas. Cleveland Park Congl. Ch., Washington, 1984-85; bd. dirs. Luso-Am. Devel. Found., 1988-90; mem. adv. bd. Portuguese-Am. Leadership Coun. of U.S. Cpl. U.S. Army, 1953-55. Recipient Bolivian Condor of the Andes, Grand Cross, 1988, Luxembourg Oaken Crown, Grand Cross, 1994, Superior Honor award, 1983, 91, Presdl. Honor award, 1988, scholar Yale U., 1949, 50, 51, 52; U. Calif. fellow, 1953; Una Chapman Cox Found. grantee, 1984. Mem. Am. Acad. Diplomacy, Am. Fgn. Svc. Assn. (v.p. 1995-97), Assn. Diplomatic Studies and Tng. (pres. 1997—), Washington Inst. Fgn. Affairs (membership com. 1999—), Stanford U. Alumni Assn., Yale U. Alumni Assn., Arena Stage Assocs., Smithsonian Assocs., The Phillips Collection, Friends of Kennedy Ctr., Cosmos Club. Avocations: photography, tennis, music. Home: 5414 Newington Rd Bethesda MD 20816-3316

ROWELL, NEVILLE ROBINSON, dermatologist, educator; b. Newcastle Upon Tyne, Eng., Nov. 3, 1926; s. Thomas and Bertha (Robinson) R.; m. Elizabeth Rachel Martin Edwards, Aug. 5, 1950; children: Christopher, Martin, Marcus. MB BS, U. Durham, Eng., 1949; MD, U. Newcastle Upon Tyne, 1966. House physician, demonstrator in pathology, med. registrar Royal Victoria Infirmary, Newcastle Upon Tyne, 1949-58; cons. dermatologist Gen. Infirmary at Leeds, Eng., 1962-90, St. James U. Hosp., Leeds, 1962-90; prof. dermatology U. Leeds, 1988-90, prof. emeritus, 1990—; cons. advisor Dept. Health and Social Security, London, 1978-88; mem. Med. Appeals Tribunal. Author: (sections) Textbook of Dermatology, 1968, 2nd edit., 1972, 3rd edit., 1979, 4th edit., 1986, 5th edit., 1992, 6th edit., 1998; contbr. more than 300 articles to profl. jours. Vice chmn. Leeds Civic Trust, 1969-92, v.p., 1992—; mem. Ct. U. Leeds, 1987-89; mem. coun. Leeds Art Collection Fund, 1984-87. Med. officer RAF, 1950-52. Fellow Royal Soc. Medicine, Royal Coll. Physicians (examiner in medicine 1980-94); mem. Brit. Med. Assn., Brit. Assn. Dermatologists (pres. 1986-87, Sir Archibald Gray medal 1989), Polish Med. Soc. (hon.), Swedish Dermatol. Soc. (hon.), French Dermatol. Soc. (hon.), German Dem. Republic Dermatol. Soc. (hon.). Avocations: golf, opera, art, antiques. Home: 15 Radlyn Oval 20 Park Ave, Harrogate HG2 9BG, England Office: Nuffield Hosp, Outwood Ln, Horsforth Leeds LS18 4HP, England

ROWE-MAAS, BETTY LU, real estate investor; b. San Jose, Calif., Apr. 2, 1925; d. Horace DeWitt and Lucy Belle (Spiker) Rowe; children: Terry Lee, Clifford Lindsay, Craig Harrison, Joan Louise. Real estate investor, Saratoga, Calif., 1968—. Mem. Nat. Trust Hist. Preservation, Smithsonian Instn., Archeol. Inst. Am., San Jose Symphony, San Jose Cleve. Ballet, San Francisco Symphony, San Francisco Ballet, M.H. de Young Meml. Mus., Santa Barbara Mus. Art, California Palice of The Legion of Honor, Loberro Theatre Found., Arlington Theater Restoration Fund; bd. dirs. Valley Inst. Theatre Arts; mem. Route 85 Task Force, 1978—, treas., 1984-89; mem. Saratoga Good Govt., 1970-89; treas. Traffic Relief for Saratoga. Mem. LWV, NOW (world affairs coun. No. Calif. chpt.), Commonwealth of Calif. Club (life), Santa Barbara Rep. Club, Toastmasters (past treas. Santa Barbara club #5). Home: 685 Mariposa Ave Mountain View CA 94041-1868

ROWEN, RUTH HALLE, musicologist, educator; b. N.Y.C., Apr. 5, 1918; d. Louis and Ethel (Fried) Halle; m. Seymour M. Rowen, Oct. 13, 1940; children: Mary Helen Rowen, Louis Halle Rowen. B.A., Barnard Coll., 1939; M.A., Columbia U., 1941, Ph.D., 1948. Mgmt. ednl. dept. Carl Fischer, Inc., N.Y.C., 1954-63; assoc. prof. musicology CUNY, 1967-72, prof., 1972—, mem. doctoral faculty in musicology, 1967—. Author: Early Chamber Music, 1948, reprinted, 1974; (with Adele T. Katz) Hearing-Gateway to Music, 1959, (with William Simon) Jolly Come Sing and Play, 1956, Music Through Sources and Documents, 1979, (with Mary Rowen) Instant Piano, 1979, 80, 83, Symphonic and Chamber Music Score and Parts Bank, 1996; contbr. articles to profl. jours. Mem. ASCAP, Am. Musicol. Soc., Music Library Assn., Coll. Music Soc., Nat. Fedn. Music Clubs (nat. musicianship chmn. 1962-74, nat. young artist auditions com. 1964-74, N.Y. state chmn. Young Artist Auditions 1981, dist. coord. 1983, nat. bd. dirs. 1989-2000, rep. UN 1991-2000), N.Y. Fedn. Music Clubs (pres.), Phi Beta Kappa. Home: 115 Central Park W New York NY 10023-4153

ROWINSKI, PAWEL MARIUSZ, hydrologist, scientist, educator; b. Warsaw, Poland, Feb. 26, 1965; s. Zygmunt and Helena (Podgorska) R.; m. Agata Maria Obara, Sept. 28, 1991; 1 child, Paulina. MSc, U. Warsaw, 1988; PhD, Polish Acad. Scis., Warsaw, 1995. Rsch. asst. Inst. Geophysics, Polish Acad. Scis., Warszawa, 1988-90, sr. rsch. asst., 1991-95, asst. prof., 1995—; vis. scientist SUNY, Stony Brook, 1991-92; translator, cons. Polish Edit. of Sci. Am., Warszawa, 1997; invited participant Ecologia Europaea, French Acad. Scis., 1998. Contbr. articles to profl. jours. Recipeint stipend for outstanding young scientists Found. for Polish Sci., 1994; grantee Polish State Com. Sci. Rsch., 1994; fellow Soros Found. and Ctrl. European U., Budapest, 1991, SUNY, Stony Brook, 1991-92. Mem. Internat. Orgn. Hydraulic Rsch., Polish Geophys. Soc., Physics of Water Sect. Polish Acad. Scis. Avocations: biographies, music, sports. E-mail: pawelr@igf.edu.pl. Fax: 48-22 6915915. Home: Marii Dabrowskiej 10 m 3, 01-903 Warsaw Poland Office: Inst Geophysics Polish Acad, Ksiecia Janusza 64, 01-452 Warsaw Poland

ROWLAND, DAVID, bank executive. Various positions Stewart Wrightson, Willis Faber; CEO, then chmn. Sedgwick Group, 1989-92; chmn. Lloyd's, 1993-97; retired, 1997; dir., deputy dir. Nat. Westminster Bank, London, 1998-99, chmn., 1999—; pres. Templeton Coll., Oxford. Office: Nat Westminster Bank, 41 Lothbury, London EC2P 3BP, England*

ROWLAND, FRANK SHERWOOD, chemistry educator; b. Delaware, Ohio, June 28, 1927; m. Joan Lundberg, 1952; children: Ingrid Drake, Jeffrey Sherwood. AB, Ohio Wesleyan U., 1948; MS, U. Chgo., 1951, PhD, 1952, DSc (hon.), 1989; DSc (hon.), Duke U., 1989, Whittier Coll., 1989, Princeton U., 1990, Haverford Coll., 1992, Clark U., 1996, U. East Anglia, 1996; LLD (hon.), Ohio Wesleyan U., 1989, Simon Fraser U., 1991, U. Calgary, 1997; laurea honoris causa, U. Urbino (Italy), 1998; DSc, Carleton Coll., 1998, Gustavus Adolphus Coll., 1997, Occidental Coll., 1998, Kanagawa Univ., Japan, 1999. Instr. chemistry Princeton (N.J.) U., 1952-56; asst. prof. chemistry U. Kans., 1956-58, assoc. prof. chemistry, 1958-63, prof. chemistry, 1963-64; prof. chemistry U. Calif., Irvine, 1964—, dept. chmn., 1964-70, Aldrich prof. chemistry, 1985-89, Bren prof. chemistry, 1989-94, Bren rsch. prof., 1994—; Humboldt sr. scientist, Fed. Republic of Germany, 1981; chmn. Dahlem (Fed. Republic of Germany) Conf. on Changing Atmosphere, 1987; vis. scientist Japan Soc. for Promotion Sci., 1980; co-dir. western region Nat. Inst. Global Environ. Changes, 1989-93; del. Internat. Coun. Sci. Unions, 1993-98; fgn. sec. NAS, 1994—, Korean Acad. Sci. Tech.; lectr., cons. in field. Contbr. numerous articles to profl. jours. Mem. ozone commn. Internat. Assn. Meteorology and Atmospheric Physics, 1980-88, hon. life mem., 1996, mem. commn. on atmospheric chemistry and global pollution, 1979-91; mem. acid rain peer rev. panel U.S. Office of Sci. and Tech., Exec. Office of White House, 1982-84; mem. vis. com. Max Planck Insts., Heidelberg and Mainz, Fed. Republic Germany, 1982-96; ozone trends panel mem. NASA, 1986-88; chmn. Gordon Conf. Environ. Scis.-Air, 1987; mem. Calif. Coun. Sci. Tech., 1989-95, Exec. Com. Tyler Prize, 1992—. Recipient numerous awards including John Wiley Jones award Rochester Inst. of Tech., 1975, Disting. Faculty Rsch. award U. Calif., Irvine, 1976, Profl. Achievement award U. Chgo., 1977, Billard award N.Y. Acad. Sci., 1977, Tyler World Prize in Environment Achievement, 1983, Global 500 Roll of Honor for Environ. Achievement UN Environment Program, 1988, Dana award for Pioneering Achievements in Health, 1987, Silver medal Royal Inst. Chemistry, U.K., 1989, Wadsworth award N.Y. State Dept. Health, 1989, medal U. Calif., Irvine, 1989, Japan prize in Environ. Sci., 1989, Dickson prize Carnegie-Mellon U., 1991, Albert Einstein prize of World Cultural Coun., 1994, Nobel Prize in Chemistry, 1995, Alumni medal U. Chgo., 1997, Nevada medal, 1997; Guggenheim fellow, 1962, 74. Fellow AAAS (pres. elect 1991, pres. 1992, chmn. bd. dirs. 1993), Am. Phys. Soc. (Leo Szilard award for Physics in Pub. Interest 1979), Am. Geophys. Union (Roger Revelle medal 1994); mem. NAS (bd. environ. studies and toxicology 1986-91, com. on atmospheric chemistry 1987-89, com. atmospheric scis., solar-terrestial com. 1979-83, co-DATA com. 1977-82, sci. com. on problems environment 1986-89, Infinite Voyage film com. 1988-92, Robertson Meml. lectr. 1993, chmn. com. on internat. orgns. and programs 1993—, chmn. office of internat. affairs 1994—, co-chmn. interacad. panel 1995—), Am. Acad. Arts and Scis., Am. Chem. Soc. (chmn. divsn. nuclear sci. and tech. 1973-74, chmn. divsn. phys. chemistry 1974-75, Orange County award 1975, Tolman medal 1976, Zimmerman award 1980, E.F. Smith lectureship 1980, Environ. Sci. and Tech. award 1983, Esselen award 1987, Peter Debye Phys. Chem. award 1993), Am. Meteorological Soc. (hon.), European Acad. Arts, Scis. and Humanities, Korean Acad. Sci. Tech., Phi Beta Kappa. Home: 4807 Dorchester Rd Corona Del Mar CA 92625-2718 Office: U Calif Irvine Dept of Chemistry 518 Rowland Hall Irvine CA 92697-0001*

ROWLETTE, HENRY ALLEN, JR., social worker; b. Phila., July 8, 1947; s. Henry Allen Sr. and Ophelia Alberta (Kilson) R.; m. Geraldine Lee Stevens, Mar. 1972 (div. Mar. 1986); children: Cessandra N., Deaeon D., Christiene A.; m. Carolyn Rowlette; 1 child, Janetta M.; m. Ann Laura Rowe, Mar. 19, 1989. BA, Cheyney State Coll., 1970; MEd, Boston U., 1981; MSW, Temple U., 1988. Cert. sch. social worker, N.J.; lic. clin. social worker; diplomate Am. Psychotherapy Assn., Nat. Bd. Cognitive Behavioral Therapists; ordained minister Bapt. Ch. Cardiac monitor technician Bapt. Med. Ctr., Little Rock, Ark., 1982-83; mental health technician The Horsham Clinic, Ampler, Pa., 1984; psychiat. technician The Lower Bucks Hosp., Bristol, Pa., 1984-90; mental health technician The Helene Fuld Med. Ctr., Trenton, N.J., 1988-90, psychiat. social worker, 1988-92; profl. sch. social worker The Willingboro (N.J.) Sch. Dist., 1990—; sch. social worker Lumberton Sch. Dist., 1998—; dist. crisis intervention team Willingboro Sch. Dist., 1994—; therapist The N.J. State Prison, Trenton, 1996, The Southwoods State Prison, Bridgeton, N.J.; clinician Kennedy Meml. Health Ctr., Cherry Hill, N.J., 1998—, The Lumberton Schs./Sch. Social Worker, Lumberton, N.J., 1998; behavioral cons. Founds. Behavioral Health, Willow Grove, Pa., 1999; mental health technician The Children's Hosp. Phila., 1999-2000. Mem. NAACP, Trenton, 1990. With U.S. Army, 1971-79. Mem. NASW, Am. Assn. Christian Counselors, Omega Psi Phi (Delta Upsilon chpt.), Phi Delta Kappa (Trenton chpt.), Am. Psychotherapy Assn., Nat. Bd. Cognitive Behavioral Therapists, Nat. Bd. Addiction Examiners, Nat. Assn. Forensic Counselors. Democrat. Baptist. Avocations: fishing, reading, computer technology/games. Home: 18 Foxchase Dr Burlington NJ 08016-3044

ROWLEY, FRANK SELBY, JR., artist; b. N.Y.C., Aug. 2, 1913; s. Frank Selby and Caroline Estelle (Bremmer) R.; m. Dorothy Folger, June 30, 1942. Student, Art Students League, N.Y.C., 1934, Nassau Inst. of Art, Hempstead, N.Y., 1935-38, U. Richmond, Va., 1952. Designer, illustrator Nina Robinson Studio, Hempstead, 1938-41; designer, muralist, 1946-49; tchr. comml. art John Marshall High Sch., Richmond, 1949-57; lectr. various art orgns. 1957—; judge art exhbns., 1957—. Exhibited in group shows at Portraits Inc., N.Y.C., 1959-87, Gallery Mayo, Richmond, Va., 1975—, Va. Mus. of Fine Arts; represented in permanent collections Va. Mus. of Fine Arts, Va. Hist. Soc., State of Va., City of Richmond, Richmond Meml. Hosp., Va. Fedn. Womens Clubs and numerous pvt. collections. Founder Richmond Concert Band, 1970; music dir., conductor Richmond Pops Band, 1977—; chmn. bd. Richmond Band Assn., 1977—; vol. art tchr. Va. Home, 1989—. Sgt. U.S. Army, 1941-45. Mem. Lions. Avocations: water color painting, music. Home: 8909 Elm Rd Richmond VA 23235-1427

ROWLEY, GLENN HARRY, lawyer; b. Hyannis, Mass., May 16, 1948; s. Harold Frederick and Olive Nellie (Jones) R.; 1 child, Brewster Westgate. BBA, U. Mass., 1970; JD with cum laude, Western New Eng. Coll., 1980. Bar: Mass. 1980, U.S. Dist. Ct. Mass. 1981, U.S. Tax Ct. 1981; cert. elder law atty. Nat. Elder Law Found./ABA. Staff mem. Cape Cod Planning and Econ. Devel. Commn., Barnstable, Mass., 1975-76; staff, estate planning tax dept. Coopers and Lybrand, Springfield, Mass., 1980-81; legal assoc. Roberts and Farrell, West Chatham, Mass., 1982-84; ptnr. Roberts, Farrell & Rowley, West Chatham, 1984-97; pvt. practice, 1997—; cons. Local Citizen Scholarship Trusts, Harwich and Chatham, Mass., 1985—. Contbr.: (weekly news column) The Cape Codder, The Enterprise, The Register, others.; contbr. articles to profl. jours. Founding mem. Brewster (Mass.) Conservation Trust, 1984; past elected mem. Brewster Hist. Dist. Com., 1975; mem. adv. bd. The May Inst., The Cape Cod Writers Ctr., Inc. With USN, 1971-74, Iceland. Recipient Am. Jurisprudence awards Lawyers Co-op. Pub. Co., 1978, 79. Mem. Mass. Bar Assn., Ocean Edge Exec. Club, Profl. Writers of Cape Cod, Cape Cod Estate Planning Coun., Nat. Acad. Elder Law Attys., Phi Delta Phi. Avocations: travel, writing. Home: Annaniases Knoll/Sheep Pond Brewster MA 02631 Office: The Marketplace PO Box 1489 26 George Ryder Rd S West Chatham MA 02669

ROWLEY, GWYN, geographer, social scientist, educator; b. Cardiff, Wales, May 24, 1938; s. Joseph and Minnie (Harris) R.; m. Glenys Kathleen White, Aug. 8, 1962; children: Lesley Lenora Jane, Jonathan Mark Douglas. BA, U. Wales, 1961, PhD, 1967, DLH, 1997; MA, Harvard U., 1989. Asst. lectr. U. Sheffield, Eng., 1964-67, lectr., 1970-73, sr. lectr., 1974-96, reader, 1996—; asst. prof. U. Nebr., Lincoln, 1967-68, Clark U., Worcester, Mass., 1968-70; cons. Ministry of Hajj, Govt. Saudi Arabia, Riyadh, 1974-97, Ferranti Computer Systems, Manchester, Eng., 1983—; bd. dirs. Chas. E. Goad Ltd. Author: Israel into Palestine, 1984, British Fire Insurance Plans, 1984; patentee in field; contbr. articles to profl. jours. Served to lt. Brit. army, 1956-58. Peabody fellow Harvard U., 1989—. Fellow Royal Geographical Soc.; meme. Inst. Brit. Geographers (com. mem. 1982-85), Assn. Am. Geographers, Brit. Fulbright Scholars Assn. (com. mem. 1985-97), Brit. Soc. Middle Eastern Studies, The Mid. East Inst. Jewish. Clubs: Sheffield Def., Univ. Sheffield. Lodge: Masons. Avocations: walking, theater, travel, gardening. Office: Sheffield U Dept Geography, Western Bank, Sheffield S10 2TN, England

ROWLEY, WILLIAM RICHARD CHARLTON, experimental physicist, consultant; b. Bath, Somerset, Eng., Mar. 11, 1935; s. Francis Bernard and Isabella (Matthews) R.; m. Cynthia Diana Garland; children: Alexandra Kate, Patrick Anderson Charlton. BS, Durham U., Eng., 1956, PhD, 1959. Chartered physicist. Sci. officer Nat. Phys. Lab., U.K., 1959-63, sr. sci. officer, 1963-68, prin. sci. officer, 1968-75, sr. prin. sci. officer, 1975-95, cons., 1995—; rapporteur Consultative Com. for Definition of Metre, 1973=93. Author: (chpt.) A Guide to the Laser, 1967; contbr. over 90 articles to profl. jours.; patentee in field. Fellow Inst. Physics. Achievements include development of first frequency stabilized laser; frequency stabilized He-Ne lasers; techniques of interferometric length measurement. Office: Nat Phys Lab, Teddington TW11 0LW, England

ROWLINSON, JOHN SHIPLEY, chemistry educator; b. Handforth, Great Britain, May 12, 1926; s. Frank and Winifred (Jones) R.; m. Nancy Gaskell, Aug. 2, 1952; children: Paul John, Stella Margaret Barczak. BA, Oxford (Eng.) U., 1947, BSc, MA, DPhil, 1950. Rsch. assoc. Naval. Rsch. Lab., U. Wis., Madison, 1950-51; rsch. fellow Manchester (Eng.) U., 1951-54, lectr., then sr. lectr. in chemistry, 1954-60; prof. chem. technology Imperial Coll., London U., 1961-73; Dr. Lee's prof. chemistry Oxford U., 1974-93; von Hofmann lectr. Gesellschaft Deutscher Chem., Bonn, Fed. Republic of Germany, 1980; Andrew D. White prof. Cornell U., 1990-96. Author: Liquids and Liquid Mixtures, 1959, 3d edit., 1982, Perfect Gas, 1963; co-author: Thermodynamics for Chemical Engineers, 1975, Molecular Theory of Capillarity, 1982, Van der Waals and Molecular Science, 1996; joint editor: Physics of Simple Liquids, 1968. Councillor Sale (Gt. Britain) Borough Coun., 1956-59. Recipient Marlow medal Faraday Soc., London, 1957. Fellow Royal Soc. Chemistry (pres. Faraday divsn. 1979-81, Faraday lectr. 1983, Meldola medal 1954), Instn. Chem. Engrs., Royal Soc. (phys. sec. and v.p. 1994-99, Leverhulme medal 1993); mem. Royal Acad. Engring., Alpine Club. Avocation: mountain climbing. Office: Phys & Theor Chemistry Lab, S Parks Rd, Oxford OX1 3QZ, England

ROXBURGH, IAN WALTER, astronomy and mathematics educator; b. Sheffield, Eng., Aug. 31, 1939; s. Walter McRonald and Kathleen Joyce (Prescott) R.; m. Diana Patricia Dunn, Aug. 20, 1960; children: Malcolm Alexander, Kathleen Mary, Patrick Rufus. BS, U. Nottingham, Eng., 1960; PhD, U. Cambridge, Eng., 1963. Asst. lectr. Kings Coll., London, 1963-64, lectr., 1964-66; reader U. Sussex, Eng., 1966-67; prof. Queen Mary & Westfield Coll., 1967—, head Sch. Math. Scis., 1983-95, dir. astronomy unit, 1983-95; bicentennial prof. U. Va., Charlottesville, 1976; vis. scientist Nat. Ctr. for Atmos Rsch., Boulder, Colo., 1966-75, U. Catania, Sicily, Italy, 1971-80; NSF fellow Goddard Space Flight Ctr., Greenbelt, Md., 1964; chmn. Com. of Heads of Depts. of Math. and Stats., U.K., 1988-93. Contbr. articles to profl. jours. Adv. Liberal Party, U.K., 1968-82; parliamentary candidate Liberal Party, 1970, Social Dem. Party, 1983. Fellow Royal Astron. Soc., Inst. Physics; mem. London Math. Soc., British Soc. for Philosophy of Sci., European Phys. Soc., European Astron. Soc., Internat. Astron. Union (pres. commn.). Avocations: economics, politics, philosophy. Office: Queen Mary & Westfield Coll, Mile End Rd, London E14NS, England

ROY, ALEC, psychiatrist. BA, Cambridge U., 1963, MB, 1966. Registrar, sr. registrar Maudsley Hosp., 1970-77; staff psychiatrist Clark Inst. Psychiatry, Toronto, Ont., Can., 1978-81, NIH, Bethesda, Md., 1982-89, Hillside Hosp., 1990-92, Vets. Affairs N.J. Health Care Sys., East Orange, 1993—. Mem. Royal Coll. Physicians, Internat. Assn. Suicide Prevention (Stengel award 1999, Am. Assn. Suicidology (Louis Dublin award 1993), Acad. Psychosomatic Medicine (2d prize, Best Jour. Paper award 1994). Office: VA NJ Health Care Sys 385 Tremont Ave East Orange NJ 07018-1023

ROY, BARIN BRIAN, travel and financial services company executive; b. Stoke-on-Trent, United Kingdom, Sept. 24, 1960; s. Bijon Behari and Tapati (Roychowdhury) R.; m. Anjana Kar, Nov. 19, 1984; children: Brian (Biswadeep), Amit. Student, St. Joseph's Coll., India, 1974-76, Thames U., London, 1978-79. Clerical asst. Dept. of Health and Social Security, London, 1978; asst. credit contr. Skyways Hotel (THF), Eng., 1979-80; overseas credit contr. Thomas Nelson & Sons Ltd., Sunbury-on-Thames, Eng., 1980; accounts batch contr. Kaynar (U.K.) Ltd., Wembly, 1980-81; unit mgr. Kabel Halsey, London, 1981-86; area mgr. Winterthur Co., Basingstoke, Eng., 1986-89; v.p. head new product devel. Europe Am. Express Europe Svcs. Ltd., London, 1989—; non-exec. bd. dirs. Am. Express Ins. Svcs. Ltd., Eng., 1992—. Fellow Inst. of Mgmt., Ins. Brokers Registration Coun. (registered broker); mem. Royal Overseas League, Chartered Ins. Inst. U.K. (assoc.). Hindu. Avocations: reading, travelling, current affairs. Office: Am Express Europe Svcs Ltd, Prestamex House Preston Rd, Brighton BN1 6BX, England

ROY, BERNARD, science educator; b. Moulins-Sur-Allier, France, Mar. 15, 1934; s. Rene and Jeanne Cherasse Roy; m. Jolivet Roy, July 15, 1957; children: Laurence, Isabelle, Solange, Patrice. Grad., Inst. Stats., Paris, 1957; DS in Math., Faculty of Scis., Paris, 1961. Sci. dir. SEMA-METRA Group, Paris, 1964-74; prof. U. Paris-Dauphine, 1972—; founder LAMSADE, Paris, 1977—, dir., 1977-99, hon. dir., 1999—; sci. advisor RATP, Paris; pres. EURO, Paris, 1985-86. Author: (books) Algèbre moderne et théorie des graphes orientées vers les sciences économiques et sociales, Vol. 1, 1969, Vol. 2, 1970, Méthodologie multicritère d'aide á la décision, 1985, Aide multicritère á la décision: Méthodes et cas, 1993, Multicritéria methodology for decision aiding, 1996. Decorated Chevalier des Palmes Académiques, 1987; recipient EURO Gold medal, 1992; named Dr. Honoris Causa, Brussels, 1978, Lieèe, Belgium, 1978, Fribourg, Switzerland, 1982, Poznan, Poland, 1992, Laval, Que., Can., 1998. Roman Catholic. Avocations: history, oenophily. Fax: 33 1 44 05 40 91. E-mail: roy@lamsade.dauphine.fr. Office: LAMSADE U Paris-Dauphine, Pl Marechal Lattre Tassigny, 75775 Paris Cedex 16, France

ROY, CHUNILAL, psychiatrist; b. Digboi, India, Jan. 1, 1935; came to Can., 1967, naturalized, 1975; s. Atikay Bandhu and Nirupama (Devi) R.; m. Elizabeth Ainscow, Apr. 15, 1967; children: Nicholas, Phillip, Charles. MB, BS, Calcutta Med. Coll., India, 1959; diploma in psychol. medicine, Kings Coll., Newcastle-upon-Tyne, Eng., 1963. Intern Middlesborough Gen. Hosp., Eng., 1960-61; jr. hosp. officer St. Luke's Hosp., Middlesborough, Eng., 1961-64, sr. registrar, 1964; sr. hosp. med. officer Parkside Hosp., Macclesfield, Eng., 1964-66; sr. registrar Moorehaven Hosp., Ivybridge, Eng., 1966; reader, head dept. psychiatry Maulana Azad Med. Coll., New Delhi, 1966; sr. med. officer Republic of Ireland, County Louth, 1966; sr. psychiatrist Sask. Dept. Psychiat. Services, Can., 1967-68; regional dir. Swift Current, Can., 1968-71; practice medicine specializing in psychiatry Regina, Sask., Can., 1971-72; founding dir., med. dir. Regional Psychiat. Ctr., Abbotsford, B.C., Can., 1972-82; with dept. psychiatry Vancouver Gen. Hosp., 1983—; cons. to prison adminstrs.; hon. lectr. psychology and clin. prof. dept. psychiatry U. B.C., clin. prof. emeritus, 2000; ex-officio mem. Nat. Adv. Com. on Health Care of Prisoners in Can.; cons. (hon.) psychiatrist Vancouver Hosp.; advisor Asian chpt. Psychosomatic Medicine, World Congress of Law and Medicine, New Delhi, 1985; appointed hon. consul for Burkina Faso, 1997; appointed auditor Med. Svcs. Com. B.C., 1997; appointed advisor mental health Govt. West Bengal, India, 1999; pres. organizing com. World Mental Health Assembly, 1999. Author: (with D.J. West and F.L. Nichols) Understanding Sexual Attacks, 1978, Hospital or Prison Memories; co-author: Oath of Athens, 1979; ; assoc. editor Internat. Jour. Offender Therapy and Comparative Criminology, 1978—; field editor Jour. of Medicine and Law; corr. editor Internat. Jour. Medicine; mem. bd. Internat. Law Medicine, 1979—; mem. editl. rev. bd. Evaluation, 1977—; contbr. articles to profl. jours. Recipient merit awards Dept. Health, Republic of Ireland, 1966, Can. Penitentiary Svc., 1974, Correctional Svcs. Can., 1983, citation by pres. U. B.C., 1983, Letten Saugstad Found. prize, Holland, 1995; knighted by Order of St. John Ecumenical Found., 1993, Awarded Order of Francisco Fajardo Gov. of Caracas, 1998, Legacy award Vancouver Travel and Conv. Ctr., 1998. Fellow Royal Coll. Psychiatry (Can.), Royal Coll. Psychiatry (Eng.), Pacific Rim Coll. Psychiatrists (founder); mem. World Psychiat. Assn. (sec., vice chmn. forensic psychiatry 1983), World Fedn. Mental Health, Internat. Coun. Prison Med. Svcs. (founding sec.-gen. 1977), Can. Med. Assn., Can. Psychiat. Assn., Internat. Acad. Legal Medicine and Social Medicine, Indian Psychiat. Assn. (life), Assn. Physicians and Surgeons Who Work in Can. Prisons (founding pres. 1974), Internat. Found. for Tng. in Penitentiary Medicine and Forensic Psychiatry (founding pres. 1980), World Psychiatry Assn., Australian Acad. Forensic Sci. (corr.), Can. Physicians Interested in South Asia (v.p. 1989, pres. 1990), Internat. Coll. Psychosomatic Medicine (adv. Asian chpt.), Internat. Conf. on Health, Culture and Contemporary Soc. (chief advisor Bombay 1989), World Psyciat. Assn. (vice chmn. forensic psychiat. sect. 1989), World Assn. Health, Culture and Environ. (sec.-gen. 1995, award 1995), Order of St. John (knight 1992), Vancouver MultiCultural Soc. (bd. dirs. 1992-93), B.C. Psychiat. Assn. (pres. 1995-96). Home: 2439 Trinity St, Vancouver, BC Canada V5K 1C9 Office: 1417-750 W Broadway, Vancouver, BC Canada V5Z 1J4

ROY, JAGAT KUMAR, developmental geneticist, educator; b. Calcutta, India, Oct. 9, 1957; s. Kartick and Alaka (Ghosh) R.; m. Smriti Ghosh, Feb. 18, 1986; children: Madhumita, Kaushik. BS, Banaras Hindu U., 1976, MS, 1978, PhD, 1983. Scientist Ctr. Cellular & Molecular Biology, Hyderabad, India, 1984-87; lectr. Banaras Hindu U., Varanasi, India, 1987—. Boyscast fellow Dept. Sci. & Technology Govt. India, 1990. Mem. Indian Soc. Cell Biology, Indian Soc. Devel. Biology. Avocations: drawing, music. E-mail: jkroy@banaras.exnet.in. Home: B/13 180A Sonarpura, 221001 Varanasi India Office: Banaras Hindu U, Dept Zoology, 221005 Varanasi India

ROY, J(AMES) STAPLETON, former secretary; b. Nanking, China, June 16, 1935; s. Andrew Tod and Margaret (Crutchfield) R.; m. Elissandra Nicole Fiore, Jan. 27, 1968; children—Andrew, David, Anthony. B.A. magna cum laude, Princeton U., 1956; postgrad., U. Wash., 1964-65, Nat. War Coll., 1974-75. Dep. dir. Office of Soviet Union Affairs Dept. of State,

Washington, 1972-74, dep. dir. Office of Chinese Affairs, 1975-78; minister counselor U.S. Embassy, Beijing, Peoples Republic of China, 1978-81, Bangkok, Thailand, 1981-84; U.S. amb. to Singapore, 1984-86; dep. asst. sec. Bur. East Asian and Pacific Affairs Dept. of State, 1986-89, spl. asst. to sec. and exec. sec., 1989-91; U.S. amb. to People's Republic of China Beijing, 1991-95; U.S. amb. to Indonesia, 1995-99; asst. sec. Bur. Intelligence and Rsch., Dept. State, 1999—. Recipient Presdl. Meritorious Service award Pres. of U.S., 1983, 88, 90, Superior Honor award Dept. State, 1977, 80. Mem. Am. Fgn. Svc. Assn., Phi Beta Kappa. Avocations: swimming; jogging; chess; computers. Office: US Dept State 2201 C St NW Rm 6531 Washington DC 20520-0001

ROY, JEAN, film critic; b. Nancy, France, Jan. 3, 1948; s. André and Annette (Mattmann) R.; m. Jacqueline Nacache, Dec. 21, 1983; children: Michael, Lucile. Doctor, U. Paris X, 1976. Gen. del. Critic's Week, Cannes, France, 1981-99; chief critic L'Humanité, Paris, 1986—; gen. sec. Syndicat Français De La Critique De Cinema, 1980-99; v.p. Internat. Fedn. Presse Cinématographique, 1983-87, 91—, Internat. Film TV Coun., 1999—. Author: Pour John Ford, 1976, Citizen Kane, 1989. Recipient Médaille D'or De La Jeunesse Et Des Sports, 1996; named Officier Des Arts Et Des Lettres, 1993. Home: 12 Blvd Poissonniere, 75009 Paris France Office: L'Humanité, 32 Rue Jean Jaures, 93528 Saint Denis France

ROY, JOAQUÍN, humanities and international affairs educator; b. Barcelona, Spain, July 9, 1943; came to U.S., 1967; s. Joaquín and Asunción (Cabrerizo) R.; m. Barbara A. Lucas; children: Núria, Alexander. JD, U. Barcelona, 1966; MS in Linguistics, Georgetown U., 1971, PhD, 1973. Instr. Georgetown U., 1968-71, Johns Hopkins U., 1969-71; asst. prof. Emory U., 1971-76; dir. Latin Am. studies U. Miami, Fla., 1980-86, from assoc. to prof. internat. studies, 1976—, dir. European Union Inst.,, 1992—, dir. Iberian Studies Inst.,, 1992—; vis. prof. U. Madrid, U. Basque County, Spain, Nat. U. of La Plata, Argentina; internat. lectr in field. Author: Cuba and Spain: relations and perceptions, 1990, Christian Democratic Thought in Latin America, 1991, The Reconstruction of Central America: the Role of the European Community, 1992, editor; contbr. articles to profl. jours. Dir. Fla. Catalan Soc., 1980—. Mem. MLA, Latin Am. Studies Assn., European Community Studies Assn., Am. Assn. of Tchrs. of Spanish and Portuguese. Roman Catholic. Avocations: tennis, soccer. Home: 443 Alcazar Ave Coral Gables FL 33134-4201 Office: U Miami Internat Studies Coral Gables FL 33124

ROY, KALYAN KUMAR, geophysics educator; b. Calcutta, India, Jan. 29, 1940; s. Subodh Ranjan and Jyotirmoyee (Dasgupta) R.; m. Padmini Sengupta, Jan. 19, 1968; children: Baishali, Debanjali. BSc with honors, Indian Inst. Tech., Kharagpur, 1962, MSc, 1964, PhD in Geophysics, 1970. Assoc. lectr. Indian Inst. Tech., Kharagpur, 1966-69, lectr., 1969-79, asst. prof., 1979-87, prof. geophysics, 1987—; bd. dirs. Internat. Lithospheric Program, 1998—; mem. programme adv. com. Dept. Sci. and Tech., New Delhi, 1991-95; mem. curricula devel. com. U. Grants Commn., New Delhi, 1987-88; mem. exec. body Assn. Exploration Geophysics, Hyderabad, 1990-96; selection com. Coun. Scientific & Indsl. Rsch., New Delhi, 1998—. Author: Deep Electromagnetic Exploration, Springer Verlag, 1998; mem. editl. bd. Jour. Assn. Exploration Geophysics, Indian Jour. Geology, Indian Jour. Earth Science, 1988-96. Postdoctoral fellow Nat. Rsch. Coun., Ottawa, Can., 1975-76; fellow Assn. Exploration Geophysicists, Hyderabad, India, 1985, Geol., Mining and Metall. Soc. India, Calcutta, 1985. Fellow Indian Geophys. Union; mem. N.Y. Acad. Scis. Hindu. Avocations: music, watch games. Office: Indian Inst Tech, Dept Geology and Geophysics, Kharagpur 721302, India

ROY, KENNETH ALFRED, editor, publisher; b. Falkirk, Scotland, Mar. 26, 1945; s. Richard and Esther (Bernard) R.; m. Margaret Henderson Campbell, June 3, 1967; children: Stephen, Christopher. Grad., Denny (Scotland) H.S., 1961. Journalist various newspapers, Scotland, 1962-69; founder, editor Scottish Theatre mag., 1969-72; anchorman BBC, Glasgow, Scotland, 1972-80; founder, mng. dir., program contr. West Sound, Ayr, Scotland, 1980-83; founder, editor, pub. The Journalist's Handbook, U.K., 1985—; TV critic, weekly columnist Scotland on Sunday, Edinburgh, 1988-94; weekly columnist The Observer, London, 1995-96; founding editor The Scottish Rev. mag., 1995—; founder Inst. Contemporary Scotland, 2000. Author: Travels in a Small Country, 1987, Conversations in a Small Country, 1989, (autobiography) The Closing Headlines, 1993, Both Sides of the Border, 1998, A Man of his Word: the life of Alastair Hetherington, 1998; editor: Dictionary of Scottish Biography, 1999. Named Critic of the Yr., Bank of Scotland Press awards, 1990, 93, Columnist of the Yr., U.K. Press Gazette Press awards, 1995. Mem. Auchinleck Boswell Soc. (hon. pres. 1998). Office: Carrick Media, 2/7 Galt House 31 Bank St, Irvine KA12 OLL, Scotland

ROY, KRIPA SHANKAR, histology and histochemistry educator; b. Gaya, Bihar, India, Dec. 20, 1946; s. Baidya Nath Roy and Navnidha Devi; m. Manju Shahi, June 6, 1971; children: Gaurav, Gautam. B in Vet. Sci. and Animal Husbandry, Bihar Vet. Coll., Patna, India, 1967; MSc in Vet. Scis., Rajendra Agrl. U., Patna, India, 1971; PhD, Punjab Agrl. U., Ludhiana, India, 1981. Vet. anatomy and histology. Asst. mgr. dept. animal husbandry Govt. of Bihar (India), 1968-72; asst. lectr. Bihar Vet. Coll., Patna, India, 1972-74; asst. prof. anatomy Coll. Vet. Scis., Ludhiana, India, 1974-82; assoc. prof. COVS, Ludhiana, India, 1982-90, prof., 1990-91, prof. cum head, 1991—. Author: Atlas of Buffalo Anatomy, 1997. Recipient Indian Coun. Agrl. Rsch. Team award for Outstanding Contribution to Animal Scis., New Delhi, 1989-90, Gold medal, 1993. Mem. Indian Assn. Vet. Anatomists (life), Punjab (India) Vet. Coun. (reg.). Hindu. Avocations: playing cricket, reading scientific books. Home: 61-A Maha Rishi Balmiki Nagar, 141001 Ludhiana Punjab, India Office: Punjab Agrl U, Ludhiana, 141004 Ludhiana Punjab, India

ROY, KULDIP KUMAR, editor; b. Lahore, Pakistan, Feb. 28, 1935; s. Ram Nath and Shanti (Devi) R.; B.A. with honours, Punjab U., 1954, J.D., 1954; D.Litt., U. Canberra (Australia), 1971; m. Vimala Goyal, July 19, 1959; 5 children. Editor, School World, 1956-58, Hosp. Digest, 1958-66, Asian and African Books Newsletter, 1966-69, Africa Letter, 1969-72, Bibliographia Asiatica, 1972-73, History of Agr., 1973-75, Library History Rev., 1975-76, Legal History, 1976-78, Asian Jour. European Studies, Multicultural Children's Lit. and Research in Tourism, 1978-81, Citizen Action, 1981-87, Computer Education, 1987-91, Security Solutions, 1991—; cons. editor univ. presses; dir. K.K. Roy Ltd., Intertrade Publs. (India) Ltd., Royson (Fire Engrs.) Pvt. Ltd. Recipient Valor award, N.Y.C., 1966; Bruce Hartmann trophy, Sydney, Australia, 1970; Edward Hartton award, London, 1971; hon. fellow Magdalen Coll., Oxford U., 1972. Fellow Royal Asiatic Soc., Theosophical Soc., Royal Soc. Medicine; mem. Internat. Assn. History Agr., Internat. Agy. Research Library History, Indian Inst. Legal History, Assn. Sci. Exports in Tourism, Indo-Latin Am. C. of C. (exec. dir.), Indo-Australian C. of C. (exec. dir.). Club: Calcutta Tennis. Author: Stray Thoughts and Other Poems; Mirza Ghalib; Waris Shah; Subramanya Bharati; The Swami and the Comrade; Living My Own Death; Old Paths, New Ruts, Promise and Poetry, Succeeding at Failure. Home: 55 Gariahat Rd, PO Box 10210, Calcutta 700 019 India Office: Suite 1-2 Presidency Ct, Gariahat Rd, Calcutta 700 019, India

ROY, N.K., chemist; b. Tangeril, Bengal, India, Feb. 5, 1935; s. J.K. and S. R.; m. Sahe S.; 2 children. BS with honors, Calcutta (India) U., 1958, MS, 1960, PhD, 1965. Prin. scientist IARI/ICAR, Delhi, India, 1970-84; head IARI/ICAR, Delhi, 1984-88, 93-94, project coord., 1984-85, prof., 1988-94, emeritus scientist, 1995—. Editor: 2 books; contbr. chpts. to books; eight patents for pesticides. Grantee Nat. Rsch. Devel. Corp. Govt. India. Fellow Instn. Chemists, Nat. Acad. Agrl. Scis., Indian sci. congr. Assn. (sectional pres.), Soc. Pesticide Sci. (pres.). Home: AN/12 C Shalimar Bagh, Delhi 110052, India Office: Divsn Agrl Chems, IARI, New Delhi 110012, India

ROY, PARTH SARATHI, forester, ecologist; b. Calcutta, India, Aug. 13, 1952; s. Nani Gopal and Chandan Rani (Karbhowmick) R.; m. Anjana Mazumdar, Jan. 16, 1981; children: Aditi, Parantap. BS, U. Campus, Gorakhpur, India, 1971, PhD, 1980; MS, St. Andrew's Coll., Gorakhpur, India, 1973. Scientist Nat. Remote Sensing Agy., Hyderabad, India, 1977-84; head forestry and ecology Indian Inst. Remote Sensing, Dehradun, 1984-98; dean Indian Inst. of Remote Sensing, Dehradun, 1998—; cons. UNESCO, Bangkok, 1981; tchr. U. Tech. Malaysia, Johur Baru, 1985; counterpart Internat. Tropical Timber Orgn./Japan Overseas Forestry Con., Tokyo, 1995-96. Author: Tropical Ecosystem, 1996, Environmental Studies in India, 1996. Recipient Vikram Sarabhai Meml. Rsch. award, 1993, B.P. Pal Nat. Environ. Fellow award, 1996. Mem. Indian Soc. Remote Sensing (life, award 1991). Avocations: cricket. Home: Maharani Bag II, 15 Shiv Vihar, Dehradun 248006, India Office: Indian Inst Remote Sensing, 4 Kalidas Rd, Dehradun 248001, India

ROY, PATRICK, professional hockey player; b. Quebec City, Que., Can., Oct. 5, 1965. Goaltender Montreal Canadiens, 1984-95, Colo. Avalanche, 1995—; mem. Stanley Cup Championship teams, 1986, 93, 96. Recipient Conn Smythe trophy as playoff MVP, 1986, William M. Jennings trophy 1986-89, 91-92, Trico Goaltender award, 1988-89, 89-90, Georges Vezina trophy, 1988-89, 89-90, 91-92; named to NHL All-Rookie Team, 1985-86, NHL All-Star Second Team, 1987-88, 90-91, NHL All-Star First Team, 1988-89, 89-90, 91-92., Sporting News All-Star Team, 1988-89, 89-90, 91-92. Achievements include playing in Stanley Cup Championships, 1986, 93. Office: Colo Avalanche 100 Chopper Pl Denver CO 80204

ROY, RANODEB, bond trader, investment banker; b. Bombay, India, Mar. 31, 1968; s. Dilip Kumar and Mala (Ghosh) R.; m. Leena Prakash, Oct. 10, 1992. BTech, Indian Inst. Tech., Kanpur, 1990; MBA, Indian Inst. Mgmt., Ahmedabad, 1992. Asst. v.p. Bank of Am., Bombay, 1992-96; assoc. dir. Peregrine Fixed Income, Hong Kong, 1996-98, Barclays Capital, Hong Kong, 1998-99; dir. Merrill Lynch, Tokyo, 1999—. Hindu. Home: 3 Old Peak Rd, 2-13-3 Tomogaya, Shibuya-Ku Tokyo Japan

ROY, ROBERT RUSSELL, toxicologist; b. Mpls., Sept. 14, 1957; s. Rudolph Russell and Arlene Charlotte (Miller) R.; m. Barbara Jane Richie, Oct. 10, 1987; children: Andrew, Katherine. BA cum laude, Augsburg Coll., 1980; MS, U. Minn., 1986, PhD, 1989. Bd. cert. in toxicology. Toxicologist, project mgr. Pace Labs., Inc., Mpls., 1989-90; toxicologist Minn. Dept. Health, Mpls., 1990-93, Minn. Regional Poison Ctr., St. Paul, 1990-97; team leader, toxicology specialist 3M, St. Paul, 1997—, team leader, sr. toxicology specialist, 2000—; lectr. U. Minn., Mpls., 1986-90, Midwest Ctr. Occupl. Health and Safety, St. Paul, 1990—, instr., 1989; clin. assoc. prof. U. Minn., 1993—; mem. grad. faculty in toxicology and pub. health U. Minn.; adj. asst. prof. emergency medicine Oreg. Health Sci. U., Portland. Mem. Mt. Carmel Luth. Ch. Coun., Mpls., 1983-85. Mem. Soc. Toxicology, Am. Indsl. Hygiene Assn., Delta Omega. Home: 6201 Near Mountain Blvd Chanhassen MN 55317-9117 Office: Corp Toxicology 3 M Ctr Bldg 220-2E-02 Saint Paul MN 55144-0001

ROY, TUHIN KUMAR, engineering company executive; b. Monghyr, India, Aug. 1, 1923; s. Rakhal Raj and Bijoyini (Gupta) R.; m. Silva Mardiste, Jan. 1, 1951; children: Dipak, Rupak, Indrek. BSc, Calcutta U., 1943, MSc, 1945; MS, MIT, 1949, ScD, 1951. Head metals rsch. Chem. Constrn. Corp., N.Y.C., 1951-54; prof., head chem. engring. Jadavpur U., 1954-56, 58-60; cons. Freeport Minerals Co., New Orleans, 1956-58; mng. dir. Indsl. Cons. Bur., New Delhi, 1960-63; sr. exec. Sci. Design Co., N.Y.C., 1963-65; mng. dir. Chem. and Metall. Design Co. Pvt. Ltd., New Delhi, 1966-89; chmn. CMDC Design Pvt. Ltd., New Delhi, 1990—; mem. rsch. adv. com. Sriram Inst. Ind. Rsch., Delhi. Inventor commercialized processes for recovering nickel and cobalt from ore leach solutions and for precipitating pure nickel powder from aqueous solutions; editor: Chemical Technology for a Better Environment, 1998; contbr. articles to profl. jours.; patentee in hydrometallurgy and chemical technology. Mng. trustee B. Jagtiani Charitable Trust; treas. Lovraj Kumar Meml. Trust. Fellow Indian Acad. Scis., Indian Nat. Acad. Enging.; mem. AIChE, Indian Inst. Chem. Engrs. (Chem. Engr. of Yr. 1983), Nat. Assn. Cons. Engrs. New Delhi (past pres.). Hindu. Home: C 6/3 Safdarjung Dev Area, New Delhi 110016, India

ROYAL, SEGOLENE, government official; b. 1953; married; 4 children. Diploma, Nat. Sch. Adminstrn. Spl. asst. Presidency of Republic, 1981-88; deputy Nat. Assembly, 1988, 93, 97; min. Ministry Environment, 1992-93; min. del. Ministry Nat. Edn., Rsch. & Tech., 1998—, Ministry for Family and Children. Office: Ministry Nat Edn Rsch Tech, 110 rue de Grenelle, 75700 Paris France*

ROYCHOUDAURY, RAJKUMAR, physicist, researcher; b. Calcutta, W. Bengal, India, Oct. 2, 1943; s. Sudhangsu Bhusan and Sneha (Roy) R.; m. Nilanjana Bhattacharyya, Feb. 26, 1977; 1 child, Anish. ISc, Moulana Azad Coll., Calcutta, 1961; BSc, Presidency Coll., Calcutta, 1963; MSc, Calcutta U., 1965; PhD, Durham (U.K.) U., 1970. Programmer in physics Durham U., 1969-70; asst. prof. West Bengal Edn. Svc., 1970-77; lectr. Indian Statis. Inst., Calcutta, 1977-82, assoc. prof., 1982-87, prof., 1987—, prof. in chg., 1994-96, head physics and applied math. unit, 1996—. Author: Engineering Mathematics, 1995; editor Acta Appl. Candae Mathematicae, 1992. Recipient Pres.'s Gold Medal, Govt. India, 1965; Govt. India Exch. fellow to Czech Republic, 1996; Govt. West Bengal State scholar, 1966. Mem. Indian Assn. Cultivation of Sci., Plasma Sci. Soc. (life). Avocations: trekking, reading, short story writing. Home: AB-91, Calcutta 700064, India Office: Indian Statistical Inst, 203 BT Rd, Calcutta 700035, India

ROYER, THOMAS JERRY, financial planner; b. Coshocton, Ohio, June 17, 1943; s. Walter H. Sr. and Francis (Guerke) R.; m. Felipa T. Pagal, Dec. 24, 1965; children: Matthew Vincent, Brian Eugene, Nicholas Alexander. Student, Xavier U., 1979, Coll. for Fin. Planning, Denver, 1986. Cert. fin. planner. Agt. Met. Life Ins. Co., N.Y.C., 1966-68, mgr., 1968-70; gen. agt. Summit Nat. Life Ins. Co., Akron, Ohio, 1970—, Community Nat., Worthington, Ohio, 1989, Life USA, 1990, Am. Life & Casualty, 1997; prin. Royer & Co., Fairfield, Ohio, 1985-88; founder, pres. Group-10 Fin., Fairfield, 1988—; founder, CEO United Group Mktg., Cin., 1993, Altamonte Springs, Fla., 1996. Mem. Inst. Cert. Fin. Planners, Nat. Exchange Club. Republican. Roman Catholic. Avocations: golf, swimming, physical fitness. Office: Group-10 Fin 2790 Mack Rd Fairfield OH 45014-5129 also: United Group Mktg 921 Douglas Ave Ste 208 Altamonte Springs FL 32714-5202

ROYERE, WILLIAM RANDOLPH, III, computer company executive; b. N.Y.C., Nov. 24, 1964; s. William Randolph Royere Jr. and Rose Marie Polisi; m. Michelle Anne Wagner, May 12, 2000. Chief sci. officer TradeRights, Isle of Man, Eng., 1997-99, Global Network Security Sys., Oxnard, Calif., 1997-99; chief info. officer MPM Pub., Oxnard, 1997-99; chief tech. officer CoreCPA, N.Y.C., 1999-2000; chief network security ResolveNet Devel. Corp., Winnetka, Calif., 1999-2000. Author, series editor Macmillan, Indpls., 1997—; author: Maximum Security: A Hacker's Guide to Protecting Your Internet Site and Network, 1998, The American Institute of Certified Public Accountants Web and Internet Security Education, Vols. I and II, 1998, Maximum Linux Security: A Hacker's Guide to Protecting Your Linux Server and Workstation, 1999, Maximum Windows 2000 Security, 2000. Mem. Federalist Soc. Mem. NRA. Republican. Anglican. Avocations: astronomy, history, ancient religions. Home: 6 N Madrid Ave Newbury Park CA 91320-3315 Office: ResolveNet 2111 Norma St Oxnard CA 93030-2259

ROYLE, ANTHONY WILLIAM, accountant; b. Corona, Calif., Dec. 22, 1956; s. William Lloyd Royle and Patricia Rae (McGahan) Magda; m. Patricia Jean Blaylcok, Aug. 13, 1977 (div. Nov. 1983); children: Nicholas Anthony, Elizabeth Marie, Michael George. BS in Acctg., Weber State U., 1979. CPA, N.Mex. Sr. tax acct. Fox & Co. CPA, Farmington, N.Mex., 1981-83; tax mgr. Cox & Co. CPA, Farmington, 1983-85; tax supr. Arthur Young, Albuquerque, 1985-87; tax supr., tax mgr. Neff & Co., Albuquerque, 1987-95, tax ptnr., 1995—; advisor for Sound Advice C. of C., Albuquerque, 1996—. With U.S. Army, 1974-76. Mem. AICPA (tax divsn.), N.Mex. Soc. CPA, Constrn. Fin. Mgmt. Assn. (Albuquerque chpt.). Avocations: reading, weight lifting, snow skiing. Office: Neff & Co LLP 7001 Prospect Pl NE Albuquerque NM 87110-4311

ROYLE, DAVID BRIAN LAYTON, television producer, journalist; b. Claygate, Surrey, England, Jan. 29, 1955; came to U.S., 1974; s. John Hardy Layton and Jessie Monica (Pringle) R.; m. Cornelia Boardman Service; children: William Brian Layton, Richard John Boardman. BA cum laude, U. N.C., 1978; MA, U. Minn., 1985. Journalist Northcliffe Newspapers, Stoke-on-Trent, England, 1979-82; news producer Ctrl. Ind. TV, Birmingham, England, 1982-83; producer Inside Story, N.Y.C., 1984-86; pres. New Atlantic Prodns., N.Y.C., 1986-89, David Royle Prodns., N.Y.C., 1989—; field prodr. Am. Detective in Russia, ABC, L.A., 1992; exec. prodr. Target: Mafia, A&E, CBS, 1993; prodr. TV Nation, NBC, BBC, 1994, Wall St. Jour. TV, 1995; pres. Pub. Media Inc., N.Y.C., 1992-97; dir. The Russian Archive, 1992—; sr. prodr. Nat. Geog. TV, Washington, 1996-98, exec. prodr., 1998—. TV shows produced include: Rupert Murdoch: Press Baron Who Would Be King, PBS, 1985 (Emmy nomination), Assignment Africa, PBS, 1986 (Emmy nomination), Senator Sam, PBS, 1988 (Ohio State award, Cine Golden Eagle), Inside Gorbachev's USSR, PBS, 1989 (George Polk award, DuPont-Columbia U. Gold Baton), (series) The Eagle and The Bear, ABC/A&E, 1993 (Cine Golden Eagle), Dr. Frank, PBS, 1994 (Cine Golden Eagle, Regional Emmy award), TV Nation, NBC/BBC, 1994 (Prime Time Emmy award), Emerging Powers: Brazil, PBS/NHK Japan, 1996, Trauma: Life and Death in the E.R., The Learning Channel, 1996, National Geographic Explorer, TBS, 1999 (2 Emmy awards, Emmy nomination). Pres. Brit. Morehead Scholarship Fund, 1993—; gov. Clifton Coll., Bristol, Eng., 1997—. Morehead scholar, 1974-78, scholar Rotary Internat., 1983, N.J. Arts Fellowship, 1995; named Hon. Citizen, Mpls., 1983; recipient excellence award U. Minn. Sch. Journalism & Mass Comm., 2000. Mem. NATAS, Soc. Profl. Journalists, Writers Guild of Am. Avocations: running, sailing, photography, reading. Office: Nat Geog TV 1145 17th St NW Washington DC 20036-4701

ROZANOV, VSEVOLOD ANATOLIYEVICH, neurochemist, biochemistry educator and researcher; b. Odessa, Ukraine, USSR, Aug. 8, 1953; s. Anatoliy Yakovlevich and Olga Akimovna (Kirilenko) R.; m. Lioudmila Vladimirovna Zhuhevich, June 27, 1976 (div. Feb. 1981); 1 child, Olga; m. Tatyana Evgenievna Reitarova, Jan. 14, 1983; children: Anphisa, Evgeniy. KandMedSci, Med. Inst., Odessa, 1976, DMedSci, 1990. Asst. Med. Inst., Odessa, 1979-89; head of lab. Rsch. Inst. of Maritime Medicine, Odessa, Ukraine, 1989-92, head exptl. dept., 1992—; lectr. in neurochemistry State U., Odessa, 1989-92; lectr. biochemistry Med. U., Odessa, 1993—; cons. Inst. Vet. Biochemistry, Odessa, 1987-93. Contbr. articles to Jour. Neurochemistry, Clin. Neuropathology, Jour. Cerebral Blood Flow and Metabolism, 1997, others. Head bd. non-govt. and non-profit orgn. Ecol. Health of the People, Odessa, 1997—; dir. Odessa regional br. Internat. Renaissance Found., 1997—. Capt. Med. Staff, Mil., 1979—. Ministry of Sci. rsch. grantee, Kiev, 1993—. Fellow European Soc. for Neurochemistry, Ukraine Soc. for Biochemistry, Ukraine Soc. Toxicology. Avocations: children, dogs and cats, home decoration. Office: Rsch Inst Med Rehab, 6 Lermontovskiy Ln, 65014 Odessa Ukraine

ROZANTINE, GAYLE LOUIS STUBBS, clinical psychologist; b. Atlanta, Dec. 1, 1944; d. William L. and Louise (Cash) Stubbs; children: Kathryn Patricia, Webb Black III, Gregory William, Benjamin Stubbs, John Paul; m. Barry Rozantine. BA in Psychology, Agnes Scott Coll., 1965; MA in Tchg., Emory U., 1966; MA in Clin. Psychology, Western Carolina U., 1990; PhD, U. Tenn., 1995. Lic. psychologist, Ga.; diplomate Am. Acad. of Experts in Traumatic Stress; cert. domestic violence counselor. Tchr. Fulton Co. Bd. Edn., Ga., 1967-68; psychology resident Med. Coll. of Ga., Augusta, 1994-95, clin. fellow, 1995-96; rsch. psychologist Pain Evaluation and Intervention Program Dept. of VA Med. Ctr., Augusta, 1995-98; staff psychologist Compass Health Systems, Miami Beach, Fla., 1998, Charter Savannah Beviroal Health System, Ga., 1999—; Mem. critical incident stress debriefing team Med. Coll. Ga.; disaster mental health response team ARC; presenter in field. Mem. Am. Psychol. Assn., Coastal Area Psychologists, Ga. Psychol. Assn., Ga. Breast Cancer Coalition and Fund, Nat. Assn. of Forensic Counselors, Nat. Register Health Svc. Providers in Psychology. Office: 1150 Cornell Ave Savannah GA 31406-2702

ROZARIO, MICHAEL, archbishop; b. Dhaka, Bangladesh, Jan. 18, 1926; s. Urban and Victoria (Peris) R. BA, U. Notre Dame, 1953; STL, Coll. Urbano, Rome. Ordained priest Roman Cath. Ch., 1956, Bishop of Dinajpur, 1968, Archbishop of Dhaka, 1978. From priest to bishop, 1956-68; archbishop Archdiocese of Dhaka, 1978—. Office: Archbishop House, 1 Kakrail Rd, PO Box 3, Dhaka 1000, Bangladesh

ROZBICKI, MICHAL JAN, American history educator; b. Gdynia, Poland, June 24, 1946; came to U.S., 1990; s. Stanislaw and Sabina (Slodowa) R.; m. Jody Annette Shol, Jan. 4, 1992. MA, Warsaw (Poland) U., 1970; PhD, Maria Curie-Sklodowska U., Lublin, Poland, 1975; habilitation, Warsaw U., 1984. Instr. Maria Curie-Sklodowska U., 1972-75, asst. prof., 1975-76; asst. prof. Am. history Warsaw U., 1976-84, assoc. prof. Am. history, 1984-92; assoc. prof. Am. history St. Louis U., 1996—; chmn. Am. Studies Ctr., Warsaw U., 1987-90, pres. Polish Assn. Am. Studies, 1989-90; assoc. dir. Polish Studies Ctr., Ind. U., Bloomington, 1990-92. Author: Transformation of English Cultural Ethos in Colonial America: Maryland 1634-1720, 1988, The Birth of a Nation, (in Polish) 1991, The Complete Colonial Gentleman: Cultural Legitimacy in Plantation America, 1998; editor: European and American Constitutionalism in the Eighteenth Century, 1990; chief editor Am. Studies, Warsaw, 1981-94. Mem. Solidarity, Warsaw, 1980-81. Am. Coun. Learned Socs. fellow, Johns Hopkins U., Balt., 1979, Oxford (Eng.) U. fellow, St. Catherine's Coll., 1984, Rockefeller Found. fellow, Italy, 1990. Mem. AAUP, Orgn., Am. Historians. Roman Catholic. Avocations: opera, painting, poetry. Office: St Louis U Dept History Saint Louis MO 63103

ROZELOT, JEAN PIERRE, astronomy educator, consultant; b. Nevers, France, Dec. 29, 1942; s. George and Alice (Masloup) R.; m. Liliane Angles; children: Helen, Jerome. BA, Jules Renard Coll., Nevers, France, 1960; MS in Electronics, Inst. Polytechnique, Grenoble, France, 1965; PhD in Physics, U. Paris VII, 1969; PhD in Econs., U. Nice, France, 1979. Registered profl. engr., France. Astronomer Pic du Midi Obs., Bagneres, France, 1965-74; sci. adviser French Embassy, Warsaw, Poland, 1974-78; dep. dir. internat. affairs Ministry of Rsch., Paris, 1978-82; dir. Ctr. Etudes et Recherches Geodynamiques et Astronomiques, Grasse, France, 1982-87; prof., astronomer CERGA Obs., Grasse, France, 1988—; vis. astronomer High Altitude Observatory/Nat. Ctr. for Atmospheric Rsch, Boulder, Colo., 1972; chmn. European Com. Sci. and Tech. Rsch., Brussels, 1986; sci. advisor Aerospatiale, Cannes, France, 1988—. Author: La Couronne solaire, 1977; coauthor: Encyclopedia of Planetary Sciences, 1995; contbr. articles to profl. jours. Recipient Gold medal Senate of Gdansk Polytechnicum, 1980. Mem. Internat. Astron. Union, N.Y. Acad. Scis. Home: 77 Che des Basses Moulieres, 06130 Grasse France Office: OCA/CERGA, Ave Copernic, 06130 Grasse France

ROZENBAUM, NAJMAN, languages educator, counselor; b. Panama, Apr. 29, 1945; s. Hersz Mayer and Ana (Baitel) R.; 1 child, Nataniel. BA, Fla. State U., 1972; MA, U. of the Pacific, 1974, EdS, 1975; DLitt, World U., 1986; PhD, Calif. U. for Advanced Studies, Petaluma, 1987. Cert. tchr., counselor N.C., N.Y., Calif. Prof. English Assn. Panama-N.Am., Panama, 1967-70, Colegio Javier High Sch., Panama, 1970, Inst. Alberto Einstein High Sch., Panama, 1971, 72, Inst. Normal Rubiano, Panama, 1973; teaching asst. Spanish U. of the Pacific, Stockton, fall 1973; teaching asst., prof. techniques of rsch. courses in edn. U. Santa Maria, Panama, 1975-76; prof. English and Spanish YMCA, Balboa, 1975-76; instr. English and Spanish various mil. bases, C.Z., 1976; prof. English and Spanish YMCA/ACJ de Balboa, Panama, 1978-94; prof. English Univ. of the Isthmus, 1995-96; instr. English Panama Canal Commn., 1980, Pan USA Ctr., 1996; pvt. practice counselor. Author: Anxieties in Adolescents, 1981, (monograph) Einstein as a Jew, 1966, (short story) The Crime, 1963; newspaper columnist Star and Herald, La Estrella de Panama. Pres. Jewish Nat. Fund, Panama, 1964-67. Mem. Nat. Geographic Soc. Avocations: reading short stories and books social issues; originator/devel. Theory of the Belts or the Bio-Social Theory of Learning, Theory of Number Nine. Home and Office: Apartado 850133, Panama City 5, Panama

ROZENBLAT, ANATOLY ISAACOVICH, manufacturing engineer, inventor; b. Moscow, Aug. 25, 1938; came to the U.S., 1990; s. Isaac Saimolovich Rozenblat and Natalie Ivanovna Fedorisheva; m. June 27, 1964 (div. 1979) children: Inna, Moshe. BS in Mech. Engring., Inst. Marine Engrs., Odessa, Ukraine, 1967; BS in Computer Sci., East-West U., 1997. Cert. mech. and mfg. engring. Adminstrv. staff Ship Repair and Shipbldg. Plant, Odessa, 1970-80; project engr. Sci. Prodn. Assn., Odessa, 1980-89;

pvt. practice scientist and inventor Chgo., 1990—; mem. Internat. Biog. Ctr., Eng., 1995, adv. bd. Am. Biog. Inst., N.C., 1996; presenter 26th Israel Conf., 1996, 27th Israel Conf., 1998. Author: Regression Analysis of Ship Speed in Waves and The Tropics, 1997, Rozenblat's Innovations For The Twenty-First Century, 1998; contbr. articles to profl. jours.; patentee in field. With Russian Air Force, 1964. Mem. ASME, Soc. Mfg. Engrs., Soc. Naval Architects and Marine Engrs., Nat. Congress Inventors Orgns. Avocations: chess, literature, music, travel, nature. Home: 1355 W Estes Ave Apt M1 Chicago IL 60626-5443

ROZENBLUM, GREGORY (GREGORY VLADIMIROVICH ROZENBLYUM), mathematics researcher, educator; b. St Petersburg, Russia, June 30, 1948; s. Vladimir and Ida (Gurevich) R.; m. Anna Yungelson, May 29, 1975; children: Elizabeth, Paul. MSc, St. Petersburg U., 1971, PhD, 1974. Asst. prof. Mordovian U., Saransk, Russia, 1974-77; rsch. fellow Rsch. Ctr. for Computer Machinery, St. Petersburg, 1977-81; sr. rsch. fellow Rsch. Ctr. for Power Industry, St. Petersburg, 1981-88; assoc. prof. Leningrad Electrotech. Inst. for Comm., St. Petersburg, 1988-95; guest prof. Aalborg U., Denmark, 1993-95; assoc. prof. Göteborg (Sweden) U., 1995-98; prof. Chalmers U. Tech., Göteborg, 1999—. Translator: Pseudodifferential Operators, 1986; author: Spectral Theory for Differential Operators, 1989 (Russian), 1995 (English); reviewer Am. Math. Soc., 1977—. Recipient Golden medal 8th Internat. Math. Olympiade, 1966. Mem. Am. Math. Soc., St. Petersburg Math. Soc., Swedish Math. Avocations: music, bridge, tourism. Home: Pianogatan 44, 42144 Göteborg Sweden Office: Dept Math, Chalmers Univ Tech, 41296 Göteborg Sweden

ROZENTAL, IOSIF LEONID, physicist, researcher; b. Moscow, Jan. 30, 1919; d. Leonid Iosif and Esfir Natan (gurevich) R.; m. Ludmila Ivah Saricheva, Feb. 12, 1950; 1 child, Sarichev Alex. PhD, State U. Moscow, 1941, D Phys.-Math. Scis., 1960. Sci. worker Phys. Inst. Acad., 1946-60; chief dept. Moscow Phys.-Injenering Inst., 1960-68; sci. worker Space Rsch. Inst., Acad. Scis., Moscow, 1968—. Author: Kinematic of Nuclear Reaction, 1959, Big Bang, Big Bounce, 1987, 88, High Energy Physics with Nuclei, 1980, 86, Theory of Multiparticle Production Processes, 1976, 88, 10 other books and 300 papers. Lt. Russian mil., 1942-45. Home: Leninskii Prospet 79-1-186, 117261 Moscow Russia Office: Space Rsch Inst, Profsousnaja Str, 117810 Moscow Russia

ROZGONYI, FERENC, medical educator, microbiologist; b. Tarcal, Zemplén, Hungary, Sept. 21, 1938; s. János and Jánosné (Mata Borbála) R.; m. Ferencné Mária Gertrúd Szécsi, Mar. 21, 1967 (dec. 1981); children: Cecilia, Viktória; m. Katalin Szitha, Mar. 31, 1984. MD, Univ. Med. Sch., Debrecen, Hungary, 1963; PhD, Hungarian Acad. Sci., Budapest, Hungary, 1978, DMSc, 1988; Dr. Med. Habil., Univ. Med. Sch., Debrecen, 1995. Cert. specialist for med. lab. investigations; specialist for med. microbiology. Asst. prof. Univ. Med. Sch., Debrecen, 1963-72, lectr., 1972-81, assoc. prof., 1981-95, prof., 1995—; chief bacteriol. diagnostic lab. Univ. Med. Sch., Debrecen, 1993-96; dir. and chmn. Inst. Microbiol. Semmelweis U. Med., Budapest, Hungary, 1996—; rsch. assoc. dept. pharmacology U. Ky., Lexington, 1969-70; vis. prof. Swedish U. Agr. Sci., Uppsala, Sweden, 1984-85, DAAD, Cologne, Berlin, 1992; vis. prof. dept. bacteriol, Royal Infirmary, U. Glasgow, U.K., 1994. Author, editor: Rapid Microbiology Diagnostic Methods for General Practitioner, 1994; editl. bd.: Jour. Chemotherapy, 1991-94, Acta Microb. Immunol., 1996—, Hungarian Venerology Archive, 1998—; contbr. articles to profl. jours. Mem. Hungaria-Helvetia Soc. (bd. dirs. 1990—). Avocations: traveling, gymnastics, music. Office: Inst Med Microbiol Semmelweis U, VIII Nagyvárad tér 4, H-1089 Budapest Hungary

ROZHANSKY, VLADIMIR ALEXANDROVICH, physicist, educator; b. St. Petersburg, Russia, Sept. 1, 1953; s. Alexander Natanovich and Sofia Yurievna (Lein) R.; m. Irina Felixovna Levinson, Nov. 3, 1973; 1 child, Igor. MS, St. Petersburg State Tech. U., 1976; PhD, Ioffe Phys.-Tech. Inst., 1979, Ioffe Phys.-Tech. Inst., 1987. Rschr. St. Petersburg State Tech. U., 1976-87, assoc. prof. physics, 1987-88, prof., 1988—; mem. sci. coun. Ioffe Phys.-Tech. Inst., St. Petersburg, 1990—; Soros prof. 1998-2000. Author: Transport Phenomena in Partially Ionized Plasma, 1988, Plasma Rotation in Tokamaks, 1996. Grantee Internat. Sci. Found., 1993-95, Swedish Inst., 1994-97, CRDF, 1997-98, Russian Acad. Sci., 1997-99, 2000—. Avocations: hiking, football. Home: 4 Krasnoarmeyskaya 2/35 48, 198005 Saint Petersburg Russia Office: St Petersburg State Tech U, Polytechnicheskaya 29, 195251 Saint Petersburg Russia

ROZHDESTVENSKIY, MIKHAIL GEORGIEVICH, aeronautical engineer; b. Moscow, Russia, Nov. 25, 1944; s. George Mikhailovich and Olga (Gavrilovna (Mosiakina) R.; m. Tamara Alexeevna Malinkina, Aug. 13, 1978; 1 child, George. M in Engring., Moscow Aviation U., 1968, D in Engring., 1985. Engr. MMHP, Moscow, Russia, 1968-78; lead engr. MMHP, Moscow, 1978-85, head dept., 1985—. Mem. Am. Helicopter Soc., Russian Helicopter Soc., Nat. Geographic Soc. Russian Orthodox. Avocations: gardening, reading. Office: Mil Moscow Helicopter Plant, Sokolnichesky Val 2, 107113 Moscow Russia

ROZHDESTVENSKY, GENNADI NIKOLAEVICH, conductor; b. Moscow, May 4, 1931; m. Victoria Postnikova. Ed. Moscow State Conservatory. Condr., Bolshoi Theatre, 1951-60, prin. condr., 1965-70; prin. condr., mus. dir. USSR Radio and TV Symphony Orch., 1960-65, 70-74, also Moscow Chamber Orch., 1974-83; prin. condr. Stockholm Philharmonic, 1974-77, 92—, BBC Symphony Orch., 1978-81; condr. Vienna Symphony Orch., 1980-83; founder, artistic dir., chief condr. State Symphony Orch. of Ministry of Culture, 1983-92; prof. conducting State Conservatoire, Moscow, 1965— artistic dir., Bolshoi Theater, Moscow; guest condr. Europe, Am., Asia. Decorated Order of Red Banner of Labour; named Merited and People's Artist R.S.F.S.R., 1966; recipient Lenin prize, 1970. Mem. Royal Swedish Acad. (hon.). Office: Bolshoi Theater, Teatralnaya Pl. 1, 103009 Moscow Russia also: care Stockholm Philharm Orch, Hotogret 8, S-111 57 Stockholm Sweden also: State Symphony Orch, Ministry of Culture, Moscow USSR

ROZINAJ, GREGOR, telecommunications engineer, educator, researcher; b. Bratislava, Slovakia, Mar. 30, 1957; s. Viktor and Helena (Bojnanská) R.; m. Viera Kosseyová, Sept. 17, 1983; children: Filip, Martin. MSc in Engring., Slovak U. Tech., Bratislava, 1981, PhD, 1990. Tchr. Slovak U. Tech., 1981-91; rschr. U. Kent, Canterbury, Eng., 1991, U. Alcatel, Stuttgart, Germany, 1992-94, U. Stuttgart, 1995-96; tchr. Slovak U. Tech., 1997—, vice dean faculty elec. engring. and info. tech., 2000—. Patentee in field of speech processing; author: Digital Signal Processing, vol. I, 1996, vol. II, 1997. Head of Bratislava I Christian-Dem. Movement, 1990-91. Roman Catholic. Office: Slovak U Tech, Ilkovičova 3, 819 19 Bratislava Slovakia

ROZŁUCKI, WIESŁAW, stock exchange executive; b. Gliwice, Poland, Dec. 9, 1947; s. Tadeusz and Karolina (Prosowska) R.; m. Grazyna, Dec. 12, 1971; children: Jerzy, Michal. MA in Econs., Cen. Sch. Planning and Stats., Warsaw, 1970; PhD in Econ. Geography, Inst. Geography and Spl. Orgn., Warsaw, 1977. Rsch. asst. Inst. Geography Polish Acad. Sci., Warsaw, 1973-79; sec. Polish com. Internat. Geog. Union, Warsaw, 1984-90; asst. prof. Polish Acad. Sci., Warsaw, 1979-89; adv. to min. finance Ministry of Finance, Warsaw, 1990; dir. capital mkt. dept. Ministry of Privatization, Warsaw, 1990-91; pres. Warsaw Stock Exch., 1991—. Office: Warsaw Stock Exchange, Nowy Swiat 6/12, 00-400 Warsaw Poland

ROZMUS, CATHY DIANE, nursing educator, graduate studies administrator; b. Bluefield, W.Va., June 25, 1953; d. William Rudolph and Virginia Elizabeth (Robinette) Leffel; m. Glenn Frank Rozmus, Aug. 4, 1974; children: Heather, Alison, Aaron. BSN, W.Va. U., 1975; MSN, Vanderbilt U., 1987; DSN, U. Ala., Birmingham, 1990. RN. Staff nurse Children's Hosp., Louisville, Ky., 1975-76; childbirth educator, 1977—; rsch. asst. Vanderbilt U., Nashville, Tenn., 1986-87; instr. Columbia (Tenn.) State C.C., 1986-90; med. ctr. fellow U. Ala., Birmingham, 1989-90; asst. prof. Belmont U., Nashville, 1990-93, assoc. prof., 1993-97, chair grad. studies, 1994; dean Sch. Nursing, Southwestern State Univ., 1997-2000; vice pres. academic affairs Georgia Southwestern State Univ., 2000—; expert witness David Smith and Assoc., Nashville, 1993—; curriculum cons. Jackson (Tenn.) State C.C., 1994. Reviewer Jour. Perinatal Edn., 1994; contbr. articles to profl. jours. Instr. HIV/AIDS, Red Cross, Nashville, 1992—; mem. Ryan White Cmty. AIDS Partnership, Nashville, 1994. Fellow Am. Coll. Childbirth Educators (cert.); mem. ANA (pres. dist. 16 1987-92), Nat. League for Nursing (dist. chair 1993—), GNA (chair cabinet nursing rsch.), 1999-2001, bd. dirs. Georgia Perinatal Assn., 1999-2001, So. Nursing Rsch. Soc., Sigma Theta Tau. Home: PO Box 1283 Americus GA 31709-1283 Office: Ga Southwestern State U 800 Wheatley St Americus GA 31709-4376

ROZNER, LEO, plastic surgeon, writer; b. Danzig, Germany, July 19, 1932; arrived in Australia, 1939; s. Chaskiel and Klara (Kleszczecki) R.; m. Katherine Jane Welk, June 8, 1954; children: Gideon, Romy; m. Judith Ur, Mar. 31, 1961 (div. 1983); children: Maya Regina, Dana Sarah. MB, BS, U. Melbourne, Australia, 1955. Resident surg. officer Royal Melbourne Hosp., 1955-61, assoc. asst. surgeon, 1959-62; asst. surgeon Sir Edward Dunlop, 1960-64; asst. plastic surgeon Alfred Hosp., Melbourne, 1964-76; sr. plastic surgeon Avenue Hosp., Melbourne, 1972—; cons. plastic surgeon Sandringham Hosp., Melbourne, 1975-84. Author: Aesthetic Plastic Surgery, 1975; contbr. articles to profl. jours. Surgeon U.S. AID, Vietnam, 1963. Recipient Vietnam Svc. medal Australian Govt., 1996. Fellow ACS, Royal Australian Coll. Surgeons, Royal Coll. Surgeons (Eng.); mem. Australian Soc. Plastic Surgeons (found.), Brit. Assn. Plastic Surgeons. Jewish. Avocations: golf, skiing, photography, music, arts. Home: 2A Verdant Ave, Toorak Melbourne 3142, Australia Office: Leo Rozner and Assocs, 31 The Avenue, 3181 Melbourne Australia

ROZOVSKIS, GREGORY, chemist, researcher; b. Kaunas, Lithuania, Nov. 10, 1929; s. Izrael and Marija (Grunkin) R.; m. Vilgelmina Grishina, Nov. 18, 1951; children: Vladimir, Natali. Grad. in chemistry, U. Vilnius, Lithuania, 1951, PhD, 1958; DSc, Inst. Chemistry, Vilnius, 1980. Rsch. scientist Inst. Agr., Vilnius, 1951-58; rsch. scientist Inst. Chemistry, Vilnius, 1958-81, head sector, 1981-90, head lab., 1990—; prof. dept. chemistry U. Vilnius, 1994—, Pedagogical U., Vilnius, 1995—. Co-author: Electroless Copper Deposition, 1966; patentee in field; contbr. over 160 articles to profl. jours. Recipient Nat. Sci. prize Govt. Lithuania, 1983. Avocations: fiction, poetry. Home: Smelio 15-1, 2055 Vilnius Lithuania Office: Inst Chemistry, A Goštauto 9, 2600 Vilnius Lithuania

RÓZSA, GYÖRGY, academy library foundation president; b. Oradea, Romania, Oct. 13, 1922; s. Rezső and Jolán (Zuckerman) R.; m. Borbála Robitsek (dec. 1967); children: Gábor, Mihály. Cert., Hungarian Inst. Internat. Rel., Budapest, 1947; Dipl. Libr. Ship, Inst. Pedagogy, Budapest, 1953; Dr. Econ., U. Econs., Budapest, 1964; DS in Econs., High Comm. Sci. Qualification, Budapest, 1988. Sec. Ministry for Fgn. Affairs, Hungary, 1947-50; libr. Ctr. for Pub. Librs., Hungary, 1952-55; chief libr. and sci. sec. Inst. Econs. Acad. Scis., Hungary, 1955-60; dir. gen. Libr. Hungarian Acad. Sci., Hungary, 1960-96; chief libr. UN Libr. at Geneva, Switzerland, 1969-75; field cons. UNESCO-UNDP, Asia, Africa. Author: Scientific Information and Society, 1973, Information from Claims to Needs, 1988, 7 other books; contbr. over 470 articles to profl. jours. Recipient medal Internat. Coun. of Archives, 1977, Librarianship Meml. medal, 1982, Pro Scientia Hungarica medal Hungarian Acad. Scis., 1996. Mem. Assn. Internat. de Bibliologie (exec. com.). Avocations: reading, tennis, fine arts. Home: XI Somloi ut 37/A, Budapest Hungary Office: Libr Hungarian Acad Scis, V Arany Janos u l, Budapest Hungary

ROZSÍVAL, PAVEL, ophthalmologist, educator, surgeon; b. Cheb, Czech Republic, Sept. 27, 1950; s. Vladimír and Věra (Matyašová) R.; m. Iva Fišerová, July 31, 1971; children: Kateřina, Pavel. MD, Charles U., Prague, Czech Republic, 1974, PhD, 1979. Sci. worker Charles U., Hradec Králové, Czech Republic, 1979-84; head dept. ophthalmology Dist. Hosp., Teplice, Czech Republic, 1984-86, Regional Hosp., Ústí n.Labem, Czech Republic, 1986-93; head dept. ophthalmology Charles U., 1993—, prof. ophthalmology, 1996—; cons. Nat. Med. Libr., Prague, 1978-92; mem. Czech Com. Ophthalmology, Prague, 1991—; mem. sci. adv. bd. Czech Chamber Physicians, 1993-98, Czech Ministry Health, 1999—; lectr. in field. Author: Ophthalmology for Family Physicians, 1994, Modern Cataract Surgery, 1995; contbr. over 180 articles to profl. jours. Mem. Am. Acad. Ophthalmology, Am. Soc. Cataract Refractive Surgery, Internat. Intraocular Implant Club, Czech Soc. Ophthalmology (pres. 1997—). Avocation: sport activities. Office: Charles Univ, Tchg Hosp, 500 05 Hradec Kralove Czech Republic

ROZSOS, ISTVÁN IMRE, general surgeon, researcher; b. Nagykanizsa, Zala, Hungary, Aug. 28, 1932; s. Antal Péter Rozsos and Irma Mária Horváth; m. Magdolna Mária Máté, Feb. 15, 1958; children: István, Tamás. MD, Med. U. Pécs, Hungary, 1957; PhD, Hungarian Acad. Sci., Budapest, 1974, DSc, 1990; D. (hon.), Pannon Agr. U., Keszthely, Hungary, 1997. Resident City Hosp., Keszthely, 1957-61; adjunct Moritz Kaposi Med. Ctr., Kaposvár, Hungary, 1961-70, head surgeon, 1970-80, chief surg. dept., 1980—; assoc. prof. Med. U. Sch., Pécs, 1985, prof. surgery, 1997—; chmn. sci. bd. Somogy County, Kaposvár, Hungary, 1978—, surg. insp., 1981—. Author: Microlaparotomy Cholecystectomy, 1998. Comdr. Com. Hungary Revolutionary, 1956. Decorated Order Hungarian Rep.; recipient Pro Patria et Liberatare World Fedn. Freedom Fighter, 1991. Mem. Club Innovators Govt., Club Acad. Roman Catholic. Achievements include invention the Synapses of Burdach's Nucleus; New Approach to gastrectomy; patent in Equipment for Micro- and Minilaparotomy in Surgery. Avocations: cultural history, moral philosophy, angling. Home: Németh I. Fasor 15, 7400 Kaposvár Hungary Office: Moritz Kaposi Med Ctr, Tallián Gy u 20-34, Kaposvár Hungary

ROZUMNYJ, JAROSLAV, literature educator, researcher; b. Honcharivka, Ukraine, Sept. 6, 1925; s. Hryhory and Anna (Parubocha) R.; m. Oksana Olha Hrycenko, Mar. 10, 1938; children: Larysa, Roman, Istan, Ruslan. BA with honors, Theol. Sem., Culemborg, Netherlands, 1950; MA, U. Ottawa, Ont., Can., 1958, PhD, 1968. Lectr. Laurentian U., Sudbury, Ont., 1960-63; asst. prof. Western Mich. U., Kalamazoo, 1963-64; asst. prof. U. Man., Winnipeg, Can., 1964-71, head dept., 1976-89, prof. lit., 1989—, sr. scholar, 1997; vis. prof. U. Ottawa, 1972, Ukrainian Cath. U., Rome, 1987; dean Faculty of Philosophy, Ukrainian Free U., Munich, Germany, 1995-96; vis. rsch. scholar Macquarie U., Sydney, 1989; mem. internat. adv. bd. U. Kiev-Mohyla Acad., 1992—, hon. prof., 1996. Editor: New Soil--Old Roots: The Ukrainian Experience in Canada, 1983; co-editor: Jubilee Collection of the Ukrainian Academy of Arts and Sciences, 1976; lit. editor: Anthology of Musical Compositions on the Poems of M. Shashkewych, 1992; editor Can. vol. Ency. of Ukrainian Diaspora, 7 vols.; editor-in-chief: Collection of Scholarly Papers, 1996; mem. editl. bd. Suchasnist, 1984-91. Pres. Ukrainian Cultural and Ednl. Ctr., Winnipeg, 1970-73; pres. Can. Friends of Rukh in Ukraine, Winnipeg, 1990-92; Can. rep. U. Kiev-Mohyla-Acad., 1992—; bd. govs. Man. Mus. Man and Nature, Winnipeg, 1976-80. Recipient Outreach Activities award U. Man., 1986, Taras Shevchenko medal Ukrainian Can. Congress, 1995. Mem. Ukrainian Acad. Arts and Scis. in Can. (pres. 1977-80, v.p. 1995—), Schevchenko Sci. Soc. U.S., Internat. Assn. Ukrainian Studies.

ROZYCKI, PAUL ANDREW, political science educator; b. Dekalb, Ill., July 18, 1944; s. Gene Conrad and Frieda Cecile (Lojewski) R.; m. Nancy Ann Lenz, Dec. 16, 1967. BA, No. Ill. U., 1966; MA, Ind. U., 1967. Instr. polit. sci. Ball State U., Muncie, Ind., 1967-69; prof. Mott Community Coll., Flint, Mich., 1969—; photography instr. U. Mich., Flint, 1980—, Flint Art Inst., 1994-98. Author: Introduction to Genesee County Legal System, 1977, Study Guide to American Government, 1984; co-author: Politics and Government in Michigan, 1983, 3d edit., 2000, A Clearer Image, 1998. Dem. precinct del., Flint, 1972—; mem. Genesee County Jury Bd., 1997—. Mem. Mich. Polit. Sci. Assn. (bd. dirs. 1982-85, 90—), Coll. Media Advisers, Community Coll. Journalism Assn. Roman Catholic. Avocations: photography, writing, travel. Home: 135 Commonwealth Ave Flint MI 48503-2151 Office: Mott Community Coll 1401 E Court St Flint MI 48503-6208

RÓŻYŁO, TERESA KATARZYNA, physician, educator; b. Tyszowce, Zamośc, Poland, Dec. 31, 1947; d. Hipolit and Władysława (Włoszczuk) Słota; m. Jan Kazimierz Różyło, Sept. 5, 1970; 1 child, Ingrid Katarzyna. Diploma physician, Med. Acad., Lublin, Poland, 1970, D in Med. Sci., 1975, DSc, assoc. prof., 1996. Med. diplomate. Physician Lublin (Poland) Hosp., 1970-72; asst. prof. Med. Acad., Lublin, 1976-96, assoc. prof., 1996—, head dept. dental and maxillofacial radiology, 1986—. Mem. Internat. Assn. Dentomaxillofacial Radiology, Polish Stomatological Soc. (vice-chmn. sect. dental radiology 1989—), Polish Phys. Radiol. Soc. Mem. Polish Farmers Party. Roman Catholic. Home: Dudzińskiego 42, 20-815 Lublin Poland Office: Acad Medicine Stomatol Br, Karmelicka 7, 20-081 Lublin Poland

ROZZELL, SCOTT ELLIS, lawyer; b. Texarkana, Tex., Apr. 12, 1949; s. George M. and Dora Mae (Boyett) R.; divorced; children by previous marriage: Stacey Elizabeth, Kimberly Marie. BA, So. Meth. U., 1971; JD, U. Tex., 1975. Bar: Tex. 1975, U.S. Dist. Ct. (so. dist.) Tex. 1975, U.S. Dist. Ct. (no. dist.) Tex. 1977, U.S. Ct. Appeals (1st, 3d, 9th cirs.) 1977, U.S. Ct. Appeals (5th and D.C. cirs.) 1976. Assoc. BakerBotts, LLP, Houston, 1975-82, ptnr., 1983-94, sr. ptnr., 1995—; mem. State of Tex. Aircraft Pooling Bd., 1997—; mem. devel. bd. U. of Tex. Health Sci. Ctr. Houston. Bd. dirs. Manned Space Flight Edn. Found., Inc., 1997—; vice chair Cancer Counseling Inc., Houston, 1991-92. Fellow Tex. Bar Found. (sustaining life), Houston Bar Found. (sustaining fellow, bd. dirs. 1991-93, chair 1993), Am. Bar Found.; mem. ABA, State Bar Tex. (bd. dirs. 1997-2000), Houston Bar Assn. (bd. dirs. 1991-95, pres. 1996-97), Fed. Energy Bar Assn., Houston Young Lawyers Assn. (bd. dirs. 1978-82, pres. 1983-84), Plaza Club (bd. dirs. 1995—). Republican. Presbyterian. Avocation: flying vintage airplanes. Home: 3121 Buffalo Speedway Apt 7309 Houston TX 77098-1859 Office: BakerBotts LLP 3000 One Shell Plz 910 Louisiana St Ste 3000 Houston TX 77002-4908

ROZZI, JAY CHRISTOPHER, mechanical engineer; b. Pitts., Sept. 30, 1966; s. Renzi Francis and Carol Ann (Csensich) R.; m. Colleen Marie Groves, Oct. 17, 1992. BS in Mech. Engring., Purdue U., 1989, MS in Mech. Engring., 1991, PhD, 1997. Rsch. asst. Purdue U., West Lafayette, Ind., 1989-91, 93-97; engr. UTC-Carrier Corp., Syracuse, N.Y., 1991-93; sr. engr. Raytheon Sys. Co., Tewksbury, Mass., 1997-99; engr. Creare Inc., Hanover, N.H., 1999—; tchg. asst. Purdue U., West Lafayette, 1996. Contbr. articles to ASME Jour. Heat Transfer, Internat. Jour. Heat and Mass Transfer, Jour. Heat Treating, Exptl. Heat Transfer, Jour. Materials Engring. and Performance, ASME Jour. Mfg. Sci. and Engring. Mem. ASME, AIAA, Soc. Mfg. Engrs., Pi Tau Sigma, Tau Beta Pi. E-mail: jcr@creare.com. Office: Creare Inc Etna Rd PO Box 71 Hanover NH 03755-0071

RUAN, MINGCHUAN, civil engineer; b. Wenzhou, China, July 31, 1965; s. Yunying Ruan and Xiangmei Lin; m. Hui Zhang, July 5, 1991; 1 child, Linda Hongzhang. BSc, Tsinghua U., 1989; MSc, Delft U. Technology, 1993, PhD, 1999. Cons. urban & regional planning Inst. Wenzhou, 1989-91; rschr. Delft U. Technology, The Netherlands, 1993-99; software developer Netherlands Orgn. for Applied Sci. Rsch., Delft, 1999—. Avocations: stock exchanges, software development. Home: Herman Gorterhof 163, 2624 XL Delft The Netherlands Office: TNO Automotive PO Box 6033, Schoemakerstraat 97, 2600 JA Delft The Netherlands

RUAN, RUN-SHENG, research scientist, otolaryntologist; b. Fuzhou, Fujian, China, Nov. 3, 1954; arrived in Singapore, 1992; s. John Ruan and Xiu-Yu Chen; m. Ling Chen, Oct. 1, 1983; 1 child, Qing-Zhao. B Medicine, Fujian Med. U., 1982; MD, Zurich U., 1991. Lectr. otolaryngology Fujian Med. U., 1982-89; vis. scholar otolaryngology Zurich U. Hosp., 1989-90, vis. scientist Cancer Rsch. Inst., 1990-91; vis. surgeon Raphel and Hislanden Hosps., Switzerland, 1991-92; sr. rsch. scientist Nat. U. Singapore, 1992. Contbr. rsch. articles to profl. publs. Rsch. grantee Nat. U. Singapore, 1993, Nat. Med. Rsch. Coun., Singapore, 1996. Avocations: swimming, dancing. Office: Nat U Singapore Dept Otolaryngology, Lower Kent Ridge Rd, Singapore 119074, Singapore

RUBASZEK, ANNA, physicist, researcher; b. Wrocław, Poland, May 21, 1951; d. Ludwik Karol Świderski and Lila (Nadel) Świderska; m. Andrzej Józef Rubaszek, Nov. 4, 1972; children: Grzegorz Erlend, Michał Jacek. MS in Math., Tech. U., Wrocław, 1973; PhD in Physics, Polish Acad. Scis., 1986, D Habilitation in Physics, 1996. Cert. engring. Jr. rschr. Inst. Math. Tech. U., Wrocław, 1973-80; adjunct sr. rschr. Polish Acad. Scis., Wrocław, 1984-97, docent, 1997—. Co-author (chpt.): Positrons at Metal Surface, 1994, Positron Spectroscopy of Solids, 1995; contbr. articles to profl. jours. Grantee Royal Soc. U.K., 1997-99; grantee Com. Sci. Rsch. Poland, 1999—. Democrat. Avocations: literature, ancient culture, fine arts. Home: Skibowa 21, 52-211 Wrocław Poland Office: Polish Acad Scis, Okólna 2, 50-950 Wrocław 2, Poland

RUBAY, JEAN ETIENNE, cardiac surgeon, educator; b. Charleroi, Hainaut, Belgium, Oct. 21, 1953; s. Jean Rubay and Raphaelle van Holderbeke. Diploma cum laude, Coll. Sacre Coeur, Charleroi, 1971; PhD magna cum laude, UCL, 1979. Surgeon UCL, St. Luc, Belgium, 1984; cons., cardiac surgeon UCL St. Luc, Brussels, 1988, prof. pediatric cardiac surgery, 1988—; associated dir. European Horograft Bank, 1991. Contbr. articles to profl. jours. Pres. Chain Hope, Belgium, 1997. Roman Catholic. Home: Ave Naurice Cesar, 1970 Wezenbeek Belgium Office: UCL St Luc, 10 Ave Hippocrate, 1200 Brussels Belgium

RUBEL, MAREK JAN, chemist, physicist, researcher; b. Warsaw, Poland, Apr. 19, 1953; arrived in Sweden, 1991; s. Stanislaw and Zofia R.; m. Elzbieta Alicja Przyborowska, July 11, 1981; children: Joanna, Jan. MSc in Chemistry, U. Warsaw, 1977; PhD in Materials Sci., Tech. U. Warsaw, 1983; docent in Plasma Physics, Royal Inst. Tech., Stockholm, 1994. PhD student Tech. U. Warsaw, 1977-82; rsch. assoc. Space Rsch. Ctr., Warsaw, 1985-90; vis. rsch. assoc. U. Ill., Urbana, 1990-91; rsch. assoc. Manne Siegbahn Inst. Physics, Stockholm, 1991-93; rsch. assoc. Royal Inst. Tech., Stockholm, 1993-97, assoc. prof., 1998—. Contbr. numerous articles to internat. scientific jours. Recipient rsch. grants Swedish Natural Sci. Rsch. Coun., and various indsl. cos. Avocations: photography, mountain climbing, canoeing, mushrooms. Office: Royal Inst Tech, Alfvén Lab, S-100 44 Stockholm Sweden

RUBEN, DAVID-HILLEL, philosophy educator, administrator; b. Chgo., July 25, 1943; arrived in U.K., 1969; s. Blair Stanley and Sylvia Toby (Ginsberg) R.; m. Alice Eyra Karlinsky, Sept. 6, 1968; children: Anna Lilian, Sophie Rachel, Simon Daniel. BA, Dartmouth Coll., 1965; PhD, Harvard U., 1971. Lectr. philosophy Glasgow (Scotland) U., 1970-75, U. Essex, Wivenhoe, U.K., 1975-79; sr. lectr. philosophy City U., London, 1979-84; prof. philosophy London Sch. Econs., 1984-98; dir. London Sch. Jewish Studies U. London, 1998-99; dir. NYU in London affiliate NYU, 2000—; senator U. London, 1991-2000. Revs. editor Mind, 1990-95; author: Marxism and Materialism, 1977, 79, Metaphysics of the Social World, 1985, Explaining Explanation, 1991; editor: Explanation, 1993; contbr. articles to profl. jours. Dep. Bd. of Deps. of Brit. Jews, London, 1991-92. Nuffield fellow Nuffield Found., London, 1989. Mem. Phi Beta Kappa. Jewish. Home: 29 Sunny Gardens Rd, London NW4 1SL, England Office: NYU in London, 6 Bedford Sq, London WC1B 3RA, England

RUBENS, ROBERT DAVID, physician, educator; b. Woking, Eng., June 11, 1943; s. Joel and Dinah (Hasseck) R.; m. Margaret Chamberlin, Oct. 30, 1970; children: Abigail, Carolyn. BSc, King's Coll., London, 1964; MBBS, St. George's Hosp., London, 1967; MD, U. London, 1974. House physician St. George's Hosp., London, 1968, house surgeon, 1968-69; house physician Brompton Hosp., London, 1969, Hammersmith Hosp., London, 1969-70; med. registrar Royal Marsden Hosp., London, 1970, St. George's Hosp., London, 1970-72; rsch. fellow Imperial Cancer Rsch. Fund, London, 1972-74; cons. physician Guy's Hosp., London, 1975—; prof. clin. oncology King's Coll., London, 1985—; dir. ICRF Unit Guy's Hosp., London, 1985-97; chmn. EORTC Breast Cancer Coop. Group, 1991-94; examiner Royal Coll. Physicians, London, 1987-94; chief med. officer merc. and Gen. Reins Co. Ltd., London, 1977-97; chief med. officer Swiss Life and Health, 1997—, Legal and Gen. Assurance Soc., 1992—. Author: (textbooks) Clinical Oncology, 1980, Bone Metastases, 1991, Cancer and the Skeleton, 2000; editor-in-chief Cancer Treatment Revs., 1992; contbr. articles to profl. jours. Dir. Lee House, Wimbeldon, Eng., 1983. Fellow Royal Coll. Physicians; mem. Soc. Apothecaries, Assurance Med. Soc. (coun. 1982), Brit. Med. Assn., Am. Soc. Clinical Oncology, Am. Assn. for Cancer Rsch., Athenaeum (London), Royal Wimbledon Golf Club. Avocations: golf, bridge. Office: Guy's Hosp, St Thomas St, London SE1 9RT, England

RUBENSTEIN, JOSHUA SETH, lawyer; b. Bklyn., Aug. 5, 1954; s. Seth and Elaine (Freedman) R.; children: Mary-Jane, Kenan, Rebecca, Marlena. BA magna cum laude, Columbia U., 1976, JD, 1979. Bar: N.Y. 1980, N.J. 1980, U.S. Dist. Ct. (ea. dist.) N.Y. 1980, U.S. Dist. Ct. (so. dist.) N.Y. 1980, U.S. Dist. Ct. N.J. 1980, U.S. Tax Ct. 1986. Assoc. Fried, Frank, Harris, Shriver & Jacobson, N.Y.C., 1979-82; assoc. Rosenman & Colin LLP, N.Y.C., 1982-88, ptnr., 1988—, mgmt. com., 1994—; chmn. trusts and estates dept. Rosenman & Colin, N.Y.C., 1995—, mgmt. com., 1994—, adv. bd. TE/DEC Systems, Inc., Jour. N.Y. Taxation; lectr. in field; adv. com. on surrogate's cts. Office of Ct. Adminstrn., 1997—; adv. coun. Columbia Law Sch. Trusts, Wills and Estate Planning, 1997—. Contbr. articles to legal publs. Dir., sec. Irvington Inst. Med. Rsch., 1991, treas., 1991-92, sec., 1992-93, co-pres., 1993-94, pres., 1994-2000, vice-chmn., 2000—; chmn. estates and trust splty. group, chmn. splty. group; task force, mem. exec. com. lawyers divsn. United Jewish Appeal-Fedn., 1989-99; mem. legis. com., devel. com., bd. governance com., Madeleine Borg com., chmn., mem. exec. com., 1994—; trustee Jewish Bd. Family and Children's Svcs., 1991—. Recipient James H. Fogelson award Lawyer's divsn. United Jewish Appeal-Fedn., 1993; named to Best Lawyers in N.Y., N.Y. Mag. Fellow Am. Coll. Trusts and Estate Counsel (state laws com.), N.Y. State Bar Found.; mem. ABA (real property and probate sect.), Internat. Acad. Estate and Trust Law (academician 1997—), Practising Law Inst. (estate adv. com., lectr. 1984—, Hadassah estate planning seminar faculty and adv. bd. 1993—), N.Y. State Bar Assn. (trust and estate law sect., treas. 1997-98, sec. 1998-99, chair elect 1999—, vice chmn. legis. com. 1988, chmn. 1988-91, co-chmn. ad hoc com. to rev. proposals of EPTL adv. com. of N.Y. State 1991—, mem.-at-large exec. com. 1992-95, liaison to legis. policy com. 1995—, Pres.'s Pro Bono Svc. award 1991, Exec. Com. award, 1992, 95, 96, treas. 1997), N.J. Bar Assn. adv. com. rels. with legis. and exec. brs., real property and probate sect.), Assn. Bar City N.Y, Phi Beta Kappa. Democrat. Jewish. Office: Rosenman & Colin 575 Madison Ave Fl 22D New York NY 10022-2511

RUBENSTEIN, LEONARD, engineering company executive; b. N.Y.C., June 18, 1931; s. William and Sylvia (Jaffe) R.; m. Reva Scharf, Jan. 1951 (div. 1960); m. Geraldine Marilyn Porper, Aug. 14, 1965; children: Alan, Elaine, Philip, Ruth, Jennie. BS in Physics, Poly. Inst. N.Y., 1964. Registered profl. engr. N.Y., N.J., Del., Ga. Equipment engr. We. Elec., N.Y.C., 1957-66; elec. engr. Gibbs & Hill, N.Y.C., 1966-69; chief engr. Kiegl Lighting, N.Y.C., 1969-72; project mgr. Stone & Webster, N.Y.C., 1972-87; v.p. engring. Laramore Douglas & Popham, N.Y.C., 1988-90; v.p., dir. engring. Gibbs & Hill, N.Y.C., 1990-92; mktr. NPS, Florham Park, N.J., 1992-95; pres., prin. Rubenstein Engring. PC, N.Y.C., 1995—; pres., CEO David Internat. Enterprise Corp., N.Y.C.; chmn. bd. HLP, N.Y.C. Contbr. articles to profl. publs. Chmn. Walt Whitman Ind. Dems., Bklyn., 1966-68, chmn. West Bklyn. Ind. Dems., 1964-66; bd. dirs. N.Y. Gilbert & Sullivan Players, N.Y.C., 1993—, 450 West End Corp, 1984-88; mem. bd. mgrs. McBurney YMCA, 1988-97. With U.S. Army, 1951-53. Mem. IEEE (sr., chmn. N.Y. sect. 1995-96, asst. editor Today's Engr. 1997-98, Region I award 1985, 94, 96), NSPE, Soc. Mfg. Engrs. (charter mem. Vision Soc., sr. mem. Robotics Internat.), Power Engring. Soc. (chmn. N.Y./L.I. chpt. 1984-85). Avocations: handball, music. Home and Office: 450 W End Ave New York NY 10024-5307

RUBENSTEIN, MICHAEL HARVEY, writer and consultant on employment law; b. Bklyn., May 13, 1943; arrived in U.K., 1964; s. Robert Samuel and Shirley Sonia (Trepel) R.; m. Barbara Stella Middleton, July 2, 1983; 1 child, Holly. BS, Cornell U., 1964; postgrad., London Sch. Econs., 1965-69. Mng. dir. Eclipse Publs., London, 1971-82; editor Indsl. Rels. Law Reports, London, 1972—, Equal Opportunities Rev., London, 1985—, Discrimination Case Law Digest, London, 1990—, ECJ Employment Law Watch, London, 1996—; cons. Commn. for European Cmtys., Belgium, 1985-92, World Bank, U.S., 1994-96; chmn. Indsl. Law Soc., U.K., 1985-89, Disability Discrimination Act Representation and Advice Project, U.K., 1996—. Author: Equal Pay for Work of Equal Value, 1985, Preventing and Remedying Sexual Harassment at Work, 1991, Fair Employment Case Law, 1996; author (report): The Dignity of Women at Work, 1998; mem. editl. com. Indsl. Law Jour., 1983—. Recipient Minerva prize (European Man of Yr.), Club of Women, Italy; named hon. v.p. Indsl. Law Soc., 1996. Mem. Inst. Employment Rights, Employment Lawyers Assn., Reform Club. Avocations: opera, theatre, American sports, travel, reading. Home: Smithwood House, Smithwood Common, Cranleigh GU6 8QY, England Office: Eclipse Group Ltd, 18-20 Highbury Pl, London N5 1QP, England

RUBEŠA, DOMAGOJ, mechanical engineering educator; b. Rijeka, Croatia, Nov. 13, 1959; s. Slobodan and Jelka (Frlan) R.; m. Dolores Deškovic, May 26, 1984; children: Ivana, Vjekoslav. BSc, Tech. Faculty Rijeka, Croatia, 1984; MSc, Faculty Mech. Engring., Ljubljana, Slovenia, 1989; PhD, U. Leoben, Austria, 1995. System analyst shipyard, Rijeka, 1984-85; univ. lectr. Tech. Faculty Rijeka, 1985-86, 87-94; rsch. fellow U. Leoben Dept. Structural and Functional Ceramics, Austria, 1994-99; R&D engr. pankl Sys., Bruck, Austria, 1999; prof. U. Applied Sci., Dept. Automotive Engring., Graz, Austria, 2000—. Author: Lifetime Prediction and Constitutive Modelling for Creep-Fatigue Interaction, 1996. With Yugoslav Army, 1986-87. Fellow German Soc. for Materials Sci. Office: Technikum Joanneum, Alte Poststr 149, 8020 Graz Austria

RUBIN, ARNOLD JESSE, aeronautical engineer; b. Bklyn., Sept. 30, 1924; s. Jack and Birdie (Reiss) R.; m. Gloria Form, June 19, 1949 (dec. Sept. 1994); children: Jacqueline Sue Rubin Grob, Mitchell Myles. B in Aero. Engring., NYU, 1949; postgrad., U. Va., 1950, Poly. Inst. Bklyn., 1960-62. Aero. rsch. scientist Langley Rsch. Ctr., NASA, Hampton, Va., 1949-51; with Fairchild Republic Co., Fairchild Industries, Inc., Farmingdale, N.Y., 1951-87; prin. aerodyn. engr. Fairchild Republic Co., Fairchild Industries, Inc., Farmingdale, 1979-82, chief aerodyns., T-46A, 1982-87. Served with USAAF, 1943-45. Fellow AIAA (assoc.); mem. Soc. Flight Test Engrs., NYU Alumni Assn., Huron Club. Home: 106 Sprucewood Dr Levittown NY 11756-3837

RUBIN, CATHY ANN, retired educator; b. Denver, July 17, 1948; d. Harry Phillip and Charlotte Ruth (Brinig) R. BA, Colo. State U., 1970; MA, U. No. Colo., 1971. Cert. tchr., Colo. Tchr. Adams County Dist. 50 Schs., Westminster, Colo., 1971-72; tchr. educationally handicapped Jefferson County Pub. Schs., Golden, Colo., 1972-98; typist, bookkeeper Kenmark-Shaw's Jewelers, Denver, 1966—. Sec.-treas. Hillel Found., Denver, 1979-81; fundraiser Women's Am. Orgn. for Rehab. through Tng., Denver, 1979—; bookkeeper Religious Coalition for Abortion Rights, Denver, 1982-90; vol. TV PBS sta., Denver, 1982—, Muscular Dystrophy Assn., Colo. AIDS Project; vol. usher DCTC, 1999—. Democrat. Jewish. Avocations: music, reading, sailing, knitting, needlepoint. Home: 3500 S Ivanhoe St Denver CO 80237-1123

RUBIN, CHANDA, professional tennis player; b. Lafayette, La., Feb. 18, 1976; d. Edward and Bernadette Rubin. Grad., Episcopal Sch. Acadiana, 1993. Mem. USTA Jr. Devel. Team, 1989, USTA Nat. Team, 1990; prof. tennis player, 1991—; player 20 tournaments and Fed. Cup with 43 wins, 19 losses, 1995, named to Olympic Team, Atlanta, 1996. Ranked 25th, 1999; recipient 3 U.S. Jr. Titles, 12 Singles, 1988, 14 Singles, 1989, 16 Indoor Doublles, 1989, Silver and Bronze medal 1995 Pan Am Games, 1995; winner U.S. nat. title and Rolex Orange Bowl 12s crown, 1988, 14 Nat., 1989, 16 Indoor Doubles, 1989, U.S. Tennis Assn. Challenge of Midland Mich.; named Most Improved Female Player, Tennis Mag., 1995, Female Athlete of Yr., U.S. Tennis Assn., 1995, Most Caring Athlete, USA Weekend Mag., 1997; singles winner Hobart, 1999, finalist, Quebec City, 1999, semifinalist, Indian Wells, 1999, Madrid, 1999; winner Doubles (with Testud) Filderstadt, 1999, finalist (with Testud) U.S. Open, 1999. Office: USTA 70 W Red Oak Ln White Plains NY 10604-3602 also: Advantage International 1751 Pinnacle Dr Ste 1500 Mc Lean VA 22102-3833*

RUBIN, HANAN, retired insurance company executive; b. N.Y.C., Mar. 9, 1927; s. Hyman and Esta (Greenberg) R.; m. Mona Klein, June 29, 1958; children: Eric Stuart, Karen Jill Rubin Dauber, Wendy Risa Rubin Axelrod. AB magna cum laude, NYU, 1948, PhD in Math., 1953. Cert. internal auditor, information systems auditor. Teaching asst. math. NYU, 1946-48, instr. math., asst. rsch. scientist Courant Inst. Math. Scis., 1948-51, instr. math., assoc. rsch. scientist, 1951-53, asst. prof. math., rsch. scientist, 1954-58, instr. Bell Telephone Labs., 1954-56; staff mathematician, cons. IBM, 1958-59, cons. analytical svcs. dept., 1959-60, asst. mgr., 1960, mgr., 1960-62; head computer group, sr. supervisory scientist TRG, 1962-64; tech. asst. to pres. Gen. Applied Sci. Labs., 1964-67; corp. staff mem., dir. edn. & tng. Computer Applications Inc., 1967-69; exec. asst. Met. Life Ins. Co., 1972-75, asst. v.p., 1975-77, v.p., 1977-91; vis. asst. prof. math. U. Tenn., 1953-54; cons. Union Carbide Nuc. Co., Oak Ridge, Tenn., 1953-66; vis. mathematician Brookhaven Nat. Lab., Upton, N.Y., 1957; co-chair Stony Brook Conf. Advances Computing SUNY, 1966; mem. bi-county task force com. computer applications medicine Nassau Heart Assn., Mineola, N.Y., 1971-72; chair ad hoc EFT com. Life Office Mgmt. Assn., 1978. Contbr. numerous articles to profl. jours. Bd. dirs. South Nassau Cmtys. Hosp., Oceanside, 1980—, treas. bd. dirs., 1985-89, 1st v.p. bd. dirs., 1989-90; bd. dirs. Winthrop South Nassau U. Health Sys., Mineola, Oceanside, 1996—. With USN, 1945-46. Rockefeller fellow NYU, 1948. Mem. Phi Beta Kappa, Tau Kappa Alpha, Sigma Xi. Avocation: computing, golf, music. Home: 359 Green Ct Oceanside NY 11572-5615

RUBIN, LAWRENCE GILBERT, physicist, laboratory manager; b. Bklyn., Sept. 17, 1925; s. Harry E. and Ruth (Feirberg) R.; m. Florence Ruth Kagan, Feb. 11, 1951; children: Michael G., Richard D., Jeffrey N. Student, Cooper Union, N.Y.C., 1943, 46-47; BS in Physics, U. Chgo., 1949; MA in Physics, Columbia U., 1950. Staff mem., physicist research div. Raytheon Co., Waltham, Mass., 1950-64; group leader Nat. Magnet Lab., MIT, Cambridge, Mass., 1964-78, divsn. head high magnetic field facility, 1978-93; advisor to high magnetic field facility, 1994-95; vis. scientist MIT, 1996—; mem. NAS adv. panel Nat. Bur. Standards, 1976-82, 85-90; bd. dirs. Lake Shore Cryotronics, Inc., Columbus, Ohio; gen. chmn. 6th Internat. Temperature Symposium, Washington, 1982, 7th Internat. Temperature Symposium, Toronto, Ont., Can., 1992, 8th Internat. Temperature Symposium, Chgo.; chmn. adv. com. Physics Today Buyers' Guide; contbg. editor Physics Today; organizer Am. Physical Soc. Tutorial program. Mem. editorial bd. Rev. Sci. Instruments, 1968-70, 79-81; contbr. articles to physics jours. With U.S. Army, 1943-46, ETO. Fellow IEEE (life), Am. Phys. Soc. (organizer and 1st chmn. instrument and measurement sci. group 1985); mem. Instrument Soc. Am. (sr.), Am. Vacuum Soc. Jewish. Home: 1504 Centre St Newton Center MA 02459-2447 Office: MIT Bldg NW14 1209 170 Albany St Cambridge MA 02139-4208

RUBIN, MARTIN N., meeting planner, consultant; b. N.Y.C., Aug. 9, 1928; s. Max and Esther (Chernow) R.; m. Shirley Anne Rubin, Aug. 22, 1954 (div. Aug. 1964); m. Karen Anne O'Brien, Sept. 21, 1981. AB, U. Mich.; AM, Miami U., Oxford, Ohio; PhD., Sussex U., Eng. Lic. psychologist. With Dayton (Ohio) Sch. System, 1951-60, West Alexandria (Ohio) Sch. System, 1961-63; instr. Wright State U., Dayton, 1961-63; with Devereux Found., Pa., N.Y. Dept. Corrections, Bklyn., 1971-73, Council for Retarded Children, Albany, N.Y., 1973-75; prin. M. Rubin & Co., Inc., Mount Vernon, N.Y., 1975—. Author: Developmentally Disabled, 1965. Candidate Dem. State Legis., 1982; adv. bd. Mt. Vernon Mental Health Bd., 1985. Master's degree scholar Miami U., 1958; Guidance Inst. grantee Miami U., 1959. Fellow Am. Assn. Mental Deficiency (pres. 1967); mem. Soc. Assn. Execs. (bd. dirs. 1985—). Lodge: Masons (sr. warden 1983). Avocations: dancing, singing.

RUBIN, NANCY ZIMMAN (NANCY RUBIN STUART), journalist, author, writer, producer; b. Boston, Nov. 25, 1944; d. Stuart Wendell and Ethel (Rabinovitz) Zimman; children: Elisabeth, Jessica. BA, Tufts U., 1966; MA in Teaching, Brown U., 1967; PhD (hon.), Mt. Vernon Coll., 1995. Playwright, dir. Equity Library Theatre, Roundabout, Joseph Jefferson and St. Clement's theaters, N.Y.C., 1971-74; freelance reporter Westchester-Gannett newspapers and mags., 1975-77, N.Y. Times, N.Y.C., 1977—; faculty affiliate Bush Ctr. in Child Devel., Yale U., New Haven, 1981-86; mem. Westchester County Women's Adv. Bd., chair, 1988; mem. faculty SUNY, Purchase, 1994-95, Fordham U., N.Y.C., 1996—. Author: The New Suburban Women; Beyond Myth and Motherhood, 1982, The Mother Mirror: How a Generation of Women is Changing Motherhood in America, 1984, Isabella of Castile: The First Renaissance Queen, 1991, American Empress: The Life and Times of Marjorie Merriweather Post, 1995, Club Dance: The Show, The Steps, The Spirit of Country, 1998; writer, assoc. prodr.: (TV series) America's Castles, 1996-99 (Best Writing Communicator award 1999) for A&E Network, The Gold Coast for The Grand Tour A & E TV, 1997; writer prodr., prodr. (TV series) Restore America, 1999—; writer/assoc. prodr. (TV show) Eccentrics, 1999 (Telly award); contbg. editor Parents mag., 1987-91, McCalls, Savvy, Travel & Leisure, Ladies Home Journal, 1980-92; theater critic Stamford Advocate, 1994-96. Recipient Washington Irving award Westchester Libr. Assn., 1993; Time, Inc.-Bread Loaf Writers' Colony scholar, 1979. Fellow MacDowell Colony; mem. Author's Guild, Am. Soc. Journalists and Authors (Author of Yr. award 1992), PEN, Nat. Arts Club. Avocations: skiing, sailing, ballet and jazz dancing, classical music.

RUBIN, ROBERT E., former secretary of treasury; b. N.Y.C., Aug. 29, 1938; s. Alexander and Sylvia (Seiderman) R.; m. Judith Leah Oxenberg, Mar. 27, 1963; children: James Samuel, Philip Matthew. AB summa cum laude, Harvard U., 1960; postgrad., London Sch. Econs., 1960-61; LLB, Yale U., 1964; DHL (hon.), Yeshiva U., 1996. Bar: N.Y. 1965. Assoc. Cleary, Gottlieb, Steen & Hamilton, N.Y.C., 1964-66; assoc. Goldman Sachs & Co., N.Y.C., 1966-70, ptnr., 1971, mem. mgmt. com., 1980, vice chmn., co-chief oper. officer, 1987-90, co-sr. ptnr., co-chmn., 1990-92; asst. to Pres. for econ. policy, head nat. econ. coun. Exec. Office of Pres., The White House, Washington, 1993-95; sec. U.S. Dept. of the Treasury, Washington, 1995-99; chmn. exec. com. Citigroup, 1999—; mem. Pres.'s Adv. Com. for Trade Negotiations, Washington, 1980-82, mem. adv. com. on tender offers SEC, Washington, 1983, Gov.'s Commn. on Trade Competitiveness, 1987, regulatory adv. com. N.Y. Stock Exch., 1988-90, adv. com. internat. capital markets Fed. Res. Bank N.Y., 1989-93, Securities and Exch. Commn. Market Oversight and Fin. Svcs. Adv. Com., 1991-93, Gov.'s Adv. Panel on Fin. Svcs., 1988-89; ptnr., bd. dirs. N.Y.C. Partnership Inc., 1991-93; bd. dirs. Ctr. for Nat. Policy, 1982-93, vice chmn., 1984; bd. dirs. N.Y. Futures Exch., N.Y.C., 1979-85, Chgo. Bd. Options Exch. Inc., 1972-76; trustee Mt. Sinai Hosp., 1977, vice chmn., 1986; trustee Sta. WNET-TV, 1985-93; mem., trustee Carnegie Corp. of N.Y., 1990-93; mem. Mayor's Coun. Econ. Advisors, 1990, Gov.'s Coun. on Fiscal and Econ. Priorities, 1990-92. Trustee Am. Ballet Theatre Found., Inc., N.Y.C., 1969-93, trustee Collegiate Sch., 1978-84; mem. bd. overseers' com. to visit econs. dept. Harvard U., 1981-87, com. on univ. resources, 1987-92; mem. fin. com. N.Y. campaign Mondale for Pres., 1983-84; mem. investment adv. coun. N.Y.C. Pension Fund, 1980-89; chmn. Dem. Congl. Dinner, Washington, 1982; Dems. for the 80s, 1985-89, Dems. for the 90s, 1989-90; chmn. N.Y.C. host com. 1992 Dem. Conv., 1989-92; mem. Commn. Nat. Elections. Recipient award Nat. Assn. Christians and Jews, N.Y.C., 1977, Disting. Leadership in Govt. award Columbia Bus. Sch., 1996, Euromoney Mag. award Fin. Min. Yr., 1996, Medal for High Civic Svc. award Citizens' Budget Com., 1997, Fgn. Policy Assn. medal, 1998, "Chmn." award Washington Greater Boys/Girls Clubs, 1998, Intrepid Sea Air Space Mus. award, 1998, Jefferson award Am. Inst. Pub. Svc., 1998, Award of Merit Yale U., 1998, Global Leadership award UN Assn., 1998, Paul Tsongas award, 1998. Mem. Phi Beta Kappa, Harvard Club (N.Y.C.), Century Country Club (Purchase, N.Y.). Jewish.

RUBIN, ROBERT JAY, toxicologist; b. Boston, Mar. 25, 1932; s. Edward and Ruth (Lichter) R.; m. Frances Stone, Sept. 5, 1954 (dec. Nov. 1981); children: Ellen Joyce, Howard Scott, Steven Glen; m. Idalea Kofsky, Aug. 28, 1983; stepchildren: David Wolfe, Jennifer Sirota, Aaron Wolfe. BA, U. Mass., 1953; MS, Boston U., 1955, PhD, 1960. Diplomate Am. Bd. Toxicology. Postdoctoral fellow Yale U. Sch. of Medicine, New Haven, Conn., 1960-64; asst. prof. pharmacology Kans. U. Med. Ctr., Kansas City, 1964; asst. prof. toxicology Johns Hopkins Sch. of Pub. Health, Balt., 1964-67, assoc. prof. toxicology, 1967-73, prof. toxicology, 1973-98, prof. emeritus, 1998—; cons. in toxicology, 1978—; adv. bd. Johns Hopkins Sch. of Pub. Health, Balt., 1985-86. Contbr. articles to profl. jours. including Toxicology and Applied Pharmacology, Jour. Toxicology and Environ. Health, Environ. Health Perspectives, many others. Pres. Stevenswood Community Assn., Balt., 1970-71; treas. Canton Square Community Assn., Balt., 1993-94. Postdoctoral fellowship NIH, Yale U., 1960-64, Career Devel. award NIH, Johns Hopkins U., 1969-74. Mem. Soc. of Toxicology (pres. Nat. Capital Area chpt. 1994-95, pres. risk assessment specialty sect. 1999-2000), Am. Soc. Pharmacology and Exptl. Therapeutics, Delta Omega (chmn. membership com. 1990-92). Avocation: travel to foreign countries. Home: 1201 S Linwood Ave Baltimore MD 21224-4869 Office: Johns Hopkins Sch Hygiene and Pub Health 615 N Wolfe St Baltimore MD 21205-2103

RUBIN, SETH ISAIAH, psychologist; b. Alexandria, LA, Mar. 6, 1945. BA, Northwestern U., 1966, MA, 1968, PhD in Psychology, 1971. Diplomate in psychoanalysis and analytical psychology; cert. profl. qualification in psychology; lic. psychologist, Pa., Calif., Ariz., Mass. Outpatient psychology fellow Hosp. U. Pa., 1978-80; tng. candidate, diploma candidate C.G. Jung Inst., Zurich, 1982-87; instr. dept. psychology Northwestern U., 1969-70; asst. prof. dept. psychology U. Ill. at Chgo. Circle, 1970-72; asst. rsch. prof. dept. psychiatry Med. Coll. Pa., 1974-75; asst. prof. dept. cmty. medicine U. Pa., 1975-76, asst. prof. dept. rsch. medicine, 1976-77, asst. prof. dept. ob-gyn., 1976-83, clin. assoc. dpet. psychiatry, 1987-88, clin. asst. prof./clin. assoc prof. psychology in psychiatry, 1987-92; allied health profl. Phila. Psychiat. Ctr., 1988-92; allied health affiliate, clin. psychologist Calif. Pacific Med. Ctr., 1994—; adj. prof. Union Grad. Sch., 1989-96, Calif. Sch. Profl. Psychology, Berkeley/Alameda, 1992—; vis. prof. psychology Saybrook Inst., 1994-95; lectr. in field. Contbr. numerous articles to profl. jours. Fellow Am. Coll. Advanced Practice Psychologists, Internat. Coll. Prescribing Psychologists; mem. APA, Internat. Assn. for Analytical Psychology, Assn. Grad. Analytical Psychologists of the C.G. Jung Inst., San Francisco Jung Inst., Soc. for Psychotherapy Rsch., othrs. Office: 2021 Webster St San Francisco CA 94115-2329

RUBIN, STUART HARVEY, computer science educator, researcher; b. N.Y.C., Mar. 18, 1954; s. Jack and Rhoda Rochelle (Lentz) R. BS, U. R.I., 1975; MS in Indsl. and Systems Engring., Ohio U., 1977; MS, Rutgers U., 1980; PhD, Lehigh U., 1988. Lectr. U. Cin., 1977-78; electronic engr. U.S. Army Rsch. Labs., Ft. Monmouth, N.J., 1980-83; assoc. prof. computer sci. Ctrl. Mich. U., Mt. Pleasant, 1988—, assoc. prof., 1996—, founder, dir. Ctr. for Intelligent Systems, 1990—; tech. cons. RCA, Princeton, N.J., 1982-83, Babcock and Wilcox Corp., Alliance, Ohio, 1990, Booz-Allen and Hamilton, Inc., San Diego, 1990-91, Adept Tech., San Jose, Calif., 1990-91; mem. rsch. coun. Scripps Clin.; cons. USAF, 1995. Contbr. articles to profl. jours.; inventor in field. Agt. United Fund Isabella County, Mt. Pleasant, 1988; supporting coach Mich. Spl. Olympics, Mt. Pleasant, 1990; event capt. San Diego Regional Sci. Olympic Competition, 1990, 92; judge 37th, 38th, 39th, 40th, 41st, 42nd, 43d, and 44th Ann. Greater San Diego Sci. and Engring. Fair, 1991-98. Recipient Am. Chem. Soc. award, 1972, U.S. Govt. Cert. of Merit, Washington, 1987, Letter of Appreciation, Gen. Charles C. McDonald, 1990; grantee NSF, Office Naval Tech., State of Mich., others, 1988—. Mem. IEEE, Am. Assn. Artificial Intelligence, Am. Soc. Engring. Edn. (ONT postdoctoral fellow 1990-93), N.Y. Acad. Scis., Internat. Assn. Knowledge Engrs., Assn. for Computer Machinery. Avocations: boating, skiing, hiking and nature. Home: 1542 La Playa Ave # 4-208 San Diego CA 92109-6328 Office: Ctrl Mich U Dept Computer Sci Pearce Hall Mount Pleasant MI 48859

RUBIN, THEODORE ISAAC, psychiatrist; b. Bklyn., Apr. 11, 1923; s. Nathan and Esther (Marcus) R.; m. Eleanor Katz, June 16, 1946; children: Jeffrey, Trudy, Eugene. BA, Bklyn. Coll., 1946; MD, U. Lausanne, Switzerland, 1951; grad., Am. Inst. Psychoanalysis, 1964. Resident psychiatrist Los Angeles VA Hosp., 1953, Rockland (N.Y.) State Hosp., 1954, Bklyn. State Hosp., 1955, Kings County (N.Y.) Hosp., 1956; chief psychiatrist Women's House of Detention, N.Y.C., 1957; mem. faculty Downstate Med. Sch., N.Y. State U., 1957-59; pvt. practice N.Y.C., 1956—; tng. and supervising psychoanalyst Am. Inst. for Psychoanalysis of Karen Horney Clinic and Ctr.; mem. faculty Am. Inst. Psychoanalytic Psychoanalysis, 1962—; pres. emeritus bd. trustees Am. Inst. Psychoanalysis. Author: Jordi, 1960, Lisa and David, 1961, Sweet Daddy, 1963, In The Life, 1964, Platzo and the Mexican Pony Rider, 1965, The Thin Book by a Formerly Fat Psychiatrist, 1966, The 29th Summer, 1966, Cat, 1966, Coming Out, 1967, The Winner's Note Book, 1967, The Angry Book, 1969, Forever Thin, 1970, Emergency Room Diary, 1972, Doctor Rubin Please Make Me Happy, 1974, Shrink, 1974, Compassion and Self-Hate, An Alternative to Despair, 1975, Love Me, Love My Fool, 1976, Reflections in a Goldfish Tank, 1977, Alive and Fat and Thinning in America, 1978, Reconciliations, 1980, Through My Own Eyes, 1982, One to One, Understanding Personal Relationships, 1983, Not to Worry, The American Family Book of Mental Health, 1984, Overcoming Indecisiveness, 1985, Lisa and David, The Story Continues, 1986, Miracle at Bellevue, 1986, Real Love, 1990, Child Potential, 1990, Anti-Semitism: A Disease of the Mind, 1990, Little Ralphie and The Creature, 1998; mem. editl. bd. Am. Jour. Psychoanalysis; also articles, columns.; co-writer (TV movie) Lisa and David, 1998. Served as officer USNR, World War II. Recipient Adolf Meyer award Assn. Improvement Mental Health, 1963. Fellow Am. Acad. Psychoanalysis; mem. N.Y. County Med. Soc., Am. Psychiat. Assn., Assn. Advancement Psychoanalysis, Authors Guild, Contemporary Authors, Writers Guild East. Office: 113 1/2 E 62nd St New York NY 10021-7301

RUBINE, ROBERT SAMUEL, lawyer; b. Rockaway, N.Y., Feb. 28, 1947; s. George and Beatrice (Simon) R.; m. Marilyn Goldberg Rubine, Aug. 15, 1970; children: Seth B., Marisa H. BA, Queens Coll., 1968; JD, Syracuse U., 1971. Bar: N.Y. 1972, Fla. 1975; U.S. Dist. Ct. (ea. and so. dists.) N.Y., 1976; U.S. Supreme Ct. 1976. Trial atty. Legal Aid Soc. Nassau County, Mineola, N.Y., 1971-77; atty. Reifman and Rubine, Jericho, N.Y., 1977-79; ptnr. Stein, Rubine and Stein, Mineola, 1979-94, Rubine and Rubine, Mineola, 1995—; adj. prof. C.W. Post Coll., Greenvale, N.Y., 1979-82. Author: (chpt.) Criminal and Civil Investigation Handbook, 1981. Dir. Legal Aid Soc. Nassau County, 1989—, pres., 1994-95, treas., 1996—. Mem. N.Y. State Bar Assn., N.Y. State Assn. Criminal Def. Lawyers, N.Y. State Defenders Assn., Nassau County Bar Assn. Avocation: golf. Home: 5 Woodland Rd Oyster Bay NY 11771-3910 Office: Rubine and Rubine PLLC 114 Old Country Rd Mineola NY 11501-4400

RUBINOFF, IRA, biologist, research administrator, conservationist; b. N.Y.C., Dec. 21, 1938; s. Jacob and Bessie (Rose) R.; m. Roberta Wolff, Mar. 19, 1961; 1 son, Jason; m. Anabella Guardia, Feb. 10, 1978; children: Andres, Ana. B.S., Queens Coll., 1959; A.M., Harvard U., 1960, Ph.D., 1963. Biologist, asst. dir. marine biology Smithsonian Tropical Research Inst., Balboa, Republic of Panama, 1964-70; asst. dir. sci. Smithsonian Tropical Research Inst., 1970-73, dir., 1973—; assoc. in ichthyology Harvard U., 1965—; courtesy prof. Fla. State U., Tallahassee, 1976—; mem. sci. adv. bd. Gorgas Meml. Inst., 1964-88; trustee Rare Animal Relief Effort, 1976-85; bd. dirs. Charles Darwin Found. for Galapagos Islands, 1977—; chmn. bd. fellowships and grants Smithsonian Instn., 1978-79; vis. fellow Wolfson Coll., Oxford (Eng.) U., 1980-81; vis. scientist Mus. Comparative Biology-Harvard U., 1987-88. Author Strategy for Preservation of Moist Tropical Forests; contbr. articles to profl. jours. Vice chmn. bd. dirs. Panama Canal Coll., 1989-93; bd. dirs. Internat. Sch. Panama, 1983-85, 90-93, Fundacion Natura, sec., bd. dirs., 1991—; bd. dirs. Ancon Panama, 1985-97, Earthwatch, 1995-97, City of Knowledge, 1996—; hon. dir. Instituto Latino Americano de Estudios Avanzados. Awarded Order of Vasco Nunez de Balboa of Republic of Panama. Fellow Linnean Soc. (London), AAAS, Am. Acad. Arts & Scis.; mem. Am. Soc. Naturalists, Soc. Study of Evolution, N.Y. Acad. Scis. Club: Cosmos (Washington). Home: Box 2072, Balboa Panama Office: Smithsonian Trop Rsch Inst Unit 948 APO AA 34002-9948

RUBINOWICZ, CLAUDE JEAN-PIERRE, financial consultant, inspector finances; b. Creteil, France, Oct. 21, 1947; s. Adolphe and Helene (Goldstein) R. Grad., Ecole Normale Superieure, Paris, 1971, E.N.A., Paris, 1979; PhD in Physics, Agrégation Faculty Scis., Paris, 1971. Sr. profl. Arthur Andersen, Paris, 1972-73; economist Crédit lyonnais, Paris, 1974-76; dep. mgr. bond markets dept. Caisse des dépots et consignations, Paris, 1979-81, mgr. investment strategy dept., 1981-83; spl. asst. Minister of Social Affairs, Paris, 1983-84; spl. asst. Minister of Economy and Fin., Paris, 1984-86, sr. advisor, spl. asst., 1988-89; exec. v.p. Crédit Lyonnais, Paris, 1989-91, sr. exec. v.p., 1991-94; ptnr. Fixage, Paris, 1995-97; pres. Finafix, Paris, 1997—; rsch. fellow Princeton U., 1971-72. Named Knight of Nat. Order of Merit, 1991. Home: 35 rue de Vaugirard, 75006 Paris France Office: Finafix, 62 rue la Boetie, 75008 Paris France

RUBINS, ANDRIS JANIS, medical educator; b. Sigulda, Latvia, Nov. 19, 1947; s. Johannes Robert Rubin and Anna Vintere Martinsone; m. Gunta Daneviča, Sept. 1, 1972; children: Sylvestrs, Janis, Davids, Maija Kar-

lis. MD, Riga (Latvia) Med. Inst., 1974; DMS, Latvian Med. Acad., 1988, Habilitation, 1992. Resident Latvian Med. Acad., Riga, 1974-75, asst., 1981-85, head sci. lab., 1984-88, asst. prof., 1984-88, prof., 1988—, chmn. dept., 1991—; physician Skin Venerology Clinic, Riga, 1976-80; pres. Derma-Pharm. Rigalid, Riga, 1993—. Author: Illustrated Handbook in Dermatovenerology, 1996; patentee in field; mem. editl. bd. Gione Internat. Dermatologia Pediatria, 1991—. Parliamentarian, Latvia, 1995-98. Mem. Dermatovenerological Assn. Latvia (pres. 1988—), Assn. Dermatovenerology Baltic States (pres. 1989—), Internat. League Dermatol. Socs., N.Y. Acad. Scis., European Acad. Dermatovenerology. Roman Catholic. Avocations: sports, table tennis, music, art, painting. Fax: 3717361615. E-mail: arubins@apollo.cv. Home: Kr Valdemara St, Riga 1013, Latvia Office: Med Acad Latvia, Dzircilma St 16, Riga 1007, Latvia

RUBINSTEIN, BORIS YAKOVLEVICH, physicist, researcher; b. Sverdlovsk, Russia, Apr. 15, 1959; arrived in Israel, 1991; s. Yakov Borisovich and Mira Ovseevna (Dinerstein) R.; m. Elena Vladimirovna Polevaya, Dec. 3, 1982; children: Semyon, Valentina. MSc, Ural Polytech. Inst., Sverdlovsk, Russia, 1982; PhD, Irkutsk State U., Russia, 1989. Rschr. Metal Physics Inst., Sverdlovsk, 1985-91; postdoctorate fellow Technion, Haifa, Israel, 1991-93, engr., 1996—; project mgr. Kernel Knowledge Ltd., Haifa, Israel, 1993-95. Author: Hebrew-Russian Dictionary of Verb Roots, 1991; author (book, computer software): Partial Differential Equations Pack, 1996; contbr. over 20 articles to profl. jours. Avocations: quizes, football, basketball. Office: Northwestern Univ Dept Engring Scis/Appl Math 2145 Sheridan Rd Evanston IL 60208-0834

RUBINSTEIN, HILARY HAROLD, literary agent; b. London, Apr. 24, 1926; s. Harold Frederick and Lena (Lowy) R.; m. Helge Kitzinger, Aug. 6, 1955; children: Jonathan, Felicity, Mark, Ben. Grad., Merton Coll., 1952. Dir. Victor Gollancz Pubs., London, 1950-63; spl. features editor The Observer, London, 1963-64; dep. editor Observer Mag., London, 1964-65; chmn. AP Watt, London, 1965-92; founder Hilary Rubinstein Books, Literary Agts., London, 1992—; coun. mem. Inst. Contemporary Arts, London, 1976-92; trustee Open Coll. of the Arts, London, 1987-96. Editor: The Good Hotel Guide, 1978 and annually until 1999, Hotels and Inns: An Oxford Anthology, 1984; editor/author: The Complete Insomniac, 1974. Home and Office: Hilary Rubinstein Books, 32 Ladbroke Grove, London W11 3BQ, England

RUBINSTEIN, ISRAEL, chemistry educator, researcher; b. Tel-Aviv, July 17, 1947; s. Nahum and Yoheved (Rapoport) R.; m. Beverly Weinberg, Jul. 20, 1978; children: Ron, Yael, Tal, Tamar. BSc, Tel-Aviv Univ., 1970, MSc, 1973, PhD, 1979. Postdoctoral assoc. Univ. Tex., Austin, 1979-81; staff scientist General Elec. R&D Ctr., Schenectady, N.Y., 1981-83; sr. scientist The Weizmann Inst. of Sci., Rehovot, Israel, 1983-88, assoc. prof., 1988-96, prof., 1996—. Editor: Physical Electrochemistry: Principles, Methods and Applications, 1995; co-editor: Electroanalytical Chemistry, 1996—; inventor in field; contbr. over 100 articles to profl. jours. With Israel Def. Forces, 1965-67. Recipient Victor L. Erlich Career Devel. award The Weizmann Inst., 1984-88, Somach Sachs Meml. award, 1987. Mem. The Electrochemical Soc., The Israel Chemical Soc., Am. Assn. Advancement of Sci., Israel Shotokan. Avocations: music, karate (black belt). Home: The Weizmann Inst Sci, 76100 Rehovot Israel Office: Weizmann Inst Sci, Dept Materials & Interfaces, 76100 Rehovot Israel

RUBIO, ANGEL, theoretical physics educator; b. Oviedo, Asturias, Spain, Sept. 27, 1965; s. Hermógenes and Maria de la Felicidad (Secades) R. B and M in Physics with honors, U. Valladolid, Spain, 1988, PhD in Physics cum laude, 1991. Rsch. fellow dept. fisica teósrica U. Valladolid, 1985-90, assoc. prof., 1991-92, prof. theoretical physics, 1993—; rsch. scientist Fritz-Haber-Inst. der Max-Planck-Gesellschaft, Berlin, 1989, Fachbereich Physik, U. Osnabrück, Germany, 1990; Fulbright and rsch. assoc. fellow dept. physics U. Calif. Berkeley and Materials Scis. Divsn. Lawrence Berkeley Lab., 1992-94; invited prof. Inst. Romand de Reserche Numérique en Physique des Materiaux, Ecole Polytechnique de Lausanne, Switzerland, 1995, U. Pais Vasco, San Sebastian, Spain, 1998, Inst. Nuclear Theory, Seattle, 1999. Editor: (with A. Loiseau and F. Willaime) Nanotubular Structures: Characterization and Simulation at the Atomic Scale, 2000; contbr. articles to profl. jours. Recipient Real Spanish Phys. Soc. prize Jóvenes Investigadores, Royal Spanish Phys. Soc., Madrid, 1992. Mem. Am. Phys. Soc., Real Spanish Phys. Soc. Avocations: travel, skiing, reading. E-mail: arubio@mileto.fam.cie.uva.es. Fax: 34-943-423013. Home: C/San Lazaro 9-2:B, E-47011 Valladolid Spain Office: U Valladolid Fac Ciencias, Prado de la Magdalena s/n, E-47011 Valladolid Spain

RUBIO, PATRICIA INES, literature educator, researcher; b. Valparaiso, Chile, Jan. 10, 1948; came to U.S., 1980; d. Florestán and Ines (Graell) R.; m. Juan Carlos Lertora, June 19, 1974; 1 child, Camila. Lic., Cath. Univ., Valparaiso, 1972; PhD, U. Alberta, Edmonton, Can., 1982. Prof. estado U. Catolica, Valparaiso, 1970-72; vis. prof. Middleburg (Vt.) Coll., 1984-85; asst. prof. Skidmore Coll., Saratoga Springs, N.Y., 1986-93, assoc. prof., 1993-2000, prof., 2000—; chair dept. fgn. langs. Skidmore Coll., 1991-92, dir. women's studies, 1999—. Author: Gabriela Mistral, 1995, Chilean Writers, 1999. Mem. MLA, Assn. Letras Femeninas (sec. 1998—), Feministas Unidas. Avocation: stamp collecting. E-mail: prubio@skidmore.edu. Office: Skidmore Coll North Broadway Saratoga Springs NY 12866

RUBLE, BERNARD ROY, minister, labor relations consultant; b. Greensburg, Ind., Apr. 4, 1923; s. Jesse Emery and Marietta (Ward) R.; B.S., Ind. U., Bloomington, 1949; postgrad. transactional analysis Midwest Inst. Human Understanding, 1972-75; m. Mary Helen Rullman, Dec. 22, 1946; children: Barry Reece, Blane Rodney. Asst. mgr. Morris 5 and 10 Stores, Greensburg, 1941; store keeper Public Service Co. Ind., Greensburg, 1941-43; asst. mgr. personnel Kroger Co., Cin., 1949-51, mgr., personnel, Madison, Wis., 1951-56, Ft. Wayne, Ind., 1956-58, Cleve., 1958-73, mgr. labor relations Erie Mktg. Area, Solon, Ohio, 1973-84; faculty Kroger Edn. Center, Cin., 1978-84; trustee Meat Cutters Health and Welfare Fund, 1971-79, Retail Clks. Union Health and Welfare Fund, Akron, 1970-88, No. Ohio Hospice Council, 1981-84. Active United Appeal Greater Cleve., Community Chest Greater Cleve., Met. Health Planning Corp.; v.p. trustee Urban League Greater Cleve., 1968-75; adv. com. Family Health Care, Washington, 1977-78; trustee Community Health Found., Greater Cleve. Interchurch Coun., 1993-99; team rep. B.R. Ruble Racing, Burton, Ohio. Served with USAAF, 1943-45. Mem. Photog. Soc. Am., Soc. for Advancement Mgmt. (trustee Madison chpt. 1952-55), Am. Soc. Personnel Adminstrn., Cleve. Personnel Assn., Indsl. Rels. Rsch. Assn. (pres.). Lodges: Masons, Sertoma (trustee Madison 1952-56, Ft. Wayne 1957-58) (charter). Home and Office: 8644 Ranch Dr Chesterland OH 44026-3132

RUBLI, FEDERICO, bank executive, educator; b. Mexico City, Oct. 30, 1954; s. Fritz and Elisabeth (Kaiser) R.; m. Ruth Ornelas, Jan. 8, 1982; 1 child, Adrian. BA, Tech. Inst. Autonome Mex., Mexico City, 1978; MA, Columbia U., 1980, MPhil, 1981. Rsch. asst. Ctr. Studies Monetarios Latin Am., Mexico City, 1977; economist Banco de Mexico, Mexico City, 1977-78, dep. mgr., 1983-92, mgr., 1994—; economist Internat. Monetary Fund, Washington, 1981-83, sr. economist, 1992-94; lectr. CEMLA, Mexico City, 1984—; prof. U. Panamericana, Mexico City, 1984-87, ITAM, Mexico City, 1984-92. Author, co-editor: Mexico Hacia la Globalización, 1992; contbr. articles to profl. jours. Study grantee Orgn. Estados Ams., N.Y., 1981. Mem. Am. Econ. Assn., Columbia U. Alumni Assn. (pres. 1988-92). Avocations: music, soccer, tennis. Office: Banco de Mexico, Apartado Postal 98-BIS, 06059 Mexico City Mexico

RUBY, KARINE, snowboarder; b. Bonneville, France, Jan. 4, 1978. Degree in commerce, IUT, Annecy, France. Snowboarder French Nat. Team, 1989—. Recipient Gold medal women's snowboard giant slalom Olympic Games, Nagano, Japan, 1998. Avocation: mountain climbing. Office: French Nat Olympic Com, 1 Ave Pierre de Coubertin, 75640 Paris Cedex 13, France*

RUCH, MARCELLA JOYCE, retired educator, biographer; b. Brutus, Mich., Sept. 20, 1937; d. Virgil Murray and Grace Milbry (Collier) Wallace; m. Robert Kirkman McMain, Aug. 29, 1956 (div. Aug. 1970); children: Melodie Froom, Kirk McMain, Nancy Hedges, Elizabeth Curran; m. Peter Jerome Ruch, Dec. 22, 1973; children: David, Dan, Michael and Justin Moore Ruch. BS, Western Mich. U., 1964; MA, U. Colo., Colorado Springs, 1973; PhD, U. Colo., Boulder, 1980. Cert. tchr., prin., counselor, Colo. Tchr. Colorado Springs Pub. Schs., 1964-69; supr. child care El Paso County Social Svcs., Colorado Springs, 1970-73; exec. dir. Antlers Day Care Ctr., Colorado Springs, 1973-77, Green Shade Schs., Colorado Springs, 1977-81, Pueblo (Colo.) Toddler Ctr., 1981-83; tchr. Penrose (Colo.) Elem. Sch., 1983-86; adminstrv. intern Cottonwood Elem. Sch., Denver, 1986-87; elem. prin. Simla (Colo.) Pub. Schs., 1987-89; tchr. Colorado Springs Pub. Schs., 1989-97; adv. bd. for early childhood edn. Pikes Peak C.C., Colorado Springs, 1970-75; child care specialist Cmty. Agencies Working Together, Colorado Springs, 1970-75. Author: The Gang of One, 1998. Founder Green Shade Schs., 1977; campaign chair United Way, Canon City, Colo., 1983-84, pres., 1984-85; chair adult coun. St. Paul's United Meth. Ch., 1994-96, ch. mission to Russia, 1997, 99. Mem. Delta Kappa Gamma (v.p. membership 1994-96), Phi Delta Kappa. Methodist. Avocations: gardening, hiking, reading, camping. Home and Office: 1111 Modes St Colorado Springs CO 80904-3242

RUCKER, DOUGLAS PENDLETON, JR., lawyer; b. Richmond, Va., Dec. 26, 1945; s. Douglas Pendleton and Margaret (Williams) R.; m. Marian F. Copeland; 1 child, Louise Meredith. BA, Hampden-Sydney Coll., 1968; JD, U. Va., 1972. Bar: Va. 1972, D.C. 1986, U.S. Dist. Ct. (ea. and we. dists.) Va. 1972, U.S. Ct. Appeals (4th cir.) 1982, U.S. Supreme Ct. 1982, U.S. Ct. Claims 1995. Assoc. Sands, Anderson, Marks & Miller, Richmond, Va., 1972-76; mem. Sands, Anderson, Marks & Miller, Richmond, 1977—. Active St. John's Episcopal Ch., mem. vestry, 1994-98, register, 1996, jr. warden, 1997, sr. warden, 1998; Lewis Ginter Bot. Garden; bd. dirs. Va. Ctr. for the Book Capital chpt. ARC; bd. dirs. James River Devel. Corp.; mem. adv. com. Richmond Renaissance. With Va. Army NG, 1968-74. Fellow Va. Law Found. (bd. dirs. 1998—), Va. Bar Assn. (constrn. law chmn. 1992, real estate and bus. law sects., exec. com. 1992-97, pres. 1996), Richmond Bar Assn. (real estate sect., bd. dirs. 1994-97), Soc. Colonial Wars in the State of Va. (gov.), Bar Assn. D.C., Am. Arbitration Assn. (comml. securities and constrn. industry panels), Met. Richmond C. of C., Commonwealth Club, Country Club Va., Downtown Club. Office: Sands Anderson Marks & Miller PO Box 1998 Richmond VA 23218-1998

RUCKER, KENNETH LAMAR, law enforcement officer, educator; b. Atlanta, July 16, 1961; s. Jack Lamar and Priscilla Anne (Anderson) R.; m. Kerri Lynn Hairston; children: Kenneth Lamar II, Kerbi Lynn. BSBA, Brenau U., 1991; MPA in Pub. Mgmt., Ga. State U., 1993; postgrad., U. Ga., 1993—. Cert. peace officer, supr., Ga., field tng. officer, law enforcement exec.; cert. supply corps, Navy Supply Corps Sch., 1997. Law enforcement officer Met. Atlanta Rapid Transit Authority, 1984-93; sch. resource officer Fulton County Bd. Edn., Atlanta, 1993-95; field facilitator Cmtys. in Schs. of Ga., Inc., Atlanta, 1995-97, field facilitator Cross Roads program, 1995-97; chief of police Fulton County Schs. Police Dept., 1997—; bd. dirs. Benefactors of Edn., Inc., Atlanta; cons. pub. security Fulton County Bd. Edn., Atlanta, 1993-95; supply corps officer Navy Supply Corps Sch. USNR, Athens, 1997. Sunday sch. tchr. Simpson St. Ch. of Christ, Atlanta, 1991—; youth motivator Atlanta Pub. Schs., 1988—. Commd. officer Supply Corps, USNR, 1995—. Doctoral fellow U. Ga. Mem. Am. Soc. Pub. Adminstrn., Internat. Assn. Chiefs of Police, Nat. Orgn. Black Law Enforcement Execs., Nat. Forum Black Pub. Adminstrs., Ga. Assn. Chiefs of Police, Benefactors of Edn., Inc. (bd. dirs. 1996-99), Brenau U. Alumni Club (bd. dirs. 1999—), Ga. State U. Alumni Club, U.S. Naval Inst., Naval Res. Assn., Res. Officer's Assn., Navy Supply Corps Assn., Pi Alpha Alpha, Pi Sigma Alpha, Omicron Delta Kappa (cir. pres. 1992-93). Avocations: computer tech., reading, photography, classical music, fitness. Home: 1835 Jenny Ln Lithia Springs GA 30122-2857 Office: Fulton County Schs Police Fulton County Bd Education 786 Cleveland Ave SW Atlanta GA 30315-7239

RUCKER, ZENA, retired flight school administrator; b. Los Mochis, Sinaloa, Mex., Dec. 25, 1929; came to U.S., 1940; d. Charles Willis Sullivan and Soledad Desmond; m. William W. Rucker, Oct. 8, 1952; children: William Charles, Michael Sullivan, Zena Lynn. AA, U. Ariz., 1951; BA, U. N. Tex., 1969. Cert. pilot, Tex. Pres. Z Yamaha, Grapevine, Tex., 1970-84, N. Tex. Aero, 1980-95; tchr. Grapevine H.S., 1984-88; ret., 1995. Precinct chair Tex. Dems., 1970-00; vol. Battered Women, Tex., 1995-00; polit. activist numerous anti-racism causes. Mem. NOW, Spanish Honorary (treas. 1970—), Ninety Nines (gen. officer 1980—). Avocations: flying, reading, traveling, studying foreign languages. Home: 650 S Carroll Ave Southlake TX 76092-8713

RUDACILLE, SHARON VICTORIA, medical technologist; b. Ranson, W. Va., Sept. 11, 1950; d. Albert William and Roberta Mae (Anderson) R.; BS cum laude, Shepherd Coll., 1972. Med. technologist VA Ctr., Martinsburg, W.Va., 1972—, instr. Sch. Med. Tech., 1972-76, assoc. coord. edn., 1976-77, edn. coord., 1977-78, quality assurance officer clin. chemistry, 1978-80, lab. svc. quality assurance and edn. officer, 1980-84, clin. chemistry sect. leader, 1984-86, staff med. technologist, 1986-94, suprvisory med. technologist, 1994-95, sr. med. technologist, 1995—; adj. faculty mem. Shippensburg (Pa.) State Coll., 1977-78, Shepherd Coll., 1977-78. Mem. Am. Soc. Med. Tech., Am. Soc. Clin. Pathologists, W.Va. Soc. Med. Technologists, Shepherd Coll. Alumni Assn., Sigma Pi Epsilon. Baptist. Home: PO Box 14 Ranson WV 25438-0014

RUDAKOV, ELISEY SERGEEVICH, physical chemist; b. Tomsk, Russia, Apr. 27, 1929; s. Sergey Dmitrievich and Lyubov Eliseevna Rechko-Retskaya; m. Radda Ilinichna Ohlopkova, Mar. 6, 1951; children: Sergey, Vladimir, Iliya, Lyubov. Engr., Inst. Fine Chem. Tech., Moscow, 1952; PhD, Inst. Organic Chemistry, Novosibirsk, Russia, 1960; DSc, Inst. Catalysis, Novosibirsk, 1968. Cert. in phys. chemistry, thermodynamics. Engr. Inst. Petrochem. Processes, Leningrad, 1952-59; sr. rsch. worker Inst. Organic Chemistry, Novosibirsk, 1959-67; head of lab. Novosibirsk State U., 1961-68, prof., head of chair of phys. chemistry, 1968-72; head of dept. Inst. Phys. Organic and Coal Chemistry, Donetsk, Ukraine, 1972—. Author: Thermodynamics of Intermolecular Interaction, 1968, Reaction of Alkanes with Oxidators, Metal Complexes and Radicals in Solutions, 1985, Molecular, Quantum and Evolutional Thermodynamics, 1998; co-author: Solubility Data Series V. 24, 1986. Named Hon. Worker in Sci. and Tech., Pres. of Ukraine, 1993; Internat. Assn. for the Promotion of Cooperation with Scientists from the New Ind. States of the Former Soviet Union grantee, 1995, 2000, Civilian R&D Found. grantee, 1997. Mem. Nat. Ukrainian Acad. Scis. (corr., Pisarzhevsky award 1982). E-mail: rudakov@infou.donetsk.ua. Office: Inst Phys Organic Coal Chem, R Luksemburg str 70, 83114 Donetsk Ukraine

RUDAS, IMRE JÓZSEF, engineering educator; b. Budapest, Hungary, Apr. 25, 1949; s. Imre and Krisztina (Dichob) R.; m. Ágnes Németh, Apr. 1, 1972; children: Erika, Andrea. B in Engring., Bánki Donát Poly., Budapest, 1971; MSc in Math., Eötvös Loránd U., Budapest, 1977; PhD in Robotics, Hungarian Acad. Scis., Budapest, 1987. Staff engr. United Electric Machine Co., Budapest, 1971-72; asst. prof. math. Bánki Donát Poly., 1972-80, prof. math., robotics, artificial intelligence, 1980-83, assoc. prof. math., 1987-90, 'ead dept. info. tech., 1987—; rschr. Inst. for Automation and Computer Sci., Budapest, 1993; vis. prof. U. Salford, Eng., 1993. Assoc. editor Control Engring. Practice, Eng., 1993—; editl. bd. Engring. Applications of Artificial Intelligence, Eng., 1998—; author, editor: Computational Intelligence: Soft Computing and Fuzzy-Neuro Integration with Applications. Mem. IEEE (sr.), Hungarian Robotics Assn., N.Y. Acad. Scis., pres. Hungarian Fuzzy Assn. Home: Kisfaludy 36/A, H-1188 Budapest Hungary Office: Budapest Polytechnic, Népszinház U 8, H-1081 Budapest Hungary

RUDD, PAULINE MARY, biochemist, researcher; b. Lymington, Hampshire, Eng., Sept. 17, 1942; d. Stanley Norman and Clarice Ruma (Taylor) Goldsmith; m. Colin Richard Rudd; children: Martin Nicolas, Simon Christopher, Hilary Claire, Jonathan Richard. BSc in Spl. Chemistry, U. London, 1964; PhD, Open U., Eng., 1995; MA (hon.), Oxon (Eng.) U., 1998. Sr. chemist R&D Wessex Biochems/Sigma, London, 1964-69; rsch. technician biochemistry dept. U. Oxford, Eng., 1981-83, rsch. asst. Glycobiology Inst., 1983-96; sr. rsch. fellow Oxford (Eng.) Glycobiology Inst., 1996—; cons. Oxford Glycosys. Ltd., Abingdon, Eng., 1994—; presenter seminars Gdansk U., 1994, 95, U. Taipei, Republic of China, 1994, Inst. Biochemistry, Bucharest, 1997, U. Shanghai, Fudan, Beijing, 1999, Croatia, 1999, Bialystok, Poland, 1998, Chataqua, 1999, State of the World Forum, 2000, Ukraine, 2000, others; participant in sci. and theology discussions Oxford and Berkeley U., Calif.; lectr. U. Oxford, Eng., 1998—; vis. prof. Shanghai Med. U., 1999-2001; vis. rsch. assoc. The Scripps Rsch. Inst., La Jolla, Calif., 1998-99. Contbr. numerous articles, revs. to profl. publs., chpts. to books; patentee tissue plasminogen activator dimer. Associate of cmty. of St. Mary the Virgin, Wantage, Eng. Mem. Ch. of England. Avocations: family, travel. Home: 29 Sadlers Court, Abingdon Oxon OX14 2PA, England Office: Glycobiology Inst, Dept Biochem South Parks Rd, Oxford OX1 3QU, England

RUDDOCK, PHILIP, government administrator; b. Canberra, Australia, Mar. 12, 1943; m. Heather Ruddock; children: Kirsty, Caitlin. BA, U. Sydney, BA, LLB. Elected Ho. of Reps., 1973; parliamentary rep. Coun. Australian Nat. U., 1976-96; spokesman ACT and Shadow Min. Asst. Opposition Leader Pub. Svc., 1983-84; shadow min. immigration & ethnic affairs Australia, 1984-85, 89-93; spokesman Ho. of Reps., Fgn. Affairs Shadow Min. Asst. Leader Ethic Affairs, 1990-93; spokesman Shadow Min. Social Security, 1993-95; min. Dept. Immigration & Multicultural Affairs, Australia, 1996—; father Ho. of Reps., 1998—; min. assisting Prime Min. for reconciliation, 1998—. Office: Parliament House Ste MF40, Canberra ACT 2600, Australia

RUDDY, FRANK, lawyer, former ambassador; b. N.Y.C., Sept. 15, 1937; s. Francis Stephen and Teresa (O'Neil) R.; children: Neil, David, Stephen. AB, Holy Cross Coll., 1959; MA, NYU, 1962, LLM, 1967; LLB, Loyola U., New Orleans, 1965; PhD, Cambridge U., Eng., 1969. Bar: D.C., N.Y., Tex., U.S. Supreme Ct. Faculty Cambridge U., 1967-69; asst. gen. counsel USIA, Washington, 1969-72; sr. atty. Office of Telecomm. Policy, White House, Washington, 1972-73; dep. gen. counsel USIA, Washington, 1973-74; counsel Exxon Corp., Houston, 1974-81; asst. adminstr. AID (with rank asst. sec. state) Dept. State, Washington, 1981-84; U.S. ambassador to Equatorial Guinea, 1984-88; gen. counsel U.S. Dept. Energy, Washington, 1988-89; v.p. Sierra Blanca Devel. Corp., Washington, 1989-92; pvt. practice Law Offices of Frank Ruddy, Washington, 1992-94; vis. scholar Johns Hopkins Sch. Advanced Internat. Studies, 1990-94; dep. chmn. UN Referendum for Western Sahara, 1994, Johnston, Rivlin & Foley, Washington, 1995-96, Rivlin & Taylor, et al, 1996-97; ptnr. Ruddy & Muir, Washington, 1998—. Author: International Law in the Enlightenment, 1975; editor: American International Law Cases (series); editor in chief Internat. Lawyer; contbr. articles to legal jours. Bd. dirs. African Devel. Found., Washington, 1983-84. Served with USMCR, 1956-61. Mem. ABA (chmn. treaty compliance sect. 1991-93), Am. Soc. Internat. Law, Internat. Law Assn., Hague Acad. Internat. Law Alumni Assn., Oxford and Cambridge Club (London), Dacor House. Republican. Roman Catholic. E-mail: global@globalltd.com. Home: 5600 Western Ave Chevy Chase MD 20815-3406 Office: Ruddy and Muir 1825 I St NW Ste 400 Washington DC 20006-5415

RUDEANU, SERGIU, mathematician, educator; b. Iasi, Romania, Feb. 9, 1935; s. Dumitru and Denisa (Botez) Rudeanu; m. Delia Mihail, May 15, 1934; 1 chld, Razvan. Degree in math., U. Bucharest, 1957, PhD in Math., 1964. Tchr. High Sch., Buftea, Romania, 1957-58; rschr. inst. math. Romanian Acad., 1958-68, scientific sec., 1967-68; assoc. prof. U. Bucharest, 1968-90, prof., 1990—. Author: Boolean Functions and Equations, 1974; co-author: Boolean Methods in Operations Research, 1968, Lukasiewicz-Moisil Algebras, 1991; contbr. articles to profl. jours. Recipient Gheorghe Titeica award Romanian Acad., 1968; grantee Deutsche Akademishce Austauschdienst, 1968. Office: Univ Bucharest Fac Math, Str Academiei 14, 70109 Bucharest Romania

RUDEL, THOMAS, researcher; b. Winnenden, Germany, Aug. 5, 1962; s. Waldemar and Elisabetha Rudel; m. Annette Gisela Willer, Mar. 19, 1988; children: Marieke Annette, Francis Luisa. Diploma, U. Tübingen, Winnenden/Bademn-Württemberg, Germany, PhD, 1994. Rschr. Max-Planck-Inst. Biology, Tübingen, 1994-95; guest scientist Scripps Rsch. Inst., LaJolla, Calif., 1995-97; rsch. group leader Max-Planck-Inst. Infections Biology, Berlin, 1997—. E-mail: rudel@mpiib-berlin.mpg.de. Fax: 49 30 28460 401.

RUDELLA, GUALTIERO, publishing executive; b. Schio, Italy, Aug. 23, 1957; s. Bruno and Luigina (Guzzonato) R.; m. Stefanie Grace Parmenter, July 8, 1990; children: Jordan Dae, Nicholas Domenico, Kristofer. B in Lang. and Lit., State Lyceum, Italy, 1976; degree in electronic engring., Rome State U., 1982. Editor in chief Gruppo Ed. Suono, Rome, 1980-85, pub., 1983-85; editor in chief Arnoldo Mondadori Editore, Milan, Italy, 1985-87, pub. mag. divsn., 1987-89; mng. dir. Mondadori Informatica, Milan, 1989-91, exec. v.p., 1991-95; mng. dir. ED. EL, Milan, 1990-92; gen. mgr. Telepiu', 1995-96; mng. dir. Pagine Italia SpA, Milan, 1997-98, dir. bus. devel., 1998-99, CEO webmond, 2000—; cons. RSO Group, Milan, 1986-89. Editor in chief: Zerouno, 1985; editor: Minisistemi, 1989, Multinet, 1990, PC Week Italy, 1987. Mem. Italian Press Fedn., Internat. Electronic Pub. Rsch. Ctr. (dir. 1990-93). Roman Catholic. Avocations: skiing, tennis. Office: Arnoldo Mondadori Editore, 20090 Segrate Milan 2, Italy

RUDENSTINE, NEIL LEON, academic administrator, educator; b. Ossining, N.Y., Jan. 21, 1935; s. Harry and Mae (Esperito) R.; m. Angelica Zander, Aug. 27, 1960; children: Antonia Margaret, Nicholas David, Sonya. B.A., Princeton U., 1956; B.A. (Rhodes Scholar), Oxford U., 1959, M.A., 1963; Ph.D., Harvard U., 1964. Instr. dept. English Harvard U., Cambridge, Mass., 1964-66; asst. prof. Harvard U., 1966-68; assoc. prof. English Princeton (N.J.) U., 1968-73, prof. English, 1973-88, dean of students, 1968-72, dean of Coll., 1972-77, provost, 1977-88, provost emeritus, 1988—; exec. v.p. Andrew W. Mellon Found., N.Y.C., 1988-91; pres. Harvard U., Cambridge, Mass., 1991—, prof. English, 1991—. Author: Sidney's Poetic Development, 1967, (with George Rousseau) English Poetic Satire, 1972, (with William Bowen) In Pursuit of the PhD, 1992. Served to 1st lt. arty. AUS, 1959-60. Hon. fellow New Coll./Oxford U., Emmanuel Coll./Cambridge U., 1991. Fellow Am. Acad. Arts and Scis.; mem. Am. Philos. Soc., Coun. on Fgn. Rels., Com. for Econ. Devel. Office: Harvard U Office of Dean 4 University Rd Cambridge MA 02138-5781

RUDERT, CYNTHIA SUE, gastroenterologist; b. Cin., Mar. 17, 1955; d. John Wayne and Hilda Wanda (Loftus) R.; children: Ronald Lamar Hilley II, Henry Byron Hilley. BS with honors, U. Ky., 1975; MD, U. Louisville, 1979. Diplomate Am. Bd. Internal Medicine, Am. Bd. Gastroenterology. Intern internal medicine Emory U., Atlanta, 1979-80, resident, 1980-82, fellow in gastroenterology, 1982-84, asst. prof. medicine, 1984-91; med. dir. Gluten Sensitive Support Group, 1997—; guest spkr. Alcoholism Conf., Kanasawa, Japan, 1987; founding mem. Celiac Standardization Group, 1999; med. advisor Gluten Intolerance Group N.Am., 1999; nat. and internat. spkr. in gastroenterology. Author: Medicine for the Practicing Physician, 3d rev. edit., 1991, (chpts.) Acute Pancreatitis, Chronic Pancreatitis, Ischaemic Hepatitis, Rudert, C.X. Alcohol Related Symptoms; editl. cons. Life in Medicine mag.; med. advisor Women in Medicine mag. Fellow ACP; mem. AMA, Am. Med. Women's Assn., Am. Assn. for Study of Liver Disease, Am. Gastroent. Assn., So. Med. Assn., Am. Liver Found., Am. Acad. Scis., Ga. Gastroent. Soc., Med. Assn. Ga., Med. Assn. Atlanta, Atlanta Women's Med. Alliance (founder). Office: 2500 Hospital Blvd Ste 210 Roswell GA 30076-4984

RÜDIGER, GÜNTHER ERHARD, astronomer, educator; b. Dresden, Saxonia, Germany, Dec. 15, 1944; s. Erhard Rüdiger and Sigrid (Forbriger) Poizl; m. Gisela Lüscher, July 30, 1971; 1 child, Sten. Degree, Gymnasium Dresden-Plauen, 1963; M in Physics, U. Jena, 1968; PhD, Acad. Scis., Potsdam, 1972. Prof. astrophysics U. Potsdam, Germany, 1995—; vis. prof. U. Göttingen, Germany, 1990, U. Newcastle, Eng., 1998. Author: Differential Rotation and Stellar Convection, 1989; editor: The Sun and Cool Stars: activity, magnetism, dynamo, 1990, The Cosmic Dynamo, 1993. Home: Rubensstr 6, D-14467 Potsdam Germany Office: Astrophysics Inst Potsdam, An der Sternwarte 16, D-14482 Potsdam Germany

RUDIN, ROBERT ALFRED, oil industry service company executive; b. Boston, Sept. 30, 1942; s. Henry S. and Marcia R.; m. Margaret S. Dunigan, June 8, 1964; children: Amanda G., Timothy N. BS, Rensselaer Poly. Inst., Troy, N.Y., 1964; MS, Rutgers U., 1966, PhD, 1969. Asst. prof. The Cooper Union, N.Y.C., 1969-74; assoc. prof. Pahlavi U., Shiraz, Iran, 1974-75, Abadan Inst. Tech., Iran, 1975-76; tng. dir. Roy M. Huffington, Inc., Balikpapan, Indonesia, 1976-78; tng. svcs. mgr. Overseas Tech. Svc., London, 1978-89, ops. dir., 1989-93; sr. v.p. ops. Baker/OTS Internat., London, 1993—; dir. 9 wholly-owned subsidiaries of Michael Baker Corp. Contbr. articles and book revs. to profl. jours. N.Y. Acad. Scis. scholar,

1970. Mem. Am. Phys. Soc. Avocation: food. Office: Overseas Tech Svc, 104 College Rd, Harrow HA1 1BQ, England

RUDLAND, PHILIP SPENCER, biochemist, educator; b. Birmingham, Eng., Jan. 2, 1946; s. Frederick William and Margaret Doris (Phillips) R.; m. Suzete de Almeida Silva, July 24, 1993. BA in Natural Sci. 1st class, Cambridge (Eng.) U., 1966, BA in Chemistry 1st class, 1967, PhD in Molecular Biology, 1971, MA (hon.), 1986. Postgrad. fellow unit molecular biology Med. Rsch. Ctr., Cambridge, 1970-71; Helen Hay Whitney fellow Salk Inst., La Jolla, Calif., 1971-73; staff mem. Imperial Cancer Rsch. Fund, London, 1974-79; head dept. cell and molecular biology Ludwig Inst. for Cancer Rsch., London, 1979-86; prof. biochemistry U. Liverpool, Eng., 1987—, head dept. biochemistry, 1988-90, head cancer and polio rsch. fund labs., 1986—; dir. Cancer and Polio Rsch. Fund, Wirral, U.K., 1994—; chmn. sci. adv. com. Clatterbridge Cancer Rsch. Trust, U.K., 1993—. Author: Medical Perspectives in Cancer Research, 1985; editor: Mammary Development and Cancer, 1997; contbr. articles to profl. publs. Gonville and Caius Coll. scholar, 1966, Salterer's Inst. Indsl. Chemistry scholar, 1967-71. Fellow Royal Soc. Sci. and Arts, Royal Coll. Pathologists, Inst. Biology. Mem. Ch. of England. Avocations: cricket, chess, table tennis, history of railways, astronomy. Office: U Liverpool Sch Biol Sci, PO Box 147, Liverpool L69 3BX, England

RUDMAN, SOLOMON KAL, magazine publisher; b. Phila., Mar. 6, 1930; s. Benjamin and Lena (Holtzman) R.; m. Lucille Steinhauer, June 29, 1958; 1 child, Mitchell. BS in Edn., U. Pa., 1951; MS in Edn., Temple U., 1957. Chmn. dept. spl. edn. Franklin D. Roosevelt Sch., Bristol Twp., Pa., 1960-68; pub. premier record/ radio trade Fri. Morning Quarterback, Cherry Hill, Pa., 1968—; bd. dirs. Variety Club, NARAS, Crime Commn., Pa., N.J., Del.; co-host Merv Griffin TV Show, 1981-82; music expert Today Show, 1981-82, Tomorrow Show, 1981-82, Tom Snyder TV Show; creator-sponsor high sch. jazz piano competition, Phila. and suburbs of Pa., with Univ. of the Arts, Phila.; sponsor-host Phila. Franklin Inst. of Sci. and Fels Planetarium mobile sci. programs, top-level entertainment shows to most Phila.-N.J. Sr. Citizens' homes, children's and vets. hosps.; co-host, talent booker Easter Seals Telethon; sponsor 47 scholarships for h.s. jazz musicians at Univ. of the Arts. Pub.: (mag.) MQB (Modern QB) for Modern Rock Music; prodr. CD's of advance hits N.Am. radio stas.; launched music trade mag. Pro QB, launched Q-Beat. Bd. dirs. Phila. Broadcast Pioneers; sponsor carillon blls Ave. of Arts, Phila., Franklin Inst. Travelling Sci. Show to Phila. elem. schs.; bd. dirs. Citizens' Crime Commn.; sponsor 1st ann. classical piano H.S. competition, Chestnut Hill Coll.; co-sponsor purchase and distbn. of dictionaries to Phila. Elem. Sch. pupils (in memory of Ennis Cosby), Robotics Competition Phila. h.s., N.J. United Cerebral palsy Marathon Dance, Rutgers U.; sponsor Franklin Inst. Time Capsule, Phila., Jewish Fedn. Atrium, Phila.; co-sponsor Succeeding By Reading Program. Recipient Lifetime Achievement award in music Phila. Music Conf., Lifetime Music Achievement award Delaware Valley Music Poll., Presdl. Citation, Citizens Crime Com.; named to Broadcast Pioneers Hall of Fame Phila.; named Penndelphia Humanitarian of Yr. Mem. Phila. Music Alliance (bd. dirs.), Nat. Arthritis Found. (bd. dirs.), NARAS (bd. dirs.), Masons, Phila. Police Commrs. Club. Office: Friday Morning Quarterback 1930 Marlton Pike E Cherry Hill NJ 08003-2150

RUDMIN, FLOYD WEBSTER, psychology educator, author; b. Lowville, N.Y., Apr. 22, 1946; s. Joseph Felix Rudmin and Josephine Luella Webster; m. Toyoko Murata, Sept. 15, 1975; children: Katrina, Christopher, Daniel. BA, Bowdoin Coll., 1971; MA, SUNY, Buffalo, 1977, Queen's U., Kingston, Ont., Can., 1982; PhD, Queen's U., Kingston, Ont., Can., 1988. Cert. in clin. competence in audiology Am. Speech and Hearing Assn. Audiologist Health Unit, Powell River, Can., 1977-78, Royal Victoria Hosp.-McGill U., Montreal, Que., Can., 1978-82; Social Scis. and Humanities Rsch. Coun. postdoctoral fellow Queen's U., 1988-90, Can. Rsch. fellow, 1990-93, vis. prof., 1993-95; prof. psychology U. Tromsø, Norway, 1995—. Author: Bordering on Aggression, 1993; co-editor: Meaning, Measure, and Morality of Materialism, 1992; issue editor Jour. Social Behavior and Personality, 1991. Chmn. Coun. Canadians, Kingston, 1990-94. Recipient C.S. Ford cross-cultural rsch. award Human Rels. Area Files, 1989. Home: 9 Gibson Ave, Kingston, ON Canada K7L 4R1 Office: U Tromsø, Dept Psychology, N-9037 Tromsø Norway

RUDNEV, BORIS IVANOVICH, marine engineer, educator; b. Vladivostok, Primorsky, Russia, July 23, 1951; s. Ivan Lucynovich and Kseniy Ignatevna (Chuchvaga) R.; m. Ludmila Stepanovna Epishkina, Mar. 25, 1972 (div. Jan. 1981); 1 child, Svetlana Borisovna; m. Nina Vasilevna Ovchnikova, Mar. 17, 1989. Diploma in engring., Tech. U., Vladivostok, Russia, 1973; PhD, Tech. U., Leningrad, USSR, 1978; DSc, Maritime Acad., St. Petersburg, Russia, 1998. Rschr. Tech. U., Vladivostok, 1973-75, assoc. prof., 1978-99, prof., 1999—; cons. shipyard, Vladivostok, 1980—. Author: Mathematical Modeling and Experimental Investigation Radiative and Convective Heat Transfer Diesels, 1995; contbr. numerous articles to sci. jours. Avocation: tennis. Home: Apt 40, 6/25 1st Marine St, Vladivostok Russia

RUDNEVA, IRINA IVANOVNA, biologist, researcher; b. Sevastopol, Crimea, Ukraine, Mar. 18, 1954; d. Ivan Semenovich Rudnev and Antonina Fedorovna (Chuprakova) Rudneva; m. Sergei Alexandrovich Titov, Sept. 21, 1991 (div. May 1997). Diploma, Simpheropol State U., 1976, Simpheropol State U., 1980; PhD, Harkov (Ukraine) State U., 1980; diploma, Moscow State U., 2000. Asst. prof. Simpheropol State U., 1980; sr. rschr. Inst. Biology So. Seas, Sevastopol, 1980—; assoc. prof. State Tech. U., Sevastopol, 1995-99, Crimean Inst. Economy and Law, Sevastopol, 1996—, Inst. Nuc. Energy, Sevastopol, 1999—. Contbr. articles to profl. jours. Russian Orthodox. Avocations: swimming, dancing, Russian modern painting. Home: Bolshaya Morshaya 16-12, 99011 Sevastopol Ukraine Office: Inst Biology So Seas, Nahimov av. 2, 99011 Sevastopol Ukraine

RUDNICK, ABRAHAM, psychiatrist, philosopher; b. Haifa, Israel, Jan. 13, 1964; s. Samuel and Ruth (Laufer) R.; m. Hana Ornoy, Mar. 18, 1989; children: Or, Niv, Lee. MD, Hebrew U., Jerusalem, 1990; M in Psychiatry, Tel-Aviv U., 1999, PhD in Philosophy, 1999. Med. officer Israel Def. Forces, 1990-94; resident in psychiatry Tel-Aviv Cmty. Mental Health Ctr., 1994-99; lectr. in behavioral scis., ethics lectr. Tel-Aviv U., 1998—; fellow in psychiatry U. Toronto, 1999—. Contbr. articles to profl. jours. including Jour. Medicine and Philosophy, Internat. Jour. Law and Psychiatry, Biol. Psychiatry, Psychosomatics. Mem. Assn. for Clin. Psychosocial Rsch., Internat. Assn. Psychiat. Rehab. Avocations: music, tai chi. Office: Whitby Mental Health Ctr, 700 Gordon St, Whitby, ON Canada L1N 5S9

RUDOBASHTA, STANISLAV PAVLOVICH, engineering educator; b. Malinovka, Donetsky, USSR, July 21, 1939; s. Pavel Matveevich Rudobashta and Taisiya Ivanovna Chapchikova; m. Ludmila Yakovlevna Chermashentseva, Dec. 29, 1964; children: Mary, Helen. Engr.-mechanic, Poly. Inst., Kharkov, USSR, 1961; Candidate, Inst. Chem. Machine Bldg., Moscow, 1967, D in Engring. Scis., 1978. Engring. diplomate. Asst. Poly. Inst., Kharkov, 1961-64; from lectr. to profl., head dept. Inst. Chem. Machine Bldg., Tambov, USSR, 1968-83; prof., head dept. heating engring. State Agroengring. U., Moscow, 1983—; sci. bationer Higher Sch., Darmstadt, Germany, 1973-74; mem., vice chmn. Sci. Methodological Coun. on Heating Engring., State Higher Sch. Com., Moscow, 1986—, mem. coordination coun. engring. disciplines, 1994—. Author: Masstransfer in Solid, 1980; co-author: Heating Engineering and Heat Application in Agriculture, 1990, Diffusion in Chemical Technology, 1993, Heat- and Water Supply of Agriculture, 1997. mem. organizing com. First, Second, Third Internat. Thermophys. Sch., Tambov, Russia, 1992, 95, 98; mem. organizing com. internat. symposium Internat. Ctr. Ednl. Sys. Functioning, UNESCO, Moscow, 1994-95. Recipient State Sci. stipendium Russian Acad. Scis., 1998-2000; named Meritorious Sci. and Technique Worker of Russia, Moscow, 1993, Honoured Worker of Higher Vocat. Edn. Russia, Moscow, 1998. Mem. Internat. Com. on Drying, Farm Edn. Acad. (academician). Avocation: swimming. Office: State Agroengring Univ, Timiryazevskaya 58, 127550 Moscow Russia

RUDOFSKY, GOTTFRIED, angiologist; b. Bischofteinitz, Czech Republic, Feb. 7, 1944; s. Gottfried and Ludmilla (Astl) R.; children: Gottfried, Katharina. MD, U. Heidelberg, 1971. Resident Country Hosp., Kipfenberg, Germany, 1969-71, Univ. Hosp., Ulm, Germany, 1971-79; asst. med. dir. Armed Forces Hosp., Ulm, 1979-89; cons. Univ. Hosp., Ulm, 1979-89; med. dir. Univ. Hosp. Angiology, Essen, Germany, 1989—. Fellow Am. Coll. Angiology; mem. Internat. Soc. Endovasculsar Surgery (assoc.), German Soc. Angiology, German Soc. Phlebology, Ind. Union of Physiology, Soc. Internal Medicine Germany, N.Y. Acad. Scis. Roman Catholic. Avocations: horseback riding, sports cars. Home: Am Ruhrstein 25b, 45133 Essen Germany Office: Universitatsklinikum Essen, Hufelandstr 55, 45127 Essen Germany

RUDOI, VALENTINE MICHAILOVICH, chemist; b. Mariupol, Donetzk, USSR, Mar. 2, 1939; s. Michail Borisovich Rudoi and Roza Abramovna Gitlin; m. Marina Nikolaevna Petrova, July 26, 1961; children: Masukevich, Tatiana, Valentinovna. Candidate Chem. Sci., Ural Polytech. Inst., Yekaterinburg, Russia, 1967, D Chem. Sci., 1985. Prof. chief elec. chemistry Ural St. Tech. U., Yekaterinburg, 1985-97, prof., 1997—. Mem. editl. bd.: Electroplating and Surface Treatment jour., 1992—; contbr. articles to profl. jours. Office: Ural State Tech U, Mira st 19/Chem Dept, 620002 Yekaterinburg Russia

RUDOLF, ANTHONY, publisher, writer; b. London, Sept. 6, 1942; s. Henry Cyril and Esther (Rosenberg) R.; divorced; children: Nathaniel David, Naomi Rebeccah. BA, Cambridge U., 1964. Pub. The Menard Press, London; Adam lectr., Kings Coll., London, 1990. Author non-fiction books, including: At An Uncertain Hour: Primo Levi's War Against Oblivion, 1990, Engraved in Flesh: A Study of Piotr Rawicz, 1996, The Arithmetic of Memory, 1999; London editor The Jerusalem Rev., Modern Poetry in Translation; translator poetry books by Yves Bonnefoy and other poets. Home: 8 The Oaks/Woodside Ave, London N12 8AR, England

RUDOLPH, EKKART, software engineer, researcher; b. Oberstdorf, Bavaria, Germany, June 25, 1942; s. Hans-Joachim and Isolde (Lenski) R. Diploma in Physics, U. Munich, Germany, 1968, PhD, 1970. Fellow Max Planck Soc., Munich, 1968-69; sci. employee Max Planck Inst. for Physics, Munich, 1970-71; fellow Royal Soc., Oxford/Cambridge, Eng., 1971-73; sci. employee Max Planck Inst. for Astrophysics, Munich, 1973-77; engring. employee Siemens/AG, Munich, 1978-95; guest scientist Tech. U., Munich, 1995—; ITU-Rapporteur, Internat. Telecomm. Union Geneva, 1990-97, expert European Telecomm. Stds. Inst., Sophia Antipolis, 1998—; developer internat. telecomm. computer lang. Contbr. numerous articles to profl. jours.; founder internat. telecomm. computer language. Violinist in Daimler Chrysler Orch., Munich. Served in Mil., 1961-62. Mem. SDL-Forum Soc. E-mail: rudolph@informatik.tu-muenchen.de. Home: Erich Kastnerstr 2, D-80796 Munich Germany Office: Tech U Munich, Arcisstr 21, D-80290 Munich Germany

RUDOLPH, PETER, material scientist, researcher; b. Gera, Thuringia, Germany, July 1, 1945; s. Erich and Hedwig (Richter) R.; m. Nila Garus, June 1969 (div. Sept. 1979); children: Rudolph, Andreas; m. Petra Platzeck, June 4, 1981. Diploma in Engring., Tech. U., Lvov, Ukraine, 1969, DEng, 1972; DSc, Humboldt U., Berlin, Germany, 1979. Sci. asst. Humboldt U., Berlin, Germany, 1973-80, lectr., docent, team head, 1980-85, prof., team head, 1985-93; prof. Inst. of Crystal Growth, Berlin, Germany, 1994—; leader Dept. Crystallography, Humboldt U., Berlin, 1976-78, head work team crystal growth, 1980-93; vis. prof. Inst. Materials Sci., Sendai, Japan, 1993-94, 98; cons. Expert Working Group of ESA, Paris, 1990-93, Eurocryst, Austria Sci. Found., Vienna, 1991-92. Author: (book) Profilzüchtung von Einkristallen, 1982; co-author: Kristallzüchtung, 1988, Recent Development of Bulk Crystal Growth, 1998, Theoretical and Technological Aspects of Crystal Growth, 1998, Ullmann's Encyclopedia of Industrial Chemistry, 2000, The Technology of Crystal Growth and Epitaxy, 2000; contbr. revs. to profl. jours. Mem. Assn. Crystallography (sec. nat. com. 1983-90, Medal 1990), German Assn. Crystallography, Assn. Crystal Growth, Internat. Orgn. Crystal Growth (coun. mem. 1989-92), Internat. Commn. on Crystal Growth of Internat. Union of Crystallography (commn. mem. 1996—). Avocations: painting, guitar playing, skiing, TV filming. Fax: 0049 30 6392 3003. E-mail: pr@ikz-berlin.de. Home: Helga-Hahnemann Str 57, 15831 Grossziethen Germany Office: Inst of Crystal Growth, Max Born Str 2, 12489 Berlin Germany

RUDOLPH, RONALD ALVIN, human resources executive; b. Berwyn, Ill., May 12, 1949; s. Alvin J. and Gloria S. (Nicoletti) R. BA, U. Calif., Santa Cruz, 1971. Sr. cons. De Anza Assocs., San Jose, Calif., 1971-73; pers. adminstr. McDonnell Douglas Corp., Cupertino, Calif., 1974-75; employment rep. Fairchild Semiconductor, Mountain View, Calif., 1973-74, 75; compensation analyst Sperry Univac, Santa Clara, Calif., 1975-78; mgr. exempt compensation div. Intel Corp., Santa Clara, 1978-79, compensation mgr., 1979-82; dir. corp. compensation Intel Corp., 1982-85; v.p. human resources UNISYS Corp., San Jose, 1985-91, ASK Group Inc., Mountain View, Calif., 1991-94, 3 Com Corp., Santa Clara, 1994-98; v.p. adminstrn. Wyse Tech. Inc., San Jose, Calif., 1999—; cons. Rudolph Assocs., Cupertino, 1982—; bd. dirs. Dynamic Temp. Svcs., Sunnyvale, Calif. Mem. Spl. Com. for Parolee Employment, Sacramento, 1973-75; bd. dirs. Jr. Achievement San Jose, 1987-88. Mem. Am. Soc. Pers. Adminstrs., Am. Compensation Assn., No. Calif. Human Resources Coun. Avocations: sailing, reading, running, camping. Office: 3 Com Corp Santa Clara CA 95050

RUDOLPH, UDO KARL, psychology educator; b. Düsseldorf, Germany, Jan. 13, 1963. PhD, U. Bielefeld, 1991; Habilitation, Ludwig-Max U., Munich, 1998. Cert. in psychology. Asst. prof. U. Munich, 1996-99; prof. Tech. U. Chemnitz, Germany, 1999—. Mem. APA, German Soc. for Psychology. Office: Tech U Chemnitz, Inst für Psychologie, 09107 Chemnitz Germany

RUDOWSKI, WITOLD JANUSZ, surgeon, educator; b. Piotrkow Trybunalski, July 17, 1918; s. Maksymilian and Stefania R.; 3 children. MD, Clandestine U., Warsaw, 1943; Dr (hon.), Poznań Med. Acad., 1975, Warsaw Med. Sch., 1979, Lodz Med. Sch., 1980, Wroclaw Med. Sch., 1982, Edinburgh U., 1983, Jagiellonian U., 1989, Bialystok Med. Sch., 1990, Lublin Med. Sch., 1993. Assoc. prof. surgery Warsaw U., 1954-61, prof. extraordinary, 1961-70, prof., 1971—; cons. surgeon, sr. rsch. worker Madame M. Curie Cancer Inst., Warsaw, 1948-64; dir., head dept. surgery Inst. Haematology and Blood Transfusion, Warsaw, 1964-88; cons. Inst. Biomed. Engring., 1988—; chmn. Sci. Coun. to Minister of Health and Social Welfare, 1970-75; expert WHO, 1975—, mem., vice-chmn. exec. bd., 1985-88; v.p. Coun. Internat. Orgn. Med. Sci., 1988. Author: Burn Therapy and Research, 1976, Disorders of Hemostasis in Surgery, 1977, Surgery of the Spleen, 1987; contbr. numerous articles in field to profl. jours. Decorated Silver Cross of Virtuti Militari, 1944, Gold Cross of Merit, 1956, comdr. Cross Order of Polonia Restituta, 1979, Medal for Warsaw, 1970, State prize 2d Class, 1972, State prize 2d Class collective, 1978, Prize, Societé Internat. Chirurgie, 1989, comdr. Cross Polonia Restituta with star, 1994, Great Cross of Polonia Restituta, 2000. Fellow ACS (hon.), Royal Coll. Surgeons Edinburgh, Royal Coll. Surgeons Eng., Royal Coll. Physicians and Surgeons Can., Royal Coll. Surgeons Ireland (hon.), Royal Australasian Coll. Surgeons, Acad. de Chirurgie, South African Coll. Surgeons, Chile Surg. Soc., Acad. Surg. Mexico; mem. Internat. Soc. Surgery (hon.), Internat. Fedn. Surg. Colls. (v.p., pres.), Coll. Dutch Surgeons (corr.), Swedish Surg. Soc. (corr.), Swiss and German Surg. Soc. (corr.), Polish Haematological Soc., Polish Assn. Surgeons, Polish Acad. Scis., North Pacific Surg. Assn., Italian Soc. Surg. Rsch., West African Coll. Surgeons (hon.), Warsaw Sci. Soc. (pres. 1995), Czech Soc. Physicians, Polish Acad. Sci., Polish Acad. Art and Sci. Office: Rsch Inst Hematology Blood Transfusion, Chocimska 5, 00 957 Warsaw Poland

RUDRAIAH, NANJUNDAPPA, academician and university administrator; b. Bellave, Karnataka, India, Aug. 18, 1932; s. Nanjundappa and Rudramma Rudraiah; m. Makkam Nanjunda Shetty Manonmani; 1 child, Jagdish B.R. BSc with honors, Mysore U., Bangalore, India, 1955, MSc, 1957; MA, Toronto (Ont., Can.) U., 1960; PhD, U. Western Ont., London, 1964. Lectr. Ctrl. Coll., Bangalore, 1957-59, lectr. in math., 1964-65; rsch. asst. in math. Toronto U., 1959-61; reader in math. Manasa Gangotri Mysore U., 1965-66; postgrad. prof. in math. Bangalore U., 1967-72, sr. prof. in math., 1972-90, coord. Univ. Grants Commn.-Dept. Spl. Assistance program, 1980-90, prin. Ctrl. Coll., 1983-90; vice chancellor Gulbarga (India) U., 1990-96; sr. nat. scientist Indian Nat. Sci. Acad., New Delhi, India, 1996-2000; hon. dir. Nat. Rsch. Inst. for Applied Math.; hon. prof. math. Bangalore U.; emeritus fellow Univ. Grants Commn., 2000—. V.p. Indian Soc. Theoretical Applied Mechs., 1976-78, pres., 1982, 83; v.p. Indian Soc. Biomechs., 1989; pres. math. sect. Indian Sci. Congress Assn., 1988-89. Nat. lectr. Univ. Grants Commn., New Delhi, 1974-75; recipient Gold medal and cash award Fedn. Indian C. of C. Industries, 1979, Rajyotsava award Govt. of Karnataka, 1986, Pro. V. V. Narkkar Meml. Lectr. award, 2000. Fellow Indian Nat. Sci. Acad., Indian Acad. Scis., Nat. Acad. Scis., Math. and Applications (U.K.). Avocations: jogging, tennis, football, yoga. Home: 492/G 7th Cross 7th Block, Kanakapura West Jayanagar, Bangalore Karnataka 560 082, India Office: Nat Rsch Inst Applied Math, 492/G 7th Cross 7th Blk W, Jayanagar Bangalore 560082, India also: Bangalore U, Dept Math, Ctrl Coll Campus, Bangalore 560001, India

RUDY, DAVID ROBERT, physician, educator; b. Columbus, Ohio, Oct. 19, 1934; s. Robert Sale and Lois May (Arthur) R.; m. Rose Mary Sims; children by previous marriage: Douglas D., Steven W., Katharine L. Rudy Hoffer, Hunter A. Elam. BSc, Ohio State U., 1956, MD, 1960; MPH, Med. Coll. Wis., 1995. Diplomate Am. Bd. Family Practice, Am. Bd. Preventive Medicine. Intern Northwestern Meml. Hosp., Chgo., 1960-61; resident in internal medicine Ohio State U. Hosp., 1963-64; resident in pediatrics Children's Hosp., Columbus, Ohio, 1964; pvt. family practice Columbus, 1964-75; dir. residency program Riverside Meth. Hosp., Columbus, 1975-85; dir. family practice residency Monsour Med. Ctr., Jeannette, Pa., 1985-88; dir. Family Practice Ctr. and residency Bon Secours Hosp., Grosse Pointe, Mich., 1988-91; prof., dept. chmn. Finch U. Health Scis., Chgo. Med. Sch., 1991-95, 97—; prof. Pomerene chair family medicine Ohio State U., 1995-97. Editor, contbr. (textbook) Family Medicine for the House Officer; author: Family Medicine Q & A: NMS Series; contbr. articles to profl. jours. Capt. flight surgeon MC., USAF, 1961-63; col. USAFR. Recipient USAF Commendation medal. Fellow Am. Acad. Family Physicians; mem. AMA, Ill. State Med. Assn. Republican. Office: Chgo Med Sch Finch U Clinic 3333 Green Bay Rd North Chicago IL 60064-3037 also: 540 Ambria Dr Mundelein IL 60060-4806

RUDY, JAMES FRANCIS XAVIER, lawyer; b. N.Y.C., Feb. 1, 1954; s. Bertrand Robert and Margaret Eleanor (Campiglia) R.; m. Mary Elizabeth Haas, Aug. 17, 1978; children: Lauren Elizabeth, James F.X. Jr. BA, U. Ariz., 1976; JD, Fordham U., 1979. Bar: N.Y. 1980, N.J. 1981, U.S. Dist. Ct. (so. dist.) N.Y. 1980, U.S. Dist. Ct. N.J. 1981, U.S. Supreme Ct. 1985. Assoc. Briger & Assocs., N.Y.C., 1979-81, Katzenbach, Gildea & Rudner, Trenton, N.J., 1981-85; ptnr. Katzenbach, Gildea & Rudner, Lawrenceville, N.J., 1985-93; ptnr. Fox, Rothschild, O'Brien & Frankel, Lawrenceville, 1993—, chmn. health law group, 1994—; twp. atty. Ewing Twp., N.J., 1992-93, atty. Rent Control Bd., 1992-93, atty. Ethical Stds. Bd., 1992-93, atty. Condemnation Bd., 1992-93. Author: University of San Francisco Law Review, 1981. Legal counsel Ewing Rep. Club, 1991-93; mem. Washington Twp. Planning Bd., Robbinsville, N.J., 1993-98; wrestling coach Washington Twp. Recreation, Robbinsville, 1993—; dist. committeeperson Ewing Twp. Rep. Com., Ewing, 1990-92; mem. Washington Twp. Town Ctr. com. 1996—. Mem. ABA, N.Y. State Bar Assn., Nat. Health Lawyers Assn., Assn. of Bar City of N.Y., N.J. State Bar Assn. , Mercer County C. of C. (bus. com. 1993-94), Ewing Twp. Kiwanis Club (dir. 1994-95), Phi Beta Kappa, Phi Kappa Phi. Republican. Roman Catholic. Avocations: golf, home improvement, wrestling, rollerblading. Home: 8 Barto Way Robbinsville NJ 08691-2422 Office: Fox Rothschild OBrien & Frankel 997 Lenox Dr Lawrenceville NJ 08648-2317

RUDY, WILLIS, historian; b. N.Y.C., Jan. 25, 1920; s. Philip and Rose (Handman) R.; m. Dorothy L. Richardson, Jan. 31, 1948; children: Dee Dee, Willis Philip, Willa. BSS, CCNY, 1939; MA, Columbia U., 1940, PhD, 1948. Instr. CCNY, 1939-49; instr., lectr. Harvard U., 1949-53, 57-58; prof. Mass. State Coll., Worcester, 1953-63; prof. history Fairleigh Dickinson U., Teaneck, N.J., 1963-82, prof. emeritus, 1982—; mem. editorial bd. Fairleigh Dickinson U. Press, 1966-77. author: The College of the City of New York, A History, 1847-1947, 1949; 1997; The American Liberal Arts College Curriculum, 1960; Higher Education in Transition, 1958, 68, 76, 97; Schools in an Age of Mass Culture, 1965; The Universities of Europe: A History, 1984; Total War and Twentieth Century Higher Learning, 1991, The Campus and a Nation in Crisis: From the Revolution to Vietnam, 1996. Mem. Orgn. Am. Historians, Phi Beta Kappa. Home: 161 W Clinton Ave Tenafly NJ 07670-1916 Office: Fairleigh Dickinson U Dept Of Hist Teaneck NJ 07666

RUDY, YORAM, biomedical engineer, biophysicist, educator; b. Tel Aviv, Israel, Feb. 12, 1946; came to U.S., 1973; s. Nahum and Yaffa (Krinkin) R. BSc, Technion/Israel Inst. Tech., Haifa, 1971, MSc in Physics, 1973; PhD in Biomed. Engring., Case Western Res. U., 1978. Asst. prof. dept. biomed. engring. Case Western Res. U., Cleve., 1981-86, assoc. prof., 1986-89, prof., 1989—, prof. combined program in biophysics and bioengring., 1991—, prof. dept. medicine, 1992—; dir. cardiac bioelectricity rsch. and tng. ctr., vis. prof. Technion/Israel Inst. Tech., 1982-83, U. Parma, Italy, 1986, 87, U. Utah, Salt Lake City, 1990, Tel-Aviv (Israel) U., 1991, Russian Acad. of Scis., St. Petersburg, 1997, U. Berne, Switzerland, 1998; mem. cardiovascular and pulmonary study sect. NIH, 1984-88. Mem. editorial bd. Jour. Electrocardiology, Jour. Cardiovascular Electrophysiology, Cardiovasc. Rsch., Cardiac Electrophysiology Rev.; contbr. articles to profl. jours. Grantee NIH, 1985—, Am. Heart Assn., 1990-95, NSF, 1987-94; recipient Gordon K. Moe Prof. award, 1997, NIH-Nat. Heart, Lung and Blood Inst. merit award, 1998. Fellow IEEE, Am. Physiol. Soc., Am. Inst. Med. and Biol. Engring.; mem. Am. Heart Assn., Biophys. Soc., Biomed. Engring. Soc. (sr.). Achievements include development of a mathematical method for noninvasive reconstruction of cardiac electrical events from electrical potentials measured on the body surface (the inverse problem of electrocardiography), of theoretical models of cardiac excitation at the cellular, sub-cellular and tissue levels; elucidation of the cellular mechanisms of cardiac arrhythmias and the role of tissue architecture in arrhythmogenesis. Office: Case Western Res U Dept Biomed Engring Cleveland OH 44106-7207

RUE, DOUGLAS MICHAEL, technical application consultant; b. Pensacola, Fla., Apr. 9, 1964; s. Barbara J. Rue; m. Andra O'Neal, 1995; 1 child, Christian Michael Rue. AA in Bus., Pensacola (Fla.) Jr. Coll., 1984, AA in Computer Sci., 1984; BS in Computer Sci. cum laude, St. Augustine's Coll., 1988; MS in Telecomms., DePaul U., 1990. Data sys. analyst Internat. Paper, Memphis, 1990-91, project analyst, 1991-94; tech. cons. Sprint, L.A., 1994—; sr. tech. applications cons. Sprint, Universal City, Calif., 1998—, Jacksonville, Fla., 1999—; instr. DeVry Inst., Pomona, Calif., 1994. With U.S. Army Res., 1985-91. Office: Sprint 7406 Fullerton St Jacksonville FL 32256-3552

RUE, NELSON B., surgical nurse; b. Dayton, Ohio, Nov. 8, 1956; s. Nelson B. Jr. and Martha Sue R.; m. Carol Ann Wear, July 1, 1978; children: Laura, Suzanne. AS in Nursing, Western Ky. U., 1977, BA, 1980; MBA, Thomas More Coll., 1999. RN. Acct. mgr. Regent Hosp. Products, Ltd., Cin., 1988-91; v.p. Commonwealth, Inc., Cin., 1991-95; sr. v.p. MedComm Fulfillment, Inc., Cin., 1995-97; sr. v.p., chief oper. officer Pinnacle Packaging & Fulfillment, Inc., Cin., 1997-2000; surg. nurse St. Elizabeth Hosp., Edgewood, Ky., 2000—. Squad comdr. Civil air Patrol, 2000—. Mem. Coun. Logistics Mgmt. (v.p. exec. com. 1994-95, pres. exec. com. 1995-96), Rotary (v.p. 1985). Republican. Presbyterian. Avocations: search & rescue, boating, scuba diving. Home: 2843 Fraternity Ct Crestview Hls KY 41017-2512 Office: St Elizabeth Hosp Dept Surgery 1 Med Village Dr Edgewood KY 41017

RUECKERT, FREDERIC, plastic, reconstructive and hand surgeon; b. Boston, Oct. 24, 1921; s. Frederic and Elizabeth (Howe) R.; m. Joan Dodge, May 31, 1947; children: Nancy Lee, Patricia, William Dodge, Carolyn. AB, Hamilton Coll., 1945; MD, Columbia U., 1947. Diplomate Am. Bd. Plastic Surgery, Nat. Bd. Med. Examiners; lic. physician, N.Y., N.H. Intern internal medicine Bellevue Hosp., N.Y.C., 1947-48; resident gen. surgery Am. U. Hosp., Beirut, 1948-50; fellow surg. pathology Columbia-Presbyn. Hosp., N.Y.C., 1950-51; resident gen. surgery Dartmouth-Hitchcock Med. Ctr., Hanover, N.H., 1953-54, staff surgeon, 1956-86; resident plastic surgery, teaching fellow plastic surgery U. Pitts. Med. Ctr., 1954-56; mem. faculty Dartmouth Med. Sch., Hanover, 1956—, prof. plastic surgery, 1974-86, prof. plastic surgery emeritus, 1986—; cons. VA Hosp., White River Junction, Vt., 1956—. Contbr. articles to profl. jours., chpts. to books. Mem. Sch. Bd. Edn., Hanover, N.H., 1964-67; bd. trustees Northfield (Mass.) Mt. Hermon

Sch., 1969-71, 80-90. With USNR, 1943-45; capt. flight surgeon USAF, 1951-53. Recipient Lamplighter award Northfield Mt. Herman Sch., 1991. Mem. AMA, ACS, Am. Assn. Plastic Surgeons, Am. Assn. Med. Colls., Am. Soc. Plastic Surgeons (bd. dirs. 1980-83, 84-86), Plastic Surgery Ednl. Found. (bd. dirs. 1978-87, pres. 1985-86), Plastic Surgeons Assn. Am. (pres. 1984-85), Internat. Confederation Plastic, Reconstructive and Aesthetic Surgeons, Am. Soc. Aesthetic Plastic Surgeons, New Eng. Surg. Soc., Northeastern Soc. Plastic Surgeons, New Eng. Soc. Plastic and Reconstructive Surgeons (pres. 1969-71), N.H. State Med. Soc., Grafton County Med. Soc. (pres. 1974-75), Univ. Club (N.Y.C.). Republican. Presbyterian. Avocations: swimming, tennis, skiing, photography, wood carving. E-mail: frjd@dartmouth.edu. Home: 18 Berrill Farms Ln Hanover NH 03755-3213

RUEDENBERG, KLAUS, theoretical chemist, educator; b. Bielefeld, Germany, Aug. 25, 1920; came to U.S., 1948, naturalized, 1955; s. Otto and Meta (Wertheimer) R.; m. Veronika Kutter, Apr. 8, 1948; children: Lucia Meta, Ursula Hedwig, Annette Veronika, Emanuel Klaus. Student, Montana Coll., Zugerberg, Switzerland, 1938-39; licence es Scis., U. Fribourg, Switzerland, 1944; postgrad., U. Chgo., 1948-50; PhD, U. Zurich, Switzerland, 1950; PhD (hon.), U. Basel, Switzerland, 1975, U. Bielefeld, Germany, 1991, U. Siegen, Germany, 1994. Research assoc. physics U. Chgo., 1950-55; asst. prof. chemistry, physics Iowa State U., Ames, 1955-60; assoc. prof. Iowa State U., 1960-62, prof., 1964-78, disting. prof. in sci. and humanities, 1978-91, disting. prof. emeritus, 1991—, sr. chemist Ames Lab., U.S. Dept. Energy, 1964-91, assoc., 1991—; prof. chemistry Johns Hopkins, Balt., 1962-64; vis. prof. U. Naples, Italy, 1961, Fed. Inst. Tech., Zurich, 1966-67, Wash State U. at Pullman, 1970, U. Calif. at Santa Cruz, 1973, U. Bonn (Germany), 1974, Monash U. and CSIRO, Clayton, Victoria, Australia, 1982, U. Kaiserlautern, Germany, 1987; lectr. univs., rsch. instns. and sci. symposia, 1953—. Author articles in field; assoc. editor: Jour. Chem. Physics, 1964-67, Internat. Jour. Quantum Chemistry; Chem. Physics Letters, 1967-81, Lecture Notes in Chemistry, 1976—, Advances in Quantum Chemistry, 1987—; editor-in-chief Theoretica Chimica Acta, 1985-97; hon. editor Theoretical Chemistry Accounts, 1997—. Co-founder Octagon Center for the Arts, Ames, 1966, treas., 1966-71, also bd. dirs. Guggenheim fellow, 1966-67; Fulbright sr. scholar, 1982. Fellow AAAS, Am. Phys. Soc., Am. Inst. Chemists, Internat. Acad. for Quantum Molecular Scis.; mem. AAUP, Am. Chem. Soc. (Midwest award 1982), Sigma Xi, Phi Lambda Upsilon. Home: 2834 Ross Rd Ames IA 50014-4030 Office: Dept Chemistry Iowa State Univ Ames IA 50011-0001

RUEEGG, WALTER H(ENRI), humanities educator; b. Zurich, Switzerland, Apr. 4, 1918; s. Walter Henri and Margarit (Braun) R.; m. Liselotte Rickenbach, Nov. 5, 1943 (dec. 1986); children: Elisabeth, Andreas, Helena; m. Irina Magyari. PhD, U. Zurich, Switzerland, 1944, privatdocent, 1950. Gymnasium tchr. Switzerland, 1941-53; guest prof. U. Cologne, Germany, 1948; reader U. Zurich, 1950-62; prof. U. Frankfurt, Germany, 1961-73, dean faculty social scis., 1964-65, rector, 1965-70; prof. U. Berne, Switzerland, 1973-86, dean faculty of law, 1975-76, prof. emeritus, 1986—. Author books in field; gen. editor: A History of the University in Europe, 1991—. Pres. Soc. Swiss Acads., 1957-62, 73—. Comdr. Ordre Palmes Academiques, France, 1970. Mem. Wissenschafliche Gesellschaft Frankfurt, Academia Scientiarum et Artium Europea, Rotary. Mem. Swiss Liberal Democratic Party. Mem. Reformed Ch. Avocations: old books, gardening. Home: Rte de Sonchax 36, CH1820 Veytaux Switzerland

RUEGER, DANIEL SCOTT, horticulture educator; b. Flint, Mich., May 16, 1957; s. William John and Barbara Jane (Ledford) R.; m. Michel Sharon Holzbach, July 22, 1989; children: Danielle Sharon, Christina Anne, Michael Scott. BS in Agr., Ohio State U., 1980, MS in Agr. Edn., 1980. Cert. profl. vocational, horticulture teacher, Ohio. Mgr. Idle R's Farms, Plain City, Ohio, 1973-77; research services worker O.M. Scott & Sons Co., Marysville, Ohio, 1977; tng. counselor Cen. Ohio Rural Consortium, Delaware, 1978; supt. parks grounds City of Delaware, 1979; tchr. horticulture Ashland (Ohio) City Schs., 1980—. Co-author: Success Handbook, 1980. Sustaining mem. Rep. Nat. Com., 1980-92; lay leader Emmanuel Meth. Ch., 1988-94; chmn. adminstrv. bd., 1990-91. Named Citizen of Yr. Citizens Commn. for the Right to Keep and Bear Arms, 1986, 87, 88, Disting. Patriot Concil for Inter-Am. Security. Mem. NEA, Nat. Assn. Agrl. Educators, Inc., Ohio Edn. Assn. (state coun. ednl. polit. action com. 1988-91, profl. devel. com. 1990-98), North Cen. Ohio Edn. Assn. (exec. com. 1986—), Ohio Assn. Agrl. Educators (hort. state chmn. 1988-92, Outstanding Agrl. Edn. Program 1992), Assn. for Career and Tech. Edn., Ohio Assn. for Career and Tech. Edn., Ashland City Tchrs. Assn. (pres. 1988-89), Ohio State U. Alumni Assn., Air Force Assn., Future Farmers Am. Alumni Assn., Orgn. for Secondary Students Enrolled in Agrl. Edn., Ohio Forestry Assn., Gamma Sigma Delta, Phi Delta Kappa. Avocations: reading, aviation, swimming, fishing, philately. Office: Ashland High Sch 1440 King Rd Ashland OH 44805-3635

RUEHLE, CHARLES JOSEPH, pathologist, military officer; b. Boone, Iowa, May 26, 1943; s. John Donald and Alta (Brown) R. DVM, Iowa State U., 1967; MD, U. Iowa, 1973, MS, 1973; m. Nellie Backus, Aug. 5, 1972. Commd. 2d lt. USAF, 1964, advanced through grades to col., sr. flight surgeon, 1984, chief flight surgeon, 1987; chief Vet. Service, Grissom AFB, Ind., 1967-69; resident in aerospace medicine Brook AFB, Tex., 1973-75; resident in pathology Wilford Hall USAF Med. Ctr., Lackland AFB, Tex., 1975-79, with div. aerospace pathology Armed Forces Inst. Pathology, Washington, 1979-88, chief div. aerospace pathology, 1982-85, chmn. dept. forensic scis., 1985-88, sec. Joint Com. Aviation Pathology, 1984-88, exec. asst. to fed. air surgeon FAA, Washington, 1988—, sr. aviation med. examiner, 1989—; adj. asst. prof. preventive medicine Uniformed Services U. Health Scis. lectr. aerospace pathology; cons. USAF Sugeon Gen., 1987. Diplomate Am. Bd. Preventive Medicine, Am. Bd. Pathology. Fellow Am. Soc. Clin. Pathologists, Aerospace Med. Assn.; mem. Am. Acad. Forensic Scis. AMA, USAF Flight Surgeons, Nat. Sojourners, Assn. Mil. Surgeons U.S., Internat. Soc. Air Safety Investigators, Air Force Assn., Alpha Zeta, Gamma Sigma Delta, Omega Tau Sigma (gov. 1967-75), Cosmos Club. Republican. Presbyterian. Home: 1000 Lower Pindell Rd Lothian MD 20711-2704 Office: Fed Air Surgeon FAA 800 Independence Ave SW Washington DC 20591-0001

RUELAS-GOMEZ, ROBERTO, electrical engineer; b. Guanajuato, Mexico, Jan. 2, 1961; s. Roberto Ruelas and Rosa E. Gomez; m. Elvia Alicia Zermeno, Sept. 17, 1988; children: Alicia, Alejandra, Roberto Jr. BS, U. Autonoma San Luis, 1982; M in Engring., McGill U., 1986. Engr. Carlingswitch Inc., Matehuala, Mexico, 1983-84; chief maintenance dept. Polimeros y Derivados, Leon, Mexico, 1986-87; owner, ptnr. Maquinaria y Controles, Leon, 1988; chief maintenance dept. Acero Preformado, Leon, 1989-90; owner, ptnr. Ruelsa, Leon, 1991—, Electrinet SA, León, 1998—. Author: Grounding Systems, 1996. Mem. IEEE (counselor UBAC student br. 1997—), Guanajuato State Edn. (bd. dirs. 2000—), Inst. Electromechanical Engrs. Guanajuato State (v. chmn. 1998-99, chmn. 1999-2000), Internat. Assn. Elec. Inspectors, N.Y. Acad. Sci. Fax: 47 144770. Home: Av Americas 819, 37370 León Mexico

RUEMLER, RUPRECHT ERNST, landscape architect, educator; b. Zeitz, Germany, Aug. 22, 1930; s. Werner and Hildegard (Koettnitz) R.; m. Ruth Leydecker, Sept. 25, 1965; children: Reinhard, Roland. Diploma, Humboldt U., Berlin, 1955; PhD, U. Aachen, Germany, 1974. Cert. landscape architect, bioengr., horticultural specialist. Landscape architect City Planning Office, Dresden, Germany, 1955-57, Marlow, Eng., 1957-58, various planning offices, various cities, Germany, 1958-67; asst. scientist Tech. U., Aachen, 1967-75; civil servant, environ. cons. Rhineland Regional Authority, Cologne, Germany, 1975-83; prof. landscape architecture and planning U. Essen, Germany, 1983-98; founding mem. Soc. Biol. Engring., Aachen, 1979; mem. Landscape Inst., Bonn, 1973-91; cons. Tng. Ctr. for German Horticulturists, Gruenberg, 1991—; cons. Rhenish Soc. Preservation of Hist. Monuments and Landscape Conservation, 1993. Mem. editl. bd. Facade Planting Guidelines, 2000; contbr. articles to profl. jours. and symposium procs.; co-author (yearbook) Nature Conservation in the Rhineland, 1993. Mem. German Soc. Dendrologists (cons. for history of parks and gardens 1988—), Profl. Assn. Architects, Friends of the Botanic Garden Cologne. Protestant. Avocations: plant use, plant identification, bioengineering, history of parks and gardens, photography. Home: Dachsweg 2, D-50859 Cologne Germany

RUEPKE, JOERG, religion historian, educator; b. Herford, Germany, Dec. 27, 1962; s. Hans Dieter and Barbara B. (Neugebauer) R.; m. Ulrike Christine Koss; 1 child, Irene. MA, U. Tuebingen, 1987, DPhil, 1989, DPhil in Habilitation, 1994. Researcher U. Tuebingen, Germany, 1990-95; dep. prof. U. Constance, Germany, 1995; prof. U. Potsdam, Germany, 1995-99, U. Erfurt, Germany, 1999—. Author: Domi militiae: Die religiöse Konstruktion des Krieges, 1990, Eduard Norden, 1993, Kalender und Oeffentlichkeit, 1995, Religion der Roemer, 2000; editor: Von Goettern und Menschen erzaehlen, 2000; co-editor: Eduard Norden, 1994, Toeten im Krieg, 1995, Roemische Reichsreligion, 1997; contbr. articles to profl. jours. Grantee Werner-Reimers-Stiftung, 1996, 98, Fritz-Thyssen-Stiftung, 1997, Deutsche Forschungsgemeinschaft, 2000. Mem. Mommsen Gesellschaft, Inst. für Historische Anthropologie, Dt Vereinigung für Religionsgeschichte. E-mail: joerg.ruepke@uni-erfurt.de. Office: U Erfurt Religionswissensch, Nordhaeuser Str 63, D-99089 Erfurt Germany

RUF, DONNIE LEE, delivery service provider, fashion model, designer; b. Ardmore, Ala., Aug. 23, 1954; s. David Eberhardt Sr. and Thelma Mae (Callahan) R.; m. Cathy Marie Paulk, Aug. 20, 1977 (div. 1986); children: Katie Leigh, Bonnie Brook. BS in Mktg., Auburn U., 1976, BS in Edn., 1976. Salesman Burroughs Corp., Huntsville, Ala., 1977; farmer, mgr. Ruf Farms, Athens, Ala., 1977-80; salesman Limestone Farmer's Coop., Athens, 1980; driver United Parcel Svc., Huntsville, 1981-2000; coord. United Way, 1981-98; model United Way Brochure, 1996; sec. Huntsville Driver Relief Fund, 1990-95; cover model Big Idea (UPS), 1989, 94; contbg. designer, Sew Beautiful, 1993, 94, Internat., Needle Arts, 1994, nat. Cover model consumer Savs. Group brochure, 1989; mem. cast (mus. prodn.) Oliver at Athens State U., 1991, contbr. article to profl. jour., contbr. designer to profl. orgns. Big bro. Big-Bros.-Big-Sisters King's Acres, Auburn, 1975-76; vol. Limestone Health Facility; model spokesperson United Way, chmn. Huntsville chpt., 1983-91; sec.-treas. Huntsville Driver Relief Fund, 1988-91; mem. United Parcel Safety Com., Huntsville, 1985-90. Named Mr. Ala. Male Am., Kansas City, Mo., 1989, Mr. Ala. N. Am., Scottsdale, Az., 1992, N.J., 1989-90, Faces Internatl., feature model, 1992, 93, Mr. Man Premiere Finalist, 1998, Person of Yr. Boys and Girls Club Limestone county, 1997, Outstanding Citizen award Jaycees, 1995, rep. to Congress Outstanding Young Alabamians, 1994; recipient Nat. Interpretaton Design Winner, Embroiders Guild of Amer., 1994, Natl. Adaption Design Winner, Embroiders Guild of Amer., 1994; Ala. United Way/UPS Leadership pin design winner, 2000. Mem. Limestone County 4-H Club, Delta Sigma Pi. Mem. Ch. of Christ. Avocations: travel, interior design, antiques. Fax #: 1-256-859-1380. Home: 26528 South Rd Athens AL 35613-3744

RUF, WERNER KLAUS, international relations and politics educator; b. Sigmaringen, Germany, Oct. 15, 1937; s. Emil and Martha (Schatz) R.; m. Annemie Schmitt, Sept. 13, 1961 (div. 1987); children: Irinell, Urs-Peter; m. Beate Jordan, Aug. 16, 1991; 1 child, Nura Dorothea. PhD, U. Freiburg, 1967. Lectr. U. Freiburg, Germany, 1965-68, 69-70; assoc. prof. Univ.-Aix-Marseille III, Aix-en-Provence, France, 1971-75; prof. sociology U. Essen, Germany, 1974-82; prof. internat. rels. U. Kassel, Germany, 1982—; sr. fellow NYU, N.Y.C., 1968-69; mem. exec. com. Univ. Ctr. Dubrovnik, Croatia, 1978-95. Author: Der Burgibismus und die Aussenpolitik des unabhängigen Tunesien, 1968, Die neue Welt-UN-Ordnung, 1994, Die algerische Tragödie, 1997; author, editor: Vom Kalten Krieg zur heissen Ordnung?, 1991; mem. editorial bd. Zeitschrift fü Kulturaustausch, 1972-86, Jour. North African Studies, 1995—. Mem. German Assn. Peace Rsch. (exec. com. 1994-98), German Assn. Polit. Sci., Fedn. Dem. Scientists, German Assn. Fgn. Policy. Fax: 49-5665-961961. E-mail: ruf@hrz.uni-kassel.de. Home: Chattenweg 32, 34295 Edermünde Germany Office: U Gesamthochsch Kassel Fach, bereich 5 NoraPlatiel Str 1, 34109 Kassel Germany

RUFEH, MARK, finance company executive. BS, Mercy Coll., 1983; MBA, Manhattan Coll., 1991. V.p. ops. and risk mgmt. First Boston Corp.; head ops. taxable fixed income divsn. Lehman Bros., Inc., N.Y.C., 1986, various sr. mgmt. positions mgmt. and corp. svcs., mng. dir., COO, mem. operating com. Office: Lehman Bors Holdings Inc World Hdqs 3 World Financial Ctr New York NY 10285-0001

RUFF, FERENC, chemist, educator; b. Budapest, Oct. 15, 1937; s. Istvan and Katalin (Maitner) R. MSc, Eotvos U., 1961, PhD, 1965; DSc, Hungarian Acad. Scis., 1991. From asst. prof. to prof. Eotvos U., Hungary, 1973—. Author: Organic Reactions, 1994; contbr. articles to profl. jours. Home: Kelenhegyi ut 50, 1118 Budapest Hungary

RUFF, HENRI-JACQUES, credit card company executive; b. France, Mar. 13, 1949; m. Eva Ruff. BSc in Econs., U. Wales, Cardiff, 1971, MSc in Econs., 1972. Lectr. Manchester (Eng.) U., 1972-74; sr. economist Barclays, London, 1974-78, bank mgr., 1978-86; bank mgr. Barclays, Paris, 1986-89; lobbyist Inst. Internat. Fin., Washington, 1989-91; head mem. risk Visa Internat., London, 1991-94, head fin. planning, 1995-97, head Euro implementation, 1997-99, econ. advisor, 1999—. Office: Visa Internat, PO Box 253, London W8 5TE, England

RUFFER, JOYCE SELLARS, poet, artist; b. Cairo, Ga., June 15, 1947; d. Oscar Odysseus and Betty Lou (Scott) Sellars; children: Charles Scott Mason, Jeffrey Dewayne Mason. Author: (poetry) Rose Moon. Named Best Poet 1994, Nat. Libr. Poetry, Poet of Yr., Internat. Soc. Poets, 1996; recipient Editor's Choice award Nat. Libr. Poetry, Poetic Achievement award, Am. Poetry Soc. Avocations: spiritual enhancement, birding, nature photography, marine ecology, feline appreciation. Fax: 707 464-7557. E-mail: Jpolli@cc.northcoast.com. Home: Thistle Dew 2426 Maher Ave Crescent City CA 95531-9137

RUFFIEUX, ROLAND, retired history and political science educator; b. Bulle, Fribourg, Switzerland, Nov. 9, 1921; s. Fernand and Léonie (Gaudard) R.; m. Eva Strumhausova, Apr. 10, 1958; children: Blaise, Jérôme, Hélène, Etienne. Lic. in letters, U. Fribourg, 1947, D in Letters in history, 1953, Habilitation, 1957, hon. prof., 1992; diploma in polit. sci., Inst. Polit. Studies, Paris, 1954, postgrad., 1955-57; hon. prof., U. Lausanne, Switzerland, 1987. Extraordinary prof. U. Fribourg, 1958-63, ordinary prof. head Inst. Contemporary History, 1963-92; dir. Swiss Nat. Libr., 1963-65; ordinary prof., head Inst. Polit. Sci. U. Lausanne, 1965-75; chmn. Pro Helvetia, Swiss Found. for Culture, 1978-86; mem. Publ. Swiss Diplomatic Documents, 1978-93, Nat. Coun. Sci. Rsch., 1981-91; mem. coun. European Sci. Found., 1984-91, Jubilee Found. of U.B.S., 1986-91, Union Bank Switzerland. Author: La Suisse de l'entre-deux-guerres, 1974, Nouvelle histoire de la Suisse et des Suisses. T.III 1848-1914, 1983; editor, contbr. Les pétitions du Jura à Berne au XIXème siècle, 1972, Histoire du canton de Fribourg, 1981, La Suisse et son avenir européen, 1989, Fribourg et ses Musées, 1992; editor: Documents diplomatiques suisses (1848-1945) T.II: 1966-72, 1976. Pres. Rencontres Suisses, 1975-86, hon. pres., 1986—; pres. Forum Helveticum, 1987-92, hon. pres., 1992—; pres. com. Mus. Art and History Fribourg, 1968-84. Mem. History Soc. Canton Fribourg (pres. 1962-68), Rotary. Avocations: collecting ancient drawings. Home: Chemin des Kybourg 3, CH-1700 Fribourg Switzerland

RUFFIN, PAUL DEAN, English language educator; b. Millport, Ala., May 14, 1941; s. David Clarence and Zealon (Robinson) R.; m. Sharon Marie Krebs, June 21, 1973; children: Genevieve, Matthew. BS, Miss. State U., 1964, MA, 1967; PhD, Univ. So. Miss., 1974. Instr. Eng. Univ. So. Miss., Hattiesburg, 1971-72, Miss. State Univ., Starkville, 1972-74; prof. Eng. Sam Houston State Univ., Huntsville, Tex., 1975—; dir. Tex. Rev. Press, Huntsville, 1992—. Author: Circling, 1996, Our Women, 1985, The Man Who Would Be God, 1993; editor: That's What I Like About the South, 1993; editor Tex. Rev., 1976—. With U.S. Army, USNG, 1959-65. Mem. Tex. Inst. Letters, Conf. Coll. Tchrs. Eng., South Ctrl. Modern Lang. Assn. Avocations: writing, gardening, woodworking. Home: 2014 Ave N 1/2 Huntsville TX 77340

RUFFING, BERNHARD, acoustics company executive; b. Landau, Germany, Apr. 9, 1957; s. Eugen F. and Gertrud (Leonhard) R.; m. Petra Munch; children: Patricia, Alexander, Thorsten. MSME, U. Karlsruhe, Germany, 1982; PhD in Mech. Engring., U. Karlsruhe, 1987. Mgr. quality Luk GmBH, Buhl, Germany, 1988-89; coord. quality mgmt. Rütgerswerke AG, Frankfurt, Germany, 1989-90; mgr. quality mgmt. CWW GmBH, Worms, Germany, 1991-93; mgmr. quality mgmt. Rütgers Automotive AG, Essen, Germany, 1994-95; mng. dir. Insonit S.A., Terrasse, Spain, 1996-97, CWW-GERKO Akustik GmbH & Co KG, Worms, 1998—; bd. dirs. Insonit S.A., Terrasse, CWW-GERKO Acoustics Inc., Gastonia, N.C. Home: Kreuzweide 6, 67551 Worms Germany Office: CWW-GERKO Akustik GmbH & Co, Weinsheimer Str 96, 67547 Worms Germany

RUFFINI, REMO JACOPO, physics educator; b. LaBrigue, France, May 17, 1942; s. Dante and Maddalena (Pettirosso) R.; m. Anna Imponente; 1 child, Jacopo. D in Physics, U. Rome, 1966. Postdoctoral fellow Mainz Acad. Scis., Hamburg, Fed. Republic Germany, 1967, Palmer Physics Lab., Princeton, N.J., 1967-68; mem. Inst. for Advanced Study, Princeton, 1968-70, 74-76; instr. Princeton U., 1970-71, asst. prof., 1971-74; prof. U. Catania, Italy, 1976-78; prof. theoretical physics U. Rome La Sapienza, 1978—; pres. Internat. Ctr. Relativistic Astrophysics, 1985—; vis. prof. Kyoto (Japan) U., 1975, U. Western Australia, Perth, 1975; mem. Coun. Ctrl. Internat. Physics, Bogota, Colombia, 1984—; mem. task force sci. use of space sta. NASA, Washington, 1975-78; chmn. Italian Sci. for Space Sta., Rome, 1986-90, Internat. Organization Com. of Marcel Grossmann Meetings, 1984—; rep. Internat. Forum Sci. Use of Space Sta., Washington, 1986-90; mem. Consiglio Rsch. Astronomy, Rome, 1987-91; co-chmn. Italian-Korean Meetings on Relativistic Astrophysics, Rome and Seoul, 1987—, William Fairbanks Meetings, 1990—; pres. Sci. Com. Italian Space Agy., Rome, 1989-93. Editor Advanced Series in Astrophysics and Cosmology-World Sci., 1986—, Internat. Jour. Modern Physics D World Sci., 1992—; co-author: (with J.A. Wheeler) Cosmology from Space Platforms, 1970, (with S. Hawking, et. al.) Black Holes, 1973, (with M. Rees and J.A. Wheeler) Black Holes, Gravitational Waves and Cosmology, 1974, Cernie Diri Gratazionnie Volni I Kosmologia, 1974, (with H. Gursky) Neutron Stars, Black Holes and Binaries Sources, 1975, (with Humitaka Sato) Black Holes, 1976, (with Fang Li Zhi) Basic Concepts Relativistic Astrophysics, 1981, (with R. Giacconi, et. al.) Physics Astrophysics of Neutron Stars Black Holes, 1978, Gamow Cosmology, 1986, (with H. Ohanian) Gravitation and Spacetime, 1994, Gravitazione e Spaziotempo, 1997; editor, co-editor numerous books; contbr. numerous articles to profl. jours. Recipient Cressy Morrison award N.Y. Acad. Scis., 1972, Space Scientist of Yr. award, 1992; Alfred P. Sloan Found. fellow, 1974-76. Fellow Am. PHys. Soc.; mem. Euorpean Phys. Soc., Italian Physical Soc. (vice dir. nuovo cimento B), Sigma Xi. Roman Catholic. Avocations: skiing, mountaineering, fishing, archeology. E-mail: Ruffini@icra.it. Home: Via Savoia 37, 00198 Rome Italy Office: ICRA Physics Dept, Piazzage A Moro 2, 00185 Rome Italy

RUFFNER, CHARLES LOUIS, lawyer; b. Cin., Nov. 7, 1936; s. Joseph H. and Edith (Solomon) R.; m. Mary Ann Kaufman, Jan. 30, 1966 (div. 1993); children: Robin Sue, David Robert; m. Nanette Diemer, Feb. 26, 1995. BSBA in Acctg., U. Fla., 1958; JD cum laude, U. Miami, 1964. Bar: Fla. 1964, U.S. Dist. Ct. (so. and Mid. dists.) Fla. 1964, U.S. Ct. Appeals (5th cir.) 1964, U. S. Ct. Appeals (11th cir.) 1984, U.S. Claims Ct. 1966, U.S. Tax Ct. 1966, U.S. Supreme Ct. 1969; cert. in taxation. Trial atty. tax divsn. Dept. Justice, Washington, 1964-67; pres. Forrest, Ruffner, Traum & Hagen, P.A., Miami, Fla., 1967-78, Ruffner, Hagen & Rifkin, P.A., Miami, 1978-81; tax ptnr. Myers, Kenin, Levinson, Ruffner, Frank & Richards, Miami, 1982-84; pres. Charles L. Ruffner, P.A., 1984—; lectr. Fla. Internat. U., Miami. Author: A Practical Approach to Professional Corporations and Associations, 4 edits., 1970, (column) Tax Talk, Miami Law Rev.; editor Miami Law Rev., 1963-64; contbr. numerous articles on taxation to law jours. Mem. ABA, Fed. Bar Assn., Fla. Bar (exec. coun. tax sect. 1967-92, 95—, amicus curiae in test case of validity profl. corps.), Dade County Bar Assn., South Fla. Tax Litigation Assn. (chmn. 1986-00), Phi Alpha Delta, Phi Kappa Phi. E-mail: cruff7117@aol.com. Office: Courvoisier Centre II 601 Brickell Key Dr Ste 507 Miami FL 33131-2652

RUFFO, MICHAEL, painter; b. Staten Island, N.Y., Mar. 9, 1954; s. Thomas Anthony and Marie (Papa) R.; m. Lorelei Ann Perez, July 5, 1995. BFA, Sch. Visual Arts, N.Y.C., 1991. Exhibited in group shows at Salmagundi Club, 1992-93, 95-99, Agora Gallery, 1998-99, World Fine Art, 1999, Knickerbocker Gallery, 1999, Hiram Blauvelt Mus., 1999, Nexus Gallery, 1999, 2000; represented in permanent collections U.S. Dept. State; patentee lockable lid support; work pub. in New Art Internat., 1999. Recipient Excellence award Manhattan Arts Internat. Competition, 1997-98, 99. Mem. Salmagundi Club (awards 1992, 93), N.Y. Artists Equity Assn., Orgn. Ind. Artists, Nexus Gallery (N.Y.C.), West Side Arts Coalition. Roman Catholic.

RUFLI, KURT, hotel executive; b. Zurich, Jan. 27, 1945; s. Fritz and Erna (Von Ah) R.; m. Maria Justina, Dec. 10, 1973; children: Tamara, Chanel, Vanessa. Diploma, Hotel Coll., Lausanne, Switzerland, 1966. Asst. mgr. Arthurs Seat Hotel, Cape Town, 1967; fin. controller Heerengracht Hotel, Cape Town, Sea Point, South Africa, 1968-71, Aga Kahn Hotels, Sardegna, Italy, 1972; gen. mgr. Nipa & Orchid Lodge Hotels, Pattaya, Thailand, 1973; group gen., mng. dir. Amari Hotels and Resorts (formerly Siam Lodge Hotels), Thailand, 1973—. With Swiss Army, 1964-65. Home: Sathorn Park Pl Duplex 35/36A, 27/2 S Sathorn Rd, 10120 Bangkok Thailand Office: Amari Hotels and Resorts, 847 Petchburi Rd Pratunam, Rajthevi Bangkok 10400, Thailand

RUGALA, KAREN FRANCIS (KAREN FRANCIS), painter, television producer; b. Memphis, Apr. 27, 1950; d. Ben Porter Francis and Marguerite K. Higginbotham; children: Sarah Helfinstein, Ben Helfinstein. BA in Communication Arts, Rhodes Coll., 1971; MA, U. Mo., 1973. Cert. tchr., Tenn. Secondary sch. tchr. Memphis City Schs., 1971-72; speech tchr. U. Ga., Athens, 1973-75; dir. computer systems installations Planning Rsch. Corp., McLean, Va., 1976-78; dir. account mgmt. TDX Systems, Cable & Wireless, Vienna, Va., 1978-80; cons. telecommunications MCI, Washington, 1985-87; producer Fairfax Cable Access, Merrifield, Va., 1991-96; owner Art Promotions, McLean, 1989—. Exhibited paintings in numerous group and one-woman shows and in cyberspace including McLean Project for Arts, 1992, Hospice of No. Va. Auction Gala, 1992, Capitol Hill Art League, Washington, 1995, Mus. Contemporary Art, Washington, 1996, Arts Coun. Fairfax County, Va., 1999, many others; paintings numerous pvt. collections. Active Family AIDS Housing Found., 1992, Hospice No. Va., 1991, 92, Friends of Vietnam Vets. Meml., 1992; founding bd. mem. Jobs for Homeless People, 1988-90; founder Non-Violence Award Program, 1998. Avocations: tennis, dancing, bridge, reading. E-mail: karen@artpro.com. Office: Art Promotions PO Box 3104 Mc Lean VA 22103-3104

RUGARN, OLOF, obstetrician-gynecologist; b. Göteborg, Sweden, Dec. 27, 1956; m. Anna Westholm, June 3, 1978; children: Jonatan, Elin, Jenny. MD, Göteborg U., 1982. Cert. specialist ob-gyn. Hosp. specialist U. Hosp., Linköping, Sweden, 1992—; tchr. Sch. Medicine, Faculty Health Scis., Linköping, 1990—. Contbr. rsch. articles to profl. jours. Lt. Swedish Army, 1989-99. Mem. Swedish Med. Assn. EFS. Avocations: sailing, running. Office: Linköping Hosp, Divsn Ob-Gyn Fac Hlth Sci, 581 83 Linköping Sweden

RUGE, MICHAEL HELMUTH, research scientist, consultant, mathematician; b. Hagen, Germany, Mar. 13, 1962; s. Helmuth and Ruth Ruge. MS, La. State U., 1986, PhD, 1989; Diplom, U. Kaiserslautern, Germany, 1988. Tchg. asst. U. Kaiserslautern, 1983-84, Fla. State U., Tallahassee, 1984, La. State U., Baton Rouge, 1984-89; sys. engr. EDS/GM, Detroit, 1990-91; rsch. sys. engr. EDS/GM, Plano, Tex., 1991; rsch. engr. tech. assessment R&D Siemens AG, Munich, 1991-94, rsch. sci. pub. comm. networks group, 1994-96, mgr. innovation field healthcare R&D, 1996-98; sr. cons. task force Y2K/Euro Siemens Bus. Svcs., Munich, 1998-99; sr. cons. mgmt. cons. Siemens Bus. Svcs., Frankfurt, Munich, Germany, 1999—; cons. Delgu Schuh- und Textilhandels GmbH, Kaiserslautern, 1993-95. Co-author: Neue Techniken in der Informationsverarbeitung, 1994; co-referee: Calculus with Analytic Geometry, 1988, Procs. Modellierung und Simulation im Umweltbereich, 1992, Procs. European Simulation Multiconf., 1993, Systems Analysis, Modelling and Simulation, Vols. 18-19, 1995; contbr. articles to profl. jours. Recipient award Studienstiftung des Deutschen Volkes, 1980; Fulbright scholar, 1984-86. Mem. Am. Math. Soc., German Math. Soc., Burschenschaft Markomannia, Phi Kappa Phi. Fax: 603-947-7242. E-mail: mhr@e-math.ams.org. Home: PO Box 1311, D-82003 U'haching Germany

RUGGERI, ANDREA PIETRO, auditor; b. Messina, Italy, Sept. 2, 1943; s. Giuseppe and Teresa (Ciraolo) R.; m. Jennifer Anne Lusby, Apr. 22,1 976; children: Alexandra Teresa, Edward Giuseppe. Bus. adminstrn. degree, U. Messina (Italy), 1968. Cert. auditor. Lectr. SDA Bocconi U., Milan, Italy, 1968, U. Florence, Genoa, Bologna and, Cagliari, LUISS, U. Pisa; auditor Deloitte, Milan, Italy, 1969-76, mgr., 1976-80; ptnr.-in-charge Deloitte, Florence, Italy, 1980-94; mem. exec. com. DRT, Milan; resp. multinats. Deloitte & Touche, Italy, mng. ptnr., chmn. mgmt. com., mem. D&T European bd., 1994. Mem. Ugolino Golf Club-Chianti, Rotary. Roman Catholic. Office: Deloitte & Touche, Via Cavour 64, 50129 Florence Italy

RUGGIE, JOHN GERARD, political science educator, diplomat; b. Graz, Austria, Oct. 18, 1944; came to U.S., 1967; s. Josef and Margaret (Macic) R.; m. Mary Zacharuk, May 21, 1965; 1 child, Andreas John. BA, McMaster U., 1967; MA, U. Calif., Berkeley, 1968; PhD, U. Calif., 1974; LLD (hon.), McMaster U., 2000. Asst. prof. polit. sci. U. Calif., Berkeley, 1974-78; prof. internat. rels. U. Calif., San Diego, 1987-91; dir. inst. global conflict and cooperation U. Calif., 1989-91; prof. polit. sci. Columbia U., N.Y.C., 1978-87, prof. polit. sci., internat. affairs, 1991—, dean Sch. Internat. and Pub. Affairs, 1991-96; asst. sec. gen. UN, N.Y.C., 1997—. Author: Winning the Peace, 1996, Constructing the World Polity, 1998; editor: 4 books; contbr. over 50 articles to profl. jours. Recipient Hubert H. Humphrey award Nitable Pub. Svc., Am. Polit. Sci. Assn., 2000; Internat. Studies Assn. Disting. scholar, 1999. Fellow Am. Acad. Arts Sci.; mem. UN Assn. (bd. dirs. 1985—), Fgn. Policy Assn. (bd. govs. 1992-95), Coun. Fgn. Rels. Avocations: skiing, scuba, tennis. Office: UN Exec Office Sec-Gen United Nations New York NY 10017

RUGGIERO, ANTHONY WILLIAM, chemical company executive; b. Mt. Vernon, N.Y., May 27, 1941; s. Jerome and Mary (Nanti) R.; m. Elaine M. Tornese, Sept. 27, 1964; children: Alicia Marie, Audrey Loren. B.S. in Econs., Fordham U., 1963; M.B.A. in Fin., Columbia U., 1964; P.M.C. in Acctg., Iona Coll., 1977. V.p. fin. E. R. Squibb & Sons, Princeton, N.J., 1969-83; sr. v.p., chief fin. officer, dir. Squibb Corp., Princeton, N.J., 1983-89; sr. v.p., contr. Bristol-Myers Squibb Co., N.Y.C., 1990; sr. v.p., CFO, Reader's Digest, Pleasantville, N.Y., 1990-95; sr. v.p., CFO Olin Corp., Norwalk, Conn., 1995-99, exec. v.p., CFO, 1999—, also bd. dirs.; dir. Primex Techs., Inc., St. Petersburg, Fla. Recipient Statistics award Am. Statis Assn., 1963. Mem. Fin. Execs. Inst. (CFO adv. coun.). Office: Olin Co PO Box 4500 Norwalk CT 06856-4500

RUGGIERO, DAVID A., neuroscientist; b. N.Y.C., May 2, 1949; s. Armand George and Margaret T. (Mirra) R.; m. Anke L. Nolting, Feb. 11, 1948. BA in Biology, Queens Coll., 1972; MA/MPhil in Human Anatomy, Columbia U., 1976, PhD in Neuroanatomy, 1977. Established investigator cert., Am. Heart Assn. Lab. instr. Coll. Physicians and Surgeons Columbia U., N.Y.C., 1974-76, 78-79; dir. and lectr. neurosci. and gross anatomy N.Y. Coll. Podiatric Medicine, N.Y.C., 1976-77; postdoctoral fellow dept. neurology Cornell U. Med. Coll., N.Y.C., 1977-79, lectr. in neurosci., 1979-80, instr. dept. neurology, 1980-81, asst. prof. dept. neurology, 1981-88, assoc. prof. neurology and neurosci., 1988-97; prof. anatomy, cell biology and psychiatry Columbia U. Med. Coll., 1998—; dir. Neurol. Rsch. Inst. of Lubec, Maine, 1993—; cons. Vets. Health Svcs. and Rsch. Adminstrn., 1990—, NSF, 1990—; mem. adv. com. Nat. Inst. on Drug Abuse, 1990, Mayo Clinic, 1996—; mem. instnl. animal care and use com. Cornell U. Med. Coll., 1988-97, Columbia U. Med. Coll., 1998—; mem. study sects. drug abuse, biomed. rsch. rev. com. Am. Heart Assn., 1987, 89; vis. prof. dept. physiology and pharmacology SUNY Health Sci. Ctr., 1998—. Contbr. over 100 articles to profl. publs. Dir. of judges Manhattan Sci. Fair, N.Y.C., 1990. Recipient Harriet Ames award N.Y. Heart Assn., 1979, cert. honor N.Y. State Westinghouse Talent Search, 1993, Neurosci. prize Am. Acad. of Neurology, 1996; named established investigator Am. Heart Assn., 1985-89; grantee NIH, 1980-96, 97—, Am. Heart Assn., 1988-91. Mem. Internat. Brain Rsch. Orgn., Am. Soc. Hypertension, Am. Assn. Anatomists, Am. Soc. Peripheral Nerve Injury, Soc. for Neurosci., Soc. for Neurosci. Rapid Response Network, Ea. Hypertension Soc., N.Y. Heart Assn., Columbia U. Alumni Assn., Sigma Xi. E-mail: david@neuron.cpmc.columbia.edu. Home: 35 Main St Lubec ME 04652-1010 Office: Columbia U Coll Physicians & Surgeons 1051 Riverside Dr # 42 New York NY 10032-1013

RUGGIERO, MARCO, molecular biologist, researcher, educator; b. Florence, Tuscany, Italy, Jan. 19, 1956; s. Aldo and Laura (Nicastro) R.; children: Carolina Kumiko, Filippo. MD, U. Florence, 1980, PhD in Molecular Biology, 1987; Specialist in Radiology, U. Siena, Italy, 1996. Intern Florence Gen. Hosp., 1980-81; scientist Burroughs Wellcome Co., Research Triangle Park, N.C., 1984-87, NIH, Bethesda, Md., 1987-89; rsch. leader Sigma Pharm., Milan, 1989-91; prof. molecular biology U. Florence, 1992—; dir. Studio Radiologico, Ruggiero, Studio Radiologico Pratese. Contbr. more than 120 articles to profl. jours. Lt. Italian Army, 1982-83. E-mail: sivispacem@yahoo.com. Office: Dept Exptl Path/Oncology, Viale Morgagni 50, 50134 Florence Italy

RÜHL, WERNER, physicist, educator; b. Remscheid, Germany, July 25, 1937; s. Karl and Emmy (Parr) R.; m. Erika Kemper, Apr. 1, 1961; children: Ute, Roland, Dorothee. PhD in Theoretical Physics, U. Cologne, 1962. Rsch. asst. Univ. Cologne, 1961-64; rsch. assoc. CERN, Geneva, Switzerland, 1964-66, Rockefeller U., N.Y., 1966-67; mem. staff CERN, Geneva, 1967-70; prof. U. Kaiserslautern, Germany, 1970—. Author: The Lorentz Group and Harmonic Analysis, 1970. Mem. Internat. Assn. Math. Physics. Office: U Kaiserslautern, PO Box 3049, 67653 Kaiserslautern Germany

RUHLIN, PEGGY MILLER, investment adviser, financial planner; b. Dayton, Ohio, May 20, 1949; d. Charles Raymond and Shirlee E. (Menke) Miller; m. John B. Ruhlin Jr., June 19, 1982; 1 child, Megan Falla. BA magna cum laude, Otterbein Coll., 1979. CPA, Ohio; Cert. fin. planner. Acct. Borden, Inc., Columbus, Ohio, 1971-72; mgr. Intraspace Planning Group, Inc., Columbus, Ohio, 1972-74; v.p. Mgmt. Media, Inc., Columbus, Ohio, 1974-80, pres., 1980-87; prin. Budros & Ruhlin, Inc., Columbus, Ohio, 1987—; adj. prof. Franklin U., Columbus, 2000—; mem. nat. adv. bd./coun. Schwab Instl., 1994-95; mem. Vanguard Group Investment Adv. Coun., 1996-97. Columnist Bus. First of Greater Columbus, 1986; commentator Sta. WCBE-FM, 1989-91, 95; contbr. articles to profl. jours. Named One of Best Fin. Advisors in U.S. Worth mag., 1996—, One of Best Fin. Advisors for Drs., Med. Econs. mag., 1998, 2000. Mem. AICPA, Assn. for Investment Mgmt. and Rsch., Fin. Planning Assn. (chpt. pres. 1989-91, nat. bd. dirs. 1992-98, pres. 96-97, chair 1997-98), Nat. Assn . Personal Fin. Advisers (Fin. Planner of Yr. award 1988), Internat. Women's Forum. Office: Budros & Ruhlin Inc 1650 Lake Shore Dr Ste 150 Columbus OH 43204-4942

RUHLMAN, HERMAN C(LOYD), JR., manufacturing company executive; b. Warren, Pa., Jan. 17, 1949; s. Herman Cloyd and Virginia Lee (Wimer) R.; divorced; children: Brian, Jason, Chad; m. Lorraine; stepchildren: Bethany, Michelle, Randy. BS in Indsl. Tech., Calif. (Pa.) State Coll., 1974. Gen. mgr. Rand Machine Products, Inc., Falconer, N.Y., 1974-80, pres., chmn. bd. dirs., 1980—; pres. Spartan Tool Co., Gerry, N.Y., 1986—. Active local Boy Scouts Am. With USAF, 1968-72. Mem. Epsilon Pi Tau. Republican. Home: PO Box 284 15 Annis St Frewsburg NY 14738-9564 Office: PO Box 72 Allen St Extension Falconer NY 14733

RUICHEK, YASSINE, physician, educator; b. Marrakech, Haovz, Morocco, Sept. 10, 1969; arrived in France, 1989; s. Rhali and Ouardia (Bellata) R.; m. Jamila El Boutaybi, Oct. 23, 1999. M in Math. Engring., Paul Sabatier U., Toulouse, France, 1992, DEA in Computer Engring., 1993; PhD in Ant. and Computer Engring., U. Lille (France) 1, 1997. Qualified computer sci., computer engring. rschr., tchr., CNU. Postdoctoral staff GRASP Lab., Phila., 1997-98; asst. prof. Lab. Ant. 13D, Lille, 1998-99, U. Bretagne Occidentale, Brest, France, 1999—; cons. EANN Conf., Helsinki, London, 1995-96, Pattern Recognition Letters Jour., 1996, Neural Sys. Jour., 1997, Real Time Imaging Jour., 1997. Authro: Road Vehicle Automation, 1997; contbr. articles to profl. jours. Avocations: soccer, traveling, reading, computer programming. Office: U Bretagne Occidentale, UFR Scis Dept Info BP 809, 29285 Brest France

RUIGROK, JAAP, electrical engineer, researcher; b. Leiden, The Netherlands, Jan. 6, 1951; s. Cor and Annabet (Jongmans) R.; m. Ada Hop, Nov. 6, 1975; children: Imke, Elmer, Anouk, Jorrit, Renske, Sven. BSc in Electronic and Radio Engring., H.T.S. voor Radiotechniek en Elektronika, Haarlem, The Netherlands, 1971; BSEE, H.T.S., The Hague, The Netherlands, 1973; MSc cum laude, Delft (The Netherlands) U., 1979; PhD, U Twente, Enschede, The Netherlands, 1988. Scientist Philips Rsch. Labs., Eindhoven, The Netherlands, 1979-91, sr. scientist, 1992-96, rsch. fellow, 1997—. Author: Short-wavelength Magnetic Recording, 1990; contbr. articles on thermally assisted rec., magnetic rec. and heads, photolithography and magnetic bubbles to sci. jours.; numerous inventions on magnetic heads; one of main inventors of digital compact cassette tech. Avocations: fitness, swimming, painting, soccer, do-it-yourself projects. Home: Margrietstraat 9, 5721 ZW Asten The Netherlands Office: Philips Rsch Labs, Prof Holstlaan 4, 5656 AA Eindhoven The Netherlands

RUIN, OLOF KRISTIAN, political science educator; b. Helsinki, Finland, Nov. 8, 1927; arrived in Sweden, 1945; s. Hans Waldemar and Karin (Sievers) R.; m. Inger Elsa Björck, Feb. 8, 1958; children: Hans, Påhl, Klas. BA, U. Lund, Sweden, 1948, MA, 1954, PhD, 1960. Editl. writer Dagens Nyheter, Stockholm, 1957-58; sec. royal com. Ministry of Edn., Stockholm, 1960-62; assoc. prof. Stockholm U., 1962-69, prof., 1970-93; dep. chancellor Swedish Univs. and Colls., Stockholm, 1978-79; vis. prof. Mich. U., Ann Arbor, 1971-72, U. Calif., Berkeley, 1981, 91; dean Stockholm U., 1974-84; chmn. Swedish Futures Studies Inst., Stockholm, 1987-95, Swedish Found. for Internat. Cooperation in Rsch. and Higher Edn., 1999; pres. Swedish Rsch. Coun. for Humanities and Social Scis., 1995-97; pres. several royal coms. on constl. matters; mem. high coun. European Univ. Inst., Florence, 1997—. Author books and articles in field. Recipient Disting. Svc. to Soc. award Royal Soc. ProPatria, 1996, His Majesty the King's Golden medal, 1997. Mem. Finnish Acad. Scis., Royal Acad. Letters, History and Antiquities. Mem. Social Dem. Party. Home: Villavägen 8 R, 182 79 Stocksund Sweden Office: Stockholm U, Dept Polit Sci, 10691 Stockholm Sweden

RUINI, CAMILLO CARDINAL, archbishop; b. Sassuolo, Italy, Feb. 19, 1931. With titular Ch. of St. Agnes; vicar gen. of Rome, titular bishop of Nepte, archbishop, 1991—, elevated to Sacred Coll. Cardinals, 1991. Office: Diocese Roman Cath Ch, P San Giovanni Laterano 4, 00184 Rome Italy*

RUISECO, JUAN MANUEL, cement company executive; b. Medellin, Colombia, July 22, 1932; s. Joaquin and Maria (Vieira) R.; m. Cecilia Gutierrez, Feb. 2, 1960; children: Maria Cecilia, Ana Cristina, Juan Manuel, Nicolas, Carolina. BSME, Marquette U., 1956; postgrad., Allis Chalmers, West Allis, Wis., 1957. Pres. Cementos Del Caribe, S.A., Barranquilla, Colombia, 1971—, also bd. dirs., 1957—; cons. bd. dirs. Cales y Cementos de Tolubiejo S.A., 1972—; pres. El Cerrejon Carboneras Ltd., 1972-73, Promotora de Siderurgicas de Colombia, 1972-73; promotor, pres. Compania Colombiana de Clinker S.A., 1974—; dir. Compania Colombiana de Carburos y Derivados S.A., Gas Natural Corp., Promigas, Pres. Inst. Colombiano de Adminstrn., 1967-68; chmn. Cia. SurAmericana de Seguros, Medellin, 1991; pres. Carbones Del Caribe, Barranquilla, 1991—, Compañia de Cemento Argos S.A., 1999; others. Hon. consul Belgium, 1975—, Finland, 1968—. Mem. Cia. De Cementos Argos (bd. dirs. 1988—). Liberal. Roman Catholic. Avocations: aviation, fishing, reading. E-mail: jmruiseco@grupoargos.com. Home: Apt 1501, Carrera 23 No 10B-91, Medellin Colombia Office: Compania de Cemento Argos, Carrero 46 No 56-11 Piso 15, Medellin Colombia

RUIZ, ANA ESTHER, zoology educator, researcher; b. Córdoba, Argentina, Mar. 9, 1958; d. César Enrique and Estela (Oberti) R.; m. Ricardo Ruben Fondacaro, Nov. 12, 1982; children: José Francisco, Maria Estela, César Rubén, Sebastián Pablo. Bachelor, Garzón Agulla, Córdoba, 1975; tchr. cert., Nat. U., Córdoba, 1982, biologist, 1983. Tchr. biology Poly. Sch., Rawson, Argentina, 1983-86; asst. prof. dept. biology Nat. U. Patagonia, Trelew, Argentina, 1986-90, prof., 1990—; mem. Commn. Hake Closed Season, Argentina, 1995-98. Contbr. articles to sci. jours. Mem. Argentine Assn. Natural Scis. (study of Pategonian Freshwater Silverside). Fax: 54-2965-481746. E-mail: fohru@cpsarg.com. Home: 9 de Julio 89, 9103 Rawson Chubut, Argentina Office: Nat U La Patagonia Biology, Roca 115, 9100 Trelew Chubut, Argentina

RUIZ, JAVIER, sales executive; b. Barcelona, Spain, Oct. 2, 1958; s. Justo and Fina (Zafon) R.; m. Paquita Blancher, Aug. 8, 1986; 1 child, Rita. B of Law, UAB, Barcelona, Spain, 1980; MBA, ESMA, Barcelona, Spain, 1986. Jud. tech. Mutua Gen., Barcelona, Spain, 1981-82, mktg. mgr., 1982-87, asst. dir., 1988-91; adminstr. Previsora Gen., Barcelona, Spain, 1988-91; mktg. mgr. Grupo Mistral, Barcelona, Spain, 1991-95, asst. dir., 1995—; instr. Mutua Gen., 1988-91, Grupo Mistral, 1991-98. Avocations: travel, reading, writing, paintings. Home: Muntaner 506 5 3, 08022 Barcelona Spain Office: Grupo Mistral SA, Avda Paisos Catalans 36, 08950 Barcelona Spain

RUIZ, JOSE FRANKLIN, health facility administrator, researcher; b. Bogota, Colombia, Feb. 17, 1956. MD, Nat. U., Colombia, 1982, MSc in Pharmacology, 1988. With new products devel. Chalver Corp., Colombia, 1988-91; med. dir. Grünenthal, Bogota, 1992—; asst. prof. pharmacology Nat. U. Medicine, 1995—. Editor Colombian Bull. Pharmacology, 1994—, Pharmacology Basis, 1996—. E-mail: franklin.ruiz@grunenthal.com. Home: CLe 151 # 29-20, Bogota Colombia Office: Grünenthal Colombiana, CLe 93 # 16-20, Bogota Colombia

RUIZ, ROBERT, physician, researcher, educator; b. Toulouse, France, May 10, 1964; s. Emile and Aurore Quirina (De la Mata) R.; m. Marie-Jeanne Delmond, Oct. 29, 1988 (div. Oct. 1995); 1 child, Mathilde. MSc, U. Paul Sabatier, Toulouse, 1986, PhD, 1991. Maitre de confs. U. Toulouse-Le Mirail, 1994—; head of sound sect. Ecole Sup. Audiovisuel, Toulouse, 1995—. Contbr. articles to profl. jours. Recipient award of Young Rschr. in Acoustics, 1992. Mem. French Soc. Acoustics, Acoustical Soc. Am., Audio Engring. Soc. Avocation: trekking. Home: 25 rue Eugene d'Hautpoul, 31400 Toulouse France Office: U Toulouse-Le Mirail/LARA, 5 Allees Antonio Machado, 31058 Toulouse France

RUIZ, ULISES, medical educator; b. Madrid, Feb. 7, 1933; s. Antonio and Encarnacion (Ferrandiz) R.; m. Liliane Loridan (div. 1982); children: David, Jaime, Elena; m. Mar Sanz (div. 1994); children: Vanesa, Violeta; m. MaAngeles Villanua. B in Philosophy, U. Poitiers, 1952; MD, Complutense U., 1958, PhD, 1983. Asst. prof. surgery Complutense U., Madrid, 1960-62; internship SUNY-Bklyn. Jewish Hosp., 1962-63; residency surgery Harvard-Beth Israel Hosp., Boston, 1964-67; assoc. prof. Complutense U. Inst. for Health Care Assessment, 1994; rsch. fellow Nat. Health Svc., Boston, 1963-64, 67-68; residency pediatric surgery Tufts-Nemch Floating Hosp., Boston, 1968-70; asst. prof. surgery Tufts Med. Sch., Boston, 1970-72; head pediatric surgery Hosp. Cruces, Bilbao, Spain, 1972—; invited assoc. prof. surgery SUNY, Stony Brook, 1982-83; CEO Insalud Hosp., Spain, 1983-85; head quality improvement plan Spanish Health Care Sys., Ministry Health and Consumer Affairs, 1985-93; mem. Nat. Bd. Pediatric Surgery, Madrid, 1986-92; assessor WHO, Copenhagen, 1989-93; expert European Union Commn., Brussels, 1989-92. Editor: Guidelines for Hospital Infection Control, 1991; author: Total Quality Plan for the Health Care System-1st Phase, 1986; coauthor: Guidelines for Self-Assessment of Healthcare Organizations, 1996; contbr. articles to profl. jours. Advisor healthcare Pres. Basque Gert., Bilbao, 1979—; rep. local govt. Hosp. Bd. Trustees, Bilbao, 1979-83; Spanish rep. COMAC-HSR D6XII, Brussels, 1987-91. Grantee Spanish Coun. Scientific Rsch., 1961, 89-91. Fellow ACS; mem. Spanish Assn. Quality (chmn. healthcare and edn. sects. 1991-93), Am. Soc. Quality (internat. counselor health care divsn.). Avocations: painting, horseback riding, sailing. E-mail: urives@eucmos.sim.ucm.es. Office: U Inst Healthcare Assessmen, Complutense U Med Sch, 28040 Madrid Spain

RUIZ-CRUCES, RAFAEL, radiology and medical physics educator, consultant; b. Malaga, Spain, Apr. 13, 1963; m. Mabel Fernandez, Apr. 23, 1994; 1 child, Ignacio Ruiz-Cruces Fernandez. Med. Degree, U. Malaga, 1988, MD, 1994. Assoc. prof. U. Malaga, 1989-94; radiologist Univ. Hosp., Malaga, 1990-93; asst. prof. U. Malaga, 1995-97, prof. radiology, 1998—; cons. on radiation protection IAEA, Vienna, 1998—; dir. X-ray Inst. Nuclear Safety Coun., Madrid, 1991; asst. dir. Group PRVMA, Malaga, 1990—; pres. IAEA Internat. Conf., Malaga. Referee jour. Physics in Medicine and Biology, U.K., 1999—; contbr. articles to profl. jours. Mem. European Radiology Soc., Spanisch Radiology Soc., Spanish Radiation Protection Soc. Roman Catholic. Avocations: sport activities (soccer, tennis, table tennis), travel, computers. Office: Radiology/Med Physics Dept, Sch Med/Campus of Teatinos, E-29071 Malaga Spain

RUIZ DE LA HERRAN, JOSE ANTONIO, engineering executive; b. Mexico D.F., Mex., Dec. 16, 1925; s. Jose Maria and Victoria (Villagomez) R.; m. Matilde Del Rio, Oct. 21 1949 (div. 1950); children: Jose, Mario. Ingenieria mecanica y electrica, Unam Mexico, 1958. Dir. of engring. Xew Radio Sta., Mexico, 1943-52, Televicentro, Mexico, 1950-60; chief prodn. metalurgist Campos Hnos., Mexico, 1960-71; designer 2 Mts. Telescope, Inst. Astronomia, Mexico, 1972-80; rsch. in reheating Centro de Instrumentos, Mexico, 1981-90; tech. cons. Museo U., Mexico, 1990-98; dir. rsch. FAGSA, Mexico, 1999—; tech. dir. Cicesa Inc., Mexico, 1952-67; cons. CCC, Mexico, 1986—, INAOE, Tonantzintla, Puebla, 1998; pres. Somedicyt, Mex., 1997. Author: Constuya Usted Su Propio Telescopio, 1992; editor: Mexico Y La Astronomia, 1994; editor Informacion Cientifica y Tecnologica. Recipient Premio Nacional de Ciencias y Artes, Mexican Govt., 1983, Sam. Sociedad Astronomica de Mex., 1987. Mem. IEEE (sr.), SME (sr.), SPIE, others. Roman Catholic. Home: Berlin 308 El Carmen, Coyocan, 4100 Mexico City Mexico

RUIZ-JARABO COLOMER, DÁMASO, international justice; b. 1949. Judge Consejo Gen. del Poder Judicial; prof. law; head Pvt. Officeof Pres. of Consejo Gen. del Poder Judicial; ad hoc judge European Ct. of Human Rights; judge Tribunal Supremo, 1996—; advocate gen. Ct. of Justice of European Cmtys., Luxembourg, 1995—. Office: Ct Justice European Cmtys, Palais de Cour de justice, Kirchberg L-2925, Luxembourg*

RUIZ SACRISTÁN, CARLOS, Mexican government official; b. Mexico City, Oct. 27, 1949. BA in Bus. Adminstrn., Anahuac U., 1972; MA in Fin., Northwestern U., Chgo., 1974. From chief of currency exch. to mgr. internat. ops. Bank of Mex., 1974-86; dir. Commn. on Exch. Rate Risk Ins., 1986-88; gen. dir. pub. credit Secretarian of Fin. and Pub. Credit, 1988-92, dep. sec. expenditures, 1992-94; dir. Gen. Mex. Petroleum "Pemex", 1994; sec. comm. and transport Govt. Mex., 1994—. Office: Xola esq Av Universidad, Cuerpo c 1er piso, 03028 Mexico City Mexico*

RUIZ-ZÚÑIGA, ANGEL, historian, philosopher of science, mathematician, educator; b. San Jose, Costa Rica, Oct. 11, 1954; s. Gerardo and Cecilia (Zúniga) Ruiz-Casas; m. Susanne Blais, Feb. 4, 1986; children: Julien, Sebastian. BS in Math., U. Costa Rica, San Jose, 1975, Lic. in Math., 1978, MA in Philosophy, 1986. Prof. U. Costa Rica, San Jose, 1975—, dir. Rsch. Ctr. on Math. and Meta-Math.; advisor for univ. devel. and nat. policies. Contbr. more than 150 articles to profl. jours.; author more than 30 books. Mem. steering com. Socialist Worker's Orgn., Costa Rica, 1976-80, People's Action Party, Costa Rica, 1980-82. Recipient Jorge Volio Philosophy award, 1995; winner essay contests. Mem. Colegio de Licenciados Y Profesores, Costa Rican Assn. Math., Latin Am. Pugwash Group, Costa Rican Assn. History and Philosophy of Sci. (chmn. 1983—), Grupo de Estudio Rodrigo Facio (chmn. 1988—), Inter-Am. Com. on Math. Edn. (sec. 1987—), Latin Am. Soc. of History of Sci. and Tech. (exec. com. 1988—). Avocations: music, films, reading, poetry, wine. Home: Apdo 1385-2100 Guadalupe, San Jose Costa Rica Office: U Costa Rica, Sch Math, San Jose Costa Rica

RUKAVINA, DANIEL, immunology and physiology educator; b. Sarajevo, Croatia, Feb. 22, 1937; s. Mile and Magdalena (Kresic) R.; m. Ida Zaputovic, May 27, 1972; 1 child, Milan. MD, Med. Faculty, Zagreb, Croatia, 1962; MSc, Med. Faculty, Rijeka, Croatia, 1968; DSc, U. Zagreb, 1972. Asst. prof. Med. Faculty, Rijeka, 1962-73, univ. docent, 1973-76, assoc. prof., 1976-81; prof. Med. Faculty, 1981—; vice dean Med. Faculty, 1977-79, 87-90, dean, 1983-87; prof. pathology, U. Pitts., 1989-97; pres. Assn. of Med. Faculties, former Yugoslavia, 1985-88; organizer, chmn., invited spkr. numerous presentations. Contbr. numerous 210 articles to profl. jours. and publs. (Ruder Boskovic state award Rep. of Croatia for Sci. 1985, award City of Rijeka 1987, others); mem. editl. bd. Am. Jour. Reproductive Immunology, Early Pregnancy Biol. and Med., Regional Immunology. Recipient award and medal Union of Physiol. Soc. of former Yugoslavia, 1988, award Acad. Sci. and Arts, Republic of Croatia, 1998, award Govt. of Austria, 1998. Mem. Alps Adria Soc. for Immunology of Reprodn. (pres. 1994-97, hon. pres. 1997), Internat. Soc. Reproductive Immunology (pres. VIII congress), Transplantation Soc. Achievements include scientific contbns. to the field of immunology of reprodn. and clin. immunology and transplantation. Office: Med Faculty/Univ Rijeka, B Branchetta 20, 51000 Rijeka Croatia

RUKEYSER, LOUIS RICHARD, economic commentator; b. N.Y.C., Jan. 30, 1933; s. Merryle Stanley and Berenice Helene (Simon) R.; m. Alexandra Gill, Mar. 3, 1962; children: Beverley Jane, Susan Athena, Stacy Alexandra. AB, Princeton U., 1954; LittD (hon.), N.H. Coll., 1975; LLD (hon.), Moravian Coll., 1978, Mercy Coll., 1984, Am. U., 1991; DBA (hon.), Southeastern Mass. U., 1979; LHD (hon.), Loyola Coll., 1982, Johns Hopkins U., 1986, Western Md. Coll., 1992; D of Fin. (hon.), Roger Williams U., 1997. Reporter Balt. Sun newspapers, 1954-65; chief polit. corr. Evening Sun, 1957-59; chief London bur. The Sun, 1959-63, chief Asian corr., 1963-65; sr. corr., commentator ABC News, 1965-73, Paris corr., 1965-66, chief London bur., 1966-68, econ. editor, commentator, 1968-73; host Wall St. Week With Louis Rukeyser PBS-TV, 1970—; nationally syndicated econ. columnist McNaught Syndicate, 1976-86, Tribune Media Services, 1986-93; frequent lectr. Author: How to Make Money in Wall Street, 1974, 2d edit., 1976 (Literary Guild selection 1974, 76), What's Ahead for the Economy: The Challenge and the Chance, 1983, 2d edit., 1985 (Literary Guild selection 1984), Louis Rukeyser's Business Almanac, 1988, 2d edit., 1991, Louis Rukeyser's Book of Lists, 1997, Right on the Money, 1998; editor-in-chief monthly newsletters, Louis Rukeyser's Wall Street, 1992—, Louis Rukeyser's Mutual Funds, 1994—. With U.S. Army, 1954-56. , Recipient Overseas Press Club award, 1963, Overseas Press Club citation, 1964, G.M. Loeb award U. Conn., 1972, Janus award for excellence in fin. news programming, 1975, George Washington Honor medal Freedoms Found., 1972, 78, N.Y. Fin. Writers Assn. award, 1980, Free Enterprise Man of the Yr. award Tex. A&M U. Ctr. for Edn. and Research in Free Enterprise, 1987, Women's Econ. Round Table award, 1990, 1st Hero of Wall Street award The Mus. of Am. Fin. History, 1998. Fin. Planning Assn. N.Y. (Malcolm S. Forbes Pub. Awareness award for Excellence in Advancing Fin. Understanding 2000). Office: 586 Round Hill Rd Greenwich CT 06831-2724

RUKHIN, ANDREW LEO, mathematics and statistics educator; b. Leningrad, USSR, Oct. 1, 1946; came to U.S., 1977; s. Lev Borisovich and Eugenia Rukhin; m. Natalie Vyshkind, Aug. 4, 1973 (div. June 1989); children: Eugenia, Andrey; m. Albina V. Afinogenova, Dec. 31, 1996. MS in Math., Leningrad State U., 1967; PhD in Stats., Steklov Math. Inst., Leningrad, 1970. Rsch. assoc. Steklov Math. Inst., 1970-74; prof. math. Purdue U., West Lafayette, Ind., 1977-87, U. Mass., Amherst, 1987-89; prof. math. and stats. U. Md., Balt., 1989—; math. statistician, NIST, Gaithersburg, Md., 1994—. Contbr. over 150 articles to profl. jours. and conf. procs. Recipient Sr. Disting. Scientist award von Humboldt Stiftung, Germany,, 1990, W.J. Youden award in interlab. testing, Am. Statis. Assn., 1998. Fellow Inst. Math. Stats., Am. Statis. Assn. E-mail: rukhin@math.umbc.edu. Office: U Md Baltimore Campus Dept Math 1000 Hilltop Cir Baltimore MD 21250-0001

RUKODZI, PATRICK SANIRO, accountant, secretary; b. Harare, Zimbabwe, June 25, 1954; s. Kenneth Chamunorwa and Ennie Chengetai (Kunaka) R.; m. Rosemary Masora, Feb. 28, 1957; children: Kenneth, Tafirenyika, Tapiwa, Nyasha. Accts. clk. Lewis Contrsn. Co., Zimbabwe, 1975-79; acct. Waddilove Inst., Zimbabwe, 1980-81; fin. contr. Jairos Jiri Assn., Zimbabwe, 1981-90; gen. mgr. Mambo Press, Zimbabwe, 1990-99; adminstrv. dir. St. Giles Med. Rehab. Ctr., 1999—; sec. Moto mag., Zimbabwe, 1995—; bd. dirs. Jairos Jim Assn., 1990—, Summit Ins. Co., 1997—. Treas. St. Mary's Cath. Ch., Gweru, Zimbabwe, 1994-98, Jairos Jiri Sch. for Deaf, Gweru, 1994—. Mem. Inst. Comml. Mgmt., Rotary Club Gweru (pres. 1998—). Roman Catholic. Home: PO Box GV61 Glenview, Harare Zimbabwe Office: PO Box A224 Avondale, Harare Zimbabwe

RUMAKER, MICHAEL, writer, English educator; b. Phila., Mar. 5, 1932; s. Michael Joseph and Winifred Marvel Rumaker. Honors degree in writing,

Black Mountain Coll., 1955; MFA, Columbia U., 1970. Lectr. writing New Sch. for Social Rsch., N.Y.C., 1967-71; tchr. writer, mem. intellectual resources pool Tappan Zee H.S., Orangeburg, N.Y., 1965-69; instr. writing workshops Rockland Ctr. for Arts, West Nyack, N.Y., 1975-78; adj. lectr. Rockland C.C., Suffern, N.Y., 1978-87; writer-in-residence CCNY, CUNY, 1969-71, adj. prof., 1985—. Author: (novels) The Butterfly, 1962 (English edit. 1968), A Day and a Night at the Baths, 1979 (German edit. 1997), My First Satyrnalia, 1981, To Kill a Cardinal, 1992, Pagan Days, 2000, (short stories) Gringos and Other Stories, 1967, 2nd edit., 1991 (German edit. 1968, English edit. (Exit 3) 1966), (memoir) Robert Duncan in San Francisco, 1996. Mem. Nat. Writers Union. E-mail: mr6213@mail.tco.com. Home: 42 6th Ave Apt 2 Nyack NY 10960-1601 Office: Harold Ober Assocs 425 Madison Ave Rm 1001 New York NY 10017-1183

RUMANE, ABDUL RAZZAK ABDUL REHMAN, electrical engineer, consultant; b. Chandve, India, June 8, 1948; s. Abdul Rehman Hasan and Rabia (Godme Rabia) R.; m. Noor Jehan Abdul Razzak Godme; children: Ataullah, Farzeen. BE, Govt. Engring. Coll., Aurangabad, India, 1972; diploma in Modern Mgmt., Brit. Career Tng. Coll., 1981; diploma in Internat. Trade, Brit. Mgmt. Assn., 1982. Trainee engr. Electro Sales, Mumbai, India, 1972-73; asst. officer Ruttonsha Electronics, Mumbai, 1973-76; asst. engr. Mandovi Pellets Ltd., Mumbai, 1976-79; engr. Crompton Greeves Ltd., Mumbai, 1979-80; officer Dynacraft Machines Co. Ltd., Mumbai, 1980-81; officer, engr. Toyo Engring. India Ltd., Mumbai, 1981-83; elec. engr. Mansour Al Subai Est., Kuwait, 1983-84, Abdullah Al Otaibi Est., Kuwait, 1984-86, Jassim Shaban & Sons Co., Kuwait, 1986-90, Al Othman Ctr. for Archtl. and Engring. Design, Al Khobar, Saudi Arabia, 1991; sr. elec. engr. Pan Arab Cons. Engrs., Bahrain, Kuwait, 1991-99, Dar Al Handasah, Kuwait, 1999—. Fellow Instn. Engrs. India; mem. IEEE (sr.), ASCE, Kuwait Soc. Engrs. E-mail: rarazak@yahoo.com. Home: PO Box 5020, Salmiya 22061, Kuwait Office: Dar Al Handasah, PO Box 1938, Safat 13020, Kuwait

RUMBAUGH, CHARLES EARL, arbitrator, mediator, educator, lawyer, speaker; b. San Bernardino, Calif., Mar. 11, 1943; s. Max Elden and Gertrude Maude (Gulker) R.; m. Christina Carol Pinder, Mar. 2, 1968; children: Eckwood, Cynthia, Aaron, Heather. BS, UCLA, 1966; JD, Calif. Western Sch. Law, 1971; cert. in advanced mgmt., U. So. Calif., 1993. Bar: Calif. 1972, U.S. Dist. Ct. (cen. dist.) Calif. U.S. Ct. Appeals (9th cir.), U.S. Supreme Ct. Engr. Westinghouse Electric Corp., Balt., 1966-68; legal counsel Calif. Dept. of Corps., L.A., 1971-77; legal counsel Hughes Aircraft Co., L.A., 1977-84, asst. to corp. dir. contracts, 1984-89, asst. to corp. v.p. contracts, 1989-95; corp. dir. contracts/pricing Lear Astronics Corp., 1995-97; pres. Ctr. for Conflict Resolution, 1998-99; arbitrator, mediator, comml., govt. contracts, internat. law, franchise, securities, torts, personal injury, real estate and constrn. panels Am. Arbitration Assn., L.A. and San Francisco; mem. arbitration and mediation panels ArbitrationWorks (formerly Arbitration and Mediation Internat.), 1994—, Nat. Assn. Security Dealers, Franchise Arbitration & Mediation Inc., Construction ADR, L.A. County Superior Ct., Santa Barbara County Superior Ct.; spkr. in field; mem. panel pvt. alt. dispute resolution neutrals U.S. Ct. Fed. Claims; mem. armed svcs. bd. of contract appeals panel of pvt. alt. dispute resolution neutrals, DLA panel of dispute neutrals, also settlement officer U.S. Dist. Ct.; mem. alternative dispute resolution panel World Bank. Mem. editl. bd. Nat. Contract Mgmt. Jour., 1996-00; contbr. articles to profl. jours. Counselor Boy Scouts Am., L.A., 1976—; mem. City of Palos Verdes Estates (Calif.) Citizen's Planning Com., 1986-90; judge pro tem L.A. County Superior Ct., L.A., 1991—. Fellow Nat. Contract Mgmt. Assn. (founder, chmn. alt. dispute resolution com., cert. profl. contracts mgr., nat. bd. advisors, nat. v.p. southwestern region 1993-95, nat. dir. 1992-93, pres. L.A./South Bay chpt. 1991-92, Fellow of Yr. award 1994); mem. ABA (dispute resolution sect., forum on franchising, forum on constrn. industry, pub. contract law sect.), Nat. Assn. Purchasing Mgmt. (chair acquisition info.), Calif. Dispute Resolution Coun. (cons. to qualifications com. 1997-99), Nat. Def. Indsl. Assn. (vice-chmn. west coast legal subcom. 1994—), Fed. Bar Assn. (pres. Beverly Hills chpt. 1992-93), State Bar Calif. (franchise law com. 1992-95, 1999—, Wiley W. Manual award 1992), LA County Bar Assn., South Bay Bar Assn., Soc. Profls. in Dispute Resolution (chmn. internat. sector com. 1996-00, past bd. dirs. L.A. chpt.), Aerospace Industries Assn. (chmn. procurement techniques com. 1987-88, 93-94), Christian Legal Soc. Avocations: camping, skiing, jogging, equestrian. Office: PO Box 2636 Rolling Hills Estates CA 90274

RUMBAUGH, MAX ELDEN, JR., professional society administrator; b. Ada, Okla., Dec. 11, 1937; s. Max E. and Gertrude (Gulker) R.; m. Joan E. Brockway; children: Maria Rumbaugh Gross, Max E. III. BS in Engring., U.S. Mil. Acad., 1960; MS in Engring. Scis., Purdue U., 1965, MBA, 1972. Instr. Purdue U., West Lafayette, Ind., 1964-65; corp. officer Midwest Applied Sci. Corp., West Lafayette, 1965-72; chief engr. advanced tech. Schwitzer div. Wallace-Murray Corp., Indpls., 1972-77, dir. research, 1977-81; mgr. engring. activities div. Soc. Automotive Engrs., Warrendale, Pa., 1981-84, v.p., asst. gen. mgr., 1984-86, exec. v.p., 1986—; pres. Performance Rev. Inst., 1991—; pres. Soc. Rsch. Adminstrs. Internat., 1973-74; chmn. Ind. sect. Soc. Automotive Engrs., 1978-79; bd. dirs., exec. com. Am. Nat. Standards Inst., N.Y.C., 1986—; bd. dirs. Intelligent Transp. Soc. of Am., 1992—, mem. exec. com., 1998—. Author mag. column Focus, 1986—. Bd. dirs. Jr. Achievement Western Pa., Pitts., 1986-98, YMCA, North Hills, Pitts., 1985-94; sec. Intelligent Transp. Soc. Am. Bd. Dirs., 2000—. 1st lt. U.S. Army, 1960-63,. Mem. ASME, Am. Soc. Assn. Execs., Coun. Engring. and Sci. Soc. Execs. (bd. dirs. 1990-97, sec. 1993-94, v.p. 1994-95, pres. 1995-96), Russian Internat. Acad. Engring., Intelligent Transp. Soc. Am. (sec. 2000—), Russian Acad. Quality Problems, Rotary (bd. dirs. 1982-84, 93-97, v.p. 1994-95, pres. 1995-96). Avocations: skiing, photography. Home: 320 Fort Duquesne Blvd Apt 25L Pittsburgh PA 15222-1141 Office: Soc of Automotive Engrs Inc 400 Commonwealth Dr Warrendale PA 15086-7511

RUMBERGER, JOHN ARTHUR, cardiologist; b. East Liverpool, Ohio, Dec. 16, 1948; s. John Arthur and Mary Alice (Duffy) R.; m. Susan L. Panzing, Dec. 15, 1973 (div. Aug. 1979); m. Suzanne Marie Rumberger, June 14, 1980; children: Meagan, Andrew. B in Aerospace/Astro Engring., Ohio State U., 1972, MSc in Engring., 1972, PhD in Engring., 1976; MD, U. Miami, 1978. Diplomate Am. Bd. Internal Medicine, Am. Bd. Cardiovascular Diseases. Rsch. assoc. Ohio State U., Columbus, 1969-76; instr. medicine Ohio State U. Hosp., Columbus, 1978-81; instr., fellow U. Iowa Sch. Medicine, Iowa City, 1981-84, asst. prof., 1984-87; prof. medicine Mayo Clinic and Found., Rochester, Minn., 1987-98; dir. cardiac rehab. Grant Hosp., Columbus, Ohio, 1998—; med. dir. Ohio Heart, LLC, Columbus, 1998—; assoc. Heartcare, Inc., Columbus, 1998—; prof. dept. internal medicine Ohio State U., Columbus, 1998—; cons. Mayo Clinic and Found., Rochester, 1987-98. Contbr. numerous articles to profl. jours. Vice chair Am. Heart Assn., Dallas, 1995-99. Fellow Am. Coll. Cardiology; mem. Tau Beta Pi. Avocations: martial arts (2nd degree black belt). E-mail: rumbj@attglobal.net. Office: Heartcare Inc/Ohio Heart 765 N Hamilton Rd Columbus OH 43230-1758 also: Ohio Heart 765 N Hamilton Rd Columbus OH 43230-1758

RÜMENAPF, GERHARD, vascular surgeon, educator; b. Dahn, Pfalz, Germany, June 4, 1957; s. Hans and Sitta (Kölln) R.; m. Nikola Burgemeister, Apr. 26, 1962; 1 child, Max. MD, U. Erlangen-Nuremberg, Germany, 1983, PhD, 1994. Resident in exptl. surgery U. Erlangen-Nuremberg, 1984-87, resident in surgery, 1987-95; chief resident in vascular surgery Rhoen-Klinikum, Bad Neustadt, Germany, 1996-99; head surgeon dept. vascular and endocrine surgery Diakoniezentrum Speyer (Germany) Krankenhaus, 1999—. Contbr. articles to profl. jours. Capt. German Med. Corps, 1983-84. Mem. Deutsche Gesellsch Chirurgie, Deutsche Gesellsch Gefaesschirurgie. Office: Diakoniezentrum Speyer, Hilgardstr 26, 67346 Speyer Germany

RUMORE, CHARLOTTE FOWLER, city official; b. Memphis, Oct. 5, 1937; d. Charles Calvin and Malinda (McDonald) Fowler; m. Marc Miller, Mar. 4, 1956 (div. Jan. 1980); children: Shai, Marc Jr., Chriss, Rachelle, Brett, Brandi; m. Anthony John Rumore, Oct. 16, 1982. Student, Sacred Heart Coll., 1968, 74, U. Ala., Huntsville, 1990, U. Ala., Tuscaloosa, 1991, 92. Dep. dir. Cullman (Ala.) County Civil Def., 1966-68; editor, co-owner The Cullman Tribune, 1968-77; reporter Cullman Times, 1978-82, Decatur (Ala.) Daily, 1983-84; sales rep., designer Monroe Bus. Equip., Huntsville, 1984-91; aide to mayor City of Madison, Ala., 1991—. Mem. Dem. Exec. Com., Cullman, 1972-76, City Coun., Cullman, 1976-80; mem. cmty. devel. com. Ala. League of Municipalities, Montgomery, 1977-80. Named Person of the Yr., Madison County Record, 1992, Outstanding Bus. Woman Bus. and Profl. women's Club, 1973. Mem. C. of C. (Leadership class 1993-94). Roman Catholic. Avocations: reading, hiking, travel. Home: 12206 Greenleaf Cir SE Huntsville AL 35803-2211 Office: 100 Hughes Rd Madison AL 35758-1110

RUMPLER, HELMUT, history researcher, educator; b. Vienna, Austria, Sept. 12, 1935; s. Franz and Juliane (Balzer) R.; m. Maria Novák, July 3, 1961; children: Agnes, Karin, Clemens. MA, U. Vienna, Austria, 1961, PhD, 1963. Sec. com. for history of Habsburg monarchy Austrian Acad. Sci., 1961-62; rsch. asst. dept. history U. Vienna, 1963-72, asst. prof. modern history, 1973-74; prof. Austrian and modern history U. Klagenfurt, Carinzia, Austria, 1975—; guest lectr. Diplomatische Akademie Wien, 1985-91, U. Ljubljana, 1993. Author: Max Hussarek. Nationalitäten und Nationalitätenpolitik in Österreich im Sommer des Jahres 1918, 1965, (Österr.) Ministerrat und Ministerratsprotokolle, 1848-1867, 1970, Die deutsche Politik des Freiherrn Ferdinand von Beust 1848-1850, 1972, Eine Chance für Mitteleuropa. Bürgerliche Emanzipation und Staatsverfall in der Habsburgermonarchie 1804-1914, 1997; editor: Kärntner Volksabstimmung, 1981, März 1938 in Kärnten, 1989, Deutscher Bund und deutsche Geschichte 1815-1866, 1990, Innere Staatsbildung und gesellschaftliche Modernisierung in Österreich und Deutschland 1867/71-1914, 1991, Kärnten (1945-1994), 1998; chief editor: Protokolle des Österreichischen Ministerrates 1848-1867, 1968-93; co-editor, Austrian corr. Austrian History Newsletter and Austrian History Yearbook, 1961-68. Recipient Kardinal Innitzer Promotion award, 1973, Austrian State award for social sci., 1990; Alexander von Humboldt-Stiftung scholar. Mem. Austrian Acad. Sci. Vienne, Slovenian Acad. Sci. and Art, Austrian Rsch. Found. Roman Catholic.

RUMYANTSEV, SERGEY NIKOLAEVICH, immunology researcher; b. Yaroslavl, Russia, Oct. 30, 1930; s. Nikolay Vasilievich and Lidia Ipatyevna (Samarina) R.; m. Dina Fiodorovna Tankopieva, Dec. 8, 1955; children: Dmitry, Olga. MD, Med. Mil. Acad., Leningrad, 1955; DPhil, Gamaleya Inst., Moscow, 1972. Sr. scientist Inst. Vaccines and Sera, Leningrad, Russia, 1966-68, head dept., 1969-72, dep. dir., 1973-75, dir., 1975-78, head dept., 1979—. Co-author: Evolution of Clostridioses, 1974, Constitutional Immunity and its Molecular Ecological Principle, 1983, Constitutional Antimicrobial Immunity, 1985; contbr. articles to profl. jours. Mem. N.Y. Acad. Scis. Home: Warsawskaya 75-59, 196240 Saint Petersburg Russia Office: Inst Vaccines and Sera, Svobody 52, 198320 Saint Petersburg Russia

RUNCIMAN, SIR STEVEN (JAMES COCHRAN STEVENSON RUNCIMAN), historian; b. Northumberland, Eng., July 7, 1903; s. 1st Viscount Runciman and Hilda Stevenson. Ed., Eton Coll., Trinity Coll., Cambridge, Eng.; LittD (hon.), Cambridge U., U. Chgo., U. Durham, U. London, Oxford (Eng.) U., St. Andrews U., Birmingham (Eng.) U., U. Salonika (Greece), U. Sofia; DD, Wabash Coll.; DLitt Hum., Ball State U. Fellow Trinity Coll., 1927-38, lectr., 1931-38; press attache Brit. Legation, Sofia, 1940-41; prof. Byzantine studies Istanbul U., 1942-45; rep. of Brit. Coun., Greece, 1945-47; chmn. Anglo-Hellenic League, 1951-67; trustee Brit. Mus., 1960-67. Author: The Emperor Romanus Lecapenus, 1929, The First Bulgarian Empire, 1930, Byzantine Civilisation, 1933, The Meddieval Manichee, 1947, History of the Crusades, 3 vols., 1951-54, The Eastern Schism, 1955, The Sicilian Vespers, 1958, The White Rajahs, 1960, The Fall of Constantinople 1453, 1965, The Great Church in Capitivity, 1968, The Last Byzantine Renaissance, 1970, The Orthodox Churches and the Secular State, 1972, Byzantine Style and Civilisation, 1975, The Byzantine Theocracy, 1977, Mistra, 1979, A Traveller's Alphabet, 1991. Pres. Friends of Mt. Athos. Created knight; decorated companion of honour, knight condr. Order of Phoenix (Greece), knight Order of Madara Horseman (Bulgaria); recipient Silver PEN award, 1969, internat. award for culture Onassis Found., 1997; apptd. by Ecumenical Patriarch, Grand Orator of GtCh., 1970; gold medal City of Athens, 1991. Fellow Brit. Soc., Brit. Acad.; mem. Acad. Athens (hon.), Royal Irish Acad. (hon.), Am. Philos. Soc. (fgn.), Royal Soc. Lit. Address: Elshieshields Lockerbie, Dumfriesshire DG11 1LY, Scotland Office: Brit Acad, 10 Carlton House Ter, London SW1Y 5ER, England

RUNCK, ROGER JOHN, editor; b. Dolores, Colo., May 24, 1912; s. Philip and Annie Elizabeth (Marsh) R.; m. Theadora May Ridgway, Oct. 16, 1934; children: Robert, Rogene, Rhonda, Robin. Student, Union Coll., Lincoln, Nebr., 1929-33; BSChemE, U. Colo., 1943; MS in Metallurgy, Stevens Inst. Tech., Hoboken, N.J., 1947. Process engr. Metal & Thermit Corp., Rahway, N.J., 1943-47; asst. div. chief Battelle Meml. Inst., Columbus, Ohio, 1947-57, mgr. def. metals info. ctr., 1957-62, dir. def. metals info. ctr., 1962-69; cons., 1970-76; govt. agt. Dept. of Energy, Laramie, Wyo., 1977-83; editor Precious Metals News Internat. Precious Metals Inst., Allentown, Pa., 1977-98; pres. Inst. Precious Metals Inst., Allentown, 1976-78. Home and Office: 1117 Fire Thorn Ct Rifle CO 81650-3706

RUND, DEBORAH GASNER, hematologist; b. N.Y.C., Nov. 19, 1949; d. Akiva and Anne (Adler) Gasner; m. Arnold Howard Rund; children: David, Eytan, Ayelet. MSW, Wurzweiler Sch. Social Work, N.Y.C., 1972; MD, Columbia Coll. Physicians &. Surgeons, N.Y.C., 1980. Diplomate Am. Bd. Internal Medicine. Assoc. prof. medicine Sch. Medicine and Hadassah U. Hosp., Jerusalem, 1987—. Mem. Am. Soc. Hematology, Israeli Soc. Hematology and Blood Transfusion.

RUNGE, DONALD EDWARD, food wholesale company executive; b. Milw., Mar. 20, 1938; s. Adam and Helen Teresa (Voss) R.; divorced; children: Roland, Richard, Lori. Grad., Spencerian Coll., Milw., 1960. Fin. v.p. Milw. Cheese Co., Waukesha, Wis., 1962-69; dir. Farm House Foods Corp., Milw., 1966-89, pres., 1966-89, CEO, treas., 1984-89, chmn., pres., 1985-89; chmn., CEO Retailing Corp. Am., Milw., 1982-89; CEO, treas. Drug Sys. Inc., Milw., 1984-89; chmn. Drug Sys. Inc. (now Retailing Corp. of Am.), Milw., 1985-89; pres. TDC, 1987-89; chmn., pres. Runge Industries, Gen. Growth, Inc., 1989—; bd. dirs. Convenient Food Mart, CasaBlanca Industries, Inc., City of Industry, Calif.; sec. The Diana Corp., Milw., 1985-86, treas. 1986—, pres. 1987-96; chmn. Economy Dry Goods Co. Inc.; treas. Fairbanks Farms Inc. Adventist.

RUNGE, KAY KRETSCHMAR, library director; b. Davenport, Iowa, Dec. 9, 1946; d. Alfred Edwin and Ina (Paul) Kretschmar; m. Peter S. Runge Sr., Aug. 17, 1968; children: Peter Jr., Katherine. BS in History Edn., Iowa State U., 1969; MLS, U. Iowa, 1970. Pub. svc. libr. Anoka County Libr., Blaine, Minn., 1971-72; cataloger Augustana Coll., Rock Island, Ill., 1972-74; dir. Scott County Libr. Sys., Eldridge, Iowa, 1974-85, Davenport (Iowa) Pub. Libr., 1985—. Bd. dirs. River Ctr. for Performing Arts, Davenport, 1983-97, Iowa State U. Rsch. Pk., 1998—; chmn. bd. dirs. Am. Inst. Commerce, 1989-98; v.p. Quad-Cities Conv. and Visitors Bur., 1992-97, Quad-Cities Grad. Study Ctr., 1992—, Downtown Davenport Devel. Corp., 1992-2000, Hall of Honor Bd. Davenport Ctrl. H.S., 1992-95, Bren ton Bank, 1995—; steering com. Quad-Cities Visions for the Future, 1987-91, Humanities Iowa, 1993-2000, chair, 1998-99; bd. govs. Iowa State U. Found., 1991—; citizens adv. coun. Iowa State U., 1998—, Leadership Iowa, 1998-99; bd. dirs. Quest Ednl. Corp., 1999—; adv. bd. mem. U. Iowa Sch. Libr. Sci., 1999—, adj. prof., 2000—; bd. dirs. Davenport One, Downtown Devel., 2000—. Recipient Svc. Key award Iowa State U. Alumni Assn., 1979, ALA/ALTA Nat. Advocacy Honor Roll award, 2000; named Quad City Panhellenic Woman of Yr., 1998. Mem. ALA (chmn. library adminstrs. and mgrs. div., fundraising section 1988), Iowa Library Assn. (pres. 1983), Pub. Library Assn. (bd. dirs. 1990-99, pres. 2000-2001), Iowa Edn. Media Assn. (Intellectual Freedom award 1984), Alpha Delta Pi (alumni service 1978). Lutheran. Office: Davenport Pub Libr 321 N Main St Davenport IA 52801-1490

RUNGE, PATRICK RICHARD, lawyer; b. Iowa City, Iowa, Oct. 25, 1969; s. Richard Gary and Sally Louise (Cozzolino) R. BSBA in Econs., U. Nebr., Omaha, 1991; JD, Creighton U., 1994. Bar: Nebr. 1994, U.S. Dist. Ct. Nebr. 1994. Prodn. editor U.N.O. Gateway, Omaha, 1990-91; graphic designer Omaha (Nebr.) Pub. Power Dist., 1991-97; intern U.S. Dist. Ct., Omaha, 1993; rsch. asst. Creighton U., Omaha, 1993; sr. cert. law student Creighton Legal Clinic, Omaha, 1994; atty. Runge Law Office, Omaha, 1994-95, Runge & Chase, Omaha, 1995—; pub. defender Winnebago Tribe of Nebr., 1996—. Disting. scholar Omaha (Nebr.) World-Herald, 1987-91; Merit scholar Creighton Law Sch., Omaha, 1991-94. Mem. Winnebago Bar Assn. Democrat. Lutheran. Office: Runge & Chase 7701 Pacific St Ste 323 Omaha NE 68114-5480

RUNGGALDIER, EDMUND, philosopher, educator; b. Ortisei, Italy, Aug. 24, 1946; arrived in Austria, 1970.; BA in Philosophy, U. Munich, 1970; MA in Theology, U. Innsbruck, Austria, 1973; PhD in Philosophy, Oxford (Eng.) U., 1977. Prof. U. Innsbruck, 1985, dean of faculty, 1993-95. Author: Carnap's Early Conventionalism: An Inquiry into the Historical Background of the Vienna Circle, 1984, Zeichen und Bezeichnetes: Sprachphilosophische Untersuchungen zum Problem der Referenz, 1985, Analytische Sprachphilosophie, 1990, Was sind Hadlungen? Eine philosophische Auseinandersetzung mit dem Naturalismus, 1996, Philosophie der Esoterik, 1996, Analysische Ontologie, 1998; contbr. numerous articles to profl. jours. Mem. Austrian Soc. Philosophy (pres. 1996—). E-mail: Edmund.Runggaldier@uibk.ac.at.

RUNGRUANGSAK TORRISSEN, KRISNA, research scientist; b. Bangkok, Jan. 1, 1950; arrived in Norway, 1980; d. Boonprung and Chalerm (Pandee) Rungruangsak; m. Ole Johan Torrissen, Apr. 17, 1980 (div. Oct. 1996); children: Jonas Kristen Torrissen, Marius Torrissen. BSc in Food Tech., Chulalongkorn U., Bangkok, 1971; MSc in Biochemistry, Mahidol U., Bangkok, 1973; PhD in Fisheries and Marine Biology, U. Bergen, Norway, 1993. Cert. biochemist and aquaculturist. Lectr. Mahidol U., Bangkok, 1973-78, asst. prof., 1979-80; rsch. fellow Inst. Nutrition, Bergen, 1978-79; scientist Inst. Marine Rsch., Bergen, 1980-89, sr. scientist, 1990-96, prin. scientist, 1997—; invited lectr. U. Bergen, 1988-91; adv. bd. feedingstuff to fish Norwegian Agrl. Inspection Svc., Ministry of Agr., Oslo, 1989-95. 1st editor: (textbook) Laboratory and Principles in Biochemistry, 1978, (book chpt.) Seafood Enzymes, 2000; contbr. articles to sci. jours. Grantee European Union Commn., 1997-99, Rsch. Coun. Norway, 1985-99. Mem. Marine Scientist Orgn. Fax: 4756366143. E-mail: krisnart@imr.no. Office: Inst Marine Rsch, Matre Aquaculture Rsch Sta, N-5984 Matredal Norway

RUNKLE, MARTIN DAVEY, library director; b. Cin., Oct. 18, 1937; s. Newton and Ilo (Neal) R.; m. Nancy Force, Aug. 7, 1965; children: Seth, Elizabeth. BA, Muskingum Coll., 1959; MA, U. Pitts., 1964, U. Chgo., 1973. Library systems analyst U. Chgo., 1970-75, head cataloging librarian, 1975-79, asst. dir. tech. services, 1979-80, dir. library, 1980—; sr. lectr. grad. library sch. U. Chgo., 1977-90. Fulbright grantee, 1965. Mem. ALA, Univ. Club Chgo. Office: U Chgo 1100 E 57th St Chicago IL 60637-1502

RUNKLE, ROBERT SCOTT, environmental company executive; b. Washington, Mar. 9, 1936; s. Lloyd Manor and Louise (Armstrong) R.; m. Betsy Grater, Mar. 26, 1960 (div. July 1983); children: Beth R. Mackey, Brynn A.; stepchildren: Lori Anne Thompson, Jay M. Thompson; m. Joan Lewis, Aug. 6, 1983 (dec. Nov. 1987); m. Mary Beth Jorgensen, July 12, 1992; stepchildren: Elizabeth Jorgensen Feild, David Jorgensen Feild. BS in Bldg. Constrn., Ga. Inst. Tech ., 1960. Draftsman Ted Englehardt AIA, Silver Spring, Md., 1960-62; engr. Research Facilities Planning BD. div. Research Service NIH, Bethesda, Md., 1962-64; vice chmn. biohazards sect. Nat. Cancer Inst., NIH, Bethesda, 1964-67; research contracts mgr. Becton Dickinson & Co., Rutherford, N.J., 1967-69; adminstrn. mgr. Becton Dickinson Research Ctr., Raleigh, N.C., 1969-73; dir. adminstrn. Huntington (Eng.) Research Ctr., 1974-75; dir. rsch. liaison Becton Dickinson Co, Rutherford, N.J., 1976-78; v.p. ops. BBL microbiology systems div., Becton Dickinson Co., Balt., 1978-85; pres., chief exec. officer, chmn. bd. Pharmplastics Closures Inc., Balt., 1985-88; v.p. EA Engring., Sci. and Tech., Inc., Balt., 1989-91; v.p. bus. devel., sr. office leader EA Labs, EA Engring., Sci. and Tech., Inc., Chgo., 1992-94; v.p. ops. Carnow, Conibear & Assocs., Ltd., Chgo., 1994-99; dir. environ. svcs. STV Inc., Chgo., 1999—; cons. Am. Inst. Biological Scis., Bethesda, 1963-67, ind., Balt., 1982-87. Author: Microbial Contamination Control Facilities, 1969, Biomedical Applications Laminar Airflow, 1973; contbr. articles to profl. jours. Mem. Assn. for Corp. Growth, Am. Chem. Soc., Bldg. Futures Coun., Ga. Tech. Nat. Alumni Assn., Raleigh (N.C.) C. of C. Democrat. Episcopalian. Avocations: photography, racquetball, swimming. Home: 838 Michigan Ave Apt 3C Evanston IL 60202-2537 Office: STV Inc 70 W Madison St Ste 2840 Chicago IL 60602-4315

RUNNICLES, DONALD, conductor; b. Edinburgh, Scotland, Nov. 16, 1954. Student, Edinburgh U., Cambridge U., London Opera Ctr.; DMus (hon.), U. Edinburgh, 1995. Music dir. San Francisco Opera, 1992—. Repetiteur Mannheim, Germany, Nat. theatre, from 1980, Kapellmeister, from 1984; prin. condr. Hanover, from 1987; numerous appearances with Hamburg Staatsoper; former gen. music dir. Stadtische Buhnen, Freiburg/Breisgau; mus. dir. San Francisco Opera, 1992—; appearances with Met. Opera include Lulu, 1988, The Flying Dutchman, 1990, The Magic Flute; condr. Vienna Staatsoper, 1990-91, Sonome, 1996; debut at Glyndebourne with Don Giovanni, 1991, Salzburg Festival with Don Giovanni, 1996, also numerous symphonic engagements; condr. London Symphony Orch., La Scale Milan Freischütz, Orch. de Paris, Israel Philharm., Rotterdam Philharm., Seattle Symphony, Pitts. Symphony, St. Louis Symphony, Chgo. Symphony, San Francisco Symphony, Cleve. Orch., New World Symphony, Bavarian Radio Symphony Orch., 2 complete ring cycles with Wiener Staatsoper; rec. Hansel and Gretel (Humperdinck), Gluck's Orphée with San Francisco Opera Orch., 1995, Tannhäuser-Bayreuth Festspick, 1995, Harvey Milk with San Francisco Opera, 1996; opened Edinburgh Festival, 1994, 96. Office: San Francisco Opera War Meml Opera House 301 Van Ness Ave San Francisco CA 94102-4509

RUNYAN, RAYMOND BRUCE, developmental biologist, educator; b. Pasadena, Calif., Aug. 27, 1950; s. Raymond Albert and Patricia Alona (Collins) R.; m. Sherry Ann Henley, Aug. 24, 1979. BA, Macalester Coll., 1972; PhD, Tex. Tech U., 1983. Electron microscope technologist Fla. State U., Tallahassee, 1975-76; lab. mgr. U. S.C., Columbia, 1976-78; rsch. assoc. U. Conn. Health Ctr., Farmington, 1983-84; rsch. assoc. M.D. Anderson Cancer Ctr. U. Tex., Houston, 1984-86; asst. prof. U. Iowa, Iowa City, 1986-92; assoc. prof. U. Ariz., Tucson, 1992-2000, prof., 2000—; mem. lung and devel. study com. Am. Heart Assn., Dallas, 1989-92. Mem. Am. Assn. Anatomists (adv. com. of young anatomists 1989-94, publs. com. 1990-94), Am. Soc. for Cell Biology, Soc. for Devel. Biology. Achievements include research in identification of tissue interaction in development of the heart, enzymatic mechanism for embryonic and cancer cell adhesion, role of transforming growth factor-beta 3 heart valve formation. Office: U Ariz PO Box 245044 Tucson AZ 85724-5044

RUOFF, A. LAVONNE BROWN, English language educator; b. Charleston, Ill., Apr. 10, 1930; d. Oscar and Laura Alice (Witters) Brown; m. Milford Anthony Prasher, Aug. 19, 1950 (div. 1964); m. Gene W. Ruoff, June 10, 1967; Stephen Charles, Sharon Louise. Student, U. Ill., Chgo., 1948-50; BS in Edn., Northwestern U., 1953, MA in English, 1954, PhD in English, 1966. From instr. to asst. prof. Roosevelt U., Chgo., 1961-66; asst. prof. English U. Ill., Chgo., 1966-69, assoc. prof., 1969-81, prof., 1981-94; prof. emeritus, 1994—; interim dir. D'Arcy McNickle Ctr. for Am. Indian History, Newberry Libr., 1999—; editor Am. Indian Lives series U. Nebr. Press, Lincoln, 1985—; mem. Am. lit. com. Internat. Exch. of Scholars, Washington, 1987-90, chair, 1989-90; NEH dir. Sumer Seminars for Coll. Tchrs. on Am. Indian Lit., 1979, 83, 89, 94. Author: American Indian Literature, 1990, Literatures of the American Indian, 1990; editor: The Moccasin Maker, 1987, 2d edit., 1998, Wynema, 1997; (with Jerry W. Ward, Jr.) Redefining American Literary History, 1990; (with Donald Smith) Life Letters and Speeches of George Copway, 1997. Bd. dirs. Am. Indian Coun. Fire, Chgo., 1980-88. Recipient Lifetime Achievement award Before Columbus Found., 1998, Lit., MLA and Assn. for Study of Am. Indian Lits. award for outstanding contbns., 1993, MELUS award for outstanding contbns. to multiethnic lit., 1986; named Writer of Yr. for Annotation/Bibliography, Wordcraft Circle of Native Writers and Storytellers, 1997; NEH fellow, 1992-93, U. Ill.-Chgo. Inst. for Humanities fellow, 1990-91; NEH Rsch. Divsn. grantee, 1981. Mem. MLA (chair discussion group Am. Indian lit., co-chair lit. of people of color com. 2000—), Am. Studies Assn., Multi-ethnic Lit. in the U.S., Assn. for Study of Am. Indian Lits. E-mail: lruoff@uic.edu. Office: Newberry Libr 60 W Walton St Chicago IL 60610-3380

RUOFF, HEINZ PETER, chemistry educator; b. Kirchheim unter Teck, Germany, May 15, 1953; s. Heinz and Hilde (Ruzicka) R.; m. Cathrine Lillo, July 26, 1974; children: Martin Ruoff-Lillo, Astrid Lillo-Ruoff. PhD, Oslo U., 1987. Rsch. asst. Oslo U., 1980-84; prof. chemistry Sch. Tech. and Sci., Stavanger (Norway) Coll., 1984—. Contbr. articles to profl. jours. Odd Hassel fellowship Norwegian Rsch. Coun., 1988-90. Mem. Am. Chem. Soc., Norwegian Chem. Soc., Sigma Xi. Achievements include rsch. on the excitability in the Belousov-Zhabotinsky reaction, theory of temperature-compensation in chem. and biological oscillators, the exptl. finding of excitability in the Belousov-Zhabotinsky reaction after theoretical prediction by Richard J. Field and Richard M. Noyes. Office: Stavanger Univ Coll, Sci Tech and Sci, N-4091 Stavanger Norway

RUOHONEN, JARKKO KALEVI, pharmaceutical researcher; b. Turku, Finland, Jan. 17, 1944; s. Kaino Kustaa and Sirkka Helena (Salonen) R.; m. Maijaliisa Jokinen, June 25, 1965; children: Sari, Saara. MSc, U. Turku, 1970, Lic Phil, 1988, PhD, 1994. Rschr. Leiras Oy, Turku, 1971-76, rsch. mgr. fine chems., 1976-94, mgr. R&D/polymer tech., 1994—. Patentee in field. Recipient Cross of Merit of Order of White Rose of Finland, 1994. Mem. Chem. Industry Fedn. Finland (sci. adv. bd. 1988-94), Am. Chem. Soc., Finnish Chem. Soc., European Chem. Soc., Controlled Release Soc., Internat. Soc. for Pharm. Engring., Turku-Samppalinna Rotary Club. Office: Leiras Oy, PO Box 415, 20101 Turku Finland

RUOKOLAINEN, JANNE TAPIO, engineer; b. Pielisjarvi, Finland, Apr. 15, 1970; s. Pentti and Kirsti Raakel (Kyyronen) R.; m. Anne Turunen, Aug. 1, 1998. MS, Helsinki U. Tech., Finland, 1995; DSc in Tech., Helsinki U. Tech., 2000. Rschr. Helsinki U. Tech., Finland, 1995—; visiting scientist Mass. Inst. Tech., Cambridge, 1997. Contbr. articles to profl. jours. Recipient O'Donnell prize World Polymer Congress, Australia, 1998. Mem. Finnish Physical Soc., Am. Chem. Soc. Avocations: kayaking, in-line skating, bodybuilding. Home: Yrttikuja 4, 02770 Espoo Finland Office: Materials Rsch Lab Univ Calif Santa Barbara Santa Barbara CA 93106

RUOZI, ROBERTO, banker; b. Biella/Vercelli, Italy, May 17, 1939; married; 2 children. Prof. econs. of banking instns. Bocconi U. Milan, rector, 1989—; dep. chmn. Banca Popolare di Milan, also bd. dirs.; with U Comerciale Luigi Bocconi, Milan; lectr. Univs. Ancona, Siena, Parma and Paris; dir. Cariplo's Ctr. for Fin. Assistance to Africa; cons. Banco Lariano, IMI, Mediocredito Regionale Lombardo, FAO, EEC and Barclays Bank Internat.; chmn. Pacchetti S.p.A., Coopers & Lybrand Consulenti di Direzione S.p.A., Gesfimi S.p.A.; bd. mem. Ciga Hotels S.p.A., Banca Popolare di Milano, Italinter Gestion S.A. Luxembourg and Saipem S.p.A.; dep. rector Bocconi U. Milan; mem. mng. com. SDA Bocconi; dir. Bocconi's Fin. Innovation Study Ctr.; gen. sec. Internat. Confedn. Farming Credit, Zurich, Switzerland; chmn. Factorit S.p.A.-Societè di Factoring delle Banche Popolar Italiane, 1978—; chmn. EGEA Edizioni Giuridiche Economiche Aziendali dell'Universita Bocconi, 1988—; chmn. Giuffrè Editori S.p.A., 1988—; bd. mem. Associazione Bancari Italiana, ASSBANK, Banque de l'Union Maritime et Financière, BAnca Popolare di Lecco, Ciba Geigy S.p.A., Finanziaria F. Ili Cerruti S.p.A., Italease S.p.A., Margraf S.p.A., Marzotto-Manifattura Lane Gaetano Marzotto & Figli S.p.A., Sogepo S.p.A., Ince S.p.A.; chmn. Europafactoring; reporter meetings in Italy and abroad. Mem. Associazione fra le Soc. di Factoring Italiane, Accademia ITaliana di Economica Aziendale, Soc. Italiana degli Economisti, Accademia dei Georgofili, Istituto Lombardo, Accademia di Scienze e Lettere, Accademia Peloritana dei Pericolanti, Rotary Club Milano Aquileia. Office: U Commerciale Luigi Bocconi, Via R Sarfatti 25, 20136 Milan Italy*

RUPE, GARY E., controller. BS, Castleton State Coll.; postgrad., U. Vt.; MSA, St. Michael's Coll. Sys. sales and support Am. Airlines, Inc.; sys. analyst Ctrl. Vt. Pub. Svc.; bus. analyst Catamount Energy; contr. Pluess-Staufer. Home: 92 Cones Point Rd Poultney VT 05764-9193 Office: Pluess-Staufer Industries Inc 61 Main St Proctor VT 05765-1178

RUPEL, DIMITRIJ, diplomat; b. Apr. 7, 1946. Degree in Comparative Lit. and Sociology, U. Ljubljana, Slovenia, 1970; PhD in Sociology, Brandeis U., 1976. Lectr., asst., assoc. prof. U. Ljubljana, 1970-92, prof., 1992—; min. Ministry Fgn. Affairs, Slovenia, 1990-93; mem. Nat. Assembly, Rep. of Slovenia, 1993-95; mayor City of Ljubljana, 1995-97; ambassador to U.S., Mex. Washington, 19972000; min. of fgn. affairs Republic of Slovenia, 2000—. Office: Ministry Foreign Affairs, Gregorciceva 25, SI-1000 Ljubljana Slovenia

RUPKE, NICOLAAS, science history educator; b. Rotterdam, Netherlands, Jan. 22, 1944; s. Christiaan and Pieternella H. (van den Heuvel) R. BSc, Groningen U., 1968; MA, Princeton U., 1970, PhD, 1972. Research fellow Smithsonian Instn., Washington, 1972-73, U. Oxford (Eng.), 1973-81, U. Tübingen, Germany, 1981-83, Wellcome Inst., London, 1983-87, Netherlands Inst. for Advanced Study, Wassenaar, 1985, Nat. Humanities Ctr., N.C., 1988-89; sr. fellow Inst. Advanced Studies, Australian Nat. U., Canberra, 1989-93; prof. history sci. and medicine Goettingen U., 1993—; dir.inst. for history of sci. Goettingen Univ., 1997—; Nelson O. Tyrone Jr. prof. Vanderbilt U., Nashville, 1997-98. Author: Great Chain of History, 1983, Richard Owen: Victorian Natuiralist, 1994; editor: Vivisection in Historical Perspective, 1987, Science, Politics and the Public Good, 1988, Ideas and Ideologies, 1994, Medical Geography in Historical Perspective, 2000; contbr. articles to profl. jours. Fellow St. Peter's Coll., Oxford, 1974-77, Wolfson Coll., Oxford, 1977-81, Humboldt Stiftung, Fed. Republic Germany, 1981-83; hon. fellow U. Coll., London, 1983-87. Fellow Geol. Soc. Am., Royal Hist. Soc. Club: Athenaeum. Avocations: painting, palmistry. Office: Inst for History of Sci, Humboldtallee 11, 37073 Göttingen Germany

RUPORT, SCOTT HENDRICKS, lawyer; b. Nov. 22, 1949; s. Fred Hendricks and Juyne (Kennedy) R.; m. Linda Darlene Smith, Sept. 12, 1970; children: Brittany Lyle, Courtney Kennedy. BSBA, Bowling Green U., 1971; JD, U. Akron, 1974. Bar: Ohio 1974, Pa. 1984, U.S. Dist. Ct. (no. dist.) Ohio 1974, U.S. Ct. Appeals (6th cir.) 1975, U.S. Supreme Ct. 1978; cert. civil trial specialist Nat. Bd. Trial Advocacy. Assoc. Schwab, Sager, Growenburgh, Rothal, Fort, Skidmore & Nukes, Akron, Ohio, 1974-76, Skidmore & George Co. LPA, Akron, 1976-79, Skidmore, Ruport & Haskings, Akron, 1979-83; ptnr. Roderick, Myers & Linton, Akron, 1983-85, Ruport Co. LPA, Akron, 1985—; instr. real estate law U. Akron, 1976-77, adj. asst. prof. constrn. tech. Coll. Engring., 1983—. Capt. Fin. Corps. USAR, 1971-79. Mem. ABA, ATLA, Ohio Bar Assn., Ohio Acad. Trial Lawyers (chmn. civil and bus. litigation sect. 1989), Akron Bar Assn., Beta Gamma Sigma, Sigma Chi. Republican. Presbyterian. Office: Ruport Co LPA 3700 Embassy Pkwy Ste 440 Akron OH 44333-8367

RUPP, GARY A., academic administrator; b. St. Cloud, Minn., Sept. 7, 1948; arrived in Thailand, 1986; s. Alvin John and Florence Ruth (Mayhew) R. BSc, St. Cloud State U., 1970; M in Edn. Adminstrn., New Eng. U., Armidale, Australia, 1981, Harvard U., 1986; EdD, Trinity U., Malaga, Spain, 1996. Lectr. in English Silpakorn U., Nakhorn Pathom, Thailand, 1986-89; asst. prin. Am. Sch. Monterrey, Mex., 1989-90, Coll. Internat. de Caracas, Venezuela, 1990-92; prin. Pattaya (Thailand) Internat. Sch., 1992-95, Ekemai Internat. Sch., Bangkok, 1995-97; dir. Bangkok Internat. Sch., 1997—; adv. Transition Edn. Adv. Com., Melbourne, Australia, 1981-82; cons. in field. Author: Innovative Work Education Project, 1982. sec.-treas., pres. Jaycees, Portland, Australia, 1975. Sport scholar U. Minn., 1968-70. Mem. Siam Soc., Rotary. Avocations: scuba diving, sailing. Office: Nana Post Office, PO Box 1182, 10112 Bangkok Thailand

RUPP, GEORGE ERIK, academic administrator; b. Summit, N.J., Sept. 22, 1942; s. Gustav Wilhelm and Erika (Braunoehler) R.; m. Nancy Katherine Farrar, Aug. 22, 1964; children: Katherine Heather, Stephanie Karin. Student, Ludwig Maximilians U., Munich, Germany, 1962-63; A.B., Princeton U., 1964; B.D., Yale U., 1967; postgrad., U. Sri Lanka, Peradeniya, 1969-70; PhD, Harvard U., 1972. Ordained to ministry Presbyn. Ch. U.S.A., 1971; faculty fellow in religion, vice chancellor Johnston College, U. Redlands, Redlands, Calif., 1971-74; asst. prof. Harvard Divinity School, Harvard U., Cambridge, Mass., 1974-76, assoc. prof., 1976-77, prof., dean, 1979-85; prof., dean acad. affairs U. Wis., Green Bay, 1977-79; prof., pres. Rice U., Houston, Tex., 1985-93, Columbia U., N.Y.C., 1993—; bd. dirs. Com. for Econ. Devel., Freedom Forum Media Studies Ctr., Martel Found., N.Y. Partnership, Pulitzer Prize Bd., Univs. Rsch. Assn., Inc. Author: Christologies and Cultures: Toward a Typology of Religious Worldviews, 1974, Culture Protestantism: German Liberal Theology at the Turn of the Twentieth Century, 1977, Beyond Existentialism and Zen: Religion in a Pluralistic World, 1979, Commitment and Community, 1989; contbr. articles to profl. jours. Bd. dirs. Amigos de las Americas, Am. Assembly, Assn. Am. Univs., Cathedral Ch. St. John Divine, Coun. on Alcohol and Substance Abuse, Inst. Internat. Edn., Nat. Assn. Ind. Colls. and Univs., YMCA of Am. Danforth Grad. fellow, 1964-71. Mem. AAAS, Am. Acad. Religion, Coun. on Fgn. Rels., Soc. for Values in Higher Edn. Office: Office of Pres Columbia U 202 Low Meml Libr MC4309 New York NY 10027*

RUPP, HENRY JACOB, physician; b. Cokato, Minn., Dec. 10, 1945; s. Victor Harry and Arletta Appolonia (Soltau) R.; m. Sandra Kaye Chase, mar. 22, 1967; children: Robinson, Wendel, Jeremy Jay, Jody Lyda, Christy Marina. BS, U. Minn., 1963, MD, 1971. Bd. cert. family practice. Phys. Shoreview Family Physicians, 1975-83; with Africa Inland Mission, Kenya, E. Africa, 1983-99; phys. Northwestern Coll., 1999-2000. Mem. Christian Med. Dental Soc. Avocations: taxidermy, fishing, camping, hunting.

RUPPEL, HOWARD JAMES, JR., sociologist, sexologist, educator; b. Orange, N.J., July 22, 1941; s. Howard J. and Lillian M. (Wordley) R.; m. Barbara Margaret Wiedemann, June 3, 1967. BA, St. Joseph's Coll., Ind., 1963; MA, No. Ill. U., 1968; postgrad., U. Iowa, 1968-76; EdD, Inst. for Advanced Study Human Sexuality, 1993, PhD, 1994. Diplomate Am. Bd. Sexology; cert. sexologist Am. Coll. Sexologists. Instr. social sci., debate coach St. Francis H.S., Wheaton, Ill., 1963-65; instr. sociology St. Dominic Coll., St. Charles, Ill., 1966-67, Cornell Coll., Mt. Vernon, Iowa, 1969-70; asst. prof. Cornell Coll., Mt. Vernon, 1970-72, lectr., 1972-73; rsch. dir. Social Sci. Rsch. Assocs., Cedar Rapids, Iowa, 1973-80; founder, co-dir. Ctr. for Sexual Growth and Devel., Mt. Vernon, 1980-95; instr. Sch. Social Work, U. Iowa, 1976-78, adj. asst. prof., 1979-81, adj. assoc. prof., 1981-96, prof., 1997—; exec. dir. Soc. for Sci. Study of Sexuality, 1988—, Found. for the Sci. Study of Sexuality, 1989-98, Am. Assn. Sex Educators, Counselors and Therapists, 1996—; prof. Inst. Advanced Study Human Sexuality, 1996—; cons. Iowa Dept. Social Svcs., Families Inc., West Branch, A&E Network (Biography); bd. dirs. The Human Outreach and Achievement Inst., Boston, 1988-90, Inst. Advanced Study Human Sexuality, 1995—. Co-editor: Sexuality and the Family Life Span, 1983; assoc. editor Ann. Rev. of Sex Rsch., 1992, 93, 94, 95, 96, 97, 98, 99; contbr. articles on complex orgns., marriage and the family, sexual attitudes and behavior, childhood and preadolescent sexuality, methodology and child care theory to profl. publs. NSF fellow, 1968. Fellow Am. Acad. Clin. Sexologists; mem. Am. Sociol. Assn., Nat. Coun. Family Rels., Iowa Coun. Family Rels. (sec. 1983-84, treas. 1985), Changing Family Conf. (bd. dirs. 1983-87), Soc. Sci. Study of Sex Inc. (bd. dirs. 1983-88, pres. Midcontinent Region 1984-85, treas. 1986-88, chmn. membership com. 1983-85, chmn. exhibits com. 1983-88, ann. meeting chmn. 1986), Am. Assn. Sex Educators, Counselors and Therapists (exec. dir. 1996—, cert. sex educator), Harry Benjamin Internat. Gender Dysphoria Assn., Coun. Assns. for Sexual Sci., Health and Edn. (del.), Inst. for the Advanced Study of Human Sexuality Alumni Assn., Alpha Kappa Delta, Alpha Sigma Lambda (hon.). Democrat. Home: 608 5th Ave N Mount Vernon IA 52314-1107 Office: 103 A Ave S Ste 2-b Mount Vernon IA 52314-1400

RUPPERT, ARMIN, sales executive; b. Ravensburg, Germany, July 21, 1967; s. Rudolf Ernst and Irmgard (Ruess) R. Apprentice sales mgr. Taylorix, Ravensburg, 1989-92; sales mgr. Westerweller, Ravensburg, 1992-93, Glas Blessing, Ravensburg, 1993-95, Rafi GmbH & Co., Berg, 1995—. Chair mem. Fanfarenzug Rauenspurg, 1998—; chmn. Fanfarenzug St. Florian, 1993-98. Mem. Fitness Club. Office: Rafi GmbH & Co KG, Ravensburgerstrasse 128-134, 88276 Berg Germany

RUPPERT, EDOUARD, auditor. Sec.-gen. European Ct. of Auditors. Office: Ct of Auditors European Cmty, 12 rue Alcide de Gasperi, 1615 Luxembourg Luxembourg*

RUPPERT, KARSTEN, historian, educator; b. Bad Bengzabern, Germany, Dec. 14, 1946; s. Karl and Elfriede (Schubert) R.; m. Edith Gemeinhardt, July 7, 1973; children: Christine, Elke. PhD, U. Bonn, Germany, 1977; D in Habilitation, U. Karlsruhe, Germany, 1990. Asst. Univ. Adminstrn. Speyer, Germany, 1978-85; lectr. U. Karlsruhe, 1990-94; repr. prof. U. Jena, Germany, 1991-92, U. Chemnitz, Germany, 1992-93, U. Regensburg, Germany, 1993-94; prof. U. Eichstaett, Germany, 1995—; rsch. dir. Commn. for Parliamentarian History, Bonn, 1987-88. Author: Die Deutsche Zentrumspartei, 1923-1930, 1992, Die Kaiserliche Friedenspolitik auf dem Westfaelischen Friedenskongress, 1977, Bürgertum und staatliche Macht in Deutschland zwischen Französischer und deutscher Revolution, 1997; editor: Protokolle der Zentrumsfraktion 1920-25, Kaiserliche Korrespondenz auf dem Westfaelischen Friedenskongress, 1645-1646, 1979. Roman Catholic. Avocations: swimming, literature, theater. Home: Am Unteren Schlittberg 9, Roemerberg D-67354, Germany Office: Catholic U, Ostenstr 26-28, Eichstaett D-85072, Germany

RURAK, ZBIGNIEW TADEUSZ, executive search consultant; b. Sept. 25, 1947. BA, Harvard U., 1969; MSc, London Sch. Econs., 1976. Cons. McKinsey & Co., Inc., Duesseldorf, Germany, 1979-82; dir. internat. mktg. Comsat Telesys., Washington, 1982-85; v.p. Leon A. Farley Assoc., Washington, 1985-87; pres. Rurak & Assocs., Inc., Washington, 1987—. Home: 3818 1/2 Huntington St NW Washington DC 20015-1928 Office: Rurak & Assocs Inc 1350 Connecticut Ave NW Ste 801 Washington DC 20036-1733

RUS, IOAN A., mathematics educator, researcher; b. Ianosda, Bihor, Romania, Aug. 28, 1936; s. Alexandru and Eva (Plumbas) R.; m. Ileana Moga, Nov. 27, 1963; children: Dana, Bogdan. BS in Math., Babes-Bolyai U., 1960, Phd in Math., 1968. Asst. prof. Babes-Bolyai U., Romania, 1960-67, lectr., 1967-72, assoc. prof., 1972-77, prof., 1977—, vice rector, 1976-84, 92-96. Author: Principles and Applications of Fixed Point Theory, 1979; editor Seminar on Fixed Point Theory Jour., 1980-97; contbr. articles to profl. jours. Office: Babes-Bolyai U, Kogalniceanu Nr 1, 3400 Cluj-Napoca Romania

RUSALOVA, MARGARITA NIKOLAEVNA, psychophysiologist; b. Moscow, Aug. 28, 1932; d. Nikolai Trofimovich and Polina Mikhailovna (Chaikova) Valuev; m. Anatoliy Ivanovich Simonov, Mar. 20, 1954 (div. June 1961); 1 child, Nikolai; m. Vladimir Mikhailovich Rusalov, Dec. 8, 1962; children: Mikhail, Yuriy. M.Physiology, Moscow U., 1961; Cand. Scis. (Physiology), Inst. Higher Nervous Activity, Moscow, 1966, ScD in Physiology, 1984. Human and animal physiologist diplomate. Sr. asst. Inst. Higher Nervous Activity and Neurophysiology, Moscow, 1962-66, jr. rschr., 1966-75, sr. rschr., 1975-88, leading rschr., 1988—. Author: Voluntary Regulation of Autonomic Functions of the Organism, 1966 (Award of Inst. Higher Nervous Activity 1966), Experimental Studies of Human Emotional Responses, 1979 (Award of Inst. Higher Nervous Activity 1979); co-author: Nervous Tension and Heart Activity, 1969, Physiological Peculiarities of Positive and Negative Emotional Reactions, 1972, Apparatus and Methodic Questions of Neurophysiological Experiment, 1970, Brain and Behavior, 1990, Individual Brain and Behavior, 1993; editor: Mechanisms of Integrative Activity of the Brain, 1981; contbr. over 80 articles to profl. jours. Russian Found. for Basic Rsch. grantee, 1999—, Russian Sci. Humanitarian Found. grantee, 1997-99; recipient Award of Coun. of Min., 1989, scholarship for outstanding scientists, 1997. Mem. Internat. Brain Rsch. Orgn. Avocation: painting. Office: Inst Higher Nervous Activ, 5a Butlerova Str, 117865 Moscow Russia

RUSAN, LAURENTIU VIRGIL, software engineer; b. Rosia-Montana, Alba, Romania, Dec. 23, 1970; s. Ioan and Maria (Goia) R.; m Luminita Moraru, Aug. 27, 1994; 1 child, Horia-Alexandru. Diploma, Mil. Tech. Acad., Bucharest, Romania, 1996, doctorand (hon.), 1996; diploma, Economic Studies Acad., Bucharest, Romania, 1998. 2d officer Mil. Topographic Dept., Bucharest, 1996-99, Mil. Gen. Staff Romanian Army, Bucharest, 1999—; univ. asst. Mil. Tech. Acad., 1998—. Mem. Romanian Cartographic Assoc. Avocations: mathematics, computer programming, swimming, skiing. Office: Ministry of Nat Def, 76482 Bucharest Romania

RUSANOV, ALEXANDER MICHAILOVICH, research scientist; b. Buzuluk, Orenburg, Russia, Feb. 13, 1947; s. Michail Ivanovich and Julia Stepanovna (Ugolkova) R.; m. Natalya Rafikovna Bakirova, Aug. 18, 1971 (div. June 1995); m. Nelly Alexeyevna Kalinkina, Dec. 4, 1996; children: Denis Alexandrovich, Maria Alexandrovna. Diploma, Moscow U., 1975; Postgrad., Dokuchayev Soil Inst., Moscow, 1981-85; Cand. Sci., Moscow, 1987; MD, Yekaterinburg, Russia, 1995. Ecologist Inst. Volgogiprozem, Orenburg, Russia, 1975-87; ecologist, head of lab. staff Inst. Plants and Animals/Ecology Ural Br. Russian Acad. Scis, Orenburg, 1987-92; chmn. scientist com. Orenburg Regional Adminstrn., 1992—; head of staff Orenburg U., 1996—; cons. agr. dept. Orenburg, 1987—. Author: (books) Humus-status of Southern Chernozems Under Natural Pastures, 1994, Influence of Erosion on the Humus State of Chernozems in the Ural Region, 1995 (co-author): Changes in Soils and Environment of the Steppe Pre-Urals Area During the Second Half the Holocene, 1996. Avocation: sports. Office: Orenburg Univ, prosp Pobedy 13, 460352 Orenburg Russia

RUSANOV, ANATOLY IVANOVICH, chemist; b. St. Petersburg, Russia, Apr. 20, 1932; s. Ivan Platonovich and Lidiya Vasilyevna (Petrova) R.; m. Vera Vasilyevna Chekh, July 9, 1963; children: Oleg, Elena. DPhil, St. Petersburg U., Russia, 1958, DS, 1963. Jr. rschr. St. Petersburg State U., Russia, 1955-60, sr. rschr., 1960-67, head lab., 1968-87, head dept. colloid chemistry, 1987—. Author: Phase Equilibria and Surface Phenomena, 1967, 78, Surface Separation of Substance, 1981, Micellization in Surfactant Solutions, 1992, 97, Interfacial Tensiometry, 1996, Physichemical Hydrodynamics of Capillary Systems, 1999. Mem. Russian Acad. Scis. (Mendeleev prize 1993), Mendeleev Russian Chem. Soc. (Volfkovich prize 1991). Avocation: philately. Office: Mendeleev Ctr, St Petersburg State U, 199034 Saint Petersburg Russia

RUSCH, GEORGE MICHAEL, toxicology and risk assessment director; b. N.Y.C., Dec. 19, 1947; s. George Warren and Emma Ellen (Whitford) R.; children: Heather Lynn, Michael. BS, Hobart Coll., Geneva, N.Y., 1963; MS, CUNY, 1967; PhD, Adelphi U., Garden City, N.Y., 1971. Rsch. assoc. NYU Med. Ctr., 1972-77; dir. inhalation toxicology Huntingdon Life Sci., East Millstone, N.J., 1977-80; mgr. inhalation toxicology Allied Signal Corp., Morristown, N.J., 1980-84, mgr. gen. toxicology, 1984-89; dir. toxicology and risk assessment Honeywell Internat., Morristown, N.J., 1989—; mem. com. of toxicology Nat. Rsch. Coun., Washington, 1997—; chair nat. adv. com. on acute exposure guidance levels, U.S. Environ. Protection Agy., Washington, 1996—. Contbr. articles to profl. jours. Adjunct prof. Rutgers U., Piscatwawy, N.J., 1997—. Recipient Herbert Stockinger award Am. Conf. of Govt. Indsl. Hygienes, Cin., 2000. Mem. Soc. Toxicology, Am. Indsl. Hygiene Assn., Emergency Response Planning Guideline Commn. E-mail: george.rusch@honeywell.com. Home: 870 Dow Rd Bridgewater NJ 08807-1179 Office: Honeywell International 101 Columbia Rd Morristown NJ 07960-4658

RÜSCHOFF, BERND, linguist; b. Essen, Germany, Oct. 14, 1953; s. Willy and Hildegard (Dunkhoefner) R.; m. Anne Vasseur, Aug. 13, 1983; children: Marie, Emily. MA, U. Alta., Edmonton, Can., 1978; PhD, U. London, 1982. Grad. tchg. asst. U. Alta., 1977-78; lectr. Poly. North London, 1979-82, European Bus. Sch., London, 1981-82; head of lang. ctr. Wuppertal (Germany) U., 1983-93; prof. Ednl. U., Karlsruhe, Germany, 1993-98; prof. didactics and tech. enhanced lang. learning U. Essen, 1998—; project evaluator, advisor German Ministry of Sci. and Rsch., 1997-98, active Lingo-Rsch. Project, 1993-96; cons., dir. of studies New-Style Workshops-Modern Lang. Projects, Coun. of Europen, Strasbourg, France; cons., advisor Ministry of Edn.-Lower Saxony, Hannover, Germany, 1986-89, mem. adv. bd., Expo 2000 ednl. cons., 1996—; cons. Fed. Inst. for Vocat. Edn., Berlin, 1995-96; vis. lectr. German Acad. Exch. Svc., Australia, 1990; active various projects Lingua/Socrates/Leonardo Bur. of European Commn., 1980s—. Author: Fremdsprachenunterricht mit computergestützten Materialien: didaktische Überlegungen und Beispiele, 1986, 88, (with D. Wolff) Fremdsprachenlernen in der Wissensgesellschaft, 1999; editor: (with A. Korsvold) New Technologies in Language Learning and Teaching, 1997; contbr. numerous articles to profl. jours. Mem. German Assn. Applied Linguistics (mem. exec. coun. 1990—), Eurocall European Assn. Tech. Enhanced Lang. Learning (mem. exec. com. 1993-2000, elected pres. 2000—). Avocations: music, arts, sports. Home: Liebigstrasse 35, D-42283 Wuppertal Germany Office: U Essen, Dept English/Didactics, D-45117 Essen Germany

RUSCIANO, DARIO, molecular biologist, researcher; b. Naples, July 10, 1955; arrived in Switzerland, 1989; s. Antonio and Rossana (Fusco) R.; m. Patrizia Lorenzoni, April 23, 1989; 1 child, Giulia. D in Biology, U. Pisa, Italy, 1979. Postdoctoral fellow U. Pisa, 1979-82; staff scientist Sclavo Rsch. Ctr., Siena, Italy, 1982-89; sr. rsch. assoc. Friedrich Miescher Inst., Basel, Switzerland, 1989—; PhD instr. U. Naples, 1989-91. Author: Cancer Metastasis: Experimental Approaches, 2000; contbr. articles to profl. jours., chpts. to books. Recipient grant European Cmty., 1994—, grant Swiss Cancer League, 1996-98, grant Basel Cancer League, 1999—. Mem. Metastasis Soc., Planetary Soc. Avocations: astronomy, astrophysics, book collection, tennis, ski. Office: Rsch Ctr Sifi SpA, Via E Patti 36, 95020 Lavinaio Catania, Italy

RUSEDSKI, GREG, tennis player; b. Montreal, Que., Can., Sept. 6, 1973. Profl. tennis player, 1991—. Avocation: basketball. Office: c/o ATP Tour 201 Atp Tour Blvd Ponte Vedra Beach FL 32082*

RUSEK, JOSEF, zoologist, educator; b. Petrovice u Karviné, Czech Republic, July 18, 1938; s. Rudolf and Anna (Lachnit) R.; m. Jitka Šťastná, Dec. 23, 1961; children: Jiři, Jarmila. MS, U. J.E. Purkyně, Brno, Czech Republic, 1961; PhD, Czechoslovak Acad. Sci., Prague, Czech Republic, 1967, DSc, 1989. Rsch. scientist Inst. Entomology Czechoslovak Acad. Sci., Prague, 1967-79; sr. rsch. scientist Inst. Landscape Ecology Czechoslovak Acad. Sci., Č. Budějovice, Czech Republic, 1979-85, sr. rsch. scientist, dir. Inst. Soil Biology, 1986—; prof. zoology U. Vienna (Austria), 1990—; prof. ecology U. S. Bohemia, Czech Republic, 1993—; mem. Internat. Com. Soil Zoology, Internat. Soc. Soil Sci., 1988—, v.p. bureau of soil biology, 1996—; vice-chair Czech Nat. Com., Internat. Geosphere-Biosphere Programme, 1990—; chair Czech Nat. Com., Sci. Com. on Problems of the Environment, Prague, 1990—. Author: The Central European Agriotes and Ectinus, 1972, Soil Fauna of Three Types of Flooded Meadows, 1984; co-editor: European Jour. Soil Biology, 1992—; contbr. articles to profl. jours. Pacific Forest Rsch. Ctr. postdoctoral fellow, 1974-75. Mem. Czech. Entomol. Soc. (treas. 1972-78), Czech Zool. Soc. (com. mem. 1983—). Avocations: music, macrophotography, scuba diving. Elaborated and defended scientific proposal for establishing of the lab. soil biology, and Inst. of Soil Biology of the Acad. of Scis. (Czech Rep.), 1985. Office: Inst Soil Biology Acad Sci, Na Sádkách 7, 370 05 Ceske Budejovice Czech Republic

RUSET, CHRISTIAN CONSTANTIN, physicist, researcher; b. Botoshani, Romania, Apr. 21, 1949; s. Constantin Ion Calota and Elena Mihai Ruset; m. Marinela Ioan Florian, Nov. 18, 1971; 1 child, Oanca Monica. Physicist, U. Al I Cuza, Iassy, Romania, 1972, PhD, 1985. Physicist Inst. Atomic Physics, Bucharest, Romania, 1972-76; rsch. fellow Joint Inst. Nuclear Rsch., Dubna, Russia, 1976-78, Inst. Physics and Tech. of Radiation Devices, Bucharest, Romania, 1978-90; sr. rsch. fellow Nat. Inst. for Laser, Plasma and Radiation Physics, Bucharest, 1990—; cons. Metaltech. Ltd., Durham, Eng., 1996; rsch. in plasma surface engring. Inventor: two Romanian patents; contbr. articles to profl. jours. Fellowship UN, Univ. Birmingham, Eng. (hon.), 1990, European Comty. Cost Program, U. Birmingham, 1994; grantee: European Comty, Copernicus Program, 1994-97; Recipient Prize for Physics Romanian Acad. Home: Apt 19 Sector 5, Calea Rahovei 317 Bl 30A, Bucharest Romania Office: Nat Inst Laser & Radi Phys, Str Atomistilor 1 Box MG 36, Magurele-Bucharest Romania

RUSH, JULIA ANN HALLORAN (MRS. RICHARD HENRY RUSH), artist, writer; b. St. Louis, Oct. 25, 1927; d. Edward Roosevelt and Flavia Hadley (Griffin) Halloran; m. Richard Henry Rush, Aug. 15, 1956; 1 child, Sallie Haywood. Student Washington U., St. Louis, 1945-47; B.A., George Washington U., 1949. One-woman shows: Fort Amador Officers Club, Panama Canal Zone, El Panama Hotel, Panama, George Washington U., Statler Hotel, Roosevelt Hotel, Washington, Newspaper Women's Club, Washington, Waukegan Library, Ill., Epworth Heights Hotel, Ludington, Mich.; exhibited in group shows: Panama Art League, Corcoran Gallery;

represented in permanent collections: U. Panama; also pvt. collections; model John Robert Powers Agy., 1950; sec.-treas., dir. N.Am. Acceptance Corp., 1956-58; v.p. Rush and Halloran, Inc., 1957-58, ptnr., 1954-57; research asst. to husband's bi-weekly newsletter Art/Antiques Investment Report, 1973—, articles in Wall St. transcript, 1971—. Illustrator: Antiques As An Investment (author Richard H. Rush), 1968; research asst.: Investments You Can Live With and Enjoy (author: Richard H. Rush), 1974, 2d. edit., 1975, 3d edit., 1976; Photographer: Automobiles as an Investment, 1982; Investing in Classic Cars, 1984. Recipient 1st prize (Panama) Newspaper Women's Club, 1953; First Prize Panama Art League, 1953. Mem. DAR, Nat. League Am. Penwomen, Florence Crittenton Circle (rec. sec. 1968-69), Kappa Kappa Gamma. Club: Washington, Royal Palm Yacht (No. Ft. Myers, Fla.), Boca West Golf and Country (Boca Raton, Fla.)

RUSH, MICHAEL DAVID, political science educator; b. Kingston, Surrey, Eng., Oct. 29, 1937; s. Wilfred George and Elizabeth May (Gurney) R.; m. Jean Margaret Telford, July 25, 1964; children: Jonathan, Anthony. BA in History and Politics with honors, U. Sheffield, Eng., 1962, PhD in Politics, 1966. From lectr. to sr. lectr. politics U. Exeter, Eng., 1964-90, reader in parliamentary govt., 1990-94, prof. politics, 1994—; vis. lectr. U. London, Ont., Can., 1967-68. Author: The Selection of Parliamentary Candidates, 1969, Parliament and the Public, 1976, The Cabinet and Policy Formation, 1984, Politics and Society, 1992; co-author: An Introduction to Political Sociology, 1971; editor: The House of Commons, Services and Facilities, 1976, The House of Commons: Services and Facilities, 1976-83, 1983, Parliament and Pressure Politics, 1990, Continuity and Change: British Government and Politics Since 1945, 1995; contbr. articles to profl. jours. With Royal Army Svc. Corps, 1957-59. Rsch. fellow Carleton U., Ottawa, Ont., 1975, 92, 99, U. Sask., 1982. Fellow Royal Soc. of Arts. Avocations: reading, theatre, classical music. Home: 2 St Loyes Rd Heavitree, Exeter EX2 5HA, England Office: Univ Exeter Dept Politics, Rennes Dr, Exeter EX4 4RJ, England

RUSH, RICHARD HENRY, financial executive, writer, lecturer; b. N.Y.C., Mar. 6, 1915; s. Henry Frederick and Bessie (Vreeland) R.; m. Julia Ann Halloran, Aug. 15, 1956; 1 dau., Sallie Haywood. BA summa cum laude, Dartmouth Coll., 1937, MCS, 1938; MBA with highest distinction, Harvard U., 1941, DCS (Littauer fellow), 1942. Dir. aviation U.S. Bur. Fgn. and Domestic Commerce, 1945-46; chief economist, chmn. planning com. All Am. Aviation (U.S. Air), 1943-45; dir. aircraft divsn. Nat. Security Resources Bd., 1948-51; Washington rep. to J. Paul Getty, 1951-52; ptnr. Rush & Halloran, 1953-58; pres., chmn. bd. N.Am. Acceptance Corp., Atlanta, also Washington, 1956-59; owner Richard H. Rush Enterprises, Greenwich, Conn., also Washington, 1953-73; prof., chmn. dept. finance and investments Sch. Bus. Adminstrn., Am. U., Washington, 1967-70, 77-79. Author: Art as an Investment, 1961, A Strategy of Investing for Higher Return, 1962, The Techniques of Becoming Wealthy, 1963, Antiques as an Investment, 1968, The Wrecking Operation: Phase One, 1972, Investments You Can Live With and Enjoy, 1976, Techniques of Becoming Wealthy, 1977, Automobiles as an Investment, 1982, Selling Collectibles, 1982, Collecting Classic Cars for Profit and Capital Gain, 1984; contbr. over 700 articles to newspapers, mags. and profl. jours.; editor series of books on starting businesses for U.S. Dept. Commerce; contbg. editor Wall St. Transcript, 1971-97, Art/Antiques Investment Report, 1972-97. Trustee, exec. com. Finch Coll., 1968-72. Recipient Pres.'s med., CCNY, 1997. Mem. Am. Mktg. Assn. (chmn. nat. com.), Am. Econ. Assn., Am. Statis. Assn., Internat. Platform Assn., AAUP, Harvard Club (N.Y.C.), Royal Palm Yacht Club (Ft. Myers), Phi Beta Kappa, Phi Kappa Phi, Omicron Delta Kappa. Episcopalian.

RUSHER, GEORGE, small business owner; b. Hanover, Pa., June 25, 1914; s. Emory Ruben and Hattie Mabel (Feeser) R.; m. Elizabeth Pauline Huchala, June 10, 1938 (dec. 1998). BS, U. So. Calif., 1938. Heater, air-conditioning svc. tech. So. Calif. Gas Co., L.A., 1938-46; pres., chief engr. Rusher Air Conditioning, Inglewood and Torrance, Calif., 1946—. Pres. N. Inglewood, Calif. C. of C., 1946, Radiant Heat Inst., L.A., 1950, Contractors Divsn. of Heating and Air Conditioning Industries, 1955. Republican. Avocation: designing, fabricating and installing innovative heating and air-conditioning systems.

RUSHING, PHILIP DALE, retired social worker; b. Carbondale, Ill., Mar. 15, 1932; S. Paul and Beulah Myrl (Benton) R.; m. Linda North, July 5, 1958 (div. July 1964); 1 child, Lisa Anne Rushing Burrow; m. Rosalie Anne Sturm, Aug. 20, 1966. BA, So. Ill. U., 1958; MSW, Washington U., St. Louis, 1960. Bd. cert. diplomate, ACSW; lic. social worker, Ill. Child welfare worker Ill. Dept. Pub. Welfare, Salem, East St. Louis, 1958-60; child welfare supr. Ill. Dept. Pub. Welfare, East St. Louis, 1960-63; field rep. Nat. Assn. for Retarded Children, Dallas, Denver, 1963-65; dir. social svcs. A.L. Bowen Children's Ctr., Harrisburg, Ill., 1965-68; asst. zone dir. for mentally retarded Ill. Dept. of Mental Health, Harrisburg, 1968-74; regional coord. for devel. disabilities Ill. Dept. of Mental Health & Devel. Disabilities, Marion, 1974-83; social work adminstr. Choate Mental Health & Devel. Ctr., Anna, Ill., 1983-95; ret., 1995; adj. asst. prof. So. Ill. U. Rehab. Inst., Carbondale, Ill., 1968-78; bd. dirs. Southeastern Ill. Pastoral Counseling Ctrs., chmn. pers. com., 1996-98. Bd. cert. diplomate ACSW; lic. clin. social worker. Bd. deacons First Presbyn. Ch., Harrisburg, 1974-77, bd. trustees, 1978-80, bd. elders, 1980-83, 96-98. With USN, 1951-55, Korea. Fellow Am. Assn. on Mental Retardation (life, chmn. social work divsn. Ill. chpt. 1973-74); mem. NASW (chmn. East St. Louis br. 1962). Home: 6542 Hwy 13 W Harrisburg IL 62946-4142

RUSIN, YEVGENIY PAVLOVICH, researcher, executive; b. Novosibirsk, Russia, Nov. 16, 1954; s. Pavel Fyodorovich and Iraida Nikolaevna (Permyakova) R.; m. Diana Mihailovna Merzlova, Nov. 6, 1981; 1 child, Pavel. MS, Novosibirsk Inst Railway Engrs, Russia, 1977; PhD, Inst. Mining, Novosibirsk, 1981. Rschr. Inst. Mining, Novosibirsk, Russia, 1981-83, 95—, head fgn. rels., 1983-88, lab. head, 1988-95; dir. Siberian Rsch. and Tech. Lab., Novosibirsk, 1991-97; head fgn. rels. Corvette Sci. Ctr., Novosibirsk, 1993—; deputy dir. devel., fgn. rels. Contrast Ltd., Novosibirsk, 1997-99; Novosibirsk rep. of World Technology Corp., Detroit, 2000—. Co-author: Pneumatic Punchers, 1991; inventor/patentee in field. Avocations: martial arts, music. Home: PO Box 138, RU630075 Novosibirsk Russia Office: Inst Mining, 54 Krasny Prospect, RU630091 Novosibirsk Russia also: Contrast Ltd, 86 Krasny Prospect, RU630005 Novosibirsk Russia

RUSKAUP, CALVIN, therapist, history professor; b. St. Louis, Feb. 5, 1939; s. Henry and Viola (Vogt) R.; m. Chandricka Maharaj, Apr. 1, 1991. BSc, U. Mo., St. Louis, 1967; PhD, Ohio State U., 1979. Diplomate Am. Psychotherapy Assn. Co-founder Cmty. Broadcasting-Sta. WFAC, Columbus, Ohio, 1975-77; lectr. Ohio State U., 1975-79; designer Trimobile Safety Car, Aspen, Colo., 1980-81; pastoral counselor UL Ch., Knoxville, Tenn., 1982-85; pres. UL Ch., Hilo, Hawaii, 1986—; spkr. World Parliament Scientists, 2000. Chmn. Commn. to Stop Violence, 1999-2000; editor Patriot Press, 1997-98; Patriot and Libertarian parties U.S. presdl. candidate, 1996. Mem. AAAS Sr. Scientists Engrs. (emeritus), Am. Anthropol. Assn., Acad. Polit. Sci., Orgn. Am. Historians, Assn. Transpersonal Psychology, N.Y. Acad. Scis., Am. Psychoanalytic Assn., Pub. Rels. Soc. Am., Nat. Press Club, Circumnavigators Club.

RUSKIN, RYAN SCOTT, packaging company executive; b. Pitts., Jan. 31, 1968; s. Stanley C. and Judith Anne (Blitzstein) R. BA, Princeton U., 1990; MBA, Northwestern U., 1994. Dir. tng. and devel. The Princeton Rev., 1987-90, nat. tng. dir., 1987-92; mgr. Vail (Colo.) Assocs., 1990-92; dir. strategic planning Sterling Lebanon Packaging Corp., Jeannette, Pa., 1992-94; assoc. A.T. Kearney, Chgo., 1994-96, sr. mgr., 1996-98; exec. v.p. Sterling Packaging Corp., Pitts., 1998-2000, pres., 2000—; advisor Coro Ctr. for Civi Leadership, Pitts., 1999—, J.L. Kellogg Sch. Northwestern U., 1994—. Mem. alumni coun. Shady Side Acad., Pitts., 1998; speech writing team, media coord. Rep. Nat. Conv., 1988; dir. Open Hand Chgo., 1999—; nat. faculty U.S. Sailing, Newport, 1990-94. Mem. Am. Soc. for Quality Control, Union League Club of Chgo., Chgo. Yacht Club, Inst. of Packaging Profls. Avocations: sailing, skiing, tennis, golf. Fax: 724-523-2476. E-mail: rruskin@spc.cc. Home: 823 W Junior Ter Chicago IL 60613-1607 Office: 1000 Thomas Ave Jeannette PA 15644-1840

RUSLI, educator electronics; b. Tanjung, Pinang, Indonesia, May 5, 1968; s. Kadam and Hatimah R. B of Engring., Nat. U. Singapore, 1991, M of Engring., 1992; PhD, Cambridge U., England, 1996. Lectr. Nanyang Tech. U., Singapore, 1996—. Mem. IEEE, Inst. Elec. Engrs. Avocation: music. Office: Nanyang Tech U, Block S2 Sch EEE Nanyang Av, Singapore 639798, Singapore

RUSLING, BARBARA N(EUBERT), state commissioner, real estate broker; b. St. Louis, Nov. 27, 1945; d. Ralph L. and Rosemary (Stroot) Neubert; m. Randolph H. Wieser, Apr. 23, 1966 (div. Nov. 1983); children: Keith, Steve, Eric; m. Robert Best Rusling, Aug. 2, 1985. BA, Vanderbilt U., 1966; postgrad., Baylor U., 1975. Lic. real estate broker. Appraisal intern Smith Real Estate, Waco, Tex., 1975; resident real estate broker Sanger Suburban Realty, Waco, 1975-81, sales mgr., 1981-83; pres., gen. mgr. Coldwell Banker Hallmark Realty, Waco, 1983-99; commr. Tex. Gen. Svcs. Commn., 1997—; mem. from dist. 57 Tex. State Ho. Reps., 1995-97. Chmn. bd. dirs. YWCA, Waco, 1976-79; dir. Leadership Waco Program, 1986-87; various positions Hist. Waco Found.; bd. dirs. Waco Civic Theatre, treas., 1999—; bd. dirs. Family Counseling Ctr., 1991-96, United Way, 1992-98, Family Abuse Ctr., 1993-2000, Waco Better Bus. Bur., 1994-99. Mem. Tex. Assn. Realtors (edn. com., strategic planning com. 1983-95, realtor lawyer com. 1985-93), Realtors Nat. Mktg. Inst. (cert.), Waco Bd. Realtors (past bd. dirs., salesman of yr. 1979), Waco C. of C. (bd. dirs. 1990-93), Am. Heart Assn. (McLennan County bd. dirs. 1997—, pres. 1999-2000), Waco Sailing Club, Kappa Delta. Home: 1635 Meandering Way China Spring TX 76633-2905 Office: Coldwell Banker 500 N Valley Mills Dr Waco TX 76710-6007

RUSLING, PAUL ALEXANDER, broadcast executive, consultant; b. Bridlington, Yorkshire, England, Nov. 17, 1953; s. David Joseph and Barbara Alice (Simpson) R.; m. Anna Pyrah, July 17, 1978; children: Dawn Crystal, Benjamin Paul. DJ, engr. Radio Caroline, various BBC locals, Radio Luxembourg, 1972-77; asst. mgr. WSRF & WSHE, 1978-89; con's engr. Radio Nova, 1980-83; ops. mgr. Laser 558, 1983-84; cons. & engr. High Adventure Ministries, Calif. & Lebanon, Voice of Hope, 1985-88, Atlantic 252, 1985, Transcom/WBC, 1986-90, Solidarity Radio, Poland, 1990-91; cons. Polish Govt., 1990-91, Radio Moscow, 1990, Lithuanian Govt., 1991-92; founder Isle of Man Internat. Broadcasting Co., 1995, CEO, 1999—; cons. in field. Author: (books) Lid Off Laser 558, 1984, Trans Frontier Radio, 1986; assoc. editor: (book) Who's Who in British Radio, 1996. Mem. Radio Soc. Great Britain, Radio Acad., Inst. of Dirs.

RUSSAKOVICH, NIKOLAI ARTEMJEVICH, physicist, educator, researcher; b. Moguilev, Belarus, Apr. 9, 1953; 1; s. Artem Mikhailovich R. and Antonina Antonovna Bronovitskaya; m. Nadezhda Lvovna Saveljeva, Aug. 26, 1976 (div. Mar. 1995); 1 child, Olga; m. Elena Nikolaevna Pankova, Mar. 17, 1995; 1 child, Artem. Degree in Physics, U. Minsk, USSR, 1975; Candidate Scis., Joint Inst. for Nuc. Rsch., Russia, 1987, DSc, 1993. Cert. physicist. Physicist Inst. Physics, Minsk, Russia, 1975-79; physicist Joint Inst. for Nuc. Physics, Dubna, Russia, dep. dir. lab. for nuc. problems, 1988-92, chief sci. sec., 1992-93, dir. lab. nuc. problems, 1993—; assoc. prof. MPTI, Moscow, 1996—. Editor: LHC Physics and Detectors, 1995. Office: Joint Inst For Nuc Rsch, Joliot-Curie 6, 141980 Dubna Russia

RUSSALOVA, MARGARITA NIKOLAEVNA, psychophysiologist; b. Moscow, Aug. 28, 1932; d. Nikolai Trofimovich and Polina Mikhailovna (Chaikova) Valuev; m. Anatoliy Ivanovich Simonov, Mar. 20, 1954 (div. June 1961); 1 child, Nikolai; m. Vladimir Mikhailovich Rusalov, Dec. 8, 1962; children: Mikhail, Yuriy. M. Physiology, Moscow U., 1961; ScD in Physiology, Inst. Higher Nervous Activity, Moscow, 1984. Sr. asst. Inst. Higher Nervous Activity and Neurophysiology, Moscow, 1962-66, jr. rschr., 1966-75, sr. rschr., 1975-88, leading rschr., 1988—. Author: Voluntary Regulation of Autonomic Functions of the Organism, 1966 (Award of Inst. Higher Nervous Activity 1966), Experimental Studies of Human Emotional Responses, 1979 (Award of Inst. Higher Nervous Activity 1979); co-author: Nervous Tension and Heart Activity, 1969, Physiological Peculiarities of Positive and Negative Emotional Reactions, 1972, Apparatus and Methodic Questions of Neurophysiological Experiment, 1970, Brain and Behavior, 1990, Individual Brain and Behavior, 1993; editor: Mechanisms of Integrative Activity of the Brain, 1981; contbr. articles to profl. jours. Recipient Award of the Coun. of Ministry, Russia, 1989; grantee Soros Found., 1996, Russian Found. for Basic Rsch., 1996-98, Russian Humanitarian Sci. Found., 1997—. Mem. Internat. Brain Rsch. Orgn. Avocation: painting. Office: Inst Higher Nervous Activit, 5a Butlerova Str, 117865 Moscow Russia

RUSSEL, RICHARD ALLEN, telecommunications consultant, aerospace engineer, nuclear engineer, electrical engineer, retired naval officer; b. Shreveport, La., Jan. 24, 1958; s. Robert Lee and Gloria Jeanette (Gile) R.; m. Kathryn Joy Koehler, Dec. 30, 1983; children: Richard Allen Russel Jr., Kammie Joyce Jeanette, Jonathan Mark, Katie Jacqueline Keala, Stephen Sungmin. BSEE, U. N.Mex., 1980; AeE in Aeros. and Astronautics, Naval Postgrad. Sch., Monterey, Calif., 1994, MSc in Astron. Engring., 1994; postgrad., Colo. Tech. U., 2000—. Commd. ensign, nuclear submarine officer USN, 1980, advanced through grades to lt. comdr., 1990; main propulsion analyst USS Puffer, Pearl Harbor, Hawaii, 1981-85; antisubmarine analyst, nuclear engr., comdr. 3d fleet USN, Pearl Harbor, 1985-87; combat systems officer USS TAUTUG, Pearl Harbor, 1987-89; navigator, ops. officer USS Indpls., Pearl Harbor, 1989-92; UHF/EHF satellite navy rep. PEO-SCS, USN, El Segundo, Calif., 1994-96; project mgr. for spacecraft comms. Booz-Allen and Hamilton, Inc., San Diego, 1996-97; dir. Space and Comm. Predicate Logic Inc., Colorado Springs, Colo., 1997-2000; dir. sys. engring. Maxim Systems Inc., Colorado Springs, Colo., 2000—; chief engr. Ctr. Y2K Strategic Stability; core systems engr. SPACE Battle Mgmt.; chief sys. engr. worldwide shared early warning program USSPACE Command. Contbr. articles to profl. jours. Pres. congregation Christ the Cornerstone Luth. Ch.; mem. sch. bd. Our Savior Luth. Sch., Aiea, Hawaii, 1986; den leader webelos Boy Scouts Am., 1995-97; bd. dirs. Children's Angelcare Aid Internat., 1998-99; chmn. bd. dirs. Christ the Cornerstone Luth. Ch.; h.s. wrestling coach; mem. telecomm. policy adv. com. Colorado Springs City Coun., 2000—; mem. telecomms. policy advisory com., Colorado Springs, 2000—, e-commerce advisory com., 2000—. Fellow Inst. for the Advancement of Engring.; assoc. fellow AIAA (vice-chair edn. L.A. sect. 1991—, dep. dir. edn. region VI 1994-97, Spl. Svc. Citation for dveloping internet capability 1996); mem. Space Nuclear Thermal Propulsion, Adventurers Club of L.A., Eta Kappa Nu. Republican. Lutheran. Achievements include design of predictive control system for thermoacoustic refrigerator, 3D laser range and orientation measuring system, navy satellite/computer secure communications systems; asynchronous transfer mode (ATM) networks; satellite and ground system design on CYBERSTAR, EHF Communications Satellite, Global Broadcast Service, Navy UHF Follow-On Satellite, GEOSAT Follow-On satellite; digital modular radio design; submarine communications support system; wireless ethernet design and installation; designed the U.S.-Russia Center for Y2K strategic stability. E-mail: rrussel@maximsys.com. Home: 1450 Branding Iron Dr Colorado Springs CO 80915-2413

RUSSELL, ALLAN DAVID, lawyer; b. Cleve., May 6, 1924; s. Allan MacGillivray and Marvel (Codling) R.; m. Lois Anne Robinson, June 12, 1947; children: Lisa Anne, Robinson David, Martha Leslie. BA, Yale U., 1945, LLB, 1951. Bar: N.Y. 1952, Conn. 1956, Mass. 1969, U.S. Supreme Ct. 1977. Atty. Sylvania Electric Products, Inc., N.Y.C., 1951-56; div. counsel Sylvania Electric Products, Inc., Batavia, N.Y., 1956-65; sr. counsel Sylvania Electric Products, Inc., 1965-71; sec., sr. counsel GTE Sylvania Inc., Stamford, Conn., 1971-76; asst. gen. counsel GTE Service Corp., 1976-80, v.p., assoc. gen. counsel staff, 1980-83; pvt. practice Redding, Conn., 1983—; sec., dir. mktg. subs. Sylvania Entertainment Products Corp., 1961-67; sec. Wilbur B. Driver Co. Dist. leader Rep. Party, New Canaan, Conn., 1955-56; sec. bd. dirs. Youth Found., Inc., 1981-83, bd. dirs., 1985—, pres., 2000—; mem. planning commn., Redding, Conn., 1987-89; mem. Redding Bd. Ethics, 1990-96, chmn., 1992-96; warden Christ Ch. Parish, Redding, 1987-89; bd. dirs. Mark Twain Libr., 1988-94, v.p., 1988-89, pres., 1990-92. With USAAF, 1943-46. Mem. SAR, Assn. of Bar of City of N.Y., Conn. Bar Assn. (exec. com. corp. counsel sect. 1986-90), Am. Soc. Corp. Secs., St. Nicholas Soc., Collie Club Am. Found., Inc. (v.p., dir. 1986-89, pres. 1989-90), Soc. Colonial Wars, Yale Alumni Assn. (sec. local chpt. 1953-56), Yale Club of Danbury (pres. 1990—), Phi Delta Phi. Home: 9 Little River Ln Redding CT 06896-2018

RUSSELL, ANDREW TARBET, materials engineer; b. Harlow New Town, U.K., Mar. 27, 1963; s. Tarbet Chalmers and Betty Anne (Reader) R. B in Engring., U. Liverpool, Eng., 1986; PhD, U. Manchester, Inst. Sci. and Tech., Manchester, Eng., 1994. Contracts mgr. Water Rsch. Ctr., Swindon Wiltshire, Eng., U.K., 1990—. Co-author: Guidance Manual for the Structural Condition Assessment of Trunk Mains, 1992, Trenchless Technology Manual, 1995, Trenchless Technology CD-Rom Database, 1996, Trenchless Technology "Local Repairs Work" Video, 1996, (CD album) Calcium Waves, 1998. Avocations: composing music, drumming, cycling, jogging, snooker. Office: Water Rsch Ctr, Frankland Rd, Swindon SN5 8YF, England

RUSSELL, BRIAN SCOTNEY, retired government administrator, consultant; b. London, May 13, 1927; s. Ben Harold and Evelyn Scotney R.; m. Jane Pauline Farmer, Jan. 31, 1959; children: Philippa, Caroline. MA, Cambridge U., Eng., 1950. Legal practice London, 1951-56; mem. legal dept. Shell Petroleum, London, 1956-59, 61-63; head, land and legal Brunei Shell Petroleum, Seria Brunei, 1959-61; legal adviser Brit. Iron and Steel Fedn., London, 1961-68; mgr. spl. projects Charterhouse Japhet, London, 1968-73; legal adviser Bates Bank, London, 1973-78, Nat. Freight Corp., London, 1978-80; prin. adminstr. U.K. Steering Com. on Local Govt. Superannuation, London, 1982-96; ret., 1996; chmn. Bar Assn. for Commerce Fin. and Industry, London, 1966-73; pres. European Club of Local Authority/Staff Pension Schemes, Bordeaux, France, 1992-93; mem. numerous legal coms. Author: The Swallows; The Brighton and Storrington Beagles, 2000; editor: Middle Eastern Commercial Law, 1969. Founder Bow Group, London, 1949. Signalman Royal Navy, 1948. Officer of the Order of the Brit. Empire, Queen Elizabeth II, London, 1994. Mem. Itchenor Sailing Club, Nat. Swallow Assn. (nat. sec. 1965-70). Conservative. Ch. of England. Avocations: yacht racing, beagling, naval history, music.

RUSSELL, CAROL ANN, personnel service company executive; b. Detroit, Dec. 14, 1943; d. Billy and Iris Koud; m. Victor Rojas (div.). BA in English, CUNY-Hunter Coll., 1993. Registered employment cons. Various positions in temp. help cos. N.Y.C., 1964-74; v.p. Wollborg-Michelson, San Francisco, 1974-82; co-owner, pres. Russell Staffing Resources, Inc., San Francisco and Sonoma, 1983-98; ret.; co-founder Workplacecentral.com, 1999—; media guest, spkr., workshop and seminar leader in field; host/cmty. prodr. Job Net program for TCI Cable T.V. Pub. Checkpoint Newsletter; feature writer/columnist The Slant; contbr. articles to profl. publs. Named to the Inc. 500, 1989, 90. Mem. Am. Women in Radio and TV, Soc. to Preserve and Encourage Radio Drama Variety and Comedy, No. Calif. Human Resources Coun., Soc. Human Resource Mgmt., Calif. Assn. Pers. Cons. (pres. Golden State chpt. 1984-85), Calif. Assn. Temp. Svcs., Bay Area Pers. Assn. (pres. 1983-84), Pers. Assn. Sonoma County, Profl. Resume Writers Am., Am. Jewish Congress.

RUSSELL, CHERYL, claims adjustor; b. Landstuhl, Germany, June 29, 1959; came to U.S., 1960; d. Robert Leigh Gross and Gail Ann Jones-Gross; m. Brent Sargent Russell, Sept. 5, 1981; children: Craig Rice, Michael, Robert. Assocs. in Office Adminstrn., Husson Coll., 1980, BBA, 1992. Cert. profl. ins. woman. Attendance sec. Fifth St. Middle Sch., Bangor, Maine, 1986-89; teller Fleet Bank Maine, Bangor, 1992-94; claims technician Sedgwick Claims Mgmt. Svcs., Inc., Bangor, 1994-95, jr. examiner, 1995-96, claims examiner, 1996—. Loaned exec. United Way Penobscot Valley, Bangor, 1993, budget com., 1994-95, allocations com. Mem. Nat. Assn. Ins. Women (pres.-elect 1998-99, pres. 1999—, Claims Profl. of Yr. 1999), No. Maine Adjuster Assn. Avocations: karaoke singing, guitar playing, camping, crafting. E-mail: crussell@sedgwickcms.com. Home: 5 J St Bangor ME 04401-2576

RUSSELL, DAVID EMERSON, mechanical engineer, consultant; b. Jacksonville, Fla., Dec. 20, 1922; s. David Herbert and Wilhelmina Russell. B-Mech Engring., U. Fla., 1948; postgrad., Oxford (Eng.) U. Registered profl. engr., Fla., Ga. Mech. engr. United Fruit Co., N.Y.C., 1948-50; civilian mech. engr. U.S. Army C.E., Jacksonville, 1950-54; mech. engr. Aramco, Saudi Arabia, 1954-55; v.p. Beiswenger Hoch and Assocs., Inc., Jacksonville, Fla., 1955-57; owner, operator David E. Russell and Assocs., Cons. Engrs., Jacksonville, 1957-98; cons. engr., 1998—. Contbr. articles to profl. jours.; patentee in field. Chmn. Jacksonville Water Quality Control Bd., 1969-73; bd. dirs. Jacksonville Hist. Soc., 1981-82; mem. Jacksonville Biocentennial Commn., 1973-79. 2d lt. AUS, 1943-46. Recipient Outstanding Svs. award City of Jacksonville, 1974. Mem. ASME (chmn. N.E. Fla. 1967-68), Nat. Soc. Profl. Engrs., ASHRAE, Fla. Engring. Soc. Univ. Club (Jacksonville), Jacksonville Humane Soc. (life). Episcopalian. Avocations: world travel, boating, classical music. Home and Office: 4720 Timuquana Rd Jacksonville FL 32210-8231

RUSSELL, DAVID L., federal judge; b. Sapulpa, Okla., July 7, 1942; s. Lynn and Florence E. (Brown) R.; m. Dana J. Wilson, Apr. 16, 1971; 1 child, Sarah Elizabeth. BS, Okla. Bapt. U., 1963; J.D., Okla. U., 1965. Bar: Okla. 1965. Asst. atty. gen. State of Okla., Oklahoma City, 1968-69, legal adviser to gov., 1969-70; legal adviser Senator Dewey Bartlett, Washington, 1973-75; U.S. atty. for Western dist. Okla. Dept. Justice, 1975-77, 81-82; ptnr. Benefield & Russell, Oklahoma City, 1977-81; chief judge U.S. Dist. Ct. (we. dist.) Okla., Oklahoma City, 1982—. Lt. comdr. JAGC, USN, 1965-68. Selected Outstanding Fed. Ct. Trial judge Okla. Trial Lawyers Assn., 1988. Mem. Okla. Bar Assn., Fed. Bar Assn. (pres. Oklahoma City chpt. 1981), Order of Coif (alumnus mem.). Republican. Methodist. Office: US Dist Ct US Courthouse 200 NW 4th St Oklahoma City OK 73102-3026

RUSSELL, DAVID WILLIAMS, lawyer; b. Lockport, N.Y., Apr. 5, 1945; s. David Lawson and Jean Graves (Williams) R.; m. Frances Yung Chung Chen, May 23, 1970; children: Bayard Chen, Ming Rennick. AB, Dartmouth Coll., 1967, MBA, 1969; JD cum laude, Northwestern U., 1976. Bar: Ill. 1976, Ind. 1983. English tchr. Talledega (Ala.) Coll., summer 1967; math. tchr. Lyndon Inst., Lyndonville, Vt., 1967-68; asst. to pres. for planning Tougaloo (Miss.) Coll., 1969-71, bus. mgr., 1971-73; law clk. Montgomery, McCracken, Walker & Rhoads, Phila., summer 1975; with Winston & Strawn, Chgo., 1976-83; ptnr. Klineman, Rose, Wolf & Wallack, Indpls., 1983-87, Johnson, Smith, Pence, Densborn, Wright & Heath, Indpls., 1987-99, Bose McKinney & Evans, Indpls., 1999—; cons. Alfred P. Sloan Found., 1972-73; dir. Forum for Internat. Profl. Svcs., 1985—, sec., 1985-88, pres. 1988-89; U.S. Dept. Justice del. to U.S. China Joint Session on Trade, Investment & Econ. Law, Beijing, 1987; leader Ind. Products Trade Fair, Kawachinagano, Japan, 1996; lectr. Ind. law Ind. Gov.'s Trade Mission to Japan, 1986, internat. law Ind. Continuing Legal Edn. Forum, 1986-96, chmn., 1987, 89, 91; adj. prof. internat. bus. law Ind. U., 1993-95; bd. dirs. Ind. ASEAN Coun., Inc., 1988-93; nat. selection com. Woodrow Wilson Found. Adminstrv. Fellowship Program, 1973-76; vol. Lawyers for Creative Arts, Chgo., 1977-83; dir. World Trade Club of Ind., 1987-93, v.p., 1987-91, pres., 1991-92; dir. Ind. Swiss Found., 1991—, Writer's Ctr., Indpls., 1999—, Asian Am. Alliance, 1999—; dir. Ind. Soviet Trade Consortium, 1991-99, sec., 1991-92; v.p., bd. dirs. Ind. Sister Cities, 1988—; dir. Internat. Ctr. Indpls., 1988-92, v.p., 1988-89; Ind. dist. enrollment dir. Dartmouth Coll., 1990-99; dir. Carmel Sister Cities, 1993—, v.p. 1995-96, pres. 1997-99, chmn., 1999—; v.p., gen. coun. Lawrence Durrell Soc., 1993—; mem. bd. advisors Ctr. for Internat. Bus. Edn. and Rsch. Krannert Grad. Sch. Mgmt. Purdue U., 1995—; dir., v.p., gen. coun. Global Crossroads Found., Inc., 1995—; mem. bd. arbitrators NASD, 1999—; mem. Ind. Dist. Export Coun., 1999—. Woodrow Wilson Found. Adminstrv. fellow, 1969-72. Mem. ABA, ACLU, Ill. Bar Assn., Ind. Bar Assn. (vice chmn. internat. law sect., 1988-90, chmn. 1990-92, co-chmn. written publs. com. 1997-99), Indpls. Bar Assn., Dartmouth Lawyers Assn., Indpls. Assn. Chinese Ams., Chinese Music Soc., Dartmouth Club of Ind. (sec. 1986-87, pres. 1987-88), Internat. Bar Assn., Zeta Psi. Presbyterian. Home: 10926 Lakeview Dr Carmel IN 46033-3937 Office: Bose McKinney & Evans LLP 2700 First Ind Plz 135 N Pennsylvania St Indianapolis IN 46204-2400

RUSSELL, DENNIS CHARLES, mathematics educator; b. Southampton, Eng., Sept. 4, 1927; came to Can. 1960; s. Henry Charles and Doris Violet (Render) R.; m. Joyce Elizabeth Margaret Brown, Dec. 21, 1951; children—Julian, Jeremy. B.Sc., U. Sheffield, Eng., 1948; M.Sc., U. London,

1952, Ph.D., 1958, D.Sc., 1972. Asst. lectr. Northampton Coll. Advanced Tech., London, 1948-52; asst. lectr., lectr. Keele U., Staffordshire, Eng., 1955-60; assoc. prof. Mt. Allison U., Sackville, N.B., Can., 1960-62; prof. math. York U., Toronto, Can., 1962-89, head dept. 1962-69, prof. emeritus 1989—; external doctoral examiner for 11 univs.; frequent lectr. U. Colloquia and Math. Confs. Contbr. articles to profl. jours.; referee for 33 internat. math. jours. Fellow Nat. Research Council Can., 1968, Canada Council, 1969, 76-77; grantee Nuffield Found. Eng., 1973, Nat. Scis. and Engring. Rsch. Coun. Can., 1968-91. Fellow Inst. Math. and Applications; mem. Can. Math. Soc. (council 1967-71, 73-75), London Math. Soc., Am. Math. Soc., Math. Assn. Am. Office: York Univ Dept Math, 4700 Keele St, Toronto, ON Canada M3J 1P3 Home: Dormy Cottage Whitwell Rd, Isle of Wight PO381LJ, England

RUSSELL, EUGENE ROBERT, SR., engineering educator, administrator; b. Cromwell, Conn., Aug. 24, 1932; s. Arland William and Annie Margaret (LeBlanc) R.; m. Mary Lou Conner, June 29, 1957; children: Theresa, Janice, Eugene Jr., Anna, Ruth, Julie, Susan, Paul, Carol, Cecilia. BSCE, U. Mo., Rolla, 1958; MS in Civil Engring., Iowa State U., 1965; PhD, Purdue U., West Lafayette, Ind., 1974. Registered profl. engr., Iowa, Ind. Asst. bridge engr. State of Calif. Pub. Works, Sacramento, 1958-62; asst. area constrn. engr. Iowa Hwy. Commn., Grinnell, 1962-63; rsch. asst. soils Iowa State U., Ames, 1963-65; asst. prof. Ind. Inst. Tech., Ft. Wayne, 1965-69; rsch. assoc. Purdue U., West Lafayette, 1969-74; assoc. prof. Kans. State U., Manhattan, 1974-80, prof. civil engring., 1980—, dir. Ctr. for Transp. Rsch. and Tng., 1990—, assoc. dir. Mid-Am. Transp. Ctr., 1995-99, Mark and Margaret Hulings prof. civil engring., 1997—. Contbr. more than 60 articles to profl. jours. With USN, 1951-53. Fellow ASCE (life mem., br. pres.), Inst. Transp. Engrs.; mem. Am. R.R. Engring. & Maintentance Assn., Transp. Rsch. Bd. (univ. rep., mem. emeritus com. A3AO5), Transp. Rsch. Forum, Am. Soc. Engring. Edn., Nat. Assn. Railroad Passengers, Roadway Safety Found., Nat. Assn. County Engrs., Am. Pub. Works Assn., Sigma Xi, Chi Epsilon. Home: 3424 Dickens Ave Manhattan KS 66503-2413 Office: Kansas State Univ Dept Civil Engring 2118 Fiedler Hall Manhattan KS 66506

RUSSELL, GEORGE, industrial investment company executive; b. Oct. 25, 1935; s. William H. and Frances A. Russell; m. Dorothy Brown, 1959; 3 children. BA with honors, Durham U., 1958; DEng (hon.), U. Newcastle upon Tyne (Eng.), 1985; DBA (hon.), Northumbria (Eng.) U., 1992; LLD, Sunderland (Eng.) U., 1995. From grad. trainee to product sales mgr. ICI, 1958-67; v.p., gen. mgr. Welland Chem. Co. Can. Ltd., 1968, St. Clair Chem. Co. Ltd., 1968; mng. dir. Alcan UK Ltd., 1976; asst. mng. dir. Alcan Aluminium (UK) Ltd., 1977-81, mng. dir., 1981-82; mng. dir., chief exec. Brit. Alcan Aluminium, 1982-86; CEO, Marley PLC, 1986-93; dir. Alcan Aluminium Ltd., 1987—; dir. 3i Group, 1992—, chmn., 1993—; bd. dirs. No. Rock Bldg. Soc.; chmn. Camelot Group plc, No. Devel. Co.; non-exec. chmn. Marley Plc; vis. prof. U. Newcastle upon Tyne (Eng.), 1978; chmn. Ind. TV News, 1987-88, Ind. TV Authority, 1988-92, Cable Authority, 1989-90. Dep. chmn. Channel Four TV, 1987-88; bd. dirs. No. Sinfonia Orch., 1977-80; mem. No. Indsl. Devel. Bd., 1977-80, Washington Devel. Corp., 1978-80, Civil Svc. Pay Rsch. Unit, 1980-81, Megaw Inquiry into Civil Svc. Pay, 1981—; mem. Widdicombe Com. Inquiry into Conduct of Local Authority Bus., 1985; trustee Beamish Develt Trust, 1985—. Mem. IBN (chmn. 1987-88), IBA chmn. (1988-92), Cable Authority (chmn. 1989-90). Avocations: tennis, badminton, bird-watching. Office: 3i Group plc, 91 Waterloo Rd, London SE1 8XP, England*

RUSSELL, GEORGE EDWARD BACHELER, management consultant; b. Gillingham, Kent, Eng., Feb. 26, 1935; s. Edward David Bacheler and Clara Emily (Craven Jones) R.; m. Suzanne Allison Billinge, Apr. 20, 1968; children: Matthew Edward Bacheler, William Alexander Bacheler, James Arthur Bacheler, Catherine Allison. MA in Engring., Cambridge (Eng.) U., 1958. Chartered engr. Grad. apprentice Ransomes & Rapier Ltd., Ipswich, Eng., 1958-60; sales staff Ransomes & Rapier Ltd., Ipswich, 1960-64; br. mgr. Holman Bros. (Nigeria) Ltd., Lagos, 1964-65, Holman Bros. (East Africa) Ltd., Dar es Salaam, Tanzania, 1966-70; cons., sr. cons. W.D. Scott & Co. Ltd., London & Johannesburg, 1970-74; prin. cons. Nat. Productivity Inst., Pretoria, South Africa, 1974-85; dir., proprietor Baileys Cons. Assocs., London & Abingdon, 1986—. Contbr. articles to profl. jours. County organizer bicycle ride Oxfordshire Historic Chs. Trust. Mem. Instn. Mech. Engrs. Anglican. Avocations: choral music, sailing, micro computers. Office: Baileys Cons Assocs, 40 Steventon Rd, Abingdon Oxfordshire OX14 4LD, England

RUSSELL, GEORGE HAW, video production company executive; b. Neosho, Mo., May 22, 1945; s. Kenneth L. and Marjorie (Haw) R.; m. Suzanne Bennett, June 1, 1967; children: Margaret Anne, Marjorie Jane, Karen Lee, George Andrew. BA, La. State U., 1967. Ednl. Video Network, Huntsville, 1990—; Ptnr. The Sam Houston Group Ltd. Liability Partnership, Huntsville, 1991—. Producer ednl. videos Nombres et Couleurs, 1988 (Silver Apple award 1988), Napoleon, 1989 (Silver Apple award 1989), Bullfight, 1990, The French Revolution, 1990; exec. producer Spain's Historic Cities, 1992, Munich's Oktoberfest, 1992, The New Nutriton Pyramid, 1992, The Visual Language of Design, 1992, Florence, 1993, Joan of Arc, 1993, New Food Guide Pyramid, 1993, Cleaning and Maintaining Your VCR, 1993, Arts and Crafts of Mexico, 1993, Understanding Geysers and Hot Springs, 1993, Thoreau at Walden Pond, 1993, French Markets, 1993, Great Zimbabwe, 1993. Bd. govs. Tex. Com. on Natural Resources, Dallas, 1979—; bd. dirs. Gibbs-Powell House Mus., Huntsville, 1984—, Natural Area Preservation Assn., Dallas, 1986—; chmn. forest practices Lone Star Sierra Club, Austin, Tex., 1984—; chmn. Fed. Forest Reform, Washington, D.C., 1991—. 1st lt. U.S. Army, 1971-74. Recipient spl. achievement award Sierra Club, San Francisco 1985, chpt. conservation award 1987, environ. heroes for centennial 1991; named Citizen of Month, Huntsville Item 1988. Democrat. Methodist. Avocations: environmental advocacy, historic building restoration, collecting antiques and folk art. Home: 1409 19th St Huntsville TX 77340-5056 Office: Ednl Video Network 1401 19th St Huntsville TX 77340-5057

RUSSELL, HENRY RICHARD, JR., business communication adviser, educator; b. St. Paul, Apr. 12, 1941; arrived in Japan, 1960; s. Henry Richard and Mary Elizabeth (Lennon) R. Student, U. Md. (Far Ea. divsn.), Ryukyu Islands, Japan, 1961-62, Sophia U., Tokyo, 1963-66. Tokyo rep. Internat. Electric Corp., Mpls., 1967-72, Internat. Travel Arrangers, St. Paul, 1973-75; overseas divsn. adviser Kyodo Printing Co., Ltd., Tokyo, 1975—, The Yamaguchi Bank, Ltd., Tokyo, 1975—, The Inst. Ea. Culture, Tokyo, 1975—, Kokusai Electric Co., Ltd., Tokyo, 1989-94, Mitsui Toatsu Chemicals, Inc., Tokyo, 1991-97, Goyo Electronics Co., Ltd. (Kokusai Electric Group), Tokyo, 1996-98; lectr. Kyoritsu Women's U., Tokyo, 1993—. With U.S. Army, 1960-63. Roman Catholic. Avocations: hiking, reading. Home: Musashino-So 5G0 3-16-2, Higashi-Cho, Kichijoji, Musashino-Shi Tokyo 180-0002, Japan Office: Kyodo Printing Co Ltd, 4-14-12 Koishikawa, Tokyo Bunkyo-ku 112-8501, Japan

RUSSELL, HORACE ORLANDO, dean of chapel, theology educator; b. Clarendon, Jamaica, Nov. 3, 1929; Came to the U.S., 1988; s. Cleveland Augustus and Rowena Nerissa (Gordon) R.; m. Beryl Joyce Redman, Aug. 31, 1957; children: Elisabeth Jennifer, Jonathan Paul Carey, Heather Dawn Marie. BD, Calabar Theological Coll., London, 1954; BA, St. Catherine Coll., Oxford, 1957; PhD, Regent's Park Coll., Oxford, 1972. Ordained Baptist min. Febr. 10, 1958. Prof. church history United Theol. Coll. W.I., U. W.I., Jamaica, 1958-76, pres., 1972-76; sr. pastor Jamaica Bapt. Union, 1976-89; dean of chapel, prof. hist. theology Ea. Bapt. Theol. Sem., Phila., 1989—; mem. faith and order commn. World Coun. of Chs., Geneva, Switzerland, 1968-90, world assoc. of Christian commn., London, 1969—; v.p. Jamaica Baptist Union, 1980; vice moderator Fund O, 1986-90. Author: (books) Five Words of Love, 1982, The Baptist Witness, 1983, Foundations and Anticipations-The Baptist Story in Jamaica 1783-1892, 1993, Jamaica Miss. W.I. to West Africa, 1999; founder, editor: (jour.) Carribean Jour. of Religious Studies, 1966. Mem. nat. commn. on unemployment Govt. of Jamaica, 1969, mem. pub. svc. commn., 1980-88, mem. nat. commn. on drug abuse, 1984-89, chair nat. heritage commn., 1988-89, mem. cultural devel. commn. 1987-88. Recipient Jamaica Prime Minister's medal Jamaican Govt., 1984, Marcus Garvey medal Marcus Garvey Internat., 1984, Jamaica Council of Churches award Churches of Jamaica, 1986. Mem. Am. Soc. of Ch. History, West Indies Group of Univ. Tchrs., Soc. for the Study of Black Religion, Hist. Soc. of Great Britain, Univ. Lodge English Masons (chaplain 1970), Oxford Soc. Baptist. Avocations: photography, creative writing. Home and Office: Ea Baptist Theological Seminary 6 E Lancaster Ave Wynnewood PA 19096-3430

RUSSELL, IAN JOHN, neurobiology educator; b. Chatham, Kent, Eng., June 19, 1943; s. Philip William George and Joan Lilian (Snook) R.; m. Janice Marion Hall, July 20, 1968; children: Simon Alexander, Charlotte Louise. BS in Zoology, U. London, 1964; MS in Zoology, U. B.C., Vancouver, Can., 1966; PhD in Zoology, Cambridge (Eng.) U., 1969. Rsch. fellow Magdalene Coll., Cambridge, 1969-72; rsch. fellow Sci. Rsch. Coun. Cambridge U., 1969-70; lectr. in neurobiology U. Sussex, Brighton, Eng., 1971-79, reader in neurobiology, 1979-87, prof. neurobiology, 1987—. Contbr. articles to profl. jours. Fellow Royal Soc. (Exch. fellow King Gustav V Rsch. Inst. in Stockholm 1970-71); mem. Physiol. Soc. London. Mem. Labor Party. Avocations: hockey, windsurfing, music, reading, gardening. Home: Little Ivy Cottage, Waldron, Heathfield, East Sussex TN21 0QX, England Office: Univ Sussex Sch Biol Scis, BN1 9QG Falmer Brighton East Sussex, England

RUSSELL, IAN MACGREGOR, accountant, utility company executive; b. Edinburgh, Scotland, Jan. 16, 1953; s. James and Christine (Clark) R.; m. Fiona Russell, Oct. 25, 1975; children: Ewan, Lindsay. B in Commerce with hons., U. Edinburgh, Scotland. Fin. dir. HSBC Asset Mgmt., Hong Kong, 1987-90; dir. fin. control Tomkins, London, 1991-94; fin. dir. Scottish Power, Glasgow, Scotland, 1994—; dep. chief exec. Scottish Power, Glasgow, 1999—. Mem. Inst. Chartered Accts. Scotland. Avocations: golf, rugby. Office: Scottish Power PLC, 1 Atlantic Quay, Strclyde Glasgow G2 8SP, Scotland

RUSSELL, IRINA, pharmacy educator; b. Johannesburg, Republic of South Africa, Aug. 3, 1946; d. Andrew Pearce and Virginia Dorothea (De Villiers) R. BSc in Pharmacy, Rhodes U., Grahamstown, Republic of South Africa, 1967, BSc in Chemistry with honors, 1968, PhD in Chemistry, 1972; BEd, U. Western Cape, Bellville, Republic of South Africa, 1980. Registered pharmacist South African Pharmacy Coun. Postdoctoral fellow McGill U., Montreal, Que., Can., 1972-73; lectr. in pharm. chemistry U. Western Cape, 1974-75, sr. lectr., 1976-80, prof. pharmaceutics, 1981—, chair dept. pharmaceutics, 1981—, head Sch. Pharmacy, 1981-89; cons. Fine Chems. Corp. (Pty) Ltd., Cape Town, Republic of South Africa, 1987-90; presenter in field. Contbr. articles to profl. publs. Fellow Pharm. Soc. South Africa; mem. Acad. Pharm. Scis. (exec. 1985-92, hon.).Third World Orgn. for Women in Sci. Avocations: travel, photography, astronomy, botany. Office: U Western Cape Sch Pharmacy, Pvt Bag X17, Bellville 7535, South Africa

RUSSELL, JOHN FINTAN, theology educator, editor; b. Springfield, Mass., July 19, 1934; s. David Joseph and Ellen Teresa (Shea) R. BA, St. Bonaventure U., 1957; STL, Lateran U., Rome, Italy, 1962; MA, Roosevelt U., 1968; STD, Cath. U., 1979. Dean of boys Carmel High Sch., Mundelein, Ill., 1962-67; dir. counseling Carmel Sem., Hamilton, Mass., 1967-70; dir. Whitefriars Hall, Washington, 1972-77; asst. prof. theology I.C.S. Sem., Mahwah, N.J., 1977-83; assoc. prof. theology Seton Hall U., South Orange, N.J., 1983-91, prof. theology, 1991—; theology cons. Nat. Office of Renew, Plainfield, N.J., 1988—. Author: (with others) Experiencing St. Therese Today, 1990; editor: Sword Mag., 1990-96; contbr. articles to profl. jours. Mem. Com. for Ednl. Excellence, Cresskill, N.J., 1983-84. Faculty rsch. grantee Seton Hall U., 1989, 94. Mem. Cath. Theol. Soc. Am. Roman Catholic. Avocations: sports, reading, travel. Home: Lewis Hall Seton U South Orange NJ 07079 Office: Seton Hall U 400 W South Orange Ave South Orange NJ 07079-1478

RUSSELL, JOHN ROBERT, neurosurgeon; b. Bloomington, Ind., Mar. 17, 1922; s. John Dale and Elsie Violet Russell; m. Jane Elizabeth Bureau, Aug. 21, 1943; children: Thomas William, John Bureau, Ann Elizabeth, Amy Catherine. BS, U. Chgo., 1941, MS, 1942, MD, 1945. Diplomate Am. Bd. Neurol. Surgery. Intern Chgo. Meml. Hosp., 1945-46, resident, 1948-50; resident Bapt. Meml. Hosp, Memphis, 1950-51; mem. faculty Ind. U. Sch. Medicine, Indpls., 1951-59; ptnr. pvt. practice neurosurgery Indpls., 1959-71; pres. pvt. practice neurosurgery Indpls. Neurosurg. Group, 1971-84; neurosurg. cons. forensic medicine Chiron/EMC, Madison, Wis., 1991-97. V.p. Neurosurg. Soc. Ind., 1976-77. Fellow ACS; mem. Am. Assn. Neurol. Surgeons (bd. dirs. 1967-70), Congress Neurol. Surgeons (sec. 1962-65, pres. 1967). Avocations: woodworking, swimming. Home: PO Box 197 Boulder Junction WI 54512-0197

RUSSELL, JOHN WILLIAM, insurance executive; b. Springfield, Mass., May 24, 1952; s. John Jacob Jr. and Helen (Mullaly) R.; m. Beronica N. Trevino, Feb. 19, 1987. BS in Indsl. Engring., Western New Eng. Coll., 1975. Registered profl. engr., Mass; cert. profl. ergonomist. Rep. loss prevention Liberty Mut. Ins. Co., Hamden, Conn., 1975-76; rep. loss prevention Liberty Mut. Ins. Co., Norwich, Conn., 1976-78, sr. loss prevention rep., 1978-80, cons. loss prevention, 1980-81, cons. indsl. loss prevention, 1981; sr. cons. indsl. loss prevention Liberty Mut. Ins. Co., East Hartford, Conn., 1981-85; tech. cons. indsl. Liberty Mut. Ins. Co., Glastonbury, Conn., 1985-88; div. tech. dir. indsl. Liberty Mut. Ins. Co., Weston, Mass., 1988-91; mgr. mfg. tech. Liberty Mutual Ins. Co., Boston, 1991—; tchr. evening div. Hartford (Conn.) State Tech. Coll., 1982-87. Contr.: Material Handling Handbook, 1985. Mem. planning com. City of Manchester, Conn., 1986-87; fin. bd. United Way, Groton, Conn., 1979; VIP com. Leukemia Soc., Hartford, 1984-85; mem. parish devel. team All Saints Episcopal Ch., East Hartford, 1987-88; mem., chmn. B11 parent com., B7, B24.1, B11.1, B11.2535 coms. ANSI. Mem. Inst. Indsl. Engrs., Am. Soc. Safety Engrs., Internat. Material Mgmt. Soc. (cert.), Cert. Safety Profls., Nat. Fire Protection Assn., Nat. Welding Soc., Mass. Soc. Profl. Engrs. (bd. dirs.), Western New Eng. Coll. Alumni Assn. (v.p. 1987, pres. 1988), Indsl. Engring. Club (pres. 1973-74), Electronics Club (pres. 1969-70). Avocations: electronics, photography, golf, exercising, reading. Home: 40 Connolly St Randolph MA 02368-1511 Office: Liberty Mut Ins Co 114 Turnpike Rd Ste 204 Westborough MA 01581-2862

RUSSELL, MARJORIE ROSE, manufacturing company executive; b. Welcome, Minn., Sept. 3, 1925; d. Emil Frederick and Ella Magdalene (Sothman) Wohlenhaus; m. Kenneth Kollmann Russell, Sept. 15, 1947 (div. May 1973); children: Jennie Rose, Richard Lowell, Laura Eloise, James Wesley. Student, Northwestern Sch., Mpls., 1944-45, St. Paul Bible Inst., 1946-47. Cook U. Minn., Mpls., 1943-45; maintenance person U. Farm Campus/N.W. Schs., St. Paul, 1945-46; clk. Kresge Corp., Mpls., 1945; cook, waitress, mgr. Union City Mission Bible Camp, Mpls., 1944-47; caterer for v.p. Gt. No. R.R., St. Paul, 1947; custodian Old Soldiers Home, St. Paul, 1946; nurse Sister Elizabeth Kenney Polio Hosp., St. Paul, 1946; seamstress Hirsch, Weis, White Stag, Pendleton, Mayfair, Portland, Oreg., 1960-72; owner, operator, contract mgr., creative designer The Brass Needle, Portland, 1972—; contractor Forrester's Sanderson Safety, Scotsco, Nero & Assocs., Gara Gear, Portland, 1972—, Columbia Sportswear; tchr. Indo Chinese Cultural Ctr., Portland, 1982; mfr. of protective chaps and vests for the Pacific Northwest hogging industry. Designer, producer Kisn Bridal Fair, 1969; composer: He Liveth in Me, 1968; prodr. Safety Chaps for Loggers. Sec. Model Cities Com., Portland, 1969; com. mem. Neighborhood Black Christmas Parade, Portland, 1970; custume designer Local Miss Jr. Black Beauty Contest, Portland, 1973; nominating com. Nat. Contract Mgmt. Assn., Portland, 1978; mem. nominating com. Multi-Cultural Sr. Adv. Com., 1988-91. Mem. NAFE, Urban League, Urban League Guild (historian 1991-92), Am. Assn. Ret. Persons, Nat. Contract Mgmt. Assn. Democrat. Mem. United Ch. of Christ. Avocations: music, swimming, painting, gardening, arts. Home and Office: The Brass Needle 2809 NE 12th Ave Portland OR 97212-3219

RUSSELL, MARY WENDELL VANDER POEL, non-profit organization executive, interior; b. N.Y.C., Feb. 6, 1919; d. William Halsted and Blanche Pauline (Billings) Vander Poel; m. George Montagu Miller, Apr. 5, 1940 (div. 1974); children: Wendell Miller Steavenson, Gretchen Miller Elkus; m. Sinclair Hatch, May 14, 1977 (dec. July 1989); m. William F. Russell, June 24, 1995 (dec. Apr. 1996). Pres. Miller Richard, Inc., Interior Decorators, Oyster Bay, N.Y., 1972—; bd. dirs. Eye Bank Sight Restoration, N.Y.C., pres., 1980-88, hon. chair, 1988—; v.p. Manhattan Eye Ear and Throat Hosp., N.Y.C., 1978-90; sec. Cold Spring Harbor Lab., N.Y., 1985-89, 92-97; mem. DNA Learning Ctr. Bd., 1991-97; bd. dirs. DNA Learning Ctr., 1997—; sec. Cold Spring Harbor Lab, 1992-97, hon. trustee, 1998—. V.p. North Country Garden Club, Nassau County, N.Y., 1979-81, 1983-85; dir. Planned Parenthood Nassau County, Mineola, N.Y., 1982-84, Hutton House C.W.Post Coll.,Greenvale, N.Y., 1982—; chair Hutton House, 1992-94. Recipient Disting. Trustee award United Hosp. Fund, 1992. Mem. Colony Club (N.Y.C.), Church Club (N.Y.C.), Piping Rock Club (Long Island), Order St. John Jerusalem (N.Y.C.). Republican. Episcopalian. Home: Mill River Rd # 330 Oyster Bay NY 11771-2733

RUSSELL, MERVYN KEITH, international marketing executive; b. Otahuhu, Auckland, New Zealand, Nov. 12, 1940; s. Williams James and Cecilia Margaret (Martin) R.; m. Audrey Emma Davidson, Oct. 26, 1963; children: John, Brian, Terry, Paul. Hand and machine typographer Wilson & Horton, Auckland, 1956-66; taxi propr. United Taxis, Papakura, 1966-68, mng. dir., 1968-70; mng. dir. Cecilia Shoes Ltd., Papatoetoe, 1970-80; sales mgr. Morrow Taylor Ltd., Auckland, 1980-87; gen. mgr. Deejays Ltd., Auckland, 1987-90; sales/mktg./export mgr. Hollywood Shoes Ltd., Auckland, 1990-92; pres. Harson Internat. Int., Auckland, 1994—; mng. dir. Russell Agys., Auckland, 1992—; cons. footwear The Warehouse, Auckland, 1992-94. Contbr. articles to profl. publs. Publicity officer Nat. Party, Papakura, 1972-75; bd. dirs. Papakura Primary Sch., 1975-78; lay preacher, elder New Zealand Presbyn. Ch., Papakura, 1963-94. Recipient award New Zealand Sch. Printing, 1959. Mem. Rotary (internat. youth dir. 1973-74). Avocations: gymnasium, cycling, music, gardening. Office: Russell Agys, 14 The Lea, Papakura Auckland, New Zealand

RUSSELL, MICHAEL, publisher, author; b. Boxmoor, United Kingdom, May 30, 1933; s. Edward Dennis and Edith Margery (Blow) R.; m. Nicole Yarde-Buller, Feb. 6, 1962; children: Lorna, Francis, Alexander. Student, Rugby Sch., 1952, Oxford Univ., 1956. Ind. publ. Michael Russell Publ. Co., 1972—. Author: Fly Fishing by J.R. Hartley, 1991, J.R. Hartley Casts Again, 1992, Golfing, 1995. With Royal Horse Guards, 1957-58. Home: Wilby Hall, Wilby Norwich, NR16 2JP Norfolk United Kingdom

RUSSELL, MICHAEL PAUL, entertainment industry executive, consultant; b. Pasadena, Calif., Aug. 8, 1956; s. Paul Russell and Ellen Geraldine Smith. BA, U. So. Calif., 1978. Editl. dir. Walt Disney Pictures, Burbank, Calif., 1978-87; exec. dir. nat. publicity Paramount Pictures, Hollywood, Calif., 1987-90; v.p. Orion Pictures, Century City, Calif., 1990-92; sr. v.p. Rogers & Cowan, Century City, Calif., 1995-97; pres. Michael Russell Group, Manhattan Beach, Calif., 1997—. Mem. Acad. Motion Picture Arts and Scis., Writers Guild Am. Democrat. E-mail: cinepoint@att.net. Office: Michael Russell Group 1601 N Sepulveda Blvd # 509 Manhattan Beach CA 90266-5133

RUSSELL, PAUL SUDHAKAR, psychiatrist; b. Nagercoil, Tamil Nadu, India, June 26, 1963; s. Raghaviah and Jessline Pushpam (David) R. MBBS, Tirunelveli Med. Coll., India, 1987; DPM, Christian Med. Coll., India, 1991, MD, 1994; DNB, Min. of Health/Govt. India, 1994. Sr. house man Moscm Hosp., Cochin, 1987; non-PG registrar Christian Med. Coll., Vellore, India, 1988-89, med. officer, 1991-92, lectr. in psychiatry, 1994-97, sr. lectr., 1997-99, reader in psychiatry, 1999—. Contbr. articles to profl. jours. Fellow Indian Assn. for Child and Adolescent Mental Health; mem. Indian Psychiat. Soc. Avocations: native flora and fauna identification, religion and philosophy, music. Office: Christian Med Coll, Bagayam, 632 002 Vellore/Tamil Nadu India

RUSSELL, ROBERT BONNELL, petroleum geologist; b. Wylie, Tex., Oct. 5, 1919; s. Vaughn Heywood and Maude Louise (Adams) R.; m. Lettye Louise Smith, Oct. 16, 1948; children: Susan Jo McDaniel, Robert Van, Robin Everett. BA in Geology, Tex. Christian U., 1953. Geologist Conoco Inc., 1953-55; petroleum geologist Conoco Inc., Midland, Tex., 1955-65; staff geologist Conoco Inc., Casper, Wyo., 1966-67; sr. geologist Conoco Inc., Denver, 1967-81; ind. petroleum geologist Lakewood, Colo., 1981—; exploration ptnr. cons. petroleum exploration cos. Served with U.S. Army, 1940-42, to 1st lt. USAAF, 1942-48, ETO, capt. USAFR, 1948-55. Mem. Fifteenth Air Force Assn., 459th Bomb Group Assn. Achievements include pioneering work in exploration for oil and gas reservoirs in buried, ancient meteorite craters (astroblemes). Home: 2696 S Ammons Way Lakewood CO 80227-3128

RUSSELL, ROBERT CHARLES, drama educator, music director, actor, theater director; b. S.I., N.Y., July 24, 1953; s. Helen (Cylek) Russell. BA in Theatre and Speech cum laude, Rutgers U., Newark, 1975; MA in Theatre, U. Denver, 1983. Theatre actor N.J., N.Y., 1970—; dir. C.C. and H.S. theatre, N.J., 1974—; theatre dir. Queen of Peace H.S., North Arlington, N.J., 1985—, educator, 1991-97; dir. music St. Joseph's Ch., East Rutherford, N.J., 1990-98; adj. prof. Kean Coll., Montclair, N.J., 1983-90. Appearances include Torch Song Trilogy, 1989, The Mystery of Edwin Drood, 1990, The Boyfriend, 1991, Into the Woods, 1992, Arsenic and Old Lace, 1993, Little Shop of Horrors, 1995, A Chorus Line, 1996, She Loves Me, 1997, Mornings at Seven, 1998, Blood Brothers, 1999, Hello, Dolly!, also in films and TV. Pastoral musician Catholic ch., N.J., 1974—; founding mem. Collaborative Arts Project, Jersey City, 1991-94; theatre dir. Don Bosco High Sch., Ramsey, N.J., 2000—. Mem. AFTRA, SAG, Actor's Equity Assn., Nat. Assn. Pastoral Musicians. Avocations: theatre, film, singer, travel. Home: 125 Elm Ave Hackensack NJ 07601-3739

RUSSELL, ROBERT JAMES, biotechnology and chemical company executive; b. London, July 13, 1955; s. James Wood and Ruth (Elliot) R.; m. Susan Helen Lee, July 28, 1984; children: Rebecca, Edward, Madeliene. BSc, Warwick U., U.K., 1980. Tech. asst. ICI, U.K., 1974-77; rsch. asst. St. Georges Med. Sch., U.K., 1980-83, tissue culture lab mgr., 1983-85; quality control technician Tissue Culture Svcs. Ltd., 1985-86, prodn. and tech. mgr., 1986-88; sales rep. Nat. Diagnositcs, East Yorkshire, Eng., 1988-92, European sales mgr., 1992-95, CEO Europe, internat. sales mgr., 1995—; dir. AGTC Bioproducts U.K.; product cons. Phillip Harris Ltd. U.K., 1998—. Mem. AAAS. Avocations: classical guitar, swimming, theater. Office: Nat Diagnostics Unit 4, Itlings Ln, Hessle, East Yorkshire HU19 3DY, England

RUSSELL, SHARON D., English educator, writer; b. Salt Lake City, May 29, 1945; d. James R. and Dorothy A. Russell; 1 child, Cadi Sharon Russell-Sauve. BA, U. Utah, 1967; MA, U. Wash., 1968. Instr. English Pierce Coll., Lakewood, Wash., 1995—. Avocations: gardening, travel, writing. E-Mail: srussell@pierce.etc.edu. Office: Pierce Coll 9401 Farwest Dr SW Lakewood WA 98498-1919

RUSSELL, SUE ELLEN, lawyer; b. Centre, Pa., Aug. 17, 1959; d. Richard Basil and Patricia Ann Glazer; m. David Tyler Russell, Oct. 6, 1990. BA with distinction, U. Va., 1981; JD, Am. U., Washington, 1987. Bar: Va. 1987, D.C. 1988, U.S. Ct. Appeals (D.C. cir.), U.S. Dist. Ct. (ea. and we. dists.) Va., Tex. Bankruptcy Ct. (cir. no. dist.). Staff asst. Rep. Stanley Lundine, Washington, 1981-84, Senator Gary Hart, Washington, 1984-85; law clk. Legal Aid Soc., Prince Georges County, Md., 1985; appellate clk. U.S. Atty's. Office, Appellate, Washington, 1986-87; jud. clk. to Chief Judge William C. Pryor, Washington, 1987-88; assoc. Brand & Lowell, Washington, 1988-94, ptnr., 1994-95; founding and mng. ptnr. Russell & Russell, PC, Falls Church, Va., 1995—; del. Jud. Conf., Washington, 1988-90. Mem. ABA (trustee Coun. on Law in Higher Edn, v.p. for student affiars), Nat. Health Lawyers Assn., Nat. Assn. Coll. and Univ. Attys., Va. State Bar, D.C. Bar, No. Va. Tech. Coun. Democrat. Avocations: sailing, hiking, swimming. Office: Russell & Russell PC 150 S Washington St Ste 101 Falls Church VA 22046-2921

RUSSELL, TIMOTHY PAUL, management consultant, engineer; b. Southend, Essex, Eng., Dec. 3, 1950; s. Ronald F. and Valerie (Nuttall) R.; m. Elizabeth F.M. Lim, Aug. 4, 1987; 1 child, Edward Timothy. BSChemE, Imperial Coll., London, 1972; BS in Psychology, Birkbeck Coll., London, 1983. Registered profl. engr., U.K. Chem. engr. Esso Petroleum, Fawley, London, 1972-73; chief tng. officer Bacie, London, 1973-77; group mgmt. devel. mgr. Ever Ready, London, 1977-79; mgmt. cons. Tim Russell Assoc., London, 1979—; co-owner Tng. Advances, Brighton, Eng., 1981-85; cons.

Australian Inst. Mgmt., Sydney, Australia, 1985—, Singapore Inst. Mgmt., 1981—, Hong Kong Mgmt. Assn., 1983—. Contbr. articles to profl. jours. Mem. Inst. Tng. and Devel., Assn. for Mgmt. Edn. and Devel., Singapore Tng. and Devel. Assn., Nat. Liberal Club, English Speaking Union. Avocations: architecture. Office: 112 Defoe House, Barbican, EC2Y 8DN London England

RUSSELL, VICTORIA ELIZABETH, solicitor, mediator, adjudicator, arbitrator; b. Tenterden, Kent, Eng., Oct. 12, 1956; d. Raymond Wycliffe and Ingeborg Elisabeth (Quade) R.; m. Stephen Thomas Lawrence, July 20, 1985; children: Thomas Russell, Edward Wycliffe. LLB with honors, Exeter U., 1977. Solicitor of the Supreme Ct.; Centre Dispute Resolution accredited mediator, 1996, Tech. and Constrn. Solicitors Assn. accredited adjudicator, 1996. Trainee solicitor Blyth Dutton, London, 1979-81; asst. solicitor Freedmans, London, 1981-85, ptnr., 1985-96; ptnr. Berrymans Lace Mawer, London, 1996-2000, Fenwick Elliott, 2000—; panel mem. Ind. Housing Ombudsman arbitration panel, London, 1994, Law Soc. Panel Arbitrators, London, 1995. Trustee Benenden Sch. Trust, Kent, Eng., 1992; bd. mem. Exeter U. Alumni Campaign Bd., Devon, Eng., 1992. Fellow Chartered Inst. Arbitrators; mem. Soc. Constrn. Law (coun. mem., vice-chmn. 1998-2000, chmn. 2000—), Internat. Bar Assn., Tech. and Constrn. Solicitors Assn., Worshipful Co. Arbitrators (liveryman, mem. ct. assts. 1992, chmn. charitable trust 1992, jr. warden 1999, sr. warden 2000), City of London Solicitors Co. (freeman 1997). Conservative. Anglican. Avocation: family activities. Home: 36 Westcroft Sq, London W6 0TA, England Office: Fenwick Elliott, 353 Strand, London WC2R 0HT, England

RUSSELL, WILLIAM MOY STRATTEN, biologist, folklorist; b. Plymouth, Devon, Eng., Mar. 26, 1925; s. Frederick Stratten and Gweneth Kate (Moy Evans) R. BA in Natural Sci. (Zoology), U. Oxford, Eng., 1948, MA, 1950, DPhil, 1952. Christopher Welch rsch. scholar dept. zoology U. Oxford, 1948-51, jr. agrl. rsch. fellow, 1951-54; fellow Univs. Fedn. for Animal Welfare Rsch., London, 1954-59; sci. info. officer Commonwealth Bur. Pastures and Field Crops, Hurley, Eng., 1964-66; lectr. dept. sociology U. Reading, Eng., 1966-71, reader, 1971-86, prof., 1986-90, prof. emeritus, 1990—; external examiner U. London Inst. Edn., 1970-80. Co-author: (with R.L. Burch) The Principles of Humane Experimental Technique, 1959, (with Claire Russell) Human Behavior: A New Approach, 1961, Violence, Monkeys and Man, 1968 (also Dutch, Swedish and German edits.), Population Crises and Population Cycles, 1999; author: Man, Nature and History, 1967 (also Italian edit.), The Barber of Aldebaran, 1995; editor: (with J.R. Porter) Animals in Folklore, 1978), (with H.R.E. Davidson) The Folklore of Ghosts, 1981; contbr. over 190 articles to profl. jours., also to 38 books. With King's Royal Rifle Corps, 1944-45. Ella Stevens Greek scholar, 1942, Classics and English Lit. scholar, 1945; recipient Smith-Kline Beechan prize for lab. animal welfare rsch. Def. Soc., London, 1994, Bronze medal Faculty of Medicine of Charles U., Czech Republic, 1997, Silver medal U. Bologna, Italy, 1999; Russell and Burch award named in his honor Humane Soc. U.S., 1990. Fellow Royal Soc. Medicine (life), Inst. Biology (chartered biologist); mem. Univs. Fedn. Animal Welfare (hon.), Folklore Soc. (hon. libr. 1977-79, pres. 1979-82, v.p. 1983-90), Pendragon Soc. Office: U Reading Dept Sociology, Whiteknights PO Box 218, Reading Berks RG6 2AA, England

RUSSEV, VESSELIN KOLEV, microbiologist, virologist; b. Stanovets, Varna, Bulgaria, Sept. 8, 1943; s. Kolyu Koltchev and Nedka Georgieva (Dobreva) R.; m. Tonca Teneva Hadjiteneva, Nov. 7, 1968; 1 child, Nelly. MD, Higher Inst. Medicine, Varna, 1969; PhD, Acad. Medicine, Sofia, Bulgaria, 1983. Gen. practitioner Cmty. Hosp., Novi Pazar, Bulgaria, 1969-73; asst. Med. U., Varna, 1973-90, assoc. prof., 1990—, head dept. microbiology and virology, 1995—, dir. sci. rsch., 1995—; cons. cmty. Hosp., Novi Pazar, Bulgaria, 1983—. Author: Medical Microbiology, 1990, Microbiology, 1990. Mem. Assn. Sci. Workers Sofia, Internat. Med. Assn. Bulgaria. Avocation: photography. Home: Complex Mladost Block 144, Entr 8 Flr 5 Flat 13, 9020 Varna Bulgaria Office: Med Univ, 55 Marin Drinov str, 9002 Varna Bulgaria

RUSSO, FRANK, lawyer; b. Camden, N.J., Nov. 23, 1953; s. Frank Orlando Russo and Ruth Marie Zebedies; m. Colleen Marie Corr; 2 children. AA, Camden County C.C., 1974; BA, U. S. Fla., 1977; JD, Southwe. U., 1982; grad. Nat. Coll. DUI Def. program, Harvard U., 1997. Bar: Fla. 1985, Colo. 1992,. Cert. legal intern then pros. atty. Office State Atty., Clearwater, Fla., 1983-86; pvt. practice St. Petersburg, Fla., 1986—; pres. Meta Progress Inc.; guest lectr. U. S. Fla., St. Petersburg Jr. Coll.; treas. Cir. Ct. Jud. Campaign, 1996. Named Leading Am. Atty. Am. Rsch. Corp., 1998. Mem. Fla. Assn. Criminal Def. Lawyers, Pinellas County Bar Criminal Def. Lawyers Assn., St. Petersburg Bar Assn. Avocations: traveling, mountain biking. Office: 11300 4th St N Ste 121 Saint Petersburg FL 33716-2939

RUSSO, GILBERTO, engineering educator; b. Rome, Aug. 23, 1954; s. Guido and Maria (Mazzoni) R. Laurea, Poly. Inst. Turin, Italy, 1975; ScD, MIT, 1980; MD, U. Chgo. Pritaker Sch. of Medicine. Pres. Studio Russo, Inc. Engring. Cons., Turin, 1970; asst. prof. Poly. Inst. Turin, 1975-80; lectr. MIT, Cambridge, Mass., 1985-91; dr. dept. plastic and reconstructive surgery U. Chgo., 1992-95; mem. dept. surgery U. Calif., San Francisco, 1995—; mem. designer selection bd. State of Mass., Boston, 1989. Contbr. articles to profl. publs., chpts. to books. Pres. Dante Alisheri Soc., Cambridge, 1986-88; treas. MIT/Poly. Alumni Assn., Turin, 1970. Fulbright fellow, 1978. Fellow Nat. Coun. Engring. Examiners; mem. Mass. Soc. Profl. Engrs. (v.p. 1991—), Tau Beta Pi (chpt. advisor 1985, Eminent Engr. 1985). Achievements include patents in solar energy collectors, development of computer aided therodynamics, computer methods for engineering, optimization of non-steady-state systems, compressible fluid flow with heat transfer, thermal dynamics models, diagnostics and surgical repair of electric/burn injuries. Address: Dept Surgery LIJ Med Ctr New Hyde Park NY 11004 Office: U Chgo Dept Plastic-Reconstrv Surg Chicago IL 60637 also: U Calif Dept Surgery Rm S-343 Box 0470 513 Parnassus Ave San Francisco CA 94122-2722

RUSSO, GIOVANNI, bioethics educator; b. Caltanissetta, Calabria, Italy, Jan. 1, 1963; s. Giuseppe and Rosaria (Patrí) R. MA in Philosophy, Salesian U., Rome, 1984; PhD in Edn., U. Messina (Italy), 1992; PhD in Theology, Lateranese U., Rome, 1992. Prof. philosophy Salesian U., Messina, Italy, 1991—; prof. bioethics Salesian U., Messina, 1992—; dir. Sch. Bioethics, 1997—; prof. sexual ethics Sch. Theology, Catania, Italy, 1993-98; dir. Ctr. Bioethics, 1993—; prof. clin. bioethics Sch. Medicine, Messina, 1993—; prof. sociology of medicine Sch. Social Scis., Messina, 1998—; vice dir. Itinerarium, Messina, 1992—; assoc. dir. Ethical Com., Messina, 1993—; cons. Gazzetta del Sud, Messina, 1994—. Author: Educare Alla Bioetica, 1994, Clinical Bioethics, 1996 (Gregorianum award 1997); editor: Bioetica Fondamentale, 1995, Report of 25 Years of Bioethics, 1997 (Itinerarium award 1997). Mem. A.I.A.D., Messina, 1995—, Progetto Culturale, Messina, 1999—. Recipient Pedagogia Clinica award Italian Soc. Clin. Pedagogy, 1994. Mem. Italian Soc. Bioethics, Hastings Ctr., Kennedy Inst., Salesian Soc. (assoc. dir. 1992—). Avocations: biking, basketball. Home: Salita Montepiselli # 24, 98121 Vaccarella Messina, Italy Office: Ist Teologico S Tommaso, Via del Pozzo 43 CP 28, 98121 Messina ME, Italy

RUSSO, ROY R., lawyer; b. Utica, N.Y., July 26, 1936; s. Chester F. and Helen L. (Gacek) R.; m. Ann M. Obernesser, Sept. 19, 1959; children: Andrew F., Susan Elizabeth. BA, Columbia U., 1956; LLB cum laude, Syracuse U., 1959. Bar: N.Y. 1959, D.C. 1967, U.S. Supreme Ct. 1969. Pvt. practice law, Washington, 1959—; atty. FCC, Washington, 1959-66; ptnr. Cohn and Marks, Washington, 1966—; spl. counsel Nat. Cath. Conf. for Interracial Justice, Washington, 1984—. Mem. editl. adv. com. The Communications Act: A Legislative History of the Major Amendments 1934-96; mem. adv. bd. Pike and Fischer Comms. Regulation. Founding chmn. Commn. on Social Ministry, Richmond (Va.) Diocese, 1970-74; v.p., bd. dirs. St. Mary's Housing Corp., Annandale, Manassas, Fredericksburg, Ashburn, Va., 1971—; pres., bd. dirs. Caths. for Housing, Inc., 1979-84, Cath. Charities, Arlington (Va.) Diocese, 1980-84. With USAF, 1960-61. Recipient Alumni medal Alumni Fedn. Columbia U., 1994. Mem. ABA, Fed. Communications Bar Assn. (co-chair mass media practice com. 1988-91, nominations com. 1991-92), Computer Law Assn., Internat. Inst. Communications, John Jay Assocs., Soc. Columbia Grads., Columbia U. Club of Washington (sr. v.p. 1989-91, pres. 1991-95), Order of Coif, Phi Alpha Delta. Democrat. Club: Columbia Coll. (Washington) (mem. steering com. 1985—, chmn. Deans' Day program 1988—). Home: 6528 Bowie Dr Springfield VA 22150-1309 Office: Cohn and Marks 1920 N St NW Ste 300 Washington DC 20036-1622

RUSSON, DAVID, library director; b. Shifnal, Eng., June 12, 1944; s. Thomas Charles and Violet (Jarvis) R.; m. Kathleen Mary Gregory, July 29, 1967; children: Katherine, Nicola, Charles Benedict. BSc, Univ. Coll. London, 1965. Rsch. scholar U. York (Eng.), 1965-69; adminstrv. officer dept. edn. and sci. Brit. Libr., London, 1969-74, with R&D dept., 1974-75; head rsch. lending div. Brit. Libr., Yorkshire, Eng., 1975-80, head forward planning, 1980-85, dir. document supply ctr., 1985-88; dir. gen. sci., tech. and industry Brit. Libr., London, 1988-96, dep. chief exec., 1996—; pres. Internat. Coun. for Scientific and Tech. Info., 1995—. Contbr. numerous articles to profl. jours. Fellow Royal Soc. Arts, Inst. Info. Scientists, Inst. of Physics; mem. Nat. Liberal Club. Home: March House, Tollerton Y06 2ET, England Office: British Libr, Boston Spa, West Yorkshire LS23 7BQ, England

RUSSOTTI, PHILIP ANTHONY, lawyer; b. N.Y.C., Mar. 24, 1948; s. Philip Armond and Yolanda (Morelli) R.; m. Mary Wolfe, Jan. 20, 1973 (div. Mar., 1996); children: Thomas, Matthew, Peter; m. Kathleen Kettles, May 25, 1996. BA, Columbia U., 1970; JD, St. John's U., Queens, N.Y., 1973. Bar: N.Y. 1974, U.S. Dist. Ct. (so. dist.) N.Y. 1974, U.S. Dist. Ct. (ea. dist.) N.Y., 1980, U.S. Ct. Appeals (2nd cir.) 1982, U.S. Ct. Appeals (D.C. cir.) 1989, U.S. Ct. Internat. Trade 1986, U.S. Supreme Ct., 1997; bd. cert. civil trial atty. Nat. Bd. Trial Advocacy, 1997. Bur. chief, Supreme Ct. trial bur. asst. dist. atty. N.Y. County Dist. Atty.'s Office, N.Y.C., 1973-80; pvt. practice N.Y.C., 1980-84; partner Russotti & Barrison, N.Y.C., 1985-89, Wingate, Russotti & Shapiro, N.Y.C., 1990—; Lectr. in the field. Gen. counsel Italian Am. Repertory Theatre, N.Y., 1985-90; mem. Prospect Park Alliance, Bklyn., 1996—. Recipient Am. Jurisprudence awards Bancroft Whitney & Lawyers Co-op, 1971, 73. Mem. ABA, ATLA, N.Y. State Bar Assn., N.Y. State Trial Lawyers Assn. Roman Catholic. Home: 433 3rd St Brooklyn NY 11215-2949 Office: Wingate Russotti Shapiro 420 Lexington Ave Rm 2750 New York NY 10170-2793

RUST, EDWARD BARRY, JR., insurance company executive, lawyer; b. Chgo., Aug. 3, 1950; s. Edward Barry Sr. and Harriett B. (Fuller) R.; m. Sally Buckler, Feb. 28, 1976; 1 child, Edward Barry III. Student, Lawrence U., 1968-69; BS, Ill. Wesleyan U., 1972; JD, MBA, So. Meth. U., 1975. Bar: Tex. 1975, Ill. 1976. Mgmt. trainee State Farm Ins. Cos., Dallas, 1975-76; atty. State Farm Ins. Cos., Bloomington, 1976, sr. atty., 1976-78, asst. v.p., 1978-81, v.p., 1981-83, exec. v.p., 1983-85, chmn., 1987—; pres., CEO State Farm Life Ins. Cos., Bloomington, 1985—; now CEO, chmn. State Farm Mutual Auto Ins. Co.; pres. and bd. dirs. State Farm Investment Mgmt. Corp., State Farm Internat. Services, Inc., State Farm Cos. Found.; chmn. State Farm Mut. Automobile Ins. Co., 1987; bd. dirs. exec. and investment coms. State Farm Annuity and Life Ins. Co., State Farm Mut. Automobile Ins. Co., State Farm Life Ins. Co., State Farm Fire and Casualty, State Farm Gen. Trustee Ill. Wesleyan U., 1985—; mem. adv. coun. Grad. Sch. Bus. Stanford U., 1987-94; mem. bus. adv. coun. Coll. Commerce and Bus. Adminstrn. U. Ill. Mem. Am. Enterprise Inst., Bus. Roundtable (chmn. edn. task force), Tex. State Bar Assn., Ill. Bar Assn., Am. Inst. Property and Liability Underwriters (trustee 1986-96), Ins. Inst. Am. (trustee 1986-96), Ins. Inst. for Highway Safety (vice chmn.), Nat. Alliance of Bus. (chmn. 1998—), Ill. Bus. Roundtable (chmn. 1998—). Office: State Farm Ins Cos 1 State Farm Plz Bloomington IL 61710-0001

RUST, JOHN NEVILLE, psychologist; b. Scunthorpe, Lincolnshire, Eng., Nov. 25, 1943; s. John Cyprian Walcot and Francis Mary (Walshaw) R.; m. Susan Esther Golombok, Feb. 22, 1978; 1 child, Jamie Carlos; 1 child by previous marriage: Naseem Azure. BSc with 1st class honors, U. London, 1970, MA in Philosophy, 1976; PhD in Psychology, Inst. Psychiatry, London, 1974. Rsch. psychologist U. London, Inst. Psychiatry, 1972-74, lectr. psychology, 1974-76; lectr. psychometrics U. London, Inst. Edn., 1976-86, sr. lectr. psychometrics, 1986, head dept. psychology, 1984—; senator U. London, 1983-87. Contbr. articles to profl. jours.; author psychol. tests; editor (jour. series) Philos. Psychology, 1987. Dir. City of Psychometrics Ltd. Inter-U. Council scholar, 1977, 78, Brit. Council scholar, 1986. Fellow Royal Statis. Soc., Brit. Psychol. Soc.; mem. Soc. for Philosophy and Psychology, Brit. Computer Soc., Am. Psychol. Assn., Licenate of Am. Bd. of Assessment Psychology. Avocation: travel. Office: U London, Goldsmiths Coll, New Cross London SE14 6NW, England

RUST, WILLIAM DAVID, JR., retired structural engineer; b. Washington, Oct. 11, 1931; s. William David and Anna Mae (Lyles) R.; m. Eunice Charles Williams, Oct. 24, 1953; children: Diann Yvonne Rust-Tierney, Cheryl Frances, William Douglas. BS in Civil Engring., Howard U., 1954; postgrad., Cath. U. Am., 1956-57; MS in Engring., George Washington U., 1962; postgrad., U. Va., 1973-74. Registered profl. engr., Mass. Naval architect Phila. Naval Shipyard, 1954; structural engr. U.S. Gen. Svcs. Adminstrn., Washington, 1956-92; ret. 1992; lectr. civil engring. Fed. City Coll. (now U. D.C.), Washington, 1973; mem. com.Interagency Seismic Safety, Washington, 1978-90, ASCE, Found. and Excavation Stds., N.Y.C., 1978-95, AISC, Steel Specification Simplification, Chgo., 1980-81; mem. coms. Fed. Constrn. Coun., Washington, 1978-90. Chmn. cub pack no. 24 Boy Scouts Am., Washington, 1968; clk. session Northminster Presbyn. Ch., Washington, 1972; commr. gen. assembly Presbyn. Ch. U.S., Ft. Worth, 1973. Lt. C.E., U.S. Army, 1954-56. Fellow ASCE; mem., NSPE, Structural Stability Rsch. Coun. (mem.-at-large), Tau Beta Pi (life). Achievements include administration of development of first nationwide microfilming of design and construction drawings system for the U.S. General Services Adminstration. Home: 7600 Alaska Ave NW Washington DC 20012-1469

RUSTAMOV, ELMAN, bank executive. Chmn. Nat. Bank Azerbaijan, Baku. Office: Nat Bank Azerbaijan, 19 Bul-Bul Ave, 370030 Baku Azerbaijan*

RUSTAN, AGNE PETER, mining engineer; b. Koping, Sweden, Feb. 21, 1941; s. Olof Kurt and Herta Mathilde (Neusteuer) R.; m. Brita Jarvhammar, July 6, 1968; children: Carolina, Sofia, Lovisa, Mattias. MS, Royal Inst. Tech., Stockholm, 1965, Tech. Licentiate, 1973; PhD in Mining, Luleå U. of Tech, Sweden, 1995. Asst. in mining Royal Inst. Tech., Stockholm, 1965-70; mine planning engr. Luossavaara-Kirunavaara, Malmberget, Sweden, 1971-74; rsch.r, tchr. Lulea U. Tech., Sweden, 1974-98; cons., 1998—. Co-author: Underground Ventilation, 1984; editor-in-chief: Rock Blasting Terms and Symbols, 1998. With Swedish Army, 1960-86. Sweden-Am. Found. scholar, Stockholm, 1970-71. Mem. Internat. Soc. Rock Mechanics (gen. sec. commn. on fragmentation by blasting), Internat. Soc. Explosive Engrs. Avocations: piano, sailing, gardening, house building, stamps. Home and Office: Lagmansvagen 20, SE-95432 Gammelstad Sweden

RUSTEN, GUNNAR, physician; b. Laerdal, Norway, Nov. 24, 1952; s. Egil Gunnar and Borgny (Søgnen) R.; m. Bente Kristin Johansen, Jan. 15, 1954; children: Harald, Birgitte, Erik. MD, U. Oslo, 1984, Splst. Family Medicine, 1992; Sports Physician, Norwegian Found. Sports Med., Oslo, 1998. Commd., advanced through grades to maj., 1999, maj. Oslo Mil. Surgery Clinic, 1999—]; pvt. practice Oslo, 1986—; supr. physician HVPU (Mentally Retarded), Oslo, 1989—; tchr. Med. Faculty U. Oslo, 1995-96; cons. physician Oslo Police Dept., 1988—, IF.Ins., Oslo, 1995—; team physician NTG-Swimming, Oslo, 1996-98, Nat. Swimming Team, Oslo, 1999—. Maj. Norwegian Army, 1989—. Mem. Norwegian Med. Assn., Norwegian Assn. Family Physicians, Norwegian Mil. Med. Assn., Norwegian Assn. Sports Physicians, Oslo Swim Club (chmn. bd. 1988—). Avocations: off road cycling, kayaking, travel. Home: Kjetilsvei 10 A, N-0494 Oslo Norway Office: Oslo Mil Surgery Clinic, Oslo Mil/Akershus, N-0015 Oslo Norway

RUSTIN, WOODROW CLEVELAND, oil industry executive, industrial engineer, educator; b. Lucedale, Miss., July 3, 1948; s. Daniel M. and Winifred L. (Leggett) R.; m. Claressa J. Parker, June 20, 1970; children: Daniel G., Carol I. BSIET, U. So. Miss., 1969, MS, 1973. Indsl. engr. Litton Ship Sys., Pascagoula, Miss., 1970; facility engr. Mitchell Engring. Co., Columbus, Miss., 1971; instr. engring. tech., adult edn. supr. Gulf Coast C.C., Perkinston, Miss., 1971-73; sr. indsl. engr. pipe and ship mgmt. Ingall's Shipbldg., Pascagoula, 1973-79; function head maintenance div. Saudi Arabia Oil Co., Dhahran, 1979-92, asst. exec. dir. indsl. svcs., 1992—; v.p., dir. Expat Corp. Tex., Austin, 1991-98. Editor: Modified Wright Theory, 1976. Regional dir. Amateur Athletic Union-USA, Mid-East Region, 1985-90; chmn. Protestant Fellowship Group, Middle East, 1988. Recipient achievement award for Desert Shield/Desert Storm, U.S. Army, 1990-92. Mem. Inst. Indsl. Engrs. (sr., chpt. pres. 1985-86, Soc. Am. Mil. Engrs. (chpt. pres. 1994-95), Am. Assn. Cost Engrs. (dir. membership and publicity 1982-83, Silver Fox com. 1998—), Planetary Soc. (new millennium com. 1994—). Republican. Baptist. Avocations: travel, reading, theater, camping, spectator sports. Home: Saudi Aramco Box 685, Dhahran 31311, Saudi Arabia Office: Saudi Arabian Oil Co, Rm 3096 Admin North, Dhahran 31311, Saudi Arabia

RUSTOMJEE, SABAR, psychiatrist; b. Avisawella, Sri Lanka, Dec. 12, 1937; arrived in Australia; d. Maneksha Rustomjee and Mehra Bapuji; m. Pirosha Framroze Rustomjee, Dec. 11, 1960; children: Hormaz, Niloufer, Pheroza. MB, BS, U. Bombay, 1961; diploma in psychol. medicine, U. Melbourne, Australia, 1972. Psychiatrist Malvern Clinic, Melbourne; cons. Cmty. Mental Health Ctr., Sandringham, Australia; cons. psychiatrist Sandringham Hosp., Royal Children's Hosp., Melbourne, Monash Med. Ctr., Melbourne; hon. sr. lectr. Monash U., 1992—; coord. master Group Analytic Studies, 1998—; pvt. practice, East Brighton, Australia. Editor: A Tribute of Freud; mem. editl. com. Psychotherapy Jour. Australia; contbr. articles to med. jours., including Group Analysis, Australian and New Zealand Jour. Psychiatry. Recipient President's award Lions Club Intenat. Fellow Royal Australian and New Zealand Coll. Psychiatrists; mem. Australian Assn. Group Psychotherapists (sec., past pres., Victorian br. com., mem. com. mgmt.), Victorian Assn. Group Psychotherapists, Internat. Assn. Group Psychotherapists (co-chmn. consultative assembly orgnl. affiliates 1992-95, treas. 1995-98, pres.-elect 1998-2000, pres. 2000-03), Am. Group Psychotherapy Assn. (clin. mem.), Lioness (pres. Camberwell, Melbourne). Zoroastrian. Avocations: tapestry, Australian rules football. E-mail: sabar@primus.com.au. Home: 2 Danielle Close, Wheelers Hill VIC 3150, Australia Office: 44 Cummins Rd, East Brighton Vic 3187, Australia

RUSTON, ALAN ROBERT, religious organization administrator, consultant; b. Hackney, Eng., Nov. 13, 1941; s. Alfred and Mabel Evelyn (Govey) R.; m. Rosemary Frances Tomlin, Sept. 3, 1970; children: Mark Robert, Jennifer Warn. BSc in Econs., U. London, 1972, diploma in religious studies, 1977. Tech. expert, cons. H.M. Customs and Excise, London, 1961-69, 72-81, 87-2000; dir. studies Civil Svc. Coll., London, 1981-86; mem. governing coun. Manchester Coll. Oxford (now Harris Manchester Coll.), 1985-88, chmn., 1988-96; rsch. assoc. New Dictionary of Nat. Biography, 2000—. Author: The Hibbert Trust: A History, 1984, The Inquirer: A History, 1992, My Ancestors Were English Presbyterians/Unitarians, 1993; editor Transactions of the Unitarian Hist. Soc., 1988—, Hertfordshire People, 1982-95. Chmn. The Essex Hall Trustees, Inc., 1991—. Mem. Brit. & Fgn. Unitarian Assn. Inc. (chmn. 1990—), Hertfordshire Record Soc. (chmn. 1996—), Hertfordshire Family and Population History Soc. (chmn. 1980-86), Hertfordshire Local History Assn. (exec. bd. 1992—). Unitarian. Avocations: genealogy, topography of London, preaching. Home: 41 Hampermill Ln, Oxhey WD1 4NS, England

RUSZKOWSKI, JANUSZ STANISŁAW, political scientist, educator; b. Pełczyce, Gorzow, Poland, July 23, 1962; s. Tadeusz and Katarzyna (Andrzejczak) R. MA, U. Szczecin, Poland, 1986, PhD in History, 1993. Asst. lectr. polit. sci. U. Szczecin, 1986-90, tutor, 1990-93, asst. prof., 1993—; inspector for transborder cooperation with Germany, Office of Voivode, Province of Szczecin, 1995—; sci. counsellor Ctrl. Com. Periodical Competition on European Union, 1994—; vice dir. European Integration House in Szczecin, 1999. Author: The Evangelical Church of German Democratic Republic 1971-89, 1995, Lexicon of European Union, 1998, European Union, 1996; co-author: Brückenschlage Zwischen West und Osteuropa, 1995; co-contbr. articles to profl. jours. Sub-lt. Polish Coast Guard, 1987-88. Mem. Soc. Polit. Sci., Soc. German Culture, Soc. European Integration. Roman Catholic. Avocations: books, music, sports. Home: ul Kruszwicka 26/b, 71-043 Szczecin Poland Office: U Szczecin Inst Phil, Pol S, ul Tarczynskiego 1, 70-387 Szczecin Poland

RUSZNÁK, ZOLTÁN GYULA, physiologist, educator; b. Nyíregyháza, Hungary, Oct. 20, 1965; s. Zoltán Miklós and Ildikó (Darvas) R.; m. Ilona Kovács, Mar. 22, 1988; children: Péter, Lili. MD, U Debrecen, Hungary, 1990, PhD, 1998. Sci. lectr. U. of Debrecen Med. and Health Sci. Ctr., Debrecen, 1990-94; asst. lectr. Debreceni Orvostudomanyi Egyetem, Debrecen, 1994—. Contbr. articles to profl. jours. Mem. Hungarian Physiol. Soc., Hungarian Neurosci. Assn., European Neurosci. Assn., The Physiological Soc. Avocations: plane spotting, computer games, bicycling, driving, traveling. Home: 17/B Alkotas u, 4225 Debrecen Hungary Office: Univ Med Sch, Nagyerdei krt 98, H-4012 Debrecen Hungary

RUTA, THOMAS V., professional sports team executive, accounting executive; married. BS summa cum laude, Fordham U., 1966; MBA with distinction, Pace U. CPA, N.Y., N.J., Minn. Founding ptnr. Behan, Ling & Ruta, N.Y.C., now chmn., pres.; ltd. ptnr. Pitts. Penguins, Pa.; ltd. ptnr. Manchester Hockey Group. Office: 358 5th Ave New York NY 10001-2209

RUTH, BRYCE CLINTON, JR., lawyer; b. Greenwood, Miss., Dec. 19, 1948; s. Bryce Clinton and Kathryn (Arant) R.; m. Martha M. Ruth; children: Lauren Elizabeth, Bryce Clinton III. BS, Delta State U., 1970; JD, Memphis State U., 1979. Bar: Tenn., 1979, U.S. Dist. Ct. (mid. dist.) Tenn. 1979, U.S. Ct. Mil. Appeals 1991, U.S. Ct. Appeals (6th cir.), 1994. Criminal investigation spl. agt. IRS, Memphis and Nashville, 1971-82; asst. dist. atty. Dist. Atty. Office, Gallatin, Tenn., 1982-89; asst. pub. defender Pub. Defender's Office, Gallatin, Tenn., 1989-90; pvt. practice White House, Tenn., 1989—; judge City of Cross Plains, Tenn., 1992—; juvenile ct. referee judge Robertson County, Tenn., 1995-98; mem. dist. investigating com. dist. VI Tenn. Bd. Law Examiners, 1989—; mem. child enforcement steering com. Asst. Dist. Atty. Office, 1983-84, chmn. legis. subcom., 1985; lectr. in field. Chmn. fin. com. White House First United Meth. Ch., 1983-88, trustee, 1988-90, chmn., 1990; trustee Vol. State Coll. Found., 1993-2000, chmn., 1998-99; bd. dirs. Crime Stoppers of Sumner County, 1989-94; bd. dirs. White House Youth Soccer, 1992-93, coach, 1987-91; bd. dirs. White House Soccer Booster Club, 1996—, pres., 1998; bd. dirs. Sumner County CASA, 1992-93; coach Jr. Pro Football, 1980-85; video cameraman for football team White House H.S., 1991—; mem. Leadership Sumner, 1989; bd. dirs. White House Men's Club, 1981-83, 85-88, v.p., 1984, 88, pres., 1985. Maj. JAGC, USAR, 1983—. Recipient Disting. Expert award for pistol marksmanship U.S. Treasury, Disting. Svc. award City of White House. Mem. NRA, Tenn. Bar Assn. (del. 1993—, mem. family law code revision commn. 1996—), Sumner County Bar Assn. (chmn. domestic rels. com. 1984-85, v.p. 1998-99, pres. 1999-2000), White House Area C. of C. (bd. dirs. 1990-95, pres. 1993-94), United C. of C. of Sumner County (pres. 1995). Avocations: scuba diving, skiing, golf, hunting, pistol shooting. Office: 3210 Hwy 31W PO Box 68 White House TN 37188-0068

RUTH, EDWARD KEITH, information systems specialist, management consultant; b. Louisville, June 28, 1960; s. William Edward and Lillian Loretta (Wyatt) R. BS in Bus. Data Processing, William Carey Coll., 1982, BA in Econs., 1982; EdD, Okla. State U., 1997; MBA, Oklahoma City U., 1990. Cert. data processor, computer prof., project mgmt., profl., Inst. Certification Computing Profls., Ill., PMP Project Mgmt. Inst., Pa. Sr. sys. analyst IV Miss. State Tax Commn., Jackson, 1982-96; sr. sys. programmer Cooper Industries, Vicksburg, Miss., 1985-86, Hertz Corp., Oklahoma City, Okla., 1986-90; applications platform mgr. Acxiom Corp., Conway, Ark., 1991-92; sr. product developer Teubner & Assocs., Stillwater, Okla., 1992-93; sr. software developer BMC Software, Austin, Tex., 1996-98; sr. info. tech. specialist IBM, Lexington, Ky., 1998—. Contbr. articles to profl. jours. Mem. Project Mgmt. Inst., Nat. Sys. Programmers Assn., Am. Vocat. Ednl. Rsch. Assn., Mgmt. Sci. Inst. Republican. Baptist. Avocations: travel, reading, music. E-mail: edruthfax@yahoo.com. Office: IBM 745 W New Circle Rd Lexington KY 40511-1807

RUTHCHILD, GERALDINE QUIETLAKE, training and development consultant, writer, poet; d. Nathan and Ruth (Feldman) Stein; m. Neil

Wolinsky, Dec. 31, 1993; 1 child, Nathaniel Gideon Wolinsky. BA summa cum laude, Queens Coll., 1977; MA in Am. Lit., Johns Hopkins U., 1980, PhD in Am. Lit., 1983. Asst. prof. Albion (Mich.) Coll., 1982-84; assoc. Investor Access Corp., N.Y.C., 1984-85; program dir. Exec. Enterprises, Inc., N.Y.C., 1985-86; pres. Ruthchild Assocs., N.Y.C., 1987-90, Exemplar, N.Y.C., 1991-95, Exemplar, Ltd., N.Y.C., 1995—; cons. J.P. Morgan & Co., Inc., MetLife, Bankers Trust Co., MasterCard Internat., Koch Industries, Inc., Chase Manhattan Bank N.A., Merrill Lynch, TIAA-CREF, Drake Beam Morin, Trans Union Corp, NatWest Bank, U.S.A., Citibank N.A., Robert Morris Assocs., Goldman, Sachs & Co., Dean Witter Reynolds, Inc., also others, 1987—. Contbr. articles, poems to profl. and lit. jours. Vol. handicapped children N.Y. Foundling Hosp., N.Y.C., 1988-90, Fgn. Visitors Desk, Met. Mus. Art, N.Y.C., 1989-97. Hopkins fellow Johns Hopkins U., 1979-80, Andrew Mellon Found. fellow, 1980-81, 81-82. Mem. ASTD, Assn. Bank Trainers and Cons., Internat. Soc. Philos. Enquiry, Phi Beta Kappa. Avocations: foreign languages, needlework, house plants. Office: Exemplar Ltd 366 N Broadway Ste 410 Jericho NY 11753-2000

RUTHERFORD, JOHN DAVID, forensic pathologist; b. Sheffield, Yorkshire, United Kingdom, Sept. 19, 1947; children: James Thomas, Emma Tamsin Lee. BSc, Sheffield (U.K.) U., 1969, M.B.,Ch.B., 1972. Registered med. practitioner, U.K.; accredited pathologist, U.K. Family physician Nat. Health Svc., Sheffield, 1973-74, hosp. physician, 1974-78; pathologist Nat. Health Svc., Manchester, U.K., 1978-94; home office forensic pathologist Manchester, 1991—. Mem. Royal Coll Physicians, Royal Coll. Pathology. Office: Ridgefield House, 14 John Dalton St, Manchester M2 6JR, England

RUTHMAN, THOMAS ROBERT, manufacturing executive; b. Cin., May 24, 1933; s. Alois H. and Catherine (Gies) R.; m. Audrey J. Schumaker, Mar. 17, 1979; children: Thomas G., Julia C., Theresa K. Grad., LaSalle U., 1970. With Ruthman Pump and Engring. Inc. (formerly Ruthman Machinery Co.), Cin., 1953—, gen. mgr., 1964-70, v.p., 1970-74, pres., 1974—, pres., owner, 1981—; pres. Gusher Pumps, Inc., Fulflo Spltys. Co., Gusher Pumps of New Castle, Cin., Williamstown (Ky.), Dry Ridge, Calif.; pres., owner, dir.Great Lakes Pump & Supply, Mich.; owner BSM Pump Corp, North Kingston, R.I.; pres., owner Birmingham (Eng.) Pump Supply, Ruthmann Pumpen, GMBH, Germany. Home: 6858 Dimmick Ct West Chester OH 45069-3930 Office: 1212 Streng St Cincinnati OH 45223-2643

RUTHVEN, KENNETH KNOWLES, English language educator; b. Bradford, Yorkshire, Eng., May 26, 1936; arrived in Australia, 1980; s. Thomas Knowles and Freda (Bennett) R.; m. Rachel Mary Bainbridge, Dec. 26, 1960; children: Simon, Guy, Patrick. BA with 1st class honors, U. Manchester, Eng., 1958, MA, 1959, PhD, 1965. From asst. lectr. to lectr. to sr. lectr. to prof. English U. Canterbury, New Zealand, 1961-79; prof. English U. Adelaide, Australia, 1980-85, U. Melbourne, Australia, 1985-99; prof. emeritus, 2000—. Author: (books) A Guide to Ezra Pound's Personae, 1969, The Conceit, 1969, Myth, 1976, Critical Assumptions, 1979, Feminist Literary Studies: An Introduction, 1984, Ezra Pound as Literary Critic, 1990, Nuclear Criticism, 1993; editor: (book) Beyond the Disciplines: The New Humanities, 1992, (jour.) So. Rev., 1981-85, (monograph series) Interpretations, 19 vols., 1993-96. Fellow Australian Acad. of Humanities. Home: 27 Fairleys Rd, Rostrevor SA 5073, Australia

RUTISHAUSER, WILHELM JAKOB, medicine educator; b. Amriswil, Switzerland, Sept. 2, 1931; s. Georg Eugen and Elsa (Ribi) R.; m. Lilly Leuener, Apr. 5, 1975. MD, Med. Fac. U., Basel, Switzerland, 1958. Specialist in internal medicine, cardiology. Pvt. docent Faculty Medicine U. Zurich, 1968-70, assoc. prof. cardiology, 1970-76; prof. cardiology and head cardiology ctr. U. Hosp., Geneva, 1976-96; pres. Swiss Heart Found., Berne, 1997—. Lt. col. General Staff, 1974-94. Recipient Goetz prize U. Zurich, 1975, Paul Morawitz prize German Cardiac Soc., 1991, Euro Crystal Globe prize, 1999. Fellow Am. Coll. Cardiology, European Soc. Cardiology (exec. scientific com. 1987-90, Silver medal 1998), Swiss Soc. Cardiology (pres. 1974-76), Swiss Heart Found. (chair sci. com. 1978-96); mem. Am. Heart Assn. (internat. fellow), World Heart Fedn. (pres. 1991-92), Internat. Soc. Cardiovascular Pharmacotherapy (pres. 1987-89). Office: Cardiology Clinic Genolier, 1272 Genolier Switzerland

RUTKEVICH, IGOR MAX, physicist, fluid mechanics researcher; b. Semipalatinsk, Kazakhstan, Russia, Apr. 6, 1944; s. Max Iakov and Judith (Bol'shinskaya) R.; m. Natalia Eidelnant, Dec. 4, 1969; 1 child, Anna. MS, Moscow U., 1966, PhD, 1971; DSc, USSR Acad. Sci., Moscow, 1988. Rschr. Inst. High Temp., Moscow, 1969-74, sr. scientist, 1974-86, leading scientist, 1986-91, prin. scientist, 1991-92; rsch. prof. Ben Gurion U., Beer Sheva, Israel, 1993—; dep. head theoretical physics dept. Inst. High Temperature, 1986-92. Author: Electric Breakdown Waves in a Bounded Plasma, 1989, Ionization Waves in Electrical Breakdown of Gases, 1994; contbr. over 100 articles to sci. jours. Grantee Israel Ministry of Scis. and Arts, Jerusalem, 1993-96, Israel Acad. Scis. and Humanities, 1996, European Commn., Brussels, 1997. Mem. N.Y. Acad. Scis. Office: Ben Gurion Univ, Dept Mech Engring, 84105 Beer Sheva Israel

RUTKOWSKI, ANTONI, food scientist, researcher; b. Poznan, Poland, Nov. 13, 1920; s. Witold and Wanda (Pokrzywnicka) R.; m. Zofia Kazmerczak, Mar. 30, 1949; children: Halina, Aleksandra. Licentiate, Agrl. H.S., Czernichow-Crakow, Poland, 1942; MSc in Food Sci., U. Poznan, 1948, PhD in Food Sci., 1951; DSc (hon.), Agrl. U. Poznan, 1983, U. Olsztyn, Poland, 1986, U. Warsaw, Poland, 1990. Asst., lectr. dept. food tech. U. Poznan, 1946-54; dir. Inst. Fats & Oils Industry, Warsaw, 1954-59; head dept. food tech. and preservation Agrl. U., Olsztyn, 1960-69; dep. dir. Inst. Gen. Chemistry, Warsaw, 1960-69, Inst. Food and Nutrition, Warsaw, 1969-73; head dept. food tech. Agrl. U., Warsaw, 1973-90; lectr. food sci. State Com. for Sci. Degrees, 1954, prof. tech. sci., 1961, 69; sci. cons. FAO, Rome, 1980; chmn. adv. coun. Ministry Food Industry and Ministry Agr., Warsaw, 1969-90. Author: Edible Vegetable Protein Concentrates and Isolates, 1981, Food Additives, 1993, Food Ingredients and Additives, 1997. Recipient Emil Baur medal German Acad. Agrl. Scis., 1986, Gold medal Czech Acad. Agrl. Scis., 1988; grantee USDA, 1965, 70, 79. Fellow Internat. Acad. Food Sci. and Tech.; mem. Polish Acad. Scis. (sci. sec. sect. agrl. scis. 1983-89, mem. of exec. 1990—, chmn. com. food chemistry and tech. 1969—, v.p. coun. of scientific socs. 1996—), Russian Acad. Agrl. Scis. (Moscow) (hon.), Inst. Food Technologists, Polish Soc. Food Engrs., Polish Food Technologists Soc. (pres. 1990-97, hon. mem. 1998), Internat. Union Food Sci. and Tech. (exec. mem., v.p. 1987-90), Hungarian Soc. Food Industry (hon.), Polish Food Coun. (v.p. 1998—). Avocations: travel, photography. E-mail: arut@ippt.gov.pl. Home: Marszalkowska 9/15 m 32, 00-626 Warsaw Poland Office: Polish Acad Scis, Palac Kultury i Nauki, 00-901 Warsaw Poland

RUTLEDGE, VIRGIE MARILYN, educator; b. Hamilton, Ohio, Jan. 23, 1950; d. Benjamin John and Virgie Jones Hann; m. Dennis Eugene Rutledge, Aug. 1, 1969; children: Brian, Aaron. BS in Edn., Miami U., Oxford, Ohio, 1988; MEd, Miami U., 1994. Elem. tchr. Hamilton City Schs., 1988—; tchr. mentor Hamilton City Schs., 1999. ch. elder Christ the King Luth. Ch., West Chester, Ohio, 2000—. Martha Holden Jennings scholar U. Dayton, 1998-99. Mem. Phi Delta Kappa Internat., Delta Kappa Gamma Soc. Internat. Republican. Avocations: reading, hiking, cooking. Office: Martha Holden J Found 710 Halle Bldg 1228 Euclid Ave Cleveland OH 44115-1831

RUTTER, ERNEST HENRY, science educator; b. Sunderland, Eng., Jan. 8, 1946; s. George William and Irene (Stevenson) R.; m. Christiane Allier, Mar. 10, 1969 (div. 1982); children: Dominic, Simon George; m. Katharine Heather Brodie, July 6, 1985; children: James Douglas Brodie, Heather Louise Brodie. BSc, Imperial Coll., London, 1967, A Royal Sch. Mines, 1967, PhD, 1970, diploma, 1970. Chartered geologist. Lectr. Imperial Coll., London, 1969-82, reader, 1982-89; reader Manchester (Eng.) U., 1989-93, prof., 1993—; cons. W. Marshall, London, 1981-83, W.S. Atkins, Epsom, U.K., 1982-85, Allott & Lomax, Manchester, 1983-85, Brit. Petroleum, London, 1989-96. Editor: Deformation Mechanisms, Rheology and Tectonics, 1990. Fellow Geol. Soc. (Wollaston Fund award 1995, Lyell medal 1999); mem. Am. Geophys. Union, European Geophys. Soc. Avocations: electronics, computing. Office: U Manchester Dept Earth Sci, Oxford Rd, Manchester M13 9PL, England

RUTTER, MARTIN KENNETH, endocrinologist, diabetologist, research physician; b. Warrington, Cheshire, Eng., Mar. 13, 1962; s. Kenneth and Irene (Cunnington) R. MBChB, Edinburgh (Scotland) U., 1985; Diploma in Med. Sci., Newcastle U., 1994. Ho. officer Western Gen. Hosp., Edinburgh, 1985-86, sr. house officer, 1986-89; registrar Queen Elizabeth Hosp., Gateshead, Eng., 1989-92, Freeman Hosp., Newcastle, 1992-93; clin. rsch. assoc. Newcastle U., 1993-94; sr. registrar Freeman Hosp., 1994-95, hon. sr. registrar, 1995-98, sr. registrar, 1998; locum cons. physician, 1998-2000; rsch. fellow Boston, 2000—; presenter in field of heart disease in asymptomatic patients and the influence of microalbuminuria; cons. endocrinologist Royal Victoria Infirmary, Newcastle Upon Tyne. Contbr. articles to med. jours. Recipient Novo Nordisk Rsch. award, 1993, Freeman Hosp. Trustees rsch. award, 1996; Northern Region Health Authority grantee, 1993; Northern Region Rsch. Tng. fellow, U.K., 1993. Mem. Royal Coll. Physicians U.K., Royal Coll. Physicians Ireland. Avocations: classical and jazz piano, local operatic society. Home: 52A Percy Gardens, Tynemouth NE30 4HH, England Office: Diabetes Rsch Ctr, North Tyneside Gen Hosp, North Shields NE29 8NH, England

RUTTY, GUY NATHAN, forensic pathologist, educator; b. Ramsgate, Kent, Eng., Nov. 27, 1963; s. Donald Arthur and Lilian Dorothy Rutty; m. Jane Elizabeth Ward, May 1993. MBBS, Royal Free Hosp. Sch. Med., London, 1987; diploma in Forensic Pathology, Royal Coll. Pathologists, 1996. House physician King Georges and Barking Hosp., London, 1987-88; house surgeon Royal Free Hosp., London, 1988; sr. house officer pathology Brook Gen. and Greenwich Hosps., London, 1988-90; registrar histopathology Mt. Vernon and Harefield Hosps., London, 1990-92; sr. registrar histopathology Leicester (Eng.) Royal Infirmary, 1992-96; lectr. forensic pathology U. Sheffield, Eng., 1996, sr. lectr., 1996-2000; trainee rep. Trent region Trent Adv. Specialist Com. in Pathology, 1993-95, Trent Histopathology Edn. Com., 1994-96. Recipient Murs Scholfield and Yehodi Gordon elective award Royal Free Hosp. Sch. Medicine, 1986, ACP Travel fellow, 2000. Mem. Royal Coll. Pathologists (trainee rep. Trent region 1995-96), Brit. Assn. Forensic Medicine (coun. mem.), Forensic Sci. Soc., Assn. Clin. Pathologists (coun. mem.), Internat. Acad. Pathology (Brit. divsn.), Path. Soc. Gt. Britain and Ireland. Avocations: walking, gardening, golf, films. E-mail: g.n.rutty@sheffield.ac.uk. Office: U Sheffield Dept Forensic, Path Medico-Legal Ctr, Sheffield S37ES, England

RUUD, ARNE ODDBJØRN, marketing professional; b. Oslo, Aug. 5, 1954. B in Mktg., Norwegian Sch. Mktg., Oslo, 1996. Sailor Fred Olsen, Oslo, 1973-76; clk. Telenor, Oslo, 1979-93; supr. Telenor, 1993—; cons. Ch.-Aid, Oslo, 1994—. Mem. Lambertseter R.C. Lutheran. Avocations: writing, skiing, social work, music, computers. Home: Feltspatvn 58, 1155 Oslo Norway

RUUD, JAY WESLEY, dean; b. Racine, Wis., Nov. 3, 1950; s. Wesley J. and Alyce Ruud; m. Cynthia Lee Kristopeit, Sept. 4, 1971 (div. Nov. 29, 1993). BA, U. Wis.-Parkside, Kenosha, Wis., 1972; MA, U. Wis.-Milw., 1974, PhD, 1981. Instr. English U. Wis.-Parkside, Kenosha, 1978-83, testing coord., 1983-84; instr. English U. Wis.-Marathon County, Wausau, Wis., 1984-85; prof. English Northern State U., Aberdeen, S.D., 1985-96, asst. dean coll. arts and scis., 1996-97, dean coll. arts and scis., 1997—; dir. NEH Inst. on Lit. of Plains Indians, Aberdeen, S.D., 1994, NEH Inst. on Chaucer's Canterbury Tales, Aberdeen, S.D., 1989. Author: Many a Song and Many a Leccherous Lay: Tradition and Individuality in Chaucer's Lyric Poetry, 1992; editor: Proceedings of the First Dakotas Conference on Earlier British Literature, 1992, Proceedings of the Seventh Northern Plains Conference on Early British, 1999; contbr. articles to profl. jours. Named Outstanding Faculty Mem. Northern State U., 1989; recipient Burlington Northern Faculty Achievement award Burlington Northern Faound. and Northern State U., 1989. Mem. New Chaucer Soc., Medieval Assn. of the Midwest. Avocation: acting in local community theater. E-mail address: ruudj@northern.edu. Fax: 605-626-2635. Office: Northern State U 1200 S Jay St Aberdeen SD 57401-7155

RUUTH, ERIK ANDERS GUSTAV, pharmaceutical industry executive; b. Vaxjo, Sweden, May 8, 1955; s. Anders Herman and Margaretha Anna (Lindholm) R.; m. Francoise Jeanne Praz, Apr. 30, 1989; childre: Julia, Lucas. MD, Umea U., Sweden, 1982, PhD, 1988. Sr. scientist Aventis Pharma, Romainville, France, 1989, group leader, 1989-90, internat. rsch. project leader, 1990-96, product expert, 1992-96, study coord., 1996-97, study mgr., 1997-99; clin. mgr. Hoechst Marion Roussel, Romainville, France, 1999—. Postdoctoral fellow INSERM, Paris, 1980-89. Mem. Am. Soc. Microbiology. Avocations: skiing, skating, music, films, books. Office: Aventis Pharma, 102 Route de Noisy, 93235 Romainville France

RUVALCABA, ROBERTO ALEJANDRO, marketing executive; b. Mexico City, Oct. 5, 1966; s. Roberto Gonzalo Ruvalcaba and Elisa Badillo. B in Actuary, U. de las Ams., Puebla, Mex., 1992; MBA, U. Iberoamericana, Mexico City, 1999. Sales The Southwestern Co., Nashville, 1988-90; trade exec. A.C. Nielsen, Mexico City, 1992-95; mgr. new bus. devel. and rsch. Reader's Digest, Mexico City, 1995—. Mem. ESOMAR, AMMD, MUNDET. Avocations: jogging, mountain biking. Home: Barcelona 114, 54020 Valle Dorado Mexico Office: Reader's Digest, Ave Lomas de Sotelo, 54020 Mexico City Mexico City

RUYBALID, LOUIS ARTHUR, social worker, community development consultant; b. Allison, Colo., Apr. 6, 1925; s. Mike Joseph and Helen Mary (Rodriguez) R.; m. Seraphima Alexander, June 12, 1949; children: Mariana, John. BA, U. Denver, 1946-49, MSW, 1951; PhD, U. Calif., Berkeley, 1970; Professor Ad-Honorem (hon.), Nat. U., Caracas, Venezuela, 1964. Social worker Ariz., Calif., Colo., 1951-62; advisor community devel. Unitarian Service Com., Caracas, 1962-64, U.S. Agy. for Internat. Devel., Rio de Janeiro, Brazil, 1964-66; area coordinator U.S. Office Econ. Opportunity, San Francisco, 1966-68; prof., dept. head U. So. Colo., Pueblo, 1974-80; licensing analyst State of Calif., Campbell, 1984—; prof. sch. of social work Highlands U., Las Vegas, N.Mex., 1988-89; cons. UN, Caracas, 1978, Brazilian Govt., Brazilia, 1964-66, Venezuelan Govt., Caracas, 1962-64. Author: (books) Favela, 1970, Glossary for Hominology, 1978, (research instrument) The Conglomerate Hom., 1976. Mem. exec. com. Pueblo (Colo.) Regional Planning Com., 1974-79, Nat. Advisory com. The Program Agy. United Presbyn. Ch., 1978-79. Served with USN, 1944-46. Recipient Pro Mundo Beneficio medal Brazilian Acad. Human Sci., Sao Paulo, 1976; United Def. Fund fellow U. Calif., Berkeley, 1961-62, Cert. World Leadership Internat. Leaders of Achievement, 1988-89. Mem. NASW (cert.), Ethnic Minority Commn., IMAGE (nat. edn. chair), Am. Hominol. Assn. (nat. pres. 1975-79), U. Calif. Alumni Assn., AARP (minority spokesperson), Phi Beta Kappa, Phi Sigma Iota. Democrat. Avocations: tennis, boxing history. Home and Office: Ruybalid Assoc Inc 129 Calle Don Jose Santa Fe NM 87501-2364

RUYECHAN, MICHAEL J., JR., writer; b. Aug. 3, 1966. Assocs., ICM Sch. of Bus., Pitts., 1986. Author: From the Pillow and Through a Dream, 1997.

RUYLE-HULLINGER, ELIZABETH SMITH (BETH RUYLE), consultant, municipal financial advisor; b. Oct. 26, 1946; d. Daniel Lester and Mae (Coley) Smith; m. Craig Harlan Hullinger, Oct. 24, 1985; children: Leigh Ann Ruyle, Clint (dec.), Bret. AA, St. Petersburg Jr. Coll., 1966; BA in English, U. Fla., 1968; MPA, U. Ga., 1975. Rsch. asst. Emory U., Atlanta, 1969-70; health planner Met. Coun. for Health, Atlanta, 1970-72; govtl. rels. coord. Atlanta Regional Commn., 1972-76, govtl. affairs coord., 1976-78; exec. dir. South Suburban Mayors' and Mgrs. Assn., Homewood, Ill., 1978-2000; pres. Chgo. Southland Econ. Devel. Alliance, 1999-2000; fin. advisor Ehlers & Assocs., Naperville, Ill., 2000—; exec. dir. South Towns Agy. Risk Mgmt., 1980-98, South Towns Area Benefits Coop., 1983-89, South Towns Bus. Growth Corp., 1983-90; cons. Planning Devel. Svc., Tinley Park, Ill., 1986—. Contbr. articles to profl. and devel. mags. Mem. World's Fair Adv. Com., Chgo., 1986, Met. Planning Coun., 1990-2000, Cook County Tax Reform adv. coun., South Suburban Arts Coun., 1987—, Coun. Urban Econ. Devel., 1986; adv. coun. Urban Innovations, Chgo., Chgo. Assembly Project; mem. Regional Partnership, 1985-2000; bd. dirs. South Suburban Hosp., 1987-96, mem. governing coun., 1999-2000; bd. dirs. Fin. Cmty. Devel. Corp., 1998-2000. Mem. Internat. City Mgmt. Assn., Ill. City Mgmt. Assn.,Met. City Mgrs. Assn., Ill. Pub. Employer Labor Rels. Assn., South Suburban Chiefs of Police Assn., Chgo. Southland C. of C., Plank Road Trail Assn., Lambda Alpha. Methodist. Home: 17255 66th Ct Tinley Park IL 60477-3501 Office: Ehlers & Assocs 1001 E Chicago Ave Ste 135 Naperville IL 60540-5500

RUYS, ANDREW JOHN, ceramics and biomaterials engineer; b. Adelaide, Australia, 1964; s. Jan and Robin Janine R.; m., 1988. B Ceramic Engring. with honors, U. NSW, Sydney, Australia, 1987, PhD in Materials Engring., 1992; Dip.B.S., Moore Coll., Sydney, 1993. Rsch. assoc. U. NSW, 1991, sr. rsch. assoc., 1992-93, rsch. fellow, 1994-96, U2000 fellow, 1997—; cons. Unisearch Ltd., Sydney, 1988—; assoc. ConsultAsia, Sydney, 1995—. Founding editor Internat. Ceramic Monographs, 1994; contbg. editor: Phase Diagrams for Ceramists, Vol. 10, 4994; editor: Proceedings of the 2nd Pacific Rim Ceramics Conference, 1996, Abstracts of the 2nd Internat. Symposium on Sol-Gel Science and Technology, 1996; mem. editl. bd. Interceram; contbr. numerous articles to profl. jours. and conf. proceedings. Elder Uniting Ch. of Australia, Turramurra, NSW, 1988-90. Postdoctoral fellow Australian Rsch. Coun., Canberra, 1994. Mem. Australasian Ceramic Soc. (sec. NSW chpt. 1992—, fed. councillor 1994-95, assoc. editor jour. 1995—), Australian Ceramic Soc. (jour. referee Composites Sci. Tech. 1997—, Ceramics Internat. 1997—). Avocations: hiking, flying, cycling, astronomy. Office: U Sydney, Dept Mech/Mechatronic Engr, Sydney NSW, Australia

RUZDJAK, VLADIMIR, astrophysicist; b. Zagreb, Croatia, Yugoslavia, Aug. 12, 1947; s. Vladimir and Ana (Pristojak) R.; m. Rajka Horvat, Feb. 13, 1948 (wid. 1975); children: Domagoj, Rajka-Smilja. Diploma, U. Zagreb, 1972, MS, 1975, PhD, 1978. Docent U. Rijeka, Croatia, 1978, U. Zagreb, Croatia, 1978; asst. Inst. Physics, Zagreb, 1973-75, sci. asst., 1975-78; sci. collaborator Hvar Observatory, Zagreb, 1978, head, 1981—; prof. U. Zagreb, Croatia, 1993—; Pres. Comm. Astron. Peoples Technic, Zagreb, 1980-86; referee Ministery for Sci., Belgrad, 1988-91. Editor: Hvar Observatory Bulletin, 1979—, (book) Lecture Notes in Physics, 1990; contbr. articles to profl. jours. Recipient award Peoples Technique, Zagreb, 1983. Mem. Croat Soc. Nat. Scis., Astron. Soc. Croat (pres. 1981-85, 2000—), Croatian Phys. Soc., Internat. Astron. Union, Am. Astron. Soc. Roman Catholic. Home: Boskoviceva 3, 10000 Zagreb Croatia Office: Faculty of Geodesy, Kaciceva 26, 10000 Zagreb Croatia

RUZICKA, MAREK CAPTAIN, naturalist; b. Sobeslav, Czech Republic, Aug. 29, 1960; s. Stanislav and Ludmila Ruzicka; m. Magdalena Zhofova, Sept. 7, 1985; children: David, Robin. MSc in Environ. Engring., Prague Inst. Chem. Tech., Czech Republic, 1984, postgrad., 1987, 88; PhD in Chem. Engring., Czech Acad. Scis., 1990. Scientist Inst. Chem. Process Fundamentals, Czech Acad. Scis., Prague, 1984—, head Group for Simple Systems, 1993—; hon. rsch. fellow U. Birmingham, Eng., 1994-95; cons. environ. engring., 1996—. Contbr.: Fractal Reviews in Natural and Applied Sciences, 1995; contbr. articles to profl. jours.; patentee in field. Mem. Union Czech Mathematicians and Physicists, 1988—. Avocations: philosophy, yoga, running. Office: Inst Chem Process Fundament, Rozvojova 135, 16502 Prague Czech Republic

RUŽIČKA, MILOŠ, general and vascular surgeon, educator; b. Brno, Moravia, Czech Republic, Dec. 9, 1950; s. Miloš and Cecilie (Wünschová) R.; m. Alena Orálková, Oct. 13, 1953; children: Hynek, Blanka, Eva, Ludvík. MUDr, Masaryk U., Brno, 1975, CSc, PhD, 1986. Registrar Regional Hosp., Dačice, Czech Republic, 1975-76; specialist 1st surg. dept. U. Hosp., Brno, 1977-90, assoc. prof., cons. 1st surg. dept., 1991-92; specialist Hamad Med. Corp., Doha, Qatar, 1992-93; assoc. prof., cons. surg. dept. U. Hosp., Brno-Bohunice, Czech Republic, 1993-95, head dept. gen. and digestive surgery, 1996-98; cons. Kuwait Cancer Control Ctr., 1996—; dep. dir., head dept. surgical oncology Masaryk Meml. Cancer Inst., Brno, 1998—. Contbr. articles to profl. jours. Capt. Czech Armed Forces, 1976-77. Mem. Internat. Soc. Surgery, Czech Surg. Soc., Gastro-Surg. Club Athens. Mem. Evangelical Ch. Avocations: sports, gardening, traveling. Home: Kroftova 98, Brno 616 00, Czech Republic Office: Univ Hosp Masaryk Meml Cancer Inst, Žluty kopec 7, Brno 656 53, Czech Republic

RWENYONYI, CHARLES MUGISHA, dentist; b. Kabale, Uganda, Apr. 4, 1955; s. Timoty and Gladys Rwenyonyi; m. Lydia Mugisha Owomugisha, June 25, 1987; children: Akanyijuka Suzan, Atukunda Sandra, Nyangoma Linda. B of Dental Surgery, Makerere U., Kampala, Uganda, 1989. Dental surgeon Makerere U. Hosp., Kampala, 1990-95; rsch. fellow Faculty of Dentistry, U. Bergen, Norway, 1995—. Contbr. articles to profl. jours. Mem. Uganda Dental Assn., Uganda Med. and Dental Surgeons Assn. Anglican. Avocations: swimming, volleyball, jogging. E-mail: mugisha.rwenyonyi@odont.uib.no. Office: U Bergen Faculty Dentistry, Aarstadveien 17, Bergen Norway N-5009

RYABININ, IGOR ALEXEEVICH, educator; b. Ilinskoe Village, Russia, June 1, 1925; s. Alexei Vasilevich and Sienaida Vasileevna (Korotkova) R.; m. Nina Danilovna Shestopalova, June 4, 1949; 1 child, Tatiana. MS, Naval Acad., St. Petersburg, Russia, 1958, DS, 1967. Tchr. Naval Acad., St. Petersburg, Russia, 1957-75, chief, 1975-89, prof., 1989—. Author: Fundamentals of the Theory of Calculation of the Reliability of Shipboard Electric Power Systems, 1967, Relaibility of Engineering Systems, Principles and Analysis, 1976; co-author: Logic-Probabilistic Methods of Research of Structure Difficult Systems Reliability, 1981, Reliability, Survivability and Safety of Shipboard Electric Power Systems, 1997, Reliability and Safety of Structurally-Complex Systems, 2000. Rear admiral Russian Navy, 1980-89. Mem. Nat. Acad. Scis. Russia, N.Y. Acad. Scis. Avocation: horticulture. Home: Nalichnaya Str 36-2-53, 199226 Saint Petersburg Russia Office: Naval Acad Viborgskaya, Naberegnaya 73/1, 197045 Saint Petersburg Russia

RYABININA, NATALIYA PAVLOVNA, university administrator, psychology educator; b. Tomsk, Tomskaya, Russia, Apr. 7, 1954; d. Pavel Aleksandrovich and Nadezda Petrovna (Mitrofanova) Z.; m. Vyacheslav Evgenyevich Ryabinin, Oct. 11, 1975; children: Maxim, Sergey. Master D in Edn., Pedagogical Inst., Chelyabinsk, Russia, 1976; PhD in Edn., State U., Chelyabinsk, Russia, 1984; docert in edn., State Com. on Edn., Moscow, 1990; DEdn, Russian Acad. of Edn., 1998. Tchr. High Sch., Chelyabinsk, 1976-79; asst. prof. State Pedagogical Inst., Chelyabinsk, 1979-89, docent, 1989-93; head scientific dept. Bimos, Chelyabinsk, 1993-95; head of chair pedagogics and psychology State Pedagogical U., Chelyabinsk, 1995—; scientific cons. State Pedagogical U., 1998—. Contbr. articles to profl. publs. Rsch. grant Min. on Econology, 1993-94. Mem. N.Y. Acad. Sci. Orthodox. Avocations: English literature. Home: Vorovsky str 79-87, 454048 Chelyabinsk Russia Office: State Pedagogical U, Lenin Av 69, 454080 Chelyabinsk Russia

RYABOV, VLADIMIR BORISOVICH, physicist, educator; b. Kharkov, Ukraine, Mar. 5, 1964; s. Boris Pavlovich and Svetlana Fyodorovna Ryabov; m. Irina Aleksandrovna Kolesnik, July 1, 1988; children: Maria, Daria. MS in Radio Physics, Kharkov State U., 1986, PhD in Physics and Math., 1991. Rsch. assoc. Inst. Radio Astronomy, Kharkov, 1991-95, doctoral fellow, 1995-98; Sci. and Tech. Agy. fellow Meterol. Rsch. Inst., Tsukuba, Japan, 1994-95; NATO fellow Paris-Meudon (France) Astrophys. Obs., 1996-97; Japan Soc. Promotion of Sci. fellow Kobe (Japan) U., 1998-2000; assoc. prof. Future U., Hakodate, Japan, 2000—. Contbr. articles to profl. jours. Grantee Soros Internat. Sci. Found., N.Y.C., 1994, rsch. grantee Internat. Assn. for the promotion of cooperation with scientists from the New Independent States of the former Soviet Union, Brussels, 1996; recipient Young Scientist award Union Radio Sci. Internat., 1989. Avocations: jazz music, skiing. Fax: 81-0138-346101. E-mail: riabov@fun.ac.jp. Home: Pioneer Mihara 305, 3-11-11 Hakodate Hokkaido, Japan Office: Future U Hakodate 116-2, Kameda Nakano-cho, 041-8655 Hakodate Hokkaido, Japan

RYAN, ALLYN CAUAGAS, writer, educator; b. Larena, The Philippines, June 2, 1938; came to U.S., 1957; d. Ignacio Fallorina Cauagas and Ignacia (Prudencia) Padayhag; m. James Edward Ryan, June 13, 1964; children: Monica Lynn Ryan-Border, Colleen Marie Ryan-Spence. BA in English, UCLA, 1959, MFA in Theater, 1964. Cert. tchr. lang. arts, lit., comm. arts, theater arts, basic edn., Calif. Adj. faculty Saddleback Coll., Mission Viejo, Calif., 1983-90, Orange Coast Coll., Costa Mesa, Calif., 1986-87, Chapman U., Orange, Calif., 1987-88, Rancho Santiago Coll., Santa Ana, Calif., 1986-98. Contbr. poetry, short stories to profl. jours. Mem. legis. adv. com. Rancho Santiago Coll., 1996-97, instructional calendar group mem., 1996-97. UCI Writing Project fellow, 1989. Mem. NEA, Calif. Tchrs. Assn., C.C.

Assn. (WHO award 1997), Continuing Edn. Faculty Assn. (Rancho Santiago Coll. chpt. pres. 1996-97, negotiations chmn. 1995-96), Romance Writers of Am. Avocations: oil painting, gourmet cooking. Home: 37261 Mojave Sage St Palm Desert CA 92211-1389

RYAN, ARTHUR FREDERICK, insurance company executive; b. Bklyn., Sept. 14, 1942; s. Arthur Vincent and Gertrude (Wingert) R.; m. Patricia Elizabeth Kelly; children: Arthur, Kelly Ann, Kevin, Kathleen. BA in Math., Providence Coll., 1963. Area mgr. Data Corp., Washington, 1965-72; project mgr. Chase Manhattan Corp. and Bank, N.Y.C., 1972-73, 2d v.p., 1973-74, v.p., 1974-75, ops. exec., 1978-82, exec. v.p., from 1982, vice-chmn., then pres., chief operating officer, 1990-94; chmn., CEO Prudential Ins. Co. Am., Newark, N.J., 1994—; mem. policy and planning com.; bd. dirs., chmn. audit com. Depository Trust Co.; past mem. exec. com., Cedel (European Depository); past chmn. steering com., program mgr. CHIPS Same Day Settlement, N.Y. Clearing House. Past bd. dirs. Urban Acad. N.Y.C. Lt. U.S. Army, 1963-65. Mem. Am. Bankers Assn. (vice chmn. ops. and automation div. and govt. rels. coun., past chmn. internat. ops. com.). Office: Prudential Ins Co Am Prudential Plaza 24th Fl 751 Broad St Newark NJ 07102-3714

RYAN, FRANCIS PATRICK, physician, writer; b. Limerick, Ireland, July 23, 1944; came to Eng., 1957; s. Francis and Mary Alice (Fitzpatrick) R.; m. Barbara Horrocks, Sept. 14, 1968; children: Catherine Jane, John Francis Malcolm. M.B., Ch.B. with honors, Sheffield U., 1970. Intern, then resident Sheffield (Eng.) Royal Infirmary, No. Gen. Hosp., 1970-75; cons. physician Bury Gen. Hosp., Lancashire, Eng., 1976, No. Gen. Hosp., 1977-94; cons., adviser Sheffield Dist. Health Authority, 1994—. Author: Sweet Summer, 1987, Tiger Tiger, 1988, The Eskimo Diet, 1990, Goodbye Baby Blue, 1990, Tuberculosis: The Greatest Story Never Told, 1992, The Forgotten Plague, 1993, The Walnut Diet, 1993, Virus X.1996, The Sundered World, 1999. Bd. dirs. Bolton Fine Arts, Lancashire, 1972-79. Fellow Royal Coll. Physicians, Royal Soc. Health; mem. Brit. Soc. Gastroenterology, Soc. Authors, M62 Club, Lansdowne Club. Avocation: patron of arts.

RYAN, FRANK SAVAGE, metallurgical engineer; b. Camp Hill, Pa., Feb. 4, 1970; s. Perry Robert and Marian Jane Ryan; m. Kim Kaso, May 25, 1997. BS in Metall. Engring., Columbia U., 1992. Assoc. engr. IBM, Yorktown Heights, N.Y., 1992-93; proces engr., lab. supr. Velie Circuits Colo., Broomfield, 1994-95; process engr. PNC Inc., Nutley, N.J , 1995-96; engring. supr. HADCO Corp., Oswego, N.Y., 1996—. Mem. N.Y. Acad. Scis. Republican. Achievements include patents in field. Avocations: youth instruction, sound recording, golf, automotive. E-mail: frryan@hadco.com. Home: 701 Front St Vestal NY 13850-1351 Office: HADCO Corp 1200 Taylor Rd Owego NY 13827-1298

RYAN, GEORGE WILLIAM, manufacturing executive; b. Sinking Springs, Ohio, Oct. 13, 1939; s. Winson Mark and Mary Edith (Smalley) R.; 1 child: Gina Kristin. Student, Wilmington Coll., 1962. Process engr. B.F. Goodrich Co., Marietta, Ohio, 1962-66; product dev. mgr. Chrysler Corp., Sandusky, Ohio, 1966-70; asst. tech. mgr. Inmont Corp., Toledo, Ohio, 1970-72; tech. mgr. Occidental Petroleum, Burlington, N.J., 1973; owner Ryan Devel. Corp., Peebles, 1973-88; prin. Straight Fork Valley Ranch, Ohio, 1986-; cons. Hooker Chem. Corp., Burlington, N.J., 1973. Bd. dirs., pres. Missionary Evang. Ch. of Christ; mem. Adams County Workforce Commn. Mem. Soc. Plastic Engrs., Peebles Ind. Inc. (sec., treas., bd. dirs., 1984-88)., Adams County Mfg. Assn. Republican.

RYAN, GERARD MICHAEL, psychologist; b. County Topperary, Ireland, Aug. 24, 1952; 010ds. Thomas Christopher and Catherine (Ryan) R.; m. Eibhlin Costigan, Jan. 7, 1977; children: Sean, Catherine, Thomas (dec.), Christina. BA, U. Coll. Dublin, 1973, MA, 1978. Psychologist St. James Hosp., Dublin, 1978-88; dir. Work Rsch. Ctr., 1988-92; assoc. prof. Copenhagen Bus. Sch., 1990-92; rsch. mgr. U. Coll. Dublin, 1994-96; scientific mgr. European Commn., 1986-98; dir. Quality Ireland, 1996—. Recipient Essay prize Coun. Europe, Ireland, 1970, Philos. prize U. Coll., Dublin, 1971; rsch. fellow U. Stockholm, 1980. Mem. APA, Brit. Psychol. Soc., N.Y. Acad. Scis. Roman Catholic. Avocations: films, literature, music, science, gardening. Home: 15 Convent Rd, Dublin Ireland Office: U Coll Dublin, Belfield, Dublin 4, Ireland

RYAN, JAMES FREDERICK, lawyer, educator; b. Boston, Mar. 11, 1928; s. James Denvir and Harriet Chenery (Bonney) R.; m. Dorothea Elizabeth Dydek, Sept. 1, 1958. AB, Harvard U., 1949, LLB, 1952. Bar: Mass. 1952, U.S. Dist. Ct. Mass. 1959, U.S. Ct. Mil. Appeals 1957, U.S. Ct. Appeals (1st cir.) 1979, Supreme Ct. Republic of Korea, 1956, U.S. Supreme Ct. 1957. Teaching fellow in law Harvard U. Law Sch., 1956-57; pvt. practice, Boston, 1958—; lectr. Suffolk Law Sch., 1958—; atty. Mass. Crime Commn., 1963-64; asst. corp. counsel City of Boston, 1968-73. Pres. alumni council Roxbury Latin Sch., 1976-78. Served with JAG Corps, USAF, 1953-56, lt. col. USAFR. Recipient Wellington prize for disting. service Roxbury Latin Sch., 1970. Mem. ABA, Mass. Bar Assn., Boston Bar Assn., Harvard Club. Author: Massachusetts Bar Examination—Questions, Answers, Comments, 1973; contbr. articles to legal jours.

RYAN, JAMES HERBERT, retired security and retail services company executive; b. Petersburg, Va., Feb. 1, 1931; s. Richard Hillsdon and Mary Orgain (Mann) R.; m. Patricia Louise Abbott, June 7, 1955; 1 child, Pamela Louise. BS, U.S. Mil. Acad., 1955; MA, U. Pa., 1962; MS, George Washington U., 1972; grad. Program for Mgmt. Devel., Harvard U., 1972; PhD, Walden U., 1984. Commd. 2d lt. U.S. Army, 1955, advanced through grades to lt. col., 1968, ret., 1972; gen. mgr. U.S. ops. Ryan Enterprises, Washington, 1970-73; pres. Ford Enterprises, Ltd., Mt. Rainier, Md., 1973-87, James H. Ryan Assocs., Inc., Petersburg, 1987-97; gen. mgr. U.S. ops. Ryan Enterprises, Washington, 1970-73; pres. Ford Enterprises, Ltd., Mt. Rainier, Md., 1973-87; pres. James H. Ryan Assocs., Inc., Petersburg, Va., 1987-97; advisor to Sec. of Army, 1975, chief of naval material, 1980-82. Mem. Pres.'s Pvt. Sector Survey on Cost Control (Grace Commn.), 1982; bd. govs. USO, 1977-86; pres. Hist. Petersburg Found., 1991-93; vestryman St. Paul's Episcopal Ch., 1994-96, 98—. Decorated Legion of Merit, Soldiers medal, Bronze Star, Air medal, Vietnamese Gallantry Cross. Mem. Am. Mgmt. Assn., Nat. Retail Fedn., Am. Soc. Indsl. Security, Internat. Assn. Profl. Security Cons. (pres. 1993-95), Ret. Officers Assn., West Point Soc. Ctrl. Va., Rotary Club of Petersburg (pres. 1993-94), Petersburg Area Art League (pres. 1997-2000, treas. 2000—). Episcopalian. Home: 1221 Woodland Rd Petersburg VA 23805-1911 Office: PO Box 2126 Petersburg VA 23804-1426

RYAN, JOHN JAMES, electronics executive, design engineer; b. Billinge, Eng., Apr. 5, 1955; s. Declan and Lois (Johnson) R.; m. Mina Sanamrad, May 29, 1979; children: Ali, Danny. BSEE, Imperial Coll., 1976. Memory evaluation engr. I.C.L., Manchester, 1978-82; test dept. mgr. Hybritech Ltd., Oldham, 1982-86, Hybrid Memory Products Ltd., Newcastle-upon-Tyne, 1986-92; sr. tech. advisor Syntaq Ltd., Newcastle-upon-Tyne, 1992-97; sr. applications engr. Mosaid Systems, Inc., Santa Clara, Calif., 1997—. Mem. IEE (assoc.). Achievements include design of memory device tester.

RYAN, JOHN PATRICK, consulting actuary, management consultant; b. Cheadle Hulme, Cheshire, England, Aug. 19, 1943; s. James Patrick and Marie Elsie (Gaines) R.; m. Verna Marguerite Mytton, Feb. 8, 1969; children: Nicholas John, Annabel Katherine, Alastair Edmund. MA, Queens Coll., Cambridge, Eng., 1965. Asst. actuary Guardian Royal Exchange, London, 1965-68; ptnr. James Capel & Co., London, 1968-76; v.p., prin. Tillinghast/Towers Perrin, London, 1976—. Chmn. Cambridge U. Conservative Assn., 1965; vice chmn. South Kensington YC's, London, 1967-68. Fellow Inst. Actuaries (coun. mem. 1987-91, 92-95, v.p. 1995—), Inst. Risk Mgmt.; assoc. mem. Soc. Investment Analysts, Casualty Actuarial Soc. Conservative Party. Office: Tillinghast/Towers Perrion Castlewood House, 77-91 New Oxford St, London WC1A1PX, England

RYAN, JOSEPH F., educator; b. N.Y.C., Jan. 27, 1949; s. Henry Martin and Anita (Vanderburg) R.; married; children: Robert M., Daniel J., Nora Jean. BA in Criminal Justice, John Jay Coll., MA in Criminal Justice, 1978; PhD in Sociology, Fordham U., 1984. Detective N.Y.C. Police Dept., 1968-91; assoc. prof. Pace U., N.Y.C., 1991—, chmn. dept. pub. adminstrn./criminal justice, 1995—; cons. Urban Inst., Washington, 1995—; peer rev. Nat. Inst. Justice, Washington, 1990—; lectr. Indian Health Svc., Albuquerque, 1991-96. Co-author 1 book; mem. editl. rev. bd. Am. Jour. Police, 1995—. Vis. fellow Nat. Inst. Justice, Washington, 1991-93. Mem. Am. Soc. Criminology. Avocations: reading, canoeing, hiking, biking, museums.

RYAN, KENNETH, research scientist; b. Bay Shore, N.Y., Jan. 20, 1960; s. Harry Joseph Ryan Jr. and Edith Muriel Kent. BS, SUNY, Stony Brook, 1982; PhD in Biol. Chemistry, Johns Hopkins U., 1992. Postdoctoral fellow, rsch. scientist U. Cambridge, Eng., 1993-96; rsch. assoc. U. Cambridge, 1996-99; jr. mem. Joseph Stores Jr. Rsch. Inst., U. Penn. Sch. Medicine, 2000—. Contbr. sci. rsch. articles to profl. jours. Grad. Sch. studentship NIH, 1985; Cancer Rsch. Campaign postdoctoral fellow, 1993. Mem. Am. Soc. for Biochemistry and Molecular Biology, Soc. for Devel. Biology, Fedn. of Am. Socs. for Exptl. Biology, N.Y. Acad. Scis. Roman Catholic. Fax: 215-590-5454. E-mail: ryank@chop.email.edu. Office: Children's Hosp of Phila/U Pa Sch Medicine, Abramson Rsch Bldg Ste 704, 34th St and Civic Ctr Blvd, Philadelphia CB2 1QR, England also: Children's Hosp of Phila/U Pa Sch Medicine Abramson Rsch Bldg Ste 704 34th St and Civic Ctr Blvd Philadelphia PA 19104

RYAN, LEO VINCENT, business educator; b. Waukon, Iowa, Apr. 6, 1927; s. John Joseph and Mary Irene (O'Brien) R. BS, Marquette U., 1949; MBA, DePaul U., 1954; PhD, St. Louis U., 1958; postgrad., Catholic U. Am., 1951-52, Bradley U., 1952-54, Northwestern U., 1950; LLD, Seton Hall U., 1988; DHL, Ill. Benedictine U., 1997. Joined Order Clerics of St. Viator, Roman Cath. Ch., 1950. Faculty Marquette U., Milw., 1957-65; dir. continuing edn. summer sessions, coord. evening divsns. Marquette U., 1959-65, prof. indsl. mgmt., 1964; prof., chmn. dept. mgmt. Loyola U., Chgo., 1965-66; adj. prof. mgmt. Loyola U., 1967-69; dep. dir. Peace Corps, Lagos, Nigeria, 1966-67; dir. Western Nigeria Peace Corps, Ibadan, 1967-68; asst. superior gen. and treas. gen. Clerics of St. Viator, Rome, 1968-69; dir. edn. Am. province Clerics of St. Viator, Arlington Heights, Ill., 1969-74; pres. St. Viator H.S., 1972-74; dean, prof. mgmt. U. Notre Dame Coll. Bus. Adminstrn., Ind., 1975-80; dean DePaul U. Coll. Commerce, 1980-88, prof. mgmt., 1980-99; Wicklander prof. profl. ethics DePaul U., 1993-94; prof. emeritus, 1999; dir. Peace Corps tng. programs Marquette U., 1962-65; adj. prof. human devel. St. Mary's Coll., Winona, Minn., 1972-74; mem. sch. bd. Archdiocese Chgo., 1972-75, vice-chmn., 1973-75, nat. edn. com. U.S. Cath. Conf., 1971-75, exec. com., 1973-75; nat. adv. bd. Benedictine Sisters of Nauvoo, 1973-83; nat. adv. coun. SBA, 1982-85, vice-chmn. minority bus., 1982-85, exec. com. Chgo. chpt., 1982-84; vis. prof. U. Ife, Ibadan, 1967-68,; chmn. trust audit com. First Bank-Milw., 1980-85, chmn. audit and examination com., 1985-90, adv. coun., 1991-93; bd. dirs. Vilter Mfg. Co., external dir. Vilter ESOP, Filbert Corp., Vilter Internat. (now Vilter Export Corp.), 1977-98, Henricksen & Co., Inc., 1978—; fin. commn. Clerics of St. Viator, 1978—, mem. provincial chpt., 1985-97, alt. mem., 1997—, devel. adv. bd. 1996—, new foundations com. 1996-98; Fulbright prof. Adam Mickiewicz U., Poland, 1993-99; vis. prof. Helsinki Sch. Econs., 1992—, Polish-Am. Ctr., U. Lodz, 1998, Poznan Acad. Econs., 1991, 99, 2000; cochair bus. and profl. com. Archdiocese of Chgo. Sesquetennial Com. Out Reach Divsn. Ctrl. Planning Group, 1993-94; vis. prof. Notre Dame, 2000, Helsinki Sch. Econs., 2000. Author: Human Action in Business, 1996, Etyka Biznesu, 1997, from Autarcy to Market: Polish Economics and Politics, 1945-1995, 1998, Students Focus on Business Ethics; mem. editl. bd. Internat. Jour. Value Based Mgmt., European Bus. Jour., Bus. Ethics Quar., Mid Atlantic Jour. of Bus. Mem. Pres.'s Com. on Employment Handicapped, 1959-65, Wis. Gov.'s Com. on Employment Handicapped, 1959-65, Wis. Gov.'s Com. on UN, 1961-64, Burnham Park Planning Commn., 1982-88; bd. dirs. Ctr. Pastoral Liturgy U. Notre Dame, 1976-79; trustee Lake Forest Grad. Sch. Mgmt., 1989-91, St. Mary of Woods Coll., 1978-81, Cath. Theol. Union, U. Chgo., 1992-95, Divine Word Coll., 1997—; regent Seton Hall U., 1981-87, mem. acad. affairs com., 1981-87, chmn., 1983-87; dir. Ctr. for Enterprise Devel., 1992-95; fellow St. Edmonds Coll. Cambridge U., 1992; mem. Cath. Commn. Intellectual and Cultural Affairs, 1992—, Cath. Campaign for Am., 1994-98; bd. dirs. Internat. Bus. Ethics Inst., Am. Grad. Sch. Internat. Mgmt., 1995-97, Assn. Profl. Ethics, 1995-96; mem. adv. com. Mgmt. Edn. in Poland, U. Md., College Park, 1995-2000. Recipient Freedom award Berlin Commn., 1961, chieftancy title Asoju Atoaja of Oshogbo Oba Adenle I, Yorubaland, Nigeria, 1967, B'nai B'rith Interfaith award, Milw., 1963, Disting. Alumnus award Marquette U., 1974, DePaul U., 1976, Tchr. of Yr. award Beta Alpha Psi, 1980, Centennial Alumni Achievement award Marquette U., 1981, Boland Meml. Disting. Alumni award, St. Louis, 1989, Disting. Alumni and Bicentennial awards Jesuit Bus. Schs., 1989, Pres.' award St. Viator H.S., 1992, Medal of Merit Adam Mickiewicz U., 1995, Excellence in Teaching award DePaul U., 1995, Via Sapentiae award, 1999, Adam Mickiewicz U., 1997, Ill. Ernst and Young Entrpreneur Supporter award, 1999, Vincentian Univs. Ethics Scholar award, 2000; Brother Leo V. Ryan award created in his honor Cath. Bus. Edn. Assn., 1962; Ryan Scholars in Mgmt. established in his honor DePaul U., 1989, Outstanding Svc. award, 1991-93, Commerce Alumni award of merit, 1997, Via Sapientiae award, 1999; DePaul Creativity Ctr. established in his honor, 1997; named hon. Life chmn. Nat. Adv. Com., Ryan Creativity Ctr., Creative Cutting Edge award, 1999; Ryan Scholarship established in his honor St. Viator High Sch., 1992, Lion award, 1997; named Man of Yr. Jr. C. of C., Milw., 1959, Marquette U. Bus. Adminstrn. Alumni Man of Yr., 1974, Tchr. of Yr. U. Notre Dame, 1980; Milw. Bd. Realtors traveling fellow, 1964, Nat. Assn. Purchasing Agts. faculty fellow, 1958, German Am. Acad. Exch. Coun. fellow, summer 1983, Presdl. fellow Am. Grad. Sch. Internat. Mgmt., 1989, vis. scholar, 1995, Malone fellow in Islamic studies, 1990, fellow Kosciuszko Found. Adam Mickiewicz U., 1990; scholar-in-residence Mgmt. Sch. Imperial Coll. Sci. and Tech. U. London, 1988; vis. scholar U. Calif., Berkeley, spring 1989; USIA Acad. Specialists grantee (3), Poland, 1991, 92, 93; fellow St. Edmund's Coll. Cambridge U., 1992; named vis. rsch. fellow Von Hugel Inst., 1992-93; scholar-in-residence Am. Grad. Sch. Internat. Mgmt., 1995; guest scholar Kellogg Inst. Internat. Studies U. Notre Dame, 1997. Mem. Cath. Bus. Edn. Assn. (nat. pres. 1960-62, nat. exec. bd. 1960-64), Assn. Sch. Bus. Ofcls. (nat. com. chmn. 1965-67), Am. Assembly Collegiate Schs. Bus. (com. internat. affairs 1977-84, chmn. 1981-84, bd. dirs. 1981-87, program chmn. 1979-80, exec. com., chmn. projects/svc. mgmt. com. 1984-86), Am. Fgn. Svc. Assn., Am. Assn. Profl. Ethics (bd. dirs. 1996-98), Allamakee County Hist. Soc. (charter life), Acad. Internat. Bus., Acad. Mgmt. (social issues div., chmn. membership com. 1990-91), Ancient Order of Hibernians, Nat. Returned Peace Corps Assn., Atomic Vets. Assn., August Derleth Soc., Chgo. Area Return Peace Corps Vols., Econ. Club Chgo., Chgo. Coun. Fgn. Rels., Coun. Fgn. Rels. (Chgo. com., diplomat cir. 1998), European Bus. Ethics Network (hon. 1998), Soc. Bus. Ethics (mem. exec. com. 1991—, pres. 1993-94, adv. bd. 1995-97), Assn. Social Econs. (life), Assn. Christian Economists, Dubuque County Hist. Soc., Iowa Hist. Soc., Iowa Postal History Soc., Fulbright Assn. (life), Internat. Assn. for Bus. and Soc. (founder), Internat. Soc. for Bus., Econs. and Ethics (charter), Internat. Trade and Fin. Assn. (founder, bd. dirs. 1989-92, 96-98, v.p. membership 1991-92, 96-97), Internat. Learned Soc. Praxiology, (hon. life, mem. internat. adv. bd. praxiology ann.), Polish Inst. Arts and Scis. in Am., DePaul Inst. Bus. and Profl. Ethics (founder 1984, adv. bd. 1984-94, Founders award 1999), Milw. Press Club (hon.), USS Mt. McKinley Reunion Assn. (hon. chaplain AGC-7 1989-96, Disting. Svc. award 1991, 96), Alpha Sigma Nu, Alpha Kappa Psi (bd. dirs. found. 1985-91, vice chmn. 1987-91, chmn. scholarship com. 1987-91, chmn. devel. com. 1987, mem. exec. com. 1990-91, Bronze Disting. Svc. award 1949, Silver Disting. Svc. award 1958), Beta Alpha Psi, Beta Gamma Sigma (co-chair 75th Anniversary com. Ill., faculty advisor DePaul chpt. 1986-92), Century Travel Club (Silver award), Delta Mu Delta, Pi Gamma Mu, Tau Kappa Epsilon.

RYAN, MATTHEW F., chemistry educator, consultant; b. Bklyn., Nov. 17, 1965; s. Mark Anthony and Dolores Mary Ryan; m. Deborah A. Ryan, Oct. 22, 1994; 1 child, Zachary Joseph. BS in Chemistry, SUNY, Oneonta, 1987; MS in Inorganic Chemistry, U. Fla., 1990, PhD in Inorganic Chemistry, 1993. Rsch. asst. U. Fla., Gainesville, 1987-93; rsch. fellow Tech. U. Berlin, Germany, 1993-94, York U., Toronto, Can., 1994-95; prof. Purdue U., Hammond, Ind., 1995—; presenter in field. Contbr. more than 20 articles to profl. jours. including Jour. Am. Chem. Soc., Bull. Japan Chem. Soc., Organometallics, among others. Grantee Purdue Rsch. Found., 1997, 2000, Purdue U., 2000. Mem. AAUP, Am. Chem. Soc. (inorganic divsn.), Am. Soc. Mass Spectroscopy, Internat. Union Pure and Applied Chemistry, Sigma Xi. Office: Purdue U 2200 169th St Hammond IN 46323-2094

RYAN, MICHAEL JOHN, finalcial analyst; b. Brisbane, Australia, Jan. 2, 1957; s. Noel and Pat R.; m. Heather; children: James, Andrew, Christopher. B, Queensland U., Brisbane, Australia, 1992; M, U. Queensland, Brisbane, Australia, 1996. Sr. tech. officer Telstra Corp., Brisbane, Australia, 1975-92, engr., 1992-96, sr. engr., 1996-2000, sr. fin. analyst, 1998-99. Dir. devel. Marist Coll, Australia, 1997-2000. Mem. IEEE, Inst. Engrs. Australia. Avocations: restoring valve radios, camping, fishing, coaching jr. sports. Office: Telstra Corp, 9/171 Roma St, Brisbane 4000, Australia

RYAN, PATRICK NELSON, lawyer; b. Indpls., Nov. 28, 1930; s. Thomas and Marie Linnie (Matthew) R.; m. Yvonne Winkler, Aug. 7, 1953; children: Geoffrey, Deborah Ryan Andrus, Valerie Ryan MacKay, Jill Anne Ryan, Matthew. BA, Butler U., 1953; JD, Ind. U., 1958. Bar: Ind. 1958, U.S. Dist. Ct. 1958, U.S. Supreme Ct. 1982. Practiced in Marion, Ind., 1958—; ptnr. Ryan, Welchons & Ryan, Marion; judge Ind. Trial Ct., Marion, 1968. Mem. sch. bd. Marion Pub. Schs., 1976-80. With U.S. Army, 1953-55. Mem. Am. Legion (dept. judge adv. 1994—), 40 and 8 (avocat 1971). Democrat. Baptist. Home: 2310 Lantern Ln Marion IN 46952-9249 Office: 112 S Boots St Marion IN 46952-3825

RYAN, PAUL RYDER, writer, journalist; b. Mineola, N.Y., Jan. 5, 1932; s. Paul Ryder Ryan and Lillian Roos; m. Ruthann Tobin, Nov. 8, 1958; children: Liane, Beth, Paul, Michael. Student, Mexico City Coll., 1955-58; BA, Harvard U., 1981. Editor Reuters, London, 1950-65, The N.Y. Times, N.Y.C. and Paris, 1965-68; asst. to new dir. RFE, Munich, 1968-69; editor The Drama Rev. NYU, 1970-75; editor Oceanus, Woods Hole (Mass.) Oceanographic Inst., 1975-92; dir. comm. Inst. for Sci. Info., Phila., 1990—; mem. adv. bd. Bangladesh Ctr. for Devel. Journalism and Comm., Dhaka, 1999-2000. Author: (non-fiction) China Daily, 1995, Bangladesh 2000, 2000, (novel) Khmer Rouge End Game, 1998. Sgt. USAF, 1950-54. Knight Internat. Press fellow, Bangladesh, 1999; Fulbright fellow, Japan, 1988-89, Indochina, 1995-96. Mem. VFW, Am. Legion. Democrat. Avocation: chess. Home: 11 Windsor Ave Cummington MA 01026-9301

RYAN, RANDEL EDWARD, JR., airline pilot; b. N.Y.C., Jan. 11, 1940; s. Randel Edward and Ann Augusta (Horwath) R.; m. Pamela Michael Wiley, May 12, 1962; children: Katherine, Gregory. BS in Sci., Trinity Coll., 1961. Quality control supr. Ideal Toy Corp., Jamaica, N.Y., 1961-62; airline pilot United Airlines, San Francisco, 1967-00. Pres. Highlands Cmty. Assn., San Mateo, Calif., 1975; chmn. Com. to Re-elect County Supr., San Mateo, 1976; mediator San Mateo County, 1986-95, mediator Pima Count, Ariz., 2000—; arbitrator Better Bus. Bur., 1988-95; rep. Highlands Cmty. Assn., San Mateo, 1970-86; coach Little League and Babe Ruth Baseball, San Mateo, 1979-83. Served to capt. USAF, 1962-68. Recipient Vandor award San Mateo PTA, 1976, awards of merit United Airlines, San Francisco, 1975, 79. Mem. Air Line Pilots Assn. (chmn. speakers panel 1983-86, cmty. rels. com. 1983-86, bd. dirs. 1986-89, 91-93, chmn. com. 34 1991-93, vice-chmn. 1986-89, founding editor newspaper The Bayliner 1984-86, mem. contract study com. 1984-86, vice-chmn. MEC grievance com. 1989-91, chmn. MEC grievance com. 1993-95, mem. nat. hearing bd. 1994—), Tucson Country Club. Democrat. Home: 2850 E Calle Sin Pecado Tucson AZ 85718-1282

RYAN, RICHARD, diplomat. Irish rep. to UN N.Y.C., 1998—. Office: Permanent Mission Ireland to UN One Dag Hammarskjold Plz 885 Second Ave 19th Fl New York NY 10017-2201*

RYAN, ROBERT J. A., investment banker; b. Sunderland, Eng., June 17, 1968; s. Richard John and Barbara Caroline (Roach) R.; m. Renata Susnjara, Oct. 26, 1996; 1 child, James Anthony. LLB with honors, U. Leicester, Eng., 1989. Trainee solicitor Allen & Overy, London, 1990-92; solicitor Allen & Overy, Tokyo, 1992-93, London, 1993-94, Tokyo, 1994-98; exec. dir., adv. fin. products CIBC Wood Gundy Securities (Japan) Ltd., 1998-99; exec. dir. asset securitisation Can. Imperial Bank of Commerce, Tokyo Br., 1999—; participant European Union's 14th Exec. Tng. Program, Japan, 1994-95; secondee capital markets dept. IBJ Securities Co. Ltd., Tokyo, 1995, projects group Nittetsu Shoji co. Ltd., Tokyo, 1995. Mem. British C. of C. in Japan, The Law Soc., Exec. Tng. Program Assn. Avocations: travel, scuba diving, music. Office: Can Imperial Bank Commerce, 2-3 Uchisaiwai-cho 2-chome, Chiyoda-ku Tokyo 100-0011, Japan

RYAN, ROY F., lawyer; b. New London, Conn., Nov. 22, 1946; arrived in Switzerland, 1987.; s. Roy and Mary Josephine (Folz) R.; m. Roseleen Patricia Desfosse, Aug. 17, 1968; children: Jessica, Katharine, Elizabeth, David. BA, Yale U., 1968; JD, U. Va. Law Sch., 1974. Assoc. Jones, Day, Reavis & Pogue, Cleveland, 1974-79, 83-86; pres. Ryan Contracting Co., Bethesda, Md., 1979-83; ptnr. Jones, Day, Reavis & Pogue, Geneva, Switzerland, 1987—. Dir. Cleveland Cmty. Food Bank, 1984-86; pres. Am. Internat. Club, 1997-98, exec. com., 1994—. Lt.j.g. U.S. Navy, 1968-71. Recipient Order of Coif U. Va. Law Sch., 1974, Michie award, U. Va. Law Sch., 1972. Mem. Internat. Fiscal Assn. Office: Jones Day Reavis & Pogue, 20 rue de Candolle, 1205 Geneva Switerland

RYAN, SUSAN SCHAFFER, electronic products developer; b. New Haven, Apr. 20, 1950; d. Eugene and Gloria Louise (Wilinski) Schaffer; m. Francis Aloysius Ryan, Sept. 13, 1981; 1 child, Mae Diana. BA, MA, U. Chgo., 1974; MBA, Northwestern U., 1981. Rsch. scientist Inst. for Juvenile Rsch., Chgo., 1974-78; with internat. mktg. dept. 1st Chgo., 1978-86; cons., bus. writer Internat. Wordsmiths, Vancouver, B.C., Can., 1986-90; corp. product mgr. Bay Bank Sys., Inc., Waltham, Mass., 1991-93; internat. product mgr. Bay Bank N.A., Boston, 1993-96; dir. global trade Baule Boston, N.A., 1996—. Mem. Shambhala Lodge (chmn. design com. 1996-98). Avocations: meditation instructor, home design, skiing, tennis. E-mail: ssryan@bbb.com. Home: 38 Maplewood Ave Newton MA 02459-2526 Office: Baybank Boston MA Mail Stop B0 A0 175 Federal St Fl 10 Boston MA 02110-2210

RYAN, TERENCE JOHN, dermatologist, educator; b. Hove, Sussex, Eng., July 24, 1932; s. Gerald John and Kathleen May (Knight) R.; m. Anne Trudie Merry; children: Josephine, James. MB BCh, Oxford (Eng.) U., 1957, MA, 1957, DM, 1977. House physician Sir George Pickering Gen. Medicine, Oxford, 1957-58; house surgeon Ear, Nose and Throat Surgery, Oxford, 1958-59; registrar in geriatrics Stoke Mandeville, Oxford, 1960-61, registrar in dermatology, 1962-65, sr. registrar, 1965-67; lectr., sr. lectr. Inst. Dermatology, London, 1968-71; physician Royal Postgrad. Med. Sch., London, 1968-71; chmn. faculty of medicine Oxford U., 1977-82, vice warden Green Coll.; cons. dermatologist Churchill Hosp., oxford, 1971—; clin. prof. dermatology, oxford U., 1992—. Contbr. more than 400 articles to profl. jours. Trustee Arts Dyslexia Trust, Fuel Initiative Resources, Strategies and Tech., Brit. Skin Found.; bd. dirs. Oxford Internat. Biomed. Ctr. Recipient Knight of the Order of St. John, Nishimaru award Japanese Microcirculation Soc., 1991. Fellow Royal Coll. Physicians, World Conf. Microcirculation (pres. 1984), European Tissue Repair Soc. (pres. 1993, gold medal 1995), Brit. Assn. Dermatology (pres.); mem. Internat. Com. Dermatology, Internat. Soc. Dermatology (pres. 1994-99), Internat. Found. Dermatology (sec.-treas. 1987-96, chmn. 1999—). Avocations: piano, watercolors. Home: Abberbury Ave, Iffley Oxford OX4 4EU, England Office: Churchill Hosp, Dept Dermatology, Churchill Hosp Headington, Oxford OX3 7LJ, England

RYBAKOV, KIRILL IGOREVICH, physicist, educator; b. Nizhny Novgorod, Russia, Apr. 30, 1967; s. Igor Nikolaevich and Natalia Ivanovna (Sokolova) R.; m. Tatiana Vadimovna Panova, Sept. 14, 1996. MS, Nizhny Novgorod State U., 1992; PhD, Russian Acad. Scis., Nizhny Novgorod, 1998. Rsch. asst. Inst. Applied Physics, Russian Acad. Scis., Nizhny Novgorod, 1989-92, rsch. trainee, 1992-93; asst. prof. Nizhny Novgorod State U., 1992-95, 96—; rsch. scientist Inst. Applied Physics, Russian Acad. Scis., Nizhny Novgorod, 1993-2000, sr. rsch. scientist, 2000—; vis. rsch. scientist U. Md., College Park, 1995-96. Contbr. articles to profl. jours. Soros grantee Open Soc. Inst., 1995, 97, 98. Avocation: amateur radio. Fax: 7-831-236-2061. E-mail: rybakov@appl.sci-nnov.ru. Office: Inst Applied Physics, 46 Ulyanov St, Nizhny Novgorod 603600, Russia

RYBALTOWSKI, ADAM, physicist, engineer; b. Bialystok, Poland, Dec. 24, 1966; s. Stanislaw and Kunegunda (Leszczynska) R. Student, Warsaw (Poland) Sch. Medicine, 1985-87; MS in Physics, U. Warsaw, 1992; postgrad., Northwestern U., 19955. Rsch. asst. Polish Acad. Scis., Warsaw, 1993, Northwestern U., Evanston, Ill., 19955; physicist Inst. Electron Tech.,

Warsaw, 1994—. Co-contbr. articles to profl. jours. Fellow Internat. Sch. Physics/Italian Phys. Soc., 1992, fellow advanced study inst. conf. on solid state lasers fellow NATO, 1992, Walter P. Murphy fellow Northwestern U., 1998-99; Travel grantee George Soros's Batory Found., Warsaw, 1995. Mem. IEEE, APS, Optical Soc. Am. Avocations: philosophy of science, music, playing piano and electric guitar, hi-fi technique, telecommunications. Home: Sienkiewicza 29 m 14, 08-110 Siedlce Poland Office: Northwestern U Dept Elec Engring Evanston IL 60208-0001

RYBICKI, KONRAD JULIAN, economist; b. Łódź, Poland, Nov. 20, 1958; s. Jerzy and Danuta (Wesolowska) R.; m. Miroslawa Sobczyk, Jan. 26, 1980; 1 child, Patryk. Student, Sch. of Chemistry; MA in Econ.-Sociol., U. Łódź. Lab didactic U. Tech., Łódź, 1980-82; sales mgr. Uniontex S.A., Łódź, 1982-89; pres. Textus Ltd., Łódź, 1990—. Author: History of Inowlodz, 1994, History of Spala, 1996, Spalski Reservation Scenery Park History of Spala and Inowlodz, 1998. Mem. Friends Soc. of Magazyn Literacki. Roman Catholic. Avocations: history, tourism, Demography. Home: Zagloby 23 M 26, 92-432 Łódź Poland

RYBKIN, VLADIMIR SEMENOVICH, research scientist; b. Kagalnitskaya, Rostov, Russia, Apr. 25, 1940; s. Semen Fedorovich and Maria Ivanovna (Panina) R.; m. Rimma Alexandrovna Glaiser, Aug. 8, 1964; children: Abrosimova, Elena, Vladimirovna. Diploma, U. Astrakhan, 1971; Doctorate, U. Saratov, 1993. Doctor Gadrud Antiplague Dept., Gadrud, 1963-64, Chernozemel Antiplague Dept., Chernozemelskiy, 1964-66; jr. rsch. asst. Rsch. Inst. on Lepra, Astrakhan, 1967-73; sr. rsch. asst. Rsch. Inst. on Lepra, Volgograd, 1974-88, head of lab, vice-dir., 1988—. Co-author: Immunoenzyme Assay in Microbiology, 1990. Mem. Russian Ecol. Acad., N.Y. Acad. of Sci., Doctor's Club. Avocation: hunting. Home: Tankistov St 8-47, 400094 Volgograd Russia Office: Antiplague Rsch Inst, Golubinskaya St 7, 400131 Volgograd Russia

RYBNÍČEK, KAMIL, botanist; b. Jihlava, Czech Republic, July 5, 1933; s. Arnošt and Karla (Hruba') R.; m. Eliška Coufalova', Apr. 29, 1957; children: Ondrej, Jan. RNDr, Masaryk U., Brno, Czech Republic, 1956; PhD, Inst. Botany Acad. Sci., Praha, Czech Republic, 1964. Rsch. asst. Geobotanical Labor, Acad. Sci., Praha-Brno, 1956-64; rschr. Inst. Botany, Acad. Sci., Pruhonice-Brno, 1964-69, sr. rschr., 1969—; asst. prof., chair botany Masaryk U., 1992—; head palaeoecol. dept. Inst. Botany, Acad. Sci., 1992-98; cons. Agy. for Nature Conservancy and Landscape Protection of Czech Republic, 1985—. Author: Die Vegetation der Moore im Südlichen Teil der Bömisch-Mährischen Höhe, 1974; co-author: Übersicht der Pflanzergesellschaften der Moore der Tschechoslowakei, 1984, (book and map) Map of Potential Natural Vegetation of the Czech Republic, 1998 (Czech Found. of Sci. Lit. award 1999); contbr. articles to profl. jours. Mem. Czech Bot. Soc., Internat. Mire Conservation Group, Czech Ramsar Com., Societas Fauna Flora Fennica (hon.). Avocations: archeology, history, nature conservancy.

RYBNIKAR, ALOIS, microbiologist, researcher; b. Rasovice, Vyskov, Czech Republic, Jan. 1, 1948; s. Alois and Anna (Knapilova) R.; m. Anna Havrankova, Sept. 8, 1973; children: Lenka, Martin. Biol. Specialist, Sci. Faculty, Brno, Czech Republic, 1971; Dr. Natural Scis., Jan Evangelista Purkyne U., Brno, 1973. Chief microbiol. lab. Bioveta, Ivanovice na Hane, Czech Republic, 1973-95, chief mycol. ctr., 1995—. Contbr. articles to profl. jours.; patentee in field. Lance-cpl. Czech Republic Army, 1971-72. Roman Catholic. Avocations: sports, nature, travel. Home: Beloruska 10, 625 00 Brno Czech Republic Office: Bioveta Ltd, Komenskeho 212, 683 23 Ivanovice na Hane Vyskov, Czech Republic

RYBOVÁ, RENATA, retired biochemist, researcher; b. Prague, Czechoslovakia, Dec. 23, 1931; d. Rudolf and Anna (Bezděková) Velden; m. Olen Ryba, Nov. 8, 1955; children: Miriam, David. MS, Charles U., Prague, 1956; PhD, Acad. Scis., Prague, 1960, DSc, 1990. Sci. asst. Acad. Sci. Inst. Microbiology, Prague, 1956-61, sci. worker, 1961-80, leading sci. worker, 1980-96; ret., 1996; supr. post-grad. students Acad. Sci. Inst. Microbiology, 1980-93. Author: (with K. Janáček) Transport Processes in Plants, 1987; contbr. articles to profl. jours. Avocations: linguistics, tourism, skiing.

RYCHETSKY, STEVE, civil and environmental engineer, consultant; b. Phoenix, Oct. 9, 1951; s. Edward and Maria (Zabroni) R.; m. Dawna Marie Strunk, June 10, 1972 (div. Oct. 1985); children: Brian, Melissa; m. Michaele Ann Turner, Dec. 28, 1986; children: Mike, Kristi, Jaye, Karly. AA in Engring., Oreg. Inst. Tech., 1972, BTech, 1976. Registered profl. civil engr., Oreg., Calif. Mgr. sales engring. Varcopruden, Turlock, Calif., 1976-79, AMCA Internat., Winston-Salem, N.C., 1979-82; civil engr. USDA Natural Resources Conservation Svc., Klamath Falls, Oreg., 1983-85; tech. advisor USDA Soil Conservation Service, Klamath Falls, Oreg., 1983-88; civil engr., tech. advisor USDA Natural Resources Conservation Svc., Redmond, Oreg., 1985—; private cons. engr. Redmond, Oreg., 1985—; pres. Civil-Engineers.com, 1997—. Active vol. cons. svcs. for environ. handicapped and children projects; bd. dirs. Tillamook Anglers, Inc., 1990-94. Democrat. Roman Catholic. Avocation: outdoor activities. E-mail: rta@civil-engineers.com. Office: Rychetsky Turner & Assocs Inc PO Box 1457 Redmond OR 97756-0402

RYCHKOV, ALEXANDER DMITRIEVICH, researcher and lecturer; b. Ulan-Ude, USSR, Oct. 19, 1942; s. Dmitri Vladimirovich and Alexandra Petrovna (Shakutina) R.; m. Elsa Sinaevna Lisovic, Mar. 21, 1968 (div. June 1977); 1 child, Olga; m. Ljudmila Ivanovna Dubrovina, May 26, 1978; children: Natalja. Grad., Tomsk State U., 1963, CandSci, 1971; DSc, Inst. of Thermophysics, Novosibirsk, 1986. Sr. rschr. Inst. Applied Math. and Mechanics, Tomsk, 1968-75, head of lab., 1975-78; prin. rschr. Inst. Theoretical and Applied Mechanics, Novosibirsk, 1978-86, head of lab., 1986-92; prof. math. State Tech. U., Novosibirsk, 1990-93; prin. rschr. Inst. Computational Techs., Novosibirsk, 1993-2000, chief rschr., 2000—; mem. sci. couns. for awarding DSc degree Inst. Thermophysics, Novosibirsk, 1989, Inst. Theoretical and Applied Mechs., 1993, State Tech. U., Novosibirsk, 1988. Author: Mathematical Modelling of Gasdynamical Processes in Channels and Nozzles, 1988, Modelling of Jet Flows in Steel-making Converters, 2000; mem. editl. bd. Jour. Thermosphysics and Aeromechanics. Recipient USSR State prize, 1985; State Sci. grantee, 1994. Avocations: reading, exercise, photography. Home: Tereshkova 10 app 12, Novosibirsk Russia 630090 Office: Inst Computational Techs, Lavrentjeva av 6, Novosibirsk Russia 630090

RYCHLAK, RONALD JOSEPH, law educator; b. Columbus, Ohio, Sept. 23, 1957; s. Joseph Frank and Lenora Pearl (Smith) R.; m. Claire Lindsey Rychlak, Oct. 26, 1985; children: Joseph Antone, Lindsey Frances, Susanna Mae, Mary Helen, Sarah Lenore. BA, Wabash Coll., 1980; JD, Vanderbilt U., 1983. Bar: Ill. 1983, U.S. Dist. Ct. (no. dist.) Ill., U.S. Ct. Appeals (5th, 6th and 7th cirs.), U.S. Supreme Ct. Law clk. to presiding judge U.S. Cir. Ct. (6th cir.), Memphis, 1983-84; assoc. Jenner & Block, Chgo., 1984-87; asst. prof. law U. Miss., Oxford, 1987-90, assoc. prof. law, 1990-95, prof., 1995—, assoc. dean for acad. affairs, 1998—; bd. dirs. Judicare of Miss., Columbus, 1989-95. Author: Real and Demonstrative Evidence: Applications and Theory, 1995, Hitler, the War, and the Pope, 2000, softcover edit., 2000; contbr. articles to profl. jours. Lilly scholar Wabash Coll., 1976-80, Andrew Ewing Scholar Vanderbilt U., 1982-83, Glen Peters fellow Peters Found., 1981, Salvatori fellow Heritage Found., 1995. Mem. Am. Assn. Law Schs. (exec. com. sect. law and sports 1988-89, 1994-95), Am. Inns. of Ct. (exec. dir. Inn III), Internat. Brotherhood Magicians, Nat. Assn. of Scholars, Federalist Soc. (state bd. advisors), Intercollegiate Scholastics Inst., Order of Coif. Roman Catholic. Avocations: jogging, softball, magic. Home: 506 College Hill Rd Oxford MS 38655-2026 Office: U Miss Law Ctr University MS 38677

RYCHLÍK, IVAN, nephrologist; b. Prague, Czech Republic, Dec. 27, 1962; s. Zdeněk and Eva R.; m. Markéta Kasalová; children: Katerina, Jan. MD, Charles U. Sch. Medicine, Prague, 1987, internal med. 1, 1990, internal med. 2, 1994, clin. nephrologist, 1996. House officer Charles U. 1st Dept. Med., Prague, 1987-90, registrar, 1990-96, clin. nephrology, 1996-99, head nephrologist, 1999—. Co-author: Vasculitides in Clin. Practice, 1994 (Book of the Yr. award), Clin. Nephrology in Czech, 1995, Nephrophathy in Type 2 Diabetes, 1999; contbr. numerous articles to profl. jours. Recipient grants in field. Fellow Internat. Soc. Nephrology; mem. Internat. Soc. Nephrology, European Renal Assn./European Dialysis and Transplant Assn., Czech Soc. Nephrology, European Vasculitis Study Group, Am. Soc. Nephrology (corr. mem.). Achievements include introduction of transjugular renal biopsy in Czechia, founding of Czech registry of renal biopsies, epidemiology of glomerulonephritis. Office: 1st Dept Med Charles U, Srobarova 50, 10034 Prague 10, Czech Republic

RYCHLÍK, JAN, historian, researcher, educator; b. Prague, Czech Republic, Nov. 26, 1954; s. Jan and Olga (Šimunek) R.; m. Magdaléna Kučerová, Mar. 4, 1978; 1 child, Terézia. BA, Charles U., Prague, 1979, MA, 1980; PhD, Kliment Ochridski U., Sofia, Bulgaria, 1985. Rschr. Mus. Agr., Prague, 1985-91, T.G. Masaryk Inst., Prague, 1991—; lectr. Charles U., Prague, 1992-98; asst. prof. Charles U., 1998—. Author: Ethnos and Folklore, 1997, Czechs and Slovaks in the 20th Century, 1997, 2d vol., 1998, History of Bulgaria, 2000; editor: The New Role of the State in the Development on Agriculture, 1995, R.W. Seton-Watson and His Relations with Czechs and Slovaks, 1906-1951, 1995, 2d vol., 1996. Avocation: skiing. Home: Dobrovskeho 40, 170 00 Prague Czech Republic Office: TG Masaryk Inst, NA Florenci 3, 110 00 Prague Czech Republic

RYCHLÍKOVÁ, MAGDALÉNA, research scientist; b. Skalica, Czechoslovakia, May 25, 1955; d. Karol and Ružena (Sasinkova) Kučera; m. Jan Rychlik, Mar. 4, 1978; 1 child, Terézia. BA, Comenius U., Bratislava, Slovakia, 1978, MA, 1980. Rschr. Za Mus., Skalica, 1978-85; rschr. Nat. Mus., Prague, Czech Republic, 1985-90, dir. Lobkovicky Palac, 1990—. Author: Folk Costumes of the Senica District. Fellow Ethnographical Soc., mem. Slovak Ethnographical Soc. Roman Catholic. Home: Dobrovského 40, 17000 Prague Czech Republic Office: Hist Exhbn Nat Mus, Lobkovicky Palac Jirska 3, 119 00 Prague-Castle Czech republic

RYCROFT, MICHAEL, physicist; b. Rickmansworth, England, July 15, 1938; s. John Lambert and Molly Elizabeth (Riglen) R.; m. Mary Cheeseright, Aug. 12, 1967; children: Matthew, David, Daniel. BS, Imperial Coll., 1960; PhD, Cambridge U., 1964. Lectr. Southamptom U., United Kingdom, 1966-79; head atmospheric scis. divsn. Brit. Antarctic Survey, Cambridge, United Kingdom, 1979-90; prof. aerospace Cranfield U., United Kingdom, 1990-94; head sch. scis. and applications Internat. Space U., Illkirch, France, 1995-99; owner CAESAR Consultancy. Editor-in-chief: Jour. Atmospheric and Terrestrial Physics, 1989-99; editor: Cambridge Ency. Space. Mem. Internat. Acad. Astronautics, Inst. Math. and its Applications (sec. 1992-95). Home: 35 Millington Rd, Cambridge CB3 9HW, England Office: Internat Space U, Blvd Gonthier d'Andernach, 67400 Illkirch France

RYDAHL, ALLAN KIM, engineering executive; b. Glostrup, Denmark, Dec. 17, 1969; s. Kim Thorkild and Elisabeth Therese Lindekron (Nielsen) R. MS, Tech. U. Denmark, Lyngby, 1994. Cert. engr. Project mgr. Calsep, Lyngby, Denmark, 1994-99; pres. Calsep, Inc., Houston, 1999—. Contbr. papers in field. Mem. Soc. Petroleum Engrs. Fax: 281 749 0847. E-mail: akr@calsep.com. Office: 11490 Westheimer Rd Ste 610 Houston TX 77077-6800

RYDBERG, ANDERS BO LARS, educator; b. Lund, Sweden, June 27, 1952; s. Bo Axel Robert and Birgit Elin Ingegard (Luumggren) R.; m. Elisabet Birgitta Pettersson; children: Natalie, Isabel. MSEE, Lund U., Sweden, 1976; PhD in Elec. Engring., Chalmers U., Goteborg, Sweden, 1988. Rsch. engr. Nat. Def. Rsch. Inst., Stockholm, 1977-78; divsn. engr. Swedish Railroads, Stockholm, 1978-79; devel. engr. Ellemtel Devel. Co., Alvsjo, Sweden, 1979-80; rsch. engr. Onsala Space Obs., Sweden, 1981-83; rsch. asst. Chalmers U. Tech., Goteborg, Sweden, 1988-90; rsch. engr. Farran Tech., Cork, Ireland, 1990-91; assoc. prof. U. Uppsala, Sweden, 1992—; prof. Uppsala U. and U. Gävle, 2000—; cons. in field. Contbr. articles to profl. jours.; patentee in field. Mem. IEEE. Avocations: amateur radio, amateur astronomy. Home: Sysslomansgatan 41C, SE-75227 Uppsala Sweden Office: Uppsala U Dept Mat Sci, Box 534, SE-75121 Uppsala Sweden

RYDBERG, INGVAR ARVID, translator, critic; b. Helsingborg, Sweden, June 14, 1940; s. Arvid and Selma (Niklasson) R. M of Polit. Sci., U. Lund, Sweden, 1966, MA, 1972, D (hon.), 1995. Author: De arabiska revolutionerna, 1975; translator (Ibn Khaldun) al-Muqaddima, 1989, Palestinsk poesi, 1972, (Fernand Braudel) Medelhavet och medelhavsvärlden på Filip II:s tid, 1997. Recipient Translator award Einar Hansen Fund, 1992. Mem. Swedish Writers Union. Home: Wrangelsgatan 18, 25439 Helsingborg Sweden

RYDBERG, SVEN, psychologist, consultant; b. Stockholm, Mar. 25, 1933; s. Nils Rydberg and Margit Lindgren; m. Mariann Fall, 1959 (div.); children: Nils G.M., Diana M.; m. Eva Fåhraeus, 1994. PhD, U. Stockholm, 1964. Cert. psychologist. Rsch. asst. Tchrs. Coll., Stockholm, 1957-59; lectr. in edn. U. Stockholm, 1960-70; docent in edn. Stockholm U. and Abo Akademi Turku, Finland, 1969—; docent in psychology U. Turku (Finland), 1969—; acting prof. edn. Abo Akademi, Turku, 1969-70; lectr. in psychology U. Stockholm, 1970—; vis. researcher inst. human learning U. Calif., Berkeley, 1973-74; acting prof. psychology Abo Akademi, Turku, 1977; chair Inst. Applied Social Scis., Stockholm, 1978—; vis. assoc. prof. psychology UCLA, 1964-66; dir. Inst. Applied Social Scis., Stockholm, 1966-77; test contstrn., cons. pers., selection, various industry, govt. and comml. orgns., Europe, 1966—. Author: Bias in Prediction, 1963; editor Nordisk Psykologi (Scandinavian), Sweden, 1961-63. Fulbright scholar, 1964. Mem. AAAS, Swedish Psychol Assn., Swedish Union Univ. Profs., Sallskapet, Soc. Club Stockholm. E-mail: sven.rydberg@cerdevo.se. Home: Hult, S-64294 Flen Sweden

RYDE, SIMON JOHN SCRIVENER, medical physicist; b. Kersey, Suffolk, Eng., Apr. 18, 1959; s. Paul Scrivener and Nora Olive (Stiff) R.; m. Stella Lee Corfield, Aug. 3, 1985; children: Eloise Clara, Holly Roberta, Dexter Edward Scrivener. BSc, Loughborough (Eng.) U., 1981; MSc, U. Surrey, Guildford, Eng., 1982; PhD, U. Wales, Swansea, 1988. Chartered physicist; state registered clin. scientist. Rschr. U. Wales, 1982-87; med. physicist Singleton Hosp., Swansea, 1987—, head radiotherapy, 1994—; mem. organizing com. Internat. Body Composition Symposia, 1988—; hon. rsch. fellow U. Wales, 1989—. Contbr. sci. articles to profl. jours. Fellow Inst. Physics and Engring. in Medicine (chmn. radiotherapy group 1996-97, sci. com. sec. 1998—, Founders prize 1994, Wis. Travel prize 1992), Inst. Physics. Avocations: music, family activities. Office: Singleton Hosp, Med Physics & Clin Engring, Swansea SA2 8QA, Wales

RYDE, ULF SIGURD BROR, theoretical chemist; b. Lund, Sweden, Dec. 9, 1963; s. Gosta Pettersson and Gunnel Ryde; m. Anna-Carin Gustafsson, Sept. 12, 1992; children: Martin, Frej, Embla, Tor. MSc, Lund U., 1986, PhD, 1991. Asst. prof. Lund U., 1992-2000, assoc. prof., 2000—. Avocations: botany, music. Office: Lund U Dept Theoretical Chm, PO Box 124, 221 00 Lund Sweden

RYDÉN, BENGT GUNNAR, stock exchange executive; b. Stockholm, Oct. 30, 1936; s. Gunnar H Rydén and Ragnhild L Soederbaum; m. Monica I.H. Tillberg, May 18, 1960. MBA, Stockholm Sch. Econs., 1960, PhD, 1972. Dep. chief economist Fedn. Swedish Industries, Stockholm, 1965-66; editor-in chief Swedish "Veckans Affärer", Stockholm, 1971-73; chief exec. Ctr. Bus. and Policy Studies, Stockholm, 1974-84; chief exec. Stockholm Stock Exch., 1985-98, exec. chmn., 1998-99; vice chmn. The Swedish Acctg. Stds. Coun., 1989—; chmn. Internat. Fedn. Stock Exchs., 1995-97, Mus. Nat. Antiquities, Sweden, 1998—, Hallvarsson & Halvarsson AB, Sweden, 1999—, Seventh Swedish Nat. Pension fund, 1999—; bd. dirs. OM Gruppen AB, Sweden, Capital Market Group, Sweden, Om Stockholm Exch., OM Fixed Income Exch., OM London Exch. Rsch. fellow Indsl. Inst. Econ. and Social Rsch., 1966-70. Fellow Royal Swedish Acad. Engring. Scis. Office: Gruppen AB, PO Box 10578, Stockholm Sweden

RYDÉN, LENNART VILHELM, retired Byzantine studies researcher; b. Sundsvall, Sweden, July 18, 1931; s. Jonas Vilhelm and Judith Maria (Persson) R.; m. Kerstin Elisabet Näslund, Aug. 11, 1956. BA, Uppsala (Sweden) U., 1955, MA, 1956, licentiate of philosophy, 1960, PhD, 1963. Assoc. prof. Ancient Greek Uppsala U., 1963-72; rschr., Byzantine studies Swedish Coun. Rsch. Humanities and Social Scis., Uppsala, 1972-80, prof. Byzantine studies, 1980-94; prof. Byzantine studies Uppsala U., 1994-96; ret., 1996; vis. fellow Dumbarton Oaks, Washington, 1972-73, 87, vis. scholar, 1998; chmn. Swedish Nat. Com. Byzantine Studies, 1983-91. Author: The Life of Symeon the Holy Fool by Leontios of Neapolis, 1963, Observations on the Life of Symeon the Holy Fool by Leontios of Neapolis, 1970, The Life of St. Andrew the Fool, I-II, 1995; editor: Aspects of Late Antiquity and Early Byzantium, 1993. Mem. Royal Soc. Humanities at Uppsala (treas. 1992—), Bollandists Soc. Brussels, Dumbarton Oaks Alumni Assn. (fgn. v.p. 1987-89). Home: Gropgränd 2A, S-75310 Uppsala Sweden

RYDER, EDWARD FRANCIS, secondary education educator; b. Lynn, Mass., Mar. 25, 1931; s. Edward W. and Theresa (Callahan) R. BSBA, Salem State U., 1954, EdM in Edn., 1973; EdM in Bus. Edn., Boston U., 1956. Cert. tchr., Mass. Bus. tchr. North Quincy (Mass.) High Sch., 1968—; owner, pub. Sunnyside Pub. Co., 1975—. Author: The Art of Playing Bingo and Winning Consistently, 1980, The Art of Entering Sweepstakes and Winning Consistently, 1981, How To Save a Fortune Using Refunds and Coupons, 1983, How to Unlock the Secrets of Winning and Good Luck, 1983, How You Can Achieve Total Success Through Self-Hypnosis, 1984, Where to Buy Everything Wholesale--A Book of Lifetime Savings, 1984, A Guide to Over 1,000 Things You Can Get--For Free!, 1984, The Art of Betting Horses and Winning Consistently, 1985, Blackjack: How to Play and Win Like an Expert, 1985, Hot Dice! How to Leave the Table a Winner, 1986, Winning Secrets of a Poker Master, 1986, Picking Winners at the Harness Races, 1987, Winning Consistently at the Greyhound Races, 1987, Lucky Slots!! How to Beat the Casino Bandits, 1988, Secrets of Winning at Casino Roulette, 1988, Keno: The Art of Playing and Winning, 1989, How to Play and Win at Casino Baccarat, 1989, Secrets of Winning at Video Poker, 1990, Winning Secrets of a Master Sports Bettor--Football, 1991, Winning Secrets of a Master Sports Bettor--Basketball, 1992, Winning Secrets of a Master Sports Bettor--Baseball, 1992; all publs. updated, 1997. Roman Catholic. Home: 28 Sunnyside Rd Lynn MA 01905-1105 Office: Sunnyside Pubs 51 Willow St # 29 Lynn MA 01901-1108

RYDER, GENE ED, retired United States Air Force training administrator; b. Canyon, Tex., Sept. 19, 1932; s. Johnny Allen and Rilda (New) R.; m. Mary Louise Wilson, Feb. 16, 1958; children: Carlyn, Katherine, Anita, Valerie. BA in Govt. cum laude, St. Mary's U., 1965; MEd, Our Lady of the Lake U., 1968; PhD in Adminstrn., The Union Inst., 1979. Instr. USAF, Scott, Keesler & Lackland AFB, 1958-65; tng. specialist USAF, Lackland AFB, Tex., 1965-69, tng. evaluator, 1969-72, curriculum coord., 1972-75, supr. curriculum devel., 1975-78, supr. tng. evaluation, 1978-83, tng. advisor, 1983-92; chief tng. policy USAF, Randolph AFB, Tex., 1992-95; ret., 1995; chmn. affiliated schs. adv. panel C.C. of Air Force, Maxwell AFB, Ala., 1984-88; co-chmn. USAF Tng. and Instrnl. Sys. Career Program, Randolph AFB, 1992-95; apptd. to Tex. State Bd. Profl. Counselors, 1995—. Author: Basics of Sunday School Leadership: A Guide for Lay Leaders, 1982. Dir. edn. Calvary Hills Bapt. Ch., San Antonio, 1981-94; coord. state scripture Gideons Internat., Nashville, 1991-94; elected mem. Tex. State Rep. Exec. Com., 1994-2000. With USAF, 1953-56. Mem. Am. Legion, Air Force Assn., Phi Delta Kappa. Home: 1502 Copperfield Rd San Antonio TX 78251-3324

RYDER, HAL, theater educator, director; b. Evanston, Ill., Aug. 21, 1950; s. Lee Sigmund and Katherine (Philipsborn) Rosenblatt; m. Caroline Margaret Ogden, Nov. 17, 1976 (div. 1991). Student, U. Ariz., 1968-72, U. Miami, summer 1971; cert. in drama, Drama Studio London, 1973; BA in Drama, U. Wash., 1987. Drama specialist Rough Rock (Ariz.) Demonstration Sch., 1971-72; artistic dir. Mercury Theatre, London, 1973-75, Fringe Theatre, Orlando, Fla., 1976-79; dir. Drama Studio London, 1980-82, interim adminstrv. dir., 1985; artistic dir. Alaska Arts Fine Arts Camp, Sitka, 1987, Shakespeare Plus, Seattle, 1983-92; instr. Cornish Coll. Arts, Seattle, 1982-98; prof., 1998—; producer theatre Cornish Coll. Arts, Seattle, 1987-97, acting-chmn. theatre dept., 1990; artistic dir., exec. dir. Open Door Theatre, 1992-98, exec. dir., 1998-00; artistic dir. Snoqualmie Falls Forest Theatre, 1992-94; founder, v.p., CEO Ednl. Arts Resource Svcs., Inc., 1996—; creative cons. Sea World Fla., Orlando, 1979; lit. mgr. Pioneer Square Theatre, Seattle, 1983; space mgr. Seattle Mime Theatre, 1986-87; pres. faculty senate, 1999—. Author: Carmilla, 1976, (with others) Marvelous Christmas Mystery, 1978; editor: Will Noble Blood Die, 1987, The New Emperor's New Clothes, 1990, Hamlet & Juliet, 1997, Pirates of Penzance, 1998; dir. over 140 stage plays; appeared in over 40 prodns. Recipient Faculty Excellence award Seafirst Bank, Seattle, 1988. Mem. SAG, AFTRA, Am. Fedn. Tchrs. (pres. faculty senate Cornish chpt. 1999—), Alpha Kappa Lamda. Democrat. Jewish. Avocations: writing, cooking, gardening, travel, scuba diving. Home: 1012 NE 62nd St Seattle WA 98115-6604 Office: Cornish Coll Arts 710 E Roy St Seattle WA 98102-4604

RYDER, KENNETH STANLEY, organist, music educator; b. London, May 22, 1940; s. Stanley Gerard and Doris Maud (Forsaith) R. Grad., Royal Sch. Music, 1961; assoc. degree, Royal Coll. Organists, 1962; diploma, Royal Acad. Music, 1963, assoc. (hon.), 1999; MA (hon.), U. East Anglia, 1998. Organ performer, 1960—, pvt. music tchr. piano and organ, 1960—; organist, master of music St. Peter Mancroft Ch., Norwich, Eng., 1963; adjudicator, Eng., 1963—, conductor, Eng., 1963—; organ performer, Bavaria, Holland, Austria, Germany, Gt. Britain, Can., 1963—. Performer CD, 1997. Mem. Inc. Soc. Musicians, Royal Acad. Music Club, Royal Coll. Organists. Anglican. Avocations: oil painting, photography. Home and Office: 56A The Close, Norwich NR1 4EH, England

RYDER, KENNETH WILLIAM, pathologist, educator; b. Mobile, Ala., May 1, 1945. BA, Knox Coll., 1967; PhD, Ind. U., 1972; MD, U. Ill., Chgo., 1975. Asst. prof. Ind. U. Sch. Medicine, Indpls., 1978-83, assoc. prof., 1983-88, prof., assoc. chair, 1986—; chief of svc. Wishard Meml. Hosp., Indpls., 1986-99; med. dir. Vencor Hosp. Lab., Indpls., 1995—; dir. chemistry labs. Clarian Health Ptnrs., Indpls., 2000—; chief pathologist VA Med. Ctr., Indpls., 2000—; med. dir. divsn. pathology Vencor Indpls., 1995—; chief pathology svc. VA Med. Ctr., Indpls., 2000—. Author: Interferographs, 1987, 2nd Edit., 1991; (with others) Difficult Diagnoses, 1991; contbr. articles to profl. jours. Fellow Coll. Am. Pathologists, 1979, Nat. Acad. Clin. Biochemistry, 1989. Office: Ind U Sch Medicine Meth Hosp 1701 N Senate Ave Indianapolis IN 46202-5306

RYDER, TIMOTHY THOMAS, classics educator; b. Claygate, Surrey, Eng., Jan. 11, 1930; s. Thomas Alfred and Enid Mary (Sanger) R.; m. Jean Ryder, Apr. 12, 1955; children: Penelope Anne Burnham, Philippa Kathryn Lea. BA, Cambridge (Eng.) U., 1952, MA, 1956, PhD, 1956. Asst. lectr. classics U. Hull (Eng.), 1955-57, lectr. classics, 1957-66, sr. lectr. classics, 1966-71, reader classics, 1971-90, dean Sch. Humanities, 1987-90; reader classics U. Reading (Eng.), 1990-95, vis. fellow, 1995—; vis. prof. history Mich. State U., East Lansing, 1966-67, vis. prof. history, 1981. Author: Koine Eirene, 1965; editor: Dictionary of World History, 1972. Mem. Soc. for Promotion of Hellenic Studies, Soc. for Promotion Roman Studies, Classical Assn. Gt. Britain. Mem. Ch. of Eng. Avocations: cricket, travel. Office: U Reading Dept Classics, Whiteknights PO Box 218, RG6 2AA Reading England

RYDER RICHARDSON, EDWARD COLIN, social services administrator; b. Aldeburgh, Suffolk, Eng., July 19, 1929; s. Edward and Glyn (Hollings) R. R.; m. Jill Balfour Hutchings, Jan. 10, 1953 (div. 1976); m. Rosemary Doris Cox, Feb. 11, 1978; children: Christopher, Sarah, Anna, Katie, Zoe. Student, Charterhouse, Surrey, Eng., 1943-47. Asst. dir. Sedgwick Group, London, 1952-88; asst. officer Civil Svc., Egham, Surrey, Eng., 1988—; hon. sec., counsellor New Approaches to Cancer, Egham, 1988—; chmn., trustee Brit. Wheel of Yoga, Sleaford, Lincoln, Eng., 1987—. Author: Mind Over Cancer, 1988, reprinted, 1994, 98. Home and Office: New Approaches to Cancer, 5 Larksfield, Egham Surrey TW20 ORB, England

RYDIN, BO GORAN, industrial executive; b. Frinnaryd, Sweden, May 7, 1932; m. Monika Aureus (dec. 1992); children: Goran, Johan, Helena, Kristina; m. Francoise Yon, 1997. MBA, Stockholm Sch. Econs., 1956, PhD in Econs. (hon.), 1992; PhD in Engring. (hon.), Lunds U., 1993. With Stockholms Enskilda Bank, 1956-57; asst. to pres. Marma Långrör AB, 1957-60; pres., CEO Gullhogens Bruk, Skovde, Sweden, 1962-71; pres., CEO Svenska Cellulosa, Aktiebolaget, Sweden, 1972-88, pres., CEO, exec. chmn., 1988—; bd. dirs. vice chmn. Svenska Handelsbanken; chmn. Industrivarden, Graninge, Skanska, Sas Assembly of Reps. Recipient King's Medal, 12th

Dimension, of Order of Seraphim. Mem. Royal Swedish Acad. Engring. Scis., Royal Swedish Acad. Agr. and Forestry, Rotary. Home: Karlavagen 3, 114 24 Stockholm Sweden Office: AB Industrivarden, PO Box 5403, 111 84 Stockholm Sweden

RYDSTROM, CARLTON LIONEL, chemist, paint and coating consultant; b. Indpls., Dec. 4, 1928; s. Carlton Lionel and Sara Ann (McNeese) R.; m. Kathleen O'Leary, Oct. 21, 1954 (dec.); children: Carlton L. III, Michael, Mary (dec.), Leslie, Patricia, Timothy, Molly. BS in Polymer Chemistry, N.D. State U., 1951; MS in Phys. Chemistry, U. Puerto Rico, Rio, Piedras, 1953. Chemist Am. Marietta Co., Kankakee, Ill., 1951-52; chemist, plant mgr. Chinamel Paints, Hato Rey, Puerto Rico, 1952-53; tech. mgr. Midwest Synthetics (Valspar), Rockford, Ill., 1953-55; mng. ptnr. Norcote Co., St. Petersburg, Fla., 1955-71; pres. C.M. Industries, Inc., St. Petersburg, 1971-74, Tuf-top/Norcote Coatings, Inc., St. Petersburg, 1974-80; owner Rydstrom Lab., Inc., St. Petersburg, 1980—; bd. dirs. Stacote Finishes, Ltd., W.I.; cons. Sch. Bds. State of Fla., 1981—, paint and adhesive industries. Pres. parish coun. St. Jude Cath. Cathedral Parish, 1977-78, 78-79, 97—, St. Vincent de Paul Pinellas Dist., St. Petersburg, 1988-91; nat. secretariat Cursillo Movement, Roman Cath. Ch., Dallas, 1985-88; dir. Cursillo Movement, Diocese of St. Petersburg, 1995—; dir. St. Vincent de Paul Food Ctr., St. Petersburg, 1988—; chmn. Waterfront Planning Com., St. Petersburg, 1959; mem. bd. dirs. St. Petersburg Cath. H.S., 1977-80; trustee N.D. State U. Devel. Found., 1998—. Fellow N.Y. Acad. Sci., Am. Inst. Chemists; mem. Nat. Assn. Corrosion Engrs., Soc. Coatings Tech. (chmn./pres. 1958-59, Disting. Svc. award 1975), Fla. Paint and Coating Assn. (treas., dir. 1959-75), St. Vincent dePaul Soc. (Top Hat award 1991), Jr. C. of C. (DSA 1960). Republican. Roman Catholic. Avocations: golf, gardening, travel, public speaking, working with needy. Home and Office: 6300 25th Ave N Saint Petersburg FL 33710-4128

RYDZYNSKI, KONRAD JOZEF, toxicologist; b. Lodz, Poland, Nov. 26, 1950; s. Zdzislaw and Waclawa (Sujka) R.; m. Aleksandra Kuzitowicz, July 1, 1974; children: Maciej, Jacek, Zuzanna. MD, Sch. Medicine, Lodz, Poland, 1974; DSc, Mil. Med. Acad., Lodz, Poland, 1978, Dr.habil., 1989. Asst. Mil. Med. Acad., Lodz, Poland, 1974-76, sr. asst., 1976-78; adj. Mil. Med. Acad., 1979-83, Polish Acad. Sci., Lodz, 1983-87; adj. Nofer Inst. Occupl. Medicine, Lodz, 1987-92, prof., head dept. toxicity and carcinogenesis, 1992—, dir. gen., 1999—. Contbr. articles to profl. jours. Mem. EUROTOX (exec. com.). Roman Catholic. Avocations: skiing, travel, politics, jogging. Home: 27 Tkacka Str, 90-156 Lodz Poland Office: Nofer Inst Occupational Medicine, Sw Teresy 8 Str, 90-950 Lodz Poland

RYE, MARCY LOUISE, graphic designer, artist; b. Feb. 6, 1968. Cert., Heinrich Heiner U., Dusseldorf, Germany, 1996; student, Corcoran Sch. Art, Washington, 1997; BA in Polit. Sci., U. Wis., 1999. Bus. devel. asst. AIG Consultants, Washington, 1991-93; membership dir. U.S. Kazakhstan Bus. Coun., Washington, 1993-94; freelance designer Arlington, Va., 1994-96; graphic designer Dos or Die, Krefeld, Germany, 1996, Staples & Charles, Alexandria, Va., 1997; art dir. Campaign Performance Group, Washington, 1998; owner FY Eye, LLC, Washington, 1999—; graphic designer A. Salon Artists Coop., 1997-98. Mentor/tutor Coll. Bound, Washington, 1998—. Mem. Am. Inst. Graphic Arts. Avocations: reading, bicycling, motorcycling, chess, learning foreign languages.

RYEO, JEOUNG DONG, association administrator; b. Seongju, Kyeongbuk, South Korea, June 29, 1933; s. Sang Min and Suk Beom (Pak) R.; m. Kyeoung Suk Ree; children: Jihwan, Tehwan, Tesun, Hwanwoo. B, Kyeongbuk U., Tegu, Republic of Korea, 1958, M in Lit., 1971. Prof. Gyeongsang, Chinju, South Korea, 1970-98, dean Humanities Coll., 1982-84, prof. emeritus, 1998—; pres. Edn. of Korean Lang. and Lit. Soc., 1993—; Mem., Kyeongnam Cultural and Arts Promotion Com., 1984—, Kyeongnam Cultural Property Com., Changwon, 1982-91. Author: History of Korean Literature, 1-2, 1997, Korean Good Son, 1991, Korean Good Sons Language, 1999, Korean Home Language, 2000 (Good Book prize Korean Govt.). With South Korean mil., 1951-52. Mem. Internat. Tae-gye Assn. in Kyeognam (chpt. pres. 1986—). Home: Apt 8-503 156 Chuyakdong, Hanju Lucky, Chinju 660-290, Republic of Korea Office: Gajadong 900, Ghyeongsang U Coll Edn, Chinji 660-701, South Korea

RYERSON, WILLIAM NEWTON, non profit organization executive; b. Phila., Mar. 9, 1945; s. W. Newton and Jean (Hamilton) R.; m. Leta C. Finch, Dec. 6, 1975. BA, Amherst Coll., 1967; M.Phil., Yale U., 1971. Dir. student intern program Population Inst., Washington, 1971-73, dir. youth and student div., 1973-79; dir. devel. Planned Parenthood Southeastern Pa., Phila., 1979-81; assoc. dir. Planned Parenthood No. New Eng., Burlington, Vt., 1981-86; pres. Ryerson & Assocs., fundraising counsel, Shelburne, Vt., 1986—; exec. v.p. Population Comm. Internat., N.Y.C., 1986-98; pres. Population Media Ctr., Shelburne, Vt., 1998—. Co-author: Population Activist's Handbook, 1974. NASA trainee in biology, Yale U., 1967-70. Mem. Phi Beta Kappa, Sigma Xi (assoc.). Home and Office: 489 Thompson Rd Shelburne VT 05482-6803

RYJACEK, ZDENEK, mathematician, educator; b. Prague, Czechoslovakia, Jan. 6, 1948; s. Jaroslav and Zdenka (Mrstikova) R.; m. Marta Klailova, Apr. 5, 1975; children: Pavel, Jan. MSc, Charles U., Prague, 1971; PhD, Czechoslovak Acad. Scis., Prague, 1985. Assoc. prof. U. West Bohemia, Pilsen, Czech Republic, 1991-97, prof., 1997—. Office: U West Bohemia Dept Math, Univerzitni 8, 306 14 Pilsen Czech Republic

RYKOV, VLADIMIR VASSILJEVICH, linguist; b. Komsomolsk-on-Amur, Russia, Sept. 11, 1947; s. Vassiliy Sezafimovich and Galina Borisovna (Kalinina) R.; m. Yelena Ivanovna Miakinina (div. 1994); children: Mikhail, Vassiliy. Degree in physics engring., Moscow Inst. Physics and Tech., 1971, PhD in Computational Linguistics, 1986. Sr. rschr. dept. computational linguistics Russian Acad. Scis., Moscow, 1990—; sr. specialist pub. TV Sta.-ORTV, Moscow, 1995—; asst. prof. Moscow Inst. Physics and Tech. Mem. N.Y. Acad. Scis. Home: 23-3-22 Garibaldi Str, 117335 Moscow Russia Office: Linguistic Inst, 1/12 Bol Kislovsky per, 103009 Moscow Russia

RYLANDER, ROBERT ALLAN, financial service executive; b. Bremerton, Wash., Apr. 8, 1947; s. Richard Algot and Marian Ethelyn (Peterson) R.; children: Kate, Josh, Erik, Meagan. BA in Fin., U. Wash., 1969; postgrad., U. Alaska, 1972-74. Controller Alaska USA Fed. Credit Union, Anchorage, 1974-77, mgr. ops., 1977-80, asst. gen. mgr., 1980-83, exec. v.p., chief operating officer, 1983—; chmn. Alaska USA Mortgage, Inc., Anchorage, 1992—, Alaska Option Svcs. Corp., Anchorage, 1983—; pres. Alaska USA Trust Co., Anchorage, 1997-2000, Alaska USA Trust Co., 2000—; bd. dirs. Alaska USA Ins., Inc., Anchorage. Served to capt. USAF, 1969-74. Avocations: audio electronics, music. Home: PO Box 220587 Anchorage AK 99522-0587 Office: Alaska USA Fed Credit Union PO Box 196613 Anchorage AK 99519-6613

RYLANDS, PHILIP BROME, museum director, art historian; b. London, Eng., Dec. 29, 1950; s. James Wolferstan and Diana Elizabeth (Goldson) R.; m. Jane Ann Turner, Nov. 25, 1972; 1 child, Augustus James George. BA, Cambridge (Eng.) U., 1973, MA, 1975, PhD, 1981. Adminstr. Peggy Guggenheim Collection, Venice, Italy, 1979-86, dep. dir., 1986-2000; dir., 2000—; sec.-treas. Internat. Torcello Com., 1979-83; Venice sec. Venice in Peril Fund, Eng., 1974-83, mem. exec. com., 1979—; lectr. U. Md. Overseas Divsn., 1974-81; overseas lectr. arch. U. Va., 1978-97; adj. dist. prof. U. Va., 1998-99. Author: Palma il Vecchio, 1988, Palma Vecchio, 1991; co-author: (with Enzo di Martino) Flying the Flag for Art, 1995; editor: (with Sir Ashley Clarke) Restoring Venice: The Church of the Madonna Dell'orto, 1977; contbr. articles to profl. jours. and catalogs. Mem. Circolo Dell'Unione, Ateneo Veneto, Garrick Club. Anglican. Office: Peggy Guggenheim Collection, 701 Dorsoduro, 30123 Venice Italy

RYLE, LILLIAN JUNE, municipal administrator; b. Grant County, Ind., June 22, 1942; d. Jack Norman and Vera Alene (Poindexter) Mann; m. Howard Lucien Ryle, Nov. 3, 1958; children: Timothy Lee, Natalie Louise, Wade Alan. Grad. h.s., Greensburg, Ind., 1966. Mem. Ind. Assn. Cities and Towns, Ind. League Mcpl. Clks. and Treas. (various coms. 1993-96, exec. dir. 1995-96, dist. dir. 1996—, historian 1997-98), Internat. Inst. Mcpl. Clks., Am. Legion Aux. (sec. 1999—). Democrat. Roman Catholic. Avocations: singing, grandchildren, cooking, cantor St. Mary's Church. Office: City of Greensburg 314 N Michigan Ave Greensburg IN 47240-1433

RYLSKI, ANDRZEJ, electrical measuring educator, researcher; b. Rzeszów, Poland, Feb. 3, 1950; s. Marian and Stefania (Betkowska) R.; m. Helena Nieplowicz, July 21, 1974; children: Aneta, Krzysztof, Przemyslaw, Bartosz. PhD in Elec. Sci., Tech. U., Wroclaw, Poland, 1986. Asst. Tech. U., Wroclaw, Poland, 1974-79, Rzeszow, 1979-83; engr. ZDZ, Rzeszow, 1983-93; tutor Tech. U., Rzeszow, 1989—. Author: Sensors and Transducers, 1994, Metrology II Alternating Current, 2000; author, editor Measurement Errors, 1997. Mem. Trade Union Solidarnosc, 1980; pres. local group ZChN party, 1992; dir. town coun., Rzeszow, 1998. Mem. Tech. Orgn. Roman Catholic. Avocations: car mechanic, gardener. Home: Struga 4, 35-328 Rzeszów Poland Office: Univ Rzeszów, W Pola 2, Rzeszów Poland

RYMILL, THOMAS MARK, lawyer; b. Penola, Australia, Feb. 19, 1950; s. Robert Riddoch and Gladys Edith (Hood) R.; m. Catherine Margaret Walters, March 10, 1979. LLB, U. Adelaide, South Australia, 1974. Enrolled legal practitioner, 1975. Prin. Rymills Law Office, Mt. Gambier, SA, 1975—. Brigade cpt. Country Fire Svc., Penola, 1977-82; v.p. Mt. Gambier C. of C., 1992-96; pres. Mt. Gambier Toastmasters Club, 1980. Recipient Nat. medal Country Fire Svc., 1986. Mem. Law Soc. of South Australia (councillor 1997). Office: Rymills Law Office, Bay Rd, Mount Gambier 5290, Australia

RYMSHA, SOFIA VITALIEVNA, psychiatrist, consultant; b. Vinnitsa, Ukraine, Sept. 26, 1956; d. Vitaliy Feliksovish and Alla Kazimirovna (Jaselsky) R.; ; m. Elena Viktorovna, Oct. 19, 1979; 1 child, Juri Viktorovna Golovenko. Candidate of Med. Sci., Med. Acad., Moscow, 1988, DMS, 1994. Lic. physician. Dr. Mental Hosp., Vinnitsa, 1979-89; asst. psychiat. dept. Med. U., Vinnitsa, 1989-95, head psychiatry chair, 1995—; cons. Mental Hosp., Vinnitsa, 1989-99. Author: (book) Mental and Somatics Disorders, 1994; contbr. articles to med. jours. Mem. Sci. Soc. Psychiatrists and Neuropathologists, N.Y. Acad. Scis. Home: Pyrogora 117a/132, 21037 Vinnitsa Ukraine Office: Med Univ, Pyrogora 54, 21018 Vinnitsa Ukraine

RYNKOWSKI, JACEK MICHAŁ, chemist, educator; b. Łódź, Poland, Feb. 6, 1948; s. Józef and Anna (Kłopotowska) R.; m. Anna Skupińska Matczak, Apr. 7, 1979; 1 child, Tomasz. MS, Tech. U., Łódź, Poland, 1970, PhD, 1978, DSc, 1988. Engring. Asst. Inst. Gen. Ecol. Chemistry, Łódź, Poland, 1970-71, lectr., 1972-78, sr. lectr., 1978-88, assoc. prof., 1989-93, dir. rsch., 1992—, prof., 1993—; rsch. fellow U. Strathclyde, Glasgow, Scotland, 1989-90. Contbr. numerous articles to scientific jours. Grantee State Com. Scientific Rsch., 1994, 95; recipient Scientific Achievement award Min. Edn., Poland, 1979, 89. Mem. Polish Catalysis Club, Polish Chem. Soc. Avocations: opera, sport. Office: Inst Gen and Ecol Chemistry, Żwirki 36, 90-924 Lodz Poland

RYSKOV, YAROSLAV GEORGIEVITCH, soil scientist; b. Stanislav, Russia, Jan. 27, 1950; s. Georgiy Nikitovich and Vera Pavlovna Ryskov; m. Nina Rudolfovna Tchaykovskaya, Apr. 20, 1974 (div. Oct. 1995); children: Eugenia Yaroslavovna, Elena Yaroslavovna, Nadegda Anatolevna, Vera Yaroslavovna; m. Elena Andreevna Arlashina, Oct. 6, 1996. BS, Moscow State U., 1972, PhD, 1997. Rschr. Inst. Agrichemistry and Soil Sci., Pushchino, Russia, 1972-80, Inst. Soil Sci. and Photosynthesis, Pushchino, 1980—. Co-author: Soil and Environment Development for the Steppe of South Ural during the Holocene Using Stable Isotope Methods, 1997. Mem. Russian Soc. Soil Scientists. Avocations: fishing, gardening, hiking. Home: 142292 Pushchino Moscow, Russia Office: Inst Soil Sci & Photosynth, Russian Acad Sci, 142292 Pushchino Moscow, Russia

RYSSEL, HEINER, electrical engineering educator; b. Plaue, Germany, Dec. 9, 1941; m. Herma Plobner, Aug. 28, 1970; children: Edna, Verena. Diploma Ing., Tech. U., Munich, 1968, Dr. Ing., 1973, Dr. habil., 1985. Rsch. fellow Inst. Tech. Electronics, Munich, 1968-72, Inst. of Solid State Technology, Munich, 1973-85; prof. elec. engring. U. Erlangen, Nuremberg, 1985—; dir. Inst. Integrated Circuits. Editor: (books) Low Implantation Techniques, 1982, Ion Implantation: Equipment and Techniques, 1983, Simulation of Semiconductor Devices and Processes, 1995; author: (books) Implantation, 1978, Ion, 1986, Microcircuit Engineering, 1993. Mem. IEEE (sr.), Bohmische Physikalische Gesellschaft, GMM, Electronic Soc., ITG, Material Rsch. Soc. Avocations: skiing, history. Office: Fraunhofer-Inst Integrated, Circuits Schottkystrasse 10, 91058 Erlangen Germany

RYSZKOWSKI, LECH, ecology educator; b. Warsaw, Poland, Nov. 18, 1931; s. Eugene and Jane (Samulak) R.; m. Grazyna Ludwiczak Ryszkowski, Apr. 7, 1969. MS, U. Warsaw, Poland, 1955, PhD, 1963, DSc, 1971. Head of animal population dept. Inst. Ecology, Warasaw, Poland, 1962-69, head of agroecology dept., 1969; dir. Rsch. Ctr. for Agrl. and Forest Environ., Poman, Poland, 1979—; prin. coord. of project Ecol. Effects of Intensive Agr., 1971-75, Natural Bases for Agrl. Landscape mgmt., 1976-80, Ecol. Bases for Agr. and Landscape Planning, 1981-85, Ecol. mgmt. and Protection of Angl. Regions, 1986-90, Ecol. Engring. of Agrl. Landscapes, 1991-94, Landscape Mgmt. in Protected Areas, 1995-98. Author: Unifying Concepts in Ecology, 1975; author, co-editor: International Biological Programme Synthesis, 1975, Dynamics of Agricultural Landscape, 1996, Landscape Diversity, 1996, Implementing Ecological Integrity, 2000; contbr. articles to profl. jours. Recipient Golden Cross of Merit, 1980 cavalier cross of merit, 1987, State Coun., Warsaw, Poland. Mem. Man and Biosphere Polish Com (v.p. 1999), INTECOL on Agroecosystems, Pornan Dist. Environ. Protection Commn. of Polish Acad. of Scis. Avocations: mediaeval history, swimming, sightseeing, book reading. Office phone: (0048) 61 847 5603. Home: Wichrowe Wzgore 26 Apt 63, 61697 Poznan Poland Office: Rsch Ctr for Agrl & Forest, Bukowska 19 Street, 60809 Poznan Poland

RYTTEL, ANNA MARTA, chemist, educator, researcher; b. Warsaw, Poland, Jan. 19, 1937; d. Henry and Julia Zofia (Krauze) Kuflewicz; 1 child, Pakosz Zofia. MSc, Tech. U. Szczecin, Poland, 1960; PhD, Tech. U. Wrocław, Poland, 1976. Technologist in industry Rzeszów, Poland, 1960-70; prof. asst. Pedagogical H.S., Rzeszów, 1970-75; adj. dept. organic chemistry Rzeszów U. Tech., 1975—. Contbr. articles to profl. jours. Mem. tchrs. Union, Warsaw, 1970-83. Mem. Polish Chem. Soc. Avocation: turistic. Home: B Krzywoustego 7/5, 35-077 Rzeszów Poland Office: Rzeszów Univ of Tech, W Pola 2, 35-959 Rzeszów Poland

RYTWO, GIORA, physical chemistry educator, researcher; b. Avellaneda, Argentina, July 14, 1958; arrived in Israel, 1971; s. Yaacov and Julia (Rizy) R.; m. Orly Bal, Mar. 14, 1989; children: Yuval, Ma'ayan. BSc, Hebrew U. Jerusalem, Rehovot, 1986, MSc, 1989, PhD in Soil Sci., 1994. Asst. instr. Hebrew U. Jerusalem, 1987-94; rschr. MIGAL, Kiriat Shmona, Israel, 1994—; prof. phys. chemistry, meteorology and soil sci. Tel Hai Acad. Coll., Doar Na Galil Elyon, Israel, 1994—; postdoctoral fellow Agrl. Rsch. Svc., USDA, Beckley, W.Va., 1996. Office: Tel Hai Acad Coll, Dept Environ Scis, 12210 Doar Na Galil Elyon Israel

RYU, CHANG-MO, physicist, educator; b. Nonsan, Choongnam, South Korea, May 31, 1952; s. Young Choon and Kuhm Soon (Ahn) R.; m. Young Hwa Rhee; children: Albert Byunglim, Byungwook. BS, Seoul Nat. U., 1975; MS, Syracuse U., 1978; PhD, Princeton U., 1983. Rsch. scientist Los Alamos (N.Mex.) Nat. Lab., 1983-85; rsch. engr. Ga. Inst. Tech., Atlanta, 1985; sr. rschr. KAERI, Daejeon, Korea, 1985-88; rsch. asst. prof. Pohang U. Sci. & Tech., South Korea, 1988-89, assoc. prof., 1989-97, prof., 1997—. Contbr. articles to profl. jours. Mem. Am. Phys. Soc, Korean Phys. Soc. Home: Jigok Prof Apt 8-1702, Pohang 790 390, South Korea Office: Pohang Univ Sci & Tech, Dept Physics, Pohang 790 784, South Korea

RYU, KWANG-SOK, Republic of Korean diplomat; b. Republic of Korea, Jan. 8, 1951; m. Joo-hee Kim; children: Hyun-ji, Hyun-woo. B Internat. Politics, Seoul Nat. U., 1973; MS in Fgn. Svc., Georgetown U., 1982. Joined Ministry Fgn. Affairs, Seoul, 1973—; 3d sec. Korean Embassy, Washington, 1976-79; mem. staff Office of the Pres., 1982-84; counselor Korea Embassy, New Delhi, 1984-87, Korean Embassy, Tokyo, 1992-95; dir. nat. security policy divsn. Am. Affairs Bur., Ministry Fgn. Affairs, 1987-92; spokesman Ministry Fgn. Afffairs, 1995, dep. dir. gen. Policy Planning Office, 1995-96, dir. gen. Asian and Pacific Affairs Bur., 1997-98; consul gen. Korean Consultate Gen., Atlanta, 1998—; vis. scholar Keio U., Tokyo, Japan, 1990-92. Recipient Presdl. citation, Republic of Korea, 1984, 98. Office: Korean Consultate Gen 229 Peachtree St NE Ste 500 Atlanta GA 30303-1600

RYU, SHIRO, telecommunications company manager; b. Ichikawa-shi, Chiba, Japan, Dec. 4, 1957; m. Mariko Ryu; children: Mayuko, Tomotaka. B in Engring., U. Tokyo, 1981, M in Engring., 1983, PhD, 1993. Rsch. engr. KDD, Tokyo, 1985-95, mgr., 1995-2000, sr. mgr., 2000—; specialist optical fiber comm. sys. Author: Coherent Lightwave Communication Systems, 1995; contbr. articles to profl. jours.; patentee in field. Mem. IEEE, Inst. Electronics, Info., and Comm. Engrs. (Best Paper award 1988, Young Scientist award 1991). Office: KDD Corp Access Sys Dept, 2-3-2 Nishi-shinjuku, Shinjuku-ku Tokyo 163-8003, Japan

RYWIK, STEFAN LUDWIK, cardiovascular epidemiologist, educator; b. Katowice, Poland, May 3, 1931; s. Ludwik and Stefania (Makomaska) R.; m. Stanisława Siemieńska, Dec. 14, 1960; 1 child, Tomasz. Physician, Acad. Medicine, Warsaw, 1956, MD, 1967, DSc, 1973. Gen. practitioner Pub. Health Svc., Warsaw, 1956-66; sr. asst. Acad. Medicine, 1966-69, asst. prof., 1969-75; assoc. prof., head dept., dep. dir. inst. Nat. Food and Nutrition Inst., Warsaw, 1975-79; assoc. prof. Nat. Inst. Cardiology, Warsaw, 1979-85, prof., 1985—, head of dept., dep. dir. inst., 1979—; mem., chmn. WHO MONICA steering com., 1984-87. Recipient award in CVD epidemiology Min. of Health, Warsaw, 1977. Fellow European Soc. Cardiology (vice chmn. working group on epidemiology 1985-89); mem. Polish Soc. Hypertension (pres. 1998—), Polish Soc. Cardiology (bd. dirs. 1986-92). Avocations: gardening, tourism. Home: Dante Str 5 m 39, 01 914 Warsaw Poland Office: Nat Inst Cardiology, Alpejska Str 42, 04 628 Warsaw Poland

RYZHAK, EUGENE, physics educator, researcher; b. Moscow, Nov. 20, 1953; s. Izmail and Diana (Mogilevskaya) R.; m. Tatyana Deryabina, Jan. 6, 1978; children: Svetlana, Alexander. MSc, Moscow Inst. Physics and Tech., Moscow, 1976; PhD, USSR Acad. Sci., Moscow, 1984. Rschr. Inst. of Physics of the Earth, USSR Acad. Sci., 1976-86, sr. rschr., 1986—; assoc. prof. Moscow Inst. Physics and Tech., 1991—. Contbr. articles to profl. publs. Recipient medal for young scientists USSR Acad. Sci., 1985. Mem. Internat. Soc. for Interaction of Mech. and Math. Avocations: ice and inline skating, ice hockey. Home: Energetischeskaya 16-2-78, 111116 Moscow Russia Office: Inst Physics of Earth RAS, B Gruzinskaya 10, 123810 Moscow Russia

RYZHAVSKII, BORIS YAKOVLEVITCH, histologist, consultant; b. Borisoglebsk, Russia, Aug. 4, 1943; s. Yakov Efimovitch and Elizaveta Romanovna (Evseeva) R.; m. Ludmila Alexandrovna Bichurina, Mar. 13, 1947; children: Dmitri, Irina. MD, Raitchikhinsk Med. Sch., Russia, 1961; MSc, Med. Inst. Blagoveschensk, Russia, 1967, D Med. Sci., 1970; DSc, Med. U. Khabarovsk, Russia, 1985. Lectr. Med. Inst., Blagoveschensk, 1970-72, asst. prof., 1972-80; head histology dept. Med. Inst. Khabarovsk, 1980—; dep. dir. Mother and Child Protection Ins., Khabarovsk, 1986-89, cons., 1989—. Author: Postnatal Ontogenesis of Adrenal Cortex, 1989, Aging, Adaptation, Reversibility, 1992, State of the Most Important Systems of Embryongenese: Remote Consequences, 1999; co-author: Structural Principles of Generative and Endocrinal Function of Ovary in Normality and Pathology, 1996; contbr. articles to Bull. Exptl. Biology and Medicine, 1981—. Soros grantee, 1997. Avocation: skiing. Home: 6 Dzerzhinskji St Apt 133, 680000 Khabarovsk Russia Office: Medical Univ, 35 Muravjov-Amurskji, 680000 Khabarovsk Russia

RYZHII, MAXIM, scientific researcher, educator; b. Moscow, Russia, Aug. 7, 1969; s. Victor Ryzhii and Nadejda Riabova; m. Elena Pedos, Apr. 10, 1993; children: Ivan, Nikita. MS, Moscow Inst. Physics and Tech., 1992. Rsch. engr. Rsch. Ctr. Microel, Moscow, 1990-93; rsch. assoc. U. Aizu, Aizu-Wakamatsu, Japan, 1993—; vis. rschr. Chalmers U. of Tech., Gothenburg, Sweden, 1998. Contbr. articles to profl. jours. Mem. IEEE, Am. Physical Soc. (life). Avocations: amateur video, travel, railway models. E-mail: m-ryzhii@ieee.org. Office: U Aizu, Fukushima, Aizu-Wakamatsu 965 8580, Japan

RYZHIKOV, GENNADY ANTONOVICH, geophysicist, researcher; b. Pskov, Russia, Feb. 26, 1945; s. Anton Zakharovich and Taisiya Ivanovna (Lebedeva) R.; m. Marina Svyatoslavovna Biryulina; children: Maxim, Alexander; stepchildren: Gleb, Slava. BSc, U. St. Petersburg, Russia, 1967; MSc, U. St. Petersburg, 1974, PhD, 1989. Sr. rschr. U. St. Petersburg, 1971-93, U. Bergen, Norway, 1993—; cons. Norwave Devel. AS, Oslo, 1997, Geminali AS, Oslo, 1998—. Author: Tomography and Remote Sensing Inverse Problems, 1994; contbr. articles to profl. jours. Avocations: tennis, chess, music, table tennis, traveling. Home: Fantoft Stud By E-210, N-5075 Bergen Norway Office: U Bergen Dept Physics, Allegaten 55, N-5007 Bergen Norway

RYZHIKOV, VLADIMIR DIOMIDOVICH, physicist, educator; b. Askania-Nova, Ukraine, Jan. 8, 1940; s. Diomid Pavlovich Ryzhikov and Vera Alexandrovna Lavrova; m. Tamara Petrovna Phiodorova (div. 1973); 1 child, Svetlana Vladimirovna; m. Helen Konstantinovna (Gurevich) Lisetskay. BS in Radiophysics, State U., Kharkov, Ukraine, 1967; MS, Inst. Single Crystals, Kharkov, DSc, 1990. Rschr. Inst. Single Crystals-Ukrainian Nat. Acad. Scis., 1973-81, head lab., 1981-96, dir. Ctr. Radiation Instruments,, 1996—. Author 3 books, also 300 papers. With rocket divsn. Ukrainian Mil., 1959-62. Mem. Russian Acad. Scis. (mem. coun. applied physics), Coun. Nondestractive Control. Avocations: literature, state and religious history, travel, mountaineering, skiing. Office: Inst Single Crystals UAS, STC RI Ave Lenin 60, 310001 Kharkov Ukraine

RYZHOV, VYACHESLAV ANATOLYEVICH, physics researcher; b. Glushenki Village, Russia, June 25, 1947; s. Anatoliy Grigorievich and Mariya Andreevna (Sidorova) R.; m. Alevtina Nikolaevna Pestereva, Mar. 6, 1970; 1 child, Dmitriy. PhD, Konstantinov Nucl. Phys. Inst., Gatchina, Russia, 1983. Engr. Inst. Pulp & Paper Industry, Leningrad, Russia, 1971-72, Br. A.F. Ioffe Phys.-Tech. Inst., Gatchina, Russia, 1972-73; jr. rschr. physics B.P. Konstantinov St. Petersburg Nuclear Physics Inst., Russia, 1973-86, sr. rschr. physics, 1986—; tchr. physics Gymnasium, Gatchina, 1993-94; tchr. physics & math. Tech. Litzey, Gatchina, 1995-96. Contbr. articles to profl. jours.; inventor in field. Mem local trade union com. Divsn. Nuclear Physics Inst., Gatchina, 1973-75, head local trade union com., 1984-86, mem. com. vol. pub. inspection, 1986-88. Grantee Russian Fund Fundamental Rsch., Moscow, 1997, 2000. Mem. N.Y. Acad. Scis. Avocations: home building, reading, walking. Office: Nuclear Physics Inst, Orlova Coppice 1, 188350 Gatchina Russia

RZEDOWSKI, JERZY, botanist, researcher; b. Lwów, Poland, Dec. 27, 1926; arrived in Mex., 1946; s. Arnold and Ernestyna (Rotter) R.; m. Graciela Calderón, July 14, 1954; children: Martha, Ernestina, Ana. Biologist, Nat. Poly. Inst., Mexico City, 1954; D in Biology, U. Nacional Autónoma Mex., Mexico City, 1961; D honoris causa, U. Autónoma Chapingo, Mex., 1995. Botanist Syntex, S.A., Mexico City, 1953-54; prof. U. Autónoma San Luis Potosí (Mex.), 1954-59, Colegio Postgrads., Chapingo, Mex., 1959-61, Nat. Poly. Inst., Mexico City, 1961-84; researcher Inst. Ecología Pátzcuaro (Michoacán, Mex.), 1984—. Decorated Ordre des Palmes Académiques (France); recipient Millenium Botany award, 1999. Mem. Bot. Soc. Mex. (diploma al mérito botánico 1972), Internat. Assn. Plant Taxonomy (mem. coun. 1981—), Am. Soc. Plant Taxonomists (corr., Asa Gray award 1995), Bot. Soc. Am. (corr.). Office: Inst Ecología AC, Apdo Postal 386, 61600 Pátzcuaro Mich, Mexico

SA, BEN-HAO, physicist, researcher, educator; b. Fuzhou, Fukien, China, May 4, 1935; s. Fu-Xuan Sa and Xue-Qing Chen; m. Yan-Ming Liu; children: Jian, Chong. BA, Peking U., Beijing, 1957. From asst. prof. to assoc. prof. China Inst. Atomic Energy, Beijing, 1957-89, prof., 1990—. Achievements include inventor disassembly of hot nuclei. E-mail: sabh@iris.ciae.ac.cn. Home and Office: PO Box 275 (18), Beijing 102413, China

SA', GERALDO MATOS DE, surgeon; b. Cajazeiras, Brazil, Jan. 21, 1934; s. Aprígio Gomes and Adalgisa Matos (Silva) S.; m. Maria Lúcia Silva;

children: Luciana, André Gustavo. DDS, U. Fed. Fluminense, Niteroi, 1955; MD, U. do Estado do Rio de Janeiro, 1960. Physician Nat. Inst. Cancer/Ministerio da Saude, Rio de Janeiro, 1961—, chief head and neck surgery, 1974-79, dir., 1985-86; pres. Found. Ary Frauzino, Rio de Janeiro, 1991-95. Editor: Residência Médica do Inca, 1995 (Best of Then award). Bd. dirs. Cons. Reg. Medicina, Rio de Janeiro, 1963, Brazilian Coll. Surgeons, Rio de Janeiro, 1989. Fellow ACS; mem. Am. Head and Neck Soc., Colegio Brasileiro. Roman Catholic. Avocations: photography, soccer, travel, popular and classical music. Office: Cath U, Rua Visconde Silve 52/605, 22271090 Rio de Janeiro Brazil

SAAB, DEANNE KELTUM, real estate appraiser, real estate broker; b. Allentown, Pa., Jan. 27, 1945; d. James A. and Agnes G. (Hanzlik) S. BA, Cedar Crest Coll., 1966; MS, U. Calif., Santa Barbara, 1973; realtors cert., Pa. State U., 1978. Cert. appraiser Assoc. Appraisal Inst., Pa., 1991; cert. sales profl. Nat. Assn. Home Builders, 1994. Tchr. Ojai (Calif.) Unified Sch. Dist., 1966-74; pvt. practice Allentown, Pa., 1978—; pres./treas. DeAnne & Assoc., Inc., Allentown, Pa., 1987—; owner Heritage Gardens, Allentown, Pa., 1981—; co-founder, treas. performance group Lehigh Valley Folk Music Soc., 1996. Mem. AAUW (various offices, Best State Newsletter award 1987), Nat. Assn. Realtors, Pa. Assn. Realtors, Allentown Lehigh Valley Assn. Realtors, Cedar Crest Coll. Alumnae Assn. (class rep., various offices), Lehigh Valley Guild Craftsmen (various offices). Avocations: gourd, herbal crafting, painting, folk music performance. Home and Office: 1360 Dorney Ave Allentown PA 18103-9731

SAAB, GHASSAN NICOLAS, insurance company executive; b. Beirut, Nov. 10, 1948; s. Nicolas Mitri and Denise Nicholas (Khabbaz) S.; m. Aida Abdulamir Dagher, Nov. 10, 1977; children: Dana, Sara. BA in Arts and Scis., Am. U. Beirut, 1973. Adminstrv. asst. ACE, Beirut, 1973-75; mgr. ACE, Kuwait City, 1976-84; risk mgr. CCC, Athens, Greece, 1985-92; gen. mgr. Bahrain Kuwait Ins. Co., Safat, Kuwait, 1993—. Trustee Lebanese Embassy, Kuwait, 1996. Home: Al Tameer Bldg Complex 207, Gulf Rd, Bneid Al Gar Kuwait Office: Bahrain Kuwait Ins Co, Ahmad Al Jaber St, 26728 Safat Kuwait

SAAD, EL SAYED MOSTAFA, electrical engineering educator, consultant; b. El Korain, Sharkia, Egypt, June 9, 1944; s. Mostafa Saad and Nafisa Mohamed Barakat; m. Magda Mohamed Hashem, Oct. 9, 1969; children: Mohamed, Walied, Amro. BSEE, Cairo U., 1967; diploma in engring., Stuttgart (Germany) U., 1977, D in Engring., 1981. Asst. engr. Higher Inst. Electronics, Menuf, Egypt, 1967-75; asst. Faculty Engring. and Tech. Helwan U., Cairo, 1976-81, asst. prof., 1981-85, assoc. prof., 1985-90, prof., 1990—; vice dean Faculty of Engring., Helwan U., 1996; cons. Arab Rep. Egypt Nat. Telecom. Orgn.-Data Traffic Project, Cairo, 1985-86, 88-89, Acad. Sci. Rsch. and Tech.-Automatic Test Equipment Project, Cairo, 1991-95, Nat. Telecom. Inst., Cairo, 1985—; expert, cons. Engring. Edn. Devel. Project, Cairo, 1993-96; supr., examiner postgrad. students. Translator: Electronic Devices and Circuits, 1994, Vocabulary for Data Processing, Telecommunications and Office Systems, 1984; contbr. articles to profl. jours.; reviewer papers in field. Served with Egyptian mil., 1969-72. Mem. Nat. Radio Sci. Com., European Circuit Soc., Egyptian Engring. Syndicate and Soc. Elec. Engring. Avocations: sports, reading. Home: Hassan Yousef St 8, 11451 Cairo Egypt Office: U Helwan Faculty Engring, 1 Sherif St, Helwan Egypt

SAAD, MASSOUD ABDEL-RAHMAN, oceanographer, researcher; b. Alexandria, Egypt, July 22, 1935; s. Abdel-Rahman Hassan Saad and Ansaf Hassan Bahgat; m. Seham Ibrahim Hambazaza, Nov. 30, 1972; children: Tarek, Sherif, Maha, Ghada. BSc in Chemistry and Biology, Alexandria U., 1957, diploma in oceanography, 1961; diploma in edn., High Inst. Edn., Egypt, 1958; PhD in Limnology, Christian Albrechts U., Kiel, Germany, 1966; DSc in Oceanography and Limnology, Czech Acad. Sci., Czechoslovakia, 1997. Lectr. Alexandria U., 1967-74, asst. prof., 1974-79, prof., 1979-81, 86-91, emeritus prof., 1991—, head oceanography dept., 1987-91; prof. King Abdul-Aziz U., Jeddah, Saudi Arabia, 1981-86, head marine chemistry dept., 1982-86; cons. Food and Agrl. Orgn., Rome, 1986-96, Environ. Resources, Alexandria, 1999-00. Contbr. articles to profl. jours. Recipient Egyptian Nat. prize, 1987. Mem. Commn. Exploration of Mediterranean Sea (20th Century award for achievements), Soc. Internat. Limnology, Estuarine and Coastal Scis. Assn. Avocations: swimming, tennis, readings, music, traveling. Home: Bahaa El-Din El-Ghatwary, 41, 15 May Sq, 21615 Alexandria Egypt Office: Alexandria U, Oceanography Dept, 21511 Alexandria Egypt

SAAD, VALERIE ANN, nursing administrator, naval officer; b. Easton, Pa., Oct. 12, 1954; d. Samuel and Josephine (Badway) S. BSN, Seton Hall U., 1976. RN, Pa., N.J.; cert. advanced trauma life support, BCLS instr., Lamaze instr. Nurse ob-gyn, operating room, newborn nursery med.-surg. ICU Easton (Pa.) Hosp., 1976-77; commd. ensign Nurse Corps, USN, 1977, advanced through grades to lt. comdr., 1989; staff nurse Naval Regional Med. Ctr., Orlando, Fla., 1977-80; intern operating rm. nursing program Mass. Gen. Hosp., Boston, 1980-81; nurse Allentown (Pa.)-Sacred Heart Hosp. Ctr., 1981-82; staff nurse MOR, charge nurse, clin. instr. Naval Hosp., Bethesda, Md., 1983-87; relief supr. ambulatory care Naval Hosp., Portsmouth, Va., 1987-89; staff nurse main operating rm. Naval Hosp., Phila., 1989-91; staff nurse perioperative nursing Naval Hosp., San Diego, 1991-97; dir. surg. svcs. Riverview Med. Ctr., Red Bank, N.J., 1997-00; dir. ambulatory surg. ctr. Holy Redeemer Healthcare Sys., Meadowbrook, Pa., 2000—. Contbr. articles to nursing jours. Mem. Phi Delta Kappa, Sigma Theta Tau. Avocations: cooking, sewing, needle point. Home: 164 Linden Ave Highlands NJ 07732-1328

SAADALLAH, FAYCEL BEN HABIB, physics educator, researcher; b. Marsa, Tunis, Tunisia, Oct. 1, 1966; s. Habib Ben Salah and M'Tira Ben Ahmed (Abdeddaïm) S. Cert. in prep. engring., Tunis, Tunisia, 1987, cert. in engring. technician, 1989; M in Physics, Sci. U., Tunis, Tunisia, 1991; D of Physics, Ecole Normal Superieure Cachan, Paris, 1993. Rschr. IPEIN, Nabeul, Tunisia, 1993—, physics educator, 1993—; cons. photothermal lab., Nabeul, Tunisia, 1994-2000. Contbr. articles to profl. jours. Mem. Soc. Tunisienne Physique. Mem. Dem. Constl. Rassemblement Pty. Avocations: fishing, swimming, photography, sci. books, drawing. Home: 13-R Okba Ben Nafaa, 5160 Eljem Mahdia Tunisia Office: IPEIN, 8000 Mrazka Nabeul Tunisia

SAADEDDINE, MONIR CAMPOS, surgeon, military officer; b. Cuiba, Brazil, Jan. 23, 1967; s. Samir and Sebastiana Maria (Campos) S.; m. Danielle Murta, Mar. 20, 1999. Med. diplomate, U. de Nova-Iguaçu, Brazil, 1993; abdominal surgery, Inst. Pós Graduação, Carlos Chagas, 1997. Asst. chmn. Unig U., Rio de Janeiro, 1989-91; postgrad. staff Estate Hosp., Rio de Janeiro, 1993, chief staff surgery, 1998—; staff surgery S.T. Lourenço Hosp., Rio de Janeiro, 1997—. Instr., 1st It. Brazilian Army, 1994—. Mem. Regional-Med. Coun., Med. Sindicate, Health Corp. Islamic. Avocations: fishing, traveling, hunting, tennis, camping. Home: Rua Sã Francisco, Xavier 395/201, 20550010 Rio de Janeiro Brazil Office: Ministerio do Exercito, Rua Salustiano Silva 455, 21745 Rio de Janeiro Brazil

SAADI, GHAZI KAMEL, journalist; b. Acre, Palestine, Nov. 14, 1934; arrived in Jordan, 1977; s. Kamel Abdel-Hamid and Jamilah Abdel-Majid Saadi; m. Kulthoum Majed Fahoum; children: Ihab, Kamel. Journalist Al-Ra'i Newspaper, Amman, Jordan, 1977—; dir. Al-Jalil Pub. House, Amman, 1978—. Author books on Israeli-Arab conflict; translator political books. Mem. Palestinian Nat. Coun. Avocations: reading, swimming, walking, writing, ping pong. Office: University St, 11121 Amman Jordan

SAAIMAN, CONRAD IZAK, psychologist; b. Bloemfontein, South Africa, Dec. 14, 1959; s. Bart and Lynette (Gribble) S. B of Libr. Sci., U. Free State, South Africa, 1982, M of Psychology, 1985, PhD, 1993; higher edn. diploma, U. South Africa, 1988. Registered psychometrist. Career counselor Civil Svc., South Africa, 1986; sch. psychologist Dept. Edn., South Africa, 1986-88; sr. lectr. Vista U., South Africa, 1989—; therapist Aurora Drug Rehab. Ctr., South Africa, 1995—; presenter in field. Contbr. articles to profl. jours. Counselor Child Welfare, Bloemfontein, South Africa, 1989-98, Goldstone Commn., South Africa, 1994. Fellow APA; mem. South African Assn. Marital and Family Therapy (pres. 1995-99), Psychol. Soc. South Africa (vice chmn. 1995-99), Internat. Family Therapy Assn. Avocations: photography, mountaineering, Dachshund breeding, squash. Home: Ockie Geyserstr 8, Bloemfontein 9301, South Africa Office: Vista U, PO Box 380, Bloemfontein 9301, South Africa

SAAIMAN, NOLAN, auditor; b. Pretoria, South Africa, Dec. 21, 1960; s. Gerhardus Bartholomeus and Louisa Anna (Meier) S.; m. Anita Myburgh, Oct. 8, 1994; children: Wikus Myburgh, Jan Albert Myburgh. BComm in Acctg., U. Pretoria, 1982; BComm with honours, U. South Africa, 1988. Cert. internal auditor; cert. info. sys. auditor; cert. fin. svcs. auditor. Sr. internal auditor Post Office, South Africa, 1981-88; acct., adminstrv. of filial Van Wyk & Louw, Inc., South Africa, 1988-99; mgr.'s asst. info. sys. audit First Nat. Bank, South Africa, 1989-92; computer audit mgr. SA Eagle, South Africa, 1992-95; info. tech. audit mgr. SA Housing Trust, South Africa, 1995-97; audit mgr. Mercedes-Benz Fin., South Africa, 1997—. Contbr. articles to profl. jours. Mem. Inst. Internal Auditors (membership sec. 1996-97), Inst. of Dirs. South Africa, Info. Sys. Audit and Control Assn., Nat Assn. Fin. Svcs. Auditors. Avocations: computers, reading, jogging, theatre, stock exchange investments. Home: 26 Retha Ct, Veglaer St, Pierre van Ryneveld Park, Centurion, Gauteng South Africa Office: Mercedes-Benz Fin, 123 Wierda Rd, PO Box 10829, Zwart Kop, Centurion 0046, South Africa

SAAKANA, AMON SABA, writer, editor; b. Port-of-Spain, Trinidad, Dec. 16, 1948; arrived in Eng., 1965; s. George Edwin and Barbara (Kippings) Clarke;m. Seheri Sujai Stroude, Nov. 27, 1979; children: Kashta, Karama, Aniba. Diploma in Higher Edn., U. East London, 1985, MA, 1988; PhD, London U., 1995; diploma in Egyptology, U. London, 1997. Cert. Egyptology, Birbeck Coll., U. London, 1996. Editor, dir. Karnak House, London, 1977—; freelance journalist London, 1969-81; mem. convocation com. U. London, 1996—; vis. lectr. Manchester (Eng.) Met. U., 1992—, U. North London, 1998-2000. Author: Sun Song, 1970, Jah Music: The Evolution of the Jamaican Popular Song, 1980, The Colonial Legacy in Caribbean Literature, 1987, Colonialism and the Destruction of the Mind: Psychosocial Issues of Race/Class, Religion & Sexuality in the Novels of Roy Heath, 1996, Not the Black and White Coon Show: European Mythological Imaging of the African on the London Stage 1908-1939, 2000. Press officer Carnival & Arts Commn., London, 1976; com. mem. Greater London Arts, 1984, Caribbean Studies Centre Commn. Goldsmiths Coll., London, 1985. Recipient Rsch. award Greater London Coun., 1985, travel grant Arts Coun. Gt. Britain, 1991. Avocations: travel, esoteric knowledge, comparative philosophy. Home and Office: Karnak House, 300 Westbourne Park Rd, London W11 1EH, England

SAAKES, MICHEL, electrochemist; b. Waalwyk, The Netherlands, Sept. 13, 1960; s. Arie and Sya (Groeneveld) S.; m. Leny Johanna Adriana Lekkerkerk, May 14, 1999. Doctoral degree, U. Utrecht, The Netherlands, 1984, PhD in Chemistry, 1991. Promovendus U. Utrecht, 1984-88; electrochemist Tolgepast Natuurvetenschappelyk Onderzoek Environ. Scis., Energy Rsch. and Process Innovation, Apeldoorn, The Netherlands, 1988—. Contbr. articles to sci. jours. Office: TNO Environ Scis Energy Rsc, Laan Van Westenenk 501, 7300 AH Apeldoorn The Netherlands

SAAKOV, VLADIMIR SEMENOVICH, plant biochemist; b. Leningrad, USSR, Aug. 8, 1935; s. Semen Grigorjevich Saakov and Katharina Grigorjevna (Schönau) Parchomenko; m. Galina Alexandrovna Shirjaeva, Aug. 30, 1964 (div. Apr. 1979); children: Dmitry, Artemy; m. Tatjana Alexeevna Petrova, Dec. 25, 1987. PhD, U. Leningrad, 1963, DSc, 1990. Lab. asst. Komarov Inst. of Botany, Acad. of Sci. USSR, Leningrad, 1958-60, postgrad. tng., 1960-63, rsch. worker, 1963-68; head dept. Siberian Inst. Plant Physiology and Biochemistry Acad. Sci. USSR, Irkutsk, 1968-71; head rsch. group Biophys. Inst. Plant Industry, Leningrad, 1971-78, Lake-Rsch. Inst. Acad. Sci. USSR, Leningrad, 1978-82; head divsn. Sechenov Inst. Evolution Physiology/Biochemistry Russian Acad. Sci., 1982—; guest assoc. prof. Ctrl. Inst. Genetics and Agr. Plants, Acad. Sci., 1969-70, 76, 88; guest prof. Nuc. Rsch. Ctr., Karlsruhe, Germany, 1990-91. Contbr. over 220 articles to profl. jours.; patentee in field. Mem. European Acad. for Environ. Affairs (corr.), Russian Soc. Plant Physiologists. Home: Torzhkovskaja St 6-25, 197342 Saint Petersburg Russia Office: Russian Acad Sci Sechenov, Inst M Thorez Av 44, 194223 Saint Petersburg Russia

SAALFELD, FRED ERICH, naval researcher; b. Joplin, Mo., Apr. 9, 1935; s. Eric Arthur and Milla (Kessler) S.; m. Elizabeth Renner, Nov. 22, 1958; 1 child, Fred E. Jr. (dec.). BS cum laude, So. East Mo. State U., 1957; MS in Phys. Chemistry, Iowa State U., 1959, PhD in Phys. Chem., 1961. Instr. Iowa State U., Ames, 1961-62; chemist Naval Rsch. Lab, Washington, 1962-63, head mass spectrometry sect., 1963-74, head physical chm. br., 1974-76, supt. chem. divsn., 1976-82; chief scientist Office Naval Rsch., London, 1979-80; dir. rsch. Office Naval Rsch., Arlington, Va., 1982-87, dir., 1987-93, dep. chief naval rsch., tech. dir., 1993-98, exec. dir., tech. dir., 1998—. Author more than 500 publications, reports, presentations on applications of mass spectrometry to fields of combustion, laser, environ. analysis. Recipient Disting. Rank awards U.S. Pres., Washington, 1989, 96, Meritorious Rank award U.S. Pres., Washington, 1986, Robert Conrad award Sec. USN, Washington, 1988, Disting. Civilian Svc. award Sec. of Def./Dept. Def., 1999; named Fed. Exec. of Yr., Fed. Exec. Inst., Washington, 1991. Fellow AAAS; mem. Am. Chem. Soc. (councilor 1973-89), Am. Soc. Mass Spectrometry (sec. 1970-74), Combustion Inst., Chem. Soc. Washington (pres. 1972). Achievements include provision for science base for life support systems used in enclosed environments; development of educational programs used by USN for scientist training. Avocations: history, woodworking, sports. Office: Office of Naval Rsch 800 N Quincy St Arlington VA 22217-0002

SAAM, NICOLE JANINE, sociologist; b. Stuttgart, Germany, June 25, 1964; m. Christian Heinrich Goetz. MA in Polit. Sci., U. Stuttgart, 1989, PhD, 1995. Ast. rsch. planner Fraunhofer Gesellschaft, Munich, 1989-92; asst. prof. Ludwig-Maximilians-U. Inst. Sociology, Munich, 1993—. Author: Computer-Supported Theory Construction in the Social Sciences, 1996; contbr. articles to profl. jours. Mem. Internat. Sociol. Assn. Office: Ludwig Maximilians U, Konradstr 6, D-80801 Munich Bavaria, Germany

SAARELA, SEPPO YRJO OLAVI, scientist, educator; b. Oulu, Finland, Oct. 5, 1949; s. Erkki Olavi and Verna Marita Saarela; m. Leena Kaarina Haro, Aug. 31, 1971; children: Elina, Matti. MSc, U. Oulu, 1974, Licentiate of Sci., 1976, PhD, 1980. Ast. U. Oulu, 1974-76, 78-84, acting assoc. prof., 1977, 84, 86-87, acting prof., 1984; postdoctoral rsch. scholar Alexander von Humboldt Found., Marburg, Germany, 1983-84; asst. U. Oulu, 1987-89, sr. asst., docent, 1990—; vis. scientist Wesleyan U., Middletown, Conn., 1992, Fla. State U., Tallahassee, 1992; vis. scientist Health Sci. Ctr. at San Antonio, U. Tex., 1993. Pres., Youth Friends Assn., Oulu, 1995—. Alexander von Humboldt Found. grantee, 1983-84; sr. scientist Acad. of Finland, 1992-93. Avocations: cross country skiing, volleyball, ballroom dancing. E-mail: seppo.saarela@oulu.fi. Office: U Oulu, PO Box 3000, Oulu Finland

SAARELMA, HANNU J., graphic arts educator; b. Finland, July 14, 1948; s. Jaakko O. and Alma A. (Leppanen) S.; m. Mirjami K. Raitanen, Sept. 22, 1971; 1 child, Risto J. MS, Helsinki U. Technology, 1973, D in Technology, 1979. Rsch. assoc., prof. Helsinki U. Technology, Finland, 1972-79; sr. rschr. Acad. Finland, 1980-81; vis. scientist MIT, Cambridge, Mass., 1983; prof. Helsinki U. Technology, 1981—. Mil. engr. Finland, 1973-74. Grantee Fulbright Found., 1983. Mem. IEEE, Soc. Motion Picture and TV Engrs., Internat. Soc. Optical Engring., Soc. Image Analysis and Pattern Recognition, Soc. Image Sci. & Technology, Soc. Info. Display, Tech. Assns. Graphic Arts Industry. Home: Kalevankatu 40A3, 00180 Helsinki Finland Office: Helsinki U Technology, 02150 Helsinki Finland

SAARI, JUHANI HEIKKI, social services administrator; b. Helsinki, Finland, Oct. 6, 1946; s. Osmo Kalevi and Rauha Hilja (Sarkkinen) S. LLM, Helsinki U., 1969. Bar: Finland 1980. Compensation lawyer State Accident Office, Helsinki, 1971-79, sect. chief, 1979-81, dept. chief, 1981-86; sec. gen. Disabled War Vets. Finland, 1987—. Author: Indemnifications for War Disabilities, 1976, 3d edit., 1987; editor-in-chief Sotainvalidi, 1987—; contbr. articles to profl. jours. With Finnish Infantry, 1970-71. Recipient Finnish Lion's Knighthood, Knighthood Finland, 1992, War Disabled's Cross of Merit, Ministry of Def., Finland, 1997, Cross of Freedom 4th class Pres. of the Republic, 1999. Mem. Union Finnish Lawyers, World Vets. Fedn. (gen. rapporteur standing com. European affairs 1988—), Invalid Found. Orton (bd. dirs. 1988—), Prosthetic Found. (auditor 1991-95), Assn. Vol. Health, Social Welfare Orgns. Finland (v.p. 1992-94). Evangelical-Lutheran. Avocations: literature, languages, skiing, jogging, bicycling. Office: Disabled War Vets Assn, Kasarmikatu 34 A, 00130 Helsinki Finland

SAARI, KAARLO MATIAS, ophthalmology educator; b. Vaasa, Finland, July 19, 1939; s. Kalle Rikhard and Aune Annikki (Heinonen) S.; m. Ritva Myllyniemi, May 27, 1967; children: Timo, Jukka. Licentiate of medicine, U. Helsinki, Finland, 1964; D in Med. Scis., U. Helsinki, 1973; docent in ophthalmology, U. Oulu, Finland, 1975. Specialist in ophthalmology, 1973. Health officer Ilomantsi, Heinävesi and Laihia Communes, 1964-67; resident Helsinki U. Eye Hosp., 1968-73; head dept. ophthalmology Selkämeri Dist. Hosp., Kristinankaupunki, Finland, 1973-74; asst. head Eye Clinic Oulu Univ. Hosp., 1974-78; prof., head Tampere (Finland) Eye. Hosp., 1978-87; prof. ophthalmology, chmn. U. Turku, Finland, 1987—; founder, pres. The First Internat. Symposium on Uveitis, Helsinki, 1984, Xth Internat. Ergophthalmol. Symposium, Tampere, 1984; examiner in ophthalmology Bd. for Specialist Examination, Helsinki, 1985—; examiner European Bd. Opthalmology Diploma examination, 1996-97; coord. basic sci. assessment test opthalmology Internat. Coun. Opthalmology, Finland, 1996—. Editor: Ophthalmology, 1982, 83, 84, 95, 2000, Acta Ophthalmologica, 1984, Excerpta Medica, 1984; mem. editl. bd. Acta Ophthalmologica Scandinavica, 1979—. Standing expert of ophthalmology Bd. Evaluating Patient Damages, Ministry of Social Affairs and Health, Helsinki, 1984—. Lt. Finnish Med. Corps, 1966—. Recipient T.F. Schlaegel Jr.-G.R. O'Connor medal Internat. Symposium on Uveitis, Helsinki, 1984, Alpo Lahti medal Finnish Ergophthalmological Soc., Helsinki, 1984, Martti Liesmaa medal Finnish Ergophthalmological Soc., Tampere, Finland, 1985, Silver medal U. Naples, Italy, 1986, Arvo Oksala medal U. Turku, Finland, 1995. Mem. Internat. Uveitis Study Group (rep. Scandinavia 1980—), Internat. Ergophthalmological Soc. (rep. Finland 1982—, treas. 1990-95), Nordic Acad. Ophthalmology (founding mem.). Avocations: sailing, skiing, tennis. Home: Vähäjärvenkatu 21, 33900 Tampere Finland Office: U Turku Dept Ophthalmology, Kiinamyllynkatu 4-8, 20520 Turku Finland

SAARIO, VIENO VOITTO, lawyer, retired Finnish chief judge; b. Turku, Finland, Sept. 13, 1912; s. Gustaf Toivo and Amanda Aleksandra (Helvaara) S.; m. Arla Mirjam Orvokki Joro, Nov. 10, 1968; 1 child, Ritva Orvokki. Juris Candidatus, U. Helsinki, 1936, Juris Licentiate, 1944, LLD (hon.), 1972; diploma, Acad. Internat. Law, The Hague, The Netherlands, 1953. Bar: Finland 1944. Pvt. practice Helsinki, 1944-55; sr. cabinet sec. Finnish Ministry Justice, Helsinki, 1951-52; judge Finnish Ct. Appeals, Helsinki, 1955-65, chief judge, 1972-82; justice Finnish Supreme Ct., Helsinki, 1965-71; mem. Finnish del. UN Gen. Assembly, N.Y.C., 1956-57, 62-63, 72-77, 80; mem. subcom. on prevention discrimination and protection minorities UN, 1957-68; Finnish rep. UN Commn. Human Rights, 1961-71; Finnish del. ECOSOC, 1972-74; chmn. ILO Inquiry Commn., 1984-86. Contbr. articles to profl. jours. 1st lt. inf. Finnish Army, 1939-44. Decorated Cross of Liberty IV; knight 1st class and comdr. 1st class Order of White Rose Finland; comdr. and grand cross Order of Lion of Finland. Mem. Finnish UN Assn. (pres. 1967-68), Union Judges Finland (pres. 1973-80), Internat. Law Assn. (pres. Finnish br. 1974-77), Finnish Lawyers Assn. (bd. dirs. 1961-72). Lutheran. Avocations: music, painting. Home: P Hesperiankatu 13 B 25, 00260 Helsinki Finland

SAASTAMOINEN, JAAKKO JUHANI, research scientist; b. Helsinki, Feb. 28, 1951; s. Jouko Hiskias Saastamoinen and Anja Marjatta (Korhonen) Heikkinen; m. Anne Kristiina Rehula, Dec. 31, 1979; 1 child, Juho. MSc, Helsinki U. Tech., 1976, D in Tech., 1987. Asst. Helsinki U. Tech., Espoo, Finland, 1977-82; sr. rsch. scientist VTT Energy, Jyväskala, Finland, 1983—. Contbr. articles to profl. jours. Office: VTT Energy, Koivurannantie 1 Box 1603, 40101 Jyväskylä Finland

SAASTAMOINEN, PIRKKO MARKETTA, plant breeder, cereal researcher; b. Keitele, Finland, Aug. 7, 1947; d. Vilho and Aino Kyllikki (Kähkönen) S. MSc in Agr. and Forestry, U. Helsinki, 1975, PhLic in Genetics, 1986, PhD in Genetics, 1988. Asst. dept. plant breeding U. Helsinki, 1975-76, rschr., 1976, 78-79; rschr. Inst. Plant Husbandry Agr. Rsch. Ctr., Vantaa, Finland, 1977; rschr. Labsystems Ltd., Helsinki, 1977-78; rschr. Inst. Plant Breeding Agr. Rsch. Centre, Jokioinen, Finland, 1979-93, dep. dir., 1992-93; plant breeder Boreal Plant Breeding, Jokioinen, Finland, 1994—, dep. dir., 1994-99; breeder of several varieties of oat and pea. Contbr. articles to Cereal Chemistry, Jour. Cereal Sci., others. Decorated knight Order of White Rose Finland. Mem. AAAS, Societas Genetica Fennica, Sci. Agr. Soc. Finland, Scandinavian Assn. Agrl. Scientists, Eucarpia. Greek Orthodox. Achievements include breeding several varieties of oat and pea. Home: Turuntie 21 A 16, FIN-30100 Forssa Finland Office: Boreal Plant Breeding, FIN-31600 Jokioinen Finland

SAATCHI, CHARLES, communications and marketing company executive; b. June 9, 1943; m. Doris Lockart, 1973. Student, Christ's Coll., Finchley. Assoc. dir. Collett Dickenson Pearce, 1966-68; dir. Cramer Saatchi, 1968-70; founder, dir. Saatchi & Saatchi, plc, 1970-94; now ptnr. M & C Saatchi Agency, 1995—. Office: 15 Lower Regent St, London SW1Y 4LR, England also: 36 Golden Sq, London W1R 4EC, England*

SAATCHI, MAURICE (LORD SAATCHI), communications and marketing company executive; b. June 21, 1946; s. Nathan and Daisy Saatchi; m. Josephine Hart, 1984; 1 son, 1 stepson. BS in Econs., London Sch. Econs. and Polit. Sci., 1967. Co-founder Saatchi & Saatchi Co., 1970; chmn. Saatchi & Saatchi Co., plc, 1984-94; co-founder, chmn. M & C Saatchi Agy., 1995—; gov. London Sch. Econ.; Chmn. Royal Opera House. Mem. Royal Coll. Art (mem. coun.). Avocations: gardens, plays. Office: 36 Golden Square, London W1R 4EE, England*

SAAVEDRA WEISE, AGUSTIN, economist, political scientist, international consultant; b. Santa Cruz, Bolivia, Nov. 19, 1943; s. Agustin Suarez and Alicia Bloomfield (Weise) S.; m. Nancy Zambrana; children: Agustin Jr., Pablo, Diego. Lic. Econs., U. Buenos Aires, 1968; lic. Liencia Politica, U. Salvador, Argentina, 1974. 1st sec. Bolivian Embassy, Buenos Aires, 1972-76; minister counselor Bolivian Embassy, Chile, 1976-78, Buenos Aires, 1978-80; ambassador Bolivian Mission, Geneva, 1980-82; minister fgn. affairs Bolivian Govt., La Paz, 1982; exec. pres. Metropolitana (Bolivia) Ltda, La Paz, 1982-85, 86-88; chmn. bd., chief exec. officer Lloyd Aereo Boliviano, La Paz, 1985-86; internat. cons. Patiño Investments, Bermuda, 1988-89; amb. Bolivian Govt., Buenos Aires, 1989-93; internat. cons., 1993—; pub. Carta Nacional e Internacional newsletter; CEO, chmn. bd. dirs. Pvt. Banker's Assn., Santa Cruz, Bolivia; chmn. bd. dirs. Genex S.A.; vice chmn. bd. dirs. Emcos S.A.; lectr. Bolivian War Coll. Author 8 books on econs., polit. sci. and internat. rels.; contbr. articles to profl. jours. Mem. Bolivian Acad. Econ. Scis., Inst. Geopolit. Studies, Diplomatic Ctr. of High Nat. Studies, Circulo de la Union, Club de La Paz, Jockey Club. Roman Catholic. Office: Calle Rene Moreno # 258, Santa Cruz Bolivia

SABA, SHOICHI, manufacturing company executive; b. Tokyo, Feb. 28, 1919; s. Wataru and Sumie (Uemura) S.; m. Fujiko Saito, 1945 (dec.); children: Hiroko, Kazuhisa (dec.), Shunji. Grad., Imperial U., Tokyo, 1941. With Toshiba Corp., Tokyo, 1942-87, mng. dir., 1972-74, exec. v.p., 1974-76, sr. exec. v.p., 1976-80, pres., CEO, 1980-86, chmn., exec. officer, 1986-87, adviser to bd., 1987—; pres. Japanese Indsl. Stds. Com., 1994—; dir. numerous cos.; adviser Japan Fedn. Econ. Orgns., 1994—. Chmn. nat. bd. govs. Nat. Assn. Boy Scouts of Nippon, 1994—; chmn., bd. trustees Internat. Christian U., 1994—. Office: Toshiba Corp, 1-1 Shibaura 1-chome, Minato-ku Tokyo 105-8001, Japan

SABABI, MANAF, physiologist, researcher; b. Ardebil, Azerbaijan, Iran, Feb. 20, 1961; s. Hassan and Karimi (Sitare) S.; m. Malahat Manafova, Mar. 20, 1992; 1 child, Elvin. BSc in Pharmacy, Pharm. Faculty, Uppsala, Sweden, 1989; PhD in Physiology, Med. U., Uppsala, Sweden, 1995. Rsch. assoc. U. Uppsala, 1995-96; postdoctoral fellow Astra zeneca, Lund, Sweden, 1996—; chemist, Apotek Algen, Gallivare, Sweden, 1989-90. Mem. Scandinavian Physiol. Soc. Home: Parternasgränd 7 18, 226 47 Lund Sweden Office: Astrazeneca, PO Box 34, 221 87 Lund Sweden

SABANCI, SAKIP, holdings company executive; b. Kayseri, Turkey, Apr. 7, 1933; s. Haci Ömer and Sadika (Sapan) S.; m. Türkan Civelek, June, 1957; children: Dilek, Metin, Sevil. D of Mgmt., U. Anatolia, Eskisehir, Turkey, 1984; LHD, Hampshire Coll., 1986. Chmn. bd. Haci Ömer Sabanci Holdings, Istanbul, Turkey, 1967—; chmn. Chamber of Industry, Adana, Turkey, 1964-74, Izmit, Turkey, 1978, 84. Author: This Is My Life, 1985, From the Gallery of My Heart, 1987, Money, 1988, From Russia to America, 1989, Wage Bargaining or Sheep Bargaining?, 1990, Changing and Developing Turkey, 1991. Recipient award Gold Mercury Internat. Com., Cairo, 1979, Spl. Friends award Edward M. Kennedy, 1983; Rank of Commodore of Order of King Leopold II, 1982; named Hon. West Virginian, Gov. of Va., 1985, Good Will Amb., Mayor of Houston, 1989. Mem. Turkish Industrialists and Businessmen's Assn. (chmn. 1986—, chmn. supreme coun. 1987-89), Turkey Kinya Petrol, lastik ve Plastik San Isverenleri Sendikosi (chmn. supreme coun.). Office: Sabanci Holdings AS, Sabanci Ctr 80745 Y Levent, 80005 Istanbul Turkey

SABAT, KHALIL YUSUF, communications educator; b. Cairo, June 3, 1919; s. Yusuf Sabat and Heneinah Boutros Beheit; m. Dolly Charles Zananiri, 1964. Student, Greek Cath. Patriarchal Coll., 1925-38, Cairo U., 1938-42; BA in French Lit., 1942, MA in Journalism, 1946, MA in Edn., 1947, PhD in Journalism, 1954. Lectr. journalism Inst. Journalism, 1950-54; from asst. to assoc. prof. dept. journalism faculty of arts Cairo U., 1954-72, prof., 1972—, vice-dean facult mass comm., prof. emeritus; seconded dept. journalism U. Baghdad; expert Nat. Ctr. Rschs.; mem. High Press Counsel, Nat. Coun. Author: (in Arabic) History of Printing in the Arab East, 1st edit., 1958, 2d edit., 1966, Press Media, 1st edit. 1959, 6th edit., 1991, Advertising, 1969, 2d edit., 1987, Freedom of the Press in Egypt, 1973, Mass Media, Origins and Developments, 1st edit., 1976, 5th edit., 1987; transl. from French to Arabic, Jean-Paul Sartre's Les Mots, 1st edit., 1965, 2d edit., 1993, Sartre-a self-portrait, 1967; contbr. articles to profl. jours. Recipient Press Union award, Chevalier, Order Nat. du Mérite, France, Order of Republic, Egypt. Mem. Journalism Grads. Assn. Cairo, Gezireh Sporting Club. Avocations: stamp collecting, classical music, reading. Home: 33 Abdel Khalekh Sarwat St, Cairo Egypt Office: Faculty Mass Comm, Cairo U, Cairo Egypt

SABATHE, EMILE, NATO official; b. Fabrezan, France, Feb. 13, 1944; m. Claude Sabathe; 3 children. Student, French Air Force Acad.; grad., Tours AFB, 1967, War Coll., Paris. Commd. French Royal Air Force, advanced through grades to gen., with 2/4 squadron, then comdr 1st flight, 1968-78; dep. squadron leader, then squadron leader 2/30 squadron French Royal Air Force, Rheims AFB, 1976-78; commdg. officer of 1/94 bomber squadron French Royal Air Force, Avord AFB, 1979-81; flight safety officer Hdqrs. Strategic Air Force Command French Royal Air Force, Taverny, 1981-83; wing comdr. Strategic Air Force Tng. unit French Royal Air Force, Bordeaux-Merignac AFB, 1983-85; gen. inspector Air Force French Royal Air Force, 1986-88, comdr. Bordeaux-Merignac AFB, 1988-90; chief ostaff Tactical Air Force and 1st Air Region Command French Royal Air Force, Metz, 1990-92; dep. for Tactical issues to Comdt. Tactical Air Force French Royal Air Force, 1992-94; comdr. French forces Operation DENY FLIGHT French Royal Air Force, Vicenza, Italy, 1993; dep. comdr. Combat Air Force Command French Royal Air Force, 1994-95; jt. command French Armed Forces French Royal Air Force, French Guyana, 1995-97; asst. chie fo staff ops. French Ministry of Def., Paris, 1997-99; now mil. rep. of France to NATO Hdqrs., Brussels, 1999—. Decorated Legion of honor. Named Comdr. Nat. Order of Merit. Avocations: swimming, hunting, playing bridge, reading. Office: NATO Hdqrs, Blvd Leopold III, 1110 Brussels Belgium*

SABATIER, JEAN-MARC ANDRÉ, biochemist; b. Fontenay-Aux-Roses, France, Jan. 20, 1961; s. Roger Joseph and Anne (Bui Thi) S.; m. Dominique Alice Trystram, July 1, 1989; children: Alexandre Roger, Florent Christian. BS in Biochemistry with honors, St. Charles U., Marseille, France, 1983, Grad. degree in Biochemistry with honors, 1984; PhD in Microbiology with honors, Luminy U., Marseille, 1988; habilitation à diriger des Recherches in biochemistry with honors, St. Charles U., Marseille, 1996. Registered profl. engr., Marseille. Asst. prof. biochemistry U. Marseille, 1988-89; sr. rschr. Ctr Nat. de la Recherche Scientifique, Marseille, 1989—; sci. dir. Devel. of SPC3 for AIDS Therapy, 1993—; head rsch. group Peptides & Proteins: Structure-Function, 1999; cons. in field. Guest editor profl. jours.; patentee (18) in field. Recipient Citizen of Yr. award Nouvel Economiste, 1994, Neosystem award, 1995. Mem. Am. Peptide Soc. (charter), Am. Soc. Microbiology, European Peptide Soc., N.Y. Acad. Scis. Avocation: photography. Home: Chemin de Campbernard, 13790 Rousset France Office: CNRS-Lab de Biochimie, UMR 6560 Bd Pierre Dramard, 13916 Marseille Cedex 20, France

SABATIER, ROBERT, writer; b. Paris, Aug. 17, 1923; s. Pierre and Marie (Exbrayat) S.; m. Christiane Lesparre, 1957. Press positions French U., 1951-64; lit. dir. editions Albin Michel, 1965-72; lectr. La Souris verte, 1990, Le Livre de la déraison souriante, 1991. Author: Alain et le negre, 1953, Le marchand de sable, 1954, Le gout de la cendre, 1955, Les fêtes solaires, 1955, Boulevard, 1956, Canard au sang, 1958, Saint Vincent de Paul, 1959, Dédicace d'un naviere, 1959, La Sainte-Farce, 1960, La mort du figuier, 1962, Dessin sur un trottoir, 1964, Les poisons delectables (poems), 1965, Le Chinois d'Afrique, 1966, Dictionnaire de la mort, 1967, Les chateaux de millions d'annees (poems), 1969, Les allumettes suedoises, 1969, Trois sucettes a la menthe, 1972, Noisettes sauvages, 1974, Histoire de la poésie francaise des origines a nos jours, 1975, Icare et autres poemes, 1976, Les enfants de l'été, 1978, Les fillettes chantantes, 1980, L'oiseau de demain, 1981; Les années secrètes de la vie d'un homme, 1984; David et Olivier, 1986, La souris verte, 1990, Le Livre de la Déraison souriante, 1991, Olivier et ses amis, 1993, Ecriture, 1994, Le Cygne Noir, 1995; producer jour. La Cassette, 1987. Recipient Grand Prix de Poesie de l'Academie francaise, 1969, Antonin-Artaud prize, Prix Apollinaire for poems Les fetes solaires, French Nat. Merit award, 1997; decorated Commandeur de la Legion d'honneur, commandeur de l'ordre national du Merite. Address: 64 blvd Exelmans, 75016 Paris France*

SABATINI, LAWRENCE, bishop; b. Chgo., May 15, 1930; s. Dominic and Ada (Piloi) S. Ph.L., Gregorian U., Rome, 1953, S.T.L., 1957, J.C.D., 1960; M.S. in Edn., Iona Coll., 1968. Ordained priest, Roman Catholic Ch., 1957, bishop, 1978. Prof. canon law St. Charles Sem., S.I., N.Y., 1960-71; pastor St. Stephen's Parish, North Vancouver, B.C., Canada, 1970-78; provincial superior Missionaries of St. Charles, Oak Park, Ill., 1978; aux. bishop Archdiocese Vancouver, B.C., Can., 1978-82; bishop Diocese Kamloops, B.C., Can., 1982-99; ret., 1999; procurator, adviser Matrimonial Tribunal, N.Y.C., 1964-71; founder, dir. RAP Youth Counseling Service, S.I., N.Y., 1969-71; vice ofcl. Regional Matrimonial tribunal of Diocese Kamloops, 1978-82; chmn. Kamloops Cath. Pub. Schs., 1982—. Named Man of Yr. Confratellanza Italo-Canadese, 1979. Mem. Can. Canon Law Soc., Canon Law Soc. Am., Can. Conf. Cath. Bishops. Office: Diocese Kamloops 612 N Western Ave Chicago IL 60612

SABATO, HILDA IRIS, historian, educator; b. Buenos Aires, Sept. 19, 1947; d. Jorge Alberto Sabato and Lydia Añez; m. Carlos Eduardo Reboratti, Aug. 6, 1971; children: Julián, Andrès. Profesora de historia, U. Buenos Aires, 1976; PhD in History, London U., 1981. Rschr. Centro Investigaciones Sociales sobre el Estado y la Adminstrn., Buenos Aires, 1978-85; full prof. U. Buenos Aires, 1985—; rsch. fellow CONICET, Buenos Aires, 1985—; mem. Inst. for Advanced Study, Princeton, N.J., 1990-91; Ctr. for Advanced Study in the Behavioral Scis., Stanford, CA, 1998-99; adv. coun. mem. Program in L.Am. Studies, Princeton U., 1993-98; com. mem. Social Sci. Rsch. Coun., N.Y., 1993-96. Author: Capitalismo y Ganadería en Buenos Aires, 1989 (Second Nat. prize for history and archeology 1992), Agrarian Capitalism and the World Market, 1990 (Bolton prize honorary mention 1991), La Politica en las Calles, 1998; co-author: Los Trabajadores de Buenos Aires, 1992, Como fue La Immigracion Irlandesa en la Argentina, 1981; editor: Ciudadania politica y formacion de las naciones, 1999; mem. editl. bd. Punto de Vista, 1983—, Desarrollo Económico, 1993-98, Latin Am. Rsch. Rev., 1986-92, Jour. L.Am. Studies, 1995—. Recipient Second prize Internat. History award José L. Romero, Buenos Aires, 1981. Mem. Am. Hist. Assn., Club de Cultura Socialista. Office: Pehesa Facultad Filos/ Letra, Puán 480 of 418, 1406 Buenos Aires Argentina

SABBAGA, JORGE, oncologist, educator; b. Sao Paulo, Brazil, Nov. 3, 1956; s. Emil and Glaucia Fonseca Sabbaga; children: Paula, Julia. MD, U. of Campinas, Brazil, 1980. Intern Hosp. das Clinicas, U. São Paulo, resident in hematology; rsch. fellow in hematology/oncology Tufts U., Boston; resident Hosp. Clinicas U. of Sao Paulo; rsch. fellow Tufts U., Boston; asst. prof. U. Sao Paulo Sch. Medicine, 1989—; med. oncologist Hosp. A.O. Cruz, Sao Paulo, 1992—; rschr. Ludwig Inst. for Cancer Rsch., Sao Paulo, 1987-89. Office: Univ Federal Sao Paulo, R Botucstu 862 8o andar, 04023-062 São Paulo Brazil

SABBAH, ALFRED, immunologist; b. Beja, Tunisia, Apr. 26, 1935; arrived in France, 1950; s. Simon and Esther (Fitoussi) S.; m. Hélène Venuat (dec. July 1965); children: Claude, Eric (dec. July 1965); m. Denise Bellaigue, July 17, 1977. MD, U. Paris, 1965; CES Hygiene of Social, Sanitary Action, Rennes, France, 1968; CES Gen. and Applied Immunology, Angers, France, 1970; CES Fundamental Immunology, Inst. Pasteur, Paris, 1971. Cert. qualification allergy, qualification internal medicine, prof. Non-resident med. student Hosp. Angers, 1961, intern, 1964, chief clin. asst., 1968, chief works asst., 1973; head dept. allergy and clin. immunology U. Hosp. Ctr., Angers, 1980—; dir. cert. immuno-allergy U. W. France, 1973—. Author: Immunologie clinique et Allergologie; editor in chief Rev. European Annals Allergy and Immunology; contbr. articles to profl. jours. Fellow Can. Soc. Allergy (hon.); mem. Assn. Medicorum Bohemoslovacorum J.E. Purkyne (hon.), European Acad. Allergy and Clin. Immunology, Am. Acad. Allergy Asthma and Immunology, Am. Coll. Allergy, Asthma, and Immunology, N.Y. Acad. Scis., Soc. Allergy and Clin. Immunology W. France (pres.), French Soc. Allergy, INTERASMA. Avocations: swimming, classical music. Fax: 011.33.2.41.35.41.24. E-mail: alsabbah@chu-Angers.fr. Home: 8 rue Montauban, Angers Maine et Loire 49100, France Office: Dept Aller and Clin Imm, U Hosp Ctr, Angers Cedex 01 49033, France

SABBAH BENSIMON, RAYMOND, marketing executive; b. Casablanca, Marocco, June 20, 1957; s. Mauricio and Denise (Bensimon) S.; m. Edna Lerner, Sept. 5, 1979; children: Yonathan, Nethali, Alma. MA, Inst. d'Etudes Politiques, Paris, 1980. Trader Onex, Madrid, 1981-88; head rsch. Inverfinanzas, Madrid, 1988-89; sales mgr. Telerate/Dow Jones, Madrid, 1989-90; gen. mgr. Efecom S.A., Madrid, 1990-95; bd. mem. Excem S.A., Madrid, 1995-99; gen. mgr. Infomedas, Madrid, 1999—. Office: Infomedas Plaza Picasso, Av SA Torre Picasso Plt 23, 28020 Madrid Spain

SABBATINI, MARCELLO, journalist, motor sports weekly director; b. Teramo, Abruzzo, Italy, Oct. 20, 1926; s. Ezio and Norina (Guerrieri) S.; m. Maria Pia Fiore, Jan. 23, 1956. Student Faculty of Law, U. Rome, 1945-49. Head sports Il Paseo, Rome, 1949-54, Paese e Paese, Rome, 1954-58; dir. Autorama, Rome, 1959-60; head sports Telesera, Rome, 1960-61, chief staff, 1961-62; asst. editor Corriere dello Sport, Rome, 1963-65; dir. Automondo, Milan, 1965; chief staff Autosprint, Bologna, Italy, 1966-68; gen. mgr. Autosprint, Bologna, 1969-81, Motosprint, Bologna, 1976-81, Rombo, Rombo TV, Bologna, 1981-90; anchorman weekly motormagazine TV Cuore Rosso di TLRC, Modena; anchor Processo F.1 weekly TV show ODEON-TV. Editor news articles in field. Recipient numerous awards. Roman Catholic.

SABDENOV, KANYSH ORAKBAEVICH, research scientist; b. Chimkent, Kazakh, Nov. 24, 1964; s. Orakbay Sabdenovich and Gulzshakhan Kuralbekovna (Zaurbekova) S.; m. Polina Fyodorovna Matveeva, Apr. 26, 1989; children: Talgat, Chingiz. Physicist-Engr., Tomsk State U., Russia, 1990. Engr. Tomsk State U., 1990-95, candidate physics and math., sci., 1999; tchr. Tomsk Architecture Reconstruction Acad., 1995-96. Sgt. Mongolian mil., 1983-85. Mem. N.Y. Acad. of Sci. Avocation: sci. fiction. Office: Tomsk State U/Phys Tech Fac, 36 Lenin Ave, Tomsk 634050, Russia

SABELIS, HUIBERT, artist; b. The Netherlands, 1942. One-person shows include Shute Inst., London, Ont., Can., 1967, 71, Philippine Nat. Mus., Manila, 1972, Isetan Gallery, Tokyo, 1974, Can. Consulate Gen., L.A., 1977, Woodstock (Can.) Pub. Art Gallery, 1980, Gallery 3, Kampen, The Netherlands, 1981, Upcake Gallery, Fairfield, NSW, Australia, 1983, Karney-Daniels Gallery, Toronto, Ont., 1986, Galerie Jan J. Albers, Apeldoorn, The Netherlands, 1989, Kasteel Groeneveld, Baarn, The Netherlands, 1991, Gallery En Suite, Apeldoorn, 1995, Vispoort, Harderwijk, The Netherlands, 1997, Galerie Peter Bax, Sneek, The Netherlands, 2000; group exhbns. include Royal Ont. Mus., Toronto, 1971, Scan '74, Vancouver, B.C., Can., 1974, 1st Fgn. Artist in Japan Exhbn., Tokyo, 1977, DF Galeria Polyforum, Mexico City, 1980, Grimsby (Can.) Pub. Art Gallery, 1982, 34th Ann. Color and Miniature Print Biennale, Seoul, 1986, Collioure Galleries des Editions Universelles, Toulouse, France, 1988, Philippine Centre Gallery, N.Y.C., 1990, Ariel Croft Studio Gallery, Mansfield, Can., 1993, Shakai Kyouiki Ctr., Kariya, Japan, 1994, Galerie Kasteel de Essenburgh, Harderwijk, 1998, M&A Gallery, The Hague, The Netherlands, 1999, Mississauga Art Gallery, Can., 2000. Fax: (905) 567-0880. E-mail: mikes@tix.com. Studio: Atelier Symphony, 1136 Bancroft Dr, Mississaugua, ON Canada L5V 1B9

SABELLI, PAOLO ANTONIO, molecular biologist, agronomist; b. Siena, Italy, June 14, 1960; s. Giuseppemaria and Nanda (Mancianti) S. Laureate in agrl. scis., U. Pisa, Italy, 1985; PhD in Molecular Biology, U. Bristol, Eng., 1994. Rsch. tng. assoc. U. Tuscia-Viterbo, Italy, 1987-88; European Econ. Cmty. fellow Rothamsted Exptl. Sta., Harpenden, Eng., 1988-90; higher sci. officer U. Bristol, 1990-94; rsch. fellow Nat. Univ. of Singapore, 1994-97; rsch. assoc. U. Ariz., Tucson, 1999—. Contbr. articles to profl. jours., chpts. to books, papers to conf. procs. Served with Italian Air Force, 1986. Rsch. tng. assoc. fellow Internat. Inst. Tropical Agr., Nigeria, 1987, rsch. fellow EEC, Belgium, 1988. Avocation: photography. Office: Dept Plant Scis U Ariz Tucson AZ 85721-0001

SABER, HAFID, structural geology educator, researcher; b. Ouled Frej, Morocco, Jan. 7, 1963; s. Aomar and En-Nakhla (Oubannaceur) S.; m. Karima Daamouch, Dec. 24, 1993; children: Sara, Idriss. Lic., Cadi Ayyad U., Marrakech, Morocco, 1985, postgrad., 1986, Doctorat, 1989; Doctorat, Chouaïb Doukkali U., El Jadida, Morocco, 1998. Rschr., educator Chouaïb Doukkali U., El Jadida, Morocco, 1989—. Contbr. articles to profl. jours. Mem. Nat. High Tchg. Syndicat, 1990-99. Avocations: fishing, jogging. E-mail: hsaber@ucd.ac.max. Office: Chouaïb Doukkali U, Scis Faculty PC 20, 24000 El Jadida Morocco

SABETIAN, MANUCHEHR, consulting surgeon; b. Teheran, Iran, Jan. 8, 1928; s. Soheil and Maryam (Sabet) S.; m. Ann Marie Le Soliec; 3 children. MB BS, Durham U., Eng., 1954; ChM, Liverpool U., 1955. Sr. surg. registrar Royal No. and St. Marks Hosp., 1990; cons. surgeon London Welbeck Hosp., 1991—; past v.p. Iranian PEN in Exile. Founder, sec. Confedn. Iranian Students in Europe, 1960. Florence Jacobsen fellow U. Liverpool, 1960. Fellow Royal Coll. Surgeons Eng., Royal Col. Surgeons Edinburgh; mem. St. Marks Hosp. Assn., World Assn. Pancreato-Hepato-Biliary Surgeons, British Assn. Urological Surgeons (assoc.), The Sportsman, The Globe. Avocations: tennis, sailing. Home: 7 Boscastle Rd, London England Office: London Welbeck Hospital, 27 Welbeck St, WIM7PG London England

SABEY, JOHN LOUIS, pianist, song composer, beekeeper; b. Honolulu, Jan. 5, 1925; s. John Samuel Sabey and Anna Kamakahukilani Kawaiaea; m. Marylyn Momi Kaakimaka, Feb. 20, 1960 (dec.); children: Scott, Mark, Hanwell (dec.), Isaiah; m. Marjorie Mae Magee Humason, June 26, 1996. Studied with Furer, Hohu,, Vetlesen, Grimes, Feurring, 1933-57; student, U. Hawaii, 1942-47. Archtl. draftsman U.S. Naval Base Pearl Harbor, Honolulu, 1943-44; engring. aide, draftsman Hon. Bur. of Plans, Honolulu, 1948-50; cartographic drafting technician State of Hawaii Tax Maps Br., Honolulu, 1952-80; realtor assoc. David Chun (R), Aaron Chaney, Inc., Honolulu, 1974-80, Herbert K. Horita Realty, Inc., Honolulu, 1980-86, Banyan Realty, Inc., Honolulu, 1989-90; piano tchr. Maunalua Acad. Music, Honolulu, 1953-56; bass, tenor singer Cen. Union Ch. Choir, Honolulu, 1956—; singer with Honolulu Gleemen, tenor Honolulu Chorale, 1983—; accompanist for Waikiki Singers, 1995, for Mrs. McKendrick's Vocal Studio, 1984. Pianist in numerous bands including Ray Andrade's Band, George Nakama's Band, Rua's Band, David Paishon's Band, Bob Kojrma's Band, Ray Tanaka's Esquires, George Takushi's Big Band, 1943—, Monday Night Band, 1975—, Randalla Band & Dance Group, 1991—, Waikiki Swingers Band, 1992—. City Coun. (primary election), 1986; Ho. of Reps. (primary election), 1988; U.S. Ho. of Reps. 1st Dist. H. (primary election), 1990; deacon Cen. Union Ch., 1985-89; ch. organist Cath. and Protestant chapel, Camp Smith, USMC, 1991. Recipient 1st prize, 1980, 2d prize Hawaiian Song Contest. Mem. Hawaiian Govt. Employees Assn., Musicians Assn. Hawaii (life), Am. Fedn. Musicians (Local 677), Hawaiian Civic Club of Honolulu. Republican. Congregationalist. Avocations: volleyball, stamp collecting, swimming, tennis, skin-diving. Home: 99-1042 Kahua Pl Aiea HI 96701-3029

SABHANEY, AARTI HARNAM, public relations executive, journalist; b. Bandung, Indonesia, May 31, 1973; d. Harnam Weromal and Soni Harnam (Punjabi) S. BS, Sydenham Coll., Mumbai, India, 1994; diploma in mass. comms., Xavier Inst. of Comms., Mumbai, India, 1997. Prodn. exec. Percept Advt., Mumbai, 1994; mgr. corp. comms. Asia TV Network, Mumbai, 1995-98; pub. rels. officer Dabhol Power Co., Mumbai, 1998—; fl. mgr. Combined Artists The Miss World World Orgn., Bangalore; active Film and TV Inst. of India, Mumbai, 1991, active fin. journalist workshop Indian Inst. of Mass Comm., Mumbai, 1998; journalist The Times of India, 1998—; Indian corr. Southasia, Asia Cable and Satellite, 1997—. Editl. coord. Indic Abroad, 1998. Active The Social Svc. League, Sydenham Coll., 1993-94. Recipient Cert. of Merit Cuffe Parade Residents Assn., 1993-94, Best Dancer award The Performing Arts Soc., 1989-94. Mem. Nat. Sports Club of India, Cricket Club of India, The Radio Presidency Club, Assn. of Youth for a Better India. Avocations: reading Indian classical dancing, swimming, meditating poetry. E-mail: aartisa@hotmail.com. Home: 193 Jolly Maker 2, Cuffe Parade, Mumbai 400005, India Office: Dabhol Power Co Wokhardt Towers, Bandra-Kurla Complex, Bandra (East) Mumbai 400051, India

SABHARWAL, RANJIT SINGH, mathematician; b. Dhudial, India, Dec. 11, 1925; came to U.S., 1958, naturalized, 1981; s. Krishan Ch and Devti (An) S.; m. Pritam Kaur Chadha, Mar. 5, 1948; children—Rajinderpal, Amarjit, Jasbir. B.A. with honors, Punjab U., 1944, M.A., 1948; M.A. U. Calif, Berkeley, 1962; Ph.D., Wash. State U., 1966. Lectr. math. Khalsa Coll., Bombay, India, 1951-58; teaching asst. U. Calif., Berkeley, 1958-62; instr. math. Portland (Oreg.) State U., 1962-63, Wash. State U., 1963-66; asst. prof. Kans. State U., 1966-68; assoc. prof. math. Calif. State U., Hayward, 1968-74, prof. math., 1974-92, prof. emeritus math., 1992—. Author papers on non-Desarguesian planes. Mem. Am. Math. Soc., Math. Assn. Am., Sigma Xi. Address: 25179 Old Fairview Ave Hayward CA 94542-1355

SABIDO, ALMEDA ALICE, mental health facility administrator; b. Blairsville, Pa., Sept. 24, 1928; d. George Jackson and Dora Irene (Byrd) McClellen; m. Frederick Lionel Harrison, Feb. 1, 1963; children: Frederick L.H., Derek M. BS in Secondary Edn., Indiana U. of Pa., 1950; MSW cum laude, U. Pitts., 1958. Staff psychiat. social worker S.I. Mental Health Soc., 1958-63, supr. psychiat. social worker, 1963-66, asst. dir. psychiat. social work, 1967-69, dir. psychiat. social work, 1969-81, acting dir. Children's Community Mental Health Ctr., 1981, dir. Children's Community Mental Health Ctr., 1982-2000. Recipient Cmty. Leader Yr. award Nat. Coun. Negro Women, 1998. Mem. NAACP, NASW, N.Y. Urban League, Nat. Coun. Negro Women, S.I. Com. on Child and Adolescent Mental Health (pres. 1984-86), S.I. Mental Health Coun. (sec. 1982-84), S.I. Mental Health Soc. (Richard M. Silberstein award 1991). Presbyterian. Avocations: writing, reading, sports, music. Home: 142 Benedict Ave Staten Island NY 10314-2315

SABIN, JOHN ROGERS, physics educator; b. Springfield, Mass., Apr. 29, 1940; s. Henry Bowman and Elizabeth (Rogers) S.; m. Claudia Ball, 1963 (div. 1978); children: Peter Bowman, Amanda Ball; m. Birgit Horn, Aug. 8, 1987; children: Lene Elizabeth Horn, Niels Kristian Horn. AB, Williams Coll., 1962; PhD, U. N.H., 1966. Asst. prof. chemistry U. Mo., Columbia, 1968-71; assoc. prof. physics U. Fla., Gainesville, 1971-77, prof., 1977—, dir. IT Coll. Liberal Arts & Scis., 1998—; adjungeret prof. Odense (Denmark) U., 1992—; guest prof. Odense (Denmark) U., 1980-92, Nordita prof., Odense, 1982-83, Fulbright prof., 1986, 91. Editor Advances in Quantum Chemistry; assoc. editor Internat. Jour. Quantum Chemistry; mem. editl. bd. Croatia Chemica Acta, 2000—. Fellow Am. Phys. Soc.; mem. Am. Chem. Soc., Danish Phys. Soc. Home: 415 NW 23rd St Gainesville FL 32607-2618 Office: Univ Florida PO Box 118435 Gainesville FL 32611-8435

SABINE, PETER AUBREY, retired geologist, consultant, researcher; b. London, Dec. 29, 1924; s. Bernard Robert and Edith Lucy (Dew) S.; m. Peggy Willis Lambert, Apr. 13, 1946; 1 child, Cedric Martin Peter. BSc ARCS, Imperial Coll., London, 1945; PhD, London U., 1951, DSc, 1970. Ch. geologist; ch. engr.; FIMM. From geologist to prin. geologist Geol. Survey and Mus., London, Eng., 1945-59; chief petrographer Geol. Survey and Mus., London, 1959-70; asst. dir. Geolog. Survey & Mus., London, 1970-77, chief geochemist, 1977, chief sci. officer, 1977-84; geol. adviser pvt. practice Gerrards Cross, Eng.; mem. chem. and minerals bd. UK Dept. Trade and Industry, London, 1973-84, minerals and geochemistry coms., European Commn., Brussels, 1975-87; bd. dirs. West European Geol. Surveys, 1978-84; chmn. Internat. Commn. Systematics in Petrology, 1984-92, vice-chmn. 1992-96. Contrubutions to profl. jours. and geol. maps. number over 150. Fellow Brit. Cartograph Soc., Mineral. Soc., Geol. Soc. (sr. fell. 1994, sec. 1959-66, v.p. 1966-67, 82-84, Lyell Fund award 1955), Royal Soc. Edinburgh, Royal Soc. Arts, Am. Mineralogical Soc.; mem. The Athenaeum London. Avocations: gardening, geology, genealogy, furniture restoration. Home: Lark Rise Camp Rd, Gerrards Cross Bucks SL9 7PF, England

SABININ, KONSTANTIN DMITRIEVICH, oceanographer; b. Krasnoufimsk, Russia, Nov. 26, 1930; s. Dmitry Anatolyevich Sabinin and Elena Grigoryevna Minina; m. Irina Alexandrovna Abramova, June 12, 1960 (div. July 1969); children: Sergey, Dmitry; m. Galina Jgorevna Kozoubskaia, Dec. 19, 1969; children: Nikolai, Lubov. Degree in oceanography, Moscow State U., 1953; PhD, Shirshov Oceanology Inst., 1960, DSc, 1978. Asst. Moscow State U., 1953-61; head lab. Andreyev Acoustics Inst., Moscow, 1961—; lead scientist Space Rsch. Inst., Moscow, 1995—; mem. acad. coun. Moscow Stat U., 1990—. Author: Waves Inside the Ocean, 1992; contbr. articles to profl. jours. Grantee U.S. Govt., 1996-98; govt. scholar, Moscow, 1994-96, 97—. Mem. Russian Acoustical Soc. Home: Vernadsky prospect 38a #83, 117454 Moscow Russia Office: Andreyev Acoustics Inst, Shvernik St 4, 117036 Moscow Russia

SABINO, LARREA ERENO, agricultural economic company executive/ researcher; b. Basauri, Basque Co., Spain, Jan. 21, 1931; s. Larrea Ibarreche Ramon and Ereno Larrinaga Justa. Lic. in econs., U. Bilbao, Spain, 1971. With fgn. divsn. Banco Bilbao, 1949-65; with rsch. dept. BBV, Bilbao, 1966-92; chmn. Asmoa AiA, SL, Galdacano, Spain, 1993—; chmn. Coop. Galdacano, 1965-82; mgr. Mut. Assurance Co., Galdacano, 1969-94. Editor: El Campo mag., 1966-92; author: Agricultura, Horizonte 2005, 1998. Mgr. Andra Mari, Galdacano, 1955-73. Mem. Internat. Assn. Agrl. Economists, Internat. Fedn. Agrl. Journalists. Roman Catholic. Avocation: sports. Home: Chimelarre 2, 48960 Galdacano Basque C, Spain Office: Asmoa AIA SL, PO Box 77, 48960 Galdacano Basque C, Spain

SABNIS, RAM WASUDEO, research chemist; b. Bombay, June 21, 1961; s. Wasudeo Shridhar and Suhasini (Kulkarni) S.; m. Seema Ram, Oct. 19, 1994. BS in Chemistry, U. Bombay, 1982, MS in Organic Chemistry, 1984, PhD in Organic Chemistry, 1990. Rsch. fellow dept. chem. tech. U. Bombay, 1985-90; indsl. postdoctoral fellow, supr. Molecular Probes Inc., Eugene, Oreg., 1990-91; scientist N.C. State U., Raleigh, 1991-93; chief chemist U.S. Textile Corp., Lancaster, S.C., 1993-94; sr. rsch. chemist Brewer Sci., Inc., Rolla, Mo., 1994—; adj. asst. prof. U. Mo., Rolla, 1999—; reviewer Biotechnic and Histochemistry, Sulfur Reports, Biochemistry and Cell Biology, and Bioorganic Chemistry; symposia presenter and spkr. Author: (with others) Methods in Cell Biology; contbr. more than 70 articles to profl. jours.; mem. editl. bd. Textile Chemists and Colorists, 1996—, Jour. Textile Assn., 1996—, Colourage, 1996—. Fellow Ciba-Geigy, 1991-93, Dianippon Ink and Chems., 1991-93, NIH, 1990-91, U. Grants Commn., 1985-90. Fellow AIC, Am. Assn. of Textile Chemists and Colorists, Soc. of Dyers & Colourists (CCol cert.); mem. Am. Chem. Soc. Achievements include patents for ultra thin organic black matrix, use of haloalkyl derivative of reporter molecules to analyse metabolic activity in cells, fluorescent haloalkyl derivates of reporter molecules well retained in cells; rschr. dyes-

tuff, heterocyclic, polymer, medicinal chemistry, and biochemistry. E-mail: ram@rollanet.org. Office: Brewer Sci Inc 2401 Brewer Dr Rolla MO 65401-7003

SABO, EDMOND, pathologist, researcher; b. Piatra-Neamt, Moldavia, Romania, June 18, 1960; arrived in Israel, 1969; s. Alexander and Deborah (Roisman) S.; m. Karen Christina Drumea. MD, Med. Sch., Iasi, Romania, 1988. Internship Nahariah Hosp., Israel; residency Bnai-Zion Med. Ctr. and Tech. Sch. Medicine, Haifa, Israel; pathologist, head Image Processing divsn. Carmel Med Ctr., Haifa, 1990—; expert in computerized histomorphometry. Contbr. articles to profl. jours. Hochfeld's Rsch. Found. grantee, 1995. Mem. N.Y. Acad. Scis., Nat. Geog. Soc. Avocations: computer science, artificial intelligence, statistics, environmental sciences, cosmology. Home: Cremieux Str 6/8, 35436 Haifa Israel Office: Carmel Med Ctr, Michal Str 7, Haifa Israel

SABOLIC, IVAN, physician, scientist; b. Kljuc, Croatia, Jan. 15, 1950; s. Karlo and Jelena (Cabrajec) S.; m. Branka Fercek, Aug. 6, 1977; children: Ivana, Petra. MD, U. Zagreb, 1973, MSc, 1976, PhD, 1980. Univ. asst. Sch. Medicine, U. Zagreb, 1973-84, asst. prof., 1984-87, prof., 1987-91; rsch. fellow Mass. Gen. Hosp., Boston, 1991-93; sci. advisor Inst. for Med. Rsch. and Occupl. Health, Zagreb, 1994—; postdoctoral fellow Max-Planck Inst. Biophysics, Frankfurt/Main, 1981-84, rsch. fellow, 1985-86; vis. prof. Harvard Med. Sch., Boston, 1989-91. Contbr. more than 150 articles to profl. jours. Recipient FIRCA award NIH, 1995, 99, Croatian State award for sci., 1999. Mem. Am. Physiol. Soc., German Physiol. Soc., Croatian Biochem. Soc. Roman Catholic. Avocation: mountain climbing. Fax: 385-1-420-398. E-mail: sabolic@imi.hr. Office: Inst Med Rsch/Occupl Health, Ksaverska cesta 2, 10001 Zagreb Croatia

SABRA, AFAF SAYED, historian; b. Suez, Egypt, Dec. 14, 1944; d. Sayed Mohamed and Fatheya Mohamed (El-Maghreby) S.; m. Mohamed Mousa El-Tanbouly, Sept. 29, 1966; children: Amr, Hossam, Faisal. BA, Cairo U., 1965, MA, 1972, PhD, 1977. Instr. Cairo U., 1961-65, lectr., 1968-77; from asst. prof. to prof. Al-Azhar U., Cairo, 1977-93; prof. Coll. of Edn., Buraydah, Saudi Arabia, 1993—; vice-dean grad. affairs Coll. of Edn., Buraydah, 1994—; cons. for hist. rsch. Cairo U., 1990-95, advisor, examiner, 1984-99; nat. awards com. Ein Shams U., Cairo, 1990-95. Author: Studies in the History of the Crusades, 1985. Mem. Eqyptian Soc. for Hist. Studies, Saudi Soc. for Hist. Studies, Arab Historian Union, Nasr City Sporting & Social Club. Avocations: reading, music, teaching, travel, crafts. Office: Coll of Edn, Al-Safraa, Buraydah Saudi Arabia

SABRA, FUAD, neurology educator; b. Beirut, Feb. 13, 1919; s. Amin and Asma (Risha) S.; m. Ellen Badr (dec. 1971); children: Amin, George, Ramzi. BS, Am. U. Beirut, 1938, MD, 1943. Fellow Columbia U., N.Y.C., 1946-47; asst. prof. neurology Am. U. Beirut, 1948-52, assoc. prof., 1952-63, prof., 1963-89, hon. prof., 1989—, chmn. dept. internal medicine, 1963-67, head div. neurology, 1963-84, pres. Mid. East med. assembly, 1962-64; vis. lectr. Harvard U., Boston, 1963; vis. prof. Johns Hopkins U., Balt., 1968. Contbr. chpts. to books. Founding mem. Lebanese Soc. for Handicapped, Beirut, 1948, World Fedn. Neurology Rehab. Commn.; mem. devel. bd. Internat. Coll., Beirut, 1968. Decorated chevalier and officer Order of Cedars (Lebanon), Order of Holy Cross (Patriarch of Constantinople). Mem. Internat. Congress Neurology (pres. sect. on neurology 1969), Alpha Omega Alpha. Avocations: classical music, English literature, tennis. Office: Am U Beirut, Dept Neurology, Beirut Lebanon

SABRI, OSAMA, nuclear medicine physician, researcher; b. Berlin, June 14, 1963; s. Mohammad and Jutta (Schott) S. MD, Freie U., Berlin, 1988. Intern Berlin, 1987; resident Aachen, Germany, 1991-96; rschr. Inst. Anatomy, U. Bonn, Germany, 1989-91, Rheinisch-Westfälische Technische Hochschule, Aachen, Germany, 1991-96. Author: Spect in Neurology and Psychiatry, 1997 (Ludo van Bogaert award 1995), Brain Spect in Psychiatry, 1995; contbr. articles to profl. jours. Instr. martial arts; instr. biomechanics, med. injuries, martial arts Sondereinsatzkommando SWAT Team Police, Germany, 1995-98. Mem. AAAS, German Assn. Nuclear Medicine (Mallinckrodt award 1999, Brahms award 1999), Soc. Nuc. Medicine. Islam. Avocations: mathematics, physics, martial arts, biomechanics. Office: RWTH Aachen Dept Nuclear Med, Pauwelsstrasse 30, D 52057 Aachen Germany

SABRY, MOHAMED MONTASER FOAD, physicist, educator; b. Damanhour, Egypt, June 8, 1946; s. Foad Aly and Ensherah Mohamed (El Gewaily) S.; m. Amira Abd El Salam El Gabaly, Jan. 31, 1980; children: Ahmed, Tarek, Sally. Bachelor, El Kanater El Khairia, Egypt, 1963; PhD in Physics, 1976. Prof. Monofia U., Shibin El Koam, Egypt, 1977-95, Cairo U., 1995—. Peace fellowship, 1985-86, Fulbright fellowship, 1994-95. Mem. Am. Phys. Soc. E-mail: m montaser sabry@hotmail.com. Home: 4 Abd El Hai St, El Kanater Khairia Egypt Office: Nat Inst of Laser Scis, Cairo Univ, Giza Egypt

SABUI, TAPAS KUMAR, medical educator; b. Calcutta, India, July 25, 1958; s. Narayan Chandra and Sarama (Mondal) S.; m. Chandana Mondal, Jan. 16, 1990; chi ldren: Abhisek, Anusruti. MBBS in child health, Calcutta Med. Coll., 1982; diploma in child health, Ramkrishna Sevapratisthan, Calcutta, 1986; MD, Post Grad. Inst. Med. Edn. and Rsch., Chandigarh, India, 1988. House physician Calcutta Med. Coll., 1983-84; resident tchg. fellow Post Grad. Inst. of Medical Edn. and Rsch., Chandigarh, 1986-88; sr. registrar PGIMER, Chandigarh, 1989; clin. tutor Calcutta Nat. Med. Coll., 1993-99; asst prof., cons. Nilratan Sarkar Med. Coll., Calcutta, 1999—; jr. cons. Nat. Med. Coll., Calcutta, 1993-99; fellow neonatology Mater Mothers' Hosp., Brisbane, Australia, 1998. Contbr. rsch. articles to profl. jours.; mem. editl. bd. The Newborn, 1999—. Scholar Nestlé Nutrition Found., Switzerland, 1998. Mem. National Neonatology Forum (sec. subcom. 1999—). Avocations: music, photography, computers. Home: 35 S B Rd, 743144 Ichapur Nawabganj India Office: Nilratan Sarkar Med Coll divsn, APC Rd, 700014 Calcutta India

SACADURA, JEAN FRANÇOIS, engineering educator; b. Lisbon, Portugal, Sept. 18, 1941; arrived in France, 1959; s. Luis Mousinho and Klara (Ody) S.; m. Josiane Marie Guillaud, Dec. 31, 1969; 1 child, Eva Elisabeth. Dipl.Ing.Mech.Engring., INSA, Lyon, France, 1963, ScD, 1980; PhD in Engring., Fac. Scis., Lyon, France, 1969. Asst. INSA, Lyon, 1963-71, maitre-asst./assoc., 1971-76, maitre-asst. 2d. class, 1976-77, prof. 2d class, 1977-83, prof. 1st class, 1983-96, prof. class except., 1996—, dir. Thermal Sci. Ctr., 1997—; mem. Nat. Univ. Coun., Paris, 1987-99; expert DSPT8, French Min. Rsch., 1996-97. Author: Initiation aux Transferts Thermiques, 1979; co-author: Mesure Temp. par Rayonnement Thermique, 1981; co-author/co-editor proc.: Heat Transfer in Semitransparent Media, 1992; editor conf. book, 1996; contbr. more than 60 articles to profl. jours. Decorated Chevalier Palmes Academiques, French Min. Edn., 1986, Officier Palmes Academiques, 1998; recipient prize Academ-INSA, Paris, 1989. Mem. French Thermal Soc. (chmn. 1997—), European Conf. Thermophys. Properties (chmn. 1993-96), Univ. Thermal Group (founding mem. Eurotherm com. 1987-97), French Nat. Com. Sci. Rsch. Avocations: sailing, skiing. E-mail: cethil@insa-lyon.fr. Office: INSA-Lyon/CETHIL, B404 20 Av A Einstein, F69621 Villeurbanne Cedex, France

SACAK, MEHMET, chemistry educator, researcher; b. Kirsehir, Turkey, Jan. 15, 1959; s. Riza and Ayse (Türk) S.; m. Zehra Demirtas, Mar. 12, 1983; children: Ufuk, Utku. BSc, Ankara (Turkey) U., 1981, MSc, 1983, PhD in Polymer Chemistry, 1986. Rsch. and tchg. asst. Ankara U., 1981-86, asst. prof. chemistry, 1986-89, assoc. prof. chemistry, 1989-98, prof. chemistry, 1998—. Avocations: painting, music. Home: 7 Sokak No 14/10, B Evler, Ankara Turkey Office: Ankara Univ Fac Sciences, Tandoğan, 06100 Ankara Turkey

SACAL MICHA, JOSÉ, sculptor, educator, consultant; b. Cuernavaca, Mex., Sept. 25, 1944; s. Alberto Sacal Costo and Alicia Micha; m. Sylvia Farca, Mar. 25, 1969; children: Albert, Alice, Jacques. Student, Morelos U., Cuernavaca, 1961-63, Regional Inst. Fine Arts, Morelos, 1962-64, 69-72, U. Autonoma Mex., Mexico City, 1964-67. Dress designer Star Dance Factory, Mexico City, 1970-81; constrn. designer Vigilantes de Construccion, Mexico City, 1981-87; sculptor, Mexico City, 1972—; art gallery cons., Mexico City, 1987—; master tchr. sculpture, Mexico City, 1988—. Prin. works include monumental cast bronze sculptures Concierto, Miskolc Nat. Theater, Hungary, 1997, Knife, Lincoln Park, Mexico City, 1997, La Nota, Ocampo Theater Mex., 1998, cast bronze sculpture Eva, Fine Arts Mus. d'Unet, France, 1998, Hermanas San Esteban Park, Monterrey, Mex., 1999; one-person shows include Dube Gallery, Barcelona, Spain, 1996, Jardín des Arts Gallery, Paris, 1997, Menache Gallery, Mexico City, 1997, Pendulum Gallery, Mexico City, 1998, Jewish Comty. Ctr., Mexico City, 1998, Wansung Fung Gallery, Beijing, 1999; exhibited in group shows at Barcelona Fair, 1997, Bienal Contemporánea, Florence, Italy, 1997, Casa Turquesa Hotel, Cancun, Mex., 1997, Cámara de Diputados de Mex., Mex., 1998, Ipprodomo Della Capannelle, Rome, 1998, Palazzo Degli Afari, Firenze, Italy, 1998, Palazzo Beccio, Firenze, 1998, La Mision de Senecu Gallery, El Paso, 1999. Recipient Lorenzo il Magnifico gold medal Biennale Internat. Arte Conteporanea, Florence, Italy, 1997, Traphe'e du Grand Prix Mondial, Internat. Acad. Fine Arts, France, 1998, President's prize European Cultural Ctr. Florence, 1998, Italia per l'arte Spl. Prize from Jury, 1998, Autumn in Venice Excellence diploma, 1998, Victory Gold medal City Hall, Paris, 1999. Mem. Found. Mexican Artists, Mexican Enologic Group, Gourmet Wine Club. Jewish. Avocations: photography, culinary arts, enology, anthropology. Fax: (525) 540-1722. E-mail: studio@josesacal.com. Studio: Sierra Paracaima 505, 11000 Mexico City Mexico

SACCO, JOHN MICHAEL, accountant; b. N.Y.C., Oct. 17, 1952; s. Anthony Carmine and Angelina (Pellegrino) S. BS, St. John's U., 1974. CPA, N.Y. Staff acct. Price Waterhouse & Co., N.Y.C., 1974-75; semi-sr. acct. Seidman & Seidman, CPAs, White Plains, N.Y., 1976-77; sr. acct. Diamond Internat. Corp., N.Y.C., 1977-79, Burns Internat. Security Svcs., Inc., Briarcliff Manor, N.Y., 1979-81; acctg. mgr. Burns Integrated Systems, Inc., Briarcliff Manor, N.Y., 1981-83; pvt. practice White Plains, N.Y., 1978—. Mem. AICPA, N.Y. Soc. CPAs. Republican. Roman Catholic. Home: 197 Upper Shad Rd Pound Ridge NY 10576-2237 Office: 3010 Westchester Ave Purchase NY 10577-2535

SACCO, RICCARDO, mathematician, researcher; b. Milan, Mar. 13, 1962; s. Franco Sacco and Eugenia Arcuria. Degree in electronic engring., Poly. Milano, 1989; PhD in Applied Math., U. degli Studi, Milan, 1993. Postdoctoral fellow Poly. Milano, 1993-94, asst. prof., 1995—; postdoctoral fellow U. degli Studi, Milan, 1994-96; cons. ST-Microelectronics, Agrate Brianza, 1989-90. Author: Matematica Numerica, 1998, 2d edit., 2000, Numerical Mathematics, 2000. Avocations: playing piano and guitar. E-mail: ricsac@mate.polimi.it. Home: Via C A Pisani Dossi 12, 20134 Milan Italy Office: Poly Milano Dept Math, Via Bonardi 9, 20133 Milan Italy

SACHANSKA, TEODORA GEORGIEVA, biochemist, educator; b. Cradetz, Burgas, Bulgaria, Mar. 19, 1937; d. Georgi Todorov and Anastasia Anesteva (Dimitrova) Korukafov; m. Salio Varbanov Sachanski, Nov. 11, 1956; children: Elisaveta Salieva, George Saliev. Diploma in Chemistry, U. Sofia, Bulgaria, 1961; PhD, Higher Med. U., Sofia, 1972, DSc, 1987. Asst. prof. Higher Med. U., Sofia, 1965-74, fellow rsch., 1974-88; assoc. prof. Ctr. Hygiene, Sofia, 1988—, prof., 1997, head lab., 1992-97; lab. of assessment of functions under extreme impacts responsible for PhD postgrad. students; leader sci. team for studying extreme impacts on organism. Inventor method for vestibular resistance, method for prognosis of individual reactivity to brain hypoxy; contbr. articles to profl. jours. Recipient awards for inventions Inst. Sci. Studies and Innovations, Sofia, 1986, 87. Mem. Barany Soc. Sweden, Neurootological Equilibrium Soc. (otoneurological sect.). Mem. Orthodox Ch. Avocations: art, classical art, literature, sports, parachute diving. Office: Nat Ctr Hygiene, 15 Dimitar Nestorov St, 1431 Sofia Bulgaria

SACHAR, DAVID BERNARD, gastroenterologist, medical educator; b. Urbana, Ill., Mar. 2, 1940; s. Abram Leon and Thelma (Horwitz) S.; m. Joanna Maud Belford Silver, Aug. 29, 1961; children: Mark Benson, Kenneth Hulbert Belford (dec.). AB magna cum laude, Harvard U., 1959, MD cum laude, 1963. Diplomate Am. Bd. Gastroenterology, Am. Bd. Internal Medicine. Intern Beth Israel Hosp., Boston, 1963-65, resident in internal medicine, 1967-68; asst. chief clin. rsch. Pakistan-SEATO Cholera Rsch. Lab., Dhaka, Bangladesh, 1965-67; resident in gastroenterology Mt. Sinai Hosp., N.Y.C., 1968-70; from instr. to prof. medicine Mt. Sinai Sch. Medicine, CUNY, N.Y.C., 1970-92, 1st Burrill B. Crohn prof. medicine, 1992-99; dir. div. gastroenterology Mt. Sinai Hosp., N.Y.C., 1983-99, vice-chmn. dept. medicine, 1992-99, dir. emeritus, 1999—; co-chmn. work group on inflammatory bowel disease NIH, 1973-75; expert adv. panel on gastroenterology and nutrition U.S. Pharmacopeial Conf., 1980-85; chmn. rsch. devel. com. Nat. Found. for Ileitis and Colitis, 1984-89; co-founder, sec.-treas. Burrill B. Crohn Rsch. Found., N.Y.C., 1984—; K.H. Koster meml. lectr. Danish Soc. of Gastroenterology, 1992; Internat. State of the Art lectr. Falk Symposia, Germany, 1996, Belgium, 1998, Brit. Soc. Gastroenterology, 1998, World Congresses Gastroenterology, Austria, 1998, Italy, 1999, Turkish Soc. Gastroenterology, 1998, Hungarian Soc. Gastroenterology, 1999, Hellenic Soc. Gastroenterology, 1999; 20th ann. Norman Tanner Meml. lectr. St. George's Hosp. Med. Sch., London, 1997, 25th ann. Nana Svartz Meml. lectr., Örebro, Sweden, 2000; mem. Gastroenterology Leadership Coun. Task Force on Fellowship Curriculum, 1994; co-chmn. 40th ann. postgrad. course Portuguese Soc. Gastroenterology, 2000. Author over 170 articles and chpts. on natural history and treatment of inflammatory bowel disease; editor 7 books and monographs on gastroenterology. Trustee Bangladesh Coun. of the Asia Soc., N.Y.C., 1972-75, Bd. Edn., Englewood Cliffs, N.J., 1973-75. Sr. surgeon, comdr. USPHS, 1965-67. Recipient Jacobi medallion for Disting. Achievement, Mt. Sinai Alumni Assn., 1994, Alexander Richman Commemorative award for humanism in medicine, 1996, Norman Tanner medal St. George's Hosp. Med. Sch., 1997, Gold Headed Cane award, 1997. Fellow ACP, Am. Coll. Gastroenterolotgy (program dirs. com. 1991—, Henry Baker Presdl. lectr. 1989); mem. Am. Gastroent. Assn. (chmn. subcom. on cert. 1987, 1st chmn. clin. tchg. project 1984-90, mem. 1990-93, 98—, nominating com. 1993-94, chmn. immuno-inflammatory disorders sectional nominating com. 1995, Disting. Educator award 1996), Crohn's and Colitis Found. Am. (grants rev. com. and coun. 1990-94, Disting. Svc. award 1991, N.Y. Govs. medal 1992, chmn. clin. rsch. subcom. Disease Classification and Measurement 1994), Internat. Orgn. for Study of Inflammatory Bowel Disease (1st Am. elected chmn. 1989-92), Phi Beta Kappa, Alpha Omega Alpha. Achievements include co-development of oral rehydration therapy for diarrhea; development of resources and standards for clinical teaching in gastroenterology. Office: Mt Sinai Med Ctr One Gustave L Levy Pl New York NY 10029

SACHAROW, BEVERLY LYNN, gerontologist; b. N.Y.C.; d. Jules and Mary (Trupine) Levy; m. Stanley Sacharow, June 18, 1961; children: Scott Hunter, Brian Evan. BA, Rutgers U., 1980, M in Gerontology Edn., 1983, cert. ednl. gerontology, 1983. Rschr. U. Pa., Robert W. Johnson Hosp., New Brunswick, N.J., 1976-81; dir. Gerontology Inst. N.J., Milltown, 1983—, Gerontology Inst. N.J., Pa., N.Y., Milltown, 1996—; tour guide, rsch. leader, del. on tour of geriatric facilities, Moscow, Kiev and St. Petersburg, Russia, 1992; invited reporter White House Conf. on Aging, Washington, 1996; conf. planner in gerontology and health; cons. assisted living industry, long term care nursing homes, start-up divsn. of social work practice. Editor (newsletter) Update on Aging, 1983; video prodr. over 300 gerontology vide tapes, 1985—. Adv. com. mem. Gov. Conf. on Aging, Trenton State Coll., 1981; mem. adv. bd. East Brunswick (N.J.) Office on Aging, 1982; planner Brandeis U. Women Study Group. Mem. Am. Soc. on Aging (mem. press for nat. conf.), Nat. Coun. on Aging (mem. press for nat. conf.), Sigma Phi Omega. Avocations: travel, golf. Office: Gerontology Inst PO Box 345 Milltown NJ 08850-0345

SACHDEV, HARSHPAL SINGH, pediatrics educator, researcher; b. New Delhi, India, Aug. 13, 1955; s. Sohinder Singh and Surjit Kaur (Oaumi) S.; m. Jagjit Narula, Mar. 1, 1981; children: Sudeep Singh, Divya. MB, BS, All India Inst. Med. Scis., Delhi, 1977, MD in Pediatrics, 1981. Pediatrician Delhi Adminstrn., New Delhi, India, 1985-86; asst. prof. pediatrics Maulana Azad Med. Coll., New Delhi, 1986-89, assoc. prof. pediatrics, 1989-94, prof. pediatrics, 1994—; cons. Integrated Child Devel. Svcs., India, 1990—, UNICEF, India, 1992, 93, 97; expert mem. Indian Coun. Med. Rsch., 1992—; advisor WHO, Geneva, 1992. Editor: (books) Principles of Pediatric and Neonatal Emergencies, 1994, Current Concepts in Pediatrics, 1994, Nutrition in Children: Developing Country Concerns, 1994, Frontiers in Pediatrics, 1996; editor-in-chief Indian Pediatrics, 1994—. Recipient H.B. Dingley award Indian Coun. Med. Rsch., 1989; grantee WHO, UNICEF, Indian Coun. Med. Rsch., US Aid, 1990-97. Fellow Internat. Med. Sci. Acad., Indian Acad. Pediatrics (exec. mem. 1987— editor-in-chief, 1994, Rsch. award 1983, 85, 91, 94); mem. Indian Soc. Med. Stats (Rsch. award 1995). Avocation: badminton. Home: E-6/12 Vasant Vihar, New Delhi 110057, India Office: Maulana Azad Med Coll, Pediatrics Dep, New Delhi 110002, India

SACHDEV, PERMINDER SINGH, neuropsychiatry educator; b. Ludhiana, Punjab, India, July 27, 1956; s. Mohindar Singh and Swarn Kaur (Pasricha) S.; m. Jagdeep Kaur Bhatia, Mar. 19, 1986; children: Sonal, Nupur. MB, BS, All India Inst. Med. Scis., New Delhi, 1979, MD in Psychiatry, 1981; PhD in Psychiatry, U. NSW, Sydney, Australia, 1991. Cons. psychiatrist Otago Hosp. Bd., Dunedin, New Zealand, 1985-87; dir. Neuropsychiat. Inst., Sydney, 1987—; assoc. prof. neuropsychiatry U. NSW, Sydney, 1993-99, prof., 1999—. Author: Akathisia and Restless Legs, 1995; contbr. articles to sci. jours. Active Alzheimer's Assn., Australia, 1990—; mem. com. Tourette Syndrome Assn. Australia, 1987—. Fellow Royal Australia and New Zealand Coll. Psychiatrists (Organon sr. rsch. award 1995); mem. Internat. Neuropsychiat. Assn. (asst. sec.-treas.). Avocations: reading, chess, squash, travel. Office: NPI, Prince of Wales Hosp, Randwick NSW 2031, Australia

SACHDEVA, SATYA PAL, retired consultant anaesthetist; b. Gujranwala, India, June 3, 1931; arrived in Great Britain, 1963; s. Nathu Mal and Kaushalya (Bagga) S.; m. Meena Kapoor, Apr. 15, 1962; children: Rajiv, Vikram, Meetali. MBBS, Med. U. Panjab, India, 1955. Mem. Royal Coll. Surgeons, London, 1964; Fellow Royal Coll. Anaesthetists, Great Britain and Ireland, 1970. Resident house officer Dist. Hosp. Jullundur, 1955-56; registrar in gen. surgery Civil Hosp., Nahan, India, 1956-57; gen. practitioner Nairobi, Kenya, 1957-63; registrar in anaesthetics various hosps., various cities, Eng., 1964-70; sr. registrar in anaesthesia Karolinska and Södertälje Hosps., Stockholm, 1970-73; cons. anaesthetist Peterborough (Eng.) Dist. Hosp., 1973-96; ret., 1996; chmn. Peterborough Hosp. Dept. Anaesthetics, 1982-85, cons.-in-charge obstetric anaesthesia, 1989-92; tutor Royal Coll. Anaesthetists of Great Britain and Ireland, Peterborough, 1985-88. Divsnl. surgeon St. John Ambulance, Peterborough, 1985-90. Fellow The Royal Soc. Medicine London; mem. Assn. Anaesthetists Great Britain and Ireland. Avocations: fitness, promoting healthy living, discouraging reckless driving. Home: 73 Holywell Way Longthorpe, Peterborough Cambs PE3 6SS, England

SACHS, FREEMAN, retired management consultant, volunteer; b. Omaha, Nov. 28, 1921; s. Charles and Anna Behrendt Sachs; m. Auguste Erika Sachs, Sept. 26, 1947; children: Michael Eduard, Martin Gregor (dec.). Grad. h.s., 1939; student, U. San Francisco, 1961, 77, U. Calif., Berkeley, 1962, 75, San Jose (Calif.) State U., 1975. With U.S. Mil., 1942-78, Internat. Exec. Svc. Corps., Stamford, Conn., 1978-88; ind. rschr., exec. vol., 1988-98; mgmt. cons. Nat. Port Authority, Liberia, 1978, Cidade U., São Paulo, 1981, Guatemala, 1982, Empressa Nat. Portuaria, Honduras, 1983, Transp. Navieros Ecuatorianos, Ecuador, 1984, Intraship Kenya Ltd., Mombasa, Kenya, 1987, Sierra Leone Nat. Petroleum Co., Ltd., 1988. Recipient 9 Outstanding Performance and Achievement awards U.S. Army, 1964-78, 24 acknowledgments Dept. Def., U.S. industry. Lutheran. Avocations: shortwave radio, gardening, parrots. Home: 772 Montecillo Rd San Rafael CA 94903-3136

SACIRBEY, MUHAMED, ambassador; b. Sarajevo, Bosnia-Herzegovina, July 20, 1956; came to U.S., 1967; s. Nedzib and Aziza (Alajbegovic) S. BA, Tulane U., 1978, JD, 1980; MBA, Columbia U., 1981. Bar: N.Y. 1981. Atty. Booth & Baron, N.Y.C., 1981-83; fin. analyst Std. & Poor's Corp., N.Y.C., 1983-85; with fin.-investment banking Trepp & Co., N.Y.C., 1985-87; with investment banking Security Pacific Merchant Bank, N.Y.C., 1987-91; ptnr., cons. Princeton Fin., N.Y.C., 1991-92; permanent rep. of Republic of Bosnia-Herzegovina UN, N.Y.C., 1992-95; fgn. minister Bosnia and Herzegovina, 1995-96; permanent rep. of Bosnia and Herzegovina to UN, 1996—. Mem. N.Y. State Bar Assn. Muslim. Office: UN Republic of Bosnia-Herzegovina Mission 866 U N Plz Rm 580 New York NY 10017-1822*

SACK, BRIAN GEORGE, hotel executive; b. Bickley, Kent, Eng., Jan. 29, 1923; s. Thomas Jacob and Stella Mae (Blake) S. Student pub. schs., London, 1937. Gen. asst. Ministry Works, London, 1947-51; hotel trainee Node Hotel, Codicote, Eng., 1951-52; propr. Sharrow Bay Country House Hotel, Ullswater, Penrith, Eng., 1952—. Served as pilot RAF, 1943-46. Decorated mem. Brit. Empire. Mem. Royal Inst. Chartered Surveyors (assoc.), Hotel Catering and Instl. Mgmt. Assn. Conservative party. Mem. Ch. of Eng. Avocations: music, tennis. Home: Swarthfield, Ullswater, Penrith CA10 2ND, England Office: Sharrow Bay Country House, Shrrow Bay Country House, Ullswater, Penrith CA10 2LZ, England

SACK, RICHARD, education policy analyst; b. N.Y.C., Dec. 8, 1939; arrived in France, 1995; s. David Sack and Clara Kastner; m. Ghislaine Deprun, Dec. 16, 1996; 1 child, Julien. PhD, Stanford U., 1972. Exec. sec. Assn. for Devel. of Edn. in Africa, Paris, 1995—; cons. in field, Paris, 1981-95; bd. dirs. Adige, Paris. Editor: (book) Formulating Education Policy: Lessons and Experiences from Sub-Saharan Africa, 1996; author: (monograph) Management/organizational Audits of National Education Ministries, 1997; contbr. articles to profl. jours. Mem. Comparative and Internat. Edn. Soc. Fax: 33 145033965. E-mail: r.sack@iiep.unesco.org. Office: Assn Devel Edn in Africa, 7 rue Eugene Delacroix, 75116 Paris France

SACK, ROBERT DAVID, judge; b. Phila., Oct. 4, 1939; s. Eugene J. and Sylvia I. (Rivlin) S.; div.; children: Deborah Gail, Suzanne Michelle, David Rivlin; m. Anne K. Hilker, 1989. BA, U. Rochester, 1960; LLB, Columbia U., 1963. Bar: N.Y. 1963. Law clk. to judge Fed. Dist. Ct., Dist. of N.J., 1963-64; assoc. Patterson, Belknap & Webb, N.Y.C., 1964-70; ptnr. Patterson, Belknap, Webb & Tyler, N.Y.C., 1970-86, Gibson, Dunn & Crutcher, N.Y.C., 1986-98; sr. assoc. spl. counsel U.S. Ho. of Reps. Impeachment Inquiry, 1974; judge U.S. Ct. Appeals (2d cir.), 1998—; lectr. Practising Law Inst., 1973-97; adv. bd. Media Law Reporter. Author: Libel, Slander, and Related Problems, 1980, 2nd edit., 1994, CD-ROM edit., 1995, Sack on Defamation -- Libel, Slander, and Related Problems, 3d edit., 1999; co-author: Advertising and Commercial Speech, a First Amendment Guide, 1999; contbr. articles to profl. jours. Chmn. bd. dirs. Nat. Council on Crime and Delinquency, 1982-83; trustee Columbia seminars on media and society Columbia U. Sch. Journalism, 1985-92, N.Y.C. Commn. on Pub. Info. and Comm., 1995-98; v.p., dir. William F. Kerby and Robert S. Potter Fund; bd. visitors Sch. of Law, Columbia U., 1999—. Fellow Am. Bar Found.; mem. ABA (bd. govs. forum com. on comm. law 1980-88), Assn. Bar City N.Y. (chmn. comm. law com. 1986-89). Office: US Cir Ct 2d Cir 40 Foley Sq New York NY 10007-1502

SACKETT, DAVID HARRISON, electrical engineer; b. Syosset, N.Y., June 2, 1971; s. Robert H. Sackett and Bonnie-Jean Rohner; m. Hien Dieu Phan, Aug. 6, 1994; children: Tiffany Holly, Brendan Harrison. BS, Rochester Inst. Tech., 1994, MS, 1996. Devel. engr. Eastman Kodak, Rochester, 1995—; owner Pro Nails and Tan, Sassy Nails and Tan. Mem. IEEE, Soc. Profl. Engring., Lasers and Electro-Optics Soc., Internat. Soc. Optical Engring., Optical Soc. Am. Achievements include 1 U.S. patent. E-mail: dsackett@ieee.org. Home: 52 Angels Path Webster NY 14580-2299 Office: Eastman Kodak 6-81-rl Mc 02008 Rochester NY 14650-0001

SACKEY, JAMES KWAO NARH, education educator; b. Somanya, Ghana, June 21, 1942; s. Kwadjo Awannor and Dede Bornyaki; m. Victoria Asuamah Osafo, Jan. 15, 1968;; children: Anthony Kwabena, Agartha Korkor, Henry Kofi, Joseph Larwer, James Kwesi, Esther Esther. BEd with honors, U. Coll. of Cardiff, U.K., 1985; MEd, U. Brunel, 1995. Instr. Ghana Edn. Svc., Obo, 1966-70; head dept. Killam Tech. Inst., Ghana, 1970-77; tutor/coord. Kumasi Adv. Tech. Tchr.'s Coll., Kumasi, 1977-95; head dept. U. Coll. Edn. of Winneba, Kumasi, Ghana, 1995-98; dean applied arts and tech. edn. UCEW, Kumasi, 1998—; SNR resident tutor, Kikam Tech. Inst., 1970-77, exams. officer, 1970-77; farm mgmr. Adv. Tech. TRS Coll., Kumasi, 1977-95; examiner WAEC, Accra, Ghana, 1986—. Author:

(textbooks) Woodwork for Senior Secondary Schools, 1991, Metalwork Technology, 1996, Woodwork Technology, 1998. Mem. Ghana Ednl. Media and Technology Assn. (founder), Univ. TRS Assn. of Ghana, Ghana Nat. Assn. Tchrs. Avocations: tchg. God;s word and witnessing for Christ.

SACKMANN, INGE-JULIANA, astrophysicist; b. Schönau, Germany, Feb. 8, 1942; came to U.S., 1971; d. Emil Sackmann and Lilly Stelter; m. Robert Frederick Christy, Aug. 4, 1973; children: Ilia Juliana Lilly Christy, Alexandra Roberta Christy. BA, U. Toronto, Ont., Can., 1963, MA, 1965, PhD, 1968. Postdoctoral fellow U. Göttingen, Germany, 1968-69, Max-Planck-Inst. for Physics and Astrophysics, Munich, 1969-71; rsch. assoc. U. Hamburg Obs., Germany, 1971, Jet Propulsion Labs., Pasadena, 1974-76; rsch. fellow Calif. Inst. Tech., Pasadena, 1971-74, sr. rsch. fellow, 1976-81, faculty assoc., 1981—. Recipient Zonta Club award in math. and physics, 1961-62, Math. and Physics Soc. prize, 1962-63, AAAS award in math. and physics, 1962-63, McLennan prize in math. and physics, 1963-64, Loudon Gold medal in math. and physics, 1963-64, Chant award, 1963-64, Alexander von Humboldt award, 1970-71; co-recipient B'nai B'rith award, 1961-62; 1st alumni scholar U. Toronto, 1959-60, 60-61, Ont. scholar, 1959-60, 1st Alumni scholar, 1962-63, Gamma Phi Beta scholar, 1963-64, Nat. Rsch. Coun. Can. scholar, 1963-64, 64-65, 66-67, 68-69, 69-70; U. Toronto Open fellow, 1965-66. Mem. Internat. Astron. Union, Am. Astron. Soc., Orgn. of Women in Sci. Achievements include scientific findings in carbon creation, preditions of lively future of the sun. Avocations: children, flower arranging, growing organic garden, horseback riding, hiking. Home: 1230 Arden Rd Pasadena CA 91106-4146 Office: U Calif Inst Tech 1201 E California Blvd Pasadena CA 91125-0001

SACKMANN, MICHAEL FRANZ, medical educator; b. Munich, Mar. 18, 1955; s. Franz and Hildegard Sackmann; m. Jnge Hiegl; children: Florian, Quirin, Sebastian. MD, U. Munich, 1985, Privatdozent, 1990. Med. diplomate; diplomate in internal medicine; diplomate in gastroenterology. Asst. physician U. Munich, 1981-90, lectr., 1990-92, assoc. prof., 1992-97, asst. prof., 1997—. Editor: (book) Baillere's Clinical Gastroenterology, 1992; contbr. articles to profl. jours. Mem. Internat. Hepato-Biliary-Pancreatic Assn., Am. Gastroenterol. Assn., German Assn. for Gastroenterology (program coun.).

SACKS, ROBERT D., educational administrator, fund raiser; b. N.Y.C., Oct. 29, 1931; s. Robert and Hortense (Saperstein) S.; divorced; children: David Robert (dec.), Michael Alan. BA, Amherst Coll., 1953; MS, Juilliard Sch., 1956; postgrad., Columbia U., 1951, 52, NYU, 1959-62, U. Paris (Sorbonne), 1962-63. Instr. SUNY, Buffalo, 1963-65; asst. prof. Antioch Coll., Yellow Springs, Ohio, 1965-69; assoc. prof. Temple U., Phila., 1969-73; dean of faculty Phila. Musical Acad., 1973-75; assoc. dir. Transactional Dynamics inst., Glenside, Pa., 1976-82; exec. dir. Keswick Theatre, Glenside, 1982-84, Delaware Valley Coun. of Am. Youth Hostels, Inc., Phila., 1993-99; Mid. States Assn. Colls. and Schs. rep. in evaluation of colls. for accreditation/renewal of accreditation, 1974-75. Vol. Hoeffel for Congress, Montgomery County, Pa., 1996, 98, 99—, U.S. Senator Harris Wofford for Re-election, 1995; chmn. Amherst Coll. Vols. for Stevenson, 1952. With U.S. Army, 1957-59. Fulbright scholar, 1962-63; grantee Danforth Found., 1966-67, Ford Found., 1966-67. Mem. Nat. Trust for Hist. Preservation, Preservation Pa. Avocations: gardening, woodworking, water sports. Home: 627 Twickenham Rd Glenside PA 19038-2034

SACKS, RUSSELL BRIAN, translator; b. Port Chester, N.Y., May 26, 1950; arrived in Spain, 1977; s. Leonard Jay and Regina (Barclay) S.; m. Maria del Mar Nogal Castellanos, Aug. 27, 1986. AB in History & Spanish magna cum laude, Lafayette Coll., 1972; MA in Spanish with honors, NYU, 1980; BS in Computer Sci. magna cum laude, U. Md., 1986. Translator Ungria Patentes y Marcas, Madrid, Spain, 1973-75; translator Interlingua Translations, Vienna, Austria, 1975-77, East Grinstead, England, 1975-77; translator Internat. Commn. Southeast Atlantic Fisheries, Madrid, 1977-86, statis. officer, 1986-90; translator text of enhanced profl. info. Mem. N.Y. Acad. Scis., Amer. Translators Assn. (accredited Spanish-to-English), Phi Beta Kappa. Fax: 34916301326. E-mail: rsacks@teleline.es. Office: PO Box 94, 28230 Las Rozas de Madrid Spain also: Elzaburu SA, Miguel Angel 21, 28010 Madrid Spain

SACKSTEDER, THOMAS MICHAEL, corporate executive, entrepreneur, writer; b. Dayton, Ohio, July 27, 1950; s. Harry Pius and Mary Kay (Liebhardt) S.; m. Teresa Ann Nevius, Oct. 12, 1968 (div. Sept. 1980); children: Lori Ann, Kristi Marie, Julie Kay. Student, Sinclair Community Coll., 1968-72, Wright State U., 1972-73, Grand Valley State Coll., 1978-79; Lourdes Coll., 19945. Installer Western Electric, Dayton, 1968-69; sales rep. Smith Corona Mcht., Dayton, 1969-70; office mgr. Indsl. Machinery, Dayton, 1970-71; advisor Bell Pub. Rels., Dayton, 1972-73; sales mgr. Washington Nat. Ins., Dayton, 1974-81, Am. Fidelity Assurance Co., 1981-95; gen. ptnr. Innovative Benefits Resource Ltd., 1995—; gen. ptnr., Annuity Compliance Specialists, ptnr., Christopher Blake Family Wellness Assn., benefits cons. Ind. State Tchrs. Assn. Ins. Trust, Indpls., 1986-91. Bd. dirs. Mental Health Assn., Dayton, 1971-75, Good Samaritan Mental Health Ctr., 1972-75; campaign mgmt. for polit. candidates and issue oriented policies, 1972—. Mem. Ohio Assn. Sch. Bus. Ofcls. (legis. com. 1993-95), Assn. of Sch. Bus. Ofcls., Natl. Tax Shelter Annuity Assn., Employers Counc. on Flexible Compensation, Natl. Assn. of Life Underwriters, Buckeye Assn. Sch. Adminstrs., Jaycees, Kiwanis. Roman Catholic. Avocations: golf, swimming, writing, research. Address: Innovative Benefits Resource Ltd Annuity Compliance Specialists PO Box 70 Holland OH 43528-0070

SACRANIE, IQBAL ABDUL KARIM MUSSA, business executive; b. Zomba, Malawi, Sept. 6, 1951; arrived in Eng., 1969; s. Abdulkarim Mussa and Mariam Mussa (Osman) S.; m. Yasmin Ismail, Jan. 30, 1976; children: Sameena, Raheena, Hamza, Abdulkarim, Muhammed. Audit clk. Clark Whitehill, London, 1973-76, audit sr., 1976-78; fin. dir. Two Diamond Clothing Co., Malawi, 1978-81; dir. Global Pharms. Ltd., London, 1982-86; chief exec. Global Group of Cos., London, 1986—. Pres., trustee Memon Assn. U.K., London, 1992-95; advisor to home sec. Home Office U.K., London, 1986—; chmn., trustee Muslim Aid, London, 1995—; chmn. bd. trustees Balham Mosque, London, 1986—; mem. Inner Cities Religious Coun., London, 1993—; joint convenor U.K. Action Com. on Islamic Affairs, 1982—; sec.-gen. Muslim Coun. Br., 1998-2000; mem. Race Rels. Forum, 1998—. Decorated Order Brit. Empire. Fellow Inst. Fin. Acctg.; mem. Inst. Adminstrv. Mgmt., Family Welfare Assn. (v.p. 1998—).

SACRIS, EDUARDO MILAN, metallurgist, consultant; b. Cebu City, The Philippines, Apr. 14, 1937; s. Ponciano A. and Rosario (Milan) S.; m. Carolina N. Nemenzo, Dec. 21, 1963; children: Leland, Yael, Lyle, Carleen. BS in Metall. Engring., U. Of The Philippines, Quezon City, 1962; MS in Metallurgy, Stanford U., 1965, PhD in Metallurgy, 1969. Registered metall. engr., The Philippines. Instr. in engring. U. of The Philippines, 1962-69; metallurgist Atlas Mining, Toledo, The Philippines, 1969-78; group/divsn./gen. mgr. Benguet Corp., The Philippines, 1978-88, v.p., 1988-91, sr. v.p., 1991-92, exec. v.p., 1992-97; chmn. Bd. Metallurgy Examiners, The Philippines, 1983-88; chmn. Petrotech Cons., Inc., The Philippines, 1994-97, cons., MARED Grp. companies, 1999—. Contbr. articles to profl. publs. Co-organizer Relocation/Aeta Project, Sister Faustina, San Marcelino, Zambales, The Philippines, 1987-96. NSF fellow, 1967-69; recipient Outstanding Tech. Profl. in Metall. Engring. award Philippine Assn. Profl. Assns., 1987. Mem. ISO-TC183 (corr. ptnr.), Soc. Metall. Engrs. of The Philippines (life, pres. 1983, 85, 87, 91), Toledo Jaycees (pres. 1972). Senator, Jaycees. Roman Catholic. Avocations: machine shop practice, fish farming, photography, table tennis, tennis. Home: 31 Mabait St Tchrs Village, Quezon City 1101, The Philippines

SADAN, NAUM, pediatrician; b. San Salvador, Argentina, Oct. 14, 1919; arrived in Israel, 1951; s. Camilo and Rosa (Gueler) Sosnitzky; m. Rosa Boguslavsky, Feb. 18, 1950; children: Ariel, Eyal. MD, U. Nat., Cordoba, Argentina, 1948. Resident pediat. U. Childrens Hosp., Cordoba, 1948-51; pediat. Health Orgn. Labour Fedn., Beer Sheba, Israel, 1952-55; sr. resident dept. pediat. Ctrl. Emek Hosp., Afula, Israel, 1955-58, dep. head dept., 1959-62; dir. dept. pediat. Meir Hosp./Sapir Med. Ctr., Kfar Saba, Israel, 1969-86, cons. dept. pediat., 1987—; bd. dirs. Health Orgn. Tel Aviv, 1969-79. Pediat. fellow Johns Hopkins U., Balt., 1966-68, NIH, 1966, U.S. Army, 1967-68. Mem. Israel Pediat. Assn., Israel Pediat. Assn. (pres. 1976-78), N.Y. Acad. Scis. Mem. Labour Party. Avocations: swimming, sailing. Home: 76 Tel Hai, 44229 Kefar Sava Israel Office: Meir Hosp, Dept Pediat, 44281 Kefar Sava Israel

SADAQA, AHMAD SAEED, surgeon; b. Ober-Lisloom, Yemen, Oct. 30, 1933; arrived in United Arab Emirates, 1977; s. Saeed Ahmad and Haleema Hassam S.; m. Rokaya Mustafa Osman, Feb. 22, 1960; children: Salwa, Bassam. MB BCH, Cairo U., 1958. Med. officer health svc. South Arabia Fedn., Arabia, 1960-67; surg. specialist Health Ministry, South Yemen, 1970-77; surg. cons. Army Med. Svc., United Arab Emirates, 1978-89, retired, 1989; tchr. surgery Inst. Health Manpower, Aden, 1970-77; anatomist Faculty Medicine, Aden U., 1975-77. Fellow Royal Coll. Surgeons Glasgow, 1976. Avocations: geology, world geography, history. Home: PO Box 70277, Abu Dhabi United Arab Emirates Office: Surgical Dept, Zayed Hosp, Abu Dhali United Arab Emirates

SADEK, ALBER ALPHONSE, metallurgical engineer, educator; b. Cairo, May 12, 1956; s. Alphonse Sadek Tadrous and Isis Melad Khelah; m. Mervien Nouh Shokry, July 16, 1985; 1 child, Elizabith. BSc, Cairo U., 1978, MSc, 1983; PhD, Osaka (Japan) U., 1994. From rsch. asst. to lectr. Ctrl. Metall. R & D Inst., Cairo, 1980-96, assoc. prof., 1996—; expert on material selection and welding tech. UNIDO, Zambia, 1998, Internat. Inst. Welding, 1996-99; cons. in field. Contbr. articles to profl. jours. Mem. Japan Welding Soc., Egyptian Orgn. for Standardization. Avocations: music, reading, swimming. Fax: à-5011185. E-mail: rucmrdi@rusys.eg.net. Home: 5-B-3-2 15 May, Cairo Egypt Office: Ctrl Metall R & D Inst, PO Box 87, Helwan Egypt

SADEK, BILAND NIAZ, marketing executive; b. Beirut, Lebanon, Jan. 30, 1971; s. Niaz Behget and Jamal Mohamed (Ghorra) S.; m. Saila Nabil Jourdi, Nov. 21, 1998. AS in Bus. Mgmt., Beirut U., 1992, BS in Bus. Mktg., 1994. Internat. sales rep. Bdier for Timber, Beirut, 1992-95; asst. media dir. Arab Reach Media, Jeddah, Saudi Arabia, 1995-97; mktg. and rsch. mgr. Tihama Media, Jeddah, 1997-99; regional mktg. mgr. Al Hayat/Al Wasat, Riyadh, Saudi Arabia, 1999—. Chief Lebanese Scouts Assn., Beirut, 1982-91; founder Hariri Found. Alumni, Beirut, 1994. Mem. Internat. Advt. Assn., Gee Advt. Assn., Lebanese Am. U. Alumni Assn. Avocations: sports, classical music, movies, reading. Home: Diplomatic Quarter, Apt # 3 Bldg # 58, Riyadh Saudia Arabia Office: Al Hayat Newspaper, Olaya Main Rd 6890, 11537 Riyadh Saudi Arabia

SADEK, HASSAN SADEK, sculptor, educator; b. Cairo, Feb. 13, 1924; s. Sadek Sadek; married; 1 child. Diploma in sculpture, Acad. Fine Arts, Cairo; PhD in Ceramic-Sculpture, Prague, Czechoslovakia. Cultural attaché, councillor Egyptian Embassy, Berlin, 1969-73; dean Acad. Fine Arts Menia U., Egypt, 1976; prof. and head dept. sculpture Helwan U., 1976-79; art cons. Helwan U. mag. Exhbns. in Egypt, Europe, U.S.A. Recipient 1st Class award Egypt's Pres., 1985, others. Mem. Permanent Com. Profs. and Asst. Profs., Supreme Coun. Univs., Sculptors Soc. Avocations: classical music, photography. Address: 17 Brazil St, Zamalek Dist, Cairo Egypt

SADEK, SAMEH SAAD EL-DIN, physician, consultant; b. Meet Ghamre, Egypt, Oct. 28, 1958; s. Yousef Saad El-Din and Sameha Hosin (Ali) S.; m. Omneya Fawzi Zein El-Din, Sept. 5, 1991; children: Karim, Nourhan. MS, Faculty of Medicine, 1987, DSc, 1995. Diplomate Ultrasonography and Obstetrics/Gynecology, Family Planning Procedures, Laparoscopic Procedures. Rotary intern Faculty of Medicine, Alexandria, Egypt, 1983-84, assoc. lectr., 1989-95, lectr. ob-gyn., 1995-2000; assoc. prof., 2000—; resident Shatby Maternity Hosp., Alexandria, 1984-87. contbr. articles to profl. jours. Served Mil. Hosp., 1984-85. Avocations: music, readings, squash. Home: 225 Abd El Salam Aaref, Alexandria Egypt Office: Shatby Maternity U Hosp, Alexandria Egypt

SADH, GULAB MOHAN, export company executive; b. Mirzapur, India, July 20, 1936; s. Phool Mohan and Atar Dei Sadh; m. Memis Lata Sadh, Feb. 20, 1954; children: Sabine Kumari, Vinit Kumar, Sunit Kumar. BSc, Banaras Hindu U., Uaranasi, India, 1955. Import/export exec. Sadh Mathuradas Lachminarain, Mirzapur, India, 1956-59, 60-67; practicant George Grotjahn & Co., Hamburg, Germany, 1959, Hans R. Luer, Hamburg, 1960, Dahm & Co., Lunebur, Germany, 1960; proprietor Ajanta Internat., Dehi, India, 1968—. Treas. Bhandarh Com., Farrukhaead, India, 1970-73, Sadh Asmbh & Samaj, New Delhi, 1995—, Pine Garden Welfare Assn., New Delhi, 1997—; founder, trustee Sadh Phoolmonan Atardei Meml. Fund, Nidelli, India, 1995. Recipient 1st prize Dist. Athletic Assn., 1949. Mem. The Club. Avocations: pen friendship, stamp collecting, traveling. Home: B-10/7483 Vasant Kuns, New Delhi 110070, India Office: Ajanta Internat, A-29 Laspat Nagar II, New Delhi 110024, India

SADIE, STANLEY (JOHN), writer, editor; b. London, Oct. 30, 1930; s. David and Deborah (Simons) S.; m. Adèle Simmons, Dec. 10, 1953 (dec. May 1978); children: Graham Robert, Ursula Joan, Stephen Peter; m. Julie Anne McCornack, July 18, 1978; children: Celia Kathryn, Matthew David. MA, PhD, MusB, Cambridge U., Eng., 1950-56; LittD (hon.), Leicester U., Eng., 1982. Music critic The Times, London, 1964-81; editor Musical Times, London, 1967-87. Author: Mozart, 1966; Handel, 1962, Handel Concertos, 1972; co-author: Opera Guide, 3d edit., 1984; Stanley Sadie's Music Guide, 1986, Mozart Symphonies, 1987; editor: New Grove Dictionary Music and Musicians, 20 vols., 1980, rev. edit. 29 vols., 2000, New Grove Dictionary of Musical Instruments, 3 vols., 1984; joint editor New Grove Dictionary of American Music, 4 vols., 1986; editor: Norton/Grove Concise Encyclopedia of Music, 1988, History of Opera, 1989, New Grove Dictionary of Opera, 4 vols., 1992, New Grove Book of Operas, 1997; co-editor: Man and Music/Music in Society, 8 vols., 1989-93, Music Printing and Publishing, 1989, Performance Practice, 2 vols., 1990; editor Master Musicians, 1976—, Wolfgang Amadè Mozart: Essays on his Life and his Music, 1996. Chmn. Handel House Trust, 1994-96, pres., 1996—. Decorated comdr. Order Brit. Empire. Fellow Royal Coll. Music (hon.); mem. Royal Acad. Music (hon.), Royal Mus. Assn. (pres. 1989-94), Am. Musicol. Soc. (corr.), Internat. Musicol. Soc. (mem. directorium, pres. 1992-97), Critics' Circle.

SADIK, NAFIS, United Nations administrator; b. Jaunpur, India, Aug. 18, 1929; d. Iffat Ara and Mohammad Shoaib; m. Azhar Sadik, 1954; 5 children. Student, Loretto Coll., Calcutta, India, Dow Med. Coll., Karachi, Pakistan, Johns Hopkins U.; LHD (hon.), Johns Hopkins U., 1989, Brown U., 1993, Duke U., 1995; LLD, Wilfrid Laurier U., 1995; DSc (hon.), U. Mich., 1996, Claremont U., 1996; LHD (hon.), Philippines U., 1997; DSc (hon.), Long Island U., 1997; LHD (hon.), Nepal Tribhuvan U., 1998; DSc, Tulane U., 1999. Intern ob-gyn. City Hosp., Balt., 1952-54; civilian med. officer in charge of women's and children's wards various Pakistani armed forces hosps., 1954-63; resident physiology Queens U., Kingston, Ont., Can., 1958; head health sect. Planning Commn. on Health and Family Planning, Pakistan, 1964; dir. planning and tng. Pakistan Ctr. Family Planning Coun., 1966-68, dep. dir.-gen., 1968-70, dir.-gen., 1970-71; tech. advisor UN Fund for Population Activities, 1971-72, chief programme divsn., 1973-77, asst. exec. dir., 1977-87, exec. dir., 1987—; under-sec.-gen. UN, 1987—; sec.-gen. Internat. Conf. on Population and Devel., 1994, Soc. for Internat. Devel. (pres. 1994-97). Writings include: Population: National Family Planning Programme in Pakistan, 1968, Population: the UNFPA Experience, 1984, Population Policies and Programmes: Making a Difference: Twenty-five Years of UNFPA Experience, 1994, Lessions learned from Two Decades of Experience, 1991, Making a Difference: Twenty-Five Years of UNFPA Experience, 1994; contbr. articles to profl. jours. Recipient Hugh Moore award; Paul Harris fellow Rotary, 1997. Fellow Royal Coll. Ob-Gyn. Avocations: bridge, reading, theatre, travel. Office: UN Population Fund 220 E 42nd St Fl 19 New York NY 10017-5806

SADIKOĞLU, YILMAZ, medical educator; b. Ordu, Turkey, Feb. 12, 1955; m. Fatma Durmaz Birsen; 3 children. Degree, Med. Faculty, 1978. Head ENT Clinic, Erzurum, 1981-83, Adana, 1983-85; dir. Medicine Hosp., Manisa, 1994-95, ENT Clinic, Manisa, 1994-95; asst. A.U. Medicine Faculty, Erzurum, 1979-82, ENT specialist, 1982; asst. prof. Celal Bayar U., Manisa, 1994. Asst. dir. Unity Wakf, Adana, 1992-94, Çukurove Sci. Wakf, Adana, 1989—. Muslim. Home: Hüdevedigar Mah, Hakikat Sok Uykar3 Apt 20/9, Bursa Turkey Office: Sultan Mehmet Bulvari, Volkan St No 5/7, Bursa Turkey

SADLER, DAVID GARY, management executive; b. Iowa City, Mar. 14, 1939; s. Edward Anthony and Elsie June (Sherman) S.; m. Karen Sadler. Student, St. Ambrose Coll., 1957-59; BS in Indsl. Adminstrn. and Prodn., Kent State U., 1961. Various mgmt. positions Ford Motor Co., Lorain, Ohio, 1962-67, Sperry-New Holland, Lebanon, Ohio, 1967-71; mgr. mfg. Allis Chalmer, Springfield, Ill., 1971-72; dir. mfg. Purolator, Inc., Fayetteville, N.C., 1972-73; v.p. mfg. farm equipment and ops. truck div. White Motor Co., Eastlake, Ohio and Chgo., 1973-78; corp. v.p. mfg. Massey Ferguson Ltd., Toronto, Ont., Can., 1978-80; corp. v.p. mfg. Internat. Harvester, Chgo., 1980-81, sr. v.p. ops. staff, 1981-82, v.p. bus. devel., 1982, pres. diversified group, 1982-83, pres. internat. group, 1983-85; pres. AMI, Inc., Chgo., 1985-86; vice chmn., chief exec. officer Savin Corp., Stamford, Conn., 1986, chmn., chief exec. officer, 1986-89, also bd. dirs.; pres. Asset Mgmt. Internat., Westport, Conn., 1989-95; chmn., CEO, Rowe Internat., Grand Rapids, Mich., 1995-2000, also bd. dirs., 2000; CEO Merisel, Inc., El Segundo, Calif., also bd. dirs. Bd. dirs. greater Chgo. Safety Coun., 1981-84; mem. adb. bd. Hellmond Assocs. Opportunity Fund II. Roman Catholic. Home: 751 Bradford Farms Ln NE Grand Rapids MI 49525-3348 Office: Merisel 200 Continental Blvd El Segundo CA 90245-0984

SADLER, JAMES BERTRAM, psychologist, clergyman; b. Albuquerque, Mar. 29, 1911; s. James Monroe and Mary Agnes (English) S.; m. Vera Ellen Ahrendt, Apr. 10, 1938. AB, U. N.Mex., 1938; BD, Crozer Theol. Sem., 1941, ThM, 1948; MA, U. Pa., 1941, EdD, 1959. Lic. psychologist, S.D.; ordained to ministry Baptist Ch., 1941. Pastor First Bapt. Ch., Mt. Union, Pa., 1941-42; chaplain USAF, 1943-48; pastor Hatboro (Pa.) Bapt. Ch., 1948-61; chmn. dept. psychology Sioux Falls (S.D.) Coll., 1961-75; pvt. practice psychology, Sioux Falls, 1975—; cons. in psychology and religion. Contbr. articles to profl. jours. Mem. ministers coun. Am. Bapt. Conv. Mem. APA, Soc. for Sci. Study Religion, Masons, Rotary (pres. 1960). Home: 4312 Glenview Rd Sioux Falls SD 57103-4935

SADO, KIMITERU, hydrologist, researcher; b. Esashi, Hokkaido, Japan, Apr. 5, 1942; s. Tsurumatsu Ōta and Setsuko (Sado) S.; m. Yasuko Moriya, Mar. 5, 1971; children: Noriko, Eriko. D of Engring., Hokkaido U., 1983. Mech. engr. Hitachi Shipbuilding Co., Inc., Osaka, Japan, 1965-67; asst. Kitami (Japan) Inst. Tech., 1967-69, rsch. assoc., 1971-72, asst. prof., 1972-73, assoc. prof., 1973-84, prof., 1984—; cons. Hokkaido River Counsellor Com., Sapporo, 1987—; committeeman Lake Abashiri Water Quality Com., Sapporo, 1987—. Recipient award Hokkaido Soc. Civil Engrs., 1982. Fellow Japan Soc. Civil Engrs. (reviewer 1995—); mem. Internat. Assn. Hydrological Scis., Japan Soc. Hydrology and Water Resources, Internat. Water Resources Assn. Avocations: hiking, skating, driving, gardening. Home: Asahimachi 48-639, Kitami Hokkaido 090-0803, Japan Office: Kitami Inst Tech, Koen-cho 165 Civil Engring, Kitami Hokkaido 090-8507, Japan

SADOFSKY, MOSHE J., biochemist; b. Phila., Aug. 16, 1956; m. Susan Eagle. BS in Kife Scis., MIT, Cambridge, 1978, BS in Chem. Engring., 1978; MD/PhD, U. Pa., 1985. Cert. anatomic pathologist Nat. Bd. Surg. Pathology. Sr. staff fellow NIH, Bethesda, Md., 1985-96; asst. prof. Med. Coll. Ga./Inst. Molecular Medicine and Genetics, Augusta, 1996—. Scholar Leukemia Soc. of Am., N.Y., 1999. E-mail: moshe@immag.mcg.edu. Office: Medical Coll of Ga Augusta GA 30912

SADOFYEV, YURI GRIGORIEVITCH, physicist; b. Ryazan, Russia, Oct. 21, 1949; s. Grigori Nikolaevitch and Anna Tikhonovna Sadofyev; m. Elena Mikhailovna Fishman, Nov. 13, 1976; children: Sergey, Anna. Degree in engring., Radioengring. Inst., Ryazan, 1972; PhD, Inst. Semiconductors, Kiev, Ukraine, 1977, DSc, 1991. Jr. rschr. Radioengring. Inst., Ryazan, 1972-75; chief lab. molecular beam epitaxy Sci. Rsch. and Tech. Inst., Ryazan, 1978-95; sr. rschr. P.N. Lebedev Phys. Inst. Russian Acad. Scis., Moscow, 1995—; prof. microelectronics Radioengring. Inst., Ryazan, 1995—; sr. rschr. Gen. Phys. Inst., Russian Acad. Scis., 1991-99. Recipient for famed Russian scientists, Pres. of Russia, Moscow, 1995—; grantee Russian Found. for Basic Rsch., Moscow, 1994—. Home: 21 Zubkovoi St Apt 228, 39048 Ryazan Russia Office: PN Lebedev Inst RAS, 53 Leninsky Prospekt, 117924 Moscow Russia

SADOUN, HENRY H., international business developer; b. Fes, Morocco, May 19, 1929; came to France, 1956; s. Simon R. Sadoun and Simy Ben David; m. Huguette Hamou, Mar. 2, 1955; children: Marc-Vidal, Thierry, Philippe. Diploma, Ecole Superieure de Commerce, Paris, 1952, M in Internat. Bus. Adminstrn., 1970. Pres. Intermark, Paris, 1971-82; gen. mgr. Micro Sys., Inc., Paris, 1982-85; dir. Cos, Inc., Paris, N.Y.C., 1985-91; owner French Internat. Consulting, Paris, 1994—; co-founder Club Repreneurs d'Affaires, Paris, 1992-94. Dir. Lettre de Paris Doyen, 1999-2000. Mem. Lions Club Internat. (sec. 1994-99, pres. 1999-2000, Outstanding award, Merit medal, Internat. Presdl. medal for internat. leadership). Avocations: painting, graphics, music, handwriting analysis, travel. E-mail: hhsadoun@club-internet.fr. Office: French Internat Consulting, 18 Rue Duret, 75116 Paris France

SADOVSKII, MICHAEL V., physicist; b. Sverdlovsk, Russia, Feb. 25, 1948; s. Vissarion D. and Iraida M. (Polyakova) S.; m. Valentina I. Panasenkova, Aug. 28, 1974; children: Alexei, Sergei. MS, Ural State U., 1971; PhD, Lebedev Phys. Inst., Moscow, 1974, DSc, 1986. Postdoctoral rschr. Lebedev Phys. Inst., Moscow, 1971-74; rschr. Inst. Metal Physics, Sverdlovsk, Russia, 1974-86; head theoretical physics lab., dep. dir., prof. Inst. Electrophysics, Ekaterinburg, Russia, 1987—. Mem. Russian Acad. Scis. (corr.). Home: 8 Marta 2-24, 620077 Ekaterinburg Russia Office: Inst Electrophysics, Russian Acad Scis, 620016 Ekaterinburg Russia

SADOWSKI, JANUSZ BOGUMIL, physiologist, researcher; b. Poznań, Poland, Apr. 18, 1937; s. Michael and Irene (Pawiński) S.; m. Jadwiga Tolak, Oct. 20, 1964; 1 child, Joanna. Degree in medicine, Warsaw (Poland) Med. Sch., 1961; D Habil. Med., Polish Acad. Scis., Warsaw, 1974, MD, 1965. Cert. in internal medicine Polish Nat. Ministry of Health. Asst. prof. Med. Rsch. Ctr., Polish Acad. Scis., Warsaw, 1966-74, assoc. prof., 1974-87, prof., 1987—; vis. asst. prof. Ind. U., Indpls., 1967-68; scholar Found. Medicine Reine Elisabeth, Brussels, 1976-77; sect. editor Acta Physiol. Polonica, Warsaw, 1984-89; dep. dir. rsch. Med. Rsch. Ctr., Polish Acad. Sci., Warsaw, 1990-96; rschr. in field. Conbr. articles to profl. jours. (award Polish Physiol. Soc. 1974, Polish Acad. Scis. 1979, 93). Dept. leader Free Trade Union Solidarity, 1980-87. Named Hon. Citizen, City of Indpls., 1973. Mem. Internat. Union Physiol. Scis., Internat. Nephrol. Soc., Am. Physiol. Soc., Hungarian Physiol. Soc. (hon.). Avocations: world literature, highland hiking, canoeing, pastel painting. Home: Pułku Baszta 7 m 42, 02-649 Warsaw Poland

SADOWSKI, TOMASZ STANISŁAW, mechanical engineering educator; b. Lublin, Poland, Apr. 6, 1954; s. Ryszard and Romana Władysława (Radzikowska) S.; m. Jolanta Aurelia Smok, Aug. 30, 1986; 1 child, Marta. MS, Tech. U., Lublin, Poland, 1978; DSc, Inst. Fundamental Tech. Rsch., Warsaw, Poland, 1985. Asst. technologist Tech. U. Lublin, 1978-85, asst. prof., 1985—, head strength materials group and lab. faculty mech. engring., 2000—; rsch. asst. U. Ill. Chgo., 1987; vis. prof. Tech. U. Munich, Germany, 1991-93. Mng. editor Archives of Applied Mechanics, 1992-97; contbr. articles to profl jours. including Mechanics of Materials, Internat. Jour. Damage Mechanics. Grantee Tempus Phare, 1997, State Com. Sci. Rsch., Poland, 1997, 99, 2000. Fellow Polish Soc. Theoretical and Applied Mechanics, Polish Soc. for Composite Materials; mem. European Structural Integrity Soc., Soc. Applied Math. and Mechanics, Polish Acad. Sci. (solid mechanics sect. mechanics com. 1994—). Roman Catholic. Avocations: classical music, painting, gardening. E-mail: tskms@archimedes.pol.lublin.pl. Office: Tech U Mech Engring Faculty, ul Nadbystrzycka 36, PL 20618 Lublin Poland

SADRUDDIN, MOE, foundation administrator; b. Hyderabad, India, Mar. 3, 1943; came to U.S., 1964; m. Azmath Ourechi, 1964; 3 children. BSME, Osmania U., Hyderabad, 1964; MS in Indsl. Engring., NYU, 1966; MBA, Columbia U., 1970. Cons. project engr. Ford, Bacon & Davis, N.Y.C., 1966; staff indsl. engr. J.C. Penney, N.Y.C., 1966-68; sr. cons. Drake, Sheahan, Stewart & Dougall, N.Y.C., 1968-70, Beech-Nut Inc. subs. Squibb Corp., N.Y.C., 1970-72; founder, pres. Azmath Constrn. Co., Englewood, N.J., 1972-77; crude oil cons., fgn. govt. rep., 1977—; pres. A-One Petroleum Co., Fullerton, Calif., 1985-99; chmn. Azhar Found., Fullerton, 1989—; govt.

advisor Puerto Rico, 1980-82, Dominica, 1983-84, St. Vincent, 1981-82, Kenya, 1983-84, Belize 1984-85, Costa Rica 1983-86, Paraguay 1984-87. Chmn. Azhar Found., 1989—; involved in bldg. 11 charitable hosps. in India in maj. cities; mem. L.A. World Affairs Coun. Mem. Internat. Platform Assn. Address: Azhar Foundation 2656 Camino Del Sol Fullerton CA 92833-4806

SADUN, ALBERTO CARLO, astrophysicist, physics educator; b. Atlanta, Apr. 28, 1955; s. Elvio Herbert and Lina (Ottolenghi) S.; m. Erica Liebman. BS in Physics, Mass. Inst. Tech., 1977; PhD in Physics, MIT, 1984. Asst. prof. Agnes Scott Coll., Decatur, Ga., 1984-90, assoc. prof., 1990—, dir. Bradley Obs., 1987-97; chmn. dept. physics U. Colo., Denver, 1997—; adj. prof. Ga. State U., Atlanta, 1986-97; rsch. affiliate NASA/Caltech Jet Propulsion Lab., Pasadena, Calif., 1988-90, summer faculty fellow, 1987, 88. Contbr. articles to Nature, Astrophys. Jour., Astron. Jour., Publ. Aston. Soc. of the Pacific, Astrophys. Letters and Communications. Mem. Am. Jewish Com., Atlanta, 1984—. Fellow Royal Astron. Soc.; mem. Internat. Astron. Union, Am. Astron. Soc., N.Y. Acad. Scis. Achievements include relocation of Agnes Scott College's telescope to Hard Labor Creek Observatory. Home: 90 S Ivy St Denver CO 80224-1023 Office: U Colo-Denver Dept Physics PO Box 173364 Denver CO 80217-3364

SADUN, LORENZO ADLAI, mathematician; b. Silver Spring, Md., Nov. 3, 1960; s. Elvio Herbert and Lina Amelia (Ottolenghi) S.; m. Anita Elizabeth Glazer, Sept. 4, 1988; children: Rina Ellen, Allan Elvio, Jonathan Richard. BS, MIT, 1981; MA, U. Calif., 1982, PhD, 1987. Rsch. instr. Calif. Tech. Math. Dept., Pasadena, 1987-89; Courant instr. Courant Inst. Math. Scis., N.Y.C., 1989-91; asst. prof. U. Tex., Austin, 1991-97, assoc. prof., 1997—. Contbr. articles to profl. publs. Home: 1706 W 30th St Austin TX 78703-1824 Office: U Tex Math Dept Austin TX 78712

SADYKOV, VLADISLAV ALEXANDROVICH, research laboratory administrator, educator; b. Kytmanovo, Altai, Russia, Feb. 4, 1951; s. Alexandr Grigoryevich and Alexandra Alexeevna (Kruglikova) S.; m. Valentina Ivanovna Mikhailova, July 11, 1972; children: Elizavela, Yana. Diploma of high edn., Novosibirsk (Russia) State U., 1973, PhD, 1979; prof. degree, 1999. Rsch. fellow Inst. Catalysis, Novosibirsk, 1973-75, jr. rschr., 1975-85, sr. rschr., 1985-91, head of lab., 1991—; asst. Novosibirsk State U., 1979-93, assoc. prof., 1993-00, prof. 2000—. Contbr. articles to profl. jours. Grantee Internat. Sci. Found., 1994, Russian Fund of Basic Rsch., 1995, INTAS, 1999; recipient Russian Govt. awd. in Sci. and Tech., 1999. Mem. Materials Rsch. Soc. Russian Orthodox. Avocations: foreign languages, gardening. Home: Tereshkovoi 2 app 48, 630090 Novosibirsk Russia Office: Boreskov Inst Catalysis, br Lavrentieva 5, 630090 Novosibirsk Russia

SADYKOVA, VERA PHILIPPOVNA, librarian, educator; b. Dneprostroy, Zaporozhie, Ukraine, Mar. 4, 1933; arrived in Kazakhstan, 1947; d. Yabtchenko and (Phesik) Philipp; m. Albert Sadykov, May, 13, 1956; children: Aleksey, Gennady. Grad., Kazakh State U., Alma-Ata, 1957, Inst. Culture, Leningrad, Russia, 1966. Cert. libr., philologist. Libr. Sci. and Tech. Libr. Kazakhstan, Almaty, 1960-62, asst. dir., 1964-65, dir., 1965-88, chief libr., 1988-94, mgr. sci.-methodical dept., 1962-64, 94—, instr. advanced courses, 1962—, head sci. rsch. sector, 1998; instr. advanced courses Kazakh State Inst. Sci. and Tech. Info., Almaty, 1962—. Author brochures; mem. editl. bd. Nautchnie i Technitcheskie Biblioteki, 1990-91; contbr. articles to profl. jours. Mem. presidium Trade Unions Com. of State Instns. Ofcls., Almaty, 1971-86. Recipient medals and hon. degree Honoured Worker of Kazakh Soviet Socialist Republic, Presidium of Supreme Soviet USSR, 1970, 83, 84, bronze medals Exhbn. Econ. Achievements of USSR, 1969, 74, 81. Avocations: collecting books, gardening. Office: Sci & Tech Libr Kazakhstan, S Mukanov 223B, 480077 Almaty Kazakhstan

SAEBO, ARVE, gastroenterological surgeon; b. Molde, Norway, Mar. 19, 1939; s. Asbjoern and Borghild (Oterholm) S.; m. Brit Olene Friestad, July 31, 1965; children: Asbjoern, Oystein, Sindre. Grad., Molde Gymnasium, 1958; MD, U. Oslo, 1966; DMS, U. Bergen, 1995. Diplomate in Gen. Surgery, Gastroenterol. Surgery. Resident Kristiansund County Hosp., Norway, 1968-70, Voss County Hosp., Norway, 1970-72, Akershus Ctr. Hosp., Nordbyhagen, Norway, 1972-76; cons. Lillestrom (Norway) Hosp., 1976-77; sr. resident Bergen (Norway) Univ. Hosp., 1977-81; cons. Bergen Casualty Dept., 1981-84, Volda County Hosp., Norway, 1984-85, Laksevag Hosp., Bergen, 1985-88, Molde County Hosp., Norway, 1988—. Cpl. Norwegian Royal Guard, 1959. Mem. Norwegian Surg. Soc., Nordic Surg. Soc., N.Y. Acad. Scis. Lutheran. Avocations: countryside cottage, photography, painting. Office: Molde County Hosp, Dept Surgery, N-6400 Molde Norway

SAEE, JOHN, social psychologist and international economics management scholar; b. Panjsher, Afghanistan, Sept. 12, 1959; arrived in Australia with family, 1962; s. Bibi Khanum and Qamardin Saee. BA in Social Scis., Flinders U., Adelaide, Australia, 1980; M in Commerce, U. New South Wales, Sydney, Australia, 1983; PhD in Internat. Bus., U. Tech., Sydney, 1998. Exec. officer NSW C. of C., Sydney, Australia, 1983-84; mgr. sys. and user support AMP, Sydney, Australia, 1984-87; group gen. mgr. Sentry and ACC Co., Sydney, Australia, 1987-88; prin. coll. dir. Australian Coll. Mgmt., Sydney, Australia, 1988-90; prof. mgmt. and internat. bus. Mgmt. and Internat. Bus. U. Western Sydney, Australia, 1990-96; internat. linkages and course dir. U. Western Sydney, Australia, 1996—; dir. Sydney Mgmt. Devel. Ctr., 1994—; chmn. Global Instn. Divsns., Assn. Mgmt. and Internat. Assn. Mgmt.-USA. Author 2 books; editl. mem. Jour. Mgmt. Sys.; sr. editor Internat. Assn. Mgmt. Jour.; contbr. over 60 articles to profl. jours. Fellow Internat. Bibliog. Assn., Australian Inst. Mgmt. (assoc.); mem. Acad. Internat. Bus. Avocations: travel, reading, cultural activation, tennis. Home: 14 Picton St Quakers Hill, Sydney 2763, Australia Office: U Western Sydney Fac Mgmt, Eastern Rd, Quakers Hill Australia

SAEED, ARSHAD, financial consultant; b. Lahore, Punjab, Pakistan, Aug. 17, 1950; s. Mohd and Zubaida Saeed; m. Lalarukh Saeed, Apr. 29, 1982; children: Mahjabeen, Maham, Sulaiman. B of Commerce, Concordia U., Montreal, Can., 1976; MBA, Nat. U., San Diego, 1981. Sr. auditor Crawford & Co., Montreal, 1976-79; cons. Govt. Alta., Edmonton, Can., 1982-85; mgr. fin. Fin. Industries, Lahore, Pakistan, 1985-90, dir., 1990-95; fin. cons. Saeed Assocs., Lahore, 1995—. Home: 1486 A-3 Nagi Rd, Lahore Cantt Punjab, Pakistan Office: 381/9 Sarfaraz Rafiqi Rd, Lahore Cantt Pakistan

SAEED, HAYDER MOHAMED, structural engineering researcher; b. Khartoum, Sudan, Oct. 7, 1962; s. Mohamed Saeed Alkoda and Asya Ali Ahmed; m. Maria Elisabetta Testa, May 11, 1988; children: Nur, Nizar, Asya. BSc in Civil and Indsl. Engring., No. Jiao Tong U., Beijing, China, 1987; PhD in Structural Engring., U. Rome La Sapienza, 1996. Cert. engr. Sudanese Engrs. Union. Asst. engr. China State Constrn. Corp., Khartoum, 1987-88; cons. ANCIFAP Spa, Rome, 1990; rsch. assoc. dept. structural engring. U. Rome, 1996-98, rschr. dept. structural engring. and geotech., 1999—. Contbr. articles to profl. jours. Postgrad. scholar Italian Govt., 1991-95. Avocations: football, basketball, Internet. Fax: 3964884852. E-mail: hayder@scilla.ing.uniroma1.it. Home: Via Dei Gracchi, 00192 Rome Italy Office: U Rome La Sapienza, Via Eudossiana 18, 00184 Rome Italy

SAEGUSA, TAKEO, engineering educator, university president; b. Tokyo, Feb. 13, 1923; s. Hyoji Shirai and Akiko Saegusa; m. Aiko Kabasawa, Oct. 16, 1964; children: Miho, Rika. Grad., Met. Tech. Coll., Tokyo, 1943; D in Engring., Tokyo Inst. Tech., 1968. Tech. officer Naval Tech. Lab., Tokyo, 1943-45; from assoc. prof. to prof. Met. Tech. Coll., Tokyo, 1946-51; from assoc. to lectr. Tokyo Met. U., 1951-56; assoc. prof., then prof. Nat. Def. Acad., Yokosuka, Japan, 1957-88, chmn., councilor, 1979-81, hon. prof., 1988—; dean, prof. Hokkaido (Japan) Info. U., 1989-98, prof., pres., dir., 1998—; p.t. lectr. Tokyo Met. Tech. Coll., 1962-85. Author: Basic Electric Measurement, 1980, Practical Use Electric Instrumentation, 1985, Introduction to Electronic Engineering, 1994, Electronic Instrumentation, 1994; inventor in field. Recipient Prize of Gov., 1951, Award of Tech. Paper, Assn. Def. Tech., 1987, Third Order of Merit medal, 1993. Fellow Internat. Biol. Assn. (life), Am. Biol. Inst.; mem. IEEE U.S. (sr.), IEE Japan (com. mgr. 1975-85), N.Y. Acad. Scis., Inst. Electrical Info. Commn. Engring. Japan (life), Soc. Inst. Cont. Engrs. Japan, Inst. Elec. Engring. (life), Assn. Japanese Tech. Edn. (com. 1978-86). Buddhist. Avocations: reciting Chinese poems, calligraphy, golf, tennis, photography. Home: 2134-3 Noba Konan-ku, Yokohama Kanagawa 234, Japan Office: Hokkaido Info U, 59-2 Nishinopporo, Hokkaido Ebetsu 069, Japan

SAEKS, ALLEN IRVING, lawyer; b. Bemidji, Minn., July 14, 1932; m. Linda J. Levin; 1 child, Adam Charles. BS in Law, U. Minn., 1954, JD, 1956. Bar: Minn. 1956, U.S. Dist. Ct. Minn. 1956, U.S. Ct. Appeals (8th cir.) 1957, U.S. Ct. Appeals (fed. cir.) 1959, U.S. Supreme Ct. 1959, U.S. Ct. Appeals (11th cir.) 1997; cert. civil trial specialist. Asst. U.S. atty. Dept. Justice, St. Paul, 1956-57; assoc. Leonard Street and Deinard, Mpls., 1960-63, ptnr., 1964—; adj. prof. law U. Minn. Law Sch., 1960-65; chmn. Lawyer Trust Account Bd., Interest on Lawyers Trust Accounts, 1984-87. Chmn. Property Tax Com., 1986-87; bd. dirs. Citizens League, Mpls., 1984-87; pres. Jewish Cmty. Rels. Coun. of Minn. and the Dakotas, 1994-96. Served to 1st lt. JAGC, U.S. Army, 1957-60. Recipient City of Mpls. award, 1996. Fellow Am. Bar Found. (life); mem. Fund for the Legal Aid Soc. (chmn. 1997-98, Law Day Testimonial award 1996), Hennepin County Bar Assn. (pres. 1983-84), ABA (commn. on interest on lawyers trust accts. 1990-93), Minn. State Bar Assn., Order of Coif, Phi Delta Phi. Office: Leonard Street and Deinard 150 S 5th St Ste 2300 Minneapolis MN 55402-4238

SAEMANN, ERNST-ULRICH, civil engineer; b. Hannover, Germany, June 19, 1949; s. Ernst and Magdalene (Halsen) S.; m. Christiane Bolte, Sept. 21, 1973; 1 child, Hedda. Diploma in Engring., U. Hannover, 1976, PhD in Engring., 1989. Scientist Tech. U., Hannover, 1976-77, rschr., 1980-89; civil servant Baubehörde, Hamburg, Germany, 1980; application engr. Brüel & Kjaer GmbH, Quickborn, Germany, 1990-91, product mgr., 1991-92, mktg. mgr., 1992-94; noise control engr. Continental, Hannover, 1995-97, test mgr. acoustics, 1997-2000, test mgr. NVH Ctr., 2000—; lectr. Tech. U., Hannover, 1990-99. Author: Brüel & Kjaer Primer (booklet), 1992; patentee in field; contbr. articles to profl. jours. and books. 2d lt. German Air Def., 1968-69. Mem. Inst. Noise Control Engring. U.S.A., Acoustic Soc. Am., German Soc. Engring., German Acoustic Soc.

SAENGER, BRUCE WALTER, consulting firm executive; b. Hanover, N.H., July 16, 1943; s. Werner Hugo and Natalie Bertha (Brown) S.; m. Cheryl Jeanne Bouchard, Nov. 6, 1976. BA, Pa. State U., 1969; postgrad. Am. Coll., Bryn Mawr, Pa., 1979, Coll. Fin. Planning, Denver, 1980; CPCU, Am. Inst., Malvern, Pa., 1981. ChFC; CLU agt., Nationwide Ins., Lansdale, Pa., 1969-73, dist. sales mgr., Springfield, Ma., 1973-75; dist. sales mgr. Am. Mut., Braintree, Ma., 1975-77; dir. mktg. Bankers Life & Casualty, Chgo., 1977-78; pres., founder Sales Tng. Techs., Southboro, Mass., 1979-81, The Saenger Orgn., Medway, Mass., 1981—; faculty Notre Dame U., South Bend, Ind., 1977-78, Northeastern U., Boston, 1984—; commr. RHU Commn., Washington, 1979-81; dir. Northeastern U. Ins. Inst., Boston, 1985-93; program dir. U. Del. Ins. Program, 1989-91; acad. cons. Mass. Soc. Lic. Ins. Advisers, 1995—; cons. in field. Author: Series 6 Study Book, 1983, Series 22 Study Book, 1984, Tax Shelter Market Guide, 1985, Marketing Mutual Funds, 1985; also articles. Bd. dirs. Lansdale Gen. Hosp., Pa., 1971-73, New Directions Theater Co., 1988-91, dir. 1988-90, Medway Bus. Coun., 1989-94, pres. 1990-92. With U.S. Army, 1960-66. Recipient Ednl. Achievement award Profl. Ins. Agts. Assn., 1983; named Outstanding Fin. Exec. of Yr., Fin. Mgmt. Assn., 1993. Fellow Soc. CLUs (ednl. adv., bd. dirs. 1987-91), Soc. CPCU's (ednl. adv.), Life Mgmt. Inst. (Outstanding Lectr. award 1984); mem. Internat. Assn. Fin. Planners (ednl. adv., bd. dirs. 1986-92, pres. 1989-91), Internat. Assn. for Fin. Planning (chmn. bd. dirs. 1990-92), Soc. Cert. Ins. Counselors (ednl. adv.), Life Underwriters Assn. (ednl. adv.), Inst. CFP (v.p. edn., bd. dirs. 1990-91), Mass. Assn. Health Underwriter (pres. 1992-93). Republican. Roman Catholic. Avocation: skiing. Home: 68 Orchard St Millis MA 02054-1018 Office: The Saenger Orgn 77 Main St Medway MA 02053-1812

SAENGER, HANNS HERMANN, retired academic administrator; b. Berlin, Aug. 16, 1919; s. Curt and Irma (Eisenhardt) S.; m. Fritzi Weil, Nov. 5, 1959 (dec. June 1974); 1 child, Ingrid. BS, Janson De Sailly, Paris, 1935. CEO Greatermans Ltd., South Africa, 1945-67, Consol. Light, Johannesburg, South Africa, 1969-75, Gresham Ltd., Johannesburg, 1975-86. Chmn. South African Jewish Trust, 1980-99; treas. South African Jewish Bd. Deps., 1972-99, hon. life pres., 1998; vice chair South African Friends of Hebrew U., 1986-99; past pres. United Hebrew Congregation Johannesburg; past chmn. Sunfield Home for Mentally Handicapped Children; mem. South African Com. for Tertiary Jewish Studies, Jewish Affairs Editl. Bd.; hon. life pres. Our Parents Home. Served in armed forces, World War II. Recipient Cert. of Honor United Hebrew Congregation, 1998; named Internat. Man of Yr., Cambridge, 1991-92; hon. fellow Hebrew U., 1996. Mem. Lansdowne Club. Democrat. Jewish. Office: SA Friends of Hebrew U, Killarney Mall, Johannesburg 2193, South Africa

SAENGER, RUDI FRED, retired superintendent; b. Berlin, July 24, 1932; naturalized, 1950; m. Inge G. Rusch, Apr. 10, 1963; children: Elisabeth, Katharina, Alexander. BS in Math./Physics, Trinity U., 1959; postgrad. various univs. including, U. Md., 1999—. Cert. tchr. Tex., 1959. Math. instr. San Antonio, Tex., 1959-60; geodesist Coast and Geodetic Survey, Washington, 1960-61; mathematician, programmer Navy Oceanographic Office, Washington, 1961-63; alternate divsn. dir. Nat. Oceanographic Data Ctr., Washington, 1963-66; dep. br. head, scientific analysis Naval Air Systems Command, Washington, 1966-71, br. head, scientific computing, 1971-81, dir., mgr. computer sci. facility, 1981-85; supt. rsch. computation divsn. Naval Rsch. Lab., Washington, 1985-93, ret., 1993; presdl. appt. U.S. Assay Commr., 1975; chmn. NAVAIR Computer-Aided Aircraft Design com., Washington, 1977-85; spl. asst. for info. resource mgmt. to chief of naval rsch., Washington, 1985-90; mem. Fed. Coordinating Coun. on Sci., Engring. and Tech., 1986-90; tech. rev. com. Naval Surface Warfare Ctr., Washington, 1996—. Contbr. articles to profl. jours. Trustee Carderock Elem. Sch., Bethesda, Md., 1970s, 1980s; mem. Avenel Homeowners Adv. Com., Potomac, Md., 1990—; mem. Tournament Players Club at Avenel, Potomac, 1990—. Recipient U.S. Navy Meritorious Civilian Svc. award, 1985. Mem. Am. Numismatic Assn. Avocations: numismatics, travel, skiing, financial investment. Fax: 301-365-0266. E-mail: saenger@bellatlantic.net. Home: 9435 Turnberry Dr Potomac MD 20854-5444

SAENGSOOK, RANGSAN, academic administrator; b. Petchaboom, Thailand, Apr. 18, 1944. LLB, Thammasat U., Thailand, MPA; PhD (hon.). Prof. law, rector Ramkhamhaeng U., Thailand, 1994—. Office: Ramkhamhaeng U, Ramkhamhaeng Rd, Huamark Bangkok 10241, Thailand*

SÁENZ, ALBERT WILLIAM, theoretical physicist, researcher, consultant; b. Medellín, Colombia, Aug. 27, 1923; came to U.S., 1941; s. Alberto Sáenz Moreno and Agnes (Williams) Sáenz; m. Pilar González García-Suelto, Sept. 7, 1957. BS, U. Mich., 1944, MA, 1945, PhD, 1949. From rsch. physicist to br. head Naval Rsch. Lab., Washington, 1950-66, br. head, 1966-76, divsn. cons., 1976-89, ret., 1989; rsch. prof. Cath. U., Washington, 1981—; vis. fellow Ind. U., Bloomington, Ind., 1951-52; vis. prof. Johns Hopkins U., Balt., 1964; vis. sr. scientist Princeton (N.J.) U., 1976-77, Max Planck Inst., Stuttgart, Germany, 1990-91, Budker Inst. Nuclear Physics, Novosibirsk, Russia, 1996; cons. Naval Rsch. Lab., Washington, 1990—. Author: (with others) Long Distance Neutrino Detection, 1979, Mathematical Methods and Applications of Scattering Theory, 1980, Coherent Radiation Sources, 1985, Relativistic Channeling, 1987, Synergetics, Order and Chaos, 1988, Essays in Classical and Quantum Dynamics, 1991, Asymptotics Beyond All Orders, 1991, others; editor numerous books; contbr. 54 articles to profl. jours. Fellow Am. Physical Soc., Washington Acad. Scis.; mem. Am. Math. Soc., N.Y. Acad. Scis., Cosmos Club. Democrat. Roman Catholic. Achievements include symmetry and degeneracy in quantum mechanics, general relativity, spin-wave theory of complex magnetic structures and spin-wave scattering of polarized neutrons, coherent radiation from electrons traversing crystals or quasicrystals, rigorous quantum mechanical scattering theory, averaging theory of periodic and nonperiodic classical dynamical systems and its quantum analogues, channeling stability studies, nonintegrability and chaos. Home: 6338 Old Town Ct Alexandria VA 22307-1227 Office: Naval Research Lab 4555 Overlook Ave SW Washington DC 20375-0001

SÁENZ, GERARDO, Mexican government official; b. Mexico City, June 4, 1959; s. Eduardo and Susana Yolanda (Garduño) S. Degree in indsl. engring., Inst. Tech. y Estudios Superiores, Monterrey, Mex., 1984, degree in civil engring., 1986; MBA, Inst. Tech. Autónomo Mex., Mexico City, 1993. Asst. to pres. Mercantil Probursa Bank, Mexico City, 1987-90; credit and bank rels. asst. Grupo ICA SA de CV, Mexico City, 1990-91, project fin. mgr., 1991-92, fin. analysis mgr., 1992-93, investor rels. dir., 1993-96; v.p. equity rsch., dir. Grupo Serfin, Mexico City, 1996-97; v.p. equity rsch. Grupo Financiero Interacciones, Mexico City, 1997-98; chief of staff to undersec. of edn. Ministry of Edn., Mexico City, 1999—. Contbr. articles to profl. publs. Mem. Partido Revolucionario Institucional Party, Mexico City, 1983, Instituto Tecnológico y de Estudios Superiores de Monterrey, Instituto Tecnológico Autónomo de México. Mem. Mex. Inst. Execs. Financiers, Mex. Soc. Analysts. Avocations: water skiing, tennis, golf, badminton.

SAENZ-RAMIREZ, ALEJANDRO, physics educator, researcher; b. San Jose, Costa Rica, Oct. 29, 1949; s. Alejandro Saenz and Maria Rosa Ramirez; m. Virginia Salazar, Mar. 14, 1975; children: Alejandro André, Cristina, Paula, Benjamin. BS in Physics, U. Costa Rica, San Jose, 1971; MS, Purdue U., 1974. Teaching asst. U. Costa Rica, San Jose, 1970-72, Purdue U., West Lafayette, Ind., 1972-74; researcher Royal Inst. Tech., Stockholm, 1975-76; instr. U. Costa Rica, San Jose, 1974-80, adj. prof., 1980-88, assoc. prof., 1988-90, full prof., 1990—. Contbr. articles to profl. jours. Mem. Assn. Costarricense de Fisica, Am. Phys. Soc., Colegio de Lic. en Letras, Cologio de Fisicos, Latin Am. Soc. Vacuum and Surface Sci. Avocation: solid state. Home: 25m Sur La Orotinense, Paso Ancho, Paso Andre San Jose Costa Rica Office: U de Costa Rica, Escuela de Fisica, San Jose Costa Rica

SAEV, NIKOLAI ILIEV, engineering executive, mechanical engineer; b. Lovech, Bulgaria, Sept. 9, 1960; s. Ilia Ivanov and Lilia Dimitrova (Popova) S.; m. Stanka Rusenova Ivanova, July 7, 1985; children: Ilian Nikolaev, Nikolai Nikolaev. Diploma, Higher Sch. Mech. Engring., Varna, Bulgaria, 1985. Computer programmer Sys. Engring., Pravets, Bulgaria, 1985-90; trading cons. Abadon Engring., Lovech, 1991-93, mgr., 1993-95; mgr. RAY Ltd., Lovech, 1995—, also bd. dirs.; ISP Bianet, 1997—. Avocations: computer programming, fishing, stamp collecting. Home: 38 Tsar Osvoboditel Ap 35, 5500 Lovech Bulgaria Office: Bianet, PO Box 226, 5500 Lovech Bulgaria

SAEVARSSON, TORFI DAN, electrical power engineer; b. Akureyri, Iceland, Sept. 2, 1960; s. Saevar Sigtysson and Sigridur Gudrun Torfadottir; m. Valgerdur Hallgrimsdottir, Dec. 31, 1983; children: Armann Snaer Torfason, Snaerun Tinna Torfadottir. Electrician diploma, Akureyri (Iceland) Tech. Coll., 1981; student, Higher Tech. Coll., Iceland, 1982, diploma in Elec. Engring., 1983; BS in Elec. Power Engring., So. Ill. U., 1987. Registered profl. engr.; high voltage registration. Lineman State Elec. Power Works, Akureyri, 1976-79, electrician, 1980-83; student worker State Elec. Power Works, Reykjavik, Iceland, 1984-86, engr., 1987-88, dept. engr., 1988-91; design engr. cons. Reykjavik, Iceland, 1991-94; instr. Lower Tech. Coll., Reykjavik, 1991-94; tech. mgr. Ind. Inspection Body, 1994-96; dep. mgr. elec. issues Icelandic Aluminium Co. Ltd., 1996-97; sr. elec. engr. Nordural, 1998—. Bd. dirs. Power com. Ind. Party of Iceland, Reykjavik, 1988—, Industry com., 1989—. Mem. IEEE. Mem. Ind. Party of Iceland. Lutheran. Avocations: skiing, weight-lifting, photography, travel. Home: Asgardur 59, 108 Reykjavik Iceland

SAFAI, BIJAN, physician, investigator; b. Ardestan, Iran, Mar. 26, 1940; came to U.S., 1968; s. Abdol-Khalegh Safai and Kanom-Sadat Sadjaddi; m. Vera Plaskon, Sept. 16, 1978; 1 child: Matthew. MD, Tehran U., Iran, 1965; DSc, U. Gutenburg, Sweden, 1981. Diplomate Am. Bd. Dermatology, Am. Bd. Internal Medicine. Intern Nassau County Med. Ctr., East Meadow, N.Y., 1968-69; resident N.Y.U. Med. Coll. VA Hosp., N.Y.C., 1969-70; resident in dermatology N.Y.U. Med. Coll., N.Y.C., 1971-73; fellow in immunology Sloan-Kettering Inst. for Cancer & Allied Diseases, N.Y.C., 1973-74; from asst. attending physician to chief dermatology svc. Meml. Hosp., N.Y.C., 1974-93; from assoc. to attending physician in dermatology N.Y. Hosp., N.Y.C., 1980-93; dir. dermatology Westchester County Med. Ctr., Valhalla, N.Y., 1993—; from asst. prof. to prof. in medicine/dermatology Cornell U. Med. Coll., N.Y.C., 1974-93; prof., chmn. dept. dermatology N.Y. Med. Coll., N.Y.C., 1993—, prof. dept. microbiology and immunology, 1994—; teaching clin. asst. in dermatology NYU Med. Coll, N.Y.C., 1973-74; adj. mem. Rockefeller U., N.Y.C., 1982-84; rsch. assoc. Sloan-Kettering Inst. for Cancer and Allied Diseases, N.Y.C., 1977-79, asst. mem., 1979-83, assoc. mem., 1983-88; assoc. mem. Memorial Sloan-Kettering Cancer Ctr., N.Y.C., 1983-88, mem. 1988-93; mem. grad. sch. med. scis. N.Y. Med. Coll., Valhalla, 1994—; mem. adv. bd. Skin Cancer Found., 1982—; sec. dermatology sect. N.Y. Acad Medicine, 1988-89, chmn. 1989-90; mem. med. adv. bd. Cancer Rsch Instn., 1997—. Mem. editl. bd. Cancer Investigation, 1984-88, AIDS Rsch. and Human Retroviruses, 1986-90, Jour. of Acquired Immune Deficiency Syndromes, 1988—; contbr. numerous articles on immunodermatology to profl. jours. Mem. AIDS adv. task force, NCI/NIH, 1982-85; mem. AIDS Etiology task force, NCI, 1982-85; mem. ad hoc study sect. for AIDS, NIH, 1982-88; mem. spl. dermatology rev. group, GM2 study sect., NIH, 1990-96; mem. spl. rev. team NCI Intramural Rev., Lab. of Tumor cell Biology, 1987, 92, Medicine br., NCI, 1996; mem. study sect. on HIV, NCI, 1996; mem. spl. rev. group FDA Intramural Rev., 1995. Mem. AMA, Internat. Soc. Tropical Dermatology, Am. Fedn. for Clin. Rsch., Am. Acad. Dermatology (mem. AIDS com. 1989-91, task force on cutaneous oncology 1988-9, mem. adv. coun. 1988-91), Am. Dermatol. Soc. for Allery and Immunology, Soc. for Investigative Dermatology, Med. Soc. of State of N.Y., Med. Soc. of County of N.Y., N.Y. State Soc. Dermatology, Dermatol. Soc. of Greater N.Y., N.Y. County Health Svs. Rev. Orgn., N.Y. Acad. Scis., N.Y. Dermatol. Soc. (pres 1990-91, sec., treas. 1989-90), Dermatology Found., Z & E Fisher Med. Found. (pres. 1993—). E-mail: safai@aol.com. Home: 340 E 64th St New York NY 10021-7503 Office: NY Med Coll Dept Dermatology Valhalla NY 10595 Office: 625 Park Ave New York NY 10021-6545

SAFARIAN, ALEK, pharmaceutical industry executive, consultant; b. Yerevan, Armenia, Oct. 12, 1964; arrived in Australia, 1982; s. Serge and Lucy (Mardirossian) S. B.Pharmacy, U. Sydney, Australia, 1987, MBA, 1995. Registered pharmacist, Australia. Pharmacist Mt. Druitt Hosp., Sydney, 1987-88; regulatory affairs officer Ciba-Geigy, Sydney, 1988-90; sci. affairs mgr. Marion Merrell Dow Australia, Sydney, 1990-95; CEO Novotech Communications, 1996—. Fellow Australian Inst. Pharmacy Mgmt.; mem. Assn. regulatory and clin. Scientists (councillor 1991-95, chmn. edn. com. 1995), Drug Info. assn., Internat. Soc. Pharmacoepidemiology. Avocations: chess, computers, travel, music. Home: 603/168 Kent St, Sydney NSW 2000, Australia Office: Novotech Communications, Level 4, 100 Harris St, Pyrmont NSW 2009, Australia

SAFER, JOHN, artist, lecturer, banker, real estate developer; b. Washington, Sept. 6, 1922; s. John M. and Rebecca (Herzmark) S.; m. Joy Scott; children: Janine Whitney, Thomas. AB, George Washington U., 1947; LLB, Harvard, 1949. chmn. NationsBank/D.C., 1980-92, Materia, 1998; chmn. exec. com. Fin. Gen. Bankshares, 1977-80; bd. dirs. Scripss Rsch. Inst., Nat. Air and Space Mus. Represented in permanent collections at Balt. Mus. Art, Corocoran Gallery Art, Folger Shakespeare Libr., Nat. Air and Space Mus., Washington Tennis Ctr., High Mus. Art, Atlanta, Milw. Mus. Art, Harvard Law Sch., Harvard Bus. Sch., Phila. Mus. Art, San Francisco Mus. Art, Duke U. Med. Ctr., Embry-Riddle Aeronautical U., Georgetown U., George Washington U., Williams Coll., Scripps Rsch. Inst., Mus. Fine Arts, Caracas, Venezuela, Royal Collection, Amman, Jordan, Royal Collection, Madrid, Am. Hosp., Paris, Embassy of U.S., London, Nassau, Beijing; pub. sculpture includes World Series of Golf Trophy, Timepiece (World's Largest Clock - Guiness Book of Records), Christa McAuliffe Meml., Bowie, Md. Served as 1st lt. USAAF, 1942-46. Clubs: Cosmos, Burning Tree, Harvard, Woodmont (Washington), Lyford Cay (Nassau), Linville Ridge (N.C.). Office: PO Box 6720 Mc Lean VA 22101

SAFFELS, DALE EMERSON, federal judge; b. Moline, Kans., Aug. 13, 1921; s. Edwin Clayton and Lillian May (Cook) S.; m. Margaret Elaine Nieman, Apr. 2, 1976; children by previous marriage: Suzanne Saffels Gravitt, Deborah Saffels Godowns, James B.; stepchildren: Lynda Cowger Harris, Christopher Cowger. AB, Emporia State U., 1947; JD cum laude, LLB cum laude, Washburn U., 1949. Bar: Kans. 1949. Pvt. practice law Garden City, Kans., 1949-71, Topeka, 1971-75, Wichita, Kans., 1975-79; U.S. dist. judge Dist. of Kans., Topeka, 1979—; county atty. Finney County,

Kans., 1951-55; chmn. bd. Fed. Home Loan Bank Topeka, 1978-79; mem. Jud. Conf. Com. on Fin. Disclosure, 1993-99. Mem. bd. govs. Sch. Law Washburn U., 1973-85; pres. Kans. Dem. Club, 1957; Dem. nominee Gov. of Kans., 1962; mem. Kans. Ho. of Reps., 1955-63, minority leader, 1961-63; mem. Kans. Corp. Commn., 1967-75, chmn., 1968-75; mem. Kans. Legis. Coun., 1957-63; Kans. rep. Interstate Oil Compact Commn., 1967-75, 1st vice chmn., 1971-72; pres. Midwest Assn. Regulatory Commn., 1972-73, Midwest Assn. R.R. and Utilities Commrs., 1972-73; trustee Emporia State U. Endowment Assn.; bd. dirs. Nat. Assn. Regulatory Utility Commrs., 1972-75. Maj. Signal Corps U.S. Army, 1942-46. Fellow Am. Bar Found., Kans. Bar Found.; mem. ABA, Kans. Bar Assn., Wichita Bar assn., Am. Judicture Soc., Delta Theta Phi. Lutheran. Fax: 785-295-2809. Office: US Dist Ct 420 Federal Bldg 444 SE Quincy St Topeka KS 66683

SAFFOLD, SYLVESTER, writer; b. Dec. 27, 1968. A in Computer Sci., Platt Jr. Coll., 1991. Writer Black Poet Ink, Kansas City, 1994—. Address: 3401 Bellefontaine Ave Kansas City MO 64128-1953

SAFFURI, KHALED AHMAD, cultural organization executive; b. Beirut, July 28, 1956; came to U.S., 1981; s. Ahmad Hasan Saffouri and Siham Sihani; m. Jeniffer Ann Hall, Aug. 28, 1994 (div. Aug. 1997). BA in Bus. Adminstrn., USIA, Calif., 1985; MA in Mgmt., U. Redlands, Calif., 1987. Dir. Mid. East affairs Am.-Arab Anti-Discrimination Com., Washington, 1987-90; asst. exec. dir. Nat. Assn. Arab-Americans, Washington, 1990-93, Am. Muslim Coun., Washington, 1994-97; exec. dir. Am. Task Force for Bosnia, Washington, 1992-98, Islamic Inst., Washington, 1998—. Co-author: (book) Islam and Free Market, 1998. Muslim. Office: Islamic Inst Found 1920 L St NW Ste 200 Washington DC 20036-5036

SAFIN, MARAT, pro tennis player; b. Moscow, Jan. 27, 1980. Mem. ATP, 1997—; winner U.S. Open, 2000, Open Seat-GODO 2000, Barcelona, Mallorca Open, Spain, 2000, Tennis Master's Series, Toronto Masters, 2000, President's Cup, Tashkent, Uzbekistan, 2000. Office: ATP Tour 201 ATP Tour Blvd Ponte Vedra Beach FL 32082*

SAFRANY, AGNES, physical chemist; b. Zombor, Yugoslavia, Feb. 25, 1954; d. Sandor and Margit (Pucher) S. BS, U. Beograd, 1978, MS in Phys. Chemistry, 1983, PhD, 1988. Rsch. asst. radiation chemistry dept. Inst. Nuclear Sci., Beograd, Yugoslavia, 1980-83, rschr., 1984-88, sr. rschr., 1989-93; rsch. fellow Japan Rsch. Inst., Takasaki, 1993-95; sr. rschr. Inst. Isotopes Hungarian Acad. Scis., Budapest, 1995—; vis. rschr. phys. chemistry dept. Hebrew U., Jerusalem, 1992, 93, 96. Contbr. articles to profl. jours. and chpts. to books. Mem. Biomaterials Soc. Office: Hungarian Acad Scis Isotope, Konkoly Thege M 29-33, H-1525 Budapest Hungary

SAFT, STUART MARK, lawyer; b. N.Y.C., Feb. 17, 1947; s. Stanley and Dorothy (Ligerman) S.; m. Stephanie C. Optekman, June 6, 1970; children: Bradley S., Gordon D. BA, Hofstra U., 1968; JD, Columbia U., 1971. Bar: N.Y. 1972, Fla. 1975, U.S. Dist. Ct. (so. dist.) N.Y. 1975, U.S. Supreme Ct. 1990. Asst. gen. counsel Joseph Bancroft & Son Co., N.Y.C., 1972-74; ptnr. Brauner, Baron, Rosenzwerz, Kligler & Sparber, N.Y.C., 1974-81, Powsner, Saft & Powsner, N.Y.C., 1981-84, Goldschmidt & Saft, N.Y.C., 1984-88; Wolf Haldenstern Adler Freeman & Herz, N.Y.C., 1988—; chmn., bd. dirs. Coun. of N.Y. Coops., N.Y.C., 1981—; chmn. bd. dirs., CEO Pvt. Industry Coun. of N.Y.C.; bd. dirs. Am. Women's Econ. Devel. Corp., Nat. Assn. Housing Coops., Nat. Coop. Bank, S.L.E. Lupus Found.; adj. asst. prof. NYU, Real Estate Inst.; chmn. N.Y. City Workforce Investment Bd. Author: Commercial Real Estate Forms, 3 vols., 1987, Commercial Real Estate Transactions, 1989, Commercial Real Estate Workouts, 1991, Real Estate Development: Strategies for a Changing Market, 1990, Commercial Real Estate Leasing, 1992, Real Estate Investor's Survival Guide, 1992, Commercial Real Estate Financing, 1993, Commercial Real Estate Forms, 2d edit., 7 vols., 1994, Commercial Real Estate Transactions, 2d edit., 1995, Commercial Real Estate Workouts, 2d edit., 1996; contbg. editor: The Real Estate Finance Jour., 1989—; contbr. articles to profl. jours. Served to capt. USAR, 1968-76. Mem. ABA, N.Y. Bar Assn., Fla. Bar Assn. Office: Wolf Haldenstein Adler Freeman & Herz 270 Madison Ave New York NY 10016-0601

SAFTA, MARIUS MIRCEA, retired organic chemistry researcher; b. Cluj, Romania, Aug. 25, 1935; s. Ioan Sabin Safta and Else Margareta Wiehe; m. Marioara Foale, July 7, 1960; children: Marius Ioan, Minerva Elena. Chem. engr., Poly. Inst., Timisoara, Romania, 1958, PhD in Tech. Chem. Scis., 1975. Cert. chem. engring. Asst. tchr. Agronomy Faculty, Craiova, Romania, 1959-64, Poly. Inst., Timisoara, 1964-77; sr. rschr. Inst. Chemistry, Timisoara, 1978-90, Inst. Chem. Scis., Timisoara, 1990-95, Inst. Electrochemistry, Timisoara, 1996-97; ret., 1997. Contbr. articles to sci. jours.; patentee in field. Mem. Planetary Soc., N.Y. Acad. Scis. Orthodox. Avocations: music, gardening, reading, playing with grandsons, learning English. Home: Str Timis Nr 6, 1900 Timisoara Romania

SAG, YESIM, engineering educator, researcher; b. Ankara, Turkey, Mar. 2, 1964; d. Erdogan and Tülin Hatice (Erkman) S. BSChemE, Hacettepe U., Ankara, 1985; MSChemE, Hacettepe U., 1988, PhD in Chem. Engring., 1993. Rsch. and teaching asst. Hacettepe U., 1986—, assoc. prof.in process and reactor design, 1994—. Contbr. articles to profl. jours. Avocations: reading books about science-fiction and literature, watching movies, listening to music. Home: Genclik cad, Ilk Sok 13-8 Anittepe, 06580 Ankara Turkey Office: Hacettepe Univ, Chem Engring Dept Faculty Engring, 06532 Beytepe Ankara, Turkey

SAGAFI-NEJAD, TAGI, business educator; b. Bainabaj, Khorasan, Iran, Dec. 19, 1941; came to U.S., 1968; s. Mir Gholam-Reza and Tayebeh Sagafi; m. Nancy Gail Black Sagafi-nejad, Nov. 22, 1967; children: Jahan Crawford Reza, David Joseph Hossein. MA, U. Pa., 1971, PhD, 1979. Lectr. U. Pa., Phila., 1974-76; asst. prof. U. Wash., Seattle, 1976-80, U. Tex., Austin, 1980-84; assoc. prof. Loyola Coll., Balt., 1984-93, prof., 1993—, dept. chair, 1995-96; cons. UN Indsl. Devel. Orgn., 1982-84, UN Ctr. on Transnational Corp., 1985—, Office of Tech. Assessment, U.S. Congress, 1983-84; lectr., spkr. in field. Editl. bd. Transnational Corp., 1993—, Competitiveness Rev., 1995—. Recipient Best Paper award Acad. of Mgmt., 1994, Pacific Asia Mgmt. Inst., U. Hawaii, 1988. Mem. Am. Competitiveness Soc. (adv. bd. 1996—), Acad. of Internat. Bus. (chair N.E. chpt. 1988-93), Iranian Scholars Assn. (founding mem., v.p. 1989-90), Middle East Studies Assn., Middle East Inst., Strategic Mgmt. Soc. Democrat. Avocations: gardening, golf, painting, walking. Office: Sellinger Sch Loyola Coll 4501 N Charles St Baltimore MD 21210-2601

SAGALOVICH, YURI LVOVICH, mathematician, researcher; b. Moscow, Aug. 10, 1924; s. Lev Josefovich and Nina Moiseevna (Pildon) S.; m. Nina Anempodistovna Kaydalova, Nov. 15, 1947 (dec. July 1995); 1 child, Marina. PhD, Leningrad (Russia) State U., 1954; D, Acad. Sci. of USSR, Moscow, 1962, DSc, 1982. Rsch. fellow Inst. Info. Transmission Problems Acad. Sci. of USSR, Moscow, 1956-66, sr. rsch. fellow, 1966-86, leading rsch. fellow, 1986—; sr. lectr. Moscow Inst. Physics and Tech., 1967-73, prof., chair, 1992—; mem. academic coun. on degree conferment. Author: States Coding and Automata Reliability, 1975, Algebra, Codes, Diagnostics, 1993; contbr. articles to profl. jours. Served with Soviet Army, 1942-45. Decorated Order of Patriotic War, 1st and 2d degrees, Red Star; grantee Pres. of Russia, 1997—. Avocation: music. Office: IITP Acad Scis of Russia, Bolshoy Karetny Str 19, 101447 Moscow Russia

SAGAN, ALEX PHILIP, history educator, consultant; b. Chgo., Feb. 21, 1962; s. Bruce and Judith (Fine) S.; m. Julie Beth Altman, Dec. 14, 1997; 1 child, Lucille. BA, Haverford Coll., 1984; AM, Harvard U., 1988, PhD, 1998. Lectr. history and lit. Harvard U., Cambridge, Mass., 1996—. Bd. dirs. Harvard Hillel, New Jewish H.S. Boston; mem. Cambridge Bicycle Com. Home: 14 Hubbard Park Rd Cambridge MA 02138-4731 Office: Harvard U Ctr for European Studies Cambridge MA 02138

SAGAR, RAM, astrophysicist, researcher; b. Baragaon, India, July 1, 1952; s. Shri Ram Nath and Basmati Devi; m. Kiran Devi, June 10, 1962; children: Sarita, Suman, Sunita, Neetu. BSc, Gorakhpur (India) U., 1971, MSc, 1973, PhD in Physics, 1981. Rsch. fellow Uttar Pradesh State Obs., Naini Tal, India, 1973-74, scientific asst., 1974-76, scientific officer, 1976-79; lectr. in physics Kumaon U., Naini Tal, India, 1979-86; reader Indian Inst. Astrophysics, Bangalore, 1986-91, assoc. prof. astrophysics, 1991-96; dir. Uttar Pradesh State Obs., 1996—; vis. scientist USSR Acad. Sci., Moscow, 1983, Royal Soc., London, 1983-84, Anglo-Australian Obs., Sydney, 1989, 95; acad. cons. Royal Obs., Edinburgh, Scotland, 1984-85; rsch. fellow Alexander von Humboldt Found., Bonn, Germany, 1989-90; mem. organizing com. IAU Com. 37, 16th and 18th scientific meetings of ASI; participant numerous internat. confs. and workshops. Contbr. numerous articles to profl. jours. and conf. procs. Awarded Royal Soc. Commonwealth bursary, 1983-84; awarded observing time on Hubble Space Telescope;. Fellow Nat. Acad. Scis. India, Laser and Spectroscopy Soc. India; mem. Astron. Soc. India (life mem., pres. 1999-00, v.p. 1997-98, assoc. editor Bull. 1992-95, Young Astronomer 1983-84), Indian Physics Assn. (life), Internat. Astron. Union, Hindi Vigyan Sahitya Parishad (life). Avocations: sports, walking. Home and Office: UP State Obs, Manora Peak, Nainital 263 129, India

SAGARA, JUNJI, editor; b. Fukuoka, Kyushyu, Japan, July 20, 1943; s. Manabu and Tatsuko Sagara; m. Masako Abe, Apr. 27, 1975; children: Takafumi, Hisanori. BA in Econs., Keio U., Tokyo, 1968, MA in Econs., 1973. Researcher The Export-Import Bank of Japan, Tokyo, 1968-71; reader dept. Econs. Keio U., Tokyo, 1971-73; journalist Nihon Keizai Shimbun, Tokyo, 1973-82; economist Japan Ctr. for Econ. Rsch., Tokyo, 1982-87, dep.-dir., 1987-89; dep. editor Nihon Keizai Shimbun Co., Tokyo, 1990-92; editor Nihon Keizai Shimbun Co., 1993—; vis. scholar U. Hong Kong, 1985-87. Active Am. C. of C., Hong Kong. Mem. Internat. Project Fin. Soc. (sec. 1988—), Japan Scotland Soc., Soong Ching Ling Meml. Found. in Japan. Home: 3-772-51 Nonoshita, Nagareyama-City 270-0135, Japan Office: Nihon Keizai Shimbun Co, News Dept, 1-9-5 Ohtemachi, Chiyoda-Ku, Tokyo 100-66, Japan

SAGARIS, LAKE, writer, journalist, translator; b. Montreal, Que., Can., Sept. 29, 1956; arrived in Chile, 1981; d. Donald Michael Batten and Lois Elizabeth McClelland. BFA in Creative Writing, U. B.C., Vancouver, Can., 1980. Writer, journalist, 1981—; Santiago corr. Bus. Week, Living on Earth, Economist Intelligence Unit, others; editor, transl. Codelco, Chilean govt., LanChile, others; participant Banff Ctr.'s Writers' Studio, 1989; spkr., reader in field. Author: (poetry collections) Exile Home/Exilio en la patria, 1986, Circus Love, 1991, Medusa's Children, 1993, (lit. nonfiction book) After the First Death: a Journey Through Chile, Time, Mind, 1996, Bone and Dream: Into the World's Driest Desert, 2000; contbr. to Sat. Night, Minn. Rev., Fiddlehead, Toronto Star, others, also to anthologies including Cuentos por latinas, Baker's Dozen, 1984 Anthology of Magazine Verse, Yearbook of American Poetry, Words We Come Home To, Frictions, Paper Guitar. Recipient 1st prize 1996 Writing Contest, Periodical Writers Assn. Can., Ont. Arts Coun. award, 1985, 86, 90, Can. Coun. Arts award, shortlisted Gov. Gen's awawrd of Can., 1996; grantee Can. Coun., 1985-87; Maclean Hunter fellow in arts journalism, 1989. Mem. Writers' Union Can. E-mail: sagaris@lake.cl.

SAGAYAMA, SHIGEKI, engineering educator; b. Wadayama, Japan, May 12, 1948; s. Jitsujiro and Fumiko (Morita) S.; m. Yuko Otsuka, Apr. 1, 1993; 1 child, Chiye. BEng, U. Tokyo, 1977, MEng, 1979, DrEng, 1998. Rschr. NTT Musashino Elec. Comm. Labs., Musashino, Japan, 1974-81, sr. rschr., 1981-83, asst. mgr. dept. 4,, 1983-85; head dept. speech processing ATR Interpreting Telephony Rsch. Labs., Kyoto, Japan, 1990-93; rsch. supr. NTT Musashino Human Interface Labs., Musashino, Japan, 1985-90, 93-95; head dept. speech recognition and synthesis NTT Musashino Human Interface Labs., Yokosuka, Japan, 1995-97; prof. Japan Advanced Inst. Sci. and Tech., Ishikawa, 1998-00, U. Tokyo Grad. Sch. Engring., 2000—. Author: Interpreting Telephony, 1994; contbr. more than 300 articles to profl. publs. and procs. Recipient Invention award Inst. Invention, Tokyo, 1991, Achievement award Sci. and Tech. Agy. Japan, 1996. Mem. Signal Processing Soc. of IEEE (mem. tech. com. 1994—), Acoustical Soc. Japan (mem. publ. bd. dirs. 1995-97), Info. Processing Soc. Tokyo, Inst. Elec. Info. Comm. Engrs. Tokyo. Avocations: classical music, chorus, hiking, travel. Home: 5-5-10 Nakamachi, Hoya-shi Tokyo 202-0013, Japan Office: U Tokyo Grad Sch Engring, Hongo, Bunkyo-ku, Tokyo 113-8655, Japan

SAGER, DONALD JACK, publisher, former librarian; b. Milw., Mar. 3, 1938; s. Alfred Herman and Sophia (Sagan) S.; m. Sarah Ann Long, May 23, 1987; children: Geoffrey, Andrew. BS, U. Wis., Milw., 1963; MSLS, U. Wis., 1964. Sr. documentalist AC Electronics divsn. GM, Milw., 1958-63; teaching asst. U. Wis., Madison, 1963-64; dir. Kingston (N.Y.) Pub. Libr., 1964-66, Elyria (Ohio) Pub. Libr., 1966-71, Mobile Pub. Libr., 1971-75, Pub. Libr. Columbus and Franklin County, Ohio, 1975-78; commr. Chgo. Pub. Libr., 1978-81; dir. Elmhurst Pub. Libr., Ill., 1982-83, Milw. Pub. Libr., 1983-91; pub. Highsmith Press, Ft. Atkinson, Wis., 1991—; sec. Online Computer Libr. Ctr., 1977-78, disting. vis. scholar, 1982; chmn. mus. com. PLA Pub. Libr., 1989-91, history com., 1993-95, chmn. investment com., 1985-89, chmn. PLA nat. conf. com., 1986-88; bd. dirs. Coun. Wis. Librs., 1982-91, Urban Librs. Coun., 1985-93, sec., 1991-93; adj. faculty U. Wis., Milw., 1984-91; cons. in field. Author: Reference: A Programmed Instruction, 1970, Binders, Books and Budgets, 1971, Participatory Management, 1981, The American Public Library, 1982, Public Library Administrators Planning Guide to Automation, 1983, Managing the Public Library, 1984, Small Libraries, 1992, 3d rev. edit., 2000; co-editor: Urban Library Management Trends, 1989; contbg. editor: Public Libraries, 1990—; contbr. articles to profls. publs. Bd. dirs. Goethe House, 1985-91; pres. Milw. Civic Alliance, 1990-91; chmn. Milw. United Way Campaign, 1984; pres. Milw. Westown Assn., 1987-90. With inf. AUS, 1956-58. Mem. ALA (coun. mem. 1995—, policy monitoring com., awards com., chmn. core values task force), Pub. Libr. Assn. (bd. dirs., v.p., pres.-elect, pres. 1982-83), Ill. Libr. Assn., Chgo. Book Clinic, Wis. Libr. Assn., Wis. Libr. Assn. Found. (chmn. 1986-88), Libr. Adminstrn. Assn. Wis. (chmn. 1987-88), Exch. Club Milw. (pres. 1988-89). Home: 590 Wilmot Rd Deerfield IL 60015-3955 Office: Highsmith Press 5527W Hwy 106 Fort Atkinson WI 53538

SAGGIO, ANTONIO, judge. Degree in Law, U. Naples. Judge Ct. of Appeal, 1960-68; legal adviser Ministry of Justice, 1974-78; head dept. diplomatic law, faculty polit. sci. U. Naples, Italy, 1971; counselor to Italian atty.-gen. European Ct. of Justice; prof. Sch. Pub. Adminstrn., Rome; judge Supreme Ct. of Cassation; pres. Ct. 1st Instance European Communities, Luxembourg, 1995-98; advocate gen. Ct. of Justice of the European Communities, Luxembourg, 1997—. Mem. Italian Soc. for Internat. Orgn., Internat. Law Assn., Italian Assn. European Jurists, Italian Soc. Internat. Law. Office: Ct of Justice, rue du Fort Niedergrünewald, L-2925 Luxembourg Luxembourg

SAGHIR, ADEL JAMIL, artist, painter, sculptor; b. Beirut, Lebanon, May 27, 1930; came to U.S., 1973; s. Jamil Khalil and Aisha Rachid (Mirii) S.; m. Jindriska Antonin Moucka, Aug. 24, 1968; children: Jamil, Ryan. BA, Am. U., Beirut, 1968, diploma in tchg., 1973; MFA, Pratt Inst., 1975; postgrad., NYU, 1976-79. Asst. prof. Fine Arts Inst., Lebanese U., Beirut, 1963-73; lectr. Am. Beirut U. Coll., 1972-73; adj. prof. Western Conn. State U., Danbury, 1988—; instr. sculpture, mural painting, art history Silvermine Sch. Art, New Canaan, Conn., 1989-98. Artist various murals and tapestries. Recipient 4th prize Alexandria Biennale, Egyptian Govt., 1963, 1st prize silk tapestries Nat. Contest Lebanon, 1965, 1st prize major sculpture monuments, 1966, 1st prize City Ctr. Sculpture Contest, 1969; Fine Arts scholar, Germany, Munic Acad., 1958-60; Fulbright-Hayes fellow NYU, N.Y.C., 1973-79. Mem. Internat. Soc. Advancement of Living Traditions in Art, Washington Pl. Artists Assn. (pres. 1977-80), Lebanese Artists Assn. (v.p. 1964-73). Avocations: gardening, fishing, upland hunting. E-mail: ajsaghir@snet.net. Home: 20 Newfane Rd New Fairfield CT 06812-4721 Office: Western Conn State U 181 White St Danbury CT 06810-6826

SAGIE-WEBER, ABRAHAM, psychologist, researcher; b. Jerusalem, Israel, Sept. 9, 1947; s. Arye and Pnina (Frenkel) Weber; s. Raaya Neuberger, Nov. 19, 1972; children: Inbal, Navit, Yoash, Shachar, Zohar. BA, Hebrew U., Jerusalem, 1972, MA, 1977; PhD, Bar-Ilan U., Ramat-Gan, Israel, 1987. Project leader Yael Software House, Ramat-Gan, 1982-84, IBS, Tel-Aviv, 1984-87; computer ctr. mgr. Aman Engrs., Tel-Aviv, 1986-87; gen.mgr. Yaad, Jerusalem, 1987-98; lectr. Sch. Bus., Bar-Ilan U., Ramat-Gan, 1988-95, dep. dir., 1995-97, dir., 1999—; cons. Israel Assn. Cmty. Ctrs., Jerusalem, 1994—, Israel Nat. Res. Authority, Jerusalem, 1988-92, Israel Postal Svcs., Tel-Aviv, 1988-92. Author: (with Meni Koslowsky) Participation and Empowerment in Organizations; guest editor Jour. Orgnl. Behavior, 1996; contbr. articles to profl. jours. Capt., Israeli Def. Forces, 1965-68. Recipient prize Israeli System Analyst Assn., 1990; Japan Soc. for Promotion Rsch. grantee, 1996; Govt. of Can. grantee, 1996. Mem. Acad. of Mgmt., Israeli Psychol. Assn., Internat. Soc. for Study of Work and Orgnl. Values (sec.-treas. 1996—). Jewish. Home: 90935 Beit Horon Israel Office: Bar-Ilan U Sch Bus, 52900 Ramat Gan Israel

SAGIR, ABUZER, agricultural engineer; b. Adiyaman, Southeast, Turkey, Feb. 25, 1949; s. Mahmut and Ayni (Akar) S.; m. Mevlude Karakas, Jan. 28, 1978; 2 children. BS, Faculty of Agr. Izmir, 1969, MS, 1974; PhD, Agean U., 1984. From head asst. to mgr. Plant Protection Inst. Dicle U., Diyarbakir, Turkey, 1979-95; head plant protection dept. Dicle U., Diyarbakir, 1995—. Home: Dicle Üniversitesi, Lojmanlari E-Blok 3 #3, 21280 Diyarbakir Turkey Office: Ziraat Fakultesi, Dicle Univ, 21280 Diyarbakir Turkey

SAGISAKA, SHONOSUKE, biologist; b. Hokkaido, Japan, Dec. 13, 1930; s. Katsuhei and Kiku (Kumeta) S.; m. Michiko Ito, Dec., 1964. BS, Tohoku U., Sendai, Japan, 1955, MS, 1957, PhD, 1960. Instr. Iwate Med. Coll., Morioka, Japan, 1960-63; asst. prof. Tohoku U., Sendai, 1963-67; assoc. prof. Hokkaido U., Sapporo, 1967-78, prof. biology, 1978-94, prof. emeritus, 1994—, dir., 1991. Contbr. articles to profl. jours. Avocations: travel, photography.

SAGLIMBENI, RODOLFO, conductor, educator; b. Barquisimeto, Venezuela, Dec. 8, 1962; s. Filippo Saglimbeni and Amalia Muñoz. Grad. Royal Schs. Music, Royal Acad. Music, London, 1985, lic., 1985, diploma in conducting, 1986. Prin. trumpet Nat. Youth Orch. Venezuela, Barquisimeto, 1977-81, prof. trumpet, 1978-80; asst. conductor Caracas (Venezuela) Philharmonic Orch., 1980-81, Venezuelan Symphony Orch., Caracas, 1988-93; prof. conducting Simon Bolívar Conservatory, Caracas, 1989—; artistic dir., prin. conductor Gran Mariscal de Ayacucho Symphony Orch., Caracas, 1989—; prof. conducting Univ. Inst. Musical Studies, Caracas, 1990—. Contbr. articles to profl. publs.; editor Orquestradivarius, 1997; co-creator video The Birth of an Orch., 1997. Bd. dirs. State Found. Nat. Sys. Children and Youth Orchs. Venezuela, Caracas, 1994—, Teresa Carreño Theatre Found., Caracas, 1994—; artistic dir. Friends of Gran Mariscal de Ayacucho Symphony, 1994—. Fellow of the Ams. John F. Kennedy Ctr. for Performing Arts, Washington, 1997; named Conductor of Yr., Art Critics Assn., Caracas, 1989, Artists House, Caracas, 1998; named to Order Jose Felix Ribas, Nat. Govt. Venezuela, 1990; recipient prize Besançon, France, 1999, prize Conductors of the Ams., 1999. Roman Catholic. Avocations: soccer, cooking, home improvement. Fax: (58) (2) 483-8354. E-mail: rodolfosaglimbeni@compuserve.com. Office: Orch Sin Gran Mar Ayacucho PO Box 25323 Miami FL 33102-5323

SAGMEISTER, EDWARD FRANK, retired military officer, business owner; b. N.Y.C., Dec. 10, 1939; s. Frank and Anna (Unger) S.; m. Anne Marie Ducker, Aug. 18, 1962; children: Cynthia Anne, Laura Marie, Cheryl Suzanne, Eric Edward. BS, U. San Francisco, 1962; MBA, Syracuse U., 1968; postgrad., Air Command and Staff Coll., 1977, Air War Coll., 1981. Commd. 2d lt. USAF, 1963, advanced through grades to lt. col., pers. officer, 1963, aide-de-camp, 1965; dir. pers. sys. Alaskan Air Command, 1968; sys. design and program analysis officer HQ USAF, The Pentagon, 1971; spl. asst. sec. Air Force Pers. Coun., USAF, 1975; dir. pers. programs and assignments HQUSAF Europe, 1979; Air Force dep. asst. inspector gen., 1982; ret. USAF, 1984; dir. devel. Am. Cancer Soc., Riverside, Calif., 1984-87; cons. Redlands, Calif., 1987-92; chmn. of bd., pres., CEO Hospitality Pub and Grub, Inc., San Bernardino, Calif., 1992—; instr. Am. Internat. U., L.A., 1987; program dir. Am. Radio Network, L.A., 1987; ptnr., owner Midway Med. Ctr., San Bernardino, 1990-91. Foreman pro-tem San Bernardino County Grand Jury, 1990-91; mem. Redlands 2000 Com., 1988; campaign cabinet mem. Arrowhead United Way, San Bernardino, 1986-87, loaned exec., 1985; exec. dir. Crafton hills Coll. Found., Yucaipa, Calif., 1988; vol. San Bernardino County Dept. Probation, 1985-88; mem. Redlands Cmty., Chorus, 1988-90; vice-chmn., charter mem. Redlands Human Rels. Commn., 1994-97, chmn., 1996-97; mem. Redlands Youth Accountability Bd., San Bernardino County, 1994-97, treas. 1996; mem. supt.'s human rels. adv. com., Redlands Unified Sch. Dist., 1996-97. Mem. Ret. Officers Assn., Nat. Soc. Fundraising Execs., (dir., charter mem. Inland Empire chpt. 1987-88), Empire Singers (v.p. 1987). Republican. Roman Catholic. Avocations: travel, music, singing, tennis, reading. Home: 503 Sunnyside Ave Redlands CA 92373-5629 Office: Hospitality Pub & Grub Inc 1987 Diners Ct San Bernardino CA 92408-3330

SAGO, HARUHIKO, obstetrician, gynecologist, geneticist; b. Gifu, Japan, Jan. 1, 1958; s. Morihiko and Tomoko (Tsubota) S.; m. Shiori Demizu, Jan. 24, 1992; children: Maiko, Maoko, Masahiko. MD, Jikei U., Tokyo, 1982; PhD, Jikei U., 1992. Med. diplomate Japanese Bd. Surgery; diplomate Japanese Bd. Obstetrics and Gynecology, Japanese Bd. Clin. Cytology. Resident Mitsui Meml. Hosp., Tokyo, 1982-86, chief resident, 1986-87; instr. Jikei U., Tokyo, 1987-93; rsch. assoc. U. So. Calif., L.A., 1993-94; postdoctoral fellow U. Calif., San Francisco, 1994-98; physician Nat. Okura Hosp., Tokyo, 1998—; asst. prof. Jikei U., Tokyo, 1999—. Contbr. articles to profl. jours.

SAGUY, ISRAEL SAM, science educator; b. Bucarest, Romania, June 8, 1946; arrived in Israel, 1950; s. Eliezer and Clara (Cohen) Siminovitch; m. Irit E. Saguy, Sept. 23, 1969; children: Ami, Dan. BSc, Technion, Haifa, Israel, 1970, MSc, 1973, DSc, 1977. Instr. food engring. MIT, Cambridge, Mass., 1977-79; sr. rsch. scientist Agrl. Rsch. Orgn., Bet Dagan, Israel, 1979-84; rsch. fellow Pillsbury Co., Mpls., 1984-89; assoc. prof. Hebrew U. Jerusalem, Rehovot, Israel, 1989-97, prof., 1997—; cons. Am. and European Food and Biotech. Industries, 1989—; mng. assoc. Moskowitz Nateev Saguy, Ltd., Tel Aviv, 1991—; vis. prof Nestlè, Switzerland, 1996-97. Editor: Computer-Aided Techniqes in Food Technology, 1983, New Product Development, 1991; contbr. over 75 articles to profl. jours.; contbr. 10 book chpts.; patentee (6) in field. Maj. C.E., Israeli Mil., 1964. Mem. Profl. Inst. Food Technologists. Jewish. Avocation; jogging. Office: Hebrew U Jerusalem, PO Box 12, 76100 Rehovot Israel

SAH, KISHORI LAL, scientist, engineer; b. Parsa, Bihar, India, Jan. 5, 1954; s. Muni Chand Sah and Sanjharia Devi; m. Siya Kumari, June 5, 1977; children: Sunita, Sunil, Subodh. BSc in Engring., Bihar Inst. Tech., Sindri, Dhanbad, India, 1982. Engring. grad. in electronics and comm. discipline. Scientist/engr. SB Indian Space Rsch. Orgn. Satellite Ctr., Bangalore, India, 1982-85, scientist/engr. SC, 1985-88; engr. SC Space Applications Ctr., Ahmedabad, India, 1988-90; scientist/engr. SE Space Applications Ctr., Ahmedabad, 1996—. Fax: 91-79-6751736. E-mail: kishorilalsah@yahoo.com. Home: 3/2 Sangam Apt, NR Ramdev Nagar, 380 015 Ahmedabad Gujarat, India Office: Space Applications Ctr, Jodhpur Char Rasta, 380 053 Ahmedabad Gujarat, India

SAH, PURUSHOTTAM, gynecologist, consultant; b. Raniganj, India, Sept. 28, 1956; s. Durga Prasad and Shanti Devi (Modi) S.; m. Manju Agarwala, May 28, 1985; 1 child, Pern. MB, BChir, Bankura Sammilani Med. Coll., Bankura, India, 1981; diploma ob-gyn., Chittaranjan Seva Sadan, Calcutta, India, 1985. Med. officer Mitra Sangh Hosp., Howrah, India, 1983-88; gynecologist Arogya Niketan Pvt. Ltd., Uttarpara, India, 1991—, Nightingale Diagnostic Ctr., Calcutta, 1997—. Mem. Indian Med. Assn. Avocations: cartoons, quizes, writing, dramatics. Home: A-2 Kishan Abason Verma Rd, Uttarpara 712 258, India Office: Arogya Niketan Pvt Ltd, Verma Rd, Uttarpara 712 258, India

SAHA, ASIS KUMAR, cardiologist; b. Calcutta, West Bengal, India, June 14, 1941; came to U.S., 1966; s. Asoke Kumar and Swarna Prabha Saha; m. Barbara Ann Bialy, June 23, 1968; children: Kamala, Tiara, Michael, Stephen. MBBS, Calcutta U., 1963. Diplomate Am. Bd. Internal Medicine and Cardiovascular Diseases. Intern Med. Coll., Calcutta U., 1963; rotating intern Willingdon Hosp., New Delhi, India, 1964-65; rotating resident Safdarjung Hosp., New Delhi, 1965-66; rotating intern St. Peter's Gen. Hosp., Rutgers U., New Brunswick, N.J., 1966-67; med. resident St. Peter's Gen. Hosp., Rutgers U., New Burnswick, N.J., 1967-69, chief med. resident, 1969-70; cardiology fellow Mt. Sinai Med. Ctr., Miami Beach, Fla., 1970-72; staff cardiologist Kissimmee (Fla.) Meml. Hosp., 1973—, chmn. dept.

medicine, 1973-87, 90—, dir. cardiopulminary dept., 1974-80, trustee, 1978—; practice medicine specializing in cardiology Kissimmee, 1973—; mem. active staff Fla. Hosp. Kissimmee and Orlando, Orlando Regional Healthcare Sys. at St. Cloud and Orlando, Osceola Regional Hosp., Columbia Pk. Med. Ctr., Orlando, Heart of Fla. Hosp., Haines City, Fla. Fellow Am. Coll. Cardiology, Am. Coll. Chest Physicians, Coun. Clin. Cardiology, Am. Coll. Angiology, Internat. Coll. Angiology; mem. ACP, Am. Soc. Echocardiology, Am. Soc. Geriatric Medicine, Am. Soc. Nuclear Cardiology (founding), Am. Heart Assn. (pres. Ctrl. Fla. chpt. 1980, lic. in nuclear cardiology), Com. of 100, Kissimmee C. of C. Democrat. Hindu. Avocations: gardening, swimming, skiing. Office: 201 Hilda St Kissimmee FL 34741-2320

SAHA, BIDHAN CHANDRA, physics educator; b. Rangunia, Bangladesh, Sept. 29, 1946; came to U.S., 1981; s. Chinta Haran and Charu Bala S.; m. Krishna Chakraborty, June 29, 1979; 1 child, Paban. BS, Dhaka U., Bangladesh, 1966; MS, Rajshahi U., Bangladesh, 1969; PhD, Calcutta U., India, 1976. Postdoctoral fellow Indian Assn. Cultivation Sci., 1976-78; rsch. assoc. Flinders U., Adelaide, Australia, 1979-80, Yale U., New Haven, Conn., 1981; rsch. scientist U. Okla., Norman, 1982-88; assoc. prof. Fla. A&M U, Tallahassee, 1994-2000. Pres. Bangladesh Assn. Tallahassee, 1998. Grantee NASA, 1997, Rsch. Cor., Tucson, Ariz., 1998, NSF-CREST, 1998; Welch Found. postdoctoral fellow Rice U., Houston, 1989-93, Indian Assn. for the Cultivation of Sci., 1976-78. Mem. Am. Phys. Soc., Indian Assn. for the Cultivation of Sci. (life), Sigma Xi. Avocations: gardening, fishing, outdoor sports. Office: Fla A&M U Dept Physics Martin Luther King Blvd Tallahassee FL 32307

SAHA, DEBASHIS, computer science and engineering educator; b. Balurghat, India, Mar. 15, 1965; s. Indulal and Ila Saha; m. Sumita Saha, Nov. 28, 1994; 1 child, Debdeep. BE, Jadavpur U., Calcutta, 1986; MTech, Indian Inst. Tech., Kharagpur, 1988, PhD, 1996. Sr. rsch. fellow Indian Inst. Tech., Kharagpur, 1988-90; lectr. Jadavpur U., Calcutta, 1990-96, reader, 1997—; joint coord. CMC-Impact Programme, Calcutta, 1995—; guest advisor S.C.G. Coll. and N.N.D. Coll., Calcutta, 1993-94, 96—; computer cons. Squarem Pvt. Ltd., Calcutta, 1990—, System Engring. Pvt. Ltd., 1996—. Co-author jour. articles, monograph, course materials and manual. Investigator, Project on Child Labour in Calcutta, 1995—, Project on Female Infertility, Calcutta, 1990—. Recipient Merit prizes Jadavpur U., 1983-85, Career award for young tchrs. All India Coun. for Tech. Edn., Govt. of India, 1997; Nat. scholar, 1980, 82; SERC vis. fellow DST, Govt. India, 1999, Boyscast fellow DST, Govt. India, 1999-2000. Mem. IEEE, IEEE Computer Soc. (sec. 1995-97), Computer Soc. India. Bengali Hindu. Avocations: reading, playing. E-mail: d.saha@vsnl.com. Office: Jadavpur U, Dept Computer Sci/Engring, 700032 Calcutta India

SAHA, MANORANJAN, chemistry educator; b. Manikganj, Dhaka, Bangladesh, Jan. 8, 1952; s. Late Bidhu Bhusan and Late Priya Bala S.; m. Kabita Saha, July 15, 1985; children: Shreshtha, Shreya. BS in Chemistry with honors, Dhaka U., 1974; MS in Chem. Engring., Azerb. Inst. Petroleum & Chem., Baku, USSR, 1977, PhD in Petroleum and Petrochems., 1982; postdoctoral, Indian Inst. of Sci., Bangalore, 1995, Indian Inst. of Petroleum, Dehradun, 1996. Asst. prof. Dhaka U., Bangladesh, 1983-90; assoc. prof. Dhaka U., 1990-94, prof., 1994—, chmn. dept. applied chemistry and chem. tech., 1998—. Inventor in field; contbr. numerous articles to profl. jours. Mem. Asiatic Soc. Bangladesh, Bangladesh Assn. for Advancement of Sci., Bangladesh Chem. Soc. Avocations: reading, gardening, playing tennis, football, cricket. Office: Dept Appl Chem/Tech, Univ Dhaka, 1000 Dhaka Bangladesh

SAHA, UJJWAL KUMAR, mechanical engineering educator; b. Nagaon, Assam, India, Jan. 25, 1963; s. Rabindra Nath and Arun S.; m. Suparna Roy, June 27, 1997. BSc (hons.), Gauhati U., Assam, India, 1984; A.M.Ae.S.I., The Aero. Soc. of India, New Delhi, India, 1989; M.E. in Rocket Propulsion, Birla Inst. Tech., Ranchi, India, 1991; PhD, Indian Inst. Tech., Bombay, India, 1996. Sr. project engr. IIT, Bombay, 1996; lectr. dept. mech. engring. North Eastern Regional Inst. Sci. and Tech., Nirjuli, India, 1996—; presenter in field at internat. confs. and nat. meetings. Contbr. articles to profl. internat. jours. Recipient Travel grant Aero. Soc. India, 1995. Mem. Nat. Soc. Fluid Mechanics and Fluid Power, Fluid Power Soc. India, Aero. Soc. India. Avocations: music, philatally, travel, movies, cooking. Home: Sankar Mission Rd 1st Ln, Nagaon 782 001, India Office: NE Regional Inst Sci & Tech, Dept Mech Engring, Itanagar 791 109, India

SAHADE, JORGE, astronomer, researcher; b. Alta Gracia, Cordoba, Argentina, Feb. 23, 1915; s. Nallib and María (Kassab) S.; m. Miriam Stella Elkin Font, Dec. 28, 1948 (dec. Nov. 1974); children: Patricia Adriana, Carlos Alberto; m. Adela Emilia Ringuelet, Oct. 9, 1975. PhD in Astron. and Related Scis., U. La Plata, Argentina, 1943; Dr.h.c., U. Cordoba, 1987; Dr. h.c., U. San Juan, Argentina, 1996; lic. land surveyor, U. Cordoba, 1937. Astronomer Cordoba Obs., 1946-53; prof. U. Cordoba, 1948-55; rsch. astronomer U. Calif., Berkeley, 1957-58; prof. U. La Plata, 1958-71; rschr. Conicet, Argentina, 1961-95, emeritus rschr., 1995—; dir. Cordoba Obs., 1953-55, La Plata U. Obs., 1968-69, Inst. of Astronomy and Space Physics, Argentina, 1971-74; hon. prof. San Marcos Nat. U., Lima, Peru, 1987; disting. fgn. scholar Mid-Am. State Univs., 1988; pres. Nat. Commn. of Space Activities, Argentina, 1991-94; sci. coord. of Argentine participation in Gemini Project, Nat. Rsch. Coun., 1996—. Co-author: (with F.B. Wood) Interacting Binary Stars, 1978; co-editor: (with M.K.V. Bappu) Wolf-Rayet and High Temperature Stars, 1973, (with G.E. McCluskey Jr. and Y. Kondo) The Realm of Interacting Binary Stars. Recipient Golden Planetarium award Friends of Planetarium and Obs., Rosario, Argentina, 1973, Konex prize, Buenos Aires, 1983, Platzeck prize Nat. Acad. Exact, Phys. and Natural Scis., Buenos Aires, 1993, Diploma of Recognition, World Cultural Coun., 1987, Plaque of recognition, NASA, 1994; asteroid named for him, 1986; 2.15-m telescope at Casleo, San Juan, Argentina named after him, 1996. Fellow Third World Acad. Scis.; mem. COSPAR (assoc.), Internat. Astron. Union (pres. 1985-88, bd. dirs. divsn. V 1997—), Nat. Acad. Scis. Cordoba (corr.), Nat. Acad. Scis. Buenos Aires (corr.), Royal Acad. Exact, Phys. and Natural Scis. Spain (corr.), Colombian Acad. Exact, Phys. and Natural Scis. (corr.), L.Am. Acad. Scis., Internat. Acad. Astronautics, Royal Astron. Soc. London (assoc.), Argentine Astron. Assn. (hon.), Rotary (pres. 1968-69). Avocations: walking, travel, music. Home: 53-448 (p11#1), B1900BAV La Plata Argentina Office: Nat Univ La Plata, Faculty Sci/Astron/Geophys, B1900CGA La Plata Argentina

SAHAGIA, MARIA CONSTANTIN, physicist, researcher; b. Brădulet, Arges, Romania, July 19, 1943; d. Constantin Ion and Filofteia Grigore (Onitoiu) Stochioiu; m. Ion Vasile Sahagia, Oct. 22, 1966; children: Calinoiu Cristina-Constanta, Marinescu, Stefania-Maria. Physicist, U. Bucharest, 1966; PhD, Inst. Physics/Nuclear Engring., Bucharest, 1978. Rschr. Inst. Physics and Nuclear Engring., Bucharest, 1966-83, sci. rschr., 1983-92, dept. head, 1992—; dept. head Nat. Inst. of R&D in Physics and Nuclear Engring., Bucharest, 1997—; internat. expert IAEA, Vienna, Austria, 1997; Romanian rep. Internat. Com. Radionuclide Metrology, 1999. Author: Radioactive Products, Present and Perspectives in IFIN-HH, 1997; contbr. articles to profl. jours.; referee editl. bd. Romanian Physics Jour., 1997—. Grantee IAEA-Vienna, 1990, IRPA-Vienna, 1996. Mem. N.Y. Acad. Sci., Internat. Radiation Protection Assn. Orthodox Christian. Avocations: reading, watching TV and radio programs. Home: Cernisoara 29-39 bl 61, Ro 77586 Bucharest Romania Office: Nat Inst R&D Phys/Nuc Eng, PO Box MG-6, RO 76900 Bucharest Romania

SAHAGUN-GODINEZ, EDUARDO, botanist, ecologist; b. Guadalajara, Jalisco, Mex., Aug. 9, 1963; s. Enrique and Guadalupe S.-G.; m. Maria Elena Romo-Limon, Nov. 17, 1995. BS in Biology, U. Autonoma Guadalajara, Mex., 1987; MS in Plant Ecology, Tex. A&M U., 1997; doctorate, U. Guadalajara, Mex., 1998—. Assoc. prof. Facultad de Ciencias Naturales y Agropecuarias U. Autonoma Guadalajara, 1990-93, prof. Facultad de Ciencias Naturales y Agropecuarias, 1994—; dir. Carlos L. Diaz-Luna Herbarium, Guadalajara, 1994—; cons. SIAFASE Environ. Impact Assessment, Guadalajara, 1995—. Illustrator of botanical line drawings, 1994—. Scholar U. Autonoma Guadalajara, 1991-93, Lamar-Fleming Fund, Tex. A&M U., 1992. Mem. Bot. Soc. Am., Assn. Tropical Biology, Soc. Bot. Mex. Roman Catholic. Avocations: photography, reading, orchids, bromeliads. E-mail: esahagun@uagunix.gdl.uag.mx. Office: Univ Autonoma Guadalajara, Av Patria 1201 Apdo 1-440, 44100 Jalisco Guadalajara Mexico

SAHASI, GURMINDER KAUR, clinical psychologist; b. Rajasthan, India, Mar. 11, 1940; arrived in U.K., 1995; d. Chandan Singh and Gurdev (Kaur) Kang; m. Khushminder Singh Sahasi; 2 children. Grad., H.M.V. Coll., Jullinder, India, 1961; MSc, U. Chandigarh, India, 1963; DM and SP, NIMHANS, Bangalore, India, 1966; PhD, U. Agra, India, 1988. Clin. psychologist All India Inst. Med. Scis., Delhi, 1976-95, Nat. Health Svc., Welwyn Garden City, Eng., 1995—. Contbr. some 20 articles to profl. jours. Vol., Save the Children Fund, 1999. Recipient Gupta award Jour. Personality Studies, 1989. Mem. APA, Brit. Psychol. Soc., IACP. Avocations: reading, crafts. Home: 9 Parkgate, Hitchin Herts SG4 9BP, England Office: 82 North Pl, Great North Rd, Hatfield, Herts AL9 5BL, England

SAHATJIAN, RONALD ALEXANDER, science foundation executive; b. Cambridge, Mass., Oct. 1, 1942; s. Vartan and Roxy (Abrahamian) S.; m. Jean Khachadoorian, July 15, 1966; 1 child, Jennifer. BS in Chemistry, Tufts U., 1964; MS in Chemistry, U. Mass., 1968, PhD in Chemistry, 1969. Scientist color photographic rsch. lab. Polaroid Corp., Cambridge, 1971-73, sr. scientist color photograhic rsch. lab., 1973-75, sr. rsch. group leader photographic/optical materials, 1976-79, program mgr. polacolor transparency projects, 1979-81, mgr. applications rsch. lab., 1980-84; dir. R & D Chem. Fabrics Corp., Merrimack, N.H., 1984-87; v.p. corp. tech. Boston Sci. Corp., Watertown, Mass., 1987—; mem. adv. bd. Franklin Inst., Boston, 1989—. Contbr. articles to Jour. Polymer Sci., Macromolecules, Radiology. Fellow Am. Inst. Chemists; mem. ASTM, Radiol. Soc. N.Am., Watertown C. of C. (bd. dirs. 1991—). Achievements include 58 U.S. and internat. patents. Home: 29 Saddle Club Rd Lexington MA 02420-2121 Office: Boston Sci Corp 1 Boston Scientific Pl Natick MA 01760-1536

SAHAY, BHAGWAN, oil and gas consultant; b. Gwalior, India, Nov. 29, 1934; s. Omrao Behari and Lakshmi Mathur; m. Shail Bala Mathur, Feb. 7, 1958; children: Anita Andley, Sahay Atul. BSc, Lucknow (India) U., 1952, MSc in Geology, 1954; PhD in Petroleum Geology, Kensington U., L.A., 1981. Geologist Std. Vacuum Oil Co., Calcutta, India, 1954-62; sr. geologist Oil and Natural Gas Corp., India, 1962-75; from dep. to supt. geologist Oil and Natural Gas Corp., Bombay, 1975-82; chief geologist Oil and Natural Gas Corp., Bombay, India, 1982-89; dy gen. mgr. Oil and Natural Gas Corp., Ahmedabad, India, 1989-92; gen. mgr./group gen. mgr. Oil and Natural Gas Corp., Ahmedabad/Delhi, 1992—; chief of geosci. GeoPetrol Internat., 2000—; mng. dir. Umrao Exploration, New Delhi, 1994—; mem. tech. bd. consultants AP Energy Petromin Asia, Singapore, 1995—; advisor on India Petro Cons., Geneva, Switzerland, 1995—, IHS Energy Group, Eng.; petroleum cons. Oil India, New Delhi, ONGC, New Delhi and Dehradun, India, 1997; worked on high pressure studies Bombay Offshore Trust; presenter in field chair tech. sessions in various confs. Author: Wellsite Geological Techniques for Petroleum Exploration, 1988, Origin and Evaluation of Formation Pressures, 1988, Petroleum Exploration and Exploitation Practices, 1994, 2d edit., 1997, Pressure Regimes in Oil and Gas Exploration, 1998-99; editor: Hydrocarbon Potential of Oceanic Reefs of the World, 1991, The Dynamic Geosphere, 1997; contbr. articles to profl. jours. Named to Internat. Hall of Fame, U.S., 1984; recipient Udyog Rattan award Inst. Econ. Studies, 1991, Udyog Jyoti award All India Econ. Forum, 1991, Udyog Gaurav award All India Orgnl. Entrepreneural Confederation, 1991, Kohinoor Ratna award Govt. India, Bangalore, 1991, Gems of India award All India Achievers Conf., Delhi, 1992, award Shiromani Inst., New Delhi, 1992, Pride of Asia Internat. and Gold medal Internat. Friendship Soc., Singapore, 1992, Pi Epsilon award, 1984. Mem. Soc. Petroleum Engrs., Russian Acad. Scis. (Kapitsa gold medal 1999). Hindu. Avocations: writing, reading, golf, music. Fax: 6136790. Home: C-9 9168 Vasant Kunj, New Delhi 70, India

SAHAY, PRADOSH PRAKASH, physics educator, researcher; b. Darbhanga, Bihar, India, Sept. 1, 1959; s. Ramji Sahai and Vijay Prabha Devi; m. Kirti Srivastava, May 2, 1994; 1 child, Ishu. MS, L.N. Mithila U., Darbhanga, 1982; PhD, Banaras Hindu U., Varanasi, India, 1992. Lectr. Tribhuvan U., Nepal, 1983-89; rsch. fellow Banaras Hindu U., Varanasi, India, 1989-92; lectr. S.L. Inst. Engring. & Technology, Sangrur, India, 1992-94; asst. prof. Regional Engring. Coll., Silchar, India, 1994—; mem. acad. com. engring. Assam U., Silchar, 1994—, mem. sch. bd. tech., 1997—; head dept. physics Regional Engring. Coll., 1994—. Contbr. articles to profl. jours. State Merit scholar Govt. of Bihar, 1979; Sr. Rsch. fellow Coun. Sci. & Indsl. Rsch., India, 1991, Sci. and Engring. Rsch. Coun. fellow Govt. India, 1998-99. Mem. Indian Soc. Tech. Edn., Indian Sci. Congress Assn., Indian Assn. Physics Tchrs. Avocations: reading, sight seeing. Home: Kaidrabad, Darbhanga 846 004, India Office: Regional Engring Coll, Dept Physics, Silchar 788 010, India

SAHEL, PIERRE, literary critic, educator; b. Algiers, France, Nov. 3, 1943; s. Leon and Marcelle (Trigano) S.; children: Jean-Jacques, Ariane. Diploma, Aix Univ., 1965; agregation, France, 1969; diplome etudes, Politiques Aix Univ., France, 1975; state doctorate, Lyon Univ., France, 1977. Asst. High Sch., Liverpool, Eng., 1963-64; tchr. High Sch., North, France, 1967-69; univ. lectr. Dakar, Senegal, 1969-70; univ. prof. Aix, France, 1970—; gen. editor C.A.R.A. Aix, 1989-92. Author: La Pensee Politique Dans Les Drames Historiques de Shakespeare, 1984; contbr. articles to profl. jours. Recipient Prix, Rotary Club, 1975. Home: Le Balcon de La Reine, 13790 Chateauneuf-le-Rouge France Office: Univ of Aix, Ave R Schuman, 13100 Aix-en-Provence France

SAHGAL, ASH, marketing professional, consultant; b. New Delhi, India, Feb. 3, 1967; arrived in U.K., 1975; s. Suraj Prakash and Kamal (Khorana) S.; m. Tarika Sahgal, Apr. 13, 1996. BA, Richmond U., London, 1994; MBA, Richmond U., 1995. Sales and mktg. mgr. Million Dollar Homes Ltd., London, 1985-87; dir. Alfirth Ltd., London, 1988-96; mktg. dfir. Adams & Assocs. (U.K.) Ltd., London, 1996—; mktg. cons. ATS Mktg. Ltd., London, 1999—. Mem. Conservative Party. Hindu. Avocations: psychometric analysis, scuba diving, puzzles, restoration of classic automobiles. Home and Office: Flat 61 Northgate, Prince Albert Rd, London NW8 7EH, England

SAHI, MUHAMMAD JAVED, electrical engineer; b. Faisalabad, Punjab, Pakistan, Aug. 13, 1957; s. Asmat Ullah Sahi. BS in Engring., U. Portsmouth, Eng., 1982; MA in Tech. Edn., W.Va. U., 1993; MS in Computer Sci., Cooks Inst. Electronic Engring., 1994. Asst. dir. Water and Power Devel. Authority, Lahore, Pakistan, 1983-85; sub-divsnl. officer Water and Power Devel. Authority, Samundri, Pakistan, 1986-87; asst. dir. Water and Power Devel. Authority, Faisalabad, Pakistan, 1987-88; sub-divsnl. officer Water and Power Devel. Authority, Jauhrabad, Pakistan, 1988-90, Lahore, 1990-91; protection engr. Water and Power Devel. Authority, Faisalabad, 1995—. Mem. IEEE, IEEE Pakistan, Instn. Engrs. Pakistan. Avocations: reading, gardening, swimming. Home: 706 Batala Colony, Faisalabad Punjab Pakistan

SAHIN, SAMI, educator; b. Kayseri, Turkey, Apr. 25, 1950; s. Ahmet and Hatice S.; m. Havva Korkmaz, May 13, 1963; children: Mehmet Fatih, Ismail Hakki, Hatice. MS, Istanbul Tech. U., Turkey, 1976, PhD, 1982. Asst. TUBITAK, Turkey, 1976-78; asst. Istanbul Tech. U., Turkey, 1978-84, tchg. lectr., 1984-86, prof., 1986—. Contbr. articles to profl. jours. With Turkish Army, 1975. TUBITAK scholar, Turkey, 1973, ETIBANK scholar, 1974, Petroleum Trust scholar, Turkey, 1976. Mem. Internat. Union Pure and Applied Chemistry, Turkish Chem. Soc., Chamber Chem. Engrs., N.Y. Acad. Scis. Islamic. Avocation: stamp collecting. Office: Istanbul Tech U, Faculty of Sci, 80626 Istanbul Turkey

SAHLER, HILDEGARD, art historian, journalist; b. Linz, Germany, Sept. 4, 1963; d. Wolfgang and Hedwig (Siebertz) S. PhD in Art History, U. Mainz, Germany, 1994. Cons. conservation of monuments Mainz C. of C., 1995-96; pvt. practice cons., 1996-98; pvt. practice journalist Conservation of Monuments, Art and Comm., Mainz, 1997-98; conservator Bavarian State Dept. Hist. Monuments, 1998—. Author: San Claudio al Chienti and the romanesque churches with inscribed-cross plan in the Marche, 1998; contbr. articles to profl. jours. Mem. Jury of Europa Nostra. Recipent award Fondazione Salimbeni per la Storia e la Critica d'Arte, 1999. Mem. Soc. Conservation of Monuments and Protection of Landscapes in the Rhineland, Assn. German Art Historians, German Castle Assn.

SAHLIN, KENT PAUL, physiologist, researcher; b. Stockholm, May 12, 1947; s. Nils Salomon and Katarina (Stenros) S.; m. Christel Birgitta Törnblom, May 17, 1975; children: Asa Sahlin, Per Jonas Sahlin, Elin Sahlin. MEng., Royal Polytech., Stockholm, 1971, PhD, 1978. Rsch. biochemist Karolinska Inst., Stockholm, 1972-79, fellow, 1980-92, assoc. prof., 1985—; lectr. U. Coll. Phys. Edn. and Sports, Stockholm, 1992—. Author: (with others) Handbook of Physiology; mem. editl. bd. Acta Physiologica Scandinavica, 1996—, European Jour. Applied Physiology, 1997—; contbr. articles to profl. jours. Mem. Am. Coll. Sports Medicine, Swedish Soc. Medicine, Am. Physiol. Soc. Office: Karolinska Inst Dept Physiol/Pharmacol, Lidingövägen 2 PO Box 5626, S-11486 Stockholm Sweden

SÄHN, SIEGFRIED, engineering educator; b. Kauffung, Schlesien, Germany, Apr. 13, 1935; s. Kurt and Elfriede (Schwarz) S.; m. Margret Teichgräber, Aug. 20, 1960; children: Michael, Matthias. Diploma in engring., Tech. U., Dresden, 1961, D in Engring., 1965, D in Engring. habilitation, 1981. Asst. Tech. U., Dresden, 1961-65, head asst., 1962-92, a.p. prof., 1992—. Author: Bruch-und Beurteilungskriterien in der Festigkeitslehre, 1989, Textbook of Fracture and Assessment Criteria in the Science of the Strength of Materials, 1992; co-author: Arbeitsbuch Höhere Festigkeitslehre, 1978, Höhere Festigkeitslehre, 1979. Named a.p. Prof., Tech. U. Dresden, 1992. Home: Wittenberger Strasse 15, D 01309 Dresden Sachsen, Germany Office: Technische Univ Dresden, Mommsen St 13, D 01062 Dresden Germany

SAHNEY, SANDEEP, pharmaceuticals executive; b. Patna, Bihar, India, Nov. 19, 1963; s. Shyam Sunder and Pushpa (Sethi) S.; m. Ritu Jhamb, Feb. 19, 1991; children: Mehak, Sarthak. BA in Econs. with honors, U. Delhi, 1984, MBA, 1986. Mgmt. trainee Ranbaxy Labs. Ltd., Delhi, 1986-87, brand mgr., 1987-91; regional mgr. Ranbaxy Labs. Ltd., Lucknow, India, 1991-93; group brand mgr. Ranbaxy Labs. Ltd., Delhi, 1993-95, mktg. mgr., 1995-97, gen. mgr., 1997-2000, dir., 2000—. Avocations: reading, music. Home: F-436 Sarita Vihar, Delhi 110044, India Office: Ranbaxy Labs Ltd, Devika Tower 6 Nehru Pl 12th Fl, Delhi 110019, India

SAHNI, O.P., business educator, management consultant; b. Feb. 16, 1941; s. Sh Jai Ram Sahni. BS, Indian Inst. Mgmt., Ahmedabad, 1961, MSc in Econs., 1965, PhD in Bus. Adminstrn., 1979. Faculty Punjab Agrl. Univ., Ludhiana, 1965—, prof. bus. mgmt., 1991—; head dept. bus. mgmt. Punjab Agrl. Univ., 5, 1995-99; vis. prof. mgmt. Asmara U., 1985-88; advisor mkt. devel. West German GTZ Team, Ctrl. Tool Room Ludhiana, 1983; bd. dirs. Nat. Fertilizers Ltd., New Delhi, Nahar Internat. Ltd., Nahar Fibres Ltd., Nahar Exports Ltd., Admath Textiles Ltd., Arihant Cotsyn Ltd., Arihant Corp. Ltd., Eastman Cast and Forge Ltd., Punj Bros. Ltd., Eastman Industries Ltd., Midland Internat. Ltd., Mangla Cottex Ltd., Ludhiana Stock Exch.; vis. faculty Jammu U., Punjab U., Chandigarth, R.A. Podar Inst. Mgmt. Jaipur, Nahar Group of Cos., Ludhiana, Oswal Group of Cos., Ludhiana, North India Tech. Cons. Orgn., others; cons. World Bank assisted project Makurdi U., 1996; lectr. in field; condr. seminars in field. Author: Farm Management, 1971, Agribusiness in India, 1977, Ludhiana Hosiery Industry, 1983, Marketing Programme for Central Tool Room, 1983; contbr. articles to profl. jours. Mem. All India Mgmt. Assn. (mem. governing coun. 1981-84), Ludhiana Mgmt. Assn. (gen. sec. 1978-82, v.p. 1982-85), Indian Mktg. Assn. (mem. steering com.). Home: Punjab Agrl Univ Campus, House 9/11, Ludhiana 141 004, India Office: Punjab Agrl Univ, Dept Bus Mgmt, 141 004 Ludhiana India

SAHNI, PRITAM SINGH, general practice physician; b. Khanpur, Punjab, India, May 11, 1933; s. Budh Singh and Ram Lubhai (Anand) S.; m. Tripat Kaur Sahni, June 25, 1961; children: Preet Inder, Binda Preet. MB, BS, U. Durham (Eng.), 1956; PhD, Oxford (Eng.) U., 1976. Cons. physician Am. Mission Hosp., Kuwait, 1964-67, sr. cons. physician, 1967—; med. examiner UN, Kuwait, 1967—. Fellow Royal Coll. Physicians and Surgeons Glasgow; mem. British Diabetic Assn., Royal Coll. Gen. Practitioners Eng., Soc. Endocrinology, Oriental Club London, United Oxford Cambridge Club. Office: PO Box 23188 SAFAT, 13092 Kuwait City Kuwait

SAHOO, MADAN MOHAN, orthopaedic surgeon, educator; b. Cuttack, Orissa, India, July 3, 1961; s. Surendra Nath and Manjusa Sahoo; m. Binodini Behera, May 22, 1991; 1 child. MB, BChir, SriRam Chandra Bhanja Med. Coll., Cuttack, India, 1984; MS in Orthopaedics, Maharaja Krishna Chandra Gajapati Med. Coll., Berhampur, India, 1989. Med. diplomate. Intern SriRam Chandra Bhanja Med. Coll. Hosp., Cuttack, 1984-85; asst. surgeon Govt. of Orissa, Kantabanji, India, 1989-90; sr. resident Safdarjang Hosp., New Delhi, 1990-93; specialist in orthopaedics Nehru Shatabdi Ctrl. Hosp., Talcher, India, 1993-96, 96—, Jawahar Lal Nehru Hosp., Bhilai, India, 1996. Contbr. articles to profl. jours.; inventor in field. Recipient 1st prize for poster presentation Coal India Med. Conf., Talcher, 1994. Mem. Orissa Orthopaedic Assn. (life), Indian Orthopaedic Assn. (life), N.Y. Acad. Scis. (life). Avocations: songs, music, writing poems. Home: Gopalpur Raghunathpur, Jagatsinghpur 754132, India

SAHOO, SUSANTA KUMAR, engineering educator, researcher; b. Puri, Orissa, India, June 28, 1967; s. Baman Charan and Pdmabati Sahoo; m. Girija Rani Giri, Oct. 20, 1997. BSc in Engring., Sambalpur U., India, 1989, MSc in Engring., 1991; PhD in Engring., Utkal U., India, 1998; MBA, Ingou, India, 1999. Sr. lectr. I.G.I.T., Sarang, India, 1991-00, R.E.C., Rourkela, India, 2000—; programme officer Nat. Svc. Scheme, India, 1998. Contbr. articles to profl. jours. Mem. Divine Life Soc., 1995. Recipient Glory of India India Internat. Frienchsip Soc., 1999. Mem. Inst. Engrs. (Meml. award 1997), Orissa Sci. Acad., Indian Soc. Tech. Edn. Avocation: story writing. Office: Regional Engring Coll, Mech Egnring Dept, 769008 Rourkela India

SAHOTA, GURCHARN SINGH, mechanical engineer; b. Talwandi Jattan, Punjab, India, Jan. 4, 1940; came to U.S., 1971; naturalized, 1980; s. Karam Singh and Amar Kaur (Nijjar) S.; m. Gurvindar Kaur Johal, May 4, 1966 (dec. Mar. 1978); 1 child, Saryadvinder Singh; m. Kamaljit Kaur Grewal, Jan. 10, 1979; children: Parmeet Kaur, Sonia K. BSME, Punjab U., 1957-61; MSME, N.J. Inst. Tech., 1975-77. Engr. Heavy Elecs., Bhopal, India, 1962-70; mfg. engr. Engelhard Industries, Union, N.J., 1974-76; from sr. plant engr. to supr. plant engring. group Am. Cyanamid Co., Stamford, Conn., 1976-93; mgr. plant engring. Cytec Industries Inc., Stamford, 1994—. Home: 34 Duke Dr Stamford CT 06905-1017 Office: Cytec Industries Inc 1937 W Main St Stamford CT 06902-4516

SAHRAWAT, KANWAR LAL, chemist; b. Delhi, India, Nov. 7, 1941; s. Jai and Samay Kaur (Udar) Lal; m. Sumitra Devi Dabas, May 6, 1964; 2 children: Dinesh, Deepak. BS in Chemistry, Punjab U., Chandigarh, India, 1962; MS in Soil Sci., Indian Agrl. Rsch. Inst., New Delhi, India, 1969, PhD in Soil Chemistry, 1973. Rsch. assoc. Internat. Crops Rsch. Inst., Hyderabad, India, 1973-75, soil chemist, 1978-88, sr. soil scientist, 1989-91; sr. soil scientist West Africa Rice Devel. Assn., Bouake, Ivory Coast, 1991—; vis. scientist U. Wis.-Madison, 1983-84; advisor Internat. Found. for Sci., Stockholm, 1998—. Editor 4 books; contbr. chpts. to books, over 120 articles to profl. jours. Post-doctoral fellow Internat. Rice Rsch. Inst., Los Baños, Philippines, 1975-78. Fellow Nat. Acad. Agrl. Sci. of India; mem. Soil Sci. Soc. Am., Am. Soc. Agronomy, Internat. Soc. Soil Sci., Assn. Rice Rsch. Workers, Indian Soc. Soil Sci. Hindu. Avocations: reading, music, writing, bird watching. E-mail: k.sahrawat@cgiar.org. Home: 92 Mahipal Pur, New Delhi 110037, India Office: West Africa Rice Devel Assn, 01BP 2551, Bouake Côte d'Ivoire

SAHU, DHARANI DHAR, English language educator, writer; b. Cuttack, Orissa, India, Sept. 15, 1948; s. Jogendra and Padmavati Sahu; m. Kanak Manjari, Feb. 19, 1975; children: Ayaskanta, Lopamudra, Monalisa. BA, Ravenshaw Coll., Cuttack, 1968, BA with honors, 1970; MA in English, Utkal U., Bhubaneswar, India, 1972, PhD, 1985. Lectr. in English, Regional Coll., Bhubaneswar, 1973-74, S.C.S. Coll., Puri, India, 1974-77, Ravenshaw Evening Coll., 1977-83, Dhenkanal (India) Coll., 1983-85; reader in English Berhampur U., 1985—, head dept. English, 1993-95; Author: Cats on a Hot Tin Roof: A Study of the Alienated Characters in the Plays of Tennessee

Williams, 1990, (novel) The House of Serpents, 1996; contbr. short stories to The New Quest, The Heritage. Avocations: music, cricket, playing the flute and banjo. Home: B/12 Profs Qtrs Berhampur U, Bhanja Bihar, 760007 Berhampur Orissa, India

SAHU, SANTOSH KUMAR, botanist; b. Berhampur, India, Apr. 1, 1965; s. Bidyadhar and Tara S. MSc in Botany, Berhampur U., 1994, PhD in Botany, 1999. With dept. botany RN Coll., Berhampur, Orissa, India, 1989—; spkr. All India Radio, Berhampur, 1998, 99. Author: Handbook of Plants, 1999; asst.: Textbook on Environment Studies, 1996, Paribesa Bigyan, 1996. Avocations: football, personal computing. Office: Berhampur U Dept Botany, Environ Toxicology Lab, 760 007 Berhampur Orissa, India

SAHU, SURENDRA NATH, physicist, researcher; b. Berhampur, Orissa, India, July 15, 1951; s. Narashinga and Jhumpa Sahu. MSc in Physics, Banaras Hindu U., India, 1973, PhD, 1984. Asst. prof. Inst. of Physics, Banaras Hindu U., India, 1991—; vis. scientist U. Uppsala, Sweden, 1986, U. New South Wales, Australia, 1986-88, U. Campinas, Brazil, 1988, U. Autonoma, Spain, 1988-90; visitor ICTP, Italy, 1989. Author: Handbook of Semiconductor Electrodeposition, 1996; contbr. some 40 articles to profl. jours. Welch fellow Internat. Union for Vacuum Sci. Tech. and Applications, 1986. Avocations: reading, sightseeing. Office: Inst of Physics, Sachivalaya Marg, 751005 Bhubaneswar Orissa, India

SAID, QABOOS BIN, Sultan of Oman, prime minister of Oman; b. Salalad, Oman, Nov. 18, 1940; s. Said bin Taimur; married. Sultan Govt. of Oman, 1970—, also prime min., min. fgn. affairs, def. and fin., also chmn. ctrl. bank; chmn. Ctrl. Bank of Oman. Decorated knight comdr. Order of St. Michael and St. George (Eng.). Avocations: reading, horse-back riding, music. Office: Office of H M The Sultan, Royal Palace, Muscat Oman*

SAIDA, TOYOYASU, chemical and biochemical engineer; b. Tokyo, Jan. 18, 1935; came to U.S., 1985; s. Tameo and Fukiko Saida; m. Mariko Itano, Jan. 16, 1961; children: Tetsuo, Miyoko Asahi, Takashi Saida. BS, U. Tokyo, 1958. Registered profl. engr. Japan. Ops. engr. Toyo Gas Chems. Corp., Niigata, Japan, 1958-59; rschr. Tokyo Inst. of Tech., 1959-61; rsch. engr. Mitsui-Toatsu Chems. Ltd., Yokohama, Japan, 1961-69, chief rsch. engr., 1969-78; mgr. process rsch. divsn. Toyo Engring. Corp., Mobara, Japan, 1978-84; adv. bd. mem. Toyo Engring. Corp., Chiba, Japan, 1984-85; sr. v.p. BW Biotec, Inc., Chgo., 1985-86; gen. mgr. Hazarmacorp Rsch. Ctr., Tsukuba, Japan, 1987-95; mng. dir. Saida & Assocs., Deerfield, Ill., 1997—. Author: Handbook of Membrane Technology, 1978, Handbook of Bioprocess, 1985, Cellulose, 1986. Recipient Excellent Invention of Yr. Sci. and Tech. Agy., 1965. Mem. Am. Chem. Soc., Soc. of Chem. Engrs. Japan. Achievements include inventor innovative new synthetic method of urea, large scale manufacturing process of single cell protein from n-paraffin, fuel alcohol manufacturing process from lignocellulosics, volume reduction method of radioactive wastes with liquid phase oxidation. Avocations: working with metallic materials, movies, computers. Home and Office: 431 Kelburn Rd Apt 315 Deerfield IL 60015-4367

SAIDI, PARVIN, hematologist, medical educator; b. Teheran, Iran, Mar. 21, 1932; came to U.S., 1946; d. Ahmad and Fatemeh (Ashouri) S.; m. Allahverdi Farmanfarmaian, May 27, 1958; children: Dellara Farmanfarmaian Terry, Kimya Farmanfarmaian Harris. BS, Smith Coll., Northampton, Mass., 1952; MD, Harvard U., 1956. Diplomate Am. Bd. Internal Medicine, subspecialty hematology and med. oncology. Intern medicine UCLA Med. Ctr., 1956-57; resident internal medicine U. Calif., San Francisco, 1957-59; NIH rsch. fellow hematology U. Calif. Hosps. and Children's Med. Ctr., San Francisco, 1959-61, 63-64; asst. prof. medicine U. Medicine & Dentistry N.J.-Rutgers Med. Sch., New Brunswick, 1968-71, assoc. prof., 1971-74; prof. U. Medicine & Dentistry N.J.-Robert Wood Johnson Med. Sch., New Brunswick, 1974—, chief divsn. hematology and oncology, dept. medicine, 1972—; chief divsn. hematology and oncology, dept. medicine Robert Wood Johnson U. Hosp., New Brunswick, 1981—; cons. internist, hematologist, oncologist St. Peter's Med. Ctr., New Brunswick, Douglass Coll., Rutgers U., New Brunswick, VA Hosp., Lyons, N.J., Muhlenberg Hosp., Plainfield, N.J., Princeton (N.J.) Med. Ctr.; dir. Melvyn H. Motolinsky Lab. Hematology Rsch., N.J. Regional Comprehensive Hemophilia Care Program; mem. Gov.'s Adv. Coun. on AIDS; chmn. N.J. Regional Comprhensive Hemophilia Care Program Adv. Bd.; chmn. HHS region II Comprehensive Hemophilia Diagnostic and Treatment Ctrs., 1984-85, 89-90, 94-95, 99-2000; chmn. med. adv. bd. Hemophilia Found. N.J.; mem. med. adv. exec. com. N.J. Blood Svcs. Cons. editor Am. Jour. Medicine; contbr. articles to profl. jours. Recipient disting. svc. award for rsch. in leukemia Melvyn H. Motolinsky Rsch. Found., 1977, Humanitarian award Hemophilia Assn. No. N.J., 1978. Fellow ACP (mem. sci. program com. N.J. region), Acad. Medicine N.J.; mem. Am. Soc. Hematology (edn. com.), N.J. Hemophilia Assn. (chmn. med. adv. com., spl. award, Dr. L. Michael Kuhn Meml. award 1996), Coop. Oncology Group N.J. (exec. com., chairperson subcom. on lymphoma), Am. Heart Assn. (coun. on thrombosis), Am. Fedn. Clin. Rsch., Royal Soc. Medicine (affiliate), Am. Soc. Clin. Oncology, World Fedn. Hemophilia, Alpha Omega Alpha, Phi Beta Kappa, Sigma Xi. Office: Robert Wood Johnson Med Sch 1 Robert Wood Johnson Pl New Brunswick NJ 08901-1928

SAIDY, AISATOU NJIE, federal official. Sec. state health, soc. and women's affairs Govt. of Gambia, 1996—, v.p., 1997—. Office: Office of Pres, State House, Banjul Gambia*

SAIED, JAMES GUY, conductor, consultant; b. Wirt, Okla., June 14, 1915; s. Oscar and Minnie (Adwan) S.; m. Helen Louella Ricker, Feb. 14, 1943; children: James Robert, Delia Ann Pierson. Ba, East Cen. U., Ada., Okla., 1936; postgrad., Vandercook Sch. Music. Cert. pub. sch. tchr. Band dir. Stroud (Okla.) Pub. Schs., 1936, Guthrie (Okla.) Pub. Schs., 1937-40, El Reno (Okla.) Pub. Schs. and Jr. Colls., 1940-42; ret.; music industry exec.; condr. of Univ., profl., mil. and community bands nationwide; cons., condr. John Sousa Concerts, 1981—. Found, condr. Oil Capitol Concert Band, Tulsa, 1959-62; condr. Tulsa Starlight Profl. Band, 1967-70; bd. dirs. Okla. Soc. Crippled Children, 1980—, Jr. Achievement, 1982-84. With U.S. Army, 1942-45, ETO. Decorated Bronze Star; named Disting. Alumnus East Cen. U., 1990; recipient Honor medal DAR, 1988, Order of Merit, John Philip Sousa Found., 1991, Nat. Good Citizen award SAR, 1992, Phi Beta Mu Internat. Outstanding award, 1990, George Washington Honor medal Freedoms Found., 1992, Will Rogers Ann. Spirit award, 1999, Outstanding Contbn. to Music Edn. award Okla. Bandmasters Assn., 1999. Mem. Nat. Assn. Music Merchants (bd. dirs. 1962-65, 71-74), Am. Bandmasters Assn. (hon. award 1988), Nat. Band Assn. (Citation of Excellence 1984, 86), Associated Concert Bands of Am., Rotary (pres. 1976-77, Outstanding Rotarian of Yr. dist. 6110 1981), Masons, Knife & Fork Club (pres. 1977-78), Kappa Kappa Psi (Disting. Svc. to Music award 1989). Democrat. Methodist. Home: 5832 S Florence Ave Tulsa OK 74105-7424 Office: PO Box 4684 Tulsa OK 74159-0684

SAIER, OSKAR, archbishop; b. Wagensteig, Germany, Aug. 12, 1932; s. Adolf and Berta S. Degree, U. Munich, U. Tübingen. Curate, 1957; asst. Kanonist Inst., U. Munich, 1963; auxilliary bishop Freiburg, Germany, 1972, archbishop, 1978—; chair pastoral comm. German Conf. Bishops, 1979-98, 2d chair, German Conf. Bishops, 1987-99; mem. Vatican Cong. for the Clergy, 1984-99. Author: Communio in der Lehre des Zweiten Vatikanischen Konzils, 1973. Named Freeman of Buchenbach, 1972, of St. Peter Black Forest, 1977, of Bethlehem, Israel, 1984, Order of El Sol del Peru, 1990, Grosses Bundesverdienstkreuz, 1992, Verdienstmedaille des Landes Baden-Württemberg, 1997. Office: Archbishop of Freiburg in Breisgau, Herrenstrasse 35, D-79098 Freiburg Germany

SAIF, ABDALLAH HASAN, bank executive. Gov. Bahrain Monetary Agy., Manama; min. of fin. and nat. economy Bahrain. *

SAIFUDDIN, ABDUL BARI, obstetrics-gynecology educator, consultant; b. Alabio, Indonesia, Apr. 6, 1940; s. Haji and Siti Fathimah (Salman) S.; m. Rosida Bari Yusuf, Sept. 6, 1968; children: Indra, Reza, Mirza. MD, U. Indonesia, Jakarta, 1965; MPH, Johns Hopkins U., 1975. Cert. ob-gyn., U. Indonesia, 1969; cert. health profns. edn., U. Ill. Med. Ctr., Chgo., 1981. Resident Jakarta, 1965-69; vice dean faculty medicine U. Indonesia, 1984-90, chmn. dept. ob-gyn., 1990-94, prof. ob-gyn., 1991—; chmn. Indonesian Coll. Ob-Gyn., Jakarta, 1996—; coun. mem. Asia-Oceanic Fedn. Ob-Gyn., Singapore, 1993-95; bd. trustees Johns Hopkins Program Internat. Edn. in Reproductive Health, Balt., 1995—. Author, editor: (textbook) Obstetrics, 1976, 2d edit., 1981, 3d edit., 1991, (textbook) Gynecology, 1982, 2d edit., 1994; editor: (reference book) National Resource Documents for Family Planning Service, 1996, National Resource Documents for Maternal and Neonatal Health Care, 2000; editor Procs. XVth AOCOG Women's Health, 1995, Safe Motherhood Modules in the Core Curriculum of Medical Education in Indonesia, 1997; editor-in-chief Indonesian Jour. Ob-Gyn., Jakarta, 1974-90, Med. Jour. Indonesia, Jakarta, 1992—. Chmn. Korps Pegawai Republik Indonesia (Indonesian Civil Servants Corp.) Faculty Medicine, U. Indonesia, 1984-90. Mem. Indonesian Assn. Secure Contraception (pres. 1988-91), Indonesian Soc. Ob-Gyn. (pres. 1990-93), Indonesian Med. Assn., Asia Pacific Scientific Editors Assn., Johns Hopkins U. Alumni Assn. Avocation: travel. Home: C221 Jalan Salemba Bluntas, Jakarta Pusat 10440, Indonesia Office: U Indonesia Fac Medicine, 6 Jalan Salemba Raya, Jakarta Pusat 10430, Indonesia

SAIFUL-ISLAM, K.M., information scientist, edcuator; b. Jessore, Khulna, Bangladesh, July 29, 1942; s. K. M. Aminul-Islam and Nurunnahar Begam. BA, Dacca Coll., Dhaka, Bangladesh, 1961; diploma in libr. sci., U. Karahci, Pakistan, 1963, MA in Libr. Sci., 1965; PhD, U. Dhaka, 1987. Catalogue libr. Karachi U. Libr., 1965-71, lectr., 1966-67; libr. Internat. Ctr. Diarrheal Diseases Rsch., Dhaka, 1972-75; lectr., asst. prof. U. Dhaka, 1975-88, assoc. prof., 1988-93, prof., 1993—; course dir. internship program Asia Found., 1988. Author: Number Building in Dewey Decimal Classification..., 1991; contbr. articles to profl. jours.; performer Radio Pakistan, 1965-70, Sta. B-TV, Dhaka, 1972—. Convenor arts fcaulty, chief, editl. com. White Party, Dhaka U., 1992-94, mem. convening com., 1993-95. Mem. Asiatic soc. Bangladesh, Bangla Acad., Karachi Univ. Profl. Librs. Assn. (gen. sec. 1967-71),. Islam. Avocations: music, hunting, photography, gardening, friendship. Office: U Dhaka Faculty Arts, Dept Libr & Info Scis., Dhaka 1000, Bangladesh

SAIFULLIN, RENAT SALYAKHOVICH, inorganic technology educator, researcher; b. Kazan, Russia, July 5, 1930; s. Salyakh Tazeevich and Gul'sum Ismahilovna (Khusnutdinova) S.; m. Rosa Galeevna Khalilova, May 5, 1955; 1 child, Adel Renatovich. Grad. in Chem. Engring., Kazan Inst. Chem. Tech., 1953, Candidate of Chem. Scis., 1958, DSc, 1970. Asst. dept. inorganic chemistry Kazan Inst. Chem. Tech., Tatarstan, 1956-61, asst. prof. dept. inorganic chemistry, 1961-71, prof. dept. inorganic chemistry, 1971-73; head dept. inorganic tech. Kazan Tech. U. (formerly Kazan Inst. Chem. Tech.), 1973—; dean chem. faculty Pub. U. Coll. Tchrs., Kazan, 1962-65; head inst. br. All Union Mendeleev's Chem. Soc., 1980-87. Author: Combined Electrochemical Coatings and Materials (in Russian), 1972, Composite Coatings and Materials (in Russian), 1977, Dispersionsschichten (in German), 1978, Inorganic Composite Materials (in Russian), 1983, Physico-Chemistry of Inorganic Polymeric and Composite Materials (in Russian), 1990, Physical Chemistry of Inorganic Polymeric and Composite Materials (in English), 1992, (with G.G. Khisameev) Explanatory Dictionary-Manual on Physics, Chemistry and Chemical Technology (in Russian, Tatar and English), 1996, (with V.A. Khusnutdinov and I.G. Khabibullin) (textbook) Equipment of Inorganic Chemicals Production (in Russian), 1987, (with L.B. Kodakova and R.T. Nabiullina) Professor Academician of Tatarstan Academy of Sciences-Essays of the Life-Past and Present (in Russian), 1997, (with A.R. Saifullin) Universal Concise Dictionary Chemistry, Physics, Technology (in English and Russian), 2000; mem. numerous editl. bds.; contbr. over 430 articles to profl. jours. Recipient medal for valiant labour Presidium of Supreme Soviet of USSR, 1970, Order of Honour, Presidium of Supreme Soviet of USSR, 1981, State prize of Tatarstan Republic on Sci. and Tech., 1994; merited Scientist and Engr. of Tatarstan, 1984, Russian Fedn., 1990. Mem. Tatarstan Acad. Scis. (elected academician 1992) and various sci. orgns. Avocations: gardening, photography, swimming, travels, good books. Home: Iskra 9 kv 16, 420045 Kazan Tatarstan Russia Office: Kazan Tech Univ, Karl Marx 68, 420015 Kazan Tatarstan Russia

SAIGOL, MUHAMMAD YOUNUS, physician; b. Sargodha, Pakistan, May 2, 1945; arrived in Eng., 1971; s. Fazal Din and Bakht (Banoe) S.; m. Maryam Khatoon, Feb. 18, 1971; children: Faisal Y., Sara M., Waqas Y. BSc, King Edward Med. Coll., Punjab, Pakistan, 1965, MB, BS, 1968; DPM, Royal Coll. Psychiatrists, London, 1973. Sr. house officer, registrar All Saints Hosp., Birmingham, Eng., 1971-75; pvt. practice Birmingham, 1975—. Mem. Brit. Med. Assn., Birmingham Med. Legal Soc., Am. Psychiatric Assn. Home: 6 Metchley Pk Rd, Edgbaston, Birmingham B15 2PG, England Office: 75-77 Cotterills Ln, Birmingham B8 3R2, England

SAI HUNG, HENRI LI, postal officer; b. Hong Kong, Oct. 4, 1951; s. Li Hing and Au Yeung Tai; m. Chan Man Kam, Sept. 4, 1983; 1 child, David Li Cheuk Hon. Cert. edn. (English), Hong Kong Exam. Authority, 1969; matriculation cert., Hong Kong Chinese U., 1971; B of English Lang. and Lit., Shue Yan Coll., Hong Kong, 1993. Cashier Hong Kong Madarin Hotel, Hong Kong, 1971; stock control and purchasing clk. Duty Free Shoppers, Hong Kong, 1972-74; postal officer Hong Kong Post, Hong Kong, 1975-94; sr. postal officer Post Office Dept., Hong Kong, 1994—; govt. translator Japanese and French, Hong Kong Govt., 1988—.

SAIKIA, NAGEN, humanities educator; b. Golaghat, Assam, India, Feb. 11, 1941; s. Umaram and Hemaprabha (Hazarika) S.; m. Lavanya Tamuli, May 11, 1965; children: Gautam, Gayatri Saikia Barua, Kausik. BA, Gauhat U., 1961, MA, 1964; PhD, Dibrugarh U., India, 1982. Tchr. DheKial High English Sch., Assam, India, 1961-64; lectr. Diphu, Jarhat, D.C.B. Coll., Assam, 1965-71, Dibrugarh U., Assam, India, 1972-82; reader Dibrugarh U., Assam, 1983-85; mem. Upper House Indian Parliament, New Delhi, 1986-92; L.N.B. prof. in Assamese lit. Dibrugarh U., 1992—. Author: Chinta Aru Charcha, 1977 (Mohan Sarma award 1980), Andharat Nizar Mukh, 1989 (Indian Sahitya Akademi award 1998); author seven collections of short stories, two collections of poems, two travelogues, one novel, eight collections of literary essays; edited 39 books. Sec. Asam Sahitya Sabha Jarhat, Anam, 1973-85; pres. Anam Sahitya Sabha, Jarhat, 1997-98, 98-99. Mem. Indian Parliamentary Group (life mem.), Comparative Indian Lit. (life). Hindu. Avocations: reading, listening to classical, modern and folk music. Office: Dibrugarh Univ, 786004 Dibrugarh/Assam India

SAINI, JOGINDAR SINGH, mechanical engineering educator; b. Harsi Pind, Punjab, India, Jan. 19, 1943; s. Nand Lal and Kesari Devi Saini; m. Veena Sharan, Feb. 24, 1970; children: Ritu, Ritesh. BSc of Engring., Punjab Engring. Coll., Chandigarh, India, 1966; M of Engring., U. Roorkee, India, 1968, PhD, 1975. Cert. engr. From lectr. in mech. engring. to reader in mech. engring. U. Roorkee, 1968-82, prof. in mech. engring., 1982—; dir. Alt. Hydro Energy Ctr., U. Roorkee, 1986-88, head mech. and indsl. engring. dept., 1995-98; cons. and rschr. in field. Contbr. rsch. papers to profl. jours. and procs. Fellow Instn. Engrs.; mem. Solar Energy Soc. India (life), Indian Soc. Heat and Mass Transfer (life). Avocation: nature. Home: 135/1 Vikas Nagar U Roorkee, 247667 Roorkee India Office: U Roorkee, Mech and Indsl Engring Dept, 247667 Roorkee India

SAINI, KULVINDER SINGH, molecular biologist, biochemistry educator; b. Ludhiana, Punjab, India, Aug. 5, 1956; arrived in Australia, 1991; s. Parkash Singh and Harkishan Kaur (Bola) S.; m. Ranjit Kaur Sahni, Aug. 7, 1991; 1 child, Anmol Simran Kaur. BS, Punjab Agrl. U., 1977, MS, 1980; PhD, Sydney (Australia) U., 1987. Rsch. fellow Punjab Agrl. U., 1980-81; postdoctoral Case Western Res. U., Cleve., 1986-87; rsch. fellow Harvard U., Boston, 1988-91; rsch. scientist Commonwealth Sci. and Indsl. Rsch. Orgn., Sydney, 1991-94; sr. scientist Princess Alexandra Hosp., Brisbane, Australia, 1994-97, Lahey Clinic, Burlington, Mass., 1998-2000; sr. scientist neurobiology divsn. Alphagene Inc., Woburn, Mass., 2000—; rsch. grant assessor Diabetes Australia Rsch. Trust; cons. FMC BioProducts, Maine, 1989-91. Contbr. articles to profl. jours. Cashier Animal Sci. Club, Punjab Agrl. U., 1977, Australian Sikh Assn., Sydney, 1984; sec. Punjabi Folk Dance Gp, Sydney, 1982-84; v.p. Punjabi Cultural Assn., Sydney, 1992. Recipient Postgrad. Rsch. award U. Sydney, 1981, Postdoctoral fellowship NIH, 1989, Sr. Rsch. fellow Princess Alexandra Hosp. Rsch. Found., 1994-97. Fellow Animal Nutrition Soc. India; mem. Am. Soc. Biochemistry, Am. Assn. Cancer Rsch. Sikh. Avocations: soccer, tennis, cricket, classical music (Indian), movies. Home: 62 Mill St Apt 6 Woburn MA 01801-2753 Office: Alphagene Inc Neurobiology Divsn 260 W Cummings Pk Woburn MA 01801

SAINI, NARINDER SINGH, veterinary surgeon; b. Singhpura, India, Nov. 1, 1961; s. Gurdev Singh and Rajinder Kaur; m. Narinderjit Kaur, Mar. 5, 1989; children: Satinder Pal Singh, Robinderpal Singh. BVS, Punjab Agrl. U., Ludhiana, India, 1985, MVS, 1987, PhD, 1996. Vet. officer Govt. of Punjab, Ludhiana, 1987-88; asst. prof. Punjab Agrl. U., Ludhiana, 1988-95, sr. asst. prof., 1996—; assoc. prof. dept. surgery and radiology Ctr. Advanced Studies, Ludhiana, 1999—. Author: Saral Science, 1996; contbr. chpt. to book, numerous articles on tendon healing and ultrasonography to sci. and profl. jours.; patentee in field. Internat. travel fellow Internat. Vet. Radiol. Assn., 1997. Mem. Indian Soc. Vet. Surgery (life), Indian Sci. Congress Assn. (life), Indian Assn. Equine Interests. Avocations: photography, sports, traveling, music. Home: 12-A Sarabha Nagar, Ludhiana 141001, India Office: Dept Vet Surgery Radiology, Punjab Agrl U, Ludhiana 141004, India

SAINI, RAM GOPAL, geneticist, researcher; b. Una, H Pradesh, India, Oct. 4, 1947; s. Om Parkash and Shanti S.; m. Santosh Paul Saini, Mar. 4, 1972; children: Manish, Shiwani. BSc in Agr., Punjab Agr. Sch., Ludhiana, India, 1967, MSc in Plant Breeding, 1969, PhD in Genetics, 1978. Rsch. asst. Punjab Agrl. U., Ludhiana, India, 1969-75; asst. prof. Punjab Agrl. U., Ludhiana, 1976-83, assoc. prof., 1984-93, prof., 1993-94; nat. fellow Indian Coun. Agrl. Rsch., New Delhi, 1995-97; head divsn. genetics Punjab Agrl. U., Ludhiana, 1998—; vis. scientist U. Sydney, Australia, 1986-87. Recipient Jawahar Lal Nehru award Indian Coun. Agrl. Rsch., 1990, Nat. fellowship, 1995, Foundation Day award, Punjab Agrl. U., Ludhhiana, 1995,. Fellow Indian Soc. Genetics and Plant Breeding; mem. Crop Improvement Soc. India (v.p.), Soc. for Enhancement of Plant Scis.. Avocations: photography, music. Home: 10/21 Punjab Agrl U Campus, Punjab Ludhiana 141004, India Office: Punjab Agrl U, Dept Genetics, Punjab Ludhiana 141004, India

SAINI, TIMO OLAVI, publishing executive; b. Helsinki, Finland, July 30, 1945; s. Pertti Olavi and Riitta-Liisa (Laakso) S.; m. Satu Sadevuori Saini, Sept. 19, 1946; children: Johanna, Jaakko, Inka. BA, Helsinki Sch. Econs., Finland, 1968; MA, 1980. Mng. dir. United Mag. Oy, Helsinki, Finland, 1983-85, Oy Crea Film & Video, Helsinki, Finland, 1985-86, Oy Talentum Ab, Helsinki, 1986-92, Oy Valitut Palat-Readers Digest Ab, Helsinki, 1992-97; regional v.p. Reader's Digest Europe, 1997-99; mng. dir. Reader's Digest Nordic, 1999—. Bd. mem. Mag. Pub. Assn., Helsinki, 1984—, Internat. Advt. Assn., Helsinki, 1983; chmn. Finnish Direct Mail Assn., 1994-97, 2000—. Lt. Navy, Finland. Avocations: sailing, cross country skiing. Home: Keskiyöntie 17A, FIN-02210 Espoo Finland Office: Oy Valitut Palat-Reader's Digest, PO Box 46, 00441 Helsinki Finland

SAINI, VASANT DURGADAS, computer software company executive; b. Bombay, Jan. 31, 1952; came to U.S., 1974; s. Durgadas D. and Pushpa (Sethi) S.; m. Sonia Juneja, May 20, 1983; children: Isha, Kaasha. B Tech. Electronics, Ind. Inst. Tech., Kharagpur, 1974; MSEE, U. Rochester, 1975, PhD in Elec. Engring., 1979. Asst. prof. elec. engring. U. Rochester (N.Y.), 1980-88; pres., CEO Advanced Computer Innovations, Inc., Pittsford, N.Y., 1988—; cons. All-Pro Printers, Rochester, 1986, W. Main Ultrasound Group, Rochester, 1986; software developer Dantec Electronics, Denmark, 1987-89, Brother Industries Ltd., Japan, 1992-93, 95-2000, Manpower Internat., USA, 1993-94, 95-96, DataEase Internat., USA, 1992-94, Wholly Genes, Inc., 1994-2000, Automated Legal Sys., Inc., 1996-2000, The Technology Group, 1996-2000, Nota Bene, 1994-2000, Expert Ease, Inc., 1997-2000, Info Access, Inc., 1997, Duxbury Sys., 1997-2000, McDonnell Douglas Helicopter Sys., 1997, U. of Rochester Med. Ctr., 1998-99. Co-author: Doppler Echocardiography, 1985, 2d edit., 1992; also articles. Mae Stone Goode Found. grantee, 1979-81. Avocations: Indo-jazz music, mathematics of music, squash. Home: 19 Roxbury Ln Pittsford NY 14534-4202

SAINOVIC, NIKOLA, prime minister of Serbia; b. 1948. BSc, Faculty of Metallurgy, Bor; MSc, Faculty of Metallurgy, Ljubljana. Pres. Mcpl. Assembly of Bor; rep. sec. Industry Energetics and Constrn.; mem. exec. coun. Assembly of Socialist Republic of Serbia; fed. min. econ. Yugoslavia; dep. prime min., former min. mining and energy Serbia; prime min. Republic of Serbia; vice-prime min. Fed. Republic of Yugoslavia, dep. prime min.; asst. prof. Faculty Mining and Metallurgy, Bor; v.p. rsch. and devel. dept. Mining and Metall. Basin, Bor.; rep. Internat. Community Copper Producing Countries. Office: Office of Prime Min, Bulevar Lenjina 2, 11070 Belgrade Yugoslavia*

SAINSBURY, DAVID JOHN, British government official; b. Oct. 24, 1940; s. Robert S.; m. Susan Carole Reid, 1973; 3 children. BA, King's Coll., Cambridge, Eng.; MBA, Columbia U., N.Y.C. With J. Sainsbury, London, 1963-73, fin. dir., 1973-90, dep. chmn., 1988-92, chmn., CEO, 1992-96, 1963-73 chmn., 1996-99; under sec. for state for sci., London, 1998—. Author: Government and Industry: A New Partnership, 1981; (with C. Smallwood) Wealth Creation and Jobs, 1987. Mem. com. to review the Post Office, 1975-77; trustee Social Democratic Part, 1982-90; mem. governing body London Bus. Sch., 1985—, chmn. 1991—. Office: Eagle House, 110 Jermyn St, London Sw1Y 6EE, England

SAINSBURY, RICHARD MARK, philosophy educator; b. London, July 2, 1943; s. Richard Eric and Freda Margaret (Horne) S.; m. Gillian McNeil Rind, June 2, 1969; children: Isabelle Miranda, William Edgar. BA, Corpus Christi Coll., Oxford U, 1964, MA, 1970, PhD, 1970. Lectr. philosophy Magdalen Coll., 1968-70, St. Hilda's Coll., 1970-73, Brasenose Coll., 1973-75, U. Essex, 1975-78; lectr. philosophy U. London, 1978-87, reader, 1987—, Stebbing prof. philosophy, 1989—; vis. prof. U. Tex., Austin, 1987. Author: Russell, 1979, Paradoxes, 1988, 95, Logical Forms, 1988, 2000; editor: Mind, 1990-2000; contbr. articles to profl. jours. Radcliffe fellow, 1987-88, L. fellow, 1995, King's Coll. fellow, 1995—, Eskine Vis. fellow, 2000, Sr. Rsch. fellow, 2000—. Fellow Brit. Acad.; mem. Aristotelian Soc. (hon. sec., editor 1982-86). Office: Kings Coll, London WC2R 2LS, England

SAINSBURY OF PRESTON CANDOVER, LORD (JOHN DAVAN SAINSBURY), food retailer executive, art patron; b. London, Nov. 2, 1927; m. Anya Linden, 1963. Student, Oxford U., fellow (hon.), 1982; LittD (hon.), South Bank, 1992; LLD (hon.), Bristol, 1993. Vice chmn. J. Sainsbury PLC, 1967-69, chmn., 1969-92, pres., 1992—. Bd. dirs. Royal Opera House, Covent Garden, Eng., 1969-85, chmn., 1987-91; bd. dirs. Royal Opera House Trust, 1974-84, 87-97, The Economist, 1972-80, chmn. Coun. Friends of Covent Garden, 1969-81, Benesh Inst. Choreology, 1986-87; chmn. bd. govs. Royal Ballet, 1987—, dir. bd. govs., 1995—; joint hon. treas. European Movement, 1972-75; trustee Nat. Gallery, 1976-83, Westminster Abbey Trust, 1977-83, Tate Gallery, 1982-83, Rhodes Trust, 1984-98; mem. Nat. Com. for Electoral Reform, 1976-85; chmn. bd. trustees Dulwich Picture Gallery, 1994—. Named Hon. Bencher Inner Temple, 1985. Fellow Inst. Grocery Distbrs.; mem. Coun. Retail Consortium, Garrick Club, Contemporary Arts Soc. (v.p. 1984—), Brit. Retail Consortium (pres. 1993-97), Friends of Nelson Mandela Children's Fund (dir. 1996—). Office: J Sainsbury PLC, 2 Queen Annes Gate Dartmouth St, SW1H 9BP London England

SAINT-AMAND, DAVID CYRIAS HOMBERTO, computer programmer, geologic consultant; b. Ridgecrest, Calif., Feb. 25, 1962; s. Pierre and Marie (Poss) Saint-A. BA in Geologic Scis., U. Calif., Santa Barbara, 1986. Programmer, analyst E.B. Assocs., Inc., Ridgecrest, Calif., 1980-94, Sci. Application Internat. Corp. Info. Svcs., Ridgecrest, 1994—; field geologist Saint-Amand Sci. Svcs., Ridgecrest, 1980—; staff geologist Gary S. Rasmussen & Assocs., Inc., San Bernardino, Calif., 1991. Mem., coord. Bicycle Safety Com., Ridgecrest, 1990; field trip leader, vol. Bur. Land. Mgmt., Bakersfield, Calif., 1996, 97, 98; sponsor Friends of the NRA, Ridgecrest, 1998, 99, 2000. Mem. NRA (sharpshooter 1975), Soc. for Creative Anachronism (conv. chmn. 1986-88, Award of arms 1989, first place poetry competition 1993), Inland Geologic Soc., Footprinters Internat. (pres. chpt. 60 1998-99, grand dir. 1999-2000). Achievements include research on theater ballistic missile defense attack operations; research on the origins of some salines and nitrates in deserts. Avocations: target shooting, history, paintball, war gaming, camping. Home: 1748 W Las Flores Ave Ridgecrest

CA 93555-8635 Office: Saint-Amand Sci Svcs PO Box 601 Ridgecrest CA 93556-0601

ST. ANTOINE, THEODORE JOSEPH, law educator, arbitrator; b. St. Albans, Vt., May 29, 1929; s. Arthur Joseph and Mary Beatrice (Callery) S.; m. Elizabeth Lloyd Frier, Jan. 2, 1960; children: Arthur, Claire, Paul, Sara. AB, Fordham Coll., 1951; JD, U. Mich., 1954; postgrad., U. London, 1957-58. Bar: Mich. 1954, Ohio 1954, D.C. 1959. Assoc. Squire, Sanders & Dempsey, Cleve., 1954; assoc., ptnr. Woll, Mayer & St. Antoine, Washington, 1958-65; assoc. prof. law U. Mich. Law Sch., Ann Arbor, 1965-69, prof., 1969—, Degan prof., 1981-98, Degan prof. emeritus, 1998—, dean, 1971-78; pres. Nat. Resource Ctr. for Consumers of Legal Svcs., 1974-78; mem. Pub. Rev. Bd., UAW, 1973—, Mich. Atty. Discipline Bd., 1999—; chmn. UAW-GM Legal Svcs. Plan, 1983-95; Mich. Gov.'s spl. counselor on workers' compensation, 1983-85; reporter Uniform Law Commrs., 1987-92; life mem. Clare Hall, Cambridge (Eng.) U. Co-author: (with R. Smith, L. Merrifield and C. Craver) Labor Relations Law: Cases and Materials, 4th edit., 1968, 10th edit., 1999; editor: The Common Law of the Workplace: The Views of Arbitrators, 1998; contbr. articles to profl. jours. 1st lt. JACG, U.S. Army, 1955-57. Fulbright grantee, London, 1957-58. Mem. ABA (past sec. labor law sect., coun. 1984-92), Am. Bar Found., State Bar Mich. (chmn. labor rels. law sect. 1979-80), Nat. Acad. Arbitrators (bd. govs. 1985-88, v.p. 1994-96, pres. 1999-2000), Internat. Soc. Labor Law and Social Security (U.S. br. exec. bd. 1983—, vice chmn. 1989-95), Am. Arbitration Assn. (bd. dirs. 2000—), Indsl. Rels. Rsch. Assn., Coll. Labor and Employment Lawyers, Order of Coif (life). Democrat. Roman Catholic. Home: 1421 Roxbury Rd Ann Arbor MI 48104-4047 Office: U Mich Law Sch 625 S State St Ann Arbor MI 48109-1215

ST. AUBYN, RONALD ANTHONY, pediatrics nurse; b. Vineland, N.J., Nov. 30, 1954; s. Richard Francis and Rita Margaret (DeFeo) St. A. BSN, Northwestern State U., Natchitoches, La., 1980. RN, La. High-risk infant homecare nurse Physicians Prescription Svcs., Shreveport, La., 1982-86; nursing dir., neonatal cons. Quality Care, Inc., Shreveport, 1985-86; poison info. specialist La. Poison Control Ctr., Shreveport, 1987; pediatric clin. supr. La. State U. Med. Ctr., Shreveport, 1988-92, pediatric edn. nurse, 1993—. Mem. ANA, La. State Nursing Assn., Soc. of Pediatric Nurses of La., Krewe Club of Aesclepius, Royalty Club, Beta Beta Beta. Home: 865 Sewanee Pl Shreveport LA 71105-2245

SAINT BLANQUAT, GEORGES M., biology educator, consultant; b. Toulouse, France, Apr. 29, 1941; s. Pierre M. and Maria A. (Sevin) Saint B.; m. Martine M. Caillard; children: Marielle, Pierre, Antoine, Anne. Lic. in biol. scis., U. Paul Sabatier, Toulouse, 1962, D in Nutrition, 1965, D in Scis., 1971. Stagiaire de recherche CNRS, Toulouse, 1965-67, attache de recherche, 1967-72, charge de recherche, 1972-86; prof. U. de Bordeaux 1, 1986—; cons. Min. Saute, Paris, 1982, Industry, 1980; v.p. IREB, 1995. Roman Catholic. Avocation: hunting. Home: Rue Demouilles 40, 31400 Toulouse France Office: U de Bordeaux 1, Ave Michel Serres, 47000 Agen France

ST. CLAIR, DONALD DAVID, lawyer; b. Hammond, Ind., Dec. 30, 1932; s. Victor Peter and Wanda (Rubinska) Small; m. Sergine Anne Oliver, June 6, 1970 (dec. June 1974); m. Beverly Joyce Tipton, Dec. 28, 1987. BS, Ind. U., 1955, MS, 1963, EdD, 1967; JD, U. Toledo, 1992. Bar: Ohio 1992, U.S. Dist. Ct. (no. dist.) Ohio 1993, U.S. Supreme Ct., 1996. Assoc. prof. Western Ky. U. Coll. Edn., Bowling Green, 1967-68; assoc. prof. U. Toledo, 1968-77, prof., 1977-92; atty., ptnr. Garand, Bollinger, & St. Clair, Oregon, Ohio, 1992-97; pvt. practice Law Offices Donald D. St. Clair, Toledo, 1997—; mem. Ohio Coun. Mental Health Ctrs., Columbus, 1978-79; dir. honors programs U. Toledo. Author: (poetry) Daymarks and Beacons, 1983, Impressions from an Afternoon in a Paris Courtroom, 1998; contbr. articles to profl. jours. Organizer Students Toledo Organized for Peace, 1970-71; mem. Lucas County Dem. Party, 1990—. With U.S. Army, 1955-57. Mem. ABA, AAU (nat. bd. dirs. 1973-74), Am. Inns of Ct., Ohio Bar Assn., Toledo Bar Assn., Ohio Acad. Trial Lawyers, Toledo Power Squadron (comdg. officer 1981), Bay View Yacht Club, Ohio Criminal Def. Lawyers Assn., Lucas County Bar Assn., Maumee Valley Criminal Def. Lawyers Assn., Ottawa County Bar Assn., Masons (32 degree), Shriners, Ancient Order Friars, Phi Alpha Delta. E-mail: stclairlaw@attglobal.net. Home: 3353 Christie Blvd Toledo OH 43606-2862 Office: 5415 Monroe St Toledo OH 43623-2800

ST GEORGE, LOURDES INGRID, obstetrician, gynecologist, consulant; b. Colombo, Ceylon, Mar. 2, 1955; arrived in U.K., 1964, Australia, 1976; d. John and Selvi Gertrude (Sinnadurai) St G.; m. Spencer Barnard White, Oct. 3, 1988; children: Phoebe, Siena, Trinity. MBBS, U. Mysore, India, 1976. Intern Mater Hosp., Newcastle, Australia, 1977-78; RMO Nepean Hosp, Penrith, Australia, 1978-80; registrar Gosford Hosp, Australia, 1981-82; registrar ob-gyn. Westmead Hosp., 1982-86; sr. registrar Bourn Hall, Cambridge, Eng., 1987-88; VMO, cons. Auburn Hosp, Ashfield & Bankstown Pvt. Hosp., Burwood, NSW, Australia, 1988—. Contbr. articles to profl. jours. Fellow Royal Australian Coll. Obstetricians and Gynecologists, Royal Coll. Obstetricians and Gynecologists; mem. AMA, Am. Soc. Ultrasound in Medicine, Soc. Laparoendoscopic Surgeons, Royal Coll. Physicians, Royal Coll. Surgeons. Roman Catholic. Avocations: music, art, aerobics, philosophy, antiques. Fax: 97475882. Office: 36 Belmore St Ste 4/36, Burwood 2134 NSW, Australia

ST. GERMAINE-LATTIG, CHARLES EDWIN, political writer; b. Rhinelander, Wis., Feb. 12, 1949; s. William St. Germaine and Ina Margaret (Lobermier) Valliere; children: Spencer Charles, Aimy Dixon. Student, SUNY, Buffalo, 1967-68, Syracuse U., 1969. Polit. writer Am. Indian Movement, 1972-79, Mpls., 1979—. Free-lance photographer, 1976—; co-hose, prodr. radio program: Living on Indian Time, KPFA, Berkeley, Calif., 1976-77; founder, editor Bay Area Indian News, Oakland, 1976-77; contbr. articles to profl. jours. Cadre mem. Am. Indian Movement, 1972-79; mem. Met. Opera Guild; tribal mem. Lac du Flambeau Band of Lake Superior Chippewa, Wis. With U.S. Army, 1971-72, Korea. Mem. Acad. Polical Sci., Nat. Audobon Soc. Avocations: wildlife and environmental preservation, astronomy, classical music, Shakespearean drama, N.E. Asian political history. Home: 2447 16th Ave S Minneapolis MN 55404-3905

ST-HILAIRE, CAROLINE, member of parliament; b. Longueuil, Can., Nov. 16, 1969; 1 child, Etienne. BA in Adminstrn., U. Quebec, 1993. With Soc. du droit de reproduction des auteurs, compositeurs et éditeurs du Can.; M.P. for Bloc Quebecois House of Commons, spokesperson on status of women's issues & amateur sport, mem. standing com. on Can. heritage; founder Soc. de Promotion Pour La Releve Musicale de l'espace Francophone. Avocation competitive figure skating. Office: House of Commons, 378 Confederation Bldg, Ottawa, ON Canada K1A 0A6

ST. HILAIRE, DAVID WILLIAM, county official, financial manager; b. Bennington, Vt., Jan. 5, 1964; s. Donald Wilfred Sr. and Gudrun Albertine St. Hilaire; m. Julie Diane Prebble, Nov. 6, 1992; 1 child, Jonathan Mathieu. BS in Bus. Econs., SUNY, Oneonta, 1986; MBA in Fin., SUNY, Binghamton, 1989; MS in Acctg., SUNY, Albany, 1995. Loan originator Bennington Savs. and Loan, 1987; fin. analyst Unisys Corp., Flemington, N.J., 1988-89; lead sr. fin. analyst Shearson Smith Barney, N.Y.C., 1990-93; sales agt. Northwestern Mut. Life, Latham, N.Y., 1993-95; dept. chief fiscal officer Rennselaer County, Troy, N.Y., 1996—. Town supr. Town of Hoosick, Hoosick Falls, N.Y., 1996-99; chmn. bd. dirs., fin. com. Hoosick Falls Ctrl. Sch. Dist., 1994-95; bd. dirs. Rensselaer County Sr. Citizen Adv. Bd., 1996-2000, Buskirk's Bridge Preservation Assn., 1998-99, Rev. Edith Craig Reynolds Found., 1996-99. Recipient Citizenship award Hoosick Falls Ctrl. Sch. Dist., 1982, Am. Hometown Leadership award Nat. Assn. Towns and Twps./Walmart, Washington, 1998, highest achievement award Dale Carnegie Course, Colonie, N.Y., 1999. Mem. Rensselaer County Suprs. Assn. (founder, organizer, chmn. 1998-99), Kiwanis (v.p. Hoosick Falls chpt. 1999), Beta Gamma Sigma. Republican. Roman Catholic. Avocations: politics, travel, outdoor activities, flying. Home: PO Box 122 4982 Rt 7 Hoosick NY 12089 Office: Rensselaer County 1600 7th Ave Troy NY 12180-3410

ST. JOHN, EVERT EUGENE, insurance company executive; b. Ft. Worth, Nov. 20, 1926; s. Warren Evert and Madeline Emily (Mount) St. J.; m. Mary Frances Wilson, June 23, 1953; children: Mary Madeline Whittinghill, James Warren, Paul Eugene. BA with hons., U. Tex., 1947. CFP, CLU, ChFC. Dir. agys. Prudential, Houston, 1960-69; v.p., founding dir. Sysco Corp., Houston, 1969-75; gen. agent Prin. Life, Des Moines, 1975—. Pres. bd. dirs. Goodwill Industries, Ft. Worth, 1998—. Lt. USNR, 1944-69. Mem. Rotary. Republican. Baptist. Avocations: creative writing, golfing. Office: St John Rigg Inc 301 Commerce St Ste 1350 Fort Worth TX 76102-4121

ST. JOHN, HENRY SEWELL, JR., utility company executive; b. Birmingham, Ala., Aug. 18, 1938; s. H. Sewell and Carrie M. (Bond) St. J.; m. J. Ann Morris, Mar. 7, 1959; children: Sherri Ann, Brian Lee, Teresa Lynn, Cynthia Faye. Student, David Lipscomb Coll., 1956-58, U. Tenn., 1958-59, U. Ala., 1962-64. Engrng. aide Ala. Power Co., Enterprise, 1960-62, Birmingham, 1962-66; asst. chief engr. Riviera Utilities, Foley, Ala., 1966-71, sec.-treas., gen. mgr., 1972—. Deacon Foley Ch. of Christ, 1975-82, elder, 1983—; active Am. Cancer Soc., chmn. bd. Baldwin County unit, 1977; bd. dirs. AGAPE of Mobile, 1977-80; treas. Christian Care Ctr., Inc., 1981—; bd. dirs. South Baldwin Civic Chorus, pres., 1979-82; bd. dirs. Baldwin County Econ. Devel. Alliance, 1997—, exec. com., 1999—, sec., 1998-99, treas. 1999—. Mem. IEEE, South Ala. Power Distbrs. Assn. (chmn. 1973-74), Ala. Consumer-Owned Power Distbrs. Assn. (chmn. 1974-75, 82-83, vice chmn. 1981, sec.-treas. 1980), S.E. Electric Reliability Coun. (assoc.), Mcpl. Electric Utility Assn. Ala. (exec. com., dir. 1971—), Ala. Mcpl. Electric Authority (bd. dirs. 1981—, vice chmn. 1981-83, chmn. 1984—), Electric Cities Ala. (bd. dirs., exec. com. 1989—, vice chmn. 2000—), United Mcpl. Distbrs. Group (bd. dirs. 1972—), Am. Pub. Power Assn. (chmn. State of Ala. mem. com. 1982—, bd. dirs. 1997—, exec. com. 1999-2000, vice chmn. com. nat. mem. 1998-99, chmn. nat. membership com. 1999-2000, com. legis. and resolutions 1972—, com. on coms. 1997-2000, bylaws com. 2000—), Pub. Gas Assn. Ala. (bd. dirs. 1987-88), South Baldwin C. of C. (pres. 1974, dir. 1972-75, 81-90, 92-95). Rotary. Clubs: Foley Quarterback (sec.-treas. 1984-85), Gulf Shores Golf (dir. 1974-75), Classic Chevy, Internat. (life), Azalea City Classic Chevy (bd. dirs., exec. com. 1989-99, v.p. 1991-92, 96-99, Chevrolet Nomad Assn. (bd. dirs. 1991—, v.p. 1993—). Home: PO Box 1817 Foley AL 36536-1817 Office: PO Box 2050 Foley AL 36536-2050

ST. JOHN, MARIA ANN, nurse anesthetist; b. Rochester, Pa., Dec. 15, 1953; d. James Edward and Evelyn Marie (Sayers) St. J.; m. Paul David Dworsky, Aug. 19, 1978 (div. Dec. 13, 1991); children: Lauren Marie Dworsky, Michael David Dworsky. BSN, U. Pitts., 1975; cert. reg. nurse anesthetist, U. Health Ctr. Pitts. Sch. Anesthesia for Nurses, 1984. Advanced RN practitioner Fla., Ohio; cert. RN anesthetist, Pa., Ohio, N.C., Ky. Nurse Presbyn. U. Hosp., Pitts., 1975-77, VA Hosp., Pitts., 1977-82; nurse anesthetist Anesthesia Assocs. of Hollywood, Fla., 1984-87, North Hills Anesthesia Assocs., Pitts., 1987-98, Queen City Anesthesiologists, Inc., Cin., 1998—. Vol. tchr. art history, fundraiser St. Alexis Sch., Wexford, Pa., 1991-97, recording sec. PT6 Bd., 1996-97, v.p. PT6 Bd., 1997-98; mem. Cranberry Twp. Athletic Assn., 1991-98, Oak Hills PTA, Cin., 1998-99, Oak Hills Athletic Boosters, 1999, PTG Springmeyer Sch. and Bridgetown Jr. H.S., Cinn., 1998-99, PTG and Athletic Boosters, Bridgetown Middle Sch., 1999—. Recipient scholarship March of Dimes, Beaver County, Pa., 1971, Pitt. scholarship, 1971-75. Mem. DAR, Am. Assn. Nurse Anesthetists, Pa. Assn. Nurse Anesthetists, Ohio Assn. Nurse Anesthetists, Fla. Assn. Nurse Anesthetists, Ky. Nurse Anesthetists, N.C. Nurse Anesthetists. Avocations: playing piano, reading, traveling, school volunteering, swimming. Home: 5646 Bridgetown Rd Apt 15 Cincinnati OH 45248-4363

ST. JOHN, SHANNON ELAINE, foundation executive; b. Orlando, Fla., Aug. 4, 1954; d. John Charles and Lorraine Margaret S.; m. Leo Thomas Barber, June 23, 1979; children: Leo T. Barber IV, John St. John Barber. BA in Econ., Emory U., 1976; MA in Sci., Tech. and Pub. Policy, George Washington U., 1981. Project dir. consumer affairs State of Ga., Atlanta, 1976-78, planner energy resources dept., 1978-79; project coord. Exec. Office of the Pres., Washington, 1980; writer and policy analyst Nat. Health Policy Forum, Washington, 1981; cons. Coopers & Lybrand, Washington, 1981-82; task force staff bd. sci. and tech. Office Gov., Raleigh, N.C., 1982-84; exec. dir. Triangle Cmty. Found., Rsch. Triangle Park, N.C., 1983—; group coord. Transatlantic Cmty. Found. network, Bertelsmann Found., Gutersloh, Germany, 1999—; Eisenhower exchange fellow, Varna, Bulgaria, 1996. Contbr. author: (book) The Role of Community Foundations in Civil Society, 1999; author: (manuals) The Philanthropic Handbook: A Guidebook to Options for Charitable Giving, 1994, The Advisor Handbook: A Manual on Charitabel Giving for Professional, 1994. Co-chmn. Coalition for Pub. Trust, Durham, N.C., 1997-98; me. The Fifty Group, Raleigh, 1997—; pres./bd. dirs. Watts Hosp.-Hillandale Neighborhood Assn., Durham, 1984-88; founding bd. mem. Cmty. Founds. of Am., Memphis, Tenn., 1999—. Recipient Tarheel of Week, New & Observer, Raleigh, 1991, Outstanding Profl. Fundraiser, Nat. Soc. Fund Raising Execs., triangle chap., Raleigh, 1991. Democrat. Avocations: travel, photography, boating. Fax: 919-990-9066. E-mail: sstjohn@trianglecf.org. Office: Triangle Cmty Found 100 Park Dr Ste 209 Research Triangle Park NC 27709

ST. LANDAU, NORMAN, lawyer; b. Vienna, Austria, Apr. 14, 1925; s. Henry M. and Anka (Nemirovska) St. L.; m. Maisie Dennis, July 18, 1942; children—Lorraine, Jon L., Norman D. B.S., A.B. with honors, U. Ill., 1941; LL.B., Rutgers U., 1948; LL.M., NYU, 1951. Bar: D.C. 1948, U.S. Supreme Ct. 1952, N.J. 1958. With Pitts. Plate Glass Co., Ohio, 1941-42; with Johnson & Johnson, New Brunswick, N.J., 1942-84, internat. counsel, 1957-84, chief trademark counsel, 1961-84; dir., officer numerous affiliates Johnson & Johnson Internat.; of counsel Lalos, Leeds, Keegan & Marsh, Washington, 1983-85, Durand, Gorman, Heher, Imbriaco & Morrice, Princeton, N.J., 1984-86, Brylawski, Cleary & Leeds, 1985-90; ptnr. Heher, Clarke & St. Landau, Princeton, 1987-97; counsel Tucker, Flyer, Lewis, Washington, 1990—; chmn. bd. Action Law Systems, Inc., 1987-90; of counsel Tucker Flyer & Lewis, Washington, 1989—; prin. Law Offices of Norman St. Landau, Princeton, 1990—; mem. adv. com. Sec. State and Commr. Patents, 1975—; bd. dirs. Nika Ltd., Pulsair Ltd., BP Johnson. Co-author: Trademark Management, 1977, Guide to Patent Arbitration, 1987; fgn. editor Les Nouvelles, 1965—. Exec. com., gen. counsel N.J. State Opera, 1958—. Mem. N.J. State Bar Assn. (v.p. patent, trademark and unfair competition sect. 1980-82, vice-chmn. immigration and nationality sect. 1988—), Nat. Fgn. Trade Council (chmn. indsl. property com.), N.J. Patent Law Assn. (past pres.), Nat. Council Patent Law Assns. (sec.-gen.), Nat. Panel Arbitrators, Am. Arbitration Assn., ABA, Am. Chem. Soc. (nat. councillor), Am. Patent Law Assn. (bd. mgrs.), Am. Immigration Lawyers Assn., Inter-Am. Assn. Indsl. Property (exec. com.), Internat. Patent and Trademark Assn., Lic. Execs. Lawyers, Nassau Club, Rotary, Hershey's Hill Club. Home: 230 Chatham Way West Chester PA 19380-6812

ST. LIFER, JANE M., art dealer, curator; b. N.Y.C., Apr. 19, 1956; d. Martin R. and Marcia (Simon) St. L. BFA, Syracuse U., 1978; MA, N.J. City U., 1996. Dir. print dept. Trail Side Galleries, Jackson, Wyo., 1978-79, Scottsdale, Ariz., 1981-85; gallery dir., Phoenix Art Press, 1980-81; dir. print dept. Hammer Galleries, N.Y.C., 1981-86; sales mgr. Gallery Urban, N.Y.C., 1986-88; dir., owner St. Lifer Fine Art, Inc., N.Y.C., 1988—; asst. dir. Grand Ctrl. Art Galleries, N.Y.C., 1991-92. Mem. Am. Soc. Appraisers, Auctioneers Assn. (sec., v.p. 1990—). Avocations: culinary arts, dog fancier, theater. Office: St Lifer Fine Art Inc 11 Hanover Sq # 703 New York NY 10005-2819

ST. LUCE, JOHN, government official; married; 5 children. Student, U. London, 1964-67. Cert. acct. audit dept. Antigua Fisheries Office, 1958-61, West Indies High Commn., 1961-64; mgr. Barclays' Bank, London, 1968, Antigua Slipway Ltd., 1968-69; asst. to gen. mgr. Antigua Sugar Estates Devel. Bd., 1969-71; pub. acct. Antigua, 1971-76; minister of agr. and supply Govt. of Antigua and Barbuda, 1976-78, minister of fin., 1978-82, 82-91, minister of info., 1991-93, minister of agr., trade, commerce, industry and consumer aff, 1994-96, min. agr., fisheries, planning and cooperatives, 1996—, min. of fin. and social security, 1996—. Chmn. Nat. Pks. Com., 1969-71; exec. mem. Antigua Labor Party, 1968—, gen. sec., 1969-92; mem. Antigua senate, 1971-76; mem. ho. of reps., 1971—; acting prime minister, several occasiona, 1978—; rep. to World Bank, IMF and Eastern Caribbean Ctrl. Bank, 1982—. Fellow Inst. Statisticians (Eng.). Office: Ministry Fin & Soc Security, High and Long Sts, Saint John's Antigua and Barbuda*

SAINT-MARTIN, ESTELLE MARIE REINE, communications executive; b. Coetquidan, France, June 15, 1967; d. Gerard and Annie Marie Marthe (Mengelle) S.-M. B French Lit., La Sorbonne, Paris, 1989. Press dir. Mayor of Lyon, France, 1990-92, Min. of Health and Social Affairs, France, 1993-96, Euro RSCG, France, 1996-98; comm. dir. Mayor of Epernay, Paris, 1992-93, DDB, Paris, 1998—; pres. dir. office for travel of His Holiness the Dalai Lama, France, 1993—. Author: Mother Teresa, 1993. Pres. St. Louis Team, Paris, 1986-89. Roman Catholic. Avocations: diving, riding, reading. Office: DDB France, 55 rue d'Amsterdam, 75008 Paris France Address: Hospital Suburbain du Bouscat, 97 avenue Georges Clemenceau, 33110 Le Bouscat France

ST-ONGE, DENIS ALDERIC, geologist, research scientist; b. Ste-Agathe, Man., Can., May 11, 1929; s. Adolphe and Jeanne M. (Ritchot) St-O.; m. Jeanne Marie Behaegel, Jan. 7, 1955; children—Marc R., Nicole J.M. B.A., Coll. St-Boniface, 1951; Lic. Sci., U. Louvain, Belgium, 1957, D.Sc., 1962; D.Sc. honoris causa, U. Man., 1990. Research scientist Geol. Survey, Ottawa, Ont., Can., 1958-68, sect. head, 1982-85; chief sub. div. Quaternary Geology, 1985-87, dir. terrain scis. div., 1987-91, sci. advisor Polar Continental Shelf Project, 1991-97; prof. geography U. Ottawa, 1968-82, chmn. geography, 1974-77, vice dean grad. studies, 1977-80, prof. emeritus, 1998—; scientist emeritus Geol. Survey Can., 1997—. Author: Geomorphologie Ellef-Ringnes Island, 1965, Quaternary Geology, Inman River Region, N.W.T. Canada, 1995; contbr. articles to profl. jours. Pres. Ont. Francophone PTA, 1967-69. Recipient Medal Queen Elizabeth II, 1989, medal of Honor U. Liege, Belgium, 1980, medal A. Cailleux, 1991, medal Can. 125, 1992, medal Royal Scottish Geog. Soc., 1994; officer Order of Can., 1996. Fellow Geol. Assn. Can. (pres. 1984-85), Royal Can. Geog. Soc. (bd. dirs. 1980-92, pres. 1992-98), chmn. Partnership Group for Sci. Engrng., 1999—, Arctic Inst. N.Am.; mem. Can. Assn. Geographers (pres. 1979-80, Svc. award 2000), Can. Quaternary Assn., Assn. Quebecoise pour l'etude du Quaternaire (hon.), Internat. Union Quaternary Rsch. (hon. life), Can. Geosci. Coun. (pres. 1996-97). Avocations: swimming; skiing; photography. Home: 1115 Sherman Dr, Ottawa, ON Canada K2C 2M3 Office: Geolog Survey of Canada, 601 Booth St, Ottawa, ON Canada K1A OE8

SAINT-PAUL, GILLES JACQUES, economist; b. Saint Etienne, France, Feb. 8, 1963; s. Michel Adolphe and Jacqueline (Escourrou) Saint-P.; m. Isabelle Catherine Rouhier, July 11, 1987; children: Thomas, Augustine. BS, Ecole Poly., Paris, 1985; MS, Ecole des Ponts, Paris, 1987; PhD in Econ., MIT, 1990; Habilitation, Ecole des Hautes Etudes Scis., Paris, 1994. Rschr. CERAS-DELTA, Paris, 1990-97; prof. econ. U. Pompeu Fabra, Barcelona, Spain, 1997-2000; prof. U Toulouse, France, 2000—; vis. prof. MIT, 1995; cons. Ministry of Planning, Lisbon, Portugal, 1989, Ministry of Labor, Madrid, 1991, Swedish Com. on Labour Market Policy, Stockholm, 1994, Internat. Monetary Fund, Washington, 1994, 95; mem. Brussels Ctr. for Econ. Policy Studies, Macroecon. Policy Group, 1998; mem. Commn. Econ. de la Nation French Ministry of Fin., 1999—. Author: Dual Labor Markets, 1997, The Political Economy of Labor Market Institutions, 2000; co-author: Some Reflections on Swedish Labor Market Policy, 1995, Unemployment: Choices for Europe, 1995; editor: Macroeconomics of Privatization in Eastern Europe, 1996. Recipient L.E. Rivot prize French Acad. Scis., Paris, 1985, IIPF prize Internat. Inst. Pub. Fin., Tel Aviv, 1996. Fellow Ctr. Econ. Policy Rsch.; mem. Soc. AMis Montherlant, European Econ. Assn. (mem. coun.). Avocation: painting. E-mail: spaul@upf.es. Office: U Pompeu Fabra, Ramon Trias Fargas 25-27, 08005 Barcelona Catalunya, Spain

ST. PIERRE, JOYCE BOURRÉ, art educator; b. Sanford, Maine, Nov. 22, 1951; d. Marcel and Josephine Bourré; m. Michael Rene St. Pierre, Feb. 4, 1953; 1 child, Daniel. BA in Humanities, Nasson Coll., 1974; MA in Edn., U. Maine, 1985. Lectr. U. Miane, Farmington, 1978-81; tchr. Farmington Schs., 1979-81; art specialist Sanford Sch. System, Maine, 1980—; tchr. adult edn. programs Sanford and Waterboro, Maine, 1981-86; lectr. U. New England, Biddeford, Maine, 1992-94; presenter in field. Contbr. articles to profl. jours. Publicity campaigner worker Jan Tockman to Sch. Bd., Sanford, Maine, 1979; vol. St. Thomas Sch., Sanford, 1998—; mediator Youth Alt., 1990-92; sec., mem. Berwick Libr. Assn., 1992—. Scholar Nasson Coll., 1970-74. Mem. Jaycees (state pres. 1986-87, editor photographer Jaycettes In Action, 1982-83), Maine Jaycee Women (v.p., program mgr. 1980-85, Outstanding Mem. award 1982). Roman Catholic. Avocations: cross-country skiing, hockey, travel, speaking. Home: 16 Keay Rd Berwick ME 03901-2308

ST. PIERRE, ROGER, communications specialist; b. Weymouth, Dorset, England, Nov. 8, 1941; s. Alexander Richard and Caroline Amelia (Borrett) St.P.; m. Lesley Constantine, Oct. 10, 1975 (div. 1982); children: Richard Alexander, Danielle Jane, Nicole Marie. Grad. high sch., Essex, Eng. Editor Ford Motor Co., Dagenham, Eng., 1962-64, Internat. Pub. Co., London, Eng., 1964-66; publicity dir. Beacon Records, Eng., 1967-68; proprietor, U.K. publicist for Marvin Gaye, James Brown, Glen Campbell and others St. Pierre Publicity, Dulwich, London, Eng., 1968—. Author 23 pub. titles including Book of The Bicycle, Rock Handbook, 1966—; editor Brit. Midland Airways Mag., 1992-98, Holiday and Leisure World, 1996—; editl. dir. Big Publishing; contbr. articles to profl. jours. Mem. Brit. Guild Travel Writers. Club: Zeus Racing (London) (sec. 1959-62), Havering Cycling (London) (sec. 1962-69). Avocations: travel, motoring, cycling, music, historical research. Home and Office: 24 Beauval Rd, London Dulwich SE22 8UQ, England

SAINTY, GUY STAIR, art dealer; b. Cuckfield, Sussex, Eng., Dec. 12, 1950; came to U.S., 1979; s. Christopher Lawrence and Virginia Cade (Stair) S.; m. Elizabeth Frost Pierson; children: Charles Henry Alastair, Clementine Virginia, Constance Della, George Christopher De Vier, Julian Phelps Stair. Student, Westminster Sch., London, 1964-68, U. Rome, 1969-71, Coll. Law, London, 1972-75. Dir. M. Newman Ltd., London, 1976-79; cons. Stair & Co., N.Y.C., 1979-82; pres. Stair Sainty Matthiesen, N.Y.C., 1982—; leader Internat. Patrons of the Arts of the Vatican Mus. Author: The Sacred Military Constantinian Order of Saint George, 1976, The Orders of Chivalry and Merit of the Bourbon Two Sicilies Dynasty, 1989, Eighty Years of French Painting, 1991, The Orders of Saint John, 1991; co-author: (exhbn. catalog) The Macchiaioli, 1984, First Painters of the King, 1985, Francois Boucher, His Circle and Influence, 1987, Romance and Chivalry: History and Literature Reflected in 19th Century French Painting, 1996, La Insigne Orden de la Toison de Oro, 1996, The Gallic Prospect: French Landscape Painting From 1785-1900. Vice grand chancellor Sacred Mil. Constantinian Order of St. George, Madrid, 1989—; historiographer Most Venerable Order St. John of Jerusalem Priory in U.S., N.Y.C., 1990—. Decorated knight of justice Most Venerable Order St. John of Jerusalem, comdr. with star Papal Order St. Gregory the Gt., grand cross of justice Constantinian Order of St. George, knight Order St. Januarius, comdr. Order of Sts. Maurice and Lazarus, officer Order of St. Joseph. Mem. Art Dealers Assn. Am., Royal Acad. Heraldry and Genealogy (Madrid, academician), Pvt. Art Dealers Assn., Nat. Assn. Papal Honorees in U.S. (acting chancellor), Turf Club (London), The Brook (N.Y.C.), Mashomark Club (Pine Plaines, N.Y.). Roman Catholic. Home: 737 Park Ave New York NY 10021-4256 Office: Stair Sainty Matthiesen 22 E 80th St New York NY 10021-0110 Home: 38 Hudson St Kinderhook NY 12106-2004

SAITO, HIDEAKI, defense official; b. Kobuchizawa, Yamanashi, Japan, Dec. 8, 1950; s. Kin-ya and Chizuko (Tanaka) S.; m. Kazuko Fujiwara, Jan. 14, 1978; children: Yu, Satsuki. B, Keio U., 1973, M in Engring., 1975, D of Engring., 1978. Cert. elec. engr. Scientist IHI Co. Ltd., Yokohama, Japan, 1978-86; sr. scientist Inst. Rsch. and Innovation, Kashiwa, Japan, 1986-90; sr. rsch. scientist Laser Lab. Japan Def. Agy., Tokyo, 1990-92, chief laser lab., 1992-96, chief E/P sys. lab., 1996—; adj. prof. Nat. Nagaoka (Japan) U., 1988-90; vis. scientist U. South Fla., Tampa, 1991. Author: Optics and Quantum Electronics, 1991; editl. steering mem. Inst. Laser Sci., Osaka, Japan, 1990—, Inst. Elec. Engring., Tokyo, 1990—; contbr. articles to profl. jours. Mem. Soc. Photo Optical Engrs., Inst. Laser Sci. Avocations: miniature drawings of birds, outdoor activities, swimming, skiing. Home: 4-18-10 Kikari Inzai-shi, Chiba 270-1359, Japan Office: Japan Def Agy Laser Lab, 2d Rsch Ctr 1-2-24 Ikejiri, Setagaya Tokyo 154, Japan

SAITO, HIDETSUNE, translator; b. Tokyo, Sept. 6, 1935; s. Rikuzo and Shino (Inomata) S.; m. Keiko Numa, Mar. 24, 1973. BA, Tokyo U., 1959. Moscow rep. Progress Trading Co., Ltd., Tokyo, 1960-64; N.Y. rep. Mit-

subishi Heavy Industries, Ltd., Tokyo, 1977-80, Moscow rep., 1988-90; interpreter, tech. translator, cons. English, Russian, Japanese, Yokohoma, 1994—. Asst. editor: World Atlas, 1996. Home: 22-83 Kami-Nagaya, 5-chome Kohnan-ku, Yokohama City 233 0012, Japan

SAITO, MAKOTO, economics educator; b. Japan, Aug. 30, 1940; s. Yoshie and Shige (Yamada) S. BA Commerce, Waseda U., Tokyo, 1967, MA Econs., 1972. Lectr. Daito Bunka U., Tokyo, 1977-81, assoc. prof., 1981-90, prof. econs., 1990—; vis. fellow Harvard U., Cambridge, 1983-84; vis. scholar U. Mich., Ann Arbor, 1982-83. Avocations: tennis, jogging, travel, arts, music. Home: Itabashi-ku, 3-27-A-1202 Nakadai, Tokyo Japan Office: Daito Bunka U, 1-9-1 Takashimadaira Itabashi-ku, Tokyo Japan

SAITO, NORIHISA, engineering researcher; b. Ashikaga, Tochigi, Japan, Apr. 18, 1953; s. Yasushi and Chiyo (Sakamoto) S. B in Engring., Tohoku U., Sendai, Japan, 1976, D in Engring., 1997; MSc, MIT, 1985. Rschr. Nippon Atomic Industry Group Co., Ltd., Kawasaki, Japan, 1976-89, Toshiba Corp., Yokohama, Japan, 1989—. Contbr. articles to profl. jours. Avocations: computers, sports. Office: PIC Toshiba Corp, 8 Shinsugita-cho Isogo-ku, Yokohama Japan

SAITO, OSAMU, law educator; b. Kobe, Hyogo-ken, Japan, Feb. 18, 1950; s. Hiromi and Yoshiko (Ishihara) S.; m. Eiko Yano, Mar. 19, 1984; children: Takashi, Makoto, Yutaka. LLB, Kansai U., Osaka, Japan, 1972; LLD, Kobe U., Japan, 1977. Full time lectr. Kobe U. Commerce, 1978-80, asst. prof. civil law, 1980-88, prof. civil law, 1988—, head dept. bus. adminstrn., 1989-91, head Grad. Sch. Bus. Adminstrn., 1989-91, chmn., pres. of faculty meeting, 1991-92. Author: Gendai Minpo Soron, 1994, 2d edit., 1999, Study on Prevention of Corruption, 1996; contbr. articles to profl. jours. Mem. Internat. Bar Assn., Japan Bar Assn., Japan Pvt. Law Soc., Japan Comparative Law Soc., Japan Assn. Traffic Law, Japan Assn. Computer Law, Japan Assn. Law Fin. Buddhism. Avocations: calligraphy, pottery, horticulture. Home: 15-3 3 chome, Tsukushigaoka Kita-ku, Kobe 651-1212, Japan Office: Kobe U Commerce 2-1 8-chome, Gakuennishimachi Nishi-ku, Kobe 651-2197, Japan

SAITO, ROBERT SHUNICHI, writer, poet; b. Alameda, Calif., Sept. 9, 1933; s. Sam Shunji Saito and Yayeko Umegawa; m. Naida Cervantes, Dec. 7, 1966. Cert., Coronado Sch. Fine Arts, 1980. Enlisted USN, 1955, advanced through grades to chief petty officer, 1971, pers. officer USS Camden, 1972-75, ret., 1975; pres. Mega Travel Inc., La Mesa, Calif., 1983-84. Author of poetry, short stories. Recipient 1st Pl. award for Batik, Coronado Art Assn., 1977. Roman Catholic. Avocations: Batik art, photography, fishing, walking, Tai-Chi.

SAITO, TAKAFUMI, humanities educator; b. Mihara, Japan, Dec. 30, 1950; s. Hiromu and Setsuko (Ikeda) S. BA, Osaka U. Fgn. Studies, Minoo, Japan, 1973; MA, Osaka U., 1977. Assoc. prof. lang. and culture Osaka U. Fgn. Studies, 1986-97, prof., 1997—; vis. prof. U. Wyo., 1988-89; vis. scholar Cambridge (Eng.) U., 1999-2000. Co-author: Cityscape As Images, 1996. Mem. The English Lit. Soc. of Japan. Avocations: travel, piano. Office: Osaka U Fgn Studies, 8-1-1 Aomatanihigashi, OsakaPre Minoo Japan

SAITO, TAKASHI, immunologist, educator; b. Tokyo, Nov. 14, 1950; s. Yasuzo and Kane (Nakazato) S.; m. Ryoko Sakaguchi, Oct. 5, 1977; 2 children. BS, Tokyo Inst. of Tech., 1975, MS, 1977; PhD, Chiba U., 1982. Postdoctoral fellow Cologne U., Germany, 1982-85; vis. assoc. NIH, Bethesda, Md., 1985-88; asst. prof. Chiba (Japan) U., 1988-89, prof., 1989—. Editor International Immunology, 1997—, Cellular Immunology, 1996—. Office: Chiba U Grad Sch Medicine, 1-8-1 Inohana Chuo-ku, Chiba 260-8670, Japan

SAITŌ, TAKASHI, emeritus political science educator; b. Tokyo, Nov. 2, 1928; s. Matajirō amd Tama S.; m. Eiko Kimizuka, May 1, 1953; children: Tatsurō, Masako. BA, U. Tokyo, 1953, MA, 1955, D of Sociology, 1967. Asst. U. Tokyo, 1955-61, lectr., 1961-62, asst. prof., 1962-70; prof. Gakushuin U., Japan, 1970-95, dean Faculty of Law,, 1979-81, prof. emeritus polit. sci., 1995—; chmn. Com. Hist. Sci., Japan, 1979-81. Author: Study of Spanish Civil War, 1966, Study of Prehistory of Second World War, 1966, History of International Relations Between the Two World Wars, 1978, Introduction of the Historical Science, 1993. Home: Takao Park Heights A 1115, T193 Hatsusawa Cho 1227-4, Hachioji Tokyo Japan

SAITO, TEIJIRO, nuclear physicist and educator; b. Tokyo, Aug. 4, 1936; s. Ichiro and Hisako Saito; m. Hiromi Inoue, Feb. 20, 1972; children: Shigeru, Akiko, Yotaro. BS, Tohoku U., Sendai, Japan, 1959, MSc, 1961, PhD, 1964. Asst. faculty of sci. Tohoku U., Sendai, 1964-66, asst. Lab. Nuclear Sci., 1966-82, assoc. prof. Lab. Nuclear Sci., 1982-2000; part-time lectr. Faculty Engring. Tohoku Gakuin U., 2000—. Editor Rsch. Report of Lab. Nuclear Sci., Tohoku U., 1972-2000. Mem. Am. Phys. Soc., Phys. Soc. Japan. Avocation: skiing. Home: 2-51 Masue, Miyagino-ku Sendai 983-0837, Japan Office: 1-13-1 Chuo, Tagajo 985-8537, Japan

SAITO, TOSHIKAZU, medical researcher, educator; b. Kobe, Hyogo, Japan, Apr. 23, 1936; s. Tokushichi and Yoshiko (Tanaka) S.; m. Itsuko Satake, May 6, 1967; children: Yuichi, Takeshi. MD, U. Tokyo, 1962, PhD, 1967. Assoc. prof. Jichi Med. Sch., Tochigi, 1974-86; prof. Jichi Med. Sch., 1987—, chmn. dept. endocrinology and metabolism, 1992—, chmn. dept. medicine, 2000—; chmn. bd. nat. exams. of medicine, 1997. Editor: Neurohypophysis, 1995. Mem. Japanese Endocrine Soc. (pres. 1998-99), Japanese Neuroendocine Soc. (pres. 1999—). Home: 2-1-26-1001 Sakura, Utsunomiya 320 0043, Japan

SAITO, WILLIAM HIROYUKI, software company executive; b. L.A., Mar. 23, 1971; s. Toshiyuki and Yoko S.; m. Yuko Saito; 2 children. BS in Biochemistry, U. Calif., Riverside, 1992; postgrad., U. Calif., 1996, 97. Cert. EMT. Programmer Merrill Lynch, Burbank, Calif., 1986-89; instr. Calif. Poly. U., Pomona, 1985-87; staff cons. computer sci. dept. U. Calif., Rancho Cucamonga, Tokyo, 1988-92; ptnr. I/O Software, Walnut, Calif., 1987-90; pres., CEO, co-founder I/O Software, Riverside, Calif., 1991—; CEO Japan I/O Software, Tokyo, 1994-97; cons. IBM, Riverside, 1986-87, Japan IBM, Tokyo, 1988-90, Japan NEC, Tokyo, 1987-89, ASCII, Tokyo, 1988-90; guest lectr. U. Calif. Anderson Sch. Bus., Riverside, 1995—; judge Ernst and Young Entrepreneur of Yr. program, 1999; keynote spkr., mem. panels, chair groups at numerous confs. including Comdex, Internet Security Conf., 1999, CardTech/Secure Tech, Washington, 1998, Chgo., 1999, Software Coun. So. Calif., San Bernardino, 1999, Nat. Info. Sys. Security Conf., Arlington, Va., 1999, Software Pubs. Assn., 1997, Assn. for Biometrics, 1998, IQPC, London, 1999, Biometrics Summit, Washington, 1999, Miami, 2000, Global Patent Strategy Briefings, London, 1999, RSA Conf., San Jose, Calif., 2000, NAFE, Peter F. Drucker Grad. Sch. Bus., Claremont, Calif., 2000, Security Industry Assn., Amelia Island, Fla., 2000, among others. Vol. medical asst. Kaiser Permanent, Riverside, 1989-92; bd. dirs. Riverside Arts Found., 1995-97, Higher Edn./Bus. Coun. City Riverside, 1998—, Riverside Cmty. On-Line, 1999—; bd. trustee UCR Found., 1998—; mem. adv. bd. Coll. Bus. San Francisco State U., 1998—, Marlan and Rosemary Bourns Coll. Engring., 1998—. Named Ernst & Young Entrepreneur of the Yr., 1998, Point of View Mag. America's 50 Top Up & Comers, 1998, one of Top 100 Computer Cos., Computer World. Mem. IEEE, AMA, AAAS, Am. Nat. Stds. Inst., Internat. Stds. Orgn., Nat. Inst. Stds. and Tech., Mensa. Republican. Roman Catholic. Avocations: fishing, tennis, skiing, stamp collecting, classical music. Office: IO Software Inc 1533 Spruce St Ste 300 Riverside CA 92507-2427

SAITO, YOSHIHIRO, systems engineer, researcher; b. Sagae, Japan, May 10, 1958; s. Yoshio and Sadako (Sato) S.; m. Yumi Ito Saito, Oct. 8, 1989; children: Shiho, Rino. MS, Tohoku U., Sendai, Japan, 1985. Fine ceramics rschr. Central Glass, Ube, Japan, 1985-89; factory auto engr. Matsusaka, Japan, 1989-92, Carlex Glass, Knoxville, 1992-93; phase shift rschr. ULCOAT, Chichibu, Japan, 1993-95; dry etch sys. rschr., 1995-98; assoc. sr. rschr. Matsusaka, 1998—; engring. mgr. Ctrl Glass Co., Ltd., Matsusaka, 1992—. Inventor in field. Avocations: scuba diving, oil painting,. Office: 1510 Ohkuchi cho, Matsusaka 515-0001, Japan

SAITOH, AKIO, association administrator retired; b. Kobe-shi, Hyogo-ken, Japan, Sept. 10, 1926; s. Masao and Sadako (toida) S.; m. Ryoko Ono, Nov.3, 1959; children: Kimiko, Junko Saitoh Hasegawa. BS, Tokyo Comml. U. (Hitosubashi), 1950. Various managerial positions Toshiba Corp., Tokyo, 1950-81; dep. sec.-gen Japanese Bus. Machine Makers Assn., Tokyo, 1981-86; sec. gen. Info. Processing Soc. Japan/Info. Tech. Stds. Commn. Japan, Tokyo, 1986-90, adviser, 1990-95; com. mem. Japanese Electronics Industry Devel. Assn., Tokyo, 1972-84; com. mem. Japanese Info. Processing Devel. Ctr., 1979-83, Japan Inst. Office Automation, 1982-83, Info. Processing Soc. Japan/Info. Tech. Stds. Commn. Japan, 1984-97. Contbr. articles to jours. in electronic processing field. Cadet Naval Acad., 1943-45. Home: Minamiyawata 4-4-17-1101, ChibaKen Ickikawa-shi 272-0023, Japan

SAITOH, MAMORU, English educator; b. Okazaki, Aichi, Japan, Jan. 1, 1935; s. Tamotsu and Kiyoko Saitoh; m. Minako Hayakawa, May 20, 1962; children: Kayoko, Yumiko. B in Engring., Nagoya U., Japan, 1958. Design engr. textile machinery div. Toyoda Automatic Loom Works Co., Kariya, Japan, 1958-71; chief design engr. Toyoda-Sulzer Mfg., Ohbu, Japan, 1971-82; chief design engr. Toyoda Automatic Loom Works Co., Kariya, 1982-84, asst. dir., 1984-95, with planning dept., 1995-99. Mem. Fuji Kani Country Club. Avocations: dancing, golf. Home and Office: 4-23 Tosakishinmachi, Okazaki 444-0849, Japan

SAITOTI, GEORGE, Kenyan government official; b. Kajido North, Rift Valley, 1944. BA, Brandeis U., 1967; MA, Sussex U.; PhD, U. Warwick, 1972. Appointed M.P., 1983; min. finance Govt. of Kenya, Nairobi, 1983, 1989-92; elected M.P., 1988—; v.p. Govt. of Kenya, Nairobi, 1989—, min. planning and devel., 1993—; tchr. Nairobi U.; chmn. Mamias Sugar Co.; chmn. Kajido branch Kenya African Nat. Union, 1988, v.p., 1989. Address: Treasury Bldg, Harambee Ave POB 30007, Nairobi Kenya*

SAIYED, SAIYEDALI AHMEDMIYA, economics educator; b. Visnagar, Gujarat, India, Oct. 21, 1953; s. Ahmedmiya Najmuddin and Shamusnnisa (Ahmedmiya) S.; m. Kulsumfatema Abbasmiya Kulsumfatema, Dec. 16, 1964; 3 children. BA in Econs., M.S. U., 1975, MA in Econs., 1977, PhD in Bus. Econs., 1998. Lectr. S.P. U., V.V. Nagar, India, 1982-83; lectr. M.S. U., Baroda, India, 1984-91, sr. lectr., 1992-97, reader, 1998—; tchr. supr. Faculty of Commerce, Baroda, 1991-93, dean of students, 1994—; pres. M.S. U. Student's Union, 1999—; mem. sen. M.S. U. Baroda. Contbr. articles to profl. jours. Gen. sec. Communical Harmony Com., Baroda, 1988—; mem. exec. com. Muslim Edn. Soc., Baroda, 1990—; mem. Gujarat Urdu Acad., Gandhinagar, 1994—; gen. sec. Bazme-Adab, Baroda City, 1990—. Home: 10-A Kalyan Soc, B/H Panigate Petrol Pump, Baroda 390 019, India Office: Faculty of Commerce, Lokmanya Tilk Rd Sayajigunj, Baroda 390 002, India

SAIZU, IOAN I., retired history educator; b. Iasi, Romania, Jan. 11, 1931; s. Ioan Neculai and Elena Mihai (Nora) S.; m. Ortansa Mihai Bejanaru, July 5, 1965; 1 child, Mihaela. Diploma, U. Iasi, Romania, 1957, D History, 1973. Rschr. Inst. History, Iasi, 1958-71, rsch. prin. III, 1971-91, rsch. prin. II, 1991-95, rsch. prin. I, 1996; ret., 1996; cons. Inst. History, Iasi, 1996-98. Author: (with others) A History of the Romanian Railways, 1977, (with others) Political Life in Romania, 1922-1928, 1979 (Acad. prize 1980), Romania's Economic Policy Between 1922 and 1928, 1981, Forgotten Pages of the Economic Culture: The Economic Congress in Romania, Jassy, 1882 and 1884, 1984, Culture and Economy, Opinions in Inter War Period, 1986, Modernization of Contemporary Romania, Interwar, 1991, (with others) The Inter-War Economic Europe, 1997 (Acad. prize 1999), Eminescu - as Eternity, 1997, Reflections and Notes Passing Through Time, 1999. Avocation: writing poetry. Home: Sulfinei 3A, 6600 Iasi Romania Office: Inst History, Lascar Catargi 15A, 6600 Iasi Romania

SAJGO, MIHALY, biochemist, educator; b. Zamardi, Somogy, Hungary, Aug. 11, 1933; s. Gyözö and Livia (Hutiray) S.; m. Klara Vukan, Aug. 11, 1956; childrenÂ Klara, Eszter. MSc, Eotvos Lorand U., 1955; PhD, Hungarian Acad. Scis., 1963, DSc, 1973. Sci. asst., officer, advisor Hungarian Acad. Scis., Budapest, 1955-81; asst. prof. U. Agr., Godollo, Hungary, 1981-82; prof. U. Agr., Godollo, 1982—, dean faculty agrl., 1990-96. Author: Textbook of Biochemistry, 1985, 2d edit., 1994; mng. editor Acta Biochem. Biophys. Acad. Sci. Hungary, 1961-85. Recipient Hungarian State award, 1973, Szent-Gyorgyi award Min. Cultural Affairs, 1993, Order of Merit, Hungarian Rep. Office Cross. Mem. Hungarian Biochem. Soc. (dep. sec. 1991-94), Nat. Rsch. Fund. Roman Catholic. Avocations: dogs, travel, computers. Home: Deak Ferenc utca 52, 1193 Budapest Hungary Office: Univ Agriculture, Pater Karoly utca 1, 2103 Godollo Hungary

SAJI, K. B., management educator, consultant; b. Trivandrum, Kerala, India, May 30, 1968; s. S. Balakrishna Pillai and N. Devaki Amma; m. Uma S. Nair, Sept. 16, 1998. BSc, U. Kerala, Trivandrum, India, 1988, B of Tech., 1992; MBA, Faculty Mgmt. Studies, Trivandrum, 1994; PhD, Indian Inst. Tech., Bombay, 1999. Cert. in engring., mktg., tech. mgmt. Advt. exec. ZPWL, India, 1992-93; sr. exec. mktg. Motorola, India, 1993-94; mgr. bus. devel. and planning LC, India, 1995-96; lectr. bus. adminstrn. U. Kerala, 1996; asst. prof. Amrita Inst. Mgmt., Coimbatore, India, 1997—; cons. Indian Rayons, Coca-Cola India, Reynolds, Carborundum, others, India, 1994-99; vis. prof. U. Madras, Bombay, 1994-99; mem. bd. studies U. Kerala, 1997; mem. acad. coun. Amrita Inst. Mgmt., 1997—; referee to internat. jours.; book reviewer books for Internat. Pubs. Contbr. rsch. papers to profl. jours. Coord. Literacy Mission, Trivandrum, 1992. Nat. Merit scholar India Govt., 1980-94. Fellow Acad. Mktg. Scis.; mem. Acad. Internat. Bus., Acad. Mgmts. Internat. Mgmt. Divsn. Hindu. Office: Amrita Inst Mgmt, Ettimadai, Coimbatore 641 105, India

SAJI, MADATHIPARAMBIL JOSEPH, orthopedist, surgeon; b. Alleppy, India, Oct. 2, 1956; s. Madathiparambil Pothen and Mary (Paul) Joseph; m. Rosy Job Saji, May 14, 1984; children: Prashant, Priyanka. MB, BChir, St. Josephs Coll., Bangalore, India, 1980; CM in Orthop., Postgrad. Inst. Med. Edn. Rsch, Chandigarh, India, 1983; postgrad., U. London, 1985. From clin. tutor to assoc. prof. St. Johns Med. Coll., Bangalore, 1983-93, prof., 1993—; head dept. orthop. Ministry of Health, Ibri, Oman, 1994-95; cons. Spastic Soc. India, Bangalore, 1988—. Contbr. articles to profl. jours. Hodgsons fellow U. Hong Kong, 1992; recipient Russell S. Hibbs award Scoliosis Rsch. Soc., Kansas City, Kans., 1992, Gold medal Assn. Otolaryngologists India, 1978. Mem. Indian Orthop. Assn., Pediat. Orthop. Assn. India, N.Y. Acad. Scis. Roman Catholic. Avocations: chess, art of bonsai. Home: Virgonagar PO, Nirmala Farm, Bangalore 560049, India Office: Ibri Regional Referal Hosp, PO Box 46, Ibri 516, Oman

SAKA, MEHMET POLAT, structural engineer, educator; b. Trabzon, Turkey, Jan. 17, 1947; arrived in Bahrain, 1984; s. Ahmet and Selcuk (Tarakcioglu) S.; m. Gulten Gulpinar, Aug. 15, 1971; children: Ayse Ufuk, Gulbanu, Cigdem. BSc, Istanbul (Turkey) Tech. U., 1968, MSc, 1969; PhD, U. Aston, Birmingham, Eng., 1975. Asst. prof. Black Sea Tech. U., Trabzon, 1975-82, assoc. prof., 1982-84; assoc. prof. U. Bahrain, Isa Town, 1984-92, prof., 1992—; coord. structures lab. U. Bahrain, Isa Town, 1984-90, sr. projects, 1984—, microcomputer lab., 1986—, MSc program civil engring., 1992—, acting head dept., 1988; cons. in field. Editor Internat. Jour. Structural Engring. Rev., 1995—, Asian Jour. Structural Engring.; contbr. articles to Proceedings Inst. Civil Engrs., Jour. Structural Engr., Jour. Structural Divsn., Jour. Computers Structures, Jour. Structural Engring., Jour. Istanbul Tech. U. Lt. Turkish Army, 1976-77. Min. Edn. Govt. Turkey scholar, 1971; UNESCO fellow, 1977, U. Aston fellow, 1977-78; Telford premium Inst. Civil Engrs., 1979. Mem. ASCE, Internat. Soc. Structural Multidisciplinary Optimization, Internat. Assn. Bridge Structural Engring., Assn. Internat. Coop. Rsch. Steel-Concrete Composite Structures, Asian Inst. Tech., Soc. Civil Engrs. Office: U Bahrain Dept Civil Engr, PO Box 32038, Isa Town Bahrain

SAKAGUCHI, MASATO, chemistry educator; b. Takikawa, Japan, Mar. 17, 1948; s. Tomekichi and Fumiko (Sasaki) S.; m. Kazuko Sato, Feb. 14, 1977; 1 child, Seiya. B in Engring., Muroran Inst. Tech., 1970; M in Engring., Hokkaido U., 1973, D of Engring., 1977. Lectr., assoc. prof. Ichimura Gakuen Coll., Inuyama, Japan, 1977-89; prof. Ichimura Gakuen Coll., Inuyama, 1990—; vis. scientist Hokkaido U., Sapporo, Japan, 1978, 79, U. Houston, 1988-89, 90; lectr. Nagoya (Japan) U., 1987—. Author: ESR Application to Polymer Research, 1973, Degradation and Stabilization of Polymer, 1975; contbr. articles to profl. jours. Mem. AAAS, Am. Chem. Soc., N.Y. Acad. Scis., Soc. Polymer Sci. Japan, Chem. Soc. Japan. Avocations: swimming, skiing, radio-ham. E-mail: sakaguch@ichimura.ac.jp. Office: Ichimura Gakuen Coll, 61 Uchikubo, Inuyama 484-8503, Japan

SAKAGUCHI, SANAE, health educator, researcher; b. Tokyo, May 10, 1952; d. Yoshiharu and Miyabi (Nakazawa) Sakaguchi; m. Takehiro Sakaguchi, Mar. 21, 1974. M of Hygiene, Kitasato U., Tokyo, 1977, Dr of Health Scis., 1980. Cert. med. technologist. Asst. prof. Kawamura Coll., Tokyo, 1983-86, assoc. prof., 1986-91; assoc. prof. Kawamura Gakuen Woman's U., Abiko, Japan, 1991-97, prof. health, 1997—; lectr. Nippon Dental U., Tokyo, 1998—, Waseda U., Tkyo, 1982—; rschr. St. Marianna U. Sch. med., Kawasaki, Japan, 1980-97. Contbr. articles to Pharmacology and Toxicology, Trace elements and Electrolytes, others. Mem. AAAS, N.Y. Acad. Scis., Japanese Soc. for Hygiene (councilor 1992—), Japan Soc. for Occupational Health (councilor 1993-96). Avocations: travel, reading. Office: Kawamura Gakuen Woman's U, 1133 Sageto, Abiko, Chiba 270-1138, Japan

SAKAGUCHI, TAKEHIRO, health educator, researcher; b. Tokyo, July 1, 1947; s. Takeichi and Kimiko (Aota) Sakaguchi; m. Sanae Sakaguchi, Mar. 21, 1974. M of Hygiene, Kitasato U., Tokyo, 1972; PhD, St. Marianna U. Sch. Medicine, Kawasaki, Japan, 1985. Lectr. dept. pub. health Kitasato U., 1972-80; asst. prof. dept. hygiene St. Marianna U. Sch. Medicine, 1980-96, assoc. prof. dept. hygiene, 1996-97; prof. dept. life sci. Kawamura Coll., Tokyo, 1997-2000; prof. dept. human environment Kawamura Gakuen Woman's U., Abiko, Japan, 2000—; lectr. Chuo U., Tokyo, 1988-97, Shizuoka (Japan) U., 1997-99, Nippon Dental U., Tokyo, 1998—. Contbr. articles to profl. jours. Mem. AAAS, Japanese Soc. Hygiene (councilor 1987—), Japan Soc. Occupl. Health (councilor 1990-96), Japanese Soc. Pub. Health (councilor 1993-96), Japanese Assn. Infectious Diseases (councilor 1997—), Japanese Soc. Bacteriology, N.Y. Acad. Scis. Avocation: travel. Office: Kawamura Gakuen Womans Univ, 1133 Sageto, Abiko Chiba 270-1138, Japan

SAKAI, AKIO, medical physiologist, educator; b. Ina, Japan, Dec. 5, 1942; m. Toshiko Akazawa, Feb. 19, 1972; children: Kenichi, Miyuki. BS in Edn., Shinshu U., Matsumoto, Japan, 1965, PhD in Medicine, 1978. Asst. Shinshu U. Med. Sch., 1965-87; rsch. fellow U. Colo. Health Scis. Ctr., Denver, 1985-86; assoc. prof. physiology Shinshu U. Med. Sch., 1987—; med. mem. Japanese Everest Skiing Expedition, Nepal, 1970; dir. Tibetan Med. Expedition, China, 1989. Contbr. articles to internat. physiol. jours. Mem. Am. Physiol. Soc., Aerospace Med. Assn. Avocation: mountain climbing. Home: Misato-mura Meisei 1171-1, Minamiazumi-gun Nagano-ken Japan Office: Shinshu U Sch Medicine, Sports Med Dept 3-1-1 Asahi, Nagano Matsumoto 390, Japan

SAKAI, AKIYOSHI, urban redevelopment consultant; b. Oguchi, Aichi, Japan, Jan. 1, 1930; s. Hisayoshi and Asako S.; m. Toshiko A. Sakai, Dec. 8, 1956; children: Seiji, Tatsuto. BS, Gitu Agrl. Coll., 1951. Microbiologist Fujisawa Pharm. Co., Ltd., Nagoya, Japan, 1951-59; pres. Takaha Archtl. Engring. Co., Ltd., Nagoya, 1960-73; chmn. Urban Dynamics Inst. Takaha Co. Ltd., Tokyo, 1974—, Toshigakaku Engring. Co., Ltd., Tokyo, 1986—; pres. C. Devel. Info. & Support Sys., 2000—. Author: Shigaichi Saikaihatsu, 1974. Mem. Regional Bus. Devel. Inst., 1994—. Mem. City Planning Assn. Japan, Urban Renewal Coord. Assn. Japan. Avocations: new thinking for intelligent creative process by subdivision and digitization. Office: Urban Dynamics Inst Takaha, 1-3-2 Nishiazabu Minato, Tokyo 106, Japan

SAKAI, HIDEYUKI, lawyer; b. Sakai-Gun, Fukui-ken, Japan, Dec. 9, 1949; s. Hidemasa and Reiko (Shigematsu) S.; m. Mieko Okamoto, Nov. 8, 1975; children: Daisuke, Chiharu, Haruka. BL, U. Tokyo, 1974; LLM, Duke U., 1982. Ptnr. Blakemore & Mitsuki, Tokyo, 1990-94; pvt. practice Tokyo, 1995—. Contbr. articles to profl. jours. Mem. Tokyo Bar Assn. (pres. com. on bankruptcy and creditor's rights 1998), Internat. Bar Assn. (mem. com. J 1985—), Inter Pacific Bar Assn., Japan Alumni Club of Duke U. Sch. Law (pres.). Avocations: rugby, music composition, reading books on sociology and cultural anthropology. Fax: 81-3-3519-8322. E-mail: sakai-law@msn.com. Office: 9th Fl Sumitomo Toranomon, Bldg 6-12 Toranomon 1-Chome, Minato-ku Tokyo 105-0001, Japan

SAKAI, HITOSHI, geochemist, scientific writer; b. Shimizu, Shizuoka, Japan, Aug. 3, 1930; s. Yoshitaro and TAke (Isozuka) S.; m. Sadako Kamiyama, Mar. 27, 1956; children: Kanako, Jun, Ken. BS, U. Tokyo, 1953, DSc, 1958. Asst. prof. U. Tokyo, 1956-61, prof., 1983-91; assoc. prof. Okayama U., Misasa, Tottori, Japan, 1962-67, prof., 1968-83; prof. Yamagata (Japan) U., 1991-96; ind. writer Tokyo, 1996—; part-time lectr. Waseda (Japan) U. Author: Ore Genesis, 1977, Chemistry of Isotopes, 1979, Stable Isotope Geochemistry, 1996, Origins of Earth and Life, 1999; editor: Biogeochemical Processes and Ocean Flux in the Western Pacific, 1996. Recipient Miyake prize Geochem. Rsch. Assn., 1981; Rsch. fellow Chinese Acad. Geol. Scis., 1992—. Fellow Geol. Soc. Am. (hon.); mem. Internat. Assn. Geochemistry and Cosmochemistry (chmn. water-rock interaction working group 1984-87, pres. 1992-96), Geochem. Soc. Japan (Shibata prize 1999). Avocation: reading. Home and Office: 1-4-7-1508 Seishin-cho, Edogawa-ku, Tokyo 134-0087, Japan

SAKAI, SHIGEKI, economist, historian; b. Tatunosi, Japan, Mar. 8, 1949; s. Takeshi and Mituko (Yamaguti) S.; m. Keiko Takemori, Mar. 21, 1977; children: Akiko, Itomi. BA, Kyoto U., 1971, MA, 1973, PhD, 1991. Prof. Kumamotogakuen U., Japan, 1976—. Author: A Study of the Financial History of Modern England, 1989, An Introduction to Economic History, 1991, Mixed Monarchy and The Tax State, 1997, Transaction of M.J. Braddick, The Nerves of State; Taxation and Financing of the English State, 1558-1714, 2000. Avocation: tennis. Office: Kumamotogakuen U, 2-5-1 Oe, Kumamotoi 862-8680, Japan

SAKAI, TAKU, metallurgist educator; b. Kaifeng, China, Oct. 14, 1942; s. Kunio and Emiko (Ikeda) S.; m. Mieko Tanaka, Dec. 9, 1972; children: Sakai, Sho, Ken. B of Engring., Yokohama (Japan) Nat. U., 1965, M of Engring., 1967; D of Engring., Tokyo U., 1978. Rsch. assoc. U. Electro-Communications, Tokyo, 1965-72, asst. prof., 1972-78, assoc. prof., 1978-86, prof., 1986—; vis. prof. McGill U., Montreal, Can., 1981-82; adv. prof. Harbin (China) Inst. Tech., 1988—; hon. prof. Northeastern U., China, 1999—; cons. NGK Insulators, Nagoya, Japan, 1985—; chmn. Rsch. Com. on Recrystallization & Texture, Tokyo, 1994-99; co-chmn. Internat. Conf. on THERMEC '97, Wollongong, Australia, 1994-97. Chief of editors: (book) Thermomechanical Processing of Steels and Other Metals, 1997, Recystallization and Related Phenomena, 1999; inventor Method of Hot Forming of Be Cu Alloy, 1989 (Award 1992, 93, 96). Mem. Japanese Inst Metals (chmn. Recrystallizatoin '99, 1999, Best Paper of 1992, 1993), Iron & Steel Inst. of Japan (Nishiyama Meml. award 1991), TMS of AIME. Avocations: reading books on history and science, music, sports. Home: Izumi 3-19-15, Suginami Tokyo 168-0063, Japan Office: U Electro-Comm Dept Mech, Engring/Integrated Systems, Chofu Tokyo 182-8585, Japan

SAKAI, YASUYOSHI, microbiologist, educator; b. Kobe, Japan, May 22, 1959; s. Yutaka and Kyoko (Tomii) S.; m. Hiromi Suetsugu, Jan. 16, 1988; children: Yumiko, Kimiko. B degre, Kyoto U., M degre, PhD. Asst. prof. Kyoto U., 1988-94, assoc. prof., 1994—; vis. prof. U. Calif., San Diego, 1996-97. Contbr. articles to profl. jours. including Jour. Cell Biology and Jour. Bacteriology. Mem. Am. Soc. Cell Biology, Soc. for Fermentation Bioengring. (mem. editl. bd. Jour. Fermentation and Bioengring.), Soc. for Biosci., Biotech., and Agrochemistry, Japan Soc. for Biochemistry. Avocation: music. Office: Kyoto U Applied Life Scis, Kitashirakawa Oiwake, Sakyo-ku Kyoto 606-8502, Japan

SAKAIDA, TAKASHI, agricultural engineer, educator; b. Yanaizu-cho, Hashima-gun, Japan, Feb. 4, 1940; s. Toichi and Akiko (Suzuki) S.; m. Kiyoko Niwa, Mar. 4, 1967; children: Masashi, Atsushi. BAgr, Tohoku U., Sendai, Japan, 1963, MAgr, 1965, DAgr, 1980. Registered profl. engineer, Japan. Breeding researcher, head researcher Enya Poultry Breeding Farm, Hozumi, Gifu, Japan, 1965-77; poultry researcher, faculty of agr. Gifu U., Yanagido, Gihu, 1977-82; assoc. prof. dept. edn. and langs. Gifu Shotoku Gakuen U., Yanaizu, Gifu, 1982-84; prof. Gifu Shotoku Gakuen U., 1984—. Author: Improving Poultry Management, vol. 1, 1983, vol. 2, 1987, Egg

Producer of High Quality and Marketing, vol. 1, 1995, vol. 2, 1999. Mem. Japan Poultry Sci. Assn. (councilor 1988—, award 1982), Japanese Soc. Zootechl Sci. (dist. councilor 1987—), Japanese Soc. Poultry Diseases, Japan Livestock Mgmt. Assn. Shin Buddhist. Avocation: poetry. Home: 138 Takakuwa, Yanaizu-cho 501-61, Gifu-ken Japan Office: Gakuen U Gifu U Edn and Langs Shotoku, Gifu Shotoku Gakuen U, 2078 Takakuwa Yanaizu-cho, Gifu-ken 501-6122, Japan

SAKAKIBARA, HISATAKA, occupational hygiene educator, researcher; b. Toki, Gifu, Japan, Sept. 27, 1953. BM, Nagoya (Japan) U., 1978, MD, 1983. Instr. indsl. hygiene Nagoya U. Sch. Medicine, 1982-87, asst. prof., 1987-97, assoc. prof., 1997-98; prof. Nagoya U. Sch. Health Scis., 1998—. Contbr. articles to med. jours., including Internat. Archives Occupl. Environ. Medicine, Am. Jour. Indsl. Medicine, Ctrl. European Jour. Pub. Health. Mem. Japan Soc. for Occupl. Health (councilor), Japanese Soc. Pub. Health, Japan. Soc. for Hygiene. Office: Nagoya U Sch Health Scis, 1-1-20 Daiko-minami Higashi, Aichi Nagoya 461-8673, Japan

SAKAKIBARA, YUZURU, medical educator; b. Takamatsu City, Kagawa, Japan, July 18, 1954; s. Hiroshi and Kazuko (Okabe) S.; m. Michiko Sato, Feb. 10, 1985; children: Masaru, Satoru. MD, U. Tsukuba, Japan, 1980; PhD, U. Tsukuba, 1988. Resident in surgery Tsukuba U. Hosp., 1980-84; rsch. fellow Mass. Gen. Hosp., Boston, 1984-85; chief resident Mitsui Meml. Hosp., Tokyo, 1985-86; asst. prof. Tsukuba U., 1986—; conductor fgn. med. practitioner Japanese Health and Welfare, Tokyo, 1991—; councilor Japanese Coll. Angiology, Tokyo, 1991—. Contbr. articles to profl. jours. Fellow Am. Coll. Angiology; mem. Soc. Thoracic Surgeons, Am. Heart Assn., Japanese Assn. Thoracic Surgery (cons. surgeon 1991—), Japanese Soc. Artificial Organs (councilor 1997—). Avocations: golfing, fishing. Home: 2-13-19 Matsushiro, Tsukuba 305-0035, Japan Office: U Tsukuba Dept Surgery, 1-1-1 Tennodai, Tsukuba 305-8575, Japan

SAKAMOTO, MUNENORI, engineering educator, researcher, chemist; b. Kita-Kyuushu, Japan, 1936; s. Masanori and Ai (Sasaki) S.; m. Kyoko Sawano, Dec. 8, 1967; children: Shigenori, Hironori. B. Engring., Tokyo Inst. Tech., 1958, MSc, 1960, DSc, 1963. Asst. Tokyo Inst. Tech., 1963-70; rsch. assoc. U. Ariz., Tucson, 1964-66; assoc. prof. Tokyo Inst. Tech., 1970-84, prof., 1984—, dir. Internat. Student Ctr., 1994-96; prof. Joetsu U. Edn., 1996—, head divsn. lit. and health sci., 2000—; mem. sci. and tech. com. Tokyo Textile Rsch. Inst., 1991. Editor Proceedings 7th Internat. Wool Rsch. Conf., 1985, Sen'i Gakkaishi, 1989-91; translator: Introdution to Reaction Injection Molding, 1983. Mem. Soc. Fiber Sci. Tech. Japan (chmn. rsch. com. on textile finishing, recipient award 1980), Chem. Soc. Japan, Soc. Polymer Sci. Japan, Am. Chem. Soc., Am. Assn. Textile Chemists Colorists. Buddhist. Home: Tsukushino 2-11-9, Machida-shi Tokyo 194, Japan Office: Tokyo Inst Tech, O-Okoyama 2-12-1, Meguro-ku Tokyo 152, Japan

SAKAMOTO, SHINJI, psychology educator, researcher; b. Yokohama, Kanagawa, Japan, June 24, 1966; s. Kohzo and Aiko (Sakuma) S. BA, U. Tokyo, 1990, MA, 1992, PhD, 1995. Domestic rsch. fellow Nat. Inst. Mental Health, Ichikawa, Japan, 1995-98; asst. prof. Otsuma Women's U., Tama, Japan, 1998—; rsch. fellow (hon.) Nat. Inst. Mental Health, Ichikawa, 1998—. Author: Self-focus and depression: Toward an interface between social and clinical psychology, 1997; contbr. articles to profl. jours. Rsch. grantee Phizer Health Rsch. Found., 1997. Mem. Japanese Assn. Ednl. Psychology, Japanese Psychol. Assn., APA. Home: 4-281 Nakamura-cho, Minami-ku, 232-0003 Yokohama Kanagawa, Japan Office: Otsuma Women's U, 2-7-1 Karakida, 206-8540 Tama Tokyo, Japan

SAKAMOTO, SHINOBU, endocrinologist, gynecologist and obstetrician, educator; b. Tokyo, Mar. 5, 1945; s. Shirou and Tsune (Sasaki) S.; m. Mayumi Okabe, May 25, 1974; children: Kaoru, Megumi, Izumi, Hitomi. MD, Tokyo Med. and Dental U., 1970, PhD (hon.), 1976. Cert. ob-gyn. Asst. prof. Tokyo Med. and Dental U., 1976-89, assoc. prof., 1989—; Chief dept. gynecology Saiwai Hosp., Kawasaki, Japan, 1988—; sch. doctor Hibiya H.S., Tokyo, 1995—. Author: Excerpta Medica, 1988, Familial Adenomatous Polyposis, 1990; contbr. articles to profl. jours. Authorized sports doctor Japan Judo Com., E. Japan, 1995—. Grant-in-Aid for sci. rsch. Ministry of Edn., Scis., Sports and Culture. Mem. Japan Endocrine Soc. (councilor), N.Y. Acad. Scis. Avocations: judo, swimming, horse riding, baseball, skiing. Fax: 03-5803-0248. Home: 5-30-22 Minamidai, Nakano-ku, Tokyo 164-0014, Japan Office: Med Rsch Inst Tokyo Med, 1-5-45 Yushima, Bunkyo-ku, Tokyo 113-8510, Japan

SAKAMOTO, TADANOBU, English literature educator; b. Kobe, Japan, July 23, 1931; s. Kazuo and Hatuno Sakamoto; m. Kazuko Yanagawa, Oct. 7, 1962; children: Kazuyoshi, Yoshihiro. BA, Osaka U., 1955, MA, 1957, DLitt, 1979. Lectr. Osaka (Japan) Inst. Tech., 1959-64, asst. prof., 1964-65; assoc. prof. English lit. Hiroshima (Japan) U., 1965-77, prof., 1977-95; prof. Hiroshima Jogakuin U., 1995—. Author: Tozasareta-Taiwa, 1969, Virginia Woolf, 1978, William Golding, 1983, Chart of Literary Creation, 1986, Collection of Short Stories, 1991, 94, Bloomsbury Group, 1995, Collection of Essays, 1995. Winner short story competition BBC World Svc., 1967; recipient prize for rising novelist Chungku-Shinbun Press, 1988, Hiroshima Lit. prize Hiroshima City Found., 1990; Brit. Coun. grantee, 1988. Mem. English Lit. Soc. Japan, English Lit. Soc. Hiroshima U., English Lit. Soc. Osaka U., Virginia Woolf Soc. Japan (pres. 1997—), Shakespeare and Modern Writers Soc. (pres. 1997—). Home: 29-7 Inokuchidai 3-chome, Nishi-ku, Hiroshima 733-0844, Japan Office: Hiroshima Jogakuin U Fac Lt, 4-13-1 Ushitahigashi, Higashi-ku Hiroshima 732-0063, Japan

SAKAMOTO, YOSHIKAZU, educator; b. L.A., Sept. 16, 1927; s. Yoshitaka and Tayoko (Hasegawa) S.; m. Kikuko Ono, June 2, 1956; children: Junko, Masako. Hogakushi, U. Tokyo, 1951. Prof. faculty law U. Tokyo, 1964-88; prof. faculty internat. studies Meiji Gakuin U., Tokyo, 1988-93; prof. emeritus U. Tokyo, 1988—; mem. scientific coun. Stockholm Internat. Peace Rsch. Inst., 1983-97; co-dir. World Order Models Project, N.Y., 1986—; mem. Jury of UNESCO Peace Edn., Prize, 1984-89; sec. gen. Internat. Peace Rsch. Assn., 1979-83. Author: Peace-Its Realities and Research, 1976, International Politics in Global Perspective, 1990, The Age of Relativization, 1997; contbg. author, editor: Strategic Doctrines and Their Alternatives, 1987, The Global Transformation, 1994, Nuclearism and Man, 1999. Fulbright grantee, 1955-56; Rockefeller fellow, N.Y., 1956-57, Eisenhower fellow, Phila., 1964, spl. fellow UN Inst. Rsch. & Tng., N.Y., 1972-74, sr. rsch. fellow Internat. Christian U., Tokyo, 1993-96. Mem. Am. Polit. Sci. Assn., Japan Peace Studies Assn. (coun. mem. 1979—). Home: 8-29-19 Shakujii-machi, Nerimaku Tokyo 177-0041, Japan

SAKANASHI, MATAO, pharmacology educator; b. Kumamoto, Japan, Oct. 16, 1943; s. Hidefumi and Mine Sakanashi; m. Yukiko Sakanashi, Nov. 29, 1970; children: Mayuko, Makiko. B in Medicine and MD, Kumamoto U., 1968, PhD, 1972. Asst. prof. Sch. of Medicine Kumamoto U., Kumamoto-City, 1973-75, instr. Sch. of Medicine, 1975-82; prof. pharmacology U. Ryukyus Sch. Medicine, Nishihara-cho, Okinawa, Japan, 1982—. Author: Peripheral Dopaminergic Receptors, 1979, Vascular Neuroeffector Mechanisms, 1983, Progress in Hypertension, 1988, Cardiovascular Disease in Diabetes, 1992, The Ischemic Heart, 1998. Ministry of Edn. grantee, 1979-80, 89-90; recipient Kanae Fund awards, 1983. Mem. Japanese Circulation Soc., Japanese Pharmacol. Soc., Japanese Coll. of Angiology, Japanese Soc. Circulation Rsch., Japanese Soc. Clin. Pharmacology and Therapeutics, Internat. Soc. Toxinology, Japanese Soc. Pharmacoanesthesiology, Internat. Soc. Heart Rsch., N.Y. Acad. Scis. Home: 2-96-1-2-302, Shuri-ishimine-cho Naha, Okinawa 903-0804, Japan Office: U Ryukyus Sch Medicine, 207 Uehara Nishihara-cho, Okinawa 903-0215, Japan

SAKANO, YUJI, psychologist; b. Osaka, Japan, Mar. 23, 1951; s. Choichi and Hatsuko (Fukui) S.; m. Fumiko Izutsu; children: Wakako, Kyoko, Etsuko. B of Edn., Kobe (Japan) U., 1973; M of Edn., Tokyo U. of Edn., 1977; PhD, Tsukuba U., Ibaraki, Japan, 1983. Lic. clin. psychologist. From asst. prof. to assoc. prof. Chiba (Japan) U., 1980-87; assoc. prof. Waseda U., Tokyo, 1987-92, prof., 1992—; vis. prof. U. S.C., Columbia, 1993-94. Author: (book) Cognitive Behavior Therapy, 1995; editor: (book) Theories and Practices of Cognitive Behavior Therapy, 1997. Mem. Japanese Assn. Behavior Therapy (exec. bd. dirs. 1995—). Avocation: skiing. Office: Waseda U Sch Human Scis, 2-579-15 Mikajima, Tokorozawa 359-1192, Japan

SAKAOKA, YASUE, artist, educator; b. Himeji-City, Hyogo-Ken, Japan, Nov. 12, 1933; came to U.S., 1953; naturalized, 1980; s. Naoshi and Sachie Sakaoka. BA, Reed Coll., 1959; Artists' Cert., Portland Mus. Sch., 1959; MFA, U. Oreg., 1963. Instr. U. Oreg., Eugene, 1961-63, Md. Coll. Art, Balt., 1963-65; asst. prof. art St. Paul's Coll., Lawrenceville, Va., 1965-77; asst. prof. sculpture and art history Mansfield State U., 1977-78; adj. prof. Ohio U., Athens, 1979-80; lectr. Ohio State U., Columbus, 1980—; vis. artist Stivers Sch. for Arts, Dayton, Ohio, 1989—; mem. minority adv. com. Ohio Arts Coun., Columbus, 1992—; mem. adv. bd. Internat. Biog. Ctr., Cambridge, Eng., 1998—; cons. in field of Japanese art and culture. Curator Dublin (Ohio) Arts Coun., 1998, 99, 2000, Fitton Ctr., Hamilton, Ohio, 1999, Sandusky Cultural Ctr., 1999; represented in permanent collections St. Helen Ch., Dayton, 1998—. mem. choir St. Stephen's Episcopal Ch., Columbus, 1993—; bd. mem. Asian Am. Cmty. Svc. Orgn., 1993—. Recipient fellowship NEH, 1976, Devel. grant Ohio Arts Coun., 1987-88, Pollock-Kvasner Found. award, 1987-88, Art Apprenticeship award Ohio Arts Coun., 1990-91, 91-92, 94-95, 97-98. Mem. Internat. Sculpture Ctr., Coll. Art Assn. Am., Ohio Desiner Craftsmen, Inc., Mid Ohio Japan Am. Assn., Wexner Ctr. for Arts, Ohio State U., Dayton Visual Arts Ctr. Avocations: gardening, music.

SAKARI-RANTALA, RITVA ELISA, physical therapy researcher; b. Paris, Dec. 3, 1957; d. Aimo Ilmari Kallio and Aino Ellen (Ryynänen) Sakari; m. Jukka Tapani Rantala, June 23, 1988; children: Vaula, Alli. Phys. therapist, Tampere (Finland) Sch. Nursing, 1980; specialized phys. therapist, Ctrl. Finland Coll. Health, Jyväskylä, Finland, 1985; MSc in Health Scis., U. Jyväskylä, 1991. Phys. therapist Health Ctr. Mänttä (Finland) Dist., 1981-83; phys. therapist Health Ctr. Keuruu (Finland) and Multia, 1983-85, rschr., 1988-91; rschr. U. Jyväskylä, asst. phys. therapy, 1998—. Contbr.: Evaluating Functional Capacity and Health of Elderly People in Two Populations, 1995 (in Finnish, with English summary). Recipient personal rsch. grants Finnish Ministry Edn., 1995, 96, 97. Mem. Finnish Soc. Growth and Aging Rsch. Avocations: piano, jogging. Office: U Jyväskylä, Dept Health Scis PO Box 35, 40351 Jyväskylä Finland

SAKATA, HIROE, civil engineer; b. Miyazaki-shi, Japan, June 13, 1940; s. Masajiroh and Tatsuyo (Nagano) S.; m. Jane Emiko Inoue, July 4, 1974; children: Ken, Eiji, Emily. BSCE, Miyazaki U., 1965; MS in Civil Engring., U. Calif., Berkeley, 1971, DEng, 1974. Registered profl. engr., Calif., Minn., Japan. Asst. engr. Pacific Consultants Co., Ltd., Tokyo, 1965-66, engr., 1966-69; field engr. Parsons, Brinkerhoff, Tudor Bechtel Co., Oakland, Calif., 1971-74; sr. engr. Harbert Corp., San Francisco, 1975-76, M.Rosenblatt & Son, San Francisco, 1976-78; resident engr. M.Rosenblatt & Son, Yokosuka, Japan, 1978-84; chief engr. CDI Marine Co., Ltd., Yokosuka, Japan, 1984-86; pres. I.C.E. Japan Co., Ltd., Yokohama, Japan, 1987—. Co-author: Underground Space Use in Japan. Mem. ASCE, Japan Soc. Civil Engrs., Soc. Naval Archs. Marine Engrs. Achievements include research in the flood control plan in Asian countries, a low flow increase for improving river environment. Home: 6-6-4 Jyomyoji, Kamakura 248-0003, Japan

SAKATA, KIMIO, aerospace engineer, researcher; b. Tokyo, Japan, Jan. 6, 1947; m. Yoko Sakata; children: Ritsuko, Kohtaro, Yoshiko. BSME, Sophia U., Tokyo, 1969; ME, Sophia U., 1972. Researcher Aeroengine div. Nat. Aerospace Lab., Tokyo, 1972-80, sr. researcher, 1980-89, head engine aerodynamics, 1989-98, leader system lab., 1997-98, supervising rschr. advanced aircraft project ctr., 1998—; visitor of Mech. Engring. Dept., Stanford (Calif.) U., 1980-81; tech. officer Agy. of Indsl. Sci. and Tech. of Ministry of Internat. Trade and Industry, Tokyo, 1982-83; dep. dir. Space Planning div. Sci. and Tech. Agy., Tokyo, 1984-86. Contbr. articles to profl. jours. Mem. AIAA, Japan Soc. Mech. Engring., Gas Turbine Soc. Japan, Japan Soc. for Aero. and Space Scis. Achievements include patent for turbine cooling, and supersonic air-intakes. Home: 5 30 2 Jindaijikita, Chofu Tokyo 182-0011, Japan Office: Nat Aerospace Lab, 7 44 1 Jindaijihigashi, Chofu 182 Tokyo Japan

SAKELLIOU-SCHULTZ, LIANA, poet, critic; b. Athens, Oct. 12, 1956; d. Athanasios and Zoi (Sotiraki) Sakelliou; m. William Roger Schultz, Jan. 12, 1985. BA, U. Athens, 1978; grad. Diploma, U. Edinburgh, Scotland, 1979; MA, U. Essex, England, 1980; PhD, Pa. State U., 1987. Tchr. Hellenic-Am. Union, Athens, 1981-82; lectr. Am. Coll., Athens, 1981-83; tchr. U. Athens, 1981-83, lectr., 1987-91, asst. prof., 1991-94, assoc. prof., 1994-97, prof., 1999—; tchg. asst. Pa. State U., State College, 1984-85. Author: Denise Levertov, 1988, Touches in the Flow, 1992, R.W. Emerson, 1992, Feminist Criticism of American Women Poets, 1994, Gary Snyder: The Poetics and Politics of Space, 1998, H.D. Introduction to Trilogy, 1999, Denise Levertov's Poetry of Revelation: 1988-98; The Mosaic of Nature and Spirit, 1999; contbr. articles to profl. jours. Fulbright scholar for Arts, 1992-93; Fulbright schoalr, 2000—; grantee Cambridge U., 1989; recipient Athenian Poets award Greek Writers Assn., 1983, Acad. of Am. Poets' award, Pa. State U., 1985. Mem. Hellenic Assn. Am. Studies, European Soc. Study of English, Women's Rsch. Ctr., Greek Ministry of Proedrias, MLA. Democrat. Mem. Christian Orthodox Ch. Avocations: photography, cinematography, classical music, Latin American dances, jazz. Home: 3 Amaryllidos St, 14565 Aghios Stephanos Attikis Greece Office: U Athens Dept English, Panepistimioupoli Zografou, 157 84 Athens Greece

SAKHAROV, VSEVOLOD I., Russian and European literature educator; b. Moscow, Feb. 22, 1946. Student, Moscow U., 1964-70; postgrad., Gorki Literary Inst., 1971-74; PhD in Philology, Russian Acad. Scis., 1977, D of Philology, 1993. Editor Prosveschenie Pub., Moscow, 1964-70; dep. chief editor hist. almanac Russian Archives, Moscow. Author: The World Renewing: Notes on Present Day Literature, 1980, Under the Canopy of United Muses: About Russian Romantics, 1984, Human Deeds: On Classical and Modern Literature, 1985, Pages of Russian Romanticism, 1988, Michail Bulgakov: Lessons of Fate, 1991, Russian Romantic Lyrics as a System of Artistic Creation, 1993, Farewell and A Fly: Life and Work of Michail Bulgakov; mem. editl. bd. Notes of Archives of Russian State Libr., Russian Archives, Slavjanin. With Russian Army, 1970-71. Mem. Union of Writers of Russia.

SAKHIBULLIN, NAIL ABDULLOVICH, astrophysicist, educator; b. Kazan, Russia, Oct. 8, 1940; s. Abdulla Gitiatullovich Sakhibullin and Nazia Zaripovna Khusnutdinova; m. Victoria Grigor'evna Kashtanova; 1 child, Rustam. PhD, Kazan U., 1970, DSc, 1987. Academician, Acad. Scis. Tatarstan, 1992. Asst. Kazan U., 1965-73, docent, 1973-88, prof. astrophysics, 1988—, head dept. astrophysics, 1988—, dean of faculty, 1988-92, dir. observatory, 1992—; sec. Acad. Scis., Kazan, 1992—; chmn. Scientific Coun., Kazan, 1995. Contbr. articles to profl. jours. Recipient award for Best Achievement in Astrophysics, Russian Acad. Scis., 1997. Mem. Internat. Astron. Union, European Astron. Soc. (founding mem.). Avocations: basketball, fishing. Office: Kazan State U, Kremlevskaya, 420008 Kazan Russia

SAKHNOVSKII, MIKHAILO YURIEVICH, optics and spectroscopy educator; b. Poltava, Ukraine, Mar. 15, 1939; s. Yuri Vladmirovich and Valentina Ivanovna (Grebets) S.; m. Svetlana Fedorovna Garkavenko, Nov. 5, 1968; 1 child, Alexander Mikhailovich. BS in Physics and Math., State U., Chernivtsi, Ukraine, 1962; PhD, State Inst., Moscow, 1990. Prof. optics and spectrometry State U., Chernivtsi, 1962—. Author: (textbook) The Principles of Polarimetrics and Ellipsometrics, 1991; contbr. over 50 articles to profl. jours. Avocations: fishing, auto travel, chess. Home: Olzhycha 5/2, 274003 Chernivtsi Ukraine

SAKIA, REMI MRUME, biometrician, educator; b. Moshi, Tanzania, Aug. 20, 1952; s. Raphael Ndetefuo and Aloisia Ndesamburo (Minja) S.; m. Gardel Leonard Teri, Feb. 7, 1981; children: Victor, Stella, Leon, Dennis. BSc with honors, Dar U., 1976; MSc, Iowa State U., 1979; PhD, Hohenheim U., 1988. Tchr. asst., lectr. Dar U., Morogoro, Tanzania, 1976-84; lectr. Sokoine U., Morogoro, 1984-94; dir. Computer Ctr., 1993; sr. lectr. U. Botswana, Gaborone, 1994—. Contbr. articles to profl. jours. Recipient scholarship Ford Found., 1976, German Acad. Exch., 1983, vis. scholar, 1992. Mem. Biometric Soc. Roman Catholic. Avocations: computers, music, soccer. Office: Botswana Coll Agr, Univ Botswana Pvt Bag 0027, Gaborone Botswana

SAKIC, JOSEPH STEVE, professional hockey player; b. Burnaby, B.C., Canada, July 7, 1969. Capt. Quebec Nordiques, 1991-95; with Colo. Avalanche, 1995—. Won WHL East Most Valuable Player Trophy, 1986-87, WHL Stewart (Butch) Paul Meml. Trophy, 1986-87, Four Broncos Meml. Trophy, 1987-88, Bob Clarke Trophy, 1987-88, Conn Smythe Trophy NHL, 1996; named to WHL All-Star Second Team, 1986-87, Can. Hockey League Player of Yr., 1987-88, WHL Player of Yr., 1987-88; played in NHL All-Star Game, 1990-94, 96. Office: c/o Colo Avalanche 1000 Chopper Cir Denver CO 80204-5809

ŠAKIĆ, KATARINA, anaesthesiologist, educator; b. Osijek, Slavonia, Croatia, Mar. 20, 1947; d. Rožo and Katica (Matošević) Zdravčević; m. Šimun Jerko Šakić, July 19, 1975; 1 child, Livija Katarina. Diploma, U. Zagreb, Croatia, 1966-72, specialization in anaesthesiology, 1973-78; post-grad., U. Zagreb, 1978-81. Head divsn. anesthesiology dept. orthopedic surgery Zagreb, 1982-97; head dept. anaesthesiology/IT Univ. Hosp. Dubrava, Zagreb, 1997—; assoc. prof. Sch. Medicine, Zagreb, 1995—. Contbr. chpt. to book and articles to profl. jours. Fellow Internat. Soc. Thrombosis and Haemostasis, European Soc. Anaesthesiologists (Croatia rep. 1997-99), European Soc. Intensive Care Medicine/Spine Surgery. Roman Catholic. Home: Mlinovi 121, 10000 Zagreb Croatia Office: Univ Hosp Dubrava, Avenija Gojka Suska 6, 10000 Zagreb Croatia

SAKKA, SAMIR GEORGE, physician; b. Koblenz, Germany, Aug. 2, 1967; s. Adib and Luise (Claes) S.; m. Nicole van Hout, Dec. 12, 1997. MD, U. Mainz, Germany, 1992. Resident I. Med. Clinic Bruederkrankenhaus, Trier, 1993-94; postdoctoral fellow in pathophysiology U. Essen, 1994-95; postdoctoral fellow in anesthesiology U. Jena, 1995—. Contbr. articles to profl. jours. Recipient scholarship DAAD, 1997; grantee German Rsch. Soc., 1999, 2000. Office: Dept Anesthes & Crit Care, Bachstrasse 18, D-07740 Jena Germany

SAKKA, SUMIO, chemistry educator; b. Osaka, Japan, Dec. 11, 1930; s. Kyoichi and Shinayo (Akitomo) S.; m. Mioko Unno, Apr. 28, 1958; children: Ikuko Mizutani, Tetsuo, Yasuo. B Engring., Kyoto (Japan) U., 1953, D Engring., 1963. Rsch. assoc. Kyoto U., 1953-63, assoc. prof., 1963-72, prof., 1983-94, dir. Inst. for Chem. Rsch., 1990-92; prof. Mie U., Tsu, Japan, 1972-83; prof. chemistry Fukui (Japan) U. Tech., 1994—. Author: New Glasses, 1987, Science of Sol-Gel Methods, 1988, Fundamentals and Applications of Glass Science, 1997; editor-in-chief Jour. Sol-Gel Sci. and Tech., 1992—. Recipient Purple Ribbon award Japanese Govt. Fellow Am. Ceramic Soc. (G. W. Morley award 1984); mem. Japan Ceramic Soc. (sci. award 1978), Chem. Soc. Japan (award 1978). Avocations: tennis, go, classical and popular music. Home: Kuzuha-Asahi 2-7-30, Hirakata Osaka 573, Japan Office: Fukui U Tech, Gakuen 3-6-1, Fukui 910-8505, Japan

SAKKOPOULOS, SOTIRIOS ANGELOS, physics educator; b. Patras, Greece, Sept. 24, 1945; s. Angelos Sotirios and Anna Stylianos Sakkopoulou; m. Rosalind Brailsford, Sept. 16, 1978 (wid.); 1 child, Angelos. BS in Physics, U. Athens, 1968; PhD, U. Patras, 1974. Rsch. and teaching asst. U. Patras, 1971-75, chief asst., 1975-76, 78-82, lectr. dept. physics, 1982-90, asst. prof., 1990—; rsch. fellow U. Leeds, England, 1976-78. Author: Thermodynamics and Statistical Physics Lessons, 1983, Lessons on Waves, 1983, Analysis of Experimental Data: Theory of Errors, 1992; co-author: Error Theory, 1985; contbr. articles to profl. jours. 2d lt. Greek Army, 1968-70. Mem. Am. Phys. Soc., Am. Assn. Physics Tchrs., Inst. Physics. Greek Orthodox. Avocations: history, philosophy of science. Home: Korinthou St 314-316, 26222 Patras Greece Office: U Patras, 25000 Patras Greece

SAKO, TEIYU, electronics executive, researcher; b. Kumamoto City, Japan, July 26, 1969; s. Takehisa and Saeko Sako; m. Hitomi Obayashi, June 27, 1998. BE, U. Tokyo, 1993, MS, 1995, PhD, 2000. Rschr. Sharp Corp., Kashiwan, 1995—. Recipient Outstanding Poster paper award Internat. Display Workshops, 1997. Mem. Internat. Liquid Crystal Soc., Japanese Liquid Crystal Soc., Japan Soc. Applied Physics. Avocation: travel. Office: Sharp Corp, 273-1 Kashiwa, Kashiwa-shi, Chiba 277-0005, Japan

SAKONG, IL, minister of finance; b. Kunwi, Kyung-buk, Korea, Jan. 10, 1940; s. Don and Jum Bun (Park) S.; m. Young Hee Lee, May 10, 1974; children: Jin, In. BA in Commerce, Seoul Nat. U., Republic of Korea, 1964; MBA, UCLA, 1966, PhD, 1969. Asst. prof. NYU, 1969-73; dir. research Korea Devel. Inst., Seoul, 1973-82; sr. economist Presdl. Council Econ. and Sci. Affairs, Seoul, 1980; sr. counsellor to Dep. Prime Minister Republic of Korea, Seoul, 1982; v.p. Korea Devel. Inst., Seoul, 1982-83; pres. Korea Inst. Econ. and Tech., Seoul, 1983; sr. sec. to pres. for econ. affairs Office of the Pres., Seoul, 1983-87; minister Ministry of Finance, Seoul, 1987-88; chmn., CEO Inst. Global Econ., Seoul, South Korea; spl. cons. to IMi, 1989—. Author: Macroeconomic Aspect of Public Enterprise, 1979, Government and Business, 1980, Korea in the World Economy, 1993; co-editor: (with C. Fred Bergsten) The Political Economy of Korea-United States Cooperation, 1995, Korea-United States Cooperation in the New World Order, 1996, The Korea-United States Economic Relationship, 1997; contbr. articles to profl. jours. Named to Order of Civil "Moran medal" Govt. of Korea, 1983, Order of Crown Kingdom of Belgium, 1986, Order of Brilliant Star with Grand Cordon Republic of China, 1987. Home: 85-702 Hyndai, Apt Abgujung Dong, 135 Seoul Republic of Korea Office: Inst Globl Econs 15P Samsung-dong, 2505 Korea World Trade Ctr, Kangnam-Ku Seoul 135-72P, Republic of Korea

SAKOU, TOSHITSUGU, dean, educator; b. Tokyo, July 30, 1934; s. Katsumi and Kiku (Ishida) S.; m. Yoko Hattori, Mar. 8, 1975; children: Akahito, Kyoko, Hiroko, Fumiko. BS, U. Tokyo, 1957, MS, 1959; PhD, Tex. A&M U., 1963. Tech. offcl. Ministry of Transp., Japan, 1959-63; asst. prof. U. Hawaii, 1963-65; affiliate prof. Tokai U., Shimizu, Japan, 1966-73, prof., 1974—, dean, 1994—. Editor: Kaiyo Gairon, 1996. Trustee Japan Marine Sci. and Tech. Ctr., 1987—, Ship and Ocean Found., 1999—, Underwater Park sassn., 1976—, DOWA, 1997—. Mem. MTS (chmn. 1997—, internat. award 1999). Home: 472 Horinishi, Hatano Kanagawa-ken Japan Office: Tokai U, 3-20-1 Orido, Shimizu Shinzuoka 424, Japan

SAKRA, TOMAS, chemistry educator and researcher; b. Pardubice, Czech Republic, Nov. 4, 1939; s. Vaclav and Milada (Pflegrova) S.; m. Jana Harvankova, Nov. 22, 1963; children: Lukas, Barbora. MSc, Tech. U., Pardubice, 1962, PhD, 1973. Asst. prof. Tech. U., Pardubice, 1963-82, assoc. prof. chemistry, 1982—, head dept. chemistry, 1986—; ct. expert in environ. protection. Co-author: Calculations in Chemical Engineering III, 1973, Chemical Engineering, parts II and III, 1983-94, Ecological Aspects of Chemical Technologies, 1987, Mehods and Apparatusses for Environment Protection, 1984, 94, others. Office: Univ of Pardubice, Nam Cs legii 565, 532 10 Pardubice Czech Republic

SAKSENA, KRISHAN PRASAD, political science educator; b. Agra, India, Oct. 25, 1929; s. Ganga Prasad and Shyam Devi; m. Urmila Johri, Feb. 27, 1962; children: Una, Jyotika, Shashank. BA, Agra Coll., 1949, LLB, 1951, MA, 1954; PhD, NYU, 1971. Lectr. in polit. sci. Agra U., 1954-56; prof. polit. sci. D.A.V. Coll., Bulandshahr, India, 1956-62; adviser Indian Mission to UN, N.Y.C., 1964-67, 68-71; cons. UN Secretariat, N.Y.C., 1967-68; prof. J.N.U., New Delhi, 1972-93; dir. Ctr. for Human Rights Edn. and Rsch. Inst. for World Congress on Human Rights, New Delhi, 1993—; expert panelist UN, Colombo, Sri Lanka, 1982, Jakarta, Indonesia, 1983; hon. cons. UNESCO, Paris, 1984-87; hon. dir. Ctr. Human Rights Tchg. and Rsch., New Delhi, 1982-93; cons., panelist, spkr. in field. Author: Constitutional Law of England, 1955, United Nations and Power Politics, 1956, United Nations and Collective Security, 1974, Cooperation in Development, 1986, Reforming the United Nations, 1993, Teaching Human Rights: A Manual for Adult Education, 1996; editor: The Teaching of Human Rights, 1985, Human Rights: Perspective and Challenges, 1994; contbr. articles to profl. publs., chpts. to books. Active in world-wide movement for civil rights; mem. confs. and workshops, N.Am., Europe, Africa and Asia; convenor World Congress on Human Rights, sec.=gen., 1990—. Fulbright grantee, 1962-64; Smith-Mundt scholar, 1962-64. Mem. Indian Soc. Internat. Law.

Avocations: gardening, sketching, painting, reading, philosophy. Home: Mayur Vihar Phase-I, 16 Samachar Noida Rd, New Delhi 110 091, India Office: Jawaharlal Nehru U, New Mehrauli Rd, New Delhi 110 067, India

SAKU, MOTONORI, surgeon, educator; b. Fukuoka, Fukuoka, Japan, Jan. 7, 1939; s. Genrin and Hisae (Saku) S.; m. Nozomi Harada, Dec. 2, 1969; children: Motoaki, Madoka. MD, Kyushu U., Fukuoka, 1963. Staff Kyushu U., 1964-74, assoc. prof., 1976-78; rsch. fellow Lund (Sweden) U., 1974-75; chief surgeon Nat. Fukuoka Ctrl. Hosp., 1979-94; chief surgeon Nat. Kyushu Med. Ctr., Fukuoka, 1995-97, dir. divsn. medicine, 1998—; clin. prof. surgery Kyushu U. Sch. Medicine, 1999—; cons. Soc. for Clin. Surgery, Fukuoka, 1995—, Soc. for Gastroent. Surgery, Fukuoka, 1995—, Kyushu Surg. Soc., Fukuoka, 1979—, Kyushu Cancer Soc., Fukuoka, 1980—. Author: (textbook) Surgery, 1994; contbr. articles to profl. jours. Judge Health Ins. Com., 1979—. Fellow Japan Surg. Soc., Japan Cancer Therapy Soc.; mem. World Hepato-Pancreato-Biliary Surgery (founding), N.Y. Acad. Sci. Avocation: golf. Office: Nat Kyushu Med Ctr, 1 8 1 Jigyohama Chuo Ku, 810-8563 Fukuoka Japan

SAKUDA, AKIRA TONY, travel agent; b. Naha, Japan, Jan. 25, 1962; s. Minoru Ray and Tomie S.; 1 child, Kenji. BBA, Chaminade U. Honolulu, 1985. Mktg. mgr. One Day Printing, Honolulu, 1986-88; banquet staff Okinawa Regent Hotel, Naha, Japan, 1989-90; mgr. Taco Time Japan, Naha, 1990-91, Okinawa Tourist Svc., 1991—. Mem. Am. C. of C. in Okinawa. Roman Catholic. Avocations: reading, swimming, travel.

SAKUMA, KAZUHIRO, aerospace engineer; b. Wakayama-shi, Japan, June 18, 1947; s. Takeshi and Isako (Kawachidani) S.; m. Noriko Ando, May 13, 1978; children: Hiroaki, Kyoko. B of Engring., Nihon U., Tokyo, 1970. Sect. chief Japan Aviation Elecs. Industry Ltd., Tokyo, 1988-91, dir., 1992—. Inventor/patentee in field. Recipient of award for devel. accelerometer Japan Def. Material Found., Tokyo, 1986. Mem. Japan Soc. Next Generation Sensor Tech. Avocations: yacht sailing, skiing, tennis, driving, gardening. Office: Japan Aviation Elecs Industry Ltd, 1-1 Musashino 3-chome, Akishima-shi Tokyo 196-8555, Japan

SAKURADA, YUTAKA, chemist; b. Kyoto, Japan, Jan. 1, 1933; s. Ichiro and Chiyoko (Okumura) S.; m. Keiko Sugimoto, May 10, 1960; children: Kazuhiro, Akihiro. BS, Kyoto U., 1956, MS, 1958, PhD, 1966. Rsch. fellow Cen. Rsch. Lab. Kuraray Co. Ltd., Kurashiki, Japan, 1958-62, 64-66; internat. fellow Stanford Rsch. Inst., Menlo Pk., Calif., 1962-64; tech. rep. N.Y. Office Kuraray Co. Ltd., N.Y.C., 1968-71; mgr. Med. Bus. Devel. Div. Kuraray, Osaka, Japan, 1974-77; gen. mgr. Med. Products Div. Kuraray, Osaka, 1977-88, gen. mgr. Corp. Rand D Div., 1988-89; mng. dir. Kuraray Plastics Co. Ltd., Osaka, 1989-91; bd. dirs. Haemonetics Corp., USA; vice chmn. Japanese Soc. for Biomaterials, Tokyo, 1987-96; pres. Haemonetics, Japan, 1991—. Recipient Technology award The Soc. Polymers, 1984, Japanese Chem. Soc., 1985. Achievements include development of ethylene vinyl alcohol copolymer hollow fiber for hemo-dialyzer; development of dental adhesives. Home: YGT2-420, 4-20-2 Ebisu Shibuya-ku, Tokyo 150-0013, Japan Office: Kyodo Bldg 3F, 16-banchi Ichibancho, Chiyoda-ku Chiyoda-ku Tokyo 102-0082, Japan

SAKURAI, TAKAHIDE, insurance company executive; b. Oct. 30, 1932; m. Motoku Sakurai. Student, Tokyo U., 1955. Chmn. Daiichi Mut. Life Ins. Co., Tokyo. Avocation: reading. Office: Daiichi Mut Life Ins Co, 1-13-1 Yuraku-Cho, Chiyoda-ku Tokyo 100-8411, Japan*

SAKUTA, MASAAKI, engineering educator, consultant; b. Kagoshima, Japan, Feb. 16, 1929; s. Masanori and Haruko (Oozato) S.; m. Akiko Shimomura, Nov. 4, 1956; children: Shigeru, Mitsuru. B of Engring., Tokyo Inst. Tech., 1952; postgrad, MIT, 1959-60; DEng, Tokyo Inst. Tech., 1966. Cert. oceanic architect, architect-engr., Japan. Rschr. Taisei Constrn. Co. Ltd., Tokyo, 1956-58, chief rschr., 1960-69; mng. dir. Fuyo Ocean Devel. and Engring. Co. Ltd., Tokyo, 1969-77; advisor Taisei Corp. Co. Ltd., Tokyo, 1978-79; prof. Nihon U., Tokyo, 1977-99, prof. emeritus, 1999—; councilor Archtl. Inst. Japan, Tokyo, 1975-76, dir., 1989-91; vice dean Coll. Sci. and Tech., Nihon U., 1978-94; vice chmn., life mem. Pacific Congress on Marine Sci. and Tech., Japan, 1990—. Author: Transportation in Ocean Space, 1975, Construction Method of Marine Structures, 1976, Introduction of Ocean Development, 1977; patentee in field of Marine structure system with soft-touched basement. Mem. Visualization Soc. Japan, Inc. (pres. 1991-92, Merit award 1992), Rotary (sr., charter). Mem. Liberal Dem. Party. Buddhist. Avocations: hiking, tennis, table tennis, painting, reading. Home: 39-723 2-2 chome Jingumae, Shibuya-ku Tokyo 150-0001, Japan Office: 9-1004 1 chome 43, Kameido, koutou-ku, Tokyo 136-0071, Japan

SAKUTA, SHIGERU, research scientist; b. Tokyo, July 13, 1961; m. Masaaki and Akiko S.; m. Yukako Sakuta; children; Akira, Reiko. B in Engring., U. Tokyo, 1985, M in Engring., 1987. Rschr. Toshiba, Yokohama, Japan, 1987-93, rsch. scientist, 1997—; vis. scientist MIT, Boston, 1993-94. Patentee in field. Avocations: judo, baseball, sumo. Office: Toshiba Mfg Engring Ctr, 33 Shin-Isogo Isogo-ku, Kanagawa Yokohama 235, Japan

SALA, EVIS, physician; b. Tirana, Albania, July 5, 1968; d. Bashkim and Valdet (Myftari) S.; m. Gezim Selenica, July 2, 1993; 1 child, Pier Ageg. MD, U. Tirana, 1991; MPhil, U. Cambridge, Eng., 1997, PhD, 1997. House officer Oncol. Inst., Tirana, 1991-92; rsch. fellow WHO, Italy, France and Denmark, 1992, Cambridge, Eng., 1996-97; trainee in gen. surgery U. Hosp. Ctr., Tirana, 1993-96; head Cancer Registry, Tirana, 1993-96; lectr. in epidemiology U. Tirana, 1995-96; rsch. assoc. U. Cambridge, 1997-2000; specialist registrar in radiology Addeubrooke's Hosp., Cambridge, England, 2000—; adviser Women's Ctr., Tirana, 1994-96, project coord., 1992-96. Contbr. articles to profl. jours. Project leader World Fedn. for Mental Health, Albania, 1995-96.. Hon. Cambridge Overseas scholar, Commonwealth Trust scholar, 1997-98; WHO fellow in cancer epidemiology, 1992, WHO fellow in cancer rsch., 1996. Mem. European Group for Breast Cancer Screening, European Network for Cancer Registries, Cambridge U. Pub. Health and Epidemiology Soc., Albanian Oncology Assn., World Fedn. Mental Health, Reflection. Avocations: travel, music, dancing, volleyball, squash. Office: Addeubrookes Hosp, Hills Rd Dept Radiology, Cambridge CB2 2Q2, England

SALA, FLORIN, agronomist, educator; b. Beius, Bihor, Romania, Nov. 11, 1962; s. Aurel and Floare (Sferlea) S.; m. Diana Claudia Cornea, Oct. 22, 1988; 1 child, Darius Gabriel. Diploma in engring., Agrl. Faculty, Timisoara, Romania, 1988; D in Agrl. Scis., U. Agrl. Scis. & Vet. Medicine, Timisoara, 1990. Cert. engr. Engr. Agrl. State Enteprise, Becicherecu, Romania, 1988-90; tutor U. Agrl. Scis. & Vet. Medicine, Timisoara, 1990-91, asst., 1991-95, lectr., 1995—; cons. Agrl. Consulting Ctr., Timisoara, 1999—. Co-author: Fertilizing and Protection, 1997, Garden Vademecum, 1997, Pesticides, 1998. With Romanian Army, 1982-83. Mem. Romanian Soc. Solar Energy, Nat. Soc. Soil Scis., Romanian Assn. Promoting Magnetic Liquids. Romanian Orthodox. Avocations: beekeeping, literature, sport, tourism, music. Office: U Agrl Scis & Vet Medicine, Calea Aradului, NR 119, Timisoara 1900, Romania

SALA, MARTIN ANDREW, biophysicist, inventor; b. Buffalo, N.Y., Sept. 6, 1957; s. Paul and Adrienne (Williams) Zahm; m. Erie Anne Wagner-Sala, Nov. 23, 1986; 1 child, Rebeckah. BA in Biophysics, SUNY, Buffalo, 1981. Dir. clin. engring. Buffalo Columbus Hosp., 1982-85; lab. inst. designer Roswell Park Cancer Inst., Buffalo, 1985-89; v.p. for R&D MBS Foundry, Brook's Grove, N.Y., 1989-96; pressetter applications engr. Nationwide Precision Prods., Henrietta, N.Y., 1996-97; sr. measurements engr. sci. and tech. disvn. Corning (N.Y.), 1997—; cons. Lotus Link Found., Buffalo, 1990—, West N.Y. Clin. Engring. Assn., Buffalo, 1989—. Author: Theory & Design of Core Memory, 1979, Purely Natural Causes, 1999; editor various periodicals, 1970—; inventor, developer Retrospex Sys. for large vehicles. With USN, 1976-81. Grantee NIH, 1990. Mem. Am. Inst. Physics, Instrument Soc. Am., AAAS, Internat. Soc. Magnetic Resonance in Medicine, Soc. for Advancement Med. Instrument Design, SPIE. Mem. Anglican Ch. Achievements include patents pending for new surgical measuring tool, facsimile design, canine surgical tool; invention of various novel scientific instruments, Retrospex Rear Vision System, patented vehicular safety devices, microscopic MRI analysis. Office: Corning Sp Td 01 Corning NY 14831-0001

SALAGEAN, MARIA N., physicist; b. Cigmau, Romania, Apr. 5, 1940; d. Nicolae G. and Maria V. (Savut) Stanciu; m. Octavian A. Salagean, July 15, 1966; 1 child, Ana Maria. Diploma, U. Bucharest, 1962. Physicist, scientific rschr. Inst. Atomic Physics, Bucharest, Romania, 1962-90; sr. scientific rschr. Inst. Physics & Nuclear Engring., Bucharest, 1990—. Contbr. numerous papers to profl. publs. Mem. Romanian Soc. Physics, N.Y. Acad. Sci. Avocations: classical music, painting. Home: Dezrobirii 12 Bl 23 ap 8, 77582 Bucharest Sector 6, Romania

SALAH, ABDULLAH AMIN, senator; b. Tulkarm, Jordan, Dec. 31, 1922; s. Amin Musleh S. and Salma (Abdulrahman) Haj Ibrahim; m. Fadwa Kamel Wafa Dajani, June 18, 1960; 1 child, Hanya. BA in Polit. Sci. with hons., Am. U., 1944; student law, Jerusalem, 1944-48. Translator Govt. of Palestine, Jerusalem, 1944-48; asst. chief census officer Unrwa, E. Jerusalem, Jordan, 1950-52; welfare officer Unrwa, Jericho, Jordan, 1952-53, Bethlehem, Jordan, 1953-54; chief edn. officer Unrwa, E. Jerusalem, Jordan, 1954-56, Amman, Jordan, 1965-62; amb. to Kuwait Kuwait, 1962-63; amb. to India New Delhi, 1963-64; amb. to France Paris, 1964-66; min. fgn. affairs Govt. of Jordan, Amman, Jordan, 1966-67, 70-72; amb. to U.S., Can., Mex., Switzerland, Austria, 1973-80; amb. from Jordan UN, N.Y.C., 1983-92; mem. senate House of Parliament, Amman, Jordan, 1971-73, 92—. Avocations: reading, music, hiking, cycling, water skiing. Office: House of Parliament, PO Box 72, Amman Jordan

SALAH, SAGID, retired nuclear engineer; b. Seoul, Sept. 2, 1932; came to U.S., 1954; s. Galim and Faiza (Sultan) Salahutdin; m. Ravile Almakay, Apr. 2, 1966; children: Shamil, Kamil, Safiye. BChemE, U. Fla., 1958, MS in Nuclear Engring., 1960, PhD in Nuclear Engring., 1964. Nuclear engr. AEC, Bethesda, Md., 1964-66; sr. design engr. Westinghouse Astronuclear Lab., Large, Pa., 1966-70; sr. sys. engr. Westinghouse Nuclear Energy Sys., Pitts., 1970-73; mem. sys. safety engring. staff U.S. Nuclear Regulatory Commn., Bethesda, 1973-93; ret., 1993; nuclear engring. cons. Oak Ridge (Tenn.) Inst. Nuclear Studies, 1963, 64; instr. U. Md., College Park, 1973-76. Contbr. articles to Nuclear Sci. and Engring. Youth coach Nat. Capital Soccer League, Vienna, Va., 1975-85. Mem. Am. Nuclear Soc. (emeritus, reviewer trans. papers 1972), Sigma Tau. Moslem. Achievements include measurements of neutron energy spectra in heterogeneous media using differential and integral methods, neutron energy spectra measurements and analysis in intermediate spectra reactors, three-dimensional transient analysis of boron dilution in PWR reactors. Avocations: astronomy, neurology, financial analysis, tennis, swimming. Home: 9302 Kilport Ct Vienna VA 22182-3426

SALAH-EL, TIYO ATTALLAH, political society executive, newsletter editor; b. West Chester, Pa., Sept. 13, 1932; s. Riley Willard and Ella Mae Jones; m. Leeda Fluellen, Aug. 8, 1954 (dec. Mar. 1975); children: Dahood, Clarance, Jaleeah, Ruby. BA, Beacon Coll., 1981, MA, 1983. Profl. musician Phila. and Washington, 1955-69; adminstr. Blackman's Devel. Ctr., Washington, 1970-72; mgr. Consolid Recovery Svc., Wilmington, Del., 1973-75; program advisor Beacon Coll., Washington, 1982-85; coord. Prison Edn. Project, Washington, 1985-93, Nat. Lawyers Guild, Dallas, Pa., 1986-93; pres. Coalition for Abolition of Prisons, Inc., Quakerstown, Pa., 1994—. Author: (musical compositions) Love of Life, 1985, Touch Me, 1985, Blues for T, 1989, Gone, 1989, (booklet) Journal of Prisoners on Prisons, 1992, (autobiography) Revolutionary Vagabond, 1998; staff writer Gay Cmty. News, Boston, 1982. Bd. dirs. Cmty. Clean Up, Media, Pa., 1964-69; mem. adv. bd. Concerned Citizens, Washington, 1970-72; co-dir. Recidivism Reducers, Dallas, Pa., 1986-89; coord. Penal Abolitionists, Dallas, 1990-93; mem. Pub. Citizen, Washington, 1990, Wider Quaker Fellowship, Phila., 1991. Sgt. U.S. Army, 1950-53, Korea. Grantee Davis-Putter Found., Chgo., 1990-91, Monty Neill/Howard Zinn Fund, Boston, 1994-99, Bread and Roses Found., Phila., 1998, North Br. Friends Meeting, Wilkes-Barre, Pa., 1999. Mem. Friends of Jazz, Internat. Conf. Penal Abolition, Alliance for Democracy (membership coord.), Pioneers (coord.), Old-Timers Health Club (instr.), John Coltrane Soc. Mem. Soc. of Friends. Avocations: classical and jazz music, exercise, reading, writing, chess. Office: Coalition for Abolition of Prisons Inc PO Box 201 Quakertown PA 18951-0201

SALAHUDDIN, AHMAD, civil engineer, educator; b. Anbala, India, Sept. 19, 1941; arrived in Zimbabwe, 1987; s. Ahmad Chaudhary Shamsuddin and Sultanta Mahmuda. BSCE, Panjab U., Lahore, Pakistan, 1961; MSc in Civil Engring., Columbia U., 1967; PhD in Structural Engring., Concordia U., Montreal, Can., 1971. Design engr. cons. industry Pakistan, 1961-65; rsch. assoc., asst. prof. Concordia U., Montreal, 1971-73, 77-81; specialist cons. Can., 1973-76, 81-83; assoc. prof. U. Bahrain, 1983-85; dir. Can. Inst. Tech. Edn., 1985-87; prof. engring. U. Zimbabwe, Harare, 1987—; editor specifications draft Standards Assn. Zimbabwe, 1993—; coord. Indsl. cons. Civil Engring. U. Zimbabwe, 1994—; mem. sci. com. Internat. Symposium Design of Structures, Germany, 1996; mem. African Structural Engring. Edn. Forum, Johannesburg, South Africa, 1996. Contbr. numerous articles to profl. jours. Fulbright-Hays fellow, Washington, 1965-67. Mem. ASCE, Internat. Assn. Shell and Spatial Sturctures, Internat. Assn. Bridge and Structural Engring. Avocations: scientific reading and writing, listening to music, computer technology. Home: 6 Montagu Ct, 142 Josiah Chinamano Ave, Harare Zimbabwe Office: Civil Engring Dept, U Zimbabwe PO Box MP167, Harare Zimbabwe

SALAITA, SHAWQI JUBRIEL, mechanical engineer; b. Madaba, Jordan, July 28, 1941; s. Jubriel Audt Allah and Zoyeeh Nicolas Salaita; m. Amal Saliba Salaita, Sept. 19, 1971; children: Shaireen, Tania, Mirna. BSME (Power), Cairo U., 1965; MSME, U. London, 1977. Chartered mech. engr., England. Mech. site engr. C.A.T. Co., Kuwait, 1965-66; head workshops divsn. Natural Resources Authority, Amman, Jordan, 1966-80; head mech. divsn. Nat. Resources Authority, Amman, Jordan, 1980-85, head of transp. divsn., 1987-90, dir. mech. and transport dept., 1990-93, advisor, dir., 1993-96, cons. in mech. engring., 1996-97; head transp. divsn. Ministry of Energy, Jordan, 1985-87; tech. dir. Al-Bassami Internat. Transp. Co., Riyadh, 1998—. Contbr. articles and studies to profl. mech. engring. jours. Mem. Instn. Mech. Engrs. (Eng.), Assn. Engrs. (Jordan), Soc. Automotive Engrs. (U.S.). Avocations: music, reading, nature sight seeing, gardening. Home: PO Box 142052 Al-Rawnak, Amman 11844, Jordan

SALAJCZYK, JANINA, Russian literature educator, translator; b. Łódź, Poland, Feb. 11, 1933; d. Marian and Jozefa Maria (Ambrozinski) Kazimierczyk; m. Henryk Wladislav Salajczyk, May 11, 1957; 1 child, Anna-Maria. MA, A. Herzen's Pedagog. Inst., Leningrad, USSR, 1955; PhD, High Pedagog. Sch., Opole, Poland, 1964. Jr. lectr. High Pedagog. Sch., 1955-68, asst. prof., 1968-71; asst. prof. U. Gdańsk, 1971-82, prof., 1982—. Author: The Theater of Leonid Leonov, 1967, The Works of Isaac Babel, 1973, Village in Soviet Russian Prose Fiction 1917-1932, 1979, The Russian Naval Prose Fiction 1917-1977, 1982, The Literary Works of Lev Luntz, 1990, The Decade of Transformations: Russian Prose Fiction of the Years 1985-1995, 1998. Mem. Polish Acad. Sci. (Slavic com.), Gdańsk Sci. Soc. Avocations: walking, sightseeing, theater. Office: U Gdańsk, Wita Strosza 55, Gdańsk Poland

SALAKHITDINOV, MAKHMUD, mathematics educator; b. Namangan, Uzbekistan, Nov. 23, 1933; s. Salakhitdin and Zukhra Shamsutdin; m. Mukharram Rasulova, Aug. 3, 1955; children: Bakhrom, Aghzam, Gulbakhor. Student, Ctrl. Asian State U., Toshkent, Uzbekistan, 1950-55, grad. student, 1955-58. Assoc. instr. Tashkent State U., 1958-59; jr. sci. fellow Inst. Math., Uzbekistan Acad. of Scis., Tashkent, 1959-60, sr. sci. fellow, 1960-64, dept. chief, 1964-66, dep. dir., 1966-67, dir., 1967-85, chief dept. differencial equations, 1974—, chmn. div. phys. and math. scis., 1994—; v.p. Uzbekistan Acad. Scis., Tashkent, 1984-85, minister higher edn., 1985-88, pres., 1988-94. Contbr. over 250 articles on differential equations to sci. jours. People's dep. Republic of Uzbekistan, Toshkent, 1986-95; active People's Dem. Party of Uzbekistan, Toshkent, 1990—. Home: G Lopatina Str Apt 70 Fl 64, Tashkent 700031, Uzbekistan Office: Inst Math, 29 F Hodijaev St, Tashkent 700143, Uzbekistan

SALAMA, ALI GAMAL EL DIN, audit firm executive, consultant; b. Port Said, Egypt, Jan. 12, 1945; s. Ahmed Abdel Aziz Salama and Fahima Khalil Kanayati; m. Mariam Hussein Ghaleb Osman, Nov. 11, 1976; children: Mahinoor, Lina, Hussein. B in Mil. Sci., Egyptian Mil. Acad., 1963, M in Mil. Sci., 1978; M in Acctg., MBA, U. Wash., 1988. CPA; cert. mgmt. acct. Officer Egyptian Army, 1963-84; cons., mgr. KPMG, Cairo, 1990-93, ptnr., 1993—; instr. Seattle U., 1988-89, City Coll., Seattle, 1988-90; mem. faculty KPMG Brussels, 1995—. EditorL Managerial Accounting, 1988, Accounting Principles, 1989; co-author: Application of International Eguyptian Accounting Standards, 1997. Col. Egyptian Army, 1963-84. Mem. AICPAs, Internat. Mgmt. Assn., Eguyptian Assn. Accts. and Auditors, Inst. Mgmt. Accts. Moslem. Avocations: field hockey, diving, tennis, bridge. Home: 14 Damascus St Maadi, 11431 Cairo Egypt Office: KPMG Hazem Hassan, 72 Mohi El Din Abu El Ezz S, 12311 Mohandeseen Egypt

SALAMA, FARID, astrophysicist, spectroscopist, research scientist; b. Paris, Jan. 28, 1957; s. Aly and Marie Rose (Garroux) S.; m. Josie Bove, July 5, 1986; 1 child, Maissa. BS in Chem. Physics, U. Paris, Orsay, France, 1981; MS in Chem. Physics, U. Pierre & Marie Curie, 1983; PhD in Physical Chemistry, U. Pierre & Marie Curie, France, 1986. Postdoctoral rsch. fellow Lawrence Berkeley Lab., Berkeley, Calif., 1987-88; rsch. assoc. Nat. Rsch. Coun./NASA, Moffett Field, Calif., 1988-90; from vis. rsch. astronomer to rsch. physicist U. Calif./NASA, Berkeley, 1990-94; prin. investigator SETI Rsch. Inst./NASA, Moffett Field, Calif., 1994-99; astrophysicist NASA, Moffett Field, 1999—; fellow Gen. Delegation Sci. Tech. Rsch., France, 1983-85; fellow NRC, 1988-90; panelist, reviewer NASA Astrophysics Rsch. & Analysis Program, 1994; speaker symposium German-Am. Frontiers Sci., 1995; reviewer Petrol. Rsch. Fund, 1996; NAS fellow German-Am. Acad. Coun., 1996. Contbr. articles to profl. jours., chpts. to books. Fellow Found. France, 1986. Mem. Internat. Soc. for Origin of Life, Astron. Soc. Pacific, Am. Phys. Soc., Am. Astron. Soc. Achievements include pioneering research in laboratory astrophysics in which the techniques of low temperature spectroscopy are applied to the study of interstellar and planetary material analogs. Avocations: reading, hiking, music, movies. Office: NASA-Ames Rsch Ctr Mail Stop 245-6 Moffett Field CA 94035

SALAMA, MOHAMED SAID, petroleum engineer; b. El Saf, Egypt, Aug. 30, 1945; s. Mohamed Said and Khadija Mohamed (El Deweeb) S.; m. Thanaa Abd Al Hakam El Deweeb. BSc in Petroleum Engring., Cairo U., 1969. Drilling engr. GPC, Egypt, 1969-78; drilling supt. EDC, Egypt, 1978-82, ops. mgr., 1983—; dir. EDC, Cairo, 1992-95. Avocations: reading, travelling, walking. Office: Egyptian Drilling Co, KM 17.5 Cairo Suez Road, Nasr City 11371, Egypt

SALAMA-BAROUM, MAGDI, management consultant; b. Cairo, Jan. 15, 1948; came to U.S., 1977; m. Maha Haddad, Aug. 24, 1997. BSc in Scis., U. Cairo, 1970; MBA, Am. U., Cairo, 1974; MSc in Bus. Mgmt., Grad. U., Arlington, Va., 1980. CEO, pres. World Trading & Investment, Vienna, Va., Internat. Group, Springfield, Va. Bd. dirs. Nat. Assn. Arab Ams., Washington, 1983-85. Democrat. Achievements include patent pending. Office: Internat Group 6388 Stagg Ct Springfield VA 22150-1183

SALAMACK, LAURICE SULLIVAN, city planner; b. Oakland, Calif., Jan. 28, 1959; d. William Joseph and Helen Ryan Sullivan; m. Joseph George Salamack, III, June 29, 1985; children: Kelly Kathleen, Allison Cecelia. BA with distinction, U. Calif., Berkeley, 1981; MS, Rensselaer Poly. Inst., 1989. Acquisition specialist Properities of Am., Williamstown, Mass., 1986-88; intern dept. econ. devel. City of Troy, N.Y., 1989; cons. Rensselaer Tech. Pk., North Greenbush, N.Y., 1989; city planner City of Piedmont, Calif., 1990—. Mem. Am. Planning Assn., Omicron Delta Epsilon. Avocation: travel. Home: 1115 Clarendon Cres Oakland CA 94610-1807 Office: City of Piedmont 120 Vista Ave Piedmont CA 94611-4031

SALAMAH, MOHAMMAD ABDUL LATIF, transportation company executive; b. Cairo, July 30, 1949; s. Abdul Latif Sulaiman and Misreya Hemaly; m. Abdul Raoof Karimah, Sept. 7, 1982; children: Karim, Loujain. BSc in Mech. Engring., Port Said U., 1973. Chief engr. East Delta Buses Co., Cairo, 1973-79; workshop mgr. Local Adminstr., Waset, Iraq, 1979-83; mgr. Salamco Est., Cairo, 1983-86; mgr. maint. Dallah Transport, Jeddah, Saudi Arabia, 1986—. Mem. Sary El Cobbah Social Svc. Soc., Ministry of Social Affairs, 1971; football referee Cairo, 1974-89; active various charitable orgns. Mem. Syndicate of Engrs., Nat. Club. Avocation: sports. Home: 36 Trabls St, Nissr City Cairo Egypt Office: Dallah Transport, PO Box 11225, Palasteen St, Jeddah 21453, Saudi Arabia

SALAMÉ, RIAD, Lebanon government official, bank executive; b. Beirut, Lebanon, July 17, 1950; s. Toufic and Renée S. Attended, Coll. Notre Dame, Jamhour; BA in Economics, Am. U. Beirut. With Merrill Lynch, Beirut, 1973-76, Paris, 1976-78, Beirut, 1978-85; sr. v.p. and fin. counsellor Merrill Lynch, Paris, 1985-93; gov. Banque du Liban, 1993—. Office: Banque du Liban, Hamra Masraf Loubnan St, PO Box 11-5544 Beirut Lebanon*

SALAMEH, RIAD JOSEPH, banker; b. Baalbeck, Bekaa, Lebanon, Sept. 5, 1935; s. Joseph Fadlallah Salameh and Eugenie Antoine Khoury; m. Hoda Rafik Nassif, Apr. 26, 1969; children: Jihad, Amani, Rim. BA, Am. U., Beirut, 1956, MA, 1958. Resident v.p. Citibank, Athens, Greece, 1969-79; mng. dir. Met. Bank, Beirut, 1979-81; asst. gen. mgr. Byblos Bank, Beirut, 1981-86; vice chmn., gen. mgr. Adcom Bank, Beirut, 1987-88; chmn., gen. mgr. Banque du Credit Populaire, Beirut, 1989-91; vice chmn., gen. mgr. Al-Moughtareb Bank, Beirut, 1992-98; bd. mem. Intra Investment Co. SAL, Beirut, 1989-93. Bd. dirs. Caritas Liban, Beirut, 1990-92; bd. mem., adv., Bank of Kuwait and the Arab World SAL, Beirut, 1990-92, exec. com. mem. Supreme Greek Cath. Coun., Beirut, 1986—. Recipient St. Sylvester medal Pope John Paul II, 1988. Avocations: reading, editing, traveling, photography. Home: Valverde St, New Naccache Lebanon Office: PO Box 70-950, Antelias Lebanon

SALAMON, MIKLOS DEZSO GYORGY, mining engineer, educator; b. Balkany, Hungary, May 20, 1933; came to U.S., 1986; naturalized, 1993; s. Miklos and Sarolta (Obetko) S.; m. Agota Maria Meszaros, July 11, 1953; children: Miklos, Gabor. Diploma in Engring., Polytech U., Sopron, Hungary, 1956; PhD, U. Durham, Newcastle, England, 1962; doctorem honoris causa, U. Miskolc, Hungary, 1990. Rsch. asst. dept. mining engring. U. Durham, 1959-63; dir. rsch. Coal Mining Rsch. Controlling Coun., Johannesburg, South Africa, 1963-66; dir. collieries rsch. lab. Chamber of Mines of South Africa, Johannesburg, 1966-74, dir. gen. rsch. orgn., 1974-86; disting. prof. Colo. Sch. Mines, Golden, 1986-98, disting. prof. emeritus, 1998—, head dept. mining engring., 1986-90; dir. Colo. Mining and Mineral Resources Rsch. Inst., 1990-94; pres. Salamon Cons. Inc., Arvada, Colo., 1995—; 22d Sir Julius Wernher Meml. lectr., 1988; hon. prof. U. Witwatersrand, Johannesburg, 1979-86; vis. prof. U. Minn., Mpls., 1981, U. Tex., Austin, 1982, U. NSW, Sydney, Australia, 1990, 91-96; mem. Presdl. Commn. of Inquiry into Safety and Health in South African Mining Industry, 1994-95. Co-author: Rock Mechanics Applied to the Study of Rockbursts, 1966, Rock Mechanics in Coal Mining, 1976; contbr. articles to profl. jours. Mem. Pres.'s Sci. Adv. Council, Cape Town, South Africa, 1984-86, Nat. Sci. Priorities Com., Pretoria, South Africa, 1984-86. Recipient Nat. award Assn. Scis. and Tech. Socs., South Africa, 1971. Fellow South African Inst. Mining and Metallurgy (hon. life, v.p. 1974-76, pres. 1976-77, gold medal 1964, 85, Stokes award 1986, silver medal 1991, 99), Inst. Mining and Metallurgy (London), Hungarian Acad. Scis. (external), 1998; mem. AIME, Internat. Soc. Rock Mechanics. Roman Catholic.

SALAND, DEBORAH, psychotherapist, educator; b. Val Dosta, Ga., July 25, 1954; d. Charles and Audrey (Horan) Gianniny. B in Profl. Studies, Barry U., 1990, MSW, 1992; D in Psychology, So. Calif. Sch. Profl. Studies, 1996. Lic. clin. social worker, Fla. Substance abuse counselor Spectrum Programs, Ft. Lauderdale, Fla., 1974-79; owner Obsession in Time, Miami, Fla., 1984-88; asst. clin. dir. Interphase Recovery, Miami, 1988-89; substance abuse counselor Transitions Recovery, Miami, 1989-91; clin. dir. level II Pathways Treatment, Miami, 1992-93; pvt. practice Inst. Human Potential, Miami, 1993—; founder Eating Disorder Tex. Program, 1997—; lectr. Addiction Traingin Inst. U. Miami, 1992, mem. faculty, 1993—; clin. supr. Transitions Recovery, Miami, 1993—, Treatment Resources, Miami, 1993-94; adj. faculty N.Y. Inst. Tech., Boca Raton, Fla., 1997—; dir. Am. Family Eating Disorder Tract, 1997-98. Contbr. articles to profl. jours. Named Spl.

Alumni Barry U., 1996. Mem. NASW, APA, Am. Group Psychotherapy Assn. (clin.), Med. Psychotherapist Am. (assoc. clin.) Nat. Bd. Cert. Counselors (counselor), Broward County Mental Health Assn. Office: Inst Human Potential 19501 NE 10th Ave Ste 305 Miami FL 33179-3502

SALANSKIS, JEAN-MICHEL, logic and epistemology educator; b. Paris, Apr. 5, 1951; s. Ilija and Simone (Poudevigne) S.; m. Brigitte Frilley, Jan. 27, 1976; 1 child, Emmanuel. Agregation of Math., U. Paris, 1973; PhD, U. Strasbourg, France, 1986. Habilitation, 1992. Rschr. CNRS, Strasbourg, 1985-93, Paris, 1993-94; prof. U. Lille, France, 1994—. Author: (books) L'Herméneutique formelle, 1991, Le Temps du sens, 1997, Heidegger, 1997, Husserl, 1998, Le constructivisme non standard, 1999; editor 4 books. Office: U Lille III, Dept Philosophy, 59653 Villeneuve d'Ascq France

SALAS, HENRY JOSEPH, environmental engineer; b. N.Y.C., Jan. 30, 1947; s. Alberto and Orestes (Martinez) S.; m. Mirna Delicia Bardalez, Oct. 22, 1991; 1 child, Henry Joseph Jr. B in Civil Engring., Manhattan Coll., 1969, M in Environ. Engring., 1970. Registered profl. engr., N.Y. Project engr. Hydrosci., Inc., Westwood, N.J., 1970-73; project mgr. Hydrosci., Inc., Westwood, 1973-79; cons. Environ. Quality Bd. P.R., San Juan, 1979-82; regional adviser in water pollution control Panamerican Ctr. Sanitary Engring. and Environ. Scis., Lima, Peru, 1982-97; regional adv. environ. impact and health Panamerican Ctr. Sanitary Engring. and Environ. Scis.; cons. Pan Am. Health Orgn., Brazil, Peru, Cuba, Uruguay, 1975-81; lectr. in field. Author: History and Application of Microbiological Water Quality Standards in the Marine Environment, 1998; co-author Manual for the Evaluation and Management of Toxic Substances in Surface Waters, 1988-94; contbr. articles to profl. jours. Mem. ASCE, Water Environ. Fedn., Chi Epsilon. Roman Catholic. Achievements include simplified mathematical model for the evaluation of eutrophication in warm-water tropical lakes/reservoirs. Home: Malecon de la Reserva, 457/1102, Miraflores Lima 18, Peru Office: CEPIS, Casilla Postal 4337, Lima 100, Peru Peru Office: Panam Ctr San Engr/Env Scis, Los Pinos 259 Urb Camacho, Lima 12, Peru

SALAS, RANDALL NOUEL, automotive company executive; b. Willemstad, Curazao, Venezuela, Oct. 20, 1945; s. Herbert and Claire (Nouel) S.; m. Silvia M. Mago, Feb. 16, 1974; children: Maria Silvia, Claudia Isabella. Student, Santiago de León, Caracas, Venezuela, 1965; BS in Indsl. Engring., Cath. U., Caracas, 1971, BA in Journalism, 1976. Pilots coordinating engr. Gen. Motors de Venezuela, Caracas, 1971-73, methods engr., 1973-76, gen. supply products facilitator, 1976-78, products facility mgr., 1978-80, prodn. mgr., 1980-81, dir. personnel, 1981-86, dir. personnel and pub. govtl. relations, v.p., 1987-97; human resources and pub. rels. v.p. Orinoco Iron-Sivensa, Caracas, 1997—; bd. dirs. Camara Automotriz de Venezuela, Caracas. Named to Labor Merit Order 1st Degree, Ministry of Labor, 1987. Mem. Coll. Engrs. Venezuela, Assn. Venezolana de Ejecutivos, Nat. Assn. Indsl. Relations Execs. Roman Catholic. Club: Lagunita Country (Caracas). Avocation: reading. Office: Sivensa Av Venezuela, Torre America Piso 14, Bello Monte Caracas 1060, Venezuela Mailing Address: c/o SDP (OI) 14505 Commerce Way Ste 700 Miami Lakes FL 33016-1514

SALATIĆ, DUŠAN, retired mineral processing educator; b. Nova Crvenka, Serbia, Yugoslavia, Mar. 3, 1929; s. Vladimir and Andja (Lazić) S.; m. Slobodanka Čolović, Mar. 15, 1964; children: Sinisha, Vladimir. DSc, Faculty Mining and Geology, Belgrade, Yugoslavia, 1965; academisian (hon.), Royal Acad. Scis., Brussels, 1999; academisian, Yugoslav Engr. Acad., Belgrade, 2000, Balkan Acad. Sci. Mineral Tech., Istanbul, 2000. Diplomate mining engring. Sect. head Coal Mine Zenica, Bosnia, Yugoslavia, 1957-58; researcher Inst. Tech. Nuclear Raw Materials, Belgrade, 1958-66; prof. Faculty Mining and Geology Tech., Belgrade, 1966-96, dir. mining dept., 1977-79, assoc. (vice) dean, 1979-81, dean, 1981-83, head mineral processing dept., 1985-96; hon. prof. Inst. Steel and Iron Tech., Anschan, China, 1989; pres. faculty coun. Faculty Mining and Geology, U. Belgrade, 1992-96, mem. univ. coun., 1992-96. Author: Flotation Reagents, 1985; editor: 45 Years of Mineral Processing Department, 1991, Technological Principles of Design of Mineral Processing Plants, 1995, Proceeding of 8th Balkam Mineral Processing Conf., 1999; contbr. over 288 articles to profl. jours. Recipient fellowship Faculte Polytech. Mons, Belgium, 1968-69. Mem. World Sci. Com. on Non-Metallic Minerals (pres. 1985—), Balkanic Mineral Processing Com. (pres. 1997—), Directory French Mineral Processing Engring. Assn., Directory Yugoslav Mining and Geol. Engring. Assn., Yugoslav Mineral Processing Com. (pres. 1983-87). Fax: 381-11-629851. E-mail: dsalatic@eunet.yu. Home: 39 Gospodar Jovanova, 11000 Belgrade Serbia, Yugoslavia Office: Faculty Mining and Geology, 7 Diušina, 11000 Belgrade Serbia, Yugoslavia

SALATICH, JOHN SMYTH, retired cardiologist, internist; b. New Orleans, Nov. 28, 1926; s. Peter B. and Gladys (Malter) S.; m. Patricia L. Mattison, Sept. 26, 1959; children: John Smyth, Elizabeth, Allison, Stephanie. BS cum laude, Loyola U., New Orleans, 1946; MD, La. State U., 1950. Diplomate Am. Bd. Internal Medicine. Intern Charity Hosp., New Orleans, 1950-51, resident, 1951-54; practice medicine specializing in cardiology and internal medicine New Orleans, 1954-92, Gen. Internal Med. Clinic, Tulane Med. Sch., New Orleans, 1992-99; dir. EKG dept. Southeastern La. Hosp., Mandeville, 1972-99; ret., 1999—; prof. clin. medicine La. State U., 1994; mem. staff Touro Infirmary, St. Charles Gen. Hosp.; chmn. dept. medicine Hotel Dieu, 1974-86; pres., New Orleans Emergency Room Corp., Physician Supplemental Services; adv. bd. Bank La., 1960-89; mem. Pres.'s Coun. Loyola U., 1990-92. Contbr. articles to profl. and bus. jours. Bd. dirs. La. Regional Med. Program, 1972. Served to capt. M.C., AUS, 1954-56; Korea. Decorated Medallion of Greek Army. Fellow Am. Coll. Chest Physicians, ACP; mem. Am. Heart Assn., La. Heart Assn., New Orleans Acad. Internal Medicine, La. Soc. Internal Medicine, AMA, La. Med. Soc., Orleans Parish Med. Soc., New Orleans Country Club, Theta Beta, Alpha Sigma Nu, Delta Epsilon Sigma. Home: 433 Country Club Dr New Orleans LA 70124-1038

SALATINO, PIERO, chemical engineering educator; b. Vinchiaturo, Italy, Aug. 19, 1959; s. Michele and Cristina (Baratta) S.; m. Stefania Acanfora, Sept. 21, 1998; children: Giulia, Michele.. Degree in Chem. Engring., U. Naples, Italy, 1982, D in Chem. Engring., 1987. Process engr. Tecnimont, Milan, 1983-84; sr. rschr. Consiglio Nazionale Ricerche-Inst. Richerche Combustione, Naples, 1985-92; prof. U. Naples, 1992—; chmn. Italian Sect. Combustion Inst., 1997—, Chem. Engring. Program, Naples, 1999—; colloquim co-chair Combustion Inst., Pitts., 1999-2000. Mem. editl. bd. Powder Tech., 1992—; contbr. articles to profl. jours. Avocation: sailing. Home: Nardones 60, 80132 Napoli Italy Office: U Napoli, Piazzale Tecchio 80, 80125 Napoli Italy

SALAZAR, CARLES, social anthropology educator; b. Badalona, Barcelona, Spain, Jan. 29, 1961; s. Joan Salazar and Josefa Carrasco. BA in Law, U. Barcelona, 1984, BA in History, 1987; MPhil in Social Anthropology, U. Cambridge, Eng., 1988, PhD in Social Anthropology, 1993. Univ. lectr. U. Barcelona, 1994-95, U. Lleida, Spain, 1994—. Author: A Sentimental Economy, 1996, De La Razón y Sus Descontentos, 1996. Office: U Lleida Dept Social Hist, Pl Victor Siurana 1, 25003 Lleida Spain

SALAZAR, OMAR MAURICIO, radiation oncologist, educator; b. Havana, Cuba, Sept. 22, 1942; came to U.S., 1959; naturalized, 1970; s. Aramis Victor and Nelida Raquel (Acosta) S.; m. Margarita Cristina Pedraza, July 7, 1979; children: Omar M., Sofia M. BS in Biology, Georgetown U., 1965; MD, U. P.R., 1969; MS, U. Rochester, 1974. Diplomate Am. Bd. Radiology. Radiotherapy resident U. P.R., Rio Piedras, 1969-72, chief resident, 1971-72; instr., fellow U. Rochester, N.Y., 1973-74, asst. prof., 1974-78, assoc. prof., 1978-81; prof., chmn. dept. radiation oncology U. Md., Balt., 1981-95; dir. radiation oncology La. State U. Med. Ctr., New Orleans, 1995-99; dir. dept. radiation oncology Oakwood Health Sys., Dearborn, Mich., 1999—; interim dir. Cancer Ctr. Excellence Oakwood Health Sys., Dearborn, 1999—; mem. CCIRC Nat. Cancer Inst., Bethesda, Md., 1980-84; coord. USA, Circulo Radioterapeutas Ibero-Latino-Americanos-L.Am. Assn. Radiation Therapy, 1981-98, v.p., 1998—; expert cons. internat. Atomic Energy Agy., Vienna, Austria, 1996—; examiner Am. Bd. Radiology, Phila., 1983-93; chmn. site cancer visit Nat. Cancer Inst., Bethesda, 1983, site visitor, 1982; co-investigator Whitaker Found., 1983. Author: Moments of Decision/Primary Brain Tumors, 1979, Bronchogenic Carcinoma, 1981; contbr. articles to profl. jours. Arthur A. Ward Trust grantee, 1981; Am. Cancer Clin. Fellowship award, 1984-86. Fellow Am. Coll. Radiology, Am. Coll. Radiation Oncology (past pres., past chmn. bd. dirs., Gold medal); mem. AMA, Radiation Therapy Oncology Group, Ea. Coop. Oncology Group (chmn. brain and lung com. 1979-80), Tex. Radiol. Soc., Mask and Bauble Dramatic Soc., Med. Chirurgical Soc., Md. Radiol. Soc., Radiol. Soc. Am., Am. Radiol. Soc., Am. Assn. Cancer Edn., Big Five Club. Roman Catholic. Address: 6402 Schaefer Rd Dearborn MI 48126-2213

SALBUCHI, ADRIAN RICARDO, insurance company executive; b. Buenos Aires, Sept. 14, 1952; s. Augusto Mario and Lidia (Pittaluga) S.; m. Susana Cristina Distefano, Apr. 16, 1977; children: Evangelina, Cecilia, Walter, Alfred. Grad. H.S., Maspeth, N.Y. With Matthews Wrightson & Co., Buenos Aires, 1968-72; clk., mgr. Stewart Wrightson Ltd., Buenos Aires, 1972-80; mgr., sec. Interior Reins. Svcs. Ltd., London, 1980-82; comml. mgr. Compania Seguros Interior SA, Buenos Aires, 1982-90; v.p. Buenos Aires, 1990-93; internat. mgr. Risk Mgmt.Co., Buenos Aires, 1993—, Aon Risk Svcs., Argentina, 1997-98; ptnr. Elite Cons., 1998—; advisor Argentine Army, Argentine Air Force, confs. for various founds. Author: World Government: Politica y Poder en el Siglo XXI, 1995, El Cerebro Del Mundo, 1995, 2d edit., 1999. Cpl. Argentine Army, 1973. Roman Catholic. Avocations: political and historical research, opera, comparative religions research. Home: Saenz Pena 445, 1854 Longchamps Buenos Aires, Argentina Office: Av Eduardo Madero 942 13 Fl, 1106 Buenos Aires Argentina

SALDANHA, LEOPOLDO FREDERICO, nephrologist, physician, educator; b. Paranagua, Parana, Brazil, Feb. 11, 1942; s. Carlos and Silvia (Neves) S.; m. Elisabeth de Medeiros, Jan. 6, 1968 (div. Sept. 1986); children: Claudine, Gabriela. BS, Santa Catarina State Coll., 1959; MD, Federal U. Sch. Medicine, 1966. Diplomate Bd. Nephrology, Bd. Internal Medicine. Resident in internal medicine Hosp. Pub. Employees of State, Rio de Janeiro, 1967-68; fellow in nephrology U. Calif. Sch. Medicine, L.A., 1970-73; rsch. fellow in nephrology med. sch. Harvard U., Boston, 1973-75; chief dept. medicine State Hosp., Florianopolis, Brazil, 1979-81; chief nephrology divsn. Charity Hosp., Florianopolis, 1981-90; assoc. prof. medicine Federal U., Florianopolis, 1987—; cons. physician State Hosp., Florianopolis, 1969-89, Charity Hosp., Florianopolis, 1969—, Telecomm. Santa Catarina, Florianopolis, 1976-99; vis. assoc. prof. U. Calif., L.A., 1991-92; rsch. scientist Cedars Sinai Med. Ctr., L.A., 1990-94. Co-author: Principles of Nephrology, 1988; contbr. articles to profl. jours. including British Med. Jour., Am. Jour. Medicine, Jour. Clin. Investigation, Trans. ASAIO, Am. Jour. Dis. Child, Am. Jour. Kidney Disease, Kidney Internat., Jour. Am. Soc. Nephrology, Nephron. Rsch. grantee Brazilian Coun., 1993, Brazilian Ministry of Edn. grantee, 1990; recipient Physician's Recognition award ACP, 1972. Mem. Am. Soc. Nephrology, Brazilian Soc. Nephrology, Brazilian Med. Assn. Avocations: classical music, films, books, Napoleonic studies, tennis. E-mail: lfsaldanha@hotmail.com. Home: Apt 1204, Av Trompowsky #227, 88015300 Florianopolis Santa Catarina Brazil

SALDARINI, GIOVANNI CARDINAL, archbishop; b. Cantu, Italy, Dec. 11, 1924. Ordained priest Roman Cath. Ch., 1947. Titular bishop of Gaudiaba, aux. bishop of Milan, 1984, archbishop of Turin, 1989, elevated to the Sacred Coll. of Cardinals, 1991, with titular ch. of the Sacred Heart. Office: Archdiocese Roman Cath Ch, Via Arcivescovado 12, 10121 Turin Italy*

SALEEM, MOHAMMAD ABDUL, hotel executive; b. Hyderabad, India, July 1, 1948; s. Mohammed Abdul Aziz and Azizunnisa Unnisa Begum; m. Merle Ann Fernandes, Jan. 11, 1979; children: Zarina, Zoheb, Zubair. P-lanning engr. Al Azam Ltd., Karachi, Pakistan, 1968-72, Tarmac Overseas Ltd., Muscat, Oman, 1973-78; mng. ptnr. Abu Dhabi (United Arab Emirates) Property Mgmt., 1978-97; mng. dir. Emirates Plz. Hotel, Abu Dhabi, Al Hamra Plz. Residence, Abu Dhabi, Howard Johnson Diplomat Hotel, Abu Dhabi, Sparkle Laundry, Scorpio Club & Restaurant, Abu Dhabi, Mayfair Hotel, Dubai, Ritz Plaza Hotel, Fujairah; cons. to Shaikh Mussalam Bin Ham; chmn. Carlton Hotel, Karachi, Pakistan. Avocations: antique collector, music, swimming, reading. Home: Flat 603, Al Wadha Twr Bldg Salam St, Abu Dhabi United Arab Emirates Office: Al Hamra Plz Residence, Zayed 1st St PO Box 4604, Abu Dhabi United Arab Emirates

SALEEM, RUBEENA, chemistry researcher; b. Lahore, Punjab, Pakistan, Sept. 8, 1965; d. Saleem Saif and Razia (Sultana) S. BS, Karachi (Pakistan) U., 1985, MS in Organic Chemistry, 1988, PhD in Chemistry, 1996. Post-grad. fellow HEJ Inst. Chemistry U. Karachi, 1990-95; sr. rsch. assoc. Humbard U., Karachi, 1995—; vis. scientist Cornell U., Ithaca, N.Y., 1998-99. Contbr. over 30 articles to profl. jours.; patentee in field. Scholar Bd. Secondary Edn., 1980-81, Fulbright scholar U.S. Edn. Found. in Pakistan, 1998-99. Mem. Pharmacol. Soc. Pakistan (life). Avocations: studying Islamic history, visiting historical places. Home: 198-A/II Adam Rd, karachi Cantt, Karachi Sindh, Pakistan Office: Humbard U, Dr HMI Inst Pharm & Herbal Scis, 74600 Karachi Sindh, Pakistan

SALEH, ALI-ABDULLAH, president; b. Beit al-Ahmer, Sanhan, Yemen, 1942; married; several children. Grad., Armor Sch., 1964. With Yemen Armed Forces, 1958, advanced through ranks marshal, 1997, dir. Armor Corps Arsenal, commandant various squadrons, battalions, brigades; commandant Taiz Governorate; mem. provisional Republican Coun.; dep.-in-chief, chief of staff Armed Forces, 1978; pres. Republic of Yemen, 1978—; comdr.-in-chief Armed Forces, 1978—; founder modern state of Yemen; sec.-gen. People's Gen. Congress, 1982; chmn. Presdl. Coun. of Republic of Yemen, 1990—. Republican award People's Constituent Assembly, 1979. Fax: 202-337-2017. Office: Embassy of Republic Yemen 2600 Virginia Ave NW Ste 705 Washington DC 20037-1905

SALEH, BRIAN BEHROOZ, aerospace executive; b. Tehran, Iran, Apr. 25, 1939; came to U.S., 1959; m. Carole Jean DeBortoli, Sept. 15, 1962 (div. 1979); children: Sharvin John, Shereen June; m. Farideh Navidi, May 12, 1983. BSEE, Northrop U., Ingelwood, Calif., 1967; MBA, Golden Gate U., San Francisco, 1973; instr. credential, Calif. C.C. Design engr. radio frequency Space Systems/Loral, Palo Alto, Calif., 1970—, mgr. GOES Comm. Subsys., 1974-76, program engr. NATO-III Satellite, 1976-79, mgr. Insat Program Engring., 1979-85; mgr. GOES Spacecraft Engring. Palo Alto, 1985-91; mgr. GOES Spacecraft Space Systems/Loral, Palo Alto, 1991-92, dir. GOES Prodn. Program, 1992-95, dir. Telstar Program, 1995-97, sr. dir. Fixed Svc. Satellite Programs, 1997-98, sr. dir. common products and planning, 1998, sr. exec. dir. CD Radio Program, 1998-99, v.p. programs, 1999—. Republican.

SALEH, HESHAM, otolaryngologist; b. Cairo, Egypt, June 10, 1961; arrived in U.K., 1987; s. Ahmed Saleh and Roufia (Tolba) S.; m. Hala Ghorab, July 1, 1995. MB BCh, Ain Shams, 1983. Intern Ain Shams U. Hosps., Cairo, 1984-85; sr. ho. officer Mataria Tchg. Hosp., Cairo, 1986-87, Nat. Health Svc., various locations, 1989-93; registrar Nat. Health Svc., South Devon, U.K., 1994-96; specialist registrar Nat. Health Svc., Dundee, U.K., 1996-98, London, 1998—; hon. clin. tchr. Dundee U., 1996-98, examiner 1998; lectr. Abertay U., Dundee, 1996-98. Contbr. articles to profl. jours. Pvt. Med. Svcs. Egyptian Army, 1985-86. Rsch. grant Scottish Otolaryngological Soc., 1997, 98, Anonymous Trust Funds, 1998. Fellow Royal Coll. of Surgeons; mem. British Assn. of Otorhinolaryngologist, British Med. Assn. Avocations: playing guitar, travel, swimming. Office: Royal Nat Throat Nose & Ear Hosp, Gray's Inn Rd, London WC1X 8DA, England

SALEH, JAIME, governor; b. Bonaire, Netherlands Antilles, Apr. 20, 1941; m. Marguerite Marie Saleh; 4 children. D, Utrecht U., 1966. Dep. prosecutor Willemstad, Curacao, 1967-71; atty. Curacao, 1971-74; judge Netherlands Antilles High Ct. of Justice, 1974-79; chief justice High Ct. of Justice, 1979-90; gov. of Netherlands Antilles Willemstad, Curacao, 1990—. Address: Fort Amsterdam 2, Willemstad Curacao, Netherlands Antilles

SALEH, JOHN, lawyer; b. O'Donnell, Tex., June 29, 1928; s. Nahum and Arslie S. BBA, U. Tex., 1950, JD with honors, 1952; cert. U.S. Army Judge Advocate Sch., U. Va., 1953. Bar: Tex. 1952, U.S. Ct. Mil. Appeals, 1953, U.S. Tax Ct. 1954, U.S. Dist. Ct. (no. dist.) Tex. 1956, U.S. Ct. Appeals (5th cir.) 1960, U.S. Supreme Ct. 1961, D.C. 1982. Pvt. practice Lamesa, Tex., 1954—; tchg. instr. legal rsch. writing U. Tex. Sch. Law, 1950-52. Assoc. editor Tex. Law Rev., 1951-52. Mem. ABA, ATLA, Tex. Law Rev. Assn. (life), Tex. Bar Assn. (spl. com. to study rev. code criminal procedure 1969-71), D.C. Bar Assn., Tex. Trial Lawyers Assn., Tex. Bar Found., Order of the Coif, The Million Dollar Advocates Forum, Phi Delta Phi. Home: 605 Doak O'Donnell TX 79351 Office: 502 N 1st St Lamesa TX 79331-5406

SALEH, KHALED J., orthopaedic surgeon, educator; b. Can., Sept. 24, 1964; s. Joinal N. and Fathi Saleh; m. Lena Saleh, July 24, 1984; children: Jasmine, Jamal, Jenine. BSc, U. Western Ont., London, Ont., Can., 1987; MD, U. Western Ont., 1991; MS, U. McMaster, Hamilton, Ont., 1995. Lic. Med. Coun. Can., Coll. Physicians and Surgeons, Commonwealth Pa. Rotating intern U. Western Ont., Victoria Hosp., 1991-92; jr. resident gen. orthopaedics and trauma U. Toronto-Toronto Western Hosp., 1992; jr. resident ICU U. Toronto-Wellesley Hosp., 1993; jr. resident gen. surgery U. Toronto-St. Joseph's Hosp., 1993; jr. resident vascular surgery, sr. resident ICU U. Toronto-Wellesley Hosp., 1993, sr. resident arthritis and gen. orthopaedics, 1993; jr. resident hand surgery U. Toronot-Toronto Western Hosp., 1994, sr. resident sports medicine, 1996-97; jr. resident orthopaedic oncology U. Toronto-Mt. Sinai Hosp., 1994; chief resident trauma orthopaedics U. Toronto-Sunnybrook Health Sci. Ctr., 1996; sr. resident pediat. orthopaedics U. Toronto-Hosp. for Sick Children, 1997; Outcome and Health Related Rsch. fellow Med. Rsch. Coun. Can., 1997-98; postgrad. fellow U. Toronto-Mt. Sinai Hosp., 1997-98; Orthopaedic Rsch. and Edn. Found. Health Svcs. fellow Am. Acad. Orthopaedic Surgeons, 1998-99; postgrad. fellow U. Cornell Med. Coll., Hosp. for Spl. Surgery, N.Y.C., 1998-99; clin. instr. Hosp. for Spl. Surgery, Cornell U. Med. Coll., N.Y.C., 1998-99; asst. prof. dept. orthopaedic surgery U. Minn., Mpls., 1999—; with Hosp. for Spl. Surgery, Osteoporosis Ctr., 1998-99; with dept. orthopaedic surgery VA Med. Ctr., Mpls., 1999—; assoc. staff South Huron Hosp., Exeter, Ont., 1992-95, Alexander Marine Hosp., Goderich, Ont., 1992-98, Mt. Sinai Hosp., Toronto, 1997-98, N.Y. Hosp., N.Y.C., 1998-99, Meml. Hosp. for Cancer and Allied Disease, 1998-99, Hosp. for Spl. Surgery, N.Y.C., 1998-99; attending physician Fairview U. Med. Ctr. VA Med. Ctr., 1999—; resident team physician Can. Nat. Ballet, 1992-97, NHL Toronto Maple Leafs, 1992-97; presenter in field. Reviewer Jour. Bone and Joint Surgery, 1999—; contbr. chpts. to books and articles to profl. jours. Grantee Am. Acad. Orthopaedic Surgery Knee Soc., 1998-99, 98-99, Arthritis Soc., 1998—, Am. Acad. Orthopaedic Surgeons and Orthopaedic Rsch. and Edn. Found., 1998-2000; scholar Nat. Sci. and Engring. Coun., 1986, 87, Med. Rsch. Coun. Can., 1997-98. Fellow Royal Coll. Surgeons Can.; mem. Am. Acad. Orthopaedic Surgeons (rsch. com. Knee Soc. 1998—, outcomes rsch. com. 1998—), Can. Orthopaedic Assn., Coll. Physicians and Surgeons Ont., Ont. Med. Assn. Fax:(612) 626-6032. Office: Dept Orthopaedic Surgery UHMC #492 420 Delaware St SE Minneapolis MN 55455-0374

SALEH, MAHMOUD ABBAS, chemistry educator; b. Cairo, Dec. 23, 1942; came to U.S., 1966; s. Abbas Saleh and Nazera Abdel Aziz; m. Fawzia Hassan Abdel Rahman, Feb. 5, 1975; children: Heidi, Ahmed, Hallah. BS in Agrl. Biochemistry, U. Cairo, 1963, MS in Agrl. Biochemistry, 1965; PhD in Organic Chemistry, U. Calif., Davis, 1971. Pesticides chemist U. Calif., Berkeley, 1975-80; prof. agrl. chemistry Cairo U., 1980-86; rsch. prof. chemistry U. Nev., Las Vegas, 1986-90; prof. chemistry Tex. So. U., Houston, 1990—. Editor: Biomarkers of Human Exposure to Pesticide, 1994, Biomarkers for Agricultural and Toxic Substances, 1996; contbr. numerous articles to profl. jours. Mem. nat. diving team, Egypt, 1962-72. Recipient nat. award for sci. achievements Acad. Sci. Rsch., Egypt, 1980, 86. Mem. Am. Chem. Soc. Moslem. Avocations: desert exploration, scuba diving, wildlife. Home: 4102 Stone Edge Ct Sugar Land TX 77479-2434 Office: Tex So U Dept Chemistry 3100 Cleburne St Houston TX 77004-4501

SALEH, MOHAMMED, diplomat; b. Manama, Bahrain, Oct. 2, 1967; s. Saleh Mohammed Saleh and Fatima Abdulla Syed Hussain; m. Khatoon Abdulla A. Salman, Aug. 11, 1995; children: Jaffer, Ali. BA in Polit. Sci., Law, Kuwait U., 1992; hon., Oxford, 1996. Third sec. Ministry Foreign Affairs, Manama, Bahrain, 1993-99; second sec. Bahrain Mission to UN, N.Y.C., 1999—; cons. UN Security Council, N.Y.C., 1998-99. Recipient Hist. award Bahrain Hist. Archeol. Soc., 1998. Avocations: collection of Poliold Polit. & religious books. Office: Bahrain Mission to the UN 866 E Second Ave New York NY 10017

SALEH, SAMEER YASIN, journalist, researcher; b. Kuwait, Dec. 28, 1956; s. Yasin Ahmad and Majeda (Husein) S.; m. Osama Ali Mousa; children: Feras, Sama'e, Shather. BA, Kuwait U., 1981. Info. officer Kuwait Petroleum Co., 1981-83; journalist Al-Seyassah Newspaper, Kuwait, 1984-87, Al A'amel Mag., Kuwait, 1987-90; journalist Al-Watan Newspaper, Kuwait, 1976-81, 83-84, mil. corr., 1991-94, spl. assignment editor, 1994—. Author: 25 Years of Sports in Kuwait, 1984; writer, co-dir. (documentary) Sports in Kuwait, 1985; rschr. (documentary) Video on the Sands, 1984; mng. editor Ibtesama Mag., 1996—, Al-Dyra Mag., 1991; script writer: (documentary) Witness Of History, 1997, O'Teen, 1997. Mem. Investigative Reporters Union. Avocations: photography, reading, snooker, collecting paintings. Home: PO Box 35236, Al-She'ab Kuwait Office: Al-Watan Newspaper, Shuwaikh 1142 13012, Safat Kuwait

SALEH, SAMIR A., lawyer, consultant, writer; b. Beirut, Lebanon, Jan. 31, 1932; arrived in Eng., 1976; s. Anis Elias and Marie (Khayat) S.; m. Josette Sara Saleh, 1958; children: Zeina, Yasmina. Degree in law, St. Joseph U., Beirut, 1952; LLM in Internat. and Air Law, McGill U., Montreal, 1954. Prin. Anis Saleh Law Office, Beirut, 1954—; lectr. law faculty Lebanese U., Beirut, 1959-69; legal advisor to His Majesty the Sultan of Oman, 1971-76; law cons. Samir Saleh & Assocs., London, 1976—; lectr. in field. Mem. Internat. C. of C. (vice chmn. ct. of arbitration Paris chpt. 1982-88),. Roman Catholic. Avocations: languages, piano, poetry, cooking. Home: Flat 5 18 Bolton Gardens, London SW5, England Office: 6 Bristol House 80 A, Southampton Row, London WC1, England

SALEH BIN, MOHAMMED AL-LUHALDAAN, judge. Chief Supreme Coun. of Justice, Saudi Arabia. Office: Supreme Ct of Justice, Riyadh Saudi Arabia*

SALEHI, MOHAMMAD, health facility administrator, educator; b. Shahre Rey, Iran, Jan. 22, 1940; s. Mohammad Hasan Salehi and Zahra Mortazavi; m. Farideh Moili, Aug. 9, 1973; children: Ali Reza, Nahal. MD, Med. U. Tehran, Iran, 1967, specialization in pediat., 1972. Intern in pediat., internal medicine, gen., plastic surgery Med. U. Tehran affiliated hosps., 1966-67; resident in pediat. Dr. Ahari Hosp. (now Med. Ctr. for Children), Tehran, 1969-72; head chest pediat. ward Rsch. Inst. Tuberculosis Lung Disease, 1977—; cons. VistaLink Travel Medicine affiliated U. Tex. Houston Med. Sch., 1999—; Editor articles in profl. jours. Fellow Internat. Coll. Pediat. Child Care (hon.), Am. Acad. Pediat. (sr.), Am. Acad. Chest Physicians Surgeons; mem. Am. Thoracic Soc. Islamic. Avocations: electronics, computers, hunting. Fax: (98-21) 7500919; office fax: 0098 21 769038. E-mail: m.salehi@dpir.com. Home: Nazari # 7 Shahid Ahmadian, Torkmanestan St Ostad Motahh Ave, Tehran 15659, Iran Office: Nat Rsch Inst TB Lung Disease, Niavaran Darabad, 19556 Tehran Iran

SALEK, SERGIO CORREA, communications engineer; b. Rio de Janeiro, Mar. 10, 1941; s. Manoel and Noemy (Correa) S.; m. Luciula Sa Freire, Apr. 30, 1966 (div. Mar. 1991); children: Lidia, Breno, Silvia. Degree in Engring., Tech. Inst. Aeronautics, São Paulo, Brazil, 1964. Registered profl. engr. Exec. Cetel, Rio de Janeiro, 1964-71; engr. Telerj, Rio de Janeiro, 1971-78, 93-94; assessor Telebras, Brasilia, 1979-80. Author: The Telephone Congestion in Rio Area of Telerj and in Embratel, 1990. Home and Office: Rua Osvaldo Pais 21 104, 22620-000 Rio de Janeiro Brazil Address: Rua General Artigas 14-102, Rio de Janeiro 22450010, Brazil

SALEM, JOSEPH JOHN, jeweler, real estate developer; b. Corpus Christi, Tex., Dec. 29, 1920; s. Sam and Victoria (Moses) S.; m. 1952; children: Chris, Joey, Sam II. LLD (hon.), U. Tex., San Antonio, 1970. Congressman State of Tex., Austin, 1968-76; jeweler Corpus Christi; apptd. Pres.'s Kennedy and Johnson Nat. Coms. on Employment of the Handicapped and Employment of Older Worker, local chmn. state of Tex. com.; past mem. mayor's com. on mental retardation Corpus Christi Police Officers Assn. Mem. Tex. and Nueces County Heart Assn., USO Exec. Com., YMCA; mem. nat. adv. com. Brand Names Found.; mem. Nueces County Dem. Orgn.; sustaining mem. Nat. Dem. Com.; past pres. West Side Pony League; past chmn. rehab. sub com. of long range planning com. UCS; past mem. mayor's com. mental retardation Task Force Com.; past pres. Better Bus. Bur. Capt. USAF, 1941-46. Recipient UMC award Outstanding Man

of Yr., Internat. Pres. award Optimists, Local Benny award Corpus Christi's Favorite Businessman, Outstanding Retailer of Yr. award Jewelers Category Brand Names Found., Cert. of Hon. Corpus Christi Classroom Tchrs. Assn., County Auditors Tex. award for Outstanding Svc., South Tex. Legislator of Yr. award Ams. in Action, Meritorious Svc. award Tex. Good Rds. and Transp. Assn., Appreciation award Tex. State Dept. of Am. Legion, Scout-A-Rama cert. Appreciation for Outstanding Work with Boy Scouts, Outstanding Svc. award Corpus Christi Police Officers and Firefighters, cert. Appreciation Boys Clubs Am., cert. Appreciation Navy Wive's Clubs Am., cert. Appreciation Lions Clubs, Kiwanis Clubs, and Civitan Clubs, award for Humanitarian Svcs. to Working People Tex. OCAW; commd. Hon. Tex. Col., Adm. in Tex. Navy, Pioneer award NAACP, 2000, Lulac Humanitarian award, 2000; Salem auditorium named in his honor Boys and Girls Club; Salem Ball Pk. named in his honor City of Corpus Christi; Salem St. named in honor; named to Vet. Hall of Fame, 1993. Mem. Corpus Christi C. of C. (mem. mil. affairs, inter-city rels. com., aviation com., Optimists (past pres.), Am. Legion (past comdr.), KC. Democrat. Roman Catholic. Avocations: golfing, boxing, weight lifting. Address: 1286 Padre Staples Mall Corpus Christi TX 78411

SALEM, SHAWKY M.A., information science educator; b. Alexandria, Egypt, July 16, 1940; s. Mahmoud Ali Salem and Zahrah Ibrahim Askar; m. Samiah A. Salem; children: Mayada S., Nesrene S. MA in Info. Sci., Cairo U., 1976, PhD in Info. Sci., 1982. Dir. Arab Ctr. for Med. Lit., 1984; prof. Alexandria U., 1995—; chmn. Alexandria Ctr. Multimedia and Librs., 1995—; tech. advisor UNESCO, WHO, The Arab League, Arab League Edn. Culture Sci. Org., United Nations Indsl. Devel. Org.; mem. internat. adv. com. 13th, 14th and 15th Internat. On-line Info. Confs.; lectr. in field. Mem. editl. bd. Jour. Info. Sci., Microcomputers for Info. Mgmt., Libr. and Info. Sci. Abstracts, Internat. Forum Info. and Documentation; author 15 books and 5 reference works; contbr. articles to profl jours. Fellow Inst. Info. Scientists U.K.; mem. YASLIB, Internat. Fedn. Libr. Assns. and Instns. (organizer Third World Countries Caucus, chmn., spl. advisor standing com. for Asia and Oceania, standing com. for biol. and med. librs., internat. com. on access to info. and freedom of expression), Internat. Fedn. for Info. and Documentation (coun. mem., pres. regional orgn. North Africa and Near East), Freedom Access to Info. and Freedom of Expression, Med. Libr. Assn., Am. Soc. Info.Sci., Microfilm Assn. Great Brit., Internat. Inst. Terminology Rsch. Office: 181-183 Ahmed Shawky St, Roushdy Alexandria Egypt

SALEM, SUSANNE FRANCES, consulting executive; b. San Francisco, Mar. 25, 1945; d. Edward L. and Mary F. (Adams) Ledinski; m. Lee C. Salem, July 14, 1979. BS, Ariz. State U., 1979. Ins. agt. Atlantic Mut. Ins. Co. and Harris & Assocs., Los Angeles, 1964-73; ptnr. Acero Enterprises, Sierra Vista, Ariz., 1973-77; lease account mgr. Truck Leasing, Phoenix, 1979-80; sales and cons. Internat. Transp., Phoenix, 1980; owner Corp. Directions Cons. & Recruiting, Phoenix, 1980-86; v.p., bd. dirs. The Prism Group, Inc., Cons., Tempe, Ariz., 1987-94; human resource leader W.L. Gore & Assocs., 1994-95; cons. Salem & Assoc., 1986—; guest speaker. Bd. dirs. Southeastern Ariz. Drug Abuse Coun., 1975-77, The Ariz. Partnership, 1989-90, adv. bd. dirs. Maricopa Skill Ctr., 1989-91. Contbr. articles to profl. jours. Mem. Am. Trucking Assns. (bd. dirs., scholar 1977-79, outstanding transp. grad. 1979), Ariz. C. of C. Office: 615 SE Linn St Unit C Portland OR 97202-7062

SALEMI, MARCO MARIA, molecular biologist, researcher; b. Caltanissetta, Sicily, Italy, Nov. 16, 1968; arrived in Belgium, 1996; s. Angelo and Maria Luisa (Grazia) S.; m. Giovanna Maria Gatti, Mar. 1, 1997. Grad., State U., Pavia, Italy, 1991; postgrad. degree, U. Milan, 1995; PhD in Scis., Cath. U. Leuven, 1999. Cert. chemist specialist biotechnology. Resident Centro Nazionale Ricerche, Pavia, 1991-95; scientist AIDS Rsch. Unit-Rega Inst., Leuven, Belgium, 1996—; rsch. assoc. U. Leuven, 1999—. Contbr. articles to profl. jours. Fellow Sorin Biomedica, Ctr. Nat. Rsch., Pavia, 1993, AIDS fellow Italian Inst. Health, CNR, Pavia, 1994-95, Marie-Curie fellow European Cmty., Leuven, 1996-98. Mem. AAAS, Internat. Soc. Molecular Evolution. Avocations: psychology, neuroscience, theater, epistemology, informatics. Office: AIDS Rsch Unit Rega Inst, Minderbroedersstraat 10, B-3000 Leuven Belgium

SALÉN, SVEN HAMPUS, trading company executive; b. Stockholm, June 2, 1939; s. Sven Gustaf and Dagmar (Mörner) S.; m. Eva Gunnel Lauritzen, June 5, 1965; children: Staffan B., Erik B. LLB, U. Stockholm, 1966. Asst. U. Stockholm, 1964-66; v.p., pres., chmn. Salén Group, 1966—; mng. dir. Whitco Marine Svcs. Ltd., London, 1972-74. Local councillor Commune of Danderyd, Sweden, 1976-82; chmn. SNS (Ctr. for Bus. and Policy Studies), Stockholm, 1979-92; vice chmn./chmn. F.R.N. Rsch. Coun., Stockholm, 1989-92; alternate mem. Swedish Parliament, Stockholm, 1988. Lt. RSN, 1966—. Decorated CBE; recipient King's medal 12th size. Fellow Chartered Inst. Transport; mem. Royal Swedish Yacht Club (commodore 1981-86, hon. 1986), Royal Ocean Racing Club (rear commodore 1974). Mem. Folkpartiet. Office: Saléna AB, PO Box 14237, 10440 Stockholm Sweden

SALEN, WAYNE LOUIS, insurance agency official, consultant; b. Hornell, N.Y., Oct. 18, 1954; s. Louis Delbert and Roselyn Ann (Muscarella) S.; children: Wesley Louis, Janelle Ashley. Cert. internat. study, Lycée Rouget de Lisle, Lons-Le-Saunier, France, 1973; BA, SUNY, Buffalo, 1977; MBA, Canisius Coll., 1986. Lic. ins. broker, N.Y.; cert. hazard control mgr., product safety mgr.; assoc. in risk mgmt. Exec. trainee Jones Chem. Co., Inc., Caledonia, N.Y., 1977-78; asst. to prodn. dir. FMC Corp., Middleport, N.Y., 1978-79; risk mgr. Twin Fair, Inc., West Seneca, N.Y., 1979-82, Peter J. Schmitt Co., Inc., West Seneca, 1987-90, Empire Soils Investigations, Inc., Middleport, 1990-91; loss control cons. Lansing B. Warner, Inc., Chgo., 1982-84; mgr., asst. to pres. Laverack & Haines, Inc., Buffalo, 1984-87; account exec. Teach, Ryan & Cable, Inc., Buffalo, 1991; risk mgr. County of Niagra, Lockport, N.Y., 1991-95, The Park Assoc., Inc., 1995—; dir. risk mgmt., mem. steering com. Food Mktg. Inst., Washington, 1988-90; cons. on risk mgmt. Mem. Royalton Hartland Cen. Sch. Bd., Middleport, 1984-89. Mem. Am. Soc. Safety Engrs. (profl.), Nat. Fire Protection Assn., Risk and Ins. Mgmt. Soc., N.Y. State Assn. Self-Insured Counties. Republican. Methodist. Avocations: Buffalo Bills, Buffalo Bisons, Buffalo Sabres. Office: 300 Gleed Ave East Aurora NY 14052-2980

SALEQUE, MD ABU, soil scientist; b. Bogra, Bangladesh, Dec. 18, 1957; s. Samir and Saleha (Begum) S.; m. Delowara Begum, Mar. 16, 1983. BS with hon., BAU, Bangladesh, 1980, MS, 1982; PhD, UPLB, Philippines, 1994. Scientific officer BRRI, Bangladesh, 1983-92; sr. scientific officer BRRI, 1992—. Recipient scholarship, USAID, Irri, Philippines, 1991, postgrad. fellowship, UPM, 1997. Office: Bangladesh Rice Res Inst, 1701 Gazipur Bangladesh

SALERNO, KERSTIN UTE, marketing professional; b. Hamburg, Germany, Oct. 16, 1966; d. Michael and Brigitte Moellers; m. Jean-Pierre Salerno, Nov. 20, 1992; 1 child, Amelie. Diploma, U. Paderborn, Germany, 1994. Salesperson EDK, Luebeck, Germany, 1986-87; sec. Draeger S.A., Paris, 1987-88; advt. mgr. dSPACE GmbH, Paderborn, 1995—; chef asst. Dale Carnegie, Paderborn, 1991; cons. sim sichermoellers, Paderbron, 1998—. Recipient Ad Q award for outstanding advt., 1998. Avocation: fitness. Fax: 49 5251 66529. Office: dSPACE GmbH, Technologiepark 25, Paderborn 33100, Germany

SALES, BRUCE HOMER, intellectual property lawyer; b. Queens, N.Y., Dec. 16, 1955. BS, Rutgers U., 1977, MS, 1980; JD, Hofstra U., 1983. Bar: N.J., Calif., D.C., U.S. Patent Office. Assoc. Lyon & Lyon, L.A., 1983-85; ptnr. Lerner, David, Littenberg, Krumholz & Mentzik, Westfield, N.J., 1985—. Home: 82 Central Ave New Providence NJ 07974-2603 Office: Lerner David Littenberg Krumholz & Mentlik 600 South Ave W Ste 300 Westfield NJ 07090-1497

SALES, EUGENIO DE ARAUJO CARDINAL, archbishop; b. Acari, Brazil, Nov. 8, 1920; s. Celso Dantas and Josefa de A. Sales; student Seminary Fortaleza City. Ordained priest Roman Cath. Ch., 1943, consecrated bishop, 1954, elevated to cardinal, 1969; Sede Plena apostolic adminstr., Natal, 1962, Salvador, 1964; archbishop, Sao Salvador, 1968-71, Rio de Janeiro, 1971—; mem. Coun. of Cardinals and Bishops in the State Sec.-2d Sect.; mem. permanent coun. CNBB-Nat. Conf. of Bishops of Brazil. Mem. Congregations, for Divine Cult, clergy, Evangelization, Oriental Chs., Couns. for Social Comm. Editor: The Pastors Voice. Address: Rua da Gloria 446, CP 1362, 20241-150 Rio de Janeiro Brazil*

SALES, JAMES BOHUS, lawyer; b. Weimar, Tex., Aug. 24, 1934; s. Henry B. and Agnes Mary (Pesek) S.; m. Beuna M. Vornsand, June 3, 1956; children: Mark Keith, Debra Lynn, Travis James. BS, U. Tex., 1956, LLB with honors, 1960. Bar: Tex. 1960. Practiced in Houston, 1960—; sr. ptnr. Fulbright & Jaworski, 1960-00, head litig. dept., 1979-99. Author: Products Liability in Texas, 1985; co-author: Texas Torts and Remedies, 6 vols., 1986; assoc. editor Tex. Law Rev., 1960; contbr. articles to profl. jours. Trustee South Tex. Coll. Law, 1982-88, 90-01, A.A. White Dispute Resolution Ctr., 1991-94; bd. dirs. Tex. Resource Ctr., 1990-97, Tex. Bar Hist. Found., 1990-99; cir. chair for membership The Supreme Ct. Hist. Soc., 1998-2000. Named among Best Lawyers in Am., 1989-2000. Fellow Internat. Acad. Trial Lawyers, Am. Coll. Trial Lawyers (state chmn. 1993-96), Am. Bd. Trial Advocates, Am. Bar Found. (sustaining life, state chmn. 1993-98), Tex. Bar Found. (trustee 1991-95, vice-chmn. 1992-93, chmn. 1993-94, chair adv. bd. for planned giving 1994—, sustaining life mem.), Houston Bar Found. (sustaining life, chmn. bd. 1982-83); mem. ABA (ho. of dels. 1984—, mem. Commn. on IOLTA 1995-97), FBA, Internat. Assn. Def. Counsel, Nat. Conf. Bar Pres. (coun. 1989-92), So. Conf. Bar, So. Tex. Coll. Trial Advocacy (dir. 1983-87), State Bar Tex. (pres. 1988-89, bd. dirs. 1983-88, chmn. bd. 1985-86), Tex. Assn. Def. Counsel (v.p. 1977-79, 83-84), Tex. Law Rev. Assn. (bd. dirs. 1996—, pres. 1999-00), Houston Bar Assn. (officer, bd. dirs. 1970-79, pres.-elect 1979-80, pres. 1980-81), Gulf Coast Legal Found. (bd. dirs. 1982-85), Bar Assn. 5th Fed. Cir., The Forum, Westlake Club (bd. govs. 1980-85), Inns of Ct. (bd. dirs. 1981-84), Order of Coif. Roman Catholic. Home: 10803 Oak Creek St Houston TX 77024-3016 Office: Fulbright & Jaworski 1301 Mckinney St Houston TX 77010-3031

SALETTA, MARY ELIZABETH (BETTY), sculptor, rancher; b. Miami, Fla., Sept. 30, 1941; d. Earl Robert and Alta Florence Cotner; m. Albert Michael Saletta, July 1, 1959; children: Tia Suzanne, Kamber Ann. Graphic artist Moore Bus. Forms Inc., Modesto, Calif., 1960-67, Live Oak Pub. Co., Oakdale, Calif., 1977-80; freelance artist U.S. Forest Svc., Modesto Irrigation Dist., Stanislaus Schs., New Don Pedro Dam Project, Calif., 1967-77; sculptor Saletta Sculpture, Oakdale, 1980—; mem. adv. bd. Calif. State U. Coll. Arts, Letters and Sci., Turlock, 1999-2000; charter mem., dir. Downtown Arts Project, Modesto, 1992-96. One-woman shows City of Oakdale Redevel. Agy., 1990, Modesto C. of C., 1996; group shows include Calif. State U. Stanislaus, Turlock, 1986, Cowboy Artist Am. Mus., Kerrville, Tex., 1988, Benson Park Sculpture Garden, Loveland, Colo., 1989, 90, 93, Danada Sculpture Garden, Chgo., 1991, 93, Tucson Mus. Art, 1995; represented in permanent collections Tucson Mus. Art, Buckaroo Hall of Fame, cities of Modesto, Oakdale, Ripon, Calif., Stockton, Calif.; sculptures include life-size pub. sculptures Yesterday Is Tomorrow, 1991, Am. Graffiti, 1997, Stockton Firefighters Meml., 1998, World War II Meml., 1999. Recipient Excellence in Fine Art award Bank Am., Stockton, Calif., 1959, Best of Show award Western Art Roundup, Winnamucca, Nev., 1987, 88, Excellence in Visual Arts award Stanislaus Arts Coun., Modesto, 1999. Mem. Nat. League Am. Pen Women, Ctrl. Calif. Art League (advisor 1991, Best of Show award 1987), Rotary (bd. dirs. Oakdale 1997-99). Democrat. Avocations: horses, skiing, mountain climbing, fishing. Fax: 209-572-4089. E-mail: salettasculpture@aol.com. Home and Studio: 4255 Wellsford Rd Oakdale CA 95361-7930

SALEWSKI, MICHAEL, educator; b. Königsberg, Germany, Jan. 2, 1938; s. Martin Helmut and Ursula (Sammesreuther) S.; two children. PhD, U. Bonn, Germany, 1964; habilitation, U. Bonn, 1970. Wiss. asst. U. Bonn, 1965-70, privatdozent, 1970-71, apl. prof., 1971-76, prof., 1976-80; prof. U. Kiel, Germany, 1980—. Ranke-Gesellschaft Vorsitzender, 1984-2000. Recipient Ernst-Reuter-Preis, Bundesregierung, Berlin, 1988. Mem. Rotary Club Eckernförde. Office: Historisches Sem der CAU, Olshausenstr 40, 24098 Kiel Germany

SALGADO-GAMA, MARIA CLARA, educational consultant; b. Rio de Janeiro, Brazil, Sept. 10, 1947; d. Antonio Augusto and Maria Thereza (Cunha) Azevedo-Sodre; m. Jorio Salgado-Gama, July 11, 1970; children: Candida, Jorio. Student, Cath. U., Rio de Janeiro, 1967-69, BA in Edn., 1985; MEd, Lesley Coll., 1988; EdD, Columbia U., 1991. Presch. tchr. The Play Group, Caracas, Venezuela, 1982-83; presch. dir. The Christian Day Nursery, Caracas, 1983-85; presch. tchr. The Am. Sch., Brazilia, 1985-86, kindergarten tchr., 1986-87; cons. Brazil, 1987—; prof. grad. program Spl. Ed. Cath. U., Rio de Janeiro, 1992—; coord. gifted and talented The Am. Sch., Rio de Janeiro, 1991—. Scholar Conselho Nacional de Desenvoluimento e Pesquisa, 1988-91. Mem. Am. Edn1. Rsch. Assn., Coun. Exceptional Children. Home: Av Ruy Barbosa 830, Rio de Janeiro Brazil

SALGO, PETER LLOYD, internist, anesthesiologist, broadcaster, journalist, lecturer, consultant; b. N.Y.C., Nov. 9, 1949; s. Michael Nicholas and Ruth F. Salgo. BA, Columbia U., 1971, MD, 1975. Diplomate Am. Bd. Internal Meidicne, Am. Bd. Anesthesiology; lic. physician, N.Y., Calif., Mass.; instrument rated comml. pilot. Internal medicine intern Columbia Presbyn. Med. Ctr., N.Y.C., 1975-76, resident in internal medicine, 1976-78; vis. faculty fellow intensive care medicine and anesthesiology, dept. anesthesiology Columbia U., N.Y.C., 1979-81; lectr. Harvard Med. Sch., Boston; clin. prof. medicine and anesthesiology Columbia P&S; mem. staff in anesthesia and medicine Mass. Gen. Hosp., Boston; attending in anesthesia and internal medicine Presbyn. Hosp., N.Y.C., assoc. vice chmn. dept. anesthesiology, chmn. inter-I.C.U. com., assoc. dir. surg. ICU; host syndicated TV broadcase Healthcare 2000; aviation med. examiner FAA; comml. pilot Instrument Rated; host nat. radio med. program Sta. PRN, 1979-81; writer, producer, host med. info. broadcast Sta. WCBS-TV, N.Y.C., 1980—; med. corr. STA WCBS News, 1981—; syndicated CBS Network Newsfeed, 1981—; corr. CBS Network Radio News, 1982-92, host Healthtalk, 1982-88; med. corr. Sta. CNBC, 1989—, CNBC TV Network, 1989-93; host The Doctor Is In, Eyada.com., 2000—; cons. to networks on med. content of TV programs; corr. Patient Info. Network, 1989—; anchor Americas Vital Signs, CNBC TV Network; lectr. in field. Recipient Leonard Pullman award Columbia U., 1971, Blakesley award Am. Heart Assn., Journalism award Medic-alert Found., Honorable Mention in Journalism, UPI, Alumni Assn. medal Columbia U. P&S, 1975, Emmy award for excellence in broadcast journalism, Journalism award Lions Eye Found. Fellow ACP; mem. AAAS, AMA, AFTRA, N.Y. State Med. Soc., N.Y. County Med. Soc., Am. Soc. Anesthesiologists. Home: Apt 33A 200 W 60th St New York NY 10023-8511 Office: Presbyn Hosp Dept Anesthesiology New York NY 10032

SALIB, MAHER BADIE, civil engineer; b. Cairo, Jan. 25, 1934; s. Badie and Latifa (Salama) S. BSCE, U. Cairo, 1957. Bridge design engr. Ministry Communications, Alexandria, Egypt, 1957-61; chief engr. design and execution French Co. Fils Barte de Jin, 1961-63; mgr. major projects State Engring. Co., Cairo, 1963-71; gen. mgr. Engring. & Contractors Co., Cairo, 1972-78, Engring. Cons. Co., Cairo, 1978—; pres. Badie & Co. GmbH, Celle, Germany, 1980-93, Am. Internat. Cons. Inc., Washington, 1993—; chmn. bd. dirs. Hudig Badie Internat., Alexandria and Cairo; pres. Free Zones Engring. Co. Hudig-Badie Internat. At Free Zones Area, Amreya, Alexandria, Egypt. Mem. ASCE, Egyptian Soc. Engrs., Gezaret Sporting Club, Celler Tennis Vereiningung. Avocations: sport, tennis, cricket, horseback riding, travel. Home: 9 Amer St, Dokki Egypt Office: Badie & Co GmbH Am Internat Cons Inc 1050 17th St NW Ste 600 Washington DC 20036

SALIBA, GEORGE, Maltese government official. Rep. to UN Govt. of Malta, 1997—; amb. of Malta to U.S., 1999—, high commr. for Malta to Can., 2000—. Office: Embassy of Malta Permanent Mission Malta to UN 2017 Connecticut Ave NW Washington DC 20008-6195

SALIBA, RICARDO ELLERA, engineering company executive, consultant; b. Belo Horizonte, Brazil, Jan. 18, 1948; s. Alberto and Julieta (Ellera) S.; m. Cláudia Silva Araujo, Mar. 3, 1972; children: Tatiana, Juliana. BS, Pontificia Univ. Catolica, Brazil, 1971; postgrad., Pontificia Univ. Catolica, 1972, 76, 77, Assn. Diplomados de Guerra, 1998. Design supr. Empresa Brasileira de Projetos Industriais, Belo Horizonte, Brazil, 1971-74; mech. dept. mgr. Companhia Brasileira de Projetos Industrials, Belo Horizonte, Brazil, 1974-80, 84-91; project engring. mgr. Milder Kaiser, Rio de Janeiro, 1980-84; dir. Unitech Engenheiros e Consultores, Belo Horizonte, Brazil, 1991—; sec. commn. Brazilian Tech. Stds. Assn., Sao Paulo, 1978-80. Dir. studies's nucleus Logosophic Found., Belo Horizonte, 1989—. Recipient Enterprise Cooperation award Cobrapi, Brazil, 1987. Mem. ASME, Conselho Regional de Engenharia, Arquitetura e Agronomia-Minas Gerais, Associaçao Brasileira de Engenheiros Mecanicos-Minas Gerais, Brazilian Assn. Mech. Engrs. (counselor 1992—), Associaçao Brasileira de Normas Tecnicas. Avocations: music, jogging. Home: Rua Canaan 88 Apto 301, Belo Horizonte 30430550, Brazil Office: Unitech Engenheiros e Consultores Ltda, Rua Padre Marinho 37-9th Fl, Belo Horizonte 30140-040, Brazil

SALIBIAN, ALFREDO, physiological and environmental sciences scientist; b. Montevideo, Uruguay, July 24, 1937; arrived in Argentina, 1942; s. Nazareth and Lydia (Djebedjian) S.; m. Maria Sara Barrera-Vidal; children: Matias, Florencia. Degree in pharmacy, U. Buenos Aires, 1959, degree in biochemistry, 1962; PhD in Biology, U. Chile, 1975. Prof. Nat. U. Lujan, Argentina, 1974—, rsch. dir., 1977—. Contbr. articles to profl. jours. Recipient To Achievements in Sci. award Internat. Rotary Club, 1995. Mem. Toxicological Assn., Assn. Advanced Sci., Soc. Biology. Office: Nat U Lujan, CC 221, B6700ZBA Lujan Argentina

SALICRU, BRUNO, radiologist; b. Nimes, Gard, France, July 4, 1958; s. Robert and Jeanne (Latour) S.; m. Marie Laure Jacqueline, July 23, 1983; children: Helene, Romain. MD, Necker Enfants Malades, Paris, 1988. House physician Hosp. Mont Pellier, France, 1981-85, asst., 1985-90; radiologist Clinique du Mail, Grenoble, France, 1990—. Mem. French Soc. Radiology (v.p. 1997). Home: 1113 Ave Joliot Curie, 38920 Crolles Isere, France Office: Clinique du Mail, 43 ave Marie Raynoard, 38100 Grenoble France

SALIH, ABD AL-MUN'IM AHMAD, Iraqi government official; b. Baghdad, Iraq, 1943. Student, Elem Tchrs. Inst., Iraq, 1959, Mustansiriyah U., 1967; MA, Baghdad U., Iraq, PhD. Asst. sec.-gen. Islamic Conf. Orgn., Baghdad, Iraq; dean Islamic Scis. Coll.; minister Awqaf and religious affairs Govt. of Iraq, Baghdad, 1993—. Office: Min Awqaf Religious Affairs, N Gate St opp Coll Engring, Baghdad Iraq*

SALIH, ALI ABDALLAH, president of Republic of Yemen; b. 1942. Security chief Taiz Province, until 1978; dep. comdr.-in-chief Armed Forces, 1978, comdr-in-chief, 1978-90; pres. Govt. of Yemen Arab Republic, 1978-90, Govt. of Republic of Yemen, San'a, 1990—; mem. Provisional Presdl. Coun. Office: Presidential Palace, Zubiary St, Sana'a Yemen*

SALIH, MUSTAFA ABDALLA MOHAMED, pediatric neurologist, educator; b. Kosti, White Nile, Sudan, Jan. 5, 1950; arrived in Saudi Arabia, 1992; s. Abdalla Mohamed Salih and Noora Elhaj Saeed. B in Surgery, U. Khartoum (Sudan), 1974, M in Pediatrics & Child Health, 1980, MD, 1982; DMS, Uppsala (Sweden) U., 1990. Clin. rsch. fellow Regional Neurol. Ctr., Newcastle Upon Tyne, Eng., 1980-82; cons. pediatrician, neurologist U. Khartoum, 1982-92; fellow dept. neurophysiology Regional Neurol. Ctr., Newcastle Upon Tyne, 1986; fellow dept. pediatrics microbiology and immunology Uppsala U., 1985-90; prof. pediatrics U. Khartoum, 1990-92; prof. pediatrics, cons. neuropediatrician King Saud U., Riyadh, 1993—; head dept. pediatrics U. Khartoum, 1990-92; pres. sci. com. Nat. Expanded Program on Immunization, Sudan, 1990-92; mem. coll. of medicine rsch. ctr. bd. King Saud U., Riyadh, 1992-98. Editor: Sudanese Jour. of Paediatrics, 1985-92; contbr. articles to profl. jours. U. Khartoum grantee, 1982-92, Postdoctoral fellow Med. Rsch. Coun., Gt. Britain, 1986, Swedish Commn. for Tech. Coop. and Med. Rsch. Coun., 1984. Mem. AAAS, Internat. Child Neurology Assn., Sudan Assn. of Paediatricians, The World Fedn. of Neurology, The N.Y. Acad. of Scis., The World Muscle Soc., Intenrat. Child Neurology Assn. Avocations: poetry, history. Office: Divsn Pediatric Neurology, King Saud U PO Box 2925, Riyadh 11461, Saudi Arabia

SALIK, FOUAD YAQUB, computer and civil engineer; b. Lahore, Punjab, Pakistan, Mar. 3, 1968; s. Muhammed Yaqub and Sajida Yaqub (Muzaffar) S. Fellow of Sci., Pakistan Internat. Coll., Riyadh, Saudi Arabia, 1985; BSCE, Purdue U., 1988, MSCE, 1990. Registered profl. engr., Pakistan. Mng. ptnr., CEO Cemcon Engrs., Lahore, Pakistan, 1993-95; design engr. Descon Engring., Lahore, 1990-93, design mgr., 1995—. Developer computer software for structural steel design. Mem. Pakistan Engring. Coun. (life), Chi Epsilon (life). Avocations: personal computers, reading, stamp collecting. Home: New Garden Town, 176/A Ahmed Block, Punjab Lahore 54600, Pakistan

SALIKHOV, KEV MINULLINOVICH, physicist; b. Krasnaya Rechka, Russia, Nov. 3, 1936; s. Minulla Salikhovich and Farhizihan Davletgareevna S.; m. Zoya Vasiljevna Shapochanskaya, July 8, 1963; children: Assia, Akim. Degree in Physics, Univ., Kazan, 1959; Degree in Science, Inst. High Molecular Compounds, Leningrad, Russia, 1963. Asst. prof. Polytechnical Inst., Karaganda, 1963; jr. rschr. IChKC, Novosibizsk, Russia, 1963-65, rschr., 1965-69, sr. rschr., 1969-86, main rschr., 1986-88; dir. Physical Tech. Inst. RAS, Kazan, Russia, 1988—; prof. Novosibirsk U., 1980-88, Univ., Kazan, 1989—. Author: (book) Electron Spin Echo and It's Applications, 1976, Spin Exchange, 1980, Spin Polarization and Magnetic Effects in Radical Reactions, 1984; editor (jour.) Applied Magnetic Resonance, 1990—. V.p. Tatarstan Acad., 1992—; vice chmn. Kazan Sci. Ctr. Russia Acad. Scis., 1990—. Recipient Lenin prize Govt. USSR, 1986, Tatarstan state prize, 1998, Gold medal Internat. Soc. Electron Paramagnetic Resonance, 1996; named Honored Scientist of Russia Pres. Russia, 1995. Fellow Wissenschafts Kolleg Zu Berlin; mem. Tatarstan Acad. Scis., Russia Acad. Scis. (corr. 1997—). Avocations: reading books, fishing, songs, gathering mushrooms. Home: Lesgaft Str. 28-15, 420043 Kazan Russia Office: Kazan Physical Tech. Inst., Sibirsky Trakt 10/7, 420029 Kazan Russia

SALIM, KASIM ABDUL, medical educator, researcher; b. Quilon, Kerala, India, Dec. 16, 1939; s. Pitcha Adima Kasim and Fathima Beevi; m. Sayyadu Fathima Salim, Nov. 14, 1962; children: Shafeek, Refeek, Ashik, Sajik. MB, BS, Trivandrumm (India) Med. Coll., 1961, MD, 1966. Tutor in medicine Trivandrum Med. Coll., 1965-68; asst. prof. medicine Kottayam (India) Med. Coll., 1968-80; assoc. prof. Calicut (India) Med. Coll., 1980-90, prof., 1990-95, chmn. dept., 1992-95; prof. King Saud U. Coll. Medicine (now King Khalid U.), Abha, Saudi Arabia, 1995—. Contbr. articles to med. jours., including Blood, Jour. Assn. Physicians India, Gastrointestinal Endoscopy, Excerpta Medica. Fellow ACP, Royal Coll. Physicians (London), Royal Coll. Pathologists (London); mem. Am. Soc. for Hematology, Brit. Soc. for Hematology. Islam. Avocations: photography, fine arts, games. E-mail: Salimka00@yahoo.com. Home: Lestershine MM Rd, Kerala Calicut 673004, India Office: King Khalid U Coll Medicine, PO Box 641, Abha Saudi Arabia

SALIM, SALIM AHMED, government official of Tanzania; b. Zanzibar, Jan. 23, 1942; s. Ahmed Salim Ali and Maryam Ali Ahmed; m. Amne Ali Rifai, Apr. 17, 1964. Cert., Lumumba Coll., Zanzibar, 1960; corr. study, U. Delhi, India, 1965-67; M of Internat. Affairs, Columbia U., 1975. Founder, 1st v.p. All Zanzibar Students Union; also sec.-gen. of youth movement, 1960; dep. chief rep. Zanzibar Office, Havana, Cuba, 1961-62; chief editor Zanzibar daily paper; also sec.-gen. All Zanzibar Journalists Rogn., 1963; ambassador to United Arab Republic, Cairo, 1964-65; high commr. to India, 1965-68; dir. African and Mid. East affairs divsn. Tanzania Min. Fgn. Affairs, 1968-69; ambassador to People's Rep. China, Dem. People's Rep. Korea, 1969; permanent rep. to UN, N.Y.C., 1970-80; pres. UN Security Coun., 1976, UN Gen. Assembly, 1979-80; also ambassador to Cuba; high commr. to Guyana, 1970-80, Barbados, 1971-80, Jamaica, 1971-80, Trinidad-Tobago, 1971-80; min. fgn. affairs Tanzania, 1980-84, prime min., 1984-85, dep. prime min., 1985-89, min. def. and nat. svc., 1985-90; chmn. UN Com. on Decolonisation, 1972-75, UN Security Coun. Com. on Sanctions against South Rhodesia, 1975—; sec. gen. Orgn. African Unity, 1989—. Mem. Tanganyika African Nat. Union and Afro-Sshirazi party. Office: Orgn African Unity Gen Secretariat, POB 3243, Addis Ababa Ethiopia

SALIMATH, PARAMAHANS VEERAYYA, food science and technology researcher; b. Mortgi, Karnataka, India, Nov. 18, 1954; s. Veerayya Veerabhadrayya and Veerawwa (Hiremath) S.; m. Bharathi Paramahans Bharathi,

Mar. 22, 1958; 1 child, Sangam P. BSc, Karnataka U., Dharwad, India, 1975; MSc, K.U.D., Dharwad, India, 1977; PhD, U. Mysore, India, 1981. Rsch. fellow Cen. Food Tech. Rsch. Inst., Mysore, 1978-81, scientist, 1984—; postdoctoral fellow Max Planck Inst., Freiburg, Germany, 1981-83; rsch. assoc. Harvard Med. Sch., Boston, 1992, Cancer Rsch. Found., La Jolla, Calif., 1993. Contbr. articles to profl. jours. Mem. Soc. of Biological Chemists India (pres. Mysore chpt. 1997-98), Assn. Microbiologists India. Home: #52 14th Cross A Block, JP Nagar, Mysore Karnataka 570008, India Office: CFTRI Dept, Biochem/Applied Nutrition, Mysore Karnataka 570013, India

SALIMONU, LEKAN SAMUSA, immunologist, researcher; b. Ibadan, Oyo, Nigeria, Mar. 31, 1939; s. Salimonu Aremu and Rabiatu Ayoka (Alagboofe) Bello; m. Sikirat Idowu Adelaja; children: Dipo, Toyosi Tunde-Akintunde, Funmi Soluade. Assoc. degree, Bromley Tech. Coll., Surrey, Eng., 1964; degree, Paddington Tech. Coll., London, 1966; MSc, Meml. U. Newfoundland, St. John's, 1976; PhD, U. Ibadan, 1980. Med. lab. scientist Queen Mary's Hosp., London, 1965-67; sr. med. lab. sci. Univ. Coll. Hosp., Ibadan, 1967-74; rsch. fellow U. Ibadan, 1976-79, sr. lectr., 1980-82, assoc. prof., 1983-89, prof., 1990—; cons. WHO, Nairobi, Kenya, 1973, project dir., Ibadan, 1990—; dir. immunology unit U. Ibadan, 1988—, dir. dept. chem. pathology, 1997—. Author: Contemporary Issues in Clinical Nutrition, 1986, Nutrition and Immunity, 1992; editor African Jour. Medicine and Med. Scis., 1992. Pres. Oktoba Club of Nigeria, Ibadan, 1975—. Fellow Can. Internat. Devel. Agy., 1974-76, UN Univ., 1986, WHO, New Delhi, 1993. Mem. Nigerian Soc. for Immunology, Internat. Union Immunological Socs., Assn. Clin. Chemists of Nigeria. Avocations: stamp collecting, photography, gardening, table tennis, reading. Home: Via Bodija, 5 Salimonu St Kongi Layout, Ibadan Nigeria Office: U Coll Hosp Coll Medicine, Dept Chem Pathology, PMB 5116 Ibadan Nigeria

SALIMULLAH, MOHAMMAD, physics educator, researcher; b. Dhaka, Bangladesh, Jan. 5, 1949; s. Mohammad Ahsanullah and Musammat Amirunessa; m. Quamrun Nahar Mily, Sept. 24, 1976; children: Rakish, Bipasha, Barsha. BSc with honors, U. Dhaka, 1970, MSc, 1973; PhD in Physics, Indian Inst Tech., Delhi, 1980; postdoc., Imperial Coll., London, 1983-84; postgrad., The Abdus Salam Internat. Ctr. for Theoretical Physics, Trieste, Italy, 1983-97, Nat. Inst. Fusion Sci., Nagoya, Japan, 1994, U. Calif. San Diego, 1998, Max Planck Inst., 2000, Ruhr Univ., Bochum, 2000, U. St. Andrews, Scotland, 2000. Rsch. fellow U. Dhaka, 1974-75; lectr. physics Jahangirnagar U., Dhaka, 1975-80, asst. prof., 1980-85, assoc. prof., 1985-88, prof., 1988—, chmn. dept., 1992-94, dean Faculty Sci., 1986-88. Contbr. over 150 articles to internat. sci. jours., including Phys. Rev., Physics Letters, Jour. Applied Physics. Recipient H.P. Roy gold medal U. Dhaka, 1981, joint award Bangladesh Acad. of Sci. and Third World Acad. of Sci., Trieste, 1986, Univ. Grants Commn. award, 1988, Kharazmi internat. prize, Iran, 1994; rsch. scholar Indian Inst. Tech., 1976-80. Mem. Bangladesh Phys. Soc. (life), Bangladesh Asn. for Advancement Sci. (life). Office: Jahangirnagar U/B-30 Staff, Quarters/Dept Physics, Dhaka 1342, Bangladesh

SALIN, JARL-GUNNAR, researcher; b. Åbo, Finland, Sept. 15, 1943; s. Jarl and Elsa (Lindroos) S.; m. Frid Solveig Hansen, Oct. 29, 1966; children: Peter, Helena. MSc in Engring., Åbo Akademi U., 1966, License in Sci. in Engring., 1973, D in Engring., 1990, docent in drying tech., 1993. Tchg. and rsch. asst. Å Akademi U., 1965-68; tech. cons. Ekono Corp., Helsinki, Finland, 1969-93; free-lance tech. cons. Esbo, Finland, 1993-95; sr. rschr. Trätek-Swedish Inst. Wood Tech. Rsch., Stockholm, 1996—; tchr. Swedish Inst. Tech., Helsinki, 1995. Contbr. articles to profl. jours.; patentee in field. Office: Trätek Swedish Inst Wood, PO Box 5609, S-11486 Stockholm Sweden

SALINGER, FRANK MAX, lawyer; b. Landau, Isar, Germany, Dec. 4, 1951; s. Karl and Ingeborg F. (Herold) S.; m. Susan Ann Wagner, May 20, 1978. Student, Columbia Union Coll., Takoma Park, Md., 1969-72; JD, U. Balt., 1975. Bar: Md. 1975, U.S. Dist. Ct. Md. 1975, U.S. Ct. Appeals (4h cir.) 1978, U.S. Tax Ct. 1978, U.S. Ct. Mil. Appeals 1978, U.S. Ct. Appeals (5th cir.) 1982, U.S. Supreme Ct. 1983, U.S. Ct. Appeals (11th cir.) 1984, U.S. Ct. Appeals (9th cir.) 1986, D.C. 1986, U.S. Ct. Appeals (3d cir.) 1989. Pvt. practice Balt., 1975-77; counsel Md. State Senate, Annapolis, 1975-76; assoc. counsel Am. Fin. Corp., Silver Spring, Md., 1977-78; govt. rels. counsel Truck Trailer Mfrs. Assn., Washington, 1978-80; v.p., gen. counsel, dir. govt. affairs Am. Fin. Svcs. Assocs., Washington, 1980-92; v.p. govt. rels. Advanta Corp., Wilmington, Del., 1992—. Co-author: (with Alvin O. Wiese and Robert E. McKew) A Guide to the Consumer Bankruptcy Code, 1989; (with Robert W. Green) State Regulations and Statutes on Consumer Credit, 1989, Federal Consumer Credit Regulations and Statutes, 1989. City councilman, Laurel, Md., 1976-78, zoning commr., 1976-78; chmn. Md. State Young Reps., 1977-78; bd. dirs. Am. Bankruptcy Inst., Washington, 1986-88. Mem. ABA (mem. com. on consumer fin. svcs., subcoms. on interest rate regulation and state regulation), Am. League Lobbyists (chair fin. svcs. sect. 1995-97), Federalist Soc. Law and Pub. Policy, Woodmore Country Club, Capitol Hill Club, Ford's Theatre Soc. Republican. Lutheran. Office: Advanta Corp One Righter Pkwy Wilmington DE 19803

SALINGER, JEROME DAVID, author; b. N.Y.C., Jan. 1, 1919; s. Sol and Miriam (Jillich) S.; m. Claire Douglas, 1953 (div. 1967); children: Margaret Ann, Matthew. Student, Valley Forge Mil. Acad., Columbia U. Author: Catcher in the Rye, 1951, Nine Stories, 1953, Franny and Zooey, 1961, Raise High the Roof Beam, Carpenters; and Seymour: An Introduction, 1963; contbr. stories to New Yorker mag. Sgt. AUS, 1942-46. Address: care Harold Ober Assocs 425 Madison Ave New York NY 10017-1110

SALINO, JEFFREY ALAN, leasing executive; b. Reading, Pa., Aug. 6, 1960; s. Joseph Frank and Lorraine Helen (Rathgeber) S.; m. Teresa Kathleen Nowak, Oct. 20, 1984; children: Sarah Eileen, Gregory Joseph, Timothy Andrew. Student, U. Vienna, 1980-81; BA in Polit. Sci. and Germanic Lang., George Washington U., 1983. Cert. comml. investment mem. Devel. asst. Stout & Teague Cos., Washington, 1983-85; dir. renewal leasing Greenhoot, Inc., Washington, 1985-87; v.p., regional leasing mgr. Heitman Properties, Arlington, Va., 1987-97; leasing and mktg. mgr. Compass Mgmt. and Leasing, 1997-98; city mgr. site acqusition Winstar Communications, Washington, 1998—. Mem. Greater Washington Comml. Assn. Realtors (comml. leasing com. 1983—), Cert. Comml. Investment Mems. (v.p. Md./D.C. chpt. 1995), Nat. Assn. Realtors, Soc. for Preservation and Encouragement of Barbershop Quartet Singing in Am. (chpt. sec. 1985-86), Internat. Brotherhood Magicians. Republican. Avocations: magic, choral singing, music, travel. Home: 7867 Vervain Ct Springfield VA 22152-3108 Office: 1850 M St NW Ste 1100 Washington DC 20036-5803

SALISBURY, EUGENE W., lawyer, justice; b. Blasdell, N.Y., Mar. 20, 1933; s. W. Dean and Mary I. (Burns) S.; m. Joanne M. Salisbury, July 14, 1950; children: Mark, Ellen, Susan, David, Scott. BA in History and Govt. cum laude, U. Buffalo, 1959, JD cum laude, 1968. Bar: N.Y. 1960, D.C. 1973, U.S. Dist. Ct. (we. and no. dists.) 1961, U.S. Ct. Appeals (2d cir.) 1970, U.S. Ct. Appeals (D.C. cir.) 1973, U.S. Supreme Ct. 1973. Ptnr. Lipsitz, Green, Fahringer, Roll, Salisbury and Cambria, Buffalo, 1960—; justice Village of Blasdell, 1961—; lectr. N.Y. Office Ct. Adminstrn., N.Y.C., 1961—; mem. N.Y. State Commn. on Jud. Conduct, 1989—, chmn., 2000—. Author: Manual for N.Y. Courts, 1973, Forms for N.Y. Courts, 1977. Capt. U.S. Army, 1948-54, Korea. Decorated Bronze Star, Purple Heart; recipient Citizen of Yr. award IRRA, 2000. Mem. ABA (del. spl. ct. sect. 1988—), D.C. Bar Assn., Erie County Bar Assn., N.Y. State Bar Assn., World Judges Assn., N.Y. State Magistrates Assn. (pres. 1973, Man of Yr. 1974), N.Y. State Jud. Conf. (chmn. 2000—), Upstate N.Y. Labor Adv. Council, 1995—. Office: Lipsitz Green Fahringer Roll Salisbury and Cambria 42 Delaware Ave Ste 300 Buffalo NY 14202-3857

SALISBURY, JONATHAN RICHARD, histopathologist, educator, consultant; b. Birmingham, Eng., June 25, 1956; s. George Richard and Patricia Doreen (Jones) S.; m. Alyson Frances Bumby, May 20, 1984; children: Elizabeth, Joseph. BSc, U. Coll., London, 1977, MB BS, 1980; MD, King's Coll., London, 1993. Sr. lectr. histopathology King's Coll., London, 1987-96, reader, 1997—, clin. dir., 1997—. Co-author, editor: Diseases of Bones and Joints, 1994, Molecular Pathology, 1997. Fellow Royal Coll. Pathologists; mem. Internat. Soc. for Diagnostic Quantitative Pathology (sec. 1992-96, treas. 1996-2000). Home: 32 Lillieshall Rd, London SW4 0LP, England Office: Kings Coll London, Bessemer Rd, London SE5 9PJ, England

SALJINSKA-MARKOVIC, OLIVERA T., oncology researcher, educator; b. Skopje, Macedonia; d. Trajko and Radmila; m. Nenad Markovic, July 9, 1961; 2 children. MD, Med. Faculty, Skopje, 1962; PhD, Med. Faculty, Belgrade, 1977; Specialist Med. Biochemistry, U. Kiril and Metodij, Skopje, 1969. Asst. prof. Med. Faculty, Skopje, 1964-79, assoc. prof., 1979-84; dir. clin. lab. U. Children's Hosp., Skopje, 1974-84; sr. rsch. assoc. Pa. State U., State College, 1984-85; sr. fellow U. Pa., Phila., 1985-88; prof. U. Belgrade, 1988-93; adj. prof. Med. Coll. of Pa., 1993-95; vis. scientist NIAMDD, NIH, Bethesda, 1976-77; vis. scientist Am. Type Culture Collection, Rockville, Md., 1995-96; dir. BioSciCon, Md., 1996—; primarius Univ. Children's Hosp., Skopje, 1983-86; head lab. for rsch. and devel., Clin. Ctr., Belgrade, 1990-93; mem. exam. com., State of Macedonia, 1980-90; adj. prof. U. Md. U. Coll., 1998, Am. U., Washington, 1999—; vis. prof. Georgetown U., Washington, 2000—. Author: Quantitative Cytoch of Enzymes, 1986; contbr. articles to profl. jours., publs. Postdoctoral intern rsch. fellowship Fogarty Internat. Ctr., NIH, Bethesda, 1971-73; recipient several rsch. grants NIH, Pharm. Co., 1984-95. Mem. Histochem. Soc., Am. Assn. Clin. Chem., N.Y. Acad. Scis., Am. Assn. Cell Biology. Achievements include inosinic acid dehydrogenase assay patent; new concept for the reversal of multidrug resistance of cancer cells to antineoplast; novel methods for cancer diagnosis and treatment. Office: BioSciCon Inc Rockville MD 20852

SALK, SUNG-HO SUCK, physics educator and researcher; b. Seoul, Korea, Apr. 14, 1939; s. Chin Sung and Jung Ja Kim Salk; m. Jung-Ja Yeon, Mar. 31, 1968; children: Tom Sang-Tae, Bob Sangki. Student, Seoul Nat. U., 1961-64; BS, Midwestern U., Wichita Falls, Tex., 1966; MS, U. Houston, 1968; PhD, U. Tex., 1972. Rsch. assoc. U. Tex., Austin, 1972-77; from asst. prof. rsch. to assoc. prof. rsch. U. Mo., Rolla, 1977-88; prof. Pohang U. Sci. and Tech., 1988—; internat. adv. mem. Internat. Conf. on Atmospheric Sci. and Air Quality, 1988; organizing com. chmn. Asian Internat. Seminar on Atomic and Molecular Physics, 1994—; conf. chmn. 15h Korean Solid State Physics Conf., 1993; co-chmn. 2d Internat. Conf. New Theories, Discoveries and Applications Superconductors and Related Materials, Las Vegas, 1999. Contbr. more than 200 articles to sci. jours. and procs. Rsch. grantee NSF, 1980-82, 83-86, 88-90. Mem. Am. Phys. Soc., Korean Acad. Sci. and Tech., Phi Kappa Phi. Home: Postech Kyosso Apt 4-1104, Pohang 790-784, Republic of Korea Office: Pohang U Sci and Tech, Dept Physics, Pohang 790-784, Republic of Korea

SALLAGAR, WALTER HERMANN, musician, educator; b. Vienna, Austria, May 27, 1935; s. Hermann Theodor F.M.L. and Sidonie (Kiendler) S.; m. Susanne Nitsch, Dec. 21, 1969 (div. 1986); children: Claudia Maria, Gabriella Konstanze, Valerie Elisabeth. Diploma, Music Acad., Vienna, 1960; degree in philosophy, U. Vienna, 1960. Bassoon soloist Vienna Baroque, 1956-62; bassoonist NOe Tonkünstler, Vienna, 1959-92; bassoonist, founder Eichendorff Quintet, Vienna, 1960-75; bassoon tchr. J. Haydn Conservatory, Eisenstadt, Austria, 1974-95; repair technician Fox Products Corp., Ind., 1989—; dir. Breiteneich Courses, Austria, 1970-85; mem. jury Internat. Competition, Colmar, France, 1970-80; pres. Haydn Fonds, Vienna, 1982-95; leader Fagottissimo workshop, 1972—; organizer ann. event Aguarell and Music, Bavaria, 1999—. Editor: Heinrichshofen's Verlag, Breiteneich Bote, 1979-86. Recipient Silver Hon. medal Govt. Lower Austria, Vienna, 1981. Mem. Bassoon Club (Vienna) (founder), Nat. Orgn. Profl. Band Instruments, Bassoon Festival at Pecs (Hungary). Roman Catholic. Avocations: natural science, horses. Office: Bassoon Club Vienna, 42 Neulinggasse, A-1030 Vienna Austria

SALLAH, AHMED SABAH, hematologist; b. Aleppo, Syria, Sept. 19, 1961; came to U.S., 1991; s. Aboud Al Jalil and Choukrie (Mardini) S. MD, Aleppo U., 1984. Rsch. asst. prof. U. N.C., Chapel Hill, 1996-97; asst. prof. medicine East Carolina U., Greenville, N.C., 1997-99, U. Tenn., Memphis, 1999—; dir. coagulation lab. U. Tenn., Memphis, 1999—; regional adv. bd. Roune Poulene Rhorer, Memphis, 1997—; sci. adv. bd. East Carolina U., Greenville, 1997-99. Recipient CD-Rom award Temple U., Phila., 1993, Scientist award East Carolina U., 1998. Mem. AAAS, Am. Soc. Hematology, N.Y. Acad. Scis., Internat. Soc. for the Study of Comparative Oncology (sci. cons. 1999—). Avocations: sports, tennis. Office: Univ Tenn 3 N Dunlap Fl 3 Memphis TN 38163-0001

SALLAH, MAJEED (JIM SALLAH), real estate developer; b. Boston, Aug. 5, 1920; s. Herbert K. and Rose (Karem) S. Student, Gloucester (Mass.) pub. schs.; m. Aline C. Powers, Apr. 10, 1970; children: Christopher M., Melissa Rose. Pres., dir. Glo-Bit Fish Co., Gloucester, 1947-48, Live-Pak of Ohio, Inc., 1947-51, Cape Ann Glass Co., Inc., Gloucester, 1950-72, Cape Ann Realty Corp., Gloucester, 1961—, Marias Restaurant, Gloucester, 1960—; pres., treas., dir. Gloucester Hot-Top Constrn. Co., Gloucester, 1967-75; pres., bd. dirs. SGF Corp., Gloucester, 1983-85, SALFAD, Inc. Rossford, Ohio; pres., treas. Points East, Inc.; trustee Christopher Investment Trust; bd. dirs. Lutsal, Inc.; bd. dirs., ptnr. Barsal, Inc., Toledo, Ohio, Hamsal, Inc., Toledo. Pres. Lebanese-Am. Bus. Men's Club; treas. Lebanese-Maronite Soc. With U.S. Army, 1942-45. Decorated Bronze Star. Mem. Gloucester Assocs., Cape Ann Investment Corp., Am. Legion, Amvets, Gloucester Fraternity Assn., Order Ky. Cols. (hon.), Lions, Elks, Moose. Roman Catholic. Home and Office: PO Box 78 56 Hilltop Rd Gloucester MA 01931-0078

SALLAI, GYULA, communications executive, educator; b. Budapest, Hungary, June 30, 1945; s. Gyula and Jolan (Lukacs) S.; m. Maria Matáé; 1 child, Kinga. MSc in Elec. Engring., Budapest Tech. U., 1968, DrUniv, 1973; PhD, Hungarian Acad. Scis., 1976, DSc, 1989, habilitation, 1997. Asst. Budapest Tech. U., 1968-75; chief rschr. Rsch. Inst. Hungarian PTT, 1975-83, dir., 1984-90; strategic exec. dir. MATAV Hungarian Telecomms. Co., 1991-93, dep. CEO, 1993-95; v.p. internat. Comm. Authority, Hungary, 1995-98; exec. v.p. Comm. Authority, 1998—; hon. prof. Tech. U., 1990-97, part-time prof., 1997—. Author, editor: Traffic Planning of Telecom Networks, 1980, Scientific Overview of Telecommunications, 1988; editor PKI Revs., 1985-95; contbr. articles to profl. jours. Recipient L. Eötvös award Hungarian Govt., 1979, G. Békésy award Hungarian PTT, 1983, Pro Comm. award Ministry for Transp. and Comm., 1998, G. Baross award Ministry for Transp. and Comm., 2000. Mem. IEEE (assoc.), Sci. for Telecom (assoc., v.p. 1996—, T. Puskas award 1994). Home: Komocsy u 50, Budapest Hungary H-1141 Office: Comm Authority, Ostrom u 23-25, Budapest Hungary H-1015

SALLAM, ISMAIL AWAD-ALLAH, government official; b. Monoufeya, Egypt, July 21, 1941. Diploma in surgery, Ain Shams U.; PhD, Glasgow U., 1955. Prof., head dept. heart surgery Ain Shams U., 1992—; head health & population com. Shura Consultative Coun., 1992—; min. Health & Population. Office: Min Health, Sharia Magles al-Sha'ab St, Cairo Egypt*

SALLAY, PETER, chemistry educator; b. Budapest, Hungary, Apr. 28, 1942; s. Janos and Janosne (Galfi Ilona) S.; m. Peterne Horvath, June 29, 1965 (wid. 1988); children: Peter, Agnes. MS, Tech. U., Budapest, 1965, PhD, 1981, Habil., 1995. Asst. prof. Tech. U., Budapest, 1965-87, assoc. prof., 1988-98, prof., 1998—. Author: Handbook of Unif Processes, 1979; inventor in field; contbr. articles to profl. jours. Avocations: history, cactus, succulent. Office: Tech U Org Chem Tech Dept, Muegyetem RKP 3, 1111 Budapest Hungary

SALLEO, FERDINANDO, Italian diplomat; b. Messina, Oct. 2, 1936; s. Carmelo and Maria Carla Stagno d'Alcontres; m. Anne Marie Riegler; children: Carmelo, Alberto. LLD, U. Rome, 1959. Enlisted Italian Fgn. Svc., Washington, 1960—; appt. to Paris, N.Y., Prage, Washington and Bonn, Germany; dir. gen. of devel. cooperation Ministry Fgn. Affairs, 1981-86; dir. gen. of econ. affairs Ministry of Fgn. Affairs, 1988; amb. OECD, Paris, 1986-88; amb. Soviet Union, 1989-93; dir. gen. polit. affairs Ministry of Fgn. Affairs, 1993, sec. gen., 1994-95; amb. of Italy to the U.S. Washington, 1995—; vis. prof. U. Florence, 1982-84; prof. Rome U. LUISS, 1985-87. Recipient Grand Cross of Order of Merit of Italian Republic, 1993. Office: Embassy of Italy 1601 Fuller St NW Washington DC 20009-5699

SALLES, CHRISTIAN, food scientist; b. Paris, Dec. 13, 1960; s. Ernest and Lucienne (Gontier) S.; m. Sylvie Helene Dupain, May 15, 1993. BS, St. Michel des Batignolles, Paris, 1979; lic. in biochemistry, U. Paris 7, 1982, M Biochemistry, 1983; D Biochemistry, U. Scis. and Techs. Languedoc, Montpellier, France, 1989. Rschr. Institut. Nat. de la Recherche Agronomique, Dijon, France, 1990—. Roman Catholic. Avocation: choral singing. Office: INRA LRSA, 17 rue Sully BV 1540, 21034 Dijon Cedex France

SALLES, GILLES, medical educator; b. Sainte-Foy-les-Lyon, France, Mar. 29, 1961; s. Jean Salles and Simone Lantieri; m. Barbara Widmer, 1992; 1 child, Simon. MD, U. Claude Bernard, Lyon, France, 1984, PhD, 1994. French Bd. cert. in internal medicine. Fellow Lyon U. Hosps., 1984-89; postdoctoral fellow Dana Farber Cancer Inst. Harvard Med. Sch., Boston, 1990-92; asst. prof. U. Claude Bernard, Lyon, 1992-96, prof. medicine, 1996—; dir. rsch. unit pathology of lymphoid cells U. Claude Bernard, Lyon, 1996—; pres. Group Etudes Lymphemes Adulte Sci. Com., France, 1997—. Contbr. articles to profl. jours. Avocation: movies. Fax: 33 478 86 65 68. E-mail: gilles.salles@chu-lyon.fr. Office: Svc Hematol Ctr Hosp Lyon S, Chemin du Grand Revoyet, Pierre Benite 69495, France

SALLMÉN, BJÖRN GUNNAR CHRISTIAN, research psychologist; b. Lund, Skåne, Sweden, Aug. 7, 1964; s. Gunnar Bertil and Gerd Eivor Hanna (Magnusson) S.; m. Susanne Monica Lück Apr. 7, 1990; children: Rebecka, Sebastian. B in Social Sci., Lund (Sweden) U., 1989, M in Social Sci., 1991, PhD, 1998. Cert. psychotherapist, rschr. and project mgr. Tchr. Lund Grammar Schs., 1984-86; emergency ward staff Clinic of Alcohol Diseases, Malmö, Sweden, 1986—; rsch. asst. Dept. Clin. Alcohol and Drug Rsch., Malmö, 1990-93; project mgr. Nat. Bd. Instnl. Care, Hvvr, Sweden, 1994-98; rsch. psychologist Nat. Bd. Instnl. Care, Stockholm, 1994—; Swedish rsch. ptnr. BIOMED II, Maastricht, 1996—; psychiat. cons. Karlsvik Rehab. Ctr., Höör; internat. trainer BIOMED II, Maastricht. Author: Compulsory Treatmentof Alcoholics: Psychiatric Comorbidity, Psychological Characterictics: Coercive Experiences and Outcome, 1998; contbr. articles to profl. jours.; composer, prodr. (music records) Idéernas Bankrutt, 1985, Journey Through a Damaged Mind, 1997. Bd. mem. Grammar Sch., Lund, 1996—. Sgt. Swedish Army, 1984-85. Recipient award for sci. and pedagocical presentation Swedish Affiliation Med. Doctors, Stockholm, 1996. Avocations: composer (multi-instrumentalist), record producer, collector of Rock-n-Roll memorabilia, multimedia production. E-mail: bjorn.salmen@swipnet.se. Fax: 46 413 29 750. Home: Kvarnstensvdgen 63, S-24336 Höör Skåne, Sweden Office: Karlsvik Rehab Ctr, Box 198, S-24323 Hö öR Skane, Sweden

SALLOWAY, JOSEPHINE PLOVNICK, school psychologist, marriage and family therapist, mental health counselor, psychology educator, college counselor; b. Brookline, Mass., July 30, 1944; d. Isadore B. and Gladys J. (Press) Plovnick; m. Richard B. Salloway, July 4, 1967; 1 child, Matthew. AB in History, Boston U., 1965, EdM in Counseling, 1966; Cert. in Human Resource Mgmt., Bentley Coll., 1980. Cert. sch. psychologist, sch. adjustment counselor, History Soc. Studies tchr.; lic. mental health counselor, lic. marriage and family therapist; nat. cert. psychologist. Counselor Boston Pub. Schs., 1966-78; counselor/sch. psychologist ednl. enrichment program Milton (Mass.) Acad., 1970-71; sch. psychologist Braintree (Mass.) Pub. Schs., 1983-89; sch. psychologist/sch. adjustment counselor Norwood Pub. Schs., 1990-92; sch. adjustment counselor Stoughton, Mass., 1993, 94; consulting sch. psychologist Waltham (Mass.) Schs., 1997—; pvt. practice Braintree, 1997—; mem. faculty psychology and child devel. Quincy (Mass.) Coll., 1997—, head counselor student support advisor, 1997—; mem. faculty psychology and early childhood edn. and devel. Massassoit C.C., 1999—; mem. faculty Program for Advancement of Learning (PAL) Curry Coll., 1999, mem. faculty psychology, 2000—, diagnostic tchr. Edn. and Diagnostic Ctr., 1999—; field supr. dept. counselor edn. Harvard U., Cambridge, Mass., Northeastern U., Boston; del. Coastline Coun. for Children, Mass., 1985—; psychometrist Mass. Gen. Hosp., Boston; asst. coord. Boston U. Counseling Clinic; diagnostic tchr. Braintree, Mass., 1999—, Mass. Edn. Reform, Tutor, Canton Pub. Schs., 2000—; mem. edn. reform Mass. Comprehensive Assessment Sys., 2000—. Pub. dir. Curtain Call Theatre, 1997; contbg. editor Gazette newsletter, 1996—. Class agt. Boston U. Alumni Assn., 1996—; ednl. dir. House of Worship, Braintree, 1994—; del. Braintree Fair Housing Commn., 1994—, Braintree Multicultural Com., 1994—; pres., bd. chmn. Cmty. Friends for Human Svcs., Inc., Boston, 1995—, chmn. edn. bd.; vol. Genesis Fund Telethon. Recipient Presdl. award Cmty. Friends for Human Svcs., Inc., 1996-97, svc. award, 1998, 99, Senatorial award, 1998; award for contbn. to svcs. for children Mass. Soc. for Prevention Cruelty to Children, 1998, 99, Senatorial award for outstanding contbn. to mental health Mass. Senate, 1998. Mem. ACA (clin.), NASP, Am. Assn. Marriage and Family Therapists (clin.), Mass. Sch. Counselors Assn., Mass. Assn. Sch. Adjustment Counselors, Mass. Assn. Marriage and Family Therapists, Mass. Assn. Mental Health Counselors, Pi Lambda Theta. Avocations: antique collecting, reading, travel, volunteer work, theatre. Home: 57 Cochato Rd Braintree MA 02184-4628

SALMAN, ROBERT RONALD, lawyer; b. N.Y., Dec. 26, 1939; s. Samuel L. and Lillian Gertrude (Sincoff) S.; m. Reva Carol Rappaport, June 16, 1963; children: Elyse D. Spiewak, Suzanne A. BA magna cum laude, Columbia Coll., 1961, LLB cum laude, 1964. Bar: N.Y. 1965, U.S. Supreme Ct. 1974, U.S. Ct. Appeals (2nd cir.) 1967, U.S. Ct. Appeals (3rd cir.) 1993, U.S. Ct. Appeals (11th cir.) 1985, U.S. Ct. Appeals (9th cir.) 1979, U.S. Dist. Ct. so. dist., ea. dist.) N.Y. 1969. Assoc. Proskauer, Rose, Goetz & Mendelsohn, N.Y.C., 1964-67; asst. corp. counsel Law Dept. N.Y., N.Y.C., 1967-69; assoc. Phillips, Nizer, N.Y.C., 1969-73; ptnr. Phillips, Nizer, Benjamin, Krim & Ballon, N.Y.C., 1973-87, Reavis & McGrath, N.Y.C., 1987-88, Carter, Ledyard & Milburn, N.Y.C., 1988-94, Phillips & Salman, N.Y.C., 1994-97, Phillips Salman & Stein, N.Y.C., 1997—; adj. prof. Seton Hall Law Sch., Newark, N.J., 1995-98. Contbr. articles to profl. jours. Pres., founder The Assn. for A Better N.J. Inc., 1991—; pres. Marlboro Jewish Ctr., 1982-84. Recipient NEGEV Builder award Israel Bonds, 1980, Award of Honor UJA Fedn., 1981. Mem. N.Y. State Bar Assn., ABA, Assn. Bar City of N.Y. Avocations: charitable and communal work, baseball, reading, writing. Office: 111 Broadway New York NY 10006-1901

SALMASI, ABDUL-MAJEED, cardiologist, consultant, hypnotherapist; b. Baghdad, Iraq, Jan. 14, 1948; s. Abdul-Hameed and Bahija (Ibrahim) S.; m. Sajida, June 17, 1975; children: Zahra, Zaynab, Najla, Huda, Yousuf. MB ChB, Med. Sch. Baghdad (Iraq), 1971; PhD, U. London, 1979. Diplomate Am. Bd. NLP. Resident Med. City Baghdad, 1972-73; sr. resident Med. City Teaching Hosp., Baghdad, 1973-75; registrar cardiology St. Mary's Hosp., London, 1978-82, sr. registrar cardiology, 1982-85, asst. dir. Irvine lab. cardiovascular investigation & rsch., 1985-90; sr. cardiac rschr. Ctrl. Middlesex Hosp., London, 1991—; diplomate Am. Bd. Hypnotherapy. Editor: Cardiovascular Applications of Doppler Ultrasound, 1989, Occult Atherosclerotic Disease Diagnosis Assessment and Management, 1991, Cardiac Output in Health and Disease, 1993, Angiology in Practice, 1996. Cardiology fellow HEART, England, 1981. Fellow Am. Coll. Cardiology (assoc.), Hypnotherapy Soc., Hypnotherapy Rsch. Soc.; mem. British Cardiac Soc. Achievements include pioneering in use of Doppler ultrasound during exercise, also cardiogenic claudication; current research includes silent myocardial ischaemia in diabetes mellitus. Avocations: travel, writing, directing plays. E-mail: amsalmasi@hotmail.com. Office: Ctrl Middlesex Hosp Cardiac Dept, Acton Ln, London NW10 7NS, England

SALMATZIDIS, IOANNIS DIMITRIOS, electrical engineer; b. Thessaloniki, Greece, Feb. 15, 1966; s. Dimitris and Lefkothea (Kalomiri) S. Diploma in elec. engring., Aristotelian U., Thessaloniki, 1988; MS, U. Md., 1991. Trainee Metropolis Computer Systems, Thessaloniki, 1989; tchg. asst. U. Md., College Park, 1990, rsch. asst., 1990-91; control engr. MLS Firmware SA, Thessaloniki, 1993-95; networks engr. LINK SA, Thessaloniki, 1995-98; tech. mgr. of info. Tech. Ctr. of Aristotle U. Thesaloniki, 1998—; cons., instr. OTE SA, Thessaloniki. With Greek Army, 1991-93. Fulbright grad. fellow, 1989. Mem. IEEE. Avocations: wine making, traveling, hiking, sailing. E-mail: jsal@auth.gr. Home: 28 A Metallinou Str, 54249 Thessaloniki Greece Office: Info Tech/Aristotelian U, 1st Flr Biology Bldg, 54006 Thessaloniki Greece

SALMENKALLIO, KAUKO ALVAR, school counselor; b. Jaakkima, Karjala, Finland, Sept. 1, 1925; s. Kaarlo Ensio and Naemi Irene (Uuskoski)

S.; m. Aino Sorja Waris, Feb. 28, 1953; children: Helena, Kirsti, Terttu, Marjatta, Katri. Theology Candidate, U. Helsinki, Finland, 1951, lic. in theology, 1979. Ordained minister Evangelical Ch., 1951; cert. sch. counselor, 1990. Student pastor U. Finland, Helsinki, 1951-56; prin. Helsingin Yksityislyseo Ja Iltalinja, Helsinki, 1957-74, Espoonlahden Yhteiskoulu, Espoo, Finland, 1974-77, Espoonlahden Lukio, Espoo, 1977-86; emeritus Espoonlahden Lukio, Espoo, 1986—; cons. in field; tchr. religion Helsingin Normaalilyseo, Helsinki, 1956-57; sch. inspector Ctrl. Bd. Schs., Helsinki, 1964; lectr., del. Internat. World Conf. on Evening Schs., Sonnenberg, Germany, 1967. Editor periodicals Etsijä, 1952-56, Hälläpyörä, 1955-58, Teinviesti, 1958-65, Oppikoulu Lehti, 1967-70, Jaakkiman Sanomat, 1967—; editor: Ihanks myö tuas tavattii, 1988; author: Matkakuvia Laatokan-Karjalasta, 1989, 2d edit., 1990. Hon. pres. Student Corp. Hämäläis-Osakunta, Helsinki, 1955-58; bd. dirs., vice chmn. Acad. Labourmarket AKAVA, Helsinki, 1967-69, 69-70; pres. Headmasters and Tchrs. Profl. Orgn., Helsinki, 1955-86; pres., mem. Ylioppilaiden Terveydenhoitosäätiö, Professori Yrjö Jahnsson Muistorahastosäätiö, Jaakkima-Säätio. Corporal Finnish Army, 1943-44. Recipient Golden Badge Karjalan Liitto/Karelian Union, 1994, 1st Order of the White Rose of Finland, 1985. Fellow Nat. Union Religious Tchrs.; mem. Rotary (charter mem. Espoonlahti club 1978-98, Espoo-Meri club 1998—, pres. 1978-79, govs. group rep. 1978-79, gen. sec. RI 75th festival, Finland 1980, Paul Harris fellow 1983), Societas Historiae Ecclestiasticae Fennica, Bibliofilinen Seura, others. Mem. Kansallinen Kokoomus Party. Evangelical Lutheran. Avocations: Karelian culture, history, genealogy, oil painting, photography.

SALMINEN, HANNU ANTERO, engineer; b. Kuhmalahti, Finland, Sept. 18, 1947; s. Antti and Annikki (Heikkila) S.; m. Sylvi Luukkonen, Sept. 1, 1984; children: Jari, Pasi. Degree in engring., U. Helsinki, 1977. Design engr. Nokia Mobira, Oulu, Finland, 1977-79; rsch. engr. Tech. Rsch. Ctr. Telecommunications Lab., Espoo, Finland, 1979—. Office: VTT Telecomm Lab, VTT Telecomms, PO Box 1202, FIN-0204 VTT Finland

SALMINEN, SIMO TAPIO, occupational health researcher; b. Helsinki, Uusimaa, Finland, Oct. 31, 1956; s. Simo Filemon and Irma Kyllikki Salminen; m. Tuija Helena Huikuri, June 25, 1982; children: Annastiina, Pekka. B of Social Scis., U. Tampere, Finland, 1979; M of Social Scis., U. Helsinki, 1982, Licenciate of Social Scis., 1987, D in Social Scis., 1997. Rschr. U. Helsinki, 1982-87, Finnish Broadcasting Co. YLE, Helsinki, 1987-88, Inst. Occupational Health, Vantaa, Finland, 1988—; mem. mng. coun. Finnish Soc. Sport Psychology, Helsinki, 1986-97. Editor: Psykologia-Jour. Finnish Psychol. Soc., 1983—. With Finland Civil Svc., 1985-86. Avocations: literature, jogging, volleyball. Office: Inst of Occupational Health, Laajaniityntie 1, 01620 Vantaa Finland

SALMIVALLI, MARJA LEENA KAARINA, occupational health physician; b. Turku, Finland, June 18, 1938; d. Aimo Aleksander and Katri Ida Marjatta (Mäkinen) Kajanen; m. Altti Juhani Salmivalli; children: Katri, Anna Mari, Lauri. Med. lic., Turku U., 1964, specialty degree in internal medicine, 1974, specialty degree in occupl. health, 1978; M Psychology, Åbo Akademi U., 1998. Asst. physician hosp., Turku, 1968-71; occupl. physician Partek, Parainen, Finland, 1971-78, Meditori, Turku, 1979-82, Fazer, Turku, 1983-90, Nokia NCE, Turku, 1991-96; occupl. health physician SEMI TECH, Turku, 1996—, Medivire Turku, 1998—. Lutheran. Avocation: environmental psychology. Home: Ruskolevänk 5, 20780 Kaarina Finland

SALMON, MICHAEL JOHN, academic administrator; b. Leeds, Eng., June 22, 1936; s. Arthur and May (Dadswell) S.; m. Angela Winstone Cookson (div. Aug., 1973); 1 child, Andrew John; m. Daphne Beatrice Bird, Aug. 17, 1973 (dec. 1996); 1 child, Christopher Michael; m. Sheila Frances Sisto, Apr. 25, 1998. BA in Econs., U. Leeds, 1956, grad. cert. in edn., 1957; MEd, U. Leicester, Eng., 1964; PhD (hon.), Anglia Poly Univ., 1995. Tchr. Letchworth Coll. Tech., Hertfordshire, Eng., 1962-65, Leeds Coll. Tech, 1965-68; tchr. N.E. London Poly., 1968-71, head. dept. acctg. and econs., 1971-77; dep. dir. Chelmer Inst. Higher Edn., Eng., 1977-83; dir. Essex Inst. Higher Edn., Chelmsford, Eng., 1983-88, Anglia Coll. Higher Edn., 1988-89, Anglia Polytech, 1989-91; vice chancellor Anglia Poly Univ., 1991-95; mem. Electricity Industry Tng. Bd., Eng., 1973-76, Council for Nat. Acad. Awards, Eng., 1979-91, Nat. Adv. Body for Higher Edn., 1982-85; chmn. higher awards com. Bus. and Technician Edn. Council, 1985-89; prof. Anglia Polytech. Univ., 1995; vis. prof. Hogeschool, Limburg, mem. gen. optical coun., 1999—; chmn. Essex Rivers NHS trust, 1995—; chmn. of govs. Norwich Sch. Art & Design, 1998—; chmn. Tending Devel. Forum, 1998—; vice chmn. InterCollege, 1998—; gov. King Edward VI Gov. Sch. Chelmsford, 1996-2000, vice-chmn., 2000—. Served as flight lt. RAF, 1957-62. Fellow Brit. Inst. Mgmt., Royal Soc. of Arts; mem. Acad. Coun. Royal Coll. Music. Baptist. Avocations: squash, climbing, walking, athletics, gardening. Home: Barberries, Runsell Ln, Danbury, Essex CM3 4NY, England Office: Essex Rivers Healthcare NHS, Turner Rd, Colchester CO4 5JL, England

SALMON, NEIL ANTHONY, research physicist; b. Nottingham, Eng., July 25, 1959; s. Derek Arthur and Pauline Patricia (Smith) S. BSc, Leeds U., South Yorkshire, Eng., 1981; MSc, Essex U., Colchester, Eng., 1982; PhD, London U., 1990. Lic. exptl. physicist. Scientist Plessey Electronic Systems Rsch., Rosmey, Eng., 1983-84; rsch. asst. London U., 1987-90; postdoctoral physicist Max Planck Inst. Plasma Physics, Munich, 1990-94; higher sci. officer Def. Rsch. Agy., Malvern, Eng., 1994—; scientist Devel. Optical/Acoustical Hardware for Def. Applications, 1983-84; rsch. asst. Devel. Millimetre Wave Radiometers for Nuc. Plasma Physics, 1987-90; postdoctoral physicist, 1990-94; sr. sci. officer R & D of Millimetre Wave Imaging Equipment and Techniques, 1994—. Contbr. articles to profl. jours. Mem. Inst. Physics (chartered physicist). Avocations: playing the piano, skiing, fitness, German language.

SALNIKOVA, EKATERINA BORISOVNA, geologist, researcher; b. Simpheropol, Crimea, Ukraine, Apr. 24, 1968; d. Boris Aphanas'evich and Nonna Borisovna (Chekasheva) S. MS, Leningrad (Russia) State U., 1990; PhD, Inst. Precambrian Geol., 1993. Cert. geologist, geochemist, petrologist. Rsch. geologist Inst. Precambrian Geology and Geochronology, St. Petersburg, 1993—. Contbr. articles to profl. jours. Recipient Govt. Stipend for Young Scientists, Russian Acad. Scis., 1994-96, 97-99, 2000-2002, stipend DAAD, Bonn, Germany, 1996; Russian Found. Basic Rsch. grantee, 1996-98, 99—; fellow INTAS, 2000—. E-mail: kate@ik4843.spb.edu. Office: Inst Precambrian Geol, Makarova emb 2, 199034 St Petersburg Russia

SALO, AHTI ANTERO, management scientist, systems analyst, educator; b. Lempäälä, Finland, June 21, 1962; s. Armas Antti and Sisko Lemmitty (Kuivasniemi) S. MS in Engring., Helsinki (Finland) U. Tech., 1987, lic. in tech., 1990, D Tech., 1992. Systems analyst Finnish PTT, 1986-87; tchg. asst. Helsinki U. Tech., 1987-88, sr. tchg. asst., 1988; rsch. asst. fellow Acad. Finland, 1989-92; vis. rsch. fellow London Bus. Sch., 1992-93; Humboldt fellow U. Mannheim, Germany, 1993-94; sr. cons. Nokia Rsch. Ctr., Helsinki, 1994-97; sr. rschr. Tech. Rsch. Ctr. Finland, Helsinki, 1997-98; prof. Helsinki U. Tech., 1998—. Contbr. articles to scientific jours. Mem. Informs, Finnish Ops. Rsch. Soc. (pres. 1999-2000), Assn. Parliament Mems. and Rschrs. (mem. bd. 1999—). Avocations: classical music, skiing. Home: Pajalahdentie 31 C 35, 00200 Helsinki Finland Office: Helsinki U Tech PO Box 1100, Sys Analysis Lab, 02015HVT Helsinki Finland

SALO, MIKA, race car driver; b. Helsinki, Finland, Nov. 30, 1966. Race car driver, 1987—. 4 Scandinavian karting championships, 1972-85 14 wins European Champion Formula Ford 1600, 1988, 6 wins, Brit. Formula 3, 1989-90, 2d pl. Grand Prix Macau, 1990. Office: Arrow Grand Prix Internat, Leafield Tech Ctr TWR Group Ltd, Witney Oxfordshire OX8 5PF, England*

SALO, VITALY IVANOVICH, physicist, researcher; b. Semipalatnisk, Kazakhstan, Ukraine, May 2, 1944; s. Ivan Minovich Salo and Eugenia Grigorievna Kopotienko-Salo; m. Svetlana Ivanovna Tkachenko, Mar. 2, 1968; children: Stanislav, Elvira. MSc in Physics, Kharkov State U., Ukraine, 1967; postgrad., Inst. Single Crystals, Kharkov, 1972-76. Cert. physicist. Engr. Inst. Electronic Materials Engring., Kaluga, USSR, 1967-68; jr. rsch. scientist Inst. Single Crystals, Kharkov, 1969-79, head group, 1980-91, head lab., 1991—; advisor Inst. Single Crystals, Kharkov, 1980—. Author: (with M. I. Kolybaeva and I. M. Pritula) MRS Symposium Proceedings Series V.329, 1993; contbr. articles to profl. jours. Grantee Sci. and Tech. Ctr. Ukraine, 1997. Mem. Ukrainian Phys. Soc. Avocations: sport, music. Fax: 380-572-320-019. Home: Apt 164, 44 Gvardeitsev Sheronintsev, 61135 Kharkov Ukraine Office: Inst Single Crystals, 60 Lenin Ave, 61001 Kharkov Ukraine

SALOGA, JOACHIM, dermatologist, allergist, researcher, educator; b. Bielefeld, Germany, Apr. 13, 1962; s. Walter K. and Marianne (Niehaus) S.; m. Annegret E.A.M. Baumann, Dec. 28, 1990; 1 dau. State Exam., U. Münster, Germany, 1988, MD, 1989; Habilitation, U. Mainz, Germany, 1996. Cert. in dermatology, allergology, environ. medicine. Rsch. assoc., postdoctoral fellow Nat. Jewish Ctr. for Immunology and Respiratory Medicine, Denver, 1990-92; intern Univ.-Hautklinik, Mainz, 1989-90, resident, 1992-95, cons. in dermatology, head allergy unit, lectr., 1995—, leader rsch. group, 1992—; organizer sci. meetings; chmn. sci. sessions; sci. presenter in field; participant sci. work groups; cons. to pharm. cos. Editor, author: Allergologie und Umweltmedizin, 1997, Allergische Rhinitis, 1998, Die Spezifische Immuntherapie—Hyposensibiliserung, 1998; contbr. numerous articles to sci. jours. With German Army, 1981-82. Recipient Herbert Herxheimer Gadaechtnispreis, German Soc. for Allergology and Clin. Immunology, 1996; scholar Nat. Scholarship Found., 1983-88; various rsch. grants. Mem. German Dermatol. Soc., German Soc. for Allergology and Clin. Immunology, Soc. for Immunology, European Soc. for Dermatol. Rsch., European Acad. Allergology and Clin. Immunology, also others. Office: Univ-Hautklinik, Langenbeckstrasse 1, 55131 Mainz Germany

SALOJARVI, PEKKA TAPANI, publishing company executive; b. Padasjoki, Finland, Mar. 29, 1940; m. Kreeta Anttalainen; children: Elina, Eero. BS in Econs., Sch. Econs., Helsinki, Finland, 1964; PhD (hon.), Jyvaskyla U., 1996. Asst. dir. Gummerus Oy, 1967-69, mgn. dir., 1970-90, chief exec. officer, 1991—. Mem. Fedn. of Printing Industry of Finland (pres. 1995-98). Office: Gummerus Pubs, PO Box 131, FIN 40351 Jyväskylä Finland

SALOLAINEN, PERTTI EDVARD, Finnish diplomat, politician; b. Helsinki, Oct. 19, 1940; m. Anja Sonninen, 1964; children: Maarit, Markus. M Econs., Helsinki Sch. Econs., 1969. Journalist Finnish Broadcasting Co., Helsinki, 1962-66; corr. Finnish Broadcasting Co., London, 1966-69; journalist Finnish sect. BBC, London, 1966; M.P. Finnish Parliament, Helsinki, 1970-96, vice chmn. parliamentary com. for social affairs, 1970-75, chmn. tax div. parliamentary fin. com., 1975-79, chmn. parliamentary fin. com., 1979-87; min. for fgn. trade Govt. of Finland, Helsinki, 1987-91, dep. prime min., 1991-95; Finnish amb. to U.K., Finnish Embassy, London, 1996—; head dept. Finnish Employers' Confedn., 1969-89; chief negotiator Finland's EU Membership; chief negotiator for Finland in GATT Uruguay-Round; mem. Helsinki City Coun., 1972-84; chmn. Helsinki dist. Nat. Coalition Party, 1973-76, mem. party exec., 1979-94, chmn., 1991-94, also chmn. fin. com.; mem. supervisory bd. Finnair, 1995—. Exhibited nature photographs in Tampere, Savitaipale, Helsinki, Bonn, Berlin, Kuusamo, Turku, 1996, Barbican Ctr., London, 1997, Edinburgh, Scotland, 1999, London, 2000. Hon. founder Worldwide Fund for Nature, Finland, 1972. Capt. Finnish Army. Recipient grand cross Order of the Finnish Lion, Grand Cross of Hungary, Germany, and Austria, Grand Cross of Swedish Nordstjerna Order, medal of merit Finnish Def. Force; recipient Internat. Conservation award World Wildlife Fund, gold medal of merit Finnish Assn. for Nature Conservation. Office: Embassy of Finland, 38 Chesham Pl, London SW1X 8HW, England

SALOMAO, TOMAS, Mozambican government official; b. Inharrime, Inhambane, Mozambique, Oct. 16, 1954; married. Degree in Econs., Eduardo Mondlane U., Mozambique. Economist, lectr.Faculty of Economy Eduardo Mondlane U., Mozambique; Sec. of State Nat. Def. Govt. of Mozambique, Maputo, dir. gen. planning, min. nat. def., dep. min. planning nat. planning commn., min. fin. and planning, 1994—, min. transport. and comms. Office: Ministry Transport & Comms, Ave Martires Ingaminga 336, C-P 276 Maputo Mozambique*

SALOMÉ, MARC LOUIS, microbiologist; b. Le Vésinet, France, Aug. 1, 1945; s. Clotaire Désiré Salomé and Louise Huguette Botti; m. Jeanine Louise Eberhard, May 29, 1982; children: Violaine, Lucas. Engring. diploma, Swiss Fed. Inst. Tech., Zurich, 1970. Asst. to dir. prodn. Henkel Cie, Germany, 1972-74; lab. head Inst. Pasteur, Garches, France, 1978-83, SANOFI Recherche, Toulouse, France, 1983—; lectr. Chimie Physique Electronique, Lyon, France, 1990—. Co-inventor and patentee in field. Fax: 33 (0)5 61 00 40 01. Roman Catholic. Avocations: rowing, philosophy. E-mail: marc.salome@sanofi-synthelabo.com. Office: Sanofi Recherche, Sanofi-Synthelab Recherche, PB 137, 31676 Labege Cedex, France

SALOMON, OSCAR DANIEL, biologist; b. Buenos Aires, Argentina, Oct. 10, 1956; m. Julia Ines Portnoy, Sept. 3, 1989. M in Pub. Health, Yale U., 1997; PhD in Biology, Buenos Aires U., 1988. Head parasitology Chagas' Disease Inst., Buenos Aires, 1994-97; dir. Nat. Ctr. Endemic & Epidemic Rsch., Buenos Aires, 1997—; scientific dir. Nat. Adminstrn. Labs. Health, Buenos Aires, 1997; rschr. Nat. Coun. Sci. & Technology, Buenos Aires, 1992—. Author novels, stories and essays. Grantee WHO, 1995—. Avocation: literature. Home: 383 Jean Jaures, Buenos Aires Argentina 1215 Office: CeNDIE, 568 Av Paseo Colsn, Buenos Aires Argentina 1063

SALOMONE, JEFFREY PAUL, surgeon, educator; b. Reno, Nev., Dec. 6, 1961; s. Joseph Anthony and Peggy Ruth (Crompton) S. BS, U. Nev., 1983, MD, 1990. Diplomate Am. Bd. Surgery; cert. surg. critical care. Resident Tulane U. Med. Ctr., New Orleans, 1990-95, fellow in critical care, 1995-96; asst. prof. Emory U., Atlanta, 1996—; cons. Nat. Registry of EMTs, Columbus, Ohio, 1996—. Fellow ACS; mem. AMA, Nat. Assn. Emergency Med. Svcs. Physicians, Am. Assn. for the History of Medicine, Soc. for Critical Care Medicine, Phi Kappa Phi. Avocations: gourmet cooking, photography, theater. Office: Emory U Dept Surgery TK Glenn Bldg Rm 312A 69 Butler St SE Atlanta GA 30303-3033

SALONEN, JARNO JUHANI, physicist; b. Masku, Finland, Sept. 14, 1967; s. Jorma and Anneli (Seilo) S.; m. Nina Anne-Maria Torpakko, Aug. 14, 1985; 1 child, Samuel. MSc, U. Turku, 1995, PhD, 1999. Mem. Finnish Phys. Soc., Materials Rsch. Soc. Home: Maenpaantie 3 AS 3, 21290 Rusko Finland

SALONEN, OILI LAILA MARJATTA, neuroradiologist, researcher; b. Kankaanpää, Finland, Nov. 20, 1950; d. Viljo Kalervo and Laila Kyllikki (Puuska) Mattila; m. Harri Artturi Salonen, July 19, 1975; children: Elina Marjatta, Mikko Artturi. MD, U. Helsinki, Finland, 1976, specialization in radiology, 1984, D in Med. Sci., 1987, docent in neuroradiology, 1996. Resident radiologist Univ. Ctrl. Hosp., Helsinki, 1978-83, sr. staff radiologist, 1984, resident neuroradiologist, 1984-86, sr. staff neuroradiologist, 1986-89, sect. head neuroradiology, 1990—; cons. radiologist, pvt. clinics, Helsinki, 1984—; cons. neuroradiologist, pvt. clinics, Helsinki, 1986—. Author: Radiology, 1991, Pediatric Neurology, 1996; contbr. articles to scientific jours. Mem. Finnish Med. Assn., Finnish Med. Soc. Duodecim, Radiol. Soc. Finland, Finnish Neuroradiol. Soc., Radiol. Soc. N.Am., Internat. Soc. Magnetic Resonance in Medicine, N.Y. Acad. Scis. Conservative. Lutheran. Avocations: family, literature. Office: Helsinki U Ctrl Hosp Radiol, Haartmaninkatu 4, 00290 Helsinki Finland

SALONIEMI, HANNU SAKARI, veterinary medicine educator, university dean; b. Helsinki, Finland, Oct. 11, 1944; s. Toivo Emil and Taimi Maria (Sarjakoski) S.; m. Hilkka Elina Inkinen, Dec. 20, 1969; children: Timo Sakari, Tiina Johanna, Mikko Tapani. DVM, Coll. Vet. Medicine, Helsinki, 1970, PhD, 1980. Asst. prof. Coll. Vet. Medicine, 1970-85; head Mastitis Lab., Nat. Vet. Inst., 1985-86; prof. animal hygiene U. Helsinki, 1987—, vice-dean Faculty of Vet. Medicine,, 1995-98, dean, 1998—; expert mem. sci. vet. com. European Union, Brussels, 1995-97. Editor Mastitis Rsch. Index, 1986-99. Recipient Golden Mark Finnish Animal Protection Assn., Helsinki, 1995, Pro Animalia award Animal Protection League, Helsinki, 1997. Mem. Internat. Soc. Animal Hygiene (pres. 1994-97), European Assn. Animal Prodn., Mgmt. and Health, Internat. Dairy Fedn., Finnish Vet. Assn. (Golden Mark 1993). Avocation: nature. Office: Fac Vet Med U Helsinki, Hameentie 57, FIN00014 Helsinki Finland

SALOOM, KALISTE JOSEPH, JR., lawyer, retired judge; b. Lafayette, La., May 15, 1918; s. Kaliste and Asma Ann (Boustany) S.; m. Yvonne Adelle Nassar, Oct. 19, 1958; children: Kaliste III, Douglas James, Leanne Isabelle, Gregory John. BA with high distinction, U. La., 1939; JD, Tulane U., 1942. Bar: La. 1942. Atty. City of Lafayette, 1948-52; judge City and Juvenile Ct., Lafayette, 1952-93; ret., 1993; of counsel Saloom & Saloom, Lafayette, 1993—; mem. jud. coun. La. Supreme Ct., 1960-64; bd. dirs. Nat. Ctr. for State Cts., Williamsburg, Va., 1978-84, adv. coun., 1984—, mem. assocs. com., 1986—; judge pro tempore La. Ct. Appeal 3d Cir., 1992; tech. adviser Jud. Adminstrn. of Traffic Cts. mem. adv. com. Nat. Hwy. Traffic Safety Adminstrn., U.S. Dept. Transp., 1977-80, Nat. Com. on Uniform Traffic Laws, 1986; mem. expert panel Drunk Driving Protection Act U.S. Congress, 1989-91. Mem. editl. bd. Tulane Law Rev., 1941; contbr. articles to profl. jours. With U.S. Army, 1942-45. Recipient Civic Cup, City of Lafayette, 1965, Pub. Svc. award U.S. Dept. Transp., 1980, Disting. Jurist award Miss. State U. Pre-Law Soc., 1987, Disting. Svc. award Nat. Ctr. State Cts., 1988, Disting. La. Jurist award La. State Bar Found., 1992, U.S. Supreme Ct. Chief Justice Warren E. Burger Soc. award, 1999. Mem. ABA (Benjamin Flaschner award 1981, vice chair JAD com. on traffic ct. program 1989-99), Am. Judges Assn. (William H. Burnett award 1982), Nat. Coun. Juvenile Ct. Judges, La. City Judges Assn. (past pres.), La. Juvenile Ct. Judges Assn. (past pres.), Am. Judicature Soc. (panel drafting La. children's code 1989-91), U.S Chief Justice Warren E. Burger Soc. (mem. award 1999), Order of Coif, Equestrian Order of Holy Sepulchre (knight comdr.), Oakbourne Country Club, Rotary (paul Harris fellow), KC. Democrat. Roman Catholic. Home: 502 Marguerite Blvd Lafayette LA 70503-3138 Office: 211 W Main St Lafayette LA 70501-6843

SALOSCHIN, ROBERT L., lawyer; b. N.Y.C., Jan. 15, 1920; s. Bruno Benedix and Edna Saloschin; m. Neita L. Saloschin, Dec. 10, 1949; children: Mary Ann, Joan Janelle. BA, Columbia Coll., 1940; JD, Columbia Law Sch., 1947. Bar: N.Y. 1947, D.C. 1960, Md. 1980, U.S. Supreme Ct. 1956. Pers. adminstr. USN, Washington, 1941-43; atty. Cahill, Gordon, Reindel, N.Y.C., 1947-49, Housing & Home Fin. Agy., Washington, 1950-52, Civil Aeronautics Bd., Washington, 1952-58; atty. Office of Legal Counsel, dir. Office Info. Law U.S. Dept. Justice, Washington, 1958-81; of counsel Lerch Early & Brewer, Bethesda, Md., 1981—; cons. standing com. on law and nat. security ABA, Washington, 1981-91; developed legal strategy for ending racial segregation in interstate bus transp., ICC; mediator for Am. athletics orgns. Olympic Games. Patentee air navigation device; editor: A Short Guide to the Freedom of Information Act, annually, 1974—; editor law rev. Columbia Law Sch., 1947. Organizer, pres. Citizens for Quality Civilization, Inc., Bethesda, 1990—; pres. West Fernwood Citizens Assn., Bethesda, 1962-65; officer North Bethesda Congress of Citizens Assocs., Bethesda, 1965-75. Lt. comdr. USN, WWII. Decorated Air medal with oak leaf cluster. Mem. Ret. Officers Assn., Herring Bay Yacht Club, Phi Beta Kappa. Avocations: coastal cruising, flying, reading, bridge, lecturing in schools. Home: 6603 Lone Oak Dr Bethesda MD 20817-1649

SALOVA, NIKOLINKA PETROVA, economics educator; b. Ticha, Bulgaria, Nov. 27, 1935; d. Petar Atanasov and Veselina Petrova (Rainova) Boncheva; m. Stoyan Salov Stoyanov, Jan. 20, 1958; 1 child, Vladimir. MBA, U. Econs., Varna, Bulgaria, 1958, DS, 1968; PhD, U. Nat. World Economy, Sofia, Bulgaria, 1980. Economist Mcpl. Coun., Varna, Bulgaria, 1958-61; asst. U. Econs., Varna, Bulgaria, 1962-71, assoc. prof., reader, 1971-82, chief dept., 1973-93, prof., 1982—, deputy rector, 1983-89; mem. acad. coun. U. Econs., 1971—, editor-in-chief ann. book, 1993—; chmn. spl. scientific coun. Coun. Ministers, Varna, 1987-95, mem., Sofia, 1978—. Author: Efficiency of Capital Investments in Home Trade in Bulgaria, 1971, Economic and Social Efficiency of Home Trade, 1983, Organization of Technology Trade, 1970, 89, Economy and Planning of Trade, 1985, 95; contbr. over 200 articles to profl. jours. and books. Bd. dirs. Popular Bank, Varna, 1996—, Union Popular Banks, Bulgaria, 1996—; chmn. bd. dirs. State-Owned Co. Lazur, Varna, 1989-92. Grantee British Coun., London, 1984, Plehanov Inst. Nat. Economy, Moscow, 1969, 76. Mem. Union Mchts. Bulgaria (mng. com. 1990—), Mchts. Trade Union Bulgaria (mng. com. 1980-92), Union Scientists Bulgaria (mng. com. 1971—, Silver Statuette 1995). Avocations: literature, travel, swimming, cinema, theatre. Office: U Econs, 77 Knyaz Boris I Blvd, 9002 Varna Bulgaria

SALT, ALEC NICHOLAS, otolaryngology educator; b. Dewsbury, Yorkshire, Eng., May 4, 1952; s. Harold and Jean Salt; m. Devina Margaret Swan, Aug. 4, 1973; children: Lisa, Anthony. BSc, U. East Anglia, Norwich, Eng., 1973; MSc, U. Birmingham, Eng., 1974, PhD, 1977. Clin. physiologist Inst. for Sound and Vibration Rsch., Southampton, Eng., 1983; rsch. asst. prof. Washington U., St. Louis, 1984-87, asst. prof., 1987-93, assoc. prof., 1993—. Contbr. articles to profl. jours. Recipient Guyot prize for otolaryngology U. Groningen, The Netherlands, 1999; rsch. grantee NIH, NIDCD, Washington U., 1992—. Mem. Assn. for Rsch. in Otolaryngology, Acoustical Soc. Am. Avocation: radio controlled flying. E-mail: salta@msnotes.wustl.edu. Fax: 314-362-7522. Office: Washington Univ Med Sch 660 S Euclid Ave Saint Louis MO 63110-1010

SALT, ALFRED LEWIS, priest; b. Hackensack, N.J., Apr. 30, 1927; s. Alfred John and Lily (Tittle) S.; m. Elizabeth May Loveland, June 18, 1949; children: Richard John, Michael Rob, Christopher William, Katharine Anne. BA with honors, Bishop's U., Lennoxville, Can., 1949, MA in History, 1951, BD, 1960; grad. advanced mgmt. program, Harvard U., 1970; D Ministry, Grad. Theol. Found., 1988. Ordained to ministry Episcopal Ch. as deacon, 1951, as priest, 1952. Incumbent St. Philip's, Sawyerville, Que., Can., 1951-52, St. John the Evangelist, Portneuf, Que., 1952-54; rector Christ Ch., Stanstead, Que., 1954-62, St. Michael's Ch., Sillery, Que., 1962-72, All Sts.' Ch., Millington, N.J., 1972-93; bishop's chaplain Diocese of Que., 1962, hon. canon, 1970; pres. Morris Convocation. Morris County, N.J., 1974-78, retreat condr., 1979—; with Victorious Ministry Through Christ, Orlando, Fla., 1981-92, dir., 1986-92, v.p., 1989-92; dir. VMTC Can., 1995—; hon. asst. Grace Ch., Port Huron, Mich., 1993-98, Trinity Ch., Lexington, Mich., 1998—. Author: Compass Book on Healing, 1996; contbr. articles to religious jour. Mem. Superior Coun. Edn., Que., 1964-70; commr. Que. Protestant Sch. Bd., 1970-72; trustee Heath Village, Hackettstown, N.J., 1974-76; mem. Passaic Twp. Welfare Bd., Millington, 1977-78, 82. With U.S. Army Air Corps Res., 1944-45; with USN, 1945-46. Mem. Blue Water Convocation, Order St. Luke (chaplain). Home: 4429 Gratiot Ave Fort Gratiot MI 48059-3926 also: 190 Chemin du Lac, North Hatley, Canada J0B 2C0

SALT, GEORGE, retired biologist; b. Loughborough, Eng., Dec. 12, 1903; s. Walter and Mary Cecilia (Hulme) S.; m. Joyce Laing, July 27, 1939; children: Michael, Peter. BSc, U. Alta., Can., 1924; SM, SD, Harvard U., 1925, 27; PhD, Cambridge (Eng.) U., 1933, ScD, 1941. Entomologist United Fruit Co., Colombia, 1926-27; Nat. rsch. fellow Harvard U., 1927-28; entomologist Imperial Bur. Entomology, Eng., 1928-31; fellow King's Coll., Cambridge, 1933—; lectr. dept. zoology Cambridge U., 1938-65, reader, 1965-71, emeritus, 1971—; vis. prof. U. Calif., Berkeley, 1966; pres. Cambridge Philos. Soc., 1970-72. Calligrapher: (formal script for illustrated manuscripts) News from Newnham, 1986-89, Faiths and Scripts, 1989-95; contbr. articles to sci. jours. Murchison grantee Royal Geog. Soc., 1951. Fellow Royal Soc. London. Avocations: calligraphy, painting (water colors and miniatures), gardening. Home: 21 Barton Rd, Cambridge CB3 9LB, England Office: King's Coll, Cambridge CB2 1ST, England

SALT, THOMAS EDGAR, neuroscientist, researcher; b. Berlin, Dec. 25, 1956. BA, U. Cambridge, Eng., 1978; MA, U. Cambridge, 1982; PhD, U. Bristol, Eng., 1982. Rsch. scientist Reckitt & Colman, Hull, Eng., 1978-79; rsch. fellow U. Birmingham, Eng., 1982-83; lectr. U. Wales, Cardiff, 1983-88; sr. lectr. Inst. Opthalmology, Univ. Coll., London, 1988-95; reader Inst. Opthalmology, London, 1995-99; prof. Inst. Opthalmology, 1999—. Mem. Physiol. Soc., British Pharmacol. Soc., Soc. Neurosci. Office: Inst Opthalmology, 11-43 Bath St, London EC1V 9EL, England

SALTMARSH, JOHN ALBERT, historian, educator; b. New Bedford, Mass., Feb. 25, 1957; s. Robert John and Dorothee (Gierich) S.; m. Gisele Marie Grenon, July 28, 1984; children: Joshua Nathaniel, Jay Cotton. BS, U. Mass., Amherst, 1979, MA, 1983; PhD, Boston U., 1989. Project dir. Campus Compact Brown U., Providence, R.I., 1998—; assoc. prof. Northeastern U., Boston, 1989—; founding chair The Good Life Ctr.,

Harborside, Maine, 1995—. Author: Scott Nearing: The Making of a Homesteader, 1991. Avocations: sailing, kayaking. E-mail: jsaltmarsh@compact.org. Home: 19 Mathews Dr Wayland MA 01778-4421

SALTYKOV, KONSTANTIN ALBERTOVICH, neurophysiologist; b. Moscow, Nov. 20, 1971; s. Albert and Elena (Alexandrova) S.; m. Irina Viktorovna Dubinina, Oct. 10, 1998; 1 child, Dimitri. MSc, Moscow State U., 1994. Scientist Inst. Higher Nervous Activity and Neurophysiology, Moscow, 1994-99. Avocations: philosophy, architecture, Russian history. Office: IHNAN, 5a Butlerova, Moscow 117865, Russia

SALTZMAN, IRENE CAMERON, perfume manufacturing executive, art gallery owner; b. Cocoa, Fla., Mar. 23, 1927; d. Argyle Bruce and Marie T. (Neel) Cameron; m. Herman Saltzman, Mar. 23, 1946 (dec. May 1986); children: Martin Howard (dec.), Arlene Norma Hanly. Owner Irene Perfume and Cosmetics Lab., Jacksonville, Fla., 1972—, Irene Gallery of Art, Jacksonville, 1973—. Mem. Cummer Mus. Art, Jacksonville, 1972—, Jacksonville Gallery of Art, 1972—; active Jacksonville and Beaches Conv. and Vis. Bur. Mem. Jacksonville C. of C. (mem. downtown coun.), Ret. Judge Advocates Assn. of USAF (hon.), First Coast Women in Internat. Trade, Cosmetic, Toiletry and Fragrance Assn., Ret. Officers Assn., Ponte Vedra Club, Jacksonville Naval Flying Club, PGA Tour Parters Club. Democrat. Episcopalian. Avocations: aviation, painting, travel, swimming, golf. E-mail: irene@ireneparfums.com. Home: 2701 Ocean Dr S Jaxville Bch FL 32250-5946

SALTZMAN, PHILIP, television writer, producer; b. Sonora, Mexico, Sept. 19, 1928; came to U.S., 1929, naturalized, 1948; s. Louis and Vanya (Liberman) S.; m. Caroline Veiller, Jan. 24, 1960; children: Jennifer, Daniel, Anthony. BA, UCLA, 1951, MA, 1953. Free lance writer, 1958-68; pres. Woodruff Prodns., Inc. Writer: TV shows Alcoa Goodyear Theater, 1959, Richard Diamond, 1959, Rifleman, 1961, Perry Mason, 1964, Dr. Kildare, 1964, Fugitive, 1964, Twelve O'Clock High, 1966; producer, writer: TV shows Felony Squad, 1966-69, F.B.I, 1969-73, Barnaby Jones, 1973-77; producer, writer, creator Intertect, 1973; producer: TV movie The FBI vs. Alvin Karpis, 1974, Attack on Terror: The FBI vs. the KKK in Mississippi, 1975, Brinks: The Great Robbery, 1976; co-writer: feature film The Swiss Conspiracy, 1975; creator-writer-producer TV movie Crossfire, 1975; exec. producer: TV shows Barnaby Jones, 1978-80, Escapade, 1978, Colorado C-I, 1978, A Man Called Sloane, 1979, The Aliens Are Coming, 1979, Freebie and the Bean, 1980; producer: TV shows Bare Essence, 1982; supervising producer-writer Partners in Crime, 1984; producer-writer Crazy Like a Fox, 1985; producer, co-writer TV movie That Secret Sunday, 1986; exec. supervising producer The New Perry Mason movies, 1987-88; exec. supervising producer, writer Jake and The Fatman, 1987-88; supervising producer Columbo, 1989-90; creator-writer The Caller, 1991. Mem. dean's coun. Coll. Letters and Sci., UCLA, Friends of English, UCLA. Mem. Writers Guild Am., West, Caucus for Writers, Producers, Dirs., Acad. TV Arts and Scis., PEN Ctr. USA West.

SALUJA, AJAY KUMAR, pharmacy educator, researcher; b. Gwalior, India, Jan. 12, 1957; s. Krishan Lal and Prakash Rani (Chabra) S.; m. Meenu Ajay Verma, May 11, 1986; 2 children. BPharm, U. Saugar, India, 1978, MPharm, 1980, PhD in Pharm. Scis., 1985. Demonstrator Lala Lajgat Rai Meml. Coll. Med. Coll., Meerut, 1980-81; lectr., rsch. fellow U. Sagar, 1981-85; lectr. S.V. Govt. Polytechnic, Bhopal, 1985-86, Ashokbhai Ramanbhai Coll. Pharmacy, Vallabh, Vidyanagar, Gujarat, India, 1986-88; assoc. prof. Ashokbhai Ramanbhai Coll. Pharmacy, Vallabh, Vidyanagar, India, 1988-96, prof., head, 1996—, rsch. guide, supr., 1989—; chmn. bd. studies Sarder Patel U., Vallabh, Vidyanagar, 1989—, mem. senate, 1996—, mem. acad. coun., 1989—; inspector, expert Pharmacy Coun. India, All India Coun. for Tech. Edn., New Delhi, 1988—. Contbr. articles to profl. jours. including Internat. Jour. Pharmacognosy, Fitoterapia, Phytotherapy Rsch., Phytotherapeutics. Fellow Indian Coun. Med. Rsch., 1981; sr. rsch. fellow U. Grant Commn., 1983. Mem. Indian Pharm. Assn. (exec. coun. 1997—), Indian Soc. for Tech. Edn. (life), Assn. Pharmacy Tchrs. (life), Indian Soc. Pharmacognosy (exec. com. 1998—). Avocations: reading, gardening, social services. Home: Professors Block 3/3, Six Bunglows, Vallabh, Vidyanagar, Gujarat 388120, India Office: AR Coll Pharmacy, Vallabh, Vidyanagar, Gujarat 388120, India

SALVAGGIO, SALVINO ANTHONY, internet strategy consultant, company director; b. Ougree, Liege, Belgium, Aug. 10, 1963; s. Giuseppe and Lucia Nicoletta (Santangino) S. BA, U. Liege, 1986; Master, U. Perugia, Italy, 1991; PhD, U. Liege, 1993. Vis. scholar U. Perugia, 1990-94; rschr. Inst. D'Etudes Socio-Historiques, Liege, 1993-95, U. Liege, 1995-96, SUNY, Buffalo, 1996-97; vis. prof. U. Quebec, Montreal, Can., 1997—; orgn. cons., Perugia, 1992-95; data base cons., Italy, 1997; info. and comm. tech. cons., Italy, Belgium, 1997-98; head dept. Internet Bus. Strategy, Belgium, 1999; info. and comm. tech. cons., 1997-99; web mktg. cons., 1998-99. Author: (novel) Au Bord De L'Amer, 1994 (1st European Mer prize 1994); sci. editor, author: N. Luhmann en Perspective, 1995, Autopoietic Systems Theory and the System of Science, 1996, Toward Post-Foundationalist Theory?, 1997, Digital Economy, 1998, Observing New Economy, 1999; editl. staff Web Mktg. Tools, Internet World-Italia. Recipient scholarship grant Italiani Residenti All'Estero, 1990-92, travel grant Inst. D'Etudes Socio-Historiques, 1995, scholarship grant U. Montreal, 1996. Mem. Internat. Sociol. Assn. (bd. dirs. 1996—). Avocations: horses, constructivist painting, cooking. Home: 76 Rue Roi Albert, 4102 Ougree Liege, Belgium

SALVANESCHI, ENRICA, humanities educator, writer; b. Genoa, Liguria, Italy, Sept. 11, 1947; d. Emilio Mario and Albertina Rosa Carolina (Rosati) S. Degree in humanities. Temp. prof. linguistics U. Chieti, 1978-79; asst. in Greek lit. U. Genoa, 1971-74, asst. in linguistics, 1974-84, temp. prof. Hebrew, 1977-78, tem. prof. Greek lang., 1979-83, assoc. prof. semantics, 1984-96, assoc. prof. comparative lit., 1997—. Author: Like That, 1990, Toward a Theory, 1992, Metopes. A Treatise on Poetics and Solitude, 1992, Centaurs?, 1992, The Other and the Nothing, 1994, Catalogue and Metamorphosis, 1996, Some Voices, 1998, Psychomachia, 1998, Poesy, 2000. Office: U Genoa Faculty of Letters, Via Balbi 4, 16126 Genoa Italy

SALVATIERRA, OSCAR, JR., transplant surgeon, urologist, educator; b. Phoenix, Apr. 15, 1935; s. Oscar and Josefine S.; m. Pamela Moss; children: Mark, Lisa Marie. B.S., Georgetown U., 1957; M.D., U. So. Calif., 1961. Intern, resident in surgery and urology U. So. Calif.-Los Angeles County Med. Center, 1961-66; practice medicine Pomona, Calif., 1968-72; chief staff Casa Colina Hosp., 1972; post doctoral fellow in transplantation U. Calif.-San Francisco, 1972-73, asst. prof. surgery and urology, 1973-75, assoc. prof., 1975-81, prof., 1981-91, chmn. transplant service, 1974-91; attending surgeon and urologist Moffitt Hosp., 1973—; exec. dir. Pacific Transplant Inst., 1991-94; prof. surgery/pediatrics, dir. pediat. renal transplantation Stanford U. Med. Ctr., 1994—, attending surgeon, urologist and pediat.; mem. study sect. NIH, 1981-85, nat. adv. bd., 1986-92, chmn. nat. adv. bd. 1990-92, chmn. spl. study sect., 1997, 99. Contbr. over 240 articles and chpts. to med. lit.; mem. editorial bd. Transplantation and Immunology, 1984—, Transplantation, 1987—, Transplantation Procs., 1990—, Pediat. Transplantation, 1998—; assoc. editor Am. Jour. Kidney Diseases, 1987-89. Mem. nat. bd. advisors Agent Orange Class Assistance Program, 1988-96. Served with M.C., U.S. Army, Vietnam, 1966-68. Decorated Army Commendation medal; recipient Chancellor's award for pub. service U. Calif., 1986, Commendation resolution Calif. State Legislature, 1990, Presdl. medal and Diploma of Honor, Argentina, 1999, Rambar-Mark award for excellence in patient care Stanford U., 1999, High Sign of Honour award Pres. of Italian Rep., 2000; NIH grantee, 1974-76, 80-83, 88-90; USPHS grantee, 1986-89. Fellow ACS (bd. govs. 1986-92); mem. Am. Surg. Assn., Am. Soc. Transplant Surgeons (bd. dirs. 1977-85, pres. 1983-84, chmn. adv. com. on issues 1984-87), Soc. Univ. Surgeons, Soc. Univ. Urologists, N.Y. Acad. Scis., Am. Soc. Nephrology, Internat. Transplantation Soc. (bd. dirs. 1984—, pres.-elect 1996-98, pres., 1998-2000), Soc. Pediatric Urology, Am. Urol. Assn., Nat. Kidney Found., Renal Physicians Assn. (bd. dirs. 1984-87), Pacific Coast Surg. Assn., San Francisco Surg. Soc., United Network Organ Sharing (bd. dirs. 1984-88, pres. 1985-86), Internat. Soc. for Organ Sharing (bd. dirs. 1991—, pres. 1993-95), Am. Soc. for Minority Health and Transplant Profls. (pres. 1992-94), Nafziger Surg. Soc. Achievements include being the prin. lay figure in passage and enactment of Nat. Organ Transplant Act, 1984. Office: Stanford U Med Ctr 703 Welch Rd Ste H2 Palo Alto CA 94304-1708

SALVATO, MATTEO, physicist; b. Salerno, Italy, July 26, 1964; s. Alfonso Raffaela (Palumbo) S. Degree in physics, U. Naples, Italy, 1992. Rschr. Ansaldo, Naples, 1992-94; rschr. dept. physics Nat. Inst. of Physics of Matter, U. Salerno, 1995—. Left Democratic. Avocation: soccer. Office: Univ Salerno Dept Physics, Via S Allende, Baronissi, 84081 Salerno Italy

SALVATORE, RICHARD JOHN, cinematographer, company executive; b. Bklyn., May 25, 1950; s. Peter Louis and Julia (Stampano) S. AA, Los Angeles Valley Coll., 1972. Artist George Whiteman & Assocs., Hollywood, Calif., 1968-72; ind. cinematographer Hollywood, 1976—; founder RJS Motion Picture and TV, Northridge, 1991—; co-founder RJS Promotions, 1993—; tchr. Prodrs. Assn., Hollywood, 1975—, Am. Film Inst., Beverly Hills, Calif., 1984—; CEO Omnicom Sys., Canoga Park, Calif., 1981—; co-owner Norman Borines World Bruce Lee Mus., Northridge, 1992—; founder RJS Comms., 1995—; bd. dirs., cinematographer Davidson Design Prodns., San Diego; cons. entertainment mktg. and advt. spl. projects (tie-ins and global exposure), 1991—; creative cons. for programming JM Entertainment, Hollywood, Calif., 1997—. Photographer: Solace, 1968 (Memorable mention Los Angeles County Fair 1968), Night Wind Dragon, 1972. Pres. Robert F. Kennedy campaign com., L.A., 1967, Gun Control Act of 1968, L.A.; dist. leader/area leader Muscular Dystrophy Assn., Los Angeles County, 1966-70. Recipient fin. grant U. Calif., 1972. Mem. Soc. Operating Cameramen (assoc.), Acad. TV Arts and Scis. (assoc.). Avocations: kung fu, collecting old movies.

SALVATORES, GABRIELE, film director; b. Naples, Italy, 1950. Works include: Sogno di una notte di mezza estate, 1983, Kamikazen: ultimo notte a milano, 1987, Marrakech Express, 1989, Turne, 1989, Mediterraneo, 1991 (Best Fgn. Lang. Film Acad. Awd), Puerto Escondido, 1993; dir., writer: Sid, 1993, Nirvana, 1997, Calcutta Chromosome, 1999. Address: c/o Tatiana Strelkoff, PO Box 13, Acilia Roma Italy*

SALVESON, MELVIN ERWIN, business executive, educator; b. Brea, Calif., Jan. 16, 1919; s. John T. and Elizabeth (Green) S.; m. Joan Y. Stipek, Aug. 22, 1944; children: Eric C., Kent Erwin. B.S., U. Calif. at Berkeley, 1941; M.S., Mass. Inst. Tech., 1947; Ph.D., U. Chgo., 1952. Cons. McKinsey & Co., N.Y.C., 1947-49; asst. prof., dir. mgmt. sci. research U. Calif. at Los Angeles, 1949-54; mgr. advanced data systems, cons. strategic planning Gen. Electric Co., Louisville and N.Y.C., 1954-57; pres. Mgmt. Scis. Corp., Los Angeles, 1957-67; group v.p. Control Data/CEIR, Inc., 1967-68; pres. Electronic Currency Corp., 1964—; chmn. OneCard Internat., Inc., 1983-92, E-currency Card.com, 1992—; founder and pres. So. Calif. Econ. Alliance, 1992-96, also bd. dirs.; founding chair Am. Soc. for Edn. and Econ. Devel., 1996-98, also bd dirs.; exec. dir. Am. Found. for Edn. and Econ. Devel.; bd. dirs. Diversified Earth Scis., Inc., Eco Rx Inc., Eexcel Enterprise Inc., Veritas et Justus Inc., Algeran, Inc., Electronic Currency Corp.; founder MasterCard System, Los Angeles, 1966; chmn. Corporate Strategies Internat.; prof. bus. Pepperdine U. 1972-85; adj. prof. U. So. Calif.; adviser data processing City of Los Angeles, 1962-64; futures forecasting IBM, 1957-61; adviser strategic systems planning USAF, 1961-67; info. systems Calif. Dept. Human Resources, 1972-73, City Los Angeles Automated Urban Data Base, 1962-67; tech. transfer NASA, 1965-70, others; mem. bd. trustees, Long Beach City Coll., 1990-95. Contbr. articles to profl. jours. Served to lt. comdr. USNR, 1941-46. Named to Long Beach City Coll. Hall of Fame; recipient Dist. Alumnus 1992 award Calif. Coll. System, 1992. Fellow AAAS; mem. Inst. Mgmt. Sci. (founder, past pres.). Republican. Club: Founders (Los Angeles Philharmonic Orch.), Calif. Yacht. Home: 130 Marguerita Ave Apt 8 Santa Monica CA 90402-1652

SALVINI, GIANPAOLO, editor, economist; b. Milan, Italy, Mar. 3, 1936; s. Sisto and Ines (Tarini) S. D in Econs., U. Cattolica del Sacro Cuore, Milan, 1964; D in Theology, U. Innsbruck, Austria, 1969. Redactor Aggiornamenti Sociali, Milan, 1969-77, editor, 1977-82; redactor Cadernos do Centro de Estudos e Acao Social, Salvador, Brazil, 1970-71; editor La Civilta Cattolica, Rome, 1985—; prof. history and geography Lic. Leone XIII, Milan, 1971-84. Mem. Soc. Jesus. Roman Catholic. Avocation: mountain climbing. Office: La Civilta Cattolica, Via di Porta Pinciana 1, 00187 Rome Italy

SALVINI, LUCA, electronics systems educator; b. Montevarchi, Italy, Feb. 9, 1958; s. Ezzelino and Giovanna (Brandi) S.; m. Monica Cherubini, Sept. 10, 1983; children: Tommaso, Giovanna. D in Physics, U. Firenze, 1985; specialist in optics, Nat. Inst. of Optics, 1988. Tchr. Ipsia G Marconi, San Giovanni, 1986, Itis G Ferraris, San Giovanni, 1986—; rschr. Nat. Rsch. Coun., Firenze, 1988-96, Nat. Inst. of Nuclear Physics, Firenze, 1997; cons. engrng. energetics dept., Firenze, 1996; tchr. Province of Arezzo, San Giovanni Valdarno, Italy, 1996-97, IAL of Toscana, San Giovanni, 1998; local edn. officer Arezzo, Italy, 1999-2000. With Opera Giogio la Pira, 1982-84. Mem. Italian Optical and Photonic Soc., European Optical Soc. Office: Itis G Ferraris, Piazza Palermo 1, 52027 San Giovanni Italy

SALYER, STEPHEN LEE, media executive; b. Lexington, Ky., July 20, 1950; s. Ralph Conley Salyer and Margaret (Greenlee) Miles; m. Martha Ingels Ruddy, Apr. 21, 1985; children: Samuel Wilmot, Duncan Davis, Clara Josephine. BA, Davidson Coll., 1972; MPA, Harvard U., 1975. Pres. Citizens' Com. on Population and the Am. Future, Washington, 1972-73; cons. Rockefeller Family Assocs., N.Y.C., 1973-75; assoc. pub. issues program Population Coun., N.Y.C., 1977-79; asst. to the pres. Ednl. Broadcasting Corp., Sta. WNET TV, N.Y.C., 1975-76, v.p. corp. affairs, 1979-80, v.p. program devel. and mktg., 1981-82, sr. v.p. edn. divsn., 1982-86, sr. v.p. mktg. and comm., 1986-88; pres., CEO Pub. Radio Internat., Mpls., 1988—, also bd. dirs.; bd. dirs. Pub. Interactive, Inc., Minn. Meeting, McPhail Ctr. for the Arts; mem. nat. adv. com. Nat. Peace Found., 1991—. Co-author: (with James J. Bausch) Toward Safe, Convenient and Effective Contraceptives, 1978. Fellow Japan Soc. U.S.-Japan Leadership, 1996; mem. Nat. Commn. on Population Growth and the Am. Future, Washington, 1970-72. Root-Tilden scholar NYU Sch. Law, 1976-79. Mem. Harvard Club (N.Y.C.), Mpls. Club. Home: 1801 Irving Ave S Minneapolis MN 55403-2822 Office: Pub Radio Internat 100 N 6th St Ste 900 A Minneapolis MN 55403-1516

SAM, RICHARD CHUNG, physicist; b. Amoy, Fukien, China, Mar. 2, 1944; came to U.S., 1967; s. Shih Mei and Mu-Cheng (Wang) Shen; m. Mary Ho Sam, Aug. 22, 1970; children: Sylvia, William. BSc, U. Hong Kong, 1966; PhD in Physics, Brown U., 1974. Staff physicist Philips Labs., Briarcliff Manor, N.Y., 1974-77; laser physicist Allied Corp., Morristown, N.J., 1977-82; sr. engr. Allied Corp. EOP, Westlake Village, Calif., 1982-86, sr. group leader, 1986-91; v.p. tech. Excel Tech. Inc., Holbrook, N.Y., 1991-92; sr. engr., sect. mgr. Spectra Diode Labs., San Jose, Calif., 1992-94; pres. Equilasers Inc., Santa Clara, Calif., 1994—; cons. Nat. Constrn. Conf., Taiwan, 1985. Author: (booklet) Solid State Lasers and Applications, Chinese edit. 1990, (chpt.) Alexandrite Laser in Solid State Lasers, 1989. Chairman, mem. exec. bd. Chinese Christian Ch. of Thousand Oaks, Calif., 1990. Republican. Evangelical. Achievements include pioneering alexandrite laser and its application in submare laser communications, developing medical solid state laser. Home: 10811 Barrington Bridge Ct Cupertino CA 95014-6401 Office: Equilasers Inc Unit 5 3350 Scott Blvd Santa Clara CA 95054-3108

SAMAD, MD ABDUS, veterinary medicine educator; b. Chapia Nawabgonj, Rajshahi, Bangladesh, Mar. 21, 1953; s. Ettaz Ali Biswas and Mosamath Ayesa Khatun; m. Mahfuza Bulbul, June 10, 1981; children: Manar Din Samad Lyric, Jadit Ettaz Samad Epic. DVM, Bangladesh Agr. U., 1974, MS, 1975; PhD, Haryana Agr. U., 1982, Cert. of Merit, 1982. Registered vet. Lectr. Bangladesh Agr. U., Mymensingh, 1976-82, asst. prof., 1982-86, assoc. prof., 1986-92, prof., 1992—; head dept. medicine Bangladesh Agr. U., 1991-92; prin. investigator haemoprotozoan diseases Bangladesh Agrl. Rsch. Coun., Dhaka, 1984-86, toxoplasmosis, Bangladesh Med. Rsch. Coun., 1994-95, torch complex, 1996-97. Author: (books) Poultry Husbandry and Medicine, 1988, 2nd edit. 1996, Animal Husbandry and Medicine, 1996, Veterinary Practitioner's Guide, 2000; editor: The Bangladesh Vet., 1984-92, Bangladesh Vet. jour., 1994—, mng. editor, 1994. Postdoctoral fellow Commonwealth Commn., U. Liverpool, London, 1989-90; NST expert fellow Min. of Sci. and Tech., Bangladesh, 1996-97, WHO fellow Mohidal U., Thailand, 1997. Mem. Bangladesh Vet. Assn. (life), Bangladesh Animal Health Soc. (life), Indian Soc. for Vet. Epidemiology and Pub. Health (life). Islamic. Office: Bangladesh Agr Univ, Dept Med, 2202 Mymensingh/Dhaka Bangladesh

ŠAMAL, MARTIN, biomedical physics educator, researcher; b. Prague, Czechoslovakia, Nov. 17, 1948; s. Václav and Jarmila (Sehrová) Š.; m. Jiřina Radotínská, Aug. 25, 1983. MD, Charles U., Prague, 1973; PhD in Biophysics and Med. Physics, Charles U., 1982; DSc in Biophysics and Med. Physics, Czechoslovak Acad. Scis., 1990. Rsch. fellow Inst. Clin. and Exptl. Medicine, Prague, 1973-78; rsch. asst. Inst. Biophys. Nuc. Medicine, Charles U., Prague, 1978-88; sr. lectr. Inst. Nuc. Medicine, Charles U., Prague, 1989—. Contbr., referee scientific articles to profl. jours. Recipient rsch. grants European Commn., Brussels, 1993, Austrian Ministry Sci. and Rsch., Vienna, 1993-95. Mem. European Assn. Nuc. Medicine, COST B2 Mgmt. Com. (nat. del. 1991-96), Soc. Nuclear Medicine. Office: Charles U Inst Nuc Medicine, Salmovská 3, CZ-12000 Prague 2, Czech Republic

ŠAMÁNEK, MILAN, pediatrics educator; b. Zborovice, Czechoslovakia, May 9, 1931; s. Miroslav and Františka (Šamánková) Š.; m. Ladislava Čevelová, Nov. 20, 1954; children: Lísková Svatava, Milan. MD, Charles U., Prague, Czech Republic, 1955, PhD, 1962, DSc, 1969. Resident in pediat. Dist. Hosp., Uh., Hradiště, Czech Republic, 1955-56; resident and sr. rsch. dept. pediat. U. Hosp., Prague, 1956-59, head cardiopulmonary lab., 1968-77; rsch. fellow Czechoslovac Acad. of Scis., Prague, 1961-62, U. Pa. Sch. of Medicine, Phila., 1964-65; dir. Ctr. Pediat. Cardiology and Cardiac Surgery, Prague, 1977-93, rsch. dir., 1993; prof. pediat. Charles U. Med. Sch., 1969; cons. WHO, 1979, mem. expert adv. panel; mem. steering com. Pediat. Cardiology and Cardiac Surgery, 1993-97. Mem. editl. bd. 6 med. jours.; author over 15 books; contbr. more than 600 articles to profl. jours. Pres. sci. com. Min. of Health, 1990-92; pres. Found. Children's Heart. Recipient Highest Sci. award Czech Govt. Fellow European Soc. Cardiology; mem. Assn. European Pediat. Cardiologists (coun. mem. 1979-86), World Heart Found. (com. sect. on cardiovasc. disease in young 1980—), Czech Med. Rsch. Coun., Czech Med. Soc. (hon. mem.), N.Y. Acad. Scis. Office: U Hosp Motol Kardiocentrum, V uvalu 84, 150 06 Prague 5, Czech Republic

SAMARA, MARIE-THERESE, bank executive; b. St. Julian's, Malta, Aug. 7, 1948; arrived in Greece, 1971; d. Joseph and Theodolinda (Cassar Torreggiani) Mifsud Bonnici; m. George Triandafilos Samaras, June 21, 1971; children: Olga, David. Student in langs., U. Malta. Pub. rels. officer, travel cons. Hotel & Tourist Enterprise, Ltd., Malta, 1965-71; reconciliations and investigations clk. Natwest Plc, Piraeus, Greece, 1974-86; asst. mgr. fgn. bus., groups liaison Natwest Plc, Athens, Greece, 1986-92, asst. mgr. premium retail, group liaison exec., 1992-96, personal banking exec., 1996-99; sr. mktg. exec. Piraeus Bank, Athens, Greece, 1999—. Roman Catholic. Office: Piraeus Bank, 5 Korai Stq, GR-10564 Athens Greece

SAMARANCH, JUAN ANTONIO (MARQUÉS DE SAMARANCH), International Olympic Committee president; b. Barcelona, Spain, July 17, 1920; s. Francisco and Juana (Torelló) S.; m. Maria Teresa Salisachs, Dec. 1955; children: Maria Teresa, Juan Antonio. Doctor honoris causa, several Internat. univs. With Spanish Olympic Com., from 1956, pres., 1967-70; pres. Internat. Olympic Com.; mem. internat. Olympic com., Lausanne, Switzerland, 1966—, v.p., 1974-78, pres., 1980—; pres. Caja de Pensiones para la Vejez y de Ahorros de Cataluña y Baleares, Spain, 1987; Spanish Ambassador to USSR and People's Republic of Mongolia, 1977-80; mcpl. councillor, Barcelona; nat. fel. for phys. edn. and sports, 1967-71; pres. Diputacion, Barcelona, 1973-77. Decorated Grand Croix. Office: Internat Olympic Com, Château de Vidy, 1007 Lausanne Switzerland*

SAMARZIJA, MIROSLAV, physician; b. Krasno, Croatia, Nov. 21, 1958; s. Nikola and Marija (Glavas) S.; m. Nada Restek, May 30, 1987; children: Luka, Filip. MD, Med. Sch. Zagreb, 1985, PhD, 1991. Rsch. asst. Med. Sch. Zagreb, 1987-89; from resident in nuclear medicine to asst. prof. medicine Zagreb U., 1989-96; internal medicine specialist, 1996—; chief postintensive care unit Univ. Hosp., Jordanov, Croatia, 1998-99; cons. Inst. Cardiac Prevention & Rehab., Zagreb, 1997-99. Author: Lung Cancer, 1998, Clinical Nuclear Medicine, 1999; contbr. articles to profl. jours. Mem. N.Y. Acad. Scis., European Soc. Cardiology, Croatian Soc. Pulmonology, Croatian Soc. Cardiology. Avocations: skiing, jogging. Home: Prilesje 49, 10000 Zagreb Croatia Office: Hosp Jordanovac, Jordanovac 104, 10000 Zagreb Croatia

SAMBANDAN, KAVITHA N., microbiologist, researcher; b. Cuddalore, Tamil Nadu, India, May 13, 1973; d. Narayanaswamy and Rajeswari Sambandan. BSc, C.K.N. Coll. for Women, Cuddalore, 1993; MSc, Presidency Coll., Chennai, Tamil Nadu, 1995; MPhil, CAS in Botany, U. Madras, Chennai, 1997, PhD, CAS in Botany, 2000. Jr. rsch. fellow Dept. Environment, Forests & Wildlife, India, 1997-99, sr. rsch. fellow, 1999—. Inventor in field. Guide Bharat Scouts & Guides, Chennai. Mem. Gedbids (ann. mem.), Acad. Plant Scis. India (ann. mem.), Indian Bot. Soc. (ann. mem.), Environ. Pollution Rsch. (ann. mem.), All India Bioethics Assn. (life mem.). Avocations: reading, plant cultivation, watching TV. E-mail: kavithans@ind5.vsnl.net.in. Office: U Madras, Guindy Campus, Chennai 600025, India

SAMBASIVAN, ESWARAN VENKAT, chemistry educator; b. Madras, India, June 8, 1947; s. Venkuaiyar and Annapurny Sambasivan; m. Sasikala Venkat Ramaswami Eswaran, May 5, 1991. BSc with honors, U. Delhi, 1966, MSc, 1968, PhD, 1973. With St. Stephen's Coll., Delhi, 1968—, head dept. chemistry, 1979-92; DAAD postdoctoral fellow Max Planck Inst. for Biochemistry, Germany, 1976-77, U. Heidelberg, Germany, 1984, U. Karlsruhe, Germany, 1984, Kluyver Lab. Biotech., Tech. U., Delft, The Netherlands, 1990-91; postdoctoral rschr. U. Göttingen, Germany, 1997, Ohio State U., Columbus, 1997. Contbr. articles to profl. jours; inventor and patentee in field. Fellow German Acad. Exch. Svc., 1976-77, 84, 97. Avocations: music, cricket, tennis. Home: A-6 St Stephens Coll, Delhi 110007, India Office: St Stephens Coll, Delhi 110007, India

SAMBASIVAN, MAHADEVA IYER, neurosurgeon, consultant; b. Trivandrum, India, May 1, 1936; s. Iyer Mahadeva and Ammal Avudai; m. Gomathy Sambasivan, May 8, 1963; children: Mahesh, Kumar, Srividya. MBBS, Trivandrum Med. Coll., India, 1955; MS in Neurosurgery, Vellore Christian Med. Coll., Trivandrum, 1960; MS in Gen. Surgery, Trivandrum Med. Coll., India, 1966. From asst. prof. to assoc. prof. Med. Coll., Trivandrum, 1966-75, prof., 1975-82, dir., 1982-91, vice prin., 1989-91; cons. neurosurgeon Cosmopolitan Hosp., Trivandrum, 1991—; sci. program dir. World Fedn. N.S. Socs., 1985-89, v.p. 1997—; dep. chmn. Neurotrauma Com. WFIVS, 1990—. Contbr. articles to med. jours. Chmn. Sankara Free Med. Ctr., Trivandrum, 1993—; v.p. Swati Tirunal Sangeetha Sabha, Trivandrum, 1994—; patron Ctr. for Human Rights Legal Aid Rsch., Trivandrum, 1994. Fellow Royal Coll. Surgeons, Acad. Med. Scis.; mem. Neurological Soc. (sec. 1981-89, pres. 1995—), World Fedn. Neurosurg. Socs. (v.p. 1997—). Avocations: Sanskrit studies, Vedie literature, nature. Home: Sivapriya Tagore Gardens, 695011 Trivandrum India Office: Cosmopolitan Hosp, Pattom, 695004 Trivandrum Kerala, India

SAMBAT, ALEXANDRE, Gabonese government official; b. Makokou, Gabon, Oct. 4, 1948. Postgrad. in chem. engring. Chem. engr.; indsl. psychologist Shell-Gabon Petroleum Co.; min. of pub. health and population Govt. of Gabon, Libreville, 1981-83, min. of labor and employment, 1983-87, min. of nat. edn., 1987, dep. min. of state to prime min. in charge of tourism, 1987, min. of environ. and nat. protection, 1988, min. of comm., postal svc. and telecomm., 1994—, min. of comm., culture, arts and popular edn., 1995—, now min. of ministry of youth sports and leisure. Office: Min Youth Sports & Leisure, BP 6, Libreville Gabon*

SAMBERGER, MICHAEL ANTONI, gynecologist, obstetrician, consultant, educator; b. Lublin, Poland, Apr. 5, 1950; s. Jozef Kazimierz and Waclawa Wanda (Glowczynska) S.; m. Teodora Wanda Majewska, Sept. 3, 1978; 1 child, Krzysztof Olaf (div.); m. Malgorzata Zofia Zawislak; 1 child, Ingrid. MD, Lublin Med. Acad., 1974, PhD, 1982, Specialist in Ob-Gyn.,

1983. Diplomate in Ob-Gyn. Asst. dept. ob-gyn. Lublin Med. Acad., 1974-83, asst. prof. dept. ob-gyn., 1983-89; observer dept. ob-gyn. U. Tex., 1984; cons. ob-gyn. ZCCM Hosp., Zambia, 1989-98; vice chmn. Country Profl. Commn., Lublin, 1983-89; organizer of introduction to mini invasive surgery/laparoscopy, Zambia, 1990—. Author: Propranolol Effect on Perfusion Pressure and Metabolism of Human Placenta, 1982; contbr. articles to profl. jours. Regional pres. Union Young Sci. Workers, Lublin, 1975-79. Mem. Internat. Soc. for Gynecol. Endoscopy, Polish Soc. Gynecology, Internat. Hosp. Fedn., Brit. Maternal and Fetal Medicine Soc. Social Democrat. Christian. Avocations: bridge, journalism, politics, skiing, tennis. Email: SAMBERGM@priv7.onet.pl. Home: PO Box 1321, Gleboka 3/22, Lublin 15, Poland Office: Ob-Gyn Centre Lublin, 4 Hempla St, 20-098 Lublin Poland

SAMBO, ABUBAKAR SANI, academic administrator; b. Zaria, Kaduna, Nigeria, July 31, 1955; s. Muhammadu Sani and A'Ishatu Sani (Mansur) S.; m. Jamila Abubakar Sambo, Aug. 8, 1982; three children. B in Engring. with first class honors, A.B.U., Zaria, 1979; PhD in Mech. Engring., U. Sussex, Eng., 1983. Registered engr. Nigeria. Grad. asst., sr. lectr. Bayero U., Kano, Nigeria, 1980-89; head mech. engring. dept. Bayero U., Kano, 1988-89, dep. dean, 1988-89; dir. Sokoto (Nigeria) Energy Rsch. Ctr., 1989-94; reader energy studies Sokoto Energy Ctr., 1989-91; exec. dir., CEO Kaduna (Nigeria) State Govt., 1994-95; vice-chancellor ATB U., Bauchi, Nigeria, 1995—; chmn. com. vice-chancellors Nigerian Univs., Bauchi, 2000—; lab. demonstrator Sch. Engring. and Applied Scis., Sussex, U.K., 1980-82; prof. energy U.D. U., Sokoto, 1991, dep. vice-chancellor, 1990-94; lectr. in field. Contbr. articles to profl. jours. Recipient Nat. Productivity award, 1997, Nat. Prodn. Order of Merit, Fed. Govt. Nigeria, 1998, Cert. of Honor, Nigerian Inst. Mgmt., 1998. Fellow Nigerian Soc. Engrs. (nat. tech. com. 1986-89, vice chmn. Kano br. 1986-87, tech. sec. Kano br. 1987-88, mem. prizes and awards com. 1988, Merit award 1997), Solar Energy Soc. Nigeria (sec.-gen. 1986-88, assoc. editor, mem. editl. bd. 1986—, pres. 1992-97), Inst. Adminstrv. Mgmt. Nigeria, Internat. Solar Energy Soc., Internat. Energy Found., World Renewable Energy Network, Nigerian Soc. Engrs. Islam. Avocations: playing squash, automobile repairs. Home: 3 Rimi Close, Bauchi Nigeria Office: Abubakar Tafawa Balewa Univ, Dass Rd, 0248 Bauchi Nigeria

SAMBROOK, PAUL JOHN, oral and maxillofacial surgeon, educator; b. Scunthorpe, Eng., Dec. 13, 1961; s. Laurence Henry and Mary Bernadette (Burke) S.; m. Heather Barbara Crosby, Mar. 24, 1990; children: Liam John Charles, Declan James Paul, Ashlinn Claire, Ciaran David Michael. B of Dental Surgery, U. Adelaide, South Australia, 1985, M of Dental Surgery, 1990, MB, BChir, 1993. House dentist South Australian Dental Svc., Adelaide, 1985; registrar Royal Adelaide Hosp., 1986-87; sr. resident Charity Hosp., New Orleans, 1988; sr. registrar Royal Adelaide Hosp., 1988-90; pvt. surg. practice Adelaide, 1990—; sr. vis. cons. Royal Adelaide Hosp., 1994—; lectr. U. Adelaide, 1994—. Note, committees of universities are not listed, per style. Recipient Lyons award for Pub. Speaking, Lyons Club, 1979. Fellow Royal Australian Coll. Dental Surgeons (accreditation com. 1991—, chair 2000—), Internat. Assn. Oral and Maxillofacial Surgeons; mem. Australian Dental Assn., Australian Med. Assn., Asian Assn. Oral and Maxillofacial Surgeons, Australian and New Zealand Assn. Oral and Maxillofacial Surgeons (sec. elect, fed. councilor). Avocation: computing. Home: 637 Greenhill Rd, Burnside 5066, Australia

SAMBUAGA, THEO LEO, government official; b. Manado, Indonesia, June 6, 1949; s. Jimmy Henry and Wilhelmine (Gontha) S.; m. Erna Soedaryati Soekardi, Nov. 18, 1952; children: Eddy Khrisna Patria, Jerry Adithya Ksatria. MIPP-SAIS, U. Indonesia, 1978; MIPP, Johns Hopkins U., 1990. Chmn. Ctrl. Bd., 1998—; sec. gen. Indonesian Nat. Youth Congress, 1978-84; chmn. ctrl. exec. bd. AMPI, 1984-89, Kosgoro, Indonesia, 1990—; min. labor Govt. of Indonesia, 1998, min. of state for housing, 1999; vice sec. gen. Ctrl. Exec. Bd. Golkar, Indonesia, 1993—; vice chmn. Working Group on Internat. Rels. Golkar, 1985-93; mem. Parliament Ho. of Reps., Indonesia, 1982—; vice chmn. Com. for Inter Parliamentary Cooperation, Indonesia, 1987-90, chmn., 1994—; vice chmn. Com. I, Indonesia, 1990-94. Avocations: swimming, tennis, cycling. Home: Salak Blok L/I Kalibata Ind, Jakarta 12750, Indonesia Office: Min Pub Housing, JL Kebun Sirih 31, Jakarta 10340, Indonesia

SAMEGY, DIVIACANTE CANTILAL GIVANE, occupational health physician; b. Inhambane, Mozambique, June 22, 1946; arrived in Portugal, 1965; s. Cantilal Givane and Iralacximibai Mathuradas; m. Maria Manuela Barbosa Dias, July 28, 1979; children: Mayur, Danil. Pub. health officer Madeira Island, 1985-90; occupl. health physician Unimed, Porto, 1990—; gen. physician CHC & Hosp. Fafe, 1993-95; gen. practice asst. Ministry of Health, Paredes, Portugal, 1995—; emergency physician Hosp. San João, Porto, 1999-2000. Mem. Portuguese Med. Assn., Portuguese Soc. Occupl. Medicine, N.Y. Acad. Sci. Avocations: cinema, music, dance, theater, gastronomy. Home: 38-4oE, Rua Nicolau Marques Gudes, 4250 333 Porto Portugal Office: Gen & Occupl Health Cabinet, R Julio Dinis 103-P, 4050 323 Porto Portugal

SAMER, BILL (FRED) CARL, poet, writer, media consultant; b. Elizabeth, N.J., Sept. 2, 1953; s. Fred Carl and Myrtle Edith (Levey) S. AA, Union Coll., Cranford, N.J., 1975; MA, Kean U. N.J., Union, 1980; BA, Concordia Coll., Bronxville, N.Y., 1994. Editor Gracevine, Union, N.J., 1975—; cons. SIS, Pine Brook, N.J., 1978—; lectr., actor. Author: Tuxedo Street, Back When We Were Young, 2000; contbr. poems to lit. jours. and audiocassettes (Editor's Choice award 1996). Del. to conv. Luth. Ch. Mo. Synod, Ridgewood, N.J., 1976; choir mem. Grace Luth. Ch., Union, N.J., 1978-79, lay minister, 1974-77; walker, CROP, Clifton, N.J., 1978; vol. I Found It TV, Campaign, N.Y., 1976, It's Just Love, 1999; librarian Garden Club, Union, 1980-82; mem. WHAT, the William Samer Activist Orgn., 1987—. Lutheran. Avocations: hiking, art, reading, volleyball, documentary photography. Home and Office: Gracevine/WHAT 936 Louisa St Union NJ 07083-6725

SAMES, KLAUS HERMANN, anatomist, gerontologist, researcher, educator; b. Kassel, Hessen, Germany, Apr. 12, 1939; s. Ernst and Margarete (Strack) S.; m. Kornelia Steinecke, Mar. 12, 1968; 1 child, Almut. MD, U. Muenster (Germany), 1971; Habilitated Dr., U. Erlangen (Germany), 1981; Prof. in Anatomy and Exptl. Gerontology, Free U. Berlin, 1987. Registered med. practitioner. Lectr. in pathology U. Heidelberg (Germany), 1971-73; lectr. in anatomy U. Heidelberg and U. Hamburg (Germany), 1973-85; sr. lectr. in anatomy Free U. Berlin, 1985-88; dep. prof. in anatomy U. Heidelberg, U. Freiburg, U. Zuerich, U. Hamburg, 1988-97; personal chair, prof. anatomy U. Hamburg and U. Berlin, 1997—. Author: (monographs) The Role of Proteoglycans and Glycosaminoglycans in Aging, 1994, Sterblich durch ein Gesetz deer Natur?, 2000; editor: (handbook) Medizinische Regeneration und Tissue Engineering, 2000; co-editor: (handbook) Kompedium Der Gerontology, 1994, Erfolgreiches Altern, 1989; contbr. numerous articles, 3 revs. to profl. jours. Grantee Deutsche Forschunggsgemeinschaft. Mem. German Soc. Gerontolgy and Geriatrics (dep. chmn. biology sect. aging 1987-91), Anatomische Gesellschaft, N.Y. Acad. Scis. Avocation: author of satiric essays. Home: Tondernstieg 6, D-22049 Hamburg Germany Office: U Hamburg U Hosp Haburg-Eppendorf, Anatomical Inst Martinstrasse 52, D-20246 Hamburg Germany

SAMES, MARTIN, neurosurgeon; b. Jablonec nad Nisou, Czech Republic, Nov. 1, 1963; s. Arnost Wilhelm and Eva Jarmila (Soulova) S.; m. Martina Vera Novakova, Nov. 21, 1962; children: Pavlina, Adela. MD, Medical Sch. Charles Univ., Prague, 1988. Diplomate Am. Bd. Neurosurgery. Resident of neurosurgy Masaryk Hosp, Usti nad Labem, Czech Republic, 1991-96, deputy chmn., 1997, chmn., 1997—; lectr. 3d Medical Sch., Prague, 1992-98, Inst. of Medicine Usti, 1992-98. Contbr. articles to profl. jours. Recipient grant Peripheral Nerve Regeneration Min. of Health, 1992-94, Normal Pressure Hydrocephalus Ministry of Health, 2000—. Mem. Czech Medical Soc., Czech Neurosci. Soc. (com. mem. 1997-98), European Assn. of Neurosurgy Soc., Nat. Geographic Soc. Avocations: music, tennis, diving, astronomy, literature. Home: Jezkova 20, 400 11 Usti nad Labem Czech Republic Office: Masaryk Hosp dept nuerosurg, Pasteurova 9, 401 13 Usti nad Labem Czech Republic

SAMHAN, MOHAMMAD JASIM, ambassador; b. Ras Al-Khaimah, United Arab Emirates, Oct. 1, 1950; married; 5 children. Cert. fundamentals in fin. and acctg., Syracuse U., 1977; BA, Goddard Coll., 1979; M in Social Scis., Syracuse U., 1981. Registered pharmacist. With Dept. Water and Electricity, Ras Al-Khaimah, United Arab Emirates, 1966-68, Nat. Oil Co., Ras Al-Khaimah, 1972-74; joined Diplomatic and Consular Svcs., 1974; 3d sec. Permanent Mission to UN, N.Y.C., 1975-76, 1st sec., 1976-77, counsellor, 1977-81; counsellor dept. polit. affairs Ministry of Fgn. Affairs, 1981; acting consul gen. United Arab Emirates Consulate, Bombay, India, 1981; min. plenipotentiary, 1981-82, dir. dept. internat. orgns. and confs., 1982-84, amb., 1984, dir. dept. Arab Homeland, 1984-87; head United Arab Emirates sect. Cairo, 1987; amb. to Tunisia, 1988-92; permanent rep. UN, N.Y.C., 1992—; permanent rep. to Arab League, 1988-90. Office: Permament Mission United Arab Emirates 747 3rd Ave Fl 36 New York NY 10017-2803*

SAMII, MASSOOD, international business educator, consultant; b. Tehran, Iran, Aug. 17, 1945; came to U.S., 1963; s. Nassar and Guity Samii; m. Farideh Namazi, Nov. 18, 1978; children: Bob, Leila. BS, U. Hartford, 1968; MBA, Western New Eng. Coll., 1970; PhD, SUNY, Albany, 1975. Chief Internat. Econ. Bur., Iranian aPlanning Ministry, Tehran, 1975-76; dir. Western Cons., Tehran, 1976-78; head fin. sect. OPEC, Vienna, Austria, 1978-87; vis. fellow Harvard U., Boston, 1987-89; prof. internat. bus., chmn. dept. N.H. Coll., Manchester, 1988—; sr. lectr. MIT, Boston, 1990—;mem. adv. bd. Office Internat. Commerce, N.H., 1995—; bd. dirs. N.H. Trade Assn., 1996—; dir. BIE project U.S. Dept. Edn., Washington, 1997-01. Contbr. over 30 articles to profl. jours. Mem. Acad. Internat. Bus., Am. Econ. Assn., Ea. Acad. Internat. Bus. (program chmn. 1998). Avocations: skiing, tennis, chess. E-mail: msamii@minerva.nhc.edu. Home: 48 Erik St Merrimack NH 03054-4592 Office: NH Coll 2500 N River Rd Manchester NH 03054

SAMIOS, NICHOLAS PETER, physicist; b. N.Y.C., Mar. 15, 1932; s. Peter and Niki (Vatick) S.; m. Mary Linakis, Jan. 12, 1958; children: Peter, Gregory, Alexandra. AB, Columbia U., 1953, PhD, 1957. Instr. physics Columbia U., N.Y.C., 1956-59; asst. physicist Brookhaven Nat. Lab., Upton, N.Y., 1959-62, assoc. physicist, 1962-64, physicist, 1964-68, sr. physicist, 1968—, group leader, 1965-75, chmn. dept. physics, 1975-81, dep. dir. for high energy and nuclear physics, 1981, dir., 1982-97; adj. prof. Stevens Inst. Tech., 1969-75, Columbia U., 1970—. Contbr. articles in field to profl. jours. Bd. dirs. Stony Brook Found., 1989, L.I. Assn., 1989. Recipient E.O. Lawrence Meml. award, 1980, award in physics and math. scis. N.Y. Acad. Scis., 1980; named AUI Disting. Scientist, 1992, W.K.H. Panofsky prize, 1993. Fellow Am. Phys. Soc. (chmn. divsn. of particles and fields 1975-76, chmn. PEP exptl. program com. 1976-78); mem. Internat. Ctr. Future Acceleration, Akademia Athenon (corr.). Achievements include being an expert in field of high energy particle and nuclear physics. Office: Brookhaven Nat Lab Bldg 510 A Upton NY 11973*

SAMKANGE, TOMMIE MARIE ANDERSON, educational psychologist, consultant; b. Jackson, Miss., Aug. 1, 1932; d. Harry and Marie (Hughes) Anderson; m. Stanlake John Thompson Samkange, Feb. 6, 1958 (dec. Mar. 1988); children: Stanlake Mudavanhu, Harry Mushore. BS, Tougaloo (Miss.) Coll., 1953; MS, Ind. U., 1955, PhD, 1958. Registered ednl. psychologist Health Professions Coun. of Zimbabwe. Psychologist, market rschr. African Pub. Rels., Harare, Zimbabwe, 1959-64; assoc. prof. Tuskegee (Ala.) Inst., 1964-67, Tenn. State U., Nashville, 1967-91; sr. tutor Harvard U., Cambridge, Mass., 1971-74; asst. prof. Tufts U., Medford, Mass., 1974-76; chief ednl. psychologist Govt. of Zimbabwe, 1981-94; ret., 1994; chairperson Ranche House Coll., Harare, 1992-96, Nyatsime Coll., Chitungwiza, Zimbabwe, 1995—, Proposed So. African Meth. U., 1997—; bd. govs. Moleli Secondary Sch., Selous, Zimbabwe, 1988—; bd. dirs. Chinyaradzo Children's Home, Zimbabwe, 1982—. Contbr.: (books) Black Woman: Myths and Realities, 1978, Hunhuism or Ubuntuism, 1980; reviewer African Dilemma Tales, 1976; contbr. articles to profl. jours. Mem. St. John's Ambulance, Harare, 1982—; cons. Zimbabwe Nat. Assn. Mental Health, 1985—; bd. dirs. Child Protection Soc., Harare, 1980—, Rusike Children's Home, Harare, 1984—. Named Outstanding Young Woman of Am. Tougaloo Coll., 1965, Am. Men of Sci., AAAS, 1968; honoree Consortium of Drs. Ltd. Women of Color in the Struggle, 1992; Mellon scholar Tufts U., 1977-78. Mem. APA, Zimbabwe Psychol. Assn., Pi Lambda Theta (life). Methodist. Avocations: music, reading. Home: The Castle Chiremba Rd, Harare Zimbabwe

SAMMAN, JUAN M., prosthodontist; b. Damascus, Syria, Nov. 4, 1953; s. Moukhtar and Souha S. BS, Am. U., Beirut, 1976; DDS, NYU, 1981; MSc, London U., 1983. Hon. clin. asst. to the Dental Hosp. Univ. Coll. Hosp., London, 1983; scientific rschr. NYU, N.Y.C., 1984-87, clin. asst. prof., 1987-93; pvt. practice Manhattan, N.Y., 1988—; assoc. N.Y. Dental Implant Restorative and Cosmetic Dentistry Ctr., 1985-87, Sam Weber, DDS, 1987-88; lectr. NYU. Contbr. articles to profl. publs. Fellow Brit. Soc. for Study of Prosthetic Dentistry, Internat. Coll. Prosthodontists, Am. Coll. Prosthdontists; mem. ADA, Internat. Assn. Dental Rsch., European Prosthodontic Assn., Acad. Osseointegration. Avocations: music, painting, travel. Office: 200 Central Park S New York NY 10019-1415

SAMMAN, SAMIR, biochemistry educator; b. Beirut, Lebanon, May 20, 1960; m. Marija B. Gavranic, July 4, 1987; children: Julia, Alexandra, Olivia. BSc, U. Sydney, Australia, 1982, PhD, 1988. Postdoctoral fellow U. Western Ont., Can., 1987-89; clin. rsch. fellow Royal Prince Alfred Hosp., Sydney, 1990; lectr. biochemistry U. Sydney, 1990-95, sr. lectr., 1995—. Office: U Sydney Human Nutrition, Dept Biochemistry, Sydney NSW 2006, Australia

SAMMER, MATTHIAS, professional soccer player; b. Dresden, Germany, Sept. 5, 1967. Defender Dynamo Dresden Football Club, East Germany, VFB Stuttgart Football Club, Germany, Inter Milan Football Club, Italy; capt., defender Germany World Cup squad; winner World Cup, 1990; defender Borussia Dortmund Football Club, Germany, 1994-99; chief coach Boriussia Dortmund, 2000Ŝ. Office: BV 09 Borussia Dortmund, Postfach 10 05 09, 44005 Dortmund Germany*

SAMMON, ALASTAIR MACNAUGHTON, surgeon, consultant; b. Edinburgh, Scotland, Sept. 23, 1947; s. John Douglas and Mary (Macnaughton) S.; m. Helen Mary Kirkman Brown, May 12, 1984; children: Alexander, Peter, Rebecca. MB, U. Glasgow, 1971, MD with honors, 1992. Surg. trainee West of Scotland Tng. Scheme, Glasgow, 1977-80; sr. surg. registrar U. Tchg. Hosp., Lusaka, Zambia, 1981; surg. specialist Umtata Gen. Hosp., Transkei, South Africa, 1981-87; sr. lectr. surgery, prin. surg. specialist Umtata Gen. Hosp., Trauskei, South Africa, 1987-88; med. officer in charge PCEA Chogoria Hosp., Kenya, 1988-95; Locum sr. lectr. U. Bristol, United Kingdom, 1995-99; cons. Gloucestershire Royal Hosp., Gloucester, Eng., 2000—. Contbr. articles to profl. jours. Alexander Walker Naddell Traveling fellow Royal Coll. Physicians and Surgeons of Glasgow, 1999. Fellow Royal Coll. Physicians, Surgeons of Glasgow; mem. British Soc. Gastroenterology, British Assn. Surg. Oncology, Christian Med. Fellow. Avocations: music, woodwork. Office: Gloucestershire Royal Hosp, Dept Surgery, Gloucestor GL1 3NN, United Kingdom

SAMMUT, JESMOND, geography educator, researcher, consultant; b. M'tarfa, Malta, May 27, 1965; arrived in Australia, 1967; s. Joseph and Janna (Grech) S.; m. Katrina Hazel Tilse, Mar. 7, 1992; 1 child, Aimee-Janna. BA with honors, U. NSW, Australia, 1988; MSc, U. NSW, 1994, PhD, 2000. Soil conservationist NSW Soil Conservation Svc., 1989-90; rsch. fellow NSW Fisheries, 1993-95; lectr. U. NSW, 1995—; cons. Unisearch, Australia, 1997; leader rsch. program Rsch. Inst. for Coastal Fisheries, Indonesia, 1997; advisor on acid sulfate soil issues various orgns. in India, Indonesia and Australia, 1995-97; workshop convenor Coll. Fisheries, Mangalore, India, 1997; mem. acid sulfate soils mgmt. adv. com.-tech. com. NSW, 1995-97. Author: An Introduction to Acid Sulfate Soils, 1996; contbr. articles to jours. in field.; mem. editl. bd. The Land, 1997. Justice of the Peace, NSW. Oyster rsch. grantee Fisheries R & D Corp., NSW, 1996—, Algae rsch. grant Australian Rsch. Coun., NSW, 1996, Waterplant and Plankton rsch. grant, 1997; postgrad. scholar Australian Ctr. for Internat. Agrl. Rsch., 1993-95. Mem. Australian Inst. Geographers, Australian Soc. Fish Biology, Australian Soc. Electron Microscopy, Internat. Land Use Soc. Avocations: recreational fishing, travel, music, humanitarian-oriented research, overseas aid work. Office: U NSW, Sch Geography, Sydney 2052, Australia

SAMODELOV, LEONID FEODOR, anesthesiologist; b. Villach, Austria, Mar. 3, 1948; s. Feodor Alexander and Valentina (Ropadin) S.; m. Gabriele Sauerland; children: Valentina, Sophia, Alexander. MS in Biology, Northeastern U., 1975; MD, U. Düsseldorf, Germany, 1984; BS in Biology, Boston Coll., 1970. Surg. orderly Mass. Gen. Hosp., Boston, 1964-70, rsch. technician respiratory ICU, 1970-75; rsch. assoc. sect. exptl. anesthesia U. Düsseldorf, 1975-83, software developer/programmer dept. anesthesiology, 1983-85, anesthesia resident, 1985-88; med. intern Mercy Cath. Med. Ctr., Upper Darby, Pa., 1988-89; anesthesia resident Albert Einstein Med. Ctr., Phila., 1989-91, Meridia-Huron Hosp., Cleve., 1991-94. Contbr. numerous articles to profl. publs. Avocations: electronic design and construction, software development, scuba diving, photography, flying. Home: 20900 Fairlane Cir Fairview Park OH 44126-2007 Office: Meridia-Huron Hosp 13951 Terrace Rd Cleveland OH 44112-4399

SAMOILOV, NAUM ALEXANDROVICH, chemist, educator; b. Tashkent, Uzbekistan, Dec. 9, 1941; s. Alexandr Izrailevich and Faina Naumovna (Reznik) S.; m. Natalia Evgenevna Remizova, July 4, 1964; children: Lubov, Julia. Canditate of scis., Poly. Inst., Kuibyshev, Russia, 1971; DSc, Oil U., Ufa, Russia, 1994. Asst. in chemistry Oil U., 1963-72, docent, 1972-94, prof., 1994—. Author: Fundamentals of Computer Application in Chemical Technology, 1986, Examples and Problems in Course of Fundamentals of Computer Application in Chemical Technology, 1995; contbr. numerous articles to sci. jours., conf. procs.; patentee in field (30). Recipient Bronze medal Averall Russian Exhbn. for Chem. Equipment, 1984; grantee Govt. of Russia, Moscow, 1996-97; Honored Inventor Republic Bachkortostan, 1998. Mem. Microbiology Soc., Mendeleev Soc., N.Y. Acad. Scis. Avocation: fine arts. Office: Ufa State Petroleum Tech U, Kosmonavtov St, 450062 Ufa Bashkir, Russia

SAMOILOV, VALERY SAMUEL, petrologist-geochemist, researcher; b. Moscow, Russia, Sept. 16, 1937; arrived in Israel, 1991; s. Samuel Isaac Shapiro and Sima Jacob (Faverman) S.; m. Jeana Ivan Kuznetzova, Nov. 21, 1964; children: Gergei, Rakhamim Julia. MSc, Moscow Geol.-Prospecting Inst., 1959; PhD, IGEM/USSR Acad. Scis., Moscow, 1967; asst. prof., Vinogradov Inst. Geochemistry, Irkutsk, USSR, 1972, DSc, 1980. Geologist USSR Ministry Geology, Moscow, 1959-62; scientist Vinogradov Inst. Geochemistry, Irkutsk, 1962-69, sr. scientist, 1969-82, chief of lab., 1982-91; rschr. Ben-Gurion U. of the Negev, Beer Sheva, Israel, 1993-99, sr. rschr., 1999—; sci. sec. Vinogradov Inst. Geochemistry, Irkutsk, 1970-72, dep. dir., 1989-90. Author: (books) Petrology, Mineralogy and Geochemistry of Carbonatites in Eastern Siberia, 1972, Carbonatites (facies and the formation conditions), 1977 (USSR Acad. Scis. award 1977), Geochemistry of Carbonatites, 1984 (USSR Acad. Scis. award 1987), Complexes of Alkaline Rocks and Carbonatites in Mongolia, 1983 (USSR Coun. Mins. award 1986). Mem. AAAS, Israel Geol. Soc., N.Y. Acad. Scis. Home: Zhabotinski 21/30, 84411 Beer Sheva Israel Office: Ben-Gurion U of the Negev, Dept Geol/Env Sc PO Box 653, 84105 Beer Sheva Israel

SAMOJLIK, EUGENIUSZ, medical educator, clinical researcher; b. Kuchmy-Bialystok, Poland, Aug. 20, 1933; s. Michael and Anastazia S.; m. Anna Morozewicz, Apr. 10, 1965; children: Dorothy, Michael. BS in Biomedicine, U. Warsaw, 1958, PhD in Reproductive Endocrinology, 1964. Rsch. asst. Maternity Inst. Dept. Pharmacology, Warsaw, 1958-62, sr. asst., 1962-66; asst. prof., chief reproductive pharmacology & toxicology Inst. Pharmacy Dept. Pharmacology, Warsaw, 1966-70; assoc. prof., chief hormone rsch. lab. Med. Acad. Dept. Clin. Endocrinology, Warsaw, 1970-73; staff rschr. II Syntex, Inc. Rsch. Divsn., Palo Alto, Calif., 1974-75; asst. prof. physiology, dir. radioimmunoassay lab. Milton S. Hershey (Pa.) Med. Ctr., Divsn. Endocrinology, 1975-80; staff endocrinologist VA Med. Ctr. Dept. Medicine, Sect. Endocrinology, East Orange, N.J., 1980-82; dir. endocrine lab. Newark Beth Israel Med. Ctr., Dept. Medicine, 1982-92; assoc. prof. medicine divsn. endocrinology U. Medicine & Dentistry-N.J. Med. Sch., Newark, 1982—; chief endocrine lab. dept. Labs. NBIMC, 1994-96; vis. researcher UCLA Sch. Medicine, Torrance, Calif., 1973; vis. scientist Nat. Inst. Child Health Human Devel., Reproductive Br., Bethesda, Md., 1973-74; lectr. in field. Mem. internat. adv. bd. Jour. Assisted Reproductive Tech. and Andrology, mem. editorial bd., 1996; contbr. articles to profl. jours. Grantee WHO, 1973-74, Ciba-Geigy, 1982-83, Nat. Cancer Inst., 1983-86, 85-88; tng. program fellow Worcester Found. Experimental Biology, Shrewsbury, Mass., 1967-69. Mem. AAAS, Am. Soc. Andrology, Am. Assn. Clin. Chemistry, Nat. Acad. Clin. Biochemistry, Acad. Medicine N.J., Endorcine Soc. Home: 73 Sykes Ave Livingston NJ 07039-1318

SAMPABLO LAURO, ITALO, physician; b. Barcelona, Spain, Oct. 3, 1963; m. Gemma Mulachs, May 9, 1992. MD, U. Autonoma Barcelona, 1987; diploma in neumology, U. Barcelona, 1992. Asst. Bellvitge Hosp., Barcelona, 1989-92; sr. med. registrar Hosp. Sant Boi, Barcelona, 1993-96; chief U. Inst. Dexeus, Barcelona, 1996—, dir. respiratory svc., 1997—; cons. Bellvitge Hosp., 1993-94, Hosp. Sant Boi, 1997—. Author: Advances in Internal Medicine, 1995; contbr. articles to profl. jours. Mem. European Respiratory Soc., N.Y. Acad. Scis. Office: Inst U Drexeus, Iradier 3, 08017 Barcelona Spain

SAMPAIO, IVAN BARBOSA MACHADO, agronomist, statistician, educator, researcher; b. Rio de Janeiro, Feb. 23, 1943; s. Dagoberto Machado and Neusa Barbosa Machado S. BSc in Agr., Fed. Rural U. Rio de Janeiro, 1966; MSc in Stats., Iowa State U., 1970; PhD in Applied Statis., U. Reading, Eng., 1988; postdoctoral in multivariate analysis, U. Poly., Madrid, 1993. Agronomist/statistician Ministry of Agr., Brasilia, Brazil, 1967-73; statistician Ministry of Health, Brasilia, Brazil, 1973; lectr., cons. Fed. U. Minas Gerais, Belo Horizonte, Brazil, 1974—; grad. courses coord., Fed. U. Minas Gerais, 1982-85; cons. com. Zoo Botanical Found., Belo Horizonte, 1991-92; vis. prof. U. Poly., Madrid, 1992-93. Editor Brazilian Jour. Vet. Medicine and Animal Sci., Belo Horizonte, 1994-96. Recipient Antonio Secundino State medal, Brazilian Agrl., 2000; grantee Overseas Rsch. Students, U.K. Com. Vice Chancellors, London, 1985; named Animal Sci. Rschr. Yr. Brazilian Soc. Animal Sci., 1996. Mem. Brazilian Soc. Animal Sci. (Rschr. of Yr. 1996). Mem. Workers' Party. Roman Catholic. Avocations: woodcarving, trekking, birdwatching, swimming. Office: U Fed Minas Gerais, Caixa Postal 567, 30123970 Belo Horizonte Minas Ge, Brazil

SAMPAIO, JORGE, president of Portugal; b. Sept. 18, 1939; m. Maria José Ritta; 2 children. Former sec.- gen. Socialist Party; former mayor City of Lisbon. Avocations: music, golf. Office: Presidencia de Republica, Palacio de Belem, 1349-022 Lisbon Portugal

SAMPAS, DOROTHY MYERS, retired government official; b. Washington, Aug. 24, 1933; d. Lawrence and Anna Cornelia (Henkel) Myers; m. James George Sampas, Dec. 8, 1962; children: George, Lawrence James. AB, U. Mich., 1955; postgrad., U. Paris, 1955-56; PhD, Georgetown U., 1970; cert., Nat. War Coll., Washington, 1987, Naval Post Grad. Sch., 1993. With Bur. Pub. Affairs Dept. State, Washington, 1958-60, analyst Bur. of Adminstrn., 1973-75, div. chief, dep. chief Office of Position and Pay Mgmt., 1979-83, div. chief Office of Mgmt., 1983-84, dir. Office of Mgmt., 1984-86; vice consul Am. Consulate Gen., Hamburg, Fed. Republic Germany, 1960-62; cons. Trans Century Corp., Washington, 1972; gen. svcs. officer Am. Embassy, Brussels, 1975-79; embassy minister-counselor Am. Embassy, Beijing, 1987-90; minister-counselor U.S. Mission to UN, N.Y.C., 1991-94; Am. ambassador to Islamic Republic of Mauritania, 1994-97, ret., 1998. Presbyterian. Home: 4715 Trent Ct Chevy Chase MD 20815-5516

SAMPAT, DHARMESH, computer consultant; b. Pune, India, Nov. 6, 1967; s. Kishansinh and Madhu Kishansinh Sampat; m. Kalindi Dharmesh, May 23, 1994; 1 child, Rohan. B of Engring., D. Y. Patil Coll. Engring., Pune, 1989; M of Engring., Victoria Jubilee Tech. Inst., Mumbai, 1993. Cert. All India Coun. Tech. Edn. Lectr. D. Y. Patil Coll. Engring., Pune, 1989-91; asst. cons. Tata Consultancy Svcs., Pune, 1993—. Avocations: surfing the Internet, watching movies. Office phone: 91-20-6711058. E-mail: dharmeshs@pune.tcs.co.in. Home: D-15 Patil Regency, Of f Karve Rd Erandwane, Pune 411 004, India Office: Tata Consultancy Svcs, 54B Hadapsar Industrial Est, Pune 411 013, India

SAMPATH KUMAR, ARAKALGUD, surgeon, educator; b. Bangalore, Karnataka, India, Apr. 15, 1946; s. A.N. and A. (Parvathamma) Anantharamiya; m. Pamela D'Souza, June 7, 1975. MBBS, Bangalore (India) Med. Coll., 1967; MS, All India Inst. Med. Sci., 1973, MCh in Cardiovasc. Surgery, 1976. Sr. resident All India Inst. Med. Sci., 1976-79, lectr., 1978-81, asst. prof., 1981-87, addl. prof., 1987-92, prof., 1992—; fellow Milw. Heart Surgery Assocs., 1979-80; Examiner in cardiovascular surgery Nizam's Inst., Bangalore U., Delhi U.; examiner, tech. expert faculty selection Sri Chitra Tirunal Inst. for Med. Scis. and Tech. Editl. cons. Indian Heart Jour., Asian Cardiovascular Thoracic Annals, Indian Jour. Med. Rsch.; editor Indian Jour. Thoracic and Cardiovasc. Surgery; contbr. articles to profl. jours. Mem. Assn. Thoracic and Cardiovascular Surgeons India, Soc. Thoracic Surgeons, Soc. for Heart Valve Disease. Avocations: photography, creative writing. Office: All India Inst Med Scis, New Delhi 110 029, India

SAMPEDRO, JOSÉ LUIS, novelist, economist; b. Spain, Feb. 1, 1917; s. Luis and Matilde (Saez) S.; m. Isabel Pellicer, July 10, 1944; 1 child, Isabel. D.Econ.Scis., Universidad Complutense, Madrid. Asst. lectr. faculty econs. U. Madrid, 1947-55, prof. econs., 1955-72; adviser Spanish Ministry Commerce, 1951-57, Ministry Fin., 1957-62; econ. adviser Banco Exterior de España, 1948-68, 77-82; v.p. Fundacion Banco Exterior, Madrid, 1982-84; rep. to OECD, Paris, 1958-62; mem. Spanish mission to UN, 1956; mem. III UNCTAD, Santiago de Chile, 1972, FMI/Banco Mundial de Tokyo, 1964. Author: (novels) Congreso en Estocolmo, 1952, El Rio que nos Lleva, 1961, Octubre, Octubre, 1981, La Sonrisa Etrusca, 1985, El Caballo Desnudo, 1970, La Vieja Sirena, 1990, Real Sitio, 1993, La Estatua de Adolfo Espejo, 1994, La Sombra de los Dias, 1994, Fronteras, 1996, El Amante Lesbiano, 2000, (play) La Paloma de Carton (Nat. prize Calderon de la Barca 1950), 1950; other plays and fiction, several works on econ. Mem. Spanish Senate, 1977-78. Mem. Royal Spanish Acad., Colegio de Economistas, Sociedad de Autores de España.

SAMPINO, ANTHONY F., physician, obstetrician and gynecologist; b. Bklyn., Jan. 13, 1965; s. Frank Paul-Joseph and Lillian Katherine (Cucinotta) S. D Osteopathic Medicine, N.Y. Coll. Osteopathic Medicine, 1991. Diplomate Am. Bd. Ob-Gyn, Am. Coll. Osteo. Bd. Ob-Gyn. Rotating intern St. Barnabas Hosp., Bronx, N.Y., 1991-92; resident ob-gyn. St. Vincents Med. Ctr. of Richmond, Staten Island, N.Y., 1992-96; with dept. ob-gyn. Good Samaritan Hosp., West Islip, N.Y., 1996—; pvt. practice Comprehensive Ob-Gyn of L.I., Massapequa Park, N.Y., 1997—; dir. osteo. internship program Good Samaritan Hosp., 1998—; clin. asst. prof. N.Y. Coll. Osteo. Medicine, 1996—. Fellow ACOG (jr., sect. chmn. 1992-94, bd. cert.); mem. AMA, Am. Osteo. Assn., Am. Coll. Osteo. Ob-gyn., Am. Soc. Colposcopy and Cervical Pathology, Am. Assn. Gynecologic Laparoscopists (Outstanding Resident in Gyn. Endoscopy 1996), Med. Soc. State of N.Y., L.I. Soc. Osteo. Physicians & Surgeons, Suffolk County Med. Soc. Home: 60 West Ln Bay Shore NY 11706-8616

SAMPLE, STEVEN BROWNING, university executive; b. St. Louis, Nov. 29, 1940; s. Howard and Dorothy (Cunningham) S.; m. Kathryn Brunkow, Jan. 28, 1961; children: Michelle Sample Smith, Elizabeth Ann. BS, U. Ill., 1962, MS, 1963, PhD, 1965; DHULL (hon.), Canisius Coll., 1989; LLD (hon.), U. Sheffield, Eng., 1991; EdD (hon.), Purdue U., 1994; DHL (hon.), Hebrew Union Coll., 1994; DL (hon.), U. Nebr., 1995. Sr. scientist Melpar Inc., Falls Church, Va., 1965-66; assoc. prof. elec. engring. Purdue U., Lafayette, Ind., 1966-73; dep. dir. Ill. Bd. Higher Edn., Springfield, 1971-74; exec. v.p. acad. affairs, dean Grad. Coll., prof. elec. eng. U. Nebr., Lincoln, 1974-82; prof. elec. and computer engring. SUNY, Buffalo, 1982-91, pres., 1982-91; pres. U. So. Calif., L.A., 1991—, prof. elec. engring., 1991—, Robert C. Packard pres.'s chair, 1995—, pres.; bd. dirs. Santa Catalina Island Co., UNOVA, William Wrigley Jr. Co., Advanced Bionics, AMCAP/AMF; vice chmn., bd. dirs. Western N.Y. Tech. Devel. Ctr., Buffalo, 1982-91; chmn. bd. dirs. Calspan-UB Rsch. Ctr., Inc., Buffalo, 1983-91; mem. Calif. Coun. Sci. and Tech., Irvine, Calif., L.A. Bus. Advisors, Nat. Acad. of Engring., 1998—; cons. in field; bd. trustees U. So. Calif., bd. overseers Keck Sch. Medicine. Contbr. articles to profl. jours.; patentee in field. Timpanist St. Louis Philharm. Orch., 1955-58; chmn. Western N.Y. Regional Econ. Devel. Coun., 1984-91; trustee U. at Buffalo Found., 1982-91, Studio Arena Theatre, Buffalo, 1983-91, Western N.Y. Pub. Broadcasting Assn., 1985-91; bd. dirs. Buffalo Philharm. Orch., 1982-91, Regenstrief Med. Found., Indpls., 1982—, Rsch. Found. SUNY, 1987-91; chmn. Gov.'s Conf. on Sci. and Engring. Edn., Rsch. and Devel., 1989-91; chair Calif. Bus.-Higher Edn. Forum; bd. dirs. L.A. chpt. World Affairs Coun., Hughes Galaxy Inst. Edn., L.A., 1991-94, Rebuild L.A. Com., L.A. Annenberg Metro Project, Coalition of 100 Club of L.A.; trustee L.A. Ednl. Alliance for Restructuring Now; trustee U. S.C., 1991—. Recipient Disting. Alumnus award Dept. Elec. Engring. U. Ill., 1980, citation award Buffalo Coun. on World Affairs, 1986, Engr. of Yr. award N.Y. State Soc. Profl. Engrs., 1985, Alumni Honor award Coll. Engring., U. Ill., 1985, Outstanding Elec. Engr. award Purdue U., 1993, Humanitarian award Nat. Conf. Christians and Jews, L.A., 1994, Hollzer Meml. award Jewish Fedn. Coun. Greater L.A., 1994; Sloan Found. fellow, 1962-63, NSF grad. fellow, 1963-65, Am. Coun. Edn. fellow Purdue U., 1970-71, NSF. Mem. Assn. of Am. Univs. (chmn. 1998-99, exec. com., tenure com.), IEEE (Outstanding Paper award 1976), Nat. Assn. State Univs. and Land-Grant Colls. (ednl. telecommunications com., 1982-83, chmn. coun. of pres. 1985-86, edn. and tech. com. 1986-87, exec. com. 1987-89), Coun. on Fgn. Rels., Assn. Pacific Rim Univs. (chmn., co-founder 1997—), Assn. Am. Univs. (vice chmn. 1997-98, chmn. 1998-99, exec. com. 1995—, tenure com. 1997—). Episcopalian. Office: U So Calif Office of Pres University Park Adm 110 Los Angeles CA 90089-0012

SAMPLES, ESTHER LOUISE HENRIETTA, political activist, animal rights activist; b. Luckey, Ohio, July 26, 1908; d. Herman Heinreich and Ida Augusta (Haase) Weber; m. Enos Joseph Stahl, Sept. 15, 1925 (dec. Sept. 1962); children: Robert Howard, Welby Herman, David Joseph, Larry Enos; m. Joseph Lilburn Samples, June 14, 1965 (dec. Dec. 1971); 1 child, Daniel Lilburn. Owner/operator Stahl Upholstery, Bloomville, Ohio, 1948-55, Bucyrus, Ohio, 1955-65; owner/operator God's Squad Upholstery, Galion, Ohio, 1965-94; co-owner, co-operator God's Squad Ministry, Galion, 1971—; pres., co-owner God's Squad Politica, Galion, 1971—. Life mem. Medic Alert Found., 1979—; charter mem. Rep. Nat. Com., 1979—. Mem. Cat Lovers of Am., Cats, Cats and More Cats. Avocations: cats, crossword puzzles, painting religious pictures. Home and Office: 5935 State Route 19 Galion OH 44833-8930

SAMPLES, STEPHEN SHAY, lawyer; b. Tuscaloosa, Ala., Sept. 18, 1951; s. John W. and Avie Lee (Lovelace) S.; m. Colleen M. Mitchell, June 19, 1982. BA, U. Ala., 1973; JD, Cumberland Law Sch., 1976. U.S. Supreme Ct., U.S. Dist. Ct. (no. and middle dists. Ala.), U.S. Ct. Appeals (5th and 11th cir.), U.S. Ct. Claims. Ptnr. Hogan, Smith, Alspough, Samples & Pratt, Birmingham, Ala., 1976-94, Hare, Wynn, Newell and Newton, Birmingham, 1994—. Fellow Internat. Acad. Trial Lawyers; mem. ATLA, ABA, Am. Bd. Trial Advocates (advocate), Birmingham Bar Assn. (mem. grievance com. 1985—, officer young lawyers com. 1983-85, exec. com. 1993-95, chmn. pub. rels. com. 1992, chmn. civil cts. com. 1998, pres. elect. 1999, pres. 2000, chmn. jud. liaison com., long range planning com. 1999), Ala. Trial Lawyers Assn. (mem. exec. com. 1985—, bd. govs. 1981-85), Birmingham Bar Found. (bd. dirs. 1995-97), So. Trial Lawyers Assn. Democrat. Presbyterian. Office: Hare Wynn Newell & Newton Massey Bldg 290 21st St N Ste 800 Birmingham AL 35203-3323

SAMPRAS, PETE, professional tennis player; b. Washington, Aug. 12, 1971; s. Sam and Georgia Sampras. mem. U.S. Davis Cup team., named to Olympic Team Atlanta, 1996. chairman ATP Tour Charities program, 1992. Winner tournaments including Phila., 1990, Manchester, 1990, U.S. Open, 1990, 1993, Grand Slam Cup, 1990, L.A., 1991, Indpls., 1991, Lyon, 1991, IBM/ATP Tour World Championship-Frankfurt, 1991, 94, U.S. Pro Indoor, 1992, Lipton Internat., 1993, Wimbledon, 1993, 94, 95, 96, 99; Australian Open, 1994, Italian Open, 1994, U.S. Open, 1996, San Jose Open, 1996, Memphis Open, 1996, ATP Tour World Championship/Hannover, Germany, 1996, Australian Open Wimbledon, 1997, Advanta Championships, 1998; ranked # 1 during 1993, 94 season, finalist Australian Open, 1995. Achievements include 1st male to win the U.S Open, Wimbledon, and the Australian Open in succession, mem. U.S. Davis Cup Team, 1991, became only the fourth player to finish as No. 1three (or more) consecutive years, 1st player to surpass $5 million in a season,all-time leader in career earnings, named ATP Tour Player of the Year, 1993-94, Jim Thorpe Tennis Player, 1993. Office: ATP Tour 420 W 45th St New York NY 10036-3503*

SAMPSON, ANTHONY PETER, pharmacologist; b. Hartlepool, Durham, England, Jan. 12, 1962; s. Peter John and Greta Patricia (Kitching) S.; m. Sally Elizabeth Green, Sept. 1, 1990; children: Rebecca Victoria, Philippa Clare, Alexander Thomas. MA, St. John's Coll., Cambridge, England, 1983; PhD, U. London King's Coll., London, 1989. Rsch. asst. Hammersmith Hosp., London, 1983-85; fellow King's Coll. Med. Sch., London, 1985-90; lectr. Royal Coll. Surgeons, London, 1990-95; sr. lecxtr., dep. dir. respiratory divsn. Univ. Southampton, England, 1995—. Contrb. articles to profl. jours. Mem. British Pharm. Soc. Avocations: literature, history, fishing, cricket. Office: Southampton Gen Hosp, Immunopharmacology 825, Southampton S016 6YD, England

SAMPSON, ANTHONY TERRELL SEWARD, author; b. Billingham, Durham, Eng., Aug. 3, 1926; s. Michael Treviskey and Phyllis Marion (Seward) S.; m. Sally Virginia Sampson, May 31, 1965; children: Katharine, Paul. Degree in English, Oxford (Eng.) U., 1950. Editor Drum Mag., Johannesburg, South Africa, 1951-55; mem. editl. staff Observer newspaper, London, 1955-74; editl. adviser Brandt Commn., 1979-83. Author: Drum: A Venture into the New Africa, 1955, The Treason Cage, 1958, Commonsense About Africa, 1960, Anatomy of Britain, 1962, Anatomy of Britain Today, 1965, Macmillan: A Study in Ambiguity, 1967, The New Europeans, 1968, The New Anatomy of Britain, 1971, The Sovereign State of ITT, 1973, The Seven Sisters, 1975, The Arms Bazaar, 1977, The Money Lenders, 1981, The Changing Anatomy of Britain, 1982, Empires of the Sky, 1984, (with Sally Sampson) The Oxford Book of Ages, 1985; editor: The Sampson Letter, 1984-86, Black and Gold, 1987, The Midas Touch, 1989, Essential Anatomy of Britain, 1992, Company Man, 1995, The Scholar Gypsy, 1997, Mandela: the authorized biography, 1999. Trustee Scott Trust, 1993-96. Fellow Royal Soc. Literature; mem. Soc. Authors (chmn. 1992-94), Beefsteak Club (London), Groucho Club.

SAMPSON, CEZLEY INTLEY, economist; b. Annotto Bay, Jamaica, Nov. 3, 1939; arrived in Tanzania, 1998; s. Walter George and Theresa (Green) S.; m. Margaret Edwards, Sept. 18, 1967 (div. 1975); 1 child, Cezley Leon; m. Faye Uklyn Thompson, May 20, 1978; children: Kavin Alexander, Melanie Melissa. Higher nat. diploma, Welsh Inst. Sci. Tech., Cardiff, 1965; cert. in engring. mgmt., Cranfield Coll. Aeronatis, 1966; MA in Mktg., Lancaster (Eng.) U., 1967. Asst. rsch. mgr. Lever Bros. & Assocs., London, 1967-68; indsl. engr., port supt. ALCAN Jamaica Co., Kingston, 1968-76, v.p., pres., chmn., 1979-87; govt. transport advisor Min. Transport, Kingston, 1976-78; mng. dir. Power and Tracter Ltd., Kingston, 1087-89; spl. advisor Min. Fin. Devel., Jamaica, 1989-91j; dir. sch. bus. U. West Indies, Kingston, 1991-98; UK DFID lead advisor Presdl. Parastatal Sector Reform Commn., Dar es Salaam, Tanzania, 1998—; chmn. Jamaica Omnibus Svcs. Ltd., Kingston, 1977-79, Agro 21 Corp. Ltd., Kingston, 1989-93, Ea. Banana Estates Ltd., Kingston, 1989-94, Airports Authority Jamaica, Kingston, 1995-98. Author: (chpt.) Competing Globally: Challenges and Opportunities, 1994, Management and Privatization: Lessons from Industry & Public Service, 1995; co-author: (chpt.) Regulations, Institution and Commitment, 1996. Rsch. fellow Liverpool U., 1974-76. Fellow Jamaica Inst. Mgmt. (chmn. 1986-88); mem. Kingston C. of C., Kingston Cricket Club. Mem. Ch. of Eng. Avocations: cricket, swimming, photography. E-Mail: csampson@ud.tz. Office: Parastatal Sector Reform Co, PO Box 9252, Dar Eses Salaam Tanzania

SAMPSON, DEBORAH, investment company executive; b. Johannesburg, Gauteng, South Africa, Feb. 6, 1965; d. Reginald and Priscilla Undene (Keyser) S. BSc, U. Witwatersrand, South Africa, 1986. Rsch. officer Market Rsch. Africa, Johannesburg, South Africa, 1987; investment analyst Old Mut. Properties, Johannesburg, South Africa, 1988-90, sr. investment analyst, 1990-92, performance mgr., 1992-94, property investments mgr., 1994-99. Avocations: squash, reading, golf. Office: Mines Pension Fund, MPF Fund House, Princess Waves Terr Parktown, 20001 South Africa

SAMPSON, JEROME MARK, pulmonologist; b. Houston. BA in Chemistry, So. Meth. U., 1977; MD, U. Tex.; MSA, Ctrl. Mich. U., 1998. Diplomate Am. Bd. Internal Medicine; cert. Am. Bd. Quality Assurance and Utilization Rev. Physicians, Am. Bd. Managed Care Medicine, Am. Coll. Physician Execs. Intern Dallas, 1981-84; fellow U. Ky., 1984-86; pulmonologist, chief of staff Dept. VA, Alexandria, La. Office: VA Med Ctr PO Box 69004 Alexandria LA 71306-9004

SAMPSON, JOHN DAVID, lawyer; b. Lackawanna, N.Y., Feb. 20, 1955; s. Hugh Albert and May (Davidson) Henderson S.; m. Carol Jasen, July 29, 1978; children: Rachel Henderson, Matthew David. BA, Canisius Coll., Buffalo, 1977; JD, Union U., Albany, N.Y., 1982. Bar: N.Y. 1983, Pa. 1998, U.S. Dist. Ct. (we. dist.) N.Y. 1983, U.S. Dist. Ct. (no. dist.) N.Y. 1996. Assoc. Damon & Morey, Buffalo, 1982-87, Lippes Silverstein Mathias & Wexler, Buffalo, 1987-88; ptnr. Walsh & Sampson, P.C., Buffalo, 1988-93, Jasen, Jasen & Sampson P.C., Buffalo, 1993-99, Underberg & Kessler LLP, Buffalo, 1999—. Paul Harris fellow, 1997. Mem. N.Y. State Bar Assn., Erie County Bar Assn., Def. Rsch. Inst., Rotary Club of Buffalo, Rotary Club of East Aurora (dir. 1993—, pres. 1995-96). Wesleyan Methodist. Avocations: golf, skiing, running. Home: 44 Elmwood Ave East Aurora NY 14052-2610 Office: Underberg & Kessler LLP 1100 Main Place Tower # 620 Buffalo NY 14202-3711

SAMPSON, STEVE, former professional soccer coach; b. Salt Lake City, Jan. 19, 1957. Graduate, San Jose State U.; MEd, Stanford U. Soccer coach Foothill Cmty. Coll., Los Altos Hills, Calif.; asst. soccer coach U. Calif., L.A., 1982-85; soccer coach Santa Clara (Calif.) U., 1986-90; asst. coach U.S. Nat. Soccer Team, Chgo., 1993-1995, head coach, 1995-98; mem. organizing com. World Cup USA 1990-91, co-chmn. U.S. Soccer Coaching com. 1990-91, v.p. competition mgmt. 1991-92. Named Nat. Coach of the Yr., 1989; earned All-America honors, Foothill Cmty. Coll., 1976. *

SAMPSON, WILLIAM ROTH, lawyer; b. Teaneck, N.J., Dec. 11, 1946; s. James and Amelia (Roth) S.; 1 child, Lara; m. Drucilla Jean Mort, Apr. 23, 1988; stepchildren: Andy, Seth. BA with honors in History, U. Kans., 1968, JD, 1971. Bar: Kans. 1971, U.S. Dist. Ct. Kans. 1971, U.S. Ct. Appeals (10th cir.) 1982, U.S. Ct. Claims 1985, U.S. Ct. Appeals (8th cir.) 1992. Assoc. Turner & Balloun, Gt. Bend, Kans., 1971; ptnr. Foulston & Siefkin, Wichita, Kans., 1975-86, Shook, Hardy & Bacon, Overland Park, Kans., 1987—; presenter legal edn. seminars and confs.; adj. prof. advanced litig. U. Kans., 1994; mem. faculty trial tactics inst. Emory U. Sch. Law, 1994, 95, 96, 97; mem. merit selection panel U.S. Dist. Ct. Kans., 1999; lectr. area law schs. Author: Kansas Trial Handbook, 1997; mem. Kans. Law Rev., 1969-71, editor, 1970-71; contbr. articles to legal jours. Chmn. stewardship com. Univ. Friends Ch., Wichita, 1984-86; bd. dirs. Friends U. Retirement Corp., Wichita, 1985-87; chmn. capital fund drives Trinity Luth. Ch., Lawrence, Kans., 1990-93, mem. ch. coun., 1990-92; bd. dirs. Lied Ctr. of Kans., 1994-97. Lt. USNR, 1971-75. Fellow Am. Bar Found., Kans. Bar Found. (chmn. Kans. coll. advocacy 1986, long-range planning, CLE com. 1987-88); mem. ABA, Assn. Def. Trial Attys., Douglas County Bar Assn., Johnson County Bar Assn. (bench-bar com. 1989-99, Boss of Yr. award 1990), Wichita Bar Assn. (bd. dirs. 1985-86), Am. Bd. Trial Advs. (pres. Kans. chpt. 1990-91, nat. bd. mem. 1990-91), Internat. Assn. Def. Coun. (faculty mem. trial acad. 1994), Def. Rsch. Inst. (Kans. state rep. 1990-97, nat. bd. mem. 1998—, Exceptional Performance citation 1990, Outstanding State Rep. 1991, 92, 94), Kans. Assn. Def. Counsel (pres. 1989-90, legis. coun. 1991, 93, William H. Kahrs Disting. Achievement award 1994), Kans. U. Law Soc. (bd. govs. 1993-96), Am. Inn Ct. (Judge Hugh Means chpt., Master of Bench), Lawrence Country Club, Order of Coif, Delta Sigma Rho, Phi Alpha Theta, Omicron Delta Kappa. Republican. Lutheran. Avocations: jogging, golf, snow skiing, travel, reading. Office: Shook Hardy & Bacon 9401 Indian Creek Pky Overland Park KS 66210-2005

SAMS, DAVID RONALD, internet marketing specialist, music producer; b. Buford, Ohio, Aug. 5, 1958; s. T. Ronald and Barbara (Donohoo); m. E. Christine Graves, (div. Dec. 1986); m. Renee T. Kenneth, Dec. 6, 1992; children: Veronica Therese, Elizabeth Ann. Student, Ohio U., 1976-77. Syndicated columnist Columbus, Ohio, 1972-75; radio announcer Stas. WCVO and WFAC, Columbus and Gahana, Ohio, 1975-76; ind. producer Sta. WSFJ-TV, Lancaster, Ohio, 1976; producer Sta. WTVN-TV (now WSYX-TV), Taft Broadcasting, Columbus, 1977-80; exec. producer, programming Sta. WBNS-TV, Columbus, 1980-82, dir. mktg., 1982-84; v.p., dir. creative affairs and mktg. King World TV, L.A., 1984-87; pres. and chief exec. officer Sams/Miller Prodns., L.A., 1987-89; chmn., chief exec. officer David Sams Industries, Inc., Beverly Hills, Calif., 1987—; mng. ptnr., co-owner TVFirst, Beverly Hills, 1994—; co-owner, founder, CEO SamsDirect Internat, 1999—; mktg. strategist The Oprah Winfrey Show, Wheel of Fortune, Jeopardy!, 1984-87; program cons. Group W/Westinghouse Prodns., Hollywood, Calif., 1987, U.S. Health Corp., 1990, Kushner/Locke Co., 1990-99, CBS-TV Network, 1990-92; syndication cons. Motown Prodns., Hollywood, 1987-89; co-founder Keep the Faith Music, 1994—; advertiser sales cons. PAX-TV Network and Christian Network, Inc., 1998—; chmn., CEO SamsDirect Internet and Spot.ccInternet, 1999—. Author: Wheel of Fortune, 1987; exec. producer, co-host Roller Games, 1989-92; creator, producer (TV shows) Pulse, 1978, Front Page Saturday Night, 1980, Trial Watch, 1990-91, Barbara DeAngelis Show, 1990-91, Life Choices, 1990, Overnight Zoo, 1990, Making Love Work, 1993-97, Rita MacNeil Show (Can.) 1995, The Platinum Collection, 1994, Keep the Faith, 1996—, ETC! Entertainment That Counts!, 1998—, The Wow Big Stage, 1998—, Top 7 Countdown, 1998—, Miracles, 1998, Gospel's Greatest Performances, 1998, other spls., 1999. Fund raiser, event producer U.S. Olympic Com., Columbus, 1983. Recipient 9 Emmy awards Acad. TV Arts and Scis., 5 Addy awards, Advt. Fedn., U.S. Olympic Medal of Appreciation U.S. Olympic Com., 1983; recipient award Nima/ERA Infomercial of Yr., 1994, Program-Length Advert. of Yr., 1995, Greensheet Best Entertainment Infomercial, 1996, Greensheet Best Self-Help Infomercial, 1995, nat. Angel awards (2) for Music and Television, 1997, 98, 99. Mem. Acad. TV Arts and Scis., Dirs. Guild Am., Gospel Music Assn., Country Music Assn., Nat. Assn. TV Program Execs. Avocations: writer, world traveler, speaker. E-mail: davidsams@samsdirect.cc. Fax: 310-772-0714. Office: David Sams Industries Inc 400 S Beverly Dr Ste 420 Beverly Hills CA 90212-4406

SAMS, ERIC, musicologist; b. London, May 3, 1926; s. Henry Sydney and Violet Lois (Hill) S.; m. Enid Mary Tidmarsh, June 30, 1952; children: Richard, Jeremy. BA, Cambridge U., 1950, PhD, 1973. Prin. officer Dept. Employment, 1950-78. Author: The Songs of Hugo Wolf, 1961, 3rd edit., 1992, The Songs of Robert Schumann, 1969, 3rd edit., 1993, Brahms Songs, 1971, 2d edit., 1989, Shakespeare's Lost Play: Edmund Ironside, 1985, 2d edit., 1986, The Real Shakespeare, 1995, 2nd edit., 1997, Shakespeare's Edward III, 1996, The Songs of Johannes, Brahms, 2000; contbr. articles to profl. jours. Served with Intelligence Corps, Brit. Army, 1944-47. Home and Office: 32 Arundel Ave, Sanderstead Surrey CR2 8BB, England

SAMS, JAMES FARID, real estate development company executive; b. Bay City, Mich., Apr. 21, 1932; s. James and Adele Sams; m. Betty Suham Hamady, Aug. 17, 1957; children: James Karl, Alicia Diane, Victoria Saab. BA, Northwestern U., 1954; JD, U. Mich., 1957; LLM, Harvard U., 1959. Com. counsel ABA spl. com. World Peace/Law, Washington, 1960-63; ptnr. Reeves, Harrison, Sams & Revercomb, Washington, 1964-69, Brown & Sams, Washington, 1969-71, Kirkwood, Kaplan, Russin, Veechi & Sams, Beirut, 1971-74; owner, prin. Am. Devel. Services Corp., Washington, 1978—; former chmn. bd. DASI, Inc., Washington, 1974-90; dir. Bristol Compressors, Inc., 1983-86, Nat. Bank Wash., 1986-91; rep. U.S. State Dept. Ams. Abroad, Washington, 1965; del. UN Com. on Internat. Trade Law, N.Y.C., 1970; adv. bd Ctr. for Internat. and Comparative Law, U. Mich. Law Sch.. Contbr. articles to profl. jours. Co-founder, dir. Am. Near East Refugee Aid, Washington, 1968-92; mem. adv. bd. Ctr. for Study of Global South, Am. U., Washington, 1983—; mem. visitors com. U. Mich. Law Sch.; mem. exec. com. Am. Task Force for Lebanon, Washington; mem. adv. bd. Ctr. Internat. and Comparative Law; former chmn., dir. Grameen Found. USA, Washington. Served to lt. U.S. Army, 1957-58. Mem. ABA, Bar Assn. of Washington, Am. Soc. Internat. Law, Nat. Assn. Arab Ams. (pres. 1981, chmn. 1983). Avocations: skiing, sports. Home: 8907 Fernwood Rd Bethesda MD 20817-3015 Office: Am Devel Svcs Corp 5454 Wisconsin Ave Ste 1260 Bethesda MD 20815-6921

SAMSIOE, GORAN NILS, obstetrician, gynecologist, educator; b. Stockholm, Sept. 14, 1945; s. Gosta and Rhoda M. (Nivene) S.; m. Ann L. Jarnfelt, Apr. 17, 1982; 2 children. B in Medicine, U. Lund, Sweden, 1966; MD, U. Göteborg, Sweden, 1971, PhD, 1974. Capt. Royal Swedish Navy, 1980-92; asst. prof. Göteborg U., 1975-78, assoc. prof., 1979-92; prof. U. Lund, Sweden, 1993—; cons. WHO, 1975-82. Author: A Profile of the Menopause, 1995. Recipient Order Internat. Fellowship, ABI. Mem. European Mewop Soc. (bd. dirs. 1993), Giovanni Lorenzini Found. (bd. dirs.). Avocations: sailing. Office: Dept Ob Gyn, Lund U Hosp, 221 85 Lund Sweden

SAMSON, MARIA ELENA, educational administrator, counseling psychologist, sociologist; b. Manila, Aug. 18, 1949; d. Jose Jesus Antonio Samson and Dolores Pascual Dela Cruz Ferguson. AB in Polit. Sci. magna cum laude, U. Santo Tomas, Manila, 1970; MS in Sociology, Asian Social Inst., Manila, 1978; MA in Psychology, Ind. U., 1984; postgrad., U. The Philippines, Quezon City, 1980-86; Phd in Applied Cosmic Anthropology, Asian Social Inst., 2000. Mem. faculty U. The Philippines, Diliman and Manila, 1980-88; head dept. social sci., mem. faculty Brent Sch., Manila, 1988-91; master mid. sch. Brent Sch., 1991-92, dir. adminstrn., 1992-95, dep. headmaster, dir. student svcs., 1995-96, dep. headmaster, dir. adminstrn., 1996—, coord. Internat. Baccalaureate, 1991—; examiner Internat. Baccalaureate Orgn., Eng., 1994-96; educator family life and sex edn. Asian Social Inst., Manila, 1972-73; lectr. in field. Anchorperson Sport Rev. Editl. ABC-TV, 1995. Cons., bd. dirs., chair edn. com., ways and means com., mem. exec. com. PhilDARE, 1993—; exec. dir. PFM Agro-Housing, Quezon Province, The Philippines, 1974-76; organizer, campaign mgr. Partido ng Masang Pilipino, Manila, 1990—; bd. dirs., barangay councilor Barangay. White Plains Homeowners Assn., Manila, 1997—. Fulbright-Hayes scholar (life mem.) Philippine Am. Ednl. Found., 1982. Mem. Quota, Internat. Manila N. (charter pres. 1997—), Polit. Psychology Assn. Philippines (founder, pres. 1999), Phi Delta Kappa Edn. Honor Soc. Roman Catholic. Avocations: interior design, acting, singing, hiking, badminton. Office: Brent Internat Sch, PSC/ULTRA Complex, Manila The Philippines

SAMSON, STEN OTTO, x-ray crystallographer, consultant, researcher; b. Stockholm, Mar. 25, 1916; came to U.S., 1953; m. Lage and Wilhelmine (Lode) S.; m. Lalli Sandström, July 3, 1948; children: Karl-Otto, Karin. FilKand, U. Stockholm, 1953, FilLic, 1956, Fil. Dr, 1968. Rsch. fellow U. Stockholm, 1947-53; rsch. fellow Calif. Inst. Tech., Pasadena, 1953-61, sr. rsch. fellow, 1961-73, rsch. assoc., 1973-80, sr. rsch. assoc., 1980-86, sr. rsch. assoc. emeritus, 1986—. Sect. editor Crystallog. Data DeterminationTables, 1973. Mem. U.S. panel U.S.-Brazil Study Group on Grad. Tng. and Rsch. in Brazil, 1974-76. Mem. Am. Crystallog. Assn. Evangelical Lutheran. Avocations: travel, hiking, photography, classical music. Home: 351 S Parkwood Ave Pasadena CA 91107-5037 Office: Calif Inst Tech Beckman Inst 139 74 Pasadena CA 91125-0001

SAMSONOV, ALEXANDER MIKHAILOVICH, physicist; b. Leningrad, Russia, Sept. 30, 1948; s. Mikhail Alexandrovich and Nina Mikhailovna (Gubareva) S.; m. Maria Georgievna Petrashen, July 27, 1974; 1 child, Anastassia. MSc, Tech. U. St. Petersburg, Russia, 1972, PhD, 1979. Jr. scientist Ioffe Inst. of Russian Acad. Scis., St. Petersburg, 1972-78, sr. scientist, 1979—, head of rsch. group, 1982—; head of lab. Inst. High Performance Computing, St. Petersburg, 1996—; overseas vis. fellow St. John's Coll., Cambridge, Eng., 1990; dir. Internat. Ctr. Nonlinear Scis., St. Petersburg, 1992—; GMD, Bonn, Germany, 1998, 99, 2000; guest prof. U. Siegen, Germany, 1995, Tech. U. Darmstadt, Germany, 1991, Cambridge (Eng.) U., 1990; convenor Intern Workshop, Hong Kong, 2000, Nowvif Symposium, St. Petersburg, 1994, Disordered Sys. Symposium, St. Petersburg, 1992; profl. expert Ministry of Scis. Russia, Moscow, 1996—. Co-author: (book) Nonlinear Waves in Solids, 1994; co-author: (book of papers) Russian Science-Withdraw and Revive, 1996 (1st prize 1996); mem. editl. bd., co-editor: Internat. Jour. Structural Optimization, 1989-94; reviewer, expert Jour. Tech. Physics, 1980—; patentee in field; contbr. articles to profl. jours. Recipient 1st prize Ioffe Inst., 1996, Solid State Electronics Divsn., 1996, prize and diploma Internat. Sci. Found. Competition, 1996; grantee Internat. Sci. Found., 1994, 95, Hughes Aircraft Co., 1994. Mem. European Rsch. Com. Flow Turbulence and Combustion (corr. mem.), Euromech. Soc.

(corr. mem.). Avocations: literature, classical music, languages, hiking. Office: Ioffe Inst Russian Acad Sci, 26 Polytechnicheskaya St, 194021 Saint Petersburg Russia

SAMSONOWICZ, HENRYK, historian; b. Warsaw, Poland, Jan. 23, 1930; s. Jan and Henryka (Krukowska) S.; m. Agnieszka Lechowska, Jan. 20, 1951; children: Anna, Jan. PhD, U. Warsaw, 1980; D honoris causa, Duquesne U., Pitts., 1981, H.S. Edn., Krakow, 1996, H.S. Edn., Torun, 1997. Tchr. U. Warsaw, 1954-71, dean Faculty history, 1969-79, rector, 1980-82; head Inst. History, Warsaw, 1975-80; Min. Edn. Poland, 1989-90. Editor: Republic of Nobles, 1984, East-Central Europe in Transition, 1986; author: Studien uber Danziger Kapital, 1972, Miasta Polskie, 1987, Polens Platz in Europe, 1996. Named Comdr. Polonia Restitutce, 1980, officer Legion d'Honneur, 1984. Mem. Polish Akademia Nauk, Academia Europea, Polish Soc. History (pres. 1978-82), Academie des Belles Lettres. Home: Wilcza 22, 00-544 Warsaw Poland Office: U Warsaw, Krakowskie Przedmiescie 26, 06-325 Warsaw Poland

SAMTER, THOMAS GUSTAV, retired pathologist, educator; b. Cairo, Egypt, Jan. 1, 1929; s. Martin and Louise (Löbl) S.; m. Hiroko Takei, Oct. 5, 1959; children: Naomi Louise, David Martin. BA, Ind. U., 1949, MD, 1952. Diplomate Am. Bd. Pathology. Pathologist Atomic Bomb Casualty Commn., Nagasaki, Japan, 1961-63; asst. prof. Ind. U. Med. Ctr., Indpls., 1963-65; pathologist St. Lukes Med. Ctr., Milw., 1965-69; pathologist Mt. Sinai Med. Ctr., Milw., 1969-97, retired; assoc. prof. Univ. Wis., Milw., 1980-97. Capt. USAF, 1955-57, Okinawa, Japan. Mem. Phi Beta Kappa, Alpha Omega Alpha. Jewish. Avocations: cycling, walking, reading japanese. Home: 5029 N Lake Dr Whitefish Bay WI 53217-5749

SAMUEL, CLINT DAVID, analytical chemist; b. Carbondale, Ill., July 9, 1969; s. David Joe and Marie Irene Samuel. BS in Chemistry, So. Ill. U., 1997, MS in Analytical Chemistry, 2000. Grad. tchg. asst. So. Ill. U., Carbondale, 1997-98, grad. rsch. asst., 1998—. Contbr. articles to profl. jours. Mensa scholar, 1994, 99. Mem. AAAS, Am. Chem. Soc., Assn. for Computing Machinery, Am. Mensa. Avocations: aerobics, weight lifting, art, cycling, creative writing. Home: 307 Texas Ave Carterville IL 62918-1430

SAMUEL, GRAEME JULIAN, entrepreneur; b. Melbourne, Victoria, Australia, May 31, 1946; s. Ralph Aaron and Shirley Samuel; m. Rose Lynne Davis, Mar. 16, 1969; children: Warren, Grant, Davina, Georgia. LLB, U. Melbourne, 1968; LLM, Monash U., Melbourne, 1977. Ptnr. Phillips Fox & Masel, Solicitors, Melbourne, 1972-81; exec. dir., dir. corp. svcs. divsn. Macquarie Bank Ltd., 1981-86; co-founder Grant Samuel & Assocs., 1988-96; Victorian councillor Taxation Inst. Australia, 1975-81, dep. chmn., 1980-81; mem. Victorian exec. Comml. Law Assn. Australia, 1978-83; gen. councillor Taxation Inst. Australia, 1979-81; vis. lectr. corp. and securities industries law and practice U. Melbourne and Monash U., 1979-86; founding chmn. bus. law sect. The Law Coun. Australia, 1980-81; coun. mem. The Law Inst. Victoria, 1980-81; commr. Australian Football League, Melbourne, 1984—; dir. Thakral Holdings, Melbourne, 1992—; chair Inner and Eastern Health Care Network, Melbourne, 1995-2000, Melbourne and Olympic Pks. Trust, 1996—; pres. Nat. Competition Coun., Melbourne, 1997—; mem. Docklands Authority, Melbourne, 1998—. Co-author: Introduction to Securities Industry Code, 1979, 82; contbr. articles to jours. and newspapers. Chmn. Playbox Theatre Co., 1983-95, Playbox Malthouse Ltd., 1985-95, Wesley Coll. Found., 1988-95, The Alfred Found., 1993-95; councillor Wesley Coll. Coun., 1990-95; pres. Victorian Employers C. of C. and Industry, 1993-95, The Alfred Healthcare Group,1 994-95, Australian C. of C. and Industry, 1995-97. Recipient Order of Australia, Australian Govt., 1998. Avocations: opera, football. Office: Nat Competition Coun, 2 Lonsdale St Level 12, Melbourne VIC 3000, Australia

SAMUEL, RALPH DAVID, lawyer; b. Augusta, Ga., May 8, 1945; s. Ralph and Louise Elizabeth (Wurreschke) S.; m. Lynn Christel Malmgren, June 12, 1971; children: Lynn Britt, Ralph Erik. AB, Dartmouth Coll., 1967; JD, Dickinson Sch. of Law, 1972. Bar: Pa. 1972, U.S. Dist. Ct. (ea. dist.) Pa. 1972, U.S. Ct. Appeals (3d cir.) 1973, U.S. Supreme Ct. 1976. Law clk. to hon. judge John P. Fullam U.S. Dist. Ct. (ea. dist.) Pa., Phila., 1972-74; assoc. MacCoy, Evans & Lewis., Phila., 1974-76; ptnr. Samuel and Ballard, P.C., Phila., 1976-98; pres., CEO Ralph D. Samuel & Co., P.C., Phila., 1998—; established Samuel Porter Fellow Dartmouth Coll., Hanover, N.H., 1994. Contbr. articles to profl. jours., poetry to publs. Trustee The George Sch., Newtown, Pa., 1983-90; chmn. bd. dirs. Stapeley in Germantown, 1985-90; mem. Chase Fund Com., 2000; chmn. budget com. Phila. Yearly Meeting of Friends, 1991-93; bd. dirs., mem. fin. com. Phila. Ranger Corps., 1992-94; pres. Cedar Park Neighbors, Phila., 1975-78, West Mt. Airy Neighbors, Phila., 1981-82. Mem. Pa. Soc., Athenaeum of Phila., Sunday Breakfast Club. Mem. Soc. of Friends. Avocations: music, writing, squash, tennis. Fax: (215) 849-6859. E-mail: RalphSamuel@lawmine.com. Office: PO Box 35185 Philadelphia PA 19128-0185

SAMUEL, ROBERT THOMPSON, optometrist; b. Kansas City, Mo., June 27, 1944; s. Manlius Thompson and Helen Evelyn (Syverson) S. BA, William Jewell Coll., 1966; postgrad., U. Mo., Kansas City, 1967; MS, U. Mo., 1968; DOptometry, U. Tenn., Memphis, 1971; postgrad., U. Mo., St. Louis, 1995, Northeastern State U., 1998. Cert. optometrist, Mo. Buyer Recco, Inc., Kansas City, Mo., 1963-67; histology lab. instr. William Jewell Coll., Liberty, Mo., 1965-66; pvt. practice optometry Gladstone, Mo., 1972—; staff doctor O.H. Gerry Optical Clinics, 1996—; panel doctor Ford Motor Co., Claycomo, Mo., 1985—, Union Pacific R.R., Kansas City, 1985—, TWA Airlines, 1990, Union Carbide, 1990. Publicity coord. Rep. Party, Kansas City, Mo., 1975-76; chmn. Save Your Vision Week, Kansas City, 1977; mem. Theatre League of Kansas City, 1976—, Kansas City Mus., 1986—, Friends of Art, 1985, Friends of Mo. Town 1955, 1980—. Recipient Outstanding Young Men of Am. award Jaycees, 1978, Good Citizens award DAR, 1962. Mem. Am. Optometric Assn., Mo. Optometric Assn., Optometric Soc. Greater Kansas City, Heart of Am. Contact Lens Congress, Am. Acad. Sports Vision, Vol. Optometric Svcs. for Humanity, Smithsonian Assocs., Lions (exec. bd. dir. Lions Eye Clinic 1974-84, bd. dirs. 1982—, Outstanding Svc. award 1973, 74, editor Lions Optometric Ctr. Quar. 1974-84), Kappa Alpha Order (treas. 1966). Republican. Lutheran. Avocations: photography, music, piano, swimming, travel. Home: 6325 N Monroe Ave Kansas City MO 64119-1923 Office: 1170 W 152 Hwy Liberty MO 64068-2035 also: 5601 NE Antioch Rd Kansas City MO 64119-2302

SAMUEL, SERGIU, quality assurance professional; b. Kisinov, Basarabia, Romania, Mar. 25, 1927; arrived in Israel, 1941; s. Albert and Luba (Schwartzberg) S.; m. Christiane Lemouzy, July 29, 1957; children: Daphne, Remi. Telecom. engr., Ecole Nat. Superieure Telecom., Paris, 1954; MSEE, MIT, 1955. Registered profl. engr., Calif. Design engr. Telemeter Magnetics, L.A., 1955-57; project mgr. Bull Co., Paris, 1957-59; tech. dir. Amron Electronics, Herzlia, Israel, 1960-62; electronics cons. Ministry of Def. and Israel Aircraft Industries, Israel, 1962-65; chief engr. electric and electronic design engring. divsn. Israel Aircraft Industries, Lod Airport, 1965-67, mgr. product assurance engring. divsn., 1967-83; dir. reliability and product assurance Israel Ministry of Def., Directorate of Def. R&D, Tel Aviv, 1983-93; adviser quality assurance and reliability Israel Ministry Def., Tel Aviv, 1993—; adj. fellow prof. Israel Inst. Tech., Haifa, 1984—; advisor for quality mgmt. Office Pers. Mgmt., Jerusalem, 1992—; presenter in field. Contbr. articles to profl. jours. Cpl. Israel Def. Forces, 1948-49. Fellow Israel Soc. Quality (head appointment and awards com., former head ethics com., former chmn., Lifetime Achievement award 1995), Am. Soc. Quality, IEEE (life); mem. Inst. Environ. Scis. (sr.), N.Y. Acad. Scis. Jewish. Avocation: music. Fax: 972-3-634-9133. E-mail: sergiu s@netvision.net.il. Office: Ministry of Def, Directorat, of Defense R&D, Hakirya, 61909 Tel Aviv Israel

SAMUELS, FERN JACQUELINE, artist, educator; b. Chgo., Feb. 16, 1931; d. Noah S. and Ann (Zager) Andrews; m. Howard Stanley Samuels, Sept. 17, 1950; children: Mitchell, Paul, David. BFA, Loyola U., 1973; MFA, Sch. Art Inst. Chgo., 1983. Instr.-coord. Mundelein Coll., Chgo., 1976-83; faculty Columbia Coll., Chgo., 1978-2000; instr. workshops Field Mus., Chgo., 1976, Lake Forest Coll., Chgo., 1976, Lincoln Park Cultural Ctr., Chgo., 1973, Ill. Inst. Tech., Chgo., 1980—, Latin Sch., Chgo., 1976; juror St. Louis Arts Guild, 1998. One-women shows include Northwestern U., 1988, Ea. Ill. U., Chgo., 1989, Countryside Gallery, 1988, Upstart Gallery, 1990, Soho 20, N.Y.C., 1993, Loyola U., 1995, Morraine Valley Coll., 1995, McDonough Mus. Art, 1997; exhibited in group shows including Smithsonian Air and Space Mus., 1983, Freeport Mus., 1995, Rockford Mus., 1996, Butler Inst. Am. Art, 1998, Lafayette Mus., 1999, Columbus Mus. Art, 2000, So. Ohio Mus., 2000, South Bend Regional Mus., 2000, Univ. Mus. S.D., 2001. Mem. LWV, Chgo., 1969—; founding mem. Alternative Fibers, Chgo., 1982; chairperson, coord. Seven Ethnic Museums, Chgo., 1986; membership chmn. ARC Gallery, Chgo., 1983-86, pres. 1988-90; bd. dirs. Artist Book Works, Chgo., 1992-93. Recipient grant Columbia Coll., 1981. Mem. Arts Club Chgo., Chgo. Soc. Arts, Am. ORT, City of Hope (Bobby Blechman chpt. founding mem.), Sch. Art Inst. East Fla. Alumni (pres.). Democrat. Avocations: reading, music, theater, excercise. Home: 84 Saint James Ct Palm Bch Gdns FL 33418-4020

SAMUELS, FRED, biotechnology company executive; b. N.Y.C., May 14, 1955; arrived in Israel, 1987; s. Nathan and Miriam (Stern) Schlofsky; m. Audrey Wolf, Sept. 9, 1979; children: Batsheva, Daniella, Chana, Rachel, Noa, Yaakov. BSc, U. Buffalo, 1977; MSc, Albert Einstein Coll. Medicine, Bronx, N.Y., 1980, PhD, 1983. Scientist Technicon, Tarrytown, N.Y., 1985-87; from project head R & D to v.p. mfg. ops. Orgenics, Yavne, Israel, 1987-2000, v.p. mfg., 1999—. Bd. dirs. Hillel Acad., Passaic, N.J., 1986-87, Ohel Shai Synagogue, Rechovot, Israel, 1992-93, 99-2000; pres. parents assn. Tzvia Jr. H.S., Rehovot, Israel, 1996-97. Rockefeller Found. fellow Harvard U., 1983-84, NIH student fellow, 1977-79, Am. Liver Found. student fellow, 1980. Mem. Am. Assn. Clin. Chemistry, Am. Microbiology Soc., N.Y. Acad. Scis., Tehilla (bd. dirs. 1986-87). Avocations: Jewish studies, basketball. Office: Orgenics, PO Box 360, 70650 Yavne Israel

SAMUELS, HANNA, artist; b. Buffalo, Apr. 26, 1908; d. Emil and Rachel (Span) S. Student, Art Inst. Buffalo, 1937-54. sr. clk. in charge of catalog Buffalo State Coll., 1966-73, vol. cons. on art. Represented in permanent collections at Erie County Hist. Mus., Vincent Price Collection, Judaic Mus., Temple Beth Zion, Buffalo, Butler Libr., Buffalo State Coll., Cox Conv. Hall, Pentecostal Temple Ch., Buffalo, Burchfield-Penny Art Ctr., Buffalo; exhibited in group shows Smithsonian Instn., Kenan Ctr., Lockport, N.Y.; exhbns. of sculpture include Burchfield-Penny Art Ctr., Buffalo, Albright, Memphis, Jr. League, Smithsonian Instn., Washington, Castellani Art Mus., Smithsonian Assocs. Nat. Mem. The Libr. of Congress. Vol. USO, Buffalo, 1942-45. Mem. Patteran Artists (rec. sec.), Castellani Art Mus. Niagara U., Libr. Congress (nat.), Smithsonian Inst. (assoc.). Democrat. Avocations: painting, music.

SAMUELSON, DOUGLAS ALAN, information systems company executive; b. Reno, Nev., July 27, 1948; s. Norman Harold and Shirley (Leder) S.; m. Francine Ruth Kimel, Jan. 7, 1979; children: Andrew, Diane. BA, U. Calif., Berkeley, 1969; MS, George Washington U., 1981, DSc, 1990. Computer systems analyst Bank of Am., San Francisco, 1972-73; cons. San Rafael, Calif., 1973-75; ops. rsch. analyst U.S. Govt., Washington, 1975-82, Evaluation Rsch. Corp., Vienna, Va., 1982-83; analyst, v.p. Micro-Zeit/Internat. Telesystems Corp., Reston, Va., 1983-88; asst. prof. Memphis State U., 1990-92; pres. InfoLogix, Inc., Annandale, Va., 1988—; prin. scientist Puma Sys., Inc., Falls Church, Va., 1997-98; chief statistician FMAS Dyncorp., Columbia, Md., 2000—; vis. rsch. scholar George Washington U., 1993-95, mem. nat. adv. coun. Sch. of Engring. and Applied Sci., 1996—; adj. assoc. prof. George Mason U., Fairfax, Va., 1994-96, vis. adj. prof., 1997-98, adj. prof., lectr. George Washington U., 1997—. Co-editor, author (with others): Human Rights and Statistics: Getting the Record Straight, 1992, Health Information and Ethics Protecting Fundamental Human Rights, 1997; author (column) The ORacle, 1986—; contbr. articles to profl. jours. Bd. dirs. George Washington U. Engr. Alumni Assn., 1994—, v.p., 1996-98, pres., 1998-2000. Mem. AAAS, Washington OR/MS Coun. (pres. 1989-90, 96-97), Am. Statis. Assn. (chair com. on scientific freedom and human rights 1985-88), Inst. for Ops. Rsch. and Mgmt. Sci. (bd. dirs. 1998-2000). Democrat. Jewish. Achievements include patent for systems for regulating arrivals of customers to servers. E-mail: dsamuel@seas.gwu.edu. Office: InfoLogix Inc 8711 Chippendale Ct Annandale VA 22003-3807

SAMUELSON, KENNETH LEE, lawyer; b. Natrona Heights, Pa., Aug. 22, 1946; s. Sam and Frances Bernice (Robbins) S.; m. Marlene Ina Rabinowitz, Jan. 1, 1980; children: Heather, Cheryl. BA magna cum laude, U. Pitts., 1968; JD, U. Mich., 1971. Bar: Md. 1972, D.C. 1980, U.S. Dist. Ct. (trial bar) Md. 1984. Assoc. Weinberg & Green, Balt., 1971-73, Dickerson, Nice, Sokol & Horn, Balt., 1973; asst. atty. gen. State of Md., 1973-77; pvt. practice Balt., 1978; ptnr. Linowes and Blocher, Silver Spring (Md.), Washington, 1979-93, Semmes, Bowen & Semmes, Washington, D.C., and Balt., 1993-95; Wilkes Artis, Chartered, Washington and Md., 1995—; spkr. in field of telecomms., fin. and leasing. Author in field. Bd. dirs. D.C. Assn. for Retarded Citizens, Inc., 1986—; bd. govs. Wash. Bldg. Congress, 1998—. Mem. ABA (chair and co-chmn. com. sect. real property, probate and trust law 1993—, moderator programs), Am. Coll. Real Estate Lawyers (moderator, spkr. programs on telecomms. and financing 1998, 99), D.C. Bar (comml. real estate com., chmn. legal opinions project and spkr. programs on real estate 1987, 89, 90), Md. Bar Assn. (real property, planning and zoning sect., chmn. environ. subcom. legal opinions project 1987-89, litigation sect. 1982-84, chmn. comml. trans. com.), Md. Inst. Continuing Profl. Edn. Lawyers (spkr.), Am. Arbitration Assn. (arbitrator and mediator), D.C. Bldg. Industry Assn. (program moderator mass transit devel. sites 1999, telecom. inside wiring 2000), Washington Assn Realtors, Inc. (moderator program on comml. leasing 1992, program on letters of intent 1996), Nat. Assn. of Corp. Real Estate Execs. (spkr. program on telecomms. transactions 1997), Civil Code Drafting Com. of the Russian Legis. (spkr. programs on leasing 1994, 95), Apt. and Office Bldg. Assn. Met. Washington (moderator of programs and spkr. 1989, 92), East Coast Builders Conf. (moderator program on financing 1990), Internat. Coun. Shopping Ctrs. (organized, cofaculty program "univ." 1988, NAFTA 1992, condemnations 1994, leasing 1997, high tech. effects 1998, com. chmn. 1998-99, pub./pvt. partnerships 1999), Montgomery County Bar Assn. (jud. selections com. 1988-90), Phi Beta Kappa, Lambda Alpha. E-mail: ksamuelson@wilkesartis.com. Office: Wilkes Artis 1666 K St NW Ste 300 Washington DC 20006-2803

SAMUELSON, M. KRISTIN, music educator; b. Milw., May 11, 1951; d. Albert C. and Jeanlyn C. (Gunderson) S.; m. Edward Allen Joffe, May 22, 1982 (div. Oct. 1996); 1 child, Janine Kirsten Joffe. BA, Denison U., 1973; MMus, New Eng. Conservatory Music, 1976; EdD, Columbia U., 1999. Acad. advisor Dean's Office New Eng. Conservatory, Boston, 1976-79; singer/soloist Nat. Opera Co., Raleigh, N.C., 1980, Enchanted Circle Concerts, Boston, 1979, 84; singer/voice tchr. Monanea Festival, Leukerbad, Switzerland, 1989-90; singer/soloist Sixth Internat. Congress of Women in Music, N.Y.C., 1990; instr. Columbia U., N.Y.C., 1994-98, N.Y.U./Lee Strasberg Theatrical Inst., N.Y.C., 1997—; adj. asst. prof. Franklin & Marshall Coll., Lancaster, Pa., 1985—; soloist Boston Symphony Orchestra, 1976, Banff Festival, Alberta, Can., 1978, 79; lectr. in field; workshop leader Symposium for Care of Profl. Voice, 1999. Contbr. articles to profl. jours. Recipient Frances Yeend's Instr. scholarship Chautauqua Inst., N.Y., 1973, Florence C. Rowe Meml. scholarship New Eng. Conservatory, Boston, 1975-76. Mem. N.Y. Singing Tchrs. Assn., Nat. Assn. Tchrs. of Singing (bd. dirs. N.Y.C. chpt.). Avocations: bicycling, travel, langs., playing piano. E-mail: kristins@prodigy.net. Office: Franklin & Marshall Coll PO Box 3003 Lancaster PA 17604-3003

SAMUELSON, PAUL ANTHONY, economics educator; b. Gary, Ind., May 15, 1915; s. Frank and Ella (Lipton) S.; m. Marion E. Crawford, July 2, 1938 (dec.); children: Jane Kendall, Margaret Wray, William Frank, Robert James, John Crawford, Paul Reid.; m. Risha Eckaus, 1981; stepdaughter, Susan Miller. BA, U. Chgo., 1935; MA, Harvard U., 1936, PhD (David A. Wells prize 1941), 1941; LLD (hon.), U. Chgo., Oberlin Coll., 1961, Boston Coll., 1964, Ind. U., 1966, U. Mich., 1967, Claremont Grad. Sch., 1967, Seton Hall U., 1971, U. N.H., 1971, Keio U., 1971, Widener Coll., 1982, Cath. U. at Riva Aguero U., Lima, Peru, 1980, Harvard, 1972, Gustavus Adolphus Coll., 1974, U. So. Calif., 1975, U. Pa., 1976, U. Rochester, 1976, Emmanuel Coll., 1977, Stonehill Coll., 1978, Indiana U. of Pa., 1993; DLitt (hon.), Ripon Coll., 1962, No. Mich. U., 1973, Valparaiso U., 1987, Columbia U, 1988; LHD (hon.), Williams Coll., 1971; DSc (hon.), U. Mass., 1972, U. R.I., 1972, Tufts U., 1988, East Anglia U., Norwich, Eng., 1966, Rennselaer Poly. Inst., 1998; D (hon.), U. Catholique de Louvain, Belgium, 1976, City U., London, 1980, New U. Lisbon, 1985, Univ. Nat. de Educacion a Distancia, Madrid, 1989, Univ. Politecnica de Valencia, Spain, 1991. Prof. econs. MIT, 1940-65, inst. prof., 1966, prof. emeritus, 1986; mem. staff Radiation Lab., 1944-45; prof. internat. econ. relations Fletcher Sch. Law and Diplomacy, 1945; cons. Nat. Resources Planning Bd., 1941-43, WPB, 1945, U.S. Treasury, 1945-52, 61-74, Bur. Budget, 1952, RAND Corp., 1948-75, Fed. Res. Bd., 1965—; council Econ. Advisers, 1960-68; econ. adviser to Pres. Kennedy; sr. adviser Brookings Panel on Econ. Activity; mem. spl. commn. on social scis. NSF, 1967-68; cons. Congl. Budget Office, Federal Reserve Bd., 1965—; Gordon Y Billard Fellow MIT, Boston, 1986—; vis. prof of polit. econ. Ctr. Japan-U.S. Bus. and Econ. Studies, NYU, 1987—; Stamp Meml. lectr., London, 1961, Wicksell lectr., Stockholm, 1962, Franklin lectr., Detroit, 1962; Carnegie Found. reflective year, 1965-66; John von Neumann lectr. U. Wis., 1971; Gerhard Colm Meml. lectr. New Sch. for Social Research, N.Y.C., 1971; Sulzbacher Meml. lectr. Columbia Law Sch., N.Y.C., 1974; J. Willard Gibbs lectr. Am. Math. Soc., San Francisco, 1974; John Diebold lectr. Harvard, 1976; Alice E. Blurneuf lectr. Boston Coll., 1981, Horowitz lectr. Jerusalem and Tel Aviv, 1984, Marschak Meml. lectr. UCLA, 1984, Tennenbaum lectr. Ga. Inst. Tech., 1985, Julis Steinberg Meml. lectr. Wharton Sch., 1986, Godkin lectr. Harvard, 1986, Woodward lectr. U. British Columbia, 1987; lectr. Harvard 350 Symposium, Harvard U., 1986, Olin lectr. U. Va., 1989, Commemorative lectr. Stonehill Coll., 1990, Lionel Robbins Meml. lectr. Claremont Coll., 1991; mem. nat. advisory com. Inst. for Rsch. on Poverty. Author: Foundations of Economic Analysis, 1947, enlarged edit., 1983, Economics, 1948-95, Readings in Economics, 1955-73, (with R. Dorfman and R.M. Solow) Linear Programming and Economic Analysis, 1958, Collected Scientific Papers, 5 vols., 1966, 72, 78, 86; co-author numerous other books; contbr. numerous articles to profl. jours.; columnist Newsweek, 1966-81; assoc. editor Jour. Pub. Econs., Jour. Internat. Econs., Jour. Fin. Econs., Jour. Nonlinear Analysis; adv. bd. Challenge Mag.; editl. bd. Procs. Nat. Acad. Scis. Chmn. Pres.'s Task Force Maintaining Am. Prosperity, 1964; mem. Nat. Task Force on Econ. Edn., 1960-61; econ. adviser to Pres. John F. Kennedy, 1959-63; mem. adv. bd. Nat. Commn. Money and Credit, 1958-60. Hon. fellow London Sch. Econs. and Polit. Sci. Guggenheim fellow, 1948-49; Ford Found. Research fellow, 1958-59; recipient David A. Wells prize Harvard U., 1941, John Bates Clark medal Am. Econ. Assn., 1947, Alfred Nobel Meml. prize , 1970, medal of Honor U. Evansville, Ill., 1970, Albert Einstein Commemorative award, 1971, Alumni medal U. Chgo., 1983, Britannica award, 1989, Gold Scanno prize, Naples, Italy, 1990; Paul A. Samuelson Professorship established in his name, MIT, 1991; recipient Nat. Medal of Sci., Washington, 1996. Fellow Brit. Acad. (corr.), Am. Philos. Soc., Econometric Soc. (v.p. 1950, pres. 1951), Am. Econ. Assn. (hon.; pres. 1961); mem. AAAS, Com. Econ. Devel. (comm. on nat. goals, research adv. bd. 1959-60), Internat. Econ. Assn. (pres. 1966-68, hon. pres.), Nat. Acad. Scis., Leibniz-Akademie der Wissenschaften und der Literatur (corr. mem. 1987—) Nat. Assn. of Investment Clubs (Disting. Svc. award in Investment Edn. 1974), Club of Econ. and Mgmt. (medal, hon. Valencia, Spain 1990), Phi Beta Kappa, Omicron Delta Epsilon (trustee). Home: 94 Somerset St Belmont MA 02478-2010 Office: MIT E52 # 383C Dept Econs Cambridge MA 02139

SAMUELSON, SIR SYDNEY WYLIE, retired film commision administrator; b. London, Dec. 7, 1925; s. George Berthold and Marjorie (Vint) S.; m. Doris, Sept. 7, 1949; children: Peter, Jonathan, Marc. Cinema projectionist various companies, Eng., 1939-43; asst. film cameraman, cameraman and camera dir. various companies, worldwide, 1947-62; founder, pres. Samuelson Film Service, Eng., 1954—. Freeman, City of London. Served with Royal Air Force, 1943-47. Recipient Comdr. Order of the Brit. Empire, apptd. First Brit. Film Commr., Brit. Govt., 1991. Mem. Brit. Soc. Cinematographers (gov. 1969-77, 1st v.p. 1976-77), Brit. Acad. Film and TV Arts (chmn. and trustee 1970—, Michael Balcon award 1985, fellow 1993); trustee Cinema TV Benevolent Fund; exec. com. Cinema TV Vets. (pres. 1980-81); fellow Brit. Kinematograph Sound TV Soc. Jewish. Avocation: vintage motoring.

SAMUELSSON, BENGT INGEMAR, medical chemist; b. Halmstad, Sweden, May 21, 1934; s. Anders and Stina (Nilsson) S.; m. Inga Karin Bergstein, Aug. 19, 1958; children: Bo, Astrid. DMS, Karolinska Inst., Stockholm, 1960, MD, 1961; DSc (hon.), U. Chgo., 1978, U. Ill., 1983. Asst. prof. Karolinska Inst., 1961-66, prof. med. and physiol. chemistry, 1972—, chmn. physiol. chemistry dept., 1973-83, dean Med. Faculty, 1978-83, pres., 1983-95; rsch. fellow Harvard U., 1961-62; prof. med. chemistry Royal Vet. Coll., Stockholm, 1967-72; mem. Nobel Assembly Physiology or Medicine, 1972—, chmn., 1990; Harvey lectr., N.Y.C., 1979; mem. Nobel Com. Physiology and Medicine, 1984-89, chmn. com., 1987-89; mem. rsch. adv. bd. Swedish Govt., 1985-88; mem. Nat. Commn. Health Policy, 1987-90; mem. European Sci. and Tech. Assembly, 1994-97; spl. adv. to commr. rsch. and edn. European commn., 1995-97; chmn. Nobel Found., 1993—. Contbr articles to profl. jours. Recipient A. Jahres award Oslo U., 1970, Louisa Gross Horwitz award Columbia U., 1975, Albert Lasker basic med. research award, 1977, Ciba-Geigy Drew award in biomed. research, 1980, Lewis S. Rosenstiel award in basic med. research Brandeis U., 1981, Gairdner Found. award, 1981, Heinrich Wieland prize, 1981, Nobel prize in physiology or medicine, 1982, award medicinal chemistry div. Am. Chem. Soc., 1982, Waterford Bio-Med. Sci. award, 1982, Internat. Assn. Allergology and Clin. Immunology award, 1982, Abraham White sci. achievement award, 1984, Gregory Pincus Meml. award, 1984, Charles E. Culpepper award, 1985, Supelco award Am. Oil Chemists Soc., 1985, Chilton lectureship award, 1986, Abraham White Disting. Sci. award, 1991, City of Medicine award, 1992, Maria Theresa medal, 1996, Medicus Magnus medal, 1997. Mem. AAAS (hon.), Royal Swedish Acad. Scis., Mediterranean Acad. Sci., Acad. Europaea (founding mem.), French Acad. Scis., Assn. Am. Physicians, Swedish Med. Assn., Am. Soc. Biol. Chemists, Italian Pharm. Soc., Acad. Nat. Medicina de Buenos Aires, Internat. Soc. Hematology, Fgn. Assn. U.S. Nat. Acad. Scis., Royal Soc. London (fgn. mem.), Spanish Soc. Allergology and Clin. Immunology, Royal Nat. Acad. Medicine Spain (hon.), Internat. Acad. Sci. (hon.), Inst. Medicine (fgn. assoc.). Office: Karolinska Inst, S-171 77 Stockholm Sweden

SAMUELSSON, MORTEN, lawyer; b. Copenhagen, Jan. 27, 1960; s. Paul Richard and Ritha Inge (Wennerwald) S.; m. Susan Lykke, Sept., 1992. Degree in law, U. Copenhagen, 1985, PhD, 1990. Admitted to Danish Bar and Supreme Ct. Denmark. Trainee European Parliament, Luxembourg, 1984; assoc. Advokaterne Bredgade 3, Copenhagen, 1985-88; ptnr. Lett & Co., Copenhagen, 1988-98; lectr., Ins. Acad., Rungsted, Denmark, 1987-93; Philip & Ptnrs., Copenhagen, 1998—; counsel Copenhagen Prosecution, 1994—; intern Haight, Gardner, Poor & Havens, N.Y.C., 1992. Author: Real Estate Agent Liability, 1989, Professional Liability, 1993, Directors and Officers Liability, 1997, Insurance Brokers, 2000. Mem. Danish Bar Assn. (litigation com. 1996—), Internat. Bar Assn., Brit.-Nordic Lawyers' Assn., Denmark-Am. Found. Office: Philip & Ptnrs, 7 Vognmagergade PO Box 2722, DK-1018 Copenhagen Denmark

SAMUKOV, VLADIMIR VASILYEVICH, chemist, research scientist; b. Ust-Kamenogorsk, USSR, Mar. 13, 1953; s. Vasily Dmitrievich and Valentina Alekseevna (Kobzeva) S.; m. Olga Alekseevna Kuznetsova; children: Darya, Vladimir, Nikolai. M in Chemistry, Novosibirsk U., 1975; PhD, Moscow U., 1980. Rsch. assoc., head lab., head dept. Inst. Molecular Biology, Novosibirsk, Russia, 1975-91; rsch. dir. Vector-BioProduct, Ltd., Novosibirsk, 1991-95, dept. head State Rsch. Ctr., 1995—. Inventor in field. Mem. N.Y. Acad. Scis. Avocation: computers. Home: 23 Ap 49, 633159 Koltsovo Russia Office: State Rsch Ctr Vektor, Nat Dept Chemistry, 633159 Koltsovo Russia

SAMWALD, HANS-JOACHIM, computer consultant; b. Krems, Austria, Mar. 18, 1948; s. Johann and Ruth (Zimmermann) S.; m. Jaroslava Jiraskova, Oct. 18, 1972; children: Nicole, Oliver, Laura. Degree, Wirtschaftsun, Vienna, 1970; MBA, Century U., L.A., 1988. Computer programmer Siemens, Munich, 1970-80; freelance cons. Munich, 1981-91, 94—; analyst Siemens, Riyadh, Saudi Arabia, 1991-93. Author: (cookbook) Arabian Cooking, 1994, (illustrated history of tattooing) Motive, 1981 (Kodak award 1982), (how-to book) Dehydration of Fruits, Mushrooms, etc., 1986; programmer/designer: (multimedia CD-ROM) Viennese for Travellers, 1997 (Brain Consult award 1997), Tattoo Today, 1998, Cyberspace der phantasie, 1998. Avocations: photography, bodybuilding, biking, travel.

SAN, NGUYEN DUY, psychiatrist, educator; b. Langson, Vietnam, Sept. 25, 1932; s. Nguyen Duy and Tran Tuyet (Trang) Quyen; came to Can., 1971, naturalized, 1977; MD, U. Saigon, 1960; postgrad. U. Mich., 1970; m. Eddie Jean Ciesielski, Aug. 24, 1971; children: Thuan Le, Megan Thuloan, Muriel Mylinh, Claire Kimlan, Robin Xuanlan, Baodan Edward. Intern, Cho Ray Hosp., Saigon, 1957-58; resident Univ. Hosp., Ann Arbor, Mich., 1968-70, Lafayette Clinic, Detroit, 1970-71, Clarke Inst. Psychiatry, Toronto, Ont., Can., 1971-72; chief of psychiatry South Vietnamese Army, 1964-68; sr. psychiatrist Queen St. Mental Health Ctr., Toronto, 1972-74; unit dir. Homewood San., Guelph, Ont., 1974-80; cons. psychiatrist Guelph Gen. Hosp., St. Joseph's Hosp., Guelph; practice medicine specializing in psychiatry, Guelph, 1974-80; unit dir. inpatient svc. Royal Ottawa (Ont., Can.) Hosp., 1980-84, dir. psychiat. rehab. program, 1985-87; asst. prof. psychiatry U. Ottawa Med. Sch., 1980-85, assoc. prof. psychiatry, 1985-87; bd. dirs. Hong Fook Mental Health Svc., Toronto, 1987—, dir. East-West Mental Health Ctr., Toronto, 1987—; chmn., bd. dirs. Access Alliance Multicultural Health Ctr., Toronto, 1988—; cons. UN High Commr. for Refugees, 1987—. Served with Army Republic of Vietnam, 1953-68. Mem. Can. Med. Assn., Can., Am. psychiat. assns., Am. Soc. Clin. Hypnosis, Internat. Soc. Hypnosis, N.Y. Acad. Scis. Buddhist. Author: Etude du Tetanos au Vietnam, 1960; (with others) The Psychology and Physiology of Stress, 1969, Psychosomatic Medicine, theoretical, clinical, and transcultural aspects, 1983, Uprooting, Loss and Adaptation, 1984, 87, Southeast Asian Mental Health, 1985, Ten Years Later: Indochinese Communities in Canada, 1988, Refugee Resettlement and Well-Being, 1989. Office: 2238 Dundas St W Ste 306, Toronto, ON Canada M6R 3A9

SANABRIA, SHERRY ZVARES, artist; b. Washington; d. Simon and Belle (Herzfeld) Zvares; m. Phillip Kasten, Aug. 31, 1958 (div. Dec. 1985); childrn: Jessica L., Alex S.; m. Robert Sanabria, Jan. 24, 1986. BA, George Washington U., 1959; MFA, Am. U., 1974. Freelance lectr. on her painting. One-woman shows include Touchstone Gallery, Washington, 1977, Phillips Collection, Washington, 1980, Baumgartner Galleries, Washington, 1981, 83, 86, 88, Genest Gallery, Lambertville, N.J., 1987, KPMG Peat Marwick, Washington, 1989, David Adamson Gallery, Washington, 1989, 91, 93, 95, Ellis Island Immigratoin Mus., N.Y.C., 1991-92, Marymount U., McLean, Va., 1992, Dorothy McRae Gallery, Atlanta, 1994, George Washington U., Ashton, Va., 1997, Washington Hebrew Congretation, 1998; exhibited in group shows, including Washington Women's Arts Ctr., 1977, So. Alleghenies Mus., Loretto, Pa., 1978, Arts Gallery, Balt., 1980, 81, Corcoran Gallery Art, Washington, 1980, Frostburg (Md.) State Coll., 1981, Art Barn, Washington, 1982, Am. Acad. Arts and Letters, N.Y.C., 1983, Williams Coll. Mus. Art, Williamstown, Mass., 1984, Cornell U., Ithaca, N.Y., 1985, FRS, Washington, 1985, 89, Washington County Mus. Fine Arts, Hagerstown, Md., 1986, Vanderbilt U., 1989, Gallery 10 ltd., Washington, 1991, Watkins Gallery, Am. U., Washington, 1992, U. Richmond, Va., 1992, Emerson Gallery, McLean, Va., 1993, U. Del., 1994, B'nai B'rith Kluznick Mus., Washington, 1996, Gallery Henock, N.Y.C., 1999, Md. Art Place, Balt., 2000; represented in permanent collections Phillips Collection, Philip Morris USA, Associated Gen. Contractors Am., Artery Orgn., First Nat. Bank Boston, Ownes and Minor Inc., Charles E. Smith Co., Ernst and Whinney, Northern Telecom., Inc., Loudoun Med. Ctr., Astrolink, McGraw Hill Pubs., Benchmark Capitol, Paul Hastings Law Firm, Carter Braxton Devel. Co., Am. Univ., others. Mem. Women's Caucus for Arts, Loudoun Arts Coun. E-mail: szspaint@aol.com.

SANADZE, TENGIZ IVANES-DZE, physicist, researcher; b. Tbilisi, Georgia, Jan. 30, 1930; s. Ivane Lukas-dze and Natalia Gerasimes-as (Efremidze) S.; m. Eleon. Konst. Zvegninceva, Feb. 15, 1955 (div. June 1975); children: Georgi, Dimitri; m. Avelina Aleksandres-as Davituliani, July 18, 1975; children: Natalia, Ekaterine. Aspirant in Physics, Tbilisi State U., 1953-56, candidate scis., 1958, DSc, 1971. Sci. worker Tbilisi State U., 1956-59, head Low Temperature Physics Lab., 1959-61, head dept. radiophysics, 1961—, prof. physics, 1971—, head acad. coun., 1973—. Discoverer Discrete Saturation phenomenon, pulsed spectroscopy of electron paramagnetic resonance; contbr. articles to profl. jours. Fellow Internat. EPR Soc.; mem. Russian Acad. Scis. (coun. on magnetism 1983—), Georgian Acad. Scis. (corr.). Avocations: classical music, downhill skiing. Home: Ateni Str 20 Apt 52, 380079 Tbilisi Georgia Office: Tbilisi State U, Chavchavadze Av I, 380028 Tbilisi Georgia

SANBAR, MOSHE GUSTAV, economist, banker; b. Kecskemet, Hungary, Mar. 29, 1926; arrived in Israel, 1948; s. Salo Salomon and Margit (Klausner) Sandberg; m. Bracha Berta Rabinovich, Nov. 1, 1951; children: Shlomit, Nava. MA in Econs., Hebrew U., Jerusalem, 1953. Project mgr. Israel Inst. for Social Rsch., Jerusalem, 1951-58; econ. advisor Ministry of Fin., Jerusalem, 1958-63, head of budget dept., 1963-68; chmn. indsl. devel. Bank of Israel, Tel Aviv, 1968-71; gov. Bank of Israel, Jerusalem, 1971-76; chmn. Bank Leumi Le'Israel, Tel Aviv, 1988-95; ind. econ. advisor, arbitrator Tel Aviv, 1995—; chmn. M.S. Internat. Fin., 1995—. Author: (book) My Longest Year, 1956 (Yad Veshem award 1958); co-author: (book) Planning and Budgeting, 1970; author, editor: (book) The Political Economy of Israel, 1986, The Local Government in Israel, 1982. Chmn. Arab Refugee Rehab. Trust, Tel Aviv, 1968-92, Habima Nat. Theatre, Tel Aviv, 1969-82, Janco-Dada Mus. of Modern Art, Ein-Hod, Israel, 1982—, Holocuast Survivors in Israel, Jerusalem, 1987—; treas. Claims Conf. Against Germany, 1992—, pres. Internat. C. of C., Israel, 1992—; bd. mem. Internat. C. of C., Paris, 1997-99; bd. dirs. World Jewish Restution Orgn., 1995—. Recipient prize of Min. of Interior for extraordinary contbn. to devel. of local govt. in Israel, 1986, Herzl prize, 1973, Internat. Humanitarian award B'nai Brith, 1995. Avocations: stamp collecting, theater.

SANBORN, ANNA LUCILLE, pension and insurance consultant; b. Bklyn., Mar. 29, 1924; d. Peter Francis and Matilda M. (Stumpp) Galligen; B.A., Bklyn. Coll., 1945; 1 son, Dean Sanborn. Head dept. benefit and estate planning Union Central Life Ins. Co., N.Y.C., 1949-51; adminstr. employee benefits Seaboard Oil Co., N.Y.C., 1952-56; with Frank J. Walters Assocs., Inc., N.Y.C., 1957—, pres., 1970—. Bd. dirs. Archdiocesan Service Corp. Mem. Am. Acad. Actuaries, Republican. Roman Catholic. Home: 58-11 Seabury St Elmhurst NY 11373-4825 Office: Frank J Walters Assocs 58-13 Seabury St Flushing NY 11373-4825

SANCHELLI, CHARLES RAYMOND (CHUCK SANCHELLI), tennis company executive; b. Decatur, Ill., June 30, 1951; s. Charles R. and Mary E. (Metzger) S.; m. Delinda A. Martinez, July 7, 1990. BS in Bus., Purdue U., 1973. Tennis dir. French Lick (Ind.) Sheraton Resort, 1973-74; with U.S. Pro Tennis Tour, 1974-75; club mgr. Newk Plus Two, Inc., New Braunfels, Tex., 1975-77, Quail Valley Tennis Club, Missouri City, Tex., 1977-79; mgr., dir. Meadow Creek Racquet Club, Missouri City, Tex., 1979-84; pres., chief exec. officer Ft. Bend Tennis Svcs., Inc., Sugarland, Tex., 1984—; engrng. technician Sonat Exploration, Inc., Houston, 1984-89; computer specialist Sonat Svcs., Inc., Houston, 1989-90; v.p., chief fin. officer Day Camp Svcs., Inc., Sugar Land, 1990—. Chmn. Greater Houston Tennis Coun., 1991—. Mem. U.S. Pro Tennis Assn. (cert. pro level I), U.S. Tennis Assn. (nat. com. 1991—, Nat. Cmty. Svc. award 1994), Tex. Profl. Tennis Assn. (chmn. 1990—, state com., Svc. award 1989), Tex. Tennis Assn. (chmn. 1989-94, state com. officer 1995—), Houston Tennis Assn. (pres. 1988-91, Svc. award 1988), Houston Profl. Tennis Assn. (founder, treas. 1988-94), Fort Bend C. of C., 1st Colony Assn. (recreation com. 1990—). Roman Catholic. Avocations: reading, tennis, music. Office: Ft Bend Tennis Svcs Inc 435 B-1 FM 1092 Stafford TX 77477

SANCHEZ, ENRIQUE PABLO, environmental pollution educator; b. Havana, Cuba, Mar. 2, 1948; s. Victor Manuel Sanchez and Martha Hernandez; m. Lissette Travieso, May 5, 1990; children: Yamnet, Annette, Lourdes. BS in Chem. Engring., ISPJAE, Havana, 1970; MSc, CNIC, Havana, 1974; PhD in Environ. Scis., VSCHT, Prague, Czech Republic, 1980. Rschr. CNIC, Havana, 1971-80, head biogas lab., 1980-88, head DECA-CNIC, 1988-95; cons. Inst. de la Grasa, Seville, Spain, 1990-95, CONACE S.A. de C.V., Mexico City, 1990-95, PROESA S.A. de C.V., Mexico City, 1994-95, various ministries and orgns. in Cuba. Contbr. articles to profl. jours.; patentee in field. Spl. fellow Alexander von Humboldt Found., Braunschweig, Germany, 1990. Mem. FAO/SREN (bd. dirs.), AIDIS Cuba. Avocations: baseball, basketball, football, volleyball. Office: Environ Cons Div Gamma SA, Min Sci Tech & Environ, Vedado Havana Cuba

SANCHEZ, ISAAC CORNELIUS, chemical engineer, educator; b. San Antonio, Aug. 11, 1941; s. Isaac Jr. and Marce (Aguilar) S.; m. Karen Patricia Horton, Aug. 7, 1976; children: Matthew, Timothy. BS with honors, St. Mary's U., 1963; PhD, U. Del., 1969. Postdoctoral Nat. Bureau Standards, Gaithersburg, Md., 1969-71; assoc. scientist Xerox Corp., Webster, N.Y., 1971-72; asst. prof. U. Mass., Amherst, 1972-77; rsch. chemist Nat. Bureau Standards, Gaithersburg, 1977-86; fellow Alcoa, Pitts., 1986-88; prof. U. Tex., Austin, 1988—; H.A. disting vis. prof. U. Akron (Ohio), 1995. Mem. editorial bd. Jour. Polymer Sci., 1986-92, Polymer, 1987—; contbr. over 100 articles to profl. jours. Lt. USN, 1963-67. Recipient William J. Murray Endowed Chair in engring U. Tex., 1997, Bronze medal U.S. Dept. Commerce, 1980, Silver medal, 1983, E.U. Condon award Nat. Bur. Standards, 1983. Fellow Am. Phys. Soc.; mem. AAAS, AIChE, Am. Chem. Soc., Nat. Acad. Engring., Materials Rsch. Soc., Soc. Plastics Engrs. (Internat. Rsch. award 1996). Avocations: golf, lay ministry. Office: Univ Tex Chem Engring Dept Austin TX 78712

SÁNCHEZ, JOSÉ SALVADOR, computer scientist, educator; b. Reus, Tarragona, Spain, Aug. 15, 1965; s. Juan and Luisa (Garreta) S.; m. Ana Isabel Marqués, July 17, 1993; 1 child, Raquel. MsC in Computer Sci., U. Politecnica Valencia, Spain, 1990; PhD in Computer Sci. Engring., U. Jaume I, Castello, Spain, 1998. Software engr. Orga, Castello, 1991-92; asst. prof. computer sci. U. Jaume I, Castello, 1992—. Contbr. articles to profl. jours. Mem. IEEE, AEPIA. Avocation: music. Office: Univ Jaume 1, Dept Computer Sci, E-12071 Castello Spain

SANCHEZ, JOSE T. CARDINAL, archbishop; b. Pandan, The Philippines, Mar. 17, 1920. Ordained priest Roman Cath. Ch., 1946. Prefect Congregation for Clergy, 1991-96; titular bishop of Lesvi, coadjutor bishop of Lucena, 1968, bishop of Lucena, 1976-82, archbishop of Nueva Segoria, 1982, resigned, 1986; sec. Congregation for Evangelization of Peoples, 1985-91; elevated to the Sacred Coll. of Cardinals, 1991, with titular ch. of St. Pius V; mem. Vatican Sec. of State Coun. of the II Session, Congregation for Bishops, Congregation for the Evangelization of Peoples, Congregation for Cath. Edn., Pontifical Commn. for the Interpretation of the Legislative Texts, Pontifical Commn. for Latin-Am., Pontifical Commn. for the Internat. Eucharistic Congress; pres. Pontifical Sanctuary of Pompei, Loreto, and Bari, Commn. Preservation Artistic and Historic Patrimony Holy See, 1991-93. Mem. Congregation for Bishops, Congregation for the Evangelization of Peoples, Congregation for Cath. Edn., Pontifical Coun. for Latin-Am., Pontifical Commn. for the Internat. Eucharistic Congress; pres. Pontifical Sanctuaries of Pompei, Loreto, Bari. Office: Congregation for the Clergy, Office of Prefect, 00120 Vatican City Vatican City*

SANCHEZ, LEONEDES MONARRIZE WORTHINGTON (HIS ROYAL HIGHNESS DUKE DE LEONEDES OF SPAIN SICILY GREECE), fashion designer; b. Flagstaff, Ariz., Mar. 15, 1951; s. Rafael Leonedes and Margaret (Monarrize) S. BS, No. Ariz. U., 1974; studied, Fashion Inst. Tech., N.Y.C., 1974-75; AA, Fashion Inst. D&M, L.A., 1975; lic., La Ecole de la Chambre Syndical de la Couture Parisian, Paris, 1976-78; certificate, La Mason de Couture, Paris, 2000. Lic. in designing. Contract designer/asst. to head designer House of Bonnet, Paris, 1976—; dress designer-in-residence Flagstaff, 1978—; mem. faculty No. Ariz. U., Flagstaff, 1978-80; designer Ambiance, Inc., L.A., 1985—; designer Interiors by Leonedes subs. Studio of Leonedes Couturier, Ariz., 1977, Calif., 1978, London, Paris, 1978, Rome, 1987, Milan, Spain, 1989, Palazzo de Leonedes, 1998; designer Liturgical Vesture subs. Studio of Leonedes Couturier; CEO Leonedes Internat., Design Consortium, Leonedes Internat. Ltd., 1999—; designer El Casillo de Nuevo Espana, Santa Fe, N.Mex.; owner, CEO, designer Leonedes Internat., Ltd., London, Milan, Paris, Spain, Ambian Ariz, Calif., Appolonian Costuming, Ariz., London, Milan, Paris, El Castillo de Leonedes, Sevilla, Spain, Villa Apollonian de Leonedes, Mykonos, Greece, Palazzo de Leoedes, Sicily; cons. House of Bonnet, Paris, 1976—, Bob Mackie, Studio City, Calif., 1974-75; CEO, designer artistical dir., Leonedes internat.; appointee commn. on religious antiquities Congregation on the Arts, The Vatican, Italy, 1998. Bd. dirs. Roman Cath. Social Svcs., 1985-86, Northland Crisis Nursery, 1985—; bd. dirs., chmn. Pine Country Transit, 1986-88; pres. Chicanos for Edn.; active master's swim program ARC, Ariz., 1979—; eucharistic min., mem. art and environ. com., designer liturgical vesture St. Pius X Cath. Ch.; vol. art tchr., instr. St. Mary's Regional Sch., Flagstaff, 1987-90, vol. art dir.; mem. Flagstaff Parks and Recreation Commn., 1994-96, citizens' adv. com. master plan, 1994-96; mem. cmty. bd. adv. com. Flagstaff Unified Sch. Dist., 1995; active Duke de Leonedes Found. de Nuevo Espana, Santa Fe, Duke de Leonedes Found. de Neuvo Espana, Santa Fe; prin. chair Duke de Leonedes Found., The Netherlands, 1995; de neuvo espana Duke de Leuedes Found., Santa Fe, N.Mex., 1996. Decorated Duke de Leonedes (Spain), 1994, His Royal Highness (Spain, Greece, Sicily), 1998; recipient Camellian Design award 1988, Atlanta. Mem. AAU (life, chairperson swimming Ariz. 1995, vice chairperson physique, mem. citizen adv. bd. parks and recreation, chairperson state of Ariz. physique, swimming, adv. to Olympic inquiry com., advisor to internat. Olympic com. on physique), Am. Film Inst., Am. Assn. Hist. Preservation, Costume Soc., Am. Nat. Physique Com., Internat. Consortium Fashion Designers, Nat. Cath. Ednl. Assn., La Legion de Honour de la Mode Parisienne, Social Register Assn., Phi Alpha Theta (historian 1972-73, pres. 1973-74), Pi Kappa Delta (pres. 1972-73, historian 1973-74). Republican. Avocations: body building, swimming. Office: El Castillo de Leonedes, Seville Spain also: El Castillo de Nuevo Espana Santa Fe NM 87501 also: Villa de Apollonian de Leonedes, Mykonos Greece

SÁNCHEZ, MARIÉ SOLEDAD, researcher; b. Madison, Wis., Dec. 21, 1965; d. Antonio Sénchez-Romeralo and Marié Soledad Martinez de Pinillos Ruiz; m. Domgoj Vucic, May 22, 1998. Licenciatura, U. Complutense, Madrid, 1988; MS, U. Calif., Santa Cruz, 1992; PhD, U. Ga., 1999. Technician Fish and Wildlife Svc., Anchorage, 1991; contractor Govt. of Navarra, Pamplona, Spain, 1993-94; postdoctoral fellow U. Calif., Davis, 1999—. Contbr. articles to profl. jours. Vol. Earthquake Relief Svcs., Santa Cruz, Calif., 1989. Regent's fellow U. Calif., 1989-90, Rsch. fellow NSF, 1999—; recipient grad. scholarship award Internat. Women's Fishing Assn. U. Calif., 1990, Travel award Marine Scis. Bd. UCSC, 1991, Student Rsch. award Friends of Long Marine Lab., 1991, James L. Carmon Scholar U. Ga. Rsch. Found., 1997, Nat. Travel award, 1998, Travel award Nat. Acad. of Scis., 2000; Rsch. grant Govt. of Navarra, 1995-97, Tgn. grantee NIH, 1997-99. Mem. Coll. Oficial de Biologos, Genetics Soc. of Am., Am. Soc. of Naturalists, European Soc. for Evolutionary Biology. Avocations: horseback riding, Flamenco. Office: Dept Environtl Sci and Policy U Calif Davis CA 95616

SANCHEZ, MARY ANNE, retired secondary school educator; b. Galesburg, Ill., Aug. 4, 1939; d. Stephen Mingare and M. Margaret Kennedy; m. J. Manuel Sanchez, Dec. 26, 1980. BS in Edn., Western Ill. U., 1961; MA, Ill. State U., 1970. Tchr. Stanford, Ill., 1962-64, Titusville, Fla., 1964-66; tchr. Montgomery County Bd. Edn., Chevy Chase, Md., 1969-72, Hillsborough County Bd. Edn., Tampa, Fla., 1972-96; ret., 1996. Mary Anne Sanchez Young Woman scholarship named in her honor by Social Studies Dept. Leto Comprehensive H.S., 1999. Mem. Nat. Coun. for Social Studies, Fla. Coun. for Social Studies, Adult Edn. Assn. Home: 2715 W Ivy St Tampa FL 33607-1922

SANCHEZ, MIGUEL RAMON, dermatologist, educator; b. Havana, Cuba, May 5, 1950; came to the U.S., 1962; s. Rodolfo and Maria Sanchez. BS, CCNY, 1971; MD, Albert Einstein Coll. Medicine, 1974. Instr. Montefiore Dept. Family Medicine, Bronx, N.Y., 1978-79; sr. med. specialist Kingsborough Psychiat. Ctr., Bklyn., 1979-80; med. dir. Ten Communities Health Ctr., Tulare, Calif., 1980-82; assoc. prof. clin. dermatology NYU, N.Y.C., 1982-83; assoc. dir. Dept. Dermatology Bellevue Hosp. Ctr, N.Y.C., 1983—; mem. Tulare County Mental Health Bd., 1980-81; mem. med. bd. Bellevue Hosp., 1990—. Contbr. articles to profl. jours. and chpts. to books; editor: (software) Derm-Rx, 1986-90, (book) Dermatology Educational Review Manual, 1993. Bd. dirs. Community Health Project, N.Y.C., 1993; mem. patient care com. community bd. Bellevue Hosp., 1990-93; co-founder, pres. Assn. Latino Faculty and Students. Recipient Testimonial of Appreciation So. Tulare County, 1981, 1st Place award Scientific Forum N.Y. Acad. Dermatology, 1985. Mem. Am. Acad. Dermatology, Acad. for Advancement Sci., Dermatologic Found. Democrat. Roman Catholic. Achievements include development of clinics for tropical dermatology, HIV skin disease, disorders of keratinization, connective tissue disease, and phototherapy; research in infectious diseases, dermatopharmacology and cutaneous manifestation of HIV infection. Office: NYU Dept Dermatology 562 1st Ave New York NY 10016-6402

SANCHEZ, NORMA GRACIELA, physicist, astrophysicist, educator; b. Buenos Aires; arrived in France, 1976; d. Antonio Luis and Norma Iris (Piccoli) S. D in Physics, U. La Plata, Argentina, 1979; Docteur d'Etat, U. Paris VII, 1979. Scientist CONICET/IAFE, Buenos Aires, 1973-76, CNRS, Paris, 1976; scientist Obs. de Paris, dir. rsch., 1990; dir. Internat. Sch. Astrophysics, Erice, Italy, 1991, Sci. Mus., Erice, 1991; dir., coord. various projects in fundamental physics European Commn.; advisor in field. Editor 20 books; contbr. articles to profl. jours. Office: Observatoire de Paris, 61 Ave de l Observatoire, 75014 Paris France

SÁNCHEZ, PABLO J., pediatrician, educator; b. Cuba, Nov. 11, 1954; s. Guillermo and Carolina (Parlade) S. BS in Biology, Seton Hall U., 1977; MD, U. Pitts., 1981. Diplomate Am. Bd. Pediats., Am. Bd. Perinatal-Neonatal Medicine, Am. Bd. Pediat. Infectious Diseases. Intern and resident in pediatrics Children's Hosp. Pitts., 1981-84; fellow in neonatology Babies Hosp. Columbia-Presbyn. Med. Ctr., N.Y.C., 1984-86; fellow in pediatric infectious disease U. Tex. Southwestern Med. Ctr., Dallas, 1986-88, asst. prof. pediats., 1988-95; assoc. prof. pediats., 1996—; mem. infection control com. Parkland Meml. Hosp., Dallas, 1988—; lectr. Columbia-Presbyn. Med. Ctr., N.Y.C., 1986, Pub. Health Dept., Dallas, 1987-93, Humana Hosp. and Med. Ctr. Dallas, 1991, Symposium on Congenital and Perinatal Infection, Chgo., 1991, Am. Acad. Pediatrics, New Orleans, 1991, Changing Role of Mycoplasma in Respiratory Diseas and Aids, Scottsdale, Ariz., 1991, Ctr. for Disease Control, Atlanta, 1991, Cirena Found., Cali, Colombia, 1993. Author: (chpts. in books) Current Therapy in Pediatric Infectious Disease, 1988, Principles and Practice of Pediatrics, 1993, Advances in Pediatric Infectious Diseases, 1992, Current Pediatric Therapy, 1993, Infectious Diseases of the Fetus and Newborn Infant, 1993; author articles and revs. Grantee U. Tex. Southwestern Med. Ctr., 1988-89, Am. Lung Assn., 1990-91, SmithKline Beecham Pharms., 1990, Ctrs. for Disease Control, 1990-91, 93-94, Pediatric AIDS Found., 1990-91, Burroughs Wellcome Co., 1993-94, NIAID/NIH, 1993—. Mem. Am. Acad. Pediatrics, Infectious Diseases Soc. Am., Pediatric Infection Soc., Tex. Med. Soc. Roman Catholic. Office: U Tex Southwestern Med Ctr 5323 Harry Hines Blvd Dallas TX 75390-7208

SANCHEZ, PEDRO LUIS, psychiatrist; b. Yarumal, Colombia, Sept. 29, 1941; s. Jaime and Susana (Gaviria) S. MD, U. Nat. Colombia, 1968; PhD, U. Santo Tomas, 1975. From psychiatrist to outpatient svc. head Hosp. Mental de Antioquia, 1971-97; pvt. practice, Medellin, Colombia, 1997—; cons. psychiat. unit rsch. UPB. Mem. Colombian Soc. Psychiatry, Antioquian Soc. Psychiatry, Decypol Forensic Psychiatry Head. Roman Catholic. Avocations: photography, music, swimming. Home and Office: Carrera 47 No 56-18 (205), Medellin Colombia

SANCHEZ, TOMASA CALVO, educator; b. Teruel, Spain, Feb. 2, 1954; d. Rafael Cawo Toran and Carmen Sanchez Villaroya. Degree in math., Valencia U., Spain, 1977. Colaborator U. Balearic Islands, Palma, Spain, 1977-78, prof., 1978—; prof. titular U. Desde, 1996. Contbr. articles to profl. jours. Mem. EUROFUSE, European Assn. Furry Logic and Tech. Roman Catholic. Avocations: swimming, reading, movies. Office: U Balearic Islands, Cnta Valldemossa 7 5, 07071 Palma Spain

SANCHEZ ALVARADO, ALEJANDRO, embryologist, molecular biologist; b. Caracas, Venezuela, Feb. 24, 1964; came to U.S., 1982; s. Delfin Orestes and Vera Antonieta (Alvarado) S. BS, Vanderbilt U., 1986; PhD, U. Cin., 1992. Rsch. asst. U. Cin. Coll. Medicine, 1987-88, grad. student, 1988-92, rsch. assoc., 1992-93; postdoctoral fellow Carnegie Inst., Balt., 1994-96, staff assoc., 1996—; sci. corr. El Nacional, Caracas, 1996; UNESCO lectr., Venezuela, 1997, 99. Editor: Regenerative Medicine; contbr. articles to Jour. Biol. Chemistry, Devel. Dynamics, Devel. Biology, Proceedings of the NAS. Recipient Marine Biol. Labs. Embryology rsch. award, 1995, Marcus Singer rsch. regeneration award, 1999. Mem. AAAS, Am. Soc. Cell Biology, Soc. Devel. Biology, Singer Soc. for Regeneration, N.Y. Acad. Scis. Achievements include research in characterizing in vitro model for vertebrate cardiogenesis; development of an invertebrate transgenic model for the molecular study of regeneration. Office: Carnegie Inst Dept Embryology 115 W University Pkwy Baltimore MD 21210-3399

SANCHEZ-CABEZA, JOAN-ALBERT, physics educator, researcher; b. Barcelona, Spain, Sept. 26, 1961; s. José Sánchez and Adoración Cabeza; m. Roser Ribalta, Jan. 4, 1986; children: Albert, Lluis. BS, Autonomous U. Barcelona, 1984, MS, 1985; PhD in Physics, U. Dublin, Ireland, 1989. Demonstrator Univ. Coll. Dublin, 1985-87; asst. lectr. physics Autonomous U. Barcelona, 1987-89, lectr. physics, rsch. dir., 1989—; tech. expert IAEA, Vienna, Austria, 1989—; data quality/mgmt. expert European Commn., Spain, 1993—. Contbr. articles to scientific jours., chpts. to books. Pres. Found. for Promotion of Self-employment, Catalan Ctr. for Promotion of Self-Employment, Barcelona, 1999. Recipient rsch. award Empresa Nacional de Residuos Radiactivos, Madrid, 1990-92, Comision Interministerial de Ciencia y Tecnologia, Madrid, 1992-95, 95-96, European Union (Nuc. Fission Safety), Brussels, 1993-95, 96-99; European Union (Marine Sci. and Technology), Brussels, 1993-95, 96-99, Empresa Nacional de Rediduos Radiactivos, Madrid, 1993-95. Mem. Royal Spanish Soc. Physics, Internat. Union Radioecology, Spanish Soc. Radiation Protection, Health Physics Soc. (plenary mem.), Commn. Internat. pour L'Exploration Scientifique de la Mer Mediterranee (marine chem. com., Monaco, 1996). Avocation: classical music. E-mail: JoanAlbert.Sanchez@uab.es. Office: Univ Auto de Barcelona, Physics Dept Bellaterra, E-08193 Barcelona Spain

SANCHEZ-CAMARA, ANTONIO ALBA, company executive, consultant; b. Madrid, May 8, 1941; s. Antonio Castaner and Siluid Ygoac (Alba) Sanchez-C.; m. Maaria Jose Madariaga Greno, June 17, 1967; children: Antonio, Inigo, aime, Luz. PhD in Elec. Engring., ICAI, Madrid, 1964; grad. in Bus. Adminstrn., Deusto, Bilbao, Spain, 1967. Mktg. and divsn. mgr. Westinghouse, S.A., Madrid, 1965-80, mng. dir., 1980-84; CEO E.N. Bazan, Madrid, 1984-95; non exec. dir. Gen. Cos., Madrid, 1995—; CEO Guindola Gestion, Madrid, 1995-97; pres. Transportes Gerposa, Sandance, Spain, 1997-99, Intermos Nets, Barcelona, Spain, 1995-99, Bermarmol, Alicante, Spain, 1996-99, Eutrasur, Cadiz, Spain, 1995-99. V.p. Colegio Ingenieros Del Icai, Madrid, 1999. Recipient Gran Cruz Merito Naval, King of Spain, 1993. Mem EACE. Office: Guindola Gestion, Avda Brasil 4, 28020 Madrid Spain

SANCHEZ-CARRILLO, JESUS, engineering educator, researcher; b. San Cristobal, Venezuela, May 11, 1923; s. Luis and Luisa (Carrillo) S.; m. Yolanda Acosta Sanchez, Dec. 8, 1963 (widowed Sept. 2, 1999); children: Irisol, Jorge. Cert. Meteorology, UCLA, 1944. Chief sect. of meteorology Min. of Agr., Maracay, Venezuela, 1944-86; prof. UCV, Caracas, Venezuela, 1958-72, assoc. prof., 1972-80, prof., 1980—. Author: Mesoclimas en Venezuela, 1980, Agroclimatologia, 1999. Mem. Coll. Venezuelian Engrs., Assn. of Profs. Home: Ave La Palmita, Caracas 1010, Venezuela

SÁNCHEZ-CASTELLI, ENGARDO PRIMO, educational services company owner, educator; b. Córdoba, Argentina, July 5, 1969; s. Jose Primo and Aroceli Edith (Castelli) Sánchez; m. Silvena Sienza, Aug. 8, 1996; children: Valentin Clive, Alma Belen. B in Bus. Adminstrn., UNC, Córdoba, 1991; MBA, Funcer, Córdoba, 1997. CEO, owner SIV SBL, Córdoba, 1990-99, Rumibo, Córdoba, 1999—; thesis dir. Funcer, Córdoba, 1999—, pres. Grad. Ctr., 1999. Avocations: live sports, basketball, running, soccer. Office: SIV SRL, Allende Rt, 5000 Cordoba Argentina

SANCHEZGIL, JOSE ANTONIO, physicist; b. Cartagena, Murcia, Spain, Aug. 8, 1965; s. Jose Antonio Sanchezgarcia and Isabel Gilsaez; m. Gema Marin, Jan. 30, 1993; 1 dau., Claudia Sanchez. BS in physics, U. Autonoma, Madrid, 1988, PhD in Physics, 1992. Postdoctoral fellow U. Calif., Irvine, 1993-94; rsch. assoc. Inst. Estructura Materia, Madrid, 1995-99, tenured scientist, 2000—; reviewer several sci. jours., 1992—. Contbr. articles to sci. jours. Grantee Caja Madrid, 1988, Min. Edn. Sci. Spain, 1989, Spanish Sci. Rsch. Coun., 1992. Mem. Optical Soc. Am. (rev. jour.), Spanish Optical

Soc. Avocations: literature, soccer, cycling, swimming, skiing. Office: Inst Estructura Materia, Serrano 121, 28006 Madrid Spain

SÁNCHEZ-GUERRERO, SERGIO ARTURO, hematologist; b. Mante, Mex., Feb. 5, 1961; s. Jorge Sánchez and Estela Guerrero; m. Maria Rocio Cárdenas, Nov. 7, 1992; children: Alejandra, Liliana. MD, U. Guadalajara, Mex., 1985; postgrad., UNAM, Mexico City, 1989, 91. Diplomate Mex. Bd. Internal Medicine, Mex. Bd. Hematology. Fellow in medicine Inst. Nat. Nutrition, Mexico City, 1986-89, fellow in hematology, 1989-91, attending physician, 1993—, chief transfusion med. svc., 1993-2000; fellow in hematology and blood bank Mt. Sinai Hosp., N.Y.C., 1991-93; assoc. prof. UNAM, 1994—; founder, prof. transfusion medicine fellowship UNAM, 2000. Contbr. articles to profl. jours. Mem. Am. Soc. Hematology, Am. Assn. Blood Banks, Assn. Mex. Estudio Hematologia. E-mail: sasanche@avantel.net. Office: Inst Nat Nutrition, Vasco de Quiroga 15, 14000 Mexico City Mexico

SANCHEZ-PALENCIA, EVARISTE, mechanics and applied mathematics researcher; b. Madrid, Jan. 3, 1941; s. Indalecio Sanchez-Palencia and Angeles Serrano; m. Jacqueline Hubert, Mar. 4, 1972; children: Bernard, Laurent. M Engring., Sch. Aero. Engring., Madrid, 1964; DS, U. Paris, 1969. Rschr. Nat. Ctr. Sci. Rsch., Paris, 1967—, dir. rsch., 1986—. Author: Non-Homogeneous Media and Vibration Theory, 1980, (with D. Leguillon) Computation of Singular Solutions in Elliptic Problems, 1987, (with J. Sanchez-Hubert) Vibration and Coupling of Continuous Systems, 1989, (with J. Sanchez-Hubert) Coques Elastiques Minces, 1997. Recipient Silver medal Ctr. Nat. Rsch. Sci., 1981, prize Inst. Français du Petrole. Mem. Acad. Scis. Paris (corr.). Office: U Paris VI, 4 Place Jussieu, 75252 Paris France

SÁNCHEZ PEÑA, RICARDO SALVADOR, researcher; b. Godoy Cruz, Argentina, Aug. 14, 1954; s. Miguel and Aida Dolores (Gallo) S.; m. Monica Maria Sallán-Mur; children: Pablo A., Lucila. Elec. engr., Univ. Buenos Aires, 1978; MSEE, Calif. Inst. of Tech., 1986, PhD in Elec. Engr., 1988. Rschr. Tech. Rsch. Ctr. of the Armed Forces, Argentina, 1977-79, Nat. Comm. Space Rsch., Argentina, 1979-84, Aeronautic and Astronautics Rsch. Inst., Argentina, 1988-87; prof. U. Buenos Aires, 1987—; rschr. Nat. Com. Space Activities, Argentina, 1994—; vis. rschr. Pa. State U., 1996, Va. Polytech. Inst., State U., 1991, Calif. Inst. Tech., 1989, vis. engr. Mobile Rocket Basis, Germany, 1979. Author: Introduction a la Teoria de Control Robusto, 1992, Robust System Theory and Applications, 1998; contbr. articles to profl. jours. Fellow Orgn. Am. States, 1984-86, Conicet, 1986-88. Mem. IEEE, Argentine Assn. Automatic Control. Avocation: playing blues on electric guitar. Office: Conae, Av Paseo Colon 751, 1063 Buenos Aires Argentina

SANCHEZ-PEREZ, ROSARIO, economist; b. Valencia, Spain, Mar. 16, 1958; d. Hondrato and Rosario (Perez) S.; m. Francisco Javier Meseguer, Nov. 6, 1991; 1 child. Diploma in econs., London Sch. Econs., 1989, MSc, 1990; PhD, U. Valencia, 1994. Asst. lectr. to lectr. econs. U. Valencia, Spain, 1996—. Fax: 34 96 3828249. E-mail: rosario.sanchez@uv.es.

SANCHEZ-POZO, ANTONIO, biochemistry educator; b. Cuevas S. Marcos, Malaga, Spain, Jan. 19, 1954. PhD in Pharmacy, U. Granada, Spain, 1980, specialization in clin. chemistry. From asst. to prof. Faculty of Pharmacy, U. Granada, prof., vice dean Faculty of Pharmacy. Author: Clinical Biochemistry, 1998. Mem. Spanish Soc. Biochemistry and Molecular Biology, Spanish Soc. Clin. Chemistry. Office: U Granada, Campus Cartuja, 18071 Granada Spain

SÁNCHEZ PROAL, ERNESTO, engineering executive; b. Torreón, Coahulia, Mex., Aug. 31, 1966; s. Ernesto Manuel Sánchez Anguiano and María de los Angeles; m. Ivonne Eunice Bernal de la Torre, Jan. 14, 1995; children: Ernesto Pablo, Daniela. Diploma in electronics engring., Inst. Tech. Estudio Sup. Occ., Guadalajara, Mex., 1988; MS in Adminstrn., Ctrl. Mich. U., 1993. Project engr. Kodak Mex., Guadalajara, 1988-89; quality engr. IBM Mex., Guadalajara, 1989-92, nat. distbn. coord., 1994-95, procurment mgr., 1995-97; devel. liaison IBM PC Co., Boca Raton, Fla., 1992-94; programs mgr. Avex Electronic Mex., Guadalajara, 1997-98; bus. unit mgr. Jabil Circuit, Guadalajara, 1998—. treas. directive bd. Condominio Vista Providencia, Guadalajara, 1997—; mem. adv. bd. coord. Coun. Devel. Electronics Industry Supply Chain, Guadalajara, 1998-99; mem. tech. bd. Cadelec, Guadalajara, 1999. Mem. IEEE (v.p. elect Guadalajara sect. 1999—). Avocations: astronomy, astrophotography, photography, mountain biking. Fax: 52-3-819-1581. Home: Pablo Neruda 3335-57, 44630 Guadalajara Mexico Office: Jabil Circuit, Avenida Valdepeñas 1993, 45130 Zapopan Mexico

SÁNCHEZ RUIZ, JORGE, physicist, educator; b. Barcelona, Spain, Aug. 4, 1966; s. Nicolás Sánchez Sánchez and Valvanera Ruiz Vera. Grad. in physics, U. Barcelona, 1989, D in Physics, 1997. Assoc. prof. U. Politècnica de Catalunya, Barcelona, 1990-91; tchr. physics and math. Aula Escola Europea, Barcelona, 1990-94; tchr. material tech. Escola de Sistemes Informàtics, Barcelona, 1995-96; assoc. prof. U. Barcelona, 1996-97, U. Carlos III, Madrid, 1997—; assoc. rschr. Inst. Carlos I de Física Teórica y Computacional, U. Granada, Spain, 1997—. Contbr. articles to profl. jours. Edn. and Rsch. fellow Fundació Aula, Barcelona, 1994-97. Mem. Am. Phys. Soc., Collegi Oficial de Doctors i Llicenciats de Catalunya, Colegio Oficial de Físicos, Nat. Geog. Soc., N.Y. Acad. Scis., Real Sociedad Matematica Espanola. Avocations: music, reading. Office: U Carlos III de Madrid, Avda de la Universidad 30, Leganés Madrid E-28911, Spain

SÁNCHEZ RUIZ, LUIS MANUEL, mathematician, researcher; b. Tetuan, Morocco, Dec. 21, 1958; s. Luis Sánchez Liebana and Carmen Ruiz Peinado; m. Teresa Viciano, Oct. 20, 1998; 1 child, Teresa del Carmen. Lic. in Math., U. Valencia, Spain, 1980, PhD, 1988. Asst. prof. U. Poly. Valencia, 1980-83, assoc. prof., 1983-91, prof., 1991—; vis. prof. U. Fla., Gainesville, 1992-99; sub-dir. internat. rels. EUITI, Valencia, 1989-91; MUST acad. coord., 1996; editl. bd. dirs. Math. Japonica, 1998—, Sci. Math., 1998—. Co-author: Metrizable Barrelled Spaces, 1995, also several textbooks; contbr. articles to profl. jours. Grantee Direccion Gen. de Investigación Científica y Técnica, 1992, 94, 95, Conselleria de Cultura, Educación y Ciencia Generalitat Valenciana, 1996, 98; recipient rsch. projects Ministry Edn., 1998—. Mem. European Assn. for Internat. Edn., Am. Math. Soc., Japan Assn. Math Scis., Real Soc. Math. Española. Avocations: motorcycles, travelling. Office: Univ Poly Valencia, EUITI Dept Applied Math, E-46071 Valencia E-46071, Spain

SANCHEZ-SOTO, PEDRO JOSE, chemist, researcher; b. Utrera, Sevilla, Spain, July 10, 1960; s. Eduardo Sanchez and Primitiva Soto. Lic. in chemistry, U. Sevilla, Spain, 1982, Grado de Licenciado, 1985, PhD in Chemistry, 1990. Pre-doctoral fellow Dept. Inorganic Chemistry, Sevilla, 1982-85, Inst. Natural Resources CSIC, Sevilla, 1986-89; postdoctoral fellow U. Fla., Gainesville, 1990-91; asst. prof. U. Sevilla, 1991-92; tenured scientist Inst. C. Materiales, 1992—. Contbr. articles to profl. jours.; patentee in field; exhibited art in various shows, 1984—. Recipient 1st place sci. photography award, Castellón, 1994, Rsch. award, Sevilla, 1996, Fundacion Domingo Martinez. Mem. Spanish Soc. Ceramics and Glasses, Am. Ceramic Soc., Internat. Conf. for Thermal Analysis and Calorimetry. Roman Catholic. Avocations: fine arts, painting, sculpture. Office: Inst Ciencia Materiales, Av Americo Vespucio s/n, 41092 Sevilla Andalucia Spain

SANCHEZ-VICARIO, ARANTXA, tennis player; b. Barcelona, Spain, Dec. 18, 1971; s. Emilio Sr. and Marisa S. Profl. tennis player, 1985—. Celebrity chairperson Children's Cancer Rsch., Spain; fundraiser Enriqueta Vilavecchia children in Spain. Recipient ESPY award for Best Female Tennis Player ESPN, 1994, ACES award Corel WTA Tour, 1995, One of Five players Players Who Make a Difference award, 1996, Infiniti Commitment to Excellence award Bausch & Lomb Tournament, 1993, Best Doubles Team, 1996, Most Improved Player award WTA, 1988, 89, Most Impressive Newcomer award, 1987. Avocations: soccer, water skiing, biking, reading. Office: Internat Mgmt Group 1360 E 9th St Ste 100 Cleveland OH 44114*

SANCHIS-ALFONSO, VICENTE, orthopaedic surgeon; b. Valencia, Spain, Aug. 28, 1961; s. Juan Sanchis-Peris and Carmen Alfonso-Ciscar. MD, Faculty Medicine, Valencia, Spain, 1985, PhD, 1991. Staff orthopaedic surgeon Hosp. Arnau Vilanova, Valencia, Spain, 1992—; assoc. prof.orthopaedic surgery U. Valencia, 1994-96. Author, editor: Knee Surgery, 1995; contbr. articles to profl. jours. Recipient Ortoimplant award Spanish Knee Soc., 1997, 98. Mem. Royal Acad. Medicine Valencia; mem. Brit. Orthopaedic Rsch. Soc.; mem. European Soc. Knee Surgery and Arthroscopy, Spanish Arthroscopy Assn., Internat. Patellofemoral Study Group. Office: Hosp Arnau de Vilanova, San Clemente 26, 46015 Valencia Spain

SAND, JOHNNY JEN-NAN, broadcasting company executive; b. Taipei, Taiwan, Republic of China, Apr. 23, 1947; s. Harry D.H. and Mabel (Dung) S.; m. Jennifer Liang-Mei Lee, Jan. 9, 1977; children: Harry S.H., Howard S.H. BA, Fu-Jen Cath. U., Taiwan, 1970; MA, U.S. Internat. U., 1974, Harvard U., 1985. Dep. dir. div. info. and protocol Govt. Info. Office, Taipei, 1980-82; mgr. dept. internat. svc. Broadcasting Corp. China, Taipei, 1985-88, mgr. dept. news, 1988-91; dir. media rels. dept. cultural affairs Kuomintang Party, Taipei, 1991-93; v.p. Po-Hsin Multimedia Inc., Taipei, 1993-96; CEO Broadcasting Devel. Fund, Taipei, 1996—. With Armed Forces, 1970-71. Mem. Harvard Club Republic of China (supr. 1996—). Office: Broadcasting Devel Fund, 13F # 15-1 Sec 1 Hang Chows Road, Taipei Taiwan, Republic of China

SANDAL, EJVIND, publisher; b. Odder, Denmark, June 17, 1943; s. Frede and Karen (Pedersen) S.; m. Lise Kirsten, Sept. 21, 1968; 1 child, Jens Ejvind. Candidate Jur., Copenhagen U., 1970. Bar: Copenhagen 1970. Lawyer Law Firm B. Helmer Nielsen, Copenhagen, 1970-88; pub., CEO Politiken Newspapers, Ltd., Copenhagen, 1988-96; lawyer Eversheds, Copenhagen, 1996—; pub. The Copenhagen Post, 1999—; chmn. Axcel, 1995—, Danish Shareholders Assn., 1998—, F.E. Bording Ltd., 1999. Bd. dirs. World Assn. Newspapers, 1988-97. 1st lt. Denmark Royal Life Guards, 1962-65. Decorated Knights Cross of Dannebrog. Mem. Danish Publ. Assn. (v.p., bd. dirs. 1988-96). Office: Eversheds, Oestergade 27, 1100 Copenhagen K 1785, Denmark

SANDBACKA, BJORN OLOF, medical facility administrator; b. Aland Islands, Finland, July 26, 1942; s. Nils-Olof and Thordis (Spiring) S.; m. Anneli Maria Tarvainen, May 28, 1966; children: Maria, Anders, Anna-Karin. MA, Abo U., 1968. Head educator Abo Acad. U., Turku, Finland, 1967-70; asst. clin. chemist U. Hosp. Turku, 1970-71; lab. dir. Regional Hosp. Jakobstad, Finland, 1971-86, Regional Hosp. Ekenas, Finland, 1986—. Mem. Finnish Assn. Chemists. Avocations: gardening, orchids, nature, boating, fishing. Home: Marknadsgränd 12, SF-10600 Ekenas Finland Office: Regional Hosp Ekenas, SF-10600 Ekenas Finland

SANDBLOM, PHILIP JOHN, retired medical educator, writer; b. Chgo., Oct. 29, 1903; arrived in Sweden, 1909; s. John Nicolaus and Ellen Therese (Chinlund) S.; m. Grace Susan Schaefer, Mar. 28, 1932; children: John, Susanna, Catherine, Carl-Louis, Gustav. MD, Karolinska Inst., Stockholm, 1930, PhD, 1944; MSc, Northwestern U., Chgo., 1934; MD (hon.), U. Glasgow, Scotland, 1965, U. Paris, 1967, U. Cordoba, Argentina, 1967; PhD (hon.), U. Lund, Sweden, 1968; MD (hon.), U. Lausanne, Switzerland, 1974; degree (hon.), Ehrenbürger Christian Albrecht Univ., Kiel, Germany. Resident Lasarettet, Örebro, Sweden, 1932-37, Serafimer Lasarettet, Stockholm, 1937-40; assoc. prof. Karolinska Inst., Stockholm, 1940-45; chmn. dept. pediat. surgery Crown Princess Louse's Children's Hosp., Stockholm, 1945-50; prof., chmn. dept. surgery U. Lund, Sweden, 1950-70; guest prof. surgery U. Calif., San Diego, 1971-72, U. Lausanne, Switzerland, 1973-80, U. Taipei, Taiwan, 1981-82; rector, pres. U. Lund, 1958-68. Author: Function of the Human Gall Bladder, 1932, Tensile Strength of Healing Wounds, 1949, The Difference in Men, 1969, Hemobilia, 1972, Creativity and Disease, 1982, 12th edit., 1999. Pres. Svensk Kirurgisk Förening, Stockholm, 1957-58, 69-70, Internat. Soc. Surgery, 1965-67; bd. dirs. Swedish Art Soc., 1943-70. Recipient Bronze medal (sailing) Olympic Games, 1928. Fellow ACS (hon.), Royal Coll. Surgeons (Eng.) (hon.), Royal Coll Surgeons (Edinburgh) (hon.), Royal Coll. Surgeons (Ireland) (hon.); mem. Am. Surg. Assn. (hon.), So. Surg. Assn. (hon.), Internat. Surg. Assn. (hon.), Surg. Assn. Sweden (hon.), Surg. Assn. Switzerland (hon.), Surg. Assn. Denmark (hon.), Surg. Assn. Gt. Britain (hon.), Surg. Assn. France (hon.), Surg. Assn. Italy (hon.), Surg. Assn.Germany (corr.), Surg. Assn. Norway (corr.), Surg. Assn. Finland (corr.). Avocations: sailing, skiing, art collecting. Home: 2 Ch des Bluets, 1009 Pully Switzerland

SANDEFER, G(EORGE) LARRY, lawyer; b. Washington, Mar. 2, 1950; s. George Hall and Mary Gray (Babers) S. BS, Auburn U., 1972; JD, U. Fla., 1978. Bar: Fla. 1978, U.S. Dist. Ct. (mid. dist.) Fla. 1978, U.S. Ct. Appeals (5th and 11th cirs.) 1981, U.S. Supreme Ct. 1982; cert. in criminal trial law Fla. Bar. Asst. state atty., criminal divsn., lead trial atty. State of Fla., Clearwater, 1977-86; sole practice Clearwater, 1986-88; assoc. Kimpton, Burke and White, P.A., Clearwater, 1988-90; pvt. practice, Clearwater, 1991—. Mem. Indian Rocks Civic Assn., 1994-2000, Leadership Pinellas; city commr. Indian Rocks Beach, 1994-00. 1st lt. USAF, 1973-75. Mem. ATLA, Pinellas County Trial Lawyers Assn., Fla. Assn. Criminal Def. Attys., Colo. Bar Assn., Fla. Bar Assn., Clearwater Bar Assn., St. Petersburg Bar Assn., Kiwanis. Avocations: tennis, skiing, boating. Address: 111 N Belcher Rd Ste 202 Clearwater FL 33765-3259

SANDEFUR, JAMES TANDY, mathematics educator; b. Madison, Ind., Apr. 25, 1947; s. James Tandy and Evelyn (Gayle) S.; m. Mary Elizabeth Epes, Sept. 6, 1969 (div. 1982); m. Helen Moriarty, Apr. 14, 1984; 1 child, Scott David. BA, Vanderbilt U., 1969; MA, U. Denver, 1971; PhD, Tulane U., 1974. Prof. math. Georgetown U., Washington, 1974—; vis. assoc. prof. Ctr. for Applied Math., Cornell U., Ithaca, N.Y., 1981-82; vis. prof. U. Iowa, Iowa City, 1988-89; math. cons. It's Academic TV show, Altman Prodns., Washington, 1985—; prin. investigator, dir. math. modelling workshop NSF, Washington, 1988-91; visitor Freudenthal Inst., Utrecht, The Netherlands, 1996; writing team Principles and Stds. for Sch. Math., 2000; mem. adv. bd. Exploratorium's Math Explorer Project; cons. Cerebellum Corp. Author: Discrete Dynamical Systems: Theory and Applications, 1990, Discrete Dynamical Modeling, 1993; adv. bd. to Annenberg/CPB math. and sci. project's Guide to Math and Science Reform; contbr. articles to math. jours. Program dir. in Instrl. Materials Devel. for Div. of Materials, Devel., Rsch. and Informal Sci. Edn.; directorate for Edn. and Human Resources NSF. NSF grantee, prin. investigator Tchr. Leadership Inst., 1993—. Mem. Math. Assn. Am. (former chmn. minicourse com.), Nat. Faculty, Nat. Coun. Tchrs. Math. (adv. panel Yearbook Discrete Math., mem. writing team for Stds. 2000), Am. Contract Bridge League (life master, chpt. bd. dirs. 1983-85). Democrat. Avocations: bridge, tennis, skiing. Office: Georgetown U Dept Math Washington DC 20057-0001

SANDELANDS, ERIC ALAN, publisher, educator, editor; b. Workington, Cumbria, Eng., June 27, 1963; s. Alan and Elizabeth Russel (Wilson) S.; m. Claire Huntley, Aug. 20, 1988; children: Luke, Chloe. DPhil, Internat. Mgmt. Ctrs.; MBA, U. Teesside, Eng., 1993; postgrad., Internat. Mgmt. Ctr., Buckingham, Eng., 1993-98. Ops. mgr. TSC, Middlesbrough, Eng., 1985-92; editor-in-chief MCB Univ. Press, Bradford, Eng., 1992-94, dir. pub., 1994-95; COO Anbar Electronic Intelligence, Bradford, 1995, CEO, 1995-96, sr. advisor, 1996-99; prin. Eric Sandelands Assocs., Middlesbrough, 1996-98; cons. Info. for Success, Bedford, Eng., 1996-98; proprietor Virtual Univ. Jour., 1996-98; dean Canadian Sch. Mgmt., 1999—, Americas Internat. Mgmt. Ctrs., 1999—. Editor Mgmt. Express, 1996-98; editor-in-chief Strategic Direction, 1992-95, Anbar Mgmt. Intelligence (info. database), 1992-95. David Sutton fellow Internat. Mgmt. Ctr., 1996, Internat. Bus. fellow U. Surrey/IMC, 1994. Mem. Inst. of Mgmt. Avocations: hiking, cinema, literature, playing squash. Home: RR # 1 553291 Grey Rd 23, Ontario, ON Canada N0C 1K0 Office: Canadian Sch Mgmt, Ste 1120 335 Bay St, Toronto, ON Canada M5H 2R3

SANDEN, CHRISTER EUGEN, company executive; b. Helsinki, Finland, Nov. 29, 1951; s. Eugen Bernhard and Marianne Gunnel (Backstrom) S.; m. Liisa Riitta Hytonen Sanden, July 30, 1977; children: Christa-Maria, Elisabeth, Nora Michaela Christine, Christian Michael Bernhard. M of Polit. Sci., Abo Akademi, Turku, Finland, 1979. Labour mkt. sec. Abo Academi, Turku, Finland, 1979-80; project mgr. MTV Oy, Helsinki, Finland, 1980-81; export mgr. Kolmeks Oy, Helsinki, Finland, 1981-84; mng. dir. Tekno-Montan Oy, Helsinki, Finland, 1984-86, Nestekniikka Oy, Vantaa, Finland, 1986—. Office: Nestekniikka Oy, Monsaksenkuja 1, 01620 Vantaa Finland

SANDER, WOLFRAM WILLY, chemist, educator; b. Heidelberg, Germany, Oct. 22, 1954; m. Marianne Elisabeth Adam, June 9, 1978; children: Julia, Tim. Chemist, U. Heidelberg, 1978, dr. rer. nat., 1982. Postdoctoral fellow UCLA, 1982-84; hochschulasst. U. Heidelberg, Germany, 1984-89; prof. chemistry Tech. U. Braunschweig, Germany, 1990-93, U. Bochum, Germany, 1993—; mem. adv. bd. Wiley-VCh. Adv. editor European Jour. Organic Chemistry; contbr. articles to profl. jours. Grantee Deutsche Fonschungssemeinschaft, 1989, Hoechst AG, 1990. Mem. Gesellschaft Deutscher Chemiker, Am. Chem. Soc. Office: Ruhr Univ Bochum, D-44780 Bochum Germany

SANDERGAARD, THEODORE JORGENSEN, information technology director; b. Chgo., Sept. 27, 1946; s. Theodore Jorgensen Sandergaard and Hilda (Roberts) Stec; m. Laraine Ann Spina, May 29, 1965 (div. 1970); 1 child, Michael James; m. Ebba Mary Janet Groth, July 12, 1980. Diploma, USAF, 1964. Data processing mgr. Leo Pharm. Products., Ballerup, Denmark, 1969-73, sr. cons., 1973-80; data processing mgr. Leo Labs. Ltd., Princes Risborough, Eng., 1980-88; dir. info. tech. Dewe Rogerson Ltd., London, 1988-94; mng. dir. Chrysoma Assocs. Ltd., Aylesbury, 1994—; cons. in field. Author: FLX Programming Language, 1979. Mem. Jr. C. of C., Ballerup, 1971. Mem. IEEE, IEEE Computer Soc., Assn. Computing Machinery, Brit. Computer Soc., Inst. Data Processing Mgmt., Inst. Dirs., N.Y. Acad. Scis. Republican. Lutheran. Avocations: history, geopolitics, reading, philately, travel. England Office: 12 Gainsborough Pl, Aylesbury Bucks HP19 8SF, England

SANDERMANN, JES, vascular surgeon; b. Copenhagen, May 2, 1953; s. Thorkil and Aase (Kjeldsen) S.; m. Lis Saxtoft Hansen, Apr. 2, 1977; children: Sigrid, Astrid. MD, Med. U., Denmark, 1980. Cert. specialist in surgery, Sweden, 1989, Denmark, 1989, specialist in vascular surgery, Denmark, 1994. Jr./sr. house officer Nat. Health Sys., Denmark, 1980-85, trainee in surg. block, 1985-87, sr. registrar surgery, 1989-91, sr. registrar in vascular surgery, 1991-96, cons. in vascular surgery, 1996—; registrar in surgery Nat. Health Sys., Sweden, 1988-89; chmn. Intenat. Med. Cooperation Com., Denmark, 1974-79; sec., chmn. Danish Assn. for Surgeons in Tng., Denmark, 1990-94; initiator to and leader of European Assn. for Vascular Surgery in Tng., 1994-96; permanent working group rep. European Bd. for Vascular Surgeons, 1996-97, offcl. Danish mem., 1997—; assessor EBSQ-VASC, 1998—. Author: Moving Analysis, 1981, 2d edit., 1998; co-author: Anatomy for Gymnastics, 1980; co-editor: Career Planning in Surgery, 1995; contbr. over 40 articles to profl. jours. Officially appointed examiner Odense (Denmark) U., 1982—. Mem. Danish Soc. for Microsurgery (sec. 1995—), Scandinavian Assn. for Vascular Surgery (editor newsletter 1996—). Avocations: golf, malt whiskeys. Home: Krattet 21, 7442 Engesvang Denmark Office: Vascular Surgery Unit, Viborg Hosp, 8800 Viborg Denmark

SANDERS, AUGUSTA SWANN, retired nurse; b. Alexandria, La., July 22, 1932; d. James and Elizabeth (Thompson) Swann; m. James Robert Sanders, Jan. 12, 1962 (div. 1969). Student, Morgan State U., 1956. RN. Pub. health nurse USPHS, Washington, 1963-64; mental health counselor Los Angeles County Sheriff's Dept., 1972-79; program coordinator Los Angeles County Dept. Mental Health, 1979-88; program dir. L.A. County Dept. Health Svcs., 1989-92; ret., 1992; apptd. by Calif. Gov. Jerry Brown to 11th Dist. Bd. Med. Quality Assurance, 1979-85; health cons., legal, 1994—; motivational spkr. Mem. Assemblyman Mike Roo's Commn. on Women's Issues, 1981-86, Senator Diane Watson's Commn. on Health Issues, 1979-85; chmn. Commn. Sex Equity L.A. Unified Sch. Dist., 1984-90; bd. dirs., sec. High Desert chpt. ARC, 1998. Named Woman of Yr., Crenshaw-Latijera Local Orgn., 1988, Wilshire Local Orgn., 1990, Victor Valley Local Orgn., 1994. Mem. NAFE, Los Angeles County Employees Assn. (v.p. 1971-72), So. Calif. Black Nurses Assn. (founding mem.), Internat. Fedn. Bus. and Profl. Women (pres. L.A. Sunset dist. 1988-89, dist. officer 1982-89, Calif. v.p. membership and mktg. 1995-96), Internat. Assn. Chem. Dependency Nurses (treas. 1990-92), Victor Valley Bus. and Profl. Women (pres. 1997-98), High Desert LWV (founder), High Desert Intercoun. Women's Orgns., Nat. Coun. of Negro Women, Am. C. of C. (adminstrn.-ednl. chmn.), Victor Valley African Am. C. of C. (edn. com.), Apple Valley C. of C., High Desert Investment Club (chmn. 1998-99), Chi Eta Phi. Democrat. Methodist. Avocations: reading, traveling, crocheting, movies, concerts, plays.

SANDERS, BARRY CYRIL, science educator; b. Drumheller, Alta., Can., July 11, 1961; arrived in Australia, 1990; s. Joseph Morris and Miriam (Freedman) S.; m. Shanno Lata Sen; children: Yuval Rishu, Sapna Lailah. BSc, U. Calgary, Can., 1985; diploma, Imperial Coll., London, 1986, 88; PhD, U. London, 1987. Rsch. assoc. U. Queensland, Brisbane, Australia, 1988-89; postdoctoral fellow U. Waikato, Hamilton, New Zealand, 1989-90; rsch. assoc. U. Queensland, Brisbane, 1990-91; lectr. Macquarie U., Sydney, Australia, 1991-92, sr. lectr., 1993-96, assoc. prof., 1997—, head dept. physics, 1997—; mem. program com. Internat. Quantum Electronics Conf., 1996; organizer local confs., 1992-96. Contbr. rsch. papers to profl. publs. Pres. Montessori Assn. Australia, 1996-97. Mem. Australian Optical Soc. (treas.), Australian Inst. Physics (postgrad. awards day organizer 1996), Optical Soc. Am. E-mail: Barry.Sanders@mq.edu.au. Office: Macquarie U, Physics Dept, Sydney NSW 2109, Australia

SANDERS, DAVID, political scientist, educator, administrator; b. Derby, Eng., Dec. 19, 1950; m. Gill Twyman; children: Joe, Ben, Rob, Lucy. BSc, Loughborough (Eng.) U., 1972; MA, Essex (Eng.) U., 1974, PhD, 1978. Lectr. polit. sci. U. Essex, 1974-89, sr. lectr., 1989-93, prof., 1994—, pro vice chancellor, 1997—. Author: Lawmaking and Cooperation, 1986, Losing an Empire, Finding a Role, 1990; editor Brit. Jour. Polit. Sci., 1991—; contbr. articles to profl. jours. Econ. and Social Rsch. Coun. rsch. grantee, 1990, 97, 99. Avocations: music, squash, tennis. Office: Univ Essex, Wivenhoe Park, Colchester CO4 3SQ, England

SANDERS, DAVID H., civil engineering educator; b. Urbana, Ill., Dec. 6, 1961. BS with honor and distinction, Iowa State U., 1984; MS, U. Tex., Austin, 1986, PhD, 1990. Asst. structural engr. Chgo. Bridge & Iron, Oak Brook, Ill., 1982; rsch. asst. Ferguson Structural Engring. Lab., Austin, Tex., 1984-89; asst. prof. dept. civil engring. U. Nev., Reno, 1990-96, assoc. prof., 1996—; vis. prof. Nat. Ctr. for Earthquake Engring. Rsch., Buffalo, 1996. Contbr. articles to profl. jours.; author reports and conf. procs.; presenter in field. Soccer coach High Sierra Soccer, Reno, 1997-99; T-ball coach Reno Continental, 1998, 99; vol. Jr. Ski Program, Reno, 1997—; scoutmaster Boy Scouts Am., Austin, 1986-89. Fellow Am. Concrete Inst. (chair earthquake resistant concrete bridge com. 1998—); mem. ASCE (treas. 1993-94, v.p. 1995-96, pres. 1996-97), Transp. Rsch. Bd., Earthquake Engring. Rsch. Inst. Avocations: skiing, golf, camping, hiking. E-mail: sanders@unr.edu. Office: U Nev Reno Dept Civil Engring 258 Reno NV 89557-0001

SANDERS, ERIC, physician; b. Bishop Aukland, Durham, Eng., Oct. 22, 1946; s. Albert and Caroline (Johnson) S.; m. Dianne Marilyn Thomas, July 10, 1971; children: Gareth Wyn, Gethyn Huw, Angharad Jane. BSc with honors, U. Wales, 1968, MB, 1971, BCh, 1971. House officer dept. surgery and medicine U. Hosp. Wales, Cardiff, 1971-74; rsch. registrar, lectr. renal disease Kruf Inst. Renal Disease, Royal Infirmary, Cardiff, 1974-80; cons. physician East Dyfed Health Authority, Carmarthen, 1980-93; dir. West Wales Diaylsis Ctr., Carmarthen, 1985-93; cons. physician North Durham NHS Trust, 1993—; trustee, treas. Kidney Rsch. Unit for Wales Found., Cardiff, 1986—; mem. coun. Wales Diabetes Rsch. Trust, 1987—. Author: Nephrology Illustrated, 1981, Clinical Atlas of the Kidney, 1991. Fellow Inst. Renal Disease, Royal Coll. Physicians (tutor 1987—); mem. Lions Club (regional officer 1982—). Anglican. Avocations: music, youth activities and assns. Home: 101 Thorntons Close, Pelton Chester W Street Co, Durham DH2 1QJ, England

SANDERS, GERALD HOLLIE, communications educator; b. Mt. Vernon, Tex., Dec. 10, 1924; s. Elmer Hugh and Velma Mae (Hollowell) S.; m. Mary Dean Crew, July 18, 1947; children: Michael Dwaine, Rose Ann, Susan Kathleen, Randall Wayne. BA, Southeastern Okla. U., 1947; MA, Tex. Tech U., 1969; PhD, U. Minn., 1974. Program dir. Sta. WEWO, Laurenburg, N.C., 1947-49; sports dir. Sta. KFYO, Lubbock, Tex., 1949-50; gen. mgr. Sta. KLVT, Levelland, Tex., 1950-51, 53-54; sports dir. Sta. KCUL, Ft. Worth, 1954-55; asst. mgr. Sta. KDAV, Lubbock, 1955-57; mgr. Sta. KCBD, Lubbock, 1957-58; owner Sta. KSEL, Lubbock, 1958-67, Sta.

KBUY, Amarillo, Tex., Sta. KERB, Kermit, Tex., Sta. KBEK, Elk City, Okla., Sta. KZZN, Littlefield, Tex.; lectr. communications The Coll. of Wooster, Ohio, 1967-68, asst. prof., 1968-75, assoc. prof., 1975-81, chmn. dept. communication, 1974-81; chmn. dept. communication Miami U., Oxford, Ohio, 1981-92, prof. emeritus comm., 1992—; disting. lectr. Jinan U., Zhong Shan U., Fudan U., Nanjing U., Beijing U., China, 1989; cons. in field, Oxford, 1982—; polit. and trial cons., 1996—. Author: Introduction to Comtemporary Academic Debate, 1983; also articles. Active Political Campaigns. Served to col. USMC, 1943-46, PTO, 1951-53, Korea. Recipient Disting. Svc. award Delta Sigma Rho-Tau Kappa Alpha, 1991, Am. Forensic Assn., 1991. Mem. Am. Forensic Assn. (pres. 1978-82), Speech Communication Assn., Speech Communication Assn. of Ohio (pres. 1976-77), Disting. Svc. award 1978), Am. Inst. Parliamentarians, Soc. Trial Cons. Presbyterian. Avocations: sports, political campaigns. Home: 200 Country Club Dr Oxford OH 45056-9050 Office: Advocacy Unltd PO Box 457 Oxford OH 45056-0457

SANDERS, JEREMY KEITH MORRIS, chemistry educator, author; b. London, May 3, 1948; m. Louise Elliott, Aug. 31, 1972; children: David, Deborah. BSc, Imperial Coll., London, 1969; PhD, Cambridge (Eng.) U., 1972. Chartered chemist, Eng. Rsch. fellow Stanford (Calif.) U., 1972-73; demonstrator Cambridge U., 1973-78, lectr. chemistry, 1978-92, reader, 1992-96, prof., 1996—, dep. head dept., 1998—, mem. coun., 1999—. Co-author: Modern NMR Spectroscopy, 1987, 2d edit., 1993, Workbook of NMR Spectroscopy, 1989, 2d edit., 1993; chmn. editl. bd. Chem. Soc. Rev., 2000—. Recipient Acad. award Pfizer PLC, 1984, 88. Fellow Royal Soc., Royal Inst. Chemistry (Meldola medal 1975), Royal Soc. Chemistry (Hickinbottom award 1981, Loschmidt award 1994, Pedler medal 1996). Office: Cambridge U Chem Lab, Lensfield Rd, Cambridge CB2 1EW, England

SANDERS, MARION YVONNE, geriatrics nurse; b. St. Petersburg, Fla., Dec. 4, 1936; d. Ira Laurey and Maude Mae Cherry Sanders; children: Dwayne Irwin Parker, Princess Charrie Ferrette, Henry, Pelote. BS, Fla. A&M U., 1959; MS, Nova U., Ft. Lauderdale, Fla., 1992. RN, Fla. Staff nurse Lantana (Fla.) TB Hosp., 1960-61, Mercy Hosp., St. Petersburg, 1961; gen. duty nurse VA, Tuskegee, Ala., 1961-62; staff nurse John Andrews Hosp., Tuskegee, 1962-63; gen. duty staff nurse Brewster Meth. Hosp., Jacksonville, Fla., 1963-65, Duval Med. Ctr., Jacksonville, 1965-66; pvt. duty nurse Dist. 2 Registry, Jacksonville, 1966-70; supr. Eartha White Nursing Home, Jacksonville, 1970; staff nurse Bapt. Hosp., Jacksonville, 1971-73, City-County Methadone Clinic, Jacksonville, 1976-78; pvt. duty nurse Home Nursing, Jacksonville, 1982-86; pvt. duty geriatric nursing and gerontology specialist Home Nursing, 1995—, Sr. Companion Svc. Corp., 1997-98; respite and relief sr. companion vol. Urban Jacksonville Cathedral Found., 1996-98. Active St. Stephen AME Ch., Jacksonville, tchr. Bible studies for youth; advocate for poor, homeless and prisoners; vol. shelter mgr. ARC, Miami, Fla., 1992-94; vol. cmty. activist, Miami, 1994; vol. Jacksonville Cmty. Rels. Bd., 1996, Jacksonville Inc. Cathederal Found., 1997—; sr. companion Svc. Corp., 1997-98, 99; mem. Ideas for Am.'s Future, 1997, 98, Brewster's and Cmty. Nurses Alumni, 1998-2000, NAACP, 1997-98; vol. Rep. Com. Fla., 1997, 98, Northside Rep. Club, 1997, 98, 99, Rep. Nat. Com., 1997-2000; vol. Rep. Senatorial Com., 1999; vol. cmty. svcs., elem. grades tutor, polit. campaigns, tchr. health edn. Recipient Cert. of Recognition, Rep. Party, Fla. and Wash., 1990, Rep. Congl. Orgn., 1988, 90, 91. Mem. ANA (mem. polit. action coms.), Fla. Nurses Assn., Women's Missionary Soc. (life). Republican. Methodist. Avocations: reading the Holy Bible, teaching Sunday school, volunteer work. Home: 4832 N Main St Apt 14 Jacksonville FL 32206-1458

SANDERS, RONALD MICHAEL, diplomat; b. Georgetown, Guyana, Jan. 26, 1948; m. Carole Lynne Lewis, Mar. 1, 1969 (div. Apr. 1974); m. Susan Idrani Ramphal, Apr. 19, 1975. BA, Boston U., 1972; MA, Sussex (Eng.) U., 1989. Program mgr. Guyana Broadcasting Svc., 1971-73, mng. dir., 1973-76; pub. affairs advisor to pres. Caribbean Devel. Bank, Barbados, 1977-78; advisor Minister Econ. Devel., Antigua, 1978-82; dep. permanent rep. for Antigua and Barbuda to UN, 1982-84; ambassador to Fed. Republic Germany Govt. of Antigua and Barbuda, 1985-87, high commr. to U.K., 1984-87; vis. fellow Queen Elizabeth House, Oxford (Eng.) U., 1987-89; cons. Inter Maritime Svcs. of Geneva, 1987-90, Atlantic Tele-Network Inc., USA, 1989-94; internat. affairs advisor Prime Minister of Antigua and Barbuda, 1994—; high commr. to U.K. London, 1995—; ambassador France and Germany, 1996—; part-time lectr. U. Guyana, 1974-76; mem. exec. bd. UNESCO, 1985-87, amb. and permanent del., 1982-83, chmn. Caribbean group of ambs., 1984-87; mem. inter-govtl. coun. Internat. Programme for Devel. of Commn., 1983-87; freelance broadcaster, writer, lectr., 1987-89; em. bd. dirs. Swiss Am. Bank Group, Antigua, Guayana Telephone and Telegraph Co., Guayana, Innovative Comms. Corp., St. Croix, U.S. V.I.; numerous govtl. delegations and confs. Author: Inseparable Humanity: An Anthology of Reflections of Shridath Ramphal, Secretary-General of the Commonwealth, 1988, Broadcasting in Guyana, 1978, Antigua and Barbuda: Transition, Trial, Triumph, 1984, Antigua and Barbuda: A Little Bit of Paradise, 1994; contbr. articles to profl. publs. Pres. Caribbean Broadcasting Union, 1974-75; bd. dirs. Caribbean News Agy., 1975-77. Decorated companion Order St. Michael and St. George. Office: Antigua and Barbarda, High Commn, 15 Thayer St, London WIM5DL, England

SANDERS, ROSS HOWARD, sports science educator; b. Sydney, NSW, Australia, Jan. 25, 1954; s. Geoffrey Howard and Alice Marion (Appleford) S.; m. Lesley Velletta Reid, Feb. 14, 1976; children: Duncan, Kimberley. Diploma in health and phys. edn., Wollongong Inst. Edn., 1976; BEd, Newcastle Coll. Advanced Edn., 1984; PhD, U. Queensland, Brisbane, Australia, 1991. Phys. edn. and health tchr. Goulburn, Australia, 1977-84; lectr. U. Otago, Dunedin, New Zealand, 1989-96; sr. lectr. Edith Cowan U., Perth, Australia, 1996-99; chair sport sci. U. Edinburgh (Scotland), 2000—. Editor: Sci. Procs. of XVII Internat. Symposium on Biomechanics in Sports, 1999, Applied Procs. of the XVII Internat. Symposium on Biomechanics in Sports, 1999; contbr. articles to profl. jours. Sch. sportsmaster Mulwaree H.S., Goulburn, 1978-82; sec. Royal Life Saving Soc., So. Tablelands Br., 1983-84. Recipient High Commendation Best Conf. Paper award in basic sci. Australian Conf. in Sports Medicine, 1993. Mem. Internat. Soc. Biomechanics in Sport (bd. dirs. 1992—, pres. 1999—). Avocations: surf life saving. Home: 14 Lakehill Gardens, Edgewater WA 6027, Australia Office: U Edinburgh, Dept Sport Phys Edn & Leisure, Edinburgh Scotland

SANDERS, TOON J.M., economist; b. Enschede, The Netherlands, Feb. 3, 1948; s. Antonius L. and Agatha (Bouma) S.; m. Hennie W.M.C. Schouwenaars, Jan. 29, 1972; children: Jasper, Remko, Meike. Degree in econs., Tilburg U., 1971. Asst. prof. Tech. U. Eindhoven, The Netherlands, 1971-72, Tilburg (The Netherlands) U., 1972-79; cons. Municipality of Eindhoven, 1979-82; mng. dir. Regional Devel. Authority of Eindhoven, 1982-89, De Lage Landen, Eindhoven, 1989—. Mem. Rotary. Home: Jac v Ruisdaelpad 5, 5062 KM Oisterwyk The Netherlands Office: De Lage Landen, Vestdyk 51, 5611 CA Eindhoven The Netherlands

SANDERS, VERONA HARBERT, special events coordinator; b. Edwards AFB, Calif., Dec. 22, 1969; d. Billie and Elizabeth (Barber) Harbert; m. Derhun Daniel Sanders, Feb. 14, 1996. Degree in hospitality mgmt., Ea. Mich. U., 1998, degree in bus. mgmt., 1998. Personnel sys. mgmt. specialist USAF, Sawyer AFB, Mich., Ramstein AB, Germany, 1989-94; owner Sanders Enterprises, Farmington Hills, Mich., 1996—. Children's ministry tchr. Dunamis Outreach Ministries, Southfield, Mich., 1996—.

SANDERS, WILLIAM JOHN, research scientist; b. Detroit, July 10, 1940; s. John William and Charlotte Barbara (Linsday) Steele; m. Gary Roberts, Sept. 12, 1961; children: Scott David, Susan Deborah. BS, U. Mich., 1962; MSEE, U. Calif., Berkeley, 1964. Sr. rsch. scientist Stanford (Calif.) U., 1967-97; pres. Sanders Data Systems, 1991—; pres. Computers in Cardiology, 1990-93. Inventor cardiac probe; contbr. articles to profl. jours. Mem. IEEE Computer Soc., Assn. Computing Machinery. Avocations: bicycling, wind surfing. Office: Sanders Data Sys 3980 Bibbits Dr Palo Alto CA 94303-4531

SANDERSON, ARTHUR NORMAN, international cultural relations specialist; b. Glasgow, Scotland, Sept. 3, 1943; s. William Roy and Annie Muriel (Easton) S.; m. Issy Halliday, July 30, 1966; children: Angus William, Emma. BA, Oxford (Eng.) U., 1966, MA, 1968; diploma in Edn., U. Edinburgh, Scotland, 1969; diploma in Mgmt., Henley Mgmt. Coll., Eng., 1993. Registered tchr., Gen. Teaching Coun. Scotland. Tutor in math. and English, Foso Tng. Coll., Ghana, 1966-68; econ. and careers master Daniel Stewart's Coll., Edinburgh, 1969-73; asst. dir. Brit. Coun., Kano, Nigeria, 1974-76; regional dir. Brit. Coun., Recife, Brazil, 1976-80; regional officer Far East and Pacific dept. Brit. Coun., London, 1980-83; asst., then acting rep. Brit. Coun., Accra, Ghana, 1983-86; regional dir. Brit. Coun., Glasgow, 1986-89; dir. Brit. Coun., Enugu, Nigeria, 1989-91, Madras, India, 1991-95, Baltic States, 1995-97; head of pub. rels. Crown Agents Customs Reform Project, Maputo, Mozambique, 1997—; chmn. Bd. Am. Sch. Recife, Brazil, 1978-80. Housing spokesman Scottish Liberal Party, Scotland, 1972-73; chmn. Edinburgh New Town Shelter Group, Edinburgh, Scotland, 1970-72; mem. Pollokshields Cmty. Coun., Glasgow, Scotland, 1987-89. Mem. Order Brit. Empire. Avocations: Scottish country dancing, choral singing, hillwalking, recreational running, languages.

SANDERSON, POLLY ELAINE, pharmaceutical company executive; b. Wilmington, N.C., Dec. 30, 1957; d. Charles Richard and Sadie Lunette (Marlowe) S.; m. Robert Fred Butz, Aug. 6, 1988; children: Sydney M. Butz, Cameron G. Butz. BA, U. N.C., Wilmington, 1981; MS, U. Wyo., 1984, PhD, 1990. Scientist Rsch. Triangle Inst., Research Triangle Park, N.C., 1984-86; clin. rsch. mgr. Glaxo, Inc., Research Triangle Park, 1987-92; assoc. dir. clin. devel. Cytel Corp., La Jolla, Calif., 1993-94; dir. product devel. Terrapin Techs., South San Francisco, Calif., 1994-97; acting v.p. devel. BioStratum, Inc., Durham, N.C., 1998—; CEO KetoPharma, Inc., Cleve., 1998-99. Contbr. articles to profl. jours. Home and Office: 6120 Penfield Ln Solon OH 44139-5936

SANDFORD, CEDRIC THOMAS, political economist and educator; b. Basingstoke, Hampshire, U.K., Nov. 21, 1924; s. Thomas and Louisa Kate (Hodge) S.; m. Evelyn Belch, Dec. 1, 1945 (dec. Mar. 1982); children: John Philip, Gillian Margaret; m. Christina Katarin Privett, July 21, 1984; 1 child, Anna Elizabeth. BA in Econs. with honors, U. Manchester, U.K., 1948, MA in Econs., 1949; BA in History with honors, U. London, 1955. Lectr. Mcpl. Coll., Burnley, U.K., 1948-58; head dept. Coll. Sci. and Tech., Bristol, U.K., 1959-65; prof. polit. economy U. Bath, U.K., 1965-87, prof. emeritus, 1987—; ind. cons., lectr., rschr. in polit. economy, 1987—; ptnr. Fiscal Publs., Bath, 1989—. Author: Taxing Personal Wealth, 1971, Hidden Costs of Taxation, 1973, Successful Tax Reform - Lessons From an Analysis of Tax Reform in Six Countries, 1993, Why Tax Systems Differ: A Comparative Study of the Political Economy of Taxation, 2000; co-author: Administrative and Compliance Costs of Taxation, 1989; contbr. articles to profl. jours. Mem. Southwestern Electricity Consultative Coun., Exeter, U.K., 1981-90; mem. Bath Dist. Health Authority, 1984-90; chmn. Bath Cancer Unit Appeal, 1983-90; mem. Wat Wessex Customer Svc. Com., 1995—. Flight sgt. RAF, 1943-46. U. Manchester grad. rsch. scholar, 1948. Mem. Econs. Assn. (pres. 1984-86). Methodist. Avocations: trout fishing, reading, gardening, walking, violin playing. Home and Office: Old Coach House, Fersfield Perrymead, Bath BA2 5AR, England

SANDFORD, HERBERT ADOLPHUS, cartographer; b. July 7, 1927; s. Sidney Bartholomew and Iris Mahala (Capon) S.; m. Ellen Frances Patricia Harvey, Apr. 23, 1949 (div. Nov. 1971); children: Andrew Paul, Freya Anne; m. Aida Caampued, May 28, 1997. BA, U. Sheffield, Eng., 1948; MA, U. London, 1966, MPhil, 1967, PhD, 1970. Educator, head dept. State Sch. System, London, 1949-68; lectr., head dept. Thomas Huxley Tchrs.' Coll., London, 1968-69; lectr., head dept. St. Mark & St. John Coll. of Higher Edn., Plymouth, Eng., 1969-78, rsch. fellow for cartopedagogy, 1978—; cons. to various publishers, 1964—; atlas cons. UNESCO, 1983—; lectr. in field. Editor: Atlas of the Environment, also numerous sch. and student atlases; contbr. articles to profl. publs., chpts. to books. Fellow Royal Geog. Soc., Linneau Soc. London, Royal Commonwealth Soc.; mem. London Natural History Soc. (mapping sec. 1966—), Internat. Geog. Union, Internat. Cartographic Assn., Geog. Assn., Brit. Cartographic Soc., others. Avocations: natural history, earth and life sciences. Home: 46 Holtwood Rd, Plymouth PL6 7HU, England Office: Ctr Cartopedagogic Studies, Atlas House, Holtwood Rd, Plymouth PL6 7HU, England

SANDHU, DAVINDER PAL SINGH, urological surgeon, consultant; b. Agra, India, July 26, 1955; arrived in Eng., 1966; s. Bhagwan Singh and Hardayal Kaur (Rai) S.; m. Punam Kaur Grewal, Dec. 26, 1982; children: Jai Nihal, Hira Omedh. MBBS, Royal Free Hosp., London, 1980; MD, Leicester (Eng.) U., 1994. House officer Royal Free Hosp., London, 1981; sr. house officer Leicester/Nottingham Hosps., 1981-85; surg. registrar Leicester Hosps., 1985-88; urology registrar U. Hosp. South Manchester, Eng., 1988-89; sr. urol. registrar Derby and Nottingham Hosps., Eng., 1990-92; urol. surgeon, cons. Leicester Gen. Hosp., 1992—, assoc. postgrad. dean for overseas doctors for South Trent. Contbr. over 35 articles to profl. jours. Fellow Royal Coll. Physicians and Surgeons (Edinburgh and Glasgow); mem. Brit. Assn. Urol. Surgeons (Surg. prize 1990; standing com. postgrad. edn. 1996—), Am. Urol. Assn. Avocations: cricket, music, literature. Home: Winkadale Uppingham Rd Bushby, Leicestershire LE7 9RP, England Office: Leicester Gen Hosp NHS, Gwendolen Rd, Leicester LE5 4PW, England

SANDHU, JAGIR SINGH, chemist; b. Marimegha, Punjab, India, July 14, 1942; s. Labh Singh and Ranjit Kaur; m. Pritam Kaur; 2 children. BSc, Chandigarh (India) U., 1962; MSc, Patiala (India) U., 1965, PhD, 1969. Asst. rsch. mgr. Ranbaxy Lab., New Delhi, 1973-76; from scientist level C to level F RRL-Jorhat, India, 1976-97, acting dir., 1997; dir. RRL-Jorhat, 1999—; postdoctoral fellow Ind. U., 1980-81; PhD guide and examiner various Indian Univs. Author 1 book; contbr. over 180 articles to profl. publs. Fellow Nat. Acad. of Sci., Nat. Sci. Acad.; mem. Learned Scientific Socs. of India. Office: Regional Rsch Lab Coun Sci, Indsl Rsch, Jorhat Assam 785-006, India

SANDHU, SARBJINDER SINGH, surgeon; b. Isleworth, Eng., Jan. 31, 1966; p. Hardyal Singh and Gurwinder Kaur Sandhu. BSc with honors, U. London, 1988, B Medicine B Surgery, 1991. Sr. house officer Royal Marsden Hosp., London, 1994-95, Princess Margaret Hosp., Swindon, Eng., 1995; clin. rsch. fellow Royal Free Hosp., London, 1995-97, SPR, 1999—; SPR Chase Farm Hosp., Enfield, Eng., 1997-98, Barnet Gen. Hosp., Hertfordshire, Eng., 1998-99; editor Urology Options, Jerusalem, 1998. Author: Computerized Tomography and Magnetic Resonance Imaging, 1999; contbr. articles to profl. jours. Pres. Jr. Drs. Royal Free Hosp., 1997, Jr. Doctors Chase Farm Hosp., 1998. Wellcome fellow, 1988; recipient award ICI Pharm. Bursary U.K., 1990. Fellow Royal Coll. Surgeons Eng.; mem. Brit. Med. Assn., Brit. Assn. Urol. Surgeons (assoc.), Brit. Soc. Endourology. Avocations: amateur dramatics, sound engineering, hiking, trekking. Office: Royal Free Hosp Dept Urol, Pond St, London NW3 2QS, England

SANDIFER, KEVIN WAYNE, archival services executive; b. Shreveport, La., Sept. 5, 1956; s. Glenn Eugene and Beverly Sue (Mauritzen) S. BS in Libr. Sci., La. State U., Shreveport, 1985, BA in History, 1987; M in Spl. Libr. Instrn., U. Arlington, 1989. Pub. Red River Press, Blanchard, La., 1985-87; pres., CEO Archival Svcs., Inc., Blanchard, La., 1988—. Author: Layman's Look at Starting a Religious Archive, 1982 (Disting. Writing award 1983), Complete Document Restoration Manual, 1986, Introduction to Religious Archival Science, 1988. 2d edit., 1998, Public Relations are an Asset for the Museum and Archives, 1986, 2d edit., 1998, Photography Simplified for the Archivist, 1990, 2d edit., 1995, Christianityn and the Ark of the Covenant, 1998, others; editor: (textbook) Oral History, 1985. Archivist Grandstone Bluff Mus., 1985-90. Named Outstanding Historian Northwest La., Shreveport Jour., 1982, Expert Archivist Shreveport Times, 1983. Fellow Soc. Am. Archivists; mem. Am. Assn. State and Local History, La. Hist. Soc., North La. Hist. Assn. Southern Baptist. Avocations: reading, writing, running track. Home and Office: 3900 Roy Rd Apt 37 Shreveport LA 71107-9631

SANDLER, BEN ZION, mechanical engineer; b. Riga, Latvia, June 26, 1932; s. Isaac and Ester (Civjan) S.; m Bluma Itkin, Mar. 22, 1935; children: Ester Zafrani, Marina Rudnicky. Degree mech. engring., Polytech. Inst., Leningrad, 1956; PhD, Polytech. Inst., Riga, 1965. Machine design engr. Rigas Audums, USSR, 1956-58; machine design engr. Meteorological Instrumentation Factory, Riga, 1958-66, head of equipment design dept., 1962-65; sr. lectr. instrumentation dept. Polytech. Inst., Riga, 1966-67, assoc. prof., 1967-72; sr. lectr. mech. engring. dept. Ben Gurion U., Beer-Sheva, Israel, 1973; assoc prof. Ben Gurion U., Beer-Sheva, 1977-85, prof., 1985—; engr. Phila. Gear Corp., 1979-80; head Inst. for Engring. Applied Rsch. Authority, Ben-Gurion U., 1982-88. Author: Probalistic Approach to Mechanisms, 1984, Creative Machine Design, 1985, Robotics: Designing the Mechanisms for Automated Machinery, 1991, 2nd edit., 1999, Computer-Aided Creativity for New Product Design and Development, 1994; contbr. articles to profl. jours. Mem. Internat. Fedn. for Theory of Machines and Mechanisms (Israeli rep. 1978). Achievements include 20 patents in field. Office: Ben Gurion U of the Negev, PO Box 653, 84105 Beer-Sheva Israel

SANDLER, BORIS, editor, writer; b. Beltz, Moldova, Jan. 6, 1950; arrived in Israel, 1992; came to U.S., 1998; s. Semyon and Yevgenia Sandler; m. Raisa Sandler, July 8, 1954; children: Arkady, Zory. Cert., Stephen Niaga Spl. Music Sch., Kishinev, Moldova, 1970; MA, G. Muzichesku Inst. Art, Kishinev, Moldova, 1975; cert., M. Gorky Inst. Lit., Moscow, 1983. 1st violinist State Symphony Orch., Kishinev, 1974-81; tchr. music Spl. Music Sch., Kishinev, 1983-89; editor "On the Jewish Street" Moldavian Nat. TV, Kishinev, 1989-92; editor Our Voice, Kishinev, 1990-92; rschr. dept. Yiddish Hebrew U., Jerusalem, 1993-98; editor-in-chief Forverts, N.Y.C., 1998—. Author: (novels) Staircase to Miracle, 1986, Regarding 5390, 1992, The Old Well, 1994, Gates, 1997, (documentary film scripts) Don't Give Up Yiddish, 1991, Where is My Home?, 1992; writer, editor Sovetish Heymland; editor Kind un Keyt. Pres. Jewish Cultural Orgn., Moldava, 1989-92. Served with Soviet mil., 1975-76. Recipient Dr. Shmuel and Rivka Hurwitz award, 1993, Jashua Rabinovich award Tel Aviv Municipality, 1993, Gershon Segal award I.L. Perez Pub. Ho., 1994, best lit. work of yr. award Di Pen, 1997. Mem. Workmen's Cir., Writer's Union of Israel, Union of Yiddish Writers and Journalists (v.p. 1996-98, Leib Melech award 1996). Home and Office: Yiddish Forverts 45 E 33d St New York NY 10016

SANDLER, HERBERT M., retired savings and loan association executive; b. N.Y.C., Nov. 16, 1931; s. William B. and Hilda (Schattan) S.; m. Marion Osher, Mar. 26, 1961. BSS, CCNY, 1951; JD, Columbia U., 1954. Bar: N.Y. 1956. Asst. counsel Waterfront Comm. N.Y. Harbor, 1956-59; ptnr. firm Sandler & Sandler, N.Y.C., 1960-62; pres., dir., mem. exec. com. Golden West Savs. & Loan Assn. and Golden West Fin. Corp., Oakland, Calif., 1963-75; co-chmn. bd., co-CEO, dir., mem. exec. com. World Savs. & Loan Assn. and Golden West Fin. Corp., Oakland, 1975—; charter mem. Thrift Instns. Adv. Coun., to Fed. Res. Bd., 1980-81; former chmn. Legis. and Regulation Com. Calif. Savs. and Loan League; former mem. bd. dirs. Fed. Home Loan Bank, San Francisco. Pres., trustee Calif. Neighborhood Services Found.; chmn. Urban Housing Inst.; mem. policy adv. bd. Ctr. for Real Estate and Urban Econs. U. Calif., Berkeley. With U.S. Army, 1954-56. Office: Golden West Fin Corp 1901 Harrison St Oakland CA 94612-3588*

SANDLER, IAN MARTIN, travel, tourism and leisure company executive; b. Johannesburg, South Africa, Oct. 17, 1957; s. Julius and Greta Sandler; m. Glenda Ruth Cohen, June 11, 1983; children: Megan, Grant. B Commerce, U. Witwatersrand, South Africa, 1979, B Accountancy, 1982. Chartered acct., South Africa. Audit mgr. Arthur Andersen, South Africa, 1980-87; corp. fin. dir. Resort Condos. Internat., Johannesburg, 1987-89, ops. dir., 1990-95, chief ops. officer, 1995-97, mng. dir., 1997-99; mng. dir. Avis-Tourism & Leisure, Johannesburg, 1999—; chmn. RCI Pacific, 1998—; dir. Avis SA, Johannesburg, 2000—; chmn. RCI SA, Johannesburg. Vice chmn. Tisa & Variety Clubs of South Africa. Mem. South African Inst. Chartered Accts., South African Inst. Dirs. Avocations: golf, tennis, reading. Office: Avis, 2A Sysie Rd PO Box 783940, Sandton 2146, South Africa

SANDLER, KENNETH BRUCE, advertising executive; b. Newark, July 24, 1942; s. Ralph M. and Mae (Ness) S.; m. Denise Ann Brooks, May 8, 1973 (div. 1988); children: Todd, Brooke. BS in Pharmacy, BS in Chemistry, Rutgers U., 1967, MBA, 1970. Registered pharmacist, N.J. Mgr. mktg. research E.R. Squibb and Sons, Princeton, N.J., 1970-73; account exec. Deltakos div. J. Walter Thompson, N.Y.C., 1973-75, exec. v.p., 1982-84; v.p., account group supr. Rolf Werner Rosenthal Inc., N.Y.C., 1975-82; pres. Sandler Comm. Inc., N.Y.C., 1984—, Sandler & Recht Comm., Durham, N.C., 1991—, Sandler Pub. Rels., N.Y.C., 1996—. Mem. Am. Pharm. Assn., Am. Mktg. Assn., Nat. Assn. Retail Druggists, Am. Soc. Hosp. Pharmacists. Office: Sandler Comm Inc 100 5th Ave Fl 9 New York NY 10011-6998 also: Sandler & Recht Comm 4364 S Alston Ave Durham NC 27713-2280

SANDLER, MARION OSHER, retired savings and loan association executive; b. Biddeford, Maine, Oct. 17, 1930; d. Samuel and Leah (Lowe) Osher; m. Herbert M. Sandler, Mar. 26, 1961. BA, Wellesley Coll., 1952; postgrad., Harvard U.-Radcliffe Coll., 1953; MBA, NYU, 1958; LLD (hon.), Golden Gate U., 1987. Asst. buyer Bloomingdale's (dept. store), N.Y.C., 1953-55; security analyst Dominick & Dominick, N.Y.C., 1955-61; sr. fin. analyst Oppenheimer & Co., N.Y.C., 1961-63; sr. v.p., dir. Golden West Fin. Corp. and World Savs. & Loan Assn., Oakland, Calif., 1963-75, vice chmn. bd. dirs., CEO, mem. exec. com., dir., 1975-80, pres., co- chief exec. officer, dir., mem. exec. com., 1980-93, chmn. bd. dirs., CEO, mem. exec. com., 1993—; pres., chmn. bd. dirs., CEO Atlas Assets, Inc., Oakland, 1987—, Atlas Advisers, Inc., Oakland, 1987—, Atlas Securities, Inc., Oakland, 1987—; mem. adv. com. Fed. Nat. Mortgage Assn., 1983-84. Mem. Pres.'s Mgmt. Improvement Coun., 1980, Thrift Insts. Adv. Coun. to Fed. Res. Bd., 1989-91, v.p., 1990, pres., 1991; mem. policy adv. bd. Ctr. for Real Estate and Urban Econs. U. Calif., Berkeley, 1981—, mem. exec. com. policy adv. bd., 1985—; mem. ad hoc com. to rev. Schs. Bus. Adminstrn. U. Calif., 1984-85; vice chmn. industry adv. com. Fed. Savs. and Loan Ins. Corp., 1987-88, Ins. Corp., 1987-88; bd. overseers NYU Schs. Bus., 1987-89; mem. Glass Ceiling Commn., 1992-93. Mem. Phi Beta Kappa, Beta Gamma Sigma. Office: Golden W Fin Corp 1901 Harrison St Fl 6 Oakland CA 94612-3588

SANDLER, MERTON, chemical pathology educator, researcher; b. Salford, Lancashire, England, Mar. 28, 1926; s. Frank and Edith (Stein) S.; m. Lorna Rosemary Grenby, Mar. 14, 1961; children: Martin, Nicholas,. Diana, Olivia. MB ChB, Manchester U., England, 1949, MD, 1962. Intern, resident, house physician Withington Hosp., Manchester, England, 1949; resident Preston Royal Infirmary, Preston, England, 1950-51; house physician Royal Manchester Children's Hosp., Manchester, England, 1950; sr. resident Royal Free Hosp., London, 1955, lectr. chem. pathology Med. Sch., 1955-58; cons. chem. pathologist Queen Charlotte's Hosp., London, 1958-73; prof. chem. pathology U. London, 1973-91, emeritus prof., 1991—; internat. chmn. 6th Internat. Catecholamine Symposium, Jerusalem, 1987. Author: The Adrenal Cortex, 1961, The Thyroid Gland, 1967, Sexual Behavior: Pharmacology and Biochemistry, 1975, Trace Amines and the Brain, 1976, Enzyme Inhibitors as Drugs, 1980, The Psychopharmacology of Alcohol, 1980, Progress Towards a Male Contraceptive, 1982, Neurotransmitter Interactions, 1986, Design of Enzyme Inhibitors as Drugs, 1986, numerous others; editor-in-chief Jour. Psychiat. Rsch., 1982-92; contbr. articles to profl. jours. Capt. Royal Army M.C., 1951-53. Recipient Anna Monika Internat. prize, 1973, Gold medal Brit. Migraine Assn., 1974; rsch. fellow Brompton Hosp., London, 1954. Fellow Royal Soc. Medicine (pres. med. sect. 1979-81, hon. libr. 1987—); mem. Brit. Assn. Psychopharmacology (pres. 1979-82), Am. Coll. Neuropsychopharmacology (fgn. corr.), Biol. Coun. (sec. 1985-91, lectr., medal 1984), Collegium Internat. Neuro-Psychopharmacologicum (councillor 1982—), Assn. Postnatal Illness (pres. 1980—), World Assn. Socs. Pathology (organizer chem. pathology sect. 1985), Migraine Trust (chmn. sci. adv. com.), Harveian Soc. London (sec. 1987-89, pres. 1990-91), Athenaeum Club, Maccabaeans Club (sec. 1974-80) (London). Jewish. Avocations: reading, music, lying in the sun. Office: Queen Charlottes Hosp, Goldhawk Rd, London W6 OXG, England

SANDLER, RON, bank executive. CEO Lloyd's of London, 1995-99, Nat. Westminster Bank, London, 1999—. Office: Nat Westminster Bank, 41 Lithbury, London EC2P 2BP, England*

SANDLIN, ANATHALEE GRAY, writer, music company owner; b. Hastings, Nebr., Nov. 12, 1945; d. Lloyd Vern and Elizabeth Powers Gray; m. John Everett Sandlin, Jr.; children: Leigh Ellen Cauthen, Kristin Ann Spain, Heidi Anathalee Wilson. Columnist Nat. Skeet Shooters Review, 1982-83; bus. mgr. Ducktape Music Prodns., Decatur, Ala., 1984—; prin.,

owner Rockin Rabbit Music Other Ducks Music, Decatur, 1986—, AGS Publishing, Decatur, 1997—; Artist-media liason various tv award shows and benefit concerts, Southeast, U.S., 1986-96; bd. dirs. Tenn. Valley Homeless Shelter, Ala.; lectr. in field. Author: When Grandma Was Really Cooking, 1989, The Decatur Daily Cookbook, 1993, The Rosary-A Treasure of Graces, 1997. Mem. ASCAP, BMI, North Ala. Songwriters Assn. (bd. dirs., chmn. 1984-86). Avocations: painting, cooking, full time grandmother. Office: PO Box 2854 Decatur AL 35602-2854

SANDOMIR, MILLER, physician; b. Manhasset, N.Y., Oct. 17, 1962; s. Richard Elliott and Griffin (Miller) S. BA, NYU, 1984; MD, Columbia U., 1990. Intern, resident Columbia Presbyn. Hosp., N.Y.C., 1990-93; staff physician North Shore Univ. Hosp., Great Neck, N.Y., 1993—; rsch. fellow Buttenweiser Inst. for Proctologic Rsch., Medford, N.Y., 1995—. Author: My Life in the Upper U.S., 1997. Del. Reform Party, Ft. Totten, N.Y., 1996. Mem. Royal Assn. for the Preservation of the Honeypot (grand high exalted mystic ruler 1995—). Buddhist. Avocations: butterfly collecting, churning butter, day trading, fire walking. Home: 6615 Thornton Pl Rego Park NY 11374-5147 Office: North Shore Univ Hosp Great Neck NY

SANDONATO, GILBERTO MARREGA, research scientist; b. Campinas, Brazil, Feb. 24, 1956; s. Gilberto Aparecido and Darcy Marrega Sandonato; m. Elizabeth Brabetz Kovacs, Sept. 21, 1981; children: Luiza, Beatriz, Debora. BS, U. Sao Paulo, 1980, MS, 1983; DS, Inst. Tech. Aeronautics, Sao Jose dos Campos, Brazil, 1993. Asst. rschr. U. Sao Paulo, 1983-84; asst. rschr. Inst. Nacional de Pesquisas Espaciais, Sao Jose dos Campos, 1985-89, sr. rschr., 1990—; cons. in field. Contbr. articles to profl. jours. Avocation: music. Fax: 55 12 345 6710. E-mail: gms@plasma.inpe.br. Home: Rua Chile 194, 12223060 Sao Jose dos Campos Brazil Office: Inst Nat Pesquisas Espacias, Av dos Astronautas 1758, 12201970 Sao Jose dos Campos Brazil

SÁNDOR, LÁSZLÓ, surgeon; b. Borota, Hungary, Oct. 31, 1946; s. Béla and Julianna (Somogyi) S.; m. Ursula Erika Kirsch, Sept. 3, 1969; children: Claudia, Viktória. MD, Med. Sch. Szeged, Hungary, 1972; postgrad. diploma in surgery, Martin Luther U., Halle-Wittenberg, Germany, 1976; postgrad. diploma in traumasurgery, Acad. Sci., Budapest, Hungary, 1979, PhD, 1982. Cert. cons. in trauma surgery. House officer Martin-Luther U., 1971-72, sr. house officer, 1973, from registrar to sr. registrar, 1974-76; med. asst. Med. Sch. Szeged, 1977-89; cons., head trauma surgery U. Szeged Faculty Medicine, 1990—; cons. Tchg. Hosp., Szeged, 2000—. Author: Traumatologie der Wirbelsäule, 1990; contbr. articles to profl. jours.; patentee in field. Assn. for Study of Internal Fixation/Arbeitsgemeinschaft für Osteosynthesefragen fellow, 1979, Humboldt fellow, 1986-87. Mem. Austrian Assn. Trauma Surgery, German Speakers Assn. Spine Surgery, N.Y. Acad. Scis. Home: Cinke U 2/3, 6726 Szeged Csongrad, Hungary Office: Med U Albert Szent Gyorgyi, Semmelweis U 6 Trauma Surgery, 6720 Szeged Hungary Office: Tchg Hosp Szeged, Kálvária sugarut 57, 6725 Szeged Hungary

SANDOVAL, MARIA OLGA, economics educator; b. Guatemala City, Guatemala, Sept. 1, 1964; d. Oscar Sandoval and Olga Recinos; m. Rolando Alfaro, Dec. 4, 1987; children: Rolando Enrique, José Daniel, Luis Andres Alfaro, María Olga Alfaro. Grad. in econs. cum laude, U. Francisco Marroquín, Guatemala City, 1986. Asst. prof. econs. Francisco Marroquín U., 1984-86, prof. math., 1986-87, prof. econs., 1987—, prof. econ. humanities faculty, 1986—, sec. econs. faculty, asst. econs. dept., 1986-87; prof. U. Mesoamericana, 1999—; prof. math. Superior Edn. Woman Inst., Guatemala City, 1986-88; cons. Nat. Econ. Rsch. Ctr., Guatemala City, 1985—. Contbr. articles to newspaper. Roman Catholic. Avocations: chess, lecturing, playing accordion, music, cooking. Home: 10 Ave 2-45 Zona 1, Guatemala City Guatemala Office: Alfaro's Office, 8 Ave 15-79 Zona 1, Guatemala City Guatemala

SANDOVAL, RIK (CHARLES SANDOVAL), broadcasting executive; b. Chgo., May 20, 1952; s. Placido Jr. and Ophelia (Lugo) S. BA in Communications, Columbia Coll., 1974. With prodn. dept. Sta. WSNS-TV, Chgo., 1971-72; dir., producer Sta. WCAE-TV, St. John, Ind., 1972-73; producer Sta. WBBM-FM, Chgo., 1973-74; prodn. mgr. Sta. WLS-TV, Chgo., 1972-76, on-air mgr., 1976-77; sr. publicist, producer Sta. KABC-TV, Hollywood, Calif., 1977-79; dir. creative svcs. Sullivan & Assocs, L.A., 1979-81; producer ABC, Hollywood, 1981-82; pres. Sandoval Prodns., Studio City, Calif., 1982-87; sr. v.p. The Agy., Studio City, 1987-88; pres. Tri-Mark Group, Inc., Studio City, 1988-92; dir. world wide ops. publicity MGM Studios, Culver City, Calif., 1992; mgr. interactive video prodn. Entergamement, Inc., L.A., 1993-94; dir. ops. GTE Interactive Media, Carlsbad, Calif., 1994-97, dir. pub. rels., 1994-97; v.p. pub. rels. and mktg. comm. Neale-May & Ptnrs., Palo Alto, Calif., 1998—; v.p. tech., sr. exec. on iMac launch Edelman Pub. Rels. World Wide, Mountain View, Calif., 1998—; v.p. publ. rels. Access Comms. Sega Dreamcast Launch and .com Strategic Svcs., 1999—; sr. dir. corp. comm. Silicon Motion, Inc., San Jose, Calif., 2000—; Judge The Clio Awards; prodr., writer Miss Hawaiian Tropic Beauty Pageant, 1992; head writer Mad Scientist Toon Club, 1993; exec. dir. Computer Game Developers Assocs., Los Altos, Calif., 1997. Producer, writer: (broadcast promotions) A.K.A. Pablo, 1984 (Silver award), Entertainment Tonight, 1984 (Silver award), Hunter, 1985, People, 1985 (Telly award, 1985, Gold Statuette award); head writer Mad Scientist Toon Club, 1993. Mem. NOSOTROS, L.A., 1987. Recipient 8 Clio nominations, 1977, 79-81, 2 Gold medals Internat. Radio Festival N.Y., 1985, 4 Bronze Telly awards, 1983-88, Silver Telly award, 1988, 2 ITVA awards, 1988, 3 Silver Telly awards, 1991, 4 Silver Telly awards, 1992, 2 Bronze Telly awards, 1992. Mem. Broadcast Promotion Mktg. Execs. (Gold medal, Silver medal 1985, 2 Bronze Telly award statuettes 1989, Silver Telly award statuette 1989, ITVA award), Nat. Assn. Broadcasters (cert. merit 1974), The Publicist Guild, Acad. TV Arts and Scis., Pub. Rels. Soc. Am. Roman Catholic. Avocations: Art Deco antiques, fine wine collector, karate, pre-Columbian artifacts, modern art collector. Home: 83 Rock Harbor Ln Foster City CA 94404

SANDOVAL IÑIGUEZ, JUAN CARDINAL, archbishop; b. Yahualica, Mar. 28, 1933. Coadjuctor bishop Cuidad Juarez, Mexico, 1988-92, bishop, 1992-94; archbishop of Guadalajara Mexico; created and proclaimed cardinal, 1994. Office: Arzobispado Guadalajara, Morelos 244, Liceo 17 San Pedro 45500, Mexico

SANDOVSKII, VLADIMIR AARON, physicist, researcher; b. Leningrad, Russia, June 24, 1934. Engr., Ural Poly. Inst., 1962; BS, Inst. Physics of Metals, 1971, Doctorate, 1990. Postgrad. fellow Inst. Physics Metals, Ekaterinburg, Russia, 1965-68, scientist, 1968-71, sr. scientist, 1971, leading scientist, 1991. Author: (with V. V. Djakin) Theory and Calculation of Superposed Eddy Current Transducers, 1981. Sr. lt. Soviet Army, 1953-56. Avocation: music. Office: Russian Acad Sci, Inst Physics Metals Ural Br, 620219 Ekaterinburg Russia

SANDS, CAMILLE, actress; b. Talladega, Ala., Aug. 7, 1946; d. Bram O. Horne and Helen Louneil. Student, Oxford U., Ala. Burlesque queen, 1969-89. Appeared in TV show Miami Vice, 1983-88; films include Where the Boys Are, 1984, Invasion U.S.A., 1987, B. L. Stryker, 1988, Smokey & the Bandit III, Porky's II, Hell Can Wait. Victims adv. battered women State Atty.'s Office, Ft. Pierce, Fla.; mem. St. Luice Hist. Soc. Avocations: martial arts, aerobics, dancing, collecting.

SANDS, CHRISTINE LOUISE, English educator; b. Johnstown, Pa., Oct. 13, 1947; d. Joseph and Margaret (Kocsis) Migut; m. Angelo Joseph Sands, Dec. 28, 1968 (div. Nov. 1989); children: Vincent, Linda. BS in German, Indiana U. Pa., 1969, BS in English, 1975; postgrad., Slippery Rock U., 1971-76. Tchg. cert. Pa. Educator New Castle (Pa.) Schs., 1969—; student advisor, judge Forensics, New Castle, 1981-96, Youngstown (Ohio) Reading Festival, 1981-95. Pres. New Castle City Coun., 1996; parish coun. St. Vitus Ch., New Castle, 1986-92; basketball referee PIAA, Mechanicsburg, Pa., 1972-91; coach New Castle H.S. Bowling, 1986-97. Democrat. Roman Catholic. Avocations: reading, traveling, sports, cooking, politics. Home: 819 E Hillcrest Ave New Castle PA 16105-2256 Office: New Castle HS 230 N Jefferson St New Castle PA 16101-2274

SANDSTROM, ALICE WILHELMINA, accountant; b. Seattle, Jan. 6, 1914; d. Andrew William and Agatha Mathilda (Sundius) S. BA, U. Wash., 1934. CPA, Wash. Mgr. office Star Machinery Co., Seattle, 1935-43, Howe & Co., Seattle, 1943-46; pvt. practice acctg. Seattle, 1945-85; controller Children's Orthopedic Hosp. and Med. Ctr., Seattle, 1948-75, assoc. adminstr. fin., 1975-81; lectr. U. Wash., Seattle, 1957-72. Mem. Wash. state Title XIX Adv. Com., 1975-82, Wash. State Vendors Rate Adv. Com., 1980-87, Mayor's Task Force for Small Bus., 1981-83; bd. dirs. Seattle YWCA, 1981—, pres., 1986-88; bd. dirs. Sr. Svcs. Seattle King Co., 1989-95, bd. dirs. Sr. Svcs. Seattle/King County, 1985, treas., 1986, pres., 1988-90; bd. dirs. Children's Orthopedic Hosp. Found., 1982-90; mem. LWV, 1997. Recipient Jefferson award for vol. svcs., 1997. Fellow Hosp. Fin. Mgmt. Assn. (charter, state pres. 1956-57, nat. treas. 1963-65, Robert H. Reeves merit award 1970, Frederick T. Muncie award 1985; mem. Wash. State Hosp. Assn. (treas. 1956-70), Am. Soc. Women Accts. (pres. Seattle chpt. 1946-48), Am. Soc. Women CPAs, Wash. Soc. CPAs, Seattle Women's Voters League, Women's Univ. Club (Seattle), City Club (Seattle, charter mem.). Home and Office: 5725 NE 77th St Seattle WA 98115-6345

SANDSTRÖM, GUNNAR EMANUEL, microbiologist; b. Lycksele, Sweden, June 1, 1951; s. Lars Åke Emanuel and Maj Dovi Helena (Holmgren) S.; m. Elsa Lillemor Johansson, May 30, 1986; children: Jörgen, Sandra. D. in Med. Sci., U. Umeå (Sweden), 1988. Asst. U. Umeå, 1970-80; asst. Nat. Def. Rsch. Establishment, Umeå, 1980-85, sr. rsch. officer, 1985-89; postdoctoral fellow US Army Med. Rsch. Inst., Ft. Detrick, Frederick, Md., 1989-90; head div. microbiology Nat. Def. Rsch. Establishment, Umeå, 1990, assoc. prof., 1991; prof. Nat. Def. Rsch. Establishment and U. Umeå, Umeå, 1994—; dir. rsch. Nat. Def. Rsch. Establishment, Umeå, 1995—, dir., 1997-2000; sr. rsch. officer NRC, Frederick, 1989-90. Contbr. tularemia articles to profl. jours.; inventor-patentee rapid diagnosis of bacteria. Chmn. Local Community Coun., Umeå, 1979-88. Mem. Rotary Internat. Avocations: music, fishing, traveling. Home: Vallmovägen 33, S 90352 Umeå Sweden Office: Nat Def Rsch Establishment, Cementvägen 20, S 901 82 Umeå Sweden

SANDU, CONSTANTINE, process development engineer; b. Costesti, Arges, Romania, Nov. 9, 1943; came to U.S. 1979, naturalized 1984; s. Dumitru and Maria (Calinoiu) S. Eng., U. Galatz, Romania, 1966; PhD, U. Wis., 1989. Plant engr. Fruit and Vegetables Co., Riureni, Romania, 1967-68; prof.'s asst. U. Galatz, Romania, 1968-75; vis. scientist Fed. Rsch. Ctr. Nutrition, Karlsruhe, Ger., 1975-77; R & D engr. Soc. for Ind. Heating & Engring., Krefeld, Ger., 1978-79; rsch. asst. U. Wis., Madison, 1979-86; sr. devel. engr. The Quaker Oats Co., Barrington, Ill., 1986-95; process devel. mgr. ConAgra Grocery Products Co., Fullerton, Calif., 1995—; adj. prof. Purdue U., W. Lafayette, Ind. 1989-95. Author: Physicomathematical Model for Milk Fouling in a Plate Heat Exchanger, 1991; editor: Fouling and Cleaning in Food Processing, 1985; contbr. articles to profl. jours. Mem. Inst. Food Technologists, Math. Assn. Am., Sigma Xi, Phi Tau Sigma. Avocations: philosophy, history, foreign languages, body building, tennis. Home: 2889 Player Ln Tustin CA 92782-1534 Office: ConAgra Grocery Products 1701 W Valencia Dr Fullerton CA 92833-3800

SANDULESCU, AURELIU EMIL, physicist, educator, politician; b. Bucharest, Romania, Feb. 11, 1932; s. Constantin and Aurora (Constantinescu) S.; m. Violette Felicia Farcas, Dec. 10, 1960. BS in Physics, U. Bucharest, 1955, PhD in Physics, 1962. Head dept. Inst. of Atomic Physics, Bucharest, 1970-74, 95—; dep. dir. Lab. Nuclear Reactions, Dubna, Russia, 1974-77; vice-dir. Jt. Inst. Nuclear Rsch., Dubna, 1983-86; v.p. Romanian Acad., Bucharest, 1994-98; vis. prof. Inst. Theoretical Physics, Helsinki, 1965-66, Max Planck Inst., Mainz, 1967-68, Sci. Inst. Niels Bohr, Copenhagen, 1968-69, Tech. Hochschule, Darmstadt, Germany, 1970-73; vis. scientist U. Frankfurt, Germany, 1978-82, 91-92, 94, 96-99, Vanderbilt U., Nashville, 1994, 96-98. Dept. Chamber of Deps., Bucharest, 1996—. Mem. Romanian Phys. Soc. (pres. 1993-98), European Phys. Soc., Romanian Acad. Bucharest. Avocation: tennis. Office: Romanian Acad, Calea Victoriei 125, 71102 Bucharest Romania

SANDULLI, ROBERTO, environmental sciences educator; b. Avellino, Italy, Sept. 30, 1956; s. Ugo and Giuliana (Giazzi) S.; m. Chiara Maria Motta, Sept. 4, 1988; 1 child, Edoardo. PhD in Environ. Scis. Scientific mgr. Cytochemia Ltd., Avellino, Italy, 1990-91; dir. rsch. ctr. Castalia Ltd., Genoa, Italy, 1991-96; prof./rschr. U. Bari, Italy, 1996—; tchg. cons. UNESCO, Brussels, 1995—; scientific cons. U. Naples, Italy, 1990—. Vol. Assn. Italiana Volotari Laici, Bari, 1999. Avocations: music, tennis, basket, tennis. E-mail: rsandulli@biologia.uniba.it. Home: Via Legniti 14, Monteforte Irpino 83024, Italy Office: Dept Zoology U Bari, Via Orabona 4, Bari 70125, Italy

SANDUM, HOWARD E., literary agent; b. Devils Lake, N.D., July 7, 1929; s. Howard E. Sandum and Gladys I. Lien; m. Evangeline M. Olson, May 12, 1955 (dec. Feb. 1972); children: Kyrie L. (dec.), Beret S. Canakes, Rachel S. Tune, Joseph H., Marn S. Turley; m. Marta R. Enebuske, July 28, 1975. BA, St. Olaf Coll., Northfield, Minn., 1951; postgrad., U. Minn., 1954-56, 60-62. Editor trade religion The Macmillan Co., N.Y.C., 1962-63, editor-in-chief Collier Books divsn., 1963-71; editor-in-chief Adult Trade divsn. The World Pub. Co., N.Y.C., 1971-73; dir. office for comm. Luth. Ch. in Am., N.Y.C., 1973-76; editl. dir. The Saunders Press (W.B. Saunders Co.), Phila., 1979-81; editl. dir. Harvest Books Harcourt Brace Jovanovich, N.Y.C. and San Diego, 1982-83; mng. dir. Sandum & Assocs. Lit. Agy., N.Y.C., 1987—; founder, dir. The Pub. Inst., U. Pa., Phila., 1980-82; dir. pub. info. The Am. Luth. Ch., Mpls., 1960-62; night editor AP, Boise, Idaho, 1956-60. Editor Scandinavian Rev., 1976-78. Lay reader, usher Ch. of Holy Trinity, N.Y.C., 1990—; planning chmn. New St. Peters Lutheran Ch. at Citicorp Ctr., N.Y.C., 1970-78. Capt. USMC, 1952-54, res. Recipient Disting. Alumnus award St. Olaf Coll., 2000. Mem. Met. Mus. Art (sustaining), N.Y. Soc. Libr. Episcopalian. Avocations: cooking, museums, urban walking. Home and Office: Sandum & Assocs a Lit Agy 144 E 84th St New York NY 10028-2004

SANDWELL, KRISTIN ANN, special education educator; b. Topeka, Kans., Jan. 13, 1955; d. Edwin C. and E. Maxine (Nelson) Henry; m. Steve Sandwell, Dec. 27, 1997; children: Dustin Grimm, Chris Creek, Brandon Grimm, Sarah Sandwell, Paul Sandwell. AA, Hutchinson (Kans.) C.C., 1986; BS, McPherson (Kans.) Coll., 1989; MEd, Wichita State U., 1992. Cert. tchr. elem., gifted. Math/parenting tchr. Flint Hills Job Corps Ctr., Manhattan, Kans., 1992; gifted facilitator Unified Sch. Dist. 353, Wellington, Kans., 1993-94, Unified Sch. Dist. 260, Derby, Kans., 1995-97; tchr. City of Wichita Summer Youth Employment Program-Edn., 1997—; gifted facilitator Unified Sch. Dist. 259, 1998—; head injury counselor, life skills trainer Three Rivers Ind. Living Ctr., Wamego, Kans., 1992; facilitator Summer Youth Employment Edn. Program, 1997-98. Epiphany Festival prodr. Trinity Luth. Ch., McPherson, 1991, 93; CASA organizer McPherson Coll., 1988-89; vol. coun. on Violence Against Persons, McPherson, 1990-92. Mem. ASCD. Avocations: reading, travel, working with disability issues.

SANDY, ARTHUR EDWARD, retired sales executive; b. Lake Forest, Ill., Mar. 13, 1929; s. Robert Edward and Emily Maud (Beacham) S.; m. Adelaide Imogene Gaertner, June 8, 1952; children: Bradley Edward, Arthur Edward Jr., Tyrrell Robert. Sales correspondent Cyclone Fence U.S. Steel Corp., North Chgo., Ill., 1947-51; head sales correspondent U.S. Steel Corp., Oakland, Calif., 1952-53; sales rep. U.S. Steel Corp., San Francisco, 1954-56, Chgo., 1957-60; sales rep. Glenbrook Labs Sterling Drug Inc., Tampa, Fla., 1961-62, dist. sales mgr., 1962-64; dist. sales mgr Glenbrook Labs Sterling Drug Inc., Chgo., 1964-65, region sales mgr., 1965-77; with sales dept. Clinical Labs., Chgo., 1977-82; sales Grant Dean Buick, Highland Park, Ill., 1982-92. Mem. Senior Cmty. Activity Team, Mission Viejo, Calif., 1999. With U.S. Army, 1946-47. Mem. Casta Del Sol Tennis Club (v.p. 2000—). Avocations: tennis, music, crossword puzzles, physical fitness. E-mail: arthure@aol.com. Home: 27704 Calle Valdes Mission Viejo CA 92692-2013

SANÉ, PIERRE GABRIEL MICHEL, international social welfare executive; b. Dakar, May 7, 1948; s. Nicolas and Thérèse Carvalho; m. Ndeye Coumba Sow, 1981; 2 children. Attended, Lycée Van Vollenhoven, Dakar, Ecole Supérieure de Commerce de Bordeaux, France, Ecole Nouvelle d'Organisation Economique et Sociale, Paris, London Sch. Econs., Carleton U., Ottawa. V.p. Fedn. of Black African Students in France, 1971-72; auditor France, 1973-77; dep. gen. mgr. Soc. Sénégalaise Pharmaceutique, 1977-78; joined Internat. Devel. Rsch. Ctr., 1978; various positions Internat. Devel. Rsch. Ctr., Ottawa, Nairobi and Dakar; regional dir. east and so. Africa Internat. Devel. Rsch. Ctr., Nairobi, until 1992; sec.-gen. Amnesty Internat., London, 1992—. Pres. PANAF 92, 1991-92, founding mem. internat. com.; active AI, 1988—. Recipient award Concours Nat. de Commercialisation, France, 1972. Avocations: reading, travelling, music, museums, arts. Office: Amnesty Internat, 1 Easton St, London WC1X 0DW, England

SANER, SALIH, petroleum geologist, educator; b. Pergamos, Cyprus, Sept. 17, 1945; s. Mehmet and Mumus (Salih) Saban; m. Zuhal Ozgenc, May 24, 1971; two children. BS, U. Istanbul, 1969, MS, 1971, PhD, 1977. Lectr. U. Istanbul, 1971-75; field geologist Mineral Rsch. & Exploration, Ankara, Turkey, 1975-76; exploration geologist Turkish Petroleum Corp., Ankara, 1976-81; rsch. scientist, prof. King Faud U. Petroleum & Minerals, Dhahran, Saudi Arabia, 1981—. Office: King Faud U Petroleum, Box 2021, 31261 Dhahran Saudi Arabia

SANETTI, STEPHEN LOUIS, lawyer; b. Flushing, N.Y., June 25, 1949; s. Alfred Julius Sanetti and Yolanda Marie (DiGioia) Boyes; m. Carole Leighton Koller, Sept. 21, 1974; children: Christopher Edward, Dana Harrison. B.A. in History with honors, Va. Mil. Inst., 1971; J.D., Washington and Lee U., 1974. Bar: Conn. 1975, U.S. Ct. Mil. Appeals 1975, U.S. Dist. Ct. Conn. 1978, U.S. Ct. Appeals (2d cir.) 1979, U.S. Supreme Ct. 1980. Litigation atty. Marsh, Day & Calhoun, Bridgeport, Conn., 1978-80; gen. counsel Sturm, Ruger & Co., Southport, Conn., 1980—, v.p., 1993—, also bd. dirs., 1998—; dir. Product Liability Adv. Coun. Tech. advisor Assn. Firearm and Toolmark Examiners; chmn. legis. & legal affairs com. Sporting Arms & Ammunition Mfrs. Inst. Served to capt., chief criminal law 1st Cavalry Div. Staff Judge Advocate, U.S. Army, 1975-78. Mem. Am. Acad Forensic Sci., Def. Rsch. Inst. Republican. Roman Catholic. Office: Sturm Ruger & Co Inc 1 Lacey Pl Southport CT 06490-1241

SANFILIPPO, HELENA MARY, development director, educator; b. Buffalo, N.Y.. BA in History, San Francisco Coll. Women, 1957; MA in History, U. San Francisco, 1967; PhD in History, U. Notre Dame, 1972. Cert. tchr. Calif. Tchr. various elem. and h.s., Calif., 1950-66; governing coun. Sisters of Mercy, Burlingame, Calif., 1972-74, archivist, 1977-87; acad. dean Russell Coll., Burlingame, 1974-82; educator King Coll., Bristol, Tenn., 1988-90, Va. Intermont Coll., 1989-90; founder, exec. dir. Tri-County (Free) Health Clinic, Richlands, Va., 1989-95; educator Chabot/Los Positas C.C. Dist., Hayward/Livermore, Calif., 1996—; devel. dir. Mercy Retirement and Care Ctr., Oakland, Calif., 1997—. Author: Inward Wealth and Outward Splendor: New England Transcendentalists View the Roman Catholic Church, 1987. Bd. govs. Cath. Healthcare West—Ariz., 1995—, Tri-County Health Clinic, Richlands, Va., 1991-95, Assn. Free Clinics, Va., 1993-95, Mercy Hosp. and Med. Ctr., San Diego, 1982-88, St. Rose Hosp., Hayward, Calif., 1981-87, Soc. Calif. Archivists, 1981-85, Mercy H.S., Burlingame, Calif., 1980-84, St. Mary's Hosp. and Med. Ctr., San Francisco, 1974-77, Mercy Retirement & Care Ctr., Oakland, Calif., 1974-77; bd. dirs. United Way of S.W. Va., Lebanon, 1993-95; cmty. outreach vol. SHARE, HelpLine, Mercy Project, Food Bank, Meals on Wheels, Water Project of Clinch Valley, Va., 1987-95. Recipient Outstanding Vol. Svc. award, Appalachian Agy. Sr. Citizens, 1995, Disting. Citizen of Yr. award, Richlands Area C. of C., 1994, Outstanding Citizen award, Woodmen of the World, 1994, Cmty. Builder's awards, Masons, 1992, 93, Gov.'s Gold award for volunteering excellence, Commonwealth of Va., 1992. Mem. Orgn. of Am. Historians, Am. Hist. Assn., Am. Cath. Hist. Soc. Roman Catholic. Avocations: volunteering, travel, crossword puzzles, reading, choral singing. Fax: 415-333-5238.

SANFORD, ANTHONY JOHN, psychology educator, researcher; b. Birmingham, Eng., July 5, 1944; s. Edwin and Winnifred Olive (Hurdman) S.; m. Valerie Anne Hines, 1966 (div. Aujg. 1986); 1 child, Bridget; m. Linda Mae Moxey, Jan. 24, 1987; children: Anthony Iain, Heather Margaret. BSc, U. Leeds, Eng., 1966; PhD, Cambridge (Eng.) U., 1969. Chartered psychologist. Med. Rsch. Coun. scholar applied psychology unit Cambridge U., 1966-69; rsch. fellow U. Dundee, Scotland, 1969-73; lectr. U. Dundee, 1973-75; sr. lectr. U. Glasgow, Scotland, 1975-81; reader U. Glasgow, 1981-83, prof. psychology, 1983—; vis. rschr. U. Bielefeld, 1992. Author: Cognition and Cognitive Psychology, 1985, The Mind of Man, 1987; co-author: Understanding Written Language, 1981, Communicating Quantities, 1993. Fellow Brit. Psychol. Soc.; mem. Exptl. Psychology Soc., Cognitive Sci. Soc. Avocations: hill walking, industrial archaeology, music, cooking. Office: U Glasgow, Dept Psychology, Glasgow G13 9YR, Scotland

SANGEETHA, PANICKER, plant pathology educator; b. Pondicherry, India, Mar. 15, 1964; d. Raghava Panicker and Saraswathi Bai; m. Rarth Muralidharan, Feb. 5, 1990; children: Abhishek, Abilash. BSc in Agr., Tamil Nadu Agrl. U., Coimbatore, India, 1986, MSc in Plant Pathology, 1988, PhD, 1996. Asst. prof. Tamil Nadu Agrl. U., Coimbatore, 1989-97, sr. asst. prof., 1997—. Author: Handbook of Horticultural Crop Diseases, 1999, A Question Bank of "Indian Administrative Service", 1999. Sgt. Indian Mil., 1980-82. Fellow Ford Found., 1986-88. Mem. Soc. Mycology and Plant Pathology. Avocations: reading, handicraft, painting, cooking. Home: 10/2 Sri Lakshmi Nagar, Coimbatore 641046, India Office: Tamil Nadu Agrl U, Dept Plant Path, Lawley Rd, Coimbatore 641003, India

SANGER, FREDERICK, retired molecular biologist; b. Rendcomb, Gloucestershire, Eng., Aug. 13, 1918; s. Frederick and Cicely Sanger; m. Joan Howe, 1940; children: Robin, Peter Frederick, Sally Joan. B.A., St. John's Coll., Cambridge U., 1940, Ph.D., 1943; D.Sc. (hon.), Leicester U., 1968, Oxford U., 1970, Strasbourg U., 1970, Cambridge U. Beit Meml. Med. Research fellow U. Cambridge, 1944-51, research scientist dept. biochemistry, 1944-61, research scientist, div. head Med. Research Council Lab. of Molecular Biology,, 1962-83. Contbr. articles in field to sci. jours. Recipient Nobel prize for chemistry, 1958, 80; Gairdner Found. ann. award, 1971, 79, William Bate Hardy prize Cambridge Philos. Soc., 1976, Copley medal Royal Soc., 1977; fellow King's Coll., Cambridge U., 1954. Mem. Am. Acad. Arts and Scis. (hon. fgn. mem.), Am. Soc. Biol. Chemists (hon.), Fgn. Assn., NAS. Home: Far Leys Fen Ln, Swaffham Bulbeck, Cambridge CB5 ONJ, England

SANGER, GARETH JOHN, autonomic neuroscientist; b. Whitehaven, Cumbria, Eng., Mar. 12, 1953; s. Glyn William and Glenys Ada (Wilson) S.; m. Yvonne Maurine Newman, Sept. 27, 1980 (div.); children: Andrew, Katie, James, Emily. BSc with honors in Physiology, U. Newcastle-Upon-Tyne, Eng., 1974; PhD in Physiology, U. Manchester, Eng., 1977, DSc, 1998. Rsch. fellow King's Coll. Hosp. Med. Sch., U. London, 1977-80; rsch. scientist Beecham Pharms., Harlow, Eng., 1980-88; dir. gastrointestinal motility rsch. Smithkline Beecham Pharms., Harlow, 1988-92, team dir. neurosci. rsch., 1992—; cons. mechanisms of emesis U.K. Palliative Care Groups, 1995—; coord. European Commn. (Biotech.) Framework IV Rsch. Group, 1996—. Co-editor: Emesis and Anti-Cancer Therapy, 1993; editor Brit. Jour. Pharmacology, 1989-95, Current Drugs, 1992-97; contbr. articles to profl. jours.; patentee in field. Framework IV grantee European Commn., Belgium, 1996; recipient Drug Discoverer's award Pharm. Rsch. and Mfrs. Am., 1998. Mem. Brit. Pharmacology Soc. (editor 1989-95), European Neurosci. Study Group, European Neurosci. Indsl. Platform (1st chmn. 1998-99). Avocations: children, collecting, voluntary work. Office: Smithkline Beecham Pharms, New Frontiers Sci Pk 3d Ave, Harlow CM19 5AW, England

SANGER, STEPHEN W., consumer products company executive; b. 1945. With General Mills, Inc., Mpls., 1974—; v.p., gen. mgr. Northstar Divsn. General Mills, Inc., 1983, v.p., gen. mgr. new bus. devel., 1986, pres. Yoplait USA, 1986, pres. Big G Divsn., 1988, sr. v.p., 1989, vice chmn. bd., 1992-96, pres., 1993-96, CEO, chmn. bd., 1996—; bd. dirs. Donaldson Co., Inc., Mpls. Treas. Guthrie Theatre Found., Mpls. Office: Gen Mills Inc One General Mills Blvd Minneapolis MN 55426

SANGHAVI, GIRISH JAYANTILAL, psychologist, hypnotherapist, sexologist; b. Bombay, June 5, 1942; s. Jayantilal Chhabildas and Priyavandna (Kothari) S.; m. Mamta Girish Shah, Dec. 25, 1969; children: Devang, Rachita. Med. graduate, Maharashtra Faculty Bd., Bombay, 1966; diploma, U. Calif., 1989; diploma in advance hypnotherapy, Am. Soc. of Clin. Hypnosis, 1998. House surgeon Sir H.N. Hosp., Bombay, 1966-67, house

physician, 1967-68; pvt. cons. Mamta Clinic, Bombay, 1969—; affiliate, dir. Asian liaison L.I. Inst. Ericksonian Hypnosis, 1996—, conf. for sexuality edn. awareness prog. Author: Road to Fulfill, Mental Health and Happiness, 1995; newspaper columnist; contbr. articles to profl. publs. Chair various coms. for various med. and social orgns. Recipient Appreciation award Lions Club of Kethwadi, 1975, Gen. Practitioners' Assn. Greater Bombay, 1978, 79, 80, 86, Bombay D-ward Med. Assn., 1980, Juhu Jaycees, 1988, Tarun Mitra Mandal, 1994, 55 Plus club, 1995, Morvi Mandal, 1995, Appreciation award Gen. Practitioners' Assn. Conf. Fellow L.I. Ericksonian Hypnosis (hon.); mem. APA (internat. affiliate status), Indian Assn. Sex Edn. Counseling and Therapy, C Ward Med. Assn., D Ward Med. Assn., GPA Med. Assn., NIMA Med. Assn. Avocations: music, travel, sports, reading. Home: 191 Pushpak Apts, 31 Alta Mount Rd, Bombay 400 026, India Office: Mamta Clinic Krishna Bldg, 34 Khetwadi 6th Ln, Bombay 400 004, India

SANGIORGI, GIORGIO, social sciences educator; b. Milan, Aug. 20, 1944; s. Massimo and Carla (Tommasina) S. Degree in Polit. Sci., U. Cattolica Sacro Cuore, Milan, Diploma in law. Dir. Scuola di Psicosociologia dell'Organizzazione, Milan, 1972—; dir. S.P.O., Milan, 1972. Mem. Internat. Coun. Psychologists, Italian Soc. Psychology, Am. Psychol. Assn. Home: Via S Eusebio 33, 20144 Milan Italy Office: Scuola di Psicosociologia, Via Washington 51, 20146 Milan Italy

SANGIOVANNI-VINCENTE, ALBERTO, engineering educator; b. Milan, June 23, 1947; m. Maria D. Di Benedetto; 1 child, Marco. Degree in elec. engrng & computer sci., Politecnico di Milan, Italy, 1971. Pof. U. Calif., Berkeley, 1976—; gen. mgr. Cadence European Labs., 1996—; vis. prof. U. Bologna, 1986, MIT, 1987, U. Pisa, 1991, U. Rome, Tor Vergata, 1992, U. Rome, La Sapienza, 1996—; with ACTEL, 1989—, Quick Turn Systems, 1990—; SGS-Thomson, 1986—; CSELT, 1986—, electronics divsn. Magneti-Marelli, 1995—, Accent, 1993—, Kawasaki, 1985—, Fujitsu Labs., 1994—, Kawasaki LSI, 1997—; sci. dir. project on advanced rsch. Architectures & Design Electronic Systems. Contbr. articles to profl. jours. Fellow IEEE (exec. v.p. circuits and systems soc. 1982-85); mem. IEEE Computer Soc., Assn. Computing Machinery, Berkeley Roundtable Internat. Economy. E-mail: alberto@eecs.berkeley.edu. Office: Univ Calif Dept EE & CS 515 Cory Hall 1770 Berkeley CA 94720-0001

SANGSUK-IAM, SUWANCHAI, engineering executive; b. Samutsakhon, Thailand, Feb. 25, 1960; s. Ha and Suwan Sangsuk-Iam; m. Nijaporn Chamnanvanakij, Jan. 16, 1993. B in Engrng., Chulalongkorn U., Bangkok, 1981; M in Engrng., U. Fla., 1983, PhD, 1987. Sr. engr. Seagate Tech., Patumthani, Thailand, 1988-89, mgr., 1989-90, sr. mgr., 1990-91; v.p. Chainavee Group of Cos., Samutsakhon, Thailand, 1991-92; chmn. electrical engrng. dept., engrng. (English) program Thammasat U., Patumthani, 1992-93, acting dir. engrng. (English) program, 1993-94; v.p. Chainavee Group of Cos., Samutsakhon, 1994—; cons. Seagate Tech., 1991-92, Chainavee Group of Cos., 1992-94; gen. sec. Chainavee Devel. Found., 1992—; adj. prof. Faculty of Engrng., Thammasat U., 1991—, Sirindhorn Internat. Inst. Tech., 1994—. Contbr. articles to profl. publs. Recipient Acad. medal King Bhumipol Adulyadech, Chulalongkorn U., 1981. Mem. IEEE, Fedn. Thai Industries (v.p. Samutsakhon chpt. 1996—). Home: Rama II Rd, Bangmod, 28/135 Chicha Village, Bangkok 10150, Thailand Office: 1258 Radpreeda Rd, Mahachai, Samutsakhon 74000, Thailand

SANGUINETI, EDOARDO, writer, Italian literature educator; b. Genoa, Italy, Dec. 9, 1930; s. Giovanni and Giuseppina (Cocchi) S.; m. Luciana Garabello, Sept. 30, 1954; children: Federico, Alessandro, Michele, Giulia. BA, U. Turin, 1956. Asst. prof. U. Turin, 1957-68, tchr., 1963-64; tchr. U. Salerno, 1968-70, prof., 1970-74; prof. Italian lit. U. Genoa, 1974-2000. Author: (novels) Capriccio Italiano, 1963, Il Giuoco dell'Oca, 1967; (poems and theatre) Laborintus, 1956, Opus metricum, 1960, Triperuno, 1964, Teatro, 1969, Storie naturali, 1971, Wirrwarr, 1972, Postkarten, 1978, Stracciafoglio, 1980, Segnalibro, 1982, Alfabeto Apocalittico, 1984, Faust un travestimento, 1985, Novissimum Testamentum, 1986, Bisbidis, 1987, Commedia dell'Inferno, 1989, Senzatitolo, 1992, Libretto, 1995, Orlando Furioso, 1996, Corollario, 1997, Cose, 1999; contbr. articles, essays to jours. Town councillor Commune Genoa, 1976-81; mem. chamber of deps. Italian Parliament, Rome, 1979-83.

SANGWAN, RAJBIR SINGH, research scientist, biotechnologist; b. Paintawas Khurd, India, Oct. 2, 1948; arrived in France, 1972; s. Kalu Ram and Harpyari (Sheoran) S.; m. Brigitte Norreel, July 25, 1975; 2 children. BS, Panjab U., Chandigarh, India, 1964, MS, 1969; DSc, U. Paris, 1981. Rsch. scholar CNRS, Paris, France, 1972-77; jr. scientist CNRS-U. Picardie, Amiens, France, 1977-83, sr. scientist, 1983-93, dir., 1993—; cons. UNIDO/FAO, Vienna, 1999, FOA/IAEA, Vienna, 1997; expert witness European Union, 1990—. Editor: Role of Technology in Agriculture, 1989. Fellow Govt. of France, 1972, sr. sci. fellow European Union, 1987. Mem. AAAS, IAPTC. Hindu. Avocation: international cultures and musics. Office: U Picardie JV Lab AEB, 33 Rue St Leu, 80039 Amiens France

SANGWAN, RAJENDER SINGH, research scientist; b. Badal, Bhiwani-Haryana, India, Aug. 24, 1958; s. Karan Singh and Kitabo Duvi (Sheoran) S.; m. Neelam Singh, Dec. 9, 1990; children: Kartikeya, Ambikeya. BSc in Biology, Kurukshetra (India) U., 1979; MSc in Biochemistry, Haryana Agrl. U., 1981, PhD in Biochemistry, 1987. Jr. rsch. fellow (BARC) Haryana Agrl. U., Hisar, 1981-82, rsch. fellow (BARC), 1983-84, sr. rsch. fellow (CSIR), 1985-86; postdoctoral rschr. Queen's U., Kingston, Can., 1990-91; scientist CIMAP (CSIR), Lucknow, India, 1986-95, sr. scientist, 1995—; mem. acad. coun. Haryana Agrl. U., Hisar, 1983-84; mem. residential instructions com., 1983-84; mem. bd. studies Coll. of Basic Scis., Hisar, 1983-84. Author: (with others) Recent Advances in Molecular and Biochemical Research and Proteins, 1992, Seed Oils for Future, 1993; contbr. articles to profl. publs. Recipient Travel award Internat. Union Biochem Molecular Biology, 1992, Young Scientist award Govt. of India, 1993; Prof. Umakant Sinha Meml. award Indian Sci. Congress Assn., 1997. Mem. Soc. for Plant Physiology and Biochemistry (life), Soc. for Plant Biochemistry and Biotechnology (life), Soc. of Biol. Chemists (life), Indian Sci. Congress Assn. (life), Am. Assn. of Plant Physiologists, Japanese Soc. of Plant Physiologists. Avocations: reading, books, farming, long driving, swimming. Home: 25/100 Sangu Marg Sect 25, Indira Nagar Extension, Lucknow 226016, India Office: CIMAP, Post Office CIMAP, Lucknow 226015, India

SANISLO, PAUL STEVE, lawyer; b. Cleve., Feb. 8, 1927; s. Paul and Bertha (Kasa) S.; m. Mary Ellen P. Conroy, May 7, 1949; 1 child, Susan J. BA, Baldwin-Wallace Coll., 1948; JD, Cleve. State U., 1961. Bar: Ohio 1961, U.S. Dist. Ct. (no. dist.) Ohio 1964. Order clk. Am. Agrl. Chem. Co., Cleve., 1948-52; safety engr. Park Drop Forge Co., Cleve., 1952-62, personnel mgr., 1954-62; assoc. then ptnr. Spohn & Sanislo, L.P.A., Cleve., 1962-81; pres., 1981-86; ptnr., pres. Sanislo, Bacevice & Assocs. LPA, Cleve., 1987-98; pres. Sanislo & Assocs. Co. LPA, 1998-2000; of counsel Stewart & Dechant, Cleve., 2000—; spl. counsel Atty. Gen. Ohio, 1971; arbitrator Am. Arbitration Assn., 1972-78; mem. Solon charter rev. commn., 2000—. Mem. Cleve. City Coun., 1964-67; trustee Cleve.-Marshall Law Sch., 1962-63; trustee Cleve.-Marshall Ednl. Found., 1963-68, pres., 1980-83; mem. Solon city Bd. Edn., Ohio, 1972-83, pres., 1974-83; chmn. Solon Charter Rev. Commn., 1971; past mem., organizer, legal adv. Solon Drug Abuse Ctr.; mem. Cuyahoga County Dem. Exec. Com.; ward leader 29th Ward Dem. Club, 1965-71, also past pres.; trustee Solon Dem. Ward Club, 1972-75. Recipient Disting. Svc. award City of Solon, 1984, Solon Bd. Edn., 1984, Solon Edn. Assn., 1984. Mem. Bar Assn. Greater Cleve. (Merit Svc. award 1978-79, chmn. workers compensation sect. 1975-96), Ohio Bar Assn., Cuyahoga County Bar Assn., Assn. Trial Lawyers Am., Cleve.-Marshall Law Sch. Alumni Assn. (pres. 1968-69), Hungarian Bus. and Tradesmen's Club (pres. 1967-68), Cleve. Assn. Compensation Attys. (pres. 1973-76). Democrat. Roman Catholic. Avocations: golf, travel. Office: Stewart & DeChant 1440 Standard Bldg Cleveland OH 44113

SANJEEVIRAJA, CHINNAPPANADAR, physics educator, researcher; b. Muhavur, Tamilnadu, India, Apr. 20, 1953; s. Narayananadar and Chinnappanadar (Thangammal) S.; m. Sanjeeviraja Thenmozhi, Oct. 24, 1957; children: Nivaskumar, Peruman. MSc, Madurai U., 1976, PhD, 1985. Lectr. V.H.N.S.N. Coll., Virudhunagar, 1981-85; lectr. Alagappa U., Karaikudi, 1985-94, reader, 1994—. Avocations: photography, collecting stamps, reading. Home: Plot 333, Karpaga Vinayagar Nagar, Karaikudi 630002, India Office: Alagappa U, Dept Physics, Karaikudi 630003, India

SANJINÉS, DIEGO IGNACIO, physicist; b. Merida, Venezuela, Oct. 30, 1962; s. Jaime and Maria Teresa (Castedo) S. Degree in engrng., ITESM, Mex., 1985; MSc, Cinuestav, Mex., 1990. Prof. ITESM, Mazlatan, Mex., 1985-86, UAM, Mexico City, 1990-91; cons. UPB, La Paz, Bolivia, 1991-92; sci. editor UASB, Sucre, Bolivia, 1992-94; tchg. asst. U. Simon Bolivar, Caracas, Venezuela, 1995—; instr. physics Grupo Escalera, Caracas, 1996. Sci. editor bull. Euromonitor, 1992-94; co-author manual: Laboratorio de Fisica I, 1997; contbr. articles to profl. jours. Recipient Einstein meda. U. Mayor San Andres, 1979; PRA scholar Orgn. Am. States, 1987, ITESM exch. student scholar U. Colo., 1983. Mem. Bolivian Phys. Soc. Avocations: history of science, writing on popular science. Home: Bao Següencoma, Av Hugo Ernst 6429 Apt 31, La Paz Bolivia Office: U Simon Bolivar, Dept Physics, 1080A Caracas Venezuela

SAN JUAN, ENRICO ABELLA, political analyst, journalist; b. Manila, The Philippines, Apr. 29, 1952; s. Epifanio P. and Ignacia Abella San Juan. BSc in Acctg., San Sebastian Coll., Manila, 1975; postgrad. in MBA program, Ateneo Grad. Sch. Bus., Makati, The Philippines, 1977. Radio commentator The Philippines, DWBL, Pasig, The Philippines; columnist Northern Times, The Philippines; dir. News Asia Group, The Philippines; freelance journalist, forum moderator The Philippines; polit. analyst San Juan & Assocs., Makati City, The Philippines; writer, mem. Philippine Coun. Fgn. Rels. Author: Marcos Legacy Revisited, Conspiracies, Controversies. Comdr. Philippine Coast Guard Aux. Mem. Rotary Internat. (dir., Paul Harris fellow), Jaycees Internat. (senator, Most Outstanding senator Asia Pacific, Kaohsiung, Taiwan, 1984, Most Outstanding senator of world, Cartagena, Colombia, 1985, Most Outstanding senator of Philippines, Cebu City), Am. C. of C. Roman Catholic. Avocations: reading, music, swimming, sports cars, motorcycles. Fax: (632) 8170709. E-mail: culdesac@info.com.ph. Office: San Juan & Assocs, Rm 1402, PDCP Bank Ctr Pas de Roxas, Makati City The Philippines

SAN JUAN, LUIS, geotechnical engineer; b. Santa Clara, Cuba, Feb. 29, 1956; s. Luis and Odelta (Suárez) San Juan; m. Elcira Sanchez, Mar. 10, 1980 (div. Nov. 1987); 1 child, Luis O.; m. Maria de Lourdes Galan, Jan. 1, 1988; 1 child, Javier. BS, Tony Stgo Jr. Coll., Villa Clara, Cuba, 1975; degree in geology and geophys. engrng., U. Bucharest, Romania, 1981. Geologist, engr. Power Projects Enterprise, Havana, 1981-82; sr. geologist Energoproyecto, Havana, 1982-87, sr. geotech. engr., 1987-90; prin. rschr. hydropower plants INEL, Havana, 1990—; prin. geologist specialist Energoproyecto, 1988-93, cons. geotech. engr., 1985-88. Co-author computer program, 1984 (High Achievement award 1984). Mem. Geol. Soc. Cuba, Nat. Union Constrn. Architects and Engrs. Avocation: fishing. Home: G St No 460-2th, 10400 Havana Cuba Office: INEL, 23 St No 105 E/OYP, 10400 Havana Cuba

SANKAR, MADHU NAINAR, surgeon; b. Viravanallur, Chennai, India, Mar. 8, 1960; s. B. Nainar and N. Rajammal; m. Jeyanthi Kamala Navaneetha Krishnan, Nov. 17, 1989. MB, BChir, Tirunelveli Med. Coll., India, 1984, MS, 1987; PhD, Nat. Rsch. Ctr. Surgery, Moscow, 1990. Diplomate Nat. Bd. Cardiothoracic Surgery. Rsch. fellow Nat. Rsch. Ctr. Surgery, Moscow, 1988-91; staff surgeon Madras Med. Mission, Chennai, 1992-95, cons., 1998—; clin. fellow St. Vincent's Hosp., Sydney, Australia, 1996, Westmead (Australia) Hosp., 1997; cons. in field. Co-author: Recent Advances in Cardiac Surgery, 1999; contbr. articles to profl. jours. Mem. Assn. Thoracic and Cardiovascular Surgeons India (life), Cardiological Soc. India (life). Hindu. Avocations: collecting stamps, reading, cricket. Home: 18-19, Sairam Street Mogappair, 600 058 Chennai India Office: Inst Cardiovascular Disease, 4 A Mogappair E, 600050 Chennai India

SANKARAN, THENEZHI MANAKKAL, science educator; b. Palakkad, Kerala, India; s. Sankaran Thenezhi Manakkal and Devaki Thenzhi Manakkal Nambudiripad; m. Naduvath Manakkal Rukmini, Sept. 2, 1972; children: Pramod Thenezhi, Sumod Thenezhi. BS, St. Thomas' Coll., Trichur, India, 1964; MS, Kerala U., 1966, cert., 1967. Rsch. asst. dept. marine scis. Cochin (India) U., 1970-75, lectr. dept. marine scis., 1975-81; assoc. prof. fisheries Kerala Agrl. U., Cochin, 1981—, head dept. mgmt. studies fisheries faculty, 1981—, prof. academic matters fisheries faculty, 1996—; network adminstr. Coll. Fisheries, 1998—, officer, assoc. patron Students' Union, 1993-96; lead expert, tng. coord. Fisheries Sector, 1999—; program officer Nat. Svc. Scheme, 1981-92. Author practical manual, 1999; editor: Souvenir, 1979; contbr. over 30 articles to profl. jours. Planning expert com. Ernakulam Dist. Panchayat, Cochin Corp., 1999; mem. Cochin U. Senate, 1980-81; acad. coun. Kerala Agri U.; pres. Changmpuzha Meml. Libr., Edappally, Cochin, 1998—; active Kerala Sastra Sahitya Parishat, Cochin, 1979—. Mem. Indian Statistical Assn., Soc. Fishery Technologists, Network of Tropical Fishery and Aquaculture Profls., Changampuzha Arts Club, Changampuzha Cult. Ctr. Hindu. Avocations: reading, cultural activities, TV.

SANKARANKUTTY, CHERUPARAMBIL, marine biology educator; b. Irinjalakuda, India, Jan. 31, 1937; arrived in Brazil, 1977; s. Kerala Varma Kunjunny Thampuran and Cheruparambil Gourikutty Amma; m. Manavazhi Meenambika, May 25, 1965 (dec. Oct. 1984); children: Ajith, Shobha; m. Sarada Ayyappath, Dec. 18, 1986. BSc, Maharajas Coll., 1956; MSc, Birla Coll. of Sci., 1958; PhD, Rajasthan U., 1964. Rsch. asst. Fisheries Inst., India, 1958-62; sr. scientific fellow Nat. Inst. Oceanography, India, 1962-66, scientist, 1967-70; assoc. prof. U. Dares Salaam, Tanzania, 1970-77; prof. Fed. U., Brazil, 1977—; cons. UNESCO, Paris, 1980; vis. prof. U. Liverpool, 1992, Smithsonian Inst., Washington, 1996, Pukyong Nat. U., 1998. Contbr. articles to profl. jours. Fellow Marine Biol. Assn. of India. Avocations: photography, snorkelling, table tennis, tennis. Home: Av Juvenal Lamartine, 978/303D, 59022020 Natal Brazil Office: Dept Oceanografia/Limnolog, Praia de Mae Luiza, 59014100 Natal Brazil

SANKI, SOHEIR, physician, surgeon; b. Khartoum, Sudan, Feb. 14, 1946; arrived in Australia, 1971; d. Joseph and Josephine Kahwati; m. Antoine Joseph Sanki, Sept. 7, 1969; children: Joseph, Amira. MB BS, Kitchener U., Khartoum, 1969. Intern Khartoum Hosp., 1969, West Middlesex Hosp., London, 1970; house officer St. James Hosp., Leeds, Eng., 1970; gen. practitioner Sydney, Austrlaia, 1971—; cons. Medisan Pty. Ltd., Sydney, 1981—; chair governing body Boulevarde Day Surg. Ctr., Sydney, 1993—. Recipinet Kitchener prize for medicine and surgery Khartoum U., 1969, prize of obgyn., 1969, prize of medicine, 1969, prize of physiology, 1966, others. Mem. Royal Coll. Surgeons London (lic.). Roman Catholic. Avocations: reading, watching cricket. Office: 200 The Boulevarde, Fairfield Heights, 2165 Sydney Australia

SAN LORENZO, CARMEN NERI, college dean; b. Bugo, Cagayan de Oro City, Misamis Oriental, The Philippines, July 16, 1928; d. Carmelino V. and Basilia F. (Velez) Neri; m. Ramon Solon San Lorenzo, Dec. 29, 1955; children: Ruben Carmel, Rene Ramon. BSN, Manila Ctrl. U., Caloocan City, Metro Manila, Philippines, 1952, postgrad., 1957; postgrad., Philippine Women's U., Metro Manila, Philippines, 1956; BS in Edn., Southwestern U., Cebu City, Philippines, 1962, MA in Edn., 1972, EdD, 1986. RN; registered midwife. Classroom tchr. Bur. Pub. Sch., Misamis Oriental, The Philippines, 1946-47; staff nurse Sacred Heart Hosp., Cebu City, The Philippines, 1952-53, head nurse, 1953-56; asst. prin., clin. instr. Coll. Nursing, Southwestern U., Cebu City, 1956-57; prin. Sch. Nursing, Southwestern U., Cebu City, 1957-63; dir. nursing Coll. Nursing, Southwestern U., Cebu City, 1963-71, dean, 1971-89, 91—; chmn. fin. com. Southwestern U., Cebu City, 1960-78, chmn. exec. com., 1983-85, chmn., 1985-87, dean of women, 1987-89, 91—. Organizer Cmty. Health Ctr. Southwestern U. Neighborhood, 1977; organizer/coord. Cmty. Health Ctr. Constrn., Lorega-San Miguel, Cebu City, 1985; treas. Barangay, Lorega-San Miguel, Cebu City, 1989-92; facilitator Cmty. Extension Devel. Program, Durano Found. Home for Elderly and Orphans, Danao City, 1991—. Mem. Philippine Nurse's Assn. (life), Integrated Registered Nurses of the Philippines, Assn. Deans Philippine, Colls. Nursing, Philippine Accrediting Assn. Schs., Colls. and Univs., Cebu Cmty. Health League Student Affiliates, Southwestern U. Alumni Assn. (treas. 1986-91, trustee 1992-99), Southwestern U. Faculty Club (treas. 1958-62). Avocations: letter writing, organizing, crocheting, collecting miniatures, gardening. Office: Southwestern U Coll Nursing, Villa Aznar Rd, 6000 Cebu City Cebu, Philippines

SAN MIGUEL, MANUEL, painter, historian, composer, poet; b. Guayama, P.R., Sept. 29, 1930; s. Manuel and Luisa (Griffo) San M.; m. Sandra Bonilla, July 12, 1969; children: Manuel, Ana. Student, U. P.R., 1947-51, U. Pa., 1966-68, Arts Students League, N.Y.C., 1968-69. Historian San Juan Nat. Historic Site, Nat. Park Svc., 1953-63; exec. sec. Acad. Arts and Scis., San Juan, 1963-64; founder of mus. and study collection El Morro Castle San Juan Nat. Hist. Site; painter, writer, musician, 1964—; cons. in field. Exhibited in U. P.R., 1958, 62, Ateneo de P.R., 1962, Pan-Am. Union, Washington, 1963, Bienal Mex., 1972, Bienal Rio de Janeiro, 1976, Orange County Schs. Mus. Art, Orlando, Fla., 1992, Mus. Modern Art, Paris, 1994, Expo of the Americas, Orlando, 1996, 98 , Gakien Santiago, San /juan, P.R., 2000, and numerous other nat. and internat. exhbns.; contbr. monographs on historical work in San Juan Nat. Historic Site to U.S. Nat. Archives, Washington; contbr. poetry to anthologies including Anthology of Latin American Poets, vol. III, 1987; rec. artist popular music of P.R.; soloist U. P.R. choir, Carnegie Hall, N.Y.C., 1949. Capt. U.S. Army, 1951-53, Korea. Decorated Bronze Star with valor clasp and oak leaf cluster, Purple Heart, Combat Infantryman Badge, others; named One of Ten Outstanding Hispanic Men, Orlando, Fla., 1991; recipient Recognition award for contbns. to Hispanic Am. Culture, Govt. P.R., 1996, Hispanic Heritage Found.; Coqui de Oro award for contbns. to Puerto Rican arts Casa de P.R., Inc., 1999. Mem. AAAS, VFW (life), Disabled Am. Vets. (life), Am. Legion, Ateneo de P.R. (bd. govs. 1959-60), Am. Biog. Inst. (bd. advisors, life mem. bd. govs.), Am. Philatelic Soc. (postal commemorative soc.), Inst. P.R. Culture (cons.), P.R. Philatelic Assn. (charter), Internat. Platform Assn., Lions (Lion of Yr. 1962-63). Achievements include documentary research in the restoration of Castillo San Marcos, St. Augustine, Fla., Castillo San Felipe de Barajas, Colombia, South Am., and restoration of San Juan fortifications and city walls. Home: 1214 Howell Creek Dr Winter Spgs FL 32708-4516

SAN MIGUEL, SANDRA BONILLA, social worker; b. Santurce, P.R., May 23, 1944; d. Isidoro and Flora (Carrero) Bonilla; m. Manuel San Miguel, July 12, 1969. BA, St. Joseph's Coll., 1966; MS in Social Work, Columbia U., 1970. Cert. social work mgr., sch. social work specialist. Case worker Dept. Labor, Migration Divsn., N.Y.C., 1966-68; clin. social worker N.Y.C. Housing Authority, N.Y.C., 1968-69, Children's Aid Soc., N.Y.C., 1969-71; sr. social worker Traveler's Aid Soc., San Juan, P.R., 1971-74; coord., supr. Dept. Addiction Control Svcs., San Juan, P.R., 1974-77; substance abuse div. dir. Seminole County Mental Health Ctr., Altamonte Springs, Fla., 1978-81; cons. pvt. practice Hispanic Cons. Svcs., Winter Springs, Fla., 1982—; adj. prof. Seminole C.C., Lake Mary, Fla., 1986-90; sch. social worker I Seminole County Pub. Schs., Sanford, Fla., 1986-91, lead sch. social worker, 1991—; pres.'s minority adv. coun. U. Ctrl. Fla., 1982—, vice-chair, 1982-86, chair, 1986-90; bd. regents EEO adv. com. State U. Sys. Fla., 1985-89; bd. dirs. Seminole Cmty. Mental Health Ctr., 1986-94, 95—, v.p., 1988-90, pres., 1990-91; adv. bd. Nat. Devereaux Found. Ctrl. Fla., 1993-98, women's adv. bd. South Seminole Hosp., Fla., 1994-96; mem. multicultural cmty. adv. com. Seminole County Pub. Schs., 1993—; mem. Fla. Consortium on Tchr. Edn. for Am. Minorities, 1990-96; mem. local com. Hispanic Info. and Telecomms. Network, 1990; mem. Seminole County (Fla.) Juvenile Justice Coun., 1993—; mem. statewide student svcs. adv. com. Dept. Edn. Fla., 1993-96, student svcs. adv. group, 1996-97. Recipient Pres.'s Outstanding Svc. award UCF, 1991, Ponce de Leon Hispanic Cmty. award, 1992, Svc. Recognition Plaque Seminole Cmty. Mental Health Ctr., 1991, Oustanding Contribution to Student Svcs. Cert. Fla. Dept. Edn., 1995, Manuel Martinez award for Outstanding Contbns. to Puerto Rican Cmty. in Ctrl. Fla., La Casa de Puerto Rico, 1999; named Ednl. Support Ctr. Tchr. of Yr., Seminole County Pub. Schs., 1999. Mem. NASW (appt. nat. sch. social work credential com. 1996-99), Nat. Network Social Work Mgrs., Fla. Assn. Sch. Social Workers (co-founder minority caucus 1988, columnist quar. newsletter Minority Corner 1988-92, bd. dirs. 1989—, sec. 1990-92, v.p. 1992-93, pres. 1993-94, Leadership Plaque 1994, Adminstr. of Yr. 1999), Sch. Social Work Assn. Am. (founding mem.), Fla. Assn. Student Svcs. Adminstrs., Collegiate Social Workers P.R., Columbia U. Alumni Assn. (nat. bd. dirs. 1997—), St. Joseph's Coll. Alumni Assn. Office: Seminole County Pub Schs PO Box 195933 Winter Springs FL 32719-5933

SANNER, GEORGE BRADLEY, bank executive; b. Balt., Sept. 20, 1953; s. George E. and Marjorie (Hohman) S.; m. Ann Margaret Tehan, Aug. 31, 1991 (div.); children: Anne, Meredith, Kimberly. BA, U. Va., 1974; MBA, Loyola Coll., Balt., 1978. Asst. v.p. Union Trust Co., Balt., 1974-82; v.p. Am. Security Bank, Washington, 1982-86; sr. v.p. Bank of Md., Towson, 1986-87; mng. dir. Provident Bank of Md., Balt., 1987-94; sr. v.p. FCNB Bank, Frederick, Md., 1994-95; pres./CEO Regal Bancorp, Owings Mills, Md., 1995—; also bd. dirs.; bd. dirs. Mid Atlantic Bus. Fin. Co., Balt., 1988-95; pres., CEO Regal Bank and Trust, 1995—. Airman USAF, 1973-75. Mem. Alpha Sigma Nu. Republican. Methodist. Avocations: golf, tennis, amateur radio. Office: Regal Bancorp 10123 Reisterstown Rd Owings Mills MD 21117-3814

SANNER, GEORGE ELWOOD, electrical engineer; b. Rockwood, Pa., Aug. 30, 1929; s. Dennis Charles and Alverda (Growall) S.; m. Marjorie Mary Hohman, July 1, 1951; children: George Bradley, Marjorie Rosalie, Cathy Ann. BS, U. Pitts., 1951; postgrad., Johns Hopkins U., 1957-59; cert. network engr., Mercer U., 1999. Registered profl. engr., Md.; cert. cost acctg. mgmt.; Microsoft cert. profl. Supervisory engr. Westinghouse Electric Corp., Balt., 1952-58, chief scientist, cons. def. and space ctr., 1964-72; chief engr., program mgr. radio div. Bendix Corp., Balt., 1958-64; engrng. mgr. jet propulsion labs. Bendix Corp., Pasadena, Calif., 1980-81; pres., gen. mgr. Santron Corp., Balt., 1972-79; v.p. engrng. M-Tron Industries div. Curtiss Wright Corp., Yankton, S.D., 1979-80; sr. engrng. specialist engrng. ctr. Litton Data Systems, New Orleans, 1981-83; cons. engrng. mgmt. AIL div. Eaton Corp., Deer Park, N.Y., 1983-87; sr. prin. engr. Am. Electronics Labs, Inc., Lansdale, Pa., 1987-92; cons. Atlanta, 1992—; rep. People to People Tour, various countries, 1978. Patentee in field. Vestryman Immanuel Ch., Sparks-Glencoe, Md., 1969-70; trustee St. Paul's Sch. for Boys, Balt., 1965-67; mem. bishop's secretariat Diocese of L.I., Garden City, N.Y., 1985-87; mem. exec. com. Scriptural Coalition, Diocese of Phila., 1990-92; mem. Rep. Nat. Com., Rep. Presdl. Trust, Nat. Rep. Senatorial Com. A.K. Mellon Found. scholar, 1947-50, Carnegie Inst. Tech. scholar, 1947-51. Mem. IEEE (life), Quarter Century Wireless Assn., Knights of Columbus. Roman Catholic. Address: 2501 Hidden Hills Dr Marietta GA 30066-5241

SANNOM, JENS, military officer; b. Copenhagen, Oct. 2, 1946; s. Vilhelm Johannes Rasmussen and Hanne (Bröchner) S.; m. Jette Jensen, July 6, 1968 (div. May 1984); 1 child, Susanne; m. Anne Margrethe Ridderstrom Hansen, Aug. 4, 1984; 1 child, Nanett. MS in Mech. Engring.-Aeronautics, Danish Defence Acad., 1978. Cadet Royal Danish Air Force Officers Sch., 1967-70, 1st lt. SAM Group, 1970-73; 1st lt., capt. Defence Command, Denmark, 1973-74, capt., 1974-78; capt., maj. Royal Danish Air Material Command, 1978-86, lt. col. chief weapons divsn., 1986-89; lt. col. Aalborg Air Base, 1989-92, NATO Def. Coll., Rome, 1992, Tactical Air Command Denmark, 1992-93; comdr. SAM Group Royal Danish Air Force, 1993-94; col. ACOS Logistics & Infrastructure Defence Command Denmark, 1994-99; col. ops. divsn. Supreme Hqrs. Allied Powers Europe, Mons, Belgium, 1999-2000, brigadier gen. ACE Resources divsn., 2000—. Avocations: aviation, military operations. Home: 74 Circuit de la Clairiere, 7331 Baudour Hainaut, Belgium Office: Supreme Hqrs Allied Powers, B-7010 Mons Belgium

SANO, EDSON EYJI, geologist, researcher; b. Echapora, Brazil, Dec. 24, 1958; s. Toyokichi and Shizu Sano; m. Nilce Renno Ribeiro; children: Naiane, David, Willian. BS, U. São Paulo, Brazil, 1983; MSc, Inst. Nat. Pesquisas Espaciais, San Jose dos Campos, Brazil, 1987; PhD, U. Ariz., 1997. Cert. in geology. Geologist Companhia Baiana de Pesquisa, Salvador, Brazil, 1986-87; cons. Sudam, Belem, Brazil, 1987-89; rschr. Embrapa, Planaltina, Brazil, 1989—. Editor: (book) GIS: Agricultural Applications, 1998; contbr. articles to profl. jours. Recipient Creativity award Rsch. Project, 1999. Mem. IEEE, RSSJ, CRSS. Home: QD 16 CJ H Casa 15, 73050160 Sobradinho Brazil Office: Embrapa Cerrados, Br-020 KM 18 CX Post 08223, 73301970 Planaltina DF, Brazil

SANO, MASAHITO, polymer physicist; b. Hikami, Hyogo, Japan, Jan. 18, 1958; s. Yaichiro and Sazako (Usui) S.; m. Reiko Nakashima, June 23, 1990; children: Chiyory, Emmry, Manary. BS in Physics, Fort Hays State U., 1981, BS in Chemistry, 1981, BS in Math., 1981; PhD in Physics, U. Wis., 1987. Postdoctoral Max Planck Inst. for Polymer Rsch., Germany, 1987-88; rschr. Japan Sci. and Tech. Corp., 1988-92, group leader, 1992—. Author: (with others) STM and AFM of Organic Molecules, 1993; contbr. articles to

profl. jours. Avocations: wine, biking. Office: Chemotransfiguration Proj, 2432 Aikawa, Kurume 839-0861, Japan

SANOU, BAWORO SEYDOU, minister of primary education of Burkina Faso; b. Kouka, Kossi, 1950; married; 3 children. Student, U. Ouagadougou, U. Caen Bishop, France. Prof. history, geography, 1976; high commissary Sourou Province, 1983-86; gen. sec. Min. Nat. Edn., 1986-87; provost marien N'Goumbi Lycee, 1989-91; dir. secondary edn., 1991-92; parliamentary People's Assembly, 1992-95; min. basic edn., mass literacy Govt. of Burkina Faso, 1995—. Office: Min Basic Edn & Mass Litera, 03 BP 7032, Ouagadougou 03, Burkina Faso*

SANSEVERINO, RAYMOND ANTHONY, lawyer; b. Bklyn., Feb. 16, 1947; s. Raphael and Alice Ann (Camerano) S.; m. Karen Marie Mooney, Aug. 24, 1968 (dec. 1980); children: Deirdre Ann, Stacy Lee; m. Victoria Vent, June 6, 1982 (div. 1995). AB in English Lit., Franklin & Marshall Coll., 1968; JD cum laude, Fordham U., 1972. Bar: N.Y. 1973, U.S. Dist. Ct. (so. dist. and ea. dist.) N.Y. 1973, U.S. Ct. Appeals (2d cir.) 1974, U.S. Supreme Ct. 1986. Assoc. Rogers & Wells, N.Y.C., 1972-75, Corbin & Gordon, N.Y.C., 1975-77; ptnr. Corbin Silverman & Sanseverino LLP, N.Y.C., 1978—, mng. ptnr., 1985—. Contbr. articles to profl. jours.; articles editor Fordham Law Rev., 1971-72. Recipient West Pub. Co. prize, 1972. Mem. ABA, Assn. Bar City of N.Y., N.Y. State Bar Assn., Twin Oaks Swim and Tennis Club (bd. dirs. 1981—, pres. 1993—). Republican. Roman Catholic. Office: Corbin Silverman Et Al 805 3d Ave New York NY 10022-7513

SANTA, KAROLY, electrical engineer, researcher; b. Debrecen, Hungary, Apr. 1, 1971; s. Karoly Santa and Katalin Kiss. MSEE, Tech. U. Dresden, Germany, 1995; PhD in Computer Sci., U. Karlsruhe, Germany, 1998. Cert. in elec. engring. Trainee Miele & Cie., Guetersloh, Germany, 1993, Siemens AG, Karlsruhe, 1994, Audi AG, Ingolstadt, Germany, 1994-95; rschr., project mgr. U. Karlsruhe, 1996-98, asst. prof., 1998—. Author: (book) Intelligent Control of Microrobots in a Micromanipulation-Station, 1998 (Klaus-Tschira prize 1999); contbr. articles to profl. jours. Avocations: badminton, swimming, dancing, biking. Fax: 49 89 244317251. E-mail: ksanta@gmx.de. Office: EnBW Energie Baden-Wuerttem, Durlacher Allee 93/Info Dpt, 76131 Karlsruhe Germany

SANTAELLA, JUAN, banker, investment advisor; b. Caracas, Venezuela, Jan. 2, 1945; came to U.S., 1993; s. Hector Santaella and Margarita Telleria; m. Alicia Zamora de Santaella, Sept. 16, 1967; children: Hector, Juan B., Maria Antonia. Degree in econs., Cath. U. Andres Bello, Caracas, 1967. Gen. mgr. Metalanca, Caracas, 1968-83; v.p. S.F. Atlantica, Caracas, 1977-80; pres., CEO Corpofin, Caracas, 1983-94, Bancor, Caracas, 1985-94; pres. Valcorp Securities, Miami, 1995—; chmn. bd. Ea. Nat. Bank, Miami, 1983-99; dir. Fedecamaras, Caracas, 1989-93, Venezuelan Banking Coun., Caracas, 1990-92; chmn. bd. dirs. Haverfield Corp., Gettysburg, Pa., 1998—; pres. Intercapital Holdings, Miami, 1999—; dir. R2 Internet Ventures, Miami, 1999—. Treas. Mus. Am. Found., Washington, 1999. Mem. Venezuelan Banking Assn. (v.p. 1992-94), Key Biscayne (Fla.) Yacht Club, Riviera Country Club. Roman Catholic. Avocations: jogging, golf, skiing. Office: Valcorp Securities 848 Brickell Ave Ste 601 Miami FL 33131-2915

SANTAMARIA CARRASCO, ALINA FABIOLA, international relations and economics educator; b. Córdoba, Argentina, Oct. 6, 1970; d. Luis Santos and Olga Mercedes Santamaria Martinez. BA in Internat. Rels., Cath. U. Cordoba, 1994; postgrad., Nat. U. Cordoba, 1996-98. English translator Peace Ctr., Cordoba, 1992—; English tchr., sec. Beverly Hills English Sch. and Ctr., Cordoba, 1994; asst. prof. internat. politics Cath. U. Cordoba, 1995-98; English tchr. Superior Langs. Inst., 1996, Maternity Hosp., 1996—, Padre Claret Sch., Cordoba, 1998—; internat. rels., econs., ethics, mgmt., fgn. trade tchr. St. Patrick's Sch., 1997—; Italian translator Radio Maria, Cordoba, 1997—; libr. Dante Alighieri Assn., Cordoba, 1997—; fgn. trade cons. Luis Santos Santamaria, Cordoba, 1995; internat. rels. cons. St. Patrick's Sch., 1997—. Author: The Falklands War, 1990, Public Sector in Argentina, 1991, International Action for Croatia's Recognition, 1994, The Balkans War, 1995, The Gulf War, 1995, The Unemployment Problem in Argentina: Causes Effects and Possible Solutions, 1995, Yugoslavia and Nationalism, 1996, Mercosur-European Union Framework Treaty, 1997, Globalization and its Implications, 1998; co-author: Argentinian Diplomatic History, 1992, The Latin American Debt Problem, 1998. Roman Catholic. Avocations: writing, ice skating, friends, travel, motorbikes. Home: Jose Verdaguer 4687, Barrio Alejandro Centeno, 5009 Cordoba Argentina Office: Avenida Valparaiso 4140, Barrio Jardin Hipódromo, 5016 Cordoba Argentina

SANTAMARTA, DAVID, neurosurgeon; b. Leon, Spain, Nov. 2, 1964; s. Genaro and Emilia (Gómez) S.; m. Teresa Ek, May 22, 1999; 1 child, Gustavo. Degree in medicine, U. Salamanca, Spain, 1989. Resident Hosp. Clinic, Barcelona, Spain, 1991-95; cons. neurosurgeon Hosp. del Rio Hortega, Valladolid, Spain, 1996-98, Hosp. Virgen de la Vega, Salamanca, Spain, 1998—. Mem. Soc. Española Neurosurgery, Soc. Castellano-Leonesa de Neurosurgery (sec. 1999—). Avocations: mountain hiking, photography. E-mail: tumbado@nexo.es. Office: Hosp Virgen de la Vega, Paseo de San Vicente 58-182, 37007 Salamanca Spain

SANTANDER, DANNY R., marketing and sales executive, consultant; b. Quito, Ecuador; s. Jorge T. Santander and Fanny M. Cedeno; m. Maria Jose Alvarez, Aug. 1994. BS, Phila. U., 1992. Adminstrv. mgr. Confecciones Linda Cia. Ltd., Quito, 1992-95, pres., 1995-97; export mktg. and sales cons. Dakini Clothing Co., Avon, Mass., 1997-98; project leader Gamanet DSCS Corp./Malden Mills Industries, Inc., Lawrence, Mass., 1998—, L.Am. sales and mktg. mgr., 1998—; bd. dirs. Centro Educativo Isaac Newton, Quito, Confecciones Linda. Founder, pres. Textile World Network, 1991. Named All-Am. scholar U.S. Achievement Acad., 1992. Avocations: languages, reading, sailing, outdoors. Fax: 978-659-5506. E-mail: santander@mediaone.net. Office: DSCS Corp/Malden Mills Industries 550 Broadway Lawrence MA 01841-2446

SANTANERA, LAURA, marketing professional, researcher; b. Turin, Italy, Aug. 3, 1971; d. Marcello S. and Scolastica Fiora. Econs., Faculty Econs., Turin, 1995. Mktg. tutor mktg. dept. Faculty Econs., Turin, 1993-95, mktg. researcher econs. and directions for enterprises dept., 1995-97; comm. and product mktg. mgr. Juvenilia Spa, Turin, 1996-99; fashion buyer La Rinascente SPA, Milan, 1999—; freelance researcher fashion sys. Author: Competition in Fashion Styling, 1999. Mem. comm. and mktg. clubs. Avocations: fashion designing, writing. Home: Via Boston 26, 10137 Turin Italy Office: La Rinascente, Strada 8 Palazzo N, 20089 Rozzano Milanofiori Italy

SANTANGELO, MARIO VINCENT, dentist; b. Youngstown, Ohio, Oct. 5, 1931; s. Anthony and Maria (Zarlenga) S.; student U. Pitts., 1949-51; D.D.S., Loyola U. (Chgo.), 1955, M.S., 1960. Instr. Loyola U., Chgo., 1957-60, asst. prof., 1960-66, chmn. dpt. radiology, 1962-70, dir. dental aux. utilization program, 1963-70, assoc. prof., 1966-70, chmn. dept. oral diagnosis, 1967-70, asst. dean, 1969-70; practice dentistry, Chgo., 1960-70; cons. Cert. Bd. Am. Dental Assts. Assn., 1967-76, VA Research Hosp., 1969-75, Chgo. Civil Service Commn., 1967-75; counselor Chgo. Dental Assts. Assn., 1966-69; mem. dental student tng. adv. com. Div. Dental Health USPHS, Dept. Health, Edn. and Welfare, 1969-71; cons. dental edn. rev. com. NIH, 1971-72; cons. USPHS, HEW, Region IV, Atlanta, 1973-76, Region V, Chgo., 1973-77; mem. Commn. on Dental Edn. and Practice, Fedn. Dentaire Internationale, 1984-92. Bd. visitors Sch. Dental Medicine, Washington U., St. Louis, 1974-76. Served to capt. USAF, 1955-57. Recipient Dr. Harry Strusser Meml. award NYU Coll. Dentistry, 1985. Fellow Am. Coll. Dentists; mem. AMA (mem. edn. work group 1982-86), Assembly Specialized Accrediting Bodies (council on postsecondary accreditation 1981-92, award of Merit 1992), Am. Assn. Dental Schs., Odontographic Soc. Chgo. (life), Am. (asst. sec. council dental edn. 1971-81, acting sec. 1981-82, sec. 1982-90, dir., 1990-92, asst. sec. commn. on dental accreditation 1975-81, acting sec. 1981-82, sec. 1982-90, dir., 1990-92, acting sec. commn. on continuing dental edn. 1981-82, sec. 1982-85), Ill., Chgo. Dental Assns. (life), Am. Acad. Oral Pathology, Am. Acad. Dental Radiology, Canadian Dental Assn. (commission on dental accreditation award of merit 1992), Am. Acad. Oral Medicine, Am. Assn. Dental Examiners (hon. 1993), Omicron Kappa Upsilon (pres. 1967-68), Blue Key, Xi Psi Phi. Contbr. articles to profl. jours. Home: 1440 N Lake Shore Dr Chicago IL 60610-1626

SANT'ANNA, ADONAI SCHLUP, physicist, mathematician, educator; b. Sao Paulo, Brazil, Sept. 2, 1964; s. Jose and Margot (Schlup) Sant'A.; m. Vilma Ana Damborowiski, Dec. 19, 1987; 1 child, Adonai. BS, Fed. U. at Parana, 1986, MS, 1989; PhD with honors, U. Sao Paulo, 1994. Postdoctoral fellow Stanford (Calif.) U., 1995-96; prof. Fed. U. at Parana, Curitiba, Brazil, 1990—; dir. Math. Soc. of Parana, 1986-87. Asst. editor: Boletim da Soc. Paranaense de Matematica, 1996-99, Math. Revs., 1998—; contbr. articles to profl. jours. Rsch. grante CAPES, Brazil, 1987, 91, CNPq, Brazil, 1995. Mem. Am. Math. Soc., Mat. Soc. Parana. Avocation: photography.

SANTA REGINA, RODRÍGUEZ IGNACIO, ecologist, researcher; b. Doñinos de Salamanca, Spain, June 20, 1953; s. Sáuches Hermógenes Santa Regina and María Rodríguez Gonzáles; m. Carmen Lorenzo Martín. Degree in biology, U. Salamanca, Spain, 1982, degree in sci., 1984, D Biology, 1987. Rschr. CSIC, Madrid, 1990—. Home: Adva Italia 14-20, 37006 Salamanca Spain Office: IRNA/CSIC, Cordel de Merinas 40, 37071 Salamanca Spain

SANTARINA, ROSITA BORJA, pediatrician; b. Cabiao, The Philippines, Sept. 4, 1928; d. D. Silvestre Matias Borja and Luis Consolacion Ortiz; m. Lorenzo De Guzman Borja Santarina, Dec. 5, 1959; 5 children. MD, U. St. Tomas, The Philippines, 1953. Diplomate Am. Bd. Pediats. Attending pediatrician Nieckja Dr. Hosp. Fellow Philippine Pediat. Soc. (pres. Cen. Iozon chpt. 1980); mem. Philippine Med. Assn., Soroptomist Club (pres. 1983), Inner Wheel Club (pres. 1982). Home: Maharlika Hwy, Cabanatuan City 4630889, The Philippines

SANTELMO, NICOLA, surgeon; b. Forlì, Italy, June 5, 1960; parents Guido Santelmo and Matilde Savini; m. Sandrine Hirschi, May 29, 1999; children: Luca, Juliette. Grad., U. Bologna, Italy, 1985, U. Modena, Italy, 1990. Asst. dept. thoracic surgery Hosp. Maggiore C.A. Pizzardi, Bologna, 1989-93; clin. fellow dept. thoracic surgery Ctr. Chirurgical Marie Lannelongue, Paris, 1994; thoracic surgery post resident U. Paris XIII, 1995-97; thoracic surgeon Avignon Hosp., France, 1997—. Mem. French Soc. Thoracic and Cardiovascular Surgery, French Thoracic Surgeons Bd. Avocations: photography, mountain biking. Fax: 33 4 90802383. E-mail: nicola.santelmo@waika9.com. Home: 11 rue de la republique, Villeneuve Avignon 30400, France Office: Ctr Hosp Avignon, 305 rue Raoul Follereau, Avignon 84902, France

SANTHANNAM, M.S., computer operator; b. Kabistalam, Tamilnadu, India, Aug. 3, 1950; s. P. Swaminathan and S. Seethalaxmi; m. S. Meera, Mar. 19, 1979; 1 child, Naveen. BSc, Vijayanagar Coll., Hospet, India, 1969; CAIBB, I.I.B., bombay, 1982; JD, Delta Inst., New Delhi, 1987; BDL, La Salle U., 1989. Clk. typist T.S.P. Ltd., T.B. Dam, India, 1969, SJS Mills, India, 1970-74; computer operator State Bank of India, CIT, Nagar, 1974—; founder, owner Reading Cir. for Children; cons. in field; C/T SBI, Hospet, 1974, inspection asst., Bombay, 1979, Madras, 1980; C/T LHO, Madras, 1982; computer operator CIT Nagar, 1999; cons. World Book Inc., Chgo. Recipient Breakfast of Champions award, 1991, Cir. of Excellence award, 1994. Avocations: reading, teaching, demonstrating, music, consulting. Home: Rams Flat No 8 I Floor, # 4 Railway Border Rd, 3720957 Kodambakkam Chennai India

SANTIAGO-FANDIÑIO, VICENTE, waste management administrator; b. Mexico City, Nov. 5, 1951; s. Federico Santiago-Escobar and Ofelia Fandiñio-Fernandez. BSc in Biology, U. Nat. Autonoma Mexico, Mexico City, 1977; MSc in Marine Biology, U. Coll. North Wales, U.K., 1979; PhD in Environ. Chem. Engring., U. Exeter, U.K., 1989. Lectr. U. Autonoma Metropolitana, Mexico City, 1977-85; dep. coord. Environ. Tng. Network Latin Am. and the Caribbean UN Environment Program, Mexico City, 1987-91; regional coord. integrated planning and instnl. devel. UN Environment Program, Caribbean Environment Programme, Kingston, Jamaica, 1991-96; project mgr. UN Environment Program, Internat. Environ. Tech. Ctr., Kusatsu, Shiga, Japan, 1996—; freshwater mgmt. and ICZM cons. Petroleos Mexicanos, Mexico City; invited curator Museo de Historia Natural de la Ciudad de Mexico, Mexico City. Mem. AAAS, Am. Mus. Natural History, N.Y. Acad. Scis., Colegio de Biologos de Mexico, Mexican Soc. Natural History. Roman Catholic. Avocations: photography, diving, mountaineering. E-mail: vstiago@unep.or.jp. Fax: (81-77) 568-4587. Home: 1091 Oroshimo-cho, Kusatsu Shiga 525-0001, Japan Office: UNEP-IETC, 1091 Oroshiomo cho, Kusatsu Shiga 525-0001, Japan

SANTIC, ANTE, electrical engineering educator; b. Novi Sad, Yugoslavia, Nov. 12, 1928; s. Spiro and Anna (Pavkovic) S.; m. Nada Saks, Mar. 14, 1953; 1 child, Anna. DiplIng, U. Zagreb, Croatia, 1953, DrSc, 1966. Rschr. Inst. of Electricity, Zagreb, 1954-59, head electronic lab., 1959-69; assoc. prof. Faculty Elec. Engring. U. Zagreb, 1969-75, prof., 1975-99, prof. emeritus, 1999—, vice dean Faculty of Elec. Engring., 1976-78, dean Faculty of Elec. Engring., 1978-80; Fulbright fellow Case Western Res. U., Cleve., 1975-76, vis. prof., 1982-84. Author: Electronic Instrumentation, 1982, 88, 93, Biomedical Electronics, 1995; editor: Biomedical Engineering Dictionary, 1986; holder 2 patents. Recipient Nikola Tesla award Republic of Croatia, 1980, Josip Loncar award Faculty Elec. Engring., 1986, award for Sci. Work, Croatian Acad. Sci., 1997, Decoration for Sci. Achievement, Pres. of Croatia, 1997. Mem. IEEE (sr.), IMEKO (TC-13 Com.), Croatian Med. and Biol. Engring. Soc. (pres.). Office: U Zagreb Elec Engring/Comp, Unska str 3, HR-10000 Zagreb Croatia

SANTILLI, NICHOLAS RICHARD, psychology educator; b. Cleve., Mar. 8, 1957; s. Richard William and Louise Mae S.; m. Sandra Lee Vanah, May 22, 1981; children: Carolyn Ann, Patrick Anthony. BA in Psychology, U. Toledo, 1979, MEd in Ednl. Psychology, 1982; PhD in Devel. Psychology, Cath. U. Am., 1986. Adj. prof. psychology Mt. Vernon Coll., Washington, 1984-86; vis. asst. prof. psychology Augustana Coll., Rock Island, Ill., 1986-87; vis. asst. prof. psychology John Carroll U., University Heights, Ohio, 1989-92, asst. prof. psychology, 1992-98; assoc. prof. John Carroll U., University Heights, 1998—, chair dept. psychology, 1995—. Editor: Social Cognition and Development in Youth: Structure and Content, 1982; contbr. articles to profl. jours. Trustee Willoughby-Eastlake Schs. Found., Ohio, 1997—; pres. bd. trustees Ravenwood Mental Health Ctr., Chardon, Ohio, 1991-93; pres. Thomas Jefferson Elem. Sch. PTO, Eastlake, 1996-98; counselor Youth Leaders Internat., Eastlake, 1997-2000; judge Northeastern Ohio Sci. and Engring. Fair, Cleve., 1994, 95, 97, 99. Grantee Ameritech Found., 1999; faculty fellow John Carroll U., 1999; recipient faculty devel. award Millersville U., Pa., 1987-88. Mem. APS, Jean Piaget Soc., Soc. for Rsch. in Child Devel., Soc. for Rsch. on Adolescence. Avocations: sports, coaching. Office: John Carroll U Dept Psychology University Heights OH

SANTINI, JEAN-JACQUES MARIE, banker; b. Boulogne, Billancourt, France, Nov. 8, 1957; s. Jacques and Colette (Breem) S.; m. Ferney Glize, June 18, 1993; children: Jean-Yves, Lauren. Grad., Inst. of Etudes Politques, Paris, 1978, Hautes Etudes Commerciales, Paris, 1980, Ecole Nat. Adminstrn., Paris, 1984; Maîtrise de Droit, U. Paris X, Paris, 1980, Lic. Sociology, 1981. Adminstr. civil Adjoint au Chef du Bureau Min. Finances, Paris, 1984-87, adminstr. civil, chef de Bureau, 1988; sous dir. Banque Nat. Paris, 1988-90, dir. adjoint, 1990-93; dir. gen. Banque Nat. Paris, Brussels, 1994-98; conseiller du Commerce Extérieur de la France, Belgium, 1994, Morocco, 1999; v.p. and treas. Chambre France de Commerce et d'Industrie, Belgium, 1994; v.p. de la sect. des Banques Etrngeres de l' Assn. Belge der Banques, 1994—; prof. Hautes Etudes Commls., 1991-94, 98—; dir. gen., bd. dirs. Banque Marocaine pour le Commerce et l'Industrie, BNP Group, Casablanca, 1998—; v.p. Conseiller du Commerce Exteriem de la France, Morocco, 2000. Author: Les Privatisations a L'Etranger, 1987, L'Economie Britannique: Le Choix Liberal, 1988, L'Economie Britannique: Le Liberalisme A L'Epreuve Des Faits, 1992. Lt. French Army, 1981. Mem. Cercle Royal Gaulois Artistique and Littéraire, Chambre France de Commerce et d'Industrie. Avocations: skiing, tennis, voile. Office: Banque Nat de Paris, MBCI Boite Postale 13573, 26 Pl des Nations Unies, Casablanca Morocco

SANTONI, RONALD ERNEST, philosophy educator; b. Arvida, Que., Can., Dec. 19, 1931; s. Fred Albert and Phyllis (Tremaine) S.; m. Marguerite Ada Kiene, June 25, 1955; children: Christina, Marcia, Andrea, Juanita, Jonathan, Sondra. BA, Bishop's U., Lennoxville, Que., 1952; MA, Brown U., 1954; PhD, Boston U., 1961; postgrad., U. Paris-Sorbonne, 1956-57. Asst. prof. philosophy U. Pacific, Stockton, Calif., 1958-61; postdoctoral fellow Yale U., New Haven, 1961-62; asst. prof. philosophy Wabash Coll., Crawfordsville, Ind., 1962-64; mem. faculty Denison U., Granville, Ohio, 1964—; prof. philosophy Denison U., 1968—, chmn. dept., 1971-73, 82-84, 92, Maria Theresa Barney chair in philosophy, 1978—; Peace lectr. Bethel Coll., 1985; vis. scholar in philosophy Cambridge U., Eng., 1986, 90, 94, 97, 99, also vis. lectr. in philosophy, 1990; vis. fellow Clare Hall, Cambridge U., 1986; vis. fellow in philosophy Yale U., 1975, 81, 93-94, 97; keynote speaker 2d Internat. Conf. on Nuclear Free Zones, Cordoba, Spain, 1985; speaker World Cong. Philosophy, Montreal, Can., 1982, Brighton, U.K., 1988, Internat. Studies Assn., London, 1989, speaker and U.S.A. co-chair Internat. Conf. Internat. Philosophers for Prevention of Nuclear Omnicide, Moscow, 1990; speaker World Congress Universalism, Warsaw, Poland, 1993; del. and raporteur UN meeting of Peace Messenger Orgns., Dagomys, Sochi, USSR, 1991; invited plenary speaker 2d Internat. Cong. Violence and Co-existence, Montreal, Can., 1992; invited participant Colloquium on Technological Risks to Environment, Montreal, Can., 1993; participant, spkr. numerous profl. confs. Contbg. author: Current Philosophical Issues, 1966, Towards an Understanding and Prevention of Genocide, 1984, Nuclear War: Philosophical Perspectives, 1985, Encyclopedic Critical Bibliography of Genocide, 1988, Just War, Nonviolence and Nuclear Deterrence: Philosophers on War and Peace, 1992, The Institution of War, 1991, Violence and Human Co-Existence, 1994, Hiroshima's Shadows, 1998, The Encyclopedia of Genocide, 1999; author: Bad Faith, Good Faith and Authenticity in Sartre's Early Philosophy, 1995; editor, contbr. Religious Language and the Problem of Religious Knowledge, 1968; co-editor Social and Political Philosophy, 1963; contbg. editor Internet on the Holocaust and Genocide; contbr. over 125 articles and revs. to profl. jours., also to The Progressive, The Human Quest, Churchman; bd. editors Jour. Peace and Justice Studies. V.p. NAACP, Licking County, 1967; co-organizer Crawfordsville Human Rels. Coun., 1962-64; mem. nat. exec. com. Episcopal Peace Fellowship, 1968-78; mem. internat. coun. Internat. Inst. on the Holocaust and Genocide, 1985—; mem. nat. coun. Fellowship of Reconciliation, 1988-89; trustee Margaret Hall Sch., Versailles, Ky., 1972-74; nat. bd. dirs. Promoting Enduring Peace, 1982—. Canadian Govt. Overseas fellow Royal Soc. Can., 1956-57; Church Soc. for Coll. Work faculty fellow, 1961-62; Yale postdoctoral rsch. fellow, 1961-62; Soc. for Religion in Higher Edn. postdoctoral fellow, 1972—; Yale rsch. fellow, 1975; guest fellow Berkeley Coll., Yale U., 1975, 81, 93-94, 97, elected assoc. fellow, 1994—; vis. fellow in philosophy Yale U., 1981, 93-94, 97; Robert C. Good faculty fellow Denison U., 1985-86, 2000—, Robert C. Good Faculty Rsch. fellow, 1993-94; elected life mem. Clare Hall, Cambridge (Eng.) U., 1986; elected mem. High Table, King's Coll., Cambridge U., 1999; recipient Mellon award for disting. faculty Denison U., 1972, Crossed Keys Faculty of Yr. award Denison U., 1986-87. Mem. Am. Philos. Assn., Ch. Soc. for Coll. Work, Soc. for Phenomenology and Existential Philosophy, Internat. Philosophers for Prevention of Nuclear Omnicide (v.p. 1983-85, v.p. cen. div. 1990-91, internat. pres. 1991-96, internat. exec. com. 1996—), Sartre Soc. of N.Am. (exec. com. 1994—), Sartre Circle (coord. 1997—), le groupe d'Etudes Sartriennes, Gandhi-King Soc., Union of Bi-Nat. Profls. Against Omnicide (v.p. 1978—), Concerned Philosophers for Peace (founding 1980—, pres. 1996-97), Fellowship of Reconciliation. Episcopalian. Home: 500 Burg St Granville OH 43023-1005

SANTOPIETRO, ALBERT ROBERT, lawyer; b. Providence, R.I., Oct. 18, 1948; s. Alfred and Marie (Epifanio) S.; m. Linda Stuart, 1994; children: Hope, Spencer, Anna. BA, Brown U., 1969; JD, U. Va., 1972. Bar: R.I. 1973, Mass. 1997, U.S. Dist. Ct. R.I. 1973, Ill. 1974, Conn. 1983, Mass. 1997. Atty. Met. Life Ins. Co., Oak Brook, Ill., 1974-75, Seligman Group, N.Y.C., 1975-76; atty. Mut. Benefit Life Ins. Co., Newark, 1976-78, asst. counsel, 1978-81; atty. Aetna Life and Casualty, Hartford, Conn., 1981-82, counsel, 1982—; assoc. counsel Conn. Mut. Life Ins. Co., Hartford, 1991-95, counsel, 1995—; 2d v.p. & assoc. gen. coun. Mass Mutual. Home: 142 Pond Brook Rd Huntington MA 01050-9620 Office: Mass Mutual 1295 State St Springfield MA 01111-0002

SANTORO, CHARLES WILLIAM, investment banker; b. N.Y.C., Apr. 20, 1959; s. Dino and Dorice (Gillick) S.; m. Vanessa Lee Bishop; 1 child, Olivia Charlotte. BA in Econs., Columbia U., 1982; MBA, Harvard U., 1984. With Morgan Stanley & Co., N.Y.C., 1984-88; sr. v.p., coord. officer European mergers and acquisitions Morgan Stanley Internat., London, 1989-90; mng. dir., head cross border investment banking Smith Barney, Inc., N.Y.C., 1991-93, head investment banking new bus. group, 1993-95; mng. dir., head. indsl. corp. finance Paine Webber Inc., N.Y.C., 1995-96, vice chmn. investment banking, 1996-2000; co-founder, mng. ptner Sterling Investment Ptnrs. LP, Westport, Conn., 2000—; co-founder, mng. ptnr. Sterling Investment Advisors, 2000—; bd. dirs. Wilmar Industries, Inc. Recipient fellowship Harvard Bus. Sch., 1983. Mem. Harvard Club of N.Y., N.Y. Athletic Club, Columbia Coll. Alumni Assn. (co-chmn. class of '82 com. 1982—), Kings Crown Rowing Assn. (trustee). Republican. Roman Catholic. Home: 3 Alden Ter Greenwich CT 06831-4422 Office: 276 Post Rd W Westport CT 06880-4703

SANTORO, MARCO, bibliography educator, researcher; b. Naples, Italy, Oct. 15, 1949; s. Mario and Eva (Pacilio) S.; m. Giovanna Bottigliero, Feb. 23, 1973; children: Gabriella, Luca. PhD, U. Naples, 1971, 2d Doctorate, 1973; hon. degree, U. Rome, 1978. Asst. U. Naples, 1972-80, assoc. prof., 1980-86; prof. U. Rome, 1986—; v.p. coun. Istituto Rinascimento, Naples, 1997—; editor (dir.) Esperienze Letterarie, Naples, 1990—, Nuovi Annali SSAB, Florence, 1990—, Accademie e Bibliote che d'Italia, Rome, 1995—. Author: La Biblioteca Oratoriana di Napoli, 1979, La Stampa a Napoli sec 400, 1984, Il Libro a Stampa. I Primordi, 1990, Storia del Libro Italiano, 1995, Libri/quotidious, 1998. Mem. Accademia Pontenious, Inst. Nazionale Sul Rinascimento Meridionale, Rotary Internat., Consiglio Nat. Beni Culturali. Avocations: bridge, tennis, golf. Office: Scuola Spec Archivisti Bibl, U Rome, Via Vicenza 23, 00815 Rome Italy

SANTOS, ARA DE JESUS, retired mathematics educator; b. Ponce, P.R., June 2, 1925; s. Claudio and Maria (Hernandez) De J.; divorced; 1 child, Richard. BS, CCNY, 1961; MA in Sci., Hofstra U., 1963; postgrad., St. Johns U., 1964-65, Stony Brook U., 1983-84. Cert. tchr., N.Y. Instr. biology William Floyd High Sch., Mastic Beach, N.Y., 1966-68; instr. chemistry and physics Wyandanch (N.Y.) High Sch., 1968-71; instr. math Cen. Islip (N.Y.) High Sch., 1972-88; pres. Sci. Biblical Research Found., Inc., West Islip, N.Y., 1985—, also writer; advisor Math Club Cen. Islip High Sch., 1977-81; conducting sci. rsch. on Shroud of Turin. Chairperson Assn. for Advancement of Puerto Rican People, N.Y.C., 1968. Recipient citation Waldemar Med. Ctr., 1969; Dept. Mental Hygiene Cen. Islip State Hosp. grantee, 1963-66. Mem. Cen. Islip Tchrs. Assn. Avocations: building homes, art. Home and Office: 34 Mill Pond Ln East Moriches NY 11940-1222

SANTOS, FILIPE DUARTE, physics educator; b. Lisbon, Portugal, Mar. 15, 1942; s. António Duarte and Regina Duarte (Branco) S.; m. Maria Do Amparo Azambuja, Dec. 18, 1965; 1 child, Sofia Azambuja Duarte. BS in Geophysics, U. Lisbon, 1963; PhD in Nuclear Physics, U. London, 1968. Rsch. fellow Atomic Energy Lab., Sacavem, Portugal, 1968-74; asst. prof. U. Lisbon, 1972-74, assoc. prof., 1974-79, prof., 1979—; vis. prof. U. Wis., Madison, 1980-81, 86, 91, U. N.C., Chapel Hill, 1982-85, 89, 97, U. Surrey, Guildford, Eng., 1984, Ludwig Maxmillian U., Munchen, Fed. Republic Germany, 1992-95; dean faculty sci. U. Lisbon, 1992—; dep. dir. Nat. Meteorol. Inst., Lisbon, 1977-88; pres. CERN, Portugese Sci. Coun., Lisbon, 1990—, chmn. dept. physics, U. Lisbon, 1982-84, 90-91; v.p. Inst. Earth and Space Scis., Lisbon, 1996—; mem. Portuguest Nat. Coun. for the Environment and Sustainable Devel., 1998—; mem. Inter-Minieterial Commn. on Climate Change, 1998—. Author: (secondary sch. text) Fisica, 1978; editor Gazeta de Fisica, 1984—; contbr. numerous articles on nuclear physics, atmospheric scis. to profl. jours.; author 1st white paper on Environment of Portugal, 1991. Advisor to Portugese Govt. Sci. Program, Lisbon, 1989, 91. Recipient Infante D. Henrique award, Lisbon, 1963; scholarships Gulbenkian Found., Lisbon, 1989, '91. Mem. Lisbon Acad. Scis., Portuguese Physical Soc. (sec. gen. 1984-90, founding mem.), European Physical Soc. (coun. 1988-90), N.Y. Acad. Scis., Am. Physical Soc., Portuguese Nat. Coun.

Environment and Sustainable Devel., Interministerial Commn. on Climate Change. Avocations: painting, drawing (4 one-man exhibits), opera, classical music, swimming. Office: U Lisbon Ctr Fisica Nuclear, Ave Gama Pinto 2, 1649-003 Lisbon Portugal

SANTOS, GABRIEL DEL PRADO, JR., geochemist; b. Manila, Jan. 22, 1937; s. Gabriel Castillo Sr.and Severina (Del Prado) S.; m. Gesilinda Magno Visperas, Mar. 4, 1963; children: Conrado, Darwin, Lana, Giselle. BS in Chemistry, U. Philippines, 1959, BS in Geology, 1960; M Nat. Security Adminstrn., Nat. Def. Coll., 1988. Lic. geologist, chemist. Geologist Acoje Mining Co., Philippines, 1960-62; nuclear rsch. asst. Philippine AEC, 1963-64, scientist, 1964-74, assoc./technologist, 1975-79, supervising specialist, technologist, 1980-88; supervising rsch. specialist Philippine Nuclear Rsch. Inst., Quezon City, 1989—; cons. Philippine Iron Mines, Manila, 1972-75, PNOC-Exploration Devel. Corp., Manila, 1978-82, Ultrana Nuclear and Mineral Co., Manila, 1980-83, The Environergy Tech., Manila, 1994—. Contbr. chpts. to books. Fellow AAECP-CSIRO, Australia, 1985, Sci. and Tech. Agy., Japan, 1991. Mem. NRC Philippines (achievement award 1994), Nat. Com. on Geol. Scis., Geol. Soc. Philippines, Mapa High Alumni (Geochemistry award 1997), Radioisotope Soc. Philippines. Roman Catholic. Home: St Ignatius Village, 9 Astoria, Quezon City 1110, The Philippines Office: Philippine Nuclear Rsch Inst, Commonwealth Ave, Quezon City The Philippines

SANTOS, JUAN LUIS, pediatrician, immunology researcher; b. Melilla, Spain, Sept. 6, 1961; s. Juan S. and Maria del Carmen Perez; m. Celia Ruiz, Sept. 15, 1985; children: Paula, Daniel. Licentiate, U. Malaga, Spain, 1985; D, U. Granada, Spain, 1994, M Pedit. Endocrinology, 1998. MD. Resident in cmty. medicine Hosp. Univ., Sevilla, Spain, 1987-89; immunology rschr. Hosp. Univ., Granada, Spain, 1990-93, pediatrician, clin. rschr., 1994—; assoc. rschr., CICYT, 1993, DICICYT, 1994; headmaster Health Zone, 2000—. Author: Laboratorio y Atlas de Citologia, 1995, Current and Future Directions for Clinical Flow Cytometry, 1995, Manual del Residente de Pediatria, 1997; contbr. articles to med. jours. Recipient Extraordinary Doctorate award Granada U., 1997. Mem. Flow Cytometry Iberian Soc. (founder), Spanish Immunology Soc., Spanish Pediats. Soc. Avocations: music, sports. Home: Per Luis Seco de Lucena, 5.18014, Granada Spain Office: Hosp Clinico, Av Dr Oloriz, 18012 Granada Spain

SANTOS, RENATO DE LIMA, pathology educator; b. Franca, Brazil, Aug. 5, 1970; s. Sicio Silveira and Rute Ferreira Lima (Lima) S.; m. Denise Amantino de Magalhaes Lima, June 11, 1994; children: Renato, Leticia. DVM, Vet. Sch. Fed. U. Minas Gerais, Belo Horizonte, Brazil, 1993, MS, 1995. Substitute prof. Fed. U. Minas Gerais, Belo Horizonte, Brazil, 1995-96, asst. prof., 1996—. Author: Reproductive Pathology of Domestic Animals, 1997; contbr. articles to profl. jours. Office: Escola Vet UFMG, Av Antonio Carlos 6627, 31161970 Belo Horizonte Brazil

SANTOS OCAMPO, PERLA D., pediatrician, educator; b. Dagupan, Pangasinan, The Philippines, July 25, 1931; m. Carlomagno G. Santos Ocampo, Apr. 4, 1956; 3 children. MD, U. the Philippines. Chancellor, prof. dept. pediatrics U. The Philippines, Manila; staff, chief multidisciplinary child and adolescent unit Philippine Gen. Hosp., Manila, 1987—; cons. several med. ctrs. Hon. pres. Assn. Pediatric Socs. S.E. Asian Region, 1974—, Internat. Soc. Tropical Pediatrics, 1986—; pres., exec. com. Internat. Pediatric Assn., 1989-92; mem. expert adv. panel on maternal and child health WHO, mem. tech. adv. group. Recipient Sci. and Tech. award IBM-DOST, 1991, Outstanding Pediatrician of Asia award 6th Asian Congress of Pediatrics, Order of Christopher Columbus, Child Health Found. medal and prize WHO, Achiever's award Philippine Med. Women's Assn., Women of Distinction award Soroptimist Internat., Zonta Internat., Gavel Award of Distinction Philippine Med. Assn., Hon. Filipino award Jaycees, Singkod Bayan award Pres. of Republic of Philippines. Fellow Philippine Pediatric Soc. (Outstanding Pediatrician), Am. Acad. Pediatrics (hon.), Japan Pediatric Soc., Australian Coll. Pediatrics; mem. Nat. Acad. Sci. and Tech. (pres.), Internat. Pediat. Assn. (past pres. 1989-92), Diarrheal Disease Study Group (chmn.), Philippine Soc. Gastroenterology and Nutrition (founding pres.), Philippines Assn. for the Gifted (founding pres., nat. rsch. coun.), Assn. of TOWNS Awardees. Home: 8 Cleveland St, Greenhills San Juan 1502, The Philippines Office: Med Ctr Manila Ste 326, 1122 Gen Luna St Box EA 100, Ermita Manila, The Philippines*

SANTURIO, JANIO MORAIS, veterinary medicine educator, researcher; b. Uruguaiana, Rio Grande, Brazil, Sept. 20, 1953; s. Edmundo P. and Neuza M. (Morais) S.; m. Cléris F. Flores, Feb. 9, 1979; children: Deise F., Roberta F. Degree vet., U. Santa Maria, Brazil, 1976; degree mycologist, U. Rio de Janeiro, 1984. Rsch. jr. Hoechst, Brazil, 1976-77; prof. U. Santa Maria, 1978—; advisor Sadia, Chapeco, Brazil, 1990-97, Frangosul, Brazil, 1996-98, Nutron, Campinas, Brazil, 1998-99, Avipal, Porto Alegre, Brazil, 1999—. Author: (with others) Micotoxinas, 1996; contbr. articles to profl. publs.; patentee in field. Soldier Brasilian Army, 1972. Mem. Isham. Lutheran. Avocations: soccer, fishing, chess. Office: U Fed Santa Maria, DMVP-Campus, 97105900 Santa Maria Brazil

SANTURJIAN, OHANES HRANT, hydraulic engineering educator; b. Sofia, Bulgaria, Feb. 21, 1938; s. Hrant Ohanes and Iskuhi Hrant (Erganian) S.; m. Evelina Radeva Ninova, Nov. 2, 1962; 1 child, Edmond. Degree in hydraulic engring., Inst. Civil Engring., Sofia, 1962, PhD, 1974; DSc, Inst. Water Problems, Sofia, 1991. Engr. Vitcha Cascade, Bulgaria, 1962-66; rsch. assoc. Inst. Water Problems, 1966-84, assoc. prof. hydraulic engring., 1984-93, prof., 1993—; head sect. Inst. Water Problems, 1988-95, dir., 1995—; mem. Nat. Com. Large Dams, Nat. Com. Irrigation and Drainage. Coauthor: Numerical Methods for Stress and Strain Determination in Hydraulic Structures, 1981; also articles. Named to 3rd Order Ciril and Methodi, State Coun., 1988. Mem. Bulgarian Assn. Sci. and Technics. Avocation: gardening. Home: Graf Ignatiev Str # 23, 1000 Sofia Bulgaria Office: Inst Water Problems, Ac G Bontchev Str, Bl 1, 1113 Sofia Bulgaria

SANYAL, SUHAS CHANDRA, microbiologist, science educator, consultant; b. Mymensingh, Bengal, India, Jan. 1, 1942; s. Sudhir Chandraand Leelaboti (Bagchi) S.; m. Kalyani Chakrabarti, May 8, 1970; children: Rubella, Rupan. MBBS, NRS Med. Coll., Calcutta, 1966; PhD, Calcutta U., 1969; MD, Banaras Hindu U., Varanasi, India, 1974. Rsch. officer NICED, Calcutta, 1969-70; lectr. Inst. Med. Scis. Banaras Hindu U., 1970-73, reader Inst. Med. Scis., 1973-79, prof., head microbiology dept. Inst. Med. Scis., 1979-95; sr. internat. scientist ICDDR, Dhaka, Bangladesh, 1981-84; sr. cons. microbiologist, dir. labs. Ministry of Health, Safat, Kuwait, 1992—; advisor Indian Coun. Med. Rsch., New Delhi, 1978-92, Coun. Scientific and Indsl. Rsch., New Delhi, 1984-92, WHO, Geneva, Switzerland, 1984-85, Ministry of Health, Govt. of India, 1977-92, Dept. Biotech., Govt. of India, 1985-92; cons. ICDDR, 1985; mem. adv. bd. Internat. Diorrhoeal Disease Info. and Documentation Ctr., Internat. Devel. Ctr., Dhaka; editl. bd. Jour. Med. Microbiology, Revs. in Med. Microbiology, Jour. Diarrhoeal Diseases Rsch.; referee Indian Jour. Med. Rsch., Indian Jour. Microbiology, Indian Jour. Exptl. Biology, Indian Jour. Veterinary Scis. and WHO Bulletin. Contbr. 194 articles to profl. jours. Recipient Sakuntala-Amirchand award Indian Coun. Med. Rsch., 1970, Dr. S.C. Agarwal award Indian Assn. Med. Microbiologists, 1989, Ranbaxy Internat. Rsch. award in Med. Scis. Rambaxy Internat., Bombay, 1991, Dr. V.R. Khanolkar Oration award Nat. Acad. Med. Scis., 1992, Dr. Bashambarnath Chopra Oration award Indian Nat. Sci. Acad., 1992, Best Original Article award Jour. Kuwait Med. Assn., 1996. Fellow Royal Soc. Tropical Medicine and Hygiene, Nat. Acad. Med. Scis., Indian Nat. Sci. Acad., Internat. Acad. Med. Scis., Royal Coll. Pathologists, Indian Acad. Scis., N.Y. Acad. Scis.; mem. Internat. Soc. on Toxinology (pres. Asia-Pacific sect. 1990-93, sec. 1987-90), Assn. Microbiologists of India (pres. 1989-90), Internat. Com. on Systemic Bactieriology, Internat. Working Group on Vibrios (founding). Avocations: reading history, socio-political writings. Office: Ibn Sina Hosp, PO Box 25427, 13115 Safat Kuwait

SANYAL, UTPAL, scientist, medical researcher; b. Calcutta, W. Bengal, India, Dec. 2, 1950; s. Bimalendu and Papri (Bhaduri) S.; m. Indrani Roy, Jan. 27, 1980; 1 child, Ishita. BSc with hons., St. Xavier Coll., Calcutta, India, 1970; MSc, Calcutta U., 1972, PhD in Sci., 1978. Jr. sci. officer Chittaranjan Nat. Cancer Inst., Calcutta, India, 1978-86; sr. sci. officer II Chittaranjan Nat. Cancer Inst., Calcutta, 1986-92, sr. sci. officer I, 1992—; head dept. anticancer drug devel. and chemotherapy Chittaranjan Nat. Cancer Inst., 1989—. Editor (chemistry sect.) Viswakosh (Bengali ency.), 1978-95; contbr. numerous articles to peer-reviewed internat. profl. jours; inventor in synthetic organic chemistry, Indian patent pending, 1996. Named Nat. Sci. Talent Search fellow, Nat. Coun. Ednl. Rsch. and Tng., Govt. India, 1967-73, Rsch. fellow Coun. Sci. and Indsl. Rsch., Govt. India, 1974-78; recipient Internat. Cancer Tech. Transfer award, Internat. Union Against Cancer, Geneva, Switzerland, 1997. Mem. Assn. UICC Fellows (Switzerland), N.Y. Acad. Sci., Indian Chem. Soc. (life), Indian Sci. Congress Assn., Indian Assn. for Cultivation of Sci. Mem. Ramakrishna Mission. Avocations: matchbox label collector, philately, origami, numismatics. Fax: 91-33-4757606. Home: 106/B S Sinthi Rd, W Bengal Calcutta 700 030, India Office: Chittaranjan Nat Cancer Ins, 37 SP Mukherji Rd, Calcutta 700 026, India

SANZ, MOLINA ALFREDO, engineering educator, researcher; b. Zaragoza, Spain, May 10, 1964; s. Feliciano Sanz and Prudencia Molina; m. Carmen Alcaine; children: Jorge, Miguel. Degree in engring., U. Zaragoza, 1989, PhD in Indsl. Engring., 1994. Project engr. U. Zaragoza, 1988-91, assoc. prof. engring., 1991-96, prof., 1996-98; founder, mgr. R&D, Bioingenieria Aragonesa, Spain, 1990—; engr. ASHORED: TIDE project, 1991-92; engr., mgr. various projects, 1994—; engr. DICE:ESPIRIT project, 1997-98. Co-author: Fuzzy Hardware, 1997, Redes Neuronales y Sistemas borrosos, 1997. Office: U Zaragoza CPS Electronica, Maria de luna 3, 50015 Zaragoza ZAR, Spain

SANZ, PERE, medical educator; b. Barcelona, Catalonia, Spain, Feb. 8, 1955; s. Pedro Sanz and Maria Gallén; m. Olga Ribas, Dec. 13, 1985; children: Albert, Elena. Licenciate in medicine, U. Barcelona, 1981, specialist in occupl. medicine, 1986, MD, 1989. Asst. prof. U. Barcelona, 1984-92, prof. postgrad. studies dept. pub. health, 1988—, prof. postgrad. studies Sch. Occupl. Medicine, 1989—, assoc. prof., 1993—, prof. master occupl. health, 1996—; Mem. group experts Generalitat de Catalunya, Spain, 1990-92, Coll. of Physicians, Barcelona, 1991-96. Author: Clinical Toxicology, 1993, Antidotes, 1996; editor: Chromium: Clinical and Toxicological Aspects, 1992, Handbook of Occupational Health, 1995. Mem. AAAS, Spanish Soc. Toxicology, Assn. Occupl. Medicine Svcs. (dir. 1990-96), N.Y. Acad. Sci. Avocations: sports, philatelic, mycology.

SANZ-GUAJARDO, DAMASO, physician, educator; b. Ibdes, Zaragoza, Spain, May 20, 1944; s. Aurelio Sanz and Carmen Guajardo; m. Pilar Sarmiento, Jan. 30, 1971; children: Damaso, Pablo, Pilar. MD, U. Zaragoza, 1967, PhD in Medicine & Neurology, 1978. Intern, resident Puerta De hierrao U. Hosp., Madrid, 1968-71; assoc. head nephrology U. Hosp., Madrid, 1972-77, clin. head nephrology, 1977-87; prof. nephrology Autonoma U., Madrid, 1987—; adviser Nat. Health Svc., Madrid, 1987—, pharm. cos., Madrid, 1987—. Author: Glomerulonephritis, 1973, Plasma Exchange, 1980, Water for Haemodialysis, 1988, Lupus Nephritis: Nephrology, 1993, Kidney in Vasculitis: Internal Medicine, 1996; contbr. articles to profl. jours. V.p. Funvida (Quality of Life Renal Patient Found.), Madrid, 1997—. Mem. Spanish Soc. Nephrology (sec. 1987-93, pres. 1996—), European Renal Assn., European Dialysis Transplant Assn., Internat. Soc. Nephrology, Santa Fe Soc. Nephrology (hon.), Iberoam. Cmty. Nephrology (hon.), Dominican Soc. Nephrology (hon.). Avocations: writing, poetry. Office: Hosp U Puerta de Hierro, San Martin de Porres 4, 28035 Madrid Spain

SAPIN, CRAIG P., lawyer; b. L.A., Aug. 5, 1956; s. Sandy Sapin and Carol (Sapin) Gold; m. Carolyn Marie Clark, June 28, 1982; children: Stephanie, Patrick. BA in Econs., U. Calif., San Diego, 1978; JD, UCLA, 1981. Bar: Calif. 1981; cert. in taxation. From assoc. to ptnr. Procopio, Cory, Hargreaves & Savitch, San Diego, 1981—. Bd. dirs. Help Disabled War Vets., San Diego, 1995—. Mem. ABA, State Bar Calif., San Diego County Bar Assn. Office: Procopio Cory Hargreaves & Savitch LLP 530 B St Ste 2100 San Diego CA 92101-4496

SAPLIN, LEONID ALEXEEVITCH, academic administrator; b. Ailino, Chelyabinsk, USSR, June 22, 1949; s. Alexei Nazarovich and Alexandra Alexeevna (Lisitsina) S.; m. Lidia Nikolaevna Novikova, Nov. 5, 1967; children: Andrey Leonidovitch, Inna Leonidovna. Elec. engr., Inst. Mechanization and Electrification of Agriculture, Chelyabinsk, USSR, 1971, Candidate of sci., 1977; reader, Higher Cert. Commn. Moscow, 1981; DSc, State Agrarian U., Russia, 2000. Asst. chair electric supply Inst. Mechanization and Electrification of Agr., Chelyabinsk, 1971-73, head chair electric supply, 1977-86, dean Electrification of Agr. Faculty, 1981-84, pro-rector, 1986-91; first pro-rector State Agro-Engring U., Chelyabinsk, Russia, 1991—. Author: Use of Power Source Resume in Agricultural Production, 1994; coauthor: Electrical Engineering, 1997. Mem. Dist. Soviet of Peoples Deps. Chelyabinsk, 1985-87, 87-89, 89-93. Recipient Badge for great successes in activities Ministry of Higher Edn. Russia, 1991. Russian Orthodox. Avocation: fishing. Office: Chelyabinsk State Agro-Engr, 75 Lenin Ave, 454080 Chelyabinsk Russia

SAPNA, GUPTA, chemist; b. Dehra Dun, India, Sept. 29, 1967; s. Davendra Kumar and Sushma G. BS, Meerut U., 1986, MS, 1988; PhD, U. Toledo, 1994. Rsch. assoc. Addis Ababa U., Addis Ababa, Ethiopia, 1988-89; tchg. asst. U. Toledo, 1989-93; postdoctoral fellow Roswell Park Cancer Inst., Buffalo, N.Y., 1993-94; postdoctoral assoc. U. British Columbia, Vancouver, Canada, 1995; asst. prof. Park Coll., Parkville, Mo., 1996—; cons. McGraw Hill, N.Y., 1999—. Contbr. articles to profl. jours. Mem. Am. Chemical Soc. (pub. affairs officer 1998—), Am. Assn. Univ. Women (mem. v.p. 1999—). Fax: 816-741-4911. E-mail: sapna@mail.park.edu. Office: Park Univ 8700 NW River Park Dr Parkville MO 64152-4358

SAPOFF, MEYER, electronics component manufacturer; b. N.Y.C., June 2, 1927; s. Benjamin and Mary (Charney) S. Student, Mohawk Coll., 1946-48, Poly. Inst. Bklyn., 1948-50, 52-53; BS in Elec. Engring. magna cum laude, Poly. Inst. Bklyn., 1950, postgrad., 1952-53; postgrad., MIT, 1951, U. Pa., 1951-52; MS in Elec. Engring., Drexel Inst. Tech., 1952. Rsch. engr. Franklin Inst. Labs., Phila., 1950-52; rsch. fellow sr. grade Poly. Inst. Bklyn., 1952-53; dir. rsch. Victory Engring. Corp., Springfield, N.J., 1953-57; dir. engring. Victory Engring. Corp., Springfield, 1957-63, v.p., 1963-69; cons., sr. staff scientist Keystone Carbon Co., St. Mary's, Pa., 1969-70; pres. Thermometrics, Inc., Edison, N.J., 1970-86, chmn. bd. dirs., 1986-93, sr. staff cons., 1993-96; pres. MS Cons., Princeton, 1993—; cons. in field, chmn. E20 Temperature com., session on thermistors 6th Symposium on Temperature, Measurement and Control in Sci. and Industry; U.S. del. to tech. com. 65 Internat. Electrotech. Commn. Contbr. articles to profl. jours.; patentee in field. Active Citizens League West Orange, 1962-75, West Orange PTA, 1960-76; trustee George St. Playhouse, New Brunswick, N.J., 1993—, fin. chmn., 1995-96, v.p. fin., 1995-98; bd. dirs. The Jewish Ctr., Princeton, N.J., 1995-98, United Jewish Fedn. Princeton Mercer Bucks, 1998—. With USN, 1945-46. Recipient Indsl. Rsch. IR-100 award, 1974; State of NYU scholar, 1948-50; Poly. Inst. Bklyn. fellow, 1953. Mem. IEEE, ASTM (mem. E20.08 med. thermometry subcom., 1st vice-chmn. E20 com. on temperature measurement 2000—, award of merit 1998), AAAS, Poly. Inst. Bklyn. Alumni Assn., Am. Ceramic Soc., Eta Kappa Nu, Tau Beta Pi. Home: 1137 Stuart Rd Princeton NJ 08540-1216 Office: 301 N Harrison St Ste 69 Princeton NJ 08540-3512

SAPORTA, MARC, author, editor; b. Constantinople, Turkey, Mar. 20, 1923; arrived in France, 1929.; s. Jaime and Simone (Nahmias) S. D. Law, U. Madrid, 1948; M.A. in Philosophy, U. Sorbonne, Paris, 1954. Research asst. UNESCO, Paris, 1948-53; lit. critic L'Express, Paris, 1954-71; dep. editor-in-chief USIS, Paris, 1954-71, editor-in-chief, 1971-84. Author: Le Furet, 1959, La Distribution, 1961, La Quete, 1961, Composition No One, 1962, Les Invites, 1964, Le Grand Defi USA-URSS, vol. I, 1967, vol. II, 1968, Le Tour des Etats-Unis en 80 Jours, 1958, La Vie Quotidienne aux U.S.A., 1972, Go West, 1976, Vivre Aux Etats-Unis, 1986, Histoire du Roman Americain, 1970, Israel, 1988, Les Erres du Faucon: Psychobiographie de William Faulkner, 1989, Le Roman Américain, 1997; editor, joint author essays: William Faulkner, 1983, Henry James, 1983, Isaac Bashevis Singer, 1984, Nathalie Sarraute, 1984, Henry Miller, 1985, Marguerite Duras, 1985, André Breton, 1988. Mem. Pen Club. Home: 9 Rue Saint Didier, 75116 Paris France

SAPPINGTON, SHARON ANNE, retired school librarian; b. West Palm Beach, Fla., Sept. 15, 1944; d. A. D. and Laura G. (Jackson) Chambless; m. Andrew Arnold Sappington III, June 11, 1966; children: Andrew Arnold IV, Kevin Sean. Student, Fla. So. coll., 1962-64; BA in Edn., U. Fla., 1966; media specialist, U. Ala., 1980. 5th grade tchr. Tates Creek Elem., Lexington, Ky., 1966-68; 4th grade tchr. Sadieville (Ky.) Elem., 1968-69; libr. media specialist A.H. Watwood Elem., Childersburg, Ala., 1980-98; ret.; guest storyteller Young Author's Conf., Winterboro, Lincoln, Sylacauga, and Fayetteville, Ala., 1982-94; vis. com. mem. Southeastern Accreditation Assn.; program presenter Internat. Reading Assn., Birmingham, Ala., 1983; guest speaker rare children's books "By the Way" TV talk show, 1983. Creator, presenter: (slide presentation) Tellers of Tales and Sketchers of Dreams, 1983, (multimedia programs) Dinosaurs, Teddy Bears, and Wild Things, 1990, Shanghaied in the Beijing Airport, 1994. Circle chmn., Sunday tchr. Grace United Meth. Ch., Birmingham, 1973, 92-95; delivery mem. Meals on Wheels, Birmingham, 1975-76; radio reader for the blind WBHM Pub. Broadcasting, Birmingham, 1980; guest speaker, program presenter Jaycees, Kiwanis, and C. of C., Childersburg, 1993-94. Title I grantee, 1991, Stutz Bearcat grantee, 1992. Mem. AAUW, ALA, Internat. Platform Assn., Am. Assn. Sch. Librs., Ala. Libr. Assn. (children's and sch. divsn. publicity chmn. 1991-93, chmn. Nat. Libr. Week 1993-94, Outstanding Youth Svcs. award 1989), People to People Internat. (libr. del. to China 1993), Kappa Delta Pi, Internat. Platform Assoc., 1997-98. Democrat. Methodist. Avocations: collector of 19th century illustrated children's literature. Home: 5131 Shore Dr Saint Augustine FL 32086-6473

SAPRA, SUNIL K., economics educator; b. New Delhi, July 15, 1953; came to the U.S., 1979; s. Chaman and Usha Sapra; m. Santosh Baghat, Jan. 16, 1986. MA in Econs., Delhi Sch. Econs., 1976; PhD in Econs., Columbia U., 1983. Asst. prof. dept. econs. SUNY, Buffalo, 1983-91; assoc. prof. dept. econs. and stats. Calif. State U., L.A., 1991-94, prof. dept. econs. and stats., 1994—; cons. Argonne Nat. Labs., 1984-87; statis. cons. Barksdale, Inc., L.A., 1994; presenter in field. Referee Econometrica, Econometric Revs., Jour. Econometrics, Jour. Applied Econometrics, Jour. Royal Statis. Soc., Explorations in Econ. History, Jour. Quantitative Econs., Jour. Bus. and Econ. Stats., Bull. Econ. Rsch., Rev. Internat. Econs., Procs. Far Ea. Econometric Soc., NSF, Acad. Internat. Bus. Grantee NSF, 1989-90. Mem. Am. Statis. Assn., Indian Econometric Soc., Western Econ. Assn. (instnl. rep.). Avocations: solving mathematical and statistical puzzles, playing cricket. E-mail: ssapra@calstatela.edu. Office: Calif State Univ Dept Econs 5151 State University Dr Los Angeles CA 90032-4226

SAPSFORD, RALPH NEVILLE, cardiothoracic surgeon; b. Bloemfontein, South Africa, Oct. 30, 1938; s. Roland Geoffrey and Doreen Inel (Cooper) S.; m. Simone Andree Evard, Jan. 13, 1962; children: Wayne, Lance, Andrea. MB, ChB, U. Capetown, Cape Province, South Africa, 1962, ChM, 1976. Resident Mpilo Hosp., Bulawayo, Rhodesia, 1963-65, various tng. hosps., Eng., 1966-67; sr. resident various cardiothoracic units, Manchester, Leeds, London, England, 1968-77; cons., sr. lectr. cardiothoracic surgery Hammersmith Hosp., London, 1977-90; hon. cons. St. Mary's Hosp., London, 1981-90; cons. cardiothoracic surgery, Wellington Hosp., London, Harley St. Clinic, Princes Grace Hosp., London, 1977—. Co-author 5 med. books; contbr. articles to profl. jours. Freeman of the City of London, 1989—; mem. Worshipful Socs. of Apothecaries, 1989—, Worshipful Soc. of Loriners, 1992—. Recipient Merit award C, Nat. Health Svc. Eng., 1983, Merit award B, 1987. Fellow Royal Coll. Surgeons, Edinburgh, London; mem. Soc. of Thoracic and Cardiovascular Surgeons, Brit. Cardiac Soc., European Soc. of Cardiothoracic Surgeons, European Cardiovascular Soc., Harlech Club, Sancta Maria Lodge. Mem. Conservative Party. Avocations: antique pistols, classic Jaguars, golf, yachting and horseback riding. Office: 66 Harley St, W1N 1AE London England

SAPSFORD, ROGER JOHN, social researcher and research methods educator; b. London, Apr. 10, 1947; s. William Arthur and Ivy Frances (Clowes) S. MA, U. Oxford, Eng., 1969; PhD, U. Coll., London, 1979. Asst. rsch. exec. AGB Rsch., London, 1969-71; sr. rsch. officer Home Office Rsch. Unit, London, 1971-78; sr. lectr. The Open Univ., Milton Keynes, U.K., 1978-98; reader in social rsch. U. Teesside, Middlesbrough, U.K., 1998—. Author: Life-Sentence Prisoners: Reaction, Response and Change, 1983; co-author: (with Pamela Abbott) Community Care for Mentally Handicapped Children, 1987, (with Pamela Abbott) Research Methods for Nurses and the Caring Professions, 1992, Survey Research, 1999; contbr. author: Data Collection and Analysis, 1996, Theory and Social Psychology, 1999. Mem. Brit. Psychol. Soc., Brit. Sociol. Assn. Office: U Teesside, Sch Social Scis, Middlesbrough TS1 3BA, England

SAQIB, MOHAMMAD, materials scientist; b. Faisalabad, Pakistan, Dec. 30, 1958; s. Mohammad and Salma (Khatoon) Sadiq; m. Sairah Hameed, May 20, 1990; children: Sameer M., Shayan M. B of Engring., Dawood Coll. Engring. & Tech., 1981; MS, U. Conn., 1984, PhD, 1987. Failure analyst P.N. Dockyard Labs., Karachi, Pakistan, 1981-82; rsch. asst. U. Conn., Storrs, 1982-87; rsch. scientist Wright State U., Dayton, Ohio, 1988-97; sr. rsch. scientist metallic materials br. NASA-Langley Ctr. Analytical Svcs. and Materials Inc., Hampton, Va., 1997—; vis. scientist Wright-Patt Airforce Base, Ohio, 1988-90; cons. Xicon Technologies, Farmington, Conn., 1996-98, Scitex Digital Printing, Dayton, Ohio, 1994-95, Acustar/Chrysler Corp., Dayton, 1994-95. Contbr. articles to profl. jours. including Material Sci. and Engring., Metallurgical and Material Transactions, Scripta Metallurgica et Materialia. Rsch. grant Xicon Technologies, 1997; U. Conn. fellow, 1985-86. Achievements include devel. of thermal protection systems for RLV and other space vehicles; rsch. in failure analysis aircraft honeycomb structures, property improvement of tianium-base high temperature materials, mechanical behavior and plastic flow of high temperature composites, ordering transformations in metal silicides. Avocations: swimming, camping, biking, chess, ping-pong. E-mail address: msaqib@larc.nasa.gov. Home: 8 Gallaer Ct Hampton VA 23666-5327 Office: NASA-Langley Rsch Ctr Ms # 188A Hampton VA 23681-0001

SAR, VEDAT, psychiatrist, educator, researcher; b. Istanbul, Turkey, June 23, 1955; s. Mehmet Cavit and Muazzez (Barut) S.; m. Ilknur Özütemiz, Oct. 24, 1983; 1 child, Meric. MD, Istanbul U., 1981; postgrad., Hacettepe U., Ankara, Turkey, 1986. Resident in psychiatry Hacettepe Univ. Medical Faculty Hosp., Ankara, 1981-86; attending psychiatrist Gümüssuyu Mil. Hosp., Istanbul, 1987-88, Sagmalcilar Correctional Ctr. Hosp., Istanbul, 1988-89; fellow Cerrahpasa Medical Faculty Istanbul U., Istanbul, 1989-90, assoc. prof. psychiatry, 1990-92; assoc. prof. psychiatry Istanbul Med. Faculty U., Istanbul, 1992-96; prof. psychiatry Istanbul U., Istanbul, 1996—; dir. Clinical Psychotherapy Unit, 1993— Istanbul Medical Faculty, Dissociative Disorders Program, 1994—. Contbr. articles to profl. jours. Recipient David Caul Meml. award Internat. Soc. Study of Dissociation, 1995, 99. Mem. Am. Psychiat. Assn. (internat. mem.), Internat. Soc. Study of Dissociation, Internat. Soc. Traumatic Stress Studies, N.Y. Acad. Scis. Office: Istanbul Tip Fakultesi, Psikiyatri Klinigi Capa, 34390 Istanbul Turkey

SARÀ, MICHELE, zoology educator, researcher; b. Naples, Fla., Apr. 27, 1926; s. Antonino and Lucia (Fletoridi) S.; m. Fiorella Ciferri, Mar. 9, 1957; children: Antonio, Franca. Grad., U. Naples, 1947, PhD in Biology, 1954. Asst. prof. U. Naples, 1949-61; prof., dir. Inst. Zoology U. Bari, Italy, 1961-69; prof. zoology U. Genoa, Italy, 1969—, dir. Inst. Zoology, 1969-94. Author: Marine Biology, 1974, General Biology, 1977, Zoology, 1990; contbr. articles to sci. jours., including Nature. Mem. Academia Europaea, Italian Union Zoology, Genoa Acad. Sci. and Letters. Avocations: painting, poetry, philosophy. Home: Via XXV Aprile 229, 16030 Pieve Ligure Genoa, Italy Office: U Genoa Dept Territory Resources, Corso Europa 26, 16132 Genoa Italy

SARAC, AHMET, governor; b. Gerede, Turkey, Oct. 20, 1961; s. Mehmet Ziya and Emine (Ozkul) S.; m. Hatice Gungor, June 5, 1990 (div. July 1992). Grad., Istanbul U. Sch. Law, Turkey, 1983. Dist. gov. Ministry of Interior, Selendi, Turkey, 1989-91, Doganyurt, Turkey, 1991-92, Semdinli, Turkey, 1992-94, Sultanhisar, Turkey, 1994-96, Viransehir, Turkey, 1996—. Pres. Social Help and Solidarity Found., 1996. Lt. Turkish Mil., 1995-97. Mem. Soc. Turkish Adminstrs., Found. Turkish Adminstrs., Nat. Geographic Soc. Muslim. Avocations: music, poetry, soccer, basketball, fishing, tennis. Home: Sanliurfa Mardin Karayolu, 63700 Viransehir Turkey

Office: Viransehir Kaymakamligi, Hukumet Konagi, 63700 Viransehir Turkey

SARAC, ARIF MURAT, surgeon; b. Ankara, Turkey, Aug. 3, 1964; s. Rahmi and Sezen (Inci) S.; m. Gulsen Esgin, Nov. 2, 1991; 1 child, Yanki Can. MD, Marmara U., Istanbul, Turkey, 1989. Med. diplomate. Dept. chief Tokat (Turkey) Health Authority, 1989-91; mem. emergency staff Yalova (Turkey) State Hosp., 1991-92; surg. residency Marmara U., Istanbul, 1992-97, Tel Aviv (Israel) U., 1995; chief staff, dir. Esma Hatun Hosp., Istanbul, 1997—. Contbr. articles to med. jours. Recipient Silver Eagle award for best rsch. Turkish Hepatoparcreatico Bilier Soc., 1997. Mem. Turkish Med. Assn., Nat. Geographic Soc., N.Y. Acad. Scis. Avocations: audio, video, fishing, football, electronics. Home: Tefvik Pasa Sok, Turkmen Apt 18/1, 81030 Istanbul Turkey Office: Esma Hatun Hosp, Lambaci Sok No 1, 81100 Istanbul Turkey

SARAI, MASAKAZU, psychiatrist, researcher; b. Maizuru, Kyoto, Japan, Apr. 15, 1949; s. Kazuo and Takae (Mimura) S. MA, Kyoto (Japan) U., 1971; MD, Osaka (Japan) U., 1980. Expert psychiatrist. Staff psychiatrist Osaka (Japan) U., 1980-81, Osaka (Japan) Prefectural Hosp., 1981-82, Osaka (Japan) Teishin Hosp., 1982-87; cons. psychiatrist Kosaka Hosp., Osaka, 1987-96; dir. Sarai Clniic, Kobe, 1996—; cons. psychaitrist Osaka Prefecture, 1985—; cons. of mental health NTT, Osaka, 1982-87. Contbr. articles to Biol. Psychiatry, Schizophrenia Rsch. and other profl. jours. Mem. AAAS, N.Y. Acad. Scis., Japanese Soc. Psychiat. and Neurology, Japanese Soc. Biol. Psychiatry, Schizophrenia Rsch. Fax: 81-078-682-8868. Office: Sarai Clinic, 1-4-6, Mikawaguchi, Hyogo-ku Kobe 652-0815, Japan

SARAIVA, PEDRO MANUEL, chemical engineering educator; b. Coimbra, Portugal, Oct. 27, 1964; s. Albano Andrade and Maria Emilia (Lopes) S.; m. Maria Isabel Rajao, June 13, 1989; children: Joana Isabel, Ana Margarida, Mariana. Diploma in chem. engring., U. Coimbra, 1987; PhD, MIT, 1993. Asst. lectr. U. Coimbra, 1987-93, asst. prof. chem. engring., 1993—, dean student affairs, 1994-96, head dept. chem. engring., 1997; rsch. asst. MIT, Cambridge, Mass., 1989-93; founder, CEO Qual-Quality Mgmt. Cons. Co., 1993—, Aiepc-Computer Learning Ctr. for Kids Co., Coimbra, 1996—. Author in field. Founder Youth Sci. Assn., Portugal, 1985, Portuguese Students Assn., Cambridge, 1992. Fulbright scholar, 1989-93, Rotary scholar, 1990; recipient Quality Feigenbaum award, Am. Soc., 1998. Fellow Portuguese Chpt. Engrs.; mem. Portugese Assn. for Quality (sect. pres. 1998—). Office: Chem Engring Dept, Polo II Da U De Coimbra, 3030-290 Coimbra Portugal

SARALEGUI, CRISTINA MARIA, journalist; b. Havana, Cuba, Jan. 29, 1948; came to U.S., 1960; d. Francisco and Cristina (Santamarina) S.; m. Marcos Avila, June 9, 1984; children: Cristina Amalia, Jon Marcos. Student mass comm., U. Miami. Features editor Vanidades Continental, Miami, Fla., 1970-73; editor Cosmopolitan Spanish, Miami, 1973-76, editor-in-chief, 1979-89; dir. enterntainment Miami Herald, 1976-77; editor-in-chief Intimidades mag., Miami, 1977-79, TV y Novelas mag., 1986-89; hostess The Cristina Show Univision Network, 1989—; keynote spkr. Union Am. Women, P.R., 1981, Legendary Women of Miami. Featured in bestseller Latin Beauty, 1982. Mem. internat. jury Miss Venezueala Pagent, 1982, Miss Columbia Pagent, 1987. Recipient Keys to City Cartagena, Colombia, 1987, Star on the Walk of Fame, 1999, Cmty. Svc. award, 2000. Mem. NAFE, Women in Comm. (key note spkr. 1986), Am. Soc. Profl. and Exec. Women, Am. Mgmt. Assn., Nat. Network Hispanic Women (Corp. Leader award), Latin Bus. and Profl. Women's Club. Republican. Roman Catholic. Office: The Christina Show 9405 NW 41st St Miami FL 33178-2301*

SARAMAGO, JOSÉ, author, poet; b. Azinhaga, Portugal, Nov. 16, 1922; m. Pilar del Río; 1 child. Doctorate (hon.), U. Turin, Italy, U. Sevilla, Spain, U. Manchester, Eng., U. Toledo, Spain, U. Brasilia, Brazil, U. Las Palmas, Spain, U. Valencia, Spain, U. Evora, Portugal, U. Rio Grande do Sul, Brazil, U. Minas Gerais, Brazil, U. Nottingham, England, U. Mass. Writings include: (fiction) Manual de pintura e caligrafia, 1976, English transl., 1994, Objecto quase, 1978, Levantado do chão, 1980, Memorial do convento, 1982, English transl., 1987, O ano da morte de Ricardo Reis, 1984, English transl., 1991, A jangada de pedra, 1986, English transl., 1994, História do Cerco de Lisboa, 1989, English transl. 1996, O Evangelho Segundo Jesus Cristo, 1991, English transl., 1993, Ensaio sobre a Cegueira, 1995, English transl., 1998, Todos os Nomes, 1997, English transl., 1999, A Caverna, 2000, (verse) Os poemas possíveis, 1966, Provavelmente Alegria, 1970, revised edit., 1985, O ano de 1993, 1975; (plays) A noite, 1979, Que farei com este livro?, 1980, A segunda vida de Francisco de Assis, 1987, In Nomine Dei, 1993; (opera libretto) Blimunda, 1990, Divara, 1993; (other writings) Deste mundo e do outro, 1971, A bagagem do viajante, 1973, O embargo, 1973, Os opiniões que o D.L. teve, 1974, As apontamentos, 1976, Viagem a Portugal, 1981, Cadernos de Lanzarote, 1994-98, Folhas Políticas, 1999, Discursos de Estocolemo, 1999; editor: O poeta perguntador, 1979. Recipient Grinzane Cavour prize, Mondello prize, Flaiano prize, Ind. prize, Luis de Camões prize, Nobel prize for literature, 1998. Office: Los Topes 3, 35572 Tias Lanzarote Canarian Spain also: Ray-Güde Mertin, 1 Friedrichstrasse, 61348 Bad Hamburg 1, Germany

SARAMBEI, NICOLAE, editor; b. Bucharest, Romania, Mar. 13, 1939; s. Constantin and Constanta (Badulescu) S.; m. Johana Valeria Linzmeier, Aug. 16, 1962; 1 child, Christian. Grad., Pedagogical Inst., Bucharest, 1966; MA, Romanian Phylology Coll., Bucharest, 1970. Journalist România Libera, Bucharest, 1966-69; columnist Fgn. Langs. Press Group, Bucharest, 1969—, editor-in-chief, 1990-91, dir., 1991—; editor-in-chief Bravo, Bucharest, 1993; contbr. Am.-Romanian Acad., Costa Mesa, Calif., 1992-97, cons. Viata Româneasca, Forum, Steaua, 1992—, Artmedia Group, Bucharest, 1993—, SEMNE '94, 1994—. Co-author: 99 Personalities of Ancient World, 1983, 97, The Great Unification, 1983, (encyclopedia) Romanians in Western Culture, 1992, 96, Romanian Philosphers for Refernece in the World of Philosophy, 1997, Who Are the Romanians?, 1997, The Illustrated History of the Romanians, 1998, Romania Brief Profile, 1999; author and coord.: The Union Strivings Along Two Millennia, 1997, Eight-Step Path of Policy Analysis (in Romanian), Pope John Paul II Blesses Romania, 1999, Romania at the Dawn of a New Millennium, 2000, 1918 and the Trianon Treaty, 2000; contbr. articles to profl. jours. Mem. Romanian Journalists Soc., Romanian Profl. Journalists, Writers' Union of Romania. Avocations: fishing, beekeeping, target shooting.

SARAN, ADARSH, business executive, finance company executive; b. New Delhi, Dec. 9, 1938; s. Pandit Shiv Saran and Pandtiani Saran (Dubey) Shakuntala; m. Neena Thapar, Apr. 26, 1943; children: Priya, Samir; m. Ranjit Chaudhri, 1994. Degree in Math. with honors, St. Stephens Coll., 1956; degree in Engring. with honors, Loughborough U., 1960. With V.E. Duncan Bros., 1960-63; gen. mgr. JCT Textiles Ltd., Phagwara, India, 1962-71; dir. Karam Chand Thapar & Bros. Group Cos. Ltd., Calcutta, 1971-79, Four Seasons Trading, London, 1980—; CEO James Greaves & Co., Eng., 1980-87; dir. Crest Internat. Trading, London, Maersk India Ltd., Bombay, Internat. Chems. Co. Ltd., Cairo. Fellow Inst. Engrs., Inst. Dirs. London. Avocations: photography, art and antiquities collecting. Home: 53/4 Hazra Rd, Calcutta 700 019, India

SARANGAPANI, JAGANNATHAN, intelligent systems and controls engineer, educator; b. Madurai, India, June 14, 1965; s. Jagannathan and Janaki (Ramaswamy) S.; m. Sandhya (Srinivasan), June 16, 1997; 1 child, Sadhika. BS, Anna U., Madras, 1987; MS, U. Sask., Can., 1989; PhD, U. Tex., Arlington, 1994. Engr. Engr. India Ltd., New Delhi, 1986-87; rsch. asst. U. Sask., Saskatoon, 1987-89; rsch. assoc. U. Man., Winnipeg, Can., 1990-91; rsch. asst. Automation and Robotics Rsch. Inst., Ft. Worth, 1992-94; cons., rsch. Caterpillar, Inc., Peoria, Ill., 1994-98; asst. prof. elec. engring., dir. intelligent sys. lab. U. Tex., San Antonio, 1998—; cons., collaborator Adv. Sensors and Controls Group, Ft. Worth, 1994-98; cons. Caterpillar Inc., 1994-98. Co-author: Neural Network Control of Robot and Nonlinear systems, 1999; contbr. chpts. to books, over 70 articles to profl. jours. Recipient several gold medals and scholarships; U. Tex. fellow, 1992-94; Sigma Xi doctoral rsch. awardee, 1994. Mem. IEEE (program chmn. Illinois Valley sect. 1994, program com. symposium on int. control), Sigma Xi, Tau Beta Pi, Eta Kappa Nu. Achievements include 10 patents and 12 patents pending; development of novel neural network methods for control and relaxation of certainty equivalence assumption, linearity in the parameters, and persistence of excitation; novel prognostic algorithms. Avocations: tennis, jogging, walking, chess, biking. Office: U Tex at San Antonio Dept Elec Engring 6900 N Loop 1604 W San Antonio TX 78249-1130

SARANIN, ALEXANDER ALEXANDER, physicist, researcher, educator; b. Porkkala-Udd, Finland, May 6, 1955; s. Alexander Isidorovich and Nina Alekseevna (Solov'eva) S.; m. Tatiana Borisovna Yarshova, July 5, 1980; children: Arseniy, Lidiya. MS, Moscow Phys.-Tech. Inst., 1978; PhD in Physics, Tech. U., St. Petersburg, Russia, 1987. Rschr. Inst. Automation and Control Processes, Vladivostok, Russia, 1978-86, sr. rschr., 1986-89, head lab., 1989—; prof. physics Far Ea. State U., Vladivostok, 1995—; vis. prof. Osaka (Japan) U., 1995, 96-97. Author: Surface Phases on Silicon, 1994. Avocations: music, cars, reading. Home: Kirova 19/1 St Apr 71, 690039 Vladivostok Russia Office: Inst Automation-Control, Processes, 5 Radio St, 690041 Vladivsotok Russia

SARANIN, VLADIMIR ALEKSANDR, physicist, educator; b. Yurla, Permskaya, Russia, Jan. 18, 1951; s. Aleksandr Ivan and Roza Melchakova A.; m. Olga Vladimir Pushkareva, Sept. 10, 1972 (div. Apr. 1977); 1 child: Evgenii; m. Roza Gabdulla Kasimova, Aug. 11, 1979; 1 child: Aleksandr. Cand. in Phys. and Math. Scis., Harkov U., Ukraine, 1984; D Phys. and Math. Scis., Perm U., Russia, 1999. Jr. sci. collaborator Machinebldg. Inst., Voroshilovgrad, Ukraine, 1973-74; asst. State Pedagogical Inst., Glazov, Russia, 1977-79, sr. educator, 1979-86, asst. prof., 1986-93, prof., 1993—, chief theoretical physics dept., 1986-88. Author: Equilibrium of Fluids and Its Stability, 1995; contbr. articles to profl. jours. Avocation: winter fishing. Office: State Pedagogical Inst, Pervomaiskaya 25, 427600 Glazov Udmurtia, Russia

SARANTOGLOU, MENELAOS HARRY, general director; b. Polygyros, Greece, May 2, 1940; s. Harry Nicolas and Anna Nicolas (Bazakos) S.; m. Maria Pan Vlamis, Dec. 30, 1967; children: Harry, Anna. Tchr. English Anglo-Am. Lang. Inst., Thessaloniki, Greece, 1966-67; tchr. English and Italian The Sarantoglou Lang. Inst., Thessaloniki, 1967-70, dir. gen., 1971-75; dir. gen. Alexander Lang. Inst., Thessaloniki, 1976-78, Recreation Assn., Thessaloniki, 1978—, Alexander Internat., Thessaloniki, 1978—, Diversified Activities, Thessaloniki, 1978—. Author English grammar books. Mem. Internat. Phonetic Assn. England, Internat. Soc. Phonetic Scis. Avocations: inventions, languages, music. Office: Alexander Internat, 27 Aetorahis St, Thessaloniki 54640, Greece

SARAPA, MILAN, pipeline engineer; b. Zagreb, Croatia, Dec. 3, 1965; s. Ilija and Marija Sarapa; m. Tanya Tasic, Oct. 18, 1997; 1 child, Zoya. B Petroleum Engring., U. Zagreb, 1991. Registered profl. engr., Croatia. Rsch. engr. MOL Plc Oil and Gas Labs., Budapest, Hungary, 1991-93; engr. gas transport INA Oil and Gas Co. Croatia, Zagreb, 1993-95; pipeline engr. Natural Gas Corp. New Zealand, New Plymouth, 1996—; project mgr. lowering of in-svc. high perssure gas pipeline in Auckland, 1999, introducing clock spring composite reinforcing sleeve for pipeline repair in New Zealand, realignment of 1300 100nb pipeline in Tauranga, New Zealand. Avocations: photography, martial arts, tramping. Fax: 64 6 755 3233. E-mail: milan.sarapa@natgas.co.nz. Home: 39 Dorset Ave, New Plymouth New Zealand Office: Natural Gas Corp NZ, 42 Connett Rd West, New Plymouth New Zealand

SARASTE, HEIKKI JUHANI, publishing executive; b. Helsinki, Finland, Jan. 3, 1952; s. Juhani and Sirkka (Ingman) S.; m. Riitta Anna Juntunen, Apr. 12, 1975; children: Anna, Jaakko. MS, Helsinki U. Tech., 1975. Pres. Helsinki Cable TV, 1981-84; gen. mgr. Sanomaprint, Helsinki, 1984-93; v.p. devel. Sanoma Corp., Helsinki, 1993-95; dir. corp. planning Telecom Finland, Helsinki, 1995-96; exec. v.p. Alma Media Corp., Helsinki, 1996—. Office: Alma Media Corp, PO Box 140, 00101 Helsinki Finland

SARASTE, JUKKA-PEKKA, conductor; b. Heinola, Finland, 1956. With Finnish Radio Symphony Orch., 1978—, prin. condr., 1987—; prin. condr. Scottish Chamber Orch., 1987-91; music dir. The Toronto Symphony Orch., 1994—. Guest condr. Helsinki Philharm., Beijing Cen. Opera Orch., Symphonic Orch. Chengdu, Rotterdam Philharm. Orch., Chamber Orch. Europe, Bavarian Radio Symphony Orch., Junge Deutsche Philharm., Detroit Orch., Minn. Orch., Vienna Symphony Orch., Rome's Santa Cecilia Orch., Cleve. Orch., Boston Symphony Orch., L.A. Philharm. Orch., others; co-founder Avanti Chamber orch.; condr. more than 39 recs. with Finnish Radio Symphony Orch. and Scottish Chamber Orch. Recipient First prize Scandinavian Conducting Competition, 1981, hon. doctorate fine arts, York U., Toronto, 1995. Office: Radio Symphony Orch, Yleisradio Ja 14, SF-00240 Helsinki 24, Finland also: Toronto Symphony Orch, 212 King St W Ste 550, Toronto, ON Canada M5H 1K5*

SARASWATHY, ARIAMUTHU, chemist, educator; b. Naraikkinar, Tirunelveli, India, Mar. 7, 1955. BSc, Madurai U., 1975; MSc, Madras U., 1977, PhD, 1987. Demonstrator in chemistry Sri Parasakthi Coll., Tirunelveli, India, 1977-78; jr. rsch. fellow Schifflon Leprosy Rsch. & Tng. Ctr., CMC, Vellore, 1978-79; from rsch. asst. to rsch. officer, capt. Srinivasa Murti Drug Rsch. Inst., CCRAS, Madras, 1979—; Guest investigator CSIR, New Delhi, 1995, Tamil U., Tanjore, 1997; participant Nat. Workshop on QC of Herbal Remedies, Jammu, 1997. Contbr. articles and revs. to profl. jours., chpts. to books; main contbr. to book: QC Standards for Certain Sid. Formulations. Recipient Hari Om Ashram Gold Medal on Herbal Rsch. Gujarat Ay. U., Jam Nagar, 1994, Gold Medal for Pioneer in Ay. Drug Standardizationn Gujarat Ay. U., 2000, Best Paper awards: Std. of Astaccurana IPC Assoc., Manipal, 1990, Need for Standardization of Sid drugs, Nat. Conf., Trivandrum, 1990, Quality Assessment Methods of Herbal Drugs in Sid System, 3rd Nat. Conf. Sid, Kerala, 1997, Micromorphological identification of Ventilago madraspatana CIMAP, 2000, Awards Royleanones and Related Quinones, Bombay, 1990, Sid Drugs and the Need to Standardize, Coun. Adv. Rural Tech., New Delhi, 1989, Tankari, a fertility regulating agt., CCRAS, New Delhi, 1999, Hon. Vis. Lectrs. Madras U., 1995, Bharathidasan U., TN Dr. M.G.R. Med. U., 1996. Mem. Herbal Acad. Bombay, Indian Pharm. Congress Assn., Siddha Pharm., Soc. for Bioscis. Muzaffar Nagar (comm. New Delhi), N.Y. Acad. Scis. Home: 22/6 HIG C Type, Anna Nagar West, 600 101 Madras India Office: CSMDRIA CCRAS, Arumbakkam, 600 106 Madras India

SARAUX, HENRY CAMILLE, academic administrator, ophthalmologist, educator; b. Niort, France, Sept. 8, 1927; s. Jean Henri and Yvonne Camille (Chaumier) S.; m. Genevieve Jeanne Oluzeau, Feb. 13, 1953; children: Jean Luc, Bertrand, Nathalie, Agnes. BS, U. Poitiers, France, 1944; MD, Paris U., 1955. Asst. prof. Paris Med. Sch., 1958-74; prof., chmn. dept. Paris St. Antoine Med. Sch., 1974-91; v.p. U. Paris VI, 1991—. Author: Anatomy of the Eye, 1960, Ophthalmology, 1970, Physiology of the Eye, 1974. Fellow Royal Coll. Ophthalmology; mem. Internat. Acad. Ophthalmology. Home: 02 Square Alboni, 75016 Paris France

SARAVACOS, GEORGE DEMETRIOS, engineering educator, researcher; b. Tiryntha, Argolis, Greece, Mar. 15, 1928; s. Demetrios and Angeliki N. S.; m. Katherine Stathakopoulos, June 22, 1961. Diploma in engring., Nat. Tech. U., Athens, Greece, 1953; MS, U. Calif, Davis, 1957; DSc, MIT, 1960. Registered profl. engr. Researcher Nuclear Rsch. Ctr., Athens, 1960-63, U.S. Army Natick (Mass.) Labs., 1963-64; from asst. prof. to assoc. prof. Cornell U., Geneva, N.Y., 1965-71; prof. Nat. Tech. U., Athens, 1971-84, dept. chmn., 1981-82, prof. emeritus, 1990—; prof. Rutgers U., New Brunswick, N.J., 1984-90. Author: Physical Separation Processes, 1976, Particle Technology, 1978, contbr. book chpt. to Engineering Properties of Foods, 1995, over 100 articles to profl. jours. Fulbright fellow, 1955-56; rsch. associateship U.S. Nat. Acad. Scis., 1963-64. Mem. AIChE, Inst. of Food Technologists, Tech. Chamber of Greece. Home: Nea Tiryntha, 21100 Nauplion Greece Office: Dept Chem Engring, Nat Tech U, 15780 Athens Greece

SARAVIITA, ILKKA JUHANI, law educator; b. Helsinki, Finland, Aug. 13, 1940; s. Jaakko Juhani; m. Leena Kaarina Yli-Kuivila, Nov. 16, 1964; children: Kristiina, Katja. LLM, U. Helsinki, 1964, LLD, 1972. Assoc. prof. U. Tampere, Finland, 1972-79; prof. U. Lapland, Rovaniemi, Finland, 1979—; legal adviser Ministry of Justice, Helsinki, 1979—, Parliament of Finland, 1980—, legal adviser delegation of Finland to UN, 1987; Jean Monnet chair U. Lapland, 1997—. Author: The Rights of Parliamentary Minorities, 1971, The Approval of the Charter of International Organizations, 1973, The Sanctions of International Organizations, 1978, The Cooperation Treaty Between Finland and Soviet Union, 1989, The Fundamental Rights, 1998. Named Knight 1st class Order of White Rose, Finland, 1987. Mem. Finnish Lawyers Union, Finnish Law-Rsch. Assn. Social Democrat. Avocation: oil painting. Home: Punavuorenkatu 1 A 8, 00120 Helsinki Finland Office: Univ Lapland, Box 122, 96101 Rovaniemi Finland

SARAZIN, LAURENT, radiologist; b. Villejuif, France, June 23, 1962; s. Jacques Sarazin and Nicole Ripoche. MD, U. Paris XI, 1988. Diplomate French Bd. Radiology. Fellow McGill U., Montreal, Que., Can., 1993-95; intern Pub. Assistance-Hosp. Paris, 1988-92, chief clinic, 1995-97, attaché, 1997—. Author: Musculoskeletal Procedures, 1996, Foot Imaging, 1997 (Fischgold prize 1998), Wrist and Hand Imaging, 1998; contbr. article to Radiographics. Mem. Radiol. Soc. N.Am., Am. Soc. Spine Radiology, French Soc. Radiology. Office: Hopital Cochin, 27 Rue Faubourg St Jacques, 75679 Paris France

SARBADHIKARI, SUPTENDRA NATH, biomedical engineer, physician; b. Calcutta, India, Dec. 25, 1965; s. Sarojendra Nath and Anima (Sinha) S.; m. Anindya Chaudhuri, May 10, 1996; 1 child, Sohini. MBBS, U. Calcutta., 1989; PhD in Biomed. Engring., Banaras Hindu U., Varanasi, India, 1995. Resident house physician Calcutta Nat. Med. Coll. Hosp., 1990-91; jr. resident Ctrl. Inst. Psychiatry, Ranchi, India, 1991; sr. rsch. fellow sch. biomed. engring., inst. tech. Banarus Hindu U., Varanasi, India, 1991-95; rsch. assoc. Indian Statis. Inst., Calcutta, 1995-97, hon. vis. scientist, 1997-98; med. practitioner Durgapur, India, 1998—; basic tchr. Bankura Sammilani Med. Coll., 1999; asst. prof. biophysics Manipal Inst. Med. Scis., Gangtok, Sikkim, India, 1999—; quizmaster All India Radio, Calcutta, 1984—; sr. class asst. physiology Calcutta Nat. Med. Coll., 1985, jr. class asst. ob-gyn., 1988; compere in health programs Doordarshan TV, Calcutta, 1990-91; assessor tropical medicine tutorial Wellcome Trust, London, 1996; spkr. in field. Cons. free clinic St. Lawrence Old Boys' Assn., Calcutta, 1990—. Mem. Indian Med. Assn. (life, editl. trainee 1990), Paribesh Unnayan Parishad (life, asst. sec. 1990-91, 95-96), Biomed. Engring. Soc. India (life). Hindu. Avocations: quizzing, reading, writing. Home: WIB R 15/6 Golf Green, Calcutta 700095, India

SARBANOV, ULAN KYTAIBEKOVICH, bank executive; b. Bishkek, Kyrgyz Republic, May 28, 1967. Diploma in econ. cybernetics, Novosibirsk State U., Russia, 1991. Rsch. asst. Inst. Econs. Siberian br. of Russian Acad. Scis., 1991-93; sr. engr. automation dept. Nat. Bank Kyrgyz Republic, 1993-94, head econ. rsch. and analysis divsn., econ. dept., 1994-97, head econ. dept., 1997, bd. dirs., 1997-99, acting. chmn. bd. dirs., 1999, chmn. bd. dirs., 1999—. Avocations: classical music, reading. Office: 101 Umetaliev St, 720040 Bishkek Kyrgyz Republic

SARBEY, OLEG GEORGIJ, physicist, researcher; b. Vladikavkaz, Russia, Oct. 3, 1933; s. Georgij Kirill Sarbey and Inna Stepanovna Morozova; m. Vera Petrovna Abramova, Dec. 27, 1962 (div. June 1965); 1 child, Natalia. Grad., State U., Rostov-na-Donu, Russia, 1955; Candidate Phys.-Math. Scis., Acad. Scis., Kiev, Ukraine, 1952, D Phys.-Math. Scis., 1970. Lab. head State U., Rostov-na-Donu, 1958-60; scientist Inst. Physics, Kiev, 1960-61, leading scientist, 1963-70, dep. head, 1971—; chair phys. sect. Nat. Coun. for Sci. and Tech., Kiev, 1993-97, State Fund for Fundamental Rsch., Kiev, 1993—; mem. High Com. for Sci. Qualification of Ukraine, Kiev, 1995-98. Co-author: Hot Electrons in Many-valley Semiconductors, 1982; contbr. over 130 articles to sci. jours.; rschr. in field. Recipient Diploma for Sci. Discovery, USSR, 1965, 84, State prize for natural scis. State Com. of Ukraine, 1986. Mem. Phys. Soc. Ukraine, Am. Phys. Soc. Avocations: playing violin, classical and modern literature, philosophy, gardening. E-mail: sarbey@iop,kiev.ua. Home: Boichenko 14/312, 252206 Kiev Ukraine Office: Inst Phys, Prospect Nauku 46, 252650 Kiev Ukraine

SARCHIO, CHAD THOMAS, lawyer; b. Wayne, N.J., Aug. 29, 1970; s. Andrew Phillip Sarchio and Lynne Christine Pedranti; m. Christina Guerola, June 20, 1998. BA, Duke U., 1992; JD, George Washington U., 1995. Bar: N.J. 1995, U.S. Dist. Ct. N.J. 1995, N.Y. 1996, D.C. 1998, U.S. Supreme Ct. 2000. Capt. U.S. Army, 1996; judge adv. Judge Adv. Gen.'s Corps U.S. Army, Ft. Bragg, N.C., 1996-97; judge adv. Judge Adv. Gen.'s Corps. U.S. Army, Tuzla, Bosnia, 1997-98, Alexandria, Va., 1998-2000; asst. U.S. atty. U.S. Atty.'s Office, Washington, 2000—. Mem. ABA, ATLA. Avocations: running, golf, acting. Office: USAO Judiciary Ctr 555 4th St NW Washington DC 20001-2733

SARDANASHVILY, GENNADI ALEKSANDRE, physicist, researcher; b. Moscow, Mar. 13, 1950; s. Aleksandre and Nadezda (Ustinova) S.; m. Aida Karamysheva, Mar. 19, 1971; children: Elena, Ira. PhD, Moscow State U., 1980, DSc, 1998. Prin. rsch. scientist Moscow State U., 1976—. Author: (with O. Zakharov) Gauge Gravitation Theory, 1992, Gauge Theory in Jet Manifolds, 1993, Generalized Hamiltonian Formalism for Field Theory, 1995; (with G. Giachetta and L. Mangiarotti) New Lagrangian and Hamiltonian Methods in Field Theory, 1997; (with L. Mangiarotti) Gauge Mechanics, 1998, (with L. Mangiarotti) Connections in Classical and Quantum Field Theory, 2000. Home: Ostrovitianova 28-1-4, 117321 Moscow Russia Office: Moscow State U, Dept Theoretical Physics, 117234 Moscow Russia

SARDENBERG, RONALDO MOTA, ambassador; b. Sao Paulo, Brazil, Oct. 8, 1940; married; 4 children. Grad., U. Brazil. Joined Ext. Rels. Ministry, 1964, advisor econ., tech. and commodities divsn., 1964-67; mem. staff Brazilian Embassy, Washington, 1967-70, Permanent Mission to UN, N.Y.C., 1970-74; polit. advisor multilateral and Afro-Asian affairs Permanent Mission to UN, 1974-76, coord. policy making, 1976-78, spl. sec. for polit. and econ. affairs internat. bilateral area, then head policy planning team, 1978-82; charge d'affaires Brazilian Embassy, Moscow, 1982, amb. to USSR, 1985-89; amb. to Spain Brazilian Embassy, Madrid, 1989-90; permanent rep. UN, N.Y.C., 1990-95; sec. strategic affairs Office of the Pres., Brasilia, 1995-98, minister for spl. projects, 1999, minister sci. and tech., 2000—. Office: Ministerio Ciencia e Tec, Bloco E 4 andar, 70067900 Brasilia Brazil

SARDÓN, JOSÉ LUIS, law and political science educator; b. Arequipa, Peru, Feb. 19, 1963; s. Luis A. Sardón Canepa and María I. de Taboada (Vizcarra); m. Sandra Bisso López de Romaña, Jan. 10, 1992; children: Sebastián, Joaquín. LLB, U. Catolica Santa María, Arequipa, 1986; MA in Polit. Sci., Am. U., 1990; diploma in internat. rels., U. Md., 1994. Exec. editor Debate mag., Apoyo S.A., Lima, Peru, 1986-88; adj. prof. U. Pacifico, Lima, 1988-89, prof., 1991-95; prof. U. San Ignacio de Loyola, Lima, 1996-99, U. Peruana Ciencias Aplicadas, Lima, 2000—; adj. prof. U. Lima, Peru, 1987-89, prof., 1998; columnist Expreso Newspaper, Lima, 1991-99, Agencia Interamericana Prensa Económica, Boca Raton, Fla., 1994—; advisor Prime Minister Alfonso Bustamante, Lima, 1993; cons. IFES/USAID, Conasev, World Bank, Presidency of the Ministry Cabinet, Lima, 1994; cons. Telecom. Commn., Lima, 1995—, Ositran, 1999. Author: Aproximaciones, 1985, Walter Piazza en el MEF, 1995, La Constitució incompleta, 1999; editor Apuntes, 1991-96. Trustee Patronato Cultural de Arequipa, Peru, 1985; congressman candidate Renovación, Peru, 1995. Recipient first prize Nat. Press Competition, Banco de Credito del Peru, 1985. Mem. Colegio de Abogados de Lima, Club Arequipa. Renovación. Roman Catholic. Avocations: music, piano, walking. Home: Ignacio Merino 740-801, Lima 18, Peru Office: Jose del Llano Zapata, 331-502 Lima 18, Peru

SARDOS, PANAYIOTIS ANTONIOU, electrical engineer; b. Larnaca, Cyprus, Jan. 3, 1949; s. Antonis Panayiotou and Elli George (Hadjifanis) S.; m. Lenia Kallis, Dec. 28, 1975; children: Lora, Antonis. BSEE, London U., 1972, MS in Elec. Machines & Power Sys., 1973, diploma of Imperial Coll., 1973; diploma in English studies, Cambridge (Eng.) U., Larnaca, Cyprus, 1988. Chartered elec. engr. Asst. engr. Electricity Authority Cyprus, Larnaca, 1974-77, engr. III, 1978-82; area sys. devel. engr. Electricity Authority Cyprus, Larnaca-Famagusta, 1982-84, area comml. engr. in mktg., 1984-92; sr. area engr. in sys. devel. Electricity Authority Cyprus, Nicosia-Kyrenia-Morphou, 1992—. Mem. bd. dirs. Welfare of Patients of Larnaca, 1990-94, Endowment Fund Evanthias Pieridou, 1990-94; pres. Friends of Pyla Movement, Larnaca, 1991—, Rotary Club Larnaca-Kition, 1994-95;

v.p. Larnaca Progressive Movement, 1992-97, pres., 1997—. Soldier Cyprus Nat. Guard, 1967-68. Mem. IEEE, Inst. Elec. Engrs., Sci. Tech. Instn. Cyprus, City and Guilds of London Inst. (assoc.). Home: 7 Eleftherias, 6030 Larnaca Cyprus Office: EAC PO Box 1413, 15 Photi Pitta Str, 1065 Nicosia Cyprus

SAREEN, TILAK RAJ, historian, researcher; b. Lahore, Pakistan, Oct. 5, 1935; s. Ram Nath and Vidya Vati (Khosla) S.; m. Anuradha Gupta, Dec. 6, 1970; children: Sumeet, Manu. BA, Panjab Univ., Chandigarh, India, 1956, MA in history, 1958, D in philosophy, 1973. Asst. archivist Nat. Archives Of India, New Delhi, 1958-63; rsch. officer Indian Inst. of Pub. Admin., New Delhi, 1963-65; archivist N.A.I., New Delhi, 1966-78; asst. dir. Nat. Archives of India, New Delhi, 1979-84; dir., sec. Indian Coun. of Historical Rsch., New Delhi, 1985-97; cons. of records mgmt. Gov. of Kenya, Narobi, Kenya, 1980-81, cons. Indian Inst. of Historical Studies, 1967-68; vis. fellow Univ. Heidelberg, 1993, Univ. Tokyo, 1993-94. Author: Indian Revolutionary Movement, 1977, Japan and the Indian National Army, 1984, Russian Revolution and Indian National Movement, 1978, Subhas Chandra Bose and Nazi Germany, 1996; contbr. numerous articles to profl. jours. Mem. Internat. Goodwill Soc. India (hon.), India and Asia Pacific Assn., India and Japan Goodwill Assn., Internat. Coun. on Archives, Assn. of Indian Archivists, Indian History Congress, South Indian History Congress, Orissa History Congress (pres.). Avocations: travelling, writing, reading, social welfare, exchange of views. Home: B 402 Kaveri Apt, 110019 New Delhi India

SAREH, MUSTAFA BIN, e-commerce entrepreneur; b. Batu Pahat, Johore, Malaysia, Mar. 22, 1963; s. Sareh Hj Tahir and Saaodah Bte Tumin. B-SChemE, U. Toledo, 1986. Tchg. asst. U. Toledo, 1984-86; mktg. exec. Delcom Svcs. Sdn Bhd, Kuala Lumpur, Malaysia, 1990-91; mktg. mgr. GEC, Petaling Jaya, Malaysia, 1991-93; sales mgr. Am. Internat. Industries, Kuala Lumpur, Malaysia, 1993-95; mktg. mgr. Mahkota Engring. Sdn Bhd, Petaling Jaya, 1996—; bd. dirs. Othman Mohammad Sdn Bhd, Segamat, Malaysia, Ideawaja Sdn Bhd, Kuala Lumpur. V.p. Bandar Country Homes Resident Assn., Rawang, 1997-99; treas. Surau An-Nur, Bandar Country Homes, 1997-99; pres. Rukun Tetangga, Bandar Country Homes, 1997—. Lt. Royal Malaysian Navy, 1986-90. Recipient Gen. Svcs. medal Malaysian Govt., 1988. Mem. Instn. Engrs. Malaysia (grad.), Bd. Engrs. Malaysia (grad.), Duta Palm Resort and Anglers Club (com. mem. 1997-98), Old Putera Assn. Avocations: golf, swimming, tennis, travel. Fax: 60-3-6923690. E-mail: mustafa@skybiz.com. Home and Office: Bandar Country Homes, 25 Jalan Desa 3/6, Rawang 48000, Malaysia

SARFRAZ, MUHAMMAD, computer scientist, educator; b. Lahore, Pakistan, May 2, 1957; s. Muhammad and Rahmat (Bibi) Nazar; m. Tayyba Sarfraz, June 21, 1985; children: Ihsan-ul-Haq, Humaira Sarfaz, Inam-ul-Haq, Ikram-ul-Haq. BSc, Govt. Coll., Lahore, 1977; MSc, Punjab U., Lahore, 1980, Brunel U., Eng., 1987; PhD, Brunel U., Eng., 1990. Lectr. U. of Engring. and Tech., Lahore, 1981-83; vis. lectr. U. Punjab, 1981-82, lectr., 1983-91, asst. prof., 1991—; asst. prof. King Fahd U. Petroleum & Minerals, Dhahran, Saudi Arabia, 1994-99, assoc. prof., 2000—; vis. faculty mem. S.A.H. Inst. Computer Sci., Lahore, 1991—. Asst. editor Punjab U. Jour. Math., 1990—; contbr. rsch. papers to profl. jours. Recipient Gold medal U. Punjab, 1980; Quaid-i-Azam scholar, 1986; sr. rsch. fellow De Montfort U. Eng.,1994—. Mem. Am. Math. Soc., IEEE Computer Soc., Punjab Math. Soc. (life; exec. mem. 1993—), Assn. Computing Machines. Home: 314 Gulsham-e-Ravi, Lahore Pakistan Office: King Fahd U Petroleum and Minerals, Dept Info & Comp Sci PO Box 1510, Dhahran 31261, Saudi Arabia

SARG, TAHA MOSTAFA, pharmacognosist, educator; b. Benha, Qualyobia, Egypt, Apr. 23, 1940; s. Mostafa Taha Ahmed and Nefesa Hassan Ali Sarg; m. Laila Osman El-Saddiki, Sept. 16, 1948; children: Marwa, Shireen, Mohamed, Maie. BSc in Pharmacy, Faculty of Pharmacy, Cairo, 1960; M in Pharmacognosy, Alexandria U., 1965, PhD of Pharmacognosy, 1969. Asst. prof. pharmacognosy Alexandria (Egypt) U., 1969-72, Riyadh (Saudi Arabia) U., 1972-76; assoc. prof. Zagazig (Egypt) U., 1977-81; rschr. sch. pharmacy U. Conn., Storrs, 1981-82; prof., head pharmacy dept. Zagazig U., 1982—; prof. pharmacognosy Tripoli (Libya) U., 1988-90. Author: Pharmacognosy, 1986. Mem. Egyptian and Am. Soc. of Pharmacognosy, Syndicate of Pharmacists. Avocations: reading, swimming, football, tennis, gymnastics. Home: Zananiri St 90 Sidi Gaber, Alexandria Egypt Office: Zagazig U Pharmacy Dept, Sharkyia Zagazig 44519, Egypt

SARGAN, DAVID RICHARD, molecular biologist, educator; b. Leeds, Eng., Nov. 23, 1955; s. John Denis and Phylis Mary (Millard) S.; m. Helen Varley, Sept. 4, 1982; children: Kate Ailsa, Sophie Elizabeth. BA with honors in Natural Sci., U. Cambridge, Eng., 1977, MA, 1981; PhD, U. Coll. London, 1981. Rsch. fellow U. Geneva, Switzerland, 1981-82, Baylor Coll. Med., Houston, 1983-85; lectr. U. Edinburgh, Scotland, 1986-93, sr. lectr., 1993-94; lectr. in molecular pathology U. Cambridge, Eng., 1994—, dir. Postgrad. Sch. Vet. and Biomed. Scis., 1997—; chair Wellcome Conf. Rsch. in Canine and Human Genetic Disease, London, 1995; mem. Wellcome Trust Vet. Interest Group, 1995-98. Contbr. numerous articles in profl. jours. Mem. Brit. Soc. for Immunology, Soc. for Gen. Microbiology, Assn. for Rsch. in Vision and Ophthalmology. Office: U Cambridge Dept Clin Vet Medicine, Madingley Rd, Cambridge CB3 0ES, England

SARGEANT, ADRIAN, marketing educator; b. Plymouth, Devon, United Kingdom, Oct. 27, 1964; s. Brian Francis and Gwendolene Doreen (Owen) S. MBA, Heriot-Watt U., 1993; PhD, Exeter U., 1996. Apprentice Devonport Dockyard, Plymouth, 1981-84; systems support officer Tunstall Telecom, Plymouth, 1984-87; bus. devel. mgr. Communication Care, Plymouth, 1987-92; lectr. Swansea (Eng.) Coll., 1993-94, Exeter (Eng.) U., 1994-97; lectr. mktg. Henley (Eng.) Mgmt. Coll., 1997—. Author: Marketing Management for Nonprofit Organizations; Contbr. articles to profl. jours. Mem. Chartered Inst. Mktg. (edn. liaison officer 1994), Inst. Mgmt., Inst. Charity Fundraising Mgrs., Inst. Direct Mktg. Office: Henley Mgmt College, Greenlands, Henley-on-Thames RG9 3AU, England

SARGENT, HERB, writer, television producer; b. Phila., July 15, 1923; m. LeGrand Council Mellon. Student, Pa. State U., 1941-43, U. Calif., L.A., 1946-48. Writer (TV series) Broadway Open House-NBC, 1950-51, Colgate Comedy Hour (Fred Allen)-NBC, 1951-52, Victor Borge Show-NBC, 1953, Tonight Show (Steve Allen)-NBC, 1954-58, Steve Allen Sunday Show-NBC, 1958-61, Tonight Show (Johnny Carson)-NBC, 1962-63, The Perry Como Show-NBC, 1963-64, That Was the Week That Was-NBC, 1964-65, The Corner Bar-ABC, 1972-73, Ivan the Terrible-CBS, 1976, The News is the News-NBC, 1983, (TV spls.) The Steve Allen Show with Peter Ustinov, Louis Armstrong and Van Cliburn-NBC, 1959, Music from Shubert Alley-NBC, 1959, Bing Crosby Special-ABC, 1961, Milton Berle Special-NBC, 1962, Annie: The Women in the Life of a Man-CBS, 1970, Lily-CBS, 1973, The Best of Saturday Night Live-NBC, 1979, The 40th Annual Emmy Awards-Fox, 1988, Diet America Challenge-CBS, 1989, Time Warner Presents: The Earth Day Special-ABC, 1990, The 43rd Annual Primetime Emmy Awards Presentation-Fox, 1991, Saturday Night Live: All the Best of the Mother's Day-NBC, 1992, The 2nd Annual Saturday Night Live Mother's Day Special-NBC, 1993; writer, script cons. Saturday Night Live-NBC, 1975-95; prodr. (TV series) That Was the Week That Was-NBC, 1964-65, The News is the News, 1983, (TV spls.) The Wonderful World of Aggravation, 1972, Alan King Looks Back in Anger-A Review of 1972, 73, Lily-CBS, 1973, The George Segal Show, 1974, Happy Endings, 1975, Love, Life, Liberty, and Lunch, 1976, (radio) NPR's Backfire!, 1992—, (screenplay) Bye Bye Braverman, 1968; co-creator (TV series) The Corner Bar-ABC, 1972-73, Ivan the Terrible-CBS, 1976, others. Writer People for the Am. Way, 1970—. Sgt. U.S. Army Air Corps, 1943-46. Recipient 6 Emmy awards, 6 Writers Guild awards. Mem. NATAS (bd. govs.), Writers Guild Am. East (coun. mem. 1985-91, pres. 1991—), Dramatists Guild, Songwriters Guild Am. Office: Writers Guild Am East 555 W 57th St New York NY 10019-2925

SARGENT, JAMES O'CONNOR, freelance writer; b. N.Y., June 15, 1918; s. Joseph Hughes and Maryann Josephine (O'Connor) S.; m. Mildred Elizabeth Clark, Apr. 19, 1949. Student, British Intelligence Sch., Calcutta, India, summer 1944, Fordham U., 1949-51. Ghostwriter, freelance writer, 1949—; founder Washington Writers Group, Washington, 1960—. Editor, rschr., writer (Bell Aircraft Co. in-house publ.) History of the Helicopter, 1952; author: (novellas) You Don't Bury on Christmas, 1960, Interregnum in a Commune, 1968, The Button Man, 1969, Moon in Pisces, 1970, Death in Saigon, 1971, Last Minuet in Washington, 1973, (MWA Anthology) Killers of the Dream, 1974; (screenplay) Queen Victoria and Lady Flora, 1993; (play) Loss of Innocence, 1994, (with Dakin Williams) Satanic Chapters, 1997; published over 1900 works. Liaison with Peiping Aviators Assn., 1995—. Maj. USAF, 1942-47. Decorated Bronze Star, Chinese medal of freedom, others; recipient 1st prize Nat. Fiction Contests, 1960, 61. Mem. 14th USAF Assn., U.S. Libr. of Congress, 528th Fighter Squadron Assn. (officer), Am. Mus. Natural History, Nat. Trust for Historic Preservation. Avocations: walking 3 miles per day, 19th and 20th Century Royal genealogy, World War I & II history, friendships. Home: 1019 Stillbrook Rd Pensacola FL 32514-1629

SARGENT, JOHN RICHARD, economist; b. Birmingham, Eng., Mar. 22, 1925; s. John Philip and Ruth (Taunton) S.; m. Anne Elizabeth Haigh, July 16, 1949 (div. 1980); children: Sara Anne, Simon David Haigh, Victoria Mary; m. Hester Mary Robinson, Oct. 18, 1980. BA, Oxford (Eng.) U., 1949, MA, 1956. Fellow, lectr. econs. Worcester Coll., Oxford U., 1951-62; econ. cons. Her Majesty's Treasury, London, 1963-65; prof. econs. Warwick U., Coventry, Eng., 1965-73; group econ. adviser Midland Bank Plc., London, 1974-84; econ. adviser Minister of Tech., U.K., 1967-69; mem. coun. of mgrs. Soc. Universitaire Recherches Financieres, the Netherlands, 1976-93, pres., 1984-87. Author: British Transport Policy, 1956; contbr. numerous articles to profl. econs. jours.; editor Midland Bank Rev., 1974-84. Mem. Doctors and Dentists Rev. Body, London, 1972-76, Armed Forces Pay Rev. Body, London, 1972-85, Pharmacists Rev. Panel, London, 1985—. Sub-lt. Royal Naval Vol. Res., 1943-46. Mem. Royal Econ. Soc. (coun. 1969-74), Am. Econ. Assn., Nat. Inst. Econ. and Social Rsch. (gov.). Avocation: gardening. Home and Office: Trentham House Fulbrook, Burford OX18 4BL, England

SARGENT, ROGER WILLIAM HERBERT, chemical engineer, retired; b. Bedford, Eng., Oct. 14, 1926; s. Herbert Alfred and May Elizabeth (Gill) S.; m. Shirley Jane Levesque Spooner, Aug. 11, 1951; children: Philip Michael, Anthony John. BSc in Chem. Engring., Imperial Coll., London, 1947, PhD, 1954, DSc in Engring., 1977; D (hon.), Inst. Nat. Poly., Nancy, France, 1987, U. Liège, Belgium, 1995; DSc (hon.), U. Edinburgh, Scotland, 1993. Asst. lectr. Imperial Coll., London, 1950-51, sr. lectr., 1958-62, prof. chem. engring., 1962-66, Courtaulds prof. chem. engring., 1966-92, prof. emeritus, sr. rsch. fellow, 1992—; design engr. Air Liquide, Paris, 1951-58; mem. process control rsch. com. Min. Tech., 1960-62; dean engring. Imperial Coll., London, 1973-76, head dept. chem. engring., 1975-88, dir. ctr. process sys. engring., 1989-92; chmn. bd. studies chem. engring. U. London, 1966-69, mem. com. acad. orgn., 1980-82; mem. adv. com. engring. tech. British Coun., 1976-89, chmn. 1984-89; mem. bd. chem. and minerals requirements Dept. Trade Industry, 1980-81, com. data requirements, 1980-81, bd. mech. elec. engring. requirements, 1981-86, com. process plant, 1980-81, chmn. 1981-87; supr. bd. nat. engring. lab., 1987-88; non-exec. dir. Prosys Tech. Ltd., 1988-91; mem. British Nat. Com. Internat. Engring. Affairs, 1987-90; Richard W. Wilhelm lectr. U. Princeton, 1994; mem. scientific counsel U. Toulouse, 1995-98; disting. rsch. lectr. chem. engring. Carnegie-Mellon U., Pitts., 1996. Assoc. editor Jour. Optimization Theory Applications, 1979—, Math. Programming, 1980-86, Soc. Indsl. and Applied Math. Jour. Optimization, 1989-93; subject editor Jour. Rsch. Devel., 1985-88; mem. editl. bd. Computers Chem. Engring., 1987—; contbr. over 110 articles to profl. jours. Mem. British-French Mixed Cultural Commn., 1985-90. Recipient Silver medal Ville de Paris, 1986, Jubilee medal Higher Inst. Chem. Tech., Sofia, 1988, Computing Chem. Engring. award AIChE, 1990. Fellow Royal Acad. Engring. (founding), Inst. Chem. Engrs. (mem. rsch. com. 1960-66, 80-85, chmn. working party process optimization 1963-66, mem. publ. com. 1961-63, chmn. 1963-72, mem. edn. com. 1984-86, mem. internat. com. 1987-88, chmn. 1988-91, v.p. 1969-73, pres. 1973-74), Inst. Math. Applications, City and Guilds London Inst. (hon.), Royal Soc. Arts; mem. U.S. Nat. Acad. Engring. (fgn. assoc.). Home: 291 A Sheen Rd, Richmond TW10 5AW, England Office: Ctr Process Systems Engring, Imperial Coll, London SW7 2BY, England

SARGIOUS, NAGY ALBEAR, pharmaceutical executive; b. Cairo, Apr. 3, 1950; s. Albear Sargious Sidhom and Helen Foad Rashidy; m. Nagwa Abbas Shaker, Feb. 27, 1978; children: Dany, Hany. BSc in Pharmacy, Cairo U., 1973; MSc in Pharmacology, Chelsea Coll., London, 1976. Gen. mgr. White Star Tours, Cairo, 1979-83, Tonsi Hotel, Cairo, 1983-85; hotel gen. mgr. Marwa Palace, Cairo, 1985; project mgr. Svcs. and Sys., Cairo, 1985-87; gen. mgr. K-Quip, 1988-92; mng. dir. STARS Group, 1992—; cons. White Stars Tours, Cairo, 1980-83, Golden Tulip Hotel chain, Cairo, 1983-85. Recipient Unitel award Ministry of Commerce, 1999. Avocations: reading, fishing, walking. Home and Office: STARS, 177 Pyramids Rd, Guiza Cairo Egypt

SARGSYAN, DAVID, library director; b. Yerevan, Armenia, Oct. 6, 1957; s. Mkrtich Sargsian and Elena Davidian; m. Valentina Alaverdian, Apr. 19, 1956. Diploma, Yerevan State U., 1979. Philologist, jr. editor Sovetakan Grogh pub. House, 1980-82, sr. editor, 1982-90; officer CC of CP of Armenia, 1990-91; dir. Hayastan Pub. House, 1991-98; head of apparatus Min. of Culture, Republic of Armenia, 1998; dir. Nat. Libr. of Armenia, 1998—. Mem. United Writers of Armenia, United Journalists of Armenia, Armenian Libr. Assn. Mem. Armenian Rev. Con. Party. Mem. Apostolic Ch. Avocations: reading, hunting. Office: Nat Libr Armenia, Terian 72, Yerevan 375009, Armenia

SARGSYAN, TIGRAN, bank executive; b. Vanadzor, Armenia, Jan. 29, 1960; married; 1 child. Diploma with honors, Fin. Econ. Inst., Leningrad, Russia, 1983, M of Econ. Scis., 1987. Head dept. of internat. econ. rels. Economy and Planning Rsch. Inst., 1987-90; coord. Standing Seminars for Bankers on Problems of Econ. Reforms, 1990-91; lectr. on banking Yerevan State U., 1993-94; chmn. standing com., parliament mem., 1990-95; dir. Transformation Soc. Rsch. Inst., 1995—; chmn. Ctrl. Bank of Am., 1998—. Contbr. articles to profl. jours. Office: Ctrl Bank of Republic, Nalbandyan str 6, Yerevan 37510, Armenia

SARHAN, MANSOOR MOHAMED, library director; b. Nuwidrat, Bahrain, Jan. 1, 1945; s. Mohamned Abdulla and Sukainah Ahmed (Ismail) S.; m. Zahra Abul Kassim Dashti, Aug. 22, 1971; children: Nazha, May, Mohamed. BA in History, Beirut (Lebanon) Arab U., 1972; B in Libr. Sci., U. Bombay, India, 1980; MA in Librarianship, Leeds (Eng.) Poly., 1985; diploma exec. mgmt., U. Bahrain, Isa Town, 1990. Tchr. for English lab. Ministry of Edn., Manama, Bahrain, 1963-73; libr. Manama (Bahrain) Pub. Libr. Ministry of Edn., 1973-82; head pub. librs. Ministry of Edn., Manama, 1982-88, dir. pub. librs., 1989—; gen. organizer Bahrain Internat. Book Fair, Manama. Author: The Book and the Libraries, 1983, Cultural Movement in Bahrain 1940-1990, 1993, Bahrain National Bibliography, 1995, Libraries in Islamic Dynasties, 1997, Survey of Cultural Movement in Bahrain during Twentieth Century, 2000, Pioneers of Bookshops in Bahrain, 2000. Lectr. schs., clubs and assns., Bahrain, 1975—; gen. organzer yearly piano concert Ministry of Edn., Bahrain, 1988—. Mem. Bahrain Libr. Assn. (pres. 1994—), Arab Fedn. for Librs. and Info., Nuwidrat Club (pres. 1966—). Avocations: reading, music, tennis, chess. Home: House 46 Rd 4301, Nuwidrat 643, Bahrain Office: Ministry of Edn, PO Box 43, Manama Bahrain

SARI, JONATHAN PAAVO, software engineer; b. Princeton, N.J., Jan. 19, 1970; s. Seppo Oliver and Elizabeth Mary (Robinson) S.; m. Sept. 12, 1992 (div. 1996). Cert. Microsoft profl. Unix cons. U. Wash., Seattle, 1988-89, sci. programmer Ctr. for Quantitative Sci., 1991-96; sci. programmer Ctr. for Process Analytical Geometry, Seattle, 1990-91; application programmer Omni Devel., Seattle, 1996; sr. software design engr. Brodie Tech. Group, Bellevue, Wash., 1996; owner, mgr. Surge Creative Cons., Shoreline, Wash., 1996-98; software arch. Excell Data Corp., Bellevue, Wash., 1987-99; software engr. perfect.com., Palo Alto, Calif., 1999—; Author freeware computer game eddie, 1992; editor Ofcl. Usenet Rose-playing Game List, 1994-99, Ofcl. Usenet Role-Playing Game Co. List, 1994-99.a. Recipient Most Colorful award Empire Hall of Fame, Internet, 1990. Democrat. Avocation: philosophy. E-mail: jonathan@perfect.com. Home: 1145 Amarillo Ave Apt 2 Palo Alto CA 94303-3711

SARIBEKIR, NUZHET ESRA, packaging company executive; b. Istanbul, Turkey, Oct. 22, 1969; d. Huseyin Necip and Guler (Ozvarnali) S. B Engring. with honors, U. Nottingham, Eng., 1990. Audit asst. Coopers & Lybrand, Istanbul, 1990; cons. asst. Andersen Cons., Istanbul, 1990-92; export and import mgr. Sarten Ambalaj, Istanbul, 1992-93, gen. sec. to bd., 1993-97, v.p. purchasing and commerce, 1997—; mem. exec. bd. Sollac Ambalaj, Istanbul, 1996-97; bd. mem. Varnaliyag, Un, Yem, Istanbul, 1998—; chmn. Silivri Park Hotel, Istanbul, 1999—; bd. mem. Petpak Ambalaj, Istanbul, 1997—. Mem. Packagers Assn. (bd. mem. 1998-2000), Tin Can Mfrs. Assn. (founder 1999). Avocations: skiing, painting, reading. Office: Sarten Ambalaj, Barbaros Bulvari No 38/7, 80700 Istanbul Turkey

SARIC, MARKO, physician, consultant; b. June 22, 1924; s. Dragutin and Pina (Kurilic) S.; m. Sonja Bartulica, Mar. 12, 1957 (dec. 1981); m. Biserka Bujas, 1983; 1 child, Lana. MD, U. Zagreb, Croatia, 1951, PhD, 1959. Physician Univ. Hosp., Zagreb, 1952-57; rschr. Inst. for Med. Rsch. and Occupl. Health, U. Zagreb, 1957-64, dir. of Inst., 1964-91, prof. occupl. health, 1964—; cons. WHO, Geneva; mem. Parliament Assembly of Yugoslavia, Belgrade, 1965-67; chmn. Council for Health and Social Welfare, Parliament, Republic of Croatia, Zagreb, 1967-74. Author: Occupational Health, 1962; co-author: Pathology of Work—Occupational Diseases in Mining, Industry and Agriculture, 1964, Occupational Medicine, 1978, 84, Working Ability, 1984; editor: Assessment of Temporary Disability, 1982; contbr. articles to sci. jours. Recipient award of City of Zagreb, City Coun. Zagreb, 1967, 78, Ruder Boskovic award Republic Com. for Sci., Tech. and Informatics of Republic of Croatia, 1977, AVNOJ award Com. for AVNOJ Awards, Fed. Assembly of Yugoslavia, 1983, Croation Nat. award life achievement field biomedical scis., 2000. Mem. AAAS, Croatian Acad. Scis. and Arts, Permanent Commn. and Internat. Assn. on Occupl. Health (bd. dirs. 1978-84), Yugoslav Assn. Occupl. Health (pres. 1969-74, bd. dirs. 1978-83), Med. Assn. Croatia (pres. sect. occupl. health 1974-91), N.Y. Acad. Sci., Am. Occupl. Med. Assn. Home: Radicevo setaliste 27, 10000 Zagreb Croatia Office: U Zagreb Inst Med Rsch and, Occ Hth Ksaverska Cesta 2, 10000 Zagreb Croatia

SARIĆ, MILOJE RADOJICA, plant physiologist, educator, researcher; b. Nemenikuce, Serbia, Yugoslavia, Sept. 12, 1925; s. Radojica Dragutin and Leposava Radomir (Životić) S.; m. Zora Stanko Toševa, Apr. 23, 1952; children: Snežana, Predrag. Grad., U. Belgrade, Yugoslavia, 1949, PhD, 1957; postgrad., U. Ill., 1953-54, U. Moscow, 1957-58. Asst. Inst. Improvement and Plant Prodn., Belgrade, 1951-58; sci. collaborator Inst. Sci. Rsch., Novi Sad, Yugoslavia, 1958-62; prof. Faculty of Agr. and Natural Scis. Univ., Novi Sad, 1962-89; mem. exec. coun. Fedn. European Socs. Plant Physiology, 1976-90, pres., 1986-88; mem. Internat. Coun. Plant Nutrition, 1978—; mem. Internat. Commn. Symposium Genetic Aspects of Plant Mineral Nutrition, 1982-92. Author: (textbook) Plant Physiology, 1963, 6th edit., 1983, General Principles of Scientific Work, 1985, 4th edit., 1996; co-author: (textbook) Plant Physiology, 1987, 3d edit., 1991, Practical Manual in Plant Physiology, 1967, 4th edit., 1990, Miloje R. Saric-Life and Work, 1995, Lives and Work of Serbian Scientists, 7 books, 1996; editor: Genetic aspects of plant mineral nutrition, 1983, Brief history of plant physiology, 1988, Medicinal herbs of SR Serbia, 1989, Flora of Serbia, 1992, Effects of phosphorous fertilizers on contamination of soil and plants by uranium, 1993; editor 23 monographs, sci. and text books. Recipient 7th of July award Exec. Coun. Socialist Republic Serbia, 1960, Liberation of Vojvodina award Exec. Coun. Vojvodina, 1977, AVNOJ award Yugoslav State, 1986. Mem. Serbian Acad. Scis. and Arts, Yugoslav Soc. Plant Physiology (founder, pres. 1966—), Serbian Biol. Soc., Yugoslav Soc. Investigation of Soil, Soc. Plant Physiology of Russian Acad. Sci. (hon.). Avocations: literature, philosophy. Office: Serbian Acad Scis Arts, Knez Mihailova 35, 11000 Belgrade Yugoslavia

SARIDIS, GEORGE NICHOLAS, electrical, computers and system engineering educator, robotics and automation researcher; b. Athens, Greece, Nov. 17, 1931; came to U.S., 1961, naturalized, 1971; s. Nicholas and Anna (Tsofa) S.; m. Panayota Dimarogona, Apr. 10, 1985. Diploma in Mech. and Elec. Engring., Nat. Tech. U., Athens, 1955; MSEE, Purdue U., 1962, PhD, 1965. Instr. Nat. Tech. U., 1955-63; instr. Purdue U., West Lafayette, Ind., 1963-65, asst. prof., 1965-70, assoc. prof., 1970-75, prof., 1975-81; prof. elec., computer and sys. engring. Rensselaer Poly. Inst., Troy, N.Y., 1981-96, dir. Robotics and Automation Lab., 1982-96, prof. emeritus, 1997—; dir. NASA Ctr. for Intelligent Robotic Systems for Space Exploration, 1988-92; engring. program dir. NSF, Washington, 1973; hon. prof. Huazhong U., Wuhan, China. Author: Self-Organizing Control of Stochastic Systems, 1977, Stochastic Processes Estimation and Control, 1995; co-author: Intelligent Robotic Systems: Theory and Applications, 1992, Reliable Plan Selection by Intelligent Machines, 1996, Design of Intelligent Control System Based on Hierarchical Stochastic Automata, 1996; also numerous articles, reports; co-author: Intelligent Robotic Sys.; co-editor, contbg. author: Fuzzy Automata, 1977; editor, contbg. author: Advances in Automation and Robotics, Vol. 1, 1985, Vol. 2, 1990. Fellow IEEE (founding pres. robotics and automation coun. 1981-84, Centennial medal 1984, Third Millennium medal 2000, Disting. Mem. award Control Sys. Soc. 1989); mem. ASME, Soc. Mfg. Engrs./Robotics Internat.-Machine Vision Assn. (sr.), Am. Soc. Engring. Edn., N.Y. Acad. Scis., Acad. Alteus (Greece). Home: 38 Loudonwood E Loudonville NY 12211-1465 Office: Rensselaer Poly Inst Dept Electrical Computer & Sys Engring Sch of Engring Troy NY 12180-3590

SARIN, SOHAN LAL, acoustician; b. Jullunder, India, May 25, 1938; arrived in The Netherlands, 1965; s. Amar Nath and Indira Prabha (Khosla) S.; m. Helle Scheving, Nov. 4, 1967; children: Sohan, Ravi. PhD, U. Tech., Delft, The Netherlands, 1968. Scientific officer KNMI, De Bilt, The Netherlands, 1968-73; sr. specialist Fokker Aircraft, The Netherlands, 1975-94, cons., 1994-96; cons. SAAB AB, Linköping, Sweden, 1996-97, specialist in aeroacoustics, 1997—; presenter in field. Contbr. articles to profl. jours. Mem. Confedn. European Aerospace Socs. (gen./tech. chair 2d aeroacoustics conf. with AIAA, mem. organizing com. 3d aeroacoustics conf., sci. com. 2d acoustics specialists' com. workshop on aircraft interior noise control). Achievements include 1 patent in field; development of new inlet design so-called spliceless inlet for more efficient attenuations of sound for aircraft applications. Office: SAAB AB, FD-SS, Linköping Sweden

SARIN, VINOD KUMAR, materials scientist; b. Jan. 29, 1944. BSMetE, U. Wis., 1965; MSMetE, U. Mich., 1966; ScD in Material Sci., MIT, 1971. Rsch. scientist Sandvik Rsch. Ctr., Stockholm, 1971-75; sr. rsch. scientist Adamas Carbide Crop, Kennilworth, N.J., 1975-77; sr. staff scientist GTE Lab. Inc., Waltham, Mass., 1977-89; prof. Boston U., 1989—; invited disting. scientist Max Planck Inst., Stuttgart, summer 1985, U. Linkoping, summer 1983, vis. prof., summer 1995; vis. prof. U. Lund, Sweden, 1996—; cons., presenter and lectr. in field. Editor Science of Hard Materials, 1988, 95, 98; mem. editl. bd. Mat. Sci. and Engring., 1988, Jour. Hard Materials, 1988—, Refractory Metals and Hard Materials, 1995, 98; author over 70 patents; contbr. articles to profl. jours. Mem. Sci. Hard Materials (conf. chmn., editor 1988, 95, 98), Am. Soc. for Metals (chmn. machinability com. 1984-86, conf. chmn. 1985), Am. Powder Metallurgy Inst., Am. Soc. for Metall. Engrs., Am. Ceramics Soc., Am. Soc. for Mfg. Engrs., Sigma Xi. Achievements include over 70 patents for surface modification, cutting tool materials, composites, materials processes. Office: Boston Univ Coll Engring 15 Saint Mary's St Boston MA 02215

SARIOLA, HANNU VEIKKO, pathologist; b. Jyväskylä, Finland, Sept. 3, 1954; s. Aarne and Elina S.; m. Anna Paula Sarjanoja; children: Salla, Reetta, Veikko, Kukka. MD, U. Helsinki, Finland, 1980, PhD, U. Helsinki, 1984. Resident in pathology U. Helsinki, 1980-84, 87, group leader devel. biology, 1993-98, rsch. dir. Inst. Biotechnology, 1999, prof. developmental biology, 2000—; postdoctoral fellow Max Planck Inst., Tubingen, Germany, 1985; sr. consulting pathologist U. Ctrl. Hosp. Helsinki, 1987, 89-92, 96. Editor Med. Jour. Duodecim, 1990-93, 97, asst. editor, 1993-96, editor-in-chief, 1998-99. Avocation: photography. Fax: 358 9 70859366. E-mail: hannu.sariola@helsinki.fi. Home: Oravatie 15, FIN00800 Helsinki Finland Office: Inst Biotech U Helsinki, Viikinkaari 9, FIN00014 Helsinki Finland

SARIS, NILS-ERIK LEO, biochemistry educator; b. Helsinki, Finland, Nov. 2, 1928; s. Eguda and Sigrid Svea Sofia (Ahlskog) S.; m. Eva Maria Wollitz, Aug. 2, 1953 (dec. June 1979); children: Paul Guenther, Gandul Helena Maria, Per Erik Joakim; m. Margita Solveig Lund, Apr. 23,

1981. MS, U. Helsinki, 1953, PhD, 1956, DS, 1964, D Medicine and Surgery (hon.), 1990. Rsch. asst. Nobel Laureate A.I. Virtanen, Helsinki, 1994; clin. biochemist Aurora Hosp., Helsinki, 1956-65; rsch. fellow U. Pa., Phila., 1958-59; prin. clin. biochemist Meilahti Hosp., Helsinki, 1965-72; prof. med. chemistry U. Helsinki, 1972-93, vice rector, 1989-92, chmn. Inst. Biomedicine, 1994; pres. Lattasaaren Tutkimuskeskus Inc., Helsinki, 1973-81, Elomit Inc., Helsinki, 1985-92; v.p. Sci. Park Heureka, Vantaa, Finland, 1989-92; mem. coun. 350 yr. anniversary U. HKI, 1994-95; bd. dirs. Found. Ann. Chemistry Congress in Finland, 1994-98. Editor: Manual of Clinical Lab, 1979, 81, IFCC Recommendations, 1985. Chmn. publ. com. Internat. Fedn. Clin. Chemistry, Geneva, 1975-88; chmn. Certifying Bd. in Clin. Biochemistry, Helsinki, 1981-95; vice chmn. Nat. Com. for Coordination of Univ. Edn. in Swedish Teaching, Finland, 1990-94. Recipient Commemorative medal of the Winter War 1939-40, Pres. of Finland, 1940; named Comdr., Order of the Finnish Lion, 1990. Mem. Assn. Finnish Chemists, Chem. Soc. of Finland, Soc. Clin. Chemistry in Finland, Societas Medicorum Fennica. Lutheran. Home: Ostra Allen 16A1, FIN-00140 Helsinki Finland Office: U Helsinki Inst Biomedicine, PB 9 Siltavuorenpenger 10, FIN00014 Helsinki Finland

SARISLEY, EDWARD F., engineering technology educator, consultant; b. New Britain, Conn., May 3, 1954. BS in Civil Engring., U. Conn., 1976, MS in Civil Engring., 1978, PhD in Structural Engring., 1989. Registered profl. engr., Conn. Structural engr. Internat. Housing Ltd., Westport, Conn., 1976-77, Maguire Group Engrs., Inc., New Britain, Conn., 1978-80; sr. structural engr. A-N Cons. Engrs. Inc., Newington, Conn., 1980-82; prof. engring. tech. Cen. Conn. State U., New Britain, 1982—; cons. U.S Naval Underwater Systems Ctr., New London, Conn., summer 1990, Close, Jensen & Miller, Wethersfield, Conn., summer 1985; sci. advisor Peoples Actions for Clean Energy; USN-Am. Soc. Engring. Edn. summer faculty rsch. assoc., 1990. Inventor prestress retention system for stress-laminated timber bridges; patentee in field. Recipient Saul Horowitz grad. fellow award Assoc. Gen. Contractors Am., 1988. Fellow ASCE; mem. Constrn. Specifications Instr., Am. Soc. Engring. Edn., Nat. Soc. Pfl. Engrs., Sigma Xi, Phi Kappa Phi, Tau Beta Pi, Chi Epsilon, Epsilon Pi tau. Avocations: sailing, skiing, model railroading. Office: Cen Conn State U Engring Tech Dept 1615 Stanley St New Britain CT 06053-2439

SARKAR, AMITENDRA NATH, geoscientist; b. Krishnanagar, India, Nov. 3, 1941; s. Rabindra Nath and Nandarani (Marik) S.; m. Pratima Majumdar, July 26, 1969; children: Suchismita, Susnigdha. BSc, Indian Inst. Tech., Kharagpur, 1962, MSc, 1964, PhD in Structural Geology, 1976; cert. on digital geog. info. sys., George Washington U., 1985; postgrad., U. Calif., Santa Barbara, 1985. Jr. geologist Geol. Survey of India, Patna, 1966-76; sr. geologist Geol. Survey of India, Calcutta, 1976-91; dir. Geol. Survey of India, Faridabad, 1991-92, 1992—; rschr. in structural geology, Indian Inst. Tech., Kharagpur, India, 1964-66; investigator geol. survey and mineral investigation Geol. Survey India, Patna, 1966-74, geosci. map compiler, 1974-91, dir., 1991—; mem. del. feasibility study of CAM systems BRGM, Orleans, France, 1989. Author: Structural and Petrological Evolution of Precambrian Rocks etc, 1982; compiler Tectonic map of India, 1999, Geotechnical map of India, 1995; contbr. articles to profl. jours. UNDP fellow, 1984-85; recipient Nat. Mineral award Govt. of India, 1992-93. Mem. Nat. Geog. Soc., N.Y. Acad. Scis. Avocations: reading scientific articles, scientific discoveries and inventions and biographies of scientists. Home: Quarter No 1050, Type V NH-IV, 121001 Faridabad Haryana India Office: NH5P NIT, Geol Survey India, 121001 Faridabad Haryana India

SARKAR, GAUTAM, science educator; b. India, Apr. 10, 1953; U.S. citizen; s. Prosanta K. and Shelly (Roy) S.; m. Shanta Bhattacharya; children: Priyanca, Preetam Sagnik. BE 1st class, U. Calcutta, India, 1975; MTech, Indian Inst. Tech., Kanpur, 1977; PhD, Marquette U., 1984. Chartered engr., Inst. Materials, U.K. Instr. Rensselaer Poly. Inst., Troy, N.Y., 1983-85; rsch. assoc. U. Fla., Gainesville, 1986-87; asst. rsch. engr. U. Calif., Santa Barbara, 1987-88; sr. devel. engr. Ferro Corp., Santa Barbara, 1988-90, rsch. cematist, 1990-94; gen. mgr. ACC-Webel Electroceramics Ltd., India, 1994-95; sr. lectr. Nanyang Tech. U., Singapore, 1995—; invited lectr. AMD Corp., Singapore, 1999; spkr. in field. Contbr. chpts. to books and articles to profl. jours.; co-patentee dielectric materials. Recipient Cert. of Tech. Excellence, AMD Corp., 1999. Mem. Internat. Microelectronic and Packaging Soc. (pres. 1998-99, Disting. Spkr. 1995, Silver Plaque 1998, Pres.'s button 1998), Electrochem. Soc., Inst. Materials. Avocation: wildlife photography. E-mail: calpolocc@hotmail.com. Home: EC 114 Sector 1 Salt Lake, Calcutta 700064, India Office: Nanyang Tech U, Sch Material Engring, Singapore 639798, Republic of Singapore Also: 101 C Nanyang View #11-05, Singapore 639670, Singapore

SARKAR, MICHAEL ROBINDRA, surgeon; b. Tübingen, Germany, Apr. 4, 1960; s. Satyabrata and Ursula (Engelmann) S.; m. Renate Erika Summ, June 4, 1988. MD, U. Tübingen, 1987. Qualified gen. and trauma surgeon. Lab. asst. Max-Planck Inst., Tübingen, 1978; rsch. fellow Lab. for Exptl. Surgery, Davos, Switzerland, 1983-84; asst. surgeon Mcpl. Hosp., Karlsruhe, Germany, 1987-93; surgeon, traumatologist Univ. Hosp., Ulm, Germany, 1994—; assisting physician dept. anesthesia Mcpl. Hosp., Karlsruhe, 1987-88, mem. gastrointestinal endoscopy unit, dept. surgery, 1992-93; mem. muskuloskeletal oncology group Univ. Hosp., Ulm, 1994—. Contbr. articles to profl. jours. Recipient Rsch. prize Assn. for Osteosynthesis, 1988, stipend Fed. Found. for Highly Qualified Students, 1980-87. Mem. Internat. Assn. Osteosynthesis (mem. soft tissue group 1995-99, head bone bank 1997—), German Traumatologists Soc., European Assn. Tissue Banks. Avocations: choir, piano, sailing, photography, cooking. Office: Univ of Ulm, Steinhövelstrasse 9, 89070 Ulm Germany

SARKAR, TAPAN KUMAR, engineering educator, researcher; b. Calcutta, Bengal, India, Aug. 2, 1948; s. Sanat K. and Mira Sarkar. B in Tech., Indian Inst. Tech., Kharapur, India, 1969; MSc, U. New Brunswick, Fredericton, Can., 1971; MS, Syracuse U., 1974, PhD, 1975; D (hon.), U. Blaise Pascal, Clermont Ferrand, France, 1998. Cert. profl. engr. Rsch. fellow Syracuse (N.Y.) U., 1972-75, assoc. prof., 1985-87, prof., 1988—; from asst. prof. to assoc. prof. Rochester (N.Y.) Inst. Tech., 1976-85; rsch. fellow Harvard U., Cambridge, Mass., 1977-78. Author 10 book; contbr. articles to profl. jours. Fellow IEEE. Home: 11 Wexford Rd De Witt NY 13214-1812 Office: Syracuse U 121 Link Hl Syracuse NY 13244-0001

SARKARI, TEHMURASP RUSTOMJI, fuel efficiency consultant; b. Bombay, Nov. 6, 1915; s. Rustomji Dhunjibhoy and Gulbanoo (Dordi) S.; m. Perin Tehmurasp Patel Sarkari, May 22, 1947; 1 child, Rita. B Mech. Engring., Coll. Engring., Poona, India, 1939, BEE, 1940. Vice prin. Polytech. Inst., Surat, India, 1934-52; asst. prof. Victoria Jublilee Engring. Coll., Bombay, India, 1952-59; prof. to sr. prof. Indian Inst. Tech., Powai, India, 1959-73; head R&D to tech. dir. Thermax Boiler Co., Poona, India, 1973-83; cons. in fuel efficiency Personal Co., Poona, India, 1983—; lectr. Polytech. Inst., Surat, India, 1940-52. Inventor software for effective fuel economy information; contbr. technical books, papers and seminars in field. Recipient Nat. award on Republic Day, 1989, Nat. Rsch. Devel. Corp., Ctrl. Govt., New Delhi, 1989. Mem. Inst. Engring., Inst. Plant Engring., Combustion Inst. Avocations: play writer, homeopathic medicine study.

SARKER, SHAMSUL ALAM, mathematics educator, researcher; b. Gaibandha, Bangladesh, Jan. 1, 1957; s. Ahmed Ali Sarker and Sarvan Nesa; m. Sultana Rajia Madhuri, May 26, 1981; children: Shamsad Parvin, A.S. Saad Ahmed. BSc, Gaibandha Coll., 1979; MSc, Rajshahi (Bangladesh) U., 1981; PhD, Banaras Hindu U., India, 1992. Lectr. Sundargonj (Bangladesh) Coll., 1982-83; sr. officer Janata Bank, Lalmonirhat, Bangladesh, 1984-86; lectr. dept. math. Rajshahi U., 1986-89, asst. prof., 1989-93, assoc. prof., 1993-99, provost Sher-E-Bangla Hall, 1996-99; prof. Rajshahi Univ., 1999—. Contbr. articles to profl. jours. Mem. Bangladesh Math. Soc. (life). Islam. Avocation: reading. Home: Dept Math, Univ Rajshahi, 6205 Rajshahi Bangladesh Office: Rajshahi U., Department Mathematics, 6205 Rajshahi Bangladesh

SARKER, SOHRAB UDDIN, wildlife biologist, educator; b. Baraghona-Ullapara, Bangladesh, Jan. 3, 1937; s. Bahadur Ali Sarker and Suraton Nessa; m. Noorjahan Sarker, Oct. 23, 1973; children: Rene-Cloude Suzan Sarker Rim, Sabrina Jahan Rim Sarker. Grad., Azizul Huq Coll., Bangladesh, 1963; BS, Rajshi Coll., Bangladesh, 1967; MS, U. Dhaka, Bangladesh, 1969; PhD, U. Bordeaux-II, France, 1978; diploma in French, VICHY, France, 1976; MD, Bogra Med. Sch., Bangladesh, 1960. Med. doctor in pvt. practice Bogra Baraghona, Bangladesh, 1963-65; h.s. sci. tchr. Bogra Matiamalipara, 1964-66; lectr. U. Dhaka, Bangladesh, 1970-73, asst. prof., 1973-83, assoc. prof., 1983-88, prof. wildlife biology, 1988—, chmn. dept. zoology, 1994-97; house tutor Shaidullah Hall Dhaka U., 1980-89; team leader NCSI Project-1 Min. of Environment and Forest, Dhaka, 1995-97. Contbr. 105 articles to profl. jours. Recipient acad. stipend Bogra Med. Sch., 1956-60; scholar French Govt., 1974-78. Fellow Zool. Soc. Bangladesh; mem. Wildlife Soc. Bangladesh, Species Survival Commn. (chmn.). Avocations: bird watching, wildlife observation, religious associations. Home: V Baraghona, PO Kuchiamara, Dist Sirajgonj Bangladesh Office: Dept Zoology, U Dhaka, Dhaka 1000, Bangladesh

SARKIS, J. ZIAD, management consultant; b. Beirut, Lebanon, July 8, 1968; arrived in France, 1975; s. Nicolas Ata and Claude (Moussalli) S.; m. Elisabeth Kalman, June 21, 1997. BAS in Anthropology, Econs. and Math. with distinction and honors, Stanford U., 1990, MS in Engring. and Mgmt., 1990; DPhil in Econs., Oxford U., Eng., 1998. Cons. McKinsey & Co., San Francisco, 1990, N.Y.C., 1991-92, Paris, 1992; co-founder, sr. ptnr., bd. dirs. Mitchell Madison Group (formerly AT Kearney FI/SP), N.Y.C., 1992—. Gen. sec. Phoenixia-X, Paris, 1993—. Greek Catholic. Office: Mitchell Madison Group 9 W 57th St New York NY 10019-2701

SARKIS, NICOLAS, oil industry research director, consultant; b. Yabroud, Syria, Dec. 28, 1934; arrived in France, 1975; s. Ata and Mountaha (Kassis) S.; m. Claude Moussalli, Jan. 12, 1941; children: Ziad, Walid-Serge, Jihad-Nicolas. Diploma in law, Beirut U., 1956; D with honors, Paris U., 1961. Dir. Arab Petroleum Rsch. Ctr., Lebanon, 1965-75, Paris, 1976-96; cons. to oil producing countries, 1966-96; guest spkr. U. Beirut, 1961-63, U. Paris, 1994-96; spkr. in field. Author: Oil and Arab Economy, 1962 (distinction award), Arab Oil and World Economy, 1976 (French award); editor: Arab Oil & Gas Directory, yearly 1974-96, (periodical) (in English, French and Arabic) Arab Oil & Gas, 1966—. Recipient award French Govt., Paris, 1975. Avocations: music, jogging, swimming. Home: 28 Rue de Franqueville, 75116 Paris France Office: Arab Petroleum Rsch Ctr, 7 Ave Ingres, 75016 Paris France

SARKISIAN, DAVID, library director; b. Yerevan, Armenia, Oct. 6, 1957; s. Mkrtich Sarkisian and Elena Davidyan; children: Mkrtich, Lusine, Andranik. Grad., High State U., Yerevan, Armenia, 1979. Editor Nairi Pub. House, 1980-81; officer CPSU of Armenia, 1991-92; dir. Hayastan Pub. House, 1992-98; head of apparatus Ministry of Culture, Republic of Armenia, 1998-99; dir. Nat. Libr. Armenia, 1999—. Mem. Union of Writers of Armenia, Union of Journalists of Armenia, Armenian Libr. Assn. Mem. Armenian Apostolic Church. Avocations: reading, hunting. Home: 28 apt, 4/3 Kievyan St, Yerevan Armenia 375028 Office: Nat Libr Armenia, Terian 72, Yerevan 375009, Armenia

SARKOMAA, PERTTI JUHANI, engineering educator; b. Jyvaskyla, Finland, June 14, 1941; m. Marjatta Elisabet Petaja, Feb. 6, 1965; children: Sari, Petri, Juha-Pekka, Anna. BS, Inst. Technology, Tampere, Finland, 1965; MS, U. Technology, Helsinki, 1970, D Mech. Engring., 1981. Prof. U. Tech., Lappeenranta, Finland, 1972—, dir. dept. energy engring., 1972-86, dir, sect. heat and fluid dynamics, 1988-95, dean dept. energy engring., 1995-98, head sect. heat transfer and environ. tech., 1995—; rsch. mgr. Nat. Fund for R&D, Finland, 1974-76; sr. rsch. Acad. Finland, 1976-77, 80, 85. Patentee in field; contbr. 180 articles to profl. and scientific publs. Maj. mil. Recipient internat. best paper award ASHRAE, 1978. Mem. TAPPI, Engring. Soc. Finland, Assn. France-Finlandaise pour la Recherche Scientific et Technique, Rotary. Home: Kuusitie 27, FIN 53810 Lappeenranta Finland Office: Lappeenranta U Tech, PO Box 20, FIN 53851 Lappeenranta Finland

SARLOS, PETER, agricultural engineer; b. Bicske, Hungary, Feb. 3, 1952; s. Jozsef and Aranka (Kapitany) S.; m. Maria Bocs, Dec. 18, 1976; two children. Bsc, Agrl. U. Mosonmagyarovar, Hungary, 1988. Asst. GYKI, Budapest, Hungary, 1970-73; tech. Hosp. Bicske, 1973-77; from tech. to rschr. Rsch. Inst. Animal Breeding & Nutrition, Herceghalom, Hungary, 1977—. Home: Kossuth 1, 2060 Bicske Fejer, Hungary

SARMA, AMARDEO CHRISTIAN, telecommunications executive; b. Kassel, Hesse, Fed. Republic Germany, Dec. 27, 1955; s. Ramnath Sundaram and Susanne Dorothea (Leicher) S.; m. Renate Kristiane Demmler, Jan. 5, 1979; children: Navina, Olivia, Dominik. B of Tech., Indian Inst. of Tech., Delhi, India, 1977; diplom.-ingenieur, Tech. Hochschule Darmstadt, Germany, 1980. Rsch. scientist Deutsche Bundespost Telekom, Darmstadt, 1981-95, head rsch. group, 1991-95; project supr. EURESCOM Heidelberg, 1995-99; head dept. engring. & methods mgmt. T-Nova Deutsche Telekom Innovationsgellschaft, Bonn, Germany, 1999—; mem. exec. coun. Com. for Scientific Investigation of Claims of the Paranormal; chmn. Internat. Telecommunications Union-Telecomm Standardization Sector (ITU-T) Study Group 10, 1996—. Co-author: SDL with Applications from Protocol Specification, 1991, SDL-Formal Object Oriented Language for Communicating Systems, 1997; co-editor SDL 93-Using Objects, SDL 95-With MSC in case, Parawissenschaften unter der Lupe, 1995. Mem. Gesellschaft for Informatik, Soc. for the Scientific Investigation of Para-Sci. (founder, hon. sec. 1987—). Social Dem. Party. Avocations: music, politics. Home: Kirchgasse 4, D-64380 Rossdorf Germany Office: Am Propsthof 10, 53121 Bonn Germany

SARMA, PULUGURTA VYAGHRESHWARA, economics educator; b. Kolanka, India, Dec. 24, 1944; s. Subba Rao and Annapoorna Pulugurta; m. Venkata Prabhavathi, 1971; two children. BA, Andhra U., 1965, MA, 1969, MSc, 1970, PhD, 1977. From lectr. in econs. and prof. econs. Andhra U., India, 1970—. Mem. Indian Soc. Agrl. Econs., Indian Soc. Regional Sci. Office: Andhra U, Econs Dept, 530003 Visakhapatnam India

SARMELA, MATTI ELJAS, anthropology educator; b. Hollola, Finland, Apr. 6, 1937; s. Vaino and Salli Sivia (Lehto) S.; m. Leena Kankare, 1962; children: Matti, Vaino. MA, U. Helsinki, 1963, Ph.Lic., 1964, PhD, 1970. Editor Atlas of Finnish Folk Culture, Helsinki, 1962-68; tchg. asst. U. Helsinki, 1969-71, mem. faculty, 1973—, prof. social anthropology, 1988—; rsch. fellow Acad. of Finland, Helsinki, 1971-73; docent cultural anthropology U. Turku, 1973—; anthrop. field work, Thailand, 1972-73, 82-83, 84-85, 97-98, 99. Author: Reciprocity Systems of Rural Society, 1969, Quantitative Methods in Ethnology, 1970, Introduction to Cultural Anthropology, 1972, Structural Change in Local Culture, 1979, Four Northern Communities, 1984, Writings in Cultural Anthropology, 1984, Information Technology and Structural Change in Local Cultures, 1987, Structural Change into Future-Postlocal Culture, 1989, The Bear in the Human Environment, 1991, Finnish Folklore Atlas, Atlas of Finnish Ethnic Culture 2, 1994 (Finlandia prize 1995). Grantee U. Helsinki, 1964, 65, 69, 70, 81, Acad. Finland, 1969, 71, 72-73, 76, 84-85, Ministry Edn., 1971, 72, Scandinavian Inst. Asian Studies, 1972, 82. Mem. Finnish Anthrop. Soc. (chmn. 1975-85), Finnish Lit. Soc. (bd. dirs. 1973-83), Kalevala Soc. (bd. dirs. 1975—), Merenkavijat Club. Mem. Green Party. Lutheran. Avocation: sailing. Home: Katajanokanranta 17 B 16, SF-00160 Helsinki, Finland

SARMENTO, ARTHUR JUNQUEIRO, NATO official; b. Lisbon, 1939; m. Maria Ana Sarmento; 4 children. Grad., Portuguese Naval Acad. Commd. 2d lt. Portuguese Navy, advanced through grades to vice-adm., 1996, early mil. assignments include jr. comm. and exec. officer; dir. Naval Radio Sta. Portuguese Navy, Azores; comdr. patrol boat Portuguese Navy, Guinea-Bissau; comm./electronics warfare officer, comdg. officer frigate Portuguese Navy, 1972-82, naval adviser to Pres. of Republic of Portugal, comdr. frigate for NATO and bilateral forces, comdg. officer patrol boat flotilla, 1987-92, head ops. dept., Naval Central Staff, 1992-93, head of Portuguese Maritime Autority, 1996-97; Portuguese mil. rep. to NATO Mil. Com. Portuguese Navy, Brussels, 1997—. Decorated Mil. Order of Aviz, Dist. Svc. Gold medal, Disting. Svc. Silver medal 92), Meritorious Svc. medal (2), others. Office: NATO Hdqrs, Blvd Leopold III, 1110 Brussels Belgium*

SARMIENTOS, PAOLO, chemical company executive; b. Naples, Italy, June 10, 1957; s. Eduardo Sarmientos and Raffaella Salzano; m. Teresa Cuocolo, July 24, 1982; children: Luca, Daria. PhD, U. Naples, 1980. Postdoctoral fellow Nat. Insts. Health, Bethesda, MD, 1980-83; rschr. Rhone-Poulenc Co., Paris, 1983-86; dir. biotech. rsch. Farmitalia, Milan, 1986-92; CEO PRIMM srl, Milan, 1992—; cons. Menarini, Florence, Italy, 1992; contract prof. U. Milan, 1990-91. Liberal. Roman Catholic. Avocations: skiing, tennis, golf. Office: PRIMM srl, via Olgettina 58, 20132 Milan Italy

SARNA, MARIAN, physics and environmental science educator, designer; b. Lubla, Rzeszów, Poland, Sept. 6, 1939; s. Stanisław and Zofia (Bigos) S.; m. Irena Leki, Mar. 27, 1967 (dec. Oct. 1988); 1 child, Ewa. M in Physics, U. Maria Sklodowska-Curie, Lublin, Poland, 1963; D in Tech., Inst. Fundamental Tech., Warsaw, 1971. Rschr. Electrostatic Precipitators Factory ELWO, Pszczyna, Poland, 1963-79; splst., 1992—; tutor Tech. U. Łodź (Poland), 1975—. Contbr. articles to profl. jours.; patentee in field. Named rector tech. U. Lodz, 1977, 78, 81, 85, 87, 88, 97, 99. Mem. Polish Soc. Theoretical and Applied Mechanics, Internat. Soc. Electrostatic Precipitators. Avocations: music, playing violin and organ. Home: Staromiejska 58, 43-200 Pszczyna Poland Office: Tech U Łódź, Willowa 2, 43-300 Bielskó-Biala Poland

SARNACKI, MICHAEL THOMAS, lawyer; b. Springfield, Mass., Nov. 13, 1965; s. Robert Michael and Jean Elizabeth S.; m. Kimberly Lynn King, Sept. 9, 1995; children: John Michael, Katherine Margaret. BA, U. Mass., Amherst, 1988; JD, We. New Eng. Coll. Law, 1992. Bar: Mass. 1992, U.S. Dist. Ct. Mass. 1994. Ptnr. Chartier, Ogan, Brady, Shute & Emm, Holyoke, Mass., 1992—. Mem. ABA, Mass. Bar Assn., Hampden County Bar Assn., Springfield Rugby Football Club (dir. 1994—), Elks, Am. Whitewater. Avocations: whitewater kayaking, rugby, running. Office: 850 High St Holyoke MA 01040-3767

SARNOFF, LILI-CHARLOTTE (LOLO SARNOFF), artist, executive; b. Frankfurt, Germany, Jan. 9, 1916; came to U.S., 1940, naturalized, 1943; d. Willy and Martha (Koch von Hirsch) Dreyfus; m. Stanley Jay Sarnoff, Sept. 11, 1948; children: Daniela Martha Bergezi, Robert L. Grad., Reimann Art Sch., Germany, 1936, U. Berlin, 1936-38; student, U. Florence, Italy, 1948-54. Rsch. asst. Harvard Sch. Pub. Health, 1955-69; rsch. assoc. cardiac physiology Nat. Heart Inst., Bethesda, Md., 1954-59; pres. Rodana Rsch. Corp., Bethesda, Md., 1959; v.p. Catrix Corp., Bethesda, Md., 1958-61. Inventor Flolite light scupltures under name Lolo Sarnoff, 1968; one-woman shows include: Agra Gallery, Washington, 1969, Corning (N.Y.) Glass Ctr. Mus., 1970, Gallery Two, Woodstock, Vt., 1970, Gallery Marc, Washington, 1971, 72, Franz Bader Gallery, Washington, 1976, Gallery K, Washington, 1978, 81-85, 87-91, (Restrospective Show) 95, Alwin Gallery, London, 1981, Galerie von Bartha, Basel, Switzerland, 1982, La Galerie L'Hotel de Ville, Geneva, 1982, Pfalzgalerie, Kaiserlautern, Fed. Republic Germany, 1985, Galerie Les Hirondelles, Geneva, 1988, Rockville (Md.) Civic Ctr., 1988, Washington Square Sculpture group, 1989, Internat. Sculpture Congress, Washington, 1990, Sculpture on the Grounds, Rockville, 1996; represented in collections: Fed. Nat. Mortgage Assn., Washington, Brookings Inst., Washington, Corning Glass Ctr. Mus., Nat. Air and Space Mus., Washington, Kennedy Ctr., Washington, Nat. Acad. Sci. Chase Manhattan Bank, N.Y.C., Israel Mus., Jerusalem, Nat. Mus. Women in Arts, Washington, Corcoran Gallery, Washington, others; transcriber: Dara Autobiography of a Chesapeake Bay Retriever, 1999. Past trustee Nat. Ballet, Mt. Vernon Coll.; founder, pres. Arts for the Aging, Inc., Bethesda, 1988—; active Washington Opera Soc., Washington Ballet Soc., bd. overseers Corcoran Gallery Art, 1991. Recipient Golda Meir award, 1995; recipient Life Commitment to the Arts ann. award Swiss Am. Cultural Exch. Coun. Gala, Corcoran Gallery Art, 1999, Path of Achievement award for Arts and Humanities, Montgomery County, Md., 2000. Home: 7507 Hampden Ln Bethesda MD 20814-1331

SAROCCHI, JEAN, education educator; b. Oran, Algeria, May 16, 1933; s. Marcel Sarocchi and Simone Blanc; m. Francoise Martinez, 1982. Doctorate, 1975. Prof. philosophy, Latin, French and Greek, 1957-62; prof. French lit. Strasbourg, France, 1962-70; scientific rschr. CNRS, 1970-75; prof. French lit. Tunisia, 1977-81, Toulouse, 1981—. Contbr. articles to profl. jours. Roman Catholic. Avocations: piano, poetry, skiing, walking. Home: 9 bis rue des Lois, 31000 Toulouse France

SARODE, DIWAKAR BABURAO, veterinarian, veterinary medicine educator; b. Karanja (Lad), India, Feb. 10, 1952; s. Baburao Govindrao and Leelabai Baburao (Harne) S.; m. Sayali Diwakar; children: Sayali, Swapnil; m. Usha Diwakar Babhulkar, May 27, 1979. BVS & A.H., Vet., Nagpur, India, 1973, MVSc (Medicine), 1975, PhD, 1987. Rsch. asst. D.R.P.K.V., Akola, India, 1975-76; asst. prof. D.R.P.K.V., Akola, 1976-78; asst. prof. D.R.P.K.V., Nagpur, 1978-92, assoc. prof., 1992-96, prof., head, 1996—, univ. head, 1994—, officer I/C Zoo, 1998-90, officer I/C Polyclinic, 1997—; asst. prof. M.A.U., Parbhani, India, 1978; pres. N.V.C., Nagpur, 1986-87, prin. investigator wild life, 1999—. Author: Diseases of Domestic Animals, 1973; contbr. articles to profl. jours. Recipient Honor Cert. I.C.A.R., 1973, Assoc. Dean N.V.C., 1990, 95. Mem. Indian Soc. Vet. Medicine (life, participant Outstanding Contbn. to Society activities 1988, Momento Citation 1988-89), I.S.V.E.P.M. (life, v.p. Chennai 1996-98), Soc. Prevention Cruelty to Animals, Nat. Geographic Soc. Avocations: academic research, extension, conferences world wide, driving, games. Home: 1/3 Janki Apt, Nagpur Gorepeth 440010 Maharashtra, India Office: Vet Coll, Dept Medicine, Nagpur 440006 Maharashtra, India

SARRAMON, JEAN-PIERRE FERNAND LOUIS, urologist, educator; b. Toulouse, France, Jan. 18, 1938; s. Henri and Jacqueline (Pellegrin) S.; m. Marie-France Lhez, Mar. 19, 1964; children: Christine, Benedicte. Baccalaureate in Lit. and Philosophy, St. Joseph Coll., Toulouse, 1956; M.D., Med. Faculty Toulouse, 1970. Intern in medicine U. Hosp., Toulouse, 1964; prosector in anatomy Med. Sch., Toulouse, 1970; chief of clinic in surgery, 1970-71, asst. prof. urology, 1972-77, assoc. prof., 1978-90, prof., 1990—; chief of svc., chmn. urology, transportation and ANDrdo U. Hosp., 1982—; dir. exptl. surgery dept. C.H.U. Purpan, Toulouse, 1985—; mem. U. Nat. Counsel, 1987; mem. faculty, lectr. European Sch. Urology. Mem. editl. bd. Les Annales d'Urologie, Archivio Italiano di Urologia, Nephrologia Andrologia, 1988, Le Progress en Urologie, 1990, Internat. Jour. Impotence Rsch., 1990; contbr. chpts. to books. Hon. officer French Armed Forces, 1975—. Mem. French Transplantation Soc., French Soc. Urology, French Coll. Urologists (mem. adminstrv. coun.), European Urol. Assn., Am. Urol. Assn. (corr.), Soc. Internat. d'Urologie, Belgium Urol. Assn., European Orgn. for Rsch. and Treatment of Cancer, European Soc. Male Genital Surgery (v.p.), Adminstrv. French Urol. Counsel, Internat. Microsurgery Soc., European Soc. Organ Transplantation, Internat. Soc. Impotence Rsch., Conseil Nat. des Univs. Roman Catholic. Avocations: riding, mountaineering, sailing, golfing, skiing. E-mail: sarramon.j.p.@chu-toulouse-fr. Home: 9 Rue Espinasse, 31000 Toulouse France Office: Urological Dept, CHU Rangueil-Chemin Du Vallon, 31000 Toulouse France

SARRAZIN, THIERRY BERNARD, medical physicist, researcher; b. Allouagne, France, Aug. 26, 1952; s. Paul and Monique (Cramez) S.; m. Nadine Michaux, Dec. 28, 1973; children: Cedric, Thibaut. MSc, U. Lille, France, 1975, DEA Solid Physics, 1976, PhD, 1978, DEA Atomic Physics, 1979. Rschr. U. Lille, 1976-78; med. physicst Clinique Louviere, Lille, 1978-92; chief dept. med. physics Ctr. Oscar Lambret, Lille, 1992—. Active Town Coun. Mouvaux, 1989-95. Mem. Nat. Trade Union French Physicists (pres. 1991—), Hosp. Physicist French Soc., Rotary (pres. 1995-96). Avocation: diving. Fax: (33) 320-29-59-72. Office: Ctr Oscar Lambret, 3 Rue F Combemale, 59020 Lille France

SARRE, WARWICK TURNER, law educator; b. Adelaide, Australia, July 25, 1955; s. Brian Robert and Winifred Grace (Turner) S.; m. Debra Anne Stuckey, Mar. 6, 1993; children: Millicent, Elliott. LLB, U. Adelaide, South Australia, 1977; MA, U. Toronto, Ont., Can., 1983. Barrister, solicitor Adelaide, 1978-88; lectr. South Australian Coll. Advanced Edn., Adelaide, 1984-91, sr. lectr., 1992; head of sch. U. South Australia, 1992-96, assoc. prof. law, 1996—; cons. South Australia Atty. Gens.' Dept., 1989; vis. prof. Graceland Coll., Iowa, 1997. Author: Leisure Time and the Law, 1977, Uncertainties and Possibilities, 1994, Exploring Criminal Justice, 1998, Considering Crime and Justice, 2000. Pres. Norwood sub-br. Australian Labor Party, 1989-95. Mem. Law Soc. of South Australia. Mem. Community of

Christ Ch. Avocation: cycling. Office: U South Australia Sch Law, PO Box 2471, Adelaide 5001, Australia

SARREALS, SONIA, data processing consultant; b. N.Y.C., Sept. 17, 1938; d. Espriela and Sadie Beatrice (Scales) Sarreals; m. Waldro Lynch, Sept. 18, 1981 (div. Oct. 1983). BA in Langs. summa cum laude, CCNY, 1960; cert. in French, Sorbonne, Paris, 1961. Systems engr. IBM, N.Y.C., 1963-69; cons. Babbage Systems, N.Y.C., 1969-70; project leader Touche Ross, N.Y.C., 1970-73; sr. programmer McGraw-Hill, Inc., Hightstown, N.J., 1973-78; staff data processing cons. Cin. Bell Info. Systems, 1978-89; sr. analyst AT&T, 1989-92; lead tech. analyst Automated Concepts Inc., Arlington, Va., 1992-96; tech. cons. Maxim Group, Fairfax, Va., 1996—. Elder St. Andrew Luth. Ch., Silver Spring, 1992-96. Downer scholar CUNY, 1960, Dickman Inst. fellow Columbia U., 1960-61. Mem. Assn. for Computing Machinery, Phi Beta Kappa. Democrat. Avocations: needlework, sewing. Home: 13705 Beret Pl Silver Spring MD 20906-3030 Office: Maxim Group 12015 Lee Jackson Hwy Fairfax VA 22033-3300

SARRIS, GEORGE ELIAS, cardio-thoracic surgeon. AB, Harvard Coll., 1978; MD, Harvard Med. Sch., 1982. Diplomate Am. Bd. Surgery, Am. Bd. Thoracic Surgery. Intern in medicine Brigham & Women's Hosp., Harvard Med. Sch., 1982-83; resident gen. surgery Stanford U., 1983-90, fellow cardiothoracic surgery & cardiopulmonary transplant, 1990-93; fellow pediat. cardiac surgery Emory U., 1993-94; asst. dir. transplant unit Onassis Cardiac Surgery Ctr., Greece, 1994-95; staff dept. pediat. and congenital heart surgery Cleve. Clinic Found., 1995-97; chief, dept. congenital heart surgery Onassis Cardiac Surgery Ctr., Athens, 1997—. Co-editor, co-author: The Stanford Manual of Cardio-Pulmonary Transplantation, 1996. Mem. Internat. Soc. for Heart/Lung Transplantation, Soc. Thoracic Surgery, European Assn. Cardiothoracic Surgery. Office: Onassis Cardiac Surg Ctr, 356 Sygrou Ave, Athens 17674, Greece

SARROPOULOS, CONSTANTIN, utilities company executive; b. Athens, Greece, Nov. 26, 1926; s. George and Kathrin S.; married, July 20, 1958; children: Kathrin, Sylvia. Degree in Civil Engring., Poly., Stuttgart, Fed. Republic Germany, 1958. Cert. engr. Engr. Krupp, Altbach, Fed. Republic Germany, 1958-60, Motor-Columbus, Baden, Switzerland, 1960-63, Ministry of Agriculture, Athens, 1963-65, Ministry of Pub. Works, Athens, 1965-66; sr. engr. Pub. Power Corp., Athens, 1966-80, sect. head, 1981-90. Mem. Cultural Soc. of Hydra (gen. sec. 1982-93), Greek Soc. of Engrs. Avocation: ancient greek philosophy. Home: Esperou 27, 145-64 Athens Greece

SARROS, P. PETER, diplomat, consultant; b. Greece, Aug. 20, 1935; came to U.S., 1949; s. Basil and Helen Sarros. BA, Hobart Coll., 1957; M in Pub. and Internat. Affairs, Princeton (N.J.) U., 1959, PhD, 1964. U.S. fgn. svc. officer Dept. of State, Washington, 1960-92, sr. fgn. affairs cons., 1992-99; spl. amb. to the Vatican, 1978; charge US Mission to the Vatican, 1975-80; acting dep. asst. sec. for Human Rights, 1980-82; adj. prof. diplomacy, George Mason U., 1992-93. U. Wilson fellow Princeton U., 1957-60; named Spl. U.S. Amb. to the Vatican Pres. Carter, 1978. Mem. Am. Fgn. Svc. Assn., Fort Myer Officers Club, Phi Beta Kappa. Avocations: bibliophile. Home: 1200 N Nash St Arlington VA 22209-3616 Office: Dept of State IRM/OPS Washington DC 20520

SARROT-REYNAULD, FRANÇOISE, internist, researcher; b. Grenoble, France, Oct. 26, 1961; d. Jean and Simone (Martin) Sarrot-R. M in Immunology and Genetics, U. Lyon, France, 1987; DEA in Cellular Biology, U. Grenoble, 1989, MD, 1989, DES in Internal Medicine, 1989; M in Stats., U. Paris VI, 1993; PhD in Med. and Biological Engring., U. Grenoble, 1999. Intern Univ. Hosp., Grenoble, 1984-89, chief resident, 1989-92, cons. internal medicine, 1992—; tchg. fellow Med. U., Grenoble, 1989-92, lectr., 1996—; sci. sec. Coll. Internistes du Centre Est, France, 1996—. Contbr. articles to profl. jours.; mem. editl. bd. Rev. de Medecine Interne, 1994—, mem. sci. com., 1996—. Founder Mutual Ins. Co., 1994. Grantee PHRC, Grenoble, 1994. Mem. French Soc. Internal Medicine. Avocation: sports. Office: BP 217, Hosp Michallon Dept Int Med, 38043 Grenoble Cedex 9, France

SARSFIELD, LUKE ALOYSIUS, school system administrator; b. Luzerne, Pa., July 29, 1925; s. Luke Aloysius and Margaret Ann (Conahan) S.; m. Nancy Ann Chiavacci, Aug. 19, 1961; 1 child, Luke Aloysius III. BA, King's Coll., Wilkes-Barre, Pa., 1952; MA, Montclair (N.J) State Coll., 1962; PhD, NYU, 1973. Diplomate Ednl. Adminstrn. Tchr. Ogdensburg (N.J) Pub. Schs., 1953-55, Luzerne Pub. Schs., 1955-60; tchr. Rutherford (N.J.) Pub. Schs., 1960-70, adminstrv. asst. to supt., 1970-72, supt. schs., 1972—. Trustee Rutherford Pub. Libr., 1972—, v.p.; trustee Williams Inst. Inc., Rutherford, 1986—, treas.; trustee Bergen County Tenn Arts, 1989—; pres. Jack Frost Jr. Racing Found., White Haven, Pa., 1987-93, South Bergen Jointure Com. With USN, 1943-46. Mem. Am. Assn. Sch. Adminstrs., N.J. Assn. Sch. Adminstrs., Bergen County Supts. Assn. (past pres.), Bergen County Assn. Sch. Adminstrs., Bergen County Audio-Visual Com., King's Coll. Alumni Assn. (past pres.), Rotary (past pres.), Phi Delta Kappa. Roman Catholic. Office: Rutherford Pub Schs 176 Park Ave Rutherford NJ 07070-2310

SARTANI, ABRAHAM, endocrinologist, researcher; b. Tel-Aviv, Israel, Nov. 28, 1946; arrived in Italy, 1978; s. Samuel and Rina (Kronheim) S.; m. Emanuela Mussio, Sept. 24, 1971; 1 child, Alessandra. MD, Sackler Sch. of Medicine, Tel Aviv, Israel, 1976; specialist in endocirnology, U. Pavia, Italy, 1982. House doctor Tel Aviv (Israel) Hosp., 1976-78; rschr. Inst. Endocrinology U. Milan, Italy, 1978-80; clin. project leader Farmitalia, Milan, 1980-83; med. dir. Farmitalia, Bern, Switzerland, 1983-84; strategic coord. Farmitalia, Milan, 1984-85; med. dir. Recordati S.P.A., Milan, 1985-88, v.p. R&D and licensing, 1988—; pres. Flora, Inc., U.S., 1994-97. Recipient Atomo D'oro Acad. Romana in Sci., Medicine and Biology, 1993; premio Galeno Prix Galien, 1994. Fellow Royal Soc. Medicine; mem. N.Y. Acad. Scis., Am. Mgmt. Assn. Home: Viale Dei Platani 20/17, 20020 Arese MI, Italy Office: Recordati SPA, Via Civitali 1, 20148 Milan MI, Italy

SARTHER, LYNETTE KAY, accountant; b. Terre Haute, Ind., Mar. 16, 1947; d. William Horace and Margaret Jane (Bennett) Alsman; m. William Patrick Sarther, June 7, 1974; children: Kristen Casey, Joseph Bennett. BS, Ball State U., 1969. CPA, Ohio. Staff acct., office mgr. Arthur Young & Co., Cin., 1969-74; ptnr. Fowler, Alsman & Co., Cin., 1974-75; sr. acct. small bus. John Sullivan, CPA, Reston, Va., 1975-77; mgr. small bus. dept. Rippe, Strickling, Kingston & Co., Cin., 1977-79; owner Lynette K. Sarther, CPA, 1979-97, ret. 1998; former bus. mgr. jour. Woman CPA; treas. market steering com. Kindervelt Children's Hosp. Aux., 1989-90; co-pres. Hinsdale Mid. Sch., 1998-99; bd. dirs. Hinsdale Central H.S. PTO, 1997-99. Mem. AICPA, Am. Soc. Women Accts. (past mem., nat. bd. dirs., past pres. Cin. chpt., past nat. editor Coordinator), Am. Woman's Soc. CPAs, Ohio Soc. CPAs. Republican. Methodist.

SARTI, PAOLO, pathologist; b. Rome, Feb. 17, 1948; s. gino and Marcella (Tozzi Condivi) S.; m. Maria Grazia Silvestrini, Feb. 2, 1949; children: Alessio, Petrodavide, Matilde. MD, U. Rome, 1972. Med. diplomate as pathologist. Physician asst. in pathology U. Rome, 1972-77, physician asst. in biochemistry, 1977-81; rschr. Ctr. of Molecular Biology, Rome, 1981-86; assoc. prof. U. of L'Aquila, Italy, 1986-90; prof. medicine U. Cagliari, Italy, 1990-96; prof. medicine U. Rome I, 1996—, vice-head dept. biochem. scis., 1998—; rsch. supr. Ctr. Molecular Biology, Rome, 1989—; dir. Inst. Biol. Chemistry, Cagliari, 1995-96. Author: Fondamenti di Chimica Sanitaria, 1994. Mem. Italian Biochem. Soc., Italian Bioenergetics Group. Avocations: tennis, football, poetry. Office: Univ Rome I Dept Biochem Sc, Piazzale Aldo Moro 5, 00185 Rome Italy

SARTOR, JOACHIM FRIEDRICH, hydraulic engineering and water resources educator; b. Traben-Trarbach, Mosel, Germany, Aug. 15, 1954; s. Heinrich Friedrich and Elsa Charlotte (Schippers) S.; m. Felicitas Maria Kien, Apr. 12, 1987; children: Helena Caroline, Linda Christine. Diploma Civil Engring., Technische Hochschule Darmstadt, Hessen, 1983; doctorate, Universität Kaiserslautern, 1995. Registered hydraulic engr. for reservoirs, rivers and sewage. Project mgr. Ingenieurbüro Conrath & Ptnr. Spiesen-Elversberg, Saarland, 1983-89; rsch. asst. U. Kaiserslautern, 1989-93; prof. Fachhochschule Trier, 1993—; cons. Ingenieurbüro für Hydrologie and Gewässerschutz, Lieser, 1994—; lectr. hydraulic engring. Fachhochschule Saarbrücken, Saarland, 1987-89. Author: Continuous Models for River Basins, 1993; co-author: Water Management and Ecology, 1994. Mem. regulation com. Abwassertechnische Vereinigung e.v., Hennef, 1994—, BWK, Düsseldorf, 1993—. With German Army, 1974-75. Mem. ASCE, Soc. Am. Mil. Engrs., Bund der Ingenieure für Wasserwirtsch, Abfallwirtsch und Kulturbau, Deutscher Verband für Wasserwirtsch und Kulturbau. Avocations: sailing, contemporary history. Home: An der Mosel 8, D-56841 Traben-Trarbach Germany Office: Fachhochschule Trier FB2, Schneidershof, D-54293 Trier Germany

SARTORIUS VON BACH, HELMKE JENS, farming economics consultant; b. Windhoek, Namibia, June 6, 1962; s. Ernst Adolf and Sigrid Elizabeth (Kiekebusch) S.; m. Dagmar Viola Paulsmeier Sartorius von Bach, Jan. 6, 1996. BS in Agr., U. Pretoria, South Africa, 1985; BS in Agr. (hon.), 1986, MS in Agr., 1990, PhD, 1992. Agrl. economist Govt. Namibia, 1985-87, sr. agrl. economist, 1988-90; lectr. U. Pretoria, South Africa, 1990-93; asst. prof., 1993-94, head dept., prof., 1995; cons. Beulah, Namibia, 1996—; rsch. fellow Alexander von Humboldt, Germany, 1993; cons. U. Pretoria, South Africa, 1991-97. Contbr. articles to profl. jours. Lt. SWATF, 1986-87, Namibia. Recipient Rsch. bursary Alexander von Humboldt, Germany, 1993, rsch. funding Ctr. for Sco. Devel., Pretoria, 1993. Mem. Agrekon. Avocations: bird watching, squash, nature. Home: Farm Beulah PO Box 29, Kunene, Kunene, Kamanjab Namibia Office: Beulah/Kamanjab Farm Beulah, Beulah/Kamanjab Farm Beulah, PO Box 29, Kunene, Kunene, Kamanjab Namibia

SARU, GEORGE, artist; b. Checea, Timis, Romania, Mar. 1, 1920; s. George and Zorca (Pavlov) S.; m. Semizaliana Brinzan, Aug. 31, 1945; children: Dorian, Horia. BFA, Acad. Fine Arts, Jassy, Romania, 1944; MFA, Acad. Fine Arts, Bucharest, Romania, 1948; Diplomate, Acad. Di Belle Arti, Perugia, Italy, 1963. editor-in-chief Arta Mag., Bucharest, 1950-64; dep. chancellor Inst. Fine Arts, Bucharest, 1966-67, prof., 1948-82. Exhibited in group shows at Biennale di Venezia, 1954, 56, Mus. of Modern Art, Szecin, Poland, 1965, 75, Vienna, Austria, 1956, Moscow, 1958, Geneva, 1961, Berlin, 1963, Paris, 1968, Leningrad, 1972, Orly, France, 1972, San Sebastian, Spain, 1973, Washington, 1973, Cairo, Egypt, 1974, Quebec, 1975, Prague, Czechoslovakia, 1979; one-man shows include Dalles Art Gallery, Bucharest, 1956, 70, 77, 81, Pushkin Mus., Moscow, 1960, LeMire Gallery, New Orleans, 1983, Alex Gallery, Washington, 1987, Morin Miller Gallery, N.Y.C., 1988, 89, 90, Dome Gallery, N.Y.C., 1991, The York Sq. Gallery, New Haven, 1995, Romanian Cultural Ctr., 1997, N.Y. Gallery @49, N.Y., 1999; represented in permanet collections The Weisman Mus. Art, Mpls., Nat. Mus. Art Romania. Recipient Nat. award for Painting, Bucharest, 1950, Laureat of the State prize Bucharest, 1951, Internat. award for Painting, 1953, Gold medal Laureat or Triennial, Sofia, Bulgaria, 1976, Aachen, Germany, 1996; named Internat. Man of Yr. Internat. Biog. Ctr. Cambridge, Eng., 1995-96. Mem. UNESCO, Fine Arts Guild of Romania, Internat. Assn. Fine Arts, Assn. Internat. Arts Plastiques. Avocations: music, sculpture, etching, travel. Home and Office: 560 Main St Apt 446 New York NY 10044-0014

SARVANTO, KARI TAPANI, management consultant, business executive; b. Helsinki, Finland, Dec. 10, 1961; s. Seppo Kalervo and Anja Orvokki (Sandell) J.; m. Marja Hannele Liimatainen, Mar. 7, 1987 (div. 1999); children: Laura Emilia Sarvanto, Salla Maria S., Sara Elisa S. Naval officer, Naval Acad., Helsinki, Finland, 1985; grad. studies, U. Turku, Finland, 1989; PhD in Bus. Mgmt., London, 1999. First officer Coastal Fleet, Turku, Finland, 1981; midshipman Naval Acad., Helsinki, Finland, 1981-85; deputy chief Logistics Co., Helsinki Naval Base, Helsinki, Finland, 1985-86; exec. officer Missile Squadron, Turku, Finland, 1986-87; mgmt. cons. Rastor, Helsinki, Finland, 1987-88; dir., corp. devel. Kotisaari-Ingman Oy, Helsinki, Finland, 1988-90, v.p., corp. devel., 1990-91; v.p., corp. devel. Ingman Foods, Helsinki, Finland, 1991-92; CEO Dynargie Oy, Helsinki, 1992-95, Do It Devel. Internat. (Nordic), Paris, 1995—; chmn. Primex Internat., 1999—; bd. mem. Pro Image Oy, Espoo, Finland, 1989-99; CEO Latvakallio Condominium, Espoo , 1989-90; mem. Strategic Mgmt. Secs., Helsinki, 1990—; assoc. dir. Groupe Dynargie, Geneva, 1992-95; bd. mem., sr. ptnr. Do It Internat. S.A., Paris, 1995—. Lt. Navy, 1981-87, commd. lt. comdr. 1996, Turku, Finland. Mem. Commd. Officers in Turku (bd. dirs.), Assn. Naval Officers, Am. Mgmt. Assn., Strategic Mgmt. Assn., French-Finnish C. of C. (chmn. bd. 1998—), Assn. Mgmt. Cons. in Finland (bd. mem.). Lutheran. Avocation: sailing. Home: Embomint 164, FIN07880 Liljendal Finland

SARWAL, VIRENDAR, cardiac surgeon; b. Chandigarh, India, Sept. 22, 1960; s. Kanahiya Lal and Daya Rani (Puri) S.; m. Rashmi Singhal, Jan. 22, 1984; children: Ridhima, Varun. MBBS, Panjabi U., Patiala, India, 1981, MS in Gen. Surgery, 1988; MCh, PGIMER, 1991. Attending cardiac surgeon Escorts Heart Inst., New Delhi, 1992-94; cons. cardiac surgeon Batra Cardiac Care Ctr., New Delhi, 1994-95; asst. prof. Pgimer, Chandigarh, India, 1995-96; assoc. cons. Apollo Heart Hosp., New Delhi, 1997-98; med. dir., sr. cons. cardiac surgeon City Hosp. and Heart Care Ctr., Chandigarh, 1998-99; sr. cons. cardia surgeon Malhatra Heart Inst. & Med. Rsch. Ctr., New Delhi, 2000—. Contbr. articles to profl. jours. Mem. Indian Assn. Cardiovascular & Thoracic Surgeons, N.Y. Acad. Scis. Avocations: playing badminton, music, writing. Home: House #1184, Sector 8-C, Chandigarh 160018, India Office: Malhatra Heart Inst Med Rsc, Ctr 14 Ring Rd, New Delhi 110024, India

SARWATA, Indonesia supreme court justice. Chief justice Supreme Ct. of Indonesia, Jakarta. Office: Mahkamah Agung, Jalan Merdeka Utara 9-13, Jakarta Indonesia 10110*

SAS, BARNABÁS, science administrator, toxicologist; b. Kálmánd, Hungary, July 2, 1944; s. Barna and Barnáné (Láng Sarolta) S. Gen. vet., U. Vet. Sci., Budapest, Hungary, 1967; expert radioisotopes, Tech. U. Budapest, 1972; vet. food toxicologist, U. Vet. Sci., 1980; PhD, Acad. Scis., Budapest, 1978; prof. food hygiene, U. Vet. Sci., 1995. Lic. gen. vet., expert radioisotopes in life scis., vet. food contaminant toxicologist. Lab. vet. Cen. Vet. Inst., Budapest, 1967-70; rsch. fellow U. Vet. Sci., Budapest, 1971-78; head biochem. dept. PHYLAXIA Co., Budapest, 1979-82; head rsch. divsn. BOSCCOP Co., Budaörs, Hungary, 1983-84; head food toxicol. dept. Cen. Vet. Food Contr., Budapest, 1985-92; exec. dir. Nat. Food Invest. Inst., Budapest, 1992—, prof. food hygiene and safety, 1999. Inventor spl. mode of microelement suppl.; contbr. articles to sci. jours. and procs. including Proc. Nucl. Activation Tech. in Life Sci., Jour. Inorganic Biochem., Proc. 5th Danube Symposium on Chromatogr., Vet. and Human Toxicology. Named Gold Medalled Inventor, Ministry Agr., Hungary, 1975. Avocations: excursions in nature, reading, music, travel. Office: Nat Food Invest Inst, Mester St 81, H-1465 Budapest 94, Hungary

SASABE, SHIGERU, theoretical physicist; b. Kyoto, Japan, Nov. 17, 1946; s. Sasabe Sotoshiro and Sasabe Haya; m. Yumiko Nakazono; 1 child, Tomohiro. PhD, Kyoto U., 1976. Instr. Tokyo Met. Coll. Tech., 1982-84; assoc. prof. Tokyo Met. Inst. Tech., 1984-93, prof., 1993—; rschr. Japan Soc. Promotion of Sci., Tokyo, 1978. Mem. N.Y. Acad. Scis., Phys. Soc. Japan, Inst. Elec. Engrs. Japan. Office: Tokyo Met Inst Tech, Asahiga-oka 6-6, Hino Tokyo 191, Japan

SASAKI, EDSON MITSUO, financial services company executive; b. Sao Paulo, Brazil, Sept. 21, 1966; s. Ioshinori and Leico (Asano) S. BSEE, Poly. U. Sao Paulo, 1990, MSME, 1996; MS in Econ. Engring. Syss. and Ops. Rsch., Stanford U., 1997. From sys. analyst to mgr. Banco Itau, Sao Paulo, 1992—. Home: R Madre Cabrini 240 apt 11, 04020000 São Paulo Brazil

SASAKI, JOHN ERIC, art company executive, artist; b. New Haven; s. Clarence and Carolyn S. BFA, Pepperdine U., 1994. Supr. Cinesite Digital Studios, Hollywood, Calif., 1994-95, composite supr., 1995-96; compositor Digital Domain, Venice, Calif., 2000—; composite supr. Manex Visual Effects, Alameda, L.A., 1998-2000; CEO John E Sasaki Inc., Pacific Palisades, Calif., 1998—. Visual effects credits include (films) Titanic, The Matrix, The Fifth Element, Armageddon, Sphere, Space Jam, Waterworld, Deep Blue Sea. Vol. Rep. Party, L.A., 1990—. Mem. Pepperdine Alumni. Salisbury Sch. Alumni (class agt.). E-mail: sasaki@gte.net. Home and Office: 16100 W Sunset Blvd Pacific Palisades CA 90272-3454

SASAKI, KENICHI, oral and maxillofacial surgeon; b. Sasebo, Japan, Sept. 11, 1953; s. Yoshiro and Michiko Sasaki; m. Mika Murayama Sasaki, Jan. 9, 1993; 1 child, Shota. PhD, Tokyo Dental Coll., Chiba, Japan, 1983. Cert. oral and maxillofacial surgeon. Lectr. Tokyo Dental Coll., Chiba, Japan, 1988—; chief Sasaki Dental Clinic, Chiba, Japan, 1988-90; chief dept. oral and maxillofacial surgery Kameda Gen. Hosp., Kamogawa, Japan, 1990—; mem. of editor: Kameda Med. Jour., Kamogawa, Japan, 1997—. Inventor: Measure tape, balloon pumping technique for temporomandibular joint arthrosis. Mem. The Planetary Soc., Pasadena, Calif., 1995. Fellow Internat. Assn. Oral and Maxillofacial Surgeons, Japanese Soc. Oral and maxillofacial Surgeons, Japanese Soc. Temporomandibular Joint. Avocations: scuba diving, golf, skiing, fishing, surfing. Home: 1296 Fujiwara, Tateyama 294-0224, Japan Office: Kameda Gen Hosp, 929 Higashi cho, Kamogawa 296-0041, Japan

SASAKI, MIKIO, trading company executive. Pres., CEO Mitsubishi Internat. Corp., N.Y.C.; CEO Mitsubishi Internat. Corp., Tokyo. Office: care Mitsubishi Internat, 2-6-3 Marunouchi Chiyoda-ku, Tokyo 100-8086, Japan

SASAKI, MIYUKI, applied linguistics educator; b. Kitakyusyu, Japan, Oct. 15, 1959; d. Yoshimasa and Noriko (Ohara) S.; m. Toru Kinoshita, May 20, 1984 (children: Tomo Kinoshita, Shou Kinoshita. BA, Hiroshima (Japan) U., 1983; MA, Georgetown U., 1986, Hiroshima U., 1987; PhD, UCLA, 1991. tech. rsch. panel mem. Test of English for Internat. Comm., Princeton, N.J., 1994-96, Ednl. Testing Svc. Author: Second Language Proficiency, Foreign Language Aptitude, and Intelligence: Quantitative and Qualitative Analyses, 1996; contbr. articles to profl. jours., including Jour. Pragmatics, Jour. 2d Lang. Writing, Lang. Learning, Lang. Testing. Avocations: travel, reading mysteries, cooking, baking, swimming. Office: Nagoya Gakuin U, 1350 Kamishinano-cho, Seto 480-1298, Japan

SASAKI, MOTOMASA, oral surgeon, educator emeritus; b. Fukuoka, Japan, Dec. 7, 1924; s. Motoji and Kishio (Nakamura) S.; m. Hisako Matsumura, Mar. 25, 1951; 1 child, Kumiko. MD, Kyushu U., Fukuoka, 1949; DDS, Tokyo Med. and Dental U., 1953; PhD in Physiology, Kyushu U., 1960. Instr. maxillofacial surgery Kyushu U., 1953-56, assoc. prof., 1956-61; prof. maxillofacial surgery Sapporo (Japan) Med. Coll., 1961-76, dir. emergency, 1971-76; prof. Nagasaki (Japan) U. Sch. Medicine, 1976-79; dean, prof. surgery Nagasaki U. Sch. of Dentistry, 1979-90, prof. emeritus, 1990—; pres. Seika Women's Jr. Coll., Fukuoka, 1990-97; dir. gen. Nagasaki Dental Technical Sch., Ohmura, 1997—. Author (with others) Double Rotation, 1976, author: Beauty in Face (Japanese), 1990; editor: Maxillo-Facial and Oral Surgery, 1995; contbr. articles to profl. jours. Recipient Med. award Hokkaido Med. Assn., 1967. Mem. Japanese Soc. of Oral and Maxillofacial Surgeons (hon.), Japanese Stomatol. Soc. (hon.), Japanese Dental Soc. of Anesthesiology (hon.), Japanese Cleft Palate Assn. (hon.), Japan Soc. for Oral Tumors (honr.). Avocations: painting, history of fine art. Home: Yayoi-machi 680-6-803, Nagasaki 850-0823, Japan

SASAKI, TEIKICHI AKIRA, materials scientist, researcher; b. Hinaimachi, Japan, May 18, 1941; s. Hidekichi and Miyo (Takamiya) S. BSc, Tohoku (Japan) U., 1964, DSc, 1969. Rschr. Japan Atomic Energy Rsch. Inst., Tokai-mura, 1969-79; sr. rschr. Japan Atomic Energy Rsch. Inst., 1979-83, prin. rschr., 1983-95, dep. dir., 1995-96, prime rschr., 1997—; guest rschr. Lawrence Berkeley (Calif.) Nat. Lab., 1977-78; guest prof. Tohoku U., 1996—, Himeji Inst. Tech., 1999—; cons. Riken, Wako-shi, Japan, 1990-91, 94-95; mem. com. Japan Synchrotron Radiation Rsch. Inst., 1994-97, Sci. and Tech. Agy., Japan, 1996-97. Contbr. articles to profl. jours. Recipient best paper prize Surface Sci. Soc. Japan, 1997. Mem. Chem. Soc. Japan, Phys. Soc. Japan. Buddhist. Avocations: travel, gardening, museums. Home: Hojo Miyano-machi 263-303, Himenji Hyogo-ken 670-0948, Japan Office: SPring-8 Mikazuki-cho, Hyogo-ken 678-5143, Japan

SASAKI, TSUTOMU (TOM SASAKI), real estate company executive, international trading company executive, consultant; b. Tokyo, July 28, 1945; came to U.S., 1979; s. Tsuneshiro and Kimiko (Fujiwara) S.; m. Yoko Katsura, Feb. 21, 1971; children: Mari, Tomoko. BA, Sophia U., Tokyo, 1969. Plant export adminstrn. Ataka & Co., Ltd., Osaka, Japan, 1969-76; officer Seattle-First Nat. Bank, Tokyo, 1976-79, AVP bus. mgr., 1982-84; AVP Japan mgr. Seattle-First Nat. Bank, Seattle, 1979-82, v.p. Japan mgr., 1984-90; owner, pres. BBS Internat., Inc., Seattle, 1990—; bd. dirs. Wired, Inc., Seattle, InterPac Devel. Inc., InterPac Mgmt., Inc., Riverplace Mgmt., Inc., BBS Bus. Svc., Inc., N.W. Club Mgmt., Inc. Bd. dirs. Adopt-a-Stream Found., Everett, Wash., 1987 ; bd. trustees N.W. Sch., Seattle. Am. Field Svc. scholar, 1963-64. Mem. Japan Am. Soc. Wash. (chmn. membership com. 1988, bd. dirs. 1997), British Am. Bus. Coun., Fairwood Golf & Country Club, Wash. Athletic Club. Avocations: golf, gardening, music, photography. Home: 4625 136th Ave SE Bellevue WA 98006-3007 Office: BBS Internat Inc 720 Olive Way Ste 1025 Seattle WA 98101-1880

SASAKI, TSUYOSHI SAMUEL, linguistics educator; b. Tokyo, Jan. 9, 1944; s. Hachiro and Fumi Sasaki; m. Michiko Yamamura (div. Mar. 1977); children: Walter, Christopher; m. Noriko Uemura, Apr. 20, 1977. BA, Internat. Christian U., Tokyo, 1967; MS in Linguistics, Georgetown U., 1971, PhD in Theoretical Linguistics, 1975. Asst. Internat. Christian U., Tokyo, 1967-69; univ. fellow Georgetown U., Washington, 1969-73, asst., 1973-74; asst. Nanzan U., Nagoya, Japan, 1973-74, lectr., 1974-83, asst. prof., 1983-98, prof., 1998—, chair dept. Am. studies and English, 1999—. Mem. AAAS, Linguistic Soc. Japan, Japan Soc. Info. and Communication Rsch., Soc. Tchg. Japanese Fgn. Lang., N.Y. Acad. Scis. Fax: 81-52-832-5330. E-mail: samsaski@ic.nanzan-u.ac.jp. Office: Nanzan U, 18 Yamazato-cho, Showa-ku Nagoya 466-8673, Japan

SASAKURA, HIROSHI, retired engineering educator; b. Bombay, Dec. 31, 1925; arrived to Japan, 1926; s. Teiichiro and Fumi (Miyanari) S.; m. Reiko Kuzuwa, Nov. 21, 1961; children: Mariko, Chizuko Inoue. BS, Osaka (Japan) U., 1947, DSc, 1961. Cert. engr. Engr. Indsl. Rsch. Inst., Osaka, 1950-69; prof. Tottori (Japan) U., 1970-90, hon. prof., 1991—; prof. Tokushima Bunri U., Takamatsu, Japan, 1991-97. Editor: Solid-State Physics, 1984; contbr. articles to profl. jours. Mem. Japanese Soc. Applied Physics. Avocations: music, piano playing, reading. Home: Koyama-cho, Minami, 2-520, Tottori 680-0945, Japan

SASAMOTO, YOICHI, ophthalmologist, immunologist; b. Sapporo, Hokkaido, Japan, May 27, 1959; s. Takejiro and Ayako (Fujikawa) S.; m. Mie Kanamori, June 10, 1984; children: Yohei, Yoshinori. MD, Hokkaido U., Sapporo, 1984, D Med.Sci., 1994. Resident Hokkaido U. Hosp., Sapporo, 1984-86, mem. staff, 1986-90, asst. prof., 1992—; vis. fellow Nat Eye Inst., NIH, Bethesda, Md., 1990-92. Mem. Japanese Ophthalmol. Soc. (specialist), Assn. for Rsch. in Vision and Ophthalmology, Japanese Soc. Immunology, Internat. Ocular Inflammation Soc. Office: Hokkaido U Sch Medicine, Kita-15 Nishi-7 Kitaku, Sapporo 060-8638, Japan

SASANE, AKINOBU, chemist, educator; b. Chita, Aichi, Japan, June 28, 1942; s. Ichimatsu and Fusako (Negoro) S.; m. Sumiko Gotoh, Mar. 12, 1967; children: Hiroshi, Akira, Ikuko. BS, Nagoya U., 1965, MS, 1967, PhD, 1972. Asst. prof. Shinshu U., Matsumoto, Japan, 1970-81; assoc. prof. Shinshu U., Matsumoto, 1981-96, prof., 1996—; rsch. fellow U. London, 1973-75. Contbr. articles to profl. jours. Mem. Chem. Soc. Japan. Avocations: orchid cultivating, classical music, go. Home: Shimo-Okada 349-1 Okada, Matsumoto 390-0313, Japan Office: Shishu U Dept Chemistry, Asahi 3-1-1, Matsumoto 390-8621, Japan

SASAYAMA, MAKOTO, food science executive; b. Tokyo, Nov. 12, 1930; s. Mikio Morimura and Yone (Yude) S.; m. Masayo Shimada, Nov. 12, 1958; children: Nobuya, Rie Shichijo. BA, Keio U., Tokyo, 1952. Pers. chief Nitto Chem. K.K., Tokyo, 1953-63; sales mgr. Nihon Unicar K.K., Tokyo, 1963-71; dir. Pfizer K.K., Tokyo, 1972-84, pres., 1984-96; cons. Morimura Brothers Co. Ltd., Tokyo, 1996—; chmn. Cultor Food Sci., Tokyo, 1996—; auditor Pfizer Seiyaku Japan, Tokyo, 1994-96; adviser Internat. Life Scis., Tokyo, 1998—. Author: Inovation of Distribution, 1991; translator: Present Knowledge in Nutrition, 7th edit., 1998. Mem. Tokyo Am. Club (v.p. 1995—), Japan Food Additive Assn. (auditor 1998—), Morimura Homei Kai (auditor 1999—), Japan Assn. for Dietary Fiber Rsch. (dir. 1997—). Avocations: golf, traveling, painting (Japanese). Home: 5-8 Osonedai, Kohoku-

ku, Yokohama 222 0004, Japan Office: Cultor Food Sci KK, 6-12-1 Nishi-Shinjuku, Tokyo 160 0023, Japan

SASE, SADANORI, agricultural engineer, researcher; b. Shibayama-machi, Chiba, Japan, Oct. 28, 1954; s. Sadao and Masa (Horikoshi) S.; m. Yumiko Sato, Oct. 28, 1981; children: Kanta, Asuka, Lico. BS, Chiba U., 1977, MS, 1979; PhD, Tokyo U., 1983. Lab. head Hokkaido Nat. Agr. Expt. Sta., Memuro, Japan, 1991-93; sr. rschr. Nat. Rsch. Inst. Agrl. Engring., Tsukuba, Japan, 1984-91; lab. head Nat. Inst. Agrl. Engring., Tsukuba, Japan, 1993—. Mem. Am. Soc. Agrl. Engring., Internat. Soc. Hort. Sci. Home: Matsushiro 4-416-202, Tsukuba 305-0035, Japan Office: Nat Rsch Inst Agrl Engring, Kannondai 2-1-2, Tsukuba Ibaraki 305-8609, Japan

SASEETHARRAN, MAHADEVA, engineering educator, researcher; b. Inuvil, Sri Lanka, June 23, 1962; arrived in Australia, 1989; s. Chelliah and Meenadchi (Thambippillai) Mahadeva; m. Sivasakthy Sivagnanasundaram, Oct. 31, 1994. B of Engring. (with honors), U. Birmingham, 1987. Tchr. Hinu Coll., Jaffna, Sri Lanka, 1981; trainee William McGeoch Ltd., Eng., 1986; tutor U. Melbourne, Australia, 1988-90; lectr. Queensland U. of Tech., Australia, 1991, U. Western Sydney, Australia, 1993-97; rschr. U. Melbourne, 1989-90, Queensland U. of Tech., Brisbane, 1991-94, U. Western Sydney, 1993-97, project supervision, 1995-97, cons. 1993-97, tchr. 1993-97, adminstr. R&D in speech tech., 1993-97; speech scientist T-Netix Inc., 1999; sr. technologist Atomic Tangeriene, Inc., 2000—; presenter internat. confs. Contbr. articles to profl. jours. Scout troop leader Hindu Coll., Trincomalee, Sri Lanka, 1973-75; active cmty., 1976-78; yoga tchr. Internat. House, Brisbane, 1991-92, contributed to Soiree, 1991-92. Govt. scholar Hindu Coll., 1974, 76; scholarship A Baur & Co., 1981; recipient Postgrad. Rsch. award U. Melbourne, 1989, Queensland U. of Tech., 1991. Mem. IEEE (sr.), Inst. of Elec. Engrs./U.K. (assoc.). Hindu. Avocations: exercising, cycling, photography, traveling, yoga. Home: 664 Morse Ave Apt 12 Sunnyvale CA 94085-3716 also: 54 Thane St, Pendlehill NSW 2145, Australia

SASIKUMAR, B., agriculture scientist, researcher; b. Sooranad, Kerala, India, Jan. 21, 1956; s. K.N. Bhaskaran Pillai and K. Saraswathi Amma; m. C. Sreedevi, Nov. 23, 1985; children: Aparna, Sabarinath. BSc, Kerala U., Trivandrum, India, 1975; MSc, Gujarat Agrl. U., Anand, India, 1979, PhD, 1983. Sr. rsch. fellow Gujarat Agrl., 1980; jr. scientist Rubber Rsch. Inst. India, Kottayam, India, 1984-85; scientist rsch. complex Indian Coun. Agrl. Rsch., Shillong, 1985-89; sr. scientist Nat. Rsch. Ctr. for Spices, Indian Coun. Agrl. Rsch., Calicut, India, 1989-98; sr. scientist Indian Inst. Spices Rsch. Indian Coun. Agrl. Rsch., Calicut, 1998—; vis. scientist Plant Biotech. Inst., NRC-Can., Saskatoon, 1994. Editor: Spices News; contbr. articles to profl. publs. Recipient ICAR Team award. Fellow Indian Soc. Genetics and Plant Breeding; mem. Indian Soc. Spices (J.S. Pruthi award 1997). Hindu. Avocations: freelance science writing, reading, films, yoga. Home: Sreevihar Kurup's Ln, Kerala Sasthamangalam 695 010, India Office: Indian Inst Spices Rsch, Marikunnu, Kozhikode Kerala 673 012, India

SASKO, NANCY ANN, insurance agent; b. Camp Lejuene, N.C., Nov. 22, 1956; d. George Michael Jr. and Margaret (Simons) S. BA in English Lit., Ind. U., 1981. Customer svc. sales rep. Apple Computer, Inc., Denver, 1982-84; owner Monitor Systems, Inc., Denver, 1984-89; sales rep. Lincoln Nat. Life, Denver, 1989-90; long term care specialist John Hancock Mut. Life, Mc Lean, Va., 1990—; long term care sales rep. GE Fin. Assurance, Carmel, Ind. Roman Catholic. Avocations: classical music, art. Fax: 317-843-5943. Office: GE Financial Assurance Long Term Care Divsn 111 Congressional Blvd Ste 118 Carmel IN 46032-5651 Address: PO Box 15482 Fort Wayne IN 46885-5482

SASLAWSKI, OLIVIER BERTRAND, pharmacist; b. Paris, Feb. 23, 1961; m. Genevieve Anne Obegi, Mar. 18, 1961; children: Amandine, Claire, Flora, Antonin. D Pharmacy, U. Paris V, 1985; MSc in Pharmacotechny, U. Paris XI, 1986, PhD, 1990. Biologist Lab. Biochemistry Herold Pediatric Hosp., Paris, 1986-87; vis. rsch. asst. Sch. Chem. Engring. Lab. Chemistry Polymers Purdue U., West Lafayette, Ind., 1988; head dept. preformulation and formulation Inst. Biopharmacy, Group Rhône-Poulenc Rorer, Vitry, France, 1989-92; dir. pedagogy European Profl. Inst. Industry, Adminstrn. and Commerce, Paris, 1992-93; head pharm. devel. and clin. supply Lipha-Merck, Lyon, France, 1993-98; dir. R&D RP Scherer, Beinheim, France, 1998—; mem. Gelatine Working Party at European Pharmacopeia. Contbr. articles to profl. jours. Recipient award Soc. Doctors of Pharmacy, Nat. Acad. Pharmacy, Paris, 1990. Mem. Am. Assn. Pharm. Scientists, Controlled Release Soc., Soc. Indsl. Galenic Pharmacy (Found. Paul Neumann award 1986), Thematic Group Rsch. on Targeting, French Soc. Pharm., Scis. and Technics, Nat. Order Pharmacy, European Pharmacopeia (mem. Gelatine working party). Achievements include development of new drug delivery systems allowing a bioavailability improvement in patient and a better compliance of treatment. Avocations: sailing, music, modern painting. Home: 10 rue des Repenties, 67500 Haguenau France Office: RP Scherer, 74 Rue Principale, 67930 Beinheim France

SASS, HEINZ GERMAN MAX KARL, geneticist, educator, researcher; b. Frankfurt an der Oder, Germany, Apr. 5, 1944; s. Heinz Kurt Eduard and Käthe Ottilie Elisabeth (Welteke) S.; m. Kristina Sylvia Maria Neugebauer, May 20, 1981; children: Sebastian Bruno Emmanuel, Ulrike Else Helene. Grad. in Biology & Chemistry, Eberhard-Karls U. Tübingen, Germany, 1973, Dr.rer.nat., 1978; habilitation, venia legendi, Johannes Gutenberg U. Mainz, Germany, 1992. Doctorate Max-Planck-Inst. for Biology, Tübingen, 1973-78; postdoctoral rsch. fellow Ruprecht-Karls U. Heidelberg, 1978-83; vis. scientist Worcester Found. Exptl. Biology, Shrewsbury, Mass., 1983-84; vis. scholar biochemistry and molecular biology Harvard U., Cambridge, Mass., 1984-85, rsch. assoc. biochemistry and molecular biology, 1985-88; rsch. assoc. in tumor suppressor genetics Johannes Gutenberg U., Mainz, 1988-92, privatdozent Dr. habil., 1992-95; prof., head dept. genetics U. Leipzig Faculty of Bioscis., Pharmacy and Psychology, Germany, 1996—. Contbr. numerous sci. articles to profl. jours. German Rsch. Found. grantee. Mem. AAAS, N.Y. Acad. Sci., Genetics Soc. of Germany, Deutscher Hochschulverband. Office: U Leipzig Inst Mikrobiologie & Genetik Lehrstuhl Genetik, Johannisalle 21-23, D-04103 Leipzig Germany

SASSE, DIETER, anatomy educator; b. Cologne, Germany, Aug. 17, 1934; Arrived in Switzerland, 1981; s. Carl and Marga (Diekamp) S.; m. Armgard von Storch, July 13, 1963; children: Bernd, Georg, Julia. MD, U. Göttingen, 1960. From asst. to lectr. Inst. Anatomy, Tubingen, Germany, 1962-72; prof. Inst. Anatomy, Freiburg, Germany, 1973-80; prof., chmn. Inst. Anatomy, Basel, Switzerland, 1981—; lectr. Inst. Anatomy. Author: Taschenbuch der Anatomie, 1995, (with L. Stammler) Anleitung zum Praeparier Kurs, 1996. Avocations: literature, history. Office: Inst Anatomy, Pestalozzistrasse 20, CH-4061 Basel Switzerland

SASSER, CHARLES WAYNE, journalist, educator, writer; b. Sallisaw, Okla., Jan. 3, 1942; s. Ben Garland and Mary Louise Sasser; m. Katherine Renee, Feb. 2, 1979 (div. Oct. 1986); 1 adopted child, Joshua Dale, children: David, Michael; m. Donna Sue Baker, Oct. 7, 1995; stepchildren: DeAnn, Darren, Michael. AA, Miami (Fla.)-Dade Jr. Coll., 1968; BA, Fla. State U., 1969; postgrad., Okla. State U., 1977-78. Police officer Miami Police Dept., 1965-68; detective Tulsa Police Dept., 1970-79; coll. instr. Tulsa Jr. Coll., 1976—; freelance journalist, 1979—; horse rancher, trainer, Mannford, Okla., 1971-78, Chouteau, Okla., 1996—; dir. criminal justice program Am. Christian Coll. Tulsa, 1974-78; profl. rodeo clown Profl. Rodeo Cowboy Assn., Okla., 1984-86. Author: No Gentle Streets, 1984, The Girl Scout Murders, 1989, The Walking Dead, 1989, One Shot-One Kill, 1990, Homicide!, 1990, The 100th Kill, 1992, Always a Warrior, 1994, Shoot to Kill, 1994, Last American Heroes, 1994, In Cold Blood: Oklahoma's Most Notorious Murders, 1994, Smoke Jumpers, 1996, First Seal, 1997, Doc: Platoon Medic, 1998, Fire Cops, 1998, At Large, 1998, Arctic Homestead, 2000, Liberty City, 2000; editor Keystone Sportsman Mag., 1975-78; contbr. articles to periodicals; actor Wagoner (Okla.) Playhouse Dinner Theater, 1997—. Pres. Keystone Crossroads Hist. Assn., Mannford, 1977; del. Creek County Reps., Sapulpa, Okla., 1977-78, Sequoyah County Reps., Sallisaw, Okla., 1984-85. With U.S. Army Spl. Forces, 1966-67, 72-83; 1st sgt. USAR, 1991-97, ret.; with USN, 1960-64. Recipient Tulsa Author's award City of Tulsa, 1992. Mem. Okla. Writers Fedn., Tulsa Nightwriters (Nightwriter of the Yr. 1990, 96). Avocations: martial arts, steer roping, scuba, parachuting, horses. Home and Office: RR 1 Box 288 Chouteau OK 74337-9617

SASSER, JAMES RALPH (JIM SASSER), ambassador, former senator; b. Memphis, TN, Sept. 30, 1936; s. Joseph Ralph and Mary Nell (Gray) S.; m. Mary Gorman, Aug. 18, 1962; children: Gray, Elizabeth. Student, U. Tenn., 1954-55; BA, Vanderbilt U., 1958, LLB, 1961. Bar: Tenn. 1961. Ptnr. Goodpasture, Carpenter, Woods & Sasser, Nashville, 1961-76; chmn. Tenn. Dem. Party, 1973-76; mem. U.S. Senate from Tenn., 1977-1994; U.S. Ambassador to China U.S. State Dept., Beijing, China, 1996-99; foreign policy advisor to vice-pres. Gore Gore 2000, Washington, DC, 2000—. Chmn. Tenn. State Dem. Exec. Com., 1973-76; so. vice chmn. Assn. Dem. State Chmn., 1975-76. Served with USMCR, 1958-65. Mem. ABA, NCCJ (dir. Nashville chpt.), UN Assn., Nashville Com. Fgn. Relations, Am. Judicature Soc. Office: Gore 2000 Inc 601 Mainstream Dr Nashville TN 37228-1203*

SASSER, WILLIAM JACK, retired federal agency administrator, consultant; b. Arcadia, Okla., Aug. 12, 1934; children: Sam, Steve, Susan, Sandra. BS in Sociology and Psychology, Okla. Bapt. U., 1956; postgrad., S.W. Bapt. Sem., 1957-60, George Washington U., 1966. Lic. comml. pilot with instrument rating. Air traffic control specialist S.W. region FAA Air Route Traffic Control Ctr., Ft. Worth, 1963-65, pers. officer, 1970-71; tech. intern FAA, Washington, 1965-66; employee devel. officer S.W. region FAA, Houston and Ft. Worth, 1966-70; chief tng. br. pers. div. Gt. Lakes region FAA, Des Plaines, Ill., 1971-73; with exec. devel. program Gt. Lakes and ctrl. regions FAA, Des Plaines, Kansas City, Mo., 1973-75; asst. chief airports div. ctrl. region FAA, Kansas City, 1975-76, mgr., 1977-87; mgr. airports div. S.W. region FAA, Ft. Worth, 1987-89, dep. regional adminstr. S.W. region, 1989-95; ret. S.W. region, 1995; pvt. cons., 1995—. Home: PO Box 162595 Fort Worth TX 76161-2595

SASSNAU, REINHOLD, veterinarian; b. Hamburg, Germany, Sept. 23, 1957. Degree in Vet. Medicine, Free U., Berlin, 1986. Pvt. practice vet. Berlin, 1988. Contbr. articles to profl. jours. Achievements include inventor and patentee of hip dysplasia gauge. Office: Südstern 2, 10961 Berlin Germany

SASSOLAS, BRUNO ANDRÉ, dermatologist, researcher; b. Nice, France, Mar. 16, 1961; s. Gabriel Marius and Agnès Marie (Deschomets) S.; m. Nathalie Marie Mattenet, June 11, 1983; children: Tanguy, Mathieu, Paul. MBChB, U. René Descartes, Paris, 1984; MD, U. Bretagne Occidentale, Brest, France, 1988; DEA in Cutaneous Biology, U. Lyon, France, 1993. Med. resident U. Hosp. Brest, France, 1985-88, hosp. asst., 1988-90, univ. asst., 1988-90, hosp. dr., 1990—; referee cons. DAP Svc., France, 1996—. Mem. direction com. Annales de Dermatology, 1996. mem. French Soc. Dermatology, Soc. Investigative Dermatology, European Acad. Dermatoloyg and Venereology. Avocations: sailing, skiing, classical music. Office: U Hosp Brest, Dept Dermatology, F-29609 Brest Cedex, France

SASSON, ARLEY ALBERTO, investment company executive; b. Mexico City; came to U.S., 1992; BS in Econs., U. Pa., 1996. Analyst emerging debt markets Goldman, Sachs & Co., N.Y.C., 1996-99, assoc. equity derivatives, 1999-2000; v.p. Donaldson, Lufkin & Jenrette, N.Y.C., 2000—. Fax: 212-892-2515. Office: Donaldson Lufking and Jenrette 277 Park Ave Fl 9 New York NY 10172-0003

SASSOON, ADRIAN DAVID, art historian, antique dealer, art advisor; b. London, Feb. 1, 1961; s. Hugh Meyer and Marion Julia (Schiff) S. Student, Wagner's, London, 1966-68, Sunningdale Sch., Berkshire, 1969-73, Eton Coll., Berkshire, 1974-78; diploma (hon.) in Fine Arts, Inchbald Sch. Design, London, 1979, Christie's Fine Arts Course, London, 1980. Curatorial asst. Dept. Decorative Arts, 1980-82; asst. curator The J. Paul Getty Mus., Malibu, Calif., 1982-84; dir. Alexander & Berendt, Ltd., 1987-92. Contbr. articles to profl. jours. Mem. French Porcelain Soc. (com. mem. 1985-95, treas. 1989-95), Lyford Cay Club (Nassau), Brook's (London).

SASSOON, ANDRE GABRIEL, lawyer; b. Cairo, Apr. 13, 1936; came to U.S., 1959; s. Gabriel and Sarine (Tawil) S.; m. Barbara Dee Freedman, Aug. 15, 1965; children: Daniel, Gabriel, Sarina. GCE, Oxford & Cambridge, England, 1953; JD, Villanova U., 1969; LLM, Harvard U., 1970. Bar: Pa. 1969, N.Y. 1970. Product mgr. Rohm & Haas Co., Phila., 1960-66; law clk. Dist. Atty.'s Office, Phila., 1968; assoc. Weil, Gotshal & Manges, N.Y.C., 1970-73; pvt. practice N.Y.C., 1973—; pres., CEO Sterimed Internat., Inc., 1999—; dir. elem. Youth in Distress, N.Y.C., 1982—; v.p., dir. internat. Anti-Drug Abuse Found., N.Y.C., 1987—; v.p., dir., mem. exec. com. Hebrew Immigrant Aid Soc., N.Y.C., 1977—; internat. sec., gov. bd. internat. govs. World Sephardi Fedn., N.Y.C., 1988—; co-pres., chmn., U.S. com., dir. internat. Jewish Com. for Sephardi '92, N.Y.C., 1989—; mem. N.Y. State Christopher Columbus Quincetenary Commn., Statewide Outreach Com., 1991—. Editor Villanova Law Rev.; contbr. articles to profl. jours. With USAR, 1960-66. Recipient Israel Trade award Govt. of Israel, 1985. Mem. ABA, Am. Arbitration Assn. (panel mem. 1971—), Am. Soc. Internat. Law, Order of the Coif, 0840 Internat. Pvt., 0860 Internat. Pub., SteriMed Internat. (pres. 1999). Home: 888 Park Ave New York NY 10021-0235 Office: 600 Madison Ave New York NY 10022-1615

SASTROWARDOYO, TERESITA MANEJAR, nurse; came to U.S., 1960; d. Timoteo and Monica (Casianan) Manejar; m. Sumarsongko H. Sastrowardoyo, June 8, 1962; children: Timoteo, Daniel (dec.), Benjamin. BSN, Ctrl. Philippine U., Iloilo, 1957; cert. operating rm. and surgical nursing, St. Luke's Hosp Ctr., N.Y.C., 1960-61. Head nurse med. unit Emmanuel Hosp., Roxas City, Philippines, 1957-58; supr. oper. rm. Brent Hosp., Zamboanga City, Philippines, 1958-60; staff nurse oper. rm. Jewish Meml. Hosp., N.Y.C., 1961-62; evening staff nurse oper. rm. Flower and Fifth Ave Hosp., N.Y.C., 1963-65; staff nurse oper. rm., charge nurse night shift St. Lukes Hosp. Ctr., N.Y.C., 1966-76; staff nurse oper. rm. South Side Hosp., Bayshore, N.Y., 1976—. Mem. N.Y. Staet Nurses Assn., Ctrl. Philippine U. Alumni Assn. N.Y., N.J. and Conn. (bd. dirs. 1994-95, 95-97). Baptist. Avocations: gardening, reading.

SASU, VOICHITA MARIA, literature educator; b. Turda, Romania, Jan. 5, 1946; d. Aurel and Victoria (Fodor) Muresan; m. Aurel Sasu, Mar. 1, 1972; 1 child, Sebastian. BA in French Lit., U. Cluj-Napoca, Romania, 1968, PhD in French Lit., 1977. Cert. of French-Romanian. Asst. faculty of letters U. Babes-Bolyai Cluj-Napoca, Romania, 1968-75, lectr. faculty of letters, 1975-91, assoc. prof., 1991-96, prof., 1998—; mem. U. Babes-Bolyai, Cluj-Napoca, Romania. Author: Destiny of Literary Ideas, 1996, L'Amour Dans Le Lyrisme Féminin, 1997, Permanent Topics in French Medieval Literature, 1997, Littérature Et Civilisation Françaises, 1997, Voix du Texte, 1999. Grantee: Tempus, Nantes, France, 1993, Aupelf-Uref, Paris, 1995-96, Canadian Studies Faculty Rsch. Award Program, Montreal, 1996. Mem. Ctr. for Canadian and Quebec Studies (chairperson, 1992—), Assn. Internat. Etudes Québécoises, Soc. Francaise d'Étude du Seizième siècle. Greek Catholic. Avocations: classical music, world literature, sports. Home: Mehedinti 4 sc II Ap 17, 3400 Cluj-Napoca Romania Office: Facultatea de Litere, Horia 31, 3400 Cluj-Napoca Romania

SATAKE, KATSUSUKE, surgeon, educator; b. Osaka, Japan, Apr. 6, 1935; s. Jutaro and Toshi (Izuma) S.; m. Michiko Kitamoto, May 28, 1967; children: Makoto, Akira, Shinobu. MD, Osaka (Japan) City U., 1961, D in Med. Sci., 1973. Intern Tachikawa USAF Hosp., Tokyo, 1961-62; resident surgery Osaka (Japan) City Univ. Hosp., 1962-69, instr. surgery, 1969-74; surg. fellow Hahnemman Med. Coll., Phila., 1970-72; asst. prof. Osaka (Japan) City U., 1974-89, assoc. prof., 1989—; chmn. surgery Osaka (Japan) Socio-Med. Ctr., 1992—; vis. prof. Kyto Univ. Sch. Medicine, 2000. Assoc. editor Pancreas, 1986; co-editor Jour. Hepato-Biliary Pancreatic Surgery, 1992; editor-in-chief Jour. of the Japan Pancreas Soc., 1999—; editor Internat. Jour. Pancreatology, 1999—. Grantee for pancreatic cancer Japanese Ministry Health and Welfare, Tokyo, 1986—, grantee for acute pancreatitis Pancreatic Rsch. Found. Tokyo Japan, 1993. Fellow ACS, Japanese Assn. Gastroenterology, Japan Pancreas Soc. (mem. coun. 1987); mem. Soc. for Surgery of the Alimentary Tract, Internat. Assn. of Pancreatology (coun. 1998), Pancreatic Rsch. Found. of Japan (coun. 1997—). Home: 4-3-9 Shinimazato Ikuno-ku, Osaka 544, Japan

SATAVA, VLADIMÍR, chemistry educator, researcher; b. Prague, Czech Rep., July 19, 1922; s. Václav and Marie (KrálL) S.; m. Jarmila Svoboda, Feb. 2, 1948. Diploma in engring., Inst. Chem. Tech., Prague, 1948, MS, 1954, PhD, 1968. Head Rsch. Inst. Czech Acad. Scis., Prague, 1961-72; asst. prof. Inst. Chem. Tech., Prague, 1948-61, prof. phys. chemistry, 1980-90, cons., 1991—. Author 4 books; contbr. articles to profl. jours. Recipient Prof. F. Stolba award Inst. Chem. Tech., 1992, Prof. E. Votocek award, 1992. Mem. Acad. of Ceramics. Evangelical. Avocations: music, playing piano, wood carving. Home: Jugoslavskych partyzanu 31, 160 00 Prague 6, Czech Republic Office: Inst Chem Tech, Technická 5, 160 00 Praha 6, Czech Republic

SATCHER, DAVID, public health service officer, federal official; b. Anniston, Ala., Mar. 2, 1941; s. Wilmer and Anna S; m. Nola; children: Gretchen, David, Daraka, Daryl. BS, Morehouse Coll., 1963; MD, PhD, Case Western Reserve Univ., 1970. Faculty mem. Sch. Medicine UCLA; faculty mem., chair dept. family medicine King-Drew Med. Ctr., interim dean, 1977-79; dir. King-Drew Sickle Cell Rsch. Ctr.; prof., chmn. dept. cmty. and family medicine Morehouse Sch. Medicine, Atlanta; pres. Meharry Med. Coll., Nashville, 1982-93; dir. Ctrs. for Disease Control and Prevention, Atlanta, 1993-98; adminstr. Agy. for Toxic Substances and Disease Registry, 1993-98; asst. sec., surgeon gen. HHS, Washington, 1998—; apptd. mem. Coun. of Grad. Med. Edn., 1986, also chair. Recipient Watts Grassroots award for Cmty. Leadership, 1978, Nat. Conf. Christians and Jews awards, 1985, Nashvillian of Yr. award, 1992, Ebony Mag. Black Achivement award, 1994, Brewslow award in Pub. Health, 1995, Dr. Nathan B. Davis award AMA, 1996. Mem. Inst. Medicine NAS, Phi Beta Kappa, Alpha Omega Alpha. Office: HHS 200 Independence Ave SW Rm 716G Washington DC 20201-0004

SATCHIT, BALAN, marketing educator; b. Cochin, Kerala, India, May 21, 1935; s. T.M. and Kutty Ammal S.; m. Susheela Krishna Pillai Chellammal, Nov. 9, 1966; children: Anand, Ajay. MBA, U. Madras, India, 1974; M Comms., Mysore, India, 1994; LLM, U. Hong Kong, 1994; PhD, Kumaun U., Nainital, India, 1997. Divsn. mgr., sales GEC of India, Ltd., 1966-76; gen. mgr. Gopi Textiles, Ltd., Hong Kong, 1976-79; mng. dir. Satchitsons, Ltd., Hong Kong, 1980-86; gen. mgr. Pan Vita, Ltd., Lagos, Nigeria, 1986-87; v.p. Siam Superior, Ltd., Hong Kong, 1988-89; asst. prof. Lingnan Coll., Hong Kong, 1989—; founder, dir. Hong Kong Inst. of Mktg.; vis. lectr. in fgn. trade, U. Madras, 1972-76; part-time lectr. on export-import bus., Chinese U. of Hong Kong, 1980-83; lectr. on export practices, Hong Kong Mgmt. Assn., 1980-81, others. Author: Export Promotion Strategies, 1997, Managing Exports, 1999; contbr. articles to profl. jours. Fellow Brit. Inst. Mgmt./London, Chartered Inst. of Secs./London, Inst. of Dirs./London, Inst. of Adminstrv. Mgmt./London, Chartered Inst. of Arbitrators/London, Inst. of Personnel and Devel./London, Chartered Inst. Mktg. U.K. (chartered marketer). Hindu. Avocations: lit., Indian music, filmmaking.

SATHANANDAN, MUTTUKRISHNA SATHA, obstetrician gynecologist; b. Jaffna, Sri Lanka, Mar. 4, 1949; arrived in Eng., 1978; s. Muttukrishna Chelvathamby and Muttukrishna Wallinayaki (Kandiah) S.; m. Kalyani Shanmugaratnam; children: Shivanthi, Krishanthi. MBBS with hons., U. Colombo, Sri Lanka, 1973; MPhil, U. Coll. London, 1989. Intern U. Colombo Tchg. Hosp., 1973-74; resident obs-gyn. Professorial Unit Desoya Maternity Hosp., Colombo, 1974-78; lectr. ob-gyn. U. Coll. London, 1982-85; postdoc. fellow U. Calif., San Diego, 1985-87; lectr. reproductive medicine U. Adelaide, Australia, 1987-88; cons. Bournhall Infertility Ctr., Cambridge, Eng., 1988-90; cons. ob-gyn. Stirling, Eng., 1990-94; cons., sr. lectr. St. Bart, London, 1995—; cons., sr. lectr. Haroldwood, London, 1995—, U. Coll. London, 1995—, Bupa Roding Invitro Fertilization Ctr., 1995—. Author: (chpt.) Bournhall Text Book of IVF, 1992, (textbook) Infertility in the NHS, 1996; assessor British Jour. Ob-Gyn., 1988—, Human Reproduction, 1988—; editor: Practical Guide to Ovulation Production, 2000. Fellow Royal Coll. Ob-gyn., Royal Coll. Surgeons. Avocations: Oriental music, traveling, swimming, meeting people. Office: Dept Gyn Haroldwood Hosp, Haroldwood RM3 0BE, England

SATHAYE, BHASKAR VINAYAK, university executive; b. Miraj, Maharashtr, India, Oct. 20, 1940; s. Vinayak Govind and Satyabhama Vinayak S.; m. Suhasini Krishnarao Desai, Dec. 28, 1969; children: Chandrasekhar, Shilpa. BAMS, Tilak Ayurved Coll., 1964, PhD, 1984; M in Ayurvedic Sci., R.A. Podar Med. Coll., Bombay, 1976. Rsch. asst. ICMR, Bombay, 1965-69, rsch. officer, 1969; prof. R.A. Podar Med. Coll., Bombay, 1969-91; dean R.A. Podar Med. Coll., 1991-95; dean govt. Ayu Coll. & Hosp., Osmanabad, India, 1996; prin. Gomantak Ayurveda Mahavidyalaya and Rsch. Ctr., Goa, India, 1996—; chmn bd. studies ayurved medicine Goa U.; mem. Ctrl. Coun. Indian Medicine, New Delhi; sec. Bd. Rsch. in Ayurved, 1991-95; nat. jury Bruhatrayi Ratna award com., Coimbator e, India, 1993-95; cons. Australian Sch. Ayurved, Adelaid, Australia, 1987-87; regional dir. All-India Sharerd Rsch. Inst., Lucknow, GOA chpt. Editl. bd. Jevaniya Arogya Prabha, Lucknow, India, 1981—; author several books in field; advisor monthly mag.: Heritage Healing Mumbai. Recipient Best Author award Bindu Madhav Found., Bombay, 1971, fellowship for rsch. U. Pune, 1975, Kayachikitsa award Khadiwale Found., Pune, 1986. Mem. Iastam working com. Avocations: Indological Rsch. Libr., yoga. Office: Rsch Ctr, Gomantak Ayurveda Mahavidyalaya, Shiroda Goa 403103, India

SATHE, TUKARAM VITHALRAO, zoology educator, researcher; b. Osmanabad, India, Dec. 27, 1953; arrived in Can., 1988; s. Vithalrao Tatyaba and Nakulabai (Vithalrao) S.; m. Mandakini Laxman Kolpe, Jan. 22, 1983; children: Asawari, Nishad, Madhuri. BSc, R.P. Coll., Osmanabad, 1975; MSc, Marathwada U., Aurangabad, India, 1977; PhD, Sangit Visharad, Aurangabad, India, 1982. Jr. lectr. R.P. Coll., Osmanabad, 1983; lectr. postgrad. dept. zoology Shivaji U., Kolhapur, India, 1984-89, sr. lectr., 1989-97, reader, 1996—; dir. BAMS exam. Shivaji U., 1999. Author: Drama in Marathi, 1981, Crop Protection from Insects, 1991, Sericultural Crop Protection, 1998, Biological Pest Control, 2000; mem. editl. bd. Hexapoda, 1999. Pres. Saraswati Gramin Kala Vikas Mandal, Osmanabad, 1985—; Sanket Shikshan Sanstha, Osmanabad, 1987—. Fellow Soc. Environ. Sci.; mem. Nat. Sci. Acad. Allahabad (life), Indian Acad. Entomology (life), Nat. Environ. Sci. Acad. (life), Indian Sci. Congress Assn. (life). Hindu. Avocations: vocal Indian classical music, acting, writing, research. Home: Tchrs Quarter, C-66 Shivaji U, 416 004 Kolhapur India Office: Dept Zoology, Shivaji U, 416 004 Kolhapur India

SATHEKGE, MACHABA MICHAEL, nuclear physician; b. Johannesburg, Gauteng, South Africa, Feb. 9, 1969; s. Alfred Mokobedu and Lizzy Moshibudi (Mokoena) S.; m. Rachel Motshwanetsi Tshukuku, Apr. 12, 1995; 1 child, Machaba Jr. MBChB, Med. U. of So. Africa, Pretonia, South Africa, 1993; MMed in Nuclear Medicine, Med. U. of So. Africa, Pretoria, South Africa, 1998. Intern GA Bangowa Hosp., Pretoria, 1993-94; registrar Med. U. of So. Africa, 1994-98, cons., 1998—; examiner Wits Tecknikon, Johannesburg, 1997, moderator, 1998—. Sec. Med. U. of So. Africa Clinic Project, Pretoria, 1993. Mem. SASNM (2006 bid com., coun. mem., nuclear med. mktg. com.). Lutheran. Avocations: television, tennis, soccer, reading. Home: Medunsa, PO Box 545, Pretonia Gauteng, South Africa Office: Dept Am Nuclear Medicine, Medunsa PO Box 83, Pretonia Gauteng, South Africa

SATHIYAMOORTHY, DAKSHINAMOORTHY, process engineering researcher; b. Pudukkottai, Tamil Nadu, India, Apr. 30, 1953; s. Dakshinamoorthy Ramasamy and Somasundaram Dakshinamoorthy Pappa; m. Sathiyamoorthy Subbiah, Feb. 22, 1984; children: Shivakumar, Srinivas. B in Tech. Chem. Engring., U. Madras, India, 1974; PhD, Indian Inst. Tech., Bombay, 1984. Sci. officer grade C-G Bhabha Atomic Rsch. Ctr., Bombay, 1975-93, head process engring. sect. Materials Processing Divsn., 1993—; rsch. fellow U. Queensland, Brisbane, Australia, 1989-90; Alexander von Humboldt fellow Tech. U. Clausthal, Germany, 1990-91; invited Japan Soc. for the Promotion of Sci., fellow Tokyo U. Agr. and Tech., 1997-98. Author: (with C.K. Gupta and D. Sathiyamoorthy) Fluid Bed Technology in Materials Processing. Mem. Indian Inst. Chem. Engrs. (life), Indian Inst. Metals (life), Indian Soc. for Heat and Mass Transfer (life), Materials Rsch. Soc. India (life), Indian Nuc. Soc. (life). Achievements include research in pyrochemical process for separation of Zr and Hf, fluidization engineering for materials processing, development of engineering scale pyrochemical process. Avocations: scientific writing, Internet surfing, old coin collecting, historical book collecting, educating kids. E-mail: dsati@magnum.bare.ernet.in.

Home: 9-B Nandadevi, Anushakti Nagar, Mumbai Bombay 400 094, India Office: Bhabha Atomic Rsch Ctr, Process Engring Sect MPD, Mumbai Bombay 400 085, India

SATHIYANARAYANAN, SRINIVASAN, engineering educator, researcher; b. Trichirappalli, Tamil Nadu, India, Aug. 18, 1966; s. Kandasamy and Srinivasan (Sundari) Srinivasan; m. Sathiyanarayanan Latha, jan. 26, 1994; 1 child, K.S. Swarna Lakshmi. B Engring., Regional Engring. Coll., Trichirappalli, 1988, M Engring., 1992, postgrad., 1999—. Mktg. exec. TNT Skypak, Trichy, India, 1989-90; area mgr. Multi Vista (Pvt. Ltd.), Chennai, India, 1990-92; owner Nat. Gasket Corp., Trichy, 1992; lectr. mech. engring. Mookambigai, Keeranur, India, 1993-96; lectr. prodn. engring. Regional Engring. Coll., Trichy, 1996—. Mem. Instn. Engrs. (assoc.), Instn. Valuers (assoc.), Indian Soc. Tech. Edn. Avocations: playing Veena, social service activities, spiritual service, playing cricket. Home: Plot 55, 5th Cross Rd, Gokula Nagar, Kattur, Trichirappalli 620 019, India Office: Regional Engring Coll, Dept Prodn Engring, Trichirappalli 620 015, India

SATIJA, MOHINDER PARTAP, library and information science educator, researcher, writer; b. Sangrur, Punjab, India, June 6, 1949; s. Ram Chand and Ram Devi (Sachdev) S.; m. Amrit Mehta, Nov. 28, 1975; children: Namarta, Puneet. BSc, Punjabi U., Patiala, India, 1970; MA in English, GND U., Amritsar, India, 1976, PhD in Libr. Sci., 1990; MLS, Punjab U., Chandigarh, India, 1980. Mem. libr. staff Guru Nanak de U., Amritsar, 1972-84, lectr., 1984—, reader, 1991—, head dept. libr. sci., 1996-97, prof., 1999—; vis. prof. Maastricht McLuhan Inst., The Netherlands, 1999. Author: S R Ranganathan and the Method of Science, 1992, Manual of Practical Colon Classification, 1995, Dewey Decimal Classification: A Practical Guide, 1996, Sears List of Subject Headings: A Practical Guide, 2000; editor: Library and Information Science: Emerging Challenges, 1996; mem. editl. advisor Harrod's Librarians' Glossary and Reference Book, 2000; contbg. editor Libr. Times Internat.; regional editl. bd. MCB U. Press. Jours. in Libr. and Info. Mgmt. Mem. Internat. Soc. for Knowledge Orgn. (coord.), Indian Assn. Tchrs. of Libr. Sci. (coun.). Avocations: reading, travel. Home: C-49 GND U, Amritsar 143005, India Office: Guru Nanak De Univ, Amritsar 143005, India

SATIN, CLAIRE JEANINE, sculptor, book artist; b. Bklyn., Jan. 9, 1942. BA, Sarah Lawrence Coll., 1956; MFA, Pratt Inst., 1968. Instr. art edn. dept. edn. Bklyn. Mus., 1958-59; instr. dept. edn. and dept. Fine Arts Broward Cmty. Coll., Ft. Lauderdale, Fla., 1971-83; dir. Broward Cmty. Coll. Gallery, Ft. Lauderdale, 1975-76; Artist rep. Vorpal Gallery, Soho, N.Y.C. Collections include Victoria and Albert Mus., London, Getty Ctr. Hist. Art and Humanities, L.A., Mus. Modern Art, N.Y.C., Mus. Art, Ft. Lauderdale, King Stephen Mus., Szekesfeherdr, Hungary, Ruth and Marvin Sackner Archive of Concrete and Visual Poetry; others; commd. works include: Chapman Chronicles, State of Alaska, U. Alaska, Fairbanks, 1992, Alphawalk, New Tampa Regional Libr., Hillsborough County, Tampa, Fla., 1997 (catalog); Alphastory, Pembroke Pines Libr., Pembroke Pines, Fla., Broward County Art in Pub. Places Program (brochure), Am. Ctrs., New Delhi, Bombay, India. Bd. dirs. Broward County Cultural Affairs Coun., Ft. Lauderdale, 1975-83, hon. chair, 1981—. Recipient S. Fla. Cult Consortium award Miami Art Mus., Fla., 1997-98; So. Arts Fedn./NEA Regional Visual Arts fellow, 1996; Fla. State Individual Artist fellow Statewide Exhbn., 1978, 97, 98; Cult Consortium fellow Miami Art Mus., 1997-98; Tiffany Found. grantee, 1968, 69. Mem. Internat. Sculpture Ctr., Am. Craft. Coun., Ctr. Book Arts, Fonteneda Soc. (bd. dirs. 1997—). Office: care ARTWORKS/ ARTSPACE 101 SW 1st St Dania FL 33004-3628

SATIN, MARK, editor, lawyer; b. N.Y.C., Mar. 16, 1946; s. Joseph Henry and Selma (Rosen) S. BA, U. B.C., Vancouver, Can., 1972; JD, NYU, 1995. Bar: D.C. 1999. Exec. dir. Toronto Anti-Draft Programme, 1967-69; freelance writer Vancouver, 1972-78; exec. dir. New World Alliance, Washington, 1979-82; editor New Options Newsletter, Washington, 1983-92; gen. ptnr. Mark Satin Prodns., LP, N.Y.C. and Washington, 1996—; gen. counsel Ctr. Visionary Law, Denver and Washington, 1998—; editor Radical Middle Newsletter, Washington, 1998—; mem. adv. bd. The Other Econ. Summit, N.Y.C., 1987-92, Elmwood Inst., Berkeley, Calif., 1986-92. Author: Manual for Draft-Age Immigrants to Canada, 1968, Confessions of a Young Exile, 1976, New Age Politics, 1979, New Options for America, 1991; contbr. article to jour. Activist U.S. Green Party, Washington, 1984-90; civil rights worker Student Non-Violent Coord. Com., Holly Springs, Miss., 1964-65. Recipient Alternative Press award for gen. excellence UTNE Reader, 1989. Mem. ABA, DC Bar Assn., Colo. Bar Assn. Avocations: jogging, cooking, art appreciation. Office: Radical Middle Newsletter PO Box 57100 Washington DC 20037-0100

SATIR, AHMET, physicist; b. Ankara, Turkey, Jan. 5, 1954; s. Ali Nafi and Nevim (Yörüker) S. BS, Mid. East Tech. U., Ankara, 1978, MS, 1980, PhD, 1994, docent in math. physics, 1996. Asst. Mid. East Tech. U., Ankara, 1978-94; physicist Soliton-Satir, Ankara, Turkey, 1998—. Contbr. articles to profl. jours.; reviewer math. reviews. Fax: 90-312-437-86-34. Home: Koza Sokak 136/1, 06670 Ankara Turkey Office: Soliton-Satir Co, Esat Caddesi 87/20, Ankara 06660, Turkey

SATKUNARAJAH, PARAMASAMY, civil and structural engineer; b. Jaffna, Sri Lanka, Apr. 9, 1949; s. Vallipuram Paramasamy and Kandiah Ratnam; m. Pathmini Panchanathan, May 17, 1978. BSCE, U. Sri Lanka, 1972; M of Structural Engring., Asian Inst. of Tech., 1976; PhD in Structural Engring., Pacific Western U., 1989. Chartered engr.; registered profl. engr.; accredited checker, Singapore. Structural engr. TY Lin, Singapore, 1976-82; sr. structural engr. Lau Downie and Ptnrs., Singapore, 1982-93; prin. cons. engr. DR Rajah & Assoc., Singapore, 1993—; instr. faculty of engring. U. Sri Lanka, 1973-74; part-time tutor Nat. U. of Singapore, 1987-89. Contbr. articles to profl. jours. Postgrad. scholarship Asian Inst. of Tech., 1974. Fellow Inst. of Structural Engrs. (U.K.), Inst. of Engrs. (Australia); mem. Inst. of Engrs. (Singapore). Avocations: cricket, tennis. E-mail: rajah@mailcityasia.com.sg. Home: 15 Peakville Walk, Singapore 487661, Singapore

SATO, CHIFUMI, physician, educator; b. Agatsuma, Japan, July 16, 1949; s. Chiharu and Keiko (Ito) S.; m. Mayumi Nakanishi, Nov. 2, 1975; 1 child. MD, Tokyo Med. and Dental U., 1975, PhD, 1983. Resident Tokyo Med. and Dental U., 1975-77, Bronx VA Med. Ctr., N.Y.C., 1977-81; sr. resident Tokyo Med. and Dental U., 1981-82, asst., 1982-90, assoc. prof., 1990-94, prof., 1994—; sr. specialist for sci. affairs Ministry of Edn., Sci. and Culture, Japan, 1987-89. Mem. N.Y. Acad. Scis., Am. Assn. for Study of Liver Disease, Am. Gastroent. Assn., European Assn. for Study of Liver. Avocation: skiing. Office: Tokyo Med and Dental U, Health Sci/1-5-45 Yushima, Bunkyo-ku Tokyo 113-8519, Japan

SATO, GLENN KENJI, lawyer; b. Honolulu, Jan. 6, 1952; s. Nihei and Katherine (Miwa) S.; m. Donna Mae Shiroma, Apr. 4, 1980 (dec. Aug. 1985); m. Nan Sun Oh, Mar. 27, 1987 (dec. Nov. 1997); children: Gavan, Allison, Garrett. BBA, U. Hawaii, 1975; JD, U. Calif., San Francisco, 1977. Bar: Hawaii 1978, U.S. Dist. Ct. Hawaii, 1978, U.S. Ct. Claims 1990. Assoc. Fujiyama, Duffy & Fujiyama, Honolulu, 1978-80, 83-87, ptnr., 1987-95; stockholder Law Offices of Glenn K. Sato, Honolulu, 1980-82; pres. ISL Svcs., Inc., Honolulu, 1983; ptnr. Sato & Thomas, Honolulu, 1995-98; pvt. practice Honolulu, 1998—; vice chmn. Pattern Jury Instrn. Com., State of Hawaii, Honolulu, 1993. Treas. Polit. Action Com., Honolulu, 1993. mem. Platform Assn., Beta Gamma Sigma. Avocations: golf, hunting, target shooting, surfing. Office: 1001 Bishop St Ste 770 Honolulu HI 96813-3481

SATO, HIDEMI, cell biologist, educator; b. Fukuoka, Japan, Sept. 17, 1926; s. Daiyu Shinoda and Kozue Sato; m. Yukiko Umeda, Aug. 1, 1927; children: Hideo, Masahiko, George Haruki. MS, Kyoto (Japan) U., 1951, DSc, 1963; MA (hon.), U. Pa., 1971. Cert. in biophys. cytology and cell biology. Asst. prof. Dartmouth Med. Sch., Hanover, N.H., 1962-66; assoc. prof. U. Pa., Phila., 1966-76; prof. Nagoya (Japan) U., 1976-90, Nagano U., Ueda, Japan, 1990-95; lectr. Grad. Sch. Waseda U., Tokorozawa, Japan, 1993-97; vis. prof. U. of the Air, Chiba, Japan, 1993-98; dir. Marine Biology Lab., Nagoya U., Toba, Mie, 1977-90; internat. cons. Internat. Marine Biology, Ile d'Yeu, France, 1988-95; mem. Nat. Com. Cell Biology, Tokyo, 1985-91. Editor: (books) Cell Motility I, 1979 (Yamada Sci. Found. award 1978), Cell Motility II, 1985 (Yamada Found. Sci. award 1982); regional editor: Cell Biology, Internat. Report, 1985; assoc. editor Biology of the Cell, 1984-95. Mem. exec. com. Internat. Cell Rsch. Orgn./UNESCO, Paris, 1984-96; convenor Indonesia-Japan Sci. Exch. Project, Dept. Higher Edn. Indonesia-Japan Soc. Promotion Sci., 1988-90; mem. internat. com. Nat. Ctr. Sci. Rsch., Paris, 1990-93. Recipient Zool. Sci. award Soc. Zoology, 1985, Hon. Citation, Internat. Corp. Assn., 1988. Fellow AAAS; mem. Marine Biol. Lab. (lifetime corp. mem., mem. Whitmann Soc.), Soc. Gen. Physiology (emeritus mem.). Mem. Friend. Soc. Avocations: visiting museums, traveling, archaeology, reading, classical music. Home: 3-24-101 Oakinishi machi, Toba Mie 517-0023, Japan Office: Sugashima Marine Biol Lab, Sugashima/Toba Mie 517-0004, Japan

SATO, HIROSHI, economics educator; b. Odawara, Japan, Feb. 17, 1928; s. Masaji and Kinu Sato; m. Keiko Kinoshita, Mar. 26, 1959; 1 child, Mikiya. BA, Hitotsubashi U., Tokyo, 1953, MA, 1955; PhD, Kansai U., Osaka, Japan, 1980. Asst. Faculty of Econs., Kansai U., Osaka, 1955-58, instr., 1958-61, assoc. prof., 1961-68, prof., 1968-98, prof. emeritus, 1998—; dean Faculty of Econs., Kansai U., 1977-78, head Gen. Edn. Rsch. Ctr., 1978-80, head of student placement, 1988-90. Author: Soviet Public Finance, 1965, Public Finance, 1966; editor: New Development of Fiscal Policy, 1980, Fiscal Theory of Quasi Public Goods, 1984, Problems of Japanese Tax System, 1998. Mem. local labor com. Osaka Prefectural Govt., Osaka, 1981, mem. loca. fin. and tax com., 1990. Mem. Japan Pub. Fin. Assn., Japan Econ. Policy Assn., Internat. Inst. Pub. Finance. Buddhist. Avocations: fishing, photography. Home: 1-9-19 Yanagawa, Takatsuki-Shi Osaka 569, Japan Office: Kansai U, 3-3-35 Yamate-Cho, Suita-Shi Osaka 564, Japan

SATO, KAZUHIKO, English educator; b. Natori, Japan, Sept. 14, 1959; s. Tomio and Kazue (Ishikawa) S. BA, Tohoku Gakuin U., 1982; MA, U. Northern Iowa, 1991. Tchr. Tohoku Gakuin Jr. and Sr. H.S., Sendai, Japan, 1982-89; instr. Miyagi Nat. Coll. of Tech., Natori, Japan, 1994-99, asst. prof., 1999—. Contbr. articles to profl. jours. Mem. TESOL, Linguistic Soc. of Am., Cognitive Sci. Soc., Linguistics Assn. Great Britain, Linguistic Soc. Japan. Avocation: amateur radio operator. Home: 9-8 Kotobukiyama, Shiroishi 989-0241, Japan Office: Miyagi Nat Coll Tech, 48 Aza Nodayama, Natori 981-1239, Japan

SATO, KAZUO, engineering educator, researcher; b. Doshimura, Japan, Mar. 15, 1932; m. Nishiki Sato, May 5, 1962; 2 children. B in Engring., Meiji U., 1957, M in Engring., 1959, DEng, 1983. Lectr., asst. prof. Shibaura Inst. Tech., Minato-ku, Tokyo, Japan, 1963-71; prof. Shibaura Inst. Tech., Minato-ku, 1971—; lectr. Meiji U., Kawasaki-shi, Japan, 1969—, chmn. dr. course com., 1998; engr. Dr. and Ph.D., Ministry of Edn., Japan, 1995. Author: Mechanical Engineering, 1975, Engine Engineering, 1991; inventor Two Cycle S.I. Engine, 1991; contbr. articles to Soc. Automotive Engrs. publ., ASME Transactions, SAE Transactions, Japan Soc. Mech. Engrs. Transactions, Japan Soc. Mech. Engrs. Internat. Jour., Japan Soc. Design Engrs. Jour., Japan Soc. Automobile Engrs. Jour., Jour. Internal Combustion Engine, numerous others; contbr. articles to profl. jours. Recipient prize by excellent rsch. in two-stroke engine, Sweden, 1992, Edn. and Rsch. prize Shibaura Inst. Tech. Japan, 1992, prize for high tech. in mech. device Fire Assn. Japan, 1993, prize by inv. in two stroke engine Kanagawa, Japan, 1994, Excellent Rsch. of Environ. Type Engines prize Internat. Biographycal Ctr. (England), 1996, Internatl. Cultural Diploma of Hon. from the Amer. Biographical Inst., 1998. Mem. Soc. Automobile Engrs., Am. Soc. Automobile Engrs., Japan Soc. Mech. Engrs., Japan Soc. Design Engrs., Japan Soc. Agrl. Machinery, Land Mfrs. Assn., Rsch. Spl. Internal Combustion. Engine work of 55 years since 1946. Avocations: fishing, reading, Japanese chess, Game of Go, Japanese wrestling. Home: Yabe 3-11-21, Sagamihara 229, Japan Office: Shibaura Inst Tech, Fukasaku 307, Omiya 330, Japan

SATO, KENJI, nutrition educator; b. Okayama City, Japan, Aug. 5, 1960; s. Masaaki and Nobuko (Akiyama) S.; m. Michiko Uemura, Nov. 17, 1989; children: Mari, Yuri; m. Noriko Higaki, Mar. 27, 2000; 1 child, Kazuki. BS, Kyoto U., 1983, MS, 1985, PhD, 1988. Asst. prof. Kyoto Prefectural U., 1989-95, assoc. prof., 1995—; lectr. Koka Women's Jr. Coll., Kyoto, 1992—. Editor: (book) Extracellular Matrix of Fish and Shellfish, 1999; contbr. articles to profl. jours. Recipient prize for chemistry Japanese Soc. of Fisheries, Tokyo, 1995. Office: Dept Food Scis/Nutrition Hl, Kyoto Prefectural Univ, Shimogamo Han/Kyoto 606-8522, Japan

SATO, MASAAKI, engineering educator; b. Sanyo, Okayama, Japan, Mar. 29, 1949; s. Yoshio and Kazue (Doi) S.; m. Yoshika Fujiwara, Mar. 20, 1977; 3 children. BS, Okayama (Japan) U., 1971; MD, Kyoto (Japan) U., 1973, PhD, 1981. Cert. in engring. From asst. prof. to assoc. prof. U. Tsukuba, Japan, 1976-92; prof. Tohoku U., Sendai, Japan, 1992—. Contbr. articles and papers to profl. jours. (Japan Soc. Mech. Engrs. medal for outstanding paper 1998, 2000). Recipient Hatakeyama award Japan Soc. Mech. Engrs., 1971. Fellow Japanese Soc. for Microcirculation, Japan Soc. of Med. Electronics and Biol. Engring. (Ann. award of original paper 1978, 81, administrv. coun.), Japan Soc. Mech. Engrs.; mem. World Coun. for Biomechanics. Buddhist. Avocations: tennis, fishing, skiing, reading books. Home: 2-19-19 Yoshinari Aoba, Sendai Miyagi 989-3205, Japan Office: Tohoku U, Aoba-yama 01, Sendai Miyagi 980-8579, Japan

SATO, MITSUO, retired philosophy educator; b. Yokohama, Japan, Nov. 2, 1929; s. Shigezo and Kikuyo (Azumi) S.; m. Tsuyako Kato, Oct. 30, 1956. BA, Tokyo U. Edn., 1954, MA, 1956, PhD, 1977. Asst. Ryutu Keizai U., Ibaraki, Japan, 1965-66, lectr., 1966-67, assoc. prof., 1967-72, prof., 1972-83; prof. Chiba U., Japan, 1983-95; part-time lectr. Tokyo U. Edn., 1963-64; dir. Assn. Italian Studies, 1998—, Assn. Italo-Giapponese, Japan, 1980—. Author: (books) The Ages of Descartes and Humanists, 1978, The Dignity of Man in the Italian Renaissance, 1981, Humanist Petrarch, 1994; editor: Banquet of Knowledges in the Renaissance, 1994. Com. of the Sci. Coun. of Japan, 1988-90, 92-93, 93-94. Avocations: Haiku, poetry. Home: 4-1-5-308 Matsuba-cho, Kashiwa 277, Japan*

SATO, MOTOAKI, geologist, researcher; b. Tokyo, Japan, Oct. 11, 1929; came to U.S., 1955, 63.; s. Iwazo and Kyoko (Ito) S.; m. Ellen B. Levinson, Feb. 11, 1961 (div. Sept. 1978); children: Emily Coates, Alice Isomé, Thomas Bartlett. BS in Geology, U. Tokyo, Japan, 1953, MS in Geology, 1955; PhD in Geology, U. Minn., 1959. Research asst. dept. geophysics Univ. Minn., Mpls., 1956-58; rsch. fellow in geophysics dept. geol. scis. Harvard Univ., Cambridge, Mass., 1958-61; assoc. prof. geology Inst. Thermal Springs Research, Misasa, Tottori, Japan, 1961-63; research geologist U.S. Geological Survey, Washington, 1963-65; geologist, project chief U.S. Geological Survey, Washington/Reston, Va., 1965-95; scientist emeritus U.S. Geological Survey, Washington/Reston, 1995—; prin. investigator Lunar Sample & Sci. Program, NASA, 1971-80. Contbg. author books and articles in profl. jours. Fulbright/Smith-Mundt fellow Inst. Internat. Edn., 1955-57, Gilbert fellow U.S. Geol. Survey, Reston, Va., 1982-83. Mem. Am. Geophysical Union, Geochemical Soc., Geological Soc. Washington (2d v.p. 1982-83), Geochemistry Div. Am. Chem. Soc. Home: 11173 Lake Chapel Ln Reston VA 20191-4308 Office: US Geol Survey 956 National Ctr Reston VA 20192-0001

SATO, NOBORU, chemist; b. Jyumonji, Akita, Japan, Oct. 13, 1953; s. tadao and Teruko (Ito) S.; m. Kazuko Sakamoto, Nov. 9, 1980; children: Nana, Takayuki. B.Engring., Yokohama Nat. U., 1976, M.Engring., 1978; Dr. Engring., U. Tokyo, 1988. Prin. engr. Honda Motor Co. Ltd., Suzuka, Mie, Japan, 1979-89; chief engr. Wako Rsch. Ctr. Honda R&D Co. Ltd., Wako, Saitama, Japan, 1990-92, mgr., 1993-94; chief engr. Tochigi R&D Ctr. Honda R&D Co., Ltd., Haga-gun, Tochigi, 1995—; lectr. Nagoya U., 1997-98. Chief editor, co-author: Corrosion engineering of Automobiles, 1992, Surface Analysis and Designing of Automobile Materials, 1995, Surface Technology Handbook, 1998; author: Chemistry of Automobile and Environment, 1995; co-author: Coating Handbook, 1996, Materials Handbook, 2000. Mem. Surface Finishing Soc. Japan (editl. staff 1994-97, Tech. award 1993), Soc. Automotive Engrs. of Japan (editl. staff 1998—), Chem. Soc. Japan. Home: 1-6-4 Oizumigakuen-cho, Nerima-ku Tokyo 178-0061, Japan Office: Honda R&D Co Ltd, 4630 Shimotakanezawa, Haga-gun Tochigi 321-3393, Japan

SATO, SHIGERU, computer research company executive; b. Kamakura, Japan, June 14, 1935; s. Ryozo and Tokuko S.; m. Junko Shimamura, Apr. 22, 1961; 2 children. B in Engring., U. Tokyo, 1958. Computer engr. Fujitsu Ltd., Kawasaki, Japan, 1958-72, mgr. computer divsn., 1972-79, gen. mgr. computer divsn., 1979-83; gen. mgr. computer divsn. Fujitsu Labs. Ltd., Kawasaki, Japan, 1983-87, bd. mem., 1987-94, pres., 1994-2000, chmn., 2000—; pres. Fujitsu Labs. of Am., Calif., 1993-2000; vis. prof. Imperial Coll., London, 1993—; invited spkr. Internat. Joint Conf. on Artificial Intelligence, Australia, 1991, 1st Pan-Pacific Computer Conf., Australia, 1985, 5th Generation World Conf., Eng., 1983. Developer computer systems and related technologies (including circuit design, packaging, and CAD), 1958-87. Fellow IEEE (sr.); mem. Info. Processing Soc. Japan (dir. 1991-93), Japan Soc. for Artificial Intelligence (vice chmn. 1993-95). Home: 3-6-3-1412 Hisamoto, Takatsu-ku, Kawasaki 213-0011, Japan Office: Fujitsu Labs Ltd, 4-1-1 Kamikodanaka Nakahara, Kawasaki 211-8588, Japan

SATO, TAKESHI (KEN SATO), retired planetarium director; b. Kyoto, Japan, Mar. 15, 1938; s. Masayoshi and Michiko (Hikida) S.; m. Saeko Ukishima, Mar. 8, 1964; 1 child, Yasuomi. B Pedagogy, Hiroshima (Japan) U., 1960. Dir. Rakurakuen Planetarium, Itsukaichi, Hiroshima, 1960-71; staff mem. Hiroshima Electric Rwy. Co., Ltd., 1971-80; dir. planetarium Hiroshima Children's Mus., 1980-98; lectr. TV and radio. Co-author: Databook for Astronomical Observers, 1970, Planet Guidebook I, 1981, Planet Guidebook II, 1981, History of Amateur Astronomy in Japan, 1994; author more than 60 planetarium stories; contbr. articles to profl. pubs.; author light pollution ordinance Town of Bisei, Okayama, Japan, 1989. Recipient award Korea Amateur Astronomers Club, 1973, All-Japan Planetarium Conf., 1991, Dir. Gen.'s award Environ. Agy. Japan, 1996, award Japan Planetarium Soc., 1998; minor planet (6884) Takeshisato named by Internat. Astron. Union, 1997. Mem. Oriental Astron. Assn. (dir. Jupiter-Saturn sect. 1960-71, bd. dirs. 1977-86, councilor 1986—), Com. Sci. Investigation Claims of Paranormal, Japan Skeptics, Soc. Tchg. and Popularization Astronomy (v.p. 1993-95), Assn. Lunar and Planetary Observers, Brit. Astron. Assn., Internat. Dark-Sky Assn., Hiroshima Astron. Soc. (advisor), Planetary Soc., Japan Spaceguard Assn. Avocations: astronomical observation. Home: 2-5-7 Sakata, Hatsukaichi 738-0001, Japan

SATO, TOSHIAKI, executive; b. Tokyo, Dec. 22, 1932; s. Tariji and Hideko S.; m. Kyoko Sato, Apr. 13, 1958; children: Chiharu, Aki. B in Comml. Sci., Chuo U., Tokyo, 1955. Cert. internal auditor. Acting mgr. acctg. NCR Japan, Tokyo, 1960-64, asst. internal audit mgr., 1965-69, internal audit mgr., 1970-75, adminstrn. mgr., 1985-87; audit supr. NCR Corp., Dayton, Ohio, 1976-85; controller Nihon MRC, Tokyo, 1987-93; pres. Daikon-no Hana Haruki Co. Ltd., 1997—. Contbr. articles to profl. jours. Mem. Inst. Internal Auditors (bd. dirs. 1976—, pres. Tokyo chpt., 1978, 83-84). Avocations: tennis, music appreciation, gardening, carpentry. Home: Higashi 1-23-5 Sekimachi, 177 Nerima-ku Tokyo Japan Office: Daikon-no Hana Haruki Co, 3-11-1 Shinjuku Shinjuku-ku, Tokyo 160-22, Japan

SATO, TSUKASA, law educator; b. Beppu, Japan, May 4, 1933; s. Kaoru and Toyo (Matuo) S.; m. Keiko Hori, Nov. 11, 1967; children: Ken, Akira. BS in Edn., Tokyo Liberal Arts U., 1958; LLM, Waseda U., 1961. Asst. prof. law Ehime U., Matsuyama, Japan, 1968-71; prof. law Kanagawa U., Yokohama, Japan, 1973—, dean faculty law, 1974-76, dean grad. sch. law, 1985-87; vis. fellow Georgetown U., Washington, 1976-77; vis. prof. Tokyo Met. U., 1992-93. Author: Ideas and Reality on Right of Education in Japan, 1986; co-author: Educational Law: Case Study, 1977; author/ editor: Modern Constitutional Law in Japan, 1986. Chmn. Extropriation Commn., Kanagawa, 1983-96; chmn. Coun. Apperation fo Pub. Access to Pub. Records, Yamoto, Japan, 1987-96; mem. spl. staff Human Dimensions of Global Environ. Change Program, 1994—. Mem. Japan Ednl. Law Assn. (bd. dirs. 1970—), Social Law Sci. Coun. Japan (bd. dirs. 1994—, chmn., chmn. environ. law and policy), Japan Dem. Lawyers Assn. (bd. dirs. 1971—), Tokyo Bar Assn. Avocations: travel, swimming, music. Home: 530-9 Issiki Hayama, Kanagawa 240-0111, Japan Office: Kanagawa U Faculty Law, Kanagawa U Faculty Law, 3-27-1 Rokkakubashi, Kanagawa 221-8680, Japan

SATO, YASUSHI, linguist, educator; b. Rikuzentakata, Iwate, Japan, Mar. 23, 1946; s. Genshi and Toyo Sato; m. Hiromi Yamamoto, Apr. 3, 1994; m. Hiroko Tajima, Oct. 20, 1970 (div. 1994); children: Miyuki, Kei. BA, Meiji Gakuin U., Tokyo, 1968, MA, 1971. Cert. in linguistics. Asst. Meiji Gakuin U. Fgn. Lang. Inst., Tokyo, 1971-73; lectr. Seisen Women's Coll., Tokyo, 1973-75; lectr. Meiji Gakuin U., Tokyo, 1975-77, assoc. prof., 1977-85, prof., 1985—. Author: (books) Current Phonetics and Phonology, 1987, Introducing Generative Grammar, 1989, English Speech Sound, 1991, Modern English Phonetics, 1997, Modern English Grammar, 2000. Fulbright fellow, 1982. Mem. English Linguistic Soc. Japan (bd. councilors 1994—), Assn. Lang. Edn. and Tech. Japan (bd. dirs. 1996—). Presbyterian. Avocations: tennis, Japanese chess. Home: 3-42-20 Fueda, 248-0027 Kamakura Kanagawa, Japan Office: Meiji Gakuin U, 1-2-37 Shirokanedai, 10808636 Tokyo Japan

SATO, YOSHINOBU, clinical pathologist, otolaryngologist; b. Kyoto, Japan, Dec. 16, 1934; s. Juhei and Aya Nakamura S.; m. Masuko Yoshida Sato; children: Mayumi Sato Morimoto, Naomi Sato Matsumoto. Grad., Kyoto Prefectural U. Med., 1961, MD, 1962, PhD Biochem. Studies, 1967. Asst. prof. Kyoto Prefectural U. Med., 1970-75; prof. clin. pathology, dep. med. tech. Kobe Tokiwa Coll., 1979-2000; cons. Biomed. and Environ. Cons., Inc., Richland, Wash., 1989—; invited guest investigator, tchg. asst. NYU Med. Ctr., 1967-68; pres. Internat. Soc. Aerosols Medicine Symposium 1990 of 3rd Internat. Aerosol Conf., 1990-91; pres. Symposium of 5th Internat. Soc. Aerosols Medicine, Tokyo, Kobe, 1984; v.p. Japan Assn. Aerosol Sci. & Tech., 1990-91; mem. exec. bd. Internat. Soc. Aerosols Medicine, 1977-95; hon. pres. Japan Soc. Aerosols Medicine, 1995—; pres. Kanto Total Health Care and Promotion Plan Clinic, 1994—, Kinki Preventive Med. Labs., Inc., 1995—. Editor Jour. Aerosol Medicine, N.Y., 1988-93. Recipient Iinoya prize Japan Assn. Aerosol Sci. and Tech., 1994, Career Achievement award Internat. Soc. Aerosols Medicine, 1997. Home: 8 Shimogamo Maehagicho, Sakyoku Kyoto 606-0833, Japan Office: Kinki Preventive Med Labs Inc, 19-9 Kojogaoka, Otsu City 521-0821, Japan

SATO, YUKIO, Japanese diplomat. Student, U. Tokyo, 1961, Edinburgh (Scotland) U., 1961-63. With Fgn. Svc., 1961—, dir. security divsn. Am. Affairs Bur., 1976-77, pvt. sec. to fgn. min., 1977-79, dir. policy coordination divsn., 1985-87, ast. vice-min. for parliamentary affairs, 1987-88, dir. gen. info. analysis, rsch. and planning bur., 1990-92, dir. gen. N.Am. affairs bur., 1992-94; permanent rep. to UN; rsch. assoc. Internat. Inst. for Strategic Studies, 1980-81; chief Prefectural Police Miyazaki Prefecture, 1984-85. Contbr. articles to profl. jours. Office: Permanent Mission of Japan 866 UN Plz 2d Fl New York NY 10017-1822*

SATOFUKA, FUMIHIKO, history of science and technology educator; b. Kobe, Hyogo, Japan, Oct. 1, 1942; arrived in Wales, 1998; m. Miyo Suzuki, May 1978; 2 children. BSc, Tokyo U., 1965, MSc, 1967, DSc in History Sci. and Tech., 1972. Prof. Sagami Women's U., Tokyo, 1978-95; vis. prof. U. Göteborg, Sweden, 1995-98; hon. rsch. fellow U. Wales, Newport, 1998-2000; prof. Musashino Womens U., Tokyo, 2000—. Home: 2-6-4-104 Yanagibashi Yamatoshi, Kanagawa 242-0022, Japan

SATOH, CHIYOKO, retired molecular geneticist; b. Hiroshima, Japan, Jan. 1, 1937; s. Takahashi Ichitaro and Mitsuko (Shimada) S.; children: Akiko, Shuhei. AB, U. Tokyo, 1960, PhD, 1968. Rsch. assoc. Tanabe Pharm. Co., Tokyo, 1960-71, Pa. State U. Sch. Medicine, Hershey, 1971-73, Atomic Bomb Casualty Commn., Hiroshima, 1973-76; sr. rsch. assoc. U. Mich. Sch. Medicine, Ann Arbor, 1976-77; lab. chief Radiation Effects Rsch. Found., Hiroshima, 1976-93, dept. chief, 1994-97, cons., 1998-99; ret. Radiation Effects Rsch. Found., 1999. Co-author: Effects of A-Bomb Radiation on the Human Body, 1995; author: (with others) Genetic Analysis of Children of Atomic Bomb Survivors, 1996; contbr. articles to profl. jours. Mem. Japan Soc. Human Genetics, Genetics Soc. Japan, Japan Radiation Rsch. Soc. Avocations: tennis, scuba diving. Home: 6-22-101 3-chome Ohtemachi, Naka-ku Hiroshima 730-0051, Japan Office: Radiation Effects Rsch Fdn, 5-2 Hijiyama Park, Hiroshima 732-0815, Japan

SATOH, TOMOHIDE, pathologist; b. Tokyo, Jan. 3, 1960; s. Shoichi and Tsuyako Satoh. DDS, Tokyo Dental Coll., Chiba, Japan, 1984, PhD, 1988. Invited scientist U. Milan (Italy), 1988-89; rsch. assoc. Tokyo Dental Coll.,

Chiba, 1990-92; rsch. assoc. Tokyo Med. and Dental U., Tokyo, 1992-93, oral pathologist, 1994-95; freelance scientist Tokyo, 1995—. Mem. AAAS, Japanese Soc. Pathology, Japanese Soc. Electron Microscopy. Avocations: playing tennis, skiing, swimming, jogging, enjoying opera.

SATOH, YASUHIRO, food products executive. CEO Kirin Brewery, Tokyo, 1996—. Office: Kirin Brewery, 2-10-1 Shinkawa Shuo-ku, 104-8288 Tokyo Japan*

SATO-ILIC, MIKA, engineering educator; b. Hokkaido, Japan, Oct. 27, 1966; d. Hiroshi and Yoko (Miyajima) Sato; m. Peter Jovan Ilic. B in Math., Hokkaido Ednl. U., Kushiro, Japan, 1989; M in Engring., Hokkaido U., Sapporo, Japan, 1991, D in Engring., 1994. Cert. engring. Lectr. Hokkaido Musashi Women's Coll., Sapporo, 1994-97; asst. prof. U. Tsukuba, Japan, 1997—; pub. chair Knowledge-based Intelligent Electronic Systems 98 Internat. Conf., Adelaide, Australia, 1998. Author: Fuzzy Clustering Models and Applications, 1997; contbg. author: Fuzzy Logic and its Applications to Engineering, Information Sciences, and Intelligent Systems, 1995, Fuzzy Logic and Soft Computing, 1995, Aggregation and Fusion of Imperfect Informations, 1998, Advances in Data Science and Classification, 1998, Data Science, Classification and Related Methods, 1998, Soft Computing in Industrial Applications, 2000; mem. editl. bd. Internat. Jour. Knowledge-based Intelligent Engineering Systems, 1996—. Grantee for sci. rsch. Ministry Edn., Sci. and Culture, Japan, 1994, 95, 96, 97, 98, 2000, 2001. Mem. IEEE Systems, Man and Cybernetics (vice-program chair internat. conf. San Diego 1998, mem. adminstrv. com. 1998—), Internat. Fedn. Classification Socs., Japan Soc. for Fuzzy Theory and Systems. Avocations: Ikebana (Japanese flower arrangement), Japanese tea ceremony. Fax: 81-298-53-5006. E-mail: mika@sk.tsukuba.ac.jp. Office: U Tsukuba Inst Policy/Scis, Tenodai 1-1-1, Tsukuba Ibaraki 305-8573, Japan

SATOLA, JAMES WILLIAM, lawyer; b. Cleve., Aug. 26, 1961; s. William John and Catherine Ann (Recek) S. BS in Zoology, Ohio State U., 1984; JD, Case Western Reserve U., 1989. Bar: Ohio 1989, U.S. Dist. Ct. (no. dist.) Ohio 1990, D.C. 1991, U.S. Ct. Appeals (6th cir.) 1992, U.S. Supreme Ct. 1993, U.S. Dist. Ct. Ariz. 1997. Med. rsch. asst. I U. Hosps. of Cleve., 1985-86; law clk to judge John M. Manos U.S. Dist. Ct. (no. dist.) Ohio, Cleve., 1989-91; assoc. Squire, Sanders & Dempsey, Cleve., 1991—. Articles editor Case Western Reserve Law Rev., Cleve., 1988-89. Mem. Celebrezze Inn of Ct. (barrister), Fed. Bar Assn. (treas., bd. dirs. no. dist. Ohio chpt.). Republican. Avocations: art, music, golf, landscaping. Home: 2608 Dysart Rd University Heights OH 44118-4409 Office: Squire Sanders & Dempsey LLP 4900 Key Tower 127 Public Sq Cleveland OH 44114-1216

SATOYOSHI, EIJIRO, neurologist; b. Tokyo, Feb. 11, 1924; s. Mitsuo and Tsunee S.; m. Mitsuko Nakamura, Oct. 1959; 1 child, Akihiko. MD, Keio U., 1946, PhD, 1955. Asst. prof. medicine Toho U. Sch. Medicine, Tokyo, 1957-68, prof. medicine, neurology, 1968-78; dir. neurology ctr. Nat. Musashi Hosp., Tokyo, 1978-86; dir. Nat. Inst. Neurosci., Tokyo, 1986-88; pres. Nat. Ctr. Neurology and Psychiatry, Tokyo, 1989-91, pres. emeritus, 1992—; bd. dirs. Japan Found. Neurosci. and Mental Health, chmn., 1991-97, pres., 1997—. Pres. VIII Internat. Congress Neuromuscular Diseases, 1994; v.p. XII World Congress of Neurology, Kyoto, Japan, 1981; v.p. World Fedn. Neurology, 1993-97. Mem. Japanese Soc. Neurology (hon., pres. 19th ann. meeting 1978), Am. Neurological Assn. (corr. mem.), French Soc. Neurology (fgn. hon. mem.), Royal Soc. Medicine. Buddhist. Avocation: tennis. Home: 4-20-33 Shimomeguro, Meguroku, Tokyo 153, Japan Office: Nat Ctr Neurology, 4-1-1 Ogawa-Higashi Kodaira, Tokyo 187, Japan

SATRIANO, GIUSEPPE SALVATORE, surgeon; b. Baragiano, Italy, June 20, 1946; s. Pietro and Maria (Alberico) S. Degree in medicine and surgery, U. Naples, Italy, 1973; degree in heart and vascular surgery, U. Naples, 1984; degree in anesthesia and intensive care, U. Catania, 1991. Med. diplomate. 1st aid surgeon S. Giovanni di Dio e Ruggi d'Aragona Hosp., Salerno, Italy, 1976, 1st aid and emergency surgeon, 1978-82, gen. surgeon, 1987-91, asst. surgeon, 1991—; fellow Italian Hosp., Buenos Aires, 1976-78; cardiovascular surgeon San Carlo Hosp., Potenza, Italy; local authority dr., Amalfi, Italy, 1974, Salerno, 1975; chief dir. emergency med. svc., Salerno, 1992-95, Salerno Emergency Med. System, 1999; cons. 1st Aid Hosp., Salerno, 1995-96; basic life support instr. Italian Resuscitation Coun.; designer devel. project Euroambulance-Third Millenium Industrias Metalomecanicas Tecnologia Avançada, Portugal; sci. dir. tng. program paramedic staff, ambulances and helicopter crews S. Giovanni Dio E Ruggi d'Aragona Hosp. Emergency Dept. Salerno; chief dir. Salerno Emergency Med. Sys., 1999. Author: (book) Protezione Civile: Che Cosa Fare e Come, 1984, (booklet) La Mia Salute, 1984, L'Elisoecorso, 2000. Founder vol. rescue team Soccorso Amico, 1974; dir. Emersalerno Emergency Med. Svc., 1992; mem. adv. coun. Dr. for Disaster Preparedness, Starke, Fla., 1988. Decorated knight comdr. Fedn. Autonomous Priories of Sovereign Order St. John of Jerusalem Knights of Malta; recipient S. Valentino d'Oro award, 1983, Gold medal Marcello Candia, Naples, 1988, Sicurezza Europea award, 1992, Pericle d'Oro award, 1996; Paul Harris fellow Rotary Internat., 1992. Mem. Italian Resuscitation Coun., Am. Civil Def. Assn. (Recognition of Excellence award 1992). Avocations: travel, collecting old medical books, scuba diving, photography, parachuting, helicopter piloting. Home: Via Giovanni Lanzalone 26, 84100 Salerno Italy Office: S Giovanni Hosp Emerg Dept, Via S Leonardo, 84100 Salerno Italy

SATSANGI, JACK, medical researcher, gastroenterologist; b. Dewsbury, Yorkshire, Eng., May 8, 1963; s. Prem Nath and Nirmal Satsangi. BSc, U. London, 1984, M.B.B.S. in Pharmacology and Pathology with distinction, 1989; DPhil, U. Oxford, 1997, MRCP, 1990. House physician St. Thomas Hosp., London, 1987; sr. house officer Radcliffe Infirmary, Oxford, Eng., 1988-90, med. registrar, 1990-92, rsch. fellow, 1993-97, clin. lectr., 1997—; prof. gastroenterology U. Edinburgh (Scotland), 2000—; tng. fellow Med. Rsch. Coun., London, 1993-97, clin. scientist, 1997-2000; prof. gastroenterology U. Edinburgh, 2000—. Contbr. articles to profl. jours. Named Sidney Truelove lectr. U. Oxford, 1997; recipient First BDF Rsch. prize, London, 1996, Clin. Scientist award European Gastrointestinal Fedn., 1996, Med. Rsch. Scientist award, London, 1997. Mem. Green Coll. Oxford, Royal Coll. Physicians. Avocations: tennis, running. Home: 35 Jack Straw's Ln, Oxford OX1 7LO, England Office: Gastroenterology Unit, Radcliffe Infirmary, Oxford OX2 6HE, England

SATTAR, ABDUL, minister of foreign affairs. Ambassador to Austria Pakistan Ministry Fgn. Affairs, 1975-78, ambassador to India, 1978-82, 90-92, ambassador to USSR, 1988-90; dir., then dir. gen. Pakistan Ministry of Fgn. Affairs, sec. for asia, 1982-86, sec. gen., 1986-88, min. fgn. affairs, 1993, 99—. Disting. fellow U.S. Inst. Peace, 1994. Office: Ministry Fgn Affairs, Shahrazad Bldg Constitution, Islamabad Pakistan*

SATTAR, ABDUS, soil microbiologist; b. Bogra, Bangladesh, Dec. 31, 1954; s. Belayet Ali Akanda and Sahar Banu; m. Nazma Akhtar, Aug. 7, 1983; children: Nahid, Sadia. BSc in Agr. with honors, Bangladesh Agrl. U., Mymensingh, 1976, MSc in Agr., 1978; PhD, Indian Agrl. Rsch. Inst., New Delhi, 1983. Officer NPS V Sonali Bank, Dhaka, Bangladesh, 1977-79; sci. officer Inst. Nuclear Agr., Mymensingh, 1979-85; sr. sci. officer Bangladesh Inst. Nuclear Agr., Mymensingh, 1985-90, prin. sci. officer, 1990-98; chief sci. officer Bangladesh Inst. Nuclear Agrl., Mymensingh, 1998—; prin. investigator BNF project BARC-BINA Joint Program, Mymensingh, 1984-91, chief sci. investigator IAEA-BINA joint BNF project, 1986-94; prin. investigator field evaluation of biofertilizer tech. project BARC-BINA, 1990-91, legume liquid inoculant formulation NifTAL-BINA joint project, 1998—, devel. phosphatic biofertilizer for maximizing crop prodn. SFFP (DANIDA)-BINA joint project, 1998—; European Econ. Commn. postdoctoral fellow Dundee U., U.K., 1991-92. Contbr. articles to profl. jours.; author: Training Manual, 1997; author, editor BINA Scientists Assn. newsletter, 1993-96, 99-2000. V.p. BINA Scientists Assn., Mymensingh, 1985-87, 89-90, 93, 94; mem. Asian Agri-History Found., Hyderabad, 1996-97. Recipient award Bangladesh Assn. for Advancement of Sci., 1990, Cert. of Achievement, Bangladesh Inst. Nuclear Agr., 1993; travel and rsch. grantee IAEA, Austria, 1986-96, 98, 99, ICRISAT, India, 1996, AusAid, Australia, 1997, TRIUMF, 1999, Internat. Isotope Soc.; 2000 NST Expert fellow Min. of Sci. and Tech., 1998-99, 99-2000. Mem. Bangladesh Soc. Microbiologists (exec. com. 1995-96), N.Y. Acad. Scis., Progressive Agriculturists (founder gen., sec. 1989-91), Bangladesh Botanical Soc., Soil Sci. Soc. of Bangladesh, Bangladesh Assn. for Environ. Devel., Crop Sci. Soc. of Bangladesh, Bangladesh Assn. Advancement of Sci., Indian Soc. for Nuclear Agr. and Biology, Bangla Acad. Islam. Avocations: reading, social welfare actitivies, writing stories and articles on science, spectator sports. Office: Bangladesh Inst Nuclear Agr, BAU Campus, 2200 Mymensingh Bangladesh

SATTAR, ABDUS, mathematician, educator; b. Dhaka, Bangladesh, Sept. 1, 1947; s. Muslehuddin Ahmed and Musammat Karimunnessa; m. Safura Begum, Feb. 4, 1971; 2 children. BSc, Dhaka U., 1967, MSc, 1969; MSc, Free U. Brussels, 1977, PhD, 1981. Rsch. fellow dept. math. Dhaka U., 1971-74, lectr. dept. math., 1974-75, asst. prof., 1984-85, assoc. prof. dept. math., 1989-93, prof. dept. math., 1993—; asst. prof. dept. math. Al-Fatah U., Libya, 1985-89. Mem. Bangladesh Math. Soc. (life). Office: Dept Math, Dhaka U, 1000 Dhaka Bangladesh

SATTAR, MOHAMMED ABDUS, research institute administrator, wood scientist; b. Dhaka, Bangladesh, May 17, 1942; s. Ahmed Ali and Nazirun Nesa; m. Husna Ara; children: Hasib, Tanim. MSc, U. Dhaka, 1963, PhD in Wood Sci., 1992; MSc, U. North Wales, 1972. Asst. to prof. U. Dhaka, 1964-65; sr. rsch. officer Bangladesh Forst Rsch. Inst., Chittagong, 1965-76, divsn. head, 1976-91, chief rsch. officer, 1992-95, dir., 1996-99, agriculture, nat. resources and environ. dir., 2000—, chmn. forest products tech. com., 1992—; instr. Bangladesh Inst. Forestry, 1976-91. Contbr. over 75 articles to nat. and internat. sci. jours. Mem. Internat. Solar Energy Soc., Internat. Network Bamboo and Rattan, Renewable Energy Network (U.K.), Bangladesh Standards Inst. (chmn. forest products tech. com.). Islam. Avocations: reading, writing, traveling. Home: Dewangonj, Jamalpur Bangladesh Office: Inst Policy Studies, House # 8/4 Block A, Dhaka 7207, Bangladesh

SATTEL, DANIEL, geophysicist; b. Bad Durkheim, Germany, June 8, 1965. Vordiplom, U. Karlsruhe, Germany, 1986; MS, Oreg. State U., 1990; Diploma, U. Tubingen, Germany, 1992; PhD, Macquarie U., Australia, 1996. Mgr. EM interpretation Fugro Airborne Surveys, Perth, Australia, 1996—. Mem. Am. Geophys. Union, Soc. Exploration Geophysicists, European Assn. Geoscientists and Engrs., Australian Soc. Exploration Geophysicists. Office: Fugro Airborne Surveys, 65 Brockway Rd, Floreat WA 6014, Australia

SATTER, RAYMOND NATHAN, judge; b. Denver, Oct. 19, 1948; s. Charles Herbert and Muriel Vera (Tuller); m. Suzanne Elizabeth Ehlers, May 28, 1977. BA, U. Denver, 1970; JD, Cath. U., 1973. Bar: Colo. 1973, U.S. Dist. Ct. Colo. 1973, U.S. Ct. Appeals (10th cir.) 1973, U.S. Supreme Ct. 1976, U.S. Tax Ct. 1981. Assoc. Wallace, Armatas & Hahn, Denver, 1973-75; ptnr. Tallmadge, Wallace & Hahn, Denver, 1975-77; pvt. practice Denver, 1978-87; Denver County judge, 1987—; gen. counsel Satter Dist., Denver, 1977-78; assoc. mcpl. judge City of Englewood, Colo., 1985-86; mem. Colo. Supreme Ct. Com. on Civil Rules. Pres. Young Artists Orch. Denver, 1985-87; sec. Denver Symphony Assn., 1985-86. Mem. Colo. Bar Assn. (ethics com.), Denver Bar Assn. (bd. trustees 1998—, Jud. Excellence award 1992, 95). Avocations: sailing, opera, classical music, fishing, bridge. Office: Denver County Ct 108 City & County Bldg 1437 Bannock St Denver CO 80202-5337

SATTERFIELD, JOHN ROBERTS, JR., retired college president and music educator; b. Danville, Va., Dec. 4, 1921; s. John Roberts and Sara Elise Council Satterfield; m. Carolyn Talley, Dec. 18, 1948; children: John Roberts III, Kenneth Scott, Keith Charles, Jean Council. BA, U. N.C., 1950, MusM, 1950, MA, 1955, PhD, 1962. Asst. prof. music Davidson (N.C.) Coll., 1953-60; assoc. prof. music Fla. Prebyn. Coll., St. Petersburg, 1960-63, prof. music, 1963-67, prof. humanities and music, 1967-68; v.p. acad. affairs, prof. humanities and music Elmira (N.Y.) Coll., 1968-70; asst. dir. N.C. Bd. Higher Edn., Raleigh, 1970-72; asst. v.p. acad. affairs U. N.C. Gen. Adminstrn., Chapel Hill, 1972, dir. Ctr. Continuing Renewal of Higher Edn., 1972; provost Kalamazoo (Mich.) Coll., 1972-75, exec. v.p., 1973-75; pres. Wagner Coll., Staten Island, N.Y., 1975-81; ret., 1981; part-time instr. music Durham (N.C.) Tech. C.C., 1997; vis. prof. music U. Ky., Lexington, 1964, U. Tex., Austin, 1966; cons. Fla. State Dept. Edn., N.Y. State Depts. Edn. and Civil Svc., U.S. Office Edn., N.C. Bd. Higher Edn., Siena Coll., Coll. St. Benedict, U. Dayton, Davidson Coll., Ohio U. Editor: Christopher Tye: The Latin Ch. Music, Part I: The Masses, 1973, Part II: The Shorter Latin Works, 1973; translator: The Technique of My Music Language (Olivier Messaien), 2 vols., 1956; chief author: Private Higher Education in North Carolina: Conditions and Prospects, 1971; contbr. numerous articles and revs. to profl. jours. and newspapers, short stories to quars., chpts. to books; composer music; keyboardist (movie) The Handmaid's Tale, 1990. Bd. mem., Empire State Found. Ind. Liberal Arts Colls., N.Y.C., 1975-81, United Meth. City Soc., N.Y.C., 1975-81. Capt., USAF, 1942-45. Decorated Bronze Star, Presdl. Citation with Cluster, Belgian Fourragere, Croix de Guerre; recipient Composers award N.C. Symphony Soc., 1951, Harbison award, the Danforth Found., 1965-66. Mem. The Melville Soc. Avocations: reading, travel, cooking. Home: 1401 Brigham Rd Chapel Hill NC 27514-3403

SATTERTHWAITE, GEORGE, II, security director; b. San Jose, Costa Rica, Apr. 18, 1935; s. Livingston Lord andAdelaide (Bristol) S.; m. Helen Marie McCann, June 28, 1958 (div. July 1982); children: Patricia Ann, Livingston Lord, Frank Lord; m. Deanna Marie Kelliher, Apr. 30, 1983; 1 child, Kelley Elizabeth. BA in Internat. Rels., U. Pa., 1957; MA in History, Johns Hopkins U., 1965. Commd. 2d lt. U.S. Army, 1957, advanced through grades to col., 1979, retired, 1987; chief indsl. security Planning Rsch. Corp., McLean, Va., 1987-89; corp. dir. security PRC Inc., McLean, Va., 1989-96; cons., 1996-98; cons., contracts officer SS1 Inc., McLean, Va., 1998—. Mem. Am. Soc. Indsl. Security. Republican. Roman Catholic. Avocations: photography, music, volks marching, travel. Home & Office: 513 Holly Rd Fort Washington MD 20744-6606

SATTERTHWAITE, JOHN STEVEN, bishop; b. Sydney, Australia, Aug. 11, 1928; s. Favel Thomas and Mabel Isobel (Stevens) S. B Engring., U. Sydney, 1949; DDiv, Lateran U., Rome, 1958. Asst. priest - Glen Innes Diocese of Armidale, NSW, 1959-61, bishop's sec., 1962-69; co-adjutor bishop Diocese of Lismore, NSW, 1969-71, bishop, 1971—. Office: Bishop's House, 6 Keen St PO Box 1, Lismore 2480, Australia*

SATTERWHITE, ROBERT LEE, library director; b. Oil city, Pa., July 16, 1941; s. Robert Linwood and Mettie Elizabeth S.; m. Mary Willis Woodruff, Aug. 12, 1972; childre: Benjamin, Elizabeth. BA in English, Hiram Coll., 1965; MA in English, U. Mich., 1966; MLS, U. Pitts., 1973. Instr. English W.Va. Inst. Tech., Montgomery, 1966-71; supr. ref. dept. Northwest Regional Libr. System, Panama City, Fla., 1973-77; regional ref. libr. Florence (S.C.) County Libr., 1977-80; dir. Vienna (W.Va.) Pub. Libr., 1980-89, Hopkinsville (Ky.) - Christian County Pub. Libr., 1989—. Recipient Pub. Svc. award Hopkinsville Human Rels. Commn., 1998. Mem. Ky. Libr. Assn.(treas. pub. libr. sect. 1994-95, sec. pub. libr. sect. 1995-96, mem. legis. com. 1996-97), Hopkinsville Civitan Club (sec. 1998-99). Avocations: creative writing, reading, guitar. Office: Hopkinsville-Christian County Pub Libr 1101 Bethel St Hopkinsville KY 42240-2051

SATTI, IDREES AHMED, physician, consultant; b. Rawal Pinki, Punjab, Pakistan, Jan. 2, 1969; s. Satti Barkhurdar and Noor Safat; m. Hajra Khatoon Satti, Nov. 20, 1992; childrne: Anam, Sanam, Salu ul din. BHMS, Rawal Pindi, Pakistan, 1994; PhD, Colombo, Sri Lanka, 1998. Physician Alnoor Rehab. Med. Ctr., Islamabad, Pakistan, 1998—; cons. Inst., Rawal Pindi, 1998—. Avocations: entertainment, ticketing, volleyball. Home: Alnoor Rehab Med Ctr, Medina Town JABA Khana Dak, IslamaBad Punjab, Pakistan Office: Fauji Found, Hosp Rawal Pindi, Rawal Pindi Punjab, Pakistan

SATULLO, GAETANO, physician; b. Messina, Sicily, Italy, May 11, 1958; s. Nicola and Teresa (Faranda) S.; m. Antonella Pustorino, Oct. 1, 1985; children: Dalila, Livia. Grad. in Medicine, U. Messina, 1982, specialization in cardiology, 1986. Rschr. U. Messina, 1987-89; asst. head physician Papardo Hosp., Messina, 1991-94, helper head cardiology physician, 1999—. Co-author: The Wisle QRS, 1989, The Disorders of Cardiac Arhythmia, 1997; contbr. articles to profl. jours. Fellow Am. Coll. Chest Physicians, Nat. Assn. Med. Cardiologists, European Soc. Cardiology; mem. Internat. Soc. Electrocardiology, Cardiac Electrophysiology Soc., N.Y. Acad. Scis. Avocation: philately. E-mail: gsatullo@tiscolinet.ct. Home: Via Lepanto 7, 98122 Messina Italy Office: Papardo Hosp Cardiology, Ctr Papardo, 98100 Messina Italy

SATYANARAYANA, BHAVANARI, mathematics educator; b. Madugula, India, Nov. 12, 1957; s. Bavanari Ramakotaiah and Bavanari (Atukuri) Anasuryamma; m. Bavanari Reddy Jaya Laksshmi, Apr. 20, 1984; children: Mallikurjuna, Satyasri, Satya Gnyanasri. BSc, Andhra U., Narasaraopet, India, 1977; MSc, Nagarjuna U., Guntur, 1979, PhD, 1985; BEd, Annamalai U., India, 1984. Jr. rsch. fellow Coun. Sci. and Indsl. Rsch., New Delhi, 1980-82, sr. rsch. fellow, 1982-85, pool officer, 1988; temp. lectr. Nagarjuna U., 1985-87, lectr., 1988-93, sr. lectr., 1993—; mem. adv. bd. jour. Sci. Promotor, 1991; referee rsch. papers Indian Nat. Sci. Acad., 1988—, Indian Math. Soc., 1993-94. Editor: Application Oriented Algebra, 1994; hon. editor Ganitha Chandrika, 1999—; patentee in field; contbr. articles to profl. jours. Grantee Univ. Grants Commn., New Delhi, 1994. Mem. Indian Math. Soc. (life), Ramanujan Math. Soc. (life), Allahabad Math. Soc. (life), N.Y. Acad. Scis., Nagarjuna U. Tchrs. Assn. (exec. mem. 1993—). Hindu. Avocations: writing general articles for youth, songs, music. Home: 3-30-3 Brundavan Gardens, Guntur Andhra Prades 522 006, India Office: Nagarjuna U, Dept Math, Nagarjunanagar AP 522 510, India

SATYANARAYANA, GAMINI MUTYA, engineering company executive, biomass systems designer; b. Tanuku, India, Feb. 10, 1950; s. Venkateswarlu and Chandramati (Kallakuri) G.; m. Subhaladevi Nagavenkata Kodati, May 26, 1972; children: Chandra Rekha, Suneeta. BME, Govt. Engring. Coll., 1971; MME, Indian Inst. of Sci., 1974. Scientist Nat. Phys. Lab., Delhi, India, 1975-82; ptnr. Associated Engring. Works, Tanuku, India, 1982-95, mng. dir., 1995—; dir. Sree Gamini Textiles Ltd., Tanuku, 1996—. Recipient Award Fedn. of A.P. C. of C. and Industry, 1996, 98, Nat. award India Govt., 1999; scholarship UN Devel. Programs, 1976. Mem. Tanuku C. of C. and Industry (v.p. 1996—), Arya Vysya Profls. Assn. (pres. 1988—), Indian Inst. of Foundrymen. Hindu. Avocations: nature watching, history, sight seeing. Home: Door No 8-49 DLK Rd, Tanuku 534 211, India Office: Associated Engring Works, Gamini Compound, Andhra Pradesh Tanuku 534 211, India

SATZIK, JULIE ANN, archivist; b. Chgo., May 12, 1965; d. Edward Max and Jeanette Kinga (Kulik) S. BA in History, Northeastern Ill. U., 1987, MA in History, 1994. Intern Mus. Broadcast Comm., Chgo., 1987; archival intern Archdiocese Chgo. Archives and Records Ctr., 1988-93, asst. rsch. archvist, 1993—. Scholar Ill. State Commn., 1983-84. Mem. Assn. Cath. Diocesan Archivists, Midwest Archives Conf., Phi Alpha Theta. Avocations: reading, old movies and TV, music, cross stitching. E-mail:jsatzik@chgo-catholicarchives@org. Office: Archdiocese Chgo Archives and Records 711 W Monroe St Chicago IL 60661-3515

SAUDI, ASHRAF HUSSEIN, retail executive; b. Kalyobia, Egypt, July 12, 1963; s. Hussein Ahmad and Ebtesam Fahmi (Ebtesam) I.; m. Maha Moawad, May 25, 1988; children: Basma, Al-Mutasem Bellah, Maha. BSW, Faculty of Social Work, 1987. Pub. rels. mgr. Bestours Internat., Cairo, Egypt, 1988-89, Kuwait Catering Co., Shuwaikh, Kuwait, 1989-90; procurement mgr. Kuwait Catering Co., Farwaniya, Kuwait, 1991—; comml. mgr. Raad Stores, Ardia, Kuwait, 1997-98, asst. gen. mgr., 1998—; comml. cons. Ebtesama Found., Salmiya, Kuwait, 1997—. Head student union Faculty of Social Work, Cairo, 1985-86, head com. 1983-85. Mem. Societal Union, Egyptian Soc. for Social Workers. Avocations: poetry, traveling, reading in different cultures, drowaing, swimming. Office: Ebtesamet Al-Gamei Found, PO Box 35023, 36051 Shabb Kuwait

SAUDREAU, MICHEL MARIE PAUL, bishop; b. Paris, Mar. 24, 1928; s. Paul and Madeleine (Laine) S. Upper philos. diploma, Paris Letters U., 1951; M of Scholastic Philosophy and Theology, Paris Cath. Inst., 1953. Tchr. theology Grand Seminaire, Issy Les Moulineaux, 1953-57; headmaster religious edn. Diocese of Paris, 1957-64; headmaster religious edn. nat., 1964-70; parish priest St. Lambert de Vaugirard, Paris, 1970-71; vicar gen. Paris Diocese, 1971-74; bishop Le Havre, France, 1974—. Office: BP 1029 17 rue Percanville, 76061 Le Havre Cedex, France

SAUER, BRIAN, molecular geneticist, researcher; b. Columbus, Wis., Sept. 18, 1949; s. Alan and V.E. Sauer. BS, U. Wis., 1972; PhD, U. Calif., Berkeley, 1979. Staff scientist Frederick (Md.) Cancer Rsch. Facility, 1982-84; prin. investigator DuPont Co., Wilmington, Del., 1984-90; sr. rsch. scientist DuPont-Merck Co., Wilmington, 1991-93; expert NIH, Bethesda, Md., 1993-98; mem./head devel. biology, dir. Transgenic Core Facility Okla. Med. Rsch. Found., Okla. City, 1998—; vis. asst. prof. Hood Coll., Frederick, 1983; adj. prof. cell biology U. Okla., 2000—. Mem. editorial bd. Analytical Biochemistry, 1994—; patentee in field. Damon Runyon-Walter Winchell Cancer Fund postdoctoral fellow Stanford U., 1979. Mem. AAAS, Am. Soc. for Microbiology, Genetics Soc. Am., Sierra Club. Office: Okla Med Rsch Found Dev Biol Prog M.S. 49 825 NE 13th St Oklahoma City OK 73104-5005

SAUER, FERNAND EDMOND, pharmaceutical evaluation organization executive; b. St. Avold, Moselle, France, Dec. 14, 1947; m. Pamela Sheppard; 3 children. Degree, U. Strasbourg, France, 1971, U. Paris II, 1977. Hosp. pharmacist, pharm. insp. Ministry of Health, 1973-79; head of pharms. European Commn., Brussels, 1985-94; exec. dir. European Agy. for Evaluation of Medicinal Products, London, 1994-2000; dir. pub. health policy European Commn., Luxemborg, 2000—. Fax: 352 43 61 24. Office: Batiment Jean Monnet, Rue Alcide de Gasperi, L-2920 Luxembourg E14 4HB, Germany

SAUER, GEORG HEINRICH, education educator; b. Altenschonbach, Bavaria, Germany, Sept. 12, 1926; s. Franz Hugo and Elfriede Clara (Kunstler) S.; m. Elisabeth Anna Grether, Aug. 4, 1961; children: Johann, Anna Maria, Katharina. ThD, U. Basel, Switzerland, 1961; U. Dozent, U. Erlangen, Germany, 1961. Univ. prof. U. Wien, Austria, 1970—. Author: Die Spruche Agurs, 1963, Jesus Sirach, 1980. Office: Univ Wien, Rooseveltplatz 10/16, A-1090 Wien Austria

SAUER, GORDON CHENOWETH, dermatologist, educator; b. Rutland, Ill., Aug. 14, 1921; s. Fred William and Gweneth (Chenoweth) S.; m. Mary Louise Steinhilber, Dec. 28, 1944; children: Elisabeth Ruth, Gordon Chenoweth, Margaret Louise, Amy Kieffer.; m. Marion Green, Oct. 23, 1982. Student, Northwestern U., 1939-42; BS, U. Ill., 1943, MD, 1945. Diplomate Am. Bd. Dermatology and Syphilology. Intern Cook County Hosp., Chgo., 1945-46; resident dermatology and syphilology N.Y.U.-Bellevue Med. Center, 1948-51; dermatologist Thompson-Brumm-Knepper Clinic, St. Joseph, Mo., 1951-54; pvt. practice Kansas City, Mo., 1954—; mem. staff St. Luke's, Research, Kansas City Gen. hosps.; assoc. instr. U. Kans., 1951-56, vice-chmn. sect. dermatology, 1956-58, assoc. clin. prof., 1960-64, clin. prof., 1964-93; clin. prof. emeritus, 1993—; head sect. dermatology U. Kans., 1958-70; clin. assoc., acting head dermatology sect. U. Mo., 1955-59, cons. dermatology, 1959-67, clin. prof., 1967—; cons. Munson Army Hosp., Ft. Leavenworth, Kans., 1959-68; dermatology panel, drug efficacy panel Nat. Acad. Sci.-FDA, 1967-69. Author: Manual of Skin Diseases, 1959, 7th edit., 1995, Teen Skin, 1965, John Gould Bird Print Reproductions, 1977, John Gould's Prospectuses and Lists of Subscribers to His Work on Natural History: With an 1866 Facsimile, 1980, John Gould The Bird Man, 1982, John Gould The Bird Man: Associates and Subscribers, 1995, John Gould The Bird Man: Bibliography 2, 1996, John Gould The Bird Man: Correspondence, Vol. 1 through 1838, 1998, vol. 2 through 1841, 1998, vol. 3, 1842-45, 1999; editor Kansas City Med. Bull., 1967-69; contbr. articles to profl. jours. Bd. dirs. Kansas City Area coun. Camp Fire Girls Am., 1956-59, Kansas City Lyric Theatre, 1969-74, Kansas City Chamber Choir, 1969-74, Chouteau Soc., 1985-97, U. Mo.-Kansas City Friends of Libr., 1988-92; bd. dirs. Mo. br. The Nature Conservancy, 1984-91. Sr. asst. surgeon USPHS, 1946-48. Named Dermatology Found. Practitioner of Yr., 1992. Fellow Am. Acad. Dermatology and Syphilology (dir. 1975-79, v.p. 1980); mem. Mo., Jackson County med. socs., Mo. Dermatol. Soc. (pres. 1974-75), Dermatology Found. (trustee 1978-83), Am. Ornithol. Union, Wilson Ornithol. Soc., Royal Australasian Ornithologists Union, Soc. Bibliography Natural History, Am. Dermatol. Assn., Alpha Delta Phi, Nu

Sigma Nu. Presbyterian. Home: 422 E 55th St Kansas City MO 64110-2454 Office: 6400 Prospect Ave Kansas City MO 64132-1180

SAUERBRUCH, TILMAN, internist, educator; b. Lauingen, Germany, July 9, 1946; s. Peter and Annemarie (v.Rosenberg) S.; m. Almuth v. Plettenberg, Aug. 13, 1973 (dec. 1987); children: Sophie, Florens, Friederike; m. Astrid V. Reitzenstein, June, 1994. MD, U. Heidelberg, 1971. Intern, resident in internal medicine U. Heidelberg, Mcpl. Hosps. Pforzheim, Munich, U. Munich, 1973-79; specialist for internal medicine and gastroenterology Munich, 1979-92; assoc. prof. internal medicine U. Munich, 1984-92; prof. internal medicine, chmn., dept. head U. Bonn, 1992—. Contbr. articles to profl. jours. Recipient Foerderpreis für die Europaischen Wissenschaften, Koerber Found., Hamburg, 1986, prize for clin. rsch. SKD, Munich, 1989. Mem. Internat. Assn. for Study Liver, Am. Gastr. Assn., Deutsche Gesellschaft für Stoffwechselkrankheiten. Office: Medizinische Univ klinik, Sigmund-Freud-Str 25, D-53105 Bonn Germany

SAUFER, ISAAC AARON, lawyer; b. Bronx, N.Y., June 16, 1953; s. Solomon and Beatrice (Kanofsky) S.; m. Debra Edith Goldberg, June 26, 1977; children: Suzanne, Nancy, Scott, Daniel, Jonathan. BA, Yeshiva U., N.Y.C., 1975; JD, Bklyn. Law Sch., 1978; LLM in Taxation, NYU, 1982. Bar: N.Y. 1979, N.J. 1986, Fla. 1986, Conn. 1987. Summer intern N.Y. County Dist. Attys. Office, N.Y.C., 1976; legal editor Prentice-Hall, Inc., Englewood Cliffs, N.Y., 1979-80; assoc. Kurzman Karelsen & Frank, LLP, N.Y.C., 1980-85, ptnr., 1986—; adj. assoc. prof. NYU Sch. Continuing and Profl. Studies, N.Y.C., 1988—; lectr. seminars, 1991, 93, 95, 97, 98, 00. Co-author: (N.Y. real property forms) Bergerman & Roth, 1986-87. Office: Kurzman Karelsen & Frank LLP 230 Park Ave Rm 2300 New York NY 10169-2399

SAUFLEY, GEORGE CLAIR, biologist, forestry technician; b. Pt. Republic, Va., Dec. 28, 1939; s. George Newton and Violet Catherine (Long) S.; m. Carol Edith Ebert, Oct. 8, 1966; children: Samuel Matthew, Michael David. BS, Ea. Mennonite U., 1964; postgrad., U. N.H., 1992. Cert. biologist. Farm hand Harrisonburg, Va., 1949-58; meat packer Swift & Co., Harrisonburg, 1958-59, Cavalier Poultry, Harrisonburg, 1962-63; machinist Space Conditioning Sys., Harrisonburg, 1964-66; forestry technician USDA-Insect & Disease Mgmt., Delaware, Ohio, 1966-70, USDA-Forest Health Protection, Durham, N.H., 1970-94; biologist USDA-FHP, Durham, N.H., 1994—; cons. inventory of forest insects and diseases USDA, Durham, 1970—. Contbr. rsch. abstracts to profl. jours. Aerobics instr. YMCA, Strafford County, N.H., 1985-87; mem. ch. coun. Resurrection Luth. Ch., sec., treas., trustee, 1970s-80s. Mem. Soc. Am. Forestry, Toastmasters Internat. (sgt. at arms 1994-95, pres. 1995-96, MCInternat. Children's Festival 1989-95). Democrat. Avocations: computers, mechanics, writing, carpentry, fitness, poetry and song writing. Home: 45 Prospect St Rochester NH 03867-2822 Office: USDA FPM PO Box 640 Durham NH 03824-0640

SAUGSTAD, OLA DIDRIK, pediatric educator; b. Baerum, Norway, Mar. 5, 1947; s. Per and Hanne (Seip); m. Anne-Margrete Frøshaug, Aug. 4, 1973; children: Andreas, Maria. MD, U. Oslo, Norway, 1973, D in Medicine, 1977. Cert. pediatrician. Rsch. fellow Norwegian Rsch. Coun., Uppsala, Sweden, 1973-74; rsch. fellow Norwegian Rsch. Coun., Oslo, 1974-76, intern, 1976-80; postdoctoral rsch. fellow NIH, San Diego, 1980-81; pvt. cons. Oslo, 1986-90; prof., dir. dept. pediatric rsch. Nat. Hosp., Oslo, 1991—; pres. 8th Internat. Workshop on Surfactant Replacement, Oslo, 1993, European Congress Perinatal Medicine 2002, 1998. Author: (in Norwegian) When the Child is Born Preterm, 1991, 2d edit., 1999, (with G. Rooth) The Roots of Perinatal Medicine, 1985; sect. editor Cardiopulmonary Phatophysiology, 1994-98; mem. editl. bd. Jour. Perinatal Medicine, 1992, Jour. Fetal and Maternal Investigations, 1992-98, Acta Paediatrica, 1993, Biology of the Neonate, 1996, Jour. Perinatology, 2000; cons. editor Pediatric Rsch., 1999; editor: Prenatal and Neonatal Medicine, 1999; contbr. 210 articles to profl. jours. Recipient Laerdal Nordic award in intensive care medicine U. Oslo, 1995, Arvo Ylppos Internat. award in neonatal medicine U. Helsinki, Finland, 1997. Fellow Royal Coll. Physicians Edinburgh; mem. Norwegian Soc. Perinatal Medicine (founder, chmn. 1987-89), Soc. Pediatric Rsch., European Soc. Pediatric Rsch. Coun. (coun. mem. 1986-89, sec. working group on neonatology 1989-92), Neonatal Soc., European Assn. Perinatal Medicine (exec. bd. 1996-2000; pres.-elect, 2000-2002), Pediat. Assn. of Hungary (hon.). Lutheran. Home: Vindernveien 22, 0373 Oslo Norway Office: Nat Hosp, Dept Pediatric Rsch, 0027 Oslo Norway

SAUKKONEN, PAULI, linguistics researcher; b. Parikkala, Finland, July 20, 1933; s. Mikko and Enni Johanna (Räsänen) S.; m. Eeva-Leena Elsinen, June 29, 1958 (div. 1982); 1 child, Panu Olli; m. Maria-Liisa Nevala, July 20, 1983. MA, U. Helsinki, 1956, PhD in Finnish Linguistics, 1966. Lexicographer Lexicography Found., Helsinki, 1958-62; rsch. asst. Acad. Finland, Helsinki, 1963-67; prof. Finnish linguistics U. Oulu, Finland, 1967-95, dean Faculty Humanities, 1972-74, 91-95; dir. Rsch. Inst. Langs. of Finland, Helsinki, 1995-98; hon. fellow U. London, 1982-83; vis. prof. U. Göttingen, Germany, 1983-85. Author books on syntax, sociolinguistics, stylistics, semantics, text linguistics, pragmatics, and vocabularies of Finnish. Mem. Finnish Acad. Sci. and Letters, Nykysuomen Seura (hon.), Internat. Quantitative Linguistics Assn. (v.p. 1998-2000). Home: Väylänrinne 4, 00830 Helsinki Finland

SAUL, ANN, public relations executive, medical writer; b. Columbia, Miss.; d. Otto and Ruth Saul. BS in Edn., Miss. Coll., 1961; postgrad., U. Louisville. Staff writer, circulation mgr. Louisville Mag. and Louisville Area C. of C., 1971-77; employee comm. staff Brown & Williamson Tobacco Corp., 1977-79; media rels. NKC Hosps., 1979-80; pub. rels. and sales promotion Am. Temp. Svcs., 1980-82; sr. account supr. Daniel J. Edelman Pub. Rels., Chgo., 1982-87; dir. comm. svcs. Nat. Easter Seal Soc., Chgo., 1987-89; v.p. Sam Huff & Assocs., Pub. Rels., Chgo., 1989-91; founder Ann Saul Pub. Rels., Phila., 1991-2000, Haddonfield, N.J., 2000—. Docent Terra Mus. Am. Art. Mem. Pub. Rels. Soc. Am., Publicity Club of Chgo. (Silver Trumpet 1985, 95, bd. dir.), Editl. Freelancers Assn., Am. Med. Writers Assn. Avocations: reading, volunteer activities, art, travel.

SAUL, IRVING ISAAC, lawyer; b. July 9, 1929; s. Israel Jacob and Jennie (Green) S.; m. Lita Brown, Dec. 29, 1950; children: Joanne Ilene, Sandra Lynn. BA, Washington and Jefferson Coll., 1949; LLB, U. Pitts., 1952; postgrad., Georgetown U., 1949, Ohio State U., 1951. Bar: Ohio 1952, U.S. Dist. Ct. (so. dist.) Ohio 1954, U.S. Supreme Ct. 1961, U.S. Ct. Appeals (6th cir.) 1966, U.S. Dist. Ct. (no. dist.) Ohio 1967, U.S. Dist. Ct. (ea. dist.) Wis. 1973, U.S. Ct. Appeals (7th cir.) 1978, U.S. Ct. Appeals (4th cir.) 1978, U.S. Ct. Appeals (fed. cir.) 1991. Pvt. practice Dayton, Ohio, 1952—; cons. in antitrust litigation; bd. advs. Fed. Civil Practice Abstracts, 1986-88, Ohio Dist. Ct. Rev., 1988—; adj. prof. complex litigation Sch. of Law U. Dayton, 1996-98; lectr. in field. Contbr. articles to profl. jours. James Gillespie Blaine scholar, 1948. Mem. Ohio Bar Assn. (chmn. fed. cts. and practice com. 1977-79, chmn. pvt. enforcement com. 1979-92, bd. govs. antitrust sect. 1982-94), Dayton Bar Assn. (chmn. fed. ct. practice com. 1976-77, 78-80, chmn. com. on judiciary 1987-88), Am. Judicature Soc., Masons (Shriner), Phi Beta Kappa. Jewish. Office: 113 Bethpolamy Ct Dayton OH 45415-2512

SAULGOZIS, JURIS, biomechanical engineer, research administrator; b. Riga, Latvia, Jan. 18, 1936; s. Žanis and Evelīna Ksenija (Dzenīte) S.; m. Rasma Sprenne, Jan. 20, 1965. MSc with honors, Latvian State Inst. Phys. Culture, Riga, 1959; MSc Inst. Polymer Mechs., Latvian Acad. Scis., Riga, 1971, PhD, 1975; MSc with honors, Inst. Polit. Sci., Riga, 1981. Lectr. Latvian State Inst. Phys. Culture, 1959-61; sr. engr. Inst. Polymer Mechanics, Latvian Acad. Scis., 1961-70, sr. rschr., 1970-86; head of lab. Latvian Sci. Rsch. Inst. Traumatology & Orthop., Riga, 1986-93, prof., head lab., 1993-94; prof., head lab. Latvian Med. Acad., Riga, 1994-97; pres. Latvian Ctr. Biomechanics, Riga, 1997—; cons. Sia Vidrižu Atvari, Latvia, 1995—. Co-author: Deformation and Destruction of Hard Biological Tissue, 1980 (1st prize Latvian Acad. Scis. 1981); contbr. articles to profl. jours. Recipient 1st prize Latvian Acad. Scis., 1975. Mem. Internat. Soc. Eye Rsch., European Assn. Vision and Eye Rsch. Avocations: history, philosophy, electronics. Fax: 371 7286938. Office: Latvian Ctr Biomechanics, PO Box 72, LV-1050 Riga Latvia

SAUNDERS, ALISON, French educator; b. Darlington, England, Dec. 23, 1944; d. Frank G. and Joan (Smith) S. PhD, Durham U., England, 1972. Lectr. Paris U., 1968-69; lectr. U. Aberdeen, England, 1970-85, sr. lectr., 1985-90, prof., 1990—. Author: The 16th Century Blason Poetique, 1981; (with D.B. Wilson) Catalogue des Poesies françaises de la Bibliothèque de l'Arsenal 1501-1600, 1985, The 16th Century Emblem: A Decorative and Useful Genre, 1988; (with A. Adams) A Bibliography of French Emblem Books of the 16th and 17th Centuries, 1999. Rsch.. grantee Brit. Acad., 1991, 99, Carnegie Trust, 1992. Mem. Renaissance Soc. Am., Bibliog. Soc. Avocations: antique books, swimming, cooking. Home: 75 Dunbar St, Aberdeen AB24 3UA, Scotland Office: U Aberdeen, Dept French, Aberdeen AB24 3UB, Scotland

SAUNDERS, BARRY WAYNE, state official; b. Roxboro, N.C., June 9, 1944; s. Charlie Clifton and Mary Louise (Mooney) S.; m. Brenda Kaye Bell, Oct. 18, 1987; children: Dara Louise Saunders Lockamy, Erin Elissa (dec.). BA, Campbell u., 1971; MEd, U. N.C., 1974; EdD, N.C. State U., 1990. Tchr. Granville County Sch. System, Oxford, N.C., 1966-69; mental health counselor Vocat. Rehab., Henderson, N.C., 1971-75; staff devel. specialist John Umstead Hosp., Butner, N.C., 1975-82; trainer, asst. mgr., mgr. tng. N.C. Dept. Transp., Raleigh, 1982—; mgr. tng. (on loan from N.C. Dept. Transp.) Gov.'s Office of Quality Improvement, 1995-96; mgr. tng. N.C. Dept. Transp., Raleigh, 1996-2000; ret., 2000; pres. Omicron Cons., Cary, N.C., 1982—. Contbr. articles to profl. jours., poems to N.C. Poetry Soc., 1981. Sec. Dem. Party, Person County, N.C., 1980-84. Mem. Nat. Mgmt. Assn. (bd. dirs. state govt. chpt. 1992-95, v.p. 1997-98), Triangle Quality Coun. (bd. dirs. 1995-96), Nat. Transp. Tng. Dirs. Assn. (v.p. 1997-2000). Methodist. Home: 3076 Helena Moriah Rd Timberlake NC 27583-9011

SAUNDERS, BRIAN KEITH, consulting company executive; b. Columbus, Ohio, June 4, 1961. BSEE, Purdue U., 1983; MBA, Dartmouth U., 1988. Asst. mgr. engring. New Eng. Telephone, Boston, 1983-85, asst. product mgr., 1985-86; assoc. Booz Allen & Hamilton, N.Y.C., 1987-90; dir. strategy and planning Pacific Bell, San Ramon, Calif., 1991-92; gen. mgr. Compus Svcs. Corp., Pleasanton, Calif., 1993-94; prin. cons., designer BKS Design, San Ramon, Calif., 1994—; sr. prin. The McKenna Group, Palo Alto, Calif., 1995-97; chief synergist The BKS Group, San Ramon, Calif., 1997-99; client ptnr. Organic Online, 1999—; instr. U. Calif.-Berkeley Extension, 1999—; bd. dirs. Children's Media Lab., Berkeley, Calif., 1993-97, Family Stress Ctr., Concord, Calif., 1995-97; mem. industry coun. Mt. Diablo Coll., Pleasant Hill, Calif., 1993-95; mem. exec. coun. Tuck MBEP Alumni Assn. Dartmouth Coll., Hanover, N.H., 1994—. Mem. Computer Game Developers Assn., Bay Area Video Coalition, MDG.org., World Future Soc. Avocations: jazz, history, science fiction, martial arts.

SAUNDERS, BRYAN LESLIE, lawyer; b. Newport News, Va., Apr. 18, 1945; s. Raymond Hayes and Lois Mae (Pair) S.; divorced; children: Kelly Brooke, Justin Lee; m. Anne Mason Dunbar, July 15, 1995. BS, East Tenn. State U., 1967; JD, U. Tenn., 1973. Bar: Va. 1973, U.S. Dist. Ct. (ea. dist.) Va. 1973, U.S. Ct. Appeals (4th cir.) 1991. Lawyer Cogdill & Assocs., Newport News, Va., 1973-76; pvt. practice Newport News, 1976—; commr. in chancery Cir. Ct. of Newport News, 1990-97. Sgt. U.S. Army, 1968-71. Decorated Bronze star, 1971; recipient Outstanding Svc. to Law Enforcement Newport News and Police Dept., 1986. Mem. Va. Bar Assn., Nat. Assn. Criminal Def. Lawyers, Va. Coll. Criminal Def. Attys., Pi Kappa Phi, Pi Gamma Mu. Avocations: chess, bridge, bowling. Office: 728 Thimble Shoals Blvd Ste C Newport News VA 23606-4546

SAUNDERS, DIANE GAIL, archive director, author; b. Nassau, Bahamas, Mar. 10, 1944; d. Edward Basil and Audrey Virginia (Isaacs) North; m. Winston Saunders, Apr. 15, 1968. BA with honors in History, U. Newcastle-upon-Tyne, Eng., 1966; MPhil in History, U. West Indies, Jamaica, 1978; PhD in History, U. Waterloo, Ont., Can., 1985. History tchr. Govt. H.S., Nassau, Bahamas, 1967-68; pub. records officer Ministry of Edn., Nassau, 1970-71; archivist Pub. Records Office, Nassau, 1971-80; chief archivist Dept. Archives, Nassau, 1980-83, dir. archives, 1983—; UNESCO cons. on govt. archives and records Govt. of Kitts & Nevis, 1979, Govt. of Antigua, 1982, Dominica, 1994; dir. Bahamas Field Sta., San Salvador, Bahamas, 1991è; bd. dirs. Internat. Rsch. & Tng. Inst. for Advancement of Women, 1991-97, pres., 1996è. Author: Bahamian Loyalists and Their Slaves, 1983, Slavery in the Bahamas 1648-1838, 1985, The Bahamas: A Family of Islands, 1988, Bahamian Society After Emancipation, 1990, 2nd edit., 1994, Social Life in the Bahamas, 1880s-1920s, 1996; co-author: Historic Nassau, 1979, Guide to the Records of the Bahamas, 1979, Sources of Bahamian History, 1991, Islanders in the Stream: A History of the Bahamian People: Islanders in the Stream: A History of the Bahamian People, Vol. I, 1992, Vol. II, 1998. Mem. preservation of hist. bldgs. com. Bahamas Nat. Trust; pres. Bahamas Hist. Soc., 1989-99; chmn. planning com. Nat. Mus., 1991—; mem. nat. coord. com. UN 1995 World Conf. for Women, 1992-95; chmn. Nat. Art Gallery of Bahamas Com. Recipient Disting. Citizen's award for govt. C. of C., 1984, Cacique award for writing Bahamas Min. Tourism, 1997, Paul Harris Fellow award Rotary Internat., 1998; named Boss of Yr., Bahamas' Sec. Assn., 1979. Mem. Caribbean Archives Assn. (pres. 1975-79, sec. 1979-89), Assn. Caribbean Historians (sec. 1986-90, v.p. 1998-2000, pres. 2000—). Anglican. Avocations: tennis, writing, painting. Home and Office: Dept Archives, PO Box N-1732, Nassau Bahamas

SAUNDERS, GEORGE LAWTON, JR., lawyer; b. Mulga, Ala., Nov. 8, 1931; s. George Lawton and Ethel Estell (York) S.; children: Kenneth, Ralph, Victoria; m. Terry M. Rose. B.A., U. Ala., 1956; J.D., U. Chgo., 1959. Bar: Ill. 1960. Law clk. to chief judge U.S. Ct. Appeals (5th cir.), Montgomery, Ala., 1959-60; law clk to Justice Hugo L. Black U.S. Supreme Ct., Washington, 1960-62; assoc. Sidley & Austin, Chgo., 1962-67, ptnr., 1967-90; founding ptnr. Saunders & Monroe, Chgo., 1990—. With USAF, 1951-54. Fellow Am. Coll. Trial Lawyers; mem. ABA, Ill. State Bar Assn., Chgo. Bar Assn., Order of Coif, Chgo. Club, Point-O'Woods Club, Quadrangle Club, Law Club, Legal Club, Phi Beta Kappa. Democrat. Baptist. Home: 179 E Lake Shore Dr Chicago IL 60611-1306 Office: Saunders & Monroe 3160 NBC Tower 455 N Cityfront Plaza Dr Chicago IL 60611-5503

SAUNDERS, GILLIAN MARGUERITE, museum curator; b. London, Dec. 14, 1956; d. Ernest and Marguerite (Hales) S. BA honors Combined Arts, U. Leicester, Leicester, England, 1978. Mus. asst. Victoria & Albert Mus., London, 1979-85; sr. mus. asst. Victoria & Albert Mus., 1985-88, rsch. asst., 1988—; sec. Wallpaper hist. Soc., Gt. Britain, 1987—. Author: G.D. Ehret's Plant Portraits, 1987, The Nude: A New Perspective, 1989, Picturing Plants: an analytical history of botanical illustration, 1995; editor, co-author: 100 Great Paintings in the V&A, 1985; co-author: Recording Britain: A Pictorial Domesday of Pre-War Britain, 1990, Apocalyptic Wallpaper, 1997. Mem. Assn. Art Historians. Office: Victoria & Albert Mus, Cromwell Rd, South Kensington London, England SW7 2RL

SAUNDERS, GRAHAM ERIC, health facility administrator; b. York, Eng., Apr. 3, 1945; s. Arthur Frank and Ivy Ethel (Short) S.; m. Valerie Barton, Dec. 20, 1969; children: Elizabeth Helen, Christopher Andrew. BSc, U. Durham, Eng., 1966. Grad. trainee Sheffield (Eng.) Regional Hosp. Bd., 1967-69; adminstr. Sunderland (Eng.) Hosp., 1969-74; gen. adminstr. Durham Health Dist., 1974-77, St. James's Hosp., Leeds, Eng., 1977-82; gen. mgr. Harrogate (Eng.) Health Authority, 1982-92; CEO Harrogate (Eng.) Health Care NHS Trust, 1992—. Justice of the Peace, Harrogate Bench, Eng., 1995—. Fellow Inst. Health Care Mgmt. (past regional chmn.). Avocations: theater, opera, good food, jogging. Office: Harrogate Dist Hosp, Lancaster Park Rd, Harrogate HG2 7SX, England

SAUNDERS, JOHN BARRINGTON, medical educator; b. Wrexham, Wales, May 14, 1949; arrived in Australia, 1984; s. William and Megan (Roberts) S.; m. Alison Margaret Lamb, Apr. 2, 1977; children: Andrew John, Jennifer Clare, Elizabeth Nicola. BA with honors, U. Cambridge, Eng., 1970, MB, BChir, 1973, MA, 1974, MD, 1986. Lectr. liver diseases King's Coll. Hosp. Med. Sch., London, 1979-83; staff specialist Royal Prince Alfred Hosp., Sydney, Australia, 1984-86, sr. staff specialist, head dept., 1986-96; assoc. prof. medicine U. Sydney, 1989-96; prof. alcohol & drug studies U. Queensland, Brisbane, Australia, 1996—; mem. expert adv. panel mental health WHO, Geneva, 1991—, co-dir. Australian Multi-Site Collaborating Ctr. Mental Health and Substance Abuse, Brisbane, 1996—; sec. Internat. Soc. Biomed. Rsch. Alcoholism, Denver, 1994—. Author: Alcoholism and Problem Brinking, 1989; editor: The Biology of Alcohol Problems, 1996; editor Drug and Alcohol Rev., 1985—; contbr. articles to profl. jours. Mem. New South Wales Drug Offensive Coun., Sydney, 1988-92. Sheldon clin. rsch. fellow West Midlands Regional Hosp. Authority, Birmingham, England, 1978-79. Fellow Royal Coll. Physicians, Royal Australasian Coll. Physicians, Australasian Faculty of Pub. Health Medicine; mem. Australian Profl. Soc. Alcohol and Drugs, Internat. Soc. Biomed. Rsch. Alcoholism. Mem. Anglican Ch. Avocations: opera, railway history. Office: U Queensland Dept Psychiatry, Royal Brisbane Hosp, Queensland 4029, Australia

SAUNDERS, JOSEPH ARTHUR, office products manufacturing company executive; b. Creston, Mont., July 9, 1926; s. Albert Henry and Edith Margaret (Rhodes) S.; m. Lois Evelyn White, June 19, 1948 (dec. Oct. 1986); children: Albert Henry II, Margaret Jean; m. Eva Homor, July 18, 1987; stepchildren: Rodney, Charmaine. Educated pub. schs., Youngstown, Ohio and Winthrop, Maine. With Saunders Mfg. Co. Inc., doing bus. as Saunders, Winthrop, 1947—, exec. v.p., 1967-77, pres., 1977-88, CEO, 1967-96, chmn. bd., 1988—; chmn. Saunders Internat. B.V., Netherlands, Graphic Utilities, 1999—, RhinoSkin, Inc., 2000—; co-founder, sec., bd. dirs. Dirigo Bank and Trust Co., Augusta, Maine, 1969-86; co-founder, dir. Cushnoc Bank and Trust Co., Augusta, Maine, 1988-94. Chmn. jour. ADL Torch of Liberty Award, 1997. With U.S. Army, 1945-47. Recipient ADL Torch of Liberty award, 1998. Mem. Maine C. of C. and Industry (bd. dirs. 1976-81, chmn. mfg. coun. 1978-82), Maine Metal Products Assn. (bd. dirs. 1983-84), Soc. Mfg. Engrs. (cert. new product engr.), Internat. Bus. Forms Industries (chmn. assocs. 1976-77, co-chmn. exhibits com. 1978-82), Order of the Black Leaf, Document Mgmt. Industries Assn., Bus. Products Industry Assn., Office Products Mfrs. Assn. (bd. govs. 1988-94, v.p. 1990), Am. Legion, Masons, Shriners, others. Achievements include patentee in field. Home: PO Box 123 Readfield ME 04355-0123 Office: Saunders Mfg & Mktg PO Box 243 Winthrop ME 04364-0243

SAUNDERS, KATHRYN A., retired data processing administrator; b. Elgin, Minn., Apr. 12, 1920; d. William P. and Mathilda M. (Mielke) Hagner; m. James L. Saunders, June 14, 1952 (dec. 1992); children: Gary, Wade, Brian. BA, U. Calif., Berkeley, 1941; cert., Coll. of Marin, Kentfield, Calif., 1948. Mem. gen. staff Fed. Res. Bank, San Francisco; with civilian pers./payroll dept. USAF, Hamilton AFB, Calif.; coord. data processing Sir Francis Drake High Sch., San Anselmo, Calif. Sec. program resource United Meth. Women, 1988—, treas., 1994-99; mem. decorations guild Marin Art and Garden Ctr., 1996—. Mem. AAUW, Calif. Sch. Employees Assn., Calif. Scholarship Fedn. (life), Nat. Assn. Ret. Fed. Employees, Coll. of Environ. Design Alumni Assn. of U. Calif. Berkeley, Order of Golden Rose of Delta Zeta. Avocations: sewing, knitting, art work, piano, volunteer work. Address: 118 Tamal Vista Dr San Rafael CA 94901-1646

SAUNDERS, KAY ELIZABETH BASS, history educator; b. Brisbane, Queensland, Australia, Aug. 19, 1947; d. Eric John and Elizabeth (Walsh) S.; m. Raymond Leslie Evans (div. 1982); 1 child, Erin. BA with honors, U. Queensland, 1970, PhD, 1975. Sr. tutor U. Queensland, 1975-88, sr. lectr., 1986-89, reader, 1990—; dir. Nat. Australian Day Coun., Sydney, 1992-96; gov. Australian War Meml., Canberra, 1994-97; mem. of coun. Australian Nat. Maritime Mus., 1994-97; chmn. Queensland Cultural Adv. Coun., Brisbane, 1997—. Author: 1901: Our Future's Past, 1997, Aboriginal Workers, 1995, Sir Paul Hasluck, 1997, Gender Relations in Australia, 1992, Race Relations in Australia, 1975, 88, 93, Identured Labour in the British Empire, 1984, Australian Masculinities, 1997. Mem. Premier Queensland's Adv. Coun. Women. Named to Australian Rsch. Coun., 1979-81, 93-94. Mem. Australia Hist. Assn. (exec. 1989-91). Avocations: reading, cooking, dancing. Office: History Dept, U Queensland, Saint Lucia QLD 4072, Australia

SAUNDERS, KENNETH BARRETT, medical educator; b. Colombo, Ceylon, Mar. 16, 1936; s. Harold Nicholas and Winifred Florence (Gadge) S.; m. Philippa Mary Harrison, Apr. 29, 1961; children: Katherine Louise, Stephen Mark. Student, Cambridge U., 1955-58, St. Thomas Med. Sch., 1958-61; MB BChir, Cantab., 1961; MA, MD, London U., 1966, DSc, 1995. Sr. lectr. in medicine Middlesex Hosp., London, 1972-80; prof. med. Med. Sch. St. George's Hosp., London, 1980-95, emeritus prof. medicine, 1995—; chmn. medicine Med. Sch., St. George's Hosp., London, 1980-90; dean of faculty of medicine London U., 1990-94; hon. cons. physician to army, 1994-97. Author: Clinical Physiology of the Lung, 1977; contbr. articles to profl. jours. Fellow Royal Coll. Physicians; mem. Royal Soc. Medicine, Brit. Thoracic Soc., Hellenic Soc. (treas.). Avocations: classical literature, especially Homer, English lit., golf, piano. Home: 77 Lee Rd Blackheath, London SE3 9EN, England

SAUNDERS, MATTHEW JOHN, architectural historian, conservationist; b. London, Apr. 12, 1953; s. John William and Joyce Mary (Day) S. MA, U. Cambridge, Eng., 1974. Editl. asst. Whitaker's Almanack, London, 1975; sec. Save Britain's Heritage, London, 1976-77; asst. sec., then sec. Ancient Monuments Soc., London, 1977-99. Author: Historic Homeowner's Companion, 1987; contbr. to books: The Architectural Outsiders, 1985, Festschrift for Sir Bernard Feilden, 1996. Hon. dir. Friends of Friendless Ch., London, 1993—; trustee Hist. Chapels Trust, London, 1993-95; mem. places of worship adv. com. Heritage Lottery Fund, 1995—, hist. bldgs. & land com. Heritage Lottery Fund, 1999—. Mem. Ecclesiological Soc. (v.p. 1994), Nat. Amenity Socs. (joint com., sec. 1982—). Avocations: music, travel, photography. Office: Ancient Monuments Soc, 2 Church Entry, London EC4V 5HB, England

SAUNDERS, ROBERT M., lawyer; b. N.Y.C., July 31, 1959; s. Herbert L. and Loretta (Tymon) S.; m. Cheryl D. Lambek, Nov. 6, 1988; children: David, Dana. BA, SUNY, Buffalo, 1980; JD, U. Chgo., 1983. Bar: N.Y. 1984, U.S. Dist. Ct. (so. and ea. dist.) N.Y. 1988, Fla. 1995, U.S. Dist. Ct. (so. dist.) Fla. 1995. Assoc. LeBoeuf, Lamb, Leiby & MacRae, N.Y.C., 1983-86, Brown & Wood, N.Y.C., 1986-88; assoc. Willkie Farr & Gallagher, N.Y.C., 1988-92, spl. counsel, 1993-95; sole practice Weston, Fla., 1995—. Office: 4300 N University Dr Ste C203 Fort Lauderdale FL 33351-6244 Address: 1300 Mancr Ct Fort Lauderdale FL 33326-2818

SAUNDERS, ROGER ALLETSON, epidemiologist; b. Neneaton, U.K., Oct. 14, 1945; arrived in France, 1992; s. Olaf Alan and Clara Alletson (Whatmough) S. DMS, Sheffield Polytech., U.K., 1975; MPhil, Bournemouth Polytech., U.K., 1985, PhD, 1987. Cert. epidemiologist. Safety edn. Coventry C.C., 1974; safety mgr. Rotherham MBC, 1974-77; prin. safety adv. South Yorkshire MBC, 1977-82; chief road safety adv. Dorset C.C., 1983-89; course dir. MSc Program Bournemouth Polytech., 1989-90; dir. Greys Group of Co., 1990-97; pres. Norstrad Group Cos., La Mothe St. Heray, France, 1997—; dir. Ctr. for Safety Studies, Bournemouth, U.K., 1985-90; prin. adv. Min. Comms., Indonesia, 1992-94; adv. WHO, EMRO, 1985-90; vis. lectr. Brighton U. Bus. Sch., 2000. Author: Handbook of Safety management, 1990, Safety For Personnel Managers, 1991, Safety Auditing, 1992, Office Safety, 1993; contbr. articles to profl. jours. Safety adv. Transp. and Gen. Workers Union, Rotherham, 1975; adv. Inst. Road Safety, U.K., 1989. Capt. UKLF 1979-85. Fellow Inst. Road Safety. Avocations: writing, reading, swimming, tennis. Office: Norstrad House, PO Box 21, 79800 La Mothe St Heray France

SAUNDERS, TERRY ROSE, lawyer; b. Phila., July 13, 1942; d. Morton M. and Esther (Hauptman) Rose; m. George Lawton Saunders Jr., Sept. 21, 1975. BA, Barnard Coll., 1964; JD, NYU, 1973. Bar: D.C. 1973, Ill. 1976, U.S. Dist. Ct. (no. dist.) Ill. 1976, U.S. Ct. Appeals (7th cir.) 1976, U.S. Supreme Ct. 1983. Assoc. Williams & Connolly, Washington, 1973-75; assoc. Jenner & Block, Chgo., 1975-80, ptnr., 1981-86; ptnr. Susman, Saunders & Buehler, Chgo., 1987-94; pvt. practice Law Offices of Terry Rose Saunders, Chgo., 1995—. Author: (with others) Securities Fraud: Litigating Under Rule 10b-5, 1989. Recipient Robert B. McKay award NYU Sch. Law. Mem. ABA (co-chair class actions and derivative suits com. sect. litigation 1992-95, task force on merit selection of judges), Ill. State Bar Assn., Chgo. Bar Assn., Order of Coif, Union League Club. Office: 30 N La Salle St Chicago IL 60602-2590

SAUR, PETRA, physician, anesthesiologist; b. Kassel, Germany, Apr. 13, 1962; d. Karl-Heinz and Helga (Knierim) S. MD, U. Goettingen, Germany, 1988, PhD, 1998. Cert. specialist in sports medicine, emergency medicine, chirotherapy, pain therapy, psychotherapy, intensive care medicine, quality management. Med. asst. U. Goettingen, 1988-98, sr. physician, 1998—, sr. physician in emergency, 1997—. Physician, Civic Sports Orgn. of Goettingen, 1992—. Recipient 1st award in pain therapy, 1994, 2nd award, 1999. Mem. German Assn. Anesthesia and Intensive Care Medicine, German Assn. Manual Medicine, German Assn. Sports Medicine. Avocation: dancing. E-Mail: psaur.gwdg.de. Home: Ritterplan 3, Goettingen 37073, Germany Office: U Goettingen/Anees Centre, Robert-Koch-Str 40, Goettingen 37070, Germany

SAURAZAS, JULIA ROBERTA, business educator; b. Toronto, Ont., Can., June 2, 1957; arrived in United Arab Emirates, 1991; d. Zigmas and Martha (Mattis) S. BA, U. Western Ont., Can., 1979; B Commerce, U. Windsor, Can., 1982; MBA, U. Queensland, Brisbane, Australia, 1987; PhD, U. Bradford, U.K., 2000. Auditor trainee Arthur Andersen & Co., Toronto, 1982-84; fin. analyst Bank of Montreal, Toronto, 1984-85; rsch. asst. U. Queensland, 1985-87; asst. to the pres. Capsule Tech. Internat., 1988-90; lectr. Grande Prairie (Can.) Regional Coll., 1990-91; supr. bus. dept., lectr. Dubai Men's Coll., United Arab Emirates, 1991—. Mem. Am. Mktg. Assn., Chartered Inst. Mktg. Avocations: aerobics, scuba diving, horse riding, travel, collecting Arabian/Asian antiques. Office: Dubai Mens Coll, PO Box 15825, Dubai United Arab Emirates

SAURO, JOSEPH PIO, physics educator; b. New Rochelle, N.Y., Apr. 4, 1927; s. Francesco Giovanni and Lucia (Arrivebene) S.; m. Elizabeth Joann Schellman, May 2, 1948; children: Brian, Michael, Joseph. BS, Poly Inst. Bkyn., 1955, MS, 1958, PhD in Physics, 1966. Dir. coll. sci. improvement program U. Mass., North Dartmouth, 1969-71, dean grad. sch., 1969-71, interim dean Coll. of Engring., 1978-80, dean Coll. Arts and Scis., 1969-80, prof. physics, 1965-93, prof. emeritus, 1995—. With USN, 1944-46. Sci. Faculty fellow NSF, 1964; State War Svc. scholar State of N.Y., 1953. Mem. Am Assn. Physics Tchr., Sigma Xi, Sigma Pi Sigma. Avocations: photography, travel, music. Home: 8 Captain Wing Rd East Sandwich MA 02537-1122 Office: U Mass North Dartmouth MA 02747

SAUTER, FRANZ FABIAN, consulting and structural engineer; b. San Jose, Costa Rica, Feb. 7, 1933; s. Federico and Hilda (Fabian) S.; m. Maria Angeles Ortiz, June 30, 1957; children: Arnold, Hans Peter, Krista Maria, Manfred, Helmuth. Engring. Degree, U. Costa Rica, 1956; postgrad., Internat. Inst. Seismology, Tokyo, 1963-64. Structural engr. Leonhardt & Andrä, Stuttgart, Germany, 1957-58; chief engr., then mgr. in charge engring. and sales Productos de Concreto S.A., San Jose, 1958-63; pres., prin. ptnr. Franz Sauter & Asociados S.A., Cons. Engrs., San Jose, 1964—; prof. structural engring. U. Costa Rica, 1958-70; mem. seismic code com. Colegio Federado de Ingenieros y Arquitectos de Costa Rica; bd. dirs World Seismic Safety Initiative, 1994-98; pres. Asociacion Centroamericana del Cemento y Concreto, 1967-72, Institucion Cultural Germano-Costarricense, San Jose, 1969-73. Co-author: Study of Earthquake Insurance, 1978; author: Introduction to Seismology, 1989. UNESCO grantee, 1963-64; decorated Bundesverdienstkreuz 1st class (Germany). Mem. ASCE, Asociacion Centroamericana Cemento y Concreto (hon.), Colegio Federado de Ingenieros y Arquitectos de Costa Rica, Earthquake Engring. Rsch. Inst., Am. Concrete Inst., Prestressed Concrete Inst., Costa Rican Assn. Structural and Seismic Engring. (hon. pres.). Address: Apartado Postal 6260-1000, San José Costa Rica

SAUTER, JOERG JOCHEN, botanist; b. Bopfingen, Germany, Mar. 23, 1937; s. Franz Josef and Hilda H.M. (Maeulen) S.; m. Helga Marie Kohring, Aug. 14, 1964; children: Antje, Birthe Christine. Diploma, U. Freiburg, Germany, 1961, D of Natural Scis., 1964; D of Natural Scis. Habilitation, U. Freiburg, 1969. From rsch. asst. to asst. prof. Freiburg U., 1961-69, asst. prof., 1972; rsch. fellow Harvard U., Cambridge, Mass., 1970-71; prof. U. Kiel, Germany, 1972—; dir. Botany Inst., Kiel, 1979—. Contbr. articles to profl. jours, chpts. to books. Rsch. fellow Harvard U., 1969, Bullard fellow, 1983; recipient faculty of sci. prizeU. Freiburg, 1964. Mem. German Botany Assn., Fedn. European Soc. Plant Physiology, Assn. German Naturforscher and Ärzte, Internat. Assn. Wood Anatomy, German Dendrol. Assn., Nat. Geographic Soc. Office: Botany Inst Kiel U, Olshausenstr 40, D-24098 Kiel Germany

SAUTIN, DMITRY, Olympic athlete; b. Voronezh, Russia, Mar. 15, 1974. Joined Soviet Nat. Team, 1990; winner Silver medal platform European Championships, 1991; winner Bronze medal springboard Barcelona, 1992; winner Gold medal platform World Championships, 1994, winner Silver medal springboard World Championships, 1994; winner Gold medal platform Atlanta, 1996; winner platform and springboard World Championships, 1998; winner Gold medal platform Sydney, 2000. First diver to win 2 medals at World Championship, 1994, first Soviet diver to win men's platform title in Olympic competition, 1996. Office: All-Russia Swimming Fedn, Luzhnitskaya Naberzhnaya o, Moscow 119270, Russia*

SAUVAN, XAVIER MARTIAL, computer scientist, consultant, researcher; b. Paris; s. Martial and Cecile (Eloy) S. MS, U. Paris VI, 1984, PhD, 1988. Cons. engr. Oracle, Inc., Paris, 1990-92; rsch. engr. U. Hosp., Zurich, 1992-96; rsch. assoc. U. Rochester, N.Y., 1996-97; rsch. engr. LIRA-DIST, Genoa, Italy, 1997-99; project mgr., cons. Software AG, Paris, 1999—; reviewer numerous internat. jours. Contbr. articles to profl. jours. including Perception & Psychophysics, Behavioural & Brain Scis., Visual Cognition, and Revs. in Neuroscis. With French Mil. Hosp., 1983. Mem. European Neurosci. Assn., N.Y. Acad. Scis. Avocations: sailing, archery, multimedia. Office: Software AG, 5 ave de Verdun, 94000 Ivry sur Seine France

SAUVÉ, CAROLYN OPAL, writer, journalist, poet; b. Columbus, N.C., Apr. 30, 1934; d. Anthony Floyd and Nina Morris Pittman; m. Joseph Ernest Sauvé, Mar. 31, 1953; children: Floyd, Kenneth, Timothy. Student, Spartanburg Meth. Coll., 1952-53; AAS, Isothermal C.C., 1976. Editor, author, photographer: History of Polk County, 1983; author, photograph APP Jour., 1999; author: Spirit of the Age, 1996. Trustee Isothermal C.C., Spindale, N.C., 1985-93; bd. dirs. Area Mental Health Bd., Spindale, 1985-91; v.p., sec., chmn. Am. Cancer Soc., Polk County, N.C., 1975-79; bd. dirs. Juvenile Justice Bd., Rutherfordton, N.C., 1978-82; chmn. Polk County Commn., Columbus, 1978-82; chmn. Polk County Rep. Party, Columbus, 1984-86, 95-98; vice chmn., dist. chmn. N.C. Rep. Women's Club, Raleigh, 1975-79; chmn World Missions Com., 1994—. Mem. Polk County Hist. Assn. (pres. 1984-86, v.p. 1996—). Presbyterian. Avocations: creative writing, boating, waterskiing, cake decorating, grandchildren. Home: RR 5 Box 2650 Columbus NC 28722-9545

SAUVÉ, GEORGES, surgeon; b. Paris, Sept. 10, 1925; s. Louis de Gonzague andMarie (Bourdon) S.; m. Monique Lemaigre, June 11, 1955; children: Frédérique, Jacques-Phillipe, Diane, Claire, Marie-Amelie, Bérengère. MD, U. Paris, 1956. Intern Hosp. de Paris, 1952-57, chief of surgery, 1975-62; practice surgery, Laval, France, 1962—. Auteur Les fils de Saint Come, 1997, De Louis XV à Poincar"248, 1989, Le Collège Stanislas, 1994. Mem. Internat. Coll. Surgeons, Lauréat Acad. Médecine, Acad. Maine, Acad. Généalogie. Roman Catholic. Avocations: music, art, literature. Home: La Templerie, 53 380 La Templerie France Office: Polyclinique du Maine, Ave Francais, Laval France

SAUVEUR, GABRIEL MARIE-JOSEPH, dental surgery educator; b. Fort-De-France, Martinique, May 3, 1936; s. Pierre and Andree (Hilaric) S.; m. Monique Courtois, Aug. 17, 1958 (div. 1969); children: Martine, Eric, Philippe, Jean-Marc; m. Christiane Diguine, Apr. 11, 1973 (div. 1987); children: Elodie, Anthony, Gabriel, Jr. Baccalaureat, Lycee Condorcet, Paris, 1957; PCB in Physics, Chemistry and Biology, Sci. Faculty, Paris, 1958; Diploma, Endodontic Sch. of Paris, 1962, Med. Faculty of Paris, 1962; DDS, Dent. Surg., 1978. Lt./dentist French Army, Bourges, France, 1962-64; dental surgeon Ormoy, France, 1964-92; asst. dentist Faculty of Dentistry, Paris, 1978-86, asst. prof., 1986—. Author: (book) Le Martiniquais-Son Alimentation-Ses Dents, 1962; co-author: (book) Manuel D'Endodontie, 1986; inventor in field. Mem. Internat. Amnesty, France, 1977-86; sec. French Odontologic Assn. for Unfortunate Children; mem. LICRA, France, 1990—; town councillor Ormoy, 1975-82. Lt. French Army, 1962-64

Recipient Silver medal Soc. for Encouragement of Progress, Paris, 1982, 1st Rsch. prize Dental Info. Jour., Paris, 1986, Silver medal of the City of Paris, 1988. Mem. Acad. Dental Surgery, French-West Indies Dental Soc. (pres. 1985—), French Soc. for Endodontic Surgery (pres. 1993—), Nat. Expert Commn. (v.p. 1997—), European Soc. Endondontics, Internat. Coll. Experts, Inst. Cons. and Internat. Experts. Avocations: sculpture, photography, poetry. Home: La Varenne Hodie, 28200 Donnemains St Mames France Office: 5 Rue Garanciere, 75006 Paris France

SAVAGE, FRANCIS JOSEPH, Governor of the British Virgin Islands; b. Preston, Lancashire, U.K., Feb. 8, 1943; s. Francis Fitzgerald and Mona May (Parsons) S. (dec.); m. Veronica Mary McAleenan, 1966; 2 children. Student, Holy Cross Convent, Broadstairs, St. Stephen's Sch., Welling, Kent, Northwest Kent Coll., Dartford. With Fgn. Office, 1961, Cairo, 1967-70, Washington, 1971-73, Aden, 1973-74; with CO, London, 1974-78; consul Dusseldorf, 1978-82; Her Majesty's consul Beijing, 1982-86; first sec. consular and immigration Lagos, 1987-90; Her Majesty's consul Benin, 1987-90; first sec. Fgn. Office, 1990-93, counsellor, 1993; Gov. of Montserrat, 1993-97; Gov. of Brit. Virgin Islands, 1998—. Decorated officer Order Brit. Empire, lt. Royal Victorian Order, companion Order St. Michael and St. George. Mem. Royal Over-Seas League, Commonwealth Trust, Catenian Assn., Kent Country Club, Peking Cricket, Royal Brit. V.I. Yacht Club. Avocations: cricket, travel, meeting people. Office: Office of Gov, Road Town, Tortola British Virgin Islands

SAVAGE, MARK RANDALL, lawyer; b. Chicopee, Mass., Mar. 10, 1959; m. Lucia Clara Savage; children: David, Ryan. BA, U. Calif., Berkeley, 1982; JD, Stanford U., 1988. Bar: Calif. Jud. law clk. to Judge James Holden North Bennington, Vt., 1988-89; mng. atty. Pub. Advocates, Inc., San Francisco, 1989—; gen. counsel Cmty. Tech. Found. Calif., San Francisco, 1998—. Contbr. articles to profl. jours. Bd. dirs. Inst. for Civic Arts and Pub. Spaces, Inc., Albuquerque, 1996—. Recipient Drum Maj. award for contbns. to peace and justice So. Christian Leadership Conf., 1998, award Diversity, Innovation and Reform in Edn., 1995, El Fuego Nuevo award for work in edn. Assn. Mex. Am. Educators, 1999, Leadership Recognition award for work in health care for immigrant cmty. Calif. Primary Care Assn., 1999, El Fuego Nuevo award for work in edn. Assn. Mex. Am. Educators, 1999, Leadership Recognition award for work in health care for immigrant cmty. Calif. Primary Care Assn., 1999. E-mail: MarkSavage@igc.org. Office: Pub Advocates Inc 1535 Mission St San Francisco CA 94103-2500

SAVAGE, MARTHA KANE, physics and geophysics educator; b. Schenectady, N.Y., June 28, 1957; arrived in New Zealand, 1995; d. Evan O'Neil and Anne Elizabeth (Bassler) Kane; m. Michael Leonard Savage, June 5, 1982; children: Patrick Evan, Kelly. BA in Physics with honors, Swarthmore Coll., 1979; MS in Geophysics, U. Wis., 1984, PhD in Geophysics, 1987. Tech. asst. Bell Labs., Murray Hill, N.J., summer 1977; participant summer rsch. program for minorities and women Bell Labs., Murray Hill, summer 1978, tech. asst., spring 1981; participant undergrad. rsch. participation program Argonne (Ill.) Nat. Labs., spring 1978; rsch. asst. U. Alaska Geophys. Inst., Fairbanks, summer 1979; field observer South Pole Station, Antarctica, 1979-80; Hertz fellow U. Wis., Madison, 1981-86, tchg. asst., 1986-87; rsch. seismologist U. Nev., Reno, 1987-89, rsch. asst. prof., 1990-94, rsch. assoc. prof., 1994-98; sr. lectr. Victoria U. Wellington, New Zealand, 1997—; vis. investigator dept. terrestrial magnetism Carnegie Inst. Washington, 1988—; assoc. seismologist Calif. Divsn. Mines and Geology, 1989; lectr. Victoria U. Wellington, 1995-96; lectr. in field. Contbr. articles to profl. jours. Active local sch. dist. coms. including sci. adv. bd.; judge sci. fairs. Mem. New Zealand Geophys. Soc. (coun. mem. 1996-99, treas. 1997-98, conf. organizer 1999), Am. Geophys. Union, Seismological Soc. Am., Inc. Rsch. Instns. for Seismology (rep., mem. data mgmt. standing com. 1993-94). Avocation: folk dancing. E-mail: Martha.Savage@vuw.ac.nz and mlsavage@the.net.nz. Home: 22 Firth Terr, Karori Wellington New Zealand Office: Victoria Univ Wellington, Box 600 Inst Geophysics, Wellington New Zealand

SAVAGE, MICHAEL JOHN, agrometeorologist, researcher, educator; b. Germiston, Gauteng, South Africa, Jan. 7, 1953; s. Ronald Dennis and Blanche Mary (Williams) S.; m. Meryl Ann Venter, Dec. 24, 1977. BSc, U. Natal, Pietermaritzburg, South Africa, 1974, BSc with honors, 1975, PhD, 1983. Lectr. U. Natal, Pietermaritzburg, 1977-81, sr. lectr., 1982-83, assoc. prof., 1985-87, ad hominem prof., 1988-89, prof. (post level 7), 1994—, prof., head dept. agronomy, 1994—; vice chmn. rsch. com. U. Natal, Durban, Pietermaritzburg, 1996-99; vis. scientist Blackland Rsch. Lab., USDA, 1984, Mich. State U., East Lansing, 1984, U. Ga., 2000; vis. scientist/prof. Tex. A&M U., College Station, 1992, U. Georgia, 2000; dir. Campbell Sci. South Africa, Stellenbosch, 1997. Co-editor and author: South African National Scientific Programs Report (monograph), 1989; contbr. numerous articles to profl. jours., chpts. to books. Preacher Christian Fellowship, Pietermaritzburg, 1994—; boardermaster St. Charles Coll., Pietermaritzburg, 1976-78. Lt. South African Army, 1976-93. Named one of Four Outstanding Young South Africans, Jr. C. of C., Johannesburg, 1990; recipient Comprehensive Rsch. award Found. for Rsch. Devel., 1985—, Cert. of Merit U. Natal, 1972, 77; Prin. Fulbright scholar Coun. for Internat. Exch. of Scholars, 1992, Satbel scholar, 1971-73; U. Natal fellow, 1996. Mem. Am. Meteorol. Soc., Agrl. Sci. Assn. Natal (pres. 1976-80, 85-86), Am. Soc. Agronomy, Internat. Soil Sci. Soc., South African Soc. Crop Prodn. (gold medal 1998), Soil Sci. Soc. South Africa (article reviewer). Pentecostal Ch. Avocations: photography, reading computer magazines. Office: U Georgia Dept Physics 1109 Experiment St Griffin GA 30223-1731

SAVAGE, MICHAEL JOHN KIRKNESS, oil company and arts management executive; b. Birmingham, Eng., Oct. 28, 1934; came to U.S., 1962, naturalized, 1981; s. Leonard W. H. and Hilda C. (Fletcher) S.; m. Elisabeth Karl, June 21, 1965 (div.); m. Virginia Hooper, Aug. 31, 1978; 1 child, Matthew Nicholas. MA in Econs. and Law with honors, Cambridge U., 1958; postgrad., Manchester (Eng.) Bus. Sch., 1965; Diploma in Arabic, Middle E. Ctr. for Arab Studies, Shemlan, Lebanon, 1967. Various positions The British Petroleum Co. Ltd., England, Kuwait, Lebanon, Abu Dhabi, Alaska, Can., U.S., 1958-82; pres. BP Alaska Inc., San Francisco, 1977, Sohio Petroleum Co., San Francisco, 1982; internat. dir. The Brit. Petroleum Co. Ltd., London, 1982; pres. Merlin Petroleum Co., San Francisco, 1983-88, Savage Petroleum Co., Sausalito, Calif., 1992-95; bd. dirs., mng. dir. San Francisco Opera, 1994-99; bd. dirs. HS Resources, Inc., San Francisco; exec. dir. Napa Valley Opera House, 2000—. Trustee Alaska Pacific U., 1982-86; trustee San Francisco Conservatory of Music, 1983—, chmn., 1990-94. Mem. Brit.-Am. Chamber (San Francisco), Belvedere (Calif.) Tennis Club (bd. dirs. 1994-96). Avocations: Music, tennis, skiing, mountain walking. Office: Napa Valley Opera House 1040 Main St Napa CA 94559

SAVAGE, RICHARD NIGEL, travel firm executive; b. Southport, England, May 15, 1948; s. Gilbert Richard and Eileen (Rowlandson) S.; m. Carol Hall, Mar. 2, 1974; children: Thomas, Katherine, Anna. BA in Natural Sci., Oxford U., England, 1969. Chmn., mng. dir. Specialised Travel Ltd., London, N.Y.C., 1980—; singing appearances, European cities, 1976—. Bd. dirs. St. Moritz Festival, Switzerland; trustee Schola Cantorum Oxford, 1985—; dir. Britten Sinfonia, David Reichenberg Arts Trust. Mem. Equity, Oxford and Cambridge Club (London). Anglican. Avocations: tennis, golf. Home: 52 Avenue Rd, Highgate, London N6 5DR, England Office: Specialized Travel Ltd, 12-15 Hanger Green Park Royal, London W5 3EL, England

SAVAGE, SEAX SCOTT, physician, educator; b. Malden, Mass., Dec. 30, 1958; s. Joseph Edward and Arlene Barbara Savage; m. Gwendolyn Kieko Uezu, July 4, 1979 (div.); m. Terri Armstrong, Apr. 2, 1998; 1 child, Colin Eric. BA, Wheaton Coll., 1983; DO, Kirksville Coll. Osteopath. Medicine, 1987. Diplomate Am. Bd. Osteopathic Medical Examiners, Am. Bd. Emergency Medicine. Commd. maj. USAF, 1988; coord. EMS svcs. Wright Patterson AFB, Dayton, Ohio, coord. disaster svcs.; attending physician Hosp. USAF Hosp., RAF Lakenheath, Eng. 1988-91, asst. dir. emergency dept., 1990-91; dir. emergency tng. we. Europe divsn USAF, RAF Lakenheath, Eng., 1990-91; flight surgeon USAF Hosp., Holloman AFB, N. Mex., 1991-92; flight surgeon Space Shuttle contingency opers. USAF, Holloman AFB, N. Mex., 1991-92; resident physician Wright State U./USAF, Dayton, 1992-95; staff physician, instr. tactical medicine USAF Hosp., Wright Patterson AFB, 1995-97, EMS dir., 1996-97; clin. instr. emergency medicine Wright State U., 1996-2000, asst. clin. prof. emergency medicine, 2000—; clin. tng. in mind-body medicine The Mind-Body Med. Inst., Deaconess-Beth Israel Hosp., Boston, 1997; staff physician New Century Physicians, Dayton, Ohio, 1997—; med. dir. Ohio Acad. Holistic Health, Dayton, 1998-99; spl. asst. Dept. Health and Human Svcs., Rockville, Md., 1986; health policy fellow U.S. Senate, Washington, 1988; chief cons. Dayton SWAT Team, 1994-96; med. dir. Ohio Acad. Holistic Health, 1998-99, Ohio Wellness Ctr., 1998-99; keynote spkr. Ohio State EMS, Columbus, 1995, Ohio Holistic Health Expn., 1998; spl. lectr. mind-body medicine Ohio Wellness Ctr.; guest lectr. grand rounds Good Samaritan Hosp., 1998; med. dir. Shelby County Emergency Med. Svcs., 2000—. Contbr. chpt.: (textbook) Emergency Medicine Reference Book, 1999. Spl. lectr. Unitarian Universalist Ch., Oakwood, Ohio, 1993; guest lectr. Rotary Club, 1999. Decorated knight Noble Co. of Rose; recipient Dir.'s award USPHS U.S. Surgeon Gen., 1987. Fellow Am. Coll. Emergency Physicians, Augustan Soc. (Order of Augustan Eagle award 2000), Toastmasters (Competent Toastmaster award 2000). Avocation: fine arts, athlete. Address: 1211 W Main St # 202 Troy OH 45373-2564

SAVAGE, TERRY RICHARD, information systems executive; b. St. Louis, Oct. 21, 1930; s. Terry Barco and Ada Vanetta (Cochran) S.; m. Gretchen Susan Wood, Sept. 26, 1964; children: Terry Curtis, Christopher William, Richard Theodore. AB, Washington U., St. Louis, 1951, MA, 1952; PhD, U. Pa., 1954. Mgr. system software IBM Rsch., Yorktown Heights, N.Y., 1956-63; dir. data processing Documentation Inc., Bethesda, Md., 1963-64; mgr. info. systems Control Data Corp., Rockville, Md., 1964-67; dir. rsch. Share Rsch. Corp., Santa Barbara, Calif., 1967-68; computer-aided acquisition and logistic support program mgr. TRW, Redondo Beach, Calif., 1968-92; ret., ind. cons. pvt. practice, 1992—; expert witness for various coms. U.S. Congress, 1981, 84, 88, 89. Contbr. articles to profl. jours. Bd. dirs. ABC-Clio Press, Santa Barbara, 1970-75, Help the Homeless Help Themselves, Rancho Palos Verdes, Calif., 1988-94, ChorusLiners, Rancho Palos Verdes, 1983—, Savage Info. Svcs., Inc., Torrance, Calif., 1992—. Mem. Cosmos Club. Home and Office: 30000 Cachan Pl Rancho Palos Verdes CA 90275-5412

SAVAGE, THOMAS JOSEPH, executive development company executive, priest; b. Medford, Mass., Oct. 28, 1947; s. Frank James and Viola Augustine (Ballou) S. B.A. summa cum laude, Boston Coll., 1971; M. City Planning, U. Calif.-Berkeley, 1973; M. Pub. Policy, Harvard U., 1982, EdD, 1985. Assoc. Cheswick Ctr., Boston, 1973, dir., 1984—; assoc. Instl. Strategies Assocs., Cambridge, Mass., 1975-87; asst. acad. v.p. Fairfield (Conn.) Univ., 1986-88; pres. Rockhurst Coll., Kansas City, Mo., 1988-96, pres. Nat. Seminars Group., Shawnee Mission, Kans., 1991—; sr. cons. William M. Mercer, Inc., San Francisco, 1998—; adj. faculty Lesley Coll., Cambridge, 1982-85; cons. Lilly Endowment, Indpls., 1983-87; chmn. planning com. Jesuits New Eng. Province, Boston, 1985-88. Author: Seven Steps to a More Effective Board, 1994, The Goverance of Catholic Health Care Institutions, Catholic Health Assn., Spring, 1988; also articles. Del. Bridges for Peace, Soviet Union, 1985; Trustee Regis U., 1989-97, U. Detroit Mercy, 1995—, St. Louis U., 1991—, Loyola Marymount, 1994—; bd. dirs. Valentine-Radford Comm., 1992—, Preferred Health Profls., 1992-97, Kauffman Found., 1993—, Menning er Clinic, 1993—; co-chair FOCUS (Comprehensive Strategic Plan for Kansas City), 1992-97; founding chmn. Brush Creek Ptnrs., 1994-96. Mellon fellow, 1971-73. Mem. Am. Planning Assn., Nat. Policy Assn., AAAS, Assn. Jesuit Colls. and Univs. (bd. dirs. 1989-96), World Future Soc., Bostonian Soc., Phi Beta Kappa. Roman Catholic. Club: Harvard. Office: William M Mercer Inc Three Embarcadero Ctr San Francisco CA 94111*

SAVAKOOR, ASHOK UMESH, company executive; b. Mumbai, India, June 28, 1939; s. Umesh Subbarao and Sumatibai Umesh (Katresuvarna) S.; m. Sonali Ashok Baindoor, Oct. 23, 1967; children: Seema, Sameer. B Elec. Engring., B.E. Coll. Sibpur, Calcutta, India, 1964. Trainee Voltas Ltd., Mumbai, India, 1965, asst. engr., 1965; sales/constrn. engr. Voltas Ltd., Chennai Tamilnado, India, 1971-77; sales mgr. Voltas Ltd., Calcutta, 1978-80; regional sales mgr. Voltas Ltd., Bangalore, Mumbai, India, 1982-84, 84-87; tech. svc. mgr. Voltas Ltd., Mumbai, 1988; dir. svc. Carrier Aircon Ltd., Gurgaon, India, 1988-90, dir. tech. edn., 1991—. V.p. Khusboo Welfare Soc.,Gurgaon, 1995. Mem. ASHRAE. Avocations: reading, photogrphy, music, film watching. Home: 42 Prithui Apts Flat No 201, 1st Fl, 3rd Main Rd, Bangalore 560003, India

SAVANIU, CRISTIAN-DANIEL, chemist; b. Bucharest, Romania, Oct. 8, 1969; s. Victor and Domnica Savaniu; m. Adina-Magdalena Cornea, June 30, 1996. BS in Chemistry and Physics, U. Bucharest, 1994; PhD in Chemistry, Romanian Acad. Sci., 1999. Rsch. scientist Nat. Inst. for R&D in Microtechnologies, Bucharest, 1994—. Contbr. articles to profl. jours. Avocations: music, sports, computers, statistics. E-mail: petrarca@altavista.net. E-mail: cristians@imt.ro. Fax: 40-1-4908238. Home: Apt 302, Bd Iuliu Maniu 67 bl 6P, RO-70600 Bucharest Romania Office: Nat Inst R&D in Microtechs, Erou Iancu Nicolae 32B, RO-72225 Bucharest Romania

SAVARIRAYAN, KANTHARAJ, oil company executive; b. Madras, India, Jan. 2, 1935; arrived in U.A.E., 1985; s. John Henry and Selvarathnam S.; m. Sarojini Moses, June 27, 1960; children: Prakash, Deepika, Udaykumar. B Eng., Coll. of Engring., Madras, 1956; cert. in bus. mgmt., Indian Inst. Mgmt., Ahmedabad, 1972. arrived in United Arab Emirates, 1985;. Ops. trainee Caltex, Bombay, 1956-59, mgr. terminals, 1966-72, mgr. supply and distbn., 1972-74, mgt. planning, supplies and distbn., 1974-76; gen. mgr. ops. Hindustan Petroleum Co., Bombay, 1976-79, gen. mgr. oil refinery, 1979-82, gen. mgr. human resources, 1082-84, gen. mgr. engring. and projects, 1984-85; mgr. ops. mktg. constrn. facilities Emirates Petroleum Co., Dubai, United Arab Emirates, 1985—; mgr. spl. projects Emirates Nat. Oil Co., Dubai, 1994—. Contbr. articles to profl. publs. Fellow Indian Instn. Engrs., Indian Inst. Plant Engrs., Indian Inst. Personnel Mgmt. Mem. Christian Ch. Avocations: tennis, badminton, basketball, music, creative writing. Office: Emirates Nat Oil Company, PO Box 6442, Dubai United Arab Emirates

SAVCHENKO, KONSTANTIN VASILYEVICH, physicist, researcher; b. Kharkov, Ukraine, May 16, 1955; s. Vasiliy Korneevich S. and Nadezhda Vasilyevna Ponomaryeva. Physicist, Kharkov State U., 1977; postgrad., Kharkov Polytech. U., 1979-82. Asst. lectr. dept. physics Kharkov Polytech. U., 1977-79, sci. rschr. dept. phys. chemistry, 1982-95; sci. rschr. Inst. Low Temperature Physics, Ukraine, 1995-96, Inst. Automatic Sys., Kharkov, 1997. Contbr. articles to profl. jours. Grantee Internat. Sci. Found., 1994, 95. Mem. Ukrainian Phys. Soc. Avocations: personal computer, esoteric sciences. Home: 58-79 Blukhera St, 61142 Kharkov Ukraine

SAVEDRA, JEANNINE EVANGELINE, art educator, artist; b. Montebello, Calif., Dec. 21, 1965; d. Robert Anthony Savedra and April Elizabeth (Sanchez) Baroth. Student, Pasadena C.C., Calif., 1985-87, Otis Art Inst./Parsons Sch., 1987-88; BA in Studio Art, Calif. State U., L.A., 1991; postgrad., 1992-93; MA in Art/Humanities, Calif. State U., Dominguez Hills, 1999; postgrad. IMMEX Inst., UCLA, 1999; postgrad., Getty Edn. Inst. for Arts. Cert. art tchr., Calif. Children's counselor Salvation Army, Pasadena, Calif., 1987-88; graphic artist Calif. State U., L.A., 1989; pvt. investigator Larry J. Larsen Investigations and Trial Preparations, L.A., 1990-93; art instr. Pasadena Unified Sch. Dist., 1994-95; studio art instr. Visual Arts and Design Acad., Pasadena, 1995—, coord./lead tchr., 1999-00; supr. mural Pasadena Playhouse Improvement Assn., 1995-96; mentor Puente program U. Calif., Berkeley, 1995—; educator Nat. Conf. Human Rels., Temescal Canyon, Calif., 1996, Annenberg Inst. Sch. Reform, Brown U., 1999—; apptd. to ednl. adv. com. Jack Scott, mem. Assembly, Calif. State Legislature, 1997—; apptd. to Sierra Madre Arts Commn., 1999; artist exch. program Cultural Min., Havana, Cuba, 2000. Co-author interactive multi-media ednl. CD-ROM. Appt. to Sierra Madre Downtown Improvement Com., 2000; founding mem. Nat. Campaign for Tolerance, Montgomery, Ala. Calif. Partnership Acad. grantee, 1996—; recipient Excellence in Visual Arts award Calif. State U., 1990. Mem. Nat. Art Edn. Assn., L.A. County Mus. Art, Mus. Contemporary Art, Nat. Soc. Women Artists, Mus. Tolerance, Pasadena Armory Ctr. for Arts, Armand Hammer Art Mus. Office: Visual Arts and Design Acad 2925 E Sierra Madre Blvd Pasadena CA 91107-1846

SAVENIJE, HUBERT H. G., water resources educator; b. Naarden, The Netherlands, June 10, 1952; s. Ben and Kitty (Van Dongen) S.; m. Heleen M. J. Van Diggele, Aug. 8, 1950; children: Afra, Laurens. MSc, Delft U. of Tech., The Netherlands, 1977, PhD, 1992. Tchr. Emmaus Coll., Rotterdam, The Netherlands, 1977-78; expert Ministry of Fgn. Affairs, The Netherlands, 1978-85; cons. Euroconsult, The Netherlands, 1985-90; lectr. Internat. Inst. Infrastruc., Hydraulic and Environ. Engring., Delft, 1990-94, prof., 1994—, vice rector, 1997—. Mem. editl. bd. Physics and Chemistry of the Earth, 1996—, Jour. Hydrology, 1994—. Office: IHE, PO Box 3015, 2601 DA Delft The Netherlands

SAVENKO, OLEG MIKHAILOVICH, physicist, educator, researcher; b. Katta-Kurgan, Uzbek SSR, Russia, Oct. 29, 1951; s. Mikhail Konstantinovich and Valentina Mikhailovna (Starikova) S.; m. Ira Alexsandrovna Shpak, Feb. 14, 1976; 1 child, Roman Olegovich. Student, Novosibirsk U., 1969-71, postgrad., 1980-83; student, Omsk Pedagogical Inst., 1971-73; PhD, Omsk U., 1995. Rsch. assoc. Omsk Pedagogical Inst., 1975-79, Novosibirsk U., 1979-84; head of lab. Omsk U., 1984—, sr. lectr., 1986-99, reader, 2000—. Home: Koroleva 12a kv 32, 644045 Omsk Russia Office: Omsk State Univ, 644077 Omsk Russia

SAVEY, LIONEL, gynecologist and obstetrician; b. Boulogne, France, May 16, 1962; s. Dominiqué and Eliane (Aubey) S.; m. Isabelle Christine Cothier, June 20, 1992; children: Paul, Jeanne. MD, U. Paris, 1991. Intern Hosp. Assitance Publique, Paris, 1987-91; chief de clinique U. Paris Ouest, 1991-93; ob-gyn. Hosp. Foch, Suresnes, France, 1993—. Contbr. articles to profl. jours. Mem. French Soc. Gynecologic Oncology, Nat. Coll. Ob-gyns. of France, Nat. Soc. Gynecology and Obstetrics of France. Avocations: skiing, golf.

SAVIC, MICHAEL I., engineering educator, signal and speech researcher; b. Belgrade, Serbia, Yugoslavia, Aug. 4, 1929; came to U.S., 1967; s. Miodrag and Jelena (Milisic) S.; 1 child, Alice. Diploma in Engring., U. Belgrade, 1955, DEng, 1965. R&D engr. Kretztechnick, Zipf, Austria, 1956-57, Tungsram, Vienna, Austria, 1957-58; asst. prof. U. Belgrade, 1958-67; rsch. assoc. Yale U., New Haven, Conn., 1967-68; prof. Western New Eng. Coll., Springfield, Mass., 1968-81; prof. elec. engring. Rensselaer Poly. Inst., Troy, N.Y., 1981—; dir. Signal and Speech Rsch. Lab.; mem. adv. bd. Am. Coll. Cryosurgery, 1977-78; cons. Milton-Bradley Co., 1970-80; chmn. adv. panel NSF, 1977. Contbr. articles to profl. jours. Recipient scholarship U.S. Govt., 1962-64. Mem. IEEE (sr., Cert. of Appreciation 1972), N.Y. Acad. Scis. Achievements include patents in areas of controlled destruction of malignant tumors, detection of gas leaks in underground and above ground pipelines, voice character transformation, detection of cholesterol deposits in blood vessels and others. Current areas of research include automatic devices for speaker recognition, signal recognition, speaker separation, language identification, voice transformation and others. Home: 39 Sweetbrier Dr Ballston Lake NY 12019-1411 Office: Rensselaer Poly Inst ECSE Dept 110 8th St Troy NY 12180-3522

SAVII, GEORGE GUSTAV, engineering educator; b. Timisoara, Timis, Romania, Apr. 8, 1949; s. Gheorghe and Silvia (Cionca) S.; m. Cecilia Marinca, Aug. 18, 1973; children: George Cristian, Simona. MSc in Engring., Politechnica U., Timisoara, 1972, PhD, 1982. Asst. prof. Politehnica U., Timisoara, 1972-78, lectr., 1978-90, sr. lectr., 1990-92, prof. dept. engring., 1992—, doctoral advisor, dir., 1994—; cons. Computer Approach SRL, Timisoara, 1993—. Author: Principles of Computer Aided Design, 1997, 3D Graphics on PC's, 1997, Artificial Intelligence Applications Development Tools, 1996, Data Processing Equipment, 1986, Air Pollution Modeling and Simulation, 1999, Modeling and Simulation, 2000, Computer Peripheral Equipment, 2000; editor-in-chief Annals U. Banat, 1999—. Named Disting. Lectr., romanian Govt., 1986. Mem. romanian Soc. Engrs., Romanian Robotics assn., Romanian Soc. for Automation and Info. Sci. Home: Bul Mihai Viteazul 18, RO-1900 Timisoara Timis, Romania Office: Politehnica Univ, Bul Mihai Viteazul 1, RO-1900 Timisoara Timis, Romania

SAVIN, RONALD RICHARD, chemical company executive, inventor; b. Cleve., Oct. 16, 1926; s. Samuel and Ada (Silver) S.; m. Gloria Ann Hopkins, Apr. 21, 1962; children: Danielle Elizabeth, Andrea Lianne. BA in Chemistry and Lit., U. Cin., 1944-46; BA in Chemistry and Literature, U. Mich., 1948; postgrad., Columbia U., 1948-49, Sorbonne, Paris, 1949-50; grad., Air War Coll., 1975, Indsl. Coll. Armed Forces, 1976. Pres., owner Premium Finishes, Inc., Cin., 1957-91; cons. aerospace and anti-corrosive coatings; inventor and owner Hyperseal Inc. Contbr. articles to profl. jours.; 15 patents in field. With USAF, 1948-55, World War II and Korea, col. Res. 1979, ret. 1986. Mem. Steel Structures Painting Coun., Nat. Assn. Corrosion Engrs., Fedn. Paint Techs., Fedn. Coatings Tech., Air Force Assn., Res. Officers Assn., Army Navy Club. Avocations: scientific development, photography, tennis.

SAVINO, GIOVANNI MARIA, telecommunication executive, educator; b. Brescia, Italy, May 17, 1941; s. Carlo and Jole (Fornari) S.; m. Carolina Nava, Oct. 24, 1970; children: Marta, Carlo, Laura. Grad., Poly. Milan, 1966; MBA, Bocconi U., Milan, 1976. Electronic telecom. sys. project mgr. Telettra, Vimercate, Italy, 1970-78, logistic mgr., 1979-80, indsl. engring. mgr., 1981-86, indsl. re-engring. mgr., 1987-90; indsl. engring. and process devel. mgr. Alcatel Telecom., Vimercate, Italy, 1991-98; cons., tchr., 1998—; instr. indsl. planning and mfg. sys. U. Bergamo, Italy, 1996-98; instr. telecom. sys. High Tech. Sch., Milan, 1970, 80; spkr. in field. Mem. APICS, Soc. Mech. Engrs. Avocations: travel, mountains. Office: Alcatel Telecom, Trento 30, 20059 Vimercate Milan Italy

SAVKO, KONSTANTIN ARKADYEVICH, geology educator, researcher; b. Voronezh, Russia, Aug. 10, 1963; s. Arkadii Dmitrievich and Tamara Konstantinovna (Sapozko) S.; m. Larisa Borisovna Prozvetova, Sept. 20, 1985; 1 child, Katherine. Engr.-geologist, State U. Voronezh, 1985; PhD, Inst. Ore Deposits, Moscow, 1992; diploma, U. Coll. Galway, Ireland, 1996; economist-mgr., State U. Voronezh, 1997. Geologist State U. Geol. Survey, Pavlovsk, Russia, 1985-88; sr. geologist State U. Geol. Survey, Voronezh, 1988-91, head geologist, 1991-92; dep. chief State Geol. Venture, Voronezh, 1992-95; asst. prof. geology State U., Voronezh, 1995—, dep. chmn., 1997-98, chmn., 1998—, prof. geology, 1999—; cons. Voronezh Region Adminstrn., 1993—; vice chief Petrographical Coun. South-Ctrl. Russia, 1995-97. Contbr. articles to profl. jours. (fin. awards 1996, 97, 99, 2000); patentee in field; editor State Geol. Maps, Bryansk-Voronezh series, 1994-97. Laureate of Competition of Young Scientists, Voronezh Region, 1995, President awrd, 2000. Mem. N.Y. Acad. Scis. Avocation: tennis (ex-champion Voronezh region, doubles champion Russia 1975). Home: Plekhanovskaya 18-41, 394018 Voronezh Russia Office: Voronezh State U, Universitetskaya pl 1, 394693 Voronezh Russia

SAVOLAINEN, REIJO ILMARI, educator; b. Rautavaara, Finland, Apr. 12, 1952; s. Pentti Kalervo and Elma (Heikkinen) S.; m. Soili Marja Jokisalo, Oct. 27, 1979; children: Olli Markus, Antti Juhani. MSc, U. Tampere, Finland, 1978, DSc, 1989. Libr. Helsinki City Pub. Libr., 1979-81, Libr. of the Acad. of Finland, 1982-88; asst. prof. U. Tampere, 1989-95, assoc. prof., 1996-98, prof., 1998—. Author of books and articles in the field of info. scis. Mem. Finnish Assn. for Libr. and Info. Sci., Finnish Assn. for Info. Studies. Office: U Tampere Dept Info Studies, PO Box 607, FIN33101 Tampere Finland

SAVOLAINEN, VESA VALTER, information systems educator, scientist; b. Ruokolahti, Carelia, Finland, Aug. 28, 1944; s. Pietari and Maria Lydia (Jäppinen) S.; m. Anneli Irene Piispa, Aug. 29, 1970; children: Simo Markus, Petri Taneli. MSc in Computer Sci., U. Tampere (Finland), 1971, Licenciate Ph., 1973, PhD, 1977. Asst. U. Tampere, 1971-72, rsch. asst., 1973-75, sr. lectr., 1976-78, acting assoc. prof., 1979; assoc. prof. Vaasa (Finland) Sch. Econs., 1980; assoc. prof. U. Jyväskylä, Finland, 1981-98, acting prof. applied math., 1982, acting prof. computer sci., info. systems, 1981-99; prof. computer sci. U. Jyväskylä, 1998-99, prof. info. sys. sci., 1999—; head of dept. U. Jyväskylä, Finland, 1980, 93-94, 96, 99; participant Internat. European Strategic Program for Rsch. and Devel. in Info. Tech., projects Office Support Systems Analysis and Design, 1986-89, Harmonized European Concepts and Tools Orgnl. Info. Systems, 1989-90. Author 5 books; contbr. over 100 articles to profl. jours., books and confs.; referee several jours. Mem. IEEE (sr.), Assn. Computing Machinery, Internat. Fedn. for Info. Processing (office systems, decision support systems). Achievements include research on graph theory, measurement theory, and information system science. Home: Luotipussi 21, FIN40630 Jyväskylä Finland Office: U Jyväskylä, Mattilanniemi PO Box 35, FIN40351 Jyväskylä Finland

SAVOLAINEN, VINCENT VESA, biologist, researcher; b. Paris, Sept. 27, 1966; arrived in Eng., 1999; s. Unto S. and Denise M.C. (Perez) S. Baccalauréat D in Math and Natural Sci., Lycée, France, 1986; BSc, Geneva (Switzerland) U., 1989, MSc, 1991, PhD, 1995. Cert. zoologist, botanist, evolutionary biologist, molecular phylogeneticist U. Geneva. Tchg. asst. U. Geneva, 1989-95; rschr. Royal Botanic Gardens, London, 1995-96, higher sci. officer, 1999—; biologist Geneva Bot. Garden, 1996-97, curator, 1997-99; first asst. U. Lausanne, Switzerland, 1996-99, prof. remplacant, 1998-99; lectr. in field. Contbr. chpts. to books and articles to profl. jours. Postdoctoral grantee Royal Soc. London, 1995, rsch. grantee Acad. Soc., Geneva, 1992, 95, 98, Swiss Nat. Sci. Found., Berne, 1998. Mem. Swiss Soc. Zoology, Swiss Soc. Botany, Soc. Systematic Biologist. Avocations: horse riding, skiing, snowboarding, French literature. Office: Royal Botanic Gardens, Kew Richmond Surrey TW9 3AB, United Kingdom

SAVON, FELIX, Olympic athlete. Winner heavyweight world jr. championship, 1985, winner of 5 consecutive World Championship titles, 1986, 89, 91, 93, 95; winner of 12 consecutive nat. championships Cuba; winner gold medal in the 201 pound heavyweight class Olympic Games, Barcelona, Spain, 1992, Atlanta, 1996; winner 201 pound heavyweight class Third Goodwill Games Championships, N.Y.C., 1998.

SAVONA-VENTURA, CHARLES, obstetrician, gynecologist; b. Cospicua, Malta, Feb. 18, 1955; s. Michael and Angelica (Ventura) Savona; m. Marylene Simler, Aug. 24, 1980; children: Kristian, Stephanie. MD, U. Malta, 1979; specialist accreditation, Cath. U. Leuven, Belgium, 1985; MRCOG, Royal Coll. Ob-gyn, U.K., 1986; PhD, Inst. Mother and Child, Warsaw, Poland, 1997; FRCOG, Royal Coll. Ob-Gyn., U.K., 2000. Trainee ob-gyn. Malta Dept. Health, 1979-84, specialist ob-gyn., 1985-98, cons. ob-gyn., 1998—; lectr. U. Malta, 1981-87, Inst. Health Care, U. Malta, 1997-99, sr. lectr., 1999—. Author: Outlines of Maltese Medical History, 1997; co-author: Prehistoric Medicine in Malta, 1999, co-editor: Proceedings: ESSAR Vth Meeting, 1988, Facets of Maltese Prehistory, 1999; contbr. numerous articles to profl. jours. Com. mem., v.p. Soc. for the Study and Conservation of Nature, Malta, 1976-81; Malta coord. Internat. Dolphin Watch, Malta, 1979-86; chmn. Natural Environment Study Sect., Malta, 1980-81; Pub. Rels. Officer, Union of Govt. Med. Doctors, Malta, 1991-92; mng. com. St. Luke's Hosp., Malta, 1998—; nat. steering com. Diabetes Prevention Care, Malta, 1998—. Recipient Craig Meml. Rsch. award U. Malta, 1988, Med. Rsch. Project award British Med. Assn./British United Pres. Assn. Ltd., Malta, 1991, Essay prize Med. Assn. of Malta, 1991. Mem. European Assn. of Gynecologists and Obstetricians, Malta Coll. of Ob-Gyn. (founder mem., archivist 1991-96), Royal Coll. Ob-Gyn U.K. (rep. com. mem. 1995-96, 2000—). Roman Catholic. Avocations: Maltese history research, natural history studies, computing, travel. Home: North Wynds, 40 Triq Antonio Zammit, Ix-Xwieki Gharghur Nxr 08, Malta Office: Dept Health, 15 Merchants St, Valletta Vlt 03, Malta

SAVOUCHKINE, SERGUEI NICK, pharmaceutical company manager; b. St. Petersburg, Russia, July 23, 1962; s. Nick Ivan and Alevtina Sergei (Limina) S. MD, St. Petersburg Med. Acad., 1984, PhD in Cardiology, 1991. Physician intensive care Cardiology Clinic St. Petersburg Med. Acad., 1984-90; head cardiology Region 5 Hosp. St. Petersburg, 1990-92; sales rep. Merck & Co., St. Petersburg, 1992-93; clin. rsch. mgr. Merck & Co., Moscow, 1993-94, mgr. mktg. dept., 1994-96; head over the counter divsn. F. Hoffman La Roche, Moscow, 1996—. Avocations: football, tennis. Office: F Hoffmann La Roche, Smolnaya str # 24, 125 445 Moscow Russia

SAVOURS, ANN MARGARET (ANN SHIRLEY), museum officer, historian, writer; b. Stoke-on-Trent, Eng., Nov. 9, 1927; d. Edgar Walter and Doris Margaret (Holt) S.; m. Laurence George Samuel Shirley, Nov. 18, 1961; children: John Alexander, Nicholas Savours. BA with honors, London U., 1949; Diplome de Civilisation Française, Sorbonne, Paris, 1950. Dept. libr. King's Coll., Aberdeen, Scotland, 1951-54; curator manuscripts, asst. libr. Scott Polar Rsch. Inst., Cambridge, Eng., 1954-66; asst. keeper Nat. Maritime Mus., London, 1970-87; hon. rsch. fellow Australian Nat. U., Canberra, 1960-61. Author: The Voyagers of the Discovery, 1992, 2d edit., 1994 (Best Book of Sea award 1992), The Search for the North West Passage, 1999; editor: Edward Wilson's (Discovery) Diary, 1901-1904, 1966; editor, author Scott's Last Voyage: Through the Antarctic Camera of Herbert Ponting, 1974; contbr. articles to profl. jours. Johnstone and Florence Stoney scholar Brit. Fedn. Univ. Women; Trans-Antarctic Assn. grantee, 1984-85, Royal Soc. grantee, 1993. Fellow Royal Geog. Soc. (coun. 1978-80); mem. Soc. Nautical Rsch. (coun. 1987, 91-95, 96-2000, hon. sec. 1987-90), Hakluyt Soc. (coun. 1980-85, 86-91, 94-98, 99—, essay contbr. 150th ann. vol. 1996), Geog. Club (London). Mem. Ch. Eng. Avocations: travel, gardening. Home and Office: Little Bridge Pl Mill Ln, Bridge Near Canterbury, Kent CT4 5LG, England

SAVOY, DOUGLAS EUGENE, bishop, religious studies educator, explorer, writer; b. Bellingham, Wash., May 11, 1927; s. Lewis Dell and Maymie (Janett) S.; m. Elvira Clarke, Dec. 5, 1957 (div.); 1 son, Jamil Sean (dec.); m. Sylvia Ontaneda, July 7, 1971; children: Douglas Eugene, Christopher Sean, Sylvia Jamila. Student, U. Portland, 1947-8; DST, D Canon and Sacred Law, Jamilian U. of the Ordained, 1980. Ordained to ministry Internat. Community of Christ Ch., 1962, bishop, 1971. Head bishop Internat. Community of Christ Ch., 1971—; lectr. in ministerial tng. studies, 1972—; pastor Univ. Chapel, Reno, 1979—; founder Jamilian Parochial Sch., 1976; chancellor, founder Sacred Coll. of Jamilian Theology; pres., founder Jamilian U. of the Ordained, 1980; pres. Advs. for Religious Rights and Freedoms; chmn. World Coun. for Human Spiritual Rights, 1984—; head Jamilian Order of Patriarchs, 1990—; engaged in newspaper pub. West Coast, 1949-56; began explorations in jungles east of Andes in Peru to prove his theory that high civilizations of Peru may have had their origin in jungles, 1967; pres., founder Andean Explorers Found & Ocean Sailing Club, Reno; expedition dir. Grand Ophir Sea Expedition; capt. Feathered Serpent III-Ophir, 1997-98. Author: Antisuyo, The Search for Lost Cities of the High Amazon, 1970, Vilcabamba, Last City of the Incas, 1970, The Cosolargy Papers, vol. 1, 1970, vol. 2-3, 1972, The Child Christ, 1973, Arabic edit., 1976, Japanese edit., 1981, The Decoded New Testament, 1974, Arabic edit., 1981, Millenium Edition, 1983, On The Trail of The Feathered Serpent, 1974, Code Book and Community Manual for Overseers, 1975, Prophecies of Jamil, First Prophecy to the Americas, vol. 1, 1976, Second Prophecy to the Americas, 1976, The Secret Sayings of Jamil, The Image and the Word, vol. 1, 1976, vol. 2, 1977, Project X—The Search For the Secrets of Immortality, 1977, Prophecy to the Races of Man, Vol. 2, 1977, Solar Cultures of The Americas, 1977, Dream Analysis, 1977, Vision Analysis, 1977, Christoanalysis, 1978, The Essaei Document: Secrets of an Eternal Race, 1978, Millennium edit., 1983, The Lost Gospel of Jesus: Hidden Teachings of Christ, 1978, Millennium edit., 1983, Secret Sayings of Jamil, vol. 3., 1978, vol. 4, 1979, Prophecy to The Christian Churches, vol. 3, 1978, The Sayings, vol. 4, 1979, Solar Cultures of Oceania, 1979, Prophecy of The End Times, vol. 4, 1980, Solar Cultures of Israel, vols. 1 and 2, 1980, Solar Cultures of China, 1980, Christotherapy, 1980, Christophysics, 1980, Christodynamics, 1980, Code Book of Prophecy, 1980, The Sayings, vol. 5, 1980, vol. 6, 1981, Solar Cultures of India, 1981, Prophecy on the Golden Age of Light and the Nation of Nations, Vol. 5, 1981, Solar Cultures of Israel, vol. 3, 1981, The Counsels, 1982, Prophecy of the Universal Theocracy, vol. 6, 1982, Prophecy of the New Covenant, vol. 7, 1982, The Book of God's Revelation, 1983, Miracle of the Second Advent, 1984, Clerical Studies in Theology, Book I, Book II, Book III, Book IV, Transformative Theology: The School of Revelation, Transformative Theology: The School of Prophecy, Liturgical Theology: Preparation for Advanced Degrees, 1993; over 400 audio tape rec. lectures, 1974—, numerous others.; dir. documentary film Adventure: Trail of the Feathered Serpent, 1970, Lost City of the Andes, 1987; wrote, dir. videos Royal Roads to Discovery, Mystery of the Essenes of Old Israel, Secrets From the High Andes of Peru, 1993, The Gran Vilaya Expeditions, 1996; contbr. articles on Peruvian cultures to mags., also articles on philosophy and religion; discoverer lost city of Incas at Vilcabamba Cuzco, numerous ancient cities in Amazonia including Gran Pajaten, Gran Vilaya, Monte Peruvia, Twelve Cities of the Condor. Trustee in Trust Head Bishop Internat. Community of Christ. Served with AS USNR, 1944-46. Decorated Order of the Grand Cross Senate of Peru, 1989; recipient Participant's medallion Seawanhaka Yacht Club, 1977; Gold medal Ministry Industry and Tourism Peru, Silver Hummingbird, 1987; Silver medal and scroll City of Ica, Peru; honored with Gene Savoy Day by City of Reno, 1996, numerous exploring awards. Mem. Geog. Soc. Lima, Andean Explorers Found., Ocean Sailing Club (Explorer of the Century 1989, Flag awards), World Coun. for Human Spiritual Rights, Advs. for Religious Rights and Freedoms, Authors Guild, Explorers Club (N.Y.C., Flag awards), L.A. Yacht Club. Home: 2025 La Fond Dr Reno NV 89509-3025 Office: 643 Ralston St Reno NV 89503-4436

SAVOY, SUZANNE MARIE, advanced practice nurse; b. N.Y.C., Oct. 18, 1946; d. William Joseph and Mary Patricia (Moclair) S. BS, Columbia U., 1970; M in Nursing, UCLA, 1978. RN, cert. neurosci. register nurse, cert. clin. nurse specialist, cert. critical care nurse. Staff nurse MICU, transplant Json Meml. Hosp., Miami, 1970-72; staff nurse MICU Boston U. Hosp., 1972-74, VA Hosp., Long Beach, Calif., 1974-75; staff nurse MIRU Cedars-Sinai Med. Ctr., L.A., 1975-77; critical care clin. nurse specialist Anaheim (Calif.) Meml. Hosp., 1978-81; practitioner, instr. Rush-Presbyn.-St. Luke's Med. Ctr. Coll. Nursing, Chgo., 1982-88; rsch. assoc. dept. neurosurgery Rush U., 1984-88; clin. rsch. assoc. Medtronic, Inc. Drug Adminstrn. Sys., Mpls., 1988-91; staff nurse crit. care Harper Hosp., Detroit, 1992-93; clin. nurse specialist, surg./trauma crit. care Detroit Receiving Hosp., 1993-95; clin. instr. Wayne State U. Coll. of Nursing, Detroit, 1991-96, adj. faculty staff, 1996-98; program coord. Crit. Care ACNP-CC MSN, Wayne State U., 1993-96; adult crit. care clin. nurse specialist Saginaw Gen. Hosp., 1996-98; interventional card. clin. nurse specialist Covenant Healthcare Sys., Saginaw, 1998—; neurosci. clinician acute stroke unit Harper Hosp., Detroit, 1989; edn. cons. Crit. Care Svcs., Inc., Orange, Calif., 1979-81. Co-author articles for profl. jours. Mem. Am. Assn. Neurosci. Nurses (treas. Ill. chpt. 1983-85, pres. 1986-87, SE Mich. chpt. 1992-98, bd. dirs., treas., program chair), Am. Assn. Crit. Care Nurses (bd. dirs. Long Beach chpt. 1981-82, treas. NEMC chpt. 1999—), Am. Assn. Spinal Cord Injury Nursing (mem. rsch. com. 1993-95), Lambda and Gamma Phi (bd. dirs. 1994-96), Sigma Theta Tau. Roman Catholic. E-mail: ssavoy@chs-mi.com.

SAVRIN, VICTOR IVANOVICH, physicist, educator; b. Chapaevsk, USSR, Dec. 4, 1944; s. Ivan Yegorovich and Lidia Timofeevna (Bobrova) S.; m. Lyudmila Arkadievna Chudakova, July 30, 1966 (div. July 1983); 1 child, Irina; m. Elena Alekseevna Shuvakina, Oct. 15, 1983; 1 child, Daria. MSc, Moscow State U., 1968; CandSci, Inst. for High Energy Physics, Protvino, 1970; Dsc, Inst. for High Energy Physics, Moscow, 1979; Prof., Moscow State U., 1998. Rschr. Inst. for High Energy Physics, Protvino, 1971-83; head divsn. Inst. Nuclear Physics, Moscow State U., 1983—, dep. dir., 1984—; head Leading Sci. Sch., Russia, 2000—. Author: Dynamical Equations, 1996; author articles. Recipient State Sci. stipendia Russian Acad. Sci., Moscow, 1994—. Avocations: family, skiing, swimming. Office: Inst Nuclear Physics, Moscow State U, 119899 Moscow Russian Federation

SAVRO, VITALIY A., physiologist; b. Mariupol, Donetsk, Ukraine, May 2, 1942; s. Alexander K. and Tamara M. (Fashkina) S.; m. Svetlana H. Bliznuk, Sept. 28, 1962; 1 child, Marina V. Sonnova. Grad., Lugansk Med. U., Ukraine, 1966; Candidate of Med. Scis. (hon.), Donetsk U., 1971; DMS, Kiev (Ukraine) U., 1990. Postgrad. fellow Lugansk Med. U., 1967-70, from asst. to reader, 1970-90, prof., 1991—; mgr. cathedra normal physiology Lugansk Med. U., 1994—. Author: (book) Evolution of Moving Centers of Spinal Cord, 1996. Mem. Acad. of Ukraine Acad. of Sci. of Nat. Progress. Home: 15 Liniya St 19/84, 348016 Lugansk Ukraine Office: Lugansk Med U, Bl 50 Let Oborova Lugansk 1, 348045 Lugansk Ukraine

SAVU, GEORGE VASILE, aerodynamicist; b. Paulis, Arad, Romania, Feb. 26, 1949; s. Vasile George and Elena Ioan (Stoi) S.; m. Daniela Popescu, Nov. 8, 1975; children: Miron, Suzana. BS, Theoretical Lyceum, Lipova, Romania, 1967; MS, Aerospace Faculty, Bucharest, Romania, 1973; PhD, Polytechnic Inst., Bucharest, 1990. Aerodynamicist Aviation Inst., Bucharest, 1973-96; aerodynamicist, space programs dir. COMOTI, Bucharest, 1996—; sci. cons. COMOTI, 1996; mem. Nat. Adv. Com. for Sci., Tech. and Innovation, Romania. Inventor in field; editor-in-chief Turbo Jour.; contbr. articles to profl. jours. Lt. Romanian Air Forces, 1975. Fellow AIAA (assoc.); mem. Romanian Physics Soc. Avocations: history of sci., biographies. Office: COMOTI, Bd Iuliu Maniu 220, 77538 Bucharest Romania

SAVVIDES, GEORGE L., barrister, legal consultant; b. Nicosia, Cyprus, Sept. 22, 1959; s. Loukis and Eroula (Michaelides) S.; m. Dora Kirzis; children: Loukis, Nicholas, Laura. LLB with honors, U. Exeter, Eng., 1982; barrister, Middle Temple, London, 1983. Advocate, mem. Cyprus Bar; Assoc. Chartered Inst. Arbitrators, London, 1992. Founder George L. Savvides Law Firm, Limassol, Cyprus, 1984-86; mng. ptnr. George L. Savvides & Co. Law Firm, Limassol, Nicosia, Cyprus, 1987—. Contbr. articles to profl. jours.; presenter in field. Mem. ABA (assoc.), Internat. Bar Assn. (chmn. com. 10c 1998—). Greek Orthodox. Home: 13 Pavlou Angelinide St, Ekali Limassol, Cyprus Office: George L Savvides & Co, 4 Rigas Fereos St POB 4098, 3720 Limassol Cyprus

SAW, HO-SUK, oncologist; b. Seoul, Korea, Apr. 29, 1949; s. Jeong-Kyu and Bok-Yul (Lee) S.; m. Sung-Hye Kim, July 10, 1982; children: Jahng-Won, Jae-Won. MD, Seoul Nat. U., 1974, MS, 1978, PhD, 1984. Cert. colposcopist, cervicography evaluator. Intern Seoul Nat. U. Hosp., 1974-75, resident in ob-gyn, 1975-79; mem. faculty Korea U. Guro Hosp., Seoul, 1983-85, asst. prof., 1985-88, assoc. prof., 1988-94, prof., chief dep. ob-gyn, 1994—; vis. prof. U. Minn., 1987-88. Co-author: Textbook of Gynecologic Oncology, 1996, Textbook of Gynecology, 1992, Textbook of Obstetrics, 1992; editor Jour. Genetic Medicine, 1997—. Maj. Seoul Dist. Hosp., 1980-83. Recipient New Century award Baron's 500, 1999; named One of 500 Leaders in New Century, Baron Co., 1999; rsch. fellow Johns Hopkins U., 1988-89. Fellow Am. Soc. Clin. Oncology, Am. Soc. Colposcopy and Cervical Pathology (liaison com. 1998—), European Soc. Gynceol. Oncology (assoc.); mem. Korean Soc. Gynecol. Oncology (sec. gen. 1993-95, coun. 1993—), Korean Soc. Med. Genetics (sec. gen. 1994-96, v.p. 1995-99, pres. 1999—), Korean Soc. Cancer (sci. coun.). Avocations: golf, piano, swimming, reading. Fax: 822-838-1560. E-mail: sawhs@kkucnx.korea.ac.kr. Home: 1-1501 Jinheung Apt, Samsung Dong, Kangnam-Gu, Seoul 135-090, Republic of Korea Office: Korea Univ Guro Hosp, 80 Guro Dong Guro Gu, Seoul 152-050, Republic of Korea

SAW, YOOSOK, engineer, telecommunications consultant; b. Seoul, Apr. 22, 1965; s. Jungbae Saw and Whaja Koo; m. Eujun Yoo; children: Kunwon, Jaewon. BSc, Sogang U., Seoul, Korea, 1987, MSc, 1989; PhD, U. Edinburgh, U.K., 1997. Rsch. engr. LG Info. and Comms., Seoul, 1989-92, sr. rsch. engr., 1993-97, head sr. rsch. engr., 1998—; rschr. Korea Inst. of Sci. and Tech., Seoul, 1992-93; rsch. fellow U. Bristol, Eng., 1997-98; vis. lectr. NgeeAnn Polytech., Singapore, 1996, cons., 1998. Author: Rate Quality Optimized Video Coding, 1999, Signal Analysis and Applications, 1998. Recipient Chevening award British Fgn. Office, 1994; scholarship British Coun. and Ministry of Sci. and Tech., 1993. Mem. IEE (assoc.), IEEE. Avocations: classical music, mountain climbing, playing football. Home: Sanbon-Dong, Kunpo 435-040, Republic of Korea Office: LG Info Comms Ltd, Hogye-Dong, Anyang 430-080, Republic of Korea

SAWADA, HIDEO, polymer chemistry consultant, chemist; b. Kyoto, Japan, Jan. 29, 1934; s. Masao and Hiroko (Ohno) S.; m. Yoshiko Kasai, May 5, 1961; children: Yukari, Jun. BS, Osaka U., Japan, 1956, DS, 1965. Rsch. mgr. Daicel Ltd. Filler Lab., Osaka, Japan, 1980-85, sr. exec. scientist rsch. ctr., 1986-89, gen. mgr. planning & devel. dept., 1989-92; chmn. tech. com. Biodegradable Plastics Soc., advisor, 1992—; convenor Internat. Orgn. for Standardization, mem. tech. com. 61, sub com. 5, working group 22, 1992—. Author: Thermodynamics of Polymerization, 1976, Encyclopedia of Polymer Science and Engineering, 1985. Mem. Am. Soc. Testing and Materials, Am. Chem. Soc., Soc. Polymer Sci. Japan, Soc. Fiber Sci. and Tech., N.Y. Acad. Scis. Zen. Home: 2534 3-chome Sayama, Osaka-Sayama 589-0005, Japan Office: Biodegradable Plastics Soc, Grande Bldg 26-9, Chuo-ku Tokyo 105-0032, Japan

SAWADA, TERUFUMI, medical researcher; b. Tokyo, Jan. 18, 1939; s. Hideichi and Kazu (Ikegawa) S.; m. Masae Ogasawara, Dec. 21, 1969; children: Norifumi, Wakako, Akifumi. MD, U. Tokyo, 1965, PhD, 1975. Intern U. Tokyo, 1965-66, faculty asst. dept. gerontology, 1966-75, 78-84, faculty lectr. dept. gerontology, 1984-91; chief dept. internal medicine Social Health Ins. Med. Ctr., Tokyo, 1984-95; vice dir. Social Health Ins. Tonan Gen. Hosp., Tokyo, 1995-99; dir. Health Promotion Ctr. Tonan Gen. Hosp., Tokyo, 1999—; nat. exam. com. for nursing licenses Min. Health, 1989-95, 97-99; lectr. Met. Hiroo Nursing Sch., 1995—, Akiba Gakuen Sch. Bus., 2000—. Co-author: Gerontologia, 1970. Joslin rsch. fellow in biochemistry Harvard U., 1975-78. Mem. Social Health Ins. Fund (receipt-reviewing com. 1990—), Internat. Soc. Nephrology, Japanese Soc. Nephrology, Japanese Soc. Gerontology, Japanese Soc. Internal Medicine, Japan Diabetes Soc., Japanese Soc. for Dialysis Therapy. Shinto. Avocations: gardening, painting, computer-programming, travel. Home: 5-16-8 Daita, Setagaya-ku Tokyo 155-0033, Japan Office: Tonan Gen Hosp Social Health Ins, 5-8-12 Higashi-Oi, Shinagawa-ku Tokyo 140-0011, Japan

SAWADA, TOSHIO, lawyer, educator; b. Tokyo, June 29, 1933; s. Stesuzo and Miyo (Ohyama) S.; m. Tomoko Koyama, Mar. 25, 1971. LLB, Chuo U., Tokyo, 1958; LLM, Columbia U., 1965; SJD, U. Mich., 1967. Bar: 1975. Analyst Econometric Inst., N.Y.C., 1959-61; counsel Hill, Betts, Yamaoka, Freehill & Longcope, N.Y.C., 1961-62; assoc. Parker Sch., Columbia U., N.Y.C., 1962-63; assoc. prof. law Sophia U., Tokyo, 1966-73, prof., 1973-99, prof. emeritus, 1999—; rep. to UN Commn. on Internat. Trade Law, 1981-87; v.p. Internat. Ct. of Arbitration, Paris, 1989—; judge adminstrv. tribunal, Asian Devel. Bank, 1995-98. Author: Subsequent Conduct and Supervening Events, 1968, International Transactions, 1982. Mem. Japanese Law Asia Assn. (bd. dirs.), 1st Tokyo Bar Assn., Japanese Coun. on Internat. Trans. (chmn. 2000—), Tokyo Club. Roman Catholic. Avocations: travel, music. Home and Office: 40-3 Jingumae 5-chome, Shibuya Tokyo 150-0001, Japan

SAWAHEL, WAGDY A., biologist, transgeneticist, educator, writer; b. El-Mahalla, Egypt, Sept. 25, 1964. BSc, Tanta U., Egypt, 1987; PhD, Leeds (Eng.) U., 1994. Chartered biologist; cert. biologist European Inst. Biology. Postdoctoral fellow UN Internat. Ctr. Genetic Engring. and Biotech., India, 1996—. Author: Transformation Technology, 1997, Plant Genetic Engineering: From A to Z, 1997, Biotechnology Development: The Asian Experience, 1997, others; contbr. articles to profl. jours.; mem. editl. bd. Internat. Jour. Cellular and Molecular Biology Letters; gen. editor International Series of Genetic Engineering and Biotechnology. Recipient Nat. Sci. award in biology Acad. Sci. Rsch. and Tech., Cairo, 3d World Acad. of Sci. prize, 1998, Nat. Rsch. Ctr. prize, 1998, Dr. Ahmed Zahran prize in sci. awareness, 1999; Brit. Coun. scholar, 1991-94. Mem. Inst. Biology U.K., European Cmty. Biologists Assn., N.Y. Acad. Scis. (internat. mem.), Genetics and Bioethics Network/Eubios Bioethics Inst. (internat. mem.), Working Group on Tech. and Agrarian Devel./Wageningen Agrl. U. (internat. mem.). Address: Nat Rsch Ctr/Genetic Engrg, Tahrir St, Dokki Cairo Egypt

SAWAYA, BASSEL E., molecular biologist, educator, researcher; b. Khiam, Lebanon, Jan. 1, 1963; arrived in France, 1990; s. Eid K. Sawaya and Nadia N. Jalbout. BA in Scis., Lebanese U., 1988; PhD in Molecular Biology, U. Paris, 1994, degree in engring., 1995. Postdoctoral fellow Thomas Jefferson U., Phila., 1995-96; postdoctoral fellow Allegheny U., Phila., 1996-97, mem. jr. faculty, 1997-99; asst. prof. Ctr. for Neurovirology and Cancer Biology Temple U., Phila., 1999—. Contbr. articles to jours. in field. Referee Italian Telethon, Phila., 1997. Mem. AAAS, Am. Soc. Microbiology, N.Y. Acad. Scis., French Soc. Biochemistry and Molecular Biology. Avocations: reading, jogging, mountain climbing, driving, archaeology. Home: 2031 South St Philadelphia PA 19146-1344 Office: Temple Univ 1500 N 12th St Philadelphia PA 19122-3308

SAWHNEY, HARJEET KAUR, obstetrician-gynecologist; b. Jullunder, Punjab, India, Dec. 15, 1953; d. Prithipal Singh and Gurbachan Kaur (Sachdev) Kalra; m. Indermohan Singh Sawhney, Mar. 8, 1981; children: Vinit, Harpreet. B Medicine B Surgery, G.G.S. Med. Coll., Punjab, India, 1978; MD, Postgrad. Inst. Med. Edn./Rsch, Chandigarh, India, 1982. Sr. resident Postgrad. Inst. Med. Edn. and Rsch., 1983-86, rsch. fellow birth control vaccine, 1986-87, sr. rsch. fellow birth control vaccine, 1987-89, asst. prof., 1989-94, assoc. prof., 1994—; cons., tchr., rschr. in field. Contbr. articles to profl. jours. Mem. Fedn. Ob.-Gyn. Socs. India, Indian Soc. Perinatology and Reproductive Biology. Avocations: music, painting. Office: Postgrad Inst Med Edn/Rsch, Dept Ob-Gyn, Chandigarh 160012, India

SAWHNEY, SHALINI HARJIT, art dealer, investment consultant; b. Nathura, India, Aug. 28, 1953; p. Gangadhar and Padna Nehta; m. Harjit Singh Sawhney; 1 child, Renuka Singh. B in Commerce, H.R. Coll., Mumbai, India, 1974, M in Commerce, 1976. Cert. assoc. Indian Inst. Bankers. Mgr. State Bank India, Bombay, 1991; owner, dir. The Guild Art Gallery, Mumbai. Mem. Bombay Presidency Club, United Svcs. Club. Avocations: collecting contemporary Indian art, horticulture, traveling, reading. Office: 10H Madhuban, 23 Cockin St Fort, Mumba 400001, India

SAWICKI, JERZY MIROSLAW, hydromechanics educator, researcher; b. Gdańsk, Poland, May 4, 1950; s. Teodor Sawicki and Waleria (Starczewska) Sawicka; m. Danuta Maria Dymarska, Dec. 25, 1974; 1 child, Sambor. MSc, Gdansk Tech. U., 1973, PhD, 1979, DSc, 1993. Asst. Gdansk Tech. U., 1973-76, sr. asst., 1976-80, adj. prof., 1980-95, prof., 1996—, dep. dean Faculty Environ. Engring. Dept., 1990-96; patentee in field. Author: Free-Surface Flows, 1998; co-author: Fundamentals of Hydromechanics and Hydraulics, 1987, 3d edit., 2000. Brit. Coun. grantee, 1986, 87; recipient award Polish Ministry Edn., 1988, 99. Mem. Internat. Assn. for Hydraulic Rsch., Internat. Assn. for Hydrol. Scis. Avocations: mountains, history, angling, collecting medals and orders, travel. Office: Tech U Faculty Environ Eng, G Narutowicza 11/12, 80-952 Gdańsk Poland

SAWICKI, PETER THADDAEUS, physician, consultant; b. Warsaw, Poland, Jan. 24, 1957; arrived in Germany, 1970; s. Ryszard and Irma (Keselring) S.; m. Ulrike Didjurgeit, July 23, 1994; children: Mark, Anna, Franziska, Sonja. MD, U. Duesseldorf, Germany, 1985, habilitation, 1994. Med. diplomate. Sr. lectr. med. dept. U. Duesseldorf, 1985-91, cons., 1991—, full prof. internal medicine, 1999—; dir. dept. internal medicine St. Franziskus Hosp., Cologne, 2000—; sec. European Hypertension in Diabetes study group European Assn. for the Study of Diabetes, 1995—, mem. coun. Nephropathy Group, 1996—; mem. exec. bd. German Nephropathy Group, 1995—. Author: Treatment of Hypertension, 1988, Diabetic Nephropathy, 1994; mem. editl. bd. Arzneimittel-Telegram, 1996—, Jour. Internat. Medicine, 1999—, Jour. Cardiovasc. Network, 1999—. Mem. Internat. Diabetes Assn. (life), German and European Diabetes Assn., Am. Diabetes Assn. Avocations: waterpolo, fly fishing, sailing. Home: Buschfeldstr 78, D-51067 Cologne Germany Office: St Franziskus Hosp, Schoenesteinstr 63, D-50825 Cologne Germany

SAWICKI, ZBIGNIEW PETER, lawyer; b. Hohenfels, Germany, Apr. 13, 1949; came to U.S., 1951; s. Witold and Marianna (Tukiendorf) S.; m. Katheryn Marie Loman, Aug. 19, 1972; children: James, Jeffrey, Jessica, Jason. BSChemE, Purdue U., 1972; MBA, Coll. St. Thomas, St. Paul, 1977; JD, Hamline U., 1980. Bar: Minn. 1980, U.S. Dist. Ct. Minn. 1981, U.S. Ct. Appeals (8th cir.) 1981, U.S. Patent and Trademark Office 1981, U.S. Ct. Appeals (fed. cir.) 1982, Can. Patent Office 1994, Can. Trademark Office 1995. Process engr. 3-M Co., St. Paul, 1973-75; process engring. supr. Conwed Corp., St. Paul, 1975-77; shareholder, bd. dirs. Kinney & Lange, Mpls., 1980—. Bd. dirs. Orono (Minn.) Hockey Boosters, 1992—. With USAF, 1970-72. Mem. ABA, Am. Intellectual Property Assn., Internat. Trademark Assn., Minn. Intellectual Property Assn. (past treas.), Am. Legion. Home: 4510 N Shore Dr Mound MN 55364-9602 Office: Kinney & Lange 312 S 3d St Minneapolis MN 55415-1624

SAWIK, TADEUSZ JAN, engineering educator; b. Wrocław, Poland, June 3, 1947; s. Jan Edmund and Marta Róża (Gałek) S.; m. Danuta Maria Nykiel, Apr. 24, 1978; 1 child, Bartosz Tadeusz. MSc in Mech. Engring. with distinction, U. Mining and Metallurgy, Cracow, 1971, PhD in Control Engring., 1976, DSc Habilitation in Ops. Rsch., 1981. Tchg. asst. U. Mining and Metallurgy, Cracow, 1971-75, asst. prof., 1976-81, assoc. prof., 1982-92, prof., assoc. dean faculty mgmt., 1994-96, prof., chmn. dept. computer integrated mfg., 1993—; assoc. prof. Cracow Poly., 1984-86; vis. prof. U. Geneva, 1991, Chuo U., Tokyo, 1992, Chalmers U. Góteborg, Sweden, 1996, U. Kagoshima, Japan, 1999; invited expert U. Mannheim, Germany, 1993. Author: Time-Optimal Control of Discrete Manufacturing Processes, 1980 (award from Min. of Scis. and Tech. 1982), Analysis and Synthesis of Multivariable Control Systems, 1984 (award of UMM Rector, 1985), Discrete Optimization in Flexible Manufacturing Systems, 1992 (Award of Min. of Edn. 1993), Production Planning and Control in Flexible Assembly Systems, 1996 (award of Min. of Edn. 1997), Operations Research for Industrial Engineers, 1998 (award of UMM Rector 1999), Production Planning and Scheduling in Flexible Assembly Systems, 1999 (award of Min. of Edn. 2000); contbr. numerous articles to profl. jours. Mem. Regional Coun. for Environ. Mgmt., Cracow, 1994-96. Rsch. grantee Komitet Badan Naukowych/Poland, 1994, 97, European Coop. Fund/European Union, 1995, Fonds Nat. Suisse de la Recherche Scientifique/Switzerland, 1996, Motorola/USA, 1999. Fellow Polish Acad. Scis. (com. on ops. rsch. and automatics 1994-96, com. on knowledge engring. and ops. rsch. 1997—), Inst. for Ops. Rsch. and Mgmt. Scis. Roman Catholic. Avocations: playing guitar, singing, hiking, travel. Home: Osiedle Urocze 1/141, 31-952 Cracow Poland Office: Univ of Mining/Metallurgy Faculty of Mgmt, Al Mickiewicza 30, 30-059 Cracow Poland

SAWKINS, JOHN, university administrator; b. Halifax, Eng., Mar. 9, 1948; s. Arthur William and Edna May Sawkins; m. Petula Anna McNamara, Apr. 22, 1972; children: Julian Mark, Kathryn Margaret. BA in Langs. with honors, London U., 1971; MEd in Edn., U. Manchester, Eng., 1982. P.G.C.E. London Inst. Edn. Tchr. langs. Dorcan Comprehensive, Swindon, Wilts, Eng., 1972-73; tchr. German Orchard Secondary Sch., Slough, Berks, Eng., 1973-75; studienrat Regino-Gymnasium, Pruem, Germany, 1975-77; head of German Stand Grammar Sch. for Boys, Whitefield, Manchester, Eng., 1977-79; head of langs. Peel Sixth Form Coll., Bury, Lancs, Eng., 1979-87; curriculum leader modern langs. Bury Coll., 1987-94; sect. leader Thurso Coll., Caithness, Scotland, 1995—; course dir. English as Fgn. Lang., Nord Anglia Internat., Manchester and York, 1982—. Avocations: song-writing, video/film. Fax: 01847 893872. E-mail: john sawkins/tc@fc.uhi.ac.uk. Office: Thurso Coll, Ormlie Rd, Thurso Caithness KW14 7EE, Scotland

SAWKO, FELICJAN, civil engineering educator; b. Wilczuki, Poland, May 17, 1937; s. Czeslaw and Franciszka (Nawrot) S.; m. Genowefa Stefania Bak, Apr. 18, 1960; children: Andrew, Barbara, Piotr, Ryszard, Paul. BSc, Leeds (Eng.) U., 1958, MSc, 1960, DSc, 1973. Chartered engr. Civil enr. Rendel, Palmer & Tritton, Eng., 1959-62; lectr. Leeds U., 1962-67; prof. Liverpool (Eng.) U., 1967-86; prof., head dept. civil engring. Sultan Qaboos U., Oman, 1986-95; ret., 1995; cons. in civl engring., 1962-86. Editor: Developments in Prestressed Concrete, 1978, Computer Methods for Civil Engineers, 1984; contbr. articles to profl. jours. Fellow Instn. Civil Engrs. Roman Catholic. Avocations: bridge, photography, numismatics, travel. Home: 23 Floral Wood, Liverpool L17 7HU, England

SAWOROTNOW, PARFENY PAVLOVICH, mathematician, educator; b. Ust Medveditskaya, Russia, Feb. 20, 1924; came to U.S., 1949, naturalized, 1965; s. Pavel Ivanovich and Anna Davidovna (Soloview) S.; student U. Graz (Austria), 1946-49; MA (Peirce scholar), Harvard U., 1951, PhD (Shattuck fellow), 1955. Teaching fellow Harvard U., 1953-54; instr. math. Cath. U. Am., Washington, 1954-57, asst. prof., 1957-62, assoc. prof., 1962-67, prof., 1967-96, prof. math. emeritus, 1997—. NSF grantee, 1967, 70; with Georgetown U. and George Washington U., 1971-77. Mem. Am. Math. Soc., Math. Assn. Am., Calcutta Math. Soc., N.Y. Acad. Scis., Sigma Xi. Mem. Eastern Orthodox Ch. Contbr. articles to and referred papers for math. rsch. jours. Home: 6 Avon Pl Hyattsville MD 20782-3328 Office: Cath U Am Dept Math 4th And Michigan Ave NE Washington DC 20064-0001

SAWTELL, OLGA, marketing executive; b. Mossman, Australia, May 30, 1944; d. Ante Yelavich and Pearl (Neda) Mijo; m. Baden Sawtell, May 15, 1976 (div. 1995); children: Emily Jane, Anthony Douglas. BA.LLB., Syndey U., 1967. Mktg. dir. Grand Metro., London, 1967-83; mng. dir. ACESAT, Syndey, Australia, 1983-91, Direct Broadcast Network, Syndey, 1991-94; CEO CBD Info. Tech., Syndey, 1994-96; gen. mgr. Edn. & Tng. Australia, Syndey, 1996-98; exec. dir. Keenfern, Pty., Ltd., Syndey; CEO Thorlock Internat. Ltd., Perth, Australia, 1998—; Bd. dirs. Industry Rsch. Devel., 1996—, chmn. com. info. and tech. coun., 1997. Roman Catholic. Avocations: swimming, tennis, reading. Office: Edn & Tng Australia, 8 Hamilton St, 6107 Cannington Australia

SAWTELLE, CARL S., psychiatric social worker; b. Boston, July 14, 1927; s. Carl Salvador and Martha (Bellamacina) S.; BA, Suffolk U., Boston, 1951; MSW, Simmons Sch. Social Work, 1953; m. Thelma Florence Ramsay, Aug. 20, 1950; children: Tracy Lynn, Lisa June. Social worker Tewksburry (Mass.) State Hosp., 1952; psychiat. social worker, head psychiat. social worker, dir. clin. social work Taunton (Mass.) State Hosp., 1953-74; 1st dir. clin. social work, Plymouth, Mass., 1974-78; co-founder, v.p. 1st legally established War On Poverty program Triumph, Inc., Taunton; co-founder 1st Greater Taunton Coun. on Alcoholism, 1972. With USCG, 1944-46. 1st lic. social worker in Mass., 1980. Mem. Nat. Assn. Social Workers (co-founder Southeast Mass. chpt. 1957, pres. 1957, Spl. Mass. Chpt. award 1978), Acad. Cert. Social Workers (chmn. 1962-72), Am. Legion, Mass. Mental Health Social Workers Assn. (co-founder, pres. 1972-74, other offices). Created innovated programs, resources, opportunities, svcs. to state mental hosp. patients and their families; mentor to young social workers; contbr. advancement of knowledge, practice quality and standards of psychiat. social work; father of licensing and registration of Social Workers in Mass. Home: 9 Tracywood Rd Canton MA 02021-3501

SAWYER, ADRIAN JOHN, taxation educator, consultant; b. Nelson, New Zealand, Feb. 16, 1967; s. Edgar Alfred and Florence Ivy May (Maindonald) S. B of Comm., LLB, U. Canterbury, Christchurch, New Zealand, 1990, M of Comm. with honors, 1993; postgrad.S.J.D., U. Va., 1998—. Chartered acct.; barrister and solicitor High Ct. New Zealand. Investigating acct. IRD, Blenheim, New Zealand, 1989-91; asst. lectr. U. Canterbury, 1991-92, lectr., 1993-97, sr. lectr., 1998—; co. acct. Marlborough Media Ltd., Blenheim, 1994-99, dir., 1994-97; cons. Inland Revenue Dept., Wellington, New Zealand, 1997-98, New Zealand Treasury, Wellington, 1993-94. Contbr. articles to profl. jours. Student pres., treas. Rochester and Rutherford Halls of Residence, Christchurch, 1986, 88; hon. auditor Canterbury Law Review, Christchurch, 1991-95, Assn. UNI Staff, Chrstchurch, 1992-96, Tenants' Protection Assn., Christchurch, 1996-97; grad. marshall U. Canterbury, 1994-98, 2000—; mem. budget com. U. Cangerbuty, 1999—; br. tax com. ICANZ, Christchurch, 1994—; deacon, treas. Christian Brethren Ch., Christchurch, 1995—; chair organizing com. AAANZ Conf., Christchurch, 1995-96. Recipient Rsch. grant New Zealand Treasury, 1994, Inland Revenue Dept., New Zealand, 1997, fellowship Coopers and Lybrand/Peter Barr, New Zealand, 1997. Mem. Acctg. Assn. Australia and New Zealand, Am. Acctg. Assn., Am. Taxation Assn., Australasian Tax Tchrs.' Assn., Australian Tax Rsch. Found., ICANZ (Inst. Chartered Accountants of New Zealand), Australasian Law Tchrs. Assn., Inst. Fiscal Studies. Avocations: squash, soccer, reading, gardening, hiking.E-mail: a.sawyer@afis.canterbury.ac.nz. Office: Univ of Canterbury Dept AFIS, Pvt Bag 4800, 8020 Christchurch New Zealand

SAWYER, THOMAS C., congressman; b. Akron, Ohio, Aug. 15, 1945; m. Joyce Handler, 1968; 1 child, Amanda. BA, U. Akron, 1968, MA, 1970. Pub. sch. tchr. Ohio; adminstr. state sch. for delinquent boys; legis. agt. Ohio Pub. Utilities Commn.; mem. Ohio House Reps., Columbus, 1977-83; mayor City of Akron, 1984-86; mem. 100th-106th Congresses from 14th Ohio dist., Washington, D.C., 1987—; mem. Transp. and Infrastructure com., com. surface transp. and infrastructure. Democrat. Office: US Ho of Reps 1414 Longworth Hob Washington DC 20515-0001

SAWYER, WILLIAM C., lawyer; b. Bangor, Maine, Aug. 26, 1929; s. Frank S. and Linda M. (Makanna) S.; m. Mary E. Eaton (div.); m. Joan N. Gardner; children: William D., Constance, Faith. AB cum laude, Harvard Coll., 1951, JD, 1954. Bar: Mass., U.S. Dist. Ct. Mass., U.S. Ct. Mil. Appeals, U.S. Supreme Ct. Assoc. Palmer & Dodge, Boston, 1958-61; ptnr. Sawyer, Burlingham, Tucker & Salloway, Boston, 1961-85, Dicara, Selig, Sawyer & Holt, Boston, 1985-90, Clarkin, Sawyer & Phillips, P.C., Boston, 1990—; bd. dirs. Jones & Vining, Inc., Ayer Sales, Inc., Applied Geographics, Inc., Applied Tech., Inc., others. Contbr. articles to profl. jours. Bd. trustees Mass. Conv. Ctr. Authority, 1991-97; pres., treas., chmn. Metro. Area Planning Coun., 1975-87; pres. Mass. Assn. Regional Planning Agys., 1980, 87; bd. dirs. Nat. Assn. Regional Couns., 1980-86; mem. Mass. Selectman's Assn., 1975—; bd. selectman Town of Action, 1967-75, chmn., 1969, 75; Rep. candidate Mass. Atty. Gen., 1990; pres. New Eng. Rep. Coun.; mem. Rep. State Com.; Rep. candidate Congress, 5th Congl. Dist., Mass., 1980. 1st lt. U.S. Army, 1955. Recipient Regional Leadership award Planning Commns. and Couns. New Eng., 1987, and others. Mem. ABA, Mass. Bar Assn., Boston Bar Assn. Avocations: tennis, painting, reading. Office: Clarkin Sawyer & Phillips PC 1 Center Plz Ste 240 Boston MA 02108-1801

SAX, DANIEL SAUL, neurologist; b. Balt., Jan. 27, 1935; s. Benjamin J. and Miriam (Helfgott) S.; m. Joan Atherton Bond, Mar. 25, 1962; children: Karen Bond, John Derek, Diana Atherton. AB, Johns Hopkins U., 1955; MD, U. Md., 1959. Diplomate Am. Bd. Psychiatry and Neurology. Intern Boston City Hosp., 1959-60, resident in neuropathology and neurology, 1961-64; resident in neurology N.E. Med. Ctr., Boston, 1960-61; asst. prof. neurology Northwestern U., Chgo., 1966-67; assoc. prof. neurology Albert Einstein Med. Sch., N.Y.C., 1967-69; assoc. prof. neurology Boston U. Sch. Med., 1969-76, prof. neurology, 1976—; chief neurology svcs. Boston VA Outpatient Clinic, 1974-90; EEG lab. dir., cons. Gifford Med. Ctr., Randolph, Vt., 1977—; cons. neurology Boston VA Med. Ctr., 1991—. Lt. comdr. USNR, 1964-66. Fellow Am. acad. Neurology; mem. AMA, Am. Neurol. Assn., Am. Assn. for Study of Headache, Am. Soc. Neuroimaging, Mass. Med. Soc., Boston Soc. Neurology and Psychiatry (pres. 1982-83, exec. com. 1985—), Multiple Sclerosis Soc. (med. adv. bd. 1977—), Huntington's Study Group, Huntington's Dx Soc. (mem. adv. bd. Mass. chpt. 1980—). Avocations: tree farmer, oenology. Office: Boston U Sch Medicine 80 E Concord St Boston MA 02118-2307

SAX, MARY RANDOLPH, speech pathologist; b. July 13, 1925; d. Bernard Angus and Ada Lucile (Thurman) TePoorten; m. William Martin Sax, Feb. 7, 1948. BA magna cum laude, Mich. State U., 1947; MA, U. Mich., 1949. Cert. clin. competence in speech and lang. pathology. Supr. speech correction dept. Waterford Twp. Schs., Pontiac, 1949-69; lectr. Marygrove Coll., Detroit, 1971-72; pvt. practice in speech and lang. pathology Wayne & Oakland Counties, Mich., 1973—; co-investigator Support Pers. Profl. Practice of Speech-Lang. Pathology; counselor to divsn. stroke liaisons Am. Heart Assn. Mich.; stroke advisor for Midwest affiliate Am. Heart Assn., 1999—; liaison between Am. Heart Assn. of Mich. and sci. coun. on stroke Am. Heart Assn., Dallas, 1996-98; adj. speech pathologist Southfield, Mich.; lectr. on stroke Mich. Spkrs. Bur., Am. Heart Assn., 1990—; pub. spkg. coach, 1989—; mem. adj. faculty SS Cyril and Methodius Sem., Orchard Lake, Mich., 1989-90; adj. St. Mary's Prep. Sch., Orchard Lake, 1990—; mem. Met. Detroit Stroke Task Force of Am. Stroke Assn., 1999—; founder, mem. Stroke Project Task Force for Detroit, 1993-98; com. mem. Charrette, study Arch. and Design for phys. restructuring Franklin, Mich., 1993; invited speech pathology del. Internat. Health Programs People to People Citizen Amb. Program, 1996. Contbr. articles to profl. jours. including Lang. and Lang. Behavior Abstracts, Lang. Speech & Hearing Svcs., Speech Lang. Hearing Jour. Active Franklinites for Responsible Govt. Recipient Svc. Recognition award Coll. Edn. Mich. State U.; grantee Inst. Articulation and Learning, 1969, others; Christian svc. commn. St. Owen, Birmingham co-chmn. blood dr. Red Cross, Franklin, Mich., 1991—. Mem. Am. Speech-Lang.-Hearing Assn. (clin. competence cert.), Mich. Speech-Lang.-Hearing Assn. (com. comty. and hosp. svcs., pvt. practitioner liaison 1991—, developer structural parameters for State Clin. Svc. award 1999—, mem. state award selection com.), Am. Heart Assn. Mich. (mem. stroke awareness seminars, continuing edn. for physicians and others profls., planning and operation edn.), Internat. Assn. Logopedics and Phoniatrics (Switzerland), Pvt. Practitioners Speech-Lang. Pathology (co-founder), Franklin Found. (mem. natural resources adv. coun. 1991—, bd. dirs. 1994—), Founders Soc. of Detroit Inst. Arts, Mich. Humane Soc., Theta Alpha Phi, Phi Kappa Phi, Kappa Delta Pi, Gamma Phi Beta. Achievements include research in language and speech acquisition in children in reference to the development of and prediction of biological speech change; research interests in developmental phonatory voice disorders, and in adult acquisition of language and speech relative to central and autonomic nervous systems. Home and Office: 31320 Woodside Dr Franklin MI 48025-2027

SAXEGAARD, FINN, retired veterinary microbiologist; b. Oslo; s. Paul Christian and Esther (Borch) Saxegaard. DVM, Norwegian Sch. Vet. Sci., Oslo, 1959; PhD, Norwegian Sch. Vet. Sci., 1989; MS, Iowa State U., 1965. Sci. asst. dept. reprodn. physiology Norwegian Sch. Vet. Sci., Oslo, 1960-63, rsch. scientist dept. microbiology, 1964-66, sr. scientist dept. microbiology, 1967-74, sr. scientist dept. food hygiene, 1975; sr. scientist bacteriology dept. Nat. Vet. Inst., Oslo, 1976-78, sr. scientist Tb dept., 1979-96, sr. rschr. bacteriology dept., 1997-2000; ret., 2000. Mem. Internat. Assn. Paratuberculosis (emeritus), Phi Kappa Phi. Avocations: classical music, literature, humanities, mountaineering.

SAXEN, ARNO ERIK ERKKI, pathologist, epidemiologist; b. Helsinki, Finland, Aug. 23, 1921; s. Arno and Katri (Palmroth) S.; m. Eva Paula Margareta Ryti, 1947; children—Irma, Anja, Aino, Tuovi. M.D., U. Helsinki, 1948, prof. pathology, 1960. Chief pathologist Central Inst. Radiotherapy, Helsinki, 1949-59; research fellow Nat. Cancer Inst., Bethesda, Md., 1951-52; prof., head dept. pathology, Lab. Pathology, U. Helsinki, 1960-86; council mem. WHO Expert Adv. Bd. Cancer, 1959—; pres. Internat. Acad. Pathology, 1983-86. Contbr. articles to profl. jours. Decorated Liberty Cross IV; recipient Hon. award Finnish Acad. Sci., 1978; Comdr. Order of Lion of Finland, 1969; Maude Abbott Lecture. Mem. Internat. Council Socs. Patology (pres.), Internat. Assn. Cancer Registries (sec.-gen. 1979-84), Suomalainen Tiedeakatemia, Finnish Cancer Registry (dir.). Home: Itainen Puistotie 3B8, Helsinki 00140 14, Finland Office: Univ Helsinki Dept Patology, Haartmaninkatu 3, Helsinki SF 00290, Helsinki

SAXENA, ALOK JAGDISH, pharmaceutical executive; b. New Delhi, India, Oct. 3, 1965; s. Jagdish and Sneh Jagdish (Talwar) S.; m. Niti Alok Kumar, Mar. 30, 1991; children: Anshita, Anshul, Arshia. BA, U. Bombay, 1987. Corp. mgr. Elder Pharms. Ltd., Bombay, 1987-90, dir. internat. divsn., 1990—; mng. dir. Indarts Exports Pvt. Ltd, Bombay, 1987—, Elder Instruments Pvt. Ltd., Bombay, 1995—; joint mng. dir. Elder Healthcare Ltd., Bombay, 1992—; dir. Elder Projects Ltd., Guhatti, India. Sec. Syed Rajwali Charitable Trust, Bombay, 1998—. Recipient Bharat Jyoti award Front for Nat. Progress, 1999, Bus. Excellence award Internat. Bus. Coun., 1999. Fellow Soc. Sales Mgmt. Adminstrs. (Eng.), Internat. Mgmt. Studies and Promotion Inst. (mgmt. program), Inst. Execs. and Mgrs. (Eng.), United Writers Assn., Inst. Profl. Mgrs. and Adminstrs. (Eng.); mem. Indian Merchants Chamber, Indian Pharm. Assn. (life), Pub. Rels Soc. India, Indian Mgmt. Assn., Inst. Comml. Mgmt. (Eng.), Soc. Bus. Practitioners (Eng.), Inst. Pub. Rels. (Eng.), Internat. Inst. Mgmt. Scis., Inst. Export Mgmt., Inst. Bus. Adminstrn., Inst. Supervision Mgmt., Inst. Mgmt. (assoc.), Inst. Sales and Mktg. Mgmt. (Eng.), Singapore Inst. Mgmt. (assoc.), Am. Inst. Mgmt. (mem. exec. coun.), Internat. Pub. Rels. Assn., Am. Mgmt. Assn., Inst. Dirs. (Eng.), Am. Mktg. Assn. (profl.), Sales and Mktg. Execs. Internat. (profl.), Internat. Pharm. Fedn., Inst. Mgmt. Splsts., Advtsg. Club (life), Bombay Mgmt. Assn. (life), Indo Japanese Soc., Indo German C. of C., Indo Italian C. of C., Indo French C. of C., Indo Am. C. of C., Maharashtra Econ. Devel. Coun., The Econ. EU C.'s of C. in India, Rotary Club Bombay (chmn. occupation info.). Avocations: reading, social work. Home: 11 Anjali behind Radio Club, Colaba Bombay 400 005, India Office: Elder Pharms Ltd 11-B, Dhanraj Mahal Apollo Bunder, Bombay 400 001, India

SAXENA, ANURAG, agronomist; b. Pantnagar, India, Nov. 29, 1965; s. Shyam Bahadur and Vimla (Devi) S.; m. Swati Kanchan, Nov. 28, 1993; children: Aayushee, Aastha. BSc in Agriculture, Coll. Agriculture, Pantnagar, 1985; MSc in Agronomy, Coll. Postgrad. Studies, Pantnagar, 1987, PhD in Agronomy, 1991. Scientist Nat. Acad. Agrl. Rsch. Mgmt., Hyderabad, India, 1991, Indian Inst. Pulses Rsch., Kanpur, India, 1991-92, Ctrl. Arid Zone Rsch. Inst., Jodhpur, India, 1992—; mem. adv. com. zonal rsch. extension Rajasthan Agrl. U., Bikaner, India, 1996—. Author: 50 Years of Arid Zone Research in India (1947-97), 1998; contbg. author: Studies in Indian Agro-Ecosystems, 1996, Desertification Control in the Arid

Ecosystems of India for Sustainable Development, 1997, Fifty Years of Agronomic Research in India, 1998, Fifty Years of Arid Zone Research in India, 1998, Predominant Cropping Systems of India: Technologies and Strategies, 1998; contbr. articles to profl. and popular publs. With N.C.C., 1983-84. Mem. Indian Soc. Allelopathy (treas. Jodhpur chpt.), Arid Zone Rsch. Assn. India, Internat. Soc. for Tropical Ecology, Satat Krishi Samanvit Gramin Vikas Samiti, Jodupur, 1997. Avocations: reading, writing, photography, tourism, table tennis. Home: IV/12 Cazri Campus, Rajasthan Jodhpur 342 003, India Office: Ctrl Arid Zone Rsch Inst, Rajasthan Jodhpur 342 003, India

SAXENA, ARJUN NATH, physicist; b. Lucknow, India, Apr. 1, 1932; s. Sheo and Mohan (Piyari) Shanker; came to U.S., 1956, naturalized, 1976; BSc, Lucknow U., 1950, MSc, 1952, profl. cert. in German, 1954; Post MS diploma, Inst. Nuclear Physics, Calcutta, India, 1955; PhD, Stanford U., 1963; m. Veera Saxena, Feb. 9, 1956; children: Rashmi, Amol, Varsha, Ashvin. Rsch. asst. Stanford U., 1956-60; mem. tech. staff Fairchild Semicondr. Co., Palo Alto, Calif., 1960-65; dept. head Sprague Electric Co., North Adams, Mass., 1965-69; mem. tech. staff RCA Labs., Princeton, N.J., 1969-71; pres., chmn. bd. Astro-Optics, Phila., 1972; pres. Internat. Sci. Co., Princeton Junction, N.J., 1973—; disting. vis. scientist Centre de Récherches Nucléaires, Strasbourg, France, 1973, 77; sr. staff scientist, mgr. engring. Data Gen. Corp., Sunnyvale, Calif., 1975-80; mgr. process tech. Signetics Corp., Sunnyvale, 1980-81; Gould AMI scientist, dir. advanced process devel. Gould AMI Semicondrs., Santa Clara, Calif., 1981-87; dir. Ctr. for Integrated Electronics, prof. dept. elec. and computer system engring. Rensselaer Poly. Inst., Troy, N.Y., 1987-96, emeritus prof., 1996—; disting. vis. scientist Inst. Microelectronics, Stuttgart, Germany, 1993-94. Treas. Pack 66, Boy Scouts Am., W. Windsor, N.J., 1970-74. Recipient Disting. Citizen award State of N.J., 1975. Mem. IEEE (life), Stanford Alumni Assn. (life). Contbr. articles on semicondr. tech., optics, nuclear and high-energy physics to sci. jours., 1953—; patentee in field. FAX: 650-856-1794. Home: 4217 Pomona Ave Palo Alto CA 94306-4312

SAXENA, ARUN KUMAR, educator, researcher; b. Kanpur, India, Sept. 18, 1936; s. Anjani Prasad and Shanti Devi (Saxena) Sarbhoy; m. Beena Saxena, Mar. 4, 1974; children: Madhumitta, Anant. MSc, U. Allahabad, India, 1962, DPhil, 1966, DSc, 1972. Pool officer Delhi U., India, 1976-78; sr. lectr. Univ. Dar E. Salaam, Tanzania, 1979-82, assoc. prof., 1982; emeritus specialist Delhi U., India, 1994—. Contbr. articles to profl. jours. Home: Flat No. 6440 Sect. B-9, 110070 Vasant Kunj New Dehli, India

SAXENA, JITENDRA KUMAR, research scientist; b. Lalganj, UP, India, Oct. 10, 1955; s. Raja Ram Singh and Sushila Devi; m. Alka Sinha. MSc in Biochemistry, Lucknow U., 1974; PhD, Kanpur U., 1979. Rsch. scientist Ctrl. Drug Rsch. Inst., Lucknow, India, 1982-92; asst. dir. Ctrl. Drug Rsch. Inst., Lucknow, 1992—. Recipient Rostsca award UNESCO, 1986. lem. Indian Soc. Parasitology (treas. 1996, assoc. editor jour. 1985, Babar Mirza award 1986, sec. 2000—), Internat. Soc. Applied Biology (assoc. editor 1991), Indian Sci. Congress Assn., Indian Soc. Immunology, Soc. Biol. Chemists India. Avocations: chess, cricket, reading. Office: Ctrl Drug Rsch Inst, PO Box 173 Chattar Manzil, UP Lucknow 226 001, India

SAXENA, NARENDRA SAHAI, physicist, educator; b. Agra, India, Nov. 25, 1948; s. Gopal Sahai and Shanti (Devi) S.; m. Tilotma Chaturvedi, Jan. 7, 1973; children: Mahima, Parul. BSc, U. Rajasthan, Jaipur, India, 1967, MSc, 1969, PhD, 1975. Lectr. Agrawal Coll., Jaipur, 1973-75; postdoctoral fellow U. Rajasthan, 1975-76, pool officer, 1976-78, asst. prof. physics, 1978-88, assoc. prof., 1988—. Co-author 4 undergrad. physics textbooks; contbr. more than 160 articles and papers to profl. jours. Mem. Nat. Acad. Scis. of India (life), Indian Sci. Congress (life), Disordered Materials Soc. India (life, sec. 1994—). Home: 378 Mahaveer Nagar, Rajasthn Jaipur India Office: U Rajasthan Dept Physics, Rajasthn Jaipur 302004, India

SAXONIS, ANTHONY, marketing executive; b. Athens, Greece, June 27, 1963; s. Nikolaos and Angelika (Iliades) S.; m. Aphrodite Petraki, Oct. 9, 1994. BBA in Mktg. Mgmt., Am. Coll. Greece, Athens, 1989. Exports supr. Kolonaki SA, Athens, 1985-87; sales supr. Kybos SA, Athens, 1989; dist. sales mgr. Delta SA, Athens, 1989-91; mktg. product mgr. Rank Xerox Greece, Athens, 1991-97; mktg. mgr. Druckfarben Hellas SA, Athens, 1997—. Sgt., Greek Army, 1987-88, Lesvos Island. Mem. Hellenic Inst. Mktg. Home: 23 Aut Irakliou Str, 15122 Marousi Greece

SAXTON, JOHN EDWIN, chemistry educator, writer; b. Rawmarsh, U.K., Mar. 19, 1927; s. John Ayliffe and Margaret Mary (King) S.; m. Joan Cicely Clark, Aug. 9, 1958; children: Helen Margaret, John Christopher Robert. BA, Oxford (Eng.) U., 1948, BS, 1949, MA, PhD, 1952. Imperial Chem. Industries rsch. fellow Oxford U., 1952-55; postdoctoral rsch. fellow Harvard U., Cambridge, Mass., 1955-56; lectr. U. Leeds, U.K., 1956-63, sr. lectr., 1963-89, sr. fellow, 1989-92, hon. lectr., 1992-95. Author: (chpts.) The Alkaloids, vols. 7, 8, 10, 12, 14, 20; editor, contbg. author: Monoterpenoid Indole Alkaloids, 1983, supplement, 1994. Avocations: several hobbies including playing piano and listening to music. Home: 30 Parklands Bramhope, Leeds LS16 9AJ, England Office: U Leeds, Leeds LS2 9JT, England

SAYAH, ELIAS BOUTROS, civil engineer, consultant; b. Saida, Lebanon, Aug. 5, 1957; s. Boutros Maroun and Hanne Hanna (Haddad) S.; m. Lena H. Haddad, Jan. 29, 1996; children: Jude-Hanne, Boutros. BS, San Diego State U., 1980; MS, U. Beverly Hills, 1984. Engr. trainee City of Chula Vista, Calif., 1980-81; asst. project engr. U. Mech., San Diego, 1981-82; sr. field engr. Flour Mid. East, Abu Dhabi, United Arab Emirates, 1982-84; gen. mgr. Gefco, Abu Dhabi, 1984-86, Gefico, Inc., San Diego, 1986-89; cons. engr. Sayah Engring. Cons. Bur., Abu Dhabi, 1989—; advisor to civil engring. higher colls. of tech., Abu-Dhabi 1991—. Warden Embassy of U.S.A., Abu Dhabi, 1993—; mem. U.S.-UAE relationship Am. Bus. Group; founder corp. mem. Am. Bus. Group, Abu Dhabi, v.p. membership, 1998—. Mem. ASCE (pres. United Arab Emirates internat. group 1991—), United Arab Emirates Soc. Engrs., Lebanese Order Engrs., Masons, Tau Beta Pi, Chi Epsilon. Republican. Mem. Maronite Christian Ch. Avocations: collecting old coins, stamps, traveling, reading, collecting books. E-mail: ebsayah@emirates.net.ae. Office: Sayah Engring Cons Bur, PO Box 2337, Abu Dhabi United Arab Emirates

SAYED, NISAR AHMAD SHAH, manufacturing company executive, consultant; b. Batala, Punjab, India, Sept. 14, 1930; arrived in U.K., 1971; s. Said Ahmad Shah and Amtal Batool Sayed; m. Eva Hornby, Dec. 23, 1961; children: Anona, Robina, Kamil, Vasil. Faculty of sci., Dyal Singh Coll., Lahore, Pakistan, 1950; diploma in textile tech., Blackburn Tech. Coll., 1954; diploma in mgmt., Brit. Inst. Mgmt., 1960. Asst. mgr. John Dugdale Textile Ltd., Blackburn, Eng., 1954-57; cost acct. Gt. Universal Stores, London, 1958-62; gen. mgr. Colony Textile Group, Nowshera, Pakistan, 1962-63; dir. adminstrn. Pakistan Coop. Devel. Bd., Lahore, 1963-66; mng. dir. Eva Hornby and Co. Ltd., Lahore, 1966-71; cons. J.R. Haworth and Co. Chartered Accts., Accrington, Eng., 1971-73, Eva Sayed and Co. Chartered Accts., Blackburn, Eng., 1973—; chmn. P. Casey Assocs., Blackburn, 1976-93, Rapid Relief Shelters Mfg. Ltd., Blackburn, 1976—, Rapid Relief Shelters Sales Ltd., Blackburn, 1976—, Ethnic Bus. Advisor Hyndburn Borough Coun., Lancashire, U.K., 1992-97; chmn. Internat. Cons. Alliance, Ltd., 1993—, Medilanta Bandages Factory Uzbek-Brit. Joint Venture, Tashkent, Uzbekistan, 1995-97; founder Uzmestbritkimbank, Uzbek-Brit. Joint Comml. Bank, 1995-97. Patentee low-cost housing for emergency relief for natural and man-made disasters throughout the world. Fellow Brit. Inst. Mgmt. (br. chmn. 1981-83), Inst. Indsl. Mgrs.

SAYEED, (ABULFATAH) AKRAM, physician; b. Jessore, Bangladesh, Nov. 23, 1935; s. Mokhles and Noor Jehan (Muncie) Ahmed; m. To Hosne-Ara Ali, Oct. 11, 1959; children: Dina Jesmine, Rana Ahmed, Reza Abu. MB BS, U. Dhaka, Bangladesh, 1958. House officer, 1958-59, rotating intern, 1960-61, sr. house officer, 1961-63; pvt. practice Leicester, Eng., 1964—; commr. Cmty. Rels. Commn., U.K., 1968-77; hon. advisor Ministry of Health, Govt. of Bangladesh, 1990—; mem. gen. optical coun., 1994-98. Co-author: Care of Asian Patients in the NHS, 1990; editl. bd. ODA News Rev., 1976-96, Asian Who's Who. Active DoH Working Groups on Ethnic Minority Health, BBC-TV and Radio Adv. Svcs. on Asian Programmes, 1972-77, Home Sec. Adv. Coun. on Race and Cmty. Rels., 1983-88. Decorated officer Brit. Empire. Fellow Royal Coll. Gen. Practitioners, Royal Coll. Physicians, Coll. Physicians and Surgeons, Royal Soc. Medicine, Overseas Doctors Assn. (gen. sec. 1975-77, v.p. 1977-86, vice chmn. 1986-90, chmn. 1993-96), Royal Inst. Health and Hygiene, Royal Soc. Health, Bangladeshi Coll. Gen. Practitioners; mem. Royal Coll. Gen. Practitioners (mem. inner city task force 1991-97, Brit. Med. Assn. (pres. 1993-94, immediate past pres. 1994-95, mem. gen. med. svcs. com. 1989-95, mem. agenda com. 1991-96), Gen. Med. Coun., EMC. Islam. Avocations: stamp collecting, gardening. Office: Ramna, 2 Mickleton Dr, Leicester LE5 6GD, England

SAYEED, MOHAMMED ABU, endocrinologist, researcher; b. Rajshahi, Bangladesh, Jan. 1, 1950; s. Mohammed Abdus Satter and Mosammet Asifa Khatun; m. Akhter Banu Minu, Mar. 10, 1974; children: Tanyeem, Nayeem, Surovi. MB, BS, Mymensingh Med. Coll., Bangladesh, 1973; postgrad., Inst. Postgrad. Medicine, 1978-79; diploma in cmty. medicine, U. Dhaka, Bangladesh, 1985, MD in Endocrinology and Metabolism, 1993. Asst. surgeon Mymensingh Med. Coll., 1973-74, asst. registrar, 1976-77, registrar, 1977-78; health adminstr. Haluaghat Health Complex, Bangladesh, 1974-75; nat. epidemiologist WHO, Bangladesh, 1975-76; tng. fellow WHO, Zagreb, Yugoslavia, 1986; med. officer Ministry Tamin, Ghadamas, Libya, 1979-83, BIRDEM, Dhaka, 1983-93; sr. rsch. officer Bangladesh Inst. Rsch. and Rehab. in Diabetes, Endocrine and Metabolic Disorders, Dhaka, 1994—. Contbr. articles to med. jours., including Bangladesh Med. Rsch. Coun. Bull., Diabetes Care, Diabetes Rsch. Clin. Practice. Pres. BIRDEM unit Doctors for Health and Environ., 1993. Travel grantee Diabetic Assn. Bangladesh, Beijing, 1994, 95, Helsinki, 1997, Internat. Diabetic Fedn., Kobe, Japan, 1994; stayment grantee European Assn. for the Study of Diabetes, Barcelona, 1998, Brussels, 1999. Mem. Nutrition Soc. Bangladesh (assoc. gen. sec. 1995-97), Bangladesh Med. Assn., Bangladesh Endocrine Soc. (v.p.), N.Y. Acad. Scis., Am. Diabetes Assn. (profl. sect. coun.). Avocations: horticulture, fish farming, tree plantatoin, free health care camp in remote villages, diabetes health care education in rural areas. Home: 129/1 South Kamlapur, Dhaka Bangladesh Office: BIRDEM, 122 Kazi Nazrul Islam Ave, Dhaka Bangladesh

SAYENKO, ELENA MIKHAILOVNA, biologist; b. Artiom, Primorye, Russia, Mar. 9, 1966; d. Mikhail Petrovich and Taissia Vasilievna (Panova) S.; m. Igor Albertovich Rodionov. Student, Far East State U., Vladivostok, Russia, 1983-88. From engr. to jr. rschr. Inst. Biology and Soil Scis., Vladivostok, 1989-98, sr. rschr., 1999—. Recipient I award Gov. Primorye Territory, Vladivostok, 1998. Mem. Russian Far East Malacological Soc. Office: Inst Biology and Soil Scis, 100let Vladivostok pr-kt159, 690022 Vladivostok Russia

SAYENKO, YURI LEONIDOVICH, electrical engineering educator; b. Mariupol, Donetsk, Ukraine, June 18, 1962; s. Leonid Arkadievich Bondarevsky and Tatiana Ivanovna Sayenko; m. Svetlana Evgenievna Fadeeva, Oct. 1, 1993; 1 child, Ivan. Elec. engr., Mariupol Metall. Inst., 1984; PhD, Inst. Electrodynamics, Kiev, Ukraine, 1986; DSc in Elec. Engring., Silesian Poly. Inst., Gliwice, Poland, 1992. Sci. rschr. Mariupol Metall. Inst., 1984-86, asst. prof., 1986-90; assoc. prof. Azov State Tech. U., Mariupol, 1990-97, prof., 1997—; dep. chief dept. Azov State Tech. U., Mariupol, 1990—. Author: (books) Matters of Probability Modeling for Calculation of Electrical Loads, 1990, Reactive Power in Electrical Supply Systems Having Nonlinear Loads, 1991, Theory of Electromagnetic Compatibility in Electrical Supply Systems, 19993, Questions of Quality of Electrical Power in Electrical Equipment, 1996. Mem. IEEE, N.Y. Acad. Scis. Avocation: satellite TV. Home: Semenishina St # 36, 87532 Mariupol Donetsk, Ukraine Office: Azov State Tech U, Republic Lane # 7, 87500 Mariupol Donetsk, Ukraine

SAYF AL-NASR, FARUQ, Egyptian government official; b. Alexandria, 1922. Mem., then chief justice Supreme Court, Cairo; min. justice Arab Republic of Egypt, Cairo, 1987—; adv. Min. Border Affairs, Min. Justice. Office: Ministry of Justice, Midan Lazoughli Nasr City, Cairo Egypt*

SAYKIEWICZ-SAJKIEWICZ, JAN NAPOLEON, marketing educator; b. Lublin, Poland, June 10, 1939; came to U.S., 1987; s. Jan Sajkiewicz and Ewa Komorowska; m. Elzbieta Katarzyna Przetacznik, Aug. 27, 1966; children: Jan Rafal, Olaf Xawery, Mateusz Konstanty. MS in Econs., Ctrl. Sch. Planning & Stats., Warsaw, Poland, 1962, PhD, 1969; post-master diploma in African studies, Oriental Inst., U. Warsaw, 1968; diploma, U. Calif., Berkeley, 1972. Cert. internat. tourism profl. Rsch. assoc. U. Calif., Berkeley, 1972-73; asst., assoc. prof. Ctrl. Sch. Planning & Stats., Warsaw, Poland, 1962-75; lectr. in mktg. Exec. Tng. Ctrs., Warsaw, 1969-88; assoc. prof. U. Warsaw, 1974-88; lectr.-prof. Warsaw Acad. Arts, 1980-87; prof. Duquesne U. Sch. Bus. Adminstrn., Pitts., 1987—; vis. prof. Fordham U., N.Y.C., 1978, Duquesne U., Pitts., 1981, No. Jiaotong U., Beijing, 1997; Fulbright prof., 2000—; expert Internat. Labor Orgn., Geneva, 1982; vice chmn., bd. dirs. Consumer Cooperative Enterprises, Warsaw, 1982-88; mem. Inter-Polcom, Chamber of Industry, Commerce, Warsaw, 1984-86; sec. gen., chief treas. Polish Mktg. Assn., 1974-81, mem. exec. bd., 1985-88. Author: Concentration of Commercial Activities, 1972, Marketing Concept in Business Management, 1975, 2nd edit., 1976, 3rd edit., 1977, Management Systems in Integrated Capitalist Business, 1975; contbr. articles to profl. jours.; transl. profl. lit. Active Solidarity Movement, Poland, 1980-81; mem. social and econ. coun., The Capital City of Warsaw, Poland, 1987-88. Vis. scholar U. Calif, Berkeley, 1972-73, Fordham U., N.Y., 1978, No. Jiaotong U., Beijing, 1997; Ford Found. fellow, 1972-73; Rsch. grantee U.S. Dept. Edn., 1993, 94; recipient Silver and Gold Crosses of Merit, Coun. of State, Poland, 1980, 82, Individual award for pedagogical performance Min. of Edn., Poland, 1981, Golden Mermaid Hon. Decoration for svc., Capital City of Warsaw, 1985. Fellow Acad. Mktg. Sci.; mem. Internat. Mgmt. Devel. Assn. (exec. v.p. 1997), Acad. Internat. Bus., Am. Mktg. Assn., Polish Inst. Arts and Scis. in Am. (bd. dirs. 1995-97). Roman Catholic. Avocations: social studies, books, travel, cognac. Home: 5853 Douglas St Pittsburgh PA 15217-2101

SAYKO, GENNADIY, physicist; b. Kiev, Ukraine, Dec. 9; s. Vladimir and Katherine (Mashovetz) S.; m. Vera Ovchinnokova, July 27, 1989; 1 child, Daniel. BS, Moscow Inst. Physics and Tech., 1987, MS with honors, 1990, PhD, 1993. Sci. rschr. Gen. Physics Inst., Moscow, 1990-93, Moscow Inst. Physics and Tech., 1988—. Contbr. articles to sci. publs. Grantee IEEE, 1992, Internat. Sci. Found., 1993, 94, NATO, 1994. Mem. Magnetic Soc. Russia, N.Y. Acad. Scis. Orthodox Christian. Avocations: history, tennis, skiing, diving. Home: Mayakovskogo Str 77-105, 02232 Kiev Ukraine

SAYLES, RONALD LYLE, computer executive; b. Waukesha, Wis., Oct. 12, 1936; s. Burton Lyall and Sophia (Lapaz) S.; m. Fumiko Soeda, Jan. 15, 1957. BS in Secondary Edn., U. Wis., Milw., 1978. Computer operator Mortgage Assocs., Milw., 1966-71, Kohl's Food Stores, Wauwatosa, Wis., 1971-83; supr. computer ops. Kohl's Dept. Stores, Menomonee Falls, Wis., 1983-86, prodn. coord., 1986-87, scheduling coord., 1987-98, ret., 1998. Contbr. articles on old time radio programs. Vol. Jim Moody for Congress, 1984, 86, 88, 90, Shirley Krug for State Assembly, 1984, 86, 88, 90, Tom Barrett for State Senate, 1990, 91, Tom Barrett for Congress, 1991, 92, 94-96, 98, 2000, Bill Clinton for Pres., 1992, 96, Al Gore for Pres., 2000. With USN, 1954-57. Mem. Milw. Area Radio Enthusiasts (sec.), Soc. to Preserve and Encourage Radio Drama, Variety and Comedy, U. Wis.-Milw. Alumni Assn. (life), Nightmare Players. Democrat. Mem. LDS Ch. Home: 4278 N 53rd St Milwaukee WI 53216-1343

SAZCI, ALI, geneticist, researcher, educator; b. Kirklareli, Turkey, June 25, 1953; s Abbas and Saffeta S.; m. Jie Wang, Sept. 23, 1992; 1 child, Gensay. BS, U. Instanbul, 1976; MS, U. Newcastle-upon-Tyne (Eng.), 1980; PhD, U. Leeds (Eng.), 1983. Instr. U. Hacettepe, Ankara, Turkey, 1984-85; prin. investigator Turkish Scientific and Rsch. Ctr., Gebze, 1985-86; asst. prof. U. Firat, Elazig, Turkey, 1986-87; vis. scholar U. Edmonton, Alta., Can., 1989-92; assoc. prof. U. Istanbul, 1992-94; genetic cons., dir. A.J. Çinpon Med. Svcs. Inc., Istanbul, 1994-97; cons., 1994—; prof. genetics U. Kocaeli (Turkey), 1997—; dir. Inst. Health Scis., Kocaeli, 1997-99. Contbr. articles to profl. jours.; reviewer, advisor Turkish Jour. Med. Scis., 1997—. Scholar Turkish Ministry of Edn., 1977-83, U. Alta., Edmonton, Can., 1987-89; grantee U. Kocaeli, 1997, 99. Mem. AAAS. Avocations: following the latest technology, classical music, travel, collectibles. Home: Funda 04 Mah Ada Sok 05 A27, Blok D.4 Bahçephir, Istanbul 34900, Turkey Office: U Kocaeli Faculty Medicine, Dept Med Biology & Genetics, Derince Kocaeli 41900, Turkey

SAZHIN, SERGEI STEPANOVICH, engineering educator; b. St. Petersburg, Russia, Feb. 4, 1949; arrived in U.K., 1988; s. Stepan Andreevich and Anna Arkhipovna (Smirnova) S.; m. Elena Mikhailovna Fomina, Sept. 11, 1980; children: Ekaterina, Anna. Diploma of Higher Edn., St. Petersburg U., 1972, Diploma of Cand. Scis., 1977; Cert. in Ednl. Studies, Sheffield (Eng.) U., 1992; Postgrad. Cert. in Tchg./Learning, U. Brighton, Eng., 1997. Chartered physicist. Rschr. Inst. Physics, St. Petersburg U., 1972-82; pvt. scientist, 1982-88; rsch. fellow dept. physics Sheffield U., 1988-92; rsch. scientist Computational Fluid Dynamics Co., Sheffield, 1992-96; sr. lectr. U. brighton, 1996—. Author: Natural Radio Emissions in the Earth's Magnetosphere, 1982, Whistler-mode Waves in a Hot Plasma, 1993; contbr. more than 170 articles to acad. and profl. jours. Founder mem. Internat. Soc. For Human Rights, St. Petersburg, 1987-88; mem. St. Gregory Found., London, 1997—. SERC/NERC(UK) fellow, 1988-92; Brit. Coun. Travel grantee, 1991. Fellow Inst. Physics U.K. Russian Orthodox Christian Ch. Avocations: walking, history. Home: 8 Brambletyne Ave, Brighton BN2 8EJ, England Office: Univ of Brighton, Sch of Engring, Brighton BN2 4GY, England

SAZONOVA, VALENTINA YEGOROVNA, ecologist, researcher; b. Tula, Russia, Oct. 26, 1937. MS, Inst. Cytology, St. Petersburg, Russia, 1973; DSc, Krasnoyarsk Agrarian U., 1996. Tchr. Tup Sch., Krasnoyarsk, 1960-61; tchr. Shira Sch., Krasnoyarsk, 1961-63, lab. asst., 1963-65; sr. rsch. worker Inst. Physics, Krasnoyarsk, 1965-81; dir. hydrobiologists group Inst. Biophysics, Krasnoyarsk, 1981-95; prof. biology Krasnoyarsk Agrarian U., 1995—. Author: Disproportional Continue Culture of Protozooa, 1976, Continue Culture Invertebrates, 1982, Disproportional Continue Culture Method in researches of the water ecosystems, 1996; contbr. articles to profl. jours.; inventor in field. Grantee Protozoologist Soc. East Siberian Dept. Russian Acad. Scis., 1996. Mem. Ecology Club Krasnoyarsk (monetary prize 1997), N.Y. Acad. Scis. Avocations: foreign languages, music, travel. Office: Krasnoyarsk Agrarian U, 88 Mira Prospect, 660049 Krasnoyarsk Russia

SCACCHETTI, DAVID J., lawyer; b. Newark, July 13, 1956; s. Edmond and Evelyn Scacchetti; m. Marcia Ellen Gessiness, Aug. 31, 1985; children: Gabriella Elise, Olivia Beth. BA in Polit. Sci. with honors, U. Cin., 1978, JD, 1981. Bar: Ohio 1982, U.S. Dist. Ct. (so. dist.) Ohio 1982, U.S. Dist. Ct. (ea. dist.) Ky. 1986, U.S. Dist. Ct. Ariz. 1997. Atty. Edward J. Utz, Esq., Cin., 1982; sole practitioner Cin., 1982-98; atty. Scacchetti & Scacchetti, Cin., 1998—. Mem. ATLA, Nat. Assn. Criminal Def. Lawyers, Greater Cin. Criminal Def. Lawyer Assn., Ohio Acad. Trial Lawyers, Ham. County Trial Lawyers Assn., Phi Beta Kappa. Avocations: writing, tennis, Tribal art, guitar, travel. Office: Scacchetti & Scacchetti 601 Main St Fl 3D Cincinnati OH 45202-2519

SCAFFIDI, JUDITH ANN, academic administrator; b. Bklyn., Aug. 2, 1950; d. Anthony William and Rose Virginia (Nocera) S. BA, SUNY, Plattsburg, 1972, MS, 1973; postgrad., Einstein Coll. Medicine, 1983; PhD (hon.), Internat. U. Bombay, 1993; HHD (hon.), London Inst. Applied Rsch., 1993. Cert. secondary edn. English. VISTA mem. ACTION, N.Y.C., 1976-77; coord. cultural resources Learning Leaders, N.Y.C., 1977-80, tng. splst. in Bklyn., 1980—; field supr., adj. faculty Coll. for Human Svcs., N.Y.C., 1984-86; adv. coun. chair Ret. Sr. Vol. Program in Bklyn., 1983-86; adv. bd. Ret. Sr. Vol. Program in N.Y.C., 1983-86. Acvive Am. Friends Svc. Com., 1994—. Recipient award for svcs. in promotion literacy Internat. Reading Assn. and Bklyn. Reading Coun., 1986, award for outstanding leadership Ret. Sr. Vol. Program, 1986, cert. of appreciation Mayor City of N.Y., 1991, cert. of appreciation for exceptional support and encouragement of volunteerism, 1998. Mem. NAFE, Cath. Tchrs. Assn. Bklyn. (del. sch. dist. 18, 1982-91), Internat. Platform Assn., World Found. Successful Women, Am. Biog. Inst. (rsch. bd. advisors 1992-93), Am. Biog. Inst. Rsch. Assn. (bd. govs. 1992—), Internat. Parliament for Safety and Peace (dep. mem. and diplomatic passport), Maisson Internat. de Intellectuels (Acad. MIDI), Cath. Alumni Club N.Y., Amnesty Internat. Roman Catholic. Avocations: foreign and domestic travel, reading, walking. Home: 2330 Ocean Ave Apt 3H Brooklyn NY 11229-3036 Office: Learning Leaders 352 Park Ave S Fl 13 New York NY 10010-1709

SCAFFIDI-ARGENTINA, FRANCESCO CONO, nuclear engineer; b. Messina, Italy, Dec. 29, 1964; s. Carmelo Scaffidi-Argentina and Giovanna Ristuccia; m. Angela Calò, Sept. 13, 1997; 1 child, Fabio. MSc in Nuclear Engring., U. Palermo, 1990; PhD in Mech. Engring., U. Karlsruhe, 1995. Trainee Joint Rsch. Ctr., Ispra, Italy, 1989-90; rsch. fellow Nuclear Rsch. Ctr. Karlsruhe, Germany, 1992-95, sr. rsch. scientist, 1995—. Roman Catholic. Avocations: sailing, swimming. Office: Forschungszentrum Karlsruhe, Hermann-von-Helmholtz Pl 1, 76344 Eggenstein Leopoldshafen, Germany

SCAGLIONE, FRANCESCO, pharmacologist, researcher; b. Cosenza, Calabria, Italy, May 5, 1953; s. Angelo Scaglione and Assunta Fusaro; m. Patrizia Malpezzi; children: Federico, Alessandro, Caterina, Riccardo. MD, State U. of Milan, Italy, 1978. Mil. doctor Italian Air Force, Milan, 1978-81; pvt. practice Milan, 1981-83; head physician INRCA Chest Hosp., Milan, 1983-86; dir. lab. Sch. of Med. U. Milan, 1986—. Author: Antibiotico Terapia Pratica, 1990, Farmacologia Clinica Pediatrica, 1991, La Scelta Dell' Antibiotico, 1995, Dialogs on Aminoglicosides, 1998; contbr. articles to profl. jours. Home: via Pusiano 13, 20031 Cesano Maderno Milan, Italy Office: U Milan Med Sch Dept Pharm, via Vanvitelli 32, 20129 Milan Italy

SCAIFE, BRENDAN KEVIN, electrical engineer; b. London, May 19, 1928; s. James Stanley and Mary Patricia (Kavanagh) S.; m. Mary Bridget Manahan, Apr. 3, 1961; children: Neil, Edmund, Lucy, Stephen. BS in Engring., Queen Mary Coll., London, 1949, PhD, 1954; DS, U. London, 1973. Assoc. prof. elecs. Trinity Coll., Dublin, 1967-72, prof. engring. sci., 1972-86, prof. electromagnetics, 1986-88, sr. fellow, 1987-88, fellow emeritus, 1988—. Author: Principles of Dielectrics, 2d edit., 1998; editor: Vol IV Mathematical Papers of Sir William Rowan Hamilton, 2000; Studies in Numerical Analysis, 1974; contbr.: Complex Permittivity, 1971. Recipient Boyle medal Royal Budlin Soc., 1992; fellow Trinity Coll., 1964-87. Fellow Inst. Elec. Engrs., Inst. Engrs. Ireland, Inst. Physics; mem. Royal Irish Acad. Home: 6 Trimleston Ave, Dublin Ireland Office: Trinity Coll, Dept Elec Engring, Dublin 2, Ireland

SCALA, RITA NADINE, polytechnic institute official, health therapist; b. Albuquerque, Aug. 13, 1936; d. William Alexander and Rosalie (Baca) Beach; m. Paul E. Pierce, Nov. 24, 1991; 1 child, Robin Reneé Scala. BS, Auburn U., 1962; MS, St. John's U., N.Y.C., 19977, Manhattan Coll., 1984; postgrad., U. N.Mex., 1996—. Adminstr., tchr. N.Y.C. Pub. Schs., 1965-90; assoc. provost N.Mex. State U., Grants, 1990-96; coord. distance edn. U. N.Mex., Albuquerque, 1996-99; distance edn. specialist Southwestern Indian Poly. Inst., Albuquerque, 1999—; owner, mgr. Victorian Tea Room and Wellness Ctr., Albuquerque. Pres. Am. Cancer Soc., Grants, 1994. Fellow U.S. Dept. Edn., 1984. Mem. AAUW (assoc.), Internat. Soc. for Performance Improvement (bd. dirs. 1996—), Rotary (pres. Grants 1994-95, mem. found. bd. Albuquerque, Paul Harris award 1995). E-mail: nscala@sipi.bia.edu. Home: PO Box 190 Tome NM 87060-0190 Office: Southwestern Indian Poly Inst Albuquerque NM 87100

SCALES, JOHN THOMAS, state official; b. Cambridge, Mass., July 5, 1935; s. Frank and Louise Adelaide (Gifford) S. Cert.-qualified law libr. Libr. clk. Harvard U. Law Sch. Libr., Cambridge, Mass., 1955-58, Assn. Bar City N.Y., N.Y.C., 1958-60, NYU Sch. Law, N.Y.C., 1960-61; law libr. Paul, Weiss, Rifkind, Wharton & Garrison, N.Y.C., 1961-69, Kelley, Drye & Warren, N.Y.C., 1969-71; editl. asst. N.J. Law Jour., Newark, 1971; reference libr. Seton Hall U., Law Sch. Libr., Newark, 1971; asst. law libr. Essex County Law Libr., Newark, 1972-80; tech. asst. legal activities State N.J. Bd. Pub. Utilities, Newark, 1981—. Roman Catholic. Avocations: opera, professional sports, public affairs. Home: 628 Arnold Ave Point Pleasant Beach NJ 08742-2531 Office: Bd Pub Utilities State NJ 2 Gateway Ctr Newark NJ 07102-5003

SCALES, JOHN TRACEY, biomedical engineering clinician, medical consultant; b. Colchester, Eng., July 2, 1920; s. Walter Laurence and Ethel Margaret (Tracey) S.; m. Cecilia May Sparrow, May 22, 1945 (dec. 1992); children: Sally Anne Cecilia, Helen Rebecca. Student Kings Coll. London., Charing Cross Hosp. Med. Sch., London, 1938-43. Casualty officer, resident anesthetist Charing Cross Hosp., 1944; house surgeon Royal Nat. Orthop. Hosp., London and Stanmore, Eng., 1944-45, house surgeon to sr. registrar, 1947-57, from lectr. to reader, 1952-74; prof. biomed. engring. Inst. Orthop., U. London, 1974-87, prof. emeritus, 1987—; hon. dir. rsch. RAFT Inst. Plastic Surgery, Mt. Vernon Hosp., Northwood, Middlesex, Eng., 1988-93; hon. dir. pressure sore prevention RAFT Inst. Plastic Surgery, Mt. Vernon Hosp., Northwood, Eng., 1994-97; hon. cons. Mt. Vernon Hosp., Northwood, 1968-97, Royal Orthop. Hosp., Birmingham, 1978-87, Royal Nat. Orthop. Hosp., London, 1958—; vis. prof. Cranfield U., 1997-98. Contbr. over 175 publs. to profl. jours. and books. Capt. Royal Army Med. Corps, 1945-47. Decorated officer Order Brit. Empire, 1988; recipient T.H. Green prize in surgery, 1943, award for contbns. to applied rsch. in biomaterials Clemson U., 1974, A.A. Griffith silver medal Inst. Materials, 1980; named to Hon. Order Ky. Cols., 1986; elected Freeman, City of London, 1995. Fellow Biol. Engring. Soc. (hon.), Inst. Physics and Engring. in Medicine (hon.), Royal Coll. Surgeons Eng. (James Berrie prize 1973), Royal Soc. Medicine (S.G. Brown award 1974), Brit. Med. Assn., Brit. Orthopaedic Assn. (sr. companion), Brit. Assn. Plastic Surgeons (hon.). Achievements include development of polymeric orthopaedic splints and appliances, 1945-51; demonstration of vascular supply of organs and preservation of tissues using polyester resins, 1949-50; development of major bone and joint prostheses and standard total joint replacements using metals and polymers, 1947-87; development of British Cuirass Respirator, female urniary apparatus, 1950-53, Airstrip dressings, air support systems for prevention of pressure sores-high air loss and low air loss beds and Verperm permeable matress, 1960-82. Avocation: china. Fax: 44 (0) 1189844945. Home: Fairbanks, Riverview Rd, Pangbourne RG8 7AU, England

SCALES, MARJORIE LAHR, pastoral counselor; b. Tampa, Fla., Oct. 6, 1935; d. E. Scott and Cecile Celeste (Rittgers) Lahr; m. Kenneth I. Scales, July 2, 1955; children: David, Daniel, Donald, Darrell, Kristofer, Kurt, Maryanne. AS, Ind. U., 1955; BA, Jacksonville (Fla.) U., 1990; M in Pastoral Studies, Loyola U., 1990; EdS, U. Fla., 1990, EdD, 1995. Cert. pastoral counseling trainer, lic. mental health counselor, Fla. Pastoral counselor Sacred Heart Ch., Jacksonville, 1990—; v.p. Ind. U. Dental Hygiene, Indpls., 1954-55; prof. Diocesan Formation Studies, Jacksonville, 1991. Contbr. articles to profl. jours. Chmn. Westside Single Cath. Adults, Jacksonville, 1988-91; facilitator Diocesan Ladies Group, 1987-90; co-dir. Contemporary Ch. Choir, Jacksonville, 1981—; treas. St. Johns Country Day Sch., Orang Park, Fla., 1980. Acad. scholar Jacksonville U., 1989-90. Mem. ACA, Nat. Bd. Cert. Counselor, Chi Sigma Iota, Phi Kappa Phi. Avocations: playing musical instruments, reading, creative writing, hiking. Office: 4116 Blanding Blvd Jacksonville FL 32210-5419

SCALISE-QUBROSI, CELESTE, lawyer; b. San Antonio, May 15, 1959; d. Robert and Edna (King) Scalise; m. James S. Boyd Jr., Oct. 6, 1984 (div. Dec. 1988); m. Marshall Bruce Lloyd, May 13, 1989 (div. July 1995); m. Khalil Qubrosi, Feb. 16, 1997. BA, U. Tex., San Antonio, 1979; JD, Tex. Tech U., 1983. Bar: Tex. 1984, U.S. Ct. Appeals (5th cir.) 1984, U.S. Dist. Ct. (so. dist.) Tex. 1985, U.S. Dist. Ct. (no. dist.) Tex. 1990, U.S. Dist. Ct. (we. dist.) Tex. 1991, U.S. Dist Ct. (ea. dist.) Tex. 1992. Field ops. asst. Bur. of Census U.S. Dept. of Commerce, San Antonio, 1980; title examiner, law clk. Lubbock (Tex.) Abstract & Title Co., 1982-83; assoc. Bonilla & Berlanga, Corpus Christi, Tex., 1983-89; sr. assoc. Heard, Goggan, Blair & Williams, San Antonio, 1989-90; assoc. Denton & McKamie, San Antonio, 1990, Joe Weiss and Assocs., San Antonio, 1990; field litigation office Cigna litigation atty. Law Offices of Sean P. Martinez, San Antonio, 1990-97; pres. Fountain Rorm, Inc.; of counsel Aaron & Quirk, San Antonio, 1997-99, Law Office of Scalise-Qubrosi, 1999—; mem. adv. group Camino Real Health Systems Agy., Inc., San Antonio, 1978-80. Mem. substance abuse adv. com. Planned Parenthood Bd., Corpus Christi, 1983-85; vice chair Nueces County Mental Health/Mental Retardation Substance Abuse Com., San Antonio, 1987-89; mem. vestry Trinity Episcopal Ch. Mem. Tex. Bar Assn. (govt. lawyers sect., ins. def.), San Antonio Bar Assn., U. Tex. at San Antonio Alumni Assn., Delta Theta Phi. Episcopalian. Avocations: photography, reading, gem and minerals collector. Home: 2130 W Gramercy Pl San Antonio TX 78201-4822 Office: Law Offices Scalise - Qubrosi 105 Furr Dr San Antonio TX 78201-4412

SCALZA, MARGARET T., publishing executive; b. Jersey City, May 27, 1936; d. Louis Patrick and Josephine M. (Cleary) Scalza; m. David Jenkins, Sept. 30, 1951 (div. 1962); children: Alison Brittain, Cynthia Higgins, Ann Jenkins Tunis;. Owner Towne House Restaurant, Hackettstown, N.J., 1963-65; pres. Kinsley Assocs., Inc., Hackettstown, N.J., 1966—; pub. purchasing guides, sch. directories, N.J., N.Y., Calif., Ill. Co-chmn. Northwestern N.J. divsn. U.S. Postal Customer Coun., 1978—. Mem. NAFE, Nat. Assn. Sch. Bus. Ofcls., North Ctrl. Jersy Assn. Realtors, Hackettstown Trade Assn. (sec.-treas., bd. dirs. 1963). Republican. Methodist. Avocations: cooking, sewing, reading, flower arranging, crabbing. Home: 9 House Wren Hackettstown NJ 07840-2815 Office: 8 Ridge Rd Hackettstown NJ 07840-4602

SCAMBLER, PETER JAMES, molecular medicine educator, researcher; b. Ormskirk, U.K., Nov. 6, 1958; s. John Dodson and Barbara (Caldwell) S.; m. Sarah Miriam Fisher, July 3, 1982; children: Christopher James, Catherine Pamela. BS in Med. Biochemistry with honors, Manchester (Eng.) U., 1979, MB, BChir, 1982, MD, 1986. House officer Hope Hosp., Salford, Eng., 1982, Victoria Hosp., Blackpool, 1983; sr. lectr. St. Mary's Hosp. Med. Sch., London, 1988-90, med. rsch. coun. human genome mapping sr. rsch. fellow, 1990-92; unit head Inst. Child Health, London, 1993—, theme leader, 1999—; cons. Axys Pharms., San Diego, 1998-2000. Contbr. articles to profl. jours. Recipient Spl. Merit award British United Provident Assn., 1993; Programme grant Brit. Heart Found., 1996. Fellow Royal Coll. Pathologists London; mem. Am. Soc. Human Genetics, Brit. Soc. Devel. Biology, Brit. Soc. Human Genetics. Avocations: soccer, running. Office: Inst Child Health, 30 Gulfordst, London WC1N 1EH, England

SCAMMELL, GEOFFREY VAUGHAN, historian, educator; b. Wallasey, Cheshire, Eng., July 11, 1925; s. Edwin and Mabel Beatrice (Vaughan) S.; m. Jean Margaret Elders, Oct. 3, 1953; 1 child, Peter Geoffrey. BA, Emmanuel Coll., 1948, MA, 1953. Research asst. U. Durham, Eng., 1949-51; lectr. U. Durham, 1951-52; fellow Emmanuel Coll. U. Cambridge, Eng., 1952-53; lectr. U. Durham, 1953-65; lectr., fellow Pembroke Coll. U. Cambridge, 1965-92, dir. studies in history, 1965-92, Leverhulme fellow Pembroke Coll., 1985-87; emeritus fellow Pembroke Coll. U., Cambridge, 1992—; mem. council Soc. Nautical Research, 1963-66, Hakluyt Soc., 1981-86; chmn. Brit. com. Internat. Maritime History Com., 1978-89. Author: Hugh Du Puiset, 1956, The World Encompassed, 1981, The Great Chartered Companies and the Sea, 1983, The First Imperial Age, 1989, Ships, Oceans and Empire, 1995; editor: Seas in History, 1991—; contbr. articles to profl. jours. Lt. Royal Navy, 1943-46. Recipient Prince Consort prize U. Cambridge, 1952, Notable Naval Book of 1982 award, U.S. Naval Inst., 1983. Mem. Little Ship Club. Club: Little Ship. Home: 137 Huntingdon Rd, Cambridge CB3 0DQ, England Office: U Cambridge, Pembroke Coll, Cambridge CB2 1RF, England

SCANCELLA, ROBERT J., civil engineer; b. Bristol, Pa., July 10, 1955; s. John Robert and MaryLou (Perkins) S.; m. Carol Ann Scannella, May 22, 1977; children: Jennifer, Dante, Joseph, John. BSCE, The Citadel, 1977; Cert. Pub. Mgr., Rutgers U., 1989. Transp. engr. Wash. Dept. Transp., Longview, 1977-80, N.J. Dept. Transp., Trenton, 1980-99; project mgr. SITE-Blauvelt Engrs., 1999—; task force mem. Constrn. Engring. Manpower Mgmt., Trenton, 1977-80; program chmn. Nat. Structural Materials Tech. Conf.; project mgr. Am. Assn. State Hwy. and Transp. Ofcls., N.J. Dept. Transp. Co-author tng. video: The Resident Engineer as a Witness, 1989; co-author manuals for N.J. Dept. Transp., 1982, 83, 86. Fellow ASCE, Am. Soc. Hwy. Engrs.; mem. Bayville Bus. Assn., KC (Grand Knight 1989-90). Republican. Roman Catholic. Home: 252 Point Pleasant Ave Bayville NJ 08721-1355

SCANIO, CHARLES JOHN VINCENT, chemist; b. Ann Arbor, Mich., June 23, 1940; s. Vincent A. and Georgette C. (Maulbetsch) S.; m. Kaaren Wellman, July 3, 1965; children: Erik W., Kurt C. BS in Chemistry, U. Mich., 1962; PhD, Northwestern U., 1966. Cert. profl. engr. Asst. prof. chemistry Iowa State U., Ames, 1966-72; staff chemist Pfizer, Inc., Groton, Conn., 1972-77; head process, research and devel. UpJohn Co., North Haven, Conn., 1977-84; corp. dir. research and devel. ChemDesign Corp., Fitchburg, Mass., 1984-86; exec. v.p. ChemSultants Internat., Inc., Winchendon, Mass., 1986-92; pres. Secant Chemicals, Inc., Winchendon, 1992—. Contbr. articles to profl. jours.; editor Jour. Radiation Curing, 1983. Mem. Planning and Zoning Commn., North Branford, Conn., 1983-84; v.p. Zoning Task Force, Winchendon, 1985-86, Indsl. Devel. Commn., Winchendon, 1985-90, Fin. Commn., Winchendon, 1989-90; mem. PCB Adv. Commn., 1990—; mem. Zoning Bd. Appeals, Winchendon, 1999—. Recipient Teaching award Iowa State U., 1969. Mem. Am. Chem. Soc., Chem. Soc. London, Sigma Xi. Republican. Achievements include 2 patents. Home and Office: PO Box 246 Winchendon MA 01475-0246

SCANLAN, JOHN OLIVER, electronic engineering educator; b. Dublin, Ireland, Sept. 20, 1937; s. John and Hannah Scanlan; m. Ann Weadock, June 20, 1961. BE, U. Coll. Dublin, 1959, ME, 1963; PhD, U. Leeds, Eng., 1964; DSc, Nat. U. Ireland, 1972. Rsch. engr. Mullard Rsch. Labs., Redhill, Eng., 1959-63; lectr. U. Leeds, 1963-68, prof. electronic engring., 1968-73; prof. electronic engring. U. Coll. Dublin, 1973—; dep. chmn. Telecom. Eireann, Dublin, 1983-97, also bd. dirs. Fellow IEEE, Inst. Elect. Engr., Inst. Engrs. Ireland, Inst. Maths. and Its Applications; mem. Royal Irish Acad. (pres. 1993-96), Academia Europaea. Office: U Coll Dublin, Dublin 4, Ireland also: Royal Irish Acad, 19 Dawson St, Dublin 2, Ireland

SCANLAN, PAPALI'I TOMMY, bank executive; b. Apia, Western Samoa, Aug. 3, 1953; s. Robert Dempsey and Tauvaga (Nive) S.; m. Carmelita Lam, Feb. 28, 1981 (div.); children: Etuale, Kristian, Tyson, Warwick, Tommy Jr., Tehania Kalei; m. Joyce Wetzedd, Feb., 1998. BS, U. Canterbury, Christ Church, New Zealand, 1977. Rsch. officer Western Samoa Treasury Dept., Apia, 1977-80; project officer Forum Secretariat, Suva, Fiji, 1981-84; energy advisor Forum Secretariat, Suva, 1984; mgr. internat. dept. Cen. Bank of Samoa, Apia, 1985-88, gen. mgr., chief exec., 1989-94, 95—; gov., 1994-95. Roman Catholic. Avocations: tennis, swimming, reading, running, golf. Home: PO Box 321, Apia Western Samoa

SCANLON, EDWARD CHARLES, clinical psychologist; b. Bradford, Pa., Dec. 3, 1931; s. Edward John Scanlan and Martha (Karlous) Charles; m. Constance Morgan, May 19, 1962 (div. Jan. 1976); 1 child, Heather Marie. AB cum laude, SUNY, Buffalo, 1954; EdM, Harvard U., 1958, EdD, 1961; postgrad., Columbia U. Lic. psychologist, Pa. Assoc. prof. Lehigh U., Bethlehem, Pa., 1961-66; acad. dean Montgomery County C.C., Conshahoken, Pa., 1966-69; acting. dir. home sch. Wilkes Coll., Wilkes Barre, Pa., 1968-71; clin. psychologist dept. human svcs. mental health and mental retardation Northampton County Dept. Human Svcs., Easton, Pa., 1972—; vis. prof. clin. psychology Clinic Mental Health and Mental Retardation, Pottsville, Pa., 1971-72. Capt. USAF, 1954-57. Thayer scholar Harvard U. Mem. APA, Pa. Psychol. Assn., Harvard Club of Phila., Lehigh Country Club, Masons, Phi Beta Kappa. Democrat. Anglican. Avocations: classic automobiles, psychoanalytic studies. Office: Bridal Path Woods D-2 Bethlehem PA 18017

SCANLON, LAWRENCE EUGENE, English language educator; b. Montclair, N.J., Sept. 12, 1927; s. Leo Dudley and Margaret Gertrude (Kennedy) S.; m. Anne Maxwell Sherrerd, Aug. 23, 1952; children: Lawrence Francis, Neal Patrick, Heidi Anne. BA, Wesleyan U., 1951; MA, Rutgers U., 1952; PhD, Syracuse U., 1958. Asst. prof. English Mount Holyoke Coll., South Hadley, Mass., 1958-63; prof. Hartford (Conn.) Coll. for Women, 1963-92. Author: First Came Commodore Perry, 1969, A Memorial of Ebensee, 1994, The Story He Left Behind Him Paddy the Cope, 1994. Justice of the peace Town of East Granby, Conn., 1970-72; v.p. Capital Region Libr. Coun., Hartford, 1970-74. With U.S. Army, 1945-46. Fulbright grantee, Austria, 1952-53, Japan, 1964-65, West Germany, 1980-81, summer grantee NEH, 1974. Avocations: writing, travel, investing. Home: 101 Holcomb St East Granby CT 06026-9531

SCANNELL, JOHN R., publishing consultant; b. Dobbs Ferry, N.Y., Dec. 23, 1947; s. John Joseph and Veronica Rose (Hannigan) S.; m. Faye Naomi Snyder, July 11, 1969; children: Michelle, Amanda, Rebecca, Benjamin. BS in Edn., Kutztown (Pa.) State Coll., 1965; MA in Speech, U. Wash., 1974. Tchr. English Nazareth (Pa.) Sch. Dist., 1969-70, Upper Dauphin Sch. Dist., Elizabethville, Pa., 1970-72; tchr. Bellevue (Wash.) Sch. Dist., 1974-85; sales rep. Macmillan Pub., Seattle, 1985-88; sr. nat. cons. social studies and lang. arts McGraw-Hill Pub., Bothell, Wash., 1988—. Pres., Our Lady of Lake Parents Club, Seattle, 1981-83; dir. Our Lady of Lake Players, Seattle, 1980, 82, 84. Recipient Wilma Grimes award U. Wash., 1972; named DECA Tchr. of Yr., Nazareth H.S., 1970. Mem. Nat. Coun. Tchrs. English, Nat. Coun. for Social Studies, Nat. Hist. Soc. Democrat. Roman Catholic. Avocation: woodworking, reading. Home: 22627 7th Dr SE Bothell WA 98021-8274

SCANNELL, THOMAS JOHN, cold metal forming company executive; b. Detroit, Sept. 11, 1954; s. Robert Michael and Mary Frances (Chadwick) S. AS, Henry Ford Community Coll., Dearborn, Mich., 1982; BME, U. Detroit, 1988. Gen. laborer Fed. Screw Works, Romulus, Mich., 1973-82, supr. tool store, 1982-84, tool design engr. III, 1984-86, tool design engr. II, 1986-88, tool design engr. I, 1988-90, mgr. tool engring., 1990-99; owner Great Lakes News Distributors, 1986—; exec. v.p. Detroit Hockey Assn. Hockey coach Detroit Police Athletic League. Mem. Soc. Mfg. Engrs. Avocations: golf, skiing, automobile restoration. Office: Great Lakes News 23440 Kean St Dearborn MI 48124-1821

SCANNELL, WILLIAM EDWARD, aerospace company executive, consultant, psychologist; b. Muscatine, Iowa, Nov. 11, 1934; s. Mark Edward and Catharine Pearson (Fowler) S.; m. Barbara Ann Hoemann, Nov. 23, 1957; children: Cynthia Kay, Mark Edward, David Jerome, Terri Lynn, Stephen Patrick. BA in Gen. Edn., U. Nebr., 1961; BS in Engring., Ariz. State U., 1966; MS in Systems Engring., So. Meth. U., 1969; postgrad. in law, Western State U., 1977, 81-82; PhD, U.S. Internat. U., 1991. Commd. 2d lt. USAF, 1956, advanced through grades to lt. col., 1972; B-47 navigator-bombardier 98th Bomb Wing, Lincoln Air Force Base, Nebr., 1956-63; with Air Force Inst. of Tech., 1963-65, 68-69; chief mgmt. engring. team RAF Bentwaters, England, 1965-68; forward air contr. 20th Tactical Air Support Squadron USAF, Danang, Vietnam, 1970-71; program mgr. Hdqrs. USAF, Washington, 1971-74, staff asst. Office of Sec. Def., 1974-75, ret., 1975; account exec. Merrill Lynch, San Diego, 1975-77; program engring. chief Gen. Dynamics, San Diego, 1977-79, engring. chief, 1979-80, program mgr., 1980-83; mgr. integrated logistics support Northrop Corp., Hawthorne, Calif., 1984-88; mgr. B-2 program planning and scheduling Northrop Corp., Pico Rivera, Calif., 1988-91; pres. Scannell and Assocs., Borrego Springs, Calif., 1991—. Author: The Nature of Motivation in Aerospace Executives, 1991. Cpl. USNG, 1952-54. Decorated DFC with three oak leaf clusters, Air medal with 11 oak leaf clusters. Mem. APA, Calif. Psychol. Assn., Soc. Indsl. and Orgnl. Psychology, Inst. Indsl. Engrs., Coronado Cays Yacht Club, De Anza Country Club, Psi Chi. Republican. Roman Catholic. Home: 37146 Turnberry Isle Dr Palm Desert CA 92211-2125

SCANNONE, JUAN CARLOS, philosophy educator, priest; b. Buenos Aires, Sept. 2, 1931; s. Juan Antonio and Rosa Fabiana (Ojuez) S. Lic. in philosophy, Philos. Faculty, San Miguel, Argentina, 1956; lic. in theology, Theol. Faculty, Innsbruck, Austria, 1963; PhD, Philos. Faculty, Munich, 1967. Prof. philosophy Univ. del Salvador, San Miguel, 1968—, dean philos. faculty, 1970-80, pres., 1992—; guest prof. Hochschule für Philosophie, Munich, 1983, 89, State U., Frankfurt, Germany, 1989, State U. Salzburg, Austria, 1992, Gregorian U., Rome, 1996—. Author: Sein und Inkarnation, 1968, Teologia de la Liberacion y Praxis popular, 1976, Teología de la liberación, 1987, Evangelización, cultura, teologia, 1990, Nuevo punto de partida en la filosofía latinoamericana, 1990, Weisheit und Befreiung, 1992. Mem. Acad. Scientiarum Europea. Roman Catholic. Home: Avenida Mitre 3226, 1663 San Miguel de Tucuman Argentina Office: U Salvador Faculty Philos, Casilla de correo 10, 1663 San Miguel de Tucuman Argentina

SCAPERDAS, AGNES COSTAS, distillery executive; b. N.Y.C., Feb. 2, 1967; d. Costas Basil and Helen Nikolaos (Papias) S.; m. Spyros Pandelis Alamanis, Feb. 14, 1993. BSc, Nat. Tech. U. Athens, Greece, 1990. Lab. rsch. asst. Ekosa, Athens, 1989-90; prodn. mgr. Entarco SA, Kiffissia, Greece, 1991-93; quality control mgr. S&E&A Metaxa Abe, Kiffissia, 1993-94, mgr. packaging devel., 1994-98, brand tech. mgr., 1998—. Mem. Tehc. Chamber of Greece, Greek Assn. Chem. Engrs. Home: 2 Macedonias/Ag Paraskevis, 14561 Kifissia Greece Office: S&E&SA Metaxa ABE, 6 A Metaxa St, 14564 Kiffissia Greece

SCARAMUZZI, FRANCO, agricultural sciences educator; b. Ferrara, Italy, Dec. 26, 1926; s. Donato and Albertina (Rovida) S.; m. Maria Bianca Cancellieri, Jan. 15, 1955; children: Donato Eugenio, Maria Oliva. PhD in Agrl. Scis., U. Bari, 1948. Asst. prof. U. Florence, 1948-59; prof. U. Pisa, 1959-69, U. Florence, 1969—; rector U. Florence, 1979-91; mem. Acad. Agrl. Sci., Moscow, 1982; pres. honor Italian Hort. Soc., 1976-83. Editor-in-chief Advances in Horticultural Sci., 1976-83. Mem. Internat. Soc. Hort. Sci. Wageningen (past pres., Holland), Acad. Georgofili (pres. Florence chpt. 1986—), Acad. Vine and Wine (pres. honor Siena (Italy) chpt. 1984—), Rotary (hon.). Home: Vle Amendola 38, 50121 Florence Italy Office: U Florence Dept Horticulture, Via Donizetti 6, 50144 Florence Italy

SCARANO, FULVIO, aerospace engineer, fluid mechanics researcher; b. Naples, Italy, Dec. 15, 1968; s. Tullio Scarano and Maria Renaudi. Lic. aerospace engr., U. Naples Federico II, 1996, PhD in Aerospace Engring., 1999; diploma course, von Karman Inst., Rhode-St. Genese, Belgium, 1997. Fulid mechanics rschr. von Karman Inst. Fluid Dynamics, Rhode-St. Genese. Contbg. author: Developments in Laser Techniques and Fluid Mechanics, 1999; contbr. articles to sci. juors., including Expts. in Fluids, Physics of Fluids. Marie Curie rsch. tng. grantee European Commn., 1998. Avocations: track and field athletics, classical and jazz music. Office: von Karman Inst, 72 Chaussee de Waterloo, B-1640 Rhode-Saint Genese Belgium

SCARBOROUGH, CHARLES BISHOP, III, broadcast journalist, writer; b. Pitts., Nov. 4, 1943; s. Charles Bishop and Esther Francis (Campbell) S.; m. Linda Anne Gross, Dec. 14, 1972; children: Charles Bishop IV, Elizabeth Anne; m. Anne Ford Uzielli, Oct. 2, 1982; m. Ellen Carol Ward, Sept. 25, 1994. B.S., U. So. Miss., 1969. Prodn. mgr. Sta.-WLOX-TV, Biloxi, Miss., 1966-68; reporter, anchorman Sta.-WDAM-TV, Hattiesburg, Miss., 1968-69; reporter, anchorman, mng. editor Sta.-WAGA-TV, Atlanta, 1969-72; reporter, anchorman Sta.-WNAC-TV, Boston, 1972-74, NBC News, N.Y.C., 1974—. Author: (novels) Stryker, 1978, The Myrmidon Project, 1981, Aftershock, 1991. Served with USAF, 1961-65. Recipient awards for journalism AP (9), 1976-92, Emmy awards (24), 1974-2000, award Aviation/Space Writers Assn., 1977, 78, 88, UPI award for journalism N.Y. Press Club award, 1988, 89, Sigma Delta Chi award, Deadline Club award, Terry Anderson Journalism award Working Press Assn. N.J., 1992. Mem. Phi Kappa Phi. Office: NBC News 30 Rockefeller Plz Fl 2 New York NY 10112-0036

SCARLAT, FLOREA, physicist, educator, research scientist; b. Radomiresti, Romania, Aug. 10, 1939; s. Ion and Floarea Scarlat; m. Rodica Candiori, Aug. 21, 1969; 1 child, Florin. Degree in engring. physics, Politechnica U., Bucharest, 1965; grad., Inst. Atomica Physics, Bucharest, 1974. Physicist engr. Inst. Atomic physics, Bucharest, 1964-67, sci. rschr. III, 1968-76, sci. rschr. II, 1977-92; sr. scientist Nat. Inst. for Laser, Plasma and Radiation Physics, Bucharest, 1993—; assoc. prof. physics Politechnica U., Bucharest, 1994-97; prof. sci. and physics Valachia State U., Targoviste, 1998—; sci. dir. Inst. for Physics and Nuclear Engring., Bucharest; dir. GEC-RON Brit.-Romanian Soc., Eng. Sublt. Romanian mil., 1964. Mem. European Phys. Soc., European Soc. for Therapeutic Radiology and Oncology, Balkan Union Oncology, N.Y. Acad. Scis. Orthodox. Avocation: chess. Office: Nat Inst Laser Plasma Rad, Atomistilor 111, R-76900 Magurele, Bucharest Romania

SCAROLA, SUSAN MARGARET, lawyer; b. Elizabeth, N.J., Mar. 19, 1948; d. Anthony and Ruth (Cohen) S. BA cum laude, Thiel Coll., 1970; JD, Rutgers-State of U. of N.J., 1976. Bar: N.J. 1976, N.Y. 1985, Fla. 1993; cert. criminal trial atty., matrimonial law atty. Law sec. to Judge Triarsi, Superior Ct. of N.J., Elizabeth, 1976-77; asst. prosecutor Union County Prosecutor's Office, Elizabeth, 1997-88; non-equity ptnr. Lomurro Davison Eastman & Munoz, Freehold, N.J., 1988-97; ptnr. Newman Scarola & Assocs., Freehold, N.J., 1997—; judge Mcpl. Ct., Twp. of Old Bridge, 1999—. Trustee Legal Aid Soc. of Monmouth County, 1992, sec., 1998—; committeewoman Old Bridge Dem. Com., 1995-99. Named Women of Yr. Women Lawyers in Monmouth County, 1994. Mem. Monmouth Bar Assn. (chair family law com. 1995-97), N.J. Bar Assn., Fla. Bar Assn., Middlesex County Bar Assn. Office: Newman Scarola & Assocs 64 W Main St Freehold NJ 07728-2142

SCARPA, ANGELA, psychology educator; b. Hoboken, N.J., May 1, 1966; d. Emilio and Rosina Scarpa; m. Bruce Howard Friedman, Aug. 10, 1997. BS, St. Peter's Coll., 1988; MA, U. So. Calif., L.A., 1990, PhD, 1993. Lic. clin. psychologist, Commonwealth Va.; diplomate Am. Bd. Psychol. Specialties, Am. Coll. Forensic Examiners. Asst. prof. psychology Ea. Wash. U., Cheney, 1994-96, U. Ga., Athens, 1996-97, Va. Poly. Inst. and State U., Blacksburg, 1997—; psychology program cons. Dept. VA Med. Ctr., Salem, 1998—. Consulting editor Jour. Clin. Child Psychology, 1999—; contbr. chpt. to book and articles to profl. jours. Mem. APA, Am. Psychol. Soc., Soc. for Psychophysiol. Rsch., Internat. Soc. for Rsch. in Agression. E-mail: ascarpa@vt.edu. Fax: 540-231-3652. Office: Va Tech Dept Psychology 5088 Derring Hall Blacksburg VA 24061

SCARPELLI, VITO, adult education educator, administrator; b. Passaic, N.J., July 17, 1946; s. Peter and Celia (Pignataro) S.; m. JoAnn Motti, Aug. 23, 1970; children: Anthony, Michele. BA in Acctg. and Edn., Montclair State Coll., 1968; MA, Kean Coll., 1984; postgrad., St. Peters, Jersey City State U., Seton Hall U., Kans. State U. Prin. Roselle Park Mid. Sch., 1996—; supr. P. Scarpelli & Sons, Nutley, N.J.; bus. adminstr. John J. Baum, Inc., Wayne, N.J.; salesman Realty World-Monaco Realty, Nutley; asst. track coach, tchr. jr. H.S. Belleville Bd. Edn., 1968-69; dir. adult edn. and summer programs Roselle Park (N.J.) Bd. Edn., 1969—; dir. Union County Summer Youth Employment and Tng., Roselle Park, 1986, asst. curriculum coord., 1992-96, dir. tech., 1993-96; adj. prof. Jersey City State Coll., 1993-96. Pres. Nutley Am. Little League, 1987—; v.p. Nutley Basketball Assn.; past pres. Lincoln Sch. PTA. Mem. NEA, N.J. Bus. Edn. Assn., N.J. Edn. Assn., Roselle Park Edn. Assn., LERN, KC (grand knight 1976). Democrat. Roman Catholic. Avocation: fishing. Home: 81 Milton Ave Nutley NJ 07110-3017 Office: Roselle Park Bd Edn 510 Chestnut St Roselle Park NJ 07204-1928

SCARPINATI, MARCO, neurosurgeon, consultant; b. Rome, Nov. 14, 1960; s. Paolo Scarpinati and Gilda Rosso; m. Piera Catalano, Oct. 4, 1993. MD, U. Rome, 1988, specialization in neurosurgery, 1993. Resident dept. neurosurgery U. Rome, 1988-93; cons. neurosurgeon Mil. Policlinic, Rome, 1993—; mem. XI Italian Antarctic Expedition, 1996, Nat. Program of Rsch. in Antarctica, 1996—; med. officer HQ NATO SFOR, Sarajevo, 1997; med. advisor Italian com. UNICER, 1998; med. dir. RC5-Pristina OSCE Kosovo Verification Mission. Contbr. articles to profl. jours. Capt. Italian Army Med. Corps, 1993—. Mem. Italian Soc. Neurosurgery, Order of Malta. Avocations: literature, golf, photography. Office: Policlinico Militare, Piazza Celimontana 50, 00184 Rome Italy

SCARPONI, CLAUDIO, laboratory administrator, consultant; b. Rome, Oct. 3, 1953; s. Mario and Valentina (Speranza) S. Mech. Engr., U. Rome, 1978. Rsch. engr. Centro Sperimentale Metallurgico, Rome, 1979-80; structural analysis engr. Aeritalia-Settore Energie Alternative, Rome, 1980-81, sys. engr., 1981-85; lab. head aerospace dept. engring. faculty Postgrad. Aerospace Sch., U. Rome, 1986; lectr. nat. and internat. meetings. Contbr. articles to profl. jours. Avocations: sailing, skiing, horseback riding, travel. Address: Piza Tuscolo 5, 00183 Rome Italy

SCARRITT, RICHARD WINN, lawyer; b. Enid, Okla., Dec. 13, 1938; s. Nathan Spencer and Rilla Fayette (Winn) S.; m. Gloria June Gaba, Nov. 7, 1966 (div. Nov. 1971); m. Deborah Louise Guillemot, Sept. 3, 1986; 1 child, Nathan Spencer IV; ward, Samantha Jo Wickizer. BA, Okla. U., 1960; JD,

Harvard U., 1963. Bar: Mo. 1963, U.S. Dist. Ct. (we. dist.) Mo. 1964, U.S. Supreme Ct. 1971. Assoc. Spencer, Fane, Britt & Browne, Kansas City, Mo., 1963-68, ptnr., chmn. real estate sect., 1969—; guest lectr. real estate law U. Mo. Extension Ctr., Independence, 1966-68; mem. panel of arbitrators Am. Arbitration Assn.; chmn. standard forms com., mem. govt. affairs, zoning law and legis. coms. Met. Real Estate Bd. Greater Kansas City; panelist Plaza West Assn., Kansas City, 1971-78. Co-author: Missouri Real Estate Forms and Practice, 1988, supplements, 1989-98. Mem. Clay County Econ. Devel. Coun.; dir. Brookside Roller Hockey League, Kansas City Jr. Blades Amateur Hockey Assn. Fellow Am. Coll. Real Estate Lawyers (attys.' opinions com., planning com.); mem. ABA (real property, probate and trust law sect., loan documentation, real estate financing and comml. fin. svcs., environ. law com. subcom. energy law and real property, corp., banking and bus. law sect., comml. fin. svcs. com.), Mo. Bar Assn. (property law com., adv. coun., energy law com.), Kansas City Met. Bar Assn. (real estate law com., chmn. com. coun.), Lawyers Assn. Kansas City, Mo. C. of C., Kansas City Club, SAR, Mensa, Phi Delta Theta. Republican. Episcopalian. Avocations: photography, collecting art, electronics, computers, youth sports. Fax: 816-474-3216. E-mail: rws@spencerfane.com. Home: 825 W 53rd Ter Kansas City MO 64112-2327 Office: Spencer Fane Britt & Browne 1000 Walnut St Ste 1400 Kansas City MO 64106-2140

SCASTA, DAVID LYNN, forensic psychiatrist; b. Austin, Tex., Dec. 13, 1949; s. Albert Ray and Helen Pearl (Hennessy) S. BA, Baylor U., 1972, MD, 1977. Diplomate Am. Bd. Psychiatry and Neurology. Staff physician U. Houston, 1977-78; adminstr. Temple U. Med. Sch., Phila., 1982-83; resident in psychiatry Temple U. Hosp., Phila., 1982; dir. consultation svcs. Grad. Hosp., Phila., 1983-84; dir. outpatient programs Phila. Psychiat. Ctr., 1983-84; pvt. practice Grad. Hosp. Phila. Psychiat. Ctr., 1984-89; med. dir. Phila. Consultation Ctr., 1987-89; attending psychiatrist Hunterdon Med. Ctr., Flemington, N.J., 1989-98, chmn. dept. psychiatry, 1996-97; pvt. practice New Hope, Pa., 1989-98; clin. assoc. prof. dept. psychiatry Temple U. Med. Sch., Phila., 1983—. Editor Jour. of Gay & Lesbian Psychotherapy, 1987-98. Dist. rep. Rep. Party of Tex., Houston, 1977, precinct sec., 1975-77; bd. dirs. Phila. Bapt. Assn., mem. exec. com. Named Ginsberg Fellow Group for Advancement of Psychiatry, 1980-82. Fellow Am. Psychiat. Assn. (pres. Caucus of lesbian, gay and bisexual mems. 1996-97); mem. AMA, Assn. Gay and Lesbian Psychiatrists (pres. 1995-97, newsletter editor 1987-94), Am. Acad. Psychiatry and the Law, Am. Coll. Forensic Examiners. Republican. Avocations: skiing, antiques. Office: Ind Psychiat Svcs 115 Commons Way Princeton NJ 08540-1507

SCATENA, LORRAINE BORBA, rancher, women's rights advocate; b. San Rafael, Calif., Feb. 18, 1924; d. Joseph and Eugenia (Simas) de Borba; m. Louis G. Scatena, Feb. 14, 1960; children: Louis Vincent, Eugenia Gayle. BA, Dominican Coll., San Rafael, 1945; postgrad., Calif. Sch. Fine Arts, 1948, U. Calif., Berkeley, 1956-57. Cert. elem. tchr., Calif. Tchr. Dominican Coll., 1946; tchr. of mentally handicapped San Anselmo (Calif.) Sch. Dist., 1946; tchr. Fairfax (Calif.) Pub. Elem. Sch., 1946-53; asst. to mayor Fairfax City Recreation, 1948-53; tchr., libr. U.S. Dependent Schs., Mainz am Rhine, Fed. Republic Germany, 1953-56; translator Portugal Travel Tours, Lisbon, 1954; bonding sec. Am. Fore Ins. Group, San Francisco, 1958-60; rancher, farmer Yerington, Nev., 1960-98; hostess com. Caldecott and Newbury Authors' Awards, San Francisco, 1959; mem. Nev. State Legis. Commn., 1975; coord. Nevadans for Equal Rights Amendment, 1975-78, rural areas rep., 1976-78; testifier Nev. State Senate and Assembly, 1975, 77; mem. adv. com. Fleischmann Coll. Agr. U. Nev., 1977-80, 81-84; speaker Grants and Rsch. Projects, Bishop, Calif., 1977, Choices for Tomorrow's Women, Fallon, Nev., 1989; presenter in field. Trustee Wassuk Coll., Hawthorne, Nev., 1984-87; mem. Lyon County Friends of Libr., Yerington, 1971—, Lyon County Mus. Soc., 1978—; sec., pub. info. chmn. Lyon County Rep. Ctrl. Com., 1973-74; mem. Marin County Soc. Artists, San Anselmo, Calif., 1948-53; charter mem. Eleanor Roosevelt Edn. Fund for Women and Girls, 1990, sustaining mem., 1992—; Nev. rep. 1st White House Conf. Rural Am. Women, Washington, 1980; participant internat. reception, Washington, 1980; mem. pub. panel individual presentation Shakespeare's Treatment of Women Characters, Nev. Theatre for the Arts, Ashland, Oreg., Shakespearean Actors local performance, 1977; mem. Nev. Women's History Project, U. Nev., 1996—; charter mem. Nat. Mus. Women in the Arts, Washington, 1987—; mem. coun., 2000. Recipient Outstanding Conservation Farmer award Mason Valley Conservation Dist., 1992, Soroptimist Internat. Women Helping women award 1983, invitation to first all-women delegation to U.S.A. from People's Republic China, U.S. House Reps., 1979; Public Forum Travel grantee Edn. Title IX, Oakland, Calif., 1977; Internat. Biog. Ctr. (Cambridge) fellow World Lit. Acad., 1993. Mem. Lyon County Ret. Tchrs. Assn. (unit pres. 1979-80, 84-86, v.p. 1986-88, Nev. State Outstanding Svc. award 1981, state conv. gen. chmn. 1985), Rural Am. Women Inc., AAUW (br. pres. 1972-74, 74-76, chair edn. found. programs 1983—, state conv. gen. chmn. 1976, 87, state sec. 1970-72, state legis. program chmn. 1976-77, state chmn. internat. rels. 1979-81, state pres. 1981-83, br. travelship, discovering women in U.S. history Radcliffe Coll. 1981, State Humanities award 1975, Future Fund Nat. award 1983, Lorraine Scatena endowment gift named in her honor for significant contbns. to AAUW Ednl. Found. 1997), Mason Valley Country Club, Italian Cath. Fedn. (pres. 1986-88), Uniao Portuguesa Estado da Calif. Roman Catholic. Avocations: writing, photography. Home: PO Box 247 Yerington NV 89447-0247

SCATURRO, PHILIP DAVID, investment banker; b. Newark, Dec. 8, 1938; s. Charles and Rose (Montino) S. BA, Williams Coll., 1960; JD, Columbia U., 1963, MBA, 1963. Analyst Ladenburg, Thalmann & Co., Inc., N.Y.C., 1964-67; v.p. Sellin, Forbes & Smith, N.Y.C., 1967; v.p. Allen & Co. Inc., N.Y.C., 1967-71, mng. dir., exec. v.p., 1977—; gen. ptnr. R&S Assocs., N.Y.C., 1972-76; pvt. investor, N.Y.C., 1976-77; bd. dirs., chmn. compensation com., exec. com. United Asset Mgmt. Co.; bd. dirs. Intrenet, Inc., Milford, Ohio, Opal Concepts, Inc., Anaheim, Calif., Asquith Ct. Ltd., London, Mass. Mus. of Contemporary Art Found., Inc., North Adams, Mass. Bd. dirs., exec. com., chmn. fin. com., treas. N.Y.C. Opera; trustee, exec. com., chmn. audit com., trustee New Sch. U., chancellor, 1999—; mem. com. on alt. investments Williams Coll. Mem. Univ. Club (N.Y.C.), Century Assn. Avocations: Opera, music, theatre, wine, fly fishing. Office: Allen & Co 711 5th Ave Fl 8 New York NY 10022-3111

SCAVARDA, DONALD ROBERT, composer, artist; b. Iron Mountain, Mich., June 18, 1928; m. Barbara Janet Regner, Nov. 13, 1965. MMus, U. Mich., 1953. co-founder, organizer Once Festival Musical Premieres, Ann Arbor, Mich., 1960-65. Composer: Groups For Piano, 1959, Sounds for Eleven, 1961, (Haiku song cycle) In the Autumn Mountains, 1961, Matrix for Clarinetist (widely recognized as the pioneering work in discovery and development of clarinet multiphonics), 1962, (piano, clarinet, 8mm film) Landscape Journey, 1963, (film score for electronic realization) Greys, 1963, (multiple film projection and tape) Caterpillar, 1965; paintings include Chamber Music, 1997, Portrait of Helen P., 1998. Fulbright scholar, 1953; recipient 1st prize for Fantasy For Violin And Orchestra BMI Inc., 1954. Home: PO Box 1908 Ann Arbor MI 48106-1908

SCEDROV, ANDRE, mathematics and computer science researcher, educator; b. Zagreb, Croatia, Aug. 1, 1955; came to U.S., 1977, naturalized, 1987; s. Oleg and Mira (Petric) S.; m. Bonnie Carol Hoke, July 23, 1983. BA, U. Zagreb, 1977; MA, SUNY, Buffalo, 1979, PhD in Math., 1981. T.H. Hildebrandt asst. prof. rsch. U. Mich., Ann Arbor, 1981-82; asst. prof. U. Pa., Phila., 1982-88, assoc. prof., 1988-92, prof., 1992—; vis. scholar U. Milan, 1982, McGill U., Montreal, 1985, U. Sydney, Australia, 1986, U. Catholique de Louvain, Louvain-La-Neuve, Belgium, 1988, U. Paris 7, 1992, Rijksuniv Utrecht, The Netherlands, 1993, CNRS Lab. de Math. Discretes, Marseille, France, 1995, Stanford U., 1995, Isaac Newton Inst. for Math. Scis., Cambridge, Eng., 1995; vis. scientist Math. Scis. Inst. Cornell U., Ithaca, N.Y., 1987; vis. fellow SRI Internat., Menlo Park, Calif., 1995; vis. assoc. prof. Stanford (Calif.) U., 1989-90; cons. Odyssey Rsch. Assocs., Ithaca, 1987, HP Labs., Palo Alto, 1990; program chair IEEE Symposium on Logic in Computer Sci., Santa Cruz, Calif., 1992, mem. organizing com., 1992-97, mem. adv. bd., 1997—, program co-chair Math. Founds. Programming Semantics, New Orleans, 1999; mem. program com. Logical Found. Computer Sci., Tver, Russia, 1992, St. Petersburg, Russia, 1994, Linear Logic Tokyo '96, 1996, Computer Sci. Logic '98, Brno, Czech Republic, 1998, Typed Lambda Calculi and Applications, L'Aquila, Italy, 1999, Category Theory in Computer Sci., Edinburgh, Scotland, 1999; plenary spkr. 2d Croatian Math. Congress, Zagreb, 2000; plenary spkr. 2d Croatian Math. Congress, Zagreb, 2000, invited spkr. Math. Founds. Programming Semantics, Oxford (Eng.) U., 1992, U. Colo., Boulder, 1996, Computer Sci. Logic, San Miniato, Italy, 1992, Internat. Summer Sch. Logic Computer Sci., Chambery, France, 1993, Proof and Computation, Marktoberdorf, Germany, 1993, Logic and Computer Sci. CIRM, Marseille-Luminy, France, 1994, Winter Sch. on Linear Logic and Applications, Lisbon, Portugal, 1995, 10th Internat. Congress on Logic, Philosophy and Methodology of Sci., Florence, Italy, 1995, Linear Logic Meeting and Spring Sch., Tokyo, 1996, Linear Logic Workshop CIRM, Marseille-Luminy, France, 1998, Constructivism in Mathematics and Computing, The Netherlands, 1999; vis. prof. Keio U., Tokyo, 1997, 2000. Author: (with P. Freyd) Categories, Allegories; editor Math. Structures in Computer Sci., 1989—, Annals Pure Applied Logic, 1993—, Perspectives in Mathematical Logic book series, 1997—; contbr. articles and rsch. papers to profl. publs. Recipient Young Faculty award Nat. Scis. Assn. U. Pa., 1987; Rsch. grantee NSF, 1985—, Office Naval Rsch., 1988—. Fellow Japan Soc. for Promotion Sci. (sr.); mem. AAAS, Am. Math. Soc. (Centennial rsch. fellow 1993-94), Assn. for Symbolic Logic (editor jours. 1988-93, chair nominating com. 1993, program com. 1988-90, coun. 1990-96, coordinating editor jours. 1994-96 exec. com. 1998—), Assn. for Computing Machinery, Math. Assn. Am. E-mail: andre@cis.upenn.edu. Office: U Pa Dept Math 209 S 33rd St Dept Math Philadelphia PA 19104-6317

ŠĆEDROV, OLEG, biochemistry, organic chemistry educator; b. Senta, Yugoslavia, Nov. 20, 1924; arrived in Croatia; s. Georgij and Maria (Halmos) Š; m. Mira Pertić, July 22, 1953 (div. Sept. 18, 1967); children: Andre, Nikola; m. Dragica Marković, Dec. 16, 1968 (div. Oct. 1974); 1 child, Ljiljana; m. Mercedes Radica, Mar. 18, 1978 (dec. Sept. 1999). BSc in Chem. Engring., U. Zagreb, Croatia, 1949, DSc in Biochemistry, 1972. Rsch. engr. Pharm. and Chem. Works Pliva, Zagreb, 1952-57; chem. dept. chief Serum Inst., Kalinovica, Croatia, 1957-66; sci. counsellor Inst. Minig & Chem. Rsch., Tuzla, Bosnia-Herzegovina, 1968-74; assoc. prof. organic chemistry Faculty Tech. U. Tuzla, 1974-76, prof. biochemistry Faculty Medicine, 1976-80, prof. emeritus, 1990—; prof. biochemistry Coll. Medicine U. Juba, Sudan, 1983-85; prof. chemistry Advanced Tech. Sch. Safety U. Zagreb, 1981-83, 85-87; prof. indsl. ecology Coll. Occupl. Safety, Zagreb, 1999—; guest prof. biochem., faculty medicine U. Tuzla, 1981-92; instr., rschr. U. Zagreb, 1954-66; cons. biotech. UN Indsl. Devel. Orgn., Vienna, Austria, 1975—; spkr. in field. Contbr. articles to profl. jours. Mem. Croatian Chem. Soc., Croatian Biochem. Soc., N.Y. Acad. Scis. Avocations: mountaineering, photography, classical music. Home: Crnojezerska 18, 10090 Zagreb Croatia

SCEIFORD, MARY ELIZABETH, retired public television administrator; b. Erie, Pa., Nov. 30, 1932; d. William Michael and Ellen Elizabeth (Laffer) S. BA, Allegheny Coll., 1954; MS, Univ. Wis., 1960; PhD, Syracuse Univ., 1969. Cert. tchr. Pa., Wis., Ohio. Kindergarten tchr. Lakewood (Ohio) Pub. Schs., 1954-56; grade one/two tchr. Madison (Wis.) Pub. Schs., 1956-59; art tchr. Mt. Lebanon (Pa.) Pub. Schs., 1960-65; tv. tchr. WQED-TV, Pitts., 1965-66; art tchr. Mt. Lebanon Pub. Schs., 1966-67; assoc. dir. Sch. Svcs. WQED-TV, Pitts., 1969-74, dir. sch. svcs., 1974-75; assoc. dir. edn. and children's tv programs Corp. for Pub. Broadcasting, Washington, 1975-96; ret.; adv. bd. Nat. Pub. Broadcasting Archives, College Park, Md., 1993—. Contbr. articles to profl. jours. Bd. trustees Allegheny Coll., 1975—; USA rep. European Broadcasting Union Youth Group, Geneva, Switzerland, 1993-96. Mem. Am. Ednl. Rsch. Assn., ASCD, Assn. Ednl. Communications & Tech., Phi Beta Kappa, Pi Lambda Theta. Avocations: walking, swimming, gardening, piano, farm work.

SCHAAD, URS B., pediatrics educator, hospital administrator; b. Herzogenbuchsee, Switzerland, June 1, 1945; s. Hans and Gertrud (Strehler) S.; m. Lilian Helen Ernst, Mar. 1, 1970; children: Christine, Michael, Sefanie. MD, Berne (Switzerland) U., 1971, specialist in pediat. infectious disease, 1981, prof. pediat., 1983. Intern, res. Univ. Children's Hosp., Berne, 1971-78; rsch. fellow pediat. infectious disease Southwestern Med. Sch., Dallas, 1978-80; chief divsn. pediat. infectious disease U. Berne, 1981-92; chmn. pediat. Univ. Children's Hosp., Basel, Switzerland, 1993—, head divsn. pediat. infectious disease, 1993—, med. dir., 1996—; mem. editl. bd. various profl. jours., including Pediat. Infectious Disease Jour., European Jour. Pediat., European Jour. Clin. Microbiology & Infectious Diseases. Author: Pediatric Infectiology, 1997, Infectious Disease Clinics of North America, 1999; contbr. over 200 articles and revs. to internat. profl. jours. and conf. procs. Fellow Infectious Diseases Soc. Am.; mem. Pediat. Infectious Diseases Soc. Am., Pediat. Infectious Diseases Soc. Germany, Swiss Soc. Infectious Diseases (founder, coun. mem. 1990—), Internat. Green Cross (v.p. 1995—), European Forum on Immunization (chmn. 1997—), European Soc. Pediat. Infectious Diseases (founder mem., Bill Marshall lectr. 1992, pres. 1995-98). Avocations: sports, culture, travel. Home: Rütiring 22, CH-4125 Riehen Switzerland Office: Univ Children's Hosp, Dept Pediatrics, CH-4005 Basel Switzerland

SCHAAL, WERNER GEORG HANS, mathematician; b. Berlin, Apr. 20, 1934; s. Gustav and Margarete (Tusk) S.; m. Ina Schuermann, 1962; children: Katharina, Kristine. Diploma in math., U. Goettingen, Fed. Republic Germany, 1959, PhD in Math, 1961; habilitation in math., U. Marburg, Fed. Republic Germany, 1966; PhD (hon.), Lomonosov U., 1995, Manchester Coll., Wilfrid Laurier U., Waterloo, Can., Lucian-Blaga U., Sibiu, Romania. Asst. U. Bonn, Fed. Republic Germany, 1961-62; C.L.E. Moore instr. MIT, Cambridge, 1962-64; asst. U. Marburg, 1964-66, dozent, 1966-70, prof. math., 1970-89, v.p., 1989-93, pres., 1994-2000; pres. Lucian-Blabga-U, Sibiu, 2000—; vis. assoc. prof. Mich. State U., East Lansing, 1968-69, vis. prof., 1978-79; hon. vis. prof. Lomonosov U., Moscow, 1993—. Contbr. articles on algebraic and analytic number theory to profl. jours. Mem. German Math. Soc., Am. Math. Soc. Home: Auf Dem Schaumrueck 28, 35041 Marburg Germany Office: Marburg U, Marburg U, 35032 Marburg Germany

SCHAAR, GÜNTER, mathematician, retired educator; b. Memel, Lithuania, Germany, Aug. 28, 1932; s. Willy and Gertrud (Jetzkus) S.; m. Gabriele Wottke, July 24, 1963. High sch. tchr., U. Leipzig, Germany, 1955; D of Natural Scis., Tech. U. Freiberg, Germany, 1962, D of Natural Scis. Habilitation, 1969. Tchr. high sch. Germany, 1954-57; asst. Tech. U. Freiberg, 1957-63, upper asst., 1963-69, docent, 1969-74, full prof., 1974-97, vice-dir. dept. math., 1972-90, dean faculty math. and natural scis., 1991, dir. inst. theoretical math., 1992-97, ret., 1997. Co-author: Hamiltonian Properties of Products of Graphs and Digraphs, 1988; contbr. more than 30 articles to profl. jours. Mem. Deutsche Mathematiker-Vereinigung, Deutscher Hochschulverband. Avocations: walking, listening to classical music, reading novels, gardening. Home: Reimannstrasse 16, D-09599 Freiberg Germany

SCHABE, HENDRIK KURT, computer scientist, consultant; b. Berlin, Feb. 28, 1958; s. Kurt Arthur and Erika (Böhme) S.; m. Marlies Christa Stoschek, Sept. 15, 1983; children: Fabian, Alexander. Dipl.phys., U. Minsk, Belarus, 1981; Dr.rer.nat., U. Minsk (Belarus), 1982; Dr.rer.nat.habil., U. Transp. & Comm., Dresden, Germany, 1987. Specialist IFA Car Factory, Ludwigsfelde, Germany, 1982-86; lectr. U. Transp. & Comm., Dresden, 1986-91; reliability mgr. ASAP, Cologne, Germany, 1991-94; specialist Inst. Software, Elecs., Railroad Tech. Tüv, Rheinland, Germany, 1995—. Contbr. articles to profl. jours. Mem. German. Statis. Soc. Office: Tüv Rheinland, ISEB, 51101 Cologne Germany

SCHABERT, TILO CARL, political studies educator, journalist; b. Gotha, Thuringia, Germany, Nov. 3, 1942; s. Caspar and Fanny (Rosendahl) S.; m. Ina Bungartz, July 31, 1969. BA in Greek and Latin, Theol. Seminary, Stuttgart, Germany, 1963; PhD summa cum laude, U. Munich, 1968; PhD (hon.), U. Perpignan, France, 1996. Asst. prof. political theory and philosophy U. Munich, 1969-70, 72-76; rsch. fellow Hoover Instn. Stanford U., 1970-72, lectr. political sci.; fellow Inst. Polit. Studies U. Bochum, Germany, 1976-78, Sr. Heisenberg Rsch. fellow German Rsch. Coun., 1978-85; prof. politics Friedrich-Alexander U., Erlangen and Nuremberg, Germany, 1986—; film dir. Bavarian TV, Munich, 1983-84; dir. Eranos Confs., Ascona, Switzerland, 1990—; pres. Assn. Eranos, Ascona, 1996-2000; mem. steering com. The Mishkenot Encounters in Religion and Culture, Mishkenot Sha'anakim, Jerusalem; sec. gen. Internat. Coun. Philosophy and Humanistic Studies, UNESCO, Paris, 1994-96; pres. Internat. Sci. Com., Internat. Jour. Humanistic Studies; staff mem. Ministry Nat. Edn., Paris, 1964-65; lectr. Munich Acad. Film and TV, 1975-76, Sch. Polit. Studies, Munich, 1981-82; planning assoc. Boston Redevel. Authority, 1981; Thyssen rsch. prof. Sci. and Politics Found., Munich-Berlin, 2000; lectr. in field. Author: Natur und Revolution, 1969, Gewalt und Humanität, 1978, Boston Politics: The Creativity of Power, 1989, Stadtarchitektur, 1990, Modernität und Geschichte, 1990, Die Architektur der Welt, 1997; editor, co-author: Der Mensch als Schöpfer der Welt, 1971, Aufbruch zur Moderne, 1974, Die Welt der Stadt, 1991; co-editor: Auferstehung und Unsterblichkeit, 1993, Die Macht des Wortes, 1996; co-editor, co-author: Strukturen des Chaos, 1994, Anfänge, 1998, Schuld, 1999; co-editor (with Erik Hornung) Eranos, vol. 1, 1993, vol. 2, 1994, vol. 3, 1995, vol. 4, 1996, vol. 5, 1997, vol. 6, 1998, vol. 7, 1999; guest editor Diogenes, 1994; co-author: (textbook) Von Gottes und von Volkes Gnaden, 1977; contbg. editor Bavarian TV, Sect. Cultural and Polit. History, 1976-78, film dir., 1983-84; contbr. articles to profl. jours. and leading European newspapers. Pres. student parliament U. Munich, 1965-66. Recipient Heisenberg fellowship German Rsch. Coun., 1978, Kennedy Meml. fellowship Harvard U., 1983; recipient grants Thyssen Found., German-French Youth Coun., French Govt., Oxford U., Stanford U., Australian Nat. U., U. Bochum, Harvard U., U. Erlangen-Nuremberg; Gulbenkian Found. professorship, 1996. Office: Univ Erlangen, Regensburger Strasse 160, 90478 Nuremberg Germany

SCHABNER, DAWN FREEBLE, artist, educator; b. Mercer, Pa., Jan. 30, 1933; d. Benjamin Frederick and Mary Emma (McElheny) Freeble; m. Donald Russell Schabner, Jan. 5, 1954; children: Donald Russell Jr., Dean Aaron. Student, Phila. Mus. Sch. Art, 1950-52; BA in Fine Arts with honors magna cum laude, Hofstra U., 1971; student, Cleve. Inst Art., 1952-53; MA in Liberal Studies, SUNY, Stony Brook, 1976. Designer Am. Greetings, Cleve., 1953; art educator Islip (N.Y.) Pub. Schs., 1967-95, Dowling Coll., Oakdale, N.Y., 1991—. One-woman shows include East Islip (N.Y.) Pub. Libr., 1977, 88, Unitarian Bay Gallery, Bellport, N.Y., 1997, L-Art Gallery, Kiev, Ukraine, 1999; group shows include Hofstra U., 1970, Patchogue-Medford Pub. Libr., 1983, East End Arts & Humanities Coun., Riverhead, N.Y., 1984, Islip Art Mus. Juried Exhibit, 1985, 87, 88, 99, Suffolk County Legis. Bldg., Hauppage, N.Y., 1988, Bennington Coll., 1989, Goat Alley Gallery, Sag Harbor, N.Y., 1989, Canio's Books, Sag Harbor, 1990, South Country Libr., Bellport, N.Y., 1991, The Parrish Art Mus., Southampton, N.Y., 1999; featured artist East End Arts and Humanities Coun., Riverhead, N.Y., 1986; featured at Clayton Liberatore Art Gallery, Bridgehampton, N.Y., 1994, 95, 97. Mem. Met. Mus. Art, East End Arts Coun., Smithtown Twp. Arts Coun., Guild Hall. Avocations: golf, bicycling, weight training, reading, attending concerts & ballet.

SCHACHNER, MELITTA, medical educator; b. Brno, Czech Republic, Apr. 4, 1943; d. Benno and Doris (Korn) Schachner; m. Iso Camartin, Mar. 24, 1974. M in Biochemistry, U. Tubingen, 1968; PhD in Biochemistry, Max-Planck Inst. Biochemistry, Munich, 1970. Postdoc. fellow Harvard Med. Sch., Boston, 1970-73, instr., 1973-74, asst. prof., 1974-76; rsch. assoc. Children's Hosp. Med. Ctr., Boston, 1973; prof. U. Heidelberg, Germany, 1976-88, Swiss Fed. Inst. Tech., Zürich, 1988-90, Ctr. Molecular Neurobiology, Hamburg, Germany, 1991—; guest prof. U. Hong Kong, 1996—. Recipient von Virchow medal U. Würzburg, 1997; Warner-Lambert lectr. U.S. Soc. Neurosci., 1997. Mem. EMBO. Home: Breitenfelder str 15, D20251 Hamburg Germany Office: Zentrum Molekulare Neurobio, Martinistr 52, D20246 Hamburg Germany

SCHACKER, SARAH ELIZABETH, educator; b. Santa Clara, Calif., Aug. 5, 1971; d. Donald Jay and Ivona Ann Schacker. BA in Anthropology and Sociology, Lewis & Clark Coll., 1993; MS in Spl. Edn., Portland State U., 1997. Cert. spl. edn. tchr. English tchr. U. Rian, Pekanbaru, Indonesia, 1991-92; rsch. asst. Internat. Refugee Ctr. Oreg., Portland, 1992-93; asst. tchr. Evergreen Sch. Dist., Vancouver, Wash., 1993-95; tchr. Parry Ctr. for Children, Portland, 1996—; mentor for beginning tchrs. Portland Pub. Schs., 1998—. Trainer, com. chair Girl Scouts Santlam Coun., Salem, Oreg., 1995—. Congress-Bundestag scholar Congress-Bundestag Com., 1987. Mem. Internat. Reading Assn. Democrat. Avocations: hiking, cross country skiing, piano, cooking. E-mail: sschacker@yahoo.com. Home: 2328 SE Tibbetts St Portland OR 97202-2150 Office: Parry Ctr Sch 3415 SE Powell Blvd Portland OR 97202-3371

SCHAD, THEODORE MACNEEVE, science research administrator, consultant; b. Balt., Aug. 25, 1918; s. William Henry and Emma Margaret (Scheldt) S.; m. Kathleen White, Nov. 5, 1944 (dec. Aug. 1989); children: Mary Jane, Rebecca Christina; m. Margot Cornwell, March 19, 1995. BSCE, Johns Hopkins U., 1939. Registered profl. engr., D.C. Staff water resources engring. U.S. Army C.E., U.S. Bur. Reclamation, Md., Colo., Oreg. Wash., 1939-54; prin. budget examiner water resources programs U.S. Bur. Budget, Exec. Office of Pres., 1954-58; sr. specialist engring. and pub. works, dep. dir. Congl. Rsch. Svc., Libr. of Congress, 1958-68; staff dir. U.S. Senate Com. Nat. Water Resources, 1959-61; exec. dir. Nat. Water Commn., 1968-73; exec. sec. Environ. Studies Bd., 1973-77; dep. dir. Commn. Natural Resources, NAS, Washington, 1977-83; exec. dir. Nat. Ground Water Policy Forum, 1984-86; sr. fellow Conservation Found., Washington, 1986-; U.S. commr. Permanent Internat. Assn. Nav. Congresses, Brussels, 1963-70, commr. emeritus, 1987—; cons. U.S. Senate Com. Interior and Insular Affairs, 1963, U.S. Ho. of Reps. Com. Sci. and Tech., 1962-65, U.S. Office Saline Water, 1965-67, A.T. Kearney, Inc., Alexandria, Va., 1979-80, Chesapeake Rsch. Consortium, 1984, Ronco Cons. Corp., 1986—, Gambia River Basin Devel. Commn., Dakar, 1986-87, Apogee Rsch. Corp., 1987—, Office Tech. Assessment, U.S. Congress, 1992-95. Contbr. articles to Ency. Brit. and profl. jours. Treas. Nat. Speleol. Found., 1961-65, trustee, 1965—; bd. dirs. Vets. Coop. Housing Assn., Washington, 1958-81, v.p., 1960-72. Recipient Meritorious Svc. award U.S. Dept. Interior, 1950, Icko Iben award Am. Water Resources Assn., 1978, Henry P. Caulfield medal, 1990, Woodrow Wilson award for disting. govt. svc. Johns Hopkins U., 1997. Fellow ASCE (treas. Nat. Capital chpt. 1952-55, v.p. 1967, pres. 1968, Julian Hinds prize 1991); mem. AAAS, Nat. Speleol. Soc., Am. Water Works Assn. (hon.), Am. Geophys. Union, Am. Acad. Environ. Engrs., Nat. Acad. Pub. Adminstrn., Permanent Internat. Assn. Nav. Congresses (commr. emeritus), Internat. Commn. Irrigation and Drainage, U.S. Com. on Large Dams, Potomac Appalachian Trail Club, Cosmos Club, Colo. Mountain Club (Denver), Seattle Mountaineers Club, Am. Alpine Club. Home: 4540 25th Rd N Arlington VA 22207-4102 Office: The Conservation Found 1260 24th St NW Washington DC 20037-1103

SCHADE, HEINZ FRITZ GEORG, physicist, fluid dynamics educator; b. Berlin, 1933; s. Friedrich and Klara (Fuchs) S.; m. Christa Rosin; children: Bernd, Lars. MS in Physics, Tech. U. Berlin, 1957, PhD in Engring., 1962, habilitation, 1964. Brit. Coun. scholar Cambridge (Eng.) U., 1958-59; rsch. asst. German Aircraft Testing Establishment, Berlin, 1959-62, 63-64, MIT, Cambridge, Mass., 1962-63; lectr. Tech. U. Berlin, 1964-69, prof. fluid dynamics, 1969-98; ret. Author: Kontinuumstheorie strömender Medien, 1970; (with Ewald Kunz): Strömungslehre, 1980, 2d edit., 1989, Tensoranalysis, 1997.

SCHADE, RICHARD ERICH, foreign language educator; b. Concord, N.H., Mar. 12, 1944; married, 1972; 2 children. BA, U. N.H., 1966, MA, 1968; PhD, Yale U., 1976. From asst. to full prof. U. Cin., 1975—; master tchr. Advanced Studies Program, Concord, N.H., 1982—; hon. consul Fed. Rep. Germany, 1996—; bd. dirs. Lessing Rsch. Inst., Kamenz, Germany, 1996—. Contbr. articles to profl. jours. Capt. U.S. Army, 1969-72. Mem. G.E. Lessing Soc. (mng. editor 1975—). E-mail: Richard.Schade@uc.edu. Office: Germany Honorary Consulate Univ Cin 734 Old Chemistry Bldg Cincinnati OH 45221-0001

SCHADE, WILBERT CURTIS, education administrator; b. St. Louis, Jan. 4, 1945; s. Wilbert Curtis and Florence Mary (Allen) S.; m. Jacqueline Siewert, May 14, 1977; children: Benjamin Allen Siewert, Timothy Knorr Siewert. BA, U. Pa., 1967; AM, Washington U., St. Louis, 1970; PhD, Ind. U., 1986. Tchg. asst. dept. romance lang. Washington U., St. Louis, 1967-68; tchr. French St. Louis Priory Sch., 1970-71; assoc. instr. dept. French and Italian Ind. U., Bloomington, 1972-74, 76-80; tchr. French Webster Groves (Mo.) H.S., 1975-76; asst. dir. admissions Beloit (Wis.) Coll., 1980-83, assoc. dir. admissions, 1983-84; dir. coll. placement and dir. admissions

Westover Sch., Middlebury, Conn., 1984-90; head upper sch. The Key Sch., Annapolis, Md., 1990-94, interim dir. devel., 1994-95; tchr. French, head lang. dept. Wasatch Acad., Mt. Pleasant, Utah, 1995-96, asst. headmaster for acad. affairs, 1996-2000; tchr., dir. of studies Internat. Seminar Series, Paris, 1999—; lectr. in field. Co-editor: African Literature in its Social and Political Dimensions, 1983; mem. editl. bd. Jour. Coll. Admission, 2000—; contbr. articles to profl. jours. including World Lit. Written in English, Studies in 20th Century Lit. Active Anne Arundel County (Md.) Task Force on Year Round Edn., 1994-95, Utah State Office of Edn.'s Fgn. Lang. Instrl. Materials and Texbook Adv. Com., 1996-98. NEH Summer Inst. on African Am. Lit. and Film grant, 1994. Mem. Nat. Assn. Coll. Admission Counseling (presenter nat. conf. 1985), Rocky Mountain Assn. for Coll. Admission Counseling (exec. bd., chief assembly del. to Nat. Assn.), African Lit. Assn. (exec. com. 1979), Phi Delta Kappa. Soc. of Friends. Avocation: tennis. Home: PO Box 3549 20 Malheur Ln Sunriver OR 97707 Office: Wasatch Acad 120 S 100 W Mount Pleasant UT 84647-1509

SCHADEWALDT, HANS, medical history educator; b. Kottbus, May 7, 1923; s. Johannes and Hedwig S.; m. Lotte, 1943. Univs. Tübingen, Würzburg and Königsberg; Lectr. U. Freiburg, 1961-63; prof. history of medicine U. Düsseldorf, 1963—, dean faculty of medicine, 1976-77. Author: Michelangelo und die Medizin seiner Zeit, 1965, Die berühmten Arzte, 1966, Kunst und Medizin, 1967, Der Medizinmann bei den Naturvölkern, 1968, Gechichte der Allergie, 1979-83, Die Chirurgie in der Kunst, 1983, Das Herz, ein Rätsel für die antike und mittelalterliche Welt, 1989, Betrachtungen zur Medizin in der bildenden Kunst, 1990, Pharmakologie bei Bayer 1890-1990, 1990, Das Bild vom Tode, 1992, die Rückkehr der Seuchen, 1994. Decorated Ordre de Mérite Culturel Monako. Mem. North-Rhine Westfalian Acad. Scis. (pres. 1994), Officer Ordre des Palmes Academiques, Grosses Bundesverdienstkreuz. Office: Inst History of Medicine, Heinrich-Heine U Moorenstr5, Düsseldorf G-40225, Germany

SCHADLBAUER, FRIEDRICH GUENTHER, geographer; b. Vienna, Austria, Dec. 7, 1939; s. Friedrich Gustav and Karoline Josepha (Pfeiler) S.; m. Eva Maria Habel, July 3, 1967; children: Friedrich Werner, Guenther Matthias. Leaving cert., Tchrs. Tng. Coll., Vienna, 1959; PhD, U. Vienna, 1967; MA, U. of the Orange Free State, Bloemfontein, Republic S. Africa, 1971. Mem. dept. econs. and social geography U. Econs. and Bus. Adminstrn., Vienna, 1964-82; researcher inst. for social and econ. rsch. U. of the Orange Free State, Bloemfontein, 1970-71; sr. lectr. dept. geography Rand Afrikaans U., Johannesburg, Republic S. Africa, 1977; freelance geographer Vienna, 1983-99; ret., 1999; part-time lectr. dept. econ. and social geography U. Econs. and Bus. Adminstrn., Vienna, 1983-91; dir. Austrian Documentation Centre for Study Abroad, Vienna, 1991-94; cons. Austrian Road Safety Bd., Vienna, 1989-94; sec. Austrian Geog. Soc., Vienna, 1972-77; chmn. Ecol. Innovation, 1989. Editor, Studies in Econ. Geography, 1972-86. Mem. Acad. of the Environment and Energy (chmn. working group village and landscape beautification scheme 1983-99). Conservative. Roman Catholic. Avocation: skiing. Home: Reumannpl 17 2 11, A 1100 Vienna Austria Office: U Econs and Bus Adminstrn, Augasse 2-6, A 1090 Vienna Austria

SCHADT, DIETER, manufacturing executive. CEO Franz Haniel, Duisburg, Germany, chmn., mng. bd. Office: Franz Haniel, Franz Haniel Platz 1, Duisburg 47119, Germany*

SCHAEBERLE, WILHELM, surgeon; b. Herrenberg, Germany, Dec. 4, 1957; s. Wilhelm and Martha (Kussmaul) S. MD, U. Tübingen, Germany, 1986, PhD, 1989. Intern, resident Kreiskrankenhaus, Böblingen, Germany, 1986, Aggertalklinik, Engelskirchen, Germany, 1987, Klinik an Eichert, Göppingen, Germany, 1988-94; surgeon Klinik am Eichert, Goeppingen, Germany, 1994-97, surgeon specializing in visceral and vascular surgery, 1997; lectr. German Fedn. of Ultrasound in Medicine, 1995. Author: Duplexsonographie in der Venendiagnostik, 1994, Ultraschall in der Gefässdiagnostik, 1998, Interventionelle Sonographie, 1999; co-editor Dr. med. Mabuse, Zeitschrift im Gesundheitswesen, 1985-93; artist in oil painting, exhbns. from 1986-94. Surgeon, Doctors Without Borders, Paris, Bonn, 1994—, instr., 1995—. Mem. German and European Fedn. of Ultrasound in Medicine. Avocations: reading, sports, music, art. Home: Georg Boehringer Weg 35, D-73033 Goeppingen Germany Office: Klinik am Eichert, Eichertstr 3, 73006 Göppingen Germany

SCHAEDELI, ULRICH P., chemist; b. Berne, Switzerland, Jan. 21, 1956; s. Philipp and Cathy (Baertschi) S.; m. Judith Boenzli, June 11, 1990; children: Lukas, Jennifer. Grad., Gymnasium Berne, 1976; diploma, U. Berne, 1981, PhD in Chemistry, 1986. Rsch. asst. U. Berne, 1982-86; postdoctoral fellow U. Ariz., Tucson, 1986-87; vis. scientist IBM, San Jose, Calif., 1987-88; rsch. chemist Ciba-Geigy, Marly, Switzerland, 1989-90, project leader, lithographic layers, 1991-98; rsch. chemist OCG, Basel, Switzerland, 1990-91; project leader, new energetic materials Nitrochemie, Wimmis, Switzerland, 1998—. Contbr. numerous articles to profl. publs.; patentee in field. Mem. Soc. Optical Engring., Polymer Group Switzerland. Avocations: skiing, hiking, travel. Home: Hubel/Geronimo, 1737 Plasselb Switzerland Office: Nitrochemie Wimmis AG, CH-3752 Wimmis Switzerland

SCHAEFER, CHARLES JAMES, III, advertising agency executive, consultant; b. Orange, N.J., Dec. 17, 1926; m. Eleanor Anne Montville, Apr. 8, 1961; 1 child, Charles James IV. AB, Dartmouth Coll., 1948, M in Comml. Sci., 1949. V.p. Dickie-Raymond, 1952-67; sr. v.p. Metromedia, 1968-69; exec. v.p., treas. The DR Group, Boston, 1969-76, pres., 1976-87; exec. v.p., dir. Needham Harper Worldwide Inc., N.Y.C., 1984-87; chmn. bd. Marcoa DR Group, Inc., N.Y.C., 1987-88; cons. Rapp Collins Marcoa, N.Y.C., 1989-92; advt. cons., 1992—. Pres. Dartmouth Class of 1948, 1998—; trustee, mem. exec. com. Direct Mktg. Ednl. Found., 1983-89; campaign chairperson United Way Millburn-Short Hills, 1994, 95, trustee, 1991-98, 2000—. With USN, 1945-46. Mem. Direct Mktg. Assn. (chmn. awards com. 1971-76, Hall of Fame com. 1978-81, ethics com. 1981-86), Assn. Direct Mktg. Agys. (pres. 1980-82, gen. chmn. Caples awards 1985, Direct Mktg. Day N.Y. 1988, N.Y. Direct Marketer of Yr. award 1987, Silver Apple award 1989, contbr. to jour.), Dartmouth Club of N.Y. (pres. 1968-70), Lotos Club (bd. dirs. 1985-88, treas. 1987-88), Canoe Brook Country Club (Summit, N.J.). Home and Office: 307 Hobart Ave Short Hills NJ 07078-2207

SCHAEFER, FRANZ STEFAN, pediatrician, research; b. Aschaffenburg, Germany; s. Heinrich A.M. and Renate (Staudt) S.; m. Susanne Wolf, June 10, 1994; 1 child, Julia. MD, U. Würzburg, Germany, 1986. Med. diplomate, Germany. Resident City Children's Hosp, Aschaffenburg, Germany, 1986-87; rsch. fellow Inst. Child Health, London, 1987, U. Heidelberg, Germany, 1987-89; trainee in pediatrics, pediatric nephrology U. Heidelberg, 1989-95; cons. in pediatric nephrology U. Heidelberg, Germany, 1995—; assoc. prof. in pediatrics U. Heidelberg, 1995—; vis. scientist U. Va., Charlottesville, 1993, 95, Stanford U., 1999-2000. Co-recipient Bierich award Pediat. Endocrinology, 1994; recipient Baxter Healthcare prize for pediat. peritoneal dialysis rsch., 1997, Recklinghausen award German Endocrine Soc., 1998. Mem. Internat. Pediatric Nephrology Assn., Internat. Soc. for Peritoneal Dialysis, European Dialysis and Transplant Assn., European Soc. for Pediatric Rsch. Roman Catholic. Avocations: jogging, skiing, travel. Office: U Heidelberg Childrens Hosp, Im Neuenheimer Feld 150, 69120 Heidelberg Germany

SCHAEFER, HANS, physiology educator, consultant; b. Düsseldorf, Germany, Aug. 13, 1906; s. Matthias Anton and Clara Juliane (Busch) S.; m. Marietta Ditgens, Sept. 16, 1931 (dec. Aug. 1993); children: Annette, Wolfgang, Anselm. MD, U. Bonn, Germany, 1931; MD honoris causa, U. Mainz, Germany, 1977. Asst. physiology U. Bonn, 1931-35, dozent physiology, 1935-39; head dept. Kerckhoff-Inst. Bad Nauheim, Germany, 1940-45, dir., 1945-50; prof. U. Giessen, Germany, 1950—, U. Heidelberg, Germany, 1951-74; speaker Bundesgesundheitsrat, Bonn, 1970-78. Author: Elektrophysiology, 1940, Das Elektrokardiogramm, 1951, Sozialmedizin, 1978, Herzinfarkt-Report, 2000, 30 other books. Recipient Adolf-Fick prize Medizinische Fakuetaet Würzburg, 1944, Albert-Schweitzer medal Landesärztekammer, 1971, Paracelsus medal Bundesaerztekammer, 1988, Grosses Bundesverdienstkreuz, Bundespräsident, 1975, Salomon Neumann medal Gesellschaft Sozialmedizin, 1987; fellow Heidelberger Acad. Wissenschaften, 1953—, Leopoldinische Acad. Naturforscher, 1957—. Mem. Deutsche Liga das Kind (pres.), Arbeitskreis Gesundheitswissenschaft (speaker 1993—), Mainauer gespräche (speaker 1979-91), Academia Scientiarum Eurpaea (hon.), N.Y. Acad. Scis. (hon. lifetime), Akademie Medizinische Ethik. Avocation: stamps. Home: Karl-Christ-Str 19, 69118 Heidelberg Germany Office: Physiologisches Inst, Im Neuenheimer Feld 326, 69120 Heidelberg Germany

SCHAEFER, HANS GUENTER, pharmacokineticist; b. Arnsberg, Germany, June 8, 1961; s. Guenter and Isolde (Leifert) S.; m. Andrea Elisabeth Huppertz, Sept. 13, 1988; children: Dominik, Julia, Sophia. MS in Pharmacy, Westf. Wilhelms U., Muenster, Germany, 1986, PhD, 1988. Rsch. scientist U. Fla., Gainesville, 1988-89, Bayer AG, Wuppertal, Germany, 1989-96; head clin. pharm. Europe Eli Lilly & Co., Windlesham, England, 1996—. Co-author: (chpt.) Handbook of Experimental Pharmacology, 1997; contbr. articles to profl. jours. Recipient Excellent Grad. award Assn. German Chem. Industry, 1991. Mem. Am. Assn. Pharmaceutical Scientists, German Assn. Clin. and Pre-Clin. Pharm and Toxicology, European Fedn. Pharmaceutical Scis., N.Y. Acad. Scis. Roman Catholic. Avocations: volleyball, tennis, cycling. Office: Eli Lilly and Co, Sunninghill Rd, Windlesham GU20 6PH, England

SCHAEFER, JUERGEN ALOIS, physics educator; b. Voelkingen, Germany, Sept. 20, 1944; s. Hans and Elisabeth (Heinen) S.; m. Helga Margarethe Koch, Oct. 15, 1971; children: Torsten, Stefanie. Diploma in physics, Tech. U. Clausthal, Germany, 1971; D of Natural Scis., U. Kassel, Hessen, Germany, 1980, privatdozent, 1990. Postdoctoral position Mont. State U., Bozeman, 1981-83, vis. assoc. prof., 1983-84; cons. AT&T Bell Labs., Murray Hill, N.J., 1984; chair tech. physics Tech. U. Ilmenau, Thueringen, Germany, 1994—; prof. King Mongkut U. of Tech., Bangkok, 1994; dir. Inst. Physics, Tech. U. Ilmenau, 1998-2000. Guest editor, author: (conf. procs.) Hydrogen in Solids and at Solid Surfaces, 1996, Nitrogen in Solids and at Solid Surfaces, 2000; patentee in field; contbr. articles to profl. jours. coach badminton Allgemeiner Deutscher Hochschulsportverband, Germany, 1971-80, other clubs; tchr., referee badminton. Grantee Deutsche Forschungsgemeinschaft, 1986—, Volkswagen, 1996—, Land Thueringen, 1996—. Mem. Deutsche Physikalische Gesellschaft, Am. Phys. Soc., N.Y. Acad. Scis. Roman Catholic. Avocations: sports, badminton, soccer. Home: Finkenstr 37, D-34225 Baunatal Hessen, Germany Office: Tech U Ilmenau Inst Physics, Weimarer Str 32, D-98684 Ilmenau Germany

SCHAEFER, MARILYN LOUISE, artist, writer, educator; b. Cedar Rapids, Iowa, Apr. 22, 1933; d. Henry Richard and Maria Augusta (Dickel) S. AA, Monticello Coll. for Women, 1953; BFA, Cranbrook Acad. Art, 1956, MFA, 1960; MA cum laude, U. Chgo., 1958; MA, St. John's Coll., Santa Fe, 1979. Rsch. asst. editor Encyclopaedia Britannica, Chgo., 1960-63; humanities editor Encyclopedia Americana, N.Y., 1964-68; acquisitions editor Litton Ednl. Pub., N.Y., 1968-70; from instr. to prof. emeritus art and advt. design dept. N.Y.C. Tech. Coll. CUNY, 1970—; contbg. editor Encyclopedia Americana, 1979—, Coll. Teaching jour., 1979. Contbr. articles to profl. pubs. including Art and Auction mag., Art and Antiques mag., Am. Artist mag., Encyclopedia Americana, 1970—. Luce Found. postgrad. study fellow St. John's Coll., 1976-79; Ingram Merrill Found. grantee, 1983-84. Mem. AAUW, CUNY Acad. Arts and Scis. Home: 306 W 76th St New York NY 10023-8065 Office: NYC Tech Coll CUNY 300 Jay St Brooklyn NY 11201-1909

SCHAEFER, MATTHIAS DIETRICH, ecology educator; b. Berlin, Apr. 23, 1942; s. Erich and Waltraut (Kroll) S.; m. Michaela Batteiger, Mar. 29, 1968; children: Nikola, Christoph, Stephan. Abitur, Nicolaus-Cusanus-Gymnasium, Bonn, 1961. Asst. U. Kiel, 1969-77; prof., head dept. ecology Zool. Inst., U. Göttingen, Ged. Repuclic Germany, 1977—. Author: Ökologie, 1992, Fauna von Deutschland, 2000; editor in chief Oecologia and Pedobiologia Jour.; contbr. articles to profl. jours. Mem. Ecol. Soc. Am., Brit. Ecol. Soc., Acad. Scis. and Lit. Mainz, Acad. Scis. Göttingen, Gesellschaft für Ökologie, Deutsche Zoologische Gesellschaft. Home: Konrad-Adenauer Str 15, 37075 Göttingen, Niedersachsen Germany Office: 2d Zool Inst U Göttingen, Berliner Str 28, 37073 Göttingen Germany

SCHAEFER, PATRICIA, librarian; b. Ft. Wayne, Ind., Apr. 23, 1930; d. Edward John and Hildegarde Hartman (Hormel) S. MusB, Northwestern U., 1951; MusM, U. Ill., 1958; MLS, U. Mich., 1963. With U.S. Rubber co., Ft. Wayne, 1951-52; sec. to promotion mgr. Sta. WOWO, Ft. Wayne, Ind., 1952, sec. to program mgr., 1953-55; coord. publicity and promotion Home Telephone Co., Ft. Wayne, 1955-56; sec. Fin Arts Found., Ft. Wayne, 1956-57; libr. asst. Columbus (Ohio) Pub. Libr., 1958-59; audio-visual libr. Muncie (Ind.) Pub. Libr., 1959-86, asst. libr. dir., 1981-86, libr. dir., 1986-95; chmn. Ind. Libr. Film Cir., 1962-63; treas. Ind. Libr. Film Svc., 1969-70, 83-85; mem. trustee adv. coun. Milton S. Eisenhower Libr., Johns Hopkins U.; mem. presdl. counsellors Johns Hopkins U., 1994—; bd. dirs. Franklin Elec. Co., Inc. Weekly columnist Libr. Lines, Muncie Evening Press, 1981-83; program annotator Muncie Symphony Orch. and Masterworks Chorale; contbr. articles to profl. jours. Bd. dirs. Muncie Symphony Assn., 1964-74, 85-91; bd. dirs. Cen. City Bus. Assn., 1986-92, Ind. Inst. Tech., Ptnrs. for the Enhancement of Cmty. Coop., Ind. Humanities Coun., 1996—; adv. coun. Coll. Fine Arts, Ball State U.; mem. bd. dirs. Sta. WIPB-TV; mem. adv. com., bookshop dir. Midwest Writers Workshop, 1976-77; sec. Del. County Coun. for the ARts, 1978-79, pres., 1979-81, bd. dirs., 1985-86; mem. pres.'s coun. Berea Coll.; bd. dirs. Muncie YWCA, 1977-82, 85-89, 95—, treas. 1981-82, 88-89; bd. dirs. ARC, Hoosier Heartland chpt.; bd. govs. Minnetrista Cultural Ctr.; gen. chmn. Ind. Renaissance Fair, 1978-79; pres. Muncie Matinee Musicale, 1965-67; past pres. Ind. Film and Video Coun.; mem. adv. bd. Cmty. Found. Muncie and Delaware County; bd. dirs. Wapehani coun. Girl Scouts U.S., 1989-96; bd. dirs. Muncie Ctr. for Arts, 1999—. Named Woman Achievement Pub. Svc., 1986; recipient Sagamore of the Wabash award Gov. State of Ind., Outstanding Libr. award Ind. Libr. Fedn., 1995, Cert. of Congrl. Recognition, 1995, Cert. of Achievement, Women's Coalition, 1996, Cert. of Appreciation, Masterworks Chorale, 1998. Mem. ALA, Ind. Libr. Assn. (pres. 1987-88), Nat. League Am. Pen Women (pres. Muncie br. 1974-78), Altrusa (pres. 1986-87, cmty. svc. award 2000), Art Students League, Riley-Jones Club, Del. Country Club, Delta Zeta, Mu Phi Epsilon. Republican. Roman Catholic. Home: 5400 W Deer Run Ct Muncie IN 47304-5775

SCHAEFER, SABINE, veterinary surgeon; b. Essen, Germany, May 21, 1966; d. Herbert Anton and Marita Schaefer. M of Vet. Medicine, U. Vet. Medicine, Vienna, Austria, 1991, D of Vet. Medicine, 1994. Univ. asst. U. Vet. Medicine, Vienna, 1994—. Mem. Austrian Soc. Veterinarians (sec. 1996—), Österreichische gesellschaft zum studium der fertilität und sterilität, universitätslehrerverband, gesellschaft der freunde der veterinärmedizinischen universität. Avocations: sports, dog walking, books. Fax: 43 2236 22475. E-mail: sabine.schaefer@vu-wien.ac.at. Home: Hauptstr 19/101, Hinterbrühl 2371, Austria Office: U Vet Medicine, Veterinäplatz 1, Vienna 1210, Austria

SCHAEFER-WEISS, DOROTHEA L., literary researcher; b. Hamburg, Germany, Mar. 17, 1933; d. Wilhelm and Maria (Deinlein) Schaefer. State exam. for high sch. tchg., Georg-August U., Göttingen, Germany, 1956, PhD in German Lang. and Lit., 1960. Rschr. German lang. and lit. UCLA, 1964-65; assoc. prof. German lang. and lit. Duquesne U., Pitts., 1965-70; rsch. asst. dept. linguistics U. Hamburg, 1972-73; contbt. to Goethe Lexicon, Acad. Scis. in Göttingen, 1975—. Author: Der Leserkontakt in den Erzählungen H.v. Hofmannsthals, 1962, Subject-Index for the Hamburger Goethe edit., 1964, Zwischen Weimar und Jena, Goethes Briefe, Tagebuecher und Gespraeche 1816-1822, 1999. Mem. MLA, Internat. Assn. for Germanic Studies, German Soc. for 18th Century Studies. Avocations: geological excursions, cross-country skiing.

SCHAEFER-WICKE, ELIZABETH, reading consultant, educator; b. Bridgeport, Conn., Mar. 30, 1941; d. William Joseph and Loretta Schaefer; m. Frederick Paul wicke, July 3, 1976. BS, U. Conn., 1963; MA, Columbia U., 1966; 6th yr. profl. diploma, U. Bridgeport, 1975. Cert. reading cons. Elem. sch. tchr. Miles Ave. Sch., Huntington Park, Calif., 1963-64, Eli Whitney Sch., Meriden, Conn., 1966-68; supr. student tchg. interns Tracey Sch., Norwalk, Conn., 1968-70; reading splst. Wolfpit Sch., Norwalk, 1970-81; remedial reading and math tchr., cons. Rowayton (Conn.) Sch., 1981—; mentor tng. program BEST, 1987—, tchr. reading recovery, 1994—. Grantee Norwalk Fund for Excellence, 1986, 87. Mem. Norwalk Fedn. Tchrs. (bldg. steward 1981—), Internat. Reading Assn., Reading Recovery Coun. Am., Delta Kappa Gamma, Phi Delta Kappa. Democrat. Roman Catholic. Avocations: writing short stories, worldwide ednl. rsch., photography, scuba diving. Home: 41 Lakeview Dr Norwalk CT 06850-2003 also: 535 Broad Ave S Naples FL 34102-7159

SCHAEFFER, BARBARA HAMILTON, retired rental leasing company executive, writer; b. Newton, Mass., Apr. 26, 1926; d. Peter Davidson Gunn and Harriet Bennett (Thompson) Hamilton; m. John Schaeffer, Sept. 7, 1946; children: Laurie, John, Peter. Student, Skidmore Coll., 1943-46; AB in English, Bucknell U., 1961-62; postgrad., Montclair State U., 1950-51, Bank St. Coll. Edn., 1959-61, Yeshiva U., 1961-62. Cert. primary, secondary tchr. N.J. Dir. Pompton Plains Sch., N.J., 1959-62; adviser Episcopal Sch., Towaco, N.J., 1968-70; v.p. Deltona-DeLand Trolley, Orange City, Fla., 1980-81; pres. Monroe Heavy Equipment Rentals, Inc., Orange City, 1981—; also Magic Carpet Travel, 1985-88; cons., founder, pres. TLC Travel Club, Orange City, 1981-88; lectr. on children's art, 1959-70. Contbr. articles to profl. publs. Mem. LWV, AAUW, Internat. Platform Assn., Small Bus. Devel. Regional Ctr. (Stetson U. chpt.), Nat. Trust Historic Preservation. Episcopalian. Avocations: restoring old homes, oil painting, piano, writing. Home: 400 Foothill Farms Rd Orange City FL 32763-5502 Address: PO Box 688 DeBary FL 32713-0688

SCHAEFFER, EVELYNE, biochemist, molecular biologist, researcher; b. Strasbourg, France, Oct. 1, 1952; d. Andre and Jeanne (Lieber) S. MS, U. Louis-Pasteur, Strasbourg, 1974, DS, 1976, PhD, 1979. Rschr. Ctr. Nat. Rsch. Sci., Strasbourg, 1977-79, Pasteur Inst. Ctr. Nat. Rsch. Sci., Paris, 1982-93, INSERM U338 Ctr. Nat. Rsch. Sci., Strasbourg, 1993—; postdoctoral rschr. U. Calif., Berkeley, 1979-82; investigator Gladstone Inst. of Virology and Immunology, San Francisco, 1999—. Contbr. rsch. articles to profl. jours. Mem. N.Y. Acad. Scis. Office: INSERM U338, 5 Rue Blaise Pascal, 67084 Strasbourg France

SCHAEFFER, HEINZ, law educator; b. Vienna, Austria, Apr. 25, 1941; s. Cyrill and Margaretha (Straszniczky) S.; m. Maria Jesus Montoro, Jan. 3, 1995. JD, U. Vienna, 1963. From asst. to prof. U. Vienna, 1963-76; min. counsellor Federal Chancellery, Vienna, 1973-76; prof. pub. law U. Salzburg, Austria, 1976—; cons. in field; pres. Austrian Assn. of Legis., 1982—; mem. Constnl. Court, 1999—. Author: Verfassungsinterpretation in Oesterreich, 1971, Theory of Legislation, 1988, Quantitative Analyses of Law, 1990; editor: Zeitschrift fur Oeffentliches Recht, Oesterreichische Verfassungsund Verwaltungsgesetz (loose leaf textbook), 4th edit., 1981—. Office: U Salzburg, U Salzburg, Kapitelgasse 5, A-5020 Salzburg Austria

SCHAEFFER, LEONARD DAVID, healthcare executive; b. Chgo., July 28, 1945; s. David and Sarah (Levin) S.; m. Pamela Lee Sidford, Aug. 11, 1968; children: David, Jacqueline. BA, Princeton U., 1969. Mgmt. cons. Arthur Andersen & Co., 1969-73; dep. dir. mgmt. Ill. Mental Health/Devel. Disability, Springfield, 1973-75; dir. Ill. Bur. of Budget, Springfield, 1975-76; v.p. Citibank, N.A., N.Y.C., 1976-78; asst. sec. mgmt. and budget HHS, Washington, 1978, adminstr. HCFA, 1978-80; exec. v.p., COO Student Loan Mktg. Assn., Washington, 1980-82; pres., CEO Group Health, Inc., Mpls., 1983-86; chmn., CEO Blue Cross of Calif., Woodland Hills, 1986—, WellPoint Health Networks Inc., 1992—; bd. dirs. Allergan, Inc., Irvine, Calif.; bd. councilors U. So. Calif. Sch. Pub. Adminstrn., 1988—; bd. dirs. exec com. Blue Cross-Blue Shield Assn., Chgo., 1986—; mem. Congl. Prospective Payment Assessment Commn., 1987-93; mem. Pew Health Professions Com., Phila., 1990-93; chmn. bd. trustees Nat. Health Found., L.A., 1992—; chmn. Nat. Inst. Health Care Mgmt., 1993—; mem. Coun. on the Econ. Impact of Health Sys. Change, 1996—; mem. adv. coun. dept. of health care policy Harvard Med. Sch., 1998—; chmn. Coalition for Affordable and Quality Healthcare, 2000. Mem. editl. adv. bd. Managed Healthcare, 1989—. Bd. govs. Town Hall of Calif., L.A., 1989—; bd. trustees The Brookings Inst., Nat. Health Mus., 2000. Kellogg Found. fellow, 1981-89, Internat. fellow King's Fund Coll., London, 1990—; recipient Citation-Outstanding Svc., Am. Acad. Pediats., 1981, Disting. Pub. Svc. award HEW, Washington, 1980. Mem. NAS, Inst. of Medicine, Health Ins. Assn. Am. (chmn. 1999), Cosmos Club, Princeton Club, Regency Club. Office: Wellpoint Health Networks Inc 1 Wellpoint Way Thousand Oaks CA 91362-3893

SCHAEFFNER, CHRISTINA, linguistics educator; b. Schlotheim, Thuringia, Germany, July 29, 1950; d. Walter and Gerta (Lang) S. Diploma, U. Leipzig, Germany, 1973, DrPhil, 1977. Tchg. asst. U. Leipzig, Germany, 1976-78, jr. lectr., 1978-82; head rsch. team Saxon Acad. Arts and Scis., Leipzig, 1982-92; lectr. Aston U., Birmingham, Eng., 1992-99, sr. lectr., 1999—, co-dir. Inst. Study Lang. and Soc., 1996—. Co-editor: (with Albrecht Neubert) Politischer Wortschatz in textueller Sicht, 1986, (with Christiane Villain-Gandossi, Klaus Bochmann, Michael Metzeltin) The Concept of Europe in the process of CSCE, 1990, (with Anita Wenden) Language and Peace, 1995, (with Andreas Musolff, Michael Townson) Conceiving of Europe - Diversity in Unity, 1996, (with Helen Kelly-Holmes) Cultural Functions of Translation, 1995, Discourses and Ideologies, 1996; editor: Gibt es eine prototypische Wortschatzbeschreibung? Eine Problemdiskussion, 1990, Translation and Quality, 1998, Translation and Norms, 1999, Analysing Political Spectres, 1997. Mem. Town Twinning Com., Birmingham, 1993—. Fellow Inst. Linguists; mem. European Soc. for Translation Studies, Soc. Lang. in Politics, German Soc. for Applied Linguistics. Office: Aston U, Aston Triangle, Birmingham B4 7ET, England

SCHAERPF, OTTO WILHELM, physicist; b. Walldürn, Germany, Aug. 8, 1929; s. Otto Albert and Maria Anna (Kuhn) S. Dr.habil., Tech. U. Braunschweig, Germany, 1977. Scientific asst. T.U. Braunschweig, Germany, 1968-73, 73-79; physicist Inst.Langevin, Grenoble, France, 1979-96; com. dir. E21 Tech. U. Munich, Germany, 1987-88. Contbr. articles to profl. jours. Mem. Deutsche Physikalisch. Gesellschaft, Acad. Sci. Europe. Roman Catholic. Achievements include development of a very efficient neutron polarizer using supermirrors, construction of a multidetector diffuse scattering instrument with plarization analysis applying this polarizer. Home: Alfred Delp Haus, Zuccalistrasse 16, 80639 Munich Germany Office: Physics Dept E13, James Franck Str 1, D-85748 Garching Germany

SCHAFER, DONNA ELIZABETH, gerontological educator, university administrator; b. Wichita, Kans., Sept. 26, 1948; d. Donald Frederick and Eunice Geneva Schafer; m. Forrest Jay Berghorn, Mar. 17, 1990. BA with distinction, U. Kans., 1970, MPhil, 1974, PhD with honors, 1984. Rsch. assoc. U. Kans., Lawrence, 1979-88; asst. prof. San Francisco State U., 1988-91, assoc. prof., 1991-2000, assoc. dean, 1994-2000; prof. Humboldt State U., 2000—, dean, 2000—; cons. Kans. Dept. Aging, Topeka, 1982, Advocacy Coun. Aging, Lawrence, 1986-88, County Coun. Aging, Johnson County, Kans., 1986, Mills-Peninsula Hosps., Burlingame, Calif., 1992-95. Author: The Urban Elderly, 1978, Reminiscence and Nursing Home Life, 1994; author, editor: The Dynamics of Aging, 1981 (Choice award 1981); contbr. articles to profl. jours. Bd. dirs. Sr. Arts Coun., Kansas City, 1977-79, Svcs. for Srs., Kansas City, 1982-85; v.p. bd. dirs. Ministry to Nursing Homes, San Francisco, 1994—. Mem. Gerontol. Soc. Am., Am. Soc. Aging, Sigma Phi Omega, Sigma Xi, Phi Beta Kappa, Phi Kappa Phi. Avocations: travel, cooking, gardening, sports. E-mail: schafer@humboldt.edn. Home: Office Rsch Grad Studies Humboldt State U One Harpst St Arcata CA 95521

SCHAFER, ELIZABETH DIANE, historian, writer; b. Opelika, Ala., Sept. 26, 1965; d. Robert Louis and Carolyn Louise (Henn) S. BA in History cum laude, Auburn U., 1986, MA in History of Sci. magna cum laude, 1988, PhD in History of Tech. magna cum laude, 1993; postgrad., Hollins Coll., 1996-98. Archivist Lee County Hist. Soc. Mus., 1988—; ind. scholar, 1993—; presenter in field. Author: Beacham's Sourcebook for Teaching Young Adult Fiction: Exploring Harry Potter, 2000; co-author: Women Who Made A Difference in Alabama, 1995; cons. editor Ency. of Sci., 1998; freelance editor various tech. docs.; editl. asst. Proceedings of the We. Soc. for French History, 1988-91, Nat. Forum: The Phi Kappa Phi Jour., 1990-91; contbr. History News Svc.; contbr. articles to profl. jours., encys., mags., chpts. to books. Recipient hon. mention poetry Writer's Digest, 1994 hon. mention children's non-fiction, 1997, children's non-fiction and fiction, 1998, Writer's Digest, Shirley Henn Meml. award Critical scholar, Hollins Coll., 1998. Mem. AAAS, AAUW, Am. Hist. Assn., Orgn. Am. Historians, Soc. History Tech., History Sci. Soc., Women's History Network, N.Y. Acad.

Scis., So. Hist. Assn., Soc. Children's Book Writers and Illustrators, Children's Lit. Assn., Ala. Writer's Forum, Assn. Gravestone Studies, Lancaster Mennonite Hist. Soc., Lee County Hist. Soc. (life mem.), Auburn U. Alumni Assn. (life mem.), Descendants Mexican War Vets., United Daus. of the Confederacy (v.p. Adm. Semmes chpt.), DAR (chmn. Light Horse Harry Lee's geneal. records com.), Daus. of Union Vets., Phi Alpha Theta (history hon.). Home and Office: PO Box 57 Loachapoka AL 36865-0057

SCHÄFER, HANS-BERND, economist, educator; b. Germany, May 25, 1943; s. Bernhard and Elisabeth S.; m. Doris Hofert, Aug. 30, 1968; children: Ilona, Anna. Diploma, U. Cologne, 1966, U. Cologne, 1967; D in Econs., U. Bochum, 1971. Staff Bank fur Gemeinwirtschaft, Frankfurt, Germany, 1970-71; asst. prof. U. Bochum, 1971-76; prof. econs. U. Hamburg, 1976—; dir. Inst. for Law and Econs., U. Hamburg, 1995—; coord. postgrad. Erasmus Program Law and Econs. Co-editor Internat. Rev. Law and Econs., 1966—. Fellow Ctr. Advanced Study Norwegian Acad. Sci.; mem. European Assn. Law and Econs., German Econs. Assn. Home: Rantzaustr 20a, Wirtschaftswissenschaften, 22926 Ahrensburg Germany Office: U Hamburg, Rechtswissenschaft II, 20146 Hamburg Germany

SCHÄFER, KAROLA, chemist, researcher; b. Mayen, Germany, Dec. 2, 1954; s. Werner and Luzia Schäfer. Degree in food chemistry, U. Bonn, 1980; PhD, Tech. U., Aachen, 1983. Group leader Deutsches Wollforschungsinstitut, Aachen, 1983—. Author: Peptides, 1987; contbr. articles to profl. jours. Mem. Deutsche Krebshilfe, Bonn, 1990, UNICEF, Cologne, 1993. Mem. Soc. German Chemists, Assn. Textile Chemists and Colorists, German Soc. Colour Sci. Roman Catholic. Office: Deutsches Wollforschunginst, Veltmanplatz 8, D-52062 Aachen Germany

SCHÄFER, LUDWIG OTTO, metallurgist, researcher; b. Albota, Bessarabia, Rumania, Jan. 24, 1938; arrived in Germany, 1940; s. Otto and Alma (Kuhn) S.; m. Gertrud Irmgard Blanke, May 5, 2000; children: Anette, Frank, Matthias, Simone. Diploma in engring., T.H. Clausthal U., Germany, 1966. Sect. leader Standard Elektrik Lorenz A.G., Esslingen, Germany, 1966-68, Forschungszentrum Karlsruhe, Karlsruhe, Germany, 1969-00. Contbr. 100 articles to profl. jours.; patentee: 3 patents. Presbyter Badische Landeskirche, Germany, 1977-95; Marburger Kreis, Germany, 1966—. Mem. Soc. German Steel Men. Home: Hagwäldle 6, 76646 Bruchsal-Hel Germany Office: Forschungszentrum Karlsruhe, PF 3640, 76021 Karlsruhe Germany

SCHAFER, RUTH ERMA, artist, educator; b. Thompson, Mo., Nov. 23, 1923; d. Lewis Maxwell and Maude Ethel (Keller) Johnson; m. Paul Linzy Starlin (dec. Jan. 1987); children: Barbara Ann White, Larry David, Stephen Paul, Paula Lynn Norris, Randal Lee; m. Justin Schafer. Student, Art Sch. of Ft. Wayne, Ind. Bus. mgr. Chevrolet Dealership, Portland, Ind.; tchr. Portland Art Sch., 1964-88. Artist oil paintings, portraits, sea scapes, landscapes, still life; exhibited in shows in Atlanta, Chgo., N.Y.C., Indpls., Ft. Wayne, Brown County Art Guild. Leader Girl Scouts U.S., Boy ScoutsAm., 4-H Club; head art booths Jay County Fairs; tchr. Sunday sch. Ch. of Christ; selected by Gov. Bowen of Ind. to serve as Ind. Arts Commn. cultural rep., 1967. Named Mother of the Yr., C. of C. of Portland, 1957; honored by Sen. Birch Bayh as one of the Ind. Artists, Washington, 1965. Mem. Ind. Fedn. Art Clubs (pres. 1975-77, treas. 1971-75), Nat. Endowment for the Arts (charter), The Hoosier Salon.

SCHAFER, WILLIAM HARRY, loss prevention consultant; b. South Portsmouth, Ky., Aug. 22, 1936; s. William Harry and Mary Minnie (Papillon) S. AS, Franklin U., 1980; BA, Capital U., 1987; MS, Greenwich U., 1992. Cert. fraud examiner; cert. protection profl.; cert. profl. mgr. With Columbus (Ohio) region Am. Electric Power (formerly Columbus So. Power), 1969-97; cons. loss prevention Columbus, 1997—. First aid instr. Franklin County ARC, Columbus, 1965-93; mem. Simon Kenton coun. Boy Scouts Am. Named Ky. Col., 1974, Ky. Adm., 1994, Hon. (Ohio) Lt. Gov., 1974; recipient Columbus Mayor's award for Vol. Svc., 1982, Outstanding Cmty. Svc. award Ohio Senate, 1982, Humanitarian Achievement award Columbus Dispatch newspaper, 1983, Silver Beaver award Boy Scouts Am., 1979, 50 Yr. Vets. award, 1997, cert. of appreciation Ohio Ho. of Reps., 1997; James E. West fellow Boy Scouts Am., 1995. Mem. Nat. Assn. Cert. Fraud Examiners (life), Acad. Security Educators and Trainers, Am. Soc. Indsl. Security, Valley Forge Hist. Soc. (life), Ky. Hist. Soc. (life), U.S. Capitol Hist. Soc. (supporting founding mem.), Nat. Safety Coun. (camping com. 1974-86), Nat. Fire Protection Assn. (edn. com. 1989-93), Children's Club-Children's Hosp. (charter), Scioto County (Ohio) Hist. Soc. (life), Masons, Shriners. Methodist. Avocations: back-packing, travel, humanities. Home: 60 Broadmeadows Blvd Apt 327 Columbus OH 43214-1152

SCHÄFERDIEK, KNUT, church history educator; b. Cologne, Germany, Nov. 11, 1930; s. Willi and Ingeborg (Krägeloh) S.; m. Helga Siermann, Mar. 9, 1962; children: Christian, Barbara. ThD, U. Bonn, Germany, 1958, cert. univ. lectr., 1966. Lectr. in ch. history U. Bonn, 1966-70, prof. ch. history, 1970-79, prof. in ordinary, 1979—. Author: Die Kirche in den Reichen der Westgoten, 1967; co-editor: Theolog Realenzyklopädie, 1976, Schwellenzeit, 1996; contbr. articles to scholarly publs. Home: Jahnstrasse 38g, D 53797 Lohmar 1, Germany Office: Evangel Theol Seminar, U Bonn Am Hof 1, D 53113 Bonn Germany

SCHÄFER-KORTING, MONIKA, pharmacology educator, university official; b. Giessen, Germany, May 7, 1952; d. Adalbert and Barbara (Ullrich) S.; m. Hans Christian Korting, Apr. 25, 1980; children: Sabine, Christina. Abitur, Herderschule, Frankfurt, Germany, 1970; pharmacist, U. Frankfurt, 1974, PhD, 1976. Jr. lectr. U. Frankfurt, Frankfurt, 1975-79, 81-92, Tech. U., Munich, 1980-81; lectr. Freie U. Berlin, 1992-94, prof., 1994—, v.p., 1997—. Contbr. articles to profl. jours. Recipient Homburg Preis Ges. ärztliche Fortbildung, Regensburg, 1979, Rsch. award La Roche Posay, 1996. Mem. Soc. for Dermatopharmacology, German Pharm. Soc., German Soc. Pharmacol. Toxicology. Roman Catholic. Avocations: classical music, mountain walking. Office: Freie U Berlin Dept Pharm, Königin Luise Str 2-4, D-14195 Berlin Germany

SCHAFFER, CANDLER GARELD, conductor, hornist, educator; b. Takoma Park, Md., June 2, 1950; s. Henry Louis and June Georgette (Schweitzer) S. MusB, U. Miami, 1972; MEd, U. Md., 1977; MFA, U. Iowa, 1991, D Mus. Arts, 1992. Dir. orchestral studies Oreg. State U., Corvallis, 1982-85, Tex. Christian U., Ft. Worth, 1985-90; music dir., condr. Fla. Space Coast Philharm., Cocoa, 1995-99, Fla. Space Coast Pops, Cocoa, 1996-99, Wichita Falls (Tex.) Symphony Orch., 1996—, Wichita Falls Chamber Orch., 1998—; mem. classical music selection panel Oreg. Arts Commn., 1984-85; grant cons. Irving (Tex.) Arts Coun., 1998; founder, bd. dirs. Camerata Winds Melbourne, Fla., 1994-96; co-founder, prin. condr. North Tex. Wind Symphony, Wichita Falls, 1997; adj. instr. horn Midwestern State U., 1996—. Bd. dirs. Willamette Arts Coun., Corvallis, 1983-85; mem. cultural execs. com. Brevard Cultural Alliance, Brevard County, Fla., 1995-96; co-founder, bd. dirs. Century Concerts, Wichita Falls, 1997—. Mem. Am. Symphony Orch. League, Am. Fedn. Musicians. Avocations: running, surfing, hiking, reading, yoga. Home: 704 Greenwood Manor Cir West Melbourne FL 32904-1914 Office: Wichita Falls Symphony Orch 4500 Seymour Hwy Ste 104 Wichita Falls TX 76309-2612

SCHÄFFER, MICHAEL RALF, physician, surgeon; b. Hannover, Germany, Oct. 16, 1965; s. Heino Ludwig and Gisela (Rössler) S.; m. Julia Hohenstein, Aug. 9, 1997; children: Leopold, Luise. MD, U. Munich, Germany, 1991. Rsch. fellow Johns Hopkins U., Balt., 1993-95; resident Univ. Hosp., Tübingen, Germany, 1991-93, Univ Hosp., Tübingen, GErmany, 1995—. Contbr. articles to profl. jours. Mem. German Soc. Surgery, European Tissue Repair Soc. Office: Chirurgische Klinic/Surgery, Hoppe-Seyler-Str 3, 72076 Tübingen Germany

SCHAFFMAN, KAREN HELEN, performing company executive; b. Hartford, Conn., Oct. 8, 1962; d. Marvin Nathan and Myrna Kaplan Schaffman; m. Jeffrey Scott Berson, July 8, 1994. BA, U. Mass., 1985, European Dance Devel. Ctr., Arnheim, The Netherlands, 1991; postgrad., U. Calif., Riverside. Tchr. Sch. New Dance & Theatre, Hannover, Germany, 1992-94; co-dir. Lower Left Dance Co., San Diego, 1995—; tchg. assoc., asst. U. Calif., Riverside, 1996-99; mentor Sushi Performance & Visual Arts, San Diego, 1998-00; guest lectr. U. Calif., Davis, 1999. Choreographer performance play by Hrostvita Von Gandersheim, Germany, 1993, San Diego Symphony Orch., 1993, World War II Meml., Germany, 1997. Vol. Am. Heart Assn., 1993-95, Sushi Performance & Visual Arts, San Diego, 1995—. Fellow Gluck Found., 1997-2000. Avocations: swimming, art, music, theatre, travel.

SCHAFFNER, CYNTHIA VAN ALLEN, writer, curator, lecturer; b. Washington, Jan. 28, 1947; d. James Alfred and Abigail Fifthian (Halsey) Van Allen; m. Robert Todd Schaffner, June 11, 1972; 1 child, Hilary Van Allen. BA, Western Coll., 1969; MAT, Simmons Coll., 1971; MA in History of Decorative Arts, Cooper Hewitt Smithsonian Instn., N.Y.C., 1999. Editor Mademoiselle mag., N.Y.C., 1972-79; dir. devel. Am. Acad. in Rome, N.Y.C., 1987-89; curator Phila. Antiques Show, 1997-98; rsch. asst. Metropolitan Mus. Art, New York, 1999—; curator Halsey House, Southampton, N.Y., 1999—. Author: Discovering American Folk Art, 1991; co-author: Folk Hearts, 1984, American Painted Furniture, 1997; contbr. articles to popular mags. Co-chair Fall Antiques Show, N.Y.C., 1979-93; trustee Mus. Am. Folk Art, N.Y.C., 1980-95. Lisa Taylor fellow, 1995-96; Smithsonian Instn. Grad. Student fellow, 1998. Mem. Coll. Art Assn., Decorative Arts Soc., Cosmopolitan Club, Victorian Soc., Lenox Hill Hosp. Aux., Southampton Hist. Mus. (trustee 1996—). Avocations: canoeing, gardening, antiquing. Home: 850 Park Ave New York NY 10021-1845

SCHAFFNER, KURT WALTER, chemistry researcher; b. Zürich, Switzerland, Oct. 6, 1931; s. Walter K. and Elis (Kaufmann) S.; m. Gertraud Lindgens, Oct. 2, 1981. D Sci. Tech., Swiss Fed. Inst. Tech., Zürich, 1957; doctorate (hon.), U. Sarriá, Barcelona, Spain, 1991. Lectr. Swiss Fed. Inst. Tech., 1963-71; prof. chemistry U. Geneva, 1971-76; dir. Max-Planck-Inst. für Strahlenchemie, Mülheim a.d. Ruhr, Fed. Republic Germany, 1976-99, emeritus, 1999—. Contbr. over 300 articles to profl. jours. Recipient Werner medal Swiss Chem. Soc., 1965, Ruzicka award Swiss Fedn. Inst. Tech., 1968, Havinga medal U. Leiden, 1990, Dewey and Kelly award U. Nebr., 1995, European Soc. for Photobiology award, 1997. Mem. European Photochemistry Assn. (pres. 1972-76), European Soc. Photobiology (founding pres. 1985-86, Award 1997), Am. Soc. Photobiology, Am. Chem. Soc., German Chem. Soc., Swiss Chem. Soc., Nordrheinisch-Westfälische Akademie des Wissenschaften (v.p. 1998-99), Gesellschaft deutscher Ärzte und Naturforscher, Deutsche Akademie der Naturforscher Leopoldina, Academia Europaea, N.Y. Acad. Scis., Rotary (local pres. 1986-87). Office: M Planck-Inst Strahlenchem, PO Box 101365, D-45413 Muelheim an der Ruhr Germany

SCHAGERL, MICHAEL, biologist, researcher; b. Vienna, Austria, Nov. 14, 1966; s. Joseph and Edith (Philipp) S.; m. Daniela Wald (div. 1989); 1 child, Florian; m. Manuela Zinöcker, Apr. 30, 1999; children: Hannah, Julia. Diploma, U. Vienna, 1989, D, 1993. Pvt. practice Austria, 1989-97; lectr. U. Vienna, 1990—, asst., 1997—; referee Internat. Rev. Hydrobiology, Germany, 1999. Contbr. articles to profl. jours. Avocations: hike, cycle, music. Office: U Vienna Inst Ecology & Con, Althanstrasse 14, 1080 Vienna Austria

SCHAICH, GEORG EBERHARD, statistics educator; b. Stuttgart, Germany, Nov. 25, 1940; s. Eugen Emil and Emma (Roehm) S.; m. Gisela Ilse Felgner, June 25, 1941; children: Christoph, Regine, Susanne. D of Polit. Econs., Ludwig-Maximilians-U., Munich, 1967, Habilitation, 1969. Office clk. Dr. Karl Thomae GmbH, Biberachriss, 1958-60; asst. prof. stats. U. Munich, 1964-70; prof. U. Regensburg, 1970-77; prof. stats. and econometrics U. Tuebingen, 1977—, pres., rector, 1999—. Author: Statistics I, II, 1993, 94, Nonparametric Statistics, 1984, Textbook Econometrics, 1999, Economic Statistics, 1995, New Demographic Faces of Europe, 2000, others. Mem. Internat. Statis. Inst., Am. Statis. Assn., Internat. Union of Sci. Study Population, Rotary. Avocations: piano, tennis. Home: Wannweiler StraBe 22, D-72138 Kirchentellinsfurt Germany Office: Wirtschaftswissenschaftlich, Seminar Mohlstrasse 36, D-72074 Tuebingen Germany

SCHAISON, GERARD SIMON, physician, researcher; b. Paris, Sept. 27, 1931; s. Geoffroy David and Germaine (Bloch) S.; m. Liliane Menkes, June 24, 1962; children: Philippe, Patrick, Olivia. MD, U. Paris, 1963. Resident Hosp. Paris, 1959-63; prof. hematology, 1972, pediatrician, 1976; head dept. pediat. hematology St. Louis Hosp., Paris, 1980-98; chmn. French Protocols Leukemia, Paris, 1980, European Sch. Hematology, 1980; emeritus U. Paris, 1998-2000. Author: Pediatric Hematology, 1990; author, editor Hematology of Children, 1995; contbr. over 700 articles to profl. jours. Recipient Legion of Honor, Paris, 1992. Avocations: painting, golf, skiing. Home: Pompe St 115, 75116 Paris France Office: St Louis Hosp, 2 Av Vellefaux, 75010 Paris France

SCHALK, PETER H., biologist, consultant; b. Haarlem, The Netherlands, Jan. 24, 1955; s. Pieter and Johanna Maria (Van Zeil) S.; m. Hilde B. Kooi, Oct. 30, 1987. D of Biology, U. Amsterdam, The Netherlands, 1982, PhD Marine Biology, 1988. Rschr. Zool. Mus., Amsterdam, 1984-88, Nioz, Texel, The Netherlands, 1986-88; sr. rschr. AWI, Bremerhaven, Germany, 1988-89; mng. dir. ETI U. Amsterdam, 1990—; editor Polar Biology jour., Springer, Germany, 1989—; chmn. SBNO, Amsterdam, 1982—; sec. Species 2000, Southampton, Eng., 1995-97, vice-chmn., 1997—. Author: Monsoon Influences on Biogeography and Ecology of Zooplankton of the Indo-Malayan Region, 1985; editor: The Expedition Antarctis VII/3 of RV Polarstern n 1908, 1989, (CD-ROM) Birds of Europe, 1994, The North Sea CD, 1997. Avocations: sailing, computer aided design, artwork. Home: Mauritskade 19, 1091 96 Amsterdam The Netherlands Office: ETI U Amsterdam, Mauritskade 61, 1092 AD Amsterdam The Netherlands

SCHALKWIJK, JOHAN PIETER, information and communication educator; b. Rijswijk, The Netherlands, Nov. 1, 1936; s. Jan and Adriana Geertruida (Beijl) S.; m. Susan alicia Farranto, Sept. 17, 1966; children: Karin, Jan, Lucy, Susanna. MSEE, Delft (The Netherlands) U., 1959; PhD in Elec. Engring., Stanford U., 1965. Scientist Nat. Def. Labs., The Hague, The Netherlands, 1961-63, Nat. Aeronautics Lab., Amsterdam, The Netherlands, 1963; sr. scientist Gen. Telephone & Electronics, Boston, 1965-68; asst. prof. U. Calif., San Diego, 1968-72; prof. U. Eindhoven, The Netherlands, 1972-98; pres. Soc. Info. and Comms. Theory in Benelux, Eindhoven, 1986-94; mem. sci. com. for applied math. and computer sci. Nat. Aeronautics and Astronautics Labs., Amsterdam, 1985—. Contbr. articles to profl. jours. 1st lt. Netherlands armed forces, 1959-61. Fellow IEEE (Best Paper award 1967, bd. govs. 1977-80); mem. Netherlands Electronics and Radio Soc. (hon., bd. dirs. 1976-84). Home: Jan Van Rotselaerlaan 4, 5581 EA Waalre The Netherlands Office: U Eindhoven, PO Box 513, 5600 MB Eindhoven The Netherlands

SCHALLER, BERNHARD JAKOB, physician; b. Liestal, Switzerland, Nov. 1, 1969; s. Jakob and Ursula (Kuster) S. MD, U. Basel, Switzerland, 1995. Resident in gen. surgery, 1995; resident in neurol. surgery Basel, 1996-98, resident in neurology, 1999—. Contbr. articles to German and English med. jours.

SCHALLER, HANS NIKOLAUS, telecommunications industry executive; b. Freiburg, Germany, Sept. 19, 1963; s. Karl Heinz and Waltraut (Fuchs) S.; m. Andrea Margrit Wolf, Apr. 26, 1996; 1 child, Katrin Susanne. MS in Engring., Tech. U., Munich, 1987; PhD, Tech. U., 1994. Scientific asst. Tech. U., 1988-95; rsch. engr. Siemens Mobile Networks, Munich, 1995; product mgr. Siemens Telephone Divsn., Munich, 1996—; rsch. project leader Tech. U., 1990-95; cons. Bavarian Dept. Interior, Germany, 1991-93; guest lectr. various univs., Japan, 1994-95; chmn. 6th Internat. DECT Congress, Rome, 2000. Author: (software) CONPAR-90/VAPPIV, 1990, WILMA SNMP Toolkit, 1991-94, Mac06, 1998-2000. With civil med. svc. Alfried Krupp Hosp., Essen, Germany, 1987-88. Mem. IEEE, GI, VDE/ITG, AMSAT DL. Avocations: sailing, dancing, skiing, amateur radio.

SCHALLER, HELMUT WILHELM, philology educator; b. Bayreuth, Germany, Apr. 16, 1940; s. Christoph and Margarete Pauline (Schmidt) S.; m. Edigne Rogl, July 30, 1974; children: Peter, Anja. PhD, U. Munich, 1965, habilitation Slavic philology, 1972, habilitation Balkan philology, 1973. Scientific asst., lectr., prof. U. Munich, 1972-82; prof. U. Marburg, Hesse, Germany, 1983—; vis. prof. U. Saarland, 1974, U. Regensburg, Bavaria, 1976-77, U. Provence, France, 1978, U. Salzburg, Austria, 1978-79; adminstr. Kleiner Balkansprachatlas, U. Marburg. Author: Die Wortstellung im Russischen Munich, 1966, Das Prädikatsnomen im Russischen, 1975, Die Balkansprachen Eine Einführung in die Balkanphilologie, 1975, many others; editor numerous profl. jours.; contbr. articles to profl. jours. Recipient Cyrill and Method award Govt. of Bulgaria, 1990. Mem. S.E. European Soc. (sci. coun. 1975), Internat. Commn. for History Slavic Studies, Internat. Commn. for Study Grammatical Structure of Slavic Langs. (pres.) , Internat. Commn. for Balkan Linguistics, Deutsch-Bulgarische Gesellschaft (pres.). Lutheran. Office: Inst für Slawische Philolog, Wilhelm-Röpke Str 6D, D-35039 Marburg Germany

SCHALLER, JOANNE F., nursing consultant; b. Columbus, Ga., July 15, 1943; d. John Frank and Ethel Beatrice (Spring) Lanzendorfer; m. Robert Thomas Schaller, Jan. 22, 1977; 1 child, Amy. BS, Pacific Luth. U., 1969; M in Nursing, U. Wash., 1971. House supr. UCLA Hosp., 1971-72; outpatient supr. Harborview Hosp., Seattle, 1973-75; outpatient clinic and emergency room supr. U. Wash. Hosp., Seattle, 1975-77; nurse specialist in hypertension, 1975—; co-author, researcher with Robert Schaller MD Seattle, 1977-87; prin. Nursing Expert-Standards of Care, Seattle, 1987—; cons. Wash. State Trial Lawyers, Wash. Assn. Criminal Def. Lawyers, 1989—, Bastyr U., 1999—; founder, CEO Present Perfect, Seattle, 1991—; appt. Breast Cancer cons. UWMC, 1995—. Contbr., editor articles to profl. jours. Bd. dirs. Pacific Arts Ctr., 1992—; vol. guardian ad litem King County Juvenile Ct., 1978—; vol. Make a Wish Found. U.S. Bank, 1984—, Multiple Sclerosis Assn., 1986—, Am. Heart Assn., 1986—, Internat. Children's Festival, 1987—, Seattle Children's Festival, 1987—, Seattle Dept. Parks and Recreation Open Space Com., 1990—, Pacific N.W. Athletic Congress, 1991—, Wash. Fed. Garden Clubs Jr. Advisor, 1992—, Fred Hutchison Cancer Rsch. Ctr., 1993—; mem. parent coun. Seattle Country Day Sch., 1986-96—, volunteer, U.S. Rowing events; mem. Photo Coun. Seattle Art Mus., 1986—, Native Am. Coun., 1989—; mem. N.W. Coun. Seattle Art Mus., 1992—, mem. NAOO Coun. Seattle Art Mus., 1989—, Plestcheeff Inst. Decorative Arts, 1992—; mem. fundraiser Children's Hosp. Med. Ctr., 1977—, Breast Cancer Fund, 1994—, Susan G. Komen Breast Cancer Found., 1994—. Named 1st Migrant Health Care Nurse, State of Wash., 1966, 1st Am. nurse visiting China, 1974. Mem. AAUW, ANA, Wash. State Nurses Assn., U. Wash. Alumni Assn. Avocations: photography, writing, gardening, hiking, music. Home and Office: 914 Randolph Pl Seattle WA 98122-5267

SCHALLER, OSKAR HEINRICH, veterinary anatomy educator, researcher; b. Linz, Austria, July 5, 1923; s. Oskar Karl and Antonia (Nagl) S.; m. Hermine Kutner, June 27, 1953; children: Thomas, Peter, Nikolaus. DVM, Vet. U. Vienna, Austria, 1951; MD, U. Vienna, 1958. Asst. Inst. Anatomy Vet. U. Vienna, 1950-62, prof. vet. anatomy, 1962—, rector, 1974-77, 81-83, 1987-91; mem. Internat. Com. Vet. Anat. Nomenclature, 1957-60, chmn. subcom., 1961-80, exec. v.p., 1963-65, pres., 1965-80. Editor, co-author: Illustrated Veterinary Anatomical Nomenclature, 1992, Spanish translation, 1996, Portuguese translation, 1999, Italian translation, 1999; chmn. editl. com. Nomina Anatomica Veterinaria, 1968. Decorated Ehrenkreuz für Wissenschaft 1st class, 1978, Grosses Goldenes Ehrenzeichen (Austria), 1992; recipient gold honor medal Cmty. of Vienna, 1989. Mem. World Assn. Vet. Anatomists, Anat. Soc., Austrian Soc. Veterinarians (pres.), European Assn. Vet. Anatomists (pres. 1974-77). Roman Catholic. Avocations: history, tennis. Home: Löwengasse 20, A-1030 Vienna Austria Office: Vet Med U, Veterinarplatz 1, A-1210 Vienna Austria

SCHALLY, ANDREW VICTOR, endocrinologist, researcher; b. Poland, Nov. 30, 1926; came to U.S., 1957; s. Casimir Peter and Maria (Lacka) S.; m. Ana Maria Comaru, Aug., 1976. BSc, McGill U., Can., 1955, PhD in Biochemistry, 1957; 18 hon. doctorates. Research asst. biochemistry Nat. Inst. Med. Research, London, 1949-52; dept. psychiatry McGill U., Montreal, Que., 1952-57; research assoc., asst. prof. physiology and biochemistry Coll. Medicine, Baylor U., Houston, 1957-62; assoc. prof. Tulane U. Sch. Medicine, New Orleans, 1962-67, prof., 1967—; chief Endocrine Polypeptide and Cancer Inst. VA Med. Ctr., New Orleans; sr. med. investigator VA, 1973-99, disting. med. rsch. scientist, 1999—. Author several books; contbr. articles to profl. jours. Recipient Van Meter prize Am. Thyroid Assn., 1969; Ayerst-Squibb award Endocrine Soc., 1970; William S. Middletown award VA, 1970; Ch. Mickle award U. Toronto, 1974; Gairdner Internat. award, 1974; Borden award Assn. Am. Med. Colls. and Borden Co. Found., 1975; Lasker Basic Research award, 1975; co-recipient Nobel prize for medicine, 1977; USPHS sr. research fellow, 1961-62. Mem. NAS, AAAS, Endocrine Soc., Am. Physiol. Soc., Soc. Biol. Chemists, Soc. Exptl. Biol. Medicine, Internat. Soc. Rsch. Biology Reprodn., Soc. Internat. Brain Rsch. Orgn., Mex. Acad. Medicine, Nat. Acad. Medicine Brazil, Acad. Medicine Venezuela, Acad. Medicine Poland, Acad. Sci. Hungary, Acad. Sci. Russia, Acad. Sci. Mex. Home: 5025 Kawanee Ave Metairie LA 70006-2547 Office: VA Hosp 1601 Perdido St New Orleans LA 70112-1207

SCHAMANEK, ANDREAS, systems theory and computer science educator; b. St. Johann in Tirol, Austria, Nov. 27, 1970. Lectr. U. Vienna, Austria, 1995—, system adminstr., 1990—. Chief editor, pub. rattenfutter, 1990—. Avocations: cybernetics, constructivism, philosophy. E-mail: andreas.schamanek@univie.ac.at. Home: Messenhausergasse 9/31, A-1030 Vienna Austria Office: U Vienna Inst Stats, Bruenner Strasse 72, A-1210 Vienna Austria

SCHAMUS, JAMES ALLAN, film producer, educator; b. Detroit, Sept. 7, 1959; s. Julian John Schamus and Clarita (Gershowitz) Karlin; m. Nancy Jean Kricorian; children: Nona Esther, Djuna Mariam. AB, U. Calif., Berkeley, 1982, MA, 1984. Co-pres., co-chmn. GOOD Machine, N.Y.C., 1990—; asst. prof. Columbia U., N.Y.C., 1991-97, assoc. prof., 1997—. Prodr., co-writer: The Wedding Banquet, 1993; assoc. prodr., co-writer: Eat Drink Man Woman, 1994; exec. prodr. various films, 1990-95; writer, prodr. The Ice Storm, 1997 (Best Screenplay, Cannes Film Festival 1997). Recipient Brian Greenbaum award, 1994. Mem. Assn. for Ind. Video and Film (bd. dirs.). Office: GOOD Machine 417 Canal St Fl 4 New York NY 10013*

SCHANDRY, RAINER DIETRICH, psychology educator; b. Jitschin, Czech Republic, June 13, 1944; arrived in Germany, 1944; s. Josef and Maria (Rolles) S.; m. Hedwig Wohlhöfner; 1 child, Niklas. Diploma in physics, U. Saarbrücken, Germany, 1972; PhD, U. Tübingen, Germany, 1978; Habilitation, U. München, Germany, 1986. Asst. prof. U. München, 1975-86, full prof., 1986—. Author: Psychophysiologie, 1989, Hypertonie und Lebensqualität, 1993, Entwicklungspsychophysiologie, 1995, From the Heart to the Brain, 1995. Mem. Deutsche Gesellschaft für Psychophysiologie (v.p. 1988-92). Avocation: sailing. Office: Univ Munich, Leopoldstr 13, D-80802 Munich Germany

SCHANFIELD, FANNIE SCHWARTZ, community volunteer; b. Mpls., Dec. 25, 1916; d. Simon Zouberman and Mary (Schmilovitz) Schwartz; m. Melvin M. Stock, Oct. 27, 1943 (dec. Apr. 1944); 1 child, Moses Samuel Schanfield; m. Abraham Schanfield, Aug. 28, 1947; children: David Colman, Miriam Schanfield Kieffer. Student, U. Minn., 1962-75. Author: My Thoughts, 1996, Son, I Have Something to Tell You, 1997, Ma, I Wrote It Down, 1997. Bd. dirs. Jewish Cmty. Ctr., Mpls., 1975-96, chairperson older adult needs, 1982-88; past pres. Bnai Emet Women's League, Mpls., 1988-90; rschr., advocate Hunger Hennepin County, Mpls., 1969-75; sec. Joint Religious Legis. Coalition; v.p., bd. dirs. Cmty. Housing Svc., Mpls., 1971-85. Recipient Citation of Honor, Hennepin County Commn., 1989, Lifetime Achievement award Jewish Comty. Ctr. Greater Mpls., 1995. Mem. NOW, Lupus Found. Minn., Internat. Soc. Poets, Hadassah (prs. 1967-69, Citation 1969). Jewish. Avocations: needlepoint, rug hooking, writing. Home: 3630 Phillips Pkwy Apt 320 Minneapolis MN 55426-3778

SCHANZ, FERDINAND ERNST, science educator; b. Zürich, Switzerland, May 10, 1944; s. Ernst and Josepha (Herzig) S.; m. Frieda Hedwig Maurer, Jan. 11, 1954; children: Monika, Martin. Tchr., Edn. Sch., Zürich, 1965; Masters, U. Zürich, 1970, PhD, 1974, lectr., 1988—. First asst. U. Zürich, 1974-98. Oberleutnant Fest Kp III/19, 1977-94. E-mail: fschanz@botinst.unizh.ch. Office: Limnolog Station, Seestr 187, CH-8802 Kilchberg Switzerland

SCHANZER, MARK JOSEPH, petroleum company executive; b. Ithaca, N.Y., Dec. 26, 1957; s. Joseph and Patricia (Bogart) S.; m. Celine Catherine Liloudis, June 20, 1980; children: James Joseph, Sarah Soh-Jung, Rebecca Byul. BS in Acctg., Canisius Coll., 1980; MBA, Averett Coll., 1992. CPA; cert. mgmt. acct. From acct. to supr. Mobil Oil Corp., Dallas, 1981-86; from fin. acct. to scheduling supr. Mobil Oil Corp., Fairfax, Va., 1986-90; trade/credit control mgr. Mobil Supply & Trading, Fairfax, 1990-92, project mgr., 1992, bus. integration team leader, 1993-96; global procurement mgr. utilities, transp. and logistics Mobil Oil Torrance (Calif.) Refinery, 1996-98; venture mgr. Extended Enterprises/Mobil Oil, Torrance, Calif., 1999; global sourcing mgr. utilities ExxonMobil, 1999—. Mem. Families Adopting Children Everywhere, Fairfax, 1991, Ch. Parish, Cypress, Calif., 1996. Mem. Nat. Assn. Accts., Inst. Cert. Mgmt. Accts., Beta Gamma Sigma. Avocations: reading, woodworking, running, boxing. Office: 601 Jefferson St Houston TX 77002-7900

SCHANZLIN, DAVID J., ophthalmology educator, researcher; b. Columbus, Ohio, Aug. 4, 1949; s. Ernest and Dorothy Schanzlin; m. Nancy Schanzlin; children: Meredith, Michael, Matthew. BA, Case-Western Res. U., 1971; MD cum laude, U. Chgo., 1975. Diplomate Am. Bd. Ophthalmology (assoc. examiner). Resident in ophthalmology U. Chgo., 1975-77, chief resident, 1977-78; Heed rellow in cornea and external diseases U. Pitts., 1978-79; Nat Eye Inst. spl. rsch. fellow in cornea-external disease U. Calif. Francis L. Proctor Found., San Francisco, 1979-80; asst. prof. dept. ophthalmology U. So. Calif. Sch. Medicine, L.A., 1980-83, assoc. prof., 1983-86, prof., 1986-87; prof., chmn. dept. ophthalmology St. Louis U., 1987-96; prof. ophthalmology, dir. Keratorefractive Surgery, U. Calif., San Diego, 1996—; acad. cons. physician Huntington Meml. Hosp., 1980-87; physician specialist U. So. Calif.-Los Angeles County Med. Ctr., 1980-87; cons. and attending staff physician cornea and external disease svc. Children's Hosp. L.A., 1982-87; attending staff physician Estelle Doheny Eye Hosp., 1985-87, St. Mary's Health Ctr., St. Louis, 1989-97, Cardinal Glennon Hosp. for Children, St. Louis, 1987-97, St. Louis U. Hosp., 1987-97, Bethesda Gen. Hosp., 1987-97, VA Hosp., La Jolla, Calif., 1997—, U. Calif.-San Diego hosps., 1996—; former chmn., pres., CEO, Anheuser-Busch Eye Inst., St. Louis U., bd. dirs., 1987-95; bd. dirs. Mid-Am. Eye and Tissue Bank, 1988-96, San Diego Eye Bank, 1997—; mem. ad hoc rev. coms. NIH; numerous invited lectures, presentations in field to hosps., med. assns., profl. meetings, 1975—. Mem. editl. bd. Refractive and Corneal Surgery, Cornea, Video Jour. Ophthalmology; contbr. over 200 articles, abstracts and book revs. to med. jours., numerous chpts. to books. Recipient numerous grants, 1980—, including Kera Vision, Inc., 1997-98, Allergan, Inc., 1997-98, Storz Ophthalmics, 1997-99, Sinskey Eye Inst., 1998-99, Coherent, Inc., Santen, Inc. Mem. AMA, AAAS, Internat. Soc. Refractive Surgeons (pres. 1999-00), Am. Ophthalmol. Soc., Am. Acad. Ophthalmology (svc. cert. 1987, honor award 1988), Assn. Proctor Fellows, Assn. for Rsch. in Vision and Ophhalmology, Am. Soc. Cataract and Refractive Surgery, Castroviejo Soc. (bd. dirs. 1985-88), Contact Lens Assn. Ophthalmologists, Ocular Microbiology and Immunology Group, Soc. Heed Fellows, Am. Assn. Eye and Ear Hosps., Internat. Soc. Refractive Surgery (bd. dirs. 1986-89, sec. for advocacy 1995-96, pres.-elect 1997-98, pres. 1999-00), Pan Am. Assn. Ophthalmology. Office: U Calif Shiley Eye Ctr Dept Ophthalmology 9500 Gilman Dr Dept 946 La Jolla CA 92093-0946

SCHAPER, DIRK WILHELM, telecommunications administrator; b. Hildesheim, Germany, Mar. 15, 1963; s. Heinrich and Ursula (Kohne) S. BSEE, FH Hannover, Germany, 1989; M of Philosophy in Elec. Engring., U. Glamorgan, Pontypridd, U.K., 1993. Part-time lectr. U. Glamorgan, 1989-91; lab. engr. FH Hannover, 1991-92; part-time lectr. U. Glamorgan, 1992-93; devel. engr. Max Stegmann GMBH, Donaueschingen, Germany, 1994; part-time lectr. Tech. Tng. Ctr., Hameln, Germany, 1995; telecom. bus. devel. mgr. Orga Kartensysteme GMBH, Paderborn, Germany, 1995-2000; mgr. tech. sales support Bluefish Techs. AG, Paderborn, 2000—. Contbr. articles to profl. jours. Vice chmn. Junge Union Sehnde, Germany, 1979-99; referee Sports Club, Sehnde, 1982-99. 1st lt. German Army, 1982-86. Mem. IEEE, Union of German Elec. Engrs. Avocation: sports. Home: Am Pfingstanger 11, D-31319 Sehnde Germany Office: Bluefish Techs AG, Bahnhofstr 27a, D-33102 Paderborn Germany

SCHAPER, JUTTA, molecular cell biologist, researcher; b. Berlin, Apr. 11, 1937; m. Wolfgang Schaper; children: Susanne, Wolfgang, Martin. MD, Düsseldorf Sch. Medicine, Germany, 1961; PhD, Justus-Liebig U., Giessen, Germany, 1980; DSc (hon.), U. Strathclyde, Glasgow, Scotland, 1995. Rsch. assoc., cardiovasc. labs. Janssen Rsch. Found., Beerse, Belgium, 1961-68, rsch. assoc. dept. electron microscopy, cardiovasc. labs., 1968-70, head dept. electron microscopy, 1970-72; lectr. ultrastructural anatomy U. Antwerp, Belgium, 1970-72; head dept. cardiovasc. cell biology Max-Planck Inst Physiol. and Clin. Rsch., Bad Nauheim, Germany, 1972—; prof. exptl. cardiology U. Giessen Med. Sch., 1980—; vis. prof. pathology, Duke U. Med. Ctr., Durham, N.C., 1982-83; mem. Lucian award com., McGill U., Montreal, Can., Einthoven Found. com., Leiden, The Netherlands. Assoc. editor Jour. Molecular and Cellular Cardiology; mem. editl. bd. (jours.) Cell and Tissue Rsch., Circulation, Jour. Thoracic Cardiovasc. Surgery, Jour. Thoracic Surgeon, Cardiosci., Circulation Rsch.; contbr. articles to profl. jours. Recipient Arthur-Weber-prize German Cardiac Soc., 1994, Gold Purkinje hon. medal Acad. Scis. Czech Republic, 1995, SPA Found. prize Nat. Found. Wetenschappelijk Onderzoek, Brussels, 1996, Albrecht Fleckenstein Basic Sci. award, Washington, 1997. Mem. Internat. Soc. Heart Rsch. (sec. European sect. 1981-92, pres.-elect 1993-95, pres. 1995-98), Hungarian Soc. Cardiology (hon.). Office: Max-Planck Inst, Benekestrasse 2, D-61231 Bad Nauheim Germany

SCHAPINK, FREDERIK WILLEM, metallurgist; b. The Hague, The Netherlands, Feb. 20, 1931; s. Andries Johan and Alberdina (Nyhoff) S.; m. Hendrika Mirande Overduyn, Sept. 26, 1955; children: Marjo Albertine, Andra Joan. MS in Physics, Leiden U., 1953; PhD, Delft U. of Technology, 1969. Rsch. physicist Shell Lab., The Netherlands, 1955-63; sr. lectr., assoc. prof. Delft U. of Technology, 1963-96; head Delft Centre for High-Resolution Electron Microscopy, 1990-96. Contbr. articles to profl. jours.; mem. editl. bd. Interface Sci., 1991—. Mem. Dutch Phys. Soc., Deutsche Ges. f. Metallkunde, Dutch Soc. for Electron Microscopy, N.Y. Acad. Scis. Achievements include the establishment of thermodynamics of vacancies in alloys in the 1960s; in the 1970s and 1980s structure determination of interfaces in metals and alloys; in recent years emphasis on interfaces in ordered alloys. Office: Delft U Tech/Lab Matls Sci, Rotterdamseweg 137, 2628 AL Delft The Netherlands

SCHAPIRO, JEROME BENTLEY, chemical company executive; b. N.Y.C., Feb. 7, 1930; s. Sol and Claire (Rose) S.; m. Edith Irene Kravet, Dec. 27, 1953; children: Lois, Robert, Kenneth. B.Chem. Engring., Syracuse U., 1951; postgrad., Columbia U., 1951-52. Project engr. propellents br. U.S. Naval Air Rocket Test Sta., Lake Denmark, N.J., 1951-52; with Dixo Co., Inc., Rochelle Park, N.J., 1954—; pres., 1966—; lectr. detergent stds., drycleaning, care labeling, consumers stds., orgns., U.S., 1968—; U.S. del. spokesman on drycleaning Internat. Stds. Orgn.,Newton, Mass., 1971, Burssels, 1972, U.S. del. spokesman on dimensional stability of textiles, Paris, 1974, Ottawa, Can., 1977, Copenhagen, 1981; chmn. U.S. del. com. on consumer affairs, Geneva, 1974, 75, 76, spokesman U.S. del. on textiles, Pairs, 1974, mem. U.S. del. on care labeling of textiles, The Hague, Holland, 1974, U.S. del., chmn. del. coun. com. on consumer policy, Geneva, 1978, 79, 82, Israel, 1980, Paris, 1981, observer Internat. Std. Orgn./Consumer Com. on Policy meeting, Kyoto, Japan, 2000; leader U.S. del. com. on dimensional stability of textiles, Manchester, Eng., 1984; fed. govtl. appointee to Industry Functional Adv. Com. on Stds., 1980-81; legal expert drycleaning techniques and procedures. Mem. Montclair (N.J.) Sch. Study Com., 1968-69; cofounder Jewish Focus, Inc., 1991, pub. Catskill/Hudson Jewish Star, 1991-98; v.p., treas. synagogue. 1st lt. USAF, 1952-53. Fellow ASTM (chmn. com. D-12 Soaps and Detergents 1974-79, mem. standing com. on internat. stds. 1980-84, hon. mem. award com. D-13 textiles); mem. AIChE, Am. Nat. Stds. Inst. (vice-chmn. bd. dirs. 1983-85, exec. com. 1979-81, 83-85, bd. dirs. 1979-85, fin. com. 1982-85, chmn. consumer coun. 1976, 79, 80, 81, mem. steering com. to advise Dept. Comerce on implementation GATT agreements 1976-77, mem. exec. stds. coun. 1977-79, internat. stds. coun., chmn. internat. consumer policy adv. com. 1978-86), Am. Assn. Textile Chemists and Colorists (mem. exec. com. on rsch. 1974-77, chmn. com. on dry cleaning 1976-88, vice-chmn. internat. test methods com. 1982-86), Am. Chem. Soc., Stds. Engring. Soc. (cert.), Internat. Stds. Orgn. (mem. internat. stds. steering com. for consumer affairs 1978-81), Nat. Small Bus. Assn. (assoc. trustee 1983-85), Masons. Jewish. Home: PO Box 771 Wurtsboro NY 12790-0771 Office: 158 Central Ave PO Box 7038 Rochelle Park NJ 07662-7038

SCHAPPELL, ABIGAIL SUSAN, speech, language, hearing and massage therapist; b. York, Pa., May 25, 1952; d. Felix and Ann (Getty) DeMoise; m. Gery Mylan Schappell, Oct. 20, 1979; 1 child, Jonathan Michael. BS with Master's equivalency, Longwood Coll., 1974; postgrad., Bloomsburg U., 1975-77; cert., Lehmann Sch Massage and Muscle, 1991, East-West Sch. Massage Therapy, 1995—. Lic. speech-lang. pathologist, Pa. Speech-lang.-hearing specialist dept. pub. welfare Hamburg (Pa.) Ctr., 1975—; judge deaf posters and essays Virginville (Pa.) Grange, 1990—, judge Pa. State Grange Conv., 1997, tchr. emergency pers. on communicating with deaf and hard of hearing, 1991, 92; leader demonstrations and workshops on sign lang. and dysphagia, non-verbal comms., active listening to various orgns., 1978—; instr. ARC; massage therapy; bd. dirs. Berks Deaf and Hard of Hearing Svcs., 2000-2003; presenter in field. Pub: (Boy Scouts Coun. manual), Scouting for the Handicapped, Hawk Mountain, 1981-82. Sign/del. to conf. Bible Sch. dir., mem. Zion's United Ch. of Christ, Windsor Castle, Pa., 1985—; rep. nat. triann. conv. Penn Laurel coun. Girl Scouts U.S., 1975; instr. ARC; vol. residential monitoring project Berks County ARC, 1998-99; bd. dirs. Berks Deaf and Hard of Hearing Svcs., 2000-03. Named Virginville Grange Comty. Citizen of Yr., 1994-95, Outstanding Young Woman of Am., 1984. Mem. AAUW, Am. Assn. Mental Retardation (presenter at state conf. 1994, regional conf. 1995, mem. Region 9 core com. for speech 1976), Pa. Speech and Hearing Assn., Schuykill Haven Bus. and Profl. Women (pres 1983-84, involvement on dist. and state level, Young Careerist local, dist. and state honors 1980-81, asst. dir. dist. 9 Pa. 1997-99, dist. 9 dir. 1999-2001, presenter local, dist. and state level workshops), Yorktown chpt. DAR, Smithsonian Assocs., Order Ea. Star (mem., chaplain Blue Mountain chpt. 1981, 82), Hamburg Area Soccer Assn. (sec. 1989-94), Young Careerist Alumni Assn. (life). Republican. Avocations: massage, signing, music. Home: 531 S 4th St Hamburg PA 19526-1307 Office: Hamburg Ctr Old RR 22 Hamburg PA 19526

SCHAPPERT, ALBERT, mathematician, researcher; b. Hanweilerhof, Germany, Apr. 11, 1959; s. Herbert and Waltrud (Doerr) S.; m. Petra Urbanski, 1984; children: Stefan, Sarah, Johanna. Diploma in math., U. Kaiserslautern, Germany, 1985, D Natural Scis., 1990. Software developer Siemens Nixdorf Info. Sys., Munich, 1991-92; dir. info. mgmt. and internet techs. Siemens AG, Munich, 1992—. Office: Siemens AG, Otto-Hahn-Ring 6, D081730 Munich Germany

SCHÄRER, HEINZ, lawyer; b. Zurich, Switzerland, Oct. 11, 1953; s. Hans and Ruth (Diggelmann) S.; m. Michaela Rathgeber; children: Cristina, Markus. Lic.iur., U. Fribourg, Switzerland, 1977, Dr.iur., 1981; MCL, So. Meth. U., 1981. Bar: Zurich. Clk. Dist. Ct. Uster, Switzerland, 1978-80; assoc. Homburger, Achermann et. al., Zurich, 1982-85, Baker & McKenzie, N.Y.C., 1986-87; ptnr. Homburger Achermann Baker McKenzie, Zurich, 1988-91, Homburger Rechtsanwälte, Zurich, 1991—; bd. dirs. Axantis Holding AG, Miracle Holding AG. Author: Representation of the Stock Corporation by its Corporate Bodies, 1989, Commentary on Loan, 1992, 96. 1st lt. Swiss Army, 1974-94. Mem. Internat. Bar Assn., Zurich Bar Assn., Swiss Bar Assn., Swiss-Am. C. of C. Office: Homburger Rechtsanälte, Weinbergstrasse 56/58, 8006 Zurich Switzerland

SCHÄRER, KARL OTHMAR, physician; b. Zürich, Switzerland, Oct. 20, 1929; arrived in Germany, 1969; s. Carl and Martha Schärer; m. Monika Olga Schwamberger, Sept. 21, 1963; children: Iria, Patrick. MD, U. Zürich, 1956. Privat dozent U. Heidelberg, Germany, 1970-73, prof., 1973-95. Contbr. numerous articles to profl. publs. Corporal Swiss Army, 1950-54.

SCHARFENBERG, MARGARET ELLAN, retired elementary educator; b. Lansing, Mich., Mar. 22, 1924; d. John Milton and Florence Lucille (Craig) Amiss; m. Howard Edward Scharfenberg, June 29, 1946; children: Ann Derr Scharfenberg White, Joan Carol Scharfenberg Anderson, John Howard Scharfenberg. Student, Oberlin Coll., 1942-44; BA, Mich. State U., 1946; MA in Teaching, Rollins Coll., 1966. Cert. tchr., elem. supr., Fla. Tchr. Hill Elem. Sch., Maitland, Fla., 1964-65, Cheney Elem. Sch., Orlando, Fla., 1965-66; reading lab. tchr. Richmond Heights Elem. Sch., Orlando, 1966-68; supr. perceptual planning, oral clinician Orange County Schs., Orlando, 1968-69; reading lab. tchr. Winter Park (Fla.) H.S., 1969-72; from perceptual trainer to exptl. reading lab. tchr. Gateway Sch., Orlando, 1972-74; tchr. of migrant children Zellwood (Fla.) Elem. Sch., 1974-93; ret., 1993; pioneer white/black sch. staffing Richmond Heights Elem. Sch., 1966-68; dir. Learning Skills Profl. Ctr., Orlando, 1971-74; speaker numerous symposia and convs. in field, 1968—; cons. in field. Author, editor (newsletter) Paper Meeting, 1968-69, (perception package) Patterns for a Purpose, 1968-69; producer films on perceptual tng., 1968-69. Archivist Oleander Garden Cir., Lakes and Hills Garden Club, also past sec.; sec. Tangerine Garden Club; historian, past v.p. and pres. Women's Soc., Tangerine Cmty. Ch., also mem. choir; vol. reader Ruleme Ctr. Nursing Home; mem. Humane Soc. U.S.A. Named Tchr. of Yr., Zellwood Elem. Sch., 1993. Mem. AAUW, NEA, Internat. Reading Assn. (sec. Orange County Coun. 1965, pres. 1969), Lions (staff mem. seminars on perception, recipient various certs. and plaques, Rsch. Found. Winter Haven chpt. 1969-74), Rosicrucian Order (A.M.O.R.C.). Republican. Presbyterian. Avocations: reading, boating, gardening, animal study. Home: 6492 Dora Dr Mount Dora FL 32757-7064

SCHARLACK, RONALD STUART, medical device company executive; b. San Antonio, Nov. 26, 1945; s. Sheppard Abraham and Sylvia Thelma (Goldinger) S.; m. Elisabeth Thresher, Apr. 11, 1970; children: Jeremy, Daniel. BS in Mech. Engring., MIT, 1967, postgrad., 1971-73; MS in Mech. Engring., Stanford U., 1968; Progam in Mgmt. Devel., Harvard U., 1985. Cons. Kelsey Hayes Co., Romulus, Mich., 1968-71; project engr. No. Rsch. Engring. Corp., Cambridge, Mass., 1973-75; mgr. Mobol-Tyco Solar Energy Corp., Waltham, Mass., 1975-78, Thermo Electron Corp., Waltham, 1978-83; program mgr. Millipore Corp., Milford and Bedford, Mass., 1983-86; tech. licensing officer MIT, Cambridge, Mass., 1986-90; mgr. Chiron Diagnostics, Medfield, Mass., 1990-98; v.p., gen. mgr. Spire Corp., Bedford, Mass., 1998-2000; v.p. ops. Atlantis Components, Inc., Cambridge, Mass., 2000—. Contbr. articles to profl. jours.; 15 patents in field. Mem. Brookline (Mass.) Town Meeting. Mem. Soc. Biomaterials, Optical Soc. Am., Sigma Xi. Avocations: windsurfing, skiing, gardening. Home: 121 Colbourne Cres Brookline MA 02445-4571 Office: Atlantis Components Inc 270 Third St Cambridge MA 02142

SCHARLE, PETER, engineering educator; b. Budapest, Hungary, Aug. 25, 1940; s. Kristof Scharle and Margit Bors; m. Erzsebet Tegzes, Aug. 8, 1964; children: Andras, Monika, Agota. Degree in Civil Engring., Tech. U. Bldg. and Transport, Budapest, 1963; Degree in Engring. and Math., Tech. U. Budapest, 1970, D in Geotechnical Engring., 1972, habilitation in civil engring., 1997; Candidate of Tech. Scis., Hungarian Acad. Scis., 1977. Structural engr. Designing Inst. for Roads and Rails UVATERV, Budapest, 1964-71; rsch. fellow Hungarian Acad. Scis., Budapest, 1971-74; head dept. Hungarian Inst. for Bldg. Sci., Budapest, 1974-84; head divsn. Ministry of Bldg., Budapest, 1985-90; gen. dir. Ministry of Transport, Budapest, 1990-94, dep. sec. state, 1994-97, chief advisor to the min., 1997-98; univ. prof. Széchenyi Istvan Coll., Györ, Hungary, 1998, Tech. U. Budapest, 1998—; titular prof. Pollack Mihaly Tech. Coll., Pécs, Hungary, 1989—. Co-author: Earth Walls, 1985. Founding mem. Hungarian Acad. Engrs., Budapest, 1989; mem. supervisory bd. Hungarian Chamber Engrs., Budapest, 1989; chair European Conf. Mins. Transport Com. of Deps., Paris, 1996; mem. strategic planning body Hungarian Pax Romana Forum, Budapest, 1998. Recipient Eötvös Lorand award Govt. Hungary, 1989. Mem. Internat. Soc. Soil Mechanics and Geomechanical Engring. (mem. tech. com. on granular materials 1988, chmn. Hungarian nat. com. 2000), Assn. for European Transports (mem. coun. 1998-99), N.Y. Acad. Scis. E-mail: h1281sch@el-la.hu and scharle@rs1.szif.hu. Fax: 36-96-503-451. Home: Meredek utca 60, 1112 Budapest Hungary Office: Széchenyi Istvan Coll, Hédervari ut 3, 9026 Györ Hungary

SCHARLIG, ALAIN RAYMOND, educator; b. Geneva, May 23, 1936; s. Ernst Rudolf and Georgette Louise (Poyet) S.; m. Anne-Lise Troesch, Mar. 21, 1959; children: Emmanuelle, Sylvie, Marie. Lic. in math., U. Geneva, 1961; D of Econs., U. Dijon, France, 1969. Dir. Remy-Martin-Switzerland, Geneva, 1957-73, gen. exec. mgr., 1973-88; editor Jour.-de-Geneve, Geneva, 1961-70, French-Swiss Television, Geneva, 1966-72; prof. U. Lausanne, Switzerland, 1982—. Author: Localisation Optimale et THeorie des Graphes, 1969, Ou Construire L'Usine, 1973, Decider sur Plusieurscriteres, 1985, Pratiquer Electre et Promethee, 1996, Faire parler les chiffres, 1997. Mem. Parliament Protestant Ch., Geneva, 1964-72. Presbyterian. Home: Chemin de Calabry 19, CH-1233 Bernex-Geneve Switzerland Office: U Lausanne, Ecole de HEC, CH-1015 Lausanne Switzerland

SCHAROLD, MARY LOUISE, psychoanalyst, educator; b. Mar. 3, 1943; d. Walter John and Louise Helen (Hartmann) Baumgartner; m. William Ballew McCollum, Aug. 23, 1964 (div. 1981); m. Harry Karl Scharold, June 19, 1982; children: Margaret Louise, Walter Ballew. BA with highest distinction, U. Kans., 1964; MD, Baylor Coll. Medicine, 1968; postgrad., Topeka Inst. Psychoanalysis, 1981. Diplomate Am. Bd. Psychiatry and Neurology. Intern Meml. Bapt. Hosp., Houston, 1968-69; resident in psychiatry Baylor Coll. Medicine, Houston, 1960-72, chief resident, 1971-72; psychoanalyst Houston, 1972—; asst. prof. Baylor Coll. Medicine, Houston, 1973-76, asst. clin. prof., 1981-84, assoc. clin. prof., 1984—; dir. Baylor Psychiat. Clinic, Houston, 1973-76; co-dir. Rice U. Psychiat. Svc., Houston, 1981-82; asst. clin. prof. U. Kans. Sch. Medicine, Kansas City, 1977-81; tchg. assoc. Topeka Inst. Psychoanalytic Inst., 1984-86, tchg. analyst, 1986-90, tng. and supervising analyst, 1990—, v.p., 1994-96, pres., 1996—. Adv. bd. Leavenworth Mental Health Assn., Kans., 1977-81. Watkins scholar U. Kans., 1961-64. Fellow Am. Psychiat. Assn. (com. quality assurance 1986-87, chair Tex. peer rev. 1984-88); mem. Am. Psychoanalytic Assn. (cert. 1982, peer rev. com. 1985-90, prof. ins. commn. 1986-93, bd. profl. stds. 1994—, CME com. 1994-96, exec. coun. 1994-96, cert. com. 1995-98, preparedness and progress com. 1998—, chair preparedness and program com. 2000—, coording com. bd. profl. stds. 2000—), Am. Group Psychotherapy Assn., Houston Psychiat. Soc. (v.p. 1984-85, pres.-elect 1985-86, pres. 1986-87), Houston-Galveston Psychoanalytic Soc. (sec.-treas. 1984-86, pres.-elect 1986-88, pres. 1988-90, alter councillor 1994-96), Houston Group Psychotherapy Soc. (adv. bd. 1984-85), Mortar Bd., Phi Beta Kappa, Delta Phi Alpha, Alpha Omega Alpha, Hilltopper, Pi Beta Phi Alumni Assn. Republican. Lutheran. Office: 2301 Westheimer Rd Houston TX 77098-1317

SCHARPING, RUDOLF, government official; b. Niederelbert/Westerwald, Germany, Dec. 2, 1947; married; 3 children. MA, U. Bonn, 1974. Chmn. Young Socialists, Rhineland Palatinate, Germany, 1969-74; mem. parliament Rhineland Palatinate, 1975; party whip Social Dems. Parliamentary Group, Rhineland Palatinate, 1979-89, chmn., 1985-91; chmn. Social Dems. orgn. Rhineland Palatinate, 1985-93; mem. Social Dems. Nat. Party Exec., 1988—; prime min. Rhineland Palatinate, 1991-94; chmn. Social Dem. Party of Germany, 1993-95; mem. Social Dem. Parliamentary Group, chmn. Social Dem. Parliamentary Party German Bundestag, 1994—; pres. Party of European Socialists, 1995—; now min. of def. Govt. of Germany. Office: Ministry of Def, Hardthohe Postfach 1328, 53003 Bonn Germany*

SCHARTEL, THOMAS, process engineer; b. Wertingen, Bayern, Germany, Oct. 29, 1962; s. Gerhard and Rosa Schartel. Diploma in Engring., Fahhochschule Ulm, Germany, 1988. Leader info. dept. Gasversorgung Filstal, Goeppingen, Germany, 1988-89; mgr. survace mount factory Tmic GmbH, Kirchheim, Germany, 1989—; pres. Microsystems for Humanity Environ., Goeppingen, 1990-93. Author: The IEC-Bus Controlled NF-Generator, 1988. Mem. Assn. of Friends and Support of Fachhochschule Ulm, Union German Engrs. Avocations: swimming, dancing, developing mcirocomputer systems. Home: Immanuel-Hohlbauch-Str 51, 73033 Goeppingen Bawü, Germany

SCHATKEN, NANCY LEAH, medical editor; b. N.Y.C., Jan. 7, 1938; d. Robert V. and Lillian Belle (Neff) S. BS, U. N.C., 1959; cert. med. tech., Albany Sch. Med. Tech., 1960. Med. tech., instr. various orgns., 1960-66; acting mng. editor Harper & Row, N.Y.C., 1966-69; assoc. editor Med. World News-McGraw-Hill, N.Y.C., 1969-70; owner, founder Mostly Med., N.Y.C., 1970-78, St. James, Barbados, 1978-98. Avocations: traveling, reading, swimming, entertaining. Address: Apt 108 212 Three Islands Blvd Hallandale FL 33009

SCHATKIN, ANDREW JAMES, lawyer; b. N.Y.C., Aug. 19, 1948; s. Sidney Bernhard and Amy Wheeler (White) S. AB cum laude, CUNY, 1969; MDiv, Princeton Theol. Sem., 1973; JD, Villanova U., 1976; diploma, U. Strasbourg, France, 1984; Cert. in Internat. Law, Acad. Internat. Law, The Hague, The Netherlands, 1985. Bar: N.Y. 1977, U.S. Dist. Ct. (so. and ea. dists.) N.Y. 1978, U.S. Dist. Ct. (no. dist.) N.Y. 1998, U.S. Ct. Claims 1991, U.S. Ct. Mil. Appeals 1991, U.S. Ct. Appeals (2d cir.) 1979, U.S. Ct. Appeals (fed. cir.) 1991, U.S. Supreme Ct. 1991. Dep. county atty. Nassau County Atty., Mineola, N.Y., 1977-81; assoc. Rivkin, Leff, Sherman and Radler, Garden City, N.Y., 1981-82; pvt. practice Bayside, N.Y., 1982-86; atty. Office of Hearings and Appeals, Social Security Adminstrn., New Haven, Conn., 1986-87; staff atty. criminal def. divsn. Legal Aid Soc., N.Y.C., 1987-94; pvt. practice Jericho, N.Y., 1994—. Author books and chpts. to books; contbr. over 120 articles to profl. jours. Named one of Outstanding Young Men of Am., 1979. Mem. ABA (criminal justice sect., family law sect., internat. law and practice sect., labor and employment law sect.), Nat. Assn. Criminal Def. Lawyers (scholarship 1994, 95), N.Y. State Assn. Criminal Def. Lawyers, N.Y. State Defenders Assn., N.Y. State Bar Assn., Suffolk County Bar Assn., Queens County Bar Assn., Nassau County Bar Assn. Republican. Lutheran. Avocations: reading, writing, classical music, travel, languages. Home: 21050 41st Ave Bayside NY 11361-1965 Office: 350 Jericho Tpke Jericho NY 11753-1317

SCHATTEN, HEIDE, science educator; b. Niederueidbach, Hesseu, Germany, Sept. 24, 1946; came to U.S., 1977; Diploma, U. Heidelberg, Germany, 1974, PhD, 1977; postgrad., U. Calif., Berkeley, 1975, 77. Rsch. asst. German Cancer Rsch. Ctr., Heidelberg, 1974-77; rsch. assoc. Fla. State U., Tallahassee, 1977-81, assoc. rsch. scientist, adj. assoc. prof., 1981-86; instr. cell biology Hopkins Marine Sta., Pacific Grove, 1989-90; rsch. assoc. prof. Sch. Dentistry, dept. oral biology U. Ala., Birmingham, 1993-96; dir. Ctr. for Electron, Microscopy U. Ill., Urbana-Champaign, 1994-96, adj. assoc. prof. dept. cell and structural biology, 1994-96; assoc. prof. dept. vet. pathobiology U. Mo., Columbia, 1996—, dir. Electron Microscopy Core Facility, 1996—; UNESCO-ICRO guest prof. cell and devel. biology, Palermo, Italy, 1984; instr. in embryology Marine Biol. Labs., Woods Hole, 1985-86; vis. scientist, instr. Centro de Investigacion DELIPN, Mexico City, 1992, Inst. Cell and Tumorbiology, German Cancer Rsch. Ctr., Heidelberg, 1992; mem. Spl. NIH Study Sects. on Shared Instrumentation, 1993-96; sr. scientist in cell biology U. Wis., Madison, 1985-96. Contbr. articles to profl. jours. NASA grantee, 1986-99. Home: 700 W Green Meadows Rd Columbia MO 65203-3008 Office: U Mo Dept Vet Pathobiology 1600 E Rollins Columbia MO 65211-0001

SCHATTENBERG, PETER-JOACHIM, retired pharmaceutical research executive; b. Berlin, Feb. 1, 1939; s. Ulrich and Ursula (Volckmar) S.; m. Angela Overgahr gen Willebrand, Dec. 1, 1972; children: Dirk-Thomas, Torsten-Børge. Biological diploma, U. Bonn, Bonn, Germany, 1970, PhD, 1972. Scientific asst. Inst. Cytology & Micromorphology U. Bonn, Bonn, 1970-71, Inst. Pathology U. Bonn, Bonn, 1972-79; monitor medical info. Bayer AG, Wuppertal, Germany, 1979-84, clinical project leader medical info., 1984-91, project leader regulatory affairs internat., 1991-93; clinical quality assurance mgr. Bayer AG Rsch. Ctr., Wuppertal, Germany, 1993-95; head quality assurance of med. affairs (ROW-med. affairs) Regions of the World, Wuppertal, Germany, 1995-99; clin. quality assurance mgr. med. dept. East Europe Regions of the World, Levevkusen, Germany, 1999-2000. With Tank Artillery, 1960-62. Scholar U. Bonn, 1971-72. Mem. German Assn. Cell Biology, German Assn. Electronmicroscopy. Lutheran. Avocations: tennis, swimming, sailing, painting.

SCHATZ, THOMAS ANDREW, nonprofit organization executive, lawyer; b. N.Y.C., Jan. 9, 1953; s. James L. and Elinor (Sloss) S.; m. Leslee Behar, June 18, 1983; children: Samantha, Alexandra. BA with honors, SUNY, Binghamton, 1974; JD, George Washington U., 1977. Bar: N.Y. 1977, D.C. 1978. Assoc. Raymond Cotton, P.C., Washington, 1978-80; legis. dir. Office Rep. Hamilton Fish, Jr., U.S. Ho. of Reps., Washington, 1980-86; dir. govt.

affairs Citizens Against Govt. Waste, Washington, 1986-88, v.p., 1988-90, sr. v.p., 1990-91, acting pres., 1991-92, pres., 1992—. Author: (with Jack Anderson) The Coming Tax Rebellion, 1997. Mem. Am. Soc. Assn. Execs., Pi Sigma Alpha. Republican. Jewish. Avocations: tennis, walking, softball, golf. Office: Citizens Against Govt Waste 1301 Connecticut Ave NW Ste 400 Washington DC 20036-1838

SCHÄUBLE, WOLFGANG, German politician, lawyer; b. Freiburg, Germany, Sept. 18, 1942; s. Karl and Gertrud (Gohring) S.; m. Ingeborg Hensle, 1969; 4 children. Ed., U. Freiburg, U. Hamburg. Regional pres. Junge Union, S. Baden, Germany, 1969-72; with tax adminstrn. Baden-Wurttemberg, 1971-72; mem. Bundestag, 1972—; exec. sec. Christian Dem. Union, Christian Social Union Parliamentary Group, 1981-84, chair com. on sport, 1976-84; regional v.p., mem. Fed. Exec. Com. Christian Dem. Union, 1989—; parliamentary leader Christian Dem. Union, Christian Social Union Parliamentary Group, 1991-2000; mem. parliament European Coun., 1975-84; min. with spl. responsibility, head of Chancellery, 1984-89, min. Interior, 1989-91; chmn. Christian Dem. Party, 1998-2000; pvt. practice Offenburg, 1978-84; chair Arbeitsgemeinschaft Europaischer Grenzregionen, 1979-82, Grosses Bundesverdienstkreuz. Decorated comdr. Ordre Nat. du Mérite, comdr. Legion of Honor. Avocations: chess, music. Office: Deutscher Bundestag, 11011 Berlin Germany

SCHAUDEL, DIETHER E., electrical engineer; b. Karlsruhe, Germany, June 27, 1943; s. Ernst and Martha (Aebischer) S.; m. Sybille Klein, Nov. 28, 1970; children: Carsten, Florian, Patrick. Diploma, U. Karlsruhe, 1968. From engr. to CEO Rsch. Inst., Wertheim, Germany, 1968-75; chief tech. officer Dr. B. Lange GmbH, Berlin, 1976-78; v.p. rsch. & devel. Endress & Hauser GmbH, Maulburg, Germany, 1978-8636; CEO Flowtec AG, Reinach, 1984-85; v.p. W.C. Heraeus GmbH, Hanau, Germany, 1985-88; chief tech. officer, chief info. officer Endress & Hauser Internat. Holding, Reinach, 1988—. Avocations: hiking, golf, photography. E-mail: diether.schaudel@t-online.de. Home: Buhlstr 32, D-79541 Loerrach Germany

SCHAUENBERG, SUSAN KAY, educational counselor, educator; b. Taylor Ridge, Ill., Oct. 23, 1945; d. Albert George and Elizabeth (Stedman) Grill; m. Robert Dale Schauenberg Jr.; 1 child, Trevor Alan. BA, Marycrest Coll., 1967; MA, U. Iowa, 1968. Prof. Black Hawk Coll., Moline, Ill., 1971—; bus. cons., Taylor Ridge, 1984—; v.p. faculty senate Black Hawk Coll., 1980-82. Author: Career Bingo, 1999. Planning com. United Way Orgn., Quad-Cities, Ill., 1981-84, agy. rels. com., 1981-82, allocations com., 1980-82; den mother Rock Island chpt. Boy Scouts Am., 1978-79; sponsor Christmas fundraiser for 100 children, yearly. Named one of Most Admired Women of the Quad-Cities, 1975; won L.I.V.E. Volunteerism honor for peer counselor-aide program, 1991. Mem. Assn. of Psychol. Type, Friends of Jung, Am. Fedn. Tchrs., Ill. Guidance and Personnel Assn. (Black Hawk chpt.), U. Iowa Alumni Assn., Phi Gamma Delta (mem. Parents Assn.). Avocations: stained glass window designer, travel. Home: 8428 104th Ave W Taylor Ridge IL 61284-9210 Office: Black Hawk Coll 6600 34th Ave Moline IL 61265-5870

SCHAUFUSS, PETER, dancer, producer, choreographer, ballet director; b. Copenhagen, Denmark, Apr. 26, 1950; s. Frank Schaufuss and Mona Vangsaae S. Student, Royal Danish Ballet Sch. Apprentice with Royal Danish Ballet, 1965; soloist Nat. Ballet Can., 1967-68, Royal Danish Ballet, 1969-70; prin. with LFB, 1970-74, N.Y.C. Ballet, 1974-77, Nat. Ballet Can., 1977-83; artistic dir. London Festival Ballet (now English Nat. Ballet), 1984-90; ballet dir. Deutsche Oper Berlin, 1990-93, Royal Danish Ballet, 1994-95, Peter Schaufuss Balletten, 1997—; guest appearances in Can., Denmark, France, Germany, Italy, Japan, U.K., U.S.A., USSR, Austria, S.Am.; presented BBC TV series Dancer, 1984; numerous other TV appearances; created roles include Rhapsodie Espagnole, The Steadfast Tin Soldier (Balanchine), Phantom of the Opera (Petit), Verdi Variations, Orpheus (MacMillan); ballets produced include La Sylphide (London Festival Ballet, Stuttgart Ballet, Roland Petit's Ballet de Marseille, Deutsche Oper Berlin, Teatro Comunale Firenze, Vienna State Opera, Opernhaus Zurich, Teatro dell'Opera di Roma, Hessisches Staatstheater Wiesbaden, Ballet du Rhin, Royal Danish Ballet, Ballet West), Napoli (Nat. Ballet Can., Teatro San Carlo, Naples, English Nat. Ballet, formerly London Festival Ballet), Folktale (Deutsche Oper Berlin), Dances from Napoli (London Festival Ballet), Bournonville (Aterballetto), The Nutcracker (London Festival Ballet, Graz Opera Ballet, Deutsche Oper Berlin), Giselle (Deutsche Oper Berlin, Royal Danish Ballet), Tchiakovsky Trilogy (Deutsche Oper Berlin), Sleeping Beauty (Deutsche Oper Berlin), Swan Lake (Deutsche Oper Berlin); staging of Romeo and Juliet (Royal Danish Ballet); producer, choreographer (Royal Danish Ballet) Hamlet, 1996; new versions of Hamlet, Swan Lake, Sleeping Beauty, The Nutcracker, Romeo and Juliet (Peter Schaufuss Balletten); prodr., choreographer The King, Manden Der Onskede Sig En Havudsigt, 1999, Midnight Express (Peter Schaufuss Balletten), 2000. Decorated officer Order of the Crown (Belgium); recipient Solo award 2d Internat. Ballet Competition, Moscow, 1973, Star of the Yr. award Abendzeitung, Munich, 1978, Evening Std. award, 1979, Soc. of West End Theatres Ballet award (now Oliver), 1979, Manchester Evening News Theatre awards-dance, 1986, Lakerolprisen, Copenhagen, 1988, Berlin Co. award for best ballet prodn. Berlinerzeitung, 1991, Edinburgh Festival Critics prize, 1991,; named Knight of the Dannebrog, 1988. Office: care Papoutsis Rep Ltd, 18 Sundial Ave, London SE25 4BX, England

SCHAUMANN, ERNST O., chemistry educator; b. Hamburg, Fed. Republic Germany, Sept. 16, 1943; s. Ernst F.F. and Helene L. S.; m. Inge, Nov. 28, 1969; children: Christina, Michael. Diploma, U. Hamburg, 1968, Doctorate, 1970, Habilitation, 1976. Asst. U. Hamburg, 1969-75, counselor, 1975-77, prof., 1977-90; prof. U. Clausthal, Fed. Republic Germany, 1990—; rsch. assoc. U. Oreg., Eugene, 1977; vis. prof. U. Wis., Madison, 1980, U. Calif., Irvine, 1986; rector U. Clausthal, 2000—. Home: Kurt-Kuechler-Str 39, 22609 Hamburg 52, Germany Office: U Clausthal, Leibnizstr 6, 38678 Clausthal Germany

SCHAUPP, JOAN POMPROWITZ, trucking company executive, writer; b. Green Bay, Wis., Sept. 29, 1932; d. Joseph and Helen Elizabeth (Vander-Linden) Pomprowitz; m. Robert James Schaupp, Sept. 4, 1956; children: Margaret Schaupp Siebert, Frederick, John Robert, Elizabeth Schaupp Sidles. BS cum laude, U. Wis., 1954; cert. in theology, St. Norbert Coll., 1979; MA, U. Wis., Green Bay, 1982; DMin, Grad. Theol. Found., 1996. Woman's editor Green Bay Press-Gazette, 1955-56; freelance writer Green Bay, 1957-75; sec.-treas., dir. L.C.L. Transit Co., Green Bay, 1962-70; dir. P & S Investment Co., Green Bay, 1982—, mgmt. cons., 1984-89, dir. strategic planning, 1992, vice chmn., 1994—; pres. The Manna Co., Green Bay, 1992—. Author: Jesus Was a Teenager, 1972, Woman Image of Holy Spirit, 1975 (Thomas Moore Book award), Elohim: A Search for a Symbol for Human Fulfillment, 1995. Master gardener De Pere (Wis.) Beautification Com., 1991-92; lector St. Francis Xavier Cathedral, Green Bay, 1991-92. Mem. Am. Acad. Religion, Nat. Fedn. Press Women, Nat. Press Club, Soc. Bibl. Lit., Equestrian Order of the Holy Sepulchre Jerusalem (lady comdr. with star), Secular Franciscan Order (vice min. Assumption Province 1991-92), Franciscans Internat. Avocations: gardening, walking, swimming. Home: PO Box 358 De Pere WI 54115-0358

SCHAUS, PHILIPPE PAUL, luxury products executive; b. Luxembourg, Luxembourg, June 6, 1963; s. Raymond and Monique Ulveling Schaus; m. Claire Josette Wehenkel, Aug. 12, 1989; children: Alice, Charlotte, Alexandre, Felix. Degree in civil engring., U. Liege, Belgium, 1987; MBA, Insead, France, 1990. Trainee J.P. Morgan & Co., Belgium, 1987-88, asst. treas., 1988-89; sr. cons. Boston Cons. Group, Germany, 1990-92; export sales mgr. Villeroy & Boch, Luxembourg, 1992-96; sales and mktg. dir. Villeroy & Boch, Luxembourg and Germany, 1997-99, pres. tableware divsn., 1999—. Mem. German Ceramics Assn. (bd. dirs. 1999—). Avocations: cycling, swimming, music. Home: 7 bvd de la Petrusse, L-2320 Luxembourg Germany Office: Villeroy & Boch AG, Rieffstrasse 46, D-66693 Mettlach Germany

SCHAUSS, ALEXANDER GEORGE, psychologist, researcher; b. Hamburg, Fed. Republic Germany, July 20, 1948; came to U.S., 1953; s. Frank and Alla S.; m. Laura Babin; children: Nova, Evan. BA, U. N.Mex., 1970, MA, 1972; PhD, Calif. Coast U., 1992. State probation/parole officer 2nd Judicial Dist. Ct., Albuquerque, 1969-73; criminal justice planner Albuquerque/Bernalillo County Criminal Justice Planning Com., 1973-75; state asst. adminstr. dept. corrections State of S.D., Pierre, 1975-77; dir. Pierce County Probation Dept., Tacoma, Wash., 1977-78; tng. officer IV Wash. State Criminal Justice Tng. Commn., Olympia, 1978-79; dir. Inst. Biosocial Rsch. City Univ. Grad. Sch., Seattle, 1979-80; exec. dir. Am. Inst. Biosocial and Med. Rsch. Inc., Tacoma, 1980—, Am. Preventive Med. Assn., 1992-94, Citizens for Health, 1992-95; dir. Citizens for Health Edn., 1994-96; assoc. prof. behavioral scis. Nat. Coll. Naturopathic Medicine, Portland, 1996-97, clin. prof. natural products rsch. dept. rsch., 1998-99; assoc. prof. rsch. S.W. Coll. Naturopathic Medicine & Health Scis., Tempe, Ariz., 1995-96, rsch. dir., 1995-96; sr. dir. rsch. S.W. Coll. Naturopathic Medicine & Health Scis., Scottsdale, Ariz., 1996-97; clin. prof. natural products rsch. Nat. Coll. Naturopathic Medicine, 1998-99, adj. rsch. prof. botanical medicine, 1999—; pres. Campaign To Label Genetically Engineered Foods, 1999—; mem. study group on health promotion WHO, Copenhagen, 1985; vis. lectr. pediats. The John Radcliffe Hosp., Oxford U., Eng., summer 1985; sec. coun. on food policy Nat. Assn. Pub. Health Policy, 1990-94, chmn., 1994-96; vis. scholar Kans. C.C. Consortium, 1982; vis. lectr. McCarrison Soc. Conf. at Oxford U., 1983; presdl. adv. bd. Bastyr U., 1979-2000, S.W. Coll. Naturopathic Medicine, 1993-97; mem. devel. planning com., Office of Dietary Supplements, Office of Disease Prevention, NIH, Bethesda, 1996-99, mem. alternative medicine adv. coun. Office Alternative Medicine, 1997-99; chmn. safety com., compliance labeling integrity com. Nat. Nutritional Foods Assn., 1996—, mem. ComPLI, 1992—. Author: Orthomolecular Treatment of Criminal Offenders, 1978, Diet, Crime and Delinquency, 1980, rev., 1995, Nutrition and Behavior, 1986, Nutrition and Criminal Behavior, 1990; co-author: Zinc and Eating Disorders, 1989, Eating for A's, 1991, Minerals, Trace Elements and Human Health, 1995, rev. edit., 1999, Anorexia and Bulimia, 1997, Cat's Claw (Una de Gato) Uncaria Tormentosa, 1996; editor-in-chief Internat. Jour. Biosocial and Med. Rsch., 1979—; reviewer U.S. Pharmacopeia Informational Monographs, 1998-99; mem. editl. bd. 14 jours. Master arbitrator Tacoma/Pierce County Better Bus. Bur., Tacoma, 1986-97; mem. Pierce County N. Area Transp. Adv. Coun., Tacoma, 1991-92; trustee Pierce County Pub. Safety Task Team, 1993, Nat. Inst. for Naturopathic Medicine, 1993-2000. Recipient Rsch. award Wacker Found., 1983-85, 88; fellow Am. Coll. Nutrition, 1986-87, Am. Orthopsychiat. Assn., 1980-95. Fellow N.Y. Acad. of Sci.; mem. Am. Chem. Soc., Acad. Eating Disorders, Internat. Assn. Clin. Nutritionists, Am. Assn. Clin. Nutritionists, Internat. Assn. Eating Disorders Profls., Am. Assn. Correctional Psychologists (pres. Citizens For Health 1995-97), Am. Found. Preventative Medicine (treas. 1992-93), Acad. Criminal Justice Scis., Am. Soc. Criminology, N.Y. Acad. Scis. (emeritus), British Soc. Nutritional Medicine (hon.), Soc. for Food Sci. and Tech., Inst. Food Technologists Soc. Food Scientists & Tech., Soc. Orthomolecular Health Medicine, Rotary (chmn. cmty. svcs. com. Tacoma chpt. 1989-90, chmn. civic affairs com. 1989-90, mem. Vladivostok com. 1991-93, mem. internat. exch. com. 1994-95, world cmty. svcs. com. 1996-97). Office: Am Inst for Biosocial and Med Rsch Inc Life Scis Divsn PO Box 1174 Tacoma WA 98401-1174

SCHAY, ZOLTAN, chemist; b. Budapest, Hungary, Aug. 31, 1942; s. Geza and Magdolna (Krocsak) S.; m. Ildiko Nemeth, Sept. 9, 1967; children: Gusztav, Daniel, Eszter. MSc, Tech. U. Budapest, 1965, PhD, 1968. Rsch. fellow High Pressure Rsch. Inst., Budapest, 1965-73; from rsch. fellow, sr. rsch. fellow Inst. Isotopes, Budapest, 1973-86, from head dept. radiochemistry to scientific advisor, 1987—. Avocations: electronics, skiing, hiking. Office: Inst Isotopes, PO Box 77, H-1525 Budapest Hungary

SCHCOLNIK, MIRIAM, language educator; b. Buenos Aires, Argentina, May 2, 1943; arrived in Israel, 1972; d. Julio and Fanny (Deli) Schurman; m. Saul Schcolnik; children: Jaime, Diana, Shai. Diploma French studies, Alliance Francaise, Montevideo, Uruguay, 1963, teaching cert., 1964; diploma Eng. studies, U. Cambridge, Montevideo, Uruguay, 1964; BA in Applied Linguistics, Tel Aviv U., 1977, tchg. cert., 1978, MA in TESOL, 1986; postgrad., Nova Southeastern U., 1998-2000. Eng., French tchr. Montevideo, Uruguay, 1964-72; Eng. tchr. Tel Aviv and Kfar Saba Schs., 1973-81; Eng. tchr., course coord., materials developer Tel Aviv U., 1981—, dir. Lang. Learning Ctr., 1989—; cons. lang. tchg., multimedia designer Calico, Q Multimedia, 1995—, Israel Ednl. TV, 1993-95; vis. scholar Brit. Coun., 1990, Duke U., Durham, N.C., 1992. Co-author: English Here and Now, 1983, 84, Enhancing Reading Comprehension in the Language Learning Classroom, 1995, Cloze for Reading Comprehension, 1988, The Junior Files, 1989, 90, 92, Beginners' Files, 1996, 98. Jewish. Office: Tel Aviv U, Ramat Aviv, 69978 Tel Aviv Israel

SCHEBESTA, INGO, physicist; b. Düsseldorf, Nordrhein-Westfalen, Germany, Jan. 19, 1964; s. Franz Emil and Karin Maria (Seiffert) S. Diploma in Physics, Westfälische Wilhelms U., Münster, Germany, 1990; D Natural Sci., U. Bremen, Germany, 1994. Tutor Westfälische Wilhelms U., Münster, 1988-90; sci. asst. U. Bremen, 1990-94; lectr. FH Dusseldorf (Germany) U., 1995—; owner SOLARIS Multimedia and 3-D Animation Films, Krefeld, Germany, 1995—; social mktg. cons. Kreditanstalt für Wiederaufbau in Kenia; knowledge mgr. Adam Opel AG, Rüsselsheim, Germany, 1999-2000; prof. computer animation and computer sci. U. Applied Scis., Emden, Germany, 2000—. Composer theatre music Gefangene Freiheit, 1992; co-author, co-prodr. TV show Moonlight, 1996; author, co-prodr. TV mag. Stop, 1998. Chmn. Stichting Pro Artis, Nijmegen, The Netherlands, 1993. With German mil., 1983-84. Grantee, Deutsche Forschungsgemeinschaft, 1994. Mem. Gesellschaft für Musikalsiche Aufführungs und Mechanische, Deutsche Physikalische Gesellschaft, 1987, Am. Phys. Soc. Avocations: music, literature, philosophy, swimming, film. Home: Burgstr 9, D-47829 Krefeld Germany

SCHEBLYKIN, IVAN GENNADEVICH, physicist, researcher; b. Moscow, Jan. 11, 1974; s. Gennady Nikolaevich Freiberg and Tatiana Petrovna Scheblykina. B. Moscow Isnt. Physics and Tech., 1995, MS, 1996, PhD, 1999. Lab. asst. Moscow Inst. Physics and Tech., 1995-97; researcher P.N. Lebedev Phys. Inst., Moscow, 1997-2000; post doctoral position Catholic Univ. of Leuven, Belgium, 2000—. Contbr. articles to profl. jours. Internat. Soros Sci. Edn. Program grantee, 1995, 96, 97, 98, 99. Mem. Moscow Club Bicyclic Tourism, Ski Team of Moscow Inst. Physics and Tech. E-mail: scheb@sci.lebedev.ru. Avocations: cross country skiing, cycling, tourism, music. Home: Leningradskoeshosse 94-3-24, 125565 Moscow Russia Office: PN Lebedev Phys Inst, Leninsky Pr 53, 117924 Moscow Russia

SCHECHTER, CLIFFORD, financial executive, lawyer; b. N.Y.C., Feb. 14, 1958; s. Howard and Diana D. (Eiss) S.; m. Niely Okonsky, June 17, 1979; children: Dana Ann, Adam Hillel, Talia Beth. BS summa cum laude, U. R.I., 1979; JD, Fordham U. Sch. Law, 1982; MBA, L.I. U., 1988. Bar: N.Y. 1983, U.S. Tax Ct. 1983, U.S. Supreme Ct. 1986, D.C. 1990, U.S. Dist. Ct. (so. and ea. dists.) N.Y. 1983; lic. gen. securities prin., fin. and ops. prin. Nat. Assn. Securities Dealers; CFP; registered investment advisor. Tax supr. Touche Ross & Co., Jericho, N.Y., 1982-86; sr. v.p., dir. taxes L.F. Rothschild & Co. Inc., N.Y.C., 1986-91, chief fin. officer, dir. adminstrn. and taxes, 1991-93; pres. Royal Fin. Svcs. Inc., San Diego, 1993-96; personal fin. counseling mgr. Ernst & Young, San Diego, 1996-99; sr. v.p., pvt. fin. advisor Bank of Am. Pvt. Bank, San Diego, 1999—; adj. prof. Adelphi U., Garden City, N.Y., 1983-91, Pace U., N.Y.C., 1991-93. Bd. dirs. P.A.D. Pub. Svc. Ctr., Washington, 1986-98, Congregation Chabad of Poway; bd. trustees San Diego Hall of Champions, 2000—. Recipient Uniroyal Found. Fellowship award, 1978, Am. Jurisprudence award Scholastic Excellence in Estate Planning, 1982. Mem. ABA, N.Y. State Bar Assn., D.C. Bar Assn., Bar Assn. Nassau County, Internat. Assn. Fin. Planning, Fin. Mgmt. Assn., Securities Industry Assn., Wall St. Tax Assn., Profl. Fraternity Assn. (bd. dirs. 1994-95, treas. 1995-96, pres.-elect 1996-97, pres. 1997-98, past pres. 1998-99), Phi Alpha Delta (internat. proctor 1986-88, marshal 1988-90, historian 1990-92, treas. 1992-94, internat. vice justice 1994-96, internat. justice 1996-98, dist. XV justice 1984-86, chmn. internat. adv. bd. 1998-2000, Outstanding Active mem. award 1982, Stan P. Jones Meml. award 1985, Outstanding Alumnus mem. Wormser chpt. 1982-85), Beta Gamma Sigma, Phi Kappa Phi. Republican. Jewish. Home: 16334 Avenida Florencia Poway CA 92064-1804 Office: Bank of America Private Bank 450 B St Ste 1700 San Diego CA 92101-8005

SCHECHTER, ROBERT SAMUEL, chemical engineer, educator; b. Houston, Feb. 26, 1929; s. Morris S. and Helen Ruth Schechter; m. Mary Ethel Rosenberg, Feb. 15, 1953; children: Richard Martin, Alan Lawrence (dec.), Geoffrey Louis. B.S. in Chem. Engring, Tex. A&M U., 1950; Ph.D. in Chem. Engring, U. Minn., 1956. Registered profl. engr., Tex. Asst. prof. chem. engring. U. Tex. at Austin, 1956-60, assoc. prof., 1960-63, prof., 1963—; adminstrv. dir. Ctr. Statis. Mechs. and Thermodynamics, 1968-72, chmn. dept. chem. engring., 1970-73, chmn. petroleum engring., 1975-78, E.J. Cockrell, Jr. prof. chem. and petroleum engring., 1975-81, Dula and Ernie Cockrell prof. engring., 1981-83, Getty prof. engring., 1984-85, Getty Oil Centennial chair in Petroleum Engring., 1985-89, W.A. (Monty) Moncrief Centennial Endowed chair in Petroleum Engring., 1989-97; prof. emeritus U. Tex., 1997; vis. prof. U. Edinburgh, Scotland, 1965-66; Disting. vis. prof. U. Kans., spring 1968; vis. prof. U. Brussels, 1969; Disting. Lindsay lectr. Tex. A&M U., 1993; cons. in field. Author: Variational Method in Engineering, 1967, (with G.S.G. Beveridge) Optimization—Theory and Practice, 1970, Adventures in Fortran Programming, 1975, (with B.B. Williams and J.L. Gidley) Acidizing Monograph, 1979, (with D.D. Shah) Enhanced Oil Recovery by Surfactants and Polymers, 1979; (with Maurice Bourrel) Microemulsions and Related Systems, 1988, Oil Well Stimulation, 1991; contbr. (with D.D. Shah) numerous articles to profl. jours. Served to 1st lt., Chem. Corps AUS, 1951-53. Decorated Chevalier Order Palmes Academique; recipient Outstanding Teaching award U. Tex., 1969, Outstanding Paper award, 1973, Gen. Dynamics award for Excellence in Engring. Teaching, Gen. Dynamics Corp., 1987, Sr. Rsch. award Engring. Rsch. Coun. of Am. Soc. Engring. Educators, 1991. Mem. AIME (Industry Edn. award 1998), AIChE (Founders award 1998), Am. Chem. Soc., Soc. Petroleum Engrs. (John Franklin Carll award 1994, Improved Oil Recovery Pioneer 1996), Nat. Acad. Engrs., Sigma Xi, Tau Beta Pi. Achievements include developing methods of measuring surface viscosity and ultra low inter-facial tensions; discovering instability of thermal diffusion. Home: 4700 Ridge Oak Dr Austin TX 78731-4724

SCHECK, FLORIAN ALFRED, physicist, educator; b. Berlin, Nov. 20, 1936; s. Gustav O. and Ernestine G. (Nitschke) S.; m. Doerte Neumann. Dipl., U. Freiburg, 1962, PhD, 1964; habil., U. Heidelberg, 1968. Vis. scientist Weizmann Inst., Israel, 1964-66; rsch. fellow CERN, Geneva, Switzerland, 1968-70; head theory group SIN/ETH, Zurich, Switzerland, 1970-76; prof. Johannes Gutenberg U., Mainz, Germany, 1976—. Author: Theor. Physik 1: Mechanik, von den Newtonschen Gleichungen zum deterministischen Chaos, 1999, Leptons, Hadrons and Nuclei, 1983, Mechanics, from Newton's equations to deterministic chaos, 1990, Electro-Weak and Strong Interactions, 1996, Theor. Physik 2: Nichtrel. Quantentheorie, Vom Wasserstoffatom zu den Vielteilchensystemen, 2000; contbr. articles to profl. jours. Mem. German Phys. Soc. Avocation: music. Office: Inst Physics, Johannes Gutenberg Univ, 55099 Mainz Germany

SCHEEL, KURT, editor; b. Hamburg, Germany, Apr. 23, 1948; s. Kurt August and Kreszentia (Stangl) S. State exam., Freie U., Berlin, 1973. Lectr. German lit. and lang. Hiroshima (Japan) U., 1977-80; subeditor Merkur, Munich, 1980-90, editor-in-chief, 1991—. Office: Merkur, Mommsenstrasse 27, 10629 Berlin Germany

SCHEEREN, THOMAS WERNER, anesthesiology educator; b. Meschede, Germany, Dec. 30, 1961; s. Hans-Werner and Anne (Jansen) S.; m. Noyan Nedret Eryilmaz, July 22, 1988; children: Turgut Alexander, Timur Rafael, Tristan Michael. MD, Heinrich Heine U., Düsseldorf, Germany, 1988, Dr Med, 1989, PhD, 1999. Specialist degree in anesthesiology and intensive care medicine. Anesthesiologist Heinrich Heine U., 1988-96, rsch. fellow, 1996-99, asst. prof. anesthesiology, 1999—, vice dir. dept. exptl. anesthesiology, 1996-99. Author: Yearbook of Intensive Care and Emergency Medicine, 1994, Oxygen Transport to Tissues, 1997, 98. Officer Bundeswehr, 1981-82. Recipient Förder prize Deutsche Gesellschaft fuer Ernaehrungs Medizin-Arbeitsgemeinschaft Klinische Ernaehrung, 1993. Mem. European Soc. Anesthesiology, Deutsche Gesellschaft fuer Anaesthesiologie and Intensivmedizin (Karl Thomas prize 1999). Roman Catholic. Avocations: playing piano, playing tennis. Home: Carl Fr Schinkel Strasse 17, D-41539 Dormagen NRW, Germany Office: Heinrich Heine U Dept Anes, Moorenstrasse 5, D-40225 Düsseldorf Germany

SCHEFFLER, BARBARA JANE, statistician, business executive; b. Phila., May 2, 1951; d. David and Elaine B. (Rothouse) Green; m. Stuart J. Scheffler, July 3, 1975. BS, Pa. State U., 1972, MS, 1973. Registered statistician. Biostatistician, sr. int. clin. info. Smith Kline Pharm., King of Prussia, Pa., 1973-78, mgr. clin. sci. adminstrn., 1985-87; v.p. clin. ops. USBiosci., Conshohocken, Pa., 1987-91, sr. v.p. clin. ops. and regulatory affairs, 1991-95, sr. v.p. project mgmt., 1995-96, sr.v.p. corp. and sci. affairs, 1996-98; pres. The Scheffler Group, Inc., 1999—; cons. Oncon, Gaithersburg, Md., 1986-88; speaker, cons. Pa. State U., University Park, 1994—, Pa. State Math. Options Program, 1993—; sec., treas. Internat. Network Cancer Treatment & Rsch., 2000—; participant in field. Fundraiser Am. Heart Assn., Villanova, Pa., 1995-96, Am. Diabetes Assn., Villanova, 1996, 99. NSF fellow, 1972-73. Mem. AAAS, Am. Statis. Assn., Am. Soc. Clin. Oncology, Drug Info. Assn., Healthcare Businesswomen's Assn., Planetary Soc., Phi Beta Kappa, Phi Kappa Phi. E-mail: bscheffler@adelphia.net Fax: 610-687-3382. Home and Office: 540 Chandler Ln Villanova PA 19085-1204

SCHEFFLER, KNUT, process engineer; b. Berlin, Oct. 26, 1938; s. Fritz Erich and Erna Käthe (Kurth) S.; m. Sigrun Ortrud Volz; Apr. 27, 1978; children: Sven, Nils, Björn, Kim Uwe. MSc, Tech. U., Berlin, 1964; PhD, Tech. U., 1968. Divsn. head Alpha-Chemie und Metallurgie GmbH, Karlsruhe, Germany, 1968-72; dept. head Nuclear Rsch. Ctr., Karlsruhe, 1972-77; project leader Deutsche Gesellschaft für Wiederaufarbeitung von Kernbrennstoffen GmbH, Mol, Belgium, 1978-86; gen. mgr. Dr. Knut Scheffler-Neue Technologien, Beckedorf, Germany, 1987-95, Golder Assoc. GmbH, Celle, 1995—. Contbr. over 30 articles to profl. publ. Mem. German Nuclear Soc., European Nuclear Soc., Soc. German Chemists. Achievements include 5 patents in nuclear waste treatment technologies. E-mail: scheffler.bec@t-online.de. Home and Office: Tulpenstrasse 14, D 31699 Beckedorf Germany

SCHEFOLD, BERTRAM, economics educator; b. Basel, Switzerland, Dec. 28, 1943; s. Karl and Marianne (von den Steinen) S.; married, Dec. 19, 1972; children: Raphael, Sarah. Diploma in math., U. Basel, 1967, PhD in Econs., 1971. Lectr. U. Basel, 1971; supr. Trinity Coll., Cambridge, Eng., 1972; rsch. assoc. Harvard U., 1973; prof. U. Frankfurt, 1974—; vis. Trinity Coll., Cambridge, 1981; vis. prof. U. Rome, 1985, 98, T.L. Heuss prof., N.Y., 1984; vis. scholar Hoover Instn., Stanford, Calif., 1990. Author: Normal Prices, Technical Charge and Accumulation, 1997, other books and articles. Wissenschaftliche Gesellschaft fellow Goethe U. Fellow Japan Soc. Promotion of Sci.; mem. Verein fur Socialpolitik, European Soc. for History of Econ. Thought (pres.). Home: Hynspergstrasse 15, D-60322 Frankfurt Germany

SCHEIBNER, HERBERT, Austrian minister for national defense; b. Vienna, Austria, Apr. 23, 1963. Student, Vienna U., 1982, Vienna Econs. U., 1982. Pvt. ins. broker, 1987-88; mgr. polit. edn. programs Austrian Freedom Party, 1988, office mgr. secretariat; chief exec. Freedom Party's Acad., 1994—; dist. councillor dist. Rudolfsheim and Fünfhaus FPO, 1987-90, nat. chmn. youth movement, 1989-93, nat. exec., 1990, sec.-gen., 1992-95, chmn. parliamentary group, 1999; del. North Atlantic Assembly, 1994; mem. Austrian Delegation to Europe, 1995; mem. assembly WEU, 1996-99; fed. min. def. Austria, 2000—. Sgt. Austrian armed forces, 1993, mem. militia inf. battalion, 1996-99. Office: Fed Ministry Nat Def, Dampfschiffstrasse 2, 1033 Vienna Austria*

SCHEICH, JOHN F., lawyer; b. Bklyn., Aug. 6, 1942; s. Frank A. and Dorothy (O'Hara) S. BA, St. John's U., N.Y.C., 1963, JD, 1966; postgrad., John Marshall Law Sch., Chgo., 1968. Bar: N.Y. 1967, U.S. Ct. Internat. Trade Admission 1969, U.S. Dist. Ct. (ea. and so. dists.) N.Y. 1971, U.S. Ct. Appeals (2nd cir.) 1971, U.S. Supreme Ct. 1975, Pa. 1980. Spl. agt. FBI, U.S. Dept. Justice, Washington, 1966-69; asst. dist. atty. Queens County, Kew Gardens, N.Y., 1969-72; pvt. practice, Richmond Hill, N.Y., 1970-76, 79-91; ptnr. Raia & Scheich, P.C., Richmond Hill, 1976-79; sr. ptnr. Scheich & Goldsmith, P.C., Richmond Hill, Hicksville, N.Y., 1991-95, Scheich, Goldsmith & Dreishpoon, P.C. Richmond Hill, Hicksville, 1996—; mortgage settlement atty. GMAC, N.Y., 1996—; lectr. estate planning Nat. Bus. Inst., 1994; mem. assigned counsel panel for indigent defendants in major felony

and murder cases 9th and 11th jud. dists. N.Y. State Supreme Ct., Queens County, 1972-94; lectr. Lawyers in the Classroom, 1979-91; chmn. arbitration panel Civil Ct. City of N.Y., 1981-90; bd. dirs. Ra-Li Brokerage Corp., v.p., 1975—; adv. bd. 1st Am. Title Ins. Co. Am., 1995—, mortage settlement atty. for Gen. Motors Acceptance Corp. N.Y. state, 1996—; trial judge St. John's U. Sch. of Law Civil Trial Inst. Editor: Conashaugh Courier, 1989-92; mem. editorial bd., 1988-92; contbg. columnist, 1981-89. Mem. Com. for Beautification of East Norwich, Nassau County, L.I., N.Y., 1983—, bd. dirs., 1993-96, pres. 1996—; mem. Holy Name Soc. of Our Lady of Perpetual Help Ch., 1963—, sec., 1965-67, v.p., 1969-71, pres., 1971-73; bd. dirs. Conashaugh Lakes Cmty. Assn., Milford, Pa., 1981-90, organizing mem. Conashaugh Lakes Lot Owners interim com., 1977-81, sec. 1981-82, v.p. 1982-84, pres. 1984-86, past pres. 1986-88; mem. St. Edward the Confessor Sch. Bd., Syosset, N.Y., 1986-90; parish coun. Our Lady of Perpetual Help Roman Cath. Ch., 1976-82, pres. 1978-80, fin. com., adv. to pastor, 1970-82, chmn. fin. com., 1979-82; bd. dirs. Northslope II Homeowners Assn., Shawnee-on-Delaware, Pa., 1988-90, 92-94, 2000—, East Norwich Civic Assn., 2000—; mem. East Norwich Rep. Club, 1982—, bd. dirs. 1984-87, 93—, v.p. 1987-89, pres. 1989-93; nat. trust and estate assoc. Meml. Sloane Kettering Cancer Ctr., N.Y.C., 1994—; active Internat. Wine Ctr., 1985-96, St. Edward the Confessor Ch., Syosset, 1982—, St. Vincent Ch., Dingman Hills, Pa., 1977—, St. Dominic's Ch., Oyster Bay, N.Y., 1982— (apptd. pastor's adv. coun. on estate planning 1998, 99, 00, mem. Legacy Soc. 1998, 99, 00), Lincoln Ctr. Performing Arts, Inc., 1985—, Nat. Rep. Senatorial Com., 1988—, Bravo Soc., 1994—, Concern for Dying, 1984—, Sea Cliff Chamber Players, 1992-99; mem. Nassau County Rep. Com., Town of Oyster Bay, 1993—, St. John Vianney Roman Cath. Ch., St. Petersburg Beach, Fla., 1994—, Non-Resident Fellow, James Beard Found., NYC, 1995—, Performing Arts Ctr. Pinellas County, St. Petersburg, 1994—, Rep. Nat. Senate Adv. Coun., 1997—, Rep. Nat. Com. Chmn.'s Honor Roll, 1997 (cert. Achievement 1998), Pact, Inc. Ruth Eckerd Hall-Richard B. Baumgardner Ctr. for Performing Arts, Clearwater, Fla., 1995—; chmn. tricentennial celebration com. Village of East Norwich, 1996-97; mem. Franciscan Ctr. Guild, Tampa, Fla., 1996—, Tilles Ctr. Performing Arts, Inc., Long Island U., Brookville, N.Y., 1997—, adv. coun. estate planning St. Dominic's Ch., 1998, St. Dominic's Legacy Soc., 1998. Recipient J. Edgar Hoover award, 1967, award of appreciation, Civil Trial Inst., St. John's U. Sch. of Law, 1991, 95, Disting. Svc. award, 1992, cert. of appreciaiton Conashaugh Lakes Cmty. Assn., 1990, Dist. Svc. award Kiwanis Club, 1992, Cert. of Merit for Disting. Svc. award Nassau County Exec. Hon. Thomas Gulotta, 1989, Presdl. Order of Merit award Pres. George Bush, 1991, Order of Merit award Nat. Rep. Senatorial Com., 1994, Cert. Achievement, Rep. Nat. Com., 1998; named one of Best Trial Lawyers in the U.S., Town and Country Mag., 1985; non-resident ow James Beard Found., N.Y.C., 1995—. Mem. ABA (cert. of appreciation Am. Bar Endowment 1992), ATLA, Pa. State Bar Assn., N.Y. State Bar Assn., Queens County Bar Assn., Nassau County Bar Assn., N.Y. State Trial Lawyers Assn., Ciminal Cts. Bar Assn., Internat. Platform Assn., John Marshall Lawyers Assn. (bd. dirs. 1992—, pres. 1992-97, treas. 1997—), Soc. Former Spl. Agts. of FBI, N.Y. State Assn. Criminal Def. Lawyers, St. John's Coll. Alumni Assn., Asst. Dist. Attys. Assn. Queens County, St. John's U. Sch. of Law Alumni Assn., St. John's Prep. Sch. Alumni Assn., Friends of the Arts of Nassau County, Inc., Cath. Lawyers Guild of Queens County, N.Y., KC, Brookhaven Wine Lovers Soc., East Norwich Civic Assn., Sun Island Assn., Phi Alpha Delta. Avocation: collecting fine wines. Home: 170 Sugar Toms Ln East Norwich NY 11732-1153 Office: Scheich Goldsmith & Dreishpoon PC 103-42 Lefferts Blvd South Richmond Hill NY 11419-2012 also: 109 Newbridge Rd Hicksville NY 11801-3908 also: 210 Conashaugh Trl Box 4042 Conashaugh Lakes Milford PA 18337

SCHEID, WERNER FRITZ, physics educator; b. Offenbach, Hessen, Germany, June 28, 1938; s. Heinrich and Rosa (Mueller) S.;m. Birgit Walter, July 24, 1973; children: Stefanie, Gabriele. Diploma Physics, Tech. U., Darmstadt, Germany, 1964; D Natural Scis., U. Frankfurt (Germany), 1967, Habilitation, 1971; Doctorate (hon.), U. Bucharest, Romania, 1993. Rsch. assoc. Va. State U., Charlottesville, 1967-68; rsch. assoc. U. Frankfurt, 1968-72, prof., 1972-76; prof. physics U. Giessen, Fed. Republic Germany, 1976—; researcher nuclear and atomic theoretical physics. Office: Inst Theoretische Physik, Heinrich-Buff-Ring 16, D-35392 Giessen Germany

SCHEIDEGGER, ALFRED, venture capitalist; b. Basel, Switzerland, Jan. 4, 1957; s. Friedrich and Annelies (Angstmann) S.; m. Ildegarda Emilia Knecht, Dec. 1, 1984; children: Jerome, Salome, Nastassja, Joel. Diploma, U. Basel, 1980, PhD in Biochemistry and Microbiology, 1984; grad. in exec. edn., Harvard U., 1997. Postdoctoral rschr. U. Kyoto, Japan, 1985-87; scientist Ciba-Geigy AG, Basel, 1987-88; project leader Ciba-Geigy (Japan) Ltd., Takarazuka, 1988-91; dir. Swiss Scientific Computing Ctr., Manno, Switzerland, 1992-95; adminstrv. dir., mem. bd. Swiss Fed. Inst. Tech. (ETH), Zürich, 1995-98; founding father Nextech Venture L.P., Zürich, 1998—; founder, pres. Indsl. Sci. and Tech. Com. Swiss C. of C. and Industry in Japan, 190-91; founder Computer and Comm. Camp, a supercomputer camp for highly-skilled h.s. scholars, 1995—. Author (book) Swiss Venture Capital Guide, 1998/99; editor: Innovation—Venture Capital—Employment: Answers to the Key Questions, 1997; patentee in field of biotech. Pres. Swiss Soc. Kansai, Japan, 1991; v.p. Agir pour demain, Switzerland, 1995-97; mem. Network for the Working Soc., Switzerland, 1996—; co-founder, mem. Com. on Innovation, Venture Capital and Employment, Switzerland, 1996—. With Swiss Tank Infantry, 1976. Grantee Holderbank Found., 1985, Monbusho, Japanese Ministry Edn., 1985-87, U. Basel, 1986. Mem. Harvard Bus. Sch. (alumni mem.), Rotary Club Zürich. Roman Catholic. Avocations: karate (3d Dan), skiing, classical music. Office: Nextech Venture AG, Scheuchzerstr 35, 8006 Zurich Switzerland

SCHEIER, IVAN HENRY, volunteer, writer; b. Plattsburgh, N.Y., Jan. 7, 1926; s. Joel Henry and Melba Gottlob S. BA in Philosophy, Union Coll., 1948; MA in Psychology, McGill U., Montreal, 1951, PhD in Psychology, 1953. Vol. coord., project dir. Boulder County Juvenile Ct., 1965-69; interim dir. Vol. and Info. Ctr. of Boulder County, 1968; exec. dir. Nat. Info. Ctr. on Volunteerism, 1967-76; pres. Assn. Voluntary Action Scholars, 1973-74; chair Alliance for Volunteerism, 1975-76; pres. Yellowfire Press, 1981-89; dir. Ctr. for Creative Cmty., 1986-95; dreamcatcher-in-residence Voluntas Retreat Ctr., 1991-95; coord. Stillpoint Self-Help Healing Ctr., 1996—; mem. faculty McGill U., 1950-51, U. Ill., 1953-58, Nat. Coll. Juvenile Justice, 1970, U. Colo. Vol. Mgmt. Cert. Program, 1973-87; mem. White House Conf. on Children and Youth, 1970, Nat. Adv. Commn. Criminal Justice Standards and Goals, 1971, Nat. Forum on Volunteerism, 1979-80; mem. adv. com. U. Colo. Vol. Mgmt. Cert. Program, 1973-77; sr. advisor Resource Devel., the Assn. for Vol. Adminstrn., 1979-80, Citizen Advocacy for Devel. Disabled, 1980-82, New Road Map Found., 1990—; mem. adv. bd. Madrid-Cerrillos Med. Clin., 1993-94; mem. youth volunteer leadership tng. project Sister Cities Internat., 1979-81. Author: Exploring Volunteer Space: The Recruiting of a Nation, 1980, Making Dreams Come True Without Much Money: The Midwifery of Dreams, 2000, When Everyone's a Volunteer, 1992, Images of the Future, 1994; pub., editor On Background, 1979-81, The Dovia Exchange, 1984—, The Restless News, 1986-89, Ex Libris, 1987-90, Madrid Muse, 1991-95. Pres. emeritus Nat. Info. Ctr. on Volunteerism, 1979—; chair com. NAACP, Urbana, Ill., 1956-59; vol. various orgns., U.S., Can., 1963—; mem. Sierra Pride Com. Turning Point, Truth or Consequences, N.Mex., 1999—; mem. policy bd. Assn. Voluntary Action Scholars, 1971-74, Nat. Ctr. for Voluntary Action, 1971-76, Nat. Info. Ctr.on Volunteerism, 1971-79, Alliance for Volunteerism, 1974-77, Nat. Orgn. Victim Assistance, 1977-79, Partners, Inc., 1979-82; bd. dirs. Madrid, N.Mex. Landowners Assn., 1993-94. Recipient Nat. Meritorious Svc. award Nat. Coun. Juvenile Court Judges, 1971, Meritorious Svc. award Province of Ont., 1976, Leadership award Alliance for Volunteerism, Inc., 1976, Disting. Svc. award State of Miss., 1982, Nat. Cmty. Svc. award Nat. Assn. on Vols. in Criminal Justice, 1987, Lifetime Achievement award Denver Dirs. of Vols. in Agys., 1997. Mem. Assn. Vol. Adminstrn. (life, Nat. Disting. Svc. award 1984, editor Volunteer Adminstrn. 1979-81), Phi Beta Kappa. Avocations: tai chi, dancing, hiking, reading, gardening. E-mail: ivan@zianet.com.

SCHEINESON, IRWIN BRUCE, insurance and investment company executive; b. Cin., Aug. 8, 1955; s. Julian and Joan (Klein) S.; married; children: Kate Marie, John Philip. BBA, U. Cin., 1978. Pres., prin. Lang-Kruke Fin. Group, Cin., 1978-97; agt. adv. liaison Community Mut. Ins. Co. (Blue Cross), Cin., 1978-80, Cen. Benefits Mut., Columbus, Ohio, 1986-88; pres. Gt. Am. Filter Co., Norwood, Ohio, 1990-98; pres., CEO Planning Works, Ltd., 1997; lectr. in field. Contbr. articles to profl. jours. Fund raiser Guilford Sch., Cin., 1985—. Mem. Internat. Assn. Fin. Planning, Nat. Assn. Health Underwriters, Nat. Assn. Life Underwriters (Nat. Sales Achievement award 1979), Cin. Assn. Health Underwriters (bd. dirs. 1984-87), Nat. Soc. CLUs and Chartered Fin. Cons., 2000 Top of the Table Million Dollar Roundtable, Crest Hills Country Club (bd. dirs. 1988-93). Republican. Jewish. Avocations: tennis, skiing, travel, golf, marathon running. E-mail: runner@fuse.net. Office: Planning Works Ltd PO Box 498007 8737 Windfield Ln Cincinnati OH 45249-3305

SCHEINMANN, PIERRE, pediatrician, educator; b. Paris, Feb. 22, 1941; s. Sigmund and Anna (Fisz) S.; m. Nicole Loubies, June 18, 1965; children: Nicolas, Renaud. MD, Necker Enfants-Malades, Paris, 1973. Resident Paris, 1967-73, fellow, 1973-78, prof., 1978—; head pulmonary allergy unit, 1991—. Author, editor several books on pediat. allergy and pediat. pulmonology including Allergologie Pediatrique, 1994, Progres En Asthme, 1995; contbr. articles to profl. jours. Lt. French Air Force, 1967-69. Office: Serv Pediat Allergol Pneum, 149 Rue Sevres, 75743 Paris 15, France

SCHEINOWITZ, MICKEY, physiology researcher; b. Petach-Tikwa, Israel, Nov. 30, 1957; s. Nachman and Dolly (Unger) S.; m. Michael Cohen, Dec. 1995; 1 child, Adi. PhD in Physiology, Tel Aviv U., 1991. Rschr. Neufeld Cardiac Rsch. Inst. Sheba Med. Ctr., 1993—; dir. exercise program Cardiostyle, Tel Aviv, 1995; chmn. Israeli Working Group on Exptl. Cardiology. Fax: 972-3-5351139. E-mail: mickeys@post.tau.ac.il. Office: Sheba Med Ctr, Neufeld Cardiac Rsch Inst, Tel-Hashower S2621, Israel

SCHEIRS, JOHN, polymer chemist, scientist; b. Melbourne, Victoria, Australia, Nov. 28, 1965; s. William Louis and Josephina Catherina (Schoormans) S.; m. Sandra Michele Fernando, Oct. 12, 1995; children: Trent Riley, Tristan Kody. BSc, U. Melbourne, Australia, 1988, PhD, 1992; post doctoral studies, U. Turin, Italy, 1994-95, U, Clermont Ferrand, France, 1995-96. Polymer chemist Exxon-Mobil J.V., Melbourne, Australia, 1991-94; cons. in polymer chemistry ExcelPlas, Melbourne, 1996-98; process mgr. Coca-Cola Amatil, Sydney, Australia, 1998—. Author: (book with Wiley) Polymer Recycling, 1998, Compositional and Failure Analysis of Polymers: A Practical Approach, 2000; editor: (books with Wiley) Modern Fluoropolymers, 1997, Metallocene-Catalyzed Polyolefins, 1999; series editor (with John Wiley and Sons, U.K.) Wiley Series in Polmer Science, 1997—; mem. editl. bd. Polymer Degradation and Stability, Elsevier Sci., U.K., 1997—. Mem. Am. Chem. Soc., Inst. Materials (UK)., Soc. Plastic Engrs. (plastics recycling divsn.) (U.S.). Achievements include assistance in the development of numerous recycled polymer products based on recycled polyethylene, scrap rubbber tires and polyethylene terephthalate such as mobile garbage bins, grocery sacks, rubber soaker hose, plastic lumber and food contact packaging. Commissioned and managed the World's first process for the closed-loop recycling of polyethylene terephthalate soft-drink bottles. Office: Coca-Cola Amatil, 23 Ash Rd, Prestons NSW 2170, Australia

SCHELDE, PER, writer, educator; b. Copenhagen, Denmark, Sept. 23, 1945; came to U.S., 1978; s. Helge Jacob Schelde and Aase Schelde (Guldager Nielsen) Jacobsen. BA, CUNY, Queens, 1981; PhD, CUNY, 1985. Actor Svalegangen, Aarhus, Denmark, 1970-73, Fiolteatret, Copenhagen, 1974-77; asst. prof. York Coll., Jamaica, N.Y., 1985-90; actor St. George Theater, Grand Canyon Shakespeare Festival, Phoenix, 1996. Author: Ibsen's Forsaken Merman: Folklore in the Late Plays, 1988, Androids, Humanoids and Other Folklore Monsters: Science and Soul in Science Fiction Films, 1993; contbr. articles to profl. jours. Fellow Royal Anthropological Soc.; mem. Am. Anthropological Soc., Phi Beta Kappa. Avocations: reading, running, tennis.

SCHELER, MANFRED, philologist; b. Veilsdorf, Thuringia, Germany, July 24, 1926; s. Gustav and Thekla (Mertz) S.; m. Ursula Fuhr; children: Christian, Michael. PhD, Free U., Berlin, 1961. Prof. English philology Free U., Berlin, 1971—. Author: Old English Loan Syntax, 1961, History of English Vocabulary, 1977, Shakespeare's English, 1982; editor: History of English Philology, 1987. Home: Goerzallee 47, 12207 Berlin 45 Germany Office: Free Berlin U, Gosslerstrasse 2-4, 1000 Berlin 33, Germany

SCHELEV, MIKHAIL YAKOVLEVICH, physicist, researcher; b. Moscow, Nov. 14, 1938; s. Yakov Stepanovich and Evdokiya Mikhailovna (Troshina) S.; m. Valentina Petrovna (Degtyareva), Sept. 18, 1965; 1 child, Irina Mikhailovna. Radioengr., Bauman High-Tech. Inst., Moscow, 1962; PhD in Tech. Scis., Moscow Phys.-Tech. Inst., 1969; DSc in Physics and Math., Lebedev Phys. Inst., Moscow, 1981; prof. in phys. electronics, Gen. Phys. Inst., Moscow, 1985. Radioengr., minor to sr. scientist, sect. head Lebedev Phys. Inst., 1962-82; picosecond photonics lab. head Gen. Physics Inst., 1983-89, photoelectronics dept. head, 1989—; vis. scientist Nat. Rsch. Coun. of Can., Ottawa, 1969-70, Comissariat Energie Atomique, Sacley, Paris, 1974-75; mem. internat. com. on high-speed photography and photonics, 1970—; program chair, organizing com. 14th and 23d Internat. Congresses on High-Speed Photography and Photonics, Moscow, 1980, 98. Author, co-author 330 publs., including 15 Russian inventions and 15 fgn. patents; contbr. numerous articles to profl. jours. and conf. procs.; mem. internat. editl. adv. bd. (jour.) Laser Focus World, 1989—. Recipient Lenin's Komsomol prize, Govt. USSR, 1971, Hubert Shardin Gold medal, German Phys. Soc., 1972, Gold Exhbn. medal, Moscow Govtl. Exhbn. Ctr., 1975, USSR State prize, 1986, Russian State Stipend for Outstanding Scientists, Moscow, 1994, 97—; named Honored Inventor of USSR, 1988, Honored Scientist of Russian Fedn., 1999, Honored Prof. of Beijing Inst. Tech., 1999. Fellow Internat. Soc. Optical Engring. (Photo-Sonics Internat. award 1988); mem. IEEE, Acad. Engring. Scis. of Russian Fedn., Acad. of Natural Scis. of Russian Fedn., Sci. Coun. Gen. Physics Inst. Avocations: gardening, swimming, cross-country skiing. Home: 12/7 Zemlyanoi Val Apt 17, 103064 Moscow Russia Office: Gen Physics Inst RAS, 38 Vavilov Str Dept Photoel, 117942 Moscow Russia

SCHELHOWE, HEIDI, computer scientist; b. Mösbach, Germany, Mar. 25, 1949; d. Georg and Johanna (Rieder) H.; m. Theodor Schelhowe, 1973; children: Anne, Steffi. Degree, U. Freiburg, 1972; diploma informatics, U. Bremen, Germany, 1989. Tchr. Bremen, 1973-81; tchr. computer sci. U. Bremen, rsch. asst., 1989-92; rsch. asst. U. Hamburg, 1992-96; tchr. & rsch. asst. Humboldt U., Berlin, 1997—; co-founder, leader of the WF Women's work and informatics Gesellschaft for Informatik, Germany, 1986-90; author Das Medium aus der Machine, 1997. Editor: Frauenwelt-Computerräume, 1986. Home: Ostendorpstr 41, D-28203 Bremen Germany Office: U Hamburg FB Informatik, HU Berlin, Unter den Linden 6, D-10099 Berlin Germany

SCHELLART-VANDEURSEN, RIKY HENDRIKA MATTHEA, artist, educator; b. The Hague, The Netherlands, Dec. 3, 1942; d. Jan Johannes Hendricus and Marie-Maria (Koevoets) vanD.; m. Paulus Aloysius Josephus Schellart-Paul, Apr. 1, 1966 (dec. June 1990); children: Sacha, Tycho, Claire. MA, Royal Acad. Art, The Hague, 1964, Acad. Art, Tilburg, The Netherlands, 1979. Art prof. H.B.O. Sch., Tilburg, 1964-79, Royal Acad., The Hague, 1979—. Author: Beeldende Kunstenaars van de VBBKZN, 1994; one-woman shows include Alkmaar de Telloor, 1993, Luyksgestel Bernice, 1993, Wassenaar de Kievit, 1994, Heerlen Hoofd Kantoor DSM, 1994, Hotel-Restaurant Merlet, 1995, Weert Hoofd Kantoor Wilma bouw, 1995, Romania Constanta Muzeului de Arta, 1995, den Haag SER bezuidenhout 60, 1996, Alkmaar de Telloor, 1996, Roemenië Piatra Neamt Muzeului de Arta, 1996, Hilvarenbeek Gemeentehuis, 1996, Romania Baia Mare Prefectura, 1996, Jasi Muzeul de Arta, 1997, Oisterwyk de Drye Swaentjes, 1997, others; exhibited in group shows at Tilburg Schouwburg, 1989, Vught Panacea, 1990, Luyksgestel Bernice, 1990, Landgraaf Agua Pictura Studio du Zavier, 1990, Oisterwyk Germeente Kantoor, 1993, Brussel residence sec. gen. WEU, 1994, Tilburg Textile Mus., 1994, Bergen op Zoom, Markiezenhof, 1996, Groot Schermer le Pignon, 1997, Holland Art Fair, The Hague, 1998, Min. Econ. Affairs, 1998, Min. Transport, 1999-2000, others, Mus. Kempenland-Eindhoven, 1998; also pvt. collections. Mem. Atlantic-Pacific Exch. Program. Avocations: painting, drawing, making sculptures, theatre, travel. Home: Friezenlaan 10, 5037KM Tilburg The Netherlands

SCHELLEKENS, MAARTEN PETRUS GODEFRIDUS, marketing consultant; b. Nymegen, The Netherlands, Apr. 5, 1963; s. Piet Godefridus and Elisabeth Maria (Verbrugge) S.; m. Frieda Geertruida Vreeman, Mar. 3, 1992; children: Menno, Nadine. Propoedeuse cum laude, Cath. U. Nymegen, 1985, doctoral degree cum laude, 1989. Asst. dept. rsch. methodology Cath. U. Brabant, The Netherlands, 1990-91; quality mgr. Schellekens & Schellekens BV, Beuning, The Netherlands, 1991; rschr. Rigo Rsch. and Advice, Amsterdam, The Netherlands, 1991-93, sr. rschr., 1994-95; cons. CSEM, Amsterdam, The Netherlands, 1995-96, sr. cons., 1997, dir. consultants, 1998; mktg. sci. specialist McKinsey & Co., Amsterdam, The Netherlands, 1999-2000; mktg. cons. McKinsey & Co., London, 2000—. Recipient Fulbright award, Fulbright Com., Amsterdam, 1989. Mem. Fulbright Alumni Assn., Amsterdam, 1990—. Avocation: composer. Home: 23 Dartnell Park Rd, West Byfleet, Surrey KT14 6PN, England Office: McKinsey & Co, 1 Jermyn St, London SW1Y 4UH, England

SCHELLENBERG, JUERGEN BERND, chemist; b. Sangerhausen, Germany, May 7, 1953; s. Gerhard and Anni (Reinhardt) S.; m. Christa Koch, Apr. 24, 1976; children: Mirco, Katrin. Chemist, Carl Schorlemmer Tech. U., 1975, PhD, 1979. Asst. Carl Schorlemmer Tech. U., Merseburg, Germany, 1975-79; rschr. Chemische Werke Buna, Schkopau, Germany, 1979-90; rsch. specialist Buna AG, Schkopau, 1990-97, Dow-BSL Olefinverbund GmbH, Schkopau, 1997—. Inventor in field; contbr. articles to profl. jours. Mem. Soc. German Chemists. Office: Dow BSL Olefinverbund GmBH, Werk Schkopau R&D, D-06258 Schkopau Germany

SCHELLENBERG, RÜDIGER, physician, researcher, therapist; b. Brotterode, Thuringia, Germany, June 6, 1952; s. Lothar and Rosa (Nimczyk) S.; m. Vera Löhr; children: Stefan, Olaf. MD, Med. Acad. Magdeburg, 1979, D med. habilitation, 1989. Physician Med. Acad. Magdeburg, Germany, 1979-81, head dept. clin. physiology, 1982-90; physician clin. physiology Jena, Germany, 1982; head clin. rsch. Pro Sci. Pvt. Rsch. Clinic, Linden, Germany, 1991-98; pvt. practice Hüttenberg, Germany, 1999—; head Inst. of Integrated Medicine and Sci., 2000—. Recipient scientific award Med. Acad. Magdeburg, 1976, 79. Mem. Internat. Brain Rsch. Orgn., Brit. Psychophysiol. Soc., German Migraine and Headache Soc., European Soc. Med. Hypnosis, German Soc. Biofeedback Therapy (pres.). Avocations: skiing, swimming, hiking. Home and Office: Talstr 29, 35625 Hüttenberg Hessen, Germany

SCHELLENBERGER, ALFRED HERMANN, biochemistry educator; b. Chemnitz, Saxony, Germany, Nov. 14, 1928; s. Martin Hilmar and Ruth (Wolf) S.; m. Ruth Bauer, 1955 (div. 1965); children: Gabriele, Thomas; m. Anneliese Litzel, July 23, 1966; children: Kerstin, Eyk. Diploma in chemistry, U. Rostock, Germany, 1952; D in Natural Scis., U. Halle, Germany, 1956, Habilitation, 1962. Asst. U. Halle, 1952-64, lectr. chemistry, 1964-67, prof. biochemistry, 1967-96, head dept. biochemistry, 1967-89, dean dept. biochemistry, 1989-94, dean sci. faculty, 1991-93, dir. Biochemistry Inst., 1989-95. Author, editor: (textbook) Enzyme Catalysis, 1988; contbr. over 150 articles to sci. publs.; patentee in applied enzymology (31). Mem. Leopoldina Acad. (v.p. 1991-2000). Avocation: music (violin). Home: Amselweg 44, Sachsen-Anhalt, D-06110 Halle Germany Office: Martin Luther Univ Halle, Weinbergweg 3, D-06120 Halle Germany

SCHELLING, THOMAS CROMBIE, economist, educator; b. Oakland, Calif., Apr. 14, 1921; s. John M. and Zelda M. (Ayres) S.; m. Corinne T. Saposs, Sept. 13, 1947 (div. 1991); children: Andrew, Thomas, Daniel, Robert; m. Alice M. Coleman, Nov. 8, 1991. AB, U. Calif., Berkeley, 1943; PhD, Harvard U., 1951. U.S. govt. economist Copenhagen, Paris, Washington, 1948-53; prof. econs. Yale U., 1953-58, Harvard U., Cambridge, Mass., 1958-90; prof. econs. and pub. affairs U. Md., College Park, 1990—, disting. univ. prof., 1990—; sr. staff mem. RAND Corp., 1958-59; chmn. rsch. adv. bd. Com. Econ. Devel., 1978-81, 84-85; mem. sci. adv. bd. USAF, 1960-64, def. sci. bd., 1966-70; mem. mil. econ. adv. panel CIA, 1980-85; trustee Aerospace Corp., 1984-93. Author: National Income Behavior, 1951, International Economics, 1958, The Strategy of Conflict, 1960, Arms and Influence, 1966, Micromotives and Macrobehavior, 1978, Choice and Consequence, 1984; co-author: Strategy and Arms Control, 1961. Recipient Frank E. Seidman Disting. award in polit. economy, 1977. Fellow Am. Acad. Arts and Scis., AAAS, Assn. for Pub. Policy Analysis and Mgmt., Am. Econ. Assn. (pres. 1991, Disting. mem. award); mem. NAS (rsch. award, 1993), Inst. Medicine, Ea. Econ. Assn. (pres. 1996). Office: Univ Md Sch Pub Affairs College Park MD 20742-0001

SCHELP, LOTHAR HEINRICH WALTER, program director, researcher; b. Minden, Germany, Sept. 6, 1941; came to Sweden, 1965; s. Heinz and Irmgard (Wehrmann) S.; m. Marianne Leila Holm, Dec. 20, 1969; children: Fredrik, Henrik. BA, U. Gothenborg, Sweden, 1970; MS, 1972; PhD, Karolinska Inst., Stockholm, Sweden, 1987. Prin. officer County Coun., Skōvde, Sweden, 1978-87; researcher Karolinska Inst., Stockholm, Sweden, 1983-84; head of divsn. Nat. Bd. Health, Stockholm, Sweden, 1987-92; dir. programs Nat. Inst. Pub. Health, Stockholm, Sweden, 1992—; assoc. prof. Karolinska Inst., Stockholm, Sweden, 1987-99, prof., 1999—; cons. Nat. Bd. health, Stockholm, Sweden, 1992—, WHO, Geneva, 1990—. Author: Epidemiology As a Basis for ..., 1987, Safety Promotion Research; contbr. articles to profl. jours. Order of Merit, Swedish Red Cross, 1990. Mem. Internat. Soc. Child and Adolescent Injury Prevention, NOMESCO. Avocations: painting, sports, nature. Home: Myggvagen 11, 54165 Skovde Sweden Office: Nat Inst Public Health, 10352 Stockholm Sweden

SCHELP, RICHARD HERBERT, mathematics educator; b. Kansas City, Mo., Apr. 21, 1936; s. Herbert and Ida Louise Schelp; m. Billie Marie Schelp, Dec. 20, 1958; children: Lisa Marie Martin, Richard John. BS in Math. and Physics, Ctrl. Mo. U., 1959; MS in Math., Kans. State U., 1961, PhD in Math., 1970. Assoc. mathematician applied physics lab. Johns Hopkins U., 1961-66; instr. math. Kans. State U., 1966-70; asst. prof. math. U. Memphis, 1970-74, assoc. prof. math., 1974-79, prof. math., 1979—; chair spl. session Fifth Hungarian Combinatorics Conf., Keszthely, Hungary, 1976, First Japan Conf. Graph Theory and Application, 1986, First China-USA Conf. on Graph and Applications, 1986, Seventh Hungarian Combinatorics, Eger, 1987; chair session Probabilistic Workshop, Budapest, Hungary, 1998; vis. rschr. Hungarian Acad. Scis.-Math. Inst., 1985, 90, Lab. Rsch. and Info., U. Paris-Sud, 1993, Hungarian Acad. Scis.-Computer and Automation Inst., 1994; presenter in field. Mem. editl. bd. Jour. Graph Theory, 1981—, co-mng. editor, 1981-86; reviewer Math. Revs.; contbr. articles to profl. jours. Named Outstanding Educators Am., 1975; NSF fellow U. Mass., summer 1968; travel grantee Internat. Rsch. and Exch., 1985, 90, grantee NSF, 1986-87, 92-95, Nat. Security Agy., 1988-91. Mem. Am. Math. Soc. (organizer spl. session 1997), Math. Assn. Am., Inst. for Combinatorics and its Applications, N.Y. Acad. Sci. E-mail: rschelp@postoffice.memphis.edu. Home: 355 Leonora Dr Memphis TN 38117-2102 Office: Dept Math Scis Univ Memphis Memphis TN 38152-0001

SCHEMMEL, RACHEL ANNE, food science and human nutrition educator, researcher; b. Farley, Iowa, Nov. 23, 1929; d. Frederic August and Emma Margaret (Melchert) Schemmel. BA, Clarke Coll., 1951; MS, U. Iowa, 1952; PhD, Mich. State U., 1967. Dietitian Children's Hosp. Soc., L.A., 1952-54; instr. Mich. State U., East Lansing, 1955-63, from asst. prof. to prof. food sci., human nutrition, 1967—. Author: Nutrition Physiology and Obesity, 1980; contbr. articles on obesity, clin. nutrition to profl. jours. Recipient Disting. Alumni award Mt. Mercy Coll., 1971, Borden award for rsch. in applied nutrition, 1986, Outstanding Alumni award U. Iowa, 1996, Outstanding Achievement award Clarke Coll., 1997. Mem. AAFCS (chair nutrition health and food mgmt. divsn. 1995-97, Outstanding Leader award 1998), Am. Soc. Nutrition Scis. (chair), Inst. Food Technologists, Am. Diet Assn. (pres. Mich. 1976-77, Lansing 1960, Outstanding Dietetic Educator award 1988), Brit. Nutrition Soc., Soc. for Nutrition Edn., Sigma Xi (sr. rsch. award 1986, pres. Mich. State U. chpt. 1983-84), Phi Kappa Phi (pres. 1994-95). Roman Catholic. Home: 1341 Red Leaf Ln East Lansing MI 48823-1339 Office: Mich State U Dept Food Sci Nutrit East Lansing MI 48824

SCHENCK, DAVID, elementary education educator, director; b. N.Y.C.; s. Ferdinand and Anna (Tuttle) S.; m. Dorothy Hall, Oct. 4, 1952; children: David, Janet, Margaret, William. BBA, U. Mich., 1948; MEd, Emory U., 1958. Tchr. Rectory Sch., Pomfret, Conn., 1954-56, Camp Waya-Awi, Rangeley, Maine, 1954-57, Ga. Mil. Acad., Coll. Pk., 1958-59; founder, tchr., dir. Schenck Sch., Atlanta, 1959—; supr. pilot program adult dyslexics Schenck Sch., Atlanta, 1999—. Bd. dirs. Hope Atlanta's Youth Fund, 1994-

99. With U.S. Army, 1942-45. Mem. Internat. Dyslexia Assn. (1st pres. Ga. br. 1990-91), Appalachian Trail Club. Democrat. Episcopalian. Avocations: hiking, painting, music. Fax: 404-252-7615. Home: 205 Ansley Villa Dr NE Atlanta GA 30324-4810 Office: Schenck Sch 282 Mount Paran Rd NW Atlanta GA 30327-4698

SCHENDA, RUDOLF WILHELM, classicist, educator; b. Essen, Germany, Oct. 13, 1930; arrived in Switzerland, 1979; s. Rudolf C. and Christine (Schmidt) S.; m. Susanne Kratschmer, 1958; children: Nicole, Catherine. PhD, U. Munich, 1959; PhD in Habilitation, U. Tübingen, Germany, 1970. Prof., dir. dept. folklore U. Göttingen, Germany, 1973-79; prof. U. Zurich, 1979-95, hon. prof., 1995—; dir. dept. folklore U. Zurich, 1991-95. Author: Folk without Books, 1970, 3d edit 1988, The Misery of Old People, 1972, Lifetimes, 1983, Fairy Tales from Sicily, 1991, From Mouth to Ear, 1993, The Alphabet of Animals, 1995, Fairy Tales from Toscana, 1996, Body Histories, 1998, G.B. Basile: Pentamerone, 2000. Recipient Premio Giuseppe Pitrè, Palermo, Italy, 1988, Festschrift: Reading, Learning, Hearing, Saying, 1995. Mem. German Soc. Folklore, Internat. Soc. Folk Narrative Rsch. E0mail: rschenda@access.ch. Home: Taegernaustr 43, CH 8645 Jona Switzerland

SCHENK, WOLFGANG OSKAR MAX, theologian, researcher; b. Jena, Thuringia, Germany, Apr. 29, 1934; s. Oskar and Erna (Wilhelm) S. Academically qualified theologian, U. Jena, Germany, 1957, ThD, 1965. Ordained reverend Luth. Sem., Eisenach, Germany, 1958. Reverend Luth. Ch., Hirschberg, Germany, 1957-67; prof. New Testament Theol. Sem., Naumburg, Germany, 1967-76; vis. prof. Free U., Amsterdam, The Netherlands, 1979; dep. prof. U. Göttingen, Germany, 1983-84, 92-93; rsch. prof. U. Bonn, Germany, 1983-85, 88-91; dep. prof. U. Bonn, 1994-95; leader Soc. Evang. Theologie, East Germany, 1969-81; chmn. Linguistic Sem. in SNTS, 1980-84; mem. Deutsche Gesellschaft für Semiotic, 1981; bd. dirs. Jüdisches Lehrhaus, Frankfurt, 1986-91; vis. prof. U. Uppsala, Sweden, 1984, U. Viena, 1997-98. Author: Der Segen im New Testament, 1967, Bibelarbeit und Bibelwoche, 1971, Der Passionsbericht nach Markus, 1974, Synopse zur Redenquelle der Evangelen, 1981, Evangelium-Evangelien-Evangeliologie, 1983, Die Philipperbriefe des Paulus, 1984, Die Sprache des Matthaus, 1987, Lima-Ökumene als Gegenaufklarung, 1990, Kommentiertes Lexikon zum 4 Evangelium, 1993, Das biographische Ich-Idiom Menschensohn, 1997. Mem. City Coun., Eppstein, Taunus, Germany, 1989-91. Mem. Internat. Fellowship of Reconciliation, Soc. N.T. Studies, Evangelische Theologie. Mem. Bündnis 90/Die Grünen Party. Mem. United Ch. Avocations: swimming, dog keeping, gardening, traveling, music. Home: Mittelstr 3, D066125 Saarbrücken Saarland, Germany

SCHENKEL, ELMAR, English educator, writer; b. Hovestadt, Westphalia, Germany, Aug. 28, 1953; s. Heinrich and Klara (Alberti) S.; m. Kumi Inada, Dec. 15, 1977; 1 child, Elena. Degree, Aldegrever Gymnasium, Germany, 1971; PhD, U. Freiburg, Germany, 1983, degree, 1991. Vis. prof. U. Mass., Amherst, 1988-89; prof. U. Freiburg, 1991, U. Konstanz, Germany, 1992-93; prof. U. Leipzig, Germany, 1993—, head English dept., 1993-95, 98-00; referee Deutsche Forschungsgem, 1997-99; pres. Foerderverein, Leipzig, Germany, 1999—. Author: (novel) Der Westfaelische Bogenschuetze, 1999, (poetry) Blauverschiebung, 1992, (travel book) Massachusetts, 1991 (H. Hesse-Foerder prize 1991), (short stories) Mauerrisse, 1985 (J. Ponto prize 1985); co-editor Chelsea Hotel Mag., 1992—; editl. bd. Inklings Yearbook, 1988—. British coord. Operation Reconciliation, Coventry, England, 1973-74. Recipient Mackensen Foerder prize Westermann, 1981; literary grantee Cultural Ministry, 1987. Mem. Soc. Lit. and Sci., Chesterton Soc., H. G. Wells Soc. Avocations: drawing, cycling. Office: U Leipzig English Dept, Bruehl 34-50, 04109 Leipzig Germany

SCHENKER, JOSEPH GEORGE, physician, obstetrics and gynecology educator; b. Cracow, Poland, Nov. 20, 1933; s. Ignacy and Anna (Greshler) S.; m. Ekaterina Idels, 1959; children: Inon, Eran. MD, Hebrew U., Jerusalem, 1959. Intern Tel Hashomer Hosp., 1958-59; resident in ob-gyn. Hadassah Med. Ctr., Jerusalem, 1962-68, temp. chief physician ob-gyn., 1965-72, permanent chief physician ob-gyn., 1973-78, chmn. dept. ob-gyn., 1978—; rsch. fellow divsn. of reprodn. U. Pa., Phila., 1972-73; dep. dir. Hadassah Med. Ctr., 1977-80; ob-gyn. lectr. Sch. Medicine Hebrew U., Jerusalem, 1968-71, sr. lectr., 1971-76, assoc. prof. ob-gyn., 1976-79, prof. ob-gyn., 1979—, chmn. com. postgrad. tng. in ob-gyn., 1973-78, exec. chief tchg., 1977-80, 82-85, mem. com. for med. edn. Med. Sch., 1981-85; chmn. directory bd. exam. in ob-gyn. State of Israel, 1979-83; chmn. adv. com. ob-gyn. Ministry of Health, State of Israel, 1979-86, chmn. com. residency tng., 1985-90, dep. chmn. sci. coun., 1985-90, chmn. com. for lic. and internship exam., 1988—, mem. pub. coun. demography, 1994—, chmn. bd. examination for med. lic. and internship, 1988—; mem. coun. for syllabus residency tng. Israel Sci. Coun., 1980-85; chmn. European Residency Exch. Program, Extended European Bd. Gyn. and Obstetrics, 1992—; mem. Internat. Sci. Adv. Bd. Jewish Physicians, 1985—; judge Ministry of Justice of Israel, Dist. Ct. of Appeals, 1986—; mem. com. on control of experiments in animals Israel Acad. Scis., 1987—; mem. adv. com. Physician Licensing, State of Israel, 1988—; mem. adv. bd. ob. interventions WHO, 1989, com. on recent advances in medically assisted reprodn., 1990, com. on assisted reprodn., 1991; chmn. FIGO Com. Study of Ethical Aspects of Human Reproduction, 1994. Editor: Recent Advances in Pathophysiol. Conditions in Pregnancy, 1984, The Intrauterine Life: Management and Treatment, 1986, Advances in Assisted Reproductive Technologies, 1990; mem. editl. bd. Human Reprodn., Internat. Jour. Gynecology and Obstets., Gynecol. Endocrinology, Asia-Oceania Jour. Ob-Gyn., Fertility and Sterility, Jour. Assisted Reprodn. and Genetics, Fetal Diagnosis and Therapy, Internat. Jour. Feto-Maternal Medicine, Global Bioethics, European Jour. Ob., Gyn., and Reproductive Biology, Early Pregnancy: Biology and Medicine, Jour. of the Russian Assn. of Human Reproduction; contbr. more than 430 articles to profl. jours. With Israel Med. Corps, 1959-62. Fellow Am. Coll. Ob. Gyn. (hon.); mem. German Soc. Ob-Gyn. (hon.), Polish Soc. Ob-Gyn. (hon.), Fertility and Sterility Soc. Peru (hon.), Rumanian Soc. Ob-Gyn. (hon.), Implantation Soc. Japan (hon.), Hungarian Soc. Ob-Gyn. (hon.), Macedonian Assn. Gynecologists and Obstetricians (hon.), Israel Med. Assn. (sci. coun. 1980-85, pres. coun. 1980-84, 84-88), Israel Soc. Ob-Gyn. (pres. Jerusalem chpt. 1976—, pres. 1984-89, 89-92, dep. pres. 1993—), Hadassah Chief Physician Orgn. (chmn. 1977-79), Hadassah Orgn. Heads of Dept. (active chmn. 1983-84), Women Coun. Israel, Fallopian Internat. Corr. Soc. (bd. dirs. 1984—), European Soc. Human Reprodn. (founder), Internat. Acad. Reproductive Medicine, Internat. Soc. for the Study of Pathophysiology of Pregnancy (founder), Internat. Soc. of the Fetus as a Patient (founder), European Soc. Reproductive and Embryology (mem. adv. com.), European Assn. Ob-Gyn. (mem. adv. com.), Asia-Oceania Soc. Ob-Gyn. (mem. adv. com.), Internat. Soc. Gynecol. Endocrinology (founder), Israel Soc. Endoscopic Surgery (founder), Am. Fertility Soc., Am. Assn. Planned Parenthood Physicians, Internat. Coll. Surgeons, Internat. Menopausal Soc., Internat. Soc. Study of Twins, Am. Assn. Laparoscopy, Soc. for Advancement of Contraception, Israel Soc. Family Planning, Israel Soc. Gerontology, Israel Soc. Endocrinology, Internat. Acad. Human Reproduction (pres. 1996), Royal Coll. Ob-Gyn. (hon.), among others. Jewish. Office: Hadassah U, Dept Ob-Gyn, 91120 Jerusalem Israel

SCHEPERS, HUUB, plant pathologist; b. Zevenbergen, The Netherlands, June 21, 1956; s. Ad and Ada (Valkenet) S.; m. Eva Kipp, Aug. 19, 1988. Degree, Agrl. U., Wageningen, The Netherlands, 1980, D, 1985. Ext. officer Ministry Agrl., Wageningen, 1985-87; tech. mgr. Hoechst Holland, Amsterdam, The Netherlands, 1987-91; occupl. hygienist Ministry Social Affairs, The Hague, The Netherlands, 1991-92; plant pathologist Ministry Agrl., Lelystad, The Netherlands, 1992—. Editor Proceedings of European Network Workshops on integrated control of late blight, 1997, 98, 99, 2000. Sgt. The Netherlands, 1980-81. Avocations: athletics, gardening. Office: Appl Rsch Sta Arable Corps, Edelhertweg 1, 8200 AK Lelystad The Netherlands

SCHEPISI, FRED, producer, director, screenwriter; b. Melbourne, Australia, Dec. 26, 1939. Student, Assumption Coll., Marcellin Coll. assessor student films Swinburne Inst. Tech., Melbourne; with govt. sponsored exptl. Film Fund; founder prodn. co. The Film Ho. Dir. films including Libido, 1973, Barbarosa, 1982, Iceman, 1984, Plenty, 1985, Roxanne, 1987, Fierce Creatures, 1997; prodr., dir. The Russia House, 1990, Mr. Baseball, 1992, Six Degrees of Separation, 1993, I.Q., 1994; screenwriter, dir., prodr. The Devil's Playground, 1976 (Best Film award Australian Film Inst.), The Chant of Jimmie Blacksmith, 1978, A Cry in the Dark, 1988 (Best Screenplay award Australian Film Inst.). Address: 315 S Beverly Dr Ste 501 Beverly Hills CA 90212-4316

SCHEPKER, RENATE, child and adolescent psychiatrist, psychoanalyst; b. Oberhausen, Germany, June 18, 1954; d. Karl Heinz and Margarete (Wehner) Blumenthal; m. Klaus Peter Schepker, Dec. 28, 1977; children: Arne, Henning. MD, Medizinische Hochschule, Hannover, Germany, 1978. Asst. Stadtische Kliniken Kinderklinik, Duisburg, Germany, 1978-79, Knappschaftskrankenhaus Psychiatry, Bottrop, Germany, 1980-84; asst. Rheinische Landes-u-Hochschulklinik, Essen, Germany, 1984-86, sr. physician, 1986-99; head child/adolescent psychiatry Westf. Inst. Hamm, 1999—; tchr. fellow Inst. Psychoanalyse, Düsseldorf, 1992—. Author: On Control Beliefs of German and Turkish Adolescents in the Ruhr area, 1995, On Indications of Forensic Assessment of Juvenile Delinquents, 1998. Recipient Bennigsen-Foerder-prize Min. Rsch. NRW, 1992; German Rsch. Coun. grant, 1992-97. Mem. German Assn. Child and Adolescent Psychiatry, German-Turkish Assn. Psychiatry (bd. dirs. 1996-98). Office: Westfaelisches Inst KJPP, Heithofer Allee 64, 59071 Hamm Germany

SCHEPP, WOLFGANG, internist; b. Aachen, Germany, Sept. 23, 1955; s. Otto and Hildegard (Buch) S.; m. Susanne Schwonzen, Apr. 1, 1958; children: Lukas, Johanna, Nicola. MD, Bonn U. Med. Sch., 1981; DSc, Munich U. Tech., 1988. Intern Bonn U. Med. Sch., Germany, 1983-84; resident Munich U. Technology, 1985-88; rsch. assoc. UCLA, 1989; cons. gastroenterologist Tech. U. Munich, 1990-97; head dept. gastroenterology Bogenhausen Acad. Tchg. Hosp., Munich, Germany, 1997—. Mem. Am. Gastroenterol. Assn., European Gastroenterology Club, German Gastroenterol. Assn., German Soc. Internal Medicine, German Cancer Assn. Avocations: classical music, sailing, mountain hiking.

SCHEPPING, WILHELM, music educator, ethnomusicologist; b. Neuss, Nordrhein, Germany, Dec. 17, 1931; s. Paul and Sophie (Hutmacher) S.; m. Annette Lüttgens, July 1, 1959; children: Christiane, Veronika, Uta, Wiltrud, Ruth. Student, Music Conservatory of Cologne, Germany, 1956, U. Cologne, 1958; PhD, U. Cologne, 1977. Lectr. Coll. Edn., Neuss, 1968-76, prof., 1976; prof. U. Düsseldorf, Germany, 1981-82, Rheinisch-Westfälische Technische Hochschule, Aachen, Germany, 1982-85; prof. music U. Cologne, 1985—; condr. Neuss Chamber Orch., 1958-88, also several univ. orchs. and choirs; concerts in diverse European countries and in Africa. Author: Die Wettener Liederhandschrift, 1978, Volksmusik und elektronische Medien, 1979, Europäische Volksmusik, 1983, Menschen seid wachsam - Widerständisches Liedgut der Jugend in der NS-Zeit, 1993; author/editor: Musik im Brauch der Gegenwart, 1988, Musikalische Volkskultur in der Stadt, 1993, Three Dekades of the Inst. for Musical Folklore, 1995, Publ. series on Musical Folklore-Materials and Analyses, 1994—; contbg. author: The Garland Encyclopedia of World Music, vol. 8, 2000. Chmn. Kommission für Lied-Musik-und Tanzforschung, Cologne, 1982-88, Landesfachgruppe Musikpädagogik NRW, Cologne, 1984-92; dir. Inst. for Mus. Folklore, U. Cologne, 1992—; mem. Commn. of Ch. Music, Archbishop of Cologne, 1986—. Recipient Ehrenmedaille, U. Nantes, France, 1983, Grosses Stadtsiegel, Stadt Neuss, 1983, Ritter des päpstlichen Gregoriusordens (Knight of Holy Gregorian Order), 1993. Mem. Rotary. Roman Catholic. Home: Kaiser-Friedrich-Strasse 18, D-41460 Neuss Germany Office: Univ of Cologne, Gronewaldstr 2, D-50931 Cologne Germany

SCHER, JOSEPH S., investment company executive; b. Chgo., Oct. 19, 1924; s. Adolph and Edith Scher; m. Lila L. Scher, Dec. 20, 1992; children: Marilyn, Mark, Julie, James. BA, U. Ill., 1947. Pres. Enterprise Cos., Chgo., 1971-79; chmn., CEO Key Ins., Peoria, Ill., 1981-95, Rips Vision Ctrs., Santa Barbara, Calif., 1983-87, Gamma Digital, Chgo., 1994-99; chmn. bd. Scher Investment Co., Santa Barbara, 1992—. Chmn. investment com. Santa Barbara City Coll., 1996—; bd. dirs. Scleroderma rsch. Found., 1988-98. Office: Scher Investment Co 4475 Vieja Dr Santa Barbara CA 93110-2075

SCHERB, HAGEN HEINRICH, mathematics, statician; b. Speyer, Germany, Jan. 6, 1951; s. Heinrich Phillip and Gertrud Kathe (Fuchs) S.; m. Eugenie Irmagard Closs, Apr. 16, 1981; children: Camilla Catharina, Anke Franziska. Diplom.math., U. Saarlandes, Germany, 1977, Dr.rer.nat., 1984. Rschr. U., Homburg, Germany, 1977-78, GSF-Nat. Rsch. Ctr. Environ. & Health, Neuherberg, Germany, 1978—. Co-author: Umwelt und Gesundheit, 1987, Gesundheitsrisiken persistenter Umwelt-Chemikalien, 1990. With German Air Force, 1969-71. Mem. Internat. Biometric Soc. Avocation: model airplane flying. Office: GSF, Ingolstaedter Landstr 1, 85764 Neuherberg Germany

SCHERBO, VITALY V., gymnast; b. Minsk, Belarus, USSR, Jan. 13, 1972; s. Viktor V. and Valentina (Chaban) S.; m. Irina Tchernilevskaya, Dec. 20, 1991; 1 child, Kristina. Diploma, Olympic Reserve Sch. of Belarus, USSR, 1990, Acad. of Sports of Belarus, Russia, 1994. prin. Scherbo, Inc., Fort Wayne, Ind., 1994—, Vitaly Scherbo Sch. of Gymnastics, Inc., Las Vegas, 1997. Recipient Honor Master of Sport Internat. Class award Goskomsport USSR, 1990, Best Athlete in the World award Trans World Sport, 1992, France Telecom award, 1993, Jesse Owens Internat. trophy, 1993, World Gymnastic All Around Title award World Gymnastics Championship, 1993, gold medal Olympic Games Barcelona all-around team, horse, rings, vault, parallel bars, 1992; bronze medal All-around competition, vault, parallel bars, horizontal bars Olympic Games, Atlanta, 1996. Avocations: fishing, reading, picking mushrooms, music, movies. Office: Internat Gymnastics Fedn 331 Rosemont Dr State College PA 16801-2532 Address: 8308 Aqua Spray Ave Las Vegas NV 89128-7432

SCHERCH, RICHARD OTTO, minister, consultant; b. Balt., Nov. 21, 1926; s. Richard Leopold and Anna Elizabeth (Finger) S.; m. Janice Marie Halbgewachs, June 24, 1951; children: Richard Paul, Leslie Carol, Lisa Beth, Jeremy Thomas. BA, Gettysburg Coll., 1948; BD, Luth. Sch. Theology, Phila., 1951; PhD, Johns Hopkins U., 1959; D Ministry, Lancaster Theol. Sem., 1975; cert. in dispute resolution recognition, Capital U., 1993. Ordained to ministry Luth. Ch., 1951. Mission developer Wichita, Kans., 1951-53; pastor Trinity Luth. Ch., Manhattan beach, Calif., 1953-57; asst. pastor 1st Luth. Ch., Balt., 1957-59; pastor St. Mark's Luth. Ch., Birdsboro, Pa., 1961-65, Zion Luth. Ch., Lebanon, Pa., 1965-71, Shiloh Luth. Ch., York, Pa., 1972-75, Christ Luth. Ch., Paramus, N.J., 1976-81; sr. pastor Emmanuel Luth. Ch., Venice, Fla., 1981-93; owner Bldg. Bridges Consultation Svcs., Sarasota, Fla., 1993—; mission developer Kansas City, Mo., 1959-61; lectr. Chautauqua (N.Y.) Inst., 1963, 64, 65; instr. Johns Hopkins U., Balt., 1957-58, U. Balt., 1958-59; dir. Consult, Inc., Lebanon, Pa.; adj. faculty mem. Luther Coll., Teaneck, N.J., 1977-78, Bergen C.C., Paramus, 1979; chmn. profl. support com. Fla. Synod Luth. Ch. Am., Tampa, Fla., 1982-87, ptnr. in evangelism, Chgo., 1985-91; cons. Fla.-Bahamas Synod, 1993—, Episcopal Diocese of S.W. Fla., 1993—; faculty Interim Ministry Tng. Network, 1997—; interim ministry cons. Tng. Network, 1997—. Comdr. USNR, 1956-77. Mem. Internat. Transactional Analysis Assn., Rotary. Republican. E-mail: dickscherch@earthlink.net.

SCHERE, DANIEL BERNARDO, laboratory and nuclear medicine executive; b. Buenos Aires, Aug. 3, 1942; s. Moises and Susana (Brener) S.; m. Maria Elena Madrid Paez, Dec. 27, 1968; children: Mariana, Daniel Ignacio, Federico Javier. Bachelor degree, Colegio Nacional Buenos Aires, 1960; MD, U. Buenos Aires, 1967. Diplomate Am. Bd. Nuclear Medicine. Resident in pediat. B.A. Children's Hosp., Buenos Aires, 1967-72, head nuclear medicine, 1977—; sci. dir. Lab. Dr. M. Schere, Buenos Aires, 1990—. Office: Lab Dr Schere, Juncal 1722, Buenos Aires 1062, Argentina

SCHERECK, WILLIAM JOHN, retired historian, consultant; b. Chgo., Dec. 22, 1913; s. Frank and Adele (Schubert) S.; m. Flora Blanch George, May 19, 1943; children: Linda, William Jr., Ralph, Florian. Student, Wofford Coll., 1950-51; BS in Sociology, U. Wis., 1952, postgrad., 1952-53. With Crawford County (Wis.) Welfare Dept., 1938-42; with State Hist. Soc. Wis., Madison, 1953-79, rsch. asst., 1954-55, field svcs. supr., 1956-59, head office local history, 1960-79, head coun. local history, 1961-79; ret.; rschr. ancient histories and religions. Author: Ghosts of the Battlefield, 1960, Guide to the History of Dane County Wis., 1970, How to Get Out of Bed, 1995, Ghosts of the Battlefield, 1995, Jonah and the Whales, 1995, Safe Karate, 1995; author, distbr. Simplified System of Cataloging Local Hist. Soc. and Mus., 1960, A Bibliography on the History of Jefferson County, Wisconsin, 1967, A Bibliography on the History of Dane County, Wisconsin, 1969; editor Quar. Newsletter Exch., 1958-79; contbr. articles to mags. and newspapers; author of poetry. Active Girl Scouts U.S.A., Spartanburg, S.C., 1947-48, Boy Scouts Am., Madison, 1956-58. 2nd lt. U.S. Army, 1942-45. Decorated Bronze Star; recipient 1st place award S.C. State Coll. Press Assn., 1951, Crusade for Freedom awards, 1951, 1st place award for Sounds of Heritage, Am. Exbhn. Ednl. Radio and TV, 1955. Mem. Am. Legion, Ret. Officers Assn., Am. Fedn. State, County and Mcpl. Employees, Am. Fedn. Police, Wis. Alumni Assn., Am. Assn. Ret. Persons. Roman Catholic. Home: W11013 W Harmony Dr Lodi WI 53555-1578

SCHERER, BARBARA ELIZABETH, publishing company executive; b. Freiburg, Germany, Mar. 2, 1958; d. Friedrich and Barbara (Lien) S. Dept. mgr. Frauhofer IRB Verlag, Germany, 1982—. Office: Fraumhofer I R B Verlag, Nobelstrasse 12, D-70569 Stuttgart Germany

SCHERER, GEORGE ROBERT, secondary education educator; b. Marion, Ill., Sept. 2, 1923; s. Herman Albert and Alice Madora (Bulliner) S.; m. Margaret Mary Brzozowski, Dec. 31, 1945; children: Marion, Anne Madora. BS in Piano, Juilliard Sch., N.Y.C., 1948; MMus in Piano, Roosevelt U., 1952; studied with Rudolph Ganz. Cert. elem. and secondary tchr., Ill. Tchr. Chgo. Bd. Edn., 1954-85; profl. chorister Chgo. Symphony Orch. Chorus, 1965-70; instr. Fenger Jr. Coll., Chgo., 1971-73; Fenger H.S. Choir appeared 4 seasons with Chgo. Civic Symphony Orchestra, 1968-71. Composer music for chorus and piano; author: Scherer "A Genealogy", 1996. Recipient (with choir) 16 superior awards in city and state contests. Mem. Am. Guild of Music Artists, Juilliard Sch. Music Alumni Assn., Roosevelt U. Alumni Assn. Avocations: genealogy, pianist. Home: 17841 Anthony Ave Country Club Hills IL 60478-4724

SCHERER, JÓZSEF, industrial designer, educator; b. Kölesd, Tolna, Hungary, July 14, 1947; s. Sándor Scherer and Ilona Bartha; m. Éva Penkala; 1 child, Petra. Diploma, Hungarian U. Craft and Design, 1971, D in Liberal Arts, 1997. Freelance designer, 1971—; lectr. Hungarian U. Craft and Design, Budapest, 1978-85, vice dir. Basic Tng. Inst., 1985-90, dir. Basic Tng. Inst., 1990—, vice rector, 1996-99; art dir. Studio for Toy Design, Budapest, 1980-81. Designer toothbrushes (Excellence in Design award 1977); editor: 100 Years of Form Studies, 1999. Curator Pesthidegkút Cultural Found., Budapest, 1995—. Recipient Dózsa Farkas András award Indsl. Designer's Assn., 1995, Ferenczy Noémy award Ministry of Culture, 1997, 3d prize Internat. Bicycle Design Competition, Japan, 1973; Japan Found. fellow, 1976-77. Mem. Hungarian Fine and Applied Artists Assn., N.Y. Acad. Scis.

SCHERINGER, MARTIN, environmental scientist, researcher; b. Aachen, Germany, June 18, 1965; s. Christian and Annemarie (Roos) S.; m. Beatrix Falch, May 15, 1998. Diploma in chemistry, U. Mainz, Germany, 1990; PhD, Swiss Fed. Inst. Tech., Zurich, 1996. Rsch. assoc. Swiss Fed. Inst. Tech., 1997—; sci. advisor Swiss Agy. of Environment, Berne, 1998. Author: Persistenz und Reichweite von Umweltchemikalien, 1999; contbr. articles to profl. jours., chpts. to books. Mem. Am. Chem. Soc., Soc. Environ. Toxicology and Chemistry, German Chem. Soc. Office: Swiss Fed Inst Tech, ETH-Zentrum, CH-8092 Zurich Switzerland

SCHERMAN, DANIEL ARIEL, biologist, pharmacologist, consultant; b. Paris, July 12, 1953; s. Pierre and Luba (Kronfeld) S.; m. Sylviane Francine Kohn, Dec. 22, 1983; children: Myriam, Michael, Jonathan, Anne-Laure, Mathias, Noémie, Ruben, Ilana. Engr., Ecole Poly., Palaiseau, France, 1975, Ecole Nat. Ponts Chaussées, Paris, 1977; D Troisième Cycle, U. Paris VII, 1980, State Doctorate, 1984. Cert. scientist in biomed. and pharm. scis. Engr. Min. Equipment, Paris, 1975-77; titular Jacques Monod grant oxygen metabolism rsch. group Ctr. Nat. de la Recherche Scientifique, 1977-80; rsch. assoc. Inst. Biologie-Physico-Chimique Ctr. Nat. de la Recherche Scientifique, Paris, 1980—, sr. scientist Physicochem. Neurobiology Lab., 1985—; 1st class dir. Joint Rsch. Unit Ctr. Nat. de la Recherche Scientifique/Rhône Poulenc-Rorer, Vitry, France, 1992—; cons. Rhône Poulenc-Rorer Co.; lectr. Ecole Polytechnique, Palaiseau, France, 1991—, Ecole Nat. Sup. de Chimie de Paris; bd. dirs. Thematic Rsch. Group on Vectors, 1999-2000; bd. dirs. non-viral vector scientific com. of Am. Soc. Gene Therapy, 2000; v.p. Groupe Thematique de Recherche sur les Vecteurs, 2000; chmn. of the non-viral vector com. of the European Soc. of Gene Therapy, 1992—, Soc. Pharmacotoxicologie Cellulaire. Author: The Biology of Stress, 1987; editor: Biology and Physiology of Blood-Brain Barrier, 1996; editl. bd. Cell Biology and Toxocology; contbr. articles to profl. jours., chpts. to books; co-inventor new methods for highly efficient DNA purification, 1995 and for gene therapy, 1996, 97, 98. Lt. French Air Force, 1972-75. Recipient grant Jacques Monod Found., 1977-80, prize inst. Biologie Physico-Chimique, Inst. de Biologie Physico-Chimique, Paris, 1982, Neurobiology award Found. de la Recherche Médicale, Paris, 1986, Rsch. Prize Phône Poulenc Group, 1998. Mem. Soc. Cellular Pharmacology and Toxicology (bd. dirs. 1994—), French Soc. Neurosci., French and European Socs. Cell Biology, French Soc. Biochemistry and Molecular Biology, Am. Soc. Gene Therapy (sci. com. 1999—). Avocations: family, reading, music, tennis. Office: Rhône-Poulenc Rorer CNRS, UMR133 13 Quai Jules Guesde, 94403 Vitry-sur-Seine Cedex, France

SCHERPE, KLAUS RÜDIGER, literature educator; b. Berlin, May 13, 1939; s. Herbert and Liselotte (Simmat) S.; m. Grethe Scherpe, Feb. 20, 1967; children: Jens, Niels. MA, Stanford U., 1963; PhD, Free U., Berlin, 1967. Lectr. Princeton (N.J.) U., 1966; asst. Heidelberg U., 1969-71; asst. Free U. Berlin, 1967-69, prof., 1973-93; vis. prof. Hamburg (Fed. Republic Germany) U., 1973, Stanford U., 1991-92, U. N.S.W., Sydney, 1988, Columbia U., 1995. Author: Gattungspoetik, 1968, Werther und Wertherwirkung, 1970, Poesie der Demokratie, 1980, Postmoderne, 1986, Unwirklichkeit der Städte, 1988, Die rekonstuiete Moderne, 1992, Literatur und Kulterwissenschaften, 1996, Responsibility and Commitment, 1996, Bilter des Holocaust, 1997, Literatur-wissenschaft und politische Kultur, 1999, Das Frende, 1999, others; editor Literatur im historischen Prozess, 1973-90, Literatur, Kultur, Geschlecht, 1991—; contbr. articles to profl. jours. Home: Jenae St 8, D-10717 Berlin Germany Office: Inst fuer Deutsch Literatur, D-10099 Berlin Germany

SCHERRER, GEORGE M., electrical engineer; b. Shawneetown, Ill., Oct. 30, 1914; s. George Bernard and Susan Scherrer; m. Ruby Nance Scherrer; children: George M. Jr., Irene, Nancy, Joyce, Fred, Jamie. BSEE, U. Ill., 1938; postgrad., Princeton U., 1944, MIT, 1945. Registered profl. engr. Farmer; ptnr. Scherrer Equipment Co., Inc.; mgr. Saline Valley Conservancy Dist.; tchr. physics Washington U., St. Louis; REA, prin. engr.; design and constrn. REA power lines A. Y. Taylor Co.; presenter in field. Bd. dirs. Ohio Valley Improvement Assn.; mem. Citizens Adv. Coun. Ohio Valley Commn., co-chmn.; pres. bd. Cath. Shrine Pilgrimage, Inc.; bd. dirs. Camp Ondessonk, 1957—. Lt. (j.g.) USNR, 1943-46. Mem. IEEE, Am. Soc. Agrl. Engrs. (sr. mem., cert.), Nat. Cattlemens Assn., Ill. Farm Bur. Democrat. Roman Catholic.

SCHERRER, PATRICK, economist; b. Berne, Switzerland, Dec. 12, 1959; s. Georg Paul and Marguerite Suzanne (Millier) S.; m. Fabienne Marie Reboul, Nov. 10, 1986; children: Florian, Felicie. Cert. in intermediate econs., Neuchatel U., 1980, M in Econs., 1982. Cert. economist. Sci. collaborator U. Neuchatel, 1980-82; devel. specialist European info. svcs. Digital Equipment Corp., Geneva, 1982-84, cons. internat. engring., 1985-86, tech. transfer mgr. software engring., 1986-89, cons. internat. engring., 1992-93, tech. dir. corp. strategic alliances, 1993-95; tech. transfer mgr. corp. rsch., mgr. European tech. Digital Equipment Corp., Evry, France, 1986-87; tech. transfer coord. corp. rsch. Digital Equipment Corp., Geneva, 1989-92; ptnr. strategic ventures devel. AT&T Internat. S.A., Geneva, 1995-96, dir. strategy and new bus. devel. value-added svcs., 1996-98; sr. assoc. Venture Ptnrs., 1998—; external auditor Fed. Inst. Tech., Lausanne, Switzerland, 1987; rep. European Computer Mfrs. Assn., Geneva, 1988-89; chmn. bd. Audiosoft, 1997-98; bd. dirs. Pollex, Global ID Com., Somm.com., others; pres. Swiss Tech. Tour, 1998. Mem. IEEE, Assn. Computing Machinery, Am. Internat. Club, European Tech Tour Assn. (v.p. 1998). Avocations: reading, swimming, skiing, jogging. Home: Rt du Col de Saxel, F-74420 Boëge France Office: Venture Ptnrs, 10 Rue du Vieux-College, 1204 Geneva Switzerland

SCHERSTEN, H. DONALD, retired oil company executive; b. Titusville, Pa., Nov. 6, 1919; s. H.J. and Clara (Brown) S.; m. Katherine Conley; 1 dau. by previous marriage, Sandra S. Hotard. B.S., Temple U., 1941; postgrad., Tulsa U., 1946-48, Columbia U., 1955. With Creole Petroleum Corp. (affiliate Exxon Corp.), 1948-69, successively dist. field chief accountant Cabimas, Venezuela, coordinator procedures, fin. statements and audits, asst. controller, 1951-62; controller Creole Petroleum Corp. (affiliate Exxon Corp.), Caracas, 1962-69; gen. auditor Exxon Corp., N.Y.C., 1969-74; coordinator math., computers, systems Exxon Corp., 1975-76; pres. H. Donald Schersten & Assocs. (Mgmt. Cons.), 1977—, R.J. Reynolds Nabisco, 1977-78; lic. real estate agt., 1985—; lic. mortgage broker, 1986-90. Pres. council Am. Ch. Caracas, 1960. Served to 1st lt. AUS, 1942-45. Named to Acct. Alumni Hall of Fame, Temple U., 1985. Mem. Am. Petroleum Inst. (chmn. audit com. 1974-76), Inst. Internal Auditors (cert.), U.S. Power Squadrons, USCG Aux. (comdr. 1983). Clubs: Internat. Safari Big Game Hunting, Toastmasters (past pres. Caracas chpt.), Los Rancheros Deep Sea Fishing. Avocations: champion/Classic Billfish Tourn. 1973, Cabo San Lucas, Mexico. Home: 4693 N Glebe Farm Rd Sarasota FL 34235-1806

SCHETTINI, SERGIO TOMAZ, pediatric surgeon, educator; b. Sao Paulo, Brazil, Jan. 7, 1946; s. Antonio and Lucinda (Guedes) S.; child from previous marriage, Monica; m. Maria Lucia Davoli, June 9, 1987; children: Ricardo, Marilia. MD, Fed. U. Sao Paolo, 1970, PhD in Pediat. Surgery, 1993. Resident in gen. surgery Sao Paulo, 1971-72, resident in pediat. surgery, 1973-74, asst. prof. pediat. surgery, 1978-86, adj. prof. pediat. surgery, 1986—. Contbr. articles to profl. jours. Roman Catholic. Avocations: jogging, watching soccer games, movies. Home: Butirapoa 111, 05059030 Sao Paulo Brazil Office: Diogo de Faria 1087, Rm 7021, 04037003 Sao Paulo Brazil

SCHEU, STEFAN, ecologist, zoologist, technical school educator; b. Stuttgart, Germany, Apr. 25, 1959; s. Hans and Ursula (Krampf) S.; m. Bettina Sostmann, Jan. 20, 1992; children: Max, Mira. Diploma in biology, U. Goettingen, Germany, 1986, D in Natural Scis., 1989, Habilitation, 1995. Lectr. U. Goettingen, 1989-97; prof. Tech. U. Darmstadt, Germany, 1997—. Editor jours., including Pedobiologia, 1996, Soil Biology and Biochemistry, 1997, Oecologia, 1998. Office: Tech U, Schnittspahn Str 3, 64287 Darmstadt Germany

SCHEULE, ALBERTUS MARIA, cardiothoracic surgeon; b. Ottobeuren, Bavaria, Germany, Mar. 6, 1965; s. Reinald and Eva-Maria (Nerdinger) S.; m. Sandra Ochs. MD, U. Ulm, Germany, 1993. Resident Med. Sch., Hannover, Germany, 1993-95, U. Tuebingen, Germany, 1995—. Avocations: soccer, cooking. Office: U Tuebingen Cardiothor Surg, Hoppe Seyler Str 3, 72074 Tuebingen Germany

SCHEURLE, JURGEN KARL, mathematician, researcher, educator; b. Schw. Gmund, Germany, Sept. 26, 1951; married; 2 children. Diploma in math., U. Stuttgart, Germany, 1974, D, 1975, habilitation, 1981. From wissmitarbeiter to privatdozent U. Stuttgart, Germany, 1975-85; assoc. prof., prof. Colo. State U., Fort Collins, 1985-87; prof. U. Hamburg, Germany, 1987-96, Munich Tech. U., 1996—. Contbr. articles to profl. jours. Mem. Internat. Soc. for Interaction of Mechanics and Math., German Math. Assn., Assn. Angew Math. and Mechanics, Math. Assn. Hamburg, Am. Math. Soc., European Mech. Soc., Soc. Indsl. and Applied Math. Roman Catholic. Office: Tech U Munich Ctr Math Scis, Arcisstrasse 21, D-80290 Munich Germany

SCHEUTZOW, MICHAEL K.R., mathematician, educator; b. Bielefeld, Germany, May 6, 1954; s. Peter F.G. and Lieselotte (Köhler) S.; m. Irmgard E. Dörr, July 23, 1982; children: Andrea, Alina, Christopher. Diploma in Math., U. Frankfurt, Germany, 1979; PhD in Math., U. Kaiserslautern, Germany, 1983, Habil., 1988. Wissenschaftlicher Mitarbeiter U. Kaiserslautern, 1979-84, asst., 1984-88; rsch. assoc. Carleton U., Ottawa, Ont., Can., 1982-83; cons. Techmath, Kaiserlautern, 1988-90; prof. Technische U., Berlin, 1990—; chmn. Graduiertenkolleg Stochastische Prozesse und Probabilistische Analysis, 1996—. Co-author: Markov-und Rainflowrekonstuktionen, 1985; contbr. articles to profl. jours. Mem. Math. Sci. Rsch. Inst. Roman Catholic. Home: Gutshofstr 31, 13465 Berlin Germany Office: Tech Univ Berlin, Fachbereich Math 3 Str 17 Juni 135, 10623 Berlin Germany

SCHEVING, LAWRENCE EINAR, anatomy educator, scientist; b. Hensel, N.D., Oct. 20, 1920; s. Einar L. and Mary (Brown) S.; m. Virginia M. Krumdick, Aug. 6, 1949; children: Lawrence, Mary, John, Jennifer, Patricia (dec.). BS in Biology, DePaul U., 1949, MS in Zoology, 1950; PhD, Loyola U., Chgo., 1957. Mem. faculty Lewis Univ., Lockport, Ill.; successively instr., asst. prof., assoc. prof., prof. and head dept. biol. sci. Lewis Univ., 1950-57; prof. anatomy Chgo. Med. Sch., 1957-67, La. State U. Med. Sch., New Orleans, 1967-70, U. Ark. Coll. Med., Little Rock, 1970-74; Rebsamen prof. anat. sci. U. Ark. Coll. Med., 1974-91, Rebsamen prof. emeritus, 1991—; vis. prof. U. Bergen, Norway, 1952, The Med. Sch. Hannover, Fed. Republic Germany, 1973; dir. chronobiology course Chautauqua series NSF, 1979; dir. NATO Advanced Study Insts., 1979, Workshop on chronobiotech. and chronobiol. engring., 1985; dir. Fedn. Am. Socs. Exptl. Biology summer research conf., Copper Mountain, Colo., 1988; mem. breast cancer task force Nat. Cancer Inst.; mem. U.S. Army med. research and devel. adv. com., 1982—; cons. to VA. Author: Biological Rhythms in Structure and Function, 1981; editor: Chronobiology, 1974, Chronobiotech. and Chronobiol. Engring. 1986, Research Advance in Chronobiology, 1987; numerous chpts. to books, over 200 articles in field of chronobiology and other biol. areas to profl. jours.; mem. editorial bd.: Chronobiologia, Chronobiology Internat., Am. Jour. Anatomy. Served to capt. AUS, 1940-45; col. Res. Decorated Bronze Star, Disting. Svc. medal, others; recipient Research award Chgo. Med. Sch. Bd. Dirs., 1962, Most Helpful Prof. award La. State U., 1968, award for Excellence in Nat. Leadership and Lifes Work, Gov. N.D., 1992; named Prof. Year Student Council Chgo. Med. Sch., 1964; recipient Golden Apple award student body U. Ark. Med. Sch., 1972; Alexander von Humboldt Sr. Scientist prize German govt., 1973, Highest Faculty award U. Ark. Med. Soc., 1987, others; spl. lecture and symposium dedicated in his honor Am. Assn. Med. and Chronotherapeutics, 1999. Mem. AAAS, Am. Soc. Anatomists, Am. Assn. Cancer Research, Am. Soc. Zoologists, Am. Soc. Photobiology, Internat. Soc. Chronobiology (hon., sec.-treas. 1971-83, pres.-elect 1983-85, pres. 1985-89, symposium dedicated in his honor 1993), So. Assn. Anatomists (past councillor), Am. Indsl. Hygiene Assn. (traditional workshifts com. 1983-89), Sigma Xi (chpt. pres. 1964-65). Roman Catholic. Home: 18255 Astor Dr Apt 102 Brookfield WI 53045-5636

SCHEWE, TANKRED, biochemist, researcher; b. Grünheide, Germany, Sept. 30, 1943; s. Horst-Helmut and Ilse Hildegard (Richter) S.; m. Christiane Schwarzlos, July 21, 1969; children: Stefanie, Martin. Grad., Humboldt U., Berlin, 1967, PhD, 1972, DSc, 1976. Scientific asst. Humboldt U., 1967-77, lectr., 1977-85, prof. in ordinary, 1985-95; scientific coworker Free U., Berlin, 1995-2000, ERTOX Inst. Nutritional Rsch. & Toxicology, Dahlwitz-Hoppegarten, Germany, 2000—; head rsch. group Humboldt U., 1977-85, head rsch. divsn., 1985-92. Contbr. over 100 articles on discovery and basic rsch on mammalian 15-lipoxygenase to profl. jours. Vice-chmn. Union for Univ. and Sci. (VHW), Germany, 1995-99. Recipient Karl-Lohmann prize German Biochemistry Soc., 1976, Rudolf Virchow prize Ministry for Health, German Dem. Rep., 1983. Avocations: natural conservation activities. Home: Friedrichstr 9C, D-15537 Erkner Germany Office: ERTOX Inst Nutritional Rsch, Rennbahnallee 110, D-15366 Dahlwitz-Hoppegarten Germany

SCHEXNAYDER, CHARLOTTE TILLAR, state legislator; b. Tillar, Ark., Dec. 25, 1923; d. Jewell Stephen and Bertha (Terry) Tillar; m. Melvin John Schexnayder Sr., Aug. 18, 1946; children: M. John Jr., Sarah Holden, Stephen. BA, La. State U., 1944, postgrad., 1947-48. Asst. editor La. Agrl. Extension, Baton Rouge, 1944; editor The McGehee (Ark.) Times, 1945-46, 48-53; editor, co-publisher The Dumas (Ark.) Clarion, 1954-85, pub., 1985-99; mem. Ark. Ho. of Reps., Little Rock, 1985-99, asst. speaker pro tem, 1995—; pres. Ark. Assn. Women, 1955, Nat. Newspaper Assn., Washington, 1991-92, Ark. Press. Assn., Little Rock, 1982, Nat. Fedn. Press Women, Blue Springs, Mo., 1977-78, Litte Rock chpt. Soc. Profl. Journalists, 1973; mem. pres.'s coun. Winrock Internat., 1990—. Editor: Images of the Past, 1991. 1st woman mem. Ark. Bd. Pardons and Parole, 1975-80; mem. Ark. Legis. Coun., 1985-92; bd. dirs. Women's Found. Ark., 1999—, Chicot-Desha Port Indsl. Com., 1999—; v.p. Desha County Mus., 1989—; dir. Dumas Indsl. Found., 1986—; mem. exec. com. Ark. Ctrl. Radiation Therapy Inst., 1991-92; mem. adv. bd. Ark. Profl. Women Achievement, 1992—; vice chair Ark. Rural Devel. Commn., 1991-96; mem. Winrock Internat. Adv. Coun., 1991—; chmn. Ark. Rural Devel. Commn., 1996-97; founding incorporator, bd. dirs. Ark. Waterways Commn., 1996—; bd. visitors Manship Sch. Comm., La. State U., 1998—; bd. dirs. Main Street Ark., 1999—, Hist. Preservation Alliance Ark., 1999—; mem. Ark. Transitional Employment Coun., 1999—; sec. Women's Found. Ark., 1999—, Dumas Area Cmty. Fund, 2000—; bd. dirs. Enterprise Corp. for the Delta, 1999—; bd. dirs. Dumas Main St., 2000%, historic Preservation Alliance Ark, 2000—; mem. Ark. Transitional Employment Assistance Bd., 2000. Named Disting. Alumnus Ark. A&M Coll., 1971, Woman of Achievement Nat. Fedn. Press Women, 1970, Outstanding Arkansan C. of C., 1986; recipient Ark. Profl. Women of Distinction award No. Bank, Little Rock, 1990, Emma McKinney award Nation's Top Cmty. Newspaper Woman, 1980, Journalist award Nat. Conf. of Christians and Jews, 1989, Lifetime Achievement award Nat. Fedn. Press Women, 1992, Outstanding Svc. award Ark. Assn. Elem. Prins., Disting. Svc. award Ark. Press Assn., 1993; named to La. State U. Alumni Hall of Distinction, 1994, Disting. Svc. award Internat. Soc. Weekly Newspaper Editors, 1996, Golden Svc. award Ark. Press Assn., 1996, State Leadership award Ark. Waterways Commn., 1996, Horizon award League Women Voters Ark., 1998; named one Top 100 Ark. Women, Ark. Bus., 1995, 96, 97, 98; named to Journalism Hall of Fame La. State U., 1998. Mem. Pi Beta Phi (Crest award 1992), Ark. Delta Coun. (chmn. of bd. dirs. 1989—). Democrat. Roman Catholic. Home: 322 Court St Dumas AR 71639-2718 Office: PO Box 160 Dumas AR 71639-0160

SCHEYD, JOSEPH FREDERICK, real estate broker; b. New Britain, Conn., Sept. 16, 1925; s. Louis F. and Mary J. S.; m. Rita Wolfer, Apr. 11, 1983; children: Gary, Ronald, Richard, Joseph D., Beth Ann, James, Sheila, Timothy. V12 Engring., Tufts U., 1945. Owner Bidway Svc., Inc., New Britain, Conn., 1946-64; real estate broker Joseph F. Scheyd Real Estate, Kensington, Conn., 1963—; assessor Town of Berlin (Conn.), 1964-85; pres. Metalform Co. Inc., New Britain, 1967-87; owner, ptnr. E.W. Realty, Kensington, 1975—. Commr. Kensington Fire Dist., 1997—; corporator Berlin Dem. Town Commn., 1959-89, New Britain Gen. Hosp., 1997—, Klingberg Children's Home, 1997—. Lt. (jg) USN, 1943-46. Mem. Am. Legion, VFW, KC (grand knight, 4th degree), Berlin C. of C. Roman Catholic. Avocations: golf, gardening, woodworking. Home: 333 West Ln Kensington CT 06037-1822 Office: Joseph F Scheyd Real Estate LLC 532 New Britain Rd Kensington CT 06037-2151

SCHIAVETTA, ALESSANDRO EDOARDO, vascular surgeon; b. Cairo Montenotte, Italy, May 9, 1962; s. Guido and Lucia (Genta) S.; m. Antonietta Rovelli, Mar. 3, 1990; children: Lorenzo Guido Giuseppe, Elisa Lucia Rossella. MD cum laude, U. Genoa, 1987. Asst. dept. vascular surgery Imperia Civil Hosp., 1992; dir. 1st level dept. vascular surgery S. Corona Hosp. of Pietra L., 1996; specialist U. Pavia, Sch. of Vascular Surgery; founder WebHospital.net, 1998. Contbr. articles to profl. jours. Scholarship Dept. Cardiac and Thoracic Surgery U. Lund, 1987, Sigma-Tau Industries, Civil Hosp. of Bergamo, Dept. of Cardiac Surgery, 1988. Mem. N.Y. Acad. Scis., Internat. Soc. Thermal Medicine and Hydrology. E-mail: nscsc@tin.it. Home: Via dello sperone 8/24, 17100 Savona Italy

SCHIAVI, RAUL CONSTANTE, psychiatrist, educator, researcher; b. Buenos Aires, Argentina, Jan. 7, 1930; came to U.S. 1956; s. Constantino and Maria (Acquier) S.; m. Michelle deMiniac, Aug. 26, 1960; children: Isabelle, Nadine, Viviane. MD, U. Buenos Aires, 1953. Diplomate Am. Bd. Psychiatry and Neurology. Fgn. asst. psychiatry U. Paris, 1955-56; resident in psychiatry U. Pa., Phila., 1956-59; instr. psychiatry U. Pa., 1959-61; assoc. College de France, Paris, 1961-63; asst. prof. psychiatry Cornell U., N.Y.C., 1963-66; assoc. prof. psychiatry SUNY, Downstate Med. Ctr., Bklyn., 1966-71; assoc. prof. psychiatry Mt. Sinai Sch. Medicine, N.Y.C., 1971-78, prof. psychiatry, 1978-96, emeritus prof. psychiatry, 1996—; fellow Found. Fund for Rsch. in Psychiatry, 1958-63; cons. NIMH, 1966-70, 77-81 (Rsch. Sci. Devel. award 1966, grantee 1976-95); dir. human sexuality program Mt. Sinai Sch. Medicine, 1973-96; advisor WHO, 1989. Author: Aging and Male Sexuality, 1999; contbr. articles to profl. jours., chpts. to books; editor-in-chief Jour. Sex and Marital Therapy, 1978-95; mem. editl. bd. Archives of Sexual Behavior, Hormones and Behavior, Psychosomatic Medicine, Revista Latinoamericana de Sexologia, Quaderni de Sessuologia Clinica, Revista Argentina de Sexualidad Humana, Annual Rev. Sex Rsch. Recipient Masters and Johnson award Soc. for Sex Therapy and Rsch., 1991; grantee NIH, 1977-80, 87-95, others. Fellow Am. Psychopathol. Assn., Psychiat. Rsch. Soc., Am. Psychiat. Assn. (life fellow, cons. 1989, Excellence in Edn. award 1992); mem. AAAS, Am. Psychosomatic Soc. (coun. 1985-88), Internat. Acad. Sex Rsch. (pres. 1995-96), Soc. Sex Therapy and Rsch. (pres. 1984-86), Sex Info and Edn. Coun. of U.S. (bd. dirs. 1979-83), Internat. Soc. Psychoneuroendocrinology, Sigma Xi.

SCHIAVO, GIAMPIETRO, laboratory administrator; b. Padua, Italy, June 25, 1962; s. Roberto and Carla (Babolin) S. Degree in chemistry & drug tech., U. Padua, Italy, 1988, PhD in Biology, 1992. Sr. scientist U. Padua, Italy, 1988-94; head lab. Imperial Cancer Rsch. Fund, London, 1997—. Recipient Chem. & Pharm. Tech. Student award, Padua, 1987; postdoctoral fellow Meml. Sloan Kettering Cancer Ctr., N.Y.C., 1994-96. Mem. Internat. Soc. Neurochemistry (Young Scientist award 1995), Biochem. Soc., Italian Soc. Biophys. & Molecular Biology. Avocation: mountaineering. Office: Imperial Cancer Rsch Fund, 44 Lincolns Inn Fields Rd, London WC2A 3PX, England

SCHIAZZA, GUIDO DOMENIC (GUY SCHIAZZA), educational association administrator; b. Phila., May 17, 1930; s. Guido and Claudina (DiPrinzio) S.; m. Irmgard Heidi Reissmueller, May 15, 1954. BA, Pa. State U., 1952; postgrad., St. Joseph's U., 1954-55, Villanova U., 1954-55, Temple U., 1955-58. Cert. tchr., Pa.; cert. clinician, ednl. specialist, instructional specialist, sch. psychologist, guidance counselor, reading specialist. Speech therapist, lang. arts instr. Commonwealth of Pa., Dept. Edn., 1956-59; founder, clinician, instr., dir., bd. pres. Communicative Arts Ctr., Inc., Drexel Hill, Pa., 1958, Communication Skills Community Resources Ctr., Inc., Drexel Hill, Pa., 1958, 1964—; charter mem. exec. bd., bd. pres. United Pvt. Acad. Schs., Assn. of Pa., Drexel Hill, 1966—; exec. bd. govs., bd. chmn. The Accrediting Commn., Drexel Hill, 1971—; charter mem. Pa. State Univ. Radio and TV Guild, University Park, Pa., 1951—; mem. legis. action com., Pa. State U., Univ. Park, 1988—; cons. communications skills, The Accrediting Commn., 1971—, United Pvt. Acad. Schs. Assn., Pa., 1966—. Founder, chmn., CEO Am. Ednl. Group, 1991—; chmn. CEO Internat. Ednl. Group, 1991—; CEO Cmty. Resources Ctr., Drexel Hill, 1991—, project coord. Energy Quest, 1992—; active Nat. Com. to Preserve Social Security and Medicare, Washington, 1986—, Am. Immigration Control Found., Monterey, Va., 1987—, English First, Springfield, Va., 1988—; mem. pres.'s coun. Rep. Nat. Com., 1989—, Nat. Rep. Senatorial Com., 1989—, Rep. Presdl. Task Force, 1989—; mem. Congrl. Legis. Agenda steering com. Empower Am., 1999. 1st Lt. Signal Corps, U.S. Army, 1952-54. Recipient Svc. award United Pvt. Acad. Sch. Assn. Pa., Monroeville, Pa., 1978, Disting. Achievement and Svc. award Bd. Govs. of the Accrediting Commn., Downington, Pa., 1980, Dr. Charles Boehm Edn. of Yr. award University Park, Pa., 1990, Loyal and Dedicated Svc. award The Accrediting Commn., 1974. Mem. NEA, Libr. Congress (chartered), Internat. Platform Assn., Pa. Edn. Assn., Jefferson Ednl. Found., World Affairs Coun. Phila., Heritage Found., Nat. Trust for Hist. Preservation, Nat. Congl. Club, Pa. State U. Nittany Lions Club, Pa. State U. Alumni Assn., Pa. State U. Football Lettermen's Club, Pa. State U. Varsity "S" Club. Republican. Roman Catholic. Avocations: music, home and garden design, automotive design, reading, golf. Office: The Accrediting Commn 436 Burmont Rd Drexel Hill PA 19026-3630

SCHICHA, HARALD, nuclear medicine physician; b. Freiberg, Germany, July 26, 1943; s. Franz and Lotte (Foerster) S.; m. Gisa Else Maria Otte, Mar. 27, 1968; children: Sebastian, Peter. MD, U. Cologne, 1969, specialist for nuc. medicine, 1979. Asst. Nuc. Rsch. Ctr., Juelich, Germany, 1969-74; sr. physician U. Hosp., Duesseldorf, Germany, 1974-77, Goettingen, Germany, 1977-85; chair and dir. nuc. medicine U. Hosp., Cologne, Germany, 1986—; mem. German Radiation Protection Commn., Bonn, Germany, 1988-98; chmn. sci. com. of the EANM, Brussels, 1994-95. Mng. editor Jour. Nuklearmedizin, 1986—; author: Nuclear Cardiology, 1983, Nuclear Medicine, 1991, 93, 97; editor Nuc. Medicine, 1994, 96. Mem. Soc. Nuc. Medicine, European Assn. Nuc. Medicine. Home: Statthalterhofallee 3, D-50858 Koeln Germany Office: Klinik Nuklear Medizin, Joseph-Stelzmann Str 9, D-50924 Koeln Germany

SCHICHLER, ROBERT LAWRENCE, English language educator; b. Rochester, N.Y., May 16, 1951; s. Alfred James and Elizabeth Johanna (Flugel) S. BA in English, SUNY, Geneseo, 1974, MA in English, 1978; PhD of English, Binghamton U., 1987. Writer, asst. administr. Artists-in-Residence Program, Rochester, N.Y., 1978-79; substitute tchr. City Sch. Dist., Rochester, 1980-82; instr. English Talmudical Inst. Upstate N.Y., Rochester, 1981-82, Binghamton (N.Y.) U., 1983-84; rsch. asst. Medieval and Renaissance Texts and Studies, Binghamton, 1985-86; adj. asst. prof. Rochester Inst. Tech., 1987-89; asst. prof. English Ark. State U., State University, 1989-94, assoc. prof., 1994-99, prof., 1999—; adj. asst. prof. Monroe C.C., Rochester, 1987-89. Author: King of the Once Wild Frontier: Reflections of a Canal Walker, 1993; editor: Lady in Waiting: Poems in English and Spanish, 1994, Abstracts of Papers in Anglo-Saxon Studies, 1988—, Ctr. for Medieval and Early Renaissance Studies, Binghamton, 1986-94, Spillway Publs., Rochester, 1992—; asst. editor: Old English Newsletter, 1986-87, Mediaevalia, Binghamton, 1988-89; contbr. articles to profl. jours. Mem. Internat. Soc. Anglo-Saxonists, Medieval Acad. Am., Modern Lang. Assn. Am., Am. Culture Assn. in the South, Popluar Culture Assn. in the South, Far West Popular Culture Assn. Home: 726 Southwest Dr Apt K-2 Jonesboro AR 72401-7043 Office: Ark State U Dept English and Philosophy State University AR 72467-1890

SCHIDLOWSKI, MANFRED, geochemist and earth sciences educator; b. Stettin, Germany, Nov. 13, 1933; m. Ingrid Piegler, 1964; 3 children. Dipl. in Geology, Freie U., Berlin, 1960, Dr.rer.nat., 1961; habilitation, Ruprecht-Karls-Univ., Heidelberg, Germany, 1968. Postdoctoral fellow dept. geology U. Pretoria, South Africa, 1961; mining geologist Anglo-Transvaal Consol. Investment Co. Ltd., Johannesburg, South Africa, 1961-63; rsch. assoc. mineralogy dept. U. Heidelberg, 1963-65, sr. rsch. assoc. mineralogy dept., 1967-68, privatdozent on staff mineralogy dept., 1968-69, adj. prof. dept. earth sci., 1976—; rsch. assoc. geology dept. U. Göttingen, Germany, 1965-67; sr. rsch. scientist dept. air chemistry/biogeochemistry Paleoenviron. Rsch. Group Max-Plack Inst. für Chemie, Mainz, Germany, 1969-98, ret., 1998; cons. and lectr. in field; hon. rsch. fellow dept. geol. sci. Harvard U., 1972-73; vis. rsch. geochemist Precambrian Paleobiology Rsch. Group, UCLA, 1979-80, Weizmann Inst. Sci., Rehovot, Israel, 1984; vis. prof. faculty scis. U. Libre Brussels, 1981; vis. lectr. USSR Acad. Sci., Petrosavodsk, 1983, Kola Sci. Ctr., 1991; vis. prof. Inst. Geology, Lanzhou br. Academia Sinica, 1988, Tsinghua U., Beijing, 1995; project leader Internat. Geol. Correlation Program, UNESCO, 1978-88; mem. adv. bd. Lab. Bioorganic Phosphorus Chemistry, Tsinghua U., Beijing, 1994—, Exobiology Sci. Team, European Space Agy., 1996-98; mem. adv. bd. Internat. Biograph. Ctr., Cambridge, Eng., 1997—. Contbr. articles to profl. jours. and books on edn.; assoc. editor Precambrian Rsch., 1977-92, Terra Nova, 1989-96, Mitt. Mus. Naturk. Humboldt U., Berlin, 1996—; editor-in-chief Terra Cognita, 1983-86; cons. editor Terra Nova, 1999—. Recipient Medaille d'Hommage, U. Libre de Brussels, 1981. Fellow Geol. Soc. South Africa, Geol. Soc. India (hon.); mem. Geochem. Soc., Internat. Soc. for Study Origin of Life (councillor 1993-96), European Union Geoscis. (councillor 1983-89), German Geol. Soc., Geol. Vereinigung, Paleontol. Soc. (councillor 1984-87), German Mineral Soc., Am. Chem. Soc., Am. Geophys. Union, N.Y. Acad. Scis., Acad. Creative Endeavors (Moscow). Home: 19 Weinbergstrasse, D-55268 Nieder-Olm Germany

SCHIEB, PIERRE-ALAIN EDOUARD, economist; b. Marseille, France, Apr. 5, 1948; s. Edouard Auguste and Gabrielle (Crozat) S. LLD, Aix. en Provence U., France, 1970, DBA, 1974; MA, Sherbrooke U., Can., 1973; PhD, Strasbourg U., France, 1981. Assoc. prof. Paris U., 1970-82, 1982-85; dean Rouen Grad. Sch. Bus., France, 1985-91; v.p. Printemps Group, France, 1991-93; prin. administr. Orgn. for Econ. Coop. and Devel. (OECD), Paris, France, 1995—; cons. BMD Internat., Strasbourg, 1976-81. Author: European Integration and Human Resource Management, 1989. Recipient Best Dissertation award, Inst. des Conseillers Adminstrn., 1974, Economics award Aix.en.Provence U., 1967. Mem. Sherbrooke Alumni Club. Office: OECD, 2 rue Andre Pascal, 75775 Paris Cedex 16, France

SCHIEDERMAIR, MANFRED LUDWIG, lawyer; b. Bonn, Germany, July 4, 1932; s. Gerhard and Imogen Elisabeth (Baum) S.; m. Waltrud Schünhoff, 1958 (div. 1986); children: Bettina, Christoph, Konrad, Martin; m. Ulrike Gerdenitsch, Oct. 5, 1990. LLB, Frankfurt U., 1961, JD, 1962; prof. of Law (hon.), Leipzig U., 1992. Ptnr. Rasor & Schiedemair, Frankfurt, 1962-89; ptnr. Boden Oppenhoff, now Oppenhoff & Rädler, Frankfurt,Cologne,Berlin, 1989—; bd. dirs. Kübler & Niethammer AG, Kriebstein. Author: Restrictive Trade Practices, 1962. Sec. Frankfurt U. Found., 1975—; bd. dirs. English Theater Frankfurt, 1980—. Recipient Disting. Svc. cross Federal Republic of Germany, 1991. Mem. Club für Handel, Industrie und Wissenschaft. Christian Democrat. Avocations: theater, opera, literature, crime stories. Office: Oppenhoff & Rädler, Mainzer Landstrasse 16, Frankfurt 60325, Germany

SCHIEFERDECKER, KLAUS JORG, science administrator; b. Meerane, Germany, Jan. 17, 1956; s. Klaus Walther and Rosa Anneliese (Bley) S.; m. Elke Gerlinde Piehler, Dec. 3, 1977; children: Romy, Christin. Diploma in engring., Dresden U., Germany, 1981, Dr.Eng.Ind., 1984, Dr.Ing. habil., 1988, docendi, 1987. Asst. prof. tech. U. Dresden, 1981-85; group mgr. Werk Fernseheletronics, Berlin, 1985-90; project mgr. Heimann GmbH, Wiesbaden, Germany, 1990-94; R&D mgr., bus. element mgr. PerkinElmer Optoelectronics, Wiesbaden, 1994-99; bus. element mgr. Perkin Elmer Optoelectronics, Wiesbaden, 1999—. Author: Handbook of Sensors, 1997; contbr. articles to profl. jours. Recipient Young Inventors award Govt. Germany, 1983. Mem. Coun. of Int. Sensor Conf., German Alpiniss Club. Avocations: mountain climbing, skiing. Office: Perkin Elmer Optoelectronics, PO Box 3007, D-65020 Wiesbaden Germany

SCHIEFFER, RUDOLF, educator; b. Mainz, Germany, Jan. 31, 1947; s. Theodor and Annelise (Schreibmayr) S. PhD, U. Bonn, Germany, 1975. Rsch. asst. Monumenta German Hist., Munich, 1975-80, pres., 1994—; prof. U. Bonn, 1980-94, U. Munich, 1994—; mem. Wissenschaftsrat, Cologne, 1984-90. Author: Die Entstehung von Domkapiteln in Deutschland, 1976, Die Entstehung Des Päpstl. Investiturverbots, 1981, Die Karolinger, 1992. Mem. Bevarian Acad. Sci. (ord.), Nordrhein-Westf. Acad. Sci. (corr.), Medieval Acad. Am. (corr.), Austrian Acad. Sci. (corr.). Office: Monumenta Germaniae Histor, Ludwigstr 16, D-80539 Munich Germany

SCHIEMENZ, ROLF BERND, business educator; b. Frankfurt, Germany, Nov. 11, 1939; s. Willi Max Paul and Anna Antonio (Noll) S.; m. Rita Maria Kollmann, Mar. 29, 1963; children: Kai Uwe, Kirsten Elena. Diploma in Econs. and Engring., Darmstadt (Germany) Inst. Tech, 1964, DrRerPol, 1969, Habilitation, 1978. Rsch. and tchg asst. Darmstadt Inst. Tech., 1964-65, 67-68; cons. OECD, Paris, 1966; prof., head Inst. for Info. Mgmt., U. Koblenz, Germany, 1990-94; asst. prof. bus. adminstrn. Philipps U., Marburg, Germany, 1969-72, prof., 1972-90, 94—; dean dept. econs. U. Marburg, Germany, 1976-77, 97-98. Author: Regelungstheorie und Entscheidungsprozesse, 1972, Automatisierung der Produktion, 1980, Betriebskybernetik, 1982, Entscheidung und Produktion, 2000; editor: Angewandte Wirtschafts- und Sozialkybernetik, 1984, Internationales Management, 1994, Interaktion, 1994. Mem. German Soc. Ops. Rsch., Soc. Econ. and Social Cybernetics (pres. 1986-99), Verband der Hochschullehrer für Betriebswirtschaft. Home: Sonnenhang 5, D-35041 Marburg Germany Office: Philipps U, Am Plan 2, D-35032 Marburg Germany

SCHIER, MARY JANE, science writer; b. Houston, Mar. 10, 1939; d. James F. and Jerry Mae (Crisp) McDonald; B.S. in Journalism, Tex. Woman's U., 1961; m. John Christian Schier, Aug. 26, 1961; children—John Christian, II, Mark Edward. Reporter, San Antonio Express and News, 1962-64; med. writer Daily Oklahoman, also Oklahoma City Times, 1965-66; reporter, med. writer Houston Post, 1966-84; sci. writer, univ. editor U. Tex. M.D. Anderson Cancer Ctr., 1984—. Recipient award Tex. Headliners Club, 1969, Tex. Med. Assn., 1972-74, 76, 78, 79, 80, 82 Tex. Hosp. Assn., 1974,

82, Tex. Public Health Assn., 1976, 77, 78, others. Mem. Houston Press Club Ednl. Found. (pres 1992—). Lutheran. Home: 9742 Tappenbeck Dr Houston TX 77055-4102 Office: 1515 Holcombe Blvd Houston TX 77030-4009

SCHIER, RUDOLF, educational administrator, educator; b. Amsterdam, The Netherlands, Mar. 4, 1937; s. Rudolf and Emilie (Jarma) S.; m. Brigitte Angele; children: Michael, Stephanie, Christopher. BA, Amherst Coll., 1959; MA, Cornell U., 1960, PhD, 1965. From instr. to asst. prof. to assoc. prof. of comparative lit. U. Ill., Urbana, 1963-79; dir. Austria-Ill. Exchange Program, Baden, 1971-79, Inst. European Studies, Vienna, Austria, 1980—. Author: Die Sprache Georg Trakls, 1970; contbr. articles to profl. jours. Grantee Am. Philos. Soc., 1970; recipient award Austrian Ministry Edn., 1976, 91, 97, Nat. Assn. Fgn. Student Affairs, 1977; named hon. mem. edn. dept. John F. Kennedy Ctr. Performing Arts, 1984. Office: Inst European Studies, Johannesgasse 7, A-1010 Vienna Austria

SCHIFANO, FABRIZIO, psychiatrist, pharmacologist; b. Padua, Italy, June 22, 1956; s. Angelo and Lia (Borsatto) S.; m. Sandra Spreafrichi, May 11, 1985; children: Nicolo, Leonardo. MD, U. Padua, 1981. Resident dept. psychiatry U. Padua, 1980-83; registrar Mil. Hosp., Padua, 1983-84, Dept. Psychiatry, Italy, 1984-87; head Addiction Treatment Unit, Conegliano, Italy, 1987-90, Addiction Treatment Unit #2, Padua, 1990-96, Addiction Treatment Unit #1, Padua, Italy, 1996—; vis. rsch. worker Dept. Clin. Psychopharmacology, London, 1988-89; chmn. European Collaborating Ctr. in Addiction Studies, 1985—; lectr. Master's Sch. Addictive Behavior Univ. of London, 1996—; contract prof. Sch. of Pharmacology Univ. Padua, 1990—. Lt. Italian Mil., 1983-84. Avocations: jogging, playing guitar. Office: Sert 1, Via Berchet 20, 35100 Padua Italy

SCHIFF, DAVID TEVELE, investment banker; b. N.Y.C., Sept. 3, 1936; s. John Mortimer and Edith Brevoort (Baker) S.; m. Martha Elisabeth Lawler, May 11, 1963; children: Andrew Newman, David Baker, Ashley Reynolds. B.Engring., Yale U., 1958. Trainee Chem. Bank N.Y. Trust, N.Y.C., 1959-62; analyst Madison Fund, N.Y.C., 1962; assoc., then partner Kuhn, Loeb & Co., N.Y.C., 1963-77; vice chmn. Kuhn Loeb & Co. Inc., 1977; mng. dir. Lehman Bros. Kuhn Loeb Inc., N.Y.C., 1977-83; also dir. Lehman Bros. Kuhn Loeb Inc.; mng. ptnr. Kuhn, Loeb & Co. (formerly KLS Enterprises), 1984—; dir., vice chmn. Am. Crown Life Ins. Co., N.Y.C., 1981-95; bd. dirs. Crown Life Ins. Co., Toronto, 1971-92; mem. lower Manhattan adv. bd. Chem. Bank, 1977-85; bd. advisors Venture Capital Fund of Am., 1998—. Trustee, chmn. bd. Wildlife Conservation Soc.; trustee Met. Mus. Art, Citizens Budget Commn., N.Y.C., Greater N.Y. coun. Boy Scouts Am., 1965-91; trustee Beekman Downtown Hosp., 1966-82, chmn., 1975-79; trustee Brooks Sch., North Andover, Mass., 1972-90, treas., 1987-90; bd. govs. Yale U. Art Gallery, 1973-97, Fed. Hall Meml. Assn.; mem. adv. bd. dirs. Outward Bound, Inc.; mem. Provident Loan Soc. N.Y.; bd. dirs. Am. Hosp. of Paris Found., N.Y.C., 1987. With U.S. Army, 1959. Mem. Econ. Club N.Y.C., Pilgrims U.S., Brook Club, Century Assn., River Club, Maroon Creek Club (Aspen, Colo.), Mill Reef Club (Antigua), Yale Club N.Y.C. Episcopalian. Home: 770 Park Ave New York NY 10021-4153 Office: 320 Park Ave 10th Fl New York NY 10022-6815

SCHIFF, JUDITH JENNY, editor, proofreader, photographer; b. Berlin, May 15, 1937; arrived in Australia, 1939; d. David Kurt and Irma (Isacson) Herman; m. Peter Schiff, June 18, 1959; children: Danny & Karen (twins), Jacqui. Exec. dir. Print Coun. Australia, Melbourne, 1975-85; editor, proofreader various advt. agys. & art studios, Melbourne, 1987-93; owner, editor, proofreader Elegant English, Melbourne, 1993—. Exhibited photography, 1990—. Active B'nai B'rith. Mem. Ctr. Contemporary Photography, Jewish Mus. Australia, Print Coun. Australia, Nat. Gallery Soc. Victoria. Jewish. Home and Office: 4 Maxwell St, Kew Victoria 3101, Australia

SCHIFFAUER, WERNER, social anthropologist; b. Lichtenfels, Germany, Dec. 6, 1951; s. Hanns and Elisabeth (Schulze) S.; m. Gertrud Hüwelmeier; children: Leonie, Jonas. Diploma, Freie U., Berlin, 1980, PhD, 1987; habilitation, U. Frankfurt Main, Germany, 1991. Jr. lectr. U. Frankfurt Main, 1983-87, lectr., 1987-93; prof. Humboldt-U., Berlin, 1993-95, European U., Frankfurt, 1995—. Author: Die Gewalt der Ehre, 1983, Die Bauern von Subay, 1987, Die Migranten aus Subay, 1991, Fremde in der Stadt—Zehn Essays über Kultur und Differenz, 1997, Die Gottesmänner Türkische Islamisten in Deutschland, 2000. Office: Europa U Viadrina, Postfach 776, 15207 Frankfurt Oder, Germany

SCHIFFER, MARCUS JOSEF, physicist, researcher; b. Biedenkopf, Germany, May 29, 1963; s. Peter and Hedwig (Zurholt) S. Univ. diploma, U. Münster, 1988, PhD in Applied Physics, 1994. Rsch. asst. U. Münster, 1989-94, postdoctoral fellow, 1994-95; tech. cons. Ruhrgas AG, Essen, Germany, 1995-97; computer cons. Schmidt, Vogel Consult AG, Bielefeld, Germany, 1997—. Contbr. rsch. articles to Phys. Rev. A and Jour. Optical Comm. Mem. IEEE, N.Y. Acad. Scis., German Phys. Soc. Roman Catholic. Home: Kirchstr 9, D-48324 Sendenhorst NRW, Germany

SCHIFFER, RANDOLPH BRENTON, physician; b. Highland Park, Mich., May 25, 1948; s. Alfred Brenton and Dolores (Aspenson) S.; m. Lynn Scott Bickley, Sept. 18, 1982; children: Brenton B., Randolph T. BA, Yale U., 1969; MD, U. Mich., 1976. Diplomate Am. Bd. Psychiatry and Neurology. Asst. prof. psychiatry and neurology U. Rochester, N.Y., 1981-87, assoc. prof. psychiatry and neurology, 1987-92; prof. neurology psychiatry and environ. medicine U. Rochester, 1993-98; Vernon and Elizabeth Haggerton prof. neurology Tex. Tech U. Health Sci. Ctr., Lubbock, 1998—, chair dept. neuropsychiatry, 1998—. Author: The Medical Evaluation of Psychiatric Patients, 1988; co-editor: Neuropsychiatry, 1996. 1st lt. USMC, 1969-72, Vietnam. Mem. Am. Neuropsychiat. Assn. (bd. dirs. 1986—), Am. Acad. Neurology, Am. Psychiat. Assn. (Falk fellow 1979-81). Home: 4515 11th St Lubbock TX 79416-4815 Office: Tex Tech U Health Scis Ctr Dept Neuropsychiat 3601 4th St Lubbock TX 79430-0001

SCHIFFLER, LUDGER, French language and literature methodology educator; b. Frankfurt, Ger., Feb. 11, 1937; s. Leonhard and Charlotte (Dichgans) S.; m. Ingrid Künstler, Feb. 15, 1965; children: Ansgar, Manuel. Prof. Dr. phil., Goethe U., 1963, Ph.D., 1969. Studiendirektor, Studienseminar, Offenbach M., 1969; full prof. Freie U. Berlin, 1971—. Author: Einführung in den audiovisuellen, Fremdsprachenunterricht, 1973; Interaktiver Fremdsprachenunterricht, 1980; Enseignement interactif des langues étrangères, 1984, Suggestopaedie und Superlearning-empirisch geprüft, 1989, Suggestopédie et Superlearning mise à l'épreuve statistique, 1992, Suggestopedic Methods and Applications, 1992, Planung des Französisch-Anfangsunterrichts, 1995, Learning by Doing im Fremdsprachenunterricht, 1998; contbr. numerous articles to profl. jours. Home: Koenigsallee 18 c, D-14193 Berlin Germany Office: Freie Univ Berlin, Habelschwerdter Allee 45, D-14195 Berlin Germany

SCHIFFMANN, DIETMAR, cell biologist, educator; b. Wiesbaden, Hessen, Germany, July 31, 1947; s. Harry and Gertrud (Kuehmichel) S.; m. Eva Reinhardt, Feb. 15, 1983; 1 child, Lisa. Dipl. biology, U. Wuerzburg, 1974, dr. rer. nat., 1978, dr. med. habil., 1991. Postdoctoral fellow, rschr. U. Wuerzburg, Germany, 1978-93; rschr. U. Rostock, Germany, 1993—, prof. cell biology and genetics, 1998—. Recipient Merit prize Found. Internat. Alternatives to Animal Experiments, Luxembourg, 1987, Surgeon Gen.'s award, Bonn, 1995. Avocations: antique books, collecting scientific instruments, skiing. Office: Inst Cell Biology/Biosys, Uniplatz 2, D-18051 Rostock Germany

SCHIFFMANN, YORAM, research scientist; b. Rehovot, Israel, Oct. 23, 1941; came to Eng., 1978; s. Jacob and Mina (Nadel) S.; m. Victoria Relisse Bratesh, Jan. 1, 1973; children—David Amir, Tamar. B.Sc. in Chemistry, Hebrew U., Jerusalem, 1965, M.Sc. in Phys. Chemistry, 1967; Ph.D. in Phys. Chemistry, U. Brussels, 1976. Research fellow U. Dundee, Scotland, 1977-82, U. Cambridge, 1982—. Contbr. articles on reaction-diffusion systems in chemistry and biology to profl. jours. Served with Israel Def. Forces, 1959-62. European Molecular Biology Orgn. long-term fellow, 1978, 79; grantee various orgns. Mem. Soc. Indsl. and Applied Math., Am. Math. Soc., Biochem. Soc. (U.K.), Cambridge Philos. Soc. Avocation: swimming. Office: U Cambridge Dept Applied Math. & Theoretical Physics/Silver St, Cambridge CB3 9EW, England

SCHIFFNER, CHARLES ROBERT, architect; b. Reno, Sept. 2, 1948; Robert Charles and Evelyn (Keck) S.; m. Iovanna Lloyd Wright, Nov. 1971 (div. Sept. 1981); m. Adrienne Anita McAndrews, Jan. 22, 1983. Student, Sacramento Jr. Coll., 1967-68, Frank Lloyd Wright Sch. Architecture, 1968-77. Registered architect, Ariz., Nev., Wis. Architect Taliesin Associated Architects, Scottsdale, Ariz., 1977-83; pvt. practice architecture Phoenix, 1983—; lectr. The Frank Lloyd Wright Sch. of Architecture, 1994, 95. Named one of 25 Most Promising Young Americans Under 35, U.S. mag., 1979; recipient AIA Honor award Western Mountain Region, 1993, Western Home awards Sunset Mag., 1989, 91, AIA Ariz. Merit award, 1993 and numerous others. Home: 5202 E Osborn Rd Phoenix AZ 85018-6137 Office: Camelhead Office Ctr 2944 N 44th St Phoenix AZ 85018-7257

SCHILBRED, CORNELIUS MATHIAS, economics educator; b. Oslo, Dec. 5, 1939; s. Cornelius Severin Scheel and Margrethe (Lomsdal) S.; m. Eli Monstad, Jan. 16, 1965 (div. Oct. 1989); children: Benedicte Elisabeth, Anne Louise, Margrethe Henriette; m. Grete Wiig, June 22, 1991. B in Bus., Norwegian Sch. Econs., Bergen, 1964, lic. degree, 1969, D in Econs., 1974. Rsch. fellow Norwegian Sch. Econs., Bergen, 1964-69, lectr., 1969-83, prof., 1983—; bd. dirs. Capital Markets Com., European Sci. Found., Centre for Econ. Policy Rsch., London, 1989-95, Harald Monstad A/S, Bergen, Scandinavian Fin. Rsch., Helsinki; chmn. Fundmix A/S, Oslo, 1989—. Author: Studies in Risk and Bond Values, 1974, Managing Short Term Currency Risk, 1990, Managerial Internat. Finance, 1996; co-author: Computer Model, 1978 (Esso prize 1981). Chmn. Soc. for the Conservation of Nature, West Norway, 1970-74; dir. Art Soc., Bergen, 1986-90; mem. com. for reorgn. Bergen Musical Festival, 1990. With Norwegian mil., 1960-85. Grantee Norwegian Am. Found., Norwestern U., 1966-67, Den norske Bank, Oslo, Hambros Bank, London, Inst. Nat. de la Statistique et des Etudes Economiques, Paris, 1971-72. Mem. Bergen Golf Club. Mem. Conservative Party. Avocations: golf, fishing, mountain hiking, skiing. Home: Ole Irgens Vei 24, N-5019 Bergen Norway Office: Norwegian Sch Econs & Bus Administrn, Helleveien 30, N-5035 Bergen Norway

SCHILCHER, HEINZ, retired pharmaceutical biology educator; b. Neuburg, Oberbayern, Germany, Feb. 21, 1930; s. Josef and Anna (Grünthaler) S.; m. Renate Fuchs, July 29, 1960 (div. 1977); 1 child, Stefan; m. Barbara Mutschler, Aug. 5, 1982. Grad. pharmacy, U. Munich, 1956, PhD, 1959. Head sci. dept. Salus Co., Munich, 1962-73; univ. prof. U. Marburg, Germany, 1973-78; head sci. dept. mgr. FINK Co., Germany, 1978-83; univ. prof. Free U., Berlin, 1983-95; dir. Inst. Pharm. Biology, 1995—; v.p. Commn. E, German Fed. Health Agy. Author 15 books about phytotherapy and herbal remedies, including Phytotherapy in Pediatrics, 1997. Roman Catholic. Avocations: skiing, canoeing, music. Address: Alfred Neumann-Anger 17, 81737 München-Perlach Germany

SCHILD, RALF LOTHAR, physician, educator; b. Saarbruecken, Germany, Oct. 29, 1961; s. Werner Johann and Waltraud (Rase) S.; m. Mandana Soltani, Dec. 30, 1992. MD, U. Saarland, Saarbrücken, Germany, 1987. Sr. house officer U. Hosp., Aachen, Germany, 1989-93, Rutherglen Maternity Hosp., Glasgow, Scotland, 1993-94; registrar L&D Hosp., Luton, Eng., 1994-96; lectr. U. Hosp., Bonn, Germany, 1996—. Contbr. articles to profl. jours. Mem. AAAS, Royal Coll. Ob-Gyn. London. Avocations: skiing, long-distance running, contemporary literature, travelling. E-mail: r.schild@uni-bonn.de. Office: U Hosp Bonn Frauenklinik, Sigmund Freud St 25, 53105 Bonn Germany

SCHILD, RAYMOND DOUGLAS, lawyer; b. Chgo., Dec. 20, 1952; s. Stanley Martin and Cassoundra Lee (McArdle) S.; m. Ellen Arthea Carstensen, Oct. 24, 1987; children: Brian Christopher, Melissa Nicole. Student, U.S. Mil. Acad., 1970; BA summa cum laude, De Paul U., 1974, JD magna cum laude, 1982; M in Life Scis., Order of Essenes, 1996. Bar: Ill. 1982, U.S. Dist. Ct. (no. dist.) Ill. 1982, U.S. Ct. Appeals (7th cir.) 1982, Idaho 1989, U.S. Dist. Ct. Idaho 1989, U.S. Ct. Appeals (9th cir.) 1989, U.S. Supreme Ct. 1990. Assoc. Clausen, Miller, Gorman, Caffrey & Witous, Chgo., 1982-84; law clk. to chief judge law divsn. Cir. Ct. Cook County, Chgo., 1984-85; assoc. John G. Phillips & Assocs., Chgo., 1985-87, Martin, Chapman, Park & Burkett, Boise, Idaho, 1988-89; pvt. practice Boise, 1989-90; pres. Martin, Chapman, Schild & Lassaw, Chartered, Boise, 1990-96; assoc. Sallaz Law Offices, Chartered, Boise, 1999—; dir., v.p. Behavioral Mgmt. Ctrs.; bd. dirs. Image Concepts Internat., Inc., Boise; lectr. on legal edn. ICLE and NBI, 1993-98. Co-host legal radio talk show KFXD, 1994; legal columnist Idaho Bus. Rev., 1988-96. Mem. adv. bd. Alliance for the Mentally Ill, Boise, 1991—, Parents and Youth Against Drug Abuse, Boise, 1991-92; fair housing adminstr. Sauk Village (Ill.) Govt., 1987-88; instr. Ada County Youth Ct., Boise, 1992—. Schmitt fellow DePaul U., 1974; recipient award of merit Chgo. Law Coalition, 1987. Mem. ATLA, Idaho Trial Lawyers' Assn., Ill. State Bar Assn., Idaho State Bar Assn., Boise Estate Planning Counsel, Shriners (temple atty. 1994—, liaison Crippled Children's Hosp.), Masons (jr. steward 1992). Avocations: tennis, trombone, writing, music. Office: 1000 S Roosevelt St Boise ID 83705-2154

SCHILDBACH, THOMAS, business administration educator; b. Bergneustadt, Germany, Mar. 8, 1945; s. Dieter and Doris (Cichy) S.; m. Maria Kawalle, Nov. 9, 1979; children: Georg, Christian. Diplom-kaufmann, U. Cologne, 1969, Dr.rer.pol., 1973, venia legendi, 1979. Rsch. fellow U. Cologne, Germany, 1969-79, lectr., 1979-81; prof. U. Passau, Germany, 1981; dean of faculty U. Passau, 1991-93. Author: Geldentwertung und Bilanz, 1969, Der Handelsrechtliche Jahresabschluss, 1987, Der Handelstrechtliche Konzernabschluss, 1991, US-GAAP, 2000; co-editor Betriebswirtschaftliche Forschung und Praxis. Home: Obersoelden 30A, D94034 Passau Germany Office: Lehrstuhl Fuer Betriebswirtschaftslehre, Innstrasse 27, D94032 Passau Germany

SCHILDBERG, FRIEDRICH WILHELM, surgery educator; b. Essen, Germany, Mar. 6, 1934; s. Wilhelm and Therese (Huesch) S.; m. Christa M. Denz, Oct. 21, 1967; children: Georg Friedrich, Claus Christof. MD, U. Freiburg, Germany, 1962; Doctorate (hon.), U. Luebeck, Germany, 1996. Med. lic.; bd. cert. in surgery, vascular surgery, and visceral surgery. Rsch. fellow in pathology U. Munich, Germany, 1961-62; rsch. fellow in physiology U. Freiburg, Germany, 1962-64; resident in surgery U. Cologne, Germany, 1964-70; surgeon on staff U. Cologne, 1970-71, asst. prof., 1971-73; assoc. prof. surgery U. Munich, 1973-78; chmn. dept. surgery U. Luebeck, 1978-89, U. Munich, 1989—. Author, editor: Surgery of Breast Cancer, 1985, Surgical Treatment of Tumor Metastases, 1986, Thoracic Surgery, 1989, Lung and Mediastinum, 1991, Host Defense Dysfunction in Trauma, Shock and Sepsis, 1994, MOF, MODS and SIRS - Basic Mechanisms in Inflammation and Tissue Surgery, 1996, Endoskopische Hernioplastik, 1997, Surgical Intensive Care, 1985, The Immune Consequences of Trauma, Shock and Sepsis, I/II, 1996. Fellow Royal Coll. Surgeons Eng.; mem. Internat. Soc. Surgery, European Surg. Assn., Austrian Surg. Soc. (corr.), Slovak Surg. Soc. (hon.), German Soc. Trauma Surgery, German Soc. Angiology, German Soc. Vascular Surgery, Bavarian Soc. Surgeons (pres. 1992), North-Western Soc. Surgeons (pres. 1983), German Soc. Surgery, German Interdisciplinary Assn. Intensive Care (gen. sec. 1993—), N.Y. Acad. Scis. Roman Catholic. Office: Klinikum Grosshadern, Marchioninistr 15, D-81377 Munich Bavaria, Germany

SCHILDERS, WILLY H.A., mathematician; b. Arnhem, Gelderland, The Netherlands, Aug. 26, 1956; s. Antonius N. and Huberta M. (Surewaard) S.; children: Erik, Roel, Koen, Tessa. MSc, Cath. U. Nymegen, 1978; PhD, Trinity Coll. Dublin, 1980. Scientist Philips CFT, Eindhoven, The Netherlands, 1980-90; sr. scientist Philips Rsch., Eindhoven, 1990—; vice-chmn. Dutch Soc. Indsl. and Applied Math., Amersfoort, The Netherlands, 1994—; mem. tech. steering com. SISPAD Conf., 1987—; referee COMPEL, London, 1984—. Author: Numerical Methods for Semiconductor Device Simulation, 2000; co-author: Uniform Numerical Methods for Problems with Initial and Boundary Layers, 1980. Mem. Wiskundig Genootschap. Roman Catholic. Avocations: analysis of stock market, number theory. Home: Elandlaan 28, 5581 CL Waalre The Netherlands Office: Philips Rsch, Prof Holstlaan 4, 5656 AA Eindhoven The Netherlands

SCHILDKRET, ARNOLD ALAN, writer; b. Feb. 14, 1935; m. Charlotte. BA, Lafayette Coll., Easton, Pa., 1956; student, NYU, Emory U. Prof. computer sci. CUNY; dir. mktg. Data Gen. Corp.; instr. New Sch. Social Rsch., N.Y.C., 1972; cons. Chancellor Bowker, Dept. Health, Edn. Welfare, Ford Found., Calif. Fed. Bank, Bank of Am., First Interstate Bank, Chevy Chase Savngs and Loan, Sanwa Bank, Honda Corp., others. Author: Bridging the Technology Gap, 1984; writer (TV shows) Computer Channel, N.Y.C., 1990; writer (stage plays and screenplays) The Patient, An American Family, The Glass Shoe Factory, 1999, (musical) The Rehearsal. With USN. Home: 4624 Maytime Ln Culver City CA 90230-5062

SCHILLER, ERICH KARL PAUL, physician; b. Hamburg, Germany, Nov. 9, 1922; s. Karl Friedrich Ernst Gustav and Else Frida Luise (Thormeyer) S.; m. Karin Beate Von Sydow, May 29, 1948; children: Ulrike Astrid, Christiane Friederike. Med. license, U. Leipzig, 1945. Med. asst. Dist. Hosp. Gelnhausen, Hesse, Germany, 1946-48; head pathol. dept. Silicosis Rsch. Inst., Homberg, Germany, 1948-62; head pathol. dept. med. inst. Air Hygiene and Silicosis Rsch., Düsseldorf, 1963-64; head med. dept. Kettelhack-Riker Co., Borken, 1965-67; dept. hygiene and indsl. medicine Ruhr U., Essen, Germany, 1967-68; head dept. exptl. pathology Cassella Co. subs. Hoechst Co. (inc. into Aventis Co.), Frankfurt, 1968-84; reader in histology U. Mainz, Rhineland-Palatinate, 1978-83. Recipient Deutsche Gesellschaft für Dokumentation, 1955. Lutheran. Home: Am Hirschgraben 8, D-63150 Heusenstamm Germany Office: German Cancer Rsch Ctr, Im Neuenheimer Feld 280, D-69120 Heidelberg Germany

SCHILLER, SOPHIE, artist, graphic designer; b. Moscow, Feb. 10, 1940; came to U.S., 1974; d. Samuel and Rebecca (Lagovier) Elinson; m. Mikhail Schiller, Apr. 29, 1960; 1 child, Maria. Student, Moscow State Art Sch., 1954-58; MA, Moscow Inst., 1964; cert. in graphic and book design, Mass. Coll. Art, 1977. Graphic artist Progress Pub. House, Moscow, 1964-70, Popular Sci. mag., Moscow, 1970-74; artist, graphic designer Boston, 1974—; freelance graphic designer Harvard Press, Boston, M.E. Sharpe Pub., N.Y., Ginn Press, Simon & Schuster, Boston, Tech. Rev., MIT, Cambridge, Mass. One person shows include Galleria del Corso, Rome, 1974, Wennigar Gallery, Boston, 1977; exhibited in group shows Taganka Exhibit, Moscow, 1962, Moscow Artists Union, 1962, Am. Painters in Paris Exhbn., 1975, Unofficial Art from Soviet Union, Washington, 1977, Mariland Gallery, St. Mary's City, 1977, Bard Coll., N.Y., 1991, Rose Art Mus., Brandeis U., Boston, 1992, Tofias Gallery, Boston, 1994, Zimmerly Art Mus., Rutgers U., N.J., 1995; group shows include The Dorland-Haight Gallery, Milton, Can., 1993. Mem. Nat. Mus. Women in the Arts. Avocations: travel, hiking, collecting children's art. Home and Studio: 63 University Rd Brookline MA 02445-4532

SCHILLING, ANDREAS JOHAN, physicist, educator; b. Wilchingen, Switzerland, Jan. 22, 1961; s. Ernst and Elisabeth (Herth) S. Diploma in physics, Eidgenössische Tech. Hochschule Zürich, Switzerland, 1987, D of Natural Scis., 1992. Postdoctorate Eidgenössisch Tech. Hochschule Zürich, 1992-95, U. Calif., Berkeley, 1995-97; asst. prof. U. Zürich, 1997—. Contbr. rsch. articles to sci. jours. Sports instr. Zürich univs. With Swiss Arty., 1981-84. Recipient award for outstanding rsch. Swiss Phys. Soc. and IBM, 1994, award for excellence for sci. achievement World Congress on Superconductivity, 1994, US-DOE Outstanding Sci. Accomplishment in Solid-State Physics award, 1997; Profil grantee Swiss Nat. Found., 1997. Mem. Am. Phys. Soc. Avocations: cooking, Bordeaux wine. Office: U Zürich Physik Inst, Winterthurerstrasse 190, 8057 Zürich Switzerland

SCHILLING, FRANKLIN CHARLES, JR., retail management professional; b. Balt., Apr. 17, 1958; s. Franklin Charles and Shirley Jean (Whitehurst) S.; children: Franklin Charles III, Tyler Kyle. Student, Dundalk Community Coll., 1975-77. Dept. mgr. Santonis Market, Inc., Balt., 1976-80; store mgr. A&P Plus Food Stores, Balt., 1980-82; area supr. Southland Corp/7-Eleven, Suitland, Md., 1982-85; mgr. retail ops. Moore Oil Co./Makin' Tracks Stores, Washington, N.C., 1986, Besche Oil Co./Quik Shop Stores, Waldorf, Md., 1987-89; dist. mgr. Cloverland Greenspring Dairy/Royal Farm Stores, Balt., 1989-97, dir. ops., 1997-98, mktg. mgr., 1999—. Mem. Rep. Nat. Com. Lutheran. Avocations: reading, sports, music. Home: 1917 August Ave Baltimore MD 21222-3015 Office: Cloverland Dairies/Royal Farm Stores 3611 Roland Ave Baltimore MD 21211-2408

SCHILLING, FREDERICK AUGUSTUS, JR., geologist, consultant; b. Phila., Apr. 12, 1931; s. Frederick Augustus and Emma Hope (Christoffer) S.; m. Ardis Ione Dovre, June 12, 1957 (div. 1987); children: Frederick Christopher, Jennifer Dovre. BS in Geology, Wash. State U., 1953; PhD in Geology, Stanford U., 1962. Registered geologist, Calif.; cert. engring. geologist, Calif.; registered environ. assessor, Calif. Computer geophysicist United Geophys. Corp., Pasadena, Calif., 1955-56; geologist various orgns., 1956-61, U.S. Geol. Survey, 1961-64; underground engr. Climax (Colo.) Molybdenum Co., 1966-68; geologist Keradamex Inc., Anaconda Co., M.P. Grace, Ranchers Exploration & Devel. Corp., Albuquerque and Grants, N.Mex., 1968-84, Hecla Mining Co., Coeur d'Alene, Idaho, 1984-86, various engring. and environ. firms, Calif., 1986-91; prin. F. Schilling Cons., Canyon Lake, Calif., 1991—. Author: Bibliography of Uranium, 1976. Del. citizen amb. program People to People Internat., USSR, 1990-91. With U.S. Army, 1953-55. Fellow The Explorers Club; mem. Geol. Soc. Am., Am. Assn. Petroleum Geologists, Soc. Mining Engrs., Internat. Platform Assn., Adventurers' Club L.A., Masons, Kiwanis, Sigma Xi, Sigma Gamma Epsilon. Republican. Presbyterian. Avocation: track and field. E-mail: faschill@pacbell.net. Office: F Schilling Cons 30037 Steel Head Dr Canyon Lake CA 92587-7460 also: 14661 Myford Rd Ste C Tustin CA 92780-7205

SCHILLING, GÜNTHER, agricultural chemistry educator; b. Leipzig, Saxony, Germany, Aug. 16, 1930; s. Friedrich and Thusnelda (Gerke) S.; m. Gudrun Linschmann, Dec. 2, 1972; children: Jörg, Stephan. Diploma in agr., Friedrich Schiller U., Jena, Germany, 1954, diploma in chemistry, 1956, Dr. agr., 1957, Dr. agr. habilitatus, 1960. Sci. asst. Friedrich Schiller U., 1957-60, univ. lectr., 1960-61, prof. plant nutrition-soil sci., dir. Inst. Agrl. Chemistry, 1961-70; prof. physiology and nutrition of crop plants Martin Luther U., Halle, Germany, 1970-95, emeritus prof., 1995—, dean Faculty Agr., 1983-90, rector, 1990-93; v.p. Rector's Conf., Bonn, Germany, 1991-95. Editor, author: Pflanzenernährung und Düngung, 3d edit., 2000; mem. editl. bd. Archives Agronomy and Soil Sci., Jour. Plant Nutrition and Soil Sci., Fertilizer Rsch., until 1996. Recipient medal and diploma 8th Internat. Fertilizer Congress, Moscow, 1976. Mem. Deutsche Akademie Naturforscher Leopoldina (Halle), Matica Srbska, Verband Deutscher Landwirtschaftlicher Untersuchungs- und Forschungsanstalten Darmstadt (v.p. 1993-96). Avocations: mountain climbing, ship travel. Office: Inst Soil Sci-Plant Nutrit, Julius Kühn Str 31, Halle Saale 06112, Germany

SCHILLING, KLAUS JÜRGEN, computer science researcher, educator; b. Bayreuth, Germany. Diploma in math., U. Bayreuth, 1981, Dr.rer.nat., 1985. Head of mission and sys. sect., dept. for sci. satellites DASA Dornier GmbH, 1985-90; prof. dept. computer sci. U. Applied Scis., Ravensburg-Weingarten, Germany, 1990—; dir. Tech. Transfer Ctr. for Applied Software and Computer Tech., Weingarten, 1992—, head MSc program in mechatronics, 1999—. Assoc. editor Control Engring. Practice; topic editor Space Tech. Jour. Recipient Postgrad. Study in Australia award Australian Govt., 1984, rsch. stay Internat. Inst. Applied Sys. Analyses, Austria, 1985. Mem. Internat. Fedn. Automatic Control (IFAC) (mem. tech. coms. aerospace and intelligent autonomous vehicles, vice chmn. TC on aerospace). Fax: 49-751-48523. E-mail: schi@ars.fh-weingarten.de. Office: Steinbeis Transferzentrum ARS, Doggenriedstrasse 42, D 88250 Weingarten Germany

SCHILLING, MARK REA, film critic, journalist; b. Zanesville, Ohio, Aug. 7, 1949; s. Vernon R. and Margaret J. (Rea) S.; m. Yuko Ono; children: Raymond, Lisa. BA, U. Mich., 1971; tchg. cert., U. of Mich., 1973. Film critic The Japan Times, Tokyo, 1989—; Japan corr. Screen Internat., London, 1990—; sports commentator NHK, Tokyo, 1992—; film critic Premiere, Tokyo, 1998—; film columnist Josei Jishin, Tokyo, 1998; spkr. in field. Author: Encyclopedia of Japanese Pop Culture, 1997, Sumo-A Fan's Guide, 1994, Tokyo After Dark, 1992, Contemporary Japanese Film, 1999; translator The Shogun's Gold, 1991, Princess Mononoke: The Art and Making of Japan's Most Popular Film of All Time; contbr. to essay collection Japan Pop!. Mem. Soc. Writers, Editors and Translators, Japan Film

Pen Club. Avocations: sumo, travel. Home and Office: 3-12-23 Chuo-cho, Higashi Kurume-shi 203-0054, Japan

SCHILLING, ULRICH CHRISTIAN, electrical engineer; b. Schwäbisch Gmünd, Germany, Apr. 9, 1964; s. Rudolf and Gerda (Rehm) S. Diploma, U. Stuttgart, 1992, doctor in engring., 1997. Rschr. U. Stuttgart, 1992-95, Robert Bosch Corp., Stuttgart, 1995—. Patentee in field. Mem. German Elec. Engrs. Office: Robert Bosch Corp, PO Box 30 02 40, 70442 Stuttgart Germany

SCHILPEROORT, SHARON ANN, secondary education educator; b. Tacoma, Wash., Apr. 25, 1947; d. Donald Earl and Ingeborg (Johnsrud) Skidmore; m. William Lester Schilperoort, Apr. 11, 1970; children: Heather Marie, Sara Ann, Andrew Michael. BS in English, Evangel Coll., Springfield, Mo., 1969; MEd in Profl. Devel., Heritage Coll., Toppenish, Wash., 1996; cert. prin., Heritage Coll., 1997. Cert. prof. educator, continuing tchr., Wash. Tchr. lang. arts grades 7 and 8 Highland Sch. Dist., Tieton, Wash., 1969-70, Mt. Adams Sch. Dist., Harrah, Wash., 1970-71; tchr. grades 6-8 Harrah Cmty. Christian, 1983-85; tchr. English grades 6-12, dept. chair West Side Christian Sch., Yakima, Wash., 1986-93; tchr. grades 6-8 OIC-Reach Mid. Sch., Yakima, 1993-94; tchr. lang. arts grade 8 Yakima Sch. Dist., 1994—. Mem. truancy bd. Yakima Sch. Dist., 1997-98; mem., bd. dirs., officer Yakima Cmty. Concert Assn., 1992-95; mem. Harrah Town Coun., 1973-80, 2000—, Parent, Tchr., Student Assn. Wilson Mid. Sch.; alt. mem., bd. dirs. Yakima County Health Dept., 1979-80; mem. admission and allocations bd. Yakima County United Way, 1975-77, bd. chmn. Lower Valley admissions and allocations bd., 1973-75. Named Outstanding Young Woman of Am., 1970. Mem. NEA, ASCD, Nat. Coun. Tchrs. of English, Wash. Edn. Assn., Yakima Edn. Assn. Avocations: travel, reading, environmental issues. Home: 3621 Harrah Rd Harrah WA 98933-9730

SCHILSON, ARNO, history of religion educator; b. Lorch, Rheingau, Germany, Jan. 19, 1945; s. Carl and Maria (Wulf) S.; m. Birgit Perschbach, 1984. Theol. Examen, Hochschule St. Georgen, Frankfurt am Main, Fed. Republic of Germany, 1969; ThD, U. Tübingen, Germany, 1973, ThD Habilitation, 1981. Asst. Cath.-Theol. Faculty, U. Tübingen, 1974-81; prof. European history of religion U. Mainz, Germany, 1981—; pres. Internat. Lessing Soc., 1993. Author: Geschichte im Horizont der Vorsehung, 1974, Theologie als Sakramententheologie, 1982, 2d edit., 1987, Perspektiven Theologischer Erneuerung, 1986, Die wahre Freude der Weihnacht, 1989, Über Religion und Theater bei Lessing, 1994; editor: Lessing, Werke 1774-78, 1989, Lessing, Werke 1778-80, 1993, Gottes Weisheit im Mysterium, 1989, Konservativ mit Blick nach vorn. Versuche zu Romano Guardini, 1994, (with J. Hake) (drama) Gottesdienst, 1998; (with H. Maier and J. Schuster) Guardini Weiterdenken II, 1999. Roman Catholic. Home: Buchenweg 9, D-55128 Mainz Germany

SCHILY, žOTTO, government official; b. Bochum, Germany. Mem. parliament Govt. of Germany, 1983—, now min. of the interior. Office: Fed Ministry of the Interior, Fed Ministry of Interior, D-10559 Berlin Germany*

SCHIMEK, MICHAEL GEORG, statistics and biometrics educator; b. Vienna, Austria, Apr. 30, 1955; s. Herbert Toni and Ingrid (Massmann) S. MA, U. Vienna, 1977, DPhil, 1979; PhD, U. Innsbruck, Austria, 1984; MPhil, U. Bath, U.K., 1991. Statistician Ludwig Boltzmann Inst. and WHO, Vienna, 1979-81; lectr. U. Innsbruck, 1981-84; lectr. U. Graz, Austria, 1985-92, assoc. prof. stats. and biometrics, 1992—; part-time lectr. U. Vienna, 1984—, U. Econs. and Bus. Adminstrn., Vienna, 1995-96; freelance cons. in stats., environ. and social scis., 1980—; vis. prof. dept. math. U. Klagenfurt, Austria, 1993, 95, Tex. A&M U., 1996; rschr. in field; chmn. Compstat Satellite Meeting on Smoothing, 1994, also editor procs. Assoc. editor CompStat Jour., 1991—, Comp. Stat. Data Analysis, 2000—; editor, author: Smoothing and Regression, 2000; contbr. chpts. to books, articles to profl. jours. Fellow Royal Statis. Soc. (chartered statistician); mem. Bernoulli Soc., Biometric Soc. (chmn. Austro-Swiss-Region computing sect. 1989-91), Internat. Assn. Statis. Computing (coun. mem. 1999—), Am. Statis. Assn. Avocations: fine arts, history of arts, photography, railway model building, sports. Office: U Graz, IMI Engelg 13, A-8010 Graz Austria

SCHIMMELPFENG, JUTTA, biologist; b. Bielefeld, Germany, Apr. 3, 1960; d. Bernd and Renate (Hoffert) S. Dr.rer.nat., U. Karlsruhe, Germany, 1989; postdoctoral fellow, Rsch. Ctr. Karlsruhe, 1989-92. Sr. scientist Rsch. Ctr. Karlsruhe, Germany, 1992-95, leader working group for devel. of cmty. female scientists, 1992-95, sr. scientist biophysics, 1996-99; sr. scientist toxicology Rsch. Ctr. Karlsruhe, 1999—, sr. scientist med. engring. and biophysics, 1999—; lectr. Rsch. Ctr. Karlsruhe Devel. Ctr., 1997—. Referee sci. jour. Bioelectromagnetics Soc., 1995-99; contbr. numerous articles to profl. jours. Mem. German Soc. for Cell Biology, Comty. of Female Artists, Soc. Biochem. & Molecular Biology, Bioelectromagnetics Soc. Avocations: public relations, advertising, psychology, medical research, fine arts. E-mail: schimmelpfeng@imb.fzk.de. Office: Forschungszentrum Karlsruhe GmbH, Hermann-von-Helmholz-Pl 1, D-76344 Eggenstein-Leopoldshafen Germany

SCHIMMELPFENNIG, JÖRG, economics educator; b. Berlin, June 17, 1955; s. Kurt Max Karl and Erika Sigrid (Penquitt) S.; m. Bärbel Engelhardt, Sept. 16, 1988; children: Laura Victoria, Larina Viviana. Diploma in math., U. Bielefeld, Fed. Republic Germany, 1979; D Polit. Sci., U. Osnabrück, Fed. Republic Germany, 1985. Sci. asst. dept. econs. U. Osnabrück, 1980-85, asst. prof. dept. econs., 1985-98. Author; contbr. articles to profl. jours. Fellow Royal Soc. Protection of Birds; mem. Inst. Fiscal Studies. Home: Pfitznerstr.9A, D-49076 Osnabruck Germany Office: Dept Econs U Osnabrück, Dept Econs U Bochum, D-44780 Bochum Germany

SCHIMPF, KLAUS, physician; b. Osterode/Harz, Germany, Aug. 12, 1923; s. Robert and Ilse (Ungewitter) S.; m. Ursula Becker, Dec. 28, 1965; children: Rainer, Birgit, Axel. State med. exam., U. Goettingen, 1953, MD, 1954; Habil, U. Heidelberg, 1965. Sci. asst. Inst. Pharmacology U Goettingen, 1953-54; resident in internal medicine U. Heidelberg Faculty Medicine, 1954-64, head blood coagulation lab., dept. internal medicine, 1964-72, sr. lectr. internal medicine, univ. hosps., 1965-73, assoc. prof., 1971-88; med. dir. Rehab. Hosp., founder Hemophilia Ctr., Heidelberg, 1972-88, ret., 1988. Author articles. Served as officer German Army, 1942-44, prisoner-of-war, 1944-48. Decorated Order of Merit (Germany). Mem. Wold Fedn. Hemophilia (med. adv. bd., med. sec. 1979-83, exec. mem. 1983-96, dir. info. clearing house 1980-96), German Hemophilia Soc. (exec. 1983-87, vice chmn. med. adv. bd. 1987-93), Internat. Soc. Thrombosis and Hemostasis, German Soc. Blood Coagulation Rsch. (chmn. 1978-79), German Soc. Hematology, German Soc. Internal Medicine, German Soc. Rehab. Home: 15 Truebner Strasse, D-69121 Heidelberg Germany

SCHINAS, CHRISTOS J., mathematician, researcher; b. Thessaloniki, Greece, Nov. 1, 1968; s. John and Vasiliki Schina. BS, Aristotle U. of Thessaloniki, 1991; MSc, U. R.I., 1992; PhD, U. Macedonia, Thessaloniki, 1998. Mathematician, rschr. dept. applied math. U. Macedonia, Greece; asst. prof. Democritus U. of Thrace, Xanthi, Greece. Contbr. articles to profl. jours. E-mail: sxoinas@macedonia.uom.gr. Home: 9 Kavalas, 554 38 Thessaloniki Greece Office: Democritus U of Thrace, Sch Engring, 67100 Xanthi Greece

SCHINDLER, ALFRED N., manufacturing executive; b. Hergiswil, Switzerland, 1949; divorced; 2 children. Matura; licentiate in law, U. Basle (Switzerland); postgrad. in bus. adminstrn., U. Pa. Cfo Notz Steeltrade, Brügg; bd. dirs. Schindler Holding AG, Hergiswil, Switzerland, 1978—, chmn., 1995—, chmn. exec. com. Office: Schindler Holding AG, Seestrasse 55, CH-6052 Hergiswil Switzerland

SCHINDLER, ANTONÍN, retired structural engineering educator; b. Plzeň, Czech Republic, Apr. 5, 1920; s. Antonín and Anna (Hollmannová) S.; m. Věra Fialková, Oct. 27, 1948; children: Antonín, Jiří. Degree in Structural Engring., Tech. U. Prague, Czech Republic, 1947, PhD, 1959, DSc, 1969. Asst. Architekt Engr. Klouda, Prague, 1940-45; design engr. Hutni Projekt, Prague, 1947-58; asst. Tech. U., Prague, 1959-61, asst. prof., 1961-72, prof., 1972-89, head dept., 1970-80, vice-dean, 1970-76, ret., 1989. Author: (with J. Bureš) Kovové mosty, 1975 (award Ministry of Edn. 1976), (with J. Bureš and J. Pechar) Navrhování ocelových mostu, 1980 (award Ministry of Edn. 1981), (with J. Bureš and J. Pechar) Kovové mosty, 2nd edit., 1990, Statical Design of the World's Greatest Steel Plate Arch Bridge, 1958 (award Ministry of Transport 1999). Active Czechoslovak Sci. and Tech. Soc., Prague, 1949-92, Internat. Assn. for Bridge and Structural Engring., Switzerland, 1973-89. Home: Na Kocince 4, CZ-16000 Prague 6, Czech Republic

SCHINDLER, CHARLES ALVIN, microbiologist, educator; b. Boston, Dec. 27, 1924; s. Edward Esau and Esther Marian (Weisman) S.; m. Barbara Jean Francois, Jan. 14, 1955; children: Marian Giffin, Susan, Neal. BS in Biology, Rensselaer Poly. Inst., 1950; MS, U. Tex., 1956, PhD, 1961. Commd. officer USAF, 1951, advanced through grades to maj., 1965; asst. dir. for biology and medicine at atomic weapons tests Armed Forces Spl. Weapons Project, Camp Mercury, Nev., 1953; rsch. scientist USAF, 1954-68; tchr. Norman (Okla.) Pub. Schs., 1968-86; asst. prof. U. Okla., Flagler Coll., 1968-86; cons., sci. supr. Oklahoma City (Okla.) Sch. Dist., 1989-93; cons. Mead Johnson Rsch. Ctr., Evansville, Ind., 1962-72. Contbr. articles to profl. jours. Coun. mem. Norman (Okla.) City Coun., 1967-81, 83-85. Fellow Charles E. Lewis Fellowship Com., Austin, Tex., 1958; rsch. grantee NSF, Norman, 1972. Mem. Soc. Gen. Microbiology, Sigma Xi. Achievements include U.S. and foreign patents on the bacteriolytic agent Lysost aphin. Avocations: electronics, photography, bridge. Home: 2000 Morgan Dr Norman OK 73069-6525

SCHINDLER, NORBERT, land use planner; b. Striegau, Silesia, Germany, July 29, 1918; s. Oskar and Anni (Obst) S.; m. Else B. Spanich (dec. 1994); 1 child, Thomas Peter. Diploma, Technische Fachhochschule, Berlin, 1953; Diploma (hon.), Technische Univ., Berlin, 1974. Leitender Senatsrat. Dir. Dept. Parks and Recreation, Mainz, Fed. Republic Germany, 1960-65; dir. gen. Dept. Open Spaces, Berlin, 1966-80; prof. Technische U., Berlin, 1974—; Author 500 articles in books, jours. in field. Recipient Verdienstkreuz I. Klasse award, Fed. Pres., Fed. Republic Germany, 1984, Diplome et Medaille d'Or de Maitrise, Ordre de Saint Fortunat L'Union Internat., Paris, 1980. Mem. Acad. Internat. de Hortis et Naturalibus Prospectibus, Roma, Deutsche Akademie fuer Staedtebau Landesplanung, Internat. Fedn. Park and Recreation Adminstrn. (pres. 1980-83). Avocation: world travel. Home: Hogenestweg 14, 12353 Berlin Germany

SCHINK, BERNHARD HERMANN LUDWIG, biologist and educator; b. Moenchengladbach, Germany, Apr. 27, 1950; s. Walther and Lotte (Mueller) S.; m. Regine M. Mailaender, Sept. 30, 1994; 2 children. Dipl.Biology, U. Goettingen, Germany, 1974, Dr.rer.nat., 1977; Dr.rer.nat.habil., U. Konstanz, Germany, 1985. Prof. biology U. Marburg, Germany, 1986-87, U. Tuebingen, Germany, 1987-91, U. Konstanz, Germany, 1991—. Contbr. more than 170 sci. articles to profl. jours. Office: U Konstanz Faculty Biology, PO Box 5560, D-78457 Konstanz Germany

SCHINNERER, ALAN JOHN, entrepreneur; b. Long Beach, Calif., June 8, 1925; s. Walter John and Esther Schinnerer; m. Barbara Elaine Daniger, Aug. 17, 1951 (div. Aug. 1971); children: Gregory, Scott, Brett, Vicky. AA, Long Beach City Coll., 1948; B of Elec. Engring., U. So. Calif., 1952, postgrad. law, 1956-57, postgrad. bus., 1958-59. Purchasing agt. McCulloch Corp., Los Angeles, 1952-56; systems engr. Hughes Aircraft Co., Culver City, Calif., 1956-59; sales engr. Gilfillan Corp., Los Angeles, 1959-61; mktg. specialist N.Am. Rockwell Corp., Downey, Calif., 1961-68; sr. project engr. Hughes Aircraft Co., El Segundo, Calif., 1968-74, dir. satellite tests, 1974-76, assoc. program mgr., 1976-84; pres., owner, founder Calif. Classic Boats, Long Beach, Calif., 1979—; founding ptnr. Looking Glass Cellars, Murrieta, Calif., 1995—. Author: (catalog) Parts for Antique and Classic Chirs-Craft, Dodge, Gar Wood and Hacker runabouts, 1979-98. Bd. dirs. Antique Powercraft Hist. Soc., 1984-85. Served with USN, 1943-46, PTO. Mem. Antique and Classic Boat Soc. (founding pres. So. Calif. chpt. 1983-86), Garwood Soc., Delta Tau Delta. Republican. Clubs: Chris-Craft Antique Boat, Porsche of Am., Tahoe Yacht, Sierra. Home: 5581 Ridgebury Dr Huntington Beach CA 92649-4825 Office: Calif Classic Boats 3267 E Grant St Long Beach CA 90804-1212

SCHINTGEN, ROMAIN, judge; b. Luxembourg, Mar. 22, 1939; m. Lucie Dui, 1974; 1 child. Grad., Athénée Grand-Ducal de Luxembourg, Faculté de Droit, Faculté de Montpellier, Faculté de Paris. Advocate Luxembourg Bar, 1964, atty.-at-law, 1967; asst. Ministry Labour, 1967, counsellor, 1974, adminstr.-gen., 1987; pres. Conseil Economique et Social, 1988-89; judge Tribunal 1st Instance European Communities, 1989-96. Author: Le Droit du Travail au Grand-Duché de Luxembourg. Comdr. Ordre de la Couronne de Chêne; recipient decorations from Germany, Portugal, Spain. Office: Ct Justice, Ctr Justice, European Communities, L-2925 Luxembourg Luxembourg

SCHINZLER, HANS-JURGEN, insurance executive; b. Madrid, Oct. 12, 1940. Mem. adminstrv. bd. Münchener Rückversicherungsgesellschaft, Munich; dep. chair Allgemeine Kreditversicherung AG, Mainz, Allianzversicherung AG, Munich; chmn. bd. mgmt. Munchener Ruckversicherungs-Gesellschaft AG. Office: Munich Re Group, Koeniginstrasse 107, 80802 Munich Germany*

SCHIODT, MORTEN, dentist, oral surgeon; b. Copenhagen, Denmark, Jan. 7, 1947; s. Gunnar and Rigmor (Ehrenreich) S.; m. Dorte Eickhardt, May 31, 1975; 1 child, Julie. DDS, U. Copenhagen, 1971, specialization in oral surgery, 1979; D of Oral Surgery, U. Hosp., Copenhagen, 1984. Asst. prof. Sch. Dentistry U. Copenhagen, 1971-80, 83-90; asst. prof. U. Hosp., 1973-90; chief surgeon Hillerod Hosp., Denmark, 1990-96, Copenhagen County U. Hosp., Glostrup, Denmark, 1996—; assoc. prof. U. Calif. San Francisco, 1985-86, 87-89. Co-author: AIDS and the Dental Team, 1986, AIDS and the Mouth, 1990; author CD-ROM Oral Medicine, 1997. Lt. Danish Navy, 1971-72. Mem. Internat. AIDS Soc., Danish Soc. Oral Surgery (pres. 1984-87, 98—), Internat. Assn. Dental Rsch. Avocations: sailing, waterskiing, skiing, butterflies. Home: Olesvej 3, 2830 Virum Denmark Office: Ringvej Dept Oral Maxil Sur, Copenhagen Co Univ Hosp, 2600 Glostrup Denmark

SCHIPANSKI, DAGMAR, physicist; b. Sättelstädt, Thuringia, Germany, Sept. 3, 1943; d. Herman and Käthe (Eichhorn) Gebhardt; m. Tigran Schipanski, 1967; children: Tankred, Agnes, Angela. Student, Magdeburg Tech. U., Germany, 1962-67, MD, 1976, PhD, 1990. Asst. Tech. U., Ilmenau, 1967-85, asst. prof., 1986-89, assoc. prof., 1990, dean of dept. elec. engring. and info. tech., 1990-94; vice-chancellor for instrn. Ilmenau Tech. U., Ilmenau, 1994, pres., 1995-96; chairwoman Sci. Coun., Cologne, Germany, 1996-98; Thuringian min. sci., rsch. and art, 1999—. Contbr. articles to profl. jours. Recipient Federal Svc. Cross, first class, 1996, Arthur Burkhardt award, 1999. Achievements include 9 patents. Office: Thüringer Ministerium für Wissenschaft, Juri-Gagarin-Ring 158, 99084 Erfurt Germany

SCHIRMANN, JEAN-PIERRE HENRI, chemist, researcher; b. Oullins, France, Mar. 28, 1939; s. Armand Joseph and Alice Marie-Louise (Thevenot) S.; m. Ana-Maria Peña-Jimenez, June 5, 1964; children: Brigitte, Remi, Nicolas. Lic. scis., U. Lyon, France, 1963; PhD, U. Lyon, 1966; degree in chem. engring., Ecole Sup. Chimie Lyon, 1963; postgrad., Roswell Park Meml. Inst., Buffalo, 1968. Scientist Ugine-Kuhlmann, Lyon, 1969-80; chief R&D dept. PCUK, Lyon, 1980-82, dep. dir. R&D, 1982-84; dir. rsch. ctr. Atochem, Lyon, 1984-91; R&D dir. ELF Atochem, Paris, 1991—; cons. CNRS, Paris, 1982-88. Author: Hydrogen Peroxide in Organic Chemistry, 1978; patentee in field; contbr. to Ullmann Encylopedia, 1978. Recipient prix scis. de l'ingenieur Acad. des Scis., 1997. Mem. French Chem. Soc. (Grand Prix de Chimie Industrielle 1988), Am. Chem. Soc. Roman Catholic. Home: 49 Chemin de la glaciere, 69600 Oullins France

SCHIRMER, WOLFGANG, retired physical chemist, researcher; b. Berlin, Mar. 3, 1920; s. Albert and Johanna (Thierfelder) S.; m. Ursula Starke, Oct. 9, 1948; children: Roland, Matthias. Diploma in chemistry, U. Berlin, 1943, habilitation, 1954; PhD, Tech. U. Berlin, Charlottenburg, 1948; PhD (hon.), U. Leipzig, Germany, 1985. Dir. enterprises Piesteritz, Lenna, German Democratic Republic, 1949-62; dir. Acad. Scis., Berlin, 1963-85; ret., 1985; rschr. in phys. chemistry; mem. JUPAC Commn. 16, 1970-78; mem. Exec. Commn. CODATA, 1976-84; mem. JIASA, Internat. Inst. Applied Sys. Analyst, Austria, 1984-90. Editor-in-chief Zeitschr. Phys. Chemistry, 1975-95. Hon. scholar Internat. Inst. Applied Sys. Analyst, 1990. Mem. European Acad. Scis., N.Y. Acad. Scis. Home: Biberpelzstr 46, 12589 Berlin Germany

SCHIRRA, WALTER MARTY, JR., business consultant, former astronaut; b. Hackensack, N.J., Mar. 12, 1923; s. Walter Marty and Florence (Leach) S.; m. Josephine Cook Fraser, Feb. 23, 1946; children: Walter Marty III, Suzanne Karen. Student, Newark Coll. Engring., 1940-42; B.S., U.S. Naval Acad., 1945; D. Astronautics (hon.), Lafayette Coll., U. So. Calif., N.J. Inst. Tech. Commd. ensign U.S. Navy, 1945, advanced through grades to capt., 1965; designated naval aviator, 1948; service aboard battle cruiser Alaska, 1945-46; service with 7th Fleet, 1946; assigned Fighter Squadron 71, 1948-51; exchange pilot 154th USAF Fighter Bomber Squadron, 1951; engaged in devel. Sidewinder missile China Lake, Calif., 1952-54; project pilot F7U-3 Cutlass; also instr. pilot F7U-3 Cutlass and FJ3 Fury, 1954-56; ops. officer Fighter Squadron 124, U.S.S. Lexington, 1956-57; assigned Naval Air Safety Officer Sch., 1957, Naval Air Test Ctr., 1958-59; engaged in suitability devel. work F4H, 1958-59; joined Project Mercury, man-in-space, NASA, 1959; pilot spacecraft Sigma 7 in 6 orbital flight, Oct. 1962; in charge operations and tng. Astronaut Office, 1964-69; command pilot Gemini 6 which made rendezvous with target, Gemini 7, Dec. 1965; comdr. 11 day flight Apollo 7, 1968; ret., 1969; pres. Regency Investors, Inc., Denver, 1969-70; chmn., chief exec. officer ECCO Corp., Englewood, Colo., 1970-73; chmn. Sernco, Inc., 1973-74; with Johns-Manville Corp., Denver, 1974-77; v.p. devel. Goodwin Cos., Inc., Littleton, Colo., 1978-79; ind. cons., 1979-80; dir. Kimberly Clark, 1983-91. Decorated D.F.C.(3), Air medal (2), Navy D.S.M.; recipient Distinguished Service medal (2) NASA, Exceptional Service medal. Fellow Am. Astronautical Soc., Soc. Exptl. Test Pilots. Home and Office: PO Box 73 Rancho Santa Fe CA 92067-0073

SCHIRREN, CARL, dermatologist, andrologist. MD, U. Kiel, Germany, 1951. Asst. in gen. practice Burg/Dithmarschen, Schleswig-Holstein, Germany, 1951; asst. clinic of endocrinology U. Hamburg, Germany, 1952, sr. asst. clinic of dermatology, 1960-87, prof. of univ., 1966, dir. dept. andrology, 1971-87, dir. reproductive medicine, prof. emeritus, 1987; hon. prof. Fujita-Gakuen U., Nagoya, Japan; editor-in-chief Andrologia, Berlin, 1969-90. Contbr. to handbooks and encyclopedias, numerous articles to profl. jours. 1st lt. German Army, 1940-45. Mem. German Soc. Andrology (hon. pres.). Lutheran. Avocations: medical history, sexual education, ethics in medicine. Home and Office: Friedrich-Kirstenstrasse 25, D-22391 Hamburg Germany

SCHIRRMACHER, THOMAS PAUL, ethics educator, publisher, periodical editor; b. Schwelm, Westfalen, Germany, June 25, 1960; s. Bernd Arthur and Ingeborg (Steinle) S.; m. Christine Ulrike Krause, July 12, 1985; children: David, Esther. BA, MTh, STH Basel, Switzerland, 1982; ThD, Theol. Hogeschool, Kampen, Netherlands, 1984; DTh, Johannes Calvijn Stichting, Kampen, 1985; PhD in Cultural Anthropology, Pac. West U., 1989; postgrad., U. Bonn, 1985-88; ThD, Whitefield Theol. Sem., 1996; DD, Cranmer Theol. Ho., 1997. Ordained Anglican by Bishop Robert H. Booth, London, 1993. Lectr. missiology, comparative religions FTA Giessen, Germany, 1983-90; lectr. in Old Testament and social ethics Bibelseminar, Wuppertal, Germany, 1984-89; lectr. social ethics and apologetics Bibelseminar, Bonn, 1993—; owner, chief editor Culture and Sci. Publ., Bonn, Germany, 1987—; head dept. STH Basel, 1991-96; prof. missiology Phila. Theol. Seminary, 1994-98; gen. dir. Inst. for World Mission, Bonn, 1984—; pres. Inst. for Islam and Christianity, Bruchsal, Germany, 1994-98; head dept. ethics, missions, religions and cultures, Free Seminary, Geneva, Switzerland, 1991-96; pres., dean, prof. Martin-Bucer Sem., Bonn, 1996—; prof. systematic theology Whitefield Theol. Sem., 1996—; prof. ethics Cranmer Theol. Ho., 1997—; external examiner U. Sough Africa, 1999—; spkr. for human rights Evang. Alliance. Chief editor Bibel und Gemeinde jour., 1988-97, Evang. Missiologie, 1997—, Jour. European Ethics, 1999—; author: Ethics, 2 vols., 1994, 2d edit., 3 vols., 2000, Der Römerbrief, 2 vols., 1993, 2d edit., 2000, Marxismus - Opium für das Volk?, 1990, Mohammed, 4th edit., 1985, 92, Galilei Legends, 1996; author/editor 40 sci. books and numerous articles to profl. jours. Pres. Bonn area PBC, Karlsruhe, 1993-96, editor; exec. bd. dirs. Kurdish Inst., Bonn, 1987-89; chmn. supervisory bd. Gebende Mande, 1995—; bd. dirs. Bibelbund, Reiskirchen, Germany, 1983-90; pres. ProMundis, Bonn, 1996—. Fellow AFEM (co-editor 1984—, chief editor 1996—), DGMW. Presbyterian. Avocations: classical music, internat. zoos. Office: Culture and Science Publ, Friedrichstr 38, D-53111 Bonn Germany

SCHLACHETZKI, ANDREAS BRUNO WILLIBALD, engineering educator; b. Breslau, Silesia, Germany, July 7, 1938; s. Johannes and Steffi (Bernatzky) S.; m. Marianne Stanke, Apr. 2, 1976; children: Constantin, Sarah. Diploma in Physics, U. Cologne, Germany, 1965, D, 1969. Rsch. assoc. Yale U., New Haven, 1970-71; tech. staff Rsch. Inst. German Post Office, Darmstadt, 1971-76; exch. scientist Nippon Telegraph & Telephone, Tokyo, 1975; prof. Tech. U. Braunschweig, Germany, 1976-84; head divsn. Heinrich Hertz Inst., Berlin, 1984-87; prof. Tech. U. Berlin, 1987—, Tech. U. Braunschweig, 1987—. Co-author: (with W.V. Muench) Integrierte Schaltungen, 1978, Halbleiterbauelemente der Hochfrequenztechnik, 1984,Halbleiter-Elektronik, 1990. Mem. Deutsche Physikalische Gesellschaft, Nachrichtentechnische Gesellschaft, Internat. Soc. Optical Engring. Roman Catholic. Office: Inst fuer Halbleitertechnik Tech U Braunschweig, Hans-Sommer-Str 66, 38106 Braunschweig Germany

SCHLACHTA-FAIRCHILD, LORETTA MARIE, nursing consultant; b. Phila., Oct. 6, 1956; d. Joseph A. and Hedwig (Bruch) S.; m. Henry B. Fairchild, July 21, 1983. BSN, U. Md., 1978; MS in Health Professions, S.W. Tex. State U., 1985; PhD in Nursing Adminstrn., Med. Coll. Ga. RN, Ga. Commd. 1st lt. U.S. Army, 1978, advanced through grades to lt. col., 1994; dir. children's ambulatory care ctr. Santa Rosa Healthcare Corp., San Antonio, 1986-88; pvt. practice healthcare cons. Heidelberg, Germany, 1988-90; telemedicine nursing cons. Ctr. for Total Access, Dept. of Def., 1994-96; clin. dir. Strategic Monitored Svcs., Inc., 1996-99; prin., founder, CEO TeleHealth Inc. Lt. col. USAR, 1987—. Recipient San Antonio Spirt award, 1987. Mem. ANA, Am. Coll. Healthcare Execs. (diplomate), Healthcare Info. Mgmt. Sys. Soc., Am. Telemedicine Assn., Assn. of Telemedicine Svc. Providers, Phi Kappa Phi, Sigma Theta Tau. Office: 6935 N Clifton Rd Frederick MD 21702-3563

SCHLACKS, STEPHEN MARK, lawyer, educator; b. Pittsburg, Kans., Oct. 13, 1955. BA, Austin Coll., Sherman, Tex., 1978; MBA, U. Dallas, 1982; JD, Baylor U., 1986. Bar: Tex. 1987, U.S. Dist. Ct. (so. dist.) Tex. 1987, (no., ea. and we. dists.) Tex. 1988, U.S. Ct. Appeals (5th cir.) 1987, (8th cir.) 1989, U.S. Supreme Ct. 1990. In mgmt. Johnson & Johnson Products, Inc., Sherman, 1978-84; assoc. atty. Wetzel & Assocs., The Woodlands, Tex., 1986-92; ptnr. Hope, Causey & Schlacks, P.C., Conroe, Tex., 1992-96, Law Office of Stephen M. Schlacks, The Woodlands, Tex., 1996-99, Schlacks, Harrison & Cox PLLC, The Woodlands, 1999—; adj. faculty North Harris County C.C., Houston, 1990—. Leon Jaworski scholar, 1984, Harcourt Brace Jovanovich scholar, 1986. Mem. Fed. Bar Assn., Montgomery County Bar Assn., Tex. Assn. Def. Counsel, Sigma Iota Epsilon, Pi Gamma Mu. Republican. Presbyterian. Home: 66 Racing Cloud Ct The Woodlands TX 77381-5203 Office: 2202 Timberloch Pl Ste 107 The Woodlands TX 77380-1163

SCHLAFLY, PHYLLIS STEWART, author; b. St. Louis, Aug. 15, 1924; d. John Bruce and Odile (Dodge) Stewart; m. Fred Schlafly, Oct. 20, 1949; children: John F., Bruce S., Roger S., Phyllis Liza Forshaw, Andrew L., Anne V. BA, Washington U., St. Louis, 1944, JD, 1978; MA, Harvard U., 1945; LLD, Niagara U., 1976. Bar: Ill. 1979, D.C. 1984, Mo. 1985, U.S. Supreme Ct. 1987. Syndicated columnist Copley News Svc., 1976—; pres. Eagle Forum, 1975—; broadcaster Spectrum, CBS Radio Network, 1973-78; commentator Cable TV News Network, 1980-83, Matters of Opinion sta. WBBM-AM, Chgo., 1973-75. Author, pub.: Phyllis Schlafly Report, 1967—; author: A Choice Not an Echo, 1964, The Gravediggers, 1964, Strike From Space, 1965, Safe Not Sorry, 1967, The Betrayers, 1968, Mindszenty The Man, 1972, Kissinger on the Couch, 1975, Ambush at Vladivostok, 1976, The Power of the Positive Woman, 1977, First Reader,

1994; editor: Child Abuse in the Classroom, 1984, Pornography's Victims, 1987, Equal Pay for Unequal Work, 1984, Who Will Rock the Cradle, 1989, Stronger Families or Bigger Government, 1990, Meddlesome Mandate: Rethinking Family Leave, 1991. Del. Rep. Nat. Conv., 1956, 64, 68, 84, 88, 92, 96, alt., 1960, 80; pres. Ill. Fedn. Rep. Women, 1960-64; 1st v.p. Nat. Fedn. Rep. Women, 1964-67; mem. Ill. Commn. on Status of Women, 1975-85; nat. chmn. Stop ERA, 1972—; mem. Ronald Reagan's Def. Policy Adv. Group, 1980; mem. Commn. on Bicentennial of U.S. Constn., 1985-91; mem. Adminstrv. Conf. U.S., 1983-86. Recipient 10 Honor awards Freedoms Found., Brotherhood award NCCJ, 1975; named Woman of Achievement in Pub. Affairs St. Louis Globe-Democrat, 1963, one of 10 most admired women in world Good Housekeeping poll, 1977-90. Mem. ABA, DAR (nat. chmn. Am. history 1965-68, nat. chmn. bicentennial com. 1967-70, nat. chmn. nat. def. 1977-80, 83-95), Ill. Bar Assn., Phi Beta Kappa, Pi Sigma Alpha. Office: Eagle Forum 7800 Bonhomme Ave Saint Louis MO 63105-1906

SCHLAG, EDWARD WILLIAM, chemistry educator; b. L.A., Jan. 12, 1932; s. Hermann and Hilda (Nolte) S.; m. Angela Gräfin zu Castell, June 15, 1955;; children: Katherine, Karl, Elisabeth. BS, Occidental Coll., L.A., 1953; PhD, U. Wash., 1958; postgrad., U. Bonn, Fed. Republic of Germany, 1958; D Philosophy honoris Causa, Hebrew U. Jerusalem, Israel, 1988. Rsch. scientist, films dept. E. I. du Pont de Nemours & Co., Buffalo, 1959; asst. prof., chemistry Northwestern U., Evanston, Ill., 1960-63; assoc. prof. chemistry Northwestern U., 1964-68, prof., chemistry, 1969-70; prof. phys. chemistry, and dir. Inst. Phys. and Theoretical Chemistry Technische Universität, Munich, Germany, 1971—; dean of the faculty of chemistry, biology and geosciences Technische Universität, 1982-84; vis. prof. U. Calif., Irvine, 1987; John Wilfred Linnett vis. prof. chem. Cambridge (Eng.) U., 1995; Woodward lectr., 1987; Fritz-Haber lectr., 1988; Ames lectr., 1990; invited lectr. Welch Found. Conf., 1994, Solvay Conf., 1995; Charles M. Knight lectr. U. Akron, 1996; Bonhoeffer-Eucken-Scheibe lectr., 1997; James-Franck lectr. Israel Acad. Scis., Jerusalem, 1998; mem. editl. bd. Coun. Sci. Info., India, Wiley Series in Ion Chemistry and Physics. Author: (with Lin, Fujimura, and Neusser) Multiphoton Spectroscopy of Molecules, 1984; author: Time of Flight Mass Spectrometry and Its Applications, 1994, ZEKE Spectroscopy, 1998; mem. editl. bd. Chem. Physics (founding editor) Chem. Physics Letters, Internat. Jour. Mass Spectrometry and Ion Processes, Jour. Phys. Chemistry, 1989, Laser Chemistry, Advances in Ion Chemistry and Physics, Trends in Chem. Physics, Accounts Chem. Rsch., Molecular Physics; contbr. over 350 articles to profl. jours. Alfred P. Sloan fellow, 1965; Recipient Gold Honorary J. Heyrovsky medal Acad. Scis. of the Czech Republic, Prague, 1993. Fellow Am. Phys. Soc.; mem. Deutsche Physikalische Gesellschaft, Fachverband Chemische Physik, Arbeitsgemeinschaft Massenspektrometrie, Bavarian Acad. Sci., Am. Chem. Soc., Am. Phys. Soc. Achievements include research in Multiphoton ionization mass spectrometry, high resolution sub-Doppler molecular spectroscopy and dynamics, spectroscopy and kinetics of molecular ions, dynamics of photoexcited states and van der Waal's molecules, synchrotron radiation experiments on molecular ions, inner shell excitation, ZEKE-Spectroscopy, patents in field. Office: Technische U München, Lichtenbergstrasse 4, 85747 Garching Germany

SCHLAGENHAUF, ULRICH, dentist; b. Albstadt, Germany, Feb. 9, 1954; s. Willi Ernst and Liselotte (Glock) S. BS, U. Tubingen, 1979, Dr. Med. Dentistry, 1984. Asst. prof. U. Tubingen, Germany, 1980-82; postdoctoral rsch. fellow U. Wash., Seattle, 1983-84; from asst. prof. to vice chmn. dept. conservative dentistry U. Tubingen, 1984—; exec. bd. Internat. Health Care Found., 1994—. Grantee NIH, 1983. Mem. IADR, DGZMK, IHCF. Lutheran. Avocations: philosophy, sports. Office: Sch Dental Medicine, Osianderstrasse 2-8, D-72076 Tuebingen Germany

SCHLAGER, WALTER AUGUST, physicist; b. Durmersheim, Germany, Jan. 16, 1964; s. Alfons and Elsa (Kuhn) S.; m. Ursula Lioba Behm, Sept. 2, 1994. Diploma in physics, U. Karlsruhe, 1989, DSc, 1994. Rsch. scientist Philips, Aachen, Germany, 1994-2000; sr. application engr. Philips Automotive Lighting, Aachen, 2000—. Roman Catholic. Office: Philips Gluhlampenwerk, Philipsstrasse 8, 52068 Aachen Germany

SCHLAGETER, KURT EDWARD, consultant; b. Chgo., June 6, 1961; s. Charles W. and Elibeth M. Schlageter; m. Stephanie Schlageter, Oct. 6, 1996. BS, U. Ariz., 1983; MS, Northwestern U., 1989, PhD, 1995. Rsch. assoc. Evanston (Ill.) Hosp. Corp., 1983-95; post-doctoral fellow Northwestern U., Evanston, 1995-98; rsch. fellow NIH, Bethesda, Md., 1998-99. Mem. AAAS, Soc. for Neurosci. E-mail: kurts@pobox.com.

SCHLAGMAN, RICHARD EDWARD, book publisher; b. London, Nov. 11, 1953; s. Jack and Shirley Ann (Goldston) S. Student, Brunel U., 1972-73. Joint chmn., mng. dir., co-founder Bush Radio Plc, 1973-86; chmn., pub. Phaidon Press Ltd., London, 1990—; pres. Judd Found., Marfa, Tex., 1999—. Fellow Royal Soc. Arts; mem. Tate Gallery Patrons of New Art (exec. com. 1994-97), Designers and Arts Dirs. Assn. U.K., Chelsea Arts Club, Queen's Club. Avocations: music, art, architecture. Office: Phaidon Press Ltd, 18 Regents Wharf All Saints St, London N1 9PA, England

SCHLAILE, HANS GERD, physicist, researcher; b. Karlsruhe, Baden, Germany, July 29, 1939; s. Wilhelm and Else (Jenet) S.; m. Sigrid Kunzmann, Oct. 10, 1970; children: Christian, Peter. Diplom Physiker, U. Karlsruhe, 1964, Dr.rer.nat., 1970. Owner Musikhaus Schlaile GmbH, Karlsruhe, 1964—; rschr. in physics U. Karlsruhe, 1970—. Contbr. articles to profl. jours. Mem. Amnesty Internat., 1970—, Uganda Hilfe E.V., 1965—; mem. coun. elders Christuskirche, 1972—, mem. ecumenical working group, 1978—. Mem. Evangelische Landeskirche Baden. Avocations: swimming, walking. Home: Jahnstr 8, D-76133 Karlsruhe Germany

SCHLÄPFER, MARTIN, performing company executive; b. Altstätten, Switzerland, Dec. 26, 1959. Studied with Marianne Fuchs and Peter Appel, 1975-77; student, Royal Ballet Sch., 1977-78. Prin. Basler Ballett, Switzerland, 1978-83, 1985-89; soloist Royal Winnipeg Ballet Can., 1983-84; dir., owner Dance Place, Basle, Switzerland, 1990-94; soloist Ballet Stadttheater, Bern, Switzerland, 1991-92, artistic dir., 1994-99; artistic dir. Staatstheater, Mainz, Germany, 1999—. Appeared in ballets 4 Temperaments, Les Patineurs, Songs of a Wayfarer, Five Tangos, Grosse Fuge, Profiteur in Green Table; co-creator ballets Fritz in Nutcracker, Till Eulenspiegel, Midsummer Night's Dream, Pierrot Lunaire, Chäs, Törless, La Fille mal gardée; choreographies for Berne Ballet, Haydn-Variations, Ruckert-Lieder, Strange Fruit, Divertimento (filmed for TV 1996), Firebird, Stabat Mater, Empty Games (filmed for TV 1997), Dritte Symphonie Martinu, Vespers, String Quartet Mendelssohn, The Four Seasons, Last Sleep Tavener; choreographies for Ballet Mainz, Orgelkonzert, Appenzellertanze, Drittes Klavierkonzert Schnittke, Mourned by the Wind, Time in Slow; appeared on cover Dance mag., 1983, Ballet Internat., 1985. Dir. found. Visions of Dance. Recipient Prix de Lausanne award, 1977. Fax: D 6131 2851129. Office: Staatstheater, Gutenbergplatz 7, D-55116 Mainz Germany

SCHLARB, BERNHARD, chemist; b. Koblenz, Germany, Mar. 31, 1958; s. Walter and Irmgard (Stegemann) S. Chemistry Diploma, Johannes Gutenberg U., Mainz, Germany, 1983, PhD, 1988. Sci. asst. Johannes Gutenberg U., 1983-84, sci. employee, 1987-88; tech. trainee Eastman Kodak Co., Rochester, N.Y., 1986; scientist BASF Aktiengesellschaft, Ludwigshafen, Germany, 1988—. Contbr. articles to profl. jours.; patentee in field. Fellow German Chem. Soc. Avocations: photography, jogging, reading. Home: Dhauner Str 15A, 67067 Ludwigshafen Germany Office: BASF Aktiengesellschaft, Polymer Rsch Lab, 67056 Ludwigshafen Germany

SCHLATTERER, BERT, biochemist, educator; b. Calw, Germany, Jan. 25, 1940; s. Albert and Olga Antonia (Scheuring) S.; m. Dorothee Gertrud Kolb, Feb. 21, 1964; children: Kathrin, Stefan, Annegret, Jörg. DVM, Ludwig-Maxim U., Munich, 1965; diploma in biochemistry, U. Tübingen, Germany, 1969; PhD, U. Stuttgart-Hohenheim, Germany, 1975. Asst. prof. U. Stuttgart-Hohenheim, 1969-75; leading scientist Fed. Health Office, Berlin, 1975-81, Fed. Environ. Office, Berlin, 1981-91; dir. Brandenburg Vet. and Chem. State Lab., Potsdam, Germany, 1992—; hon. prof. Justus-Liebig U. Giessen, 1991—. Editor: Environmental Chemical Risk Factors of Cancer, 1991; contbr. articles to profl. jours. Univ. scholar Volkswagenwerk Found., 1965-69. Mem. Soc. German Chemists, German Vet. Soc., Soc. Environ. Toxicology and Chemistry. Liberal Party. Avocations: fencing, general sports, theater. Home: Hüninger Str 12, D14195 Berlin Germany Office: Vet and Chem State Lab, Pappelallee 20, D14469 Potsdam Germany

SCHLECHTWEG, MICHAEL, electrical engineer, researcher; b. Kassel, Germany, Jan. 10, 1958; s. Otto and Johanna Renate (Quelle) S.; m. Sabine Wangart, Aug. 6, 1993; 1 child, Luise Caroline. Dipl.Ing., Tech. Hochschule Darmstadt, Germany, 1982; Dr.Ing., U. Kassel, 1989. Rsch. asst. U. Kassel, 1983-89; rsch. scientist Fraunhofer Inst. Angewandte Festkörperphysik, Freiburg, Germany, 1989-94; group leader Fraunhofer Inst. IAF, Freiburg, Germany, 1994-96, dept. leader, 1996—; lectr. Eurochip, Berlin, 1994-95, Europractice, Berlin, 1996; mem. Conf. Orgn. Network, Sindelfingen, Germany, 1992-93. Contbr. articles to profl. jours. Recipient Fraunhofer Soc. prize, 1993, European Microwave Assn. prize, 1998. Mem. IEEE, Microwave Theory and Techniques Soc., Electron Devices Soc. Avocations: badminton, hiking, biking. Home: Kappler Str 34, D-79117 Freiburg Germany Office: Fraunhofer Inst IAF, Tullastr 72, D-79108 Freiburg Germany

SCHLEE, WALTER, mathematician, educator; b. Schwandorf, Bavaria, Germany, Sept. 12, 1942; s. Walter Konrad and Babette Maria (Birner) S.; m. Walburga Koessler, Mar. 15, 1974. Student, Technische U. Munich, Diplom-Mathematiker, 1967, Dr.rer.nat., 1970. Rschr., mem. faculty dept. math. Technische U. Munich, 1967—. Author works on math. optimization, graph theory and nonparametric stats. in English, French, German; contbr. articles and revs. to profl. jours. Fellow Royal Statis. Soc.; mem. Am. Statis. Assn., Deutsche Statistische Gesellschaft, Soc. Française de Statistique. Office: Arcisstrasse 21, D-80333 Munich Germany

SCHLEGELMILCH, BODO BERND, marketing educator; b. Wipperfürth, NRW, Germany, Jan. 8, 1955; s. Erich and Cilly (Kienert) S.; m. Irene M. Michalcewicz; 1 child, Roger. BSc, FH-Köln, Germany, 1979; MSc, U. Manchester, U.K., 1981, PhD, 1983. Stock adviser Deutsche Bank, Cologne, Germany, 1973-76; bd. mgmt. Procter and Gamble, Frankfurt, Germany, 1983-84; with U. Edinburgh, Scotland, 1984-88; asst. prof. U. Calif., Berkeley, 1984-88; British rail chair of mktg. U. Wales, U.K., 1989-93; prof. mktg. Thunderbird, Phoenix, 1993-97; chair internat. mktg. and mgmt. Vienna U., Austria, 1997—; dir. Canyon Cons., Phoenix, 1997—; adj. prof. U. Minn., Mpls., 1999—, U. Otago, New Zealand, 1999, U. Innsbruck, Austria, 1994; adj. prof. mktg. U. Miami, Fla., 1992-93; vis. mktg. scholar U. Köln, Germany, 1989. Author: Marketing Ethics: An International Perspective, 1998; editl. bd. Jour. Internat. Mktg., Jour. Internat. Bus., Jour. of World Bus.; contbr. articles to profl. publs. Rsch. grant U. Edinburgh, The Carnegie Trust, The Higher Edn. Funding Coun. for Wales, British Rail, The Charity Aid Found., The U.S. Dept. of Edn., City of Vienna. Fellow Chartered Inst. of Marketing; mem. Am. Mktg. Assn., European Mktg. Assn., Acad. of Internat. Bus., Acad. of Internat. Bus., Market Rsch. Soc., Assn. of Consumer Rsch., Acad. of Mktg. Sci., Inst. of Mktg. Sci., European Bus. Ethics Network, Soc. for Bus. Ethics and Verband der Hochschullehrer für Betriebswirtschaft. Avocation: windsurfing. Fax: 43-1-31336-793. E-mail: bodo.schlegelmilch@WU-Wien.AC.AT. Office: Wu-Wien Internat Mktg/Mgmt, Augasse 2-6, 1090 Vienna Austria

SCHLEGELMILCH, REUBEN ORVILLE, electrical engineer, consultant; b. Green Bay, Wis., Mar. 8, 1916; s. Raymond Adolf and Emma J. (Schley) S.; m. Margaret Elizabeth Roberts, Aug. 22, 1943; children: Janet R., Raymond J., Joan C., Margaret Ann. BS in Elec. and Agrl. Engring., U. Wis., 1938; MS in Elec. and Agrl. Engring., Rutgers U., 1940; postgrad. in elec. engring., Cornell U., 1940-41, Poly Inst. Bklyn., 1947-51, U. Ill., 1941-42; SM in Indsl. Mgmt., MIT, 1955; postgrad. in elec. engring., Syracuse U., 1956-59, Fed. Exec. Inst., 1982. Registered profl. engr., N.J. Dir. rsch. and devel. Rome Air (Elec.) Devel. Ctr., N.Y., 1955-59; tech. dir. def./space Westinghouse Elec. Corp. Hdqrs., Washington, 1959-63; mgr. adv. tech. and missiles Fed. Sys. IBM, Owego, N.Y., 1963-68; gen. mgr., pres. Schilling Industries, Galesville, Wis., 1968-71; mgr. sys. design U.S. Army Adv. Sys. Concepts Agy., Alexandria, Va., 1971-74; mgr. gun fire control sys. Naval Sea Sys. Command, Washington, 1974-80; tech. dir. office R&D U.S. Coast Guard Hdqrs., Washington, 1980-86; cons. in field, 1986—; govt. cons. electronics, Dept. Def. R & D Bd., 1949-54; indsl. cons. missile/space Aerospace Industries Assn., 1959-63; chmn. profl. sci. com. Rome Air Devel. Ctr., 1956-59; mem. nat. com. Engring. Mgmt. Inst. Elec. Engring., N.Y.C., 1956-59. Author tech. reports and articles; patentee target position indicator. Vol. Annandale Christian Cmty. for Action (Va.), 1973—; mem. winterset Civic Assn., Annandale, 1971—. Fellow Alfred P. Sloan Found. MIT, 1954-55. Mem. IEEE (sr. life, sec., vice chmn., chmn. 1956-59, Recognition award 1959), Am. Def. Preparedness Assn.(chmn. So. Tier Empire Post 1967-68, recognition award 1968), NSPE, N.Y. Acad. Scis., Soc. Sloan Fellows MIT, Mason, Rotary, Shriners. Home: PV203 7442 Spring Village Dr Springfield VA 22150-4444

SCHLEIFER, KARL HEINZ, microbiologist; b. Freising, Bavaria, Germany, Feb. 10, 1939; s. Karl and Else (Weissler) C.; m. Gerti Radlmair, Feb. 1, 1969; children: Bernd, Susanne. PhD, Tech. U., Munich, 1967; Habilitation, U. Munich, 1971. Asst. prof. Tech. U., Munich, 1967-69, prof., 1974—, head, dept. microbiology, 1974—; postdoctoral fellow Rockefeller U., N.Y.C., 1969-70; assoc. prof. U. Munich, 1971-74. Editor/co-editor five books; contbr. numerous articles to profl. jours. Recipient Koerber prize for European Scientific Rsch., 1995. Mem. Am. Acad. Microbiology, Acad. Scis. Goettingen, Royal Acad. Vet. Scis. (Madrid). Office: Tech U Dept Microbiology, Am Hochanger 4, D-85350 Freising Germany

SCHLEIFER, THOMAS C., management consultant, author, lecturer. BS in Constrn. Mgmt., E. Carolina U., 1989, MS in Constrn. Mgmt., 1990; PhD, Herriot-Watt U., 1994. Owner Schleifer Bros., Inc., Hanover, N.J., 1964-75; owner, founder, pres., internat. cons. firm CMA Cons. Group, Morristown, N.J., 1976-86; dir. appropriate tech., vol. Habitat for Humanity, Americus, Ga., 1987-88; assoc. prof. Ariz. State U., Tempe, 1990-92; eminent scholar Del E. Webb Sch. Constrn., Ariz. State U., 1993-94; vis. prof. East Carolina U., 1989-90; former chmn. continuing edn. com. Associated Gen. Contractors Am.; lectr. and presenter in field. Author: Construction Contractors' Survival Guide, 1990, Glossary of Suretyship and Related Terms, 1981; contbr. articles to profl. jours. Bd. advisors Habitat for Humanity Internat., 1989—. Mem. Am. Inst. Constructors (bd. dirs. 1990-93), Am. Arbitration Assn. (N.J. adv. coun. 1968-75), Am. Concrete Inst. (edn. com. 1972-76), Associated Gen. Contractors Am. (chmn. continuing edn. com. 1970-76), Assn. Advancement 3d World (internat. adv. coun. 1988-91). Home and Office: 5625 N 75th Pl Scottsdale AZ 85250-6471

SCHLEIFFENBAUM, BORIS EUGEN, hematologist; b. Bochum, Germany, Aug. 14, 1956; s. Horst and Eva (Hannelore) S.; m. Verena Maria Husler, Apr. 29, 1983; children: Lea, Eva-Maria. MD, U. Munich, 1983. Intern medicine Kantonsspital Luzern (Switzerland), 1984-85; intern medicine U. Zurich, 1989-91, intern hematology, 1992-93, chief resident, 1993-99; med. dir. Bern Blood Bank and Transfusion Ctr., 2000—. Pathology fellow U. Munich, 1983-84, Rsch. fellow, 1985-89, Harvard/Dana-Farber Cancer Inst. Rsch. fellow, Boston, 1991-92; recipient 1st prize Swiss Soc. Hematology, 1991, Habilitation award, 1996. Office: Bern Blood Bank, Wankdorfstr 10, CH-3014 Bern Switzerland

SCHLENKER, CLAIRE, physicist, educator; b. Grenoble, France, Sept. 8, 1940; d. Samuel and Anna (Sapetti) Schnaider, m. Michel Schlenker, Dec. 21, 1963; children: Martine, Jean-Marc, Philippe. Licence de Physique, U de Grenoble, France, 1963, 3éme cycle, 1963, Doctorat, 1970. lectr. statistical physics, irreversible thermodynamics, quantum mechanics, elec. and magnetic properties of matter, transport phenomena, solid state physics, superconductivity. Author of more than 180 publs., editor of 6 books, reviewer for Jour. Physique-France, Solid State Comm., J. of Solid State Chemistry, Zeitschrift für Physik. Dir. Lab. Et Propr. Electronique Solides du CNRS, Grenoble, 1985-88, Ecole Nat. Sup. de Physique, INPG, Grenoble, 1997—, couns. Ministry Higher Edn., 1993-96. Decorated chevalier Legion of Honor. Mem. Société Française de Physique Bureau Matière Condensée, Conseil Nat. Achievements include rsch. in condensed matter physics including metal/non-metal transition. low dimensional conductors-charge density waves, transition metal oxides, superconductivity, creation of the Higher European Rsch. Course for users of Large Exptl. Sys. (Hercules), Grenoble, 1997—. Home: 22 Domaine des Plantées, 38330 Biviers France Office: Ecole Nat Sup de Grenoble, Rue de la Houille Blanche, 38402 Saint Martin d'Heres Cedex, France Office: CNRS-LEPES, BP 166, 38042 Grenoble Cedex 9, France

SCHLENKER, MARK FREDERICK, lawyer; b. Des Moines, May 20, 1954; s. Ralph Frederick and Charlotte Jane (Peterson) S.; m. Leila C. Badre, Oct. 10, 1987; children: Hannah, Paul. BS in Econs., Iowa State U., 1975; JD, Creighton U., Omaha, Nebr., 1978. Bar: Iowa 1978, U.S. Dist. Ct. (no. and so. dist.) Iowa 1978, U.S. Tax Ct. 1978, U.S. Supreme Ct. 1992. Asst. atty. gen. Iowa Dept. Justice, Des Moines, 1978-79; ptnr. Hall-Schlenker, Indianola, 1980—; hon. consul Fed. Rep. of Germany in State of Iowa, 1994—. Editor Environmental Law Manual, 1992-94. Mem. Rotary (chpt. pres. 1991). Republican. Methodist. Avocation: amateur radio operator. Office: Hall-Schlenker 115 S Howard St Indianola IA 50125-2513

SCHLENSKA, GÜNTER KUNO, neurologist; b. Cologne, Mar. 7, 1944; s. Johann and Ilse (Sommerlade) S.; m. Karin Kratz, Feb. 9, 1973; children: Katrin, Anke. Dr. med., U. Hamburg, 1969. Asst. physician U. Marburg, 1969-76, neurologist, 1976-79, asst. med. dir., 1979-80; head physician dept. neurology Nieders. Landeskranken-haus, Hildesheim, 1980—; head physician stroke unit St. Bernward Krankenhaus Hildesheim, 1999—; prof. neurology Medizinische Hochschule Hannover, 1991—. Contbr. articles to profl. jours. Mem. Deutsche Gesellschaft für Neurologie, Deutsche Gesellschaft für Klinische Neurophysiologie. Home: Blauer Kamp 23, 31141 Hildesheim Germany Office: Nieders Landeskrankenhaus, Goslarsche Landstr 60, 31135 Hildesheim Germany

SCHLENSKER, GARY CHRIS, landscaping company executive; b. Indpls., Nov. 12, 1950; s. Christian Frederick and Doris Jean (Shannon) S.; m. Ann Marie Tobin, Oct. 27, 1979; children: Laura Patricia, Christian Frederick II. Student, Purdue U., 1969-71, 73; A Bus. Adminstrn., Clark Coll., 1979; cert. emergency med. technician, Ind. Vocat. Tech. Inst., Lafayette, 1974. Salesman Modern Reference, Indpls., 1971; orthopaedic technician St. Elizabeth Hosp., Lafayette, 1973-75, asst. mgr. ambulance service, 1975; sales asst. Merck, Sharpe & Dohme, Oakbrook, Ill., 1975-77; v.p. Turfco, Inc., Zionsville, Ind., 1977-84; pres. Turfscape, Inc., Zionsville, 1984—; speaker Midwest Turf Conf., 1991. With U.S. Army, 1971-73. Mem. ASTM (erosion control subcom.), BBB, Nat. Fedn. Ind. Bus., Midwest Turf Found., Ohio Turf Found., Internat. Erosion Control Assn. (bd. dirs Gt. Lakes chpt. 1998—), U.S. C. of C., Ind. C. of C., Zionsville C. of C., Phi Kappa Psi. Presbyterian. Avocations: woodworking, golf.

SCHLEPPY, CHARLES-ANDRE, pharmacist; b. Le Locle, Neuchatel, Switzerland, Dec. 22, 1946; s. Charles Schleppy and Georgette Schleppy-Dubois; m. Genevieve Jaccoud, Aug. 31, 1991. Diploma in pharmacy, U. Neuchatel, Lausanne, Switzerland, 1971; D in Pharmacy, U. Lausanne, 1975. Asst. pharmacist U. Lausanne, 1971-74; pharmacist Galencia S.A., Berne, Switzerland, 1974-77; head pharmacist Hosp., La Chaux-de-Fonds, Switzerland, 1978—; clin. pharmacist Hosp., La Chaux-de-Fonds, 2000—. Contbr. articles to profl. jours. Recipient First prize of interpretation Societe Suisse de Pedagogie Musicale, 1962, 64. Mem. Gesellschaft schweizerischer Amts- und Spitalapotheker, Soc. Sci. Orgn. Pharmacy Switzerland, Soc. Suisse de Pharmacie, N.Y. Acad. Scis. Avocations: organ, piano, Harpischord. E-mail: schleppyca@bluewin.ch and Charles-Andre.Schleppy@ne.ch. Fax: 032 967 21 78. Office: Hosp Pharmacy, Chasseral 20, 2300-CH La Chaux-de-Fonds Switzerland

SCHLESINGER, ARTHUR (MEIER), JR., writer, educator; b. Columbus, Ohio, Oct. 15, 1917; s. Arthur M. and Elizabeth (Bancroft) S.; m. Marian Cannon, 1940 (div. 1970); children: Stephen Cannon, Katharine Kinderman, Christina, Andrew Bancroft; m. Alexandra Emmet, July 9, 1971; 1 son, Robert Emmet Kennedy. AB summa cum laude, Harvard U., 1938, mem. Soc. of Fellows, 1939-42; postgrad. (Henry fellow), Cambridge (Eng.) U., 1938-39; hon. degrees, Muhlenberg Coll., 1950, Bethany Coll., 1956, U. N.B., 1966, New Sch. Social Rsch., 1966, Tusculum Coll., 1966, R.I. Coll., 1969, Aquinas Coll., 1971, Western New Eng. Coll., 1974, Ripon Coll., 1976, Iona Coll., 1977, Utah State U., 1978, U. Louisville, 1978, Northeastern U., 1981, Rutgers U., 1982, SUNY-Albany, 1984, U. N.H., 1985, U. Oxford, 1987, Akron U., 1987, Brandeis U., 1988, U. Mass., Boston, 1990, Hofstra U., 1991, Adelphi U., 1992, Dominican Coll., 1992, Mt. Ida Coll., 1993, Middlebury Coll., 1994, Roosevelt U., 1995, Lynn U., 1996, No. Ill. U., 1996, City U. N.Y., 1999. With OWI, 1942-43, OSS, 1943-45; assoc. prof. history Harvard U., 1946-54, prof., 1954-62; vis. fellow Inst. Advanced Study, Princeton, N.J., 1966; Schweitzer prof. humanities CUNY, 1966-95; cons. Econ. Cooperation Adminstrn., 1948, Mutual Security Adminstrn., 1951-52; spl. asst. to Pres. of U.S., 1961-64; mem. jury Cannes Film Festival, 1964; mem. Adlai E. Stevenson campaign staff, 1952, 56; chmn. Franklin Delano Roosevelt Four Freedoms Found., 1983—; trustee Robert F. Kennedy Meml., Twentieth Century Fund.; adv. Arthur and Elizabeth Schlesinger Library. Author: Orestes A. Brownson, 1939, The Age of Jackson, 1945 (Pulitzer prize for history 1946), The Vital Center, 1949, (with R.H. Rovere) The General and the President, 1951, The Age of Roosevelt Vol. I: The Crisis of the Old Order 1919-1933, 1957 (Francis Parkman prize Soc. Am. Historians 1957, Frederic Bancroft prize Columbia U. 1958), The Age of Roosevelt Vol. II: The Coming of the New Deal, 1958, The Age of Roosevelt Vol. III: The Politics of Upheaval, 1960, Kennedy or Nixon: Does It Make Any Difference?, 1960, The Politics of Hope, 1963, (with John Blum) The National Experience, 1963, A Thousand Days, 1965 (Pulitzer prize for biography 1966, Nat. Book award 1966), The Bitter Heritage, 1967, The Crisis of Confidence, 1969, The Imperial Presidency, 1973 (Sidney Hillman Found. award 1973), Robert Kennedy and His Times, 1978 (Nat. Book award 1979), The Cycles of American History, 1986, The Disuniting of America, 1991, A Life in The 20th Century: I, Innocent Beginnings, 2000; contbr. articles to mags. and newspapers; film reviewer: Show mag, 1962-64, Vogue, 1967-72, Saturday Rev., 1977-80, Am. Heritage, 1981-82; editor: Harvard Guide to American History, 1954, Guide to Politics, 1954, Paths to American Thought, 1963, The Promise of American Life, 1967, The Best and the Last of Edwin O'Connor, 1970, History of American Presidential Elections 1789-1972, 1971, 1972-1984, 1986, The Coming to Power, 1972, The Dynamics of World Power: A Documentary History of United States Foreign Policy 1945-1973, 1973, History of U.S. Political Parties, 1973, Congress Investigates, 1975, Running for President, 1994; screenwriter: (teleplay) The Journey of Robert F. Kennedy. Served with AUS, 1945. Decorated comdr. Order of Orange-Nassau (The Netherlands), Ordem del Libertador (Venezuela); recipient Nat. Inst. and Am. Acad. Arts and Letters gold medal in history and biography, 1967, Ohio Gov.'s award for history, 1973, Eugene V. Debs award in edn., 1974, Fregene prize for lit. (Italy), 1983, U. Thant award for Internat. Understanding, 1998; Guggenheim fellow, 1946; Am. Acad. Arts and Letters grantee, 1946. Mem. Am. Hist. Assn., Orgn. Am. Historians, Soc. Am. Historians (pres. 1989-92), Am. Acad. and Inst. Arts and Letters (pres. 1981-84, chancellor 1984-87), Am. Philos. Soc., Mass. Hist. Soc., Colonial Soc. Mass., Russian Acad. Scis., Franklin and Eleanor Roosevelt Inst. (co-chmn. 1983—), ACLU, Coun. Fgn. Rels., Ams. for Dem. Action (nat. chmn. 1952-54), Century Assn., Knickerbocker Club, Phi Beta Kappa. Democrat. Unitarian. Home: 455 E 51st St New York NY 10022-6474

SCHLESINGER, HELMUT FRANZ, banker; b. Penzberg, Bavaria, Germany, Sept. 4, 1924; m. Carola Mager, 1949; 4 children. Dr., U. Munich, 1951; D (hon.), Johann Wolfgang Goethe U., Frankfurt am Main, 1981, Georg August U., Göttingen, 1981, U. St. Gallen, 1993. With Ifo Inst. Econ. Rsch., Munich, 1949-52; mem. staff Bank deutscher Länder (now Deutsche Bundesbank), Frankfurt, Germany, 1952—, head rsch. and stats. dept., 1964-72, mem. bd., 19725, dep. gov., 1980-91, gov., 1991-93; bd. dirs. METRO AG; hon. prof. U. Adminstrv., Speyer; guest prof. Princeton U. and Humboldt U., Berlin, 1995-98; mem. sci. adv. coun. Ministry of Econs. With German mil., 1943-45. Recipient Ludwig Erhard Prize, 1981, Grand Cross, Order of Merit of Federal Republic of Germany and Order of Merit of Land Hesse, high decorations from the heads of state in and outside of Europe. Avocations: art, music, mountaineering. Home: An der Heide 25, 61440 Oberursel 50, Germany

SCHLESINGER, IZCHAK M., psychology educator; b. Cologne, Germany, Aug. 25, 1926; s. Simon S. and Paula (Schloss) S.; m. Avigail Glickman, Apr. 13, 1959; children: Shlomo-Shimon, Ayala, Noam-Eliahu. BA, Hebrew U., Jerusalem, 1955, PhD, 1964; MA, NYU, N.Y.C., 1958. Sr. rsch. assoc. Israel Inst. Applied Social Rsch., Jerusalem, 1966-82;

from lectr. to sr. lectr. Hebrew U., Jerusalem, 1966-71, assoc. prof., 1971-77, prof., 1977—; prof. emeritus, 1994—. Co-author: A New Dictionary of Sign Language, 1977; contbr. articles to profl. jours. Recipient Joseph H. and Belle Braun Chair in Psychology, 1990. Mem. Internat. Assn. for Study Child Lang. (v.p. 1981-89). Office: Hebrew U Psychology Dept, Mt Scopus, 91905 Jerusalem Israel

SCHLESINGER, JAMES RODNEY, economist; b. N.Y.C., Feb. 15, 1929; s. Julius and Rhea (Rogen) S.; m. Rachel Mellinger, June 19, 1954; children: Cora K., Charles L., Ann R., William F., Emily, Thomas S., Clara, James Rodney. A.B. summa cum laude, Harvard U., 1950, A.M., 1952, Ph.D., 1956. Asst. prof., then assoc. prof. U. Va., 1955-63; sr. staff mem. RAND Corp., 1963-67; dir. strategic studies, 1967-69; asst. dir. Bur. Budget, 1969, acting dep. dir., 1969-70; asst. dir. Office Mgmt. and Budget, 1970-71; chmn. AEC, 1971-73; dir. CIA, Feb.-July 1973; U.S. sec. def., 1973-75; vis. scholar Johns Hopkins Sch. Advanced Internat. Studies, 1976-77; asst. to Pres., 1977; sec. Dept. Energy, 1977-79; counselor Ctr. for Strategic and Internat. Studies, Georgetown U., 1979—; sr. adv. Lehman Bros., 1979—; cons. in field. Author: The Political Economy of National Security, 1960, America at Century's End, 1989; co-author: Issues in Defense Economics, 1967. Frederick Sheldon prize fellow Harvard U., 1950-51. Mem. Phi Beta Kappa. Republican. Presbyterian. Office: Lehman Bros 800 Connecticut Ave NW Ste 1200 Washington DC 20006-2709*

SCHLESINGER, JOHN RICHARD, film, opera and theater director; b. London, Feb. 16, 1926; s. Bernard Edward and Winifred Henrietta (Regensburg) S. B.A., Balliol Coll., Oxford U., 1950. Dir. BBC TV, 1958-60. Dir. feature films including Terminus, 1961 (Golden Lion award Venice Film Festival, Brit. Acad. award), A Kind of Loving, 1962 (Golden Bear award Berlin Film Festival), Billy Liar, 1963, Darling, 1965 (N.Y. Critics award, Acad. nomination), Far From the Madding Crowd, 1967, Midnight Cowboy, 1968 (Acad. award best dir., best film, Brit. Acad. award best dir., best film), Sunday Bloody Sunday, 1970 (David di Donatello award), Day of the Locust, 1974, Marathon Man, 1976, Yanks, 1978 (Nat. Bd. Rev. award, New Std. award), Honky Tonk Freeway, 1980, The Falcon and the Snowman, 1983, The Believers, 1986, Madame Sousatzka, 1988, Pacific Heights, 1991, The Innocent, 1993, Cold Comfort Farm (BBC/ Thames), 1994, Eye for an Eye, 1995, Sweeney Todd, 1997, TV films including Separate Tables, 1982, An Englishman Abroad (BBC), 1983 (David Wark Griffith award for best TV film, Brit. Acad. award, Best Single Drama, Broadcasting Press Guild award, Best Single Drama, Best Fiction Film, Barcelon Film Festival), A Question of Attribution (PBS), 1992 (Brit. Acad. award best single drama); plays including Days in the Trees, 1966, I and Albert, 1972, Heartbreak House, 1975, Julius Caesar, 1977, True West, 1981, Separate Tables, 1982, operas including Les Contes d'Hoffmann, 1980-81 (Soc. West End Theatre award), Der Rosenkavalier, 1984-85, Un Ballo in Maschera, 1989 (Salzburg Festival); assoc. dir. Nat. Theatre, London, 1973-80. Served with Royal Engrs., 1943-48. Recipient David di Donatello Spl. Dir. award, 1980, Shakespeare prize, 1981, The Hamptons Internat. Film Festival Disting. Achievement award, 1995; BAFTA fellow, 1995. Office: United Talent Agy Attn Andrew Cannava 9560 Wilshire Blvd Ste 500 Beverly Hills CA 90212-2427

SCHLESINGER, KARL-GEORG, mathematician, researcher; b. Berlin, Feb. 27, 1968; s. Günter and Anneliese (Böhmer) S. Diploma in math., U. Wuppertal, Germany, 1993; PhD in Math., U. Wuppertal, 1996. Rschr. U. Wuppertal, 1996-97, 99—, Erwin Schroedinger Inst., Vienna, Austria, 1997-98, 99, Inst. des Hautes Etudes Scientifique, Paris, 1999. Author: Generalized Manifolds, 1997; contbr. articles to profl. jours. Postdoctoral fellow German Acad. Exch. Svc., Bonn, 1997. Mem. Internat. Assn. for Math. Physics, German Math. Soc., Austrian Math. Soc., N.Y. Acad. Scis. Avocations: attending opera performances, concerts and theatre, alpine hiking. Home: Stuttbergstr 12, 42107 Wuppertal Germany Office: Univ Wuppertal, Gaussstr 20, 42097 Wuppertal Germany

SCHLESINGER, PHILIPPE, cardiologist; b. St. German Enlaye, France, Nov. 17, 1950; s. Jena Pieree and Elisabeth (Gruel) S.; m. Marie Christine Muscat, Aug. 9, 1973; children: Thomas, Anne-Lise. Sport medicine, Tours, France, 1977; cardiologie, Paris, 1980; D in medicine, Tours, France, 1981. Intern Tours, 1976-79; resident Lab. Ifsen, Paris, 1982; cardiologist Paris, 1982-95, Cabinet, Bastia, France, 1995—. Mem. Group de Rsch. in Cardiology (pres. 1996), Assn. Cardiologists Implanteures de Pacermaker Bastia (gen. sec. 1997). Home: 113 Marina di Fiori, 20137 Porto-Vecchio France Office: Cabinet de cardiologie, 5 Rue Jean Pierre Gaffory, 20600 Bastia France

SCHLESINGER, SANFORD JOEL, lawyer; b. N.Y.C., Feb. 8, 1943; s. Irving and Ruth (Rubin) S.; children: Merideth, Jarrod, Alexandra; m. Suzanne Beth Mangold, 1994; 1 stepchild, Mariel Mangold. BS in Govt. with hons., Columbia U., 1963; JD, Fordham U., 1966. Bar: N.Y. 1966, U.S. Dist. Ct. (so. and ea. dists.) N.Y. 1967, U.S. Ct. Appeals (2d cir.) 1968, U.S. Ct. Internat. Trade 1969, U.S. Tax Ct. 1993, U.S. Supreme Ct. 1978. Assoc. Frankenthaler & Kohn, N.Y.C., 1966-67; asst. atty. gen. trusts and estates bur. charitable found. div. State of N.Y., N.Y.C., 1967-69; ptnr. Rose & Schlesinger, N.Y.C., 1969-81, Goldshmidt, Oshatz, Powsner & Saft, N.Y.C., 1981-85; ptnr., head trusts and estates dept. Shea & Gould, N.Y.C., 1985-93; ptnr., head wills and estates dept. Kaye, Scholer, Fierman, Hays & Handler, LLP, N.Y.C., 1993—; ptnr. co-chair family owned bus. practice group Kaye, Scholer, Fierman, Hays & Handler LLP, N.Y.C., 1993—; adj. faculty Columbia U. Sch. Law, 1989-94; adj. prof. N.Y. Law Sch., 1978—; adj. prof. grad. program in estate planning U. Miami Grad. Sch. Law, 1995—; mem. estate planning adv. com. Practising Law Inst., 1990—; bd. advisors and contbrs. Jour. of S Corp. Taxation, 1989-96; lectr. in field; condr. workshops in field. Author: Estate Planning for the Elderly Client, 1984, Planning for the Elderly or Incapacitated Client, 1993; columnist, mem. editl. bd. Estate Planning mag., 1995—; contbr. articles to profl. jours. Mem. adv. bd. Inst. Fed. Taxation NYU, 1988-96, chmn., 1993-94; mem. legis adv. com. Scarsdale (N.Y.) Sch. Bd., 1981-83, mem. nominating com., 1979-82; pres. dist. 17 N.Y.C. Cmty. Sch. Bd., 1970-71; mem. fin. and estate planning adv. bd. Commerce Clearing House, 1988—; mem. adv. bd. Tax Hotline, 1997—. Fellow Am. Coll. Trust and Estate Counsel; mem. ABA (chmn. social security and other govt. entitlements com. 1990-91, chmn. probate and trust com.-estate planning, drafting charitable giving coms., 1992-94), Internat. Acad. Estate & Trust Law (Academician 1992—), Nat. Acad. Elder Law Attys., Bklyn. Bar Assn., Assn. of Bar of City of N.Y., N.Y. State Bar Assn. (treas. trusts and estates sect. 1991-92, sec. trusts and estates sect. 1992-93, chmn. trusts and estates sect. 1994-95, chmn. exec. com. 1st jud. dist. 1987-91, jour. bd. editors 1995—). Avocations: baseball, writing. Office: Kaye Scholer Fierman Hays & Handler LLP 425 Park Ave New York NY 10022-3506

SCHLEUSING, MICHAEL, anesthesiologist; b. Chemnitz, Saxony, Germany, Apr. 1, 1934; s. Adalbert and Sabine (Böhme) S.; m. Rosemary Müller, Oct. 6, 1965; children: Eva, Bettina. MD, Düsseldorf (Germany) U., 1962; PhD, Leipzig (Germany) U., 1991. SHO Inst. Pathology, Chemnitz, 1958-60, Dist. Hosps. in Ludwigsburg, Hall and Rottweil, Germany, 1962-64, Clin. for Thoracical Surgery, Zschadrass, Germany, 1965-66, Univ. Tchg. Hosp., Berlin-Buch, Germany, 1967; cons. Dist. Hosp., Pasewalk, Germany, 1968-69, Altenburg, Germany, 1970-91; cons. Altenburg, Germany, 1992—; dir. Emergency Ambulance Svc., Altenburg, 1979-91. Contbr. articles to profl. publs. Mem. East German Parliament, 1990. Mem. NAW Arztebund (chmn. Thuringia), German Acad. Acupuncture. Mem. Christian Democratic Party. Evangelical Lutheran. Avocation: photography. Home: Riegenstr 7, D-04600 Altenburg Germany Office: Wettiner Str 2, D-04600 Altenburg Germany

SCHLICH, ROLAND EMILE, research director; b. Metz, Moselle, France, Jan. 17, 1932; s. Adolphe Francois and Camille Mignon (Boehm) S.; m. Michelle Binder, Apr. 26, 1958; children: Josiane, Pascal, Thomas. Lic. Scis. Physiques, U. Strasbourg, France, 1955; diploma engring., Inst. Physique du Globe, Strasbourg, 1956; Doctorat d'Etat, U. Paris VI, 1974; Prix Tchihatchef, Acad. Scis., Paris, 1975; Prix Barrabé, Geol. Soc. France, Paris, 1976; Prix Léon Lutaud, Acad. Scis., Paris, 1996. Cert. geophysicist. Mem. French Antarctic Expdn., 1956-58; attaché de recherche Nat. Ctr. Sci. Rsch. (CNRS), Paris, 1958-65; chargé de recherche CNRS, Paris, 1965-73, maître de recherche, 1974-76, dir. recherche, 1977-81; dir. recherche titulaire CNRS, Strasbourg, 1981-97, dir. recherche émérite, 1998—; dir. Ecole et Observatoire de Physique du Globe, Strasbourg, 1980-96; dep. dir. Institut de Physique du Globe, Paris, 1975-79; dir. Marine Geophys. Lab., Paris-Strasbourg, 1975-96. Author: Structure et âge de l'océan Indien, 1975; author, editor: Proceedings of the Ocean Drilling Program, 1972-74, 1989-92; contbr. articles to internat. jours. Recipient Chevalier de l'Ordre de l'Etoile Noire, 1958, Chevalier-Officier de l'Ordre Nat. du Mérite, 1968-85, Chevalier de la Légion d'Honneur, 1994. Mem. European Union Geoscis. (treas. 1981—, chief exec. 2000—), Com. Nat. Français de Géodésie et Géophysique (treas. 1972—), Sci. Com. Antarctic Rsch. (chmn. fin. com. 1990—, v.p. 1998——), Am. Geophys. Union, Sci. Com. Oceanographic Rsch., Commn. Nat. Française pour l'UNESCO. Roman Catholic. Avocations: music, oenology, stock exchange. Office: Ecole et Observatre Physiq du Globe, 5 rue René Descartes, 67084 Strasbourg France

SCHLICHT, EKKEHART JOHANNES, economics educator; b. Kiel, Germany, Apr. 30, 1945; s. Robert Ferdinand and Meta Anna (Zilz) S.; m. Gerlinde Schlicht, May 25, 1996; children: Robert, Philipp, Emmi, Lotte. Diploma in econs., U. Regensberg, Fed. Republic Germany, 1969, D in Econs., 1971. Asst. prof. U. Regensberg, 1969-75; prof. econs. U. Bielefeld, Fed. Republic Germany, 1976-80; mem. Inst. for Advanced Stdy, Princeton, N.J., 1985-86; prof. econs. Tech. U. Darmstadt, Fed. Republic Germany, 1980-93, U. Munich, Fed. Republic Germany, 1993—; fellow Inst. for Advanced Study, Berlin, 1997-98, Instnl. and Theoretical Econs., 1993-99. Home: Pettenkoferstr 17, 80336 Munchen Germany Office: U Munich, Schackstr 4, 80539 Munchen 22 Germany

SCHLICHTING, FRANK, physicist, researcher; b. Jesteburg, Hamburg, Germany, Apr. 26, 1968; s. Werner and Astrid (Mauerhoff) S.; m. Vanessa Irit Landschoof, July 22, 1993; 1 child, Celina Miriam. Diploma in physics, Tech. U., Darmstadt, Germany, 1995; Dr-Ing/PhD in Electron Spectroscopy, Tech. U. Berlin, 1999. Programmer, software cons. Daimler-Benz, Darmstadt, 1989-95; sys. analyst process and IT/IS mgmt./chief coord. tech watch Volkswagen Autostadt GmbH, Wolfsburg, Germany, 2000—; rschr. Tech. U., Darmstadt, 1989-95, U. Calif., Berkeley, 1993; instr. physics, network and software cons. Tech. U., Berlin, 1995-2000. Group leader, organizer Student's Lang. Exchange program, Winsen, Germany, 1985-91. With German Army, 1987-88. Mem. German Physics Assn., German Assn. for Electronmicroscopy. Achievements include the co-development and construction of a miniaturized Moessbauer spectrometer for extraterrestrial missions, Mars in 1998. Home: Parksiedlung Spruch 4, 12349 Berlin Germany

SCHLICKE, PAUL VAN WATERS, English educator, writer; b. Charleston, S.C., Apr. 21, 1943; arrived in Scotland, 1971; s. Carl Paul and Hilda Meek (Hinckley) S.; m. Priscilla Adelaide Smith, June 14, 1967 (div. Jan. 1966); children: Edward Carl Laurence, Alexander Paul; m. Judith Ross Napier, April 26, 1996; 1 child, Frances Ross. BA, Stanford U., 1965; student, U. Wash., 1965-67; postgrad., U. Calif., San Diego, 1967-71; PhD, U. Wash., 1971. Lectr. U. Aberdeen, Scotland, 1971-89, sr. lectr., 1989—. Author: Dickens and Popular Entertainment, 1985, The Old Curiosity Shop: An Annotated Bibliography, 1988; editor: Oxford Reader's Companion to Dickens, 1999. Rsch. fellow Nat. Def. Edn. Act, 1967-70, U. Aberdeen, 1993-94, Arts and Humanities Rsch. Bd., 1999-00. Mem. Dickens Soc. (pres. 1994), Dickens Fellowship, Soc. for Theatre Rsch. Avocation: athletics. Home: Hill Cottage, Thainstone Inverurie, AB51 5NT Aberdeen Scotland Office: Dept English Univ Aberdeen, AB24 2UB Aberdeen Scotland

SCHLIFFER, WOLFGANG, computer scientist; b. Darmstadt, Germany, Apr. 16, 1935. Dipl-Ing, Tech. U., Darmstadt, 1964. Computer scientist Deutsches Rechenzentrum, Darmstadt, 1964-73, Gesellschaft für Mathematik und Datenverarbeitung, Darmstadt, Germany, 1973-74; head Computer Ctr. U Würzburg, Germany, 1974—. Mem. Assn. for Computing Machinery, Gesellschaft für Informatik Germany, Arbeitskreis der Leiter Wissenschaftlicher Rechenzentren Germany. Office: Rechenzentrum U Wuerzburg, Am Hubland, Wuerzburg 97074, Germany

SCHLINDWEIN, FERNANDO SOARES, engineer, educator; b. Porto Alegre, Brazil, Mar. 26, 1956; arrived in Eng., 1992; s. Edvino and Maria de Lourdes (Soares) S.; m. Walkiria Santos Silva, Sept. 26, 1985; 1 child, Alexandre Santos. B Engring., Fed. U. Rio Grande de Sul, Brazil, 1979; MS, Fed. U. Rio de Janeiro, 1982; DSc, Fed U. Rio De Janeiro, Eng., 1992; PhD, U. Leicester, Eng., 1990, DSc, 1992. Cert. in biomed. engring. Lectr. Fed. U. Rio de Janeiro, 1982-92, U. Leicester, 1992—; mem. sci. program com. World Congress of Biomed. Engring., Rio de Janeiro, 1994. Mem. internat. editl. bd. Brazilian Jour. Biomed. Engring.; contbr. articles to profl. jours. Overseas rsch. scholar Com. of vice-chancelors and principals, 1986-89, Rsch. Coun. of Brazil scholar, 1986-90. Mem. Inst. Physics and Engring. in Medicine, British Med. Ultrasound Soc., Brazilian Soc. Biomed. Engring. Roman Catholic. Avocation: football. Office: U Leicester Dept Engring, University Rd, LE1 7RH Leicester L-shire, England

SCHLINK, BERNHARD, lawyer, writer; b. Grossdornberg, Bielefeld, Germany, July 6, 1944. State exam. referendar, Baden-Württemberg, 1968; state exam. assessor, Baden-Württemberg, 1972; JD, Ruprecht Karl U., Heidelberg, 1975; Privatdozent, Albert-Ludwigs-U., Freiburg, 1981. Bar: Germany. Prof. Rheinische Friedrich-Wilhelms-U., Bonn, Germany, 1982-91, J. W. Goethe U., Frankfurt, Germany, 1991-92, Humboldt-U., Berlin, Germany, 1992—; cons. in field. Author: Abwägung im Verfassungsrecht, 1976, Gewaltenteilung in der Verwaltung, 1982, Staatsrecht II Grundrechte, 1985, 16th edit., 2000. Justice of Constnl. Ct. Nordrhein-Westfalen, Germany, 1988—. Office: Humboldt U, Unter den Linden 6, D-10099 Berlin Germany

SCHLOBACH, JOCHEN, French literature educator; b. Liegnitz, Feb. 6, 1938; s. Erich and Annemarie (Koch) S.; m. Ursula Gressung, July 12, 1948; children: Katja, Stefan. PhD, U. Saarbrucken, Germany, 1964. Asst. prof. U. Saarbrücken, 1964-74, prof., 1974—; associated prof. Paris III/Sorbonne Nouvelle, 1975-76; assoc. prof. U. Nice, 1979-80; vis. prof. U. Mo., 1992; dir. Inst. of Romance Langs., Saarbrücken; dean Dept. of Modern Langs., Saarbrücken, 1979-80. Author: Geschichte und Fiktion bei Roger Martin du Gard, 1965 (Strasbourg prize 1966), Zyklentheorie und Epochenmetaphorik, 1980; editor various publs. Mem. Internat. Soc. for Eighteenth-Century Studies (pres. 1995-99). Home: Richard-Wagner Str 87, D 66125 Saarbrucken Germany Office: U Saarlandes, D 66123 Saarbrucken Germany

SCHLOGL, KARL, administrator; b. Vienna, Austria, Jan. 28, 1955. MA in Polit. Sci. & History, 1991. Sec. of youth then cultural & organization sec. SPO, 1978-92; mem. Upper House Parliament, 1987-91, Nat. Assembly, 1991-94; mayor Lower Austrian Town Purkersdorf, 1989-97; min. Ministry State Fed. Chancellery, 1995-97, Ministry Interior, Vienna, 1997—. Office: Ministry Interior, Herrengasse 7, A-1014 Vienna Austria*

SCHLOTFELDT, WILLIAM WEST (BILL SCHLOTFELDT), real estate investor; b. Des Moines, July 9, 1925; s. Dale William and Agnes Bertha (Klewer) S.; m. Marjorie Alyce Signs, Aug. 11, 1946; children: Deborah Sue Jackson, Judith Ann Sample. Grad. H.S., Newton, Iowa. Svc. mgr., gen. mgr. Schlotfeldt Olds & Cadillac, Newton, 1946-56; sales mgr., exec. v.p. R.N. Duffy & Co. Real Estate, Houston, 1956-61; pres., gen. mgr. First Fannin Realty, Houston, 1961-79; ind. real estate investment broker Houston, 1979-91; buying, remodeling, leasing, selling Bay Area homes Bayou Vista, Tex., 1991—. Life dir. Houston Livestock Show & Rodeo, Houston, 1956-99, Houston Farm & Ranch Club, 1956-99; mem. bd., exec. com. Bill Williams Capon Charity Dinner, Houston, 1957-94. With USMC, 1942-46, South Pacific, 1950-52, Korea. Mem. Nat. Auto Dealers Assn. (v.p. young execs. 1952-56), Nat. Apt. Assn. (hon. life), Tex. Apt. Assn. (hon. life), Houston Apt. Assn. (hon. life pres.), 1st Marine Divsn. Assn. (dir., past co-chmn. nat. reunion 1980-99), Masons, Rotary (past pres.). Home and Office: 1200 Sailfish St Hitchcock TX 77563-2712

SCHLOTZHAUER, VIRGINIA HUGHES, parliamentary consultant; b. Washington, July 24, 1913; d. William and Secy Alice (Royston) Hughes; m. Elbert O. Schlotzhauer, May 16, 1936; children: Carol Schlotzhauer Hinds, Jean Schlotzhauer Sumner, Jude Schlotzhauer Wilson. AB in LS, George Washington U., 1934. Mem. libr. staff George Washington U., Washington, 1934; various clerical positions U.S. Govt., ARC, Washington, Phoenix, mid-1930s; cons. parliamentarian Washington, 1967—; cons. Nat. Parliamentarian Edn. Project for Colls. and Univs. sponsored by Am. Inst. Parliamentarians funded by William Randolph Hearst Found., 1993-95; presenter seminars. Author: A Parliamentarian's Book of Limericks, 1984; (with others) Parliamentary Opinions, 1982, Parliamentary Opinions II, 1992; primary contbr./cons. column Parliamentary Jour.; contbr. articles to profl. publs. Mem. steering and bylaws coms., sec. Nominating Conv. for Endorsement of Candidates for Bd. Edn., Montgomery County, Md., 1966; election reporter ABC-LWV, Prince George's County, Md., 1970s; v.p., bylaws com. Planned Parenthood Am., Prince George's County, late 1960s and 70s; group leader, bd. dirs., sec., trustee Potomac Area coun. Camp Fire Girls, Md. and D.C. area, 1940s and 50s; participant nonpartisan and Dem. polit. campaigns; judge various contests Future Bus. Leaders Am., Washington, 1970s. Co-recipient (parliamentary book in Spanish) Las Asociaciones y Normas Procesales para sus Asambleas Deliberativas by Lcda Dominga Rivera-Rivera dedicated in her honor, 1996. Mem. AAUW (life, named gift Bethesda-Chevy Chase br. 1962, named gift Md. divsn. 1972), Am. Inst. Parliamentarians (cert. profl. parliamentarian, mem. adv. coun. or bd. dirs. 1966—, pres. D.C. chpt. 1966-68, opinions com. 1974—, chmn. 1974-89, cons., name changed to Virginia Schlotzhauer D.C. chpt. 1984), Nat. Assn. Parliamentarians (ret. profl. registered parliamentarian), D.C. Assn. Parliamentarians (founding pres., 1st hon. pres., Achievement award 1976), Westerners. Avocations: travel, writing, poetry, gardening, Spanish language and culture. Home and Office: 9819 Indian Queen Point Rd Fort Washington MD 20744-6904

SCHLUMBERGER, JEAN FRANCOIS, pharmaceutical company administrator; b. Tonnerre, France, May 29, 1938; s. Jean and Marland Denise Schlumberger; m. Genevieve De Marcellus, June 16, 1967; children: Ulrich, Benoit, Delphine, Gregoire. MD, Faculty Medicine, Paris, 1970. Cardiologist, clin. rsch. dir. Lab. Delalande, Paris, 1970-77; internat. clin. rsch. dir. Pharmuka, Paris, 1978-83; med. dir. Schering, Paris, 1984-98; adminstr., bd. Oeuvres Hospitalières Françaises de l'Ordre de Malte, Paris, 1998—; part-time cardiologist asst. Broussais Hosp., Paris, 1967-82. Contbr. articles to profl. jours. Adv. bd. mem. Provie, Paris, 1984. Named Knight Malta Order. Mem. N.Y. Acad. Scis., Soc. Francaise de Cardiologie, Soc. Therapie (adv. bd. 1980-96). Avocations: golf, music, opera. Home: 17 Ave Theophile Gautier, 75016 Paris France Office: 92 rue du Ranelagh, 75016 Paris France

SCHLUMPF, FELIX, business analyst; b. Zurich, Switzerland, Feb. 27, 1964; s. René and Rosmarie (Burgbacher) S.; m. Priska Rueegg, Apr. 22, 1989. MS in Physics, ETH, Zurich, 1989; PhD, U. Zurich, 1992. Rsch. asst. U. Zurich, 1989-92; rsch. assoc. Stanford (Calif.) U., 1992-94, U. Md., College Park, 1994-95; actuary Swiss Re, Zurich, 1995-97, underwriter, 1997-99, mgr., 1998—, bus. analyst, 1999—. Contbr. articles to profl. jours. Rsch. grantee Swiss Nat. Sci. Found., 1989, 92. Mem. Am. Phys. Soc., Swiss Phys. Soc. Avocations: swimming, photography. Office: Swiss Re, Mythenquai 50/60, 8022 Zurich Switzerland

SCHLUNDT, JØRGEN, microbiologist; b. Copenhagen, Nov. 23, 1953; s. Erik and Mette (Jacobsen) S.; m. Jytte Schlundt, Aug. 24, 1985; children: Jakob, Marie, Katrine, Søren. DVM, Royal Vet. and Agr. U., Copenhagen, 1978, PhD, 1983. Lectr. Royal Vet. and Agr. U., Copenhagen, 1978-83; cons. Danish Environ. Agy., Copenhagen, 1983-85; bacteriologist Vet. Rsch. Lab., Harare, Zimbabwe, 1985-87; microbiologist Nat. Food Agy., Copenhagen, 1987-93, head microbiology sect., 1994-97; head divsn. microbiol. safety Vet. and Food Adminstrn., Copenhagen, 1997-99; coord. food safety program WHO, Geneva, 1999—; cons. Danish Aid, Harare, 1994-95. Co-author: Gene-Technology and Risk Assessment, 1992. Mem. Am. Soc. Microbiology. Avocations: coaching and refereeing basketball, tennis. E-mail: j.schlundt@libertysurf.fr. Home: 1771 bis Rue du Jura, 01170 Cessy France Office: WHO, 20 Ave Appia, CH1211 Geneva 27 Switzerland

SCHLUSSEL, JOSEPH LAZAR, diamond dealer, publisher; b. Munkacs, Czechoslovakia, Apr. 19, 1935; came to U.S., 1951; s. Charles C. and Fanny Schlussel; m. Rose Ickowitz, June 16, 1960; children: Fay, Amy. Student, Bklyn. Coll., 1954-55, CCNY, 1956-59. Mgr. Gemcutters, N.Y.C., 1960-61; broker Diamond Dealers Club, N.Y.C., 1961-69; pres. The Diamond Registry, N.Y.C., 1969—; editor and publisher The Diamond Registry Bulletin, 1969—; cons. Nat. Westminster Bank USA, E.A.B., Merchants Bank, Bankers Trust, Solomon Bros. Columnist Nat. Jeweler, 1978, Jewel Mag., 1988—; lectr. in field; guest on NBC Today, 1978; quoted in many major publs. as leading authority in field. Mem. Gemological Assn. Gt. Britain, Jewelry Industry Coun., Jewelers Vigilance Com., Jewelers Bd. of Trade, Diamond Dealers Club. Office: The Diamond Registry 580 5th Ave New York NY 10036-4701

SCHLUTER, GERALD EMIL, economist; b. Carroll, Iowa, June 9, 1942; s. Emil and Violetta Marie (Witt) S.; m. Carolyn Jean Finnell, Apr. 27, 1968; 1 child, Deborah Jean. BS, Iowa State U., 1964, MS, 1966, PhD, 1971. Rsch. asst. econs. Iowa State U., Ames, 1964-66, rsch. assoc. econs., 1966-70; agrl. economist USDA Econ. Rsch. Svc., Washington, 1970-84, supervisory economist, 1984—; econs. instr., Washington, 1983—, USDA Grad. Sch., Washington, 1979-83. Editor Agrl. Econs., 1984-87; author: (econs. series) Food & Fiber System, 1972; contbr. articles to profl. jours. Property com. Bethany Luth. Ch., Alexandria, Va., 1983-88; coach Lee-Mt. Vernon Soccer Assn., Alexandria, 1982-83. Mem. Am. Agrl. Econs. Assn., So Regional Sci. Assn. (coun. 1992-95), Am. Econ. Assn., Western Agrl. Econs. Assn., Northeastern Agrl. and Resource Econs. Assn., Food Distbn. Rsch. Soc. Avocations: fishing, youth soccer, personal computers. Home: 3877 Manzanita Pl Alexandria VA 22309-1479 Office: USDA Econ Rsch Svc 1800 M St NW Rm 2122 Washington DC 20036-5802

SCHLUTER, ROBERT ARVEL, physicist; b. Salt Lake City, Aug. 27, 1924; s. Arvel R. and Florence (Leach) S.; 1 child, Jonathan R. BS, U. Chgo., 1947, PhD, 1954. Rsch. assoc. U. Chgo. Inst. for Nuclear Studies, 1954; from instr. to asst. prof. MIT Lab. for Nuclear Studies, Cambridge, Mass., 1955-60; assoc. physicist Argonne (Ill.) Nat. Lab., 1961-72; prof. physics and astronomy Northwestern U., Evanston, Ill., 1961-92, emeritus, 1992—; guest scientist Brookhaven (N.Y.) Nat. Lab., 1955-70, Lawrence Radiation Lab., U. Calif., Berkeley, 1958-60; guest appointee Aspen Inst. for Humanities, 1967. Contbr. chpts. to books. Served with C.E., U.S. Army, 1943-46. Grantee AEC NSF, Dept. Energy, NASA, others. Mem. Am. Phys. Soc., Nat. Assn. Scholars. Achievements include first observation of K-Mesic X-rays, first measurement of Lambda Hyperon Magnetic Moment, first observation of 2d and 3d excited states of the proton. Avocations: mountain climbing and exploration, study of history. Home: 241 N Vine St Apt 902E Salt Lake City UT 84103-1971 Office: Northwestern U Dept Physics and Astronomy 2145 Sheridan Rd Dept And Evanston IL 60208-0834

SCHMADL, FRANZ WILHELM, financial management executive; b. Munich, Germany, Apr. 19, 1958; s. Balthasar And Rosemarie (Sartori-Graf) S.; m. Claudia Melinda Sandmann, May 30, 1987; children: Laura Antonela Rosalin, Stella Pamina Claudine, Melinda Franziska Maximiliane, Celia Amathea Christin, William Guy Lorenz Balthasar. MS, U. Munich, 1984. Rsch. analyst Dresdner Bank Frankfurt, Germany, 1984-85; head currency mgmt. ABDI Internat. Mgmt. Corp., Frankfurt and N.Y.C., 1985-86; mng. dir. Matuschka & Co., Frankfurt and Greenwich, Conn., 1987-92; mngr. gen. ptnr. OSV Ptnrs., Boston and Frankfurt, 1992-96; CEO, CIO OSV Ptnrs., Bad Homburg and Greenwich, 1996—; fin. advisor to ctrl. banks and govts., 1992-93. Contbr. articles to jours. and mags.; developer of currency overlay bus. as separate asset mgmt. discipline. Recipient Best Narrator award Bavarian Edn. Ministry, Munich, 1970. Mem. Polo Club Frankfurt, Union Internat. Club Frankfurt. Roman Catholic. Avocations: book collecting, literature, painting, jogging, polo. Home: Ernst-Moritz-Arndt-Strasse 12, 61348 Bad Homburg Germany Office: OSV Fin Mgmt GmbH, Tannenwaldallee 2, 61348 Bad Homburg Germany

SCHMAEHL, WINFRIED ARTHUR, economist, educator; b. Liegnitz, Silesia, Germany, May 31, 1942; s. Arthur and Hildegard (Melzer) S.; m. Johanna E. Nicolai, May 31, 1963; 1 child, Andreas. Diplom-Volkswirt, U.

Frankfurt, 1967, Dr.rer.pol., 1972, Habil.Econs., 1976. Asst. prof. econs. U. Frankfurt/Main, 1973-76; prof. econs. Free U. Berlin, 1976-89, U. Bremen, Germany, 1989—; dir. dept. econs. Ctr. for Social Policy Rsch. U. Bremen, 1989—; chmn. Adv. Coun. on Pension Policy, German Fed. Govt., 1986-2000, mem. Commn. on Pension Policy, 1996-97, mem. Commn. on Report of Living Conditions for the Aged, 1998-2000; mem. Commn. on Demographic Changes, German Fed. Parliament, 1992-94, 95-98, 99—. Author/editor: Future of Public and Private Pension Schemes, 1991, Old Age Security and Income Distribution, 1977, Social Policy in the Process of the German Unification, 1992, Minimum Social Security in Old Age, 1993, European Social Policy, 1997, Firmbased Social and Personell Policy, 1999. Decorated Officer's Cross Order of Merit, Germany; recipient 1st prize for pubs. on social mkt. economy Wolfgang-Ritter Found., 1991. Office: U Bremen Ctr Social Policy Rsch, Parkallee 39, D-2809 Bremen Germany

SCHMALBROCK, GERD, journalist; b. Essen, Germany, Apr. 18, 1930; s. Theo and Henriette (Kassner) S.; m. Gertrud Haltermann, Febr. 4, 1956; children: Bernd, Barbara, Urban, Sibylle, Beate. Student, Folkwang Coll., Essen, 1948-50. Editor IKC Presse, Gladbeck, Germany, 1956—, Ihr Programm, Gladbeck, Germany, 1975—; writer, 1972—; radio drama writer, 1966-71. Author: (radio drama) Der liebe Verstorbene, 1966, Der letzte Zug, 1967, Zum Nachtisch Mord, 1967, Impromptu oder die Vielheit des Herrn Rot, 1969, Der mörderische Chef vom Dienst, 2000. Home and Office: Mendelssohn St 10, 45966 Gladbeck Germany

SCHMALE, WOLFGANG, historian; b. Wuerzburg, Germany, Apr. 4, 1956; s. Franz-Josef and Ott Irene Else S.; m. Katharina Anna Swiniarski, Mar. 20, 1981 (wid. Jan. 1997); children: Julia Yonne, Clemens-Ekkehard; m. Katrin Keller, Aug. 24, 1999. PhD, U. Bochum, 1984. Maitre de confs. U. Tours, France, 1987-88; scientific asst. U. Bochum, 1989-93, U. Munich, 1993-95; prof. U. Braunschweig, Germany, 1995-96, U. Graz, Austria, 1997-98, U. Munich, 1998, U. Vienna, Austria, 1999—. Editor: (book) Human Rights and Cultural Diversity, 1993, (book series) Innovations, 1997—; co-author: (book) L'An I des droits de l'homme, 1989; author: (book) Archeology of Fundamental and Human Rights in Early Modern Period, 1997, French Military, 2000. Roman Catholic. Avocations: climbing, hiking, painting. Office: Inst Geschichte U Vienna, Dr Karl-Lueger-Ring, A-1010 Vienna Austria

SCHMALISCH, GERD HEINZ, biophysicist, researcher; b. Poessneck, Germany, Apr. 26, 1951; s. Heinz Herbert and Ilse Olga (Pfeifer) S.; m. Petra Rentke Bürger, Aug. 21, 1976 (div. Nov. 1978); 1 child, Henrik; m. Cornelia Jähne, July 19, 1984; children: Josephine, Juliane, Sebastian. Cert. Engr., Tech. U., Dresden, Germany, 1973, Dr-Ing, 1979; DrScNat, Humboldt U., Berlin, 1990. Asst. Tech. U., Dresden, 1973-78, Humboldt U., Berlin, 1978—. Contbr. articles to Jour. Applied Physiology, Biol. Neonate, Intensive Care Medicine, European Respiration Jour., others. Mem. European Respiratory Soc., Pediatic Pulmonology Soc. (Germany), Perinatal Medicine Soc. (Germany), N.Y. Acad. Scis. Mem. Evangelic Ch. Avocations: horticulture, music. Office: Humboldt U Dept Neonatology, Schumann Str 20/21, D-10098 Berlin Germany

SCHMALZ, GOTTFRIED, dentist; b. Zwickau, Germany, Oct. 13, 1946; s. Hans and Johanna Schmalz; m. Christiana Weigelt, Feb. 24, 1978; 1 child, Fabian. DrMedDent, U. Tubingen, 1966-71, DDS, 1979. Instr. dept. operative dentistry and periodontology U. Tûbingen, Germany, 1973-77, sr. instr. dept. operative dentistry, 1977-83; dir. clinic, prof. and chmn. dept. operative dentistry U. Regensburg, Germany, 1983—; postdoctoral rsch. assoc. Materials Sci. Toxicology Lab. U. Tenn., Memphis, 1974-75; adj. prof. U. Tex., Houston, 1998—. Contbr. more than 200 articles to profl. jours. Rsch. grantee Deutsche Forschungsgemeinschaft. Mem. Assn. Operative Dentistry Germany (pres. 1984-88), Assn. Profs. of Dentistry Germany (pres. 1990-92), Internat. Assn. for Dental Rsch. (pres. 1986-87), German Sci. Assn. for Dentistry (pres. 1993-97). Office: Univ of Regensburg, Dept Operative Dentistry, and Periodontology, Regensburg 93042, Germany

SCHMAUDER, SIEGFRIED KARL, materials scientist; b. Gutenberg, Germany, Nov. 23, 1956; s. Friedrich Karl and Elfriede Christiane (Bohnacker) S.; m. Annegret Meissner, Jan. 19, 1957; children: Katharina, Christian. Diploma in math., U. Stuttgart, 1981, D, 1988. Rep. group leader Max Planck Inst., Stuttgart, 1988-89; fellow U. Tokyo, 1989-90; rsch. asst. U. Calif., Santa Barbara, 1990-91; group leader Max Planck Inst., Stuttgart, 1990-94; prof. U. Stuttgart, 1994—. Mem. ASME, Soc. Applied Math. and Mechanics, German Materials Rsch. Soc. Avocations: skiing, piano, tennis. Office: U Stuttgart, Pfaffenwaldring 32, D-70569 Stuttgart Germany

SCHMAUS, SIEGFRIED H. A., engineering executive, consultant; b. Muelheim/Ruhr, W. Ger., Dec. 23, 1915; s. Wilhelm Friedrich and Hedwig (Flader) S.; student Staatliche Ingineur Schule, Duisburg, W. Ger., 1940-41, Esslingen, W. Ger., 1945-46; m. A. Babette Schmid, Aug. 17, 1946. Apprentice-designer Demag A.G., Duisburg, 1930-36; designer/supr. Meissner, Cologne, W. Ger., 1936-38; designer aircraft engines Daimler-Benz A.G., Stuttgart, W. Ger., 1943-45; designer Fischer & Porter, Warminster, Pa., 1948-53, Ametek Inc., Sellersville, Pa., 1954-65; staff rsch. engr. Fischer & Porter, Warminster, 1966-80; pres. Sensor Devel. Inc., Broomall, Pa., 1977—, Sensor Rsch. Inc., Phila., 1980-90. Patentee in field. V.p. Friends Hist. Rittenhouse Town. Served with German Luftwaffe, 1938-42. Recipient Hess Ingenuity award, 1962. Mem. Franklin Inst. (sr., silver mem.), Instrument Soc. Am. (sr.), Am. Soc. Mfg. Engrs., German Soc. Pa. (v.p. 1984, Founders medal 1987, Officer's Cross of the Gov. of Germany 1988), Masons. Republican. Lutheran. Home and Office: Penfield Downs 806 Powder Mill Ln Wynnewood PA 19096-4037

SCHMEHL MORLEY, SUSAN LINDA, performing arts educator; b. Sheffield, Mass., Aug. 29, 1949. BFA, U. Mass., Amherst, 1971; postgrad. in grad. studies, Studio Art Ctr. Internat., Florence, Italy. With Peace Corps, 1973-76; studio arts, Spanish tchr., 1976—; chair of fine and performing arts Berkshire Sch., Sheffield, Mass., 1997—. Mem. Ind. Sch., Art Instrs. Assn. Home: 245 N Undermounatin Rd Sheffield MA 01257

SCHMEICHEL, PETER, professional soccer player; b. Gladsaxe, Denmark, Nov. 18, 1963. With Gladsaxe Football Club, Hvidovre Football Club, 1984-86, Brondby IF Football Club, 1987-91, Manchester United Football Club, 1991-99; goal keeper Sporting Lisboa, Portugal, 1999, Denmark; winner Danish 1st Divsn. Championship, 1987-88, 90-91, Danish Cup, 1989, F.A. Cup, 1993, 95, Premiership Championship, 1992, 93, 95-96, European Championship, 1992. Recipient Nat. Title at Sp. Lisboa, 2000; named Best Keeper of the World, 1992, 93. Office: Danish Football Assn, Idraettens Hus Brondy St 20, 2605 Brandby Denmark*

SCHMEIDLER, FELIX BERNHARD, astronomer; b. Leipzig, Germany, Oct. 20, 1920; s. Bernhard and Emmy (Windscheid) S.; m. Marion Pampe, Oct. 28, 1965; children: Renate, Martin. Dr. rer. nat., U. Munich, 1941. Asst. Universitatssternwarte, Munich, 1943-57, prof. astronomy, 1957—, asst. dir., 1979-86. Author: Nikolaus Copernicus, 1970; editor edition of works of Hevelius, 1969, Regiomontanus, 1972; contbr. numerous articles to profl. jours. Recipient Silberne Medaille, U. Helsinki, 1968, Kulturpreis, Landsmannschaft Westpreussen, Munster/Westfalen, Fed. Rep. Germany, 1973; named Hon. Citizen Stadt Konigsberg in Bayern, Fed. Rep. Germany, 1982. Fellow Royal Astron. Soc. London; mem. Astronomische Gesellschaft, Internat. Astron. Union, AltpreuBische Gesellschaft Wissenschaft, Kunst and Lit. Home: Mauerkircherstrasse 17, 81679 Munich Germany Office: Museuminsel 1, 80538 Munich Germany

SCHMEIDLER, KAREL ROBERT, architect, sociologist; b. Ivancice, Czechoslovakia, Feb. 27, 1951; s. Karel and Drahomira (Netopilova) S.; m. Sylva Talpová Schmeidlerova, Apr. 8, 1978 (div. 1987); children: Katerina, Sylva. MS in Architecture, Tech. U. Brno, 1976, PhD in Architecture, 1980; MS in Sociology, Masaryk's U., Brno, 1984; PhD in Architecture, Tech. U. Brno, 1980; PhD in Sociology, Masaryk's U., Brno, 1988. Profl. cert. Min. Higher Edn., Prague, 1990, City Coun. Brno, 1995. Tchr. Civil Engring. Faculty, Brno, Czech Republic, 1979-80; rschr. Faculty of Architecture, Brno, Czech Republic, 1980-85; sr. rschr. Fellow Faculty Architecture, Brno, 1986-97; assoc. prof. Urban Planning Inst. TU, Brno, 1997—; freelance architect faculty arch. Tech. U. Brno, Czech Republic, 1976-97; planning cons. Stern, Brno, Czech Republic, 1990-97; rsch. fellow Rsch. Inst. for Architecture and Planning, Brno, Czech Republic, 1990-93, Ga Rep Rsch. Inst., Brno, Czech Republic, 1996—; vis. prof. U. Ctrl. England, Birmingham, 1999. Author: Sociology in Architecture and Planning, 1997; co-author: Human Sciences in Architecture and Urban Planning, 1995, Environmental Sciences Education for Architects, 1995. Head Young Architects Orgn., Brno, 1976-78, Prukopnik Housing Coop., Brno, 1978-79; mem. Trade Union Branch Edn., Brno, 1976-97; nat. rep. Assn. European Schs. of Planning, Brussels, 1994-97. Grantee: Rsch. Support Scheme Ctrol. European U., Prague, 1994-96, Min. Edn., Prague, 1995, Tech. U., Brno, 1997. Mem. Assn. Urban Planning and Urban Design., Masaryk Sociological Soc., Union of Czech Architects, Udalosti na Tech. U. Brno. Avocations: skiing, tennis, travel, computers, swimming. Fax: 0042-05-42142125. Home: Ondrouskova 14, CZ63500 Brno Czech Republic Office: Tech U Brno, Urban Plng Inst Porici 5, CZ-63900 Brno Czech Republic

SCHMELLER, NIKOLAUS THEODOR, surgeon, educator; b. Munich, Bavaria, Germany, Aug. 3, 1952; s. Theodor and Lore (Cron) S.; m. Ulrike Margarethe Eltze, Sept. 20, 1980; children: Ferdinand, Katharina, Emily. MD, Ludwig-Maximilians U., Munich, 1978. Prof. urology Ludwig-Maximilians U., Munich/Bavaria, 1992—. Mem. Hungarian Assn. of Urology (hon.). Office: LKH Salzburg Urologische, Muellner Hauptstr 48, 5020 Salzburg Austria

SCHMELZ, BERND, anthropologist; b. Bamberg, Franken, Germany, Jan. 11, 1959; s. Kurt and Liselotte (Funck) s.; m. Esther Romero, Apr. 5, 1991. MA, U. Bonn, Germany, 1987; DPhil, U. Marburg, Germany, 1992. Cert. anthropologist. Ind. sci. investigator Peru, 1989-90, Germany, 1991-93; asst. Mus. Anthropology, Hamburg, 1993-95, head of dept. of Europe, 1995—; asst. prof. Latin Am. Studies U. Hamburg, 1995—; investigator Dept. Archaeology Würzburg, 1982. Author: Kontinuität und Wandel religiöser Feste in Peru, 1992, Lope de Atienza-Misionero y Etnógrafo, 1996; editor: Drache, Stern, Wald und Gulasch—Europa in Mythen und Symbolen, 1997, Hexerei, Magie und Volksmedizin, 1997; co-editor: Auf Drachenspuren, 1995, Estudios Sobre el Sincretismo en America Central y En Los Andes, 1996; co-editor: Ethnographie Afrikas, Ethnographische Photographie, 1999, Das gemeinsame Haus Europa, 1999, Unser Europa, 1999, Das gemeinsame Haus-Fundgrube Europa, 1999, Indianer der Plains und Prärien, 1999. Mem. Bonner Amerikanistische Studien, Asociacion de Historiadores Latino Americanistas, Deutsche Gesellschaft für Völkerkunde. Home: Braunschweiger Str 12, D-21614 Buxtehude Germany Office: Mus für Völkerkunde, Binderstr 14, 20148 Hamburg Germany

SCHMID, ALFRED ALLAN, economist; b. Dawson, Nebr., Mar. 12, 1935; s. Alfred E. and Florence A. Schmid; m. Alice B. Todd, 1956 (dec.); children: Elizabeth, John; m. Kay A. Schmid, 1985. BS, U. Nebr., 1956; MS, U. Wis., 1957, PhD, 1959. Asst. prof. Mich. State U., East Lansing, 1959-64, assoc. prof., 1964-68, prof., 1968-98, Univ. Disting. prof., 1998—; vis. scholar Resources for the Future, Washington, 1964-65; mem. World Bank Mission to Romania, 1993. Author: Property, Power and Public Choice, 1978, 2d edit., 1987, Law and Economics, 1980, Benefit-Cost Analysis, 1989; editor: Beyond Agriculture and Economics, 1997; mem. edit. bd. Land Econs., 1969-71, Jour. Econ. Issues, 1972-75, Am. Jour. Agrl. Econs., 1978-80. Mem. East Lansing Planning Commn., 1973-75. Mem. Am. Agrl. Econs. Assn. (Quality of Comm. award 1992), Am. Econs. Assn., Assn. for Evolutionary Econs. Avocations: travel, writing. E-mail: schmid@msu.edu. Office: Mich State Univ Dept Agr Econs East Lansing MI 48824

SCHMID, BERNHARD HELMUT, hydrologist, consultant; b. Steyr, Austria, Mar. 19, 1960; s. Helmut and Eugenie Karoline (Pfaffenlehner) S.; m. Margareta Ottel, June 6, 1992. Diploma in Engring., Tech. U. Vienna, Austria, 1983; D of Tech., 1986. Sr. hydrologist Danube Hydro Austria, Vienna, Austria, 1983-93; lectr. Tech. U. Vienna, Austria, 1988-91; sr. lectr., 1992—; ind. cons. Vienna, Austria, 1992—. Author: Zur math. Modellierung der Abflussentstehung an Haengen, 1986, A Study on Kinematic Cascades, 1990; contbr. articles to profl. jours. Recipient Pres.'s Ring of Honor, Austria, 1986. Mem. ASCE, Internat. Assn. for Hydraulic Rsch., Am. Geophys. Union. Avocations: foreign languages, history of art, skiing. Home: Vegagasse 16, A-1190 Vienna Austria Office: Tech Univ Vienna, Karlsplatz 13 E223, A-1040 Vienna Austria

SCHMID, FRIEDERIKE GERTRUD, physicist, researcher; b. Stuttgart, Germany, Apr. 23, 1966; d. Christhard and Ursula S. Degree, U. Munich, 1983; PhD, U. Mainz, Germany, 1991. Postdoc. fellow U. Wash., 1992-94; rsch. asst. U. Mainz, 1995-98; group leader Max-Planck-Inst. for Polymers Rsch., Mainz, 1999-2000; prof. physics U. Bielefeld, Germany, 2000—. Contbr. articles to profl. jours. Recipient Studienstiftung des deutschen Volkes fellowship, 1985-89, Heisenberg fellowship, 1998, Gerhard Hess award, 1998. Office: U Bielefeld Dept Physics, Universitätstrasse 25, 33615 Bielefeld Germany

SCHMID, GARY BRUNO, psychotherapist, physicist; b. Cleve., Dec. 23, 1946; arrived in Switzerland, 1985, Swiss citizenship, 1994; s. Bruno Joseph Schmid and Bertha Januska; m. Rebecca Dian Howe, June 15, 1969 (div. June 1974); m. Marion Louise Wagner, Apr. 15, 1979; children: Marie-Hélène Talaya, Cendrine Chandra. BSc, Ohio State U., 1968; PhD, U. Ariz., 1977; diploma, C.G. Jung Inst., Zürich, 1988. Cert. psychotherapist Canton Zuerich, Switzerland. Rsch. assoc. U. Colo., Boulder, 1977-80, Hahn-Meitner Inst., Berlin, 1979-80, U. Karlsruhe, Germany, 1980-85, Psychiat. U. Clinic, Zürich, Switzerland, 1985-95; pvt. practice psychotherapist, hypnotherapist Zürich, 1988—; head psychotherapist Cantonal Psychiat. Clinic, Rheinau, Switzerland, 1995—. Author: Death by Imagination, 2000; contbr. articles to profl. jours. Grantee NSF, Case-Western Res. U., 1964-65; Fulbright scholar Deutsche Acad. Austauschdienst, Karlsruhe, 1970-71. Mem. Internat. Assn. for Analytical Psychology, Swiss Psychotherapists Orgn., Swiss Soc. for Med. Hypnosis, N.Y. Acad. Scis. Avocations: creative writing, blues harmonica, juggling. E-mail: gbschmid@bli.unizh.ch. Fax: 41 52 304 9391. Home: Trittligasse 2, CH-8001 Zürich Switzerland Office: Cantonal Psychiat Clinic, CH-8462 Rheinau Switzerland

SCHMID, HANS HEINRICH, theology, educator, educational administrator; b. Zurich, Switzerland, Oct. 22, 1937; s. Gotthard and Erika (Hug) S.; m. Christa Nievergelt, Jan. 6, 1962; children—Anna Regula, Konrad Heinrich, Ulrich Martin, Verena Elisabeth. Dr. Theol., U. Zurich, 1965; Dr. Theol. honoris causa, U. Leipzig, 1991. Asst. prof. U. Zurich, 1967-69, prof. Old Testament studies, 1976-88, rector, 1988—; prof. Kirchliche Hochschule Bethel, Bielefeld, Fed. Republic Germany, 1969-76. Author books, including: Wesen und Geschichte der Weisheit, 1966; Gerechtgkeit als Weltordnung, 1968; Altorientalische Welt in der alttestamentlichen Theologie, 1974; Der Sogenannte Jahwist, 1976. Mem. Wissenschaftliche Gesellschaft fur Theologie (pres. 1984-90), Schweizerische Gesellschaft fur Orientalische Altertums wissenschaft (bd. dirs. 1976-89), Gelehrte Gesellschaft, others. Mem. Freisinnig-demokratische Partei; recipient Golden Order of Merit Republic of Austria, 1996. Presbyterian. Home: In der Halden 11, CH 8603 Schwerzenbach Switzerland Office: U Zurich, Rämlstrasse 71, CH-8006 Zurich Switzerland*

SCHMID, HANS-PETER, biochemistry educator, researcher; b. Riedlingen, Fed. Republic Germany, Nov. 8, 1950; came to France, 1989; s. Eugen Josef and Auguste (Broska) S.; m. Claudia Kreutzer, July 9, 1988; children: Tania, Marco. Diploma, U. Stuttgart, Fed. Republic of Germany, 1976, PhD, 1982, Tchg. Cert., 1987. Asst. U. Stuttgart, 1978-83, asst. prof., 1984-89; assoc. prof. U. Clermont, France, 1989-92, prof., 1992—. Author: Dangerous Animals of the Sea, 1985, Underwater Guide Red Sea, 1987, Underwater Guide Sinai, 1992. Mem. N.Y. Acad. Scis., European Soc. Cell Biology, Senckenberg Soc., Assn. United Diving Instrs. (hon.), European Proteasome Assn. (founder pres.). Achievements include discovery of prosome (proteasome). Avocations: scuba diving, photography, writing. Office: Univ Clermont Fd II, 24 Avenue des Landais, 63177 Aubiere France

SCHMID, HOLGER, psychologist; b. Freiburg, Baden, Germany, Sept. 24, 1962; s. Wolfgang and Elisabeth (Birkenberger) S. Diploma in Psychology, U. Freiburg, 1990; PhD, U. Fribourg, Switzerland, 1995. Cert. psychologist. Asst. in clin. psychology U. Fribourg, 1990-94; project dir. rsch. dept. Swiss Inst. for Prevention of Alcohol and Drug Problems, Lausanne, 1996-97. Mem. Swiss Fedn. of Psychology, Swiss Psychol. Soc., Swiss Soc. Health Psychology. Office: Swiss Inst Prev Alcohol &, Drugs/Av de ruchonnet 14, 1001 Lausanne Switzerland

SCHMID, HUBERT MARTIN, software developer; b. Friedrichshafen, Germany, Apr. 15, 1957; s. Franz and Johanna (Brielmaier) S. BS, U. Ulm, 1982, MS, 1982. Tech. advisor, software specialist U. Ulm, Germany, 1980-82, Kumatronik, Friedrichshafen, 1982—; with Dornier, Friedrichshafen, 1986-90, AEG, Konstanz, Germany, 1986-90; self-employed, Friedrichshafen. Roman Catholic. Home: Steinaecker 6, 88048 Friedrichshafen Germany

SCHMID, INGOBERT CHRISTIAN, mechanical engineering researcher, educator; b. Stuttgart, Germany, May 12, 1936; s. Christian and Lydia (Zeeb) S.; m. Sigrid Gudrun Reiniger; children: Ingrun Christiane, Katharina Sybille. Dipl.ing., Tech. U., Stuttgart, Germany, Dr.ing. Rsch. engr. Fried Krupp, Essen, Germany, 1961, Vehicle Rsch. Inst. U. Stuttgart, Germany, 1961-65; chief motor vehicle divsn. Battelle Inst., Frankfurt, Germany, 1965-75; full prof., head Automotive Rsch. Inst. IKK U. German Forces, Hamburg, Germany, 1975—; dean mech. engring. faculty U. German Forces, Hamburg, 1979, 95; cons. in field. Author: Deutsche Kraftfahrt und Strassenverkehrsforschung, Der Landschaftsmater Otto Reiniger, 1982, Fritz Lang - Maler und Holzschneider, 1992; contbr. sci. articles to profl. jours. Mem. Internat. Soc. Terrain Vehicle Systems (gen. sec. Europe 1992-94, bd. dirs. 1996—), Verein Deutscher Ingenieure (chmn. vehicle group Frankfurt 1972-75, coun. bd. VDI-FVT 1997-98), Wissenschaftliche Gesellschaft fur Kraftfahrzeug-und Motorentechnik e.v. (chmn. 1997-98, bd. dirs. 1999—), Automobiltechnische Zeitschrift (coun. bd. 1997-98), Motortechnische Zeitschrift (coun. bd. 1997-98). Office: U German Forces, Holstenhofweg 85, 22043 Hamburg Germany

SCHMID, KARL HERMANN, mathematician, educator; b. Schwaebisch Gmuend, Germany, Oct. 30, 1937; s. Hermann Klemens and Maria Anna (Hiller) S.; m. Ingrid Schmitz, July 22, 1976; children: Matthias Christoph, Andreas Felix. BS, U. Stuttgart, Germany, 1958, MS, 1961, Cert. in Edn., 1963, PhD, 1964. Tchr. trainee High Schs., Stuttgart, Germany, 1962-63; asst. prof. U. Stuttgart, Germany, 1963-65, 67-68, Calif. State U., Hayward, 1965-67; advisor math. methods UNESCO, U. Cape Coast, Ghana, 1970-71; chmn. Landesfachschaft Mathematik, Bden Wuerttemberg, 1986-89; prof. math. Paedagogische Hochschule, Schwaebisch Gmuend, 1968—; in-service courses for teachers, 1970—; part-time lectr. math. and computer sci. U. Md. European Div., 1981-85; dir. Ctr. of Continued Edn. for Tchrs., 1991-99. Contbr. articles to profl. jours. Mem. Sixth Form Math. Project Group Ghana. Roman Catholic. Home: Am Scheuelberg 10, D-73540 Heubach Germany Office: Paedagogische Hochschule Schwaebisch Gmuend, Oberbettringerstr 200, D-73525 Schwaebisch Gmuend Germany

SCHMID, LYNETTE SUE, child and adolescent psychiatrist; b. Tecumseh, Nebr., May 28, 1958; d. Mel Vern John and Janice Wilda (Bohling) S.; m. Vijendra Sundar, June 13, 1987; children: Jesse Christopher Mikaéle, Eric Lynn Kalani, Christina Elizabeth Ululani. BS, U. Nebr., 1979; MD, U. Nebr., Omaha, 1984; postgrad., U. Mo., 1984-89. Diplomate Am. Bd. Med. Examiners, Am. Bd. Psychiatry and Neurology. Child and adolescent psychiatrist Fulton (Mo.) State Hosp., 1990-91, Mid-Mo. Mental Health Ctr., Columbia, Mo., 1991-96; owner Fairview Motel, Kemmerer, Wyo., 1996—; clin. asst. prof. psychiatry U. Mo., Columbia, 1990-96. Contbr. articles to profl. jours. Mem. Am. Psychiat. Assn., Am. Acad. Child and Adolescent Psychiatry, Ctrl. Mo. Psychiat. Assn. (sec.-treas. 1992-93, pres.-elect 1993-94, pres. 1994-95), U. Nebr. Alumni Assn., Phi Beta Kappa, Alpha Omega Alpha. Republican. Avocations: walking, reading, studying scripture.

SCHMID, RUDI (RUDOLF SCHMID), internist, educator, scientist; b. Switzerland, May 2, 1922; came to U.S., 1948, naturalized, 1954; s. Rudolf and Bertha (Schiesser) S.; m. Sonja D. Wild, Sept. 17, 1949; children: Isabelle S., Peter R. BS, Gymnasium Zurich, 1941; MD, U. Zurich, 1947; PhD, U. Minn., 1954. Intern U. Calif. Med. Center, San Francisco, 1948-49; resident medicine U. Minn., 1949-52, instr., 1952-54; research fellow biochemistry Columbia U., 1954-55; investigator NIH, Bethesda, Md., 1955-57; assoc. medicine Harvard Med. Sch., 1957-59; asst. prof. Harvard U., 1959-62; prof. medicine U. Chgo., 1962-66; prof. medicine U. Calif., San Francisco, 1966-91, prof. emeritus, 1991—, dean Sch. Medicine, 1983-89, assoc. dean internat. rels., 1989-95; cons. to U.S. Army surgeon gen., USPHS, VA; hon. prof. Peking Union Med. Coll., Shanghai Soc. Med. U. Mem. editl. bd. Jour. Clin. Investigation, 1965-70, Blood, 1962-75, Gastroenterology, 1965-70, Jour. Investigative Dermatology, 1968-72, Annals Internal Medicine, 1975-79, Procs. Soc. Exptl. Biology and Medicine, 1974-84, Chinese Jour. Clin. Scis., Jour. Lab. Clin. Medicine, 1991—, Hepatology Rsch. (Japan), 1993—; hon. editor-in-chief World Jour. Gastroenterology, China, 1996—; cons. editor Gastroenterology, 1981-86. Served with Swiss Army, 1943-48. Master ACP; fellow AAAS, N.Y. Acad. Scis., Royal Coll. Physicians; mem. NAS, Am. Acad. Arts and Scis., Assn. Am. Physicians (pres. 1986), Am. Soc. Clin. Investigation, Am. Soc. Biol. Chemistry and Molecular Biology, Am. Soc. Hematology, Am. Gastroenterol. Assn., Am. Assn. Study Liver Disease (pres. 1965), Internat. Assn. Study Liver (pres. 1980), Swiss Acad. Med. Scis. (mem. senate), Leopoldina, German-Am. Acad. Coun. (exec. com.). Achievements include research in biochemistry, metabolism of hemoglobin, heme, prophyrins, bile pigments, liver and muscle. Home: 211 Woodland Rd Kentfield CA 94904-2631 Office: U Calif Med Sch Office Dean PO Box 0410 San Francisco CA 94143-0410

SCHMID, STEFAN, international management educator; b. Augsburg, Germany, Mar. 19, 1967; s. Martin and Gertraud (Gaar) S. Vordiplom, U. Augsburg, 1990; diploma in bus., European M in Mgmt., European Sch. Mgmt., Paris, 1993; PhD in Internat. Bus., Cath. U., Eich Staett-Ingolstadt, Germany, 1996. Asst. prof. internat. mgmt. Cath. U. Eichstaett-Ingolstadt, Germany, 1993—; lectr. Banking Acad., Frankfurt, Germany, 1993—. Author: Cultural Diversity in Multinational Corporations, 1996. Grantee Studienstiftung des deutschen Volkes, 1992-93. Mem. Assn. MBAs, European Internat. Bus. Acad. Brussels, Acad. of Internat. Bus. Roman Catholic. Home: Theresienstrasse 28, 85049 Ingolstadt Germany Office: Cath U Eichstaett, Auf der Schanz 49, 85049 Ingolstadt Germany

SCHMIDBAUER, GEORG SEBASTIAN, surgeon, researcher; b. Straubing, Germany, Jan. 17, 1959; s. Josef and Edeltraud Ottilie (Buchner) S.; m. Inge Schäfer-Schmidbauer, June 16, 1990; 1 child, Isabel Sophie. MD, Ludwig-Maximilians-U., Munich, 1984, PhD, 1985; Privatdozent, Justus-Liebig-U., Giessen, Germany, 1996. Resident in pathology Ludwig-Maximilian-U., 1986; resident in surgery Justus-Liebig-U., 1986-90; rsch. fellow Brigham & Women's Hosp./Harvard U., Boston, 1990-92; resident in surgery Justus-Liebig-U., 1992-95, resident in traumatic surgery, 1995-97, surg. assoc., 1998—; chief dept. surgery Evangelisches Krankenhaus Johannisstift, Münster/Westfalen, Germany, 1999. Author: Treatment with SK&F 105685 and Rapamycin in a Rat Heart Allotransplantation Model, 1997; co-author: Immunosuppressive Drugs, 1994; contbr. articles to profl. jours. Rsch. grantee Deutsche Forschungsgemeinschaft, Bonn, 1990. Mem. Study Group for Promotion of Surg. Rsch. Avocations: sports, art. Office: Evangelisches Krankenhaus, Wichernstrasse 8, 48147 Münster Germany

SCHMIDBAUR, HUBERT, chemistry educator, consultant; b. Landsberg, Bavaria, Germany, Dec. 31, 1934; s. Johann B. and Katharina (Ehelechner) S.; m. Rose-Marie Fukas, Oct. 16, 1962; children: Hans Christian, Karolin Elisabeth. Diploma in chemistry, U. Munich, 1958, Dr. rer.nat., 1960; Habilitation, U. Marburg, 1964. Asst. prof. chemistry U. Munich, 1960-62; asst. prof. chemistry U. Marburg, Germany, 1962-64, lectr., 1964-65; lectr. U. Würzburg, Germany, 1965-67, prof., 1967-73; prof. chemistry Tech. U. Munich, 1973—; vis. prof. U. Edinburgh, Scotland, 1970, Kyoto (Japan) U., 1967, MIT, Cambridge, 1974, U. Melbourne, Australia, 1987, U. Hiroshima, Japan, 1992, U. Auckland, New Zealand, 1992, U. Western Ont., London, 1995,U. Calif., Berkeley, 1997; curator Fonds der Chemischen Industrie, Frankfurt, Fed. Republic Germany, 1981-87. Editor 12 jours; contbr. numerous articles to chem. jours. Senator Deutsche Forschungsgemeinschaft, Bonn., 1988-92. Recipient prize Verband der Chem. Industry, Frankfurt, 1966, F.S. Kipping award Am. Chem. Soc., 1973, A Stock prize Gesellschaft Deutscher Chemiker, 1982, Dwyer medal, U. NSW, 1987, Bailar medal U. Ill., 1988, Leibniz prize Deutsche Forschungsgemeinschaft, Bonn,

1987, Wacker Silicon prize, Munich, 1996, Birch medal Australian Nat. U., 1998, Chemistry prize U. Bonn, 1998. Fellow Royal Soc. Chem. London (L. Mond medal); mem. Gottingen Acad. Sci. (corr.), Finnish Acad. Sci. (Helsinki), Leopoldina Acad. (Halle), Bavarian Acad. Sci., Order of Merit. Roman Catholic. Home: Koenigsberger Strasse 36, D-85748 Garching Germany Office: Tech U Munich, Lichtenbergstrasse 4, D-85748 Garching Germany

SCHMID-BORTENSCHLAGER, SIGRID, humanities educator; b. Wels, Austria, Feb. 28, 1946; d. Wilhelm and Maria (Wiesmayr) Bortenschlager; m. Georg Schmid, May 28, 1971. PhD, U. Salzburg, 1974. Asst. U. Salzburg, Austria, 1974-83, assoc. prof., 1983—; prof. U. Utrecht, 1998-99; prof. U. Paris VIII, 1995; dir. rsch. project Austrian Rsch. Fund, 1979-81, 89-91, Acad. Sci. Austria, 1989-92. Author: Dynamik und Stagnation, 1980, Ost. Schriftstellerinnen 1880-1938, 1982, Konstruktive Literatur, 1985; editor: Zwischenbilanz, 1976, Totgeschwiegen, 1982, Die Bessere Halfte, 1995, Eigensinn und Widerstand. Schriftstellerinnen der Habsburgermonarchie, 1998. Recipient Theodor-Korner award, 1982, Sandoz Award for Humanities, 1985. E-mail: sidgrid.schmidt@sbg.ac.at. Office: Univ Salzburg, Akademiestr 20, A 5020 Salzburg Austria

SCHMIDER, MARY ELLEN HEIAN, American studies educator, academic administrator; b. Chippewa Falls, Wis., Apr. 17, 1938; d. A. Bernard and Ellen Dagmar (Gunderson) Heian; m. Michael Heaton Leonard, June 16, 1962 (div. Oct. 1969); 1 child, William Gunerius Leonard; m. Carl Ludwig Schmider, June 17, 1970; 1 child, Dagmar Heian Schmider. BA in English Lit. magna cum laude, St. Olaf Coll., Northfield, Minn., 1960; MA in English Lit., U. So. Calif., 1962; PhD in Am. Studies, U. Minn., 1983. Mem. founding faculty in English, Calif. Luth. Coll., Thousand Oaks, 1961-64; instr. dept. English U. Vt., Burlington, 1964-70; instr. univ. writing program U. R.I., South Kingston, 1973-77; grad. asst. dept. rhetoric U. Minn., Mpls., 1975-76; dir. continuing edn./cmty. svcs. Moorhead (Minn.) State U., 1977-86, dean grad. studies and grad. faculty, 1983-95; U.S. Fulbright lectr. Lanzhou U., Peoples Republic of China, 1997—; bd. dirs. Luth. Brotherhood, Mpls., 1988—; mem. bd. higher edn. and schs. Evang. Luth. Ch. in Am., Chgo., 1987-95; mem. bd. pensions Luth. ch. in Am., Mpls., 1982-87; certificate coll. mgmt. Carnegie Mellon U., 1987; lectr. U. Medicine, U. Coll. Medicine, Europe, Heidelberg, Germany, 2000—. Author biog. sketches Biog. Dictionary of Social Welfare. Mem. exec. commn. Minn. Humanities Commn., St. Paul, 1983-89, chair, 1987-88. Bush Leadership fellow, 1987. Mem. U.S. Fulbright Assn., Am. Studies Assn., Phi Beta Kappa, Phi Kappa Phi. Lutheran. Avocations: swimming, clothing design, music, international travel, family activities. Home: 7701 180th St Chippewa Falls WI 54729-6440

SCHMIDHAMMER, ROBERT HOWARD, environmental executive, engineering consultant; b. Altoona, Pa., May 13, 1931; s. Leo Anselm and Audrey Norma (Dibert) S.; m. Elaine Carol Jones, Dec. 18, 1954 (dec. Nov., 1986); children: Linda K., Raymond J.; m. Patricia M. Burgess, Feb. 29, 1996. BSME/ BSCE, Finlay Engring. Coll., Kansas City, Mo., 1958; grad. studies Engring. & Constrn. Mgmt., Various Schs., 1960-72. Constrn. mgr., consulting engr. Developers and individuals, different locations, 1960-87; sr. project mgr. Marcor Environ. Corp., Rochester, N.Y., 1987-90; engring. cons., environ. svcs. AAC Contracting, Inc., Rochester, N.Y., 1990—; cons. pvt. practice, Rochester, 1990—; bd. dirs. 3 non-pub. corps. Contbr. articles to environ. jours. Bd. dirs. various civic orgns. With USAF, 1950-53, Korea. Mem. Rochester Engring. Soc. (fin. cons.), Rochester Host Lions Club (pres., dir.), Rochester C. of C., Assn. Facilities Engrs., Cert. Hazardous Materials Mgr. (Finger Lakes chpt.), Construction Specifications Inst. (dir.), VFW, Am. Legion, Bldg. Owners and Mgmt. Assn. Republican. Roman Catholic. Avocations: travel, cmty. svc. work. Home: 36 Rogers Ave Rochester NY 14606-1827 Office: AAC Contracting Inc Engring and Environ Svcs Rochester NY 14611

SCHMIDHEINY, THOMAS, industrialist; b. Balgach, Switzerland, Dec. 17, 1945; s. Max S. and Adda Scherrer; m. Suzanne Lise Mireille Weber; 4 children. Degree in Mech. Engring., Swiss FEd. Inst. Tech.; MBA, IMEDE, Lausanne, Switzerland, 1972; D in Bus. Adminstrn. (hon.), Tufts U., 1999. Tech. mgr. Cementos Apasco, Mexico, 1970-71; mng. dir. Swiss cement cos. Holderbank Financière Glaris Ltd., 1975, chmn. exec. com., 1978—, dep. chmn. bd. dirs., mng. dir., 1980-84, pres., 1984—; bd. dirs. Credit Suisse Group, SAir Group, vice chmn. Avocations: sailing, shooting. Office: Holderbank, Financiere Glaris Ltd, CH-8750 Glaris Switzerland*

SCHMID-HEMPEL, PAUL, evolutionary ecologist; b. Zurich, Switzerland; s. Hermann and Berta (Baumann) Schmid; m. Regula Hempel, Oct. 19, 1979. MS in Engring., ETH, Zurich; MS in Biology, U. Zurich, 1979, DPhil in Biology, 1982. Rsch. fellow Swiss Nat. Sci. Found., Oxford, Eng., 1983, Royal Soc. London, Oxford, 1984; asst. prof. U. Basel, Switzerland, 1984-88; rsch. prof. Swiss Nat. Sci. Found., Basel, 1988-91; prof. exptl. ecology ETH Zurich, 1991—; vis. prof. Simon Fraser U., Vancouver, B.C., Can., 1991. Author: Foraging in Individually Searching Ants, 1983; contbr. over 100 articles to profl. publs.; assoc. editor Jour. Evolutionary Biology, 1986-88; co-editor Behavioral Ecology, 1995-99. Mem. Swiss Zool. Soc. (pres. 1988-92, v.p. 1992-94), Internat. Soc. for Study of Behavioral Ecology (treas. 1990-94), European Soc. Evolutionary Biology (councillor 1998—), Brit. Ecol. Soc. Achievements include research on efficiency of ecologically relevant behaviors, studies on maintenance of genetic variability, on evolutionary ecology of host-parasite interactions. Office: ETH Exptl Ecology, ETH-Zentrum NW, CH-8092 Zurich Switzerland

SCHMIDLI, KEITH WILLIAM, vocational education administrator, educator, researcher; b. Niagara Falls, N.Y., Oct. 11, 1952; s. Duane Irving and Jennie Mary (Schultz) S.; m. Jaquline Barbara Irish, May 27, 1978 (div. Jan. 3, 1982). AA in Liberal Arts and Scis., Niagara County C.C., Sanborn, N.Y., 1972; journeyman cert. auto/diesel mechanics, Trott Vocat. Sch., 1982; BS in Vocat. Tech. Edn. summa cum laude, SUNY, Buffalo, 1992, MS in Edn. summa cum laude, 1993; PhD magna cum laude, U. Buffalo, 1999; MBA, DBA, Cambridge State U., 1995. Cert. tchr., N.Y.; cert. career devel. facilitator; cert. coord. for diversified coop. work-study programs. Maintenance mechanic, operating engr., machinist Gt. Lakes Carbon Corp., Niagara Falls, N.Y., 1973-82; owner, mgr. Apt. Rental Units, Niagara Falls, 1975-88; mechanic Tracy-Luckey Co. Inc., Andalusia, Ala., 1984-85; mechanic, operating engr. Niagara Falls Country Club, Lewiston, N.Y., 1985-86; millwright Custom Maintenance, Buffalo, 1986-87; pipefitter John Martin Plumbing, Niagara Falls, 1987; engring. technician Precious Plate, Niagara Falls, 1987-90; grad. adminstrv. asst. SUNY, Buffalo, 1993-94; adminstr. Niagara County C.C., Sanborn, N.Y., 1995-96; faculty selection com. Dept. Tech. SUNY, Buffalo, 1992-94; tchg./curriculum cons. LaSalle Sr. H.S., Niagara Falls, 1992—; grad. student selection com. U. Buffalo, 1994-95, rsch. symposium com., 1994-95, acad. stds. com., 1995-99. Author: Increasing Enrollment in Secondary Vocational Eduction Programs Through Teacher-Based Promotion, 1993, Career Education: Exploring the Unfinished Agenda of Providing Applied Practical Knowledge and Skills Needed in a Changing Economy, 1999, Career Readiness and Employees Expectations, 2000; contbr. articles to profl. jours. Vol., donor Red Cross Western N.Y., Buffalo, 1991-95; vol. Am. Heart Assn., Buffalo, 1996, Dept. Comty. Edn./Resource Devel., Niagara Falls, 1992. Mem. ASCD, ASME, Assn. Study of Higher Edn., Coun. Exceptional Children, Am. Soc. Quality, Soc. Mfg. Engrs., Libr. Congress Assoc., Am. Mus. Natural History, Postal Commemorative Soc., Alpha Sigma Lambda (charter pres. 1993-94), Kappa Delta Pi. Avocations: guitar playing, songwriting, camping, hunting, home remodeling. Home: 209 Sabre Park Niagara Falls NY 14304-1754 Office: SUNY Coll at Buffalo 109 Bacon Hall Buffalo NY 14222

SCHMIDPETER, ALFRED, chemistry professor; b. Munich, Germany, Dec. 14, 1929; s. Michael and Maria (Hammerstingl) S.; m. Gerlinde Bayer, 1956; children: Stephan, Barbara, Gregor. D degree, U. Munich, 1960. Prof. U. Munich, 1975—. Mem. editl. bd. Phosphorus, Sulfur and Silicon, N.Y.C., 1971—; European editor Heteroatom Chemistry, N.Y.C., 1989—; author nearly 300 rsch. papers and revs. in profl. jours. Mem. ICMGC, Gesellschaft Deutscher Chemiker. Home: Attersestrasse 10, D-81241 Munich Germany Office: Dept Chemie U, Butenandtstrasse 5-13 HausD, D-81377 Munich Germany

SCHMID-SCHONBEIN, GEERT WILFRIED, biomedical engineer, educator; b. Albstadt, Germany, Jan. 1, 1948; came to the U.S., 1971; s. Ernst and Ursula Schmid; m. Renate Elisabeth Schmid-Schonbein, July 3, 1976; children: Philip, Mark, Peter. MS, U. Calif. San Diego, La Jolla, 1973, PhD, 1976. Staff assoc. Columbia U., N.Y.C., 1976-77, sr. staff assoc., 1977-79; asst. prof. U. Calif. San Diego, La Jolla, 1979-84, assoc. prof., 1984-89; prof. U. Calif. San Diego, 5, 1989—; founding fellow Am. Inst. Med. and Biol. Engring., Washington, 1991. Editor: Physiology and Pathophysiology Leukocyte Adhesion, 1995; contbr. articles to profl. jours. Cadent sgt. Bundeswehr, 1967-69. Recipient Melville medal ASME, 1990, Ratchow medal European Soc. Phlebology, Bremen, Germany, 1999; named hon. mem. Am. Venous Forum, San Diego, 1992. Fellow Am. Heart Assn., Am. Physiol. Soc., Biomed. Engring. Soc. (sr., pres. 1991-92); mem. World Coun. on Biomechanics, Microcirculatory Soc. (coun. mem. 1990-93), N.Am. Soc. Biorheology (pres. 1998-99). Avocation: hiking. E-mail: gwss@bioeng.ucsd.edu. Office: U Calif San Diego Dept Bioengring 9500 Gilman Dr La Jolla CA 92093-5004

SCHMIDT, ALBRECHT, bank executive; b. Leipzig, Germany, 1938. JD. With Bayerische Vereinsbank, 1967-79, mem. bd., 1979-89; mem. bd. mgmt. Bayerische Vereinsbank, Munich, 1989—, CEO; mem. supervisory bd. Vereins-und Westbank AG, Hamburg. Mem. Bayerischer Bankenverband (pres. 1990—). Office: Bayerische Hypo-und Vereinsbank, Am Tucherpark 16, 80538 Munich Germany also: Kardinal-Fullhaber Str 1, POB 100101, 8000 Munich Germany*

SCHMIDT, ALFRED, chemistry educator; b. Vienna, Austria, Dec. 31, 1928; s. Heinrich Georg and Maria K. (Leski) S.; m. Ottilie K. Hoellrigl, May 18, 1956; children: Gundula, Alfred. Diploma in engring., Tech. U. Vienna, 1952, D of Tech., 1954. Head dept. chem. engring. Tech. U. Vienna, 1973-97, 1997—; with rsch. dept. Chemie Linz (Austria) AG, 1954-73; exec. com., chmn. bioenergy agreement Internat. Energy Agy., 1982-86, mem. Austria chpt., 1982-97. Author 3 books; contbr. numerous articles to sci. jours. Mem. Austrian Chem. Soc. (pres. 1991-96), Austrian Acad. Sci. (corr.), Rotary Club Vienna. Office: Tech U Vienna, Getreidemarkt 9, A-1060 Vienna Austria

SCHMIDT, ANDREAS, pastor; b. Hannover, Germany, Apr. 19, 1960; s. Gerhard Schmidt and Margarete Flader-Schmidt. Abitur, Integrierte Gesamtschule, Hannover, Germany, 1980. Wissenschaftliche Hilfskraft U. Göttingen, Germany, 1987-88; vicar Evangelisch-Lutherische, Kirche Hannovers, 1988-91, pastor, 1991—; mem. Internat. Q Project, Claremont, 1991—. Contbr. articles to profl. jours. Mem. Assn. Internat. Papyrologues, Am. Acad. Religion, Soc. Bib. Lit. Avocations: soccer, music, traveling, studying New Testament.

SCHMIDT, AXEL, general practice physician, mycologist, researcher; b. Krefeld, Northrhine Westfalia, Germany, May 29, 1962; s. Eckhard C.F. and Juliane (Blehs) S.; m. Doris Bade, July 19, 1969; 1 child, Julia Maria. Abitur, Gymnasium Fabritianum, Krefeld, Germany, 1981; Candidate Philosophy, U. Düsseldorf, Germany, 1987, MD, 1988. Cert. MD, clin. microbiologist. Clin. microbiologist U. Hosp., Düsseldorf, Germany, 1988-93; dir. Bayer Pharma Rsch., Wuppertal, Germany, 1993—; assoc. prof. U. Witten/Herdecke, Witten, Germany, 1997—; pres. North-Rhine Westfalia Union of German Clin. Microbiologists, Germany, 1995—; mem. bd. curators Manfred Plempel Stipendium for Med. Mycology, 1997—, Dorothy Hegarty award, 1997—. Editor: (book series) Contributions to Microbiology, 1996—; mem. editl. bd. Chemotherapy, 1996—, Drug Rsch., 1996—, Haut, 1996—, Alternatives to Lab. Animals, 1997—, Mikrobiologe, 1998—, Luft, 1998—; mem. sci. bd. (jour.) Progress in Medicine, 1996—, Skin, 1997—, Mycoses, 1998—; reviewer New Eng. Jour. Medicine, 1997—; contbr. numerous sci. papers; patentee in field. Recipient 20th Century Achievement award Am. Biog. Inst., 1998. Mem. Union German Clin. Microbiologists, German Soc. Mycology, German Hygiene and Microbiology Assn., German Assn. Natural Scis. and Art, Virology Assn., Paul Ehrlich Assn., French Soc. Med. Mycology, Internat. Soc. Human/Animal Mycoses, Robert Koch Found. Christian Democrat. Roman Catholic. Avocations: chamber music, clarinet, hunting, mineralogy. E-mail: axel780961@aol.com. Home: Bahnstr 118, D-42327 Wuppertal Germany Office: Pharma Rsch Antiinfectives, Bayer AG PO Box 101709, D-42096 Wuppertal Germany

SCHMIDT, DOMINIQUE, lawyer, educator; b. Strasbourg, France, June 5, 1942; s. Paul and Betty (Reeb) S.; m. Geneviève Dohr, July 3, 1967. Lic. in law, U. Strasbourg, 1963, D en Droit, 1967; Agrégation en Droit, U. Paris, 1970. Assoc. ASA Avocats Assoc., Paris, 1964—; prof. U. Strasbourg, France, 1970—; arbitrator various litigations. Author: Les droits de la minorité dans la société anonyme, Les conflits d'intérêts das la société anonyme (Best Bus. Law Book of Yr. 1999); contbr. articles to profl. jours. Dir. Droit et Commerce, Paris, 1993. Lt. French Army, 1964. Mem. Assn. des Cabinets d'Avocats à Vocation Internat. (chmn.). Roman Catholic. Avocation: skiing. E-mail: dominique.schmidt@wanadoo.fr. Office: 12 rue de Bourgogne, 75007 Paris France

SCHMIDT, EDWARD CRAIG, lawyer; b. Pitts., Nov. 26, 1947; s. Harold Robert and Bernice (Williams) S.; m. Elizabeth Lowry Rial, Aug. 18, 1973; children: Harold Robert II, Robert Rial. BA, U. Mich., 1969; JD, U. Pitts., 1972. Bar: Pa. 1972, U.S. Dist. Ct. (we. dist.) Pa. 1972, U.S. Ct. Appeals (3d cir.) 1972, U.S. Ct. Appeals (D.C. cir.) 1975, U.S. Supreme Ct. 1981, U.S. Ct. Appeals (9th cir.) 1982, U.S. Ct. Appeals (4th cir.) 1982, U.S. Ct. Appeals (6th cir.) 1987, U.S. Ct. Appeals (11th cir.) 1990, U.S. Ct. Appeals (2d cir.) 1992, U.S. Ct. Appeals (4th cir.) 1994. Assoc. Rose, Schmidt, Hasley & Di Salle, Pitts., 1972-77, ptnr., 1977-90, Jones, Day Reavis & Pogue, Pitts.; mem. adv. com. Superior Ct. Pa., 1978-80; NITA instr. Duquesne U., 1998—. Co-editor; Antitrust Discovery Handbook-Supplement, 1982; asst. editor: Antitrust Discovery Handbook, 1980; contbr. articles to profl. jours. Bd. dirs. Urban League, Pitts., 1974-77, NITA instr., Duyuesne U., 1998. 99. Mem. Supreme Ct. Hist. Soc., Pa. Bar Assn., D.C. Bar Assn., Allegheny County Bar Assn. (pub. rels. com. coun. civil litigation sect. 1977-80), Internat. Acad. Trial Laywers, Acad. Trial Lawyers Allegheny County (bd. govs. 1985-87), U. Pitts. Law Alumni Assn. (bd. govs. 1980), Western Res. Acad. Alumni Assn. (trustee 1998—). Clubs: Rolling Rock (Ligonier, Pa.), Duquesne (Pitts.), Longue Vue (Pitts.). Republican. Home: 159 Washington St Pittsburgh PA 15218-1351 Office: Jones Day Reavis & Pogue One Mellon Bank Ctr 31st Fl 500 Grant St Pittsburgh PA 15219-2502

SCHMIDT, ERWIN ROBERT, genetics educator; b. Bellmuth, Hessen, Germany, Mar. 29, 1949; s. Karlheinz and Erika Gisela (Feyh) S.; m. Agnes Viest, Mar. 29, 1978; children: Esther Eva, Claudius Alexander. Abitur, Aufbaugymnasium, Friedberg, 1967; Diplombiologe, Giessen U., 1973, PhD, 1975; habilitation, Ruhr U., Bochum, Germany, 1985. Postdoctoral Ruhr-Univ., DFG Developmental Physiology, Bochum, 1975-78; wiss. assistent Ruhr-Univ., Inst. Genetics, Bochum, 1978-85, asst. prof., 1985-89; prof. Johannes-Gutenberg U., Mainz, 1989-92, U. Hohenheim, Inst. Gen. Genetics, Stuttgart, 1992, U. Mainz, Inst. Genetics, 1993-94; dir. Inst. Molecular Genetics and Biosafety Rsch. & Cons., 1994—; founder & CEO Genterprise Biotech. Co. Editor Molekular & Zellbiologie, 1985, Chromosoma, 1989. Mem. Deutsche Zoologische Gesellschaft, Deutsche Gesellschaft für Genetik, Gesellschaft für Biologische Chemie, Am. Soc. Microbiology, Am. Soc. Cell Biology, Am. Genetical Soc. Home: Robert Koch Str 6, D-55270 Ober-Olm Germany Office: Johannes Gutenberg U, Saarstr 21, D-55099 Mainz Germany

SCHMIDT, FRANK BROAKER, executive recruiter; b. Shamokin, Pa., Aug. 8, 1939; s. Frank Wilhelm and Doris (Maurer) S.; children by previous marrage: Susan E., Tracie A.; m. Elizabeth Mallen, Mar. 18, 1989; children: Alexandra M., Frank W.M., Drake M. BS, U. Pa., 1962; MBA, Case Western Res. U., 1969; cert. brewmaster, Siebel Inst. Brewing Tech., Chgo., 1964. With Carling Brewing Co., Cleve., 1964-69, mgr. sales and advt. div., brand mgr., 1969-70; advt. and merchandising mgr. The Pepsi-Cola Co., Purchase, N.Y., 1970-73, dir. mktg. programs, then dir. mgmt. devel., 1973-74; dir. sales and mktg. The Olga Co., Van Nuys, Calif., 1974-75; pres. F.B. Schmidt, Internat., L.A., 1975-95; mng. dir. Stanton Chase Internat., 1995—; chmn. Mediterranean Properties, 1994—. Author: Draft Beer Manual, 1967, Assn. Nat. Advertisers Computerized Media System, 1970. Chmn. Morrison Ranch Estates Homeowners Assn., 1993-96. Mem. Calif. Exec. Recruiters Assn., Wharton Alumni Assn., Personnel Cons. Am. (region chmn. 1981-83, chmn. 92-95), Am. Mktg. Assn. Republican. Avocations: sports cars, flying, marathon bicycling, racing. Office: 30423 Canwood St Ste 239 Agoura Hills CA 91301-4318

SCHMIDT, GERHARD HERBERT, entomology educator, researcher; b. Deutsch-Krone, Germany, Feb. 20, 1928; s. Josef Martin and Martha (Hasenleder) S.; m. Ursula Gertrud Stirnberg, May 16, 1959; children: Wolfgang, Annette, Sabine, Ludger. Sci. auxiliary, Mus. Naturkunde, Münster, Westfalen, Germany, 1948-49; D in Nat. Scis., U. Münster, Westfalen, Germany, 1954; habil., U. Würzburg, Bayern, Germany, 1965. Rsch. officer Deutsches Inst. für Fettforschung, Münster, Westfalen, Germany, 1954-57; sci. asst. U. Würzburg, Bayern, Germany, 1957-69; sr. sci. asst. U. Würzburg, 1969-75; wissenschaftlicher Rat und prof. U. Hannover, Niedersachsen, Germany, 1975-78; prof. U. Hannover, 1978-95; vis. scientist U. Pavia, Italy, 1959, U. OECD, Zürich, Switzerland, 1964, U. Firenze, Italy-Somalia, 1974, Regional Rsch. Lab., Jammu-Tawi, India, 1978; dir. Univ. (Zoology-Entomology) Hannover, 1978-95, dean of faculty, 1988-89; project coord. European Comty., Brussels, 1991-97; sci. cons. U. Lisbon, Portugal, 1995—. Author: (books) Pesticide und Umweltschutz, 1986, Geographische Verbreitung der Oedipodinae (Orthopteroidea, Caelifera, Acrididae) in Europa und Randgebieten, 1997; editor: (books) Sozialpolymorphismus bei Insekten, 1974, 2d edit., 1987, On the Biology and Control of Thaumetopoea (Lepidoptera, Insecta), 1990. Recipient Aristoteles award Internat. Organizing Com. for Devel. Bee Keeping in Greece, U. Patras, 1993. Mem. German Zoological Assn., German Assn. Gen. Application Entomology, Internat. Union for Study of Social Insects, Leuven Belgium. Avocation: gardening (holds Orthopteran collection). Home: Brakenweg 5, D-31535 Neustadt, Niedersachsen Germany Office: U Hannover Entomology Sect, Herrenhauser Strasse 2, D-30419 Hannover Niedersachsen, Germany

SCHMIDT, GLEN KEVIN, finance director; b. Stoke-on-Trent, Eng., Oct. 4, 1964; s. Guido Erich and Jenetta Jessy (Reed) S. BSc in Chemistry with 1st class honors, U. London, 1986. Chartered acct. ICAEW. Jr. asst. mgr., audit mgr. KPMG, London, 1986-91; sr. internal auditor DHL, Brussels, 1991-93; fin. dir. Elan U.K., Birmingham, Eng., 1993; fin. reporting and planning mgr. Europe/Africa DHL, Brussels, 1993-97; change mgr. European Rim DHL, Vienna, Austria, 1997-99; fin. and change mgr. DHL, Vienna, 1999—. Avocations: golf, skiing, football, cycling, mountain walking. E-mail: gschmidt@at.dhl.com. Home: Stiege II Flat 18A, Mariahilfer Strasse 51, 1060 Vienna Austria Office: DHL Internat, Steingasse 6-8, 1030 Vienna Austria

SCHMIDT, GUSTAV FRIEDRICH, political science educator; b. Berlin, Germany, Nov. 22, 1938; s. Gustav Walter and Luise (Rennemann) S.; m. Heide-Irene Windschiegl, Aug. 17, 1971; children: Sandra Sophia, Sabine Beate, Sonja Andrea. Staatsexamen, Free U. Berlin, 1961, DrPhil, 1963; Habilitation, Westf. Wilhelms U., Münster, Fed. Republic Germany, 1971. Rsch. asst. Inst. Polit. Sci., Berlin, 1963-65; sci. asst. dept. history Münster U., 1965-71, prof. history internat. rels., 1972-76; prof. internat. politics Ruhr U., Bochum, Fed. Republic Germany, 1976—; vis. prof. St. Antony's Coll., Oxford (Eng.) U., 1979*80, Emory U., Atlanta, 1984, U. Toronto, (Ont., Can.), 1985-86, Cornell U., 1990-91. Author: Deutscher Historismus, 1964, England in der Krise, 1981, Der europäische Imperialismus, 1985; editor: Konstellationen internationaler Politik (USA and Western Europe 1924-32, 83), Britain and Europe-Britain in Europe, 1989, Changing Perspectives on European Security and NATO's Search for a New Role, 1998, Amerikas Option für Deutschland und Japan, 1996, Zwischen Bündnissicherung und privilegierter Partnerschaft: Die deutsch-britischen Beziehungen und die USA, 1955-63, 1995, Ost-West-Beziehungen: Konfrontation und Détente, 1945-89, 3 vols., 1993-95, Deutschland-Grossbritannien-Europa, 1992, NATO-The First 50 Years, 3 vols., 2000. Chmn. Arbeitskreis Deutsche Eng.-Forschung, 1981-88. Fellow Britisch-Deutscher Historikerkreis, Deutsche Gesellschaft für Politische Wissenschaft, Deutsche Gesellschaft für Auswärtige Politik. Avocations: mountain climbing, jazz. Home: Am Ossenbrink 2a, D-58313 Herdecke Federal Republic of Germany Office: Ruhr U Internat Politics, Universitätsstrasse 150, D-44780 Bochum Federal Republic of Germany

SCHMIDT, HANS-JÜRGEN REINHOLD, mathematician; b. Berlin, Feb. 15, 1956; s. Reinhold and Ingeborg (Dirksen) S.; m. Renate Reichstein, Oct. 22, 1977; children: Markus, Theodor, Mareike. Diploma math., U. Greifswald, Germany, 1978, D Natural Sci. in Topology, 1980; D Natural Sci. in Astrophysics, Acad. Scis., Berlin, 1987; D Natural Sci. Habilitation, U. Potsdam, Germany, 1992. Scientist Inst. Astrophysics, Potsdam, 1979-90, leader rsch. group, 1991; lectr. dept. physics Tech. U., Berlin, 1990-91; lectr. dept. astronomy Münster (Germany) U., 1991-92; leader rsch. group dept. math. U. Potsdam, Germany, 1992—; mem. evangelische Forschungsakademie, Berlin, 1988—, Kuratorium, 1996—; guest scientist Inst. H. Poincaré, VI U., Paris, 1990, Inst. Cosmic Rsch., Acad. Scis., Moscow, 1986, Osservatorio Romano, Rome, 1992; guest scientist dept. physics Free U. Berlin, 1999-2000; visitor State U., Kyoto, Japan, 1991, N.Y., 1996, Princeton, N.J., 1996, Hebrew U., Jerusalem, 1997, Inter-U. Ctr. for Astronomy and Astrophysics, Poona, India, 1997; speaker WIP-Astronomie, Potsdam U., Rat Deutscher Sternwarten, München, 1992-94. Co-author: Lexikon der Mathematik, 5 vols., 2000—; editor Gen. Relativity and Gravitation, 1995—; co-editor (with M. Rainer): Current Topics in Mathematical Cosmology, 1998; contbr. articles to profl. jours. Mem. group preparing found. of Potsdam U., 1990-91; co-founder Arbeitskreis Astronomiegeschichte, Astronomische Gesellschaft, 1992; leader Potsdam dist. Aktion Sühnezeichen in Evangelic Ch., 1979-89; leader trade union group Astrophys. Inst., Potsdam, 1989-90. Recipient C.F. Gauss medal Acad. Scis. German Democratic Republic, Berlin, 1977. Mem. Internat. Soc. Gen. Relativity and Gravitation. Home: H Sachs Str 13, 14471 Potsdam D, Germany Office: Potsdam U Dept Math, Am Neuen Palais 10, 14415 Potsdam D, Germany

SCHMIDT, HARTMUT, chemist, researcher; b. Salzwedel, Germany, Dec. 21, 1941; s. Werner and Annemarie (Gebhardt) S.; m. Rocio Perez Ramirez; 1 child, Anja. Diploma in chemistry, U. Frankfurt, 1967, PhD, 1969, Habilitation, 1977. From sci. asst. to docent U. Frankfurt, 1968-80, prof. in biophys. chemistry, 1994—; sci. collaborator Carl Zeiss, Oberkochen, 1980; rsch. head Braun Melsungen AG, Melsungen, 1981-82; rsch. dir. Tetra Werke, Melle, 1983—. Contbr. articles to profl. jours. Home: Schauenroth 28, D-49124 Georgsmarienhutte Germany Office: Tetra Werke, Herrenteich 78, D-49304 Melle Germany

SCHMIDT, HARTMUT, banking and finance educator; b. Halle, Germany, Oct. 27, 1941; 1 child, Luis. Diploma, Kaufmann, 1966; diploma Handelslehrer, U. Saarland, Germany, 1967, PhD in Econs., 1969. Lectr. Syracuse (N.Y.) U., 1969-70, asst. prof., 1970-73, assoc. prof., 1973-74; prof. banking and fin. Hamburg (Germany) U., 1974—; bd. dirs. European Capital Markets Inst., Hanseatische Wertpapierbörse, Hamburg, Germany, Deutsche Gesellschaft für Finanzwirtschaft, Germany, pres., 1999; investment com. Ring-Fonds DWS, Germany, 1994—. Author: Advantages and Disadvantages of an Integrated Market Compared with a Fragmented Market, 1977, Wertpapierbörsen, 1988; co-author, editor: Special Market Segments for Small Company Shares, 1984; co-author: Corporate Governance in Germany, 1997; co-editor Zeitschrift für Bankrecht und Bankwirtschat, 1989—. Office: Inst Geld-und Kapitalverkehr, Univ Hamburg Von-Melle-Park 5, 20146 Hamburg Germany

SCHMIDT, INGO LOTHAR OTTOKAR, retired economics educator; b. Breslau, Silesia, Germany, May 30, 1932; s. Lothar Bruno and Emmy Martha Selma (Jaersch) S.; m. Hilde-Lore Fischer, Aug. 28, 1959; children: Cornelia, Felix. Diploma in econs., Free U. Berlin, 1958, D in Econs., 1961; Habilitation, Ruhr U., Bochum, Fed. Republic Germany, 1972. Civil servant Bundeskartellamt, Berlin, 1962-73, Senator für Wirtschaft, Berlin, 1973-77; prof. U. Hohenheim, Stuttgart, Fed. Republic Germany, 1977-99. Author: The Suitability of Concentration Measures for European Competition Policy, 1983, A Critical Evaluation of the Chicago School of Anti-trust Analysis, 1989.

SCHMIDT, JOANNE (JOSEPHINE ANNE SCHMIDT), language educator; b. N.Y.C., June 7, 1950; d. Joseph William and Maria Esther (Morazzani) S. BA, Chestnut Hill Coll., Phila., 1972; MA, U. Va., 1974, PhD, 1980. Tchg. asst. U. Va., Charlottesville, 1973-76, Lycée Marie Curie,

Sceaux, France, 1976-77; lectr. U. Va., Charlottesville, 1977-79; asst. prof. Cedar Crest Coll., Allentown, Pa., 1981-84; asst. prof. Calif. State U., Bakersfield, 1984-88, assoc. prof., 1988-94, prof., 1994—, chair dept., 1998—; freelance translator, Bklyn., 1979-81, Allentown, Pa., 1981-84, Bakersfield, Calif., 1984—. Author: (book) If There Are No More Heroes There Are Heroines: A Feminist Critique of Corneille's Heroines, 1987, (jour.) San Jose Studies, 1987, (poetry book) (author as Teresita Bosch) Portraits, 1991; assoc. editor: (jour.) Coll. Tchg., 1985-89. V.p. Women, Inc., Allentown, 1983-84; pub. spkr. Alliance Against Family Violence, Bakersfield, Calif., 1985-90. Fulbright Hays grantee Fed. Govt., 1976-77, Affirmative Action grantee Calif. State U., 1985, 87, 91. Mem. MLA, NOW, Am. Assn. Tchrs. of French, Nat. Women's Studies Assn., Calif. Lang. Tchrs. Assn., Delta Kappa Gamma. Democrat. Avocations: carpentry, golf, creative writing, family history, oral history. Office: Calif State U Modern Langs & Lit Dept 9001 Stockdale Hwy Bakersfield CA 93311-1022

SCHMIDT, KARSTEN, law educator; b. Oschersleben, Germany, Jan. 24, 1939; s. Eberhard and Karla (Hamann) S.; m. Inga Syassen, Mar. 28, 1967; children: Frauke, Hilke. 1st legal exam., Kiel (Germany) U., 1965; 2d legal exam., Hamburg (Germany) U., 1969; JD, Bonn (Germany) U., 1972. Asst. Kiel U., 1966-67, Bonn U., 1969-75; prof. law Göttingen U., 1976-77, Hamburg (Germany) U., 1977-97; dir. Comml. Law Inst., Bonn, Germany, 1997—; v.p. Bucerius Law Sch., Hamburg, Germany, 1999—; cons. expert German Rsch. Orgn., Bonn, 1987-95. Author: Cartel Law Procedure, 1977, Company Law, 1986, 3d edit., 1997, Commercial Law, 1980, 5th edit., 1999; editor Comml. Law Jour., 1980—; contbr. over 300 articles to legal jours., chpts. to books. Mem. Orgn. Civil Law Profs. (pres. 1993-99), European Acad. Sci. and Lit., Zeit Found. (pres. 1985—), Argentine Acad. Scis., Overseas Club Hamburg (v.p. 1986—). Avocations: violin, skiing, tennis, literature. Home: Pikartenkamp 44, D-22587 Hamburg Germany Office: Comml Law Inst, Adenauerallee 24-42, D-53113 Bonn Germany

SCHMIDT, KLAUS D., mathematician, educator; b. Glückstadt, Germany, Feb. 25, 1951; s. Walter and Anneliese (Schütt) S.; m. Livia Grass. Diploma, U. Zürich, Switzerland, 1975; PhD, U. Mannheim, 1980. Asst. U. Zürich, 1975-76, Ecole Polytechnique Federale, Lausanne, Switzerland, 1976-79; teaching asst. U. Mannheim, Germany, 1979-84, univ. asst., 1984-90, lectr. math., 1990-93; prof. math. T.U. Dresden, Germany, 1993—; lectr., vis. prof. Univs. Darmstadt, Mannheim, Saarbrücken, Münster, Dresden. Author: Amarts and Set Function Processes, 1983, Jordan Decompositons of Generalized Vector Measures, 1989, Lectures on Risk Theory, 1996, Mathematik (Grundlagen fuer Wirtschaftswissenschaftler), 1998. Mem. Deutsche Mathematiker-Vereinigung, Deutsche Gesellschaft für Versicherungsmathematik, Schweizer Vereinigung der Versicherungsmathematiker, Internat. Statis. Inst.

SCHMIDT, KLAUS WALTER, fiber manufacturing company executive; b. Berlin, July 19, 1938; s. Walter J. and Elisabeth H. (Förster) S.; m. Ulla M. Mendelsohn, July 30, 1967; children: Dirk, Christian. Diploma physics, U. Frankfurt, Germany, 1963; D, U. Frankfurt, 1967; Philosophicum, U. Munich, 1961. Rschr. U. Frankfurt, 1964-67; prof. agregado U. de los Andes, Merida, Venezuela, 1967-69; rschr. Kernforschungs Zentrum, Karlsruhe, 1970; group leader process/product devel. Carl Freudenberg Nonwovens, Weinheim, Germany, 1971-79; mgr. process devel. Spunweb Freudenburg, Kaiserslautern, Germany, 1980-82; tech.dir. Freudenberg Spunweb Co, Durham, N.C., 1983-87; dir. internat. ops. Freudenberg Spunweb Co, Kaiserlautern, 1988—; bd. dirs. Freudenberg Spunweb, Durham, 1990, Colmar, France, 1992; dir. internat. support ops. The Freudenberg Nonwovens Group. Contbr. articles to profl. jours.; patentee in field. Presbyter ch., Kaiserslautern, 1988—. Mem. Insead Alumni (Sigma challenge 1988). Avocations: ball games, squash, tennis, raquetball, soccer, golf. Office: Carl Freudenberg Sparte Spinnvliesstoff, Freudenberg Vliesstoffe KG, D-69465 Weinheim Germany

SCHMIDT, L(AIL) WILLIAM, JR., lawyer; b. Thomas, Okla., Nov. 22, 1936; s. Lail William and Violet Kathleen (Kuper) S.; m. Diana Gail (div. May 1986); children: Kimberly Ann, Andrea Michelle; m. Marilyn Sue, Aug. 11, 1990; stepchildren: Leland Darrell Mosby, Jr., Crystal Rachelle Mosby. BA in Psychology, U. Colo., 1959; JD, U. Mich., 1962. Bar: Colo. 1962, U.S. Dist. Ct. Colo. 1964, U.S. Tax Ct. 1971, U.S. Ct. Appeals (10th cir.) 1964. Ptnr. Holland & Hart, Denver, 1962-77, Schmidt, Elrod & Wills, Denver, 1977-85, Moye, Giles, O'Keefe, Vermeire & Gorrell, Denver, 1985-90; of counsel Hill, Held, Metzger, Lofgren & Peele, Dallas, 1989—; pvt. practice law Denver, 1990—; lectr. profl. orgns. Author: How To Live-and Die-with Colorado Probate, 1985, A Practical Guide to the Revocable Living Trust, 1990; contbr. articles to legal jours. Pres. Luth. Med. Ctr. Found., Wheat Ridge, Colo., 1985-89; pres. Rocky Mountain Prison and Drug Found., Denver, 1986—; bd. dirs. Luth. Hosp., Wheat Ridge, 1988-92, Bonfils Blood Ctr. Found., 1995—, Planned Giving Adv. Group of Nat. Jewish Hosp., Denver, 1996-98, St. Joseph Hosp. Found., 1999—; planned giving advisor Aspen Valley Med. Found., 1997—; mktg. and gifts adv. com. The Denver Found., 1998—. Fellow Am. Coll. Trust and Estate Counsel (Colo. chmn. 1981-86); mem. ABA, Am. Judicature Soc., Denver Estate Planning Coun., Rocky Mtn. Estate Planning Coun. (founder, pres. 1970-71), Greater Denver Tax Counsel Assn., Am. Soc. Magicians, Denver Athletic Club, Phi Delta Phi. Republican. Baptist. Avocation: magic. Office: 1050 17th St Ste 1700 Denver CO 80265-2077 also: Law Offices Robert L Bolick Ltd 6060 Elton Ave Ste A Las Vegas NV 89107-0100

SCHMIDT, LAJOS, lawyer; b. Budapest, Hungary, Apr. 23, 1920; s. Lajos Schmidt and Gisella Adorjan; m. Shirley M. Formell, Feb. 21, 1961 (dec. Aug. 1978); children: Anne, Christina, Catherine; m. Maria Bartakovics Rudolf-Schmidt, Aug. 4, 1999. PhD, Ludwig Maximilian U., Munich, 1942; JD, St. Elizebeth U., Pécs, Hungary, 1943; 2d JD, Ill. Inst. Tech., 1954. Bar: Budapest, 1947, readmitted 1992; cert. officer Supreme Ct. Ill., 1954. Supr. Armeria del Exercito Ciudad Trujillo, Dominican Republic, 1948-51; ptnr. Baker & McKenzie, Chgo., 1952-93, chmn. policy com., 1979, 82; mng. dir. Internat. Strategic Cons., Budapest, 1993—; chmn. bd. Messer Hungarogaz Kft, 1989—. Author: Munchener Volkswirtschaftliche Studien, 1943; contbr. articles to profl. jours. Bd. dirs. Am. Hungarian Found., New Brunswick, N.J., 1990; chmn. emeritus bd. overseers Ill. Inst. Tech. Chgo./Kent Coll. Law, 1974—; trustee Ill. Inst. Tech., Chgo., 1974, 90; mem. bd. Found. for the Support of the Internat. Exbhns. of the Mus. Fine Arts, Budapest, 1996—; pres. Friends of the Mus. of Fine Arts, 1996. Recipient George Washington award Am.-Hungarian Found., 1999. Mem. Beirat German Hungarian C. of C. Roman Catholic. Avocations: horseback riding, restoring antiques. Home: Petofi Ter 3 B/II 6, H-1052 Budapest Hungary Office: Internat Strategic Cons, Petofi ter-3, H-1052 Budapest Hungary

SCHMIDT, LAWRENCE KENNEDY, philosophy educator; b. Rochester, N.Y., Oct. 2, 1949; s. Paul Frederick Schmidt and Rebecca Jane Gilford; m. Monika Reuss, Sept. 2, 1984; 1 child, Kassandra Gaya Reuss-Schmidt. BA, Reed Coll., 1972; MA, U. N.Mex., 1978; PhD, U. Duisburg (Germany), 1983. Instr. Philosophy U. Duisburg, Duisburg, 1979-83, U. N.Mex., Albuquerque, 1984; asst. prof. Philosophy Hendrix Coll., Conway, Ark., 1984-89, chair dept. Philosophy, 1987-92, 97—, assoc. prof. Philosophy, 1989-99, prof. philosophy, 1999—; bd. dirs. Marshall T. Steel Ctr. for the Study of Religion and Philosophy. Author: (book) The Epistemology of H-G Gadamer, 1985, 2d edit., 1987; editor: (book) The Specter of Relativism, 1995; translator: (book) Hans-Georg Gadamer on Education, Poetry, and History, 1992; contbr. articles to profl. jours. Fulbright scholar, Duisburg, 1977-79, Fulbright sr. scholar Heidelberg, 1999; faculty rsch. grantee Hendrix Coll., 1985, 88, 91, 93, 96. Mem. AAUP (pres. Hendrix chpt. 1987-91, 95—), Ark. Philos. Assn., Am. Philos. Assn., Phi Beta Kappa. Avocations: travel, skiing, hiking. Office: Hendrix Coll Conway AR 72032

SCHMIDT, LYNDA WHEELWRIGHT, psychotherapist; b. Beijing, July 29, 1931; came to the U.S., 1931; d. Joseph Balch and Jane Byers (Hollister) Wheelwright; m. Klaus Dieter, May 8, 1930; children: Karen Calley, Claudia Lewis. BA, U. Calif., Berkeley, 1965, MSW, 1968. Cert. Jungian analyst; bd. cert. diplomate Am. Bd. Examiners Clin. Social Work. Staff psychiat. social worker Pacific Med. Ctr., San Francisco, 1968-71; pvt. practice psychotherapy and Jungian analysis San Francisco, 1971-87, Brooklin, Maine, 1985—; tng. analyst CG Jung Inst., San Francisco, 1978—; mem. certifying com. CG Jung Inst., San Francisco, 1980-84; cons. and lectr. in field. Author: Time Out of Mind: Trekking the Hindu Kush, 1978, The Long Shore, A Psychological Experience of the Wilderness, 1991; contbr. articles to profl. jours. Fellow Calif. Soc. Clin. Social Workers; mem. NASW, Acad. Cert. Social Workers, Inc., CG Jung Inst. (chair certifying com. 1980-84), Alpha Phi Sorority. Democrat. Avocations: books, horses, travel, music. Home and Office: PO Box 2426 North Conway NH 03860-2426

SCHMIDT, MAARTEN, astronomy educator; b. Groningen, Netherlands, Dec. 28, 1929; came to U.S., 1959; s. Wilhelm and Antje (Haringhuizen) S.; m. Cornelia Johanna Tom, Sept. 16, 1955; children: Elizabeth Tjimkje, Maryke Antje, Anne Wilhelmina. BSc, U. Groningen, 1949; PhD, Leiden U., Netherlands, 1956; ScD, Yale U., 1966. Sci. officer Leiden Obs., The Netherlands, 1953-59; postdoctoral fellow Mt. Wilson Obs., Pasadena, Calif., 1956-58; mem. faculty Calif. Inst. Tech., 1959-95, prof. astronomy, 1964-95, exec. officer for astronomy, 1972-75, chmn. div. physics, math. and astronomy, 1975-78, mem. staff Hale Obs., 1959-80, dir. Hale Obs., 1978-80, emeritus prof. astronomy, 1996—. Co-winner Calif. Scientist of Yr. award, 1964. Fellow Am. Acad. Arts and Scis. (Rumford award 1968); mem. Am. Astron. Soc. (Helen B. Warner prize 1964, Russell lecture award 1978), NAS (fgn. assoc., recip. James Craig Watson Medal, 1991), Internat. Astron. Union, Royal Astron. Soc. (assoc., Gold medal 1980). Office: Calif Inst Tech 105 24 Robinson Lab Pasadena CA 91125-0001

SCHMIDT, MARTHA BUBECK, educator, counselor; b. Cadott, Wis., Sept. 28, 1912; d. Karl Christian and Lydia Sarah (Keller) Bubeck; m. Eugene Milton Schmidt, Sept. 11, 1943; children: Eugene Karl, Fredric John. BS, U. Wis., Stout, 1934; MPhil, U. Wis., Madison, 1947, M in Psychology and Behavioral Studies, 1959. Tchr. home econs. Barron (Wis.) High Sch., 1934-37; supr. student teaching U. Wis., Stout, 1937-38; state supr. home econs. edn. Wis. State Bd. Vocat. Edn., Madison, 1938-48; instr. adult evening sch. Madison Area Tech. Coll., 1949-69; guidance counselor Madison Met. Schs., 1959-79; coord. AARP and Wis. Ret. Tchrs. Assn., Madison, 1986-90; state chmn. health/long term care action group AARP, Wis., 1990-91; coord. health advocacy svcs. AARP, 1991—; founder Future Homemakers of Am., 1943, past advisor; condr. fgn. study programs, Europe, Asia, Australia, 1971-88. Bd. dirs. Madison Oakwood Retirement Ctr., 1983-89, mem. resident care com., 1992—; com. mem. Wis. Legis. Study Elderly Abuse, 1985-88. Recipient Disting. Educator award, U. Wis., Stout, 1998. Mem. AARP, Wis. Ret. Tchrs. Assn. (rec. sec. 1983-89, found. bd. dirs. 1998), AAUW, Nat. Honor Soc. Home Econs., Luth. Women Missionary League, Valparaiso U. Guild (state pres. 1981-85), Madison Civics Club, Rotary (Sr. Svc. award 1998). Lutheran. Avocations: travel, volunteering. Home: 3709 Zwerg Dr Madison WI 53705-5229

SCHMIDT, MARTIN, nephrologist; b. Kassel, Germany, Feb. 25, 1970; s. Eberhard and Anita (Weber) S. MD, Göttingen, 1997. Avzt im Praktikum Uni-Klinik, Munich, 1997-98, asst., 1998—. Contbr. articles to profl. jours. Avocations: philosophy, sports. Home: Klenzestr 44, 80469 Munich Germany

SCHMIDT, MICHAEL FRIEDRICH GEORG, molecular biologist, educator; b. Langenselbold, Germany, Aug. 13, 1946; s. Friedrich Georg and Magdalene (Pagel) S.; m. Margaret Judith Burgin, May 31, 1974; 1 child, Christopher Easthope. Diploma, U. Giessen, Germany, 1972, Dr.rer.nat., 1975. Rsch. asst. U. Giessen, 1972-77; rsch. fellow Wash. U., St. Louis, 1977-79; asst. prof. U. Giessen, 1980-86; assoc. prof. Kuwait U. Faculty of Medicine, 1986-90; prof. Free U. Dept. of Virology, Berlin, 1990-93; dir. Dept. of Immunology and Molecular Biology Free U., Berlin, 1993—; cons. Biochem. Jour., London, 1994, Med. Prin. Practice, Kuwait, 1993—, various rsch. funding agencies internat., 1990—; vice dean rsch. Faculty of Vet. Scis., Free U., Berlin, 1999—. Author books; contbr. articles to profl. jours. Mem. Faculty Coun., Berlin, 1993—. Grantee German Rsch. Coun., 1980—, Kuwait U., 1986-90. Mem. Biochem. Soc., German Soc. of Virology, German Soc. of Biol. Chemistry, Gesellschaft f. Naturund Heilkuude. Avocations: tennis, skiing, classical music. Office: Free Univ Dept Immun/Molec Biology, Luisenstr 56, Berlin 10117, Germany

SCHMIDT, NANCY ANNE, psychotherapist; b. Jersey City, July 18, 1958; d. William John Lawrence and Ruth Martha (Morant) S. BA summa cum laude, Fordham U., 1986; MA summa cum laude, N.J. City State U., 1990; cert. pastoral counselor, World Christianship Ministries, 1994. Cert. social worker, criminal justice specialist, hypnotherapist, addiction counselor, eating disorders specialist; cert. domestic violence counselor, cert. crisis counselor. Adj. prof. N.J. City State U. (formerly Jersey City State Coll.), 1988-91, adj. prof. psychology, 1990-94; pvt. practice West New York, 1990—; counselor Substance Abuse Treatment Ctr., Union City, N.J., 1994-96; substance abuse program dir. Sr. Treatment and Edn. Program, Union City, 1994-96; staff psychotherapist North Hudson Cmty. Action Corp. Mental Health Ctr., West New York, 1996-98, dir. mental health, addictive svcs., social work, psychiatry, 1998—; bd. dirs. Hudson Health Care Partnership, Jersey City; bd. dirs. Hudson County Healthy Families 2000, mem. Hudson County Task Force on Women & Addiction, co-dir. Union City Police Dept./NHCAC Domestic Violence Outreach Program, Union City Police Dept. stress reduction cons.; presenter in field. Mem. APA, Am. Counseling Assn., Am. Assn. Family Counselors (cert.), Nat. Assn. Alcohol and Drug Abuse Counselors, Am. Assn. Christian Counselors, Am. Psychotherapy Assn., Alpha Sigma Lambda, Phi Kappa Phi, Psi Chi. Avocations: swimming, walking, reading, writing, poetry. Office: North Hudson Cmty Action Corp Mental Health Addictive Svc 5301 Broadway West New York NJ 07093-2622

SCHMIDT, OTTO, molecular biologist; b. Karlsruhe, Germany, July 20, 1947; m. Waltraud Kellenberger, Aug. 18, 1971; 1 child, Rolf. PhD, U. Freiburg, Germany, 1977. Rsch. asst. U. Freiburg, 1975-77, asst. prof., 1982-88; postdoctoral fellow Yale U., New Haven, 1978-80, rsch. assoc., 1980-81; vis. scientist Stockholm U., 1989-91; prof. molecular biology, head dept. U. Adelaide, Australia, 1992—. Office: U Adelaide, Waite Rd, Glen Osmond SA 5064, Australia

SCHMIDT, PAUL GERHARD, humanities educator; b. Mar. 25, 1937. PhD, U Gottingen, 1962. Prof. U. Marburg, Fed. Republic Germany, 1978-89, U. Freiburg, Fed. Republic Germany, 1989—; vis. fellow Oxford U., Eng., 1977, Florence, Italy, 1997. Author: Supplemente lateinischer Prosa, 1964; editor: Johannes de Hauvilla, Architreni(u)s, 1973, Visio ThurKilli, 1978, Otloh von St. Emmeran, Liber vision(u)m, 1989, Johannes von Magdeburg, Vita Margarete Contracte, 1992, Karolellus, 1996, Visio Alberici, 1997, Humanismus im deutschen suedwesten, 2000. Office: Freiburg U, Werthmann Platz 1-3, D-79085 Freiburg Germany

SCHMIDT, PAUL JOEL, lawyer; b. Milw., Nov. 25, 1961; s. Joel Schmidt and Mary Bierlein. BA, Colo. Coll., 1985; postgrad., U. Mich., 1986-88; JD, U. Colo., 1992. Bar: Colo. 1992, U.S. Dist. Ct. Colo. 1993. Assoc. Crane, Leake, Casey et al, Durango, Colo., 1993-95; dep. dist. atty. 6th Jud. Dist., Durango, 1995—. Actor Project A Jacky Chan H.K., 1983. Regional coord. Access Fund, Four Corners, 1993-95. Chinese Studies fellow U. Mich., 1987-88. Avocations: mountaineering, rock climbing, hiking, mountain-biking, skiing. Office: Office Dist Atty 1060 E 2d Ave Durango CO 81301

SCHMIDT, ROBERT, retired mechanics and civil engineering educator; b. Ukraine, May 18, 1927; came to U.S., 1949, naturalized, 1956; s. Alfred and Aquilina (Konotop) S.; m. Irene Hubertine Bongartz, June 10, 1978; children: Ingbert Robert. Student, UNRRA-Univ., Munich, 1946-47, Technische Hochschule Karlsruhe, Germany, 1947-49, Vorpruefung; BS, U. Colo., 1951, MS, 1953; PhD, U. Ill., 1956. Tech. draftsman Kalisch, Poland, 1943-45; rsch. asst. U. Ill., 1953-56; asst. prof. mechanics U. Ill., Urbana, 1956-59; assoc. prof. U. Ariz., Tucson, 1959-63; prof. mechanics and civil enging. U. Detroit, 1963-99, chmn. civil enging. dept., 1978-80; ret., 1999; lectr. Oakland U., 1997-98; rschr. in linear and nonlinear theory of elasticity, theories of arches, plates, and shells, and approximate methods of analysis. Editor: Indsl. Math., 1969—; book reviewer Applied Mechanics Rev., Indsl. Math. Jour.; contbr. numerous articles to profl. jours. With C.E., U.S. Army, 1951-52. Grantee NSF 1960-78. Mem. AAUP, ASCE, ASME (cert. recognition 1972), Am. Acad. Mechanics (a founder), Indsl. Math. Soc. (pres. 1966-67, 81-84, 1st Gold award 1986), Sigma Xi. Avocations: biosophy, walking, bicycling, swimming.

SCHMIDT, ROBERT FRANZ, physiologist, educator; b. Ludwigshafen, Germany, Sept. 16, 1932; s. Richard and Maria (Leistenschneider) S.; m. Lotte Lambrecht, 1969; children: Sabine, Christian, Christoph. Med. student, Heidelberg U., 1959; PhD, Australia Nat. U., Canberra, 1963; habil., Heidelberg U., 1964; DSc (hon.), U. NSW, Sydney, 1996. Asst. scientist Heidelberg U., 1963-65; scientist Rat Physiol. Inst., Heidelberg, 1966-70, SUNY, Buffalo, 1970-71; prof., dir. Physiol. Inst. U. Kiel, 1971-82; prof. Vorst Physiol. Inst. U. Würzburg, 1982. Home: Oberer Dallenbergweg 6, D-97082 Würzburg Germany

SCHMIDT, ROBERT MILTON, physician, scientist, educator, administrator; b. Milw., May 7, 1944; s. Milton W. and Edith J. (Martinek) S.; children Eric Whitney, Edward Huntington. AB, Northwestern U., 1966; MD, Columbia U., 1970; MPH, Harvard U., 1975; PhD in Law, Medicine and Pub. Policy, Emory U., 1982; MA, San Francisco State U., 1999. Diplomate Am. Bd. Preventive Medicine. Resident in internal medicine Univ. Hosp. U. Calif.-San Diego, 1970-71; resident in preventive medicine Ctrs. Disease Control, Atlanta, 1971-74; commd. med. officer USPHS, 1971; advanced through grades to comdr., 1973; dir. hematology div. Nat. Ctr. for Disease Control, Atlanta, 1971-78, spl. asst. to dir., 1978-79, inactive res., 1979—; clin. asst. prof. pediatrics Tufts U. Med. Sch., 1974-86; clin. asst. prof. medicine Emory U. Med. Sch., 1971-81, clin. assoc. prof. community health, 1976-86; clin. assoc. prof. humanities in medicine Morehouse Med. Sch., 1977-79; attending physician dept. medicine Wilcox Meml. Hosp., Lihue, Hawaii, 1979-82, Calif. Pacific Med. Ctr., San Francisco, 1983—; dir. Ctr. Preventive Medicine and Health Research, 1983—, dir. Health Watch, 1983—; sr. scientist Inst. Epidemiology and Behavioral Medicine, Inst. Cancer Research, Calif. Pacific Med. Ctr., San Francisco, 1983-88; prof. hematology and gerontology, dir. Ctr. Preventive Medicine and Health Rsch., chair health professions program San Francisco State U., 1983-99, prof. medicine, 1983—, prof. emeritus, 1999—; dir. Health Watch Internat., 1997—; cons. WHO, FDA, Washington, NIH, Bethesda, Md., Govt. of China, Mayo Clinic, Rochester, Minn., Northwestern U., Evanston, Ill., U. R.I., Kingston, Pan Am. Health Orgn., Inst. Pub. Health, Italy, Nat. Inst. Aging Rsch. Ctr., Balt., U. Calif., San Diego, U. Ill., Chgo., Columbia U., N.Y.C., Brown U., Providence, UCLA, U. Calif., San Francisco, Harvard U., Stanford U., Boston, U. Chgo., Emory U., Atlanta, Duke U., N.C., U. Tex., Houston, Ariz. State U., U. Hawaii, Honolulu, U. Paris, U. Geneva, U. Munich, Heidelberg U., U. Frankfurt, U. Berlin, Cambridge (Eng.) U., U. Singapore, others; vis. rsch. prof. gerontology Ariz. State U., 1989-90; mem. numerous sci. and profl. adv. bds., panels, coms. Mem. editorial bd. Am. Jour. Clin. Pathology, 1976-82, The Advisor, 1988—, Generations, 1989—, Contemporary Gerontology, 1994—, Alternative Therapies in Health and Medicine, 1995—, Aging Today, 1997—; book and film reviewer Sci. Books and Films, 1988—, many other jours.; author: 17 books and manuals including Hematology Laboratory Series, 4 vols., 1979-86, CRC Handbook Series in Clinical Laboratory Science, 1976—; assoc. editor: Contemporary Gerontology, 1993—; contbr. more than 300 articles to sci. jours. Alumni regent Columbia U. Coll. Physicians and Surgeons, 1980—. Northwestern U. scholar, 1964-66; NSF fellow, 1964-66; Health Professions scholar, 1966-70; USPHS fellow, 1967-70; Microbiology, Urology, Upjohn Achievement, Borden Rsch. and Virginia Kneeland Frantz scholar awards Columbia U., 1970; recipient Am. Soc. Pharmacol. and Exptl. Therapy award in pharmacology, 1970, Commendation medal USPHS, 1973, Meritorious Performance and Profl. Promise award, 1989, Student Disting. Teaching and Svc. award Pre-Health Professions Student Alliance, 1992, Leadership Recognition awards San Francisco State U., 1984-89, 91-96, Meritorious Svc. award, 1992. Fellow ACP (commentator ACP Jour. Club/Annals of Internal Medicine 1993—), AAAS (med. scis. sect.), Royal Soc. Medicine (London), Gerontol. Soc. Am., Am. Geriatrics Soc., Am. Coll. Preventive Medicine (sci. com.), Am. Soc. Clin. Pathology, Internat. Soc. Hematology; mem. AMA, APHA, Am. Med. Informatics, Internat. Commn. for Standardization in Hematology, Am. Soc. Hematology, Internat. Soc. Thrombosis and Hemostasis, Acad. Clin. Lab. Physicians and Scientists, Am. Assn. Blood Banks, Nat. Assn. Advisors for Health Professions (bd. dirs.), Am. Assn. Med. Informatics (chair prevention and health evaluation informatics WG), Calif. Coun. Gerontology and Geriatrics, Am. Coll. Occupl. and Environ. Medicine, Assn. Tchrs. Preventive Medicine (edn. com., rsch. com.), Am. Soc. Microbiology, Am. Soc. Aging (editl. bd. 1990—, Dychtwald Pub. Speaking award 1991), N.Y. Acad. Scis., Calif. Med. Assn., Internat. Health Evaluation Assn. (v.p. for Ams. 1992-94, bd. dirs. 1992—, pres. 1994-96), Cosmos Club, Golden Key (hon. faculty mem.), Army and Navy Club (Washington), Harvard Club (N.Y.), Havard Club (San Francisco), Knight of Malta, Sigma Xi, others. Fax: 415-956-8950. E-mail: rmschmidtmd@aol.com. Home: Whaleship Plaza 25 Hinckley Walk San Francisco CA 94111-2303 Office: Health Watch Med Ctr PO Box 7999 San Francisco CA 94120-7999

SCHMIDT, SASCHA LEONARD, strategic management consultant; b. Hagen, Germany, Feb. 8, 1971; s. Lieselotte Anderfuhr Schmidt. BBA, U. Essen, Germany, 1993; diploma in Bus. Adminstrn. summa cum laude, U. Zurich, Switzerland, 1996, DBA summa cum laude, 1999. Cert. first aid instr. German Red Cross, Unna, Germany, 1991. Rsch. asst., lectr. Inst. for Rsch. in Bus. Adminstrn., Zurich, Switzerland, 1994-98; lectr. for strategic mgmt. Kaderschule Zurich, Zurich, 1997-98; mgmt. cons. McKinsey & Co., Zurich; rsch. assoc. Harvard Bus. Sch., Boston, 1995, vis. scholar, 1999—. Author: Qualitaet und Effizienz als strategische Herausforderung im Gesundheitswesen, 1997; editor: (with Heinz Galli) Neuorientierung im Gesundheitswesen, 1998, Megamerger in der Pharmaindustrie, 2000. Avocations: tennis, skiing, theatre. E-mail address: sascha schmidt@mckinsy.com. Fax: 41.0.1876.9322. Home: Kinkelstr 10, CH-8006 Zurich Switzerland Office: McKinsey and Co, Alpenstr 3, Ch-8065 Zurich Switzerland

SCHMIDT, SEBASTIAN MARTIN, physicist, researcher; b. Stralsund, Germany, June 6, 1967; s. Martin Kurt and Ingrid Anita (Kruse) S.; m. Kerstin Doris Selkmann, June 19, 1998; 1 child, Greta Carlotta. Diploma in physics, Rostock (Germany) U., 1993, PhD in Nuclear Physics, 1995. Postdoctoral rschr. Tel Aviv U., 1995-96, Argonne (Ill.) Nat. Lab., 1999—; rsch. assoc. Rostock U., 1997-98; referee Phys. Rev.; spkr. in field. Contbr. numerous articles to profl. jours. Recipient Minerva stipend, 1995-96, A.v. Humboldt stipend, 1999—, Studientstiftung des Deutschen Volkes award, 1992. Mem. German Phys. Soc. Mem. Christian Dem. Union. Avocations: literature, sports, travel.

SCHMIDT, SIGURD OTTOVICH, historian, educator, researcher; b. Moscow, Apr. 15, 1922; s. Otto Yulievich Schmidt and Margarita Emmanouilovna Golosovker. Grad., Moscow State U., 1944; Candidate of History, U. Moscow, 1949. Chief editor History of USSR, 1956-60; rsch. fellow Inst. Russian History, Moscow, 1956—; prof. The Hist.-Archival Inst., Moscow, 1979—; chmn. Archeographical Commn., 1968—. Author: Stanozlenie Rossiiskogo Samoderjavstva, 1973, Rossiiskoe Gosudarstvo Vscreoline, 1984, Kraevednie i Documentalnii Pamyatniki, 1992, Local History and Doument Monuments, 1992, At the Beginning of the Absolutism, 1996, Put Istorika, 1997, Archeography, 1997, Rossia Ivana Groznogo, 1999; chief editor (ency) Moscow, 1994-97. Mem. presidium CIBAL UNESCO, 1976-91. Recipient prize Govt. Russian Fedn., 1998, Pushkin medal, 1999; named Honored Scientist, 1987. Mem. Russian Acad. Edn., Acad. Scis. Poland (fgn.), Union Local Historians (chmn. 1991—). Home: Krivoarbatsky 12 cv 8, 121002 Moscow Russia Office: Archeographiceskaya Komissa, ul Dmitria Ulianova 19, 117096 Moscow Russia

SCHMIDT, TERRY LANE, health care executive; b. Chgo., Nov. 28, 1943; s. LeRoy C. and Eunice P. Schmidt; children: Christie Anne, Terry Lane II. BS, Bowling Green State U., 1965; MBA in Health Care Adminstrn, George Washington U., 1971; DHA, Med. U. S.C., 2000. Resident in hosp. adminstrn. U. Pitts. Med. Center, VA Hosp., Pitts., 1968-69; adminstrv. asst. Mt. Sinai Med. Center, N.Y.C., 1969-70; asst. dir. Health Facilities Planning Council of Met. Washington, 1970-71; asst. dir. dept. govtl. relations A.M.A., Washington, 1971-74; contract lobbyist and govtl. rels. Wash. Reps. in Health, Washington, 1974-87; pres. Terry L. Schmidt Inc. Physician Svcs. Group, San Diego, 1987-99, Washington Actions on Health, 1975-79; partner Washington Coun. Medicine and Health, 1979-81; pres. Recreational

Enterprises, Inc., Washington, 1977-78; v.p. Crisis Communications Corp. Ltd., 1982-90; pres. Med. Cons. Inc., 1983-84, Ambulance Corp. Am., La Jolla, Calif., 1984-87; exec. dir., chief operating officer Emergency Health Assocs. P.C., Phoenix, 1989-91, Charleston Emergency Physicians, Inc., S.C., 1990-94, Joplin Emergency Physican Assocs., 1991-92, Big Valley Med. Group, 1991-92, Blue Ridge Emergency Physicians, P.C., 1992-94, Berkeley Emergency Physicians, P.C., 1992-94; chmn., pres. Univ. Inst., 1992—; asst. dir. Dept. of Emerg. Med., Med. U.S.C., 1999—; bd. dirs., Univ. Inst., 1997—, lectr., instr. dept. health svcs. adminstrn. George Washington U., 1969-83, preceptor, 1975-84; adj. prof. grad. sch. Pub. Health San Diego State U., 1996—, preceptor, 1989—, guest lectr. health care adminstrn. Nat. U. San Diego, 1992-93; guest lectr. Bus. Adminstrn. U.S. Internat. U., San Diego, 1994—; instr. Nat. Naval Sch. Health Care Adminstrn., 1971-73; faculty Civil Svc. Commn. Legis. Insts., 1972-76; fac. Am. Assn. State Colls. and U. Health Tng. Insts., 1975-78; mem. adv. com. ambulatory care standards Joint Commn. Accreditation of Hosps., 1971-72, pres., Recreational Enterprises, Inc., Wash., 1977-78, guest lectr., Coll. of Med. & dept. Health Admin. & Pol., Med. U.S.C., 1998-99, preceptor, 1999—, assoc. prof., Coll. of Health, Med. U.S.C., 1999—. Author: Congress and Health: An Introduction to the Legislative Process and the Key Participants, 1976, A Directory of Federal Health Resources and Services for the Disadvantaged, 1976, Health Care Reimbursement: A Glossary, 1983; mem. editl. adv. bd. Nation's Health, 1971-73; contbr. articles to profl. jours. Bd. dirs. Nat. Eye Found., 1976-78. Mem. Med. Group Mgmt. Assn., Health Care Fin. Mgmt. Assn., Assn. Venture Capital Groups (bd. dirs. 1984-89), Amer. Coll. of Health Execs., Amer. Coll. of Med. Prac. Exec., Soc. for Acad. Emerg. Med., Assn. of Univ. Progs. in Health Admin., San Diego Venture Group (chair 1984-87), Univ. Club (life), Natl. Rep. Club, Nat. Dem. Club (life), Capitol Hill Club (life), Alpha Phi Omega (pres. Bowling Green alumni chpt. 1967-70, sec.-treas. alumni assn. 1968-71). Office: Terry L Schmidt Inc 7770 Regents Rd Ste 113 San Diego CA 92122-1967

SCHMIDT, VOLKER HERMANN, social scientist; b. Itzehoe, Germany, Dec. 23, 1959; s. Hermann and Inge (Moeller) S. Diploma in Sociology, U. Bielefeld, Germany, 1987; PhD, U. Bremen, Germany, 1995. Rsch. assoc. U. Bremen, Germany, 1989-95; vis. fellow U. Oxford, U.K., 1992; asst. prof. U. Mannheim, Germany, 1995—; vis. fellow Harvard U., Cambridge, Mass., 1997-98. Co-author: Neue Technologien - verschenkte Gelegenheiten?, 1991, Lokale Gerechtigkeit in Deutschland, 1997; author: Politik der Organverteilung, 1996, Bedingte Gerechtigkeit, 2000. Mem. N.Y. Acad. Sci., Akademie fuer Ethik in der Medizin, Deutsche Akademie fuer Transplantationsmedizin. Office: U Mannheim Faculty Soc Sci, Seminargebaeude A5, 68131 Mannheim Germany

SCHMIDT, VOLKER REINHARD, chemist; b. Unna, Germany, Mar. 21, 1956; m. Junko Kamakura, Apr. 7, 1995. BSc, Coll. Engring., Aachen, Germany, 1981; MSc, U. Bremen, Germany, 1986, PhD, 1989. Sr. rsch. asst. U. Bremen, 1987-88; rsch. fellow Riken Inst., Wako-Shi, Japan, 1986; lab. mgr. Beiersdorf/tesa, Hamburg, Germany, 1989-92; R & D mgr. Asia/Pacific Beiersdorf/tesa, Yokohama, Japan, 1993-95; head adhesive devel. Beiersdorf/tesa, Hamburg, 1996—. Office: Beiersdorf AG, Dept 2217, D-20245 Hamburg Germany

SCHMIDT, WALDEMAR ADRIAN, pathologist, educator; b. L.A., Aug. 22, 1941; s. Waldemar Adrian and Mary Charlotte (Parker) S.; m. Karmen LaVer Bingham, Feb. 1, 1963; children: Rebecca, Sarah, Waldemar, Diedrich. BS, Oreg. State U., 1965; PhD, U. Oreg., 1969, MD, 1969. Intern U. Oreg. Hosps. and Clinics, Portland, 1969-70, resident, 1970-73; pathologist LDS Hosp., Salt Lake City, 1973-77; prof. pathology U. Tex. Med. Sch., Houston, 1977-91; prof. pathology Oreg. Health Sci. U. and VA Med. Ctr., Portland, 1991—, chief pathology and lab. medicine svc., 1997—, vice chair pathology, 1997—. Author: Principles and Techniques of Surgical Pathology, 1982; editor Cytopathology Annual, 1991-94, Revs. in Pathology-Cytopathology, 1994-99. Asst. scoutmaster Boy Scouts Am., Houston, 1982-91. Maj. U.S. Army, 1970-76. Fellow Am. Soc. Clin. Pathologists, Coll. Am. Pathologists; mem. Internat. Acad. Cytology, Am. Coll. Physician Execs., Sigma Xi, Alpha Omega Alpha. Avocations: photography, silviculture, apiculture. Office: VA Med Ctr 3710 SW Us Veterans Hospital R Portland OR 97201-2964

SCHMIDT, WILLIAM MAX, management consultant, business executive; b. Danville, Pa., Nov. 23, 1947; s. Frank Wilhelm and Doris Savilla (Maurer) S.; m. Marylea O'Reilly, Sept. 20, 1980. BS, U. Pa., 1969; MBA, Northwestern U., 1971. Mktg. specialist Moody's Investors Svc., Inc., N.Y.C., 1971-72; cons. William E. Hill & Co. Inc., N.Y.C., 1972-74; product supr. Internat. Paper Co., N.Y.C., 1974-79; dir. market analysis U.S. Industries, Inc., Stamford, Conn., 1979-82, mgr. corp. devel., 1982-84; dir. corp. mktg. Combustion Engring., Inc., Stamford, Conn., 1984-86; v.p. mktg., planning Combustion Engring., Inc., Union, N.J., 1986-91; pres. Pragmatics, Basking Ridge, N.J., 1991—. Author: (newsletter) Think Again, 1995. Bd. dirs. Curbing Hunger, Inc., Basking Ridge, N.J., 1995—; adv. Jr. Achievement, N.Y.C., 1976-78. Mem. TAPPI, Exec. Forum, Strategic Leadership Forum, Univ. Club, Sons of the Revolution, Wharton Club (N.Y.C.), Sigma Chi. Republican. Mem. United Ch. of Christ. Avocations: tennis, astronomy, canoeing, community service, numismatics. Home and Office: 46 Quincy Rd Basking Ridge NJ 07920-2245

SCHMIDT, WOLF-DIETER, veterinarian; b. Posen, Poland, Aug. 22, 1944; s. Rolf and Eleonore (Pfeiff) S.; m. Karin Stradtmann, July 4, 1970; 1 child, Christiane. Degree in vet. medicine, U. Hannover, Germany, 1973, DVM, 1974. Asst. vet. practice Hamburg, Germany, 1974-75; pvt. vet. medicine practice Wolfsburg, Germany, 1975—; tchr. postgrad. studies in field. Author: Publications of Behavior Therapy, 1995, 97. Lt. German Navy, 1965-67. Mem. German Animal Behaviour Therapists, European Soc. Vet. Clin. Ethology, German Animal Vet. Assn., German Vet. Dermatol. Soc., Internat. Radiographic Vet. Assn. Avocations: sailing old ships, riding, reading political literature. Office: Friedrich Ebert Str 61-63, 38440 Wolfsburg Germany

SCHMIDT-ASSMANN, EBERHARD, law educator; b. Celle, Germany, Feb. 13, 1938; s. Julius and Anna (Assmann) S.-A.; m. Ulrike Knoke, May 23, 1969. JD, U. Goettingen, Germany, 1967, D in Legal Education, 1971. Prof. U. Bochum, Germany, 1972-79, U. Heidelberg, Germany, 1979—. Author: Constitution, 1969, Urban Planning Law, 1972, Administrative Law, 1982, Environmental Law, 1991, 2nd vol., 1994, Local Government, 1995, Administrative Procedure Law, 1996, General Principles of Administrative Law, 1998. Mem. Vereinigung der Deutschen Staasrechtlehrer, Berl. Akademie der Wissenschaften. Avocation: literature. Office: U Heidelberg, Friedrich-Ebert-Anglage 6-10, 69117 Heidelberg Germany

SCHMIDT-BIGGEMANN, WILHELM, philosophy educator, dean; b. Olpe, Germany, June 23, 1946; s. Karl and Paula (Biggeymann) Schmidt; m. Cordula Lütticke, June 16, 1947; children: Damian, Cosima, Benedikt. PhD, Ruhr U., Bochum, Germany, 1974; Habilitation, Freie U. Berlin, 1987. Head dept. Herzog August Bibliothek Wolfenbüttel, Germany, 1975-79; asst. prof. Freie U. Berlin, 1979-85, rsch. dir., assoc. prof., 1985-89, dir., prof. Inst. Philosophy, 1989-92, dean Inst. Philosophy, 1992-95. Author: Maschine Und Teufel, 1975 (prize 1975), Topica Universalis, 1983, Theodizee und Tatsachen, 1988, Sinn-Welten-Welten-Sinn, 1992, Philosophia Perennis, 1998, Blaise Pascal, 1999. Mem. election bd. Deutscher Akademischier Austauschdienst, Fgn. Ministery, Germany, 1992—. Recipient Comenius medal Comenius Mus., 1991, Golden medal Carls U. Prague, 1993. Home: Feldstr 28, 12207 Berlin Germany Office: Inst Philosophie FU, Inst Philosophie FU, Habelschwerdter Allee 30, 14195 Berlin Germany

SCHMIDT-JORTZIG, EDZARD, former member of parliament. Min. justice Fed. Ministry Justice, Bonn, Germany, 1999. Office: Bundeshaus, D-53113 Bonn Germany

SCHMIDTKE, HANS-HERBERT, chemistry educator; b. Rastenburg, Germany, July 9, 1929; s. Robert Emil and Asta (Pietsch) S.; m. Helga Kühnel, Jan. 13, 1962; children: Jacqueline, Hans-Jürgen. Diploma, U. Frankfurt, Fed. Republic Germany, 1956, PhD, 1958; habilitation, U. Frankfurt, 1967; postgrad., Northwestern U., 1959-60. Scientist Max Planck Inst., Munich, 1960-61, Cyanamid Rsch. Inst., Geneva, 1961-68; prof. U. Frankfurt, 1969-73, U. Düsseldorf, Federal Republic Germany, 1974—; dir. U. inst. Theoretical Chemistry, Düsseldorf, 1974-94, prof. emeritus, 1994—. Author: Quantum Chemistry, 1987, 2d edit. 1994. Grantee Deutsche Forschungsgemeinschaft, 1970-94. Mem. Deutsche Bunsengesellschaft. Avocations: tennis, classical music. Office: Heinrich-Heine-U, Universitätsstr 1, D-40225 Düsseldorf Germany

SCHMIDTKE, JÖRG, geneticist, educator, administrator; b. Braunschweig, Germany, July 8, 1946; s. Gotthard and Elsa (Weinlich) S.; m. Veronika Sieben, 1972 (div. 1993); children: Adrian, David, Benjamin; m. Bettina Pape; 1 child, Claudia. Exam., U. Freiburg, 1973, MD, 1974; Dr.med.habil., U. Göttingen, 1981. Asst. prof. U. Göttingen (Germany) Dept. Human Genetics, 1977-81, sect. leader, 1983-88; sect. leader Free U. Dept. Human Genetics, Berlin, Germany, 1988-90; head Dept. Human Genetics, Med. Sch., Hannover, Germany, 1990—; co-chair Human Gene Mapping Workshops, 1988-91; cons. in field. Author: DNA-Fingerprinting, 1994, 98, Vererbung und Ererbtes; author/editor: Gentherapie, 1995, 97. Heisenberg fellow Deutsche Forschungsgemeischaft, 1981. Mem. Am. Soc. Human Genetics, Human Genome Orgn., German Bd. Med. Genetics (pres. 1993-97), German Soc. Human Genetics (pres. 1998-2000), European Soc. Human Genetics (bd. dirs. 1997—). Office: Dept Human Genetics, Medizinische Hochschule, D-30623 Hannover Germany

SCHMIDT-TRUCKSÄSS, ARNO, internist; b. Hannover, Germany, May 17, 1960; s. Bernhard and friedel (Bähre) S.; m. Michaela Trucksäss; 1 child, Senta. MD, PhD, Univ. Hosp. Göttingen, Germany, 1986. Clinician, rschr. dept. preventive, rehab., sports medicine Ctr. for Internal Medicine, Univ. Hosp. Freiburg, Germany, 1996—. Contbr. articles to profl. jours. Maj. German Army. Mem. Am. Coll. Sports Medicine, German Soc. Sports Medicine, German Soc. Internal Medicine. Avocations: jogging, classical music, European history. Office: Univ Freiburg Clinic, Hugstetter Str 55, 79106 Freiburg Germany

SCHMIECHEN, MICHAEL, retired hydromechanical systems researcher; b. Reinbek, Germany, Mar. 22, 1932; s. Richard S.W. and Helene F.J. (Ruess) S.; m. Susanne E.M. Loeper, Dec. 23, 1958; children: Catharina, Henriette, Johanna, Carl Philipp. Diploma in engring., Tech U. Berlin, 1958; postgrad., Imperial Coll. Sci. and Tech., London, 1958-59; PhD in Engring., Tech U. Berlin, 1964; postdoctoral Max-Kade rsch. fellow, MIT, 1968-69; habilitation for hydromech. systems, Tech U. Berlin, 1970. Scientific officer to dep. and acting dir. The Berlin Model Basin (VWS), Berlin, 1959-97; privatdozent and adj. prof. hydromech. systems Tech. U. Berlin, 1974-97; ret., 1997; vis. prof., Indian Inst. Tech., Madras, 1973, Tokyo U., 1973, Ship Scientific Rsch. Ctr., Wuxi, China, 1996; sec., exec. com. Internat. Towing Tank Conf., Berlin and Ottawa, Can., 1969-75, mem. and sec. symbols and terminology group, 1975-96; mem. and dep. chmn. ship hydromechanics com., Schiffbau-Technische Gesellschaft, Berlin/Hamburg, Germany, 1985—. Editor Procs. 13th Internat. Towing Tank Conf., 1972; author, organizer, presenter and editor 1st and 2d Internat. Workshop, Rational Theory of Ship Hull-Propeller Interaction, Berlin, 1991; contbr. articles to profl. jours. Elder, Kaiser Friedrich Luth. Ch., Berlin-Tiergarten, 1978-93. Mem. Soc. Naval Archts. and Marine Engrs., Verein Deutscher Ingenieure. Avocations: hiking, travel, theory, philosophy and history of science. E-mail: m.schm@t-online.de. Home: Bartningallee 16, Tiergarten Berlin D-10557, Germany

SCHMIEDEKNECHT, MARTIN ERICH LUDWIG, microbiologist, researcher; b. Saalfeld, Thuringia, Germany, Jan. 8, 1927; s. Albert Erich Ludwig and Ida Margarethe Ernestine (Enge) S.; m. Lisa Schmiedeknecht Neubauer, May 22, 1954; children: Angela, Uta. Diploma in Biology, U. Jena, Germany, 1953, D Natural Sci., 1955, Habilitation, 1963. Sci. asst. U. Jena, 1953-55; rschr. Inst. Phytopathology, Aschersleben, Germany, 1955-66; chief rschr. Inst. Cereal Breeding, Hadmersleben, Germany, 1966-72, Inst. Phytopathology, Aschersleben, Germany, 1972-81; custodian Herbarium Haussknecht, U. Jena, 1981-91; rschr., 1992—; participant as mykologist and phytopathologist biol. expdn. through Mongolia and Gobi desert, 1964, Cuba and eastern coastal lowland of Mexico, 1967-68, highland of Armenia and Caucasia, 1975, lowland of Turan and surrounding mountain chains, 1985, coastal B.C., 1994, Palestine and the Nile valley, 1998, Zimbabwe, Namibia, Botswana, South Africa, 2000; collector, determinator voluminous collections of exsiccated fungi from Mongolia, Cuba, Mexico and Caucasus; discoverer, descriptor, author numerous new taxa of microscopic fungi from Ctrl. Asia and Mid. Am; initiator virulence frequency monitoring system for cereal rusts and mildews in East European countries. Co-author: Phytopathology and Plant Protection, Vol. I and II, 1964, 2d edit., 1974, Urania Plants Kingdom, 1974, 2d edit., 1977, 3d edit., 1991, transl. in Hungarian, 1975, The Problem of Species and Races in Fungi, 1964, Production of Cereals, 1970, Hindrance and Promotion of Phytopathogenic Microorganisms in the Soil, 1961, Problems of the Physiology of Disease Resistance, 1963, General Mykology, 1993; contbr. articles to profl. jours. Mem. Soc. Mycology and Lichenology Germany. Avocations: ethnology, formative arts. Home: Halberstädter Strasse 22, D-06449 Aschersleben Germany

SCHMIEDING, HOLGER, economist; b. Papenburg, Lower Saxony, Germany, Jan. 10, 1958; s. Lothar and Anneliese (Lechtenberg) S.; m. Simone Ferling, May 5, 1992; children: Hannes, Malte, Lasse. Vordiplom, U. Munich, 1980; Diploma in Econs., U. Kiel, Germany, 1984, D in Social Scis., 1992. Journalist Westfaelische Nachrichten, Muenster, Germany, 1976-78; economist Kiel Inst. of World Econs., Germany, 1986-93, Internat. Monetary Fund, Washington, 1993; chief economist Merrill Lynch, Frankfurt, Germany, 1993-97; chief economist Europe Merrill Lynch, London, 1998—. Co-author: (book) The Fading Miracle, 1992; author: (book) Europe After Maastricht, 1992. Mem. Mont Pelerin Soc. Roman Catholic. Office: Merrill Lynch, 25 Ropemaker St, London EC2Y, England

SCHMIED-KOWARZIK, WOLFDIETRICH, philosophy educator; b. Friedberg, Hessen, Germany, Mar. 11, 1939; s. Walther and Gertrud (von den Brincken) S.; m. Iris von Gottberg, Mar. 3, 1966; children: Anatol, Daria, Robin. Dr.phil., U. Vienna, 1963; Habil., U. Bonn, 1970. Wiss. asst. U. Bonn, 1964-71; prof. philosophy U. Kassel, Germany, 1971—; dir. Interdisz. Arbeitsgruppe Philosophische Grundlagenprobleme, Kassel, 1979—. Author: Fragments on the Dialectic of Philosophy, 1974, A Dialectical Philosophy of Education, 1974 (Portuguese edit. 1983), The Dialectic of Social Action, 1981, The Dialectic in the Relationship of Human Beings and Nature, 1984, Education, Emancipation and Morality, 1993, Richard Hoenigswald's Philosophy of Education, 1995, Schelling's Philosophy of Nature, 1996, Thinking as a Responsibility to History, 1999; editor 26 books; contbr. more than 200 articles to profl. jours. Recipient Bundesverdienstkreuz Bundespräsident d Bundesrepublik Deutschland, 1999, Festschrift zum 60. Geburtstag "Kritik und Praxis", 1999. Mem. Ulrich Sonnemann Gesellschaft (dir.), Internat. Fichte Gesellschaft, Internat. Schelling Gesellschaft, Internat. Hegel Gesellschaft, Allgem. Gesellschaft für Philosophie, others. Office: U Gesamthoschschule Kassel, Nora-Platiel-Str 1, D-34109 Kassel Germany

SCHMINCKE, HANS ULRICH, educator; b. Detmold, Germany, Oct. 21, 1937. MA, Johns Hopkins U., 1962, PhD, 1964. Postdoctoral U. Heidelberg, Germany, 1965-69; asst. prof. U. Bochum, Germany, 1969-76, assoc. prof., 1976-89; prof. U. Kiel, Germany, 1990—. Author 4 books; contbr. articles to profl. jours. Recipient Bowen award Am. Geophys. Soc., Leibniz prize Deutsche Forschungs Gemeinschaft, 1991, Thorarinsson medal Internat. Assn. Volcanology.

SCHMITT, BERND HERBERT, business educator; b. Heidelberg, Germany, Oct. 22, 1957; s. Herbert Scmitt and Anna Gefaeller; m. Hisako Fujii, Sept. 14, 1996. Diploma, U. Heidelberg, 1994; PhD, Cornell U., 1998. Prof. Columbia U., N.Y.C., 1988—; head mktg. CEIBS, Shanghai, China, 1996—; dir. Ctr. Global Brand Leadership, N.Y.C., 1998—; cons. Co-author: Marketing Aesthetics, 1997; author: Experiential Marketing, 1999. Avocations: opera, travel, art collecting. Fax: 212-864-8762. Office: Columbia U Sch Bus 510 Uris Hall New York NY 10025

SCHMITT, CHRISTIAN KARL W., romance linguist, educator; b. Mosbach, Germany, Mar. 27, 1944; s. Karl Martin and Herta Anna Clara (Fiehn) S.; m. Danielle Blanche Fouache, Aug. 1, 1970; children: Frank, Jens. Staatsexamen, U. Heidelberg, Germany, 1968, PhD, 1973, Dr. phil. habil., 1977. Wissenschaftlicher asst. U. Heidelberg, Germany, 1969-77, privatdozent, 1977; prof. U. Hamburg, Germany, 1977-79, U. Bonn, Germany, 1979-83; full prof. U. Heidelberg, Germany, 1984-88; full prof. U. Bonn, Germany, 1988—, dir. Seminary of Romance Langs., dean, 1992-96; dir. Heidelberg Inst. Translatology, 1984-88, Romanisches Seminar Bonn, 1988—; dir. Internat. Bd. of Univs. for Translators and Interpreters, 1985-87; mem. Kuratorium Deutsch-Französisches Jugendwerk, 1992-98. Editor Romanistisches Jahrbuch, 1988—; editor, author: Handbook of Romance Linguistics, 1988—; author: The Linguistic Areas of Galloromania, 1974, Dictionary of Industries: French/German, German/French, 1993, Contributions to Developmental Linguistics, 1988, New Methods in Translation, 1990, Andrés Bello, 2000. Recipient Preis der Neuphilologischen Fakultät Heidelberg, 1973. Mem. Soc. de Linguistique Romane, Deutscher Romanistenverband, Deutscher Hispanistenverband. Avocations: chess-game, handball, music, folklore, athletics. Home: Bennauerstrasse 33, 53115 Bonn Germany Office: U Bonn, Am Hof 1, 53113 Bonn Germany

SCHMITT, HANS JUERGEN, physics educator, researcher; b. Dortmund, Germany, Aug. 3, 1930; s. Alfred and Lieselotte (Thiemann) S.; m. Ilse Gerwig, Aug. 31, 1956; children: Sabine, Mathias, Christine, Justine. Diploma in Physics, U. Göttingen, Germany, 1954, D in Nat. Scis., 1955. Asst. prof. Harvard U., Cambridge, Mass., 1956-63; staff mem. Sperry-Rand, Sudbury, Mass., 1963-65; group leader Philips Rsch. Lab., Hamburg, Germany, 1965-67; dept. head Philips Rsch. Lab., Hamburg, 1967-80; prof. Rheinisch Wesf. Tech. HochSchul, Aachen, Germany, 1980-96; prof. emeritus Rheinisch Wesf. Tech. HochSchul, Aachen, 1996—; chmn. European Microwave Conf., Hamburg, 1975, MMCom., Hamburg, 1976-77, Fakultaetentag Elektrotechnik, Aachen, 1989-91; dir. Rheinisch Wesf. Tech. Hochschul Inst. HF Technique, Aachen, 1980-95; vertrauensdozent Studienstiftung d Deutschen Volkes, Bonn, Aachen, 1981—. Author, co-author over 200 sci. papers as articles in profl. jours. or presentations at sci. confs.; inventor with 25 patents. Recipient fellowship Guggenheim Found., N.Y., Europe, 1961. Fellow IEEE (treas. German sect. 1997—, treas. region 8 1998—); mem. Verband Deutscher Elektrotechniker-Aachen (beisitzer 1994). Avocations: tennis, writing. Home: Hangstr 34, 52076 Aachen Germany Office: Rheinisch Wesf Tech HochSch, Melatener Str 25, 52056 Aachen Germany

SCHMITT, JACKY, biotechnologist, researcher; b. Bischwiller, France, Oct. 27, 1961; s. Arsène and Jacqueline (Hoff) S.; children: Thomas, Philippe. MS, U. Louis Pasteur, Strasbourg, France, 1985, Doctor, 1993. Engr. EMBL, Heidelberg, Germany, 1985-89, rsch. asst., 1989-93; postdoctoral fellow Max-Planck-Inst. for Immunobiology, Freiburg, Germany, 1993-95; group leader P&U Diagnostics, Freiburg, Germany, 1995—. Avocation: music. Office: Pharmacia and Upjohn, Munzingerstrasse 7, 79111 Freiburg Germany

SCHMITT, JÜRGEN MARTIN, biology educator; b. Weinheim, Germany, Aug. 20, 1948; s. Friedrich and Ruth (Reinemuth) S. Staatsexamen, U. Heidelberg, Germany, 1973; dr. rer. nat., U. Düsseldorf, Germany, 1978; habil., U. Würzburg, Germany, 1986. Rsch. scientist U. Düsseldorf, Germany, 1978-79; postdoctoral fellow Carlsberg Labs., Copenhagen, 1979-80; asst. U. Würzburg, Germany, 1980-89; prof. Freie U., 1989—. Avocation: audiophile. Office: Freie U Pflanzenphysiol, Königin Luise Str 12-16, 14195 Berlin Germany

SCHMITT, KARL M., political scientist; b. Säckingen, Baden, Germany, June 4, 1944; s. George M. and Josefine M. (Meffert) S.; m. Dorothea Kaehler, 1983; children: Peter, Paul, Klara. PhD, U. Freiburg, Germany, 1977, Dr. Habil., 1985. Asst. prof. U. Freiburg, 1972-86; prof. U. Cologne, Germany, 1986-92; prof. polit. sci. dept. U. Jena, Germany, 1992—. Editor: Die Verfassung des Freistaats Thueringen, 1995; contbr. articles to profl. jours. Mem. Deutsche Gesellschaft fur Politikwissenschaft (pres.). Roman Catholic. Office: Inst Politikwissenschaft, Univ Jena, D-07740 Jena Germany

SCHMITT, RALPH GEORGE, manufacturing company executive; b. Tarrytown, N.Y., Aug. 8, 1944; s. Alfons George and Otillie Lucie (Mehler) S.; m. Kathleen OShaughnessy; children: Ralpha Scott, Carrie Lee, Kurt Ryan. BS, MIT, 1966, MS, 1967; MS, U. Calif., 1970. Engr. McDonnell Douglas, Huntington Beach, Calif., 1967-70, Rockwell Internat., Downey, Calif., 1970-72; pres., chmn. bd. TPG Industries, L.A., 1972-74; gen. mgr. Columbia Yacht divsn. Whittaker Corp., Chesapeake, Va., 1975-76; v.p. ops., dir. R&G Sloane Mfg. Co., L.A., 1976-83; dir. mgr.-plastics Sweetheart Products Group Ft. Howard Paper Co., Wilmington, Mass., 1983-86; v.p., gen. mgr. PHI, City of Industry, Calif., 1986-90; v.p. ops. Dowty Aerospace, L.A., 1991-93; v.p. ops. Applied Sys. divsn. York (Pa.) Internat., 1993-96, v.p. product engring. and mfg. tech., 1996-99; v.p., gen. mgr. Airside Products, 1999-2000, Chillers, 2000—. Mem. MIT Alumni Assn. (nat. selection com. 1991-93), Tau Beta Pi, Sigma Xi, Sigma Gamma Tau, Sigma Alpha Epsilon. Home: 1730 Wyndham Dr York PA 17403-5913 Office: York Internat PO Box 1592-361C York PA 17405

SCHMITT, ROBERT LEE, computer scientist; b. Astoria, N.Y., Oct. 1, 1948; s. Edward and Margaret Louise (Gleason) S.; m. Elsy Evagelene Burnett, June 1999; stepchildren: Eric Jason Marin, Alexis Michelle Marin. AAS in Data Processing, SUNY, Farmingdale, 1972; student, Hofstra U., 1972-73; BS in Computer Sci., SUNY, Stony Brook, 1974, MS in Computer Sci., 1975; postgrad., U. Md., 1979-80, 94-96; grad. diploma in strategic sci., U.S. Naval War Coll., 1991. Cert. computer programmer, data processor. Computer programmer U.S. Army Environ. Hygiene Agy., Aberdeen Proving Ground, Md., 1976; data systems programmer Dept. Def., Ft. George G. Meade, Md., 1976-78; data systems analyst Dept. Def., Ft. George G. Meade, 1978-83, computer systems analyst, 1983-85, sr. computer systems analyst, 1985-86, computer scientist, 1986-89, sys. acquisition mgr., 1989-94, dep. dir. for tech. fellow, 1994-95, sr. computer scientist, 1995-96, stds., tng. and verification engr., 1996-97, systems engr., 1997-99, yr. 2000 compliance mgr., 1999, sys. arch. implementation engr., 2000—; with Va. Summer Inst. for Math. Tchrs., 1995-96, dir. 1996-2000. With USNR, 1968-79. Home: 3002 Viburnum Pl Olney MD 20832-3073 Office: 9800 Savage Rd Fort George G Meade MD 20755-6000

SCHMITT, ROLAND WALTER, retired academic administrator; b. Seguin, Tex., July 24, 1923; s. Walter L. and Myrtle F. (Caldwell) S.; m. Claire Freeman Kunz, Sept. 19, 1957; children: Lorenz Allen, Brian Walter, Alice Elizabeth, Henry Caldwell. BA in Math, U. Tex., 1947, BS in Physics, 1947, MA in Physics, 1948; PhD, Rice U., 1951; DSc (hon.), Worcester Poly. Inst., 1985, U. Pa., 1985; DCL (hon.), Union Coll., 1985; DL (hon.), Lehigh U., 1986; DSc (hon.), U. S.C., 1988, U. Tech. De Compeigne, 1991; DL (hon.), Coll. St. Rose, 1992, Russell Sage, 1993, Hartford Grad. Ctr., 1995, Ill. Inst. Tech., 1996, Rensselaer Polytechnic Inst., 1997. With GE, 1951-88; R & D mgr. phys. sci. and engring. GE, Schenectady, 1967-74; mgr. energy sci. and engring. R & D GE, 1974-78, v.p. corp. R & D, 1978-82, sr. v.p. corp. R & D, 1982-86, sr. v.p. sci. and tech., 1986-88, ret., 1988; pres. Rensselaer Poly. Inst., Troy, N.Y., 1988-93; ret., 1993; bd. dirs. Blasch Precision Ceramics, Reveo Corp., VRex, GlobalSpec.com, Logical Net, Value Innovations; bd. advisors LearnLinc, 1996—; tech. adv. bd. Chrysler Corp., 1990-93; tech. adv. coun. Mobil Corp., 1997-99; past pres. Indsl. Rsch. Inst.; energy rsch. adv. bd. U.S. Dept. Energy, 1977-83; mem. Nat. Sci. Bd., 1982-94, chmn., 1982, 84-98; chmn. CORETECH, 1988-93; mem. Com. on Japan, NRC, 1988-90, Comml. Devel. Ind. Adv. Group, NASA, 1988-90; exec. com. Coun. on Competitiveness, 1988-93; chmn. NRC Panel on Export Controls, 1989-91; mem. Dept. Commerce Adv. Commn. on Patent Law Reform, 1990-92; adv. bd. Oak Ridge Nat. Lab., 1993-98; chmn. Motorola's Sci. Adv. Bd., 1995-99; chmn. rsch. priority panel for NRC Future of Space Sci., 1994-95. Trustee N.E. Savs. Bank, 1978-84; bd. advisors Union Coll., Schenectady, 1981-84, Argonne Univs. Assn., 1979-82, RPI, 1982-88; bd. govs. Albany Med. Ctr. Hosp., 1979-82, 88-90; bd. dirs. Sunnyview Hosp. and Rehab. Ctr., 1978-86, Coun. on Superconductivity for Am. Competitiveness, 1987-89; mem. exec. com. N.Y. State Ctr. for Hazardous Waste Mgmt., 1988-89; chmn. Office of Tech. Assessment adv. panel on industry and environment; mem. Nat. Commn. Ill. Inst. Tech., 1993-94. With USAAF, 1943-46. Recipient RPI Community Svc. award, 1982, award for disting. contbns. Stony Brook Found., 1985, Rice U. Disting. Alumni award, 1985, IRI Medalist award, 1989, Royal Swedish Acad. of Engring. Sci., 1990, Arthur M. Bueche award Nat. Acad. of Engring.,1995; named Fgn.

Assn. of Engring. Acad. of Japan, U. Albany Found. Acad. Laureate, 1997; named to Jr. Achievement Capital Region Bus. Hall of Fame, 1996. Fellow AAAS, IEEE (Centennial medal 1984, Engring. Leadership award 1989, Founders medal 1992, Hoover medal 1993), Am. Phys. Soc. (Pake award 1993), Am. Acad. Arts and Scis.; mem. NAE (coun.), Am. Inst. Physics (chmn. 1993-98), Coun. Sci. Soc. Pres. (chair 1993-97), N.Y. Acad. Scis. (pres. coun. 1993—), Dirs. Indsl. Rsch., Rensselaer Alumni Assn. (Disting. alumni award 1993), Eta Kappa Nu. Office: PO Box 240 Rexford NY 12148-0240

SCHMITT, WILLIAM ALLEN, lawyer; b. Louisville, Aug. 29, 1909; s. Michael Joseph and Naoma Katherine Schmitt; m. Dorothy S. Turner, June 12, 1936 (dec. Feb. 1998); 1 child, Selene S. Kaelin. Grad., U. Louisville, 1933. Bar: Ky. 1936, U.S. Dist. Ct. (we. dist.) Ky. 1936, N.C. 1997. Pvt. practice law Louisville, 1936—; assoc. atty. Schmitt & Schmitt, Louisville, 1936-60; judge Jefferson County Probate Ct., Louisville, 1962-70; alcohol beverage control adminstr. Jefferson County Govt., Louisville, 1962-70; law ptnr. Schmitt & Sandmann, Louisville, 1968-74; pvt. practice law Louisville, 1974—. Author: Kentucky Probate, 1980, 2nd edit., 1997; contbr. articles to profl. jours. Election poll judge various gen. elections, Louisville; active Muir Chapel United Meth. Ch.; pres. Wildwood Country Club, 1964, Legal Aid Soc., Louisville, 1968. Lt. USN, 1944-46. Inductee Ky. Tennis Hall of Fame, 1993. Mem. ABA, ATLA, Am. Arbitration Assn. (arbitration panelist 1983—, cert. mediator 1985—), Nat. Assn. Securities Dealers (arbitration panelist 1990—, cert. mediator 1994—), Am. Coll. Trust and Estate Counsel (state chmn. 1978-83), Ky. Bar Assn. (life, spkr. at seminars and convs. 1960-80, pres. 1970-71, chmn. probate com. 1974-79, trustee 1979-84, clients indemnity fund), N.C. State Bar Assn., N.C. State Bar, Fla. Acad. Cert. Mediators, Louisville Bar Assn. (spkr. at seminars 1960-80, pres. 1966, chmn. probate com. 1974-79, various meritorious svc. awards 1966-75). Avocation: tennis. Home: 109 Sagewood Rd Jamestown NC 27282-9489 Office: PO Box 997 Jamestown NC 27282-0997 Office: 500 Ky Home Life Bldg 239 S 5th St Louisville KY 40202-3213

SCHMITT, WOLFGANG GEORG I HUBERTUS, radiologist; b. Worms, Rhine, Germany, Oct. 27, 1945; s. H.S. and Buxbaum G.H. Schmitt; m. Monika M. Willburger; children: Robert, Hannes, Eva. MD, Wuerzburg, 1971. Cons. U. Heidelberg, U. Tuebingen, U. Cologne and Bochum, 1972-87; prof., head of dept. Juliusspital Wuerzburg, 1987—. Author: 100 Jahre Roentgen, 100 Raetsel, 1975; contbr. articles to profl. jours.; patentee in field. Stabsarzt Sanitatsdienst d. Bundeswehr, 1971-72. Mem. German Roentgenology Soc. Avocation: painting. Home: Eisenmannstr 1, D97074 Wuerzburg Germany Office: Juliusspital Radiology, Juliuspromenade, D-97070 Wuerzburg Germany

SCHMITZ, CHARLES EDISON, evangelist; b. Mendota, Ill., July 18, 1919; s. Charles Francis Schmitz and Lucetta Margaret (Foulk) Schmitz Kaufmann; m. Eunice Magdalene Ewy, June 1, 1942 (dec. Mar. 2000); children: Charles Elwood, Jon Lee. Student, Wheaton Coll., 1936-37, 38, 39; BA, Wartburg Coll., Waverly, Iowa, 1940; BD, Wartburg Theol. Sem., Dubuque, Iowa, 1942, MDiv, 1977. Ordained to ministry Am. Luth. Ch., 1942. Founding pastor Ascension Luth. Ch., L.A., 1942-48, Am. Evang. Luth. Ch., Phoenix, 1948-65; dir. intermountain missions, founding pastor 14 Evang. Luth. Parishes, Calif., Ariz., N.Mex., Fla., 1942-89; evangelist Am. Luth. Ch., Mpls., 1965-73; sr. pastor Peace Luth. Ch., Palm Bay, Fla., 1973-89; pastor-at-large Am. Evang. Luth. Ch., Phoenix, 1989—; charter mem. Navajo Luth. Mission, Rock Point, Ariz., 1960—; chmn. Greater Phoenix Evangelical Ministers Assn., 1998-99; pastoral advisor Ariz. Luth. Outdoor Ministry Assn., Prescott, 1958-65, 89—; Kogudus Internat. Retreat master and chaplain, Fla., Berlin and Marbach, Germany, 1990; mem. transition team Fla. Synod, Evang. Luth. Ch. Am., 1985-89. Author: Evangelism for the Seventies, 1970; co-author: ABC's of Life, 1968; assoc. editor Good News mag., 1965-71. Founder, chmn. Ariz. Ch. Conf. on Adult and Youth Problems, 1956-65; vice chmn. synod worship & ch. music com. Am. Luth. Ch., Mpls., 1960-66; chmn. Space Coast Luth. Retirement Ctr., Palm Bay, Fla., 1985-89; chaplain Ariz. chpt. Luth. Brotherhood, 1991-2000. Named Citizen of Yr., Palm Bay C. of C., 1979. Mem. Nat. Assn. Evangelicals, Greater Phoenix Assn. of Evangelicals (pres.), German Am. Nat. Congress (nat. chaplain 1970), Lions (life mem., officer Phoenix and Palm Bay clubs 1952—, Ariz. Dist. 21A chaplain 1994-95, Melvin Jones fellow 1995), Kiwanis (bd. dirs. L.A. chpt. 1942-48). Republican. Home: 12444 W Toreador Dr Sun City West AZ 85375-1926

SCHMITZ, DOLORES JEAN, primary education educator; b. River Falls, Wis., Dec. 27, 1931; d. Otto and Helen Olive (Webster) Kreuziger; m. Karl Matthias Schmitz Jr., Aug. 18, 1956; children: Victoria Jane, Karl III. BS, U. Wis., River Falls, 1953; MS, Nat. Coll. Edn., 1982; postgrad., U. Minn., Mankato, 1969, U. Melbourne, Australia, 1989, U. Wis., Milw., 1989, Carroll Coll., 1990, Cardinal Stritch, 1990. Cert. tchr., Wis. Tchr. Manitowoc (Wis.) Pub. Schs., 1953-56, West Allis (Wis.) Pub. Schs., 1956-59, Lowell Sch., Milw., 1960-63, Victory Sch., Milw., 1964; tchr. Palmer Sch., Milw., 1966-84, 86-94, unit leader, 1984-86; ret., 1994; co-organizer Headstart Tchg. Staff Assn., Milw., 1968; insvc. organizer Headstart and Early Childhood, Milw., 1969-92; pilot tchr. for Whole Lang., Hi-Scope and Math. Their Way, 1988-93; bd. dirs. Curriculum Devel. Ctr. of Milw. Edn. Ctr., 1993-94. Author: (curriculum) Writing to Read, 1987, Cooperation and Young Children (ERIC award 1982), Kindergarten Curriculum, 1953. Former supporter Milw. Art Mus., Milw. Pub. Mus., Milw. County Zoo, Whitefish Bay Pub. Libr., Riveredge Nature Ctr.; vol. fgn. visitor program Milw. Internat. Inst., 1966-94, holiday folk fair, 1976-94, Earthwatch, 1989; lobbyist Milw. Pub. Sch. Bd. and State of Wis., 1986-93; coord. comty. vols., 1990-94. Grantee Greater Milw. Ednl. Trust, 1989. Mem. NEA (life), ASCD, Milw. Kindergarten Assn. (rec. sec. 1986-93), Nat. Assn. for Edn. of Young Children, Tchrs. Applying Whole Lang., Wis. Early Childhood Assn., Milw. Tchrs. Ednl. Assn. (co-chmn. com. early childhood 1984-86), Assn. for Childhood Edn. Internat. (charter pres. Manitowoc chpt. 1955-56), Milw. Educating Computer Assn., Alpha Psi Omega. Roman Catholic. Avocations: bicycling, nature, world travel. Home: 1355 Pinellas Bayway S Apt 22 Tierra Verde FL 33715-2140

SCHMITZ, GERHARD, mechanical engineer; b. Dortmund, Germany, Feb. 10, 1955; s. Albert and Käthe (Panzer) S.; m. Monika Zerbach, Feb. 19, 1982; children: Thomas, Eva Maria. Dipl. engr., Ruhr U., Bochum, Germany, 1980; D of Engring., Ruhr U., 1985. Rschr. Gaswärme Inst., Essen, Germany, 1980-86; dept. leader Gaswärme Inst., Essen, 1986-91; prof. Hamburg (Germany)-Harburg Tech. U., 1991—. Author: Optimierung des Energieverbrauch in mit Gas beheizten industriellen Chargenöfen, 1985. Mem. Deutscher Verein des Gas und Wasserfachs, Verein Deutscher Ingenieure. Social Democrat. Avocation: piano playing. Fax: +49 40 42878 2632. E-mail: schmitz@tu-harburg.de. Home: Rönneburger Kirchweg 16b, 21079 Hamburg Germany Office: Hamburg-Harburg Tech U, Denickestrasse 17, 21073 Hamburg Germany

SCHMITZ, HEINRICH WALTER, communications educator; b. Setterich, Germany, July 15, 1948; s. Josef and Marta (Zillessen) S.; m. Petra Quirmbach, July 24, 1970; 1 child, Jan David. MA in Anthropology, U. Bonn, Germany, 1973; PhD in Comm. Sci., U. Bonn, 1977. Rsch. asst. inst. anthropology U. Bonn, 1973-74, rsch. asst. inst. comm. rsch. phonetics, 1975-78, asst., 1978-89; vis. prof. comm. sci. U. Essen, Germany, 1989-92; prof. comm. sci. U. Essen, 1992—, dean faculty of lit. and linguistics, 1994-98. Mem. German Soc. Semiotics, Maatschappij der Nederlandse Letterkunde, Royal Dutch Acad. Scis. (fgn.). Office: U Essen FB 3, Univ St 12, D 45117 Essen Germany

SCHMITZ, HERMANN, philosophy educator; b. Leipzig, Saxony, Germany, May 16, 1928. PhD, U. Bonn, 1955; Habilitation, U. Kiel, 1958. Prof. U. Kiel, Germany, 1965-93, ordenlicher prof., 1971—, dir. Philos. Inst., 1971-93. Author 33 philos. books including Hegels Logik, 1992, Die Liebe, 1993, Adolf Hitler inder Geschichte, 1999, Der Spielraüm der Gegenwart, 1999, 10 vol. sys. of philosophy; contbr. many papers to profl. jours. Home: Steinstrasse 27, D-24118 Kiel Germany Office: Philos Seminar de Univ, Leibnizstrasse 6, D-24098 Kiel Germany

SCHMITZ, JUSTUS MICHAEL, textile company executive; b. Emsdetten, Germany, Dec. 3, 1947; s. Carl-Hinderich and Heidi (Beusch) S.; m. Sae Hyun Chung, Sept. 12, 1980; 1 child, Rudolf. Grad., U. Hamburg, 1978. Atty. Elring Dichtungswerke, Fellbach, Germany, 1978-80; export mgr. Schmitz Werke, Emsdetten, Germany, 1980-87, sales dir., 1987-89, pres., 1989—. Inventor in field. Bd. dirs. Textilverband Nord-West, Munster, Germany, 1994—. With German Mil., 1967-69. Fellow Rotary Club; mem. Verband der deutschen Heimtextilien Industrie, Verband der Nord-Westdeutschen Textilindustrie (pres.). Avocation: golf. Office: Schmitz Werke, Hansestr 87, D-48270 Emsdetten Germany

SCHMITZ, M. LIENHARD, molecular biologist, researcher; b. Tübingen, Baden-W., German, Feb. 16, 1961; s. Erhard and Elisabeth (Buurman) S.; m.. Susanne Bacher, Aug. 15, 1997; children: Johannes, Simon. MS, U. Göttingen, Germany, 1982; diploma, U. Freiburg, Germany, 1986, PhD, 1990, Habilitation, 1997. Postdoctoral fellow Max Planck Inst. for Biochemistry, Martinsried, Germany, 1990-93; asst. prof. U. Freiburg, 1993-95; vis. scientist U. Ghent, Belgium, 1996; group leader German Cancer Rsch. Ctr., Heidelberg, 1997—; referee several founds. and sci. jours. Contbr. numerous articles to sci., jours., chpts. to books. Grantee European Union, 1996, 2000, German Cancer Rsch. Ctr., 1997, U. Heidelberg, 1998. Mem. German Soc. for Immunobiology, Assn. for Biochemistry and Molecular Biology, N.Y. Acad. Scis. Home: Häusserstrasse 42, 69115 Heidelberg Germany Office: German Cancer Rsch Ctr, Neuenheimer Feld 280, 6912 Heidelberg Germany

SCHMITZ, RUDOLF PETER, physicist; b. Düren, Germany, Dec. 21, 1953; s. Josef and Agnes (Kirschsiefen) S.; m. Gabriele B. Hugot, Aug. 6, 1982; children: Guido, Rebecca, Rahel. D of Natural Scis., Rheinisch Westfälische Technische Hochschule, Aachen, Germany, 1981, Habilitation, 1988. Rsch. assoc. Rockefeller (N.Y.) U., 1982-83, Tech. U., Aachen, 1983-88, U. Fla., Gainesville, Fla., 1989; privat dozent U. Düsseldorf, Germany, 1990-95, U. Mainz, 1996—; vis. prof. MIT, Cambridge, Mass., 1990; apl. prof. RWTH Aachen, 1998. Heisenberg fellow Deutsche Forschungs-Gemeinschaft, 1990-95. Mem. Am. Phys. Soc., German Phys. Soc. Avocation: piano playing. Home: Karlstr 6, 52080 Aachen Germany

SCHMITZ, SHIRLEY GERTRUDE, marketing and sales executive; b. Brackenridge, Pa., Dec. 19, 1927; d. Wienand Gerard and Florence Marie (Grimm) S. BA, Ariz. State U., 1949. Tchr., guidance counselor Mesa (Ariz.) H.S., 1949-51; area mgr. Field Enterprises Ednl. Corp., Phoenix, 1951-52, dist. mgr., 1952, regional mgr., 1953-55; br. mgr. Field Enterprises Ednl. Corp., Montreal, 1955-61; nat. supr. Field Enterprises Ednl. Corp., Chgo., 1961-63, asst. sales mgr., 1963-65, nat. sales mgr., 1965-70; v.p., gen. sales mgr. F.E. Compton Co. divsn. Ency. Brit., Chgo., 1970-71, exec. v.p., dir. sales, 1971-73; pres. CHB Port-A-Book Store, Inc., 1973-76; gen. mgr. Bobbs-Merrill Co., Inc., Indpls., 1976-82; v.p. sales U. S. Telephone Comms. of Midwest, Inc., Indpls., 1982-83; exec. v.p. sales and market devel. Entertainment Publs. Corp., Birmingham, Mich., 1983-89; sr. v.p. mktg. and sales Entertainment Publs. Corp., Troy, Mich., 1989-92; prin. S.G. Schmitz and Assocs., Chgo., 1992—; bd. advisors, founder Ctr. Advanement of Small Bus., Ariz. State U. Sch. Bus.; bd. dirs. Spectral, Inc.; mem. pres.'s cabinet capital fund raising campaign Ariz. State U. Recipient Elizabeth Cutter Morrow award Internat. Bd. YWCA, 1978, Disting. Achievement award Ariz. State U., 1995, Angel award Ariz. chpt. Nat. Assn. Women Bus. Owners, 1996, Bus. Achievement award Beta Gamma Sigma, 1998. Home: 93 Miller Rd Hawthorn Wds IL 60047-1395 Office: SG Schmitz and Assocs Lake Zurich IL 60047

SCHMOCH, ULRICH ERNST, engineer, researcher; b. Mulheim/Ruhr, Germany, Apr. 20, 1954; s. Otto Richard and Edith Kathe (Kropp) S.; m. Sylvia Ilse Bottcher, Oct. 8, 1982; children: Thomas, Christina. Degree in engring., U. Grenoble, 1974; diploma in mech. engring., U. Hannover, 1977, PhD, 1983. Rsch. asst. Inst. for Turbo-Machines U. Hannover, 1978-80; patent engr. Patent Atty.'s Office Peerbooms, Wuppertal, 1983-85; sr. rschr. Fraunhofer Inst. for Sys. and Innovation Rsch., Karlsruhe, 1986-90, dep. head, 1991—; lectr. Polytech. Sch., Karlsruhe, 1987-88, U. Karlsruhe, 1998-99. Author: Technology Forecast by Patent Indicators, 1988 (Joseph von Fraunhofer award 1988), Competitive Advantage through Patent Information, 1990 (Joseph von Fraunhofer award 1990); editor, author: Organization of Science and Technology at the Watershed, 1996, Technology Transfer Systems in the United States and Germany, 1997. Mem. Applied Econs. Assn. (conf. organizing com. 1996—), Internat. Assn. Prodrs. and Users of Online Patent Info., German Assn. for Sci. and Tech. Rsch., German Assn. for Sociology. Avocations: jogging, playing the clarinet. Office: Fraunhofer Inst Sys Innov/Research, Breslauer Str 48, D-76139 Karlsruhe Germany

SCHMOECKEL, J. MICHAEL, cardiac surgeon; b. Stuttgart, Germany, Jan. 2, 1963; s. Dieter and Rotraut (Mayer) S.; m. Ingrid Oostendorp, Sept. 19, 1992; children: Felix, Pia. MD, U. Munich, 1989, PhD, 1999. Registrar cardiac surgery Klinkum Grosshadern, Munich, 1990-96; rsch. fellow dept. cardiothoracic surgery Papworth Hosp./U. Cambridge, Eng., 1996-97; team leader surgery Imutran Ltd., Cambridge, Eng. Contbr. articles to profl. jours. With German Army, 1989-90. Recipient Rsch. award German Heart Found., 1996; rsch. fellow German Rsch. Coun., 1996-97. Mem. German Assn. Thoracic, Cardiovasc. Surgery (Ernst-Derra award), Internat. Soc. Heart Lung Transplantation. Lutheran. Avocations: tennis, skiing, sailing, surfing.

SCHMOLKE, CORDULA, physician, anatomical researcher and educator; b. Bremerhaven, Germany, Feb. 10, 1955. Med. state exam., U. Duesseldorf, Germany, 1980, MD, 1982; postgrad., U. Bonn, Germany, 1991. Cert. specialist in anatomy. Postdoctoral fellow Anat. Inst. U. Bonn, 1981-92, asst. prof. Anat. Inst., 1992-98; extraordinary prof. Anat. Inst., asst. dr. in Rheinische Kliniken, Bonn, 1998—. Contbr. articles to Exptl. Brain Rsch., Anatomy and Embryology, Jour. of Anatomy., Oral Maxillofacial Surgery, Cerebal Cortex. Mem. Anatomische Gesellschaft, European Neurosci. Assn., Neurowissenschaftliche Gesellschaft. Achievements include research in cerebral cortex, masticatory apparatus. Office: Rheinische Kliniken Bonn, Kaiser Karl Ring 20, D-53111 Bonn Germany

SCHMOLL, HANS JOACHIM, internal medicine, hematology, oncology educator; b. Hannover, Germany, June 21, 1946; s. Johannes and Edeltraut (Schneider) S. MD, Med. U. Hannover, 1970, PhD, 1982. Rsch. assoc. Med. U., Hannover, 1971-84, prof. medicine and hematology-oncology, 1984-95; prof. medicine and hematology, chair hematology/oncology Martin Luther U., Halle-Wittenberg, Germany, 1996—. Author, editor: Kompendium Intern Onkologie, 1986, 3d edit., 1999. Home: Ludwig Barnay Strasse 9, D-30175 Hannover Germany Office: Martin Luther Univ, Dept Hematol/Oncol Int Med IV, D-06120 Halle Germany

SCHMUCKER, PETER, anesthesiologist; b. Nürnberg, Germany, Oct. 9, 1947; s. Walter and Emilie (Krämer) S. m. Rita Weirather, Aug. 6, 1973; 1 child, Katherina. MD, U. Munich, 1973. Privat dozent U. Munich, 1984; prof. Free U. Berlin, 1986—; dir., prof. Inst. Anaesthesiology of Heart Inst., Berlin, 1986-90; dir., prof. clinic of anesthesiology Med. U. Lübeck, Germany, 1990—. Avocations: literature, early music, reed instruments. Office: Med U Lübeck, Clinics for Anesthesiology, 23538 Lübeck Germany

SCHMUTH, GOTTFRIED PETER FRANZ, orthodontist; b. Vienna, Austria, June 29, 1926; arrived in Germany, 1955; s. Franz and Maria (Weigelsperger) S.; m. Ursula Muhlenbruch, Feb. 28, 1952; children: Axel, Thomas, Christof, Matthias. MD, U. Vienna, 1949; MD in Dentistry, U. Dusseldorf, Germany, 1955, Priv. Docent, 1957; Full Prof., U. Bonn, Germany, 1967. Head orthodontics dept. U. Cologne, Germany, 1960-67; adviser Bundeswehr. Deutscher Zahnazte U. Cologne, 1968-76; dir. Dental Sch. U. Bonn., 1967-91; prof. emeritus U. Bonn, 1992—; vis. prof. Inst. Odontol. Paulista, Sao Paulo, 1984; mem. NRS Bd. Orthodontists, Dusseldorf, 1962-67; coun. mem. Vereingung d. Hochschullehrer ZMK, 1970-74; coun. mem. Deutsche Gesellsh. Zahn-Mund-Kierferheilkd. 1971-79, European Orthodontists Soc., 1980—, pres. 1982; dean med. faculty U. Bonn, 1977-78; pres. Deutsch Gesellschaft Orthodontists, 1981-87. Author: Kieferorthopädie Thieme Verlag Stuttgart seit, 1973; editor: Praxis der Zahnheilkunde, 12 vols., 1968. Hon. mem. Verein Österreichischer Zahnärzte, Peruvian Orthodontists Soc., Deutsche Gesellsch. f. Kieferorthop., Acad. di Antropometria Oro-faciale, Rotary Club (pres. Bonn club 1991-92); hon. pres. Türkish Orthodont. Soc. Avocations: sports, music. Home: Am Kottenforst 33, D 53125 Bonn Germany

SCHNABEL, ECKHARD JOHANNES, theologian, educator; b. Stuttgart, Germany, May 9, 1955; s. Paul and Elsbeth (Blattner) S.; m. Barbara Cornelia Duerrschmidt, Sept. 11, 1981; children: Mirjam, Benjamin. ThM, FETA, Basel, Switzerland, 1979; PhD, U. Aberdeen, Scotland, 1983. Asst. prof. N.T. Asia Theol. Sem., Manila, The Philippines, 1985-88; lectr. Wiedenest Bible Coll., Bergneustadt, Germany, 1989-94; head N.T. dept. German Theol. Sem., Giessen, Germany, 1994-98; assoc. prof. N.T. Trinity Internat. U., Deerfield, Ill., 1998—; mem. exec. com. Arbeitskreis für evangelikale Theologie, Germany, 1991-98. Author: Law and Wisdom From Ben Sira to Paul, 1985, Inspiration und Offenbarung, 1986, Das Reich Gottes als Wirklichkeit und Hoffnung, 1993, Sind Evangelikale Fundamentalisten?, 1995, Die Gemeinde des neuen Bundes, 1996, Jesus and the Beginnings of the Mission to the Gentiles, 1994, Studium des Neuen Testaments, 2 vols., 1999-2000; contbr. articles to profl. jours. Mem. Soc. N.T. Studies, Tyndale Fellowship, Soc. of Bibl. Lit., Evangelical Theol. Soc., Inst. for Bibl. Rsch. Office: Trinity Internat U Half Day Rd Deerfield IL 60015

SCHNABEL, RALF PAUL HELMUT, neuropathologist, pathologist; b. Leipzig, Germany, May 31, 1928; m. Christa Else Rückardt, Dec. 5, 1964; children: Bettina, Rena. MD, U. Leipzig, Germany, 1952; Dr.med.habil., Med. Acad., Magdeburg, Germany, 1962. Sr. physician, chief dept. neuropathology Inst. Pathology, Magdeburg, 1955-64; chief sect. exptl. endocrinology German Acad. Scis., Jena, 1964-74; sr. physician Inst. of Pathology, Mcpl. Hosp., Bielefeld, Germany, 1978-79; dir. Inst. Neuropathology Bodelschwingh Hosp., Bielefeld, 1981-93; guest prof. U. Munich, 1993—; prof. Westfälische Wilhelms U., Muenster, Germany. Contbr. numerous articles to profl. jours. Mem. German Soc. for Neuropathology and Neuroanatomy, Internat. Soc. for Neuropathology, Internat. Brain Rsch. Orgn. of UNESCO, N.Y. Acad. Scis. Avocations: bibliophily, classical music, botany./. Home: Berliner str 34, D-80805 Munich Germany Office: Ludwig-Maximilians U Inst of Neuropathology, Thalkirchner Str 36, D-80337 Munich Germany

SCHNABEL, RONALD WOLFRAM, electrical engineer; b. Berlin, Apr. 12, 1963; s. Wolfram and Hildegard S.; m. Heike Schnabel. Engring. degree, Tech. U., Berlin, 1988, PhD, 1996. Scientific staff mem. Heinrich Hertz Inst., Berlin, 1988-97; mem. ops. support sys. staff Arcor AG & Co., Eschborn, Germany, 1997-2000; bus. cons. UMTS head dept. Motorola GmbH, Wiesbaden, Germany, 2000—. Roman Catholic. Avocations: violincello, basketball. Office: Hagenauer Str 47, 65203 Wiesbaden Germany

SCHNADER, JEFFREY Y., physician, educator; b. N.Y.C., Sept. 7, 1953. BA in Physics, Columbia Coll., 1975; MD, McGill U., 1979. Intern in medicine SUNY, Stony Brook, 1979-82; fellow in pulmonary medicine Johns Hopkins Sch. Medicine, Balt., 1983-87, fellow in environ. physiology, 1983-87; asst. prof. medicine U. Pa. Sch. Medicine, Phila., 1987-91; attending physician Hosp. U. Pa., Phila., 1987-91; asst. prof. medicine Cornell U. Med. Coll., N.Y.C., 1991-96; assoc. prof. medicine, physiology and biophysics Wright State U. Sch. Medicine, Dayton, Ohio, 1996—, chief pulmonary and critical care medicine, 1996—; chief pulmonary and critical care medicine, dir. med. ICU Dayton VAMC, Dayton, Ohio, 1996—. Mem. editl. bd. Chest, 1998—, deptl. editor, 1998—; contbr. more than 30 articles to profl. jours. Mem. adv. bd. Am. Lung Assn. Ohio, Dayton, 1999—; mem. fgn. lang. adv. bd. Oakwood Bd. Edn., Dayton, 1999—; boys team soccer coach Miami Valley Youth Soccer Assn., Dayton, 1998—. Fellow Am. Coll. Chest Physicians (nominating com., edn. com. 1998—, mktg. com., program com. 1998—); mem. Am. Thoracic Soc. (program com. 1995—), Ohio Thoracic Soc. (v.p. 1999-2000, pres.-elect 2000—), Am. Physiol. Soc. Avocations: soccer, fluency in French. Office: Dayton VAMC (111) 4100 W 3rd St Dayton OH 45417-1443

SCHNAGL, ROGER DIETER, microbiology educator, virologist, researcher; b. Reitendorf, Austria, Oct. 10, 1944; Heinz Günther and Elfriede Gerhild (Prandstetter) S.; Heather York Syme, Feb. 25, 1978. BSc, U. Melbourne, 1968, BSc (honors), 1969, PhD, 1975. Postdoctoral rsch. fellow microbiology dept. U. Melbourne, 1975-78; lectr. dept. Microbiology LaTrobe U., Melbourne, 1979-86, sr. lectr. dept. microbiology, 1987—, head of dept. microbiology, 1993—; demonstrator, tutor U. Melbourne, 1968-77; tutor Ormond Coll., 1970-77, St. Hilda's Coll., 1978-80; virol. cons. Alice Springs (Australia) Hosp., 1976—; rsch. grant reviewer Nat. Health and Med. Rsch. Coun. Australia, Canberra, 1982—; mem. human ethics com. LaTrobe U., 1987-94, dep. chair, 1991-94. Contbr. articles to profl. jours. Numerous rsch. grants and awards, 1979—. Fellow Australian Soc. for Microbiology; mem. N.Y. Acad. Scis., Rich River Golf Club, Royal Automobile Club of Victoria. Avocations: squash, tennis, scuba diving, philately. Office: LaTrobe U Dept Microbiology, Plenty Rd, Bundoora 3083, Australia

SCHNAPF, ABRAHAM, aerospace engineer, consultant; b. N.Y.C., Aug. 1, 1921; s. Meyer and Gussie (Schaeffler) S.; m. Edna Wilensky, Oct. 24, 1943; children: Donald J., Bruce M. BSME, CCNY, 1948; MSME, Drexel Inst. Tech., 1953. Registered profl. engr., N.J. Devel. engr. on lighter-than-air aircraft Goodyear Aircraft Corp., Akron, Ohio, 1948-50; mgr. fire control system def. electronics RCA, Camden, N.Y., 1950-55, mgr. airbourne navigation system, aerospace weapon system, 1955-58; program mgr. TIROS/TOS weather satellite systems RCA Astro-Electronics, Princeton, N.J., 1958-70, mgr. satellite programs, 1970-79, prin. scientist, 1979-82; cons. Aerospace Systems Engring., Willingboro, N.J., 1982—; lectr., presenter on meteor. satellites, space tech., communication satellites. Sgt. USAF, 1943-46. Recipient award Nat. Press Club Washington, 1975, award Am. Soc. Quality Control-NASA, 1968, Pub. Svc. award NASA, 1969, cert. of appreciation U.S. Dept. Commerce, 1984, RCA David Sarnoff award; inducted into Space Tech. Hall of Fame, 1992; named to 5000 Personalities of the World, named Internat. Man. of Yr. 1992-93. Fellow AIAA; mem. Am. Astro. Soc., Am. Meterol. Soc., Space Pioneers, N.Y. Acad. Scis. (mem. think tank week sessions 1980's), N.J. Arbitration Soc.

SCHNAPP, ROGER HERBERT, lawyer; b. N.Y.C., Mar. 17, 1946; s. Michael Jay and Beatrice Joan (Becker) S.; m. Candice Jacqueline Larson, Sept. 15, 1979; 1 child, Monica Alexis. BS, Cornell U., 1966; JD, Harvard U., 1969; postgrad. Pub. Utility Mgmt. Program, U. Mich., 1978. Bar: N.Y. 1970, U.S. Ct. Appeals (2d cir.) 1970, U.S. Supreme, 1974, U.S. Dist. Ct. (so. dist.) N.Y. 1975, U.S. Ct. Appeals (4th and 6th cirs.) 1976, U.S. Ct. Appeals (7th cir.) 1977, U.S. Dist. Ct. (so. dist.) N.Y. 1975, U.S. Dist. Ct. (no. dist.) Calif. 1980, U.S. Ct. Appeals (8th cir.) 1980, Calif., 1982, U.S. Dist. Ct. (cen. dist.) Calif. 1982, U.S. Ct. Dist. (ea. dist.) Calif., 1984. Atty. CAB, Washington, 1969-70; labor atty. Western Electric Co., N.Y.C., 1970-71; mgr. employee rels. Am. Airlines, N.Y.C., 1971-74; labor counsel Am. Electric Power Svc. Corp., N.Y.C., 1974-78, sr. labor counsel, 1978-80; indsl. rels. counsel Trans World Airlines, N.Y.C., 1980-81; sr. assoc. Parker, Milliken, Clark & O'Hara, L.A., 1981-82; ptnr. Rutan & Tucker, Costa Mesa, Calif., 1983-84, Memel, Jacobs, Pierno, Gersh & Ellsworth, Newport Beach, Calif., 1985-86, Memel, Jacobs & Ellsworth, Newport Beach, 1986-87; pvt. practice Newport Beach, 1987—; bd. dirs. Dynamic Constrn., Inc., Laguna Hills, Calif., 1986—; commentator labor rels. Fin. News Network; commentator Sta. KOCN Radio, 1990-91; lectr. Calif. Western Law Sch., Calif. State U.-Fullerton, Calif. State Conf. Small Bus.; lectr. collective bargaining Pace U., N.Y.C.; lectr. on labor law Coun. on Edn. in Mgmt.; N.E. regional coord. Pressler for Pres., 1979-80. Author: Arbitration Issues for the 1980s, 1981, A Look at Three Companies, 1982; editor-in-chief Indsl. and Labor Rels. Forum, 1964-66; columnist Orange County Bus. Jour., 1989-91; contbr. articles to profl. publs. Mem. Bus. Rsch. Adv. Coun. U.S. Dept. Labor; trustee Chapman U., 1991-95. Mem. Calif. Bar Assn. (chmn.), Labor Law Consulting Group, Calif. Bd. of Legal Specialization, Balboa Bay Club, The Ctr. Club, Club 33. Republican. Jewish. Office: PO Box 9049 Newport Beach CA 92658-1049

SCHNARRENBERGER, CLAUS, plant physiologist, educator; b. Karlsruhe, Germany, Aug. 6, 1939. Degree, U. Freiburg, 1966, D, 1969; habilitation, U. Kaiserslautern, 1974. Rsch. asst. Mich. State U., East Lansing, 1970-71; asst. prof. U. Kaiserslautern, Germany, 1972-78; prof. Free U., Berlin, 1979—; guest prof. Saga (Japan) Med. Sch., 1991-92, U. Ariz., 1995; guest scientist Nat. Inst. Basic Biology, Okazaki.

SCHNAUS, PETER, musical history educator; b. Berlin, Apr. 17, 1936; s. Kurt and Ilse (Grünbaum) S.; m. Ursula Grünbaum, Dec. 22, 1967; children:

Christian, Andrea, Susanne. Assessor, Studienseminar Hannover, Germany, 1968; PhD, U. Freiburg, Germany, 1976. Tchr. Hannover H.S., 1966-70; asst., tchr. Musikhochschule, Hannover, 1970-82, prof. music history, 1982—; mem. Senat Musikhochschule, Hannover, 1979-99, spkr. dept. instrumental edn., 1979—, v.p., 1986-90. Author: E.T.A. Hoffmann als Beethoven—Rezensent der Allgemeinen Musikalischen Zeitung, 1977; editor, author: Europäische Musik in Schlaglichtern, 1990; contbg. author: Kunst und Kultur, Vols. 3, 4 and 5, 1998-99; contbr. articles to profl. jours. Home: 4 Mendelssohnstrasse, D-30173 Hannover Germany Office: Hochschule für Musik, Emmichplatz 1, D-30175 Hannover Germany

SCHNEBELEN, PIERRE, resort planner and developer, consultant; b. Mulhouse, Alsace, France, June 10, 1935; s. Emile and Renee (Gingelwein) S.; children: Stephanie, Mathieu; m. Francois E. Roetynck, June 1, 1985; children: Yvan, Sophie, Wendy, Thomas. Diploma in engring., Ecole Nat. d'Arts et Metiers, Paris, 1958; MS, MIT, 1960. With Mobil Oil Internat., N.Y.C., 1961; founder, chief exec. officer SEFCO, 1965-73, Soc. des Telepheriques de la Grande Motte, 1967-87, SEGMO, 1974-88; founder, pres. SEPARFI, SEGMO IMMOBILIER; founder, dir. Soc. de reprentacoes et de participacoes, Sao Paulo, Brazil, 1977—; pres., chief exec. officer Piersen SA, 1989—; founder, pres. P.S.I. Resorts, Paris, 1988—; founder, pres. Soc. des telepheriques de Valfrejus, 1983-88, societa delle Funivie del Frejus, 1983-88; founder, dir. SEGMO Vacances; CEO West Rock Assocs. LLC, Boise, Idaho, 1998—; pres., CEO Athlon Fin. Corp., L.A., 1995—. Avocations: skiing, tennis, squash. Home: 20 El Oro Ln Pacific Palisades CA 90272-2813 Office: Athlon Resorts 1801 Ave Of Stars Los Angeles CA 90067-5902

SCHNECKER, NIELS, lawyer; b. Bucharest, Romania, Jan. 1, 1960; s. Kurt and Ruth (Dankner) S. LLM, U. Paris, 1982, PhD, 1987; MBA, Nat. Sch. Bus. Studies, Washington, 1990. Floor trader Merrill Lynch Pierce Fenner & Smith, London, 1982-83; mgr., v.p. Degefa Reisen, Frankfurt, Germany, 1983-85; assoc. Chula & May, Santa Anna, Calif., 1985-85; v.p., pres., ceo Internat. Investment Bankers Group, Colorado Springs, 1986-90; gen. mgr. rsch. & devel. Federal Express, Johannesburg, 1990-91; mng. sr. ptnr. Schnecker Van Wyk & Pearson, Johannesburg, 1991—; of counsel The White House, Washington, 1986-87; chief counsel Phemelo Found., African Nat. Congress, Johannesburg, South Africa, 1991-93; counsel Romanian Parliament, 1993—; Romanian Govt. counsel, 1993-96. Nat. com. U.S. Rep. Party, 1985—. Mem. Am. Mgmt. Assn., Am. Bank Attys. Assn., Inst. Dirs., Chartered Inst. Bankers, Jewish Lawyers Assn., Crans Montana Forum. Avocations: music, flying, skiing. Address: Ion Ionescu de la Brad 4, Schnecker Van Wyk 7 Pearson, Bucharest 1, Romania

SCHNEIDER, CALVIN, physician; b. N.Y.C., Oct. 23, 1924; s. Harry and Bertha (Green) S.; m. Elizabeth Gayle Thomas, Dec. 27, 1967. AB, U. So. Calif., 1951, MD, 1955; JD, LaVerne (Calif.) Coll., 1973. Intern L.A. County Gen. Hosp., 1955-56, staff physician, 1956-57; pvt. practice medicine West Covina, Calif., 1957—; staff Inter-Community Med. Ctr., Covina, Calif.; cons. physician Charter Oak Hosp., Covina, 1960—. With USNR, 1943-47. Mem. AMA, Calif. Med. Assn., L.A. County Med. Assn. Republican. Lutheran.

SCHNEIDER, CARL CHRISTOPH, pharmaceutical company executive; b. Leipzig, Germany, June 12, 1935; s. Carl and Ingeborg (Pohrt) S.; m. Gisela Stephan, Sept. 27, 1984; children: Carl Philipp, Sibylle, Andreas. PhD in Microbiology, U. Cologne, Germany, 1961; diploma, Inst. Tropical Disease, Hamburg, Germany, 1965. Postdoctoral fellow Columbia U., N.Y.C., 1961-62; rsch. assoc. Inst. Tropical Diseases, 1962-65; exptl. immunologist Biol. Inst., Cologne, 1965-72; dir. exptl. rsch. Madaus Pharm., Cologne, 1972-88; v.p. corp. projects Madaus AG, Cologne, 1988—; instr. Chamb. Ind. Comm., Cologne, 1966-73. Editor: Pharmacodynamics Procs., 1974; contbr. articles to sci. jours. Fellow N.Y. Acad. Scis.; mem. Lic. Execs. Soc., German Assn. Sci., German Assn. Tropical Medicine. Avocation: archaeology. Office: Madaus AG, Ostmerheimer Strasse 198, D-51109 Cologne Germany

SCHNEIDER, CARLOS RODOLFO, manufacturing company executive; b. Joinville, Brazil, Nov. 25, 1951; s. Carlos Frederico Adolfo Schneider and Theodora Isolde Odebrecht; m. Eliane Rassweiler, May 31, 1985; children: Hugo Carlos, João Rodolfo. BBA, EAESP/FGV, São Paulo, 1974, MBA, 1976. Dir. Granville, São Paulo, 1976-81; dir. Ciser, Joinville, 1981-85, v.p., 1985—; v.p. Hacasa, Joinville, 1985—; v.p. Sinpa, São Paulo, 1990—; counselor ACIJ, Joinville, 1986—. Contbr. articles to profl. jours. Mem. Consulate, Joinville, 1997—; counselor Desenville, Joinville, 1997—, Hosp. São José, Joinville, 1998-99, Sociesc-Sch., Joinville, 1990—. Named Outstanding Cmty. Mem., Assn. Comercial Indso. Joinville, 1996. Mem. Soc. Harminoa Lira, Joinville Tennis Club. Avocations: water sports, travel, reading. Office: Ciser, Cachoeira 70, 89205070 Joinville Brazil

SCHNEIDER, CYNTHIA PERRIN, ambassador, art history educator; b. Pa., Aug. 16, 1953; m. Thomas J. Schneider; 2 children. BA in Fine Arts magna cum laude, Harvard U., 1977, PhD in Fine Arts, 1984. Asst. curator European paintings Mus. Fine Arts, Boston, unitl 1984; asst. prof. art history Georgetown U., Washington, 1984-90, assoc. prof., 1990—; amb. to The Netherlands, Am. Embassy, The Hague, 1998—; lectr. on Rembrandt and Dutch art in U.S. and Europe. Author: Rembrandt's Landscapes; organizer, writer catalog for internat. loan exhbn. Rembrandts Landscapes: Drawings and Prints, Nat. Gallery Art, Washington, 1990; contbr. numerous articles on 17th Century Dutch art to profl. jours. Former vice chmn. President's Com. on Arts and Humanities, mem. steering com. for Creative Am. and millenium planning group, also chmn. fed. design subcom.; corrd. arts policy Clinton-Gore Campaign, 1992; former mem. bd. dirs. Nat. Mus. Women in Arts, Australian-Am. Leagership Dialogue. Office: Dept State Am Amb To The Netherlands Washington DC 20521-0001

SCHNEIDER, DENNIS EUGENE, manufacturing company executive; b. Bellevue, Ohio, Dec. 27, 1957; s. Vernon Edwin and Marquerite Mary (Best) S.; m. Sandra Lynn Seavolt, June 26, 1982; 1 child, Elaina Amanda. BS, Bowling Green State U., 1981; MBA, Rockford Coll., 1995. Buyer Teledyne Continental Aviation and Engring. Co., Toledo, 1981-84; div. purchasing mgr. Tappan Appliances, Mansfield, Ohio, 1984-85; corp. purchasing mgr. Marathon Electric Mfg. Corp., Wausau, Wis., 1985-88; materials mgr. Pacific Sci. Corp., Rockford, Ill., 1988-90; group materials mgr. Case Corp., Racine, Wis., 1990-93, ops. mgr., 1993-95, dir. global logistics, 1995-97, dir. supply chain Europe, Africa and Middle East, 1997; v.p. supply chain Allied Signal, Tempe, Ariz., 1998-2000; sr. v.p. supply chain and ops. World Kitchens, Elmira, N.Y., 2000—. Vol. Toledo Bid Bros./Big Sisters, 1982-85. Mem. Am. Prodn. and Inventory Control Soc., Nat. Assn. Purchasing Mgmt., Coun. Logistics Mgmt., Internat. Platform Assn., Ducks Unltd., Am. Chesapeake Club, KC. Republican. Roman Catholic. Avocations: history, dog tng., music, backpacking, wildlife art. Home: 213 Lincoln Rd Horseheads NY 14845-2267 Office: World Kitchens One Pyrex Pl Elmira NY 14902-1555

SCHNEIDER, DENNIS RAY, microbiology educator; b. Sinton, Tex., June 10, 1952; m. Cynthia Diane Schatte; 2 children. BA with honors, U. Tex., 1974, PhD, 1978. Post-doctoral fellow Behringwerke AG, Marburg/Lahn, West Germany, 1978-79, U. Mo. Med. Sch., Columbia, 1980-81; rsch. microbiologist New Eng. Nuclear, N. Billerica, Mass., 1981-82; R&D dir. Austin (Tex.) Biol. Lab., 1982-88; adj. assoc. prof. U. Tex., Austin, 1986—; R&D devel. dir. Micro-Bac Internat., Austin, 1988-94; v.p. Micro-Bac Internat., Round Rock, Tex., 1994—. Author: Bioremediation: A Desktop Manual for the Environmental Professional; author chpt. Microorganism Adaptation to Host Defense. Grantee NASA, 1988, 92, 93. Mem. AAAS, Am. Soc. for Microbiology, Mensa, Profl. Assn. Dive Instrs. Avocations: scuba diving, writing. Office: Micro-Bac Internat 3200 N I H 35 Round Rock TX 78681-2410

SCHNEIDER, DIETER, business administration educator; b. Striegau, Silesia, Germany, Apr. 2, 1935; s. Walter and Lina (Wolff) S.; m. Marlene Jakobs, 1971. Diploma, U. Frankfurt, 1957, D in Bus. Econs., 1960; D (hon.), U. Duisburg, 1992, U. Bayreuth, 1992, U. Wurzburg, 1992, U. Gottingen, 1995. Prof. bus. econs. U. Munster, 1965-70, U. Frankfurt, 1970-73, U. Bochum, 1973-2000; v.p. Verein für Social Politik, Germany, 1994-96. Author: Investition, Finanzierung und Besteuerung, 7th edit., 1992, Betriebswirtschaftslehre Vol. 1: Grundlagen, 2d edit., 1995, Vol. 2 Rechnungswesen, 2d edit., 1997, Vol. 3, Theorie der Unternehmung, 1997, Vol. 4 Geschichte und Methoden, 2000; co-editor Zeitschrift für Betriebswirtschaftliche Forschung, Steuer und Wirtschaft. Avocation: classical and chamber music. Home: Hofleite 12, 44795 Bochum Germany Office: Ruhr-U Bochum, Universitatsstrasse 150, 44780 Bochum Germany

SCHNEIDER, EUGENE SAUL, microbiologist, laboratory administrator; b. N.Y.C., Apr. 28, 1920; s. Isreal and Gertrude (Mendelsohn) S.; m. Bertha Gollan, Feb. 18, 1945; 1 child, Myles Gordon. BS in Microbiology, Cornell U., 1942. Cert. med. technologist, microbiologist. Microbiologist 50th Gen. Hosp., 1942-45, Morrisania City Hosp., Bronx, N.Y., 1946; rsch. microbiologist Coll. Phys. and Surg., N.Y.C., 1946; microbiologist Tacoma Gen. Hosp., 1946-48; lab. dir. Pierce County Hosp., Tacoma, 1948-52, St. Helens Med. Labs., Tacoma, 1952-68, Nat. Health Labs., Kent, Wash., 1985-92, Meridian Valley Lab., Kent, 1992—; founding pres. Wash. State Soc. Med. Tch., 1947-48, Wash. Soc. AMTs, 1963-66; mem. Stae Commn. on Alcoholism. Contbr. articles to profl. jours.; presenter in field. Mem. Tacoma Coun. on Alcoholism, 1961-75. 1st lt. U.S. Army, 1949-52. Recipient Disting. Citizen award, Olympia, Wash., 1972, Order of Golden Microscope, AMT, 1963. Mem. Anaerobic Soc. of the Ams. Democrat. Jewish. Avocations: painting, model railroading. Home: 6810 Opal Ln SW Tacoma WA 98498-6410 Office: Meridian Valley Clin Lab 515 W Harrison St Kent WA 98032-4403

SCHNEIDER, FRANK, psychiatrist; b. Wetzlar, Germany, Jan. 22, 1958; s. Robert H. and Christel (Kolberg) Mueller; m. Elisabeth L. Ruehl, Mar. 28, 1981; children: Julia Kim, Isabella, Magdalena. MD, U. Giessen, Germany, 1987; PhD in Psychology, U. Tuebingen, Germany, 1988, Habilitation, 1993. Lic. psychologist, physician, psychiatrist, psychotherapist. Resident and scientific fellow U. Tuebingen, 1986-91, assoc. prof. psychiatry, 1993-95, prof. clin. psychology, 1995; prof. of psychiatry U. Duesseldorf, Germany, 1996—; vis. assoc. prof. U. Pa., 1991-93; sr. physician Hosp. of the U. Tuebingen, 1993-95; head dept. clin. psychology U. Tuebingen, 1995; head outpatient svc. Psychiat. Hosp. of the U. of Duesseldorf, 1996—. Editor: (book) Perspectives of Psychiatry, 1991; author: (book) Psychophysiological Nonspecifity of Schizophrenic Illnesses, 1992, Victim Care in Court, 2000. Studienstifung des Deut Volkes scholar, Germany, 1980-86; NATO Sci. Com. fellow, 1992-93, MacArthur Found. fellow, 1991-93; recipient Attempto award, 1990, Rsch. award German Psychiat. Assn., 1990, Hans Roemer award Psychosomatics, 1996.

SCHNEIDER, GISBERT, research biochemist; b. Fulda, Germany, Oct. 10, 1965; s. Helmut and Brigitte (Förster) S.; m. Petra Kleineberg, June 11, 1993. Diploma in biochemistry, Free U. Berlin, 1991, PhD, 1994. Rschr. Tech. U. Berlin, 1991-92; staff scientist Free U. Berlin, 1992-93, Benjamin Franklin Clinics, Berlin, 1993-94; with AG Bioinformatics, Berlin, 1994-96; Boehringer-Ingelheim Fonds fellow MIT, U. Stockholm, 1995-96; with Max-Planck-Inst. Biophysics, Frankfurt, Germany, 1996-97; rschr. F. Hoffmann-La Roche Ltd., Basel, Switzerland, 1997—; lectr. Free U. Berlin, 1994-97, Freiburg (Germany) U., 1998—. Editor: Concepts in Protein Engineering and Design, 1994, Virtual Screening for Bioactive Molecules, 2000. Mem. German Chem. Soc., Qsar & Modeling Soc.

SCHNEIDER, GÜNTER, zoologist, educator, retired; b. Berlin, May 13, 1918; s. Berthold and Frieda S.; m. Renate Löhr, Mar. 28, 1953; children: Marianne, Andrea, Iris. D in Natural Scis., Göttingen, Würzburg, Fed. Republic Germany, 1953; habil., U. Würzburg, 1961. Sci. asst. Zoolog. Inst. U. Würzburg, Fed. Republic Germany, 1953-61, asst. prof., 1961-66; prof. Zoolog. Inst. U. Düsseldorf, Fed. Republic Germany, 1966-83, prof. emeritus, 1983—; dean Faculty of Scis., U. Düsseldorf, 1968-69. Mem. Deutsche Zoologische Gesellschaft, Verband Deutscher Biologen. Home: Nikolausstrasse 79 A, 40589 Düsseldorf Germany Office: U Düsseldorf Inst Zoologie, Universitätstrasse 1, 40225 Düsseldorf Germany

SCHNEIDER, HANS JULIUS, philosophy educator; b. Freiburg, Germany, June 27, 1944; s. Julius and Ferdinande (Gocke) S. Abitur, Erich-Hoepner Gymnasium, Berlin, 1963; PhD, U. Erlangen, Germany, 1970; Habiliation, U. Constance, Germany, 1975. Wissenschaftlicher asst. U. Constance, 1970-77, Heisenberg fellow, privatdozent, 1978-83; prof. of philosophy U. Erlangen, 1983-96; prof. chair philosophy U. Potsdam, Germany, 1997—; exch. student U. Tex., Austin, 1965-66; vis. prof. U. Ga., Athens, 1989; v.p. Gesellschaft Analytische Philosophie, 1992-94. Editor: Metapher, Kognition, Kuenstliche Intelligenz, 1996; author: (book) Pragmatik als Basis von Semantik und Syntax, 1975, Phantasie und Kalkuel, 1992; co-editor: Enteignen uns die Wissenschaften?, 1993, Deutsche Zeitschrift fur Philosophie, 1993—, Mit Sprache Spielen, 1999; contbr. articles to profl. jours. Mem. Allgemeine Gesellschaft Philosophie in Deutschland, Gesellschaft Analytische Philosophie, Am. Philos. Assn. Avocation: painting. Office: Inst Philosophie U Potsdam, Am Neuen Palais 10, D-14415 Potsdam Germany

SCHNEIDER, IMRE GYULA FERENC, dermatologist, educator; b. Temesvár, Romania, June 23, 1930; s. Joseph and Jolán (Knisz) S.; m. Györgyi Berkó, Aug., 1968; children: Peter, György. MD, U. Med. Sch., Szeged, Hungary, 1956, PhD, 1974. Physician dept. anatomy Univ. Med. Sch., Szeged, 1956-61, physician dept. dermatology, 1961-76; physician dept. dermatology Univ. Cologne, Germany, 1975; chmn. dept. dermatology County Hosp., Szombathely, Hungary, 1976-82; chmn. dept. dermatology U. Pécs, Hungary, 1982-95, chmn. sci. sessions, 1987-91, prof. dermatology, 1995—; sec. Bd. Diseases of Sense Organs, Hungarian Acad. Scis., Budapest, 1990-96. Editl. bd. Jour. Hungarian Dermatol. Soc., 1990. Mem. Hungarian Soc. Dermatology (mem. leaders, medal of prof. M. Kaposi 1990, pres. 1995-98), European Soc. Dermatol. Rsch., French Dermatol. Soc. (corr.), German Dermatol. Soc. (hon.), European Soc. Pediatric Dermatology, European Acad. Dermatology and Venereology, Soc. Investigative Dermatology. Avocations: classical music, novels, excursions. Office: Univ Med Sch Dept Dermatology, Kodály Z u 20, 7624 Pécs Hungary

SCHNEIDER, JAYNE B., school librarian; b. Cin., Nov. 9, 1950; d. Neil Kendrick and Edith (Dilworth) Bangs; m. James R. Bronn, June 9, 1973 (div. 1979); m. Arthur Schneider, July 11, 1986; 1 stepdaughter, Heather. BS in Elem. Edn., Ea. Ky. U., 1973; MA in Libr. Sci., Spaulding U., 1978. Tchr., 1st & 2d grades Fort Thomas (Ky.) Pub. Schs./Ruth Moyer Elem., 1973; libr. Lassiter Middle Sch., Ky., 1973-2000; presenter Nat. Middle Sch. Assn., St. Louis, 1988, Denver, 1989, Assn. of Ind. Media Educators, 1992. Mem. Ky. Hist. Soc., Friends of the Libr.; co-capt. Block Watch. Recipient Outstanding Media Librarian award Jefferson County, 1998; named Superstar Ky. Ednl. TV; Owen Badgett grantee Louisville Community Grant, 1988. Mem. NEA, ALA, AASL, PTSA (life), Nat. Mid. Sch. Assn., Jefferson County Sch. Media Assn. (treas. 1982-83, sec. 1991-92, newsletter editor 1992-93, pres.-elect 1993-94, pres. 1994-95, nomination chairperson 1996-97, bd. dirs. 1997-2000, named Jefferson County's Outstanding Sch. Media Librarian 1998), Ky. Sch. Media Assn. (bd. dirs. 1994-95, 97-98). Presbyterian. Avocations: genealogy, collecting antique glass, knitting. Home: 2553 Kings Hwy Louisville KY 40205-2646 Office: Lassiter Mid Sch 8200 Candleworth Dr Louisville KY 40214-5599

SCHNEIDER, MANFRED, chemical and pharmaceutical company executive; b. Bremerhaven, Germany, Dec. 21, 1938; married; 1 child. Student, U. Freiburg, U. Hamburg, U. Cologne; doctorate, Tech. U. Aachen, Germany. With orgn., auditing and cost acctg. dept. Bayer AG, Leverkusen, Germany, 1966-71, head dept. regional coordination, internal auditing and controlling, 1984-87, chmn. mgmt. bd. com. logistics and svcs., mem. bd. coms. R&D, investment and tech., spokesman West-European activities, 1987-92, chmn. bd. mgmt., 1992—; head divsn. fin. and accounting, then chmn. bd. mgmt. Duisburger Kupferhütte subs. Bayer AG, 1971-81. Office: Bayer AG, D-51368 Leverkusen Germany

SCHNEIDER, MARGARET PERRIN, writer; b. N.Y.C., Dec. 31, 1923; d. Sam and Peggy (Flood) Perrin; m. Paul Schneider, Apr. 10, 1950; children: Peggy Lee, Peter-Lincoln, Ann Rose. BA in Psychology and Edn., UCLA, 1949. Gen. elem. tchg. credential, Calif. Tchr. L.A. City Schs., North Hollywood, 1944-55; script writer MGM Studios, 1957-75; staff writer Universal Studios, 1957-75; head writer CBS Studios, N.Y.C., 1975-76; participant Women in Film, L.A., 1975; chmn. Writers Craft Conf., Arrowhead, Calif., 1975. Mem. Writers Guild Am. (freelance writers com. 1985), Dems. for Action. Avocations: wild flower photography, birding, gardening, traveling. Home: PO Box 65 54386 Village View Idyllwild CA 92549

SCHNEIDER, MARTIN MAX, energy executive; b. Zurich, Switzerland, June 20, 1959; s. Max Karl Schneider and Erika Elsa Vollenweider; m. Xiaoye Yin, June 19, 1990. MS, Swiss Fed. Inst. Tech., 1984, U. Calif., Davis, 1987; MBA, Stanford U., 1993. Engr. Motor-Columbus Consulting Engrs. Inc., Baden, Switzerland, 1984-88; mgr. Holinger Ltd., Baden, 1988-93, ABB Power Generation Group Ltd., Baden, 1993-96; asst. v.p. ABB Power Generation Group Ltd., Zurich, 1996-98; v.p. ABB Alstom Power Ltd., Baden, 1998—; lectr., Switzerland, 1994—. Author, prodr. Multivision Shows, 1980-90; author, editor Power & Money, 1994-95. Mem. polit. program com. Jungreisinnige Partei der Stadt Zuerich, 1983-86; mem. Swiss Ho. Owner Assn., 1994—. Major Swiss Army, 1980—. Scholar Swiss Fed. Inst. Tech., 1991. Mem. Swiss Liberal Party. Avocations: golf, tennis, travel, music. Fax: 41 56 205 84 60. Home: Zuerichstr. # 5, 8700 Kuesnacht Switzerland Office: ABB Alstom Power Ltd, Haselstrasse, 8700 Baden Switzerland

SCHNEIDER, PAUL, writer; b. Passaic, N.J., Aug. 4, 1923; s. Solomon Peter and Rose (Levine) S.; m. Margaret Flood Perrin, Apr. 10, 1951; children: Peggy Lee, Peter Lincoln, Ann. BA, Harvard U., 1945. Writer N.Y.C., Hollywood, Calif., 1954-91; staff writer Universal City Studios, North Hollywood, Calif., 1967-74; head writer Love of Life CBS Studios, N.Y.C., 1974-76. Writer: (TV) Star Trek, 1954-85, Bonanza, 1954-85, Marcus Welby, M.D., 1954-85, (movies) The Looters, 1957, Ride the Wind, 1966, (plays) Effigy, 1983, Acrimonious, 1962. Mem. Writers Guild Am. (chmn. violence com. 1980-81), Harvard Alumni Assn., Dems. for Action. Avocations: hiking, mountain trails, travel, Zen. Home: PO Box 65 Idyllwild CA 92549-0065

SCHNEIDER, PETER, veterinarian; b. Dettum, Germany, Mar. 20, 1950; s. Kurt and Käthe Schneider; m. Liesel Breitländer, Dec. 28, 1982. Diploma in biology, Johannes Gutenberg U., 1974; PhD, U. Hannover, 1981; DVM, Hannover Vet. Sch., 1987. Pvt. practice Germany, 1984-86; sci. rsch. Inst. Hygiene and Tech. of Milk Hannover Vet. Sch., 1986-90; acad. counselor Inst. Food Sci. Justus Liebig U., Giessen, 1991—; head dept. vet. medicine Schaper & Brummer GmbH & Co., KG, Salzgitter Ringelheim, 1992-97; sales mgr./head scientific dept. Sanum-Kehlbeck GmbH & Co., Hoya, Germany, 1998—; prof. vet. medicine and food sci. Cath. U., Cuenca, Ecuador, 1991; assoc. prof. Higher Inst. Zootechnics and Vet. Medicine, Stara Zagora, Bulgaria, 1994. Patentee in field; contbr. articles to profl. jours. Recipient Rsch. award Fed. Govt. Germany, 1981; named Specialist for Milk Hygiene Vet. Bd. Hessen, 1991. Mem. AAAS, Internat. Soc. Animal Husbandry, German Soc. Vet. Medicine, German Soc. Milk Sci., German Cancer Soc. Home: Johann Beckmann Str 35, D-27318 Hoya Germany Office: Sanum-Kehlbeck, Hasseler Steinweg 9-12, D-27318 Hoya Germany

SCHNEIDER, PETR, chemical engineer, scientist; b. Praha, Czechoslovakia, Nov. 3, 1933; s. Richard and Olga (Vogelova) S.; m. Kveta Sitinova, 1960; 1 child, Petra. Diploma ing., Inst. Chem. Tech., Praha, 1957; PhD, Czechoslovak Acad. Scis., Praha, 1961; DSc, Acad. Scis., Praha, 1973. Scientist Inst. Chem. Process Fundamentals Czechoslovak Acad. Scis., Praha, 1965—. Author: Chemical Kinetics for Engineers, 1978. Mem. Chem. Soc., Sci. Tech. Soc. Home: Sladkovicova 1306, 142 00 Praha 4, Czech Republic Office: Czech Acad Scis, Rozvojova 135, 165 02 Praha 6, Czech Republic

SCHNEIDER, RICHARD A., lawyer; b. Bklyn., Mar. 10, 1954; s. Robert Thomas and Nancy Ann (James) S.; m. Helen D. Schroll; children: Heather Elizabeth, Kristin Anne. Student, U.S. Naval Acad., 1975-77; BA, Auburn U., 1978; JD, Mercer U., 1981. Bar: Ga. 1981, U.S. Ct. Appeals (11th cir.), U.S. Supreme Ct. 1991. Litigator King & Spalding, Atlanta, 1981-88, ptnr., 1988—. Bd. dirs. UNICEF, Atlanta, 1991—. With USN, 1973-77. Mem. 191 Club, Atlanta Soc. Avocations: writing, songwriting. Home: 1014 Brookhaven Ln NE Atlanta GA 30319-4702 Office: King & Spalding 191 Peachtree St SW Atlanta GA 30303-3637

SCHNEIDER, SAMUEL JAMES, JR., retired ceramic engineer; b. St. Louis, Sept. 11, 1930; s. Samuel and Dorothy Helen (Pins) S.; m. Joan Carolyn McMahon, Aug. 6, 1955; children: Steven, Michael, Sandra. BS in Ceramic Engring., U. Mo., Rolla, 1952, Profl. Ceramic Engr., 1975. Ceramic engr. Laclede Refractory Co., St. Louis, 1952-53; phys. scientist ceramics Nat. Bur. Stds., Gaithersburg, Md., 1955-74, asst. to dir. Inst. Materials Rsch., 1974-81, dep. chief. ceramics divsn., 1981-84; sci. advisor to dir. Inst. Materials Sci. and Engring. Lab. Nat. Inst. Stds. & Tech., Gaithersburg, 1984-97; pvt. cons., guest rschr. Nat. Inst. Standards and Technology, 1997; ret., 1997; bd. trustees Orton Found., Columbus, Ohio, 1986-98; chmn. TC 206 Internat. Stds. Orgn., Geneva, 1994—; exec. sec. materials tech. subcom. Office Sci. and Tech. Policy, Washington, 1991-98. Editor: Handbook on Advanced Ceramics, ASM Engineering Series, 1993; contbr. articles to profl. jours. Elder Rockville (Md.) United Ch. With CIC, U.S. Army, 1953-55. Recipient silver medal/Rosa award Dept. Commerce, Washington, 1970, 88, internat. prize Japan Fine Ceramics Assn., 1994; named Academian Internat. Acad. Ceramics, Italy, 1994. Fellow ASTM (award of merit 1984, Cavanaugh award, life mem., 1996), Am. Ceramic Soc. (Refractories award 1985); mem. Nat. Inst. Ceramic Engrs., Lakewood Country Club. Republican. Presbyterian. Achievements include research on phase equilibria-high temperature techniques, energy, materials, issues R&D policy; coordination of interagency materials R&D program among 10 federal agencies-materials standard; instrumental in the development of international standard for ceramics. Avocations: golf, skiing. Home: 5 Marlin Ct Rockville MD 20853-3611 Office: Nat Inst Stds & Tech Gaithersburg MD 20899

SCHNEIDER, SHARON M., systems administrator, information technologist; b. Detroit, Mar. 15, 1958; d. Peter and Mary S.; m. Wesley A. Comes, May 23, 1987. BS, Kutztown U., 1990; MS, MSIS, Drexel U., 1998. Reference and info. asst. Bucks County Free Libr., Doylestown, Pa., 1988-94; computer sys. tech. Cedar Crest & Muhlenberg Colls., Allentown, Pa., 1994-95; sys. adminstr., info. technologist Cedar Crest Coll., 1995—. Mem. ALA, Am. Soc. Info. Sci., Assn. Computing Machinery, World Future Soc.

SCHNEIDER, SUSAN ELLEN, Judaism and Kaballah educator, writer, scientist; b. St. Louis, Aug. 4, 1951; arrived in Israel, 1981; d. Gene Martin and Betty Jean (Spasser) Schneider; divorced. BA in Molecular, Cellular, Devel Biology, U. Colo., 1975; pvt. studies metaphysics and meditation, 1973—; student, Neve Yerushalaim Coll. Women. Cert. tchr., Israel. Lab. rschr. Celestial Seasonings, Boulder, Colo., 1975-79; freelance writer Taos, N.Mex., 1979-81; writer Gal Ayrai Inst. Kaballastic Studies, Jerusalem, Israel, 1981-84; writer, founder, dir. A Still Small Voice, Jerusalem, 1985—; spiritual counselor, 1985—; meditation instr., Jerusalem, 1990—. Author: Eating as Tikon, MoonLore: Kabbalistic Writings on the Fall and Rise of the Shethina; author weekly essays on Jewish mysticism. Vol. counselor Heritage House, Jerusalem, 1992—. Jewish. Avocation: wilderness backpacking. Office: A Still Small Voice, PO Box 14503, 91141 Jerusalem Israel

SCHNEIDER, UWE, physicist; b. Selb, Franken, Bavaria, Feb. 2, 1964; s. Burkard and Edda (Reinel) S. M in Physics, U. Bayreuth, Bavaria, 1989; PhD, Swiss Fed. Inst. Tech., 1994. Rsch. asst. U. Bayreuth, 1988-89; med. physicist Hosp. Bayreuth, 1989-91; rsch. asst. Paul Scherrer Inst., Switzerland, 1991-94; asst. prof. U. Munich, 1994-95; chief med. physicist City Hosps., Zurich, 1995—; expert in med. physics equipment Min. of Health, Berne, Switzerland, 1995—. Author: Ion Beam Therapy, 1994, Hadron Therapy in Oncology, 1994; contbr. articles to profl. jours. Recipient Poster prize German Med. Physics Soc., 1993, Med. Physics award Swiss Soc. for Radiation Biology and Medical Physics, 1994. Mem. Am. Assn. Physicists in Medicine, Inst. Phys. Scis. in Medicine, German Soc. Med. Physicists. Home: Spielberg 39, D-95100 Selb Germany Office: City Hosp Dept Radiation On, Divsn Med Physics, Ch-8063 Zurich Switzerland

SCHNEIDER, VALERIE LOIS, speech educator; b. Chgo., Feb. 12, 1941; d. Ralph Joseph and Gertrude Blanche (Gaffron) S. BA, Carroll Coll., 1963;

MA, U. Wis., 1966; PhD, U. Fla., 1969; CAS, Appalachian State U., 1981. Tchr. English and history, dir. forensics and drama Montello (Wis.) H.S., 1963-64; instr. speech U. Fla., GAinesville, 1966-68, asst. prof. speech, 1969-70; asst. prof. speech Edinboro (Pa.) State Coll., 1970-71; assoc. prof. speech East Tenn. State U., Johnson City, 1971-76, prof. speech, 1976-97; instr. newspaper course Johnson City Press Chronicle, 1979, Elizabethton Star, Erwin Record, Mountain City Tomahawk, Jonesboro Herald and Tribune, 1980; mem. investor panel USA Today, 1991-92. Editor East Tenn. State U. evening and off-campus newsletter, 1984-91; assoc. editor Homiletic, 1974-76; columnist Video Visions, Kingsport Times-News, 1984-86; book reviewer Pulpit Digest, 1986-90; contbr. articles to profl. jours. Chmn. AAUW Mass Media Study Group Com., Johnson City, 1973-74. Recipient Creative Writing award Va. Highlands Arts Festival, 1973; award Kingsport Times News, 1984, 85, Tri-Cities Met. Advt. Fedn., 1983, 84; Danforth assoc., 1977; finalist Money mag. contest, 1994. Mem. AAUW (v.p. chpt. 1974-75, pres. 1975-76), Speech Comm. Assn. (Tenn. rep. to states adv. coun. 1974-75), So. Speech Comm. Assn., Tenn. Speech Comm. Assn. (exec. bd. 1974-77, publs. bd. 1974-78, pres. 1977-78), Religious Speech Comm. Assn. (Best Article award 1976), Tenn. Basic Skills Coun. (exec. bd. 1979-80, v.p. 1980-81, pres. 1975-76), Bus. and Profl. Women's Club (chpt. exec. bd. 1972-73, v.p. 1976-77), Johnson City Book Club (1st v.p.), Mensa, Delta Sigma Rho, Tau Kappa Alpha, Phi Delta Kappa, Pi Gamma Mu. Presbyterian. Home: 3201 Buckingham Rd Johnson City TN 37604-2775 Office: East Tenn State U PO Box 23098 Johnson City TN 37614-1310

SCHNEIDER, WOLFGANG ERICH, psychologist, educator, dean; b. Voelklingen, Germany, June 19, 1950; s. Karl Ludwig and Helga Sofie (Woelflinger) S.; m. Elisabeth Maria Schaaf, Dec. 23, 1977; children: Christof, Felix. MA, U. Heidelberg, Germany, 1975, PD, 1979; Habil, U. Munich, Germany, 1988. Ast. prof. U. Heidelberg, 1977-81; vis. scholar Stanford (Calif.) U., 1981-82; sr. rschr. Max Planck Inst., Munich, 1983-88, assoc. rsch. prof., 1989-90; prof. dept. psychology U.Würzburg, Germany, 1991—, dean faculty philosophy, edn. and social scis., 1996-98; founding dean U. Erfurt, Germany, 1991-92. Author: The Development of Metamemory, 1989, Memory Development Between 2 nd 20, 1989, 2d edit., 1997; editor: Inventory of European Longitudinal Studies, 1990, Memory Performance and Competencies, 1995, Individual Development from 3 to 12, 1999. Volkswagen Found. grantee, 1981-82. Avocations: tennis, soccer, piano. Office: U Würzburg, Wittelsbacherplatz 1, D-97074 Würzburg Germany

SCHNEIDER, WOLFGANG JOHANN, biochemical educator, biochemist; b. Vienna, Apr. 5, 1949; s. Rudolf and Herta (Zeilinger) S.; m. Lieselotte Frauendorf, Mar. 18, 1974; 1 child, Jeannine. Dipl.Ing., Tech. U., Vienna, 1973, Dr.rer.techn., 1975. Asst. prof. U. Tex. S.W. Med. Ctr., Dallas, 1981-85; assoc. prof. U. Alberta, Can., 1985-89, prof., 1989-91; chair dept. molecular genetics U. Vienna, 1991—; adj. prof. U. Graz, Austria, 1986—; investigator Am. Heart Assn., 1982-85; med. scientist Alberta Heritage Found. Med. Rsch., 1989-91. Reviewer, editor, contbr. articles and book chpts. to profl. jours. Recipient Curt Adam prize Soc. Continuing Edn. Physicians, Germany, 1987, Gabor Szasz prize Soc. Clin. Investigation, Germany, 1987, Heinrich Wieland prize H. Wieland Soc., Germany, 1991. Mem. Am. Soc. Biol. Chemistry and Molecular Biology, Am. Soc. Cell Biology, Austrian Atherosclerosis Soc. (v.p.). Avocation: painting. Office: Dept Mol Gen Biocenter, Dr Bohr-Gasse 9/2, A-1030 Vienna Austria

SCHNEIDER GOWER, CINDY ELAINE LONES, electronic technician; b. Springfield, Ohio, Nov. 27, 1960; d. James K. Lones and Catherine May (Dellinger) Oldfield; m. George W. Gower Jr., July 11, 1981 (div. 1986); children: Natasha May, Matthew W.; m. Brian J. Schneider, Nov. 27, 1999. AAS in Electronic Engring., Columbus State C.C., 1993. HVAC electronic control tech. Creative Control Designs, Inc., Columbus, 1993-96; owner Schneider's Tax and Bookkeeping Svc., Columbus, 1992—, SurepayCollect; tax and fin. cons. ePartner with eCollect Inc., 1999—. Mem. Nat. Assn. Tax Profls., Am. Inst. Profl. Bookkeepers, WIBC. Republican. Avocations: pencil drawing, reading, bowling, electronics, philosophy. Office: 1632 Harrisburg Pike Columbus OH 43223-3614

SCHNEIDERKA, PETER, physician, biochemist; b. Holesov, Czech Republic, June 11, 1941; s. Ludvik and Marie (Horakova) S.; m. Olga Stiborova, 1968; children; Jan, Eva. MD, Charles U., Prague, Czech Republic, 1964, PhD, 1985. Rschr. Mil. Inst. Hygiene, Epidemiology and Microbiology, Prague, 1964-69; lectr. dept. med. biochemistry 1st Med. Faculty, Prague, 1969-84, head dept. clin. biochemistry, 1990-99; head dept. clin. biochemistry Hosp. Benesov, Czech Republic, 1985-90, Faculty Hosp., Olomouc, Czech Republic, 2000—; assoc. prof. biochemistry Charles U., 1993; auditor Czech Accreditation Inst., Pr ague, 1997—; lectr. Inst. Chem. Tech., Prague, 1992-2000; ptnr. Sekk Co. Ltd., Pardubice, Czech Republic, 1996—; chmn. orgn. com. 14th European Congress Clin. Chemistry, Prague, 2000—. Author: Medical Chemistry and Biochemistry, 1981, Estimation of Analytes in Clinical Biochemistry, 1998; co-author: Medical Chemistry and Biochemistry, 1990; author, editor chpts. in textbooks, 1998. Recipient Hon. medal Charles U., 1998. Mem. Czech Soc. Clin. Biochemistry, Czech Soc. Biochemistry and Molecular Biology, Czech Soc. Microbiology, Czech Soc. Immunology, Am. Assn. Clin. Chemistry. Office: Hosp Olomouc Clin Biochem, I P Pavlova 6, 775 20 Olomouc Czech Republic

SCHNEIDER-MUNTAU, HANS JÖRG, mechanical engineering, academic administrator; b. Neisse, Germany, June 13, 1935; s. Günther and Ruth Schneider-Muntau; m. Annie Marie Pierre; children: Stephan, Philippe, Stephanie, Barbara, Alexandra. BS, Tech. U., Stuttgart, Germany, 1958, MS in Engring., 1962; PhD in Engring., Technische Hochschule, Munich, 1967. Scientist Max Plack Inst. for Plasmaphysik, Garching, Germany, 1962-67; head devel. lab. European Space Rsch. Inst., Frascati, Italy, 1967-72; chief engr. Max Plack Inst. Festkörperforschung, Grenoble, France, 1972-91; dir. magnet sci. and tech. Nat. High Magnetic Field Lab, Fla. State U., Tallahassee, Fla., 1991-97; dep. dir. Nat. High Magnetic Field Lab, Fla. State U., Tallahassee, 1991—; prof. mech. engring. Coll. Engring., Fla. State U./Fla. A&M U., Tallahassee, 1991—. Editor: High Magnetic Fields: Applications, Generation, Materials, 1997. Fellow Am. Phys. Soc. E-mail: smuntau@magnet.fsu.edu. Office: Nat High Magnetic Field Lab 1800 E Paul Dirac Dr Tallahassee FL 32310

SCHNEIDEWIND, JANA-MARIA, nephrologist; b. Leipzig, Germany, July 17, 1965; d. Ulrich Franz Oskar and Eva-Maria Gertrud (Herzberg) S. MD, U. Rostock, Germany, 1991; postgrad. mgmt. in healthcare sys., Cologne, Germany; postgrad., Malmö Univ. Hosp., 1999, Harvard Med. Sch., 2000. Physician U. Rostock, Germany, 1991-93, Southern Clinic, Rostock, Germany, 1994-96; splst. Inst. Blood Purification, Homburg, Germany, 1996, Dialysis Cmty. North, Rostock, Germany, 1996-97, Charité Campus Virchow Humboldt U., Berlin, Germany, 1997-98; nephrologist CreaTief & Care LLC, Rostock, Germany, 1998-99; head physician CreaTief & Care GmbH, 1999—. Contbr. articles to profl. jours. Mem. Internat. Soc. for Apheresis, European Renal Assn.-European Dialysis and Transplant Assn., Soc. German Internists,. Avocations: running, swimming, music. Office: CreaTief Care GmbH, Rigaer Strasse 21, D18107 Rostock Mecklenburg Germany

SCHNEIDLER, JON GORDON, lawyer; b. Seattle, Oct. 22, 1938; s. J. Gordon and Mary Louise (Bartholomew) S.; m. Linda Gilmore White, June 27, 1964 (div. June 1988); children: Kristina Richards, Jolie Wolcott, Andrew Schneidler, Peter Schneidler; m. Elizabeth Ann Nairn, Apr. 2, 1989; 1 stepdaughter: Jessica Albright. BA, U. Wash., 1962, JD, 1968. Bar: Wash.; U.S. Ct. Appeals (9th Cir.), U.S. Dist. Ct. (we. dist.) Wash. CEO Schneidler Industries, Inc., Seattle, 1968-70; ptnr. Cartano, Botzer & Chapman, Seattle, 1970-86; dir., CEO 4100 Assocs., Seattle, 1989—; sec. Transiplex Internat., Inc., Seattle; mem. adv. bd. Pacific Legal Found., Sacramento; trustee Ehrlich Donnan Found., Seattle. Co-author: (book) Real Property Deskbook, 1981, 2d edit. 1986; patentee Air Structure Systems, 1969. Bd. dirs. North Kitsap Sch. Bd., Poulsbo, Wash., 1984, Friends of Youth, Renton, Wash., 1974; founder, dir. Tchr. of Yr. Found., Poulsbo, 1988—. 1st lt. USAF, 1962-66. Decorated Air Force Commendation medal; recipient Baker scholar George F. Baker Foun., 1957-60. Fellow Paul Harris Found.; mem. ABA, Wash. State Bar Assn., King County Bar Assn., Coll. Club (trustee, treas. 1998—), Rotary. Avocations: fly fishing, competitive bridge, sailing, gardening. Office: 999 3rd Ave Ste 4100 Seattle WA 98104-4084

SCHNEITER, ROGER, biochemist; b. Aarau, Switzerland, Dec. 10, 1962; s. Peter and Elisabeth (Fritschi) S.; m. Rita Maria Gaehler, Oct. 4, 1992; children: Matthaeus, Joab. Diploma, Swiss Fed. Inst. Technology, Zurich, 1987; PhD, U. Zurich, 1992. Postdoctoral rschr. Case Western Res. U., Cleve., 1993-95, Graz U. Technology, Austria, 1995—. Fellow Austrian Soc. Genetics. Office: Graz U Tech Inst Biochem, Petersgasse 12, A-8010 Graz Austria

SCHNELL, ROGER THOMAS, business owner, retired state official and career officer; b. Wabasha, Minn., Dec. 11, 1936; s. Donald William and Eva Louise (Barton) S.; m. Barbara Ann McDonald, Dec. 18, 1959 (div. Mar. 1968); children: Thomas Allen, Scott Douglas. A in Mil. Sci., Command and Gen. Staff Coll., 1975; A in Bus. Administn., Wayland Bapt. U., 1987. Commd. 2d lt. Alaska N.G., 1959, advanced through grades to col., 1975; shop supt. Alaska N.G., Anchorage, 1965-71, personnel mgr., 1972-74, chief of staff, 1974-87, dir. logistics, 1987; electrician Alaska R.R., Anchorage, 1955-61, elec. foreman, 1962-64; dir. support personnel mgmt. Joint Staff Alaska N.G., 1988-92, ret.; personnel mgr. State of Alaska, 1992; asst. commr. dept. mil. and vets. affairs State of Alaska, Ft. Richardson, 1992-95, dep. commr. dept. mil. and vets. affairs, 1995-98; owner RTS Enterprises, Anchorage, 1999—; ind. bus. owner internat. health and preventive health-care corp. RTS Enterprises, 1999—. Bd. dirs. Meth. Trust Fund. Mem. Fed. Profl. Labor Relations Execs. (sec. 1974-75), Alaska N.G. Officers Assn. (pres. 1976-78, bd. dirs. 1988—), Assn. U.S. Army (corp.), NG Assn. U.S. (life, retiree rep. from Alaska 1993—), Am. Legion, Amvets. Republican. Methodist. Lodge: Elks. Avocations: traveling, photography. Home and Office: Huntwood Park Estates 6817 Queens View Cir Anchorage AK 99504-5203

SCHNELL, SANTIAGO, mathematical & theoretical biologist, consultant; b. Caracas, Venezuela, Oct. 6, 1971; s. Hans and Cristina (Cortiñas) S.; m. Mariana Rodriguez-Ortiz; Mar. 14, 1997. BS, St. Thomás de Villanueva Sch., Caracas, Venezuela, 1989; Degree in Biology, Simón Bolivar U., Valle de Sartenejas, Venezuela, 1996; P.R.S., U. Oxford, Eng. Lib. asst. The Brit. Coun., Caracas, Venezuela, 1989-91; rsch. asst. Inst. Advanced Studies, Vallede Sartenejas, Venezuela, 1991-95; acad. visitor Math. Inst. U. Oxford, Eng., 1996; sr. rsch. asst. Procter & Gamble, Caracas, Venezuela, 1997-98; José Gregorio Hernández Scholar and Lord Miles U. Oxford, Eng., 1998—; vis. collaborator Venezuelan Inst. Sci. Investigations, Altos de Pipe, Venezuela, 1995—; referee to several profl. jours. Author proceedings; contbr. articles to profl. jours. Mem. bioethical com. Nat. Coun. Sci. and Technol., Caracas, 1996. IDEA Found. grantee Internat. Inst. Advance Studies, Valle de Sartenejas, 1991; José Gregorio Hernández Fellow Venezuelan Acad. Med./Pembroke Coll., Oxford, 1998, Overseas Rsch. Student award, Com. Vice-chancellors and Prins. of Univs. of U.K. Lord Miles, 1998, Sr. Scholar award in sci.Pembroke Coll., Oxford, 1999; Nat. Coun. Sci. and Tech. sr. scholar, 1998. Mem. Soc. for Math. Biology, Soc. for Indsl. and Applied Math., European Soc. Math. and Theotical Biology, Am. Math. Soc. Avocations: philosophy, reading lit., writing poetry, cinema, tennis. Fax: 44(0) 1865 276418. E-mail: schnell@maths.ox.ac.uk. Home: Pembroke Coll, Oxford OX1 1DW, England Office: Ctr Math Bio and Math Inst, 24-29 St Giles', Oxford OX1 3LB, England

SCHNEPEL, BIRGIT, pianist, educator; b. Meldorf, Germany, Jan. 28, 1960; d. Otto Rudolf and Helga Margarethe (Schümann) S. Music-pedagogue-diploma, State U. Music, Lübeck, Germany, 1982, artistic-diploma, 1985, concert-pianist-diploma, 1987. Leader piano sect. State Sch. Music, Norderstedt/Hamburg, Germany, 1993, vice-mgr., 1996. Pianist various performances and solo concerts; author, graphic artist, musician multimedia project on 7 poems of Sylvia Plath. Mem. Folio Soc. London. Avocations: literature, reading, music. Home: Buckhoerner Moor 9, 22846 Norderstedt Germany

SCHNEPEL, ROLAND, English educator; b. Ahlsen, Germany, Mar. 4, 1957; s. Rudolf and Annemarie (Wiatshoch) S. Teaching cert., U. Bielefeld, Germany, 1982; MA, Pa. State U., 1985. Teaching asst. No. Ireland Edn. Bd., Coleraine, 1982-83; instr. German Pa. State U., 1983-85; tchr. Real/Hauptschule Eslohe, Arnsberg, Germany, 1985-87; fgn. lang. mng. asst. Kuper Machine Factory, Rietberg, Germany, 1988-90; tchr. English, geography and Protestant religion Gymnasium Helmholtz, Bielefeld, Germany, 1991-99, head geography dept., 1993-99; tchr. Liceul Diaconovici-Tietz, Resita, Romania, 1999—; leader, pres. Studentenmission Bielefeld, 1981-82; judo trainer TV Arnsberg (Germany) 1861, 1985-87. Recipient Scholarship, German Acad. Exch. Svc., Bradford, Eng., 1979-80. Mem. MLA, Am. Assn. Tchrs. German, Phi Sigma Iota, Delta Phi Alpha. Home: Str M Kogalniceanu 2a, 1700 Resita Romania Office: Liceul Diaconovici-Tietz, Str M Vitezul 34, 1700 Resita Romania

SCHNIBBE, STEVEN C., media consultant; b. Yonkers, N.Y., Sept. 15, 1950; s. Robert J. and Anne F. Schnibbe; m. Virginia M. Shipman, July 23, 1984; children: Robert F., Juliane E. BA, SUNY, Albany, 1973. Pres., CEO Schnibco, Inc., Saranac Lake, N.Y., 1976—; pres. Blue Sky Entertainment, Gardiner, N.Y., 1985—; mem.-at-large Assn. Internet Profls., N.Y.C.; dir., editor Schnibco's List, Saranac Lake. Mem. Webmaster's Guild. E-mail: webmaster@park-avenue.com. Office: Schnibco Inc 70 Park Ave Saranac Lake NY 12983-1117

SCHNITZER, MOSHE, exporting company executive; b. Czernowitz, Israel, Jan. 21, 1921; s. Menahem and Ethel (Neumann) S.; m. Varda Reich, Aug. 13, 1946; children: Hana, Shmuel, Etty. D (hon.), Hebrew U., Jerusalem, Bar Ilan U., Tel Aviv. Ptnr. Diamond Export Enterprise, 1953—; pres. Israel Exporters' Assn. of Diamonds, 1962—; chmn. Israel Diamond Inst., 1966—; mem. bd. dirs. Bank Leumi Le-Israel, Tel Aviv, 1988-98; pres. Israel Diamond Exch., 1966-92, hon. pres., 1992—. Author, editor: Diamonds. Mem. cons. com. to min. of commerce, 1968—. Served with Israel Army. Named Most Disting. Exporter of Israel, 1964. Mem. World Fedn. Diamond Bourses (hon. pres.). Home: 4 Uri St, Tel Aviv Israel Office: M Schnitzer & Co Diamonds, 1 Jabotinsky Rd, Ramat Gan 52520, Israel

SCHNITZLER, GAVIN REINHARDT, biochemist, researcher, educator; b. Milw., July 22, 1965; s. Roger G. and Melissa A. Schnitzler. BA in Biochemistry and Psychology, Swarthmore Coll., 1987; PhD in Biology, U. Calif., San Diego, 1993. Resch. fellow molecular biology Mass. Gen. Hosp., Boston, 1994-99; asst. prof. Tufts U., Sch. Medicine, Boston, 1999—. Contbr. articles to profl. jours. Vol. Boys & Girls Club, Somerville, Mass., 1998, 99. Recipient Annual award Am. Chem. Soc., 1986; Post-doctoral fellow Helen May Whitney Found., 1995-98. Mem. Phi Beta Kappa, Sigma Xi (assoc. mem.), Phi Lambda Upsilon (mem. at large). Avocations: art, bird watching, sailing, games, guitar. E-mail: gschni01@emerald.tufts.edu. Office: Tufts Univ Sch Medicine Dept Biochem 136 Harrison Ave Boston MA 02111-1800

SCHNITZLER, GÜNTER HEINZ, German literature educator, music educator; b. Mönchengladbach, Germany, June 16, 1946; s. Hans and Josephine (Dommers) S.; m. Eva Fischbach, June 12, 1977; children: Daniel, Leon. Student, Cologne (Germany) U., 1966, Bonn (Germany) U., 1966-68, Freiburg (Germany) U., 1968-71; Staatsexamen, Freiburg (Germany) U., 1971, PhD, 1979, D habilitation, 1988. Asst. Freiburg U., 1980-87, pvt. docent, 1987-94, prof., 1994—; publ. cons. Rombach Pub. House, 1988—; dept. mgr. Studium Gen. of Freiburg U., 1972-89. Author: Zur Philosophie des Wiener Kreises, 1980, Erfahrung und Bild Die.dichterische Wirklichkeit des Charles Sealsfield, 1988; editor and co-editor books, year-books, jours.; contbr. articles to profl. jours. Rsch. scholar German Forschungsgemeinscheft, 1987-88. Mem. N.Y. Acad. Scis., Assn. for Music and Ästhetik, Montagsgesellschaft, Heinrich Heine Assn., Hugo von Hofmannsthal Assn., Karl May Assn.. Roman Catholic. Avocations: performing arts, history of arts and philosophy. Home: Bayernstr 10, D 79100 Freiburg Germany Office: Deutsches Seminar II, Werthmannplatz, D 79085 Freiburg Germany

SCHNITZLER, JÖRG-PETER, biologist; b. Bad Urach, Germany, Feb. 14, 1961; s. Walter and Erika Frieda Schnitzler; m. Constanze Schmid, May 15, 1996. Diploma in biology, Eberhard-Karls U., Tübingen, Germany, 1988. Postdoctoral Rsch. Ctr. Environment and Health, Munich, 1992-94; work group leader Fraunhofer Inst. Atmospheric Environ. Rsch., Garmisch-Partenkirchen, Germany, 1994—; chmn. UV-B rsch., Rsch. Ctr. Environment and Health, Munich, 1993-94, coord. German Tropospheric Rsch. Program projects, Ministry Edn., Rsch. and Tech., Berlin, 1997—. Obergefreiter, Field Arty., 1980-81, Pfullendorf, Germany. Grantee Landesgraduierten-Förderung Baden-Württenberg, Stuttgart, Germany, 1989-91. Mem. German Bot. Soc., Bordeaux (France) Polyphenols Group. Mem. Evangelical Ch. Avocations: bird watching, trekking. Office: Fraunhofer Inst Atmos Rsch, Kreuzeckbahnstr 19, D-82467 Garmisch-Partenkirch Germany

SCHNÖCKEL, HANSGEORG, chemist, educator; b. Marienburg, Germany, May 9, 1941; s. Willi and Eva (Borrmann) S.; m. Margret Hassheider, June 18, 1970; two children. Diploma in chemistry, U. Münster, 1967, MD, 1970. From asst. to prof. U. Münster, 1970-89; prof. U. Munich, 1989-93, U. Karlsruhe, 1993—. Office: U Karlsruhe Inst Inorgchemistry, Engesserstrasse, D-76128 Karlsruhe Germany

SCHNOHR, PETER, health facility administrator; b. Copenhagen, June 10, 1941; s. Edgar and Lisa (Jansen) s.; m. Britt Waldö, Sept. 12, 1969; children: Josephine, Christina, Alexander. MD, U. Copenhagen, Denmark, 1968; gen. med. specialist, U. Copenhagen, 1980, cardiovascular disease specialist, 1984. Intern, resident, chief resident Copenhagen (Denmark) Hosp., 1968-85; med. dir. Clin. Prevention Health Examinations, Lagernes Test Ctr., 1987—; med. sec. Danish Heart Found., 1971-85, chief physician, 1985-87; co-founder, leader The Copenhagen City Heart Study, 1976—. Editor Ischaemic Heart Disease-The Strategy of Postponement, 1977; contbr. articles to profl. jours. Founder Danish jogging campaign Eremitage-race, 1969; with Danish Sports Rsch. Coun., 1970-96, Nordic Countries Sports Rsch. Coun., 1974-96. Recipient Prof. A. Tybjerg Hansens Honorable award The Danish Heart Found., Copenhagen, 1991. Fellow Am. Coll. Cardiology; mem. d'Honneur de Fedn. de Cardiologie Française, Copenhagen Ski Club (hon. mem.), Copenhagen Athletic Club (hon. mem.). Avocations: jogging, tennis, food and wine, art. Home: Rømersgade 3, DK-1362 Copenhagen Denmark

SCHNUDA, DANIEL NASR, internist, pathologist; b. Luxor, Egypt, Dec. 20, 1938; came to U.S., 1961; s. Daniel Schnuda and Zahia Girgis; children: Charles, Peter. MB, MD, Faculty of Medicine, Cairo, 1959; MS, Ohio State U., 1966. diplomate Am. Bd. Pathology. Resident in pathology Ohio State U., Columbus, 1963-66, mem. faculty, 1966-67; rsch. fellow immunology Toronto (Can.) Western Hosp., 1967-68; rsch. fellow electron microscope Banting Inst. U. Toronto, 1968-71; asst. prof. pathology Wayne State U., Detroit, 1971-76; chmn. dept. pathology, dir. of labs. Edgewater Hosp. Mazel Med. Ctr., Chgo., 1976-79; assoc. prof. Chgo. Med. Sch., 1977-81; pres. N.W. Internal Medicine S.C., Palatine, Ill., 1981—; attending physician N.W. Cmty. Hosp., Arlington Heights, Ill., 1983—, med. dir., leader, 1996—; attending physician Good Shephard Hosp., Barrington, Ill., 1989—, St. Alexis Hosp., 1981; pres. Chgo. Internat. Corp. Ltd., 1987—. Contbr. articles to profl. jours.; patentee in field. CEO Internat. Med. Coun. Ill., 1996—; founder Crops for the World, 1998; founding bd. dirs. Assn. Am. Physicians and Surgeons, 1998. Fellow Coll. Am. Pathologists; mem. ACP, Ill. State Med. Soc. (del. 1988—), Chgo. Med. Soc. (coun. mem. 1998—), Mich. Soc. Pathologists. Achievements include work conducting agriculture projects to convert desert land to fertile land, achieved in the Egyptian desert and the Chinese desert using newly invented patented product "fertile desert." Avocation: growing desert crops to alleviate hunger in 3d world countries.

SCHNUR, JAMES A., real estate executive; b. Chgo., May 5, 1960; s. Jacob J. and Ellen D. Schnur; m. Ellen L. Rang, Aug. 20, 1988; children: Jacob, Michael. BBA, U. Iowa, 1982. Store mgr. Jewel Food Stores, Melrose Park, Ill., 1978-84; mdse. mgr. Warehouse Club, Niles, Ill., 1984; gen. svcs. mgr. Hewlett-Packard Co., St. Paul, 1985-89, area ops. mgr., 1989-92; regional project mgr. real estate and facilities Hewlett-Packard Co., Chgo., 1992-95, U.S. field real estate and facilities project mgr., 1995-99; global real estate mgr. Agilent Techs., Inc., Chgo., 1999—. Avocations: golf, coaching, boating, skiing. E-mail: jim schnur@agilent.com. Office: Agilent Techs Inc 25 NW Point Blvd Elk Grove Village IL 60007-1056

SCHNURR, LEWIS EDWARD, telecommunications educator; b. Colorado Springs, Colo., Apr. 12, 1936; arrived in the U.K., 1962; s. Clark Edward and Mary Magdalene (Lewis) S.; m. Jennifer Wood Gateaux, Aug. 1, 1964 (div. July 1977); children: Daniel, Emily, Christopher. BSEE, Colo. State U., 1961; MPhil in Electronic Engring., London, 1968; DSc in Info. Sys., Columbia Pacific U., 1986. Registered profl. engr., Colo.; chartered engr., U.K., Europe. Engr. RCA, Inc., Cape Canaveral, Fla., 1957-58; chief engr. Regional Broadcasting Corp., Loveland, Colo., 1958-61; rsch. engr. Sci. Radio Products, Loveland, 1961-62, Standard Telephones and Cables, London, 1962-65; lectr. Mid-Essex Tech. Coll., Chelmsford, U.K., 1965-68, sr. lectr., 1968-77; reader in telecomms. Essex Inst. of H.E., Chelmsford, 1977-80; prof., chair telecomms. Anglia U., Chelmsford, 1980—; founding dir. and CEO Network Planning and Maitenance Ltd., 1989—; tech. advisor Conf. European Posts & Telecomms., Geneva, 1984-89; tech. coord. PSTN stds. U.K. Govt. Dept. Trade and Industry, Westminster, 1985—; advisor European Commn., Brussels, 1992—; adj. prof. N.Y. Law Sch., 1990—; mem. Electronics Sector Applications Group, NEDO, 1990-92; chmn. European editl. bd. Horizon House, Inc., Boston, 1982-84; mem. venture capital adv. bd. Imperial Life of Can., London, 1982-83; tech. advisor to CEO Mod-Tap Sys., Harvard, Mass., 1982-86. Author 4 books on telecomms. and related subjects; contbr. over 150 articles to profl. publs; over 30 patents in field. Gov. secondary schs. Essex County Coun. Edn. Authority, 1975-86; lead gov. Thurstable Sch., Essex County Coun./U.K. Dept. Edn., 1989—; assoc. St. George's House, Windsor Castle, U.K., 1982—. With USNG, 1953-62. Adj. scholar Adam Smith Inst., London, 1983—. Mem. IEEE, Internat. Inst. Comms., Brit. Inst. Mgmt., Instn. Elec. Engrs., Pacific Telecoms. Coun., U.K. Inst. Dirs., N.Y. Acad. Scis., Brit. Stds. Inst. (chmn. telecomms. stds. and policy com. 1980—), Law Soc. of Eng. and Wales (registered expert witness). Avocations: politics, sports, classic cars, amateur radio. Office: Anglia U Ctrl Campus, Victoria Rd South, Chelmsford Essex CM1 1LL, England

SCHNYDER, PATTY, professional tennis player; b. Basel, Switzerland, Dec. 14, 1978. Profl. tennis player USTA, 1994—; reached Grand Slam quarterfinals U.S. Open, 1998; reached quarterfinals Australian Open, Sydney, 1997, Italian Open, 1997. Winner 6 World Tennis Assn. singles titles, 1 doubles title, 3 Internat. Tennis Fedn. Women's Circuit singles titles, 1995 Futures/Cureglia, 1995 Futures/Presov, 1995 Futures/Nitra, 1998 Palermo, 1998 Maria Lankowitz, 1998 Madrid, 1998 Hannover, 1998 Hobart, 1999 Gold Coast; ranked one of top 15 in the world. Achievements include being a mem. Swiss Fed Cup Team, 1996-98, Swiss Olympic Team, 1996. Office: c/o USTA 70 W Red Oak Ln White Plains NY 10604-3602*

SCHOBINGER, JUAN, retired archaeology educator; b. Lausanne, Switzerland, Feb. 18, 1928; arrived in Argentina, 1931; s. Jacques and Elsa (Huber) S.; m. Liliana Schickendantz, Dec. 15, 1980; children by previous marriage: Juan Cristian, Verena. Prof. History, U. Buenos Aires, 1951, PhD, 1954. Prof. anthropology U. Nacional de Cuyo, Mendoza, Argentina, 1956-73, prof. archaeology, 1956-94, dir., 1956-92, prof. emeritus, 1995—; assessor Consejo Nacional de Investigaciones Cientificas and Tecnicas, Buenos Aires, 1969-78. Editor: La Momia del Cerro El Toro, 1966; author: Prehistoria de Sudamerica, 1969, 2nd edit., 1988, Estudios de Arqueologia Sudamericana, 1982, (with C. Gradin) Cazadores de la Patagonia y Agricultores Andinos, 1985, The First Americans, 1994, Arte Prehistorico de America, 1997. Fellow Coll. de Graduados en Antropologia; mem. Internat. Assn. for Study of Prehistoric Religions (founding), Internat. Com. for Rock Art, Internat. Union Prehistoric and Protohistoric Scis. (mem. permanent coun., mem. exec. coun. 1987-96). Home: Videla Castillo 1968, Mendoza Argentina 5500 Office: Univ Nacional de Cuyo, Inst de Arquelogia PO Box 345, Mendoza Argentina 5500

SCHOCHOR, JONATHAN, lawyer; b. Suffern, N.Y., Sept. 9, 1946; s. Abraham and Betty (Hechtor) S.; m. Joan Elaine Brown, May 31, 1970; children: Lauren Aimee, Daniel Ross. BA, Pa. State U., 1968; JD, Am. U., 1971. Bar: D.C. 1971, U.S. Dist. Ct. D.C. 1971, U.S. Ct. Appeals (D.C. cir.) 1971, Md. 1974, U.S. Dist. Ct. Md. 1974, U.S. Ct. Appeals (4th cir.) 1974, U.S. Supreme Ct. 1986. Assoc., McKenna, Wilkinson & Kittner, Washington, 1970-74; assoc. Ellin & Baker, Balt., 1974-84; ptnr. Schochor, Federico & Staton, Balt., 1984—; lectr. in law; expert witness to state legis. Assoc. editor-in-chief American U. Law Rev., 1970-71. Mem. ABA, Assn.

Trial Lawyers Am. (state del. 1991, state gov. 1992-95), Am. Bd. Trial Advocates (membership com. 1994—), Am. Bd. Trial Advocates, Am. Judicature Soc., Md. State Bar Assn. (spl. com. on health claims arbitration 1983), Md. Trial Lawyers Assn. (bd. govs. 1986-87, mem. legis. com., 1985-88, chmn. legis. com. 1986-87, sec. 1987-88, exec. com. 1987-92, v.p. 1987-88, pres.-elect 1989, pres. 1990-91), Balt. City Bar Assn. (legis. com. 1986-87, spl. com. on tort reform 1986, medicolegal com. 1989-90, circuit ct. for Balt. City task force-civil document mgmt. system 1994-95), Bar Assn. D.C., Internat. Platform Assn., Phi Alpha Delta. Office: Schochor Federico & Staton PA 1211 Saint Paul St Baltimore MD 21202-2783

SCHOCK, AXEL, magazine editor, writer; b. Nekarbischofsheim, Germany, Sept. 11, 1965; s. Artur and Renate (Staebler) S.; m. Ulf Meyer, Aug. 2, 1968. Magister, Freie U., Berlin, 1994. Editor Radio 100, Berlin, 1985-92, Magnus Mag., Berlin, 1991-96. Author: I'm Crazy for Das Holzfallerhemd, 1995, Der schwule Sprachfuhrer, 1996, Das Queer Quiz Buch, 1996,; editor Schreib-Spuren, 1993 (with Ulf Meyer) Die Regenbogenseiten, 1997, Die Bibliothek von Sodom, 1998, Wir Dich ouch! Das Guildo-Horn-Kultbuch, 1999, Die acapickels drucken sich aus, 2000, Die Casso-Story, 2000, Out Now, 2000. Recipient Scheffel prize Scheffel Gesellschaft, 1985. Avocations: literature, theatre, movies, riding. Home: Keithstrasse 13, D-10787 Berlin Germany

SCHOECK, GUNTHER C., physics researcher; b. Tuttlingen, Germany, Jan. 8, 1928; arrived in Austria, 1971; s. Alfred and Johanne (Tesdorpf) S.; 2 children: Markus, Pamina. Dr. rer. nat., Tech. U., Stuttgart, Germany, 1954. Cert. univ. prof. physics. Rsch. scientist Westinghouse Rsch., Pitts., 1954-59; sci. advisor Nat. Rsch. Coun., Argentina, 1959-61; sci. cons. Gen. Atomic, La Jolla, Calif., 1961-62; prof. physics Centro Atomico, Bariloche, 1962-70, U. Vienna, Austria, 1971—; vis. prof. Tech. U., Stuttgart, 1964-66, Rice U., Houston, 1968-69, U. Campinas, Brazil, 1976, U. Mex., 1979, U. Merida, Venezuela, 1980, U. Rome, 1987. Author: Dislocation in Solids, vol. 3, 1980; contbr. numerous articles to sci. publs. Mem. N.Y. Acad. Sci. Avocations: skiing, climbing, paragliding, adventure tours. Home: Paradisgasse 27, 1190 Vienna Austria Office: Inst Materials Physics, Boltzmanngasse 5, 1090 Vienna Austria

SCHOEFFMANN, RUDOLF, consulting engineer; b. Linz, Austria, May 25, 1926; s. Rudolf and Anna (Hartl) S.; m. Herta Buttinger, Apr. 20, 1954; children: Monika M.B., Margit M.A., Rudolf M.G. Ing., Engring. Sch. Linz, 1944; Dipl.Ing., Tech. U. Vienna, Austria, 1951. Constructor Vôest, Linz, 1951-55, constrn. group leader, 1955-65, mgr., 1959-65, divsn. mgr., 1965-72; cons. Allis Chalmers Corp., Milw., 1972-81; dir. and cons. Rokop-Davy, Stockton, Eng., 1980-82; pvt. cons. engr. Linz, 1973—. Contbr. articles to profl. jours. Recipient Silver Cross of Merit, Pres. of Austria, 1969. Mem. Club of Engrs. and Architects, Chamber of Cons. Engrs., Golf Club of Linz. Roman Catholic. Achievements include 18 patents. Avocations: golf, skiing, swimming, chess.

SCHOEFS, BENOIT, plant physiologist; b. Liège, Belgium, July 28, 1965; s. Joseph and Mariette (Marnette) S. BS, U. Liège, 1989, M in Plant Sci., 1990, PhD, 1994; Habilitation, U. South Bohemia, Ceske Budejovice, Czech Republic, 1999; Habil., U. Lille, France, 2000. Prof. French Adminstrn. of Liége City, 1987-96; rschr. U. Que., Montreal, Can., 1990, U. Lille, France, 1991-93, U. Liège, Belgium, 1993-97; asst. prof. U. South Bohemia, 1997-99, assoc. prof., 2000—; lectr. in cell biology U. Lille, 1992, lectr. biochemistry photosynthetic pigments, 1998-2000; vis. scientist U. Lille, 1995-97, 99, U. Stockholm, 1996, 98, U. Liège, 1998, 99, 2000, Ecole Normale Supérieure, Paris; organizer Internat. Sch. on Biochemistry, Biophysics and Molecular Biology, Liège, Belgium, 1996, Minisymposium on Structure and Spectroscopy of Pigment-protein Complexes, Ceske Budejovice, Czech Republic, 1998; cons. in pigments for food, feed, beverage and pharm. products. Editor Procs. of the Internat. Sch. on Biochemistry, Biophysics and Molecular Biology; contbr. chpts. to books, articles to profl. jours.; referee for varjous jours. in sci. field including Jour. Chromatography and Tree Physiology. Recipient D. Clos prize Academie des Scis., Inscriptions et Belles-Lettres of Toulouse, France; laureate travel competition Edn. Ministry of the French Cmty. of Belgium, 1990, annual competition Belgian Royal Acad., 1998. Mem. French Soc. Biochemistry and Molecular Biology, Inst. for Sea and Air-Water Interactions, Nat. Geog. Soc., N.Y. Acad. Scis., European Soc. for Photobiology, Belgian Soc. for Plant Physiology, Fedn. European Biochem. Socs., Friends of the Liège U., Internat. Soc. Photosynthesis. Avocations: stamp collector, cycling, informatics, reading. Office: Lab Dynamique Membranes Vegetale, 46 rue d'Ulm, 7523 Paris Cedex 05, France

SCHOELLER, WOLFGANG WILHELM, chemistry educator; b. Illertissen, Bavaria, Germany, Mar. 7, 1947; s. Franz and Eleonore (Rettich) S.; m. Johanna Stabler; children: Sebastian, Friederike. Diploma in Engring., Tech. Sch., 1963; Diploma in Chemistry, U. Stutgart, 1966, Doctorate, 1969. Postdoctoral fellow U. Tex., Austin, 1969-71; scientific asst. U. Bochum, Germany, 1971-77; prof. chemistry U. Bielefeld, Germany, 1978—. Mem. Chem. Soc. of Germany. Office: U Bielefeld/Fac Chem, Postfach 100131, 33615 Bielefeld Germany

SCHOEN, ALLEN HARRY, retired aerospace engineering executive; b. N.Y.C., Mar. 10, 1936; s. Harry Alfred and Dorothy Julia (Browne) S.; m. Patricia Alice O'Madigan, June 1, 1958 (div. 1989); children: Theresa Mary, James Allen, Karen Linda. SB in Aero. Engring., MIT, 1958, postgrad., 1989. Aerodynamicist Douglas Aircraft Co., Santa Monica, Calif., 1958-61, United Aircraft Co., Farmington, Conn., 1961-66; with Boeing Helicopters, Phila., 1966-98, tech. mgr., 1980-84, dir. tech., 1984-86, dep. tech. dir. V-22 Osprey joint program, 1986-88, dir. preliminary design, 1988-92, dir. devel. engring., 1992-95, dir. devel. program, 1995-98; ret., 1998; aero. adv. com. NASA, Washington, 1985-90. Patentee propulsion sys.; contbr. articles to profl. jours. Fellow AIAA (assoc.), Am. Helicopter Soc. (hon., pres. Phila. chpt. 1983-84, v.p. Mideast region 1986-88, dir.-at-large 1988-90, Paul E. Haueter meml. award 1999). Republican. Episcopalian. Avocations: photography, gardening, woodworking, woodcarving.

SCHOEN, J. CHRISTOPHER, investment banker; b. Evanston, Ill., July 5, 1966; s. John William Schoen and Michelle Arden Johnson; m. Melissa Anne Kelly, June 5, 1993; children: Jessica Morgan, John Christopher Jr. BS in Math./Computer Sci., Hampden-Sydney (Va.) Coll., 1988. Mgr. Deloitte & Touche, N.Y.C., 1988-91; dir. Prudential Securities, N.Y.C., 1991-95; v.p. Smith Barney, N.Y.C., 1995-2000; sr. v.p. PaineWebber, N.Y.C., 1996—. Republican. Avocations: skiing, boating, golfing. Office: PaineWebber 1285 6th Ave Fl 11 New York NY 10019-6028

SCHOEN, JOHANN, university administrator; b. Grossensterz, Bavaria, Germany, Feb. 16, 1940; s. Franz and Maria (Bayer) S.; m. Christl Helmerich, 1968; children: Hans, Susanne. Diploma in agrl. engring., Tech. U., Munich, 1963; D Agr., U. Giessen, Germany, 1970; D (hon.), Pannon Agrar U., Hungary, 1995. Adviser Ministry Agr., Munich, 1963-66; asst. Inst. Agrl. Engring., Giessen, 1966-70; sr. acad. adviser Inst. Agrl. Engring. Technologie, Freising-Weihenst, Germany, 1970-78; dir. Fed. Rsch. Ctr., Braunschweig, Germany, 1978-90; dir., head Inst. Agrl. Engring., Freising, 1990—. Author: Elektronik und Computer in der Landwirtschaft, 1993, Landtechnik Bauwesen, 1998; contbr. articles to profl. jours. Mem. Kuratorium Technik und Bauwesen in der Landwirtschaft (pres.), Wiss. Beirat des Inst. for Agrartechnik, Bornim Wiss. Beiret Nachr., Rohstoffe, Bonn, Bayerische Acad. Ländlicher Raum Munich. Office: Tech U Munich Inst Agr Tech, Am Staudengarten 2, 85354 Freising Bavaria, Germany

SCHOEN, MICHAEL DAVID, manufacturing executive; b. Milw., July 4, 1960; s. John Russel and Virginia Helen S.; m. Tammy Lynn, Sept. 6, 1986; children: Matthew, Stephanie. BSME, Marquette U., 1982; MBA, Keller Grad. Sch. Mgmt., 1995. From mfg. engr. to v.p. internat. ops. Briggs & Stratton, Milw., 1983-96, v.p. internat. ops., 1996—. Commr. Okauchee (Wis.) Lake Mgmt. Dist., 1997—; vol. firefighter Okauchee Fire Dept., 1987-96. E-mail: schoen.mike@basco.com. Office: Briggs & Stratton PO Box 702 Milwaukee WI 53201-0702

SCHOENAU, ECKHARD, pediatrician, endocrinologist, consultant; b. Kiel, Germany, June 12, 1958; s. Herbert and Minna (Kiel) S.; m. Magitta Lumbeck, May 27, 1983; children: Mareike, Henrike, Ineke. MD, U. Erlangen, 1986; Habilitation, U. Cologne, 1994. Pediat. physician Erlangen, 1980-86; pediat. physician Luebeck, 1986-89, med. specialist in pediats., 1989-91; asst. med. dir. U. Cologne, 1991—. Editor: Paediatric Osteology, 1996; contbr. article to profl. jours. including Lancet, Clin. Chemistry, among others. With German Mil., 1977-79. Grantee Wilhelm-Sander Stiftung, 1989, German Rsch. Soc., 1997. Mem. Am. Soc. for Bone and Mineral, European Soc. for Pediat. Rsch., European Soc. for Pediat. Endocrinology. Avocations: sports, tennis, music. Office: Childrens Hosp U Cologne, Joseph-Stelzmannstr 9, 50924 Cologne Germany

SCHOENBOHM, JOERG, government executive; b. Bao, Germany, Sept. 2, 1937; s. Horst Eberhard and Elisabeth (Asselborn) S.; m. Eveline Ella Martha Kueu, Dec. 30, 1959; children: Lyne, Hendrik, Arne. Chief gen. army Ministry of Defense, Bonn, Germany, 1991-92; state sec. Ministry of Defense, Bonn and Berlin, Germany, 1992—. Author: Two Armies and the Futureland, 1995. With German Mil., 1959-89. Mem. rotary (sec. 1980-87). Avocations: history, politics, opera, tennis, jogging.

SCHOENBORN, BENNO P., biophysicist, educator; b. Basel, Switzerland, May 2, 1936; came to U.S., 1955; s. Wilhelm and Maria (Dobler) S.; m. Catherine Cowie Kay, Oct. 26, 1962. BA, UCLA, 1958; PhD, U. New South Wales, Australia, 1962; DSc (hon.), N.J. Inst. Tech., 1982. Teaching fellow U. New South Wales, Sydney, 1958-61; postdoctoral fellow U. Calif., San Francisco, 1962-63, asst. prof. dept. pharmacology, 1964-66, assoc. prof. dept. pharmacology and biochemistry, 1967; biophysicist dept. biology Brookhaven Lab., Upton, N.Y., 1968-74, sr. biophysicist dept. biology, 1974-92, assoc. chmn. dept. biology, 1984-90; head ctr. structural biology, 1984-91; sr. fellow Los Alamos (N.Mex.) Nat. Lab., 1992—; adj. prof. biochemistry Columbia U., N.Y.C., 1978-93; vis. scientist Molecular Biology Lab., Cambridge, Eng., 1964-66; adj. scientist biophysics SUNY, Stony Brook, 1988-92; mem. editorial bd. Biophys. Jour., 1977-80; mem. Reactor Safety Com., 1972-79. Editor: Neutrons in Biology, 1976, 84, 96; contbr. articles to profl. jours.; patent in multilager monochromator, 1975. Recipient E.O. Lawrence award Dept. of Energy, 1980. Mem. Nat. Com. for Crystallography, Biophys. Soc. (coun. mem. 1976-79). Republican. Avocation: sailing. Home: 816 Stagecoach Dr Santa Fe NM 87501-1144

SCHOENE, ARMIN JOACHIM, engineering educator; b. Reichenbach, Silesia, Fed. Republic Germany, June 15, 1932; s. Rochus and Anna Emilie (Engel) S.; children: Heralt, Egbert. Diploma in engring., Tech. U., Munich, 1954; DEng, Tech. U., Aachen, 1965, Habilitation, 1969. Sci. collaborator, mng. employee Bayer AG, Leverkusen, Fed. Republic of Germany, 1955-69; head devel. Elastogran GmbH, Lemförde, Fed. Republic of Germany, 1970-71; pres. Chemie Elektronik und Verfahrenstechnik GmbH, Lemförde, 1970-72; privat dozent Tech. U. Aachen, Fed. Republic of Germany, 1969-76; prof. Polytechnic of Bielefeld, 1974-83, Tech. U. Aachen, 1976—, U. Bremen, 1983—; pres. FWBI Forschungsges.m.b.h., 1997—. Author: Dynamisches Verhalten von Wärmeaustauschern, 1966, Prozessrechensysteme der Verfahrensindustrie, 1969, Regeln und Steuern, 1971, Prozessrechensysteme, 1981, Digitaltechnik. . . , 1984, Regelungstechnik I, 1986, 2d edit., 1993, Regelungstechnik II, 1987, 2d edit., 1997, Messtechnik, 1994, 2d edit., 1997, Einführung in die Regelungs und Steuerungstechnik, 1995; editor, co-author: Simulation Technischer Systeme, 1974-76. Mem. German Forschungsvereinigung f. Mess-, Regelungs- and System technik (pres. 1992—), Verein Deutscher Ingenieure, Verband German Elektrotechniker, Assn. Informatik, German Werkbund, European Soc. Engring. Edn., Verein Geschichte und Landeskunde von Osnabrück. Avocation: history, tournament chess. Office: U Bremen, U Bremen, Postfach 33 04 40, D 28334 Bremen Germany

SCHOENE, KATHLEEN SNYDER, lawyer; b. Glen Ridge, N.J., July 24, 1953; d. John Kent and Margaret Ann (Bronder) Snyder. BA, Grinnell Coll., 1974; MS, So. Conn. State Coll., 1976; JD, Washington U., St. Louis, 1982. Bar: Mo. 1982, U.S. Dist. Ct. (we. and ea. dists.) Mo. 1982, Ill. 1983. Head libr. Mo. Hist. Soc., St. Louis, 1976-79; assoc. Peper, Martin, Jensen, Maichel & Hetlage, St. Louis, 1982-88, ptnr., 1989-98; ptnr. Armstrong Teasdale LLP, St. Louis, 1998—; bd. dirs. Legal Svcs. of Eastern Mo. Author: (with others) Missouri Corporation Law and Practice, 1985, Missouri Business Organizations, 1998; contbr. articles to profl. jours. Trustee Grinnell (Iowa) Coll., ex officio voting mem., 1991-93; bd. dirs. Jr. League St. Louis, 1995-96, Leadership Ctr. Greater St. Louis, 1995-96, FOCUS St. Louis, 1996—, mem. exec. com., 1997-99; active St. Louis Forum, 1997—, Herbert Hoover Boys and Girls Club, St. Louis, 1999—. Mem. ABA, Nat. Conf. Bar Founds. (trustee 1996-2000, pres. elect 1997-98, pres. 1998-99), The Mo. Bar (bd. govs. 1997-99), Ill. State Bar Assn., Bar Assn. Met. St. Louis (treas. 1991-92, sec. 1992-93, v.p. 1993-94, pres.-elect 1994-95, pres. 1995-96, chairperson small bus. com. 1987-88, mem. exec. com. 1988-96, chairperson bus. law sect. 1988-89, mem. exec. com. young lawyers sect. 1988-90), St. Louis Bar Found. (bd. dirs. 1994-2000, v.p. 1995-96, pres. 1996-98). Home: 7824 Cornell Ave Saint Louis MO 63130-3701 Office: Armstrong Teasdale One Metropolitan Sq Saint Louis MO 63102

SCHOENER, GEORGE FRANCIS, JR., lawyer; b. Phila., Oct. 17, 1954; s. George Francis Sr. and Irene Louise (Nocito) S.; m. Patrice Irene Cipressi, Nov. 24, 1984; children: Michael James, Kristin Elizabeth, Stephen Christopher. BS, Rensselaer Poly. Inst., 1975; JD, Villanova U., 1978. Bar: Pa. 1978, U.S. Dist. Ct. (ea. dist.) Pa. 1978, U.S. Ct. Appeals (3d cir.) 1983, U.S. Supreme Ct. 1987; bd. cert. civil trial advocate Nat. Bd. Trial Advocacy. Assoc. Kessler & Sorin P.C., Phila., 1978-81; assoc. M. Mark Mendel Ltd., Phila., 1981-86, shareholder, 1986-95; pres. George F. Schoener Jr., P.C., Phila., 1995—; seminar presenter in the field. Author: (with M.D. Zingarini and R.B. Goss) Civil Trial Procedures in Pennsylvania, 1992; co-author: Two New Products Liability Courses, 1995, Products Liability Practice Update, 1996, Products Liability Update, 1997, 99. Mem. ABA, FBA, Assn. Trial Lawyers Am., Pa. Bar Assn., Phila. Bar Assn., Pa. Trial Lawyers Assn., Phila. Trial Lawyers Assn., Justinian Soc., Nat. Italian-Am. Bar Assn. Avocation: long distance running. E-mail: gfs@schoenerlaw.com. Fax: (215) 564-9187. Office: Eight Penn Center Plz #1301 1628 John F Kennedy Blvd Philadelphia PA 19103-2125

SCHOENFELD, MICHAEL P., lawyer; b. Oct. 17, 1935; s. Jack and Anne Schoenfeld; m. Helen Schorr, Apr. 3, 1960; childrne: Daniel, Steven, Tracy. BS in Acctg., NYU, 1955; LLB, LLD, Fordham U., 1958. Bar: N.Y. 1959, U.S. Supreme Ct. 1963. Coun. Am. Home Assurance Co., N.Y.C., 1958-62; ptnr. Schoenfeld & Schoenfeld, Melville, N.Y., 1959—; v.p. Interstate Brokerage Corp., 1965-84, pres., 1984—; ptnr. Melville Realty Co., 1977—; legal adv. various bus. orgns. V.p., trustee Temple Beth David, Commack, N.Y., 1972-75; chmn. Cmty. Action Com. of Dix Hills and commack, 1970-72, Dix Hills Planning Bd., 1972-74; treas. Dix Hills Rep. Club, 1976-80; mem. Huntington (N.Y.) Zoning Bd. Appeals, 1980-91, chmn., 1986-89. Recipient United Jerusalem award Israel Bond Drive, 1977, City of Hope Svc. award, George Bacon award Fordham Law Sch. Mem. N.Y. State Bar Assn., Suffolk County Bar Assn. Home: 14 Clayton Dr Dix Hills NY 11746-5517 Office: 999 Walt Whitman Rd Melville NY 11747-3007

SCHOENFELD, NILI AVIVA, biochemist, researcher; b. Salzburg, Austria, Oct. 6, 1947; arrived in Israel, 1949; d. Zerach and Blima (Fein) Strauch; m. Tommy Moshe Schoenfeld, Aug. 28, 1969; children: Lilach, Limor. BSc in Biology, Tel Aviv U., 1969, MSc in Biochemistry, 1973, PhD in Physiology and Pharmacy, 1983. Rschr. Lab. Biochem. Pharmacology Beilinson Med. Ctr., Petah-Tikva, Israel, 1969-77, asst. head, 1979-91, rschr., dir. Porphyria Reference Lab., 1991—; rsch. fellow Sch. Medicine U. So. Calif., L.A., 1978-79; prof. dept. clin. biochemistry faculty medicine Tel Aviv U., 1998—. Contbr. over 100 articles to sci. jours., chpts. to books, internat. meetings. With Israel Air Force, 1965-67. Mem. N.Y. Acad. Scis., Internat. Assn. Clin. Biochemistry. Avocations: graphology, gardening, painting, literature. Home: 28 Lochamei-Hagetto St, 49651 Petah Tiqwa Israel Office: Beilinson Med Ctr, Porphyria Reference Lab, 49100 Petah Tiqwa Israel

SCHOENFELD, THEODORE MARK, industrial engineer; b. N.Y.C., July 10, 1907; s. Emil and Serena (Kertesz) S.; widowed; 1 child, Edward Lawrence. BS, CCNY, 1930; Grad. Cert. Pub. Adminstrn., NYU, 1938; Grad. Cert. Indsl. Engring., Stevens Inst. Tech., 1945. Profl. engr., Calif. Newspaperman Daily News Record, Christian Sci. Monitor, N.Y.C., 1930-33; asst. dir. methods and systems City of New York, 1934-41; adminstrv. officer U.S. Dept. of State, N.Y.C., 1944-45; chief indsl. engr. MGM Internat. Films Corp., N.Y.C., 1945-48; indsl. engr. and mgmt. cons. George S. May Co., N.Y.C., Park Ridge, Ill., 1949-73; exec. v.p. Ramco Mfg. Co., Roselle Park, N.J., 1974-91; vol. medicare counselor, chmn. outreach com., cert. lectr. CHIME, Princeton, N.J., 1992—. Author: The Safety Shield Story, 1984; contbg. author: Worldwide Multi-National Symposium, 1976. Dir. U.S. Peace Corps Aux., N.Y.C. and L.I., 1968-69; v.p. Bklyn. Soc. for Ethical Culture, N.Y.C., 1964-79, pres., 1980-85. With field artillery U.S. Army, 1943-44. Recipient Legis. commendation N.J. Senate, 1982, Nat. Chem. award with honors Chem. Processing Mag., 1980, with highest honors, 1982; named Disting. Engr. of U.S., Engring. Joint Coun., 1983; named to Cambridge/Oxford list of persons who in the course of history have contributed to the advancement of sci., 1985; recipient Medicare Nat. Beneficiary Services award of Merit, 1998. Award of Merit U.S. Govt. Outstanding Medicare Counselor in the U.S., 1998. Fellow Am. Inst. Chemists, N.J. Inst. Chemists (mem. gov. coun. 1988—); mem. Am. Inst. Indsl. Engrs. (nat. divs. dir. 1974-75), Princeton Ethical Humanist Fellowship (pres., 1986-87, treas. 1989—, founder). Democrat. Achievements include inventing the Spra-Gard - most widely used safety device against hazardous chemical fluids used by chemical and atomic plants throughout the world; inventing the first safety shield to protect against hydrofluoric acid, first effective safety shield for expansion joints, "Gain Sharing Plan" used by automobile dealer service departments throughout the U.S.; creating secondary distribution pattern for flowers resulting in sales of flowers by supermarkets and green grocers throughout the U.S. Home: 86C Empress Plz Monroe Township NJ 08831-3810

SCHOENFELD, WILLIAM PATTON, aerospace mechanical engineer; b. N.Y.C., Jan. 10, 1946; s. William August and Vira (Patton) S.; m. Dawn Marie Cifani, Oct. 9, 1976 (div. 1979). BSME, Villanova U. Sr. aerodynamics, aerothermal test engr. Holloman High Speed Test Track, Holloman AFB, N.Mex.; rocket sled aerodynamics, rocket performance analyst Schoenfeld Engring., Cloudcroft, N.Mex.; sr. aerodynamics, rocket ballistics and missile test engr. Standard Missile Co., McLean, Va.; sr. aerodynamicist Conatec Inc., Greenbelt, Md. Recipient numerous awards for excellence in engring. and contbns. to DOD and NASA Programs. Mem. IEEE, AIAA, ASME, N.Y. Acad. Scis. Democrat. Episcopal. Avocations: flying, sailing, football, teaching. Office: Schoenfeld Engring PO Box 458 Cloudcroft NM 88317-0458

SCHOENFELDER, EVA LUISE, ergonomics and organization business educator; b. Dresden, Germany, Dec. 12, 1951; d. Edgar Herbert and Erika Luise (Huebner) Schneider; m. Thomas Alfred Schoenfelder, Nov. 6, 1970; children: Olaf, Uwe. Diploma in engring., Tech. U. of Dresden, 1974; D of Polit. Sci., U. Karlsruhe, Baden, Germany, 1991. Engr. for workstudy Feinmess Dresden, Saxony, Germany, 1974-76; project leader engrs. office Ingenieurbüro Beton, Dresden, 1978-80; asst. lectr. U. Karlsruhe, Baden, 1987-92; expert for tchrs. tng. Refa Inst., Darmstadt, Germany, 1992-93; prof. Maerkische Fachhochschule Iserlohn, North Rhine, Germany, 1994—; cons. U. Philippines, Manila, 1988-90; lectr. Vocat. Coll., Karlsruhe, 1988-91. Author: Development of a Procedure to Asssess Shift Systems. Avocations: travelling, skiing, visiting cultural events. Office: Maerkische Fachhochschule, Frauenstuhlweg 31, 58644 Iserlohn Germany

SCHOENING, RUTH IRENE, retired music educator, musician; b. Moline, Ill., Mar. 23, 1922; d. Karl John and Cora Irene (Reynolds) Wilhelmsen; m. Raymond Edward Schoening, Apr. 28, 1945; children: Stephen Ray, Carol Irene Haertel, John Edward. MusB Edn., U. Wis., 1945, MusM, 1979. Cert. music tchr. Pvt. piano instr. Racine, Wis., 1945—; music instr. Racine Christian Sch., 1960-75; workshop presenter Music Educators Nat. Confs., 1975-82; instr. music U. Wis.-Parkside, Racine, 1985-90, 95, 98. Author, editor: From Sound to Symbol, 1969, Can You Do This?, 1984, Shortcuts for the Older Beginner, 1987. Organist Luth. Ch. Resurrection, Racine, 1960—; accompanist Racine Symphonic Chorus, 1987-98; vol. accompanist Racine Pub. Schs., 1983-93, Park High Sch. Concert Choir, 1998—; active vol. Christian Coalition, Chesapeake, Va., 1990—, nat. and state Rep. coms., 1993—. Mem. Am. Guild Organists, Music Tchrs. Nat. Assn. Avocations: reading, walking, computers, entertaining. Home: 923 Illinois St Racine WI 53405-2223

SCHOENTGEN, FRANÇOISE MARIE LAURE, biochemist, researcher; b. Paris, Mar. 21, 1946; d. Maurice Charles Schoentgen and Marie LeMoine. B.T.S., Ecole Nat. de Chimie, Paris, 1966; maitrise, U. Paris VI, 1974; PhD, U. Paris VII, 1984. Tech. asst. Pharm. Industry, Paris, 1966-67; technician CNRS, Paris, 1967-76, engr., 1976-84, rsch. engr., 1986-87, rschr., 1987-95, rsch. dir., 1995—; UFR mem. U. Paris V, 1992-95. Referee FEBS Letters, European Jour. Biochemistry. Mem. AAAS, Protein Soc., Soc. Française de Biochimie et Biolojie Moleculaire. Avocation: classical music. Office: CNRS UPR 4301, rue Charles Sadion, 45071 Orleans Cedex 2, France

SCHOEPE, KLAUS BERNHARD, chemist, pharmacist; b. Cologne, Germany, Jan. 31, 1954; s. Ernst August and Dietlinde (Rogge) S.; m. Renate, Apr. 22, 1977; 1 child, Carl Philipp. Diplomchemiker, U. Freiburg, Germany, 1979; PhD, U. Heidelberg, Germany, 1984, cert. pharmacist, 1986. Rsch. asst. German Cancer Rsch. Ctr., Heidelberg, 1979-83, rsch. scholar, 1983-86; group leader Boehringer Mannheim (Germany), 1986-88, product mgr., 1988-92, dir., 1992-97; v.p. Internat. Project Mgmt. Therapeutics, 1997-98; global head planning and fin., global project mgmt. Hoffmann-La Roche, Ltd., Basel, Switzerland, 1998-99, head project mgmt. and controlling, strategic mktg. and bus. devel., 1999—; vis. rschr. dept. pharmacology Baylor Coll., Houston, 1983. Mem. Gesellschaft Deutscher Chemiker, Gesellschaft Biologische Chemie, Deutsche Pharmazeutische Gesellschaft. Home: Draisstr 34-36, D-68169 Mannheim Germany Office: Hoffmann-La Roche Ltd, PBP Bldg 74/4th Fl East, CH-4010 Basel Switzerland

SCHOFIELD, CAREY, writer; b. Grayshott, Eng., Dec. 29, 1953; d. James Edward and Cecilia Mary (Carter) S.; m. Laurence Richard King, June 14, 1985. BA with honors, Clare Coll., Cambridge, Eng., 1976. Writer: Mesrine, 1980, Jagger, 1984, Russia at War 1941-45, 1987, Inside the Soviet Army, 1991, The Russian Elite: Inside the Airborne Forces and Spetznaz, 1993. Fellow The Atlantic Coun.; mem. Internat. Inst. for Strategic Studies, Royal United Svc. Inst. for Def. Studies. Roman Catholic. Home: 6 St Martins Rd, London SW9 0SW, England

SCHOFIELD, MALCOLM, philosopher educator; b. St. Albans, Eng., Apr. 19, 1942; s. Harry and Ethel (Greenwood) S.; m. Elizabeth Virginia Milburn, Aug. 17, 1970; 1 child, Matthew. BA, U. Cambridge, Eng., 1964; PhD, U. Oxford, Eng., 1970. Asst. prof. Cornell U., Ithaca, N.Y., 1967-69; jr. rsch. fellow Oxford (Eng.) U., 1970-72; lectr. U. Cambridge, Eng., 1972-89, reader, 1989-98; prof., 1998—; fellow St. John's Coll., Cambridge, Eng., 1972—. Author: (book) An Essay on Anaxogaras, 1980, The Stoic Idea of the City, 1991, Saving the City, 1999; co-author: (book) The Presocratic Philosophers, 2d edit., 1983; co-editor: (book) Justice and Generosity, 1995, The Cambridge History of Hellenistic Philosophy, 1999; editor Phronesis: A Jour. for Ancient Philosophy, 1987-92. Fellow Brit. Acad.; mem. The Classical Assn. (hon. sec. 1989—). Office: Saint John's Coll, Cambridge CB2 1TP, England

SCHOFIELD, ROGER SNOWDEN, historical demographer, research director; b. Leeds, Yorkshire, Eng., Aug. 26, 1937; s. Ronald Snowden and Muriel Grace (Braime) S.; m. Elizabeth Mary Cunliffe, Sept. 3, 1961 (div. Nov. 1999); 1 child, Melanie. BA, U. Cambridge, Eng., 1959, PhD, 1963. Fellow Clare Coll., Cambridge, Eng., 1962-65, 69—; asst. dir. rsch. of U.K. Social Sci. Rsch. Coun., Cambridge, Eng., 1966-73, rsch. unit dir. of U.K., 1974-94; mem. computing and stats. com. Social Sci. Rsch. Coun., London, 1970-78; mem. Population Investigation Com., London, 1976-97, treas., 1987-97; mem. hist. demography com. study of population Inst. Union for Sci., London, 1983-93, pres., 1987-91; sr. rsch. assoc. U.K. Social Sci. Rsch. Coun., 1994—. Co-author: The Population History of England, 1981, English Population History from Family Reconstitution, 1997; editor: Population Studies, 1979-97; co-editor: The State of Population Theory, 1986, Famine, Disease and the Social Order in Early Modern Society, 1989; contbr. articles to profl. jours. Sherman Fairchild Disting. scholar, 1984-85, 89. Fellow Royal Hist. Soc., Royal Stats. Soc., British Acad.; mem. Brit. Soc. for Population Studies (council 1979-87, treas. 1981-83, v.p. 1983-85, pres. 1985-87), Soc. de Demographie Historique. Home: Clare Coll, Cambridge CB2

1TL, England Office: Econ & Social Research Council, 27 Trumpington St, Cambridge CB2 1QA, England

SCHOGOLEV, IGOR VLADIMIR, ornithologist, researcher; b. Athens, Attika, Greece, Nov. 29, 1952; came to Russia, 1960; s. Vladimir George and Georgia Ioannou (Vamvakidou) S.; m. Galina Leonida Bikofska, May 15, 1982; children: Eugene, Sergio. Biologist, U. Odessa, Ukraine, 1974. Engr. Zool. Instn., Kiev, Ukraine, 1975-92, U. Odessa, 1993-95; field ornithologist WWF, Hellas, Greece, 1995; cons. ornithologist Hellenic Ornithol. Soc., Athens, 1996—, The Goulandris Natural History Mus., Athens, 1995—. Contbr. articles to profl. jours. Mem. Ecol. Union, Odessa, 1989-95. Capt. Ukraine Mil., 1973-74. Mem. Rumanian Ornithol. Soc. Avocation: tennis. Home: Meandrou 78, GR-14233 Athens Perissos, Greece Office: The Goulandris Nat His Mus, Levidou 13, GR-14562 Athens Kifissia, Greece

SCHOKNECHT, GUENTER, medical physicist, educator; b. Berlin, Mar. 10, 1930; s. Wilhelm and Elisabeth (Wieczorek) S.; m. Benita von Knobloch, May 10, 1967. Diploma in Physics, Free U., Berlin, 1954; D Natural Scis., Tech. U., Berlin, 1957. Head lab. Auguste-Viktoria Hosp., Berlin, 1958-70; dir., prof. Fed. Health Office, Berlin, 1970-94, Fed. Inst. Drugs and Med. Devices, Berlin, 1994-95; prof. med. physics Free U., Berlin, 1984—; mem. adv. bd. Phys. Tech. Fed. Inst., Braunschweig, Germany, 1982-97; vice head INst. Social Medicine and Epidemiology/Fed. Health Office, 1984-94. Author: X-Ray Analysis of Crystals, 1957, Application of Computers in Radio Therapy, 1970, Breath Alcohol Analysis, 1992. Mem. German Soc. Med. Physics (chmn. 1973-74), German Roentgen Soc., German Soc. Physics. Avocations: photography, history. Home: Muehlen Str 5, 14167 Berlin Germany

SCHOLES, EDISON EARL, army officer; b. McCaysville, Ga., Aug. 16, 1939; s. Alvin L. and Marie (Plemmons) S.; m. Elva E. Bussey, June 4, 1961; children: Juana Kimberly Scholes, Tracy Michele Scholes Heller, Michael Lee. BS in Physics cum laude, No. Ga. Coll., 1961; MS in Ops. Rsch., Naval Postgrad. Sch., 1970; postgrad., Army War Coll., 1980, Harvard Def. Policy Seminar, 1991. Commd. 2d lt. U.S. Army, 1961, advanced through grades to maj. gen., 1991; comdr. A Detachment, 10th Spl. Forces Group, 1st Spl. Forces U.S. ArmyEurope, 1963-66; comdr. Co. D, 2d Bn.(Abn.), 8th Cav., 1st Cav. Div. U.S. Army, Republic of Vietnam, 1967-68; comdr. 1st Bn., 23d Inf., 2d Inf. Div. U.S. Army, Republic of Korea, 1976-77; comdr. 2d Tng. Bn., Sch. Brigade, U.S. Army Inf. Sch. U.S. Army, Ft. Benning, Ga., 1978-79, comdr. 1st Inf. Tng. Brigade, U.S. Army Infantry Tng. Ctr., 1983-85; dep. commanding gen. chief of staff 3d U.S. Army/U.S. Army Cen. Command U.S. Army, Ft. McPherson, Ga., 1986-88; asst. div. comdr. 82d Airborne Div. U.S. Army, Ft. Bragg, N.C., 1988-89, chief of staff XVIII Airborne Corps, 1989-90; chief of staff joint task force-south, Op. Just Cause U.S. Army, 1989-90; dep. commanding gen. XVIII Airborne Corps, Operation Desert Shield/Desert Storm U.S. Army, Saudi Arabia, Iraq, 1990-91; dep. commanding gen. XVIII Airborne Corps U.S. Army, Ft. Bragg, 1991-93; dep. comdr. Allied Land Forces, S.E. Europe NATO, 1993-95; postgrad. Harvard Def. Policy Seminar, 1991; program gen. mgr. Saudi Arabia N.G. Modernization Program, Vinnell Arabia, 1995—. Decorated Dept. Def. Disting. Svc. medal, Army Disting. Svc. medal with oak leaf cluster, Silver Star, Legion of Merit with oak leaf cluster, Bronze Star with V device and 4 oak leaf clusters, Purple Heart with oak leaf cluster, 6 Air medals, Army Commendation medal with V device and oak leaf cluster, Armed Forces Expeditionary medal, Vietnam Svc. medal with 6 campaign stars, Southwest Asia Svc. medal with 3 campaign stars, Combat Infantry badge, Expert Infantry badge, Army Gen. Staff badge, Meritorious Svc. medal, Nat. Def. Svc. medal with oak leaf cluster, Kuwait Liberation medal; Cross of Gallantry with Silver and Bronze Stars and Palm (Republic of Vietnam), S.W. Asia Svc. medal with 3 stars; numerous other domestic and foreign awards and skill badges. Mem. 82d Airborne Divsn. Assn., Spl. Forces Assn. (chpt. XXXIV), U.S. Army Ranger Assn., Assn. of U.S. Army, Spl. Ops. Assn., VFW. Baptist. Avocations: running, reading, camping, fishing. Office: Vinnell Corp Unit 61322 Box A2-R APO AE 09803-1322

SCHOLES, MYRON S., law educator, finance educator; b. 1941. BA, McMaster U., 1962, MBA, 1964; PhD, U. Chgo., 1969. Instr. U. Chgo. Bus. Sch., 1967-68; prof. U. Chgo., 1976-83; asst. prof. MIT Mgmt. Sch., Cambridge, 1968-72, assoc. prof., 1972-73; assoc. prof. U. Chgo., 1973-75, prof., 1975-79, Edward Eagle Brown prof. fin., 1979-82; dir. Ctr. for Rsch. in Security Prices U. Chgo., 1975-81; prof. law Stanford (Calif.) U., 1983-96, Frank E. Buck prof. emeritus fin., 1996—; sr. rsch. fellow Hoover Instn. Stanford U., 1988—; mng. dir. Salomon Bros., 1991-93; prin. Long-Term Capital Mgmt., Greenwich, Conn., 1994-98. Co-recipient Nobel prize for econs., 1997. Office: Arbor Investors 2775 Sand Hill Rd Ste 220 Menlo Park CA 94025-7019

SCHOLES, ROBERT THORNTON, physician, research administrator; b. Bushnell, Ill., June 24, 1919; s. Harlan Lawrence and Lura Zolene (Camp) S.; m. Kathryn Ada Tew, Sept. 3, 1948; 1 child, Della. Student, Knox Coll., 1937-38; BS, Mich. State U., 1941; MD, U. Rochester, 1950; postgrad., U. London, 1951-52, U. Chgo., 1953. Intern Gorgas Hosp., Ancon, C.Z., 1950-51; lab. asst. dept. entomology Mich. State U., 1940-41; rsch. asst. Roselake Wildlife Exptl. Sta., 1941; rsch. assoc. Harvard U., 1953-57; served to med. dir. USPHS, 1954-71; med. officer, dep. chief health and sanitation divsn. U.S. Ops. Mission, Bolivia, 1954-57; chief health and sanitation divsn. U.S. Ops. Mission, Paraguay, 1957-60; internat. health rep. Office of Surgeon Gen., 1960-62; br. chief, rsch. grants officer, acting assoc. dir. Nat. Inst. Allergy and Infectious Diseases, NIH, Bethesda, Md., 1962-71; co-founder, pres. The Bioresearch Ranch, Inc., Rodeo, N.Mex., 1977—; cons. Peace Corps, 1961, Hidalgo County Med. Svcs., Inc., 1979-99, N.Mex. Health Sys. Agy., 1980-86, N.Mex. Health Resources, Inc., 1981-93, Luna County Charitable Found., 1993—. Contbr. articles to profl. publs. Capt. USAAF, 1942-45. Commonwealth Fund fellow, 1953. Mem. AAAS, AMA, APHA, Am. Ornithologists Union, N.Y. Acad. Sci., Sembot Hon. Soc. Achievements include research, writing and field test of first health survey indices detailing anthropological parameters; institution of first country wide malaria control project in Paraguay. Home and Office: PO Box 117 Rodeo NM 88056-0117

SCHOLTES, BERTHOLD, engineering educator; b. Nalbach, Saar, Fed. Republic Germany, Sept. 15, 1950; s. Felix Scholtes; m. Kornelia Maria, Apr. 1975; children: Susanne Katharina, Jan Felix. Engring. diploma, U. Karlsruhe, Fed. Republic Germany, 1975, D. in Engring., 1980. Rsch. engr. U. Karlsruhe, 1975-93, lectr., 1980-93; prof. U. Kassel, Germany, 1993—. Author: Eigenspannungen in mechanisch randschichtverformten Werkstoffen, 1991. Mem. deutsche Gesellschaft für Materialkunde, Arbeitsgemeinschaft für Wärmebehandlung und Werkstofftechnik, Deutscher Verband für Materialprüfung, Am. Soc. Materials Internat. Home: Langenhofsweg 69, 34134 Kassel Germany Office: U Kassel, Mönchebergstr 3, 34109 Kassel Germany

SCHOLTISSEK, KLAUS LUDWIG, theologian; b. Kelkheim, Germany, Mar. 15, 1962; s. Ruprecht and Margret (Pellens) S. Diplomtheologe, U. Muenster, 1986, Dr.Theol., 1990; Habilitation, U. Wuerzburg, Germany, 1999. Ordained priest Roman Catholic Ch., 1991. Scholar Cusanuswerk, Bonn, Germany, 1983-89; chaplan Dioezese Muenster, Germany, 1991-94; scholar Univ. Chgo., 1996; chaplan Roman Catholic Ch., Warendorf, Germany, 1991-94; scholar Bayerisches Kultusministerium, Germany, 1996-99; dean of studies theol. sch., Jerusalem, 2000. Author: Die Vollmacht Jesu, 1992, Vollmacht im Alten Testament und Judentum, 1993, Jesus Gestalt und Geheimnis, 1994, Christologie in der Paulus-Schule, 1999, In ihm sein und bleiben, 2000; contbr. articles to profl. jours. Mem. Goerresmegellschaft Koeln, Soc. Bibl. Lit.

SCHOLTZ, JOHANN WILLEM, lawyer; b. Windhoek, Namibia, Nov. 13, 1962; arrived in S. Africa, 1964; s. Willem Skalk and Aletta (Van Zyl) S.; m. Jacqueline Heaton, Jan. 2, 1988. Bachelor of Civil Law, U. Pretoria, South Africa, 1984, LLB, 1986; LLM, Cambridge (Eng.) U., 1988. Admitted as atty. High Ct. South Africa 1991; admitted as notary 1991. Jr. lectr. U. South Africa, Pretoria, 1984-85; articled clk. Webber Wentzel Bowens, Johannesburg, South Africa, 1989-90, profl. asst., 1991, assoc. ptnr., 1992-93, ptnr., 1994—. Contbr. articles to legal jours. Recipient Grotius medal Pretoria Bar Coun., 1986, Atty.'s Scholar award Atty.'s Fidelity Fund, 1987. Mem. Internat. Bar assn. (com. vice-chmn. 1996-00), Transvaal Law Soc. (Pres.'s medal 1990), Assn. Banking Lawyers of South Africa (chmn.), Rand Club. Avocations: reading, military history, traveling, tennis. Office: Webber Wentzel Bowens, 60 Main St, 2107 Johannesburg Gauteng, South Africa

SCHOLZ, HANS-JOACHIM, linguistics educator; b. Goerlitz, Germany, Apr. 1, 1927; s. Hans and Charlotte (Klemt) S.; m. Dorel Dresler, June 8, 1957; children: Ekkehart, Gundula, Frederun. PhD, Univ., Cologne, Federal Republic of Germany, 1971. Tchr. primary, secondary and spl. schs., Cologne, 1960-67; asst. prof. Tchr.'s Coll., Cologne, 1967-72; prof. Tchr.'s Coll., Reutlingen, Fed. Republic Germany, 1972-75; prof. and dir. dept. logopedics Seminar Sprachbehindertenpädagogik U., Cologne, 1980—. Author books on speech disorders and development; contbr. articles to profl. publs., 1969—. Mem. Internat. Soc. Applied Psycholinguistics. Home: 112 Am Schmidtgrund, D-50765 Cologne Germany Office: University, 4 Frangenheimstr, D-50931 Cologne Germany

SCHOLZ, HASSO, pharmacologist, educator; b. Stettin, Germany, Aug. 24, 1937; s. Hans Friedrich and Ruth (von Langendorff) S.; m. Elke Ries, 1962; children: Kristin, Inken. MD, U. Mainz, Germany, 1966. Prof. pharmacology U. Mainz, 1972-75; prof., head dept. biochem. pharmacology Med. Sch., U. Hannover, Germany, 1976-81; prof. pharmacology U. Hamburg, Germany, 1982—; head div. pharmacology Univ. Hosp. of Eppendorf, U. Hamburg, Germany, 1982—. Contbr. numerous articles to profl. publs. Mem. German Soc. Pharmacology and Toxicology (pres. 1987-90), German Cardiac Soc. (pres. 1991-92). Home: Fuhlsbuetteler Weg 28, D-22453 Hamburg Germany Office: Univ Hosp Dept Pharmacology, Martinistrasse 52, D-20246 Hamburg Germany

SCHOLZ, OTFRIED, academic administrator; b. Berlin, Oct. 7, 1945; s. Oswald and Erika (Schmidt) S.; m. Rosemarie Brüning, May 18, 1987; 1 child, Christoph. PhD, Freie U., Berlin, 1978. Acad. collaborator Historische Kommission, Berlin, 1971; asst. lectr. Päd Hochschule, Berlin, 1971-74; acad. collaborator Rsch. Project Prof. Büsch, Berlin, 1974-76; student tchr. Coll. of Edn./Gymnasium Steglitz, Berlin, 1976-78; acad. employee Hochschule der Künste, Inst. Hist. & Comparative Art Edn., Berlin, 1978, 80—, leader, 1985—; mem. organizing com. Insea World Congress XXVI, Hamburg, Germany, 1985-87; cons. Jour. Art and Design Edn., Liverpool, England, 1988. Contbr. articles to profl. jours.; editor and co-editor anthologies. Bd. dirs. Trade Union Edn. and Sci., Berlin, 1979-84; mem. Trade Union Pub. Svcs., Traffic and Transport, Berlin, 1990—. Mem. Bund Deutscher Kunsterzieher, Werkbundarchiv, Deutsche Gesellschaft für Erziehungswissenschaft. Avocations: foreign languages, international relations, traveling. Home: Albrechtstr 27, D-12167 Berlin Germany Office: Hochschule der Kunste, Hochschule der Künste, Postfach 120544, D-10595 Berlin Germany

SCHOLZ, ROLAND W., environmental science educator; b. Halle/Saale, Germany, Apr. 15, 1950; s. Werner E. and Thea (Wabner) S.; m. Maya Urbatzka; children: Christian Emanuel, Soeren Willibald, Nanja. Diploma in math., U. Marburg, Germany, 1976; PhD, U. Mannheim, Germany, 1979, Habilitation, 1987. Rsch. asst. U. Mannheim, 1976-78; rsch. assoc. U. Bielefeld, Germany, 1978-93; prof. natural and social environ. sci. Swiss Fed. Inst. Tech., 1993—; dir. Orgn. and Decision Making Cons. (GOE), Zurich, Switzerland, 1993—. Author: Dyadic Bargaining, 1981, Decision Making Under Uncertainty, 1983, Cognitive Strategies in Stochastic Thinking, 1987; editor various books and jours. Mem. City Forum, Zurich, 1996. Avocations: bicycling, skiing, classical music, farming.

SCHOLZ, UWE, ballet director, choreographer, stage director; b. Jugenheim, Germany, Dec. 31, 1958; s. Erwin and Elsbeth (Buchler) S. Student, Wurttembergischen Staatstheatr, 1973-76, Sch. Am. Ballet, 1976, John-Cranko Ballet Acad., 1976-79. Dancer Stuttgart Ballet, 1979-80, choreographer, 1976-82, resident choreographer, 1982-85; ballet dir., chief choreographer Operahouse Zurich, 1985-91, Leipzig (Germany) Opera, 1991—; choreographer Frankfurt Opera, 1980-84, Teatro Comunale, Florence, 1984, Royal Ballet, Stockholm, 1984; hon. prof. choreography Felix Mendelssohn Coll., Leipzig. Stage dir. Testimonium Festival, Jerusalem and Tel Aviv, Israel, 1983, La Scala, Milan, 1986, Vienna State-opera, Monte Carlo, 1984, Ballet de Zaragoza, 1990, 93, Vienna State Opera, 1994, Ballet B.C. (Can.), 1993, Nederlands Dance Theatre, 1986, Teatro Mcpl. Santiago de Chile, 1988, Komische Opera Berlin, 1990, Bavarian State Ballet, Munich, 1991, Aterballetto, Reggio Emilia, Italy, 1993, Les Ballets de Monte-Carlo, 1993, Teatro Alla Scala, Milan, 1995, Semper Opera, Dresden, 1995, Stuttgart Ballet, 1990, 91, 96, Ankara State Ballet, 1997. Decorated cross Order of Merit (Germany); recipient Omaggio Alla Danza Dance award, Bavarian Theater awrd, 1998, German Dance award, 1999. Avocations: music, literature. Office: Leipzig Ballet, Augustusplatz 12 PSF 35, D-04109 Leipzig Germany

SCHOLZ, WOLF-ULRICH, psychologist, consultant; b. Frankfurt am Main, Germany, Sept. 6, 1950. Diploma in psychology, Goethe Univ., Frankfurt am Main, 1978, diploma in ednl. scis., 1991. Cert. clin. psychologist, 1984, supr., 1994, psychol. psychotherapist, 1999, trainer in suggestopedia, 1994, clin. hypnosis, 1987. Counseling psychologist pvt. practice, Frankfurt am Main, 1980—; acad. tutor Goethe U., 1985-91; trainer, instr. FIRST, Frankfurt am Main, 1990—; lectr. clin. psychology cognitive behavior therapy and hypnosis, health promotion Deutsche Psychologen Akademie, Bonn, 1989—; trainer Didactic Ctr., Goethe U., 1990-97; pers. cons. Goethe U., 1999—. Author: Hypnose und Hypnotherapie, 1994, Die List der Vernunft, 1999; co-author: FIRST Papers in REVT, 1995. Mem. Psycholog. Arbeitskreis für Autogenes Tng. and Progressive Relaxation (sci. advisor 1995-96), Berufsverband Deutscher Psychologen (substitute del. 1996-98, del. 1999—). Achievements include development of metalogue theory for the practical use of rational-emotive behavior therapy and counseling, symbolization approach of rational-emotive behavior therapy and counseling, symbolization theory for the context of the fostering of development. Office: FIRST, Sandweg 53, D-60316 Frankfurt am Main Germany

SCHOMBURG, EIKE DIETER, neurophysiologist; b. Berlin, Dec. 14, 1940; d. Erich Karl and Gertraut (Groth) S.; m. Waltraud Lattermann, Nov. 4, 1972; children: Jana, Jens. Student, U. Göttingen, Federal Republic of Germany, 1960-61, 63-65, MD, 1965. Intern Hosps. in Waldsassen and Berlin, 1966-67; rsch. assc. U. Göttingen, 1967-71, 74-78; rsch. fellow U. Göteborg (Sweden), 1971-72; from lectr. to prof. physiology U. Göttingen, 1974; leader rsch. group, 1974—; guest prof. U. Copenhagen, 1992. Contbr. articles to profl. jours. Mem. German Physiol. Soc., Scandinavian Soc. for Physiology, European Neuroscience Assn., Soc. for Neurosci., Physiol. Soc. Avocations: music, sports, ornithology. Office: U Gottingen Dept Physiology, Humboldtallee 23, D-37073 Göttingen Germany

SCHOMMERS, WOLFRAM, physicist, educator; b. Wuppertal, Germany, Jan. 15, 1941; s. Matthias and Hilde (Moethe) S.; m. Gisela Anna Fritz, Mar. 12, 1976; 1 child, Stephanie. Diploma in physics, U. Muenster, 1968; PhD, U. Karlsruhe, 1972. Theoretical physicist Brown Boveri Krupp, Germany, 1968-69; scientist Forschungszentrum, Karlsruhe, Germany, 1969—; prof. U. Patras, Greece, 1996—. Author: Structure and Dynamics of Surfaces I and II, 1986, 87, Space and Time, Matter and Mind, 1994, Symbols, Pictures and Quantum Reality, 1995, Zeit und Realitaet, 1997; editor, author: Quantum Theory and Pictures of Reality, 1989, The Visible and the Invisible, 1998, Elemante des Lebans, 2000. Achievements include research in foundations of physics (quantum theory, space and time, philosophical implications), solid state physics, and statistical mechanics. Office: Forschungszentrum, PO Box 3640, D-76021 Karlsruhe Germany

SCHON, ISABEL, library science specialist, educator; b. Mexico City, Jan. 19; d. Oswaldo and Anita S.; m. Richard R. Chalquest, Oct. 7, 1977; 1 child: Vera. Attended, U. Nat. Autonoma de Mex., 1967-70; BS cum laude, Mankato State U., 1971; MA in Elem. Edn., Mich. State U., 1972; PhD in Edn., U. Colo., 1974. Founding dir. ednl. media ctr. Am. Sch. Found., Mexico City, 1958-72; ednl. evaluator sch. bus. administrn. Nat. U. Mex., 1972; evaluator bilingual ednl. materials U. Colo., 1973; asst. prof. dept. ednl. tech. and libr. sci. Ariz. State U., Tempe, 1974-79, assoc. prof., 1979-83, prof. reading edn. and libr. sci., 1983-89; dir. ctr. study books in Spanish for children and adolescents Calif. State U., San Marcos, 1989—, prof. edn., 1989—; vis. prof. U. Ams., Mex., 1972, Am. Schs., Guayaquil and Quito, Ecuador, 1971; adminstrv. asst. Materials Dissemination Ctr. Kettering Found., 1966; evaluator libr.-media ctrs., 1960-72, evaluator Southwestern Coop. Ednl. Lab., Albuquerque, 1967, Nat. Indigenous Inst., Chiapas, Mex., 1972; cons. bilingual-bicultural edn. Mex., Argentina, Chile, Venezuela, Spain, Ecuador, U.S., 1971—; editl. cons. Macmillan Pub. Co., 1985, 87, Holt, Rinehart and Winston Inc., 1994, Harcourt Brace & Co., 1997—, Monterey Bay Aquarium, 1997—; columnist Booklist, 1989—; mem. adv. bd. Santillana Pub. Co., 1991-94, Parents' Choice, 1989—; mem. lang. adv. bd. Scholastic Inc., 1992-94. Author: A Hispanic Heritage: A Guide to Juvenile Books about Hispanic People and Cultures, 1991, Books in Spanish for Children and Young Adults, 1993, Contemporary Spanish-Speaking Writers and Illustrators for Children and Young Adults: A Biographical Dictionary, 1994, Tito Tito: Rimas, adivinanzas y juegos infantiles, 1994, Latino Heritage: A Guide to Juvenile Books about Latino People and Cultures, 1995, Introduccion a la literature infantil y juvenil, 1996, A Guide to the Best Juvenile Books about Latino People and Cultures, 1997, Recommended Books in Spanish for Children and Young Adults 1991-95, 1997, many others; contbr. chpts. to 7 books; contbr. over 200 articles to profl. jours.; mem. editl. bd. The Reading Tchr., 1998—, The New Advocate, 1995—, PBS Svc. para la familia, 1997—; contbg. Spanish editor Sch. Libr. Jour., 1984-87; referee, reviewer Sch. Libr. Media Quarterly, 1993-95; reviewer Libr. Sci. Annual, 1986—, Am. Edn. Rsch. Jour., 1983-85, Jour. Nat. Assn. Bilingual Edn., 1982-85, NEH, 1981—. Judge libr. essay contest San Diego Pub. Libr., 1998, 99, Arroz con Leche Children's Lit. Contest, 1994—, Nat. Libr. Writing Competition Am. Libr. Assn., 1977; chair internat. bd. books for young people Asahi Reading Promotion Award Com., 1997—. Grantee Ariz. State U., 1974-75, 75-76, 77-78, 79-80, 81-82, 82-83, 85-86, Santillana Pub. Co., 1992, Office Edn. Dept. Health, Edn., Welfare, 1978-79, Ariz. Dept. Edn., 1980-81, Am. Libr. Assn., 1982-83, Ariz. State Libr. Assn., 1983-84, 84-85; recipient U.S. Role Model in Edn. award U.S. Mex. Found 1992, Women's Book award Women's Nat. Book Assn., 1987, Herbert W. Putnam Honor award Am. Libr. Assn., 1979, Grolier Found. award, 1986, Denali Press award, 1992. Avocation: tennis. Fax: 760-750-4073. E-mail: ischon@mailhost1.csusm.edu. Office: Calif State U Ctr Study Books Spanish Chi San Marcos CA 92096-0001

SCHÖNBERGER, WINFRIED JOSEF, pediatrics educator; b. Wiesbaden, Hessen, Germany, Apr. 2, 1940; s. Josef Adam and Thea (Brechmann) S.; m. Gisela Schönig, Apr. 8, 1971. MD, Gutenberg U., Mainz, Germany, 1966. Asst. prof. U. Mainz, 1972-75, pvt. docent, 1975-77, prof. pediatrics, 1977—. Author 2 books, 100 papers. Recipient Ann. award German Soc. Dentistry, 1977, Prize, Boehringer Preis, Ingelheim, 1980. Mem. German Soc. Pediatrics, South German Soc. Pediatrics, German Soc. Endocrinology. Home: Pfahlerstr 43, D-65193 Wiesbaden-Sonnenberg Hessen, Germany Office: Johannes Gutenberg U, Langenbeckstr 1, D-55131 Mainz Germany

SCHONER, WILHELM, biochemist; b. Nurenberg, Germany, May 26, 1935; s. Konrad and Anne Marie (Degel) S.; m. Karin Walther. MD, Univ. Mainz, Germany, 1962; PhD, Univ. Gottingen, 1969. Med. asst. Univ. Clinics, Mainz, 1961-63; asst. Inst. Physiol. Chemistry, Frankfurt, Germany, 1963-68; asst. Inst. Physiol. Chemistry, Goettingen, 1968-69, 1st asst., 1969-71; dir., chmn. Inst. Biochemistry & Endocrinology Univ., Giessen, Germany, 1972—, dean Vet. Faculty, 1986-86, 98-99; dir. Inst. Biochemistry Endocrinology Univ. Giessen, 1972-96. Editor: The Sodium Pump, 1993. Mem. Gesellschaft für Biochemie und Molekularbiologie, Gesellschaft für Zellbilogie, Gesellschaft Deutscher Chemiker. Office: U Giessen, Franfurter Str 100, D-35392 Giessen Germany

SCHÖNFELD, ECKART ALBERT ROBERT, physicist, researcher; b. Berlin, Nov. 20, 1937; s. Walter Wilhelm Fritz and Dorothea Anna Emilie (Baldin) S.; m. Ursula Elisabeth Hein, Sept. 4, 1970; children: Kristina, Sabine, Dörte. Diploma in physics, Humboldt-U. Berlin, 1964; DS in Physics, Tech. U. Dresden, Germany, 1983. Sci. asst. German Bd. Standardization, Metrology and Goods Testing, Berlin, 1964-90; sci. asst. Physikalisch-Tech. Bundesanstalt, Braunschweig, Germany, 1991-93, head lab. environ. radioactivity, 1994-96, head lab. of activity unit, 1997—. Contbr. articles, report to profl. publs. Achievements include explanation of numerical value of Sommerfeld's fine-structure constant alpha. Home: Traunstrasse 37, D-38120 Braunschweig Germany Office: PTB, Bundesallee 100, D-38116 Braunschweig Germany

SCHONFELD, WALTER TIBOR, retired jewelry importer, writer; b. Vienna, Austria, May 14, 1917; came to U.S., 1951; s. Ferdinand Schonfeld and Irma Pollatschek; m. Beth Bond Valentine, Sept. 22, 1990. Student, Charles U., Prague, Czechoslovakia, 1939. Prosecutor War Crimes Trials, Nuremberg, Germany, 1945-49, case editor, 1949-51; importer Sterling, Sheffield, London, 1952-56; jewelry salesman Balt., 1957-75; freelance writer Onancock, Va., 1976-88; writer, author Onley, Va., 1989—. Author: Nazi Madness Highlighted in Nuremberg. Mem. Country Yacht Club. Republican. Presbyterian. E-mail: lilbuff@visinet.com. Home: PO Box 536 Onley VA 23418-0536

SCHONHORN, HAROLD, chemist, researcher; b. N.Y.C., Apr. 2, 1928; s. Benjamin and Dorothy (Gitlin) S.; m. Esther Matesky, Jan. 17, 1954; children: Deborah, Jeremy. BS, Bklyn. Coll., 1950; PhD, N.Y. Polytech. U., 1959. Mem. tech. staff Bell Labs., Murray Hill, N.J., 1961-84; v.p. R & D Polyken Tech. div. Kendall Co., Lexington, Mass., 1984-93; pres. Schonhorn Consultants, 1993—. Contbr. over 100 articles to profl. jours. Pres. B'nai B'rith Lodge, Summit, N.J., 1970. With U.S. Army, 1953-55, Korea. Mem. Am. Chem. Soc. Achievements include 15 patents. Fax: (617) 738-4742.

SCHÖNING, UWE, computer scientist, educator; b. Ulm, Germany, Dec. 28, 1955; s. Uwe Hans and Hannelore Elise (Krutz) S.; m. Anna Regina Trinder, Jan. 30, 1982; children: Saskia, Verena. Diploma, U. Stuttgart, Germany, 1980, PhD, 1981, Habilitation, 1985. Asst. U. Stuttgart, 1980-85; assoc. prof. U. Koblenz, Germany, 1985-89; prof. computer sci. U. Ulm, 1989—, dean faculty computer sci., 1991-93. Author: Logic for Computer Scientists, 1987, Theoretical Computer Science, 1992, The Graph Isomorphism Problem, 1993; editor: Complexity Theory, 1994. Office: Univ of Ulm Dept of Computer Sci, James-Franck-Ring, D-89069 Ulm Germany

SCHONPFLUG, WOLFGANG MICHAEL, psychology educator; b. Berlin, Mar. 31, 1936; s. Fritz Ludwig and Kate (Mendel) S.; m. Ute Josepha Moll, Nov. 20, 1964; children: Tobias, Daniel. MA in Psychology, U. Frankfurt, 1958, diploma in psychology, 1961, PhD, 1962. Asst. U. Frankfurt, 1963-65; asst. Ruhr U., Bochum, Germany, 1966-67, lectr., 1967-73; prof. psychology Free U. Berlin, 1974—. Author: Psychologie, 1995, Geschichte und Systematik der Psychologie, 2000; contbr. articles to profl. jours. Mem. Deutsche Gesellschaft fur Psychologie, Berufsverband Deutscher Psychologen, Internat. Assn. Applied Psychology, Deutscher Arbeitsring fur Larmbekampfung, Gesellschaft fur Informatik Hochschulverband. Home: Ringstrasse 13, D-12203 Berlin Germany Office: Freie Univ, Habelschwerdter Allee, D-14195 Berlin Germany

SCHÖNWIESE, CHRISTIAN-DIETRICH, climatologist, educator; b. Breslau, Germany, Oct. 7, 1940; s. Alex J. and Ursula A. (Leitzke) S.; m. Marianne Zilleken, Jan. 24, 1975; children: Ralf U., Alexa C. Diploma in meteorology, U. Munich, Germany, 1968, D in Natural Sci., 1974. Mem. adv. bd. Weather Svc., Germany, 1970-81; prof. environ. rsch. and climatology Univ.-Inst. for Meteorology and Geophysics, Frankfurt, Germany, 1981—; bd. dirs. Univ. Ctr. for Environ. Rsch., Frankfurt. Author: Climate Variations, 1979, Applied Statistics, 1985, Climatic Change, 1992, Climatology, 1994; co-editor Theoretical and Applied Climatology, 1985; contbr. articles to profl. jours. Mem., reviewer sci. working group UN Intergovtl. Panel on Climate Change, Geneva, 1989—; rapporteur for statis. climatology UN World Meteorol. Orgn., Geneva, 1994—. Mil. duties, 1961-63, Germany. Recipient German Environ. Book award for Treibhauseffekt, City of Hürth, Germany, 1989. Mem. German Meteorol. Soc. (mng. bd. 1974—), Austrian Meteorol. Soc., Am. Meteorol. Soc., European Geophys. Soc. Office: Univ Inst Meteorology & Geo, PO Box 11 19 32, D-60054 Frankfurt Germany

SCHOOLEY, VERN DEAN, lawyer, real estate developer; b. Reed City, Mich., Sept. 26, 1937; s. Clinton D. and Agnes Schooley; m. Tricia M. Reschke, Nov. 27, 1976; 1 child, Kelly Ann. BSME, Mich. State U., 1961; JD, U. San Diego, 1966. Bar: Calif., U.S. Patent Office. Design engr. Boeing Aircraft, Renton, Wash., 1962, Gen. Dynamics Astronautics, San

Diego, 1962-66; assoc. Fulwider, Patton, Lee & Utecht, LLP, Long Beach, Calif., 1966-73, ptnr., mgr., 1973—. Mem. Long Beach Bar Assn. (bd. govs. 1986-87, pres. 1990, Atty. of Yr. 1996), Inn of Ct. (pres. Joseph A. Ball/Clarence S. Hunt chpt.), Am. Inn of Ct. (bd. trustees 1998, 2000). Avocations: tennis, snow skiing. E-mail: vschooley@fulpat.com. Office: Fulwider Patton Lee & Utecht LLP 200 Oceangate Ste 1550 Long Beach CA 90802-4335

SCHOONOVER, JACK RONALD, judge; b. Winona, Minn., July 23, 1934; s. Richard M. and Elizabeth A. (Hargeisheimer) S.; student Winona State Coll., 1956-58; LLB, U. Fla., 1962; m. Ann Marie Kroez, June 18, 1965; children: Jack Ronald, Wayne J. Bar: Fla. 1962. Atty. Wotitzky, Wotitzky & Schoonover, 1962-69, Schoonover, Olmsted & Schwarz, 1969-75; spl. asst. state's atty., State of Fla., 1969-72; city atty. City of Punta Gorda, Fla., city judge, 1973-74; judge 20th Jud. Cir. Ct., Ft. Myers, Fla., 1975-81, 2d Dist. Ct. Appeal, 1981-97, chief judge, 1990-92, ret. 1997; atty. Charlotte County Sch. Bd., 1969-75, Charlotte County Zoning Bd., Charlotte County Devel. Authority; mem. unauthorized practice law com. 12th Jud. Cir., mem. grievance com. 20th Jud. Cir.; adj. prof. Edison C.C. Tchr. Charlotte County Adult Edn. Assn. Served with USAF, 1952-56. Mem. Am. Legion. Home and Office: 14380 Olde Hickory Blvd Fort Myers FL 33912-0816

SCHOPPER, ERWIN WILHELM, retired physicist; b. Heilbronn, Germany, June 26, 1909; s. Gottlob Friedrich and Pauline (Auweter) S.; m. Eleonore Maria Bachner, May, 1937 (dec. Feb. 1951); m. Elfriede Bartschat, Mar., 1952; 1 child, Susanna. Dr.rer.nat., U. Tübingen, 1934. Asst. prof. Tech. Hochschule, Stuttgart, Germany, 1934-37; from asst. prof. to assoc. prof. Tech. Hochschule, Stuttgart, 1945, 50-56; dept. leader ctrl. lab. IG-Farbenindustrie, Wolfen, 1937-45; sr. scientist, mem. Inst. Physik d. Stratosphäre Max-Plank-Gesellschaft, Friedrichshafen, Weissenau, Germany, 1940-56; leader Inst. Physik d. Stratosphäre Dept., Hechingen, Germany, 1952-56; ret.; prof. nuclear physics, dir. Inst. for Kernphysik U., Frankfurt/Main, 1956-79; extern mem. Max Planck Inst. Aeronomie Lindau, Katlenburg, 1958—; mem. German Atomic Commn., Bonn, 1961-71. Co-author: (with G. Joos) Grundriss d. Photographie, 1958, (with E. Lohrmann and G. Mauck) Hdbch Physik Cosmic Rays, 1967; contbr. articles to profl. jours.; inventor in field. Mem. directory Goethe-Inst., Munich, 1959-68. Recipient Bundesverdienstkrenz I, Fed. Republic Germany, 1984. Mem. Deutsche Physikal. Gesellschaft, Wissenschaftl. Gesellschaft, European Phys. Soc. Home: Forststr 17, D 65812 Bad Soden 2, Germany Office: U Inst Kernphysik, August-Eulerstr 6, D 60486 Frankfurt am Main Germany

SCHOPPMANN, MICHAEL JOSEPH, lawyer; b. N.Y.C., May 17, 1960; s. Fred Richard and Dorothy Ann (Wood) S.; m. Marlene Elizabeth Macbeth, Nov. 21, 1987; children: Michael, Steven. BS, St. John's U., 1982; JD, Seton Hall U., 1985. Bar: N.J. 1985, U.S. Dist. Ct. N.J. 1986, U.S. Supreme Ct. 1992, D.C. 1993, N.Y. 1994. Assoc. Baker Garber Duffy & Baker, Hoboken, N.J., 1985-87; counsel Johnstone Skok Loughlin & Lane, Westfield, N.J., 1987-90; prin. Kern Augustine Conroy & Schoppmann, Bridgewater, N.J., 1990—. Author, editor: (text) Basic Health Law, 1993; author: New Legal Threats in Managed Care, New Criminals for the Millenium?, Physician Unions - The Myth and One Important Truth. Mem. ATLA, N.J. Bar Assn. (chmn. adminstrv. law sect. 1994-98), N.Y. State Bar Assn., D.C. Bar Assn., Somerset County Bar Assn. E-mail: schoppmann@drlaw.com. Office: Kern Augustine Conroy & Schoppmann 1120 Us Highway 22 Ste 8 Bridgewater NJ 08807-2972

SCHOR, SUZI, lawyer, psychologist; b. Chgo., Feb. 1, 1947; d. Samuel S. and Dorothy Helen (Hineline); 1 child, Kate. BSBA, Ind. U., 1964; JD, Northwestern U., 1970; JD, U. Palmer's Green, London, 1971; PhD in Fine Arts (hon.), U. Nev., PhD in Clin. Psychology, 1989; PhD in Clin. Psychology, Kensington U., 1989. Bar: Ill., 1971. Pvt. practice L.A., 1971-80; v.p. legal affairs Little Gypzy Mgmt., Inc., Beverly Hills, Calif., 1980—; trust officer, pvt. fiduciary svcs. Bank of Am., L.A.; mem. Pres.'s Coun. on Alcoholism. Author: 13th Step to Death, 1995; contbg. author Wine and Dine Mag.; contbr. articles to profl. jours. Bd. dirs. Nat. Ctr. for Hyperactive Children, L.A., 1989-91, sec. Rainbow Guild Cancer Charity, L.A., 1985-89, ind. cons. Jewish Legal Aid, L.A., 1988—; campaign coord. advisor Dem. Nat. Campaign, L.A., 1990, 94, 2000; donor mem. L.A. Coun. on World Affairs. Recipient Poet of Yr. award Nat. Libr. and Assn. of Poetry, 1995, 98. Mem. ABA (criminal justice com. 1994), AAUW, NAADAC, CAADAC, L.A. Breakfast Club (chmn. entertainment 1988-90), Rotary, Mensa, Beverly Hills Bar Assn., Century City Bar Assn. Jewish. Avocations: singing, skiing, writing.

SCHORI, PIERRE, Swedish government official; b. Norrköping, Sweden, 1938. MA, U. Lund, 1962. Sec. for labor Social Dem. Party, Stockholm, 1966-71; adminstrv. chief Internat. Devel., Stockholm, 1971-72, Polit. Dept., Stockholm, 1972-73; dep. asst. undersec., undersec. of state Ministry. Fgn. Affairs, Stockholm, 1973-76, 82-94; internat. sec. Social Dem. Party Bd., Stockholm, 1976-82; min. Internat. Devel. Coop. & Ea. and Ctrl. European Affairs Swedish Govt., Stockholm, 1994—; dep. min. fgn. affairs (aid and migration); vice-chmn. Com. on Fgn. Affairs, 1991—. Office: Dep Min Fgn Affairs, Gustav Adolphs torg 1, S-103 23 Stockholm Sweden*

SCHORPION, WILFRIED ANNA, information systems specialist; b. Hasselt, Belgium, Aug. 18, 1965; d. Jan Pieter and Philomene (Houben) S. Kandidaat Natuurkunde in Physics, Limburgs U. Centrum, Diepenbeek, Belgium, 1985; Licentiaat Natuurkunde, Katholieke U., Leuven, Belgium, 1987. Tchr. secondary schs., Belgium, 1988-89; tech. mgr. Barco Digital Cinema, Kuurne, Belgium, 1989—. Belgian military, Brussels, 1988-89. Mem. Soc. Optical Engrs., Gilde der Loonse Wynluyden. Avocations: wine tasting, beekeeping, motorcycling, photography. Home Phone: 056/428556. E-mail: wilfried@schorpion.com.

SCHORR, MARTIN MARK, forensic examiner, psychologist, educator, screenwriter; b. Sept. 16, 1923; m. Dolores Gene Tyson, June 14, 1952; 1 child, Jeanne Ann. Student, Oxford (Eng.) U., 1945-46; AB cum laude, Adelphi U., 1949; postgrad., U. Tex., 1949-50; MS, Purdue U., 1953; PhD, U. Denver, 1960; postgrad., U. Tex. Diplomate in psychology, Am. Bd. Profl. Disability Cons., Am. Bd. Forensic Examiners, Am. Bd. Forensic Medicine; lic. clin. psychologist. Chief clin. psychol. svcs. San Diego County Mental Hosp., 1963-67; clin. dir. human services San Diego County, 1963-76; pvt. practice San Diego, 1962—; forensic examiner superior, fed. and mil. cts., San Diego, 1962—; prof. abnormal psychology San Diego State U., 1965-68; chief dept. psychology Center City (Calif.) Hosp., 1976-79; cons. Dept. Corrections State of Calif., Minnewawa, 1970-73, Disability Evaluation Dept. Health, 1972-75, Calif. State Indsl. Accident Commn., 1972-78, Calif. Criminal Justice Adminstrn., 1975-77, Vista Hill Found., Mercy Hosp. Mental Health, Foodmaker Corp., Convent Sacred Heart, El Cajon, FAA Examiner; screenwriter KT Entertainment, 4-Sq. Prodns. of San Diego. Author: Death by Prescription, 1988; dir. Alpha Centauri Prodns., San Diego. Recipient award for aid in developing Whistle Blower Law Calif. Assembly, 1986, Man of Yr. award, 1995. Fellow Internat. Assn. Social Psychiatry, Am. Coll. Forensic Examiners (life); mem. AAAS, PEN, APA, Am. Acad. Forensic Scis. (qualified med. evaluator), Internat. Platform Assn., World Mental Health Assn., Mystery Writers Am., Nat. Writers Club, Mensa. Home: University City 2970 Arnoldson Ave San Diego CA 92122-2114

SCHOSEHINA, ELENA VASILYEVNA, phycologist, researcher; b. Onega, Russia, Jan. 2, 1956; d. Vasiliy Aleksandrovich and Klavdia Vasilyevna (Rasheva) S.; 1 child, Schoschin Maxim. Grad., Leningrad (Russia) State U., 1978. Biol. diplomate. Rschr. Polar Inst. Fishery and Oceanography, Archangelsk, Russia, 1978-82; sr. rschr. Murmansk (Russia) Marine Biol. Inst., Russian Acad. Scis., 1982—; tchr. Murmansk State Tech. U., 1998—. Contbr. articles to profl. jours. Mem. Bot. Soc. Home: Chalatina 11-71, 183037 Murmansk Russia Office: Murmansk Marine Biol Inst, Vladimirskaya 17, 183010 Murmansk Russia

SCHOTT, HEINZ GUSTAV, history of medicine educator, author; b. Bergzabern, Rheinland, Germany, Aug. 8, 1946; s. Heinz Ludwig and Ruth (Geilert) S.; m. Elisabeth Margarete Rosemarie Schmidt-Glintzer, Aug. 27, 1973; children: Kai, Mareile, Johannes. MD, U. Heidelberg (Germany), 1974, PhD, 1978. Asst. Inst. for the History of Medicine, Freiburg, Germany, 1978-82, asst. prof., 1982-87; chair Medico-Hist. Inst., Bonn, Germany, 1987—. Author in field. Cand. for Lord Mayor of Bonn, 1994, 99. U. Glasgow grantee, 1969-70, State grantee, 1972-73. Fellow Soc. for History Sci.; mem. German Soc. for History Medicine, Sci. and Tech. (pres. 1991-94), European Acad. Scis. and Arts (Salzburg). Avocations: cycling, piano playing. Home: Haager Weg 17, 53127 Bonn Germany Office: Medizinhistorisches Inst, Sigmund Freud Str 25, 53105 Bonn Germany

SCHOTT, JOHN (ROBERT), international consultant, educator; b. Rochester, N.Y., Jan. 30, 1936; s. John and Ellen (Waite) S.; m. Diane Elizabeth Dempsey, June 19, 1963; children: Elizabeth Anne (dec.), Jennifer, Jared Reed, George Kermit Alexander. BA magna cum laude, Haverford Coll., 1957; postgrad., Oxford U., 1957-59; PhD, Harvard U., 1964. Resident tutor in govt. Eliot House, Harvard Coll., Cambridge, Mass., 1960-64; inst. polit. sci. Wellesley (Mass.) Coll., 1964-66; policy planning specialist AID, Washington, 1966-67; chief Title IX div. AID, Washington, 1967-68; vis. prof. polit. devel. Fletcher Sch. Law & Diplomacy, Tufts U., Medford, Mass., 1968-70; sr. v.p. Thunderbird Grad. Sch. Internat. Mgmt., Phoenix, 1970-71; cons. internat. affairs Francestown, N.H., 1971-74; pres. Schott & Assocs., Inc., Jaffrey Center, N.H., 1974-93; mem. U.S. Del. World Assembly Internat. Secretariat for Voluntary Service, New Delhi, 1967; advisor Office Prime Minister Royal Thai Govt., Bangkok, 1978-80, Minister Cooperatives Govt. of Indonesia, Jakarta, 1983-84; research asst. spl. appointment The Brookings Inst., Washington, 1960-61;. Author: Kenya Tragedy: European Colonization in East Africa, 1964, Frances' Town: History of Francestown, N.H., 1972, 98, A Five-Year Comprehensive Plan for Development of Agricultural Cooperatives in Thailand, 1979, Recana-Komprehensip Pengembangan Kud, Jakarta, Indonesia, 1985, also various govt. reports and articles in profl. jours. and regional publs.; editor: An Experiment in Integrated Rural Development, 1978. Bd. of Selectmen, Francestown, N.H., 1975-78; trustee Spaulding Youth Ctr., Tilton, N.H., 1971-82, 85-89, pres. bd. trustees, 1972-75; trustee Internat. Inst. Rural Reconstrn., N.Y.C., 1979-89, mem. exec. com., 1985-89, bd. trustees N.H. Pub. Radio, 1990-96, chmn., 1993-95; mem. spl. study commn. Coop. Extension Svc. State of N.H., 1980-81, also mem. scenic and cultural by-ways com., 1993-96; forestry rep. County Extension Coun., Hillsboro County, N.H., 1979-82; pres. N.H. Timberland Owner's Assn., 1989-90, bd. dirs., 1988-91; chmn. N.H. chpt. The Nature Conservancy, 1990-93, hon. trustee, 1993—, chmn. N.H. Timber-Tourism Coalition, 1990-94; vice-chmn, Foresters Lic. Bd. State of N.H., 1990-95; bd. trustees Cheshire Med. Ctr., 1992-94, RiverMead Retirement Cmty., Peterborough, N.H., 1992—, chmn., 1996—; mem. bd. overseers comty. econ. devel. program N.H. Coll., 1997—, chmn., 1997-2000. Rotary Found. fellow, 1957-58, Coslett Found. fellow, 1958-59, Harvard Arts & Scis. fellow, 1959-60, Fulbright scholar, 1962-63; recipient award for svc. to humanity Haverford (Pa.) Coll., 1999. Mem. Am. Forestry Inst. (cert. tree farmer). Home and Office: Schott & Assocs PO Box 660 Jaffrey NH 03452-0660

SCHOTT, JOHN WILLIAM, psychiatrist; b. LaSalle, Ill., July 2, 1940; s. Joseph William and Anne Marie Schott; m. Sarah Purdy, June 4, 1966; children: Anne Rutherford, Hannah Elizabeth, Lilly Hamilton. AB, Johns Hopkins U., 1962; MD, Harvard U., 1966. Clin. dir. Dorchester Mental Health, Boston, 1970-73, Westboro (Mass.) State Hosp., 1973-75; chmn. dept. psychiatry Leonard Morse Hosp., Natick, Mass., 1975-91, MetroWest Med. Ctr., Framingham & Natick, Mass., 1991—; clin. instr. Harvard Med. Sch., Boston, 1991—; portfolio mgr. Steinberg Global Asset Mgmt., Boston, 1993—; treas. AEMS Corp., Natick, 1990—; pres. Cochituate Enterprises, Natick, 1991—. Author: Mind Over Money, 1998; assoc. editor Jour. of Psychology and Fin. Markets, 2000—; writer, publisher The Schott Letter, 1983—. Dir. Learning Ctr. Deaf Children, Framingham, 1977—; chmn. bd. trustees Dover (Mass.) Ch., 1978-80. Mem. Am. Psychoanalytic Assn., Am. Psychiat. Assn., Mass. Med. Soc., Boston Psychoanalytic Soc. (treas. 1983-90, chmn. bd. trustees 1986-90), East Chop Tennis Club, East Chop Beach Club. Mem. United Ch. of Christ. Avocations: croquet, chess, gardening. Home: 120 Centre St Dover MA 02030-2411 Office: Leonard Morse Hosp 67 Union St Natick MA 01760-6089

SCHOTT, RÜDIGER, ethnology educator; b. Bonn, Germany, Dec. 10, 1927; s. Albert and Beatrice (von Kryger) S.; m. Helga von Notz, Aug. 13, 1958; children: Inge, Brigitte, Gisela, Ulrike. PhD, U. Bonn, 1954, Habilitation, 1964. Asst. rsch. project. German Rsch. Assn. (DFG), Bonn, 1954-58; asst. Arnold-Bergstraesser Inst., Freiburg/Breisgau, Germany, 1961-64; prof. ethnology U. Münster, Germany, 1965-93; prof. emeritus, 1993. Author: Anfänge der Privat-und Planwirtschaft, 1955, Aus Leben und Dichtung eines westafrik. Bauernvolkes, 1970, Afrik. Erzählungen als religionsethnol. Quellen, 1990, Folktales of the Bulsa in Northern Ghana, 1993, 96; co-editor: The Present-Day Importance of Oral Traditions, 1998. Mem. Nordrhein-Westfäl. Acad. Scis. Fax: 49-228-2421514. E-mail: Schott.R@uni-bonn.de. Home: Nachtigallenweg 56, D-53115 Bonn Germany

SCHOTTE, JAN P., cardinal; b. Beveren-Waregem, Belgium, Apr. 29, 1928; s. Marcel Schotte and Rhea Duhou. Degree, Sacred Heart Diocesan Coll., Waregem; CICM, Scheut-Brussels and Katholieke U., Leuven. Asst. prof. canon law Catholic U., Leuven, 1955-62; rector I.H.M. Sem. Catholic U. Am., Washington, 1963-66; sec. gen. Congregation Immaculate Heart Mary, Rome, 1967-72; attaché Internat. Orgns. Secs. State, Vatican City, 1972-80; v.p. Pontifical Com. Justice and Peace, 1980-85; sec. gen. World Synod Bishops, 1985—; mem. pontifical com. Catechism Cath. Ch., 1986-92; pres. labor office Apostolic See, Vatican, 1989—; counsellor pontifical com. Latin Am., 1989—; mem. Congregation Bishops, 1985—; mem. joint working group Holy See-WCC, 1983—; mem. Interdisciplinary Com. Universal Catechism, 1992—; mem. Congregation for Evangelization of Peoples, 1995—; titular Bishop Silli, 1984; archbishop, 1985; made Cardinal, 1994; mem. Supreme Tribunal Apostolic Signatura, 1997—, Supreme Ct. Appeal of Vatican City State, 1998—. Decorated Lègion d'honneur, France, Ordre Leopold II, Belgium, Knight Grand Cross Ordre of Holy Selpuchre, Bailiff Knight Grand Cross Constantinian Order St. George. Office: Palazzo del Bramante, 00120 Vatican City The Vatican Address: Sinodo dei Vescovi, 00120 Vatican City Vatican City

SCHOULER, ANGELIKA PETRA, lawyer; b. Werncent, Germany, Apr. 4, 1960; arrived in France, 1989; d. Wilhelm and Katharina (Czerny) Ryschawy; m. Benoit André, June 24, 1989; children: Sabrina, Frederik, Clare. LLB, U. Munich, Germany, 1985, LLM, 1988; postgrad., Sorbonne U., Paris, 1993. Lawyer Law Firm Dr. Schmitt-Rolfes, Köster and Assocs., Munich, 1985-88; legal dir. Atlantique Prodns. S.A., Paris, 1989-92; lawyer Law Firm Henri Choukroun, Paris, 1992-93; counselor internat. affairs SACEM, Paris, 1993—; with French-Am. Cultural Cinema Fund, Paris, 1996—. Avocations: cinema, opera, tennis, skiing. Home: 32 rue Danton, 92150 Suresness France Office: SACEM, 225 Ave Clarlet de Saulk, 92521 Neuilly-Aux-Seine France

SCHOUPS, JOZEF JAN, Belgian army officer; b. Sint Truiden, Limburg, Belgium, May 13, 1940; s. Jean and Berthe (Vrancken) S.; m. Alexa Helena Baeten, July 14, 1970; children: Johan, Elisabeth. Grad., Royal Mil. Acad., Belgium, 1961, War Coll., Belgium, 1973, U.S. Army Command and Gen. Staff Coll., 1974. Commd. officer Belgian Army, 1961, advanced through grades to lt. gen.; bn. comdr. 1st Cav. Rgt., Arolsen, Germany, 1982-85; comdr. Reconaissance Brigade, Arolsen, 1988-91, Ace Mobile Force, Heidelberg, Germany, 1991-94, Army Operational Command, Brussels, 1997-98; chief staff Hdqs. AFNORTH, NATO, Brunssum, The Netherlands, 1998—. Decorated King's Sword, grand officer Order of Leopold II (Belgium), Redom Nikole Sbiča Zrinskog (Croatia). Avocations: swimming, bicycling, mountain climbing, travel. Home: Bosstraat 40, B-3060 Bertem Brabant, Belgium Office: RHQ AFNORTH, PO Box 270, 6440 AG Brunssum Limburg, The Netherlands

SCHOURUP, LAWRENCE CLIFFORD, linguist, educator; b. La Jolla, Calif., Oct. 16, 1947; s. William Harvey and Yvonne Mary (Mierlot) S. BA, U. Calif., San Diego, 1970; MA, Ohio State U., 1972, PhD, 1982. Fgn. expert Shaanxi Normal U., Xi'an, China, 1982-83; lectr. Kobe (Japan) U., 1985-90; assoc. prof. Osaka (Japan) Women's U., 1990-92, prof., 1992—; visitor U. Coll. London, 1995-96. Author: Common Discourse Particles in English Conversation, 1985, English Connectives, 1988, From Text to Context, 1990, Dictionary of Iconic Expressions in Japanese, 1996, Onomatopoeia: Form and Meaning, 1999. Mem. Linguistic Soc. Am., Linguistic Soc. Japan, Internat. Pragmatics Assn., Am. Dialect Soc. Buddhist. Home: Residence Okura A407 Mibu, Fuchida-cho 12 Nakagyoku, Kyoto 604-8855, Japan Office: Osaka Womens U, 2-1 Daisen-cho, Sakai-shi 590-0035, Japan

SCHRADE, ROBERT WARREN, classical pianist, educator; b. Walden, N.Y., Dec. 2, 1924; s. Louis J. and Elizabeth M. (Eitner) S.; m. Rolande M. Young, Dec. 21, 1949; children: Robelyn, Rhonda Lee, Rolisa M., Randolph R.A., Rorianne C. MusB, Manhattan Sch. Music, 1948, MusM, 1948. Mem. piano faculty Manhattan Sch. of Music, N.Y.C., 1949-56, 68-89; mem. music faculty, artist-in-residence Chapin sch., N.Y.C., 1948-89; pres., artistic dir. Sevenars Concerts, Inc., Worthington, Mass., 1976—; lectr. in field. Appeared in frequent piano concerts, N.Y.C., Europe, including Carnegie Hall, Lincoln Ctr., 1977, 81, 86, with Schrade Family Pianists, 1980-93, Lincoln Ctr., N.Y.C., 2000; soloist symphony orchs. throughout Europe and South Pacific; ann. solo concerts Sevenars Music Festival, Sevenars Music Festival, Worthington, Mass., Berkshires; featured on radio and TV shows including PM Mag. film, NBC Today Show, Radio New Zealand; 50th anniversary of N.Y. adult debut Liederkranz Found. (Town Hall), N.Y.C. Cpl. USAAC, 1942-45. Avocations: tennis, fishing. Home: 30 East End Ave New York NY 10028-7053 Address: Rte 112 at Ireland St S South Worthington MA 01098

SCHRADE, ROLANDE MAXWELL YOUNG, composer, pianist, educator; b. Washington, Sept. 13; d. Harry Robert and Isabelle Martha (Maxwell) Young; m. Robert Warren Schrade, Dec. 21, 1949; children: Robelyn, Rhonda Lee, Rolisa, Randolph, Rorianne. Pupil, Harold Bauer, N.Y.C., Vittorio Giannini; student, Manhatten Sch. Music, Juilliard Sch. Music. Debut as concert pianist Town Hall, N.Y.C., 1953, Nat. Gallery, Washington, 1954; concert pianist Constitution Hall, Washington, 1972; founder, dir. ann. performances Sevenars Concerts, Inc., Worthington, Mass., 1968—, music dir., 1975—, also broadcasts, 1984, 85; recitalist Radio Sta. WGMS-FM, Washington; mem. music faculty Allen-Stevenson Sch., N.Y.C., 1968-69; co-founder, v.p., treas. Sevenars Music House, Inc., N.Y.C., 1968—. Concerts include Lincoln Ctr., Alice Tully Hall, 1980, 93, Sevenars Concerts, Inc., 1968—, Lincoln Ctr., 2000!; tour, N.Z., 1982, 84; featured NBC Today Show with Schrade family pianists, 1993; named to Steinway Piano Co. Global Artist List; appearances PM Mag., TV, 1980-81; composer, pub., recs. of more than 100 songs; albums include America 76, Original and Traditional Songs for Special Days, 1988; editor: songs of Carrie Jacobs Bond, Boston Music Co.; TV feature film With Schrade Family Pianists, 1997; performed in Shrade-James Family Concert Lincoln Ctr., N.Y.C. Mem. ASCAP, DAR (Bicentennial award 1972), Mut. Artists Mgmt. Alliance (founder, bd. dirs.). Episcopalian. Home and Office: 30 E End Ave Ste 3A New York NY 10028-7053 Office: Sevenars Concerts Ireland St S at Rte 112 Worthington MA 01098

SCHRADER, KEVIN KINRADE, microbiologist, researcher; b. Johnson City, Tenn., June 29, 1963; s. John Ellsworth Schrader and Marita Cole Garin. BS, Auburn U., 1986, PhD, 1995. Postdoctoral fellow Miss. State U., Stoneville, 1996-97; rsch. scientist USDA, Oxford, Miss., 1997—. Rsch. grantee So. Regional Aquaculture Ctr., 1998. Mem. Internat. Assn. Water Quality, Am. Soc. Microbiology, Soc. Indsl. Microbiology, Sigma Xi. Avocations: tennis, fishing, stamp collecting, sports collectibles. Office: PO Box 8048 University MS 38677-8048

SCHRADER, MICHAEL EUGENE, columnist, editor; b. Jersey City, Apr. 3, 1938; s. Eugene Charles and Anne Veronica (Kane) S. BA in Latin, NYU, 1961, MA in English, 1963; postgrad., UCLA, 1965-67, 68-69, Trinity Coll., Dublin, 1967-68, U. Copenhagen, Denmark, 1970. Asst. editor Macmillan Co., N.Y.C., 1962-64; teaching asst. U. Ill., Urbana, 1964-65; teaching asst., rsch. asst. UCLA, 1965-67, 68-69; sr. copy editor Dell Pub. Co., N.Y.C., 1971-72; copy chief Sat. Rev. mag., N.Y.C., 1972-76, Penthouse mag., N.Y.C., 1976-82; assoc. editor Med. Econs. mag., Oradell, N.J., 1982; sr. copy editor Woman's World mag., Englewood, N.J., 1983-84; book reviewer, sr. copy editor Nation's Restaurant News, N.Y.C., 1985—. Columnist: From the Bookshelf, in Nation's Restaurant News, 1988—. Friend of Bobst Libr., Soc. of Torch, NYU, 1994—, established Anne Kane Schrader Cookbook and Nutrition Collection. Recipient Danish Marshall award U. Copenhagen, 1970; Fulbright scholar, 1967-68. Fellow James Beard Found. (judge food and beverage book awards 1991-94); mem. Soc. of the Torch (charter), Internat. Assn. Culinary Profls. Democrat. Roman Catholic. Avocations: reading fiction and poetry, growing house plants, travel, movies, theater. Home: 30 Waterside Plz Apt 33H New York NY 10010-2627 Office: Lebhar-Friedman Inc Nation's Restaurant News 425 Park Ave New York NY 10022-3549

SCHRAEDER, PETER KLAUS, orthopaedic surgeon, educator; b. Neuwied, Germany, Feb. 28, 1967; s. Rudolf Wendelin and Margrit Anna (Jung) S.; m. Nicole Annette Maerz, May 21, 1994; 1 child, Luise Katharina. MD, U. Zuerich, Switzerland, 1994. Asst. Free U. Berlin, 1993-95; rschr. AO Rsch. Inst., Davos, Switzerland, 1995; asst. prof. dept. orthopaedics U. Ulm, Germany, 1995—; rsch. fellow AO Rsch. Inst., Davos, 1996, Schulhess Clinic, Zuerich, 1997. Author: (book chpt.) Lehrbuch der Geriatrie, 1999; contbr. articles to profl. jours. Mem. Lions Club, Leo Club (pres. 1988-89), Efort Fellow Club (pres. 1999—, traveling fellow 1997). Roman Catholic. Avocations: reading, gardening. Home: Goethe Str 32, 89278 Nersingen Germany Office: U Ulm Dept Orthopaedics, Oberer Eselsberg 45, 89081 Ulm Germany

SCHRAMM, ANDREAS, microbiologist, researcher; b. Augsburg, Bavaria, Germany, July 14, 1970; s. Georg Siegfried and Siegrid Maria (Bartussek) S.; m. Doris Elisabeth Hafner, June 5, 1996; children: Anne Magdalena, Miriam Elisabeth. Diploma in biology, Tech. U., Munich, 1995; PhD, U. Bremen (Germany), 1998. Rsch. asst Tech. U., Munich, 1995-96; rsch. asst Max Planck Inst. Marine Microbiology, Bremen, Germany, 1997-98, postdoctoral rschr., 1999; rsch. assoc. BITOEK, U. Bayreuth, Germany, 1999—. Contbr. articles to prof. jours., including Applied and Environ. Microbiology, Biotech., Water Sci. and Tech. Recipient Otto-Hahn medal Max-Planck Soc., 1998. Avocations: music, hiking, reading. Home: Bayreuther Str 5, D 95473 Haag Bavaria, Germany Office: BITOEK U Bayreuth, Dr Hans Frisch Str 1-3, D 95440 Bayreuth Bavaria, Germany

SCHRAND, RICHARD HENRY, broadcaster; b. Cin., Nov. 1, 1957; s. Edward August and Jane Marie (Scheib) S.; m. Deborah Fortner, 1979 (div. 1985); 1 child, Cynthia Lanette; m. Sharon Lynn Lassandro, Dec. 24, 1986; children: Courtney Lynne, Richard Jr., Brandon Ian. Student, Ohio State U., 1975-76, No. Ky. U., 1976-77. Intern Sta. WCPO-TV, Cin., 1971-75; producer Sta. WKRC-TV, Cin., 1975-79; pub. affairs dir., reporter, anchor Sta. WCSC-TV, Charleston, S.C., 1979-83; actor Phila. Experiment, L.A., 1984; asst. promotion dir. Sta. WLWT-TV, Cin., 1983-86; spl. projects coord. Sta. KXAS-TV, Dallas/Ft. Worth, 1986-87; mgr. media svcs. NBC TV Network, Burbank, Calif., 1987-89; pres. Cyn-Court Enterprises, Burbank, 1989-91; mktg. dir. Sta. WPTA-TV, Ft. Wayne, Ind., 1991-92; v.p., gen. mgr. Branson (Mo.) Broadcasting Corp., 1992-95; dir. spl. projects/nat. media, graphics and advt. creator Jim Owens & Assocs., 1995-98; gen. mgr. Jim Owens Radio, Inc., Nashville, 1995-98; pres. GRFX ByDesign, Nashville, 1996—; v.p. Komodo Studios, L.A., 1999-2000; instr., spkr. Graphic Design Tour, 2000—. Author: Canoma Visual Insight, 2000, 3D Creature Workshop vol. 2, 2000, Macromedia Web Design Handbook, 2000, Adobe Golive 5F/X & Design, 2000, Adobe Live Motion Visual Jumpstart, 2000, Adobe Photoshop 6 Visual Jumpstart, 2000; contbr.: Pixels: 3D Book, 1999, Mastering Pixels: 3D; writer Poser 4 Book, 1999, Adobe PhotoshopVisual Jumpstart, 2000; webmaster Crook & Chase Theater. Bd. dirs. Project Graduation, Dallas/Ft. Worth, 1986-87; mem. Muscular Dystrophy Assn., Charleston, 1980-83; publicist Housing Now, L.A., 1988. Recipient Regional Emmy award NATAS, 1975, award Broadcast Promotion and Mktg. Exec., Seattle, 1992. Avocations: guitar, writing, singing, golf. E-mail: grfx.pro@home.com.

SCHRANK, SHIRLEY ANN, artist; b. Nunda, N.Y., Jan. 30, 1933; d. Ward Donald and Norma Mae (Kelley) Crane; m. John Roberts McKalip Jr., Oct. 8, 1966 (dec. May 1974); children: Catherine, William Ward; m. William Thomas Schrank, Nov. 24, 1976 (dec. Aug. 1993). Degree in nursing, U. Rochester, 1954, BSN, 1960, MS in Nursing Edn., 1961. Staff nurse dept. psychiatry U. Rochester, N.Y., 1954-56; team leader dept. medicine U. Rochester, 1956-60; instr. in pediatric nursing Genesee Hosp.,

Rochester, 1960-61; staff nurse eye surgery Children's Hosp. San Francisco, 1961; nurse pvt. duty surg. patients Presbyn. Med. Ctr., San Francisco, 1962; instr. medicine, surg. and ICU nursing Samuel Merritt Hosp. Sch. Nursing, Oakland, Calif., 1963-67, ret., 1967; with The Sculpture Group Gallery, Danville, Calif., 1995—, East Bay Women Artists, Oakland, Calif., 1993-99. Stephen min., Stephen tchg. leader, choir and ensemble. Mem. AAUW. Republican. Presbyterian. Avocations: camping, traveling, singing, needle-point. Home: 609 Maureen Ln Pleasant Hill CA 94523-2719

SCHRAUB, SIMON, oncologist, educator; b. Bordeaux, France, Jan. 9, 1940; s. Benjamin and Cécile (Zwiebel) S.; m. Aurore Anklewicz, Aug. 20, 1969; children: karin, David, Mickael. MD, U. Strasbourg, France, 1966. Intern U. Hosp. of Strasbourg, France, 1962-64, resident, 1964-67; prof. oncology U. Besançon, France, 1970-97; head comprehensive cancer ctr. Ctr. Paul Strauss, Strasbourg, head radiotherapy dept.; prof. oncology U. Strasbourg; nat. cons. of unproven methods in oncology. Author: La Magie et la Raison, 1987. Adminstr. Adminstrn. Coun. Univ. Hosp., 1989-94, Nat. French Anti-Cancer League, Paris, 1981. With French Armed Forces, 1967-68. Recipient Chevalier de la légion d'Honneur, 1994. Mem. Rotary. Fax: 33 3 88 252458. E-mail: schraub@strasbourg.fnclcc.fr. Office: Ctr Paul Strauss, 67085 Strasbourg France

SCHRAUFNAGEL, TONY, artist, educator; b. Dallas, Sept. 3, 1968; s. William Anthony and Loretta Joan S.; m. Caitlin Schraufnagel, Nov. 11, 1995. BFA, U. North Tex., 1992, MFA, 1996. V.p. Aesthetic Design Source, Krum, Tex., 1996—; pres. 500X Gallery, Dallas, 1999—; asst. prof. Tex. Tech. U., Lubbock, 2000—; mem. adj. faculty Brookhaven Coll., Farmers Branch, Tex., 1997-99, U. North Tex., Denton, 1998-2000. Mem. Tex. Fine Arts Assn., Coll. Art Assn., Internat. Sculpture Ctr. E-mail: tschraufnagel@hotmail.com.

SCHREDELSEKER, KLAUS, finance educator; b. Mannheim, Germany, Mar. 26, 1943; s. Kurt and Otti (Hübinger) S.; m. Carola Bielfield, 1978; children: Johann Paul, Theresa. MBA, U. Mannheim, 1967; PhD, U. Munich, 1974. Scholar U. Milan, 1968-69; asst. prof. U. Munich, 1969-76; assoc. prof. U. Wuppertal (Fed. Republic Germany), 1976-85; prof. finance U. Innsbruck (Austria), 1986—, chmn. dept. fin., 1987—; prof. U. Siena (Italy), 1989—; chmn. Internat. Mgmt. Program, Innsbruck, 1988—. Author: Eigentümer Kontrolle, 1976, Publizität yund Unternehmensvefassung, 1986. Mem. Am. Econ. Assn., Am. Fin. Assn., European Fin. Assn., European Fin. Mgmt. Assn. (pres.), German Econ. Assn. Home: Hohenstrasse III, A-6020 Innsbruck Austria Office: U Inssbruck Dept Fin, Universitaetsstr 15, Innsbruck Austria

SCHREDL, MICHAEL, researcher; b. Wiesloch, Germany, Sept. 14, 1962; s. Eberhard Schredl and Maria Mayer. Diploma in engring., U. Karlsruhe, Germany, 1986; diploma in psychology, U. Mannheim, Germany, 1991, PhD, 1998. Tchr. adult edn. VHS Mannheim, 1989—; bio-engr. Sleep Lab. of Ctrl. Inst. Mental Health, Mannheim, 1991-92, dream rschr., 1992—. Author: Hör Auf Deine Träume, 1996, Die nachtliche Traum welt, 1999; contbr. articles to profl. jours. Mem. Assn. for Study of Dreams, German Sleep Soc. Avocations: juggling, lucid dreaming. Home: Hölderlin Str 46, 68259 Mannheim Germany Office: Ctrl Inst Mental Health, Sleep Lab PO Box 122120, 68072 Mannheim Germany

SCHREFF, DAVID JONATHAN, marketing professional; b. New Haven, Conn., July 8, 1955; s. Michael C. and Anita L. Schreff; m. Melissa Hoskins, July 29, 1984; children: Benjamin, Daniel, Rebecca. BA in Polit. Sci., Wesleyan U., 1977; MBA in Mktg., U. Conn. Dir. affiliate mktg. Viacom Internat./Showtime Networks, N.Y.C., 1982-85; v.p. Walt Disney Co./Disney Channel, Burbank, Calif., 1985-90; pres. mktg. and media group Nat. Basketball Assn., N.Y.C., 1990-96; pres., COO Marvel Entertainment, N.Y.C., 1996-98; pres., founder Bedare Entertainment LLC, Greenwich, Conn., 1998-00; mng. ptnr. Food Innovation Ptnrs. LLC, Greenwich, 1999—; mng. ptnr. WOWEE LLC, Tarrytown, N.Y., 1999—; bd. dirs. Bottle Rocket, N.Y.C., Gizmox.com, N.Y.C.; pres., COO Notara.com, 2000—. Contbr. articles to profl. jours. Scoutmaster Boy Scouts Am., Greenwich, 1997. Mem. Young Pres. Orgn. Republican. Jewish. Avocations: oboe music performance, writing children's books, scoutmaster, youth sports coaching. E-mail: david.schreff@notara.com. Office: Notara Inc 257 Park Ave S New York NY 10010-7304

SCHREIBER, ANTON, engineering educator; b. Reichstadt, Sudetenland, Czechoslovakia, Sept. 22, 1925; s. Josef and Anna (Nentwich) S.; m. Waltraud Müller, July 12, 1958; children: Heidemarie, Angelika. Student in econs., U. Rostock, German Dem. Republic, 1953; M in Econs., U. Leipzig, German Dem. Republic, 1957, Dr.rer.oec. (hon.), 1963, Dr.sc. (hon.), 1971. Comml. apprenticeship Oppelt-Hess Ltd., Reichstadt, 1941-1943, clk., 1943-45; adminstrv. clk. Social Security Ins., Weimar, Gotha, Erfurt, German Dem. Republic, 1946-53; sr. asst. Tech. U. Ilmenau, German Dem. Republic, 1957-69, lectr., 1969-71, prof., head sci. and rsch. prod. process section device engring., 1971-91, v.p. rsch. section device engring., 1971-74, head section device engring., 1974-91; Head Assn. Support Mech./Engring. Faculty, Tech. U., 1991-97. Contbr. 40 articles to sci. and tech. mags. Mem. peace-coun. German Dem. Republic, Berlin, 1973-89; mem. Peoples Assn. War Memls., Kassel, 1995—. Mem. Assn. German Univs., Assn. German Engrs. Roman Catholic. Avocations: reading, history, traveling. Home: Geschwister Scholl St 4c, 98693 Ilmenau Thuringia, Germany

SCHREIBER, EILEEN SHER, artist; b. Denver, 1925; d. Michael Herschel and Sarah Deborah (Tannenbaum) Sher; m. Jonas Schreiber, Mar. 27, 1945; children: Jeffrey, Barbara, Michael. Student, U. Utah, 1942-45, NYU ext., 1966-68, Montclair (N.J.) State Coll., 1975-79; also pvt. art study. Exhibited Morris Mus. Arts and Scis., Morristown, N.J., 1965-73, N.J. State Mus., 1969, Lever House, N.Y.C., 1971, Paramus (N.J.) Mus., 1973, Newark Mus., 1978, 1991-92, Am. Water Color Soc., Audubon Artists, N.A.D. Gallery, N.Y.C., Pallazzo Vecchio Florence, Italy, Art Expo 1987, 1988, India Mus., 1994, 95, Athens (Greece) Mus., 1996, 97; represented in permanent collections Tex. A&M U., Telesoft Inc., Phoenix, State of N.J., Morris Mus., Seton Hall U., Bloomfield (N.J.) Coll., Barclay Bank of Eng., N.J., Somerset Coll., NYU, Morris County State Coll., Broad Nat. Bank, Newark, Ind. Cmty. Bank, Consulting Actuaries, Internat., IBM, Am. Tel. Co., RCA, Johnson & Johnson, Champion Internat. Paper Co., Sony, Mitsubishi, Celanese Co., Squibb Corp., Nabisco, Nat. Bank Phila., Data Control, Ind. Cmty. Bank, Sperry Univac, Ga. Pacific Co., Pub. Svc. Co. N.J., Diane Levine Gallery, Boston, S.W. Gallery, Long Beach Island, N.J., others; also pvt. collections. Recipient awards N.J. Watercolor Soc., 1969, 72, 1st award in watercolor Hunterdon Art Ctr., 1972, Best in Show award Short Hills State Show, 1976, Tri-State Purchase award Somerset Coll., 1977, Art Expo, N.Y.C., 1987, 88, numerous others. Mem. Nat. Assn. Women Artists (chmn. watercolor jury, Collage award 1983, Marian Halpren Meml. award 1995), Nat., N.J. Artists Equity, Printmaker Coun. Visual Artists (1st award in printmaking 1996), Women Visual Artists (Fla.). Home: 22 Powell Dr West Orange NJ 07052-1337

SCHREIBER, ERNST RUDOLF, horticultural educator, researcher; b. Quedlinburg, Germany, Sept. 18, 1938; s. Johannes and Waltraud (Kloeppel) S.; m. Hanna Maria Gerdom, May 31, 1967; children: Jan Patrik, Max Philipp. Journeyman degree, Chatelaine Horticulture Sch., Geneva, 1962; diploma in horticulture, Technische U. Hannover, Germany, 1966; Dr. Agr., Tech. U., Berlin, 1978. Rschr. Schering AG, Berlin, 1967-68; cons. in Portugal Govt. Germany, Bonn, 1968-71, cons., rschr. in Morocco, 1971-74; prof. horticulture Technische Fachhochschule, Berlin, 1974—; cons. for German Govt. in Brazilia and Senegal, 1983, in Thailand, 1985, in Pakistan, 1986, in Jordan, 1992, in Georgia/Russia, 1994. Author: Biologie, Importance et Moyens de Controle du Nematode des Tiges sur Feves au Maroc, 1978. Mem. German Soc. Horticultural Sci. Evangelist. Avocations: foreign languages (Italian, Portuguese, English, French), swimming, windsurfing. Office: Tech-Fachhochschule-Berlin, Luxemburger Str.10, D-13353 Berlin Germany

SCHREIBER, GERHARD HANS, biochemistry educator; b. Berlin, Oct. 28, 1932; m. Margot Thon, May 18, 1957; 3 children. MD, U. Mainz & U. Freiburg, Germany, 1959. Registrar dept. medicine U. Kiel, Germany, 1964; dozent biochemistry U. Freiburg, Germany, 1970, deputy mng. dir. biochemistry, 1970-71, mng. dir. biochemistry, 1971-73; chair biochemistry U. Melbourne, Australia, 1973-97; prof. emeritus U. Melbourne, 1998—. Postdoctoral fellow McArdle Lab. Cancer Rsch., Madison, Wis., 1965. Home: 17 Graham Rd Rosanna, Melbourne 3084, Australia Office: U Melbourne, Dept Biochemistry & Molec Bio, Parkville 3052, Australia

SCHREIBER, HARRY, JR., management consultant; b. Columbus, Ohio, Apr. 1, 1934; s. C. Harry and Audrey (Sard) S.; m. Margaret Ruth Heinzman, June 12, 1955; children: Margaret Elizabeth Schreiber Yeager, Thomas Edward, Amy Katherine Schreiber Garcia. BS, MIT, 1955; MBA, Boston U., 1958. CPA, N.Y. Acct. truck and coach divsn. Gen. Motors Corp., Pontiac, Mich., 1955; instr. MIT, 1958-62; pres. Data-Service, Inc., Boston, 1961-65, Harry Schreiber Assocs., Wellesley, Mass., 1965; mgr., nat. dir. merchandising cons. Peat, Marwick, Mitchell & Co., N.Y.C., 1966-70; ptnr. Peat, Marwick, Mitchell & Co., Chgo., 1970-75; chmn. bd. Close, Martin, Schreiber & co., 1975-83; ptnr. Deloitte Haskins & Sells, 1983-85; chmn. bd. Harry Schreiber & Assocs., Ltd., 1985—; mem. staff Work Simplification Conf., Lake Placid, N.Y., 1959-60; Tobe retailing lectr. Harvard Bus. Sch., 1964; lectr. indsl. engring. Northeastern U., 1958-61; lectr. info. sys. Babson Coll., 1962; lectr. Bridgeport Engring. Ins., 1962, Western Mich. U., 1975. Pub., Retail Working Papers, 1991—. Treas., Emmanuel Episcopal Ch., Chestertown, 1999—. 1st lt. AUS, 1956-58. Served to 1st lt. AUS, 1956-58. Mem. Am. Inst. Indsl. Enrs. (chmn. data processing divsn. 1964-66, chpt. v.p. 1961, 65, chmn. retail industries divsn. 1976-78), Com. Internat. Congress Transp.Confs., Assn. for Computing Machinery, Assn. for Sys. Mgmt., Inst. Mgmt. Scis., Retail Rsch. Soc., Retail Fin. Execs., Nat. Retail Fedn. (retail sys. specifications com., acctg. stds. com.), Food Distbn. Rsch. Soc. (dir. 1972-78, pres. 1974), Japan-Am. Soc. Chgo., MIT Faculty Club, Hidden Creek Country Club (Reston, Va.), Chester River Yacht and Country Club (Chestertown, Md.), Army and Navy Club (Washington), Plaza Club (Chgo.). Republican. Home: 105 High St Chestertown MD 21620-1515

SCHREIBER, JUDY ANN, counselor; b. St. Marys, Pa., Apr. 22, 1952; d. Francis John and Agnes (Meyer) S. BS in Edn./Music, Edinboro U. Pa., 1974, MA in Counseling, 1991; postgrad., Notre Dame U., 1981-82; grad. nursing program, Erie Tech./Hamot Hosp., 1979. Cert. music tchr., elem. sch. counselor, secondary sch. counselor, school psychologist. Tchr. Erie (Pa.) Diocese, St. Mary's, 1974-77, Clearfield, Pa., 1977-78; missionary Young People Who Care Ctr., Clearfield, 1977; sr. mem. Mercy, Erie, Pa., 1977-86; nurse Hamot Hosp./DuBois Hosp., Erie and DuBois, Pa., 1978-81; tchr., coord. pastoral music St. George Parish Sch., Erie, 1981-87; tchr. Millcreek Sch. Dist., Erie, 1987-91, sch. counselor, 1991—; cert. sch. psychologist Millcreek Sch. Dist., 1996-99; dir. liturgy and music St. George Parish, 1999—; dir. guidance St. George Sch., 1999—; mem. Erie Philharmonic Chorus, 1987-89, Presque Isle Choral, 1991—; soloist Erie Parishes, 1974—; cantor St. George Ch., Erie, 1981—; musician Erie Playhouse, 1990—; cons. Mem. Great Erie Excellence Coun., 1990—; mem. Community Awareness Coun., J.S. Wilson Mid. Sch., Erie, 1991. Nominee for Pa. Tchr. of Yr. award, 1990-91. Mem. Music Educators Nat. Conf., Am. Sch. Counselors Assn., Erie County Sch. Counselors Assn., Nat. Pastoral Musicians (hon. chair 1999). Roman Catholic. Avocations: music, running, playhouse. Office: Millcreek Schs Westlake Mid Sch 4330 W Lake Rd Erie PA 16505-1416

SCHREIBER, MARTIN FRITZ BRUNO, computer scientist; b. Helmstedt, Germany, June 9, 1955; s. Hans and Hellita (Kroos) S.; m. Regine Abel; children: Pascal, Rafael. Examen in Maths., U. Hamburg, Germany, 1984. Tchr. U. Lüneburg, Germany, 1988-94, head computing dept., 1994—. Avocations: sports, handworks. Home: Haesefeld 1, 21406 Barnstedt Germany Office: U Lueneburg Rechenzentrum, Scharnhorststr 1, 21332 Lueneburg Germany

SCHREIBER, STEFAN WOLFGANG, gastroenterologist, immunologist; b. Berlin, June 25, 1962; s. Wolfgang Roland and Gisela Ruth (Koninski) S.; m. Birte Ingrid Groessner, Aug. 13, 1988; 1 child, Nicholas Stefan. MD, U. Hamburg, Germany, 1986. Rsch. asst. U. Hamburg, 1986-88; rsch. assoc. Washington U., St. Louis, 1988-90; asst. prof. medicine U. Pa., Phila., 1990-91; rsch. asst. U. Hamburg, 1991, Humboldt U., Berlin, 1995-98; assoc. prof. medicine Christian-Aebechts-Univ., Kiel, Germany, 1998—; invited lectr. numerous sci. meetings. Ad. hoc reviewer Jour. Cell Biology, Digestion, Gastroenterology, Jour. Immunology; contbr. chpts. to med. textbooks, more than 130 articles to profl. jours. Asche fellow, Germany, 1988; Mercke, Sharp & Dohme awardee, 1990; recipient Frerichs award German Soc. Internal Medicine, 1994. Fellow Am. Coll. Gastroenterology; mem. Am. Gastroenterol. Assn., European Soc. Clin. Investigation, Am. Soc. for Cell Biology, Deutsche Gesellschaft fuer Verdauungs-und Stoffwechselkrankheiten. Lutheran. Avocations: skiing, pinao playing, opera. Office: Christian-Aebechts U 1st Dept Medicine, Schittenhelm Str 12, 24105 Kiel Germany

SCHREIBER, VRATISLAV, clinical physiology educator; b. Prague, Czech Republic, June 29, 1924; s. Josef and Jarmila (Hrouzková) S.;m. Olga Cechová, June 28, 1950; 1 child, Michal. MD, Charles U., Prague, Czech Republic, 1954. Intern First Med. Sch., Gen. Hosp., Prague, 1955-57, sci. worker, leading sci. worker, 1957—; prof. clin. physiology 1st Med. Sch., Charles U., Prague, 1991—; pres. Coun. for Popularisation of Sci., Czech. Acad. Sci. Major Czech Army, 1955. Recipient prizes Sci. Coun. Ministry of Health, 1964, Soc. Occupational Medicine, 1951, Endocrinology Soc., 1956, 60, Physiol. Soc., 1964, Nat. prize, 1967, 87. Mem. Czech Endocrinology Soc. (pres.). Home: Zitomirská 39, 101 00 Prague 10, Czech Republic Office: Charles U 1st Sch Med Lab Endocrin Metab, U nemocnice 1, 128 21 Prague 2, Czech Republic

SCHREIER, GUNTER, remote sensing data specialist, researcher; b. Düsseldorf, Germany, July 19, 1958; s. Günter and Rosel (Rinio) S.; m. Martina E. Büchel, July 26, 1986; children: Michael, Elisabeth. Diploma in geophysics, U. Munich, 1983. Researcher U. Munich, 1982-85; scientist German Aerospace Ctr. Establishment, Oberpfaffenhofen, 1985-87; project mgr. German Aerospace Rsch. Establishment, Oberpfaffenhofen, 1987—; mem. Com. Earth Observation Satellites, Washington, 1987—, chmn. aux. data sets group, 1991—; chmn. working group GEOSAR, 1988—; project head global change video Space Agys. for Internat. Space Yr., Munich and London, 1991; lectr. Synthetic Aperture Radar Geocoding, 1988, 90, 92, 96, 2000; mgr. German Processing and Archiving Facility for Earth Observation Satellites, ENVISAT project mgr., 1993—; project mgr. European Commn. Ctr. Earth Obs., 1996, head mktg., commercialization, 1996; v.p. definiens AG, 2000. Mem. IEEE, German Geophys. Soc. Avocations: reading, his children. Office: definiens AG, Rindermarkt 7, D-80331 Munich Germany

SCHRELL, UWE MARTIN HEINRICH, neurosurgeon, educator, researcher; b. Hameln, Germany, Mar. 10, 1950; m. Maria Eva Reitmeier, Oct. 21, 1981; children: Constanze Maria Laetitia, Catherina Eva Felicitas. Degree, Ludwig-Maximilians U., Munich, 1983; MD, U. Munich, 1985; habil., U. Erlangen-Nuremberg, Germany, 1994. Tng. in neurosurgery U. Erlangen-Nüremberg, 1983-90, sr. neurosurgeon Neurosurg. Clinic, 1991, lectr., 1994—. Contbr. articles to profl. jours., chpts. to books. Recipient Career Devel. award Ria Frifrau von Fritsch Stiftung, 1993. Mem. Deutsche Gesellschaft Endokrinologie, Deutsche Gesellschaft Neurochirurgie, Deutsche Krebsgesellschaft. Office: Euromed Clinic Neurochirur, Europa-Allee 1, 90763 Füth Germany

SCHREMPF, DETLEF, professional basketball player; b. Leverkusen, Germany, Jan. 21, 1963. Student, U. Washington. Forward Dallas Mavericks, 1985-89, Indiana Pacers, 1989-93, Seattle Supersonics, 1993-99, Portland Trailblazers, 1999—; player West German Olympic Team, 1984, 92. Recipient Sixth Man award NBA, 1991, 92; mem. NBA All-Star team, 1993.

SCHREMPP, JÜRGEN, automotive executive; b. Daimler-Benz, Stuttgart, Germany, Sept. 15, 1944. Various positions Daimler Benz, Stuttgart, Germany, 1974-80, dep. mem. bd. of mgmt., pres., CEO, 1989-95, CEO, chmn. bd., 1995—; apptd. pres. EUCLID Inc., Cleve., 1984; apptd. dep. chmn. mgmt. bd. EUCLID Inc., 1985, apptd. chmn. mgmt. bd., 1987; chmn. mgmt. bd. Daimler Chrysler AG, Stuttgart. Office: Daimler Chrysler AG, Epplestrasse 225, 70546 Stuttgart Germany*

SCHRENK, GARY DALE, foundation executive; b. San Jose, Calif., Apr. 29, 1949; s. Robert Shepard and Katherine Mildred (Grant) S.; m. Rhonda Lynn King, Oct. 9, 1981 (div. Jan. 1989); children: Stephen, Kristen, James. BA in Comm., Am. U., 1970; postgrad., Regis U., 1990—. TV dir. WTOP (now WUSA), Washington, 1971-73, KBTV (now KUSA), Denver, 1973-75; with Denver Area Boy Scouts Am., 1975-80; regional dir. St. Jude Children's Rsch. Hosp., Memphis, 1980-83; dir. devel. Denver Art Mus., 1983-85; asst. dir. devel. The Children's Hosp., Denver, 1985-87; pres. North Colo. Med. Ctr. Found., Greeley, 1987—; dir., instr. Fast Start Course, 1985—; pres. Monfort Children's Clinic, Greeley, 1994—. Pres. Vision Together, Weld County, Colo., 1994-95; chmn., founding dir. Weld Citizen Action Network, 1995-98, 2000—; founding dir. First Steps Weld County, 1993-99; chmn. Weld Cmty. Health Coalition, 1992—; chmn. pub. support com. Team Colo. ARC, 1997—. Recipient Disting. Citizen award Highlanders, Denver, 1974. Mem. Nat. Soc. Fund Raising Execs. (mem. nat. found. bd. 1998—, nat. assembly 1994-98, bd. dirs. Colo. chpt. 1979—, pres. 1984), Colo. Assn. Nonprofit Orgns. (founding dir. 1987-92), Rotary, Greeley Country Club, Tahosa Alumni Assn. (past pres., past chair). Methodist. Avocation: golf. Home: 4956 13th St Greeley CO 80634-2215 Office: North Colo Med Ctr Found 1801 16th St Greeley CO 80631-5154

SCHREUDER, DERYEK M., academic administrator; arrived in Australia, 1976; Former deputy vice-chancellor Macquarie U.; former vice-chancellor U. We. Sydney; vice-chancellor, pres. U. We. Australia, 1998—; chmn. numerous Australian Rsch. Coun. coms. and panels; dir. Bus. Higher Edn. Round Table and IDP, Australia; former prof. in Canada. Author numerous books in field. Rhodes scholar to Oxford; Kennedy fellow at New Coll., Oxford. Mem. Australian Acad. of Humanities (past pres.), Australian Hist. Assn. (former pres.), African Studies Assn. of Australasia and the Pacific (former pres.). Office: Univ Western Australia, Nedlands WA 6907, Australia

SCHREUDER, RINO HERMAN CHRISTIAAN, publisher, consultant; b. Deventer, The Netherlands, Jan. 29, 1957; s. Gerard H. and Umbgrove Constance M.C. (van Lulofs) S.; m. Yvonne M.A. Kuysters, Sept. 3, 1988; children: Bastiaan, Merel. BA, Nijenrode U., The Netherlands, 1979; MBA, Erasmus U., Rotterdam, The Netherlands, 1981. Cons. Krekel WW, Rotterdam, 1981-83; mng. dir. Kluwer Study Ctr., Maarssen, The Netherlands, 1983-88, Dutch Nat. Mktg. Inst., Amsterdam, The Netherlands, 1988-91; HRD mgr. Bührmann-Tetterode, Amsterdam, The Netherlands, 1991-92; mng. dir. European Mgmt. Devel. Centre, Huizen, The Netherlands, 1992—; non-exec. dir. Logion, Rotterdam, 1995—; mem. adv. bd. Rotterdam Sch. Mgmt., 1991—, Dutch Ctr. for Postgrad. Studies in Bus. Adminstrn., Utrecht, The Netherlands, 1990—. Editor-in-chief: (anm. ref. books) European Management Education Directory, 1994—, Asian Management Education Directory, 1995—; chief editor Jour. Mgmt. Devel., 1993—. Vice chair Dutch Young Liberal Dems., Amsterdam, 1977-79. Mem. European Found. for Mgmt. Devel., Dutch Inst. Dirs., Internat. Fedn. Tng. and Devel. Orgns. Fax: 31 35 695 1900. E-mail: mail@emdcentre.com. Office: EMD Centre, Naarderstraat 296, NL1272NT Huizen The Netherlands

SCHREUR, BARBARA, computer science educator; b. Neuendettelsau, Germany, Jan. 4, 1944; came to U.S., 1952; d. Franz and Elsbeth (Gasner) Fischer; m. Julian Jay Schreur, June 4, 1966; children: Alex, George. BA, Manhattanville Coll., 1964; MA, U. Ariz., 1969; PhD, Fla. State U., 1979. Physicist CBS Labs., Stamford, Conn., 1965-66; grad. assist. U. Ariz., Tucson, 1967-70; tchr. Valdosta (Ga.) H.S., 1971-74; grad. assist. Fla. State U., Tallahassee, 1974-80; asst. prof. Tex. A&M U., Kingsville, Tex., 1980-86; assoc. prof. Tex. A&M U., Kingsville, 1986-97; prof. Tex. A&M Coll., Kingsville, 1997—; cons. Coastal Bd. Coun. of Govts., Corpus Christi, Tex., 1990-93; creator software reuse libr., NASA, 2000—. Recipient Summer faculty fellowship, NASA, 1993, 94, 95, presentation of shuttle hardware and software, NASA, 1996-98, software engring. initiative NASA, Huntsville, Ala., 1998-99. Mem. IEEE, Am. Computing Machinery, Tex. Acad. Sci, Am. Astron. Soc. (divsn. Dynamical Astronomy). Avocations: reading, golf. E-mail: bschreur@ieee.org. Home: 555 Elizabeth St Kingsville TX 78363-6741 Office: Tex A&M U-Kingsville MSC Box 192 Kingsville TX 78364-0192

SCHREY, HEINZ PETER, soil scientist; b. Viersen, Germany, June 28, 1958; s. Heinz and Cathy (Rath) S.; m. Christiane Hesse, 1985; children: Moritz Cajetan, Elisabeth Dorothea, Charlotte Sophie. Diploma, Tech. U., Hannover, Germany, 1982, D in Horticulture, 1987. Project mgr. GLA NRW, Krefeld, Germany, 1987-95, adminstr. soil info. system and computer cartography, 1995—. Roman Catholic. Avocations: philosophy, reading, hiking. E-mail: schrey@gla.nrw.de. Office: Geologisches Landesamt NRW, De-Greiff-Str 195, D-47803 Krefeld Germany

SCHREY, MANFRED, lithography educator; b. Rheydt, Rhineland, Germany; s. Wilhelm and Mathilde Johanna (Potz) S.; m. Hannelore Russ, May 10, 1986; m. Martha Lilia Alba, Nov. 11, 1991; 1 child, Lara Carina. Diploma in Physics, RWTH-Aachen (Germany), 1971, D Natural Scis., 1977. Asst. Inst. Phys. Chemistry RWTH-Aachen, 1971-77; asst. prof. Inst. Phys. Chemistry U. Duisburg, 1977-78; dir. dept. Photoresists Hunt Chem., St. Niklaas, Belgium, 1978-81; procurist MIT Halbleiter Chemie, Solingen, Germany, 1981-82; prof. microlithography dept. photoengring. U. Applied Scis., Cologne, Germany, 1982—; guest rsch. scientist Inst. Ctr. Instruments, U. Mexico City, 1991-94. Author: Nasschemisches Ätzen, 1981, Reprofotografiehelfe, 1997, Microchip Production, 1994. Chmn. Die Grünen Köln, 1988-91; mem. VDI, Düsseldorf, 1971—, GDPh, Cologne, 1996. Avocations: sailing, tennis, windsurfing. Home: Osterriethweg 27, 50996 Cologne Germany Office: Polytechnique Cologne, Betzdorfer Str 2, 50679 Cologne Germany

SCHREYER, WILLIAM ALLEN, retired investment firm executive; b. Williamsport, Pa., Jan. 13, 1928; s. William L. and Elizabeth (Engel) S.; m. Joan Legg, Oct. 17, 1953; 1 child, DrueAnne Frazier. BA, Pa. State U., 1948. With Merrill Lynch, Inc. and predecessors, N.Y.C., 1948-93; CEO Merrill Lynch & Co., N.Y.C., 1984-92, chmn., 1985-93; chmn. emeritus, 1993—; exec. com. AEA Investors, Inc. Trustee Ctr. for Strategic and Internat. Studies, Pa. State U., 1986—, chmn. bd. trustees, 1993-96. With USAF, 1955-56. Mem. Econ. Club N.Y., River Club, Links Club, Saturn Club, Springdale Golf Club, Bedens Brook Club, Eldorado Country Club, Georgetown Club, Met. Club, Old Baldy Club, Tournament Players Club, Nassau Club, The Carnegie Club at Skibo Castle, Knights of Malta. Roman Catholic. Office: Merrill Lynch & Co Inc 800 Scudders Mill Rd Plainsboro NJ 08536-1606

SCHRIBMAN, SHELLEY IRIS, database engineer, consultant; b. Weehawken, N.J., July 29, 1944; d. George and Mildred (Kamen) Shulman; m. Marshall Melvin Schribman, Aug. 26, 1979. BFA cum laude, Art Inst. Chgo., 1966; MBA, Simmon Coll. Grad. Sch. Mgmt., 1982. Asst. dir. Advanced Inst. Devel. Am. Repertory Theatre, N.Y.C., 1970-71; ptnr. Sir Charles Cleaning Co., Boston, 1982-83; owner SIS Internat., Boston, 1984-87; database developer (freelance) Boston, 1995—; cons. Boston Computer Soc., 1995-96, Catchpole Corp., Wellesley, Mass., 1996-97, Ptnrs. In Home Care Inc., Missoula, Mont., 1996-97; designer, developer Shulman Bankruptcy Program, 1998-99. Pres. Orgn. for Rehab. Through Tng., Boston, 1986-88; mem. LWV, Boston (housing specialist 1989-91, pres. 1990-91, nat. credentials chairperson 1991-92). Mem. Belmont Dramatic Club, Alumni Theatre, Lexington Players. Jewish. Avocations: acting, composing music. Home and Office: 8 Whittier Pl Boston MA 02114-1402

SCHRICK, JERRY L., minister; b. Riverside, Calif., Dec. 29, 1959; s. Marvin and Patricia Mae (Taitt) S.; m. Debra Lynn Schrick, July 23, 1983; children: Rebecca, Andrea, Catherine, Jeremiah. BA, Christian Heritage Coll., El Cajon, Calif., 1984; postgrad., Dallas Theol. Sem., 1984-89; MDiv, Biola U., LaMirada, Calif., 1991. Ordained to ministry, Bapt. Ch., 1992. Min. Calvary Cmty. Ch., Beaumont, adrif., 1992—; officer, bd. trustees S.W. Bapt. Conf., West Covina, Calif., 1997-2000, chair ch. svcs. coord. com., 1994-95; reserve chaplain Riverside County Fire Dept., 1995-97. Co-author: (booklet) Guidelines for Designing HIV/AIDS Policy for the Local Church, 1995. Republican. Avocations: singing, reading. Office: Calvary Cmty Church 1252 Beaumont Ave Beaumont CA 92223-1506

SCHRIEFERS, HERIBERT JOHANNES, psychology educator; b. Schiefbahn, Rhineland, Germany, Mar. 13, 1956; s. Herbert Theodor and Marianne (Overberg) S. MA in Psychology, U. Bonn, 1981; PhD in Psychology, Nijmegen U., 1985. Rschr. Max-Planck Inst. for Psycholinguistics, Nijmegen, The Netherlands, 1981-90; asst. prof. Free U., Berlin, 1990-94; prof. cognitive psychology Nijmegen U., 1994—; chmn. bd. Nijmegen Inst. for Cognition and Info., Nijmegen, 1996—. Contbr. articles to profl. jours. Office: NICI Nijmegen Univ, PO Box 9104, 6500 HE Nijmegen The Netherlands

SCHRIEFFER, JOHN ROBERT, physics educator, science administrator; b. Oak Park, Ill., May 31, 1931; s. John Henry and Louise (Anderson) S.; m. Anne Grete Thomsen, Dec. 30, 1960; children: Anne Bolette, Paul Karsten, Anne Regina. BS, MIT, 1953; MS, U. Ill., 1954, PhD, 1957, ScD, 1974; ScD (hon.), Tech. U., Munich, 1968, U. Geneva, 1968, U. Pa., 1973, U. Cin., 1977, U. Tel Aviv, 1987, U. Ala., 1990. NSF postdoctoral fellow U. Birmingham, Eng., also; Niels Bohr Inst., Copenhagen, 1957-58; asst. prof. U. Chgo., 1958-59; asst. prof., then assoc. prof. U. Ill., 1959-62; prof. U. Pa., Phila., 1962-79; Mary Amanda Wood prof. physics U. Pa., 1964-79; Andrew D. White prof. at large Cornell U., 1969-75; prof. U. Calif., Santa Barbara, 1980-91, Chancellor's prof., 1984-91, dir. Inst. for Theoretical Physics, 1984-89; Univ. prof. Fla. State U., Tallahassee, 1992—, Univ. Eminent Scholar prof., 1995—, chief scientist Nat. High Magnetic Field Lab., 1992—; pres.'s com. Nat. Medal of Sci., 1996—. Author: Theory of Superconductivity, 1964. Mem. Pres.' Com. on Nat. Medal of Sci., 1996. Guggenheim fellow Copenhagen, 1967; Los Alamos Nat. Lab. fellow; Recipient Comstock prize Nat. Acad. Sci.; Nobel Prize for Physics, 1972; John Ericsson medal Am. Soc. Swedish Engrs., 1976; Alumni Achievement award U. Ill., 1979; recipient Nat. Medal of Sci., 1984; Exxon faculty fellow, 1979-89. Fellow Am. Phys. Soc. (v.p. 1994, pres.-elect 1995, pres. 1996, past pres. 1997, Oliver E. Buckley solid state physics prize 1986); mem. NAS (coun. 1990—), Am. Acad. Arts and Scis., Coun. Nat. Acad. Sci., Royal Danish Acad. Scis. and Letters, Acad. Sci. USSR, Nat. Medal Sci. com. Office: Fla State Univ NHMFL 1800 E Paul Dirac Dr Tallahassee FL 32310-3748

SCHRIEVER, FRED MARTIN, management consultant, financial investor; b. N.Y.C.; s. Samuel and Sara S.; m. Cheri G. Spatt; children: Melissa Ann, Elizabeth Ellen. BME, Poly. U. N.Y., 1956, MME, 1958. Registered profl. engr., N.Y., Wash.; cert. mgmt. cons. Chief engr. divsn. Sperry Corp., N.Y.C., 1956-64; ptnr. Booz, Allen and Hamilton, N.Y.C. and Washington, 1964-71; sr. v.p. Reliance Group Holdings, Inc., N.Y.C., 1971-96; chmn., pres. RCG Internat. Inc., N.Y.C., 1971-96; bd. dirs. Nat. Exec. Svc. Corps., Hagler, Bailly, Inc.; cons. in field. Fellow Inst. of Dirs., Inst. Mgmt. Consultants U.K.; mem. ASME, Inst. Mgmt. Cons., Chemists Club. Home: PO Box 32 Westport CT 06881-0032

SCHRIMP, ROGER MARTIN, lawyer; b. Stockton, Calif., May 26, 1941; s. Clarence and Mary Helen (Martin) S; m. Delsie Louise Canapa, July 7, 1963; children: Angela and Christine. AA with honors, Stockton C.C., 1961; AB with honors, U. Calif., Berkeley, 1963, JD, 1966; LLM, U. Pacific, 1982. Bar: Calif. 1966, U.S. Dist. Ct. (no., ctrl., and ea. dist.) Calif. 1967, U.S. Tax Ct. 1978, U.S. Supreme Ct. 1978, U.S. Claims Ct. 1981. Ptnr. Law Offices of Stockton & Schrimp, Modesto, Calif., 1966-86; private practice Law Offices of Roger M. Schrimp, Modesto, 1986-90; ptnr. Law Offices of Damrell, Nelson, Schrimp, Pallios & Ladine, Modesto, 1990—; bd. gov.s Calif. C.C., pres., chmn. econ. Devel. and vocat. edn. com., 1996—; founder, chmn. bd. Oak Valley Cmty. Bank, Oakdale, Calif. 1991—; chair Joint Adv. com. Vocational Edn., Calif. Bd. Edn.; mem. Calif. State U. Joint Standing com. Yosemite area council bd. Boy Scouts Am., 1967—, nat. council, 1986-93, council pres., 1986-87, exec. bd. mem., 1967—, western region bd. mem., 1990-98, area III v.p., 1990-95, area III pres. 1995—, western region exec. bd. 1995—; exec. com. Oak Valley Dist. Cmty. Hosp. Found., 1976-94, bd. trustees, 1970-94; chmn. Oakdale Airport Commn., 1974-88, commn. mem. 1970-88; bd. trustees Oakdale Elem. Sch. Dist., 1972-80; bd. dir. Am. Cancer Soc., Stanislaus/Tuolumne Br., 1967-80, pres., 1970-71; vice-chmn. culture commn. City of Modesto, 1989-93, mem., 1986-93; mem. Calif. Postsecondary Edn. Commn. (western region v.p. finance 1998—). Mem. ABA (com. agr., taxation section), State Bar Calif., Assn. Trial Lawyers Am., Calif. Trial Lawyers Assn., Stanislaus County Bar Assn. (pres. 1993-94), Am. Judicature Soc., Northern Calif. Assn. Def. Counsel, Def. Rsch. Inst., Lawyers-Pilot Assn., Oakdale Rotary Club (pres. 1980-81), Medesto Lions "500" Club (pres. 1973-74), Rancheros Visitadores, El Viage de Portola, Oakdale Shrine Club (pres. 1975), Oakdale Dinner Club (pres. 1970-71), Calif. Cattlemen's Assn. (bd. dir. 1994-97), San Joaquin/Stanislaus Cattlemen's Assn., Knights Ferry Lodge #112, Morning Star Lodge #68, McHenry Mansion Found., McHenry Mus. Found., Modesto Shrine Club, Internat. Order St. Hubertus, Univ. Calif. Alumni, Million Doallar Advocates Forum, Univ. Calif. Berkeley Boalt Hall Alumni Assn. (bd. dir. 1994—), Airplane Owners and Pilots Assn., Oakdale Sportsmen's Club. Republican. Office: Damrell Nelson Schrimp Pallios & Ladine 1610 I St Fl 5 Modesto CA 95354-1122

SCHROCK, FLETCHER, lawyer; b. Washington, N.C., Oct. 4, 1952; s. John J. and Linda Marslender Schrock; m. Lynn Gehringer, Mar. 5, 1977 (div. Jan. 1985); m. Bonnie Workman, Mar. 14, 1987; children: Ashley Nicole, Hannah Whitney, Elizabeth Ann, Wesley Robert McMurry. BA with high distinction, U. Ky., 1974, JD, 1976. Bar: Ky. 1977. Assoc. McMurry & Livingston Law Firm, Paducah, Ky., 1977-81; ptnr. McMurry & Livingston Law Firm, Paducah, 1982—; moot ct. bd. U. Ky. Coll. Law, Lexington, 1977. Chmn. adv. bd. Salvation Army, Paducah, Ky., 1987—; co-chmn. Walk Am. Campaign, March of Dimes, Paducah, 1994-95. Mem. ABA, Ky. Bar Assn., McCracken County Bar Assn. (v.p. 1979-80), Phi Beta Kappa. Avocations: reading, snow skiing, basketball, kick boxing. E-mail: fletch@ml-lawfirm.com. Home: 252 Alben Barkley Dr Paducah KY 42001-4466 Office: McMurry & Livingston 7th Fl 333 Broadway St Ste 7 Paducah KY 42001-0761

SCHRÖDER, HEINZ CHRISTOPH, biochemistry educator, researcher; b. Ingelheim, Germany, Sept. 13, 1951; s. Wilhelm and Anneliese (Schneider) S. Diploma, U. Mainz, Germany, 1977, PhD, 1980, Med. Exam., 1981, MD, 1983. Asst. U. Mainz, 1981-82, Liebig stipendium, 1982-84, lectr. biochemistry, 1984-85, prof., 1985—; Liebig fellow Max-Planck-Inst. for Biophys. Chemistry, Gottingen, Germany, 1982-83. Contbr. over 200 articles to sci. jours. Recipient award Boehringer Ingelheim, 1980, Louise-Eylmann-Stiftung prize, 1985, Max-Bürger prize German Soc. for Gerontology, 1988. Mem. Acad. Scis. and Lit. (advisor 1990—), German Soc. for Aging Rsch. (sec. gen. 1990—). Office: U Mainz Inst Physiol Chem, Duesbergweg 6, 55099 Mainz Germany

SCHRODER, HOBE JOHANNES, physiologist, educator; b. Rostock, Germany, Oct. 5, 1942; s. Jurgen and Gertrud (Putz) S.; m. Jutta Scherz, Aug. 10, 1968; children: Tilmann, Momme, Mathis. MD, U. Hamburg, 1968, PhD, 1976. Prof. U. Hamburg, Germany, 1984—. Contbr. articles to profl. jours. Mem. Soc. for Gynecologic Investigation, Deutsche Physiologische Gesellschaft. Office: Univ Hamburg U Frauenklinik, Martinistr 52, 20246 Hamburg Germany

SCHRÖDER, J. MICHAEL, neuropathologist, medical educator; b. Hamburg, Germany, Nov. 12, 1937; s. Hans R.J. and Katharina (Lenssen) S.; m. Monika Katharina Blut, Oct. 29, 1971. MD, U. Mönchen, 1962. Medizinalassistent Berlin and Köln, Germany, 1962-64; sci. asst. Max Planck Inst., Köln-Merheim, Germany, 1964, Frankfurt, Germany, 1966-74; rsch. fellow Harvard U. Med. Sch., Boston, 1965-66; prof. divsn. neuropathology Inst. Pathology, U. Mainz, 1974-81; prof. neuropathology U. Hosp. of Rheinisch-Westfälische Technische Hochschule, Aachen, Germany, 1981—; mem. exec. com. rsch. group on neuromuscular diseases World Fedn. Neurology, 1981; project sec. Internat. Soc. Neuropathology, 1994—. Author: Pathologie der Muskulatur, 1982, Pathologie heriphere Nerven, 1999; contbr. over 236 articles to profl. jours. Recipient Duchenne-Erb-Preis, 1991; Deutsche Forschungsgemeinschaft grnatee, 1976-85, 98—. Mem. Deutsche Gesellschaft für Neuropathologie und Neuroanatomie, Deutsche Gesellschaft für Pathologie, Deutsche Gesellschaft für Elektronenmikoskopie, Deutsche Gesellschaft für Muskelkranke, Peripheral Nerve Soc., World Muscle Soc., Brit. Soc. Neuropathology, Royal Soc. Medicine, Rotary. Home: Eberburgweg 55, 52076 Aachen Germany

SCHRÖDER, TOM MARTIN, surgeon; b. Helsinki, Finland, Mar. 3, 1950; s. Nils Henning and Eva Regina (Lagus) S.; m. Rita Maria Qvickström, Mar. 30, 1972; children: Anna, Ola, Vilhelm. Med. cand., Helsinki U., 1973, MD, 1976, PhD, 1981. Chief Laseri Hosp., Helsinki, 1990—, Silmälaseri, Helsinki, 1996—; lectr. Helsinki U., 1984; prof. Kuopio (Finland) U., 1990; vis. prof. U. Cin., 1984-85; sr. rschr. Finnish Acad., Helsinki, 1989-91, head surgery divsn. Deaconess Hosp., Helsinki, 1991-93. Contbr. articles to profl. jours.

SCHRÖDER, WOLFGANG PETER, biochemist researcher; b. Nybro, Sweden, Sept. 26, 1958; s. Kurt E. and Marianne. BS, U. Lund, Sweden, 1983, PhD in Biochemistry, 1989, assoc. prof. in biochem., 1995. Postdoctoral fellow CNRS, Gif sur Yvette, France, 1990-91, Max-Volmer-Inst., Berlin, Germany, 1991-92; sr. lecturer biochemistry Stockholm, 1995-96; vis. fellow ANU, Canberra, Australia, 1997; sr. lecturer Södertörns Högskola, Sweden, 1998—. Avocations: golf, fencing, jogging. Home: Torphagsvagen 16, S-10405 Stockholm Sweden Office: Södertörus Högskol, Bipontus Box 4101, SE-14104 Huddinge S-141 86, Sweden

SCHRÖDL, MICHAEL, zoologist; b. Munich, May 7, 1967; s. Richard and Renate (Brunnbauer) S.; m. Rebecca Oberhauser; 1 child, Theresa. MS, Ludwig-Maximilians U., 1993, PhD, 1999. Postgrad. U. Concepcion, Chile, 1991-92; postdoctoral rshr. Zool. State Collection, Munich, 1998—, asst. curator, 1997-99, curator mollusc, 1999—; scientific expert Diverse Jours., 1997—; hon. ranger, cons., Munich, 1990—. Contbr. articles to profl. jours. Cons. Authorities of Munich, 1992—. Postgrad. grant Ministry of Edn., 1991-92; rsch. grant German Acad. Exch. Svc., 1996-98. Mem. Soc. German Biologists, Landesbund für Vogelschutz, hon. mem., Chilean Nalacological Soc. Roman Catholic. Avocations: scuba-diving, paragliding, mountaineering, travelling. Office: Zoologische StaatssammlungMünchen, Münchhausenstr 21, 81247 Munich Germany

SCHRÖECKE, HELMÜT HEINRICH, mineralogist, geologist, physical chemist, educator; b. Zwickau, Germany, June 18, 1922; s. Ernst Kürt and Doris Schröcke; married Dec. 22, 1952; children: Wolfram, Rotaud, Roswitha, Volker. BS in Geology, Bergakademie, Freiberg, Germany, 1950, PhD, 1951; DSc, U. Heidelberg, Germany, 1958. Rsch. asst. U. Göttingen, Germany, 1951-54; sci. asst. U. Heidelberg, Germany, 1954-64; konservator U. Munich, 1964-66, sci. lectr., 1966-67, ausserplanmäsiger prof., 1967-70, chmn. dept. crystallography, 1964—. Author: Grundlagen der magmatogenen Lagerstättenbildung, 1970, Die Entstehung der endogenen Erzlagerstätten, 1986, Siebenbürgen, Menschen, Städte, Kirchenburgen, 1987, Aufl. II, 1999, Germanen—Slawen, Vor—und Frühgeschichte des ostgermanischen Raumes, 1996, Aufl. II, 1999, Kriegsursachen-Kriegsschuld, 1997, Aufl. II, 2000; co-author: Mineralogie, Naturwissenschaftliche Tafelwerke, 1969, Mineraux, Naturwissenschaftliche Tafelwerke, 1972, Mineralogie, ein Lehrbuch auf systematischer Grundlage, Aufl. I, 1981, Aufl. II, 1992. Home: Am Hohen Weg 22, 82288 Kottgeisering Germany Office: U Munich Inst Crystallography, Theresienstrase 41 d, Munich Germany

SCHROEDER, ALFRED CHRISTIAN, electronics research engineer; b. West New Brighton, N.Y., Feb. 28, 1915; s. Alfred and Chryssa (Weishaar) S.; m. Janet Ellis, Sept. 26, 1936 (dec.); 1 dau., Carol Ann Schroeder Castle.; m. Dorothy Holloway, Nov. 21, 1981. BS, MIT, 1937, MS, 1937. Mem. tech. staff Sarnoff, Inc., Princeton, N.J., 1937-2000; ret. Contbr. articles to profl. jours. Recipient RCA Lab. awards, 1947, 50, 51, 52, 57, 70. Fellow IEEE (Vladimir Zworykin award 1971); mem. AAAS, Optical Soc. Am., Soc. Motion Picture and TV Engrs. (David Sarnoff Gold medal 1965), Soc. Info. Display (Karl Ferdinand Braun prize 1989), Sigma Xi. Quaker. Achievements include 75 patents for color TV products including shadow mask tube. Home: Pennswood Village Apt I-114 Newtown PA 18940-2401

SCHROEDER, BARBET G., director; b. Teheran, Iran, Apr. 26, 1941. Film critic Cahiers du Cinema, L'air de Paris, 1958-63; owner, prin. Films du Losange, 1963—; dir. CAA, 1991—. Film dir.: More, 1969, The Valley, 1972, General Idi Amin Dada, 1974, Maitress, 1975, Koko, Talking Gorilla, 1978, Cheaters, 1983, The Charles Bukowski Tapes, 1985, Barfly, 1987, Reversal of Fortune, 1990 (Acad. award nominee best dir. 1990, Golden Globe award nominee best dir. film 1990), Single White Female, 1992, Kiss of Death, 1995, Before and After, 1996, Desperate Measures, 1997; film prodr.: La Boulangerere de Monceau, 1962, La Carriere de Suzanne, 1963, Mediterrannee, 1964, Six in Paris, 1968, My Night at Maud's, 1968, The Collector, 1966, Claire's Knee, 1971, Chloe in the Afternoon, 1972, (with Tchalgadjieff), Out One, 1972, (with Pierre Cottrell) The Mother and the Whore, 1973, Celine and Julie Go Boating, 1974, Flocons d'or, 1975, Perceval, 1978, Improper Conduct, 1983, La Carriere de Suzanne, Mediterranee, Tu Imagines Robinson, Out One, The Marquise of O, 1975, Le Passe-Montagne, 1977, The Rites of Death, Le Navire Night, Le Pont du Nord; asst. to dir. Jean-Luc Goddard for The Soldiers, 1968; coprodr.: Chinese Roulette, 1977, The American Friend, 1977; appeared in films The Soldiers, 1960, Six in Paris, 1965, The Mother and the Whore, 1973, Celine and Julie Go Boating, 1974, L'amour Par Terre, Roberte, 1978, The Golden Boat, 1990, Beverly Hills Cop III, 1994, La Reine Margot, 1994, Mars Attack!, 1997; screenwriter: (with Paul Gegauff) More, 1969, (with Gegauff) The Valley, 1972, Maitress, 1975, Cheaters, 1983. Office: CAA 9830 Wilshire Blvd Beverly Hills CA 90212-1804

SCHROEDER, BENT, information technology executive; b. Soenderborg, Denmark, Sept. 30, 1959; s. Karl Andreas and Signe (Nielsen) S.; m. Ingeborg Elisabeth Jacobsen, May 4, 1984; children: Ann, Emma, Cilla, Laura. BSME, Soenderborg Teknikum, Denmark, 1982; mgmt. diploma, Henley Mgmt. Coll., U.K., 1993. Cert. in prodn. and inventory mgmt. Am. Prodn. and Inventory Control Soc., 1995. Sys. specialist Danfoss A/S, Nordborg, Denmark, 1984-89, info. tech. mgr., 1989-92, mgr. bus. logistics, 1994-95, project dir., 1995—; cons. Hewlett-Packard, Palo Alto, Calif., 1992-94; external examiner Soenderborg Teknikum, 1987-92, 94—; cons., spkr., lectr. in field. Founder, chmn. Stolbrolykke Windmills, Als, Denmark, 1990—. Avocations: computers, reading. Office: Danfoss A/S, A 324, 6430 Nordborg Denmark

SCHROEDER, ERIC PETER, lawyer; b. Floral Park, N.Y., July 20, 1970; s. Fredric G. and Linda M. Schroeder. BA, Duke U., 1992; JD, Vanderbilt U., 1996. Bar: Ga. 1997, U.S. Dist. Ct. (no. dist.) Ga. 1997, U.S. Ct. Appeals (11th cir.) 1998. Law clk. Hon. William C. O'Kelley, U.S. Dist. Ct. (no. dist.) Ga., Atlanta, 1996-97; atty. Powell, Goldstein, Frazer & Murphy, Atlanta, 1997—; mem. planning com. Ga. Bar Media Jud. Conf., 1999, 2000. Articles editor Vanderbilt Law Rev., 1995-96; mem. editl. bd. INTA The Trademark Reporter, 2000—. Active Boys and Girls Club of Am., Atlanta, 1998-00; vol. Ga. Vol. Lawyers for the Arts, Atlanta, 1998; lawyer Anti-Defamation League, Atlanta, 1998. Mem. Atlanta Bar Assn., U.S. Copyright Soc., Internat. Trademark Assn., Order of Coif, Lamar Inn of Ct. Home: 935 Greenwood Ave NE Apt C Atlanta GA 30306-4701 Office: Powell Goldstein Frazer & Murphy 191 Peachtree St Atlanta GA 30303

SCHROEDER, ERICH CHRISTIAN, educator; b. Elberfeld, Germany, July 3, 1925; s. Erich and Ida (Schniewind) S.; m. Karin Mueller, Oct. 4, 1935; children: Peter, Martin, Christian. DPhil, U. Cologne, 1954. Asst. U. Cologne, 1956-60; prof. Ednl. U. Bielefeld (Germany), 1961-65, Ednl. U. Westfalen-Lippe (Germany), 1965-80, U. Bielefeld, 1980—; pres. Ednl. U. Westfalen-Lippe, 1967-69, 78-80; v.p. U. Bielefeld, 1980-83. Author: Die Moral bei Nietzsche, 1954, Abschied von der Metaphysik?, 1969; editor: Meditationes by Descartes, 1956; contbr. articles to profl. jours. Chmn. U. Extension Bielefeld, 1972-74. Fellow Allgemeine Gesellschaft Philosophie Deutschland, Deutsche Gesellschaft Phaenomenologische Forschung. Evangelical. Avocation: music. Home: Heinrichstrasse 8, D-33818 Leopoldshoehe Germany Office: U Bielefeld, Universitaetsstrasse 25, D-33501 Bielefeld Germany

SCHROEDER, FRIEDRICH-CHRISTIAN, criminal law and procedure educator; b. Güstrow, Germany, July 14, 1936; s. Walter and Maria (Hagemeister) S.; m. Ute Behrendt; children: Henning, Antje, Hans-Kaspar, Marieke. DrJur, U. City of Munich, Germany, 1963; DrHabil, U. Munich, 1968; Dr. honoris causa, U. Breslau, Germany. Asst. U. Munich, 1961-68; prof. law U. Regensburg, Germany, 1968—; dir. Institut für Ostrecht München, 1973—. Author: Der Tater hinter dem Tater, 1964, Der Schutz von Staat und Verfassung im Strafrecht, 1970, 74 Jahre Sowjetrecht, 1992, Strafprozessrecht, 2d edit., 1997; editor Jahrbuch für Ostrecht, 1971—. Mem. Assn. for Penal Law, Deutsche Gesellschaft für Osteuropakunde (head dept. law 1973—). Home: Steinmetzstr 14, 93049 Regensburg Germany Office: U Regensburg, Universitatsstr 31, 93053 Regensburg Germany

SCHROEDER, GERHARD FRITZ KURT, chancellor of Germany; b. Mossenberg, Germany, Apr. 7, 1944; m. Doris Koepf(div.), m. Doris Koepf; two children. Degree in law, Goettingen U., 1971. Lawyer Hanover, Germany, 1976-80; chmn. Young Social Dems., 1978-80; legislator German Bundestag, 1980-86; leader of the opposition State Parliament of Lower Saxony, 1986—; prime min. Lower Saxony, Germany, 1990-98; chancellor Govt. of Germany, 1998—. Contbr. articles to numerous profl. publs. Office: Office of the Fed Chancellor, Office Fed Chancellor, Schlossplatz 1, D-10178 Berlin Germany*

SCHROEDER, HUBERT ERNST, dentist, researcher; b. Königsberg, Germany, Feb. 17, 1931; came to Switzerland, 1958; s. Ernst Richard and Ruth Ottilie (Wollschläger) S.; m. Jutta Gretlies Schilling, Aug. 8, 1961; children: Alice Gabriele, Ulla Friederike. DDS, Goethe U., Frankfurt, 1956, Dr med. dent., 1957; Dr. Odontol. h.c. (hon.), U. Aarhus, Denmark, 1983, U. Lund, Sweden, 1992. Rsch. fellow, sr. rsch. assoc. Dental Inst., U. Zurich, Switzerland, 1961-72; rsch. fellow Inst. Dental Rsch., NYU, 1965; rsch. assoc. Royal Dental Coll., U. Aarhus, 1965-66, Harvard U. Med. Sch., Boston, 1971; prof., chmn. dept. oral structural biology U. Zurich, Switzerland, 1972-94; rsch. affiliate Forsyth Dental Ctr., Boston, 1976—; vis. researcher Dept. Pathology, U. Wash., Seattle, 1980; prof., dir. Inst. for Oral Structural Biology U. Zurich, 1994-97; mem. med. faculty promotion com., Zurich, 1990-96. Author: Formation and Inhibition of Dental Calculus, 1969 (Dr. R. Jaccard 1st prize Inter. Arbeitsgemeinschaft Paradontologie 1969), (with Dr. M. Listgarten) Fine Structure of the Developing Epithelial Attachment of Human Teeth, 1971, (with Dr. R. Page) Periodontitis in Man and Other Animals, 1982; Differentiation of Human Oral Stratified Epithelia, 1981, (handbook) The Periodontium, 1986, (textbooks) Oral Structural Biology, 1976, 5th edit., 2000, Pathobiology of Oral Structures: Teeth, Pulp, Periodontium, 1983, 3d edit., 1997; contbr. 200 articles to profl. jours. Recipient rsch. grants Swiss Nat. Found. Sci., 1968-72. Fellow Royal Micros. Soc.; mem. Internat. Assn. Dental Rsch. (pres. periodontal rsch. group 1964-65, Rsch. award 1972), Schweiz Zahnärztegesellschaft (hon., editor 1987-95), Schweiz Gesellschaft Parodontologie (hon. 1988—), German Acad. Natural Scientists: Leopoldina. Avocations: classical lit., music, history lit., gardening. Fax: 0041 1 8104415.

SCHROEDER, JOYCE KATHERINE, state agency administrator, research analyst; b. Moline, Ill., Apr. 1, 1951; d. Reinhold J. and Miriam-May Schroeder. BS in Math., U. Ill., 1973, MA in Ops. Rsch., 1978. Underwriter, programmer Springfield, Ill., 1973-76; ops. rsch. analyst Ill. Dept. Transp., Springfield, 1976-78, data analyst, 1978-80, team leader, fatal accident reporting sys., 1980-83, mgr. safety project evaluation, 1983-92, mgr. accident studies and investigation, 1992—; sys. engring. del. to China China Assn. for Sci. and Tech., 1986; mem. staff Driving While Intoxicated Adv. Coun. and Task Force, State of Ill., 1983-86, 89-92, Gov. Task Force on Occupant Protection, 1988-90, Ill. Traffic Safety Info. Sys. Coun., 1993-95. Vol. Animal Protective League, Springfield; leaderbd. co-chairperson LPGA Rail Classic, Springfield, 1983-87; amb. of goodwill Lions of Ill. Found., 1993, trustee, 1995-99. Lions Clubs Internat. Melvin Jones fellow, 1993, Lions of Ill. Found. fellow, 1995. Mem. Lions of Ill. Found. (amb. of goodwill 1993, trustee 1995-99, treas. found. bd. 1996-97, v.p. found. bd. 1997-98, pres. found. bd. 1998-99, chmn. long range planning com. 1997—), Springfield Lincoln Land Lions Club (charter pres. 1988-90, treas. 1993-95, news editor 1995—), Lions Club (dist. gov. Ill. 1992-93, state membership coord. 1994-96, Melvin Jones fellow 1993), Past. Dist. Gov. Assn. (sec.-treas. 1993—), Lions of Ill. (endowment fund bd. 1998-99), Phi Kappa Phi, Kappa Delta Pi. Avocations: dogs, travel, music, sports, humanitarian svc. Office: Ill Dept Transp 3215 Executive Park Dr Springfield IL 62703-4514

SCHROEDER, KIMBERLY HUDSON, financial auditor; b. Oklahoma City, Dec. 24, 1973; d. Richard Kenneth and Conchieta Sue Hudson; m. Kevin Michael Schroeder, Dec. 12, 1998. BBA, U. Okla., 1996. CPA, Okla. Fin. auditor Grant Thornton, Oklahoma City, 1996-98, PricewaterhouseCoopers, Houston, 1998—. Mem. AICPA, Okla. Inst. CPAs. Home: 4925 W 43d St Houston TX 77092

SCHROEDER, KLAUS H., Romance philology educator; b. Schwerin, Germany, Oct. 13, 1932; s. Walter and Ilse (Davids) S.; m. Renate Döhlemeyer. Degree of Doctor, Free U. Berlin, 1961, Univ. Prof., 1971. Prof. Romance philology Free U. Berlin, 1971—, head dept., 1972-73. Author: Die Medialen Verben im Neufranzosischen, 1961, Einfuhrung in das Studium des Rumanischen, 1967, Davids' Enkel, 1991, Geschichte der franzosischen Sprache, 1996, others. Mem. German Assn. Romance Philology. Home: Johann-Sigismund-Strasse 16, 10711 Berlin Germany

SCHROEDER, MANFRED ROBERT, physics educator; b. Ahlen, Westphalia, Germany, July 12, 1926; s. Karl and Hertha (Kraemer) S.; m. Anny Menschik, Feb. 25, 1956; children: Marion, Julian, Alexander. Vordiploma math., U. Göttingen, Germany, 1949, diplom physiker, 1951, Dr.rer.nat.physics, 1954. Mem. rsch. staff Bell Labs., Murray Hill, N.J., 1954-58; head acoustics rsch. Bell Labs., Murray Hill, 1958-63, dir. acoustics and speech rsch., 1963-69; dir. Drittes Phys. Inst., U. Göttingen, 1969-91, prof. physics, 1970—. Author: Number Theory in Science and Communication, 1984 (Lord Rayleigh medal 1987), Fractals, Chaos, Power Laws, 1990 (Helmholtz medal 1995), Computer Speech: Recognition, Compression, Synthesis, 1999; editor: Speech and Speaker Recognition, 1985; patentee in field. Recipient Gold medal Audio Engring. Soc., N.Y.C., 1972, Gold medal Acoustical Soc. Am., 1991, Niedersachsenpreis, Lower Saxony, Hannover, Germany, 1992, First Prize Internat. Computer Graphics competition Assn. for Computing Machinery, 1969. Fellow Am. Acad. Arts and Scis., N.Y. Acad. Scis.; mem. Nat. Acad. Engring., Göttingen Akademie der Wissenschaften. Avocations: photography, computer graphics, cycling, skiing. Office: Drittes Physikalisches Inst, Bürgerstr 42-44, D-37073 Göttingen Germany

SCHROEDER, ROLF ROBERT, chemical engineer; b. Cleve., July 19, 1934; s. August C.G. and Adele A. (Siemer) S.; m. Gail A. Erickson, Feb. 5, 1956 (div. Jan. 1986); children: Mark, Susan, Eric; m. Joyce M. Wilkins, Oct. 5, 1989. BS in Chem. Engring., Ill. Inst. Technology, Chgo., 1956, MS, 1961, PhD, 1963; MBA, La. State U., 1977. Sr. engr. Esso Rsch. & Devel. Labs., Baton Rouge, La., 1963-69; sr. analyst Esso Internat., N.Y.C., 1969-71; dir. rsch. Howe-Baker Engrs., Tyler, Tex., 1971-75; engring. assoc. Exxon Rsch. & Devel. Labs., Baton Rouge, 1975-86; prin. engr. Kerr McGee Oil Co., Oklahoma City, 1987-90; advanced sr. refining engr., tech. mgr. Marathon Ashland Petroleum Co., Garyville, La., 1990—. Home: 3127 E Lakeshore Dr Baton Rouge LA 70808-2852

SCHROEDER, WILFRIED, geophysicist. chmn. history commn. Internat. Assn. Geomagnetism/Aeronomy, 1987-91, chmn. European sect. of the geophys. history commn. Author: Historical Events and People in Geosciences, 1983, Aurora Borealis, 1984, Göttingen Academy of Science and Development of Physics, 1985, History of Göttingen Academy of Sciences, 1985, Advances in Geosciences, 1987, Noctilucent Clouds, 1989, Solar-Terrestrial Physics and Global Change, 1991, History Geomagnetism and Aeronomy, 1991, Ertels Potential Vorticity and Geophysical Hydrodynamics, 1991, Solar-Terrestrial Physics, 1993, Earth Sciences, 1993, Noctilucent Clouds, 1997, Aurora Borealis, 1999, Long and Short Term Variability in Sun's History, 1999; editor IAGA History Newsletters, Acta Historica Geophysicae. Fellow Royal Meteorol. Soc.; mem. Internat. Commn. on the History of Geol. Sci., German Geophys. Soc. (sec. geophys. history commn., editor comms. geophys. history commn.), Am. Geophys. Union, Tensor Soc.

SCHROER, SILVIA, religious studies educator; b. Munster, Germany, Dec. 29, 1958; arrived in Switzerland, 1980; Diploma in theology, U. Fribourg, 1983, D in Theology, 1986, Habilitation, 1989. Asst. Bibl. Inst. Fribourg, 1983-86; chief sec. Swiss Bible Assn., 1987-92; prof. theology U. Berne, 1997—. Author: Die Körpersymbolik der Bibel, 1998, Feminist Interpretation, 1998, Die Weisheit hat ihr Haus gebaut, 1996, I Die Göttin auf den Stempelsiegeln aus Palästina Israel, 1989. Mem. Swiss Cath. Exegetes (pres.

1994—). Office: U Berne Evang Theol Fac, Langgassstr 51, 3000 Bern 9, Switzerland

SCHROETTER, HEINZ WILHELM, physics educator; b. Gablonz, Czechoslovakia, Aug. 8, 1931; arrived in Germany, 1946; s. Johann and Irma Milada (Watzek) S.; m. Erika Rita Frase, Aug. 12, 1960; children: Barbara, Bernd, Ursula. Dr.rer.nat., Ludwig-Maximilians U., Munich, 1960, privatdozent, 1972. Post-doctoral fellow Nat. Rsch. Coun. Can., Ottawa, Ont., 1960-61; asst. Max-Planck Inst. für Kohlenforschung, Mülheim, Germany, 1961-64, Ludwig-Maximilians U., Munich, 1964-74; assoc. prof. LM Univ., Munich, 1974-78, prof., 1978—. Contbr. chpt. in book and articles on linear and nonlinear Raman spectroscopy to profl. jours. Mem. Deutsche Physikalische Gesellschaft. Office: Sektion Physik der LMU, Schelling Str 4, D-80799 Munich Germany

SCHRÖGER, ERICH, psychologist; b. Munich, Bavaria, Germany, Nov. 11, 1958; s. Johann and Elfriede (Brandner) S.; m. Heike Adolphs, Aug. 10, 1993; children: Anna, Luise. PhD, Ludwig-Maximilians U., Munich, 1991. Prof. psychology U. Leipzig, Munich, 1987—. Author: Konstanz und Laurtheit, 1991; contbr. articles to profl. jours. Mem. Soc. Psychophysiological Rsch. Office: U Leipzig, Seeburg St 14-20, D-04103 Leipzig Germany

SCHRÖTER, ULRICH HANS, philologist, educator, researcher; b. Waltershausen, Germany, Apr. 14, 1933; m. Dorothea Ruth Goldfriedrich, May 16, 1959. Grad., U. Halle (Germany), 1958; PhD, Acad. Scis., Berlin, 1974; Facultas Docendi, U. Berlin, 1981. Secondary sch. tchr. Königs Wusterhausen, Germany, 1958-60; from asst. to sci. collaborator Acad. Scis., Berlin, 1960-93; sci. collaborator U. Potsdam, Germany, 1994-96; lectr. Humboldt U., Berlin, 1974-87. Contbr. articles to Jacob and Wilhelm Grimm Deutsches Wörterbuch-Neubearbeitung, 1960-88; also essays and articles to other literary publs. Recipient diploma Henning-Kaufmann-Siftung. Mem. Brüder Grimm Gesellschaft Kassel. Home: Flerderstrasse 17, 15732 Eichwalde Brandenbg Germany

SCHROTH, PETER W(ILLIAM), lawyer, management and law educator; b. Camden, N.J., July 24, 1946; s. Walter and Patricia Anne (Page) S.; children: Laura Salome Erickson-Schroth, Julia James. AB, Shimer Coll., 1966; JD, U. Chgo., 1969; M in Comparative Law, U.Chgo., 1971; SJD, U. Mich., 1979; postgrad., U. Freiburg, Fed. Republic Germany, Faculté Internationale pour l'Enseignement de Droit Comparé; MBA, Rensselaer Poly. Inst., 1988; DHL, Shimer Coll., 2000. Bar: Ill. 1969, N.Y. 1979, Conn. 1985, Mass. 1990; solicitor Supreme Ct. England and Wales 1995. Asst. prof. So. Meth. U., 1973-77; fellow in law and humanities Harvard U., 1976-77, vis. scholar, 1980-81; assoc. prof. N.Y. Law Sch., 1977-81; prof. law Hamline U., St. Paul, 1981-83; dep. gen. counsel Equator Bank Ltd., 1984-87; v.p., dep. gen. counsel Equator Holdings Ltd., 1987-94, v.p., gen. counsel, 1994-2000; adj. prof. law U. Conn., 1985-86, Western New Eng. Coll., 1988—, adj. prof. of mgmt. Rensselaer Poly. Inst., 1988-98, prof., 1999—, dir. Internat. Ctr. for Global Bus. Studies, 2000—. Author: Foreign Investment in the United States, 2d edit., 1977; (with Stiefel) Products Liability: European Proposals and American Experience, 1981, Doing Business in Sub-Saharan Africa, 1991; bd. editors Am. Jour. Comparative Law, 1981-84, 91—; mem. editl. bd. Conn. Bar Jour., 1988—, sr. editor, 1993-2000, editor-in-chief, 2000—; mem. editl. bd. N.Y. Internat. Law Rev.; mem. editl. rev. bd. Jour. Bus. in Developing Nations, 1996-2000, editor, 2000—; contbr. articles to profl. jours. Mem. ABA (editor in chief ABA Environ. Law Symposium 1980-82), Am. Soc. Comparative Law (bd. dirs. 1978-84, 91—), Am. Fgn. Law Assn., Internat. Bar Assn., Internat. Law Assn. (com. multinat. banking), Acad. Internat. Bus., Conn. Civil Liberties Union (bd. dirs. 1985-92), Environ. Law Inst. (assoc.), Columbia U. Peace Seminar (assoc.), Hartford Club (bd. govs. 1995-98), Am. Corp. Counsel Assn. (pres. Conn. chpt.1997-2000), Conn. Bar Assn. (chair sect. of internat. law 1997-2000). Office: Rensselaer Poly Inst Lally Sch Mgmt and Tech 275 Windsor St Hartford CT 06120-2910

SCHROTTA, WERNER, newspaper publisher; b. Asch, Austria, May 13, 1935; s. Franz and Emma (Swoboda) S.; m. Hanni Klima, July 21, 1960; children: Karin, Walter, Margit, Barbara, Christian. Diplomkaufmann, U. Commerce, Vienna, Austria, 1957; Dr., U. Commerce, 1960. Mng. dir. LKB-Data Processing, Vienna, 1960-67, Wochenpresse news mag., Vienna, 1964-78; pub. OOE Nachrichten, Linz, Austria, 1978-98; lectr. U. Vienna, 1969-79, U. Salzburg, Austria, 1977-79. Bd. dirs. IFRA, Darmstadt, Fed. Republic Germany, 1980-91. Fulbright scholar U.S. Fulbright Commn., 1957; recipient Goldenes Ehrenzeichen Republik OÖsterreich, 1982, Silbernes Ehrenzeichen des Landes Oo 1995, Kommeizielrat, 1997. Mem. Austrian Pubs. Assn. (bd. dirs. 1967-97, pres. 1991-97), Austrian Press Agy. (bd. dirs. 1978-98), European Newspaper Pubs. Assn. (bd. dirs. 1995—, pres. 1998—), Rotary. Lutheran. Avocations: skiing, sailing, reading, music. Home and Office: Prandtauerstrasse 8 10, A 4040 Linz Austria

SCHUALLER, ULRICH CHRISTOPH, physician, researcher; b. Krouach, Bavaria, Germany, May 24, 1968; s. Gerhard Johannes and Halgard Alunt Janausuheck S. MD, Med. Sch., Munich, 1996. Intern Eye Hosp., Munich, 1997-98, resident, 1998—. Contbr. articles to profl. publs. Mem. VCG, Arvo. Lutheran. Avocations: trumpet, golf, climbing. Office: Univ Eye Hosp, Mathildewstr 8, 80336 Munich Germany

SCHUBERT, AXEL, computer scientist; b. Munich, Germany, Oct. 10, 1949; s. Gerhard and Martha (Behne) S. BA, U. Cambridge, Eng., 1974, MA, 1978. Rsch. asst. Med. High Sch. Hannover, Germany, 1975-76; programmer, sr. cons. Softlab GmbH, Munich, 1976-85; project mgr., quality del. IM (CTS), Compaq (formerly Digital Equipment), Munich, 1985—. Co-author: Human Factors. . ., 1985. Mem. Assn. for Computing Machinery, Gesellschaft fuer Informatik. Christian. Avocations: music, walking. Address: Belgradstr 9, D-80796 Munich Germany

SCHUBERT, GUENTHER ERICH, pathologist; b. Mosul, Iraq, Aug. 17, 1930; s. Erich Waldemar and Martha Camilla (Zschitzschmann) S.; children: Frank, Marion, Dirk. MD, University, Heidelberg, Germany, 1957; pvt. docent in pathology, University, Tuebingen, Germany, 1966. Asst. med. dir. University Tuebingen, Fed. Republic of Germany, 1966-76; prof. pathology, 1972; head Inst. Pathology, Wuppertal, Fed. Republic of Germany, 1976-96; chair of pathology U. Witten-Herdecke, Fed. Republic of Germany, 1985-96. Co-author: Coloratlas of Cytodiagnosis of the Prostate, 1975, Pathologie 1984, 97, Endoscopy of the Urinary Bladder, 1989, Pathologie, 1984, 2d edit., 1997; author: Textbook of Pathology, 1981, 87. Mem. Wissenschaftlicher Beirat, Bundesarztekammer, Bonn, Germany, 1976-85; pres. Medizinisch Naturwissenschaftliche Gesellschaft, Wuppertal, 1984-85, Onkologischer Schwerpunkt, Wuppertal, 1985-93, OSP Bergisch-Land, 1992-95, Bergische Arbeitsgemeinschaft fur Gastroenterologie, Wuppertal, 1987-88, 90-91, 94-95. Mem. Deutsche Gesellschaft fur Pathologie, Deutsche Gesellschaft fur Nephrologie, Deutsche Gesellschaft fur Urologie, Internat. Acad. of Pathology, N.Y. Acad. Scis., Lions. Avocations: music, diving, photography. Office: Inst of Pathology, Am Anschlag 71, 42113 Wuppertal 2, Germany

SCHUBERT, INGO ARMIN, geneticist, researcher; b. Crostau, Saxony, Germany, Mar. 23, 1947; s. Joachim Paul and Rosl Berta (Pohl) S.; m. Rita Heidi Plewa, Feb. 9, 1968; children: Edger, Stephan, Edda. Diploma, Ernst-Moritz-Arndt U., Greifswald, Germany, 1970; PhD, Martin-Luther-U., Halle, Germany, 1975; Dr.habil., Acad. Scis., Gatersleben, Germany, 1982. Sci. co-worker Zentralinstitue für Genetik und Kulturpflanzenforschung, Gatersleben, 1970-90; head cytogenetics divsn. Inst. für Genetik und Kulturpflanzenforschung, Gatersleben, 1990-91, head cytogenetics dept., 1992—. Mem. editl. adv. bd. Chromosome Rsch., 1995—. Recipient Correns medal Biologische Gesellschaft der DDR, 1982. Avocations: fencing, gymnastics, history, traveling. Office: Inst Pflanzengenetik, Corrensstr 3, 06466 Gatersleben Germany

SCHUBERT, KURT HEINRICH, engineering educator; b. Pirna-Jessen, Saxony, Germany, Jan. 23, 1926; s. Richard Kurt and Selma Martha (Schulze) S.; m. Johanna Annekatrin Krüger, Apr. 4, 1953; children: Andreas, Thomas. D. in Engring., Bergakademie Freiberg, German Dem. Rep., 1951, Dr.Ing., 1956, Dr.sc.techn., 1971; D. (hon.), U. Heavy Industry, Miskolc, Hungary, 1987; D.(hon.), TU, Leuna-Merseburg, 1988. Asst. prof. Bergakademie Freiberg, 1951-52; engring. mgr. VVB-NE-Metalle, Eisleben, German Dem. Rep., 1952-59; prorector Bergakademie Freiberg, 1963-75, dean, 1980-91, prof., 1960-91; hon. prof. U. Wuhan, China, 1989. Mem. Internat. Mineral Processing Congresses (vice-chmn. internat. sci. com. 1988-91). E-mail: schuberh@mvtat.tu-freiberg.de. Home: 14 Johann Sebastian Bach St, D-09599 Freiberg Saxony, Germany Office: Tech U Bergakademie, Agricolastr 1, D-09596 Freiberg Saxony, Germany

SCHUBERT, PER JOHAN FREDRIK, computer scientist; b. Täby, Sweden, Oct. 30, 1960; s. Per-Åke and Vivianne H. (Bäckström) S. MSc, Royal Inst. Tech., Stockholm, 1986, lic. engring., 1993, PhD, 1994. Rsch. engr. Def. Rsch. Establishment, Stockholm, 1987, scientist, 1987-96, sr. scientist, 1996—. Contbr. articles to profl. jours. Mem. Internat. Soc. Info. Fusion, European Network Uncertainty Tech. Devel. Use Info. Tech., Swedish Artificial Intelligence Soc., Royal Inst. Tech. Alumni. Avocations: opera. Office: Def Rsch Establishment, SE 17290 Stockholm Sweden

SCHUBERT, ULRICH, chemistry educator; b. Regensburg, Bavaria, Fed. Republic Germany, May 26, 1946; s. Josef and Gertraude (Soph) S.; m. Gudrun Braun; children: Dominik, Simone. Diploma in chemistry, Technische U., Munich, 1972; D. in Natural Scis., Technische U., 1974, D. Natural Scis. Habilitation, 1980. Rsch. asst. Technische U. Munich, 1972-80, lectr., 1980-82; prof. inorganic chemistry U. Würzburg, Fed. Republic Germany, 1982-94; rsch. coord. Fraunhofer Inst. für Silikatforschung, Würzburg, 1989-94; prof. inorganic chemistry Tech. U. Vienna, 1994—. Author: Synthesis of Inorganic Materials, 2000; editor: Advances in Metal Carbene Chemistry, 1989; contbr. articles to profl. jours. Mem. German Chem. Soc., Austrian Chem. Soc. (v.p. 1998—), Am. Chem. Soc., Material Rsch. Soc., Austrian Acad. Sci. (corr.). Office: Inst Anorganische Chemie Techn U Vienna, Getreidemarkt 9/153, A-1060 Wien Austria

SCHUBERTH, ERWIN ARTHUR, physicist, educator; b. Straubing, Bavaria, Germany, Jan. 11, 1945; s. Arthur and Aloisia (Paulus) S.; m. Regina G. Giera, May 10, 1974; children: Christian, Bernhard. Diploma, Tech. U. Munich, Germany, 1970; PhD, U. Regensburg, 1976; habilitation, Tech. U. Munich, 1996. Univ. asst. U. Regensburg, 1971-78; postdoctoral rsch. asst. U. Fla., 1978-79; sr. scientist Bavarian Acad. Sci., Munich, 1980—; lectr. Fachhochschule, Munich, 1984-96; private dozent Tech. U. Munich, 1996—; vis. rsch. faculty Gainesville, Fla., 1999. Contbr. articles to profl. jours. Mem. Am. Physical Soc. Avocations: rowing, skiing, gymnastics, hiking, theater. Office: Walther Meissner Inst, Walter Meissner Str. 8, D-85748 Garching Germany

SCHUBIGER, PIUS AUGUST, radiopharmacy educator, consultant; b. Uznach, St. Gallen, Switzerland, May 19, 1945; m. Johanna Kulling, Mar. 17, 1968; children: Madeleine Minh Irang, Raffael August. Diploma chemistry, U. Zurich, 1969, PhD, 1972. Expert Internat. Atomic Energy Agy., Brazil, 1973-74; postdoctoral Max-Planck Inst., Heidelberg, Germany, 1974-76; rschr. Paul Scherrer Inst., Villigen, Switzerland, 1976-79; group leader Radiopharmacy, Villigen, Switzerland, 1979-89, head dept., 1989-97; head Ctr. Radiopharm. Sci. Swiss Fed. Inst. Tech., Zurich, Switzerland, 1997—; cons. bd. Forschungszentrum Rossendorf, Germany, 1995—; chmn. European Cost Program, Brussels, 1999—; mem. Exec. Bd. of Profs. ETH, Zurich, 1997—. Editor Roche series; patentee in field. Mem. Soc. Nuclear Medicine, European Soc. of Nuclear Medicine, Soc. Radiopharmacists (bd. dirs.). Roman Catholic. Avocations: gardening, mountain hiking. Office: Paul Scherrer Inst, CH-5232 Villigen Switzerland

SCHUCHERT, ANDREAS, medical educator; b. Dusseldorf, Germany, Aug. 9, 1959; s. Josef and Gertrud (Gunther) S. MD, Heinrich-Heine U., Dusseldorf, Germany, 1984, D, 1986. Med. asst. Med. Clinic, Ratingen, Germany, 1985-86; med. asst. dept. cardiology U. Hosp. Med. Clinic, Hamburg, Germany, 1986-94, assoc. prof. dept. cardiology, 1994—. Co-author: Therapie - Handbuch, Klinik der Gegenwart, Checklists EKG; contbr. articles to profl. jours. Mem. Deutsche Gesellschaft Kardoiologie, German Working Group Pacemaker Therapy. Roman Catholic. Avocations: running, biking. Office: U Hosp Eppendorf, Martinistr 52, 20246 Hamburg Germany

SCHUCK, MARJORIE MASSEY, publisher, editor, author's consultant; b. Winchester, Va., Oct. 9, 1921; d. Carl Frederick and Margaret Harriet (Parmele) Massey; m. Ernest George Metcalfe, Dec. 2, 1943 (div. Oct. 1949); m. Franz Schuck, Nov. 11, 1953 (dec. Jan. 1958). Student, U. Minn., 1941-43, New Sch., N.Y.C., 1948, NYU, 1952, 54-55. Mem. editl. bd. St. Petersburg (Fla.) Poetry Assn., 1967-68; co-editor, pub. Poetry Venture mag., St. Petersburg, 1968-69, editor, pub., 1969-79; co-editor, pub. Poetry Venture Quar. Essays, Vol. I, 1968-69, Vol. II, 1970-71; pub., editor poetry anthologies, 1972—; founder, owner, pres. Valkyrie Press, Inc. (now Valkyrie Pub. House), 1972—; cons. designs and formats trade publs., ann. reports, lit. books and pamphlets, 1973—; founder Valkyrie Press Roundtable Workshop and Forum for Writers, 1975-79; established Valkyrie Press Reference Libr., 1976-80; pub., editor The Valkyrie Internat. Newsletter, 1986-96; exec. dir. Inter-Cultural Forum Villanor Ctr., Tampa, Fla., 1987-94; dir. edn. The Villanor Mus. Fine and Decorative Arts, Tampa, 1994, St. Petersburg, 1994-98; pres. Found for Human Potentials, Inc., Tampa, 1988-94; rep. distbr. Marg Art Publs. of India (Bombay), 1992-98; mem. pres. coun. U. South Fla., 1993-95; lectr. in field; judge poetry and speech contests Gulf Beach Women's Club, 1970, Fine Arts Festival dist. 14 Am. Fedn. Women's Clubs, 1970, South and West, Inc., 1972, The Sunstone Rev., 1973, Internat. Toastmistress Clubs, 1974, 78, Beaux Arts Poetry Festival, 1983, 89, 92-99, 2000; judge poetry contest Fla. State conf. Nat. League Am. Pen Women, 1989, Tampa Bay Poetry Coun., 1994-98; judge Fla. Gov.'s Screenwriters Competition, 1984-96. Author: Speeches and Writings for Cause of Freedom, 1973; contbr. poetry to profl. jours. Corr.-rec. sec. Women's Aux. Hosp. for Spl. Surgery, N.Y.C., 1947-59; active St. Petersburg Mus. Fine Arts (charter), St. Petersburg Sister City Com., St. Petersburg Arts Ctr. Assn.; mem. Com. of 100 of Pinellas County, Inc., exec. bd., 1975-77, membership chmn., 1975-77; pub. rels. chmn. Soc. for Prevention Cruelty to Animals, 1968-71, bd. dirs., 1968-71, 75-77; founder, mem. Pinellas County Arts Coun., 1976-79, chmn., 1977-78; mem. grant rev. panel for lit. Fine Arts Coun. of Fla., 1979; mem., bd. dirs. Tampa Bay Poetry Found., Inc., 1995-98, lectr., 1995-98, adv. bd., 1998-00. Named One of 76 Fla. Patriots, Fla. Bicentennial Commn., 1976; recipient 1st ann. People of Dedication award Salvation Army, Tampa, 1984; named to Poetica Hall of Fame, Tampa Bay Poetry Coun., 1994, Hall of Fame, St. Petersburg, 1997; presented with the keys to the City of St. Petersburg, 1997. Mem. Acad. Am. Poets (founder), Fla. State Poets Assn., Fla. Suncoast Writers' Confs. (founder, co-dir., lectr. 1973-83, 97-98, adv. bd. 1984-96), Coordinating Coun. Lit. Mags., Friends of Libr. of St. Petersburg, Suncoast Mgmt. Inst. (exec. bd., chmn. Women in Mgmt. 1977-78), Pi Beta Phi. Republican. Episcopalian. Home and Office: 8245 26th Ave N Saint Petersburg FL 33710-2857

SCHÜCK, OTTO, nephrologist, researcher; b. Prague, Czech Republic, Aug. 26, 1926; s. Pavel and Marie (Sedlačková) S.; m. Ladislava Čizková, Aug. 16, 1950. MD, Charles U., Prague, 1950, PhD, 1956, DSc, 1966. Rsch. fellow First Med. Clinic, Prague, 1950-61; asst. dir. Inst. for Exptl. Therapy, Prague, 1962-65; rsch. fellow Med. Clinic, Manchester, Eng., 1966-67; dir. Clinic of Nephrology, Prague, 1967-85; researcher Inst. for Clin. Exptl. Medicine, Prague, 1985—; head dept. nephrology Postgrad. Med. Sch. Prague, 1976-92; cons. Nat. Med. Care, Prague, 1994-97. Author: Examination of Kidney Function, 1984 (medal Czech Soc. Internal Medicine 1985), Clinical Nephrology, 1995 (Cilag Found. award 1996); contbr. articles to profl. jours. Recipient Bruno Watschinger award Danube Symposia for Nephrology, 1987, Purkynje award Czech Soc. Medicine, 1996. Mem. Czech Soc. Nephrology (hon. pres. 1996, medals 1962, 72), N.Y. Acad. Scis., Gesselschaft für Nephrologie). Avocations: music, swimming. Home: Kratochvilova 4, 162 00 Prague Czech Republic Office: Inst Clin Exptl Medicine, Videnska 800, 140 00 Prague Czech Republic

SCHUCKMAN, NANCY LEE, retired principal; b. Bklyn., June 3, 1939; d. Abraham Benjamin and Sophie (Kalefsky) S. BA, Bklyn. Coll., 1961, MS, 1964, postgrad., 1965-69; postgrad., Hofstra U., 1970-72, Columbia U., 1979-80. Tchr. N.Y.C. Bd. Edn., 1961-69; adminstr. N.Y.C. Bd. Edn., Bklyn., 1969-77, prin., 1977-97; ednl. consultant East New Yorker, East N.Y. Devel. Corp., Bklyn., 1974-76, Starrett City Sun, Bklyn., 1975-76; co-owner Lanah Ednl. Toys, Bklyn., 1975-76. Mem. Thomas Jefferson Dem. Club, Bklyn., 1978—, Kings County Dem. Com., 1981-97; polit. campaign coord. John F. Kennedy Dem. Club, Bklyn., 1974-76, mem. exec. bd., 1974-75; mem. adv. bd. Prin.'s Ctr. at Bklyn. Coll., 1989-95. Recipient City Coun. proclamation N.Y.C. Coun., 1987, Legis. Resolution, N.Y. State Assembly/Senate, 1997, Congrl. Record Recognition, U.S. Congress, 1997. Mem. ASCD, Nat. Assn. Elem. Sch. Prins., Coun. Suprs. and Adminstrs. (Ednl. Leadership Recognition award N.Y.C. Dist. 19, 1997, conv. registration chmn. 1985-88), Adminstrv. Women in Edn., Am. Assn. Sch. Adminstrs., N.Y.C. Elem. Prins. Assn. (Svc. Appreciation award 1997), Bklyn. Reading Coun. Democrat. Jewish. Avocations: education law, journalism, oil painting, traveling, sports. Home: 122 Crispell Rd Krumville NY 12461-5408

SCHUDEL, ALEJANDRO ANIBAL, research scientist; b. Rosario, Santa Fe, Argentina, July 7, 1942; s. Alejandro Anibal and Josefa Toledo Ibarguren Schudel; m. Viviana Echenique, May 13, 1971; children: Viviana Elisa, Carolina Ines, Alejandro Federico, Martin Eduardo. Perito Mercantil, Florentino Ameghino, Santa Fe, 1959; DVM, U. Nat. Plata, Argentina, 1965, MS in Animal Sci., 1972, PhD, 1977. Prof. FCV-UNLP, La Plata, 1965-68; rsch. assoc. Regional Poultry Rsch. Lab. USDA, East Lansing, Mich., 1968-70; rsch. fellow CONICET, East Lansing, 1968-70; prin. rschr. CONICET, Argentina, 1970—; rsch. assoc. Rush Presbyn. St. Luke's Med. Ctr., Chgo., 1973-75; fellow WHO, Chgo., 1973-75; rsch. mem. INTA, Castelar-Buenos Aires, Argentina, 1978—; dir. Inst. Virology, Moron, Argentina; prof. virology FLU-UBA, 1996—; vis. scientist U. Zurich, 1982-83; cons. FAO, Latin Am., Italy, 1980-86, IICA-FAO, Latin Am., 1985-89, IAEA-FAO, Latin Am., 1989-91. Recipient Wilfrid Baron award Acad. Nat. Agr. and Vet., Argentina, 1987, Remonta y Vet., Ejercito Argentino, 1981, B. Hussay award CONICET, 1987, Konex award Konex Found., Argentina, 1993. Mem. AAAS, Soc. Med. Vet., Assn. Argentina Microbiology, Nat. Acad. Agronomy and Vet. Sci. Roman Catholic. Avocation: sailing. Home: G Flaubert 1211, Bella Vista 1661, Argentina Office: Inst Investig Ciencias Vete, rinarias UBA Chorroarin 280, Buenos Aires 1447, Argentina

SCHUDER, JOHN CLAUDE, biomedical engineer; b. Olney, Ill., Mar. 2, 1922; s. Charles Claude Schuder and Louise Ella Muench; m. Retha Elizabeth Schuder, July 23, 1946; children: Linda Lee Brown, Charles Wayne, Jonna Elizabeth. BSEE, U. Ill., 1943; MSEE, Purdue U., 1951, PhD, 1954. Jr. engr. Westinghouse Rsch., East Pittsburgh, Pa., 1943-44; from instr. to asst. prof. Purdue U., West Lafayette, Ind., 1949-56; assoc. prof. Doane Coll., Crete, Nebr., 1956-57; fellow, asst. prof. U. Pa., Phila., 1957-60; assoc. prof. emeritus U. Mo. Sch. Medicine, Columbia, 1960—; cons. Hewlett-Packard, Medtronics, GE, Physio Control, NIH, others. Mem. editl. bd. PACE, 1991—; contbr. numerous articles to profl. jours. Peace activist, anti-death penalty activist Columbia Fellowship of Reconciliation, local and nat., 1960—. Recipient numerous grants NIH, Am. Heart Assn., Mo. Heart Assn., others. Mem. AAUP, IEEE Engring. in Medicine and Biology Soc. (life), Am. Soc. Artificial Internal Organs,. Quaker. E-mail: schuderj@health.missouri.edu. Home: 105 Manor Dr Columbia MO 65203-1727 Office: U Mo Dept Surgery Columbia MO 65212-0001

SCHUDER, RAYMOND FRANCIS, lawyer; b. Wickford, R.I., Dec. 27, 1926; s. Rollie Milton and Selma (Ball) S.; AB, Emory U., 1949, JD, 1951; m. Betty Jo Williams, Mar. 14, 1948; children: Gregg Williams, Glen Arva. Bar: Ga. 1951. With Trust Co., Ga., Atlanta, 1951-54; assoc. firm Wheeler, Robinson & Thurmond, Gainesville, Ga., 1954-59; pvt. practice law, Gainesville, 1959-70, 76-96; ptnr. Schuder & Brown, Gainesville, 1971-76; Mcpl. ct. judge, Gainesville, 1956-60, 73-75, Magistrate ct. judge, 1985—. Supr. Upper Chattahoochee Soil and Water Conservation Dist., 1971-74; chief exec. officer, bd. dirs. Charles Thompson Estes Found., Inc., Gainesville. Cpl. USMCR, 1944-50; 1st lt. USAR, ret. Mem. State Bar Ga. (gov. 1966-70), Gainesville-Northeastern (pres. 1969-70) Bar Assn., Am. Legion, V.F.W., Elks. Methodist. Home: 2224 Riverside Dr Gainesville GA 30501-1232

SCHUEMCHEN, ANDREAS, editor, educator; b. Gelsenkirchen, N Westphal, Germany, Jan. 20, 1964; s. Winfried and Ilse (Iwan) S. MA, Berlin U. of Tech., 1990. Freelance rschr. Sender Freies Berlin, Berlin, 1987-90; mgr. AV Studio Berlin, 1990-91; editor Medien Bull., Munich, Germany, 1992-94; chief editor Medien Bull., Munich, 1994-97, Grimme, Marl, Germany, 1998—; guest lectr. Acad. Film Making, Baden-Wuerttenberg, Ludwigsburg, Germany, 1995, Eichstätt U., 1998, Bavarian TV Acad., 1998—; prof. journalism Bonn-Rhein-Sieg U., 2000—. Author: Karriere in den Medien-Video und TV, 1995, Shooting in Germany, 1997. Mem. Soc. Motion Picture and TV Engrs., Fernseh und Kinotechnische Gesellschaft. Home: Hesseloher Strasse 9, D-80802 Munich Germany Office: Bonn-Rhein-Sieg U, D-53754 Sankt Augustin Germany

SCHUEPBACH, EVI, environmental scientist, consultant; b. Muehlethurnen, Berne, Switzerland, June 15, 1958; d. Hansrudolf and Alice (Marti) S. MSc, U. Berne, 1988; PhD, U. East Anglia, U.K., 1994. Asst. Dept. Interior, Switzerland, 1979-80; dep. leader Swiss Nat. Sci. Found., 1988-90; rsch. assoc. U. East Anglia, U.K., 1994-2000; asst. prof. U. Berne, 1994—; reviewer Am. Geophys. Union, 1997—; mem. steering com. TOR-2/Trap 45 in Eurotrac-2, Germany, 1997—; coord. mentoring project U. Berne, 1999—, asst. coord. EU project, 1996-98. Editor: (books) Meteorologie und Luftchemie in Waldbestanden, 1991, Luftschadstoffe und Lufthaushalt in der Schweiz, 1991; contbr. sci. articles and papers to profl. jours. Pres. Assn. Geography students, U. Berne, 1982-85. Recipient Philips prize, 1986, Sir Winston Churchill award Brit. Coun., 1990, Jubilee award Swiss Fedn. Univ. Women, 1992, Fgn. and Commonwealth award, 1991. Mem. Swiss Meteorol. Soc., Internat. Fedn. U. Women. Avocations: fitness, yoga, opera and musicals, piano playing, travel, nature.

SCHUESSEL, WOLFGANG, Austrian chancellor; b. Vienna, Austria, June 7, 1945; married; 2 children. Grad., Schottengymnasium, Vienna, 1963; PhD, Vienna U., 1968. Sec. Parliamentary Austrian People's Party Group, 1968-75; sec. gen. Austrian Econ. Fedn., 1975-89; MP Govt. Austria, Vienna, 1979, leader Econ. Fedn. parliamentary dels., dep. chmn. Parliamentary Austrian People's Party, 1987-89, dept chmn. parliamentary fin. com., 1987-89, min. Econ. Affairs, 1989-95; vice chancellor, min. fgn. affairs Govt. of Austria, Vienna, from 1995, chancellor; leader People's Party of Austria. Office: Office Federal Chancellor, Ballhausplatz 2, A-1014 Vienna Austria*

SCHUETH, DOROTHEE, mathematician, educator, researcher; b. Bonn, Germany, Nov. 2, 1965; d. Heinrich Wilhelm Arnold and Ruth (Fischer) S.; m. Georgios Vrazitulis, Nov. 17, 1995; children: Elena, Michael. Diploma in math., U. Bonn, Germany, 1991, diploma in Turkish & Arabic translation, 1992, PhD in Math., 1993, habilitation in Math., 2000. Tchg. asst. U. Bonn, 1990-93, sci. asst., 1993-94, 1995—; rsch. fellow Dartmouth Coll., Hanover, N.H., 1994-95. Contbr. articles to profl. jours. Recipient prize Soc. Friends and Supporters of U. Bonn, 1994; rsch. fellow Deutsche Forschungsgemeinschaft, 1994. Mem. German Math. Soc., European Women in Math. Avocations: Greek, Turkish, Arabic and Russian languages. Home: Masurenweg 3, D-53119 Bonn Germany Office: U Bonn Math Inst, Beringstr 1, D-53115 Bonn Germany

SCHUHBAUER, HEIDI, scientist; b. Neuendeltelsau, Germany, June 5, 1969; d. Hans and Hildegard (Popp) Meyer; m. Walter and Schuhbauer, May 23, 1998. Diploma in bus. mgmt. & computer sci., Friedrich-Alexander U., Nurnberg, Germany, 1996, D, 1999. Programmer DATEV, Nurnberg, Germany, 1988-91; scientist FORWISS, Elangen, Germany, 1996—. Office: FORWISS, Am Weidiselgaulen 7, 91058 Evlangen Germany

SCHÜHLEN, HELMUT, cardiologist; b. Sindelfingen, Germany, Feb. 15, 1958; s. Albrecht Johannes and Anneliese Schühlen. MD, Ludwig-Maximilians U., Munich, 1986. Fellow med. clinic U. Munich, 1986-87; rsch. fellow cardiology Cedars-Sinai Med. Ctr., L.A., 1987-89; fellow med. clinic III U. Freiburg, Germany, 1990-93; staff med. clinic I Tech. U. Munich, 1993—. Contbr. articles to profl. jours. Deutsche Forschungs Gemeinschaft grantee, 1988, 89. Fellow European Soc. Cardiology; mem. Am. Heart Assn.

(coun. on circulation 1989—), German Soc. Cardiovascular Rsch. Office: Tech U Munich Med Clinic I, Ismaningerstr 22, 81675 Munich Germany

SCHUIJT, CHRIS, pharmaceutical executive; b. Zaandam, The Netherlands, Aug. 12, 1942; s. Chris and Ida (Busch) S.; m. Marianne Thijs, Sept. 22, 1970; children: Kirsten, Martinus. PhD, State U., Leiden, The Netherlands, 1978. Staff mem. pharmacochemistry State U., Leiden, 1973-77; clin. rsch. mgr. Boehringer Ingelheim, Haarlem, The Netherlands, 1977-80; mktg. dir. Boehringer Ingelheim, Alkmaar, The Netherlands, 1980-84; mng. dir. Boehringer Ingelheim, Copenhagen, 1984-91; head corp. clin. quality assurance Boehringer Ingelheim, Ingelheim, Germany, 1991—. Contbr. articles to profl. jours. Bd. dirs. Copenhagen Internat. Sch., 1985-89. Cpl. Dutch Army, 1965-67. Mem. Dutch Bus. Club (chmn. 1987-89, 93-94), Drug Info. Assn., Assn. Clin. Rsch. Profls., European Forum Good Clinical Practice. Avocations: history of chemistry, travel. Home: Kurhausstr 50, 65719 Hofheim am Taunus Germany Office: Boehringer Ingelheim GmbH, PO Box 200 Bingerstrasse, D-55216 Ingelheim Germany

SCHUISKI, LARRY LEROY, information scientist; b. L.A., Jan. 5, 1950; s. Leroy Hillis Duitsman and Charleen Edna (Nelson) Sager; m. Larissa Schuiski, June 17, 1988. BS in Physics with honors, U. Washington, 1972. Architect Boeing Computer Svcs., Seattle, 1978-88; dir. Trident Sys., San Francisco, 1988-92, View Star Corp., Alameda, Calif., 1993-95; v.p. Moore Document Solutions, Lake Forest, Ill., 1995-97; sr. cons. The Concours Group, Kingwood, Tex., 1997-99; sr. v.p. Attachmate corp., Bellevue, Wash., 1999—.

SCHUKLENK, UDO, bioethics educator; b. Waltrop, Germany, May 19, 1964; s. Walter R. and Inge (Sindermann) S.; m. Saul Garcia Lopez. PhD, Monash U., Melbourne, Australia, 1995. Gen. sec. German Young Dems., Bonn, 1990-91; rsch. officer Bremen (Germany) U., 1991-92; lectr. U. Ctrl. Lancaster, Preston, U.K., 1996-97, Monash U., 1997-99; assoc. prof. bioethics, head of dept. U. Witwatersrand, Johannesburg, South Africa, 1999—. Joint editor Bioethics jour. of Internat. Assn. Bioethics; author: Access to Experimental Drugs in Terminal Illness, 1998; editor: AIDS: Society, Ethics and Law, 2000; founding editor: (jour.) Developing Word Bioethics; contbr. over 100 articles to profl. publs. City councilor, Waltrop, Germany, 1990-95. Mem. Green Party. Avocations: swimming, cycling. Office: U Witwatersrand, Faculty Health Scis, Johannesburg South Africa

SCHULENBURG, ROSAMUNDE MARIA GRAEFIN VON DER (ROSAMUNDE NEUGEBAUER), art historian, educator; b. Augsburg, Germany, Aug. 29, 1958; d. Walter and Maria Theresia (Knoller) Neugebauer; m. Stephan Schulenburg Graf von der, Apr. 23, 1991. MA, U. Heidelberg, Germany, 1986, PhD, 1992. Diplomate painting & sculpture restoration, 1980. Rschr., curator various exhibitions Univ. Libr., Heidelberg, 1985-93, Mus. Applied Arts, Frankfurt/Main, Germany, 1990-92; asst. prof. U. Mainz, Germany, 1993—; freelance historian Dr. Tenner Auction House, Heidelberg, 1983-85, co-mgr. Marsilius Antiquarian Bookshop, Speyer, Germany, 1984-85. Author: Erlesen gestiftet, 1991, George Grosz, Macht und Ohnmacht satirischer Kunst, 1993; co-author: Matthaeus Merian d. Ae., 1993; editor: Aspekte der literarischen Buchillustration im 20. Jahrhundert, 1996. Home: Neuhofstrasse 39, D-60318 Frankfurt/Main Germany Office: Inst fuer Buchwissenschaft, Johannes-Gutenberg-Univ, D-55099 Mainz Germany

SCHULER, ALISON KAY, lawyer; b. West Point, N.Y., Oct. 1, 1948; d. Richard Hamilton and Irma (Sanken) S.; m. Lyman Gage Sandy, Mar. 30, 1974; 1 child, Theodore. AB cum laude, Radcliffe Coll., 1969; JD, Harvard U., 1972. Bar: Va. 1973, D.C. 1974, N.Mex. 1975. Assoc. Hunton & Williams, Richmond, Va., 1972-75; asst. U.S. atty. U.S. Atty.'s Office, Albuquerque, 1975-78; adj. prof. law U. N.Mex., 1983-85, 90, 98—; ptnr. Sutin, Thayer & Browne, Albuquerque, 1978-85, Montgomery & Andrews, P.A., Albuquerque, 1985-88; sole practice Albuquerque, 1988—. Bd. dirs. Am. Diabetes Assn., Albuquerque, 1980-85, chmn. bd. dirs., 1984-85; bd. dirs. June Music Festival, 1980-95, pres., 1983-85, 93-94; bd. dirs. Albuquerque Conservation Trust, 1986-90, N.Mex. Osteo. Found., 1993-96; chairperson Albuquerque Com. Fgn. Rels., 1984-85; mem. N.Mex. Internat. Trade and Investment Coun., Inc., 1986—; mem. coun. St. Lukes Luth. Ch., 1976-80, 82-84, 91-96, v.p., 1978-80, 82-84, pres., 1994-95, chartered org. rep. troop 444, Boy Scouts Am., 1997—, mem. nominating com., mem.-at-large dist. com. Sandia dist., 1998—, dist. vice chmn., 1999—. Recipient Award of Merit, Sandia Dist., 2000, Tng. award, 2000. Mem. Fed. Bar Assn. (coord.), ABA, Va. Bar Assn., N.Mex. Bar Assn. (chmn. corp., banking and bus. law 1982-83, bd. dirs. internat. and immigration law sect. 1987-95, chmn. 1993-94), Harvard U. Alumni Assn. (mem. fund campaign, regional dir. 1984-86, v.p. 1986-89, chmn. clubs com. 1985-88, chmn. communications com. 1988-91), Radcliffe Coll. Alumnae Assn. Bd. Mgmt. (regional dir. 1984-87, chmn. comms. com. 1988-91), Harvard-Radcliffe Club (pres. 1980-84). Home: 632 Cougar Loop NE Albuquerque NM 87122-1808 Office: 4300 San Mateo Blvd NE Ste B380 Albuquerque NM 87110-8401

SCHULER, HANS, chemical and process engineer; b. Biberach, Fed. Republic Germany, Dec. 24, 1950; s. Konrad and Sofie (Voelkle) S.; m. Angela Frank, 1982. Diploma in Mech. Engring., U. Stuttgart, 1975, PhD in Chem. Engring., 1982. Sci. asst. U. Stuttgart, Fed. Republic Germany, 1975-82; chem. engr. BASF A.G., Ludwigshafen, Fed. Republic Germany, 1982—. Recipient Heinz Maier Leibnitz award German Ministry Culture and Sci., 1985, Dechema award Max Buchner Rsch. Found., 1992, 93. Mem. IEEE, AICE, Verein Deutscher Ingenieure, Deutsche Gesellschaft fuer Chemisches Apparatewesen, Gesellschaft Verfahrenstechnik und Chemie Ingenieur Wesen, Gesellschaft Mess-und Automatisierungstechnik.

SCHULER, HEINZ FRIEDRICH, psychologist, educator; b. Vienna, Austria, June 6, 1945; s. Willi and Erika I. (Stetzenbach) S.; m. Karin Kohl, Oct. 11, 1968; children: Benjamin, Julia. Diploma in psychology, U. Munich, 1970; Dr. rer.pol., U. Augsburg, Fed. Republic Germany, 1973; Dr. habil., U. Augsburg, 1978. Prof. psychology U. Erlangen-Nürnberg, Fed. Republic Germany, 1979-82, U. Hohenheim, Stuttgart, Fed. Republic Germany, 1982—. Author 20 books, including The Employee's Picture, 1972, 2d edit., 1974, 3d edit., 1980, Personality, 1974, 2d edit., 1978, Attraction and Influence in Groups' Decisions, 1974, Decision Processes in Groups, 1976, Dynamics of Group Decisions, 1978, Ethical Problems in Psychological Research, 1980, Psychology in the Economy and Public Administration: Practical Experience with Concepts in Organizations Psychology, 1982, Organizational Psychology and Corporate Practice: Perspectives for Cooperation, 1985, Biographical Questionnaires as a Method for Personnel Selection, 1986, 2d edit., 1990, Assessment Center as a Method for Personnel Development, 1987, 2d edit., 1992, Assessment and Promotion of Vocational Success, 1991, Personnel Marketing, 1993, Organizational Psychology, 1993, 2d edit., 1995, Personnel Selection and Assessment: Individual and Organizational Perspectives, 1993, Personnel Selection in European Comparison, 1993, Revised General Clerical Test, 1994, Personnel Selection in Research and Development, 1995, Psychological Personnel Selection, 1996; contbr. over 250 articles to sci. jours., books; editor sci. jours. Mem. nat. and internat. sci. assns. Office: U Hohenheim, Lehrstuhl Psychol 540, D-70593 Stuttgart Germany

SCHULER, WALTER E., lawyer; b. Memphis, Tenn., Sept. 8, 1962; s. James D. and Clare A. Schuler. BBA magna cum laude, U. Memphis, 1993; JD cum laude with cert. in health law with hons., St. Louis U., 1996. Bar: Tenn. 1996, U.S. Dist. Ct. (Western Dist.) Tenn. 1996, U.S. Ct. Appeals (6th cir.), 1998. Assoc. The Bogatin Law Firm, PLC, Memphis, Tenn., 1996—. Contbr. articles to profl. jours., chpt. to book. Sgt. (E-5), U.S. Army, 1985-90, staff sgt. (E-6) USAR, 1990-93. Recipient Commendation Medal-1st Oak Leaf Cluster, U.S. Army, 1989, Army Achievement Medal-2nd Oak Leaf Cluster, 1989, Nat. Def. Svc. Med., 1992. Mem. Am. Health Lawyers Assn., ABA, Tenn. Bar Assn., Memphis Bar Assn. Office: Bogatin Law Firm PLC Ste 300 International Place Dr Memphis TN 38120

SCHULERI, ERWIN WILHELM, physician, consultant; b. Deva, Romania, Feb. 4, 1933; arrived in Germany, 1979; s. Wilhelm Friedrich Schuleri and Ida (Breckner) Baltres; m. Liane Gilda Schuster, June 10, 1959; children: Ingo, Jessie. Diploma dr. med., Med.-Pharm. Inst., Cluj, Romania, 1958; Diploma in Philosophy, Babes-Bolyay U., Cluj, 1974. Paediatrician Govt. Med. Sta., Baita, Deva, Romania, 1958-63; asst. physician pathology County Hosp., Deva, 1963-67, med. specialist, head dept., 1967-79; asst. physician pathology Town Hosp., Pforzheim, Germany, 1979-81, head physician, 1981-83; head physician Town Hosp., Schweinfurt, Germany, 1983-87, head dept. pathology, 1987-98. Contbr. articles to profl. jours. Capt. Romanian Reserve Army, 1952-55. Mem. N.Y. Acad. Scis. Avocations: fishing, travelling, literature on history, philosophy and art. Home: Alstadtstr 26, 97422 Schweinfurt Germany

SCHULHOF, ROBERT J., medical association administrator; b. L.A., Jan. 2, 1942; s. Max and Betty Claire Schulhof; m. Margaret Ellen Schulhof, Apr. 15, 1994; children: Lisa, Eric. AB, UCLA, 1964, MA, 1966. Mem. tech. staff Hughes Space Sys., El Segundo, Calif., 1964-67; mgr. equipment evaluation Litton Data Sys., Van Nuys, Calif., 1967-69; pres. Rocky Mountain Info. Svcs., Van Nuys, 1969-83; dir. orthodontic svcs. Databill, Woodland Hills, Calif., 1984-88; v.p. mktg. Patient Centered Mgmt. Sys., Mpls., 1988-89; pres. Solution Providers, Acton, Calif., 1990-95; v.p. orthodontics Pentegra Dental Group, Phoenix, 1999—; mem. Found. for Orthodontic Rsch., L.A. Co-author: BioProgressive Therapy, 1976, Orthodontic Diagnosis and Planning, 1982; contbr. articles to profl. jours. Avocation: writing. E-mail: bschulhof@uswest.net.

SCHULHOFF, KAREN L., information specialist; b. Long Island City, N.Y., Dec. 11, 1959; d. Edward and Eleanor (Gillespie) S. MLS, CUNY, 1993. Tng. program coord. Chem. Bank, N.Y.C., 1983-90; libr. Katharine Gibbs Sch., N.Y.C., 1990-92; cons. Pfizer, N.Y.C., 1993—. Mem. NAFE, Am. Mgmt. Assn. Roman Catholic. Office: Pfizer 235 E 42nd St New York NY 10017-5755

SCHULIEN, SIGURD, physicist, educator; b. Hemmersdorf, Saarland, Germany, Mar. 22, 1935; s. Jakob and Amalie (Kohl) S.; m. Renate Pietsch; children: Stefan, Henriette. Diploma, U. Bonn, Germany, 1963; vordiploma, U. Göttingen, Germany, 1969. Scientific collaborator Deutsche Edelstahlwerke, Germany, 1963-65, Leybold, Germany, 1965-70; head of vacuum dept. Dornier, Germany, 1970-73; prof. Fochhochschule Wiesbaden, Wiesbaden, Germany, 1973—. Contbr. articles to profl. publs.; patentee in field. E-mail: sschulien@aol.com. Home: Erbes-Büdesheimer Str 21, D-55232 Alzey Germany Office: Agafe, Am Brückweg 26, D-65428 Rüsselsheim Germany

SCHULLER, GERALD DIEDRICH THOMAS, electrical engineer; b. Neuenstein, Germany, Oct. 8, 1961; s. Thomas Schuller and Renate Mingers-Schuller. MS, Tech. U. Berlin, 1989; PhD, U. Hannover, Germany, 1997. Intern AEG, Berlin, 1987, Hahn-Meitner-Inst., Berlin, 1988-89; rsch. asst. Tech. U. Berlin, 1990-92; tchg. asst. Ga. Inst. Technology, Atlanta, 1993; rsch. asst. U. Bonn, Germany, 1994, U. Hannover, 1995—, Bell Labs., Lucent Techs., Murray Hill, N.J., 1998—. Inventor in field; contbr. articles to profl. jours. Mem. IEEE, Deutscher Amateur Radio Club. Avocation: amateur radio. Office: Lucent Techs 600 Mountain Ave New Providence NJ 07974-2008

SCHULMAN, CLAUDE CHARLES, urologist, educator; b. Brussels, Apr. 30, 1943; s. Abram and Fary S.; m. Mireille Weinstein, Aug. 22, 1970; children: Julie, Nicolas. MD, U. Brussels, 1968, PhD, 1979. Intern, resident Brussels U. Hosps.; asst. dept. urology U. Brussels, 1968-72, assoc. prof. urology, 1972-78, chmn. dept. urology, 1979, prof. urology, 1985; chief dept. of Urology Univ. Brussels, 1978—; editor-in-chief European Urology Jour.; chmn. Publ. Office European Assn. Urology, pres. congress 2000. Author: Advances in Diagnostic Urology, Urologie Pediatrique, Precursors Prostate Cancer, Chemoprevention Prostate Cancer; contbr. some 500 articles to profl. jours. Mem. European Assn. Urology, 20 Internat. Soc. Office: Erasme Hosp Dept Urology U Clinic Brussels, Rt de Lennik 808, Brussels Belgium 1070

SCHULMAN, SAM, hematologist; b. Stockholm, Feb. 29, 1952; arrived in Israel, 1992; s. Jim and Anita (Gachnoch) S.; m. Doris Rose Lederman, July 8, 1979; children: Melissa, Jacqueline, Rafael. MD, Karolinska Inst., Stockholm, 1977, Dr.Med.Sci., 1985. Specialist in internal medicine, specialist in hematology. Intern Vasteras (Sweden) Ctrl. Hosp., 1977; resident in internal medicine Huddinge (Sweden) Hosp., 1978-81, 82-83, McMaster U. Hosps., Hamilton, Ont., Can., 1981-82; cons. dept. medicine Karolinska Hosp, Stockholm, 1984-92, dir. coagulation unit dept. medicine, 1996—; cons. Nat. Hemophilia Ctr., Tel Hashomer, Israel, 1992-96; editor, chmn. info. bd. Med. Students Union, Stockholm, 1974-75. Mem. editl. bd. Haemophilia, 1995—, Thrombosis Rsch., 1995—. Recipient Hemophilia Ctr. Twin of the Yr. award, 1997. Mem. World Fedn. Hemophilia, Internat. Soc. Thrombosis and Haemostasis, Swedish Soc. Medicine. Avocations: philately, jogging. Office: Karolinska Hosp, Dept Medicine, SE-17176 Stockholm Sweden

SCHULT, MARC, physician, researcher; b. Lueneburg, Germany, Apr. 2, 1968; s. Walter Johann and Alma Lore S.; m. Heike Schult-Sikorsky, Jan. 23, 1997; 1 child, Ole. MD, U. Luebeck, Germany, 1995. Med. diplomate. Physician Hannover Med. Sch., Hannover, Germany, 1995-98, Westfalian Wilhelms U., Muenster, Germany, 1998—. Contbr. articles to med. jours., including Transplantation, Am. Jour. Physiology, others. Mem. German Surg. Soc. Office: Dept Gen Surg W Wilhelms U, Waldeyerstr 1, D-48129 Muenster Germany

SCHULTE, JURGEN, physics educator; b. Kamen, Germany, Nov. 8, 1958; arrived in Australia, 1996; MSc in Physics, Tech. Hochschule Darmstadt, Germany, 1985; DSc in Physics, U. Oldenburg, Germany, 1990. Rsch. assoc. U. Oldenburg, 1986-89; rsch. assoc. Tex. A&M U., College Station, 1990-92, asst. prof., 1992-93; asst. prof. Mich. State U., East Lansing, 1993-95; sr. rschr. Hitachi Ltd., Tokyo, 1995-96; lectr. U. Tech., Sydney, 1996—; bd. dirs. Indus Media, Inc., McKinney, Tex., Indus Media Internet Info. Svcs. Pvt. Ltd, Madras, India, Silicon Dune Pty. Ltd., Sydney, Australia. Editor: Ultra High Dilution-Physics and Physiology, 1994, Fundamental Research in Ultra High Dilution and Homeopathy, 1998; mem. internat. editl. bd. Brit. Homeopathy Jour., London, 1998; patentee in field. Grantee Hitachi Ctrl. Rsch., Tokyo, 1996. Mem. Australian Homeopathy Assn.

SCHULTE-HILLEN, GERD, business executive; b. Menden, Germany, Oct. 1, 1940; married; four children. From asst. to mgn. dir. to head printing divsn. Gruner & Jahr AG (divsn. Bertelsmann AG), 1969-81, CEO, 1981—, chmn. Office: Druck und Verlagshaus, Am Baumwall 11, D-20459 Hamburg Germany*

SCHULTE-NOELLE, HENNING, insurance company executive; b. Essen, Germany, Aug. 26, 1942. Student, U. Tübingen, U. Bonn, U. Cologne, U. Edinburgh, U. Pa. With Allianz Versicherungs-AG, 1975-84; head regional office Allianz Versicherungs-AG, North Rhine-Westphalia, 1984-88; mem. bd. mgmt. Allianz Versicherungs-AG, Munich, 1988-91, chmn. bd. mgmt., 1991—; mem. bd. mgmt. Allianz Lebensversicherungs-AG, Stuttgart, Germany, 1988-91, chmn. bd. mgmt., 1991—; now CEO Allianz Lebensversicherungs-AG; chmn. Allianz AG; dep. chmn. supervisory bd. MAN AG, Munchener Ruckversicherungs-Gesellschaft AG; dep. chmn. Riunione Adriatica di Sicurta SpA. Office: Allianz Lebensversicherungs-AG, Postfach 106002, 70178 Stuttgart Germany also: Konigin str 28, 80802 Munich Germany*

SCHULTESS, LEROY KENNETH, lawyer, consultant; b. Garrett, Ind., May 7, 1907; s. George Mathias and Elizabeth (Lehmbeck) S.; m. Sarah Mildred Atwater, Apr. 28, 1942. AB, Mich. U., 1929; JD, Northwestern U., 1932. Bar: Ind. 1933. Practice law, LaGrange, Ind.; pres. Creek Chub Bait Co., Garrett, Lure, Inc., Garrett; hon. dir. Farmers State Bank, LaGrange. Recipient Meritorious awards Farmers State Bank, VFW, Boy Scouts Am., Am. Lung Assn. Mem. U. Mich. Alumni Assn., LaGrange C. of C., ABA, Ind. Bar Assn. (Golden Anniversary award), LaGrange County Bar Assn. (Outstanding and Dedicated Svc. awards), Sigma Chi, Phi Delta Phi, Rotary (LaGrange) (pres. 1956-7), LaGrange Country. Lodges: Shriners, Masons. Office: Farmers State Bank Bldg 220 S Detroit St Lagrange IN 46761-1808

SCHULTZ, ARTHUR LEROY, clergyman, educator; b. Johnstown, Pa., June 14, 1928; s. Elmer Albert Robert and Alice Lizetta (Flegal) S.; m. Mildred Louise Stouffer, Nov. 29, 1948; children: Thomas Arthur, Rebecca Louise. BA, Otterbein Coll., 1949; MDiv, United Theol. Sem., 1952; MEd, U. Pitts., 1955, PhD, 1963. Sr. min. Albright United Meth. Ch., Pitts., 1952-56; dir. pub. rels. Otterbein Coll., Westerville, Ohio, 1956-65, adj. prof. religion and philosophy, 1990-98; pres. Albright Coll., Reading, Pa., 1965-77, Ashland (Ohio) Coll., 1977-80; exec. dir. Cen. Ohio Radio Reading Svc., Columbus, 1980-84; parish min. Ch. Master United Meth., Westerville, 1984-89; min. of visitation Ch. Messiah United Meth., Westerville, 1991—; pres. Pa. Assn. Colls. & Univs., Harrisburg, 1974-75. Trustee Reading Hosp., 1967-77, Wyoming Sem., Kingston, Pa., 1971-80; v.p. Found. for Ind. Colls. Pa., Harrisburg, 1972-73; pres. Pa. Coun. on Alcohol Problems, Harrisburg, 1968-76; pres. Westerville (Ohio) Hist. Soc., 1986-89, Westerville Area Ministerial Assn., 1992-93. Named Outstanding Young Man of the Year Jr. C. of C., Westerville, Ohio, 1960. Mem. Brookstone Cmty. Assn. (sec. bd. trustees 1994-99, v.p. 1999—), Rotary (charter pres. 1959, dist. gov. 1965-66, dist. sec.-treas. 1982-93), Masons, Shriners, Torch Club. Republican. Methodist. Avocations: collecting post cards, golf, tennis, travel. Home: 151 Sandstone Loop Westerville OH 43081-4599

SCHULTZ, BARBARA MARIE, insurance company executive; b. Chgo., Sept. 9, 1943; d. Edwin and Bernice (Barstis) Legner; m. Ronald J. Schultz Sr., May 1, 1965; 1 child, Ronald J. Grad. high sch., Chgo. Account rep. Met. Ins. Co., Aurora, Ill., 1981—; qualifier Met. Life Leaders Conf., 1990. Fellow Nat. Assn. Life Underwriters (edn. chmn. 1988-91, nat. quality award Robert L. Rose award 1990), Life Underwriters Tng. Coun. (chmn. 1986-88, citation 1987), South Cook County Assn. Life Underwriters (edn. chmn. 1988-91). Roman Catholic. Avocations: boating, aerobics, fishing. Office: Met Ins Co 15255 94th Ave Orland Park IL 60462-3800

SCHULTZ, DENNIS BERNARD, lawyer; b. Detroit, Oct. 15, 1946; s. Bernard George and Madeline Laverne (Riffenberg) S.; m. Andi Lynn Leslie, Apr. 18, 1967; 1 child, Karanne Anne. BS, Wayne State U., 1970; JD, Mich. State U., 1977. Bar: Mich. 1977, U.S. Dist. Ct. (ea. and we. dist.) Mich., U.S. Ct. Appeals (6th cir.), U.S. Dist. Ct. (we. dist.) Pa. V.p. Barkay Bldg. Co., Ferndale, Mich., to 1976; law clk. Hon. George N. Bashara, Mich. Ct. Appeals, Detroit, 1977; shareholder Butzel Long, Detroit, 1978—. Editor Detroit Coll. Law Rev., 1977. Detroit Coll. Law Alumni Assn. scholar, 1976, Mich. Consolidated Gas Co. scholar, 1977. Mem. Detroit Bar Assn., Mich. Bar Assn. Republican. Roman Catholic. Avocations: boating, biking, golf.

SCHULTZ, EVELYN ECALE, artist; b. Chgo., Nov. 28, 1931; d. George Ecale and Marie Elise Bauermeister; m. Robert Frank Schultz, Dec. 19, 1925; children: Kenneth M., Robin C. Brower, Karen M. Rantis, Jennifer B. Kaiser, Erik K., Steven E., Jason Robert. Attended, U. Ill., 1949-54, Coll. DuPage, Glen Ellyn, Ill., 1995-2000, numerous art workshops. Owner, operator ECALE Studio, Villa Park, Ill., 1997—; represented by Ill. Artisans Shop, Chgo., Artists Exch., Elmhurst, Ill., Wallscapes Gallery, Elmhurst Art. Mus. Gallery, DuPage Art Gallery and Sch.; del. W. Suburban Fine Arts Alliance, Oakbrook Terrace, Ill., 1995-97; judge U. Ill., Coop. Ext. Svc., DuPage County, Triton Coll., River Grove, Ill., Naperville Art League, Ill., Henry Hyde Congressional Art Exhbn., Elmurst Art Mus., local guilds and leagues, others. One-woman shows include Loyola Med. Ctr., Maywood, Ill., Navy Pier, Chgo., Hinsdale Libr., Ill., DuPage Gallery, Wheaton, Ill., Wallscapes Gallery, Elmhurst, Jason's on York, Elmhurst, Riverside Art Exhbn., West Suburban Bank, Villa Park; group shows include Chgo. Cultural Ctr., 1999, Elmhurst Art Mus., 1999, Ill. State Profl. Art Exhbn., Springfield, ICARUS, Nags Head, N.C., St. Charles Art and Music Festival, Ill., numerous juried art shows and nat. and internat. exhbns.; represented in permanent collections Neville Mus., Green Bay, Wis., Elmhurst Art Mus., Beverly Art Ctr. Mus., Chgo., Drury Lane Theater, Oakbrook, Ill., DuPage County Bar Assn., Wheaton, Ill., Pegasus Assocs., Chgo., Elk Grove Village Libr., Villa Park Libr., numerous pub. and pvt. collections; subject of numerous articles in newspapers, mags. Mem. Econ. Devel. Commn., Elmhurst; sec., exec. bd. Elmhurst Art Mus., 1998-99. Named Best of Show Beverly Arts Ctr., Chgo., 1999, DuPage Art League and Gallery, 1997, 98, 99, Elmhurst Artists Guild, 1997; recipient Grumbacher medallion and award of excellence No. Colo. Art Assn., 1998, Merit award Ill. Watercolor Exhbn., 1999, 1st place Christian Art Exhbn., College DuPage, 1997, 98; numerous other nat. and internat. awards. Signature mem. Water Color Soc. (Midwest, Ga., Mont., Pa., Tex., Ill., Niagara Frontier, We. Colo.), Taos Soc. Watercolorist; mem. Watercolor Soc. (Phila., Okla., W. Tex., La., Colo., Ky., Ala.), Art Inst. Chgo., Elmhurst Artists Guild (hon. life, pres. 1995-2000), Addison Art Guild, Chgo. Artists Coalition, Sr. Art Network, Oil Painters Am., DuPage Art League. Roman Catholic. Avocations: opera, German studies, museum studies, travel, books. Home: 550 Edgewood Ave Elmhurst IL 60126-4140 Studio: 320 Ardmore Villa Park IL 60181

SCHULTZ, FINN PEDER, paper company executive; b. Copenhagen, May 7, 1942; s. Albert and Helene Marie (Christensen) S.; m. Benedikte Braa Holm, July 7, 1991; children: Helene Sophie, Peter Broberg; 1 foster child, Frederik Bockhahn. Grad., Copenhagen Bus. U., 1961. Asst. gen. mgr. East Asiatic Co., Morovia, Liberia, 1964-67; br. mgr. IBM Corp., Copenhagen, 1980-81; ops. mgr. IBM Europe, Paris, 1982-85; mng. dir. Nashua Corp., Copenhagen, 1986-90, Gestetner PLC, Stockholm, 1990-91, Internat. Paper, Copenhagen, 1991—; mng. dir. Internat. Paper, Stockholm, 1992—, gen. mgr. Nordic, Denmark, Norway, Finland, Iceland, Sweden, 1993. Lt. Danish Army, 1961-63. Mem. Rotary. Avocations: tennis, golf, bridge. Home: 15 Digesmuttevej, 2970 Hörsholm Denmark Office: Internat Paper, Gadelandet 18, DK-2700 Bronshoj Denmark

SCHULTZ, HELGA, historian, educator; b. Schwerin, Germany, Aug. 16, 1941; d. Peter and Gerda (Grospitz) Grimm; m. Ludwig Schultz (div. 1976); children: Ulrike Himmelsbach, Anne Schützler. Staatsexamen, U. Rostock, Germany, 1964, Diplom Hist., 1965, PhD, 1969, Habilitation, 1978. Rschr. Acad. Scis., Berlin, 1977-91; prof. Europa U. Viadrina, Frankfurt V/Oder, Germany, 1993—; asst. U. Rostock, 1965-77. Author: Social and Political Conflicts in Rostock During the 18th Century, 1973, Rural Handicraft in the Transformation from Feudalism to Capitalism, 1984, Berlin 1650-1800 - Social History of a Residence, 1992, Artisans, Merchants and Bankers - European Economic History in Early Modern Times, 1997; editor: Frankfurt Border Region Studies, 1996—. Recipient Robert Kuczynski Preis award Jahrbuch Wirtschaftsgeschichte, 1983. Mem. Frankfurt Inst. for Transformation Studies. Home: Pl Vereinten Nationen 25, 10249 Berlin Germany Office: Europe U Viadrina, El Pb 1786, 15207 Frankfurt V/Oder Germany

SCHULTZ, JAN ROGER, computer scientist, software engineer; b. Detroit, Jan. 24, 1942; s. Pierce Schultz and Clara Ruth (Cantor) Diamant; m. Sue Diane Burton, Nov. 25, 1989. BS, U. Ill., Champaign, 1962; MS, U. Ill., 1964. Rsch. assoc. Dept. Medicine Case Western Res. U., Cleve., 1966-68; asst. prof, engring, bus. adminstrn. and computer sci. U. Vt., Burlington, 1976-78, rsch. assoc., dir. computer devel. PROMIS lab. Dept. Medicine, 1969-80; dir. programming and application devel. Promis Info, Systems, Inc., South Burlington, Vt., 1981-86; owner, prin. JRS Computer Cons., Burlington, 1987-90; dir. bus. and info. svc. Univ. Health Ctr., Inc., Burlington, Vt., 1991-94; pres., sr. v.p. engring. and devel. Step Soft, Inc., Burlington, 1994-97; dir. devel. IDX Systems Corp., 1997—; site visitor Can. Govt. Health, 1972, Ill. Regional Med. Program, Chgo., 1975; programmer, music mentor workstas., 1989. Contbr. chpts. to books. Mem. Burlington Econ. Devel. Coun., Burlington, 1982-83; chmn. Burlington Electric Commn., 1985, commr., 1984-90; bd. dirs. Burlington Revolving Loan Fund Bd., 1983-84; com. mem. in info. tech. workforce needs Nat. Acad. Scis., 1999—. Grantee Nat. Ctr. for Health Svcs. Rsch., 1967-75. Mem. Assn. Computing Machinery. Avocations: bicycling, cross country skiing, electronic music, reading. Home: 17 Bayview St Burlington VT 05401-4017 Office: 1400 Shelburne Rd Burlington VT 05403-7754

SCHULTZ, KLAUS, theater administrator; b. Bad Kissingen, Bavaria, Germany, May 20, 1947; s. Ernst and Maiken (v. Busch) S.; m. Corinna Ponto; children: Yorck Philip, David. Dramaturg Frankfurt (Germany) Opera House, 1973, 74-77; chief dramaturg State Opera, Munich, 1977-82; musikdramaturg Berlin Philharm. Orch., 1980-84; generalintendant Stadttheater, Aachen, Germany, 1984-92, Nationaltheater, Mannheim, Germany, 1992-96; staatsintendant Staatstheater am Gärtnerplatz, Munich, 1996—; exec. pres. Bayer Theaterakademie, 1999; lectr. Staat Hochschule, Frankfurt, 1975-77, U. Frankfurt, 1975-77, Acad. Bildenden Künste,

Munich, 1977-78, U. Heidelberg, Germany, 1993-96; prof. Hochschule Bremen, 2000. Contbr. articles to jours. in field. Office: Staatstheater, Gärtnerplatz 3, 80469 Munich Germany

SCHULTZ, PATRICIA BOWERS, vocal music educator, performer; b. Gomer, Ohio, Apr. 26, 1941; d. Paul Edward and Blodwen (Watkins) Bowers; m. Charles Albert Schultz; children: Todd Matthew, Vaughn Andrew, Cynthia Kristine. BS in Edn., French & Music, Miami U., Oxford, Ohio, 1963; MEd in Counseling, U. Ill., 1964; D of Musical Arts in Vocal Performance, U. Mo-Kansas City, 1984. Cert. K-12 music educator, Ohio, Mo.; cert. secondary sch. counseling, Ohio, Mo., ; cert. secondary sch. French, Ohio. Music educator, counselor Northmont Pub. Schs., Dayton, Ohio, 1964-66; French educator Bowling Green (Ohio) H.S., 1967-68; performer freelance USA and Europe, 1969—; instr. music and French Dickinson (N.D.) State U., 1972-74; instr. voice Ctrl. State U., Wilberforce, Ohio, 1975-76; dir. choral activities Savannah (Mo.) H.S., 1979-80; prof. music N.W. Mo. State U., Maryville, 1981—; contest judge MO. State H.S. Activities Assn., Columbia, 1976—; dir. music First United Meth. Ch., Maryville, 1977-88; tour mgr. Jenny Lind Ensemble, 1978—; musical dir. N.W. Mo. State U., Maryville, 1981—. Accomplishments in music include author, lead role in music drama Encore for Jenny Lind, 1976— (London Premiere 1992); conductor choral music Welsh Gymanfoedd Ganu, 1989— (Nat. Selection 1993); Coloratura soprano recitals and concerts throughout U.S.; soloist European tour Cin. Symphony, 1969; presentator Am. Assn. Higher Edn. Teaching Learning & Tech. Conf., 1997. Pres. Univ. Women, Maryville, 1978-79; first judge of vocal competition Nat. Glenn Miller Scholarship Competition, Clarinda, Iowa, 1992, 94; pres. Faculty Senate N.W. Mo. State U., 1993-95; organizer, charter mem. Mo. Assn. Faculty Senates, Springfield, Mo., 1993-94. Named Faculty Fellow Mo. Coordinating Bd. for Higher Edn., Jefferson City, 1997-98, Outstanding Alumnae Conservatory of Music, U. Mo.-Kansas City, 1990; grantee Mo. State Coun. on Arts, 1991-95. Mem. AAUW, Am. Assn. Higher Edn., Am. Coun. on Edn./Nat. Identification Program, Nat. Assn. Tchrs. Singing (Teacher of regional state and chpt. winners in Mo., Nebr. and eight state region 1986, 88, 90, 92, 97, 98), Am. Choral Dirs. Assn., Coll. Music Soc. Avocations: gardening, reading, travel. Home: 1004 W Cooper St Maryville MO 64468-2005 Office: NW Mo State Univ Dept Music 800 University Dr Maryville MO 64468-6015

SCHULTZ, WOLFRAM, neurobiologist, educator; b. Meissen, Germany, Aug. 27, 1944; arrived in Switzerland, 1977; s. Robert and Herta (Beegen) S.; m. Gerda Baumann, May 19, 1972; children: Johannes, Thomas, Carolina. MD, U. Heidelberg, Germany, 1972. Rsch. assoc. sect. neurobiology Max-Planck Inst. Biophys. Chemistry, Göttingen, Germany, 1973-75; rsch. asst. prof. lab. neurobiology dept. physiology SUNY, Buffalo, 1975-76; Swedish Med. Rsch. Coun. vis. scientist dept. histology Karolinska Inst., Stockholm, 1976-77; chef de Travaux Inst. Physiology, U. Fribourg, Switzerland, 1977-81, asst. prof., 1986-96, prof. neurophysiology, 1996—. Contbr. articles to profl. jours. Recipient Ellermann prize Swiss Socs. Neurology, Neurosurgery and Neuropathology, 1984, Theodore Ott prize Swiss Acad. Med. Sci., 1997. Mem. Internat. Basal Ganglia Soc. (councilor 1992-95, 98—), European Brain and Behavior Soc. (councilor 1996-99, pres. 2000—). Achievements include processing of reward in basal ganglia and frontal cortex. Office: U Fribourg, Inst Physiology, 1700 Fribourg Switzerland

SCHULTZE, HANS-PETER E.R., paleontology educator, researcher; b. Swinemünde, Usedom, Germany, Aug. 13, 1937; s. Erich and Irmgard (Quesseleit) S.; m. Renate Reif, Aug. 6, 1965 (div. 1980); children: Juergen, Sabine, Ulrike; m. Gloria E. Arratia Fuentes, Oct. 21, 1980. MS in Geology, U. Tübingen, Germany, 1962, PhD, 1965; Dr. habil., U. Göttingen, Germany, 1971. Postdoctoral fellow Naturhistoriska Riksmuseet, Stockholm, 1965-67; from asst. to assoc. prof. U. Göttingen, Germany, 1967-78; from asst. to assoc. prof. U. Kans., Lawrence, 1978-87, prof., 1987-94, chmn. dept. systems and ecology, 1988-90; dir., prof. dept. paleontology Mus. Natural History, Berlin, 1994-99, dir., 1999—; leader expdns. to Can. Arctic, 1975, 95, 97. Author: Dipnoi-Fossilium Catalogus, Pars 131, 1992; editor: (series) Handbook of Paleoichthylogy, 1978—; co-editor Origins of the Higher Groups of Tetrapods-Controversy and Consensus, 1991, Devonian Fishes and Plants of Miguasha, Quebec, Canada, 1996. Mem. Palaeontologische Gesellschaft, Soc. Vertebrate Paleontology, Soc. Sys. Biology. Avocations: Middle Age architecture, stamp collecting, hiking. Home: Türkenstrasse 17, D-13349 Berlin Germany Office: Mus Natural History, Invalidenstrasse 43, D-10115 Berlin Germany

SCHULTZE, JOACHIM WALTER, chemistry educator; b. Jena, Germany, Jan. 23, 1937. Habilitation, Freie U., West Berlin, 1972. Prof. phys. chemistry Freie U., West Berlin, 1972; ord. prof. Heinrich-Heine-Univ., Dûsseldorf, Fed. Republic Germany, 1979; dir. AGEF eV.-Inst. an der HHU Düsseldorf. Author over 300 sci. publs. in field of phys. chemistry and electrochemistry; editor: Gundlagen von Elektrodenreaktionen, 1986. Recipient fellowship Japanese Soc. for Promotion of Sci., Sapporo, 1989. Fellow Electrochem. Soc.; mem. F.D.P., Fed. European Chem. Soc. (mem. coun. 1992-99), Internat. Soc. Electrochemistry (pres.-elect 1993, pres. 1995-96). Office: Heinrich-Heine-U Universitätssr 1, Geb 26 32, D-40225 Dûsseldorf Germany

SCHULZ, EKKEHARD, business executive. Chmn. exec. bd. Thyssen Krupp AG; chmn. supervisory bd. Thyssen Krupp, Eisen-und Krupp Thyssen Stinless GmbH, Thyssen Krupp Materials and Svcs. AG, Thyssen Krupp; bd. dirs. Budd Co., Thyssen Inc.; mem. supervisory bds. Commerzbank AG, Hapag Lloyd AG, MAN AG, Energie AG, Strabag AG; pres. Eurofer; com. mem., bd. Wirtschaftsvereinigung Stahl, VDEh. Office: Thyssen Krupp AG, August Thyssen Str 1, 40211 Düsseldorf Germany*

SCHULZ, GEORG EBERHARD, biochemistry educator, researcher; b. Berlin, Aug. 24, 1939; s. Max and Helene S.; m. Elsa Schulz, Apr. 28, 1964; children: Annette, Dorothee, Sebastian. Dipl., U. Heidelberg, Germany, 1964, PhD, 1966, prof., 1979. Asst. U. Heidelberg, 1967; rsch. fellow Yale U., New Haven, Conn., 1967-68; rsch. assoc. Max Planck Inst., Heidelberg, 1969-73, ind. rschr., 1974-83; prof. biochemistry Albert Ludwigs U., Freiburg, Germany, 1984—. Mem. Deutsche Akademie Leopoldina. Office: Inst Organische Chemie Biochemie, Albertstr 21, 79104 Freiburg Germany

SCHULZ, GERHARD JOHANN ERNST, historian, educator; b. Sommerfeld, Germany, Aug. 24, 1924; s. Kurt Ernst Albert and Elise Johana (Dvorak) S.; m. Cornelia Anna Katharina Popitz, Nov. 29, 1952 (dec. Sept. 1987); children: Cornelius Gerhard, Johannes Heinrich. PhD, Free U., Berlin, 1952, Habilitation, 1960. Asst. Deutsche Hochschule für Politik, Berlin, 1952-55; sr. asst. Inst. for Polit. Sci. Free U. Berlin, 1955-60, head of history dept., 1960-62; prof. history U. Tübingen, Germany, 1962-90; prof. emeritus U. Tübingen, 1990—; dir. Seminar fur Zeitgeschichte, Tübingen, 1962-90; cons. mem. Kommission fur Geschichte des Parlamentarismus, Bonn, 1963-93, Wissenschaftlicher Beirat des Inst. f. Zeitgeschichte, 1983-93. Author: Das Zeitalter der Gesellschaft, 1969, Revolutionen und Friedensschlüsse 1917-1920, 1967, 6th edit., 1984, Swiss edit., 1969, English transl., Revolutions and Peace Treaties, 1917-1920, 1972, Zwischen Demokratie und Diktatur, 1963, 2d edit., 1987, 92, Faschimus-Nationalsozialismus. Versionen und theoretische Kontroversen, 1922-72, 1974, Aufstieg des Nationalsozialsozialismus, 1975, Einführung in die Zeitgeschichte, 1992; co-author: Die nationalsozialistische Machtergreifung, 1960, 3d edit., 1974. Pvt. Infantry, 1943-44.

SCHULZ, HOLGER FRITJOF, physiologist; b. Cologne, Germany, July 4, 1957; s. Heinz Helmut and Ruth Lieselotte (Klinke) S.; m. Anne Ulrike Hillebrecht, Mar. 20, 1992. MD, Albertus-Magnus U., Cologne, Germany, 1986; Habilitation, Ludwig-Maximilians U., Munich, Germany, 1996. Rsch. asst. Max-Planck Inst., Goettingen, Germany, 1984-88; anesthesiologist Albertus Magnus U., Cologne, Germany, 1988-89; rsch. assoc. Inst. Inhalation Biology Nat. Rsch. Ctr. for Environ. Health, Munich, Germany, 1989-94; dep. dir. inst. inhalation biology Nat. Rsch. Cen. for Environ. Health, Munich, 1995—; lectr. Ludwig-Maximilians U., Munich, 1996—. Co-Author: (book) Particle-Lung Interactions, 1999; contbr. articles to profl. jours. Mem. German Pneumol. Soc. (bd. dirs.), Internat. Soc. Aerosols in Medicine, European Respiratory Soc. Avocations: jogging, hiking, photography, music, bird-watching. Office: Nat Rsch Cen Environ/Health, Ingolstaedter Landstr 1, D-85758 Neuherberg Germany

SCHULZ, LAURA JANET, writer, retired secretary; b. Alba, Tex., Aug. 12, 1931; d. Joseph Clifton and Laura Oza (Carruth) English; m. Gordon Robert Schulz, Dec. 4, 1953; children: LeAnn Clarinda Schulz Barclay, Peggy Gaynell Schulz Lingbloom. Grad. h.s., Denison, Tex., 1948. Sec. history dept. Tex. Christian U., Ft. Worth, 1948-49; continuity editor Sta. KDSX, Denison, 1949-51; clk., typist Perrin AFB, Sherman, Tex., 1951-55; acctg. clk. England AFB, Alexandria, La., 1955; sec. Emile R. Jardine, CPA, Stockton, Calif., 1957-59; tchr. Little Meth. Pre-Sch., Lodi, 1968-69; sec. Heather, Sanguinetti, Caminata & Sakai, CPAs, Stockton, 1983-92; sec., feature writer, photographer Lodi (Calif.) Dist. C. of C., 1993-97. Author: Katy's Children, 1990, Little Rocky's True Adventures, 1991, Depot Days, 1999. Hon. life mem. Wesleyan Svc. Guild Trinity Meth. Ch., Denison, 1955—, Calif. Congress of PTA, 1984—; pres. PTA Needham Sch., Lodi, 1968-70; leader Camp Fire, Lodi, 1974-82; vol. advisor, tchr. Grapevine Newspaper Vinewood Sch., Lodi, 1974-82; tchr. First United Meth. Ch., Lodi, 1961-80, circle chair. Recipient Appreciation award Vinewood Sch., Lodi Unified Sch. Dist., 1974-82. Mem. Nat. League Am. Pen Women, Sierra Club. Democrat. Methodist. Avocations: photography, reading, walking, camping, nature. Home: 1910 W Tokay St Lodi CA 95242-3440

SCHŬLZ, LEO-CLEMENS, pathologist; b. Gŭttstadt, Germany, Aug. 22, 1923; s. Clemens and Anna (Hoenig) S.; m. Brigitte Meister, Mar. 20, 1958; children: Jan-Michael, Sabine. Approbation, Tierarztliche Hochschule, Hannover, Germany, 1952, Doctor summa cum laude, 1953, grad. in Edn., 1959; D (hon.), U. Cordoba, Spain, 1975, U. Gent, Belgium, 1977, Med. Sch. Hannover, 1982. Asst. Inst. Vet. Pathology, Hannover, 1952-60; prof. State U., Chile, 1961-63; dir. Inst. Vet. Pathology, Hannover, 1964-86; rector Tierarztliche Hochschule, 1968-70, head spl. team in rheumatoid diseases, 1968-78. Author: Two-phases Concept of Rheumatoid Inflammation, 1981, Biological Phenomena as Bridge to Art, 2000; editor: General Veterinary Pathology, 1980, ed edit., 1990, Special Veterinary Pathology, 1991; contbr. over 175 articles to profl. jours. Recipient Carol Nachman prize in rheumatology, Wiesbaden, Germany, 1981, Martin Lerche prize in comparative pathology, Nauheim, Germany, 1990. Mem. Comparative Neuropathology (corr. mem.), Deutsche Akademie der Naturforscher-Leopoldina, Halle, N.Y. Acad. Scis. Avocations: natural philosophy, drawing, alpinist. Home: 20a von Graevemeyerweg, D-30539 Hannover Germany

SCHULZ, MARTIN WILHELM, pharmacologist; b. Hamburg, Germany, Dec. 14, 1959. Degree in pharmacology, U. Hamburg, 1983, D in Natural Scis., 1988. Clin. pharmacist Hosp. St. Adolf-Stift, Reinbek, Germany, 1983-84; head drug info. Fed. Union German Assns. Pharmacists, Frankfurt, 1988—; vice chmn. Commn. on Drugs of German Pharmacists, Eschborn, 1991—; com. mem. Commn. on Processing Drugs in Neurology/Psychiatry, 1989-94. Author: Drug Profiles, 1991, Osteoporosis, 1991; editor, author: Self-Medication, 1992, Self-Therapy, 1994, 4th supplement, 1996-99, Pharmaceutical Care, 1999, (Health Base Found. award 1999); contbr. articles to profl. jours. Mem. AAAS, German Soc. Pharmacology and Toxicology, Am. Assn. Pharm. Scientists, Am. Coll. Clin. Pharm., Am. Coll. Clin. Pharmacology, Am. Soc. for Clin. Pharmacology and Therapeutics. Office: c/o ABDA, Carl-Mannich-Str 26, D-65760 Eschborn Germany

SCHULZ, MAX JOACHIM, physics educator; b. Nuremberg, Germany, May 17, 1939; s. Max E. and Gretel (Leder) S.; m. Telse Jebens, Aug. 26, 1938. Diploma in Physics, Tech. U., Braunschweig, Germany, 1964, D Natural Scis., 1966; Habilitation, U. Freiburg, Germany, 1972. Rsch. fellow U. Essex, Eng., 1967-69; rschr. Fraunhofer Gesellschaft, Freiburg, 1969-72, sect. head, 1972-78; prof., chair applied physics U. Erlangen, Germany, 1978—, dean math. and physics, 1995-97, vice rector, 2000—; vis. prof. Stanford U., 1982-83; cons. prof. Jiaotong U., Xian, China, 1980—; dist. vis. scientist Jet Propulsion Lab., Pasadena, Calif., 1988; sci. head ZAE Bayern, Erlangen, 1993—. Author, editor: (handbook series) Landolt-Börnstein Semiconductor Data, 1982, (textbook series) Applied Physics, 1985. Office: U. Erlangen Applied Physics, Staudtstr 7, D-91058 Erlangen Germany

SCHULZ, PABLO CARLOS, chemist, educator; b. Bahia Blanca, Argentina, July 9, 1943; s. Fernando Rodolfo and Berta (Becker) S.; m. Marta Susana Curvetto, Sept. 21, 1971; children: Pablo Gaston, Erica Patricia, Eduardo Nicolas. B, Coll. Nat., Bahia Blanca, 1962; lic. chemistry, U. Nat. Del Sur, Bahia Blanca, 1969, lic. biochemistry, 1970, D in Chemistry, 1977. Asst. prof. U. Nat. del Sur, Bahia Blanca, 1976-88, assoc. prof., 1988-91, titular prof., 1991—; asst. prof. U. Tech. Nat., Bahia Blanca, 1984-87; prof. officers Sch. Argentine Navy, Puerto Belgrano, 1980-86; vis. prof., rschr. U. de Guadalajara, Mex., 1988-90, 96, 98; chief dept. rsch. Univ. Inst. Naval and Maritime Studies. Author: Espectroscopia Infrarroja, 1990, Surfactantes, 1990, Seguridad en Laboratorios, 1999; contbr. articles to profl. jours. Lt. Argentine Navy, 1977-87. Mem. Assn. Argentina Para la Investigacion Fisicoquimica, Am. Chem. Soc. Democrat. Roman Catholic. Avocations: archeology, history. Home: Alvear 147, 8000 Bahia Blanca Argentina Office: U Nat del Sur, Av Alem 1253, 8000 Bahia Blanca Argentina

SCHULZ, RAINER MARIA, physician, clinical pharmacologist; b. Kelheim, Bavaria, Fed. Republic Germany, Sept. 16, 1955. MD, U. Tübingen, Fed. Republic of Germany, 1981; postgrad. in Clin. Pharmacology, U. Tübingen, 1984-88. Diplomate German Bd. Clin. Pharmacology. Instr., staff rsch. scientist Inst. Pharmacology, U. Tübingen, 1984-85; staff physician Human Pharmacology Inst. CIBA-GEIGY Corp., Tübingen, 1985-88; rsch. scientist CIBA-GEIGY Corp., Summit, N.J., 1988-90; sr. physician CIBA-GEIGY Corp., Tübingen, Germany, 1990-91; physician clin. pharmacology Hoffmann-LaRoche, Basel, Switzerland, 1991-94; head Inst de Pharmacologie Clinique, Strasbourg, France, 1994-99; gen. mgr. Quintiles, Freiburg, Germany, 1999—. Capt. German Army Med. Corps, 1982-84. Fellow Royal Coll. Physicians U.K. (faculty of pharm. medicine), N.Y. Acad. Scis., Am. Coll. Clin. Pharmacology, German Assn. Pharmacologist and Toxicologists, German Assn. Clin. Pharmacology.

SCHULZ, RALPH-HARDO, mathematician, educator; b. Metz, France, Sept. 15, 1942; s. Carl Conrad and Auguste L. (Terkatz) S. DiplMath, U. Mainz, Germany, 1967, DrRerNat, 1968. Tchr. Gymnasium Boppard, 1969; mem. faculty U. Tuebingen, Germany, 1969-74; prof. math. and math. edn. Free U. Berlin, 1974—. Author: Codierungstheorie, 1991, Repetitorium Mathematik, 1994; editor Math. Aspekte d.angewandten Informatik, 1994. Studienstiftung des Deutschen Volkes grantee. Mem. German Math. Soc., Berlin Math. Soc. Office: II Math Inst Free U Berlin, Arnimallee 3, Berlin 14195, Germany

SCHULZ, RITA, space scientist; b. Dortmund, Germany, Mar. 13, 1961; arrived in The Netherlands, 1997; d. Edmund E.F. and Wally A. Gengalaiti S.; m. Joachim A. Stüwe, Oct. 18, 1991; children: Viviane, Michael. Diploma in Physics, Ruhr U., Bochum, Germany, 1987; Dr.rer.nat., Ruhr U., Bochumlger, 1991, Diploma in Chemistry, 1991. Rsch. asst. Forschungez., Julich, Germany, 1988, RUB, Bochum, 1988-91; European Space Agy. fellow U. Md., College Park, 1992-93; rsch. asst. MPAE, Lindau, Germany, 1994-96; space scientist European Spage Agy./ESTEC, Noordwijk, The Netherlands, 1997—; mem. rev. panel NASA, Washington, 1993, ESO, OPC, Garching, Germany, 1996-98, 99—, European Space Agy., Paris, 1996, dep. project scientist, Rosetta, Noordwijk, 1997—. Contbr. articles to profl. jours. Mem. Am. Astron. Soc. (divsn. for planetary sci.), European Astron. Soc. Office: ESA Space Sci Dept, Keplerlaan 1, 2200 AG Noordwijk The Netherlands

SCHULZ, WILFRIED, educator; b. Schwenningen, Fed. Republic Germany, Sept. 9, 1939; s. Wilhelm and Eugenie (Mueller) S.; m. Ursula Schulz, Oct. 22, 1965 (dec. Mar. 1989); children: Ralph Jimmy, Mirjam Susanne. Dipl. V(olks)w., U. Tuebingen, 1965; PhD, U. Calif., Berkeley, 1966; Dr.rer.pol., U. Freiburg. Univ. asst. U. Freiburg, 1965-75; univ. prof. U. Bundeswehr, 1975—. Author: Steuerwirkungsvergleiche, Mikroökònomie, 4 vols., Verbraucherverhalten, Mathematik für Wirtschaftswissenschaftler, 8th edit.; editor: Struktur und Dynamik der Wirtschaft, Theories of Regional Competition. With mil. Home: Sauerbruchweg 2, 85521 Ottobrunn/Munich Germany Office: Werner Heisenberg-Weg 39, 85577 Neubiberg/Munich Germany

SCHULZE, ANDREAS J., pharmaceutical company executive; b. Stuttgart, Germany, Apr. 11, 1962; arrived in Switzerland, 1996; s. Friedrich and Marianne (Sribe) S.; m. Karin Lobeck, Nov. 4, 1995. Diploma in biology, U. Stuttgart-Hohenheim, 1990; PhD, Tech. U. Munich, 1993; indsl. engr., Akad Bus. Sch., Zurich, Switzerland, 1999. Postdoctoral fellow Pasteur Inst., Paris, 1994-95; rsch. sci. postdoctoral Marion Merrell Dow Rsch., Strasbourg, France, 1995-96; group leader R&D Pentapharm Ltd., Basel, Switzerland, 1996-99, v.p. R&D, 1999—. Contbr. articles to profl. jours.; patentee in field. Mem. Internat. Soc. Thrombosis and Haemostasis, Gesellschaft fur Thromosis and Haemostaseforsdung, Gesellschaft Deutscher, Chemiker. Avocations: literature, classical music, scuba diving. Office: Pentapharm Ltd, Engelgasse 109, 4002 Basel Switzerland

SCHULZE, ERIC WILLIAM, lawyer, legal publications editor, publisher; b. Libertyville, Ill., July 8, 1952; s. Robert Carl and Barbara (Mayo) S. BA, U. Tex., 1973, JD, 1977. Bar: Tex. 1977, U.S. Dist. Ct. (we. dist.) Tex. 1987, U.S. Ct. Appeals (5th cir.) 1987, U.S. Dist. Ct. (ea. and so. dists.) Tex. 1988, U.S. Dist. Ct. (no. dist.) Tex. 1989, U.S. Supreme Ct. 1989; bd. cert. civil appellate law Tex. Bd. Legal Specialization, 1990—. Rsch. asst. U. Tex., Austin, 1978; legis. aide Tex. Ho. of Reps., Austin, 1979-81; editor Tex. Sch. Law News, Austin, 1982-85; assoc. Hairston, Walsh & Anderson, Austin, 1986-87; ptnr. Walsh, Anderson, Brown, Schulze & Aldridge, Austin, 1988—, mng. ptnr., 1993—; editor Tex. Sch. Adminstrs. Legal Digest, Austin, 1986-92, co-pub., 1991—, mng. editor, 1992—. Editor: (legal reference books) Texas Education Code Annotated, 1982-85; editl. adv. com. West's Edn. Law Reporter, 1996—. Del. Tex. State Democratic Conv., 1982, Travis County Dem. Conv., 1982, 84, 86. Recipient Merit award for pubs. Internat. Assn. Bus. Communicators-Austin br., 1983, Merit award for authorship Coll. of State Bar Tex., 1992. Mem. Fed. Bar Assn., Am. Bar Assn., Tex. Bar Assn., Travis County Bar Assn., Bar Assn. of 5th Cir., Defense Rsch. Inst., Nat. Council Sch. Attys., Tex. Council Sch. Attys., Edn. Law Assn., Toastmasters (pres. Capital City chpt. 1995). Home: 3416 Mount Bonnell Cir Austin TX 78731-5745 Office: Walsh Anderson Brown Schulze & Aldridge PO Box 2156 Austin TX 78768-2156

SCHULZE, JUERGEN HELMUT, engineering executive; b. Brockwitz, Germany, June 16, 1939; s. Helmut Bruno and Marianne (Kowalski) S.; m. Barbara Rueger; children: Henrik, Eric. BSME, Coll. Engring., Esslingen, 1963; MBA, Columbia U., 1972. Sales mgr. Worthington Corp., Harrison, N.J., 1963-67; sr. cons. Peat, Marwick, Mitchell & Co., N.Y.C., 1968-72; gen. mgr. Rank Xerox, Dusseldorf, Germany, 1973-81; mng. dir. Lonza Werke, Waldshut, Germany, 1982-91; chmn., CEO Deutz motor, Cologne, Germany, 1991-99; prof. mktg. U. Wuppertal, Germany, 1982—; bd. dirs. No. Tech. Corp., Mpls., Kirloskar-Deutz, Pune, India, Deutz Corp., Atlanta, KHD Deutz Ltd., U.K.; chmn. Helmut Schulze GmbH, Saarbrucken, Germany. Pres. Support Orgn. Free Dem. Party, Bonn, 1983—; founding mem. Children Aids Found., Dusseldorf, 1986; mem. adv. bd. Handelshoch-Schule, Leipzig. Mem. INSEAD Alumni Orgn. Avocation: golf. Home: Habichtweg 2, 40670 Meerbusch Germany Office: Helmut Schulze GmbH, Hasichtweg 2, D 40670 Meerbusch Germany

SCHULZE, MARTIN SAMUEL PAUL, English and American studies educator; b. Kohlfurt-Dorf, Silesia, Germany, June 11, 1928; s. Alfred and Hildegard Anna (Malz) S.; m. Karin Ursula Brinkmann, Sept. 25, 1954; 1 child, Rainer Martin. Staatsexamen, U. Halle, 1951, DrPhil, 1955. Cert. secondary sch. tchr. English and Russian. Referent adminstr. for lit. and pub. affairs East Berlin, 1952-55; polit. prisoner East Germany, 1955-60; students' counsellor Internat. Union of Social Work, Frankfurt, Germany, 1961-63; journalist Frankfurter Rundschau and several radio cos., 1961—; prof., dirs. Inst. U. Giessen, 1970-72; full prof. U. Kassel, Fed. Republic Germany, 1972—, dean, 1983-84; mem. commn. Wissenschaftstrat, Bonn, Federal Republic Germany, 1976-78; guest prof. U. Wis., 1984-85, Radford (Va.) U., 1988, 91; acad. counseler, guest prof. reconstn. Martin Luther U., Halle-Wittenberg, 1991-94. Author: Ways of American Literature, 1968, Literary Criticism Alexander Puschkin, 1963, History of American Literature, 1999; editor: American Short Stories, 1957; co-editor: Kasseler Arbriten fur Sprache und Literatur, 1973—, Festschrift Tangenten, 1996. Congress for Freedom of Culture scholar, Paris, 1961; named Hon. Citizen, City of New Britain, 1985. Mem. Anglistentag, Deutsche Gesellschart für Amerikastudien, European Assn. for Am. Studies, Lions Club (mem. Cabinet for Student Esch. with U.S.). Home: Kohlenstr 63, D-3500 Kassel Hessen, Germany Office: U Kassel, Georg-Forster-Strasse 3, D-3500 Kassel Hessen, Germany

SCHULZE-HAGENEST, DETLEF, physicist, researcher; b. Hamburg, Germany, Sept. 13, 1947; s. Rolf and Martina (Reissenberger) S.-H.; m. Elisabeth Kaiser, June 8, 1973; children, Till, Felix. Diploma, U. Hamburg, 1974; PhD, U. Kaiserslautern, Germany, 1980. Tchr. physics and chemistry Hamburg Eidelstedt H.S., 1974-75; mem. staff R&D, Pelikan Info. Tech., Hamburg, 1980-82, dir. R&D,, 1982-83; mgr. R&D electronic printing techs. BASF Lacke & Farben AG, Stuttgart, Germany, 1983-88; mgr. R&D spl. chems. Michael Huber Munich GmbH, Kirchheim, Germany, 1988-99; sr. engr. advanced tech. NexPress GmbH, Kiel, Germany, 1999—; session chmn. 9th Internat. Congress Advances in Non-Printing Technology, Japan, 1993. Contbr. prof. articles to sci. pubs. including Symposium of Atomic Spectroscopy, others. Bd. dirs. Waldorf Sch., Ismaning, Germany, 1992-99. Mem. Soc. Image Sci. and Tech. Achievements incldue 5 patents and 4 patents pending in field of materials for electrophotography. Office: NexPress GmbH, Siemenswall, 24107 Kiel Germany

SCHULZKE, JÖRG-DIETER, gastroenterologist, educator; b. Berlin, Oct. 9, 1957; s. Bodo and Helga (Reichert) S.; 1 child, Barbara. MD, Free U., Berlin, 1983. Rsch. asst. clin. physiology Berlin, 1982-83, rsch. asst. biochemistry and molecular biology, 1984-85, rsch. asst. internal medicine, 1986-91, faculty dept. medicine, 1992—; dozent dept. medicine, 1991; sabbatical dept. medicine E. Carolina U., 1989-90; bd. dirs. Sonnenfeld-Stiftung, Berlin. Mem. Deutsche Gesellschaft für Verdauungs und Stoffwechselkrankheiten, Deutsche Physiologische Gesellschaft. Avocations: tennis, golf. Office: Med Klinik I UKBF, FU Berlin Hindenburgdamm 30, 12200 Berlin Germany

SCHULZRINNE, HENNING G., computer science educator; b. Cologne, Germany. PhD, U. Mass., 1992. Assoc. prof. Columbia U., N.Y.C., 1996—. Mem. IEEE. Office: Dept Computer Sci Columbia Univ New York NY 10027

SCHUMACHER, MICHAEL, race car driver; b. Huerth-Hermuehlheim, Germany, Jan. 3, 1969. Race car driver, 1990—. Winner F3 German Championship, 1990, Belgian Grand Prix, 1992, 95, 96, 97, Portuguese Grand Prix, 1993, San Marino Grand Prix, 1994, Hungarian Grand Prix, 1994, Drivers' World Championship, 1994, 95, Monaco Grand Prix, 1994, 95, 97, French Grand Prix, 1994, 95, 97, Pacific Grand Prix, 1994, 95, Brazilian Grand Prix, 1994, 95, European Grand Prix, 1994, 95, Spanish Grand Prix, 1995, 96, Japanese Grand Prix, 1995, 97, German Grand Prix, 1995, Italian Grand Prix, 1996. *

SCHUMACHER, PAUL MAYNARD, lawyer; b. Columbus, Nebr., Apr. 4, 1951; s. Maynard Mathew and Rita Bell (Jarosz) S.; m. Michele Suzanne Gassé, June 26, 1976; children: Nicole Suzanne, Kristen Paulette. AA, Platte Coll., 1971; BS, Fort Hays U., 1973; JD, Georgetown U., 1976. Bar: Fla. 1976, Nebr. 1977, U.S. Dist. Ct. Nebr. 1977. Mem. staff U.S. Senate, Washington, 1974-76; sole practice Miami, Fla. and Columbus, 1976—; v.p. Community Lottery Systems, Inc., Columbus, 1990-92, pres., 1992—; v.p. Megavision Corp., Columbus, 1976—. Treas. prin. Rep. campaign com. U.S. Senate Candidate, Lincoln, Nebr., 1978-79; atty. Platte County, Columbus, 1979-87; chmn. Platte county Reps., 1988-94; mem. Nebr. Rep. State Ctrl. Com., 1994-96, 2000—; CEO Lotto Nebr., 1992—; CEO Cmty. Internet Sys., Inc., 1995-98, bd. dirs., 1995—. Mem. Nebr. Bar Assn., Fla. Bar Assn., Platte County Bar Assn. (pres. 1992-93), Internat. Platform Assn., N.Am. Gaming Regulators Assn. (internat. gaming com.), Rotary, Elks. Roman Catholic. Avocation: physics. Home: 6255 Meyer Rd Columbus NE 68601-8044 Office: PO Box 122 Columbus NE 68602-0122

SCHUMACHER, RALF, race car driver; b. Hürth-Hermülheim, Germany, June 30, 1975. Race car driver, 1993—. 2d pl. finisher ADAC Formula Jr., 1993, 3d pl. German Formula, 1994-95, champion Formula Nippon, 1996. *

SCHUMACHER, STEFAN, medical educator; b. Arnsberg, Germany, June 19, 1964; s. Alfons and Sigrid (Berghoefer) S. MD, U. Mainz, Germany, 1991. Resident U. Hosp., Mainz, Germany, 1991-94, 95-96, Marien Hosp., Arnsberg, Germany, 1994-95; head neuro-urology lab. U. Hosp., Mannheim, Germany, 1996-97; assoc. prof. U. Hosp., Bonn, Germany, 1998—; cons. and presenter in field. Author: Innovations in Urologic Surgery, 1997, Ausgewaehlte urologische Techniken, 1997, Advances in Bladder Research, 1999; contbr. articles to profl. jours.; patentee in field. Recipient 3d prize Exptl. Urological Soc., Germany, 1998; Med. Rsch. fellow Hyogo Coll. Medicine, Japan, 1993. Mem. German Urological Assn. (Bard prize 1997), European Urological Assn., Internat. Continence Soc. Roman Catholic. Office: U Bonn, Sigmund Freud Str 25, 53105 Bonn Germany

SCHUMACHER, STEPHEN JOSEPH, lawyer; b. L.A., Feb. 5, 1942; s. Joseph Charles and Theresa Isabel (Flynn) S.; m. Jeanne Keller Schumacher, Sept. 29, 1990; children by previous marriage: William Scott, Stacey Elizabeth. AB, U. So. Calif., 1963; JD, Hastings Coll. Law, U. Calif., 1967; LLM in Taxation, NYU, 1969. Bar: Calif. 1968. Assoc. Stephens, Jones, LaFever & Smith, L.A., 1967-68, Wenke, Kemble & Burge, 1970-73; ptnr. Wenke, Taylor, Schumacher & Evans, Santa Ana, Calif., 1974-79, Schumacher & Evans, Costa Mesa, Calif., 1979-87; sole practice Orange County, Calif., 1987—; instr. real estate taxation U. Calif.-Irvine, 1980-83. Bd. dirs. Orange County Opportunities Industrialization Ctr., 1973-75. Mem. ABA, Calif. Bar Assn., Orange County Bar Assn., Balboa Bay Club. Office: 4340 Campus Dr Ste 100 Newport Beach CA 92660-1812

SCHUMANN, DEBRAOH KAY, construction company executive; b. Tomball, Tex., Apr. 22, 1957; d. Erwin Herman Joe and Agnes Marie Mazac Seydler; m. Jerome A. Schumann, July 11, 1970; children: Richard Peter, Jerome Jr. AS, San Antonio Coll., 1994. Owner Double-D Cedar Yard, New Braunfels, Tex., 1983, Schumann Constrn., New Braunfels, 1945—. Inventor auto windshields, children's gameboards. Recipient Editor's Choice award Nat. Libr. Poetry, 1998. Mem. The McNay Arts, Toastmasters, Women's Power Group for CEO's, NAFE. Avocations: deer hunting, writing mysteries, golfing, fishing, hiking. Home: 403 River Bend Dr New Braunfels TX 78130-8964

SCHUMANN, HANS, research chemist; b. Muelheim, Germany, June 6, 1962; s. Herbert and Anna Sophie (Schulze) S.; m. Iris Rischmueller, Aug. 18, 1990. Diplom.Chem., U. Duisburg, 1988; Dr.rer.nat., U. Bielefeld, 1990. Rsch. chemist Bayer AG, Leverkusen, Germany, 1990-91; habilitand Fakultaet f. Chemie ACI-U. Bielefeld, 1991-92; coord. R & D era Beschichtung, Stolzenau, Germany, 1993—. Author: Gmelin Handbook of Inorganic Chemistry: Organoiron, vols. 15, 16b, 17, Organomolybdenum, vols. 6, 7, 8, 9, 12, 13/. Grantee Studienstiftung d. Deutschen Volkes, 1986-88, Fonds d. Chem. Industrie, 1988-90; recipient Heinz-Meier-Leibnitz prize BMFT, 1991, Liebig stipend, 1991-92. Office: era Beschichtung GmbH & Co, era Beschichtung GmbH & Co, Grosse Brinkstrasse 13, D 31592 Stolzenau Germany

SCHUMANN, NILS, Olympic athlete. Winner Gold medal 800 meter Sydney, 2000. Office: European Athletic Assn, Postfach 710316, Frankfurt 60493, Germany*

SCHUMPE, ADRIAN, chemistry educator; b. Bevensen, Germany, May 14, 1953; s. Alexander and Elisabeth (Löffler) S.; m. Gabriele Mönsters, Aug. 25, 1978; children: Inga, Birga. Diploma in chemistry, U. Hannover, Germany, 1978, D Natural Sci., 1981; Habilitation in Chem. Engring., U. Oldenburg, Germany, 1988. Rschr. U. Hannover, 1978-81, U. Oldenburg, 1982-86, Soc. for Biotech. Rsch. mbH, Braunschweig, Germany, 1986-91; rsch. assoc. U. Pitts., 1981-82; prof. chemistry U. Erlangen, Nürnberg, Germany, 1991-94, Tech. U. Braunschweig, 1994—. Editor: Three-Phase Sparged Reactors, 1996; patentee for method of isolating polysaccharide producing bacteria. Grantee Deutsche Forschungsgemeinschaft, 1985. Mem. Deutsche Gesellschaft fur Chemisches Apparatwesen, Chemische Technik und Biotechnologie, Gesellschaft Deutscher Chemiker, Gesellschaft Verfahrenstechnik und Chemieingenieurwesen/Verein Deutscher Ingenieure. Office: Tech U Inst for Chem Tech, Hans-Sommer Strasse 10, D-38106 Braunschweig Germany

SCHUMPELICK, VOLKER, surgeon, educator; b. Jena, Germany, Oct. 12, 1944; s. Walter and Antje Schumpelick; m. Gabriele Dilthey, 1971; 1 child, Felix. MD (hon.), U. Hamburg, Germany; MD, U. Moscow. Resident, surgeon, prof. surgery Univ. Clinic Hamburg, Germany, 1971-85; dir., chmn. surg. clinic U. Aachen, Germany, 1985—. Author 22 books, 16 sci. videos; presenter in field; contbr. numerous articles to profl. jours. Recipient Hermann-Kümmel prize, 1975, Hamburgische Wiss Stiftung prize, 1976, Doktor-Martini prize, 1976, Förderpreis Intensivmedizin Deutsch Ges. f. Chirurgie, 1992. Mem. ACS, Internat. Gastrosurg. Club, Deutsche Gesellschaft fur Chirurgie (Exptl. sect. 1980—), Nordwestdeutsche Gesellschaft fur Chirurgie, Berufsverband Deutscher Chirurgen, Hamburgische Krebsgesellschaft, Niederrheinisch-Westfalische Vereinigung der Chirurgen, Vereinigung der belgisch niederlandisch deutschen Grenzland-Chirurgen, Soc. Internat. Chirurgie, Berliner Chirurgische Gesellschaft. Office: Univ Aachen Surg Clinic, Pauwelsstreet, 52057 Aachen Germany

SCHUN, LAURENT ANDRÉ, export company executive; b. Chatenay-Malabry, France, Mar. 29, 1966; s. Arsene and Claudine (Nicolas) Schun; m. Francesca Geilager, June 4, 1994; 1 child, Laura. B, Lycee Passy-Buzenval, Rueil-Malmaison, France, 1984; MBA, Ecole Supérieure Scis. Econs. Commls., Cergy-Pontoise, France, 1987. Product mgr. Cusenier, Paris, 1989-92; sr. product mgr. Ricard, Marseilles, France, 1992-94, export area manager, 1996-98; export dir. PR Larios, Madrid, 1998—. Avocations: travel, cinema, wines, tennis. Office: PR Larios, Arturo Soria 97, 28027 Madrid Spain

SCHÜNGEL, PAUL, retired theology educator; b. Bergheim/Erft, Germany, May 24, 1938. Theology educator Marienschule Euskirchen, Bonn, Germany, 1966-69, Gymnasium Fredien, 1969-76, Gymnasium Rheinbach, 1976-86; ret., 1986. Author: Schule des Betens, 1974, revised edition, 1988, Kraft des Ursprungs, 1992; contbr. articles to scholarly and profl. jours. Home: Waldauweg 20, D-53127 Bonn Germany

SCHUNICHT, SHANNON ANTHONY, retired army officer, politician; b. Miami, Nov. 17, 1961; s. Wayne Anthony Schunicht and Suzanne Chatin (Tindell) Fast. *While in the Army, Mr. Schunicht was involved in a mid-air collision rendering him unconscious for three weeks. Everything had to be relearned, as nursing actions were reported having been displayed on awakening from the extended unconsciousness (19 days). Studies while in recovery brought about some pragmatic discoveries to compensate for the residual memory deficits. The most valuable discovery was having each vowel represent a mathematical sign, i.e. "A" multiplication implying "@"; "O" for division implying "over"; "I" for subtraction implying "minus"; "U" for addition implying "plus"; and "E" implying "equals". Most constants and variables are consonants, e.g. C=speed of light, R=time/rate variable.* BA in Philosophy/Polit. Sci., Fla. State U., 1983; BS in Microbiology, Tex. A&M U., 1994, BA in Biology, 1994. Lic. real estate agt., Tex. With U.S. Army, 1983-90. Mem. Internat. Leprosy Assn., Am. Soc. for Microbiology. E-mail: shannon@alpha1.net. Home: 309 1st St College Station TX 77840-1231 Office: Maroon and While Properties Ste B 209 University Dr East College Station TX 77840-1793

SCHUNKE, HILDEGARD HEIDEL, accountant; b. Indpls., Nov. 24, 1948; d. Edwin Carl and Hildegard Adelheid (Baumbach) S. BA, Ball State U., Muncie, Ind., 1971, MA in German/English, 1973, MA in Acctg., 1975. CPA, Ind., Calif. Exch. tchg. grad. asst. Padagogische Hochschule, Germany, 1971-72; tchg.ing grad. asst. in German and acctg. Ball State U., 1972, 74-75, asst. prof. acctg., 1975-78; investing rschr. Family Partnership, Muncie, 1977-83; staff acct. Am. Lawn Mower Co., Muncie, 1984-88, G&J Seiberlich, CPAs, St. Helena, Calif., 1988-89, R.A. Gullotta, MBA, CPA, Sonoma, Calif., 1989-90; plant acct. Napa (Calif.) Pipe Corp., 1990—. ESOL instr. Napa County Project Upgrade, 1988-92; ticketing and refreshments com. North Bay Philharm. Orch., Napa, 1988—, North Bay Wind Ensemble, Napa, 1988— ; mem. TC 207 Tag Team. Mem. AICPA, Calif. Soc. CPAs (continuing edn. instr. Redwood City 1990, bd. dirs. East Bay chpt. 1998-2000), Inst. Internal Auditors, Environ. Auditing Roundtable, Am. Soc. for Quality. Avocations: gardening, transcribing, translating and reading German. Home: 1117 Devonshire Ct Suisun City CA 94585-3343 Office: Napa Pipe Corp 1025 Kaiser Rd Napa CA 94558-6257

SCHUPP, RONALD IRVING, clergyman, missionary, civil and human rights leader; b. Syracuse, N.Y., Dec. 10, 1951; s. George August and Shirley Louise (Mitchell) S. Ordained ministry, Old Country Ch., 1972; ordained Bapt. ministry, 1976; cert., Moody Bible Inst., 1986, 1988; advanced cert., Evang. Tng. Assn., 1992; cert., Emmaus Bible Coll., 1996, 97. Missionary, asst. pastor The Old Country Ch. Inc., Chgo., 1972-76; missionary Solid Rock Bapt. Ch., Chgo., 1976-89, Marble Rock Missionary Bapt. Ch., Chgo., 1990—; asst. dir. Uptown Community Orgn., Chgo., 1974-76; dir. Chgo. Action Ctr., 1978-80; bd. dirs. West Englewood United Orgn./Clara's House Shelter, 1991-95 (Recipient Appreciation award, 1992), assoc. chaplain, 1991-95; mem. steering com. 1st Congl. Dist. Ministerial Assn., Chgo., 1993-95, chair housing com., 1993-95; missionary Jesus People, U.S., 1997—, percussionist Worship Band, 1997—. Contbr. articles and poems to periodicals; peace art represented in permanent collections at Chgo. Hist. Soc., Peace Mus., Chgo., Smithsonian Instn. Mem. Nat. Coalition for the Homeless, 1991—, Nat. Union of the Homeless, 1992—, Chgo. Coalition for the Homeless, 1988-99, vol. organizer, 1988-94, mem. empowerment adv. com., 1991-94; mem. Homeless on the Move for Equality, 1990-92, bd. dirs. 1991-92; mem. Chgo. Peace Coun., 1984-87; active Pledge of Resistance, Chgo., 1985-90; rep. Chgo. Welfare Rights Orgn., 1986-88; activist Chgo. Clergy and Laity Concerned, 1981-87; founding mem. People's Campaign for Jobs, Housing and Food, Chgo., 1992-98, chaplain, 1992-98; founding mem., missionary People's Ministry Without Walls, Chgo., 1993-98; rep. Lakota Nat. Organizing Com., 1993—, Lakota Nat. Govt., 1993—, League of Indigenous Sovereign Nations of Western Hemisphere, 1993—; supporting mem. Autonomous Chgo. chpt. Am. Indian Movement of Ill., 1994—, Chgo. Native Am. Urban Indian Retreat, 1994—; pres., co-founder Citizens Taking Action, Chgo., 1995-97, chair, steering com., 1995-97, 99—, mem. action com., bd. dirs., 1995—; organizer Chgo. People's Conv. Coalition, 1996; mem. steering com. Raising Issues to Demand Everyone's Right to Svc., 1997-98; mem. Ams. Disabled for Attendant Programs Today, 1997—, affiliate, Radio Emergency Associated Communications Teams internat. (REACT), 2000—. Recipient letter of commendation Chgo. Fire Dept., 1983, proclamations Mayor Richard M. Daley, Chgo., 1991, 92, 93, 94, 97, 99, Mayor Joan Barr, Evanston, Ill., 1993, Mayor Lorraine H. Morton, Evanston, 1994; commendation resolution Chgo. City Coun., 1993, South African elections vigil support resolution Chgo. City Coun., 1994, Tibet vigil support resolution Chgo. City Coun., 1999, 00; tribute in congl. record Congressman Bobby L. Rush, 1993, Sen. Carol Moseley Braun, 1994, Congressman Luis V. Gutierrez, 1998, 00; initiated Wa-kin-ya-wicha-ho Thunder Voice by trad. Lakota Elders, 1993; Appreciation Cert. Nuclear Energy Info. Svc., 2000; portfolio on file at Smithsonian Instn., Nat. Civil Rights Mus., UN Libr., Vatican Libr., Nat. Liberation Archives. Mem. SCLC (life), Operation Push, Inc. (citation 1990), NAACP (life), ACLU, Chgo. Free South Africa (steering com. 1984-94), Am. Indian Movement (rep., nat.), Internat. Campaign for Tibet, Tibetan Alliance Chgo., North Am. Shortwave Assn. Democrat. Avocations: poetry, radio, kayaking. Home and Office: 6412 N Hoyne Ave Apt 3A Chicago IL 60645-5655

SCHUPP, VOLKER, literature educator; b. Karlsruhe, Germany, Feb. 12, 1934; s. Josef and Maria (Herr) S.; m. Renate Richter, Aug. 9, 1967; children: Stefan, Christian, Bettina. PhD, U. Freiburg, Germany, 1962; PhD (hon.), U. Jassy, Romania, 1994. Asst. U. Freiburg, 1963-69, prof., 1978—, rector, 1983-87; prof. U. Bochum, 1974-78. Author: Siebenzahl u Bauform, 1964; Studien zu Williram v. Ebersberg, 1978; editor: Deutsches Rätselbuch, 1972, Emil Gött, 1992, Ywain and Schloss Rodenegg, 1996; co-editor: Poetica Zeitschrift Für Sprach-und Literaturwissenschaft. Office: Albert Ludwigs U, Werthmannpl, D-79085 Freiburg Germany

SCHUPP, WILFRIED JOHANNES, physiatrist, neurorehabilitation specialist; b. Saulgau, Germany, Nov. 27, 1955; s. Albert and Klara Johanna (Bautz) S.; m. Centa Maria Hoesle, Mar. 28, 1984,. MD, U. Ulm, 1981. Diplomate Neurology and Psychiatry, Bavarian Chamber of Physicians, 1987, Social medicine, 1989, Physiatrist, 1993. Asst. mem. Psychiatric Clinic Reichenau, Konstanz, Germany, 1981-82; mem. Max Planck Inst. Psychiatry, Munich, Germany, 1982-84, Dept Neurology, Fachklinik Enzensberg, Füssen, Germany, 1984-86; med. vice head dept. neurology Fachklinik Enzenberg, Füssen, 1987-90, med. head dept. neurology, 1990-96; mem. Neurological Univ. Clinic, Munich, 1986-87; med. head dept. neurology Fachklinik Herzogenaurach, Germany, 1996—; assoc. mem. Ctr. for Neuromuscular Diseases, Erlangen; lectr. rehab. and sports medicine U. Erlangen, 1998—; mem. adv. com. for rehab. Fedn. German Pension Ins. Insts., Frankfurt, 1988-91, leader of adv. bd. on neurorehab., 1991—; vice leader adv. bd. on neurorehab. Fedn. Bavarian Social Health Insurances, Munich, 1994—; adviser Bavarian Chamber of Physicians, Munich, 1994—; advisor Fed. German Assn. for Rehab. of Disabled, Frankfurt, 1998—. Co-author: (books) Posture and Gait, 1990, Rehabilitation of the Disabled, 1992, EMG-Biofeedback in Neuromuscular Diseases, 1994, Rehabilitation and Care for Neurologically Disabled Patients in Germany, 1995, Rehabilitation Medicine--Rehabilitation of Neurological Diseases, 1995, 2d edit., 1998, Stroke (and its Rehabilitation), 1996; also jour. articles. Mem. German Soc. for Neurology, German Soc. for Neurorehab., German Soc. for Neurotraumatology and Clin. Neuropsychology, German Soc. for Phys. and Rehabilitative Medicine (Award of Yr. 3d prize 1996), German Soc. for Muscular Ills, Internat. Soc. for Innovation Mgmt., Internat. Assn. for Study of Pain (German sect., Award of Yr. 3d prize 1999), World Muscle Soc., Rotary Club. Roman Catholic. Avocations: mountain sports, modern arts, cultural life, cooking and wines, travel. Office: Fachklinik Herzogenaurach, In der Reuth 1, D-91074 Herzogenaurach Bavaria, Germany

SCHUPPAN, DETLEF BRUNO, physician; b. Essen, Germany, Aug. 9, 1954; s. Walther and Helga (Pahnke) S.; m. Fatuma Isaak, Oct. 21, 1959; three children. PhD in Biochemistry, L. Max U., Munich, 1981; MD, Free U., Berlin, 1986, Habilitation in Biochemistry, 1991, Habilitation in Medicine, 1996. Rschr. in biochemistry Max-Planck-Inst., Munich, 1979-81, U. Marburg, Germany, 1981-82; rschr. Free U., Berlin, 1982-86, intern, resident, fellow to assoc. prof., 1986-97; full prof. U. Erlangen, Nurnberg, Germany, 1997—; cons. gastronetrology, Berlin, 1994-97; dir. Rsch. Labs., Free U., 1991—; cons. various pharm. cos. worldwide, 1991—. Inventor in field; contbr. articles to profl. jours. Rsch. grantee German Rsch. Assn., 1987—, German Cancer Fund, 1995—, Industry, 1984—. Mem. Am. Gastroenterol. Assn., Am. Assn. Study of Liver Diseases, Am. Soc. Cell Biology, European Assn. Study of Liver Diseases (sec. 1999—), Similar Nat. Socs. Avocations: langs., practicing music, cello. Office: Medizinische Klinik I mit Poliklinik der Friedrich-Alexander, U Erlangen, Nuremberg Germany

SCHURE, ALEXANDER, university chancellor; b. Can., Aug. 4, 1920; s. Harry Joshua and Bessie (Ginsberg) S.; m. Dorothy Rubin, Dec. 8, 1943 (dec. June 1981); children: Barbara, Matthew, Louis, Jonathan; m. Gail Doris Strollo, Sept. 12, 1984. AST in Elec. Engring, Pratt Inst., 1943; BS, CCNY, 1947; MA, NYU, 1948, PhD, 1950, EdD, 1953; D in Engring. Sci., Nova U., 1975; DSc, N.Y. Inst. Tech., 1976; LLD, Boca Raton Coll., 1976, L.I. U., 1983; LHD, Columbia Coll., Calif., 1983; D of Pedagogy, N.Y. Chiropractic Coll., 1985. Asst. dir. Melville Radio Insts., N.Y.C., 1945-48; pres. Crescent Sch. Radio and TV, Bklyn., 1948-51, Crescent Electronics Corp., N.Y.C., 1951-55; pres., CEO N.Y. Inst. Tech., Bklyn., 1955-82; chancellor, CEO, N.Y. Inst. Tech., 1982-91, chancellor emeritus, 1991—; pres., CEO, chancellor The Univ. Fedn., Inc., 1995—; founder Computer Graphics Lab NY Inst. Tech., 1970-91; chancellor, CEO Nova U., 1970-86; mem. Fla. State Bd. Ind. Colls. and Univs., 1991—; pres. Vidbits, Inc., 1992; cons. N.Y. State Dept. Edn., U.S. Office Edn., UNESCO; mem. Regents Regional Coordinating Council for Post-Secondary Edn. in N.Y.C., 1973—, Nassau County Consortia on Higher Edn., L.I., 1971—, Alfred P. Sloan Found. adv. com. for expanding minority opportunities in engring., 1974; rep. to Nat. Assn. State Adv. Council, 1975—; chmn. N.Y. Title IV Adv. Council, 1975-77; mem. steering com. L.I. Regional Adv. Council, 1974—; chair Regents Adv. Council on Learning Techs., 1986-88; mem., trustee exec. com. Commn. Ind. Colls. and Univs.; mem. adv. council learning technologies N.Y. State Dept. Edn., 1982—; mem. Accreditation Task Force for Council on Postsecondary Accreditation/SHEEBO Project on Assessing Long Distance Learning Via Telecommunications (Project ALLTEL), 1982—; mem. N.Y. State Motion Picture and TV adv. bd., chairperson tech. com.; dir. numerous research projects; expert witness Ho. Reps. com. of Commn. on Sci. and Astronautics; mem. adv. coun. Fla. State Bd. Ind. Colls. and Univs.; vis. tech. exec. Hofstra U., L.I., N.Y., 1998, 99. Author and-or editor textbooks, film producer; designer automatic teaching machine; built one of first computer-controlled anthropomorphic speech devices, 1959; patentee in field. Pres. bd. dirs., trustee L.I. Ednl. TV Coun., Garden City; bd. dirs. Coun. Higher Ednl. Instns., N.Y.C., 1973-83. Served with Signal Corps AUS, 1942-45. 1st inductee Fine Arts Mus. of Long Island's Computer Hall of Fame, 1986. Mem. IEEE (L.I. sect. Gruenwald award 1988), N.Y. Acad. Sci., Am. Inst. Engring. Edn., N.E.A., Electronic Industries Assn. (chmn. task force curriculum devel.), Phi Delta Kappa, Delta Mu Delta, Eta Kappa Nu.

SCHUREK, HANS JOACHIM FRANZ, nephrologist; b. Stuttgart-Bad Cannstatt, Germany, Jan. 28, 1941; s. Adalbert Heinrich Eugen and Frieda Anna Emma Hedwig (Freitag) S.; m. Marianne Ursula Elisabeth Bialetzki, Aug. 25, 1967; children: Jens-Uwe, Eva-Maria. MD, U. Tuebingen, Germany, 1968; Habilitation, Medizinische Hochschule, Hannover, Germany, 1982. Researcher, clinician Freie U./U. Klinikum Benjamin Franklin, Berlin, 1969-75; researcher, clinician Medizinische Hochschule, Hannover, 1975-79, cons., researcher, 1979-86, head physician, researcher, 1986-88; chief nephrology St. Bonifatius Hosp., Lingen, Germany, 1988—; cons. Medizinische Hochschule, Hannover, 1979-86; guest researcher physiology U. Zurich, Switzerland, 1988. Contbr. articles to profl. jours.; patentee in field. Grantee Deutsche Forschungsgemeinschaft, 1974-89. Mem. Internat. Soc. Nephrology, Am. Soc. Nephrology, European Renal Assn., N.Y. Acad. Scis. Roman Catholic. Avocations: music, painting, Pedersen-cyclist, journeys. Office: NZE at St Bonifatius Hosp, Gymnasialstrasse 6, D-49808 Lingen Germany

SCHÜRER, W(ILFRIED) RALPH, physician; b. Ehrenfriedersdork, Germany, May 30, 1957; s. Wilfried Martin and Sigrid Helen (Weber) S. Physician Diploma, Humboldt U., Berlin, 1981; MD, Acad. Med. Sci., Berlin, 1987. Asst. dr. Berlin, 1981-88, asst. med. dir., 1989-90, pvt. practice, 1991—; instr. sports medicine U. Potsdam, 1994. Pres. Heart Groups Potsdam, 1990. Mem. Pain Assn. Brandenburg (v.p. 1993), IABS (chmn. dept. chronical pain 1993). Avocations: traveling, nature, friends. Home: Laplacering 36, 14480 Potsdam Germany Office: An der Pirschheide 28, 14471 Potsdam Germany

SCHURIG, FRANK VOLKER, chemistry educator, researcher; b. Dresden, Germany, Feb. 16, 1940; s. Günther and Elisabeth (Gebler) S.; m. Adina Levi, Mar. 29, 1975; children: Rona Veronique, Jonathan David. Diploma in chemistry, U. Tübingen, Germany, 1966, D of Chemistry, 1968, Habilitation, 1975, Prof., 1980. Cert. in organic chemistry and stereochemistry. Postdoctoral fellow Weizmann Inst. Sci., Rehovot, Israel, 1969-71, U. Houston, 1971-72; prof. chemistry U. Tubingen, Germany, 1973—; guest prof. Weizmann Inst. Sci., Rehovot, 1983; fellow Inst. Advanced Studies, Jerusalem, 1995-96; permanent com. mem. Symposium Series Chiral Discrimination. Founding editor Enantiomer; co-editor Jour. Chromatography A; contbr. articles to sci. publs.; patentee in field. Sen. U. Tübingen, 1984-88. Mem. German Chem. Soc. Avocations: musical composition, jazz piano. Office: Inst Organic Chemistry, Morgenstelle 18, 72076 Tübingen Germany

SCHURIG, KLAUS, lawyer, educator; b. Berlin, May 1, 1942; s. Waldemar Schurig and Christel Moritz Leibstein; m. Ursula Unger, Aug. 27, 1965; children: Jacqueline, Marcel. JD, U. Koln, Germany, 1974, Habilitation, 1980. Wissenschaftlicher asst. U. Koln, 1969-80; sub. prof. U. Hamburg, 1980; prof. ord. for civil law, pvt. internat. law and comparative law U. Passau, Germany, 1981—; dir. Inst. for Internat. and Fgn. Law, U. Passau, 1986—. Author: Vorkaufsrecht im Privatrecht, 1975, Kollisionsnorm und Sachrecht, 1981, Colmmentary on German pvt. internat. Law Soergel, B6B, Vol. 10, 12th edit., 1996, (with G. Kegel) Internationales Porvatrecht 8th edit., 2000; co-editor: Festschrift fuer G. Kegel, 1987; contbr. articles to profl. jours. and festschriften. Office: U Passau, Faculty of Law, D-94030 Passau Germany

SCHÜRMANN, HANS WERNER, physicist, educator; b. Bielefeld, Westfalia, Germany, Dec. 11, 1938; s. Werner and Hedwig (Hummert) S.; m. Anne Köhne, Dec. 21, 1963; children: Ruth, Max. D Natural Scis., U. Münster, Germany, 1965. Asst. Inst. Theoretical Physics, U. Münster, 1965-67; prof. H. Alfeld, Germany, 1968-72, U. Hildesheim, Germany, 1972-97, U. Osnabruck, Germany, 1997—. Author: Theorie bildung und Modell bildung, 1977; (with E. Schwarzer) Chemical Thermodynamics, 1981; contbr. articles to profl. jours. Mem. Deutsche Physikalische Gesellschaft, Optical Soc. Am. Home: Gut Stockhausen, D32312 Lübbecke Germany Office: U Osnabruck Dept Physics, Barbarastr 7, D49069 Osnabrück Germany

SCHURZ, FRANKLIN DUNN, JR., media executive; b. South Bend, Ind., May 22, 1931; s. Franklin Dunn and Martha (Montgomery) S.; m. Robin Rowan Tullis, Nov. 22, 1975 (div. 1985). A.B., Harvard U., 1952, M.B.A., 1956, A.M.P., 1984. Exec. asst. South Bend Tribune, 1956-60, dir., 1961-76, sec., 1970-75, assoc. pub., 1971-72, editor, pub., 1972-82, exec. v.p., 1975-76, pres., 1976-82; asst. pub. Morning Herald and Daily Mail, Hagerstown, Md., 1960-62; pub. Morning Herald and Daily Mail, 1962-70, editor, 1966-70; pres. Schurz Communications, Inc., 1982—, treas., 1983-89; bd. dirs. Atlantic Salmon Fedn. Chmn. Ind. Arts Commn., 1979-81; bd. regents St. Marys Coll., Notre Dame, Ind., 1977-83; chmn. adv. coun. Coll. Arts and Letters Notre Dame U., 1980-82; bd. dirs. Ind. Endowment Ednl. Excellence Inc., Indpls., 1987-90; mem. pres.'s coun. Ind. U., Bloomington, 1988-94; bd. dirs. C-Span, 1997—. 2d lt. U.S. Army, 1952-54. Recipient Presdl. Award of Merit Nat. Newspaper Assn., 1965, Frank Rogers award Rotary, South Bend, 1980. Mem. Am. Press Inst. (bd. dirs. 1985-94), AP (chmn. audit com. 1979-84), Chesapeake AP Assn. (past pres.), Md.-Del.-D.C. Press Assn. (past pres.), Hoosier State Press Assn. (past pres.), Newspaper Advt. Bur. (past bd. dirs.), South Bend Mishawaka Area C. of C. (pres. 1980-82), Am. Soc. Newspaper Editors, Am. women in Radio and TV (Found. hon. trustee 1996—), Inland Press Assn., Inst. Newspaper Fin. Execs. (past pres.), South Bend Country Club, Nat. Press Club, Soc. Profl. Journalists. Presbyterian. Home: 1329 Erskine Manor Hl South Bend IN 46614-2186 Office: Schurz Communications Inc 225 W Colfax Ave South Bend IN 46626-1000

SCHUSSER, FRANTIŠEK, construction executive; b. Kaplice, Czech Republic, May 16, 1960; s. František and Hana (Říhová) S.; m. Dagmar Vajsábelová, Apr. 19, 1986; children: Pavel, Šimon. MA, Charles U., Prague, Czech Republic, 1984, PhD, 1990. Mgr. asst. Omnipol, Prague, 1984-88; mgr. for project Martimex Martin, Slovakia, 1988-91; comml. mgr. Gamex, Č.Budějovice, Czech Republic, 1991-94; regional Asia mgr. Strojexport, Prague, 1996—. Contbr. articles to profl. jours. Founder African-Czech Friendship Club, Prague-Harare, 1988, Vietnamese-Czech Friendship Club, Hanoi, 1994; mem. Czecho-Arab Cooperation, Prague, 1990. Avocations: canoening, jogging, fishing. Home: U tří lvu 12, 370 01 Budějovice Czech Republic

SCHUSTER, BERTRAM, recruiter, management consultant, publisher; b. N.Y.C., Jan. 7, 1940; s. Harry and Lillian (Grossfield) S.; m. Zohara Teena Glassman, Mar. 16, 1980. BA, CUNY, 1986; postgrad., U. Pa. Sales dir. Franklin Mint, Franklin Center, Pa., 1971-74; nat. dir. AMR Internat., N.Y.C., 1974-77; pub., COO Vital Mag., Chgo., 1977-79; v.p. Morgan Stanley Dean Witter, Chgo., 1980-86; mng. dir. Robbins Trading Co., Chgo., 1986-91; pub., COO Futures Mag., Cedar Falls, Iowa, 1992-94; mgmt. cons. George S. May Internat., Inc., Park Ridge, Ill., 1994-96; pub., CEO Traveler Pub. Corp., Chgo., 1996-97; exec. v.p. DHR Internat., Chgo., 1998—. Author: The Insider's Edge, 1985; contbr. articles to profl. publs. Bd. dirs. Human Capital, Director's Monthly; bd. dirs. Winston Tower 1 Condominiums, pres., 1997-99, Director's Weekly. With U.S. Army, 1963-69. Mem. Managed Futures Trade Assn. (founding bd. dirs. 1985-88). Avocations: reading, music, race car driving, photography, swimming. Home: 6933 N Kedzie Ave Apt 316 Chicago IL 60645-2891 Office: DHR Internat Inc 10 S Riverside Plz Ste 2220 Chicago IL 60606-3703

SCHUSTER, MARVIN MEIER, physician, educator; b. Danville, Va., Aug. 30, 1929; s. Isaac and Rosel (Katzenstein) S.; m. Lois R. Bernstein, Feb. 19, 1961; children: Roberta, Nancy, Cathy. BA, BS, U. Chgo., 1951, MD, 1955. Diplomate Am. Bd. Internal Medicine. Intern Kings County Hosp., Bklyn., 1955-56; resident Balt. City Hosps., 1956-58, Johns Hopkins Hosp., Balt., 1958-61; founder divsn. digestive disease Balt. City Hosps.;

Janssen, Strauss Halbreich prof. emeritus medicine and psychiatry Johns Hopkins U. Sch. Medicine, Balt., 1976-97, chief digestive disease divsn.; dir. Marvin M. Schuster Ctr. for Digestive and Motility Disorders, Balt. Author: Gastrointestinal Disorders: Behavioral and Physiological Basis for Treatment; Keeping Control: Understanding and Managing Fecal Incontinence; editor: Gastrointestinal Motility Disorders, 1981, Atlas of Gastrointestinal Motility, 1994; mem. editl. bd. Gastroenterology, 1978-81, Gastrointestinal Endoscopy, 1979-81, Psychosomatics, 1979—, Am. Jour. Gastroenterology, 1993—; contbr. chpts. to textbooks and articles to profl. jours. Bd. dirs. Beth El Congregation, 1961-76, Am. Cancer Soc., 1975—, pres., 1984-86; chmn. med. adv. bd. Balt. Ostomy Assn., 1966—; chmn. phys. divsn. Assoc. Jewish Charities, 1961-76. Recipient St. George Disting. Svc. award Am. Cancer Soc., 1979. Fellow ACP, Am. Psychiat. Assn., Am. Gastroent. Assn. (chmn. audiovisual com. 1975-78); mem. AAUP, Am. Soc. Gastrointestinal Endoscopy (governing bd. 1975-78), Am. Coll. Gastroenterology (pres. 1996), Am. Physiol. Soc. Democrat. Jewish. Achievements include research on gastrointestinal motility and application of biofeedback to gastrointestinal control. Home: 10 Red Cedar Ct Baltimore MD 21208-6305 Office: Schuster Ctr Digestive/Motility Disorders Johns Hopkins Bayview MC 4940 Eastern Ave Baltimore MD 21224-2735

SCHUSTER, REINHARD GOTTFRIED, mathematician, researcher; b. Leipzig, Saxony, Germany, Apr. 28, 1956; s. Gottfried Willy and Gertraud Irmgard (Geissler) S.; m. Heidrun Cornelia Friedrich, Mar. 22, 1986; children: Martin Reinhard, Fabian Gerhard. Diploma in math., U. Leipzig, 1980, D in habilitation, 1992, Dr.rer.nat., 1993. Asst. U. Leipzig, 1980-94; rschr. Med. Svc., Lübeck, Germany, 1995-96; dir. North German Biometrical Ctr., Lübeck, 1997—; pvt. dozent U. Lübeck, 1997—; cons. Med. Svc., Lübeck, 1997—. Author: Introduction to Biomathematics, 1995; co-editor, author: Hospital Report, 1998; co-editor (CD to book) Kiel List of Essential Medicaments, 1997; inventor in field. Lt. German Arty., 1974-76. Recipient 3rd prize Internat. Math. Olympiade, Internat. Com., Moscow and Erfurt, Germany, 1973, 74. Mem. Schlaraffia (Ritter award 1995). Avocations: skiing, mountaineering. E-mail: Reinhard.Schuster.Luebeck@t-online.de. and reinhard.schuster@mdk-shide. Fax: 49-0451-4803300. Home: Rittersporнweg 12 E, D-23566 Lübeck Germany Office: North German Biometrical Ct, Katharinenstr 11a, D-23554 Lübeck Germany

SCHUSTER, ROBERT PARKS, lawyer; b. St. Louis, Oct. 25, 1945; s. William Thomas Schuster and Carolyn Cornforth (Daugherty) Hathaway; 1 child, Susan Michele. AB, Yale U., 1967; JD with honors, U. Wyo., 1970; LLM, Harvard U., 1971. Bar: Wyo. 1971, U.S. Ct. Appeals (10th cir.) 1979, U.S. Supreme Ct. 1984, Utah 1990. Dep. county atty. County of Natrona, Casper, Wyo., 1971-73; pvt. practice law Casper, 1973-76; assoc. Spence & Moriarity, Casper, 1976-78; ptnr. Spence, Moriarty & Schuster, Jackson, Wyo., 1978—. Trustee U. Wyo., 1985-89; Wyo. Dem. nominee for U.S. Ho. of Reps., 1994; polit. columnist Casper Star Tribune, 1987-94; pres. United Way Natrona County, 1974; bd. dirs. Dancers Workshop, 1981-83; chair Wyo. selection com. Rhodes Scholarship, 1989-98; mem. bd. visitors Coll. Arts and Scis., U. Wyo., 1991-2000; mem. Dem. Nat. Com., 1992-2000; chair Wyo. Pub. Policy Forum, 1992-98; mem. Wind River Reservation Econ. Adv. Coun., 1998-99. Ford Found. Urban Law fellow, 1970-71. Mem. ABA, ATLA, Wyo. Trial Lawyers Assn. Home: PO Box 548 Jackson WY 83001-0548 Office: Spence Moriarity & Schuster 15 S Jackson St Jackson WY 83001

SCHUSTER, WILLY GOTTFRIED, plant physiologist, virologist, educator; b. Meissen, Saxony, Germany, Apr. 21, 1923; s. Reinhold Willy and Martha Elisabeth (Schmieder) S.; m. Gertraud Geissler, Dec. 11, 1954; children: Reinhard, Michael. Diploma, U. Leipzig, Fed. Republic of Germany, 1951; Dr.'s diploma, U. Leipzig, 1954, Dr. rer. nat. habilitation, 1960. Asst. Inst. Phytopathology, U. Leipzig, 1951-54, head asst., 1954-55; head asst. Div. Agrl. Botany, U. Leipzig, 1955-60, lectr., 1960-62, prof. mit Lehrauftrag, 1962-64, prof. mit vollem Lehrauftrag, 1964-68; prof. dept. bioscis., plant physiology, microbiology U. Leipzig, 1969-89, rsch. prof. dept. bioscis., plant physiology, microbiology, 1989—; vice dean Agrl. faculty of U. Leipzig, 1964-68, vice dir. Dept. Bioscis., 1972-78, dir. Dept. Bioscis., 1978-83. Author: Virus and Virus Diseases, 1957, 4th rev. edit., 1988, Methods and Approaches for the Physiological-Chemical Virus Diagnostic, 1962, Viruses in the Environment, 1997; (manuals) Plant Cytology and Morphology, 1963, Plant Morphology, 1963, Plant Physiology Part I, 1963, Plant Physiology Part II, 1964, Instructions for Bot. Exercises, 1964; editor: Antiphytoviral Compounds, 1982, New Results and Trends of the Plant Physiology, 1987. Avocations: horticulture, tourism. Office: U Leipzig Div Plant Physiology Microbiology, Talstrasse 33, D-04103 Leipzig Germany

SCHUTJES, CORNELIS PIETER MAARTEN, research scientist; b. Eindhoven, The Netherlands, July 24, 1947; s. Josephus and Maria Anna (Appelhof) S.; m. Antonia C.P.M. de Bruijn, Oct. 9, 1976; children: Jacqueline, Roland. Chem. engr., Eindhoven U. Technology, 1978, PhD, 1983. Rschr. St. Johns Hosp., Eindhoven, 1970-79; rsch. scientist Eindhoven U. Technology, 1979-83; rsch. scientist Akzo Nobel Ctrl. Rsch., Deventer, The Netherlands, 1983-84, sect. head chromatography, 1984—; cons. Ysselland Coll., Deventer, 1990—, Overgelder Coll., Deventer, 1986-98. Soldier Paramedics, 1967-68. Mem. Royal Dutch Chem. Soc. Avocations: technical applications and programming of computers, photography, bicycling. Office: Akzo Nobel Polymer Chem Lab, Zutphenseweg 10, 7400AA Deventer The Netherlands

SCHUTZ, BERNARD FREDERICK, physics educator, astrophysics researcher; b. Paterson, N.J., Aug. 11, 1946; arrived in Wales, 1974; s. Bernard Frederick and Virginia Mae (Lefebure) S.; m. Susan Whitelegg, Sept. 16, 1977 (div. Jan. 1983); m. Siân Lynette Pouncy, Dec. 22, 1983; children: Rachel Grace, Catherine Virginia, Annalie Eileen. BS, Clarkson Coll. Tech., 1967; PhD, Calif. Inst. Tech., 1972. Postdoctoral fellow Cambridge U., Eng., 1971-72; postdoctoral fellow Yale U., New Haven, 72-73, instr., 1973-74; lectr. Univ. Coll., Cardiff, Wales, 1974-76, reader, 1976-84, prof., 1984-88; prof. U. Wales Coll. Cardiff, 1988—; dir. Max Planck Inst. Gravitational Physics Albert Einstein Inst., Golm, Germany, 1995—; mem. editorial bd. Jour. Classical & Quantum Gravity, Bristol, Eng., 1988-90, Revs. in Math. Physics, Singapore, 1988—. Author: Geometrical Methods of Mathematical Physics, 1980, A First Course in General Relativity, 1985; editor: Gravitational Wave Data Analysis, 1989; contbr. numerous articles to profl. jours. Grantee Sci. and Engring. Rsch. Coun., Swindon, U.K., 1976—. Fellow Inst. Physics, U.K.; mem. Royal Astron. Soc. (coun. 1990-92), Icosahedron. Avocations: skiing, singing. Office: Max Planck Inst Gravitational Physics, Albert Einstein Inst, 14476 Golm Germany

SCHUTZ, EMILE, Kiribati government official; b. Tarawa, Kiribati, Jan. 23, 1962; m.; 1 child. Owner Royal Crown Enterprises; elected Island Constituency, 1994, Abaiang Island, 1994; min. of works and energy Govt. of Kiribati, Tarawa Atoll, 1994—. Mem. Maneaban Te Mauri Party. Office: Ministry of Works Energy, PO Box 498, Baetio Tarawa Atoll Kiribati*

SCHÜTZ, GUNTER MARKUS, physicist, researcher; b. Friedberg, Hessen, Germany, Mar. 11, 1961; s. Karl and Liesel Lydia S.; m. Beate Speier, Aug. 24, 1989; children: Carmen Ronit, Colin Raimund. Diploma, Bonn (Germany) U., 1987, DSc in Physics, 1991. Postdoctoral rsch. fellow Weizmann Inst., Rehovot, Israel, 1991-93, U. Oxford, Eng., 1993-96; rsch. fellow Forschungszentrum Jülich, Germany, 1996—; vis. prof. U. Nancy, France, 1996, U. Essen, Germany, 1999. Editor Evangelium und Wissenschaft, 1997—; contbr. more than 50 articles to sci. jours. Recipient Gustav Hertz prize in physics, 2000. Mem. German Physics Assn., Karl Heim Assn. (curator 1991—). Avocations: photography, tennis. Office: Inst Festkörperforschung, Forschungszentrum Jülich, 52425 Jülich Germany

SCHÜTZ, HELMUT GEORG, art educator; b. Woellstadt, Hessen, Germany, 1938; children: Indira, Raju Helmut, Lennart Urban Alexander; m. Helga Angela Wandke, Dec. 8, 1984. Lehramtspruefung, Paedagogisches Institut, Darmstadt, Germany, 1962; postgrad., U. Mainz, Germany, 1967-68; DrPhil, U. Frankfurt, Germany, 1974. Tchr. Parkschule, Ruesselsheim, Germany, 1963-67; dozent Paedagogische Hochschule Esslingen, Baden-Wuerttemberg, Germany, 1974-77; prof. Paedagogische Hochschule Esslingen, Baden-Wuerttemberg, 1977-80; prof. art edn. Paedagogische Hochschule Karlsruhe Karlsruhe U. Edn., Germany, 1980—. Author: Kunstpaedagogische Theorie, 1973, Didaktische Aesthetik, 1975, Pragmatische Kunstpaedagogik, 1979, Sphinx Beckman, 1997, Die Kunstpadagogik öffnen, 1998; editor: Kunstpaedagogische Einsichten, 1987; contbr. chpts. to books, numerous articles to profl. jours. Office: Paedagogische Hochschule Karlsruhe, Bismarckstrasse 10, D-76133 Karlsruhe Germany

SCHUTZ, JOHN ADOLPH, historian, educator, former university dean; b. L.A., Apr. 10, 1919; s. Adolph J. and Augusta K. (Gluecker) S. AA, Bakersfield Coll., 1940; BA, UCLA, 1942, MA, 1943, PhD, 1945. Asst. prof. history Calif. Inst. Tech., Pasadena, 1945-53; assoc. prof. history Whittier (Calif.) Coll., 1953-56, prof., 1956-65; prof. Am. history U. So. Calif., L.A., 1965-91; chmn. dept. history U. So. Calif., 1974-76, dean social scis. and communication, 1976-82. Author: William Shirley: King's Governor of Massachusetts, 1961, Peter Oliver's Origin and Progress of the American Rebellion, 1967, The Promise of America, 1970, The American Republic, 1978, Dawning of America, 1981, Spur of Fame: Dialogues of John Adams and Benjamin Rush, 1980, A Noble Pursuit: A Sesquicentennial History of the New England Historic Genealogical Society, 1995, Legislators of the Massachusetts General Court, 1691-1780, 1997; joint editor: Golden State Series; contbg. author: Spain's Colonial Outpost, 1985, Generations and Change: Genealogical Perspectives in Social History, 1986, Making of America: Society and Culture of the United States, 1990, rev. edit., 1992, Encyclopedia Britannica. Trustee Citizens Rsch. Found., 1985-99. NEH grantee, 1971; Sr. Faculty grantee, 1971-74; U. Calif. fellow, 1944-45. Mem. Am. Hist. Assn. (pres. Pacific Coast br. 1972-73, sec.-treas. 1951-88, 95-96), Am. Studies Assn. (pres. 1974-75), Mass. Hist. Soc. (corr.), New Eng. Hist. Geneal. Soc. (trustee 1988—, editor, author intro. book Boston Merchant Census of 1789, 1989, rec. sec. 1995—), Colonial Soc. Mass. (corr.). Home and Office: 1100 White Knoll Dr Los Angeles CA 90012-1353

SCHUTZ, ROBERT RUDOLPH, retired editor; b. Bixby, Minn., July 22, 1915; s. Walter Valentine and Myrtle Esther Lois (Burns) S.; m. Marie Hayes, Jan. 22, 1949; children: David, Margaret, Roberta, Karla. BS in Horticulture, U. Minn., 1939, MS in Plant Genetics, 1941; PhD in Econs., U. Calif., Berkeley, 1952. Lectr. U. Calif., Berkeley, 1946-53; pub. affairs dir. KPFA, Berkeley, 1949-56; economist Fed. Res. Bank, San Francisco, 1957-59; lobbyist Lobby for Peace, No. Calif., Berkeley, 1960-63; exec. dir. Am. Soc. for Eastern Arts, Berkeley, 1963-68; editor-in-chief Annual Revs., Palo Alto, Calif., 1969-74; ret. Author: The $30,000 Solution, 1996, (pamphlet) How to Make Capitalism Fair to People and Benign to the Earth, 1990; contbr. articles to profl. jours. Co-founder Monan's Rill, Santa Rosa, Calif., 1970-94, treas., 1972-76; co-founder Friends House, Santa Rosa, 1984—. Lt. USNR, 1943-46. Avocations: writing, reading, gardening, walking. Home and Office: 684 Benicia Dr Apt 70 Santa Rosa CA 95409-3069

SCHUTZ, ROBERTA MARIA (BOBBI SCHUTZ), social worker; b. Smithtown, N.Y., July 19, 1962; d. Robert N. S. and Janice (Sharpe) Taylor. BS, U. Utah, 1988, MSW, 1996. Lic. clin. social worker, Divsn. Occupl. and Profl. Licensing, Utah. Intern Salt Lake Rape Crisis Ctr., 1987-88, VA Med. Ctr., 1992, East Valley Mental Health, 1994-95, Obs. & Assessment.Divsn. Youth Corrections, 1995-96; behavior/employment specialist Columbus Cmty. Ctr., Salt Lake City, 1986-88; skills instr. Project TURN/Possibilities, Salt Lake City, 1987-90; indsl. unit supr. South Valley Tng. Co., Sandy, Utah, 1988-90; case mgr. Office Social Svcs./Divsn. Svcs. People with Disabilities, Midvale, Utah, 1990-91; DD/MR home & cmty.-based waiver specialist Dept. Human Svcs./Renevue Mgmt. Unit, Salt Lake City, 1991-93; case mgr. Dept. Human Svcs./Divsn. Svcs. People with Disabilities, Murray, Utah, 1993-96, social worker, 1996-97; social worker Utah State Prison Dept. of Corrections, Draper, 1997—. Author of poems. Mem. NASW (Utah PACE com. 1995—, Utah bd. dirs. 1995-2000, Salt Lake City rep. 1996-98), Am. Assn. Mental Retardation (Utah bd. dirs. 1996-98), Am. Correctional Assn. Democrat. Avocations: running, stamp collecting, lacrosse, reading, writing poetry. Home: 3503 Blair Cir Salt Lake City UT 84115-4609 Office: Dept Corrections Utah State Prison PO Box 250 Draper UT 84020-0250

SCHUTZE, MICHAEL JOHANNES, research institute director; b. Ottendorf Okrilla, Germany, Oct. 23, 1952; s. Johannes and Sieghild (Claus) S.; m. Renate Pick, Apr. 26, 1986; children: Dagmar, Christian. Engring. diploma, Friedrich Alexander U., Erlangen, 1978; D in eng. sci., Rheinisch West Tech. Hochschule, Aachen, 1983. Rsch. assoc. Dechema Karl-Winnacker Inst., Frankfurt, Germany, 1978-83; asst. group head Dechema Karl-Winnacke Inst., Frankfurt, Germany, 1983-91, group head, 1991-96, inst. dir., 1996—; prof. engring. sci. Rheinisch West Tech. Hochschule, 1998—. Author: Die Korrosionsschutzwirkung oxidischer Deckschichten, 1991, Protective Oxide Scales and Their Breakdown, 1997, Oxidation of Intermetallics, 1997; inventor in field. Recipient Friedrich Wilhelm award RWTH, 1991. Mem. ASM, Inst. of Materials, VDI. Avocations: hiking, biking, skiing, sailing, golf. Office: Dechema e v, Theodor Heuss Allee 25, 60486 Frankfurt Germany

SCHUURMAN, HENDRIK JAN, medical researcher; b. Enschede, The Netherlands, July 11, 1950; s. Boudewijn J. and Marcella H.G. (Slijper) S.; m. Marieke Vander Heyden; 3 children. Diploma in chemistry, U. Utrecht, The Netherlands, 1974, PhD, 1977. Staff mem. dept. medicine U. Hosp., Utrecht, The Netherlands, 1979-92; cons. Nat. Inst. Pub. Health, The Netherlands, 1988-92; head lab. Sandoz Pharma Preclin. Rsch., Basel, 1992-96; head transplantation unit Novartis Pharma Rsch., Basel, Switzerland, 1997-99, Imutran Ltd., Cambridge, Eng., 1999—; cons. in field. Mem. Dutsch Soc. Immunology, Brit. Soc. Immunology. Home: 9 Speedwell Close, Cambridge CB1 4YS, England Office: Imutran Ltd, PO Box 399, Cambridge CB2 2YP, England

SCHUYLER, ROBERT L., anthropologist, archaeologist; b. New Haven, Conn., Sept. 13, 1941. BA, U. Ariz., 1964; MA, U. Calif., Santa Barbara, 1968; PhD, U. Calif., 1974. Registered profl. archaeologist. Lectr. U. Md., College Park, 1969-70; instr. City Coll. N.Y., N.Y.C., 1970-74, asst. prof., 1974-79; assoc. prof., assoc. curator U. Pa., Phila., 1980—. Editor: Historical Archaeology: A Guide to Substantive and Theoretical Contributions, 1978, Archaeological Perspectives on Ethnicity in America: Afro-American and Asian American Culture History, 1980; founding editor North Am. Archaeologist, 1979-82. Mem. Soc. Historical Archaeology (pres. 1982), Coun. for Northeast Historical Archaeology (pres. 1980). Democrat. E-mail: schuyler@sas.upenn.edu. Office: Univ Pa Museum 33rd and Spruce Sts Philadelphia PA 19104

SCHUZ, JOACHIM CHRISTOPH, epidemiologist; b. Darmstadt, Germany, Mar. 31, 1967; s. Peter Christoph and Hannelore S.; m. Katja Weissgerber, July 24, 1998. Diploma, U. Heidelberg, 1993; PhD, U. Mainz, 1997. Computer scientist Tumor Ctr., Mainz, 1993-97; epidemiologist U. Mainz, 1998—. E-mail: schuez@imsd.uni-mainz.de.

SCHWAB, ADRIJANO, scientist, researcher, physician; b. Postojna, Slovenia, Feb. 21, 1965; s. Elio and Emilija (Obrecht) S; m. Wilhelmina Gugliemina Renata Vilma; children: Sabina, Irma, Angelo/Silvan, Elio. MD, Med. Faculty, Ljubljana, Slovenia, 1991, DSc, 1995. Profl. rep. Eli Lilly (Suisse) S.A., Ljubljana, Slovenia, 1995; mktg. coord. Eli Lilly (Suisse) S.A., Ljubljana, 1995-96, med. coord., 1996-97. Fellow Am. Biog. Inst. Rsch. Assn. (20th Century award for achievement); mem. Slovene Med. Soc., Planetary Soc. N.M.C., N.Y. Acad. Scis. (hon. DSc.), Nat. Geog. Soc., N.Y. Acad. Scis. Avocations: art history, tennis, chess, windsurfing, diving. Home: Na Grivi 61, 1351 Dragomer Slovenia

SCHWAB, CHARLES R., brokerage house executive; b. Sacramento, 1937; m. Helen O'Neill; 5 children. Stanford U., 1959, Postgrad., 1961. Formerly mut. fund mgr. Marin County, Calif.; founder brokerage San Francisco, 1971; now chmn., CEO Charles Schwab & Co., Inc. Author: How to be Your Own Stockbroker, 1984. Republican. Office: Charles Schwab & Co Inc 101 Montgomery St San Francisco CA 94104-4175*

SCHWAB, GEORGE DAVID, social science educator, author; b. Nov. 25, 1931; s. Arkady and Klara (Jacobson) S.; m. Eleonora Storch, Feb. 27, 1965; children: Clarence Boris, Claude Arkady, Solan Bernhard. BA, City Coll. N.Y., 1954; MA, Columbia U., 1955, PhD, 1968. Lectr. Columbia Coll. N.Y.C., 1959, CUNY, 1960-68; asst. prof. history, 1968-72, assoc. prof. history, 1973-79, prof., 1980—; mem. Columbia U. Seminar on History of Legal and Polit. Thought and Institutions; dir. Conf. History and Politics CUNY; with Nat. Com. Am. Fgn. Policy. Author: Dayez: Beyond Abstract Art, 1967, Enemy oder Foe, 1968, Switzerland's Tactical Nuclear Weapons Policy, 1969, The Challenge of the Exception: An Introduction to the Political Ideas of Carl Schmitt, 1970, 2nd edit., 1989, Appeasement and Detente, 1975, 81, Carl Schmitt: Political Opportunist?, 1975; translator: The Concept of the Politcal with Comments by Leo Strauss (Carl Schmitt), 1976, 96, Legality and Illegality as Instruments of Revolutionaries in Their Quest for Power, Remarks Occasioned by the Outlook of Herbert Marcuse, 1978, The German State in Historical Perspective, 1978, Ideology: Reality or Rhetoric, 1978, Ideology and Foreign Policy, 1978, 81, The Decision: Is the American Sovereign at Bay?, 1978, State and Nation Toward: A Further Clarification, 1980, American Foreign Politics at the Crossroads, 1980, Carl Schmitt: Through a Glass Darkly, 1980, From Quantity and Heterogeneity to Quality and Homogeneity: Toward a New Foreign Policy, 1980, Toward an Open-Society Bloc, 1980, Eurocommunism: The Idoelogical and Political Theoretical Foundations, 1981, American Foreing Policy at the Crossroads, 1982, A Decade of the National Committee on American Foreign Policy, 1984, trans. Political Theology: Four Chapters on the Concept of Sovereignty (Carl Schmitt), 1985, 88, RB: The Destruction of a Family, 1987, Elie Wiesel: Between Jerusalem and New York, 1990, The Broken Vow, The Good Obtained, 1991, Thoughts of a Collector, 1991, Carl Schmitt Hysteria in the United States, 1992, Contextualizing Carl Schmitts's Concept of Grossraum, 1994; (translation) The Leviathan in the State Theory of Thomas Hobbes (Carl Schmitt), 1996, Carl Schmitt, A Note on a Qualitative Authoritarian Bourgeois Liberal, 2000, The National Committee on American Foreign Policy's Focus on Russia, 2000; editor Am. Fgn. Policy Interests; series Global Perspectives in History and Politics. Trustee, pres. mem. exec. com. Nat. Com. Am. Fgn. Policy. Recipient Ellis Is. medal of honor. Office: Nat Com Am Fgn Policy 320 Park Ave New York NY 10022-6815

SCHWAB, HAROLD LEE, lawyer; b. N.Y.C., Feb. 5, 1932; s. Harold Walter and Beatrice (Braverman) S.; m. Rowena Vivian Strauss, June 12, 1953; children: Andrew, Lisa, James. BA, Harvard Coll., 1953; LLB, Boston Coll., 1956. Bar: N.Y. 1957, U.S. Ct. Mil. Appeals 1958, U.S. Dist. Cts. (so. and ea. dists.) N.Y. 1967, U.S. Dist. Ct. (no. dist.) N.Y. 1974, U.S. Dist. Ct. (we. dist.) N.Y. 1988, U.S. Dist. Ct. Conn. 1995, U.S. Dist. Ct. (ea. and we. dists.) Ark. 2000, U.S. Ct. Appeals (2d cir.) 1971, U.S. Ct. Appeals (D.C. cir.) 1986, U.S. Ct. Appelas (11th cir.) 1988, U.S. Ct. Appeals (5th cir.) 1991, U.S. Supreme Ct. 1971. V.p. H.W. Schwab Textile Corp., N.Y.C., 1959-60; assoc. Emile Z. Berman & A. Harold Frost, N.Y.C., 1960-67, ptnr., 1967-74; sr. ptnr. Lester Schwab Katz & Dwyer, N.Y.C., 1974—; lectr. N.Y. State Bar Assn., N.Y. County Lawyers Assn. Contbr. articles to legal jours.; mem. editl. bd. Jour. Products and Toxics Liability, 1976-96. Served to lt. col. USAFR. Fellow Internat. Acad. Trial Lawyers; mem. ABA, ASTM, SAE, Assn. Advancement of Automotive Medicine, Product Liability Adv. Coun., N.Y. State Bar Assn. (chmn. trial lawyers sect. 1980-81, editor sect. newsletter 1981-84), Am. Bd. Trial Advs. (pres. N.Y. chpt. 1982-83), Fedn. Ins. and Corp. Counsel (v.p. 1979-80), Assn. Bar of City of N.Y., N.Y. County Lawyers Assn., N.Y. State Trial Lawyers Assn., Def. Assn. N.Y., Harvard Club N.Y., Downtown Assn. Home: 205 Beach 142 St Neponsit NY 11694 Office: Lester Schwab Katz & Dwyer 120 Broadway Fl 38 New York NY 10271-0071

SCHWAB, NELSON, JR., lawyer; b. Cin., July 19, 1918; s. Nelson Sr. and Frances Marie (Carlile) S.; m. Elizabeth Bakhaus (div.); m. Sylvia Lambert; children: Nelson III, Richard O. BA, Yale U., 1940; LLB, Harvard U., 1943. Bar: Ohio 1947. Ptnr. Graydon Head & Ritchey, Cin., 1947-95; sr. counsel, 1995—; bd. dirs. Rotex, Inc., Ralph J. Stolle co., Security Rug Cleaning Co., Yoder Die Casting Corp. Grants Review Com. The Greater Cin. Found.; mem. Cin. Pub. Schs. Degration Task Force; former chmn. bd. Vol. Lawyers for the Poor Found.; trustee Cin. Scholarship Found., FISC; adv. bd. Cin. Playhouse in the Park; ; past mem., sec. Cin. Bus. Com., 1977-88, mm. Schs. Task Force; past mem. Cin. City Mgr.'s Working Rev. Com. 2000 Plan, chmn. Reconstituted 2000 Plan Rev. Com., 1990; pres. Greater Cin. C. of C., 1973; chmn. Greater Cin. Ednl. TV, 1965-70, hon. trustee; chmn. Cincinnati and Hamilton County Am. Red Cross, 1955-57, hon. trustee; incorporator United Appeal, 1955; mem. Cin. Sch. Bd., 1959-64. Honoree Greater Cin. Region NCCJ, 1990; Great Living Cincinnatian Grater Cin. C. of C., 1991. Mem. 6th Cir. Jud. Conf., Cin. Country Club (past bd. dirs., sec.), Commonwealth Club (past pres.), Comml. Club, Recess Club (past pres.), Gyro Club (past pres.), Queen City Club, Queen City Optimists (past pres.), Cin. Yale Club (past pres.), Lincoln's Inn Soc., Delta Kappa Epsilon. Home: 2470 W Rookwood Ct Cincinnati OH 45208-3321 Office: Graydon Head & Ritchey 511 Walnut St # 53D Cincinnati OH 45202-3115

SCHWAB, ULRICH, theology educator; b. Nuremberg, Germany, Oct. 18, 1957; s. Walter and Lieselotte (Sengfelder) S.; m. Anne Loreck, Apr. 24, 1985; children: Thaddaeus, Viktoria, Felicitas. MA, U. Munich, Germany, 1983, Dr.theol., 1991, Dr.theol.habil, 1994. Asst. min. Evang.-Luth. Ch., Bavaria, Germany, 1985-87; min. Evang.-Luth. Ch., Bavaria, 1987-88; asst. U. Munich, 1988-94; min. Evang.-Luth. Ch., Bavaria, 1994-95; prof. U. Marburg, Germany, 1995—. Author: Evangelische Jugendarbeit in Bayern, 1800-1933, 1992, Familienreligiosität, 1995. Office: Philipps U, Lahntor 3, D-35037 Marburg Germany

SCHWAB, WILFRIED GEORG, food chemist; b. Remlingen, Bavaria, Germany, Apr. 2, 1961; s. Georg Johann and Ferdinande Elisabeth (Aurich) S.; m. Elisabeth Maria Schoch, July 5, 1990; children: Jonathan, Melissa. Grad., Julius-Maximilians U., Wurzburg, Germany, 1985, Doctorate, 1989; Habilitation, Julius-Maximilians U., 1999. Lab leader Hoechst AG, Frankfurt, Germany, 1991-93, Agrevo, Frankfurt, 1993-94; rsch. asst. U. Wurzburg, Germany, 1994—. Mem. Lebensmittelchemische Assn., Soc. German Chemists. Lutheran. Avocation: volleyball. Home: Rupert Mayer 7, D-97828 Marktheidenfeld Germany Office: Dept Food Chemistry, U Wurzburg Am Hubland, D-97074 Würzburg Germany

SCHWABACH, AARON, law educator. BA, Antioch Coll., 1985; JD, U. Calif., Berkeley, 1989. Bar: Calif. 1989, Fla. 1993. Assoc. prof. Thomas Jefferson Sch. Law, San Diego, 1994—. E-mail: aarons@tjsl.edu. Office: Thomas Jefferson Sch Law 2121 San Diego Ave San Diego CA 92110-2986

SCHWABE, RAINER, mathematical statistician; b. Mainz, Germany, Nov. 26, 1954; s. Walter and Paula (Neumann) S.; m. Helga Rothe, May 16, 1988; children: Jonas, Philipp. Diploma in math., Free U. Berlin, 1982, D in Math., 1985. From scientist to sci. asst. Free U. Berlin, 1983-93; vis. scientist Uppsala U., Sweden, 1994; sr. rschr. Exptl. Design Rsch. Group, Berlin, 1994-98; sr. lectr. Tech. U. Darmstadt, Germany, 1996-97, U. Mainz, Germany, 1997-98; sr. lectr. in med. biometry U. Tubingen, Germany, 1999—. Author: Optimum Design in Multi-Factor Models, 1996; contbr. articles to scientific jours. Mem. Inst. Math. Stats., German Math. Assn., Bernoulli Soc., German Stats. Assn., Internat. Biomed. Soc. Home: Welzenwiler Str 3, 72074 Tübingen Germany Office: Univ Tubingen Dept Med Biom, Westbahnhofstr 55, 72070 Tubingen Germany

SCHWABE, WALTER WOLFGANG, plant physiology researcher, horticulture educator; b. Berlin, June 1, 1920; arrived in England, 1938; s. Walter and Anne Emilie (Lagershausen) S.; m. Valerie Bramley, Nov. 15, 1958 (div.); children: Fiona, Ruth, John. BSc, Assn. Royal Coll. of Sci., London U., 1945, PhD, Diploma Imperial Coll., 1949, DSc, 1957; DAg (hon.), Agrl. U., Ås, Norway, 1984. Sci. officer Inst. Plant Physiology, Imperial Coll., London (Eng.) U., 1945-58; prin. sci. officer Agrl. Rsch. Coun., Imperial Coll., London (Eng.) U., 1958-65, acting dir. unit plant morphogenesis and nutrition, 1963-65; prof. horticulture Wye Coll., London (Eng.) U., 1965-85; prof. emeritus London U., 1985—; mem. governing body exec. com. Glasshouse Crops Rsch. Inst., Littlehampton, U.K., 1970-80, East Malling (U.K.) Rsch. Sta., 1971-86, Nat. Vegetable Rsch. Sta., Wellesbourne, 1971-89; chmn. biol. program adv. com. Palm Oil Rsch. Inst., Kuala Lumpur, Malaysia, 1981-87. Editor Jour. Exptl. Botany, 1981-88; assoc. editor Physiologia Plantarum, 1985-94, Jour. Horticultural Sci., 1984—, Elais, 1988—, Jour. Biol. Sys., 1991—; contbr. chpts. to books and articles to profl. jours. Mem. Ashford (Kent) Sch. Coun., 1980-99. Avocations: hill walking, gardening, skiing. Office: Dept Horticulture, Wye Coll London Univ, Wye TN25 5AH, England

SCHWABER, EVELYNE ALBRECHT, psychiatrist; b. Vienna, Austria, Sept. 17, 1934; d. Henry and Augusta Albrecht; m. Jules R. Schwaber, Apr. 29, 1956; children: Carl S., Jeff M., Mitchell S., Glen I.A. AB, Radcliffe Coll., Cambridge, Mass., 1955; MD, Albert Einstein Coll. Medicine, Bronx, N.Y., 1959. Faculty Boston Psychoanalytic Inst., 1973—; tng. and supervising analyst Psychoanalytic Inst. New Eng., East Needham, Mass., 1983—; speaker in field. Author: more than 60 publs. on aspects of clinical listening with translations published in several foreign languages. Recipient Jour. prize, Am. Psychoanalytic Assn., 1985, Samuel G. Hibbs award Am. Psychiatric Assn., 1992. Mem. Psychoanalytic Assn. of New Eng., East Boston Psychoanalytic Inst. and Soc., Am. Psychoanalytic Soc. (cert.), Am. Psychiatric Assn., Internat. Psychoanalytical Assn., Mass. Med. Soc., Norfolk Dist. Med. Soc., New Eng. Coun. of Child Psychiatry. Avocations: grandparenting, music.

SCHWABL, FRANZ, educator; b. Zell a See, Austria, June 24, 1938; s. Franz and Maria (Weinmeyer) S.; 1 child, Birgitta. PhD, U. Vienna, 1962. Prof. Theoretical Physics U. Linz, Austria, 1973-82, Tech. U., Munich, 1982—. Author: Quantenmechanik, 1988, 4th rev. edit., 1993, 5th rev. edit., 1998, Quantum Mechanics, 1991, 2d rev. edit., 1995, Quantenmechanik für Fortgeschrittene, 1997, Advanced Quantum Mechanics, 1999, Statisstische Mechanik, 2000. Mem. German Phys. Soc., Austrian Phys. Soc., Am. Phys. Soc. Office: Tech U Munich, James-Franck-Strasse, 85747 Garching Germany

SCHWADE, JAMES GARY, radiation oncologist; b. Milw., Dec. 14, 1946; s. Leonard and Esther S.; m. Karyn Karl, July 4, 1982; children: Loryn, David, Jonathan. AB cum laude, Washington U., St. Louis, 1969; MD, Med. Coll. Wis., Milw., 1973. Diplomate Am. Bd. Med. Examiners, therapeutic radiology Am. Bd. Radiologists. From intern to resident in radiaton oncology U. Calif., San Francisco, 1973-77, chief resident radiaiton oncology, 1976-77, instr., 1977-78; acting head radiology sect. radiation oncology br. divsn. cancer treatment, Nat. Cancer Inst., Bethesda, Md., 1978-81; assoc. clin. prof therapeutic radiology U. Miami (Fla.) Sch. Medicine, 1981-87, prof., chmn. dept radiation oncology, 1987-94; assoc. dir. clin. rsch. program Sylvester Cancer Ctr., Miami, 1989-94; med. dir. radiation oncology AMI Palmetto Gen. Hosp., Oncology Treatment Ctr., 1994-95; dir. radiation oncology, Gamma Knife unit Miami Neuro Sci. Ctr., Health South Doctor's Hosp., Coral Gables, 1994—; sr. v.p. for medicine and sci. Proton Therapy Corp. of Am., 1995-97; chmn., CEO Quality Oncology, Ft. Lauderdale, Fla., 1994-98; spl. asst. for radiation oncology, cancer therapy evaluation program, Divsn. Cancer Treatment, Nat., Cancer Inst., Bethesda, 1977-78; cons. Nat. Naval Med. Ctr., Bethesda, 1978-81; chief dept. radiation oncology, med. dir. regional cancer treatment ctr., Baptist Hosp. Miami, 1981-87; chief radiation oncology svc. Jackson Meml. Hosp., VA Hosp., UMHC/SCCC, Miami, 1981-87; lectr. and presenter in field. Contbr. articles to profl. jours., chpts. to books; assoc editor Internat. Jour. of Radiation Oncology, Biology, Physics, 1991-97; revewer ASTRO, Sci. Program 1989-92, Internat. Jour. Oncology. Mem. Am. Cancer Soc., chmn. task force on prostate cancer, Fla. Divsn, mem. rsch. peer rev. subcom; chmn. spl. com. and Fla. com. for Health Care Reform, 1991-92; mem. adv. coun. on radiation protection, Fla., HRS, 1985-94, vice chmn. 1988-90, chmn. subcom. on emergency preparedness; chmn. Nat. Assn. for Proton Therapy, 1992. Recipient Order of Red Sword, Am. Cancer Soc., Dade County Unit, Fla., 1988—; grantee Alpha Therapeutic Corp., Inter Am. Pharms. Ltd., Radiation Therapy Oncology Group, Nat. Cancer Inst. Fellow Am. Coll. Radiology; mem. AMA, Fla. Med. Assn., Dade County Med. Assn., Fla. Radiol. Soc. (legis. com. 1984), Am. Radium Soc., Coun. of Affiliated Regional Radiation Therpy Socs. (counselor-at-large Am. Coll. of Radiology ann. mtg. 1988), Am. Soc. for Therapeutic Radiology and Oncology, Fla. Soc. Clin. Oncology (bd. dirs. 1988-91, legis., legal and ethics com. 1989-90). Fax: 305-347-5187. E-mail: drschwade@aol.com. Home: 10 Edgewater Dr Apt 15A Coral Gables FL 33133-6968 Office: 1221 Brickell Ave Ste 917 Miami FL 33131-3224

SCHWAHN, DIETMAR GERHARD JÜRGEN, physicist; b. Potsdam, Germany, July 19, 1943; s. Gerhard Schwahn and Jutta (Reichardt) Schroth; m. Roswitha Renn, Dec. 3, 1971; children: Alexander, Julius. Dr. rer. nat., Univ., Bochum, Germany, 1976. Scientist Solid State Div. of Forschungszentrumtz, Jülich, Germany, 1976—. Contbr. numerous articles on metal and polymer physics to profl. publs. Mem. Deutsche Physikalische Gesellschaft, Am. Phys. Soc. Home: Peter Schall Str 20, D52152 Simmerath NRW, Germany Office: Solid State Div of KFA, Postfach 1913, D-52425 Jülich Germany

SCHWAIGHOFER, KLAUS, law educator; b. Innsbruck, Austria, Jan. 23, 1956; s. Hans and Elisabeth (Epp) S.; m. Edith Kleissner, Oct. 30, 1982; children: Julia, Lukas, Johannes, Andreas, Teresa. Dr. iur, U. Innsbruck, 1979. Vis. prof. U. Graz, Austria, 1994-95; prof. U. Innsbruck, 1996—; def. lawyer, 1980—; expert, cons. for criminal law matters, 1988—. Author: Auslieferung und Internationales Strafrecht, 1988, Das Strafrechtsanderungsgesetz, 1996, 97, (textbook) Oesterreichisches Strafrecht Besonderer Teil I und II, Das Neue Suchtmittelrecht, 1997, Das Neue Suchtmittelrecht Ergänzungsband, 1998; contbr. articles to profl. jours. Office: Univ Innsbruck Inst Strafrecht, Innrain 52, 60 20 Innsbruck Austria

SCHWALB, HARRY, artist; b. Pitts., July 2, 1924; s. Adolf and Maria (Bruder) Schwalb; m. Myrna Kline, Dec. 28, 1958 (div. May 1989); 1 child, Adam. Student, Pa. State U., 1940-42; BS summa cum laude, U. Pitts., 1947, MA, 1949. Creative dir. Fisher Sci. Co., Pitts., 1951-93; U.S. corr. ARTnews Mag., N.Y.C., 1988—; editor The Lab. Mag., Pitts., 1960-93; art critic Pitts. Mag., 1977-95; dean Ivy Sch. Profl. Art, Pitts., 1970-72; juror, curator and cons. for arts orgns. in U.S. and Can. Illustrator: Of Long Ago, 1949, A Western Journal, 1951; one man shows include Collectors Gallery, N.Y.C., 1960, Arnot Art Gallery, Elmira, N.Y., 1962, Carnegie Mus. Art, Pitts., 1965, Westmoreland Mus. Am. Art, Greensburg, Pa., 1965, 99, Mendelson Gallery, Pitts., 1995, 98; represented in permanent collections Carnegie Mus. Art, Westmoreland Mus. Am. Art. Recipient Critical Writing Silver medal U. Kans., 1990, Golden Quill award Pitts. Press Club, 1990-95; ann. Harry Schwalb award established in 1996 Pitts. Mag. Avocations: lecturing, writing essays. Home and Office: 166 N Dithridge St Pittsburgh PA 15213-2647

SCHWALLIE, JOHN ALAN, media company executive, certified public accountant; b. Westfield, Mass., Apr. 4, 1963; s. Harvey Frederick and Barbara Schade; m. Lisa Renee Auerbach, Sept. 6, 1997. BA, Skidmore Coll., 1986; MBA, Cornell U., 1992. CPA, N.Y. Auditor Urbach Kahn & Werlin, Glens Falls, N.Y., 1986-89; restaurant owner Provincetown, Mass., 1989-90; advisor to fin. dir. Prague Breweries, Czech Republic, 1992-93; fin. dir. NOVA TV, Prague, Czech Republic, 1994-95; CFO Ctrl. European Media Enterprizes, London, 1995—. Office: Ctrl European Media Enterpr, 18 D'Arblay St, London WIV 3FP, England

SCHWAN, LEROY BERNARD, artist, retired educator; b. Dec. 8, 1932; s. Joseph L. and Dorothy (Papenfuss) S.; children from previous marriage: David A., Mark J., William R., Catherine L., Maria E. Student, Wis. State U., River Falls, 1951-53, Southeastern Signal Sch., Ga., 1954; BS, U. Minn., 1958, MEd, 1960, postgrad., 1961-64; postgrad., No. Mich. U., 1965, Tex. Tech. U., 1970, So. Ill. U., 1978, U. Iowa, 1980; EdD (hon.), U. Iowa, 1988. Head art dept. Unity Pub. Schs., Milltown, Wis., 1958-61; instr. art Fridley Pub. Schs., Mpls., 1961-64; asst. prof. art No. Mich. U., Marquette, 1964-66; asst. prof. art Mankato (Minn.) State Coll., 1966-71, assoc. prof., 1971-74; tchr. off-campus grad. classes Northeast Mo. State U., John Wood Cmty. Coll.; dir. Art Workshop Educultural Ctr., 1968; dir. art edn. Quincy (Ill.) Pub. Schs., 1974-78, art tchr., 1978-88, ret., 1988; tchr. art to mentally retarded children, Faribault, Minn., Owatonna, Minn., Mankato, Lake Owasso Children's Home, St. Paul; dir. art workshops, Mankato, 1970, St. Paul, 1972, 73, 74, 75; dir. workshops tchrs. mentally retarded Mankato, 1971, Faribault, 1972, Omaha, 1972-73, Quincy, 1974, 79, 82, 84-86, asst. adj. Ill. VA Home, 1980—. Author: Art Curriculum Guide Unity Public Schs., 1961, Portrait of Jean, 1974, Schwan's Art Activities, 1984, Poems of Life, 1995; co-author: Bryant-Schwan Design Test, 1971, Bryant-Schwan Art Guide, 1973; contbr. articles to profl. jours., poems to Am. Poetry Assn. publs., 1984-94, Nat. Libr. Poetry publs., 1991-96, 97, 98, Internat. Soc. Poets, 2000; one-man shows: Estherville Jr. Coll., 1968, Mankato State Coll., 1968, 71, 73, 97, Farmington, Wis., 1970, 71, 91, Good Thunder, Minn., 1972, Quincy, 1975, 77, 84, Mankato, Minn. 1975, Western Ill. U., 1979, St. Croix River Valley Arts Coun. Gallery, Osceola, Wis., 1993, 94, 95, 96, The Northern Ctr. for the Arts, Amery, Wis., 1994, Health Ptnrs. Gallery, Woodbury, Minn., 2000; exhibited in group shows: Pentagon, Washington, 1955, U. Minn., 1958, No. Mich. U., 1965, St. Cloud State Coll., 1967, Moorhead State Coll., 1967, Bemidji (Minn.) State Coll., 1967, MacNider Mus., Mason City, Iowa, 1969, 72, 73, 74, Gallery 500, Mankato, Minn., 1970, Rochester, Minn., 1972, Minn. Mus., St. Paul, 1973, Hannibal, Mo., 1976, 77-78, Quincy, Ill., 1976, 77, 85, Ill. Art Educators Show, 1984-85, Tchrs. Retirement Art Show, Springfield, Ill., 1987, Phipps Ctr. Arts, Hudson, Wis., 1997-98, 99, 2000; prodr. ednl. TV series, 1964-65, also 2 shows Kids Komments, Sta. WGEM, Quincy; mural commd. Gem City Coll., 1977. Weblos leader Twin Valley council Boy Scouts Am., 1968-69; bd. dirs. Polk County Hist. Soc., 1993—. Served with Signal Corps., AUS, 1954-56. Recipient cert. of accomplishment Sec. Army, 1955, Golden Poet award, 1985, 86, 88, 90, 91, Silver Poet award 1989. Mem. Nat. Art Edn. Assn., Ill. Art Edn. Assn., Cath. Order Foresters, Am. Legion, Phi Delta Kappa. Home: 849 County Road H New Richmond WI 54017-6209

SCHWANAUER, FRANCIS, philosopher, educator; b. Zsámbék, Hungary, Jan. 20, 1933; came to U.S., 1959; s. Georg and Maria (Keller) S.; m. Johanna Maria Koelln, Sept. 29, 1957; children: Stephan Michael, Miriam Frances. Maturum, Ulrich von Hutten Gymnasium, Korntal, Germany, 1954; PhD, U. Stuttgart, Germany, 1959. Asst. prof. Lebanon Valley Coll., Annville, Pa., 1960-62, U. Maine, Orono, 1962-65; asst. prof. U. So. Maine, Portland Gorham, 1965-67, assoc. prof., 1967-72, prof., 1972—. Author: Truth is a Neighborhood with Nothing in Between, 1977, Those Fallacies by Slight of Reason, 1978, No Many is not a One (For the Case is Comparison), 1981, The Flesh of Thought is Pleasure or Pain, 1982, To Make Sure is to Cohere, 1982, Philosophical Fact and Paradox, 1987, Fables from the Fox, 1991; abstracts, 1997, 98, 99, 2000; contbr. articles to profl. publs. Grantee John Anson Kittredge Ednl. Fund, 1991, 93. Mem. New England Philos. Assn., Internat. Platform Assn. Democrat. Roman Catholic. Avocation: fishing. Home: 4 Woodmont St Portland ME 04102-2709

SCHWANK, JOHANNES WALTER, chemical engineering educator; b. Zams, Tyrol, Austria, July 6, 1950; came to U.S., 1978; s. Friedrich Karl and Johanna (Ruepp) S.; m. Lynne Violet Duguay; children: Alexander Johann, Leonard Friedrich, Hanna Violet, Rosa Joy. Diploma in chemistry, U. Innsbruck, Austria, 1975, PhD, 1978. Mem. faculty U. Mich., Ann Arbor, 1978—, assoc. prof. chem. engring., 1984-90, acting dir. Ctr. for Catalysis and Surface Sci., 1985-90, prof., interim chmn. dept. chem. engring., 1990-91, assoc. dir. Electron Microbeam Analysis Lab., 1990—; chmn. dept. chem. engring., 1991-95; prof. chem. engring. U. Mich., Ann Arbor, 1995—; vis. prof. U. Innsbruck, 1987-88, Tech. U. Vienna, 1988; cons. in field. Patentee bimetallic cluster catalysts, hydrodesulfurization catalysts and microelectronic gas sensors; contbr. over 100 articles to sci. jours. Fulbright-Hays scholar, 1978. Mem. AAAS, Am. Chem. Soc., Am. Inst. Chem. Engrs., Mich. Catalysis Soc. (sec.-treas. 1982-83, v.p. 1983-84, pres. 1984-85), Am. Soc. Engring. Edn. Home: 2335 Placid Way Ann Arbor MI 48105-1295 Office: U Mich Dept Chem Engring 2300 Hayward St Ann Arbor MI 48109-2136

SCHWANTES, ROBERT SIDNEY, international relations executive; b. Beetown Township, Wis., July 11, 1922; s. Kurt John and Lillian Ellen (Walker) S.; m. Marion Laura Miles, July 15, 1943; children: Virginia, Janet, Ingrid. AB summa cum laude, Harvard U., 1943; MA, U. Colo., 1947; PhD, Harvard U., 1950. Instr. in history Harvard U., Cambridge, Mass., 1950-52; Carnegie resch. fellow Coun. on Foreign Rels., N.Y.C., 1952-54; various positions The Asia Found., San Francisco and Tokyo, 1954-66; dir. of programs The Asia Found., San Francisco, 1966-69, v.p. for programs, 1969-84, exec. v.p., 1984-88; vis. rsch. scholar Hoover Inst., Stanford, 1988—; mem. Am. adv. com. Japan Found., Tokyo, 1984-86, vis. History lectr. Harvard U., 1958. Author: Japanese and Americans, 1955, What Did You Do in the War, Daddy?, 1998; contbr. articles to profl. jours. Vestryman St. Paul's Episcopal Ch., Burlingame, Calif., 1993-95. Lt. (j.g.), USNR, 1942-46, PTO. Assn. Asian Studies, World Affairs Coun. No. Calif. Democrat. Avocations: reading, travel. Home: 1432 Benito Ave Burlingame CA 94010-5550

SCHWARCZ, STEVEN LANCE, law educator, lawyer; b. N.Y.C., Nov. 10, 1949; s. Charles and Elinor Schwarcz; m. Susan Beth Kolodny, Aug. 24, 1975; children: Daniel Benjamin, Rebekah Mara. BS summa cum laude, in Aero. Engring., New York U., 1971; JD, Columbia U., 1974. Bar: N.Y. 1975, U.S. Dist. Ct. (so. dist.) N.Y. 1975. Assoc. Shearman & Sterling, N.Y.C., 1974-82, ptnr., 1983-89; ptnr., chmn. structured fin. practice group Kaye, Scholer, Fierman, Hays & Handler, 1989-96; adj. prof. law Yeshiva U., Benjamin N. Cardozo Sch. Law, N.Y.C., 1983-92; vis. lectr. Yale Law Sch., 1992-96; lectr. in law Columbia Law Sch., 1992-96; prof. law Duke U. Sch. Law, 1996—; dir. Duke Global Capital Markets Ctr., 1997—. Contbr. articles to profl. jours. Chmn. Friends of the Eldridge St. Synagogue, N.Y.C., 1979—, Legis. Drafting Rsch. Fund. Recipient First Prize award Pub. Speaking Contest, NYU, 1971; George Granger Brown scholar, 1971; NSF grantee in Math., 1969. Fellow Am. Coll. Commercial Fin. Lawyers; mem. Am. Law Inst., Assn. of Bar of City of N.Y. (environ. law com. 1975-78, nuclear tech. com. 1979-81, sci. and law com. 1985—, chmn. 1987—), Am. Law and Econs. Assn., Tau Beta Pi, Sigma Gamma Tau. Jewish. Office: Duke U Sch Law Box 90360 Science Dr & Towerview Rd Durham NC 27708

SCHWARTING, RAINER KARL WILLI, psychologist; b. Berlin, Germany, July 27, 1955; s. Karl and Ursula Eva Maria (Möller) S.; m. Georgia Schlöder. Apr. 28, 1990; children: Alessa, Mona. MS in Psychology, U. Düsseldorf, Germany, 1982, PhD, 1987, habilitation, 1993. Asst. prof. Inst. Physiol. Psychology, Düsseldorf, Germany, Heisenberg fellow, 1994-98; prof. gen. and physiol. psychology, 1999—; mem. Biologisch-Medizinisches Forschungszentrum, U. Dusseldorf, mem. grad. program.; edtl. bd. Neurotoxicity Rsch., 1999—. Mem. editorial bd. Neuropsychobiology, 1994—. Recipient Rsch. grants Deutsche Forschungsgemeinschaft, Bonn, Germany, 1992-94, 94-96, 96—. Mem. German Soc. for Psychology (treas. 1994—), Soc. for Neurosci., N.Y. Acad. Scis., European Behavioral Pharmacology Soc. Home: von Stauffenberg Str 27, 41352 Korschenbroich Germany Office: Philipps-Univ Marburg, Gutenbergstr 18, 35032 Marburg Germany

SCHWARTZ, A(LBERT) TRUMAN, chemistry educator; b. Freeman, S.D., May 8, 1934; s. Albert and Edna Kaufman Schwartz; m. Beverly Beatty, Aug. 12, 1958; children: Ronald Eric, Katherine Schwartz Herrmann. BA, U. S.D., 1956, Oxford (Eng.) U., 1958; MA, Oxford (Eng.) U., 1960; PhD, MIT, 1963; DSc, U. S.D., 1991. Rsch. chemist Procter & Gamble Co., Cin., 1963-66; asst. prof. Macalester Coll., St. Paul, 1966-72, assoc. prof., 1972-78, prof., 1978-83, DeWitt Wallace prof., 1983—, dean faculty, 1974-76, chair dept. chemistry, 1980-88, 94-95; vis. rschr. U. Lund, Sweden, 1968, U. Mass., Amherst, 1972-73; vis. prof. U. Wis., Madison, 1979-80; hon. vis. prof. U. York, Eng., 1994; dep. dir. tchr. preparation and enhancement NSF, Washington, 1986-87. Author: Chemistry: Imagination and Implication, 1973; sr. author: Chemistry in Context: Applying Chemistry to Society, 1994, 2nd edit., 1997; co-editor: Motion Toward Perfection: The Achievement of Joseph Priestley, 1970; contbr. articles to profl. jours. Mem. selection com. Rhodes Scholarship Trust, 1963—, sec. Minn. and Midwest dist. coms., 1993. Recipient Catalyst award in chem. edn. Chem. Mfrs. Assn., 1982, Coll. Sci. Tchr. of Yr., Minn. Sci. Tchrs. Assn., 1988; Rhodes scholar Rhodes Trust, Oxford U., 1956-58. Fellow AAAS; mem. Am. Chem. Soc. (chair divsn. chem. edn. 1989, chair Minn. sect. 1992-93, mem. various coms., Conn. Sect. award 1991, Brasted award 1996, James Flack Norris award 1997). Avocations: music, photography, travel, cooking. E-mail: schwartz@macalester.edu. Home: 68 Otis Ave Saint Paul MN 55104 Office: Macalester Coll 1600 Grand Ave Saint Paul MN 55105-1801

SCHWARTZ, ALEXANDER, translator, interpreter; b. Budapest, Hungary, May 22, 1926; came to US, 1937; s. William and Elizabeth (Weinberger) S.; m. Miriam Kleinman, Aug. 31, 1947; children: Daniel Glenn, Lawrence Lee, Annette Lynne La Due. BA in Engring. and Langs., Columbia U., 1950; MS in Math., NYU, 1956. Mathematician to sr. mathematician Reeves Instrument Corp., N.Y.C., 1951-62; staff analyst (math.) Gen. Precision Aerospace, Little Falls, N.J., 1962; translator to sr. reviser UN, N.Y.C., 1962-86; self-employed translator, interpreter N.Y.C., 1986—. Translator: (books) Spl. Topics in Number Theory, 1964, Celestial Mechanics, 1966, Refaire l'ONU!, 1988, The New Law of the Sea, 1988. Sgt. U.S. Army, 1944-46. Named the Greatest U.S. Linguist Guinness Book of Records. Mem. Am. Translators Assn., N.Y. Circle of Translators. Jewish. Home: 3299 Cambridge Ave Bronx NY 10463-3623

SCHWARTZ, BERNARD JULIAN, lawyer; b. Edmonton, Alberta, Can., July 29, 1960; came to U.S., 1982; s. Sol and Anne (Motkovich) S. BA, U. Alberta, 1981; JD, McGeorge Sch. Law, 1986. Bar: U.S. Supreme Ct. 1991. Atty. Ropers, Majeski, San Francisco, 1987-88, Riverside County Pub. Defenders, Riverside, Calif., 1988-89; pvt. practice Riverside, 1990—. Coach Riverside County H.S. Mock Trial Team, 1990, 96, 97. Mem. Calif. Attys. Criminal Justice, Calif. Pub. Defenders Assn., Riverside County Bar Assn. Home: 6157 Hillary Ct Riverside CA 92506-2139

SCHWARTZ, CAROL ANN, investment company executive; m. Michael D. Schwartz, Jun., 1985; children: Matthew, Allison, Elana. B in Bus. Adminstrn., U. Cinn., 1983; M in Bus. Adminstrn., Finance, Xavier U., 1984; graduate, Grad. Real Estate Inst., 1992. Lic. real estate sales agent. Asst. v.p. Fifth Third Bank, 1984-91; exec. v.p. Morris Investment Co., 1991—. Mem., Adath Israel Sisterhood (Torah Fund-Residence Halls luncheon com. 1994, 97, 99, donor com. 1994, 95, v.p. membership 1995-97, v.p. programming 1999-2000, publicity com. 1995-99, pres., 1999—), Adath Israel Synagogue (bd. mem. 1992—, fin. sec. 1994-96, corr. sec. 1999-2000, budget and fin. com. 1994-95, 95-96, 98—, religious svcs. analysis com. 1991-92; dues analysis com. 1993, publicity chair 1994—, Night of Rising Stars chair, 1996, advt. book com. 1991-97, 99, advt. book chair 1994, 95, baker 1995, 96, Adath Israel 2000 Campaign com., 150th ann. com.), Cin. Bus. and Profl. Women (Cin. chpt. long range planning com. 1985-88, 95-96, chair, 1986-88, Nat. Bus. Women's Week Dinner com. 1986-88, conveener of judges 1990, program chair 1988-90, first v.p. 1988-90, pres.-elect 1990-91, pres., 1989-91, 93, Meet Profl. Women Role Model 1985-90, 92-94, endowment com. 1991-93, adv. com. chair 1993-94, program spkr. 1990, 94, 95, bd. tng./leadership tng. facilitator 1995; regional chpt. long range planning chair 1986-87, nom. com. chair 1992-94, first v.p. 1994-95; state chpt. conv. attendee 1985, 90, 91, 92, 93, nom. com. 1993, 94), Fin. Women Internat. (Cin. chpt. pub. affairs chair 1984-85, 85-86, sponsor's chair 1984-85, 85-86, v.p. 1985-86, pres. 1986-87, mem. of Yr. 1988; state chpt. state conf. attendee 1985, 86, 87, 88, program spkr., bd. mem. 1986-88, state conf. chair 1987-88, mem. of Yr. 1987), Greek Affairs Coun. U. Cin. (bd. mem. 1985-94, awards com. 1991-94, nom. com. 1990, 91, 93, 94, sec. 1990-94), Hadassah Ya'al Group (hosp. chair 1992-93, bulletin co-chair 1992-93, chair 1994-99, bd. mem. 1992—, co-coord. 1992-93, pres. 1995-97, community svc. coord. 1997—) Hadassah Cin. chpt. (winter mtg. com. 1992-93, bd. mem. 1993—, donor com. publicity 1992-93, 96-97, pre-donor brunch chair 1992-93, chair 1993-94, donor book 1994-96, jewels and memorials 1995-97, 98-99, cons., 1999-2000, budget chair 1995-97, com. 1997—, regional conf. attendee 1993, 96, 97, 98, 99, leading gifts divsn. co-chair 1996-97, pres. 1997-99) Hadassah Regional (fundraising conf. coord. 1993, regional conf. com., spkr. 1997, regional conf. 1998, bd. mem. 1995-96, 96-97, 97-98, 98-99, 99-2000, Nat. Young Leaders Adv. coun. rep. 1999-2001), Hadassah Midwest Area Coop. (fundraising conf. attendee 1993, pres. tng. attendee, 1997, young womens' co-chair, 1999-2000) Hadassah National (young women/young leaders mission to Israel 1997, Nat. Conv. chat room facilitator 1998, 99, Nat. Young Leaders Adv. Coun. 1999-2000, conv. attendee 1996, 97, 98, 99), Hillel (bd. mem. 1998—, alumni com. 1998-99, 99-2000, auction com. 1998-99, 99-2000), Jewish Fedn. of Cin. (leadership coun. group 1987-92, solicitor 1991, 92, lect. series com. 1989, kickoff party com. 1990, women's divsn. group 1992—, campaign co-chair 1996-97, bus. and profl. women co-chair 1998-99, Israel programs cabinet 1998-99, chair 1999-2000, campaign cabinet program co-chair, 1999-2000, bd. dirs. 1999-2001), Jewish Nat. Fund (hostess liquid assets luncheon, 1993, bd. mem. 1995—, v.p. edn. 1996-97, 97-98, 98-99, tchrs. edn. day chair 1997-98, 98-99, four star dining com. 1998-99, 1999-2000, trade and industry dinner com. 1997, 98, Green Sunday com. 1996—, Walk for Water com. 1998—), Jewish Women's Auxiliary (life 1995—), Jr. Achievement (group adv. 1984-85, 85-86), March of Dimes (vol. neighborhood coord., solicitor 1993-97, 98—), Nat. Conf. Christians and Jews (1993 awards dinner com.), Nat. Coun. Jewish Women (life 1993—, bus. and profl. group program com. 1990-91, 91-92, 92-93; chpt. legis. com. 1991-92, pub. affairs com. 1992-93, computer analysis com. 1992-93, fin. analysis com. 1993-94), Orgn. Rehabilitation and Tng. Blue Chip chpt. (lox box com. 1993, 95, 96), United Appeal (group fundraiser 1986-89), United Jewish Cmtys. Nat. Young Leadership Cabinet, 2000—, U. Cin. Coll. Bus. Adminstrn. (guest spkr. career devel. 1990, 91, 94), Yavneh PTA (bd. mem 1995-96, 96-97, Sukkot decorating com., Rosh Hashanah Treats co-chair, Tu'Bishvat spkr. 1997, Tu'Bishvat Seder com. 1998), Yavneh Day Sch. (v.p. fundraising 2000—, bd. mem. 1997—, Friends of Yavneh Campaign chair, 1998-99, 99-2000). Recipient State Member of Yr. Fin. Women Internat., 1987, Cin. chpt. Mem. of Yr., 1988, Nat. Leadership award Cin. chpt. Hadassah Ya'al Group, 1994, Clara Geller Young Leadership award Jewish Fedn. Cin.; named among Outstanding Women of Am., 1985, The Cincinnati Business Courier's Who's Who Among Women in Bus. in Cin., 1992, Top 40 Women in Bus., 1993. Mem. AAUW, Cin. Bd. of Realtors (mem. svcs. com. 1992-93), Ohio Assn. Relators (conv. attendee), Nat. Assn. Realtors (conv. attendee), Comm. Indsl. Real Estate Industry (CCIM designate), Cin. Art Mus., Cin., Historical Soc., Cin. Playhouse in the Park, Contemporary Arts Ctr., Nat. Assn. Female Execs., Nat. History Mus., U. Cin. Alumni Assn. (life mem. 1986—), Women's City Club, World Jewish Cong., Xavier U. Alumni Assn. (life).

SCHWARTZ, CHARLES ROBERT, JR., photographer; b. Beckley, W.Va., Jan. 3, 1951; arrived in Italy, 1982; s. Charles Robert Schwartz and Reva Geraldine (Plumley) Sydnor; m. Delia Montero, Sept. 25, 1971 (div. Aug. 1979); 1 child, Melani. Student, Rochester Inst. Tech., 1968-69, U. Hawaii, 1980-81, U. Md., Naples, Italy, 1984-86. Owner Bob Schwartz Photography, Honolulu, 1974-82, Naples, 1982-85, Milan, 1985—; cons. Edicat, Milan, 1996-97. Photographer: Il Gatto, Amico Mio, 1990, The Eukanuba Cat Book, 1997, Barron's Cat Encyclopedia, 1997; photographer, editor, graphic design artist FIFe News, 1995-97, Colours and Patterns, 1998. Mem. TAU Visual. Avocations: creating web pages, stamp collecting, traveling, aquariums, reading. Home and Office: via Mario Franza 3, 10010 Lessolo TO, Italy

SCHWARTZ, CHARLES WALTER, lawyer; b. Brenham, Tex., Dec. 27, 1953; s. Walter C. and Annie (Kuehn) S.; m. Kay Anne Kern, Sept. 24, 1996. BS, U. Tex., 1975, MA, 1980, JD, 1977; LLM, Harvard U., 1980. Bar: Tex. 1977; bd. cert. civil appellate law Tex. Bd. Legal Specialization. Law clk. U.S. Ct. Appeals (5th cir.), Austin, Tex., 1977-79; assoc. Vinson & Elkins L.L.P., Houston, 1980-86, ptnr., 1986—. Contbr. articles to law revs. Fellow Coll. State Bar Tex. (dir.); mem. ABA, State Bar Tex. (former chmn. grievance com. 1993-99), Tex. Bar Found., Houston Bar Found., Houston Bar Assn., Am. Law Inst., Tex. Law Rev. Assn., Bar Assn. 5th Cir. Home: 2825 Albans Rd Houston TX 77005-2309 Office: Vinson & Elkins LLP 2300 First City Tower 1001 Fannin St Houston TX 77002-6760

SCHWARTZ, GEORGE R., physician; b. Caribou, Maine; m. Kathleen Schwartz; children: Ruth, Rebekah, Rachel, Moses, Abigail, John Gabriel, Aaron. BS in Chemistry with honors, Hobart Coll., 1963; MD magna cum laude, SUNY, Bklyn., 1967. Diplomate Am. Bd. Family Practice, Am. Bd. Emergency Medicine; cert. CPR instr. Intern King County Hosp., Seattle, 1967-68; instr. dept. medicine U. Wash., Seattle, 1967-68; resident in psychiatry Hillside Hosp., Glen Oaks, N.Y., 1968-69; resident in surgery Ind. U. Med. Ctr., Indpls., 1971-72; instr. emergency medicine Med. Coll. Pa., Phila., 1972-76, dir. emergency svcs., asst. dir. emergency medicine program, 1972-74; dir. emergency medicine West Jersey Hosp., 1974-76; pvt. practice, 1977; assoc. prof., dir. divsn. emergency medicine U. N.Mex., Albuquerque, 1978-83; staff mem. emergency medicine Heights Gen. Hosp., Albuquerque, 1983-85; with Los Alamos (N.Mex.) Med. Ctr., 1985-90; vis. assoc. prof. Med. Coll. Pa., 1991—; co-founder Allied Genomics. Author: Geriatric Emergencies, 1984; Co-author: (with Tandberg) Emergency Medicine Continuing Edn. Rev., 1981, 2d edit. 1984, (with Bosker) Geriatric Emergency Medicine, 1990; editor: Principles and Practice Emergency Medicine, 1978, 3d edit., 1992, 4th edit., 1999; co-editor Trauma Rounds, 1973-75; editorial bd. Annals Emergency Medicine, 1972-81, Resident and Staff Physician, 1978—, Emergency Med. Abstracrts, 1978-85, Med. Exam. Publ. Co., 1981-87; contbr. articles to profl. jours., chpts. to textbooks. Med. dir. The Bridge

Counselling Ctrs., Los Alamos, N.Mex., 1988-91, N.Mex. Poison Ctr., 1978-83; dir. planning com. disaster exercise Phila. Internat. Airport, 1974, Camden County Poison Ctr., 1974-76. Recipient Gallup award, 1973, Giraffe award, 1990. Mem. AAAS, AMA, Am. Coll. Emergency Physicians (charter mem.; pres. N.Mex. chpt. 1980-81), N.Mex. Med. Soc., Univ. Assn. Emergency Physicians (chmn. socio-econ. com. 1976-77), Internat. Emergency Care Assn., Am. Trauma Soc. (founding mem.), Am. Acad. Clin. Toxicology, Am. Acad. Emergency Medicine (founding mem., sec. 1994, bd. dirs. 1998—), Internat. Assn. for Study of MSG and Food Additives (pres. 1988). Achievements include patent for use of a pharmaceutical agent in male impotence; research on computer applications in medicine, new medical diagnostic instruments; patentee in cerebral hypothermia field; partner, Brain Resuscitation Research LLC, neuropoietin research through Healing Research Institute. Address: PO Box 1968 Santa Fe NM 87504-1968

SCHWARTZ, GERALD, public relations and fundraising agency executive; b. N.Y.C., June 22, 1927; s. George and Martha F. S.; m. Felice P. Schwartz, June 25, 1950: children: Gary R., Gregg R., Wendy L. Student N.C. State U., 1944-45; AB, U. Miami, Fla., 1949, BS, 1950, postgrad., 1966-67. Staff writer Miami Herald, 1941-44; publicity dir. U.S. Army in Europe, 1946-48; editor Miami Beach Sun, 1950-51; fund raising and pub. rels. counselor, Miami, 1952-58; press sec. to Gov. Nebr., 1959-60; exec. v.p. Bar-Ilan U., Ramat Gan, Israel, Israel, 1960-61; prin. Gerald Schwartz Agy., Miami, Fla., 1962—. Dep. chmn. Dem. Midwest Conf., 1958-60; pres. Am. Zionist Fedn. So. Fla., 1970-73, 86-92; nat. v.p. Am. Zionist Fedn., 85-89, 91-93; pres. Pres.'s council Zionist Orgn. Am., 1983-85; bd. dirs. Temple Emanu-El of Greater Miami, Papanicolaou Cancer Research Inst., Miami, 1962-80; vice chmn. Urban League of Greater Miami, 1983-87; vice chmn. City of Miami Beach Planning Bd., 1953-55; bd. dirs. Greater Miami Symphony, 1982-87, Miami Beach Taxpayers Assn., 1988-98; pres. Civic League Miami Beach, 1985-87; nat. chmn. Friends of Pioneer Women/Na'amat, 1984-98; pres. Greater Miami chpt. Assn. Welfare of Soldiers in Israel, 1983-86; chmn. City of Miami Beach Hurricane Def. Com., 1978-86, 90-97; trustee South Shore Hosp. and Med. Ctr., Miami, 1987—; exec. vice chmn. South Shore Med. Ctr. Found., 1989—; bd. govs. Barry U., 1985-86; chmn. Econ. Devel. Coun. City of Miami Beach, 1985-91; bd. dirs. Crimestoppers of Dade County, 1991-94; bd. dirs., adminstrv. com. Jewish Nat. Fund of Am., 1995—, v.p. Greater Miami Region, 1996-97; mem. exec. bd. State of Israel Bonds Orgn., 1996—. Served with U.S. Army, 1944-46. Recipient Jerusalem Peace award State of Israel Bonds, 1978., Jerusalem 3000 award State Of Israel, 1996. Mem. Pub. Rels. Soc. Am. (accredited; treas. So. Fla. chpt. 1962-64), Am. Pub. Rels. Assn. (pres. chpt. 1960-61), Am. Assn. Polit. Cons, Nat. Assn. Fund Raising Execs. (pres. chpt. 1977-78), Miami Beach Taxpayers Assn. (bd. dirs. 1994—), Miami Internat. Press Club (bd. dirs. 1991—), Miami Beach C. of C. (v.p. 1978-80, 81-84, 86-87, pres.-elect 1988-90, trustee 1990—), Lead and Ink, Tiger Bay Club (pres. 1986-88), Prime Minister's Club of State of Israel (Greater Miami chmn. 1997—), B'nai B'rith (pres. lodge 1964-66), Theta Omicron Pi, Omicron Delta Kappa, Alpha Delta Sigma (pres. chpt. 1965-67), Zeta Beta Tau. Office: Gerald Schwartz Agy 600 Alton Rd Miami FL 33139-5502*

SCHWARTZ, GERALD WILFRED, financial executive; b. Winnipeg, Man., Can., Nov. 24, 1941; s. Andrew O. and Lillian Arkin (Leith) S.; m. Heather Reisman, May 15, 1982; children: Carey, Jill, Andrea, Anthony. B.Commerce, U. Man., 1962, LLB, 1966; MBA, Harvard U., 1970. V.p. Estabrook & Co., Inc., N.Y.C., 1970-73, Bear Stearns & Co., N.Y.C., 1973-77; pres., dir., mem. exec. com. CanWest Capital Corp., Winnipeg, 1977-83; chmn., pres., CEO ONEX Corp., Toronto, 1984—; bd. dirs. Sky Chefs Inc., Celestica Internat. Holdings Inc., Bank of N.S. Bd. dirs. Can. Coun. Christians and Jews; vice chmn., bd. dirs., gov., mem. exec. com. Mt. Sinai Hosp. of Toronto; dir. bd. of assocs. Harvard Bus. Sch.; trustee Simon Wiesenthal Ctr.; mem. adv. coun. Dancer Transition Ctr.; nat. bd. dirs. Ben-Gurion U. of the Negev; hon. trustee Starlight Found. With RCAF, 1958. Office: Onex Corp, 161 Bay St 49th Fl PO Box 700, Toronto, ON Canada M5J 2S1

SCHWARTZ, GORDON FRANCIS, surgeon, educator; b. Plainfield, N.J., Apr. 29, 1935; s. Samuel H. and Mary (Adelman) S.; m. Rochelle DeG. Krantz, Sept. 5, 1959; children—Amory Blair, Susan Leslie. AB, Princeton U., 1956; MD, Harvard U., 1960; MBA, U. Pa., 1990. Intern N.Y. Hosp.-Cornell Med. Ctr., N.Y.C., 1960-61; resident in surgery Columbia-Presbyterian Med. Ctr., N.Y.C., 1963-68; instr. surgery Columbia U., N.Y.C., 1966-68; assoc. in surgery U. Pa., Phila., 1968-70; dir. clin. services Breast Diagnostic Ctr., Jefferson Med. Coll., Phila., 1973-78, asst. prof. surgery, 1970-71, assoc. prof., 1971-78, prof., 1978—; practice medicine specializing in surgery and diseases of breast, Phila., 1968—; founder, chmn. acad. com. Breast Health Inst., 1990—; edtl. bd. The Breast Jour., 1994—. Author: (with R.H. Guthrie, Jr.) Reconstructive and Aesthetic Mammoplasty, 1989, (with Douglas Marchant) Breast Disease: Diagnosis and Treatment, 1981; mem. editl. bd. The Breast-Ofcl. Jour. of the European Soc. of Mastology, 1996—, Cancer, 1997—; co-editor Seminars Breast Disease, 1997; mem. editl. bd. ONE, Oncology Econs., 1999—; contbr. numerous 170 articles to profl. jours. Mem. Pa. Gov.'s Task Force on Cancer, 1976-82; mem. breast cancer task force Phila. chpt. Am. Cancer Soc.; mem. clin. investigation rev. com. Nat. Cancer Inst., 1992-95. Served to capt. AUS, 1961-63. NIH Cancer Control fellow, 1968-69. Mem. ACS, AMA, AAUP, Assn. for Acad. Surgery, Allen O. Whipple Surg. Assn., Soc. Surg. Oncology, Internat. Cardiovasc. Soc., Soc. for Surgery Alimentary Tract, Am. Soc. Clin. Oncology, Soc. for Study Breast Diseases (pres. 1981-83), Soc. Internat. Senologie (treas. 1982-90, v.p. 1990-92, sci. com. 1992—), Pa. Med. Soc., Am. Soc. Transplant Surgeons, N.Y. Acad. Scis., Am. Soc. Artificial Internal Organs, Am. Radium Soc., Philadelphia County Med. Soc. (chmn. com. on econs. 1999-2000, bd. dirs. 1999-2000), Italian Soc. Senology (hon.), Greek Surg. Soc. (hon.), The Phila. Club, Union League, Locust Club, Princeton Club (pres. Phila. 1989-91), Princeton Club (N.Y.C.), Princeton Terrace Club, Nassau Club, Phi Beta Kappa, Sigma Xi, Alpha Omega Alpha, Nu Sigma Nu. Republican. Jewish. Office: 1015 Chestnut St Ste 510 Philadelphia PA 19107-4305

SCHWARTZ, GREGORY JOHN, lawyer, business and investments transactions specialist; b. Rochester, Pa., Oct. 10, 1958; s. Louis Frederick and Helene (Kardasz) S.; m. Ann Elizabeth Salazar, Aug. 20, 1988. BA in Govt. and Politics cum laude, U. Md., 1981; JD, Cath. U. Am., 1985; postgrad., Georgetown U., 1990-93. Bar: Md. 1986, U.S. Dist. Ct. Md. 1986, D.C. 1987. Assoc. Williams and Huffman, Chevy Chase, Md., 1985-87, Conroy, Fitzgerald, Ballman and Dameron, Gaithersburg, Md., 1987-90; mng. ptnr. Gregory J. Schwartz, Profl. Law Corp., Gaithersburg, 1990—. Contbr. articles to profl. jours. Mem. ABA (former program Ctrl. and Ea. European Law Initiative), Md. Bar Assn., D.C. Bar Assn., Montgomery County Bar Assn., Washington Fgn. Law Soc. (former bd. dirs., rapporteur), Suburban Md. Internat. Trade Assn. (former pres. and bd. dirs.), Internat. Trade Networking Group of Washington (founder), Jaycees (bd. dirs. and legal counsel Washington br. 1987-90), Lowry Alumni Investors Club, Phi Alpha Delta, Sigma Alpha Epsilon, Omicron Delta Kappa, KC. Avocations: horsemanship, tennis, golf, magic, flying. Office: International Sq 1825 I St NW Ste 400 Washington DC 20006-5415

SCHWARTZ, HEDWIGA, physician; b. Beius, Bihor, Romania, Oct. 15, 1932; arrived in Israel, 1975; d. Bela and Piroska (Neumann) Pless; m. Carol Schwartz; 1 child, Richard. MD, CLUS, Romania, 1959; specialist internal medicine, Bucharest, Romania, 1961. Capacity of labour internal Oradea, Romania, 1961-75; gen. practice Petach Tikva, Petach Tikva, 1976-81, Makabi, Petach Tikva, 1981—. Mem. N.Y. Acad. Scis. Home: 66 Salant, Petah Tiqwa Israel Office: Macabi, 24 Hertzl Str, Petah Tiqwa Israel

SCHWARTZ, ILANY CALONIMUS, mathematician, institute director; b. Bucarest, Romania, July 4, 1948; arrived in Israel, 1960; s. Mayer and Esther (Mittelmann) S.; m. Odetta Schwartz, Sept. 9, 1994. MSc, Grand Ecole Poly., Paris, 1974, PhD in Physics and Maths., 1978. Oriental medicine diplomate; master of Chinese acupuncture. Dir. pain dept. Shiba Hosp. - T.A., 1975-78; dir. Homac Internat. Ltd., Tel-Aviv, 1986—; dir. pain clinic Asaf Harofe Hosp., Tel-Aviv, 1994-97. Author: Zone Therapy, 1993, Standardized Auricular Acupuncture Points, 1994, Laser Therapy, 1996, Pain Relief by Auric Medicine, 1997; inventor in field; contbr. articles to profl. jours. Recipient Gold medal Russian Acad. Sci., Moscow, 1992. Mem. AAAS, AIAA, Royal Aero. Soc. (assoc., Silver medal 1994), Israel Med. Soc. Acupuncture, Can. Med. Acupuncture Soc., Internat. Assn. Auricular Medicine, Danish Med. Assn. Acupuncture, The Planetary Soc., Pilots Interant. Assn. Inc., Israel Med. Assn., Med. Soc. Acupuncture, N.Y. Acad. Sci. (gold medal 1995). Avocations: helicopters, mathematics, aerospace news, physics. Office: Homac Ltd, 22 Helsinki St, 62996 Tel Aviv Israel

SCHWARTZ, ILENE, psychotherapist; b. Phila., June 19, 1942; d. Israel Gerson and Jean Schiffman. BS, Temple U., 1970; MEd, Antioch U., 1990. Crisis counselor Phila., 1972-82, pvt. practice counseling, 1978—; cons., crisis counselor in field; instr. psychology and edn., 1974-79. Mem. ACA, AAUW, Freud Friends.

SCHWARTZ, JOHN J., association executive, consultant; b. New Rochelle, N.Y., Aug. 28, 1919; s. Edwin Benner and Marjorie Helen (James) S.; m. Katharine S. Sprackling, Jan. 6, 1942; children: Christopher Louis. Grad. high sch., New Rochelle; student, Mercersburg Acad., 1938. Campaign dir. John Price Jones Inc., N.Y.C., 1946-50; dir. pub. relations and fund raising Travelers Aid Soc. N.Y., N.Y.C., 1950-55; dir. devel. Community Service Soc., N.Y.C., 1955-57, Near East Found., N.Y.C., 1957-60; v.p. G.A. Brakeley & Co. Inc., N.Y.C., 1960-61; dir. devel. Fgn. Policy Assn., N.Y.C., 1962-64; founding pres. Greater N.Y. Nat. Soc. of Fund Raising Execs., 1964; asst. v.p. for crusade Am. Cancer Soc., N.Y.C., 1964-66; exec. dir. Am. Assn. Fund Raising Counsel, N.Y.C., 1966-68, exec. v.p., 1968-72, pres., 1972-87; founding bd. mem. Ind. Sector, Washington, 1980-85, mem. com. to measurably increase giving; mem., former pres. Com. on Nat. Ctr. for Charitable Stats.; spl. cons. to Com. on Pvt. Philanthropy and Pub. Needs., 1973; chair pvt. adv. group Nat. Assn. Attys. Gen. Model Law Project. Author: Modern American Philanthropy; A Personal Account, 1993. Mem. adv. bd. mgmt. fund-raising cert. program NYU; mem. adv. coun. Grad. Sch. Mgmt. and Urban Professions, New Sch. Social Rsch.; active formation of 5 borough coalitions Daring Coals for Caring Soc., N.Y.C., 1987; cons. Ind. U. Ctr. on Philanthropy, 1988-91, Cmty. Counselling Svc. Co., Inc., 1988-91; pres. Nat. Philanthropy Day, 1988-90, mem. hon. com., 1981; bd. dirs.-at-large USA World Fund Raising Coun., 1993; immediate pres. Friends of Westport Libr., 1995-98; bd. dirs. Norwalk Sr. Ctr., 2000. Capt. USAAF, 1941-46; PTO. Recipient Disting. Profl. Service to Philanthropy award Am. Assn. Fund-Raising Counsel, N.Y., 1976, Outstanding Agy. Profl. award United Way Am., Alexandria, 1982, Henry A. Rosso Lifetime Achievement in Ethical Fundraising award Ind. U. Ctr. on Philanthropy, 1997. Mem. Nat. Charities Info. Bur. (bd. dirs. 1978-94), Nat. Soc. Fund-Raising Execs. (bd. dirs. 1964-90, past pres.), Fairfield County Nat. Soc. Fund-Raising Dirs. (bd. dirs. 1992-2000, bd. dirs. emeritus 2000—), Am. Assn. Ret. Persons (bd. dirs. Andrus Found. 1983-90), 501C-3 Soc., Princeton Club (N.Y.C.), VFW. Democrat. Unitarian. Avocations: writing history, ship models.

SCHWARTZ, LEONARD JAY, lawyer; b. San Antonio, Sept. 23, 1943; s. Oscar S. and Ethel (Eastman) S.; m. Sandra E. Eichelbaum, July 4, 1965; 1 child, Michele Fay. BBA, U. Tex., 1965, JD, 1968. Bar: Tex. 1968, Ohio 1971, U.S. Supreme Ct. 1971, U.S. Dist. Ct. (no., ea., wes. and so. dists.) Tex., U.S. Dist. Cts. (no. and so. dists.) Ohio, U.S. Dist. Ct. Nebr., U.S. Ct. Appeals (5th, 6th, 7th and 11th cirs.). Assoc. Roberts & Holland, N.Y.C., 1968-70; ptnr. Rigely, Schwartz & Fagan, San Antonio, 1970-71; staff counsel ACLU of Ohio, Columbus, 1971-74; ptnr. Schwartz & Fishman, Columbus, Ohio, 1974-79; elections counsel to sec. of state State of Ohio, Columbus, 1979-80; ptnr. Waterman & Schwartz and successor firms, Austin, Tex., 1981-85; mng. dir. Schwartz & Eichelbaum, P.C., Austin, 1985-99, 2000—, shareholder, 1985—; gen. counsel various sch. dists.; adj. prof. law U. Tex. Sch. Law, Austin; labor and employment law cons. and sch. law Tex. Assn. Sch. Adminstrs; condr. workshops in field; mem. com. on fed. judiciary relations Tex. Bar. Contbr. articles to profl. jours. Mem. chancellor's coun. U. Tex. Sys.; mem. U. Tex. Pres.'s Assocs., Littlefield Soc., Sch. of Law Keeton Fellows. Recipient Outstanding Teaching Quiz Master award U. Tex. Sch. Law, 1968. Fellow Tex. Bar Found.; mem. ABA, Tex. Bar Assn., Bar Assn. 5th Cir., Fed. Bar Assn., Phi Delta Phi. Democrat. Jewish. Office: Schwartz & Eichelbaum PC One Commodore Plz 800 Brazos St Ste 870 Austin TX 78701-2507

SCHWARTZ, LORI BETH, psychologist, educator; b. Des Moines, May 11, 1961; d. Albert M. and Miriam L. Schwartz; 1 child, Jon Bryan Goodwin, Aug. 26, 1995. BA in Psychology, U. Kans., 1983; MA in Counseling and Guidance, U. Mo., Kansas City, 1985, PhD in Counseling Psychology, 1990. Grad. tech. asst. Cmty. Counseling Svc., Kansas City, 1985-88; psychologist Counseling Psychologists and Assocs., Kansas City, 1990—; adj. prof. U. Mo., Kansas City, 1989-96; instr. Longview C.C., Kansas City, 1989-96, Avila Coll., Kansas City, 1990—; prof. Johnson County C.C., Overland Park, Kans., 1990—; outreach seminars provider Reorganized Ch. LDS Ch., Independence, Mo., 1997—, Johnson County C.C., 1998—, Ct. Apptd. Spl. Advs. Vols., Kansas City, 1999—, Kans. Pediat. Dental Soc., Wichita, 1999. Bd. mem. U. Mo. Kansas City Sch. Edn. Alumni Bd., 1998—. Mem. APA, Mo. Psychol. Assn., Greater Kansas City Psychol. Assn. (ethics and profl. affairs chair 1999). Avocations: theatre, movies. E-mail: lbsphd@aol.com. Office: 4901 Main St Ste 401 Kansas City MO 64112-2635

SCHWARTZ, LOUIS WINN, ophthalmologist; b. Pa., Apr. 19, 1942; s. Edward and Sylvia Beatrice (Winn) S.; m. Linda Weinberg, June 14, 1964; children: Joanne Karen, Geoffrey Paul. AB, Bowdoin Coll., 1963; MD, Jefferson Med. Coll., 1967. Diplomate Am. Bd. Ophthalmology. Intern Phila. Gen. Hosp.-U. Pa., 1967-68; resident in ophthalmology Wills Eye Hosp., Phila., 1970-73; ophthalmologist Ophthalmic Assocs., Lansdale, Pa., 1973—; attending surgeon Wills Eye Hosp. Glaucoma Svc., Phila., 1984—; clin. assoc. prof. ophthalmology Jefferson Med. Coll., Phila., 1984—; sec.-treas. Wills Eye Hosp., 1998-2000, v.p., 2000—; chief ophthalmology North Penn Hosp., 1995—. Co-author: Laser Therapy of Anterior Segment, 1988, 7 other books; assoc. editor Contact Lens Assn. Ophthalmology Jour., 1988; contbr. articles to profl. jours. Recipient Honor award Am. Acad. Ophthalmology, 1988. Mem. AMA, Am. Glaucoma Soc., Pa. Acad. Ophthalmology, InterCounty Ophthalmol. Soc. (pres. 1985-86), Ophthalmic Club Phila. (pres. 1985-86). Office: Ophthalmic Assocs 1000 N Broad St Lansdale PA 19446-1138

SCHWARTZ, MELVIN, physics educator, laboratory administrator; b. N.Y.C., Nov. 2, 1932; s. Harry and Hannah (Shulman) S.; m. Marilyn Fenster, Nov. 25, 1953; children: David N., Diane R., Betty Lynn. A.B., Columbia U., 1953, Ph.D., 1958, DSc honoris causa, 1991. Assoc. physicist Brookhaven Nat. Lab., 1956-58; mem. faculty Columbia U., N.Y.C., 1958-66; prof. physics Columbia U., 1963-66, Stanford U., Calif., 1966-83; cons. prof. Stanford U., 1983-91; chmn. Digital Pathways, Inc., Mountain View, Calif., 1970-91; assoc. dir. high energy and nuclear physics Brookhaven Nat. Lab., Upton, N.Y., 1991-94; prof. physics Columbia U., N.Y.C., 1991-94, I.I. Rabi prof. physics, 1994—. Co-discoverer muon neutrino, 1962. Bd. govs. Weizmann Inst. Sci. Recipient Nobel prize in physics, 1988, John Jay award Columbia Coll., 1989, Alexander Hamilton medal Columbia U., 1995; Guggenheim fellow, 1968. Fellow Am. Phys. Soc. (Hughes award 1964); mem. NAS. Home: PO Box 5068 Ketchum ID 83340-5068 Office: Columbia U Dept Physics New York NY 10027

SCHWARTZ, MICHAEL, university president, sociology educator; b. Chgo., July 29, 1937; s. Norman and Lillian (Ruthenberg) S.; m. Ettabelle Slutsky, Aug. 23, 1959 (div. Jan. 1998); children: Monica, Kenneth, Rachel; m. Joanne Rand Whitmore, Nov. 10, 1998. BS in Psychology, U. Ill., 1958, MA in Indsl. Rels., 1959, PhD in Sociology, 1962; LLD (hon.), Youngstown State U., 1990. Asst. prof. sociology and psychology Wayne State U., Detroit, 1962-64; asst. prof. sociology Ind. U., Bloomington, 1964, assoc. prof. sociology, 1966-70; prof., chmn. dept. sociology Fla. Atlantic U., Boca Raton, 1970-72, dean Coll. Social Sci., 1972-76; v.p. grad. studies and rsch. Kent (Ohio) State U., 1976-78, interim pres., 1977, acting v.p. acad. affairs, 1977-78, v.p. acad. and student affairs, 1978-80, provost, v.p. acad. and student affairs, 1980-82, pres., 1982-91; pres. emeritus and trustee's prof. Kent State U., 1991; trustee Ctrl. State U., 1996-97; acting dir. Inst. for Social Rsch., Ind. U., 1966-67; tng. cons. Operation Head Start in Ind., 1964-70; cons. Office of Manpower, Automation and Tng., U.S. Dept. Labor, 1964-65. Cons. editor, Sociometry, 1966-70, assoc. editor, 1970; reader Am. Sociol. Rev. papers; author: (with Elton F. Jackson) Study Guide to the Study of Sociology, 1968; contbr. articles to profl. jours., chpts. to books. Chmn. Mid-Am. Conf. Coun. Pres.; rep. Nat. Coll. Athletic Assn. Pres.'s Commn.; chmn. divsn. I, 1988; corps evaluators North Ctrl. Assn. Colls. and Schs.; mem. bd. visitors Air U., USAF; mem. Akron (Ohio) Regional Devel. Bd., N.E. Ednl. TV of Ohio, Inc., N.E. Ohio Univs. Coll. Medicine; trustee Akron Symphony Orch. Assn.; mem. State of Ohio Post-Secondary Rev. Entity, 1995; mem. Assn. of Governing Bds. Commn. on Strengthening the Presidency. Recipient Disting. Tchr. award Fla. Atlantic U., 1970-71, Meritorious Svc. award Am. Assn. State Colls. and Univs., 1990; Michael Schwartz Ctr., Kent State U., named in his honor, 1991. Mem. Ohio Tchr. Edn. and Cert. Adv. Commn., Press Club, Pine Lake Trout Club. Office: Kent State U 405 White Hl Kent OH 44242-0001

SCHWARTZ, MICHAEL, historian; b. Recklinghausen, Germany, Apr. 23, 1963; s. Dieter and Elfriede (Rocktaschel) S. PhD, Westfalische Wilhelms U., 1995. Fellow Westfalische Wilhelms U., Munster, Germany, 1992-93; fellow Inst. F. Zeitgeschichte, Potsdam, Germany, 1994-96, Berlin, 1996—; lectr. Westfalische Wilhelms U., Munich, Humboldt U., Berlin. Author: Bernhard Bavink, 1993, Socialist Eugenics, 1995. Office: Inst Fur Zeitgeschichte, Finckensteinallee H85/87, 12205 Berlin Germany

SCHWARTZ, MICHAEL LEE, computer software engineer; b. Buffalo, N.Y., Nov. 7, 1950; s. Robert Donald and Annette S.; m. Bonni Lynne Jacobs, Dec. 30, 1978; children: Jeremy L., Melody L. BA in Math. Sci./Elec. Engring., Rice U., 1973, M in Elec. Engring., 1973. Software programmer, analyst Tex. Instruments, Houston and Austin, 1973-79; engr. Sperry/Honeywell, Phoenix, 1979—. Recipient Life Giver Pheresis Donor award United Blood Svcs., 1992. Mem. Assn. Computing Machinery (voting, treas. Phoenix chpt. 1991—), AzTec Freenet (supporter). Jewish. Office: Honeywell 5353 W Bell Rd Glendale AZ 85308-3900

SCHWARTZ, PERRY LESTER, information systems engineer, consultant; b. Bklyn., July 29, 1939; s. Max David and Sylvia (Weinberger) S.; m. Arlene Metz, Jan. 24, 1960; 3 children. BEE, CUNY, 1957-62; MS in Indsl. Engring. and Computer Sci., NYU, 1967. Registered profl. engr., N.J., profl. planner, N.J.; cert. mediator and arbitrator, expert witness comm. Microwave engr. Airbourne Inst. Lab., Deer Park, N.Y., 1962-63; ITT Fed. Labs, Nutley, N.J., 1963-64; program mgr. Western Electric Co., N.Y.C., 1964-69; dept. head RCA, Princeton, N.J., 1970-71; dir. engring. Warner Comms. Inc., N.Y.C., 1972-74; cons. engr. Intertech Assocs., Freehold, N.J., 1974—; adj. faculty CCNY, 1962-71, Ocean County Coll., Toms River, N.J., 1981-83, Rutgers U., New Brunswick, N.J., 1984-87; lectr. N.J. Dept. Edn., 1994, 95. Mem. steering com., trustee Intelligent Bldgs. Found., 1982-89. Mem. IEEE (sr.), Am. Cons. Engrs. Coun., Nat. Soc. Profl. Engrs., Nat. Assn. Radio and Telecom. Engrs. (sr. mem. charter mem., cert. master engr. in wire and RF, Cert. of Distinction 1994-95), Cons. Engrs. Coun. N.J., N.Y. Acad. Sci., Zeta Beta Tau (chpt. founder 1958), K. P. Office: Intertech Assoc 77-55 Schanck Rd Ste B-9 Freehold NJ 07728

SCHWARTZ, RICHARD FREDERICK, electrical engineering educator; b. Albany, N.Y., May 31, 1922; s. Frederick William and Mary Hoyle (Holland) S.; m. Ruth Louise Feldman, Oct. 25, 1945 (div. Oct. 1977); children: Kathryn Gail, Frederick Earl, Karl Edward, Eric Christian, Frieda Diane; m. Margaret Camp Boes, May 29, 1982. BEE, Rensselaer Poly. Inst., Troy, N.Y., 1943, MEE, 1948; PhD, U. Pa., 1959. Registered profl. engr., Pa., Mich. Instr. Rensselaer Poly. Inst., Troy, 1946-48; engr. Radio Corp. Am., Camden, N.J., 1948-51; instr. U. Pa., Phila., 1951-53, rsch. assoc., 1953-59, asst. prof. electrical engring., 1959-62, assoc. prof. electrical engring., 1962-73; prof. elec. engring. Mich. Tech. U., Houghton, 1973-85, dept. head, 1973-79; prof. elec. engring. SUNY, Binghamton, 1985-95, prof. emeritus, 1995—; pvt. practice Endicott, N.Y., 1999—; vis. asst. prof. U. Mich., Ann Arbor, 1960; cons. Pa. Bar Assn. Endowment, Armstrong Cork Co., Am. Electronics Labs., Inc., IBM, RCA, City of Phila., GE. Co-author: The Eavesdroppers, 1959; contbr. 40 papers to various pubs. Active Delaware County Symphony, Pa., 1967-72, Keweenaw Symphony Orch., Houghton, 1973-85, Vestal Cmty. Band, 1993—, Ctr. for Tech. and Innovation, Endicott, N.Y., 1995—, Broome County Peace Action, 1995—, sec. bd., 1998—; active Broome County Interfaith Caregivers, 1997—; mentor Schs. to Careers Partnership. With U.S. Army, 1942-46. Fellow Acoustical Soc. Am.; mem. IEEE (sr., life, vice chmn. Binghamton chpt. 2000—), AAAS (life), NSPE (life), Am. Soc. Engring. Edn. (life), N.Y. Soc. Profl. Engrs. (Broome chpt., Engr. of Yr. 1995, Contbns. to Edn. award 1996), Audio Engring. Soc. (life), Catgut Acoustical Soc., Order of the Engr., Sigma Xi, Eta Kappa Nu, Tau Beta Pi. Democrat. Unitarian. Achievements include patents for tuning sys., 1954, oscillator frequency control, 1954, transistor amplifier with high undistorted output, 1954. Home and Office: 2624 Bornt Hill Rd Endicott NY 13760-8231

SCHWARTZ, ROBERT WILLIAM, management consultant; b. N.Y.C., Oct. 23, 1944; s. Edward and Bertha R. S.; m. Gail Beth Greenbaum, Mar. 18, 1967; children: Jill, Evan. BS, Cornell U., 1967; postgrad., SUNY, Albany, 1970. Assoc. IBM, 1967-68; cons. Peat, Marwick, Mitchell & Co., Albany, 1970-71; v.p. Security Gen. Svcs., Inc., Rochester, N.Y., 1971-73; v.p. fin. and adminstrn. Gardenway Mfg. Co., Troy, N.Y., 1973-77; exec. v.p. United Telecommunications Corp., Latham, N.Y., 1977-79; pres. United Telecommunications Corp., Latham, 1980-82; also bd. dir. United Telecommunications Corp.; pres., chmn. Winsource, Inc., Albany, 1982-85, Schwartz Heslin Group, Inc., 1985—; bd. dirs. Blasch Ceramics, Inc., Albany, Docucon, Inc., San Antonio, GoZPay.com, Inc., Troy, N.Y., LBO Capital Corp., Detroit; N.Y. State Zone Capital Corp, Albany, 6ozpay.com, Inc., adj. prof. Rochester Inst. Tech., 1971-73, U. Albany, SUNY Albany, 1998—. Bd. dirs. United Cerebral Palsy of Capital Dist., 1973—; trustee Newman Found., Rensselaer Poly. Inst., 1974-78, Gov. Clinton coun. Boy Scouts Am., SUNY Found. Mem. Am. Mgmt. Assn., Esarco Internat., N.Am. Tel. Assn., Assn. for Systems Mgmt., Ft. Orange Club, Econ. Club, Corenell Club (N.Y.C.). Republican. Home: 2 Myton Ln Albany NY 12204-1310 Office: 8 Airport Park Blvd Latham NY 12110-1441

SCHWARTZ, SORELL LEE, pharmacologist, toxicologist, educator; b. Buffalo, Sept. 13, 1937; s. Jacob M. and Rosalind (Greenberg) S.; m. Marsha Kohlenstein, June 9, 1963; children: Joanne Beth, Rebecca Lynn. BS, U. Med., 1959; PhD, Med. Coll. Va., 1963. Pharmacologist U.S. Naval Med. Rsch. Inst., Bethesda, Md., 1963-66; head pharmacology divsn., toxicology, applied pharmokinetics Georgetown U. Sch. Medicine, 1968-98, prof. emeritus pharmacology, 1998—; sci. dir. Ctr. for Environ. Health and Human Toxicology, Washington, 1983-96; prin. Internat. Ctr. for Toxicology and Medicine, Rockville, Md., 1996—. Contbr. numerous articles to sci. jours. Seved with UNSR, 1963-66. Mem. Am. Soc. Pharmacology and Exptl. Therapeutics, Soc. Toxicology, Am. Coll. Toxicology, Am. Acad. Clin. Toxicology, Soc. Risk Analysis, Soc. Law, Medicine and Ethics. Jewish. Achievements include research in mathematical modeling of biological systems, risk assessment and management, methods for causality assessment and uncertainty judgments. Address: Georgetown U Dept Pharmacology Sch Medicine Washington DC 20007

SCHWARTZ, STEPHEN LAWRENCE, composer, lyricist; b. N.Y.C., Mar. 6, 1948; s. Stanley Leonard and Sheila Lorna (Siegel) S.; m. Carole Ann Piasecki, June 6, 1969; children—Scott Lawrence, Jessica Lauren. Student, Juilliard Sch. Music, 1960-64; BFA, Carnegie-Mellon U., 1968. Works include: title song for play and film Butterflies Are Free, 1969; (theatre) music and new lyrics Godspell, 1971, four songs, adaptation and direction Working, 1978, music for 3 songs Personals, 1985, (with Leonard Bernstein) English texts for Leonard Bernstein's Mass, 1971, music and lyrics Pippin, 1972, The Magic Show, 1974, The Baker's Wife, 1976, Children of Eden, 1991, lyrics Rags, 1986, (films) Pocahontas, 1995 (Acad. award for best original score 1996, Acad. award for best original song 1996), The Hunchback of Notre Dame, 1996; (music and lyrics) The Prince of Egypt, 1998 (Acad. award for best original song 1999); (TV, music and lyrics) Geppetto, 2000, (juvenile) The Perfect Peach, 1977, The Trip, 1983, (recording) Reluctant Pilgrim, 1997. Recipient Drama Desk awards, 1971, 78, Grammy awards, 1971, 96, Golden Globe award, 1996, Broadcast Film Critics award, 1999. Mem. ASCAP, Nat. Acad. Rec. Arts and Scis., Am. Motion Picture Arts Soc.

SCHWARTZ, THOMAS A., military officer. BS, U.S. Mil. Acad.; MS in Psychology Counseling, Duke U.; MS in Pers. Mgmt., Salve Regina; grad.,

Armed Forces Staff Coll.; MA in Nat. Security & Strategic Studies, U.S. Naval War Coll. Commd. 2d lt. U.S. Army, 1967, advanced through grades to gen., 1998; tactical officer staff and faculty U.S. Mil. Acad., West Point, N.Y., 1973-76; pers. mgmt. officer U.S. Army Mil. Pers. Command, Alexandria, Va., 1978-81; divsn. inspector gen. 1st armored divsn. VII Corps U.S. Army Europe and 7th Army, Germany, 1982-83; comdr. 1st Bn. 6th Inf., 1st Armored Divsn., Illesheim, Germany, 1983-85; chief infantry br., combat arms br. U.S. Army Mil. Pers. Ctr., Alexandria, 1986-88; comdr. 1st brigade, 4th infantry divsn. Ft. Carson, Colo., 1988-90; chief staff 4th Inf. Divsn., Fort Carson, Colo., 1990-91; chief of staff combined field army U.S. Forces, Korea, 1991-92; asst. divsn. commdr. 2d infantry divsn. 8th U.S. Army, Korea, 1992-93; commdg. gen. 4th Inf. Divsn., Fort Carson, Colo., 1993-95; comdg. gen. III Corps Ft. Hood, Tex., 1995-98; commdg. gen. U.S. Forces Command, Ft. McPherson, Ga., 1998-99; comdr. in chief UN Command/Combined Forces Command U.S. Forces Korea, Yongsan, South Korea, 1999—. Decorated Disting. Svc. medal, Silver Star, Def. Superior Svc. medal, Legion of Merit with 3 oak leaf clusters, Bronze Star, Purple Heart, Air medal. Office: US Army Forces Command PSC 303 Box 45 APO AP 96205-0045

SCHWARTZ, WILLIAM, lawyer, educator; b. Providence, May 6, 1933; s. Morris Victor and Martha (Glassman) S.; m. Bernice Konigsberg, Jan. 13, 1957; children: Alan Gershon, Robin Libby. AA, Boston U., 1952, JD magna cum laude, 1955, MA, 1960; postgrad., Harvard Law Sch., 1955-56; LHD (hon.), Hebrew Coll., 1996, Yeshiva U., 1998. Bar: D.C. 1956, Mass. 1962, N.Y. 1989. Prof. law Boston U., 1955-91, Fletcher prof. law, 1968-70, Roscoe Pound prof. law, 1970-73, dean Sch. of Law, 1980-88, dir. Ctr. for Estate Planning, 1988-91; univ. prof. Yeshiva U., N.Y.C., 1991—; of counsel Swartz & Swartz, 1973-80; v.p. for acad. affairs, chief acad. officer Yeshiva U., N.Y.C., 1993-98; counsel Cadwalader, Wickersham and Taft, N.Y.C., Washington, Charlotte, London, 1988—; mem. faculty Frances Glessner Lee Inst., Harvard Med. Sch., Nat. Coll. Probate Judges, 1970, 77, 78, 79, 88; gen. dir. Assn. Trial Lawyers Am., 1968-73; reporter New Eng. Trial Judges Conf., 1965-67; participant Nat. Met. Cts. Conf., 1968; dir. Mass. Probate Study, 1976—; chmn. spl. com. on police procedures City of Boston, 1989, 91; bd. dirs. UST Corp., chmn. of co., 1993-94, chmn. bd. dirs., 1996-2000; bd. dirs. Viacom Inc., Viacom Internat. Inc.; mem. adv. com. WCI Steel, Inc.; mem. legal adv. bd. N.Y. Stock Exch. Author: Future Interests and Estate Planning, 1965, 77, 81, 86, Comparative Negligence, 1970, A Products Liability Primer, 1970, Civil Trial Practice Manual, 1972, New Vistas in Litigation, 1973, Massachusetts Pleading and Practice, 7 vols., 1974-80, Estate Planning and Living Trusts, 1990, The Convention Method: The Unused Amending Superhighway, 1995, Jewish Law and Contemporary Dilemmas and Problems, 1997, Does Time Heal All Wrongs?, 1999, others; note editor: Boston U. Law Rev., 1954-55; property editor: Annual Survey of Mass. Law, 1960—; contbr. articles to legal jours. Bd. dirs. Kerry Found.; trustee Hebrew Coll., 1975—, Salve Regina Univ.; rep. Office Public Info., UN, 1968-73; chmn. legal adv. panel Nat. Commn. Med. Malpractice, 1972-73; examiner of titles Commonwealth of Mass., 1964—; spl. counsel Mass. Bay Transp. Authority, 1979; trustee Yeshiva U.; pres. Fifth Ave. Synagogue, N.Y.C., 1997—. Recipient Homer Albers award Boston U., 1955, John Ordronaux prize, 1955; Disting. Service award Religious Zionists Am., 1977; William W. Treat award; William O. Douglas award. Fellow Am. Coll. Probate Counsel; mem. ABA, Am. Law Inst., Mass. Bar Assn. (chmn. task force tort liability), N.Y. State Bar Assn., Assn. Bar City N.Y., Nat. Coll. Probate Judges (hon. mem.), Phi Beta Kappa. Office: 100 Maiden Ln New York NY 10038-4818

SCHWARTZ, YVES RAYMOND, philosopher, educator; b. Marseille, France, Sept. 8, 1942; s. Daniel and Yvonne (Berr) S.; m. Elisabeth Dechery, Dec. 21, 1966; children: Laure, Pierre, Claire. BS, Lycée Louis le Grand, 1963. With Ecole Normale Supérieure, Paris, 1963-68; asst. U. d'Aix Marseille, Aix en Provence, 1968-75, maître asst., 1975-88, prof., 1988—; sr. mem. Inst. U. France, 1993—; mem. jury agregation de Philosophie, Paris, 1991-93; dir. Analyse Pluridisciplinaire des Situations de travail, 1991—; expert Communauté Européenne, Brussels, 1997—. Author: Experience et Connaissance du Travail, 1988, Travail et Philosophie, Convocations Mutuelles, 1992, Reconnaissances du Travail, 1997. Mem. nat. exec. Syndicat Nat de l'Enseignement Supérieur, Paris, 1973-79. Mem. Societe des Amis de J.Cavailles, Revue de Philosophie Ecomonique. Office: APST Univ de Provence, 29 Av R Schumann, 13621 Aix en Provence France

SCHWARTZBERG, DAVID B., chemical industry executive; b. N.Y.C., Feb. 8, 1946; s. Morris and Anne S.; m. Susan R. Schwartzberg, Nov. 25, 1967; children: Robert, Mindy, Frank, Lauren. BSCHe, Polytechnic Inst. of N.Y., 1967; MBA, Fairleigh Dickinson U., 1973. Gen. mgr. indsl. chem. divsn. M&T Chems., Inc., Woodbridge, N.J., 1988-89; gen. mgr. plastic additives divsn. Elf Atochem NA (name now Atofina Chems. Inc.), Phila., 1989-90, pres. mineral products divsn., 1990-93, v.p. performance products, 1993-95, v.p. remediation, 1995-98, v.p., health, environ. and safety, 1998—; adv. bd. Hazardous Substance Mgmt. Rsch. Ctr., Newark, N.J., 1996—. Office: Atofina Chems Inc 2000 Market St Philadelphia PA 19103-3231

SCHWARTZE, PETER HEINRICH, physician, researcher; b. Salzuflen, Germany, May 23, 1931; s. Heinrich Emil and Margarete (Staudt) S.; m. Hannelore Grete Köhler; children: Ulrike, Thomas. MD, U. Leipzig, Germany, 1957, D Habilitatus, 1968. Med. asst. Dist. Hosp., Freiberg, Germany, 1958-62; rsch. asst. Inst. Physiology U. Leipzig, Germany, 1962-72, lectr., 1972-78; prof. pathophysiology-physiology Inst. Physiology U. Leipzig, 1978-92; head dept. pathophysiology Inst. Physiology U. Leipzig, Germany, 1978-80, head physiology, 1980-92, ret., 1992—; mem. Coun. Med. Rsch., Berlin, 1980-90. Author: (with Hannelone Schwartze-Köhler) Fetal, Neonatal and Child Physiology, 1977; editor: Physiology and Pathophysiology of Development, 1990; mem. editl. bd. dirs. Pediatrics and Related Topics Jour., 1990—, Internat. Tinnitus Jour., 1990—; contbr. articles to profl. jours. Active Volkskammer of the GDR, 1980-90. Mem. Soc. Exptl. Rsch. (v.p. 1978-81). Avocations: history of physiology, entomology, music. Home: Obertriebeler Str 37, D-08606 Triebel Germany

SCHWARTZE-KÖHLER, HANNELORE G., retired pathophysiologist; b. Dresden, Saxony, Germany, Aug. 3, 1933; d. Bernhard P. and Grete (Stieper) Köhler; m. Peter H. Schwartze, Dec. 28, 1957; children: Ulrike Schwartze-Diez, Thomas. BS, U. Greifswald, Germany, 1954; MD, U. Leipzig, Germany, 1957, D in Med. Sci., 1977. Resident Freiberg Hosp., 1958-60, resident in pediats., 1960-63; resident in physiology U. Leipzig, 1964-66, specialist in physiology, 1967-76, head divsn. Inst. Physiology, 1977-80, lectr. pathophysiology Inst. Physiology, 1981-84, prof. pathophysiology, 1984-93; ret.; head dept. pathophysiology U. Leipzig, 1981-84, dir. Inst. Pathophysiology, 1984-93. Author: (with P. Schwartze) Physiologie des Foetal Säuglings-und Kindesalters, 1977; contbr. over 100 articles to profl. jours. Mem. Trade Union, Leipzig, 1967-90. Rsch. grantee German Govt., 1964-93. Mem. Cmty. Medicine & Soc. Berlin, N.Y. Acad. Sci. Avocations: fine arts and literature, music, family life, travel. Home: Obertriebeler Strasse 37, D-08606 Triebel Germany

SCHWARTZMAN, MICHAEL ISAAC, investment management firm executive; b. Kutais, Krasnodar, USSR, Oct. 23, 1945; came to U.S., 1974; s. Isaac and Esther S.; m. Natalie Vera Belikhova, 1967 (dec.); children: Elya, Anthony; m. Lynn Rosenhoover, 1998. MS in Computer Sci., Novosibirsk U., USSR, 1970. Researcher Acad. Scis., USSR, 1970-73, Columbia U., N.Y.C., 1974-75; cons. Chase Manhattan Bank, N.Y.C., 1975-76; mgr. Digital Equipment Corp., Maynard, Mass., 1976-78, Prime Computer, Inc., Natick, Mass., 1978-79; pres., chmn. bd. Lang. Processors, Inc., Framingham, Mass., 1979-87; mng. ptnr. ENT Capital Mgmt., Acton, Mass., 1987-92, Carlisle Capital Mgmt., Acton, Mass., 1992-94, ValueSearch Capital Mgmt., Swampscott, Mass., 1994—. Pres. Jewish Migration and Family Reunification Coun., Swampscott, Mass., 1988—; bd. dirs. Jewish Vocat. Svc., Boston, 1989-90. Avocations: skiing, bicycling, sailing. Office: ValueSearch Captial Mgmt 29 Galloupes Point Rd Swampscott MA 01907

SCHWARZ, BARBARA RUTH BALLOU, elementary school educator; b. East Orange, N.J., Aug. 8, 1930; d. Robert Ingram Ballou and Ruth Edna Sweeney; m. Eugene A. Schwarz, Jr., Dec. 24, 1954 (div. 1977); children: Ruth Ellen, Eugene A. III. BS, Trenton State Coll., 1952. Tchr. West Orange N.J. Schs., 1952-54, Franklin Sch., Ft. Wayne, Ind., 1955-56, Parliament Place Sch., North Babylon, N.Y., 1965-91; trustee welfare trust fund North Babylon Tchrs. Orgn., N.Y., 1988-91. Vol. Safe Home, L.I. Women's Coalition, Bayshore, N.Y., 1979-90; sec. Victims Info. Bur., Suffolk, 1987-88, v.p., 1989-90, pres. bd. dirs., 1990-94, rep. to Women's Equal Rights Coalition, Suffolk County Human Rights Commn., 1989-94; mem. adv. bd. Suffolk County Women's Svcs., 1990-96, vice-chair, 1991-93; bd. dirs. Suffolk Abortion Rights Coun., 1992-96; mem. Suffolk-Nassau Abortion Def., 1991-94; pub. affairs com. Planned Parenthood Suffolk County, 1990-92; mem. adminstrv. bd. Babylon Meth. Ch., 1992-93; mem. Long Islanders for Fairness and Equality 1994-97; mem. subcom. Islip Presbyn. Ch. on Legis. Com. of N.Y. State Coalition Against Domestic Violence, 1999—; steering com. Save Our Svcs., Long Island, 1998—. Women's History Month Community Svc. honoree Town of Babylon, 1997. Mem. AAUW (mem. v.p. Islip area br. 1982-84, pres. 1984-88, legis. chair 1988-93, mem. com. promoting individual liberties Nassau-Suffolk dist. VI 1989-91, pro-choice coord. N.Y. state 1990-92, rep. to women on job task force 1986-98, chair dist. VI inter-br. 1991-92, chair N.Y. state pub. policy 1992-96, rep. on L.I. and N.Y. State Pro-Choice Coalitions, chair N.Y. state voter edn. campaign, 1995-98, assoc. pub. policy com. 1996-98, L.I. Achievement award 1996), Com. Against Domestic Violence (pres. chpt. Islip), N.Y. State Ret. Tchrs. Assn., Western Suffolk Ret. Tchrs. Assn., Coalition Ret. Tchrs. L.I., North Babylon Tchrs. Orgn. (retirees chpt.). Republican. Avocations: lobbying, reading, handcrafts, gourmet cooking, volunteer activities. Home: 23 Wyandanch Ave Babylon NY 11702-1920

SCHWARZ, CARL A., JR., lawyer; b. N.Y.C., Apr. 27, 1936; s. Carl A. and Genevieve C. Byrne; m. Maryellen McG., Apr. 30, 1966; children: Peter Thomas, Elizabeth Anne. BS, Fordham U., 1957, JD, 1960. Bar: N.Y. 1960, U.S. Dist. Ct. (so., ea., we. and D.C. dists.) N.Y. 1960, U.S. Ct. Appeals (2d cir.) 1960, U.S. Supreme Ct. 1965. Ptnr. Schwarz & DeMarco, Garden City, N.Y.; chmn., bd. trustees N.Y. Sch. Interior Design. Trustee Cath. Charities; Capt. USAF, 1961-65. Mem. Manhasset Bay Yacht Club (vice commodore), Order of Malta. Roman Catholic. Office: Schwarz & DeMarco LLP 1225 Franklin Ave Garden City NY 11530-1691

SCHWARZ, DOMINIK JOHANNES, physicist; b. Vienna, Austria, Jan. 15, 1968; s. Gottfried and Elisabeth (Aistleitner) S.; m. Petra Renate Lutter, June 3, 1994; children: Maximilian, Constantin. Diploma in Physics, Tech. U. Wien, 1991, DSc, 1995; privatdoznt, U. Frankfurt, 2000. Libr., rsch. asst. Inst. Theoretical Physics Tech. U. Wien, 1989-95; fellow Inst. Theoretical Physics ETH-Zurich, Switzerland, 1995-97, U. Frankfurt, Germany, 1997-99, Tech. U. Wien, Austria, 1999—. Alexander v. Humboldt fellow Inst. Theoretical Physics U. Frankfurt, 1997-99; APART fellow Austrian Acad. Scis., 1999—. Mem. Austrian Phys. Soc.

SCHWARZ, FREDERICK AUGUST OTTO, JR., lawyer; b. N.Y.C., Apr. 20, 1935; s. Frederick August Otto and Mary Delafield (DuBois) S.; m. Marian Ladd, June 19, 1959; children: Frederick August Otto III, Adair L., Eliza Ladd; m. Frederica Perera, May 11, 1996. BA in History magna cum laude, Harvard Coll., 1957, LLB magna cum laude, 1960; LLD (hon.), N.Y. Law Sch., 1987, CUNY, 1993. Bar: N.Y. 1961, U.S. Dist. Ct. (so. dist.) N.Y. 1963, U.S. Ct. Appeals (2nd cir.) 1978, U.S. Ct. Appeals (9th cir.) 1972, U.S. Ct. Appeals (10th cir.) 1973, U.S. Supreme Ct. 1973. Law clk. to chief judge J. Edward Lumbard U.S. Ct. of Appeals, 2d Circuit, 1960-61; asst. commr. for law revision Govt. of No. Nigeria, 1961-62; assoc. firm Cravath, Swaine & Moore, N.Y.C., 1963-68; ptnr. Cravath, Swaine & Moore, 1969-75, 1976-81, 87—; chmn. N.Y.C. Charter Revision Commn., 1989; corp. counsel City of N.Y., 1982-86; chief counsel Senate Select Com. on Intelligence, 1975-76; speaker in the field. Author: Nigeria: The Tribes, The Nation, or the Race, 1966; Editor Harvard Law Sch. Law Review. Contbr. articles to profl. jours. Chmn. Fund for the City of N.Y., 1977-81, 87-97; pres. Vera Inst. Justice, 1978-81, chmn. 1987-98; mem. bd. overseers Harvard U., 1977-83; mem. Com. to Visit Harvard Coll., N.Y.-N.J. Citizens Commn. on AIDS; trustee Experiment in Internat. Living, 1965-82; bd. dirs. NAACP Legal Def. Fund. Constl. Edn. Found., Manhattan Bowery Corp., 1970-81, Lawyers for the Public Interest, 1976-81, FAO Schwarz, 1970-85; chair leadership N.Y. Adv. Coun., 1989—; trustee Nat. Resources Def. Coun., 1987-92, chmn., 1992—, Legal Action Center, 1973-81, N.Y.C. Criminal Justice Agy., 1977-81, Town Sch., 1972-80, Am. Com. on Africa, 1965-79, Milton Acad., 1960's, NAACP Legal Def. Fund, Constitutional Edn. Found., William Nelson Cromwell Found.; trustee The A Theater Found., 1992—. Recipient Liberty award Lambda Legal Def. and Edn. Fund, 1987, The Louis Lefkowitz award Fordham Urban Law Jour. 1990, Civic Leadership award Citizens Union City of N.Y., 1990, The Whitney North Seymour Pub. Svc. award Fed. Bar Coun., 1991,. Fellow N.Y. Bar Found.; mem. ABA, Assn. of Bar of City of N.Y. (mem. exec. com. 1986-90, coun. on criminal justice, chmn. juvenile justice com. 1980-81, chmn. nominating com. 1983, Cardozo lectr. 1991), Am. Law Inst., Harvard Law Sch. Assn. of N.Y.C. (pres. 1983-84), N.Y. State Bar Assn., N.Y.C. Bar Assn. Office: Cravath Swaine & Moore 825 8th Ave Fl 38 New York NY 10019-7475

SCHWARZ, GERHARD E., journalist; b. Hard, Vorarlberg, Austria, Apr. 19, 1951; arrived in Switzerland, 1969; s. Alois and Herma (Gasser) S.; m. Doris Dürrenberger, Mar. 1978; children: Christina, Claudia, Kathrin. Lic. oec., U. St. Gallen, Switzerland, 1973; dr. oec., U. St. Gallen, 1980; postgrad., Harvard U., 1996. Tchg. asst. U. St. Gallen, 1973-79; mktg. rschr. Hilti AG, Liechtenstein, 1980; journalist Neue Zürcher Zeitung, Zurich, Switzerland, 1981-82; corr. Neue Zürcher Zeitung, Paris, 1983-86; economics editor Neue Zürcher Zeitung, Zurich, 1987-93, head econ. and bus. sect., 1994—; lectr. U. Zürich, Switzerland, 1989—. Author: Auslandische Direktinvestitionen und Entwicklung, 1980, Die "Soziale Kalte" des Liberalismus, 3d edit., 1996; editor: Wo Regelnbremsen, 1988, Das Soziale der Marktwirtschaft, 1990. Mem. Mont Pelerin Soc., Am. Econ. Assn., Progress Found. (mem. bd.), St. Gallen Found. Internat. Studies (mem. bd.), Swiss Inst. Internat. Studies (bd. dirs.), Internat. Inst. Austrian Econs. Avocations: skiing, bridge. Office: Neue Zurcher Zeitung, Falkenstr 11, CH-8021 Zurich Switzerland

SCHWARZ, JOACHIM, preventive medicine physician; b. Stuttgart, Germany, Jan. 11, 1954; s. Paul and Elisabeth Schwarz; m. Cordula Bayer, Sept. 12, 1984; children: Judith, Jasmine, Jens, Jonathan. MD, U. Heidelberg, Germany, 1982. Intern in internal medicine U. Heidelberg, Germany, 1981-82; preventive medicine physician Allgemeine Ortskrankenkasse Pforzheim, Germany, 1987-97, Sabbath Rest Advent Ch., Dickendorf, Germany, 1998—. Contbr. articles to med. jours. Adventist. Avocations: family, history. Home: In den Schmitten 13, 57520 Dickensdorf Germany Office: Sabbath Rest Advent Church, Waldstrasse 37, 57520 Dickendorf Germany

SCHWARZ, MARKUS J., psychiatrist, neurochemist; b. Ingolstadt, Germany, Apr. 16, 1966; s. Georg and Maria (Riemer) S.; divorced; 1 child, Marie Sophie. Diploma in medicine, U. Munich, Germany, 1996; MD, Ludwig-Maximilian U., Munich, 1998. Physician Ludwig-Maximilian U., 1996-97; rsch. asst. dept. neurochemistry psychiat. Hosp., Munich, 1998—; sec. sect. on immunology and psychiatry WPA, N.Y. and Washington, 1999—, external project ptnr. Expo 2000 for Psychoneuroimmunology, Hannover, Germany, 1997—; mem. core group of reviewers European Psychiatry, 1999—. Patentee in field. With German Mountain Inf., 1986-87. Fellow European Coll. Neuropsychopharmacology, 1999, Arbeitsgem Neuropsychopharmacology, 1999. Fellow World Psychiat. Assn. (sec. immunology and psychiatry sect. 1999—); mem. Am. Psychiat. Assn., European Coll. Neuropsychopharmacology (poster award), German Soc. Immunology. Roman Catholic. Avocations: mountain biking, travel, opera, walking, skiing. Office: U Munich Psychiat Hosp, Nussbaumstr 7, D-80336 Munich Germany

SCHWARZ, MICHAEL, lawyer; b. Brookline, Mass., Oct. 19, 1952; s. Jules Lewis and Estelle (Kosberg) S.; m. Rebecca Handy; 1 child, Patrick Joshua Charles. BA magna cum laude, U. No. Colo., 1975; postgrad., U. N.Mex., 1977, JD, 1980; reader in Negligence Law, Oxford U., 1978; diploma in Legal Studies, Cambridge U., 1981. Bar: N.Mex. 1980, U.S. Dist. Ct. N.Mex. 1980, U.S. Ct. Appeals (10th, D.C., and Fed. cirs.) 1982, U.S. Ct. Internat. Trade, 1982, U.S. Tax Ct. 1982, N.Y. 1987, U.S. Supreme Ct. 1983. Vol. VISTA, Albuquerque, 1975-77; rsch. fellow N.Mex. Legal Support Project, Albuquerque, 1978-79; supr. law Cambridge (Eng.) U., 1980-81; law clk. to chief justice Supreme Ct. N.Mex., Santa Fe, 1981-82; pvt. practice Santa Fe, 1982—; spl. pros. City of Santa Fe, 1985, spl. asst. atty. gen., 1986-88; mem. west editl. adv. com. Social Security Reporting Svc., 1983-95. Author: New Mexico Appellate Manual, 1990, 2d edit., 1996; contbr. articles to profl. jours. Vice dir. Colo. Pub. Interest Rsch. Group, 1974; scoutmaster Great S.W. Area coun. Boy Scouts Am., 1977-79; mem. N.Mex. Acupuncture Lic. Bd., 1983. Recipient Cert. of Appreciation Cambridge U., 1981, Nathan Burke Meml. award, 1980, N.Mex. Supreme Ct. Cert. Recognition, 1992, 93, 95. Mem. ABA (litig. com. on profl. responsibility, litig. com. on pretrial practice and discovery, 10th cir. editor 1998, mem. Ctr. Profl. Responsibility), ATLA, ACLU, Bar Assn. U.S. Dist. Ct. Dist. N.Mex., State Bar N.Y., N.Mex. State Bar (bd. dirs. employment law sect. 1990-96, chmn. 1990-91, chmn. family law sect. 2000—, bd. dirs. 1999—). Home and Office: PO Box 1656 Santa Fe NM 87504-1656

SCHWARZ, PAUL WINSTON, judge; b. Sacramento, Sept. 24, 1948; s. Egon Ferdinand and Louise (Fulcher) S.; m. Virginia Adams, July 12, 1987; children: Austin Winston, Julie Adams. BA in Philosophy, Calif. State U., San Jose, 1971; JD, Santa Clara U., 1974. Bar: Pa. 1975, U.S. Supreme Ct. 1978, D.C. Ct. Appeals 1987, Va. 1992. Commd. 2d. lt. U.S. Army, 1971, advanced through grades to lt. col., 1992; corp. counsel Oracle Corp., Bethesda, Md., 1992-93; sec., v.p. and corp. counsel Oracle Complex Systems Corp., Arlington, Va., 1992-93; counsel McAleese & Associates, P.C., Washington, DC, 1993-94; apptd. U.S. adminstrv. law judge, 1994. Author: A Roadmap into the World of Federal Contracts, 1989. Decorated Legion of Merit, U.S. Army Gen. Staff Badge award. Mem. ABA (chmn. com. on pub. contract law gen. practice sect. 1991, vice-chmn. judiciary com. 1995), Army and Navy Country Club, Army and Navy Club Washington D.C., Nat. Soc. SAR. Episcopalian. Avocations: swimming, pistol. Home: 5336 Sugar Hill Dr Houston TX 77056-2028

SCHWARZ, RAINER, economics educator; b. Leipzig, Germany, Nov. 26, 1941; s. Helmut and Margarete (Kretschmar) S.; m. Gabriele Greiner; children: Robert, Jochen. Diploma in physics, U. Leningrad, 1966; PhD, Humboldt U., Berlin, 1970; D of Econ. Scis., Bus. Sch. Rahnsdorf, Berlin, 1979. Rsch. fellow Bus. Sch. Rahnsdorf, Berlin, 1970-79, asst. prof., 1979-89; full prof. Acad. Scis., Berlin, 1989-91; rsch. fellow Sci. Ctr., Berlin, 1990-94; full prof. Brandenburg Tech. U., Cottbus, Germany, 1994—; prof. Pvt. Acad. for Mgmt., Poland, 1999—. Author: Chaos or Order, 1995; co-author: Input-Output-Techniques, 1982, Basic Concepts of System Analysis, 1988. Mem. Am. Econ. Assn., Deutsche Assn. Operation Rsch. Office: Brandenburg Tech U Cottbus, Universitaetsplatz 3-4, 03044 Cottbus Germany

SCHWARZ, SIGFRID ALFRED, chemist; b. Eisenberg, Germany, Apr. 9, 1933; m. Brigitte Erna S.; children: Birgit, Beatrix. Diploma in chemistry, Friedrich-Schiller-U., Jena, Germany, 1959, D in Chemistry, 1968. From scientific asst. to head dept. chem. rsch. Jenapharm, Jena, 1959-98; prof. natural chemistry Friedrich Schiller U., Jena, 1986—. Contbr. articles to profl. jours.; patentee in field. Office: Jenapharm GMBH Divsn Rsch & Devel, Otto-Schott-Str 15, D-07745 Jena Germany

SCHWARZ, SUSAN DECKER, development officer; b. Chgo., Jan. 17, 1938; d. Ted Silas and Marion Gene (Popper) Decker; m. Wolfgang Schwarz, May 12, 1976; children: Jaime Bartholomew, Noah. BA in History, Chatham Coll., Pitts., 1960. Account exec. Gilbert Jonas Co., 1965-69; dir. fin. Howard Samuels gubernatorial campaigns, N.Y. State, 1970, 74; asst. to chmn., pub. affairs officer Joseph E. Seagram & Sons, Inc., 1970-74; asst. dir. Bklyn. Mus., 1975; pres. Decker-Klaris Assocs., N.Y.C., 1975-77; pub. affairs cons. 1977—; cons. Westchester affiliate Am. Acad. Bd. Cert. Psychologists; bd. dirs. Pub. Affairs Coun., 1971-78. Trustee Meml. Fellowship Polit. Responsiveness of Nat. Ctr. Urban Ethnic Affairs, 1974-81; ofcl. LWV of New Castle, Westchester and N.Y. State; dir. ann. giving and alumni affairs Purchase Coll., 1997—; mem. Westchester County Fair Campaign Practices Com.; bd. dirs. Foster Parents Plan (U.S.A.), Inc., 1975-78, N.Y. Artists in Exbhn., 1975-76, The Bridge, Inc., 1967-69. Address: 81 Paulding Dr Chappaqua NY 10514-2818

SCHWARZACHER, SEVERIN PAUL, physician, consultant; b. Vienna, Dec. 15; s. Severin Schwarzacher and Elisabeth Menges; m. Theresa Josephine Volpini de Maestri, Aug. 31, 1991; children: Gregory, Teresita. MD, U. Vienna, 1989; internal medicine degree, U. Innsbruck, 1997, cardiology bd. cert., 1999. Fellow Dept. Cardiology U. Vienna, 1990-91, Dept. Pharmacology U. Vienna, 1991-92, Dept. Cardiology Internat. Medicine, Vienna, 1992-94, Dept. Cardiology Stanford U., 1994-97; attendant co-dir. Dept. Cardiology U. Innsbruck, 1997—; dir. Lab for Intracoronary Diagnostics Dept. Cardiology, Innsbruck, 1987—; cons. MSD, 1997—. Sr. editor: Intravascular Imaging, 1996—; patentee in field; contbr. articles to profl. jours. Recipient Cardiology Sci. award, 1993. Mem. Internat. Soc. Heart Rsch., Austrian Cardiology Soc., German Cardiology Soc., European Heart Assn., Stanford Flying Club, Sovereign Order Malta (MSD rsch. award 1994), St. Johns Club (Vienna). Roman Catholic. Avocations: aviation, horseback riding, water ski, jogging. Office: U Innsbruck Dept CardSchMed, Anichstr 35, A-6020 Innsbruck Austria

SCHWARZE, JOCHEN, applied computer science educator; b. Braunschweig, Fed. Republic Germany, Aug. 8, 1937; s. Paul and Luise (Abel) S.; m. Margot Brössel, Apr. 1, 1966; children: Stephan, Melanie. Diploma in bus., U. Göttingen, Fed. Republic Germany, 1963, D. in Mgmt. Sci., 1967; Habilitation, U. Münster, Fed. Republic Germany, 1972; Hon. Prof., Beijing Agrl. Engring. U., 1987, Internat. U. Kyrghyszstan, 1997. Apprentice Miag Mühlenbau GmbH, Braunschweig, 1957-59; asst. prof. U. Göttingen, 1964-67, U. Münster, 1967-72; prof. stats. Tech U., Braunschweig, 1972-90; prof. applied computer sci. U. Hannover, Fed. Republic Germany, 1990—, also head Institut für Wirtschaftsinformatik, 1990—; pres. Acad. for Mgmt. and Adminstrn., Leer, Fed. Republic Germany, 1970-91, Leibnizakademie, Hannover, 1991-94. Author 25 books; contbr. numerous articles to profl. jours. Office: Inst Wirtschaftsinformatik, Königsworther Platz 1, 30167 Hannover Germany

SCHWARZKOPF, DIETRICH GUENTER, television program director; b. Stolp, Pomerania, Germany, Apr. 4, 1927; s. Walter and Dorothea (Ernst) S.; m. Hildegard Irene Stallmach, Dec. 30, 1959. MA, U. Minn., 1951; State Law Exam., Free U., Berlin, 1954. Journalist Der Tagesspiegel, Berlin, 1952-55; parliamentary corr. Der Tagesspiegel, Bonn, Fed. Republic Germany, 1955-62; head Bonn office Deutschlandfunk nat. radio, Bonn, 1962-66; TV program dir. Norddeutscher Rundfunk, Hamburg, Fed. Republic Germany, 1966-74; dep. dir. gen. Norddeutscher Rundfunk, Hamburg, 1974-78; TV progam dir. Deutsches Fernsehen/ARD, Munich, 1978-92; v.p. European Cultural Channel, Strasbourg, 1991-94; chmn. German Sch. of Journalism, Munich, 1980—. Author: Atomherrschaft, 1969; co-author: Chancen für Deutschland, 1964; editor: Rundfunkpolitik in Deutschland, 1999. Fellow Internat. Coun. NATAS; mem. Journalisten-Verband Berlin, Assn. Cath. Journalists, Press Club Munich, Herrenclub, Rotary. Christian Dem. Union. Roman Catholic. Home: 1A Prinzenweg, 82319 Starnberg Germany Office: Deutsche Journalisten-Schule, 3 Altheimer Eck, 80331 Munich Germany

SCHWARZKOPF, H. NORMAN, retired army officer, public speaker; b. Trenton, N.J., Aug. 22, 1934; s. H. Norman and Ruth (Bowman) S.; m. Brenda Holsinger, July 6, 1968; children: Cynthia, Jessica, Christian. BS in engring., U.S. Mil. Acad., West Point, N.Y., 1956; MME, U. So. Calif., Los Angeles, 1964; student, U.S. Army War Coll., Carlisle Barracks, Pa., 1972-73; LHD (hon.), U. S. Fla.; D. in Leadership (hon.), U. Richmond; D. in Pub. Svc. (hon.), U. Miami, U. Fla. Commd. 2nd lt. U.S. Army, 1956, advanced through grades to gen., 1988; platoon leader, exec. officer 2nd Airborne Battle Group, 1957-59; platoon leader 6th Inf., Fed. Rep. Germany, 1959; aide-de-camp Berlin Command, Fed. Rep. Germany, 1960-61; assoc. prof. Dept. Mechanics, U.S. Army Military Acad., West Point, NY, Ga., 1965; advisor U.S. Army, Vietnam, 1965-66; commander 1st Battalion, 6th Inf., 198th Inf. brigade, 23rd Inf. Div., Vietnam, 1969-70; chief, Prof. Devel. Section, Inf. branch Office Personnel Operations, Washington, D.C., 1970-72; military asst. Office Asst. Sec. Army, Washington, D.C., 1973-74; dep. comdr. 172d inf. brigade Ft. Richardson, Alaska, 1974-76; comdr. 1st brigade 9th Inf. div., Ft. Lewis, Wash., 1976-78; dep. dir. plans U.S. Pacific Command, Camp Smith, Hawaii, 1978-80; asst. div. comdr. 8th inf. div. (mechanized) U.S. Army Europe, Fed. Republic Germany, 1980-82; dir. mil. personnel mgmt. Office Dep. Chief Staff for Personnel, Washington,

1982-83; comdg. gen. 24th inf. div. (mechanized) Ft. Stewart, Ga., 1983-85; dep. comdr. U.S. forces in Grenada operation, 1983; asst. dep. chief staff ops. Hdqrs. Dept. Army, Washington, 1985-86; comdg. gen. I corps Ft. Lewis, Wash., 1986-87; dep. chief staff for ops. and plans Hdqrs. Dept. Army, Washington, 1987-88; comdr. in chief U.S. Cen. Command, MacDill AFB, Fla., 1988-91, U.S. Forces in Ops. Desert Shield, Desert Storm, Saudi Arabia, 1990-91; ret. U.S. Army, 1992; lecturer, 1993—; contbr. and analyst NBC News, 1995—; chair Starbright Found., 1995—. Author: (with Peter Petre) It Doesn't Take a Hero, 1992. Chair Starbright Found., 1995—. Decorated Def. D.S.M., D.S.M. with two oak leaf clusters, D.S.M. for USN, D.S.M. for USAF, D.S.M. for USCG, Silver Star with two oak leaf clusters, Def. Superior Svc. medal, Legion of Merit, D.F.C., Bronze Star with three oak leaf clusters, Purple Heart with oak leaf cluster, Combat Infantryman badge, Master Parachutist badge, Gen. Staff Identification badge, Joint Staff Identification badge, Dept. Def. Identification badge, Presdl. Medal of Freedom; Nat. Order of Legion of Honor, hon. pfc. French Fgn. Legion (France); Order of Leopold (Belgium); knight Hon. Order of the Bath (U.K.); Decoration 1st degree (Bahrain); Sash of Independence (Qatar); Medal of Independence (United Arab Emirates); officer Order of King Abd Al Aziz 1st class (Saudi Arabia), Order of Kuwait with Sash of Most Excellent Order (Kuwait); named Father of the Yr., 1991, Toastmaster Internat. Best Spkr., 1992, Humanitarian of the Yr. United Cerebral Palsy, 1993, Living Legends M. D. Anderson Found., 1996; recipient Am. Patriot medal, 1993, Gilda Radner award Courage, 1995, N.J. Disting. Svc. medal, 1995, Vince Lombardi award Excellence, 1995, James Ewing Layman award Soc. Surg. Oncologists, 1997, Oliver R. Grace award, 1998, Ambassador Hope award, 1998, Spirit of Hope award, 1999, Leadership award Multiple Myeloma Rsch. Found., 1999, Inspirational award U. Pitts. Med. Ctr., 2000, Harry S. Truman Good Neighbor award, 2000. Avocations: hunting, fishing, skeet, trap and sporting clays. Office: care Internat Creative Mgmt Inc 40 W 57th St New York NY 10019-4001 Office: 400 N Ashley Dr Ste 3050 Tampa FL 33602-4314

SCHWARZTRAUBER, SAYRE ARCHIE, former naval officer, maritime consultant; b. Zion, Ill., June 23, 1929; s. Archie Douglas and Eleanor Miriam (Sayrs) S.; m. Beryl Constance Stewart, June 27, 1953; children: Sayre Archie, Beryl Ann, Heidi, Holly. BS cum laude, Maryville Coll., 1951; MA, Am. U., 1964, PhD, 1970. Commd. ensign USN, 1952, advanced through grades to rear adm., 1976; comdr. River Squadron 5, Vietnam, 1968-69, U.S.S. Decatur guided missile destroyer, 1970-71, Navy Recruiting Area 4, 1974-76; dep. chief staff Supreme Command Atlantic (NATO), 1976-79; co-dir. U.S.-Spanish Combined Staff, Madrid, 1979-81; dir. Inter-Am. Def. Coll., Washington, 1981-83; ret., 1983; apptd. rear adm. U.S. Maritime Svc., 1984; mem. Sec. of Navy Adv. Com., 1986-90; nat. and internat. lectr. strategic naval and maritime matters, 1973—. Author: The Three-Mile Limit of Territorial Seas, 1972, Schwarztrauber, Stewart and Related Families, 1995; editor Mass. Maritime Mag., 1987-90; contbr. articles, essays and revs. to profl. jours. Ruling elder Presbyn. Ch. U.S.A., 1965-86. Decorated Def. Disting. Svc. Medal, Legion of Merit, Cross of Gallantry (Vietnam), Gran Cruz de Merito (Spain); recipient Alfred Thayer Mahan award Navy League, 1974. Mem. SAR (pres. Cape Cod chpt. 1993-95, state pres. and genealogist 1992—, state pres. 1998-99, nat. trustee 1999-2000), Gamewardens of Vietnam, Nat. Geneal. Soc., U.S. Naval Inst., Am. Legion, Masons, VFW, Mil. Order World Wars, Mensa, Phi Kappa Phi, Pi Gamma Mu, Pi Sigma Alpha, Theta Alpha Phi. Home and Office: PO Box 589 Osterville MA 02655-0589

SCHWEBEL, RENATA MANASSE, sculptor; b. Zwickau, Germany, Mar. 6, 1930; came to U.S., 1940, naturalized, 1946; d. George and Anne Marie (Simon) Manasse; m. Jack P. Schwebel, May 10, 1955; children: Judith, Barbara, Diane. BA, Antioch Coll., 1953; MFA, Columbia U., 1961; student, Arts Students League, 1967-69. Cartographer Ecostate Inc., Ridgewood, N.J., 1949; display artist Silvestri Inc., Chgo., 1950-51; asst. Mazzolini Art Found., Yellow Springs, Ohio, 1952. One-woman shows include Columbia U., 1961, Greenwich Art Barn, Conn., 1975, Sculpture Ctr., N.Y.C., 1979, Pelham Art Ctr., N.Y., 1981, New Rochelle Libr. Gallery, N.Y., 1980, Outdoor Installations Katonah Gallery, 1986, 89, Berman/Daferner Gallery, N.Y.C., 1992-93; exhibited in group shows Stamford Mus., Conn., 1967, 96, Hudson River Mus., Yonkers, N.Y., 1972, 74, Wadsworth Atheneum, Hartford, 1974, Silvermine Art of the Northwest U.S. A. Anns., 1972, 76, 80, 95, 98, Silvermine Gallery, 1986, 91, 2000, New Britain Mus. Am. Art, Conn., 1974, Sculptors Guild Anns., 1974—, Imprimatur Gallery, St. Paul, 1985, Bergen County Mus., N.J., 1983, Sculpture Ctr., N.Y.C., 1978-88, Katonah Gallery, N.Y., 1986-90, Cast Iron Gallery, N.Y.C., 1991, 93, Kyoto (Japan) Gallery, 1993; traveling show exhibited in Am. cultural ctrs. in Egypt and Israel, 1981, 3 Rivers Art Festival, Pitts., 1994, FFS Gallery, N.Y.C., 1994, 95, exhibition, Russian consulate, N.Y.C., 1998, Long Beach Island Found. of the Arts and Scis., N.J., 1999, Grounds for Sculpture, Hamilton, N.J., 1999, Chesterwood Mus., Stockbridge, Mass., 2000; represented in permanent collections S.W. Bell, Columbia U., Colt Industries, Am. Airlines, Comcraft Industries, Nairobi, Grüber Haus, Berlin, Mus. Fgn. Art, Sofia, Bulgaria. Bd. dirs. Fine Arts Fedn., N.Y., 1985-87; trustee Sculpture Ctr., 1980-88, chmn. exhbn. com., 1986-88; mem. adv. bd. Pehlham Art Ctr., 1982. Mem. Sculptors Guild (bd. dirs. 1975-94, 95—, pres. 1980-83), Antioch Coll. Assn. (bd. dirs. 1971-77), Ams. for Peace Now (bd. dirs. 1991—), Nat. Assn. Women Artists (Willis Meml. prize 1974, Medal of Honor 1981, Paley Meml. award 1979), Audubon Artists (Chaim Gross award 1980, medal of honor 1982, Rennick award 1986, 90, 92, 95), Conn. Acad. Fine Arts, N.Y. Soc. Women Artists, Artists Equity N.Y., Katonah Gallery (artist mem. 1986-90). Home: 10 Dogwood Hills Rd Pound Ridge NY 10576-1508

SCHWEBEL, STEPHEN MYRON, judge, arbitrator; b. N.Y.C., Mar. 10, 1929; s. Victor and Pauline (Pfeffer) S.; m. Louise Ingrid Nancy Killander, Aug. 2, 1972; children: Jennifer, Anna. BA in Govt. magna cum laude with highest honors in govt., Harvard U., 1950; postgrad., Cambridge (Eng.) U., 1950-51; LLB, Yale U., 1954; LLD (hon.), Bhopal (India) U., 1983, Hofstra U., 1997. Bar: N.Y. 1955, U.S. Supreme Ct. 1965, D.C. 1976. Dir. UN hdqrs. office World Fedn. UN Assns., 1950-53; lectr. Am. fgn. policy various univs. U.S. State Dept., India, 1952; research, drafting asst. to Trygve Lie for writing of In the Cause of Peace, 1953; assoc. White & Case, N.Y.C., 1954-59; asst. prof. law Harvard U., Cambridge, Mass., 1959-61; asst. legal advisor U.S. Dept. State, Washington, 1961-66, dep. legal advisor, 1973-81; exec. dir. Am. Soc. Internat. Law, Washington, 1967-72; Burling prof. internat. law Sch. of Advanced Internat. Studies, Johns Hopkins U., Washington, 1967-81; pres. Adminstrv. Tribunal Internat. Monetary Fund., 1994—; judge Internat. Ct. Justice, The Hague, The Netherlands, 1981-2000; v.p. Internat. Ct. Justice, The Hague, 1994-97, pres., 1997-2000; jurist-in-residence John's Hopkins Sch. Adv. Internat. Studies, 2000—; spl. rep. Micronesian claims U.S. Dept. State, 1966-71; legal adviser U.S. del. 16th-20th and 4th Spl. Gen. Assemblies UN; U.S. assoc. rep. Internat. Ct. Justice, 1962, U.S. dep. agt., 1979-80, U.S. counsel, 1980; U.S. rep., chmn. U.S. del. to 1st session UN Spl. Com on Principles Internat. Law concerning friendly relations and cooperation among states, Mexico City, 1964; U.S. rep. on adv. com. UN Program Assistance in Teaching, Study, Dissemination and Wider Appreciation Internat. Law, 1966-74; U.S. counsel Franco-Am. Air Arbitration, 1978; legal adv. U.S. del. to 32d and 33d WHO Assemblies, Geneva, 1979-80; vis. prof. internat. law Australian Nat. U., Canberra, 1969; U.S. rep., chmn. del. 3d session UN Spl. Com. on Question Defining Aggression, Geneva, 1970; counselor internat. law U.S. Dept. State, 1973; U.S. rep., chmn. del. 2d and 4th sessions UNCTAD Working Group on Charter Econ. Rights and Duties of States, Geneva, 1973, Mexico City, 1974; U.S. alt. rep. UN Econ. and Social Council, Geneva, 1974; legal adviser U.S. del. Conf. Internat. Econ. Coop., Paris, 1975; mem. U.S. Tripartite Adv. Com. on Internat. Labor Standards, 1980, Internat. Law Commn., UN, Geneva, 1977-81; spl. rapporteur internat. watercourses Internat. Law Commn., UN, 1977-81, chmn. drafting com., 1978; chmn. or party-apptd. arbitrator internat. comml. arbitration tribunals, 1982—, arbitral tribunal Eritrea-Yemen Arbitration, 1996-99; pres. So. Bluefin Tuna Arbitration (Australia and New Zealand vs. Japan), 2000; mem. exec. com. Commn. Study Orgn. Peace, 1948-61; adv. joint com. law internat. transactions Am. Law Inst. and Am. Bar Assn., 1959-61; nat. chmn. Collegiate Council for UN, 1948-50; pres. Internat. Student Movement for UN, 1950-51; undergrad. orator Harvard U. Commencement, 1950; mem. adv. bd. Ctr. Oceans Law and Policy U. Va., 1975-81; vice chmn. Sec. State's Adv. Com. Pvt. Internat. Law, 1978-79, chmn., 1979-81; hon. fellow Cambridge U. Ctr. for Rsch. in Internat. Law, 1983—, mem. bd. electors Whewell Professorship in Internat. Law U. Cambridge, 1983—; mem. overseers' com. to visit Harvard U. Law Sch., 1991-97; cons. Ford. Found., 1990; chmn. supervisory bd. Telders Internat. Law Moot Court Competition, The Hague, Netherlands, 1993-98, chmn. Hauser Scholars Selection Bd., N.Y.U. Law Sch., 1997—; hon. bencher Gray's Inn, London, 1998—, vis. lect. Cambridge U., 1957, Carnegie Lectr. Hague Acad. Internat. Law, 1972, Inst. Universitaire de Hautes Etudes Internationales, Geneva, 1980; Brown lectr. Cath. U., 1983; Lauterpacht. lectr., Cambridge U., 1983; jurisprudential lectr. U. Wash., 1985; Otto Walter Internat. Fellow, N.Y. Law Sch., 1987; Sherrill lectr. Yale U., 1988; Centennial Morris vis. prof. Chgo.-Kent Coll. of Law, 1988; Page Disting. vis. jurist U. Kans., 1988; Allison lectr. Suffolk Law Sch., 1989; Regents' lectr. U. Calif. Berkeley, 1990; Wing-Tat Lee lectr. Loyola U., 1990; Ford Found. lectr. U. N.Mex., U. Wash., U. Ind., Vanderbilt U., U. Minn., 1991, U. Calif., L.A., U. Houston, U. Miami, Emory U., Notre Dame U., 1992, U. Iowa, U. Pitts., 1993; Ben C. Green lectr. Case Western Res. U., 1992; Blaine Sloan lectr. Pace U., 1993; Hauser lectr. NYU Law Sch., 1994; Goff lectr., Hong Kong City U., 1994; Freshfields lectr. U. London, 1996, F. A. Mann lectr., 1998; jurist-in-residence Touro Coll. Law Sch., 1999; lectr. U. Balt., 2000. Author: The Secretary-General of the United Nations, 1952, International Arbitration: Three Salient Problems, 1987, Justice in International Law, 1994; editor: The Effectiveness of International Decisions, 1971; mem. editorial bd. Am. Jour. Internat. Law, 1967-81, hon. mem., 1996—; chmn. editorial adv. com. Internat. Legal Materials, 1967-73. Frank Knox fellow Harvard U., 1950-51, Hallows Jud. fellow Marquette U. Law Sch., 2000; recipient Gherini prize Yale Law Sch., 1954, medal of Merit, 1997, Pres. medal Johns Hopkins U., 1992, Harold Weill medal NYU, 1992, Wolfgang Friedmann award Columbia U., 1998. Mem. ABA, Am. Soc. Internat. Law (exec. v.p. 1967-73, hon. v.p. 1982-95, hon. pres. 1996—, Manley O. Hudson medal 2000), Internat. Law Assn., Inst. Droit Internat., Coun. Fgn. Rels., Acad. of Experts (v.p. 1995—), Harvard Club (N.Y.C.), Athenaeum (London), Haagsche Club (The Hague), Cosmos Club (Washington), Phi Beta Kappa. Avocation: music.

SCHWEDES, JOERG, university administrator, consultant; b. Berlin, Feb. 26, 1938. Diploma in Engring., U. Karlsruhe, Germany, 1964, D of Engring., 1971. Head R&E group mech. process engring. Bayer AG, Leverkusen, Germany, 1971-76; prof., head Inst. Mech. Process Engring. Tech. U., Braunschweig, Germany, 1976—; v.p. Tech. U., 1982-84, head dept. mech. engring., 1989-91, dean faculty mech. and elec. engring., 1997-99; cons. on bulk solids tech., 1991—; cons. in commination tech., 1996—. Contbr. over 200 articles to profl. jours. Office: Tech Univ, Volkmaroder Str 4/5, D-38104 Braunschweig Germany

SCHWEGLER, HELMUT, theoretical physics educator; b. Munich, Dec. 21, 1938; s. Michael and Johanna (Seidinger) S.; m. Christel Schamoni, Jan. 14, 1963; children: Thomas, Ursula, Johannes. Diploma in physics, Tech. U. Munich, 1963; D Natural Scis., Tech. U. Darmstadt, Germany, 1966, Habilitation in Natural Scis., 1970. Prof. physics Tech. U. Darmstadt, 1971; prof. theoretical physics and biophysics U. Bremen, Germany, 1972—, dir. Inst. Theoretical Neurophysics/Ctr. for Cognitive Scis. Mem. German Physics Soc., German Soc. for Biophysics, European Phys. Soc., Wittheit zu Bremen. Home: Bergius Strasse 87, D-28357 Bremen Germany Office: U Bremen, PO Box 330440, D-28334 Bremen Germany

SCHWEHR, UDO, cardiologist, internist; b. Kenzingen, Germany, May 22, 1957; s. August and Susanne Schwehr; m. Angelika Koesler, May 4, 1991. MD, U. Freiburg, Germany, 1982. Resident dept. internal medicine Gen. Hosp., Karlsruhe, Germany, 1984-87; resident dept. gastroenterology Dist. Hosp., Heppenheim, Germany, 1987-90; resident dept. cardiology RHZ Bad Krozingen, Germany, 1990-92; pvt. practice Seelbach, Germany, 1993—; del. Hartmann-Bund. Served to maj. German Air Force, 1982-84. Mem. Interdisciplinaire Gesellschaft Umweltmealizin, Deutsche Gesellschaft Ultraschaft in der Medikin, Am. Heart Assn., Arbeitskreis niedergel. Kardiologen, Berufsverband dt. Internisten Wiesbaden, Ges. Dt. Naturforscher u. Aerzte Leverkusen, Deutsche Hochdruckliga Heidelberg, Ges. fuer Praev. u. Rehabil. Koenigsfeld, Studienstiftung des deutschen Volkes, Ges. fuer Herz- und Kreislaufforschung, Greenpeace Germany, Ski Assn., Tennis Assn. Roman Catholic. Avocations: skiing, tennis, travel. Home and Office: Litschentalstrasse 7, 77960 Seelbach Germany

SCHWEICKART, RUSSELL LOUIS, communications executive, astronaut; b. Neptune, N.J., Oct. 25, 1935; s. George L. Schweickart; children: Vicki Louise, Russell and Randolph (twins), Elin Ashley, Diana Croom; m. Nancy Kudriavetz Ramsey; step-children: Matthew Forbes Ramsey, David Scot Ramsey. B.S. in Aero. Engring, Mass. Inst. Tech., 1956, M.S. in Aeros. and Astronautics, 1963. Former research scientist Mass. Inst. Tech. Exptl. Astronomy Lab.; astronaut Johnson Manned Spacecraft Center, Houston, lunar module pilot (Apollo 9, 1969); dir. user affairs Office of Applications, NASA; sci. adv. to Gov. Edmund G. Brown, Jr. State of Calif., 1977-79; chmn. Calif. Energy Commn., 1979-83, commr., 1979-85; pres., founder Assn. Space Explorers, 1985-98; pres. NRS Communications, San Francisco, 1991-94; exec. v.p. CTA Comml. Systems, Rockville, Md., 1994-96; pres., CEO, Aloha Networks, Inc., San Francisco, 1996-98, exec. v.p., 1998; pres. NRS Comms., 1985-98; ret., 1998; cons. and lectr. in field. Trustee Calif. Acad. Sci. Served as pilot USAF, 1956-60, 61; Capt. Mass. Air N.G. Recipient Distinguished Service medal NASA, 1970, Exceptional Service medal NASA, 1974, De La Vaulx medal FAI, 1970, Spl. Trustees award Nat. Acad. TV Arts and Scis., 1969. Fellow Am. Astronautical Soc.; mem. AIAA. Club: Explorers. *

SCHWEICKERT, RICHARD JUSTUS, psychologist, educator; b. Madison, Wis., July 19, 1946; s. Carl E. and Marie E. (Dilzer) S.; m. Carolyn M. Jagacinski, Dec. 27, 1980; children: Patrick, Kenneth. BS in Math., U. Santa Clara, 1968; MA in Math., Ind. U., 1972; PhD in Psychology, U. Mich., 1979. Statistician Bellevue Psychiatric Hosp., N.Y.C., 1969-71; asst. prof. Purdue U., West Lafayette, Ind., 1978-83; assoc. prof. Purdue U., West Lafayette, 1984-91, prof., 1992—; adv. panel on human cognition & perception NSF, 1993-96. Author: (with others) Handbook of Human Factors, 1987; editor: Jour. Mathemat. Psychology; assoc. editor Psychol. Bull. and Rev., 1993-98; mem. editl. bd. Jour. Exptl. Psychology; Learning, Memory & Cognition, 1985-89, 91-94, Jour. Math. Psychology, 1986-94; contbr. articles to profl. jours. Grantee NSF, 1981-84, 92-2000, NIMH, 1983-89. Fellow AAAS, Am. Psychol. Soc.; mem. Soc. for Math. Psychology (pres. 1990-91, bd. dirs.), Psychonomic Soc., Informs. Office: Purdue U Dept Psychol Scis Purdue University IN 47907

SCHWEID, ELIEZER, philosopher; b. Jerusalem, Israel, Sept. 7, 1929; s. Zvi and Osnath (Rosen) S.; m. Sabina Fuchs, Oct. 14, 1953; three children. PhD, Hebrew U., 1962. Prof. Hebrew U., Jerusalem, 1984—. Recipient Israel prize Israeli Ministry Edn., 1994.

SCHWEIGER, ULRICH, psychiatrist, psychotherapist; b. Steinhoring, Germany, Sept. 18, 1955; s. Hermann and Elfriede (Weinfurtner) S.; m. Marion Werner, Aug. 6, 1982; children: Janina, Julietta, Jonathan. MD, Ludwig-Maximilians U, Munchen, Germany, 1983. Physician, rschr. Max-Planck Inst. Psychiatrie, Munich, Germany, 1983-94; asst. med. dir. Klinik Roseneck, Prien, Germany, 1995-98, Klinik Psychiatry, Medizinische U., Lubeck, Germany, 1999—. Editor: The Menstrual Cycle and Its Disorders, 1989; contbr. articles to profl. jours. Recipient Otto-Hahn-Medaille Max-Planck Gesellschaft, 1986. Mem. Endocrine Soc., Deutsche Gesellschaft Psychiatrie, Psychotherapie und Neurologie. Office: Medizinische Univ, Klinik Psychiatrie, D-23538 Lübeck Germany

SCHWEIKER, ULRICH, management consultant; b. Osnabrueck, Germany, July 20, 1955; s. Hans-Georg and Ingeburg (Goetting) S.; m. Waltraud Ospelt, July 18, 1980. BA, U. Munster, 1976, MA, 1979, PhD, 1983. Sr. expert Ctr. for Info. and counseling U. Erlangen-Nuremberg, 1983-85; sr. expert Team and Orgn. Devel. Volkswagen Corp. Exec. Devel., Wolfsburg, 1985-88; head corp. human resources planning and devel. Bilfinger & Berger Corp., Mannheim, 1988; head corp. exec. devel. Krupp Corp., Essen, 1988-90; ptnr. House of Mgmt., Mannheim, 1991-94; v.p. total quality mgmt., global human resources mgmt. Sulzer Metco Holding, Wohlen, Switzerland, 1995-97; assoc. ptnr. Andersen Consulting, Zurich, 1997—; vis. scholar U.S. Internat. U., San Diego, 1982-83. Contbr. articles to profl. jours. Mem. APA, Internat. Orgn. Devel. Assn., European Consortium for the Learning Orgn., European Found. for Mgmt. Devel. Avocations: travel, people, cultures, piano. Home: Flurweg 3, CH-5430 Wettingen Aargau, Switzerland Office: Andersen Consulting, Fraumuensterstrasse 16, CH-8001 Zurich Switzerland

SCHWEIKHARD, LUTZ CHRISTIAN, physics educator; b. Ingelheim, Germany, June 3, 1959; s. Ernst Christian and Hildegard (Hessel) S.; m. Johanna Sischka, Oct. 19, 1989; children: Frank Philipp, Thomas Matthias. Student, U. Mainz (Germany), 1978-80, U. Colo., Boulder, 1980-81; Dipl. in Physics with highest honor, U. Mainz, 1985, PhD, 1990, Habil., 1996. Teaching asst. U. Mainz, 1983-90, sci. assoc. Inst. Physics, 1985-90; sci. assoc. CERN, Geneva, 1986-90; sci. assoc. Inst. Physics U. Mainz, 1992-96, temporary prof. experimental physics, 1996-99; physics educator Heisenberg Stipendiary Deutsche Forschungsgemeinschaft, 1999—. Contbr. articles to profl. jours. Postdoctoral fellow The Ohio State U., Columbus, 1990-92, Mattauch-Herzog prize, Arbeitsgemeinschaft Massenspektrometrie, 1995, Rudolf Kaiser prize, 1999. Mem. German Phys. Soc., European Phys. Soc., Am. Phys. Soc., Am. Soc. for Mass Spectrometry. Office: U Mainz Inst Physics, Staudinger Weg 7, D-55099 Mainz Germany

SCHWEINFURTH, ULRICH, geography educator; b. Detmold, Germany, Feb. 6, 1925; s. Julius and Suse (Werther) S.; m. Heidi Marby; 1 child, Dagmar. D in Natural Scis., U. Bonn, Fed. Republic Germany, 1956. Instr. U. Bonn., 1963; found. chmn., head dept. geography S. Asia Inst., U. Heidelberg, Fed. Republic Germany, 1964-93; emeritus prof. U. Heidelberg, 1993—. Author: The Horizontal and Vertical Distribution of the Vegetation in the Himalayas, 1957, Studies in the Plant Geography of Tasmania, 1962, New Zealand Observations and Studies on Plant Geography and Ecology of the antipodean Island Group, 1966; editor: Yearbook of the South Asia Inst., Heidelberg U., 1968-69, 1969, Studies in the Climatology of South Asia, 1970. Mem. Royal George Soc. London (hon.). Achievements include research in Ceylon I-III, 1971, 81, 89; geoecological research since 1972. Office: S Asia Inst U Heidelberg/Geog, PO Box 103066, 69020 Heidelberg Germany

SCHWEINS, MICHAEL JOSEF, physician, surgeon; b. Kaiserslautern, Germany, July 29, 1958; s. Bernd M. and Josefine (Wallrafen) S.; m. Birgit Maria Dolle, June 19, 1961; children: Julian Benedikt, Moritz Michael, Felix Simon. MD, U. Cologne, Germany, 1984; PhD, U. Cologne. Diplomate in surgery and trauma surgery. Fellow in intensive care U. Cologne, 1984-85, fellow in surgern, 1985-90, surgeon cons., 1990-93; chief and owner Outpatient Clinic for Surgery, Orth. Surgery and Sports Med., Cologne, 1993—. Author: Sonografie in Surgery, 1988, Hygiene Procedures in German Hospitals, 1993; editor: Hygiene Procedures in Surgery, 1993; contbr. articles to profl. jours. Cpl. Air Def., German Army, 1977-78. Mem. German Soc. Surgery, German Soc. Orthopedic Surgery, Orgn. Ambulatory Surgery (bd. mem.). Roman Catholic. Avocations: sports (skiing, golf, tennis), hunting, collecting modern art. Office: Outpatient Clinic Surgery, Frankfurter Str 589, 51107 Cologne Germany

SCHWEITZER, CARL-CHRISTOPH, political science educator; b. Potsdam, Germany, Oct. 3, 1924; s. Carl Gunther and Paula (Vogelsang) S.; m. Therese Christians, Dec. 1949; children: Helmuth, Georg. BA, Oxford U., 1946; PhD, U. Freiburg (Germany), 1949. Founding officer Fed. Office Edn. in Citizenship, Bonn, 1951-61; advisor Pres. Fed. Republic, Bonn, 1961-63; prof. polit. sci. Berlin U., 1963-69, U. Bonn, 1969—; mem. German Fed. Parliament, 1972-76, 80; internat. coord. Europe 12-Action and Rsch. Com. on the EC; vis. prof. Duke U., Oxford U., U. Toronto. Author: Amerikas Chinesisches Dilemma, 1969, Die deutsche Nation von Bismarck bis Honecker, 1976, The Political System of the Federal Republic of Germany, 1984, 95, The Changing Analysis of the Soviet Threat, 1990, others; author: Gains and Losses of EC Membership, 1990. Mem. German Polit. Sci. Assn., Aktion Gemeinsinn (chmn.). Social Democrat. Lutheran. Avocations: tennis, alpine skiing, music. Home: Roettgenerstr 186, 53127 Bonn Germany Office: Aktion Gemeinsinn, 53113 Bonn Germany

SCHWEITZER, LOUIS, automotive industry executive; b. Geneva, July 8, 1942; s. Pierre-Paul and Catherine (Hatt) S.; m. Agnès Schmitz, Dec. 20, 1972; children: Zoé, Marie. BA in Polit. Sci., U. Paris, JD; postgrad., École Nationale d'Administration, 1968-70. Inspector fins. Govt. France, 1970—, dep. office dir. gen. pub. assistance, 1970-71, dep. office gen. inspection fins., 1971-74, dep. office budget mgmt., 1974-79, under dir. office budget mgmt., 1979, dir. cabinet of Laurent Fabius, min. budget, min. industry, P.M., 1981-86; v.p. for fin. and planning Régie Renault, 1986-88, exec. v.p., 1989-90, pres., COO, 1990-92, chmn., CEO, 1992—; prof. Paris Inst. Polit. Studies, 1982-86. Bd. dirs. French Inst. Internat. Rels., Pechiney, Banque Nationale de Paris, EDF, Philips. Decorated officer Legion of Honor, officer Nat. Order Merit (France). Home: 1 rue Dauphine, 75006 Paris France Office: Renault, 13-15 quai Alphonse Le Gall, F-92513 Boulogne France

SCHWEITZER, MARCELL, economics and business administration educator, researcher; b. Radautz, Rumania, Oct. 18, 1932; arrived in Germany, 1940; s. Franz Ferdinand and Anna (Biborosch) S.; m. Hildburg Charlotte Müller, May 12, 1961; 1 child, Marcus. Student in Indsl. Econs., Hannover, Germany, 1954; MBA, Free U. of Berlin, 1959, PhD in Bus. Adminstrn., 1963, Habilitation for Bus. Adminstrn., 1968. Cert. Bus. Adminstrn. Lectureship Free U. of Berlin, 1961-66; lectr. Acad. Econs., Berlin, 1961-66; guest prof. U. Tuebingen, Germany, 1968-69, prof. econs. and bus. mgmt., 1969—; dean Faculty Econs. and Bus. Mgmt., U. Tuebingen, Germany, 1972-73, 81-82, dir. Rsch. Dept. Indsl. Mgmt, 1972-73, 74—, treas. Faculty Econs. and Bus. Mgmt., 1992-94; dir. Acad. Pub. and Bus. Adminstrn., Stuttgart, Germany, 1984—; guest prof. Jiao Tong U., Shanghai, China, 1988—; cons. Ministry Econs., Baden-Wuerttemberg, 1990-91, State Ministry, Baden-Wuerttemberg, 1992-93; evaluator German Rsch. Community, Germany, 1992—, Higher Edn. Coun., Germany, 1994—. Author: Probleme der Ablauforganisation in Unternehmungen, 1964, Struktur und Funktion der Bilanz: Grundfragen der betriebswirtschaftlichen Bilanz in methodologischer und entscheidungstheoretischer Sicht., 1972, Japanese edit., 1992, Einführung in die Industriebetriebslehre, 1973, 2d edit., 1994, (with others) Produktions- und Kostentheorie der Unternehmung, 1974, 2nd edit., 1996, Systeme der Kostenrechnung, 1976, Japanese edit., 1978, Indonesian edit., 1991, 7th edit., 1998, Entscheidungen in Industrieunternehmungen, 1977, Break-even-Analysen: Grundmodell, Varianten, Erweiterungen, 1986, 2d edit., 1998, Japanese edit., 1991, N.Y. edit., 1991, Chinese edit., 1993, 2nd edit., 1996, Allgemeine Betriebswirtschaftslehre, vols. 1-3, 8th edit., 2000; co-editor: Handbook of German Bus. Mgmt. Vols. 1-2, Handworterbuch des Rechnungswesens, 3d edit., 1993; contbr. to numerous handbooks, jours. and revs. Mem. Verband der Hochschullehrer für Betriebswirtschaft, Verein für Socialpolitik, Schmalenbach-Gesellschaft, European Acctg. Assn. Avocations: music, painting, sports. Home: Ammertalstr 6, D-72108 Rottenburg/Neckar Germany Office: Eberhard-Karls-Universitaet, Nauklerstrasse 47, D-72074 Tuebingen Germany

SCHWEITZER, WOLF, physician, forensic medicine specialist; b. Münich, Germany, Sept. 24, 1967. MD, U. Zürich, 1994. Registrar Inst. für Rechtsmedizin der Univ. Zürich, 1992-93, Ospidal Sch.d'Engiadina, Bassa, Switzerland, 1994-95; registrar, rsch. fellow Inst. für Pathologie, Müüsterlingen, Switzerland, 1995-97, Victorian Inst. Forensic Medicine, Melbourne, Australia, 1997-98; with Inst. f Rechtsmedizin, Bern, Switzerland, 1998—.

SCHWEIZER, ANETTE, limnologist, researcher; b. Baienfurt, Germany, May 12, 1962; d. Paul Adolf and Irene Rose (Kleebauer) S. D of Natural Scis. in Biology, U. Konstanz, Germany, 1990. Rschr. Inst. für Seenforschung Landesanstalt für Umweltschutz and U. of Konstanz, 1991-96. Author, editor: (book) Jubiläumsband 75 Jahre Institut für Seenforschung, 1996; contbr. articles to profl. jours. Nurse Ravensburg Hosp., 1981; 1st violinist Baienfurt Orch., 1979-85. Avocations: classical music, mountain climbing, cooking, reading, art history.

SCHWEIZER, EDWARD SOWERS, insurance agency owner; b. Houston, May 6, 1938; s. John Mel Jr. and Alicia Lucille (Sowers) S.; m. Suzan Lee Peterson, June 20, 1964; children: Edward Jr., Sally, Elizabeth. Degre superieur, U. Paris, 1957; BA, Occidental Coll., 1961; MA, Pepperdine U., 1978. Cert. surface warfare officer USN. Owner ESS Ins. Svcs., Camarillo,, Calif., Chesapeake City, Md., 1989—; mem. bd. Laguna Beach Pageant of the Masters; mem. adv. bd. San Diego Found., 1998-99, Orange County

Register Grants Bd., Santa Ana, Calif., 1998-99. Commr. City of Mission Viejo, 1990-92, 97-99, Parks and Recreation Com., Chesapeake City, 2000—. Capt. USN, 1962-88. Decorated Meritorious Svc. medal. Mem. Ret. Officers Assn., Res. Officers Assn., Naval Res. Assn., KC (Grand Knight 1989-90), Navy League of the U.S. Republican. Roman Catholic. Avocations: civic affairs, fine art, international traveling, running, ocean swimming, skiing. Home: 504 Bohemia Ave Chesapeake City CA 21915-0711

SCHWELLA, ERWIN, management educator, consultant; b. Bloemfontein, South Africa, Nov. 6, 1953; s. Terence and Anna Gysberta Schwella; children: Heinrich, Johann, Lindi; m. Lynette Monk. BA in Law, U. Stellenbosch, South frica, 1975, BA in Sociology cum laude, 1984, MPA, 1983, PhD, 1988. Registered pers. practitioner. Clk. of ct., state prosecutor Dept. Justice, South Africa, 1975-77; pers. officer South African Def. Force, 1977-79; tng. officer Cape Town (South Africa) City Coun., 1979-80; lectr. U. Stellenbosch, 1981-92, prof., dir. Sch. Pub. Mgmt. and Planning, 1992—; dir., cons. Consultus Programme for Pub. and Devel. Sector Capacity Bldg., Bellville and Stellenbosch; dir., trustee Joint Univs. Pub. Mgmt. and Ednl. Trust, South Africa; sr. vis. fellow Brit. Civil Svc. Coll., Sunningdale, Eng., 1993-94; vis. acad. U. Leuven, Belgium, Kennedy Sch. Govt./Harvard U., Inst. Social Studies, The Hague, Netherlands; sr., cons. all spheres of South African govt. Co-author: Public Management, 1991, Public Resource Management, 1996, Reflective Public Administration, 1999; mem. editl. bd. Jour. Pub. Affairs Edn., Jour. Comparative Policy Analysis, Pub. Productivity and Mgmt. Rev.; contbr. articles to profl.jours. Mem. South African Inst. Mcpl. Mgmt. Avocations: cricket, rugby, reading, travel. E-mail: erwin.schwella@sopmp.sun.ac.za. Office: U Stellenbosch Sch Mgmt, Bellville Pk/PO Box 610, Bellville 7353, South Africa

SCHWEPKER, CHARLES HENRY, JR., marketing educator; b. St. Charles, Mo., Jan. 21, 1963; s. Charles Henry Sr. and Mary Regina (Halter) S.; m. Laura Ann Pirrone, Dec. 1992; 1 child, Charles Henry III. BSBA, S.E. Mo. State U., 1984, MBA, 1988; PhD, U. Memphis, 1992. Asst. mgr. WalMart, Lubbock, Tex., 1985; prof. mktg. Cen. Mo. State U., Warrensburg, 1992—; mktg. cons.; ad hoc reviewer Jour. of Personal Selling and Sales Mgmt., 1991, 92. Mem. editl. rev. bd. Jour. Personal Selling and Sales Mgmt., 1993—, Jour. Mktg. Theory & Practice, 1993—, Jour. Bus. and Indsl. Mktg., So. Bus. Rev.; contbr. articles to profl. jours. and books; co-author: Sales Management: Analysis and Decision Making, Professional Selling: A Trust Based Approach. Chpt. advisor for Student Am. Mktg. Assn. at Ctrl. Mo. State U., 1992—, internat. study tour coord. Recipient Excellence in Reviewing award, Jour. Mktg. theory and Practice, 1996, Award for Jour. Personal Selling and Sales Mgmt., 1996. Mem. Am. Mktg. Assn., Acad. Mktg. Sci., So. Mktg. Assn. (procs. reviewer 1991), Atlantic Mktg. Assn. (procs. reviewer 1991, nat. conf. in sales mgmt. procs. reviewer 1993, 94, 95, 96, 97). Roman Catholic. Avocations: golf, basketball, camping, fishing. Office: Ctrl Mo State U Coll Bus & Econs Dept Mktg and Legal Studies Warrensburg MO 64093

SCHWERTMANN, UDO, soil scientist, researcher; b. Stade, Germany, Nov. 25, 1927. MSc, U. Hannover, Germany, 1952, PhD, 1959, habilitation, 1961; Doctorate (hon.), U. Kiel, Germany, 1996. Head soils dept. Tech. U., Berlin, 1964-70, Munich, 1970-95; reviewer German Sci. Found., 1988-96. Author: (textbook) Bodenkunde, 10 edits., 1960-96, (handbook) Soil Erosion, 1987, (lab. book) Iron Oxides in the Laboratory, 1991, 2d edit., 2000, The Iron Oxides, 1996. Mem. Acad. Leopoldina, Clay Mineral Soc. (named Pioneer in Clay 1992, Disting. mem. 1997), Soil Sci. Soc. Germany (honor mem.). Home: Lintnerstr 4A, D-85354 Freising Bavaria, Germany Office: Tech Univ, D-85350 Freising Bavaria, Germany

SCHWERY, HENRI CARDINAL, bishop; b. St. Leonard, Switzerland, June 14, 1932. Ordained priest Roman Cath. Ch., 1957, ordained bishop, 1977. Rector Coll. Sion, 1972-77; elevated to cardinal with titular Ch. of Holy Protamartyrs, 1991; elevated to Sacred Coll. Cardinals, 1991. Office: Diocese of Roman Cath Ch, CP 2334, CH-1950 Sion 2, Switzerland*

SCHWIER, PRISCILLA LAMB GUYTON, television broadcasting company executive; b. Toledo, Ohio, May 8, 1939; d. Edward Oliver and Prudence (Hutchinson) L.; m. Robert T. Guyton, June 21, 1963 (dec. Sept. 1976); children—Melissa, Margaret, Robert; m. Frederick W. Schwier, May 11, 1984. B.A., Smith Coll., 1961; M.A., U. Toledo, 1972. Pres. Gt. Lakes Comms., Inc., 1982-97; vice chmn. Seilon, Inc., Toledo, 1981-83, also dir. Contbr. articles to profl. jours. Trustee Wilberforce U., Ohio, 1983—, Planned Parenthood, Toledo, 1979-83, Maumee Valley Country Day Sch., Toledo; bd. dirs. N.W. Ohio Hospice, 1991-98. Episcopal Ch., Maumee, Ohio, 1983—; bd. trustees Toledo Hosp., Maumee Country Day Sch., 1986-92; pres. Edward Lamb Found., 1987—. Democrat. Episcopalian. Home and Office: 345 E Front St Perrysburg OH 43551-2131

SCHWIETZ, ROGER L., bishop. Ordained priest Roman Cath. Ch., 1967, consecrated bishop, 1990. Bishop Diocese of Duluth, Minn., 1989-99; archbishop Archdiocese of Anchorage, 1999—. Home: 2830 E 4th St Duluth MN 55812-1501 Office: Archdiocese of Anchorage 225 Cordova St Anchorage AK 99501-2409

SCHWILK, BERNHARD, physician, researcher; b. Kaisersbach, Baden-Württemberg, Germany, Feb. 3, 1952; s. Walter and Maria Eva (Rothweiler) S.; m. Christina Säps Ernst, Aug. 23, 1985; children: Max, Nora. Examin as Phys., U. Ulm, Germany, 1982. Resident Karl-Olga-Krankenhaus, Stuttgart, Germany, 1982-85; resident in anaesthesiology U. Ulm, 1986-91, sr. physician anaesthesiology, 1991-98, sr. physician, asst. prof. anaesthesiology, 1998—. With German Army, 1971-72. Mem. Physicians Prevention Nuc. War, European Soc. Intensive Care Medicine, N.Y. Acad. Sci., European Soc. Computing and Tech. in Anaesthesiology and Intensive Care (gen. sec. 1996—, founding mem. 1989), Bd. German Anaesthesiologists (mem. commn. quality assurance 1993—), Bd. Physicians (vice-chair coun. quality assurance anaesthesiology in Baden-Württemberg 1998—). Avocations: anthropology, economics, ethical discussions. Office: Anaesthesiology U Hosp, Steinhovelstr 9, D-89070 Ulm Baden-Württemberg, Germany

SCHWIND, HANS-DIETER, criminology educator; b. Tokyo, May 31, 1936; s. Martin Georg and Eva (Klamroth) S.; m. Ortrud Roswitha Haas; children: Elke, Maike, Volker. Diploma, U. Hamburg, U. Munich. Tech. asst. U. Göttingen, Germany; prof. U. Ruhr, Bochum, Germany, 1974—, dean Faculty Law, 1982-83; min. justice Ministry Justice, Hannover, 1978-82; chmn. violence com. Commn. of Fed. Govt., 1987-90. Author: Kriminalitätsatlas, 1975, Kriminologie, 10th edit., 2000, (with others) Kommentar z. Strafvollz., 3d edit., 1999, (rsch.) Dunkelfeld Bochum I, 1975, II, 1986, III, 2000. Decorated Great Fed. Svc. Cross, 1981, bú-lé-merite Orden, 1984. Mem. German Criminol. Soc. (pres. 1984-89), New Criminol. Soc. (v.p. 1989—). Lutheran. Home: Bismarckstrasse 19, D-49076 Osnabrück Germany Office: Ruhr U, Universitässtrasse 150, 44801 Bochum Germany

SCHWINGELER, THOMAS HEINRICH, banker; b. Bonn, Germany. BA in Econs., Yale U., 1990; MBA, Harvard U., 1995. Assoc. cons. Bain & Co., London, 1990-91; fin. analyst Goldman Sachs, London, 1991-93; assoc. Merrill Lynch, N.Y.C., 1995-98; v.p. Goldman Sachs, N.Y.C., 1998—.

SCHWINGHAMER, ERWIN AMBROSE, retired microbial geneticist; b. Albany, Minn., Sept. 5, 1920; s. Isidor and Elizabeth (Funk) S.; m. Joyce Elizabeth Kempenich, Sept. 10, 1949; children: Mark Wayne, Jane Elizabeth, Glenn Matthew. BSc, U. Minn., 1949, PhD, 1954. Rsch. asst. U. Minn., Mpls., 1949-52; plant pathologist U.S. Dept. Agrl., Fargo, N.D., 1952-55; assoc. plant pathologist Brookhaven Nat. Lab., Upton, N.Y., 1955-61; sr. rsch. fellow Divsn. of Plant Industry, CSIRO, Canberra, Australia, 1961-64, prin. rsch. scientist, 1969-83, ret., 1983; assoc. prof. radiation geneticist Oreg. State U., Corvallis, 1965-69. Contbr. 37 articles to profl. publs. Staff sgt. Army Air Force, 1943-46. Recipient Career Devel. award NIH, 1965-69. Mem. Probus Club, Pambula-Merimbula Golf Club, Centenary Inst. Med. Rsch. Found., Narooma Golf Club, Belconnen Bowls Club. Achievements include research on mode of inactivation of fungal spores by ionizing radiation, host-induced modification of bacteriophage in Rhizobium, use of biochemical mutants for study of symbiotic ability in Rhizobium. Home: 7 Marqua Pl, 2614 Hawker Canberra, Australia

SCHWISTER, JAY EDWARD, portfolio manager; b. Milw., Apr. 16, 1962; s. Jerome Charles and Carol Christina (Keeler) S.; m. Sara M. Schlaudecker. BS in Fin. cum laude, Marquette U., 1984. Chartered fin. analyst. Sr. investment officer First Wis. Trust Co., Milw., 1984-87; sr. v.p., sr. portfolio mgr. Putnam Investments, Boston, 1987—; fin. com. mem. Hills Bd. Trustees, Wayland, Mass., 1990—; pres. coun. Marquette U., Milwaukee, Wis., 1990—. Chmn. fund raising com. Marquette U. Alumni Fund, Boston, 1989—. Mem. Assn. for Investment Mgmt. and Rsch., Boston Security Analysts Soc., Inc., Bond Analysts Soc., Inc., Beta Gamma Sigma. Avocations: golf, tennis, travel, woodworking, music. Home: 83 Hillside Dr Wayland MA 01778-3826 Office: Putnam Investments 1 Post Office Sq Fl 7 Boston MA 02109-2106

SCHWOERER, JOHN ARNOLD, mechanical engineer; b. Phila., Apr. 9, 1954; s. Frank and Lois Katherine (Green) S.; m. Virginia Mary Tierney, Apr. 13, 1991; children: Emma Anne, Charles Francis. AB in Physics, Dartmouth Coll., 1976; MSME, MIT, 1979, ScDME, 1985. Engr. transient/control analysis GE Aircraft Engines, Lynn, Mass., 1984-87, staff engr. transient/controls, 1987-93; staff engr. screw compressor Carrier Carlyle Compressor, Syracuse, N.Y., 1993-95; sr. engr. technology Jacobs Vehicle Systems, Bloomfield, Conn., 1995-99, prin. engr., analysis team leader, 1999—; software cons. Neutron Products, Inc., Dickerson, Md., 1974-83; engring. cons. Carrier Carlyle Compressor, Syracuse, 1996-97. Contbr. articles to profl. jours. including Advances in Cryogenic Engring., AIAA Jour. of Energy, Symposium on the Engring. Aspects of MHD. Mem. ASME, Soc. of Automotive Engrs. Achievements include developing real-time simulation approach for digital control development at GE Aircraft Engines; developed approach for performance rating of screw compressors; developed state-of-the-art hydraulic simulation capability and lead the selection and customization of engine performance analysis software at Jacobs Vehicle Systems for the design of new technology diesel engine retarding and variable actuation systems. Avocations: home improvement projects, swimming, tennis, small sailboat racing, cross-country skiing. Office: Jacobs Vehicle Systems 22 E Dudley Town Rd Bloomfield CT 06002-1440

SCHWYN, CHARLES EDWARD, accountant; b. Muncie, Ind., Oct. 12, 1932; s. John and Lela Mae (Oliver) S.; m. Mary Helen Nickey, May 25, 1952 (dec.); children: Douglas, Craig, Beth; m. Madelyn Steinmetz, June 26, 1993. BS, Ball State U., 1957. CPA, Calif., D.C. With Haskins & Sells, Chgo., Orlando, Fla., 1958-67; mgr. Deloitte, Haskins & Sells, Milan, Italy, 1967-70, San Francisco, 1970-80; with Deloitte, Haskins & Sells (now Deloitte & Touche), Oakland, Calif., ptnr. in charge, 1980-92, ret., 1992. Bd. dirs. Jr. Ctr. Art and Sci., 1982-89, pres., 1987-88; bd. dirs., trustee Oakland Symphony, 1982-86, 89-91; bd. dirs. Oakland Met. YMCA, 1984-89, Oakland Police Activities League, 1981-91, Joe Morgan Youth Found., 1982-91, Summit Med. Ctr., 1989-94, 96-99, Marcus A. Foster Ednl. Inst., 1986-95, pres., 1991-93; bd. dirs. Greater Oakland Internat. Trade Ctr., 1996-97; mem. adv. bd. Festival of Lake, 1984-89, U. Oakland Met. Forum, 1991-99; co-chmn. Commn. for Positive Change in Oakland Pub. Schs., 1989-91; mem. campaign cabinet United Way Bay Area, 1989; bd. regents Samuel Merritt Coll., 1993—; chmn., bd. regents, 1996—; chief of protocol, City of Oakland, 1996-97; mem. Calif. Coun. of the Oakland Mus. of Calif. Found., 1997—; docent Pt. Sur Hist. Lighthouse, 2000—. With USN, 1952-56. Recipient Cmty. Svc. award Kiwanis Club, Cert. Recognition Calif. Legis. Assembly, 1988, Ctr. for Ind. Living award, Oakland Bus. Arts award for outstanding bus. leader Oakland C. of C., 1992; honoree Schwyn Endowment fund for cancer rsch. Bay Area Tumor Inst., 1998; date of job retirement honored in his name by Oakland mayor; named Knight Order of St. John of Jerusalem Knights Hospitaller. Mem. AICPA (coun. 1987-90), Oakland C. of C. (chmn. bd. dirs. 1987-88, exec. com. 1982-89), Oakland Met. C. of C., pres., 1996, Calif. Soc. CPAs (bd. dirs. 1979-81, 83-84, 85-87, pres. San Francisco chpt. 1983-84), Nat. Assn. Accts. (pres. Fla. chpt. 1967), Claremont Country Club (treas., bd. dirs. 1989-97), Lakeview Club (bd. govs. 1987-92), Oakland 100 Club (pres. 1994), Rotary (bd. dirs. Oakland club 1986-88, 91-92, treas. 1984-86, pres. 1991-92), Golf Club at Quail Lodge.

SCIALABBA, DAMIAN ANGELO, lawyer; b. Bklyn., May 16, 1963; s. Dominick Anthony and Elmerinda Gilda (Caccavo) S.; m. Brenda Jean Carpenter, Apr. 24, 1993; children: Dominick Antonio, Emily Marion. BS, Ursinus Coll., 1984; JD, St. Johns U., 1987. Bar: N.J. 1987, U.S. Dist. Ct. N.J. 1987, NY 1988. Law clk. to Hon. Jared Honigfeld and Hon. B. Thomas Leahey N.J. Superior Ct. (Essex County), Newark, 1987-88; assoc. Sellar, Richardson, Stuart & Chisholm, Roseland, NJ, 1988-91, Mongello & Marshall, P.A., South Plainfield, NJ, 1991-96; ptnr. Mongello, Marshall & Scialabba, LLC, South Plainfield, NJ, 1996—. Judge Voice of Democracy competition VFW, N.J., 1995. Mem. ATLA, N.J. State Bar Assn., N.Y. State Bar Assn., Middlesex County Bar Assn., Phi Delta Phi, Psi Chi, Pi Gamma Nu, Alpha Phi Omega. Office: Mongello Marshall & Scialabba LLC 1550 Park Ave Ste E South Plainfield NJ 07080-5565

SCIAME, JOSEPH, university administrator; b. Bklyn., Sept. 9, 1941; s. Joseph and Sophie (Pintacuda) S. EdB, St. John's U., 1971. Fin. aid officer, asst. to dean of admissions St. John's U., Jamaica, N.Y., 1967-71, dir. fin. aid, 1971-82, dean fin. aid, 1982, v.p. fin. aid and student svcs., 1982-94, v.p. for govt. and community rels., 1994—; mem. Gov. Commn. on Sch. Achievement, 1971—, chairperson, 1993—; pres. N.Y. Assn. Student Fin. Aid Adminstrn., 1980-82, Ea. Assn. Student Fin. Aid Adminstrn., 1986-87. Chmn. bd. ethics Town of North Hempstead, N.Y., 1984—; nat. chmn., bd. dirs. Garibaldi-Meucci Mus., N.Y., 1987-93, 97—; mem. Providence Rest Found., 1995—; bd. dirs. St. John's Prep, 1996—. Decorated cavaliere del Merito della Repubblica Italiana, Cavaliere Ufficiale Order Merit House of Savoy; recipient Lifetime Membership award Ea. Assn., 1995, Achievement award N.Y. State Fin. Aid Adminstrs., 1982, Congl. Record award, 1979, 91, 93, 94, 95. Mem. Nat. Assn. Student Fin. Aid Adminstrs. (chmn. 1987-88, Disting. Svc. award 1988, Leadership award 1994), Assn. Equestrian Order Holy Sepulchre (knight grand cross 1991, knight invested 1980), Order Sons of Italy in Am. (lodge pres. 1974-75, state pres. 1993-97, nat. v.p. 1997—), Futures in Edn. Found. (vice chair 1991-93, chair 1994-97), Jamaica C. of C. (bd. mem. 1998—). Roman Catholic. Avocations: walking, cooking, gardening, reading, lecturing. Home: 6 Jones St New Hyde Park NY 11040-1616 also: Trout Ln Southampton NY 11968 Office: St John's Univ Off Vp Govt & Community Rels Jamaica NY 11439-0001

SCIANCE, CARROLL THOMAS, chemical engineer; b. Okemah, Okla., Feb. 16, 1939; s. Carroll Elmer and Winifred (Black) S.; m. Anita Ruth Fischer, Jan. 30, 1960; children: Steven, Frederick, Thomas, Erica. BS in Chem. Engring., U. Okla., 1960, M in Chem. Engring., 1964, PhD, 1966. With E.I. duPont de Nemours & Co., Inc., 1966-95; planning mgr. nylon intermediates divsn., petrochem. dept. E.I. duPont de Nemours & Co., Inc., Wilmington, Del., 1978-80; tech. mgr. E.I. duPont de Nemours & Co., Inc., Wilmington, 1980-83, dir engring. rsch., engring. dept., 1983-87, prin. cons. corp. rsch. and devel. planning divsn., 1987-89; mgr. petroleum products R&D divsn. Conoco, Inc., 1989-93; pres. Sci. Cons. Svcs., Inc., 1995—; sr. lectr. U. Tex., Austin, 1996—; mem. Travis County (Tex.) Appraisals Rev. Bd., 1999—; mem. math. scis. and edn. bd. NRC, 1987-89; mem. adv. bd. for chem. sci. and tech. NIST, 1988-94. Served as officer USAR, 1961-63. Fellow AIChE (bd. dirs. material engring. and scis. divsn. 1986-92, chmn. new tech.com. 1990-92, govt. rels. com. 1993-96); mem. Fedn. Materials Socs. (v.p. 1988-92, pres. 1993-94), Am. Chem. Soc. (mem. environ. R&D com. 1995—), N.Y. Acad. Scis., Sigma Xi. Home: 16658 Forest Way Austin TX 78734-1110

SCIANNAMEO, FRANCO LUDOVICO ORLANDO, music educator; b. Maglie, Apulia, Italy, Aug. 5, 1942; came to the U.S., 1968; s. Donato and Noemi (De Donno) S.; m. Louise G. Cavanaugh, Oct. 26, 1984; 1 child, Nicholas. Diploma (prof. music), Conservatorio Santa Cecilia, Rome, 1963; MA in Hist. Musicology, U. Pitts., 1996, MA in Cultural Studies, 1996. Solo player I Solisti di Roma, Rome, 1963-68; prof. music Nazionale Academia Santa Cecilia, Rome, 1967; faculty The Hartford (Conn.) Conservatory, 1968-79; assoc. concertmaster Ft. Worth Symphony, 1980-83; dir. publs. L.F.S. Publs., Inc., Ann Arbor, Mich., 1984-89; faculty Carnegie Mellon U., Pitts., 1990—; faculty The Chautauqua (N.Y.) Instn., 1996—. Author: Scoring Fellini, 1996, Giacinto Scelsi, 1998, Filippo Traetta, 1998, Roman Soundtrack, 1999; editor The Violexchange, 1986-92; editor sheet music Rarities for Strings, 1970-86. Office: Carnegie Mellon Univ Sch Music 5000 Forbes Ave Pittsburgh PA 15213-3890

SCICLUNA, CHARLES JUDE, priest; b. Toronto, Ont., Can., May 15, 1959; arrived in Malta, 1960; s. Emmanuel and Carmen (Falzon) S. LLD, U. Malta, 1984, Lic. Theology, 1986; D Canon Law, Pontifical Gregorian U., Rome, 1991. Ordained priest Roman Catholic Ch., 1986; lic. canon lawyer. Defender of bond Metro. Tribunal, Malta, 1990-95; lectr. canon law and pastoral theology U. Malta, 1991-95; vice rector Roman Cath. Major Sem., Malta, 1994-95; substitute promoter of justice Supreme Tribunal Apostolic Signature, Vatican City, 1996—; prof. jurisprudence Pontifical Gregorian U., Rome, 1999—. Author: The Essential Definition of Marriage According to the 1917 and 1983 Codes of Canon Law, 1995; mem. editl. bd. Forum, 1990—; contbr. articles and book revs. to profl. jours. Avocations: reading literature, classical music concerts, walks in the country. Home: Via Di Monserrato 45, 00186 Rome Italy

SCIRIHA AQUILINA, IRENE, mathematics educator, researcher; b. Tarxien, Malta; d. Joseph and Carmen (Magro) Aquilina; m. Joseph P. Sciriha; children: Bertrand, Gabriella. BSc, Royal U. Malta, 1969, MSc, 1971; PhD in Math, Reading (Eng.) U., 1999. Tech. sch. tchr. Govt. Edn. Dept., Hamrun, Malta, 1969-71; jr. coll. lectr. Royal U. Malta, Valleta, 1971-74; head math. dept., 6th form lectr. DeLaSalle Coll., Cottonera, Malta, 1974-90; part-time lectr. U. Malta, Msida, 1987-90, full-time lectr., 1990—; referee Publs. of Math. Inst., Belgrade, Yugoslavia, 1997; chair, exam. setter and marker, Malta Matriculation Examining Bd., 1990—; vis. lectr. for doctoral program, U. Messina, Italy, 2000—. Contbr. articles to profl. jours. Treas. Malta Students' Movement; com. mem. Tarxien Preyouth Helpers, Malta. Fellow Inst. Combinatorics and Its Applications (assoc.); mem. Am. Math. Soc., European Women in Math (regional coord. 1996—, dep. convenor 1997-99, convenor/chmn. 1999—, participant meeting EU commn. Fifth Framework Program), European Math. Soc. (mem. women's sci. com.). Avocations: swimming, reading, crafts and design, theory of music, computer programming. Fax: 00356-333908. E-mail: is-cil@um.edu.mt. Home: Troika, G Montebello St, PLA 12 Tarxien Malta Office: U Malta, Dept Math Faculty Sci, Msida Malta

SCIUNNACH, DARIO ANDREA, geologist; b. Milan, Italy, Oct. 12, 1967; s. Franco and Giovanna (Rinoldi) S.; children: Marta Beatrice, Paolo Aurelio. BA, Liceo Scientifico G.B. Vico, Cologno Monzese, Italy, 1986; MSc, Milan U., 1992, PhD, 1996. Cons. Mus. Natural History, Lugano, Switzerland, 1993-96, Town Cologno Monzese, 1995-96; ofcl. geologist Regione Lombardia, Milan, 1996—. Translator: (from English) Marihuana, The Forbidden Medicine (L. Grinspoon and J. B. Bakalar), 1995; (from Russian) numerous papers and book chpts. E-mail: dario sciunnach@regione.lombardia.it. Fax: 39-0 2-67654620.

SCLAFANI, ANTHONY PAUL, plastic surgeon, educator, biomedical researcher; b. Bklyn., Oct. 3, 1963. BA, Columbia U., 1985; MD, U. Pa., 1989. Diplomate Am. Bd. Otolaryngology, Am. Bd. Facial Plastic and Reconstructive Surgery. Intern in gen. surgery Beth Israel Med. Ctr., N.Y.C., N.Y., 1989-91; resident in otolaryngology, head and neck surgery N.Y. Eye and Ear Infirmary, N.Y.C., 1991-95, assoc. prof., dir. facial plastic surgery, 1996—; fellow in facial plastic and reconstructive surgery St. Louis U. Sch. Medicine, 1995-96; pvt. practice, N.Y.C., N.Y., 1996—, Chappaqua, N.Y., 1998—. Contbr. articles to profl. jours. Fellow ACS, Am. Acad. Facial Plastic and Reconstructive Surgery (Sir Harold Delf Gillies award 1996); mem. Am. Acad. Otolaryngology and Head and Neck Surgery. Office: NY EE Infirm/Facial Pl Surg Dept Otolaryng/Head Neck 310 E 14th St 6th Fl New York NY 10003-4201 also: 59 S Greeley Ave Chappaqua NY 10514-3321

SCOATES, WESLEY MARVIN, mining company executive; b. Jacksonville, Fla., Apr. 21, 1938; s. Harry William and Orlene (Buffkin) S.; m. Patty Ann Flora, 1958 (div. 1969); children: Teresa, Lesa, Leslie, Randall; m. Anneliese Marie Knorlein, May 11, 1970; children: Stephen, Cherry. B in Mech. Engring., U. Dayton, 1962; MBA, Fla. Internat. U., 1983. Commd. 2d lt. U.S. Army, 1962, advanced through grades to lt. col., 1982; artillery officer U.S. Army, Ft. Sill, Okla., 1962-65; mech. engr. U.S. Army Corps of Engrs., Jacksonville, 1965-66; artillery officer U.S. Army, Republic of Vietnam, Republic of Korea, Federal Republic of Germany, 1968-76, refrad, 1975; project engr. U.S. Gypsum Co., Jacksonville, 1966-67; div. chief City of Jacksonville, 1976-78; asst. equipment supt. Metro Dade County, Miami, Fla., 1978-79; asst. service mgr. Kelly Tractor Co., Miami, 1979-81; maintenance supt. Vulcan Materials Co., Miami, 1981-87, area mgr., 1987-91; equipment mgr. Lowell Dunn Co., Miami, 1991-92; ops. mgr. Ind. Aggregates, Inglis, Fla., 1992-93; dir. mining ops. Marcona Ocean Industries Ltd., Jacksonville, Fla., 1993—; ret. U.S. Army, 1999; CGSOC instr. USAR Sch., 1979-88. Contbr. articles to army logistician mag. With USAR, 1975-90. Decorated Bronze Star with oak leaf cluster, Air medal, Army Commendation medal with oak leaf cluster, Meritorious Svc. medal. Mem. Acad. Polit. Sci., Coun. on Fgn. Rels., Am. Def. Preparedness Assn., Am. Assn. Individual Investors, Sunshine Via De Cristo (lay dir.), Ret. Officers Assn. Republican. Methodist. Avocations: fishing, singing, photography. Office: Marcona Ocean Ind Ltd 366 E Graves Ave Orange City FL 32763-5216

SCOBIE, GEOFFREY EDWARD WINSOR, psychologist, clergyman; b. Plymouth, Eng., July 13, 1939; s. Edward Albert and Lily Elsie (Winsor) S.; m. Enid Diane Jago Scobie, Aug. 19, 1961; children: Karen, Rachel, Kelvin. BS in Psychology, U. Bristol, 1962; postgrad., Tyndale Hall Theol. Coll, Bristol, 1962-64; MS in Psychology, U. Bristol, 1967; MA in Theology, U. Birmingham, 1970; PhD in Psychology, U. Glasgow, 1977. Cert. Ch. Eng. Ministry Ordination; assoc. fellow, chartered psychologist Brit. Psychol. Soc. Ground wireless mechanic Royal Air Force, Gibraltar, 1957-59; curate Christ Ch., Birmingham, Eng., 1965-66, St. Anne's Moseley, Eng., 1966-67; lectr., sr. lectr. U. Glasgow, Scotland, 1967—; chief adviser of studies U. Glasgow, 1991-95, dir. Glasgow Interface Ctr. of Evaluation, 1988—; external examiner Aberdeen (Scotland) U., 1987-90; rector Scottish Episcopal Ch., St. Silas Episcopal Ch., Glasgow, 1983-88; asst. minister 1971-83, 88-98; assoc. priest St. James the Less, Bishoppbriggs, 1999—; Brit. rep. Psychology of Religion Europe, 1989—. Author: Psychology of Religion, 1975; contbr. Jour. Theory of Soc. Behavior, 1998, Jour. Psychology and Christianity, 1999, Archiv Fur Religions, 1994, others. Burgh councillor Bishoppbriggs Burgh Coun., Glasgow, 1971-74; lectr. Scottish Retirement Coun., Glasgow, 1975—; candidate General Election, Moray, Nairn, 1979; chmn. Bishopbriggs H.S. PTA, Glasgow, 1980-84; edn. convenor Scottish Episcopal Ch. Grantee NCR (AT&T), Glasgow, 1988-94, Honeywell Bull, Glasgow, 1989-93, NCDL, Glasgow, 1994, edn. grantee, 1993-98. Fellow Royal Soc. for Encouragement of Arts Manufactures and Commerce; mem. Scottish Brit. Psychol. Soc. (vice chmn.). Achievements include application of psychological principles to product evaluation, investigations in the psychology of religion, exploring the psychology of forgiveness and it's measurement. Office: Dept Ednl Studies U Glasgow, 8 University Gardens, Glasgow G12 8QQ, Scotland

SCOFIELD, LOUIS M., JR., lawyer; b. Brownsville, Tex., Jan. 14, 1952; s. Louis M. and Betsy Lee (Aiken) S.; children: Christopher, Nicholas, Emma. BS in Geology with highest honors and high distinction, U. Mich., 1974; JD with honors, U. Tex., 1977. Bar: Tex. 1977, U.S. Dist. Ct. (ea. and so. dists.) Tex., U.S. Ct. Appeals (5th cir.) 1981, U.S. Supreme Ct. 1984. Ptnr. Mehaffy & Weber, Beaumont, Tex., 1982—; spkr. CNA Ins., Dallas, Jefferson County Ins. Adjusters, S.E. Tex. Ind. Ins. Agts., Gulf Ins. Co., Dallas, Employers Casualty Co., Beaumont, Tex. Employment Commn., Jefferson County Young Lawyers Assn., Jefferson County Bar Assn., South Tex. Coll. of Law, John Gray Inst., Lamar U., 1991, Tex. Assn. Def. Counsel, 1991; cert. arbitrator Nat. Panel of Consumer Arbitrators; arbitrator BBB; presenter Forest Park H.S., Martin Elem. Sch., St. Anne's Sch. Contbr. articles to profl. jours.; columnist Jefferson County Bar Jour. Patron Beaumont Heritage Soc., John J. French Mus.; bd. dirs. Beaumont Heritage Soc., 1983-84, mem. endowment fund com., 1988; chmn. lawyers divsn. United Appeals Campaign, 1984; grand patron Jr. League of Beaumont, 1989, 90. Fellow Tex. Bar Found., State Bar of Tex. (mentors com. 1995); mem. ABA (contbg. editor newsletter products, gen. liability and consumer law com., vice chmn. of com.), Assn. Def. Trial Attys. (Tex.

state membership chmn., Central U.S. region chmn. 2000—, exec. coun. 1999-2002, U.S. ctrl. regional chmn.), Tex. Assn. Def. Counsel (dir. at large 1986-87, v.p. 1987-89, adminstrv. v.p. 1989-90, program chmn. San Diego 1989), Def. Rsch. Inst., Am. Judicature Soc., Jefferson County Bar Assn. (disaster relief project 1979, outstanding young lawyer's com. 1980), Beaumont Country Club, Tower Club of Beaumont, Phi Beta Kappa. Democrat. Episcopalian. Avocations: golf, reading, fishing. Home: 4790 Littlefield St Beaumont TX 77706-7748 Office: Mehaffy & Weber PO Box 16 Beaumont TX 77704-0016

SCOFIELD, PAUL, actor; b. Jan. 21, 1922; m. Joy Parker; 2 children. Trained, London Mask Theatre Drama Sch., Birmingham Repertory Theatre, 1941, 43-46, Stratford-on-Avon, Shakespeare Meml. Theatre, 1946-48, Arts Theatre, 1946, Phoenix Theatre, 1947. With H.M. Tennent, 1949-56; assoc. dir. Nat. Theatre, 1970-71. Has appeared in Adventure Story, Chekhov's Seagull, Anoilh's Ring Round the Moon, Gielgund's prodn. Much Ado About Nothing, Charles Morgan's The River Line, Richard II, The Way of the World, Venice Preserved, Time Remembered, A Question of Fact, Hamlet, Power and the Glory, Family Reunion, A Dead Secret, Expresso Bongo, The Complaisant Lover, A Man For All Seasons, Stratford Festival, Ont., Can., 1961, Coriolanus, Don Armado, N.Y., 1961-62, A Man for All Seasons, London, 1962-63, King Lear, N.Y.C., Moscow and Ea. Europe, 1964, Timon, 1965, Staircase, 1966, The Government Inspector, 1967, Macbeth, 1968, The Hotel in Amsterdam, 1968, Uncle Vanya, 1970, The Captain of Kopenik, 1971, Rules of the Game, 1971, Savages, 1973, The Tempest, 1974, 75, Dimetos, 1976, Volpone, 1977, The Madras House, 1977, The Family, 1978, Amadeus, 1979, Othello, 1980, Don Quixote, 1982, A Midsummer Night's Dream, 1982, I'm Not Rappaport, 1986-87, Heartbreak House, 1992, John Gabriel Borkman, 1996; films: The Train, 1962, A Man For All Seasons (Oscar and N.Y. Film Critics award, Moscow Film Festival and Brit. Film Acad. awards), King Lear, 1970, Scorpio, 1972, Bartleby, 1980, A Delicate Balance, A Potting Shed, 1981, If Winter Comes, 1981, Song at Twilight, 1982, Come into the Garden Maud, 1982, 1919, 1985, Anna Karenina, 1984, Mr. Corbett's Ghost, 1986, The Attic, 1987, Why the Whales Came, 1989, Henry V, 1990, Hamlet, 1990, UTZ, 1991, Quiz Show, 1994, Martin Chuzzlewit, 1994, The Little Riders, 1995, The Crucible, 1996. Decorated comdr. Brit. Empire. Address: The Gables, Balcombe Sussex RH17 6ND, England

SCOGGINS, FRANK STEPHEN, JR., nuclear specialist; b. Warner Robins AFB, Ga., Aug. 14, 1958; s. Frank Stephen Sr. and Barbara Ann (Glassman) S.; m. Rhonda Yvette Brown, Feb. 14, 1987; 1 child, Roy Stephen. AS in Indsl. Electricity, Brevard C.C., Cocoa, Fla., 1981; AS in Nuc. Engring. Tech., Aiken (S.C.) Tech. Coll., 1985. Health physics technician level 1 Ga. Power Co., Plant Hatch, Baxley, 1985-86, health physics technician level 2, 1986-87; health physics technician level 2 Ga. Power Co., Plant Vogtle, Waynesboro, 1987-90, nuc. specialist level 2 radwaste shipper, 1990-92, nuc. specialist level 1 radwaste shipper, 1992-96; nuc. specialist level 1 radwaste shipper So. Nuc. Oper. Co., Plant Vogtle, Waynesboro, 1996—. E-4, USMC, 1976-80, Cherry Point, N.C. Mem. Amateur Radio Club of Augusta, Ga. (dir. 1998, pres. 1997, Vol. of Yr. 1996). Avocation: amateur radio. Fax: 706-826-3787. E-mail: ks4oc@yahoo.com, fsscoggi@southernco.com. Office: So Nuc Oper Co Plant Vogtle PO Box 1600 7821 River Rd Waynesboro GA 30830

SCOGIN, TROY POPE, publishing company executive, accounts executive; b. Manchester, Ala., Oct. 31, 1932; s. James David and Thelma Katie (Helton) S.; m. Katie Elizabeth Bates, May 26, 1956; children: Norma Kay, Joyce Marie. BA, Howard Coll., 1955; MDiv, So. Baptist Theol. Seminary, Louisville, 1959; MA, Samford U., 1972. Ordained to ministry Baptist Ch., 1956. Pastor West Port (Ky.) Baptist Ch., 1956-58, Providence Baptist Ch., Bellevue, Ohio, 1958-61; chaplain/capt. USAF, Lincoln, Nebr., 1961-64; pastor Sycamore (Ala.) Baptist Ch., 1964-65; sales rep. Houghton Mifflin Co., Boston, 1965-74, regional mgr., 1974-89, spl. asst. to exec. v.p. coll. div., 1989-90, v.p., 1984—, nat. accounts exec., 1990-92; pastor Ross Ave. Bapt. Ch. Intercity Mission, Dallas, 1993-98; prof. Wake Tech. C.C., Raleigh, N.C., 1998—; adv. bd. dirs. Ross Ave. Ctr.; faculty Eastfield Coll., 1992-98. Chmn. bd. deacons Ross Avenue Bapt. Ch., Dallas, 1991. Mem. Am. Mgmt. Assn., Am. Soc. Tng. Devel., Nat. Coun. Tchrs. English, Tex. Jr. Coll. Tchrs. Assn., Phi Kappa Phi, Omicron Delta Kappa (nat. leadership fraternity pres. 1954), Alpha Phi Omega (nat. svc. fraternity pres. 1952). Democrat. Avocations: bowling, swimming, fishing, tennis, golf. Home: 7202 Hidden Ridge Dr Apt 104 Raleigh NC 27613-3967

SCOGLAND, WILLIAM LEE, lawyer; b. Moline, Ill., Apr. 2, 1949; s. Maurice William and Harriet Rebecca S.; m. Victoria Lynn Whitham, Oct. 9, 1976; 1 child, Thomas. BA magna cum laude, Augustana Coll., 1971; JD cum laude, Harvard U., 1975. Bar: Ill. 1975, U.S. Dist. Ct. (no. dist.) Ill. 1975. Assoc. Wildman, Harrold, Allen & Dixon, Chgo., 1975-77, Hughes Hubbard & Reed, Milw., 1977-81; from assoc. to ptnr. Jenner & Block, Chgo., 1981—. Author: Fiduciary Duty: What Does It Mean?, 1989; co-author Employee Benefits Law, 1987. Mem. Phi Beta Kappa, Omicron Delta Kappa. Republican. Office: Jenner & Block One IBM Plz Fl 4000 Chicago IL 60611-7603

SCOGNAMIGLIO, CARLO, economics and finance educator, financial consultant; b. Verese, Italy, Nov. 27, 1944; s. Luigi and esther (Pasini) S.; m. Cecilia Pirelli, May 28, 1980; children: Filippo, Elisabetta Thea. D.Econs., U. Bocconi, Milan, Italy, 1968; spl. student, London Sch. Econs., 1970-71. Asst. prof. U. Bocconi, 1968-73, prof., 1973-79; prof. U. Rome-Luiss, 1979—, dean and rector, 1984—; senator Constituency of Milan, 1992—, pres. of senate, acting pres. of Republic, 1994-96, defense minister, 1998-99; pres. Corriere della Sera, 1983, Aspens Inst. Italia, 1995—. Author: The Stock Exchange, 1973, Industrial Crises, 1976, Industrial Economics, 1987, Theory of Finance, 1987, The Liberal Project, 1996. Winner prize for econs. French Acad., 1988. Office: Senato della Repubblica, 00100 Rome Italy

SCOLEDES, ARISTOTLE GEORGIUS MICHALE, retired science and technology educator, research consultant; b. N.Y.C., Feb. 22, 1929; s. Michael George and Soultanitsa (Hadtzifoca) S.; m. Anne-Marie Furchtenicht, Sept. 7, 1957 (dec. Nov. 1970); children: Alexander Michael, Alexandra Anne; m. Barbara Lynn Sterling, Aug. 14, 1977; 1 child, Dylan. AB, Syracuse U., 1951; MSE, Johns Hopkins U., 1953; ScD, MIT, 1957; PhD, Stanford U., 1965. Fellow appl. laser beams for airborne guidance sys. Johns Hopkins U., Silver Springs, Md., 1951-53; rsch. fellow U. Chgo., 1953-54, MIT, Cambridge, Mass., 1955-59; exec. engr., project coord. Apollo-Gemini Mission program Philco Western Devel. Labs./Ford-Aerospace, Sunnyvale, Calif., 1960-62; asst. prof. philosophy of sci. Alfred (N.Y.) U., 1962-63; assoc. prof. philosophy of sci. and theoretical biology SUNY, Buffalo, 1963-68; prof. philosophy sci. and tech. Ga. Inst. Tech., 1968-72; sr. cons. sponsored minorities program Econ. Opportunity Atlanta/CETA, U.S. Govt., Atlanta, 1972-77; project mgr., dir. Consulting Consortium U.S./Stanford/MIT, Stanford, 1977-95; mem. MIT/Stanford Venture Lab. Contbr. articles to profl. jours. Recipient Rsch. Svcs. Recognition award Offices of Naval Rsch. and Chief of Naval Ops., 1984; hon. fellow AIAA, 1971. Mem. AAUP, Nat. Space Soc., The Planetary Soc., Democritos Soc., History of Sci. Soc., Air Force Assn., Philosophy of Sci. Assn., Am. Philos. Assn. (life), Sigma Xi (hon.), Tau Beta Pi. Avocations: public speaking, drawing, philately, numismatics. E-mail: variari@aol.com. Home: 84 Roosevelt Cir Palo Alto CA 94306-4218

SCOLES, GIACINTO, chemistry educator; b. Torino, Italy, Apr. 2, 1935; came to Can., 1971; to U.S., 1987; s. Mario and Maria (Fiorio) S.; m. Giok-Lan Lim, Oct. 20, 1964; 1 child, Gigi. Degree in chemistry, U. Genoa, Italy, 1959, Libero Docente, 1968. Asst. prof. U. Genoa, 1960-61, 64-68, assoc. prof., 1968-71; research assoc. U. Leiden, The Netherlands, 1961-64; prof. chemistry and physics U. Waterloo, Ont., Can., 1971-86; Donner prof. sci. Princeton (N.J.) U., 1987—. Editor: Atomic and Molecular Beam Methods, 1987; contbr. numerous articles to profl. jours. Killam fellow Sci. Council Can., 1986; Ellis R. Lippincott Awd., 1995, Optical Soc. Am. Fellow The Chem. Inst. Can.; mem. Can. Assn. Physicists, Am. Phys. Soc., Am. Chem. Soc., Optical Soc. Am. Office: Princeton U 10A Frick Chemistry Lab Princeton NJ 08544-0001*

SCOLL, EULALIE ELIZABETH, writer, researcher; b. Vancouver, Wash., Mar. 6, 1920; d. Frederick and Elizabeth (Williamson) Laws; m. James Leslie Hildebrand; children: James, Frederick. BS, Women's U. Tex., 1941; MS, Salve Regina U., 1989, PhD, 1996. Engring. draftsman for Dr. Urey Manhattan Project, N.Y.C.; high fashion designer N.Y.C.; interior decorator. Author: The Role and Abuse of Women as Portrayed in Three Dostoevsky's Major Novels, 1989, Nietzsche Journal of Antichrist Tibetan Buddhism Versus Christianity, 1991, Dostoevsky's Sonya and Martha: Fiction and Reality, 1996. Mem. AAUW, Am. Assn. Advancement Slavic Studies, Nat. Trust for Historic Preservation, Nat. Mus. Women in the Arts, Am. Soc. Phys. Rsch., Inc., The Authors Guild, Inc., Newport Preservation Soc., Newport Hist. Soc., Asian Soc., Naval War Found., Internat. Dostoevsky Soc., Bailey's Beach Oldest Beach Club Am. Home: Cave Cliff 11 Chastellux Ave Newport RI 02840-3811

SCOREI, ION ROMULUS, biochemist, educator; b. Tirgu Jiu, Gorj, Romania, Apr. 4, 1953; s. Ion and Margareta Scorei; m. Vilma Negoianu, June 29, 1976; children: Mihai, Iulia. Degree in biochemistry, U. Bucharest, 1977, PhD, 1997. Biochemist DoljChim, Craiova, 1985-90; prof. chemistry U. Craiova, 1990—; pres. Bioex sa Craiova, 1990—. Mem. Internat. Soc. for the Study of Origin of Life, European Cell Biology Orgn. Avocations: study of origin of life, sports, travel. Office: Bioex SA/AI Cuza St, No 19 Bloc Patria Scb Apt 3, 1100 Craiova Romania

SCOTT, ADAM, telecommunications consultant, educator, clergyman; b. Devizes, Wiltshire, Eng., May 6, 1947; s. Fraser and Bridget Penelope (Williams) S.; m. Oona MacDonald Graham, Sept. 30, 1978. BA, Oxford (Eng.) U., 1968, MA, 1972; MSc, City U., London, 1979. Barrister, Eng. and Wales, 1972; ordained priest Anglican Ch., 1976. Intellectual property lawyer Eng., 1972-80; corp. planner Brit. Telecomms., London, 1981-86, dir. pvt. office, 1986-88, dir. internat. affairs, 1988-92, cmn. BT Apparatus, 1992-94, divsn. dir., 1994-97; fellow Salzburg Seminar, 1983; hon. curate St. Michael's, Blackheath Park, Eng., 1975—; speaker in field. Columnist Jour. of the Lawyers Christian Fellowhip; contbr. chpt. to book, articles to profl. jours. Mem. U.K. del. CSCE, London, 1989; trustee BT Benevolent Fund, 1984-94; fellow Brit.-Am. Project, 1989—; dean Woolwich Episcopal Area, 1990-2000; mem. Appeal Tribunals U.K. Competition Commn., 2000—. Decorated Territorial decoration (U.K.); U. St. Andrews fellow. Fellow IEE; mem. Cannons. Avocations: opera, gardening, walking, aerobics. Home: 19 Blackheath Park, Blackheath London SE3 9RW, England Office: U St Andrews/The Scores, St Katharine's West, St Andrews, Fife KY16 9AL, Scotland

SCOTT, ALEXANDER ROBINSON, engineering association executive; b. Elizabeth, N.J., June 15, 1941; s. Marvin Chester and Jane (Robinson) S.; m. Angela Jean Kendall, July 17, 1971; children: Alexander Robinson, Jennifer Angela, Ashley Kendall. B.A. in History, Va. Mil. Inst., 1963; M.A. in Personnel and Counseling Psychology, Rutgers U., 1965. Sales mgr. Hilton Hotels, 1967-70; meetings mgr. Am. Inst. Mining Engrs., N.Y.C., 1971-73; exec. dir. Minerals, Metals and Materials Soc., 1973—. Served with U.S. Army, 1965-67. Decorated Bronze Star. Mem. Am. Soc. Assn. Execs. Republican. Baptist. Home: 107 Staghorn Dr Sewickley PA 15143-9506 Office: TMS 184 Thorn Hill Rd Warrendale PA 15086-7514

SCOTT, ALLEN JOHN, public policy and geography educator; b. Liverpool, England, Dec. 23, 1938; came to U.S., 1980; s. William Rule and Nella Maria (Pieri) S.; m. Nga Thuy Nguyen, Jan. 19, 1979. BA, Oxford (Eng.) U., 1961; PhD, Northwestern U., 1965. Prof. geography UCLA, 1980—, dir. Lewis Ctr. for Regional Policy Studies, 1990-94, assoc. dean Sch. Pub. Policy and Social Rsch., 1994-97; Professeur associé U. Paris, 1974; André Siegfried chair Inst. d'Etudes Plitiques, Paris, 1999. Author: Combinatorial Programming, 1971, Urban Land Nexus, 1980, Metropolis, 1988, New Industrial Spaces, 1988, Technopolis, 1993, Regions and the World Economy, 1998, The Cultural Economy of Cities, 2000. Fellow Com. on Scholarly Communication with People's Republic China, 1986. Croucher fellow U. Hong Kong, 1984; Guggenheim fellow, 1986-87. Fellow Brit. Acad. (corr.). Office: UCLA Sch Pub Policy Social Rsch Los Angeles CA 90095-0001

SCOTT, BARBARA ANN, sociology educator, feminist, peace activist; b. N.Y.C., Jan. 3, 1937; d. Richard W. and Lia (Varell) Scott; m. Josiah Bartlett Page, June 8, 1958 (div. 1975); children: Evan Bartlett, Eric Scott. BA magna cum laude, Pembroke Coll., Brown U., 1958; MA in Sociology Grad. Faculty, New Sch. for Social Rsch., 1972, PhD in Sociology, 1979. Elem tchr. The Harley Sch., Rochester, N.Y., 1958-61, Poughkeepsie (N.Y.) Day Sch., 1968; instr. sociology SUNY, New Paltz, 1973-79, asst. prof., 1979-84, assoc. prof., 1984—; co-organizer, co-chmn. intercollegiate conf. Liberal Arts in a Time of Crisis, 1981; vis. scholar Ctr. Def. Info., Washington, 1986-87, mem. adv. bd., cons.; mem. bd. adv. editors Sociol. Inquiry, 1990—; spkr. FLACSO U. Havana, Cuba, 1993, Camaguey, Holguin, Cuba, 1994. Author: Crisis Management in American Higher Edn., 1983 (Albert Salomon Meml. award 1980); editor: The Liberal Arts in a Time of Crisis, 1991; contbr. articles to profl. jours. Founder, coord. Mid-Hudson chpt. Educators for Social Responsibility, 1983-87; trustee Shoreline Found. for Folk Lit. and Art, Branford, Conn., 1983—; alumni spkr. Grad. Faculty New Sch. for Social Rsch., 1977; del. Salvador/U.S. women-to-women dialogue sponsored by Found. for Compasionate Soc., Cuernevaca, Mex. 1989, del. conf. on Media in a Time of Crisis, Sweden, 1989, expert group of U.N. Divsn. of Advancement of Women, meeting on women in pub. life, Vienna, 1991; spkr. various symposia. Recipient 2nd prize Quest for Peace Essay contest Citizen Edn. for Peace Project, 1988; rsch. grantee Am. Coun. Learned Socs., 1990—, SUNY Rsch. Found., 1984, 86, 87, 89, 90, 91, 96, 2000; bd. adv. Radio for Peace Internat., Costa Rica, 1990—, Women for Mutual Security Internat., 1989—. Mem. AAUW (Issue Focus grant 1988-89), NOW, SANE/FREEZE, Internat. Peace Rsch. Assn. (chair N.Am. sect., women and peace commn. 1990-91, del. to 25th Ann. Conf. Netherlands 1990, Malta 1994), War Resisters League, World Federalist Assn., Soc. Study Social Problems, Am. Sociol. Assn., Assn. for Humanist Sociology, N.Y. State Sociol. Assn. (bd. dirs. 1974-75), Ea. Sociol. Soc. (com. undergrad. tchg. 1974-76), Women's Internat. League for Peace and Freedom, Women Strike for Peace, Greenpeace, Internat. Action Ctr., Phi Beta Kappa. Home: 160 Hurley Rd Salt Point NY 12578-3140 Office: SUNY Sociology Dept New Paltz NY 12561

SCOTT, BOB, insurance company executive. CEO CGNU, London. Office: St Helens, 1 Undershaft, London EC3P 3DQ, England

SCOTT, BRENDA D., writer; b. Tampa-Sneads, Fla.; d. Alonzie III and Felicia (Lopez) S. Diploma in child guidance, Lively Vocat. Tech. Ctr., Tallahassee, 1987; AA in Sci. Edn., Tallahassee C.C., 1993; BS in Reading Edn., Fla. State U., 1995; AA in Criminal Justice, 2000. Contbr. poetry to mags., other publs including Internat. Women's Writing Guild; author: (screenplay) Surprise (Guild Membership movie), 1998, Mrs. Jellie Mae's Store, 1999, poetry book, Down-Home-News, 2000. Mem. West Fla. Literary Assn., Am. Black Book Writers Assn., Acad. Am. Poets, Internat. Soc. Poets, Women Ministering Biblically. Democrat. African Meth. Episcopalian. Avocations: reading, writing, movies, church activities, sports. Home and Office: PO Box 64 Sneads FL 32460-0064

SCOTT, CHARLES TOLBERT, elementary educator, health care interviewer; b. Agra, Okla., July 20, 1933; s. Tolbert Grover and Cyril Georgia (russell) S.; m. Phyllis Jeraldine Chappa, 1957 (div. 1971); m. Ann Marie Holland, July, 18, 1981; children: Stephen Charles, Paul Tolbert. BA, Fresno State U., 1959; MA, San Diego State U., 1967. Cert. elem. tchr. Elem. tchr. La Mesa (Calif.)-Spring Valley Sch. Dist., 1969-76, Nadaburg Sch. Dist., Wittmann, Ariz., 1976-78; realtor Fred Lamb Elec. Assn., Phoenix, 1978-79; detention officer Maricopa County Sheriff's Office, Phoenix, 1979-84; courier Madison Sch. Dist., Phoenix, 1984-88; elem. tchr. St. Jerome Elem. Sch., Phoenix, 1988-89; eligibility interviewer Maricopa County Health Dept., Phoenix, 1989-96. singer. With USN, 1952-55. Mem. KC (recorder 1977—). Republican. Roman Catholic. Avocations: teaching guitar, traveling, speaking spanish and japanese. E-mail: amtscott@access1.com. Home: 106 W Ruth Ave Phoenix AZ 85021-4547

SCOTT, DAVID, real estate professional; b. Helselden, U.K., Jan. 28, 1947; arrived in New Zealand, 1978, Australia, 1989.; m. Louise Anne Scott; children: Norna, Pippa. BS in Civil Engring. with hons., U. Nottingham, 1968, PhD, 1971. Chartered profl. engr. Mgmt. cons. to staff of dir. of med. svcs. Govt. Botswana, 1971-72; mgmt./engring. cons. Wesley/Guild Hosp., Ilesha, Nigeria, 1974-75; lectr. in dept. of civil engring. U. Nottingham, 1972-74, 75-76; assoc. prof. of constrn. engring., mgmt. Asian Inst. Technology, Bangkok, 1976-78; sr. lectr. dept. civil engring. U. Canterbury, Christchurch, New Zealand, 1978-89; prof., head of Sch. of Constrn. Mgmt. Queensland U. of Technology, Brisbane, Australia, 1989-93; prof., chair dept. of bldg. and real estate Hong Kong Polytechnic U., Hunghom, Kowloon, Hong Kong, 1993—; adv. prof. Tongji U., 1996—, Beijing U. Aeronautics and Astronautics, 1999; hon. prof. Jilin Archtl. and Civil Engring. Inst., 1995; vis. prof. Shanghai Inst. of Urban Constrn., 1995, external examiner/adv. com. mem., 1995; hon. vis. prof. Harbin U. of Architecture and Engring., 1994; vis. prof. U. Reading. UK, 1998.; com. mem. Bd. Exam., UK Inst. Builders, 1997-2000; mem. Engr. Panel of Rsch. Grants Coun, 1999-2000. Contbr. articles to profl. jours./publs. Fellow Australian Inst. of Bldg., 1989, Instn. of Engrs. Australia, 1989. Fellow Hong Kong Instn. Engrs., Hong Kong Inst. Builders; mem. Instn. Civil Engrs. (London), Chartered Inst. Bldg. (U.K.).

SCOTT, DAVID IRVIN, minister; b. Yakima, Wash., Dec. 5, 1947; s. Jack Phillip and Betty Lucille (Paronto) S.; m. Jill Louise Baker, June 23, 1982 (div. May 1991). AA, Monterey Peninsula Coll., Calif., 1975. Accredited resident mgr., Inst. Real Estate Mgmt., 1987. Courier Gallery Hawaii, Inc., Honolulu, 1981; acting resident mgr. Fairway Gardens, Honolulu, 1981; resident mgr. Waimalu Park, Honolulu, 1981-83, Waikiki Skyliner, Honolulu, 1983-84, Bishop Gardens, Honolulu, 1985-86, Plaza Landmark, Honolulu, 1986-88, Westlake Apts., Honolulu, 1988, Fairway Gardens, Honolulu, 1988—; condo mgmt. cons.; pres. Inner Man Ministries. Mem. Inst. Real Estate Mgmt., Alpha Gamma Sigma. Avocations: vocalist, archery, billiards, fishing, community theater. Office: Inner Man Ministries PO Box 2141 Pearl City HI 96782-9141

SCOTT, DAVID KNIGHT, physicist, university administrator; b. North Ronaldsay, Scotland, Mar. 2, 1940; married, 1966; 3 children. BSc, Edinburgh U., 1962; DPhil in Nuclear Physics, Oxford U., 1967. Rsch. officer nuclear physics lab. Oxford U., 1970-73; rsch. fellow nuclear physics Balliol Coll., 1967-70, sr. rsch. fellow, 1970-73; physicist Lawrence Berkeley Lab. U. Calif., 1973-75, sr. scientist nuclear sci., 1975-79; prof. physics, astronomy and chemistry Nat. Superconducting Cyclotron Lab. Mich. State U., East Lansing, 1979-93; Hannah disting. prof. physics, astronomy and chemistry Mich. State U., East Lansing, 1979-86, assoc. provost, 1983-86, provost, v.p. acad. affairs, 1986-92; Hannah Disting. prof. learning, sci. and soc. Nat. Superconducting Cyclotron Lab. Mich. State U., East Lansing, 1992-93; chancellor U. Mass., Amherst, 1993—. Fellow Am. Phys. Soc. Office: U Mass Office of Chancellor 374 Whitmore Adminstrn Bldg Amherst MA 01003

SCOTT, DAVID RICHARD ALEXANDER, finance director, accountant; b. Oakham, Rutland, Eng., Aug. 25, 1954; s. Robert Irwin Madden Scott and Daphne (Alexander) Weston; m. Rosalind Mary Baraclough, Aug. 1, 1981; children: Alexander John Barraclough, Arabella Dorinda. Student, Wellington Coll., 1967-72. Acct. Peat Marwick Mitchell, London, 1972-81; dir. fin. Channel 4 TV Co. Ltd., Eng., 1981-97, Channel 4 TV Corp., Eng., 1993—; non-exec. dir. Brit. Screen Fin. Ltd., Eng., 1985-91; bd. dirs. Channel 4 Internat. Ltd., Film Found. Ltd. Fellow Inst. Chartered Accts. in Eng. and Wales. Mem. Ch. of Eng. Avocations: opera, ballet, bridge, cinema, country pursuits. Office: Channel 4 TV Corp, 124 Horseferry Rd, London SWIP 2TX, England

SCOTT, DEBBIE ANN, recreational facility executive; b. Washington, Mar. 22, 1956; d. Dewey L. and Udra L. Barnwell; m. Jeffery W. Scott, Nov. 1, 1980; children: Amy Beth, Brennan Marshall. BA in Psychology, U. New Orleans, 1984; M in Gerontology, Baylor U., 1987; M in Religious Edn., Southwestern Bapt. Sem., 1989. Youth and children dir. Corace Temple Bapt., Waco, Tex., 1984-87; activity coord. Asbury Meth. Village, Gaithersburg, Md., 1988-90; activity dir. Wayside Farm Nursing, Akron, Ohio, 1990; social worker Laural Lake Retirement, Hudson, Ohio, 1990-95; children and sr. adult dir. Colonial Ave Bapt., Roanoke, Va., 1999—. Avocations: crafts, sewing. Office: Colonial Ave Bapt 6143 Colonial Ave Roanoke VA 24018

SCOTT, DEREK BRIAN, music educator; b. Birmingham, Midlands, Eng., Feb. 28, 1950; s. Harry and Barbara Jean (Alcock) S.; m. Sara Margaret Dodd, May 1, 1992. BA, U. Hull, Eng., 1972, MMus, 1978, PhD, 1991, cert. edn., 1975. Head music dept. Brunel U. Coll., London, 1990-93; dir. music U. Coll., Salford, Eng., 1993-95; dir. music U. Salford, 1996—, chmn. music, 1997—. Author: (book) The Singing Bourgeois, 1989; author (with others) Blackwell History of Music in Britain, Vol. 6, 1995, Music, Culture and Society, 2000; contbr. articles to profl. jours. Office: Univ Salford, The Crescent, Salford M3 6EQ Manchester, England

SCOTT, DONALD MICHAEL, educational association administrator, educator; b. L.A., Sept. 26, 1943; s. Bernard Hendry and Barbara (Lannin) S.; m. Patricia Ilene Pancoast, Oct. 24, 1964 (div. June 1971); children: William Bernard, Kenneth George. BA, San Francisco State U., 1965, MA, 1986. Cert. tchr. Calif. Tchr. Mercy High Sch., San Francisco, 1968-71; park ranger Calif. State Park System, Half Moon Bay, 1968-77; tchr. adult div. Jefferson Union High Sch. Dist., Daly City, Calif., 1973-87; dir. NASA-NPS Project Wider Focus, Daly City, 1983-90; dir. Geo.S. Spl. Projects Wider Focus, San Francisco, 1990—; also bd. dirs. Wider Focus, Daly City; nat. park ranger/naturalist Grant-Kohrs Ranch Nat. Hist. Site, Deer Lodge, Mont., 1987-88; nat. park ranger pub. affairs fire team Yellowstone Nat. Park, 1988; nat. park ranger Golden Gate Recreation Area, 1988-92; rsch. subject NASA, Mountain View, Calif., 1986-90; guest artist Yosemite (Calif.) Nat. Park, 1986; nat. park ranger Golden Gate Nat. Recreation Area, Nat. Park Svc., San Francisco, 1986, nat. park svc. history cons. to Bay Dist., 1988-94; adj. asst. prof. Skyline Coll., 1989-94, Coll. San Mateo, 1992-94; aerospace edn. specialist NASA/OSU/AESP, 1994—; cons. Friends of Ea. State Penitentiary Project, Phila., 1993. Contbr. articles, photographs to profl. jours., mags., chpts. to books. Pres. Youth for Kennedy, Lafayette, Calif., 1960; panelist Community Bds. of San Francisco, 1978-87; city chair Yes on A com., So. San Francisco, San Mateo County, Calif., 1986; active CONTACT Orgn., 1991—, bd. dirs. 1995—; mem. edn. working group Case for Mars VI, Boulder, 1996. Mem. Nat. Assn. for Interpretation (founding mem.), Yosemite Assn. (life), Wider Focus, Friends of George R. Stewart, Nat. Sci. Tchrs. Assn., Nat. Coun. of Tchrs. of Math., Internat. Tech. Edn. Assn., Smithsonian Planetary Soc. (charter mem.), Mars Soc. (founding), Orange County Space Soc., Mars Soc. Ednl. Task Force. Avocations: photography, hiking, camping, travel. Home and Office: NASA Ames Rsch Ctr MS 253 2 Moffett Field CA 94035-1000

SCOTT, FREDERICK ISADORE, JR., editor, business executive; b. Balt., Oct. 27, 1927; s. Frederick Isadore and Rebecca Esther (Waller) S.; m. Viola Fowlkes, Feb. 4, 1949. B.E. in Chem. Engring, Johns Hopkins, 1950; M.S. in Mgmt. Engring, Newark Coll. Engring., 1956. Chem. process engr. in research and devel. RCA, Harrison, N.J., 1951-59; with Kearfott div. Gen. Precision Aerospace, Little Falls, N.J., 1960-62; asst. sales mgr. Isotopes, Inc., Westwood, N.J., 1964-66; mgr. capacitor sect. Wellington Electronics, Inc., Englewood, N.J., 1967-68; owner F.I. Scott & Assos. (med. equipment), Montclair, N.J., 1968-80; tech. product mktg. and editorial svcs. F.I. scott & Assocs., Check, Va., 1980-86; editor instrumentation publ. Am. Lab. and Internat. Lab., Fairfield, Conn., 1968-80, cons. editor, 1980—; pres. Group Tech., Ltd., 1979—; editor Am. Clin. Lab., 1990—. Served with AUS, 1946-47. Mem. Am. Chem. Soc. (sr.), AAAS, N.Y. Acad. Sci., IEEE (editor newsletter No. N.J. sect. 1957-58, chmn. publs. com. 1958-59), N.Y. Micros. Soc. Home and Office: 1 E Chase St Apt 410 Baltimore MD 21202-2597

SCOTT, GENEVA LEE SMITH, nursing educator; b. Codell, Kans., Nov. 2, 1943; d. Lester Lee and Lennicejean Leota (Lynch) Smith; m. Dennis G. Scott, Feb. 20, 1965; children: J.D., Shane, Deminy. BS, Fort Hays Kans. State Coll., 1965; BS in Nursing, Fort Hays State U., 1979; MS in Nursing, West Tex. State U., 1986. Charge nurse Hadley Regional Med. Ctr., Hays, Kans.; sch. nurse Borger (Tex.) Ind. Sch. Dist.; clin. and classroom instr. North Cen. Kans. Area Vocat. Tech. Sch., Hays; nursing instr. St. Philip's Coll., San Antonio; sch. nurse Bryan Ind. Sch. Dist., 1993-97; instr. nursing edn. Blinn Coll., Bryan, Tex., 1997-98; instr. nursing edn. Weatherford (Tex.) Coll., 1998, vocat. nursing instr., 1998-2000, instr. associates degree in

nursing program, 2000—. Scholarship grant, 1983. Mem. Am. Nurses Assn., Phi Delta Kappa, Beta Sigma Phi (membership chairperson, Girl of Yr. 1978). Home: 405 W Spring St Weatherford TX 76086

SCOTT, GEORGE GALLMANN, accountant; b. Hattiesburg, Miss., July 8, 1928; s. John Havers and Rebecca Evelyn (Gallmann) S.; m. Patsy T. Womack, June 27, 1953; 1 child, George Gallmann. BS, Millsaps Coll., 1949. Accredited bus. acct., tax advisor, 1992; accredited in acctg. and taxation Nat. Accreditation Coun. for Accountancy. Clk. Spanish Trail Transport, Mobile, Ala., 1949-50, asst. auditor, 1953-55; bookkeeper Met. Engraving & Electrotype Co., Richmond, Va., 1952-53; chief clk. Mobile (Ala.) office Ctrl. Truck Lines of Tampa, Fla., 1955-56; gen. auditor M.R.&R. Trucking Co., Crestview, Fla., 1956-66, sec.-treas., 1967-77; pub. acct. enrolled to represent taxpayers before IRS, 1979—; mem. data processing adv. com. Okaloosa-Walton C.C., Niceville, Fla., 1965- 66, 72-73; mem. Okaloosa County Gen. Advisory Com. for Devel. Vocat. Edn., 1973, 79. Bd. dirs. Okaloosa Cmty. Concert Assn., 1982-87; chmn. Crestview Downtown Devel. Bd., 1988-89; bass-baritone soloist, 1953—, choir dir. Meth. Ch., 1966-83, chmn. ofcl. bd., 1971-73, chmn. fin. com., 1974-75, 79-81, audit com., 1977-86, mem. com. on lay personnel, 1979-87, chmn., 1983-87, 89-90, mem. com. on pastor-parish rels., 1980-86, coun. on ministries, 1985, trustee, 1985-87, treas., 1990-95. With U.S. Army, 1950-52. Mem. Nat. Assn. Accts., Nat. Assn. Enrolled Agts., Am. Trucking Assn. (nat. acctg. and fin. coun. 1956-77), Southeastern Acctg. and Fin. Coun. (bd. dirs. 1974-77), Fla. Assn. Enrolled Agts., Crestview Downtown Mchts. Assn. (bd. dirs. 1980-84, treas. 1980-84), Greater Crestview C. of C. (chmn. bus. ethics com. 1973-74, bd. dirs. 1981-83, treas. 1982-83), Fla. Accts. Assn. (bd. govs. 1979-80, pres. N.W. Fla. chpt. 1979-80), Kiwanis (past treas., past sec., past pres.), Pi Kappa Alpha. Home: 244 Seminole Trail Crestview FL 32536-2326

SCOTT, GERALD, chemistry, educator; b. North Shields, England, July 28, 1927; s. Andrew George and Eleanor Freda (Richardson) S.; m. Gwendoline Law; children: Ian Christopher, Robin David, Keith Michael. BA, Balliol Coll., Oxford, 1951, MSc, 1952, DSc, 1983. Mgr. Polymer Chemicals Rsch. ICI, Manchester, 1959-65; head works R & D Polymer Chemicals Rsch. ICI, Grangemouth, 1965-67; prof. chemistry Aston U., 1967-89, prof. emeritus, 1989—; cons. polymer industry. Author: Atmospheric Oxidation and Antioxidants, 1993, Degradable Polymers: Principles and Applications, 1995, Antioxidants in Science, Technology, Medicine and Nutrition, 1997, Polymers and the Environment, 1999; contbr. articles to profl. jours. Fellow Royal Soc. Chemistry, Inst. of Materials; mem. N.Y. Acad. Scis., Materials Life Soc., Russian Acad. of Creative Endevours. Avocations: mountain climbing, photography. Email: scott@rogat.fsnet.co.uk. Office: Aston Univ, 0121 359 Birmingham United Kingdom

SCOTT, GERALD WESLEY, retired American diplomat; b. Oklahoma City, Aug. 7, 1940; s. Charles Wesley and Dorothy Bernadine (Heidlage) S.; m. Frances Helen Gardner-Brown, Aug. 9, 1975; children: Charles Alan, Michael Tacon. BS in Fgn. Svc., Georgetown U., 1962; MA, Johns Hopkins U., 1969, Naval War Coll., 2000. Commd. fgn. svc. officer, 1969; vice consul Am. Consulate Gen., Danang, Viet Nam, 1973-75; polit. officer Am. Embassy, Rome, 1980-83; advisor polit. and security affairs U.S. Mission to UN, N.Y.C., 1983-85; dep. chief of mission Am. Embassy, Mbabane, Swaziland, 1985-88; polit. counselor Am. Embassy, Kinshasa, Zaire, 1988-92, Nairobi, Kenya, 1992-93; dep. chief of mission Am. Embassy, Kinshasa, 1993-95; ambassador to The Gambia, Banjul, 1996-98; internat. affairs advisor Naval War Coll., Newport, R.I., 1998-2000; ret., 2000; cons. internat. and security affairs, 2000—. Lt. USNR, 1962-67. Decorated Air medal, Navy Commendation medal. Mem. Am. Fgn. Svc. Assn. (William R. Rivkin award 1992), SAR, Sons of the Revolution, Lotos Club (N.Y.C.), Army and Navy Club (Washington). Roman Catholic. Office: Naval War Coll PO Box 430 Duncan OK 73534

SCOTT, GORDON RAMSAY, veterinarian, virologist; b. Arbroath, Scotland, July 6, 1923; s. William and Margaret Ann Ramsay (Jackson) S.; m. Joan Henderson Walker, July 15, 1947; children: Ann, Andrew, Margaret. BSc, Edinburgh U., Scotland, 1946, PhD, 1959; MS, Wis. U., 1953. Asst. Scotland, 1946-49; virologist Veterinary Rsch. Lab., Kenya, 1950-52; head divsn. virus diseases East African Veterinary Rsch. Orgn., 1956-62; acting dir. East Africam Veterinary Rsch. Orgn., 1959, 62; lectr. Tropical Veterinary Medicine U. Edinburgh, 1963-67; sr. lectr. Topical Veterinary Medicine U. Edinburgh, 1967-78, reader, 1978-90, reader emeritus, 1990—. Author: Diagnosis of Rinderpest, 1967, Rinderpest Eradication Campaign in South Asia, 1986, Global Eradication of Rinderpest, 1992, others; contbr. articles to profl. jours. Reservist Kenya Police, 1953-56. Decorated Officer Order of Brit. Empire for svcs. to tropical vet. medicine. Fellow Royal Coll. Vet. Surgeons; mem. Kenya Veterinary Assn. (chmn. 1955), Assn. Veterinary Tchrs. & Rsch. Workers (exec. mem. 1970-80), Assn. Veterinary Tchrs. (hon. life), Animal Diseases Rsch. Adminstrn. (hon.). Home: 2/12 Craufurdland, Edinburgh EH4 6DL, Scotland

SCOTT, H. LEE, retail store company executive. With Wal Mart Stores, 1979—, various mgmt. positions, pres., CEO, 1999—; vice chmn., COO Wal Mart Stores, Inc., 1999—. Office: Wal Mart Stores 702 SW Eighth St Bentonville AR 72716*

SCOTT, HOWARD WINFIELD, JR., temporary help services company executive; b. Greenwich, Conn., Feb. 24, 1935; s. Howard Winfield and Janet (Lewis) S.; m. Joan Ann MacDonald, Aug. 12, 1961; children: Howard Winfield III, Thomas MacDonald, Ann Elizabeth. BS, Northwestern U., 1957. With R.H. Donnelly Corp., Chgo., 1958-59; sales rep. Masonite Corp., Chgo. and Madison, Wis., 1959-61, Manpower Inc., Chgo., 1961-63; br. mgr. Manpower Inc., Kansas City, Mo., 1963-65; regional mgr. Salespower divsn. Manpower Inc., Phila., 1965-66; asst. advt. mgr. soups Campbell Soup Co., Camden, N.J., 1966-68; pres. PARTIME, Inc., Paoli, Pa., 1968-74; dir. mktg. Kelly Svcs., Inc., Southfield, Mich., 1974-78; pres. CDI Temporary Svcs., Inc., Southfield, Mich., 1978-91, Dunhill Pers. Sys., Inc., Woodbury, N.Y., 1991-94; v.p. SOS Temporary Svcs., Salt Lake City, 1994; COO SOS Staffing Svcs., Salt Lake City, 1995-97, CEO, 1997; COO Empire Staffing Svcs., LLC, N.Y.C., Tempositions Group of Cos., N.Y.C. With AUS, 1957-58. Mem. Nat. Assn. Temporary Svcs. (sec. 1970-71, pres. 1971-73, bd. dirs. 1982-91), Kappa Sigma. Republican. Home: 400 E 84th St Apt 14C New York NY 10028-5609 also: 1204 Annapolis Sea Colony E Bethany Beach DE 19930 Office: Empire Staffing Svcs LLC 161 William St New York NY 10038-2607 also: Tempositions Group of Cos 420 Lexington Ave New York NY 10170-0002

SCOTT, IAN JAMES, accountant; b. Glasgow, Scotland, Feb. 10, 1930; s. Wilfrid Henry and Violet Margaret Handasyde (Mackay) S.; m. Aileen Rennie Wright, June 14, 1961; children: Charles Roderick, Carolyn Louise Hermione Lorna, Lorne Hamilton Mackay. Chartered Acct., Inst. Chartered Accts Scotland, Glasgow, 1958. Ptnr. R.A. Clement & Co., Glasgow, 1960-74, Ian J. Scott & Co., Helensburgh, Scotland, 1974-95; cons. Hammond & Co., Helensburgh, 1995—; dir. A.W.D. Shipping, Glasgow; dep. chmn. T.S.B. Scotland, Edinburgh, 1986. Collector of the House Trades House of Glasgow, 1995-96; deacon Incorporation of Gardeners, Glasgow, 1993-94; deacon convener Trades of Glasgow, 1997-98; freeman City of London, 1995; mem. Worshipful Co. of Gun-makers, London, 1995. Recipient Silk Cut Nautical award for svcs. to nat. yachting, 1986, Corinthian award for svcs. to nat. yachting, 1993. Mem. Insolvency Practitioners Assn., Soc. Practitioners of Insolvency, Royal Yacht Assn. (judge 1990—), Clyde Corinthian Yacht Club (hon. commodore), Sandyford Burn Club (v.p. 2000), Patrick Curling Club (pres. 2000). Conservative. Mem. Ch. of Scotland. Avocations: sailing, curling, shooting. Home: The Little House, Pier Rd, Rhu Arqyll & Rule G84 8LH, Scotland

SCOTT, JAMES HUNTER, JR., investment executive; b. Balt., Jan. 28, 1945; s. James Hunter and Marialice (Short) S.; m. Katheen Ann Bilderback, Sept. 1, 1973; children: Andrew James, Elizabeth Ann. BA, Rice U., 1967; MS, Carnegie Mellon U., 1970, PhD, 1975. Instr. Carnegie Mellon U., Pitts., 1969-71; rsch. fellow Fed. Res. Bank of Cleve., 1971-72; asst. prof. U. Wis., Milw., 1972-75; from asst. prof. to prof./divisional rep. fin. Columbia U., N.Y.C., 1975-87; mng. dir. Prudential Ins. Co., Newark, 1987-97; chmn. PTC Svcs., Newark, 1991—; CEO Prudential Diversified Investment Strategies, Short Hills, N.J., 1994-97; sr. mng. dir. Prudential Investments, 1997—; vis. asst. prof. Stanford (Calif.) U., 1974-75, assoc. prof., 1979; adj. prof. grad. sch. bus. Columbia U., 1988—; dir. Inst. for Quantitative Rsch. in Fin., N.Y.C., 1995—; with Goldman, Sachs, Kinsey & Co., 1981-82; trustee adminstrv. com. Eastern Air Lines Pilots Investment Plan, Miami, 1985-91; dir. Prudential Trust Co., 1996—. Bd. editors Fin. Analysts Jour., 1998—; contbr. over 25 articles to profl. jours. Pres. bd. trustees Alpine (N.J.) Cmty. Ch., 1986-89, v.p., 1998—; v.p. bd. trustees Tenafly (N.J.) Bd. Edn., 1998—; mem. Grad. Sch. Indsl. Adminstrn. Coun. on Fin., Carnegie Mellon U. Mem. Am. Econ. Assn., Am. Fin. Assn. Methodist. Office: Quantitative Mgmt Prudential Investments 2 Gateway Ctr Fl 4 Newark NJ 07102-5003

SCOTT, JOHN ERNEST, chemical morphologist; b. Macclesfield, Eng., Nov. 14, 1930; s. John Alfred and Henrietta (Bradley) S.; m. Margaretha Bergman, Apr. 5, 1961 (div. 1973); 1 child, John Peter. BSc, Manchester (Eng.) U., 1951, MSc, 1953, PhD, 1956, DSc (hon.), 1965. Leverhulme fellow St. Mary's Hosp., London, 1958-60; Empire Rheumatism fellow Med. Rsch. Coun., Taplow, Eng., 1961-63, staff mem. rheumatism unit, 1963-76; prof. chem. morphology Manchester U., 1976—; cons. to various firms, including CSIRO, Australia, Fidia, Italy, Boehringer, Germany. Founder, sec. Fedn. European Connective Tissue Socs., Cambridge, Eng., 1968. Officer RAF, 1956-58. Hon. fellow Massey U., New Zealand, 1995; recipient Robert Feulgen prize Gesellschaft Histochemie, Basle, Switzerland, 1987, Citation Classic award Inst. Sci. Informatics, 1993. Mem. Biochem. Soc. (Gold medal 1973), Brit. Connective Tissue Soc. (hon.), Anat. Soc. Gt. Britain and Ireland (hon.), Purkinje Soc. (hon.), Italian Histochem. Soc. (hon.). Achievements include establishment of the study of chemical morphology. Avocations: chess, music, travel. Office: Manchester U, Manchester U, Dept Chem Morphology, Manchester M13 9PL, England

SCOTT, JOHN PAUL, medical educator; b. Kamunting, Malaysia, June 26, 1956; came to U.S., 1991; s. Joseph and Agnes (Beldon) S.; m. Lesley Carol Poole, Dec. 5, 1981; children: Christopher Michael, Elizabeth Mary, David Matthew. MB ChB, Otago U., Dunedin, New Zealand, 1979, MD, 1990; MS, Cambridge U., England, 1992; MS in Econs., U. London, 1999; LLB (hon.), U. Wolverhampkan, 2000. Resident Otago U., Dunedin, New Zealand, 1979-83; assoc. prof. transplantation Mayo Clinic, Rochester, Minn., 1991-96, prof., 1996—; internat. advisor, 2000—. Contbr. articles to profl. jours. Fellow dept. pulmonary medicine Otago U., 1984-85, Cambridge U., 1985-88, sr. fellow, 1988-91. Fellow Royal Coll. Physicians (internat. advisor 2000—), Royal Australian Coll. Physicians, Am. Coll. Physicians, Royal Statis. Soc.; mem. Am. Thoracic Soc. (Minn. rep. 1993-96), Royal Soc. New Zealand, Internat. Soc. Philosophical Enquiry, Mayo Thoracic Soc. (pres. 1996-99). Avocations: philosophy, economics, chess, climbing, travel. Office: Mayo Clinic 200 1st St SW Rochester MN 55905-0002

SCOTT, JOYCE M. C., academic administrator; b. N. Plainfield, N.J., Feb. 17, 1924; d. Charles Chester Sr. and Martha England Murphey Yost; m. William Scott, Jan. 8, 1952; children: Elizabeth V. K. Hartzell, Terry L., Jyothi J., Shanti J. BA in Bibl. Edn., Columbia Internat. U., 1946; MA in Missions cum laude, Ea. Bapt. Theol. Sem., Phila., 1972, LittD (hon.), 1993; DD (hon.), Internat. Inst. Ch. Mgmt., Madras, India, 1991. Ordained Am. Bapt. Ch., 1990. Clin. lab. supr. Christian Hosp., Karimnagar, India, 1961-66; corr., treas. Mission Mid. Sch., Tchr. Tng. Sch., Andhra, India, 1966-75; supr. Clin. Lab. Clough Meml. Hosp., Ongole, India, 1966-75; supr., treas. dept. youth Christian Edn., Ongole, 1972-75; corr., mgr. Edn. and Rehab. Handicapped Children, Ongole, 1972-75; corr., bursar New Life Ctr. Children, Narasarapoet, India, 1972-75; bursar, advisor adult literacy program Samavesham Telugu Bapt. Chs., India, 1976-77; exec. asst. India Bible Lit., 1975-86; dir. World Home Bible League, 1980-83; dir., founder adult literacy program Literacy India Trust, 1984—; assoc. gen. dir. India Bible Lit., 1973—. Author: Happiness - An Illustrated Flip Chart, 1979, Great Bible Truths, 1981, Discovering Bible Truths, 1983, Beyond Doubt, 1994; contbr. articles to profl. jours. Recipient Mother Edn. award Tharigoppula Welfare Soc., 1989; named Disting. Alumnus Columbia Internat. U., 1995. Republican. Avocations: music, reading, pets. Home: 116 Fairview Ave Dover PA 17315-1316 Office: Scipture Ministries India 22 S Main St Dover PA 17315-1506

SCOTT, KAREN ANN, dentist; b. Gary, Ind., Jan. 7, 1957; d. Jay R. and Bernadette (Hogan) S. BS, U. Notre Dame, 1979; BSD, U. Ill., Chgo., 1983, DDS, 1985. Pvt. practice dentistry Chgo., 1985—. Active Alliance Francaise de Chgo., Grant Park Concert Soc.; mem. adv. bd. Chgo. Archtl. Found.; mem. Chgo. Cares, Habitat for Humanity. Notre Dame scholar, 1975-79; recipient Achievement award Internat coll. Dentists, 1985. Mem. ADA, Ill. Dental Soc. (sci. presenter 1987), Chgo. Dental Soc., Internat. Vis. Ctr., Chgo. Architecture Found. (adv. bd. Cathedral High Sch.), Notre Dame Club Chgo., Alliance Francaise de Chgo., Pets Are Worth Saving (PAWS), Young Variety Club (Chgo.), Young Internat. Club, Ill. Club for Cath. Women, Alpha Epsilon Delta, Omicron Kappa Upsilon. Home: 1301 N Dearborn Pkwy Apt 503 Chicago IL 60610-6093 Office: 55 E Washington St Ste 3102 Chicago IL 60602-2206

SCOTT, KENNETH EUGENE, lawyer, educator; b. Western Springs, Ill., Nov. 21, 1928; s. Kenneth L. and Bernice (Albright) S.; m. Viviane H. May, Sept. 22, 1956 (dec. Feb. 1982); children: Clifton, Jeffrey, Linda; m. Priscilla Gay, July 30, 1989; children: Ashley, Shaler. BA in Econs., Coll. William and Mary, 1949; MA in Polit. Sci., Princeton U., 1953; LLB, Stanford U., 1956. Bar: N.Y. 1957, Calif. 1957, D.C. 1967. Assoc. Sullivan & Cromwell, N.Y.C., 1956-59, Musick, Peeler & Garrett, L.A., 1959-61; chief dep. savs. and loan commr. State of Calif., L.A., 1961-63; gen. counsel Fed. Home Loan Bank Bd., Washington, 1963-67; Parsons prof. law and bus. Stanford (Calif.) Law Sch., 1968-95, emeritus, 1995—; sr. rsch. fellow Hoover Instn., 1978-95, emeritus, 1995—; mem. Shadow Fin. Regulatory Com., 1986—, Fin. Economists Roundtable, 1991—; bd. dirs. Am. Century Mut. Funds, Mountain View, Calif., Dresdner RCM Capital Funds, San Francisco. Author: (with others) Retail Banking in the Electronic Age, 1977; co-editor: The Economics of Corporation Law and Securities Regulation, 1980. Mem. ABA, Calif. Bar Assn., Phi Beta Kappa, Order of Coif, Pi Kappa Alpha, Omicron Delta Kappa. Home: 610 Gerona Rd Stanford CA 94305-8453 Office: Crown Quadrangle Stanford Law Sch Stanford CA 94305-8610

SCOTT, KERRIGAN DAVIS, private investor, philanthropist; b. Magdalene, Fla., Sept. 26, 1941; s. Thurman Thomas and Jacqueline (Glenister) S.; children: Katherine, Stephanie, Jennifer. N.D. U. Va., 1964. Pvt. investor, Hilton Head Island, S.C., 1965—. Aide-de-camp to gov. of Tenn. with rank of col. Recipient Presdl. Legion Merit, Shield of Valor medal, White House Letter Commendation. Author: Aristocracy and Royalty of the World, 1983, Hereditary Baron in the Nobility of France. Mem. bd. regents Liberty U., Lynchburg, Va.; bd. dirs. Aid to Hospitalized Vets.; assoc. Library of Congress; pres. The Cittanova Found. Recognized as His Royal Highness, Prince of Cittanova by Govts. of Albania and San Marino (Italy). Episcopalian. Club: Shipyard Plantation Racquet. Home: Hilton Head Plantation 10 Windflower Ct Hilton Head Island SC 29926-1704

SCOTT, LOLITA JEAN, social worker; b. Owensboro, Ky., Apr. 21, 1957; d. James Thomas Jr. and Jewell Dean (Walls) Howard; m. Lindsey Scott, Aug. 15, 1980; 1 child, Latavia Seneca Scott. AA, Ea. Ky. U., 1980, BSW, 1993; MA in Marriage and Family Therapist, Louisville Theol. Sem., 1999. With child protective svcs. Ky. Dept. Social Svcs., Richmond, 1993, 94-95; social worker sr. placement Richmond Family Resource Ctr., Richmond, 1993; asst. tchg. parent Spring Meadows, Louisville, 1994; sr. case mgr. Seven Counties Svcs., Louisville, 1995—; clin. therapist assoc. Ctr. for Family Ministries, Archdiocese of Louisville, 1996—; mem. adoption-foster care rev. bd., 1998-99. Singer Ea. Ky. Ensemble, 1975-78, Tommy Jones workshop Cmty. Choir, 1995-96; vol. tutor Ky. Dept. Adult Edn. and Literacy, Richmond, 1993; vol. Women's Abuse Ctr., Owensboro, Ky., 1989, Telford Cmty. Ctr., Richmond, 1991. Mem. Am. Assn. Christian Counselors; Am. Assn. Marriage and Family Therapy, Ky. Assn. Marriage and Family Therapy, Omega Psi Phi Pearl. Democrat. Baptist. Avocations: bicycling, volleyball, movies, reading, dancing. Home: 8703 Big Tree Cir Apt B Louisville KY 40220-5853 Office: Seven Counties Svcs 2225 W Broadway Louisville KY 40211-1087

SCOTT, LOTTIE BELL, retired civil rights administrator; b. Ridgeway, S.C., Nov. 5, 1936; d. Joe and Estelle (Stone) Bell; m. Charles Wright, 1961 (div. 1965); 1 child, Clyburn. AS, Mohegan Community Coll., Norwich, Conn., 1982; B of Gen. Studies, U. Conn., Storrs, Conn., 1986. Clk.-typist Conn. Dept. of Mental Health, Norwich, 1962-70; neighborhood resource worker Conn. Commn. on Human Rights & Opportunities, Norwich, 1970-73, investigator, 1973-79, regional mgr., 1979-92; owner LBS Human Resource Cons., Norwich, 1992—. Dir. Thames Valley Coun. for Cmty., Jewett City, Conn., 1965-68; br. sec. NAACP, Norwich, 1967-74, br. pres., 1974-80; asst. sec. Conn. State Conf. of the NAACP, 1971-73, v.p., 1973-79; bd. dirs. Conn. Civil Liberties, Hartford, 1972-76; vice chmn. Norwich Redevelopment Agy., 1974; vice moderator, Unitarian Universalist Ch., 1977-81; bd. dirs. United Cmty. Svc., 1977-80, 85-88; com. chmn., bd. dirs. William W. Backus Hosp. Long Range Planning, 1981-88, chmn. bd. dirs., 1988-90; bd. dirs. Conn. Hosp. Assn., Wallingford, Conn., 1990-92, YMCA, Norwich, 1991-97. Mem. Rotary. Democrat. Avocations: dancing, musicals, drama, reading, walking. Office: LBS Human Resource Cons 85 Church St Norwich CT 06360-5001

SCOTT, MARIE EVELYN, publisher, journalist; b. High Wycombe, Bucks, Eng., Oct. 3, 1940; d. Mark and Irene Marion (Bainsfair) S. Student, U. Westminster, 1960-62. Fashion editor Tailor and Cutter, 1962-65; editor The Maker-Up, 1965-70, Jr. Age, 1970-71; fashion editor Style, 1971-75; editor Sir Internat., 1975-78; ptnr. Style Publs. Ltd., 1978-85; editor Menswear Weekly, 1985-87; ptnr. Scott Taylor Ltd, 1987—. Pub. British Style, Savile Row Style, 1999—. Mem. Gerry's, English Spkg. Union. Avocations: lunch, champagne, dog walking. Office: Scott Taylor Ltd, Brit Style 2 Beacon Hill, London N7 9LY, England

SCOTT, MAURICE FITZGERALD, economist; b. Dublin, Ireland, Dec. 6, 1924; s. Gerald Chaplin and Harriette Geraldine (FitzGerald) S.; m. Eleanor Warren Dawson, Mar. 30, 1953 (dec. Feb. 1989); children: Alison, Sheila, Jean. MA, Oxford U., 1948, BLitt, 1953. Economist OEEC, Paris, 1949-5l; econ. adviser statis. sect. Office of Prime Minister, London, 1951-53; econ. adviser Cabinet Secretariat, London, 1953-54; rsch. officer Nat. Inst. for Econ. and Social Rsch., London, 1954-57; fellow in econs. Christ Church, Oxford (Eng.) U., 1957-68, Nuffield Coll., 1968-92; fellow emeritus Nuffield Coll., 1992—; economist Nat. Econ. Devel. Office, London, 1962-63; fellow Devel. Ctr., OECD, Paris, 1967-68. Author: A Study of United Kingdom Imports, 1963, Can We Get Back to Full Employment?, 1978, A New View of Economic Growth, 1989, Peter's Journey, 1989, (with Little and Scitovsky) Industry and Trade in Some Developing Countries, 1970. Temp. capt. Royal Engrs., 1943-46. Fellow Royal Econ. Soc. (coun. 1984-88), Brit. Acad.; mem. Polit. Economy Club. Office: Nuffield Coll Oxford U, Oxford OX1 1NF, England

SCOTT, NANCY ELLEN, psychologist; b. El Paso, Tex., Nov. 1, 1960; d. Robert Churchill and Annie Jo (Schmidt) S. BS, U. Tex., El Paso, 1982; MS, Springfield Coll., 1985; MA, Columbia U., 1987, EdM, 1989; PhD, Fordham U., 1996. Cert. tchr., Tex., cert. clin. hypnotherapy; lic. psychologist, N.Y. Assoc. Occupl. Health Consulting Inc., West Nyack, N.Y., 1985-88; psychiat. rehab. counselor Met. Hosp., N.Y.C., 1988-91; psychotherapist Met. Ctr. for Mental Health, N.Y.C., 1991-96; psychology intern Albert Einstein Coll. of Medicine, Bronx, N.Y., 1991-92; psychologist Albert Einstein Coll. Medicine, Bronx, N.Y., 1992-94, Bronx Psychiat. Ctr., Bronx, N.Y., 1994-95; assessor Assessment Sys., Inc., N.Y.C., 1995; pvt. practice N.Y.C., 1995—; neuropsychologist Burke Med. Rsch. Inst., White Plains, N.Y., 1996-99, dir. neuropsychol. assessment program, 1999—. Contbr. articles to profl. jours. Mem. APA. Fax: 914-597-2757. E-mail: nscott@burke.org. Office: Burke Med Rsch Inst 785 Mamaroneck Ave White Plains NY 10605-2523

SCOTT, PAMELA, secondary education educator; b. Marshall, Mo.; d. Lester Henry and Dorothy Ann (Reno) Langewisch; m. Robert Ray Scott, Dec. 20, 1969; children: Christopher Alan, Shalishea Elizabeth. BSE, Emporia State U., 1985, MS, 1999. Owner-operator P.S. etc. Craft Store, Burlington, Kans., 1980-83; tchr. Highland Park H.S., Topeka, 1985-86, Burlington H.S., 1986—. Active human and civil rights commn. Kans. Nat. Educators Assn., Topeka, 1998—. Mem. NEA, Kans. Nat. Educators Assn. (sunflower uniserve adv. bd. 1998—), Burlington Unified Tchrs. Assn. (pres. 1996-98), Nat. Art Educators Assn., Beta Sigma Phi (pres., sec.). Republican. Lutheran. Avocations: photography, travel, arts, crafts. E-mail: pammysuescott@hotmail.com. Home: 804 Sanders St Burlington KS 66839-1159 Office: Burlington High Sch 830 Cross St Burlington KS 66839-1103

SCOTT, PETER BRYAN, lawyer; b. St. Louis, Nov. 11, 1947; s. gilbert Franklin and Besse Jean (Fudge) S.; children: Lindsay W., Sarah W., Peter B. Jr. AB, Drury Coll., 1969; JD, Washington U., St. Louis, 1972, LLM, 1980. Bar: Mo. 1972, Colo. 1980; diplomate Ct. Practice Inst.; accredited estate planner, advanced wealth specialist planner. Pvt. practice St. Louis, 1972-80; assoc. McKie and Assocs., Denver, 1980-81; ptnr. Scott and Chesteen, P.C., Denver, 1981-84, Veto & Scott, Denver, 1984-92; pvt. practice Denver, 1992—; tchr. Denver Paralegal Inst., Red Rocks C.C. Mem. Evergreen Christian Ch., Disciples of Christ. Capt. USAR, 1971-79. Mem. ABA, Mo. Bar Assn., Colo. Bar Assn., 1st Jud. Dist. Bar Assn. Republican. Home: 6305 W 6th Ave Unit C18 Lakewood CO 80214-2359 Office: Ste 2-103 777 S Wadsworth Blvd Lakewood CO 80226

SCOTT, PETER DALE, writer, retired English language educator; b. Montreal, Jan. 11, 1929; s. Francis Reginald and Marian Mildred (Dale) S.; m. Mary Elizabeth Marshall, June 16, 1956; children: Catherine Dale, Thomas, John Daniel; m. Ronna Kabatznick, July 14, 1993. BA, McGill U., Montreal, Que., Can., 1949, PhD, 1955; postgrad, Inst. d'Etudes Politiques, Paris, 1950, Univ. Coll., Oxford, Eng., 1950-52. Fgn. service officer Canadian Dept. External Affairs, Ottawa, Ont., 1957-61; asst. prof. speech U. Calif., Berkeley, 1961-66, from asst. prof. to assoc. prof. English, 1966-80, prof., 1980-94; ret., 1994. Author: The War Conspiracy, 1972, Crime and Cover-Up, 1977, Coming to Jakarta, 1988, Listening to the Candle, 1992, Deep Politics and the Death of JFK, 1993, Crossing Borders, 1994, Deep Politics Two, 1995, Drugs, Contras, and the CIA, 2000, Minding the Darkness, 2000; co-author: The Assassinations, 1976, The Iran-Contra Connection, 1987, Cocaine Politics, 1991. Fellow Internat. Ctr. Devel. Policy (Freedom award 1987). Mem. Assn. for Responsible Dissent (bd. dirs. 1988). Avocation: birdwatching. Office: U Calif Dept English Berkeley CA 94720-0001

SCOTT, QUINCY, JR., dean, clergy; b. Norfolk, Va., Jan. 11, 1944; s. Quincy Sr. and Josephine Delores Scott; m. Constance LaVern Scott, Feb. 6, 1972; children: Toya Williams, Quincy III, Derek Thomas. AB, Shaw U., 1965; MDiv, Vanderbilt U., 1968; D in Ministry, Howard U., 1978. Ordained to ministry Baptist Ch.; cert. clin. pastoral counselor. City recreation specialist City Pks. and Recreation, Norfolk, 1963-65; commd. lt. U.S. Army, advanced through grades to col., chaplain, 1968-95; dean chapel Shaw U., Raleigh, N.C., 1995—; dir. freshman yr. Shaw U., Raleigh, 1996—. Commr. Boy Scouts, Pisa, Italy, 1980-84; trustee Chesapeake Hospice, Crownville, Md., 1993-94. Decorated Bronze Star, Cross of Gallantry, Legion of Merit. Mem. Assn. Pastoral Counselors, Retired Army Officers Assn., Nat. Theol. Fraternity, Kappa Alpha Psi. Avocations: sports, music, arts. Office: Shaw U 118 E South St Raleigh NC 27601-2399

SCOTT, RALPH C., physician, educator; b. Bethel, Ohio, June 7, 1921; s. John Carey and Leona (Laycock) S.; m. Rosemary Ann Schultz, June 26, 1945; children: Susan Ann, Barbara Lynne, Marianne Elizabeth. BS, U. Cin., 1943, MD, 1945. Diplomate: Am. Bd. Internal Medicine (subspecialty cardiovascular disease). InternUniv. Hosps. U. Iowa, 1945-46; resident, asst. dept. pathology Coll. Medicine U. Cin., 1948-49, fellow internal medicine Coll. Medicine, 1949-53, fellow cardiology Coll. Medicine, 1953-57, mem. faculty Coll. Medicine, 1950—, prof. medicine Coll. Medicine, 1968—; staff clinics Cin. Gen. Hosp., 1950-75, clinician in internal medicine, 1952-75, dir. cardiac clinics, 1965-75, attending physician med. service, 1958—; staff VA Hosp., Cin. 1954-86, 1992—, cons., 1961-86, 92—; attending physician Med. Svc., Christian R. Holmes Hosp., Cin., 1957-86; attending staff USAF Hosp., Wright Patterson AFB, 1960—; staff Good Samaritan Hosp., Cin., 1961—, cons., 1967—; staff Jewish Hosp., Cin., 1957—, cons., 1968—; cons. Children's Hosp., Cin., 1968—; attending physician Providence Hosp., Cin., 1971—, dir. cardiology, 1971-94. Contbr. articles to med. jours.; editorial bd. Am. Heart Jour, 1967-79, Jour. Electrocardiology, 1967—; editor: Electro-Cardiographic-Pathologic Conf., Jour. Electrocardiology, 1967—, Clin. Cardiology and Diabetes, 5 vols, 1981. Capt. AUS, 1946-48. Nat.

Heart Inst. grantee, 1964-68, 67-74, 76-82, 1985-90. Fellow ACP, Am. Coll. Cardiology, Am. Coll. Chest Physicians, Coun. Clin. Cardiology, Coun. Clin. Epidemiology and Prevention; mem. Ohio State Med. Assn., Cin. Acad. Medicine, Cen. Soc. Clin. Rsch., Am. Heart Assn., Cin. Soc. Internal Medicine, Heart Assn. Southwestern Ohio, Am. Fedn. for Clin. Rsch., Internat. Cardiovascular Soc., Am. Soc. Preventive Cardiology, Sigma Xi, Alpha Omega Alpha, Phi Eta Sigma, Phi Chi. Home: 2955 Alpine Ter Cincinnati OH 45208-3407 Office: U Cin Med Ctr Divsn Cardiology PO Box 670542 Cincinnati OH 45267-0001

SCOTT, REBECCA ANDREWS, biology educator; b. Sunny Hill, La., June 4, 1939; d. Hayward and Dorothy (Nicholson) Andrews; m. Earl P. Scott, June 8, 1957; children: Stephanie Scott Dilworth, Cheryl L. BS, So. U., 1962; MS, Eastern Mich. U., 1969. Biology thr. Detroit, 1966-68; sci. tchr. Ann Arbor (Mich.) Pub. Schs., 1968-69; biology tchr. North H.S., Mpls., 1972—, coord. math., sci. tech. magnet, 1986—, advisor Jets Sci. Club. Mem. LVW (pres. 1981-83, 87-89, treas. 1989-94), NSTA, Minn. Sci. Tchrs. Assn., Minn. Acad. Sci., Nat. Assn. Biology Tchrs., Iota Phi Lambda (pres. 1995-99, fin. sec., 1999—). Democrat. Baptist. Home: 3112 Wendhurst Ave Minneapolis MN 55418-1726 Office: 1500 James Ave N Minneapolis MN 55411-3161

SCOTT, RICHARD ELTON, health facility administrator; b. St. Louis, Oct. 3, 1934; s. Earl Ray and Celest (Roark) S.; m. Carol Jenkins, Apr. 3, 1960; children: Suzanne Scott Abbe, Richard E. Jr. BA, Baylor U., 1971; MS, Trinity U., 1978. Cert. healthcare exec. Am. Coll. Healthcare Execs. Various positions Hillcrest Bapt. Med. Ctr., Waco, Tex., 1961-78, asst. adminstr., 1973-78, v.p., 1978-90, exec. v.p., 1990-92, pres., CEO, 1992—; adminstrv. resident Scott & White Clinic, Temple, Tex., 1973-78; chmn. VHA S.W., Inc., Dallas, 1997-98; pres. Bapt. Hosp. Assn., 1999—. Pres. exec. com., bd. Dr. Pepper Museum, Waco, 1996; chmn. Waco Bus. League, 1999; chmn. bd. trustees First Bapt. Ch., Waco, 2000. Named Vol. of Yr. United Way Waco-McLennan County, 1991, CEO of Yr. Red Cross Blood Campaign, 1995; recipient Leondard A. Duce award Trinity U. Healthcare Alumni Assn., San Antonio, 1997. Mem. Waco Rotary, Masonic Grand Lodge Tex.(Cmty. Builder award 1998). Baptist. Avocations: snow skiing, water skiing. Fax: 254-202-4420. E-mail: rscott@hillcrest.net. Office: Hillcrest Health Sys 3000 Herring Ave Waco TX 76708-3239

SCOTT, ROBERT ALLYN, academic administrator; b. Englewood, N.J., Apr. 16, 1939; s. William D. and Ann. F. (Waterman) S.; children: Ryan Keith, Kira Elizabeth. BA, Bucknell U., 1961; PhD, Cornell U., 1975. Mgmt. trainee Procter & Gamble Co., Phila., 1961-63; asst. dir. admissions Bucknell U., Lewisburg, Pa., 1965-67; asst. dean Coll. Arts and Scis. Cornell U., Ithaca, 1967-69, assoc. dean, 1969-79, anthropology faculty, 1978-79; dir. acad. affairs Ind. Commn. for Higher Edn., Indpls., 1979-84, asst. commr., 1984-85; pres. Ramapo (N.J.) Coll., 1985-2000, Adelphi U., 2000—; cons. Sta. WSKG Pub. TV and Radio, 1977-79, also to various colls. and univs., pubs., 1966—; mem. curriculum adv. com. Ind. Bd. Edn., 1984-87, Lilly Endowment Think Tank, 1984-86; mem. nat. adv. panel Ind. 21st Century Schooling Project, 1990-92; U.S. rep. to creation of U. Mobility Asian-Pacific, 1993—; U.S. rep. to meetings of Coun. European Rectors, 1991—; sr. advisor to U.S. State Dept. on Higher Edn. in Unesco European Region, 1997—; U.S. del. to UNESCO N.Am. and World Confs. on Higher Edn., 1998; sr. cons., chair N.J. Higher Edn. Restructuring Team, 1994; bd. dirs. iRV, Internet Minute. Author books and monographs; editorial bd. Cornell Rev., 1976-79; book rev. editor Coll. and Univ., 1974-78; cons. editor Change mag., 1979—; cons. editor Jour. Higher Edn., 1985—; exec. editor Saturday Evening Post book div. Curtis Pub. Co., 1982-85; contbr. articles to sociols., ednl. and popular publs. Trustee Bucknell U., 1976-78, First Unitarian Ch., Ithaca, 1970-73, 78-79, chmn., 1971-73, Unitarian Universalist Ch. of Indpls., 1980-85. With USNR, 1963-65. Spencer Found. rsch. grantee, 1977; recipient Sagamore of the Wabash award, 1986, Prudential Found. Leader of Yr. award, 1987, Disting. Svc. award West Bergen Mental Health Ctr., 1991, NYU Presdl. medal, 1994, Sci. and Edn. award Boy Scouts Am., 1993. Fellow Am. Anthrop. Assn.; mem. Am. Sociol. Assn., Am. Assn. Higher Edn., Coun. on Liberal Arts and Scis. (chair 1990-93), Am. Coun. on Edn. Commn. On Internat. Edn. (chair 1991-93), Global Kids, Inc., Higher Edn. Colloquium (chmn. 1982-84, 96-98), N.J. Assn. of Coll. and Univs. (chair 1991-92), Bucknell U. Alumni Assn. (bd. dirs. 1971-80, pres. 1976-78, Outstanding Achievement 1991), Indian Trail Club, Phi Kappa Psi, Phi Kappa Phi. Office: Adelphi U Garden City NY 11530

SCOTT, ROBERT ELLIS See ROBERTS, MARK

SCOTT, ROBERT HAYWOOD, JR., lawyer; b. Hazelton, Pa., Mar. 27, 1941; s. Robert Haywood and Marjorie Jane (Briggs) S.; m. Sandra Lou Carroll, June 6, 1966; children: Paige Carroll, Robert Haywood. AB magna cum laude, Kenyon Coll., 1963; JD with distinction, Duke U., 1966. Bar: Mo. 1969, Kans. 1966, Ohio 1972. Assoc. Hoskins King Springer McGannon and Hahn, Kansas City, Mo., 1970-72; operating v.p., sr. counsel Federated Dept. Stores, Cin., 1972-83; ptnr. Roberts Fleischaker & Scott, Joplin, Mo., 1983-88; chief exec. officer W&S Mfg., Inc., Joplin, 1988-92, also chmn. bd. dirs.; CEO Robert Scott Investment Banking, 1988—; chmn. Deep Sea Archaeology Rsch. Coun., 1994—. Contbr. articles to profl. jours. Served to capt. USAF, 1966-70. Mem. Mo. Bar Assn., Order of the Coif, Phi Beta Kappa. Republican. Episcopalian. Home: 1330 Valle Dr Joplin MO 64801-1074

SCOTT, SIDNEY BUFORD, financial services company executive; b. Richmond, Va., Mar. 3, 1933; s. Buford and Mary (Nixon) S.; m. Susan Elder Bailey, Sept. 19, 1959; children: Sidney Buford Jr., Elizabeth Scott Cech, George Reily Bailey. Student, Yale U., 1951-53; BA, U. Va., 1955; LLD (hon.), St. Paul's Coll., 1982. Chmn. Scott & Stringfellow Inc., Richmond, 1974—; bd. dirs. Ethyl Corp.; mem. regional firms adv. com. N.Y. Stock Exch., 1982-85; chmn. bd. trustees Securities Industry Found. for Econ. Edn., 1976-86; trustee Va. Retirement Sys., 1984-94; dir. Nat. Coun. Econ. Edn. Bd. dirs. Atlantic Rural Expn., Hollywood Cemetery, Police Benevolent Assn., Richmond Renaissance, Va.; trustee, chmn. Elk Hill Farm, Inc.; bd. visitors U. Va., 1987-94; former vice rector, bd. visitors Va. Commonwealth U.; past chmn. United Way Greater Richmond; vestryman, past sr. warden St. Paul's Episcopal Ch.; bd. dirs., past pres. Sheltering Arms Hosp; past bd. dirs., v.p. Big Bros. Am.; past bd. dirs., chmn. Big Bros. Richmond, Met. Found., also others. Sgt. U.S. Army, 1956-58. Recipient Outstanding Young Man of Yr. award Richmond Jr. C. of C., 1964, outstanding svc. award Va. Coun. on Econ. Edn., 1976, 80, Brotherhood award NCCJ, 1981, George P. Baker medal Joint Coun. on Econ. Edn., 1986, Bd. Mem. of Yr. award Va. Assn. Children's Homes, 1987. Mem. Securities Industry Assn. (governing coun. 1976-78), Raven Soc., Beta Gamma Sigma. Democrat. Home: 4919 Lockgreen Cir Richmond VA 23226-1748 Office: PO Box 1575 Richmond VA 23218-1575

SCOTT, STANLEY DEFOREST, real estate executive, former lithography company executive; b. Hudson County, N.J., Nov. 2, 1926; s. Stanley DeForest and Anne Marie (Volk) S.; m. Mary Elizabeth Hazard, Dec. 30, 1953. BA, U. So. Calif., 1950. Gen. mgr. Alfred Scott Pubs., N.Y.C., 1951-56; chmn., pres. S.D. Scott Printing Co., Inc., N.Y.C., 1956-92; gen. ptnr. 145 Hudson St. Assocs.; co-chmn. mus. and art com. Fraunces Tavern Mus., 1973-87, chmn., 1998; assoc. J. Carter Brown Libr.; former mem. Mayor's Industry Adv. Com.; former bd. dirs., Bus. Relocation Com. With USNR, 1944-46. Frick Collection fellow. Mem. Soc. Mayflower Descs., Soc. Colonial Wars, Pilgrims U.S., S.R. (bd. mgrs. 1969—, treas. 1972-73, 3d v.p. 1975-77, 2d v.p. 1977-79, 92-94, 96-98), Am. Numismatic Soc., English-Speaking Union U.S. (patron), Royal Oak Found., Am. Assocs. Royal Acad. Arts, Am. Friends English Heritage, Am. Friends of the Brit. Mus. (patron), Sir John Soane's Mus. Found. (patron), Met. Mus. Art, Mus. Modern Art, Morgan Libr., Am. Mus. in Brit. (coun. 1986—), N.Y. Hist. Soc., Mt. Vernon Ladies Assn. (adv. com), Grolier Club, Knickerbocker Club, Union Club, Downtown Athletic Club, The Church Club of N.Y., Merchants Club (v.p. 1985-94). Republican. Episcopalian. Home: One Sutton Pl South New York NY 10022-2471 Office: 145 Hudson St New York NY 10013-2103

SCOTT, STEPHEN GREGORY, telecommunications company executive; b. Bklyn., Oct. 28, 1956; s. James and Frances S.; m. Margaret R. Narleski, Jan. 14, 1978; two children. AAS, County Coll. Morris, 1982; BS, Thomas Edison State Coll., 1990. Rsch. asst. ITT Rayonier, Whippany, N.J., 1977-79; sales rep. Metro. Life Ins. Co., Morristown, N.J., 1979-81; tutor County Coll. Morris, Randolph, N.J., 1981-82; tech. assoc. Bell Tel. Labs., Morristown, N.J., 1982-86; sr. tech. assoc. AT&T Bell Labs., Whippany, 1986-91; MIS dir. Star Semicondr., Warren, N.J., 1991-92; cons. Pinkerton Computer Cons., Iselin, N.J., 1992-95; tech. staff mem. AT&T, Holmdel, N.J., 1995-98; regional svc. mgr. AT&T, Middletown, N.J., 1998—. Mem. IEEE, Assn. Computing Machinery, Sys. Adminstrs. Guild, KC. Office: D1-2B25 200 S Laurel Ave Middletown NJ 07748-1914

SCOTT, STEVEN JAMES, purchasing engineer; b. Iowa Falls, Iowa, July 28, 1955; s. James Harold and Ann (Hauberg) S.; m. Pamela Jane, Apr. 7, 1984; children: William Steven, Rachel Elizabeth. BS in mech. engring., U. Ill., Champaign, 1977; MBA, U. Iowa, 1984. Registered profl. engr., Ill.; cert. purchasing mgr., Ill. Coop. engr. Deere & Co., Moline, Ill., 1975-77, engr., 1977-84, sr. engr., 1984-88, mgr., 1988-89, team leader, 1999—. E-mail: scottstevenj@johndeere.com. Home: 1326 25th Ave Moline IL 61265-5203 Office: Deere & Co 1 John Deere Pl Moline IL 61265-8010

SCOTT, STUART L., real estate company executive; b. Montreal; s. David George and Jean (Lothian) S.; m. Anne O'Laughlin, Nov. 26, 1982; children: Alexis L., Sarah Scott Tornes, Charity A., Fiona L., Christopher G., Phoebe B. BA in Enlish Lit., Hamilton Coll., 1961; JD, Northwestern U., 1964. Atty. SEC, 1964-66; sr. v.p., asst. to chmn., bd. dirs. Arthur Rubloff & Co., 1966-73; pres. Equity Assocs., Inc. div. LaSalle Ptnrs., Inc., Chgo., 1973-75; pres. LaSalle Ptnrs., Inc., Chgo., 1975-90, co-chmn., 1990-92, chmn., CEO, 1992-99; chmn., CEO Jones Lang LaSalle Inc., Chgo., 1999—; bd. dirs. Hartmarx Corp., LaSalle Hotel Properties. Bd. dirs. Rehab. Inst. Chgo., chmn. 8 yrs.; charter trustee Hamilton Coll., Clinton, N.Y.; trustee Lyric Opera Chgo. Named Real Estate Exec. of Yr. 1998, Comml. Property World. Mem. Chgo. Club, Econ. Club Chgo., Comml. Club Chgo., Old Elm Club. Office: Jones Lang LaSalle Inc 22 Hanover Sq London W1A 2BN, England

SCOTT, SUSAN, research demographer; b. Liverpool, Eng., Oct. 20, 1953; d. William Francis Scott and Alice Carr. BA, Liverpool John Moores U., Eng., 1990; PhD, Liverpool U., 1995. Admissions officer Sch. Biol. Scis. U. Liverpool, 1971—. Author: Human Demography and Disease, 1998, Biology of Plagues, 2000; contbr. articles to sci. jours. Fellow Royal Soc. Arts.; mem. Inst. Biology. Avocations: family history, reading, painting. Office: Liverpool U Sch Biol Scis, Derby Bldg, Liverpool L69 3BX, England

SCOTT, THOMAS GORDON, chemistry educator, writer; b. Laconia, N.H., Nov. 27, 1941; s. William Stafford and Jeanne Richardson Scott; m. Elizabeth Mary Winterberg, Mar. 11, 1995. AB, U. Pa., 1963; BA with honours, Cambridge (Eng.) U., England, 1965, MA, 1970; PhD, U. Ill., 1969. Profl. tchg. cert., Pa. Tchg. asst. U. Ill., Champaign-Urbana, 1965-66; asst. prof. chemistry Oberlin (Ohio) Coll., 1969-70; lectr. biochemistry U. Calif., Santa Barbara, 1971; cons. Sci-Math Cons., Uniontown, Pa., 1972-75; supr. secondary studies Westminster Acad., Carmichaels, Pa., 1975-79; asst. prof. chemistry Alderson-Broaddus Coll., Philippi, W.Va., 1981-84; assoc. prof. chemistry Bryan Coll., Dayton, Tenn., 1984-86, Knoxville (Tenn.) Coll., 1987-89, Union Coll., Barbourville, Ky., 1989-91, Jarvis Christian Coll., Hawkins, Tex., 1992-98; with Chem. Edn. Cons. USA, Hawkins, Tex., 1998-2000; instr. math. Winona (Tex.) Ind. Sch. Dist., 1998-99; instr. math Pittsylvania County (Va.) Schs., 2000—; rsch. assoc. DuPont Chem. Co., Inc., Phila., 1963, EPA, Phila., 1988, Edgewood-Aberdeen Rsch. U.S. Army, Aberdeen Proving Ground, Md., 1993; vis. prof. La. Coll., Pineville, 1992; cons. with Transition State Assocs., Danville, Va.; adj. assoc. prof. biology Danville C.C., Va., 1999—. Author: (with others) Synthetic Procedures in Nucleic Acid Chemistry, 1968, Spectroscopic Model Studies of NAD, 1969; contbr. articles to Jour. Am. Chem. Soc., 1967, 1970, 1972. Thouron fellow John R.H. Thouron Found., 1963-65; grantee NSF, 1996-97, Army Rsch. Orgn., 1993-95, Robert A. Welch Found., 1996-98. Mem. Am. Chem. Soc., Cambridge U. Chem. Soc., Am. Sci. Affiliation (dir. 1998), Rotary Internat. (chmn. internat. edn. com. 1977-81). Avocations: kayaking, exploring ideas, swimming competitively, Renaissance music (treble and tenor blockflute), astronomy. Office: Transition States Assocs USA 281 Golden Ln Sutherlin VA 24594-2010

SCOTT, WILLIAM CORYELL, medical executive; b. Sterling, Colo., Nov. 22, 1920; s. James Franklin and Edna Ann (Schillig) S.; m. Jean Marie English, Dec. 23, 1944 (div. 1975); children: Kathryn, James, Margaret; m. Carolyn Florence Hill, June 21, 1975; children: Scott, Amy Jo, Robert. AB, Dartmouth Coll., 1942; MD, U. Colo., 1944, MS in OB/GYN, 1951. Cert. Am. Bd. Ob-Gyn., 1956, 79, Am. Bd. Med. Mgmt., 1991. Intern USN Hosp., Great Lakes, Ill., 1945-46, Denver Gen. Hosp., 1946-47; resident Ob-Gyn St. Joseph's Hosp., Colo. Gen. Hosp., Denver, 1946-51; practice medicine specializing in Ob-Gyn Tucson, 1951-71; assoc. prof. emeritus U. Ariz. Med. Sch., Tucson, 1971—; v.p. med. affairs U. Med. Ctr., Tucson, 1984-94. Contbr. articles to med. jours. and chpt. to book. Pres. United Way, Tucson, 1979-80, HSA of Southeastern Ariz., Tucson, 1985-87; chmn. Ariz. Health Facilities Authority, Phoenix, 1974-83. Served to capt. USNR, 1956-58. Recipient Man of Yr. award, Tucson, 1975. Fellow ACS, Am. Coll. Ob-Gyn, Pacific Coast Ob-Gyn Soc., Ctrl. Assn. of Ob-Gyn; mem. AMA (coun. on sci. affairs 1984-93, chmn. 1989-91), Am. Coll. Physician Execs., Ariz. Med. Assn. Republican. Roman Catholic. Avocations: golf, gardening, photography. Address: HC 1 Box 923 Sonoita AZ 85637-9705

SCOTT, WILLIAM RAYMOND, accountant, financial director; b. United Kingdom, Jan. 7, 1948; s. William Chalmers and Margaret Ellen S.; m. Janet Scott, Feb. 5, 1994: children: Lauren, Amanda, Helen. BSc, U. Edinburgh, Scotland, 1969. Apprentice Touche Ross & Co., Edinburgh, 1969-73; cost acct. Tullis Russell & Co., Markinch, Fife, Scotland, 1973-74; mgmt. acct. Tate & Lyle Ltd., London, 1974-78; fin. dir. Mutual of Omaha Ins. Internat. Ltd., London, 1978-86; sr. cons. KPMG, Leicester, Eng., 1986-87; fin. dir. Walsh UK Ltd., Loughborough, Eng., 1987-92, Walsh Europe, Brussels, Belgium, 1992-93; gen. mgr. Walsh Italia, Milan, Italy, 1993-98; fin. dir. Source Internat., Loughborough, 1987—, Omnibus Sys. Ltd., Loughborough, Eng., 1998—; lectr. Bus. Studies De Montfort U., Leicester, Eng., 1986. Mem. Inst. Chartered Accts. Scotland. Mem. Conservative Party. Mem. Salvation Army. Avocations: athletics, fell running, skiing, reading. Office: Omnibus Sys Ltd, Stanford House, Leics Loughborough LE12 5PY, England

SCOTT-BUCZAK, ALMA, human relations executive; b. Phila., May 29, 1952; d. Thomas Harrison Scott and Georgia Belle Neal; m. William Myron Buczak, July 2, 1983; 1 child, Derrick. AB in Econs., Lafayette Coll., 1974; MA in Human Resources Mgmt., New Sch. U., 1987. Rsch. analyst Pfizer, N.Y.C., 1974-75, mgr. human rels., 1981-89, dir. human rels., 1989—; ops. analyst Fed. Res. Bank of N.Y., N.Y.C., 1975-76, mgmt. recruiter, 1976-78, supr. compensation and benefits, 1978-81. Mem. adv. panel to bd. trustees Lafayette Coll., Easton, Pa.; bd. advisors New Sch., N.Y.C.; v.p. bd. dirs. Coun. on Adoptable Children, N.Y.C.; dir. religious edn. Victory Tabernacle FBH Ch., Teaneck, N.J. Named Nlack Achievers in Industry, Harlem YMCA, 1989; Lubin scholar New Sch., 1987. Mem. NAFE. Republican. Avocations: family activities, working with youth, reading. E-mail: almascottbuczak@aol.com. E-mail: scotta@pfizer.com. Fax: 201-886-8073. Office: Pfizer Inc 235 E 42nd St New York NY 10017-5755

SCOTT-CARROLL, KEVIN MICHAEL, conference interpreter; b. Shipley, Yorkshire, Eng., July 29, 1951; s. Kevin Scott-Carroll and Eileen Mary Jordan; m. Theresa Jacqueline Scott, Jan. 1975. BA, London Sch. Econs., 1974. firefighters diploma, Dale Carnegie diploma. Employee export dept. Colibri, London, 1974; employee Export Co., France, 1974-77; conf. interpreter Assn. Internat. des Interprhtes de Confirence, Paris, 1977—; advisor CCAQ, UN, Geneva, Switzerland, 1999; regional treas. AIIC-France, Paris, 1997—. Author glossaries: Oil Pollution Glossary, 1986, Computer Generated Imagery, 1984. Mem. Internat. Assn. Conf. Interpreters (regional treas. 1997—). Conservative. Roman Catholic. Avocations: VFR pilot, archaeology. E-mail: kscottcarroll@compuserve.com. Home and Office: Blue Sky Navigators, 2 rue Albert Camus, 75010 Paris France

SCOULAR, ROBERT FRANK, lawyer; b. Del Norte, Colo., July 9, 1942; s. Duane William and Marie Josephine (Moloney) S.; m. Donna V. Scoular, June 3, 1967; children—Bryan T., Sean D., Bradley R. B.S. in Aero. Engring., St. Louis U., 1964, J.D., 1968. Bar: Mo. 1968, Colo. 1968, N.D. 1968, U.S. Supreme Ct. 1972, Calif. 1979. Law clk. to chief judge U.S. Ct. Appeals (8th cir.), 1968-69; ptnr. Bryan, Cave, McPheeters & McRoberts, St. Louis, 1969-89; mng. ptnr. Bryan, Cave, McPheeters & McRoberts, Los Angeles, 1979-84, exec. com., 1984-85, sect. leader tech., computer and intellectual property law, 1985-89; ptnr. Sonnenschein, Nath, Rosenthal, Chgo., 1990—; mng. ptnr. Sonnenschein, Nath, Rosenthal, L.A., 1990—, mem. policy and planning com., 1995—; co-leader intellectual property practice, 1990-98; dir. Mo. Lawyers Credit Union, 1978-79. Contbr. articles to profl. jours. Bd. dirs. St. Louis Bar Found., 1975-76, 79; bd. dirs., vice chmn. L.A. Area Coun. Boy Scouts Am.; league commr. Am. Youth Soccer Orgn.; mem. alumni coun. St. Louis U., 1979-82; hon. dean Dubourg Soc. Recipient Nat. Disting. Eagle Scout award. Mem. ABA (nat. dir. young lawyers div. 1977-78), Am. Judicature Soc., Bar Assn. Met. St. Louis (v.p. 1978-79, sec. 1979, chmn. young lawyers sect. 1975-76), Los Angeles County Bar Assn., Assn. Bus. Trial Lawyers, Calif. Bar. Assn., Mo. Bar (chmn. young lawyers sect. 1976-77, disting. svc. award), Computer Law Assn., Fed. Bar Assn., Dubourg Soc. (hon. dean). Home: 1505 Lower Paseo La Cresta Palos Verdes Peninsula CA 90274-2066 Office: Sonnenschein Nath & Rosenthal 601 S Figueroa St Ste 1500 Los Angeles CA 90017-5720

SCOZZARI, ALBERT, portfolio manager, inventor; b. Chgo., BA, Northeastern Ill. U., 1973; MPA, Ill. Inst. Tech., 1974; PhD, Columbia Pacific U., 1986. Cons. World Bank Group, 1987-99; adj. prof. bus. studies. Ill. Inst. Tech., 1975, Columbia Pacific U., 1986; artist-in-residence Ariz. Coun. Fine Arts, 1999. Author: Mass Communications in Politics, 1978, Managing for Effectiveness, 1986, Management in the 90s, 1990, Vietnam Faces, 1995, Field Cross, 1996, The Mountain, 1997, The Trail, 1997, A Collection of Verses and Poems, 1997. Pres. Homeowners Assn., Phoenix, 1992-96, Scozzari Meml. Scholarship Fund, 1991—. With USNR, 1961-66, ret. ANG, 1979-87. Mem. Am. Fedn. Musicians (life), Assn. Stage and Film Actors (life), Am. Poets and Writers Guild (life), Am. Mensa Assn. (life), Vietnam Vets. Am. (life), Adventurers Club. (life). Home: PO Box 7445 Chula Vista CA 91912-7445

SCRIBA, JOHANNES HERMANN, academic dean; b. Inadi, Natal, Republic of South Africa, Jan. 25, 1938; s. Friedrich Heinrich and Emma (Schmidt) S.; m. Maria Katharina Stern, Sept. 1, 1962; children: Hermann, Hans, Ernst. BA, U. South Africa, 1965, BA with honors, 1971; Diploma, Saasveld Coll., Republic of South Africa, 1958; MA cum laude, Stellenbosch U., Republic of South Africa, 1984. Forestry lectr. Swartkop Forestry Sch., Republic of South Africa, 1958-68; forester dept. forestry Republic of South Africa, 1969-72; forestry lectr. Saasveld Forestry Coll., Republic of South Africa, 1972-80, prin., 1981-85; dir., dean faculty Forestry Port Elizabeth Technikon, George, Republic of South Africa, 1986—; forestry cons. SADC and Commonwealth Secretariat, London, 1996-97; mem. Nat. Forestry Advisory Coun., Minister of Forestry, Republic of South Africa, 1996-98; mem. Found. of Rsch. Devel. Evaluations, Found. for Rsch. Devel., Pretoria, 1995-98. Mem. South African Inst. of Forestry (br. chmn. 1985-86, 96-98). Lutheran. Avocations: Cycad Cultivation, popular articles, photography, family genealogy. Office: Faculty of Forestry/Saasvld, Port Elizabeth Tec/ Boz 1708, 6530 George South Africa

SCRIPPS, DOUGLAS JERRY, music educator, conductor, director; b. Grand Rapids, Mich., Aug. 25, 1942; s. Kenneth Witvoet and Marguerite F. (Rottier) S.; m. Betty Ann Broersma Porter, July 24, 1963 (div. Aug. 1974); children: Elisabeth Ann Scripps Blue, Theodore Jon; m. Merilee Evelyn Collins, Apr. 5, 1975; children: Daniel Collins, Taylor Douglas, Adam Rottier. Student, Eastman Sch. Music, 1961, 62; BA, Calvin Coll., 1965; MM, U. Mich., 1970. Prin. trumpet player Grand Rapids Symphony Orch., 1961-65, assoc. conductor, 1976-85; dir. music Grand Rapids City Coll., 1967-78; conductor Lake St. Clair Symphony, Detroit, 1970-72, Alma (Mich.) Symphony Orch., 1985—; music dir. Grand Rapids Ballet, 1979-99; asst. prof. music Ctrl. Mich. U., Mt. Pleasant, 1981-84; prof. music, dept. chair Alma Coll., 1985—; guest condr. Interlochen Ctr. Arts, Joffrey Ballet, Bay View Music Festival, Blue Lake Fine Arts Camp; vis. prof. Grand Valley State U., Calvin Coll., 1977-81; adjudicator various midwest comps., 1968-95. Am. Heritage Assn. study abroad lectr., Vienna, 1999. Mem. Am. Symphony Orch. League, Internat. Soc. Verdi Studies, Nat. Assn. Schs. Music. Avocations: reading, travel, sailing. Office: Alma Coll 614 W Superior St Alma MI 48801-1511

SCRIVEN, JANE KATHERINE, solicitor; b. Copthorne, Sussex, Eng., Oct. 5, 1959; d. Peter Walter and Elspeth Felecia (Macintosh) Gibbings; m. Simon Charles Guy Scriven, June 13, 1987; children: Harriet Clare, Frederick Charles Guy. LLB, Kings Coll.-London U., 1981. Asst. solicitor Norton Rose, London, 1985-86; comml. mgr. Elders IXL, Hong Kong, 1986-89; strategy and investment mgr. Elders IXL, London, 1989-91; group company sec. Geest PLC, Spalding, Eng., 1991-98, legal and svcs. dir., 1990-98, devel. dir., 1998—; bd. dirs. Kent Property Investments, London. Mem. Law Soc. Avocations: competitive equestrianism, gardening, tennis. Office: Geest PLC, West Marsh Rd, Spalding Lnclnshr, England

SCROGGS, DEB LEE, communications professional; b. Norton, Va., Sept. 27, 1953; d. Jennings Eugene and Edith Marie (Harris) S.; m. John L. Price, Apr. 1, 1984. AAS in Acctg., C.C. of Denver, 1981; BSBA magna cum laude, Regis Coll., 1987; MSS in Applied Comms., U. Denver, 1992. Bookkeeper Am./Trayer, Inc., Bristol, Va., 1972-74; assessment transcriber Dept. of Interior, Bristol, 1974-78; supr. computer asst. Dept. of Labor, Mine Safety and Health Adminstrn., Lakewood, Colo., 1978-82; lead tech. writer OAO Corp., Lakewood, 1982-83; tech. writer, editor Tele-Communications, Inc., Denver, 1984-85, Integrated Svcs., Inc., Aurora, Colo., 1985-87; sr. documentation specialist AT&T Customer Edn. Tng., Denver, 1988-89; sr. project mgr. AT&T Customer Edn. and Tng., Denver, 1989-94; tng. facilitator AT&T Customer Edn. Tng., Denver, 1993-94; resource/dept. mgr. AT&T Customer Edn. & Tng., Whippany, N.J., 1994; customer tng. and info. products tech. svcs. mgr. Lucent Technologies, Whippany, N.J., 1996—. Contbr. articles to profl. jours., publs. Vol. Art Reach of Denver, 1988-94, Channel 6 TV, Denver, 1989-94, Jersey Cares, 1996—; amb. U.S. Citizen Amb. Program's Tech. Comm. Delegation to China, 1995—. Mem. AAUW, Internat. Soc. for Performance Improvement, Soc. Tech. Comm. (Achievement award for user manual 1986, Achievement award for mktg. brochure 1986, Merit award for user manual 1988, spk. nat. conf. 1991, 93, 95-96, 98, networking lunch coord./nat. conf. 1992-95). Avocations: weight training, jogging, golf, reading. Office: Lucent Tech 67 Whippany Rd Rm 14j-323 Whippany NJ 07981-1425

SCRUTON, ROBERT, accountant, management consultant; b. Grimsby, Eng., Apr. 6, 1952; s. George Henry Kirman and Kitty (Van der Vord) Scruton. BSc with honors, U. Kent, Canterbury, Eng., 1973; MSc, Open U., Milton Keynes, Bucks, Eng., 1990. Mgr. Reeves & Neylan, Canterbury, 1973-80, fin. and computer ptnr., 1980-98, chmn., 1995-98; chmn. S.W. Mount and Sons Ltd., Canterbury, 1999—; dir. Jenson Tech Group Ltd., Bristol, Avon, Eng., 1993-2000; external examiner Mid Kent Coll., Chatham, 1993-96; dir. Kent Ambulance NHS Trust. Councilor Womenswold (Canterbury) Parish Coun., 1983-99; coun. mem. Nat. Assn. Local Couns., London, 1992—; v.p. Rural Cmtys. Charity for Eng., Cirencester, Gloucestershire, Eng., 1993—; trustee Canterbury Hosp. Broadcasting Network, Canterbury, 1987-92; commr. Local Govt. Commn. for Eng., London, 1993-98; vice chmn. St. Martin's Emmaus, Dover, 1997—; chmn. Kent Assn. Parish Couns., 1992-94, v.p. 1994-98, pres., 1998—; chmn. Kent Rural Cmty. Coun., 1999—; v.p. Nat. Assn. Local Couns., 1994—. Recipient Silver medal Royal Soc. for Arts, 1970. Fellow Inst. Chartered Accts. in Eng. and Wales; mem. Soc. Trust and Estate Practitioners, London Math. Soc., U. Kent at Canterbury, Inst. of Dirs., Royal Over-Seas League. Avocations: badminton, skiing, flying. Home: 17 Sea View Ave, Birchington CT7 9LU, England Office: Reeves & Neylan, 327 Chelsea Cloisters, London SW3 3EE, England

SCRUTON, ROGER VERNON, aesthetics educator, writer; b. Feb. 27, 1944; s. John and Beryl Clarys (Haynes) S. BA, Cambridge U., 1965, MA, 1967, PhD, 1973. Bar: Inner Temple, 1978. Rsch. fellow Peterhouse, 1969-71; lectr. in philosophy Birkbeck Coll. U. London, 1971-79, reader, 1979-85, prof. aesthetics, 1985-91; prof. U. Boston, 1992-95. Author: Art and Imagination, 1974, The Aesthetics of Architecture, 1979; The Meaning of Conservatism, 1980, From Descartes to Wittgenstein, 1981, Fortnight's Anger, 1981, The Politics of Culture, 1981, Kant, 1982, A Dictionary of

Political Thought, 1982, The Aesthetic Understanding, 1983, (with Baroness Cox) Peace Studies: A Critical Survey, 1984, Thinkers of the New Left, 1985, Sexual Desire, 1986, Untimely Tracts, 1987, The Philosopher on Dover Beach, 1990, Franesca, 1991, A Dove Descending, 1991, Xanthippic Dialogues, 1993, Modern Philosophy, 1994, On Hunting, 1999, Perictone in Colophon, 2000; co-author: Education and Indoctrination, 1985; editor Salisbury Rev., 1982—; contbr. articles to The Times, Guardian, others. Avocations: music, literature, architecture.

SCRUTTON, NIGEL SHAUN, biochemistry educator; b. Batley, U.K., Apr. 2, 1964; s. Donald and Annie Scrutton; m. Nia Roberts, Sept. 9, 1989; children: Samuel David, Victoria Anne, Robert Michael. BS with honors, London U., 1985; PhD, U. Cambridge, Eng., 1988. Rsch. fellow St. John's Coll., U. Cambridge, 1989-92, rsch. fellow, 1991-99; rsch. fellow U. Leicester, U.K., 1991-99; tchg. fellow Churchill Coll., U. Cambridge, 1992-95; lectr. U. Leicester, 1995-97, reader, 1997-99, Lister Inst. rsch. fellow, prof., 1999—; chair molecular enzymology group com. Biochem. Soc. U.K., 1998—; mem. coun. U.K. Biochem. Soc., 1998—; mem. various sci. adv. groups Biotechnology and biol. Scis. Rsch. Coun., U.K. Co-editor: Enzyme Catalysed Electron and Radical Transfers; contbr. over 100 articles to profl. jours. Recipient Henry Humphreys Rsch. prize U. Cambridge, 1989, Colworth medal U.K. Biochem. Soc., 1999. Fellow Royal Soc. Chemistry. Avocations: Victorian college philately, association football. Office: U Leicester Dept Biochem, University Rd, Leicester LE1 7RH, United Kingdom

SCUCCIMARRA, ANTONIO TOMMASO GABRIELE, physician, researcher; b. Pescara, Abruzzo, Italy, June 10, 1948; s. Nicola Antomo Luigi and Santa Aurora Libia (Melchiorre) S.; m. Antonietta Maria Teresa Matone, Aug. 14, 1976; children: Gennaro-Italo-Erik, Valeria Santa, Tommaso Bonaventura. MD, U. Bologna, Italy, 1973. Asst. U. Padova, Italy, 1975-78; chief nueurosurgeon Hosp., Reggio, Italy, 1978-96; mgr. neurosurgery Hosp., Pescara, Italy, 1996—; cons. neurologist USL, Giolatauro, Italy, Tauranova, Italy, ASL, Lanciano, Italy, 1999—. Contbr. articles to profl. jours.; patentee in field. Artilleryman Italian Army, 1974. Mem. SISUM (counsellor 1977-78), SNO, ISNU. Avocation: sculpting. Home: Via Chieti 5i, 65100 Pescara Italy Office: Pvt Study, Via Sirolli 70, 66040 Archi Italy

SCUDDER, CHARLES A., primary and secondary education educator; b. Madison, Ind., Aug. 8, 1916; s. Earl and Laura (Phillips) S.; children: Gary, Sharon, Shirlene. BS, Ctrl. Normal U. Comdr. USN. Mem. Masons. Republican. Baptist. Home: 350 Ponca Pl # 470 Boulder CO 80303-3802

SCUDLA, VLASTIMIL, hematology educator; b. Sternberk, Czech Republic, Feb. 13, 1946; s. Josef and Marie (Sychrova) S.; m. Marie Vecerova Scudla, June 29, 1974; children: Eva, Miroslav. Student, Palacky U. Med. Faculty, Czech Republic, 1963-69. Physician 1st dept. internal medicine Faculty Hosp., Olomouc, Czech Republic, 1970-73, 1st asst., 1973-81, co-chief 1st dept. internat medicine, 1981-87, assoc. prof., 1987-88, prof., 1988—; 1st asst. Palacky U., Olomouc, 1973-81, head 3d dept. internal medicine, 1988—. Author: Vnitrni Lekarstvi, 1985, Folia Haematologica, 1991. Mem. Internat. Soc. Haematology, IGCI, European Soc. Haematology. Avocations: tourist, skiing, classical music. Home: Na Strelnici 38, 77200 Olomouc Czech Republic Office: 3rd Dept Internal Medicine Faculty Hosp, Fac Hosp 3d Dept Int Med, IP Pavlova 6, 77520 Olomouc Czech Republic

SCULFORT, JEAN-LOU, chemistry and physics educator, researcher; b. Liesse, Picardie, France, June 20, 1944; s. Jean and Bernadette (Desson) S.; m. Françoise Hardy, Nov. 12, 1966; 1 child, Philippe. BS, U. Champagne, France, 1966; PhD in Physics, U. Paris, 1972, DSc, 1976. Asst. prof. U. Amiens, France, 1966-76, lectr., 1976-87; lectr. U. Paris, 1983-87; prof. U. Reims, 1987—; cons. C.N.R.S. Lab., Meudon, 1970—. Inventor photo-electrochem. cell; contbr. 80 articles to profl. jours. Served with French Marines, 1970-71. Mem. Am. Electrochem. Soc., France Chem. Soc., Am. Vacuum Soc., France-Swedish Assn., Am. Inst. Physics, I.U.P.A.C., Internat. Photochem. Soc., France Phys. Soc., European Phys. Soc. Avocations: golf, bridge. Email: jean lou.sculfort@wenadoo.fr. Address: Lycee Chrestien de Troyes, 3 Rue de Québec, 10000 Troyes France Office: Inst U Tech, 9 Rue de Quebec, F-10026 Troyes France also: Pole U, Leonard DeVinci, 92916 Paris La Defense Cedex, France

SCULLY, JOHN ROBERT, oral and maxillofacial surgeon; b. N.Y.C., Mar. 2, 1949; s. Frank Edward and Helen Veronica (Sawyer) S.; m. Bonnie Diane Baron, Aug. 28, 1971; children: Amanda Rose, John Robert Jr. BS in Chemistry, Spring Hill Coll., 1970; DDS, Med. Coll. Va., 1974; MS, U. Iowa, 1980. Diplomate Am. Bd. Oral and Maxillofacial Surgery. Resident in oral and maxillofacial surgery U. Iowa, 1977-80; pvt. practice oral and maxillofacial surgery Asheville, 1980—; chief oral and maxillofacial surgery St. Josephs Hosp., Asheville, 1984—, Meml. Mission Hosp., 1984—; cons. Pardee Hosp., Hendersonville, N.C., 1983—; bd. trustees St. Joseph's Hosp. Found.; adv. bd. Sleep Medicine Ctr. Contbr. chpt. to book; also articles to profl. jours. Capt. USAF, 1974-77. USAF Merit scholar, 1972-74. Fellow Am. Coll. Oral and Maxillofacial Surgery, Am. Assn. Oral and Maxillofacial Surgery, Internat. Assn. Oral and Maxillofacial Surgeons; mem. ADA, N.C. Dental Soc., Southeastern Soc. Oral and Maxillofacial Surgeons, N.C. Soc. Oral and Maxillofacial Surgeons, Am. Trauma Soc., Buncombe County Dental Soc., Asheville C. of C., Zebulon Vance Debating Soc., Internat. Platform Assn., Asheville Country Club, Delta Sigma Delta. Avocations: music, rock and folk guitar, dance, tennis, auto racing. Home: 450 N Griffing Blvd Asheville NC 28804-2814 Office: 5 Rockcliff Pl Asheville NC 28801-4510

SCURLOCK, RALPH GEOFFREY, cryogenics educator, consultant; b. Southampton, U.K., Aug. 21, 1931; s. Walter Howard and Linda May (James) S.; m. Maureen Mary Oliver, Aug. 7, 1956; children: Jonathan, Robin, Timothy, Alexander. BA, Oxford (Eng.) U., 1954, MA, DPhil, 1957. Chartered engr. Lectr. dept. physics U. Southampton, 1959-66, sr. lectr. dept. physics, 1966-68, reader dept. physics, 1968-85, dir. Inst. Cryogenics, 1979-96, prof. cryogenic engring., 1985-96, emeritus prof., 1996—; chmn. Brit. Cryogenics Coun., London, 1979-82, 91-94; vice chmn. Internat. Cryogenic Engring. Com., 1988-90, 98—; exch. visitor Royal Soc., Republic of China, 1979, 87; vis. lectr. Inst. Petroleum, Boumerdes, Algeria, 1982, Korea Gas Corp., 1992; cons. prof. Sian Chiao-Tung U., Republic of China, 1985—; cons. Boc, Oxford Instruments, AERE, others; hon. chmn. Czech Internat. Cryogenic Com. Author: Low Temperature Behaviour of Solids, 1966, History and Origins of Cryogenics, 1993; editor Cryogenic Monographs; adv., editor (periodical) Cryogenics; contbr. over 200 articles to profl. jours. Chmn. Parent's Assn., Southampton, 1968-78; trustee Residents Gardens Trust, Southampton, 1992—; gov. King Edward VI Sch., Southampton, Bedales Sch., Petersfield. Recipient Samuel C. Collins award for outstanding contbns., 1999. Fellow Instn. Mech. Engrs., Inst. Physics. Achievements include 10 patents in field; notable rsch. findings in vapour cooled shields, convective behaviour of cryogenic liquids in large scale storage, liquid helium behaviour in large diameter rotors at 3000 RPM, frostproof and cryogenic concretes, cold electronic instrumentation, engineering of ceramic superconductors. Avocations: music, ballet, tennis, gliding. Home: 22 Brookvale Rd, Southampton S0171QP, England

SCUTAREANU, PETRU GAVRIL, biologist, researcher; b. Malini, Romania, June 23, 1931; arrived in The Netherlands, 1990, naturalized, 1995.; s. Gavril and Ecaterina (Iacob) S.; m. Viorica A. Hutu, July 10, 1955 (div. 1973); 1 child, Calin. Diploma in engring., U. Brasov, Romania, 1955; diploma qualified population dynamics, Internat. Agrl. Ctr., Wageningen, The Netherlands, 1972; PhD in Entomology, Acad. Agrl. Forest Sci., Bucharest, Romania, 1977. Forest chief diplomat engr. Dept. of Forestry, Campulung, Romania, 1955-58; prin. scientific rschr. Forest Rsch. Inst., Bucharest-Cluj, Romania, 1958-90; guest rsch. scientist U. Amsterdam, The Netherlands, 1991—; cns. specialist forest protection Forest Rsch. Sta., Cluj, 1960-90; assoc. prof. Agronomic Inst., Cluj, 1982-88. Contbr. articles to profl. jours. With Romanian Army, 1953, 55. Fellow Royal Entomol. Soc.; mem. Internat. Union Forest Rsch. Orgns.-Working Party, Netherlands Entomol. Soc., European Entomol. Soc. Avocations: classical music, travel, museum. Office: U Amsterdam Sect Pop Biol, Kruislaan 320, 1098 SM Amsterdam The Netherlands

SCZAKIEL, GEORG ALOIS, biochemist; b. Kaiserslautern, Germany, July 7, 1956; s. Johannes and Friederike (Nadler) S.; m. Jutta Schmitt, Dec. 16, 1988; children: Henrike-Lisa, Julian-Mathias. Diploma in chemistry, U. Freiburg, Germany, 1983; PhD, Max-Planck-Inst., Heidelberg, Germany, 1986. Rschr. Max-Planck-Inst., 1986; rschr. German Cancer Rsch. Ctr., Heidelberg, 1987-93, head ind. group, 1994-2000; co-founder and CEO A3D GmbH Antisense Design & Drug Devel.; prof., dir. Inst. Molecular Medicine U. Lübeck, Germany, 2000—; lectr. theoretical medicine U. Heidelberg, 1993-2000; scientist Nat. Inst. Biosci. and Human Tech., Tsukuba, Japan, 1994, NIH, Tokyo, 1996; mem. editl. bd. Antisense and Nucleic Acid Drug Development, 1995—; chmn. Gene Therapy Network, Heidelberg, 1996-2000; project leader Steinbeis-Transferzentrum for genome informatics, Heidelberg; founder DGS Cons. Editor: Advances in Hematopoietic Stem Cell Transplantation and Molecular Therapy, 1997; contbr. over 75 articles to profl. jours.; patentee in field. Mem. German Assn. Chemistry, European Working Group on Human Gene Transfer and Therapy, Assn. Biol. Chemistry. Avocations: vineyard owner, wine prodr. Office: Lubeck Inst Mol Medicine, Ratzeburger Allee 160, D-23538 Lubeck Germany

SCZUDLO, WALTER JOSEPH, lawyer; b. Fairbanks, Alaska, May 28, 1953; s. Walter and Dolores J. Sczudlo; children: Lauren Hall, Elizabeth Fairbanks, Walter Christopher; m. Rebecca Grey Tucker, Mar. 8, 1996. AB, Middlebury Coll., 1975; JD, Golden Gate U., 1979; LLM, Georgetown U., 1987; postgrad., U. Calif., Santa Barbara, 1972, Tulane U., 1971-72, Vt. Law Sch., 1976-77. Bar: Alaska 1979, Calif. 1980, D.C. 1986, U.S. Ct. Appeals (9th cir.) 1980, U.S. Ct. Appeals (D.C. cir.) 1986, U.S. Dist. Cts. (no., cen., ea. and so. dists.) Calif., U.S. Dist. Ct. Alaska, U.S. Ct. Claims, U.S. Tax Ct. Law clk. to presiding justice Alaska Supreme Ct., 1978-79; assoc. atty. Merdes, Schaible, Staley and Delisio, Anchorage, 1979-82; legis. dir., gen. counsel U.S. Senator Murkowski, Washington, 1982-84; sr. tax assoc. Schramm and Raddue, Santa Barbara, Calif., 1984-85; dir. congl. rels., counsel Natural Gas Supply Assn., Washington, 1985-88; Washington counsel Shell Oil Co., 1988-96; v.p., Washington counsel Intercontinental Energy Corp., 1996-99; gen. counsel, vice pres. pub. affairs and comms. Nat. Soc. Fund Raising Execs., Washington, 1999—; prin. ptnr. WEBK Broadcasting 105.3 FM, Killington, Vt., 1985—; dir. Sun's Edge, Inc., Santa Barbara, 1987—, Natural Gas Roundtable, Washington, 1987—. Author: (with other) Washington Legal Foundation, 1988. Com. chmn. Steve Cowper for Gov., Anchorage, 1982. Recipient Am. Jurisprudence award Bancroft-Whitney Pub. Co., 1978. Roman Catholic. Avocations: mountaineering, cross-country skiing, tennis. Home: 6700 Loring Ct Bethesda MD 20817-3148 Office: NSFRE 1101 King St Ste 700 Alexandria VA 22314-2944

SEAB, CHARLES GREGORY, astrophysicist; b. Ft. Benning, Ga., May 26, 1950; s. James A. and Ruby (Jones) S.; m. Peggy R. McConnell, May 9, 1979; 1 child, Jenna R. McConnell-Seab. BS in Physics, La. State U., 1971, MS in Physics, 1974; PhD in Astrophysics, U. Colo., 1982. Engring. analyst, programmer Mid. South Svcs., New Orleans, 1974-77; NRC rsch. assoc. NASA Ames Rsch. Ctr., Mountain View, Calif., 1983-85; rsch. scientist U. Calif., Berkeley, 1985, Va. Inst. Theoretical Astronomy, Charlottesville, 1985-87; vis. asst. prof. U. New Orleans, 1987-89, asst. prof., 1989-91, assoc. prof. astrophysics, 1991-96; prof., 1996—; bd. dirs. Freeport McMoran Obs., New Orleans, 1991—. Author: Astronomy, 1994, Study Guide for Universe, 1997; contbr. articles to profl. jours., chpts. to books. Capt. USAR, 1971-80. Nat. Merit scholar, 1967-71. Mem. Am. Astron. Soc., Astron. Soc. Pacific, Pontchartrain Astronomy Soc., Planetary Soc., Phi Kappa Phi, Sigma Pi Sigma. Avocations: amateur astronomy, tennis. Office: U New Orleans Physics Dept Lakefront Frnt New Orleans LA 70148-0001

SEABRA LOPES, LUIS FILIPE DE, engineering educator; b. Sangalhos, Portugal, May 28, 1967; s. Américo L. Cândido and Maria Helena R. de Seabra. Licenciado, U. Nova Lisboa, Portugal, 1990; postgrad., U. Nova Lisboa, 1992-97. Rschr. U. Nova Lisboa, 1990-91; tchr. Inst. Nat. Adminstrn., 1990-96; asst. prof. U. Aveiro, Portugal, 1997-98; auxiliar prof. U. Aveiro, 1998—. Contbr. articles to profl. jours. Mem. IEEE, Appia, Assn. Portuguesa Casas Antigas, Assn. Portuguesa Rosa (founding). Roman Catholic. Avocations: history, archeology. Home: Sao Joao Azenha, 3780 Anadia Portugal Office: Dept Elec Telecomm, Univ Aveiro, 3810 Aveiro Portugal

SEACHRIST, WILLIAM EARL, holding company executive; b. Columbia, Pa., Jan. 31, 1931; s. Simon Earl and Madelyn Grace (Stiger) S.; m. Marjorie Leone Raab, June 20, 1953; children: Frederick, Sibyl, David, Eric, Marjorie. AB in Polit. Sci., Franklin and Marshall Coll., 1952; M of Govt. Adminstrn., U. Pa., 1958. City mgr. City of Ridgway, Pa., 1958-62; pres. Kent (Ohio) Industries, Inc., 1966-82; pres., prin. W.E. Seachrist Assocs., Lancaster, Pa., 1967-83; pres. Seachrist Real Estate, Kent, 1968-83; pres., chief exec. officer Tekcore, Inc., Hudson, 1982—, also bd. dirs.; pres., CEO Adventek Corp., Hudson, 1982-89; chmn., CEO, Prodex, Inc., Hudson, 1987-94, also bd. dirs.; chmn., Brandywine Internat. Ltd., also bd. dirs., 1995; adj. instr. Franklin & Marshall Coll., Kent State U.; chmn. bd. Adventek Corp., Hudson, 1989—. Author: The Role of the State Planning Agency, 1953; contbr. articles to profl. jours. Cons. State of Pa., Harrisburg, 1959-61; bd. dirs. United Fund, Kent, 1963; sr. warden Episcopal Ch., Kent, 1972; trustee, overseer Franklin and Marshall Coll., Lancaster, Pa., 1972—, chmn. bd. trustees; chmn. bd. Hourglass Found., 1999—; bd. dirs. Pa. Acad. Music, Lancaster Symphony. Served to lt. USN, 1953-57. Recipient Alumni Disting. Service Medal award Franklin and Marshall Coll., 1984; Fels fellow U. Pa., 1953. Mem. Am. Acad. Polit and Social Sci., Acad. Polit. Sci., Soc. Plastic Engrs., N.Y. Acad. Scis., Internat. City Mgrs. Assn., Nat. Assn. Scholars, Akron City Club, Lancaster Country Club, Hamilton Club, Penn. Club, Masons, Beta Alpha Psi. Republican. Avocations: reading, music. E-mail: wseachrist@aol.com.

SEADLER, STEPHEN EDWARD, business and computer consultant, social scientist; b. N.Y.C., 1926; s. Silas Frank and Deborah (Gelbin) S.; children: Einar Austin, Anna Carin; m. Christine J. Majewski, Dec. 1, 1998. AB in Physics, Columbia U., 1947, postgrad. in atomic and nuclear physics, 1947; postgrad. with George Gamow in relativity, cosmology, and quantum mechanics, George Washington U., 1948-50. Electronic engr. Cushing & Nevell, Warner Inc., N.Y.C., 1951-54; seminar leader, leader trainer Am. Found. for Continuing Edn., N.Y.C., 1955-57; exec. dir. Medimetric Inst., 1957-59; mem. long range planning com., chmn. corporate forcasting com., mktg. rsch. dir. W.A. Sheaffer Pen Co., Ft. Madison, Iowa, 1959-65; founder Internat. Dynamics Corp., Ft. Madison and N.Y.C., 1965, pres., 1965-70; originator DELTA program for prevention and treatment of violence, 1970; founder, pres. ID Ctr., Ft. Madison, now N.Y.C., 1968—; mgmt. cons. in human resources devel. and conflict reduction, N.Y.C., 1970-73; pres. UNICONSULT computer-based mgmt. and computer scis., N.Y.C., 1973-76; speaker on decision support systems, internat. affairs and ideological arms control; author/speaker (presentation) Holocaust, History and Arms Control; originator social sci. of ideologics and computer based knowledge systems sci. of ideotopology; spl. works collection accessible via On-line Computer Lib. Ctr. Instr. polit. sci. Ia. State Penitentiary, 1959-62; guest speaker on radio and television. Author: Holocaust, History and Arms Control II, 1990; contbr. Ideologics and ideotopology sects. to Administrative Decision Making, 1977, Societal Systems, 1978, Management Handbook for Public Administrators, 1978, Statement on ideological arms control in Part 4 of Senate Fgn. Rels. Com. hearing on Salt II Treaty, 1979, Principia Ideologica: A Treatise on Combatting Human Malignance, 1999; Ideologics Extended to treat ethnic, racial, religious conflict, 1992, with first call for Abrahamic Reformation at Morristown N.J. Unitarian Ch., 1993; contbr. articles to profl. jours. Served with AUS, 1944-46. Recipient 20th Century Achievement Award medal Internat. Biographical Ctr., U.K., 1995; named to The Wisdom Hall of Fame by The Wisdom Soc., 1997. Mem. IEEE, Am. Phys. Soc., Am. Statis. Assn., Acad. Polit. Sci., N.Y. Acad. Scis., Am. Sociol. Assn., Am. Mgmt. Assn. (lectr. 1963-68), Fgn. Policy Assn., Forum on Physics and Soc., Union of Concerned Scientists, Scottish Rite, Shriners. Unitarian. Office: 521 5th Ave Ste 1700 New York NY 10175-0003

SEAFORD, JOHN NICHOLAS, clergyman, dean; b. Middlesbrough, Eng., Sept. 12, 1939; s. Nicholas and Kathleen (Longbotham) S.; m. Helen Marian Webster, Aug. 2, 1967; children: Nicholas, Charles, Katherine. BA, Durham (Eng.) U., 1967, diploma in theology, 1968. Ordained to ministry Anglican Ch., 1968. Curate St. Mark's Ch., London, 1968-71, St. Luke's Ch., Winchester, Eng., 1971-73; vicar Chilworth and North Baddesley, Hampshire, Eng., 1973-78, Highcliffe and Hinton Admiral, Dorset, Eng., 1978-93; rural dean Christ Ch., Dorset, 1988-93; rector St. Helier Ch., Jersey, Channel Islands, 1993—; dean of Jersey, 1993—. Mem. States of Jersey. Fax: (01534) 617488. Home and Office: The Deanery, David Pl, Saint Helier Jersey JE2 4TE, Channel Islands

SEAGER, DAUNA GAYLE OLSON-STOKES, speech therapist; b. Logan, Utah, Sept. 22, 1925; d. Helmar Alexander and La Rena Barnes (Jones) Olson; m. Arch Jr. Stokes, Aug. 5, 1943 (dec. Apr.il 1970); children: Jeffrey David, John Phillip, Jeannette; m. Floyd W. Seager, July 7, 1973 (dec. Oct. 1996). AS, Weber State U., 1964; BS, Utah State U., 1969, MS in Audiology Speech Pathology, 1969. X-ray ech., physician asst. Robins X-Ray, Ogden, Utah, 1946-52; asst. to supt. Lyman (Wyo.) Pub. Schs., 1952-60; clinic supr. Utah State U., Logan, 1965-69; speech, language, hearing therapist Weber/Davis Sch. District, Ogden, Farmington, Utah, 1969-73, various, Utah, 1970-90; co-founder, coord. Clinic at O.R.M., Ogden, Utah, 1988—; bd. dirs. Weber County DUP Mus., Ogden. Author: Pioneer Settlers, 1990; contbr. articles to profl. jours. Co-founder Seager Indigent Clinic, Ogden Mission, Utah, 1988—; organized Stroke Club for Families of CVA Support Group, Ogden, 1972-74, Stroke Unit St. Benedict's Hosp., Ogden, 1972-74, Parent Child Tchr. Group, Ogden, 1970-73; mem. Ogden Sesquicentennial Com., OgSesqui, 2000—, Weber County Sesquicentennial, 2000; co-chair Ogden Mayor's Cemetery Enhancement Commn. Fellow Utah State U., Logan, 1967-68, 68-69. Mem. Aglaia Club, Altrusa Internat., Weber Far South Ctr. Co., Weber County Women's Legis. Coun. and Rep. Women, Fedn. Ogden Bus. Profl. Women Internat., Ogden Mayors Project (Cemetery Com., Sesquicentennial Com.), DAR, Daus. of Utah Pioneers. Mem. LDS Ch. Avocations: historian/lecturer, writer, golfer, bridge, swimmer, ballroom dance instr. Home and Office: 4046 South 895 East Ogden UT 84403-2416

SEAGLE, J. HAROLD, lawyer; b. Marion, N.C., May 9, 1947; s. Rufus James and Alma Rhoda (McMahan) S.; m. Linda Jean Cranford, June 3, 1967; 1 child, James Mark. BA, U. N.C., 1973, JD, 1977. Bar: N.C. 1977, U.S. Dist. Ct. (ea., middle, w. dists.) N.C. 1977, 88, 92; U.S. Ct Appeals (4th cir.) 1982; U.S. Supreme Ct. 1982. Assoc. atty. Rountree & Newton, Wilmington, N.C., 1977-79; ptnr. Rountree & Seagle, L.L.P., Wilmington, N.C., 1979—; past pres. Fifth Jud. Dist. Bar. Bd. trustees and bd. deacons Winter Park Baptist Ch.; past moderator Wilmington Baptist Assn.; bd. dirs. Rescue Mission of Cape Fear; past adv. Bd. Coastal Bioethics Network; past chmn. annual fund drive Am. Cancer Soc.; past sect. chmn. Cape Fear United Way. Mem. New Hanover County Bar Assn. (co-chair grievance com.), N.C. Bar Assn., N.C. State Bar, N.C. Acad. Trial Lawyers, N.C. Coll. of Advocacy, Southeastern Admiralty Law Inst. (officer), Maritime Law Assn. of U.S. (proctor), N.C. Bar Coun. of Pres., Wilmington Inns of Ct. (exec. com., master). Avocations: acoustic guitar, motorcycle racing. Office: Rountree & Seagle LLP 2419 Market St Wilmington NC 28403-1135

SEAGULL, KEITH ALLEN, lawyer; b. Milw., Apr. 19, 1957; s. Louis and Helen Ann S.; m. Asma Parveen, Nov. 20, 1994; 1 stepchild, Samia; 1 child, Sasha Y.; BS, U. Wis., Milw., 1977; JD, Southwestern U., L.A., 1981; cert. atendance, Cambridge U., 1981. Bar: Calif. 1990; cert. specialist workers' compensation State Bar Calif. Bd. Legal Specialization. Law clerk Law Offices Steven M. Hanna, Fullerton, Calif., 1981-85; asst. office mgr. Joe Kay Design & Constrn., Fullerton, Calif., 1985-89; adjuster Wausau Ins., Pasadena, Calif., 1989-90; atty., adjuster Springfield Ins., Covina, Calif., 1990-91; atty. Law Offices Rose, Klein & Marias, L.A., 1991, Stephen G. Krutzsch & Assocs., ITT Hartford Ins., Brea, Calif., 1991-94, Law Office James Max Stewart, Temecula, Calif., 1994-95; prin. Law Offices Keith A. Seagull, Pomona, Calif., 1995—. Mem. ABA, Calif. Applicants' Attys. Assn., Eastern Bar Assn. L.A. County, Masons. Avocations: sailing, scuba diving, walking, music, politics. Home: 4920 Toronto Ave Fontana CA 92336

SEAL, JOHN S., JR., manufacturing company executive; b. Phila., May 20, 1944; s. John S. Sr. and Gertrude Eva (Abbott) S.; m. LoriAnn LaBonte; children: Kathryn, Ashley and Kristen (twins), Heather, Stephen, Spencer, Mackenzie, Riley. BS in Econs., Drexel U., 1967; MBA, Dartmouth Coll., 1971. CPA, N.Y. Asst. to exec. v.p. fin. Gould Inc., Chgo., 1971; dir. electronics group fin. planning Gould Inc., Newton Upper Falls, Mass., 1972-73; pres., treas., CEO Nat. Comms. Industries Co., Greenwich, Conn., 1973-76, chmn., 1973-79; exec. v.p. Boyerton (Pa.) Burial Casket Co., 1976-77; v.p., gen. mgr. comms. products divsn. FSC Corp., Pitts., 1977-79; sr. v.p. Butcher and Singer Inc. subs. Butcher and Co. Inc., Phila., 1979-85; pres. Sovereign Group Inc. subs. Butcher and Co. Inc., Phila., 1983-85, Seal Devel. Co., Phila., 1985-88; mng. dir. Essex Fin. Group, Phila., 1988-97; CFO telecoms. Spiraduct, Inc., Montgomeryville, Pa., 1997-00; bd. dirs. RTG Svcs., Inc., 1992—, Rittenhouse Sq. Fitness Club, Phila., 1983-89. Trustee Please Touch Mus., Phila., 1987-90; bd. dirs. alumni bd. Drexel U., Phila., 1983-92. With U.S. Army, 1967-68. Mem. AICPA, N.Y. Soc. CPAs, Conn. Soc. CPAs. Republican. Mem. Ch. of Christ. Club: Union League (Phila.). Avocations: helicopter pilot, boating, traveling. Fax: (561) 741-7875. Home: 18210 SE Ridgeview Dr Tequesta FL 33469-8124 Office: Spiroduct Inc 170 Keystone Dr Montgomeryville PA 18936-9637

SEAMAN, ARLENE ANNA, retired musician, educator; b. Pontiac, Mich., Jan. 21, 1918; d. Roy Russell and Mabel Louise (Heffron) S. BS, life cert., Ea. Mich. U., 1939; MMus, Wayne State U., 1951; postgrad., Colo. Coll., 1951-52, Acad. Music, Zermatt Switzerland, 1954, 58, U. Mich. guest conductor Shepherds and Angels, Symphonie Concertante, 1951; asst. conductor Detroit Women's Symphony, 1960-68; adjudicator Mich. State Band and Orch. Festivals, Solo and Ensemble Festivals, 1950-70, Detroit Fiddler's Band Auditions, 1948-52, Mich. Fedn. Music Clubs, 1948-55; tchr. Ea. Mich. U., 1939-42, Hartland Sch. Music, 1939-42, Pontiac (Mich.) Pub. Schs., 1942-45, Detroit Pub. Schs., 1945-73, pvt. studio, 1973-90. Performer cello South Oakland Symphony, 1958-65, Detroit Women's Symphony, 1951-68, Riviera Theatre Orch., 1959, 60, Masonic Auditorium Opera, Ballet Seasons, 1959-65, Toledo Ohio Symphony, 1963-70, others; performer trumpet Detroit Brass Quartet, 1974-78; piano accompanist various auditions, recitals, solo and ensemble festivals; composer: Let There Be Music, 1949, Fantasy for French Horn and Symphonic Band, 1951. Mem. Quota Internat., Delta Omicron. Home: 14650 N Alamo Canyon Dr Tucson AZ 85737-8812

SEAMAN, DARYL KENNETH, oil company executive; b. Rouleau, Sask., Can., Apr. 28, 1922. BSME, U. Sask., 1948, LLD (hon.), 1982; LLD (hon.), U. Calgary, 1993. Cert. mech. engr. CEO Bow Valley Industries Ltd., Calgary, Alta., Can., 1962-70, 85-91, chmn., chief exec. officer, 1970-82; chmn. Box Valley Industries Ltd., Calgary, Alta., Can., 1982-85; pres. Bow Valley Industries Ltd., Calgary, Alta., Can., 1985-87; chmn. Bow Valley Industries Ltd., 1991-92; bd. dirs. Tetonka Drilling Inc., Far West Mining Ltd., Renaissance Energy Ltd., Calgary, Potash Corp. Sask. Inc., Encal Energy Ltd., CCR Techs. Ltd., Pure Techs. Ltd., Alta. Basic Industries Ltd. (formerly known as Basic Industries Corp.), Bow Valley Energy Ltd.; co-owner, bd. dirs. Calgary Flames Hockey Club; chmn., pres. Dox Investments, Inc. Mem. Royal Commn. Econ. Union and Devel. Prospects for Can., 1982-85; active numerous coms. for fundraising U. Sask.; hon. chmn. The Western Heritage Centre Soc.; chmn. nat. adv. com. Banff Sch. Mgmt. Served with RCAF, 1941-45, North Africa, Italy. There is no repetition since it is indicated as an award you received and as a membership. Mem. Assn. Profl. Engrs., Geologists and Geophysicists (hon. life, Frank Spragins award, 1985, McGill Mgmt. Achievement award, 1979), Order of Canada 1993, Western Heritage Centre Soc., Ranchmen's Club, RAF Club, Earl Grey Golf Club, Calgary Petroleum Club, Calgary Golf and Country Club, U. Calgary Chancellor's Club. Progressive Conservative. Mem. United Ch. Can. Avocations: ranching, golf, hunting, skiing. Home and Office: Dox Investments Inc 500 333 5th Ave SW, Calgary, AB Canada T2P 3B6

SEAMAN, GERALD ROBERTS, musicology educator, writer; b. Leamington Spa, Eng., Feb. 2, 1934; arrived in N.Z., 1965; s. Leslie Roberts and Lilian Alice (Heath) S.; m. Lorna Vivien Johnston, Dec. 21, 1964 (dec. 1993); children; Julia (dec. 1997), Cleone; m. Katherine Helena Fairchild, Apr. 28, 1995. BA, Oxford (Eng.) U., 1957, MA, DPhil, 1962. Lectr. music Nottingham (Eng.) Tchrs. Tng. Coll., 1962-64; temp. lectr. musicology U. Western Australia, 1964-65; sr. lectr. musicology U. Auckland, New Zealand,

1965-69, assoc. prof., 1970-98; free-lance lectr., writer, 1999—; tchr. Liverpool U., 1999, Oxford and Surrey U., 2000; past sr. assoc. St. Antony's Coll., Oxford, 1972—. Author: History of Russian Music, 1968, Orchestral Scores, 1984, Rimsky-Korsakov, 1988. With Royal Navy, 1952-54. Mem. Internat. Assn. Music Librs. (pres. N.Z. br. 1981-82, 90-93), Am. Musicological Soc., Brit. Soc. for 18th Century Studies, Royal Mus. Assn., Internat. Musicological Soc., Royal Commonwealth Soc. Mem. Conservative Party. Anglican. Avocations: languages, travel. Office: St Antonys Coll, Oxford OX2 6JF, England

SEAMAN, JEROME FRANCIS, actuary; b. Oak Park, Ill., Nov. 4, 1942; s. William Francis and Bernice Florence (Haughey) S.; m. Jacquelyn Ann Robinson, Aug. 22, 1970; children: Carolyn, John. BA, U. Notre Dame, 1964; MA, Northwestern U., 1991. Asst. actuary Combined Ins. Co. of Am., Chgo., 1966-73; v.p., actuary United Equitable Life Ins. Co., Skokie, Ill., 1975-77; mgr. Peat Marwick Mitchell & Co., Chgo., 1973-75, 77-78; nat. dir. actuarial svcs. Arthur Young & Co., Chgo., 1978-83; pres., cons. actuary Jerome F. Seaman & Assocs., Northfield, Ill., 1983—; dir. Polysystems, Inc., Chgo., 1987-91. Contbr. articles to profl. jours. Recipient Commendation for Svc. Pres. Ronald Reagan, 1982. Fellow Soc. of Actuaries, Conf. of Cons. Actuaries; mem. Am. Acad. Actuaries (task force on risk based capital health orgns. 1993-95). Democrat. Unitarian Universalist. Avocations: hiking, classical music, opera, baseball. Home: 2107A Sherman Ave Evanston IL 60201-6116 Office: Jerome F Seaman & Assocs 2107 A Sherman Ave Evanston IL 60201-6116

SEAMANS, ANDREW CHARLES, editorial and public relations consultant, columnist, author; b. Hillside, N.J., Sept. 10, 1937; s. Thomas Randall and Marie Josephine (Mazur) S.; m. Marion Gloria Lufbery, Aug. 25, 1956 (div. June 1986); children: Andrew Charles, Darryl Wayne, Marion Gloria Seamans Raynor, Dawn Louise. AS cum laude, No. Va. Community Coll., Annandale, 1989. Lic. real estate salesman, Va. Editorial writer U.S. Press Assn., McLean, Va., 1968-70; pub. rels. asst. Nat. Right to Work Com., Washington, 1970; assoc. editor Human Events, Washington, 1970-81; mng. editor Heritage Features Syndicate, Washington, 1981-91; syndicated columnist The Answer Man Creators Syndicate, L.A., 1985—; chief copy editor The Hill Newspaper, Washington, 1996—; bd. dirs., pub. rels. cons. Marine Learning Inst., St. Louis, 1980—. Author: Who, What, When, Where, Why In the World of American History, 1991, Who, What, When, Where, Why In the World of World History, 1991, Who, What, When, Where, Why In the World of Nature, 1992; co-author: Whose FBI?, 1974. Bd. dirs. McLean Little League Baseball, Inc., 1975-83, pres., 1982-83; pres. Rahway (N.J.) Young Rep. Club, 1964-66; chmn. platform com. Union County Young Reps., N.J. Young Reps., various other Rep. orgns. Recipient cert. of appreciation McLean Little League Baseball, 1978, named to Hall of Fame, 1985. Mem. Pub. Rels. Soc. Am., Soc. Profl. Journalists (bd. dirs. D.C. chpt. 1986-87, membership dir. 1986-87, 89-90, dir. pub. info. 1988), No. Va. Assn. Historians, Va. Hist. Soc., Internat. Platform Assn., Nat. Press Club. Episcopalian. Home and Office: Horizon House 603 1300 Army Navy Dr Arlington VA 22202-2054

SEAMANS, ROBERT CHANNING, JR., astronautical engineering educator; b. Salem, Mass., Oct. 30, 1918; s. Robert Channing and Pauline (Bosson) S.; m. Eugenia Merrill, June 13, 1942; children: Katherine (Mrs. Louis Padulo), Robert Channing III, Joseph, May (Seamans Baldwin), Daniel M. BS, Harvard U., 1939; MS, MIT, 1942, ScD, 1951; grad. exec. program bus. adminstrn., Columbia U., 1959; DSc, Rollins Coll., 1962, NYU, 1967; DEng, Norwich Acad., 1971, Notre Dame U., 1974, Rensselaer Poly. Inst., 1974, U. Wyo., 1975, George Washington U., 1975, Lehigh U., 1976, Thomas Coll., 1980, Curry Coll., 1982. Successively instr. dept. aero. engring., staff engr. instrumentation lab., asst. prof., project leader instrumentation lab., asso. prof. Mass. Inst. Tech., 1941-55; chief engr. Project Meteor, 1950-53, dir. flight control lab., 1953-55; mgr. airborne systems lab., chief systems engr. airborne systems dept. RCA, 1955-58, chief engr. missile electronics and controls div., 1958-60; asso. adminstr. NASA, 1960-68, dep. adminstr., 1965-68, cons., 1968-69; vis. prof. MIT, 1968, Hunsaker prof., 1968-69; sec. air force, 1969-73; pres. Nat. Acad. Engring., 1973-74; adminstr. ERDA, Washington, 1974-77; Henry R. Luce prof. environment and pub. policy MIT, 1977-84, sr. lectr. dept. aeros. and astronautics, 1984-96, dean Sch. Engring., 1978-81; mem. sci. adv. bd. USAF, 1957-62, assoc. adviser, 1963-67. Bd. overseers Harvard U., 1968-74; trustee Mus. Sci., Boston, Sea Edn. Assn.; trustee emeritus Nat. Geog. Soc., Carnegie Inst., Washington, Woods Hole Oceanographic Inst. Recipient naval ordnance devel. award 1945, Godfrey L. Cabot award Aero Club New Eng., 1965, disting. svc. medal NASA, 1965, 69, Robert H. Goddard meml. trophy, 1968, disting. pub. svc. medal Dept. Def., 1973, exceptional civilian svc. award Dept. Air Force, 1973, Gen. Thomas D. White U.S. Air Force Space Trophy, 1973, Ralph Coats Roe medal ASME, 1977; achievement award Nat. Soc. Profl. Engrs., Thomas D. White Nat. Def. award, 1980, exceptional svc. award Dept. Air Force, 1985. Fellow Am. Acad. Arts and Scis., Am. Astron. Soc., IEEE, AIAA (hon., Lawrence Sperry award 1951); mem. Internat. Acad. Astronautics, Am. Soc. Pub. Adminstrn., Nat. Acad. Engring. (Arthur M. Bueche Award, 1994, Daniel Guggenheim award 1996), AAAS, Air Force Acad. Found., Fgn. Policy Assn., Coun. on Fgn. Rels., Sigma Xi. Clubs: Harvard (Boston); Manchester Yacht (Mass.); Essex County (Mass.); Chevy Chase, Metropolitan (Washington); Cruising of Am. (Boston Sta.).

SEARA, INES MARTINS, business executive; b. Waterbury, Conn., Feb. 9, 1958; d. Sicuerio Santos and Maria Arlete (Fiel) Martins; m. Fernando Roberedo Sera, Jan. 8, 1983; 1 child, Alexandre. Degree in econs., U. Catolica, Lisbon, 1982; MBA, U. Nova, Lisbon, 1983. Tchr. U. Internacional, Lisbon, 1984-87; mem. tech. staff ANEOP, Lisbon, 1984-87; dir. Banco ESSI, Lisbon, 1987-94; mng. dir. M. Central P. Mos, Porto de Mos, 1994—. Mem. AMBA, Assn. Ant. Arunos U. Catolica, Am. Club. Office: Marmores Ctrl de Porto Rem, Manjozo Porto de Mos, 2480 Porto de Mos Portugal

SEARLE, EDWARD, retired analytical chemist; b. Herne Bay, Kent, U.K., Oct. 9, 1940; s. Edward Charles and Doris Evelyn (Tilley) S. BSc in Spl. Chemistry, London U., 1964, PhD in Organic Chemistry, 1967. Chartered chemist. Asst. chemist UKAEA, Harwell, U.K., 1960-61; chemist BDH Ltd., London, 1967-70; sr. chemist William Ranson & Son, Ltd., Hitchin, U.K., 1970-73; chemist Sterling Winthrop Ltd., Newcastle Upon Tyne, U.K., 1974-75; mgr. London Underground Ltd., 1975-93; tech. advisor to London Underground Ltd. PHDS Ltd., London, 1993-94, ret., 1994. Contbr. articles to profl. jours. Mem. Royal Soc. Chemistry. Avocations: amateur radio, travel, video photography. Home: 203 Church Rd, Earley, Reading RG6 1HW, England

SEARLE, ROBERT FERGUSON, minister; b. Auburn, N.Y., July 13, 1951; s. Loren Rawson and Esther Lucille (Ferguson) S. BS, Cornell U., 1973; MDiv, Princeton Theol. Sem., 1977; cert. pastoral care, Gordon D. Hoople Inst., Syracuse, N.Y., 1981; DMin, Asbury Theol. Sem., 1997. Ordained deacon United Meth. Ch., 1978, ordained elder, 1980. Cln. pastoral edn. Ancora Psychiat. Hosp., Hammonton, N.J., 1977; cln. pastoral educator Bethany Med. Ctr., Kansas City, Kans., 1977-78; pastor of Blodgett Mills Freetown and McGraw (N.Y.) United Meth. Ch., 1978-84; pastor Pennsylvania Ave. United Meth. Ch., Pine City, N.Y., 1984-98; chaplain resident Duke U. Med. Ctr., 1998-99; chaplain U.S. Army Res., 1991—; pastor Clyde United Meth. Ch., 1999—; mem. bd. Ordained Ministry, Syracuse, N.Y., 1980-84, mem. conf. bd., 1980-85, dist. youth dir., Syracuse, 1981-84; mem. Cortland County Youth Bur., 1980-81; mem. hosp. com. Cortland County Coun. of Chs., 1980-84. Mem. McGraw Bd. Edn., 1981-84; bd. dirs. Meals on Wheels, Elmira, 1985-88; bd. dirs. CPC, Elmira, 1985-93; mem. edn. and rsch. instl. rev. bd. Arnot Ogden Hosp., Elmira, 1995-98; mem. cmty. bd. Southport Correctional Facility, 1987-98; spiritual dir. Spiritual Exercises, 1986-98, 99—, Walk to Emmaus, Rome, N.Y., 1993. Mem. Am. Assn. Christian Counselors, Charles Wesley Soc., Marathon Lodge #438, Royal Arch Mason (Elmira chpt. # 42), Royal and Select Masters (So. Tier coun. # 16), Knights Templar (St. Omers Commandery # 19). Republican. Avocations: reading, exercise, travel, music. Home: 5905 Draper St Wolcott NY 14590-1148

SEARLE, ROGER CLIVE, geophysicist educator; b. St. Ives, Huntingdon, U.K., Oct. 24, 1944; s. Eric Thomas and Marjorie Emily Louise (Evenden) S.; m. Margery Joan McGuckin, Sept. 27, 1969; children: Rupert, Ben, Jonathan. BA, Cambridge U., U.K., 1966, MA, 1970; PhD, Newcastle Upon Tyne, U.K., 1969. Asst. prof. Haile Sellassie I U., Addis Ababa, Ethiopia, 1970-73; sr. sci. officer Inst. Oceanographic Scis., Wormley, U.K., 1973-78, prin. sci. officer, 1978-88, sr. prin. sci. officer grade 6, 1988-89; prof. geophysics U. Durham, U.K., 1989—; vis. scientist Scripps Instn. of Oceanography, San Diego, 1982-83; chmn. Nuclear Energy Agy. Seabed Working Group, 1981-83, Interridge Internat. Rsch. Programme, 1994-96. Contbr. numerous rsch. papers to profl. publs.; editor Marine Geophys. Researches, 1986-92. Com. mem. Natural Environment Rsch. Coun., Swindon, U.K., 1985-88, 92-97. Grantee Natural Environment Rsch. Coun., 1989—, NSF, 1990-92, European Community, 1988-90, 96-98; Royal Soc. Maurice Hill fellow, 1982, Sir Derman Christopherson rsch. fellow Durham U., 1996-97; named NATO Sr. Scientist, 1982. Fellow Royal Astron. Soc. (London); mem. Am. Geophys. Union. Avocation: listening to music, hill-walking, cooking, reading, theatre. Office: Dept Geol Scis, South Rd, Durham DH1 3LE, England

SEARLES, EDNA LOWE, artist, illustrator; b. Minden, La., Sept. 10, 1936; d. Prentiss W. Lowe; m. Thomas D. Searles; children: Dan, Laura, Carol, Prentiss. AA, Mont. Coll., 1975; BA in Edn., La. Poly., 1958. Tchr. pub. sch. La. & Ga., 1958-65; guest curator Delaphine Visual Art Ctr., Frederick, Md., 1995, East Meets West. Illustrator: Soy for the 21st Century, 1984, ABC Coloring Book 1994, Mind Children, 1995, Mind Travel, 1998, About You, 1998, Choose Life, 2000; one-woman shows include Arnot Art Mus., Elmira, N.Y., 1988, Va. Tech State U., 1989, Gwinnett Coun. of the Arts Gallery, Ga., 1990, VA Honorarium, 1990, Janice Aldridge Gallery, Georgetown, Washington, 1996, Sculpture on the Ground, Md., 1994, 99, The Artist's Gallery, Frederick, Md., 1997—, The Garden Gallery, Carlisle, Pa., 1999—, Nancy Stamm's Galleria, Carlisle, Pa., 1999, Millinneum Exhibit Music for the Eyes, 1999-00, Musicians and All that Jazz, Frederick, Md., 2000, Gallery of Modern Masters, Olney, Md., 2000—. Past pres. Clarksburg (Md.) Comty. Assn. Recipient Juror's award for painting Montgomery County Art, 1993, Internat. Gold medal for painting Academia Italia, 1973; named Wilson Wims Citizen of Yr. Clarksburg Comm. Assn., 1974. Mem. DAR (Pleasant Plains of Damascus chpt.), Nat. League of Am. Pen Women (past pres. Chevy Chase chpt.). Methodist. Avocations: hammered dulcimer, harp, piano, composing music.

SEARLES, THOMAS DANIEL, society administrator; b. New Orleans, Aug. 6, 1937; s. Eugene Harve and Mary Louise (Swan) S.; m. Edna Winifred Lowe, Mar. 10, 1956; children: Thomas Daniel II, Laura Louise, Carol Gay, Prentiss Eugene. BS, La. Tech. U., 1960; postgrad., Montgomery Coll. Field rep. So. Pine Inspection Bur., Pensacola, Fla., 1960-65, Am. Lumber Std. Com., Germantown, Md., 1965-70; pres. Am. Lumber Std. Com., Germantown, 1970—; U.S. rep. to lumber com., UN ECE, Geneva, 1974-82; appointee to Industry Sector Adv. Com., Sec. Commerce, Washington, 1986—, Industry Functional Adv. Com., Sec. Commerce, Washington, 1986—. Vice pres. Clarksburg (Md.) Community Assn., 1988. Mem. Am. Soc. Assn. Execs., Standard Engring. Soc., Greater Washington Soc. Assn. Execs. Republican. Methodist. Office: Am Lumber Standard Com PO Box 210 Germantown MD 20875-0210

SEARS, JOHN WINTHROP, lawyer; b. Boston, Dec. 18, 1930; s. Richard Dudley and Frederica Fulton (Leser) S.; m. Catherine Coolidge, 1965 (div. 1970). AB magna cum laude, Harvard U., 1952, JD, 1959; MLitt, Oxford U., 1957. Bar: Mass. 1959, U.S. Dist. Ct. Mass. 1982. Rep. Brown Bros. Harriman, N.Y.C., 1959-63, Boston, 1963-66; mem. Mass. Ho. Reps., 1965-68; sheriff Suffolk County, Mass., 1968-69; chmn. Boston Fin. Commn., 1969-70, Met. Dist. Commn., 1970-75; councilor-at-large Boston City Coun., 1980-82; trustee Sears Office, Boston, 1975—. Contbr. articles to profl. jours. Apptd. bd. dirs. Fulbright Scholarship, 1991-93; trustee Christ's Ch., Longwood, Brookline, Mass., 1965—, Sears Trusts, Boston, 1975—; hon. trustee J. F. Kennedy Libr., 1991—; bd. dirs. Am. Mus. Textile Heritage, 1987-97, Shirley-Eustis Assoc., Environ. League, Mass., 1994-97; Rep. candidate Sec. State, Mass., 1978, Gov. of Mass., 1982; vice chmn. Ward 5 Rep. Com., 1965-69, 75-85; chmn. Rep. State Com., 1975-76, mem., 1980-85; del. Rep. Nat. Conv., 1968, 76, State Conv., 1966-92; mem. U.S. Electoral Coll., 1984; bd. dirs. United South End Settlements, 1966—, chmn., 1977-78. Lt. comdr. USNR, 1952-54, 61-62. Recipient Outstanding Pub. Servant award Mass. Legis. Assn., 1975; Rhodes scholar, 1955. Mem. Mass. Bar Assn., New Eng. Hist. and Geneal. Soc. (bd. dirs., councillor 1977-82), Mass. Hist. Soc., Handel and Haydn Soc. (gov. 1982-87), Signet Soc., Boston Atheneum, Tennis and Racquet Club, Somerset Club, The Country Club (Brookline), St. Botolph Club, Wednesday Evening Club of 1777, Thursday Evening Club of 1846 (pres. 1999), Spee Club (Cambridge chpt., pres., trustee), Phi Beta Kappa. Republican. Home: 7 Acorn St Boston MA 02108-3501

SEARS, SANDRA LEE, computer consultant; b. Rochester, N.Y., Apr. 25, 1952. AB with distinction, Cornell U., 1974; MA, U. Conn., 1976, postgrad., 1976-81. Cert. in data processing. Tng. cons. Ins. Crime Prevention Inst., Westport, Conn., 1977-78; systems analyst Data Directions, Bloomfield, Conn., 1978-79; prin. S. S. Prindle Consulting, Manchester, Conn., 1979-81; dir. info. svcs. Conn. Attys. Title Ins., Rocky Hill, Conn., 1981-85; mgr., systems, programming Community Health Care Plan, Inc., Wallingford, Conn., 1985-87; assoc. dir. Mass. Mutual Life Ins., Springfield, Mass., 1987-91; cons. mgr. Coopers & Lybrand Cons., East Hartford, Conn., 1991-96; dir. info. architecture and data warehousing CIGNA Healthcare, Bloomfield, Conn., 1996-97; divsn. dir. advanced devel. solutions divsn. Advanced Computing Techniques, Glastonbury, Conn., 1997-98; practice dir. data warehousing and knowledge mgmt. PRT Group, Inc., Windsor, Conn., 1998-99; sr. mgr. KPMG Cons., Hartford, 1999—; adj. faculty U. New Haven, West Haven, Conn., 1976-77, Eastern Conn. State U., Willimantic, 1986—, Manchester C.C., 1989—; participant Tex. Instruments' Case Satellite Seminar, 1989. Mentor Career Beginnings, Hartford, 1991-95. Presdl. scholar Nat. Merit Program, 1970, William Stout scholar Cornell U., 1973, AAUW fellow U. Conn., 1981. Mem. Cornell Club of Greater Hartford (mem. admissons vol. programs alumni adv. com., exec. bd., book award chair 1987—), Cornell Alumni Admissions Amb. Network (chair 1983-86), Mortar Board, Phi Kappa Phi, Pi Mu Epsilon. Office: KPMG LLP City Place II Hartford CT 06103-4103

SEARS, WILLIAM REES, engineering educator; b. Mpls., Mar. 1, 1913; s. William Everett and Gertrude (Rees) S.; m. Mabel Jeannette Rhodes, Mar. 20, 1936; children—David William, Susan Carol. BS in Aero. Engring, U. Minn., 1934; Ph.D., aeronautics, Calif. Inst. Tech., 1938; DSc (hon.), U. Ariz., 1987. Asst. prof. Calif. Inst. Tech., 1939-41; chief aerodynamics Northrop Aircraft, Inc., 1941-46; dir. Grad. Sch. Aero. Engring., Cornell U., Ithaca, N.Y., 1946-63; dir. Center Applied Math., 1963-67, J.L. Given prof. engring., 1962-74; prof. aerospace and mech. engring. U. Ariz., Tucson, 1974-88, prof. emeritus, 1988—; F. W. Lanchester lectr. Royal Aero. Soc., 1973, Gardner lectr. MIT, 1987, Guggenheim lectr. Internat. Congress Aero. Scis., 1988; cons. aerodynamics. Author: The Airplane and its Components, 1941, Stories from a 20th-Century Life, 1994; editor: Jet Propulsion and High-Speed Aerodynamics, vol. VI, 1954, Jour. Aerospace Scis., 1956-63, Ann. Revs. of Fluid Mechanics, Vol. I. Recipient Vincent Bendix award Am. Soc. Engring. Edn., 1965, Prandtl Ring Deutsche Gesellschaft für Luft- und Raumfahrt, 1974, Von Karman medal AGARD (NATO), 1977, ASME medal, 1989, NAS Award in Aeronautical Engrng Nat. Acad of Sciences, 1995; named to Ariz. Aviation Hall of Fame, 1996. Fellow AIAA (hon., G. Edward Pendray award 1975, S.A. Reed Aeros. award 1981, Von Karman lectr. 1968, Daniel Guggenheim medal 1996); mem. NAE, NAS, Am. Acad. Arts and Scis., Nat. Acad. Engring. Mex. (fgn.), Am. Phys. Soc. (Fluid Dynamics prize 1992). Home: Santa Catalina Villas 8202 7500 N Calle Sin Envidia Tucson AZ 85718-7300

SEARSON, JOHN ERIC, stockbroker; b. Ripley, Derbys, Eng., July 10, 1929; s. Eric and Grace Edwick (Chamberlain) S.; m. Daphne Elizabeth Ridgway, June 20, 1953; 1 child, Fiona. 1st honors ceramics, Staffordshire U., Stoke-on-Trent, Eng., 1952. Works mgr. Associated Clay Industries, Horwich, Lancs, Eng., 1952-57; gen. mgr. ceramics Lilleshall Co., Telford, Eng., 1957-62; mng. dir. Searson Masonry, Birmingham, Eng., 1962-67, C.A.E.C. Howard, Bedford, Eng., 1967-72; exec. Ed Bates, London, 1972-74; ptnr. Searson Assocs., Birmingham, 1974-85; dir. Devel. Capital Group, Birmingham, 1983-85; ptnr. Harris Allday Lea & Brooks, Birmingham, 1985-93, Brook Corp. Fin., Birmingham, 1993—; dir. Oakland Elevators Ltd., Leicester. Chmn. South Staffordshire Conservative Assn., 1981-84, West Staffordshire and Congleton Conservative European Assn., Stafford, 1994-99. Capt. Royal Arty., 1947-52. Named Mem. Brit. Empire, Her Majesty the Queen, 1992. Fellow Inst. Materials; mem. Securities Inst., Chartered Inst. Mktg., Inst. Clay Tech. Conservative. Avocations: private pilot, golf, bridge, travel. Office: Brook Corp Fin Ltd, 33 Great Charles St, Birmingham B3 3JN, England

SEARY, LAWRENCE ANTHONY, cinematographer, news assignment editor; b. N.Y.C., June 13, 1951; m. Phyllis Cole, Oct. 2, 1976; children: Tara Ann, Paul Anthony. BFA, NYU, 1973. News cameraman, assignment desk supr., prodr. NBC, N.Y.C., 1974—. Bd. dirs. Believe in Me Found. Recipient N.Y. State Broadcast award UPI, 1987. Mem. NATAS (bd. govs. 1996-2000, Emmy award nominations 1978, 82, 94, 95, Emmy award 1978), N.Y. Press Photographers Assn., Mensa, N.Y. Press Club (bd. trustees, Feature Video award 1994). Democrat. Roman Catholic. Office: NBC 30 Rockefeller Plz Rm 728E New York NY 10112-0002

SEASE, LYNN D., mortgage company executive; b. L.A., Mar. 24, 1943; d. Stephen Francis O'Donnell and Janice Audrey Redmond-Flanagan; m. Gerald W. Couch, July 15, 1960 (div. 1961); 1 child, Stephen Wayne Couch; m. Dewayne Sease, July 1, 1970 (div. May 1976); children: Brian Douglas Sease, Jason Patrick Sease. Grad. h.s., L.A. Pres. Miracle Mortgage, Inc., Denver, 1994—. E-mail: lsease@sprintmail.com. Office: Miracle Mortgage Inc 1842 S Parker Rd Unit 3 Denver CO 80231-2927

SEATON, ALBERTA JONES, biologist, educator, consultant; b. Houston, Dec. 31, 1924; d. Charles Alexander and Elizabeth (Polk) Jones; m. Earle Edward Seaton, Dec. 24, 1947 (dec. Aug. 1992); children: Elizabeth Wamboi, Dudley Charles. BS in Zoology and Chemistry, Howard U., 1946, MS in Zoology, 1947; ScD in Zoology, U. Brussels, 1949. Asst. prof. Spelman Coll., Atlanta, 1953-54; assoc. prof. biology Tex. So. U., Houston, 1954-60, prof. biology, 1960-72, 91-95; adminstr. Ministry Edn., Bermuda, 1973-76; lectr. biology Bermuda Coll., Devonshire, 1976-78; prof. anatomy Sch. Allied Health U. Tex. Health Ctr., Houston, 1979-80; cons. sci. sect. Nat. Inst. Pedagogy Ministry of Edn. Sci., Victoria, Seychelles, 1980-89; head dept. biology Wiley Coll., Marshall, Tex., 1950-51; dir. NSF Summer Sci. Inst. Tex. So. U., 1957-59, gen. studies program, 1970-72, undergrad. and grad. rsch. in biology, 1954-72; mem. Univ. Honors Program Com., Tex. So. U., 1960-70; chair self-study com., Tex. So. U., 1969-71, ednl. policies com., 1968-72; lectr. biology U. Md., USN Air Sta., Bermuda, 1972-78; supr. adminstrn. and budget Office of the Minister Ministry Edn., Bermuda, 1973-76; lectr. in field. Author, editor: Conserving the Environment, Part 1, 1984; editor: Reprints of Agrinews, 1982; co-author, co-editor: Conserving the Environment, Part 2, The Seychelles, 1986, Conserving the Environment, Part 3, Focus on Aldabra, 1991; contbr. articles to profl. jours. Evaluator grant proposals NSF, 1957-72; active regional meetings Com. on Undergrad. Edn. in Biol. Sci., 1967-72, AAC-AAUP confs. on curriculum improvement, 1970-72; chair nurses licensing bd., Hamilton, Bermuda, 1973-75; mem. Endangered Species Com., Hamilton, 1974-77. Postdoctoral fellow Calif. Inst. Tech., Pasadena, 1959-60, NSF postdoctoral fellow Roscoe B. Jackson Lab., Bar Harbor, Maine, 1959, U. Brussels, 1965-66. Mem. AAAS, AAUP (apptd. to ad hoc coms. 1968-71, sec.-treas. Tex. State Conf. 1968-70), AAUW, Am. Assn. Zoologists, Assn. des Anatomistes, Assn. Women in Sci., Tex. Acad. Sci., Beta Kappa Chi, Beta Beta Beta. Episcopalian. Home and Office: 3821 Gertin St Houston TX 77004-6503

SEATON, ANTHONY, environmental and occupational medicine educator; b. London, Aug. 20, 1938; s. Douglas Ronald and Julia (Harrison) S.; m. Jillian Margaret Duke, Apr. 4, 1964; children: Ronald Andrew, Jonathan Edward. BA, Cambridge (Eng.) U., 1956, MB, BChir, 1962, MD, 1972. Asst. prof. medicine U. W.Va., Morgantown, 1969-71; cons. physician Univ. Hosp. of Wales, Cardiff, 1971-77; dir. Inst. of Occupational Medicine, Edinburgh, Scotland, 1978-90; prof. environ. and occupational medicine U. Aberdeen, Scotland, 1988—; chmn. U.K. Dept. Environ. Com. on Air Quality Standards, 1992—; mem. U.K. Dept. Health Com. on Effects of Air Pollution, 1992—. Co-author: Occupational Lung Diseases, 1975, 86, 95, Respiratory Diseases, 1989, 2000, Practical Occupational Medicine, 1994; editor: (jour.) Thorax, 1977-81; contbr. articles to med. jours. Decorated CBE. Fellow Faculty Occupl. Medicine, Royal Coll. Physicians London and Edinburgh, Acad. Med. Scis.; mem. Brit. Thoracic Soc. (pres. 1999). Avocations: opera, keeping fit. Home: 8 Avon Grove, Cramond Edinburgh EH4 6RF, Scotland Office: Med Sch Dept Environ Occupl Med, Foresterhill, Aberdeen AB25 2ZD, Scotland

SEAVER, JEFFREY MARK, SR., lawyer; b. Hartford, Conn., Feb. 4, 1960; s. Herbert Lawrence and Mary Muriel S.; m. Brenda Colette Seaver, June 23, 1983; children: Arielle, Lunden, Jared. B in Gen. Studies, La. Tech. U., 1988; JD, So. Univ. Law Ctr., Baton Rouge, 1997. Bar: La. 1997. With USAF, 1977-89, advanced through grades to tech. sgt., 1987; inflight refueling technician USAF, Barksdale AFB, La., 1977-89; dir. tng. FDIC, Washington, 1990-94; mng. ptnr. Seaver Law Firm, Baton Rouge, 1997—; bd. dirs. Krewe of Orion, Baton Rouge. Author: Career Transition and Placement Training Manual, 1994. Recipient pro-bono award Baton Rouge Bar Assn., 1998. Mem. ABA, Assn. Trial Lawyers Am., La. Trial Lawyers Assn., La. State Bar, Baton Rouge Bar, Baton Rouge C. of C. Republican. Roman Catholic. Avocations: hunting, fishing. E-mail: jeff-seaver@seaverlawfirm.com. Home: 10919 Major Oaks Dr Baton Rouge LA 70815-5445 Office: Seaver Law Firm LLC 2833 Brakley Dr Ste A Baton Rouge LA 70816-2329

SEAVER, ROBERT LESLIE, retired law educator; b. Brockton, Mass., June 13, 1937; s. Russell Bradford and Lois (Marchant) S.; m. Marjorie V. Rote, Aug. 21, 1960 (div. 1974); children: Kimberly, Eric, Kristen; m. Elizabeth A. Horwitz, May 22, 1984. AB cum laude, Tufts U., Medford, Mass., 1958; JD, U. Chgo., 1964. Bar: Ohio 1964, U.S. Ct. Appeals (6th cir.) 1964, U.S. Dist. Ct. (so. dist.) Ohio 1965. Assoc. Taft, Stettinius and Hollister, Cin., 1964-66; v.p., sec., gen. counsel IDI Mgmt. Inc., Cin., 1966-74; pvt. practice Cin., 1974-75; prof. law emeritus No. Ky. U. Salmon P. Chase Coll. Law, Highland Heights, 1975—; of counsel Cors & Bassett, Cin., 1993-99; ret., 1999; cons. in field, 1975—. Author/editor: Ohio Corporation Law, 1988; contbr. chpts. to books. Advisor subcom. on pvt. corps of Ky. Commn. on Constl. Rev., 1987. With USMC, 1958-61. Recipient Justice Robert O. Lukowsky award of Excellence Chase Law Sch. Student Bar Assn., 1986. Mem. Ohio Bar Assn., Cin. Bar Assn., No. Ky. Bar Assn. Republican. Unitarian. Avocations: duplicate bridge (life master), history. Home: 826 Woodscene Ct Cincinnati OH 45230-4334 Office: Northern Kentucky U Salmon Chase Coll Law Highland Heights KY 41099

SEAY, TAMMY ELAINE, product design engineer; b. Madison, Wis., Oct. 12, 1965; d. Mack Seay and Shelba Jean Mistek; 1 child, Rebbeca Rachel. Degree in mech. engring., U. Wis., 1989, degree in profession engring., 1997. Lic. engr. in tng., Wis. Product design engr. John Deere, Horican, Wis., 1990-94; mech. engr. Rayovac, Madison, Wis., 1997-98, dept. engr., 1998-99; cons. Solutions Engring. Co., Madison, 1999—. Avocations: artist, photographer. Home: 2342 Chalet Gardens Rd Apt 3 Madison WI 53711-6031

ŠEBA, PETR, physicist, researcher; b. Melnik, Czech Republic, Jan. 30, 1957; s. Jiri and Eva (Wankova) Š; m. Jana Kurfirstova, Nov. 12, 1982; children: Frantisek, Vojtech, Martin. PhD, Charles U., Prague, 1986, DSc, 1992. Cert. theoretical physicist. Rschr. Czech Acad. Scis., Prague, 1982-92, leading rschr., 1992—; head, dir. Czech Cath. Charity, Hradec Kralove, 1991-95. Editor 3 vols. procs.; contbr. articles to profl. jours. Coord. German Cath. Charity, 1990. Alexander von Humboldt fellow. Home: Slemeno 33, 51601 Rychnov Czech Republic Office: Czech Acad Sci, Inst Nuclear Physics, 25068 Rez Czech Republic

SEBASTIAN, SIR CUTHBERT MONTRAVILLE, governor general; b. Oct. 22, 1921. BSc, Mount Allison U., Can., 1953; MD, M of Surgery, Dalhousie U., Can., 1958. Pharmacist, lab. technician Cunningham Hosp., St. Kitts, 1942-43, med. supt., 1966; med. supt. Joseph N. France Gen. Hosp., 1967-80; CMO St. Christopher and Nevis, 1980-83; pvt. med. practitioner, 1983-95; gov. gen. St. Christopher and Nevis, 1996—. Active Royal Air Force, 1944-45; capt. surgeon St. Kitts Nevis Def. Force, 1958-60.

Mem. Rotary of St. Kitts. Avocations: farming, reading, dancing. Office: Govt House, Basseterre Saint Kitts*

SEBASTIAN, NJARAKAD JOSEPH, librarian; b. Shertallai, India, Feb. 6, 1951; s. Varkey and Thresiamma Joseph; m. Elizabeth Michael, Sept. 23, 1979; two children. BA, St. Thomas Coll., 1971; MA, Maharaja's Coll., 1973; B in Libr. Sci., U. Delhi, 1976, M in Libr. Sci., 1977. From asst.libr. to libr. Nat. Coun. Applied Econ. Rsch., New Delhi, 1981—; Fulbright intern Syracuse U, 1992-93; mem. standing com. IFLA Social Sci. sect.; mem. exec. com. Internat. Com. for Social Sci. Info. and Documentation. Fax: 91-11 3327164; e-mail: njsebastian@ncaer.org. Office: Nat Coun Applied Econ Rsch, Parisila Bhawan II IP Estat, 110002 New Delhi India

SEBASTIAN, PHYLIS SUE, real estate broker; b. Childersburg, Ala., Jan. 24, 1945; d. Albert Freeman and Era Mae (McGowin) Ingram; m. Robert Emmett Martin, March 31, 1965 (div. Sept. 1976); children: Connie, Michael, Toni, Robert; m. Thomas Haskell Sebastian III, June 26, 1985; stepchildren: Shellie, Tabitha, Cherie, Thomas IV. Lic. real estate broker, Am. Sch. Real Estate, St. Louis, Mo., 1989. Owner, broker Phylis Sebastian Real Estate, Farmington, Mo, 1989-97, U.S. Auto Sales, Park Hills, Mo, 1993-96; owner Bus. Legal Svs., Park Hills, Mo., 1997. Author: Marriages in Madison County Missouri 1848-1868, 1998, 1910 Census for Madison County Missouri, 1998; contbr. articles to newspapers. Co-founder Astrological Assn., St. Louis, 1976-77, Mo. Mental Health Consumer Network, 1989-93 (Mineral Area chpt. 1989-93). Mem. Nat. Realtors Assn., Mo. Realtors Assn., Mineral Area Realtors Assn., Nat. Gardening Club, Libr. Congress, Smithsonian, Nat. Hist. Soc., Geneal. Assn. Madison County, Mo. Mem. LDS Ch. Avocations: geneology, astrology, reading, walking, gardening. E-mail: morrisbaby@hotmail.com. Home: 5231 West 72 Highway Fredericktown MO 63645 Office: Second Step Inc Auction & Real Estate Corp 315A W Russell St Ironton MO 63650-1316

SEBASTIANELLI, MARIO JOSEPH, internist, nephrologist, health services administrator; b. Jessup, Pa., Sept. 14, 1935; s. Carlo and Antonia (Antonelli) S.; m. Alena Marie Drazdauskas, June 26, 1993; children: Mario, Alexa, Marco. BS in Biology, U. Scranton, 1958; MD, Jefferson Med. Coll., 1962. Diplomate Am. Bd. Internal Medicine. From sr. instr. to assoc. prof. medicine Hahnemann U., Phila., 1969-87; pvt. practice Scranton, Pa., 1971—; chief nephrology, founding dir. hemodialysis Moses Taylor Hosp., Scranton, 1972-76; founding med. dir. Pa. Regional Tissue Bank, Scranton, 1983-91; dir. inpatient hemodialysis svcs. Comty. Med. Ctr., Scranton, 1996—; mem. senateconfirmed gov. apptd. Govs. Renal Disease Adv. Com., Harrisburg, Pa., 1973-76; creator, owner Comprehensive Health Svcs. Ctr., Dunmore, Pa., 1979—; founding med. dir. Diagnostic Lab., Dunmore, 1981-95. Contbr. sci. rsch. articles to profl. publs. Bd. dirs. Scranton Lackawanna Human Devel. Agy., Scranton, 1977-82. Lt. USN, 1963-65. Fellow ACP; mem. AMA, Am. Soc. Internal Medicine, Am. Soc. Nephrology, Internat. Soc. Nephrology, Renal Physicians Assn., KC (4th degree), Alpha Omega Alpha. Republican. Roman Catholic. Avocations: fishing, swimming, traveling, sports cars, reading. Office: Comprehensive Health Svcs Ctr 1416 Monroe Ave Ste 100 Dunmore PA 18509-2477

SEBASTIANI, LUCA, plant biotechnologist; b. Pietrasanta, Lucca, Italy, Aug. 4, 1964; s. Carlo and Angela (Balderi) S.; m. Rosella Cantone, Sept. 26, 1992; 1 child, Elena. Diploma in Agrl. Sci., U. Pisa, Italy, 1991; PhD, SSSUP S. Anna, Pisa, 1996. Postdoctorate fellow Scuola Superiore di Studi U. e di Perfezionamento S Anna, Pisa, 1996-98, asst. prof. pomology, 1998—. With Aeronautics, Pisa, 1991-92. Recipient Comett grant European Commn., 1995, award G. Spitali Found., 1998; Swedish Rsch. Coun. grantee, 1996, 97, Italian Rsch. Coun. grantee 1997. Mem. Italian Orticultural Soc., Italian Soc. Plant Physiology. Office: SSSUP S Anna, Carducci 40, 56127 Pisa Italy

ŠEBEK, MICHAEL, research scientist, entrepreneur; b. Prague, Czech Republic, Jan. 25, 1954; s. Antonín and Jana (Hanzlová) S.; m. Ivana Ornestová, Nov. 21, 1992; children: Michael, Natalie. Diploma in elec. engring., Czech Tech. U., Prague, 1978; PhD, Czech Acad. Scis., Prague, 1981, DSc, 1995. Scientist Inst. Info. Theory and Automation, Prague, 1981-88, sr. scientist, 1988-90, chief scientist, chmn. of Control Theory Dept., 1991-98, head Control Theory Dept., 1998—; vis. prof. Swiss Fed. Inst. Tech., Zurich, 1994-95; mem. policy com. Internat. Fedn. Automatic Control, 1993—; project leader Internat. Project Polynom Algorithms in Control, European cmty., 1994—; mem. various internat. coms.; coord. of EUROPOLY (Europen Network of Excellence for Indsl. Applications of Polynomial Methods 1998; co-founder and CEO of PolyX, Ltd. (world-wide producer of software for polynomial methods in systems, signals and control), 1998; rsch. group leader in Trnka Lab for Automatic Conrol, Czech Tech. U. Prague, 1998; lectr. in field. Asst. Editor. European Journal of Control; Contbr. numerous articles to profl. jours. Mgr., coach Medicina Baseball Club, Prague, 1985-90. Recipient Czech Nat. prize Czech Parliament, 1989. Mem. IEEE (sr., mem. exec. com. Czech sect. 1996—), IEEE Control Sys. Soc. (mem. conf. editl. bd. 1994—, chmn. Czech chpt. 1996—), Am. Math. Soc., N.Y. Acad. Scis. Avocations: jogging, baseball, photography. Home: Jarní 4, 16000 Prague 6, Czech Republic Office: Inst Info Theory & Automation, 18208 Prague 8, Czech Republic

ŠEBEK, MICHAEL, psychologist, educator, psychoanalyst; b. Prague, Czech Republic, Oct. 18, 1946; s. Jaroslav and Zdenka (Filounkova) Š.; m. Jana Burková, Dec. 14, 1973; children: Kamila, Helena. PhD, Charles U., 1971, CSc, 1986. Clin. psychologist Nat. Health Inst., Prague, 1971-77, 86-91; rschr. Child Psychiat. Clinic Charles U., Prague, 1977-85, asst. prof. 2d Med. Sch., 1991—; dir. Psychoanalytic Inst., Prague, 1990-99; cons. Organ Transplantation Fund, Prague, 1995-98. Author: The Hyperactive Children, 1990, I, Your Pupil, You, My Teacher, 1988; mem. internat. editl. bd. Psychoanalytic Inquiry, 1993—; contbr. articles to profl. jours. Mem. Czech Soc. Psychoanalytic Psychotherapy (pres. 1993-99), Internat. Psychoanalytical Assn., Internat. Assn. for History of Psychoanalysis (corr.), Czech Psychoanalytic Soc. (pres. 1999—). Avocations: classical music, theater, gardening. Home: Korunovačni 18, 17000 Prague Czech Republic Office: Charles U 2d Med Sch, Vuvalu 84, 150 00 Prague 5, Czech Republic

ŠEBENIK, ANTON, education educator; b. Brezovica, Slovenia, Jan. 11, 1941; s. Alojz and Uršula (Mrak) Š.; m. Marija Jemec, May 6, 1972; children: Gregor, Gorazd. BS of Chemistry, U. Ljubljana, Slovenia, 1967, MS of Chemistry, 1973, PhD, 1976. Rschr. Donit, Medvode, Slovenia, 1965-71, head rsch. dept., 1971-76; sr. rschr. Nat. Inst. Chemistry, Ljubljana, 1976-82; prof. U. Ljubljana, 1982—; sr. rschr. NSF, 1976-84, 86-89. Contbr. articles to profl. jours. Mem. Slovenian Chem. Soc. (sec. 1982-86). Home: V Radno 62, 1351 Brezovica Slovenia Office: Univ Ljubljana, Aškerčeva 5, 1001 Ljubljana Slovenia

SEBEOK, THOMAS ALBERT, linguistics educator; b. Budapest, Hungary, Nov. 9, 1920; came to U.S., 1937, naturalized, 1944; s. Dezso and Veronica (Perlman) S.; m. Eleanor Lawton, Sept. 1947; 1 child, Veronica C.; m. Jean Umiker, Oct. 1972; children: Jessica A., Erica L. B.A., U. Chgo., 1941; M.A., Princeton, 1943, Ph.D., 1945; PhD honoris causa, U. Budapest, Hungary, 1990; Dr. honoris causa, U. Nacional de Rosario, Argentina, 1991; DSc honoris causa, U. So. Ill., 1991. Mem. faculty Ind. U., Bloomington, 1943-91, Disting. prof. linguistics, 1967-78, Disting. prof. linguistics and semiotics, 1978-91, Disting. prof. emeritus, 1991—, prof. anthropology, prof. Uralic and Altaic studies, fellow Folklore Inst., mem. Russian and East European Inst., chmn. Research Center for Lang. and Semiotic Studies, 1956-91, chmn. emeritus Grad. Program in Semiotic Studies, 1991—; mem.-at-large NAS-NRC, also mem. various coms.; lectr. various acads. and univs., U.S. and abroad; vis. prof. U. Mich., 1945, 58, U. P.R., 1949, U. N.Mex., 1953, U. Ariz., 1958-59, U. Vienna, 1963, U. Besançon, 1965, U. Hamburg, 1966, U. Bucharest, 1967, 69, U. Ill., 1968, U. Colo., 1969, Stanford U., 1971, U. South Fla., 1972, Linguistic Soc. Am. prof., 1975, Internat. Christian U., Tokyo, 1985, U. Quebec, 1985, El Colegio de Mexico, 1987, U. of Republic, Montevideo, Uraguey, 1987, others; Disting. vis. prof. Internat. Summer Inst. for Semiotic and Structural Studies, 1980-88; cons. Ford Found., Guggenheim Found., Wenner-Gren Found. for Anthrop. Research, U.S. Office Edn., NSF, fellowship div. Nat. Acad. Scis., Can. Council; panel mem. for linguistics Nat. Endowment for Humanities, 1966-67; mem. U.S. del. to permanent council Internat. Union Anthrop. and Ethnol. Scis., 1970-73; U.S. del. Comité International Permanent des Linguistes, 1972—; mem. internat. sci. council Royaumont Center for Sci. of Man, 1973—; exch. prof. NAS-USSR Acad. Scis., 1973; Regents fellow Smithsonian Instn., 1983-84; adj. fellow Woodrow Wilson Internat Ctr. for Scholars, 1983-84, mem. program on history, culture and soc., 1986-87. Author: Perspectives in Zoosemiotics, 1972, Structure & Texture: Selected Essays in Cheremis Verbal Art, 1974, The Play of Musement, 1981, others; editor-in-chief: Semiotica, 1968—, Current Trends in Linguistics, 1963—, Approaches to Semiotics, 1968-74; editor: Studies in Semiotics, 1974—, others; gen. editor: Advances in Semiotics, 1974—, others; contbr. numerous articles to profl. and scholarly jours. Mem. vis. com. Harvard U., 1973, Simon Fraser U., 1975, Georgetown U., 1977, Vanderbilt U., 1977-78. Recipient Pres.'s medal of excellence Ind. U., 1991, Profl. Achievement citation U. Chgo., 1992; John Simon Guggenheim Meml. Found. fellow, 1958-59, 81-82, Ctr. for Advanced Study in Behavioral Scis. fellow, 1960-61, 66-67, 71, NSF sr. postdoctoral fellow, 1966-67, NEH fellow, 1973-74, 80-81, Netherlands Inst. for Advanced Study fellow, 1973-74, Nat. Humanities Ctr. fellow, 1980-81, Smithsonian Instn. Regents fellow, 1983-84, Rsch. Assoc., 1984-87, Woodrow Wilson Internat. Ctr. for Scholars adj. fellow, 1983-84, Com. for Sci. Investigation of Claims of Paranormal fellow, 1983—; Fulbright grantee Germany, 1966, 71, Italy, 1969, 71, 87, Argentina, 1987, Uruguay, 1987, Am., Am. Coun. Learned Socs. grantee, Ford Found., Wenner-Gren Found. Anthrop. Rsch., USIA, other fed. agys. Fellow Am. Anthrop. Assn. (disting. service award 1984), Am. Folklore Soc., Soc. Cultural Anthropology, AAAS, Explorers Club, also fgn. linguistic socs.; mem. Internat. Assn. Semiotic Studies (editor-in-chief 1968—, exec. com. 1969—), Linguistic Soc. Am. (sec.-treas. 1969-73, v.p. 1974, pres. 1975, asso. dir. Linguistic Inst. 1958, 75, dir. 1964), Central States Anthrop. Soc. (pres. 1956), Am. Assn. Machine Translation and Computational Linguistics (exec. bd. 1964-66), Animal Behavior Soc. (exec. bd. 1968—), Semiotic Soc. Am. (sec.-treas. 1975, exec. dir. 1976-85, pres. 1984), Sigma Xi, others. Clubs: Cosmos (Washington); University (Chgo.); Princeton (N.Y.C.) ; Internat. House (Tokyo). Home: 1104 Covenanter Dr Bloomington IN 47401-6043 Office: Indiana U PO Box 10 Bloomington IN 47402-0010

SEBESTA, VLADIMIR VRATISLAV, electrical engineer, educator; b. Predin, Moravia, Czechoslovakia, Oct. 7, 1938; s. Vladimir Wenzel and Vratislava (Drlikova) S.; m. Helena Marketa Belusova, Aug. 1, 1964; 1 child, Vladimir. MSc, Czech Tech. U., Prague, 1961; PhD, Tech. U. Brno, Czech Republic, 1973. R&D engr. Tesla, Prelouc, Czechoslovakia, 1962-63; asst. Tech. U. Brno, 1963-80, assoc. prof. elec. engring., 1980-95, prof., 1995—, faculty senate chmn., 1991-93; mem. Univs. Coun., Czech Republic, 1991-93; mem. sci. coun. faculty electrical engring. Tech. U. Brno, 1997-98; mem. sci. coun. faculty Air Forces, Brno Mil. Acad., 1999—. Co-author: Electronics and Data Transmission, 1985 (prize of chancellor 1985); author: Data Transmission Theory, 1987 (prize of chancellor 1987). Ministerial grantee Signal Lab., 1995, univ. grantee Band-pass Gap Signal Reconstrn., 1995, ministerial grantee Digital Signal Processing Lab., 1997-2000. Mem. IEEE. Office: Brno U Tech Inst Radio Electronics, Purkynova 118, 612 00 Brno Czech Republic

SEBRING, MARJORIE MARIE ALLISON, former home furnishings company executive; b. Burnsville, N.C., 1926; d. James William and Mary Will (Ramsey) Allison Shockey; 1 child, Patricia Louise Banner Krohn. Student, Mars Hill Coll., 1943, Home Decorators Sch. Design, N.Y.C., 1948, Wayne State U., 1953; cert. home furnishings rep., U. Va., 1982. Dir. decorating divsn. Robinson Furniture, Detroit, 1949-57; head buyer Tyner Hi-Way House, Ypsilanti, Mich., 1957-63, Town and Country, Dearborn, Mich., 1963-66; instr. Nat. Carpet Inst., 1963-71; owner Adams House, Inc., Plymouth, Mich., 1966-72; exec. v.p. mktg. and sales, regional sales and mktg. mgr. Triangle Industries, L.A., 1972-89; co-owner Markham-Sebring, Inc., St. Petersburg, Fla., 1983-89; dir. contract divsn. Kane Furniture, 1984-85; co-owner Accessories, Etc., 1985-89; chmn. bd. Heritage Lakes, U.S. Home; co-owner, dir. Talamanca Pipeline Ltd., Costa Rica. Vol. coord. Pasco County Clk. Ct., Suncoast Theatre; mem. adv. bd. Webster Coll.; charter mem. Presdl. Task Force; pres. Presbyn. Ch. Seven Springs; bd. dirs. Fla. Health and Human Svc., Fla. Presbyn. Homes; chmn. bd. dirs. Two Westminster Condominium Assn.; mem. Tampa Bay Presbytery Rev. and Evaluation. Recipient recognition for work with youth and aged; named to Fla. Finest List, Gov. of Fla., 1994. Mem. Internat. Home Furnishings Assn., Fla. Home Furnishings Rep. Assn. (officer), Am. Security Coun. (coun.), Williamsburg Found., USCG Aux., Nat. Audubon Soc., Internat. Platform Assn. Republican. Avocations include contbr. creative display to Better Homes & Gardens, 1957-64. Fax: 727 375-7702. Home: 4902 Cathedral Ct New Port Richey FL 34655-1486

SECHER, NIELS HENRY, anesthesiologist; b. Fredericksberg, Denmark, June 24, 1946; s. Ole Vilhelm S. and Lili Sue (Kiersgaard) Secher; m. Lisbeth Gudrun, Jan. 3, 1991; children: Anne Camilla, Anne Katherine, Erik, Frederik, Christian. MD, U. Copenhagen, 1975, Dr., 1984. Med. tng. Bispebjerg Hosp., Denmark, 1977-80; surg. tng. Frederiksberg, Denmark, 1980-83; anesthesia tng. Rigshospitalet, Copenhagen, 1983-90, with, 1990—; mem. Copenhagen Muscle Rsch. Ctr., 1994—. Author: The Physiology of Rowing, 1984; editor: The Physiology of Sports, Exercise and the Circulation in Health and Disease, 1999. Bd. dirs. REE LEGAT, 1985—. Rsch. fellow Gentofte Hosp., Denmark, 1975-76, Herlev Hosp., Denmark, 1976-77. Mem. Nordic Anesthesiology Soc., Scandinavian Soc. Physiology, Am. Physiol. Soc. Avocation: rowing. Office: Dept Anesthesia, Rigshospitalet 2041, DK-2100 Copenhagen Denmark

SECHMAN, ANDRZEJ, agricultural studies educator; b. Cracow, Poland, Nov. 19, 1960; s. Adam and Helena (Pitala) S.; m. Sept. 23, 1982; children: Anna, Natalia. MS, U. Agr., Cracow, 1984, PhD, 1990. Asst. prof. U. Agr., Cracow, 1984-92, tutor, 1992—. Contbr. articles to profl. jours. Grantee Polish Com. for Sch. Rsch., 1999—. Mem. ESNA. Home: Mogilany 131, 32-031 Mogilany Poland Office: Univ Agr, Al Mickiewicza 24/28, 30-059 Cracow Poland

SECHOVSKY, VLADIMIR, physicist; b. Mseno, Czech Republic, July 15, 1946; s. Hynek and Jirina (Ikadlikova) S.; m. Miluska Vodickova, Sept. 22, 1972; children: Katerina, Stepan, Karolina. MSc, Charles U., 1970, PhD, 1975; DSc, 1991. From jr. scientist to prin. researcher Charles U., Prague, 1975-98, prof., 1998—. Alexander von Humboldt Found. fellow, 1976-87, Japan Soc. for Promotion of Sci. fellow, 1990. Mem. Am. Physical Soc., Union Czech Mathematicians & Physicists, European Phys. Soc. Avocations: sports, travel. Home: U Bazantnice 375, 159 00 Prague 5 Czech Republic Office: Charles U, Ke Karlovu 5, 121 16 Prague 2 Czech Republic

SECHREST, LARRY J., economist, educator; b. Detroit, Oct. 12, 1946; s. Howard J. and Frances C. Sechrest; m. Donna R., May 6, 1971; children: J. Kyle, R. Tara. BA in History, U. Tex., Arlington, 1968, MA in Econs., 1985, PhD in Econs., 1990. Instr. U. Tex., Arlington, 1985-90; prof. econs. Sul Ross State U., Alpine, Tex., 1990—; adj. scholar Ludwig von Mises Ins., Auburn, Ala., 1996—; found. scholar Found. Advancement of Monetary Edn., 1996—; mem. editl. bd. Quar. Jour. Austrian Econs., 1996—; mem. bd. advisors Jour. Ayn Rand Studies, 1999—. Author: Free Banking, 1993; contbr. chpt. to book, articles to profl. jours. Fellow Inst. Humane Studies, Fairfax, Va., 1987-88; listed Guide to Pub. Policy Experts, Heritage Found., Washington, 2000. Mem. Nat. Assn. Scholars, Am. Statis. Assn., The Hist. Soc., Soc. Devel. Austrian Econs., Internat. Maritime Econ. History Assn., So. Econ. Assn., N.Y. Acad. Scis. Libertarian. Avocations: maritime history, yacht design, firearms, marine art, golf. E-mail: larrys@sulross.edu. Office: Sul Ross State U 400 N Harrison St Alpine TX 79832-8300

SECK, MAMADOU MANSOUR, ambassador, career officer; b. Dakar, Senegal, July 3, 1935; children: Ndeye, Safi, Makura, Astou Dior, Sonia Penda. Attended, St. Cyr Milit. Acad., France, Salon Air Force Acad., French Air War Coll., Institut des Hautes Etudes de la Def. Nat. Commanding officer 1st Senegalese Air Force Squad, 1966; comdr. 1st Senegalese Air Force, 1972; dep. chief gen. staff, 1980-84, spl. chief of staff to Pres. of Republic of Senegal, chief of staff of Sene-Gambia Confedn., 1984, gen. chief of staff, gen. chief Confedn., 1988; chmn. Joint Chiefs of Staff of Senegal, 1988-93; amb. to U.S. Govt. of Republic of Senegal, 1993—; amb. to Mex., Argentina, Jamaica, Haiti, Trinidad and Tobago, Barbados, 1993—. Decorated Senegal, France, Gabon, Hollan, Luxembourg. Office: Embassy of Republic of Senegal 2112 Wyoming Ave NW Washington DC 20008-3926

SECKLER, MAX, apologetics educator; b. Westerhofen, Germany, Sept. 23, 1927; s. Isidor and Anna (Pfitzer) S. PhD, U. Tübungen, Germany, 1957, ThD, 1958; postgrad., U. Munich, 1960, habilitation, 1964. Ordained priest Roman Cath. Ch., 1952. Priest Stuttgart, Germany, 1952-55, Tübingen, 1957-60; asst. prof. U. Munich, 1960-62, sr. lectr., 1964; lectr. U. Passau, Germany, 1962; prof. apologetics U. Tübingen, 1964-93, head dept., 1964-93, prof. emeritus, 1993—. Contbr. numerous articles on sys. theology and philosophy to profl. jours. Home: Sommerhalde 5, D-72070 Tübingen Germany Office: Univ Tübingen, Liebermeisterstr 12, D-72070 Tübingen Germany

SECOLA, JOSEPH PAUL, lawyer; b. Hartford, Conn., May 18, 1959; s. Pasquale Anthony and Anna Maria; m. Mary Alice Ipavich, June 20, 1982; children: Peter, Sharon, Mary Joy, Timothy, Paul, Andrew. BA in History, Fairfield U., 1981; JD, Oral Robert U., 1984. Bar: Conn. 1984, N.Y. 1985, U.S. Dist. Ct. Conn. 1985, Va. 1986, U.S. Dist. Ct. (so. dist.) N.Y. 1988, U.S. Ct. Appeals (2d cir.) 1989, U.S. Supreme Ct. 1990, U.S. Dist. Ct. (we. dist.) N.Y. 1996. Pvt. practice Brookfield, Conn., 1984—. Mem. bd. edn. City of Milford, Conn., 1989-90, Greater Danbury (Conn.) Cath. Elem. Schs., 1992-96. Mem. Nat. Employment Lawyers Assn., Am. Trial Lawyers Assn., Conn. Trial Lawyers Assn., Conn. Bar Assn., Conn. Employment Lawyers Assn., Litchfield County Bar Assn., Greater Danbury Bar Assn. Republican. Roman Catholic. Avocations: sports, N.Y. Yankees. E-mail: secola.law@snet.net. Fax: (203) 740-2355. Office: Ste 500 67 Federal Rd Bldg A Brookfield CT 06804-2538

SECOR, WILLIAM ROBERT, writer; b. Indpls., Nov. 8, 1937; m. Mary Lou Mohler, Apr. 5, 1980; children: Patricia A., Michael P. BA in History, Ind. U., 1978, MS in Edn., 1979. Tchr. Denver Pub. Schs. Author: Who Knows?, 1999. Home: 15241 W Domingo Ln Sun City West AZ 85375-2946 also: 2677 S Xanadu Way Unit A Aurora CO 80014-2223

SECREST, JAMES SEATON, SR., lawyer; b. Middletown, Ky., Dec. 9, 1930; s. Elmer S. and Linney (Witherbee)S.; m. Mary Sue Corum, Sept. 2, 1950; children: James Seaton, Lynne Suzanne. J.D., U. Louisville, 1954. Bar: Ky. 1954. Ptnr. Goad & Secrest, Scottsville, Ky., 1955-62; solo practice Scottsville, Ky., 1962-77; ptnr. Secrest & Secrest, Scottsville, 1977—. City judge pro tem Scottsville, 1955-58; judge Allea County, 1958-61; city atty. Scottsville, 1962-66; atty. Allen County, 1966-89, dep. judge-exec., 1990-99; bd. dirs. Barren River Area Devel. Dist., 1970, mem. regional bd. ethics; mem. adv. bd. dirs. Starbank, Scottsville, 1998; bd. dirs. Commonwealth Health Corp. Mem. Scottsville C. of C. (pres. 1962), Ky. County Attorneys Assn. (pres. 1973), Ky. Assn. Counties (bd. dirs. 1985-86), ABA, Ky. Bar Assn. Republican. Methodist. Club: Rotary (pres. 1960). Home: 10055 New Glasgow Rd Scottsville KY 42164-9534 Office: Secrest & Secrest PO Box 35 210 W Main St Scottsville KY 42164-1123

SECRETO, GIORGIO, health science association administrator; b. Erba, Como, Italy, May 4, 1944; s. Giuseppe Secreto and Vincenzina Terrone; m. Maria Grazia Secchi, Apr. 6, 1972; 1 child, Guido. MD, U. Milan, 1969; specialization in endocrinology, U. Turin, 1974. Resident Montefiore Hosp., N.Y.C., 1981; intern dept. gynecology Nat. Cancer Inst., Milan, 1967-70, intern, 1967-70, asst., 1970; resident Montefiore Hosp., N.Y.C., 1981; vice-dir. Nat. Cancer Inst., Milan, 1990—; dir. unit endocrinology Nat. Cancer Inst., Milan, 1980—; tchr. Italian Sch. Senology, Orta S. Giulio, Italy, 1988—; cons. tchr. U. Milan, others. Contbr. over 60 articles to profl. jours. Mem. AAAS, N.Y. Acad. Sci., Attive come prima (bd. dirs., scientific com.). Avocations: classical music, enigmatography, fishing. Office: Nat Cancer Inst Endocrin, Via Venezian 1, 20133 Milan Italy

SEDA, ANTHONY KAREL, mathematics educator, researcher; b. Wolverhampton, Eng., Oct. 31, 1945; arrived in Ireland, 1972; s. Karel Joseph and Barbara Muriel Helen (Roberts) S.; m. Martine Marie-Aline Guillaume, Aug. 5, 1978. BSc with 1st class honors, U. Wales, Aberystwyth, 1969; MS, U. Warwick, Coventry, Eng., 1970; PhD, U. Wales, Bangor, 1974. Lectr. Univ. Coll., Cork, Ireland, 1972-78, sr. lectr., 1979-87, 1988—; vis. prof. Inst. des Hautes Etudes Sci., France, 1978-79, Tulane U., New Orleans, 1979, U. Bristol, Eng., 1987-88. Reviewer: Math. Revs., 1977-87, Zentralblatt fur Mathematik, 1977-87, Fundamenta Informaticae, 1995—, Jour. of Logic Programming, 1996—, Theoretical Computer Sci., 1998—, Jour. Logic and Computation, 1999—; mem. editl. bd. Jour. Info.; contbr. articles to profl. jours. and procs. Sr. vis. fellow Royal Irish Acad., 1978. Fellow Inst. Math. and its Applications; mem. European Assn. for Logic, Lang. and Info., European Assn. for Theoretical Computer Sci., N.Y. Acad. Scis. Methodist. Office: Univ Coll Cork, Dept Math, Cork Ireland

SEDACCA, ANGELO ANTHONY, police officer, scholar, notary; b. Bronx, N.Y., Mar. 14, 1971; s. Joseph and Marie Ann (Rella) S; m. Diane Bockino; children: Christopher Michael, Nicholas Anthony. BA in French Studies, Fordham U., 1993, BA in Italian Studies, 1993; MA in French Lang. and Civilization, NYU, 1995; postgrad. Inst. Religious Studies, St. Joseph's Sem. Professed mem. Secular Franciscan order. Asst. martial arts instr. U.S.A. Martial Arts Ctr., 1991-94; tchr. Italian, St. Raymond's H.S., Bronx, 1994; translator Legal Lang. Svcs., N.Y.C., 1994-97, Franciscans Internat., N.Y.C, 1995—; tchr. theology and Italian, Salesian H.S., New Rochelle, N.Y., 1995-96; tchr. Latin Our Lady of Solace Sch., Bronx, 1996; fin. officer premium financing A.I. Credit Corp., N.Y.C., 1996-97; bartender Pelham Country Club, New Rochelle, N.Y., 1997-98; police officer NYPD, 1998—; translator Magnificat Mag., Yonkers, N.Y., 1999—; police officer Acad., 1998-99, 40th Precinct NYPD, 1999—, vol. translator Ops. Unit, 1999—; cert. expert Marijuana/Hashish Field Testing, 2000—; translator Magnificat Mag., Yonkers, N.Y., 1999—. Mem. bd. govs. Fordham Prep. Sch. Alumni Assn., 1995-98; mem. young alumni com. Fordham U., 1993-98; eucharistic min. and lector, 1990—. Recipient Internat. Sash of Academia, Internat. Cultural Diploma of Honor, Man of Yr. medals, 1998, 99. Fellow Am. Biog. Inst. (life; dep. gov., continental gov.), Internat. Biog. Ctr. (life, dep. dir. gen.); mem. Cath. League, KC (4th degree), N.Y./NJ Bartenders' Assn., Am. Soc. Notaries, Fraternal Order Police, Internat. Police Assn., N.Y. Police Dept. Holy Name Soc., N.Y. Police Dept. Columbia Assn., N.Y. Police Dept. Anchor Club, Korean Martial Arts Instrs. Assn., Black Belts of the Faith Internat., Knights of Pythias, Order of Malta Aux., Order of Internat. Fellowship, Noble Order Internat. Ambassadors. Roman Catholic. Avocations: martial arts, philosophy, civil and canon law, country music, theater. Home: Apt 5B 1650 Hutchinson River Pkwy E Bronx NY 10461-4314

SEDAGHATI, RAMIN, manufacturing consultant, researcher; b. Tehran, Iran, Feb. 18, 1965; s. Arsalan Sedaghati and Efat Karimai. BS, Tehran Poly., 1988, MS, 1990; PhD, U. Victoria, B.C., Can., 2000. Tech. master Shahid Hasan Bagheri Co., Tehran, 1988-92; tech. advisor Heavy Machine Tools Prodn. Factory, Tehran, 1991-93; lectr. Islamic Azad U., Tehran, 1993-95, Iran Islamic Republic of Airline, Tehran, 1993; expert Sap Co., Tehran, 1994-96; cons., project mgr. Hoveyzeh Co., Tehran, 1996—; master expert renovation and devel. Orgn. of Iranian Industries, Tehran, 1996—; rschr., instr. U. Victoria; rschr. Tehran Poly., 1994—. Avocations: mountain climbing, swimming, studing. Home: 1804 Jade Pl, Victoria, BC Canada V8P 3E4 Office: U Victoria, Dept Mech Engring, Victoria, BC Canada V8W 3P6

SEDAGHATIAN, MOHAMAD REZA, pediatrician, neonatalogist; b. Shiraz, Fars, Iran, Feb. 11, 1938; s. Habib and Roghayeh (Hodjati) S.; m. Nezhat Khalili, Sept. 4, 1970. MD, Shiraz (Iran) Med. Sch., 1964. Diplomate Am. Bd. Pediatrics, Am. Bd. Neonatal Perinatal Medicine. Pediatric resident Tulane U., 1969-71; neonatal fellow U. Ariz., Phoenix, 1972; asst. prof. pediatrics Shiraz Med. Sch., 1973-79, assoc. prof. pediatrics, 1979-84, prof. pediatrics, 1984; sr. cons. Ministry of Health, Abu Dhabi, United Arab Emirates, 1985—; dir. Neonatal Units, Shiraz, 1973-85; dir. pediatric residency Shiraz U., 1981-85; head Dept. Neonatal Medicine and Surgery, Abu Dhabi, 1985-2000. Contbr. articles to profl. publs.; founder Sedaghatian congenital lethal metaphyical chontrodysplasian syndrome. 1st lt. Health Corp., 1966-68. Fellow Am. Acad. Pediatrics, United Arab Emirates Med. Assn., Tulane Pediatrics Alumni Assn., Am. Perinatal Assn., Emirate Perinatal Soc. (pres.). Avocations: tennis, movies, music, table tennis, volleyball. Home and Office: PO Box 2951, Abu Dhabi United Arab Emirates

SEDANO, LUIS ANGEL, physics educator, researcher; b. Aviles, Asturias, Spain, Aug. 13, 1964; s. Manuel Sedano and Teresa Miguel; m. Monica Torre. Lic. in physics, U. Barcelona, Spain, 1988, M Material Sci., 1990; PhD in Physics, UPC, Barcelona, 1997. Prof. math. Barcelona, 1989-92; doctoral fellow Commissariat Atomic Energy, Saclay, France, 1992-96; European Union sci. agt. Inst. Advanced Materials Joint Rsch. Ctr., Ispra, Italy, 1996-98, European Union fellow, 1998-00; prof. physics UPV-EHU, Bilbao, Spain, 1999—; invited prof. U. Basque Country, Bilbao. Contbr. articles to sci. jours., including Jour. Nuclear Materials, Fusion Tech. Recipient To a Young Rschr. award Govt. of Catalonia, Barcelona, 1982. Achievements include patent in field.

SEDAR, WARREN THOMAS, lawyer; b. Casper, Wyo., Mar. 21, 1954; s. Bob Thomas Cedar and Mary Lou Knox; m. Pam E. Doby (div.); children: Tera, Cheri, William, Sara, Mary; m. Charlene D. Sedar, Aug. 22, 1992. Pvt. practice Caspar, Wyo.; mem. staff Trial Lawyers Coll., Dubois, Wyo., 1999-2000; dean People's Law Sch., Casper, 1995—. Avocations: painting, writing fiction, fly fishing. E-mail: tsedar@ibm.net. Office: Law Office of Tom Sedar PC 254 N Center St Casper WY 82601-1927

SEDDON, PRISCILLA TINGEY, painter; b. Boston, Apr. 1, 1938; d. Richard Hume and Mildred Gurina (Lundgren) Tingey; m. James Alexander Seddon, Jr., Nov. 28, 1959; children: Amy, Sarah, Carroll, Alice. BFA, Tufts U., 1989; Cert., Sch. of the Mus. of Fine Arts, Boston, 1990, Postgrad. 5th Yr., 1991. Associated with Imagining Angels: World AIDS Day Show, Howard Yezersky Gallery, Boston, 1995, others. Exhbns. include: U. Bridgeport, Conn., 1997, Gallery 84, N.Y.C., 1996, Erector Square Gallery, New Haven, Conn., 1996, Harvard U., Cambridge, Mass., 1996, Art-sWorcester Gallery, Worcester, Mass., 1995, Wellesley Coll., Mass., 1994, Grove Street Gallery, Worcester, 1993, Carvajal Sculpture Gallery, Boston, 1992; works include metal work, paintings and sculptures. Grantee MIT Coun. for Arts, Cambridge, 1988, Firstnight, Inc., Boston, 1991, Hingham Edn. Found., Mass., 1993. Mem. Womens Caucus for Art, Visual AIDS. Avocation: watercolour.

SEDDON, RICHARD HARDING, artist; b. Sheffield, Yorkshire, Eng., May 1, 1915; s. Cyril Harding and Mary (Booth) S.; m. Audrey Madeline Wareham, Aug. 17, 1946. AA, Royal Coll. of Art, London, 1939; PhD, U. Reading, Eng., 1946. Staff tutor in fine art U. Birmingham, U.K., 1946-48; dir. city art galleries Sheffield, U.K., 1948-64; dir. art history and liberal studies Buckinghamshire Coll. of Higher Edn., U.K., 1964-80; art corr. The Guardian, U.K., 1961-64; art columnist Sheffield Telegraph, U.K., 1961-64; London art critic, Birmingham Post, U.K., 1964-72, Yorkshire Post, U.K., 1974-91, Nat. Art Collections Fund Rep. for Yorkshire, 1954-64. Author: The Academic Technique of Painting, 1961, A Hand Uplifted: Memoirs of a War Artist, 1963, Art Collecting for Amateurs, 1965, The Artist's Studio Book, 1983; (with Kimberley Reynolds) A Dictionary of Art Terms, 1981; artist 11 war pictures in The Imperial War Mus., London, 6 pictures in the Victoria and Albert Mus., London, various pictures in pub. and pvt. collections; exhibitor Royal Acad., Royal Watercolour Soc., London, Internat. Exhbn. Watercolour in Seville, Barcelona, Madrid, 1992. Lance corp. Royal Army Ordnance Corps, French 10th Army, 1940; intelligence officer (lt.) Home Guard, 1941-44. Recipient Civic medal Neufchatel, Normandie, France, 1978. Fellow Royal Soc. Watercolour (sr. mem., treas. 1974-86, pres. 1995-96). Avocations: photography, gardening. Home: Arlesey Close, Lytton Grove, SW15 2EX London England

SEDDON-BROWN, WILLIAM GEOFFREY, environmental services company executive; b. Manchester, Eng., June 29, 1941; s. Geoffrey James and Irene Seddon-Brown m. Victoria Sybille Mikolajczak, July 18, 1973; children: Fiona, Stephanie, Leslie, James. Student in natural scis., Cambridge U.; diploma in internat. mktg., Ctr. d'Etude Internat., Geneva; student in pub. and govtl. affairs, U. Calif., Pomona. With Lansil Ltd., Germany and Italy, 1961-63; supr. indsl. engring. and svcs. Monsanto Co., Luxembourg, 1964-68; sr. mktg. mgmt. trainee Monsanto Co., U.S., 1968-69; mgr. Monsanto Co., Brussels, 1969-77; area mgr. Monsanto Co., Romania, 1978-81, Yugoslavia, 1981-84; comml. mgr. Monsanto Co., China, 1984-87; mgrn. pub. affairs Europe-Africa Monsanto Co., Brussels, 1987-91; dir. European Govt. Affairs Waste Mgmt. Internat. plc, Brussels, 1992—; pres. Policy Options and Devel. Strategy sprl; bd. dirs. Vanro S.A. Belgium, European Environ. Coun., conf. Bd. Europe; chmn. European Energy-from-Waste Coalition; lectr. European Ctr. for Pub. Affairs. Photographs exhibited in Hong Kong; contbr. articles to profl. publs. Former bd. dirs. Internat. Sch., Bucharest, Internat. Sch. Burssels; former treas. Belgian Squash Rackets Fedn.; former dep. chmn. Crop Chems. Internat. Comms. Group; former mem. pub. rels. com. Brit. Agrochem. Assn., agrochem. industry water com. Natural Sci. County scholar. Mem. Am. C. of C. in Belgium (bd.dirs., chmn. com., former chmn. environ. health and safety subcom., chmn. eu com.), European Energy Waste Coalition (pres.), European Coun. of Am. C. of C. (chmn.). Avocations: tennis, squash, golf, piano, painting. Address: Ave de la Pelouse 46, 1150 Woluwe-Saint-Pierre Belgium

SEDEI RODDEN, PAMELA JEAN, therapist; b. Johnstown, Pa., Jan. 31, 1956; d. Joseph and Betty Ruth (Watkins) Sedei; m. William Eugene Rodden, Dec. 4, 1982; 1 child, Gretchen Jean. BA, Southwestern Coll., Winfield, Kans., 1977; MS, Pittsburg (Kans.) State U., 1979; PhD, Western Colo. U., 1983. Llic. profl. counselor, Colo., Wyo.; diplomate in psychotherapy; cert. cognitive behaviour therapist; nat. cert. counselor; cert. domestic violence counselor; cert. criminal justice splst. Staff psychologist Autumn Manors Inc., Florence, Kans., 1982-83; clin. psychologist Richmond (Tex.) State Hosp., 1984-86; unit psychologist Wheat Ridge (Colo.) Regional Ctr., 1986-89, acting unit dir., 1989; dir. behavioral svcs. Colo. State Divsn. Devel. Disabilities, Denver, 1989-97; dir. Forensic Mental Health Svcs., Boulder, Colo., 1997—; dir. Rodden Cons., Longmont, Colo., 1986-96. Co-author: A Model for Interdisciplinary On Site Evaluation of People Who Have Dual Diagnosis, 1991. Fellow Am. Coll. Forensic Examiners; mem. Nat. Assn. Dual Diagnosis (bd. dirs. 1994—, pres. Columbine chpt.), Assn. Treatment of Sexual Abusers (clin. mem.), Am. Counseling Assn. Republican. Roman Catholic. Avocations: playing accordian, sewing, reading. Office: Forensic Mental Health Svcs 2741 Iris Ave Ste D Boulder CO 80304-2437 also: 315 W Oak St Ste 204 Fort Collins CO 80521-2724

SEDELMAIER, J. J., filmmaker; b. Chgo., Mar. 11, 1956; s. John Josef and Marie S.; m. Patrice Estella Masters, Nov. 4, 1981. Student, Millikin U., 1974-75; BS in Art, U. Wis., 1979. Asst. animator Perpetual Motion Pictures, N.Y.C., 1981-82; asst. animator, animator Buzzco Prodns., N.Y.C., 1982-84; asst. animator, animator The Ink Tank Corp., N.Y.C., 1984-85, producer, 1985-86, exec. producer, 1986-88, assoc. dir., dir., exec. producer, rep., 1989-91; pres., producer, dir. J. J. Sedelmaier Prodns., White Plains, N.Y., 1991—; launched Beavis and Butthead for MTV-(Art Dirs. Club gold medal, BDA awards, Comm. awards, Hatch awards; subject of retrospectives: Ottawa Animation Festival, 1997, Cinematique Quebecoise, 1997; acclaimed series of cartoons for "Saturday Night Live", animated peacocks for NBC, Captain Linger series for Cartoon Network; prodr. (3 episodes) Schoolhouse Rock; vis. artist Sch. Visual Arts. Prodr., dir. Saturday TV Funhouse. Recipient Annecy Film Festival, France, N.Y. Festivals, Annie award, Mobius award, medal Multiple N.Y. Festivals, Multiple Worldfest. Mem. Am. Inst. Graphic Artists, Assn. Internat. Film Animation, Art Dirs. Club (2 Gold medals), Shore Line Interurban Hist. Soc., Chgo. Transit Posters. Avocations: collecting illustrations, animation art, animation film cons. Office: 199 Main St White Plains NY 10601-3200

SEDGWICK, MARK JOHN, historian, educator; b. London, July 20, 1960; arrived in Egypt, 1987; s. John Reginald and Susan Grace (Hedges) S.; m. Lucy Hope Seton-Watson, Jan. 19, 1996; children: Laila, Zahra. BA, Oxford (Eng.) U., 1981, MA, 1986; postgrad., U. St. Andrews, Scotland, 1991-92; PhD, U. Bergen, Norway, 1999. Audit sr. Arthur Andersen & Co., London, 1981-86; cons. MSCC, London, 1986-87; core coord. Am. U., Cairo, 1989-96, instr., 1987—. Author: Sufism: The Essentials, 2000. Fellow Inst. Chartered Accts. Eng. and Wales; mem. Am. Hist. Assn., Middle East Studies Assn., World History Assn., Am. Acad. Religion. Muslim. Avocations: modern history of Islam, Sufism, new religious movements. Home: 8 Salamlik St Apt 61, Garden City Cairo, Egypt Office: Am U, PO Box 2511, Cairo Egypt

SEDGWICK, (IAN) PETER, merchant banker; b. Liverpool, Eng., Oct. 13, 1935; m. (Verna) Mary Churchward, 1956. Mgr., asst. dir., dir. J. Henry Schroder Wagg & Co. Ltd., London, 1969-89; CEO Schroder Investment Mgmt. Ltd., London, 1985-94; chmn. Schroder U.K. Growth Fund, London, 1994—; non-exec. dir. Schroder & Co., Inc., N.Y.C., 1991-99, chmn., 1996—; non-exec. dir. The Equitable Life Assurance Soc., London, 1991—; pres., chief exec. Schroder US Holdings Inc., N.Y.C., 1996—; chmn. INVESCO City and Comml. Investment Trust plc, London, 1992—; dep. chmn., chmn. del. Schroders plc, London, 1995—; dep. chmn. Schroder Ventures Internat. Investment Trust plc, 1995—, Schroder Internat. Ltd., 1995—. Avocation: golf. Office: Schroders plc, 120 Cheapside, London EC2V 6DS, England

SEDIYAMA, CARLOS SIGUEYUKI, agronomist, educator; b. Maria da Fe, Brazil, Dec. 9, 1947; s. Yuto and Sumie S.; m. Elizabete Zanuncio, Jan. 3, 1976; children: Andre, Ricardo, Camilla. BS, Fed. Univ. Vicosa, 1970, MS in Plant Sci., 1972; PhD in Genetics, N.C. State U., 1980. From aux. tchr. to prof., vice rector Fed. U. Vicosa, Brazil, 1972—. Mem. Brazilian Superior Agrl. Edn. Assn., Phi Kappa Phi. Roman Catholic. Avocations: chess, soccer, reading. Home: Rua Vaz de Melo 91/402, Vicosa 36570000, Brazil Office: U Fed Vicosa, Campus Universitario, Vicosa 36571000, Brazil

SEDLÁČEK, DALIBOR, immunologist, educator; b. Karlovy Vary, Czech Republic, Oct. 24, 1957; s. Svatomír and Markéta (Höhligová) S.; m. Romana Penelová, June 6, 1998. MD, Charles U., Czech Republic, 1983, PhD, 1989. Intern Charles U. Hosp., Plzen, Czech Republic, 1983-86; resident Charles U. Hosp., Plzen, 1986-88; asst. prof. Med. Faculty Charles U., Plzen, 1988—; dep. head immunol. lab. Univ. Hosp., Plzen, 1984-89; cons. infectious diseases Charles U. Hosp., 1989—, head AIDS ctr., 1994—. Contbr. articles to profl. jours. Mem. Infectious Diseases Soc., Travel and Tropical Medicine Soc., Czech Immunol. Soc. Avocations: mountain biking, skiing, hunting, angling. Home: Majakovského 28, 323 19 Plzen Czech Republic Office: Charles U Hosp AIDS Ctr, Benese 13, 305 99 Plzen Czech Republic

SEDLACEK, JAN, engineering executive, consultant; b. Plzen, Czech Republic, Apr. 30, 1949; s. Bohumil and Jirina (Sedivec) S.; m. Marcela Sedlak, Dec. 12, 1974; 1 child, Jan. Ing., Tech. U., Plzen, Czech Republic, 1972; PhD, Tech. U., Prague, 1983. Rschr. Skoda Rsch., Plzen, Czech Republic, 1972-83, head dept., 1983-90, dep. dir., 1991—; cons. U. Plzen, Czech Republic, 1980—. Contbr. articles to profl. jours.; inventor in field. Home: Rojikova 17, 31214 Plzen Czech Republic Office: Skoda Rsch, Tylova 57, 31600 Plzen Czech Republic

SEDLAK, ANTONIN, radiation biophysicist researcher; b. Benesov, Prague, Czech Republic, Mar. 27, 1944; s. Antonin and Marie (Merhautova) S. Master's Degree, Faculty of Natural Scis., Prague, Czech Republic, 1966, Doctor's Degree, 1968; PhD, Czechoslovak Acad. Scis., Brno, 1975. Rschr. worker Inst. Radiation Hygiene, Prague, Czech Republic, 1966-70; grad. rschr. worker Inst. Hygiene and Epidemiology, Prague, Czech Republic, 1971-90; sr. rschr. worker Nat. Inst. Pub. Health, Prague, 1991-94; ind. scientist Nat. Radiation Protection Inst., Prague, 1995—; lectr. Faculty of Nuclear Scis. and Phys. Engring., Prague, 1986—. Author: (book) Mikrodozimetrie, 1989 (Creative Prize 1990). Mem. N.Y. Acad. Scis. Avocation: computers. Office: Nat Radiation Protect Inst, Srobarova 48, 100 00 Prague Czech Republic

SEDLAK, JAMES WILLIAM, organization administrator; b. Tarrytown, N.Y., Nov. 17, 1943; s. Jacob Frank and Catherine Eva (Sedlak) S.; m. G. Michaeleen Bizub, June 17, 1967; children: Frank George, Jeanette Michele Sedlak Veltri, Terri Lynn Rose Sedlak Ferrara. BS in Physics, Manhattan Coll., 1967; MS in Indsl. Adminstrn., Union Coll., Schenectady, 1975. Customer engr. IBM, N.Y.C., 1963-67; semicondr. engr. IBM, East Fishkill, N.Y., 1967-80; sr. engr. IBM, Harrison, N.Y., 1980-92; co-founder, nat. dir. Stop Planned Parenthood, La Grangeville, N.Y., 1986-93; pres., writer, editor The Ryan Report, STOPP (Stop Planned Parenthood) Internat., La Grangeville, 1994-98; v.p. pub. policy and edn. Am. Life League, Inc., Stafford, Va., 1998—; Former guest lectr. med. ethics Mt. St. Mary's Coll., Newburgh, N.Y.; guest lectr. ethics Vassar Coll., Poughkeepsie, N.Y., 1986-92. Author: Quarterly Dividends, 1975, Parent Power!!, 1990, Deadly Deception, 1996; co-author: Title X: The Six Billion Dollar Scam, 1997; contbr. to pro-life publs. Past pres. PTO; mem. bd. advisors Am. Life League, Inc.; former mem. faculty Apostles of Life Leadership Acad., Human Life Internat.; cons. to nat. and internat. pro-life groups; speaker numerous state-wide pro-life convs. and events, U.S., Can., Mex., Italy, Australia, No. Ireland, Eng. and New Zealand; workshop presenter nat. convs. Concerned Women for Am., Human Life Internat., Am. Life League; numerous apprearances on radio and TV. Recipient Dutchess County Right to Life Pro-Lifer of Yr. award, 1984, Expectant Mother Care N.Y. Pro-Life Champion award, 1987, family life award Parent's Roundtable, 1987, Unsung Hero award Am. Life League, 1988, Disting. Svc. to Life award Grand Haven (Mich.) Pro-Lifers, 1993, also others. Mem. KC (3d degree). Roman Catholic. Office: Am Life League Inc PO Box 1350 Stafford VA 22555-1350

SEDLAK, JOSEPH ANTHONY, III, lawyer; b. Cleve., Feb. 22, 1952; s. Joseph Anthony Jr. and Winefred Veronica (Nantell) S.; m. Susan Ann Dill, Oct. 1, 1983; children: Joseph Anthony IV and John Warrior Sedlak (twins). BA, Ohio State U., 1974; JD, St. Mary's U., San Antonio, 1977. Bar: Tex. 1977, Colo. 1980, U.S. Dist. Ct. Colo. 1980, U.S. Ct. Appeals (10th cir.) 1980. Assoc. Law Offices of Grady L. Roberts, Piersall, Tex., 1977-80, LoBato, Bliedt & Bliedt, Lakewood, Colo., 1980-81, Vranesic & Visciano, Denver, 1981-85; pres. Sedlak & Vogel P.C., Denver, 1985-91, Sedlak & Assocs. P.C., Denver, 1991—. Mem. Colo. Bar Assn., Denver Bar Assn., Am. Trial Lawyers Assn., Denver Jud. Adminstrn. Com., Denver C. of C., Racquet World Club, Denver Petroleum Club. Roman Catholic. Avocations: skiing, golf, hunting. Office: 621 17th St Ste 2655 Denver CO 80293-2601

SEDLÁK, MIKULÁŠ, ambassador, educator; b. Kojšov, Slovakia, Sept. 18, 1928; s. Mikulášand Irena (Hausová) S.; m. Anna Perželová, Oct. 18, 1952; 1 child, Mikuláš. MBA, Sch. Econs., Bratislava, Slovakia, 1951; PhD, Sch. of Econs., Prague, Czech Republic, 1957. Assoc. prof. Sch. of Econs., Bratislava, Slovakia, 1960-65, dean of faculty, 1960-63, prof., 1965, v.p., 1966-69, pres., 1969-70, prof., 1970-90, dean faculty, 1990, pres., 1991-94, prof., 1994-98; amb. Embassy of the Slovak Republic in Tokyo, Japan, 1998—. Author: Organization of the American Firms and Managers, 1967, Production Organization of the Enterprises, 1971, Organization Structure Development of the Industrial Enterprises, 1988, Managment, 1997, 98, 2000 (in Slovakia). Chmn. Slovak Assn. of the Scientific Mgmt., Bratislava, 1967-71; mem. Econ. Coun. of Govt., Bratislava, 1990-93. Mem. Slovak Internat. Rels. and Understanding Soc. (v.p. 1994-99), Ind. Assn. of Economists of Slovakia (pres. 1995-99), N.Y. Acad. Scis., Fgn. Corr. Club of Japan, Internat. Friendship Exch. Com., City Club Tokyo. Avocations: music, fine arts, tourism, reading belles-letters. Home: Hiroo Residence No 301, 3-12-24 Hiroo Shibuya-ku, Tokyo Japan Office: Emb of the Slovak Republic, 2-16-14 Hiroo Shibuya-ku, Tokyo 150-8691, Japan

SEDLAK, S(HIRLEY) A(GNES), freelance writer, novelist; b. Chgo., Sept. 6; d. Frederick Jesse and Agnes (Baum) Machacek; m. Harold Otto Sedlak; 1 child, Linda Carol. Student, Morton Jr. Coll., Cicero, Ill. Editor children's books Benefic Press subs. Harcourt Brace Jovanovich, Westchester, Ill., 1973-75; publicity and pub. rels. The Nat. League of Am. Pen Women, Inc., Chgo. br., 1987-89. Author: Bury Her Gently, 2000. Home: 2226 S 9th Ave No Riverside IL 60546-1110

SEDLAR, MILAN, mathematician; b. Sumperk, Czech Republic, Mar. 15, 1960; s. Milan and Vera (Stoklasek) S.; m.Marta Vymazal, Dec. 23, 1965; children: Petr, Dana. MS, Palacky U., Olomouc, Czech Republic, 1984; PhD, Acad. Scis., Prague, Czech Republic, 1994. Rschr. SIGMA Rsch. Inst., Olomouc, 1984-89; ind. rschr. Pump Rsch. Inst., Olomouc, 1989-96, rsch. scientist, 1996-97; sr. rsch. scientist SIGMA R & D Inst., Lutin, Czech Republic, 1997—; lectr. Palacky U., 1989—, Tech. U., Brno, Czech Republic, 1993—. Contbr. papers to profl. pubs. Recipient award of Sec. of State for Edn. and Sci. Dept. Edn. and Scis. Czech Republic, 1984. Mem. Czech Mech. Engring. Soc. (Babuska award 1994). Avocations: swimming, sports, painting. Home: Dvorakova 529, CZ-75101 Tovacov Czech Republic Office: Sigma R&D Inst, Jana Sigmunda 79, CZ-78350 Lutin Czech Republic

SEDO, ALEKSI, scientist, physician; b. Helsinki, Finland, June 18, 1961; s. Karel and Jirina Sedo; m. Liliana Raquel Liberoff, June 14, 1985; 1 child, Clara. MD, Charles U., Prague, Czech Republic, 1986, PhD, 1990. Specialist in internal medicine Govt. Inst. Edn. of Physicians. Rsch. fellow Rsch. Inst. Respiratory Diseases, Prague, 1986-91; rsch. fellow Inst. Mutagenesis, Pisa, Italy, 1992, vis. prof., 1993; rsch. fellow Inst. Curie, Paris, 1994-95; asst. prof. Charles U., 1995-96, assoc. prof. biochemistry, 1996—; sr. scientist corp. rsch. and devel. Europe Procter and Gamble, Frankfurt, Germany, 1996—; sr. scientist Acad. of Scis., Prague, 1995—, head Acad. Sci. and Charles U. Joint Lab. of Biology of Cancer Cells, 1999—. Contbr. numerous articles to profl. jours.; patentee in field. Grantee Grant Agy. of Czech Republic, 1993-95, 96-98, Grant, Charles Univ., 1999—, Assoc. Recherche et Partage, France, 1994, CNR Italy/Charles U. Prague, 1993-94; recipient Gold medal EXPO Invention Exhbn., 1991. Mem. Biochem. Assn. Prague, Assn. Physicians Prague, Internat. Com. on Proteolysis, N.Y. Acad. Scis., European Tissue Regeneration Soc. Roman Catholic. Avocations: music, literature, painting. Home: Dominova 2470, 155 00 Prague 5, Czech Republic Office: 1st Dept Med Chem, Katerinska 32, 121 08 Prague 2, Czech Republic

SEEBOLD, ELMAR, retired educator; b. Stuttgart, Germany, Sept. 28, 1934; s. Eugen and Maria (Engelhardt) S.; m. Hertha Margarete Dilger, Aug. 14, 1964 (dec. 1999); children: Ulrich, Hildegard, Irmtraud, Almut. DPhil, U. Tubingen, 1964; PhD, U. Cologne, 1970. Asst. U. Tubingen, Germany, 1965; asst. U. Cologne, 1965-71, asst. prof., 1970; assoc. prof. U. Fribourg, Switzerland, 1971-74, prof., 1974-83; assoc. prof. U. Munich, 1983-2000; dean faculty U. Fribourg, 1978-79, U. Munich, 1987-89. Author etymological dictionaries of German and other Germanic langs. Home: Muhlstr 18, Andechs D-82346, Germany

SEED, JENNY (CECILE EUGENIE SEED), children's writer; b. South Africa, 1930. Author: Peter the Gardener, 1966, To the Rescue, 1966, Tombi's Song, 1966, Timothy and Tinker, 1967, The River Man, 1968, Canvas City, 1968, The Voice of the Great Elephant, 1968, Kulumi the Brave, 1970, The Prince of the Bay, 1970 (published in U.S. as The Vengeance of the Zulu King), The Great Thirst, 1971, The Broken Spear, 1972, The Red Dust Soldiers, 1972, The Shy Green Lizard, 1973, The Bushman's Dream, 1974, The Unknown Land, 1976, Strangers in the Land, 1976, The Year One, 1981, The Policeman's Button, 1981, Gold Dust, 1982, The New Fire, 1983, The Spy Hill, 1984, Place Among the Stones, 1987, Hurry, Hurry, Sibusiso, 1988, Old Grandfather Mantis, 1992, The Hungry People, 1992, A Time to Scatter Stones, 1993, Lucky Boy, 1995, The Strange Large Egg, 1996. Office: 10 Pioneer Cres Northdene, Queensburgh Kwazulu Natal 4093, South Africa

SEED, MICHAEL PETER, rheumatologist, researcher; b. Sydney, N.S.W., Australia, Sept. 3, 1957; m. Janet Margaret Bentham, Sept. 29, 1990; children: Christina Janet, Patrick Michael. BSc in Pharmacology with hons., U. Bath, Avon, U.K., 1980, PhD, 1984. Chartered biologist. Lectr. Bath U., Avon, 1984-86; scientist Hoechst (UK) Ltd., Milton Keynes, 1986-87; sr. scientist Roussel Labs Ltd., Swindon, 1987-90; rsch. fellow, hon. lectr., head angiogenesis rsch. St. Bartholomews Hosp. Med. Sch., London, 1990-97; mng. dir. Panceutics Ltd., Swindon, 1998—, Nutrasense Europe Ltd., 1999—; prin. Futurebiotics Ltd., 2000—; vis. fellow St. Bartholomew's Hosp. Med. Sch., 1998—. Asst. editor European Jour. Rheumatology and Inflammation, London, 1992-95; U.K. editor: Inflammation Rsch. jour., 1995-2000, HBSA/NRA Heritage Arms Catalogue; mem. editl. bd. Angiogenesis Jour.; contbr. articles to profl. jours. Fellow Royal Soc. Medicine; mem. European Inflammation Soc., Inst. Biology (U.K.), Brit. Pharmacol. Soc., Brit. Soc. for Rheumatology, Brit. Inflammation Rsch. Assn. (com. mem. 1995-00), N.Y. Acad. Sci., Hist. Breech Loading Small Arms Assn. (life, coun. mem. 1998—, chmn. rsch. and scholarship standing subcom. 2000—), NRA U.K. (life), North London Rifle Club (pistol capt. 2000—, Gold jewel award 1999, Silver Jewel award 1993, Bronze jewel award 1997), Inst. Advanced Motorists and High Performance Club, British Alpine Rifles. Avocations: British military, civilian and target pistols, roadcraft. Office: Panceutics Ltd, PO Box 1358, Swindon SN3 4GP, England

SEEDAT, YACKOOB KASSIM, medical educator; b. Durban, Natal, South Africa, Feb. 7, 1934; s. Kassim Mohammed and Hajira Mohammed (Ebrahim) S.; m. Zuleka Cassim Mahomedy, Apr. 6, 1966; children: Riaz, Ziad. MB BChir., BA in Obstetrics, Nat. U. Ireland, 1957, MD, 1967; diploma, Sastri Coll., Durban; PhD in Med. Sci. (hon.), U. Durban-Westville, 1991. Intern in surgery Univ. Coll., Dublin, Ireland, 1950-56; various positions King Edward VIII Hosp., 1958-78; acad. registrar Royal Infirmary, Manchester, U.K., 1967-68; prof., head medicine U. Natal, Durban, South Africa, 1978-94, prof. medicine, rsch., 1995—; presenter in field; pres. So. African Hypertension Soc., 1981-83; chmn. faculty of physicians Coll. of Medicine of South Africa, 1992-95; internat. adviser Internat. Coll. Nutrition. Mem. editorial bd. numerous jours., including Blood Pressure, South African Med. Jour., Modern Medicine, Update, Internat. Jour. of Artificial Organs, Cardiovascular Risk Factors, Jour. Human Hypertension, Jour. Ethnicity and Health, Am. Biographical Inst.; contbr. over 350 articles to profl. publs., chpts. to books. Decorated officer Order St. John of Jerusalem; recipient Spl. award for rsch. Med. Rsch. Coun. of South Africa, State Pres.'s Order for Meritorious Svc., 1990, Silver Rsch. award Med. Assn. South Africa, 1994; hon. fellow Coll. Medicine of South Africa, 1998. Fellow Coll. Medicine of South Africa, Uruguayan Cardiac Soc. (hon.), Med. Grad. Assn. U. Natal (hon. life fellow), Royal Coll. Physicians London, Royal Coll. Physicians Ireland, Royal Coll. Physicians South Africa, Am. Coll. Cardiology,Coll. Chest Physicians, Am. Coll. Angiology, Internat. Coll. Angiology, I.C.N., N.Y. Acad. Scis., Royal Soc. Sci. South Africa; mem. Med. Assn. of South Africa (fed. coun. 1974-81, 94-98), Nat. Kidney Assn. South Africa (mem. com.), Rsch. Assn. (bd. govs.), Coun. Coll. Medicine (exec. mem. 1989-95, chmn. coll. of physicians 1992-95, 98—), Internat. Soc. Hypertension, Internat. Soc. Nephrology, South African Med. Assn. (nat. councillor 1998—), Health Profl. Coun. Muslim. Avocations: reading, music, writing, travel, walking. Home: 41 Devon Terr, Westville 3630, South Africa Office: U Natal, PO Box 17039, Congella 4013, South Africa

SEEDORF, CLARENCE, soccer player. Midfielder Real Madrid Soccer Club, Inter, Italy. Address: Inter Head Office, Via Durini 24, 20122 Milan Italy*

SEEDS, ALWYN JOHN, opto-electronics researcher, educator; b. Amersham, Eng., July 24, 1955; s. Harry and Margaret Mary (Ferguson) S.; m. Angela Carolyn Williams, Oct. 11, 1986; 1 child, Caroline Emily Margaret. BSc, U. London, 1976; PhD, Univ. Coll. London, 1980. Staff mem. Lincoln Lab., MIT, Lexington, 1980-83; lectr. telecom. Queen Mary Coll., London, 1983-86; lectr. Univ. Coll. London, 1986-91, sr. lectr., 1991-93, reader, 1993-95, prof. opto-electronics, 1995—; cons. U.K. Ministry of Def., 1994—, Lincoln Lab., MIT, 1995-96; European Community, 1993, European Space Agy., Noordwijk, The Netherlands, 1987, Bell No. Rsch. Europe, Harlow, Eng., 1991-94, GE Co., Eng., 1992-99, BBC, London, 1985. Patentee in field; contbr. articles to profl. publs. Rsch. grantee U.K. Engring. and Phys. Scis. Rsch. Coun., 1985—, European Space Agy., 1991-92, Royal Soc., 1989-90, USAF Office Sci. Rsch., 1993-99, U.S. Army, 1995-97; travel grantee U.S. Army, Royal Soc., Royal Acad. Engring. Brit. Coun. Fellow IEEE, Inst. Elec. Engrs. (chartered, mem. optical devices and systems profl. group 1989-95); mem. Microwave Theory and Techniques Soc. of IEEE (chmn. light wave com. 1999—), Internat. Union for Radio Sci. (chmn. commn. D 1999—). Anglican. Avocations: amateur radio, music, opera, architectural history. Office: Univ Coll, Torrington Pl, Dept Electronic/Elec Engrng, London WC1E 7JE, England

SEEGENSCHMIEDT, HEINRICH MICHAEL, radiation oncologist; b. Erlangen, Germany, June 10, 1956; s. Friedrich Johann and Adelheid (Fricke) S.; m. Marion Elisabeth Wuermeling, Apr. 12, 1980; children: Sebastian, Johannes, Andreas, Emanuel, Victoria. MD, U. Würzburg, Germany, 1982. Lic. in radiation/oncology, Germany. Fellow in pathology U. Würzburg, 1983-84; resident in internal medicine, hematology/oncology Nürnberg (Germany) Cmty. Hosp., 1984-85, resident in radiation diagnos-

tics, 1989-90; resident/fellow in radiation oncology Hahnemann U., Phila., 1985-87; resident in radiation oncology U. Erlangen-Nürnberg, Germany, 1987-89, instr., then sr. instr., 1987-90, jr., then sr. attending physician in radiation oncology, 1991-96, assoc. prof., 1994-96; prof., head dept. radiation oncology, therapeutic radiology and nuc. medicine Alfried-Krupp Krankenhaus, Essen, Germany, 1996—; instr. dept. radiation oncology and nuclear medicine Hahnemann U., 1985-87, vis. prof., 1990—; mem. allied health professions com. in internal medicine U. Erlangen-Nurnberg, 1988, mem. allied health professions com. on radiation oncology, 1990, mem. quality assurance and other coms.; Lund Sci. clin. hyperthermia investigator, 1988—; organizer nat. and internat. profl. symposia, 1987, 88, 91, 93, 95, 97, 98, 99, 2000; active many profl. confs. and workshops, 1987—. Editor: (textbook) Interstitial and Intracavitary Thermoradiotherapy, 1993, Thermoradiotherapy and Thermochemotherapy, vol. 1, 1995, vol. 2, 1996, Treatment Side Effects in Oncology, 1998, Current Concepts of Radiation Therapy for Non-Malignant Diseases, 1998, 99, 2000, Radiation Oncology Sequelae, 2000; contbr. numerous articles to sci. jours.; mem. rev. bd. Internat. Jour. Hyperthermia, 1988—, Internat. Jour. Radiation Oncology Biology Physics, 1988—, Radiother. Oncol., 1993—, Acta Oncologica, 1995—, others; mem. rev. bd. Am. Jour. Clin. Oncology, 1989—, mem. editl. bd., 1992—. German Cancer Aid Found. rsch. fellow/scholar, 1985-87, German Rsch. Found. rsch. fellow/scholar, 1991-93, 93-95; scholar Hundhammer Found., Munich, 1976-82, Konrad Adenauer Found., Bonn, Germany, 1978-82; recipient Erwin Braun prize Erwin Braun Found., Basel, Switzerland, 1991, Rsch. Travel award Sophie Wallner Cancer Rsch. Found., 1988, 92, 94, Deutsche Forschungsgemeinschaft, 1989, 91, 95, Anna Hamann Found., 1992, 94, Deutscher Röntgenpreis German Radiol. Soc., 1994. Mem. Am. Soc. Therapeutic Radiology and Oncology, Radiation Rsch. Soc., N.Am. Hyperthermia Group, Cir. of Radiotherapeutics Ibero Latin Am., German Med. Assn., Bavarian Med. County, German Radiology Soc., German Cancer Soc. (quality assurance com.), European Soc. Therapeutic Radiology and Oncology, European Soc. Hyperthermic Oncology, German Soc. Radiation Oncology (quality assurance com.), Radiol. Soc. N.Am., German Soc. Palliative Medicine. Avocations: sports, volcanoe climbing, photography, music/piano. Home: Hans-Niemeyer-Str 4, 45133 Essen Germany Office: Alfried-Krupp Krankenhaus, Alfried-Krupp Str 21, 45117 Essen Ruttenscheid, Germany

SEEGER, DAVID OWEN, electrical engineer, consultant; b. Feb. 25, 1974. B Elec. Engring., Ga. Inst. Tech., 1997. Analyst, cons. Andersen Consulting, Atlanta, 1997—. Home: 20 Pellbridge Rd Hopewell Junction NY 12533-6229

SEEGER, MELINDA WAYNE, realtor; m. Robert Charles Seeger; 1 child, Jeffrey Wayne. Chief occupl. therapy Rehab. Inst. Oreg., Portland, 1964-66; supr. phys. disabilities and gen. medicine and surgery occupl. therapy Mpls. VA Hosp., 1966-68; supr. phys. disabilities occupl. therapy Nat. Naval Med. Ctr., Bethesda, Md., 1968-71; assoc. chief rehab. svcs., dir. occupl. therapy UCLA Med. Ctr., 1974-85, cons., prin. investigator rheumatology divsn. dept. medicine, 1985-86; realtor Merrill Lynch Realty, L.A., 1987-95, Re/Max Estate Properties, Beverly Hills, Calif., 1995-96, Nelsoden Shelton & Assocs., Beverly Hills, 1996—. Author, editor articles in field. Mem. utilization rev. com. Vis. Nurse Assn. L.A., 1975-85, mem. profl. adv. com., 1979-80; mem. exec. com. Allied Health Professions sect. Arthritis Found., 1980-85, chmn. edn. com., 1982-85, mem. profl. edn. com.; bd. dirs. Calif. Occupl. Therapy Found., 1984-85, Westwood-Holmby Hills Homeowners Assn.; mem. adv. bd. Save Westwood Village L.A. Recipient Spl. Achievement award Nat. Naval Med. Ctr., 1971, Outstanding Performance award, 1971, Spl. Performance award UCLA, 1980, 84, Addie Thomas Svc. award for outstanding svc. to rheumatology cmty. Arthritis Found., 1986, Cert. of Appreciation award, 1989; mem. Million Dollar Club. Mem. Am. Occupl. Therapy Assn., Occupl. Therapy Assn. Calif., Allied Health Professions Assn. (chmn. edn. com. 1982—), L.A. Bd. Realtors, San Fernando Valley Bd. Realtors, West L.A. C. of C., Million Dollar Club, Blue Diamond Club. Office: 355 N Canon Dr Beverly Hills CA 90210-4704

SEEGER, THOMAS, chemical engineering scientist; b. Essen, Germany, June 1, 1962; s. Herbert and Doris (Pollmer) S.; m. Astrid Sandkühler, Oct. 2, 1987; children: Katrin, Jan. Diploma in physics, U. Essen, 1989; D of Engring., U. Erlangen-Nürnberg, Erlangen, Germany, 1994. Rsch. asst. Ruhr U., Bochum, Germany, 1989; rsch. asst. U. Erlangen-Nürnberg, Erlangen, 1989-94, asst. prof., 1994—. Contbr. articles to profl. jours. Mem. German Phys. Soc., German Soc. Engrs. Roman Catholic. Office: LST Tech Thermodynamics, Am Weichselgarten 8, 91058 Erlangen Germany

SEEHAUSEN, RICHARD FERDINAND, architect; b. Indpls., Mar. 17, 1925; s. Paul Ferdinand and Melusina Dorothea (Nordmeyer) S.; m. Phyllis Jean Gates, Dec. 22, 1948; children: Lyn, Dirk. Student, DePauw U., 1943-44, Wabash Coll., 1944, State U. Iowa, 1944; BArch, U. Ill., 1949. Registered profl. arch. Ptnr. Johnson, Kile, Seehausen & Assocs., Inc. archs., engrs., Rockford, Ill., 1955-82, pres., 1974-82; pres. Richard F. Seehausen-Arch., Inc., Rockford, Ill., 1983—; mem. com. jail planning and constrn. stds. Bur. Detention Facilities, Ill. Dept. Corrections, 1970-73; analyst Dept. Def., 1962-66; analyst Fed. Fall-Out Shelter, 1962—. Prin. works include No. Ill. U. Ctr., also Health Svc. Bldg., DeKalb, Winnebago County Courthouse, Rockford, St. Mark Luth Ch., Rockford, Christ Meth. Ch., Rockford, 1st Presbyn. Ch., Rochelle, Ill., Forest Hills Free Ch., Rockford, Ill., Messiah Luth. Ch., Rock Falls, Ill., Ch. of the Nazarene, Freeport, Ill., McHenry County Ct. House, Woodstock, Ill., Stephenson County Courthouse, Freeport, Ogle County Pub. Safety Bldg., Oreg., DeKalb H.S., Page Park Spl. Edn. Sch., Rockford, Oak Crest Retirement Ctr., Sycamore/DeKalb, Ill., Social Security bldgs. in Racine, Sheboygan, Oshkosh and Janesville, Wis., Freeport YWCA Bldgs., renovation Carroll County Ct. House, DeKalb Area Retirement Ctr.; renovation Old Winnebago County Courthouse, Rockford, Rockford Mut. Ins. Home Office Bldg., renovation Court Street Meth. Ch., Rockford, Willows Personal Care Ctr., Rockford, others. Bd. dirs. Rockford Boys Club, Lincoln Pk. Boys Club, past dir.; trustee Emmanuel Luth. Ch., Rockford, 1989-92; mem. Nat. Trust Hist. Preservation, 2000—. Served with USNR, 1943-45, Lt. USAF, 1949-55. Mem. AIA (dir. No. Ill. chpg. 1966-68, 75-77, pres. chpt. 1978-79), Ill. Coun. of Am. Inst. Archs., U. Ill. Alumni Assn., Mason (Shriner), Kiwanian, Forest Hills Country Club (gov. 1970-72), Saddle Brooke Country Club, Lamdba Chi Alpha. Lutheran. Office: Richard F Seehausen Arch Inc 65297 E Emerald Ridge Dr Tucson AZ 85739-1434

SEELA, TORSTEN, library educator; b. Gorlitz, Germany, Feb. 14, 1948; s. Heinz Alfred and Gerda Lucie (Czieselsky) S.; m. Petra Susanne Spies, Apr. 15, 1972; 1 child, Christiane. Diploma in libr., Humboldt U., Berlin, 1975, PhD, 1990. Tchr. Coll. Libr., Leipzig, Germany, 1970-92; prof. HTWK, Leipzig, Germany, 1992—. Author: Buecher und Bibliotheken in nationalsozialistischen Konzentrationslagern, 1992; contbr. articles to profl. jours. Mem. Verein Deutscher Bibliothekare. Roman Catholic. Avocation: philately. Home: Kroikstr 5, D-04157 Leipzig Germany Office: Hochschule Techn Wirtsch, Bertolt-Brecht-Str 1, D-04347 Leipzig Germany

SEELBACH, KARL ULRICH, foreign language educator, literary historian; b. Giessen, Hessen, Germany, Oct. 23, 1952; s. Karl-Ernst and Helga (Schwarz) S.; m. Sabine Heimann, Feb. 10, 1992; children: Karl, Martin. MA, Free U. Berlin, 1980, PhD, 1984, habilitation, 1997. Assoc. prof. dept. German Free U. Berlin, 1997—; Mem. com. for early modern lit. German Working Group for Scholarly Editing, 1990, mem. com. for computer editing, 1992—; guest prof. Medieval German Lit. U. Osnabrueck, 1998-99. Author: Bibliographie zu Wernher der Gartenaere, 1981, Arbeiter-, Soldaten- und Bauernraete im Kreis Giessen, 1983, Spaethoefische Literatur im spaeten Mittelalter, 1987, Kommentar zum Helmbrecht, 1987; editor: Erzehlungen aus den Mittlern Zeiten, 1985, Wernher der Gartenaere: Helmbrecht, 1987, Joerg Muelich: Reisebericht, 1993; co-editor: Daniel Czepko. Werke (8 vols.), 1988-97, Johann Fischart. Werke, 1991—, Wilhelm Salzmann: Octavianus, 1993, Ludus lectoris Studien zum idealen leser Johann Fischarts, 2000; editor Daphnis, 1985—. Home: Gemenweg 57, 48149 Münster Germany Office: Fachbereich Philosophy Free, U Habelschwerdter Allee 45, 14195 Berlin Germany

SEELENBERGER, SERGIO HERNAN, clinical and diagnostic company executive; b. Santiago, Chile, Oct. 3, 1942; s. Gustav Julius and Sonia (Posternack) S.; m. Annabella Farba, Apr. 6, 1968 (separated 1993); m. Miriam Linetzky, Sept. 7, 1996; children: Martha, Alberto, Alexander. Diploma in Architecture, Cath. U., Santiago, 1967, M in Regional Planning, 1968; M in City Planning, U. Calif., Berkeley, 1970. Registered profl. architect. Researcher U. Calif., Berkeley, 1969-70; prof. Cath. Univ., Santiago, 1970-73; chief planning advisor Sec. of State of Transp., Rio De Janeiro, Brazil, 1973-79; rsch. dir. Ibam-Brasil, Rio De Janeiro, 1975-81; prof. Federal Univ.-Coppe, Rio De Janeiro, 1975-77, Getulio Vargas Found., Rio De Janeiro, 1977-81; ptnr., dir. Planpur Ltd., Rio De Janeiro, 1977-81, Icham Ltd., Santiago, 1983-90, Clinitest Ltd./Labatria S.A., Santiago, 1985—; ptnr., dir., pres. Biomerieux Chile S.A., Santiago, 1993-95; dir. Biogen S.A., Santiago, 1995-96; ptnr., dir. S. Seelenberger & Sons Holding Co., Santiago, 1992—; cons. InterAm. Devel. Bank, Washington, 1988-90, World Bank, Washington, 1988-89, UN/Cepal, Rio de Janeiro, 1980-82. Author: Low Income Housing National Contest-Brasil, 1975 (Negrao de Lima prize 1976); contbr. articles to profl. jours. Internat. v.p. B'nai B'rith Internat., Washington/Santiago, 1990-92, pres. dist. 27, Chile-Bolivia, 1988-90, mission officer for help to Russian Refuseniks, Leningrad-Moscow, 1989; policy advisor Ministry of Housing, Santiago, 1970. Recipient grad. scholarship Cath. U., 1967, grad. studies grant Ford Found., Berkeley, 1968-70, rsch. grant Govt. Brasil, 1976. Mem. AAAS, InterAm. Planning Soc., Am. Inst. Planners, Am. Planning Assn., Am. Assn. for Clin. Chemistry. Jewish. Avocations: social work, chess, computer graphics, soccer, tennis. Home: Carolina Rabat 920 Apt 11, Vitacura Santiago Chile Office: Clinitest Ltd, Ricardo Lyon 1899, Santiago Chile

SEELENFREUND, ALAN, distribution company executive; b. N.Y.C., Oct. 22, 1936; s. Max and Gertrude (Roth) S.; m. Ellyn Bolt; 1 child, Eric. BME, Cornell U., 1959, M. in Indsl. Engring., 1960; PhD in Mgmt. Sci., Stanford U., 1967. Asst. prof. bus. adminstrn. Grad. Sch. Bus. Stanford U., Palo Alto, Calif., 1966-71; mgmt. cons. Strong, Wishart and Assocs., San Francisco, 1971-75; various mgmt. positions McKesson Corp., San Francisco, 1975-84, v.p., chief fin. officer, 1984-86, exec. v.p., chief fin. officer, 1986-89, chmn., CEO, 1989-97, chmn., 1997-99, also bd. dirs., chmn., 1997—; bd. dirs. McKesson HBOC, Inc., San Francisco, 1999—. Bd. dir. Golden Gate Nat. Park Assn. Mem. World Affairs Coun. No. Calif., Bay Area Coun., Nature Conservancy, World Wildlife Fund, St. Francis Yacht Club, Villa Taverna Club, Pacific Union Club. Avocations: sailing, skiing. Office: McKesson Corp 1 Post St Ste 3275 San Francisco CA 94104-5292

SEELOS, CHRISTIAN, scientist, consultant; b. Innsbruck, Austria, Jan. 3, 1964; s. Otto Max Seelos and Gudrun (Gritsch) Liener. MSc, U. Vienna, 1990, PhD, 1993. Rsch. assoc. Baylor Coll. Medicine, Houston, 1990-92; sr. cons. UN Spl. Commn., N.Y.C., 1994-99; assoc. prof. U. Vienna, 1992—. Author: DNA Tumor Viruses, 1996. Lt. col. Austrian Army, 1997-99. Decorated medal in the svc. of peace UN, 1999. Avocations: skiing, guitar, piano, cooking.

SEELY, ROBERT DANIEL, physician, medical educator; b. Woodmere, N.Y., Nov. 4, 1923; s. Harry and Ethel (Weil) S.; m. Marcia Ann Wells, June 19, 1953; children: Ellen Wells, Anne Wells. B.S., NYU, 1943; M.D., Columbia U., 1946. Intern Mt. Sinai Hosp., N.Y.C., 1946-47, asst. resident in medicine, 1950-51, resident in pathology, 1951-52, chief resident in medicine, 1952-53; Sara Welt fellow in cardiovascular research Presbyn. Hosp., N.Y.C., 1953-54; instr. dept. physiology, cardiovascular research Western Res. U., Cleve., 1947-48; chief rheumatic heart disease clinic Mt. Sinai Hosp., N.Y.C., 1961-70, attending physician medicine and cardiology, 1978—, chief of service dept. medicine, 1979—, clin. prof. medicine, cardiology Sch. Medicine, 1970—; practice medicine specializing in cardiovascular disease N.Y.C., 1953—. Contbr. articles to profl. jours. Served to capt. M.C. AUS, 1948-50. Recipient Solomon Berson Meml. award Mt. Sinai Hosp., 1977. Fellow Am. Coll. Cardiology, ACP; mem. N.Y. Heart Assn., AMA, N.Y. County Med. Soc., Soc. Cert. Internists N.Y., Phi Beta Kappa, Alpha Omega Alpha, Beta Lambda Sigma. Office: 49 E 96th St # 11D New York NY 10128-0782

SEELY, STEPHEN, design engineer, researcher; b. Budapest, Hungary, Oct. 11, 1909; arrived in United Kingdom, 1939; BS, U. Edinburgh, U.K., 1942. Design engr. GE, Manchester, U.K., 1942-71; rsch. fellow U. Manchester, U.K., 1980-92. Author: Diet-Related Diseases: The Modern Epidemic, 1985; Contbr. articles to profl. jours. Mem. AAAS, The N.Y. Acad. Scis. Avocation: bridge. Home: 3 Truro Dr, Sale M33 5DF, United Kingdom Office: Dept Cardiology, University of Manchester, Manchester United Kingdom

SEEMAN, PHILIP, pharmacology educator, neurochemistry researcher; b. Winnipeg, Man., Can., Feb. 8, 1934; s. Jacob and Fanny (Wigdor) S.; m. Mary V. Szwarc; children: Marc, Bob, Neil. BS, McGill U., Montreal, Can., 1955, MS, 1956, MD, 1960; PhD, Rockefeller U., 1966. Prof. pharmacology U. Toronto, Can., 1967—, chmn. dept. pharmacology, 1977-87. Author over 300 publs. on dopamine receptors, their discovery, and their changes in brain diseases. Recipient Upjohn award Can. Pharmacology Soc., 1980, John Dewan award Ont. Mental Health Found., 1981, Heinz Lehmann award Can. Coll. Neuropsychopharmacology, 1985, Lieber award Nat. Alliance for Rsch. in Schizophrenia and Depression, 1990, Dean award Am. Coll. Psychiatrists, 1990, Tanenbaum Schizophrenia Rsch. award Can. Psychiat. Rsch. Fedn., 1991, Prix Galien Can., 1994, Pasarow award in Neuropsychiatry, 1995, Killam award Can. Coun., 1996, Lifetime Achievement award Soc. Biol. Psychiatry, 1996. Fellow Royal Soc. Can.; mem. Am. Soc. Pharmacology, Soc. Neurosci., Am. Coll. Neuropsychopharmacology. Home: 32 Parkwood Ave, Toronto, ON Canada M4V 2X1 Office: U of Toronto Med Scis Bldg, Dept of Pharmacology, Toronto, ON Canada M5S 1A8

SEEMANN, ROSALIE MARY, international business and foreign policy association executive; b. St. Louis, July 30, 1942; d. Ulysses Sylvester and Helen Maire (Hootselle) Simon; m. Richard Vaughn, Jan. 20, 1968 (dec.); 1 child, Heather Elizabeth. Student, Lindenwood Colls., St. Charles, Mo., 1973-76, Harris Tchrs. Coll., St. Louis, 1961, U. Fla., Gainesville, 1964. Vol. U.S. Peace Corps, Brazil, 1964-66; tech. analyst, group leader Conductron-Mo., St. Charles, 1966-71, bus. mgr., 1971-77; maintenance engr. McDonnell Douglas Astronautics, St. Louis, 1977-78; mgr. supply support Northrop Def. Systems Divsn., Rolling Meadows, Ill., 1978-80; logistics mgmt. cons. Logistic Support Svcs., Spring Grove, Ill., 1980-85; mgr. reliability, maintanability, integrated logistic Recon/Optical, Inc., Barrington, Ill., 1985-90; v.p., exec. dir. Mid-Am. Com. Internat. Bus. & Govt. Coop., Chgo., 1991-97; exec. dir. World Affairs Coun., St. Louis, 1997-99; founder, pres. Mid-West Inst. Internat. Exch., 1999—; v.p. global initiatives World Trade Ctr., St. Louis, 1999—; bd. dirs. Libr. Internat. Rels., Chgo.-Kent Coll. Law, Prime Med. Products. Bd. dirs. U. Mo.-St. Louis Chancellor's Coun., internat. affairs com.; bd. dirs. World Affairs Coun. Am.; mem. women's bd. Goodman Theatre, Chgo.; active Girl Scouts U.S.A. Recipient commendation Conductron-Mo., 1967, pres. award Recon-Optical, 1989. Mem. Am. Soc. Assn. Execs. (internat. sect. coun. 1996—), Nat. Coun. Internat. Visitors, Am. Women Internat. Understanding, Soc. Logistics Engrs. (Mem. of Yr. award, sr. mem.), English Speaking Union, Japan Am. Soc., Chgo. Coun. Fgn. Rels. (Chgo. com.), Assn. Old Crows, Coun. Women Leaders, Execs. Club Chgo., Arts & Edn. Coun. Greater St. Louis, Internat. Trade Assn., Senate Constantine Prophyrogenetus Internat. Assn. (Greece, hon. pres.), Inst. Mid. East Studies Al-Mamun. Fax: 314-646-0419. E-mail: rseemann@worldnet.att.net.

SEEMANOVÁ, EVA, geneticist, consultant; b. Louny, Czech Republic, Apr. 3, 1939; d. Jan and Alžběta (Schindler) Petřík; m. Jiří Seeman, Apr. 22, 1964; children: Pavel, Tomáš, Jana. MD, Charles U., Prague, 1962; PhD, Acad. Scis., Prague, 1974. Physician Hosp. Benešov, Benesov, Czech Republic, 1962; physician inst. molecular biology and genetics Acas. Scis., Benesov; head Rsch. Inst. Devel. Children, Prague, 1969-89; head dept. clin. genetics Charles U. Hosp., Prague, 1990—. Author: Účinky pokrevního příbuzenství rodičů, 1971 (Hálek prize 1973), Familial Microcephaly with Normal Intelligence, Immunodeficiency and Risk for Lymphoreticular Malignancies, 1985 (Purkyně Assn. prize 1986), Hereditary Syndromes and Medical Genetics, 1986 (Purkyně Assn. prize 1988). Recipient Hálek prize, 1973, Trapl medal, 1991, Purkyně medal, 1994. Mem. Presidium Assn. Czech Med. Socs. Roman Catholic. Avocations: history, antiquity. Home: Rasinovo Nabr 66, CZ 12000 Prague Czech Republic Office: Charles Uni 2nd Med Faculty, V Uvalu 84, 150 06 Prague Czech Republic

SEETHARAMU, KANKANHALLY NARASIMHASASTRY, mechanical engineering educator; b. Kankanhally, Karnataka, India, Aug. 22, 1939; s. Kankanhally Lakshmi Narasimhabhatta Narasimhasastry and Gudemaranahllly Sivaramaiah Lakshamma; m. Subhrahamanyasastry Uma, May 5, 1969; 1 child, K.S. Anil. BE, U. Coll. Engring., Bangalore, 1960; ME, Indian Inst. Sci., Bangalore, 1962; PhD, Indian Inst. Tech., Madras, 1973. Cert. mech. engr. Asst. engr. Sirpur Paper MIlls, Kaghaznagar, India, 1962-65; asst. prof. Birla Inst. Tech., Ranchi, India, 1965-68; lectr. Indian Inst. Tech., Madras, 1968-73, asst. prof., 1973-80, prof. mech. engring., 1980—; prof. Sch. Mech. Engring. U. Sci., Malaysia. Author: Finite Element Method in Heat Transfer Analysis, 1996; editor: Finite Element Methods in Engineering Design, 1988; chief editor Internat. Jour. Engring. Analysis and Design, 1994; mem. editl. bd. Internat. Jour. Numerical Methods in Engring., Internat. Jour. Numerical Methods in Heat and Fluid Flow, 1989, 90. Recipient Best Paper award Fluid Mechanics and Fluid Power Conf., Hyderabad, 1994, Madras, 1995. Mem. IndianSoc. Heat and Mass Transfer (life), Indian Soc. Technical Edn. (life), Indian Soc. Wind Engring. (life), Internat. Microelectronics and Packaging Soc. (sec. Malaysia). Hindu. Avocations: reading, listening to music, meeting friends. Home: 1095/1203 8 Cross II Phase, Girinagar, Bangalore 560085, India Office: IIT Madras, Mech Engring Dept, Madras 600036, India

SEEVINCK, EVERT, engineering scientist; b. Doetinchem, Gelderland, The Netherlands, Apr. 15, 1945; s. Jan Hendrik and Berendina Aleida (Beijering) S.; m. Bernadette Elizabeth Teulings, Aug. 12, 1972; children: Saskia, Michael, Peter. BSc, U. Pretoria, South Africa, 1966, BSc in Engring., 1970, BSc in Electronics cum laude, 1975, DSc, 1981. Registered profl. engr., South Africa. Design engr. Philips Semiconductors, Nijmegen, The Netherlands, 1970-72; cons. engr. Philips Components, Johannesburg, South Africa, 1973-74; rsch. engr. CSIR, Pretoria, South Africa, 1975-81; design engr. Philips Semiconductors, Eindhoven, The Netherlands, 1981-83; prof. U. Twente, Enschede, The Netherlands, 1983-89; rsch. scientist Philips Rsch. Lab., Eindhoven, 1985-96; design cons. Circuit Rsch. Internat., Eersel, Netherlands, 1996—; prof. U. Pretoria, 1996—. Author: Analysis and Synthesis of Translinear Integrated Circuits, 1988; co-author: Analogue IC Design: The Current-Mode Approach, 1990; contbr. articles to profl. jours.; inventor in field. Recipient Philips Rsch. Invention award, 1996. Mem. IEEE (sr.). Democrat. Avocations: motorcycle riding, classical music, inventing new paradigms. Home: Pikhoek 6, 5521JX Eersel The Netherlands

SEFFER, ISTVÁN, surgeon, plastic surgeon; b. Nagyatád, Somogy, Hungary, Apr. 20, 1953; s. István and Mária (Rompos) S.; m. Adrienne Renner, June 20, 1980; children: István Jr., Gergö. MD, Med. Sch., Pécs, Hungary, 1977; PhD in Medicine, Sci. Acad., Budapest, Hungary, 1995. Resident surgery Med. Sch., Pécs, 1977-81; resident plastic surgery Med. Postgrad. U., Budapest, 1985-87; head physician Mór Kaposi County Hosp, Kaposvár, Hungary, 1990-96, Am. Hosp., Rome, 1990-91; propr., founder Seffer-Renner Pvt. Clinic, Kaposvár, 1992-96; sci. programs coord. Hungarian Soc. Plastic, Reconstructive & Aesthetic Surgeons, Budapest, 1994-96; head physician plastic surgery Transdanubia, 1996—. Author: Breast Reconstruction, 1994; contbr. articles to profl. jours. Recipient Dr. Miklós Arató meml. leaf, 1984, Hon. worker Hungarian Coun. Mins., 1988, Pala Artificialis Comitatus Somogy, 1994. Mem. Civil Casino, European Plastic Reconstructive Aesthetic Surgery, Internat. Plastic Reconstructive Aesthetic Surgery, Hungarian Soc. Plastic Reconstructive and Eesthetic Surgeons, Hungarian Soc. Surgeons. Avocations: conditional training, International practice shooting, angling, swimming, cycling. Office: Seffer-Renner Pvt Clinic, 7 Szent Imre, 7400 Kaposvár Somogy, Hungary

SEFFNER, WOLFGANG, veterinary pathologist; b. Plauen, Germany, Jan. 7, 1931; s. Max and Margarete (Schneider) S.; m. Marianne Fahndrich, July 13, 1960; children: Martin, Reinhard. DVM, U. Leipzig, 1954, DSc, 1970. Asst. Veterinary Investigation Ctr., Halle, Germany, 1955-64; from asst. to docent Inst. Veterinary Pathology, Leipzig, 1964-81; head dept. Inst. Hygieny & Microbiology, Bad Elster, Germany, 1980-90; fellow Inst. Water, Hygiene & Soil, Berlin, 1990—. Author: Dissection of Domestic Animals, 1970; co-author: Infectious Diseases of Domestic Animals, 1974, Internal Diseases of Domestic Animals, 1985, Compendium of Veterinary Pathology, 1986, Cat Diseases, 1989, Udder Diseases, 1986. Mem. European Soc. Veterinary Pathology, Soc. Toxicol. Pathology, Rotary. Lutheran. Avocations: history, bee farming, travel. Home: Querstrasse 27, D-04463 Brosspösna Saxonia, Germany Office: Fed Health Office, Heinrich Heine Strasse, 08645 Bad Elster Saxonia, Germany

ŠEFR, ROMAN JOSEF, surgeon, endoscopist; b. Brno, Czech Republic, Feb. 8, 1963; s. Josef and Anna (Machová) S.; m. Dana Klempusová, Apr. 30, 1994; 1 child, Roman. MD, Masaryk U., Brno, 1988, PhD, 2000. Cert. surgeon, Czech Republic. Resident Trauma Hosp., Brno, 1988-93; head surg. endoscopy Bakes Surg. Hosp., Brno, 1993—; cons. surgeon Automotodrom Brno, 1989—; clin. observer Meml. Sloan-Kettering Cancer Ctr., N.Y.C., 1998. Contbr. articles to med. jours., including Jour. Japan Surg. Soc., Surg. Endoscopy, Internat. Surgery. 2d lt. Czech Army, 1988-89. Surg. fellow Olga Havel Found., Montreal, Que., Can., 1993, Fulbright travel fellow, Orlando, Fla., 1995. Mem. European Assn. for Endoscopic Surgery, Internat. Gastro-Surg. Club, Internat. Ascites Club. Avocations: tennis, golf, road racing. Office: Bakes Surg Hosp, Zluty Kopec 5, 60200, Brno Czech Republic

SEGAL, DAVID ROBERT, sociology educator; b. N.Y.C., June 22, 1941; s. Harry and Daisy Rose Segal; m. Mady Wechsler, Dec. 25, 1976; 1 child, Eden Heather. BA, Harpur Coll., 1962; MA, U. Chgo., 1963, PhD, 1967; DHL (hon.), Towson U., 1991. From asst. prof. to assoc. prof. U. Mich., Ann Arbor, 1966-75; tech. area chief U.S. Army Rsch. Inst., Arlington, Va., 1973-75; prof. U. Md., Coll. Pk., 1975—; dir. Ctr. Rsch. Mil. Orgn., Coll. Pk., 1995—; vis. rsch. fellow U. Bonn, Germany, 1971; guest scholar Brookings Inst., Washington, 1981-84; disting. vis. prof. U.S. Mil. Acad., W. Point, N.Y., 1988-89; mem. bd. visitors U.S. Army War Coll., Carlisle, Pa., 1997-00. Co-editor: The All-Volunteer Force, 1977, Recruiting for Uncle Sam, 1989, Peace Keepers and Their Wives, 1993, The Postmodern Military, 2000. Spl. asst. peace ops. Chief Staff U.S. Army, Washington, 1993-95; mem. task force Def. Sci. Bd., Washington, 1998-00. Fellow Inter-Univ. Sem. Armed Forces and Soc. (pres. 1995—); mem. Am. Sociol. Assn. (chair sect. peace and war 1991-92), D.C. Sociol. Soc. (pres. 1994-95, Morris Rosenberg award 1997). Avocations: tennis, astronomy. Office: U Md Dept Sociology College Park MD 20742-0001

SEGAL, GARY STEPHEN, investment and venture capital company executive; b. Vancouver, B.C., Can., Sept. 18, 1952; s. Joseph and Rosalie (Wosk) S.; m. Nanci Ann Golick, Aug. 30, 1979; 4 children. BA, U. B.C., 1974; LLB, U. We. Ont., London, 1979. Bar: B.C. Articled student Freeman & Co., Vancouver, 1979-80, assoc. lawyer, 1980-85; v.p. Kingswood Capital Corp., Vancouver, 1985—; pres. Kingswood Venture Capital Corp., Vancouver, 1990—; bd. dirs. E-Z-Rect Mfg. Inc., North Vancouver, Stork-Craft Mfg. Inc., Richmond, B.C., Sterling Shoes Inc., Richmond, Arteif Furniture Mfg. Inc., Edmonton, Alta. Mem. Can. Bar Assn., Vancouver Bd. Trade, Vancouver Lawn Tennis and Badminton Club, Richmond Golf and Country Club, Simon Fraser U. Pres.'s Club. Avocations: tennis, basketball, piano, languages. Office: Kingswood Capital Corp, 701 W Georgia St Ste 520, Vancouver, BC Canada V7Y 1A1

SEGAL, GERALDINE ROSENBAUM, sociologist; b. Aug. 26, 1908; d. Harry and Mena (Hamburg) Rosenbaum; m. Bernard Gerard Segal, Oct. 22, 1933; children: Loretta Joan Cohen, Richard Murry. BS in Edn., U. Pa., 1930, MA in Human Rels., 1963, PhD in Sociology, 1978; MS in Libr. Sci., Drexel U., 1968; LittD (hon.), Franklin & Marshall Coll., 1990. Social worker County Relief Bd., Phila., 1931-35; sociologist Phila., 1935—; cons. and lectr. in field. Author: In Any Fight Some Fall, 1975, Blacks in the Law, 1983. Bd. dirs. NCCJ, 1937-47, 82—, sec., 1983-91; bd. overseers U. Pa. Sch. Social Work, 1983-97; bd. dirs. Juvenile Law Ctr., 1984-98; chair Phila. Tutorial Project, 1966-68; 1st v.p. U. Pa. Alumnae Assn., 1967-70. Co-recipient Nat. Neighbors Disting. Leadership in Civil Rights award, 1988; recipient Drum Major award for Human Rights, Phila. Martin Luther King, Jr. Assn. for Nonviolence, 1990, Brotherhood Sisterhood award

NCCJ, 1994. Democrat. Jewish. Home: 2401 Pennsylvania Ave Apt 19c44 Philadelphia PA 19130-3003

SEGAL, JOSYLYN CHAN, cross-cultural clinical psychologist, musician; b. N.Y.C., Feb. 7, 1958; d. Gerald and June Carol (Thompson) Segal. BS, Beacon Coll., Boston, 1984, Brandeis U., 1980; MS, San Francisco State U., 1984; PhD, The Wright Inst., Berkeley, Calif., 1998. Cert. marriage/family therapist. Lectr. New Coll. of Calif., San Francisco, 1987-92, City Colls. of Chgo. Overseas, Brussels, 1987-92; staff therapist AIDS Family Project, San Francisco, 1989-93; secondary edn. coord. Holocaust Ctr. No. Calif., San Francisco, 1989-91; diversity trainer/educator various, San Francisco Bay Area, Calif., 1989-95; marriage/family therapist Oakland and San Francisco; cross-cultural psychologist Berlin, Germany, 1996-98; intercultural comm. cons. Germany, 1998—; prin. Temple Beth Abraham, Oakland, Calif., 1984-88. Contbr. articles to profl. jours. Mem. APA, Internat. Assn. Cross Cultural Psychologists, Verband Binationaler Familien und Partnerschaften. Avocations: composing music, camping, trekking. E-mail: djcsegal@aol.com.

SEGAL, RODICA, science educator; b. Satu-Nou, Ismail, Romania, June 6, 1938; d. Mihai and Vasilica (Anghel) Gheorghui; m. Brad Segal, Oct. 18, 1962; 1 child, Mugur. Degree in engring., Inst. Poly., Galati, Romania, 1961; MSc, U. Dunarea de Jos, Galati, 1971, PhD, 1971. Asst. prof. Inst. Poly., Galati, 1961-68, lectr., 1968-90; prof. U. Dunarea de Jos, Galati, 1990—. Author (with B. Segal, V. Teodoru, V. Gheorghe) Nutritional Value of Food Products, 1983, (with I. Mincu, B. Segal) News Orientation in Nutrition, 1997, (with G. Popa, B. Segal, S. Dumitrache) Toxicology of Food Products, 1987 (award Romanian Acad. 1989); editor (with G.M. Costin) Functional Foods, 1999. Mem. Acad. Agrl. Sci. (corr.), Romanian Soc. Biochemistry and Molecular Biology. Avocations: travels, recreational activities. Home: Eroilor 32A, 6200 Galati Romania Offic: U Dunarea de Jos, Domneasca 47, 6200 Galati Romania

SEGAL, RONALD MICHAEL, author, editor; b. Cape Town, Republic of South Africa, July 14, 1932; s. Leon and Mary (Charney) S.; m. Susan Wolff, 1962; children: Oliver, Miriam, Emily. BA, U. Cape Town, 1951, Trinity Coll., Cambridge, 1954. Dir. faculty and cultural studies Nat. Union South African Students, 1951-52; founder African South Quar., 1956-61; gen. editor Penguin African Libr., 1961-84; with Pluto Crime Fiction, 1983-86; pres. U. Cape Town Council Univ. Socs., 1951; Philip Francis duPont fellow U. Va., 1955-56; founder Africa South quar., 1956-61; gen. editor Penguin African Library, 1961-84, Pluto Crime Fiction, 1983-86. Author: (novel) The Tokolosh, 1960; (non fiction) Political Africa: A Who's Who of Personalities and Parties, 1961, African Profiles, 1962, Into Exile, 1963, The Anguish of India, 1965, The Race War: The World-Wide Clash of White and Non-White, 1966, America's Receding Future, 1968, The Struggle Against History, 1971, Whose Jerusalem?, 1973, The Decline and Fall of the American Dollar, 1974, Leon Trotsky: A Biography, 1979, The Black Diaspora, 1995; (with Michael Kidron) The State of the World Atlas, 1981, The New State of the World Atlas, 1984, The Book of Business, Money and Power, 1987; editor: South-West Africa, Travesty of Trust, 1967, Sanctions Against South Africa, 1964. Helped launch econ. boycott, South Africa, 1959; banned by South African govt. from all meetings, July 1959; in Eng. with Africa South in Exile, 1960-61; hon. sec. South African Freedom Assn., 1960-61; convenor Internat. Conf. on Econ. Sanctions against South Africa, 1964, Internat. Conf. on S.W. Africa, 1966; chair Ruth First Meml. Trust, 1983—. Vis. fellow Ctr. for Study Democratic Instns., Santa Barbara, Calif., 1973, Philip Francis duPont fellow U. Va., 1955-56. Mem. The Walton Soc. (founding chmn. 1975-79, pres. 1979—). Home: Old Manor House, Manor Rd, Walton-on-Thames Surrey, England

SEGAL, VLADIMIR M., metallurgist, researcher; b. Barashi, USSR, Oct. 3, 1936; came to U.S., 1989; s. Miron S. and Rahei N. (Volfovich) S.; m. Galina M. Freidlina, Feb. 20, 1962; children: Svetlana, Leonid. MSME, Tech. U., 1959, Phd in Metallurgy, 1965; ScD in Metallurgy, Acad. Scis., 1974. Devel. engr. Minsk Tractor Plant, Minsk, Buelorussia, 1959-65; sr. scientist Acad. Scis., Minsk, Buelorussia, 1965-86; prof. Engring. Inst., Lygansk, Ukraine, 1986-89; design engr. Interstate Forging Industry, Navasota, Tex., 1990-92; rsch. engr. Texas A&M U., College Station, Tex., 1992-95; principal rsch. scientist Honeywell Electronics, Spokane, Wash., 1996—. Author: 8 books in Russian, 1966-95. Achievements include invention of new metalworking techniques for materials processing for properties; over 50 patents in field. Home: 1906 S Sonora Dr Veradale WA 99037-8011 Office: Honeywell Electronics 15128 E Euclid Ave Spokane WA 99216-1801

SEGAL, YOSSI, biochemist, association executive; b. Shaar Ha-Amakim, Israel, Sept. 14, 1946. PhD, Hebrew U., Jerusalem, Israel, 1976. Asst. prof. Harvard Med. Sch., Boston, 1980-85; sr. lectr. Hebrew U., Jerusalem, 1986-91; rsch. assoc. Karolinska Inst., Stockholm, 1990-91; sec. natural scis. Israel Acad. Scis. and Humanities, Jerusalem, 1994—. Office: Israel Acad Sci and Humantieis, PO Box 4040, IL-91040 Jerusalem Israel

SEGAWA, DAISUKE, surgeon; b. Osaka, Japan, July 21, 1961; s. Akira and Seiko (Kobayashi) S.; m. Mami Segawa, Apr. 27, 1992; 2 children. Grad., Nat. Def. Med. Coll., Japan, 1987, MD, 1998. Jr. resident Nat. Def. Med. Coll., Japan, 1987-89, sr. resident, 1991-94, postgrad., 1994-98, instr., 1998—; co. comdr. med. svc. unit Ground Self Def. Force, Japan, 1989-91; rschr. Nat. Def. Med. Coll., Japan, 1994-98. Contbr. articles to profl. jours. Maj. Japan Ground Def. Force, 1987—. Mem. Japanese Surg. Soc., Japanese Assn. Thoracic Surgery. Avocations: rugby football, ski, traveling, conjuring tricks. Fax: 81-42-996-5206. Home: 3-9-7-305 Tagara, 179-0073 Nerimaku Tokyo, Japan Office: Nat Def Med Coll Dept Surg, 3-2 Namiki, 359-8513 Tokorozawa Saitama 359-8513, Japan

SEGEL, KAREN LYNN JOSEPH, lawyer, taxation specialist; b. Youngstown, Ohio, Jan. 15, 1947; d. Samuel Dennis and Helen Anita Joseph; m. Alvin Gerald Segel, June 9, 1968 (div. Sept. 1976); 1 child, Adam James. BA in Soviet and East European Studies, Boston U., 1968; JD, Southwestern U., 1975. Bar: Calif., 1996, U.S. Tax Ct., 1996, U.S. Dist. Ct. (cen. dist.) Calif., 1996, U.S. Ct. Appeals (9th cir.), 1997. Adminstrv. asst. Olds Brunel & Co., N.Y.C., 1968-69, U.S. Banknote Corp., N.Y.C., 1969-70; tax acct. S.N. Chilkov & Co. CPA's, Beverly Hills, Calif., 1971-74; intern Calif. Corps. Commr., 1975; tax. sr. Oppenheim Appel & Dixon CPA's, L.A., 1978, Fox, Westheimer & Co. CPA's, L.A., 1978, Zebrak, Levine & Mepos CPA's, L.A., 1979; ind. cons. acctg., taxation specialist Beverly Hills, 1980—; settlement officer L.A. County Superior Ct., 2000; law student mentor Southwestern U., 1996-2000, tax moot ct. judge, 1997; settlement officer Beverly Hills Mcpl. Ct. Editorial adv. bd. Am. Biog. Inst. High sch. amb. to Europe People-to-People Orgn., 1963. Mem. Calif. State Bar, Women's Inner Circle of Achievement, Calif. Young Lawyers Assn., Beverly Hills Bar Assn., Complex Litig. Inns of Ct., L.A. County Bar Assn, Beverly Hills Tinseltown Rose Soc. Avocations: collecting seashells, lhasa apso dog breeding, art, traveling, music.

SEGER, MARTIN, geography scientist; b. Moedling, Austria, Jan. 27, 1940; s. Josef and Berta (Schramek) S.; m. Elizabeth Seger, July 15, 1967; children: Christopher, Barbara, Bernhard. MSc, U. Vienna, 1965, PhD, 1969. Lectr. U. Vienna, 1965-72, asst. prof. geography, 1973-77; full prof. U. Klagenfurt, Austria, 1978—; head dept. geography U. Klagenfurt, 1992—. Author: Teheran: an Urban Study, 1978, Austria: Space-Society-Economy, 1984; editor: Borderline Iron Curtain, 1993; chief editor Jour. of Austrian Geographic Soc., 1994. Mem. Austrian Acad. Scis. (corr.). Home: Goritschitzenweg 5, A 9073 Klagenfurt Austria Office: U Klagenfurt Dept Geography, U Klagenfurt Dept Geography, University St 65, A9020 Klagenfurt Austria

SEGERS, HENDRIK HERWIG, zoologist, researcher; b. Kortrijk, Belgium, July 27, 1964. Lic., U. Gent, Belgium, 1986, PhD in Zoology, 1995. Asst. U. of Gent, Belgium, 1990-96, doctoral asst., 1996—; postdoctoral asst. Acad. Natural Scis., Pa., 1995. Rotifera 2: The Lecanidae, 1995 (Schouteden award Royal Belgian Acad. Scis. 1996), World Records of Lecanidae, 1995, Rotifera Monogononta in Six Zoogeographical Regions after Publications Between 1960-1992, 1997; contbr. numerous articles to profl. jours., chpts. to books. Mem. Royal Belgian Zool. Soc., Societas Inst. Limnologiae. Office: U Gent Dept Biology, K L Ledeganckstraat 35, 9000 Gent Belgium

SEGETH, KAREL, mathematician; b. Praha, Czech Republic, May 10, 1943; s. Karel and Ludmila (Zavadilova) S.; m. Jitka Klanska, Apr. 14, 1966; children: Jitka, Jana. MS, Charles U., 1964; PhD, Acad. Sci. Praha, 1972. From rsch. asst. to dir. Math. Inst. Acad. Sci. Praha, 1966—; asst. prof. Charles U., 1975-82, 90-96, assoc. prof., 1996—. Co-author: Mathematical Modeling in Electromagnetic Prospecting Methods, 1982, Survey of Applicable Mathematics, 1994. Mem. Union Czech Mathematicians and Physicists. Office: Math Inst Acad Sci, Zitna 25, CZ 11567 Praha 1, Czech Republic

SEGGERMAN, ANNE CRELLIN, foundation executive; b. Los Angeles, May 13, 1931; d. Curtis Vergil and Yvonne (LaGrave) Crellin; m. Harry G.A. Seggerman, Apr. 14, 1951; children: Patricia, Henry, Marianne, Yvonne, Suzanne, John. Studies with Albert Levesque, Paris, 1948-50; Student, Sch. Decorative Arts, Paris, 1950, Sch. of the Louvre, Paris, 1950, Albertus Magnus Coll., 1951; D.H.L. (hon.), Sacred Heart U., 1980. French tchr. Beverly Hills, Calif., 1958-60; translator World Affairs Council, Los Angeles, 1958-60; staff mem. West Side Sch. Gifted Children, Beverly Hills, 1958-60; pres. Huxley Inst. for Bio-Social Research, Fairfield, Conn., 1972—, 4th World Found. Interfaith Media Action, Fairfield, 1977—, Steiner Prodns., Fairfield, 1981—; founder The Com. for Guadalupe Research, Fairfield, 1982—; bd. dirs. Anuk, Inc. co-founder Christian/Jewish Ctr. Understanding Sacred Heart U., Fairfield, Conn.; active Pres. Reagan's Health Task Force Resources Com. on Health Adv. Couns. of U.S. Dept. Health and Human Svcs.; mem. Pres.'s Com. Mental Retardation, 1981-86, Com. Housing Handicapped Families, 1989; mem. Nat. Coun. on Disability, 1992-95; bd. dirs. Easter Seal Rehab. Ctr., Fairfield, Internat. Coll. Applied Nutrition, World Health Med. Group, Cath. League for Religion and Civil Rights. Recipient Am. Assn. Sovereign Mil. Order of Malta, 1991, Cmdr. of Equestrian Order of Holy Sepulchre of Jerusalem, 1991. Mem. Nat. Health Fedn., The Inst. for Study of Human Knowledge, Am. Holistic Med. Inst., Internat. Acad. Preventive Medicine, Calif. Orthomolecular Soc., Am. Phys. Rsch., Fairfield County Organic Gardeners.

SEGGEV, MEIR, radiologist, educator; b. Burgas, Bulgaria, Jan. 23, 1939; came to U.S., 1969, naturalized, 1976; s. Bouco and Helen (Bejerano) S.; m. Ruth Lerner, Dec. 30, 1964 (div. Apr. 1978); 1 child, Yael.; m. Sandra Lee Slarsky, Apr. 7, 1979. MD, Hebrew U. Hadassah, Jerusalem, 1969. Diplomate Am. Bd. Radiology. Resident in radiology Harvard Med. Sch., Beth Israel Hosp., Boston, 1970-73; radiologist Peter Bent Brigham Hosp., Boston, 1973-74, Hale Hosp., Haverhill, Mass., 1974—; assoc. radiologist Beth Israel Hosp., Boston, 1974—; clin. instr. radiology Harvard Med. Sch., Boston, 1973—. Mem. AMA, Am. Inst. Ultrasound in Medicine, Am. Roentgen Ray Soc., Radiol. Soc. N.Am., Am. Coll. Radiology, Mass. Med. Soc., Harvard Club. Home: 236 Fairview Rd Palm Beach FL 33480-3320

SEGNER, HELMUT ERICH, biologist; b. Tauberbischofshein, Baden, Germany, Sept. 10, 1954; s. Erich and Elisabeth (Lind) S.; m. Eveline Christeler, Aug. 8, 1986; 1 child, Johann. Diploma, U. Heidelberg, 1982, doctor, 1985. Rsch. asst. U. Heidelberg, 1982-86; rschr. Tetra Co., Melle, Germany, 1986-87; asst. prof. U. Karlsruhe, Germany, 1988-92; group head Nat. Rsch. Ctr., Leipzig, Germany, 1992-2000; prof. fish and wildlife health U. Berne Inst. Animal Pathology, Switzerland, 2000—; head Ctr. for Fish and Wildlife Health U. Berne Inst. Animal Pathology, 2000—. Editor: Ecotoxicology and Ecophysiology, 1993; contbr. articles to profl. jours. Lt. German Army, 1973-75. Recipient Environtl. award Elec. Power Co., 1986. Mem. Soc. of Environtl. Toxicology and Chemistry, European Aquaculture Soc., Tissue Culture Assn./Soc. ofor Ucho Biology. Avocation: fine arts. Home: Muehlenweg 28, 04827 Machern Germany Office: Ctr for Fish & Wildlife, Laenggass Str 122, CH-3012 Berne Switzerland

SEGRE, CESARE, romance philology educator; b. Verzuolo, Italy, Apr. 4, 1928; s. Franchino Segre and Vittorina Cases; m. Maria Luisa Meneghetti, June 8, 1981. MA, U. Turin, Italy, 1950; PhD, U. Italy, 1954; PhD (hon.), U. Chgo., 1976, U. Geneva, 1986, U. Turin, 1998. Assoc. prof. U. Trieste, Italy, 1954-56; assoc. prof. U. Pavia, Italy, 1956-60, prof. romance philology, 1960—. Author: Semiotics and Literary Criticism, 1973, Structures and Time, 1979, Introduction to the Analysis of the Literary Text, 1988, Per Curiosità, 1999. With arty. Italian Army, 1951-52. Recipient Premio Tevere award Municipality of Rome, 1987, Prix Lagrange Acad. Inscriptions Belles Lettres, Paris, 1988, Premio Feltrinelli award Acad. del Lincei, Rome, 1990. Mem. Accademia Nat. Lincei, Accademia della Crusca, Acad. Royal de Belgique. Office: U Pavia Faculty Letters, Strada Nuova 65, 27100 Pavia Italy

SEGRE, SANDRO, sociologist, educator; b. Sao Paulo, Brazil, Nov. 1, 1945; s. Silvio Segre and Annette Holzer; m. Alessandra Arrigoni, Dec. 12, 1987; 1 child. Grad., U. Bocconi, Milan, 1970; MS, NYU, 1972, PhD, 1978. Prof. sociology U. Bocconi, 1978—; asst. prof. sociology U. Genova, Italy, 1991—; rsch. dir. FIAT, Turin, Italy, 1979-81. Author: Max Weber and Capitalism, 1983, Weber and Simmel, 1987, Weber and Sombart, 1989, Juvenile Delinquency, 1996, Drug Policies in Sweden, United States and Italy, 2000. Mem. Internat. Sociol. Assn., Italian Sociol. Assn., Am. Sociol. Assn. Home: Via G Rasori 13, 20145 Milan Italy Office: Dept Polit/Social Sci, U Genoa Largo Zecca 8/18, 16124 Genoa Italy

SEGUI, MELISSA PAULA REYES, psychologist; b. Manila, June 30, 1969; d. Jose Udarbe and Murita (Reyes) S. BS in Psychology cum laude, Assumption Coll., Manila, 1990; MS in Psychology, De La Salle U., Manila, 1998. H.S. guidance counselor Assumption Coll., 1990-94, sr. psychometrician, rschr., 1995-98, coll. guidance dir., 1998—; human resources asst. Monterey Farms Corp., Manila, 1994-95; prof. Assumption Coll., 1996-98. Poll watcher Nat. Citizens Movement for Free Elections, Manila, 1986-88. Mem. Psychol. Assn. of The Philippines. Avocations: travel, reading, dancing, badminton. Home: 745 Remedios St Malate, Manila 1004, The Philippines

SEGURA, FRANCISCA SOLEDAD, geographer, educator; b. Xert, Spain, Apr. 29, 1959; d. Francisco Segura and Adoracion Beltran; m. Vicent Beltran; children: Anna, Lara Maria. Lic. in geography and history, 1982, PhD in Geography and History, 1987. Rsch. fellow Ministry of Edn. and Sci., Valencia, 1983-86; lectr. U. Valencia, 1987-91, prof., 1991—. Author: Las Ramblas Valencianas, 1990; contbr. articles to profl. jours. Mem. N.Y. Acad. Scis., Spanish Assn. for Study of Quaternary, Spanish Assn. Geomorphology. Home: Plaza del Raco de L'Horta 3, 3 Pta 9, 46020 Valencia Spain Office: Faculty Geography & History, Avda Blasco Ibañez 28, 46010 Valencia Spain

SEHGAL, AMAR NATH, sculptor; b. Campbellpur, West Pakistan, Feb. 5, 1922; s. Ram Asra Mal and Parmeshwari Devi; m. Shukla Dhawan, 1954; 2 children. Ed. Punjab U., Govt. Coll., Lahore, and NYU; M.A. Hon. art cons. to Ministry Community Devel., Govt. India, 1955-66; participant Sculpture Biennale, Musee Rodin, Paris, 1966, UNESCO Conf. on role of art in contemporary soc., 1974; organizer Internat. Children's Art Workshop, UNESCO, Paris, 1979. One-man shows: N.Y., 1950-51, Paris, 1952, East Africa, India, (retrospectives) Nat. Gallery Modern Art, New Delhi, 1972, City Hall, Ottawa, Ont., Can., 1975, Aerogolf, Luxembourg, 1975, India House, N.Y.C., 1976, Rathaus, Fransheim, W.Ger., 1977, Frankfurt Airport, 1977, Neustadt, 1978, Brenners Park, Baden-Baden, 1979, Luxembourg, 1980, Arpana Art Gallery, 1999, Habitat Ctr., 1999; group shows: Dubai, Abu Dhabi, 1980, Jeddah, 1981, Chaux de Fond, Switzerland, 1982, Cercle Munster, Luxembourg, 1987, Berne, 1988, Gold Sculptures, Luxembourg, 1990; represented in permanent collections: Vigyan Bhawan (India's Internat. Conf. bldg.), White House, New Delhi Airport, also in Jerusalem, Vienna, Paris, Berlin, Antwerp, Luxembourg, Conn., New Delhi; works include: Voice of Africa (Ghana), 1959, A Cricketer, 1961, Mahatma Gandhi, Amritsar, To Space Unknown bronze, 1963, Conquest of the Moon bronze, 1969, Anguished Cries bronze monument, 1971, Gandhi monument, Luxembourg, 1971, Monument to Aviation, 1972, Rising Spirit, 1978, The Crushing Burden, 1984, Victims of Torture designed for U.N., Monument to Freedom Fighters of Namibia, Vienna, 1986, Int. Year of Peace, Head with Horns, 1986, NARI Monument to Women, Int. Womens Day, 1986, Monument to Nehru, 1989, Flute Player Gift of Children of India to UNICEF, 1986, The Captive at Polais des Human Rights, Geneva, 1999; sculpture exhbns., Belgarde, 1964, Musee d'Art Moderne, Paris, 1965, Paulskirche Frankfurt, 1965, Haus am Lutzoplatz West Berlin, 1966, Musees Royaux D'Art et Histoire, Brussels, 1966, Musee Etat Luxembourg, 1966, Wiener Secession, Vienna, 1966, Flemish Acad. Arts, 1967, Tokyo Internat. Fair, 1973, Nat. Gallery of Modern Art, New Delhi, 1993; author: Arts and Aesthetics; Organising Exhibitions in Rural Areas; (poetry) Der Innere Rhythmus, 1975, also poetry in English, French and Arabic; Folio of Graphics, 1981; Folio on Ganesha, 1991; Lonesome Journey, 1997, Awaiting a New Dawn, 1998. Recipient Sculpture award Lalit Kala Acad., 1957, Pres.'s award (donated to Prime Minister Nehru during Chinese invasion), 1958. Fellow Lalit Kala Akademy. Home: J-23 Jangpura Ext, New Delhi 110014, India Office: The Creative Fund, 1 Montée de Clausen, L-1343 Luxembourg Luxembourg

SEHGAL, JAGJEET SINGH, trading company executive; b. Mandalay, Burma, Oct. 31, 1928; arrived in Singapore, 1952; s. Hem Singh and Daya Wanti Sehgal; m. Harsimran Kaur Bedi; children: Jasbir Singh, Johnny, Mike. BA with honors, Punjab U., Lahore, Pakistan, 1946. Mgr. Rose & Co. Ltd., Singapore, 1952-56; dir. BMR Pte. Ltd., Inchcape Group, Singapore, 1958-78; mng. dir. Stockland (S) Pte. Ltd., Singapore, 1978—; patron Singapore Cycle and Motor Traders Assn., 1978-93; rep. Chamber of Asian Japan Econ. Coun. and Singapore Metrication Bd. Chmn. Cen. Sikh Gurdwara Bd., Ministry Comty. Devel., Singapore, 1990—, Telok Kurau East Sch. Adv. Com., Singapore, 1970-84, St. Patrick's PTA, Singapore, 1982-84; pres. Sri Guru Nanak Sat Sang Sabha, 1992-93; trustee Singapore Sikh Edn. Found., 1995—, Singapore Sikh Welfare Coun., 1995—. Recipient Pub. Svc. medal Pres. Singapore, 1984, Pub. Svc. star Pres. Singapore, 1996, Sikh Comty. award BG Lee Hsien Loong, Dep. Prime Min. Singapore, 1996, Arch of India Gold award SH Bhajan Lal Chief Min. Haryana, India, 1994. Mem. Singapore Khalsa Assn. (life), Singapore Indian Assn. (life, pres. 1990-91), Singapore Indian Edn. Trust (life), Automobile Assn. Singapore (life). Home: MA 1/5-3D Garden Estate, Mehrouly-Gurgaon Rd, 122002 Gurgaon Haryana, India Office: Stockland (S) Pte Ltd, 136J Koon Seng Rd, Koon Seng House Singapore 427065, Singapore

SEHILI, MAHMOUD, artist; b. Tunis, July 27, 1931; m. Gabriele Buth, Apr. 11, 1959; children: Thouraya, Lilia, Raouf. Student, Fine Arts Sch., Tunis; diploma supérieur des arts plastiques, Ecole des Beaux-Arts, Paris. Tchr. Inst. Technol. d'Art, d'Arch. et d'Urbanisme, Tunis; dir. Irtissem Art Gallery, Tunis, 1977—. Recipient Golden medal Cagnes sur Mer, 1st prize Town of Tunis, 1963, others. Avocations: music, playing the luth, composition of Arabic music, fishing. Home: 4 Rue Victor Hugo, Carthage Tunisia

SEHNAL, FRANTISEK, administrator; b. Olomucany, Czech Republic, Sept. 11, 1938; s. Frantisek and Anna (Zarubova) S.; m. Jana Hrozna, Mar. 17, 1964 (div. Feb. 1984); children: Borek, Anna, Stepan. MS, Purkyne U., Brno, Czech Republic, 1960, Purkyne U., Brno, Czech Republic, 1966; PhD, Czech Acad. Sci., 1966. Lectr. Palacky U., Olomouc, Czech Republic, 1960-62; rschr. Inst. Entomology, Acad. Sci., Praha, Czech Republic, 1968-90; v.p. U. South Bohemia, Budejovice, Czech Republic, 1992-95; dir. Inst. Entomology, Acad. Scis., Budejovice, Czech Republic, 1995—; vis. prof. U. Calif., Irvine, 1991; cons. in field. Co-editor: Regulation of Insect Development and Behavior, 1981, 2 others; contbr. articles to profl. jours., chpts. to books; patentee in field; mem. editl. bd. Archives of Insect Biochemistry and Physiology, European Jour. Entomology, Jour. Insect Physiology. Sec. Found. Support Sci., Czech Republic, 1992-98; mem. Sci. Coun., Praha, 1994-97, U. South Bohemia, 1995—. 2d lt. Czech Army, 1962. Postdoctoral fellow Case Western Res. U., Cleve., 1966-68; recipient JSPS award Fgn. Specialists, 1987; Roentgen Professorship, U. Wuerzburg, Germany, 1999; hon. scientist, Korea, 1999. Fellow European Soc. Comparative Endocrinologists (coun. mem.), Coun. Internat. Entomological Congress. Avocations: skiing, travel. E-mail: Sehnal@entu.cas.cz. Home: Bezdrevska 15, 370 11 Ceske Budejovice Czech Republic Office: Czech Acad Sci, Branisovska 31, 370 05 Ceske Budejovice Czech Republic

SEHNAL, JIŘÍ, musicologist; b. Radslavice, Czech Republic, Feb. 15, 1931; s. František and Marie (Oherova) S.; m. Helena Dudešková, Aug. 15, 1957. PhD, Masaryk U., Brno, Czech Republic, 1967. Libr. U. Libr., Olomouc, Czech Republic, 1955-58, Rsch. Inst. Vegetables, Olomouc, Czech Republic, 1958-64; archivist Inst. Music History, Moravian Mus., Brno, Czech Republic, 1964-94, head, 1978-94; ret., 1994; prof. Masaryk U., Brno, 1997—, Palacky U., Olomouc. Author: Music Literature in the Library of Kroměříži, 1960, Music in the Olomouc Cathedral in the 17th and 18th Century, 1988, Pavel Vejvanovsky, 1993, Musik des 17. Jahrhunderts und Pavel Vejvanovsky, 1994, (with others) Caroli de Liechtenstein-Castelcorno episcopi Olomucensis operum artis musicae collectio Cremsirii reservata, 1998; editor ancient music, contbr. The New Grove Dictionary of usic and Musicians; contbr. articles to profl. jours. Mem. Zentralinstitut für Mozart-Forschung, Gesellschaft zur Herausgabe der Tonkunst Österreich, Joseph Haydn Inst. Roman Catholic. Avocation: mountain touring. Home: Filipinskeho 3, 615 00 Brno Czech Republic

SEHRING, ADOLF, artist, sculptor; b. Urupinsk, Russia, June 8, 1930; came to the U.S., 1949; s. George Henry M. and Clair (Burstin) S.; married, 1992; children: Nina, Marc. Student, Acad. Fine Arts, Germany, 1946-49. Pres. A. Sehring Studio Inc., Orange, Va., 1970—, Am. Artist Portfolio Inc., Orange, 1987—; lectr. in field, 1970—. Commd. by the Vatican to paint the ofcl. portrait of Pope John Paul II, Hearst Castle, Calif., to sculpt Pocahontas bronze, Town of Gloucester, Va., bronze in collection of Pres. Bush; works collected in Chrysler Mus., Am. Embassy, Stockholm, Bayly Mus., Victoria and Albert Mus. and major pvt. collections; represented in 10 galleries. Served with U.S. Army, 1951-53, Korea. Decorated 14 combat medals; recipient Stalin medal for art, 1937, Rias award, 1946. Avocations: antiques, gardening, birds. Home: Tetley Plantation Tetley Dr Somerset VA 22972 Office: A Sehring Studio Tetley Plantation Somerset VA 22972

SEIBEL, WILFRIED, science association director; b. Korbach, Hessen, Germany, Feb. 6, 1930; s. Wilhelm and Else (Decker) S.; children: Christiane, Ulrich, Martin. MS in Agr., Justus-Liebig U., Giessen, Germany, 1953, PhD in Agr. Chemistry, 1956; Senator of honour, Fachhochschule Lippe, Lemgo, Germany, 1991. Cereal chemist Fed. Rsch. Ctr. for Cereal, Potato and Lipid Rsch., Detmold, Germany, 1956-62; mng. dir. Meneba Mills, Rotterdam, Netherlands, 1962-68; head Inst. for Milling and Banking Fedn., Detmold, 1968-95, Fed. Rsch. Ctr. for Cereal, Potato and Lipid Rsch., Detmold, 1989-95. Editor Getreide Mehl und Brot, 1970—. Recipient Silberner Max-Eyth-Gedenk-Münze, German Agr. Soc., Frankfurt, 1977, Clyde H. Bailey medal Internat. Assn. for Cereal Sci. and Tech., Vienna, Austria, 1982, P.F. Pelshenke medal German Agr. Soc., Frankfurt, 1985, Sprengel-Liebig Medal in gold Assn. Agrl. Rsch. and Testing, Darmstadt, Germany, 1988. Home: Alter Postweg 19, 32756 Detmold Germany

SEIBERLICH, CARL JOSEPH, retired naval officer; b. Jenkintown, Pa., July 4, 1921; s. Charles A. and Helen (Dolan) S.; m. Trudy Germi, May 29, 1952; children: Eric P., Heidi M., Curt A. B.S., U.S. Mcht. Marine Acad., 1943; grad., Armed Forces Staff Coll., 1959. Commd. ensign U.S. Navy, 1943, advanced through grades to rear adm., 1971; designated naval aviator, 1947; comdg. officer Airship ZPM-1, 1949, Air Anti-Submarine Squadron 26, 1961, U.S.S. Salamonie, 1967, U.S.S. Hornet, 1969; dir. recovery astronauts Apollo 11 and 12 lunar missions, 1969; comdr. anti-submarine warfare group 3 Flagship U.S.S. Ticonderoga, 1971; comdr. task force 74 Viet Nam Ops., 1972; asst. dep. chief naval ops. for air warfare Navy Dept., 1975-77; dep. chief naval personnel, 1977-78; comdr. Naval Mil. Personnel Command, 1978-80; with VSE Corp., 1980-82; pres. U.S. Maritime Resource Ctr.; dir. mil. program Am. Pres. Lines, 1983-95, TranSystems Corp., Reston, Va., 1996—; co-chmn. intermodal task force Nat. Rsch. Coun., Transp. Bd.; mem. NAFTA Info. Exch. & Automation working group. Vice pres. Naval Aviation Mus. Found.; active Boy Scouts Am. Decorated Legion of Merit (6), Air medal; recipient Harmon Internat. trophy for devel. 1st variable depth towed sonar, 1951; Vincent T. Hirsch Maritime award Navy League, 1995. Mem. VFW, AIAA, Am. Soc. Naval Engrs., Soc. Naval Architects and Marine Engrs., Am. Helicopter Soc., U.S. Naval Inst., U.S. Naval Sailing Assn. (commodore 1979), Am. Angus Assn., Tailhook Assn., Navy Helicopter Assn., Naval Airship Assn., Early and Pioneer Naval Aviators Assn., Nat. Def. Transp. Assn., Navy League U.S. (maritime affairs com.), Propeller Club, Order of Daedalians, U.S. Mcht. Marine Acad. Alumni Assn., Assn. Naval Aviation, Am. Legion, N.Y. Yacht Club, Nat. Space Club, Delta Sigma Pi. Clubs: N.Y. Yacht, Nat. Space. Home: Seagate

Farm 1510 Loudoun Dr Haymarket VA 20169-1120 Office: TranSystems Corp 2100 Reston Pkwy Ste 202 Reston VA 20191-1200

SEIBERT, ALBERT FRANK, chemical engineer; b. Houston, Oct. 29, 1958; s. Albert Frank and Cecilia Ruth (Williams) S. BSChemE, U. Houston, 1982; MSChemE, U. Tex., Austin, 1984, PhD in Engring., 1986. Rsch. assoc. Separations Rsch. Program, Austin, 1986-92, rsch. engr., 1993, tech. mgr., 1993—; cons. J.L. Humphrey & Assocs., Austin, 1987—. Author: Fluid Mixture Separation Technologies for Cost Reduction and Process Improvement, 1986; contbr. articles to profl. jours. Getty Oil scholar, 1981-82; recipient Excellence award ARCO, 1982. Mem. AIChE, N.Am. Membrae Soc. Achievements include applied research in liquid and supercritical extraction, distillation packings and trays; discovery use of high pressure carbon dioxide for cleaning oily water in a column contactor; contributed to the development of the membrane extractor and high capacity coflo distillation tray. Office: U Tex CES Bldg 133 10100 Burnet Rd Austin TX 78758-4445

SEIDEL, BASTIAN TOBIAS, engineering consultant; b. Freikeh, Metn, Lebanon, June 11, 1968; s. Frank Ferstl and Gertrud Siglinde Seidel; m. Stephani Elisabeth de Clercq, July 31, 1999. Diploma in engring., Tech. U., Munich, Germany, 1996. Cert. in engring. Cons. Rolf Bodo Szylagie, Munich, 1994, Deutsche Gesellschaft für Mittelstandsberatung, Munich, 1996—. Avocations: trekking, cooking, basketball, traveling.

SEIDEL, JOAN BROUDE, stockbroker, investment advisor; b. Chgo., Aug. 16, 1933; d. Ned and Betty (Treiger) Broude; m. Arnold Seidel, Aug. 18, 1957; children: David, Craig. BA, UCLA, 1954; postgrad., N.Y. Inst. Fin. Registered prin., investment advisor Morton Seidel & Co. Inc., L.A., 1970-74, v.p., 1974-93; pres., 1993—; also bd. dirs. Morton Seidel & Co. Inc., L.A.; instr. UCLA Extension, 1979-84. Treas. City of Beverly Hills, Calif., 1990—, chmn. rent adjustment bd., 1989-90, mem., 1983-89; mem. investment com. YWCA, L.A., 1987—, treas. Greater L.A., 1992-95; bd. dirs. Discovery Fund for Eye Rsch., L.A., 1987—, treas., 1999—; corp. dir. Queen's Care. Named Citizen of Yr. Beverly Hills C. of C., 1993. Fellow Assn. for Investment Mgmt. and Rsch.; mem. Am. Technion Soc. (v.p. 1998—), Nat. Assn. Security Dealers (dist. bus. conduct com. 2S 1993-95, 98—, small firm adv. bd. 1998—, chair dist. 2 1999-2000), L.A. Soc. Fin. Analysts, Orgn. Women Execs., Bond Club, Rotary, Phi Sigma Alpha. Avocations: reading, travel. Home: 809 N Bedford Dr Beverly Hills CA 90210-3023 Office: Morton Seidel & Co Inc 8730 Wilshire Blvd Ste 530 Beverly Hills CA 90211-2792

SEIDEL, SELVYN, lawyer, educator; b. Long Branch, N.J., Nov. 6, 1942; s. Abraham and Anita (Stoller) S.; m. Deborah Lew, June 21, 1970; 1 child, Emily. BA, U. Chgo., 1964; JD, U. Calif., Berkeley, 1967; Diploma in Law, Oxford U., 1968. Bar: N.Y. 1970, U.S. Dist. Ct. (so. and ea. dists.) N.Y. 1970, D.C. Ct. Appeals, 1982. Ptnr. Latham & Watkins, N.Y.C., 1984—; adj. prof. Sch. Law, NYU, 1974-85; instr. Practicing Law Inst., 1980-81, 84. Bd. dirs. Citizen Scholarship Fund Am., 1995—. Mem. ABA, New York County Bar Assn., N.Y.C. Bar Assn. (mem. fed. cts. com. 1982-85, internat. law com. 1989-92, 95-96, art law com. 1997—), Boalt Hall Alumni Assn. (bd. dirs. 1980-82), Contbr. articles to profl. jours. Office: Latham & Watkins 885 3rd Ave Fl 9 New York NY 10022-4834

SEIDEL-DREFFKE, BJÖRN BIRGIT, Slavist, educator; b. Schlema, Germany, Nov. 25, 1963; s. Fritz and Ingetraud Dreffke; m. Thomas Seidel, May 28, 1988. Diploma in Russian Lang. and Lit., U. Kazan, 1987. Scientific asst. Acad. of Scis., Inst. of Lit., Berlin, 1987-91, Rsch. Program for Acad. Workers, Berlin, 1991-94; scientific asst., lectr. U. Potsdam Inst. of Slavistics, Germany, 1994—; scientific sec. rsch. group of Russian lit., Berlin, 1991; mem. rsch. group Russian philosophy, 1995. Author: The Main Tendencies of Gogol'-Investigations in the 20th Century, 1992, The Way of the White Flower, 1998; editor: E.P. Blaratskaja: Stories and Traveller Notes, 1999; contbr. articles to profl. jours. Home: Neubrandenburger Str 58, D-13059 Berlin Germany Office: Inst of Slavistics Univ Potsdam, Postfach 60 1553, D-14415 Potsdam Germany

SEIDELL, JACOB CAESAR, epidemiologist, nutritionist; b. Weert, The Netherlands, Nov. 3, 1957; s. Johan Frans and Grietje (Broekhuizen) S.; m. Moniqa Eva Bergholm, May 1, 1989 (div. June 1994); m. Ruth Wouters, Sept. 1, 1995; 1 child, David. MSc, Wageningen U., The Netherlands, 1983, PhD, 1986. Rsch. asst. Wageningen U., 1983-86; sr. rsch. fellow Royal Acad. Sci., Amsterdam, 1987-92; head dept. chronic disease epidemiology Nat. Inst. Pub. Health, Bilthoven, The Netherlands, 1993—; hon. prof. medicine Glasgow U., Scotland; prof. human nutrition Faculty of Medicine, Free U. of Amsterdam, 1999—. Editor European Jour. Clin. Nutrition. Recipient bi-ann. nutrition prize Netherlands Ctr. for Nutrition, 1999. Mem. European Assn. for the Study of Obesity (pres. 1996—). Home: Herenlaan 55, 3701 AS Zeist The Netherlands Office: RIVM/CCM, PO Box 1, 3720 BA Bilthoven The Netherlands

SEIDEN, BEATRICE RABIN, artist; b. Bronx, N.Y., May 5; d. Joseph and Sophie Rabin; m. Arthur Seiden, Aug. 1947; 1 child, Jessica. BFA, Pratt Inst., 1940; BA, Queens Coll., 1972; MFA, L.I. U., 1975. Cert. H.S. tchr., N.Y. Works on display at Nat. Acad. of Design, N.Y.C., and numerous galleries nationwide. Mem. Audubon Artists, Art Students League of N.Y. (life). Jewish. Avocations: jewelry design, sculpture.

SEIDEN, HENRY (HANK SEIDEN), advertising executive; b. Bklyn., Sept. 6, 1928; s. Jack S. and Shirley (Berkowitz) S.; m. Helena Ruth Zaldin, Sept. 10, 1949; children: Laurie Ann, Matthew Ian. BA, Bklyn. Coll., 1949; MBA, CCNY, 1954. Trainee Ben Sackheim Advt. Agy., 1949-51; nat. promotion mgr. N.Y. Post Corp., 1951-53; promotion mgr. Crowell-Collier Pub. Co., Inc., 1953-54; copy group head Batten, Barton, Durstine & Osborn, Inc., 1954-60; v.p., creative dir. Keyes, Madden & Jones, 1960-61; sr. v.p., assoc. creative dir. McCann-Marschalk, Inc., 1961-65, chmn. plans bd., 1964-65; creative dir., dir., prin. Hicks & Greist, Inc., N.Y.C., 1965—, sr. v.p., 1965-74, exec. v.p., 1974-83, COO, 1983—, pres., 1986—; CEO Ketchum/Hicks & Greist Inc., 1987-89; chmn., CEO Ketchum Advt., 1989-91; exec. v.p. Ketchum Comm. Inc., also bd. dirs.; vice chmn. Jordan, McGrath, Case & Taylor, Inc., 1992—; chmn., CEO The Seiden Group, Inc.; bd. dirs. Ketchum Internat. Inc.; guest lectr. Bernard M. Baruch Sch. Bus. and Pub. Adminstrn., CCNY, 1962—, Baruch Coll., 1969—, New Sch. Social Scis., 1968, 72,73, Sch. Visual Arts, 1979, 80—, Lehman Coll., CCNY, 1980—, Ohio U., 1981, Newhouse Grad. Sch., Syracuse U., 1981, NYU, 1983; cons. pub. rels. and comm. to mayor City of New Rochelle, N.Y., 1959—; cons. mktg. dept. Ohio State U.; cons. to pres. N.Y.C. City Coun., 1972-73; cons. Postmaster Gen. U.S., 1972-74; comm. advisor to commr. N.Y.C. Police Dept., 1973—, hon. dept. commr., 1991—, spl. cons. to commr., 1992—. Author: Advertising Pure and Simple, 1976, Advertising Pure and Simple: The New Edition, 1990; contbg. editor: Madison Ave. mag, 1966—, Advt. Age, Mag. Age; guest columnist: N.Y. Times, 1972. Vice commr. Little League of New Rochelle; bd. dirs. Police Res. Assn. N.Y.C., 1973—, pres. exec. com.; bd. dirs. Cancer Rsch. and Treatment Fund, Inc., pres., 1992—, Transmedia Network, Inc.; bd. dirs., pres. New York's Finest Found., 1975—, pres., 1996; bd. dirs., sr. v.p. Drug Enforcement Agy. Found., 1995—. Recipient award Four Freedoms Found., 1959, award Printers Ink, 1960, promotion award Editor and Pub., 1955, Am. TV Comms. Festival award, 1963-69, Effie award Am. Mktg. Assn., 1969, 70, award Art Dirs. Club N.Y., 1963-70, award Am. Inst. Graphic Arts, 1963, Starch award, 1969, spl. award graphic art lodge B'nai B'rith Greater N.Y., 1971, 87, award of highest honor FBI Nat. Acad., 1994. Mem. NATAS, Am. Inst. Mgmt. (assoc.), Drug Enforcement Agts. Found. (sr. v.p. 1995), Advt. Club N.Y. (exec. judge Andy awards, award 1963-65), Advt. Writers Assn. N.Y. (Gold Key award for best newspaper and mag. advts. 1962-640, Copy Club (co-chmn. awards com., Gold Key award for best TV comml. 1969), Alpha Phi Omega. Home: 1056 5th Ave New York NY 10028-0112 Office: The Seiden Group 708 3rd Ave New York NY 10017-4201

SEIDENFUS, HELLMUTH STEPHAN, retired economics educator; b. Mannheim, Germany, May 5, 1924; s. Stephan and Hedwig (Boehm) S.; m. Gisela Orthmann, Apr. 3, 1956; children: Christoph, Florian, Valentin. Asst. U. Cologne, Germany, 1953-60; prof. econs. U. Giessen, Germany, 1960-63; prof. econs. U. Münster, Germany, 1963-89, prof. emeritus, 1989—; adviser Ministry Transport, Bonn, Germany, 1960-96. Author: Consequences of Traffic Control, 1968, Unsolved Issues of Fundamental Importance for Transport Policy, 1995; also articles. Mem. German Soc. Transp. Econs. (pres. 1983-91, hon. mem. 1992—), European Soc. Transp. Insts. (hon. pres. 1994—), Acad. Scis. Brescia, Hungarian Acad. Transp. Scis., Austrian Acad. Transp. Scis. Avocations: golf, sailing, piano, organ. Home: Parkallee 19A, D-48155 Münster Germany Office: U Münster, Am Stadtgraben 9, D-48143 Münster Germany

SEIDENSPINNER, GUNDOLF O(TTO), social science educator, writer; b. Landsberg/Lech, Germany, June 20, 1939; s. Otto Martin and Maria Louise (Scharold) S.; m. Gerlinde Renate Mueller, May 4, 1964; children: Utta, Sonja, Bastian. Diploma in econs., U. Ludwig-Maximilians, Munich, 1965; DPhil in Polit. Sci., U. Salzburg, Austria, 1969. Office leader Africa-Archives, Munich, 1966-69, Allianz-Assecuration, Munich, 1969-70; chmn. advising team Ludwig-Maximilians U., 1970-78, Tech. U. Munich, 1978-79; dir. youth adminstrn. City of Munich, 1979-83; prof. sci. Fachhochschule, 1983-98; dir. Horizonte e.V. Akademie fuer Fort-u. Weiterbildung, Landshut, 1993—; dir. Inst. fur Soziale Praxis, Munich, 1991—; chmn. Freunde und Foerderer der Deutschen Studentenschaft, Munich, 1969—. Author and editor numerous books. Mem. Com. for Univs. and Rsch., Bonn, 1974—. Mem. Time Share Clubs (Saalfelden and Saalbach, Austria). Home: Untere Hausbreite 11, D-80939 Munich Germany Office: Fachhochschule Landshut, Am Lurzenhof 1-2, D-84036 Landshut Germany

SEIDENSTICKER, EDWARD GEORGE, Japanese language and literature educator; b. Castle Rock, Colo., Feb. 11, 1921; s. Edward George and Mary Elizabeth (Dillon) S. B.A., U. Colo., 1942; M.A., Columbia U., 1947; postgrad., Harvard U., 1947-48; LittD (hon.), U. Md., 1991. With U.S. Fgn. Service, Dept. State, Japan, 1947-50; mem. faculty Stanford U., 1962-66, prof., 1964-66; prof. dept. Far Eastern langs. and lit. U. Mich., Ann Arbor, 1966-77; prof. Japanese Columbia U., 1977-85, prof. emeritus, 1986—. Author: Kafu the Scribbler, 1965, Japan, 1961, Low City, High City, 1983, Tokyo Rising, 1990, Very Few People Come This Way, 1994; transl.: (by Murasaki Shikibu) The Tale of Genji, 1976. Served with USMCR, 1942-46. Decorated Order of Rising Sun Japan; recipient Nat. Book award, 1970; citation Japanese Ministry Edn., 1971; Kikuchi Kan prize, 1977; Goto Miyoko prize, 1982; Japan Found. prize, 1984; Tokyo Cultural award, 1985; Yamagata Banto prize, 1992. Home: 1350 Ala Moana Blvd Apt 3103 Honolulu HI 96814-4229

SEIDL, GUNTHER BERNHARD, organic-pharmaceutical chemist; b. Burghausen, Bavaria, Fed. Republic Germany, Mar. 12, 1931; s. Karl and Anna-Maria (Ruhland) S.; m. Ingeborg E. Bruch, Mar. 13, 1960; children: Marie-Luise, Christine, Markus, Barbara. D. in Natural Scis., U. Munich, 1958. Dir. R&D medicinal chemistry Hoechst AG, Frankfurt, Fed. Republic Germany, 1973-77, dir. pharm. R&D, 1977-88, dir. sci. coordination corp. rsch., 1988-93; chmn. expert group biotech. Verband der Chem. Industry, 1991-93; ret., 1993; prof. U. Mainz (Fed. Republic Germany), 1981; lectr. in field. Contbr. articles to profl. jours.; patentee in field. Mem. Gesellschaft Deutscher Chemiker, Gesellschaft für Biologische Chemie (treas. 1992-93), N.Y. Acad. Scis., Am. Chem. Soc. Avocations: travelling, cooking.

SEIDLER, GRZEGORZ LEOPOLD, historian, educator; b. Stanislawow, Poland, Sept. 18, 1913; s. Teodor and Eugenia (Dawidowicz) S.; m. Alina Jadwiga Bogusz, Mar. 1, 1969. MA, Jagiellonian U., 1935, PhD, 1938; PhD (hon.), Maria Curie Sklodowska U., Lublin, Poland, 1970, Acad. Econs., Cracow, Poland, 1975, Lock Haven U., 1990. Lectr. Jagiellonian U., Cracow, 1945-50; prof. Marie Curie Sklodowska U., 1951-83; dir. Polish Cultural Inst., London, 1969-71; vis. prof. U. Kiel, 1980-81; vis. fellow Clare Hall Cambridge U., 1981-82. Author: The Emergence of the Eastern World, 1968, Przedmarksowska Mysl Polityczna, 1974, Rechtssystem und Gesellschaft, 1985, O Istocie I Akceptacji Wladzy Panstwowej, 1995. Mem. Polish Parliament, Warsaw, 1985-89. Decorated comdr.'s cross with star Order of Polonia. Mem. Am. Soc. 18th Century Studies, Rotary Club Lublin, United Oxford and Cambridge Univ. Club. Avocation: walking, studying European intellectual traditions. Home: Ul Raabego 7 m 17, 20-030 Lublin Poland

SEIDMAN, GLENN ELLIOTT, sales and marketing professional; b. June 18, 1953; m. Charlene Goldberg, 1988; children: Brooke, Michelle. BA, CUNY, 1975; MA, NYU, 1977. Asst. dir. student activities Columbia U., N.Y.C., 1978-83; assoc. dean students Poly. U., Bklyn., 1983-88; territory mgr. Quality Products & Svcs., Reading, Pa., 1988—. Mem. Queens Coll. Alumni Assn. (pres. 1987-89). Home: 5 Yates Ave Jericho NY 11753-1418

SEIF AL NASR, WALEED MEHMOUD, advertising, communication and marketing executive; b. Cairo, Maadi, Egypt, Aug. 6, 1969; arrived in Saudi Arabia, 1994; Mehmoud Seif Al-Nasr Salem and Nazly Ahmed Zahran; m. Dalia Ismail Al Kattan. BS in Tourism and Mgmt., Hellwan U., Cairo, 1990; Pre-Masters in Mass Comm., Am. U., Cairo, 1992. Advt. and promotion exec. Pub. Promotion Svcs., Cairo, 1988-90; account exec. Search Mag., Cairo, 1991-94, Ara Media, Jeddah, Saudi Arabia, 1994-98; account dir. TMI-JWT, Jeddah, 1998—. Active Rotary Club, Egypt, 1992, Leons, Egypt, 1992, Internat. Advertising Assn., N.Y., 1998. Avocations: reading, golf, tennis, traveling, music. Fax: 9662-6697055. Office: TMI JWT, PO Box 13823, 21414 Jeddah Saudi Arabia

SEIFER, MARC JEFFREY, psychology educator; b. Far Rockaway, N.Y., Feb. 17, 1948; s. Stanley Cyclone and Thelma (Imber) S. BA, U. R.I., 1970; postgrad., New Sch. for Social Rsch., 1970-72, Sch. Visual Arts, 1971; MA, U. Chgo., 1974; PhD, Saybrook Inst., 1986. Cert. handwriting expert. Investigator neurol. study hand writing of schizophrenics Billings Hosp., Chgo., 1972-73; coll. instr. Providence Coll. Sch. of Continuing Edn., 1975-90, U. R.I. Extension, Providence, 1975-80, Bristol C.C., Fall River, Mass., 1980—, C.C. of R.I., Warwick, 1988—; expert handwriting neurol. investigation epileptic split brain writers UCLA, 1986; handwriting expert U. R.I. Crime Lab, Kingston, 1974-75; assoc. editor Jour. of Occult Studies, Providence, 1977-79; editor MetaScience, Kingston, 1979—, Jour. Am. Soc. Profl. Graphologists, Bethesda, Md., 1989—; dir. MetaSci. Found., Kingston, 1979—; handwriting expert Dept. Social Svcs. and R.I. Atty. Gen.'s Office, Providence, 1990—; lectr. on Tesla, U.S. Mil. Acad., West Point, N.Y., 1982, Colo. Coll., Colorado Springs, 1984, CCNY, 1984, Zagreb, Yugoslavia, 1986, Colorado Springs, 1992, 96, UN, 1997, L.A., 1999, Mesa, Ariz., 2000; lectr. on graphology, Jerusalem, Israel, 1985, U. Vancouver, B.C., Can., 1986, Oxford (Eng.) U., 1987, Santa Fe, 1991, Cambridge (Eng.) U., 1992, Ann Arbor, Mich., 1994, N.Y.C., 1997, 2000, Brandeis U., 2000; lectr. on consciousness U. Ariz., Tucson, 1996; cons. Inventors Series Discover Channel and Koch TV, 1994, The American Experience, PBS and Elevator Pictures, 1995, BBC, 1995, Biography A&E, 1998, Good Morning America, 2000. Author: Startez Encounter, 1988, The Man Who Harnessed Niagara Falls, 1991, Handwriting and Brainwriting, 1992, (screenplay) Tesla: The Lost Wizard (performed at Producer's Club Theater, 1996, video docudrama 1997), 1992, video, 1984, Hail to the Chief, 1991, Mr. Rhode Island: The Stephen Rosati Story, 1994, Wizard: The Life and Times of Nikola Tesla, 1996 (designated as a book of unusual interest and merit, Publishers Weekly, 1996, designated as serious piece of scholarship, Sci. Am., 1997, high recommendation AAAS, 1997); contbr. chpts. to books; contbg. editor: Extraordinary Science, 1996, 2000, The Tesla Journal, 1997, Wired, 1998, Jour. Conscientology, 1999, Civilization, 2000; contbr. articles to profl. jours. and publs. including The N.Y. Times. Fellow Am. Coll. Forensic Examiners (bd. dirs. 1992-93); mem. APA, Am. Soc. Profl. Graphologists (bd. dirs. 1989—), Tesla Soc., Nat. Bur. Document Examiners, Nat. Soc. for Graphology. Avocations: snorkeling, bridge. Home: PO Box 32 Kingston RI 02881-0032

SEIFERT, EBERHARD, phoniatrician; b. Muenster, Germany, Oct. 20, 1961; s. Ulrich Hans and Lieselotte (Buzer) S.; m. Ruth Singel, Sept. 13, 1986; children: Malte, Marijke. Dr.med., Duesseldorf U., 1988; PhD, Muenster U., 1999. Sr. physician ENT clinic U. Heidelberg, Mannheim, Germany, 1987-93; sr. physician dept. phoniatrics and pediatric audiology Westphalian Wilhelms U., Muenster, Germany, 1993-99; head dept. phoniatrics Univ. of Bern, Switzerland, 2000—. Co-author: Diffential Diagnosis of Speech-Voice and Hearing Disorders, 1997. Mem. Internat. Assn. of Logopedics and Phoniatrics, Sir Charles Bell Soc., Deutsche Krebs-Gesellschaft. Office: Dept Phoniatrics ENT Clinic, Inselspital, 3010 Bern Switzerland

SEIFERT, JAROSLAV, biochemist; b. Jicín, Czechoslovakia, July 10, 1932; s. Jaroslav and Marie (Ulrichová) S.; m. Marie Meňovská, Feb. 5, 1935; children: Marie, Klára. Rerum nat dr, Charles U., Prague, Czechoslovakia, 1956; PhD, Acad. Scis., Prague, Czechoslovakia, 1962. Asst. Acad. Scis., Prague, 1956-65, head of group, 1965-68, head dept., 1968-92; head inst. Inst. Pharmacology, Prague, 1992—. Contbr. articles to profl. jours. Mem. Internat. Soc. Immunopharmacology (mem. com. 1993), N.Y. Acad. Scis. Avocation: botany. Home: U Ladronky 23/1338, 169 00 Prague 6 Czech Republic Office: Inst Pharmacology AS CR, Videnska 1083, 142 20 Prague Czech Republic

SEIFERT, LUKE MICHAEL, lawyer; b. Smyrna, Tenn., Apr. 8, 1957; s. Donald R. and Joan (Clemas) S.; m. Kathleen Louise Schaffer, Aug. 1, 1980; children: Joseph, Nicholas, Peter, Rachel. BA, Creighton U., 1979; JD, William Mitchell Sch. of Law, St. Paul, 1983. Bar: U.S. Dist. Ct. Minn., Minn. Page Minn. Ho. of Reps., St. Paul, 1980, com. adminstr., 1981-82; assoc. Holmen Law Office, St. Cloud, Minn., 1983-87; pvt. practice St. Cloud, 1987-98; assoc. Quinlivan Law Firm, 1998—. Mem. ABA, Minn. Bar Assn., Minn. Trial Lawyers Assn., Minn. Def. Lawyers Assn., Stearns Benton Bar Assn. (sec., treas. 1986-87, v.p. 1987-88, pres. 1988-89), K.C. (guard 1986-87, advocate 1987-90), Delta Theta Phi. Home: 1305 W Oakes Dr Saint Cloud MN 56303-0741 Office: Quinlivan Hughes Law Firm 600 Norwest Ctr Saint Cloud MN 56303

SEIFERT, PATRICIA CLARK, cardiac surgery nurse, educator, consultant; b. Springfield, Mass., Apr. 4, 1945; d. Thomas W. and Kathleen E. (O'Malley) Clark; m. Gary F. Seifert, Sept. 10, 1966; children: Kristina S. Glenn, Philip A. BA in History, Trinity Coll., 1967; ADN, No. Va. Community Coll., 1976; MS in Nursing, Cath. U. Am., 1988. RN, Va., D.C.; cert. oper. rm. nurse, first asst. nurse. Head nurse cardiac surgery Fairfax Hosp., Falls Church, Va., 1976-88; adminstrv. dir. Washington Hosp. Ctr., 1988-89; oper. room coord. cardiac surgery Arlington (Va.) Hosp., 1989-97, coord. cardiovasc. svcs., 2000—; oper. room coord. cardiac surgery Alexandria (Va.) Hosp., Daytona Beach, Fla., 1995-97; mgr. open heart surgery Halifax Med. Ctr., Daytona Beach, Fla., 1997-98; coord. cardiovasc. svcs. Arlington (Va.) Hosp., 2000—; lectr./cons. in field. Author: (books) Clinical Assessment Tools for Use with Nursing Diagnosis, 1989, Cardiac Surgery, 1994; contbr. chpts. to Alexander's Care of the Patient in Surgery, 11th rev. edit., 1999, Cardiovascular Nursing, 7th rev. edit., 1991, Perioperative Care Planning, 2d rev. edit., 1996, The RN First Assistant: An Expanded Perioperative Role, 3d rev. edit., 1999, Core Curriculum for the RN First Assistant, 3d rev. edit., 1999, CNOR Study Guide, rev. edit., 1999; contbr. numerous articles to profl. jours. Fellow Am. Acad. Nursing; mem. AACN, N.Am. Nurses Nursing Diagnosis Assn., Am. Orgn. Nurse Execs., Am. Heart Assn. Coun. on Cardiovasc. Nursing, Assn. Perioperative RN's (cert. perioperative nurse, RN 1st asst., nat. bd. dirs. 1994-98, pres. No. Va. chpt. 1994-95, nat. pres.-elect 1998-99, nat. pres. 1999-2000, numerous scholar awards, Nat. Pres.'s award 1992, nat. nominating com. 1991-93), Am. Assn. for History of Nursing, Assn. Perioperative RN's Found. (trustee), Am. Soc. Perianesthesia Nurses, Va. Nurse's Assn. (dist. 8 bd. dirs. 1987-91, Nurse of Yr. 1984), Sigma Theta Tau (pres. Eta Alpha chpt. 1990-92, Virginia Henderson fellow). Fax: 703-237-1259. E-mail: seifertpc@aol.com. Home: 6502 Overbrook St Falls Church VA 22043-1942

SEIFERT, THOMAS LLOYD, lawyer; b. Boston, June 6, 1940; s. Ralph Frederick and Hazel Bell (Harrington) S.; m. Ann Cecelia Berg, June 19, 1965. BS cum laude, Ind. U., 1962, JD cum laude, 1965. Bar: Ill. 1965, Ind. 1965, N.Y. 1979. Assoc. law firm Keck, Mahin & Cate, Chgo., 1965-67; atty. Essex Group, Inc., Ft. Wayne, Ind., 1967-70, Amoco Corp., Chgo., 1970-73; assoc. gen. counsel, asst. sec. Canteen Corp., Chgo., 1973-75; sec., gen. counsel The Marmon Group, Inc. (and predecessor cos.), Chgo., 1975-78; v.p., gen. counsel, sec. Hanson Industries, Inc., N.Y.C., 1978-82; sr. v.p. law, chief fin. officer Petrie Stores Corp., N.Y.C., 1982-83; mem. Finley, Kumble, Wagner, Heine, Underberg, Manley, Myerson & Casey, N.Y.C., 1983-87, Paul, Weiss, Rifkind, Wharton & Garrison, N.Y.C., 1987-91; gen. counsel, chief legal officer Sterling Grace Capital Mgmt., L.P. and affiliated cos., N.Y.C., 1991—. Note editor Ind. Law Jour., 1964-65. Named to Ind. Track and Cross Country Hall of Fame, 1993. Mem. ABA, N.Y. State Bar Assn., Order of Coif, The Creek, Beta Gamma Sigma. Home: Museum Tower 15 W 53d St Apt 31 E New York NY 10019-5401 Office: Sterling Grace Capital Mgmt 515 Madison Ave Ste 2600 New York NY 10022-5403

SEIFF, ERIC A., lawyer; b. Mt. Vernon, N.Y., Apr. 25, 1933; s. Arthur N. and Mathilde (Cohen) S.; m. Sari Ginsburg, June 26, 1960 (div. Oct. 1983); children: Judith C., E. Kenneth, Dean A.; m. Meredith Feinman, Jan. 15, 1984; children: Abigail, Sarah. BA, Yale U., 1955; LLB, Columbia U., 1958. Bar: N.Y. 1958, U.S. Dist. Ct. (so. dist.) N.Y. 1960, U.S. Dist. Ct. (ea. dist.) N.Y. 1981, U.S. Ct. Appeals (2d cir.) 1965, U.S. Supreme Ct. 1967. Assoc. Bower and O'Connor, N.Y.C., 1959-60, Yellin, Kramer & Levy, N.Y.C., 1961; asst. dist. atty. N.Y.C. Dist. Atty.'s Office, 1962-67; asst. counsel Agy. for Internat. Devel., Washington, 1967-70; counsel Agy. for Internat. Devel., Rio de Janeiro, 1970-72; gen. counsel N.Y. State Divsn. Criminal Justice Svcs., 1972-74; dep. chief atty. Legal Aid Soc. Criminal Def., N.Y.C., 1974-75; first dep. commr. N.Y. State Investigation Commn., 1975-77; chmn. N.Y. State Investigation Commn., N.Y.C., 1977-79; ptnr. Seiff, Kretz & Maffeo (formerly Scoppetta & Seiff), N.Y.C., 1981—; spl. dist. atty. Bronx County, 1986-89; spl. asst. atty. gen. State of N.Y., Gov.'s Task Force Investigating Conduct of Attica Prosecutions, 1975. Bd. dirs. Legal Aid Soc., N.Y.C., 1994—; Prisoners' Legal Svcs., N.Y.C., 1989—, Lawyers Fund for Client Protection, N.Y., 1980—. Recipient Frank S. Hogan Meml. award Frank S. Hogan Assn., 1994. Mem. N.Y. Criminal Bar Assn. (bd. dirs. 1980—, past pres.), Bar Assn. City N.Y. (chmn. project on the homeless 1999—). Office: Seiff Kretz & Maffeo 645 Madison Ave New York NY 10022-1010

SEIFF, STEPHEN S., ophthalmologist; b. L.A., Sept. 30, 1925; s. Max and Minnie F. (Feldman) S.; m. Gloria Louise Holtzman, Apr. 16, 1950; children: Stuart R., Sherri Seiff Sloane, Karen Seiff Sacks. AA, UCLA, 1945; AB, U. Calif., Berkeley, 1946; MD, U. Calif., San Francisco, 1949. Diplomate Am. Bd. Ophthalmology. Intern County Gen. Hosp., L.A., 1949-50; fellow in anesthesiology Lahey Clinic, Boston, 1950-51; resident in ophthalmology U. Calif., San Francisco, 1952-55; clin. prof. dept. ophthalmology UCLA, 1956—; pvt. practice Beverly Hills, Calif., 1955—; clin. chief divsn. ophthalmology Cedars/Sinai Med. Ctr., L.A., 1957—; attending ophthalmologist Children's Hosp., L.A., 1956-94; lectr. in field; assoc. examiner Am. Bd. Ophthalmology. Collaborating author: Clinical Anticoagulant Therapy, 1965; contbr. articles to profl. jours. Bd. dirs. That Man May See Inc., San Francisco; former exec. com. mem. UCLA Hosp. Lt. M.C. USNR, 1950-52. Recipient Sr. Honor award UCLA Dept. Ophthalmology, 1994. Fellow ACS, Am. Acad. Ophthalmology; mem. L.A. Soc. Ophthalmology (past pres.), Frederick Cordes Eye Soc. (past nat. pres.), Calif. Med. Assn., Am. Soc. Cataract and Refractive Surgery (founding mem.). Avocation: sailing. Office: 435 N Roxbury Dr Ste 107 Beverly Hills CA 90210-5003

SEIFFER, NEIL MARK, photographer; b. Bklyn., July 18, 1960; s. Martin Henry and Eileen S. AAS in Bus. Adminstrn., County Coll. Morris, 1980; BS, Montclair State Coll., 1984. Spl. projects photographer Billboard Pubs., 1987-95; beauty-event photographer Lancome, Elizabeth Arden, Christian Dior, Chanel, 1988-91; celebrity/entertainment photographer, West Paterson, N.J., 1984—, N.Y.C., 1995—; official photographer 1st annual Touchstone Awards for Women in Music, 1997. Author: Photographic Guidelines for Performing and Recording Artists, 1987, Model's Guide/What You Need to Know About a Modeling Career, 1994, Neil Seiffer's Photographic Guidelines for the Performing Artist, 1995, Neil Seiffer's Photo Tips for Actors, 1996; photographer spl. project include Billboard Publs., 1987-95, Lancome, Elizabeth Arden, Chanel, and Christian Dior, 1988-91, Dunn & Bradstreet, 1995; inventor photo adjustable-platform to increase productivity for still-life comml. photographers. Achievements include invention of photo adjustable platform to increase productivity for commercial still-life photographers. Home: 147 Overmount Ave Apt A West Paterson NJ 07424-3221

SEIFTER, NORBERT, mathematics educator; b. Judenburg, Styria, Austria, June 25, 1956; s. Norbert and Waltraud (Stickler) S.; m. Sabine Müller, Jan. 11, 1986; children: Georg, Florian, Katharina. Dipl. ing., Tech. U., Graz, Austria, 1978, D Tech., 1981. Asst. prof. math. Montan U. Leoben, Austria, 1980-86, assoc. prof., 1986—. Contbr. articles to internat. math.

jours. Mem. City Coun., Judenburg, 1995—. Mem. Am. Math. Soc., Austrian Math. Soc. (prize 1996), Univ. Tchrs. Union (chmn. Leoben 1985-86, 95-96). Mem. Social Democratic Party. Home: Strettwegerweg 2, 8750 Judenberg Styria, Austria Office: Montan U Leoben, Franz Josef Strasse 18, 8700 Leoben Styria, Austria

SEIGEL, ARTHUR MICHAEL, neurologist, educator; b. Rochester, N.Y., Oct. 9, 1944; s. Hyman and Judith (Hyman) S.; m. Ellen May Streitfeld, June 1, 1969; children: Daniel Aaron, Mark Louis. Diplomate Am. Bd. Psychiatry and Neurology; cert. instrument comml. pilot, 1994. Intern SUNY, Affiliated Hosps., Buffalo, 1970-71; resident Yale-New Haven Hosp., 1973-76; asst. prof. pediatrics and neurology Yale U. Sch. Medicine, New Haven, 1976-77, clin. instr., 1977-81, clin. asst. prof., 1981—; cons. in neurology Gaylord Rehab. Hosp., Wallingford, Conn., 1976-86; practice medicine specializing in neurology, New Haven, 1977—; attending physician Hosp. St. Raphael, New Haven, Yale-New Haven Hosp. Pres., bd. dirs. Orch. New Eng. Served with USPHS, 1971-73. Fellow Royal Soc. Medicine, Am. Acad. Neurology; mem. Conn. Neurol. Soc. (v.p. 1987-2000), Conn. Med. Soc., New Haven County Med. Soc., Yale Neurology Alumni (pres. 1994-2000). Home: 38 Vineyard Ave Guilford CT 06437-3235 Office: 60 Temple St New Haven CT 06510-2716

SEIGEL, JAN KEARNEY, lawyer; b. Bayonne, N.J., Feb. 7, 1947; s. Max and Margaret (Kearney) S.; m. Judy L. Mascuch, Aug. 29, 1971; children: Margaret, Emily, Jonas, Luke. BSBA, Georgetown U., 1968, JD, 1971; LLM in Taxation, NYU, 1974. Bar: N.J. 1971, D.C. 1972, Ga. 1972, U.S. Ct. Appeals (3d cir.) 1979, U.S. Supreme Ct. 1979. Law sec. to Hon. Theodore Rosenberg Superior Ct. of N.J., Paterson, 1971-72; asst. prosecutor Passaic County Pros.'s Office, Paterson, 1972-76; pvt. practice Ridgewood, 1976-98; sr. ptnr. Seigel & Mongiardo, P.C., Ridgewood, N.J., 1990—; mem. faculty William Paterson Coll., 1974-79; lectr. N.J. Inst. for Continuing Edn., 1981—, N.J. State Bar and various county bar assns. Recipient Police Hon. Legion award Police Chiefs Assn. of N.J., 1980. Mem. ABA (rep. of N.J. young lawyers divsn. 1980-82), N.J. State Bar Assn. (Young Lawyer of Yr. award 1983, bd. trustees 1978-79), Passaic County Bar Assn. (bd. trustees 1973-81), Bergen County Bar Assn. Office: Seigel & Mongiardo 505 Goffle Rd Ridgewood NJ 07450-4027

SEIGEL, LEILA RUTH, activist organization representative, advocate; b. N.Y.C., June 1, 1918; arrived in Switzerland, 1962; d. Charles G. and Charlotte (Brenner) S. BA, NYU, 1939; M in Social Scis., New Sch. for Social Rsch., N.Y.C., 1944. Rep. Office of War Info., London, Brussels, 1944; N.Y. corr. Le Peuple, Brussels, 1947-50, Le Populaire, Paris, 1952-55; organizer Cmty. and Social Agys. Union Loc. 1707, N.Y.C., 1955-62; pub. rels. dir. World ORT Union, Geneva, 1962-74; non-govtl. rep. UN Internat. Coun. Jewish Women, Geneva, 1975—, pres., 1984-87. Polit. activist Ams. for Dem. Action, N.Y.C., 1946-62. Mem. Mu Sigma Hon. Soc. Democrat. Jewish. Avocations: music, fine arts, travel.

SEIGELL, MAN MOHAN, marketing professional; b. Rawalpindi, Pakistan, Dec. 10, 1933; s. Gokal Chand and Sumitra Devi (Baggo) S.; m. Usha Seigell, June 21, 1961; children: Poonam, Chetna, Radhika. BCom, St. John's Coll., 1953; postgrad., AMC Inst., 1960; doctor homoepathy, Mavelil Homoeo Mission, 1998. Exec. Godrej & Boyce, New Delhi, 1953-58; mktg. mgr. Gestetner, India, 1958-69; zonal mgr. Kores, India, 1969-78; pres., CEO Top Jours., New Delhi, 1978—; cons. Godrej & Boyce, New Delhi, 1955; sales trainer Gestetner, India, 1965-67; product devel. profl. Kores, India, 1974-75; with sales promotion Top Jours., India, 1978—. Editor Gestetner News, 1966 (Best Layout 1966). Area warden, New Delhi, 1962. Sgt. maj. Coll. Mil. Tng., 1952. Mem. Consumer Forum Delhi, Women's Consumer Assn. (advisor 1997-98), Delhi Publisher's Soc. Avocations: reading, writing, gardening, stamp and coin collecting, yoga. Home and Office: SFS 97A Pkt A Sukhdev Vihar, Mathura Rd, 110 025 New Delhi India

SEIGNEURIN, FRANÇOIS, research engineer; b. Tours, France, May 26, 1957; s. Yvon and Jacqueline (Gonda) S.; children: Pierre, Caroline, Grégeire. BAC E, Lycée Grandmont, Tours, 1977; Deug. Scis., U. Rabelais, Tours, 1980, Licence, 1981, Maitrise, 1982. Engr. SYSAAF, Nouzilly, France, 1982—. Office: SYSAAF, SRA-INRA, 373880 Nouzilly France

SEIGNORET, SIR CLARENCE (HENRY AUGUSTUS SEIGNORET), former president of Commonwealth of Dominica; b. Roseau, Dominica, Feb. 25, 1919; s. Clarence Augustus and Violet (Riviere) S.; m. Judith Laronde, Apr. 11, 1950; children: Joseph Phillip, Gilbert Karol Theodore. Student, Balliol Coll., Oxford U. Civil servant Roseau, 1936-77; permanent sec. Govt. of Dominica, 1956-67, sec. to cabinet, head Civil Svc., 1967-77; pres. of Dominica, 1983-93; exec. sec. Dominica Assn. Industry and Commerce, Roseau, 1979-83. Decorated officer Order Brit. Empire, knight Grand Cross Order of Bath, knight comdr. Grand Cross of Grace, Sovereign Mil. and Hospitalier Order St. John, Jerusalem, Knights of Malta; recipient Dominica award of honor, collar of the Order of the Liberator.

SEIGO, SATORU NISHI, artist, educator; b. Sukumo, Japan, Sept. 6, 1955; s. Toshio and Ruriko (Hijiya) Nishi; m. Momoko Kudo, Dec. 31, 1986; children: Kurumi, Anzu. AA, Cuesta Coll., 1978; BFA, Calif. Coll. Arts & Crafts, 1981; MFA, Acad. Art Coll., 1985. Instr. Obunsha LL Sch., Kochi, Japan, 1987-88; dir. Art Studio Seigo, Kochi, 1988—; art instr., instr. Tosajuku Jr. and H.S., 2000—. One-man shows include Bokushin Gallery, Tokyo, 1994, 95, 96, Gallery Cocteau, Kyoto, Japan, 1991, 92, 93, Gallery Fumi, Tokyo, 1990, Gallery Andante, Ashiya, 1992, Gallery Tanaka, Tokyo, 1997, 98, 99, Gallery Jin, Tokyo, 1998, 2000; exhibited in group shows at Sakaide Mus., 1990, Ino Paper Mus., 1990, Petit Musee, 1992, Mus. of Art, Kochi, 1995, Ueno Royal Mus., 1995. Recipient Merit award Art Quest '86, 1986, Best Work award Berkeley Art Ctr. Comp., 1986, Mr. T award Outdoor Sculpture Exbhn., Kochi, 1983; Holbein Art scholar, 1996-97. Avocation: tennis. E-mail: czg13126@nifty.ne.jp. Home: 2-12-31 Hattan-cho, Kochi 780, Japan Studio: 2-12-31 Hattan-Cho, Kochi 780-0912, Japan

SEIKE, ATSUSHI, labor economics educator; b. Tokyo, Apr. 11, 1954; s. Kiyoshi and Yuki (Iwamoto) S.; m. Kyoko Imamura, Oct. 6, 1981; children: Hiroshi, Takashi, Satoshi. BA, Keio U., Tokyo, 1978, MA, 1980, PhD, 1993. Cert. in labor econs. Asst. prof. Keio U., Tokyo, 1980-85, assoc. prof., 1985-92, prof., 1992—; vis. scholar UCLA, 1987-88; cons. Rand Corp., Santa Monica, Calif., 1987-90; vis. spl. rschr. Japan Inst. Labor, Tokyo, 1993-99; vis. sr. rschr. Econ. Planning Agy., Tokyo, 1995-97. Author: Employment System Reform for the Aging People, 1992 (Keio-Gijuku Acad. prize 1992), Labor Market in the Aging Society, 1993 (Kagami Meml. award 1993, Commendation of Excellent Labor Related Pubs. 17th prize 1994), Beyond the Life-time Employment, 1998. Mem. Japan Econs. Assn., Japan Statis. Soc., Japan Indsl. Rels. Rsch. Assn. Home: 3-8-2 Higashi-yukigaya, Ohta-ku Tokyo 145-0065, Japan Office: Keio U, 2-15-45 Mita Minato-ku, Tokyo 108-8345, Japan

SEIL, KONRAD ANTON, physicist, educator; b. Schwaz, Tyrol, Austria, Dec. 2, 1951; s. Anton and Erna (Hoetzl) S.; m. Maria Johanna Julia Leichter, May 23, 1980; children: Christian, Johannes. PhD, U. Innsbruck, 1978. Asst. U. Innsbruck, 1979-81; lens designer Swarovskioptik Absam, 1981—, mem. tech. office, 1990—; prof. HTL-Optometrie, Hall, Austria, 1983—. Contbr. articles to profl. publs. Mem. Soc. Photo-optical Instrumentation Engrs., Österreichische Physikalische Gesellschaft. Avocations: soccer, jogging, mountain biking. Home: St Martin 7A, 6131 Schwaz, Tyrol Austria Office: Swarovski Optik KG, Swarovskistrasse 70, 6067 Absam, Tyrol Austria

SEILER, CHARLOTTE WOODY, retired English language educator; b. Thorntown, Ind., Jan. 20, 1915; d. Clark and Lois Merle (Long) Woody; m. Wallace Urban Seiler, Oct. 10, 1942; children: Patricia Anne Seiler Bootzin, Janet Alice Seiler Sawyer. AA, Ind. State U., 1933; AB, U. Mich., 1941; MA, Ctrl. Mich. U., 1968. Tchr. elem. schs. Whitestown, Ind., 1933-34, Thorntown, Ind., 1934-37, Kokomo, Ind., 1937-40, Ann Arbor, Mich., 1941-44, Willow Run, Mich., 1944-46; instr. English divsn. Delta Coll., University Center, Mich., 1964-69, asst. prof., 1969-77, ret., 1977; organizer, dir. Delta Coll. Puppeteers, 1972-77. Mem. Friends of Grace A. Dow Meml. Libr., 1974—, treas., 1974-75, 77-79, corr. sec., 1975-77; mem. Midland Art Assn.; adv. bd. Salvation Army, 1980-91, sec., 1984-87; leader Sr. Ctr. Humanities program Midland Sr. Ctr., 1977—. Mem. AAUW (fellow 1979), Mich. Libr. Assn., Midland Symphony League, Tuesday Rev. Club (pres. 1979-80), Seed and Sod Garden Club (v.p. 1986-87, pres. 1987-88), Pi Lambda Theta, Chi Omega. Presbyterian. Home: 5002 Sturgeon Creek Pky Midland MI 48640-2284 also: 652 Blackburn Blvd Harbor Cove North Port FL 34287

SEILER, DIETER JOSEF, chemist, clinical pathologist; b. Karlsruhe, Germany, May 7, 1941; s. Emil G. and Elisabeth M. Seiler; m. Margot E. Schneider, Oct. 15, 1966; 1 child, Michael J. Diploma chemiker, U. Heidelberg, Germany, 1965, PhD, 1967, MD, 1973, prof. clin. biochemistry, 1975. Cert. clin. chemist, 1973, cert. clin. pathologist, 1977. Asst. chemist Chem. Inst. U., Heidelberg, 1965-67; asst. physician Klinikum U., Heidelberg, 1968-77; head dept. clin. chemistry Klinikum, Ludwigshafen, Germany, 1977—; head Klinikum, Ludwigshafen, 1989—. Contbr. articles to profl. jours. Mem. Am. Assn. Clin. Chemistry, Deutsche Gesellschaft For Klinische Chemie, Deutsche Gesellschaft für Laboratoriumsmedizin, N.Y. Acad. Scis. Roman Catholic. Avocations: sports medicine, long distance running. Office: Klinikum der Stadt, Bremserstr 79, 67063 Ludwigshafen am Rhein Germany

SEILER, ERNST FRIEDRICH, pianist; b. Munich, Germany, Sept. 6, 1934; arrived in Japan, 1961; s. Johannes and Charlotte (Springer) S.; m. Mie Ogiso, Sept. 16, 1959 (div. Mar. 1976); children: Yuri, Naomi, Mayumi, Midori; m. Kazuko Masada, Mar. 3, 1976; children: Kio, Oto. Diploma, Juilliard Sch. Music, 1959, postgrad. diploma, 1960. Prof. Kobe (Japan) Coll., 1961-67; head prof. City Music Coll., Kyoto, Japan, 1961-67; lehrauftrag Mozarteum, Salzburg, Austria, 1968-72; prof. Bunri U., Tokushima, Japan, 1974-96, Senzoku U., Tokyo, 1983-85; adv. Yamaha Music Found., Tokyo, 1961-68; chmn. Kayabuki Ongaku-do Competition for Piano Duet, Japan, 1998, 2000. Co-author: Seiko-Uso, 1992; CDs include Encores from Kayabuki, 1994, The Seasons of Japan, 1995. Bd. dirs. Kyoto Prefecture Internat. Ctr., Kyoto, 1996—. Recipient 1st prize Colony Club, 1959, Disting. Svcs. award Hiyoshi County, Japan, 1995, Kyoto Prefecture, 1995, Disting. Svcs. award, Japan, 1997. Mem. Piano Instrs. Assn., Japan Piano Tchrs. Assn. (founding mem.), Juilliard Alumni Assn. Avocations: farming, collecting music. Home: Iwagakaki Uchi-cho 30, 603 Kyoto-Kitaku Japan

SEILER, FRIEDRICH, fluid mechanics engineering researcher, lecturer; b. Karlsruhe, Germany, May 2, 1946; s. Friedrich Herrmann and Hedwig Klara (Pfeifer) S.; m. Irene Schleicher, Apr. 27, 1979; children: Sebastian, Anja, Daniel. MSc in Physics, U. Karlsruhe, 1975, PhD in Engring., 1980, habilitation, 1992. Rschr., lectr. in physics and engring. U. Karlsruhe, 1975-80; rsch. leader French-German Rsch. Inst. St.-Louis, France, 1980-96; head aerothermodynamics and shock tube dept. French-German Rsch. Inst. St.-Louis, 1997—; prof. U. Karlsruhe, 1998—; lectr. U. Karlsruhe, 1993—, cons., 1980—; cons. several rsch. insts., Germany and France, 1980—. Author: Shock Structures, 1979, Optical Measuring Techniques, 1990; contbr. articles to 200 scientific publs. Gefreiter, German Army, 1967-68, Munich. Conservative. Evangelical. Achievements include development of a unique optical measuring technique called "Doppler Picture Interference Velocimetry" (DPV) for visualizing worldwide first the gas velocity distribution in an image; inventing and patenting a new gasdynamic accelerator and a new projectile flight control system. Office: French-German Rsch ISL, 5 rue du Gen Cassagnou, F-68301 Saint-Louis Alsace, France

SEILER, JAMES ELMER, judge; b. LaCrosse, Wis., Sept. 2, 1946; s. Elmer Bernard and Margaret Theresa (Mader) S.; m. Sonia Gonzales, Feb. 9, 1968; children: Rebecca, Cristina. BA, U. Wis., LaCrosse, 1968; JD, U. Wis., 1973. Bar: Wis. 1973, Minn. 1981, U.S. Supreme Ct. 1985, Mo. 1986. Pvt. practice Balsam Lake, Wis., 1973-81; in-house counsel Farm Credit Banks, St. Paul, 1981-85; corp. counsel Hussmann Corp., St. Louis, 1985-94; adminstrv. law judge Social Security, Evansville, Ind., 1994-95, Office of Hearings and Appeals, Creve Coeur, Mo., 1995—; chief adminstrv. law judge Hearing Office, Creve Coeur, Mo., 1997—. Candidate Dist. Atty., Polk County, Wis., 1980. With U.S. Army, 1969-71. Avocations: soccer coach, swimming, water skiing, running. Home: 18 Harbor Point Ct Lake Saint Louis MO 63367-1336 Office: 11475 Olde Cabin Rd Saint Louis MO 63141-7130

SEILER, OTTO J., retired shipping company executive; b. Hamburg, Germany, May 9, 1929; s. Friedrich-Wilhelm and Charlotte (Komnick) S.; m. Ilse Gertrud Dankert, Oct. 11, 1937; children: Anne-Kathrin, Joachim, Christine. Grad. pub. schs. Trainee J.A. Reinicke, Hamburg, 1950-53; clk. Aug. Bolten, Wm. Mill. Nachf., Hamburg, 1953-54; mgr. Hamburg-Am. Line, Hamburg, 1955-70; dep. dir. internat. shipping affairs Hapag-Lloyd AG, Hamburg, 1972-79; dir. corp. planning, 1980-82, v.p. shipping policy and planning, 1983-90, ind. publ., 1991—; cons. in field. Author: A Century of Liner Shipping to the Far East, 1986, A Century of Liner Shipping to Australia, 1986, Bridge Across the Atlantic, 1991, Crossing the Tracks of Columbus: German Shipping to Latin America, The Caribbean and Pacific Coast of North America Down the Years, 1992, Kurs Sudamerika—125 Years of Hamburg South America Line, 1996, The Influence of Sea Power upon German History 1890-1945: a critical review, 1998. Mem. Clausewitz Gesellschaft. Avocations: history, politics, music, wild life protection, hiking. Home: Henseweg 13J, D-22359 Hamburg Germany

SEILER, ROBERT KURT, textile company executive, consultant; b. Vilsbiburg, Bavaria, Germany, Feb. 6, 1958; s. Kurt Wilhelm and Elfriede Maria (Knopf) S. Diploma Kaufmann, U. Munich, 1986; diploma Engineering, Tech. U., Munich, 1982. Bus. lectr. U. Munich, 1986-91; CEO Seiler Consulting, Munich, 1986—, Caro Systems, Munich, 1991—, Textil Holding Gmbh, Emmendingen, Germany, 1995—, Ramie-Seiler AG, Emmendingen, 1995—; mem. supervisory bd. Ramie-Seiler AG, Emmendingen, 1986-95, Textil-Holding, Emmendingen, 1986-95. Author Handbook of Project Management, 1989. Publisher student newspaper U. Munich, 1982-83. Mem. Internat. Neural Network Soc. Office: Ramie-Seiler AG, Box 1580, 79305 Emmendingen Germany

SEILER, WOLFGANG, atmospheric chemist; b. Remscheid, Germany, Jan. 22, 1940; s. Paul and Bertel (Lingelbach) S.; m. Hannelore Wild; children: Birgit, Dirk. M in Meteorology, U. Mainz, Germany, 1967, PhD, 1972. Rsch. asst. U. Mainz, 1967-69; sr. scientist Max Planck Inst., Mainz, 1969-85; dir. Fraunhofer Inst., Garmisch, Germany, 1986-98; prof. U. Augsburg, Germany, 1998—; mem. climate adv. bd. Govt. of Germany, Bonn, 1988-96; mem. Enquete commn. German Parliament, Bonn, 1987-95; chmn. scientific environ. adv. bd. German Bahn AG, 1995—; mem. coun. experts Global Environ. Aspects BMBF, 1999—. Office: Fraungifer Inst Atm Env R, Kreuzeckeckbahn Str 19, D-82467 Garmisch-Partenkrchn Germany

SEINGRY, GEORGES-FRANCIS, publishing company executive; b. Metz, France, Aug. 12, 1946. BA Modern Languages, Sorbonne, Paris, 1971; LLM, U. Paris, 1972. Lectr. U. Dakar, Senegal, 1972-73; local resident Hotel Industry, Dakar, 1973-76; chmn. Editions Delta, Brussels, Belgium, 1976—. Office: Editions Delta SA, Rue Scailquin 55, B-1210 Brussels Belgium

SEIPELT, MARIA UTA, physician; b. Dresden, Sachsen, Germany, Dec. 27, 1968; d. Hubertus and Uta Hanna (Zippe) Lantsch; m. Peter Friedrich Seipelt, Sept. 5, 1997; 1 child, Johannes Emil. Approbation/physician, Humboldt U., Berlin, Germany, 1995; MD, Georg-August U., Göttingen, Germany, 1999. Intern Inselspital Dept. Neurology, Bern, Switzerland, 1993, Charité Dept. Neurology, Berlin, Germany, 1994, Charité Dept. Neurosurgery, Berlin, Germany, 1994; resident Creutzfeldt-Jakob Rsch. Group, Göttingen, Germany, 1995, Uniklinikum Dept. Neurology, Göttingen, Germany, 1996-97, Uniklinikum Dept. Neuroradiology, Göttingen, Germany, 1997-99. Contbr. articles to profl. jours. Mem. Soc. for Prevention of Cruelty to Animals, Soc. Physicians Against Experimentation with Animals. Catholic. Avocations: astronomy, painting, music. Home: Stadtpark 3, D-16303 Schwedt Brandenburg, Germany

SEITELBERGER, FRANZ, neurologist, emeritus educator; b. Vienna, Austria, Dec. 4, 1916; s. Franz and Bertha (Heuritsch) S.; m. Erika Weber, July 7, 1945; children: Edda, Linda, Rainald. MD, U. Vienna, 1940. Cert. specialist in neurology and psychiatry. Asst. Neurol. Inst. U. Vienna, 1951-54, docent Neurol. Inst., 1954-59, dir. Neurol. Inst., 1959-87, prof., 1959-87, dean med. faculty, 1974-75, rector, 1975-77, prorector, 1977-78, prof. emeritus, 1987—; dir. Inst. Brain Rsch., Vienna, 1970-90. Author: Brain, Consciousness and Cognition, 1988; contbr. 430 articles to sci. jours. and chpts. to books. Named to Order of Sacred Treasure, Emperor of Japan, 1989. Mem. Austrian Acad. Scis. (Schrödinger award 1987), Hungarian Acad. Sci. (hon.), Mex. Med. Acad. (hon.), Max Planck Soc., Deutsche Akademie der Naturforscher Leopoldina. Roman Catholic. Home: Weimarerstrasse 97, 1190 Vienna Austria

SEITELMAN, MARK ELIAS, lawyer; b. N.Y.C., Apr. 14, 1955; s. Leo Henry and Pearl (Elias) S. BA, Bklyn. Coll., 1976; JD, Bklyn. Law Sch., 1979. Bar: N.Y. 1980, U.S. Dist. Ct. (ea., so., and we. dists.) N.Y. 1980, U.S. Supreme Ct. 1995, U.S. Ct. Mil. Appeals, 1995. Law asst. Criminal Ct., Bklyn., 1979; law clk. to Hon. Justice Aaron D. Bernstein N.Y. Supreme Ct., Bklyn., 1980; assoc. Lester, Schwab, Katz & Dwyer, N.Y.C., 1981-87, Weg and Myers, 1987-88, Kroll & Tract, 1988-90; pvt. practice N.Y.C., 1990—. Appeared on WABC TV Eyewitness News; interviewed by N.Y. Daily News, N.Y. Newsday. Mem. ABA, ATLA (sustaining mem. motor vehicle and small practice sect.), N.Y. State Bar Assn., N.Y. County Bar Assn. (ins. and supreme ct. coms.), N.Y. State Trial Lawyers Assn. (sustaining mem., bd. dirs., mem. spkrs. bur., conv. com., legis. com., contbg. editor Trial Lawyers Quar.), N.Y. State Trial Lawyers Inst. (CLE program chmn., lectr.), Bklyn. Bar Assn. (legis. com., employment law com.). Office: 233 Broadway Rm 901 New York NY 10279-0999

SEITZ, GUNTHER H. R., pharmaceutical chemistry educator; b. Hamburg, Fed. Republic Germany, Mar. 8, 1936; s. Hans and Else (Sydow) S.; m. Edith Boos; children: Christina, Angela, Birgit. Appr. Pharmacist, 1961; Diploma in chemistry, U. Marburg, Marburg, Fed. Republic Germany, 1962; D., U. Marburg, 1965, Habilitation, 1968. Acad. councillor U. Marburg, 1970-72; prof. chemistry dept. chemistry Vet. Medicine Coll., Hannover, Fed. Republic Germany, 1972-77; prof. pharm. chemistry U. Marburg, 1977—. Author papers and treatises on chem. and pharm. rsch. Recipient Lesmüller medal German ABDA, 1999. Mem. German Pharm. Soc. (pres., Carl-Mannich medal 1999), Soc. German Chemists (pres.), Am. Chem. Soc. Home: Hubgraben 8, 35041 Marburg Lahn Germany Office: Inst Pharm Chemistry, Marbacher Weg 6, 35032 Marburg Germany

SEITZ, RÜDIGER JÜRGEN, neurology educator; b. Hamburg, Germany, May 9, 1956; s. Dieter Rudolf and Elisabeth (Ziese) S.; m. Inès Louise Freiin von Uslar-Gleichen, Aug. 29, 1981; children: Richard, Bernhard, Christiane, Friedrich. Dr med, U. Hamburg, Germany, 1981; PhD, U. Düsseldorf, Germany, 1991. Cert. MD. Residency U. Düsseldorf, Germany, 1982-87; rsch. fellow Karolinska Inst., Stockholm, Sweden, 1987-89; cons. U. Düsseldorf, Germany, 1990—; head Neuro-Imaging Rsch. Lab., U. Düsseldorf, 1990—, assoc. prof., 1996; chmn. 5th Internat. Conf. on Functional Mapping of the Human Brain, Düsseldorf, 1999. Contbr. to profl jours. Recipient Hugo Spatz prize German Soc. Neurology, 1992, Rsch. award German Curatorium ZNS, 1997. Mem. German Soc. Clin. Neurophysiology, Internat. Soc. Cereb. Blood Flow Metabolism, Soc. Neuroscience, German Soc. Neuropathology, German Soc. Neurology. Avocations: skiing, sailing. Office: U Düsseldorf, Moorenstrasse 205, D-40225 Düsseldorf Germany

SEKADDE-KIGONDU, CHRISTINE BERTHA, biochemist, researcher; b. Kampala, Uganda, Aug. 23, 1946; came to Kenya, 1980.; d. Yutuko Mukasa Sekadde and Namuyiga Samali; m. John Giceha Kigondu, Oct. 29, 1979; children: Sanyu, Elizabeth, Wangu. BSc, Purdue U., 1970; PhD, SUNY, Buffalo, N.Y., 1974. Lectr. Makerere U., Kampala, Uganda, 1974-77; sr. lectr. U. Liberia, Monrovia, 1977-80; assoc. prof. U. Nairobi, Kenya, 1995—; cons. USAID, Kenya, 1995, World Health Orgn., Geneva, 1994. Editor Jour. Ob-gyn East and Central Africa, 1980-92. Mem. WHO, Third World Acad. Sci. (Kenya chpt.), Kenya Assn. U. Women, Assn. Clin. Chemists (asst. chmn. 1993-97). Avocations: sewing, swimming, science clubs for girls, travel. Office: U Nairobi Dept PO Box 19676, Nairobi Kenya

SEKE, JOSIP, physicist, educator; b. Sombor, Vojvodina, Yugoslavia, June 9, 1949; arrived in Austria, 1968; s. Mihalj and Jelisaveta Seke. PhD in Physics, Vienna Tech. U., 1979. Postdoctoral fellow SUNY, Albany, 1981; vis. mem. Courant Inst. NYU, N.Y.C., 1981-82; rsch. physicist, lectr. Vienna Tech. Univ., 1983-86, docent, 1986; prof. theoretical physics Vienna Tech. U., 1993—. Contbr. more than 140 articles to profl. jours. Office: Inst Theoretical Physics Tech U, Wiedner Hauptstr 8-10/136, A-1040 Vienna Austria

SEKERIS, CONSTANTINE EVANGELOS, biochemistry educator; b. Nauplia, Argolis, Greece, June 12, 1933; s. Evangelos G. and Polyxeni E. (Eulambiou) S.; 1 child, Evangelos. Diploma, U. Athens (Greece), 1962; MD, U. Munich, 1962. Rsch. asst. Med. Sch. U. Munich, 1962-64; asst. Med. Sch. U. Marburg, Germany, 1964-66, sr. asst., 1966-69, assoc. prof., 1969-73; head. sect. molecular biology of cell German Cancer Rsch. Ctr., Heidelberg, 1974-78; dir. Inst. Biol. Rsch. Nat. Hellenic Rsch. Found., Athens, 1979—, v.p., 1986-93; prof. biochemistry U. Athens, 1979—; hon. prof. U. Heidelberg, 1980. Contbr. articles to profl. jours. 2nd lt. med. unit Greek mil., 1957-59. Mem. Hellenic Biochemistry Biophys. Soc. (past pres.), Hellenic Soc. Biology Rsch., Assn. Biology and Chemistry, Biochem. Soc., European Molecular Biology Orgn., Assn. Cell Biology, Am. Soc. Cell Biology, European Acad., Serbian Acad. Scis. and Arts (fgn.). Greek Orthodox. Home: Ithakis 9, 11369 Athens Greece Office: U Athens Med Sch, Goudi, 11635 Athens Greece

SEKHON, BHUPINDER SINGH, chemistry educator, researcher; b. Sanehwal, Punjab, India, May 6, 1947; s. Pritam Singh and Amir Kaur (Somal) S.; m. Nirmal Kaur Grewal, Feb. 22, 1976; children: Harjot Singh, Romal Kaur. MSc, Punjab Agrl. U., Ludhiana, 1970, PhD, 1974. Asst. prof. biochemistry Punjab Agrl. U., 1974-84, assoc. prof. chemistry, 1985-93, prof., 1993—. Contbr. articles to profl. jours. Postdoctoral fellow dept. chemistry U. Coll. Dublin, Belfield, Dublin, Ireland, 1980-82. Mem. N.Y. Acad. Scis. Office: Punjab Agrl U, Dept Chemistry, Ludhiana 141004, India

SEKI, HUMITAKE, microbiology educator, martial artist; b. Okayama City, Japan, Dec. 14, 1937; s. Masaji and Sakae (Sentou) S.; m. Atsuko Yamamoto, May 31, 1970; children: Junko, Tsunetake. B in Agr., U. Tokyo, 1961, M in Agr., 1963, PhD in Agr., 1966. Rsch. assoc. U. Tokyo, 1966-76; postdoctoral fellow NRC of Can., B.C., 1967-69; lectr. Waseda U., Tokyo, 1973-75; assoc. prof. microbiology U. Tsukuba, Japan, 1976-89, prof., 1989—, dean master's program in biosys. studies, 1998—; 19th headmaster, Kashima-shinryu Martial Arts Assn.; councilor U. Tokyo, 1992-96, 98—; mem. com. cons. Ministry of Edn., Tokyo, 1994-96; sec. gen. ann. meeting Oceanographic Soc., 1997. Author: Organic Materials in Aquatic Ecosystems, 1982, The Kashima-Shinryu and Samurai Martial Culture, 1997; mem. editl. bd. Water, Air, and Soil Pollution, 1980—, Aquatic Living Resources, 1991—. Recipient Okada prize Oceanog. Soc., 1966, Disting. Svc. awards Pacific region Dept. of Def. Dependent Schs., U.S., 1983, ann. Waka column prize Mainichi newspaper, 1984, Oceanog. Soc. prize, 1996. Mem. Japan Sci. Coun. (com. 1991-2000), Societe Franco-Japanaise d'Oceanographie (2000 Prix), Oceanographic Soc. Japan, Am. Soc. for Microbiology (emeritus mem.). Shintou. Avocations: traditional martial arts of Japan, haiku, waka. E-mail: seki@bsys.tsukuba.ac.jp. Home: Takezono 3-207-3, Tsukuba Ibaraki 3050032, Japan Office: U Tsukuba Inst Biol Scis, Tennoudai 1-1-1, Tsukuba Ibaraki 3050006, Japan

SEKI, MASAHARU, patent lawyer; b. Tokyo, Nov. 20, 1944; s. Tadao and Miyo (Nagao) S.; m. Emiko Egashira; children: Yasuharu, Shigeharu, Atsuko. BS, Tokyo U., 1967. Cert. patent atty., supr. for treatment of radioisotope, supr. for preventions against water pollution, Japan. Control engr. Teijin Ltd., Osaka, Japan, 1967-74, instrument rschr., 1979-87; control engr. Japan Oil Engring. Co., Tokyo, 1974-79; asst. Kitamura Patent Office, Osaka, 1987-89; patent atty. Asamura Patent Office, Tokyo, 1990-95, Seki Patent Office, Tokyo, 1995—. Co-author: Study on Examples of Software Relating Patents, 1994. Mem. Soc. Instrument and Control Engrs., Japan Patent Attys. Assn., Japan Radioisotope Assn. Home: 11-3 Makuharihongo 2-chome, Hanamigawa, Chiba 262-0033, Japan Office: Seki Patent Office, Saiwai Bldg 4 Fl 4 Gobancho, Chyda-ku Tokyo 102-0076, Japan

SEKI, YASUSHI, nuclear scientist, researcher; b. Shanghai, Apr. 11, 1943; s. Morisaburo and Ruriko (Kimura) S.; m. Mamiko Shirahata, Oct. 29, 1972; children: Kensuke, Daisuke, Yuko. BS in Nuclear Engring., U. Tokyo, 1967, D Engring., 1977. Rschr. Japan Atomic Energy Rsch. Inst., Tokaimura, 1967-80, sr. scientist, 1980-86; prin. scientist Japan Atomic Energy Rsch. Inst., Naka-machi, 1986-92, head Fusion Reactor Sys. Lab., 1992-98, dep. dir. dept. fusion engring. rsch., 1998-2000, dir. Nuclear Tech. and Edn. Ctr., 2000—; vis. scientist Oak Ridge (Tenn.) Nat. Lab., 1977-78; sr. engr. UCLA, 1986; vis. prof. Ibaraki U., Hitachi, Japan, 1998; chmn. exec. com. Internat. Energy Agy. Implementing Agreement on Environ., Safety and Econ. Aspects Fusion Power, 1997-2000. Recipient Tech. award Atomic Energy Soc. Japan, Tokyo, 1982. Mem. Am. Nuclear Soc., Atomic Energy Soc. Japan (mem. planning com. 1984-85), Japan Soc. Plasma Sci. and Nuclear Fusion Rsch. Avocations: tennis, books, go. Office: Nu Tech Atom Energy Rsch 2-, 28-49 Honkomagome Bunkyo-ku, 113-0021 Tokyo Japan

SEKIMOTO, MAYAKA, English literature educator; b. Tokyo, Jan. 15, 1930; d. Kanzo and Misao (Tusumura) Mori; m. Takahiro Sekimoto, Apr. 16, 1956; children: Masakazu, Sumito, Misako. Student, Tusda Coll., Tokyo, 1950; BA, Waseda U., Tokyo, 1953; MA, Tokyo U., 1956. Lectr. Seijo U., Tokyo, 1959-65, assoc. prof., 1965-74, prof. English lit., 1974—. Author: The Duchess of Malfi: Study of J. Webster, 1965; contbr. articles to lit. publs. Mem. English Lit. Soc. Japan, Malone Soc. Avocations: travel, reading books, playing and listening to music, attending plays. Home: 1-29-6 Higashi Yukigaya, Ohta-ku Tokyo 145-0065, Japan

SEKIMOTO, MAYAKO, professor; b. Tokyo, Jan. 15, 1936; d. Kanzo and Misao (Tusumura) Mori; m. Tadahiro Sekimoto, Apr. 16, 1956; children: Masakazu, Sumito, Misako. address: 1 29 6 Higashi Yukigaka, Ohta-Ku Tokyo 145 0065, Japan

SEKIMOTO, TADAHIRO, electronics company executive; b. Nov. 14, 1926; s. Taichiro and Tomi (Katayama) S.; m. Mayako Mori, Apr. 16, 1956; children: Masakazu, Sumito, Misako. BS in Physics, U. Tokyo, 1948, D Engring., 1962. With NEC Corp., Ltd., 1948-65, 67—, dir., 1974—, assoc. sr. v.p., then sr. v.p., 1974-78, exec. v.p., 1978-80, pres., 1980-94, chmn. bd., 1994—, sr. mem. bd., 1998—, chmn. emeritus, counselor, bd. dirs., 2000—; mgr. comms. process lab. COMSAT, 1965-67. Decorated officier de l'Ordre Nat. de Légion d'Honneru Commandeur (France), Grand Cordon of the Order of the Sacred Treasure; hon. knight comdr. Most Excellent Order of Brit. Empire, Dato Setia Diraja Kedah, Malaysia, comdr. Nat. DeLa Legion D'Honneur (France); hon. friendship amb. Chinese People's Assn. Friendship with Fogn. Countries; recipient Japanese Govt. prize, 1976, Dato'Setia Diraja Kedah (Malaysia), Purple Ribbon medal, 1982, Blue Ribbon medal, 1989, Aerospace Comms. award AIAA, 1992, Eli Whitney Productivity award SME, 1994. Fellow IEEE (life, Edwin Haward Armstrong Achievement award, 1982, Alexander Graham Bell medal 1996, Satellite Hall of Fame award); mem. NAE (fgn. assoc.). Home: 29-6 Higashi Yukigaya 1-chome, Ohta-ku Tokyo 145-0065, Japan Office: NEC Corp, 7-1 Shiba 5-Chome, Minato-ku Tokyo 108-8001, Japan

SEKINE, HIDEKI, aeronautics educator; b. Tokyo, Mar. 22, 1943; m. Yukimi Sekine. D in Engring., Tohoku U., Sendai, Japan, 1977. Assoc. prof. Tohoku U., 1980-87, prof., 1987—. Author: Theory of Elasticity, 1983; patentee in field. Recipient prize Mining and Materials Processing Inst. Japan, 1985, Yamazaki prize Soc. Materials Engring. for Resources, 1992, 99. Mem. Japan Soc. for Composite Materials (bd. dirs. 1991—, v.p. 1999—, prize 2000). Home: 7-9-904 Itsutsu-bashi 2 chome, Aoba-ku Sendai 980-0022, Japan Office: Tohoku U, Aoba-yama 01, Sendai 980-8579, Japan

SEKINE, JOJI GEORGE, oral and maxillofacial surgeon; b. Nagasaki, Japan, Feb. 18, 1961; s. Takeshi and Kyoko (Sugamura) S. DDS, Fukuoka Dental Coll., Japan, 1989; PhD, Nagasaki U., 1996. Accredited oral and maxillofacial surgeon. Postgrad. second dept. oral anatomy Fukuoka Dental Coll., Japan, 1989-90; resident second dept. oral and maxillofacial surgery Nagasaki Univ. Sch. of Dentistry, 1990-91, resident dept. anesthesiology, 1991-92; resident ICU Nagasaki U. Med. Hosp., 1992; asst. prof. second dept. oral and maxillofacial surgery Nagasaki U. Sch. of Dentistry, 1991-99, lectr. second dept. oral and maxillofacial surgery, 1999—. Contbr. articles to profl. publs. Mem. AAAS, Japanese Soc. of Oral and Maxillofacial Surgeons, accredited oral & maxillofacial surgeon, Japanese Assn. of Anatomists, Internat. Assn. Oral and Maxillofacial Surgeons, Internat. Coll. Surgeons, Internat. Soc. Preventive Oncology. Avocation: yacht racing, teddy bear collecting. Home: 3-5-11 Izumi, Nagasaki 852-8151, Japan Office: Nagasaki U Sch Dentistry, 1-7-1 Sakamoto, Nagasaki 852-8588, Japan

SEKINE, MASAHIKO, environmental engineering educator; b. Osaka, Japan, Aug. 10, 1958; s. Michihiko and Jyunko (Kawabata) S.; m. Nobue Tanaka, Nov. 26, 1983; children: Masahiro, Satomi, Yoshimi. B.Engring., Kyoto U., 1981, M.Engring., 1983, Dr.Engring., 1991. Rsch. assoc. Yamaguchi U., Ube, Japan, 1983-93, lectr., 1993-95, assoc. prof., 1995—; vis. scientist Nat. Water Rsch. Inst., Burlington, Can., 1996-97. Co-author: Sustainable Development in the Seto Inland Sea Japan, 1997; contbr. articles to profl. jours. Com. mem. Com. of Solid Waste Disposal Site, Hiroshima, 1993, Com. of Frukou River Restoration, Yamaguchi, 1995, Com. of Ichinosaka River Restoration, Yamaguchi, 1996; project mem. Project of Inspection for Solid Waste Disposal Site, Ube, 1994; com. mem. comprehensive countermeasure for river water pollution, Found. River and Watershed Environment Mgmt., 1999-2000. Mem. Japan Soc. Civil Engring. (mem. environ. sys. com. 1997—), Japanese Soc. fisheries Sci., Internat. Soc. Ecol. Modelling. Avocations: skiing, scuba diving. Office: Yamaguchi Univ, 2-16-1 Tokiwadai, Ube 755-8611, Japan

SEKINE, YASUJI, science educator; b. Tokyo, Dec. 7, 1931; s. Tainojo and Haru (Shitara) S.; m. Hideko Nakaji, Apr. 26, 1936; 1 child, Yoko. BS, U. Tokyo, 1954, MS, 1956, D of Engring., 1959. Lectr. U. Tokyo, 1959-60, from assoc. prof. to prof., 1960-92; prof. Sci. U. Tokyo, 1992—; v.p. Cen. Rsch. Inst. Elec. Power Industry of Japan, 1993—; hon. prof. Xian Jiatong U., China, 1984, Harbin Inst. Tech., China, 1986; advisor Tokyo Electric Power Co., 1992—. Author: (books) Power Systems Engineering, 1966 (Outstanding Book prize 1968), Theory of Power Systems Analysis, 1971 (Outstanding Book prize 1972), Introduction to Energy Engineering, 1996, Mathematical Programming, 1976. Fellow Inst. Elec. and Electronic Engrs. (life); mem. Conf. Internat. Grand Reseaux Elec. a Haute Tension (hon., treas. 1996—), Inst. Elec. Engrs. Japan (pres. 1989-90, Disting. Contbn. award 1990, Disting. Power Engr. medal 1974, Centennial Anniversary award 1988), Power Sys. Computer Conf. (pres. 1990—), Royal Swedish Acad. Engring. Scis. Avocations: gardening, reading books, movies, walking. Home: 5-22-7 Kataseyama, Fujisawa Kanagawa 251-0033, Japan Office: Sci U of Tokyo, 1-3 Kagurazaka Shinjuku, Tokyo 162-0825, Japan

SEKIZAWA, TADASHI, computer and data processing executive; b. Tokyo, Nov. 6, 1931; m. Misako Sekizawa; 2 children. Student, Tokyo U. Joined Fujitzu Ltd., 1954, various mgmt. positions, 1954-82, gen. mgr. switching sys. group, 1982-84, bd. dirs., 1984—, mng. dir., 1986-88, exec. dir., 1988-90, pres., rep. dir., 1990—; chmn. Fujitsu Ltd. Mem. Comm. Industry Assn. Japan (vice chair 1990—), Japan Electronic Industry Devel. Assn. Avocations: lit., travel, motoring. Office: Fujitsu Ltd, 1-6-1 Marunouchi Chiyoda-ku, Tokyo 100-8211, Japan*

SEKIZAWA, TSUYOSHI, medical educator, physician, neurologist; b. Ohfumato, Iwate, Japan, Apr. 24, 1942; s. Ryohichi and Fukuko (Konno) S.; m. Naoko Machida, Apr. 16, 1972; children: Satoko, Koh, Yukiko. MD, Tohoku U., Sendai, Japan, 1977. Rschr. Tohoku U., Sendai, 1970-77, neurologist, rschr., 1980-96; prof. Yamagata (Japan) Coll., 1997—; vis. scientist NIH, Bethesda, Md., 1977-80; cons. for patients with interactable diseases, Sendai City, 1996. Contbr. articles to profl. jours. including Sci., Jour. Virology, Jour. Infectious Diseaes, Jour. Neurol. Sci. Mem. Japan Neurol. Assn. (councilor 1995—). Avocation: music appreciation. Home: Kaigamori, Sendai Miyagi 981-0942, Japan Office: Yamagata Coll Health Sci, Kamiyanagi 260, Yamagata 990-2212, Japan

SEKULIC, ANTE, educator; b. Tavankut/Subotica, Backa, Nov. 16, 1920; s. Sime and Julka (Pavlic) S.; m. Ruza Crnkovic, Aug. 24, 1954; 1 child, Ante. Secondary Sch. degree, U. Zagreb, Croatia, 1945, ScD, 1947. Secondary sch. tchr., 1946-67; dep. dir. secondary sch. Delnice, Croatia, 1959-66; prof., chmn. dept. Slavic langs. Rijeka U., 1969-72; author, lectr., cons., 1972—. Author: Zovna bjeline, 1947, Hrvatski realizam, 1957, Knjizevnost backih Hrvata, 1970, Drevni Bac, 1978, Tragom franj. ljetopisa u Subotici, 1978, Narodni zivot i obicaj backih Bunjevaca, 1981, Marijanske poboznosti podunavskih Hrvata, 1985, Remete, 1986, Backi Bunjevci i Sokci, 1989, Backi Hrvati, 1991, Olimje v XVII. i XVIII.stoljecu, 1993, Hrvatski toponimi u Backoj zupaniji, 1993, Hrvatska knjizevnost u juznoj Ugarskoj do XVIII, 1993, Filozofska ucilista u Srijemu, 1994, Hrvatska preporodna knjizevnost u ugarskom Podunavlju do 1918, 1994, Hrvatski backi mjestopist, 1994, Hrvatska knjizevnost podunavskih Hrvata u XX st 1996, Juraj Utisinovic, 1996, Hrvatski baraniski miestonisi, 1996, Hrvatski srijemski mjestopisi, 1997. Recipient award Matica suboticka, 1940. Mem. Philol. Soc. Croatia, Soc. Croatian Authors, Soc. ord. Acad. Marianna, Rome, Soc. Scrib. Acad. Croatica. Home and Office: 133 Vlaska, 10000 Zagreb Croatia

SELANNE, TEEMU, professional hockey player; b. Helsinki, Finland, July 3, 1970. Hockey player Winnipeg Jets Nat. Hockey League, 1992-95, hockey player Phoenix Coyotes, 1995-97, hockey player Anaheim Mighty Ducks, 1997—; played in All-Star Game, 1996, 94, 93. Named Rookie of Yr. Sporting News, 1992-93, All Rookie team, 1992-93; Recipient Calder Meml. Trophy, 1992-93. Office: Mighty Ducks PO Box 61077 2695 E Katella Ave Anaheim CA 92803-6177

SELAOLO, EDSON TSIABABA, hydrogeologist; b. Thamaga, Kweneng, Botswana, Aug. 8, 1956; s. Sebakele and Serepudi (Kenyafetse) S.; m. Tjongabangwe Macha, Dec. 12, 1989; 1 child, Karabo. Diploma in Mining Tech., Haileybury Sch. Mines, Ont., Can., 1980; BSc in Geology, U. N.B., Can., 1984; MSc in Hydrogeology, U. London, 1985; PhD in Hydrogeology, Free U. Amsterdam, The Netherlands, 1998. Asst. hydrogeologist Geol. Survey, Lobatse, Botswana, 1984-85, hydrogeologist, 1985-87, sr. hydrogeologist, 1987-90, prin. hydrogeologist, 1990-92, rsch. hydrogeologist, 1992-97, chief hydrogeologist, 1998—. Author: Tracer, Studies and Groundwater Recharge Assessment, 1998; contbr. articles to profl. jours. Mem. Botswana Geoscientist Assn. (editor newsletter 1986-87), Internat. Assn. Hydrogeologists. Baptist. Avocations: squash, jogging, swimming, tennis, weight lifting. Office: Dept Geol Survey, P/Bag 14, Lobatse Botswana

SELBERG, DANIELA, freelance writer, editor; b. Karlsruhe, Baden, Germany, Feb. 24, 1954; d. Emil Speck and Ruth (Kroh) Hoffmann; m. Matthias Friedrich Müller, Aug. 7, 1981 (div. Jan. 1988); children: David, Rebecca; m. Oliver Selberg, May 17, 1991; children: Robin, Lorenz, Leo, Marc Samuel, Cedric Oliver. BA, U. Freiburg, Germany, 1979; proficiency cert. in English, Cambridge (Eng.) U., 1989. Registered chief sec., Heidelberg, Germany. Mng. dir. Tennis Enterprises, Eberbach, Germany, 1974-84. Contbr. interviews to Am Markt. Hon. tchr. Integrated sch., Hannover, Germany, 1997-98. Mem. N.Y. Acad. Scis. Mem. Social Democrat. Party. Home: Klabundestrasse 29, 30627 Hannover Nieders, Germany

SELBERG, OLIVER, physician; b. Hamburg, Germany, May 20, 1960; s. Werner Julius Emil Adolf and Gerda Marie Elisabeth (Jepp) S.; m. Daniela Speck, May 17, 1991; children: David, Rebecca, Robin, Lorenz, Leo, Marc Samuel, Cedric Oliver. MD, U. Hamburg, 1990. Rsch. asst. Nutrition Team Med. Sch., Hannover, Germany, 1989-91, pathological biochemist, 1992—. Contbr. articles to profl. jours. Postdoctoral fellow Med. Sch., Hannover, 1992. Mem. N.Y. Acad. Sci. Avocation: stamp collecting. Office: Med Sch Hannover, Med Sch Hannover, Carl-Neuberg Str 1, 30625 Hannover Germany

SELBERG, TIMOTHY SCOTT, artist; b. Pontiac, Mich., Nov. 6, 1959; s. Jack Donald and Joyce Maxine S.; m. Lorna Elaine Rinehart, July 12, 1986; children: Elise Nichole, Lukas Eldon. Diploma, Waterford Kettering, Mich., 1978; cert., Ctr. Creative Studies, Detroit. Graphic artist Delta Faucet, Southfield, Mich., 1986-87; owner Selberg Studios, Inc., Leonard, Mich., 1987—. Mem. Internat. Assn. Amusement Parks and Attractions, Internat. Ventriloquist Assn., Nat. Assn. Am. Ventriloquists. E-mail: selberg@concentric.net.

SELBERHERR, SIEGFRIED, university dean, educator, researcher, consultant; b. Klosterneuburg, Austria, Sept. 3, 1955; s. Johannes and Josefine (Henninger) S.; m. Margit Leonhard, Oct. 12, 1979; children: Andreas, Julia. Dipl., Ing. Tech. U., Vienna, Austria, 1978, Dr. techn., 1981, venia docendi, 1984. Research assoc. Tech. U., Vienna, 1978-79, asst. prof. microelectronics, 1979-84, prof. computer-aided design, 1984-88, dean microelectronics, 1988—; cons. to bus. and industry. Author: Analysis and Simulation of Semiconductor Devices, 1984; editor Jour. Transactions of the Soc. for Computer Simulation, 1983—, Jour. Electrosoft, 1988-92, Jour. Mikroelektonik, 1986—, book series Computational Microelectronics, 1985—; contbr. articles to profl. jours. Recipient Dr. Ernst Fehrer award Tech. U. Vienna, 1983, Heinz Zemanek award Austrian Computer Soc., 1987, Dr. Herta Firnberg Fed. award Republic of Austria, 1986, Wilhelm-Exner medal Austrian Bus. Assn., 1994, Sci. award Land Niederösterreich, 1999. Fellow IEEE; mem. Assn. Computing Machinery, Soc. Indsl. and Applied Math., Nachrichtentechnische Gesellschaft (award 1985). Home: Fasanstrasse 1, A 3430 Tulln Austria Office: Tech U Vienna, Gusshausstrasse 27-29, A 1040 Vienna Austria

SELBMANN, HANS KONRAD, medical information processing educator; b. Stuttgart, Germany, Dec. 11, 1941; s. Hans and Hildegard (Gerster) S.; m. Karin Kraft, Jan. 30, 1970; children: Anke, Dorrit. Diploma in Math., Stuttgart U., 1966; D in Human Biol. Sci., Ulm (Germany) U., 1972, habilitation in med. stats. and data processing, 1976. Mathematician Du Pont, Frankfurt, Germany, 1966-70; rschr. U. Ulm, 1970-74; prof. Inst. Med. Info. Processing and Biomath., U. Munich, 1974-84; chmn. Inst. Med. Info. Processing U. Tübingen, Germany, 1984—, dean med. faculty, 1994-95; mem. expert coun. health care Fed. Health Ministry, Bonn, Germany, 1988-91; mem. health rsch. coun. Fed. Ministry for Rsch. and Tech., 1990-99, chmn. com. on health rsch., 1992-99. Editor 25 books; contbr. articles to profl. jours. Mem. Soc. Quality Mgmt. in Health Care (chmn. 1993-97), Soc. Med. Info., Biometry and Epidemiology (chmn. 1985-87). Office: Inst Med Info Processing, Westbahnhofstr 55, D-72070 Tübingen Germany

SELBY, JEROME M., mayor; b. Wheatland, Wyo., Sept. 4, 1948; s. John Franklin and Claudia Meredith (Hudson) S.; m. Gloria Jean Nelson, June 14, 1969; children: Tyan, Cameronn, Kalen. BS in Math., Coll. Idaho, 1969, MA in Ednl. Adminstrn., 1974; MPA, Boise State U., 1978. Assoc. engr. Boeing Co., Seattle, 1969-71; dir. evaluation WICHE Mountain States Regional Med. Program, Boise, 1971-74; dir. rsch., evaluation Mountain States Health Corp., Boise, 1974-76, with health policy analysis and accountability, 1976-78; dir. health Kodiak (Alaska) Area Native Assn., 1978-83; mgr. Kodiak Island Borough, 1984-85, mayor, 1985-98, bus., mcpl. and fisheries cons., 1998—; regional dir. planning and devel. Providence Health System, 1998—; proprietor Kodiak Tax Svc., 1978—, Registered Guide, Kodiak, 1987—; cons. Nat. Cancer Inst., Washington, 1973-78, others. Contbr. articles to profl. jours. Treas. ARC, Kodiak, 1978-93, bd. dirs., 1978-95, chmn., 1989-90, mem. western ops. hdqrs. adv. bd., 1986-92, mem. group IV and V nat. adv. coj., 1986-89, nat. bd. govs., 1989-95, chmn. chpt. rels. com., 1994-95; pres. S.W. Alaska Mcpl. Conf., Anchorage, 1988-89, v.p., 1986-87, treas., 1996-98, bd. dirs., 1986-98; pres. Alaska Mcpl. League Investment Pool, Inc., 1992-98; v.p. Alaska Mcpl. League, 1988-90, pres., 1990-91, bd. dirs., 1988-98; bd. dirs. Alaska Mcpl. League Jt. Ins. Assn. Bd., 1995—, v.p., 1996-98, pres., 1998—; mem. Alaska Resource Devel. Coun., 1987—, exec. com., 1989-2000; mem. policy com. of outer continental shelf adv. bd. U.S. Dept. Interior, 1990—, vice chair, 1996-98, chair, 1998—; co-chair Alaska Task Force, 1995—; mem. Com. on Oil Pollution Act, 1995; mem. Nat. Assn. Counties, Cmty. and Econ. Devel. Steering Com., 1990-98, Alaska govtl. roles task force, 1991-92; mem. Alaska state/local govt. task force, 1996-98; chmn. Kodiak Island Exxon Valdez Restoration Com., 1991-95; dir. Kodiak Health Care Found., 1992—, v.p. 1992—; co-chmn. Arctic Power, 1993—; bd. dirs. Western Interstate Region Nat. Assn. of Counties, 1993-98; bd. dirs. Alaska Oceans, Seas, Fisheries Rsch. Found., 1998—, pres., 1998—; mem. environment, energy and land use steering com. Nat. Assn. Counties., 1997-98; mem. grad. med. edn. com. Alaska Family Practice Residency, 2000—. Paul Harris fellow, 1987, 88, 91, 92, 96; recipient Outstanding Contbn. award Alaska Mcpl. League, 1994, Disting. Alumni award Albertson Coll. of Idaho, 1997, Lifetime Achievement award Alaska Mcpl. League, 1998. Mem. Alaska Conf. Mayors, Nat. Soc. Tax Profls., Acad. Polit. Sci., Alaska Mcpl. Mgrs. Assn., Kodiak C. of C. (dir. 1983-99), Rotary (bd. dirs. 1989-97, treas. 1989-93, v.p. 1993-94, pres.-elect 1994-95, pres. 1995-96). Office: Providence Health Systems PO Box 196604 3200 Providence Dr Anchorage AK 99519-6604

SELBY, ROY CLIFTON, JR., neurosurgeon; b. Little Rock, Sept. 28, 1930; s. Roy Clifton Sr. and Annie Mae (Bular) S.; m. Marilyn Triffler, May 12, 1960; children: Brian M.T., Bretta L.T. BSc, MSc, La. State U., 1952; MD, U. Ark., Little Rock, 1956. Diplomate Am. Bd. Neurol. Surgery. Intern Montreal Gen. Hosp., 1956-57; resident VA Hosp., Little Rock, Ark., 1957-58, U. Ill. Depart. Neurology and Neurosurgery, Chgo., 1958-61; sr. fellow Neurosurgery Lahey Clinic, Boston, 1961-62; dir. dept. neurosurgery Ministry Health Gen. Hosp., Kuala Lumpur, Malaysia, 1963-70; chmn. dept. neurosurgery Cook County Hosp., Chgo., 1970-74; practice medicine specializing in neurosurgery Texarkana, Tex., 1974-86; assoc. clin. prof. neurosurgery U. Ill., Chgo., 1970-74; prof. Cook County Postgrad. Sch. Med., 1970-74; vis. assoc. prof. Rush Presbyn. Med. Ctr., 1970-74; lectr. dept. psychology E. Tex. U., Texarkana, 1986—. Author short stories; contbr. chpts. to books. Fellow Royal Soc. Medicine; mem. Am. Assn. Neurol. Surgeons, N.Y. Acad. Scis., Soc. Neurol. Lange Francaise, N.Y. Acad. Medicine, French Soc. History of Medicine, Am. Physiolog. Soc., Acad. Medicine (Paris), Internat. Soc. Surgery, Am. Osler Soc., Ark. Hist. Soc., Soc. Neurosci., Cen. Neuropsychiat. Soc., Am. Physiol. Soc., Inst. Charles DeGaulle, Ala. Hist. Soc., La. Hist. Soc., Sigma Xi, Alpha Omega Alpha. Avocations: reading, writing, gardening. Home: 3619 Garrison Rd Little Rock AR 72223-9673

SELCHER, WAYNE A., political science educator. BA in Spanish magna cum laude, Lebanon Valley Coll., 1964; MA in L.Am. Studies, U. Fla., 1965, PhD in Polit. Sci., 1970. Tchr. Elizabethtown (Pa.) Coll., 1969—, chair dept. polit. sci., 1970-96, prof. internat. studies, 1984—, dir. internat. studies, 1983-98; scholar-analyst U.S. Dept. State, 1981-86; exec. com. mem. Pa.-Bahia Brazil Com., Ptnrs. of the Ams., 1990-97; vis. rsch. prof. grad. program Sch. Adminstrn., Fed. U. Bahia, Salvador, Brazil, 1996. Author: The Afro-Asian Dimension of Brazilian Foreign Policy, 1956-72, 1974, Brazil's Multilateral Relations: Between First and Third Worlds, 1978; editor, contbr.: Brazil in the International System: The Rise of a Middle Power, 1981, Political Liberalization in Brazil: Dynamics, Dilemmas, and Future Prospects, 1986; contbr. chpts. to books and articles to profl. jours. Fulbright-Hays dissertation grantee, 1968, Howard Heinz Endowment grantee, 1984, Fulbright Lecturing grantee Coun. for the Internat. Exch. Scholars, 1989, Fulbright faculty rsch. abroad grantee, 1979, 90. Mem. Internat. Studies Assn., L.Am. Studies Assn., MIddle Atlantic Coun. L.Am. Studies, Brazilian Studies Assn. (exec. com. 1997-98). E-mail: selchewa@etown.edu. Office: Dept Polit Sci Elizabethtown Coll Elizabethtown PA 17022

SELES, MONICA, professional tennis player; b. Novi Sad, Yugoslavia, Dec. 2, 1973; came to U.S., 1986; d. Karol and Esther Seles. Profl. tennis player, 1989—. Winner Houston, 1989, 91, 92, Oakland, 1990, 92, L.A., 1990, 91, Tampa, 1990, 91, U.S. Hardcourts, 1990, Lipton, 1990, 91, Roland Garros, 1990, 91, 92, Italian Open, 1990, German Open, 1990, French Open, 1990, 91, 92, Va. Slims, 1990, 91, 92, Phila., 1991, Milan, 1991, Tokyo Nichirie, 1991, 92, U.S. Open, 1991, 92, Australian Open, 1991, 92, 93, 96, Italian Open Doubles (with Kelesi) 1990, (with Capriati) 1991, (with Sukova), 1992, Essen, 1992, Indian Wells, 1992, Barcelona, 1992, Chgo., 1993, Can. Open, 1995, 96, Amelia Island, 1999; finalist Dallas, 1989, Brighton, 1989, Palm Springs, 1991, U.S. Hardcourts, 1991, Hamburg, 1991, Italian Open, 1991, San Diego, 1991, Oakland, 1991, Wimbledon, 1992, Italian Open, 1992, L.A., 1992, Can. Open, 1992, Paris indoors, 1993, U.S. Open, 1995, Can. Open, 1999, Tokyo Cup, 1999; singles semifinalist , New Orleans, 1988, Roland Garros, Washington, 1989, European indoors, 1989, Washington, 1990, Australian Open, 1999, French Open, 1999, New Haven Open, 1999; doubles semifinalist (with A. Smith) Australian Open, 1991, (with Nagelsen), Chgo., 1993; named Yugoslavia's sportwoman of yr., 1985, World #1 ranked player, 1991, 92, #3 players in terms of career titles as a teenager, 1993; ranked 9th, 1999; recipient 1990 Rado Topspin award, Ted Tinling Diamond award Va. Slims, 1990, Grand Slam Title, 1996; named Tennis Mag./Rolex Watch Female Rookie of Yr., 1989, World Champion, 1991, 92, Comeback Player of Yr. Tennis mag., 1995, Profl. Female Athlete by Yr., 1995. Achievements include 3rd player in the Open-era to capture the Australian and Roland Garros in same calendar year; named youngest #1 ranked player in tennis history for women and men at 17 years, 3 months, 9 days; has won a total of 44 Singles events throughout professional tennis career. Office: care Internat Mgmt Group 1 Erieview Plz Cleveland OH 44114-1715*

SELEZOV, IGOR TIMOTHY, mechanics educator; b. Nevel, Pskov Regn, USSR, June 30, 1930; s. Timothy Naum and Olga Ignat (Savitskaya) S.; m. Ludmila Vasilij Jakovleva, Oct. 20, 1961. Engineer, Aviation Inst., Kharkov, USSR, 1954; CSc, Polytech. Inst., Kiev, USSR, 1961; DSc, Kiev U., 1971. Engr. Antonov Aviation Bureau, Kiev, 1954-57; sr. rsch. assoc. Inst. Mechanics, Kiev, 1960-63, Inst. Cybernetics, Kiev, 1963-73; prof., dept. head Inst. Hydromechanics, Kiev, 1973—; cons. Med. Surg. Soc. Bologna, Italy, 1997, Euromech., Cambridge, England, 1988-96; prof. Kiev U., 1979—; vis. prof. Nat. Rsch. Council Italy U. Bologna, 1995, 97. Author: Waves in Magnetohydroelastic Media, 1975, Wave Diffraction by Symmetric Inhomogeneities, 1978, Transformation of Waves in Shelf Coastal Zone, 1983, Wave Scattering by Local Inhomogeneities in Continuous Media, 1985, Modelling of Wave and Diffraction Processes in Continuous Media, 1989, Nonstationary and Nonlinear Waves in Electrically Conducting Media, 1991. Soros Humanitarian Found. grantee Am. Physical Soc., U.S.A., 1993, Soros prof. Internat. Soros Sci. Edn. Program, N.Y., 1994-96. Mem. Internat. Soc. Biorheology, Internat. Soc. for Cardiovasc. Medicine and Sci., Gesellschaft für Anewandte Mathematik und Mechanik. Avocations: knowledge and modelling of nature, physical training. Home: 11 Dobrokhotov St Apt 37, 03142 Kiev Ukraine Office: Inst Hydromech Nat Acad Sci, 8/4 Sheliabov St, 03057 Kiev Ukraine

SELF, DANA R., museum curator; b. Ft. Lauderdale, Fla., June 5, 1959; d. Charles Thomas and Joy A. Self. BA, Stephens Coll., 1981; MA, U. Kans., 1984; student, Oxford (Eng.) U., 1980. Asst. curator John Michael Kohler Arts Ctr., Sheboygan, Wis., 1993-94; curator Edwin A. Ulrich Mus. Art Wichita State U., 1994-96; curator Kemper Mus. Contemporary Art, Kansas City, Mo., 1996—; adj. instr. art history Johnson County C.C., Overland Park, Kans., 1991-93; peer reviewer IMLS, Washington, 1999; mem. panel CAA, Toronto, Can., 1998, N.Y.C., 2000; juror Kansas City Artists Coalition, 1998. Author: Chihuly Over Venice: The Spectacle of Beauty, 1996, Intimate Landscapes: The Canyon Suite of Georgia O'Keeffe, 1997, (exhbn. catalogue) Subversive Domesticity, 1996, Out of Eden, 1997. Commr. Commn. on the Status of Women, Wichita, 1995-96; mem. PEO, Kansas City, 1977—; mem. Overland Park Orch., 1985-93, 96—. Mem. Am. Assn. Mus., Coll. Art Assn. Avocations: reading, running, playing cello. Office: Kemper Mus Contemporary Art 4420 Warwick Blvd Kansas City MO 64111-1821

SELF, MARK EDWARD, communications consultant; b. Tyler, Tex., Dec. 6, 1955; s. Edward and Ruby (Rogers) S.; m. Dianne Logan; children: Patricia Bartlett, Marcile Christine. Student, Tenn. Tech. Sch., 1973-76. Gen. mgr. Gulf Telephone Inc., Beaumont, Tex., 1980-82; gen. sales mgr. CSC Telephone Inc., Tyler, Tex., 1982-83; v.p. sales Teleci Inc., Irving, Tex., 1983-85; cons. Self & Assocs., Grapevine, Tex., 1985—; pres. S&A Equipment Co., Grapevine, 1990—; v.p. mktg. Hicom, Inc., Euless, Tex., 1994—. Fundraiser Freedom Ride Found., Dallas, 1987. Named Outstanding Young Men of Am., 1985. Mem. Am. Hotel and Motel Assn., Nat. Office Machine Dealer Assn., Nat. Fedn. Ind. Bus., Dallas C. of C., Masons. Avocations: fishing, hunting, woodworking. Home: 3442 Spring Willow Dr Grapevine TX 76051-6516 Office: Self & Assocs 1114 S Airport Cir Ste 130 Euless TX 76040-6842

SELFRIDGE, CALVIN, lawyer; b. Winnetka, Ill., Dec. 20, 1933; s. Calvin Frederick and Violet Luella (Bradley) S. BA, Northwestern U., 1956; JD, U. Chgo., 1960. Bar: Ill. 1961. Trust officer Continental Ill. Nat. Bank & Trust Co., Chgo., 1961-71; pvt. practice Chgo., 1972-76, 79—; mem. How-

ington, Elworth, Osswald & Hough, Chgo., 1976-79; pres., dir. Northwest Newspapers Corp., 1977—, Des Plaines (Ill.) Pub. Co., 1977-90. Pres., bd. dirs. Scholarship Fund Found., 1965-99; trustee, pres. Lawrence Hall Youth Svcs., 1982—; trustee, vice-chmn. Ill. Soc. Colonial Wars. With AUS, 1959. Mem. Chgo., Am., Ill. Bar Assn., Law Club Chgo., Legal Club Chgo., Chi Psi, Phi Delta Phi, Attic Club (gov., past pres.), Univ. Club, Racquet Club (Chgo.), Balboa Club (Mazatlan, Mex.), Indian Hill Country Club (Winnetka, Ill.), Mid Day Club (Chgo.). Republican. Congregationalist. Home: 1325 N State Pkwy Apt 16D Chicago IL 60610-6124 Office: 208 S Lasalle St Ste 786 Chicago IL 60604-1006

SELIEM, MOHAMED ABDEL-HAMID, pediatric cardiologist; b. Beba, Egypt, Mar. 9, 1953; s. Abdel-Hamid Hamdy and Monera Mohamed (Mosa) S.; m. Amina Al-Khaiat, July 29, 1982; children: Monera, Ahmed, Karema, Mostafa. MB BcH, Cairo U., 1977. Intern Cairo U. Hosp., 1978-79; gen. pediatrician pvt. practice, Cairo, 1980-83; resident Georgetown U. Hosps., Washington, 1983-86; fellow in pediat. cardiology Children's Meml. Hosp., Chgo., 1986-89; asst. prof. pediatric cardiology The Children's Hosp. Phila., 1989-92; cons. pediatric cardiologist SAMSO, Saudi Arabia, 1992—; adj. asst. prof. pediatrics Children's Hosp. Phila., 1992-95. Contbr. articles to profl. jours. With Egyptian Mil., 1979-80. Pediatric cardiology fellow Children's Meml. Hosp., Chgo., 1986-89. Fellow Am. Coll. Cardiology; mem. Am. Heart Assn., Am. Soc. Echocardiology, Am. Bus. Assn. Avocations: jogging, swimming, writing. E-mail: seliemma@aramco.com.sa. Home: Saudi Aramco Box 1939, Dhahran 31311, Saudi Arabia Office: Dhahran Health Ctr, R A-406 Box 76, Dhahran 31311, Saudi Arabia

SELIG, KARL-LUDWIG, language and literature educator; b. Wiesbaden, Germany, Aug. 14, 1926; naturalized, 1948; s. Lucian and Erna (Reiss) S. BA, Ohio State U., 1946, MA, 1947; postgrad., U. Rome, Italy, 1949-50; PhD, U. Tex., 1955. Asst. prof. Romance langs. and lit. Johns Hopkins U., Balt., 1954-58; assoc. prof. U. N.C., Chapel Hill, 1958-61, U. Minn., Mpls., 1961-63; vis. prof. U. Tex., Austin, 1963-64, prof. Romance langs. and lit., 1964-65; Hinchliff prof. Spanish lit. Cornell U., Ithaca, N.Y., 1965-69; dir. grad. studies in Romance lit. Cornell U., Ithaca, 1966-69; prof. Spanish lit. Columbia U., N.Y.C., 1969—; Brown Found. fellow, vis. prof. Spanish and comparative lit. U. of the South, Sewanee, Tenn., 1990; vis. prof. U. Munich, 1963-64, U. Berlin, 1967; vis. prof. U. Greifswald, Germany, 1991-96, hon. prof., 1996—; cons. prof. Ohio State U., Columbus, 1967-69; vis. lectr. U. Zulia, Maracaibo, Venezuela, 1968; dir. summer seminar NEH, 1975, cons., 1975-77; vis. scholar Ga. U. Sys., 1977; vis. rsch. scholar Fondation Hardt, Vandoeuvres, Switzerland, 1959, Herzog August Bibliothek Wolfenbüttel, Fed. Repubic Germany, 1979—; mem. com. grants-in-aid Am. Coun. Learned Soc., 1969-73; chmn. Comparative Lit. Program and Colloquia, Columbia Coll., 1976-88. Author: The Library of Vincencio Juan de Lastanosa, Patron of Gracián, Geneva, 1960, Studies on Alciato in Spain, 1990, Studies on Cervantes, 1992; also numerous articles, revs.; editor: (Thomas Blundeville) of Councils and Counselors, 1963, (with A. G. Hatcher) Studia Philologica et Litteraria in Honorem L. Spitzer, 1958, (with J. E. Keller) Essays in Honor of N. B. Adams, 1966, (with R. Brinkmann) Theatrum Europaeum. Festschrift E. M. Szarota, 1982, (with S. Neumeister) Theatrum Mundi Hispanicum, 1986, (with R. Somerville) Florilegium Columbianum: Essays in Honor of Paul Oskar Kristeller, 1987, (with E. Sears) The Verbal and the Visual: Essays in Honor of William Sebastian Heckscher, 1990, Polyanthea Essays on Art and Literature in Honor of William Sebastian Heckscher, 1993; assoc. editor Modern Lang. Notes, 1955-58; mng. editor Romance Notes, 1959-61; editor: U. N.C. Studies in Comparative Lit, 1959-61, Bull. Comediantes, 1959-64, assoc. editor 1964-68, mem. editl. bd., 1979-88; co-editor Yearbook of Comparative Lit., Vol. IX, 1960; editorial bd. Colección Támesis, London, 1962-79, Romanic Rev., 1969-89, Teaching Lang. Through Lit, 1978-88; assoc. editor Hispania, 1969-74, Ky. Romance Quar, 1973-85; gen. editor Revista Hispánica Moderna, 1971-86; mem. nat. adv. bd. MLA Internat. Bibliography, 1978-88; editorial bd. Yale Italian Studies, 1976-80. Recipient Mark Van Doren award Columbia, 1974, spl. citation Columbia Coll. Alumni Assn., 1991, Festschrift, Über Texte, 1997; fellow Fulbright Found., Rome, 1949-50, Newberry Libr., 1958, Folger Shakespeare Libr., 1959, 63, Belgian Am. Ednl. Found., 1961, 62; sr. fellow Mediaeval and Renaissance Inst. Duke U., 1978; Fulbright rsch. scholar Utrecht, The Netherlands, 1958-59; DAAD rsch. grantee, 1979. Mem. MLA (sec., then chmn. Romance sect. 1965-66, chmn. comparative lit. 1973, James Russell Lowell prize com. 1989-90, chmn. 1990), Internat. Assn. Hispanists, Am. Comparative Lit. Assn., Coll. Art Assn., Acad. Lit. Studies, Am. Friends Herzog August Bibliothek (bd. dirs. 1996—), Phi Beta Kappa (hon.). Home: 30 E 37th St Apt 8J New York NY 10016-3054

SELIGMAN, DELICE, lawyer; b. Worcester, Mass.; m. Frederick Seligman. AB, Clark U., MA; JD, NYU, 1971. Bar: N.Y. 1972, U.S. Dist. Ct. (so. and ea. dists.) N.Y. 1973, U.S. Supreme Ct. 1979. Assoc. Legal Aid Soc. Nassau County, Mineola, N.Y., 1972-76; ptnr. Seligman, Stein & Abromowitz, Garden City, 1976-86, Seligman & Seligman, N.Y.C., N.Y., 1986—; legal counsel Contemporary Sculptors, Roslyn, N.Y., 1987-90, Artists Network Great Neck, N.Y., 1987-90, Woodstock Animal Rights Movement, Legal Action for Animals, Stop Graffiti Now, Inc.; pres. Wildlife Legal Action, Inc. Bd. dirs. For Our Children and Us, Hicksville, N.Y., 1985—. Mem. Nassau Women's Bar Assn. (pres. 1982-83), Bar Assn. Nassau County (chairperson arts com. 1984-85), Phi Alpha Delta. Home: Runge Rd Shokan NY 12481 Office: 26 Broadway New York NY 10004-1703 also: Seligman & Seligman 70 Main St Kingston NY 12401-3802

SELIGMAN, LYNN, literary agent; b. N.Y.C., Feb. 25, 1947; d. Siegbert and Kay Reis Seligman; div. Apr. 6, 1996; children: Samuel Patterson, Emma Patterson. BA, Goucher Coll., 1967; MA, Columbia U., 1970. ESL tchr. N.Y.C. Schs., 1976-77; asst. sub. rights Thomas Y. Crowell, N.Y.C., 1977-79; mgr. serial rights Doubleday & Co. (now BDD), N.Y.C., 1979-81; assoc. dir. sub. rights Simon & Schuster, N.Y.C., 1979-81; ind. lit. agt. Julian Bach Lit. Agy., Inc. (now Internat. Mgmt. Group), N.Y.C., 1981-85, Upper Montclair, N.J., 1985—. Woodrow Wilson scholar, Woodrow Wilson Found., 1968. Mem. Women's Media Group, Other Agt.'s Group, Phi Beta Kappa. Democrat. Jewish. Avocations: reading, ballet, cooking, Scrabble. Home and Office: 400 Highland Ave Montclair NJ 07043-1102

SELIGMAN, RAPHAEL DAVID, lawyer; b. Dublin, Ireland, Nov. 29, 1919; s. Ephraim and Esther (Wigoder) S.; m. Lorna Duke, Aug. 19, 1962; children: Arthur, Helene, Edgar. BA (with honors), Trinity Coll., U. Dublin, 1939, LLB (with honors), 1940, MA, 1960. Admitted solicitor Supreme Ct. of Ireland 1942; bar: Bahamas 1967, Turks ans Caicos Islands 1966, Grays Inn London, 1996, Lincolns Inn London, 1997. Practiced in Dublin, 1942-57; internat. legal cons. Nassau, Bahamas, 1957-67; stipendiary magistrate, circuit justice Nassau, 1962-67; of counsel firm Seligman, Maynard & Co., Nassau, 1971-86, Graham, Thompson & Co., 1986-96, Harry B. Sands and Co., 1996—; apptd. Queen's Counsel, 1996; hon. consul gen. of Israel in Bahamas, 1974—, Turks and Caicos Islands, 1985—. Contbr. articles to legal jours. Fellow Inst. Dirs. (London); mem. Internat., Bahamas Bar Assn., Lodge: Masons (33 deg., Supreme Council of Israel, past dist. grand master Bahamas and Turks, Grand Lodge of Eng., past grand sr. deacon Grand Lodge of Ireland, mem. Mahi Shrine Miami); Clubs: Lyford Cay, Royal Nassau Sailing, Naval and Mil. (London), Kildare St. Univ. Club (Dublin). Home: PO Box N7776 Lyford Cay, Nassau Bahamas Office: Sassoon House, 50 Shirley St PO Box N624, Nassau Bahamas

SELIGMANN, HERVÉ, ecology researcher; b. Esch/Alzette, Luxembourg, Mar. 8, 1966; arrived in Israel, 1983; s. André Jacques and Marion (Bernard) S.; children: Sa'an, Yahev. BS, Hebrew U., Jerusalem, 1988, MS, 1991, postgrad., 1994—. Tchg. asst. in zoology and ecology Hebrew U., Jerusalem, 1996—; researcher Regional Ctr. Rsch. and Devel., Judean Desert, 2000—. Contbr. articles to profl. jours. Acad. officer Israel Def. Forces, 1991—. Avocations: hiking, archery. Office: Hebrew U Jerusalem, Dept Evol, Syst and Ecol, 91904 Jerusalem Israel

SELIGMANN, WILLIAM ROBERT, lawyer, author; b. Davenport, Iowa, Oct. 10, 1956; s. William Albert and Barbara Joyce (Carmichael) S.; m. Carole Lee Francis; children: D Anna, Matthew. BA, U. Calif., Santa Barbara, 1979; JD, Santa Clara U., 1982. Bar: Calif. 1983, U.S. Dist. Ct. (no. dist.) Calif. 1983. Assoc. Office of J.R. Dempster, Cupertino, Calif., 1983-85; city atty. City of Campbell, Calif., 1985—; ptnr. Dempster, Seligmann & Raineri, Los Gatos, Calif., 1985—; judge pro tem, Santa Clara County, 1992—. Bd. dirs. Los Gatos C. of C. Mem. Santa Clara County Bar Assn. (civil practice com., judiciary com.). Avocations: cross country skiing, scuba diving, swimming, writing, Aikido. Office: Dempster Seligmann & Raineri 455 Los Gatos Blvd Ste 111 Los Gatos CA 95032-5523

SELINGER, ANDREW JOSEPH, ice and roller rink development company executive; b. Seattle, Oct. 3, 1966; s. Edward and Nancy S. BA, Harvard U., 1988; JD, UCLA, 1991. Airline exec. Trans Con., Orlando, Fla., 1991-94; developer Hockey World, Marina Del Ray, Calif., 1994—. Office: Hockey World 333 Washington Blvd Ste 235 Marina Del Rey CA 90292

SELIVANOV, VASYL, internist; b. Fashchevka, Ukraine, Apr. 2, 1961; s. Fedor and Nina S.; m. Svetlana Nikokosheva, June 5, 1985; children: Marianna, Kristina. MD, Donetsk State Med. U., 1984; PhD, Kharkov State Med. U., 1993. Intern, ship doctor, internist casualty ward Asoz Sea Basin Ctrl. Hosp., Mariupol, Ukraine, 1984-88, internist internal medicine dept., 1990-97; pvt. practice Mariupol, 1997—; head internal medicine/pulmonology dept. Azov Sea Basin Ctrl. Hosp., 1999—; leading pulmonologist. Mem. N.Y. Acad. Sci. Office: Azov Sea Basin Ctrl Hosp, 114-116 Gagarina, Mariupol 341000, Ukraine

SELIVERSTOV, VLADIMIR MIKHAILOVICH, pediatrician; b. Nizhny Novgorod, Russia, Jan. 6, 1946; s. Mikhail I. and Anastasia Pavlovna S.; m. Nina Pavlovna Sveshnikova, Dec. 9, 1970; children: Pavel, Elena, Irina. Degree in pediatric medicine, Gorky State Med. U., Russia, 1971. State cert. pediatrician, Russia. Dist. pediatrician Children's Clinic, Zima, Russia, 1971-75; rergional chief pediatrician Khasin Dist. Health Dept., Magadan Oblast, Russia, 1975-81; head dr. Ctrl. Policlinic, Sayansk, Russia, 1981-86; dep. dir. Irkutsk (Russia) Oblast Health Dept., 1986-90; chief dr. Irkutsk Oblast State Children's Hosp., 1990—. Bd. mem. Oblast Health Dept., Irkutsk, Russia, 1975—. Recipient The Sign of Honour Govt. Russian Fedn., Moscow, 1986; named Honoured Dr. of Russian Fedn. Govt. Russian Fedn., Moscow, 1996. Mem. Pediatric Assn. Irkutsk Oblast. E-mail: pav@omi.irk.ru. Fax: 7 (3952) 243565. Office: Irkutsk Oblast State Children's Hosp, 4 Gagarin Blvd, 664022 Irkutsk Russia

SELKIRK, ALEXANDER MACDONALD, JR., lawyer; b. Jamaica, N.Y., Oct. 2, 1943; s. Alexander MacDonald and Anne (Roth) S.; m. Joanne Patrician Diskant, July 21, 1974; children: Marianne C., Victoria L. BA in Polit. Sci., St. Johns U., Jamaica, 1965; JD, N.Y. Law Sch., 1970; LLM in Trade Regulation, NYU, 1973. Bar: N.Y. 1971, U.S. Dist. Ct. (so. and ea. dists.) N.Y. 1972, U.S. Ct. Appeals (2d cir.) 1972, U.S. Supreme Ct. 1976, Fla. 1991. Sr. staff atty. Hartford Ins. Co., N.Y.C., 1971-74; assoc. Richard C. Mooney, Esq., Hempstead, N.Y., 1974-77; sr. trial atty. Home Ins. Co., Huntington Sta., N.Y., 1978-80; asst, county atty. Suffolk County, Hauppauge, N.Y., 1980-88; assoc. Garcia & Stallone Esqs., Melville, N.Y., 1988-90, CIGNA Ins. Co., Woodbury, N.Y., 1990-95; trial counsel Martin Fallon Mulle, Huntington, N.Y., 1995—; arbitrator Suffolk County Dist. Ct. 10th Jud. Dist., 1982-88; instr. N.Y. State JAG's Sch., 1997—. Feature writer Ronkonkoma Rev., 1986-90; contbr. articles to legal publs. Committeeman Suffolk Country Rep. Com., Ronkonkoma, N.Y., 1977-92; del. 10th Jud. Dist. Conv. Suffolk County, 1981-84; v.p. Holbrook Rep. Club, 1979-81, pres., 1981-83; bd. dirs. Holbrook Youth Devel. Corp., 1985-91; pilot legal officer Nassau sr. squadron CAP, 1978-84; counsel. Com. for A Drug Free Holbrook, 1988-90. Maj. JACG, N.Y. Army N.G., 1983—. Mem. Am. Arbitration Assn. (comml. arbitrator), N.Y. State Bar Assn., Internat. Platform Assn., Suffolk Country Bar Assn., NYU Alumni Assn., Holbrook C. of C. (bd. dirs. 1981—, v.p. 1987-89, pres. 1984-91, 92-93), Gt. Neck (N.Y.) Sportsman's Club, KC (adv. 1981-84, 87—, trustee 1984-87), Lions (bd. dirs. 1985-86, v.p. 1986-87, pres. 1987-88). Roman Catholic. Home: 12 Glen Summer Rd Holbrook NY 11741-5006 Office: Martin Fallon Mulle 100 E Carver St Huntington NY 11743-3593

SELKIRK, KEITH EDWARD, mathematician; b. Wirral, Merseyside, Eng., Jan. 28, 1936; s. Cyril and Bertha Mabel (Jones) S.; m. Jennifer Anne Birch, July 29, 1961; children: Stephen, Katherine, Timothy. BA, Oxford U., Eng., 1960, MA, 1964; PhD, Nottingham U., Eng., 1984. Tchr. Bedford (Eng.) Sch., 1960-65; head dept. Croesyceiliog Grammar Sch., Cwmbran, Gwent, Eng., 1965-71; lectr. Nottingham (Eng.) U., 1971-86, sr. lectr., 1986-93. Author: Pattern and Place, 1982, Teaching Mathematics, 1984; editor: Assessment at Sixteen, 1988, Fifty Per Cent Proof, 1989, Longman Mathematics Handbook, 1991, (with P. Pool and A. Graham) Nuffield Nationa, 1996, Curriculum Mathematics State 5; contbr. articles to profl. and scholarly jours. Named Fell Exhibitioner and Honorary Scholar Christ Ch., Oxford, 1958. Mem. Math. Assn., Assn. Univ. Math. Edn. Tchrs. (sec. 1978-81, chmn. 1982-85). Anglican. Avocations: reading, travel. Home: 1 Fairfax Ave, Menston Ilkley, West Yorkshire LS39 6EP, England

SELKOWITZ, LUCY ANN, security officer; b. Pitts., Oct. 15, 1956; d. Thomas Francis and Matilda Margaret (Carlini) Donato; m. Jeremiah Anthony Barry, Jan. 10, 1976 (div. July 1979); 1 child, Jeremiah; m. Stanley Irwin Selkowitz, Aug. 19, 1987; children: Lori, Lee, Mattie. Grad., William Boyd, 1974. Cert. EMT, Pa. Owner, buyer Tillie's Antiques, Pitts., 1972-86; legal aide Selkowitz & Assoc., Pitts., 1986-94; armed security officer Wackenhut Corp., Pitts., 1994—. Dance performer Shade Sisters, 1992—. Counselor troubled youths, Clairton, Pa., 1986—; active PTA, chair 1995—. Mrs. Am. Finalist, 1990-91. Avocations: jet skiing, camping, animal care, onstage dance performer. Home: 100 Farm Ln Jefferson Hills PA 15025-3362 Office: Wackenhut Inc Rt 88 Castle Shannon PA 15234

SELLA DI MONTELUCE, BINA INDURKUMAR, real estate developer; b. Bombay, India, Jan. 13, 1949; d. Indurkumar Hassamal and Lakshmi (Sipihimalani) Shivdasani; m. Nicolo Umberto Giovanni Sella di Monteluce, Apr. 28, 1979; 1 child, Indoo-Domenico. A Levels (advanced cert. edn.), Cheltenham Ladies' Coll., 1966. Pres. Residential Property Devel., London, 1970-79, Comml. Property Devel., London, 1979-85, Comml. Real Estate Devel., L.A., Chgo., Atlanta, Orlando, Dallas, Houston, 1980—; chmn. Island Devel. Corp., Washington; mem. neurobiology com. Harvard Med. Sch., 1999—. Gov. Sussex Ho. Sch., adv. coun. Atlantic Coll., Wales, 1989—; trustee Inlaks Found., Leichtenstein, 1979—, Sella di Monteluce Found., U.K., 1985—, Nat. Symphony Orch., Washington, Duke of Edinburgh's award fellow, 1989-99. Mem. World Pres.'s Orgn. Conservative. Hindu.

SELLAR, ROBIN JOHN, neuroradiologist, magnetic resonance consultant; b. Paisley, Renfrew, Scotland; s. Robert Milne and Monica Mary (Mott) S.; m. Elizabeth Anne Crow, Mar. 11, 1996. BSc, Bedford Coll., London, 1973; MB, BS, St. Thomas Hosp., London, 1975; diploma in med. radio diagnosis, U. Edinburgh, Scotland, 1982. Registrar in renal medicine Adden Brookes Hosp., Cambridge, Eng., 1977; intern in chest medicine London Chest Hosp., 1978; intern in cardiology Brompton Hosp., London, 1978-79; registrar cardiology Edinburgh, Scotland, 1979-80; sr. lectr. U. Edinburgh, Scotland, 1981-85; con. neuroradiology NHS, Edinburgh, Scotland, 1986—; chmn. dept. clin. neuroscis. Western gen. Hosp., Edinburgh, Scotland, 1993—; cons. Alliance Med., Banbury, Eng., 1997. Co-author: Myelographic Technique, 1988 (Kodak prize 1988); author: Imaging of the Blood Vessels of the Head and Neck; editor-in-chief Neuro Interventionist; rschr. in field. Chmn. Scottish Youth Adventure Ctr., Edinburgh, 1992. Mackie scholar, 1985. Fellow Royal Coll. Radiology (Eng.), Royal Coll. Surgeons, Royal Coll. Physicians (Eng.); mem. Brit. Soc. Neuroradiology (intervention rep. 1995—), Brain Interface Group (chmn. 1996-97); adv. to WHO on new variant Creutzfeld-Jacob Disease. Avocations: tennis, golf, parties, literary theory, white burgundy. Home: 82 Inverleith Pl, Edinburgh EH3 5PA, Scotland Office: Western Gen Hosp, Dept Clin Neuroscis, Edinburgh EH4 2XU, Scotland

SELLER, TIMOTHY JOHN, academic administrator, zoology educator; b. Twickenham, Eng., Sept. 8, 1946; s. John Arthur and Mabel Joan (Bradford) S.; m. Jennifer Ann Hunter, July 5, 1969; children: Christopher Adrian, Kathryn Rebecca. BSc, U. London, 1967, PhD in Pharmacology, 1971. Rsch. worker Inst. Psychiatry U. London, 1967-70; lectr. Imperial Coll., London, 1970-89, dir. inernat. office, 1989—; exec. com. UKCosa, London, 1992—; gov. Cranleigh (Eng.) Sch., 1997—; deputy chair Brit. Coun. Edn. Counselling Svcs., 1999—. Editor, author: Bird Respiration, 1987; spkr. in field. Mem. Ch. of Eng. Fellow Zool. Soc. London; mem. Soc. Exptl. Biology, Brit. Ornithologists Union (hon.), Brit. Trust for Ornithology, Brit. Ornithologists Club. Avocations: walking, gardening, classical music, golf. Office: Internat Office, Imperial Coll, London SW7 2AZ, England

SELLERS, GREGORY JUDE, physicist; b. Far Rockaway, N.Y., June 20, 1947; s. Douglas L. and Rita R. (Dieringer) S.; m. Lucia S. Kim, Nov. 26, 1983; 1 child, Kristin Kim. AB in Physics, Cornell U., 1968; MS, U. Ill., 1970, PhD, 1975. Sr. scientist B-K Dynamics, Inc., Rockville, Md., 1974-76; with Allied-Signal Corp., Morristown, N.J., 1976-88, applications physicist, 1977-88; product supr. Amphenol Fiber Optic Products, Naperville, Ill., 1985-88; mgr. Cinch Connectors, Elk Grove, Ill., 1988-91; pres. Forss, Inc., Naperville, 1991-96, Fotron, Inc., Naperville, 1995—; bd. dirs. Thermo-Tek, Inc., N.J., Fotron. Mem. AAAS, IEEE, Am. Phys. Soc. Achievements include development and commercialization of electronic connectors and fiber optic products; development of applications for polymeric materials and glassy metals in the electrical and electronics arena. Co-inventor adhesive bonding metallic glass, electromagnetic shielding, testing of thermal insulation, amorphous antipilferage marker, amorphous spring-shield, multiple fiber positioner for optical fiber connection. Home and Office: Fotron Inc 7S 515 Oak Trails Dr Naperville IL 60540

SELLERS, PETER HOADLEY, mathematician; b. Phila., Sept. 12, 1930; s. Lester Hoadley and Therese (Tyler) S.; m. Lucy Bell Newlin, June 21, 1958; children: Mortimer, Therese, Mary, Lucy Bell. BA, U. Pa., 1953, MA, 1958, PhD, 1965. Math. tchr. Kangaru Sch., Embu, Kenya, 1961-63; programmer U. Pa., Phila., 1958-61; mem. faculty Rockefeller U., N.Y.C., 1966—; Johnson Found. postdoctoral fellow, 1963-65. mem. editl. bd. Genomics, 1986-97; author: Combinatorial Complexes, 1979; contbr. articles to profl. jours. Trustee Coll. of the Atlantic, Bar Harbor, Maine, 1985-96; curator Rockefeller Hist. Instrument Collection, 1997—. Lt (j.g.) USNR, 1953-55. Mem. Am. Math. Soc., Math. Assn. Am., Soc. Indsl. and Applied Math. Democrat. Episcopalian. Avocation: boat building. Home: 413 W Stafford St Philadelphia PA 19144-4407 Office: Rockefeller Univ 1230 York Ave New York NY 10021-6399

SELLES, ROBERT HENDRIKUS, actuary, consultant; b. Amsterdam, Nov. 8, 1938; came to U.S., 1969; s. Albertus Hendrikus and Jansje Suzanna (Cordes) S.; m. Manuela Ioana Cazaban Sava-Goiu Comnene, Aug. 26, 1966 (div. Mar. 1978); 1 child, Melina Joanna. B in Commerce with honors, U. Manchester, 1961. Actuarial asst. Can. Premier Life Ins. Co., Winnipeg, Manitoba, Canada, 1961-62; asst. actuary Sun Life Assurance Co. Can., Montreal, 1962-69; sr. v.p. Hay/Huggins Co., Inc., Phila., 1969-75, 77-79, 1991—, Boston, 1975-77, San Francisco, 1979-84, 87-91, 1991—, N.Y.C., 1984-87. Fellow Soc. Actuaries; mem. Conf. Cons. Actuaries, Am. Acad. Actuaries, Internat. Benefits Found., Western Pension and Benefits Conf., Actuaries Club San Francisco, Netherlands Soc. Phila. (pres. 1993-96, 99-2000, bd. dirs. 1991—, Netherlands Am. Assn. Delaware Valley (bd. dirs. 1993-96), Gavel Soc., Rainbow River Inc. (pres. 1995—). Home: 1420 Locust St Apt 24N Philadelphia PA 19102-4214

SELLEY, RICHARD CURTIS, geology educator; b. Effingham, Surrey, Eng., Sept. 21, 1939; s. Harry Westcott and Dorothy Joan (Curtis) S.; m. Pauline Fletcher, May 15, 1965; children: Helen, Andrea. BSc, U. London, 1961, PhD, 1963; DIC, Imperial Coll., London, 1963. Chartered geologist. Lectr. sedimentology Imperial Coll., London, 1966-69; sr. sedimentologist Oasis Oil Co., Tripoli, Libya, 1969-71; sr. geologist Conoco Europe, London, 1971-74; reader petroleum geology Imperial Coll., London, 1971-90, prof. applied sedimentology, 1990—, head dept. geology, 1988-93; mng. dir. R.C. Selley & Co. Ltd., Dorking, Eng., 1982—; dir. Tooting Constl. Club Ltd., London, 1972—; disting. lectr. Petroleum Exploration Soc. Australia, 1978. Author: Ancient Sedimentary Environments, 1970, 4th edit., 1996, Elements of Petroleum Geology, 1984, 2d edit., 1998, Applied Sedimentology, 1988, 2d edit., 2000. Justice of the Peace, S.E. Surrey Petty Sessional Divsn., 1981—; dep. chmn., 1999—. Fellow Geol. Soc. London (v.p. 1992-94, sec. fgn. and external affairs 1994—, Murchison Fund 1975); mem. Petroleum Exploration Soc. Gt. Britain (dir. 1977), Coun. Sci. and Tech. Insts., Coun. European Fedn. Geologists, Am. Assn. Petroleum Geologists (cert. of merit 1977). Avocations: archaeology, desert travel. Home: Clare Hill Deepdene Park Rd, Dorking RH5 4AW, England Office: Imperial Coll Dept Geology, Imperial Coll Royal Sch, Mines Prince Consort Rd, London SW7 2BP, England

SELLI, CESARE, urologist, researcher; b. Perugia, Italy, Feb. 27, 1950; s. Mario Selli and Giuseppina Pascoletti. MD, Pisa U. Med. Sch., Italy, 1974. Fellow in urology SUNY, 1976-77; rsch. fellow Florence U., 1977-81, 82-87; fellow in urologic surgery Duke U., Durham, N.C., 1981-82; assoc. prof. urology Rome U., 1987-91; assoc. prof. Florence U., 1991-96; chmn. urology Udine U., 1996—. Cons. Acta Urologica Italica, 1992—; referee European Urology, 1995, Urology, 1995. Mem. ACS, Am. Urolog. Assn., European Urolog. Assn., Soc. Internat. Urology. Roman Catholic. Avocations: skiing, fishing.

SELLS, KEVIN DWAYNE, marine engineer; b. Bridgeport, Conn., Sept. 20, 1958; m. Ketruthai Houngsatjakul, July 14, 1986; children: Corey A., David H. III, Vidhya Sarah. AS in Quality Assurance, Ft. Steilacoom C.C., Tacoma, 1984; BS in Marine Engring., Pierce Coll., 1987. Nuc. shipfitter elec. boat divsn. Gen. Dynamics, Groton, Conn., 1976-79; quality assurance surveyor Tacoma Boatbuilding Co., 1979-81, marine constrn. planner, 1981-84; sr. logistics engr. F.E. Basil, Washington, 1984-86; ship repair engr. C. Long Assocs., Bangkok, Thailand, 1987-89; sr. logistics analyst C. Long Assocs., Tucson, 1989—. Mem. Soc. Naval Architects, Am. Archeology Soc., Smithsonian Inst., Libr. Congress. Achievements include research and implementation of modular shipbuilding techniques; revamped Saudi Arabian naval supply system. Avocations: auto mechanics, photography, hiking, archeology. Office: C Long Assocs 718 W Hatfield St Tucson AZ 85706-7606

SELLS, ROBERT ANTHONY, surgeon; b. Leamington, England, Apr. 13, 1938; s. William Blyth and Eleanor Mary S.; m. Paula Gilchrist, Nov. 5, 1977; children: Rupert, Henry, Catherine, Edward, Patrick. MB, BS, U. London, Guy's Hosp., 1962, MRCS, LRCP, 1962. House officer Guy's Hosp., London, 1961-62, rsch. asst. dept. medicine, 1962-63, asst. lectr. dept. anatomy, 1963-65, lectr., surgery, 1967-68; asst. dir. rsch. dept. surgery U. Cambridge, 1968-69; sr. lectr. dept. surgery U. Liverpool, 1971-74, prof. immunology and surgery; dir. Mersey Regional Transplant Unit, cons. gen. surgeon Royal Liverpool Hosp., 1972—; v.p. Transplantation Soc., chmn. ethical com. Editor: Transplantation Today, 1983, Organ Transplantation-Current Clinical and Immunoloogical Concepts, 1989. Conductor Crosby Symphony Orch., Liverpool, 1985—. Travelling scholar Harvard Med. Sch., Dept. Surgery, Boston, 1970-71. Mem. Brit. Transplantation Soc. (past pres.), Surg. Rsch. Soc., Am. Soc. Transplant Surgeons, Moynihan Chirurgical Travelling Club, XX Club (pres.), Liverpool Med. Instn. (past pres.). Avocations: music, model bldg. Office: Royal Liverpool Hosp, Prescot St, L7 8XP Liverpool England

SELMAJ, KRZYSZTOF WOJCIECH, neurology educator, researcher; b. Lodz, Poland, Apr. 3, 1955; s. Wladyslaw A. and Eugenia (Matuszewska) S.; m. Maria-Assunta W. Michalska, Sept. 17,1977; children: Hubert, Igor. MD, Med. Acad. Lodz, 1980, PhD, 1983, DSc, 1988. Asst. prof. dept. neurology Med. Acad. Lodz, 1980-88, assoc. prof., 1988-93, prof., 1993—, chmn. dept., 1995—; vis. prof. Albert Einstein Coll. Med., N.Y.C., 1993, La Trobe U., Melbourne, Australia, 1995. Mem. editl. bd. Jour. Neuroimmunology, 1993—, Archiuum Immunolology and Therapeutics Expt., 1995—, European Jour. of Neurology, 1999—. Recipient award in medicine Polish Acad. Sci., 1991, Found. for Polish Sci., 1994. Mem. Internat. Soc. Neuroimmunology (exec. bd. dirs. 1993—), European Fedn. Neurology (v.p. 1999—). Avocations: skiing, sailing. Home: Malachowskiego St, 90-158 Lodz Poland Office: Med Acad Lodz, Med Univ Lodz, 22 Kopcinskiego St, Lodz 90-153, Poland

SELMAN, PAUL HARRY, environmental planner, educator; b. Manchester, Eng., Feb. 18, 1951; s. Neville Andrew and Bessie Gourlay (Shaw) S.; m. Jill Robertson Pirie, Mar. 17, 1975; children: Peter, Christopher. BSc, U. East Anglia, Norwich, 1973; MSc, Heriot-Watt U., Edinburgh, 1975; PhD, U. Stirling, 1985. Chartered town planner. Planner Falkirk Dist. Coun., 1975-76; lectr. Glasgow Sch. of Art, 1976-78, U. Ctrl.

Eng., Birmingham, 1978-81, U. Stirling, 1981-90; reader Cheltenham & Gloucester Coll., 1990—, prof., 1995—. uthor: Ecology and Planning, 1981, Local Sustainability, 1996, Environmental Planning, 2000; editor: Countryside Planning in Practice, 1988; editor Landscape Rsch., 1994—; contbr. articles to profl. jours. including Town Planning Rev., Jour. Environ. Mgmt., Jour. Environ. Planning & Mgmt., and Land Use Policy. Grantee Econ. and Social Rsch. Coun., Natural Environment Rsch. Coun., among others. Mem. Inst. Ecology & Environ. Mgmt., Royal Town Planning Inst. Mem. Labour Party. Anglican. Avocations: exploring the British countryside, guitar, church activities. Office: Cheltenham-Gloucester Coll, Countryside-Cmty Rsch Unit, Gloucester GL50 4AZ, England

SELMECZI, JOSEPH, retired philosopher, researcher; b. Makó, Csongrad, Hungary, Feb. 16, 1929; s. Frank and Helena (Erdei) S.; m. Victoria Levin, Aug. 24, 1954; children: Matthias, Julia. PhD, U. Leningrad, Russia, 1953; Cand.Philosophy, Acad. Sci., Budapest, 1967. Lectr. Inst. of Lenin, Budapest, 1953-57; rsch. worker Inst. Philosophy, Acad. Hungary, Budapest, 1957-60; sr. mem. U. Econs., Budapest, 1960-90; ret.; sr. mem. U. Lomonosow, Moscow, 1984-85, Inst. Philosophy Acad. Russia, 1971-73, 87. Author: Lenin's Period of Marxistic Philosophy, 1957, Chapters of History of Political theories, 1991, genesis of Philosophical and Political Pluralism, 1992; contbr. articles to profl. jours. Mem. Com. of Hungarian Dem. Jouth Orgn., Makó, 1945; mem. com. Autonom Univ.'s Student Orgn., Budapest, 1947; mem. trade Union of Pedagogues, Budapest, 1953—. Lt. Air Def. Hungary, 1995. Hungarian Socialist Party. Calvinist. Home: I Jobb Fszt 4, Villányi ut 55-65, 1118 Budapest Hungary

SELOILWE, GAORALALWE SEITEO, marketing professional; b. Botswana, Botswana, Apr. 4, 1952; s. Magoanaga and Mokopa S.; m. Esther Salang Ziyanwe-Mahlanza, Sept. 23, 1977; 1 child, Mothusi. BA in Econs., UBLS, Roma, Lesotho, 1975; BPhil in Econs., U. Nairobi, Kenya, 1978; Diploma in Fiscal Studies, Bath U., U.K., 1982; MBA in Mktg., Morgan State U., 1992. Cert. chartered marketer Inst. Mktg. Mgmt. Fin. officer Botswana Govt., 1975-80; student devel. fellow U. Botswana, 1980-83; project acct. Botswana Power Corp., 1983-86; lectr., cons. Inst. Devel. Mgmt., Botswana, 1986-93; prin. mktg. cons. IDM, Botswana, 1997-98, acting dir., 1996, lectr., cons., 1986-93, sr. cons., 1993-97, acting dir., 1996, prin. mktg. cons., 1997-98; cons. in field; former acting country dir. Botswana. Treas. U. Alumni Assn., Botswana, 1976, Botswana Civil Svc. Assn., 1978-80, sec. 1985-90; vol. Botswana Family Assn., 1996-98. Fellow Acad. Mktg. Sci.; mem. Dijammogo Social Soccer Club, Chartered Inst. Mktg. (chartered marketer), Inst. Mktg. Mgmt. Avocations: soccer, karate, athletics, boxing, farming. Office: Inst Devel Mgmt, 1357 Gaborone Botswana

SELOVER, WILLIAM CHARLTON, corporate communications and governmental affairs executive; b. Long Beach, Calif., Dec. 12, 1938; s. John Jesse and Myrtis Charlton (Holmes) S.; m. Mary-Louise Hutchins, Jan. 5, 1963 (div. 1985); children: Victoria, Edward. BA, Principia Coll., 1960; MA, U. Va., 1962. Editl. staff Christian Sci. Monitor, from congl. corr. to diplomatic corr., 1964-71; spl. asst. to sec. of the navy USN, 1971; mem. White House Coun. on Internat. Econ. Policy, Washington, 1971-72; history and archives divsn. chief Cost of Living Coun., Exec. Office of the Pres., Washington, 1973-74; asst. to adminstr. U.S. EPA, Washington, 1974-75, 77-78; from staff mem. White House Domestic Coun. to asst. to V.P. Nelson Rockefeller White House, Washington, 1975-76; speechwriter Pres. Gerald R. Ford, Washington, 1976; pub. affairs exec. Ford Motor Co., Detroit, 1978-88; pub. affairs mgr. diversified products ops. Ford Motor Co.; regional pub. affairs mgr. Ford Motor Co., L.A., 1988-91; v.p. corp. comms. and govtl. affairs USL Capital Corp. (subs. Ford Fin. Svcs. Group), 1991-96; prin. The Chaparral Working Group, San Francisco, 1997—. Speechwriter for chmn. and CEO of Ford Motor Co., Henry Ford II; editor autobiography former Pres. Richard M. Nixon, 1977. Helen Dwight Reid Found. fellow, Carnegie Found./Maxwell Grad. Overseas fellow, 1962. Mem. Conference Bd. (coun. corp. comm. execs.), Nat. Press Club, Press Club Detroit, Press Club L.A., Motor Press Guild, Internat. Motor Press Assn., Leadership Detroit Alumni Assn., Am. Polit. Sci. Assn. Address: 1257 Union St San Francisco CA 94109-1922

SELŠEK, CVETKA, stock exchange executive. Chmn. bd. dirs., pres. mgmt. bd., CEO Ljubljana Stock Exch., Inc., Slovenia. Office: SKB Banka Inc, Ajdovščina 4, 1000 Ljubljana Slovenia

SELTEN, JEAN-PAUL CONSTANT JEROEN, psychiatrist, researcher; b. Tilburg, Holland, Oct. 27, 1955; s. Jan and Elisabeth (Baggen) S.; m. Alida Gerarda van Ree, Aug. 12, 1987; children: Berber, Jasmijn. MD, U. Amsterdam, The Netherlands, 1983; PhD, U. Groningen, The Netherlands, 1995. Registered psychiatrist, The Netherlands. Psychiatrist U. Nijmegen, The Netherlands, 1988-89, Rosenburg Hosp., The Hague, The Netherlands, 1989-95; assoc. prof. U. Utrecht, The Netherlands, 1995—. Author: Evidence Against MAternal Influenza as a Risk Factor for Schizophrenia, 1994. Recipient, Honours: Janssen-Cilag, Schizophrenia Rsch. Awd., 2000. Office: Univ Hosp Utrecht, PO Box 85500, 3508 GA Utrecht The Netherlands

SELTEN, REINHARD, retired economist, educator; b. Breslau, Germany, Oct. 5, 1930; s. Adolf and Kåthe (Luther) S.; m. Elisabeth Amalie Laugreiner, Feb., 1959. Diploma in math., Frankfurt U., 1957, PhD, 1961, habilitation in econs., 1968; PhD in Econs. (hon.), U. Bielefeld, Germany, 1989, Johann-Wolfgang-Goethe U., Frankfurt, Germany, 1996, U. Graz, Austria, 1996, U. Breslav, Poland, 1996; hon. doctoral degree in econs., U. Norwich, Eng., 1997; hon. doctoral degree, ENS Cachan, 1998, U. Innsbruck, Austria, 2000. Asst. Frankfurt (Germany) U., 1957-67, private docent, 1968-69; vis. prof. U. Calif., Berkeley, 1967-68; prof. Free U. Berlin, 1969-72, U. Bielefeld, Germany, 1972-84, U. Bonn, Germany, 1984-96; prof. emeritus, 1996; hon. prof. Jiaotong U., Shanghai, China, 1996; hon. p. Author: Models of Strategic Rationality, 1988, (with J. Harsanyi) A General Theory of Equilibrium Selection in Games, 1988. Recipient Nobel Prize in econs., 1994. Fellow Econometric Soc.; mem. NAS (fgn. assoc.), North-Rhine Westfalian Acad. Scis., Am. Acad. Arts and Scis. (fgn. hon.), Berlin-Brandenburgian Acad. Scis., European Econ. Assn. (pres.), Am. Econ. Assn. (hon.). Home: Hardtweg 23, Königswinter D-53639, Germany Office: Lab Wirtschaftsforschung, U Bonn Adenauerallee 24-42, 53113 Bonn Germany

SELTING, MARGRET, linguistics educator, researcher; b. Rhede, Germany, May 25, 1955; d. Erwin and Anna (Sieverdingbeck) S. PhD, U. Bielefeld, Germany, 1985. Jr. lectr. U. Oldenburg, 1984-87, sr. lectr., 1987-93, asst. prof., 1993-94; prof. U. Potsdam, Germany, 1994—. Author: Problems of Understanding, 1987, Prosody in Conversation, 1995; editor: Style and Stylization, 1989, Prosody in Conversation-Interactional Studies, 1996, Speech and Conversational Styles, 1997; contbr. articles to profl. jours. Recipient Heisenberg grant Deutsche Forschungsgemeinschaft, 1993. Mem. German Soc. for Linguistics, Internat. Pragmatics Assn., other linguistic socs. Office: Univ Potsdam Inst Germanistik, Postfach 601553, 14415 Potsdam Germany

SELTZER, MITCHELL SHERMAN, hotel executive; b. Abington, Pa., June 10, 1948; s. Larry and Mary Ellen (Gallagher) S.; m. Laura Ann Hayhurst Seltzer; 1 child, M. Babe. BA, Pa. State U., 1971. Chef Valley Forge Hilton Hotel, King of Prussia, Pa., 1974-77, Cutillo's Restaurant, Pottstown, Pa., 1977-79; gen. mgr. Unisys Edn. Ctr., Malvern, Pa., 1984-88; gen. mgr. Dave Thomas Ctr. Duke U., Durham, N.C., 1988-90; gen. mgr. Am. Coll. Marriott Corp., Bryn Mawr, Pa., 1990-92; gen. mgr. Certain-teed Corp. World Hdqr. Marriott Corp., 1992-94; gen. mgr., operating ptnr. First Noah's Corp., 1994-97, Hospitality Staff Phila., 1997-98; gen. mgr. Profl. Edn. and Conf. Ctr., Kent State U., 1999—. Avocations: skiing, golf. Home: 2219 Applegrove St NW North Canton OH 44720-6252

SELTZER, VICKI LYNN, obstetrician, gynecologist; b. June 2, 1949; d. Herbert Melvin and Marian Elaine (Willinger) S.; m. Richard Stephen Brach, Sept. 2, 1973; children: Jessica Lillian, Eric Robert. BS, Rensselaer Poly. Inst., 1969; MD, NYU, 1973. Diplomate Am. Bd. Ob-Gyn. Intern Bellevue Hosp., N.Y.C., 1973-74, resident in ob-gyn., 1974-77; fellow gynecol. cancer Am. Cancer Soc., N.Y.C., 1977-78, Meml. Sloan Kettering Cancer Ctr., N.Y.C., 1978-79; assoc. dir. gynecol. cancer Albert Einstein Coll. Medicine, N.Y.C., 1979-83; assoc. prof. ob-gyn. SUNY, Stony Brook, 1983-89; prof. ob-gyn. Albert Einstein Coll. Medicine, 1989—; v.p. women's health svcs. North Shore-L.I. Jewish Health Sys., 199—; chair ob-gyn. North Shore Univ. Hosp., 1999—; chair ob-gyn. L.I. Jewish Med. Ctr., 1993—; dir. ob-gyn. Queens Hosp. Ctr., Jamaica, N.Y., 1983-93, pres. med. bd., 1986-89. Author: Every Woman's Guide to Breast Cancer, 1987; editor-in-chief: Primary Care Update for the Ob-Gyn, 1993—; editor: Women's Primary Health Care, 1995, 2d edit., 2000; mem. editl. bd. Women's Life mag., 1980-82, Jour. of the Jacobs Inst. Women's Health, 1990-95; contbr. numerous articles to profl. jours.; host Weekly Ob-Gyn. TV Program, Lifetime Med. TV. Chair health com. Nat. Coun. Women, N.Y.C., 1979-84; mem. Mayor Beame's Task Force on Rape, N.Y.C., 1974-76; bd. govs. Nat. Coun. Women's Health, 1985-94; chair Coun. on Resident Edn. in Ob-Gyn., 1987-93. Recipient citation Am. Med. Women's Assn., 1973, Nat. Safety Coun., 1978, Achiever award L.I. Ctr. Bus. and Profl. Women, 1987; Galloway Fund fellow, 1975. Fellow N.Y. Obstet. Soc. (pres. 1999-2000), Am. Coll. Ob-Gyn. (v.p. 1993-94, pres.-elect 1996-97, pres. 1997-98, gynecol. practice com. 1981, examiner Am. Bd. Ob-Gyn. 1988—); mem. Women's Med. Assn. (v.p. N.Y. 1974-79, editl. bd. jour. 1985—, resident rev. com. for ob-gyn. 1993-98), Am. Med. Women's Assn. (com. chair 1975-79, editl. bd. jour. 1986—), N.Y. Cancer Soc., NYU Sch. Med. Alumni Assn. (bd. govs. 1979—, v.p. 1987-91, pres. 1992-93), Alpha Omega Alpha. Office: LI Jewish Med Ctr New Hyde Park NY 11040

SELVANAYAGAM, ZACHARIAH EMMANUEL, zoologist, toxicologist, researcher; b. Madras, Tamil Nadu, India, Oct. 10, 1963; s. Paulraj Rajam and Devanesan Zachariah; m. David Parvatha Vathani, July 5, 1996; children: Evangeline, Emmanuel. BSc in Zoology, U. Madras, MSc in Zoology, MPhil in Zoology, PhD in Forensic Scis.-Zoology. Rsch. assoc. Indian Inst. Sci., Bangalore, 1995-96; rsch. asst. dept. anatomy Nat. U. Singapore, 1996-99, rsch. fellow, 1999—, coord. Microarray Facility, 1999—. Contbr. articles to sci. jours., including Fitoterapia, Toxicon, others; presenter confs.; patentee in field. Grantee various insts., Singapore; Indian Govt. fellow Ministry of Health, 1991-94. Fellow Indian Chem. Soc.; mem. Assn. Biomed. Scis., Indian Pharm. Assn., Soc. Biol. Chemists India, Indian Immunology Soc. Avocations: reading, watching T.V., exercise. Office: NUS Faculty Sci Dept Chem, 3 Science Dr 3, Singapore 117543, Singapore

SELVARAJ, PONNUSWAMI, fishery economics educator, consultant; b. Asaripallam, Tamil Nadu, India, May 24, 1943; s. Zacharias Ponnuswami and Michael (Annam) S.; m. Kulandaiswami Chellam, Nov. 26, 1970; children: Annie Vathana, Antony Pon Vijay. BSc in Agr., Agrl. Coll., Coimbatore, India, 1964, MSc in Agr., 1966; PhD in Agr., Tamil Nadu Agrl. U., Coimbatore, India, 1985. Asst. lectr. Tamil Nadu Agrl. U., Coimbatore, 1966-74, asst. prof., 1974-80, assoc. prof., 1980-89, prof., 1989—. Mem. Gideons Internat. India, Tuticorin, 1995—. Recipient Best PhD award Rotary Club, 1985. Mem. Assn. Economists Tamil Nadu and Pondicherry, Soc. Social Economists South India, Soc. Fishery Technologists (India), Vols. Agrl. and Regional Devel. Studies Group (hon. coord.). Avocations: reading, writing, public speaking, collage, editing articles and papers. Home: A Fisheries Coll, Staff Quarters, Tuticorin Tamil Nadu 628008, India Office: Fisheries Coll & Rsch Inst, Harbour Bypass Rd, Tuticorin 628008, India

SELVEY, ANTHONY ROCHFORD, publishing executive; b. London, May 2, 1944; m. Christine Florence Pearce, Dec. 2, 1969; children: Amanda Jayne, Mark Rochford. Chief exec. Taylor and Francis Group plc, London. mem. accreditation panel Hempshire (Eng.) Tng. Enterprise Coun., 1994-95. Fellow Chartered Assn. Cert. Accts., Brit. Inst. Mgmt. (companion), Inst. Dirs. Avocations: golf, tennis. Office: Taylor & Francis Group plc, 11 New Fetter Ln, London EC4P 4EE, England

SELWYN, ZACHARY STEPHEN, disc jockey; b. Apr. 3, 1975. BA in Broadcast Journalism, U. So. Calif., 1997. Writer 28th Street mag., L.A., 1993-99; disc jockey You Should Be Dancing, L.A., 1997—.

SELYPES, ANDRAS GERGELY, cytogeneticist; b. Szeged, Hungary, July 29, 1950; s. Andras and Julianna (Gal) S. MD, Szent-Gyorgyu U. Med. Sch., 1974. From asst. to first asst. Univ. Med. Sch., Szeged, 1974-88; chief chem. labs. Inst. Pub. Health, Miskolc, Hungary, 1988-94; asst. Univ. Med. Sch., Pècs, 1994-2000; supr. Nat. Health Ins. Co., Szeged, 2000—. Mem. N.Y. Acad. Scis. Avocations: chess, classical music. Home: 28 Arviz, 6724 Szeged Hungary Office: Univ Med Sch, Co Office Nat Hlth Ins Co, 17-21 Bal Sasov, 6726 Szeged Hungary

SELYUGIN, OLEG VIKTOROVICH, physicist; b. Taldom, Moscow, Russia, May 31, 1946; s. Viktor Sidorovich and Rufina Ivanovna Selyugin; m. Galina Valentinovna Grusha, Oct. 29, 1971 (div. Nov. 1987); children: Svetlana, Iliya; m. Tatyana Vladimorovna Moroz, Dec. 30, 1987; 1 child, Anna. Degree in physics, Moscow State U., 1970; PhD, JINR, Dubna, Russia, 1982, DSc, 1999. Lab. asst. Heat Engring. Inst., Chelyabinsk, 1961-63; rschr. Joint Inst. Nuclear Rsch., Dubna, 1970—; invited prof. Pierre et Marie Kyuri U., Paris, 1994. Contbr. articles to profl. jours. including Physics of Atomic Nuclei, Phisica A., Phys. Letters, Internat. Jour. Modern Physics A, Phys. Red. D. Avocations: yachting, windsurfing, skiing, canoeing. Office: BLTP JINR, 141980 Dubna Moscow, Russia

SEM, RICHARD JORGEN, banker; b. Oslo, Norway, June 7, 1972; s. Gunnar and Hilary (McDougal) S.; m. Sonia Diaz, Sept. 12, 1998. BSc, Imperial coll., London, 1994, MBA, 1995. Mem. Assn. of MBAs, Securities and Futures Assn. Corp. fin. officer Banque Paribas, London, 1995-97, Paribus, Paris, 2000—. Avocations: yachting. Office: 250 Bishopsgate, London EC2M 4AA, England

SEMBER, JUNE ELIZABETH, retired elementary education educator; b. Apr. 3, 1932; d. Charles Benjamin and Cora Emma (Miller) Shoemaker; m. Eugene Sember, Oct. 18, 1975. BS with honors, Ea. Mennonite, 1957; post-grad., Columbia U., 1958, U. W.Va., 1960. Tchr. grades 1-6 Cross Roads Pvt. Sch., Salisbury, Pa., 1953-55; tchr. grade 5 Connellsville (Pa.) Area Schs., 1957-58, tchr. grade 2, 1958-66, tchr. grade 1, 1967-92, classroom vol., 1992—; supervising tchr. California (Pa.) U., 1970-90. Mem. Delta Kappa Gamma (pres. 1978-80). Presbyterian. Avocations: writing, traveling, reading nonfiction. Home: 1125 Pittsburgh St Scottdale PA 15683-1630 Office: Connellsville Area Schs 7th Ave Connellsville PA 15425

SEMENCHINSKY, SERGEY GEORGIEVICH, physicist, metrologist; b. Moscow, Sept. 9, 1948; s. Georgiy Victorovich and Olga Sergeevna (Tat'yanko) S.; m. Natalia Vladimirovna Vershinina, June 19, 1981 (div. May 1996); 1 child, Anastasiya. Degree in engring., Moscow Inst. Physics and Tech., 1972; candidate of sci., Rsch. Inst. Metrological Svc., Moscow, 1979; DSc, Kapitza Inst. Phys. Problems, Moscow, 1987. Yang rschr. Inst. for Crystallography, Acad. Sci., Moscow, 1972; rschr. Rsch. Inst. Metrological Svc., 1979, head lab., 1989—; sci. keeper of std. Rsch. Inst. Metrological Svc., 1989—; mem. sci. coun. Russian Rsch. Ctr. for Surface and Vacuum, 1990-95; prof. physics Moscow Inst. Physics and Tech., 1991-93; vis. prof. Šafarik U., Kosice, Slovakia, 1994; vis. scientist NRC, Ottawa, Ont., Can., 1990, Inst. Physics, Prague, Czech Republic, 1994—. Co-creator initial quantum resistance std. in USSR and Ea. Europe, 1987 (legislated 1989); contbr. over 60 articles to sci. jours. Rsch. grantee Internat. Sci. Found., 1994; named Sr. Scientist, USSR High Attestation Commn., 1988, Hereditary Hon. Citizen, Senate of Russian Empire, 1909. Avocations: computers, travel. Office: Rsch Inst Metrological Svc, 46 Ozernaya, 119361 Moscow Russia

SEMENESCU, GHEORGHE, chemistry educator; b. Vaideeni, Valcea, Romania, Mar. 21, 1950; s. Gheorghe Constantin and Elena Constantin (Marcu) S.; m. Floarea Ion Bratu, Apr. 3, 1979; children: Ileana-Andreea, Florina-Cristina. BCh, Faculty, Bucharest, Romania, 1973; Specialist, Bucharest U., 1974. Chemistry diplomate. Probational Petro-Chem. Works, Pitesti, Romania, 1974-79; scientific rsch. Inst. for Nuclear Power Reactors, Pitesti, 1979-91; chief dept. chemistry surfaces, dep. chief corrosion/matls. Inst. Nuclear Power Reactors, 1983-91; assoc. prof. Pitesti U., 1991—, chemistry/physics chair, 1992—. Contbr. articles to profl. jours. Mem. Romanian Chemistry Soc., N.Y. Acad. Scis. Orthodox Ch. Avocations: neurophysiology, bioreceptors, mountaineering. Home: Calea Bucuresti, bloc U 1 etaj 2 apt 7, 0300 Pitesti Jud Arges, Romania Office: U Pitesti Facultatea de Stiinte, Gh Doja 41, 0300 Pitesti Arges, Romania

SEMENOV, ALEXANDR MIKHAILOVICH, research scientist; b. Nihjne-Devick Region, Voronehj, Russia, Oct. 26, 1951; s. Mikhail Dmitrievich Semenov and Mariya Emel Oblastyanovna (Agaphonova) Semenova; m. Elena Vladimirovna Gogoleva, Aug. 26, 1976; 1 child, Vicktoria. M, Moscow State U., 1978; PhD, Russian Acad. Sci., 1987. Probationer, rschr. Inst. Microbiology Russian Acad. Scis., 1978-80, jr. rsch. scientist, 1980-88, sr. rsch. scientist, 1989-98; sr. rsch. scientist Moscow State U., 1999—; vis. scientist U. Calif., Davis, 1996-99; cons. Biotec, Russia, 1993—. Co-author: Advances of Microbiology Ecology, 1992; contbr. articles to profl. jours.; patentee in field. Recipient grant USDA, 1997-99, grant NATO, 1997-98, Russian Fedn. Govt., 1993-98. Mem. Am. Microbiological Soc., Russian Microbiological Soc. Home: h 4 f 44, Prospect Leninskogo Komsoma, 142700 Vidnoe Russia Office: Dept Microbiology Biol Fac, Moscow State U Vorobevy Gory, 119899 Moscow Russia

SEMENOV, ANDREW GRIGORIEVICH, physicist; b. Moscow, Apr. 11, 1943; s. Grigory Julievich Schteinbock and Nadezhda Sergeevna Semenova; m. Lilia Davidovna Gorelik, Dec. 8, 1973 (div. Apr. 1980); children: Andrew, Eugene, Veronika; m. Irena Vladislavovna Zubko, Feb. 7, 1986. MSc in Theoretical Nuclear Physics, Moscow Phys. Engring. Inst., 1966; PhD, Russian Acad. Sci., 1972. Engr. investigator N.N. Andreev Acoustics Inst. Russian Acad. Scis., Moscow, 1966-69, rsch. scientist, 1969-72, sr. rsch. scientist, 1973-82, sr. fellow rsch. scientist, 1983—; founder, pres. Invac Internat. Corp. Ltd., Moscow, 1996—; cons. Ctrl. Hydro Aerodynamics Inst., Moscow, 1976-80, Mando Machinery Corp., Seoul, Republic of Korea, 1997—; expert State Invention Com., Moscow, 1978-83; reviewer jour. Acoustical Physics, Moscow, 1985—. Patentee in field; contbr. articles to profl. jours. Named Hon. Inventor of Russia, 1984; grantee Internat. Sci. Found., 1993-94, 94-95, Russian Fundamental Sci. Found., 1995-96, 97—. Mem. Acoustic Soc. Russia, N.Y. Acad. Scis. Democrat. Mem. Russian Christian Ch. Avocations: classic fiction, poetry, music, jazz, swimming, wrestling. Home: Bldg 3 Apt 54, 182 Prospect Mira, Moscow 129366, Russia Office: NN Andreev Acoustics Inst, 4 Shvernik St, Moscow 117036, Russia

SEMENOV, SEMEN NICOLAEVICH, researcher; b. Zaporozhzhje, Ukraine, Feb. 28, 1951; s. Nikolaj Ivanovich and Olga (Zaika) S.; m. Lora Ivanovna Alekseeva, May 27, 1972; children: Olga, Timofej. Engr. Degree in Semiconductor Physics, Moscow Steel and Alloys Inst., 1973; Candidate in Physico-Math. Sci., Moscow State U., 1987. Engr. Factory of Electrovacuum Devices, Zaprudnia, Moscow, Russia, 1973-74; sr. engr. Inst. Chem. Physics, Acad. Sci. USSR, Moscow, 1974-79, jr. rschr., 1979-86; rschr. Inst. Chem. Physics, Acad. Sci. Soviet Union, Moscow, 1986-89, sr. rschr., 1989-96; sr. rschr. Inst. Biochem. Physics, Russian Acad. Sci., Moscow, 1996-99, leading rschr., 1999—; translator of patents Gorodlsskij and Ptnrs., Moscow, 1993—. Contbr. articles to profl. jours. Recipient award for most outstanding and innovative presentation Sci. Com. 5th Symposium on Hyphenated Techniques in Chromatography, Bruges, Belgium, 1998; rsch. grantee European Commn., Brussels, 1998, NSF, 1993, Internat. Sci. Found., 1995. E-mail: mgta@mail.ru. Fax: 095-137-4101. Home: Microdistrict B, Home 34 Apt 77, 142092 Troitsk Moscow, Russia Office: Inst Biochem Physics RAS, Kosygin St 4, 117977 Moscow Russia

SEMENOV, VLADIMIR, geophysicist; b. Moscow, May 17, 1946; s. Yury Sergey and Vera Pavel (Isaeva) S.; children: Viktor, Natalia, Ekaterina. G-rad. in engring., Geol. Inst., Moscow, 1970; PhD in Geophysics, Inst. Terrestrial Magnetism, Troitsk, Russia, 1976. Engr. Mineralogy Rsch. Inst., Moscow, 1970-72; rschr. Inst. Terrestrial Magnetism, 1972-80; sr. scientist Geol. Inst., 1980-83, Geophys. Ctr., Moscow, 1983-97; docent Inst. Geophysics, Warsaw, Poland, 1996—. Author: Data Processing for Magnetotelluric Sounding, 1985; contbr. articles to profl. jours. Office: Inst Geophysics, Ks Janusza 64, 01452 Warsaw Poland

SEMENOVA, TATIANA PAVLOVNA, neurophysiologist, researcher; b. Kujbyshev, Russia, May 28, 1940; d. Pavel Andreevich and Valentina Pavlovna (Egorova) S.; m. Mikhail Borisovich Zykov; 1 child. PhD, Moscow State U., Russia, 1969, DSc, 1990. Rsch. scientist Inst, Higher Nervous Activity and Neurophysiology, Moscow, 1966-68; from rsch. scientist to sr. rsch. scientist Dept. Memory Problems, Puschino, Russia, 1968-94; leading scientist Inst. Cell Biophysics, Puschino, 1990—; UN assoc. mem. Internat. Acad. Sci. of Informatisation, Moscow, 1996; Mem. Sci. Coun. for Memory Rsch., Puschino, Russia, 1969-76, Sci. Coun. for Neurobiology, Puschino, 1978-86, Russian Acad. Scis., com. memory mechanisms, St. Petersburg, Russia, 1989-95; vis. prof. physiology U. Tex. Health Sci. Ctr., San Antonio, 1991; mem. sci. coun. biophysics, 1998—.. Author: (book) Optimization of the Learning and Memory Processes, 1992; also articles in profl. jours. Mem. Star Alliance Global Found., Berkeley, Calif., 1991-97; v.p. of bd. Road of Survival and Freedom, Corpus Christi, Tex., 1992-97. Grantee: Russian Found. Fundamental Investigation, Moscow, 1995-96, 98—, Internat. Sci. Found., Moscow, 1996, State Sci. Stipendium, Moscow, 1997-2000. Avocations: classical music, archery, fine art. E-mail: tsemenova@venus.iteb.serpukhov.su. Home: Microregion G 23-53, 142290 Puschino Moscow R, Russia Office: Acad Scis Inst Cell Biophys, Institutskaya 3, 142292 Puschino Moscow R, Russia

SEMENZA, GIORGIO, biochemistry educator; b. Milan, June 23, 1928; s. Carlo and Clementina (Gerli) S.; m. Berit Andersson, May 30, 1958; children: Christina, Jan C., André. MD, U. Milan, 1951; PhD (hon.), Autonomous U. Madrid, 1984; MD (hon.), U. Nice, France, 1999, U. Copenhagen, 1999. Asst. and then oberassistent dept. biochemistry U. Zurich, Switzerland, 1956-61, with, 1961-64, asst. prof., 1964-69; prof. biochemistry Fed. Swiss Inst. Tech., Zurich, 1969-95, dean Faculty Natural Scis., 1980-82; prof. biochemistry U. Milan Med. Sch., 1995—; vis. prof. Chgo. Med. Sch., 1965, U. Padua, 1985-86, U. Parma, 1987-88, U. Rome, 1988-89; prof. gen. physiology U. Milan, 1967-69. Contbr. over 250 articles to sci. jours.; mng. editor Fedn. European Biochem. Socs. Letters, 1985-99; editor: Of Oxygen, Fuels, and Living Matter, 1981; editor, co-editor 6 vols. of personal recollections in comprehensive biochem. series. Recipient Internat. prize Modern Nutrition, 1975, Iorio-Rustichelli prize Italian Union against Vivisection, Milan, 1985, Gold Purkiň medal 14th Internat. Congress Biochemistry, Prague, 1988. Mem. Italian Soc. Exptl. Biology, Acad. Sci. and Letters, Spanish Biochem. Soc., Acadl Europaea. Avocations: literature, fine art. Office: ETH Zentrum, Postfach 35, CH 8092 Zurich Switzerland also: U Milan Dept Chem and Bio, Via Saldini 50, I 20133 Miland Italy

SEMERDJIEV, TZVETAN ATANASOV, laboratory administrator; b. Pazardjik, Bulgaria, July 5, 1949; s. Atanas and Maria Kostadinova (Georgieva-Avishai) S.; m. Julia Petrova Hinkova, June 21, 1981; 1 child, Atanas Tzvetanov. MSc in Avionics, Zhukovsky AF Engring. Acad., Moscow, 1973, PhD, 1977; DSc, High Mil. Acad. G.S. Rakovsky, Sofia, Bulgaria, 1986. Cert. prof. radar systems, navigation and multisensor data fusion. Engr. radar dept. Inst. Spl. Electronics, Sofia, 1977-80, sr. rschr., head dept., 1981-83, dir., 1983-88; head lab. Bulgarian Acad. Scis., Sofia, 1988-92; head R&D projects Ctrl. Lab. Parallel Info. Processing, Sofia, 1993-95, head R&D group, 1995—; prof. gen. staff faculty High Mil. Acad., Sofia, 1996—; prof. air traffic control systems Sofia Tech. U., 1996—; mem. Mil. Sci. Couns., Sofia, 1986-90, Mil. Sci. Commn., Sofia, 1987-90; sr. advisor Presidency of Republic Bulgaria, Sofia, 1990; mem. High Testimony Commn. of Coun. of Mins., Sofia, 1990-92, Expert Commn. Ministry Sci. and Edn., 1990-93. Editor Series books in radar and navigation, 1991-97; author: Radar Data Automated Processing, Vols. 1, 2, 3, 1991. With Bulgarian Air Force, 1967-92. Mem. IEEE, AFCEA, Internat. Acad. Info. Processes and Techs. (academician 1986). Home: Velchova Zavera PO Box 89, Sofia Bulgaria Office: Acad G Bonchev, Str bl 25 A, 1113 Sofia Bulgaria

SEMERGIDIS, THEMISTOCLES GEORGE, oral maxilofacial surgeon; b. Athens, Dec. 21, 1959; s. George Themistocles and Sophia Anastasios (Mazloumidu) S. DDS, Dental Sch., 1983; D of Public Health, Sch. of Public Health, 1984; MD, Med. Sch., 1987; PhD, Athens U., 1994. Cert. oral maxillofacial surgeon. Assoc. OMFS Clinic Accident's Hosp., Athens, 1984-87, fellow, 1993-94, attending, 1995-97; resident in oral maxillofacial surgery Athens U., 1987-93; fellow divsn. plastic maxillofacial surgery U. Pitts., 1994-95; chief OMFS Clinic Gen. Hosp., Larissa, Greece, 1997—, OMFS Clinic Univ. Hosp., Larissa, 1999—; cons. Physician Nikaia Gen. Hosp., 1989-94. Contbr. articles to profl. jours. Air Force physician 251 Air Force Hosp., 1983. Mem. European Assn. CMFS, Internat. Assn.

OMFS, Nat. Assn. Implants Biomaterials (exec. bd.). Avocations: martial arts, tennis, sailing, golf. Office: Larissa Univ Hosp, 41 110 Larissa Greece

SEMIKINA, TATIANA VICTOROVNA, scientist, educator, musician; b. Kiev, Ukraine, Apr. 24, 1968; d. Victor Artemovich Karpenko and Lyudmila Nikolaevna Shmyryeva; m. Sergey Victorivich Semikin, Oct. 14, 1989 (div. May 1997); 1 child, Julia. MSc, Nat. Tech. U. Ukraine, 1991; Diploma, Musician Sch., Kiev; postgrad., Kiev Poly. Inst., 1994-97; student, U. Bristol (Eng.) Lang. Ctr., 1997-99. Engr.-investigator Kiev Poly. Inst., 1991-94, 99—; advisor Kiev Poly. Inst., 1993-99, translator, 1994-99. Author articles and poetry; singer and performer. Laureate of Music Competition, Kiev, 1987, 89. Avocations: science, physics, music, religion, psychology. E-mail: semikina@ee.ntu-kpi.kiev.ua and semikina@mail.ru. Home: Prospect Pobeda 27 ap 80, Kiev Ukraine 03055 Office: Kiev Politech Inst, Prospect 37, Kiev Ukraine 03055

SEMIOKHIN, IVAN ALEXANDROVICH, chemistry educator and researcher; b. Spassk Riazanskii, Russia, Aug. 28, 1923; s. Alexandr Vladimirovich and Efrosinia Kouzminichna (Kouliukhina) S.; m.Antonina Fedorovna Krasiukova, July 7, 1949; children: Victor, Helen. PhD, Moscow M.V. Lomonsov State U., 1952, DSc, 1970. Rschr. Moscow M.V. Lomonosov State U., 1952-54; assoc. prof. Moscow State U., 1955-77; prof. chemistry Moscow M.V. Lomonosov State U., 1978—; chief of chair Royal Tech. U., Pnom-Penh, Cambodia, 1966-67. Author: Elementary Processes in Low-Temperature Plasma, 1988, Physical Chemistry for Geologists, 1991; co-author: Kinetics of Elementary Reactions, 1985, Kinetics of Homogeneous Chemical Reactions, 1986 (D.I. Mendeleev Chem. Soc. prize 1988), Kinetics of Chemical Reactions, 1995; editor: Chemical and Biochemical Applications of Lasers, vol. V, 1983; contbr. articles to profl. jours. Mem. N.Y. Acad. Scis. Home: Michurinsky Prospect 54-17, 117 192 Moscow Russia Office: Moscow MV Lomonosov State U, Dept Chem Vorobiovy Gory, 119899 Moscow Russia

SEMKIN, DMITRI NIKOLAEVICH, physicist, lecturer; b. Cheboksary, Russia, May 22, 1968; s. Nina Victorovna Semkina. Diploma, Chuvash State U., 1990; D in Physics, Sanct-Petersburg State U., 1996. Programmist computer ctr. Chuvash State U., Cheboksary, 1990-91, asst. constrn. faculty, 1992-94, sr. lectr. constrn. faculty, 1995-96, asst. prof. constrn. faculty, 1997—, dep. dean constrn. faculty, 1996—; chamber concert, opera singer art faculty Chuvash State U., 1999—. Contbr. articles to profl. jours. Concert singer, Cheboksary, 1996—, mem. trade union com., 1999—. Fellowship INTAS, 1995-96, Russian Acad. of Scis., 1997—; grantee Russian Ministry of Edn. St. Petersburg U., 1998—. Avocations: computer technologies, education, pedagogics, classical vocal music, theatre. Fax: 7 (8352) 214252. E-mail: semkin@chuvsu.ru. Home: Leningradskaya str 16-45, 428032 Cheboksary Russia Office: Chuvash State U, Moskovsky prosp 15, 428015 Cheboksary Russia

SEMOUCHKINA, ELENA, physicist, researcher; b. Tomsk, Russia, May 1, 1956; came to U.S., 1997; m. George Semouchkin, Apr. 26, 1985; children: Alex, Vassilissa. A in German, Tomsk State U., 1974, A in Modern Dance, 1978, MS in Engring. with highest distinction, 1978, PhD in Physics and Math., 1986; PhD in Materials, Pa. State U., 2000. Rsch. asst. Physics-Tech. Inst., Tomsk, 1979-83, sr. rschr., 1984-92; sci. cons. NEOS Co., St. Petersburg, Russia, 1992-94; sr. rschr. State Tech. U., St. Petersburg, 1994-97; rsch. asst. Pa. State U., University Park, 1997—. Contbr. articles to sci. jours., including Soviet Physics Jour., Microwave and Optical Tech. Letters, others. Recipient Young Siberian Scientist award, 1985; Lenin scholar Tomsk State U., 1974-78. Russian orthodox. Avocations: downhill skiing, dancing, reading, drawing, painting. E-mail: eas203@psu.edu. Home: 544 Easterly Pkwy State College PA 16801-6403 Office: Pa State U Materials Rsch Lab University Park PA 16802

SEMPE, HENRI JEAN, economics educator; b. Toulouse, France, Dec. 1, 1933; s. Robert Auguste and Lea Odette (Vieu) S.; m. Michelle Louise Bauthier, Sept. 27, 1967 (dec. May 1991); children: Laurent, Nathalie. AB, U. Toulouse, 1956, D in Polit. Economy, 1957, D in Econs., 1958. Asst. prof. U. Toulouse, 1958-61, head dept., 1963-66, prof., 1968—; dir. Ctr. Econ. Fin., Toulouse, 1978, European Bank and Fin., 1992. Author: Treatise on Public Finance, 2d edit.; contbr. articles to profl. jours. With French mil., 1961-63; col. Air Commissary, 1992-98. Decorated Nat. Merit Order Def., 1986; recipient Acad. Palms Order, Nat. Edn. Toulouse, 1976. Mem. Econ. Doctor Nat. Assn., Nat. Assn. Commissary. Avocations: jogging, bridge, literature. Office: U Toulouse, 1 Pl Anatole France, 31042 Toulouse France

SEMPLE, MARGARET OLIVIA, arts education director; b. London, July 30, 1954; d. Robert Henry and Olivia Victorine (Shuffler) S. Advanced diploma in edn., London U., 1981; MA, Sussex U., 1986. Cert. tchr. Tchr. Inner London Edn. Authority, 1975-79, adv. tchr., 1979-80, head faculty arts, 1980-87, dep. prin., 1987-88; dir. Arts Coun., Gulbenkian Found., Commn. for Racial Equality, London, 1989-90; head of edn. Arts Coun. of Gt. Britain, London, 1991—; dir. learning experience The Dome, 1997—, Liverpool Inst. for Performing Arts, 1997; patron Coun. for Dance Edn. & Tng., Essex, Eng., 1987—; external examiner Laban Ctr., London, 1986—; dir. Liverpool Inst. for Performing Arts, 1997; bd. dirs. Tchr. Tng. Agy. Choreographer (dance) Grace & Glitter, 1987, So. Arts. Assn., Bracknell, Eng., 1988, Ea. Arts Assn., Ipswich, Eng., 1988; performer Danger Women at Work, 1988. Rsch. dir. Extemporary Dance Theatre, London, Kent, Eng., 1988; trustee Bararoo's Charity, 1998, Rambert Dance Co., 1998, Royal Soc. Arts, 1999, Sadlers Wells Theatre, 1998; mem. All Souls Group, Oxford, Windsor Leadership Trust, Brit. Am. Project. Mem. Nat. Curriculum Dept. Edn., Sci. Phys. Edn. Working Group, Phonis Bird Choreographic Awards U.K.; fellow Royal Soc. of Arts, 1992, Laban Guild, U.K., 1992 (pres.). Avocations: dancing, reading. E-mail: msemple@newmill.co.uk. Home: 110 Playford Rd, Islington, London N4 3NL, England Office: The Arts Coun New Millennium Experience, The Dome Drawdock Rd, London SEIO 0AK, England

SEMPLICINI, ANDREA, therapeutics educator; b. Venice, Italy, Dec. 10, 1949; s. Rodolfo and Clory (Guazzo) S.; m. Federica Pirrone, June 23, 1976; children: Luca, Claudio. Diploma in classic studies, 1968; MD, U. Padova, Italy, 1974, specialized in internal medicine, 1979; specialized in clin. pharmacol., U. Padova, 1983. Lectr. clin. medicine U. Padova Med. Sch., 1974-77, clin. asst., 1977-81, rsch. asst., 1981-92, asst. prof. therapeutics, 1992—, sr. clin. asst., 1989—, head of secondary hypertension unit, 1996—. Author: L'Ipertensione Arteriosa, 1996, La cardiopatia ipertensiva, 1997, L'endotelio, 1998; contbr. articles to profl. jours. Mem. Padova Ospitale Assn. (v.p. 1996—), Italian Soc. Hypertension (sec. Triveneto br. 1996—), Italian Soc. Internal Medicine (sec. Triveneto br. 1999—), Internat. Soc. Hypertension, Am. Soc. Hypertension, European Soc. Hypertension. Roman Catholic. Avocations: travel, music, photography. Home: Via San Mattia 20, 35121 Padova Italy Office: Clin/Expt Med Policlinico U, Via Giustiniani 2, 35128 Padova Italy

SEMPLINER, JOHN ALEXANDER, artist; b. Grosse Pointe, Mich., Jan. 4, 1953; s. Arthur William and Elaine Marie (Wood) S.; m. Lorraine Ann Fraser, May 24, 1986. BA, George Washington U., 1974; MFA, Pratt Inst., 1976. Lectr. Am. Coll. in London, 1985—, Archtl. Assn., 1989-97. One-man shows Ward-Nasse Gallery, N.Y.C., 1976, Bucknell U. Gallery, Lewisburg, Pa., 1978, Olshonsky Gallery, Washington, 1981, Crucial Gallery, London, 1988, 89, Grosvenor Gallery, London, 1993, Philharmonic Ctr. for Arts, Naples, Fla., 1995, Consell Comarcal, La Seu d'Urgell, Spain, 1999. Mem. Savile Club, Chelsea Arts Club, Royal Automobile Club, Queens Club, St. Hubert Club, Marylebone Cricket Club, Sigma Chi (pres. Epsilon chpt. 1973-74, sec. N.Y.C. alumni chpt. 1976-77). Libertarian. Mem. Ch. of England. Avocations: real tennis, rackets, fishing, shooting, stalking. Home: 134 Westbourne Terrace Mews, London W2, England Studio: Britannia Works, Dace Rd, London E3, England

SEMPRINI, AUGUSTO ENRICO, physician, researcher; b. Milan, Sept. 28, 1953; s. Ezio and Luciana (Campana) S. Degree in Medicine, U. Milan, 1979. Diplomate Italian Bd. Immunology and Allergic Diseases, Italian Bd. Ob-gyn., Tropical and Infectious Diseases. Fellowship in reproductive immunology U. Mich., 1986; sr. rsch. scholar dept. ob-gyn. U. Milan, 1990—; cons. dept. ob-gyn. U. Milan, 1980-94; hon. cons. Chelsea & Westminster Hosp., London, 1999. Contbr. over 37 articles to profl. jours.; author 30 book chpts. Recipient Rsch. grant Inst. Clinic Perfezionamento, Milan, 1981, grantee Consiglio Nazionale Delle Ricershe, Milan, 1983; hon. rsch. lectr. U. Coll. London, 1999. Mem. Italian Soc. Ob-gyn., Italian Jour. Obgyn. Avocations: sailing, skiing, Cordon Bleu cooking. Home and Office: Via Crivelli 20, 20-122 Milan Italy Office: Hosp L Sacco Dept Ob-Gyn, Via G B Grassi 76, 20157 Milan Italy

SEMPSEY, JAMES JOHN, III, information director; b. Ventnor, N.J., June 18; s. James John and Geraldine Sempsey; m. Agata Karolina Nowak, Mar. 12, 1999. BA, Temple U., 1988, MEd, 1993, PhD, 1998. Faculty Temple U., Phila., 1993-98; pres. FJS Internet Svcs., Wyndmoore, Pa., 1996-99; dir. info. Able Soft Corp., Pennsauken, N.J., 1999—; cons. Phila. Franklin Inst., Phila., 1996-98. Editor in chief: Jour. Virtual Environments, 1999—. Mem. APA, Mensa. Avocation: musician. E-mail: jamesiii@netaxs.com.

SEMPUKU, TAKEO, orthopedist; b. Osaka, Japan, Sept. 27, 1958; s. Shigeji and Teruko (Ishibashi) S.; m. Kazuko Tanioku, Mar. 31, 1992; children: Mika, Lisa, Chie. B in Medicine, Nara Med. U., 1984, MD, 1984, PhD, 1992. Resident Nara Med. U., Kashihara, Nara, Japan, 1984, 86, Kagawa Med. Sch., Miki, Kagawa, Japan, 1984-85; med. staff Ohmiwa Hosp., Sakurai, Nara, Japan, 1986-88, Nara Prefectural Gojoh (Japan) Hosp., 1988-90, Saiseikai Chuwa Hosp., Sakurai, Nara, 1990-92, 94-96; rsch. fellow Hosp. Spl. Surgery, N.Y.C., 1992-93; chief orthop. surgeon Nat. Sanatorium Fukui Hosp., Mikata, Fukui, Japan, 1996, Saiseikai Chuwa Hosp., Sakurai, 1996—. Author: Bioceramics Vol. 8, 1995; contbr. articles to profl. jours. Mem. Japanese Orthop. Assn., Japanese Soc. Surgery of Hand, Japanese Soc. Reconstructive Microsurgery, Japanese Soc. Bone and Mineral Rsch., Japanese Soc. Bone Morphometry, Japanese Soc. Biomaterials, Japanese Soc. Orthop. Biomechanics, Ctrl. Japan Soc. Orthop. Surgery and Traumatology. Office: Saiseikai Chuwa Hosp, 323 Abe, Sakurai Nara 633-0054, Japan

SEMYONOV, ALEXEY VLADIMIROVICH, immunologist, researcher; b. Yoshkar-Ola, The Mari, USSR, May 26, 1963; s. Vladimir Mikhailovich and Raisa Ivanovna (Titova) S. Grad. specialist in pediatrics, 2d State Med. Inst., 1986; MD, N.F. Gamalei Rsch. Inst., Moscow, 1991; PhD, Minstry Medicine-Med. Industry, Moscow, 1995; grad. specialist in clin. lab. diagnostics, The Russian Med. Acad. of Post Dipl. Edn., 1997, grad. specialist in allergy and immunology, 1997. Children's physician Ctrl. Dist. Hosp., Balashikha, USSR, 1986-87; jr. rsch. worker Moscow Rsch. Inst. Pediat. and Pediat. Surgery, 1987-91, sr. rsch. worker, cons. Lab. Immunology, 1991—, lab. physician, 1995—. Contbr. articles and abstracts to med. jours., including Immunology Letters, Internat. Jour. Immunorehab., European Jour. Allergy and Clin. Immunology. Mem. All-Union and Russia Sci. Soc. Immunologists, Inst. Immunology, Russia Sci. Soc. Allergologists. Orthodox. Achievements include research on role of actin filaments in pathogenesis of allergie reactions. Home: Bykovsky St 10 Apt 48, 143907 Balashikha 7 Moskoy Region, Russia Office: Moscow Rsch Inst Pediatrics, Taldomskaya St 2, 127412 Moscow Russia

SEMYONOV, VIKTOR, federal official; b. 1951. Head Belaya Dacha Farm; min. Agr. and Food Prodn., Moscow, Russia, 1998-99; dep. head State Duma Com. for Econ. Policy & Bus., Moscow, 2000—; chief Dep. Food Council, Moscow, 2000—. Office: Ministry Agr Food Prodn, Orilkov per 1/11, Moscow 107139, Russia*

SEN, AMARTYA KUMAR, economist, educator; b. Santiniketan, India, Nov. 3, 1933; s. Ashutosh and Amita Sen. BA, Calcutta U., 1953, Cambridge (Eng.) U., 1955; PhD, 1958; DLitt (hon.), U. Sask., 1979, Visva-Bharati U., 1983, U. Essex, 1984, Georgetown U., 1989, Jødavpur U., 1990, Kalyani U., 1990, Athens U. Econs. and Bus., 1991, Williams Coll., 1991, London Guildhall U., 1991, New Sch. Social Rsch., 1992, Calcutta U., 1992, Oberlin Coll., 1993, Syracuse U., 1994, Wesleyan U., 1995, Oxford, 1996; DSc (hon.), U. Bath, 1984, U. Edinburgh, 1995; D (hon.), U. Caden, 1987, Louvain, 1989, U. Valencia, 1994, U. Zurich, 1994, U. Antwerp, 1995, U. Stockholm, 1996; dottore ad honorem, U. Bologna, 1988; LLD (hon.), U. Tulane, 1990, Queen's U., 1993. Prof. econs. Jadavpur U., Calcutta, 1956-58; fellow Trinity Coll., Cambridge U., 1957-63; prof. econs. Delhi U., 1963-71, London Sch. Econs., 1971-77; prof. econs. Oxford (Eng.) U., 1977-80, Drummond prof. polit. economy, 1980-88; prof. econs. and philosophy Harvard U., Cambridge, Mass., 1987-98, Lamont univ. prof., 1988-98, vis. prof., 1968-69; master Trinity Coll. Cambridge U., 1998—; vis. prof. U. Calif., Berkeley, 1964-65; Andrew D. White prof.-at-large Cornell U., Ithaca, N.Y., 1978-84; chmn. expert group role advanced skill and tech. UN, 1967; hon. fellow Trintiy Coll., Cambridge Inst. Social Studies, The Hague, Inst. Devel. Studies, U. Sussex, London Sch. Econs., U. London. Author: Choice of Techniques, 11960, Collective Choice and Social Welfare, 1970, Growth Economics, 1970, On Economic Inequality, 1973, Employment, Technology and Development, 1975, Poverty and Famines: An Essay on Entitlement and Deprivation, 1981, Utilitarianism and Beyond, 1982, Choice, Welfare and Measurement, 1982, Resources, Values and Development, 1984, Commodities and Capabilities, 1985, On Ethics and Economics, 9187, The Standard of Living, 1987, Hunger and Public Action, 1989, Inequality Reexamined, 1992, Quality of Life, 1993, India: Economic Development and Social Opportunity, 1995; contbr. articles to profl. jours. Recipient Agnelli Internat. prize, 1990, Alan Shawn Feinstein World Hunger award, 1990, Nobel prize in econ. scis., 1998; co-recipient Wassily Leontief prize for advancing frontiers econ. thought Tufts Global Inst. for Environ. and Devel., 2000. Fellow Brit. Acad., Econometric Soc. (past pres.); mem. AAAS (fgn. hon.), Am. Econ. Assn. (past pres.), Indian Econ. Assn. (past pres.), Royal Econ. Soc. (v.p.), Indian Econometric Conf., Devel. Studies Assn. (past pres.), Internat. Econ. Assn. (pres. 1986-89, hon. pres.). Office: Cambridge U Trinity Coll, Trinity St, Cambridge CB2 1TQ, England*

SEN, ANANDA, communications senior executive; b. Calcutta, W Bengal, India, Nov. 1, 1953; d. Sumil Kumar and Minakshmi S.; m. Reena Sen, Nov. 19, 1980; 1 child, Amarita. BE, IIT, 1982; MBA, Ignou, 1999. Jr. exec. Army, India, 1974-84; middle level exec. Army, 1984-94, dir., 1994-97, sr. gen. mgr., 1997—; techno comml. evaluator India, 1997—. Col. Corps of Signals, India 1997—. Avocations: music, mountaineering, visiting historical places, computer technology.

SEN, PABITRA N., physicist, researcher; b. Calcutta, India, Sept. 5, 1944; came to U.S., 1968; s. Bibudh N. and Uma (Sen) S.; m. Susan Shu, Feb. 18, 1984; children: Indra, Maya. MS, Calcutta U., 1966; PhD, U. Chgo., 1972. Mem. profl. staff Xerox, Palo Alto, Calif., 1973-76; sr. scientist Xonics, Santa Monica, Calif., 1976-78; sci. adv. Schlumberger, Ridgefield, Conn., 1978—; vis. prof. U. de Provence, Marseille, France, 1985, Hong Kong U. Sci. & Tech., 1997; guest rsch. fellow Royal Soc., Eng., 1988-89; vis. scientist MIT, 1999-2000. Fellow Am. Phys. Soc., Inst. Physics. Achievements include explanation of laws of conduction and diffusion in porous media, explanation of huge dielectric constants in rocks and tissues, introduction of elastic and continuum percolation theories, new methods of probing porous media by nuclear magnetic resonance. Home: 52 Woodlawn Dr Ridgefield CT 06877-5120 Office: Schlumberger Doll Rsch-Lib Old Quarry Rd Ridgefield CT 06877

SEN, SAMDECH HUN, prime minister Cambodia; b. Kompong, Cham Prov, Cambodia, 1951. Courier Khmer Rouge, 1967; comdr. Guerilla Regiment, Ea. Zone, 1969; deserted, exile in Viet Nam Khmer Rouge, 1977; co-founder, mem. CC/Cambodian Front for Nat. Salvation, 1978; fgn. min. Cambodia, 1985-91; vice-chmn., 2d prime min., 1993—. Office: Office of Prime Minister, Khemarin Palace, Phnom Penh Cambodia*

SENAC, PATRICK GABRIEL, computer science educator; b. Toulouse, Haute, France, Jan. 21, 1958; s. Rene and Jeanine (Galibert) S.; m. Christine Dours; 1 child, Florence. MA, University Paul Sabatier, Toulouse, 1981, PhD, 1996; Engr., ENSEEIHT, 1983. Head of computer sci. lab. Ensica, Toulouse, 1985-90, prof., 1990-96. Editor: (book) Multimedia Modeling, 1996; author: (book) Lectures Notes in Computer Sciences, 1996; contbr. articles to profl. jours. Mem. IEEE, N.Y. Acad. Scis., AACE. Avocation: tennis. Office: Ensica, 1 Place Emile Blouin, 31056 Toulous France

SENANI, RAJ, electronics and communication engineering educator, researcher; b. Budaun, India, Mar. 14, 1950; s. Jagan and Girija (Devi) Ram; m. Santosh Chandel; 1 child, Namrata. BS, Lucknow U., India, 1966; BS in Engring., Harcourt Butler Technol. Inst., Kanpur, India, 1971; M of Engring. with honors, M.N.R. Engring. Coll., Allahabad, India, 1974; PhD, Allahabad (India) U., 1988. Lectr. M.N.R. Engring. Coll., 1975-87, reader, 1987-88; asst. prof. Delhi (India) Inst. Tech., 1988-90; prof. Delhi Inst. Tech. (now Netaji Subhas Inst. Tech.), 1990—; dir. Delhi Inst. Tech., 1996-97, dean (acad.), 1996-97, dean (postgrad. studies and rsch.), 1993-96, dean (adminstrn.) and dean (rsch.), 1997—. Contbr. more than 80 articles to profl. jours. Mem. Indian Soc. Tech. Edn. (life.). Avocations: music, reading. Home: C-6/12/2, Safdarjung Devel Area, Hauz Khas, New Delhi 110 016, India Office: Netaji Subhas Inst Tech, Azad Hind Fauj Marg Sect 3, Dwarka, New Delhi 100 045, India

SENANI, SWARAJ, animal nutritionist, researcher; b. Budaun, India, July 1, 1957; s. Jagan Ram and Girija Devi Pali; m. Anjana Senani, Jan. 23, 1990; 1 child, Urja. BSc, Kulbhaskar Ashram Coll., Allahabad, India, 1979; MSc, Govind Ballabh Pant City U., Nainital, India, 1985; PhD in Animal Nutrition, Indian Vet. Rsch. Inst., India, 1993. Mgmt. trainee Pradeshik Coop. Dairy Fedn., Lucknow, India, 1985-86; sr. rsch. fellow Indian Vet. Rsch. Inst., Bareilly, 1986-90; scientist Indian Coun. Agrl. Rsch., New Delhi, India, 1995—; head, Divsn. Animal Scis. Cen. Agrl. Rsch. Inst., Port Blair, India, 1997—; milk procurement mgr. Pradeshik Coop. Dairy Fedn. Ltd., Lucknow, India, 1985-86; rsch. scholar Indian Vet. Rsch. Inst., Bareilly, 1986-90; rschr. Indian Coun. Agrl. Rsch., New Delhi, 1990—; head Divsn. Animal Science Cen. Agrl. Rsch. Inst., Port Blair, 1997—. Contbr. articles to scientific jours. Recipient Fakhruddin Ali Ahmad award in animal sci. rsch., 1994-95. Mem. Animal Nutrition Soc., Orgn. Andman Sci. Assn. Mem. Bhartiya Janata Party. Hindu. Avocations: Indian classical music, reading, games, sports, travelling. E-mail: ssenani@hotmail.com. Home: 6/30 Ticket Ganj, 243601 Budaun India Office: Cen. Agrl. Rsch. Inst., Garacharma, 744001 Port Blair India

SENDA, KEI, aerospace engineering educator; b. Shinminato, Toyama, Japan, Aug. 17, 1963; s. Akio and Masako (Miwa) S.; m. Yoko Matsui, May 3, 1991; 1 child, Narisuke. BS, Osaka Prefecture U., Sakai, 1986, MS, 1988, PhD, 1993. Rsch. assoc. Osaka Prefecture U., Sakai, 1988-94, lectr., 1994, assoc. prof., 1994—; vis. prof. Mich. State U., East Lansing, 1996-97; invited prof. Inst. Space and Astronautical Sci., 2000—. Contbr. articles to profl. jours. including AIAA (Best Presentation award 1992) and Transactions of Inst. of Sys. Control and Info. Engring. (Best Paper award 1994). Mem. AIAA (Guidance Navigation and Control tech. com.), Inst. Sys., Control, and Info. Engrs., Japan Soc. Aero. and Space Scis., Japan Space Utilization Promotion Ctr., Robotics Soc. Japan (councilor). Avocations: playing soccer, skiing. Office: Osaka Prefecture U Grad Sch, Engring, 1-1 Gakuen-cho, Sakai Osaka 599-8531, Japan

SENDA, TAKASHI, economics educator; b. Tsuyama, Okayama, Japan, Nov. 19, 1964; s. Jun-ichi and Mikiko (Yorinobu) S. BA, Kobe (Japan) U., 1988, MA, 1990; PhD, Johns Hopkins U., 1998. Asst. prof. faculty econ. Hiroshima U., Higashi-Hiroshima, Japan, 1998—. Co-author: Introduction to Monetary Economics, 1998. Mem. Japan Soc. Monetary Econ., Am. Econ. Assn. Office: Hiroshima U Faculty of Econ, 1-2-1 Kagamiyama, Higashi Hiroshima 739-8525, Japan

SENDAK, MAURICE BERNARD, writer, illustrator; b. Bklyn., June 10, 1928; s. Philip and Sadie (Schindler) S. Student, Art Students League, N.Y.C., 1949-51; LHD, Boston U., 1977; hon. degree, U. So. Miss., 1981, Keene State Coll., 1986. Window display artist Timely Svc., N.Y.C., 1946; display artist FAO Schwartz, N.Y.C., 1948-51; co-founder, artistic dir. The Night Kitchen, 1990—. One-man shows include Gallery Sch. Visual Arts, N.Y.C., 1964, Rosenbach Found., Phila., 1970, 75, Trinity Coll., 1972, Galerie Daniel Keel, Zurich, 1974, Ashmolean Mus., Oxford, 1975, Am. Cultural Center, Paris, 1978, Pierpont Morgan Library, N.Y.C., 1981; author, illustrator: Kenny's Window, 1956 (Spring Book Fesitval honor book 1956), Very Far Away, 1957, The Acrobat, 1959, The Sign on Rosie's Door, 1960, The Nutshell Library (contains Chicken Soup with Rice, One Was Johnny, Alligators All Around, Pierre: A Cautionary Tale), 1962, Where The Wild Things Are, 1963 (N.Y. Times Best Illustrated Book award 1963, Caldecott medal 1964, Lewis Carroll Shelf award 1964, Internat. Bd. on Books for Young People award 1966, Art Books for Children award 1973, 74, 75, Best Young Picture Books Paperback award Redbook Mag. 1984, Children's Choice award 1985), Hector Protector and As I Went Over the Water: Two Nursery Rhymes, 1965, Higglety, Pigglety, Pop!; or, There Must Be More to Life, 1967 (Am. Book award nomination 1980), In the Night Kitchen, 1970 (N.Y. Times Best Illustrated Book award 1970, Caldecott medal nomination 1971, Art Books for Children award 1973, 74, 75, Redbook Mag. award 1985), Ten Little Rabbits: A Counting Book with Mino the Magician, 1970, Pictures by Maurice Sendak, 1971, Maurice Sendak's Really Rosie, 1975, Some Swell Pup; or, Are You Sure You Want A Dog, 1976, Seven Little Monsters, 1977, Outside Over There, 1981 (N.Y. Times Best Illustrated Book award 1981, Boston Globe/Horn Book award 1981, Caldecott medal nomination 1982, Am. Book award 1982), We Are All in the Dumps with Jack and Guy, 1993, Tsippi, 1994, Moishe, 1994, Max, 1994; illustrator: Atomics for the Millions, 1947, Good Shabbos, Everybody!, 1951, The Wonderful Farm, 1951, A Hole is to Dig, 1952 (N.Y. Times Best Illustrated Book award 1952), Maggie Rose: Her Birthday Christmas, 1952, The Giant Story, 1953, Hurry Home Candy, 1953, Shadrach, 1953, A Very Special House, 1953 (Caldecott medal nomination 1954), I'll Be You and You Be Me, 1954 (N.Y. Times Best Illustrated Book award 1954), Happy Hanukkah, Everybody, 1954, The Tin Fiddle, 1954, Magic Pictures, 1954, Mrs. Piggle-Wiggle's Farm, 1954, The Wheel on the School, 1954, Charlotte and the White Horse, 1955, The Little Cow and the Turtle, 1955, Singing Family of the Cumberlands, 1955, What Can You Do With a Shoe?, 1955, Happy Rain, 1956, The House of Sixty Fathers, 1956, I Want to Paint My Bathroom Blue, 1956 (N.Y. Times Best Illustrated Book award 1956), Birthday Party, 1957 (N.Y. Times Best Illustrated Book award 1957), Circus Girl, 1957, You Can't Get There From Here, 1957, Little Bear, 1957, Along Came a Dog, 1958, No Fighting, No Biting!, 1958, Somebody Else's Nut Tree, 1958, What Do You Say, Dear?, 1958 (N.Y. Times Best Illustrated Book award 1958, Caldecott medal nomination 1959), The Moon Jumpers, 1959 (Caldecott medal nomination 1960), Father Bear Comes Home, 1959 (N.Y. Times Best Illustrated Book award 1959), Seven Tales, 1959, Dwarf Long-Nose, 1960, Little Bear's Friend, 1960, Open House for Butterflies, 1960 (N.Y. Times Best Illustrated Book award 1960), Let's Be Enemies, 1961, The Tale of Gockel, Hinkel and Gackeliah, 1961, What Do You Do, Dear?, 1961, Little Bear's Visit, 1961 (Caldecott medal nomination 1962), Schoolmaster Whackwell's Wonderful Sons, 1962, Mr. Rabbit and the Lovely Present, 1962 (Caldecott medal nomination 1963), The Singing Hill, 1962 (N.Y. Times Best Illustrated Book award 1962), Nikolenka's Childhood, 1963, She Loves Me, She Loves Me Not, 1963, The Bat-Poet, 1964 (N.Y. Times Best Illustrated Book award 1964), How Little Lori Visited Times Square, 1964, Pleasant Fieldmouse, 1964, Lullabies and Night Songs, 1965, The Animal Family, 1965 (N.Y. Times Best Illustrated Book award 1965), Zlateh the Goat, 1966 (N.Y. Times Best Illustrated Book award 1966), The Golden Key, 1967, Poems from William Blake's Songs of Innocence, 1967, The Big Green Book, 1968, Griffin and the Minor Canon, 1968, A Kiss for Little Bear, 1968 (N.Y. Times Best Illustrated Book award 1968), The Light Princess, 1969 (N.Y. Times Best Illustrated Book award 1969), The Bee-Man of Orn, 1971, Sarah's Room, 1971, The Juniper Tree and Other Tales from Grimm, 1973 (N.Y. Times Best Illustrated Book award 1973), Fortunia: A Tale by Mme. D'Aulnoy, 1974, Fly by Night, 1976 (N.Y. Times Best Illustrated Book award 1976), King Grisly-Beard: A Tale from the Brothers Grimm, 1978, The Nutcracker, 1984 (N.Y. Times Best Illustrated Book award 1984), In Grandpa's House, 1985, The Children's Books of Randall Jarrell, 1988, Dear Mili, 1988, I Saw Esau, 1992, The Ubiquitous Pig, 1992; author: Fantasy Sketches, 1970, Collection of Books, Posters, and Original Drawings, 1984, The Love for Three Oranges: The Glyndebourne Version, 1984, Posters, 1986, Caldecott & Co.: Notes on Books and Pictures, 1988, Maurice Sendak Book and Poster Package: Wild Things, 1991; editor: Maxfield Parrish Poster Book, 1974, The Disney Poster Book, 1977; contbr.: The Publishing Archive of Lothar Meggendorfer, 1975, Babar's Anniversary Album, 1981, Masterworks of Children's Literature, Vol. 7, 1984, Victorian Color Picture Books, 1985, Winsor McCay: His Life and Art, 1987, Mickey Mouse Movie Stories, 1988; dir., lyricist: Really Rosie, 1975; lyricist, set designer: Really Rosie, 1978; lyricist, set designer,

costume designer: Where the Wild Things Are, 1980, Higglety, Pigglety, Pop!, 1984; set designer, costume designer: The Magic Flute, 1980, The Cunning Little Vixen, 1981, Love for Three Oranges, 1982, The Goose of Cairo, 1984, Idomeneo, 1988, L'Enfant et les Sortileges, 1989, L'Heure Espagnol, 1989, It's Alive!, 1994, So, Sue Me, 1994; photographer: The Cunning Little Vixen, 1985; designer: (film) The Nutcracker, 1986. Recipient Chandler Book Talk Reward of Merit, 1967, Hans Christian Andersen Internat. medal, 1970, Laura Ingalls Wilder award Assn. Libr. Svc. to Children, 1983, Nat. Medal Arts, 1997. Office: Harper Collins Childrens Divsn 1350 Ave of the Americas New York NY 10019*

SENDI, RICHARD, land use planner, researcher, architect; b. Kampala, Buganda, Uganda, May 28, 1950; arrived in Slovenia, 1972; s. Asaph and Victoria S.; m. Vida Čepirlo, Aug. 29, 1987; 1 child, Maja. BArch, Ljubljana (Slovenia) U., 1979, MS in Urban Design, 1983; PhD in Urban Design, Edinburgh (Scotland) U., 1987. Project architect Medicoengring., Ljubljana, 1979-80; project architect Gradben Podjetje, Grosuplje, Slovenia, 1988-91; rsch. assoc. Urban Planning Inst. Slovenia, Ljubljana, 1991-96; sr. rschr. Urban Planning Inst. Slovenia, 1996—; cons. Ministry Sci. and Tech., Slovenia, 1993—, Ministry of the Environment, Slovenia, 1994—. Contbr. articles to profl. jours. Pres. Uganda Students' Assn. in Yugoslavia, 1976-79; pres. African Students' Union in Slovenia; mem. bd. govs. Vič Primary Sch., Ljubljana, 1994-97. Recipient Rowntree Found. scholarship Edinburgh U., 1984. Avocations: football, tennis, swimming, cycling, indoor family games. Home: Iga Grudna 19, 1000 Ljubljana Slovenia Office: Urban Planning Inst, Trnovski Pristan 2, 1000 Ljubljana Slovenia

SENDOV, BLAGOVEST HRISTOV, mathematician, educator; b. Asenovgrad, Plovdivska, Bulgaria, Feb. 8, 1932; s. Hristo Stoev and Marushka (Blagova) S.; children from previous marriage: Marushka, Ana; m. Anna Marinova, July 4, 1951; 1 child, Blagovest. PhD in Math., Sofia (Bulgaria) U., 1964; DSc in Math., Moscow U., 1967, LHD (hon.), 1977. Prof. math. Sofia U., 1968, rector, 1973-79; v.p. Bulgarian Acad. Scis., 1981-88, 1988-91; pres. Com. for Sci., Sofia, 1986-88. Mem. parliament Nat. Assembly, Sofia, 1975-90, pres. 1995-97, v.p., 1997—. Recipient Dimitrov's prize Bulgarian Govt., 1969. Mem. Am. Math. Soc., Bulgarian Math. Union, Internat. Assn. Univs. (v.p. 1980-85, hon. pres. 1985—), Internat. Fed. Info. Process (pres. 1988-93, hon. pres. 1999—), Internat. Found. for Survival and Devel. on Mankind (bd. dirs. 1987-93), World Fedn. Nat. Math. Competitions Com. (pres. elect 1994, pres. 1995-96), Internat. Coun. Sci. Unions (extraordinary v.p. 1990-93). Avocation: tennis. E-Mail: bsendov@argo.bas.bg.

SENE, IBRAHIMA, diplomat; b. Mlomp, Senegal, Nov. 2, 1945; s. Adama Sene and Khardiata Ndiaye; m. Khadidiatou Samb, Apr. 14, 1974; children: Dieynaba-Papa, Adama-Khadidiatou, Mame soce. Diploma in diplomacy, Ctr. for Diplomacy Tng., Dakar, Senegal, 1971; B Comml. Scis., Superior Inst. Commerce, Brussels, 1981; MPA, U. D.C., Washington, 1989. Second sec. fin. High Commn. Senegal, Banjul, Gambia, 1972-76; head bur. litigation Ministry Fgn. Affairs, Dakar, 1976-77, dep. chief divsn. fin., 1981-85; 1st sec. Embassy of Senegal to European Econ. Cmty., Brussels, 1977-81; second counselor trade Embassy of Senegal to U.S., L.Am. and Caribbean, Washington, 1985-91; chief divsn. mgmt. Ministry Fgn. Affairs, Dakar, 1991-93; consul immigration, social affairs and pub. rels. Embassy of Senegal to U.S., L.Am. and Caribbean, Washington, 1993—; rsch. asst. U. D.C., 1988; freelance cons. in French lit. Contbr. articles to profl. publs. Advisor African Coalition for Islamic Edn., Washington, 1997—. named Knight of the Senegalese Order of Merit, Ministry Fgn. Affairs, 1985. Mem. Amicale des Cadres du ministére des Affaires Etrangeres, Senegal Support Soc. (hon.), Africare (Washington chpt.), Washington D.C. Consular Corps. (pub. rels. com. 1990-91), U. D.C. Alumni Assn. Muslim. Avocations: internet, foreign travel, movies, music. E-mail: gunar1@hotmail.com. Home: 5523 Burnside Dr Rockville MD 20853-2458 Office: Embassy of Senegal 2112 Wyoming Ave NW Washington DC 20008-3999

SENECAL, JEAN, retired medical educator; b. Iares, France, June 29, 1916; s. Marcel and Susanne (Chaumeil) S.; m. Jeanne Demont-Vivot, 1940 (dec. 1965); children: Claudine, Catherine, Christine; m. Barbara Schellenberg, Oct. 28, 1966; children: Sabine, Nathalie. MD, Med. Fac. Paris, 1945. Chef de clinique Faculty of Medicine of Paris, 1945-47; prof. pediat. Faculty of Medicine of Kabul, Afghanistan, 1947-50; prof. Faculty of Medicine, Dakar, Senegal, 1951-61; dir. Nat. Sch. Pub. Health, Rennes, France, 1961-66; prof., lectr. Faculty of Medicine, Rennes, 1966-85, dir., instr. maternal and child health, 1970-94; cons. OMS, 1961-80. Mem. French com. UNICEF, 1985. Served with French mil. Named Commdr. Legion of Honor, France, 1988, commdr. Palmes Academiques, France, 1985. Mem. Nat. Acad. Medicine, Nat. Children's Com. (v.p.). Avocations: football, tennis. Home: 4 rue St Martin, 35700 Rennes France Office: Inst Mere Enfant, Annexe Pediat Hosp Sud D256129, 35056 Rennes France

SENECHAL, THIERRY J., economist, finance expert; b. Brest, France, Oct. 4, 1964; s. Georges and Micheline (Cadiou) S.; m. Marie Naudet, Aug. 12, 1988; children: Jeanne, Clemence. BA in Econs. and Philosophy magna cum laude, Columbia U., 1992; MS in Fin. Econs., London Bus. Sch., 1995. Fin. fraud expert Seri Experts, Paris and London, 1992-97; sr. expert Security Coun. UN, Geneva, 1997—; mng. dir. Federalist Paper, N.Y.C., 1989-91. Contbr. numerous articles to internat. jours. Mem. St. Anthony's Hall, N.Y.C. Mem. Phi Beta Kappa. Avocations: sailing, Russian literature, environmental issues, music. Home: 15 rue de Buci, Paris 75006, France Office: UN Palais des Nations, Villa la Pelouse, Geneva 10, Switzerland 1211

SENEL, SEVDA, pharmacist, educator; b. Ankara, Turkey, Oct. 15, 1959; s. Tevhit Senel and Avniye Babilik; 1 child, Can Us. MSc in Pharmacy, U. Ankara, 1984; PhD in Pharmacy, Hacettepe U., Ankara, 1989. Cert. pharmacist, Turkey. Rsch. asst. Hacettepe U., 1980-89, postdoctoral fellow, 1989-91, asst. prof., 1992-94, assoc. prof., 1994—; postdoctoral fellow Leiden (The Netherlands) U., 1991-92; rschr. U. Paris-Sud, 1994, 95, U. Strathclyde, Glasgow, 1998; prin. investigator Dental Sch., U. Iowa, 1998. Contbr. numerous articles to profl. jours., chpts. to books; editor book in field. Grantee NATO, Brussels, 1997, 99, Brit. Coun., 1997, French Govt., 1994, 95. Mem. Internat. Microencapsulation soc., Internat. Chitin Soc., Controlled Release Soc. Fax: 90-312-3114777. E-mail: sevda@tr-net.net.tr. Office: Hacettepe U, Faculty Pharmacy, 06100 Ankara Turkey

SENER, BURCIN, physician, microbiology educator; b. Ankara, Turkey, Feb. 9, 1965; d. Mehmet Güngör and Hurside (Emiroğlu) Dirican; Nüvit Sener, May 27, 1989; 1 child, Cansu. MD, physician, Hacettepe U., Ankara, 1988. Cert. med. physician. Rsch. asst. faculty medicine dept. clin. microbiology Hacettepe U., Ankara, 1988-92, asst. prof. faculty medicine dept. clin. microbiology, 1993-1998, assoc. prof. faculty medicine dept. clin. microbiology, 1999—. Editor, account mgr. Microbiology Bull., 1996. Mem. Ankara Microbiology Soc. (account mgr.), Klimik Soc. Moslem. Avocations: decorative painting, house decoration. Home: Mesrutivet cad. Atac Sok. 64/5, 06420 Ankara Kizilay, Turkey Office: Hacettepe U Sch Medicine, Dept Clin Microbiology, 06100 Ankara Sihhiye, Turkey

SENER, KAYA, business executive; b. Sivas, Turkey, Oct. 12, 1946; s. Recep and Sebahat (Ekenel) S.; m. Ergul Alpteker, July 2, 1973; children: Basar, Basak. MS in Chem. Engring., Tech. U. Istanbul, 1972; MBA, Marquette U., 1974; Degree in Internat. Mgmt., INSEAD, France, 1995. Various managerial positions Unilever Group, Turkey, 1976-82; gen. mgr. Akril Chems., Turkey, 1982-86, Tuborg Breweries, Turkey, 1986-89, Henkel-Turyag, Turkey, 1989-98, Intermart A.S., Istanbul, 1998—. Trustee Turkish Edn. Found., Istanbul, 1990—. Mem. Turkish Industrialist and Businessmen Assn. Office: Intermart AS, Untel Sokak No 12, Umraniye, Istanbul Turkey

SENER, SIDDIK, civil engineering educator, consultant; b. Cemisgezek, Turkey, Apr. 1, 1950; s. Abdulkadir and Hikmet (Akin) S.; m. Sulin Gulsun Unal, Oct. 26, 1979; children: H. Duygu, K. Can, Cansu. Diploma in civil engring., Black Sea Tech. U., Trabzon, Turkey, 1973; PhD in Civil Engring., Istanbul (Turkey) Tech. U., 1983. Asst. to asst. prof. civil engring. Istanbul Tech. U., 1974-88; vis. prof. civil engring. Northwestern U., Chgo., 1985-86, Tokai U., Shimizu, Japan, 1987; assoc. prof. civil engring. Gazi U., Ankara, Turkey, 1988-93, prof. civil engring., 1993—; vis. prof. U. Wales, Cardiff, 1996; design engr. Ministry Pub. Works, Ankara, 1973-74. Contbr. articles to profl. jours. Recipient prize European Sci. Exch. Programme Royal Soc., 1996; Istanbul Tech. U. fellow, 1985-86. Mem. Turkish Soc. Civil Engrs., Turkish Assn. Bridge and Structural Engring., Turkish Numismatic Soc. Moslem. Avocations: coins, walking, swimming, hiking. Home: Akyuz Sokak, 24/6 K. Esat, 06660 Ankara Turkey Office: Gazi U, Dept Civil Engring, 06571 Ankara Turkey

SENESE NEUMANN, ENNIO R., management consultant; b. Amsterdam, Oct. 21, 1961; s. Mario Senese and Betty Hubertine Belinfante; m. Selma Maria Smulders Idem, Sept. 5, 1995; 1 child, Giuliano Serafino. BSc, Textile and Commerce U., Amsterdam, 1985; BSc in Philosophy Bus. Mgmt., Amsterdam U., 1987, BSc in European Law, 1995; PhD, Australian U., 1995. Diplomate banking & fin. European standards. Jr. fin. and banking mgr. Trestellco, Amsterdam, 1981-83; project mgr. GabbianiSel, Italy, 1983-86; fin. and banking mgr. P&O Cruises, 1986-87; mng. dir. Italco Exploration, The Netherlands, 1987-93; CEO Orca BV/Global Mgmt. BV, The Netherlands, 1993—, Project Fin. Invest S.A., Switzerland, 1995—; sr. v.p. Proudfoot Consult, U.K., 1996-98; v.p. Taylor & Co. Cons., 1998-2000; mng. cons. Compendium E. Procurement Europe, 2000—; pres. Global Mgmt. Securities; chmn. World Travel Found., The Netherlands, 1996—; cons. Millenium Found., 1995—. Mem. Italian Acad. Culinary Art, 1993—, Italian C. of C., European Assn. Fin. Consultancy, Dutch C. of C. E-mail: ennio@wxs.nl. Home: Postbus Orca 5218, 2000GE Haarlem The Netherlands Office: Heereweg 349, 2161 CA Lisse The Netherlands

SENESH, DAVID, clinical child psychologist, educator; b. Haifa, Israel, July 18, 1954; s. George and Ginosra (Abramson) S.; m. Ilana Weiser; children: Omer, Odie. BA cum laude, Hebrew U., Jerusalem, 1979; PhD, U. Calgary, Alta., Can., 1988. Cert. supr. in psychotherapy, Ministry of Health, Israel; cert. clin. psychologist Ministry of Health, Israel. Predoctoral intern Albera Children's Hops., Calgary, 1985-86, Portag Path Cmty. Mental Health, Akron, Ohio, 1988-89; instr. psychology Levinsky Coll. Edn., Tel Aviv, 1995—; instr. clin. criminology Bar Ilan U., Ramat-Gan, Israel, 1996—; psychotherapist Cmty. Mental Health, Rishon Le Zion, Israel, 1989-95, Pvt. Clinic, Rishon Le Zion & Tel Mond, Israel, 1992—. Contbr. articles to profl. jours. Bd. dirs. Israeli Assn. for Protection of Children, Tel Aviv, 1991—; mem. Amnesty, Tel Aviv, 1993—. Capt. Israeli Air Force, 1990—. Recipient Rsch. grant Alta. Sr. Citizens Secretariat, 1987. Mem. APA (internat. affiliate), Israeli Assn. Psychologists (clin. sect.). Jewish. E-mail: senesh@hotmail.com. Home and Office: PO Box 645, 13 Bat Hen St, 40600 Tel Mond Israel

SENESI, GUGLIELMO CESARE, engineer, engineering executive; b. Rome, Lazio, Nov. 25, 1925; s. Attilio Emilio S. and Eleonora Maria D'Inzeo; m. Loredana Cristiani, Jan. 12, 1956; children: Silvia, Glauco. Lic. liceale, Convitto Nazionale, Rome, 1943; Engring. Degree, U. "La Sapienza", Rome, 1953. Asst. prof. U. Rome, 1954-61; owner, civil engr. Studio Senesi, Rome, 1961—. Contbr. articles to profl. jours. Patent for prestressed concrete pool, 1970. Mem. Engring. Soc. Rome (mem. structural bd.), Club Aviazione Populare Venegono, Exptl. Aircraft Assn. Avocations: boating, experimental aviation. Office: Studio Senesi, 34 Piazza Medagle d'Oro, 00136 Rome Lazio, Italy

SENF, LOTHAR, chemistry; b. Zeitz, Germany, July 10, 1942; s. Erich and Gertrud Eleonore Luise (Kretzschmar) S.; m. Erika Elfriede Nuese Berthold, Sept. 23, 1972 (div. Sept. 1987); children: Stefan Erich, Franziska Gertrud. Diploma in chemistry, U. Halle, Germany, 1970, D in Nat. Scis., 1973; Habilitation, U. Jena, Germany, 1981. Pedagogue Chem. Plant, Leuna, 1963-70; aspirant U. Acad. Scis., Halle, 1970-73; lectr. in chemistry, biochemistry, and clin. chemistry Med. Sch., Efrurt, 1973-94; leader isotope lab. Hosp., Efrurt, 1973-2000, clin. chemist, 2000—. Author: Biophysical Analysis of Plant System, 1977; contbr. articles to profl. jours. Home: Koernerstrasse 2, D-99099 Erfurt Germany

SENFT, GUNTER, psycholinguistics researcher, educator; b. Kaiserslautern, Germany, July 19, 1952; s. Emil and Emmy (Juncker) S.; m. Barbara Schlaefer, Apr. 16, 1982; children: Frauke, Sebastian. PhD summa cum laude, Frankfurt (Germany) U., 1982. Rsch. asst. German Rsch. Soc., 1976-78; fellow Max-Planck-Soc., Nijmegen, The Netherlands, 1978-81; rsch. asst. Human Ethology Unit, Seewiesen, Germany, 1981-91; sr. rsch. fellow Max-Planck-Inst., Nijmegen, 1991—; prof. Tech. U. Berlin, 1992-94; prof. Cologne (Germany) U., 1994-98, extraordinary prof., 1998—; adv. bd. NWO ISIR-Irian Jaya Project, Leiden, The Netherlands, 1992-00. Author: Kilivila—The Language of the Trobriand Islanders, 1986, Classificatory Particles in Kilivila, 1996, Sprachliche Varietat und Variation im Sprachverhalten, 1982; editor: Referring to Space, 1997, Systems of Nominal Classification, 2000; co-editor (jour.) Pragmatics, 1992—. Mem. Linguistic Soc. Am., Am. Anthrop. Assn., European Soc. Oceanists (founding mem., bd. mem. 1992—), Soc. Endangered Langs. (v.p. 1997—). Avocations: music, art, photography, literature. Home: Holthuisenbosch 1, D-47574 Goch Germany Office: MPI for Psycholinguistics, PB 310, NL6500AH Nijmegen The Netherlands

SENFT, RALPH, biomedical engineer; b. Mannheim, Germany, Jan. 23, 1962; s. Dieter O. and Helena (Friebe); m. Sabine Stengl, Aug. 29, 1997. Diploma, U. Karlruhe, Germany, 1988. R&D project mgmt. Dornier Medizintechnik, Germany, 1989-96; application rsch. Dornier Surgical Systems, Germany, 1996-97, program mgmt., 1997-98, project mgmt. imaging, 1998-99, dir. program mgmt., 1999—. Contbr. articles to profl. jours. Home: Horemansstr 24a, 80636 Munich Germany Office: Dornier Medizintechnik GmbH, Argelsrieder Feld 7, 82234 Wessling Germany

SENGERS, JAN VINCENT, physicist; b. Heiloo, Netherlands, May 27, 1931; came to U.S., 1963; s. Adriaan and Cornelia Alida (Van Schie) S.; m. Johanna M.H. Levelt, Jan. 21, 1963; children: Rachel Teresa, Adriaan Jan, Maarten Willem, Phoebe Josephine. PhD cum laude, U. Amsterdam, Netherlands, 1962; D honoris causa, Tech. U. Delft, 1992. Teaching asst. U. Amsterdam, 1952-53, rsch. asst., 1953-55, rsch. assoc., 1955-63; physicist Nat. Inst. Stds. and Tech., Gaithersburg, Md., 1963—; assoc. prof. physics U. Md., College Park, 1968-74, prof., 1974—, dir. chem. physics, 1978-85, affiliate prof. chem. engring., 1991-94, prof., chair chem. engring., 1994-99, disting. prof., 1997-99, rsch. prof., 2000—; vis. prof. Tech. U. Delft, Netherlands, 1974-75. Mem. editl. adv. bd. Physica A, Amsterdam, 1975—; assoc. editor Internat. Jour. Thermophysics, 1989-99; U.S. editor Jour. Nonequilibrium Thermodynamics, 1994-2000; mem. editl. bd. Molecular Physics, 1999—; contbr. over 200 articles to profl. jours. Recipient Touloukian medal ASME, 1991. Fellow AAAS, ASME, AIChE, Am. Phys. Soc.; mem. Discalced Carmelite Secular Order, Cath. Com. on Intellectual and Cultural Affairs, Royal Netherlands Acad. Sci. (corr.). Roman Catholic. Achievements include research in transport properties of gases, exptl. studies of static and dynamic critical phenomena of fluids, nonequilibrium fluctuations in fluids; development of nonclassical equations for the thermodynamic and transport properties of fluids in the critical region. Home: 110 N Van Buren St Rockville MD 20850-1861 Office: U Maryland Inst Phys Sci And Tech College Park MD 20742-0001

SENGHAS, KARLHEINZ, retired university administrator; b. Stuttgart, Germany, Apr. 7, 1928; s. Karl and Elisabeth (Jacob) S.; m. Irmgard Spresert, Dec. 29, 1956; children: Werner, Ulrich, Gunther. D Natural Scis., U. Heidelberg, Germany, 1956. Asst. U. Heidenberg, 1956-60, kustos, 1960-80, acad. dir., 1980-93. Author: Flora von Deutschland u.a., 1956-2000; author, editor: Die Orchideen, 4 vols., 1972-2000; editor Die Orchidee, 1973—; contbr. articles to profl. jours. Mem. German Orchid Soc. (mem. bd., pres. 1973-78, hon. pres.). Avocations: music, floristic, art history. Home: Schilerstr 1, D-69251 Gaiberg Germany Office: U Heidelberg, Im Neuenheimer Feld 340, D-69120 Heidelberg Germany

SENGLAUB, KONRAD, retired zoologist, educator; b. Leipzig, Germany, Mar. 15, 1926; s. Konrad and Martha (Jahns) S.; m. Gerda Baehr, Aug. 12, 1950; children: Axel, Ralph. Dipl.Biol., U. Leipzig, 1951, Dr.rer.nat., 1956, Dr.habil., 1961. Asst. U. Leipzig, 1955-61; prof. zoology U. Berlin, 1962-81; dir. Zool. Mus. Berlin, 1962-74. Author: Wildhunde-Haushunde, 1978, 2d edit., 1980; editor: Exkursionsfauna von Deutschland, 1979-96, (with J. Jahn and R. Loether) Geschichte der Biologie, 1985. Home: Falkenbergerstr 160, 13088 Berlin Germany

SEN-GUPTA, NANDA DULAL, retired atomic science researcher; b. Rangpur, India, Apr. 30, 1918; s. Shyam Lal and Amiya Bala (Das-Gupta) S-G.; m. Latika Sen-Gupta; June 4, 1958. BSc in Physics with honors, U. Rangpur, India, 1938; MSc in Physics, Calcutta (India) U., 1940. Rsch. scholar Calcutta U., 1941-45, rsch. assoc., 1945-47; prof. physics Ruia Coll., 1949-62; vis. mem. Tata Inst. Fundamental Rsch., Bombay, 1962-64, emeritus scientist, 1978—; sci. officer Bhabha Atomic Rsch. Ctr., 1964-78. Contbr. over 100 articles to profl. jours; reviewer jours. in field. Mem. Calcutta Math. Soc. (life, past pres.), Indian Assn. for Cultivation of Sci., Indian Sci. Congress, Sci. Soc. of Bengal, Internat. Assn. Math & Physics (founder), Am. Math. Soc. Office: Tata Inst Fundamental Rsch, Bombay 400005, India

SENIOR, CARL, research scientist; b. Gibraltar, July 10, 1970; s. Martin Senior and Marie-Laura Lavanga. BSc in Cognitive Sci. with honors, U. Westminster; MS in Cognitive Neuropsychology, U. London; PhD in Psychology, Inst. of Psychiatry. Rsch. scientist Depersonalisation Rsch. Unit, London. Mem. APA (internat. affiliate), Brit. Psychology Soc., Cognitive Neurosci. Soc. Office: Depersonalisation Rsch Unit, 103 Denmark Hill, London SE5 8A2, England

SENIOR, ROXY, physician; b. Calcutta, W Bengal, India, May 13, 1953; s. Rex and Aparna (Lahiry-Chowdhury) S.; m. Purnima Muliyil, Mar. 7, 1987; children: Sunetra, Natasha. MBBS, Nat. Med. Coll., Calcutta, 1980; MD, NRS Med. Coll., Calcutta, 1983; DM in Cardiology, Postgrad. Med. Sch., Calcutta, 1987. Sr. house office Nat. Med. Coll., 1979-80; registrar NRS Med. Coll., 1981-83; sr. registrar Postgrad. Med. Sch., 1985-87; registrar Northwick Park Hosp., Harrow, U.K., 1989-93, sr. registrar, 1993-95, cons., 1995—; reviewer for profl. jours. Contbr. articles to profl. jours. Recipient Gold medal Calcutta U., 1977, medal Am. Soc. Nuclear Cardiology, 1995. Fellow Royal Coll. Physicians (London); mem. Brit. Cardol. Soc., Brit. Soc. Echocardiography, Brit. Cardol. Nuclear Soc. Avocations: cricket, football, reading novels, music, art. Home: 23 Churchill Ave, HA30AX Middlesex Harrow, United Kingdom Office: Northwick Park Hosp, HA13UJ Middlesex Harrow, United Kingdom

SENITSKY, YURY EDUARDOVICH, civil engineer; b. Smolensk, Russia, Apr. 21, 1933; s. Eduard Petrovich and Natalia Vladimirovna (Fox) S.; m. Natalia Aleksandrovna Golovko, Nov. 13, 1954; 1 child, Aleksandr. Degree in engring., Inst. Civil Engring., Kuibyshev, Russia, 1956; Cand. Tech. Scis., Poly. Inst., Kuibyshev, 1965; D. tech. Scis., Bldg. Structures Inst., Moscow, 1988. Asst. Inst. Civil Engring., 1956-62, sr. instr., 1962-65, assoc. prof., 1965-73; head dept. Acad. Arch. and Civil Engring., Samara, Russia, 1973—, prof. engring. mechanics, 1989—; sci. cons. Inst. Rsch. Devel. and Operation of Oil Pipes, Kuibyshev, 1971-79, All Union Rsch. and Design Inst., Atomenergoproect, Moscow, 1980-90, Rsch. and Design Inst., 1991-99. Author: Investigation of the Elastic Deformation of Construction Elements under Dynamic Actions by the Method Finite Integral Transforms, 1985; contbr. articles to profl. jours.; editor-in-chief jour. Materials, Technology, Structures in Constrn., 1999. Named Honored Scientist of Russia, 1998. Mem. Russian Soc. Civil Engrs. (chmn. dept. 1998-99), N.Y. Acad. Scis. Avocation: playing jazz piano. Home: Osipenko St 14-18, 443110 Samara Russia Office: Acad Arch and Civil Engring, ul Molodogvardeiskaya 194, 443001 Samara Russia

SENKARIK, MIKKI, oil painter; b. Oak Ridge, Tenn., Dec. 2, 1954; d. GEorge and Cleta (VanMarter) S. BFA, U. South Fla., 1976; MS in Med. Illustration, Med. Coll. Ga., 1979. Freelance med. illustrator, San Antonio and Corsicana, Tex., 1979-90; mem. adv. bd. LOOPS Internat., Odessa, Tex., 1990—; bd. dirs. Flying Horse Ltd., Virginia Beach, Va. Guest Contbr. Equine Images, Ft. Dodge, Iowa, 1990—, Equus, Gaithersburg, Md., 1991—; one-woman shows include Lyon Gallery, Scottsdale, Ariz., Forms Gallery, Del Ray Beach, Fla., Pitzer's of Carmel (Calif.); represented by Marcus Gallery, Santa Fe. Fundraiser/voter registration Rep. Women's Party, 1976—; fin. contbr. Shelter of Abused Women, Galveston, Tex., 1994—. Recipient award of excellence Assn. Med. Illustrators, 1983, 85, 87, 88, 91. Avocations: travel, writing. Office: 301 E 5th Ave Corsicana TX 75110-5342

SENN, HANS-JOERG, science center administrator; b. Zurich, Mar. 28, 1934; s. Oskar and Hedwig (Witschi) S.; m. Irene Luscher; children: Christoph, Andrew, Mathias. MD, U. Zurich, 1961; PhD, U. Basel, Switzerland, 1970. Asst. Kantonsspital Schaffhausen, Switzerland, 1960-61; resident St. Luke's Hosp., Jacksonville, Fla., 1961-62; asst. Tiefenau-Spital, Bern, Switzerland, 1962-66; sr. staff mem. U. Med. Poliklinik, Basel, Switzerland, 1968-72; chief dept. medicine and cancer ctr. Kantonsspital, St. Gallen, Switzerland, 1973-97; dir. Ctr. for Tumor Detection and Prevention, St. Gallen, 1998—; assoc. prof. medicine and oncology U. Basel, 1978; chmn. Swiss Group Clin. Cancer Rsch., Bern, 1987-95, Internat. Breast Cancer Study Group, Bern, 1993-95, scientific adv. com. EORTC, Brussels, 1992-94. Editor-in-chief Recent Results in Cancer, 1985—, Supportive Care in Cancer, 1992—, European Jour. Cancer, 1995-2000. V.p. German speaking br. Euorpean Sch. Oncology, St. Gallen, 1996—. Lt. col. Swiss Army. Mem. Rsch. Foun. Ea. Switzerland (pres. 1986—), Am. Soc. Clin. Oncology, European Soc. Clin. Oncology. Avocations: hiking, swimming, golf, skiing. Office: Ctr Tumor Detection-Prev, Rorchacherstrasse 150, CH-9006 Saint Gallen Switzerland

SENN, RICHARD ALLAN, environmental safety professional; b. LaCrosse, Wis., Dec. 20, 1946; s. Hugo and Evelyn Ruth (Winters) S.; m. Denise Marie Corriveau, May 6, 1989; 1 stepchild, Danelle Marie Wiersma. BS in Chemistry and Bus., U. Wis., 1970, BS in Environ. Scis., 1975; MBA in Mgmt., U. Wis., Whitewater, 1980. Cert. hazardous materials mgr., 1990, chem. hygiene officer, 1998. Analytical chemist Warf Inst., Madison, Wis., 1970-75; scientist Warf Inst., Madison, 1975-77; scientist II Raltech Scientific Svcs., Madison, 1977-78, herbicide sect. leader, 1978-82; environ. chemist III U. Wis., Madison, 1982-84; pres. 4 Lakes Volleyball Assn., Madison, 1981-83; owner Sports Mgmt. Svcs., Madison, 1981-83; lab/safety mgr. Agracetus, Madison, 1984-86; environ. health safety mgr. Agracetus, Middleton, Wis., 1984-97; pres. 4 Lakes Enterprises (formerly 4 Lakes Recreation Inc.), Verona, Wis., 1984-98; instr. U. Wis. Ext. Engring., 1993—; co-owner Howling at the Moon, 1997—. Author: (with others) Waste Minimization in Research and Academic Institutions, 1995; mem. editl. adv. bd. Lab. Safety and Environ. newsletter, 1998—; assoc. editor Desk Reference on Hazardous Materials Mgmt. Vol. WHA-Pub. TV, Madison, 1991—; grad. asst. Dale Carnegie. Mem. Fedn. Environ. Techs. (Madison chpt. program chmn. 1986—, pres., founder 1990-92), Acad. Cert. Hazardous Materials Mgrs. (bd. dirs. Greater Wis. chpt. 1993—, pres. 1996, nat. bd. dirs. 1998—), U. Wis. Madison Volleyball Booster Club (bd. dirs. 1987-95). Avocations: photography, camping, travel, volleyball, investments. Home: 6066 Whalen Rd Verona WI 53593-9274 Office: Agracetus Campus Monsanto Co 8520 University Grn Middleton WI 53562-2508

SENNAROGLU, ALPHAN, physics educator; b. Nicosia, Cyprus, Nov. 10, 1966; s. Ozdemir Mustafa and Aydin (Behcet) S.; m. Figen Ecer, Oct. 14, 1995; 1 child, Canan. BS, Cornell U., 1988, MS, 1990, PhD, 1994. Asst. prof. physics Koc U., Istanbul, 1994—; assoc. prof. optoelectronics Higher Edn. Coun. of Turkey, 1997; prin. investigar Turkish Sci. and Rsch. Coun., Koc U., 1996-98, mem. core curri culum com., 1996-97, rschr. lab. optoelectronics and laser sci., 1994—. Contbr. articles to sci. jours. Sage fellow, Cornell U., 1988-89. Mem. IEEE, Optical Soc. Am., Tau Beta Pi, Eta Kappa Nu. Avocations: violin, photography, reading. Office: Koc U Optoelectronics Lab, Cayir Caddesi #5 Istinye, 80860 Istanbul Turkey

SENNETT, PAUL WILLIAM GERVASE, bank executive; b. Harrow, Middlesex, Eng., Aug. 29, 1962; s. John Mead and Alice Lawson (Haworth) S.; m. Carol Mary Tarr, Oct. 18, 1986. BA in Economic History, Durham (Eng.) U., 1980-83. M.d. Bankers Trust Internat., London, 1983-99, Deutsche Bank, London, 1999—. Mem. Bow Group, London, 1985—. Mem. The Securities Assn., Royal Yachting Assn., Wine Soc. Conservative. Methodist. Avocations: wine collecting, sailing, deep sea fishing, the Arts. Home: 1 Waterside, Radlett WD7 7DY, England Office: Bankers Trust Internat, Deutsche Bank, 23 Great Winchester St, London EC2N 2DB, England

SENSIBA, WINIFRED J., lighting designer; b. Milw., Mar. 1, 1934; d. Reuben F. Sensiba and Margaret M. Milokovic. BS, U. Wis., Milw., 1959; postgrad. Sch. of Drama, Yale U., 1960-61. Lighting designer, scenic designer Marquette Theatre Marquette U., Milw., 1956-60; lighting designer Beckford-Sensiba Assocs., N.Y.C., 1962—, N.Y.C. Swedish Cottage Marionette Theatre, 1963-99; instr. archtl. lighting Queens (N.Y.) Coll., 1980-82, 87-93; lighting designer Winn Sensiba, N.Y.C., 1999—. Mem. Designers Lighting Forum, Illuminating Engrng. Soc. (N.Y. sect.), Internat. Assn. Lighting Designers, U.S. Inst. Theatre Tech. (sec. 1973). Avocations: music, walking my dog. Home: 30 W 10th St New York NY 10011-8712

SENTER, TERENCE ARTHUR, art and design history educator; b. King's Lynn, England, Nov. 29, 1940; s. James and Olive (Watts) S.; m. Gillian Wendy Nunneley, Aug. 26, 1989 (div. Dec. 1998); children: Laura, Gemma, Abigail. BA, U. Durham, 1963; MPhil, U. Nottingham, 1976. Lectr. Coll. Art and Design, Nottingham, England, 1967-77; sr. lectr. The Nottingham Trent U., England, 1977—; cons. in field, 1981—. Avocations: music, theatre. Office: Nottingham Trent U, Burton St, NG1 4BU Nottingham England

SENZIA, MUSA SAIDI, laboratory technologist, consultant; b. Mwanga, Tanzania, Oct. 4, 1937; s. Saidi Kimomwe Senzia and Hadija Saidi Mashombo; m. Rukia Saidi, May 20, 1962. Lab. technician Ministry of Health, D'Salam, Tanzania, 1960-95, RC Mission Hosp., Bagamoyo, 1996—; rechr. in field. Avocations: reading, photographing, working in lab. doing some investigations and health care to the public. Office: RC Mission Bagamoyo, Dept of Lab, Bagamoyo Tanzania

SEO, DAE-SHIK, electrical engineer; b. Cheonan-city, Korea, Dec. 16, 1963; parents Mu-Deok Seo and Hyeon-Hee Choi; m. Jeong-Hyeon Noh, May 31, 1998; 1 child, Ji-Eun Seo. BS, Tokyo U. Agriculture & Tech., 1989, MSc, 1991, PhD, 1994. Rsch. Japan Soc. Promotion Sci., Tokyo, 1993-94, Kent (Ohio) State U., 1994-95; asst. prof. Soongsil U., Seoul, 1995—. Mem. Korean IEEE, Korea Info. Display Soc., Soc. Info. Display U.S., Japan Liquid Crystal Soc., Internat. Liquid Crystal Soc. Office: Cheongdam-dong Kangnam-ku, Seoul 135-100, Korea

SEO, DONG WAN, internist; b. Daejeon, Choongnam, Korea, Jan. 12, 1963; s. Ho-Jin and Hyang-Sup (Kim) S.; m. Hye-Kyung Lee; children: Jung-Hee, Jae-Duk. BS, Seoul Nat. U. Med. Coll., 1987; MS, U. Ulsan, Seoul, 1995, MD, 1997. Korean med. diplomate with qualification for gastroenterology bd., gastrointestinal endoscopy. Dir. Boeun Sanitary Ctr., Seoul, 1988-90; resident Asan Med. Ctr., Seoul, 1991-94, fellow in gastroenterology, 1995-96; instr. Asan Med. Ctr./U. Ulsan, Seoul, 1997-98, prof. medicine, 1999—. Contbr. articles to profl. jours. Recipient Young Investigator's award Asian Pacific Congress of Gastroenterology, 1996, Internat. Jour. Pancreatology, 1998, Korean Min. Health, 1998-99. Mem. Am. Gastroenterol. Assn., Am. Soc. Gastrointestinal Endoscopy, Internat. Assn. Pancreatology. Achievements include research in MR spectroscopy, cholangioscopy/gastrointestinal endoscopy. Avocations: golf, travel, sports. Home: Apt Pungnapdong Songpagu, 102-1101 Hyundai, Seoul 138-040, South Korea Office: Asan Med Ctr Div Gastroent, 388-1 Pungnapdong Songpagu, Seoul 138-736, South Korea

SEO, TORU, medical doctor; b. Amagasaki, Japan, Feb. 3, 1961; s. Setsu and Harumi (Inatome) S.; m. Miwako Takemoto, Feb. 4, 1993; children: Mikako, Minako. MD, Hyogo Coll. Medicine, Nishinomiya, Japan, 1986, PhD, 1994. Diplomate med. doctor. Asst. prof. Hyogo Coll. Medicine, Nishinomiya, Japan, 1993—. Office: Hyogo Coll Medicine, 1-1 Mukogawa-cho, Nishinomiya 663-8501, Japan

SEOANE, RODOLFO EDUARDO, electronic company executive, consultant; b. Buenos Aires, Sept. 9, 1954; s. Rodolfo Francisco and Olga Josefina (Rodriguez) S.; m. Maria Victoria Romanelli, Dec. 9, 1994; children: Maria Constanza, Federico Edwardo. Student, Inst. Evangelico Am., Buenos Aires, 1966, COM-11 H.S., Buenos Aires, 1972; grad. in Programming, Estudios Superiores Buenos Aires, Buenos Aires, 1990; mech. engr., U. Manila Mercante, 1999. Co-owner, sr. programmer Boot Ltd., Buenos Aires, 1990—. Comdr. Argentinian Navy, 1976-98. Recipient Gold medal COM-11, Buenos Aires, 1972. Mem. Radio Club Argentino, Lighter Than Air Assn. Avocations: electronics, computers. Home: Nazca 3153, Buenos Aires 1417, Argentina Office: Boot SRL, Tinogasta 3010 2o 4, 1417EHN Buenos Aires Argentina

SEOL, DONG-IL, meteorologist, researcher; b. Kongju, Republic of Korea, Nov. 11, 1961; s. Yeong-Sam and Jae-Sook (Kim) S.; m. Gab-Soon Choi, Dec. 25, 1988; children: Ju-Hwan, Ji-Hee. BS, Korea Maritime U., Pusan, 1985, MS, 1992; PhD, Hokkaido U., Sapporo, Japan, 1998. Deck officer Korea Shipping Co., Seoul, 1985-89; asst. Korea Maritime U., Pusan, 1989-92, part-time instr., 1992-94; fgn. rschr. Hokkaido U., 1998-99; instr. Korea Maritime U., Pusan, 1999—. Contbr. articles to Jour. Korean Inst. Nav., Geophys. Rsch. Letters, Jour. Meteorol. Soc. Japan, others; also author procs. Mem. Korean Inst. Nav., Meteorol. Soc. Japan. Avocations: climbing, fishing.

SEONG, JINSIL, physician, researcher; b. Seoul, Korea, June 15, 1959; d. E-Chun and Kyung-Sun (Chung) S.; m. Kwang-Hyub Han, Jan. 22, 1983; children: Sojung, Sowoon. MD, Yonsei U., Seoul, Korea, 1983, PhD, 1993. Instr. Yonsei U., Seoul, 1987-90, 92-93, asst. prof., 1993-98, assoc. prof., 1999—; vis. scientist M.D. Anderson Cancer Ctr., Houston, 1990-92, 95-96. Contbr. articles to profl. jours. including Internat. Jour. Radiation Oncology, Anticancer Drug. Recipient Most Outstanding Paper award Korean Assn. Therapeutic Radiology and Oncology, 1994, Korean Assn. Sci. and Tech., 1996. Mem. European Soc. for Therapeutic Radiology and Oncology, Radiation Rsch. Soc., Am. Soc. for Therapeutic Radiation and Oncology. Avocations: swimming, oil painting. Office: Yonsei U Med Coll Rad Oncol, Shinchon-dong 134, Seoul 120-752, Korea

SEOW-CHOEN, FRANCIS, colorectal surgeon; b. Singapore, May 6, 1957; s. Hong-Teng and Lay-Keng (Kong) Seow; m. Ching-Peng Siow, May 28, 1983; children: Isaac, Samuel, Olivia. M.B.B.S., Nat. U. Singapore, 1981. House surgeon Ministry of Health, Singapore, 1981-82, orthopaedic resident, 1984-87; med. officer Ministry of Def., Singapore, 1982-84; registrar in surgery Singapore Gen. Hosp., 1987-89, registrar in colorectal surgery, 1989, sr. registrar coloproctology, 1989-92, cons. surgeon, 1992-95, head, sr. cons., 1996—; rsch. fellow St. Mark's Hosp., London, 1989-90; head and sr. cons. surgeon Singapore Gen. Hosp., 1995—, clin. assoc. prof., 1998—; dir. surg. oncology Nat. Cancer Ctr.; instr. advanced trauma life support ACS, 1992-94; officer in charge operating theatre Singapore Navy, 1990-94; dir. Endoscopy Ctr., Singapore, 1994—; officer-in-charge med. flight Rep. of Singapore Air Force, 1982-83; chmn. 1st Clin. Nutrition Meeting, 1994; treas. 25th Combined Surg. Meeting, 1992, vice chmn. 26th, 1992, chmn. 28th, 1994; sci. chmn. 28th Malaysia-Singapore Congress, 1994. Mem. editl. bd. Techniques in Coloproctology, Brit. Jour. Surgery, Colorectal Diseases, Diseases of the Colon and Rectum, 1990—, Indian Jour. Coloproctology; contbr. articles to med. jours. Vol. aftercare officer Singapore Anti-Narcotics Assn., 1977-79; organizing com. Steering Com. on Trauma Mgmt., Singapore, 1992, Practice Guidelines of Endoscopists, Singapore, 1992. Capt. Singapore Navy, 1982-94. Beecham scholar Nat. U. Singapore, 1980-81; Manpower Devel. Plan fellow Ministry of Health, Singapore, 1989-90, Overseas Fund fellow Royal Coll. surgeons, Edinburgh, 1989, Internat. Travel fellow Am. Soc. Colon and Rectal Surgeons, 1993. Fellow Acad. Medicine Singapore (sec. 1992-94). Ch. of Eng. Avocations: taxonomy of stick-insects, entomology, writing. Home: 54 Mimosa Walk, Singapore 2880, Singapore Office: Singapore Gen Hosp, Singapore Gen Hosp., Dept Colorectal Surgery, Singapore 0316, Singapore

SEPAROVIC, ZVONIMIR PAUL, law educator, politician; b. Blato, Croatia, Sept. 14, 1928; s. Franko and Betina (Lipovac) S.; m. Branka Oklobdzia, Apr. 10, 1990; children: Borut, Duska Maria. LLB, U. Zagreb, Croatia, 1953, LLM, 1961; PhD, U. Ljubljana, Slovakia, 1967; Academician, European Acad. Sci. and Arts, Salzburg, 1994. Journalist Radio Zagreb, 1949-51; judge Dist. Ct., Zagreb, 1955-61; prof. law Law Sch., Zagreb, 1961—; min. fgn. affairs Govt. Croatia, 1991-92, amb. to UN, 1992; prof. emeritus U. Zagreb, 1998—; min. justice govt. Croatia, 1999-2000; dean Sch. Law, U. Zagreb, 1985-87, rector, 1989-91; senator European Acad. Sci. and Arts, 1994—. Author: Criminology and Social Pathology, 1981 (Bk. of Yr. award 1983), Limits to Risk (Bioethics), 1985 (Bk. of Yr., Yugoslavia 1985), Victimology-Study of Victims, 1985. Pres. World Soc. Victimology, Munster, Germany, 1985-88, permanent rep. to ECOSOC, Vienna, Austria, 1988—; hon. pres. Hands of Cain (Abolition of Death Penalty by 2000), 1990. Recipient Safety award Mo. Safety Ctr., 1973, Humboldt scholarship (Germany), 1965, 79, Fulbright scholarship, 1972-73, Hans v. Hentig award WSV (Montreal), 2000; named Hon. Citizen, City of New Orleans, 1992. Mem. Croatian Soc. Victimology (pres. 1990—), Croatia-Indian Friendship Soc. (pres. 1995-97), Almae Matris Alumnae Croatice, U. Zagreb (pres. 1991-92). Roman Catholic. Avocations: chess, swimming, classical music, books. Home: Cesari 12, 10040 Zagreb-Dubrava Croatia Office: Law School, Pravni fak 14, 10000 Zagreb Croatia

SEPPALA, MARKKU TAPIO, gynecologist, obstetrician, eductor; b. Helsinki, Finland, May 16, 1936; s. Aate Ensio and Annikki (Partanen) S.; m. Maija Leena Peltonen, Aug. 26, 1961; children: Jussi Markku P., Kalle Thomas. MD, U. Helsinki, 1964, D in Med. Sci., 1965; PhD (hon.), U. Leège, Belgium, 1995. Intern dept. surgery U. Ctrl. Hosp., Helsinki, 1964, resident, 1966-69, chair dept. I ob-gyn., 1980—, adminstrv. chmn. dept. I and II ob-gyn., 1983-84, 87-90, 1993-94; sr. lectr., asst. prof. U. Helsinki, 1970-75, assoc. prof., 1976-78, chair ob-gyn., 1979—; rsch. prof. Acad. of Finland, 1978-80; vis. prof. St. Bartholomew's Hosp. Med. Ctr., London, 1979-80; examiner ob-gyn. Nat. Bd. Health, Finland, examiner gynecol. and reproductive endocrinology, adviser, 1984-89; advisor Nat. Bd. Social Affairs and Health, 1990-92, Nat. Agy. for Welfare and Health, 1993—. Editor books; editor Acta Endocrinologica, 1980-85, Acta Obstetrica et Gynecologica Scandinavica, 1984-89; assoc. editor Obstetrical and Gynecol. Survey, 1981—, Tumor Biology, 1987-90, Human Reproduction Update, 1995—; mem. editl. bd. Zentralblatt fur Gynakologie, 1980—, Oncoldevel. Biology and Medicine, 1980-86, Jour. In Vitro Fertilization and Embryo Transfer, 1984-91, Human Reproduction, 1986-92, assoc. editor, 1993-97, Internat. Jour. Gynecology and Obstetrics, 1986—, Current Opinion in Ob-gyn, 1988—, Jour. Assisted Reproduction and Genetics, 1992—, European Jour. Ob-gyn., 1993—, Clin. Endocrinology, 1994-98; mem. adv. bd. Archives of Ob-gyn., 1988-97, Fertility Sterilization, 1998; contbr. articles to profl. jours. Bd. dirs. Cancer Soc. Finland, 1982; congress pres. III World Congress of In Vitro Fertilization and Embryo Transfer, 1984, XIV meeting Internat. Soc. Oncodevel. Biology and Medicine, 1986; congress pres. VII Congress on Human Reproduction,1990, VII European Congress on Gynaecology and Obstetrics, 1992, XVI World Congress of Gynecology and Obstetrics, Washington, D.C., 2000. Recipient Matti Ayrapaa prize Finnish Med. Soc. DuoDecim, 1981, Wissenschafts prize, Deutscheprechende Professoren, Luzern, Switzerland, 1971. Fellow N.Y. Acad. Sci., Royal Coll. Ob-Gyn. (U.K.), Brit. Fertility Soc. (hon.), Am. Coll. Ob-Gyn. (hon.), Soc. Gynecol. Obesity (hon.), Chilean Soc. Gynecological Obesity (hon.), Brazilean Federation Gynecological Obesity (hon., Chgo. Soc. Gynecological Obesity (hon.); mem. Internat. Soc. Oncodevelopmental Biology and Medicine (dir.), Population Coun. N.Y. (bd. trustees), Finnish Med. Found. (bd. trustees), European Assn. Gynecologists and Obstetricans (sec. gen. 1985-88, pres. 1994-97), Internat. Fedn. Gynecology and Obstetrics (exec. bd., pres. 1997-2000), Hungarian Gynecol. Soc. (hon.). Lutheran. Address: Pihlajatie 20B 15, 00270 Helsinki 27, Finland

SEPPÄLÄ, MATTI KULLERVO, physical geography educator; b. Vaasa, Finland, Sept. 5, 1941; s. Risto Kullervo and Lea Kaarina (Seppä) S.; m. Raija Anneli Merila, July 8 1967; children: Uula Matti, Salla Tuulikki O'Donoghue, Oula Mikko, Malla Anneli. MSc, U. Turku, Finland, 1967, licentiate of philosophy, 1969, PhD, 1971. Rsch. asst. Acad. Finland, Turku, 1970-72; asst. prof. U. Turku, 1972-73; assoc. prof. U. Oulu, Finland, 1973-78; acting prof. U. Turku, 1975; assoc. prof. U. Helsinki, Finland, 1978-98, prof., 1998—; vis. fellow U. Cambridge, U.K., 1994-95, U. Durham, U.K., 1995; docent U. Turku, 1972—; project leader Ministry of Environment, Helsinki, 1983-84; mem. editorial bd. Geography physique et Quaternaire, 1983-90, Permafrost and Periglacial Processes, 1989-93; visiting lectr. over 25 foreign univs. Co-author: Relief and Landforms in Atlas of Finland, 1986, Advances in Periglacial Geomorphology, 1988; contbr. over 100 articles to profl. jours. Recipient sr. scientist fellowship Acad. Finland, 1976, 85, 90, 92, A.V. Humboldt fellowship, 1981-82, Emil Aaltonen Found. fellowship, 1986-87, Erskine fellowship U. Canterbury, 1991; decorated Order of the Lion of Finland. Mem. Geog. Soc. Finland (editor Fennia 1984-85, pres. 1984, Ragnar Hult medal), Internat. Glaciological Soc. (corr. 1980-92, br. pres. 1974-76), Arctic Inst. North Am. Avocations: photography, check. Office: Univ Helsinki, Siltavuorenpenger 20A, Helsinki 00014, Finland

SEPPÄLÄ, MATTI TAPIO, neurosurgeon; b. Kotka, Finland, Dec. 14, 1958; s. Olavi Viljam and Terttu Johanna (Tuomela) S.; m. Mervi Elina Penttilä, June 8, 1984; children: Tapio Markus, Tuulikki Elina, Terho Olavi. MD, Helsinki (Finland) U., 1983, degree in neurosurgery, 1990, PhD, 1998. Gen. practitioner Primary Health Care, Hanko, Finland, 1984; registrar neurology Helsinki City Hosp., 1985; registrar neurosurgery Helsinki U. Hosp., 1985-90, cons. neurosurgery, 1990—. Contbr. articles to profl. jours. Mem. Finnish Neurosurgical Assn. (cashier 1993-95), Scandinavian Neurosurgical Assn. Avocations: family, gardening, nature photography. Office: Helsinki U Hosp Dept Neurosurgery, Topeliuksenkatu 5, 00260 Helsinki Finland

SEPPALA, PENTTI OLAVI, retired medical director, physician; b. Uskela, Finland, May 16, 1933; s. Toivo Johannes and Elli Vilhelmiina (Takala) S.; m. Anneli Helena Haroma, June 6, 1958; children: Olli-Pekka, Anna-Leena. MD, U. Turku, Finland, 1958, D Med. Scis., 1964. Instr. in med. chemistry U. Turku, 1955-61, asst. physician dept. medicine, 1961-64, acting assoc. prof., 1964-65, chief physician Student Health Svc., 1965-69, docent internal medicine, 1970-96; assoc. chief physician dept. medicine U. Ctrl. Hosp., Turku, 1970-92, med. dir., 1993-96; chief physician Cancer Soc. Southwest Finland, 1986—; ret.; sr. rsch. fellow Dept. Connective Tissue Rsch. Inst. Biology and Med. Scis., Boston, 1966-67. Contbr. articles to profl. jours. Chmn. bd. Student Health Svc. of Turku, 1970-75, 96—, Collegium for Med. Edn./U. Turku, 1975-77, Diabetes Bd. for Dist. of Univ. Ctrl. Hosp. of Turku, 1983-93; bd. dirs. med. faculty U. Turku, 1975-78, Diabetes League in Finland, 1982-90, Cancer Soc. for South-West Finland, 1982—. Recipient Silver medal Student Health Svc., 1976, Golden medal Diabetes League of Finland, 1990, Bronze medal Soc. Ins. of Finland. Mem. Finnish Soc. Internal Medicine (sec. 1969-71), Finnish Soc. Rheumatology, Finnish Soc. Encodrinology, Finnish Soc. Clin. Chemistry, Finnish Med. Soc. Duodecim, Finnish Soc. Gastroenterology. Home: Saunakatu 1, 20720 Turku Finland

SEPPALAINEN, UGI GERHARD, journalist; b. Helsinki, Finland, July 6, 1928; s. Gerhard Kristian and Elina Vilhelmina (Juur) S.; m. Rauni Lis Ronkainen, Dec. 16, 1961. Freelance film journalist, 1948-52; Helsinki city editor Social Democrat, Helsinki, 1960-61, chief editor fgn. divsn., 1961-68; editl. sec., columnist Social Democrat, 1968-74; freelance journalist, 1974—. Contbr. numerous articles to Social Dem. mag., Metal Workers Union mag. Govt. mem. Journalist Soc. Helsinki, 1968. Recipient Fgn. Leader Fulbright grant U.S. Govt., 1964, Kordelin Fund grant Helsinki, 1965. Social Democratic Party of Finland. Avocations: history, literature. Home: Kaskilaaksontie 5 B 19, 02360 Espoo Finland

SEPPANEN, HANNELI KIRSTI, chemical company executive; b. Kajaani, Finland, Apr. 10, 1952; d. Mauri and Anja (Mustonen) Katavisto; m. Reijo Kalevi Seppanen, Dec. 26, 1975; 1 child, Emilia. Lic. in Phil., Helsinki U., 1985, MPhil, 1978. Lab. supr. Suomen Sokeri, Finland, 1978; rschr. Tech. Rsch. Inst., Finland, 1979-80; rschr. Neste Chems., Finland, 1981-86, devel. engr., 1986-90, rsch. and devel. mgr., 1990-94; application mgr. Borealis, Finland, 1994-97, application devel. mgr., 1997-99, market devel. mgr., 1999—. Patentee in polymer chemistry and applications; speaker in field. Mem. Soc. Plastics Engrs. Avocations: reading, Native Americans, stones.

SEPPONEN, RAIMO ERIK, educator, laboratory administrator; b. Lahti, Finland, Aug. 4, 1950; s. Mauno Erik and Mrijam Ruth Sepponen; m. Ulla Kaarina Jokinen, 1875; children: Jan-Erik, Eila Mirjam. MSc, Helsinki U. Tech., Espoo, Finland, 1974, LicSc, 1979, DSc, 1986. R&D mgr. Oy Esmi Ab, Helsinki, 1975; project mgr. Instrumentarium Corp./Datex, Helsinki, 1976-77; mgr. new devel. Instrumentarium Corp., Helsinki, 1979-81; product group mgr. Instrumentarioum Corp./Palomex, Helsinki, 1982-83; devel. mgr. Palomex-Instrumentarium Corp., Helsinki, 1984-87; clin. applications mgr. Instrumentarium Corp./Imaging Divsn., Helsinki, 1988-91; entrepreneur Increa Ltd., Helsinki, 1992-94; prof. Helsinki U. Tech., Espoo, 1994—. Contbr. articles to profl. jours. Recipient Engring. Achievement awrd, 1986. Mem. AAAS, Finnish Tech. Soc., Soc. for Med. Physics and Tech., Hellenic Radiol. Soc. (hon.), Radiol. Soc. N.Am. (corr.). E-mail: Raimo.sepponen@hut.fi. Office: Helsinki U Tech, Otakaari 5 A, Espoo Finland

SEPULCHRE, RODOLPHE JUAN, engineering educator; b. Brussels, Apr. 2, 1967; s. Jacques and Michele (Cassiers) S.; m. Nathalie Petit, Sept. 8, 1990; children: Edith, Simon, Camille. PhB, Cath. U. Louvain, Belgium, 1990, Engrng. degree, 1990, PhD in Engrng., 1994. Cert. engr. Rsch. fellow U. Calif., Santa Barbara, 1994-96; rsch. assoc. Cath. U. Louvain, 1996-97; prof. U. Liege, Belgium, 1997—. Author: Constructive Nonlinear Control, 1997. Fellow Belgian Am. Ednl. Found., 1994. Mem. IEEE. Avocations: music, philosophy. Home: Rte de Strivay 1, 4122 Plainevaux Belgium Office: Inst Montefiore, B 28, B-4000 Liege Belgium

SEPULVEDA, EDUARDO SOLIDEO, chemical engineer; b. Loay, Philippines, Jan. 5, 1945; came to U.S., 1981; m. Consuelo S. Araneta, May 18, 1977; children: Edward, Josephus, Blaise. BSChE, De La Salle U., 1966; M of Chem. Engrng., U. Philippines, 1972. Lic. profl. engr., Calif. Instr. U. Philippines, Quezon City, 1968-70; sr. instr. De La Salle U., Manila, Philippines, 1970-71, asst. prof., 1971-73; process engr. Philippines Petroleum Corp., Makati, 1973-74, sr. process engr., 1974-75, mgr. tech. svc., 1975-81; sr. engr. C F Braun & Co., Alhambra, Calif., 1981; prin. engr. Brown & Root Braun, Alhambra, Calif., 1987-94, L.G. Engineering Co., Ltd., Seoul, Korea, 1994-96; supervising process engr. Parsons, Martinez, Calif., 1997—; reviewer chem. bd. De La Salle U., 1970-79. Mem. St. John Corregidor Lodge, Manila, 1979. Mem. AICE, Project Mgmt. Inst., Phi Kappa Phi. Achievements include designed and engineered a fluid catalyst transport system to hydrocracker reactor. Home: 3700 Oaklawn Ln Pico Rivera CA 90660-5941 Office: Parsons 2000 Marina Vista Ave Martinez CA 94553-1301

SEQAT, MOHAMED, banker. Gov. Bank of Morocco. Office: Banque Al-Maghrib, 277 ave Muhammad V BP 445, Rabat Morocco

SERA, BOZENA, botanist, researcher, educator; b. Jindrichuv Hradec, Czech Republic, Apr. 8, 1966; m. Michal Sery. MSc, Charles U., Prague, Czech Republic, 1990, RNDr, 1990; postgrad., South Bohemia U., Ceske Budejovice. Tchr. h.s., Prague, 1990-91; botanist Protected Landscape Area Blansky Les, Cesky Krumlov, 1991-92; tchr. South Bohemia U. Faculty Agr., Ceske Budejovice, 1996—; botanist Inst. Landscape Ecology, Acad. Scis. of Czech Republic, Ceske Budejovice, 1998—; authorized expert South Bohemia Ct. of Law, 1998. Mem. Czech Bot. Soc., 1990—. Avocations: horticulture, photography. Office: Inst Landscape Ecology Acad Sci Czech Republic, Na Sadkach 7, 370 04 Ceske Budejovice Czech Republic

SERA, KOICHIRO, physicist, educator; b. Sendai, Miyagi, Japan, Jan. 13, 1952; s. Terushiro and Mieko Sera; m. Michiko Kon, Oct. 9, 1982; children: Shuntaro, Daishiro. PhD, Tohoku U., Sendai, 1981. Instr. engring. Tokohu U., Sendai, 1974-90; assoc. prof. Iwate Med. U., Morioka, Japan, 1990-2000; vice-dir. Cyclotron Rsch. Ctr./Iwate Med. U., 2000—. Editor Internat. Jour. PIXE, 1996—; Contbr. articles to profl. jours. Mem. Japan Particle Induced X-ray Emission Assn. (mem. organizing com. 1992—). Avocations: violin, mountain-climbing, painting. Fax: 81-19-688-6072. Home: 4-21-6 Kitamatsuzono, Morioka 020-0105, Japan Office: Iwate Med U, 348 Tomegamori, Takizawa 020-0173, Japan

SERALINI, GILLES-ERIC, molecular biology educator, researcher; b. Bone, Algeria, Aug. 23, 1960; s. Gilbert and Liliane Josephine (Schembri) S.; m. Soline Lise Pabiot Seralini, Sept. 17, 1988; children: Harmonie, Alexandre. PhD, U. Montpellier, France, 1987. Fellow U. Nice, Montpellier, France, 1983-87; vis. scientist U. London, 1987-89; fellow U. Quebec, 1990-91; prof. molecular biology U. Caen, France, 1991—; lab. dir. U. Caen, France, 1991—; expert commn. Genie Biomolecular F. and Com. de Biovigilance, Biochemistry and Molecular Biology, France, 1996-2000. Author: (poetry) Ciel A Bruler, 1986, Il N'est Source Que Bonheur, 1990; (science) L'Evolution de la Matiere, 1994, Le Sursis de L'Espece Humaine, 1997, Genie Genetique, 1997, Transgénique le Temps des Manipulations, 1998. Corr. mem. French Poets Soc., France, 1988—, Biol. Soc., France, 1996—; sec. Young Rschrs. in Biochemistry and Molecular Biology, France, 1996-98. Decorated comdr. Order de l'Etoile de l'Europe. Mem. Endocrine Soc., Biochemical Molecular Biology. Avocations: poetry, writing. Office: U Caen IBBA, Esplanade de La Paix, 14032 Caen France

ŠERBEDŽIJA, NIKOLA, computer scientist; b. Belgrade, Yugoslavia, Apr. 17, 1953; s. Bogdan Nikola and Zora Darinka (Živanovič) Ž.; m. Marija Luka Scepanovic, Dec. 30, 1978; children: Borko, Vojin. BA in Math., U. Belgrade, 1976, MSc in Computer Sci., 1981, PhD in Computer Sci., 1989. Rschr. Mihajlo Pupin, Belgrade, 1977-86; guest scientist GMD, Karlsruhe, Germany, 1986-88; lectr. U. Belgrade, 1989-91; scientist cons. Mihajlo Pupin, 1989-91; sr. rschr. GMD, Berlin, 1991—; mem. Univ. Coun., Belgrade, 1989-91; cons. Mihajlo Pupin, 1991—; lectr. Tech. U. Berlin, 1992—; vis. prof. U. Tech. Sydney, 1999-2000, Berlin U. of Arts, 2000—. Author: (monograph) Asynchronous Process Communication, 1990; contbr. articles to profl. jours. Recipient grant/stipends Yugoslavia Sci. Found., U. So. Calif., L.A., 1983, Serbian Acad. Sci., Arts, 1986. Avocations: literature, theater, film, sports. Office: GMD First, Kekuléstr 7, D-12489 Berlin Germany

SERCHUK, IVAN, lawyer; b. N.Y.C., Oct. 13, 1935; s. Israel and Freda (Davis) S.; children: Camille, Bruce Mead, Vance Foster. BA, Columbia U., 1957, LLB, 1960. Bar: N.Y. 1961, U.S. Dist. Ct. (so. dist.) N.Y. 1963, U.S. Ct. Appeals (2d cir.) 1964, U.S. Tax Ct. 1966. Law clk. to judge U.S. Dist. Ct. (so. dist.) N.Y., 1961-63; assoc. Kaye, Scholer, Fierman, Hays & Handler, 1963-68; dep. supt., counsel N.Y. State Banking Dept., N.Y.C. and Albany, 1968-71; mem. Berle & Berle, 1972-73; spl. counsel N.Y. State Senate Banks Com., 1972; mem. Serchuk & Zelermyer LLP, White Plains, 1976—; lectr. Practising Law Inst., 1968-71. Mem. Assn. of Bar of City of N.Y., N.Y. State Bar Assn. Home: Mead St Waccabuc NY 10597 Office: Serchuk & Zelermyer LLP 81 Main St White Plains NY 10601-1711

ŠERCL, MIROSLAV, radiologist; b. Olomouc, Moravia, Czechoslovakia, July 19, 1948; s. Miroslav and Božena (Vlasáková) S.; m. Ladislava Vondroušová, June 9, 1973; children: Miroslav, Dana. MD, Charles U., Czechoslovakia, 1972, PhD, 1986. Physician Univ. Hosp., Hradec Králové, Czech Republic, 1972-80, cons. in neuroradiology, 1980-87, dep. head dept. radiology, 1987—, cons. neuroradiology, 1990—; regional med. officer East Bohemia, Czech Republic, 1986-90; vis. cons. tomography Radiol. Dept., Rychnov, 1991—. Contbr. articles to profl. publs. Mem. Neuroradiologic Soc., Czech Med. Soc., Czech Med. Assn. (cons.). Avocation: sailing. Home: Husova 591, 500 08 Hradec Králové Czech Republic Office: Univ Hosp, Dept Radiodiagnostics, 500 05 Hradec Králové Czech Republic

SERDYUK, ALEXANDER DMITRIEVICH, rector; b. Kharkov, Ukraine, Feb. 4, 1944; s. Dmitry Ivanovich Serdyuk and Alexandra Stepanovna Solomachina; m. Tatjiana Alexeevna Kozub, Dec. 13, 1973; children: Alexey, Dmitry. BS, Kharkov State U., 1966, PhD in Physics and Math., 1976. Asst. lectr. of exptl. physics Kharkov (Ukraine) State U., 1967-69, from asst. lectr. to asst. prof. higher math., 1972-96, prof., 1996—; rector Kharkov Inst. of Mgmt., 1998—; head higher math. and info. sci. dept., Kharkov Inst. Mgmt., 1993—; asst. dean of faculty for fgn. students, Kharkov State U., 1980-82. Author: Economic Dictionary-Thesaurus, 1999; edotor: Economy, Society, Market, 1998; contbr. articles to profl. jours. Mem. Internat. Personnel Acad., Assn. of Rectors, Assn. of Pvt. Ednl. Instns. of Ukraine. Avocations: books, music, travel. Office: Kharkov Inst Mgmt, Shevchenko St 24, 61013 Kharkov Ukraine

SEREBROV, VLADIMIR YURIEVICH, biochemist, educator; b. Tomsk, Russia, Dec. 10, 1952; s. Yuri Vladimirovich and Irina Grigorievna (Lobina) S.; m. Marina Anatolievna Volkova, Dec. 12, 1980; 1 child, Tihon. MD, Med. U. Siberia, Tomsk, 1976, PhD, 1980, DMS, 1995. Asst. prof. Med. U. Siberia, Tomsk, 1979-82, sr. lectr., 1982-85, docent, 1985-95, prof., 1995—,

head dept. biochemistry, molecular and cell biology, 1998—; mem. coun. Tomsk House of Scientists, 1985-93; vis. prof. London U., 1993; head internat. relations dept. Med. U. Siberia, 1994—; sci. rschr. expert Tomsk Region Adminstrn., 1996—. Author: Thymus at the System of Endocrine Regulation of Metabolism, 1987, The Endocrine Role of Thymus, 1993; contbr. over 100 articles to profl. jours. Editor Tomsk TV Radio Sta. Co., 1987—; bd. dirs. pub. orgn. Harmony, 1995. Internat. Sci. Found. grantee, 1995. Mem. N.Y. Acad. Sci., Russian Biochemistry Soc. Moscow, Russian Clin. Biochem. Soc. Democrat. Avocations: music, arts, TV and radio journalism, cars, traveling. FAX: (3822)233309. Office: Med U Siberia, Moscowski Trakt Ave 2, 634050 Tomsk Siberia, Russia

SEREBRYANY, ANDREY NINELOVICH, physical oceanographer, researcher; b. Severomorsk, USSR, Apr. 5, 1953; s. Ninel Semenovich and Irina Il'inichna (Shishkina) S.; m. Nataliya Nickolaevna Deeva, Apr. 27, 1991 (div. June 1995). MSc in Engring and Physics, Moscow Inst. Electronic Equip., 1977; PhD in Phys. and Math. Scis., Marine Hydrophys. Inst., Sevastopol, USSR, 1988. Engr. N.N. Andreyev Acoustics Inst., Moscow, 1977-84, jr. rschr., 1984-88, rsch. scientist, 1988-92; sr. rsch. scientist N.N. Andreyev Acoustics Inst., 1992—; guest scientist U. NSW, Canberra, Australia, 1994; mem. acad. coun. N.N. Andreyev Acoustics Inst., 1998 —; participant in 19 marine and oceanic rsch. cruises worldwide, 1971—. Contbr. 40 articles to profl. jours., 17 papers to internat. confs.; inventor in field in oceanographic instrumentation. Grantee Internat. Sci. Found., 1993, Russian Found. Basic Rsch., 1998-99; Recipient Inventor of USSR badge State Com. of Inventions, Moscow, 1990. Mem. Am. Geophys. Union, Nat. Geographic Sc., Russian Acoustical Soc. Avocation: alpine skiing. Home: Akademik Pavlov Str 30, Apt 55, 121 552 Moscow Russia Office: NN Andreyev Acoustics Inst, Shvernik Str 4, 117 036 Moscow Russia

SEREGARD, STEFAN BJORN, ophthalmologist, pathologist; b. Stockholm, May 2, 1957; s. Ingvar Bror and Kerstin Ingegerd (Kallhammar) S.; m. Marie Karin Pers, Sept. 2, 1989; children: Louise Karin Viktoria, Caroline Karin Elisabet. MD, Karolinska Inst., 1983, PhD, 1995. Resident dept. ophthalmology Karolinska Hosp., 1986-91; fellow in ophthalmic pathology Inst. of Optholmology, London, 1991; staff mem. St. Eriks Eye Hosp., Stockholm, Sweden, 1991-95, dir. ophthalmic pathology and oncology svc., 1995—; assoc. prof., chmn. retina dept. Karolinska Inst., 1997—. Contbr. articles to scientific jours. Mem. Assn. for Rsch. and Vision in Ophthalmology, European Orgn. for Rsch. and Treatment of Cancer, European Ophthalmic Pathology Soc., European Assn. Vision and Eye Rsch., Internat. Soc. for Orbital Disorders, Internat. Soc. of Ophthalmic Pathology, Am. Acad. Ophthalmology. Home: Oxenstiernsgatan 25, S-11527 Stockholm Sweden Office: St Eriks Eye Hosp, Polhemsgatan 50, S-11282 Stockholm Sweden

SEREGIN, PAVEL PAVLOVICH, physics educator; b. Riga, Lathvia, Dec. 6, 1940; s. Pavel Grigorievich and Mariya Nikitichna (Shurygina) S.; m. Larisa Nikolayevna Shlyugaeva, Dec. 30, 1963; 1 child, Nikita. Grad., State U., Leningrad, 1963. Rschr. Inst. Semiconductors, Leningrad, Russia, 1968-70, Phys.-Tech. Inst., Leningrad, Russia, 1971-92; prof. State Tech. U., St. Petersburg, Russia, 1993—. Author: Application of Emission Mossbauer Spectroscopy, 1982, Application of Mossbauer Effect in Amorphous, 1989, Mossbauer Effect and Photoelectronic Spectroscopy, 1991, Electronic Phenomena in Chalcogenide Semiconductors, 1996. Home: Apt 82 Bldg 86, Moskovskiy Prospect, 196084 Saint Petersburg Russia Office: State Tech U, Bldg 29 Polytechnicheskaya, 194251 Saint Petersburg Russia

SERENELLI, GIOVANNA, pathologist, researcher; b. Foligno, Perugia, Italy, Dec. 27, 1953; d. Abramo and Elisena (Rustici) S. MD in Medicine and Surgery, Perugia U., 1980; PhD in Gen. Surgery, Trieste U., 1986. House physician Hosp. Assisi, 1980-81; emergency room surgeon Hosp. Gorizia, 1981-83; rsch. scientist U. Perugia, 1983—; collaborator Yahoo.it; expert collaborator Xagena.it. Contbr. articles to profl. jours. including Internat. Jour. Oncology, European Jour. Histochemistry, Yahoo.it, News in Medicine, Xagena.it, General Oncology. Mem. WWF, 1989, Accademia Properziana del Subasio, Assisi, 1994. Recipient award Accademia Anatomico Chirurgica, 1980. Mem. N.Y. Acad. Sci., Flow Cytometry Italian Orgn., Italian Soc. Cytology, among others. Avocations: ethology, animal husbandry, ecology, gardening. E-mail: serengio@krenet.it. Office: Istituto Patologia Generale, Policlinico Monteluce, 06100 Perugia Italy

SERES, LASZLO, chemistry educator; b. Mindszent, Csongrad, Hungary, Jan. 10, 1939; s. Istvan and Veronika (Takacs) S.; m. Edit Magocsi, July 23, 1964; children: Laszlo, Ildiko. Degree in chemistry, U. Szeged, Hungary, 1962, PhD, 1973; DSc, Hungarian Acad. Scis., Budapest, 1994. Asst. lectr. Szeged U., 1962-67, asst. prof., 1967-74, assoc. prof., 1974-91; prof. Tchrs. Tng. Coll., Szeged, 1991—; guest rschr. Nat. Bur. Stds., Washington, 1971; cons. chemist Chinoin Pharm. Co., Budapest, 1974-84, MOL Oil and Gas Co,. Szazhalombatta, 1974-84. Co-author: FORTRAN Programs for Solution of Physical Chemistry Problems, 1978; contbr. articles to profl. jours. including Jour. Am. Chem. Soc., Jour. Phys. Chemistry, among others. Recipient Disting. Worker of Edn. award Ministry of Edn., 1975, Order of Work award, 1983, Szent-Gyorgyi Albert award, 1988. Mem. Chemometrics Soc. Office: Juhasz Gyula Tchrs Tng Coll, Boldogasszony Sgt 6 POB 396, H-6701 Szeged Csongrad, Hungary

SERFLING, EDGAR ALBERT ERNST, pathology educator; b. Hermsdorf, Germany, Feb. 7, 1944; s. Ernst and Ilse (Gäbler) S.; m. Karin Thoma Petzold, May 23, 1980; children: Sebastian, Julia. Diploma biology, U. Halle, Germany, 1968, Dr.rer.nat., 1972; Dr.sc.nat., Acad. of Scis., Berlin, 1982; Dr.habil.med., U. Würzburg, Germany, 1982. Group leader Zentral Inst. Genetik, Gatersleben, Germany, 1976-82; sr. rsch. Inst. of Molecular Biology II, Zürich, Switzerland, 1983-85; group leader Inst. of Virology and Immunobiology, Würzburg, 1985-92; head of dept. Inst. of Pathology, U. Würzburg, 1992—. Author: Struktur und Expression der Gene höherer Organismen, 1982. Recipient Leibniz medal Acad. Scis., 1976. Achievements include research on structure of eukaryotic enhancers, transcriptional regulation of lymphokine genes. Home: Am Wirtsgarten 10, D-97241 Oberpleichfeld Germany Office: U Würzburg Inst Path, Josef-Schneider Strasse 2, D-97080 Würzburg Germany

SERGEEV, VICTOR I., engineering executive, researcher; b. Voronezh, Russia, May 14, 1963; s. Igor V. and Ludmila A. (Melnik) S.; m. Elena A. Muravieva, May 24, 1989; 1 child: Igor V. Sergeev II. Student, Kemerovo Higher Mil. Sch., Russia, 1980-83; MSc in radioengring., Voronezh Politechnical Inst., Russia, 1986; PhD, Novosibirsk Electrotechnical, Russia, 1992; DSc, Russian Acad. of Scis., Moscow, 1997; MSc (justice), Russian Acad. State Svc., Moscow, 1999. Locksmith assembler Excavater Plant, Voronezh, 1983-84; engr. Constrn. Bur. of Radiocomm., Voronezh, 1984-86, 89, Irkutsk, Russia, 1987-89; radio operator, antenner Lenskaja Oil-Gas Prospecting Espdn., Settlement Verhne Markovo, 1986-87; chief Voronezh Constrn. Bur. Antenna Design, 1989—; dir. coun. Comml. Bank, Voronezh, 1992; chair sect. applied radiophysics Russian Acad. Natural Scis., Voronezh, 1996, mem. extended presidium, Moscow., 1996—. Author: Parametrical Antennas, 1995, Receiving Antennas of cm-Band, 1997; discovered phenomenon of parametrical absorption, 1996; inventor radiolocation method, 1994 (gold medal Brusseles-Eureka 1994), radioholographic retranslation, 1993 (gold medal Brussels-Eureka 1994), method microcollaptique deformation, 1996 (gold medal Brusseles-Eureka 1995), antennas system (bronze medal Brusseles-Eureka 1995), method of energy bunches formed (diploma Brusseles-Eureka 1996). Named Hon. Academician Internat. Acad. of Inventional, Moscow, 1998, Hon. Radio Operator of Russia, 1993; recipient Russian Govt. prize, 1997;,Goskomoboronprom of Russia prize winner, 1995. Mem. Engring. Coun. (chartered, U.K.), Inst. Elec. Engrs. (U.K.), N.Y. Acad. of Scis., Russian Acad. Natural Scis., Russian Lord Coun., Alliance of Princes of Russia, Knights of Malta. Mem. Monarch party. Dzen. Avocations: classical music, philosophy, poetry, recreational activities, fantastic literature. Office: VCB AD, Tekstiltchikov Str 1, 394026 Voronezh Russia

SERGEEV, YURI ALEXANDROVICH, mathematician, educator; b. Molodechno, Belarus, Dec. 9, 1947; arrived in Eng., 1995; s. Alexander Dmitriyevich and Taissia Petrovna (Tarassova) S.; m. Larissa Alexandrovna Proddubnyak, Oct. 27, 1970; 1 child, Irina Yurievna. MSc, Moscow State U., 1971; PhD, Inst. Problems in Mechanics, Moscow, 1977; DSc in Physics/Math. (hon.), Russian Acad. Sci., 1993. Chartered mathematician, U.K. Rsch. fellow Inst. Problem Mechanics, Moscow, 1972-80, sr. scientist, 1980-91, head lab., 1991-94, rsch. prof., 1994-95; part-time prof. Moscow Inst. Physics and Tech., 1994-95; prof., head of dept. U. Newcastle, Newcastle-upon-Tyne, 1995—; cons. Shell Rsch., Amsterdam, 1993-95. Contbr. articles to profl. jours. Grantee Internat. Sci. Found., 1994-95, Engring. and Phys. Scis. Rsch. Coun. U.K., 1996-99. Mem. London Math. Soc., N.Y. Acad. Scis., Inst. Math. and its Applications U.K., Soc. Rheology of Am. Inst. Physics. Office: U Newcastle Engring Math, Claremont Rd Stephenson Bld, Newcastle-upon-Tyne NE1 7RU, England

SERGEYER, IGOR DMITRIYERICH, federal official; b. Verkhnyu, Ukraine, Apr. 20, 1938. PS Nakhimov Black Sea Higher, Naval Tech. Sch.; FE, Dzerzhinsky Mil. Acad. Army officer various commands in strategic missile troops, until 1992; min. of def. Moscow, 1997—. Office: Ministry of Def, ul Znamenka 19, 103160 Moscow Russia*

SERGEYEV, IGOR DMITRIYEVICH, federal official; b. Verkhnyu, Ukraine, Apr. 20, 1938. Student, Naval Tech. Sch., F.E. Dzerzhinsky Mil. Acad., Mil. Acad. Gen. Staff. Army officer including various commands Strategic Missile Troops; min. def. Moscow, 1997—. Office: ul Myasnitskya 37, 103175 Moscow Russia*

SERGI, CONSOLATO, pediatric pathology researcher; b. Rome, June 24, 1965; arrived in Germany, 1994; s. Filippo Sergi and Maria Occhiuto; m. Julia Benstz; 1 child. MD, U. Genoa, Italy, 1989; specialty degree in pediat., U. Genoa, 1993. Scientific group coord. G. Fornaroli Hosp., Magenta, Italy, 1993-94; pathologist, sci. asst. Ruprecht-Karls-U., Heidelberg, Germany, 1994—; postmortem examiner fetal-pediat. autopsies, organizer fetal/pediat. clinico-pathol. meetings, U. Heidelberg, 1996—. Contbr. articles to profl. jours. Served with Italian Red Cross. Molecular biology fellow Zeneca-Wellcome Corp., 1994. Fellow Italian Soc. Pediat.; mem. Internat. Acad. Pathology, Am. Acad. Pediats. Avocations: bicycling, collecting old books of teratology and pediatric pathology, translating from Latin to other languages. E-mail: consolato sergi@med.uni-heidelberg.de. Office: Inst Pathology, Im Neuenheimer Feld 220, D-69120 Heidelberg Germany

SERGIEVA, SONJA BORISSOVA, oncologist; b. Sofia, Bulgaria, Sept. 18, 1964; d. Boris Sergiev Stoilov and Liljana Stephanova Vassileva. MD, Med. Acad., Sofia, 1990; postgrad., Nat. Oncology Ctr., Sofia, 1994, nuclear medicine specialty, 1994, MD, PhD, 1994. Jr. asst. Nat. Oncology Ctr., Sofia, 1994-96, sr. asst., 1996-98, main asst., 1998—. Contbr. papers to profl. jours. Point 2 award in Creative Works, Bulgarian Found. Against Cancer, 1994. Mem. European Assn. of Nuclear Medicine, European Assn. for Cancer Rsch., European Soc. for Med. Oncology, Bulgarian Assn. Radiology and Nuclear Medicine (Point 1 award in creative works 1995), Am. Acad. Sci. Avocations: modern music, theater, cinema. Home: kv Krasno Selo bl 212 vA, 1618 Sofia Bulgaria Office: Nat Oncology Ctr, 6 Plovdivsko Pole St, 1756 Sofia Bulgaria

SERGIN, VLADIMIR YAKOVLEVICH, cybernetician, brain scientist; b. Archangelsk, Russia, May 21, 1935; s. Yakov Michailovich and Anna Leontievna (Scherbinina) S.; m. Nina Michailovna Tuganova, Oct. 14, 1969; children: Natalia Vladimirovna, Alexei Vladimirovich. Diploma in engring., Mil. Engring. Acad., Moscow, 1960-65, Candidate Engring. Scis., 1968; D Physico-Math. Scis., USSR Hydrometeorogical Ctr., Moscow, 1975. Prof. Moscow Physico-Tech. Inst., Dolglprudnii, Russia, 1968-70; dir. lab. Pacific Inst. Geography, Far East divsn. USSR Acad. Scis., Vladivostok, Russia, 1971-80; dir. lab. Inst. Control Scis., USSR Acad. Scis., Moscow, 1980-84; sci. adviser Main Naval Staff, Moscow, 1984-87; dir. lab. Neuroinformatics Lab., Far Ea. divsn. Russian Acad. Scis., Petropavlovsk-Kamchatsky, 1987—; expert Internat. Conf. Experts Global Atmospheric Rsch. Program-Climate, Stockholm, 1974; invited scientist program on exch. scientists between USSR and U.S.A., Climatic Rsch. Inst., Oreg. State U., Corvallis, 1978; invited scientist Nat. Ctr. for Atmospheric Rsch., Boulder, Colo., 1978; expert Internat. Conf. Experts, Internat. Inst. for Applied Sys. Analysis, Laksenburg, Austria, 1980; mem. adv. bd. Journal Higher Nervous Activity, 1998—. Author: Systems Analysis of the Problem of Large-Scale Oscillations of the Climate and Glaciations of the Earth, 1978, The Nature of Global Geological Cycles: Thermodynamical Mechanism, 1994; contbr. articles to sci. jours., including Jour. Geophys. Rsch., Jour. Higher Nervous Activity, Internat. Jour. Computing Anticipatory Sys., chpts. to books. Named Honored Scientist of Russian Fedn., Pres. of Russian Fedn., 1999. Mem. Russian Acad. Natural Scis. (corr.). Avocations: hiking, swimming. E-mail: volcan@kcs.iks.ru. Home: Leningradskoye Shosse 15/227, 125171 Moscow Russia Office: Russian Acad Scis Far Ea, Neuroinfo Lab 9 Piyp Ave, 683006 Petropavlovsk-Kamchatsky Russia also: Russian Acad Scis, Inst Num, Numerical Math, Gubkin St 8, 117334 Moscow Russia

SERI, ISTVAN, physician, researcher; b. Szombathely, Hungary, Apr. 15, 1951; came to U.S., 1986; s. Istvan and Katalin (Orszagh) S.; m. Eva Novoszel, Oct. 11, 1975; children: David, I. Adam. MD, Semmelweis Med. Sch., Budapest, 1976; PhD, Hungarian Acad. Scis., Budapest, 1985. Resident in pediatrics Semmelweis Med. Sch., Budapest, 1976-79, instr. in pediatrics, 1979-84, asst. prof. in pediatrics, 1984-91; rsch. fellow Karolinska Inst., Stockholm, Sweden, 1984-86; rsch. fellow in nephrology Harvard Med. Sch., Boston, 1986-88, fellow in neonatology, 1988-91, instr. in pediatrics, 1991-94; asst. prof. in pediatrics U. Pa., Phila., 1994-00, assoc. prof., 2000—; clin. dir. neonatal svcs. Children's Hosp. Phila., U. Pa., 1994—. Editor Prenatal and Neonatal Medicine, 2000—; contbr. over 50 articles to profl. jours. Recipient Janeway award Children's Hosp. Boston, 1991-92, CHRC award NIH, Washington, 1991-92, Clin. Investigator award NIH, 1992-94, Blockley-Osler tchg. award U. Pa., 2000, Faculty Tchr. of Yr. Children's Hosp. of Phila., 1999-2000. Fellow Am. Acad. Pediatrics; mem. AAAS, Am. Heart Assn., Hungarian Med. Assn., Soc. Pediat. Rsch., European Soc. Pediat. Rsch. Avocations: soccer, tennis, bridge. Office: Children's Hospital Phila 34th St & Civic Ctr Blvd Philadelphia PA 19104

SERIU, MASAFUMI, physicist; b. Kyoto, Japan, Sept. 23, 1964; s. Yoichi and Ikuko (Ogiso) S. BS, Kyoto U., 1987, MS, 1989, DS, 1992. Rsch. fellow dept. physics Kyoto U., 1992-93; postdoctoral fellow Inter-Univ. Ctr. for Astronomy and Astrophysics, Pune, India, 1993-95; Yukawa Meml. fellow Yukawa Inst. for Theoretical Physics, Kyoto, 1995, JSPS Rsch. fellow, 1996; assoc. prof. Fukui U., Japan, 1996—; vis. rsch. assoc. Inst. Cosmology, Tufts U., 1999—. Contbr. articles to profl. jours. Rsch. award Inoue Fund for Scic.,1993, recipient 3d prize in Silver Jubilee Essay Competition, Indian Assn. for Gen. Relativity and Gravitation, India, 1994, Honda Heihachiro Meml. scholarship Japan Assn. for Math. Sci., 1994, 95, Yukawa Meml. fellowship, 1995, JSPS Rsch. fellowship, 1996, Inamori Found. Grant-in-Aid, 1998. Mem. Japan Phys. Soc., Japan Astron. Soc. Office: Fukui Univ, Bunkyo 3-9-1, Fukui 910-8507, Japan

SERKOVSKAYA, GALINA STEPANOVNA, physics educator, researcher; b. Moscow, June 15, 1938; d. Stepan Ivanovich and Anastasia Petrovna (Bachyrina) S.; m. Aleksandr Vasilevich Sergeev, Jan. 1966 (div.); 1 child, Korchagina Anna Aleksandrovna. Diploma in Physics and Elec. Engring., Moscow Pedagogical State Inst., 1963; PhD in Biology Sci., Russian Acad. Med. Sci., Moscow, 1975; Tchg. Cert., Moscow Inst. Increase Qualification, 1997. Jr. sci. rschr. Oncology Sci. Ctr., Russian Acad. Med. Sci., 1964-93, sci. rschr., 1993—. Contbr. articles to profl. jours. including Chemistsry and Tech. Fuels and Oils, 1995-2000 (translated from Russian). Brigadier of agitators in election Supreme Soviet of USSR. Home: St Pivchenkova dom 5 kv 63, 121108 Moscow Russia Office: Russian Acad Med Sci, Kachirskoe Rd 24, 115478 Moscow Russia

SERLACHIUS, GUSTAF FREDRIK, forest industry company executive; b. Mänttä, Finland, June 16, 1935; s. Ralph Erik and Ellen Brita Lisa (Idman) S.; m. Eva Mortensen, 1967 (dec. 1986); m. Birgitta Holmberg, 1988. BBA, Helsinki Sch. Econs., Finland, 1959; student, U. Wis., 1956-57; postgrad., Centre d'Etudes Industrielles, Geneva, 1959-60. Dept. head G.A. Serlachius Corp., Finland, 1961-68, asst. gen. mgr., gen. mgr. Kangas Paper Mill, chmn. bd. dir., 1968-86, mem. adminstrv. bd., 1978-86; chmn. bd. Metsä-Serla Oy, Finland, 1987—; mng. dir. G.A. Serlachius Corp., 1969-86; chmn. adminstrv. bd. dirs. and mgmt. The Gosta Serlachius Fine Arts Found., Mantta; bd. dirs. Cen. Assn. Finnish Forest Industries, The Finnish Adv. Bd. Insead, others; vice chmn. bd. UPM-Kymmene Corp., 2000—; governing bd. Pension-Varma Mut. Ins. Co., 1986—, Indsl. Mut. Ins. Co., 1971—, Finnish Marine Ins. Co. Ltd., 1976-90. Mem. Finnboard (chmn. 1990-91), Employers' Assn. of Finnish Forest Industries, Finnish Employers' Assn. (adminstrv. bd. 1972—), Finnish Fgn. Trade Assn., Finnish-Soviet C. of C., Helsinki Stock Exch. Coop. Home and Office: Ehrenströmintie 10A6, 00140 Helsinki Finland

SERMONTI, GIUSEPPE, geneticist; b. Rome, Oct. 4, 1925; s. Alfonso and Letizia (Marchesano) S.; m. Isabella Spada, June 11, 1953; children: Andrea, Fabio, Valeria. Degree in agrl., Pisa (Italy) U., Pisa, Italy, 1947; degree in biology, Rome U., Rome, 1953. Rsch. worker Health Inst., Rome, 1950-67; prof. Camerino (Italy) U., Camerino, 1967, Palermo (Italy) U., Palermo, Italy, 1967-74; prof. Perugia (Italy) U., Perugia, Italy, 1974-85, ret., 1986. Author: Genetics of Antibiotic-Producing Microorganisms, 1969, Fables of Moon, 1986, Fables of Underground, 1989, Fables of Flowers, 1992; co-author: Forgetting Darwin, 1999; editor Rivista di Biologia/Biology Forum, 1980—. V.p. XIV Internat. Congress Genetics, Moscow, 1978; chmn. Internat. Commn. Genetics Indsl. Microorganisms, 1979-88. Mem. Italian Genetical Soc. (pres. 1970-73), Osaka Group (exec. 1987-97). Avocations: astronomy, archeology, tennis. Home: Via Annone 6, 00199 Rome Italy Office: Rivista di Biologia, CP 7214 Roma Nom, 00100 Rome Italy

SERNA ARISTIZABAL, JUAN ALBERTO, business owner; b. El Santuario, Colombia, Aug. 22, 1962; s. Leoncio Alberto and Eumelia (Aristizabal) Serna Salazar. Degree, U. Autonoma Latin Am., Medellin, Colombia, 1987. Mgr. Comml. Ctr., Medellin, 1983-86; pvt. practive fin. assessor Medellin and Bogota, Colombia, 1986-88; owner Cacherreria Noulousa, Medellin, 1988—; dir. Del Periodico Provincial of El Santuario, 1986-89. Counselor Liberal Party, Sl Santuario, 1991. Home: Calle 51 N 49-52, El Santuario Colombia

SERNICKI, JAN KAZIMIERZ, electronic engineer; b. Warsaw, Poland, Apr. 7, 1943; s. Kazimierz Poluchowicz-Sernicki and Anna Dębicka Sernicka; m. Krystyna Elzbieta Łysakowska, July 9, 1970. Master's, Tech. U., Warsaw, 1969, postgrad., 1971-75, DEng, 1976. Electronic engr. Inst. Nuclear Rsch., Swierk, Poland, 1969-71, rsch. engr., 1976-78; sci. worker Joint Inst. Nuclear Rsch., Dubna, Russia, 1978-81; specialist The Andrzej Sołtan Inst. Nuclear Studies, Swierk, 1981—. Contbr. articles to profl. jours. Avocations: recreational activities. Home: Saska 99-4, 03-914 Warsaw Poland Office: The Andrzej Sołtan Inst, Nuclear Studies Nuc Spectro, 05-400 Otwock Swierk, Poland

SERÔDIO, ILÍDIO DE AYALA, civil engineer; b. Pangim, India, Nov. 21, 1945; s. Francisco António and Maria Francisca Diniz (de Ayala) S.; m. Anna Eva Peggy Lundström, June 19, 1970 (div. 1979); m. Maria João Saraiva de Menezes, June 26, 1993; children: Vanessa, Ines, Bernardo. Degree civil engring., Inst. Superior Tech., Portugal, 1969; MS in Civil Engring., Purdue U., 1971; MBA, U. Geneve, 1979. Traffic engr. Junta Autónoma de Estradas, Lisbon, Portugal, 1969-72; head divsn. Junta Autónoma de Estradas, Luanda, Angola, 1972-75; asst. prof. U. Luanda, 1972-75; pres. Consulplano SA, Lisbon, 1975—; dir. Parkman Cons., U.K., 1982-86, AsiaConsult, Macau, 1982-98; gen. mgr. Asia Cons. Pacific Ltd., Hong Kong, 1990—, Global Infocentre Hong Kong Ltd., 1991-94; pres. Profabril SA, Lisbon, 1993—; group pres. PCG Profabril Cons. Group, Lisbon, 1996—; dir. PCG Engring., U.S., 1997—; dir., pres. Proman, Lisbon, 1998—; dir. Cobrapi Engring., Profabril Engring., Brazil, 1998—, China Corp. Ltd., Hong Kong, 2000—; mem. adv. bd. Nat. Computer Ctr. Luanda, 1972-75, Banco Privado Portugues, 1996-99; chmn. AsiaConsult Straits, Malaysia, 1996-97. V.p. Portuguese-Chinese C. C. and Industry, Lisbon, 1996—. Lt. Portuguese Mil., 1972. Recipient O'Farril Hwy. Outstanding award Internat. Rd. Fedn., Washington, 1971. Mem. ASCE, Inst. Transp. Engrs. Am. Club Lisbon, Profl. Engrs. Assn. (bd. dirs.), AIP Portuguese Industry Assn. (bd. dirs. 1997—), Proforum Assn. for Engring. Devel., Lisbon (bd. dirs. 1995—). Avocations: skiing, tennis, golf. Office: Profabril SA, P Alvalade 6, P-1700-076 Lisbon Portugal

SEROK, SHRAGA, retired psychologist, social worker, educator; b. Ostrolenka, Poland, Apr. 10, 1929; arrived in Israel, 1949; s. Eliezer David and Chaya (Shafran) Serok; m. Frieda Novick, Oct. 11, 1955; children: Varda, Liora, Sigal. Diploma Social Work, Tel Aviv Sch. Social Work, 1956; BA in Psychology, Tel Aviv U., 1967, postgrad., 1969-71; PhD, Case Western U., 1975. Diploma gestalt therapist Gestalt Inst. Cleve., 1975. Youth probation officer, supr. Israeli Govt., Tel Aviv, 1956-70; lectr. Tel Aviv U., 1975-81; dir. Faye Ratner Gestalt Program, 1982-2000; lectr. Gen Gurion U., Beer Sheva, Israel, 1982-98; pvt. practice psychotherapy Rishon Lezion, 1975-2000; ret., 2000; cons. group dynamics Israeli Def. Forces, 1975-82; instr. Inst. Productivity Tel Aviv, 1967-72; expert supervision ctrativity and human potential in couples. Author: Human Potential Challenge, 1984, Innovative Applications of Gestalt Therapy, 2000; contbr. articles to profl. jours. Mem. Israeli Union Social Workers, Israeli Assn. Psychotherapy, Am. Psychol. Assn., Internat. Assn. Play Therapy, Cert. Cons. Internat., N.Y. Acad. Scis. Address: 8 Shimshon St, 75270 Rishon Le Zion Israel

SEROTA, NICHOLAS ANDREW, art gallery director; b. Apr. 27, 1946. BA, Cambridge (Eng.) U., 1968; MA, Courtauld Inst. Art, London, 1970. Regional art officer, organizer exhibitions Arts Council Gr. Britain, 1970-73; dir. Mus. Modern Art, Oxford, Eng., 1973-76, Whitechapel Art Gallery, London, 1976-88, Tate Gallery, London, 1988—; mem. visual arts adv. com. Brit. Coun., 1976—, chmn., 1992—; mem. adv. com. Carnegie Internat. Pitts., 1985, 88. Author: Autumn, 1996, Experience or Interpretation: The dilemma of Museums of Modern Art, 1996. Trustee Pub. Art Devel. Trust, 1983-87, Architecture Found., 1991—. Office: Tate Gallery, Millbank, London SW1P 4RG, England*

SEROTA, WENDY ELLEN, tax officer; b. Phila., May 25, 1974; d. Ted K. and Tina R. (Saltzburg) S. BBA in Acctg. and Bus. Law, Temple U., 1996, MBA in Risk Mgmt. & Ins., 1999; postgrad., Bucknell U. Sec., tchr.'s asst. Superior Beginnings, Voorhees, N.J., 1989-95; tax asst., intern First Fidelity (First Union) Bancorp, Phila., 1996; tax officer PNC Pvt. Bank, NA, Phila., 1996—; treas. Temple U. Young Alumni Adv. Coun., Phila., 1997—. Active Phila. Mus. Art, 1996—, U.S. Holocaust Mus., Washington, 1996—; vol. mem. Phila. Flower Show, Pa. Horticulture Soc./PNC Bank, NA, 1997, 98; vol. mem. Summer at the Mann, Phila. Orch./Mann Ctr., 1997, 98. Mem. NAFE, Am. Choral Dirs.' Assn., Banker's Tax Assn., Young Leadership Coun.-So. NJ Fedn., Phila. Estate Planning Coun. (corp.), Pi Alpha Delta (charter). Democrat. Jewish. Avocations: travel, reading, writing short stories and articles, singing in choirs, leisure time at the shore. Home: 1504 Dogwood Dr Cherry Hill NJ 08003-3120 Office: Isdaner & Co LLC Three Bala Plz Bala Cynwyd PA 19004-3484

SEROUR, ALEYA ALY, publishing executive, literary agent; b. Cairo, Mar. 28, 1940; d. Aly and Zeinab Mahmoud Serour; m. Mohamed Wahba Emara, Apr. 19, 1984. BA, Cairo U., 1963; MA in Mass Comm., Am. U. in Cairo, 1978. Editor Franklin Book Programs, Cairo, 1964-68; asst. to dir. Am. U. in Cairo Press, 1969-95, asst. pub. dir., 1995-98, assoc. pub. dir., 1998—; agt. to Nobel Laureate Naguib Mahfouz, Cairo, 1985—; mem. resources com., Am. U. in Cairo, 1979-83; transcriber various confs. Co-author, editor: Cairo Guide, 1975—. Mem. Com. for Dokki (dist. of Cairo) Cmty. Devel., 1993—. Mem. Gezira Sporting Club. Avocations: reading, writing, travel. Office: American U in Cairo Press, 113 Kasr El Aini St, 11511 Cairo Egypt

SÉROUX, PATRICE JEAN, finance company executive; b. Fontainebleau, France, Apr. 10, 1954; s. Jean and Yvette A. (Roubault). MS in Math., U. Bordeaux, 1975, ENSERB degree of engr. in electronics, 1976, DS in Ops. Rsch., 1976; MBA, U. Paris, 1977. Cons. Arthur Andersen, Chgo., 1978, Paris, 1978-81; mgr. Europe hdqrs. DuPont De Nemours, Geneva, Barcelona, Wilm., Del., 1982-89; mng. ptnr. KPMG Peat Marwick, Geneva, 1989—; equity portfolio mgr. London Bus. Sch., 1994; with exec. program strategic cost mgmt. INSEAD, Paris, 1995, with exec. program internat. mktg., 1999. Mil. svc. with French Ministry of Def., Paris, 1977. Office: KPMG, 14 Chemin de Normandie, CH-1211 Geneva 25, Switzerland

SEROV, EDWARD AFANASJEVICH, conductor; b. Moscow, USSR, Sept. 9, 1937; s. Afanasiy Alexeevich and Alexandra (Nikiforova) S.; m. Guenrietta Alexeevna, June 29, 1961; children: Yuriy, Alexey. Student,

Sveshnikov Sch., Moscow, 1944-54, Gnessin Inst., Moscow, 1954-59, Tschajkovsky Conservatory, Kiev, USSR, 1958-61, Rimsky-Korsakov Conservatory, Leningrad, USSR, 1961-64. Condr. Leningrad Philharm., 1961-68, 85-90; founder, chief condr. Uljanovsk (USSR) Philharm., 1968-77, Leningrad Chamber Orch., 1974-85, Volgograd (Russia) Symphony Orch., 1987—; chief condr. Odense (Denmark) Symphony Orch., 1991-96; prof. Leningrad Conservatory (now St. Petersburg Conservatory), 1987—; chief condr. Saratov Philharm., Russia, 1995—. Named People's Artist of Russia by Pres. Russia, Moscow, 1990. Avocations: basketball, mountain climbing. Home: Warschavskaja str 124 kw 95, 196 240 Saint Petersburg Russia Office: Volgograd Rechnoj woksal-131, Central Concert Hall, 400018 Saint Petersburg Russia*

SEROV, VIKTOR ANGUELOV, engineering executive; b. Sofia, Bulgaria, May 2, 1954; s. Angel Georgiev and Tsvetanka Petrova (Damianova) S.; m. Rositza Grozdanova Nikolova, Aug. 12, 1984 (div. 1993); 1 child, Alexander Viktorov; m. Boriana Bojidarova Alexova, Feb. 25, 1995; children: Angela Viktorova, Michel Viktorova. Diploma in engring., Tech. U., Sofia, 1979; magistrar, Econ. U., Sofia, 1985; Doctorate, Mgmt. Acad., Sofia, 1989. Expert Izot Svc., Sofia, 1979-80; chief info. dept. Youth Orgn., Sofia, 1980-85, Municipality of Sofia, 1985-89; chief electronic dept. Nat. Agy. of Quality, Sofia, 1989-90; pres. Vi-Vesta, Sofia, 1990—. Capt. Bulgarian Army, 1972-74. Recipient medals Bulgarian Govt., 1983-85, decorations Bulgarian Army, 1993-94, hon. diploma Israel Inst. Pub. Opinion Mgmt. award, 1997. Mem. Oxford Club (chmns. circle). Avocations: swimming, skiing. Office: Vi Vesta Spa, 16 Lavele St, 1000 Sofia Bulgaria

SERRA, JOSÉ, Brazilian government official; b. 1943; married; 2 children. PhD in Econs., Cornell U. Prof. U Campinas, Sao Paulo, 1978—; economy and planning sec. Govt. of Brazil, Sao Paulo, 1983-86; senator Nat. Assembly, 1986; min. of planning and budget Govt. of Brazil, 1995-96, min. of health, 1998—. Pres. Nat. Union Students, 1963-64; mem. Popular Action; economy and planning sec., 1983-86, dep. Nat. Assembly; sen., Sao Paulo; min. planning, Brazil, 1994—. E-mail: infoasaude.gov.br. Office: Ministry of Health, BL G 5o andar, 70058900 Brasília Brazil

SERRAGLIO, MARIO, architect; b. Bassano, Veneto, Italy, Apr. 13, 1965; came to U.S., 1972; s. Luciano G. and Maria P. (Bellon) S. BS in Architecture, Ohio State U., 1988. Real estate agent Four Star Realty, Columbus, Ohio, 1984—; treas. Columbus Masonry, Inc., 1985-86; v.p. Serraglio Masonry, Inc., Columbus, 1986-87; pres. Serraglio Constrn., Columbus, 1987—; residential designer Gary A. Bruck, SGR, Inc., Columbus, 1988-89, Sullivan Gray Ptnrs., Columbus, 1989-92; project mgr. John Regan Archs., Columbus, 1992-93; prin. Architettura Serraglio, Inc., Reynoldsburg, Ohio, 1995—. Mem. AIA, Nat. Assn. Realtors. Office: Architettura Serraglio 7404 E Main St Reynoldsburg OH 43068-2166

SERRANO, IVONNE, human resources specialist; b. Chihuahua, Mex., Oct. 23, 1960; d. Horacio Serrano and Martha Rodriguez; m. Jose Luis Castro, Nov. 17, 1985; children: Michelle, Paola. Degree in psychology, Chihuahua, 1983; cert. in human resources, ITESM, Juarez, Mex., 1996, cert. in mgmt. devel., 1999. Prodn. supr. Delphi, Juarez, 1984-86, quality coord., 1986-88, tng. supt., 1988-89, prodn. supt., 1989-92; prodn. supt. Cadimex, Juarez, 1993-94, human resources mgr., 1994—; program coord. Day Care Ctr., Chihuahua, 1980-81; vocat. asst. Sec.Tec., Chihuahua, 1981-82; pub. rels. tchr. Tec. Turism, Chihuahua, 1982-83. Recipient Target for Excellence award GM Co., 1985, Leader Auditor award Perry Johnson, 1997. Mem. CANACINTRA, AMAC. Baptist. Avocations: swimming, baking, travel, music, dancing. Office: Cadimex SA de CV, Av Henequen 1269 Parque Ind, Salvacar Juarez Chihuahua 32690, Mexico

SERRANO-MOLINA, JOSE S., pharmacologist; b. San Roque, Cadiz, Spain, Dec. 25, 1933; s. Francisco and Maria (Molina) S.; m. Carmen Martino; children: Maria Isabel, Jose Julian, Miguel Francisco, Maria Del Carmen. MD, Med. Sch. Cadiz, Spain, 1962; PhD in Pharmacology, Marquette U., Milw., 1968. Instr. Med. Sch. Cadiz, 1960-61; asst. prof. Med. Sch. Cali, Colombia, 1962-64; instr. med. sch. Marquette U., Milw., 1965-68; asst. prof. Med. Sch. Valladolid, Spain, 1969-70, assoc. prof., 1971-72; prof. pharmacology, chmn. Med. Sch. Murcia, Spain, 1973-78; dean Med. Sch., Murcia, Spain, 1975-78; prof. pharmacology, chmn. Med. Sch. Seville, Spain, 1979—, vice dean, 1983-86; clin. pharmacol. unit head U. Hosp., Seville, 1979—. Author: Pharmacological Analysis of Myocardial Actions of Beta-Adrenergic Blockers, 1977, (with others) Home Medicine Cases in an Andalousian Urban Population, 1987, Pharmacological Therapy in Geriatry, 1988, Pharmacology Outlines for Students, 1990-98; contbr. chpts. to books including Velázquez Farmacologia; contbr. over 100 articles to profl. jours. Mem. AAAS, Spanish Pharm. Assn. (pres. 1989), Spanish Clin. Pharm. Assn., Brit. Pharm. Soc., Royal Soc. Medicine (London), N.Y. Acad. Scis., Soc. France Pharm. Clin. Roman Catholic. Avocations: reading, swimming, stamp collecting, music listening. Home: Adva Kansas City 34-2-6, Seville 41007, Spain Office: Depto Farmacologia Fac Med, Ave Sanchez Pizjuan 4, Seville 41009, Spain

SERRATTO, MARIA E., pediatric cardiologist, educator; b. Genoa, Italy, Mar. 30; came to U.S., 1962; d. Tito and Gemma (Macaluso) S.; m. Riccardo Benvenuto. MD summa cum laude, U. Genoa, 1955. Diplomate Am. Bd. Pediatrics, Am. Bd. Pediatric Cardiology, Italian Bd. Cardiology. Intern U. Genova (Italy) Hosp., 1955-56; resident Northwestern U., Chgo., 1957-63; mem. attending staff Cook County Children's Hosp., Chgo., 1971—; prof. pediat. (cardiology) U. Ill., Chgo., 1981—, Rush Med. Sch., Chgo., 1994-96; coord. pediatric cardiology Nat. Ctr. for Advanced Med. Edn., Chgo., 1975-98, trustee, 1994-97, dir. pediatric cardiology compass med. edn., 2000—; cons. cardiologist Cardiothoracic Ctr. Monaco, Monte Carlo, 1988—; attending Rush-Presbyn.-St. Luke's Med. Ctr., Chgo., 1994—; trustee Hektoen Inst. for Med. Rsch., Chgo., 1995—, mem. exec. com. bd. dirs., 1998—; attending staff U. Ill. Hosps. Chgo., 1981—, Michael Reese Hosp., Chgo., 1995—, Mercy Hosp., Chgo. Contbr. over 150 articles to med. jours., chpts. to books. Recipient cert. of meritorious svc. Am. Heart Assn., 1965, 84. Fellow Am. Coll. Cardiology, Am. Acad. Pediat., Am. Coll. Chest Physicians; mem. Am. Pediatric Soc., Am. Fedn. for Clin. Rsch., Soc. Pediatric Echocardiography, N.Y. Acad. Scis., Italian Soc. Pediatric Cardiology (hon.), Mario Negri Rsch. Inst. (Milan, rep. for N.Am. internat. heart sch., mem. sci. coun. cardiologia, mem. sci. coun. leadership medica), Sigma Xi Soc. Roman Catholic. Avocations: sailing, opera, concerts, travel. Office: Cook County Children's Hosp 700 S Wood St Chicago IL 60612-3834

SERRE, THIERRY JACQUES, physicist, astronomer, researcher, consultant; b. Rognac, France, Feb. 15, 1964; s. Yves Alexis and Monique (Betti) S. Lic. in physics, Marseilles (France) U., 1986, M Physics, 1987; Diploma of State in Astronomy, Paris Obs., 1989, PhD, 1992. Scientist U. Fla., Gainesville, 1991, rsch. asst., 1993-94; rsch. cons. Paris Obs., 1995-96; spkr. Enrico Fermi Sch. of Physics, Varenna, Italy, 1996. Contbr. articles to sci. jours. including Astronomy and Astrophysic, Phys. Rev. Letters, Astrophys. Jour. With French Air Force, 1988. Rsch. grantee French Rsch. Ministry, 1993, U. Fla., 1994. Mem. Planetary Soc. Avocation: astronomical and science fiction painting. Home: 14 Rue Jean Giono, 13580 La Fare Les Oliviers, France

SERRIE, HENDRICK, anthropology and international business educator; b. Jersey City, July 2, 1937; s. Hendrick and Elois (Edge) S.; m. Gretchen Tipler Ihde, Sept. 3, 1959; children: Karim Jonathan, Keir Ethan. BA with honors, U. Wis., 1960; MA, Cornell U., 1964; PhD with distinction, Northwestern U., 1976. Dir. Solar Energy Field Project, Oaxaca, Mex., 1961-62; instr. U. Aleppo, Syria, 1963-64; asst. prof. Beloit (Wis.) Coll., 1964-69, Calif. State U., Northridge, 1969-70, Purdue U., West Lafayette, Ind., 1970-72, New Coll./U. South Fla., Sarasota, 1972-77; tchr. Pine View Sch., Sarasota, 1978; prof. anthropology, internat. bus. Eckerd Coll., St. Petersburg, Fla., 1978—; dir. internat. bus. overseas programs Eckerd Coll., 1981—; sr. rsch. assoc., Human Resources Inst., St. Petersburg, 1988—. Author, editor: Family, Kinship, and Ethnic Identity Among the Overseas Chinese, 1985, Anthropology and International Business, 1986, What Can Multinationals Do for Peasants, 1994, The Overseas Chinese: Ethnicity in National Context, 1998; writer, dir. films: Technological Innovation, 1962, Something New Under the Sun, 1963; contbr. articles to Wall Street Jour. and Wall Street Jour. Europe. Tchr. Sunday sch., North United Methodist Ch., Sarasota, 1977—. Exxon scholar, So. Ctr. for Internat. Issues, Atlanta, 1980-81; Presdl. fellow Am. Grad. Sch. Internat. Mgmt., 1991; recipient Leavy award, Freedoms Found., Valley Forge, Pa., 1989. Fellow Am. Anthropol. Assn., Soc. Applied Anthropology; mem. So. Ctr. Internat. Issues, Acad. Internat. Bus., Tampa Bay Internat. Trade Coun., Internat. Soc. Intercultural Edn., Tng. and Rsch. Republican. Avocations: singing, drawing, beach walking, cycling, sailing. Home: 636 Mecca Dr Sarasota FL 34234-2713 Office: Eckerd Coll Dept Internat Bus Saint Petersburg FL 33733

SERRY-KAMAL, MORDU, political science/public administration educator; b. Kambia, Sierra Leona, Aug. 25, 1948; came to U.S., 1971; s. Bai Sebora Kamal II and Dora Kamal. BA in Econs., Howard U., 1977, MA in Pub. Affairs, 1979, PhD in Polit. Sci., 1988. Cert. tchr., Ga. Asst. to min. Ministry of Fin., Sierra Leone, 1970-71; salesman The Regal Co., N.Y.C., 1972-74, Washington, 1974-86; adj. prof. Bowie (Md.) State U., 1986-90; grad. prof. Savannah (Ga.) State U., 1991-97, Ga. So. U., Statesboro, 1991-95; tchr. Savannah-Chatham Edn. Bd., 1997—; assoc. grad. faculty mem. Coll. Grad. Studies U. Ctrl. Mich.; referee Southeastern Polit. Review, Ga. State U., 1991-97; mem. com. Savannah State/Ga. So. U., Statesboro, 1991-97; advisor student govt. elections Savannah State U., 1992; mem. adv. bd. Elite/Dushkin Pub., Guilford, Conn., 1996—. Author: American Government, 1996; contbr. articles to profl. jours. Advisor, counselor Univ./H.S., Savannah, 1991—; fin. contbr. United Way, Savannah, 1991-97; "Buddy Bear" mem. Hesse Elem. Sch., Savannah, 1996-97. Recipient Patricia Roberts-Harris grant Housing and Urban Devel., 1992, Cert. of Appreciation, Grad. Assn. Pub. Adminstrn., 1993, Cmty. Work-Study grant Housing and Urban Devel., 1997. Mem. African Polit. Sci. Assn., Ga. Polit. Sci. Assn., Conf. Minority Pub. Adminstrn. Democrat. Avocations: academic discussions, short-wave D-xing, listening to music, helping others solve problems. Home: 249 Bordeaux Ln Savannah GA 31419-2869

SERUDIN, MOHAMMED ZAIN BIN, Brunei government official; b. Aug. 30, 1936. BA in Islamic Laws, al-Azhar U., Cairo, 1963; PhD, IAIN, Jakarta, 1987. Dep. chief Kadi, 1963-65, chief, 1967-70; sec. religious affairs Govt. of Brunei, 1965-67, state religious affairs officer, 1970-86, min. religious affairs, 1986—. Office: Min Religious Affairs, Jalan Elizabeth II, Bandar Seri Begawan 1180, Brunei*

ŠERUGA, MARIJAN, food science educator; b. Bednja, Croatia, Sept. 20, 1947; m. Barnarda Lazanin, Feb. 13, 1971; children: Martina, Matea. Degree in chem. engring., U. Zagreb, Croatia, 1970, MSc in Chemistry, 1975, PhD in Chemistry, 1977; postgrad., U. Manchester, Eng., 1979. Asst. faculty food tech. U. Osijek, Croatia, 1972-78, asst. prof. food tech., 1978-96, assoc. prof., 1996-99, prof., 1999—, vice dean faculty food tech., 1979-83, head dept. chemistry, 1996-97, vice rector, 1997—. Rsch. grantee Ministry of Sci. of Croatia and German Govt., 1996, Austrian Govt., 1998. Mem. Internat. Soc. Electrochemistry (nat. sec. 1997—), Croatian Soc. Chem. Engrs., Croatian Chem. Soc., Nat. Geog. Soc. Avocations: literature, sports, travel. Home: Sjenjak 34, HR-31000 Osijek Croatia Office: U Osijek Dept Chemistry, Kuhačeva 18 POB 709, HR-31000 Osijek Croatia

SERVANT, CHRISTOPHER TERENCE JACKSON, orthopaedic surgeon; b. Croydon, Surrey, Eng., July 3, 1965; s. Terence Edward Henry and Marion Jackie (Jackson) S. BSc with honors, U. London, 1987, MB, BChir, 1990. Sr. ho. officer Royal Nat. Orthopaedic Hosp., Stanmore, Eng., 1992-93, Royal United Hosp., Bath, Eng., 1995-96; specialist registrar Royal United Hosp., Bath, 1996—; med. officer Bath Rugby Club, 1996—. Author: Examination Schemes in Surgery and Orthpaedics, 1999. Fellow Royal Coll. Surgeons Eng.; mem. Brit. Orthopaedic Assn., Brit. Orthopaedic Sports Trauma Assn., Brit. Assn. Sport and Medicine. Home: 19 Symes Park, Bath BA1 4PA, England Office: Royal United Hosp Combe Pk, Bath BA1 3NG, England

SERVENTY, CAROLINE MARY, cultural organization administrator; b. Perth, Australia; d. Alfred William and Mary Ethel (Tolland) Darbyshire; m. Vincent Serventy, Sept. 1, 1955; children: Natasha, Catherine, Matthew. BA, U. Western Australia, 1952. Pres. Australian Fedn. Friends of Mus., 1989-95, World Fedn. Friends of Mus., 1997—; trustee Australian Mus., Sydney, 1976-86; coun. mem. Nat. Mus. Australia, Canberra, 1982-92. Author: (book) Rolf's Walkabout, 1970; co-author: (books) Australian Birds, 1981, Australian Landforms, 1981, Australian Wildlife, 1981, Koalas, 1989. Named to Order of Australia, Commonwealth Govt., 1980. Avocations: reading, camping, traveling, walking. Home and Office: 36 Diamond Rd, 2256 Pearl Beach NSW, Australia

SERVIEN, LOUIS-MARC, COMTE DE BOISDAUPHIN, LORD OF QUENDON, finance company and import-export executive; b. Yverdon-les-Bains, Switzerland, Jan. 8, 1934. Doctorate, Accad. Tiberina, Rome, Italy. Pres., mng. dir. Soc. de Financement SA, Geneva, Compagnie des Grands Crus SA. Author: Mutual Funds, Why Not? A Survey of International Investment Funds, 1968; "Gibraltar: Tax on the Rock" (Revue Premier Monte Carlo, Monaco, No. 17, 1985-86); several publications in German, French, Italian & Spanish; contbr. articles to profl. publs., journalist. Named hon. col. Confederate Air Force, Midland, Tex., Commendatore of the Concordia Order, Brazil, 1974, Commedador of Imperial Orden Hispanica de Carlos V, Spain, 1992. Mem. Internat. Tax Planning Assn., Manorial Soc. Gt. Britain, Diplomat Club Geneva, Chow Chow Club Paris. Home and Office: Quendon Hall, 23 chemin du Levant, CH 1005 Lausanne Switzerland

SERWITZ, MARSHALL DAVID, finance company executive; b. N.Y.C., June 11, 1947; s. Paul and Helen Francis (Dolch) S.; m. Jewel Mondshine Safren, Nov. 4, 1979 (div. Jan. 1991); m. Barbara June Chappell; children: David, Rebecca; step-children: James, Andrew, Robert, Katherine. BS, NYU, 1969. Exec. v.p. Columbia Corrugated Container Corp., Syosset, N.Y., 1969-79; founder Child Rsch. Devel. Inst., Palo Alto, Calif., 1982-88; chmn., co-founder Sullivan & Serwitz, Los Altos, Calif., 1989—. Author: Developing Child/Developing Parent, 1987; contbr. articles to med. jours. Office: 779 Altos Oaks Dr Los Altos CA 94024-5430

SESÉ, LUIS MARIANO, chemistry educator, researcher; b. Madrid, Sept. 18, 1955; s. Mariano and Maria del Carmen (Sánchez) S.; m. Mercedes Mejías, May 11, 1992; 1 child Luis. BS, U. Complutense, Madrid, 1976, MS with honors, 1978, PhD, 1983. Ayudante U. Complutense, 1978-80, encargado, 1980-81; encargado Nat. U. for Distance Edn., Madrid, 1981-82, colaborador, 1982-84, lectr., 1985-87, permanent lectr., 1987—; cons. Amilco, S.A., Coslada, Spain, 1982-84. Author: Metodos Teoricos de la Quimica Fisica, Vol. I, 1990, reprinted, 1994, (with M. Criado) Termodinamica Quimica Molecular, 1990; contbr. articles to profl. jours. With Spanish Coast Artillery, 1978-79. Grantee Nat. Inst. Assistance and Promotion of Students, Madrid, 1977, 78. Mem. Planetary Soc., N.Y. Acad. Scis. Office: Univ Nacl Educ Dist, Fac Scis/U Nacl Educ Dist, C/Senda del Rey 9, 28040 Madrid Spain

SESHAMANI, VENKATESH, economics educator; b. Mumbai, India, June 8, 1947; s. Venkatesh Seshaiyer Shekharipuram and Janaki Sarma Venkatesh; m. Lalitha Lingam, May 5, 1976; children: Sharmishtaa, Shreyas. BA in Econs., U. Bombay, Mumbai, 1968, MA in Econs., 1970; MS in Ops. Rsch., Stanford U., 1974. Lectr., sr. lectr. U. Bombay, Mumbai, 1970-77; sr. lectr., assoc. prof. U. Daressalaam, D'Salaam, Tanzania, 1977-81; assoc. prof., prof. U. Zambia, Lusaka, 1982—; cons. UNICEF, Lusaka, 1986-90, UN Econ. Commn. for Africa, Addis Ababa, Ethiopia, 1987-90, World Bank, Washington, 1993-96, UN Devel. Program, Lusaka, 1996—, Internat. Labor Office, Geneva, 1996. Co-editor: Economic Management in Sub-Saharan Africa, 1997; contbr. articles to profl. jours. Econs. discussant Zambia TV, Lusaka, 1988-93; budget analyst U. Zambia/Swedish Internat. Devel. Agy., Lusaka, 1993—; moderator Interparty Debate, Zacci, Lusaka, 1996. H.H. the Pope scholar U. Bombay, Mumbai, 1968-70; Fulbright fellow Dept. State, U.S. Govt., Calif., 1973-74; vis. rsch. fellow Inst. Developing Econ., Tokyo, 1997. Mem. Zambia-India Friendship Assn., Zambia Tamil Arts and Cultural Assn., Econs. Assn. Zambia. Hindu. Avocations: television viewing, yoga, meditation. Office: Univ Zambia, Great East Rd Box 32379, Lusaka Zambia

SESHAN, SURYA VENKATA, pathologist; b. Rajahmundry, India, Sept. 3, 1952; came to U.S., 1976; d. Lakshminarayana Sastry and Ramana Venkata (Hota) Lanka; m. Thirumoorthi Venkata Seshan, Feb. 23, 1975; children: Karthik Siva, Nandini Lakshmi. Grad., Govt. Med. Coll., 1969, B of Medicine and Surgery, 1974. Intern Med. Coll. Affiliated Hosps., Mysore, India, 1974-75, K.R. Hosp., Mysore, India, 1975; physician Johnston-Willis Hosp., Richmond, Va., 1977-78; resident pathology N.Y. Hosp. Coll., Met. Hosp. Ctr., N.Y.C., 1978-82, chief resident anatomic pathology, 1979-80, chief resident clin. pathology, 1981; assoc. clin. prof. Mt. Sinai Sch. Medicine; clin. prof., dir. labs. U. Medicine and Dentistry N.J., Paterson, N.J.; guest lectr. and cons. in field. Chief editor: Classification of Tubulointerstitial Diseases, 1999; editor: The Kidney in Collagen-Vascular Diseases, 1993; mem. writing com. Classification of Glomerular Diseases, 2d edit., 1994; contbr. articles to profl. jours. Rsch. fellow Renal Pathology fellow Barnert Hosp., 1982-84, Vis. fellow Mt. Sinai Hosp., 1982-84. Fellow Am. Soc. Clin. Pathology, Coll. Am. Pathologists; mem. AMA, Am. Soc. Nephrology, Renal Pathology Soc., Nat. Kidney Found., Internat. Acad. Pathology, Women in Nephrology, N.J. Soc. Pathology. Avocations: Indian classical music, lang. analysis, reading, table tennis. Office: Barnert Hosp Dept Pathology 680 Broadway Paterson NJ 07514-1422

SESHANARAYANA, KOLAR NAGARAJAN, radiologist, consultant; b. Bangalore, Karnataka, India, Apr. 1, 1939; s. Kolar S. Nagarajan and Kolar N. Lalithamma; m. Kolar S. Nirmala, May 26, 1971; children: Balasubramanya. Shivakumar. MBBS, Bangalore Med. Coll., 1962. Resident in radiology Norfolk (Va.) Gen. Hosp., 1964-67; lectr. radiology Bangalore Med. Coll., 1963-64; instr. radiology U. Va. Sch. Medicine, Charlottesville, 1967-68, asst. prof., 1968-69; cons. radiologist C.S.I. Hosp., Bangalore, 1970-83, Sindhi Charitable Hosp., Bangalore, 1984-94, Lakeside Med. Ctr. & Hosp., Bangalore, 1983—. Mem. Indian Radiol. and Imaging Assn. (life, sec. 1977-78, 78-79, pres., 1981-82, Karnataka State Med. Assn., Karnataka State Cricket Assn. Home and Office: X-Ray Ctr, Wilson Gardens, 15 (11/12) 4th Cross, Bangalore 560 027, India

SESOW, PETER ALFRED, social services administrator; b. Springfield, Vt., Jan. 14, 1933; s. John Karol and Vinnie Ola Sesow; m. Beverly Jean Fish, Dec. 19, 1954; children: Patricia, Diane. Ednl. specialist, Ariz. State U., 1969; BS, Castleton State U., 1954; MS, Ariz. State U., 1966, Doctorate, 1978. Cert. edn. Vt., N.Y., Ariz. Tchg. prin. Castleton (Vt.) Schs., 1956-60; tchr. Rutland (Vt.) Schs., 1961-63, Avondale (Ariz.) Schs., 1963-66; tchr. Agua Fria H.S., Avondale, 1966-68, prin., 1972-76; tchr., adminstr. East Greenbush (N.Y.) Schs., 1968-71; prin. Dysart H.S., Peoria, Ariz., 1976-81; ptnr. Hohokam Investments, Avondale, 1981-83; exec. dir. C. of C., Avondale, 1983-87, Cottonwood, Ariz., 1987—; team mem. North CTrl. Evaluation, Phoenix, 1972-79; v.p. Phoenix Metro Group, 1985; pres. Chamber Execs., Phoenix, 1988-89, Travel Industry Assn., Phoenix, 1995, Intra-State Tourism Com., Phoenix, 1996-97; rep. Hwy. Enhancement, Phoenix, 1995—. Author: Instrument for the Observation of Teaching Activites Workshop Coordinators Handbook, 1971, Iinstrument for the Observation of Teaching Activities Director/Consultants Handbook, 1971. sec. New West Twenty, Avondale, 1984; charter mem. Estrella Toastmasters, Avondale, 1984; acitve West Valley Jr. Chamber's, Avondale, 1984; chmn. Am. Cancer Jail-A-Thon, Cottonwood, 1987, 90; vice chmn. Yavapai County United Way, Prescott, Ariz., 1992-93; pres. Family Network Coun., Cottonwood, 1995; bd. mem. Rainbow Acres, Camp Verde, Ariz., 1997—. With U.S. Army, 1955-56. Named Hon. Chpt. Farmer, Dysart H.S., Peoria, 1979. Mem. Verde Valley Rotary Club (pres. 1987-2000, Paul Harris fellow 1989), Phi Delta Kappa. Republican. Baptist. Avocations: hunting, fishing, traveling. E-mail: cottonwoodchamber@sedona.net. Home: 4015 Pueblo Rd Cottonwood AZ 86326-5738 Office: Cottonwood C of C 1010 S Main St Cottonwood AZ 86326-4606

SESSA, SALVATORE, orthopaedic surgeon; b. Naples, Italy, Aug. 27, 1960; s. Amedeo and Maria (Ricciardi) S. MD, U. Naples, 1984. Resident Orthopaedics Dept., Naples, Italy, 1984-88, Nancy, France, 1988-92; orthopaedic surgeon Paris, 1993—; cons. in field. Fellow Pediatric Orthopaedics Dept., Nancy, 1989-91, Orthopaedic Dept., 1992. Mem. SOFCOT, ESDS, GES. Roman Catholic. Avocations: tennis, football, collecting model cars. Home: 122 Rue De Villiers, 92300 Levallois Perret, France Office: 19 Rue Théodore Banville, 75017 Paris France

SESSIONS, BARBARA C., business development director, lawyer; b. St. Johns, Mich., Jan. 23, 1961; d. John C. and Patricia H. (Hyland) Cary; m. Rex. L. Sessions, Oct. 10, 1989; 1 child, Isabel P. BA in English, U. Mich., 1983; JD, DePaul U., 1986. Bar: Ill. Comml. litigator Hinshaw & Culbertson, Chgo., 1986-90; sr. acct. exec. Edelman Pub. Rels. Worldwide, N.Y.C., 1990-91; mgr. mktg. and comms. Skadden, Arps, Slate, Meagher & Flom, N.Y.C., 1991-94; dir. bus. devel. Winston & Strawn, Chgo., 1994—. Mem. Jr. League, N.Y.C. 1990-94, Chgo., 1989-99. Mem. Law Mktg. Assn. (pres., pres-elect 1998, bd. dirs. 1996—), Info. Innovators (editl. bd.). Fax: 312-558-5700. Office: Winston & Strawn 35 W Wacker Dr Chicago IL 60601-1614

SESSIONS, DAVID FRANCIS, retired insurance industry executive; b. Reading, Berkshire, Eng., Oct. 11, 1934; s. Francis Arthur and Florence Elizabeth (Young) S.; m. Patrice Ernestine Phyllis Farnsworth, July 17, 1965; children: Kevin Francis John, Christopher Leslie Farnsworth, Mark Stephen Paul, Patrick David Miles. From jr. clk. Sun Life Assurance Soc., Reading, Eng.; supr. clk. Sun Life Assurance Soc., London; chief clk. Sun Life Assurance Soc., Bradford, Eng., 1968-76; supt. Sun Life Assurance Soc., Bristol, Eng., 1976-86, jour. editor, 1986-92, ret., 1992—. Author: The Early Rapid Cancelling Machines of Canada, 1982, Philatelic Fantasies of British North America 1860-1910, 1999; editor: Maple Leaves jour., 1986—, Stamp News jour., 1991-93. Fellow Royal Philatelic Soc., Can. Philatelic Soc. Gt. Britain (jour. editor 1986—); mem. Chartered Ins. Ins. (assoc.), Worthing Philatelic Soc. (pres. 1997-99). Avocations: philately, postal history. Home: 31 Eastergate Green, Rustington BN16 3EN, England

SESSIONS, JUDITH ANN, librarian, university library dean; b. Lubbock, Tex., Dec. 16, 1947; d. Earl Alva and Anna (Mayer) S. BA cum laude, Cen. Fla. U., 1970; MLS, Fla. State U., 1971; postgrad., Am. U., 1980, George Washington U., 1983. Head libr. U. S.C., Salkehatchie, 1974-77; dir. Libr. and Learing Resources Ctr. Mt. Vernon Coll., Washington, 1977-82; planning and systems libr. George Washington U., Washington, 1981-82, asst. univ. libr. for adminstrn. svcs., acting head tech. svcs., 1982-84; univ. libr. Calif. State U., Chico, 1984-88; univ. libr., dean of libr. Miami U., Oxford, Ohio, 1988—; cons. Space Planning, S.C., 1976, DataPhase Implementation, Bowling Green U., 1982, TV News Study Ctr., George Washington U., 1981; asst. prof. Dept. Child Devel., Mt. Vernon Coll., 1978-81; mem., lectr. U.S.-China Libr. Exch. Del., 1986, 91; lectr., presenter in field; mem. coord. com. OhioLink Adv. Coun., 1995—, v.p., 1996, 97, chair, 1998-2000; mem. gov. bd. OhioLink, exec. com., 1998—; mem. OCLC Users Coun., 1998—; convenor Pub. Acad. Libr. Group, 1999-2000. Contbr. articles, book revs. to profl. jours. Trustee Christ Hosp., Cin., 1990-94, Deaconness Gamble Rsch. Ctr., Cin., 1990-94, OhioNet, 1990-94, treas. 1993; bd. dirs. Hamilton (Ohio) YWCA, 1994-98, pres., 1995-96, v.p., 1996-97, 97-98; mem. OCLC user's coun., 1998—. Recipient award for outstanding contbn. D.C. Libr. Assn., 1979; rsch. grantee Mt. Vernon Coll., 1980; recipient Fulbright-Hayes Summer Travel fellowship to Czechoslovakia, 1991. Mem. ALA (Olofson award 1978, councillor-at-large policy making group 1981-94, coun. com. on coms. 1983-84, intellectual freedom com. 1984-88, directions and program rev. com. 1989-91, fin. and audit subcom. 1989-90, mem. exec. bd. 1989-94, mem. del. to Zimbabwe Internat. Book Fair 1997), Assn. Coll. and Rsch. Librs. (editorial bd. Coll. and Rsch. Librs. jour. 1979-84, nominations and appointments com. 1983-85, faculty status com. 1984-86), Libr. and Info. Tech. Assn. (chair legis. and regulation com. 1980-81), Libr. Adminstrn. and Mgmt. Assn. (bd. dirs. libr. orgn. and mgmt. sect. 1985-87), Calif. Inst. Librs. (v.p., pres. elect 1987-88), Mid-Atlantic Regional Libr. Fedn. (mem. exec. bd. 1982-84), Jr. Mems. Round Table (pres. 1981-82), Intellectual Freedom Round Table (sec. 1984-85), Freedom to Read Found. (trustee 1984-88, v.p. 1985-86, treas. 1986-87, pres. 1987-88), Rotary, Beta Phi Mu. Home: 45 Waters Way Hamilton OH 45013-6324 Office: Miami U Edgar W King Oxford OH 45056

SESSLER, GERHARD MARTIN, communications technology educator; b. Rosenfeld, Germany, Feb. 15, 1931; s. Martin and Else (Fischer) S.; m.

Renate Brigitte Schulz, Dec. 9, 1961; children: Cornelia, Christine, Gunther. Diplom, U. Goettingen, 1957, DrRerNat, 1959. Mem. tech. staff Bell Labs., Murray Hill, N.J., 1959-65, supr., 1965-75; prof. electroacoustics Tech. U. Darmstadt, W.Ger., 1975—, dean dept. elec. comms., 1976-77, 89-90. Editor: E;ectrets, 1980, 3d edit., 1999, Procs. of 5th Internat. Symposium on Electets, 1985; contbr. articles to profl. jours.; inventor electret microphone, 1962. Recipien Callinan award Electrochem. Soc., 1970, Patent Recognition award AT&T, 1992, Heimholtz award German Acoustical Soc., 1983, Helmholtz-Rayleigh Interdisciplinary medal Acoustical Soc. Am., 1997; inducted into Nat. Inventors Hall of Fame, Akron, Ohio, 1999. Fellow IEEE (Sr. award 1971, Thomas W. Dakin award 1986), Acoustical Soc. Am., Am. Phys. Soc.; mem. Dielectrics Soc. (Gt. Britain), German Phys. Soc., Nachrichtentechnische Gesellschaft, Deutsche Gesellschaft fuer Chemisches Apparatewesen. Home: Fichtestrasse 30 B, D-64285 Darmstadt Germany Office: Tech U Darmstadt, Merckstrasse 25, D-64283 Darmstadt Germany

SESSOMS, ALLEN LEE, academic administrator, former diplomat, physicist; b. N.Y.C., Nov. 17, 1946; s. Albert Earl and Lottie Beatrice (Leff) S.; m. Csilla Manette von Csiky, Apr. 18, 1990; children: Manon Elizabeth, Stephanie Csilla. BS, Union Coll., Schenectady, N.Y., 1968; PhD, Yale U., 1972; DSc (hon.), Union Coll., 1998. Sci. associate CERN, Geneva, Switzerland, 1973-78; asst. prof. physics Harvard U., Cambridge, Mass., 1974-81; sr. tech. advisor OES, State Dept., Washington, 1980-82; dir. Office Nuclear Tech. & Safeguards, State Dept., Washington, 1982-87; counselor for sci. and tech. U.S. Embassy, Paris, 1987-89; polit. minister, counselor U.S. Embassy, Mexico City, 1989-91, dep. chief of mission, 1991-93; exec. v.p., v.p. for acad. affairs U. Mass. Sys., Boston, 1993-95; pres. CUNY Queens Coll., Flushing, N.Y., 1995—; mem. adv. com. U.S. Sec. Energy; mem. NCAA Pres. Coun., 1996-2000. Contbr. articles to profl. jours. Adv. com. mem. U.S. Sec. of Energy; bd. dirs. Milestone Fund, Drawing Ctr., Big Apple Circus; mem. adv. coun. Toda Internat. Ford Found. travel/study grantee, 1973-74; Alfred P. Sloan Found. fellow, 1977-81; recipient Wilbur Cross medal Yale Grad. Sch. Alumni, 1999, Medal of Highest Honor, Soka U., 1999; officer dans l'Order des Palmes Académiques, 1999. Mem. AAAS, Am. Phys. Soc., N.Y. Acad. Sci., Cosmos Club.

SESTA, HILARY SOPHIA, actress, writer; b. London, Aug. 19, 1931; d. Don and Lily (Rosenberg) S.; m. Norman Bernard Moss, July 21, 1963; children: Paul, Tony. Matriculation, Burlington, London, 1948; student, The Studio Drama Sch., London, 1949-51. Freelance journalist New Society, 1985, Observer Mag., 1995, Observer Newspaper, 1996, Guardian Newspaper, 1998, Observer Newspapers, 1996, O. Actress under contract Nottingham (Eng.) Playhouse, 1997, Large Scale Films, Leicester, Eng., 1999, Big Bear Films, Eng., 1999, Ind. TV, Eng., 1999; 2000; films include Jabberwocky, Same Dog Whitewashed, Esther Kahn, 2000, Night Creatures, 2000; tv films include Darling Buds of May, 1998, Oliver TWist, 1999, Last of the Summer Wine, Jonathan Creek, 2000, Mother Teresa; commercials. Elected mem. Cmty. Health Coun., London, 1976. Mem. Brit. Actors Equity (mem. com. 1995-2000), Actors' Ctr. Liberal Democrat. Jewish. Avocations: reading, theatre, cinema, tv. Office: c/o June Epstein, 62 Compayne Gans, NW6 3RY London England

ŠESTÁK, JAROSLAV, chemistry educator, scientist; b. Drzkov, Jablonec, Czech Republic, Sept. 25, 1933; s. Antonín and Zofie (Havlova) S.; m. Věra Zelenkóva, June 1, 1969; children: Elizabeth, Pavel. BSc, Chemistry Coll., Praha, Czech Republic, 1957; M in Engring., Inst. Chemistry, Praha, Czech Republic, 1962; PhD, Inst. Physics, Praha, Czech Republic, 1967; DSc, Inst. Chemistry, Praha, Czech Republic, 1990. Guest scientist Nuclear Ctr., Studsvik, Sweden, 1968-69; asst. prof. U. Mo., Rolla, 1969-70; prin. scientist Inst. Physics, Praha, 1971-77, sr. scientist, 1977—; program chair Internat. Conf. Thermal Analysis, Bratislava, Slovakia, 1985; prof. Pardub (Czech Republic) U., 1993—; vis. prof. Cordoba (Argentina) U., 1992, Kyoto (Japan) U., 1996; prof. Charles U., Praha, 1996—; vice dir. Inst. Fundamental Studies Charles U., Praha, 1998—; vis. prof. NYU in Prague, 2000—; lectr. in field. Author: Thermophysical Properties, 1984, Teoreticeskij Analyz, 1987; co-author: Kinetic Phase Diagrams, 1991; editor: Specialni Technologie, 1993, Crystallization of Glasses, 1996; editor Thermochimica Acta, 1971-97, Jour. Thermal Analysis, 1986—, Jour. Mining and Metallurgy; contbr. articles to profl. jours. Councilor Internat. Fedn. Thermal Analysis, 1988—; city councilor City Govt., Praha, 1994-98. Recipient Mettler award in thermal analysis N.Am. Thermal Analysis Soc., 1974, Kurnakov medal in Chemistry, Moscow, 1985, Bodenheimer award in chemistry, Jerusalem, 1988, Internat. Fed. Thermal Analysis and Calorimetry/Thermal Analysis award in thermal analysis, Hatfield, Eng., 1992, Hanus medal in chemistry, Praha, 1997, Heyrovsky medal in chemistry Acad. Sci., 1999. Fellow Internat. Fedn. on Thermal Analysis; mem. Czech Chem. Soc. Conservative. Czechoslovak Husite. Avocations: mountaineering, photography. Home: 3 V Strani, 15000 Praha Czech Republic Office: Acad Scis, 10 Cukrovarnicka, 16253 Praha Czech Republic

ŠESTÁK, JIŘÍ VLADIMÍR, mechanical engineering educator; b. Brno, Czechoslovakia, Oct. 4, 1930; s. Antonín and Vlasta (Bumbalová) S.; m. Alena Komárková, Nov. 4, 1959; 1 child, Petra. MSc, Czechoslovakia Tech. U., Prague, 1954, PhD in Mech. Engring., 1965. Asst. prof. mech. engring. Czechoslovakia Tech. U., Prague, 1955-68, assoc. prof., 1969-88, dean faculty of mech. engring., 1990-91; mem. Czech Com. for Sci. Degrees, Govt. of Czech. Republic, Prague, 1990—; vis. prof. U. Toronto, Ontario, Can., 1982-83. Author, co-author, editor, books, textbooks, jour. articles in field. Sworn interpreter of English lang. Mcpl. Ct., Prague, 1967—. Named Sr. Rsch. fellow, Ford Found. U. Toronto, Can., 1966-67; recipient Felber Gold medal Czech Tech. Univ. in Prague, 1990. Mem. Czecoslovak Group of Rheology (chmn. 1982—), Czech. Soc. for Adv. Tech. Lit. (vice chmn. 1991—), Soc. Rheology U.S. Roman Catholic. Office: Fakulta strojni Czech Tech U, Technická 4, 166 07 Prague Czech Republic

SESTÁK, ZDENĚK, plant physiologist; b. Prague, Aug. 4, 1932; s. Frantisek and Marie (Kotorova) S.; m. Milada Vojkovska, Apr. 4, 1964 (dec.); children: Jana, Jiri, Alena. BS, Dr. Charles U., 1956; DSc, Czechoslovak Acad. Sci., 1981. Sci. documentalist Czech. Acad. Agrl. Sci., Prague, 1956-57; scientist Inst. Exptl. Botany, Czech. Acad. Sci., Prague, 1961—; dept. head Czech. Acad. Sci., Prague, 1987-99, dep. dir., 1990-94; lectr. Charles U., Prague, 1966-76, 94—, South Bohemian U., Ceske Budejovice, 1994—, Masaryk U., Brno, 1998—. Exec. editor: Photosynthetica, 1967-90, editor-in-chief, 1991—; author, editor: Metody Studia Fotosyntheticke Produkce Rostlin, 1966, Plant Photosynthetic Production: Manual of Methods, 1971, Photosynthesis During Leaf Development, 1985, Photosynthesis Bibliography Vols. 1-25, 1974-98, Jak Psat a Prednaset o Vede, 1999; contbr. articles to profl. jours. Fellow Europaische Akademie fur Umweltfragen, Club of Friends of Arts Czech Republic (exec. com.); mem. Am. Soc. for Photobiology, European Assn. Sci. Editors. Roman Catholic. Avocations: arts and crafts, travel, world history. Home: Zvonkova 2884, CZ-10600 Prague 6 Czech Republic Office: Inst Exptl Botany Acad Sci Czech Republic, Na Karlovce 1A, CZ16000 Prague 6 Czech Republic

ŠESTÁKOVÁ, VĚRA, physical technologist; b. Praha, Czech Republic, Apr. 17, 1945; d. Vladimir and Zdeňka (Viznerova) Zelenka; m. Jaroslav Šesták, Sept. 25, 1938; children: Elizabeth, Pavel. M in Engring., Inst. Chemistry, Praha, 1968; MS, Mo. U., 1971. Rschr. Nuclear Ctr., Studsvik, Sweden, 1969; scientist Inst. Physics, Praha, 1971-82, prin. scientist, 1982—; bus. asst. Mumieipale House of Prague, 1998—; bus. asst. Motorola, Praha, 1995—. Co-author: Specialni Technologie, 1993. Roman Catholic. Avocations: mountaineering, dancing. Home: 3 V Strani, 15000 Praha Czech Republic Office: Acad Scis, 10 Cukrovarnicka, 16200 Praha Czech Republic

SESTAN, BRANKO, orthopedic surgeon, consultant; b. Rijeka, Croatia, Sept. 30, 1961; s. Anton and Milena Sestan; m. Loredana Misgur, Aug. 2, 1986; children: Marko, Mia. MD, Med. Faculty, Rijeka, Croatia, 1986, MS, 1992; DSc, Med. Faculty, 1994; postgrad., Oxford U., 1992-93; specialist in orthopedic surgery, Zagreb U., 1996. Med. doctor Emergency Svc., Rijeka, 1986-89; resident in orthopedic surgery Orthopedic Clin. Hosp., Rijeka, 1991-92; resident Oxford U. Nuffield Orthopedic Center, 1992-93; resident Orthopedic Clin. Hosp., Zagreb, 1994-96, cons. in orthopedic surgery, 1996—, head of hosp. dept., 1997—, asst. prof., 1998—. Patentee in field. Girdlestone Meml. scholarship in Orthopedic Surgery, 1992-93; scholarship Austrian Ministry of Scis. Mem. N.Y. Acad. Sci., Girdlestone Orthopedic Soc., Croatian-Austrian Soc., Croatian Orthopaedic Soc., Croatian Soc. for Children's Orthopedics, Croatian Med. Soc. Avocation: yachting. Office: Orthopaedic Clin Hosp, M Tita 1, HR-51415 Lovran Croatia

SESTIER, ANDRÉS, mathematician, educator; b. Nogales, Vera Cruz, Mexico, July 23, 1939; s. Jacques and Yvonne (Bouclier) S. B of Math., Nat. U. Mexico, 1963; M of Math., Poly. Inst. of Mexico, 1968. Instr. U. Mexico, 1962-63; asst. U. Md., 1963-64; prof. Nat. Poly. Inst. of Mexico, 1966-71, U. de los Andes, Venezuela, 1971-72, U. Anahuac, Mexico, 1984; translator, cons. Compañia Editorial Continental, Mexico, 1970-80; prof. U. Autonoma Metropolitana, Iztapalapa, Mexico, 1980—; translator Fondo de Cultura Economica, Mexico, 1986. Author: Historical Documents of Mathematics, 1981, History of Mathematics, 1987; contbr. articles to profl. math. jours. Mem. Am. Math. Soc., Mexican Math. Soc. Avocations: literature, movies, mountain climbing, travel, swimming. Home: Dakota 422 Dept 1, 03810 Mexico City DF, Mexico Office: U Autonoma Metropolitana, Dept Math, Iztapalapa Mexico City DF, Mexico

SESTRIC, ANTHONY JAMES, lawyer; b. St. Louis, June 27, 1940; s. Anton and Marie (Gasparovic) S.; m. Carol F. Bowman, Nov. 24, 1966; children: Laura Antonette, Holly Nicole, Michael Anthony. Student, Georgetown U., 1958-62; JD, Mo. U., 1965. Bar: Mo. 1965, Minn. 1996, U.S. Ct. Appeals (8th cir.) 1965, U.S. Ct. Appeals (7th cir.) 1984, U.S. Dist. Ct. Mo. 1966, U.S. Dist. Ct. (no dist.) Tex. 1985, U.S. Dist. Ct. Ill. 1994, U.S. Tax Ct. 1969, U.S. Supreme Ct. 1970, U.S. Claims Ct. 1986. Law clk. U.S. Dist. Ct., St. Louis, 1965-66; ptnr. Sestric, McGhee & Miller, St. Louis, 1966-77, Fordyce and Mayne, 1977-78, Sestric & Garvey, 1978-96, Sestric Law Firm, St. Louis, 1996—; spl. asst. to Mo. atty. gen., St. Louis, 1968; mem. Fed. Jud. Selection Commn., 1993, U.S. Jud. Selection Commn., 1993-94; gen. chmn. 22nd jud. cir. bar com., 1995. Contbr. articles to profl. jours. Hearing officer St. Louis Met. Police Dept.; active St. Louis Air Pollution Bd. Appeals and Varience Rev., 1966-73, chmn., 1968-73; active St. Louis Airport Commn., 1975-76; dist. vice-chmn. Boy Scouts Am., 1970-76; bd. dirs. Full Achievement, Inc., 1970-77, Legal Aid Soc. St. Louis, 1976-77, Law Libr. Assn. St. Louis, 1976-78, Thomas Dunn Memls., 1995-98, Marquette Learning Ctr., 1995-98; v.p. bd. St. Elizabeth Acad., 1985-86;. Mem. ABA (state chmn. judiciary com. 1973-75, cir. chmn. com. condemnation, zoning and property use 1975-77, standing com. bar activities 1982-88), Nat. Conf. Bar Pres.'s (exec. coun. 1987-90), Mo. Bar Assn. (vice-chmn. young lawyers sect. 1973-76, bd. govs. 1974-77, chmn. law practice mgmt. com. 1997-99), Bar Assn. Met. St. Louis (chmn. young lawyers sect. 1974-75, exec. com. 1974-83, 94-95, pres. 1981-82, bd. govs. 1995-98, chmn. survey com. 1999). Home: 3967 Holly Hills Blvd Saint Louis MO 63116-3135 Office: Sestric Law Firm 801 N 2nd St Saint Louis MO 63102-2560

SETFORD, GEORGE A., information systems company executive; b. New Rochelle, N.Y., July 13, 1948; s. George John and Cecelia (Guida) S.; m. Alida Russo, July 3, 1970 (div. 1999); 1 child, Jessica Lyn. BA, Fairleigh Dickinson U., 1970, MA, 1972. Sales mgr. Eden Inc., N.Y.C.; ptnr., v.p. Transaction Info. Sys., N.Y.C. Avocations: golf, chess, antiques. Office: 115 Broadway Fl 20 New York NY 10006-1604

SETH, ANDREW, industry executive, educator, writer; b. Cardiff, South Wales, May 21, 1937; arrived in England, 1957; s. George and Jessie May (Dods) S.; m. Edith Agnes Elizabeth Howlin, Sept. 17, 1962; children: Patrick, Christopher, Stephen, Toby. MA, Jesus Coll., Oxford, England, 1960; student, Harvard U., 1981-82; D in Bus. Studies (hon.), Kingston (England) U., 1993. Exec. v.p. mktg. Lever Brothers., N.Y.C., 1982-86; chmn., CEO Lever Brothers, England, 1992-95; COO Unilever Detergents, London, 1986-90; dir. Lever Europe, Brussels, Belgium, 1990-92; non-exec. dir. Added Value Cons., Hampton, England, 1995—; exec. dir. Richmond (England) Events, 1996—, Tempus PLC, London, 1996—; chmn. Kingston (England) U., 1995—; v. chmn. Dulwich Coll. Govs., England, 1998—; bd. dirs. Coop. Ireland. Author: The Grocers, 1999; broadcaster BBC Radio/TV, 1994-2000; lectr. in field; contbr. articles to profl. jours. Gov. Royal Shakespeare Theatre, England, 1997—. Fellow Royal Soc. Arts; mem. Consumers Assn. of Great Britain (bd. coun. 1995-97), Nat. Campaign for Learning (United Kingdom chpt., bd. mem. 1994-97), United Oxford and Cambridge Univ. Club, Royal Blackheath Golf Club, Beckenham Cricket Club, Marylebone Cricket Club. Mem. Ch. of England. Avocations: reading, theatre, family, travel, sports. Home: Great Bainden Picidally Ln, SE39SQ Mayfield, E. Sussex England Office: Added Value Rivermead, 6 Lower Teddington Rd, KT14ER Hampton Wick England

SETH, CHANDER MOHAN, forestry researcher; b. Jammu, India, Mar. 2, 1949; s. Thaker Dass and Krishna Devi (Padha) S.; m. Asha Devi, Feb. 28 1979; children: Rishav, Saruti. BSc, GGM Sci. coll., Jammu, India, 1969; MSc, Kashmir U., Srinagar, India, 1975; PhD, Jammu U., 1994. Divsnl. mgr. S.F.C., Doda, India, 1987-90; divsnl. forest officer Dept. Forestry, Nowshera, India, 1990-93; jt. dir. SFRI Dept. Forestry, Jammu, 1993-96, dir. SFRI, 1996, chief forester working plan, 1996-97, chief forester rsch., 1997-98; chief forester West Cir. Jammu, 1998—. Contbr. articles to profl. jours. Recipient FNRS award Internat. Soc. Conservators and Explorers, 1995, Prof. William Schlich award Oxford (Eng.) U., 1977. Mem. Indian Inst. Pub. Adminstrn. (life), World Wide Fund for Nature-India (dir. 1995—), Commonwealth Forestry Assn. (life), Helpage India (life), Lion's Club Internat. Jammu Tawi (v.p. 1997-98, pres. 1998-99, immediate past pres. 1999-2000, region chmn. environment dist. 321-D 1999), Youth Hostel Assn. India (life, state coord. environment 1999). Sufi. Avocations: mountaineering, photography, horseback riding, painting, gardening. Home: 59 A/B Gandhi Nagar, Jammu 180004, India Office: State Jammu Kashmir Dept, Forestry Dogra Hall Exch Rd, Jammu 180001, India

SETH, SHASHIKANT SURAJMAL, plastic industry executive; b. Bombay, June 27, 1944; s. Surajmal Shankarlal and Sohanben S.; m. Rajshree Seth, May 8, 1970; children: Shrish S., Harish S., Manish S. Ptnr. Platic Mfg. Unit, Bombay, 1965—.

SETHI, NARESH, property investor, accountant, management consultant, educator; b. New Delhi, Oct. 22, 1952; arrived in Eng., 1969; s. Yash Dev and Shanta (Multani) S.; m. Rohini Sahi, Dec. 11, 1981 (div. Aug. 1996); 1 child, Ishaan Yash. BSc with honors, Newcastle (Eng.) U., 1975, MSc, 1979; MBA, Cranfield U., 1984. Trainee acct. Levy Gee, London, 1979-82; propr. Investland, London, 1984-89; mng. dir., property developer London, 1985-89; prin. N. Sethi, London, 1990—; mng. dir. Alfacrest Ltd., London, 1995-98; part-time lectr. Schiller Internat. U., London, 1996—. Fellow Inst. Cost and Exec. Accts. (assoc.); mem. Inst. Dirs. Inst. Mgmt. Mem. Labor Party. Hindu. Avocations: swimming, walking, traveling, chess, cinema. Home and Office: 31 Leyborne Ave, W Ealing London W13 9RA, England

SETHI, PRAHLAD KUMAR, neurologist, consultant; b. Pindigheb, Cambelpur, India, Oct. 14, 1939; s. Ram Prakash and Veera Wali (Sahani) S.; m. Shashi Kala Bhushan, Sept. 8, 1967; children: Neetika, Nitin. MBBS, All India Inst. Med. Scis., 1962, MD, 1969; DSc, Shiva Ji U., India, 1998. Resident in neurology SUNY, Buffalo, 1971-73; neurologist Command Hosp., Lucknow, India, 1973-77, Calcutta, India, 1977-83; neurologist, head. dept. Army Hosp., Delhi, India, 1983-86; sr. cons., coord. tchg., chmn. Sir Gangaram Hosp., 1986—; chmn. neurology Vimans, New Delhi, 1993-95. Contbr. articles to profl. jours. Pres. Indian Epilepsy Trust, 1998—. Lt. col. Indian Army, 1963-83. Recipient Vishist Sewa medal Pres. India, 1960. Mem. Def. Svcs. Officers Inst., Habitat Ctr. Avocations: reading, writing. Home: 104 Nav Jiwan Vihar, New Delhi 110017, India Office: Sir Gangaram Hosp, Sir Gangaram St, New Delhi 110060, India

SETHI, RAJINDER SINGH, chemist; b. Nowshera, India, Feb. 1, 1938; arrived in U.K., 1966; s. Attar Singh and Nikki (Madan) S.; m. Harbans Kaur Ahuja, Jan. 12, 1969; children: Janet, Rushmi. BS in Chemistry with honors, Delhi U., 1960, MS in Chemistry, 1962, PhD in Phys. Chemistry, 1966. Chartered chemist. Rsch. fellow Delhi U., 1962-66; postdoctoral fellow Imperial Coll., London, 1966-70; sr. scientist Plessey Co. Ltd., Northants, U.K., 1970-73, prin. scientist, 1973-76, sr. prin. scientist, 1976-84, chief chemist, 1984-90; chief chemist GEC-Marconi Material Tech., Northants, U.K., 1990-98; sr. rsch. assoc. inst. biotechnology U. Cambridge, Cambridge, U.K., 1998—; indsl. advisor Sch. of Natural and Environ. Scis., Coventry (U.K.) U., 1993-96, indsl. PhD supr., 1985-94; indsl. ptnr. Inst. Biotech., U. Cambridge, U.K., 1984-91, Brunel U., West London, U.K., 1992-96. Author: (chpt.) Special Polymers for Electronics and Optoelectronics, 1995; contbr. articles to profl. jours.; patentee in field. Mem. Protcol, Northampton, U.K., 1972—. Fellow Royal Soc. Chemistry U.K. (chartered), UK Parliament Soc. Link (hon. rep.); mem. Electrochem. Soc. USA, Internat. Union Pure and Applied Chemistry. Avocations: photography, table tennis, jazz music, gardening. Office: Inst. Biotech. U. Cambridge, Tennis Ct Rd, Cambridge CB2 1QT, England

SETHI, RAMESH KUMAR, accountant; b. Nairobi, Kenya, Dec. 27, 1943; arrived in U.K., 1965; s. Pyare Lal and Shanti Devi (Bhalla) S.; m. Suresh Kumari Parmar, Oct. 7, 1965; children: Ashwin Kumar, Sunita, Punam, Rajesh Atul. Chartered cert. acct.; registerd auditor; chartered mgmt. acct. Sr. asst. auditor Midlands Electricity Bd., Birmingham, Eng., 1966-67; sr. auditor South Wales Electricity Bd., Cardiff, 1967-70; cost acct. Anglo Am. Corp., Chingola, Zambia, 1970-73; sys. auditor Forward Trust Group Ltd., Birmingham, 1973-79, audit mgr., 1979-81, chief internal auditor, 1981-86, dir. divsn. audit, 1985-87; head internal audit U.K. Banking, Midland Bank, 1987-88; fin. dir. Halfords, 1988-90; exec. v.p., group fin. dir. Transax Fin. Svcs. Ltd., 1990-91; prin. Sethi Assocs., CPAs, 1990-92; mng. ptnr. Sethi and Sethi, 1992—. Contbr. articles to profl. jours. Fellow Chartered Inst. Mgmt. Accts. (accredited; dist. exec. com. 1979—, chmn. dist. soc. Birmingham 1990-92, pres. Birmingham dist. br. 1992-94, v.p. 1994-96, CIMA Inst. plaque 1996), Assn. Chartered Cert. Accts.; mem. Inst. Chartered Secs. and Adminstrs. (chartered sec.), Inst. Mgmt. Svcs. (chmn. Birmingham dist. 1979-82), Brit. Inst. Mgmt., Inst. Internal Auditors (U.K. coun. 1982-84, dist. chmn. 1982-83), Assn. Internat. Accts. (hon. sec. Midlands region 1974-85), Orgn. Methods Soc. Zambia (founder 1970, chmn. 1970-73), Civil Justice Assn. (pres. 1965), Chingola Hindu Assn. (hon. sec. 1972), Shri Geeta Bhawan Mandir (life; hon. auditor 1975-91, chmn. bd. trustees 1991-96, pres. 1998—), Greenlands Assn. of Henley Mgmt. Coll. (life), Egbaston Priory Club. Hindu. Home: 9 Woodbourne Rd Edgbaston, Birmingham B153Q2, England Office: Sethi & Sethi, 143 Sandon Rd, Edgbaston Birmingham B17 8HA, England

SETHI, SANDEEP, environmental engineer; b. New Delhi, India, Jan. 27, 1969; came to U.S., 1991; s. Satish Kumar and Champa (Bhasin) S. BS in Civil Engring. with honors, Birla Inst. Tech. & Sci., Pilani, India, 1991; MS in Environ. Engring., Rice U., 1994, PhD in Environ. Engring., 1997. Engr. Nat. Informatics Ctr., New Delhi, 1991; rsch. asst. Rice U., Houston, 1991-97; sr. engr. Metcalf & Eddy, Inc., Atlanta, 1997-99; project and rsch. engr. Carollo Engrs., Santa Ana, Calif., 1999—; chair, invited spkr. membrane technology sessions ASCE 1999 Conf.; lectr. Calif. State U., Long Beach, 2000. Contbr. articles to internat. and profl. jours.; reviewer: Jour. Environ. Engring., Jour. Am. Water Works Assn. Mem. Water Environment Fedn., Am. Water Works Assn. (invited spkr. 1999 conf.), N.Am. Membrane Soc., Santa Ana River Basin Sect. Calif. Water Environment Assn. (rsch. achievement award com. 1999). Avocations: music, computer programming, literature, photography, traveling. Achievements include: development of unified model for performance of membrane filtration processes, incorporating multiple transport mechanisms, which can predict the observed minimum in permeate flux with particle size; first researcher to simulate comparison of constant pressure and constant flux modes of operation in ultrafiltration and microfiltration based on detailed mathematical modeling; developer of cost model for membrane processes incorporating separate correlations for major system components and a changing economy of scale with the design mix; optimization of hollow-fiber membrane design; optimization of membrane system operation; optimization of single and integrated nanofiltration systems; developer of computer software package for membrane systems for the U.S. EPA; rsch. contributions in numerical simulation, sensitivity analysis, and optimization of non-linearly constrained systems and application of advanced computational techniques to solve complex research engineering problems. Office: Carollo Engrs 3100 S Harbor Blvd Ste 200 Santa Ana CA 92704-6810

SETHI, SURESH P., management educator, researcher; b. Ladnun, Rajashtan, India, July 8, 1945; came to the U.S., 1967; s. Gulab Chand and Manak Bai Sethi; m. Andrea Sethi, May 25, 1988; children: Chantal Angelina, Anjuli Sulochana. B in Tech. with honors, Indian Inst. Tech., Bombay, 1967; MBA, Wash. State U., 1969; MS in Indsl. Adminstrn., Carnegie Mellon U., 1971, PhD, 1972. Instr. fin. Carnegie Mellon U., Pitts., 1969-70; asst. prof. mgmt. sci. Rice U., Houston, 1972-73; from asst. prof. to assoc. prof. U. Toronto, Ont., Can., 1973-77, prof. ops. mgmt., 1978-92, prof., dir. lab. mfg., 1992-97; Ashbel Smith prof. U. Tex. Dallas, Richardson, 1997—; vis. assoc. prof. Carnegie Mellon U., Pitts., 1977-78. Author: Optimal Control Theory, 1981, 2d edit., 2000, Hierarchical Decision Making in Stochastic Manufacturing Systems, 1994, Optimal Consumption and Investment with Bankruptcy, 1997; assoc. editor Inst. Ops. Rsch. and Mgmt. Scis., 1994-96, Jour. Math. Analysis and Applications, 2000—. Founder Gulab Chand Sethi Charitable Trust, Ladnun, India, 1980; sci. fair judge Plano (Tex.) Ind. Sch. Dist., 1999, dist. sci. fair judge, 2000. Fellow IC2 Inst., Royal Soc. Can., N.Y. Acad. Scis.; mem. AAAS, IEEE, Inst. Ops. Rsch. and Mgmt. Scis., Can. Operational Rsch. Soc. (chair awards com. 1996-98, award Merit 1996). Avocations: photography, jogging, travel, art. Fax: 972-883-2089. Home: 4428 Longfellow Dr Plano TX 75093-3217 Office: U Tex Dallas 2601 N Floyd Rd Richardson TX 75080-1407

SETHY, ANDREAS THOMAS, retired electronic engineer; b. Budapest, Hungary, Aug. 27, 1932; arrived in Austria, 1956; s. Béla and Kornelia (Firtay) S.; m. Christiane Maria Schall-Riaucour, Sept. 27, 1969; children: Gabrielle, Johanna, Anton, Franz. M in Engring., Tech. U. Budapest, 1955; M, Diplom Engr., Tech. U. Vienna, Austria, 1958; DSc in Polit. Sci., U. Vienna, Austria, 1966. Devel engr. Geophys. Co., Budapest, 1954-56, Goerz Co., Vienna, 1956-58; consulate diploma U. Vienna, 1964; chief rsch. lab. Siemens, Vienna, 1961-67; head dept. Elec. Inst., Vienna, 1967-94; prof. Tech. Coll., Mödling, Austria, 1973-96; ret., 1996; cons. rsch. policy, hunting, forest policy, tennis; v.p, Austrian Assn. Info. Tech., Vienna, 1991-97; v.p., chmn. working party for modem testing Internat. Telecomm. Union, mem. consultative com. internat. for telegraphy and telephone, Geneva, 1971-93; expert Internat. Electrotech. Commn., Geneva, 1987-92, Austrian Electrotech. Assn., Vienna, 1975—; chief First European Measurements of Surface of MAGMA, 1955; internat. expert for signalling safety of rwy. traffic, 1980-94. Author: Research Policy for Austria, 1969, Basic Considerations for Hungary's Development Policy, 1993, Memoirs, 1997, Taid 1998, 99, Confessional Dialog to Millennium, 2000, others; developer of first autocorrelation vocoder, 1965. Recipient First Class Merit Cross for Scis. Republic of Austria, 1994, Officer Cross for Merit Maltesian Order, 1977, Big Merit Cross Austrian Govt., 1990. Mem. IEEE (sr.), German Electrotech. Assn., Austrian Elec. Assn. (life hon. mem.). Roman Catholic. Home: Liechtensteinstrasse 32/6, A-1090 Vienna Austria

SETIADI, SORAYA ANGGRAINI, marketing research consultant, educator; b. Kudus, Indonesia, Apr. 17, 1954; d. Mohammad Zainal Arifin and Oeperti Roemiati Soerjosoebroto; m. Franky Setiadi; children: Edwin Pradana, Evan Dwiarta. M Bus. Mgmt., Cath. U. of Parahyangan, Bandung, Indonesia, 1978. Rsch. exec. PT Unilever Indonesia, Jakarta, 1978-79, group head, 1980-83; dir. PT Reka Cipta Akarsana, Jakarta, 1983—; lectr. Cath. U. of Parahyangan, 1991—. Avocations: music, piano. Home: Rempoa Permai Housing, Jl Merak 3, Jakarta 12330, Indonesia Office: PT Reka Cipta Akarsana, Jl Bintaro Utama DD12/13, Sektor 3A Jakarta Bintaro Jaya 12330, Indonesia

SETIEN, EDWARDO, artist; b. Cde Avila, Cuba, May 24, 1952; came to the U.S., 1980; s. Mario Martinez and Angela Setien. Degree in Acctg., U. Miami, 1985. Exhibited in group shows ACCA, Miami, Fla., 1995 (1st prize painting 1995), Municipalities Fair, Miami, 1998 (1st prize sculpture 1998), Gallery 421, Ft. Lauderdale, Fla., 1999 (1st prize painting 1999). Mem. South Fla. Art Ctr. E-mail: circl@east.com. Home and Studio: 60 NW 32nd Ct Miami FL 33125-4909

SETLIN, ALAN JOHN, entrepreneur; b. N.Y.C., Oct. 27, 1933; s. Samuel and Alyce (Inginito) S.; children: Susan Marie, Peggy Ann, Gina Marie, Alycia Ruth, Alana Jean; m. Deborah Ann Kozlowski, Oct. 14, 1986. Student, U. Miami. CLU. V.p. Figurette, Ltd., Miami, Fla., 1956-60; ptnr. Robins & Clarke, N.Y.C., 1960-63; leading agt. Equitable Life Ins. Co., N.Y.C., 1963; gen. agt. Madison Life Ins. Co., N.Y.C., 1963-66, Beneficial Nat. Life Ins. Co., N.Y.C., 1967-72; pres., chief exec. officer Alliance Assoc.,

Inc., Beverly Hills, Calif., 1972—; ptnr. McMutry & Bell, Inc., Beverly Hills, 1982—; chief exec. officer Emergency Help, Inc., Beverly Hills, 1989-91; COO, dir. Clinica Medica Familiar, L.A., 1993-96; COB, CEO Futurenet On-Line, Inc., Valencia, Calif., 1996—; bd. dirs. Six Million Dollar Forum, 1979-80. Mem. Rep. Senatorial Inner Circle, 1988-90. Sgt. AUS, 1952-54. Mem. Nat. Assn. Life Underwriters (fed. legis. chmn. Western States div. 1980-81, pres. L.A. chpt. 1979-80), CLU Assn. (pres. county chpt. 1979-80), Million Dollar Round Table (life), Golden Key (nat. com.). Roman Catholic. Avocations: weightlifting, boxing, skiing, white water rafting, motorcycling. Office: Futurenet On-Line Inc 12711 Ventura Blvd Ste 480 Studio City CA 91604-2456

SETO, WILLIAM RODERICK, public accounting company executive; b. N.Y.C., July 2, 1954; s. James and Dorothy (Tsang) S. BS, U. Pa., 1976; JD, Cornell Law Sch., 1979. Bar: N.Y. 1980; CPA. Ptnr. Ernst & Young, Atlanta; S.E. area dir. internat. tax, 1986—; mem. bd. advisors Fgn. Sales Corp./Domestic Internat. Sales Corp. Tax Assn., 1994-95; lectr. in field. Mem. editl. bd. Atlanta Internat. Mag., 1992-94. Mem. Leadership Atlanta. Named one of Top Tax Advisors in U.S., Internat. Tax Rev. mag., 1995. Mem. ABA, AICPA, N.Y. Bar Assn., Internat. Fiscal Assn. Office: Ernst & Young 2800 Nations Bank Plz 600 Peachtree St NE Ste 2800 Atlanta GA 30308-2215

SETTER, TIMOTHY LOUIS, agricultural and environmental scientist; b. Albany, Ga., July 4, 1950; s. Louis Claire and Ruth W. (Goodenough) S.; m. Margaret Ann Bridgeman, June 11, 1977; children: Michael Timothy, Danielle Sheree, Tiffany Margaret. BSc in Botany, U. Okla., 1971; MSc in Agr., U. Western Australia, Nedlands, 1979, PhD in Plant Physiology, 1983; diploma in Environ. Impact Assessment, Murdoch (WA) U., 1999. Postdoctoral fellow U. Western Australia, Nedlands, 1982-84, sr. postdoctoral fellow, 1982-84, lectr., 1987-89, sr. lectr., 1987-89; head plant physiology group Internat. Rice Rsch. Inst., Los Banos, The Philippines, 1991-96; sr. cereal scientist Agr. Western Australia, South Perth, 1996-2000, discipline leader crop agronomy and crop physiology, 2000—; rsch. scientist dept. agr. Australian Centr. Internat. Agr. Rsch., Thailand, 1984-87; regional resource scientist Internat. Rice Rsch. Inst., India, 1992-95, rainfed rice program cons., 1996; postgrad. workshop supr. Crawford Fund Australia, Vietnam and The Philippines, 1995-97; lectr. in field. Contbr. chpts. to books and articles to profl. jours. Sci. advisor Western Australia Parliament, 1997-98; tech. advisor State Agrl. Biotechnology Ctr., Murdoch U., 1998—; nat. agrl. rsch. reviewer Australian Rsch. Coun., 1998—. Co-recipient Best Sci. Paper award Crop Sci. Soc. The Philippines, 1997; rsch. grantee in field. Mem. Internat. Assn. Impact Assessment, Internat. Soc. Plant Anaerobiosis (sec. 1991-95), Australian Soc. Plant Physiology. Roman Catholic. Avocations: developing collaborative research between developed and developing countries, environmental policy analysis, scuba divemaster, photography, amateur builder. Office: Agr Western Australia, 3 Baron-Hay Ct, South Perth WA 6151, Australia

SETTERS, PAULA LOUISE HENDERSON, physics educator; b. Kay Jay, Ky., July 18, 1949; d. Louis and Lora (Bruce) H.; m. Charles Mullikin Setters; children: Philip Bennett, Lora Elizabeth. BS in Physics, Western Ky. U., 1970, postgrad., 1992; MA in Sci. Edn., U. Ala., 1974. Cert. secondary tchr. Tchr. Warren Ctrl. H.S., Bowling Green, Ky., 1970-71, Homewood (Ala.) H.S., 1971-75; tchr. LaRue County H.S., Hodgenville, Ky., 1976-99, ret., 1999; adj. prof. Campbellsville U., 1998—; profl. devel. presenter AEL, Charleston, W.Va., 1995-98, Ky. Instrnl. Tech. Leaders, Frankfort, Ky., 1994-98; rsch. asst. Dept. of Energy TRAC at Los Alamos (N.Mex.) Nat. Lab., 1991; strategic planning com. LaRue County Bd. Edn., 1992-99; site-based coun. LaRue County H.S., 1996-99. Chair spl. programs United Meth. Women, Hodgenville, 1990, pres., 1980-82, LaRue Co. Relay for Life, 2000; pres., chmn. Hodgenville Elem. PTO, 1980-81; chair LaRue County Run for Life, 2000. Mem. NEA, Nat. Sci. Tchrs. Assn., Am. Assn. Physics Tchrs., Ky. Sci. Tchrs. Assn., Ky. Assn. Physics Tchrs. Ky. Edn. Assn., LaRue County Edn. Assn. Republican. Methodist.

SETTIS, SALVATORE, archaeologist, art historian; b. Rosarno, Italy, June 11, 1941; s. Rocco and Carmela (Megna) S.; m. Chiara Frugoni, Dec. 9, 1965 (div. 1982); children: Silvano, Andrea, Marta; m. Maria Michela Sassi, Jan. 4, 1984; children: Bruno, Nicola. Grad., U. Pisa, Italy, 1963; PhD, Scuola Normale Superiore, Pisa, 1965. Asst. prof. U. Pisa, 1965-69, lectr., 1969-75, prof., 1976-84, dean Faculty Letters and Philosophy, 1978-81; prof. Scuola Normale Superiore, Pisa, 1984—, dean Faculty Letters and Philosophy, 1986-91; dir. Getty Rsch. Inst. for History Art and Humanities, Santa Monica, Calif., 1994-99, Scuola Normalé Superiore, Pisa, 1999—. Author: La Tempesta Interpretata, 1978, La Colonna Traiana, 1988, I Greci, 4 vols., 1996-98, Laocoonte Fama e stile, 1999. Office: Scuola Normale Superiore, Piazza dei Cavalieri 7, 56100 Pisa Italy

SETTIVARI, NAGARJUNA, scientist, researcher; b. Somala, India, May 10, 1961; s. Settivari Sambaiah and Settivari Chennamma; m. Latha Kusuma, Oct. 21, 1988; children: Kum. S. Susmitha, S. Jagadeesh. BTech., Banaras Hindu U., Varanasi, India, 1984, PhD in Metall. Engring., 1996. Engr. trainee Mishra Dhathu Nigam, Hyderabad, India, 1984-85; scientist Def. Metall. Rsch. Lab., Hyderabad, 1985—. Recipient Young Metallurgist award Govt. of India, Ministry of Steel. Mem. Indian Inst. Metals (life), Materials Rsch. Soc. India (life). Avocations: music (sitar), photography, reading. Office: Def Metall Rsch Lab, Kanchanbagh-PO, 500 058 Hyderabad India

SETTNES, OSVALD PETER, medical microbiology educator; b. Copenhagen, Aug. 4, 1936; s. Harald Aksel and Bertha Johanne (Olsen) Jedlnsen; m. Anné Margrethe Jarlstrup, June 12, 1960; children: Annette, Marianne. DVM, U. Copenhagen, 1961, PhD, 1973. Gen. practice vet. medicine, 1961-62; rschr. pathology Royal Vet. H.S., 1962-67; rschr. med. microbiology U. Copenhagen, 1967-73, assoc. prof., 1973—, head Inst. Med. Microbiology, 1985-91. Avocations: farming, piano playing and composing. Home: Kalholm Brodeskovvej, 3400 Hillerod Denmark Office: Inst Md Micro U Copenhagen, Blegdamsvej 3, DK-2200 Copenhagen Denmark

SETTUR, SREENATH, electronics and telecommunications engineer; b. Settur, Andhra Pradesh, India, Mar. 21, 1962; s. Narasimhamurthy and Saradamma S.; m. Annapurna Yajamanam, Nov. 15, 1987; 1 child, Srikar. B in Tech., Jawaharlal Nehru Technol. U. Coll. Engring., Anantapur, India, 1983; PGD in M&SM, Bharatiya Vidya Bhavan, Bangalore, India, 1989; diploma in mgmt., All India Mgmt. Assn., New Delhi, 1990; MSc in Engring., Indian Inst. Sci., Bangalore, 1993. Engr. ISRO Satellite Ctr., Bangalore, India, 1984-85; tech. staff quality and vendor devel. Ctr. Devel. Telematics, Bangalore, 1985-87, group leader, program mgr. quality and vendor devel., 1988-92, sr. program mgr. reliability and project mgmt., 1993-95, sr. program mgr. computer aided design/computer network ops., 1995-2000, chief adminstrv. officer material mgmt., 2000—; mem. agripec com. adv. group on reliability info. for profl. electronic components Dept. Telecom, Govt. India, Bangalore, 1988-94, BIS components com. Bur. Indian Stds., 1988-95, LCSO panel electronic components standardisation orgn. Dept. Def., 1988-99. State Merit scholar Govt. Andhra Pradesh, 1973-76; Nat. Merit scholar Govt. India, 1976-83. Fellow Inst. Electronics and Telecomm. Engrs. Orgn. (life, Bangalore chpt.); mem. Internat. Microelectronics and Packaging Soc. (life, India chpt.), Inst. Standards Engrs. (life, Bangalore sect.), Indian Inst. Sci. Alumni Assn. (life, Bangalore sect.). Hindu. Avocations: reading, listening to music. Fax: 001-908-771-8645. Home: GA 175 Srikrishna Apts Kamala Nagar, Sri Gruhalakshmi Layout II Stage, Bangalore 560079 Karnataka, India Office: Ctr Devel Telematics, 71/1 Sneha Complex Millers Rd, Bangalore 560052 Karnataka, India

SETTY, M.G. ANANTHA PADMANABHA, oceanographer; b. Huliyar, Karnataka, India, Sept. 19, 1926; s. Minha Gangadhar and Meenakshamma Setty; m. Lalitha Bhoopalam (dec. June 1971); children: Ravi Kiron, Jyothi Priyadarshini; m. Vimala Kumari, June 8, 1972. BSc with honors, U. Mysore, Bangalore, India, 1949, MSc, 1950; PhD, U. Utah, 1963. Lectr. U. Mysore, 1954-59; tchg. and rsch. asst. U. Utah, Salt Lake City, 1959-64; rsch. geologist internat. Indian Ocean expdn. UNESCO, Kerala, 1964-65; sci. officer Coun. Sci. and Indsl. Rsch., New Delhi, 1965-67; head geologist Nat. Inst. Oceanography, Goa, India, 1968-77, asst. dir., 1977-86; geology field worker, faculty U. Mysore, 1955-59, 60-62; rsch. scientist INS Kistna & RV, 1964, 67; chief scientist RV Gaveshani, 1977-84; vis. prof. U. Bombay, U. Roorkee, U. Andhra, U. Baroda, U. Cochin, U. Lucknow, 1968-86; invited scientist Internat. Geol. Congress, New Delhi, 1964, UN Environ. Program, U.S. EPA, Washington, 1984, UNESCO, Paris, Hobart, Australia, 1986; cons. disaster control, mgmt. of oil spills off Karnataka Coast, Arabian Sea, 1992. Contbr. more than 85 articles to profl. jours. in U.S., Can., France, Spain, Italy, Australia, others; editor Sr. Citizens Club Mag., Bangalore, 1995. Youth leader Indian Nat. Congress, Bangalore, 1943-46; sec. Indo-Am. Assn., Bangalore, 1966-67; bd. dirs. Sr. Citizens Club Bangalore, 1992—, Sr. Citizens Welfare Forum, Bangalore, 1997—. Fellow Geol. Soc. India (sec. 1949-50); mem. AAAS, Sigma Xi, Sigma Gamma Epsilon. Avocations: billiards, snookers. Home: Shangri-la 130 V Main IV, Blk II Phase Banashankari, III STG Bangalore 560085, India

SETTY, VISWANATH B. R., chemical company executive; b. Hindupur, India, Apr. 2, 1952; s. Rathnaiah B.V. and Lalithamma R. Setty; m. Muktha V. Setty; children: Karthik, Adithya. B in Commerce, St. Joseph's Coll. Commerce, 1973. Pres. Sankranthi Export House, Bangalore, India; regional chmn. Basic Chems., Pharmas. and Cosmetics Export Promotin coun., Bangalore. Pres. Vasavi Ednl. Trust, Bangalore, 1989—. Recipient Udyog Rattan award Inst. Econ. Studies, 1993. Mem. Karnataka Chamber of Exports (pres. 1997-98), Fedn. Karnataka Chamber of Commerce and Industry (mng. com. 1996-97), Greater Mysore Chamber of Industry (mng. com. 1996-97), Rotary (dist. gov. 1988-89). Avocations: travel, golf, tennis, swimming. Home: VIII Block, Rathna 295 39th Cross, 560-082 Bangalore India Office: Sankranthi Export House, 30 T Mariyappa Rd II Block, 560-011 Bangalore India

SETUA, GOPAL CHANDRA, research scientist; b. Lowada, India, Jan. 4, 1951; s. Satish Chandra and Susama (Dey) S.; m. Mithua Chowdhury, Jan. 16, 1981; 1 child, Sutapa. BS in Botany with honors, Bhadrak (India) Coll., 1972; MS in Botany, Ravenshaw Coll., Cuttack, India, 1974; PhD in Botany, Kalyani (India) U., 1984. From jr. rsch. fellow to sr. rsch. fellow Kalyani U., 1977-82; sr. rsch. asst. Ctrl. Silk Bd., Bihar, India, 1982-90, sr. rsch. officer, 1990—. Co-author: Perspective of Mycology, 1986, Temperate Fruits, 2000; contbr. articles to profl. jours. Nat. scholar Govt. India, 1967-69, Rsch. scholar Govt. Orissa, India, 1975. Avocations: yoga, reading, gardening. Home: Lowada, 721136 Midnapore India Office: Central Silk Bd, Berhampore, 742101 Murshidabad India

SETZEKORN, WILLIAM DAVID, retired architect, consultant, author; b. Mt. Vernon, Ill., Mar. 12, 1935; s. Merrett Everet and Audrey (Ferguson) S.; m. Georgia Sue Brown, Feb. 4, 1958 (div. 1968); children: Jeffrey Merle, Timothy Michael. BArch, Kans. State U., 1957; cert. in computer graphics, Harvard U., 1968; BA with MA equivalency in Humanities, Western Ill. U., 1982. Registered arch., Calif. Coord. design and constrn. Cal-Expo, Sacramento, 1968; pvt. practice, Los Altos and Redding, Calif., Seattle, 1968-85; cons. Contra Costa County, Martinez, Calif., 1985-89, El Dorado County, Placerville, Calif., 1985-89, Somerset, Calif., 1989—; cons. Fed. Emergency Mgmt. Agy., The Presidio, San Francisco, 1989-95, Gov. Keating's task force for disaster recovery, Oklahoma City, 1995; apptd. Calif. State Grand Jury, 1996—. Author: Formerly British Honduras: A Profile of the New Nation of Belize, 1975, 4 other titles; contbr. articles to mags. Recipient Ofcl. Commendation, State of Calif., 1968, U.S. Presdl. Medal of Merit, Ronald Reagan, 1988. Fellow Augustan Soc. (bd. dirs. 1994-96); mem. Noble Co. of the Rose (knight 1979, lt. magister rosae 1995—), Mil. and Hospitaller Order of St. Lazarus (comdr.), numerous other internat. orders of chivalry, Family Setzekorn Assn. (prin. officer 1979—), San Leandro (Calif.) Yacht Club (founding), Kiwanis. Republican. Unitarian. Avocations: genealogy, medieval history, heraldry, travel. Home and Office: 4224 Crestline Ave # 5 Fair Oaks CA 95628-7178

SEUÁNEZ, HÉCTOR NICOLÁS, geneticist, educator; b. Montevideo, Uruguay, Mar. 15, 1947; s. Hector Seuanez Olivera and Ana Abreu; m. Maria Helena Salgado, Sept. 7, 1974; children: Maria Jose, Pablo, Ana Helena. BSc, Gonzaga U., 1967; MD, U. Montevideo, 1974; PhD, U. Edinburgh, 1978. Rschr. Inst. Ciencias Biologicas, Montevideo, 1972-74; fellow MRC Clin. Cytogenetics Unit, Edinburgh, Scotland, 1974-78; assoc. prof. U. Fed. Rio de Janeiro, Brazil, 1978—; fellow genetics dept. U. Montevideo, 1970-74; scientist Instituto Nacional de Cancer, Rio de Janeiro, 1984—; vis. scientist Nat. Cancer Inst. NIH, Frederick, Md., 1987-91; cons. in field. Author: The Phylogeny of Human Chromosomes, 1979; contbr. articles to profl. jurs.; assoc. editor Jour. Heredity, 1996—, Am. Jour. Primatology, 1988-92. Fulbright scholar, 1965-67. Mem. Acad. Ciencias Am. Latina, Brazilian Soc. Genetics, Brazilian Acad. of Scis. (corr. mem.). Avocations: reading, classical music. Home: Aquarela do Brasil 333/Apt 1703, Rio de Janeiro Brazil Office: Inst Nat Cancer, Genetics Sect, 20230130 Rio de Janeiro Brazil

SEUFERT, CHRISTOPHER J., lawyer; b. East Bridgewater, Mass., Aug. 12, 1959; s. Lawrence D. and Pauline W. (Lussier) S.; children: Christopher J., Megan. BA, U. Mass., Dartmouth, 1981; JD, Suffolk U., Boston, 1984. Bar: N.H. 1985, Mass. 1985, N.C. 1995, U.S. Dist. Ct. (1st cir.) 1987, U.S. Dist. Ct. N.H. 1985, U.S. Dist. Ct. Mass. 1985, U.S. Supreme Ct. 1988. Atty. Seufert Profl. Assocs., Franklin, N.H., 1985—; bd. dirs. N.H. Redevel. Inc., Franklin. Served with USCG, 1979-85. Mem. Franklin KC, Andover Lions Club. Republican. Roman Catholic. Office: Seufert Profl Assocs 59 Central St Franklin NH 03235-1134

SEUFERT, JANET ARLENE, small business owner, consultant; b. Baumholder, Germany, Sept. 23, 1967; (parents Am. citizens); d. Edward Cecil and Shirley Ann (Pratt) S. BS, U.S. Mil. Acad., 1989; MBA, U. Md., 1999. Commd. 2d lt. U.S. Army, 1989, advanced through grades to capt., 1993; platoon leader Battery A, 2-52 Air Def. Art. (HAWK) U.S. Army, Ft. Bragg, N.C., 1990=91; with Desert Shield/Desert Storm U.S. Army, 1991; instr., course dir. U.S. Army Adj. Gen. Sch., Ft. Jackson, S.C., 1993-97; resigned, 1997; owner, mgr. Higher Pursuits, Columbia, Tenn., 1999—; asst. dir. Camp $tart-Up, Ind. Means, Inc., Santa Barbara, Calif., 1998, 99, 2000. Decorated Valorous Unit award, Meritorious Svc. medal, Army Commendation medal, Army Achievement medal, Nat. Def. medal, Liberation of Kuwait medal, Def. of Saudi Arabia medal, S.W. Asia medal with two bronze stars, Parachutist badge. Avocations: backpacking, canoeing. E-mail: jseufert@aol.com. Home: 116 7th Ave Columbia TN 38401-2852 Office: Higher Pursuits 211 3d Ave Columbia TN 38401-2915

SEUL, HEINRICH LORENZ, agricultural engineer; b. Burgbrohl, Fed. Republic Germany, July 6, 1960. Diploma Agrl. Engring., U. Kassel (Germany), 1988. Rschr. dept. ecol. chemistry U. Kassel, 1983-85; cons. on ecol. forest and land mgmt. in Brazil Cote d'Ivoir and Ghana, 1985-90. Author: (books) Ecological Sound Rainforest Management for Rubber and Brazilnut, 1988, Amazonia-an Indian Cultural Landscape, 1988, The Future of Amazonia, 1988; film editor for German, British, and U.S. TV, 1990-95; sr. assoc. of CREAM Cons., 1995-98; pres. CREAM Cons., 1999—. Avocations: piano, horse breeding, tennis, golf. Home and Office: Gut Fahrenbach, D-37216 Witzenhausen Hessen Germany

SEUL, KWANG-WON, engineer, researcher; b. Seoul, South Korea, July 13, 1960; s. Kyong-Jin Seul and Ok-Lim Lee; m. You-Sun Han, Apr. 5, 1989; children: Kun-Woong, Tae-Woong. BS, Yonsei U., Seoul, South Korea, 1984; MS, Korea Advanced Inst. Sci/Tech., Seoul, 1986, PhD, 1991. Rschr. Korea Inst. Nuclear Safety, Taejon, 1991-96, project mgr., 1997—. Contbr. articles to profl. jours. Mem. ASME. Avocations: reading, history, painting. Office: Korea Inst Nuclear Safety, PO Box 114, Yusung-Gu Taejon 305-600, South Korea

SEVASTIANOV, SERGEY VASSILYEVICH, mathematician; b. Petropavlovsk, Russia, Jan. 15, 1953; s. Vassiliy Pavlovich and Yelena Petrovna (Stolbovskaya) S.; m. Anastassiya Yegorovna Belonogova, May 5, 1978; children: Yevgeniya, Kseniya. MSc, Novosibirsk State U., 1975; PhD, Inst. of Math., 1981. Lab. asst. Inst. of Math., Novosibirsk, 1974-75, probationer, 1975-76, jr. rschr., 1976-86, rschr., 1986-91, sr. rschr., 1991—; asst. Novosibirsk State U., 1982-89, assoc. prof., 1989—. Contbr. articles to profl. jours. Recipient 1st Prize Siberian Contest of Young Rschrs. Presidium of the Siberian Br. Acad. Sci. USSR, 1982; long-term rsch. grant Internat. Sci. Found., 1994; fellowship EC programme human capital and mobility Commn. of the European Cmty., 1995. Avocations: hockey, chess. Home: Lesosechnaya 3-184, 630060 Novosibirsk Russia Office: Inst of Math, Pr Koptjuga 4, 630090 Novosibirsk Russia

SEVASTIANOV, VIKTOR IVANOVICH, biophysicist, researcher; b. Novo-Kuznetsk, Russia, Aug. 28, 1945; s. Ivan Nikolaevich and Valentina Kirillovna (Girdyuk) S.; m. Irina Alekseevna Shvilkina, Aug. 24, 1968; children: Irina, Victoria. MSc in Biophysics, 2nd Med. Inst., Moscow, 1969; Candidate of Sci. in Phys. Chemistry, Inst. Chem. Physics, Moscow, 1973; DS in Biophysics, Rsch. Inst. Transplantology, 1985. Prof. biophysics; cert. testing biomaterials rschr. Jr. rschr. dept. kinetics of chem. and biol. processes Inst. Chem. Physics, USSR Acad. Sci., Moscow, 1969-78; sr. rschr. biomaterials group Inst. Transplantology and Artificial Organs, Moscow, 1978-84, head of lab. of blood compatible biomaterials, 1984-86, head state ctr. for rsch. of blood compatible biomaterials, 1986—; instr. math. Russian Polytech. Inst., Moscow, 1969-81; prof. dept. physics of living sys., faculty physico-chem. biology Moscow Physico-Tech. Inst., 1986—; head State Testing Lab. for Blood Compatible Biomaterials, 1996—; chmn., organizer All-Union Workshop on Blood Compatible Biomaterials, Kiev, 1986, Moscow, 1988, 90. Co-editor, founder: Internat. Jour., Biomaterial-Living Sys. Interactions, 1993-95; author: (book chpt.) High-Performance Biomaterials: A Comprehensive Guide to Medical and Pharmaceutical Applications, 1991; co-author: (book chpt.) Proteins at Interfaces II, 1995; editor, co-author: Biocompatibility, 1999; mem. editl. bd. Jour. Biomed. Materiasl Rsch., 1989—, Jour. Advanced Materials, 1994—, Jour. Transplantology and Artificial Organs, 1994—. Sci. sec. problem com. Presidium of USSR Acad. Med. Sci., 1980-91; mem. Internat. Union Pure and Applied Chemistry Working Party, 1985-92; mem. USA/Russia Scientist Exch. Program of Heart, Lung, and Blood Inst., NIH, 1981-93. Mem. Internat. Soc. for Artificial Organs, Am. Soc. for Artificial Organs, N.Y. Acad. Scis. Avocations: carpentry, cross-country skiing. Office: Inst Transp/Artifical Orgns, 1 Schukinskaya str, 123182 Moscow Russia

ŠEVČÍK, JAN, pharmacologist, researcher; b. Prague, Czech Republic, Mar. 5, 1960; s. Jan and Blanka (Kavanova) S. MD, Charles Univ., Prague, 1985; PhD, Acad. Scis., Prague, 1989. Postgrad. Inst. Pharmacology, Prague, 1985-89, asst., 1989-90; rsch. fellow Humboldt Found., Freiburg, Germany, 1991-92; rsch. worker Inst. Pharmacology Acad. Scis. Czech Republic, Prague, 1993—; mem. sci. bd. Inst. Pharmacology Acad. Scis. Czech Republic, Prague, 1993—. Contbr. articles to profl. jours. Mem. Czech Med. Soc., Internat. Brain Rsch. Orgn. Avocations: chess, literature, tourism, nature. Home: Polska 1547/50, 120 00 Prague 2 Czech Republic Office: Inst of Pharmacology AV CR, Videnska 1083, 142 20 Prague 4 Czech Republic

SEVERDIA, ANTHONY GEORGE, chemistry researcher; b. Sharon, Pa., Sept. 20, 1946; s. George Anthony and Angela Mary (Tomich) S. BS, Pa. State U., 1968; MS, Case Western Reserve U., 1971, PhD, 1974. Rsch., teaching assoc. Rensselaer Poly. Inst., Troy, N.Y., 1975-77; chemist N.Y. U., 1977-79, 82-83, Columbia U., N.Y.C., 1979-82; analytical chemist Mallinckrodt Group, Terre Haute, Ind., 1983-92; sr. chemist analytical sci. Sanofi Rsch., Gt. Valley, Pa., 1992—. Contbr. articles to profl. jours.; presenter in field. Recipient Summer fellowship NSF, Cleve., 1971. Mem. Am. Chem. Soc. (exec. com., treas. Terre Haute sect. 1991-92), Soc. Applied Spectroscopy, The Internat. Soc. for Optical Engring. Home: 301 Pritchard Ln Wallingford PA 19086-6104

SEVERIN, CECILE FRANCOISE, retired protective services official; b. La Plaine, Dominica, Dec. 29, 1937; s. Benoit Reuter and Virginia Christina (Alexander) S.; m. Eulyn Veronica Alexander, July 20, 1985 (div. Apr. 1991); children: Cadmus, twins Cleve, Joanne Francess Ajetunmobi. Student, Agrl. Dept. Roseau and St. Joseph, Dominica, 1955-57. Cert. agriculturist. Tchr. Primary Sch., La Plaine, Dominica, 1953-55; estate overseer Pvt. Sector Stowe Estate, Dominica, 1957-59; police constable Police Dept., Roseau, Dominica, 1959-70, police cpl., 1970-75; police sgt., staff sgt. Police Dept., Roseau, Grand Bay, La Plaine, Castle Bruce, St. Joseph, Wesley, Coliha, ut, Laplaine, Dominica, 1975-90; police inspector Police Dept., Roseau, St. Joseph, Mahaut, Salisbury, Coulibistrie, Dominica, 1990-97; magistrate's ct. prosecutor Police Dept. police stations, Grand Bay Village, La Plaine Village, Castle Bruce Village, St. Joseph Village, Wesley Village, Colihaut Village, Roseau Magistrates Cts. # 1 and 2, Dominica, 1977-97; lectr. Police Tng. Sch., Roseau, Dominica, 1993-94. Recipient award for meritorious svc. Govt. Dominica, 1994. Mem. Endeavours Group (sec. 1998-99). Roman Catholic. Avocations: farming, rearing pets, cricket, hunting, reading. Home: 3648 10th St, Canefield Dominica

SEVERIN, DOROTHY SHERMAN, Spanish language and Hispanic studies educator; b. L.A., Mar. 24, 1942; d. Wilbur B. and Virginia L. (Tucker) sherman; m. Giles Timothy Severin, Mar. 24, 1966 (div. Apr. 1979); 1 child, Ida. AB summa cum laude, Harvard U., 1963, AM, 1964, PhD, 1967. Tutor Harvard U., Cambridge, Mass., 1964-66; vis. lectr. U. W.I., 1967-68; asst. prof. Vassar Coll., Poughkeepsie, N.Y., 1968-69; lectr. Westfield Coll., London, 1969-82; prof. Spanish, head dept. Hispanic studies Liverpool U., England, 1982-89, also Gilmour prof., 1982—, also pro vice chancellor, 1989-92; vis. prof. Harvard U., 1982, Columbia U., N.Y.C., 1983, Yale U., New Haven, 1985, U. Calif., Berkeley, 1996. Author: Memory in La Celestina, 1970, The Cancionero de Martinez de Burgos, 1976, Tragicomedy and Novelistic Discourse in Celestina, 1989, Cancionero de Onate, 1990 Witchcraft in Celestina, 1995; co-author: Animals in Celestina, 1999; editor: Fernando de Rojas, La Celestina, 1969, 87, Diego de San Pedro, La Pasion Trobada, 1973, La Lengua de Erasmo, 1975, Celestina with the Translation of James Mabbe (1631), 1987, Two Spanish Songbooks, 2000; co-editor: Diego de San Pedro, Obras Completas III, 1979, Cosas Sacadas de la Cronica del Rey Don Juan II, 1982, ADMYTE: Paris Cancioneros, 1993, 99; editor Bull. Hispanic Studies. Ann Radcliffe scholar, 1956-60; Woodrow Wilson fellow, 1963-64, 66-67; grantee Am. Philos. Soc., 1969, Leverhulme Found., 1987-91, Br. Acad., 1975, 88, 92. Fellow Soc. Antiquaries; mem. Internat. Courtly Lit. Soc. (past pres. Br. br.), Modern Humanities Rsch. Assn. (com.), N. Ireland Higher Edn. Coun., Internat. Assn. Hispanists, Assn. Hispanists of Great Britain and Ireland, Assn. Hispanica Lit. Medieval. Office: Liverpool U, Dept Hispanic Studies, Liverpool L69 3BX, England

SEVERIN, VLADIMIR SVYTOSLAVOVYCH, physicist; b. Donesk, Ukraine, July 12, 1949; s. Svytoslav Ivanovich and Catherine Petrovnar (Omsharnskary) S.; m. Olgar Anartolievnar Skripschenko, Sept. 10, 1988 (div. Aug. 1992). Degree in physics, Kiev (Ukraine) State U., 1971. Engr. Kiev Arsenal Plant, 1971-72; scientist Inst. Semiconductors-Ukrainian Acad. Scis., Kiev, 1972-73, 75-94; tchr. Kiev State Tech. U. Constrn. & Arch., 1995-96; tchr. gen. and theoretical physics Kiev Internat. U. Civil Aviation, 1996—. Sr. lt. Soviet Army, 1973-75. Mem. N.Y. Acad. Scis. Home: B Hmelnitzkogo Str 39 Flt 38, 01030 Kiev Ukraine Office: Kiev Internat U Civil Avia, Cosmonavta Komarova av 1, 03058 Kiev Ukraine

SEVERN, MICHAEL JASON, urologic implantable sales specialist; b. Texarkana, Tex., Mar. 12, 1965; s. Walter Michael and Polly Jean (Carver) S.; m. Kristi Leigh Richardson, May 4, 1996; 1 child, Madison Kirkey. BBA in Mktg., Tex. Tech. U. Buyer, mktg. adminstr. PhD Southwest, Dallas, 1989-90; medical surgical device sales Davis & Geck, Lubbock, Okla. City, Tex., Okla, 1990-92; regional sales mgr. Laserscope Inc., Dallas, 1992-97; urologic implantable sales Medtronic, Inc., Dallas, 1997—. Author: Sales Protocol, 1994. Mem. Ducks Unlimited (Tex. chpt.). Republican. Baptist. Avocations: boating, fitness, golf, fishing, finance. Home: 405 High Meadow Ln Heath TX 75032-5851

SEVERS, WILLIAM FLOYD, actor; b. Britton, Okla., Jan. 8, 1932; s. Harry Lysander Fletcher and Katherine Lucinda (McAuliffe) S.; m. Mary Anne Proctor, Jan. 18, 1964 (div. 1971); 1 child, Pilar; m. Barbara Alice Schonger, Sept. 9, 1978; children: Katherine Meghan, Erin Christine. AA, Pasadena Playhouse Coll., 1956. Appeared on Broadway in Cut of the Axe, 1959-60, On Borrowed Time, 1991-92, nat. tour Look Homeward, Angel, 1960; co-star nat. tour Spoon River, 1964; actor Secret Storm, All My Children, One Life to Live, Guiding Light, Texas, Search for Tomorrow, Another World, Loving, 1963-93; other TV appearances include Armstrong Circle Theatre, 1963, The Defenders, 1964, World War II, A GI Diary, 1978, Nurse, 1980, Muggable Mary, 1986, Law and Order, recurring role as Hon. Henry Fillmore, 1990-99, Hallmark Hall of Fame, Grace and Glorie, 1998;

appeared in films, including Funny Farm, 1988, Regarding Henry, 1991, Meet the Parents, 2000, Revolution #9, 2000; actor European tour West Side Story, 1990-91, 94, Asian tour West Side Story, 1999; actor, voice artist numerous commls., 1964—. Staff sgt. USAF, 1946-53. Mem. SAG, AFTRA, Actors Equity Assn., Pasadena Playhouse Alumni Assn. Democrat. Avocations: reading, golf. Home: 10 Waterside Plz Apt 6F New York NY 10010-2610 Office: Michael Hartig Agency Ltd 156 5th Ave New York NY 10010-7002

SEVÓN, LEIF JÖRGEN ARVIDSSON, judge; b. Helsinki, Oct. 31, 1941; s. Enzio Arvid and Ulla Ingalill (Melart) S.; m. Guje Agneta Lindberg, 1965 (div. 1996); children: Staffan, Pia. ML, U. Helsinki, 1965, Licentiate of Laws, 1969; Dr.jur (h.c.), U. Stockholm, 1999, U. Helsinki, 2000. Asst. U. Helsinki, 1966-71, asst. prof., 1971-74; counsellor of legislation Ministry Justice, 1973-78, dir. legislation, 1980-86, dir. gen. dept. legislation, 1986-91; sr. judge, chamber pres. City Ct. Helsinki, 1979-80; judge Supreme Ct. Justice, 1991—, Ct. of Justice European Cmtys., 1995—; counsellor Dept. Trade Ministry Fgn. Affairs, 1991-92; pres. European Free Trade Assn. Ct., 1994; mem. negotiation delegation, c-chmn. drafting group EEA Agreement; mem. Nordic Com. High Officials for Cooperation in the Legal Field, 1975-91. Author: Consumer Protection, 1978, Sale of Goods Act, 1987, Transport Law, 1988, Act on Interests, 1983; contbr. articles to profl. jours.; translator books, articles. Mem. Bd. Compensation to Victims of Criminal Offenses, Consumer Complaints Bd., Compensation for Carriage of Goods Bd., Bd. Compensation to Patients for Injuries Due to Med. Treatment. Mem. Internat. Inst. Unification Pvt. Law (mem. govning. coun. 1989—), UN Commn. Internat. Trade Law (mem. Finnish delegation, mem. working groups internat. shipping legislation, internat. sale of goods, chmn. working group New Internat. Econ. Order), Internat. Maritime Orgn., Internat. Civil Aviation Orgn., Coun. Europe, OECD, The Hague Conf. Internat. Pvt. Law. Office: Ct Justice, 2925 Luxembourg Luxembourg

SEWARD, GEORGE CHESTER, lawyer; b. Omaha, Aug. 4, 1910; s. George Francis and Ada Leona (Rugh) S.; m. Carroll Frances McKay, Dec. 12, 1936 (dec. 1991); children: Gordon Day, Patricia McKay (Mrs. Dryden G. Liddle), James Pickett, Deborah Carroll (Mrs. R. Thomas Coleman). BA, U. Va., 1933, LLB, 1936. Bar: Va. 1935, N.Y., Ky., D.C., U.S. Supreme Ct. With Shearman & Sterling, N.Y.C., 1936-53, Seward & Kissel, N.Y.C., 1953—; founder, hon. chmn. Internat. Capital Markets Group of Internat. Fedn. Accts., Fedn. Internat. des Bourses de Valeurs, Internat. Bar Assn.; dir. Witherbee Sherman Corp., 1952-66, pres. 1964-66, Howmet Corp., 1955-75, Chas. P. Young Co., 1965-72, Howmedica Inc., 1970-72, Benson Mines, Inc., 1980-85; trustee Benson Iron Ore Trust, 1969-80. Author: Basic Corporate Practice, 1977, Seward and Related Families, 1994; co-author: Model Business Corporation Act Annotated, 1960, We Remember Carroll, 1992. Trustee Arts and Scis. Coun. U. Va., 1983-93, pres., 1991-93; trustee Edwin Gould Found. for Children, 1955-96, Nature Conservancy of Ea. L.I., 1969-80, N.Y. Geneal. and Biog. Soc. Named to Louisville Male H.S. Alumni Assn. Hall of Fame, 1991; recommd. Ky. Col., 1993. Fellow Am. Bar Found. (chmn. model corp. acts com. 1956-65), N.Y. State Bar Found.; mem. Internat. Bar Assn. (hon. life pres., hon. pres., founder sect. on bus. law, lectr. series named in his honor, New Delhi 1988, Lisbon 1992, Budapest 1993, Geneva 1994), ABA (chmn. bus. law sect. 1958-59, chmn. sect. com. corp. laws 1952-58, chmn. sect. banking com. 1960-61, mem. ho. of dels. 1959-60, 63-74, mem. joint com. with Am. Law Inst. on continung legal edn. 1965-74), Athenaeum Lit. Assn. (Louisville), Downtown Assn. (N.Y.C.), Knickerbocker Club, N.Y. Yacht Club, Univ. Club (Chgo.), Met. Club (Washington), Bohemian Club (San Francisco), Gardiner's Bay Country Club (Shelter Island, N.Y.), Greencroft Club (Charlottesville, Va.), Cum Laude Soc., Raven Soc., Order of Coif, Phi Beta Kappa Assocs. (pres. 1969-75), Phi Beta Kappa, Theta Chi, Delta Sigma Rho. Home: 48 Greenacres Ave Scarsdale NY 10583-1436 Office: Seward & Kissel One Battery Park Plz New York NY 10004 also: Internat Bar Assn, 271 Regent St, London W1R 7PA, England

SEWARD, JAMES PICKETT, internist, educator; b. N.Y.C., Oct. 14, 1949; s. George C. and Carroll Frances (McKay) S. AB, Harvard U., 1971; M of Pub. Policy, U. Calif., Berkeley, 1977; MD, U. Calif., San Francisco, 1977. Diplomate Am. Bd. Internal Medicine, Am. Bd. Occupational Medicine, Am. Bd. Med. Mgmt. Resident U. Calif. Hosps., San Francisco, 1977-80; Robert Woods Johnson postdoctoral fellow U. Calif., San Francisco, 1980-82; med. dir. health svcs. Lawrence Livermore Nat. Lab., 1994—; dir. preventive medicine residency U. Calif., Berkeley, 1991-95; assoc. clin. prof. U. Calif., San Francisco, 1983—; assoc. clin. prof. Sch. Pub. Health U. Calif., Berkeley, 1986—. Fulbright scholar, 1972-73. Fellow Am. Coll. Preventive Medicine, Am. Coll. Occupl. and Environ. Medicine, Am. Coll. Physicians Execs., Calif. Acad. Preventive Medicine (pres.), We. Occupl. and Environ. Med. Assn. (bd. dirs.). Office: HSD L723 LLNL PO Box 808 Livermore CA 94551-0808

SEWELL, JEFFERY PETER, barrister; b. Sydney, NSW, Australia, Dec. 26, 1955; s. Peter John and Margaret Valerie (Jeffery) S.; m. Victoria Anne Nutman; children: Belinda Victoria Sewell, Michelle Marie Sewell. LLB, B in Commerce, U. NSW, Sydney, Australia, 1979. Barrister, Supreme Ct. NSW, Supreme Ct. ACT, High Ct. Australia. Solicitor, Sydney, 1979-89; barrister Supreme Ct. NSW, ACT, High Ct. Australia, Sydney, 1989—; case law reporter Butterworths Ltd., Sydney, Australia, 1979-85, editor, author, case law annotator Butterworths Family Law Svc., 1980-84. Contbr. articles to profl. jours. Pres. Monkees Fan Club, Sydney, 1967; cricketeer NSW Chs. League, 1970-79. Recipient Bronze Medallion and bar, NSW Life Saving Assn., 1969, Bronze Cross, 1970. Mem. NSW Bar Assn., LEADR Comml. Law Assn. Australia, Australian Mus. Soc., Australian Maritime Mus., Zoo Friends, Tattersalls Club, Olympic Club, NSW Leagues Club, Kirribilli Ex-Serviceman's Club. Anglican. Avocations: cricket, football, golf, swimming. Office: Garfield Barwick Chambers, 11/53 Martin Pl 11th Fl, Sydney NSW 2000, Australia

SEWELL, JOHN ISAAC, electronic engineer, educator; b. Kirkby Stephen, England, May 13, 1942; s. Harry and Dorothy (Brunskill) S.; m. Ruth Alexandra Baxter, May 6, 1989; children: Elizabeth Anna, Deborah Ruth. BSc, U. Durham, 1963; PhD, U. Newcastle-upon-Tyne, 1966; DSc, U. Durham, 1995. From lectr. to reader electronic sys. U. Hull, England, 1968-85; prof. electronic sys. U. Glasgow, 1985—, dean engring., 1990-93; vis. rsch. prof. U. Toronto, 1995. Fellow IEEE, Instn. Elec. Engrs. Avocations: walking, swimming. E-mail: sewell@elec.gla.ac.uk. Home: 16 Paterson Pl, Bearsden Glasgow G61 4RU, Scotland Office: U Glasgow, Dept Elec Engring, G12 8LT Glasgow Scotland

SEWELL, RODNEY MILTON, biologist; b. Frederick, Md., July 5, 1946. BS in Psychobiology, Hood Coll., 1974. Operating room tech. USN, 1967-70; biologist NIMH/LBEB, 1974-79; systems integrator LAMDA, 1983—. Mem. IEEE Computer Soc., N.Y. Acad. Scis., AAAS, Am. Chem. Soc., Am. Psychol. Soc., Soc. Photo-Optical Instrumentation Engrs. Achievements include research in developmental and comparative aspects of neurobiology and behavior, computer-assisted learning devices. Office: Lab Med Devices PO Box 30634 Bethesda MD 20824-0634

SEWELL, RUFUS, actor; b. Twickenham, England, Oct. 29, 1967; s. William and Jo Sewell. Student, Ctrl. Sch. Speech & Drama, London. Actor theatrical debut As You Like It, Shefield's Crucible Theatre, (miniseries) Middlemarch, 1994, Arabian Nights, 1999, (films) Twenty-One, 1991, Dirty Weekend, 1993, Cold Comfort Farm, 1995, Hamlet, 1996, Dark City, 1998, Dangerous Beauty, 1998, In a Savage Land, 1999, Bless the Child, 1999. Office: UTA 9560 Wilshire Blvd Ste 500 Beverly Hills CA 90212-2427

SEWELL, WILLIAM GEORGE, III, electronics engineer; b. Roanoke, Va., Dec. 14, 1950; s. William George Jr. and Elizabeth Marie (Morrison) S.; m. Verna Landry, Aug. 25, 1970 (div. 1974); children: Ronald Allen, Bryan Joseph; m. Colleen Rose Gaynor, May 15, 1981. BS in Engring., U. Ill., Chgo., 1980; PhD, Calif. U., Modesto, 1983. Electronic technician 928 Airlift Group, Chgo., 1972-74; with FAA, Chgo., 1974-85; staff engr. FAA, Wheeling, Ill., 1980-82; regional nav. and landing systems engr. FAA, Chgo., 1982-85; with Jerry Thompson & Assocs., Kensington, Md., 1987-88; v.p. Navcom Systems, Inc., 1988-89, B2 Software, Inc., 1988-89; v.p., CEO The Thinkk Corp., 1988-89; founder, CEO Software Coalition, 1989—; dir. comm. and info. systems group SEMA, Inc., 1990-93; dir. comm. solutions, Jacobs Facilities, Inc., 1993—, Sverdrup fellow, 1998; cons. engr. W.G. Sewell & Assocs., Internat., Niles, Ill., 1981-88; chair TIA Indsl. Telecom Standards Body. Contbr. articles to tech. publs. Mem. Chgo. Coun. Fgn. Rels., 1976-80. Served with USAF, 1970-72, Vietnam. Recipient 1st prize Am. Soc. Electro-Surgery, 1982. Mem. IEEE (chair telecomm. industry assoc. indsl. stds. group), Soc. Automotive Engrs., Aircraft Owners and Pilots Assn. Achievements include invention of high speed turn control for land vehicles, 1980; co-inventor child's hidden identification and location device, 1990. Office: 1300 Wilson Blvd Ste 500 Arlington VA 22209-2307

SEXSON, STEPHEN BRUCE, education writer, educator; b. Silver City, N.Mex., May 29, 1948; s. Ralph Dale and Wanda Claudean (McMahan) S.; m. Barbara Jane Davis, May 24, 1968; children: David Paul, Linda Carol. BA in Rhetoric and Pub. Address, Pepperdine U., 1969, MA in Pub. Comm., 1975; PhD in Higher Edn., Okla. State U., 1990. Asst. to supt. Morongo Unified Sch. Dist., 29 Palms, Calif., 1973-77; corp. trainer Merrill Lynch Realty, Dallas, 1979-81; sch. psychologist Texhoma (Tex.) Sch. Dist., 1982-83; assoc. prof., dir. Christian Student Ctr. Okla. Panhandle State U., Goodwell, 1982-84; rsch. resident Okla. State U., Stillwater, 1984-87; mem. spl. programs staff L.A. Unified Sch. Dist., 1987-93; dir. Edwest Edn. Rsch., Burbank, Calif., 1991—; lectr. Chapman U., 1998—; guest lectr. edn. Okla. State U., Stillwater, 1993-94, U. Tulsa, 1993-94; conv. spkr. Merrill Lynch Realty-Relo, Atlanta, 1979; prof. Chapman U., 1998—. Author: The Magic Classroom, 1995, The Values Rich Teacher, 1996; contbr. articles to profl. jours. Mem. ASCD, Am. Assn. Sch. Adminstrs., Nat. Assn. of Sch. Psychologists, Lions Club, Phi Delta Kappa. Avocations: computing, travel, theatre. Home: PO Box 1853 Twentynine Palms CA 92277-1250 Office: Chapman U Coachella Valley Campus 333 N Glassell St Orange CA 92866-1099

SEXTON, DAVID FARRINGTON, lawyer, investment banking executive; b. Montclair, N.J., Aug. 20, 1943; s. Dorrance and Marjorie (McComb) S.; m. Ann Hemelright, Feb. 27, 1971; children: James, Ashley, Christopher. AB cum laude, Princeton U., 1966; JD cum laude, U. Pa., 1972. Bar: N.Y. 1972. Assoc. Sullivan & Cromwell, N.Y.C., 1972-77; with First Boston Corp., N.Y.C., 1977-90; v.p., gen. counsel First Boston Corp., 1980-83, mng. dir., gen. counsel, 1983-86; mng. dir., pres. First Boston Internat. Ltd., 1986-90; sr. exec. v.p., dir. Yamaichi Internat. (America), Inc., N.Y.C., 1990-95, vice-chmn., 1995-98; pres., CEO The Farrington Group, LLC, N.Y.C., 1998—; bd.dirs. Yamaichi (Am.) Holdings, Inc., Yamaichi (Am.) Fin., Inc.; adj. prof. law Fordham U., 1985-86; mem. U.S.-Japan Friendship Commn., Washington, 1990-94, chmn. fin. adv. com., 1994—. Lt. USNR, 1966-69. Mem. Assn. Bar City N.Y., Racquet and Tennis Club, N.Y. Yacht Club, Ivy Club, Bucks Harbor Yacht Club (bd. govs. 1991—), The Nat. Assn. of Japan Am. Socs. (bd. dirs. 1998—). Republican. Presbyterian.

SEXTON, JOSEPH PATRICK, sales executive; b. Owensboro, Ky., Mar. 12, 1964; s. Cecil and Margie (Hamilton) S.; m. Tracy F. Shoemaker, May 17, 1986; children: Brittany, Zachary. Computer mgmt., ICM Sch. Bus., Pitts., 1992. Ins. sales Met LIPG, Pitts., 1988-92; help desk Genix Corp., Pitts., 1992-93; sr. account mgr. Black Box Corp., Pitts., 1993-98; supr. reseller sales Black Box Corp., 1998—; strategic account mgr. fed. Marconi Comm., 2000—. Rep. committeman, 1996—. Cpl. U.S. Army, 1985-88. Mem. Moose, Lions. Roman Catholic. Avocations: golf, investments, boating. E-mail: BBoxJoe@yahoo.com. Home: 1825 Realty Ave Pittsburgh PA 15216-3611 Office: Black Box 1000 Park Dr Lawrence PA 15055-1018

SEYA, HIROMICHI, glass products company executive; b. Oct. 7, 1930. Degree in engring., Tokyo U., 1954. With Nippon Carbide Chem. Ind. Co.; with Asahi Glass K.K., Tokyo, 1954, various mgmt. positions, 1954-85, mng. dir., 1985—, former pres., CEO; former pres. Asahi-Olin Ltd., Tokyo; pres. Sanritto Industries; chmn., CEO Asahi Glass Co. Ltd., Tokyo. Office: Asahi Glass Co Ltd, 1-2 Marunouchi 2-chome, Chiyoda-ku Chiyoda-ku Tokyo 100-8305, Japan also: Asahi-Olin Ltd, 25 Oasu Higashi Wada Kamisumachi, Ibaragi Prefecture, Tokyo 104, Japan*

SEYBOLD, KLAUS DIETER, theology educator; b. Heidenheim, Germany, Apr. 28, 1936; arrived in Switzerland, 1979; s. Jakob and Margarete (Hofmann) S.; m. Gisela Vetterlein; children: Bernhard, Dietrich. D of Theology, U. Kiel, Germany, 1968, habilitation in theology, 1972. Vicar Nat. Evang. Ch. Württemberg, Germany, 1961-64; asst. scholar U. Kiel, Faculty of Theology, 1964-72, docent, 1972-77, prof. theology, 1977-79; prof. Old Testament studies U. Basel, Switzerland, 1979—. Author: Das davidische Königtum im Zeugnis der Propheten, 1972, Das Gebet des Kranken im Alten Testament, 1973, Der aaronitische Segen, 1977, Krankheit und Heilung, 1978, Die Wallfahrtspsalmen, 1978, Sickness & Healing, 1981, Die Psalmen—Eine Einführung, 1986, Introducing the Psalms, 1990, Der Prophet Jeremia, Leben und Werk, 1993, Die Psalmen, Handbuch zum Alten Testament, 1996, Studien fur Psalmenauslegung, 1998, Die Sprache der Propheten, 1999; editor Theologische Zeitschrift, Basel, 1980—. Mem. Soc. Bibl. Lit., German Soc. Palestine, Schweizerische Gesellschaft für orientalische Altertumskunde SGOA, Internat. Orgn. of Study of the Old Testament IOSOT. E-mail: klaus.seybold@.unibas.ch. Home: Bruderholzrain 62, CH-4102 Binningen Switzerland Office: Leonhardsgraben 3, CH-4051 Basel Switzerland

SEYFERT, WAYNE GEORGE, secondary education educator, anatomy educator; b. Roslyn Park, N.Y., Nov. 23, 1947; s. George William Seyfert and Helen Francis (Weiss) Marks; m. Kathleen A. Kearns, May 23, 1970 (div. 1980); children: Sean Francis, Kerry Noelle, Adam Wayne. BS in Biology, SUNY, Cortland, 1969; MS in Biology, L.I. U. at C.W. Post, 1973; profl. diploma in sch. adminstrn., CUNY at Queen's Coll., N.Y.C., 1988. Cert. biology and secondary sci. tchr., N.Y.; cert. sch. adminstr. and supr., N.Y.; cert. sch. dist. adminstr., N.Y. Jr. h.s. sci. tchr. Port Washington (N.Y.) Schs., 1969-70; sci. tchr. Lawrence (N.Y.) Pub. Schs., 1970—; instr. North Shore Sci. Mus., Plandome, N.Y., 1973-75; adj. prof. human anatomy and physiology Nassau C.C., Garden City, N.Y., 1975—, N.Y. Inst. Tech., N.Y., 1994—; summer program dir. Sci. Mus. L.I., Plandome, 1976-85; environ. cons. Town of Brookhaven, L.I., 1978-80. Contbr. articles to profl. publs. Membership chmn. Boy Scouts Am., Sunrise dist., N.Y., 1978-79; mem. conservation adv. coun. Town of Brookhaven, 1977-79; mem. L.I. Sci. Congress exec. bd., 1985-98. Recipient Ednl. Leadership award Lawrence Ednl. Found., 1998, named L.I. Educator of Month, Hofstra U./TV Channel 12, L.I., 1995, Person of the Yr., Nassau Herald, 1998, STANYS Nassau County H.S. Sci. tchr. of yr., 1998. Mem. AAAS, Am. Fedn. Tchrs., Adj. Faculty Assn., Nat. Sci. Tchrs. Assn., Nat. Biology Tchr. Assn., Am. Philatelic Soc., Am. 1st Day Cover Soc., Am. Revenue Assn., Am. Perfin Soc., Am. Precanceled Stamp Soc., United Postal Stationary Soc., Meter Stamp Soc., State Revenue Assn., Am. Airmail Soc., Aerogramme Soc., Christmas Seal and Charity Seal Soc., N.Y. Acad. Scis., N.Y. State United Tchrs., Sci. Tchrs. Assn. N.Y. State, L.I. Cover Soc., Lawrence Tchrs. Assn. (1st v.p. 1984—), MACUB Soc. for Neutobiology. Achievements include writing first history of America's first prairie and performance of first environmental study to trace an area's environmental change since first European encroachment. Home: PO Box 116 Woodmere NY 11598-0116 Office: Lawrence HS 2 Reilly Rd Cedarhurst NY 11516-1002

SEYITOGLU, GUROL, structural/tectonic geologist, educator; b. Istanbul, Turkey, July 30, 1960; s. Rahmi and Necmiye (Aydinbeyli) S.; m. Emine Gul Kapci, Oct. 27, 1990; 1 child E. U. Akay. BSc, Istanbul Tech. U., 1982, MSc, 1984; PhD, Leicester (Eng.) U., 1992. Rsch. asst. Istanbul Tech. U., 1986-87; hon. rsch. fellow Leicester (Eng.) U., 1993; asst. prof. Ankara (Turkey) U., 1996-98, assoc. prof., 1998—; cons. BHP Minerals, Herndon, Va., 1992-93. Contbr. articles to profl. jours. Recipient Encouragement award Sci. and Tech. Rsch. Coun. Turkey, Ankara, 1998; rsch. grantee Sci. and Tech. Rsch. Coun. Turkey, Ankara, 1994, PhD grantee Turkish Ministry Edn., Ankara, 1989. Mem. Chamber Geol. Engrs. Turkey (Golden Hammer rsch. award 1997), Internat. Assn. Structural/Tectonic Geologists, Internat. Assn. Volcanology and Chemistry Earth's Interior. Avocations: swimming, walking. Home: 1 Cadde, 25 Sokak 2/15, Ankara TR-06680, Turkey Office: Ankara U Dept Geol Engring, Tandogan, Ankara TR-06100, Turkey

SEYMOUR, GEORGE EDWARD, research scientist, consultant; b. Newark, Feb. 27, 1939; s. George Francis Seymour and Ava Bernadette Simon; m. Janet Lee Perkowski, June 25, 1965 (div. 1974); children: George Earl Charles, Debora Lee Ann Curry. BA, San Diego State U., 1969, MA, 1973; PhD, U. Mo., 1978. Prof. Calif. State U., Northridge, 1979-81; cons. Walt Disney, Inc., Anaheim, Calif., 1982-83, Sys. Info. Resources, San Diego, 1982-85; rsch. psychologist Navy Pers. R&D Ctr., San Diego, 1986-95; rsch. scientist Space and Naval Warfare Sys. Ctr., San Diego, 1995—. With USN, 1958-62. Mem. APA, Human Factors and Ergonomics Soc., Acad. Mgmt., Sigma Xi. Avocation: Internet. E-mail: drgeorge@home.com and seymour@spawar.navy.mil. Home: PO Box 84990 San Diego CA 92138-4990

SEYMOUR, JEFFREY ALAN, governmental relations consultant; b. L.A., Aug. 31, 1950; s. Daniel and Evelyn (Schwartz) S.; m. Valerie Joan Parker, Dec. 2, 1973; 1 child, Jessica Lynn. AA in Social Sci., Santa Monica Coll., 1971; BA in Polit. Sci., UCLA, 1973; MPA, 1977. Councilman aide L.A. City Coun., 1972-74; county supr.'s sr. dep. L.A. Bd. Suprs., 1974-82; v.p. Bank of L.A., 1982-83; prin. Jeffrey Seymour & Assocs., L.A., 1983-84; ptnr. Morey/Seymour & Assocs., L.A., 1984—; mem. comml. panel Am. Arbitration Assn., 1984 . Chmn. West Hollywood Parking Adv. Com., L.A., 1983-84; chm. social action com. Temple Emanuel of Beverly Hills, 1986-89, bd. dirs. 1988-93, v.p. 1990-93; v.p. Congregation N'Vay Shalom, 1994-95; mem. Pan Pacific Park Citizens Adv. Com., L.A., 1982-85; bd. dirs. William O'Douglas Outdoor Classroom, L.A., 1981-88; regent designate, bd. regents U. Calif., 2000 . Recipient plaques for svcs. rendered Beverlywood Cheviot Hills Dem. Club, L.A., 1981, Jewish Fedn. Coun. Greater L.A., 1983, certs. of appreciation, L.A. Olympic Organizing Com., 1984, County of L.A., 1984, City of L.A., 1987, Santa Monica Mountains Conservancy, 1999; commendatory resolutions, rules com. Calif. State Senate, 1987, Calif. State Assembly, 1987, 96, County of L.A., 1987, City of L.A., 1987. Mem. Am. Soc. Pub. Adminstrn., UCLA Alumni Assn. (mem. govtl. steering com. 1983 , bd. dirs. 1995 , chair bd. dirs. 1995-97, pres. 1998-2000); exec. sect. Calif. Fedn. Young Dems., 1971; mem. Calif. Dem. Cen. Com., 1979-82; pres. Beverlywood-Cheviot Hills Dem. Club, L.A., 1978-81; co-chmn. Westside Chancellor's Assocs. UCLA, 1986-88; mem. L.A. Olympic Citizens Adv. Com.; mem. liaison adv. commn. with city and county govt. for 1984 Olympics, 1984; v.p. comty. rels. metro region, Jewish Fedn. Coun. of L.A., 1985-87, co-chmn. urban affairs commn., 1987-89, vice chmn., 1989-90, sub-com. chmn. local govt. law and legislation commn., 1990 , chmn. campus outreach task force, 1994 ; mem. adv. bd. Nat. Jewish Ctr. for Immunology & Respiratory Medicine, 1991-93; bd. dirs. Hillel Coun. of L.A., 1991 ; mem. platform on world peace and internat. rels. Calif. Dems., 1983; pres. 43d Assembly Dist. Dem. Coun., 1975-79; arbitrator BBB, 1984 ; trustee UCLA Found., 1989-97; pres. UCLA Jewish Alumni, 1992-95; mem. Santa Monica Mountains Conservancy adv. com., 1996-99; mem. cabinet Jewish Cmty. Rels. Com. Greater L.A., 1994 , chair campus outreach task force, 1994-95, govtl. rels. commn., 1995-96, v. chair Jewish Cmty. Rels. com. Jewish Fedn. Coun. Greater L.A., 1998 ; mem. bd. dirss., Century City C of C, 1998 , adv. bd. L.A. Peace Now. Office: Morey Seymour Assocs 233 Wilshire Blvd Ste 290 Santa Monica CA 90401-1217

SEYMOUR, JOHN FRANCIS, medical oncologist; b. Melbourne, Australia, Aug. 25, 1963; s. James Patrick and Wendy Marie (Hankin) S.; m. Helen Symeopoulos, Apr. 28, 1991; children: James Dionysios, Gabriel John. MB, U. Melbourne, 1987, MB, BS, 1987; PhD, Inst. Cancer Rsch., 1998. FRACP. Intern St. Vincent's Hosp., Melbourne, 1988-91; fellow in med. oncology MD Anderson Cancer Ctr., Houston, Tex., 1992-93; oncology registrar Royal Melbourne Hosp., 1994, sr. med. oncologist dept. clin. haematology and med. oncology, 1995-98; sr. med. oncologist dept. med. oncology Austin and Repatriation Med. Ctr., Melbourne, 1995-97; cons. hematologist, head protocol devel. leukemia/lymphoma Peter MacCallum Cancer Inst., Melbourne, 1998-99, head leukemia/lymphona svc. divsn. hematology, med. oncology, 1999—; hon. hematologist, St. Vincent's Hosp., Melbourne, 1998—, hon. vis. med. oncologist Royal Melbourne Hosp., 1998—; treas., mem. Australasian Leukemia and Lymphoma Group, 1999—; councilor Australian and New Zealand Apheresis Assn., 1998—; mem. Victorian Med. & Sci. Com. Leukemia Found. Australia, 1999—, clin. rsch. com., Institutional Biorepository Mgmt. com., Antibiotic Issues Group, Peter MacCallum Cancer Inst., 1998—; presenter in field. Contbr. numerous articles to profl. jours., chpts. to books. Fellow Royal Australian Coll. of Physicians, 1994; recipient advanced cardiac life support cert. Am. Heart Assn., 1992, clin. rsch. award MD Anderson Cancer Ctr., 1993, 94, Travel award Am. Soc. of Hematology, 1993, 97, Haematology Soc. of Australia, 1998, Med. Postgrad. Rsch. scholar Australian Nat. Health and Med. Rsch. Coun., 1995-98. Mem. Australian Leukemia Study Group, Australian and New Zealand Lymphoma Group, Australian and New Zealand Apheresis Assn., Am. Assn. Cancer Rsch., Am. Soc. Clin. Oncology, Am. Soc. Hematology, Australasian Leukemia and Lymphoma Group, Australian Med. Assn., Australasian Radiaton Oncology Lymphoma Group, U. Melbourne Med. Soc., Med. Oncology Group of Australia, Med. Wine Soc. Victoria, Clin. Oncol. Soc. Australia, European Haematology Assn., Royal Australasian Coll. Physicians, Haematology Soc. Australia and New Zealand. E-mail: jseymour@petermac.unimelb.edu.au. Office: Peter MacCallum Cancer Inst, St Andrews Pl, East Melbourne Vic 3002, Australia

SEYMOUR, MARY FRANCES, lawyer; b. Durand, Wis., Oct. 20, 1948; d. Marshall Willard and Alice Roberta (Smith) Thompson; m. Marshall Warren Seymour, June 6, 1970; 1 foster child, Nghia Pham. BS, U. Wis., LaCrosse, 1970; JD, William Mitchell Coll., 1979. Bar: Minn. 1979, U.S. Dist. Ct. Minn. 1979, U.S. Ct. Appeals (8th cir.) 1979, U.S. Supreme Ct. 1986. With Cochrane and Bresnahan, P.A., St. Paul, 1979-94, Loper & Seymour, P.A., 1994—. Mem. ABA, Minn. Bar Assn., Ramsey County Bar Assn. Office: Loper & Seymour PA 24 4th St E Saint Paul MN 55101-1002

SEYMOUR, RICHARD DEMING, technology educator; b. Shelby, Ohio, Oct. 3, 1955; s. G. Deming and Elizabeth (Peterson) S.; m. Vicki Stebleton; 1 child, Ryan. BS in Edn., Ohio State U., 1978; MA, Ball State U., 1982; EdD, W.Va. U., 1990. Tchr. Crestview Sr. High Sch., Ashland, Ohio, 1978-81; from instr. to assoc. prof. Ball State U., Muncie, Ind., 1982—; vis. instr. W.Va. U., Morgantown, 1985, Oreg. State U., 1990-91. Co-author: Exploring Communications, 1987, rev. edit., 2000; co-editor: Manufacturing in Technology Education, 1993. Advisor 4-H Clubs, Richland County, Ohio, 1978-81; dir. tech. in-svc. workshops Ind. Dept. Edn., Indpls., 1988-2000. Named technology tchr. educator of yr. Coun. on Technology Tchr. Edn., 1998. Mem. Internat. Tech. Edn. Assn. (bd. dirs. 1992-94, chmn. internat. conf. 1999, Award of Distinction 1999), Soc. Mfg. Engrs., Coun. on Tech. Tchr. Edn., Ind. Math., Sci., Tech. Alliance (bd. dirs. 1994—), Tech. Educators Ind. (pres. 1995-96), Am. Soc. Engring. Edn., Tech. Edn. Collegiate Assn. (internat. advisor 1990-92), Epsilon Pi Tau, Phi Delta Kappa. Methodist. Avocations: model railroads, sports, travel. Office: Ball State U Dept Industry Tech Muncie IN 47306-0001

SEYRANIAN, ALEXANDER PARUIR, mechanical engineering and mathematics educator; b. Moscow, Feb. 15, 1947; s. Paruir Abraham Seyranian and Zinaida Vasilievna Shipova; m. Eleonora Andreevna Saakian, Aug. 23, 1975; children: Gayane, Andrei. MS, Moscow Phys.-Tech. Inst., 1971; PhD, Russian Acad. Scis., Moscow, 1977, DSc in Aerospace and Mech. Engring., 1988. Engr. Ctrl. Aero-Hydrodynamic Inst., Moscow, 1971-73; rschr. Inst. for Problems in Mechanics-Russian Acad. Scis., Moscow, 1977-91; guest prof. Tech. U. Denmark, 1991-92; leading rschr. Moscow State Lomonosov U., 1993—; bd. dirs. Aerospace Ctr., Moscow; hon. adv. Nat. Lab., Dalian U. Tech., China, 1994—. Co-author: Optimization Methods for Aviation Structures, 1989, Structural Optimization under Stability and Vibration Constraints , 1989; contbr. over 100 articles to profl. jours. and conf. procs.; mem. adv. bd. Internat. Jour. Theoretical and Applied Mechanics, Yugoslavia. Mem. N.Y. Acad. Scis., Internat. Soc. of Structural and Multidisciplinary Optimization. Office: Moscow State Lomonosov U Inst Mechanics, Michurynski pr 1, 117192 Moscow Russia

SEZER, AHMET NECDET, president of Turkey; b. Afyon, 1941. Head Constitutional Court, 2000—. Office: Cumhurbaskanligi Kökü, Cankaya, Ankara Turkey*

SEZNEC, ALAIN, university dean, foreign language educator; b. Paris, Mar. 20, 1930; came to U.S., 1941; s. Jean Joseph and Genevieve (Dunan) S.; m. Janet E. Grade, June 15, 1950; children: Anne, Peter J., Catherine G., Dominique M., Michael A. Licence es lettres, U. Paris, 1951, Diplome d'Etudes Superieures, 1953. Instr. French Harvard U., Cambridge, Mass., 1953-55, 57-58; asst. prof. Cornell U., Ithaca, N.Y., 1958-63, assoc. prof.,

1963-69, prof., 1969—, assoc. dean Coll. Arts and Scis., 1969-73, vice provost for humanities and performing arts, 1970-73, chmn. dept. Romance studies, 1976-78, dean, 1978-86, Carl A. Kroch Univ. librarian, 1999—, prof. Romance studies emeritus, 1996—. Editor: Princesse de Cleves (de Lafayette), 1961; author: Diderot and Pope's Essay on Man, 1975. Trustee Wells Coll., 1998—. Served with French Army, 1955-57. French Nat. fellow, 1965; recipient Clark award Cornell U., 1968. Mem. Modern Lang. Assn., Am. Assn. Tchrs. French. Home: 131 Kline Rd Ithaca NY 14850-2114 Office: Cornell U 210 Olin Library Ithaca NY 14853-5301

SFEIR, NASRALLAH PIERRE CARDINAL, archbishop; b. Reyfoun, Lebanon, May 15, 1929. D in Theology and Philosophy, St. Joseph U. Ordained priest, 1950. Parish priest Reyfoun, 1951-56; sec. of Maronite Archdiocese Damascus, 1956; gen. sec. Maronite Patriarchate; ordained bishop, 1961; patriarch Patriarch of Antioch for Maronites, Lebanon; elevated to cardinal Roman Cath. Ch., 1994. Office: Patriarchate Antioch & All East, Patriarcat Maronite, Bkerké Lebanon*

SFINIAS, JOHN, data systems company executive; b. London, May 27, 1965; s. George Sfinias and Penelope Tsaousopoulou. MA in Polit. Terrorism (hon.), Aberdeen (Scotland) U., 1989. Cert. in polit. studies and internat. rels. Spl. advisor to min. Ministry of Nat. Economy, Athens, Greece, 1992-93, chmn. bimisterial com. on denationalisation, 1993; dealer Telesis Securities, Athens, 1994; mktg. vice-dir. Minoan Lines, Athens, 1995-96; mng. dir. 1st Data Sys., Athens, 1997—. Founding mem. Liberals Polit. Party, Athens, 1999. Master sgt. Greek Paratroopers Regiment, 1990-91. Avocations: bridge, squash, reading, scuba diving.

SFORNA, MARINO, utilities/energy executive; b. Rome, Dec. 22, 1959. PhD in Elec. Engring., U. Rome, 1985. Power sys. expert ENEL, Rome, 1982-89; prin. rschr. ENEL, Milan, 1990-97; mgr. Italian ISO, Milan, 1998—; asst. prof. U. Rome, 1997—. Contbr. articles to profl. jours. Lt. Italian Army, 1985-86. E-mail: sforna.marino@grtn.it. Office: Italian ISO, Viale Edison 18, Sesto San Giovanni 20099, Italy

SFORZA, MARIO VITO, newspaper writer, retired surgeon; b. Milan, May 20, 1933; s. Francesco and Natalia (Stropeni) S.; m. Valsecchi Maria Antonia; children: Chiarella, Cristina, Caterina, Francesco, Ermanno. Doctorate, U. Milan, 1957, cert., 1965; cert., U. Milan, 1972. Head svc. City Hosp., Oggiono, Italy, 1976-85, Lecco, Italy, 1985—; now writer. Author: Tumoral Metastasis, 1962, ECG in Urgen Gen. Surgery, 1965, Breast Tumors, 1967. Mayor Mandello Municipality, 1970-78; pres. Mountain Community, Lecco, 1972-78, Med. Coun., Lecco, 1978-81. Decorated Knight, Italy. Roman Catholic. Home: Aquileia, 23900 Lecco Italy

SGALL, PETR, linguist, educator; b. Budějovice, Czechoslovakia, May 27, 1926; s. Oskar Sgall and Ružena (Hüblová) Sgallová; m. Eva Zahelová, 1950 (div. 1952); 1 child, Ivan; m. Květuše Hofbauerová, 1958; children: Jiří, Alena. PhD, Charles U., Prague, Czechoslovakia, 1949, CSc, 1955, DrSc, 1966; Dr. Honoris Causa, INALCO, 1995, U. Hamburg, 1998. Sr. rsch. worker Charles U., 1962-67, rsch. prof., 1967-90, prof., 1990-92, prof. emeritus. Author: Infinitive im Rigveda, 1958; author (with others): Functional Approach to Syntax, 1969, Topic, Focus and Generative Semantics, 1973, Meaning of Sentence, 1986, Topic-focus Articulation, Tripartie Structures and Semantic Context, 1998. Recipient Humboldt Rsch. prize, 1992. Mem. Soc. Linguistica Europaea (internat. com. of computational linguistics), Czech Linguistic Soc., Cybernetic Soc., Prague Linguistic Cir. Home: Ortenovo n 24, 17000 Prague 7, Czech Republic Office: Charles U Fac Math/ Physics, Malostranske nam 25, 11000 Prague 1, Czech Republic

SGANGA, JOHN B., furniture holding company executive; b. Bronx, N.Y., Nov. 21, 1931; s. Charles and Marie (Crusco) S.; m. Evelyn Joan Battilana, Jan. 19, 1957; children: Mark, John B. Jr., Matthew. BS in Acctg. cum laude, Bklyn. Coll., 1961; postgrad., Bernard Baruch Coll. Systems analyst DIVCO, Wayne, N.Y., 1965-67; mgr. mgmt. cons. svcs. Coopers & Lybrand, CPAs, N.Y.C., 1967-74; sr. v.p. fin. and adminstrn. Aurora Products Co. subs. RJR Nabisco, West Hempstead, N.Y., 1974-79; contr. Gt. Lakes Carbon Corp., N.Y.C., 1979-80, v.p., 1980-81, sr. v.p. fin., CFO, 1981-86; v.p. Cunard Line, Ltd., N.Y.C., 1988; exec. v.p. CFO Consolitated Furniture Corp. (formerly Mohasco Corp.), N.Y.C., 1989—, also bd. dirs. Contbr. articles to profl. jours.; editl. adv. to Financial Management mag. Served with USNR, 1950-54. Mem. Inst. Cert. Mgmt. Cons. (a founder), Inst. Mgmt. Accts., Fin. Execs. Inst. (past chmn. com. M.I.S.), Treas.'s Club. Home: 21312 Tarraco Mission Viejo CA 92692-5921 Office: Consolidated Furniture Corp One Commerce Ctr 445 Park Ave Fl 9 New York NY 10022-2606

SHA, WEI, materials science educator; b. Beijing, June 13, 1964; arrive in Eng., 1988; s. Yong-an and Wen-pei (Duan) S. B Engring., Tsinghua U., Beijing, China, 1986; PhD, Oxford U., 1992. Rsch. assoc. Imperial Coll., London, 1991-92, Cambridge (Eng.) U., 1992-95; lectr. Queen's U. Belfast, Northern Ireland, 1995-99; reader Queen's U., Belfast, No. Ireland, 1999—; mem. steering com. Centre for High Temperature Superconductivity, London, 1991-92; 2d consulting engr. Steel Constrn. Inst., Eng., 1997; vis. prof. Harbin Inst. Tech., China, 1997—. Contbr. articles to profl. jours. Mem. Steel in Fire Forum, Chinese Materials Assn. (co-dir. 1994-96). Avocation: sports. Home: 5 Sandhill Gardens, Belfast BT5 6FF, Northern Ireland Office: Queens U Belfast, Sch Civil Engring, Belfast BT7 1NN, Northern Ireland

SHA, ZHEN-QUAN, marketing educator; b. Shanghai, China, Nov. 12, 1959; s. Xiang Sha and Yue-Ying Yang; m. Ruo-Ying Gu; 1 child, Si-Yun. BS, East China Normal U., Shanghai, 1982; M Engring., South China U. Tech., Guangzhou, China, 1991. Tchg. asst. South China U. Tech., 1982-86, lectr., 1987-93, assoc. prof., 1994—; rsch. fellow Chinese Mgmt. Rsch. Ctr., City U. Hong Kong, 1997-99; cons. Guangzhou Taxi Co., 1992-97. Author: Chain Operations in China, 1998; contbr. articles to profl. jours. Mem. Chinese People's Polit. Consultative Conf., 1998. Rsch. grantee Nat. Natural Sci. Fund, China, 1994, Guangdong Soft Sci. Fund, China, 1999. Mem. Guangdong Chain Ops. Assn. Mem. Chinese Guo-ming-Dang Revolutionary Party. Avocations: reading, table tennis, cooking.

SHA, ZONG, professional society administrator, educator; b. Rui-Chang, Hunan, China, Aug. 15, 1926; s. Sheng Ting and Dong Rui (He) Kong; m. Jian Zhou; children: Sha Lin, Sha Yin. BS, Nat. Wuhan U., China, 1949. Group leader Rsch. Inst. Electronics, Beijing, China, 1949-60; dir. Propagation Rsch. Lab., Sijiazhuang, China, 1960-65; dir. gen. China Rsch. Inst. Radiowave Propagation, Xinxiang, Henian, China, 1965-85; dep. sec. gen. Chinese Inst. Electronics, Beijing, 1985-96, v.p., 1996—; con. prof. Shan-Xi U., Taiyuan, China, 1993—; chmn. IEE Beijing Ctr., 1994—; vice chair IEEE Beijing Sect., 1993—. Named Best Rschr. Nat. Scientific Congress, Beijing, 1978. Fellow IEEE, IEE (based in U.K.), Chinese Inst. Electronics. Home: Lugu Rd #74, 100040 Beijing China Office: Chinese Inst Electronics, PO Box 165, 100036 Beijing China

SHAABAN, AZIZ MAHMOUD, physicist; b. Sidi Salim, Egypt, Oct. 19, 1949; s. Mahmoud and Ansaf Mohamed Hussein S.; m. Zeinab Medhat El Marasy, Sept. 26, 1976; children: Ahmed, Mohamed, Mostafa. BS in Physics, Assiut U., 1972; MS, London U., 1977, PhD, 1980. Asst. Assiut U., 1972-76, assoc. lectr., 1977-80; asst. and rsch. student London U., 1976-79; lectr. nuclear physics Mansoura U., Egypt, 1981-89, assoc. prof., 1990-96; prof. exptl. physics Mansoura U., 1997—; scientific cons. Helipolis Electronic, Cairo, 1983-88, Electro-Combined Opers., Cairo, 1988-97, United Arab Co., Cairo, 1997—. Contbr. articles to profl. jours. Avocations: bridge, chess, stamp collecting. Office: Mansoura Univ, 35516 Mansoura Egypt

SHAARAWI, AMR MOHAMED, engineering educator; b. Giza, Egypt, June 12, 1956; s. Mohamed Aly Shaarawi and Latifa Mohamed Ossman; m. Maria Cristina Chieli, Sept. 21, 1988; children: Sara Amr, Jihan Amr. BSc in Elec. Engring., Cairo U., 1978, BSc in Physics, 1980; MSc, Va. Poly. Inst. and State U., 1984, PhD, 1989. Instr. Cairo U., 1978-82, assoc. prof., 1989-99; tchg. and rsch. asst. Va. Poly. Inst. and State U., Blacksburg, 1982-87, rsch. fellow, 1987-89; assoc. prof. Am. U., Cairo, 1999—; investigator, rsch. fellow, rsch. asst. various projects. Contbr. numerous rsch. articles to profl. jours. Sr. Scholar fellow Binat. Fulbright Commn., 1996-97. Mem. Egyptian Syndicate for Engrs., Optical Soc. Am. Phi Kappa Phi. Office: Am U in Cairo, 113 Kasr El Aini St PO 2511, 11511 Cairo Egypt

SHAATH, AHMED AMER, human resources management specialist; b. Neunkirchen, Saarland, Germany, Dec. 13, 1966; s. Amer Juma and Tamam Kamel Shaath; m. Mervat Khader Abu Haseera, Apr. 8, 1998. BSc, Pacific Western U., 1995; diploma in mgmt., Coll. Profl. Mgmt., London, 1996; MBA, Pacific Western U., 1997. Chartered bus. adminstr. Sr. adminstr. Ministry of Health, United Arab Emirates, 1989-91; adminstrn. head Saqaya Group, United Arab Emirates, 1991-95; dir. internat. rels. Ministry of Youth, Gaza, 1995; mgr. Gulf Comml. Group, United Arab Emirates, 1995-96; gen. coord. Hamriya Free Zone, Sharjah, United Arab Emirates, 1997—; instr. Emirates Cultural Ctr., Abu Dhabi, United Arab Emirates, 1992-94, 96—; cons. Nat. Found. for Devel., Jerusalem, 1994-95. Author: (poetry book) The Forgotten Beach, 1996 (Arab Knights award 1996). Recipient Achievement award Thiga Club, 1998, Best Participation award Emirates Cultural Forum, 1994. Fellow Chartered Inst. Bus. Adminstrs.; mem. Acad. Internat. Mgmt. Avocations: bowling, playing oud, air travel. Office: Hamriyah Free Zone Auth, PO Box 27010, Sharjah United Arab Emirates

SHABAKA, NABIL EL-MONGY MUHAMMAD, library director; b. Mansoura, Egypt, Oct. 14, 1942; arrived in Can., 1994; m. Faika Hosny Kamel, Feb. 8, 1970; children: Mohammed, Dalia, Ahmed, Dina, Thamer. BA in Libr. Sci., Cairo (Egypt) U., 1964; MA in Libr. Sci., Clarion (Pa.) U., 1983. Libr. Faculty of Commerce, Mansoura (Egypt) U., 1964-70; from libr. to sr. libr. Ministry of Edn., Kuwait, 1970-79, lectr. in libr. sci., 1979-80, inspector of sch. librs., 1980-81; libr. dir. Al-Sudairy Found. Pub. Libr., Sakaka, Saudi Arabia, 1984—; cons. audio video collection Police Coll., Kuwait, Instructional Materials Ctr., Cairo (Egypt) U.; mem. Com. on Kuwait Nat. Bibliography, 1980-81; supr. press clippings svc. Ministry of Interior, Riyadh, Saudi Arabia, 1984—. Feature columnist Weekly Jour., Al-Balagh, Kuwait, 1970-81; contbr. articles to (newspaper) Al-Bilad, Jeddah, 1984-86, Al-Madina, Jeddah, 1988—; co-author (books) Courses of Study, Ministry of Edn., Kuwait, 1979, 82.; co-translator (book) Desert Frontier of Arabia, 1995. Mem Egyptian Libr. Assn., Am. Libr. Assn., Kuwait Libr. Assn. Office: Al-Sudairy Found Pub Libr, Malk Fahd Rd PO Box 458, Sakaka Al Jawf, Saudi Arabia

SHABANA, EL-HASSAN, dentistry educator; b. Foa, Egypt, May 25, 1952; arrived in France, 1987; s. Husien Shabana and Fatima Ali; m. Francoise Poiraud, 1983; 1 child, Marwan. BDSc, Alexandria U., 1975, MSc, 1979; PhD, Eastman Dental Hosp., London, 1986; habilitation á dirigé recherches, U. Paris 7, 1997. Cert. in dentistry. Dentist M. Health, Tanta, Egypt, 1975-76; from asst. lectr. to lectr. Faculty of Dentistry, Mansoura, Egypt, 1977-87; lectr. faculty of sci. U. Paris 7, 1991—; pvt. practice as dentist, Alexandria, 1977-80; rschr. Lab. Biology-Odontology, Paris, 1987-99. Editor: (jour.) Microscopy Rsch. and Technique, 1998; contbr. articles to profl. jours. Soldier Med. Corps, 1976-77. Mem. European Assn. Cell Biology, French Soc. Cell Biology, French Soc. Cancer. Avocations: painting, sculpture, calligraphy, gardening.

SHABOT, DAVID M., personnel specialist; b. Bklyn., May 27, 1952; s. Murray D. and Lily S.; m. Michelle M. Drescher, Feb. 19, 1977; children: Cari, Mollie, Michael. BA in Sociology, SUNY, Stony Brook, 1974, MS in Health Svcs. Adminstrn., 1976. Logistics mgr. NYU Med. Ctr., N.Y.C., 1976-77; asst. prof. Framingham (Mass.) State Coll., 1979-80; dir. Health Planning Coun. Greater Boston, 1977-78, Southeastern Mass. Hosp. Coun., Burlington, 1978-84, Met. Boston Hosp. Coun., Burlington, 1981-84; v.p. managed care Mass. Hosp. Assn., Burlington, 1984-86; mng. dir. Korn/Ferry Internat., Boston, 1988-96; office mng. dir. Korn/Ferry Internat., Phila., 1996—. Contbr. articles to profl. jours. Bd. dirs. Tiferet Bet Israel, Blue Bell, Pa., 1997—. Mem. World Affairs Coun. Jewish. Avocations: cooking, running. Home: 910 Wooded Pond Rd Ambler PA 19002-1871 Office: Korn/Ferry Internat 11 Penns Ct Philadelphia PA 19144-2912

SHACHMUROVE, YOCHANAN, economics educator; b. Tel Aviv, Oct. 10, 1951; s. Emanuel and Victoria Shachmurove; m. Yochanan Shachmurove, 1978; 3 children. BA magna cum laude, Tel Aviv U., 1975, MBA magna cum laude, 1977; MA, U. Minn., 1980, PhD, 1983. Prof. Ind. U., Indpls., 1982-84, Bar-Ilan U., Ramat-Gan, Israel, 1985-90; prof. econs. U. Pa., Phila., 1991—; assoc. prof. CCNY, 1996-99, prof., 2000—; internat. advisor Harvard Inst. for Internat. Devel., Ukraine, 1996-99. Assoc. editor Internat. Jour. Bus., 1997—; contbr. articles to profl. jours., chpts. to books. Maj. Israel Def. Forces, 1969-72. Grantee NSF, 1996, Harvard Inst. for Internat. Devel., 1996-97, New Econ. Sch., Moscow, 1996. Mem. Am. Econ. Assn. (assoc. editor Am. Economist 1996—). Home: 56 Trent Rd Wynnewood PA 19096-3707 Office: U Pa Dept Econs 3718 Locust Walk Philadelphia PA 19104-6209

SHACKLETON, KEITH HOPE, artist, naturalist; b. Weybridge, Surrey, Eng., Jan. 16, 1923; s. William Stancliffe and Constance Mary (Hope) S.; m. Jacqueline Tate, Sept. 14, 1951; children: Sarah, Jason, Jasper. Student pub. schs., Oundle, Eng.; LLD (hon.), U. Birmingham, Eng., 1987. Dir., pilot Shackleton Aviation Ltd., London, 1946-59; freelance painter and writer, 1959—. Author, illustrator: Tidelines, 1951, Wake, 1953, Wildlife and Wilderness: An Artist's World, 1981, Ship in the Wilderness, 1989, Keith Shackleton: An Autobiography in Paintings, 1998. With RAF, 1941-46. Fellow Geog. Soc., Zool. Soc. London; mem. Royal Soc. Marine Artists (pres. 1974-79), Soc. Wildlife Artists (pres. 1979-84), Artists League Gt. Britain (pres. 1980-85). Avocations: small boat sailing, exploration, fieldwork. Home and Studio: Woodley Wood Farm, Woodleigh, Kingsbridge TQ7 4DR, England

SHACKLETON, RICHARD JAMES, lawyer; b. Orange, N.J., May 24, 1933; s. S. Paul and Mildred W. (Welsh) S.; m. Katharine L. Richards, June 16, 1956; children: Katharine Margaret, Julia Anne, Forrest Maxwell. Student, Kalamazoo Coll., 1957; JD, Rutgers U., 1961. Bar: N.J. 1961, U.S. Dist. Ct. N.J. 1967, U.S. Dist. Ct. (ea. dist.) N.Y. 1987, U.S. Dist. Ct. (so. dist.) N.Y. 1986, U.S. Dist. Ct. (we. and no. dists.) N.Y. 1997, U.S. Ct. Appeals (3rd cir.) 1983, U.S. Ct. Appeals (4th cir.) 1986, U.S. Supreme Ct. 1969, Fed. Bar Coun. N.J. 1988. Ltd. atty. Berry Whitson & Berry, 1961; practice Ship Bottom, N.J., 1961—; sr. ptnr. Shackleton, Hazeltine & Dasti, Ship Bottom, 1965-84, Shackleton, Hazeltine & Bishop, 1984—. Pres. Beach Haven Inlet Taxpayers Assn., 1958-68, Ocean County Vis. Homemakers Assn., 1966-72, Brodhead Watershed Assn., 1997-98; mem. hist. soc. U.S. Dist. Ct. N.J. Mem. ABA (litigation sect., product liability com.), Am. Judicature Soc., Fed. Bar Coun. N.Y., N.J. Bar Assn., N.Y. Bar Assn., Ocean County Bar Assn., Def. Rsch. Inst. (mem. med. device and products sect.), Ocean County Lawyers Club, Henryville Conservation Club (chmn. bd.), Henryville Flyfishers Club (pres.), The Anglers' Club Phila., Phila. Gun Club, Sandy Island Gun Club (life), NRA (life), Brodhead Protectice Assn. (bd. dirs.), Brodhead Watershed Assn. (bd. dirs., pres. 1997-98), Ancient Inc. Order of the Beefeater. Home: 5614 West Ave Beach Haven NJ 08008-1059 Office: 22d St at Long Beach Blvd Ship Bottom NJ 08008

SHACKLETON, ROBERT JAMES, accounting executive; b. Louisville, Aug. 21, 1936; s. Robert James and Annelle (Barrett) S.; m. Mary Randall, Dec. 21, 1963; children: Scott Randall, David Eric, Nancy Lynne. BSc, U. Louisville, 1958; MBA, U. So. Calif., 1969. Acct. audit dept. KPMG Peat Marwick, L.A., 1961-69, audit ptnr., 1969, ptnr. in charge San Fernando Valley, 1970-71, mem. profl. practice review com., 1974-76, SEC reviewing ptnr., 1976-97; ptnr. in charge audit dept. KPMG Peat Marwick, Orange County, Calif., 1976-88, ptnr. in charge profl. practice, 1988-97; mng. ptnr. Shackleton & Co., Orange County, 1998—. Co-Author: Audits of Airlines, 1981. Chmn. L.A. Jr. C. of C., 1967-68, dir., 1968-70, pres. Arts Found., 1970-71, trustee Arts Found., 1970-75; dir. L.A. Master Chorale So. Calif. Choral Music Assn., 1968-69; treas. Jr. Achievement So. Calif., 1972-74, bd. dirs., 1972-80, treas. Orange County chpt., 1989-93; bd. dirs. Newport Harbor Area C. of C., Calif., 1979-91, CFO, 1983-84, pres. orgnl. affairs divsn., 1988, vice chmn. bd. dirs., 1989, chmn. bd. dirs., 1990; exec. bd. dirs. Orange County coun. Boy Scouts Am., 1981-99, chmn. Scout-O-Rama, 1982, chmn. camp promotion, 1986, dist. chmn. Rancho Del Mar, 1984-85, advisor Order of Arrow, 1984-86; bd. dirs. Orange County Lincoln Club, 1992; mem. Calif. State Bd. Accountancy, 1992, chmn. profl. conduct com. and bd. liaison to qualifications com., 1992-94, mem. enforcement program mgmt. com., 1993-95, mem. article 9 task force, 1993-94, v.p., 1995, pres., 1996-97; assoc. mem. Calif. Rep. State Ctrl. Com. Lt. USN, 1958-61. Mem. AICPA (mem. fed. govt. panel advisors 1973-80, mem. subcom. civil aeronautics 1973-80), Nat. Assn. Accts. (bd. dirs. San Fernando Valley chpt. 1971-72), Nat. Assn. State Bds. Accountancy (mem. rels. with govt. agys. com. 1992-95, mem. legal liability task force 1992-95, chmn. privity subcom. 1992-95, mem. CPA adv. panel 1995-96, mem. audit com. 1995-98, mem. future licensing, litig. and legis. com. 1995-98, bd. dirs. 1997-98), Fin. Mgrs. Soc. Savs. Insts. (assoc. mem.), Calif. Soc. CPA (chmn. aerospace and electronics industry com. L.A. chpt. 1972-74, mem. state savs. and loan com. 1980-92, chmn. savs. and loan conf. 1985, cert. in estate planning, 1998), Balboa Bay Club, Ctr. Club, Newport Harbor Yacht Club (bd. dirs. 1989-90, treas. 1990), Am. Legion Yacht Club, St. Francis Yacht Club, Marin Yacht Club. Presbyterian. Avocations: boating, collecting nautical artifacts, collecting Presidential memorabilia. Office: Shackleton & Co 102 Linda Isle Newport Beach CA 92660-7210

SHACKLEY, DOUGLAS JOHN, fire alarm company executive; b. Oakland, Calif., Sept. 21, 1938; s. Floyd H. and Margqret I. Shackley; m. Chloe Jeanne Olson, Sept. 11, 1965; children: Derek Todd, Darren James, Daniel John, Christina Louise. Student, San Jose State U., 1957, Chabot Coll., 1962-63; diploma in bus. mgmt., LaSalle Extension U., 1972. Officer mgr. service dept. Am. Dist. Telegraph Co. (ADT), Oakland, 1961-67; office mgr. Pacific Aux. Fire Alarm Co., San Francisco, 1967-69, mgr., 1969-73, pres., gen. mgr., 1973—, also dir. Contbg. mem. Alarm Industry Telecommunications Com. Pres., Chabot Sch. Dad's Club, 1969-70, Chabot Sch. Parent's Club, 1971-72; moderator Eden United Ch. of christ, 1980-81, vice moderator, 1987-88; mem. Eden Area YMCA, San Francisco YMCA, Boy Scouts Am.; sustaining mem. Calif. Republican Com.; mem. Rep. Presdl. Task Force, 1994-95. Served with USMC, 1957-61. Recipient Art Kane Meml. award, CAFAA, 2000. Mem. Nat. Fire Preventnion Assn., Calif. Automatic Fire Alarm Assn. (bd. dirs. 1986-87, 94, 95, pres. 1988-89, v.p. for No. Calif. 1987-88, 96-2000, Art Kane Meml. award 2000), Lake Mont Pine Home Owner Assn. (bd. dirs. 1988-89), San Francisco C. of C. (code com.), Rotary. Home: 1380 Carlton Pl Livermore CA 94550-6400 Office: Pacific Aux Fire Alarm Co 95 Boutwell St San Francisco CA 94124-1903

SHADAREVIAN, PAUL, solicitor; b. London, July 18, 1958; s. Sarkis Sahag and Jeanette Linda (West) S.; m. Elizbaeth Ann Williams, Nov. 10, 1988; 1 child, Tobias Alexander. BA with honors, U. Essex, 1980; diploma in law, City U., London, 1981. Sr. rsch. officer dept. govt. U. Essex, England, 1981-83; barrister-at-law, 1984-89, solicitor, 1989-96; ptnr. Norton Rose, London, 1991-96. Consulting editor, jt. author: Butterworths Planning Law Svc. Fellow Royal Soc. Arts; mem. Environ. Bar Assn. (planning com.). Mem. Ch. of England. Avocations: music, sailing, writing, fencing, cycling. E-mail: paul@shadarevian.F9.co.uk. Office: Norton Rose, Kempson House Camomile St, London EC3A 2AY, England

SHADAYDEH, MAHA, engineering educator; b. Damascus, Syria, May 20, 1968; parents Sami Mansour Shadaydeh and Shamieah Diyab Al-Mousa. BSEE, Damascus U., 1990; M of Engring., Toyohashi U. Tech., 1996; PhD in Elec. and Comm. Engring., Tohoku U., Sendai, Japan, 1999. Engr. High Inst. Applied Scis. and Tech., Damascus, 1990-91; instr. Computer Engring. Inst. Damascus U., 1991-92, asst. lectr. faculty mech. and elec. engring., 1992-93, lectr. faculty mech. and elec. engring., 1999—. Contbr. papers to profl. jours. Mem. IEEE, Inst. Electronics, Info. and Comm. Engrs. Avocation: basketball. E-mail: shadayde@scs-net.org.

SHADDOCK, PAUL FRANKLIN, SR., human resources director; b. Buffalo, Apr. 7, 1950; s. William Edmund and Rhea (Riester) S.; m. Linda Jeannine Bauer, July 19, 1980; children: Paul Jr., Jessica. BS, State U. Coll. N.Y., Buffalo, 1973; MBA, SUNY, Binghamton, 1975. Warehouse mgr. Ralston Purina Co., Denver, 1976-77; prodn. supr. Samsonite Corp., Denver, 1978-79, labor rels. rep., 1979-83; dir. human resources NBI, Inc., Denver, 1984-89, United Techs. Corp., Colorado Springs, Colo., 1990-95, Rockwell Semiconductor Sys., Newport Beach, Calif., 1995-96; v.p. human resources CSG, Systems, Inc., Denver, Colo., 1996—. Mem. Colo. Alliance of Bus., Denver, 1983-85, 90—, exec. com. U. Colo., Colorado Springs, 1990—. Mem. Assn. of Quality Participation, Am. Personnel Assn., Colo. Human Resource Assn., Human Resource Electroncis Group, Mountain States Employers Coun., S. Metro C. of C. Republican. Roman Catholic. Avocations: swimming, tennis, skiing. Home: 5744 S Lima St Englewood CO 80111-4145

SHADE, DEBRA L., biomedical researcher; b. Quincy, Ill., Aug. 12, 1961; d. Elvin D. and Virginia L. Starman. BS, Quincy Ill., 1983; postgrad., U. North Tex., 1994. Rsch. technician Washington U., St. Louis, 1984-86; rsch. asst. U. Tex. Southwestern Med. Sch., Dallas, 1986-89; assoc. scientist Alcon Labs., Ft. Worth, 1989-90, scientist I, 1990-93, scientist II, 1993-97, sr. scientist I, 1998—. Patentee in field of neuroprotection. Mem. AAAS, Soc. for Exptl. Biology and Medicine. Achievements include patent in field. E-mail: debra.shade@alconlabs.com. Home: 5021 Timbercreek Dr Apt 132 Arlington TX 76017-0960 Office: Alcon Rsch Ltd Glaucoma Rsch R3-24 6201 South Fwy Fort Worth TX 76134-2001

SHADE, KERRYN VINCENT, city manager; b. Frankston, Victoria, Australia, Dec. 19, 1946; s. Eric Vincent and Rachel Rosemary (Manuel) S. Student, Royal Melbourne Inst. Tech., Australia, 1972. Cert. mcpl. clk. Clk., adminstrv. officer City of Frankston, Melbourne, 1965-75; chief clk. City of Shepparton, Australia, 1975-77; dep. shire sec. Shire of Romsey, Australia, 1977-78; shire sec. Shire of Arapiles, Natimuk, Australia, 1978-86, Shire of Warracknabeal, Australia, 1986-95; CEO Horsham (Australia) Rural City Coun., 1995—. Justice of the peace, Victoria, 1983; bail justice, Victoria, 1990. Fellow Australian Inst. Mgmt., Inst. Mcpl. Mgmt., Local Govt. Profls.; mem. Internat. Inst. Mcpl. Clks., Lions Internat. Anglican. Avocations: philately, horse racing, reading, football. Home: 4 Bullen Ct, Horsham VIC 3400, Australia Office: Horsham Civic Ctr, Roberts Ave, Horsham VIC 3400, Australia

SHADRICK, BETTY PATTERSON, university administrator, consultant; b. Kansas City, Mo., Nov. 5, 1945; d. Purvis and Ernestine (Murray) Patterson; m. Henry Fredrick Shadrick, Dec. 12, 1970; children: Erik Fanon, Sean Fitzgerald. BS, Grambling State U., 1971; MS, SUNY, Albany, 1972, EdS, 1983, EdD, 1995. Cert. K-9 tchr., N.Y. Head Start tchr. Schenectady (N.Y.) Pub. Schs., 1972; program specialist Title I N.Y. State Edn. Dept., Albany, 1973-75; edn. counselor Capital Dist. Equal Opportunity Ctr., Troy, N.Y., 1975; dir. ednl. opportunity Schenectady County C.C., 1975-79; dir. talent search Carver Cmty. Ctr., Schenectady, 1980-86; asst. dean SUNY, Albany, 1986-92, asst. v.p., 1992—; mem. adv. coun. Upper Hudson Libr. Fedn., Albany, 1984-90; founding mem. Black Faculty Profl. Staff Assn., SUNY, Albany, 1993—; cons./supr. Assn. Investment Mgmt. & Rsch., Charlotteville, Va., 1994—; bd. dirs. SUNY Aux. Svcs., Albany, 1996—. Mem. Soroptomist Internat., Schenectady, 1980-86; mem. Albany Dist. Links Inc., 1996—; bd. dirs. Family and Children Svc. Inc., Albany, 1991-93, Hamilton Hill Arts Ctr., Schenectady, 1997—, Nat. Black Child Devel. Inst., 1998—. Quality of Work Leave grantee SUNY, Albany, Chancellor's Award Excellence Profl. Svc., 1995. Mem. United Univ. Professions, AAUW, Assn. Equality and Excellence in Edn. (treas. 1984-85, v.p. 1985-86), Alpha Kappa Alpha (grad. advisor 1993-95). Dem. Baptist. Avocations: pub. speaking, golf, fitness tng., gardening, reading. Home: 223 Vincenza Ln Schenectady NY 12303-5646 Office: SUNY at Albany 1215 Western Ave # Ad121 Albany NY 12222-0001

SHADRIN, ARKADIY PETROVICH, heat power engineer, educator; b. Yakutsk, Russia, Aug. 1, 1941; s. Petr Nikolaevich and Vera Dmitrievna (Okhlopkova) S.; m. Lyudmila Gavrilyevna Savvina, Apr. 25, 1975; 1 child, Mila. Grad., Poly. Inst., Tomsk, Russia, 1966; CandTechScis, Poly. Inst., St. Petersburg, Russia, 1974. Engr., heat physicist Yakutian Br. of Acad. Scis. USSR, Yakutsk, Russia, 1967-69; sci. rschr. Inst. Physics/Siberian Br. of Acad. Scis. USSR, Yakutsk, 1972-78, head lab. on heat energy, 1978—; asst. prof. heat physics U. Yakutsk/Sakha, 1978—, asst. prof. heat supply, 1996—, asst. prof. electricity supply, 1997—; lectr. soc. Knowledge, Yakutsk. Author: Atomic Power Stations on Far North, 1983, Energy Facility: Problems and Forecasts, 1983, Optimization of Heat-Supplying Systems on Yakutia, 1987, Energy of Russia in Transitional Period, 1996;

editor newspaper Tech. of North. Mem. Russia Nucleus soc., Acad. of North Forum. Avocations: cars, the cosmos. Home: Kirova 7/2 ap 44, Yakutsk Russia 677007 Office: Russia Acad Scis/Physics, 1 Oktyabrskaya str, Yakutsk 677891, Russia 677891

SHAFAEDDIN, MEHDI, economist, educator; b. Yazd, Iran, July 21, 1945; s. Hossein and Zahra (Sadr) S.; m. Shahnaz Owrang, Aug. 28, 1970; children: Negar, Bahar. BA, Tehran U., 1969, MA, 1971; DPhil, Oxford U., 1980. Acting chief rsch. and planning Ministry of Economy Inst. Std. and Indsl. Rsch., Tehran, 1970-71; asst. prof. Abu-Rihan U., Tehran, 1971-73; econ. affairs officer UN Conf. on Trade and Devel., Geneva, 1981-88, trade policy advisor, 1988-94, editor bull. and chief policy coord., 1994-96, sr. economist, 1996—; sr. lectr. Webster U., Geneva, 1992-96; lectr. Tehran U., 1972, Rasht (Iran) U., 1972-73; cons. Min. of Agr., Tehran, 1972. Author: Fallacies in Trade and Industrial Policy; contbr. articles to profl. jours. Brit. Coun. scholar, 1973-76, Tehran U. scholar, 1964-68, 76-78. Mem. Devel. Assn., European Devel. Rsch. Inst. E-mail: mehdi.shafaeddin@unctad.org. Office: UNCTD, Palais des Nation, 1211 Geneva Switzerland

SHAFEEN, ISMAIL, Maldivian government official; b. Malé, Maldives, May 15, 1955; s. Ahmed Zaki and Fathimath Ibrahim Didi; m. Aishath Nadira; children: Fathimath Nabreesa, Ahmed Samuel. BA in Econs., Macquarie U., NSW, Australia, 1976; Hubert Humphrey fellow, Boston U., 1984-85. Dir. planning Ministry of Planning and Environ., Malé, Maldives, 1989, dep. min., 1989-90; min. Ministry of Planning and Environ., Malé, 1991-93, Ministry of Tourism, Malé, 1990-91, Ministry Planning, Human Resources and Environ., Malé, 1993—; now min. Ministry of Transp. and Comms., Malé, 1996—, min. home affairs, housing, and environment; min. Ministry of Tourism, Malé, 1990-91; chmn. Nat. Coun. for Protection and Preservation of Environ., Malé; gov. Asian Devel. Bank, Manila, The Philippines. Active Vols. for Environ. and Social Harmony and Improvement, Malé. Home: Orchid Maage, Amir Ahmed Magu, Malé 20-05, Maldives Office: Min Planning Human Rscs Environ/Trans Comms, Huravee Bldg, Malé 20-05, Maldives*

SHAFER, BYRON EDWIN, American government educator; b. Hanover, Pa., Jan. 8, 1947; s. Byron Henry and Doris Marguerite (von Bergen) S.; m. Wanda Kathleen McErn, Aug. 22, 1981. BA, Yale U., 1968; PhD, U. Calif., Berkeley, 1979; MA, Oxford U., 1985. Andrew W. Mellon prof. Am. govt. Oxford (Eng.) U., 1985—. Author: Presidential Politics, 1983, Quiet Revolution, 1983, Bifurcated Politics, 1988, Is America Different?, 1991, The End of Realignment?, 1991, The Two Majorities, 1995, Postwar Politics in the G-7, 1996, Present Discontents, 1996, Partisan Approaches to American Politics, 1998. Resident scholar Russell Sage Found., N.Y.C., 1977-85; recipient Schattschneider prize Am. Polit. Sci. Assn., 1980, Burdette prize, 1990. Mem. Phi Beta Kappa. Lutheran. Avocations: gardening, livestock management, furniture restoration. Home: Briar Post, Stratford Rd, Drayton nr Banbury Oxon OX15 6EG, England Office: Nuffield Coll, New Rd, Oxford OX1 1NF, England

SHAFER, ROBERT TINSLEY, JR., judge; b. Cin., Sept. 11, 1929; s. Robert Tinsley and Grace Elizabeth (Welsh) S.; m. Barbara Jean Hough, Dec. 27, 1950; children: Richard Hough, Janet Lee Shafer Davis, Charles Welsh. BA, Coll. of Wooster, 1951; JD, U. Cin., 1956. Bar: Fla. 1956, U.S. Ct. Appeals (5th cir.) 1963, U.S. Dist. Ct. (so. dist.) Fla. 1961, U.S. Supreme Ct. 1965. Asst. trust officer 1st Nat. Bank, Ft. Myers, Fla., 1956-57; ptnr. Henderson, Franklin, Starnes & Holt, P.A., Ft. Myers, 1957-77; cir. judge 20th Jud. Cir. State of Fla., Ft. Myers, 1977-92, chief cir. judge, 1985-89, sr. judge, 1992—; mem. com. for ret. and sr. judges Nat. Conf. State Trial Judges. Contbr. article to Corp. Law, 1955-56 (Goldsmith Corp. Law prize, 1956). Elder Covenant Presbyn. Ch., 1982-85; mem. jud. commn. Fla. Presbyn. Synod, 1960-63; chmn. Lee County chpt. Red Cross, Ft. Myers, 1963; chair Permanent Judicial Commn., Peace River Presbytery, Presbyn. Ch. U.S.A. 2nd lt. USMCR, 1951-53, PTO, Korea. Mem. ABA, Fla. Conf. Cir. Judges (exec. com. 1986-88), Fla. Bar Assn. (bd. govs. Jr. Bar sect. 1961-64), Lee County Bar Assn. (pres. 1968), Am. Judges Assn., Am. Judicature Soc., Nat. Conf. Met. Cts. Calusa Inn of Ct. Republican. Avocations: running races, bicycle racing, bicycle touring, travel, reading. Home: 2704 Shriver Dr Fort Myers FL 33901-5931

SHAFER, THOMAS W., real estate executive; b. Wenatchee, Wash., Dec. 3, 1941; 1 child, Katrina M. Broughton. BS, Wash. State U., 1965; MS, San Diego State U., 1972. Cons. Mex. Devel., 1972-80; devel. mgr. Am. Diversified, Encino, Calif., 1976-82; v.p. Pilchers Ltd., London, 1982-90, MGM Fin., San Diego, 1997—; mng. dir. M&T Investment Bankers, San Diego, 1990-97. Author: Real Estate and Economics, 1976, Urban Growth and Economics, 1978. With USN, 1965-70, Vietnam. Office: MGM Fin 1027 10th Ave San Diego CA 92101-5541

SHAFFER, ANITA MOHRLAND, counselor, educator; b. Racine, Wis., Apr. 5, 1939; d. Milton Arthur and Gudrun Amanda Stoffel. BS magna cum laude, U. Wis., 1961; MEd, U. Wash., 1966; postgrad., Ariz. State U., 1971-76. Cert. in elem. edn., social sci. secondary edn., spl. edn., Tex., Ariz.; lic. profl. counselor, Tex.; diplomate Internat. Acad. Behavioral Medicine, Counseling and Psychotherapy. Tchr. Racine Unified Dist. 1, 1961-63, Edmonds Sch. Dist. 15, Lynnwood, Wash., 1963-70, Ariz. Dept. Corrections, Phoenix, 1971-77; tchr. spl. edn. Pasadena (Tex.) Ind. Sch. Dist., 1977-78, spl. edn. counselor, 1978-90, elem. counselor, 1990-98; univ. supr. U. Houston, 1998—; ednl. cons., 1998—. Mem. ACA, NAFE, Internat. Platform Assn., Mus. Fine Arts Houston (patron), Beta Sigma Phi, Pi Lambda Theta. Home: 260 El Dorado Blvd # 801 Webster TX 77598-2244

SHAFFER, CLARENCE F., retired electronics executive; b. Williamsport, Pa., Sept. 19, 1910; s. Howard Edward and Zita Agnes (Gonsman) S.; m. Gertrude Alice Gray, Dec. 16, 1933; 1 child, Nancy Shaffer Ivanski. Student, Pa. State Coll., 1929-30, Harvard U., 1961. Pres., owner Shaffer Constrn. Co., Williamsport, 1930-39; dist. sales mgr., v.p. Pitney Bowes, Stamford, Conn., 1939-55; v.p., gen. sales mgr. Harris Intertype Co., Cleve., 1960-61; gen. mgr. bus. machines divsn. Fairchild Camera & Ins. Co., 1961-63, v.p., 1963-65; pres., owner Distbrs. Leasing and Sales, Cleve., 1966-75. Contbr. over 500 articles to computer mags. or books; holder 18 patents on bldg. industry products, including centerline sawing sys. Mem., pres. task force, mem. steering com. Rep. Nat. Com.; mem. Nat. Rep. Senatorial Com. Recipient silver medal Olympics; heavyweight champion Golden Gloves (oldest living champion). Mem. N.Am. Yacht Racing Union, Interlake Yachting Assn., Cleve. Yachting Club, Boater Luncheon Club (pres. 1949-97), Masons (32d degree), Shriners. Methodist. Avocations: painting, photography, yacht racing, computers, writing. Home: 19757 Roslyn Dr Rocky River OH 44116-1643

SHAFFER, DAVID JAMES, lawyer; b. Springfield, Ohio, July 30, 1958; s. Frank James Shaffer and Martha Isabelle (Hardman) Matthews; m. Julie Renee Cohen, Oct. 8, 1995; children: Brynn Danielle, Jedediah Clay. BA, Wittenberg U., 1980; JD, Stanford U., 1983. Bar: Calif. 1984, U.S. Dist. Ct. (no. and ea. dists.) Calif. 1984, U.S. Ct. Appeals (9th cir.) 1984, U.S. Dist. Ct. (so. dist.) Calif. 1985, U.S. Dist. Ct. (we. dist.) Wash. 1986, D.C. 1988, U.S. Dist. Ct. D.C. 1988, U.S. Ct. Appeals (D.C. cir.) 1988, U.S. Dist. Ct. (no. dist.) Tex. 1991, U.S. Supreme Ct. 1993, Md. 1994, U.S. Dist. Ct. Md. 1997. Supr. field ops. U.S. Census Bur., Columbus, Ohio, 1980; legal intern Natural Resources Def. Coun., Inc., San Francisco, 1982-83; assoc. Gibson, Dunn & Crutcher, San Jose, Calif., 1983; law clk. to Judge Betty B. Fletcher, U.S. Ct. Appeals for 9th Cir., Seattle, 1983-84; assoc. Gibson, Dunn & Crutcher, San Jose, 1984-87, Arnold & Porter, Washington, 1987-92; ptnr. Semmes, Bowen & Semmes, Washington, 1992-94, Arter & Hadden, Washington, 1995-99, Thelen Reid & Priest LLP, Washington, 1999—. Campaign mgr. Clark County Dem. Party, Springfield, 1978-80; organizer Citizens for Sensible County Planning, Fairfax, Va., 1989-94. Alumni scholar Wittenberg U., 1976. Mem. ABA, FBA (chmn. EEO com. 1992-94, individual rights and responsibilities 1994-95, co-chmn. alt. dispute resolution 1995-96, mem. governing bd. labor law and labor rels. sect., editor newsletter Labouring Oar, Outstanding Svc. award 1992), D.C. Bar Assn., Calif. Bar Assn., Order of Coif. Avocations: music, hiking, nature study. Office: Thelen Reid & Priest LLP 701 Pennsylvania Ave NW Washington DC 20004-2608

SHAFFER, DOROTHY BROWNE, retired mathematician, educator; b. Vienna, Austria, Feb. 12, 1923; d. Hermann and Steffy (Hermann) Browne; arrived U.S., 1940; m. Lloyd Hamilton Shaffer, July 25, 1943 (dec. 1978); children: Deborah Lee, Diana Louise, Dorothy Leslie. AB, Bryn Mawr Coll., 1943; MA, Harvard U., 1945, PhD, 1962. Mathematician, MIT, Cambridge, 1945-47; tchg. fellow, research asso., Harvard U., Cambridge, 1947-48; asso. mathematician Cornell Aeronautical Lab, Buffalo, N.Y., 1952-56; mathematician Dunlap & Assoc., Stamford, Conn., 1958-60; lectr. grad. engring. U. of Conn. at Stamford, 1962; prof. math Fairfield (Conn.) U., 1963-92, prof. emeritus, 1992—; vis. prof. Imperial Coll. Sci. and Tech., London, fall 1978, U. Md., College Park, spring 1981; vis. prof. U. Calif.-San Diego, summer 1981; vis. scholar, 1986; NSF faculty fellow IBM-T.J. Watson Research Center, Yorktown Heights, N.Y., 1979. Contbr. numerous papers in math. analysis. Mem. Am. Math. Soc., Math. Assn. of Am., Assn. for Women in Math., London Math. Soc. Achievement include patent in Viscosity Stabilized Solar Pond. Home: 156 Intervale Rd Stamford CT 06905-1311 Office: Fairfield U Dept Math & Computer Sci Fairfield CT 06430

SHAFFER, DOUGLAS D., lawyer; b. Cin., Oct. 16, 1957; s. Harold and Ruth (Noble) S.; m. Leslie, June 8, 1992; 1 child, William. BS, Ohio State U., 1980; JD, Pepperdine Sch. Las, 1984. Atty. Luce, Forward, Hamilton & Scripps, San Diego, 1984-87, O'Melvery & Myers, L.A., 1988-90, Sanford Gage, esq., Beverly Hills, Calif., 1990-93, Michael Pwze, Esq., L.A., 1993-97, Law Offices of Douglas Shaffer, Santa Monica, Calif., 1997—; expert witness. Scholar Pepperdine Sch. Law, 1982-84. Democrat. Avocations: triathlons, road races. E-mail: DSHAFLAW@AOL.COM. Office: Law Office of Douglas Shaffer 1299 Ocean Ave Ste 900 Santa Monica CA 90401-1042

SHAFFER, ELINOR SOPHIA, English/comparative literature educator, writer; b. Boston; arrived in Eng., 1968; d. Vernon Cecil Stoneman; m. Brian Myer Shaffer; children: Mark Jeremy, Milo Peter. BA with honors, U. Chgo., 1954; BA in English with honors, Oxford (Eng.) U., 1958, MA, 1962; PhD in English and Comparative Literature, Columbia U., 1966; MA, Cambridge (Eng.) U., 1968. From instr. to asst. prof. U. Calif., Berkeley, 1963-64; rsch. fellow Cambridge U., 1968-71; lectr. U. East Anglia, Norwich, Eng., 1971-77, reader, 1977-95; dir. rsch. Sch. Advanced Study, U. London, 1977—; vis. prof. Brown U., Providence, 1983-84, Stanford U., Palo Alto, Calif., 1988, KTH Stockholm, 2000—; exch. lectr. Free U., Berlin, 1979; vis. lectr. U. Zürich, Switzerland, 1986; vis. fellow All Souls Coll., Oxford, 1996; lectr. Brit. Coun., 1981, 93; adv. bd. on European cultures DeGruyter, Berlin, 1991—; fellow European Humanities Rsch. Ctr., Oxford U., 1995—. Author: Kubla Khan and the Fall of Jerusalem, 1975, Samuel Butler as Painter, Photographer, Art Critic, 1988; editor: Comparative Criticism, 1979—, The Third Culture, 1996; series editor Critical Traditions: The Reception of British Authors in Europe; contbr. articles to books and profl. jours. Lizette A. Fisher fellow, u. fellow, Columbia U., 1961-63, Study fellow Am. Coun. Learned Soc., 1971, Faculty fellow Leverhulme Trust, Berlin, 1976, Rsch. fellow Humanities Rsch. Ctr., Canberra, Australia, 1982; fellow U. Calif. Humanities Rsch. Inst., 1991, Leverhulme Trust sr. fellow, 1998-2000. Fellow Brit. Acad. (elected 1995); mem. Internat. Comparative Lit. Assn. (rsch. dir. 1978-94), Internat. Lit. Theory Com. (founding mem. 1986-96), Brit. Comparative Lit. Assn. (founding mem., exec. com. 1975—), European Prof. English (elected mem. 1995).

SHAFFER, MARY LOUISE, art educator; b. Blufton, Ind., Nov. 23, 1927; d. Gail H. and Mary J. (Graves) S. AB, Northwest Nazerene U., 1950; MA, Ball State U., 1955; EdD, MS, Ind. U., 1964. Art and music tchr. Kuna (Idaho) H.S., 1950-55; asst. prof. art Northwest Nazarene U., Nampa, Idaho, 1955-56, head art dept., 1971-98, dir. Friesen Art Galleries, 1997-2000, faculty emeritus, 1998; asst. prof. art Pasadena (Calif.) U., 1956-61; prof. art Olivet Nazarene U., Kankakee, Ill., 1964-71; dir. music Kankakee Congl. Ch., 1964-71, Nampa Christian Ch., 1971-76, Nampa Meth. Ch., 1976-81; juror Nampa Art Guild Painting Show, 1994; head art policy coun. Northwest Nazarene U.; speaker various civic clubs and confs., 1965-81. One-woman show Friesen Art Galleries, 1999; participant European Images Art Show, 1989; cover artist Nazarene Internat. Mag., 1989; painting retrospective, 1999. Dir. music Van Nuys (Calif.) Nazarene Ch., 1957-60. E.I. Lilly grantee, 1961-62; women's singles tennis champion Kankakee, Ill., 1966, 67, 68, Boise (Idaho) Racquet and Swim Club, 1973, Idaho Sr. Tennis champion Sun Valley, 1984; watercolor Sun Valley Mountain selected to go to moon on Endeavour Space Shuttle, 1992. Mem. NAFE, Nat. Art Edn. Assn., Idaho Arts Edn. Assn., Nat. Assn. Univ. Women, Nat. Mus. Women in the Arts, Boise Racquet Swim Club, Boise Art Mus. Avocations: travel, music, renovating buildings, watercolor painting, tennis. Home: Shaffer Studios 4755 E Victory Rd Meridian ID 83642-7011 Office: NW Nazerene U Holly at Dewey Nampa ID 83686

SHAFFER, PETER LEVIN, playwright; b. Liverpool, Eng., May 15, 1926; s. Jack and Reka (Fredman) S. BA, Cambridge U., Eng., 1950. Conscript coal mines, Eng., 1944-47; with N.Y. Pub. Libr., N.Y.C., 1951-54, Bosey & Hawkes, London, 1954-55; lit. critic Truth, 1956-57; music critic Time and Tide, 1961-62; freelance playwrite, 1957—; vis. prof. contemporary drama Oxford (Eng.) U., 1994-95. Author: (plays) Five Finger Exercise, 1958 (Evening Standard Drama award 1958, N.Y. Drama Critics Cir. award 1960), The Private Ear, 1962, The Public Eye, 1962, It's About Cinderella, 1963, The Royal Hunt of the Sun, 1964, Black Comedy, 1965, The White Liars, 1967, The Battle of Shrivings, 1970, Equus, 1973 (Best Play Tony award 1975, Outer Critics Cir. Best Play award 1975), Amadeus, 1979 (Evening Standard Drama award 1979, London Drama Critics award 1979, Best Play Tony award 1980, Plays and Players Best Play award 1980), Yonadab, 1985, Lettice and Lovage, 1987 (Evening Standard Drama award 1988), The Gift of the Gorgon, 1992, Whom Do I Have the Honor of Addressing?, Chicketer Festival Theatre, 1996, (screenplays) Follow Me!, 1971, Equus, 1977 (Acad. award nomination for best screenplay adaptation 1977), Amadeus, 1984 (Acad. award for best screenplay adaptation 1984), (TV plays) The Salt Land, 1955, Balance of Terror, 1957, (radio plays) The Prodigal Father, 1955, Whom Do I Have the Honor of Addressing?, 1989, (novels, with Anthony Shaffer) The Woman in the Wardrobe, 1951, How Doth the Little Crocodile?, 1952, Withered Murder, 1955. Decorated comdr. Order Brit. Empire, 1987; recipient Hamburg Shakespeare prize, 1987, William Inge award for disting. achievement in Am. theatre, 1992. Fellow Royal Soc. Lt. (London chpt.). Address: The Lantz Office 200 W 57th St Ste 503 New York NY 10019-3211

SHAFFNER, RANDOLPH PRESTON, shop owner, educator, writer; b. Winston-Salem, N.C., Jan. 17, 1940; s. Emil Nathaniel and Anna Jackson (Preston) S.; m. Margaret Farmer Rhodes; children: Eric Randolph, Edward David, Joseph Andrew, Thomas Matthew, Jackson Rhodes. Student, Davidson Coll., 1958-60; BA in English with honors in writing, U. N.C., 1962, MA in Comparative Lit., 1969, PhD, 1973. Surveyor's lineman Joyce Mapping Co., Winston-Salem, 1955-58, 62; counselor, scoutmaster Camp Sequoyah, Weaverville, N.C., 1959; track repairman Alaska R.R., Anchorage, 1960; case handler Emard Packing Co., Anchorage, 1960, AYR Canneries, Seldovia, Alaska, 1961; tchr. U.S. Peace Corps., Chiengrai, Thailand, 1963-65, St. Christopher's Sch., Richmond, Va., 1969-71; instr. U. N.C., 1968-69, 71-73; asst. prof. Fairfield U., Conn., 1973-78, Western Carolina U., 1984, 87, Continuing Edn. program World Materpieces, Highlands, N.C., 1987-89; moderator Highlands lecture series Western Carolina U., 1989-92; editor John F. Blair Pub., Winston-Salem, 1966-68; bookseller, owner Cyrano's Bookshop, Highlands, N.C., 1978—; asst. to dean Sch. Libr. Scis. U. N.C., Chapel Hill, 1973-74; literary mag. adv., mem. various subcoms. Dept. Eng. Fairfield Univ., 1973-78. Author: Apprenticeship Novel, 1984, Tree Ordinance for Town of Highlands, 1987, Good Reading Material, Mostly Bound and New: The Hudson Library 1884-1994, 1994, (with others) Nineteenth Century Literature Criticism, Vol. 21, 1989; contbr. poetry to N.C. Poetry Soc. anthology Here's to the Land, 1992; contbr. short stories to mags; contbr. Heritage of Macon Co., N.C., Vol. 2, 1999. Lectr. with Alexander, String Quartet, Words & Music, 1989, 92, 94, for Western Carolina U., Highlands lectr. series, 1991, 92, 93, 2000; chmn. ARC Disaster Svcs., Fairfield, 1974-78, Zoning Bd. of Adjustment, Highlands, 1981-83, 85-90; pres., bd. trustees Hudson Libr., Inc., Highlands, 1987-90, 99—, chmn. libr. com., 1995-99; trustee Hudson Libr. Bascom-Louise Art Gallery, 1987-90, 95-99, Highlands Land Trust, Inc., 1995-96; bd. dirs. Highlands Cultural Art Ctr., 1987; fundraisingcom. Highlands Permanent Endowment Scholarships, 1987-89; Town of Highlands Millennium Com., 1999; historian Highlands Hist. Soc., Inc., 1999—; vice chmn. bd. missions Greenfield Hill Congl. Ch., Fairfield, Conn., 1977, chmn. scholarship co., 1975-77; bd. dirs. ARC, Fairfield, 1974-78; chaperon Am. Inst. for Fgn. Study, Grenoble, France, 1970. Recipient God and Country award, 1955, Outstanding Pres. and Trustee award Hudson Libr. and Bascom-Louise Gallery, 1990; Goethe Inst. scholar German Embassy, Munich, Fed. Rep. Germany, 1965, Univ. Besançon, France, 1965. Mem. Internat. Comparative Lit. Assn., Am. Comparative Lit. Assn., Writers' Workshop, N.C. Poetry Soc., Am. Acad. Poets, Am. Booksellers Assn., Southeastern Booksellers Assn., Highlands Merchants Assn. (chmn. fin. com., treas. 1984-87, chmn. tree com. and beautificatio com. 1984-89), Highlands Biol. Found. (exec. com. 1986—, bd. trustees 1981—, bd. dirs. 1981—, environ. protection com. 1986—, fund raising com. 1986, treas. 1990—, adv. com. on Nature Ctr. 1992—), Highlands C. of C., Clan Morrison Soc., Nat. Peace Corps Assn., Trail Hikers Am., Lambda Iota Tau (founder, faculty moderator Delta Omicon Ch. 1975-80), Rotary (Outstanding Vol. award 1989). Democrat. Moravian. Avocations: construction, reading, travel, hiking, camping. Home: Hickory St PO Box 765 Highlands NC 28741-0765 Office: Cyrano's Bookshop Main St Highlands NC 28741

SHAFI, MUHAMMAD, geographer, educator; b. Jaunpur, India, Aug. 1, 1924; s. Husain Ali and Mariam Ali; married; 5 children. BA, Allahabad U., 1945; MA, Aligarh U., 1947; PhD, London U., 1956. Lectr. geography Aligarh (India) Muslim U., 1947-56, reader, 1956-62, prof., 1962-84, sr. prof., 1965-84, prof. emeritus, 1984—, dir. acad. programs, 1972—; head dept. geography, 1962-84, provost residential hall, 1959-62, dean Faculty Sci., 1967-70, mgr. univ. schs., 1967-75, chief Univ. Employment Bur., 1972, provice-chancellor univ., 1974-79, vice chancellor, 1979-80, pro-chancellor, 1992—; mem. Internat. Commn. on Applied Geography, 1964—, Internat. Commn. on Agrl. Typology, 1963-72; dep. chmn. Internat. Commn. on Agrl. Productivity and World Food Resources, 1976—; mem. Indian Coun. Social Scis. Rsch.; chmn. Indian nat. com. in geography Internat. Geog. Union, 1978—, also liaison mem. to FAO; chmn. nat. com. Internat. Geog. Congress, 1978; chmn. Internat. Geog. Commn. on Comparative Rsch. in Food Systems of World; mem. All India Bur. for Promotion of Urdu; chmn. All India Univ. Grants Commn. Geography Panel. Author: (monograph) Land Utilization in Eastern Uttar Pradesh; Studies in Applied and Regional Geography; Agricultural Productivity and Regional Imbalances, Spectrum of Modern Geography, Dryland Agriculture in India Food Systems of the World, Forest Ecosystems of the World, The Geography of Environment: Issues and Challenges, South Asia: Agricultural Geography, Central Asian States: Economic Cultural Resources, India; contbr. over 110 articles to profl. jours.; editor Geographer (jour.); Land Use in Developing Countries. Recipient medal for pioneering work on land use U. Liege (Belgium), Gold medal Ministry of Higher Edn., Syria, 1981, membership award Coun. Royal Geographic Soc., London (v.p. 1984-88, 88-92), Diploma Merit, World Cultural Coun. Mex., 1989; recipient 1st prize essay contest UNESCO, 1979. Mem. Nat. Assn. Geographers India (pres.), Russian Acad. Scis. (fgn. mem. inst. geography). Home: Shafi Manzil Doodhpur Medical Rd, Aligarh 202001 Uttar Pradesh India

SHAFI, NUSRAT, chemist, researcher; b. Haripur, Pakistan, July 29, 1954; d. Mohammad Shafi. BSc, Peshawar (Pakistan) U., 1976, MSc in Chemistry, 1979, PhD in Pharm. Scis., 1989. Sci. officer Pakistan Coun. Sci. and Indsl. Rsch., Peshawar, 1979-84, sr. sci. officer, 1984—; investigator Chem. and Pharm. Orgn., Peshawar, 1979—, Narcotics Testing Labs., 1979-98; prin. investigator Medicinal Botanic Ctr., Peshawar, 1989—. Contbr. articles to profl. jours. S&T scholar Sch. of Pharmacy, Glasgow, Scotland, 1985-89. Mem. Chem. Soc. Pakistan, U. Strathclyde Alumni Assn. Avocations: reading, traveling. Office: Pakistan Coun Sci Indsl Rsc, Jamrud Rd Peshawar U, Preshawar 25120, Pakistan

SHAFIQ, MUHAMMAD, surgeon, consultant, lecturer; b. Lahore, Punjab, Pakistan, June 10, 1935; arrived in Eng., 1964; s. Khan M. and Hamida Begum; m. Surriya Din, Mar. 18, 1961 (div. Feb. 2, 1978); 2 children; m. Sandra Fay Woodington, July 12, 1978; 2 children. MB, BS, Nishtar Med. Coll., Pakistan, 1957. Cert. Higher Surg. Tng., Licenentiate of medicine and surgery Soc. Apothacaries. House surgeon Nistar Med. Coll. and Hosp., Multan, Pakistan, 1957-58; med. officer Gen. Hosp., Deri Ghazi Khan, Pakistan, 1958-60; demonstrator anatomy Nistar Med. Coll. and Hosp., Multan, Pakistan, 1960-63; registrar surgery Nistar Med. Coll. and Hosp., Multan, 1963-64; sr. house officer Princess Beatrice Hosp., London, 1964, King Edward VII Hosp., Warwick, Eng., 1964-65; registrar cardiac sur. Chest Hosp., Southampton, Eng., 1966-68, sr. registrar, 1968-70; sr. registrar surgery North Manchester (Eng.) Gen. Hosp., 1972-74, cons. surgeon, 1974—. Fellow Royal Coll. Surgeons (Hallett prize 1964), Royal Coll. Surgeons Edinburgh; mem. Brit. Med. Assn., Hosp. Cons. and Specialist Assn. (county chmn. 1996—), Pakistan Med. Soc., Pakistan Med. Assn. Avocations: skiing, photography, travel. Home: 6 Kenwood Ave, WA15 9DE Altrincham Cheshire, England Office: N Manchester Med Splsts, Roselands 4 Middleton Rd, M8 5DS Manchester England

SHAFTESBURY, ANTHONY, former British government executive, company executive; b. London, May 22, 1938; s. Anthony Ashley-Cooper and Francoise Claudine (Ashley) Soulier; m. Christina Eva Montan, Dec. 15, 1976; children: Anthony Nils Christian Ashley, Nicholas Edmund Anthony Ashley-Cooper. Student, Eton Coll., Berkshire, Eng., 1951-56, Oxford (Eng.) U., 1958-59. Banker Kleinwort Benson Ltd., London, 1961-64; mem. Ho. of Lords, London, 1961—; chmn. St. Giles Farms Ltd., Dorset, Eng., 1961—, Shaftesbury Estate of Lough Neagh Ltd., Belfast, No. Ireland, 1961—, Ashurst Investments Ltd., Dorset, 1978—; dir., vice chmn. P.K.L. Group Ltd., London, 1989-96; pres. Dorset F.W.A.G., 1993-96. Chmn. London Philharm. Orch. Coun., 1966-80, Internat. Musicians Seminar, London, 1980-86; pres. Hawk and Owl Trust, 1996—; v.p. Brit. Butterfly Conservation, 1992—. Lt. Brit. Royal Armoured Corps, 1956-58. Recipient 1st prize Duke of Cornwall's Nat. award for Forestry and Conservation Royal Forestry Soc., 1992; named Hon. Citizen, State of S.C., 1967. Mem. Shaftesbury Soc. (pres. 1961-96). Conservative. Mem. Ch. of Eng. Avocations: mountaineering, music, wildlife conservation, tennis. Home: St Giles's House, Wimborne, Dorset BH21 5NA, England Office: PKL Group Ltd, Moulin D'Herechou, 32450 Faget-Abbatial, Gers France

SHAGAM, MARVIN HÜCKEL-BERRI, private school educator; b. Monongalia, W.Va.; s. Lewis and Clara (Shagam) S. AB magna cum laude, Washington and Jefferson Coll., 1947; postgrad., Harvard Law Sch., 1947-48, Oxford (Eng.) U., 1948-51. Tchr. Mount House Sch., Tavistock, Eng., 1951-53, Williston Jr. Sch., Easthampton, Mass., 1953-55, Westtown (Pa.) Sch., 1955-58, The Thacher Sch., Ojai, Calif., 1958—; English dept. head Kurasini Internat. Edn. Centre, Dar-es-Salaam, Tanzania, 1966-67; dept. head Nkumbi Internat. Coll., Kabwe, Zambia, 1967-68; vol. visitor Prisons in Calif., 1980-95, Calif. Youth Authority, 1983-93; sr. youth crisis counsellor InterFace, 1984-94. With U.S. Army, 1942-46, 1st lt. M.I. res.,1946-57. Danforth Found. fellow, 1942; Coun. for the Humanities fellow, Tufts U., 1983. Mem. Western Assn. Schs. and Colls. (accreditation com.), Great Teaching (Cooke chair 1977—), Phi Beta Kappa, Delta Sigma Rho, Cum Laude Soc. Republican. Avocations: hiking, camping, travel. E-mail: mshagam@thacher.org. Fax: 808-646-9490. Office: The Thacher Sch 5025 Thacher Rd Ojai CA 93023-9001

SHAGAN, STEVE, screenwriter, novelist, film producer; b. N.Y.C., Oct. 25, 1927. Film technician Consol. Film, Inc., N.Y.C., 1952-56, RCA, Cape Canaveral, Fla., 1956-59; asst. to publicity dir. Paramount Pictures, Hollywood, Calif., 1962-63. Prodr.: (TV series) Tarzan, 1966; prodr., writer movies for TV, Universal and CBS, Hollywood, Calif., 1968-70; writer original screenplay: Save the Tiger, 1972 (Writers Guild award, Acad. award nominee 1973); prodr. film, author screenplay: City of Angels (produced as movie Hustle), 1975, novel, screenplay The Formula, 1979, screenplay Voyage of the Damned, 1976 (Acad. award nominee); writer, prodr. film The Formula, 1980; author: (novels) Save the Tiger, 1972, City of Angels, 1975, The Formula, 1979, The Circle, 1982, The Discovery, 1985, Vendetta, 1986, Pillars of Fire, 1989, A Cast of Thousands, 1993, (screenplays) Primal Fear, 1996, Gotti, 1996 (Emmy nominee Best Screenplay). Served with USCG, 1944-46. Mem. Writers Guild Am. (bd. dirs. West chpt. 1978-82).

SHAGINYAN, LEONID ROBERTOVICH, physicist, researcher; b. Samarkand, Uzbekistan, Mar. 30, 1949; s. Robert Petrovich Shaginyan and Valentina Alexsandrovna Savich; m. Svetlana Ivanovna Vlaskina, Mar. 30, 1971 (div. Apr. 1992); two children; m. Jeanne Alekseevna Khropataya, July 12, 1995. MS in Physics, State U., Samarkand, USSR, 1971; Candidate

Scis., PhD, Inst. Problems Material Sci., Kiev, USSR, 1974. Sr. engr. Inst. Problems Material Sci., Kiev, 1976-77, minor rschr., 1977-82, sr. rschr., 1982—, rsch. mgr., 1978—. Contbr. articles to profl. jours. Active Ukrainian Mil., 1974-75. Recipient Sr. Rschr. diploma Nat. Acad. Scis. Ukraine, Kiev, 1993; grantee Nat. Acad. Scis. Ukraine, Kiev, 1997-2000. Avocations: Eastern philosophy, literary work, hatha yoga. Office: Inst Problems Material Sci, 3 Krzhyzhanovsky St, 252142 Kiev Ukraine

SHAGINYAN, VASILY, physicist; b. Samarkand, USSR, Jan. 14, 1952; s. Robert and Valentina (Savich) S.; m. Tatiana Dreval, Nov. 15, 1974; children: Maria, Margarita. MS, Leningrad State U., 1974; PhD, Leningrad Nuclear Physics, Inst., 1981, DSc, 1990. Jr. rschr. Leningrad Nuclear Physics Inst., Gatchina, USSR, 1974-83, rschr., 1983-90, sr. rschr., 1990-92; leading rschr. Petersburg Nuclear Physics Inst., Gatchina, 1992—. Contbr. articles to profl. jours. Fax: 007-812-7146096. Office: Petersburg Nuclear Phys, Orlova Roscha Gatchina, Leningrad District 188350, Russia

SHAH, AASHIT AMRITLAL, automotive executive; b. Moshi, Tanzania, June 15, 1962; s. Amritlal Nemchand and Indu Amritlal Shah; m. Nita Aashit Keshavlal, Aug. 3, 1986; children: Kush Aashit, Aashna Aashit. BSc in Mgmt. Sci., Warwick U., U.K., 1985. Mng. dir. Melaplas Ltd., Nairobi, Kenya, 1985-94; dir. L.G. Harris (E.A.) Ltd., Nairobi, 1987, 90, 92, Harris Products Ltd., Nairobi, 1993-95, Marble Ore Products Ltd., Nairobi, 1993-95, Tyre Merchants Ltd., Nairobi, 1993-96, Treadsetters Tyres Ltd., Nairobi, 1987—. Mem. Parklands Sports Club, Kiambu Sports Club, Muthaiga Golf Club. Avocations: golf, tennis, cycling, aerobics, attending self improvement and leadership seminars. Office: Treadsetters Tyres Ltd, Baba Dogo Rd PO Box 45242, Nairobi Kenya

SHAH, AASHIT K, neurologist; b. Baroda, India, Feb. 19, 1964; m. Jigna Shah; children: Aashka, Ananya. MBBS, N.H.L. Mcpl. Med. Coll., Gujarat, India, 1987. Diplomate Am. Bd. Neurology. Intern Interfaith Med. Ctr., Bklyn., 1988-89; res. Wayne State U. Detroit Med. Ctr., 1989-92, fellowship, 1992-93; staff neurologist Hutzel Hosp., Detroit, 1993, Harper Hosp., Detroit, 1993, Detroit Rec. Hops., 1993; asst. prof. Wayne State U., 1993. Office: 8A-UHC/Dept Neur 4201 Saint Antoine St Detroit MI 48201-2153

SHAH, CHITTRANJAN, automobile company executive; b. Bharuch, India, Oct. 26, 1928; s. Anantlal and Lilavati (Chokshi) S.; m. Madhurika Tolat, May 5, 1954; children: Nayan, Meera, Manjari, Kanan, Mita. B in Commerce, Sydenham Coll., Mumbai, India, 1949. Dir. Bhailal Group Ltd., Mumbai, 1950-52; dir., mgr., bd. dirs., exec. dir. Ctrl. Automobiles, Mumbai, 1952—; chmn.-dir. Madhuchitt Hi-Tech Svcs., Mumbai, 1988—. Trustee Shri Kamnath Madhadev Navgrah Mandir, 1994—; chmn. Himgiri Coop. Housing Soc. Ltd., Mumbai, 1999—; trustee Fam Charitable Trust, Mumbai, 1991—, A.T.S. Aujs Hosp., Bharuch. Mem. Maharashtra Motor Parts Dealers' Assn. (pres. 1977, 78, 81, 82, 86, 87, 90-92, mem. coms.), Fedn. Assn. Maharashtra (v.p. 1985-95, 99—, mem. coms.), Indo-Polish Friendship Assn. (v.p. 1991-95), Fedn. All India Automobile Spare Parts Dealer's Assn. (com. 1993-96), Indian Merchants' Chamber Internal Trade & Consumers Affairs Com. (vice chair 1994-96, 99-2000), Assoc. C. of C. and Industries, Rotary. Avocations: reading, writing, indoor games. Home: 14 Himgiri 755-56 Peddar Rd, 400 026 Mumbai India

SHAH, JASHWANT CHIMANLAL, solicitor; b. Malwan, India, June 20, 1932; s. Chimanlal and Vimala S.; m. Jyotsna Chimanlal; children: Deepika, Paresh, Kalpana, Kavita. BSc, Jai Hind Coll., Bombay, India, 1955; LLB, Law Coll. Bombay, 1961. Asst. Amin Desai, Bombay, 1961-63; ptnr. Rustomji & yinwala, Bombay, 1963-66; sr. ptnr. Shah & Sanghavi, Bombay, 1966—. Avocations: golf, music, reading, traveling, drama. Home: C Rd Swadhini Sadavi, 400020 Bombay India Office: Shah & Sanghavi, 114A Mittal Ct, 400021 Bombay India

SHAH, JIGISH K., advertising executive; b. Ahmedabad, Gujarat, India, Sept. 6, 1957; s. Kanaiyalal J. and Chandrika K. Shah; m. Uma Jigish Patel, Apr. 29, 1983; children: Devna, Aashil. BCom, Abad, India, 1977. Salesman Chaise Mktg., Ahmedabad, India, 1980-81; sales exec. Grace Paper Ltd., Abad, 1981-83; asst. mgr. Sugam Advt., Abad, 1983-84; CEO Sanket Advt., Ahmedabad, 1984—; dir. Raipath Club Ltd, Abad, 1991-99; pres. Ahmedabad Advt. circle, Abad, 1996-97, hon. sec., 1994-96; dir. Gujarat C. of C. and Industry, 1999—. Avocations: travel, photography. Home: Ravija 3, Nilgiri Byanglows Satellite, Ahmedabad 380 015, India Office: Sanket Advt 305 Aditya, Nr SP Seva Samaj Mithkaali, Ahmedabad 380 006, India

SHAH, JOYOTSNABEN MANHARLAL, consultant; b. Visanagar, India; s. Natwarlal J. and Champaben N. S.; m. Manharlal R., Apr. 27, 1971; 1 child. BA, Gujarat U., India, 1972. Sec. Gujarat Electricity Bd., India, 1986—. Home: Plot No 791/D/4 Shreeji Apt, Panch Sheel Pk Sector 21, Gandhinagar 382021, India

SHAH, KAVITA, biochemist, educator, researcher; b. Varanasi, India, Nov. 6, 1968; d. Rai Sushil Kumar and Shubha Agarwal; m. Mukul Kumar Shah, Jan. 25, 1991; 1 child. BSc, Banaras Hindu U., Varanasi, 1989, MSc, 1991, EdB, 1992, PhD, 1995. Jr. rsch. fellow dept. biochemistry Banaras Hindu U., 1993-95, sr. rsch. fellow, 1995-96, rsch. assoc., 1996—; postdoctoral rsch. fellow Nat. Inst. Health Scis., Tokyo, 1998—; cons. Ministry of Environment, India. Inventor in field. Served with Indian Nat. Cadet Corps, 1984-88. Sta fellow Japan Sci. and Tech. Corp., Tokyo, 1998—. Mem. Indian Sci. Congress Assn. (life), Soc. Biol. Chemists (India) (life). Avocations: painting, reading, handicrafts, games. Home: B-27/65-1 Durgakund, Varanasi 221005, India Office: Dept Biochemistry, Faculty of Sci BHU, Varanasi 221 005, India

SHAH, MADHU CHINUBHAI, textiles executive, risk management consultant; b. Ahmedabad, Gujrat, India, Dec. 7, 1944; s. Chinubhai Chimanlal and Kusum Chinubhai (Shah) S.; m. Meena Madhu Jhaveri, Dec. 5, 1967; children: Akshay, Aditi. Diploma in Journalism, I.R. Inst., N.Y.C., 1979. Ops. chief Global Trading Co., Chgo., 1979-89; pres. Meena Textiles, Ahmedabad, India, 1980—; bd. dirs. A.M. Drape, Ahmedabad-Bombay, 1994—; mem. Control Mgmt. Strategy Intelligency Svcs., Eng. Co-op. mem. Gondhia Hosp., Rajkot, India, 1994—; feeder assoc. Jonas Inst., Rajkot, 1995—; trustee Young Men's Gandhian Assn., Rajkot. Mem. Internat. Airlines Passengers Assn., Sports Club Ahmedabad (life). Home: Satyagraph 236/12 Sector 6, Ahmedabad 380054, India Office: 5701 New Cloth Mkt, Ahmedabad 380002, India

SHAH, MANHARLAL RASIKLAL, engineering executive; b. Kalol, India, Mar. 26, 1946; s. Rasiklal Hargovindas and Shardaben (Rasiklal) S.; m. Jyotsnaben Monharlal Shah, June 27, 1971; children: Ambarishkuma, Nimishaben. B of Elec. Engring., Gujarat U., Ahmedabd, India, 1967. Supr. engr. G.E.B., Dhumarian, India, 1971—. Avocations: reading, collecting stamps and coins, visiting holy places. Home: Plot 791/D 4 Shreeji Appt, Panch Sheel Park Sector 21, Gandhinagar 382021, India Office: GE Board, GTPS, Gandhinagar 382 041, India

SHAH, MEHUL KIRIT, information technology company executive; b. Surendranagar, Gujarat, India, Apr. 14, 1973; s. Kirit Yirji Rambhia and Sushila Kirit (Dharod) S. Diploma in computer software, Mumbai U., 1992. Prin. Mehul Enterprise, Mumbai, 1991—, cons., 1996—. Recipient Sci. Fair Activity award City Edn. Bur., 1987. Mem. World Wildlife Fund. Avocations: science, nature conservation, traveling, experiments, explorations. Home: A-2 Navin Manju Zaver Rd, Mulund Mumbai 400080, India Office: Mehul Enterprise, B-6 Navin Manju SL Rd, Mulund Mumbai 400080, India

SHAH, MUHAMMAD AZHER ZAFAR, international relations educator; b. London, Nov. 15, 1956; s. Mohammad Mueenuddin Zahangir Shah and Begum (Rahima) Zahangir; m. Firdousi Kohinoor, Sept. 6, 1985 (div. July 1988); m. Kazi Mansura Huda, Jan. 1, 1989. BSc in Econs. with honors, London Sch. Econs., 1977; MPhil in Internat. Rels., U. London, 1982. Asst. prof. internat. rels. U. Dacca, Bangladesh, 1978-95, assoc. prof., 1995—; bd. dirs. Z. Shah and Co. Ltd., Bangladesh. Author: India and the Super Powers, 1983; columnist Holiday Weekly, Bangladesh, 1980—. Cen. v.p. Natun Bangla Jubo Sanghati, govt. youth front, Bangladesh, 1983-86. Mem. Asiatic Soc. Bangladesh (life), Bangladesh Red Crescent Soc. (life), Bangladesh Lions Found. (life), Lions (bd. dirs. Dacca 1988—). Islam. Avocations: swimming, jogging, reading, debating. Home: Z Shah House 120A, Motijheel CA, Dacca 1000, Bangladesh Office: U Dacca Dept Internat Rels, Dacca Bangladesh

SHAH, MUKHTAR HAMID, surgeon; b. Chakwal, Punjab, Pakistan, Nov. 8, 1939; s. Karam and Phoolan (Bibi) S.; m. Asia Bano, Dec. 15, 1963; children: Mohammad Zahid Mukhtar, Mohammad Tauseef, Mohammad Taufeeq. Lic. Medicine & Surgery, Liaquat Med. Coll., Jamshoro, Hyderabad, 1963; M Surgery, U. Punjab, Lahore, 1972; On-Job Tng. in Nepho-Urology, Inst. Urology, London, 1977. Med. officer Govt. of West Pakistan Health Dept., 1963-67; registrar urology ward Mayo Hosp., Lahore, 1967-70, sr. registrar urology ward, 1971; surgeon Pakistani Armed Forces, Pakistan, 1971-72, cons. urologist and transplant surgeon, 1973-86; cons. urologist and transplant surgeon Kidney Ctr., Rawaldindi, 1987—. Author book in field of dialysis. Col. Army Med. Corps, 1973-86. Mem. Asian Soc. Transplantation, Internat. Soc. Nephrology, Asian Colliquium in Nephrology, Pakistan Soc. of Nephro-Urology (past v.p.), Pakistan Soc. Urology. Achievements include pioneering of many urol. procedures in Pakistan, dialysis in Pakistan, 1969, kidney transplantation in Pakistan, 1979; performed 1462 kidney transplant operations (highest number performed by one single surgeon in the world). Office: Kidney Ctr, 1 Hill Park/Jehlum Rd, Rawalpindi/Punjab Pakistan

SHAH, NARENDRA M., Nepalese diplomat. Amb. from Nepal to UN, N.Y.C. Office: Perm Mission of Nepal to UN 820 2d Ave 17B Fl New York NY 10017-4504*

SHAH, NITIN VINAYCHAND, paper company executive; b. Nairobi, Kenya, July 9, 1957; s. Vinaychand Manekchand and Kanta Vinaychand (Dhanani) S.; m. Suhani Nitin, Feb. 14, 1988. Diploma in bus. studies, Watford Coll., 1978; diploma in mktg., Nairobi, 1983; MBA, Calif. Coast U., 1988. Sales rep. Kensta, Nairobi, 1979-81, asst. sales mgr., 1981-82, sales mgr., 1982-90, sales & mtkg. dir., 1990-97, regional sales dir., 1998—; dir. Surya Agencies Ltd., Nairobi, 1993—, Transpaper Ltd., Nairobi, 1984-96. Pub. rels. Neighborhood Watch, Parklands Nairobi, 1995-97; mem. mgr. com. Oshwal H.S., Parklands Nairobi, 1996-97, Oshwal Sports Complex, 1996-97. Hindu. Home: PO Box 32642, Nairobi Kenya Office: Kensta, PO Box 46309, Nairobi Kenya

SHAH, PANKAJKUMAR CHANDRAKANTBHAI, physicist, researcher; b. Limbdi, Gujarat, India, June 7, 1965; s. Chandrakantbhai Ranchhoddas and Vasantiben Muljibhai Shah. BS, Kotak Coll., Rajkot, India, 1986; MS, Saurashtra U., Rajkot, India, 1988, PhD, 1992. Instr. Vijay Tech. Inst., Rajkot, 1983-84; rsch. fellow dept. physics Saurashtra U., 1988-89; lectr. Kotak Sci. Coll., Rajkot, 1989-92, Virani Sci. Coll., Rajkot, 1992—; cons. Ravi Prakashan, Rajkot, 1995—. Author: Textbook on General Physics, 1996; editor: Textbook of Physics, 1996; author, editor: Textbook of Physics for Second Year Undergraduate Sci., 1997; contbr. articles to profl. jours. Sec. Prof.'s Union, Virani Sci. Coll., 1995. Recipient Nat. Merit scholarship Govt. India, 1986-88, Rsch. fellowship Dept. Atomic Energy, Bombay, 1988-89. Mem. Rajkot Chess Club. Avocations: games (chess, swimming, cricket), reading history and philosophy, metal treatment. Home: 1 Haridham Soc, Alkapuri Main Rd Raiya Rd, Rajkot 360 001, India Office: M and N Virani Sci Coll, Kalawad Rd, Rajkot 360 005, India

SHAH, RAJESH CHIMANLAL, mathematics educator; b. Jalgaon, Maharashtra, India, Oct. 3, 1968; s. Chimanlal Hiralal and Kantaben Chimanlal S.; m. Mayuri Rajesh, June 16, 1997; 1 child. BS, Maharaja Sayajirao U., Baroda, India, 1990, MS second rank, 1992, BEd, 1993; M.Phil., Sardar Patel U., V.V. Nagar, India, 1995; PhD, South Gujarat U., Surat, India, 1997. Lectr. Maharaja Sayajirao U., Baroda, 1994-95, Sardar Vallabhbhai Regional Coll., Surat, 1995-97; lectr. in maths., head dept. applied sci. humanities Vyavasai Vidya Pratishthan Engring. Coll., Rajkot, India, 1997—; in charge info. libr. Vyavasai Vidya Pratishthan Engring. Coll., Rajkot, 1998—, in charge info. tech. dept., computer ctr., 1999—. Contbr. articles to profl. jours. Mem. Gujarat Ganita Mandal (life). Avocations: reading, writing, playing, singing, public speaking. Home: Manjalpur, 9-B Trilok Kunj Soc, 390 011 Baroda Gujarat, India Office: VVP Engring Coll, Kalavad Rd, 360 005 Rajkot Gujarat, India

SHAH, SHANTILAL JAMNADAS, accountant, educator; b. Bombay, Sept. 12, 1935; s. Jamnadas Motichand and Chandanmani Jamnadas (Darbari) Juthani; m. Kumudini Shantilal Bhagat, Feb. 17, 1960; children: Paresh, Mayank, Surbhi, Pinki, Pragna. B Commerce with honors, U. Bombay, 1955, LLB, 1968; Parangat, Tatwagnan Vidyapith, Bombay, 1985. Chartered acct., India. Mem. mng. com. Western India Regional Coun., Chartered Accts. India, Mumbai, 1979-82; mem. mng. com. Bombay Chartered Accts. Soc., Mumbai, 1966—, sec., 1970-71, treas., 1977-78, pres., 1979-80; head acctg. dept. Akbar-Peerbhoy Coll. Commerce & Econs., Mumbai, 1972-95; mem. bd. studies in acctg. U. Bombay, Mumbai, 1982-99, chmn., 1990-95, mem. acad. coun., 1990-93; mem. bd. studies in acctg. S.N.D.T. U., Mumbai, 1995-99. Author: (with J.S. Thacker, I.M. Attarwalla) Accounting and Financial, 1977; (with J.S. Thacker, S.P. Ved) Accounting and Financial Management II, 1978; (with I.M. Attarwalla, A.N. Jagasheth) Accounting and Financial Management I, 1991; (with L.N. Chopde, D.H. Choudhari) Cost Accounting III, 1996. V.p. trustee Bombay Adult Edn. Assn., Mumbai, 1978-99; mem. mng. com. Consumer Guidance Soc. India, Mumbai, 1986-95. Recipient Best Tchr. award Anjuman-I-Islam, Mumbai, 1995. Fellow Inst. Chartered Accts. India (A.F. Ferguson prize 1958, N.M. Shah prize, 1958); mem. Inst. Cost and Works Accts. India. Swadhyaya. Avocations: reading, travel, swimming, music. Home: Wadala Rd 198/18, 400-031 Mumbai India Office: Shantilal Shah & Co 29/314, Walchand Hirachand Marg, 400-001 Mumbai India

SHAH, SHIRISH KALYANBHAI, computer science, chemistry and environmental science educator; b. Ahmedabad, India, May 24, 1942; came to U.S., 1962, naturalized, 1974; s. Kayyanbhai T. and Sushilaben K. S.; m. Kathleen Long, June 28, 1973; 1 son, Lawrence. BS in Chemistry and Physics, St. Xavier's Coll. Gujarat U., 1962; PhD in Phys. Chemistry, U. Del., 1968; cert. in bus. mgmt., U. Va., 1986; PhD in Cultural Edn. (hon.), World U. West, 1986. Asst. prof. Washington Coll., Chestertown, Md., 1967-68; dir. quality control Vita Foods, Chestertown, Md., 1968-72; asst. prof., assoc. prof. sci., adminstr. food, marine sci. and vocat. programs Chesapeake Coll., Wye Mills, Md., 1968-76; assoc. prof., prof. sci., chmn. dept. tech. studies C.C. of Balt., 1976-91; assoc. prof. chemistry Coll. Notre Dame of Md., 1991—; advisor to Young Republicans, 1992—; chmn. computer sys. and engring. techs., 1982-89, project facilitator telecom. curriculum and lab., 1985-89, coord. tech. studies, 1989-91; adj. prof. Phys. Sci. Coppin State Coll., 1996-98; mem. Balt. City Adult Edn. Adv. Com., 1982-89, Distance Learning Task Force, 1996-97; chmn. Coll. wide computer user com., 1985-91; coun. mem. Faculty R&D, 1994-97; adj. prof. chemistry Towson U., 1998—, Morgan State U., 1999—; cons. joint apprentice com. Baltimore City Govt., 1980-91. Contbr. articles to profl. jours. Permanent mem. Rep. Senatorial Com.; charter mem. Rep. Presdl. Task Force; mem. Congl. Adv. Com., 1983—. Recipient Phoenix award Am. Chem. Soc., 1996, 97, Pub. Rels. award, 1996, Sci. Policy award, 2000. Fellow Am. Inst. Chemists; mem. IEEE, APHA, Am. Lung Assn. (mem. com. 1971-80), Am. Lung Assn. Md. (bd. dirs. 1971-80), Am. Chem. Soc. (chmn.-elect Md. Sect. 1995-96, chmn. 1996-98, chair kids and chemistry program of Md. sect. 1996-99, bd. dirs. 1971-80), Assn. Indsl. Hygiene (chmn. com. govt. rels. Md. sect. 1998—), Data Processing Mgmt. Assn., Nat. Environ. Tng. Assn., Nat. Sci. Tchrs. Assn., Nat. Assn. Indsl. Tech. (dir. local region, bd. accreditors 1989-95), Am. Vocat. Assn., Am. Tech. Edn. Assn., Am. Fedn. Tchrs., Md. State Tchrs. Assn., Md. Assn. Cmty. and Jr. Colls. (v.p. 1977-78, pres. 1978-97), Sigma Xi, Epsilon Pi Tau, Iota Lambda Sigma Nu. Roman Catholic. Home: 5605 Purlington Way Baltimore MD 21212-2950 Office: Coll Notre Dame Dept Chem 4701 N Charles St Baltimore MD 21210-2404

SHAH, SYED ALI N., engineer; b. Hyderabad, Sindh, Pakistan, Jan. 1, 1959; s. Shah Nawaz and Kalsoom Shah; m. Neelofer Shah, Oct. 12, 1995. B Engring., Mehran U. Engring. and Tech., Jamshoro, Pakistan, 1984. Cert. engring. Engr. Karachi (Pakistan) Lubricants, 1985-86; participant tng. course NOVA Gas Internat., Canada; sr. engr. Sui So. Gas. Co., Karachi, 1987—. Mem. ASME, USA, Pakistan Engring. Coun. Home: Arif House, F/33-98 Laj-Pat Rd, Sindh Hyderabad 71000, Pakistan

SHAH, VIRENDRA PADAMSEY, insurance adjuster; b. Bombay, June 2, 1932; s. Padamsey Premchand and Jaya (Padamsey) S.; m. Bharati Virendra Kapadia, Mar. 10, 1955 (dec. Sept. 1996); children: Sandeep, Purvi, Kiran. B in Commerce, Sydenham Coll., Bombay, 1951, BA, 1953; LLB, Govt. Law Coll., Bombay, 1954. Ptnr. Padamsey P. Shah and Co., Bombay, 1951-66, Mehta and Padamsey, Bombay, 1967-73; dir. Mehta and Padamsey (P) Ltd., Bombay, 1973-84; proprietor Virendra Padamsey Shah, Bombay, 1984—. Fellow Inst. Ins. Surveyors and Adjusters, Inst. Risk Mgmt.; mem. Internat. Inst. Loss Adjusters, Indian Coun. Arbitration, Willingdon Sports Club, Wiaa Club, Radio Club, Nat. Sports Club India. Jain. Avocation: bridge. Office: 123 TV Industrial Estate, SK Ahire Marg, Bombay Maharashtra 400025, India

SHAHABUDDEEN, MOHAMED, judge, international arbitrator; b. Vreed-en-Hoop, Guyana, Oct. 7, 1931; s. Sheikh Abdul and Jamillah Hamid; m. Bebe Sairah; children: Faid, Sieyf, Shalisa. BSc in Econs., LLM, PhD; LLB, U. London; LLD (hon.), U. West Indies. Bar: Middle Temple, London, 1954. Pvt. practice, 1954-59, magistrate, 1959; magistrate Crown Counsel, 1959-62; solicitor gen. London, 1962-73, atty. gen., 1973-88; min. justice Govt. Guyana, 1978-88, acting fgn. min., 1978-88, v.p., 1983-88; Q.C. judge Internat. Ct. Justice, The Hague, The Netherlands, 1988-97; v.p. Internat. Tribunal for the former Yugoslavia, 1997-99; mem. bd. electors Whewell Professorship of Internat. Law of Cambridge U.; mem. Guyana del. to numerous internat. confs.; judge Appeals Chamber Internat. Criminal Tribunal for Rwanda, 1997—. Mem. adv. bd. European Jour. Internat. Law; author of books, articles to profl. jours. Recipient Cacique's Crown of Honor; named Hon. Bencher Middle Temple, to Order of Excellence, Order of Roraima. Mem. Inst. Internat. Law (1st v.p.), Internat. Law Assn. (hdqrs.), French Soc. Internat. Law (hon.), Am. Soc. Internat. Law (hon.), African Soc. Internat. Law (adv. bd.), Indian Soc. Internat. Law (hon. life), Internat. Acad. Comparative Law (assoc.). Office: Internat Criminal Tribunal, Churchillplein 1, 2517 JW The Hague The Netherlands

SHAHABUDIN, SYED AHMAD MAHMUD, government official; b. Kulim, Kedah, Malaysia, May 4, 1925. Mem. Fed. Legis. Coun., 1955-59, The Kedah State Assembly, 1959-77, The Fed. Senate, 1959-67, Menteri Besar Kedah State, 1967-77, Timbalan Menteri Dalam Negeri, 1977-81; high commr. for Malaysia in Singapore, 1981-85; Gov. of Melaka Malaysia, 1985—; pres. The Assn. Justices of Peace of Malaysia, 1980—. Office: Yang di-Pertua Negeri, Melaka 75692, Malaysia*

SHAHALAM, ABULBASHER MOHAMMED, environmental engineering educator, researcher, consultant; b. Sengarchar, Commilla, Bangladesh, Dec. 31, 1942; came to U.S., 1969; s. Osman Ghani and Qulthum Nessa; m. Dilara Parveen, Mar. 9, 1965; children: Shahnaz, Shahriar, Shahjabin, Shahreaj Alam. BSc in Civil Engring., Bangladesh U. Engring. and Tech., Dhaka, 1963; MS in Civil Engring., Carnegie Mellon U., 1970; MS, U. Pitts., 1972; PhD, U. Toledo, Ohio, 1976. Registered profl. civil engr., Ohio. Asst. chief planner Bangladesh Water & Power Devel. Auth., Dhaka, 1964-68; project engr. Green Internat. Inc., Swickley, Pa., 1969-71; sr. engr. The Chester Engrs., Coraopolis, Pa., 1971-77; prin. engr. Schneider Engrs., Bridgeville, Pa., 1977-79; sr. engr. Michael Baker Engrs., Beaver Falls, Pa., 1979-80; prof. Jordan U. Sci. and Tech., Irbid, 1980-91, Am. U. Beirut, Lebanon, 1992-96, Ohio State U. Rsch. Ctr., Coshocton, 1997-98; head dept. civil engring. Sultan Qaboos U., Muscat, Oman, 1998—; cons. Pitts. Wastewater Treatment Plant, 1976-77; coord. grad. study program Jordan U. Sci. & Tech., Irbid, 1980-84; rschr. Rsch. Inst. KFUPM, Dhahran, Saudi Arabia, 1985-87. Author 78 rsch. papers published in profl. jours. and conf. procs.; reviewer manuscripts for profl. jours.; patentee portable toilet system. Mem. Save the Environment, Jordan, 1988-92. Recipient best rsch. award Govt. Saudi Arabia, 1988. Fellow ASCE; mem. Internat. Assn. Water Quality (Eng.) (specialist group health-related water microbiology 1993—), Sigma Xi. Muslim. Avocations: tennis, hiking, cycling. Home: 1100 Tyndall St Pittsburgh PA 15204-2337

SHAHAM, NATHAN, writer; b. Tel Aviv, Jan. 29, 1925; s. Eliezer and Varda (Brisman) Steinman; m. Ktina Panitch, 1952; children: Boaz, Orit, Yavin. Cultural officer Palmach, Israel, 1947-49; sec. Kibbutz, Betalfa, Israel, 1952-53, 68-69, 1983-85; vice chmn. Israel Broadcasting Authority, Jerusalem, 1968-75; cultural attachee State of Israel, N.Y.C., 1977-80; mem. Press Coun., Tel Aviv, 1983—; dir. gen. Sifriat Pualim Pub. Ho., Tel Aviv, 1985-99, editor-in-chief, 1999—. Author 43 books including, The Rosendorf Quartet, 1993; author 9 plays. Chmn. lit. dept. Israel Arts Coun., 1995-99. Mem. Chamber Music Assn. Avocation: viola. Office: Sifriat Poalim, PO Box 37068, 61369 Tel Aviv Israel

SHAHBAZIAN, GAGIK, government official; b. Yerevan, Armenia, July 27, 1955; married; 1 child. Degree in Mech. Engring., Armmenian Agrl. Inst. Jr., sr. sci. assoc. Sci. Prodn. Assn. Armeslkhozmekhanizatsiya of Min. of Agr., 1977; rector Armenian Higher Sch. of State Com. Agro-Indsl. Complex, 1985-87; dep. chief Gosagroprom's Main Adminstrn. for Sci. Support, 1987-89; 1st dep. chmn. Republic Ctr. for Sci. Support for Gosagroprom, 1989-91; dep. chmn. State Com. on Econ., 1991; min. of state, min. agr. Govt. of Armenia, Yerevan, 1991-93, min. of state, 1993-95, min. rels. with CIS, the European Union, Internat. Econ.Orgn., 1995-98, min., chief staff govt., 1998-99, min. of agr., 1999—. Office: Ul Nalbandian 48, Yerevan 375010, Armenia*

SHAHI, SUSHIL KUMAR, research scientist; b. Saharanpur, India, Sept. 7, 1973; s. Sri Ram and Kamala Shahi. ISc, Govt. Inter. Coll., Lalitpur, India, 1990; BSc, Maharaj Singh Degree Coll., Saharanpur, India, 1993; MSc, Maharani Lal Kuwari Coll., Balrampur, India, 1995; PhD, Allahabad (India) U., 1997. Rsch. assoc. U. Allahabad, 1997—. Contbr. articles to profl. jours. including Current Sci., Skin Pharmacology. Recipient awards Indian Bot. Soc., 1996, Indian Phytopathol. Soc., 1998, Def. Rsch. and Devel. Orgn., 1998, Best awards Soc. for Plant Rsch., 1999. Mem. Indian Sci. Congress. Avocations: new discovery, singing, nature. E-mail: shahi.sk@usa.net. Office: U Allahabad Biol Prod Lab, Dept Botany, Allahabad 211002, India

SHAHI, VINOD KUMAR, chemist, researcher; b. Fazilnagar, Uttar Pradesh, India, July 12, 1964; s. Raj Kumar and Shivdhari Devi (Rai) S.; m. Madhulika, Rai, June 6, 1987; children: Bhavya, Heemanshi, Anmol. Intermediate, P.N.M.I. Coll., Fazilnagar, 1981; MS, U. Gorakhpur (India), 1986, PhD, 1991. Jr. rsch. fellow U. Gorakhpur, 1987-90, rsch. assoc., 1992-97; lectr. U.N.P.G. Coll., Padrouna, India, 1991-92; scientist pool Ctrl. Salt and Marine Chems. Rsch. Inst., Bhavnagar, India, 1997-98; scientist Ctrl. Salt and Marine Chems. Rsch. Inst., Bhavnagar, 1999—. Contbr. articles to scientific jours. Mem. Indian Nat. Desalination Assn. Avocations: cooking, Hindustani music, linguistic research. Home: Fazilnagar, 274401 Kushinagar Uttar Pradesh, India Office: CS&MCRI, Gijubhai Badheka Marg, 364002 Bhavnagar Gujarat, India

SHAHID, MUHAMMAD HANIF, agrarian consultant; b. Jhang, Punjab, Pakistan, Mar. 3, 1962; s. Aziz-Ud-Din and Shahida Khatoon; m. Zarina Hanif Zareen, Oct. 12, 1982; children: Wajahat Hanif, Zohaib Hanif, Wajeeha Hanif. Intermediate, Govt. Coll., Jhang, Pakistan, 1979; BSc in Agr. with honors, Agr. U., Faislabad, Pakistan, 1984. Mobile credit officer Agrl. Devel. Bank Pakistan, Sialkot, 1985-93, 93—; extra asst. dir. Agrl. Devel. Bank Pakistan, Sialkot, Pakistan, 1985-92; asst. dir. Agrl. Devel. Bank Pakistan, Sialkot, 1993—. Social worker BLC, Sialkot, 1995. Named Cricket Best Player Dist. Bd. Jhang, 1978. Mem. Nat. Stars Soc. Pakistan (pres. 1975-85). Mem. Pakistan Peoples Party. Mem. Pakistan Awami Tehreek. Avocations: tourism, general knowledge, music, friends. Home: St # 7-A Mohallah, Madina Masjid Pacca Gharrah, Sialkot Punjab 51330, Pakistan Office: Agrl Devel Bank Pakistan, Kotli Loharan, Sialkot Punjab 51210, Pakistan

SHAHID, NIGAR SAYEM, epidemiologist; b. Dhaka, Bangladesh, Nov. 24, 1950; d. Abusadat Mohammad and Khojesta (Ahmed) Sayem; m. Qazi Shahidul Alam, Jan. 18, 1974; children: Naureen Shahid, Qazi Munirul Alam, Rudabeh Shahid. MBBS, Dhaka (Bangladesh) Med. Coll., 1976;

MSc, London Sch. Hygiene, 1980; MPH, Johns Hopkins U., 1986. Med. officer Dhaka Med. Coll., 1976, Red Lion Sun Soc., Tehran, Iran, 1976-79; asst. scientist Internat. Ctr. Diarrhoeal Disease Rsch., Dhaka, 1981-87, Internat. Ctr. for Diarrhoeal Disease Rsch., Bangladesh; assoc. scientist Internat. Ctr. Diarrhoeal Disease Rsch., Dhaka, 1987-92, scientist, 1993—; mem. editorial bd., sci. com. Bangladesh Med. Rsch. Coun., 1996-98; chmn. Human Devel. Program, Khulna, Bangladesh, 1997—. Contbr. numerous articles to profl. jours. Mem. Nat. Adv. Com. on AIDS, Dhaka, 1996—, cons. AIDS awareness program, 1996—; mem. ethical rev. com. Internat. Ctr. for Diarrhoeal Disease Rsch., Bangladesh, 1998—. UN Univ. scholar, Tokyo, 1985-86; recipient Commonwealth Fellowship award, 1997. Mem. Brit. Med. Assn., Fedn. Univ. Women, Advocacy for Women's Health, Bangladesh Environ. Soc. (sec. gen. 1999—). Avocations: classical Indian music, photography. Home: 669-A Dhanmondi RA Rd 32, Dhaka 1209, Bangladesh Office: Internat Ctr Diarrhoeal, Disease Rsch Mohakhali, Dhaka 1212, Bangladesh

SHAHIDI, FREYDOON, mathematician, mathematics educator; b. Tehran, Iran, June 19, 1947; came to U.S., 1971; s. Manoochehr and Aghdas (Shahidi) S.; m. Guity Ravai, Sept. 21, 1977; children: Alireza, Amir. BS, Tehran U., 1969; PhD, Johns Hopkins U., 1975. Vis. mem. Inst. for Advanced Study, Princton, N.J., 1975-76, 83-84, 90-91; vis. asst. prof. Ind. U., Bloomington, 1976-77; asst. prof. Purdue U., West Lafayette, Ind., 1977-82, assoc. prof. math., 1982-86, prof. math., 1986—; vis. asst. prof. U. Toronto, 1981-82; vis. prof. U. Paris VII, 1990, U. Chgo., 1988, Katholische U. Eichstätt, 1993, Ecole Normale Superieure, 1995, Calif. Inst. Tech., 1997, U. Iowa, 1998, Tata Inst. Fundamental Rsch., Bombay, India, 1999; vis. mem. MSRI, Berkeley, 1994. Co-author: Analytic Properties of Automorphic L-functions; contbr. articles to jours. including Am. Jour. Math., Compositio Mathematica, Duke Math. Jour., Mathematische Annalen, Inventiones Mathematicae, Annals of Mathematics. Served to 2d lt. C.E., Iran, 1969-71. NSF grantee, 1977-79, 79—; XL grantee Purdue Rsch. Found., 1981; Japan Soc. Promotion Sci. fellow Kyoto U., 1993, 96. Mem. Am. Math. Soc. Moslem. Avocation: music. Home: 3219 Elkhart St West Lafayette IN 47906-1159 Office: Purdue U Dept Math Purdue University IN 47907

SHAHIN, ADEL BASYOUNY, zoology educator; b. Quesna, Egypt, Mar. 23, 1960; s. Abdel Aleem Basyouny Shahin and Fekryia Ibraheem Abu Elsououd; m. Mervat Gamal Hussein, Aug. 8, 1989; children: Amr, Radwa, Nouran. Magester, Faculty Sci., Minia, Egypt, 1987; PhD, Minia U., 1993. Asst. lectr. faculty sci. Minia U., 1982-87, lectr. faculty sci., 1987-93, asst. prof. faculty sci., 1999—; rschr. in field. Officer Traf. Commn., Egypt, 1982-84. Mem. Minia Nat. Club (honor prize 1997). Avocations: reading, football, basketball, swimming, tennis. Office: Fac Sci Dept Zoology, Minia Univ, El Minia 61519, Egypt

SHAHIN, M. MOUNIR AHMED (LORD OF STRANTON), engineering educator, researcher; b. Egypt, May 21, 1943; arrived in U.K., 1974; s. Ahmed Shahin; m. Samya Wahid Ibrahim, Mar. 29, 1969; children: Tamer, Sally. B of Engring., Ain-Shams U., Cairo, 1964; Diploma in Bus. Adminstrn., Kuwait U., 1974; PhD in Engring., U. Wales, 1977. Chartered profl. engr., U.K. Univ. demonstrator and devel. engr., min. of transp. Ain-Shams U., Cairo, 1964-68; UNESCO instr., head automobile sect. Tech. Coll., Kuwait, 1968-74; rsch. fellow U. Wales, 1974-77; postdoctoral sr. rsch. fellow Atomic Energy Authority, Brit. Nuclear Fuels Ltd., Risley and Windscale, 1977-85; assoc. prof. U. Qatar, Doha, 1985-90, prof., chmn. dept. mech. engring., 1990-98; prof. engring., ICT cons. London, 1998-2000; internat. cons. specialist Project Assist Program, Washington, summer 1992; prodr., presenter TV and radio programs on nuclear energy Qatar, 1988, 98. Author: (textbooks) Automotive Internal Combustion Engines, 1972, Automotive Chassis and Transmission Units, 1973, Dynamics of Clutch Engagement, 1977; designer new cropping blade for elimination of sparks inside nuclear reprocessing plants, 1980; innovator new debris reduction technique for elimination of hazardous nuclear radiation levels, 1982; contbr. articles to profl. jours. Pres. Egyptian Soc., Swansea, Wales, 1977; founder Egyptian Assn. in Gt. Britain, London, 1997. Ain-Shams Univ. Disting. Student scholar, Egypt, 1960-64; grantee Atomic Energy Authority, U.K., 1981, Brit. Nuclear Fuels Ltd., U.K., 1983; named Lord of Stranton, U.K., 2000. Fellow Inst. Mech. Engrs. (London); mem. Landed Gentry Soc. Nobles in Gt. Britain (hon.). Avocations: music (keyboards), tennis, swimming. E-mail: mshahin@emil.com. Office: 48 Bowes Rd, London W3 7AB, United Kingdom

SHAHIN, MAGDY MOHAMED, physicist, educator; b. Nahtay, Egypt, Jan. 21, 1957; s. Mohamed Abdul Salam Shahin and Shalabia Nasr Al-Gamal; m. Fatma Hassan Taher, Sept. 4, 1991; children: Omar Magdy Shahin, Sherif Magdy Shahin. BSc, Mansoura (Egypt) U., 1978, MSc, 1985, PhD, 1989. Demonstrator Mansoura U., 1978-85, asst. lectr., 1985-89, lectr., 1989-96, asst. prof., cons. prof., 1996—; asst. prof. Presidency for Girls Edn., Al-Kharj, Saudi Arabia,, 1994-99. Contbr. numerous articles to profl. jours. With Egyptian Army, 1978-79. Grantee Egyptian Govt., 1987-89, Brit. Govt., 1992. Mem. Internat. Orgn. Physics, Optical Soc. Am., Inst. Physics U.K. Avocations: reading, scientific research, travel, computer science. Home: Flat 7 Bldg 7, St 304 New Maadi, Cairo Egypt Office: Physics Dept Faculty of Sci, Mansoura U PO Box 69, Mansoura 35516, Egypt

SHAHIN, REDA RAGAB MOHAMED, soil chemistry educator, researcher; b. Al-Mahala Al-Kobra, Egypt, Sept. 1, 1949; s. Ragab Mohamed Shahin and Rashida Mohmoud Al-Wazan; m. Fatma Ibrahim Al-Wazan, Oct. 8, 1974; children: Yosra Reda, Mahmoud R. BSc in Agr., Cairo U., 1971, MSc in Agr., 1975, PhD in Agr., 1980. Demonstrator in agr. Cairo U., Giza, Egypt, 1971-75, lectr., 1975-80, asst. prof., 1980-85, assoc. prof., 1985-90, prof., 1990—; prof. King Saud U., Bureidah, Saudi Arabia, 1994-99; vis. prof. Ghent U., Belgium, 1985, U. Calif., Riverside, 1987-88, McGill U., Montreal, Can., 1989; cons. Al-Manar Cons., Giza, 1985-89; mem. rsch. team Acad. Sci. and Tech., Cairo, 1985-88. Author: (in Arabic) Basic Physics and Agricultural Meteorology, 1990, Soil Chemistry, 1992; contbr. articles to profl. jours. Mem. Environ. Svcs. Cmty. Group, Giza, 1978-94. Recipient State award of Sci., Acad. Sci. and Tech., Egypt, 1989, Presdl. Excellence medal Pres. of Egypt, 1995; Peace fellow U.S. AID, 1987-88. Mem. Soil. Sci. Soc. Egypt, Saudi Soc. Life Sci. Avocations: photography, painting, poetry, camping. Home: 57 Al-Rasheed St Al-Agouza, Giza Egypt Office: Cairo U, Faculty Agr, Giza Egypt

SHAHMIRI, SOHEILA, chemist, educator; b. Tehran, Iran, Mar. 8, 1958; d. Abolfazl and Afsar (Payandeh) Shahmiri. BSc, Beheshti U., Tehran, 1984; MSc, Islamic Azad U., Tehran, 1993, PhD, 1997. Chemist Pharm. R & D, Tehran, 1984-85, quality control chemist, 1991-92; lab. instr. Beheeshti U., Tehran, 1987-91; asst. prof. Islamic Azad U., Tehran, 1996—. Contbr. articles to profl. jours. Mem. ACS (Pres. Club). Avocations: swimming, mountain hiking. Home: 213/C Saman Bldg, Tehran 14358, Iran Office: Islamic Azad U, Shariati, Zafar Tehran Iran

SHAIK, SASON, chemist, educator; b. Bagdad, Iraq, Dec. 17, 1948; arrived is Israel, 1951; s. Shalom and Nazima (Zadik) S.; m. Sara Yadid, 1980; 1 child, Yfaat. BSc, MSc, Bar-Ilan U., Ramat-Gan, Israel, 1974; PhD, U. Wash., 1978. Lectr. Ben-Gurion U., Beer-Sheva, Israel, 1980, sr. lectr., 1980-84, assoc. prof., 1984-88, prof., 1988-92; prof. dept. organic chemistry Hebrew U., Jerusalem, 1992—; dir. The Lise-Meitner Minerva Ctr. for Computational Quantum Chemistry, Jerusalem, 1997—. Contbr. over 200 articles to profl. jours. Sgt. Israeli Def. Forces, 1966-69. Recipient The Bergman Rsch. prize Israel Acad. Scis., 1996, the Alexander Von Humboldt Sr. Rsch. award, 1996; Fulbright fellow Am. Israeli Edn. Found., 1974-79. Mem. AAAS, Israel chem. Soc. (Outstanding Young Israeli Investigator 1987), Am. chem. Soc., N.Y. Acad. Scis. Avocations: poetry, palmistry. Office: Hebrew Univ, Dept Organic Chemistry, 91904 Jerusalem Israel

SHAIKH, ASGHAR AHMED, electrical engineering consultant; b. Digri, Sindh, Pakistan, Apr. 1, 1965; s. Datar Dino Shaikh and Alman Khatoon Shaikh; m. Zubia A. Shaikh. B in Engring., Mehran U. Engring. & Tech., 1989. Elec. engr., cons. Rastek (Pvt) Ltd., Karachi, 1989-91, Gatron (Ind.) Ltd., Lasbeela, 1991-92; sr. elec. engr., cons. Techred (Pvt) Ltd., Lahore, 1992-99; gen. mgr. North Desert Trading, Muscat, Oman, 1999—. Author: Design: Star Oil Immersed Natural Cooled Power Transformer, 1988 (award 1988), The Design, Control and Protection of 132/11 KV Grid Station, 1990 (award 1990); contbr. articles to profl. jours. Recipient shield Pakistan Nat. Cadet Corps, 1982. Mem. ASME (assoc.), IEEE (assoc.), Pakistan Engring. Coun., Divine Jaycees (dir. Hyderabad chpt. 1985). Mem. Pakistan Peoples Party. Avocations: golf, playing cricket, cards, badminton. Home: 98 Defence Ave, 7 Tariq Rd, Hyderabad Sindh, Pakistan Office: PO Box 3962, 112 Muscat Oman

SHAIKH, GHULAM HUSSAIN, physicist; b. Hyderabad, Sindh, Pakistan, May 6, 1950; s. Maqbool Hussain and Jannat Maqbool; m. Kulsum Bano Shaikh, 1955; children: Aftab Alam, Farhana, Shahina, Rizwana. Intersci., Govt. Coll., Hyderabad, Pakistan, 1968, BS, 1970; MS, U. Sindh, Jamshoro, Pakistan, 1972. Scientific officer PCSIR Labs., Karachi, 1974-89, sr. scientific officer, 1989—, group leader, 1994—. Contbr. articles to academic and profl. jours. Mem. Pakistan Stds. Instn. (chmn. sect. com. acoustics, 1998—), Pakistan Assn. Scientists and Scientific Profls., Karachi Physics Soc., Inst. Noise Control Engring. Avocations: writing, reading, cricket. Office: Applied Acoustics Grp, PCSIR Lab/Off University Rd, Karachi 75280, Pakistan

SHAIKH, SAAD, physician; b. Reading, Pa., Aug. 23, 1973; s. Mohammed Ainuddin and Shahnaz (Qureshi) S.; m. Naazli Mohsin, June 19, 1998. BS summa cum laude in Biochemistry, UCLA, 1993; MD, U. Calif., Davis, 1997. Medical intern Univ. Calif., Irvine, Calif., 1997-98; resident ophthalmologist Stanford Univ. Medical Ctr., Stanford, Calif., 1998—. Contbr. articles to profl. jours. Recipient Dunn prize in biochemistry, 1992, Merck award for excellence in chemistry, 1993. Mem. Phi Beta Kappa. Avocations: basketball, literature, rollerblading.

SHAIKHET, LEONID EFIMOVICH, mathematician, researcher; b. Donetsk, Ukraine, Feb. 17, 1948; s. Efim Leontievich and Raisa L'vovna (Murrey) S.; m. Iryna Mikhailovna Zeldina, Dec. 23, 1977; children: Gennadiy, Alina. Grad., Donetsk State U., 1971; Candidate of Sci., Kiev (Ukraine) Inst. Math., 1981; DSc, Kiev State U., 1991. Rschr. Inst. Mining Mechanics, Donetsk, 1971-92; head math. dept. Donetsk State Acad. Mgmt., 1992—; lectr. Donetsk State U., 1979-87; prof. Donetsk Poly. Inst., 1991-92, Donetsk State Acad. Mgmt., 1995. Author: Control of Hereditary Systems, 1992, Control of Systems with Aftereffect, 1996; contbr. articles to profl. jours. Grantee Soros Sci. Found., 1993. Mem. GAMM, Ukraine Acad. Mgmt., Ukraine Acad. Informatics, N.Y. Acad. Sci. Fax: 0038-062-337-71-08. E-mail: leonid.shaikhet@usa.net; leonid@dsam.donetsk.ua. Home: Postysheva St 122 55, 83055 Donetsk Ukraine Office: Donetsk State Acad Mgmt, Chelyuskintsev St 163-a, 83015 Donetsk Ukraine

SHAIN, YOSSI, political scientist, educator; b. Tel Aviv, Sept. 21, 1956; s. David and Hana Shain; m. Nancy Schnog, June 7, 1987; children: Eytan, Emily. BA, Tel Aviv U., 1981, MA, 1983; MPhil, MA, Yale U., 1986, PhD, 1988. Lectr. Tel Aviv U., 1989-93, sr. lectr., 1993-97, head dept. polit. sci., 1996—, prof., 1997—; vis. prof. Middlebury (Vt.) Coll., 1991-92, Fletcher Sch. of Law, Boston, 1994; vis. prof., sr. fellow St. Antony's, Oxford, Eng., 1995; Aaron and Cecile Goldman vis. prof. dept. govt. Georgetown U., 1999-2000; Fulbright vis. prof. Yale U., 1991; vis. asst. prof. Wesleyan U., Middletown, Conn., 1986-87. Author: The Frontier of Loyalty: Political Exiles in the Age of the Nation-State, 1989 (Helen Dwight Reid award Am. Polit. Sci. Assn. 1989), Marketing the American Creed Abroad: Diasporas in the U.S. and Their Homelands, 1999 (Best of Yr. award); co-author: (with Juan J. Linz) Between States: Interim Governments and Democratic Transitions, 1995; editor: Governments in Exile in Contemporary World Politics, 1991; co-editor: (with Aharon Klieman) Democracy: The Challenges Ahead, 1997; mem. editl. bd. Diaspora, 1991—. Sgt. Israeli Army, 1974-77. Alon fellow Israeli Higher Edn. Com., Jerusalem, jr. fellow St. Antony's Coll., Oxford, Eng.; Fulbright scholar Am. Learned Soc., N.Y.C. Mem. Am. Polit. Sci. Assn. Office: Tel Aviv U, Dept Polit Sci, Ramat Aviv Israel

SHAINE, FREDERICK MORDECAI, newspaper executive, consultant; b. Cambridge, Mass., Feb. 5, 1916; s. Joseph and Mollie (Prescott) S.; m. Sylvia Pollack, Mar. 21, 1944; 1 child, Frederick Mordecai Jr. (Rick). Student, U. Vt., 1934-35; BA, Columbia U., 1970. From copy boy to advt. sales rep. Boston Herald, 1933, 36-41; advt. rep. O'Mara & Ormsbee, N.Y.C., 1946-58; advt. dir. Book Rev. N.Y. Herald Tribune, 1958-63; bus. mgr. Book Week Nat. Sun newspaper supplement, 1963-66; bus. mgr. Book World, Sun. book rev. Washington Post/Chgo. Tribune, N.Y.C., 1966-72; dir. N.Y. ops. European Stars and Stripes, N.Y.C., 1972-95; cons. to Armed Forces Info Svcs., Dept. Def., 1996-97; transl. from Italian: And No Quarter, 1972; reviewer and translator various publs. Mem. adv. coun. Casa Italiana, Columbia U., 1967-70. With USCG, 1941-45. Mem. Soc. for Italian Hist. Studies, Columbia Club. Avocations: reading, travel, translating, bridge. Home: 930 5th Ave Apt 12F New York NY 10021-2651 also: PO Box 473 Shelter Island Heights NY 11965-0473

SHAIWALLA, ALIASGER YUSUFALI, computer scientist, educator; b. Mumbai, India, Sept. 20, 1966; s. Yusufali Sharafali and Zainab Yusufali (Jarwala) S.; m. Tasneem Aliasger Andheriwala, Oct. 31, 1993; 1 child, Munira. B of Engring., U. Mumbai, 1988; M of Tech., Indian Inst. of Tech., Mumbai, 1996. Lectr. Thadomal Shahani Engring. Coll., Mumbai, 1988-96, asst. prof., 1996—; cons. Persistent Svcs., Mumbai, 1996—, Fortune Harvest Ltd., Mumbai, 1997—; mem. bd. studies for engring., U. Mumbai, 1996—. Contbr. articles to profl. jours. Mem. IEEE (Bombay sect. com. 1998—), IEEE-TSEC (student branch counselor 1997—), Inst. of Elec. and Electronics, Indian Soc. for Tech. Edn. (life), Instn. of Engrs. (assoc.),. Avocations: reading, travel. Home: 8 St Johns Apts Church Rd, Mumbai 400059, India Office: Thadomal Shahani Engring Co, PG Kher Marg TPSIII, 400050 Mumbai India

SHAKELY, JOHN BOWER (JACK SHAKELY), foundation executive; b. Hays, Kans., Jan. 9, 1940; s. John B. and Martha Jean (Gaston) S.; 1 child, Benton. BA, U. Okla., 1962. Vol. Peace Corps., Costa Rica, 1963-64; editor publs. Dept. Def., 1967-68; dir. devel. U. Okla., 1968-70, Resthaven Mental Health Ctr., L.A., 1970-74; pres. Jack Shakely Assocs., L.A., 1974-75; sr. adv. Grantsmanship Ctr., L.A., 1975-79, Coun. on Founds., Washington, 1979; pres. Calif. Community Found., L.A., 1980—; lectr. in field. Bd. dirs. Emergency Loan and Assistance Fund, 1985—, chair bd. dirs., 1988-93; mem., vice chair L.A. Am. Indian Commn.; bd. dirs. So. Calif. Assn. Philanthropy, 1980—, Comic Relief, 1987—; chmn. bd. dirs. Nonprofit Channel. Served to 1st lt. U.S. Army, 1965-68. Decorated Army Commendation medal; named Nat. Philanthropy Day Outstanding Exec., L.A. Com. Nat. Philanthropy Day, 1989. Office: 445 S Figueroa St Ste 3400 Los Angeles CA 90071-1638

SHAKER, GHASSAN I., business executive, banker. Student, Victoria Coll., Alexandria, Egypt, 1944-56, Cambridge (Eng.) U., 1956-59. Chmn. Ibrahim Shaker Co., Saudi Arabia, Saudi Tng. & Distbn. Co., Hussein Aoueini & Co., Saudi Specialist Constrn. Co., Saudi Electronic Switchgear Co., Arab Eastern Ins. Co., Bahrain; dir. Gulf Conversion Co., Ajman, United Arab Emirates, Transmediterranean, S.A.L., Lebanon, Banorabe, Paris, Banorabe, Paris, Holding du Liban et d'Outre Mer, Lebanon, Banque du Liban et d'Outre Mer, Lebanon, Izmir Hilton Golf and Country Club, Izmir, Turkey. Decorated Grand Officier de la Legion d'Honneur (France), Cavalieri di Gran Croce (Italy), Grand Order of the Rep. (Egypt), Grand Order of the Rep. (Tunis), Grand Order of the Renaissance (Jordan), Grand Order of the Sultanate (Oman), Grand Order of Yek Homayoun (Iran), Grand Order of the Star (Jordan), Grand Order of the Renaissance (Oman), Grand Order of Civil Merit (Spain). Muslim. Avocations: swimmnig, shooting. Office: PO Box 50, Jeddah Saudi Arabia

SHAKER, WILLIAM HAYGOOD, marketing professional, public policy reformer; b. Downey, Calif., Apr. 22, 1938; s. Elmer S. and Marylee (Watts) S.; m. Joanna (Drummond) Shaker, Jan. 28, 1966; children: Catherine Patricia, Marylee, Marcus, Matthew. BS in Engring., U. So. Calif., 1964; MS in Engring., U. Mich., 1969. Registered profl. engr., Calif. Exec. Dow Chem. Co., Midland, Mich., 1966-78; v.p. Nat. Legal Ctr. for the Pub. Interest, Washington, 1979; exec. v.p. Nat. Tax Limitation Com., Washington, 1980-86; pres. Am. Coun. for Health Care Reform, Arlington, Va., 1982—, Heart to Heart Found., Arlington, Va., 1982—; CEO Washington Mktg. Group, Arlington, Va., 1987—; pres. Health PAC, Arlington, Va., 1994—, RepublicanPac.com, 2000—; chmn. Nat. Energy and Comm. Co., 2000—; chmn. Nat. Energy and Comms. Co., 2000—; pres. RepublicanPac.com, 2000—. Author: Health Care Reform, 1994, also legis. and govt. publs.; editor: Electric Power Reform, 1979; editor, pub. millennium edit. The Man of Galilee, 1999; contbr. articles to profl. jours. Founder, chmn. Taxpayers United, Mich., 1972-84. Mem. Govtl. Rsch. Assn. (most effective presentation of govtl. rsch. award 1973), Direct Mktg. Assn. (echo awards 1982-97, maxi awards 1987-97), Pub. Rels. Soc. (silver anvil 1979), Am. Conservative Union (health care reform award 1995). Republican. Lutheran. Office: Washington Mktg Group 5155 37th St N Arlington VA 22207-1824

SHAKIBANASAB, LAUREN VORWERK, music director, educator; b. Chattanooga, Nov. 17, 1959; d. Norman Thomas and E. Harlsie Vorwerk; m. Reza Shakibanasab, Nov., 15, 1961; children: David Reza, Joseph Reza, Alexander Reza, Samuel Reza. MusB, Converse Coll., 1981; postgrad., Coll. Charleston, 1981-83; MusM, So. Ill. U., 1995; pvt. piano study, Paris, 1984. Piano tchr. Shakibanasab Studio, Summerville, S.C., 1985—; music dir. Knightsville United Meth. Ch., Summerville, 1995-98, Midland Park United Meth. Ch., North Charleston, S.C., 1999—; accompanist St. Luke's Children's Ctr., Summerville, 1999—; freelance accompanist; spl. events coord. Piccolo Spoleto, 1990, 91, performer, 1982. Music dir.: Rejoice, The Lord King, 1998, Prime Time Christmas, 1999, Shepherds, Stars and a Savior, 1999, Walk In The Light, 1999. Mem. Music Tchrs. Nat. Assn., Am. Guuild Organist, S.C. Piano Festival Assn. Episcopalian. Avocations: gardening, swimming. Home: 215 W Carolina Ave Summerville SC 29483-4356

SHAKIR, SAAD A. W., pharmacologist, physician, researcher; b. Baghdad, Apr. 27, 1953; arrived in Eng., 1980; s. Abdulwahab Shakir; m. May Shakir; children: Tamarah, Sufyan. MB, ChB, Baghdad U., 1976. Cert. drug safety physician. Rsch. fellow Western Infirmary, Glasgow, Scotland, 1989-90; sr. med. officer Medicines Control Agy. U.K., 1990-91; head safety evaluation group Glaxo Wellcome U.K., 1994-97; v.p. pharmacovigilance and pharmacoepidemiology Rhone-Paulene Rorer, Antony, France, 1997-99; dir. Drug Safety Rsch. Unit, Southampton, Eng., 1999—. Fellow Royal Coll. Physicians (Glasgow and Edinburgh), Faculty Pharm. Medicine (London); mem. Soc. Pharm. Medicine (v.p. 1994-99, chmn. pharmacovigilance working party 1994-99), European Soc. Pharmacovigilance (exec. com. 1996—). Avocations: reading modern history, skiing, easy walking. Home: 38 Lorne Gardens Shirley, Croydon CR0 7RY, England Office: Drug Safety Rsch Unit, Bursledon Hall, Blundell Ln, Southampton SO31 1AA, England

SHAKUSHO, RIN, civil law educator; b. Taipei, Taiwan, July 23, 1935; s. Rin Shi an Rin Chang Pizhl; m. Rin Shi Alen, Mar. 9, 1966; children: Yoshiho Rin, Masatoshi Rin. B in Law, Chung Shing U., 1958; MA, Nagoya (Japan) U., 1967. Asst. Nagoya U., 1971-73; asst. prof. Momoyama Gakuin U., Osaka, Japan, 1974-80, prof., 1980—, dean econs. faculty, 1982-84, councilor, 1986-92, human rights com., 1987-89. Avocations: tennis, music, travel. Home: 8-284-7 Otori Nakamati, Sakai Osaka 593-8327, Japan Office: Momoyama Gakuin U, 1-1 Manabino, Izumi Osaka 590-1198, Japan

SHALALA, DONNA EDNA, federal official, political scientist, educator, former university chancellor; b. Cleve., Feb. 14, 1941; d. James Abraham and Edna (Smith) S. AB, Western Coll., 1962; MSSC, Syracuse U., 1968, PhD, 1970; 38 hon. degrees, 1981-91. Vol. Peace Corps, Iran, 1962-64; asst. prof. polit. sci. CUNY, 1970-72; assoc. prof. politics and edn. Tchrs. Coll. Columbia U., 1972-79; asst. sec. for policy devel. and research HUD, Washington, 1977-80; prof. polit. sci., pres. Hunter Coll., CUNY, 1980-87; prof. polit. sci., chancellor U. Wis., Madison, 1987-93; sec. Dept. HHS, Washington, 1993—. Author: Neighborhood Governance, 1971, The City and the Constitution, 1972, The Property Tax and the Voters, 1973, The Decentralization Approach, 1974. Bd. govs. Am. Stock Exch., 1981-87; trustee TIAA, 1985-89, Com. Econ. Devel., 1981-93; bd. dirs. Inst. Internat. Econs., 1981-93, Children's Def. Fund, 1980-93, Am. Ditchley Found., 1981-93, Spencer Found., 1988-93, M&I Bank of Madison, 1991-93, NCAA Found., 1991; mem. Trilateral Commn., 1988-93, Knight Commn. on Intercollegiate Sports, 1990-93; trustee Brookings Inst., 1989-93. Ohio Newspaper Women's scholar, 1958, Western Coll. Trustee scholar, 1958-62; Carnegie fellow, 1966-68; Guggenheim fellow, 1975-76; recipient Disting. Svc. medal Columbia U. Tchrs. Coll., 1989. Mem. ASPA, Am. Polit. Sci. Assn., Nat. Acad. Arts and Scis., Nat. Acad. Pub. Adminstrn., Coun. Fgn. Rels., Nat. Acad. Edn. (Spencer fellow 1972-73). Office: Dept Health and Human Svcs Office of Sec 200 Independence Ave SW Rm 615F Washington DC 20201-0004

SHALEV, BARUCH ABA, geneticist; b. Jerusalem, Israel, Feb. 20, 1936; s. Zwi and Hana (Cherstien) Shwieg; m. Rina Cohen, Sept. 13, 1965; children: Ofra, Zwi, Itay. BS, Hebrew U., Jerusalem, 1961; MS, U. Calif., Davis, 1962; PhD, U. Reading, England, 1977. Sr. supr. Goldman's Egg City, Moorpark, 1962-63; geneticist Min. Agrl., Israel, 1963-99, statistician in charge experiments, 1965-99, rschr., 1965-99, in charger computer unit, 1977-99, sr. geneticist, 1977-99; ret., 1999, pvt. cons., 2000—; lectr. Hebrew U., Israel, 1970-74; cons. FAO, UN, Rome, 1990-92; cons. in field. Author: Poultry Genetics, 1980, Poultry Production, 1995, Field Experiments in Poultry, 1996; developer 2 genetic lines of geese; contbr. over 200 articles to profl. jours. Brit. Coun. fellow, 1974-77. Mem. European Poultry Genetics Working Group (prize of excellence 1989). Avocations: swimming, music, stamp collecting, aerobics. Home: 23 Hameginim St, 46686 Herzliyya Israel

SHALEV, SARIEL, archaeometallurgist, archaeologist; b. Tel-Aviv, July 3, 1952; s. Yehuda Shlichter and Susi Loewe Shalev; married, 3 children. BA with honors, Tel Aviv U., 1979, MA with honors, 1986, PhD, 1993; postdoctoral, Oxford (U.K.) U., 1992-96. Area supr. Tel Michael Excavations, Israel, 1978-80, Tel Gerisa Excavations, Israel, 1981-84; asst. dir. Tel Qasileh Excavations, Israel, 1983; sr. rsch. fellow Christ Ch., Oxford, 1995-96; sr. lectr. Haifa (Israel) U., 1996—; sr. scientist Weizmann Inst. of Sci., Rehovot, Israel, 1996—; lectr. Tel Aviv U., 1980-92; dir. restoration and conservation Tel Michal Excavations, 1979-81; curator spl. exhbn. Ashmolean Mus., Oxford, 1994-95. Contbr. chpts. to books and numerous articles to profl. publs. Maj. IDF, 1970-74. Scholarship Coun. for Higher Edn., 1990-92, British Coun. Oxford U., 1992-93, Wingate Found. Oxford U., 1993-94, others. Office: Weizmann Inst Sci, Dept Environtl Scis, 76100 Rehovot Israel

SHALHOUB, MICHAEL See SHARIF, OMAR

SHALIF, RUTH, English educator; b. Manchester, U.K., Mar. 30, 1929; d. Norman Myer and Sybil (Wolfe) Jacobs; m. Avia Shalif, Apr. 17, 1951; children: Jesse, Esther, Gad, Michal. BA with honors, U. Manchester, 1949; MA, Hebrew U., 1952. Sch. tchr. Manchester Edn. Com., 1953-55, Ctrl. H.S. for Girls, Manchester, 1955-56; pvt. tchr. Haifa, Israel, 1956-58; English tchr. Haifa Municipality, 1956-58; univ. lectr. Technion Israel Inst. of Tech., Haifa, 1958-68; univ. sr. tchr. Barilan Univ., Ramat Gan, Israel, 1968-94; head of EFL unit Bar Ilan U., Ramat Gan, Israel, 1969-75, 88-89, head of pre-acad. unit, 1980-84, head of translation unit, 1976-78. Author: A Reader in Mechanical Engineering, 1972. Treas. Faculty Assn., Ramat Gan, 1983—. Mem. Israel Geneal. Soc. Jewish. Avocation: family history research. Home: POB 2336, 17 Habrosh St, 56-530 Savyon Israel

SHALIKASHVILI, JOHN MALCHASE, retired military career officer; b. Warsaw, Poland, June 27, 1936; s. Dimitri and Maria (Ruediger) S.; m. Gunhild Bartsch, Apr. 18, 1963 (dec. Aug. 1965); m. Joan E. Zimpelman, Dec. 27, 1966; 1 child, Brant. BSME, Bradley U., 1958; attended, Naval War Coll., 1969-70, U.S. Army War Coll., 1977-78; MA in Internat. Affairs, George Washington U., 1970; LLD (hon.), U. Md., 1993, Bradley U., 1994. Joined U.S. Army, 1958, advanced through grades to gen., 1992—, various troop and staff assignments Alaska, U.S., Fed. Republic of Germany, Vietnam, Korea, 1959-75; commdr. 1st bn. 84th field arty. U.S. Army, Ft. Lewis, Wash., 1975-77; dep. chief of staff ops. So. European Task Froce U.S. Army, Vicenza, Italy, 1978-79; comdr. div. arty., 1st Armored Div. U.S. Army, Nuernberg, Fed. Republic of Germany, 1979-81; chief., politico-mil div., later dep. dir. ODCSOPS U.S. Army, Washington, 1981-84; asst. div. comdr. 1st. Armored div. U.S. Army, Nuernberg, Fed. Republic of Germany, 1984-86; dir. strategy, plans, policy ODCSOPS U.S. Army, Washington, 1986-87; comdg. gen. 9th inf. div. Ft. Lewis, Wash., 1987-89; dep. comdr.-in-chief Hdqrs. USAREUR and 7th Army, Heidelberg, Fed. Republic of Germany, 1989-91; asst. to chmn. Joint Chiefs of Staff, Wash-

ington, 1991-92; Supreme Allied Comdr. Europe, Comdr.-in-Chief U.S. Forces Europe, 1992-93; chmn. Joint Chiefs of Staff, 1993—. Bd. trustees Bradley U.; mem. Buffalo Soldier Meml. Hon. Com. Decorated Def. D.S.M. with 3 oak leaf clusters, D.S.M. (Army) with oak leaf cluster), D.S.M. (Navy), D.S.M. (Air Force), D.S.M. (Dept. Trans.), Legion of Merit with 2 oak leaf clusters, Bronze Star medal with V device, Meritorious Svc. medal with 3 oak leaf clusters, Air medal, Joint Svc. Commendation medal, Army Commendation medal, Nat. Def. Svc. medal with bronze svc. star, Armed Forced Expeditionary medal, Republic of Vietnam Svc. medal with silver service star, S.W. Asia Svc. medal with bronze svc. star, Humanitarian Svc. medal, Army Svc. Ribbon, Overseas Svc. Ribbon with bronze Arabic numeral 5, Inter-Am. Def. Bd. medal, Kuwait Liberation medal, Order of Combat Infantryman badge, Parachutist badge, Joint Chiefs of Staff Identification badge, Army Staff Identification badge, Brazilian Order of Mil. Merit with 1st and 2d award, French Grand Officer of Nat. Merit, Belgian Grand Cordon of Order of Leopold, German Order of Merit with star and sash, Japanese Order of Rising Sun, Argentine Order of May in Grade of Gt. Cross for Mil. Merit, Korean Order of Nat. Security Merit, Tong-IL medal, Bintang Yudha Dharama Utama Hon. Decoration (Indonesia), Kuwait Def. medal, Grand Cross of Royal Norwegian Order of Merit, Grand Cross of Mil. Merit medal of Portuguese Republic, Republic of Vietnam Gallantry Cross with 2 silver and 1 bronze star, Republic of Vietnam Armed Forces Honor medal 1st class, Republic of Vietnam Armed Forces Honor medal 1st class, Republic of Vietnam Campaign medal, Republic of Vietnam Chung My medal 2d class, Tng. Svc. medal 1st class, Netherlands Comdr. Order Orange Nassau with swords, Mexican U.S. Mil. Merit 1st class, Great Cross Repub. Poland; recipient Chilean Bernardo Higgins award, Dwight D. Eisenhower Dist. Svc. award Vets. Fgn. Wars, Dist. Alumni Achievement award George Washington U. Mem. Assn. U.S. Army, Field Arty. Assn., Armed Forces Benefit Assn., Ret. Officers Assn., SHAPE Officers' Assn., Coun. Fgn. Rels., Am. Acad. Achievement, Mil. Order of Carabao, Army and Air Force Benefit Assn.

SHALIMOV, VLADIMIR NIKOLAEVICH, science educator; b. Novograzhdanskaya, Russia, Feb. 7, 1954; s. Nikolai Fyodorovich and Zinaida Alexeyevna (Dorozhkina) S.; m. Natalia Stepanovna Kuprik, July 28, 1979 (dec. Feb. 1992); children: Alina, Marianna; m. Zinaida Kuzminichna Pervushina, Jan. 7, 1993. Degree in engring., Novocherkassk Poly. Inst., Russia, 1976; D, Novocherkassk Poly. Inst., 1979. Jr. rschr. Novocherkassk Poly. Inst., 1979-80, asst. instr. Volgodonsk (Russia) br., 1980-84, sr. instr., 1984-89, docent, 1989—. Contbr. articles to profl. jours.; patentee in field. Dep. advisor Russian Parliament, Moscow, 1994-96; chmn. Volgodonsk br. Dem. Vybor Rossii Party, 1993—, Social-Ecol. Union Rostov region, Volgodonsk, 1996—, Volgodonsk br. Coalition of Right-Wing Forces, 1999; dep. Mcpl. Coun., Volgodonsk, 1990-93. Mem. N.Y. Acad. Scis., Social Com. on Elimination of Results of Terrorist Act in Volgodonsk. Avocations: soccer, amateur poetry writing, reading, outdoor activities. Home: Mira Ave 37/143, 347383 Volgodonsk Russia Office: Volgodonsk Inst Novocherkassk Tech Univ, Lenina St 73/94, 347360 Volgodonsk Russia

SHALIT, HANOCH, imaging scientist, executive; b. Tel-Aviv, July 1, 1953; came to U.S., 1982; s. Mordechai and Yael (Bryskier) S.; m. Cleri Machlouzarides, May 17, 1992; children: Antonia, Alexander. BSc with honors, Poly. of Cen. London, 1978; PhD in Physics, London U., 1981. Asst. photographic scientist John Hadland Ltd., Bovingdon, Eng., 1977-78; demonstrator London U., 1978-81; asst. prof. Rochester (N.Y.) Inst. of Tech., 1981-82; sr. photographic scientist Chemco Photo Products, Glen Cove, N.Y., 1982-83, sr. rsch. project mgr., 1984-87; dir. of photographic sci. Fonar Corp., Melville, N.Y., 1987-88; pres. IMATEC Ltd., N.Y.C., 1988—; mem. stds. com. Digital Image Comm. in Medicine. Contbr. articles to profl. jours; patentee in field. With M.C. Israeli Army, 1971-74. Recipient scholarship, London U., 1978-81. Mem. Soc. for Imaging Sci. and Tech., Brit. Assn. for Crystal Growth, Soc. Motion Picture and TV Engrs. (voting mem., subcom. on med. imaging), Am. Coll. of Radiology, Nat. Elec. Mfg. Assn. Home: 245 E 63rd St Apt 34B New York NY 10021-7400

SHALITA, ALAN REMI, dermatologist; b. Bklyn., Mar. 22, 1936; s. Harry and Celia; m. SImone Lea Baum, Sept. 4, 1960; children: Deborah (dec.) and Judith (twins). AB, Brown U., 1957; BS, U. Brussels, 1960; MD, Bowman Gray Sch. Medicine, 1964; DSc (hon.), L.I. U., 1990. Intern Beth Israel Hosp., N.Y.C., 1964-65; resident dept. dermatology NYU Med. Ctr., 1967-68, NIH tng. grant fellow dept. dermatology, 1968-70, instr. dermatology, 1970-71; asst. prof. NYU, 1971-73, Columbia U., N.Y.C., 1973-75; assoc. prof. medicine, head divsn. dermatology SUNY Downstate Med. Ctr., Bklyn., 1975-79, prof., 1979—, head divsn. dermatology, 1979-80, chmn. dept. dermatology, 1980—, asst. dean, 1977-83; acting dean Queens campus SUNY Downstate Med. Ctr., 1983-84; assoc. dean clin. affairs SUNY Health Sci. Ctr., Bklyn., 1989-92, assoc. provost for clin. affairs, 1992-93, assoc. v.p. clin. affairs, 1993—; disting. tchg. prof. SUNY Health Sci. Ctr., Bklyn., 1996—; asst. attending in dermatology Univ. Hosp., N.Y.C., 1970-73, Bellevue Hosp. Ctr., 1970-73, Manhattan VA Hosp., 1971-73, Presbyn. Hosp., 1973-75; mem. med. bd. Kings County Hosp. Ctr.; cons. dermatology Bklyn. VA Hosp., 1975—; chief dermatology Brookdale Med. Ctr., 1977-90; chief dermatology Univ. Hosp. of Bklyn., 1975—; chief dermatology Kings County Hosp. Ctr., Bklyn., 1975—, acting med. dir., 1989-92; med. dir. Univ. Hosp. Bklyn., 1992-96. Pres. Temple Shaaray Tefila, N.Y.C., 1982-86, chmn. bd. trustees, 1987-95. Lt. M.C. USNR, 1965-67. Recipient Torch of Liberty award Anti-Defamation League, 1987, Surg. and Pediatric awards Beth Israel Hosp., N.Y.C., 1965, Leah Dickstein Man of Good Conscience award, Women's Med. Assn. of N.Y., 1999, Leadership in Urban Med. Edn. award Arthur Ashe Inst. for Urban Health, 1999; spl. fellow NIH, 1970-73. Mem. AMA, AAAS, Am. Acad. Dermatology (bd. dirs. 1983-87, v.p. 1995-96), Soc. Investigative Dermatology, Dermatology Found. (past trustee), Am. Dermatol. Assn. (sec.-treas. 1996—), Am. Soc. Dermatol. Surgery (past bd. dirs.), Soc. Cosmetic Chemists, Assn. Profs. Dermatology (sec.-treas. 1988-94, pres. 1996-98), Internat. Soc. Dermatology, N.Y. Acad. Scis., N.Y. State Med. Soc., N.Y. Acad Medicine, N.Y. State Dermatol. Soc., Dermatol. Soc. Greater N.Y. (pres. 1980-81), N.Y. Dermatol. Soc. (pres. 1989-90), Brit. Assn. Dermatologists, Soc. Francaise de Dermatologie et Syphilagraphie, Spanish Acad. Dermatology (hon.), Argentina Dermatology Soc., Polish Dermatology Soc. (hon.), Venezuelan Dermatology Soc., Alpha Omega Alpha. Republican. Home: 70 E 77th St New York NY 10021-1811 Office: 450 Clarkson Ave Brooklyn NY 11203-2056

SHALKOVSKY, VOLODYMYR VALENTINOVICH, diplomat; b. Kiev, Ukraine, Sept. 26, 1976; s. Valentin Volodymyrovich and Ludmila Dmitrievna Shalkovsky. M of Econs., Kiev U., 1998; grad., George C. Marshall European Ctr. Security Studies, Germany, 1998; Candidate, Kiev Inst. Internat. Rels., 1999. Mgmt. cert. Asst. dir. Ministry of Fgn. Affairs of Ukraine, Kiev, 1996-98, 3d sec., 1998—. Avocations: reading, fishing, fitness. Home: pr-t Obolonsky 13, 04205 Kiev Ukraine Office: Ministry Fgn Affrs Ukraine, 1 Mikhaylivska Sq, Kiev Ukraine

SHALL, BASIL, systems analyst; b. Klerksdorp, Transvaal, South Africa, Oct. 2, 1956; arrived in England, 1977; s. Emanuel and Jaqueline (Rosin) S.; m. Vivienne Ruth Swerdlow, July 4, 1982; children: Emma, Kate. BSc in Bldg., U. Witwatersrand, Johannesburg, South Africa, 1977; MSc in Bus., London Bus. Sch., 1981. Bus. sys. mgr. Levi Strauss, London, 1984-85; mgmt. cons. Price Waterhouse, London, 1985-89; bus. planning mgr. Guinness PLC, London, 1989-94; head info. sys. strategy Post Office Counters Ltd., London, 1994-95; head info. sys. planning The Post Office, London, 1995—, info. sys. dir. retail banking, 1999—. Mem. Glycogen Storage Disease Assn. (info. sys. officer 1994—). Jewish. Home: 46 Howard Walk, London N2 0HB, England Office: Post Office, 148 Old St, London EC1V 9HQ, England

SHALLENBERGER, GARVIN F., lawyer; b. Beloit, Wis., Jan. 7, 1921; s. Garvin D. and Grace (Hubbell) S.; m. Mary L., May 5, 1945; children: Diane, Dennis Clark. BA in Pre-law, U. Mont., 1942; JD, U. Calif., Berkeley, 1949; LLD (hon.), Western State U., Fullerton, Calif., 1988. Bar: Calif. 1949, U.S. Dist. Ct. (cent. dist.) Calif. 1949, U.S. Ct. Appeals (9th cir.) 1949, U.S. Supreme Ct. 1961, U.S. Dist. Ct. (no. and so. dists.) Calif. 1963. Of counsel Rutan & Tucker, Costa Mesa, Calif.; chmn. spl. adv. com. state bar legal svcs. program, 1979-89, pub. law ctr Orange County, 1979-90. Recipient distinguished svc. award Boalt Hall (U. Calif. Berkeley), Judge Learned Hand Human Rel. award Nat. Jewish Com., 1990, Outstanding Alumnus award, U. Mont., 1999. Fellow Am. Coll. Trial Lawyers; mem. Am. Bd. Trial Advs. (a founder and 1st sec.),Calif. Bar Assn. (bd. govs. 1975-76, pres. 1977-78; mem. com. on jud. nominees 1978-79, pres. 1980), mem. Orange County Bar Assn. (bd. dirs. 1970-71, pres. 1972, Franklin West award 1979). Democrat. Avocations: tennis, writing. Office: Rutan & Tucker PO Box 1950 Costa Mesa CA 92628-1950

SHALTIEL, SHMUEL, biochemist, researcher, educator; b. Thessaloniki, Greece, Jan. 12, 1935; s. Sabetay and Renée (Bourla) S.; m. Sarah Mass, May 10, 1956 (dec. July 1997); children: Orna, Ruth. MSc, Hebrew U., Jerusalem, 1960; PhD, Weizmann Inst., Rehovot, Israel, 1964. Rsch. assoc. U. Wash., Seattle, 1964-66; mem. faculty Weizmann Inst. Sci., 1964—, prof., 1975—, head chem. immunology dept., 1992-95, head biol. reg. dept., 1995—; dep. pres., acting pres. Weizmann Inst., 1985-88, bd. govs., 1988—, dean Feinberg Grad. Sch., Rehovot, 1978-84, chmn. sci. coun., 1976-77; mem. planning and budgeting com. Israeli Coun. for Higher Edn., Jerusalem, 1992-98; vis. prof. U. Calif., Berkeley, 1972-73, ETH, Zurich, Switzerland, 1992; Fogarty scholar-in-residence NIH, Bethesda, Md., 1981-83, 99. Co-author: New Horizons in Science, 1974; editor: Metabolic Interconversion of Enzymes, 1976; co-editor: Current Topics in Cellular Regulation: Modulation by Covalent Modification, 1985; author: The Biochemical Revolution in Medicine, 2000; inventor hydrophobic chromatography; co-editor sci. column Haaretz Daily, Israel, 1963-78; mem. adv. bd. European Jour. Biochemistry, 1974-80; mem. editl. bd. Analytical Chemistry, U.S., 1980-90, Archives of Biochemistry and Biophysics, 1995-1999; editor FEBS letters, 1989—. Chmn. bd. dirs. U.S.-Israel Ednl. Found., 1975-78; mem. Nat. Coun. for Higher Edn., Jerusalem, 1978-81; mem. sci. adv. panel Novartis (Ciba) Found., London, 1990—. With Israel Def. Forces, 1958-60. Fulbright grantee U.S.-Israel Edn. Found., 1964; Brainin fellow Weizmann Inst. Sci., 1968; recipient Landau prize in natural scis. Mifal Hapayis, 1980, Biochem. analysis prize German Soc. Clin. Chemistry, 1978, Weizmann prize in the exact scis. Tel Aviv Municipality, 1984, biology prize Rothschild Found., 1994. Mem. Israel Biochem. Soc. (Shlomo Hestrin prize 1971), Am. Biochem. Soc., Spanish Biochem. Soc., Israel Immunol. Soc., German Soc. Clin. Chemistry, European Molecular Biol. Orgn., Am. Soc. Biochem. and Molecular Biology (hon.). Home: Neveh Matz 7, 76306 Rehovot Israel Office: Weizmann Inst Sci, Dept Biol Regulation, Rehovot 76100, Israel

SHAM, SAMUEL YAT-WAH, oil and transport executive, trade executive; b. Hong Kong, Oct. 18, 1952; s. How Ying Chow; m. Rebecca Yeun-mei Lee, 1976; children: Sophia, Shirley, Susan. BSc in Engring. with honors, U. Hong Kong, 1974. Chartered Engr., Eng. Various managerial and exec. positions Esso Petroleum, Hong Kong and Singapore, 1974-89; from gen. mgr. to mng. dir. Wickland Oil Asia, Singapore, China, 1989-93, 95-97; gen. mgr. Louis Dreyfus Energy, Singapore, China, 1993-95; dir., gen. mgr. Wilson Group, Hong Kong, 1997—; dir. Kai Tak Refuellers, Hong Kong, 1982-84, Wilson Parking, Hong Kong, 1997—, TsingMa Mgmt., Hong Kong, 1997—, China Tollways, Hong Kong, 1997—, Autotoll/Hong Kong Parking, 1997—. Pres. Tsuen Kwai Ch., Hong Kong, 1978-84; supr. Tsung Tsin Sch., Hong Kong, 1978-84. Mem. Hong Kong Instn. Engrs., Inst. Marine Engrs. Avocations: golf, tennis, squash. Office: Wilson Group Rm 2601-3, 280 Gloucester Rd, Hong Kong Hong Kong

SHAMA, MOHAMED ABDEL FATTAH, dean, engineering educator; b. Alexandria, Egypt, May 3, 1938; s. Abdel Fattah Mohamed S.; m. Laila Mohamed Nassef, Feb. 29, 1968. BSc, Alexandria (Egypt) U., 1960; PhD, Glasgow (Scotland) U., 1965. Lctr. Faculty of Engring., Alexandria, Egypt, 1966-72; assoc. prof. Faculty of Engring., Alexandria, 1972-77, prof. naval engring., 1977—, head dept., 1988-92, vice dean, 1992-95, dean, 1995-98; vis. prof. U. Basrah, Iraq, 1976-79; rsch. surveyor Lloyds Register, London, 1969-71. Inventor in field; contbr. articles to profl. jours. Grantee Sci. Rsch. Coun., 1979; recipient State prize for engring. sci., 1974, others. Mem. ISSC, Egyptian Soc. of Marine Engrs. and Shipbuilders (bd. dirs.), Internat. Maritime Assn. of Mediterranean Sea, Ency. of Life Support System (hon.), Semouha Sporting Club, Almontada, U. Staff Club. Avocations: travel, reading, walking. Office: Faculty Engring, Alexandria Egypt

SHAMBAUGH, STEPHEN WARD, lawyer; b. South Bend, Ind., Aug. 4, 1920; s. Marion Clyde and Anna Violet (Stephens) S.; m. Marilyn Louise Pyle (dec. 1993); children: Susan Wynne Shambaugh Hinkle (dec. 1998), Kathleen Louise Shambaugh Thompson. Student, San Jose State Tchrs. Coll., 1938-40, U. Ark., 1951; LLB, U. Tulsa, 1954. Bar: Okla. 1954, Colo. 1964. Mem. staff Reading & Bates, Inc., Tulsa, 1951-54; v.p., gen. mgr., legal counsel Reading & Bates Drilling Co. Ltd., Calgary, Alta., Can., 1954-61; sr. ptnr. Bowman, Shambaugh, Geissinger & Wright, Denver, 1964-81; sole practice Denver, 1981-97; now ret.; dir., fin. counsel various corps. Col. USAF ret. Mem. Colo. Bar Assn., Okla. Bar Assn., P-51 Mustang Pilots Assn., Masons, Elks, Phi Alpha Delta.

SHAMDASANI, HARESH RAMCHANDRA, export company executive; b. Bombay, Oct. 26, 1948; s. Ramchandra Hassomal and Devi Ramchandra (Advani) S.; m. Erika Christine Lohmann, Sept. 2, 1976; 1 child, Sonia. Textile degree, Bradford U., Eng., 1973. Mng. dir. Ea. Express Co. Ltd., Hong Kong, 1973-80, Shelsham Trading Co. Ltd., Hong Kong, 1980—. Active The Shamdasani Found., Hong Kong and Bombay. Mem. Rotary.

SHAMEEL, MUSTAFA, marine botany educator, researcher; b. Rudauli, Lucknow, India, July 3, 1941; arrived in Pakistan, 1952; s. Syed Amirul Hasan and Muhammadi Begum Quadri; m. Suraiya Quadri, July 18, 1964; children: Simin, Naushin. BSc, U. Karachi, Pakistan, 1960, MSc, 1962; PhD, U. Kiel, Germany, 1972, postgrad., 1977. Lectr. dept. botany U. Karachi, 1962-72, asst. prof., 1972-73, asst. prof. Inst. Marine Biology, 1973-78, assoc. prof., 1978-79, assoc. prof. dept. botany, 1979-85, prof., 1985-99, prof. grade 21, 1999—; chmn. landscape and gardening coun. U. Karachi, 1985-86, chmn. mktg. com., 1987-88, mem. bd. govs. Ctr. of Excellence in Marine Biology, 1992-95, dir., 1999—, dir. Inst. Marine Scis., 1994-98, mem. bd. studies, 1985—, faculty of sci., 1978-79, 85—, acad. coun., 1985—, bd. advanced studies and rsch., 1997—, senate, 1985—. Editor-in-chief Pakistan Jour. Marine Biology, 1999—; mem. editl. bd. Pakistan Jour. Botany, 1986—, Pakistan Jour. Marine Scis., 1992, Marine Rsch., 1992-95, Biol. Rsch. Jour., 1994-95; contbr. 120 rsch. papers to jours. in field. Gen. sec. Karachi U. Tchrs.' Soc., 1985-86, pres., 1988-89; mem. bd. studies Pakistan Marine Acad., 1994—, U. Sindh, Jamshoro, Pakistan, 1997—; pres. Karachi U. Employment Coop. Housing Soc., 1999—. Recipient Agha Hasan Abedi Gold medal in botany Pakistan Acad. Sci., 1998, Izaz-e-Kamal Civil award Pres. of Pakistan, 2000; DAAD scholar German Acad. Exch. Svc., Bonn, Germany, 1967-72, sr. rsch. fellow Alexander von Humboldt Found., Bonn, 1976-77; 4 species of plants named in his honor. Mem. Pakistan Bot. Soc. (life, v.p. 1985-91, 96—), Unikarians, Pakistan Assn. Scientists. Avocations: reading, pop and classical music, films, TV. Home: B-26 Staff Town, U Karachi, Karachi 75270, Pakistan Office: Ctr Excel Marine Biology, U Karachi, Karachi 75270, Pakistan

SHAMGAR, MEIR, judge; b. Danzig, Aug. 13, 1925; came to Israel, 1939; s. Eliezer and Dina (Bonfeld) Sterenberg; children: Anat, Ram, Dan. Grad., Govt. Law Sch., Jerusalem, 1950; D honoris causa, Weizman Inst. Sci., 1987, Hebrew U., Jerusalem, 1990, Ben Gurion U., Beer Sheva, 1995, Tel Aviv U., 1997, Bar Ilan U., 1998; Disting. Fellowship, Open Univ. Israel, 1993. Commd. officer Israeli Army, 1948, advanced through grades to brig. gen., 1968, mil. advocate gen., 1961-68; atty. gen. Israel, 1968-75; justice Supreme Ct. of Israel, Jerusalem, 1975—, pres., 1983-95; mem. Internat. Ct. Arbitration of the Hague, 1988; lectr. Hebrew U., Tel-Aviv U., 1961-67; chmn. commn. inquiry Hebron Massacre, 1994, Assassination Prime Min. Rabin, 1995. Author, editor: Military Government in the Territories Governed by Issrael, 1982; contbr. articles to profl. jours. Mem. Internat. Soc. Mil. Law and Law of War (conseil de direction 1964—). Recipient Issrael prize for svc. to state and cmty., 1996, Ben Gurion prize, 1997. Mem. World Jurist Assn. (mem. coun. 1977—), Internat. Assn. Supreme Adminstrv. Jurisdictions (coun. mem. 1985—). Office: Supreme Ct, S Mishpat Str Kiriat Ben-Gurion, Jerusalem Israel

SHAMIM, MAH TALAT, chemist; b. Karachi, Pakistan, Sept. 7, 1952; came to U.S., 1976; d. Syed Hasan and Askaribi (Nuzhat) Akhtar; m. A. Najm Shamim, Dec. 20, 1975. BS in Chemistry, Karachi U., 1972, MS in Chemistry, 1973; MS in Chemistry, Howard U., 1981, PhD in Chemistry, 1983. Postdoctoral fellow NIH, Bethesda, Md., 1983-89, sr. staff fellow, 1989-91; chemist EPA, Washington, 1991-93, sect. chief environ. fate and effects divsn., 1993-97, chief environ. risk br. environ fate and effects divsn., 1997—; panelist U.S. Merit Sys. Protection Adv. Bd., Washington, 1996—; mem. internat. environ. fate workgroups. Co-author: Rejection Rate Analysis: Environmental Fate Guidelines, 1995; contbr. articles to profl. jours. Mem. Am. Chem. Soc., Assn. Asian-Pacific Ams. Avocations: gardening, writing poetry, writing short stories, oil painting, sewing. Achievements include development of highly selective adenosine receptor antagonists which are used as effective probes in studying the nature of this class of receptors; designed and developed a wide range of heterocycles which show cardiac stimulant, behavioral stimulant and tracheal stimulant activities; contributed significantly in the development and harmonization of OECD environmental fate guidelines for environmental fate studies for pesticides which are required by international regulatory agencies for the registration of pesticides. Office: Environ Protection Agy 401 M St SW Washington DC 20024-2610

SHAMIR, YITZHAK (YITZHAK YEZERNITSKY), statesman, former Israeli prime minister; b. Ruzinoy, Poland, Oct. 15, 1915; arrived in Palestine, 1935; married; 2 children. Degree, Warsaw U. Law Sch., Hebrew Univ. of Jerusalem; Dr. (hon.), Hebrew Union Coll., 1991, L.A. Jewish Inst. Religion, 1991. Mem. Irgun Zvai Leumi (Jewish Mil. Orgn.), 1937; founder, leader Lohamei Herut Yisrael (Stern Group), 1940-41; arrested British Mandatory Authority, 1941, escaped, 1942; exiled Eritrea, Africa, 1946, escaped, 1947; given political asylum France; returned Israel, 1948; sr. post Civil Svc., 1955-65; mgr., dir. various bus. concerns, 1965—; mem. Herut Movement, 1970—, chmn. exec. com., 1975-92; mem. Knesset, 1973-96, speaker, 1977-80; min. Ministry of Fgn. Affairs, 1980-83, 84-86; dep. prime min. Israel, 1984-86, prime min., 1983-84, 86-92; leader Likud, Israel, 1983-93; former Min. Labor and Social Affairs; acting min. Ministry Interior, 1987-88. Author: Summing Up, 1992. Address: 8 Shaul Hamelech Blvd, 64733 Tel Aviv Israel

SHAMRIKOV, BORIS MIKHAILOVICH, aviation educator, researcher, engineer; b. Magnitogorsk, Russia, Apr. 17, 1941; s. Mikhail Ilyich and Anna Mikhailovna (Volkova) S.; m. Lubov Georgievna Tolstova, Aug. 14, 1964; 1 child, Ilyia. Graduate, Chelyabinsk Poly., 1963; candidate degree, Aviation Inst. Moscow, 1968, PhD, 1973. Engr. Rsch. Inst. Automation, Sverdlovsk, 1964-66; rschr. Aviation Inst. Moscow, 1968-75, assoc. prof., 1975-77, prof., 1977—. Co-author: (with others) Accurate Methods in Analysis of Non-Linear Control Systems, 1971, Oscillation in Digital Control Systems, 1983, Digital Systems and Stepwise Adaptive Control, 1999; author: Automatic Digital Control Basic Theory, 1985, (with others) Automatic Control Basic Theory, 1985. Avocations: lawn tennis, fishing. Office: Moscow Inst Aviation, 125871 Moscow Russia

SHAMSAVARI, ALI, economist, researcher, lecturer; b. Mahabad, Iran, May 24, 1944; s. Hoseingholi and Tuba (Asaf) S.; m. Fazrad Amai, Mar. 13, 1967; children: Seena, Sara. BA in Econs., Nat. U., Tehran, 1966; MA in Econs., Vanderbilt U., 1970, PhD in Econs., 1973. Researcher, advisor Indsl. Devel. Bank, Tehran, 1966-67; rsch. asst. Vanderbilt U., Nashville, 1968-70, teaching asst., 1970-71; asst. prof. Ala. A&M U., Huntsville, 1971-74; lectr. Humboldt State U., Arcata, Calif., 1975-76; assoc. prof. Jundi Shapur U., Ahvaz, Iran, 1976-81; sr. researcher Ministry of Planning, Rio de Janeiro, 1981-82; sr. lectr. Kingston (Eng.) U., 1982—; part-time lectr. Univ. Coll., London, 1985-86; vis. prof. Vanderbilt U., Nashville, summer 1985; part-time lectr. Schiller Internat. U., London, 1982—. Author: Dialectics & Social Theory, 1991, Einfach/Komplex: entry in Critical/Historical Dictionary of Marxist Concepts, vol. 3, Argument, Berlin, 1998. Mem. Royal Econ. Soc., Assn. Polytech. Tchrs. in Econs., Greenpeace, Friends of the Earth, Action Aid. Mem. Brit. Labour Party. Avocations: chess, tennis, music, walking, biking. Home: 4 Moresby Ave, Surbiton Surrey KT5 9D5, England Office: Kingston U, Pennhyn Rd, Kingston KT1 2EE, England

SHAMSAVARY, PARISIMA, academic adminstrator, educator; b. Mahabad, Azebaiejan, Iran, Mar. 3, 1942; d. Hossain Goli and Tuba (Assef) S.; m. Houshang Shams; children: Parinaz, Farnaz. BA, U. Tabriz, Iran, 1963; MEd, Goucher Coll., 1964; MA, U. London, 1967, PhD, 1972. Cert. secondary, elem. and primary tchr. Rsch. officer Iran Ctr. for Edn. Rsch., Tehran, 1973-74; asst. prof. edn. U. Tabriz, Tehran, 1972-74, dep. dean faculty of edn., 1972-74; head dept. social and philos. found. of edn., faculty edn. Tehran U., 1974-85; lectr. Schiller Internat. U. London, 1987—; head EAL dept. St. Paul's Way Cmty. Sch., London, 1989—. Contbr. articles to profl. publs. Tchr. Gov. Behishti Sch., Tehran, 1978-85, St. Paul's Way, London, 1995-99. active Iran Women's Orgn., 1973-79. Fulbright scholarship Goucher Coll., 1963-64; Ministry Edn. scholarship London U., 1964-70. Mem. Comparative Edn. Soc., Internat. Fedn. of Women, Comparative and Internat. Edn. Soc. Muslim. Avocations: reading, swimming, travelling. Office: St Pauls Way Cmty Sch, Shelmerdine Close, London E3 4AN, England

SHAMS-UD DOHA, AMINUR RAHMAN, publisher, editor-in-chief; b. Murshidabad, India, Jan. 24, 1929; s. Abu Hamid Mohammad and Hamida (Ghazi) S.; m. Wajiha Moukaddem, June 29, 1981. BSc with honors, Calcutta U., 1948; BA, Dhaka U., 1955. Commd. artillery, 1952, advanced through grades to maj.; stationed Ft. Sill, Okla., 1957-58; gen. staff officer ops. Pakistan Army, 1967; stationed Royal Coll. Sci. and Tech., Shrivenham, U.K., 1964-65; ret., 1968; gen. sec. Awami League, Rawalpindi, 1969-71; editor, pub. Interwing Rawalpindi, 1969-71; amb. Bangladesh, Yugoslavia and Romania, 1972-74, Iran and Turkey, 1974-77; high commr. U.K., 1977-82; min. of info. Govt. of Bangladesh, Dhaka, 1982, min. of fgn. affairs, 1982-84; founder, chmn., editor-in-chief Dialogue Publs. Ltd., 1989. Chmn. Fgn. Ministers Conf., Orgn. of Islamic Conf., 1983-84; leader Delegation to Non-Aligned Conf., 1982-84, OIC Con., Niamey, Nigeria, 1982, Unga, N.Y., 1983; chmn. Commonwealth Fund for Tech Coop., Montreal, 1978, Malta, 1979. Named Yugoslav Order of Lance and Flag, 1974; recipient Gwanha medal South Korean Order of Diplomatic Svc., 1983. Mem. Internat. Inst. of Strategic Studies, English Speaking Union, Officers and Golf Club, Royal Overseas League, London. Avocations: 1948 trials for London Olympic games, football, tennis, gardening. Home: Farm View Indira Rd, Tejgaon Dhaka 1215, Bangladesh

SHAN, JIE (JEFFREY SHAN), science educator; b. Jiang su, Jiansu, China, Oct. 28, 1961; s. Zhitong Shan and Jingxian Qu; m. Jijun Lei, Oct. 25, 1989; 1 child, David. PhD, Wuhan U., 1989. Rsch. fellow Stuttgart (Germany) U., 1995-96; sr. lectr. U. Gävle, Sweden, 1997-98; faculty sch. civil engring. Purdue U., West Lafayette, Ind., 1998—. Author: Combined Adjustment of Photogrammetric and non photogrammetric Observations, 1993; contbr. over 50 articles to profl. jours. Recipient Nat. Excellent Youth award Assn. Sci. and Tech. China, 1991, Humboldt Stiftung, 1995. Mem. Am. Soc. Photogrammetry and Remote Sensing, Am. Congress Surveying and Mapping, Am. Geophys. Union. E-mail: jshan@ecn.purdue.edu. Fax: (765) 496-1105.

SHANAHAN, BRENDAN FREDERICK, professional hockey player; b. Mimico, Ont., Canada, Jan. 23, 1969. Formerly with St. Louis Blues; with Hartford Whalers, 1995-97; forward Detroit Red Wings, Detroit, MI, 1997-. Played in NHL All-Star Game, 1994, 96; named to NHL All-Star First Team, 1993-94. Office: care Detroit Red Wings 600 Civic Center Dr Detroit MI 48226-4408

SHANAHAN, DANIEL AUGUSTUS, foreign language educator; b. Ft. Lee, Va., Nov. 22, 1947; arrived in France, 1989; s. Daniel A. and Mary E. (Leary) S.; m. Irena Pohorská, Mar. 20, 1986 (div.); children: Gabriel, Marc. BA, Calif. State U., Sacramento, 1971, MA, 1973; MA, Stanford U., 1974, PhD in English, 1978. Prof. Monterey (Calif.) Inst. Internat. Studies, 1980-91, Ecole Hautes Etudes Commls., Paris, 1989—; sr. Fulbright lectr. U. Split, Yugoslavia, 1979-80, Charles U., Prague, Czech Republic, 1987-88; vis. scholar U. Calif., Berkeley, 1996-97; vis. scholar, Ctr. for Theoretical Studies, Prague, 2000. Author: Toward a Genealogy of Individualism, 1991; contbr. articles to profl. jours. Rsch. fellow Can. Ministry of External Affairs, 1982, 85, 88, Quebec Ministry Intergovtl. Affairs, 1983. Mem. MLA. Home: 35 ruedes Bergers, 75015 Paris France Office: Groupe HEC, 78351 Jouy-en-Josas France

SHANAHAN, KATHLEEN MARIE, public relations executive; b. Calif., Aug. 16, 1958; d. Michael Shanahan and Shirley Lorenz. BA, U. Calif., San Diego, 1981; Exec. MBA, NYU, 1999. Staff asst. Nat. Security Coun., Washington, 1982-85; spl. asst. to v.p., dep. security staff Office of V.P. George Bush, Washington, 1985-89; sr. v.p., chief of staff to pres. and CEO Hill & Knowlton, Washington, 1990-92; sr. v.p. Wexler Group, Washington, 1989-90, 92; dep. sec. econ. devel. Calif. Trade & Commerce Agy., Sacramento, 1993-94; sr. v.p. govt. rels. and pub. affairs Paine Webber Inc., N.Y.C., 1996—; exec. dir. Paine Webber Fund for Better Govt., N.Y.C., 1996—; former advisor PW Diversity Coun., N.Y.C.; polit. cons., 1985—; campaign dep. to Republican Convention and Dir. Adminstrn. George Bush for Pres., Washington, 1988; dep. campaign dir. Bush-Quayle, 1992, dep. campaign mgr. Gov. Wilson re-elect, Sacramento, 1994. Active Jr. League, Washington, Sacramento. Republican. Roman Catholic. Office: Paine Webber 14th Fl 1285 Ave of Americas New York NY 10019

SHANAMAN, FRED CHARLES, JR., business consultant; b. Tacoma, June 21, 1933; s. Fred Charles and Marjorie Blanch (Jeffries) S.; m. Jane Francis Aram, July 7, 1962; children: Fred C. III, Mara Shanaman Burke. BA, Dartmouth Coll., 1957; postgrad., U. B.C., Vancouver, 1958. Sales rep. Air Reduction Co., San Francisco, 1958-62; pres. Bulk Distbrs., Tacoma, 1962-75, Pyrodyne Corp., Tacoma, 1964-75, Toys Galore, Tacoma, 1964-75, Youth Entrepreneurship Corp., Tacoma, 1978-86; pres., owner Rainier Mgmt. Corp., Tacoma, 1970—; bd. dirs. Puget Sound Bancorp., Tacoma, Bellingham (Wash.) Nat. Key Bank of Wash., Tacoma Rockets Hockey Club, Puget Sound Hockey Ctrs.; presdl. appt. to commerce sec. Elliot Richardson's Regional Rep. in N.W., 1975-77; sec. of commerce spokesman and prin. liaison, 1975-77; mem. Commerce Dept. rep. Fed. Regional Coun. and Pacific N.W. River Basins Commn., 1975-77. Author: 101 Money Making Ideas for Young Adults 10 to 18 Year of Age, 1980, The First Official Moneymaking Book for Kids of All Ages, 1983, The Best is Yet to Come: Retirement A Second Career, 1984. Chmn. NCAA Womens Final Four, Tacoma, 1988-89; commr. Ice Hockey Goodwill Games, Seattle, 1990; past bd. dirs. Annie Wright Sch., Faith Home, United Way, Tacoma Symphony, Bellarmine Preparatory Sch., Greater Lakes Mental Health Clinic, Tacoma Actors Guild, Assn. of Washington Bus., Mary Bridge Hosp., Tacoma Leukemia Soc., Vt. Acad., and others. Mem. Tacoma Country Club, Canterwood Country Club, Elks, Lakes Club, Gyro Club, Le Mirador (Switzerland). Republican. Episcopalian. Avocations: fishing, skiing, antique collecting, Christmas decoration collection.

SHAND, WILLIAM STEWART, surgeon; b. Derby, Eng., Oct. 12, 1936; s. William Paterson and Annabella Kirkland Stewart (Waddell) S.; m. Caroline Anne Dashwood Charvet, Aug. 26, 1972; children: Claire, Sophie, Tom, Robert, James. MA, Cambridge U., 1961, MD, 1970. Cons. surgeon Hackney & Homerton Hosps., London, 1973-94, King Edward VII Hosp. for Officers, London, 1995-97; hon. consulting surgeon St. Bartholomew's Hosp., Royal London Hosp., 1998—; vis. consulting gen. surgeon for diseases of the colon and rectum St. Mark's Hosp., London, 1980-97; cons. surgeon St. Bartholomew's Hosp., London, 1973-96. Co-author: The Art of Dying - The Story of Two Sculptors' Residency in a Hospice, 1989; contbr. chpts. in books. Mem. Presbyn. Ch. Wales, Ch. Eng., lic. reader, 1996—. Recipient Nat. Art Collections fund award, 1992. Fellow Royal Coll. Surgeons Eng. (Penrose May tutor 1980-85, tchr. 1986—, Ct. of Examiners 1985-91, hon. curator ceramics 1980—), Royal Coll. Surgeons Edinburgh (bd. examiners 1985-97), Royal Soc. Medicine of London; mem. Harveian Soc. London, Assn. Surgeons Gt. Britain and Ireland, Hunterian Soc., Traveling Surg. Soc. Gt. Britain and No. Ireland (pres. 1994-97). Avocations: dry-fly fishing, skiing, walking, watercolor painting, stained glass window making. Home: Dan-y-Castell, Castle Rd, Crickhowell Powys NP8 1AP, England

SHANDYBA, ALEXANDER BORISOVICH, water-resources engineer, researcher; b. Kharkov, Ukraine, June 3, 1955; s. Boris Stepanovich and Galina Grigorivna (Pavlenko) S.; m. Valentina Petrovna Klimova, Sept. 3, 1977; children: Nadia, Iren. BS, Civil Engr. Inst., Kharkov, Ukraine, 1977; PhD, Kiev (Ukraine) Tech. U., 1990. Water resources engr. Chemprom Inc., Sumy, Ukraine, 1977-79; pipelines engr. Build Design Inst., Sumy, 1979-83; water resources engr. EnergoSteel, Inc., Kharkov, Ukraine, 1983-88; sr. rschr. Sumy State U., 1988-95, head projects, 1989-97, asst. prof., 1991-95, head dept., 1999—; assoc. prof. Agrl. U., Sumy, 1995—; cons. New Tech. Inst., Sumy, Ukraine, 1991-96, Success Co., Sumy, 1996-97, Head Projs. pos. at Sumy State U., 1989-97. Contbr. articles ot profl. jours.; inventor in field. Recipient 20th Century award for achievement Internat. Biog. Ctr., Cambridge, 2000. Mem. N.Y. Acad. Scis. Avocations: biking, fishing. E-mail: root@pharm.sumy.ua. Home: Marko Vovchok St 5 apt 17, 40007 Sumy Ukraine Office: Sumy Agrl U, Kirova St 160 St 57, 40021 Sumy Ukraine

SHANE, ROBERT SAMUEL, chemical engineer, consultant; b. Chgo., Dec. 8, 1910; s. Jacob and Selma (Shayne) S.; m. Jeanne Felice Lazarus, Aug. 21, 1936; children: Stephen H., Susan R., Jacqueline G. SB, U. Chgo., 1930, PhD, 1933. Plant supt. Amecco Chems., Rochester, N.Y., 1941-42; plant chemist Bausch & Lomb Optical Co., Rochester, 1942-46; project supr. Wyandotte (Mich.) Chems. Corp., 1952-54; assoc. dir. rsch. Davis & Geck div. Am. Cyanamid, Danbury, Conn., 1954-55; mgr. chem., ceramics, powder metals Westinghouse Atomic Power, Forest Hills, Pa., 1955-57; nucleonics specialist Bell Aircraft Co., Niagara Falls, N.Y., 1958-59; mgr. parts, materials, process engrng. GE, Valley Forge, Pa., 1959-69; staff cons. Nat. Materials Adv. Bd., Washington, 1969-80; prin. Shane Assocs., Stuart, Fla., 1980-96; cons. in field; editor material engrng. Marcel Dekker, Inc., N.Y.C., 1983—. Author, editor: Space Radiation Effects on Materials, 1962, Predictive Testing, 1972, Materials and Processes, 1985; author: Technology Transfer & Innovation, 1982; editor: Testing for Prediction of Material Performance, 1972; contbr. articles to profl. jours. Adult leader Boy Scouts Am.; organizer Literacy Coun., Ardmore, Pa., 1988. Recipient Joseph Stewart award Am. Chem. Soc., 1987, medal Swedish Royal Acad. Engring., 1972; named to space tech. hall of fame NASA, 1995. Fellow ASTM (award of merit 1973, F-15 com. on consumer product stds.), AIChE; mem. Am. Chem. Soc. (emeritus), Am. Soc. for Metals Internat. (life), Sigma Xi. Home and Office: 1904 NW 22nd St Stuart FL 34994-9270

SHANE, WILLIAM WHITNEY, astronomer; b. Berkeley, Calif., June 3, 1928; s. Charles Donald and Mary Lea (Heger) S.; BA, U. Calif., Berkeley, 1951, postgrad., 1953-58; ScD, Leiden (The Netherlands) U., 1971; m. Clasina van der Molen, Apr. 22, 1964; children: Johan Jacob, Charles Donald. rsch. assoc. Leiden U., 1961-71, sr. scientist, 1971-79; prof. astronomy, dir. Astron. Inst., Cath. U. Nijmegen, The Netherlands, 1979-88; guest prof. astronomy Leiden U., 1988-93; C.H. Adams fellow Monterey (Calif.) Inst. Rsch. Astronomy, 1994—. With USN, 1951-53. Fellow AAAS; mem. Internat. Astron. Union (commns. 33, 34), Am. Astron. Soc., Astron. Soc. Netherlands, Astron. Soc. of the Pacific, Phi Beta Kappa. Achievements include research on structure and dynamics of galaxies, observational astronomy. Home: 9095 Coker Rd Prunedale CA 93907-1401 Office: Monterey Inst Rsch Astronomy 200 8th St Marina CA 93933-6002

SHANEFIELD, DANIEL JAY, ceramics engineering educator; b. Orange, N.J., Apr. 29, 1930; s. Benjamin and Nan (Leichter) S.; m. Elizabeth Davis, June 28, 1964; children: Alison, Douglas. BS in Chemistry, Yale U., 1952; PhD in Chemistry, Rutgers U., 1962. Sr. project engr. ITT Group, Nutley, N.J., 1962-67; sr. mem. tech. staff AT&T Bell Labs., Princeton, N.J., 1967-86; disting. prof. Rutgers U., New Brunswick, N.J., 1986—; adv. panel NSF, 1990—; course dir. Ctr. for Profl. Advancement, U.S. and The Netherlands, 1993—; cons. in field; presenter at profl. confs. Author: Organic Additives and Ceramic Processing, 1996; co-author: Defects in Gold Plating, 1981, Industrial Electronics for Engineers, Chemists and Technicians, 2000; contbr. 4 chpts. to tech. books, articles to profl. jours.; co-inventor 17 patents; assoc. editor Jour. Am. Ceramic Soc., 1987-99. With U.S. Army, 1952-54, Korea. Fellow Am. Inst. Chemists, Am. Ceramic Soc. (Best Paper award); mem. IEEE (chmn. stds. com. 1984-99), Am. Chem. Soc., Ceramic Assn. of N.J. (Man of Yr. award 1996). Republican. Avocations: modifying sports cars, writing audio, stereo articles. Fax: 732-445-3258. E-mail: shanefie@rci.rutgers.edu. Office: Rutgers U Ceramics Engring Dept 607 Taylor Rd Piscataway NJ 08854-8065

SHANER, BRONWYN MARIAN, elementary education educator; b. Buffalo, Aug. 12, 1937; d. Warren Eugene and Myfanwy Rosetta (Murray) Boone; m. Byrns William Long, Mar. 4, 1961 (dec. Sept. 1983); 1 child, Karen Anne Long Clark; m. Richard Leroy Shaner, Mar. 30, 1991. BS in Edn., SUNY, Buffalo, 1960, MS in Edn., 1989. Cert. tchr., N.Y. Tchr. art Brittonkill Ctrl., Troy, N.Y., 1960-61; tchr. spl. and elem. edn. Buffalo Pub. Schs., 1961-66, tchr. elem., 1990—; ret., 1999; dir. advt. Cayuga Mfg. Corp., Blasdell, N.Y., 1981-83. Actress, costume designer, stage hand East Aurora Children's Theater, 1971-74. Bd. dirs. LWV, Kenmore, East Aurora and Clarence, N.Y., 1967-90; bd. deacons 1st Presbyn. Ch., Clarence, 1991-93. Mem. DAR, NEA. Republican. Avocations: reading, cooking, sailing. Home: 10186 Pine Ledge Dr S Clarence NY 14031-1536 Office: Buffalo Pub Schs Sch 74 126 Donaldson Rd Buffalo NY 14208-1629

SHANG, ER-CHANG, physicist; b. Sheng Yain, Liaonin, China, Feb. 5, 1932; came to U.S., 1986.; BS in Theoretical Physics, Peking U., Beijing, China, 1958; PhD equivalent, Inst. Acoustics, Acad. Sinica, Beijing, 1982. Asst. prof. Inst. of Acoustics, Beijing, 1958-62, assoc. prof., 1962-75, prof., 1975-82, dep. dir., 1982-86; sr. rsch. assoc. AOML/NOAA, Miami, Fla., 1983-84, Wave Propagation Lab./NOAA, Boulder, Colo., 1987-88; NRC postdoctoral advisor Wave Propagation Lab./NOAA, 1991—; rsch. assoc. CIRES/U. Colo./NOAA, Boulder, 1988-91, rsch. prof., supervisor, 1991—; vis. scientist Scripps Inst. Oceanography, U. Calif. San Diego, La Jolla, 1982-83; vis. prof. U. Wis., Madison, 1983, Yale U., New Haven, 1986-87. Author: Underwater Acoustics, 1981; editor-in-chief Jour. Computational Acoustics. Recipient Nat. award for sci. Nat. Com. of Sci, Beijing, 1982, 89. Fellow Acoustical Soc. Am. Achievements include new method of source localization in ocean waveguides--matched mode processing; modal ocean acoustic tomography and applied for El Nino monitoring; impact of mode-coupling on modal travel time in ocean waveguide; modal theory in shallow water acoustics. Office: ETL/NOAA 325 Broadway St Boulder CO 80305-3337

SHANGGUAN, WENFENG, chemist, educator; b. Shuichang, Zhejiang, China, Oct. 11, 1959. MSc, Wuhan (China) U. Tech., 1983, 88; PhD, Nagasaki (Japan) U., 1996. Cert. sci. rschr. Asst. Wuhan U. Tech., 1983-88, lectr., 1989-93; postdoctoral rschr. Kyushu Nat. Indsl. Rsch. Inst., Tosu, Japan, 1996-2000; assoc. prof. Shanghai Jiao Tong U., 2000—; presenter Internat. Symposium on Zeolites and Microporous Crystals, Tokyo, 1997, Internat. Conf. on Energy and Environment, Shanghai, 1998, 10th Internat. Symposium on Intercalation Compounds, Okazaki, Japan, 1999, Twelfths JAcques Gartier Meetings-Clean Processes & Environment, Lyon, France, 1999. Contbr. articles to profl. jours.; inventor in field. Mem. AAAS, Internat. Assn. for Hydrogen Energy, Chem. Soc. Japan, Catalysis Soc. Japan. Fax: 81 942 830850. E-mail: wfshangguan@hotmail.com. Office: Sch Power & Energy Engring, Shanghai Jiao Tong U, Shanghai China

SHANI, ARNON, chemist, researcher; b. Ramat-Gan, Israel, Apr. 19, 1935; s. Matityahu and Habiba (Katz) S.; m. Mira Miriam Bar-Zur, Sept. 28, 1955; children: Osnath, Merav, Michal, Mati. MSc, Hebrew U., Jerusalem, 1961; PhD, Weizmann Inst., Rehovot, Israel, 1965. Postdoctoral fellow U. Chgo., 1965-67; rsch. assoc. Hebrew U., 1967-69; asst. prof. Ben-Gurion U., Be'er Sheva, Israel, 1969-73, assoc. prof., 1973-82, prof. chemistry, 1982—, chmn. chemistry dept., 1971-73, 78-80, dep. rector, 1984-86, dir. applied rsch. inst., 1989-93; mem. 7th Coun. for Higher Edn. Israel, 1987-91; Israeli nat. rep. com. on tchg. chemistry IUPAC, 1983-86; sci. cons., Israel, 1971-73, 80-84, 93-95. Contbr. over 90 articles to profl. publs. Recipient E.D. Bergmann award for applied rsch. Synthesis and Prodn. of Pheromones, 1980; rsch. grantee various Israeli and internat. orgns., 1977—. Mem. Internat. Soc. Chem. Ecology (councilor 1987-90), Israel Chem. Soc. (mem. coun. 1984-86, pres. 1997—), Sci. and Tech. Edn. in Israel, others. Jewish. Avocation: archaeological digging. Office: Ben-Gurion U, Dept Chemistry, 84105 Beer-Sheva Israel

SHANI, ESTHER, medical sociologist, researcher; b. Haifa, Israel, Jan. 5, 1941; d. Mordechai and Dina (Shpiro) Rosenfeld; m. Gideon Shani; children: Shirly, Dana. BA, Hebrew U., Jerusalem, 1967, MA cum laude, 1986; PhD, Ben-Gurion U., Beersheba, 1994. English tchr. H.S., Beersheba, 1967-79; English lectr. Ben-Gurion U., Beersheba, 1977-79, rschr., 1987—; dir. U. Ctr., Beersheba, 1998—. Contbr. articles to profl. jours.; author: Play it Safe, 1988; Anti-Sun, 1998; editor: (20mm video film) Play it Safe, 1995. Mem. Negev Coexistence Forum, Beersheba, 1999. Sgt. Israeli Engring. Forces, 1959-61. Rsch. grantee Israel Cancer Assn., 1989, Min. Edn., 1994-99, Min. Labor, 1996-97. Mem. Israeli Women's Network, Israeli Sociol. Soc. Home: Eshel 84, Omer Israel Office: Soroka Med Ctr, Plastic Surgery, Beersheba Israel

SHANIN, TEODOR, sociology educator; b. Wilno, Poland, Oct. 29, 1930; s. Meir Matvei and Rebeka Zajdsznur; m. Naomi, div.; m. Shula Ramon, 1970; children: Anna, Aelita. BA in Sociology/Econs., Hebrew U., Jerusalem, 1963; PhD in Sociology, U. Birmingham, 1969; MS in Social Scis., U. Manchester, Eng., 1975. Cert. social worker. Lectr., sociology U. Sheffield, Eng., 1965-70; sr. lectur. Haifa U., Israel, 1970-71, assoc. prof., 1971-73; sr. fellow St. Antony's Coll., Oxford, Eng., 1973-74; prof. sociology U. Manchester, Eng., 1974—, head sociology dept., 1976-85; rector Moscow Sch. Social and Econ. Scis., 1995—. Author: The Awkward Class, 1972, Peasants and Peasant Societies, 1987, Russia as a Developing Society, 1985, Russia 1905-7; Revolution as a Moment of Truth, 1986 (Deutscher Meml. prize 1988); editor: Informal Economy: Russia and the World, 1999. Recipient awards Econs. Social Rsch. Coun., Brit. Acad., Wilson Ctr., Washington, U. Wis. and others. Fellow Russian Acad. Agrl. Scis.; mem. Assn. Univ. Tchrs., British Sociol. Assn. Avocations: hill walking. Office: Moscow Sch Social Econ Scis, Vernadsky Prospect 82/2, 117571 Moscow Russia

SHANK, RUSSELL, librarian, educator; b. Spokane, Wash., Sept. 2, 1925; s. Harry and Sadie S.; m. Doris Louise Hempfer, Nov. 9, 1951 (div.); children: Susan Marie, Peter Michael, Judith Louise. BS, U. Wash., 1946, BA, 1949; MBA, U. Wis., 1952; DrLS, Columbia U., 1966. Reference libr. U. Wash., Seattle, 1949; asst. engrng. libr. U. Wis.-Madison, 1949-52; chief pers. Milw. Pub. Libr., 1952; engring.-phys. scis. libr. Columbia U., N.Y.C., 1953-59; sr. lectr. Columbia U., 1964-66, assoc. prof., 1966-67; asst. univ. libr. U. Calif.-Berkeley, 1959-64; dir. sci. libr. N.Y. Met. Reference and Rsch., 1966-68; dir. librs. Smithsonian Instn., Washington, 1967-77; univ. libr. prof. UCLA, 1977-89, asst. vice chancellor for libr. and info. svcs. planning, 1989-91, univ. libr., prof. emeritus, 1991—; cons. Indonesian Inst. Sci., 1970; bd. cons. Pahlavi Nat. Library, Iran, 1975-76; pres. U.S. Book Exchange, 1975; bd. trustees Freedom to Read Found., 1989—. Trustee OCLC, Inc., 1978-84, 87, chmn., 1984; mem. library del. People's Republic of China, 1979; bd. dirs. Am. Council on Edn., 1980-81. Served with USNR, 1943-46. Recipient Disting. Alumnus award U. Wash. Sch. Librarianship, 1968, Role of Honor award Freedom to Read Found., 1990, Disting. Alumnus award Columbia U. Sch. Libr. Sci., 1992; fellow Coun. on Libr. Resources, 1973-74. Fellow AAAS; mem. ALA (pres. 1978-79, coun. 1961-65, 74-82, exec. bd. 1975-80, chmn. internat. rels. com. 1980-83, pres. info. sci. and automation div. 1968-69), Assn. Coll. and Rsch. Librs. (pres. 1972-73, Hugh Atkinson award 1990), Assn. Rsch. Librs. (bd. dirs. 1974-77), Beta Phi Mu. Home: 12919 Montana Ave Apt 101 Los Angeles CA 90049-4843

SHANK, SUZANNE ADAMS, lawyer; b. Kansas City, Mo., Nov. 13, 1946; d. Howard Howe and Bettie Ann (Winkler) Hettick; m. Martin Smoler, May 18, 1991. BJ, U. Mo., 1972; MPA in Health Adminstrn., U. Mo., Kansas City, 1982, JD, 1982. Bar: Mo. 1982, U.S. Dist. Ct. (we. dist.) Mo. 1982. Journalist U. Kans. Med. Ctr., Kansas City, 1972-73; asst. editor Am. Family Physician, Kansas City, Mo., 1973-75; exec. dir. Lambert Med. Clinic, Kansas City, Mo., 1975-80; assoc. Shughart, Thomson & Kilroy, Kansas City, 1982-85; v.p. GE/Employers Reins. Corp., Overland Park, Kans., 1985—. Mem. Friends of Zoo, Kansas City, Mo., 1981—, Menorah Med. Ctr. Aux., Kansas City, 1982—, Women's Vision Internat., Kansas City, Mo., 1999—; mem. Internat. Rels. Coun., 1999—. Mem. ABA, Mo. Bar Assn., Kansas City Bar Assn. (chmn. ins. law com.), Soc. Profl. Journalists, Soc. CPCU (rsch. com.), Com. to Protect Journalists, Kappa Tau alpha. Home: 2703 W 66th Ter Shawnee Mission KS 66208-1810 Office: Employers Reins Corp PO Box 2991 Shawnee Mission KS 66201-1391

SHANKARKUMAR, UMAPATHY, research scientist; b. Virudhunagar, Tamil Nadu, India, Apr. 1, 1964; s. Umapathy and Janagamani Shankarkumar; m. Geetharamani Shankarkumar, Aug. 24. 1994. BSc, Madurai Kamaraj U., India, 1982, MSc, 1987, PhD, 1994. Rsch. scholar Madurai Kamaraj U., 1987-94; lectr. Virudhunagar (India) Hindu Nadars Senthikumara Nadar Coll., 1994-95; rsch. officer Inst. Immunohaematology, ICMR, Mumbai, India, 1995—. Home: Flat # 704 Nestle III A, PB Marg Worli, Mumbai 400013, India Office: Inst Immunohematology 13 Fl, NMS Bldg KEM Hosp Campus, Parel Mumbai 400012, India

SHANKHAPAL, KAMALAKAR VISHWANATH, microbiologist, educator; b. Varkhed, India, Apr. 22, 1950; s. Vishwanath and Yashoda (Choudhary) S.; m. Alka Wat, May 29, 1978; children: Smita, Shraddha. BS, Nagpur U., 1970, MS, 1972, PhD, 1976. From lectr. to prof. biochemistry Nagpur U., India, 1978—. Vol. Soc. Oppressed, Suppressed and Depressed, Nagpur, 1985-87. Mem. Assn. Microbiologists of India, Soc. Biol. Chemists, Soc. Pure & Applied Scis. Avocations: music, service to disabled, adventure, meditation. Home: 17 Chaitanya Pub Colony, Sahakarnagar, Nagpur 440025, India

SHANKLIN, DOUGLAS RADFORD, physician; b. Camden, N.J., Nov. 25, 1930; s. John Ferguson and Muriel (Morgan) S.; m. Virginia McClure, Apr. 7, 1956; children: Elizabeth, Leigh, Lois Virginia, John Carter, Eleanor. Student, Wilson Tchrs. Coll., 1949; AB in Chemistry, Syracuse U., 1952; MD, SUNY, Syracuse, 1955. Intern in pathology Duke U., 1955-56, resident, 1958; resident in pathology SUNY, Syracuse, 1958-60; practice medicine specializing in pathology Gainesville, Fla., 1960-67, 78-83; mem. faculty U. Fla., 1960-67; prof. pathology, ob-gyn. U. Chgo., 1967-78; prof. dept. pathology U. Tenn., Memphis, 1983—, prof. obstetrics, 1986—, vice chmn. dept. pathology, 1983-90; vis. prof. U. Okla., 1967, Duke U., Mich. State U., 1969, Leeds U., Dundee U., Karolinska, 1974, Leeds U., 1978, 85, Emory U., 1980, London U., Edinburgh U., 1981, 85, U. Brit. Coll., 1987; jr. investigator Marine Biol. Lab., Woods Hole, Mass., 1951-54, sr. investigator, 1966—, mem. corp., 1970—; parliamentarian, 1990-94; mem. Marine Resources Adv. Com., 1988-90, mem. election com., 1994—; chmn. nat. adv. com. W-I-C evaluation U.S. Dept. Agr., 1979-86; lectr. Coll. Law U. Fla., 1963-67, 77-83; cons. Pan Am. Health Orgn., 1973-89; sr. cons. Santa Fe Found., 1976-79, exec. dir., 1979-83; course dir. Ctr. Continuing Edn., U. Chgo., 1980-82. Author: Syllabus for Study of Gynecologic-Obstetric-Pediatric Disease, 1961, Diseases of Woman, Pregnancy, Child, 1964, Maternal Nutrition and Child Health, 1979, 2nd edit., 2000, Tumors of Placenta and Umbilical Cord, 1990; editor Interscience Devel. Disorders, 1971-80; assoc. editor Jour. Reproductive Medicine, 1968-70, 79-85, editor in chief, 1970-75; contbr. articles to profl. jours. Trustee Coll. Light Opera Co., Falmouth, Mass., 1970—, Hippodrome Theatre, Gainesville, 1975-83, Opera Memphis, 1989-92. With M.C., USNR, 1956-58. Recipient Best Basic Sci. Tchg. award U. Fla., 1967; named freeman citizen of Glasgow, 1981. Fellow Royal Soc. Medicine (London); mem. AAAS, Am. Soc. Exptl. Pathology, Am. Soc. Molecular Marine Biology and Biotech., Am. Chem. Soc., Astronom. Soc. Pacific Am., Hosp. Assn., Am. Coll. Rheumatology (spl. study com. 1995-96), Soc. Pediat. Rsch., Internat. Acad. Pathologists, Math. Assn. Am., So. Soc. Pediat. Rsch., So. Med. Assn., N.Y. Acad. Scis., Am. Coll. Ob-gyn., Physicians Social Responsibility, Internat. Physicians for Prevention Nuc. War, Coll. Physicians and Surgeons Costa Rica, Pediat. Pathology Club (sec.-treas. 1970-75, pres. 1981-82), Navy League, Cosmos Club, Phi Beta Kappa, Sigma Xi. Home: 1238 NW 18th Ter Gainesville FL 32605-5370 Office: 134 Grove Park Cir Memphis TN 38117-3115

SHANKS, IAN ALEXANDER, electrical engineer, educator; b. Glasgow, Scotland, June 22, 1948; s. Alexander and Isabella Affleck (Beaton) S.; m. Janice Smillie Coulter, May 14, 1971; 1 child, Emma Jane. BSc in Elec. Engrng. with honors, Glasgow U., 1970; PhD, Coun. for Nat. Acad. Awards, 1976. Projects mgr. Scottish Colorfoto Labs., Ltd., Alexandria, 1970-72; rsch. student Portsmouth Poly., 1972-73; jr. rsch. fellow to prin. sci. officer Royal Signals and Radar Establishment, Malvern, Eng., 1973-82; from sr. scientist to prin. scientist/sr. mgr. Unilever Rsch., Sharnbrook, Bedford, Eng., 1982-86, sci. advisor, 1994—; chief scientist Thorn EMI plc, Hayes, Middlesex, Eng., 1986-94; mem. optoelectronics adv. com. The Rank Prize Funds, London, 1985—; vis. prof. dept. elec. and electronic engring. Glasgow U., 1985—. Contbr. over 40 articles to profl. jours.; over 70 patents in field. Vice pres., coun. mem. The Royal Soc., London, 1989-91; ind. mem. Adv. Bd. for the Rsch. Couns., London, 1990-93; chmn. Interag. Com. for Marine Sci. and Tech., London, 1991-93; chmn. def. costs study K-Meteorol. Office, Ministry Def., 1994. Freeman, Worshipful Co. of Clockmakers. Fellow Royal Soc., Royal Acad. Engring., Royal Soc. Edinburgh, Royal Soc. Arts, Instn. Elec. Engrs. Avocations: music, antique clocks and watches, antiques. Home: Kings Close, 11 Main Rd Biddenham, Bedford MK40 4BB, England Office: Unilever Rsch, Colworth House Sharnbrook, Bedford MK44 1LQ, England

SHANMAN, JAMES ALAN, lawyer; b. Cin., Aug. 1, 1942; s. Jerome D. and Mildred Louise (Bloch) S.; m. Marilyn Louise Glassman, June 11, 1972; 1 child, Ellen Joan. BS, U. Pa., 1963; JD, Yale U., 1966. Bar: N.Y. 1967, U.S. Ct. Mil. Appeals 1971, U.S. Supreme Ct. 1971, U.S. Ct. Appeals (2d cir.) 1972, U.S. Dist. Ct. (so. and ea. dists.) N.Y. 1972, U.S. Ct. Internat. Trade 1976, U.S. Ct. Appeals (fed. cir.) 1987, U.S. Dist. Ct. (ea. dist.) Mich. 1989, U.S. Ct. Appeals (7th cir.) 1999. Assoc. Cahill Gordon & Reindel, N.Y.C., 1971-74, Freeman, Meade, Wasserman, Sharfman & Schneider, N.Y.C., 1974-76; mem. firm Sharfman, Shanman, Poret & Siviglia, P.C., N.Y.C., 1976-95; ptnr. Camhy Karlinsky & Stein LLP, N.Y.C., 1995-96; mem. firm Sharfman, Siviglia, Poret, Kook, Ross & Shanman, P.C., N.Y.C., 1996-98; ptnr. Edwards & Angell, LLP, N.Y.C., 1998—; speaker on reins. law topics. Capt. USAF, 1966-71. Mem. ARIAS.US (cert. arbitrator), ABA, N.Y. State Bar Assn., Assn. of Bar of City of N.Y. (com. ins. law 1985-88, 90-92, 98—, com. profl. liability ins. 1988-92, com. on assn. ins. plans 1989—), Am. Arbitration Assn. (comml. panel arbitrators 1980—). Office: Edwards & Angell LLP 750 Lexington Ave New York NY 10022-1253

SHANMUGAM, GANAPATHY, geologist, researcher; b. Sirkali, Tamilnadu, India, Apr. 23, 1944; came to U.S., 1970; s. Ganapathy Mudaliar and Sambooranam; m. Jean Marie Barham, Aug. 21, 1976. BSc in Geology and Chemistry, Annamalai U., South India, 1965; MSc in Applied Geology, Indian Inst. Tech., Bombay, 1968; MS in geology, Ohio U., 1972; PhD in Geology, U. Tenn., 1978. Rsch. geologist Mobil Exploration & Product Tech. Ctr., Dallas, 1978-82, sr. rsch. geologist, 1982-84, assoc., 1984-85, rsch. assoc., 1985-89, sr. rsch. assoc., 1989-93, assoc. geol. rsch. advisor, 1993-96, geol. scientist, 1996-2000; adj. prof. geology U. Tex., Arlington, 2000—; conf. chmn. Geol. Soc. London, 1996; debate panelist Am. Assn. Petroleum Geologists, Dallas, 1997. Author: Dimensions and Geometries of Deep-Water Systems, 1998; contbr. over 75 articles to profl. jours. Geology adv. bd. U. Tenn., Knoxville, 1985-89. Recipient Silver medal Indian Inst. Tech., 1968; Penrose grantee Geol. Soc. Am., 1976-78; recipient best Paper award Nigerian Assn. Petroleum Explorationists, 1995. Mem. Soc. Sedimentary Geology (nominating com. 1993), Nat. Geog. Soc., Sigma Gamma Epsilon (v.p. 1976-77). Achievements include questioning of the deep-water turbidite paradigm and advocation of sandy debris flows in forming deep-water petroleum reservoirs. Avocation: photography. Office: U Tex Arlington Dept Geology PO Box 19049 Arlington TX 76019-0001

SHANNON, JOE, JR., lawyer; b. Nov. 9, 1940; s. Joe and Juanita Elizabeth (Milliorn) S.; children: Kelley Jane, Joseph Patrick, Shelley Carol. BA, U. Tex., 1962, LLB, 1963. Bar: Tex. 1963, U.S. Supreme Ct. 1977, U.S. Dist. Ct. (no. dist.) Tex. 1970, U.S. Ct. Appeals (5th cir.) 1977, U.S. Dist. Ct. (we. dist.) Tex. 1998; cert. family law Tex. Bd. Legal Specialization, matrimonial arbitrator. Ptnr. Shannon & Shannon, Ft. Worth, 1963-72; adminstrv. asst. to spkr. Tex. Ho. of Reps., Austin, 1970; chief criminal div. Tarrant County Dist. Atty., Ft. Worth, 1972-78; pvt. practice Ft. Worth, 1978-99; ptnr. Snakard & Gambill, Ft. Worth, 1986-90; chief econ. crimes Tarrant County Dist. Atty., 1999—; adj. prof. Tex. Weslyan Sch. Law. Mem. Tex. Ho. of Reps., 1964-70. Fellow Tex. Bar Found., Am. Acad. Matrimonial Lawyers (cert.); mem. ABA, State Bar of Tex. (adv. com. family law, state bd. legal specialization 1985-99, dist. grievance com. 1973-76, chmn. 1975-76, 95—, sec. 2d ct. appeals adv. com. 1995—), N. Tex. Family Law Specialists, Tarrant County Family Law Bar Assn. (pres. 1998), Tarrant County Bar Assn. (dir. 1999—), Phi Alpha Delta, Masons, Shriners. Office: 1701 River Run Fort Worth TX 76107-6579

SHANTAROVICH, VICTOR PETROVICH, physicist; b. Leningrad, Russia, Apr. 4, 1938; s. Peter Semenovich and Polina Kuz'minichna (Voronova) S.; m. Ol'ga Borisovna Tarasova, Nov. 23, 1963; children: Helen, Ann. PhD in Physics and Math., Phys. Engring. Inst., Moscow, 1966; D of Physico-Math. Scis., Inst. Chem. Physics, Moscow, 1980. Jr. rschr. Inst. Chem. Physics Russian Acad. Scis., Moscow, 1966-69, sr. rschr., 1969-89, head of lab., 1989—, prof., 1991. Co-author: Modern Physics in Chemistry, 1976, Physics of the 20th Century, History and Outlook, 1987; contbr. articles to jours. in field. V.G. Khlopin grantee Acad. Scis. of the USSR, Moscow, 1978. Mem. Russian Acad. Natural Scis. (corr.). Office: Russian Acad Sci Inst Chem Physics, Kosygin St 4, 117334 Moscow Russia

SHAPIRA, AMOS, law educator; b. Petach Tikva, Israel, Jan. 17, 1937; s. Nathan and Rachel (Kerman) S.; m. Yocheved Lustgarten; children: Limor, Sigal, Efrat. LLM, Hebrew U., Jerusalem, 1962; M Comparative Law, Columbia U., 1963; DS in Law, Yale U., 1968. Bar: Israel. Mem. faculty of law Tel Aviv U., 1968—, prof. law, 1974—, acad. chmn. overseas students program, 1979-80, dean faculty of law, 1980-85, incumbent Lubowski chair law and biomed. ethics, 1985—, dir. Cegla Inst. for Comparative law, 1991-97, dir. Minerva Ctr. for Human Rights, 1997—; disting. prof. Nat. Autonomous U. Mex., 1987; dep. pres. Israel Press Coun., Tel Aviv, 1990—; mem. Contbr. numerous books and articles in Hebrew, English and other langs. on pvt. internat. law, law and biomed. ethics and constnl. law. Bd. dirs. Tel Aviv Performing Arts Ctr. With Israel Def. Forces, 1954-57. Mem. Internat. Law Assn. (mem. com. on civil and comml. litigation 1998—), Internat. Assn. Jewish Lawyers and Jurists (exec. bd. 1998—), Am. Law Inst., Israel Democracy Inst. (bd. dirs.). Jewish. Home: 5 Brazil St Apt 25, Ramat Aviv 69460, Israel Office: Tel Aviv U, Facult of Law, Ramat Aviv 69978, Israel

SHAPIRA, JOSEPH, electomagnetics/communications engineer; b. Tel Aviv, Israel, Sept. 1, 1937; s. Eliezer and Haia Shapira; m. Ruth Karger, Aug. 9, 1961; children: Shye, Ayelet, Gali, Omer. BSc, Technion, Haifa, Israel, 1961, MSc, 1967; PhD, Polytech. U., N.Y.C., 1974. Head electromagnets dept. Rafael, Israel, 1974-79; dep. dir. guidance divsn. Rafael, 1984-88; sr. fellow Rafael (ADA), Haifa, Israel, 1989; staff engr. Qualcomm, San Diego, Calif., 1990-91; pres. Qualcomm Israel, Haifa, 1992-94; cons. Haifa, 1995-97; pres. Celletra Ltd., 1997—; pres. Israel Nat. Com. for Radio Sci., 1981-99; organizer Internat. Sci. Conf. Commsphere, 1991, 95, 97. Recipient Best Paper award, IEEE, 1974, A.D. Bergman prize, Pres. Israel, 1980. Fellow IEEE; mem. Internat. Union for Radio Sci. (v.p. 1996-99, 99—). Home: 23 Sweden St, 34980 Haifa Israel

SHAPIRO, ALAN MEYER, meteorology educator, researcher; b. Seattle, Sept. 28, 1962; s. Bernard and Isabel Jane (Gallagher) S.; m. Sandra Jean Diez-Luckie, Aug. 12, 1991. BS, Cornell U., 1983; MA, Johns Hopkins U., 1985, PhD, 1987. Postdoctoral scientist Nat. Meteorol. Ctr., Camp Springs, Md., 1987-89; postdoctoral scientist Ctr. for Analysis and Prediction of Storms, Norman, Okla., 1990, rsch. scientist, 1991-92, sr. rsch. scientist, 1993-95; asst. prof. meteorology U. Okla., Norman, 1996—. Contbr. articles to profl. jours. Mem. AAAS, Am. Meteorol. Soc., Am. Math. Soc., Am. Geophys. Union, Soc. for Indsl. and Applied Math. Avocations: origami, hiking, sailing. E-mail: ashapiro@ou.edu. Home: 2821 Astor Dr Norman OK 73072-2262 Office: U Okla 100 E Boyd St Rm 1310 Norman OK 73019-1015

SHAPIRO, ALVIN DALE, lawyer; b. N.Y.C., Apr. 30, 1930; s. Samuel and Fannie (Korman) S.; m. Patricia Nan Swaden, Nov. 8, 1959; children: Peter, Julia, Molly, Anthony. BS, U. Mo., 1951; LLB, Yale U., 1958. Bar: Fla. 1958, Mo. 1959, U.S. Supreme Ct. 1966. Assoc. Sams, Anderson & Assocs., Miami, Fla., 1958-59; ptnr. Stinson, Mag & Fizzell, Kansas City, Mo., 1959-80; sole practice Kansas City, 1980-95; ptnr. Shapiro, Manson & Karbauk, Kansas City, 1996—; mem. Yale Law Sch. Exec. Com., 1982-87. Exec. bd. dirs., v.p. Hyman Brand Hebrew Acad., Kansas City, 1966—; bd. dirs. Beth Shalom Congregation, Kansas City, 1970—. Served with USN 1951-55. Mem. ABA, Mo. Bar Assn., Fla. Bar Assn. Democrat. Jewish. Club: Yale. Home: 816 W 52nd Ter Kansas City MO 64112-2322 Office: 1200 Main St Kansas City MO 64105-2122

SHAPIRO, BORIS ISAAKOVICH, chemist, educator; b. Yaroslawl, Russia, Aug. 5, 1937; s. Isaak Solomonovich and Anna Vasilievna Shapiro; m. Irina Naumovna Tevzadze, Oct. 18, 1986; 1 child, Tekla. PhD with honors, Leningrad (Russia) Tech. Inst., 1959; DSc, Moscow Inst. Fine Chem. Tech., 1966; DSc in Chemistry, State Rsch. Inst. Photo-Chem., Moscow, 1985. Asst. Yaroslavl (Russia) Tech. Inst., 1959-62; scientist Moscow Inst. Fine Chem. Tech., 1966-70, prof. chemistry, 1999—; head lab. State Rsch. Inst. Photo-Chem. Industry, Moscow, 1971-96; head lab. sci. ctr. Niikhimfotoproekt, Moscow, 1996—; dir. edn. ctr. Niikhimfotoproekt, Moscow Inst. Fine Chem. Tech., 1990—. Author: The Theoretical Foundation of the Photographic Process, 1999 (Russian Found. for Basic Rsch. award 1999); contbr. articles to profl. jours. Recipient State prize USSR, 1983. Mem. Russian Soc. Photographic Sci. and Tech. (pres. 1995—), Soc. Imaging Sci. and Tech., Optical Soc. Am. Fax: 007(095)333-11-04. Home: Michlukcho-Machlaya, 117279 Moscow Russia Office: Niikhimfotoproekt, Leningradsky Prosp 47, 125167 Moscow Russia

SHAPIRO, BORIS Z., mathematician; b. Moscow, June 9, 1957; arrived in Sweden, 1991; s. Zalman F. and Tamara A. (Sholomova) S.; m. Natalia A. Malinovskaya, Sept. 5, 1982 (div. Sept. 1989); 1 child, Sonya; m. Uliana G. Nikulina, Dec. 28, 1989; 1 child, Jakob. MsD in Math., Moscow R.R. Inst., 1979; PhD in Math., U. Stockholm, 1990. Rsch. scientist VNIIBI, Moscow, 1984-90; vis. prof. U. Wis., Madison, 1990-91; rsch. fellow U. Stockholm, 1991-94, assoc. prof., 1994—. Contbr. articles to profl. jours. Jewish. Avocations: jogging, languages. Office: Univ of Stockholm, Dept Math, S-10691 Stockholm Sweden

SHAPIRO, DAVID L., lawyer; b. Corsicana, Tex., May 19, 1936; s. Harry and Alice (Laibovitz) S. BA, U. Tex., 1967; JD, St. Mary's U., 1970. Bar: Tex. 1970, U.S. Dist. Ct. (we. dist.) Tex. 1972, U.S. Supreme Ct. 1975, U.S. Ct. Appeals (5th cir.) 1981. Assoc. Law Office Jim S. Phelps, Houston, 1971; pvt. practice Austin, 1972—; spl. counsel com. human resources Tex. Ho. Reps., Austin, 1973-74; counsel subcom. health svcs. Tex. Senate, Austin, 1983-87. With U.S. Army, 1959-61. Mem. State Bar Tex. (chmn. lawyer referral svc. com. 1980-82, adminstrn. of justice com. 1990-93, jury svc. com. 1998—, contbr. Media Law Handbook supplement 1986), Travis County Bar Assn. (sec.-treas. 1977-78, dir. 1979, pres. family law sect. 1980-81), Coll. of State Bar of Tex., Austin Criminal Def. Lawyers Assn., Travis County Bar Assn. Democrat. Avocations: automobiles, reading. Office: 1200 San Antonio St Austin TX 78701-1834

SHAPIRO, EDWARD MURAY, dermatologist; b. Denver, Oct. 6, 1924; s. Isador Benjamin and Sara (Berezin) S.; student U. Colo., 1941-43; m. Ruth Young, Oct. 14, 1944; children: Adrian Michael, Stefanie Ann; m. Dorothy Rosmarin, July 22, 1990. AB with honors, U. Tex., 1948, MD, 1952. Intern, Jefferson Coll. Medicine Hosp., Phila., 1952-53; resident in dermatology U. Tex. Med. Br., Galveston, 1953-55; resident in dermatology Henry Ford Hosp., Detroit, 1955-56, asso. in dermatology div. dermatology, 1956-57; clin. instr. dermatology Baylor U. Coll. Medicine, Houston, 1957-68, assoc. clin. prof., 1968—; staff Ben Taub Gen. Hosp., Houston, 1958—; active staff Columbia Bayshore Hosp., 1962—, Meml. Hosp., Pasadena, 1958—. Served with USAAF, 1943-46. Henry J. N. Taub research grantee, 1958-60; diplomate Am. Bd. Dermatology. Fellow Am. Acad. Dermatology; mem. AMA, Tex. Med. Assn., Tex. Dermatol. Soc. (pres.-elect 1988, pres. 1989-90), South Cen. Dermatol. Assn. (bd. dirs. 1987-88), Harris County Med. Assn. (pres. S.E. br. 1968-69), Houston Dermatology Assn., Houston Art League, Gulf Coast Art Soc., Am. Physicians Art Soc. (v.p. 1993). Jewish. Clubs: B'nai B'rith, Rotary Internat. (Paul Harris fellow 1995, 97). Contbr. articles in field to med. jours. Office: 1020 Pasadena Blvd Pasadena TX 77506-4700

SHAPIRO, HAROLD TAFLER, academic administrator, economist; b. Montreal, Que., Can., June 8, 1935; s. Maxwell and Mary (Tafler) S.; m. Vivian Bernice Rapoport, May 19, 1957; children: Anne, Marilyn, Janet, Karen. BComm, McGill U., Montreal, 1956; PhD in Econs. (Harold Helm fellow, Harold Dodds sr. fellow), Princeton U., 1964. Asst. prof. econs. U. Mich., 1964-67, assoc. prof., 1967-70, prof., 1970-76, chmn. dept. econs., 1974-77, prof. econs. and pub. affairs, from 1977, v.p. acad. affairs, 1977-79, pres., 1980-87; research adv. Bank Can., 1965-72; pres. Princeton U., 1988—; bd. dirs. Dow Chem.; trustee Univs. Rsch. Assn., 1988—; mem. exec. com. Assn. Am. Univs., 1985-89, N.J. Commn. on Sci. and Tech., 1988-91; mem. Pres.'s Coun. Advisors on Sci. and Tech., 1990-92; chmn. com. on employer-based health benefits Inst. Medicine, 1991; bd. overseers Robert Wood Johnson Med. Sch., 2000—. Editor: (with William G. Bowen) Universities and Their Leadership, 1998. Trustee Alfred P. Sloan Found., 1980—, Interlochen Ctr. for Arts, 1988-95, U. Pa. Med. Ctr., 1992—, Ednl. Testing Svc., 1994—; dir. Am. Coun. Edn., 1989-92; chmn. Spl. Presdl. Com., The Rsch. Librs. Group, 1980-91; mem. Gov.'s High Tech. Task Force, Mich., 1980-87; mem. Gov.'s Commn. on Jobs and Econ. Devel. (Mich.), 1983-87; mem. Carnegie Commn. on Coll. Retirement, 1984-86; mem. Pres. Bush Coun. Advisors on Sci. and Tech., 1990-92; chair Nat. Bioethics Adv. Commn., 1996—; chair Inst. Medicine's Com. on Employer-Based Health Benefits; trustee Univ. Corp. for Advanced Internet Devel., 2000—; mem. Ednl. Testing Svc., 1994-2000. Recipient Lt. Gov.'s medal in commerce McGill U., 1956. Fellow Am. Acad. Arts and Scis., Mich. Soc. Fellows (sr.); mem. Inst. Medicine of NAS, Am. Philos. Soc., Nat. Bur. Econ. Rsch. (bd. dirs.). Office: Princeton U Office of Pres Princeton NJ 08544-0001

SHAPIRO, IRWIN IRA, physicist, educator; b. N.Y.C., N.Y., Oct. 10, 1929; s. Samuel and Esther (Feinberg) S.; m. Marian Helen Kaplun, Dec. 20, 1959; children: Steven, Nancy. A.B., Cornell U., 1950; A.M., Harvard U., 1951, Ph.D., 1955. Mem. staff Lincoln Lab. MIT, Lexington, 1954-70; Sherman Fairchild Distinguished scholar Calif. Inst. Tech., 1974; Morris Loeb lectr. physics Harvard, 1975; prof. geophysics and physics MIT, 1967-80, Schlumberger prof., 1980-84; Paine prof. practical astronomy, prof. physics Harvard U., 1982-97; sr. scientist Smithsonian Astrophys. Obs., 1982—; dir. Harvard-Smithsonian Ctr. for Astrophysics, 1983—; prof. Harvard U./Timken, 1997—; cons. NSF, NASA. Contbr. articles to profl. jours. Recipient Albert A. Michelson medal Franklin Inst., 1975, award in phys. and math. scis. N.Y. Acad. Scis., 1982, Einstein medal Einstein Soc. Bern, 1994; Guggenheim fellow, 1982. Fellow AAAS, Am. Geophys. Union (Charles A. Whitten medal 1991, William Bowie medal 1993), Am. Phys. Soc.; mem. AAAS, NAS (Benjamin Apthorp Gould prize 1979), Am. Astron. Soc. (Dannie Heineman award 1983, Dirk Brouwer award 1987, Gerard Kuiper award 1997), Am. Philos. Soc., Internat. Astron. Union, Phi Beta Kappa, Sigma Xi, Phi Kappa Phi. Home: 17 Lantern Ln Lexington MA 02421-6029 Office: Harvard-Smithsonian Ctr Astrophysics 60 Garden St Cambridge MA 02138-1516

SHAPIRO, ISADORE, materials scientist, consultant; b. Mpls., Apr. 25, 1916; s. Jacob and Bessie (Goldman) S.; m. Mae Hirsch, Sept. 4, 1938; children: Stanley Harris, Jerald Steven. BChemE. summa cum laude, U. Minn., 1938, PhD, 1944. Asst. instr. chemistry U. Minn., 1938-41, rsch. fellow, 1944-45; rsch. chemist E. I. duPont de Nemours and Co., Phila., 1946; head chem. lab. U.S. Naval Ordnance Test Sta., Pasadena, Calif., 1947-52; dir. rsch. lab. Olin-Mathieson Chem. Corp., 1952-59; head chemistry Hughes Tool Co., Aircraft div., Culver City, Calif., 1959-62; pres. Universal Chem. Systems Inc. 1962—, Aerospace Chem. Systems, Inc., 1964-66; dir. contract rsch. HITCO, Gardena, Calif., 1966-67; prin. scientist Douglas Aircraft Co. of McDonnell Douglas Corp., Santa Monica, Calif., 1967; prin. scientist McDonnell Douglas Astronautics Co., 1967-70; head materials and processes AiResearch Mfg. Co., Torrance, Calif., 1971-82, cons., 1982—; inaugurated dep. gov. Am. Biog. Inst. Rsch. Assn., 1988; dep. dir. gen. Internat. Biog. Ctr., 1989, Eng. Rater U.S. Civil Svc. Bd. Exam., 1948-52. Served 1st lt. AUS, 1941-44. Registered profl. engr., Calif. Fellow Am. Inst. Chemists, Am. Inst. Aeros and Astronautics (assoc.); mem. AAAS, Am. Ordnance Assn., Am. Chem. Soc., Soc. Rheology, Soc. Advancement Materials and Process Engring., Am. Inst. Physics, AIM, Am. Phys. Soc., N.Y. Acad. Sci., Am. Assn. Contamination Control, Am. Ceramic Soc., Nat. Inst. Ceramic Engrs., Am. Powder Metallurgy Inst., Internat. Plansee Soc. for Powder Metallurgy, Sigma Xi, Tau Beta Pi, Phi Lambda Upsilon. Author articles in tech. publs. Patentee, discoverer series of carborane compounds; created term carborane; formulator of universal compaction equation for powders (metals, ceramics, polymers, chemicals). Home: 5624 W 62nd St Los Angeles CA 90056-2009

SHAPIRO, JAMES ANTHONY, lawyer; b. N.Y.C., June 20, 1959; s. Edwin Stanley and Sandra Isabel Shapiro; m. Laura Beth Miller, Sept. 25, 1988; children: Kevin Miller, Allison Miller. AB, Trinity Coll., Hartford, Conn., 1981; JD, William and Mary, 1985. Bar: Ill. 1985. Assoc. Hinshaw & Culbertson, Chgo., 1985-88, D'Ancona & Pflaum, Chgo., 1988-89; asst. U.S. atty. U.S. Attys. Office, Chgo., 1989-95; pvt. practice Chgo., 1996-98; of counsel Applegate & Valauskas, Chgo., 1998-2000; ptnr. Shapiro & Schwartz, Chgo., 2000—; adj. prof. Loyola U. Law Sch., Chgo., 1995-98; hearing officer Atty. Registration and Disc. Comm., Chgo., 1996—. Treas. Ind. Voters Ill.-Ind. Precinct Orgn., Chgo., 1999-2000. Mem. Chgo. Inn of Ct. (barrister). Avocations: golf, tennis, softball. E-mail: jashapiro@earthlink.net. Office: Shapiro & Schwartz 134 N Lasalle St Ste 1426 Chicago IL 60602-1104

SHAPIRO, JERALD STEVEN, scientist, bank executive; b. Dec. 3, 1943; s. Isadore and Mae (Hirsch) S. BS, UCLA, 1964, student, 1970. Lic. real estate broker, Calif.; cert. review appraiser, real estate broker, mortgage banker, escrow officer, investment broker, investment specialist; registered mortgage underwriter. Mgr. process engring., quality control Aerospace Chem. Sys., Inc., Gardena, Calif., 1963-66; chem. engr. HITCO, Gardena, Calif., 1966-67; materials and process engr. McDonnell Douglas Corp., Long Beach, Calif., 1967-70; chemist L.A. county Sanitation Dist., 1971-74; staff scientist TRW Def. and Space Sys. Group, Redondo Beach, Calif., 1975—; cons. Century 21 Beverlywood Realty, Inc., L.A.; pres. Nationwide Mortgage Corp., L.A., Heritage Realty Group, L.A.; adv. bd. 1st Women's Bank of Calif., 1977-78; JSK Capital Group, Inc. Beverly Hills, 1990-94; trustee, prof. Internat. Coll. of Calif., Irvine, 1991-93; bd. dirs. Western Advanced Tech. Systems, Inc., Environ. Protection Polymers, Inc. Author: Aware and Beware Guide to Intelligent Home Buying, 1974; co-inventor particle discriminator, 1964. Bd. dirs. Internat. Wellness Inst., Beverly Hills, 1992-93. Mem. Nat. Assn. Mortgage Bankers, Nat. Assn. Rev. Appraisers and Mortgage Underwriters, Chem. Soc., Century 21 Investment Soc. (charter), Mortgage Bankers Assn., Calif. Escrow Assn., Calif. Assn. Realtors, L.A. Bd. Realtors, Alpha chi Sigma. Office: 2800 S Robertson Blvd Los Angeles CA 90034-2406

SHAPIRO, JEROME FRANKLIN, educator; b. San Francisco, Dec. 17, 1958; s. Harry and Helen Suzanne (Chaban) S.; m. Tomoko Yabe, Dec. 27, 1993; children: Dixon Takashi, Sydney Kozue. BA, Calif. State U., Long Beach, 1985; MA, U. Calif, Irvine, 1987, PhD, 1991. Adj. prof. Orange Coast Coll., Costa Mesa, Calif., 1989-90, U. Calif., Irvine, 1989; lectr. Kyoto (Japan) U., 1991-94; adj. prof. Kyoto Sangyo U., 1993-94, Hiroshima (Japan) Shudo U., 1996-98; assoc. prof. cinema & comparative cultures Hiroshima U., 1994—; presenter to com. on CR3 State Assembly, Calif., 1986; com. mem. U. Calif. Pres. Com. on Handicapped, Berkeley, Calif., 1987, U. Calif. Chancellor's Adv. Com., Irvine, 1987-90; coord. Fulbright-Hays Japan Seminar, Hiroshima, 1997; keynote spkr. Klutznick Symposium, Creighton U., Omaha; spkr. various clubs. Collaborator origina play Hiroshima (Crucible of Light, 1995; contbg. editor Hiroshima Sign Post Mag., 1996-98; contbr. articles to profl. jours. Advisor Historicale Cultural Found., Orange County, Calif., 1988. Recipient lang. program fellowship Johns Hopkins U., Japan Found., Washington, 1986, dissertation fellowship U. Calif. Regents, Berkeley/Irvine, 1990, rsch. fellowship Fulbright, Japan, 1991. Mem. Am. Studies Assn. (panel organizer 1991). Avocations: flower arranging, Kashou. Home: 4216-7 Jike Saijo-Cho, Higashi-Hiroshima 739-0041, Japan Office: Hiroshima U, 1-7-1 Kagamiyama, Higashi-Hiroshima 739-8521, Japan

SHAPIRO, LAURIE GWEN, writer, filmmaker; b. N.Y.C., July 8, 1966; d. Julius and Jeanette Shapiro; m. Paul Garan O'Leary, May 25, 1995. BS, Syracuse (N.Y.) U., 1988. Author: The Unexpected Salami, 1998; co-dir.: Once I Was a Cannibal, 2000; prodr.: McCourts of Limerick, 1998; co-prodr.: McCourts of New York, 1999. Mem. Authors Guild, Ind. Film Project. Jewish. Avocations: writing, films, rock music, cartooning, storytelling. Home: 473 Fdr Dr Apt K2103 New York NY 10002-2029

SHAPIRO, MAURICE MANDEL, astrophysicist; b. Jerusalem, Israel, Nov. 13, 1915; came to U.S., 1921; s. Asher and Miriam R. (Grunbaum) S.; m. Inez Weinfield, Feb. 8, 1942 (dec. Oct. 1964); children: Joel Nevin, Elana Shapiro Ashley Naktin, Raquel Tamar Shapiro Kislinger. B.S., U. Chgo., 1936, M.S., 1940, Ph.D., 1942. Instr. physics and math. Chgo. City Colls., 1937-41; chmn. dept. phys. and biol. scis. Austin Coll., 1938-41; instr. math. Gary Coll., 1942; physicist Dept. Navy, 1942-44; lectr. physics and math. George Washington U., 1943-44; group leader, mem. coordinating council of lab. Los Alamos Sci. Lab., U. Calif., 1944-46; sr. physicist, lectr. Oak Ridge Nat. Lab., Union Carbon and Carbide Corp., 1946-49; cons. div. nuc. energy for propulsion aircraft Fairchild Engine & Aircraft Corp., 1948-49; head cosmic ray br. nucleonics div. U.S. Naval Research Lab., Washington, 1949-65, supt. nucleonics div., 1953-65, founder, chief scientist Lab for Cosmic Physics, 1949-82, apptd. to chair of cosmic ray physics, 1966-82, chief scientist emeritus, 1982—; lectr. U. Md., 1949-50, 52—, assoc. prof., 1950-51, vis. prof. physics and astronomy, 1986—; vis. prof. physics and astronomy U. Iowa, 1981-84; vis. prof. astrophysics U. Bonn, 1982-84; vis. scientist Max Planck Inst. für Astrophysik, W. Ger., 1984-85; cons. Argonne Nat. Lab., 1949; cons. panel on cosmic rays U.S. nat. com. IGY; lectr. physics and engring. Nuclear Products-Erco div. ACF Industries, Inc., 1956-58; lectr. E. Fermi Internat. Sch. Physics, Varenna, Italy, 1962; vis. prof. Weizmann Inst. Sci., Rehovoth, Israel, 1962-63, Inst. Math. Scis., Madras, India, 1971; Inst. Astronomy and Geophysics Nat. U. Mex., 1976; vis. prof. physics and astronomy Northwestern U., Evanston, Ill., 1978, exec. dir.Astrophysics assocs.(non profit corp.) 1995—; cons. space rsch. in astronomy Space Sci. Bd., Nat. Acad. Scis., 1965; cons. Office Space Scis., NASA, 1965-66, 89; prin. investigator Gemini S-9 Cosmic Ray Expts., NASA, 1964-69, Skylab, 1967-76, Long Duration Exposure Facility, 1977—; mem. Groupe de Travail de Biologie Spatiale, Council of Europe, 1970—; mem. steering com. DUMAND Consortium, 1976—, mem. exec. com., 1979-82, mem. sci. adv. com., 1982—; lectr. Summer Space Inst., Deutsche Physikalische Gesellschaft, 1972; dir. Internat. Sch. Cosmic-Ray Astrophysics, Ettore Majorana Centre Sci. Culture, Erice, Italy, 1977—; chmn. U.S. IGY com. on interdisciplinary research, mem. nuclear emulsion panel space sci. bd.; Nat. Acad. Scis., 1959—; chief U.S. rep., steering com. Internat. Coop. Emulsion Flights for Cosmic Ray Research; cons. CREI Atomics, 1959—; vis. com. Bartol Research Found., Franklin Inst., 1967-74; mem. U.S. organizing com. 13th and 19th Internat. Confs. on Cosmic Rays; mem. sci. adv. com. Internat. Confs. on Nuclear Photography and Solid State Detectors, 1966—; mem. Com. of Honor for Einstein Centennial, Acad. Naz. Lincei, 1977; mem. Internat. Organizing com. Tex. Symposia on Relativistic Astrophysics, 1976—; Regents lectr. U. Calif. Riverside, 1985; Edison lectr. Naval Rsch. Lab award, 1990. Mem. editorial bd. Astrophysics and Space Sci., 1968-75; assoc. editor: Phys. Rev. Letters, 1977-84; editor (NATO) ASI Series on Cosmic-Ray Astrophysics; contbr. to Am. Inst. Handbook of Physics, various encys. Recipient Disting. Civilian Svc. award Dept. Navy, 1967, medal of honor Soc. for Encouragement au Progrés, 1978, Sr. U.S. Scientist award Alexander von Humboldt Found., 1982, Profl. Achievement citation U. Chgo., 1992; Guggenheim fellow, 1962-63. Fellow Am. Phys. Soc. (chmn. organizing com. div. cosmic physics, chmn. 1971-72, com. on publs. 1977-79), AAAS, Washington Acad. Scis. (past com. chmn., Disting. Career in Scis. award, 1993); mem. Am. Astron. Soc. (exec. com. div. high-energy astrophysics 1978—, chmn. 1982), Philos. Soc. Washington (past pres.), Am. Technion Soc. (Washington bd.), Alexander von Humboldt Assn. of Am. (pres. Washington area chpt. 2000—), Assn. Los Alamos Scientists (past chmn.), Assn. Oak Ridge Engrs. and Scientists (past chmn.), Fedn. Am. Scientists (past mem. exec. com., nat. council), Internat. Astron. Union (organizing com. commn. on high-energy astrophysics), Internat. Conf. on Cosmic Rays (Victor Hess Meml. lectr., Rome, 1995), Phi Beta Kappa, Sigma Xi (Edison lectr. 1990). Club: Cosmos (Washington). Achievements include patents in field; discovery of first definitive evidence for production of cosmic ray secondaries in the interstellar medium; first determination of the source composition of cosmic rays; research in cosmic radiation, composition, origin, propagation, and nuclear transformations; in high-energy astrophysics; in particles and fields; in nuclear physics, neutron physics and fission reactors; in hydrodynamics and gamma-ray and neutrino astronomy. E-mail: shapiro@sigmanet.net. Office: 205 S Yoakum Pkwy Apt 1514 Alexandria VA 22304-3838

SHAPIRO, MICHAEL, engineering educator, researcher; b. St. Petersburg, USSR, Aug. 13, 1951; arrived in Israel, 1979.; s. Victor and Tamara (Shulman) S.; m. Galina Kantor, Oct. 7, 1974; children: Michael Jr., Daniela, Jonathan. Engr.-Physicist, Poly. Inst., St. Petersburg, USSR, 1974; DSc in Mech. Engring., Technion, Haifa, Israel, 1984. Rsch. engr. Inst. Mining Industry, Haifa, Israel, 1979-80; instr. Technion, Haifa, 1980-84, sr. lectr., 1986-91, assoc. prof., 1991-99; Bantrel postdoc. fellow MIT, Cambridge, Mass., 1984-86; prof. Technion, 1999—; dir. rsch. Nat. Scientific Rsch. Ctr., Poitiers, France, 1993-94; mem. steering com. Forum Bulk Solids Handling, Israel, 1994—. Contbr. articles to profl. jours.; mem. editl. bd. Jour. Aerosol Sci., 1992—; asst. to editor: Internat. Jour. Multiphase Flow, 1997—. Igal Alon fellow Ministry Edn., Israel, 1986-89, Bat-Sheva de Rothschild fellow Rothschild Found., Israel, 1988-90; recipient M. Smoluchowski award European Assn. Aerosol Rsch., 1995. Mem. Israel Assn. Aerosol Rsch. (pres. 1996-97), Internat. Aerosol Rsch. Assembly (del., chair awards com. 1990—), European Aerosol Assn. (bd. dirs.). Avocations: yacht sailing, skiing, European history. Office: Technion-Israel Inst Tech, Faculty Mech Engring, 32000 Haifa Israel

SHAPIRO, PHILIP ALAN, lawyer; b. Chgo., May 14, 1940; s. Joe and Nettie (Costin) S.; m. Joyce Barbara Chapnick, May 29, 1966; children: David Ian, Russell Scott, Mindi Jennifer. AA, Wilson Coll., 1960; BS in Fin., So. Ill. U., 1965; MBA in Mktg. with distinction, San Diego State U., San Diego, 1977; JD, Western State U., 1985, Western State U., 1985. Bar: Calif. 1988. Spl. agt. U.S. Secret Svc., Washington, 1965-67, Chgo., 1967-77; mgr. divsn. sales Roche Labs. divsn. Hoffman-La Roche, Inc., Chgo.; account exec. Cellular Comm., Inc., San Diego, 1985; with Complete Comm., San Diego, 1983—; assoc. Law Office Jeffrey S. Schwartz, 1988-91; pvt. practice, 1991—; chair gen. and solo practice section State Bar of Calif.; editor law rev. Western State U. Coll. Law. editor law rev. Western State U. Coll. Law. Mem. Spreckes Elem. Sch. Adv. Bd., San Diego, 1976-77; mem. University City Town Coun., San Diego, 1977; pres. Congregation Beth El, La Jolla, Calif., 1976-79. With USMC, 1958-60. Recipient Award of Merit, U.S. Treasury Dept., 1965, Israel Solidarity award, 1977, U. of Judaism award, 1978, Wiley W. Manuel award State Bar Calif., 1990, 91. Mem. ABA (vice chmn. gen. practice sect.), Calif. Trial Lawyers Assn., San Diego County Bar Assn., San Diego Trial Lawyers Assn., State Bar Calif. (exec. com. gen. practice sect.), San Diego Bus. Referrals (pres. 1998-99). Fax: 858-483-4639. E-mail: pshaplaw@san.rr.com. Office: PO Box 178475 San Diego CA 92177-8475

SHAPIRO, ROBERT B., manufacturing executive; b. N.Y.C., Aug. 4, 1938; s. Moses and Lilly (Langsam) S.; m. Berta Gordon, Mar. 27, 1964; children: James Gordon, Nina Rachel. A.B., Harvard U., 1959; LL.B., Columbia U., 1962. Bar: N.Y. 1963. Assoc. in law Columbia U., 1962-63; atty. firm Poletti Freidin Prashker Feldman & Gartner, N.Y.C., 1963-67; spl. asst. to gen. counsel and undersec. U.S. Dept. Transp., Washington, 1967-69; assoc. prof. law Northeastern U., Boston, 1969-71; asst. prof. law U. Wis., Madison, 1971-72; v.p., gen. counsel Gen. Instrument Corp., N.Y.C., 1972-79, G.D. Searle & Co., Skokie, Ill., 1979-82; pres. NutraSweet Group div. G.D. Searle & Co., Skokie, Ill., 1982-85; chmn., pres., chief exec. officer Nutra Sweet Co. subs. Monsanto, Skokie, Ill., 1985-95, also bd. dirs, 1992—; now chmn., CEO Monsanto Co., St. Louis, 1995-2000; chmn. Parmacia Corp., St. Louis, 2000—. Mem. Mass. Gov.'s Transp. Task Force, 1970-71; mem. com. on procedure CAB, 1975-76; mem. bus. adv. com. White House Domestic Policy Rev. on Indsl. Innovation, 1978-79; Nat. Bd.. Trustees Boys Clubs of Am. Recipient John R. Miller award as outstanding corporate mktg. exec., 1984; Outstanding Achievement award Sales and Mktg. Mgmt. Mag., 1984. Mem. Am. Bar Assn. (vice chmn. com. on corp. counsel 1981-82), U.S. C. of C. (council on antitrust policy 1981-82), N.Y. State Bar Assn. Home: 20 E Cedar St Chicago IL 60611-1198 Office: Pharmacia Corp 800 N Lindbergh Blvd Saint Louis MO 63167-0001

SHAPIRO, ZALMAN MORDECAI, chemist, consultant; b. Canton, Ohio, May 12, 1920; s. Abraham and Minnie (Pinck) S.; m. Evelyn Greenberg, June 24, 1945; children: Joshua, Ezra David, Deborah Esther. BA, Johns Hopkins U., 1942, MA, 1945, PhD, 1948. Rsch. assoc. Johns Hopkins for Nat. Rsch. Coun., Balt., 1942-45; instr. chemistry Johns Hopkins U., 1946-48; sr. engr. Westinghouse Electric Corp., Pitts., 1948; mgr. phys. chemistry, mgr. chem. metallurgy AEC Bettis Naval Nuc. Power Lab., Westinghouse,

West Mifflin, Pa., 1949-56; asst. divsn. mgr. pressurized water reactor divsn. AEC Bettis Naval Nuc. Power Lab., Westinghouse, West Mifflin, 1956-57; pres., chmn. bd. Nuc. Materials and Equipment Corp., Apollo, Pa., 1957-70; pres., chmn. of bd. Numec Instruments and Controls Corp., Apollo, Pa., 1960-70, Numec Decontamination Corp., Apollo, 1961-70, Isotope & Radiation Enterprises, Israel, 1964-70; pres. Assoc. Tech. and Bus. Consultants, Pitts., 1970—; v.p. Arco Chem. Co., Phila., 1967-70. Contbr. 2 chpts. to books; patentee in field. Mem. Govs. Sci. and Tech. Coun., Harrisburg, 1963-64; cons. Pa. Subcom. on Atomic Energy, Harrisburg, 1970-71; founder, vice-chmn., Ams. for Energy Independence, Washington, 1975—; organizer Project Pacesetter, Allegheny County, 1976. Named hon. fellow Technion Israel Inst. Tech., Haifa, 1988. Fellow Am. Nuc. Soc. (citation of merit); mem. AAAS, Am. Soc. Metals, Am. Chem. Soc., Phi Beta Kappa, Sigma Xi. Avocations: sailing, wood working. Home: 1045 Lyndhurst Dr Pittsburgh PA 15206-4535 Office: ASTECH 6334 Forbes Ave Pittsburgh PA 15217-1717

SHAPOSHNIK, IGOR IOSIFOVICH, cardiologist; b. Bendery, Moldova, Nov. 1, 1949; s. Josif Israelevich and Clara Solomonovna (Kaplevackaya) S.; m. Olga Dmitrievna Ushakova, July 30, 1983; 1 child, Maria. Resident Chelyabinsk State Med. Inst., Russia, 1974; therapeutist, cardiologist Chelyabinsk City Hosp., Russia, 1974-79; asst. prof. dept. internal diseases propedeutics Chelyabinsk State Med. Inst., Russia, 1979-87, head of dept. internal diseases propedeutics, 1992—, prof., 1994—; chief cardiologist Chelyabinsk Region, 1994—. Contbr. articles to profl. jours.; inventor diagnostic method of cardiomyopathy. Mem. Chelyabinsk Region Cardiology Assn., Chelyabinsk Region Therapeutic Assn., N.Y. Acad. Sci. Avocation: travelling. Office: Chelyabinsk State Med Inst, 16 UL Vorovskogo, 454092 Chelyabinsk Russia

SHAPOSHNIKOV, YAKOV DAVID, gastroenterologist; b. USSR, July 4, 1944; came to U.S., 1987; s. David Solomon and Dvora Bruchas (Chapovetsky) S.; m. Lilian Tandeitnik, Aug. 30, 1974; 1 child, Rimma. MD, Pavlov Med. Sch., 1967; PhD, Petrov Inst. Oncology, 1971. Diplomate Am. Bd. Internal Medicine. Intern Millard Fillmore Clinic, Buffalo, 1989-90; resident SUNY-Buffalo Hosp., 1990-92; fellow in gastroenterology U. Buffalo, 1992-95; attending physician Millard Fillmore Hosp., Buffalo, 1995-97, Kenmore Mercy Hosp., Buffalo, 1996-97, Buffalo Gen. Hosp., 1996-97; pvt. practice Las Vegas, 1997—; clin. instr. SUNY, Buffalo. Contbr. over 100 articles to profl. jours. Fellow ACP; mem. Am. Coll. Gastroenterology. Jewish. Address: 1612 Hidden Springs Dr Las Vegas NV 89117-5427 Office: 121 E Flamingo Rd Las Vegas NV 89109-4543 also: 1706 Bearden Dr Las Vegas NV 89106-4107

SHAPOVALOVA, VIKTORIYA ALEXEEVNA, pharmaceutical company executive; b. Krasnij Luch, Lugansk, USSR, Sept. 6, 1957; d. Aleksey Vasiljevich Vasin and Olga Kirillovna Zotova; m. Valeriy Vladimirovich Shapovalov, June 17, 1983; 1 child, Valentin. D in Pharmacy, Ukrainian Pharm. Acad., Kharkov, 1996, prof., 1998. Cert. 5th World Congresses on Innovations in Psychiatry. Head lab. Ukrainian Pharm. Acad., Kharkov, 1988-95, prof. pharm. chemistry chair, 1996-98; v.p. sci. Kharkov State Pharm. Enterprise Zdorovye Narodu, 1998-99; head forensic pharmacy chair Nat. Pharm. Acad. Ukraine, 1998—; mem. pharmacol. com. Ministry Health in Ukraine, Kiev, 1996—, mem. pharmacopea com., 1996—; dir. sci. Joint Stock Co. Zdorovye, Kharkov, 1999—. Author: (monograph) Handbook on Judicial and Forensic Pharmacy, 1997; author, editor: (monographs) Drugs in Psychopharmacology, 1997, Drugs in Clinical Surgery, 1998, Over-the-Counter Medicines, 1998. Active mem. Alliance of Lawyers in Ukraine, Kiev, 1999; sci. sec. Zakhyst, Kiev, 1999. Named Honored Inventor of the USSR, 1985. Mem. Internat. Acad. Ecology, Man and Nature Protection Scis., N.Y. Acad. Scis. Avocations: fitness, tennis, scientology, classical music. E-mail: valentin@euroseek.com. Fax: 380 572 160347. Office: Open Joint Stock Co Zdonovy, Shevchenko St 22, 61013 Kharkov Ukraine

SHARAN, MAITHILI, mathematician, educator; b. Kaman, Rajasthan, India, Jan. 4, 1953; s. Khem Chand and Ganga Dai; m. Suman Gupta, May 9, 1984; children: Umang, Upma. BSc, U. Rajasthan, Jaipur, India, 1972, MSc in Math., 1974; PhD, Indian Inst. Tech., 1982. Lectr. in math. Govt. Coll., Nathdwara, Rajasthan, India, 1974-75; rsch. fellow, asst. Indian Inst. Tech., Delhi, 1975-82, lectr., 1982-87, sr. sci. officer grade I, 1987-90, asst. prof., 1990-95; prof. Ctr. for Atmospheric Scis., Delhi, 1995—; vis. rsch. fellow U. Tech., Compiegne, France, 1979-81; postdoctoral fellow Johns Hopkins Sch. Medicine, Balt., 1986-87; vis. scientist U. Ala., Huntsville, 1990, Nat. Inst. Resources for Environment, Tsukuba, Japan, 1994; vis. prof. U. Ala., Huntsville, 1995, 96, Johns Hopkins U., Balt., 1999; vis. scientist Johns Hopkins U., Balt., 2000. Contbr. articles to profl. pubis. Recipient Gold medal Bhartiya Kala Sansthan, 1989, Young Scientist award Indian Nat. Sci. Acad., 1984, Shanti Swarup Bhatnagar Math. Scis. award Coun. of Sci. and Indsl. Rsch., 1992. Fellow Indian Nat. Sci. Acad., Nat. Acad. Scis. India; mem. Indian Math. Soc. (life), N.Y. Acad. Scis., Indian Sci. Congress Assn. (life). Office: Indian Inst Tech, Ctr Atmospheric Scis, Delhi 110016, India

SHARAN, RAJESHWAR NATH, molecular biology; b. Bettiah, Bihar, India, July 8, 1956; s. K. N. and Urmila (Verma) S.; m. Vibha Sinha; children: Amrita, Ankur. BSc, Patna U., 1975; MSc, Jawaharlal Nehru U., Delhi, India, 1978, MPhil, 1979, PhD, 1983. From rsch. assoc. to scientific pool officer Jawaharlal Nehru U., 1983-84; from asst prof. to assoc. prof., head dept. North-Eastern Hill U., Shillong, India, 1984—. Editor: Perceptions in Science, 1985, Trends in Radiation and Cancer Biology, 1998, Recent Aspects of Cellular and Applied Radiobiology, 1999. Mem. Indian Soc. Radiation Biology (v.p. 1996-97, pres. 2000—), Indian Assn. Cancer Rsch., Indian Complex Sys. Soc. Avocations: sports, reading, classical music. Office: North-Eastern Hill U, Dept Biochemistry, Shillong 793022, India

SHARANSKY, NATAN (ANATOLY SHARANSKY), human rights activist, mathematician, computer programmer; b. Donetsk, Soviet Union, Jan. 20, 1948; s. Boris and Ida (Milgrom) Sharansky; m. Avital Stieglitz; children: Rachel, Hana. Grad. in cybernetics, Moscow Phys. Tech. Inst. Computer programmer Moscow Rsch. Inst. for Oil and Gas; assoc. editor The Jerusalem Report, 1990-95; founder (polit. party) Yisrael ba-Aliya, 1996—; Min. Industry & Trade Govt. Israel, 1997-99, Min. Interior, 1999-2000; vis. prof. Brandeis U., Waltham, Mass. Author: Fear No Evil. Co-founder Moscow Helsinki Watch, 1976; pres. Soviet Jewry Zionist Forum, 1988-96. Polit. prisoner, USSR, 1977-86. Office: Knesset, 91950 Kiryat Ben-Gurion Israel*

SHARBAUGH, W(ILLIAM) JAMES, plastics engineer, consultant; b. Pitts., Apr. 13, 1914; s. Oliver Michael and Sarah Marie (Wingenroth) S.; m. Eileen Carey, May 14, 1938; children: William James Jr., Eileen Sharbaugh Pinkerton, Susan Sharbaugh Coté. BS in Engring., Carnegie Inst. Tech., 1935. Project engr. MSA Corp., Pitts., 1935-46; founder, gen. mgr. ENPRO, Inc., St. Louis, 1947-62; mgr. plastics div. Vulcan Rubber and Plastic, Morrisville, Pa., 1962-67; v.p. engring. and mfg. FESCO div. Celanese, Pitts., 1967-72; exec. v.p. plastics div. Lenox, Inc., St. Louis, 1970-72; div. mgr. Crown Zellerbach, Inc., San Francisco, 1972-77; pres. Plastics Assocs., Cons., Newport Beach, Calif., 1977—; founder ISOBET USA, Inc., Newport Beach; dir. devel. and tech. Crown Zellerbach, Inc.; pres. Western Plastics Pioneers; cons. nat. and internat. plastics cos.; pres. Plastics Assocs., Inc., 1996—; founder Advanced Bldg. Tech., 1995. Author tech. papers, reports. Mem. Soc. of Plastics Engrs. (first pres. Pitts. sect.), Soc. Plastics Industry (industry profl. witness, forensics of plastic product failures). Republican. Roman Catholic. Achievements include patents for military products, consumer items and the development of ISOBET construction materials. Fax: (949) 651-0261. E-mail: plastx@juno.com. Office: Plastics Assocs Inc 37 Morena Irvine CA 92612-1719

SHARE, RICHARD HUDSON, lawyer; b. Mpls., Sept. 6, 1938; s. Jerome and Millicent S.; m. Carolee Martin, 1970; children: Mark Lowell, Gregory Martin, Jennifer Hillary, Ashley. BS, UCLA, 1960; JD, U. So. Calif., 1963. Bar: Calif. Sup. Ct. 1964, U.S. Dist. Ct. (cen. and so. dists.) Calif., U.S. Supreme Ct. 1974. Field agt. IRS, 1960-63; mem. law divsn., asst. sec. Avco Fin. Svcs., 1963-72; founder Frandzel and Share, L.A., 1972-99, Richard Hudson Share & Assocs., 1999—; lectr. Nat. Bus. Inst., Creditor's Rights; adj. prof. Loloya Law Sch., 1999. Mem. Calif. Bankers Assn. E-mail: sharelaw@aol.com. Office: PO Box 1003 Pacific Palisades CA 90272-1003 also: 150 N Santa Anita Ave Ste 530 Arcadia CA 91006-3127

SHARETT, ALAN RICHARD, lawyer, environmental litigator, mediator and arbitrator, law educator; b. Hammond, Ind., Apr. 15, 1943; s. Henry S. and Frances (Givel) Smulevitz; children: Lauren Ruth, Charles Daniel; m. Cherie Ann Vick, Oct. 15, 1993. Student, Ind. U., 1962-65; JD, DePaul U., 1968; advanced postgrad. legal edn., U. Mich. and U. Chgo., 1970-71; post-grad., Fla. Internat. U., 1999-2000; cert. mediator, Am. Arbitration Assn., 1994; cert. tng. and human resource devel., Fla. Internat. U., 2000. Bar: Ind. 1969, N.Y. 1975, U.S. Ct. Appeals (2d cir.) 1975, U.S. Ct. Appeals (7th cir.) 1974, U.S. Supreme Ct. 1973. Assoc. World Peace Through Law Ctr., Washington, 1967-68, Call, Call, Borns and Theodoros, Gary, Ind., 1969-71; judge protem Gary City Ct., 1970-71; environ. dist. atty. 31st Jud. Cir., Lake County, Ind., 1971-75; counsel Dunes Nat. Lakeshore Group, Ind., 1971-75; mem. Cohan, Cohan and Smulevitz, 1971-75; town atty. Independence Hill, Ind., 1974-75; judge pro tem Superior Ct., Lake County, Ind., 1971-75; pvt. practice Flushing, N.Y., 1980-82, Miami Beach, Fla., 1988—; lead trial counsel, chmn. lawyers panel No. Ind. ACLU, 1969-71; liaison trial counsel Lake County and Ind. State Health Depts., and Atty. Gen., 1971-75; professorial dir. NYU Pub. Liability Inst., N.Y.C., 1975-76; speaker, guest lectr., adj. faculty ATLA, Purdue U., NYU, Ind. U., De Paul U., Valparaiso U., St. Joseph Coll., U. Miami; coll. paralegal instr., 1970-89; adj. faculty prof. constl. law Union Inst., Miami, Cin., 1990-92; adj. prof. environ. litigation and alternative dispute resolution Ward Stone Coll., Miami, 1994; guest prof. internat. environ. law Dept. Internat. and Comparative Law, U. Miami, 1992—; mem. adv. panel, seminar speaker on internat. environ. law Interam. Dialogue on Water Mgmt., 1993; speaker on environ. transactions and litigation, North Dade county Fla. Bar Assn., 1995—; seminar speaker on environ. politics, U. Miami Dept. Environ. Sci., 1995—; mem. Nat. Dist. Attys. Assn., 1972-75, mem. environ. protection com.; pres. ESI Group, Nat. Environ. Responsibility Cons. Inc. Editor-in-chief DePaul U. The Summons, 1967-68; mem. staff DePaul Law Rev., 1968; contbr. articles to profl. jours. Gen. counsel Marjory Stoneman Douglas Friends of Everglades, 1992-93; asst. atty. gen., chair fed. and constnl. practice litigation group N.Y. State, N.Y.C., 1976-78; mem. Coalition Fla. Save Our Everglades Program; diplomate, vice chancellor Law-Sci. Acad. Am., 1967. Recipient Honors award in forensic litigation Law-Sci. Acad. Am., 1967. Mem. ABA (nat. article editor law student divsn. 1967-68, nat. com. environ. litigation, com. fed. procedures, com. toxic torts, hazardous substances and environ. law, com. energy resources law, com. internat. environ. law, com. internat. litigation, environ. interest group, sect. natural resources, energy and environ. law, judge negotiation competition championship round., law student divsn., midyr. meeting 1995, sect. sci. and tech., biotech. com., environ. law and pub. heath com., standing com sci. evidence, spl. com. legal edn., nat. toxic and hazardous substances and environ. law com., sect. tort and ins. practice, corp. gen. counsel com., non-profit orgns. com., media law and defamation torts com., tort and hazardous substances and environ. law com.), AAAS (physics, math, astronomy) , Judicature Soc., Nat. Orgn. Social Security Claimants Reps. (sustaining), Am. Arbitration Assn. (cert. program in mediation 1993), Am. Soc. Tng. and Devel., Soc. Human Rource Mgmt., Assn. Bar City of N.Y., N.Y. County Lawyers Assn. (com. on fed. cts. 1977-82), ATLA (nat. coms. toxic, environ. and pharm. torts, environ. litigatin), Environ. Law Inst., Am. Immigration Lawyers Assn., Ill. State Bar Assn. (staff editor 1967-68), N.Y. State Bar Assn. (environ. law sect., family law sect.), Ind. State Bar Assn. (environ. law sect., internat. law sect., trial practice sect.), Nat. Fla. Assn. Environ. Profls., Greater Miami C. of C. (trustee 1993-94, com. environ. awareness, environ. econs., biomed. exch., planning and growth mgmt., internat. econ. devel., bus. and industry econs. devel., govtl. affairs, ins., internat. banking, Europe/Pacific), N.Y. Acad. Sci., Astron. Soc. of Pacific, Am. Acad. Poets, So. Cross Astron. Soc. Office: ESI Group Nat Environ Responsibility Cons Inc 14630 Bull Run Rd Ste 213 Miami Lakes FL 33014-2017

SHARF, STEPHAN, automotive company executive; b. Berlin, Dec. 30, 1920; came to U.S., 1947; s. Wilhelm and Martha (Schwartz) S.; m. Rita Schantzer, June 17, 1951. Degree in Mech. Engring., Tech. U., Berlin, Fed. Republic Germany, 1947. Tool and die maker Buerk Tool & Die Co., Buffalo, 1947-50; foreman Ford Motor Co., 1950-53; gen. foreman Ford Motor Co., Chgo., 1953-58; with Chrysler Corp., Detroit, 1958-86, master mechanic Twinsburg stamping plant, 1958-63, mfg. engring. mgr., 1963-66, mrg. prodn. Twinsburg stamping plant, 1966-68, plant mgr. Warren stamping plant, 1968-70, plant mgr. Sterling stamping plant, 1970-72, gen. plants mgr. stamping, 1972-78, v.p. Engine and Casting div., 1978-80, v.p. Power Train div., 1980-81, exec. v.p., mfg., dir., 1981-85, exec. v.p. internat., 1985-86, also bd. dirs.; pres. SICA Corp., Troy, Mich., 1986—; bd. dirs. Integral Vision Inc. Columnist Ward's Auto World Common Sense mag., 1987—. Bd. dirs. Jr. Achievement, Detroit council Boy Scouts Am.; trustee, v.p. Oakland U. Mem. Soc. Auto Engrs., Detroit Engring. Soc. Club: Wabeek Country. Home: 966 Adams Castle Dr Bloomfield Hills MI 48304-3713 Office: SICA Corp PO Box 623 Troy MI 48099-0623

SHARIF, KHALID, educational association administrator; b. Lahore, Pakistan, May 2, 1936; m. Farhat, Sept. 20, 1970; 3 children. Diploma, Inst. Affaires Internat., Paris, Academia Argentina Diplomacia, Mem. Caricom, Carribbean States; PhD (hon.), Addison State U., World Acad. Assn. Masters Univ, Monchengladbach, Germany, Australian Inst. Coord. Rsch., Victoria; LLD, London Inst. Applied Rsch., Third World Coll. Internat., Paris. Sec. Pakistan Students Fedn., London, 1956-58; gov. Lewisham Inst. Adult Edn., London, 1987-90; sch. gov. Waverley Girls high Sch., Peckham Rye Sch., London, 1987-90; mem. Amnesty Internat., 1992-98; Lord of Rock Island County Rosecommon, Ireland, 1997—; Lord Manor Gt. Pollicott, 1999, Manor Gt. Linton, 2000. Cmty. devel. worker Wandsworth Anglo-Indian Welfare Assn., London, 1970-72; mem. mgmt. com. Southwark Coun. Cmty. Rels., London, 1972-75, treas., 1985-86, Southwark Coun. Vol. Svc., London, 1975-78, King's/Southwark Cmty. Health Coun., London, 1983-85, three boroughs project Commn. Racial Equality, London, 1988-91; cmty. rep. Southwark Police Consultative Group, London, 1981-84, Bromley Cmty. Police Consultative Group, 1988-92, Lewisham Police Consultative Group, London, 1994-95; mem. help on arrest scheme juveniles, lay vis. Southwark Police Stas., London, 1981-84; gen. sec. Southwark Asian Cmty. Orgn., London, 1981-84; trustee Camberwell Consokidated Charities, London, 1983-85; vice chmn. race subcom. Southwark Borough Coun., London, 1984-86; chmn. sch. gov. body Ivydale Primary Sch., London, 1983-86, Robert Browning Primary Sch., London, 1983-85; ind. chmn. tenancy agreements Southwark Arbitration Tribunals, London, 1984-86; mem. bd. vis. HM Prison, Wandsworth, London, 1984-92; mem. S.E. London Valuation Cmty. Charge Tribunals, London, 1984-92; chmn. Bromley Asian Cmty. Orgn., London, 1988-92, Lewisham Asian Cmty. Orgn., London, 1992-95; founder, chmn. Day Ctr., Lunches Club Sr. Citizens, Bromley, Kent, Eng., 1988-91; gov. Brockley Sch., Lewisham Edn. Authority, London, 1994-95, Kilmorie Sch., 1994-95, mem. edn. appeals tribunal, 1995—; mem. edn. appeals tribunal Southwark Edn. Authroity, London, 1995—; senator Coun. States Protection Life, Palermo, Italy, 1995—. Named Lord of Camster, Baron, Royal Order Bohemian Crown, Count, Order of San Ciriaco, Knight Commdr., Lofsensic Urninius Order, Knight, Grand Prior Templar Order, Order of Holy Grail, Circulo Nobilario Los Caballeros Universals, Capt., Order Eagle of Sea, Knight of Yr., Internat. Assn. Writers Artists, 1995. Fellow Australian Inst. Coord. Rsch.; mem. Maison Internat. Intellectuals, Monarchist League. Address: 11 High St, London SE20 7HJ, England

SHARIF, MAHMUD SAYID AHMAD, Egyptian government official. PhD in Surgery, Univ. Cairo, 1957. Prof. surgery, 1974-91; minister local adminstrn. Govt. Egypt, Cairo, 1991—. Office: Embassy of Egypt 3521 Internat Ct NW Washington DC 20008-4010*

SHARIF, MOHAMMAD NOWAZ, former prime minister of Pakistan; b. Lahore, Pakistan, Dec. 25, 1948; s. Mian Mohammad sharif; married, 1971; 4 children. Student, Govt. Coll of Lahore; grad. in law, U. of Punjab. With Ittefax faction indsl. group, 1969; min. of fin. Province of Punjab, Pakistan, 1981-85; chief min. Govt. of the Punjab, Pakistan, 1985-90; prime minister Islamic Republic of Pakistan, 1990-99. Pres. Pakistan Muslim League, Punjab, 1985, Islami Jamhoori Ittehad, 1988. Avocations: social work, photograpgy, hunting, cricket. Address: Office of Prime Min, Islamabad Pakistan*

SHARIF, OMAR (MICHAEL SHALHOUB), actor; b. Alexandria, Egypt, Apr. 10, 1932; s. Joseph and Claire (Saada) Shalhoub; m. Faten Hamama, Feb. 5, 1955; 1 child, Tarek. Attended, Victoria Coll., Cairo. Appeared in numerous Egyptian, French and Am. films including (debut) Ciel d' enfer, 1953, The Mamluks, The Blazing Sun, Goha, Lawrence of Arabia, 1962 (Golden Globe award for best supporting actor), Behold a Pale Horse, 1964, The Fall of the Roman Empire, 1964, Genghis Khan, 1965, The Yellow Rolls Royce, 1965, Doctor Zhivago, 1966 (Golden Globe award best actor), Night of the Generals, 1967, More Than a Miracle, 1967, Funny Girl, 1968, Mayerling, 1969, Che!, 1969, MacKenna's Gold, 1969, The Appointment, 1969, The Horsemen, 1970, The Last Valley, 1971, The Burglars, 1972, The Tamarind Seed, 1974, The Mysterious Island of Captain Nemo, 1974, Juggernaut, 1974, Funny Lady, 1975, Crime and Passion, 1975, Ace Up The Sleeve, The Pink Panther Stikes Again, The Right To Love, Ashanti, 1979, Bloodline, 1979, Oh Heavenly Dog, 1980, The Baltimore Bullet, 1980, Green Ice, Chanel Solitaire, Top Secret, 1984, The Rainbow, 1989, Mountains of the Moon, 1990, Journey of Love, 1990, (voice) Umm Kulthum, 1996, Heaven Before I Die, 1997, The 13th Warrior, 1998, Mysteries of Egypt, 1998, The 13th Warrior, 1999; TV appearances include S*H*E*, Pleasure Palace, The Far Pavillion, Mrs. 'arris Goes to Paris, 1992; (TV movie) Lie Down with Lions, 1994; (TV miniseries) Peter the Great, 1986, Anastasia: The Mystery of Anna, 1986, Grand Larceny, Gulliver's Travels, 1996, Katharina die Grote, 1995, also Omar Sharif Returns to Egypt, The Mysteries of the Pyramids (host). Author: The Eternal Male, 1977; author syndicated columns on bridge. Office: William Morris Agy care Ames Cushing 151 S El Camino Dr Beverly Hills CA 90212-2775

SHARIFY, NASSER, educator, author, librarian; b. Tehran, Iran, Sept. 23, 1925; came to U.S., 1953, naturalized, 1972; s. Ebrahim and Eshrat (Saghafy) S.; m. Homayoun Taslimy, June 14, 1950 (div. 1978); children: Sharareh, Shahab. Licencie es Lettres, U. Tehran, 1947; M.S., Columbia U., 1954, Dr. L.S., 1958. Editorial staff Teheran jours. Rah-e Now, Jahan-e Now, Saba, Jonb va Jush, 1943-51; translator, announcer All India Radio, 1948-49; librarian, dep. dir. Library of Parliament Iran, Tehran, 1949-53; cataloger Library of Congress, 1954-55; program asst. libraries devel. sect. UNESCO, Paris, 1959-61; acting chief servicing sect. Dept. Edn., 1962-63; dir. gen. Ministry Edn., Tehran, 1961-62; asst. prof. library and info. scis. and internat. edn. U. Pitts., 1963-66; founder, dir. Internat. Library Info. Center, 1964-66; vis. lectr. SUNY Albany Sch. Library Sci., summer, 1966; dir. internat. librarianship and documentation, internat studies and world affairs SUNY, Oyster Bay, 1966-68; dean, prof. grad. sch. library and info sci. Pratt Inst., Bklyn., 1968-87, chmn. inst. research council, 1971-89, disting. prof., dean emeritus sch. computer, info. and library scis., 1987—; pres. B.E.L.T., Inc., internat. planning cons., 1981—; Dir. Grad. Library Tng. Program, UNESCO Mission, Nat. Tchrs. Coll., Tehran, 1960; Iran's Ofcl. del. to UNESCO Conf. Ednl. Pubs., Geneva, 1961, SE Asia Edn. Secs. Conf., Murree, Pakistan, 1961, Internation Conf., on Cataloging Prins., Paris, 1961, CENTO Libr. Devel. Conf., Ankara, Turkey, 1962; chmn. standing com. for preparation reading materials for new literates UNESCO, Tehran, 1961-62; mem. U.S. AID Mission, Turkey, Iran, Pakistan, 1966; dir. Conf. on Internat. Responsibility Coll. and Univ. Librarians, Oyster Bay, 1967; U.S. del. 33d Conf. and Internat. Congress on Documentation, Tokyo, 1967; ALA del. UN Conf. on Non-Govtl. Orgn., 1969; cons. U.S. AID, Conf. on Book Devel., 1967; mem. adv. bd. Ency. Libr. and Info. Scis., 1969—; chmn. Pre-Am. Library Assn. Conf. Inst. on Internat. Libr. Manpower, Edn. and Placement in N.Am., Detroit, 1970; mem. Am. del. Internat. Fedn. Libr. Assn. Conf., Liverpool, Eng., 1971, Budapest, 1972, Grenoble, France, 1973, Washington, 1974, Brussels, 1977, Montreal, 1982, Chgo., 1985, Barcelona, 1992; bldg. cons. Learning Resources Center, Nat. Tchrs. Coll., Iran, 1972-73, cons. campus planning, 1972-73; UNESCO cons. missions to plan and evaluate Nat. Sch. Info. Sci., Morocco, 1973-74, 79-81, 89; cons. U.S. Info. Agy., Morocco, 1991, 92, 95; chmn. Conf. on Orgn. and Control of Info for Islamic Research, 1982; chmn. bd. cons. to Nat. U. Iran, 1974-75, Pahlavi Nat. Library of Iran, 1975-77; speaker Symposium Internat. sur l' information Economique, Casablanca, Morocco, 1990; inaugural speaker Ctr. Documentation et D'Information Multimedia, Rabat, Morocco, 1995. Author: cataloging of Persian works Including Rules for Transliteration Entry and Description, 1959, Book Production, Importation and Distribution in Iran, Pakistan and Turkey, 1966; Beyond the National Frontiers: The International Dimension of Changing Library Education for a Changing World, 1973; The Pahlavi National Library of the Future, 17 vols., 1976, other books; contbr. to Ency. of Library and Info. Sci., 1969, ALA World Ency. Library and Info. Services, 1980, 86, library jours., 1973—, Bookmark, 1972, Library Education in the Middle East, 1991, Remembering Rangathan: A Sentimental Reflection, 1992; contbr. poetry to various jours. and anthologies, 1947-51, 67, 91-93 lyrics to Iranian motion pictures and recs., 1948-52; works on display at Archieves of Hoover Inst. on War Revolution and Peace, Stanford U.; Contbr. to: film script for motion picture Morad, 1951-52. Trustee Bklyn. Public Library, 1970-82; pres. Maurice F. Tauber Found., 1981—. Recipient Taj (crown) medal and citation for disting. svc. Mohammad Reza Shah Pahlavi, Shah of Iran, 1978, Kaula Gold medal and citation for disting. svc. to internat. librarianship, 1985; named for Annual Nasser Sharify Lecture Series, Sch. of Computer Info. and Libr. Scis., Pratt Inst., 1988—; writings by and about Nasser Sharify are preserved at Archives of Hoover Instn. on wars, revolutions and peace., Stanford U., Stanford, Calif. Mem. ALA (chmn. com. equivalencies and reciprocity 1966-71, mem. UNESCO panel, mem. nominating com. 1970-71, chmn. Pakistan, Iran, Turkey, Morocco, and Middle East Resource panels, internat. library edn. com. 1973—, mem. com. internat. library schs. div. library edn. 1968-72, coordinator country resources panels, internat. library edn. com. library edn. div. 1973-78), N.Y. Library Assn. (dir. library edn. sect. 1969-72), Pub. Library Assn. (task force on internat. relations 1981-86), Am. Assn. Library Schs. (chmn. govtl. relations com., 1984-88), Am. Soc. Info. for Sci., Spl. Librarian Assn., Internat. Fedn. Library Assns. (adv. group library edn. 1971-73, v.p. library schs. sect. 1973-77). Home: 252 Jericho Tpke Westbury NY 11590-1213 Office: Pratt Inst Sch Info and Libr Sci 200 Willoughby Ave # 4 Brooklyn NY 11205-3899

SHARIPOV, ILGIZ ZUFAROVICH, physicist, researcher; b. Sterlitamak, Bashkortostan, USSR, Nov. 25, 1961; s. Zufar Salyakhetdinovich and Rashida Davletgareevna (Kutusheva) S.; m. Galina Aleksandrovna Beskhlebnova, Nov. 26, 1983; children: Irina, Margarita, Tamara. Diploma Thesis, Moscow State U., 1985; PhD, Inst. Metal Superplast Problems, Ufa, USSR, 1997. Scientific worker Bashkir State U., Ufa, Russia, 1985-92, Int. Met. Superplast Problems, Ufa, 1992—. Contbr. articles to profl. jours. Office: Inst Metal Superplasticity, 39 Khalturina St, 450001 Ufa Russia

SHARKANSKY, IRA, political science educator; b. Fall River, Mass., Nov. 25, 1938; arrived in Israel, 1975; s. Eugene L. and Beatrice R. (Mines) S.; m. Ina S. Goldberg, Aug. 21, 1960 (div. 1982); children: Stefan, Erica; m. Varda Horn, Sept. 30, 1982; children: Tamar, Mattan. BA, Wesleyan U., Middletown, Conn., 1960; MS, U. Wis., 1961, PhD, 1964. Asst. prof. Ball State U., Muncie, Ind., 1964-65, Fla. State U., Tallahassee, 1965-66, U. Ga., Athens, 1966-68; assoc. prof. U. Wis., Madison, 1968-71, prof. polit. sci., 1971-83; prof. polit. sci. Hebrew U., Jerusalem, 1975—. Author: Israel and its Bible, 1996, Governing Jerusalem, 1996, Policy Making in Israel, 1997, Rituals of Conflict, 1996, Ambiguity, Coping and Governance, 1999, The Politics of Religion and the Religion of Politics, 2000. With Israel Def. Forces, 1981-91. Office: Hebrew Univ Dept Polit Sci, Mt Scopus, 91905 Jerusalem Israel

SHARKEY, LEONARD ARTHUR, automobile company executive; b. Detroit, May 21, 1946; s. Percy and Lillian (Peros) S.; m. Irene Johnson, Aug. 9, 1969 (div. Nov. 1991); children: Michelle, Wesley Tucker (step-son). Cert. pvt. pilot. Tool and diemaker Ford Motor Co., Dearborn, Mich., 1965-85; indsl. hazardous substance educator Ford Motor Co., Dearborn, Mich., 1985-86, indsl. health, safety and energy control educator, 1987-88, tool and diemaker leader, 1989—; non-fiction author Individual Initiative, Brighton, Mich., 1989—. Author: Journey Into Fear (reprinted title Split Decision, 1997), 1995, Hidden Shadows - An Opening to the Windows of the Mind, 1996. Mem. Mich. Rep. Party. Mem. Nat. Geog. Soc., Livingston Players, Nat. Rifle Assn., Boat U.S., Drummond Island Sportsman's Club, Mich. United Conservation Clubs. Avocations: boating, shooting sports, political awareness studies, Biblical prophetic studies, theater.

SHARKEY, MICHAEL FRANCIS, literature educator; b. Sydney, Australia, Aug. 1, 1946; s. James Anthony and Patricia Clare (Cashman) S.; m.

Maureen Joan Drumm, Dec. 31, 1969 (div. 1982); children: Amanda, Sarah; life ptnr. Winifred Anne Belmont. BA, Sydney U., 1972; PhD, U. Auckland, New Zealand, 1976. Tchg. fellow Sydney U., 1972-73, Auckland U., 1976; tutor U. New Eng., Armidale, Australia, 1977-82; sr. lectr. U. New Eng., 1992-97; lectr. U. So. Queensland, Toowoomba, Australia, 1983-84, Melbourne U. Technology, Australia, 1985-87; asst. prof. Bond Univ., Gold Coast, Australia, 1990-91; editor/cons. Kardooarir Press, Armidale, 1980-88. Editor: Ulitarra Mag., Australia, 1997-2000; author: Look, He Said, 1994, Strange Journey, 1995, Waiting for Rain, 1996, Park, 2000. Chmn. New Eng. Writers' Ctr., Armidale, 1994-97. Fellowship Australia Coun., 1989. Mem. Australian Soc. of Authors. Avocation: writing. Office: Univ New Eng, NSW Armidale 2351, Australia

SHARKEY, PAUL MARTIN, electrical engineer; b. Dublin, Leinster, Ireland, Oct. 3, 1962; arrived in England, 1988; s. John Brendan and Brid (Nolan) S.; m. Karen Yvonne Meynink, Dec. 30, 1991; children: Liam, Eoin, Conall. Diploma in elec. engring., Dublin Inst. Tech., 1985; BSc in Engring., U. Dublin, 1985, MA, 1991; PhD, U. Strathclyde, Glasgow, Scotland, 1988. Chartered engr. Rsch. engr. U. Strathclyde, Glasgow, 1985-88; rsch. fellow U. Oxford, Eng., 1988-93; dir., cons. Oxford Mechatronics Ltd., 1991—; lectr. U. Reading, Eng., 1993-97, sr. lectr., 1997-98, dir. virtual reality rsch. group, telerobotics rsch. group, 1994-97, dir. interactive systems rsch. group, 1997—, reader of interactive systems, 1998-99; prof. cybernetics U. Reading, 1999—; chair rsch. com. Sch. Computer Sci., Cybernetics and Electronic Engring., 1999—; program chair European Confs. on Disability, Virtual Reality and Associated Techs., 1995—; internat. program com. mem. Mechatronics Confs., 1995—, Mechatronics and Machine Vision in Practice Confs., 1996—; mem. program com. IEEE Internat. Conf. on Robotics, Automation, 1998; mem. organizing com. Mechatronics, 1998. Author: (with others) The Mathematics of Control Theory, 1992; (with others) Active Vision, 1992, Real-Time Computer Vision, 1994; content editor Internat. Jour. Virtual Reality, 1998—; mem. editl. adv. bd. Knowledge Transfer Jour., 1988—; contbr. articles to profl. jours.; patentee in field. Mem. IEEE (sr. mem.), Inst. Elec. Engrs., Coun. of Engring. Avocations: photography, music, travel, walking, car building. Office: U Reading dept Cybernetics, Whiteknights, Reading RG6 6AY, England

SHARKOV, EUGENE ALEXANDER, physicist, educator; b. Moscow, July 29, 1942; s. Alexander Michail and Antonia Andreevna (Mitina) S.; m. Alla Evgenievna Chepigus, July 24, 1979; children: Olga, Alexander. Diploma in physics, Moscow State U., 1965, PhD in Physics, 1968; D of Phys. & Environ. Sci., Space Rsch. Isnt., Moscow. Sr. rschr. Space Rsch. Inst., Moscow, 1968-89, head remote sensing lab., 1989—; mem. editl. bd. Jour. Earth Obs. Remote Sensing, Moscow, 1997—; prof. Moscow Phys. & Tech. Inst., 1970—, Moscow U. Geodesy & Cartography, 1994—; mem. COSPAR sci. commn. Am. Geophys. Union; cons. to industry. Author: Remote Sensing of Tropical Regions, 1998, Catalogue of Tropical Cyclones and Tropical Disturbances of the World Ocean for 1983-1998, 1999; contbr. articles to profl. jours. Recipient Acad. Scis. Hon. award, Moscow, 1979, 99, Pres. Russian Fedn. Outstanding Scisntists award, Moscow, 1994-96. Office: Space Rsch Inst, Profsouznaya str 84/32, 117810 Moscow Russia

SHARLAND, DESMOND EDWARD, physician, anatomy educator; b. London, Apr. 13, 1929; s. Edward Harry and Beatrice Ursula (Gleeson) S.; m. Edna Guscott, June 9, 1965 (dec. Apr. 1974); children: Stephen William, Sarah Jane; m. Dulcie Newboult, Apr. 12, 1986. BSc, London U., 1950, MD, 1967; MB, BS, London Hosp., 1953. House physician The London Hosp., 1953; registrar Ctrl. Middlesex Hosp., London, 1960-64; sr. registrar Univ. Coll. Hosp., London, 1964-66; cons. physician Whittington Hosp., London, 1966-94, lectr. in human anatomy, 1975—. Fellow Royal Coll. Physicians. Roman Catholic. Avocation: ballroom dancing. Home: Church Path Woodside Ln, London N12 8RH, England

SHARMA, ARJUN DUTTA, cardiologist; b. Bombay, June 2, 1953; came to U.S., 1981; s. Hari D. and Gudrun (Axelsson) S.; m. Carolyn D. Burleigh, May 9, 1981; children: Allira, Eric, Harrison. BSc, U. Waterloo, Ont., Can., 1972; MD, U. Toronto, Ont., 1976. Intern Toronto Gen. Hosp., 1976-77, resident in medicine, 1978-80; resident in medicine St. Michael's Hosp., Toronto, 1980-81; residency medicine Toronto Gen. Hosp., 1977-78; Rsch. assoc. Washington U., St. Louis, 1981-83; asst. prof. pharmacy and toxicology U. Western Ont., London, 1985-89, asst. prof. medicine, 1983-89, assoc. prof. medicine, 1989-90; dir. interventional electrophysiology Sutter Meml. Hosp., Sacramento, 1990-95; abstract reviewer, faculty of ann. sci. sessions N.Am. Soc. for Pacing and Electrophysiology, 1993-97; assoc. clin. prof. U. Calif., Davis, 1990-96, clin. prof. medicine, 1997—; cons. Medtronic Inc., Mpls., 1985-2000, Telectronics Pacing Sys., Inc., 1990-94, Ela Med., 2000—, Guidant, 2000—; mem. rsch. com. Sutter Inst. Med. Rsch., 1991-97; mem. exec. com. Sutter Heart Inst., 1992; program dir. Update in Tachyarhythmia Mgmt., Palm Springs, 1996, Pacing Defibrillation and Electrophysiology, Squaw Valley, 1997; mem. atrial fibrillation adv. bd. Guidant Inc. Reviewer profl. jours., including Circulation, Am. Jour. Cardiology; contbr. articles to profl. publs. Mem. coun. for basic sci. Am. Heart Assn., chmn. ann. sci. session, 1989. Recipient John Melady award, 1972, Dr. C.S. Wainwright award, 1973-75, Rsch. prize Toronto Gen. Hosp., 1979, 80, Ont. Career Scientist award Ont. Ministry of Health, 1983-89; Med. Rsch. Coun. Can. fellow, 1981-83. Fellow ACP, Am. Coll. Cardiology; mem. Am. Fedn. Clin. Rsch., Canadian Cardiovasc. Soc., N.Y. Acad. Scis., Sacramento Eldorado Med. Soc. Avocations: skiing, tennis, philately. Office: 3941 J St Ste 260 Sacramento CA 95819-3633

SHARMA, BHAVENDER PAUL, biotechnologist; b. Patiala, Punjab, India, Oct. 22, 1949; s. Tribhawan Nath and Parkash Wati Sharma; m. Kathryn Ann Bilinski, Aug. 15, 1973; children: Anjana, Nealinder. BSc in chem. engring., Punjab U., India, 1969; MPhil, Rutgers U., 1974, PhD, 1977; MBA, Syracuse U., 1985. Instr. Rutgers U., New Brunswick, N.J., 1975-76; sr. project engr. Corning (N.Y.) Inc., 1976-83; dir. tech. and strategic planning Genencor Internat., Inc., South San Francisco, Calif., 1983-91; pres. InterSpex Products, Inc., Foster City, Calif., 1991-94; exec. dir. CV Therapeutics, Inc., Palo Alto, Calif., 1994—; editor newsletter and web site INSAF, West Orange, N.J., 1996—. Mem. AIChE, Am. Assn. Pharm. Scientists, Parenteral Drug Assn., Am. Chem. Soc. Fax: 650-570-5215. E-mail: bob sharma@cvt.com. Office: CV Therapeutics Inc 3172 Porter Dr Palo Alto CA 94304-1212

SHARMA, CHANDRA SHEKHAR, editor, mathematics educator; b. Kishanganj, India, June 17, 1933; arrived in Eng., 1960; s. Mahendra Prasad Sinha and Chandradhana (Devi) S.; m. Margaret Anthea Grubb, Sept. 21, 1974. BSc (hons.), Sci. Coll., Patna, India, 1953; MSc, Patna Univ., 1955, MSc math., 1960; D Phil, Wadham Coll., Oxford U., Eng., 1963. Lectr. in chem. Patna Univ., 1955-60; lectr. in math. Birkbeck Coll., London, 1962-69, reader in math., 1970-79, prof. math., 1979-98; reviewer Math. Reviews, Ann Arbor, Zentralblatt für Math., Berlin. Author: Mathematical Foundations of Non Relatinstic Quantum Theory, 1992, Mathematical Foundations of The Special Theory of Relativity, 1993, Mathematical Foundations of Elementary Mechanics, 1994, Mathematical Foundations of Electrodynamics, 1995, Mathematical Foundations of the General Theory of Relativity, 1996; editor, pub.: Jour. Natural Geometry, 1992—. Recipient Imam Gold medal Patna Univ., 1953, McPherson Gold medal, 1953, Univ. Gold medal, 1955. Fellow Royal Astromonical Soc.; mem. London Math. Soc., Am. Math. Soc. Avocations: hill walking, photography.

SHARMA, DEVINDER KUMAR, development and environment administrator; b. Pragpur, Punjab, India, Nov. 25, 1947; s. Talakam Chand and Narbada Devi S.; m. Usha Rani Sharma, Feb. 8, 1972; children: Charu, Atul. BS, Punjab Agr. U., Ludhiana, India, 1968, MS in Stats., 1970. Lectr. Punjab Agr. U., Ludhiana, 1970-71; statis. asst. Govt. of Himachal Pradesh, India, 1972-76, rsch. officer, 1976-80, sr. rsch. officer, 1980-83, dist. dir., 1983-85, dir., 1985-86, adviser planning, 1986-98; prin. advisor Govt. of Himachal Pradesh, 1998—; UN fellow UNCRD, Nagoya, Japan, 1987; cons. NORAD, Delhi/Oslo, Norway, 1993-94, Govt. of India/World Bank, 1995; mem. First State Fin. Commn., Shimla, India, 1994-96, State Planning Commn., Shimla, 1991—; mem., sec. Second State Fin. Commn. Author/editor several books and publs. in field. Avocations: trekking, reading, social work. Home: House No 18 Type V, Govt Colony/Kasumpti, PIN17100 Himachel Pradesh India Office: State Planning Dept, Govt Himachal Pradesh, PIN 171002 Himachel Pradesh India

SHARMA, DHARMA DUTTA, English educator; b. Patna, India, Jan. 3, 1936; s. Kewal Pati Sharma and Ram Rati Devi; m. Daya Moyee; children: Manoranjan, Aneeta, Reeta, Kiran. BA, Patna U., 1955, MA in English, 1957; PhD, Edinburgh U., 1966. Lectr. Bihar U., India, 1958-67; reader Lucknow U., India, 1967-77; prof. English Lucknow U., 1977-96, dean arts, 1991-94, pro vice chancellor, 1993-95; vis. prof. English Sanaa U., Yemen, 1989-91, Taiz U., Yemen, 1996-98. Home: C-65 Butler Palace Colony, 226 001 Lucknow UP, India

SHARMA, GAURI DUTT, microbiologist, researcher; b. Ghaziabad, India, Oct. 1, 1950; s. Natuhu Singh and Bhagnan Devi Sharma; m. Sharda Rani Sharma, May 11, 1971; children: Indu, Nicky, Vicky Varun. BSc, Meirut (India) U., 1971, MSc, 1973; PhD, Northeastern Hill U., Shillong, India, 1981; postdoctoral fellow (hon.), Sheffield U., U.K., 1991. Sr. lab. technican Northeast Hill U., Shillong, 1976-79, temp. lectr., 1979-81, lectr., 1981-87, sr. lectr., 1986-88, reader, 1988—; vis. scientist Sheffield U., 1991. Contbr. articles to profl. jours., chpts. to books. Founder, sec. Northeastern Hill U. Book Coop, Shillong, 1983-85, joint sec. teaching assn., 1983-86; sec. NEHUTSA, Shillong, 1980-81. Recipient Dr. Narsimhan Medal award for best rsch. paper, 1994, medal, Indian Phytopathol. Soc., 1995; INSA/Royal Soc. U.K. fellow, 1991. Fellow Bot. Sci. Soc., Conservation Natural Resources Soc.; mem. Meghalaya Sci. Soc. (joint sec. 1982-84). Hindu. Avocations: Yoga, meditation. Home: Northeastern Hill Univ, Northeastern Hill Univ, Qr No 29, Shillong 793022, India Office: Sch Life Scis, Assam U, Silchar 788011, India

SHARMA, GURUMAYUM JITENDRA, biologist, researcher; b. Imphal, Manipur, India, Mar. 1, 1951; s. Gurumayum Amusana S. and Gurumayum Ongbi Pishak Devi; m. Aribam Indira Devi, July 1973; 4 children. BS with honors, Gauhati (India) U., 1971; MS, Banaras Hindu U, Varanasi, India, 1973; MPhil, Jawarharlal Nehru U., New Delhi, 1974, PhD, 1983; C Biol., Inst. Biology, London, 1989. Asst. prof. Manipur U., Imphal, India, 1976-84, assoc. prof., 1984-92, prof., 1992—, head dept. life scis., 1993-94; mem. basic scis. com. II Bd. Rsch. in Nuclear Scis., Dept. Atomic Energy, Govt. of India, Mumbai, 1997—. Contbr. over 40 articles to scientific jours., chpts. to books. Rsch. fellow Univ. Grants Commn., Govt. of India, 1973-76, tchr. fellow, 1979-82, Commonwealth Academic Staff fellow Assn. Commonwealth Univs., London, 1989-90. Mem. Indian Soc. Radiation Biology, Inst. Biology, N.Y. Acad. Scis., Indian Soc. Cell Biology. Avocations: reading, music, nature watching. Home: Khongman Mangjil, 795003 Imphal Manipur, India Office: Manipur U, Dept Life Scis, 795003 Imphal Manipur, India

SHARMA, HARBANS LAL, nuclear medicine researcher, educator; b. Lahore, Punjab, India, Oct. 21, 1944; s. Bal Kishan and Maya Wati Sharma; m. Kussum Sharma, Aug. 9, 1976 (div. 1994); children: Puja, Neera; m. Jaswinder Sharma, Apr. 8, 1994. BSc, Punjab U., India, 1964, MSc, 1966; PhD, U. Minn., 1974; DSc, Manchester (Eng.) U., 1993. Lectr. in physics Punjab U., 1966-70; rsch. asst. U. Minn., Mpls., 1970-74; rsch. assoc. Manchester U., 1974-76, lectr., 1976-85, sr. lectr., 1985—. Mem. Soc. Nuclear Medicine, Brit. Nuclear Medicine Soc., European Nuclear Medicine Soc., N.Y. Acad. Scis. Avocations: reading, cooking, badminton, travelling, photography. Home: 67 Gleneagles Rd, Cheshire SK 8 3EN, England Office: U Manchester Dept Med Biophysics, Oxford Rd, Manchester M13 9PT, England

SHARMA, HARI CHAND, entomologist; b. Behra, Bilaspur, India, June 15, 1954; s. Moji and Mahanti (Devi) S.; m. Veena Sharma, Nov. 23, 1980; children: Anu, Ankita. BSc in Agr., H.P. U., Shimla, India, 1974, MSc in Entomology, 1976; PhD, IARI, New Delhi, 1979. Scientist I Internat. Crops Rsch. Inst. Semi-Arid Tropics, Patancheru Andhra, India, 1979-86, scientist II, 1987-93, sr. scientist, 1993-96, 97—; rsch. scientist U. Wis., Madison, 1986-87; vis. scientist ODPI, Toowoomba, Australia, 1996-97; scientist ICAR, Nagpur, 1979. Editor Indian Jour. Plant Protection, 1988-95, Pests and Pest Mgmt. in India: The Changing Scenario, 1994, Plant Protection and Environment, 1997, Internat. Sorghum and Millets Newsletter, 1997; contbr. articles to profl. jours. Recipient Lal Bahadur Sastir Meml. gold medal, 1979, H.P. U. Merit Gold Medal, 1974, N.N. Mohan Meml. Gold Medal, 1978, others. Fellow Entomol. Soc. India, Plant Protection Assn. India; mem. Entomol. Soc. Am., Acad. Environ. Biology. Avocations: flute, walking, swimming, track. Home: 10A 1 Crisat, AP Patancheru 502 324, India Office: ICRISAT, Asia Ctr, Patancheru Andhra 502324, India

SHARMA, KAMAL KISHORE, surgeon; b. Haridwar, India, July 9, 1946; s. Girdhari Lal and Bhagwati Devi S.; m. Suman, Jan. 21, 1972 (dec. Aug. 1987); children: Amit, Sumit.; BSc, Govt. Coll. Punjab, India, 1963; MBBS, S.N. Med. Coll., Agra, India, 1968, MS, 1973. Registrar surgery S.N. Med. Coll., Agra, 1971-73; dir. primary health care Adampur Doaba, Jalandhar, India, 1974-76; surg. specialist Dist. Civil Hosp., Punjab, 1976-79; sr. med. officer, dir. civil hosp. Punjab Civil Med. Svc., 1979-86, Dasuya, 1986-87; owner, dir. K&K Nursing Home, Punjab, 1987—. Vol. Lions, Hoshiarpur, Punjab, 1976-88. Fellow Indian Coll. Laparascopic Surgeons; mem. Indian Med. Assn., Assn. Surgeons India. Avocations: music, travel. Home: 38-L Model Town, 146001 Hoshiarpur Punjab, India Office: K&K Nursing Home, Bassi Khawaju, 146001 Hoshiarpur India

SHARMA, KAMALESH, diplomat. Rep. from India UN, N.Y.C. Office: Permanent Mission of India 235 E 43rd St New York NY 10017-4703

SHARMA, KRISHAN KUMAR, retired computer company executive, physicist, oncologist, immunotherapist; b. Paprola, India, Oct. 20, 1936; arrived in Eng., 1968, naturalized, 1978; s. Khazana Ram and Kirpi Devi Sharma; m. VEronica Ann Edge, June 16, 1964; children: Ravi, Priya. BSc in Physics with honors, Delhi U., 1959; MSc in Physics, Nagpur U., India, 1968; M of Homeopathy, Calcutta Med. Inst. Sci. asst. India Meteorol. Dept., 1959-68; rsch asst. U. Lancaster, Eng., 1969-70; engr. Internat. Computer Ltd., Kidsgrove, Stoke-on-Trent, Eng., 1971-77, prin. engr., 1977-81, sr. mgr. printed cir. test assemblies, 1982-87; ind. bus., 1988-90, homeopathic cons., 1991-96; homeopathic cons. in gen. and on internet med. forums, 1997—; rschr. on homeopathy; fine art, antique dealer, Stoke-on-Trent, 1987—. Author: Stress in High Technical Society; contbr. rsch. articles to India Meteorol. Jour. Rsch., 1964-68. Hindu. Avocations: research in old oil paintings, chess, stock market studies, camping, sathya sai baba. E-mail: sharmahomoepath@aol.com. Home: 14 Bradeley Rd, Haslington, Crewe, Cheshire CW1 5PW, England

SHARMA, LAXMINARAIN, language educator; b. Kaithal, Haryana, India, Mar. 12, 1943; s. Hansraj and Ganpati Sharma; m. Santosh K. Sharma, Nov. 25, 1969; children: Vibhu, Divya, Apara. BA, Radha Krishma Sanatan Dharma, Kaithal, India, 1964; MA, Kurukshetra U., India, 1966, PhD, 1971; D Litt, U. Magadha, India, 1989; D Spiritualism (hon.), Internation Meditation Inst., Kullu, India, 1985. Lectr. RKSD Coll., 1966; rsch. fellow Kurukshetra U., 1967; lectr., reader Panjab U., Chandigarh, India, 1967—, chmn., head Hindi dept., 1993-96; vis. prof. Humboldt U., Berlin, 1988; spl. duty officer Indira Gandhi Nat. Open U., New Delhi, 1986-87; vis. prof. U. St. Augustine, Trinidad and Tobago, 1989-93; 1st sec. High Commn. India, Port of Spain, Trinidad and Tobago, 1989-92; rschr. supr. Panjab U., 1973-2000. Author: Contemporary and Eternal, 1989 (1st prize Philosophical Book award 1979), Concept of Time and Poetry, 1986 (Best Book of Yr. Haryana Govt. 1987), The Space Eternal, 1983 (Internat. Meditation Inst. award 1988), Sriramayana Katha: The Ancient Ritual, 1999, Sarbhaum Sriram, 2000, (poetry) Vatsala, 1987 (ICCSR award of the Decade 1992), others. Recipient 1st prize Supreme Ct. India, 1972; named Hon. Chancellor U. Supreme Divinity, 1994—. Mem. Internat. Meditation Inst. India (dir. gen. 1992, life mem.), Soc. Working for Advancement Hindu Aspirations of Trinidad (life), Indian Coun. for Cultural Studies and Rsch. Avocations: lecturing on human values, culture and mythology. Home: 239 Sector 37-A, Chandigarh 160036, India Office: Panjab U, Hindi Dept, Chandigarh 160014, India

SHARMA, MADAN LAL, pharmacologist, researcher; b. Jammu, India, Feb. 11, 1938; s. Chhaju Ram and Umavati Sharma; m. Vishno Khajuria, Apr. 24, 1962; children: Jyoti, Shakti, Manisha, Anu. BS, Govt. G.M. Sci. Coll., Jammu Tawi, India, 1959; MS, U. Jammu, 1979, PhD in Zoology, 1991. Sr. sci. asst. Regional Rsch. Lab. (CSIR), Jammu Tawi, 1965-76, jr. sci. officer scientist A, 1976-81, sr. sci. officer scientist B, 1981-86, sr. sci. officer scientist C, 1986-91, asst. dir. scientist EI, 1991-96, sr. asst. dir. scientist EII, 1996-98; project leader R&D Regional Rsch. Lab. (CSIR), Jammu Tawi, 1970-78, 79-86, 86-98. Co-author: (book) Chemistry and Pharmacology of Vascine, A New Oxytocic and Abortifacient Agent, 1980; patentee in field; contbr. numerous rsch. papers to profl. jours. Mem. Indian Pharmacol. Soc. Hindu. Avocations: gardening, reading, yoga, games. Home: 234/9-Shakti Nagar, 180 001 Jammu Tawi India Office: Regional Rsch Lab, Canal Rd, 180-001 Jammu Tawi India

SHARMA, MANOJ, health educator, research physician; b. New Delhi, Nov. 24, 1963; came to U.S., 1992; s. Basant L. and Shakuntala Sharma; m. Sulekha Sharma, Feb. 3, 1991; children: Ankita Anna, Malvika Molly. MB BChir, U. Delhi, New Delhi, 1987; MS, Minn. State U., 1994; PhD, Ohio State U., 1997. Lic. Med. Coun. India; cert. in health and family welfare mgmt., health edn. specialist; diploma in tng. and devel. Resident in internal medicine Safdarjang Hosp., New Delhi, 1987-88; program officer cmty. health Vol. Health Assn. India, New Delhi, 1988-92; rsch. asst. health sci. Minn. State U., Mankato, 1992-94; rsch. & tchg. assoc. health edn. Ohio State U., Columbus, 1994-95; health promotion supr. Columbus Health Dept., 1995-97; asst. prof. cmty. health edn. U. Nebr., Omaha, 1997—; cons. health and medicine Plan Internat., New Delhi, 1989-92; expert tech. resource devel. consortium NIH Family Welfare Mgmt., New Delhi, 1991-92; guest lectr. population demographic St. Mary's Coll., St. Paul, 1992-93; cons. evaluation Assn. Italiana Amici di Raoul Follerea, Bologna, Italy, 1997—. Author: (book) Practical Stress Management, 1995; contbr. rsch. articles to profl. jours. Mem. adv. bd. Am. Cancer Soc., Omaha, 1998—, World Gym Fitness Ctrs., Columbus, 1995-97; mem. membership com. Indian Soc. for Tng. and Devel., New Delhi, 1989-92. Health Promotion grantee Ctrs. for Disease Control and Prevention, 1995-97, Weight Control Program grantee Omaha Tribe, 1997-98, Evaluation of Smoking Cessation Programs in Nebr. grantee Nebr. Health & Human Svcs., 1999-2000, Asthma Prevention grantee EPA, 1999-2001; Lead Prevention grantee EPA, 1999—. Fellow Am. Inst. Stress, Soc. Pub. Health Educators (Best Dissertation 1997); mem. APHA, Am. Sch. Health Assn. (life, Best Dissertation 1997), Indian Sci. Congress Assn. (life), Indian Assn. Preventive and Social Medicine (life), Eta Sigma Gamma (life). Hindu. Avocations: yoga, meditation, stamp and coin collection, traveling. E-mail: manoj sharma@unomaha.edu. Office: U Nebr at Omaha 6001 Dodge St Omaha NE 68182-0001

SHARMA, MOHAN DATT, seismology mathematics educator, researcher; b. Sahghwal, Punjab, India, Oct. 1, 1961; s. Dina Nath and Sandhya (Devi) S.; m. Anju Shard, Nov. 19, 1993; children: Niyati, Saurik. BSc, DAV Coll., Dasuya, India, 1981; MSc, Panjab U., Chandigarh, India, 1983, MPhil, 1985; PhD, Kurukshetra (India) U., 1989, cert. in yoga, 1997. Jr. rsch. fellow Kurukshetra U., 1985-87, sr. rsch. fellow, 1987-89, rsch. assoc., 1990-91, rsch. scientist, 1991-92, lectr. dept. atmospheric scis., 1992-96, reader, 1996—. Contbr. articles to sci. jours., including Jour. Acoustical Soc. Am., Bull. Seismol. Soc. Am., Internat. Jour. Solids and Structures, Geophys. Jour. Internat. Pres. Body Care Club, Kurukshetra, 1990-94. Nat. scholar Univ. Grants Commn., 1981; Commonwealth fellow Commonwealth Scholarship Commn., London, 1997. Avocations: healthcare activities, organizing beauty contests. Office: Kurukshetra U, Dept Math, Kurukshetra 136 119, India

SHARMA, MOTILAL, senior education specialist; b. Sardar Shahr, Rajasthan, India, Feb. 10, 1942; s. Ramlal and Naraini (Devi) S.; m. Shanti Devi, Apr., 1959; children: Mohani, Kanak, Vimala, Kamala, Naju, Omprakash. MEd, Rajasthan U., 1966, MA in Polit. Sci., 1968; PhD in Edn., U. Baroda, Gujarat, 1973; B.Phil, U. Birmingham, Eng., 1976. Tchr. dept. of edn. Rajasthan, 1960-73; rsch. officer Directorate Primary & Secondary Edn., Bikaner, India, 1973-76; reader in edn. South Gujarat U., Surat, India, 1976-84, prof. edn., 1985-86; edn. specialist Asian Devel. Bank, Manila, 1983-89, sr. edn. specialist, 1990-92, sr. evaluation specialist, 1993-95, sr. edn. specialist, 1996—; chmn. bd. studies of philosophy South Gujarat U., 1980-83; mem. internat. adv. bd. Open U. Hong Kong, 1996—; mem. adv. bd. Colombo Plan Staff Coll., Philippines, 1998—; chmn. Asian Devel. Bank staff coun., Manila, Philippines, 2000-2001. Author: Diagnosing School Personality, Schools in Context, Technical Handbook for SOCDQ, Diagnosing School Climate, Planning and Evaluating Non-Formal Education: A Systems Approach, Report of National Seminar on Non-formal Education; editor: Distance Education-Report of a Regional Seminar, vol. I and II, Distance Education (A Report of Round Table on Distance Education for South Asian Countries, Systems Approach in Education, Systems Approach: Its Application in Education, others; contbr. numerous articles to profl. jours., chpts. to books. Trustee, edn. advisor Jain Visawaharti, Ladnun, India, 1976—. U. Grants Commn. fellow, 1970, Commonwealth fellow, 1975. Mem. Ctr. for Peace Devel. Edn. (U.S., internat. adv. bd. 1985—), Found. Internat. Tele-Edn., Nat. U. Teleconf. Network, U.S. Nat. Greening Movement Found. (trustee Phillipines chpt. 1988—), Indian Assn. Ednl. Tech. (treas. 1977-83), Global Village Referral Network (assoc.). Home: Tapasya Naya-bas, Sardar Shahr Rajasthan, India Office: Asian Devel Bank, No 6 ADB Ave Mandaluyong, Manila The Philippines

SHARMA, NEERAJ K., computer engineer, educator; b. Allahabad, India, Mar. 7, 1965; came to U.S., 1999; m. Mamta; children: Suyash, Aman. BSEE, U. South Ala., 1987; MSEE, U. Akron, 1989, PhD, 1992. From lectr. to sr. lectr. La Trobe U., Melbourne, Australia, 1993-98; assoc. prof. Clarkson U., Potsdam, N.Y., 1999—. Mem. IEEE, Eta Kappa Nu, Pi Mu Epsilon.

SHARMA, NIVEDITA, microbiologist, researcher, educator; b. Mandi, India, June 9, 1964; d. Somesh Chand and Chanderkanta Sharma; m. Bhanu Neopaney; 1 child, Moksharthi. BSc, H.P. U. Shimla, India, 1983, MSc, 1985, MPhil in Microbiology, 1987, PhD in Microbiology, 1991. Rschr. Himachal Pradesh U. Shimla, India, 1991-92, U. Horticulture and Forestry, Solan, India, 1992-95; prof. U. Horticulture and Forestry, Solan, 1995—; asst. prof. Gesellscaft fü Biotechnologische Forschung mbH, Braunschweig, Germany, 1994. Nat. Merit scholar Govt. India, 1979-83; rsch. fellow H.P. U. Shimla, 1985-91; fellow Indian Coun. Agrl. Rsch., 1992-95. Mem. Assn. Microbiology India, GBF Club. Avocations: reading, listening to music, gardening, traveling, nature. Home: H 167/3 Bhagwati Niwas, Mandi 175 001, India Office: U Horticulture & Forestry, Dept Basic Scis, Solan 173 230, India

SHARMA, NIYAM CHARAN, pharmaceuticals company executive; b. Mandanpur, India, June 17, 1940; s. Bhupal Dev and Jay Devi Sharma; m. Sheila, May 18, 1964; three children. BSc, Rajasthan U., 1960, MSc, 1962; PhD, All India Inst Med. Scis., 1973. Asst. prof. U. Utah Med. Sch., Salt Lake City, 1979-83; prin. scientific officer Nat. Inst. Immunology, New Delhi, 1983-88; from gen mgr. to sr. gen. mgr. biotechnology Lupin Labs. Ltd., Bhopal, India, 1988-94; from chief scientist to v.p. biotechnology Cadila Pharms. Ltd., Ahmedabad, India, 1994—; hon. prof. microbiology Bhopal U., 1994—. Contbr. over 60 articles to profl. jours., chpts. to books. Mem. Internat. Brain Rsch. Orgn., Indian Acad. Vaccinology & Immunology. Office: IRM House, Off CG Rd, Navarangpura Ahmedabad 380 009, India

SHARMA, PANKAJ, clinician scientist; b. New Delhi, India, Aug. 24, 1964; s. Kewal Krishan and Janak Sharma. MBBS, Royal London Hosp., 1988; diploma in History of Medicine, Soc. Apothecories, London, 1989; PhD, Cambridge (Eng.) U., 1997. House officer prof. surg. unit Royal London Hosp., 1989; sr. house officer-rotation Addenbrooker Hosp., Cambridge, 1990-91; med. registrar rotation St. Georges Hosp., London, 1992-94; clinician scientist Cambridge U., 1997—; neurology registrar Nat. Hosp. for Neurology, Queen Square, London, 1997-98. Contbr. articles to profl. jours. Pres. Gonville Hall Debating Soc., Cambridge U., 1995-97. Fulbright scholar Harvard U./Mass. Gen. Hosp. Mem. Royal Coll. Physicians London. Avocations: collecting anitquarian medical books, theatre, tennis, fencing, debating. Office: Cambridge U Clin Pharm Unit, Addenbrookes Hosp, Cambridge CB2 2ZQ, England

SHARMA, PAWAN KUMAR, publishing executive; b. Pilani, Rajasthan, India, Mar. 12, 1957; s. Prahlad Rai and Sharda S.; m. Asha Sharma, June 26, 1980; children: Shipra, Swati, Tanay. B in Comm., Jodhpur (India) U., 1978, LLB, 1981. Mktg. United Book Traders, Jodhpur, 1981-83; pub. in

charge Scientific Pub., Jodhpur, 1984-90, mng. ptnr., 1991—, editor, 1996—. editor Jour. Econ. Tax. Botany, 1996—, Sci. Rev. Arid Zone, 1996—, Jour. Plant Anatomy Morphology, 1990—. Fellow Lok Kalyan Samiti (pres. 1996), Rajgopal Trust (sec. 1997); mem. Lions (1st. pres. 1997—, Outstanding Lion 1997). Avocations: traveling, religious literature. Home: Palace Rd Ratanada, Sharda Sadan Subash Colony, Jodhpur India Office: Scientific Pub, 5/A New Pali Rd PO Box 91, Jodhpur 342001, India

SHARMA, P.C., electronics engineer; b. Rajahmundry, India, Nov. 19, 1961; s. Suryanarayana and Savithri S. PhD, Indian Inst. Tech., Bombay, 1995. Vis. rechr. U. Calif., L.A., 1996—; rsch. cons. Rsch. & Devel. Labs., Culver City, Calif., 2000; sr. rsch. engr. Elec. Engring. Indian Inst. Tech., 1993-96; tech. cons. Garage.Com, Palo Alto, Calif., 1999. Cont. to profl. jours. Mem. IEEE, Am. Phys. Soc., Am. Vaccuum Soc. Avocations: trivia games, travel, wildlife. E-mail: pcsharma@ee.ucla.edu. Office: Electrical Engineering U Calif Los Angeles CA 90095-0001

SHARMA, PREM SAGAR, foreign language educator; b. Delhi, India, Apr. 20, 1950; s. Bishan Dass and Sushila Devi Sharma; m. Surekha Sharma, Dec. 30, 1979; 1 child, Aseem. MA in Russian, Jawaharlal Nehru U., New Delhi, 1973; PhD in Russian, Guru Nanak Dev U., Amritsar, India, 1987, cert. in Japanese, 1989, diploma in French, 1992. Interpreter Kasimpur Power House, Aligarh, India, 1973; tchr. Jawaharlal Nehru U., 1975-76, tech. asst., 1977; prof., head Guru Nanak Dev U., 1997—. Avocations: reading, cricket, badminton, TV, travel. Home: Tchr Flat 15, Guru Nanak Dev U, Amritsar 143 005, India Office: Guru Nanak Dev U, Dept Fgn Langs, Amritsar 143 005, India

SHARMA, RAJEEV KUMAR, fire and safety engineer, educator, consultant; b. Moradabad, U.P., India, Mar. 31, 1964; s. Shyamendra Prakash and Chitra (Shukla) S.; m. Shalini Gaur, Nov. 8, 1987; children: Ravi, Aadrika. BSc, Hindu Coll., Moradabad, India, 1981, MSc, 1983; BE in Fire Engring., Nat. Fire Svc. Coll. Nagpur U., 1986; post grad. diploma Indsl. Pollution Mgmt, 1992. Sta. officer, sci. officer Bhabha Atomic Rsch. Ctr., Bombay, India, 1987-88; head of fire and safety dept. India Glycols Ltd., Kashipur, India, 1988—; vis. cons. Nat. Safety Coun., Kanpur, India, 1991—, vis. auditor, faculty mem., 1995—. Presentation at sci. confs.; contbr. profl. jours. Recipient II prize at state level State Sci. Exhibition, Allahabad, 1974, Cert. B Nat. Cadet Corps Sr. Army Wing, 1979, Merit scholarship Ministry Home Affairs Govt. of India, 1983-86. Fellow Indian Chem. Soc.; mem. Nat. Inst. Ecology (life), Nat. Fire Protection Assn., Indian Inst. Chem. Engrs. (life), Indian Soc. Indsl. Hygine (life), Nat. Safety Coun. (life), Loss Prevention Assn. India Ltd. (life), Indian Assn. for Environ. Mgmt. (life), British Safety Coun., Instn. Fire Engrs., Instn. Fire Engrs. India, Instn. Indsl. Safety Profls. India (life), Adminstrv. Staff Coll. of India Alumni Assn. (life), Internat. Safety Coun., Vigyan Parished-Allahabad (life), Internat. Inst. Risk and Safety Mgmt. of Nat. Safety Ctr./U.K. Avocations: reading, painting, sculpture, book collecting, article writing. Fax: 91 05947 75315. E-mail: rajeevsharma rk@yahoo.com. Home: 2/3 Swadeshi Beema Nagar, Civil Lines Agra 282002UP, India Office: India Glycols Ltd, A-1 Indsl Area, Kashipur 244713UP, India

SHARMA, RAMESH CHANDRA, environmental science educator; b. Kalyanpur, India, Jan. 1, 1954; s. Kishan Lal and Maya (Devi) S.; m. Vineet Ghildial, June 16, 1982; children: Spandan, Sankalp. BSc with honors, Meerut (India) U., 1972, MSc in Zoology, 1975; DPhil, HNB Garhwal U., Srinagar, India, 1982, DSc, 1992. Lectr. zoology K.N. Govt. Postgrad. Coll., Gyanpur, India, 1975-77; lectr. zoology HNB Garhwal U., Srinagar, 1977-83, sr. lectr, 1983-89, reader in environ. biology, 1989-94, head dept. environ. studies, 1994—; head dept. zoology Tehri campus HNB Garhwal U., India, 1977-85; advisor Himalayan Environ. Conservation Nature Club, 1996-99; hon. animal welfare officer Animal Welfare Bd. India. Contbr. articles to profl. jours. Recipient fellowship Soc. Bioscis., 1996. Mem. Asian Fisheries Soc., Zool. Soc. (convenor 1978-85). Avocations: reading, writing articles, social work, listening to music, conduction of extension work on environment. Office: HNB Garhwal U Post Box 67, Dept Environ Studies, Srinagar-Garhwal 246174, India

SHARMA, RAMESH DUTT, nutritionist; b. Agra, India, Nov. 5, 1930; s. Jugal Kishore and Bhavani (Devi) Dixit; m. Yashoda Devi Tiwari, July 7, 1956; children: Rajeev, Kalpana, Sadhana. BSc, Agra Coll., 1948, MSc, 1956; PhD, S.N. Med. Coll., Agra, 1962. Asst. rsch. officer Indian Coun. Med. Rsch., New Delhi, 1956-68, rsch. officer, 1969-76; sr. rsch. officer Nat. Inst. Nutrition, Hyderabad, India, 1976-84, asst. dir., 1985-90; guide theses of MD and PhD postgrad. dept. medicine S.N. Med. Coll., Agra, 1960-76; cons. referee Food Tech. Mysore, India, 1980-90. Author: Diet and Diabetes, 1991; contbr. articles to profl. jours., chpt. to book. Recipient award for diabetes work Shree Bhagwati Devi Rastogi Trust Vishakha Pattam, India, 1991, P.P. Surya Kumari prize Indian Pharmocological Soc., 1988, Best Paper award Nutrition Soc. India, 1987. Home: 56/113-A P&T, Colony Cantt Phatak Agra, Agra 282001, India Office: Nat Inst Nutrition, Hyderabad, Agra 500007, India

SHARMA, SHASHI K., engineer; b. Ludhiana, India, Aug. 28, 1951; s. Harbans Lal and Shanti Devi S.; m. Aruna Kumari, Oct. 17, 1977; children: Suchi, Akash. BSME, Panjab U., Chandigarh, India, 1972; MSME, U. Dayton, 1982; PhD, Ohio State U., 1997. Engr. Shriram Pistons and Rings, Ghaziabad, India, 1972-73, Panjab State Electricity Bd., Bhatinda, Panjab, India, 1973-79; design engr. Process Equipment Co., Tipp City, Ohio, 1979-81; project engr. Tech Devel., Inc., Dyton, Ohio, 1981-83; scientist Universal Energy Systems, Dayton, 1983-84; assoc. mech. engr. U. Dayton Rsch. Inst., 1984-87; mech. engr. Materials Directorate/Wright Rsch. and Devel. Ctr., Wright-Patterson AFB, Ohio, 1987-90; materials rsch. engr. Materials and Mfg. Directorate, Air Force Rsch. Lab., Wright-Patterson AFB, 1990—; engring. cons. Enginetics Corp., Tipp City, 1983. Sports dir. India Club of Greater Dayton, 1989. Recipient Gold medal for Outstanding Performance in BSME, Panjab U., 1972, Guru Nanek Engring. Coll., India, 1972, Scientific Achievement award USAF, Washington, 1992. Mem. Soc. Tribologists and Lubrication Engrs. (sec. treas., vice-chmn. 1987—), ASME. Hindu. Avocations: tennis, table tennis. Office: Air Force Rsch Lab AFRL/MLBT 2941 P St Rm 136 Wright Patterson AFB OH 45433

SHARMA, SHUK DEV, education educator; b. Faridkot, Punjab, India, July 24, 1943; s. Vidhi Raj and Rachani Sharma; m. Pushap Bhardwaj, Jan. 18, 1975; children: Manu, Kanu. BA, P.U., Chandigarh, India, 1965; MA in Sanskrit, P.U., Hoshiarpur, India, 1968; PhD, K.U., Kurukshtra, India, 1972. Rsch. asst. V.V.I.S. & I.K. P.U. Hoshiarpur, 1962-69; rsch. fellow K.U. Kurukshetra, 1969-72; lectr. Govt. Coll., Hisar, India, 1972-73; lectr. Guru Nanak Dev U., Amritsar, India, 1973-82, assoc. prof., 1983-95, prof., 1995—, chmn. dept. Sanskrit, 1987-90, 93-96, mem. senate, 1996-97, 2000—, chmn. bd. studies in Sanskrit, 1987-90, 93-96; mem. rsch. bd. dept. Sanskrit, Kurukshtra U., India, 1989—, Punjabi U., Patiala, India, 1989—, Punjab U., Chandigarh, India, 1992-93. Author: Sanskrit Gadya Kanika, 1982, Sanskrit Natymanjari, 1983, (commemorative volumes) Brahmagavi, 1998, Saptasapti, 1999. Rsch. fellow K.U.K., 1969-71. Mem. Pranolok (bd. dirs. 1999-2000), V.V.R.I. (bd. dirs., life mem.). Avocations: reading, writing, poetry, travel, music. Office: Guru Nanak Dev U, Dept Sanskrit, Amritsar 143 005, India

SHARMA, SITA RAM, agriculturist, veterinarian; b. Tataher, India, Sept. 14, 1966; s. Bansi Lal and Burfi Devi Sharma; m. Hem Nalini Sharma, May 18, 1996; 1 child, Bhavika Sharma. B of Veterinary Sci./Animal Husbandry, Veterinary Coll. of Nagpur, India, 1988, M of Veterinary Sci., 1991; PhD in Veterinary Medicine, Indian Veterinary Rsch. Inst., 1994. Veterinary officer HP State Animal Husbandry Dept., Simla, India, 1990-91; sr. rsch. fellow Coun. Sci. and Indsl. Rsch., New Delhi, 1992-94; scientist Indian Coun. Agrl. Rsch., New Delhi, 1994—; vis. scientist McGill U., Montreal, Can., 1997-98. Contbr. articles to profl. jours. Recipient gold medal merit award Nat. Acad. Agrl. Rsch. and Mgmt., 1994, HARI OM Trust award Indian Coun. Agrl. Rsch., 1995-96; BOYSCAST fellow Ministry of Sci. and Tech., 1997-98. Mem. Indian Soc. Veterinary Medicine (life, appreciation award 1994-95), Indian Assn. Advancement of Veterinary Rsch. (life). Avocations: gardening, cricket, badminton, music. Office: North Temperate Reg Sta, Garsa Via Bhuntar, Kullu 175141, India

SHARMA, TARUN, physician, consultant; b. Patiala, Punjab, India, May 1, 1959; s. Kirti Chander and Chandra Kanta S.; m. Sitalakshmi, Nov. 12, 1986; 1 child, Abhishek. MBBS, Govt. Med. Coll., Patiala, Punjab, 1982. Lic. ophthalmogist. Sr. cons. Sankara Nethralaya, Chennai, Tamil, Nadu, 1991—, cons., 1986-91, sr. rsch. officer, 1986-89; vis. scholar The Chinese U. of Hong Kong, 1997-98; bd. dirs. Vision Rsch. Found., Chennai, hon. sec./treas. Office: Sankara Nethralaya, 18 College Rd, Chennai/Tamil Nadu 600 006, India

SHARMA, T.L., communications executive; b. Ludhiana, Punjab, India, May 6, 1942; s. N.R. and Parsinni Devi Sharma; m. Neena Arora, Mar. 20, 1972; 1 child, Nidhi. B Tech. in Telecomms. and Electronics, Jawahar Lal Nehru U., New Delhi, 1970; M Tech. in Telecomms. and Electronics, Mil. Coll. Telecomms., Mhow, India, 1979; MBA, Indian Inst. Mgmt., Indore, 1991. Officer Corps of Signals Indian Army, 1962-94; v.p. mktg. Kalani Industries Ltd., New Delhi, 1993-94; chief project mgr. e-mail Mekaster Telecom Ltd., New Delhi, 1994; asst. v.p. Presicion Electronics Ltd., Noida, India, 1994-97; v.p. mktg. Zamana Cons. Pvt. Ltd., New Delhi, 1997-2000; v.p. Tripoint Global, New Delhi, 2000—; cons. AP Inst. Tech., New Delhi, 1995-97; cons., advisor, organizer seminar Wisitex Found., New Delhi, 1996-97; vis. faculty Def. Svcs. Staff Coll., Wellington, india, 1981; prof., head faculty Mil. Coll. Telecom. Engring., Mhow, India, 1981-83, 88-91. Lt. col. India Army, 1962-94. Fellow Inst. Engrs. (India); mem. All India Mgmt. Assn., Computer Soc. India, Inst. Electronics and Telecom Engrs. (mem. coun. Calcutta region 1973-75). Hindu. Avocations: golf, bridge. Home: 138 Sector 28 Arun Vihar, Noida 201303, India Office: Zamana Cons Ltd, C2/52 Safdarjang Devel Area, 110016 New Delhi India

SHARMA, VASUDENA SUBRAMONIA, literature educator, dean, editor; b. Suchindrum, Kerala, India, Mar. 12, 1936; s. Subramonia Vasudeva Sharma and Parvathy Antharjanam. BA, India, 1958; MA, Kerala U., India, 1960, MLitt, 1968, PhD, 1975, DLitt, 1982. Editor Malyale Rajyam, Quilon, India, 1961-62; rsch. K. U., Trivandrum, India, 1962-68; lectr. S.K.V. Coll., Tricur, India, 1968-69; lectr. Kerala U., Trivadnum, 1969-75, reader, prof., head, dean, 1990-96; chief editor Amba Prasadem, Trivadnum, 1999—; hon. dir. Ullur Meml., Trivandum, 1990—; chmn. Kerala Kala Memlalam, 1993-96; spkr. in field. Recipient Nat. Akashvani award, 1984; Sr. fellow Govt. India, fellow Tatz Found. Mem. Kathakali Club. Home: Sasthamangalam, Niveditha, Trivandrumy 695010, India Office: Dept Malayalam, Univ Kerala, Trivandum 695010, India

SHARMA, VIJAY KUMAR, biologist; b. Calcutta, India, Sept. 29, 1967; s. Laximi Narayan and Kamala Sharma. BS, Calcutta U., 1987, MS, 1990; MPhil, North Eastern Hill U., Shillong, India, 1993, PhD, 1997. Jr. rsch. fellow North Eastern Hill U., 1991-93, sr. rsch. fellow, 1993-95; resource person Madurai (India) Kamaraj U., 1995-96; rsch. assoc. Jawaharlal Nehru Ctr. for Advanced Sci. Rsch., Bangalore, India, 1996-98, fellow, 1998-99; faculty fellow Jawaharlal Nehru Ctr. for Advanced Sci. Rsch., Bangalore, 1999—; guest rschr. NTNU, Norway. Gen. sec. Gyan Bhaskar Pustakalaya, Titagarh, India, 1984-91; pres. Rsch. Scholars Welfare Assn., Shillong, 1992-94. Recipient Young Scientists medal, Indian Nat. Sci. Acad., India, 1998. Mem. Indian Soc. Complex Sys. (life), Indian Acad. Sci. (assoc.). Hindu. Avocations: music, games, poetry. Office: J N Ctr Adv Sci Rsch, Jakkur PO, Bangalore 560064 Karnataka, India

SHARMAN, DIANE LEE, secondary school educator; b. Harvey, Ill., May 12, 1948; d. Eric Melvin and Josephine A. (Kut) Van Patten; m. Richard Lee Sharman, Nov. 3, 1973; children: Daria Lee, Deedra Lee. BS, Purdue U., 1970; MBA, U. Chgo., 1973. Cert. secondary sch. math. tchr., Tex. Computers sales rep. GE, Chgo., 1970-73; mgr. sold equipment Xerox Corp., Rochester, N.Y., 1973-81; mgr. fin. ops. analysis worldwide Xerox Corp., Stamford, N.Y., 1981-84; math. tchr. Conroe (Tex.) Ind. Sch. Dist., 1993—. Mem. DAR, Nat. Coun. Tchrs. of Math., Assn., Tex. Profl. Educators, Purdue Alumni Assn. (life), Nat. Charity League, U. Chgo. Alumni Assn. Avocations: golf, horseback riding. Home: 26 Fernglen Dr The Woodlands TX 77380-3955 Office: Knox HS 12104 Sawmill Rd The Woodlands TX 77380-2133

SHARON, MAHESHWAR, chemistry educator; b. Chapra, Bihar, India, Jan. 10, 1941; s. Prasad Bhrigunath and Kuar Jagrani; m. Madhuri Sharon, July 4, 1965; children: Manisha, Chetna. Diploma in nuc. power, Stratch Clyde U., Glasgow, Scotland, 1962; diploma Radiochemistry, Leicester (Eng.) Poly., 1964, PhD in Solid State Chemistry, 1967. Cert. chemistry. Rsch. assoc. Leicester Poly., 1964-67; postdoctoral fellow Bolton (U.K.) Inst. Tech., 1967-69, Manchester (U.K.) U., 1969-70; assoc. prof. Himachal Pradesh (India) U., 1970-73; reader Pune (India) U., 1973-78; prof. in chemistry Indian Inst. Tech., Mumbai, India, 1978—. Editor: Photoelectrochemical Solar Cell, 1983. With Nat. Cadet Corps India, 1957-60. Fellow Royal Soc. Chemistry London, Electro Chem. Soc. India; mem. NAS (life). Hindu. Achievements include research in solar energy, electrochemistry of semiconductor, carbon nano materials. Avocations: painting, music. Fax: 00 91 22 5767152. Office: Chemistry Dept, Indian Inst Tech, Mumbai India

SHARON, MOSHE, Islamic history educator; b. Haifa, Israel, Dec. 18, 1937; s. Abraham and Victoria (Zeide) S.; m. Judith Howitt; 6 children. BA, Hebrew U., Jerusalem, 1961, MA, 1964, PhD in Islamic History, 1971. Lectr. Hebrew U., Jerusalem, 1971-74, sr. lectr., 1974-81, assoc. prof., 1981-89, prof., 1989—; prof. U. Witwatersrand, Johannesburg, South Africa, 1988-93, Barllan U., Ramat Gan, Israel, 1989-97; advisor on Arab affairs to Israel's premier, 1977-79, established chair for Bahá'í studies Hebrew U., 1999, first incumbent; affiliated prof. religion Landegg Acad., Switzerland. Author: Black Banners From the East I, 1983, Black Banners From the East II, 1990, Judaism Christianity and Islam, 1989, Judaism in the Context of Diverse Civilizations, 1993, Corpus Inscriptionum Arabicarum Palaestinae (CIAP), 1997, 99. Mem. Israel's Film Rating Bd., Jerusalem, 1985—. Col. (res.) Israeli Def. Force. Rsch. grantee Israel Acad. Scis., Jerusalem, 1989, 93-95, 96-99, Getty grantee Getty Found., L.A., 1995. Home: 9 Midbar Sinai, 97805 Jerusalem Israel Office: Hebrew U, Mount Scopus, 91905 Jerusalem Israel

SHARON, NATHAN, biochemist; b. Brisk, Poland, Nov. 4, 1925; arrived in Israel, 1934; m. Rachel Itzikson, 1948; children: Esther, Osnat. MS, Hebrew U., Jerusalem, 1950, PhD, 1953; Dr. (hon.), U. Rene Descartes, Paris, 1990. Rsch. asst. Agrl. Rsch. Sta., Rehovot, Israel, 1949-53; rsch. asst. dept. biophysics Weizmann Inst. Sci., Rehovot, Israel, 1954-57, rsch. assoc. dept. biophysics, 1957-60, sr. scientist dept. biophysics, 1960-65, assoc. prof. dept. biophysics, 1965-68, prof. dept. biophysics, 1968-90; prof. emeritus, 1991—; vis. scientist numerous univs. and colls. Author: Complex Carbohydrates: Their Chemistry, Biosynthesis and Functions, 1975; co-editor: Biotechnological Applications of Proteins and Enzymes, 1977, The Lectins: Properties, Functions and Applications in Biology and Medicine, 1986; co-author: Lectins, 1989; contbr. over 400 articles to profl. jours. Recipient Laundau prize Mifal Hapyis, Israel, 1973, Weizmann prize in exact scis. City of Tel Aviv, 1977, Olitzki prize Israel Soc. Microbiology, 1989, Datta lectureship award Fedn. European Biochem. Socs., 1987, Bijvoet medal Utrecht U., 1989, Israel Prize in Biomedical and Medical Research, 1994. Mem. Am. Chem. Soc., Biochem. Soc. Eng., Am. Soc. Biol. Chemists (hon.), European Molecular Biology Orgn., Israel Acad. Scis. and Humanities, Academia Europaea, Internat. Sci. Writers Assn., Israel Biochem. Soc. (pres. 1969-70), Soc. for Complex Carbohydrates, Fedn. European Biochem. Socs. (chmn. 1980-81), Internat. Glycoconjugate Orgn. (pres. 1989-91). Avocation: swimming. Home: 77 Mishmeret, Afeka Tel Aviv 69012, Israel Office: Weizmann Inst Sci, Biol Chemistry, Rehovot 76100, Israel

SHAROV, ALEXANDER NICK, financial exchange executive; b. Putivl, Ukraine, Oct. 17, 1954; s. Nick Zakhar and Valentine Mitrophan (Peerohova) S.; m. Tanya Dmitry Sheshneva, Oct. 6, 1953; 1 child, Diana. MA in Econs., Inst. Nat. Economy, Ternopil, Ukraine, 1976; PhD in Econs., Inst. World Economy, Moscow, 1983; DSc in Econs., Inst. Europe, Moscow, 1995. Mgr. Stroy-bank, Ternopil, 1978-84; asst. prof. Inst. Nat. Economy, Ternopil, 1984-92; dep. gov. Nat. Bank of Ukraine, Kiev, 1992-93; 1st v.p. Ukrainian Fin. Group, Kiev, 1993-97; v.p. Inst. Banking, Kiev, 1997-98; chmn. Gold Bullion Exch., Kiev, 1998—; CEO Nat. Depository, Kiev, 1999—; cons. parliament, Kiev, 1991-92; alt. gov. IMF, Washington, 1992-93; vis. prof. Trianandra, Jakarta, Indonesia, 1994; pres. Vito Bank, Kiev, 1995-97; prof. Inst. Nat. Economy, Ternopil, 1992—; chief arbiter Interbank Exch., Kiev, 1995—; academician Entrepreneurial Acad., Moscow, 1996. Author: Currency Convertability, 1995; author, editor: Gold Bullion Markets, 1998; mem. editl. com. Nat. Bank Rev., 1995—, World of Money, 1997—. Fellow Assembly Nobilities, Kiev, 1997. Served with Ukrainian mil., 1976-77. Avocations: tennis, travel, history. Office: Gold Bullion Exch Inst, 1 Mizhgirska Str, 254070 Kiev Ukraine

SHARP, CHRISTOPHER, occupational physician; b. London, Mar. 3, 1952. MB BS, London U., 1975. Sr. med. officer Royal Air Force, 1978-95; head med. dept. Nat. Radiol. Protection Bd., U.K., 1995-99; group med. adviser Anglian Water, 1999—; co. med. officer Brit. Nuclear Fuels, Sellafield, 1993; cons. Internat. Atomic Energy Agy., Vienna, 1995-99; hon. sr. clin. lectr. Oxford U., 1995-99. Fellow Royal Coll. Physicians; mem. Royal Coll. General Practitioners, Faculty Occupl. Medicine, Royal Aero. Soc. Avocations: computers, aviation. Office: Anglian Water, Ambury Rd, Huntingdon PE18 6NZ, England

SHARP, DAVID HOWLAND, physicist; b. Buffalo, N.Y., Oct. 14, 1938; s. Russel Howland and Margaret (Dorries) E.; m. Gloria Evanitsky, Jan. 9, 1982; children: Lisa E., Michelle L.; stepchildren: Brian P. Riepe, Michael A. Riepe. AB, Princeton U., 1960; PhD, Calif. Inst. Tech., 1964. Fellow Los Alamos (N.Mex.) Nat. Lab., 1984—. Fellow AAAS, Am. Phys. Soc. Home: 174 Laguna St Los Alamos NM 87544-2603

SHARP, DOUGLAS ANDREW, secondary school educator; b. Austin, Tex., July 19, 1945; s. Jack Weston and Jean Ernestine (Beeman) S.; m. Marylin Gene Martin, Jan. 20, 1977. BA in Math., Tex. A&M U., 1967, MS in Math., 1970, postgrad., 1969-71; EdD, La Salle U., Mandville, La., 1993. Teaching fellow dept. math. Tex. A&M U., College Station, 1967-71; chmn. math. dept., asst. coach/coach athletics dept. Southfield Sch., Shreveport, La., 1972-73; coach athletics dept. St. John's Sch., Houston, 1975, chmn. math. dept., 1981-93, master teaching chair math., 1987-89; disting. vis. lectr. U. Houston, 1989-90, adj. prof., 1990. Contbr. articles to profl. jours. Recipient Excellence in Teaching award Fin. Dept. U. Houston, 1993, Outstanding Tchr. award Tandy Technol. Scholars, 1993-94. Mem. Am. Math. Soc., Am. Soc. Composer, Authors and Pubs., Am. Statistical Assn., Math. Assn. Am. (Edyth May Stiffe award 1991, 97), Calculus and Elem. Analysis Tchrs. Houston, Nat. Coun. Tchrs. Math., Cum Laude Soc. Office: St John's Sch 2401 Claremont Ln Houston TX 77019-5897

SHARP, J(AMES) FRANKLIN, finance educator, investment portfolio manager; b. Johnson County, Ill., Sept. 29, 1938; s. James Albert and Edna Mae (Slack) S. B.S. in Indsl. Engring., U. Ill., 1960; M.S., Purdue U., 1962, Ph.D., 1966, cert. mgmt. acctg., 1979. Chartered fin. analyst, 1980; cert. in fin. mgmt., 1997. Asst. prof. engring., econs. Rutgers U., New Brunswick, N.J., 1966-70; assoc. prof. NYU Grad. Sch. Bus., N.Y.C., 1970-74; supr. bus. research AT&T, N.Y.C., 1974-77, dist. mgr. corp. planning, 1977-81, dist. mgr. fin. mgmt. and planning, 1981-85; prof. fin. Grad. Sch. Bus. Pace U., N.Y.C., 1975-91; chmn. Sharp CFA Rev. & Inst. for Investment Edn., 1987-96, Sharp Seminars, 1996—; speaker, moderator meetings, 1965—; cons. Sharp Investment Mgmt., 1967—. Contbr. numerous articles to profl. publs.; corr.: Interfaces, 1975-78; fin. editor: Planning Rev., 1975-78. Mem. N.Am. Soc. Corp. Planning (treas. 1976-77, bd. dirs. at large 1977-78), Inst. Mgmt. Sci. (chpt. v.p. acad. 1972-74, chpt. v.p. program 1974-75, chpt. v.p. membership 1975-76, chpt. pres. 1976-77), Internat. Affiliation Planning Socs. (coun. 1978-84), N.Y. Soc. Security Analysts (CFA Rev. 1985-87), Ops. Rsch. Soc. Am. (pres. corp. planning group 1976-82), AAUP (v.p. Pace U. chpt. 1988-90), Theta Xi. Republican. Office: 315 E 86th St Apt 7H New York NY 10028-4740

SHARP, PAUL MARTIN, genetics researcher; b. Heanor, Derbyshire, U.K., Dec. 9, 1957; s. Maurice Hicking and Wendy Joyce Griffiths Sharp; m. Bridget Ellen Smith, Sept. 12, 1996. BSc, U. Edinburgh, Scotland, 1979, PhD, 1982. Lectr. in genetics Trinity Coll., U. Dublin, Ireland, 1982-92, assoc. prof., 1992-93; prof. U. Nottingham, U.K., 1993—. Editor: Evolution of Microbial Life, 1996; assoc. editor Molecular Biology and Evolution, 1993-97; contbr. over 100 articles to profl. jours. Mem. European Molecular Biology Orgn., Royal Irish Acad. Avocation: cricket. Office: Inst Genetics U Nottingham, Queens Med Ctr, Nottingham NG7 2UH, United Kingdom

SHARP, PHILLIP ALLEN, biologist, educator; b. Ky., June 6, 1944; s. Joseph Walter and Katherin (Colvin) S.; m. Ann Christine Holcombe, Aug. 29, 1964; children: Christine Alynn, Sarah Katherin, Helena Holcombe. BA, Union Coll., Barbourville, Ky., 1966, LHD (hon.), 1991; PhD, U. Ill., 1969; DSc (hon.), U. Ky., 1994, Bowdoin Coll., 1995, U. Tel Aviv, Israel, 1996, Albright Coll., 1996; hon. degree, U. Glasgow, 1998, U. Uppsala, 1999, Thomas Moore Coll., 1999. NIH postdoctoral fellow Calif. Inst. Tech., 1969-71; sr. research investigator Cold Spring Harbor (N.Y.) Lab., 1972-74; assoc. prof. MIT, Cambridge, 1974-79, prof. biology, 1979-99, Inst. prof., 1999—, head dept. biology, 1991-99, dir. Ctr. Cancer Rsch., 1985-91; co-founder, mem. sci. bd., dir. BIOGEN, 1978—, chmn. sci. bd., 1987—; mem. Pres.' Adv. Coun. on Sci. and Tech., 1991-97; trustee Alfred P. Sloan Found., 1995—; mem. presdl. appt. Nat. Cancer Adv. Bd., NIH, 1996—; chmn. GM Cancer Rsch. Found. Awards Assembly, 1994—; mem. sci. bd. Ludwig Inst., 1998—; founding dir. McGovern Inst. for Brain Rsch., 2000—. Mem. editl. bd. Cell, 1974-95, Jour. Virology, 1974-86, Molecular and Cellular Biology, 1974-85, RNA, 1995—. Co-recipient Nobel Prize in Physiology or Medicine, 1993; recipient awards Am. Cancer Soc., 1974-79, awards Eli Lilly, 1980, awards Nat Acad. Sci./U.S. Steel Found., 1980, Howard Ricketts award U. Chgo., 1985, Alfred P. Sloan Jr. prize Gen. Motors Research Found., 1986, award Gairdner Found. Internat., 1986, award N.Y. Acad. Scis., 1986, Louisa Horwitz prize, 1988, Albert Lasker Basic Med. Rsch. award, 1988, Dickson prize U. Pitts., 1990, Benjamin Franklin medal Am. Philos. Soc., 1999; awarded Class of '41 chair, 1986-87, John D. MacArthur chair, 1987-92, Salvador E. Luria chair, 1992-99, Benjamin Franklin medal, 199. Fellow AAAS; mem. Am. Chem. Soc., Am. Soc. Microbiology, NAS (councilor 1986), Am. Acad. Arts and Scis, European Molecular Biology Orgn. (assoc.), Am. Soc. Biochemistry and Molecular Biology (elected mem. coun.), Am. Philos. Soc. (elected mem.), Inst. of Medicine of NAS (elected mem.). Home: 36 Fairmont Ave Newton MA 02458-2506 Office: MIT Ctr for Cancer Rsch 40 Ames St Rm E17529B Cambridge MA 02142-1308

SHARPE, DAVID THOMAS, plastic surgeon, consultant; b. Gravesend, Kent, England, Jan. 14, 1946; s. Albert Edward and Grace Emily (Large) S.; m. Patricia Lillian Meredith, Jan. 23, 1971; children: Timothy Richard Briney, Katherine Anna, Caroline Louise. BA in English Lit. with honors, Cambridge U., Eng., 1967; MA MB BChir, Cantab, 1970. House surgeon Radclifee Infirmary, Oxford, Eng., 1970-71; with accident svc. pathology dept. Radclifee Infirmary, Oxford, 1972-73; sr. officer in plastic surgery Churchill Hosp., Oxford, 1971-72; gen. surgery Royal United Hosp., Bath, Eng., 1973-75; registrar in plastic surgery Chepstow, 1976-78; with Canniesburn Hosp., Glasgow, Scotland, 1978-80; sr. registrar in plastic surgery Leeds and Bradford, 1980-84; cons. plastic surgeon Bradford Royal Hosp. and Huddersfield Infirmary, Eng., 1985—; prof. plastic reconstructive surgery Bradford U., 1997—. Contbr. numerous articles to profl. jours. Recipient Prince of Wales award for Innovation and Technology, 1988, awards Design Coun. Fellow Royal Coll. Surgeons; mem. Brit. Assn. Aesthetic Plastic Surgeons (pres. 1997-98), Brit. Assn. Plastic Surgery, Brit. Helicopter Adv. Bd. Avocations: flying, shooting. Office: The Yorkshire Clinic, Bradford Rd, Bingley West Yorkshire BD16 1TW, England

SHARPE, DONALD CHARLES, service manager; b. Durham, N.C., July 28, 1956; s. Lawrence Albright and Virginia Ann (Pacofsky) S. Electrician, ICS Corr. Schs., Scranton, Pa., 1983. Cert. chlorofluorocarbons, motor vehicle air conditioning, pool and spa operator, notary pub., N.C., 1997; lic. real estate agt., N.C. Electrician USN, 1974-88; maintenance engr. Holiday Inn Exec. Ctr., Virginia Beach, Va., 1988-94; ind. contractor Virginia Beach, 1994-95; maintenance asst. Sterling Forest Apts. Grubb Mgmt., Raleigh, N.C., 1995; svc. supr. Sterling Brook Apts. Grubb Mgmt., Carrboro, N.C., 1995-98; svc. mgr. Four Seasons Apartments, Raleigh, N.C., 1998-2000, Summit Properties, Durham, N.C., 2000—. Republican. Christian. Avocations: rare collectibles and books, archaeology, biblical research, history.

SHARPE, KENNETH JOSEPH, financial services executive; b. Dunfermline, Fife, Scotland; s. William and Henrietta Bryden (Wallace) S.; m. Margaret Georgina Prince, FEb. 17, 1968; 4 children. Gard. h.s.,

Dunfermline. Cert. fin. planner. Clerical officer Civil Svc., Dunfermline, 1964-68; asst. mgr. Provident Clothing & Supply Co. Ltd., Edinburgh, Scotland, 1968-71; prison officer Civil Svc., Edinburgh, 1971-73; area mgr. United Friendly Ins. Co. Ltd., Scotland, 1973-92; mgr. Citibank Fin. Svcs., Scotland, 1992-93; sr. mgr. Caesar & Howie, Solicitors, Bathgate, West Lothian, Scotland, 1993-97; propr. Total Mortgage Solutions, Bathgate, 1997—. Avocations: sports, gardening, holiday, travel. Home and Office: 87 Whitelaw Rd, Dunfermline KY11 4BN, Scotland

SHARPE, ROBERT KENT, writer, director, producer, photographer; b. Chgo., Nov. 17, 1930; s. Byron C. and Helen Lee S.; m. Mary Kahn, 1955 (div. 1971); children: Steven W., Sharon E., Jonathan K., Julia A.; m. T. Tina Ditta, Apr. 26, 1980. BA in English, Brown U., 1953. Writer, dir. Ford Found., N.Y.C., 1956-57, CBS, N.Y.C., 1957-58; writer, dir. NBC Spl. Projects Dept., N.Y.C., 1959-61, free-lance dir., 1962-63; pres. Robert K. Sharpe Prodns., Inc., Ardsley, N.Y., 1965—, Hastings on Hudson, N.Y., 1965—; pres. RKS Devel. Corp., Ardsley, 1963-75. Producer, writer, dir.: (documentary) Before the Mountain Was Moved, 1969 (awards 1969-70); writer, dir.: (shorts) Night in a Pet Ship, 1959 (awards 1959-60), producer, writer, dir. (shorts) Pancho, 1966-67 (awards 1966-67), Joe, 1965 (awards 1965), Face of Excellence, 1962, The Forgotten, 1958 (awards 1958-59); screenwriter: (films) WFAT, 1982, The Long Night, 1962, Barbero, 1983, A Dead Issue, 1963, Computer, 1965, A Letter Home, 1965, Squaw Gap Speaking, 1976; dir.: (television) The Twentieth Century Series, 1962-63, Keep It Cool, Rhodes Scholar, The Jazz of Dave Brubeck, The Songs of Harold Arlen, Fire Brand on Ice - Stan Mikita, Here is New York, Buildings for Business and Government, Call it Courage, Equestrianism, others; staff writer, dir.: (television) Wisdom Series, 1959-61, The Ordeal of Woodrow Wilson as Told by President Herbert Hoover, The Seven Lively Arts Series, Omibus Series, 1956-57; producer, dir. (films) The Great Debate, 1963; writer, dir. (films) Light as You Like It, 1958; photographic series Assisi, 1953, Spanish Patterns, 1990, Interplay, 1998, The Unseen, 1999. Mem. Am. Soc. Media Photographers, Dirs. Guild Am., Photographic Adminstrs., Inc., Phi Beta Kappa. Democrat. Jewish. Avocations: photography, amateur radio, HI-FI & electronics, wood working. Home and office: 765 N Broadway Apt 15E Hastings Hdsn NY 10706-1056

SHARPE, WILLIAM FORSYTH, economics educator; b. Cambridge, Mass., June 16, 1934; s. Russell Thornley Sharpe and Evelyn Forsyth (Jillson) Maloy; m. Roberta Ruth Branton, July 2, 1954 (div. Feb. 1986); children: Deborah Ann, Jonathan Forsyth; m. Kathryn Dorothy Peck, Apr. 5, 1986. AB, UCLA, 1955, MA, 1956, PhD, 1961; DHL honoris causa, DePaul U., 1997. Economist Rand Corp., 1957-61; asst. prof. econs. U. Wash., 1961-63, assoc. prof., 1963-67, prof., 1967-68; prof. U. Calif., Irvine, 1968-70; Timken prof. fin. Stanford U., 1970-89, Timken prof. emeritus, 1989-92; prin. William F. Sharpe Assocs., 1986-92; prof.fin. Stanford U., 1993-95, STANCO 25 prof. fin., 1995-99, emeritus, 1999—; chmn. Financial Engines, Inc., 1996—. Author: The Economics of Computers, 1969, Portfolio Theory and Capital Markets, 1970; co-author: Fundamentals of Investments, 1989, 2d edit., 1993, 3d edit., 2000, Investments, 6th edit., 1999. With U.S. Army, 1956-57. Recipient Graham and Dodd award Fin Analysts' Fedn., 1972, '73, '86-88. Nicholas Molodovsky award, 1989. Nobel prize in econ. scis., 1990, UCLA medal, 1998. Mem. Am. Fin. Assn. (v.p. 1979, pres. 1980), Western Fin. Assn. (Enduring Contbn. award 1989), Ea. Fin. Assn. (Disting. Scholar award 1991), Am. Econ. Assn., Phi Beta Kappa.

SHARPLES, THOMAS DAVY, retired mechanical engineer; b. West Chester, Pa., Sept. 3, 1916; s. Philip M. and Jean Watt (Davy) S.; m. Renate Adele Backhausen, Sept. 20, 1948; children: Thomas D. Jr., Hendrik W. Student, Calif. Inst. Tech., 1935-37, Swarthmore Coll., 1937-39. Owner Art Tech. Studio and Sch. of Photography, South Pasadena, Calif., 1939-42; dir. rsch. Sharples Corp., Phila., 1948-51, mgr. product design, 1952-65; chief mech. engr. Beckman Instruments, Inc., Palo Alto, Calif., 1966-74; mgr. product design Beckman Instruments, Inc., Palo Alto, 1974-84, engring. staff specialist, 1985-88, mgr. engring. rsch., 1988-91; owner Sharples Engring., Junction City, Oreg., 1991—. Patentee in field. Capt. U.S. Army, 1942-46, North Africa, ETO. Named Beckman fellow, 1991. Mem. Photographic Soc. of Am., Soc. Mfg. Engineers, Am. AAAS, History of Science Soc. Republican. Soc. of Friends. Avocations: antique scientific books and instruments, microscopy, glass blowing, machine shop. E-mail: TDSENG@aol.com. Home: 128 Heather Dr Atherton CA 94027-2120 Office: Sharples Engring 91448 Steinmetz Rd Junction City OR 97448-9540

SHARPLES, WINSTON SINGLETON, automobile importer and distributor; b. Springfield, Mass., Oct. 24, 1932; s. Winston Singleton and Carmela (Parrino) S.; m. Jeanette Williams, July 1961 (div. Apr. 1981); children: John, Hadley, Gillian; m. Ruth Emily Lissak, June 26, 1981. BA, Harvard Coll., 1953; postgrad. drama, Yale U., 1956-57; MFA, Carnegie Mellon U., 1959; postgrad., Univ. Md., 1978-80. Freelance writer, 1959—; producer, dir. Mon. Valley Playhouse, Charleroi, Pa., 1959, Robin Hood Theater, Arden, Del., 1960-61; pres., film and music editor Synchro-Sound Inc., N.Y.C., 1961-71; prof. CUNY, N.Y.C., 1969-74, Temple Univ., Phila., 1974-76, U. Md., College Park, 1978-79; adminstr. film preservation and documentation Am. Film Inst., Washington, 1976-78; prof. Howard Univ., Washington, 1978-80; pres. Cantab Motors, Ltd., Purcellville, Va., 1984—. Author: (with others) A Primer for Film-Making, 1971—; supr. Am. Film Inst. Catalog of Feature Films, 1960-69, 77; editor, music editor films and cartoons; contbr. articles to profl. jours. and mags. With U.S. Army, 1953-56. Nat. Endowment for the Humanities grantee, 1977. Mem. ASCAP, Archeol. Soc. Va., Am. Studies Assn., Univ. Film Assn. (v.p. 1975-76), Soc. for Cinema Studies, Soc. Automotive Engrs., Washington Automotive Press Assn., Morgan Car Club, Land Rover Owners Assn. Va., British Automobile Mfrs. Assn., Harvard Club (N.Y.C.). Democrat. Avocations: forestry, archeology. Home: 16657 Tree Crops Ln Round Hill VA 20141-2236 Office: Cantab Motors Ltd Valley Indsl Park 37251 E Richardson Ln Purcellville VA 20132-3505

SHARPLESS, JOSEPH BENJAMIN, former county official; b. Takoma Park, Md., Feb. 4, 1933; s. William Raiford and Julia Maude (Rouse) S.; m. Nancy Kathleen Steffen, July 28, 1962 (dec. Feb. 1988); 1 child, Carole Marie. BA, Earlham Coll., 1955; MS, Pa. State U., 1960. Instr. recreation Montgomery County Recreation Dept., Rockville, Md., 1957-58; from program supr. to dir. Recreation and Parks Dept., Livingston, N.J., 1959-70; chief recreation svc. Md.-Nat. Capital Park and Planning Commn. Prince George's County, Riverdale, Md., 1970-77, parks and recreation div. chief, 1977-95; ret., 1995—. Contbr. articles to profl. jours. V.p. Montpelier Cmty. Assn., South Laurel, Md., 1983-84, pres., 1985; mem. Md. Sports Adv. Com., 1988-92; Md. State Games Commr., 1986-91; bd. regents, instr. Sch. Sports Mgmt., N.C. State U., 1989-92; nat. volleyball chmn. AAU, 1966-69, 72, volleyball chmn. N.J. chpt. 1961-70, volleyball chmn. Potomac Valley chpt., 1971-73; U.S.A. volleyball nat. commr., 1976-81; mem. volleyball games staff 1996 Olympic Games, Atlanta; staff World Volleyball Congress, Atlanta, 1996; dir. volleyball Spl. Olympics Internat., 1994—, tech. del. Spl. Olympic World Summer Games, 1999; trustee U.S. Volleyball Edn. Found., 1976—, sec., 1996—; pres. NJAAU, 1968-70. Recipient Pioneer award AAU, 1998. Fellow Nat. Recreation Parks Assn. (Berman Profl. Citation award Mid-Atlantic Regional Coun. 1995, Disting. Svc. award 1995); mem. U.S. Volleyball Assn. (bd. dirs. 1973—, mem. exec. com. 1976-80, 85-89, 92-96, v.p. 1973-90, 96—, regional commr. 1965-78, nat. ofcl. 1967-96, exec. cons. 1989-91, corp. sec. 1992-96, mng. editor pubs. 1994-98, numerous awards), Nat. Intercollegiate Soccer Ofcls. Assn. (sec. 1966-68, treas. 1968-70), Am. Park and Recreation Soc. (bd. dirs. 1977-80, nat. coun., coun. affiliate pres.), N.J. Recreation and Pks. Assn. (sec. 1965, v.p. 1966, pres. 1967), Md. Recreation and Pk. Assn. (v.p. 1975-77, pres. 1977-78, Mem. of Yr. 1975, Citation 1985), Ret. Life Profl. (Disting. Fellow award 1996), Sch. and College Soccer Officials Assn. (sec., treas. 1965-70), N.J. Soccer Ofcls. Assn. (sec./treas. 1966-70), Nat. Capitol Area Bd. Volleyball Ofcls. (sec. 1985-89). Republican. Mem. Soc. of Friends. Home: 26205 S Cedarcrest Dr Sun Lakes AZ 85248-7206

SHARPS, JOHN GEOFFREY, retired psychologist, author; b. Weaverham, Northwich, Eng., July 29, 1936; s. John Richard and Nellie (Street) S.; m. Heather Acheson, Aug. 19, 1966; children: Rosalind Helen May, Paul George John. MA in English (hons.), U. Edinburgh, Scotland, 1958; MEd in Psychology, Queen's U. Belfast, Northern Ireland, 1963; MLitt in English, U. Oxford, Eng., 1964; BTh (hons.), U. Hull, Eng., 1992. Chartered psychologist, chartered ednl. psychologist. Part-time lectr. Mid-Cheshire Ctrl. Coll. Further Edn., Hartford, Cheshire, Eng., 1963-64; lectr. North Riding Coll. Edn., Scarborough, Eng., 1964-71, sr. lectr., 1971-87. Author: Mrs. Gaskell's Observation and Invention: A Study of Her Non-Biographic Works, 1970. Fellow Royal Soc. Arts, Royal Geog. Soc., Royal Econ. Soc.; assoc. fellow Brit. Psychol. Soc. Mem. Liberal Democratic Party. Anglican. Avocations: reading, television, films, theatre, book collecting. Home: 25 Cornelian Dr, Scarborough N Yorksh YO11 3AL, England

SHARROCK, JOHN TIMOTHY ROBIN, editor; b. Alphington, Devon, Eng., Dec. 6, 1937; s. John Norman and Maisie Flora (Storey) S.; m. Erika Marion Otte, Aug. 4, 1961 (div. Apr. 1997); children: Lorna Wendy, John Kieran Clive. BSc, U. Southampton, Eng., 1959, PhD, 1967. Rschr. Potato Mktg. Bd., Bedfordshire, Eng., 1963-66; head of survey sect. Nat. Inst. Agrl. Engring., Bedfordshire, 1966-69; nat. organizer Breeding Bird Atlas Brit. Trust for Ornithology, Tring, Hertfordshire, Eng., 1969-76; mng. editor British Birds, Blunham, Bedford, 1976—; mem. coun. Cape Clear Bird Obs., 1970—, pres.; pres. Bedfordshire Bird Club, 1996—. Author: The Atlas of Breeding Birds in Britain and Ireland, 1976, Scarce Migrant Birds in Britain and Ireland, 1973, The Birdwatchers' Quiz and Puzzle Book, 1976; editor/author: The Natural History of Cape Clear Island, 1974. Mem. Brit. Trust for Ornithology (hon.), Brit. Ornithologists' Union (past coun. mem.). Mem. Liberal Democrats Party. Avocations: birdwatching, bridge, good food, spectator of speedway. Home and Office: Fountains, Park Ln Blunham, Bedford MK44 3NJ, England

SHARROW, MARILYN JANE, library administrator; b. Oakland, Calif.; d. Charles L. and H.Evelyn Sharrow; m. Larry J. Davis. BS in Design, U. Mich., 1967, MALS, 1969. Libr. Detroit Pub. Libr., 1968-70; head fine arts dept. Syracuse (N.Y.) U. Librs., 1970-73; dir. libr. Roseville (Mich.) Pub. Libr., 1973-75; asst. dir. librs. U. Wash., Seattle, 1975-77, assoc. dir. librs., 1978-79; dir. librs. U. Man., Winnipeg, Can., 1979-82; chief libr. U. Toronto, Can., 1982-85; libr. U. Calif., Davis, 1985—; chair bd. North Regional Libr. Facility, 1999—. Recipient Woman of Yr. in Mgmt. award Winnipeg YWCA, 1982; named Woman of Distinction, U. Calif. Faculty Women's Rsch. Group, 1985. Mem. ALA, Assn. Rsch. Librs. (bd. dirs., v.p., pres.-elect 1989-90, pres. 1990-91, chair sci. tech. work group 1994-98, rsch. collections com. 1993-95, 2000—, preservation com. 1997-99), Online Computer Libr. Ctr.-Rsch. Librs. Adv. Com. (vice-chair 1992-93, chair 1993-94), Calif. State Network Resources Libr. Com. Office: U Calif Shields Libr 100 NW Quad Davis CA 95616-5292

SHARTLE, STANLEY MUSGRAVE, consulting engineer, land surveyor; b. Brazil, Ind., Sept. 27, 1922; s. Arthur Tinder and Mildred C. (Musgrave) S.; m. Anna Lee Mantle, Apr. 7, 1948; 1 child: Randy. Student, Purdue U., 1947-50. Registered profl. engr., land surveyor. Ind. chief dep. surveyor Hendricks County (Ind.), 1941-42; asst. to hydrographer Fourteenth Naval Dist., Pearl Harbor, Hawaii, 1942-44; dep. county surveyor Hendricks County (Ind.), Danville, 1944-50, county engr., surveyor, 1950-54, county hwy. engr., 1975-77; staff engr. Ind. Toll Rd. Commn., Indpls., 1954-61; chief right of way engring. Ind. State Hwy. Commn., Indpls., 1961-75; owner, civil engr. Shartle Engring., Indpls., 1977-89; prin. Parsons Cunningham & Shartle Engrs., Inc., Indpls., 1990—; right of way engring. cons. Gannett Fleming Transp. Engrs., Inc., Indpls., 1983-88; part-time lectr. Purdue U. for Ind. State Hwy. Commn., 1965-67. Prin. works include residential subdiv., 1989 (named Indiana's Most Successful Ind. Bus. Jour., 1989); author: Right of Way Engineering Manual, 1975, Musgrave Family History, 1961, 95, Shartle Genealogy, 1955; contbr. tech. articles in sci. jours. Ex-officio mem., charter mem. exec. sec. Hendricks County (Ind.) Plan Commn., 1951-54; mem. citizen adv. com. Hendricks County Subdivision Control Ordinance, 1988—; citizens adv. com. transp. Indpls. Met. Planning Area. Recipient Outstanding Contbn. award Hendricks County Soil and Water Conservation Dist., 1976; Stanley Shartle Day proclaimed by Hendricks County, Ind., 1997. Mem. Am. Congress Surveying and Mapping (life), Nat. Soc. Profl. Surveyors, Ind. Soc. Profl. Land Surveyors (charter, life, bd. dirs. 1979), Nat. Geneal. Soc. (Quarter Century club), Ind. Toll Road Employees Assn. (pres. 1959-60), Internat. Right of Way Assn. (charter, founder chpt. 10), Geog. and Land Info. Soc., Indpls. Scientech Club. Republican. Avocations: astronomy, genealogy, geodesy. Home and Office: 6575 Kings Ct Avon IN 46123-9075

SHARVIT, URI, music educator; b. Jerusalem, Oct. 24, 1939; m. Bruria Pasternak. Diploma, Rubin Acad. Music, Jerusalem, 1965; BA, Hebrew U., Israel, 1968; MA, Columbia U., 1971, PhD, 1977. Prof. music Bar-Ilan U., Ramat Gan, Israel, 1973—; prof. ethnomusicology Rubin Acad. Music, 1975—; chmn. jury Internat. Klezmers Festivals, Safed, Israel, 1990-93; dir. ethnic music master classes Jerusalem Music Ctr., 1996-99. Author: A Treasury of Jewish Yemenite Chants, 1981, Chassidic Tunes from Galicia, 1995; composer Passacaglia for symphony orch., 1971 (League Israeli Composers, Authors and Publishers 1st prize 1971), Tehila for a capella chorus, 1980 (League Israeli Composers, Authors and Publishers 1st prize 1980). Mem. music bd. Nat. Coun. for Culture and Art, 1994—. Mem. Internat. Orgn. Jewish Studies, League Israel Composers, Internat. Coun. Traditional Music. Home: 10 Tsemah St, 96190 Jerusalem Israel Office: Bar-Ilan U, Music Dept, 52900 Ramat Gan Israel

SHARY, SERGEY PETROVICH, mathematician; b. Semipalatinsk, USSR, Mar. 24, 1962; m. Irene Alexandrovna Sharaya; children: Anastasiya, Maria, Svetlana. MS, Novosibirsk (Russia) State U., 1985; PhD in Math. and Mechanics, Russian Acad. Scis., Ekaterinburg, 1992; DSc in Computer Math., Russian Acad. Scis., Novosibirsk, 2000. Rschr. Computer Ctr. Siberian br. Russian Acad. Scis., Krasnoyarsk, 1985-95; sr. rschr. Inst. Computational Techs. Siberian br. Russian Acad. Scis., Novosibirsk, 1995—. Office: Russian Acad Scis, Inst Computational Tech, 630090 Novisibirsk Russia

SHASHIDHARA, PRASAD J., physics educator; b. Thimmasandra, Karnataka, India, Nov. 18, 1947; s. D. and Savithramma Javaregowda; m. Revathi Kallegowda, Sept. 10, 1973; 1 child, Shivasundara Sathyendra. BSc, Yuvaraja Coll., Mysore, India, 1966; MSc in Physics, U. Mysore, 1968, PhD in Physics, 1972. Chartered physicist. Lectr. U. Mysore, 1971-75, reader, 1975-84, prof. physics, 1984—, chmn. dept., 1989-91, dean faculty sci., 1989-91, syndicate mem. exec. body, 1993—, acting vice-chancellor, 1990, coord. dept. environ. sci., 1996—; Commonwealth fellow Oxford (Eng.) U., 1976-77; participant various confs.; PhD, MSc bd. examiners Karnatak U.; MSc bd. examiners Mysore U., PhD, MPhil Bd. Examiners, Nagarjuna U.; external expert faculty sci. Gulbarga U., Mangalore U.; external expert faculty sci. Cochin U.; MSc bd. examiners Mangalore U., Kakatiya U., PhD bd. examiners IISc, Bangalore, Burdwan U., Calcutta U., Gulbarga U., Jadavpur U., U. Pondicherry; mem. mgmt. adv. com., rsch. adv. com. IACS, Calcutta; mem. mgmt. adv. com. IIT, Kanpur and IIT, Bombay, X-ray com. RSIC, IIT, Madras; mem. mgmt. adv. com. Ctrl. U., Hyderabad; presenter papers at confs. and seminars. Translator: An Introduction to Solid State Physics (C. Kittel); referee Indian Jour. Pure and Applied Physics; editor Semi-popular Sci. Jour. U. Mysore; chief editor Mysore U. Sci. Jour.; contbr. articles to profl. jours. and encys. Pres. Sri Kuvempu Vidhya Vardhaka Trust, Mysore, 1995—; sec. Dejagow Trust, Mysore, 1989—. Nat. Career awardee U. Grants Commn. India, 1980-83. Fellow Inst. Physics; mem. Indian Assn. Physics Tchrs., Indian Physics Assn., Am. Inst. Physics, Optical Soc. Am., Australian Inst. Physics, Am. Phys. Soc., Internat. Liquid Crystal Soc. (mem. bd.), Indian Liquid Crystal Soc. (mem. coun.). Avocations: yoga and meditation, reading. Home: 49/2 5th Main 3rd Block, Jayalakshmipuram, Mysore 570012, India Office: U Mysore, Dept Studies in Physics, Manasagangothri, Mysore 570 006, India

SHATA, AL-SYED SALEH AHMED, research scientist; b. Makkah, Saudi Arabia, Sept. 25, 1955; s. Ahmed and Rogaiah S.; m. Fatema Omar Waly, 1979; children: Ahmed, Abdul Aziz, Lulwah, Ibrahim, Lotita. BSME, King Fahd U. of Petroleum, and Minerals, 1978. Gen. mgr. Saudi Basic Tech., Jeddah, Saudi Arabia, 1979—, Nargis Flowers, Jeddah, Saudi Arabia, 1979—; dir. Azheathrow Chauffeurs, Ltd., London, 1998—, Saudi Basic Technologies, Ltd., London, 1998—. Mem. IAPA. Office: Saudi Basic Technologies, 209 Kaki Ctr/PO Box 18686, 21425 Jeddah 21425, Kingdom of Saudi Arabia

SHATROV, ANDREY BORISOVICH, biologist; b. Leningrad, Russia, Aug. 28, 1954; s. Boris and Tamara S.; m. Alla Kushnir, Mar. 22, 1979; 1 child, Shatrova. Grad., Leningrad State U., 1978, PhD, 1983; DSc, Zoological Inst., St. Petersburg, Russia, 1995. From asst. to sr. rschr. Zool. Inst. Acad. Sci. Russia, Leningrad, 1972-95; leading rschr. Zool. Inst. Acad. Sci. Russia, St. Petersburg, 1995—. Mem. Russian Entomol. Soc., St. Petersburg Parasitol. Soc. E-mail: chigger@mail.ru. Office: Zool Inst Russian Acad Sci, Universitetskaya nab 1, 199034 St Petersburg Russia

SHATROV, VLADIMIR ANATOLJEVICH, immunologist, researcher; b. Yalta, Ukraine, Sept. 22, 1958; s. Anatoliy Aleksandrovich and Ninel Ivanovna (Bulgakova) S. MD with honors, Crimean Med. Inst., Simferopol, Ukraine, 1981; PhD in Med. Sci., Kiev (Ukraine) Med. Inst., 1985, DSc in Immunology, 1992. Head lab. of allergology Sechenov Rsch. Inst., Yalta, 1985-87; rsch. group leader Crimean Med. Inst., 1987-92; vis. scientist German Cancer Rsch. Ctr., Heidelberg, 1993-96; sr. scientist Inst. Gustave-Roussy, Villejuif, France, 1996—. Contbr. articles to profl. jours. Rsch. grantee German Cancer Rsch. Inst., 1993-95. Mem. AAAS, European Bioelectromagnetics Assn., Ukrainian Soc. Immunologists, N.Y. Acad. Scis. Russian Orthodox. Avocations: hiking, swimming, scuba diving, classical music, literature. Office: U-487 INSERM, 39 rue Camille Desmoulins, 94805 Villejuif France

SHATS, VLADIMIR YAKOV, retired physician, researcher; b. Retchiza, Yomel, USSR, Dec. 1, 1932; arrived in Israel, 1980; s. Yakov Abraham and Ludmila Moshe (Sobolev) S.; m. Juna Uark Korostoshevskaua, Oct. 7, 1960; 1 child, Leonid. MD, Med. U., Omsk, USSR, 1956; PhD, Inst. Oncol. Leningrad, USSR, 1969. Physician Clin. Hosp., Kurgan, Russia, 1956-59, Regional Hosp., Leningrad, 1960-64; researcher Inst. Oncol. Leningrad, 1964-74; sr. biostatician Med. Genetic Ctr., Leningrad, 1974-81; sr. physician Hosp. Safed, Israel, 1981-98; ret., 1999. Author: The Problem of the Sex Formatin in Oncology, 1969, Population Screening for Cancer, 1971, Modern Methods of Treatment in Oncology, 1972, Early Detection of Cancer in Prophylactic Screening, 1975; reviewer Jour. Hazefah, 1997-99; patent for diffusion chamber for inhibition of the second set tumor growth, 1992. Med. officer (jr. lt.) Israeli Def. Forces, 1982-86. Grantee head scientist Min. Health, Safed, Israel, 1987. Mem. Gerontol. Soc. Mem. Merez. Avocations: internet. Home: Str Megido 5/9, 21950 Kazmiel Galil, Israel

SHATSOVA, RAHIL BORISOVNA, astronomer, educator, researcher; b. Homel, Byelorussia, Jan. 24, 1922; d. Boris Notanovich and Sarra Samuilovna (Monastyrskaya) S.; m. Boris Ivanovich Shimchuck, Aug. 18, 1951 (dec. July 1987); 1 child, Galina Borisovna. Higher edn., State U., Leningrad, 1944, postgrad., 1947; D in Physics and Math. Sci. (hon.), State U., Moscow, 1975; prof. theoretical physics chair (hon.), Higher Cert. Commn., Moscow, 1976. Lectr., docent Tchg.-Tng. Coll., Tambov, Russia, 1947-56; docent Tchg.-Tng. Coll., Rostov-on-Don, Russia, 1956-76; prof. State Pedagogical U., Rostov-on-Don, 1976—, chief postgrad., 1962—; docent State U., Rostov-on-Don, 1963-68. Author: Planck's Stellar Velocity Distribution Near the Sun, 1965; editor: Applied Questions of Physics, 1974, The Problems of Astronomical Training for Students in Pedagogical Institute, 1990; contbr. articles to profl. jours. Recipient medal for the totality of sci. works Ministry Higher Edn., 1975; Newton grantee State U., Leningrad, 1943-45. Mem. Russian Astron. Soc., North Caucasus Acad. Informative Edn., N.Y. Acad. Scis, All-Union Astron.-Geodesical Soc. (chmn. Rostov sect. 1963—). Avocation: gardening. E-mail: rozina@rspu.edu.ru. Home: Dneprovsky 124/5-79, 344065 Rostov-on-Don Russia Office: Rostov State Pedagogical U, Dneprovsky 116, 344065 Rostov-on-Don Russia

SHATTOCK, MICHAEL JONATHAN, physiologist, researcher; b. Newtownards, Northern Ireland, Aug. 23, 1958; s. Leonard Charles and Eileen (McCarthy) S.; m. Alison Christine Cave. BSc, U. London, 1979, PhD, 1984. Rsch. asst. St. Thomas Hosp., London, 1979-81, PhD student, 1981-84; postdoctoral rsch. fellow U. Calif., Riverside, 1985-88; sr. rsch. fellow St. Thomas Hosp., 1988-90, lectr. in physiology, 1990-93, sr. lectr. in physiology, 1993-99, reader in cardiac physiology, 1999—; mem. Wellcome Trusts Foresight Study Group on Policy Rsch. in Sci. and Medicine, 1993. Contbr. chpt. to Methods in Neurosciences, Vol. 4, Electrophysiology and Microinjection, 1990; contbr. articles to (jour.) Circulation Rsch., (jour.) Cardiovasc. Rsch., and Am. Jour. Physiology. Recipient Upjohn Young Investigator award Internat. Soc. Heart Rsch., 1989,, Brit. Lab. News award for sci., 1989. Mem. Am. Physiol. Soc., Brit. Cardiac Soc. (abstract reviewing panel 1993—), European Soc. Cardiology (nucleus group on cellular biology 1996—), Physiol. Soc., Internat. Soc. Heart Rsch. Office: St Thomas' Hosp Rayne Inst, Cardiovasc Rsch, London SE1 7EH, England

SHATTUCK, MAYO ADAMS, III, investment bank executive; b. Boston, Oct. 7, 1954; s. Mayo Adams Jr. and Jane (Bergwall) S.; m. Molly Anne George, Sept. 29, 1997; children: Mayo Adams IV, Kathleen Elizabeth, Spencer George. BA, Williams Coll., 1976; MBA, Stanford U., 1980. Analyst Morgan Guaranty Trust Co., N.Y.C., 1976-78; mgr. Bain & Co., Menlo Park, Calif., 1980-83; v.p. to mng. dir. and head of corp. fin. Alex Brown & Sons, San Francisco, 1985-91; pres. and COO Alex Brown & Sons, Balt., 1991-97; co-chmn., CEO BT Alex Brown Inc., from 1997; vice chmn. Bankers Trust N.Y., from 1997; now co-chmn., co-CEO, GA Bank Alex Brown Inc., Balt.; bd. dirs. BGE Corp. Trustee Noble & Greenough Sch.; adv. dir. U. Md., Balt., 1992—, U. Md. Balt. County. Mem. Young Pres. Orgn. Avocations: tennis, golf. Office: GA Baml Alex Brown Inc 1 South St Baltimore MD 21202-3298

SHAUL, ROGER LOUIS, JR., health care consultant, software executive, researcher; b. Hartford, Conn., Jan. 12, 1948; s. Roger Louis Shaul Sr. and Margot (Bradley) Vinson; m. Michele Marie Morland, Dec. 21, 1974; children: Lisa Marie, John Benjamin, Robert Louis. AA, Palm Beach Jr. Coll., Lake Worth, Fla., 1968; BS, U. Fla., 1970, MBA, 1974; cert., Yale U., 1981, U. N.C., 1984, Harvard U., 1998. Adminstrv. resident Univ. Hosp. of Jacksonville, Fla., 1974-79; dir. rev. svcs. Capital Health Sys. Agy., Durham, N.C., 1979; dir. Sun Alliance, Charlotte, N.C., 1979-83; v.p. Sun Health, Inc., Charlotte, 1983-87; pres. Preferred Med. Mktg. Corp., Charlotte, 1987—; adj. faculty, lectr. Duke U., Durham, 1974-78, U. N.C., Chapel Hill, 1974-78; cons. in field. Contbr. articles to profl. jours. Com. mem. Mecklenburg County chpt. ARC, Charlotte, 1985, bd. dirs. Durham County chpt., 1976-79, chmn. fin. com., 1979; mem. missions com. Myers Pk. United Meth. Ch., Charlotte, 1989-95. Mem. Am. Hosp. Assn., Am. Coll. Healthcare Execs., Am. Assn. Preferred Provider Orgn., Healthcare Fin. Mgmt. Assn., Mecklenburg Entrepreneurial Coun., Civitan (pres., v.p., sec. Durham chpt. 1976-79). Republican. Methodist. Avocations: boating, skiing. Office: Preferred Med Mktg Corp Ste 240 7400 Carmel Executive Park Dr Charlotte NC 28226-8415

SHAUMAN, WENDELL L., farmer; b. Monmouth, Ill., Oct. 19, 1945; s. John M. and Ruth L. (Meyer) S.; m. Janet Mae Agan, Aug. 20, 1967; children: Austin, Janelle, Michael. BA in Chemistry, Monmouth Coll., 1967; MS in Agronomy, U. Nebr., 1970, PhD in Genetics, 1971. Rsch. asst. U. Nebr., Lincoln, 1967-71; rsch. scientist Funk Seeds Internat., Inc., Bloomington, Ill., 1971-75; operator Shauman Farms, Kirkwood, Ill., 1975—; dir. Ill. Farm Bur., Bloomington, Country Cos. Ins. Group, Bloomington. Bd. dirs. Yorkwood Sch. dist. 225, Monmouth, Ill., 1985—; mem. fertilizer rsch. and edn. coun., Ill. Dept. Agr., Springfield, 1990-95, 97-99, youth and exec. coun. Warren Co. Ext., Monmouth, 1978-84; treas. Ill. Agrl. Assn. Found., Bloomington, 1997—. Mem. Am. Soc. Agronomy, Ill. Soybean Assn., Coun. for Agrl. Sci. and Tech., Sigma Xi. Presbyterian. E-mail: wshauman@maplecity.com. Office: Shauman Farm 313 Us Highway 34 Kirkwood IL 61447-9756

SHAVER, JUDSON RAYFORD, academic administrator; b. Riverside, Calif., July 29, 1949; s. John Robert and Carol Jean Shaver; m. Deborah Page Boyer, Aug. 27, 1988; children: Nathan Robert, Sarah Margaret. BA, So. Calif. Coll., 1975; MA, U. Notre Dame, 1979, PhD, 1984. Asst. prof. Wheeling (W.Va.) Jesuit Coll., 1980-85; assoc. prof. Seattle U., 1985-90; dean, assoc. prof. Regis U., Denver, 1990-95; provost, v.p. acad. affairs, prof. Iona Coll., New Rochelle, N.Y., 1995—. Author: Torah and the Chronicler's History Work, 1989; contbr. author: Exra and Nehemiah: On the Theological Significance of Making Them Contemporaries, 1992, Passover Legislation and the Identity of the Chronicler's Law Book, 1990; co-author: Understanding the Sunday Readings, 1980. Still fellow, 1983, Fulbright

fellow, 1988, Danforth fellow, 1979, NEH, 1985. Mem. Am. Acad. Religion, Soc. Bibl. Lit., Soc. Values in Higher Edn., Larchmont Shore Club. Roman Catholic. Avocations: golf, theatre. E-mail: jshaver@iona.edu. Office: Iona Coll 715 North Ave New Rochelle NY 10801-1830

SHAVITSKY, ZIVA, Hebrew language and literature educator; b. Tel Aviv, Israel, Mar. 7, 1937; arrived in Australia, 1954; d. Simon Sam and Annie Shiff; m. Maxwell Shavitsky, Dec. 20, 1960; children: Daniel Isaac, Adrian Jonathan, Leora Bella. BA, U. Melbourne, Australia, 1960, MA with 1st class honors, 1969, PhD, 1978. Tutor in Hebrew lang. and lit. U. Melbourne, 1957, 59-60, 1965-78, acting lectr. Hebrew lang. and lit., 1957-58, tutor in Mid. Eastern studies, 1975-78, lectr. in modern Hebrew lang. and lit., 1979-93, Israel Kipen lectr. in modern Hebrew lang. and lit., 1996—, head Jewish studies program, 1997—; vis. scholar Oxford (Eng.) U., Monash U., Melbourne, Hebrew U., Jerusalem, 1996; head state excm. bd. coms. for Hebrew, Victorian Curriculum Assessment Bd., Victorian Inst. Secondary Edn., Civtorial Bd. Studies, Melbourne, 1964-92. Author: Biblical Lexicon, 1987-90; contbr. articles to profl. publs. Mem. Nat. Adv. Com. on Arabic and Mid. Eastern Studies, Melbourne, 1994—; mem. Coun. for Chaplaincy in Tertiary Instns., Australia, 1999—; bd. dirs. Australian br. Golda Meir Fellowship Com., 1990—. Commonwealth scholar Australian Govt., 1956, 66; grantee Melbourne U., 1966, 93-99, Australian Rsch. Coun., 2000. Mem. Nat. Assn. Profs. Hebrew, World Union Jewish Studies, Australian Friends of Hebrew Com. (exec.-acad. com. chair 1989—). Avocations: concerts, opera, walking, croquet. Fax: 61-3-94160382. E-mail: z.shavitsky@language.unimelb.edu.au. Home: Sky Apts, 29 Queens Rd Apt 17C, Melbourne VIC 3004, Australia Office: U Melbourne, Grattan St, Melbourne VIC 3010, Australia

SHAVITT, YUVAL, researcher; b. Jan. 12, 1964. BSc, Technion Israel Inst. Tech., Haifa, 1986, MSc, 1992, DSc, 1996. Rschr. Bell Labs, Lucent Techs., Holmdell, N.J., 1997—. Office: Lucent Techs Rm 4g-627 101 Crawfords Corner Rd Holmdel NJ 07733-1900

SHAW, BERNARD, television journalist; b. Chgo., 1940; m. Linda Shaw; children: Anil, Amar. Corr. Washington bur. CBS News, 1971-77; fgn. corr., bur. chief ABC News, 1977-80; anchor Cable News Network, Washington, 1980—, co-anchor Inside Politics. Served with USMC. recipient, Cable Ace award: Best Newscaster, 1994. Office: CNN 820 1st St NE Washington DC 20002-4243

SHAW, CHENG-KUANG, dentist, epidemiologist, educator, administrator; b. Taipei, Taiwan, China, Feb. 12, 1959; s. Dao-An and Yu-Jen (Kuan) S.; m. Li-Zen Wang, Sept. 28, 1988; children: Ryan, Rachel. DDS, Nat. Yang-Ming U., Taipei, 1983; MPH, Nat. Taiwan U., Taipei, 1985; D in Pub. Health, U. Mich., 1993. Assoc. prof. Tzu Chi Coll. Medicine, Hualian, China, 1993-99, prof., chmn. dept. pub. health, 1999—; exec. officer Tzu Chi Marrow Donor Registry, Hualian, 1995—. Contbr. articles to profl. jours. Lt. Mil. Hosp., 1985-88. Recipient Ann. Rsch. award Am. Coll. Epidemiology, 1991, Ann. Paper award Tzu Chi Med. Rsch. Found., 1995. Fellow Assn. Pub. Health Taipei. Avocations: go game, reading historical books. Office: Tzu Chi Coll Medicine, 701, Sec 3, Chung Yung Rd, Hualien Taiwan, China

SHAW, COLIN DON, retired professional society adminstrator, writer; b. Liverpool, Eng., Nov. 2, 1928; s. Rupert Morris and Enid Fryer (Smith) S.; m. Elizabeth Ann Bowker, Apr. 25, 1955; children: Tessa, Susan Soul, Giles. BA in English Lit., Oxford (Eng.) U., 1952, MA, 1956; barrister-at-law, Inner Temple, 1960. Various posts BBC, Eng., 1953-76; dir. TV Ind. Broadcasting Authority, Eng., 1977-83; dir., programming planning secretariat Ind. TV Coys. Assn., Eng., 1983-87; dir. Broadcasting Standards Coun., London, 1988-96; ret. Author plays. Fellow Royal TV Soc., Royal Soc. Arts. Avocations: walking, writing letters, theatre.

SHAW, DANNY WAYNE, secondary education educator, consultant; b. Detroit, Jan. 18, 1947; s. George L. and Nina Margarete (Smith) S.; m. 2d Nancy Rivard Shaw, Feb. 29, 1980; 1 child, Christina Marie. BS, Wayne State U., 1973, MusM, 1975, EdS, 1979, PhD, 1982. Tchr. Dearborn (Mich.) Pub. Schs., 1973-74, Lincoln Park (Mich.) Schs., 1974-98; pres. System Support Services, Lincoln Park, Trenton, Mich., 1982-98; rsch. asst. Wayne State U., 1980-81, now adj. faculty; adj. faculty Marygrove Coll., Detroit, 1984. Mem. music adv. panel mich. Coun. Arts, 1976-84; mem. cultural commn. city of Trenton, 1997—; mem. Leadership Beaufort Class 2000. With USMC, 1965-68, Vietnam. Decorated Vietnam Svc. medal, Nat. Def. Svc. medal, Presdl. Unit citation, Campaign medal Rep. Vietnam; recipient cert. for outstanding acad. achievement Mich. Ho. Reps., 1975. Mem. NEA, Masons, Phi Delta Kappa. Home: 22 Brisbane Dr Beaufort SC 29902-5296

SHAW, DENNIS FREDERICK, retired library director, chartered physicist, consultant; b. Teddington, Middlesex, Eng., Apr. 20, 1924; s. Albert and Lily Florence (Hill) S.; m. Joan Irene Chandler, June 25, 1949; children—Peter James, Margaret Denise, Katherine Joan, Deborah Mary. B.A. in Physics, U. Oxford, 1945, M.A., 1950, D.Phil. Nuclear Physics, 1950. Sr. research officer Oxford U., Eng., 1950-75, tutor in physics Keble Coll., 1956-75, professorial fellow, 1977—, keeper of sci. books, 1975-91; vis. scientist CERN, Geneva, 1960-61; vis. prof. U. South Tenn., 1974; ; chmn. IFLA Sci. and Tech. Librs., 1987-91, hon. treas. spl. librs. div., 1991-93, mem. cons., 1993—; mem. Home Office Sci. Adv. Council, London, 1966-78; mem. Home Def. Sci. Adv. Com., London, 1978-95; mem. Hebdomadal Council, Oxford U., 1980-89; mem Com. for the Internat. Coun. of Sci. Unions Press, 1991-96, mng. editor electronic pub., 1997—. Contbr. articles to profl. jours. Gov. Christ's Hosp., London, Almoner, 1980-98, chmn. edn. com., 1993-96; mem. Oxford City Council, 1963-67. Decorated Comdr. Brit. Empire, 1974. Freeman of City of London, 1998. Fellow Inst. Physics, Zool. Soc.; mem. Am. Inst. Physics (sr.), Internat. Assn. Tech. Univ. Librs. (hon., sec. 1983-85, pres. 1986-90, chmn. pub. bd. 1991-93), N.Y. Acad. Sci. Anglican. Club: Oxford and Cambridge. Home: 29 Davenant Rd, Oxford OX2 8BU, England Office: Keble Coll, Parks Rd, Oxford OX1 3PG, England

SHAW, GRACE GOODFRIEND (MRS. HERBERT FRANKLIN SHAW), publisher, editor; b. N.Y.C.; d. Henry Bernheim and Jane Elizabeth (Stone) Goodfriend; m. Herbert Franklin Shaw (dec. 1992); 1 son, Brandon Hibbs. Student, Bennington Coll.; BA magna cum laude, Fordham U., 1976, MS, 1991. Reporter Port Chester (N.Y.) Daily Item; editorial coordinator World Scope Ency., N.Y.C.; assoc. editor Clarence L. Barnhart, Inc., Bronxville, N.Y.; freelance-writer for reference books; editing supr. World Pub. Co., mng. editor, sr. editor; mng. editor Peter H. Wyden Co., N.Y.C., 1969-70; assoc. editor Dial Press, N.Y.C., 1971-72; sr. editor Dial Press, 1972, David McKay Co., N.Y.C., 1972-75, Grosset & Dunlap, 1975-79; chief editor Today Press (Grosset), 1977-79; sr. editor, coll. dept. Bobbs-Merrill, N.Y.C., mng. editor, exec. editor trade div., 1979-80; pub. Bobbs-Merrill, 1980-84; mng. editor Rawson Assocs. div. Macmillan Pub., 1985-91; pres. Grace Shaw Assocs., Scarsdale, N.Y., 1991-97; profl. respite provider Westchester Jewish Cmty. Svcs., N.Y., 1997—. Home and Office: 85 Lee Rd Scarsdale NY 10583-5212

SHAW, HELEN ROSEMARY, communications director; b. Dublin, Ireland, Feb. 24, 1962; d. Walter H. and Rose P. (O'Reilly) S. BA with honors, U. Coll. Dublin, 1982, MA with honors, 1993; higher diploma in Journalism, DCU, 1983. Reporter Irish Times, Dublin, 1984-88; prodr. Radio Telefis Eireann, Dublin, 1988-95, dir., 1997—; editor current affairs BBC, Belfast, Northern Ireland, 1996-97; observer Apso, South Africa Elections, 1994. V.p. Ireland Internat. Womens Forum, 1999-2000; v.p., radio committer EBU, 1999—. Journalist in Europe fellowship, 1990-91; recipient Gold Sony, 1997. Avocations: poetry, theatre, music, books, travel. Office: Radio Telefis Eireann, Donnybrook, Dublin 4, Ireland

SHAW, HENRY, chemical engineering educator; b. Paris, Oct. 25, 1934; came to U.S, 1947; s. Joseph B. and Sadie (Milstein) S.; m. Evelyn Goodman, Aug. 11, 1963; children: Laura Rachel, David Michael, Jessica Anne. PhD, Rutgers U., 1967; MBA, Rutgers U., Newark, 1976. Nuclear chem. engr. Babcock & Wilcox Co., Lynchburgh, Va., 1957-60, Mobil Oil Co., Princeton, N.J., 1961-65; instr. Rutgers U., New Brunswick, 1965-67; environ. mgr. Exxon Rsch. and Engring., Florham Park, N.J., 1967-86; prof. N.J. Inst. Tech., Newark, 1986—; invited mem. Nat. Commn. on Air Quality, Washington, 1980, com. mem. Nat. Rsch. Coun., Washington, 1980-93; chmn. of bd. Engring. Found., N.Y.C., 1988-90; chmn. adv. com. Oak Ridge (Tenn.) Nat. Lab., 1984-87. Developer university courses on design of non-polluting chemical processes; adv. bd. Jour. Clean Products and Processes, Environ. Progress. Capt. U.S. Army, 1958. Recipient Larry K. Cecil award in Environ. Chem. Engring. AIChE, 1997, Frank Dittman award in cmty. svc. and engring. achievement AIChE, 1992; rsch. grantee NSF, EPA, DOE, DOD, Hazardous Substance Rsch. Ctr., Newark, 1989-92, EPA, DOE, DOD, Linden, N.J., 1973-80, fellowship, Allied Corp., Florham Park, N.J., 1966, Lucent Tech. Indsl. Ecology fellow, 1994-96. Fellow AIChE (chair rsch. com. 1981-82, chair environ. divn. 1998-99); mem. AAAS, Am. Chem. Soc., Engring. Found. (bd. mem., chmn. 1988-90). Achievements include development of air pollution control methods treating nitrogen oxides from power plants and gas turbines; 4 patents; plasma production of fine powders, control of particulates, catalytic NOx control, NOx scrubbing. Home: 2 Gary Ct Scotch Plains NJ 07076-2007 Office: NJ Inst Tech 138 Warren St Newark NJ 07103-3515

SHAW, IAN CHARLES, toxicologist, educator; b. Birmingham, England, Mar. 25, 1956; s. William Charles and Audrey Joan (Furber) S. BSc with 1st class honors, U. Bath, 1978; PhD in Biochemistry, U. Birmingham, 1981. Lectr. in toxicology U. Coll., London, 1981-85; sr. clin. scientist Boeringer Ingelheim Ltd., Bracknell, U.K., 1985-87; head toxicology Ministry of Agriculture, Fisheries and Food, Weybridge, 1987-91; prof. toxicology U. Ctrl. Lancashire, Preston, U.K., 1991—; vis. cons. toxicologist Royal Preston Hosp., 1993—; Food Safety Prog. Mgr., Environmental Sci. Rsch., Christchurch Sci. Ctr., Christchurch, New Zealand, 1999, chmn. Working Party on Pesticide Residues (formerly U.K. Pesticide Residues Com.), 1995—, mem. adv. com. pesticides, 1997-2000; external examiner London Sch. Pharmacy, 1995-99, U. North London, 1993-98; vis. prof. Institut Teknologi Bandung, Indonesia, 1999. Author: (with Chadwick) Principles of Environmental Toxicology, 1998; contbr. articles to profl. jours. Justice of the Peace Borough of Wyre in Lancashire, 1988-2000. Fellow Royal Soc. Chemistry, Inst. Biology (adv. com. animal feed stuffs 1999-2000), New Zealand Inst. Chemistry. Avocations: collecting antiques, walking, music. Fax: 64-3 351-0010. E-mail: ian.shaw@esr.cri.nz. Office: ESR Christchurch Sci Ctr, 27 Creyke Rd Ilam PO Box 29-181, Christchurch New Zealand

SHAW, JAMES DEREK, farmer, agribusiness company executive; b. Belfast, No. Ireland, Feb. 21, 1941; s. Samuel and Margaret Elizabeth (Paterson) S.; m. Ann Forrest Stewart, June 3, 1967; children: Catherine, Jane, Christopher. Nat. diploma in agr., Seale Hayne Coll., Newton Abbot, Eng., 1962, diploma in farm bus. adminstrn.-mgmt., 1963. Mng. ptnr. Shaw Partnership, Gilford, No Ireland, 1963-74; CEO Colly Farms Pty. Ltd., NSW, Australia, 1979-84, chmn., mng. dir., 1984-88; chmn., CEO, Barbour Campbell Group Ltd., Lisburn, No. Ireland, 1989-94, Elmfield Farms Ltd., Gilford, 1974—, Shaw Farms Ltd., Gilford, 1979—; chmn. Ulster Farmers Investments Ltd., No. Ireland, 1988—, Linden Food Ltd., No. Ireland, 1994—, Armagh & Dungannon Health Trust, No. Ireland, 1996—; vice chmn. Lendu Plc, Tunbridgewells, Eng., 1990—; dir. Indsl. Devel. Bd. No. Ireland, 1997—. Internat. hockey player, Ireland, 1963-72. Fellow Royal Agr. Soc., Inst. Dirs.; mem. Internat. Agribus. Mgrs. Assn., Farmers Club, Reform Club. Avocations: tennis, skiing, gardening. Home: Elmfield Castle, Moyallon BT63 5JX, Northern Ireland Office: Shaw Farms Ltd, Moyallon, Portadown BT63 5JX, Northern Ireland

SHAW, JOHN BEAUMONT, civil engineer; b. London, June 13, 1929; s. George Beaumont and Gwendoline (Coles) S.; m. Janette Claire Kerr, Mar. 30, 1957 (dec. Mar. 24, 1970); children: Alison Jane, Douglas Beaumont, Robert William George, Fiona Mary Elizabeth; m. Lena Mathers, June 10, 1972. BSc, U. Bristol (Eng.), 1952. Grad. asst. City Engr. of Bristol, 1952-54; site engr., agt. Turiff Constrn. Corp., Warwick, Eng., 1954-56; design engr. C.S. Allott and Son, Manchester, Eng., 1956-60; project mgr. Walker Sons & Co. Ltd., Colombo, Sri Lanka, 1960-63; engr. Rendel Palmer & Tritton, London, 1963-66; prin. engr. Brian Colquhoun & Ptnrs., London, 1966-76; contracts mgr. Hong Kong Mass Transit Railway Corp., Hong Kong, 1976-81; engr.'s rep. Rendel Palmer & Tritton, Tripoli, Libya, 1981-86; asst. fin. contr. Eurotunnel, London, Eng., 1987-91; project contracts mgr. London Underground Ltd., London, 1991-96; ind. cons. engr. John B. Shaw, Bognor Regis, Eng., 1996—. With Nat. Svc. Brit. Army, 1947-49. Fellow ASCE, Instn. Civil Engrs.

SHAW, JOSEPHINE, training consultant; b. Coventry, Eng., Aug. 15, 1930; d. James Henry and Gwendoline Mabel (Baker) S. Student, Birmingham Secretarial Coll., 1977-78. Edn. mgr. Speedwriting Ltd., London, 1963-65; advisor Internat. Labour Office, Geneva, 1965-75; mng. dir. Teaching Aids Ltd., New Milton, Eng., 1976-88; chmn., mng. dir. Teaching Aids Ltd., New Milton, 1988-94; moderator Bus. Edn. Coun., London, 1979-83; tng. cons. Josephine Shaw Assocs., dir., 1994—. Author: Retail Distribution for the Junior Certificates, 1970, Teach Yourself Office Practice, 1972, Essential Secretarial Studies, 1974, Secretarial Management—A Guide to the Effective Use of Staff, 1977, Office Organization for Managers, 1978, West African Office Practice, 1978, Administration in Business, 1981, ILO Training Packages, 1981, Training Techniques for Word Processing and Computer Trainers, 1988, Business Administration, 1991; co-author: Caribbean Office Procedures, 1983, 3d edit., 1998. Hon. sec. St. John Ambulance Assn., Uganda, 1956-62. Recipient Serving Sister award Order of St. John Jerusalem, London, 1960. Fellow Inst. Dirs., Inst. Mgmt.; mem. Chartered Inst. Pers. Devel. Anglican. Avocations: photography, classical music, needlework. Office: Josephine Shaw Assocs, PO Box 22, Lymington Hampshire SO41 0ZQ, England

SHAW, JOYCE M., librarian; b. Gulfport, Miss., Mar. 4, 1955; d. Philip Walker and Marion Joyce (Bendler) S.; 1 child, Oliver Shaw Kuttner. BA, U. New Orleans, 1978; MA, Roosevelt U., 1982; M Libr. and Info. Sci., Rosary Coll., River Forest, Ill., 1994. Libr. asst. Times Picayune Publs., New Orleans, 1976-78, Roosevelt U., Chgo., 1978-80, Field Mus. Natural History, Chgo., 1980-83; libr. Lincoln Park Zool. Gardens, Chgo., 1983-94, Shaw/Walker Archs., Gulfport, Miss., 1994-95; head libr. Gulf Coast Rsch. Lab., Ocean Springs, Miss., 1995—; mem. adv. bd. nature connections Chgo. Pub. Libr., 1984-86. Contbr. articles to profl. jours., including Spl. Librs., Jour. Miss. Acad. Scis., Ill. Librs. Conservation grantee Inst. Mus. Svc., 1986. Mem. Spl. Librs. Assn., Soc. for Conservation Biology, Internat. Assn. Marine Sci. Librs. and Info. Ctrs., Miss. Acad. Scis. Presbyterian. Avocation: reading. E-mail: joyce.shaw@usm.edu. Office: Gulf Coast Rsch Lab 708 E Beach Blvd Ocean Springs MS 39564

SHAW, MAXWELL KENNETH, Christian school administrator; b. Newcastle, NSW, Australia, May 22, 1938; s. Kenneth Clement and Edith Emily (Bridge) S.; m. Elva Carole Dean, Sept. 8, 1962; children: Kirstin, Carole, Kenneth, Fionna, Elizabeth, Felicity. BS, U. Queensland, Brisbane, Australia, 1960, MS, 1964; PhD, U. Calif., Davis, 1966; BEd, Christian Heritage Coll., Brisbane, 1999. Rsch. assoc. NH & MRC, Brisbane, 1959-60; rsch. scientist CSIRO, Brisbane, 1960-70; group mgr. rsch. & devel. Mauri Bros & Thomson Ltd, Sydney, Australia, 1970-77; chief cons. Shaw Consulting Svcs., Sydney, 1977-83; headmaster Redeemer Bapt. Sch., Sydney, 1983—; exec. sec. Australian Indsl. Rsch. Group, Sydney, 1978-83; chmn. biol. registration Nat. Assn. Testing Authorities, Sydney, 1975-83. Contbr. over 10 articles to profl. jours. Fellow Australian Inst. Food Sci. and Tech. (life) (sec. 1978-83), Royal Soc. Chemistry; mem. Australian Soc. Microbiology, Assn. Executives of Christian Schs. (sec. 1988-89). Avocations: church elder, reading, music. Home: 14 Brisbane Rd, NSW Castle Hill 2154, Australia

SHAW, MICHAEL JOSEPH, research physicist, educator; b. Glasgow, Scotland, Feb. 13, 1970; s. Patrick Derek and Hilary Joan (Hewlett) S.; m. Allison Rosalind Keillor, July 30, 1994; children: Alexander Thomas, James Patrick. BSc with honors, U. Manchester, Eng., 1990; PhD, U. Newcastle Upon Tyne, Eng., 1993. Rsch. assoc. U. Newcastle Upon Tyne, 1993—. Contbr. articles to profl. jours. Mem. Inst. Physics (grad. mem.). Office: Dept Physics, Univ Newcastle Upon Tyne, Newcastle Upon Tyne NE1 7RU, England

SHAW, PETER JAMES, cell biologist, researcher; b. Oxford, Eng., Dec. 5, 1951; s. Dennis Frederick and Joan Irene (Chandler) S.; m. Christina Helen Pimlett, Oct. 1, 1976; children: Genevieve Rebecca, Felix Oliver. BA, Trinity Coll., Cambridge, Eng., 1972; PhD, Bristol (Eng.) U., 1976. Postdoctoral fellow U. Birmingham, Eng., 1975-76, U. Bristol, 1976-79; staff scientist John Innes Ctr., Norwich, Eng., 1979—; vis. rschr. U. Calif., San Francisco, 1987; hon. reader U. East Anglia, Norwich, 1994—; organizer various sci. confs., U.K., 1987—; mem. various grant assessment panels, U.K., E.C. Mem. editl. bd.: Jour. Cell Sci., Current Opinion Plant Sci., Bioimaging, Plant Molecular Biology; contbr. numerous sci. papers to profl. jours., numerous chpts. to sci. books. Recipient Pres.'s medal Soc. for Exptl. Biology, 1986; rsch. grantee various orgns., 1987—. Fellow Royal Micro. Soc.; mem. AAAS, Brit. Soc. Cell Biology, Brit. Biophys. Soc. Office: John Innes Ctr, Colney, NR4 7UH Norwich England

SHAW, RANDY LEE, human services administrator; b. Revenna, Ohio, Oct. 18, 1945; s. Robert and Dorothy Mae (Turner) S.; m. Terri Marie Richardson, July 4, 1988; 1 child, Garrett Samuel. BTh, Ridgedale Sem., 1975, ThM, 1977. Cert. social worker, addictions counselor. Exec. dir. Boy's Recovery Home, Detroit, 1979; clin. dir. Boniface, Detroit, 1979-83; unit dir. Problem Daily Living, Detroit, 1983-84; clin. dir. Calvin Wells, Detroit, 1984-86; exec. dir. Children Youth Equal Rights Adv. House, Pontiac, Mich., 1986-87, Touch of Hope, Hartford, Mich., 1988-89; program supr. New Ctr. Community Mental Health, Detroit, 1989-91; exec. dir. Nat. Inst. Hypertension Studies, Detroit, 1979-88. Local rep., magician for Make-A-Wish Found.; exec. dir. Magicians Against Gangs, Ignorance, and Crime Intervention Program, M.A.G.I.C., 1991—. Mem. Soc. Am. Magicians (local pres. 1993-94), Magic Circle, Internat. Brotherhood of Magicians (local pres. 1993-94), Supreme Magic Club of U.K., Psychic Entertainers Assn. Fax: 760-281-7066. E-mail: majorshaw@yahoo.com. Home and Office: 5375 Antoinette Dr Grand Blanc MI 48439-4310

SHAW, RICHARD GLENN, financial analyst; b. Queens, N.Y., Oct. 11, 1956; s. Martin and Patricia Ann (Landes) S. BA, Jacksonville U., 1978. CFP, Registry of Certified Financial Planning Practitioners. Ins. agent Guaranty Security, Jacksonville, Fla., 1978-80; mgr. real estate devel. firm, 1980-84; owner mktg. corp., 1985-88; fin. advisor Lincoln Fin. Group, Overland Park, Kans., 1988—. Bd. dirs., trustee U. Mo., Kansas City, Kans. Conservatory Music, Kansas City. Mem. Internat. Assn. Fin. Planning, Estate Planning Soc. Kansas City, Internat. Baseball Fedn. Office: Lincoln Fin Group 9225 Indian Creek Pkwy Overland Park KS 66210-2009

SHAW, ROLAND CLARK, oil company executive; b. Boston, Oct. 22, 1921; s. Adrian Vere and Helen (Halter) S.; m. Felicitas von Frankenberg und Proschlitz, 1952 (dec. 1995); children: Alexandra, Victoria. BA, Princeton U., 1947; MSc, London Sch. Econs., 1949. Chmn. Shaw Oil & Gas Ltd., London. Capt. USAF, 1940-45. Office: Shaw Oil & Gas Ltd, 10 Storeys Gate, London SW1P 2AY, England

SHAW, RONALD, mathematical physics educator; b. Stoke, Staffordshire, Eng., Sept. 5, 1929; s. Samuel Potts and Maud Emma (Frost) S.; m. Marion Rutherford, July 20, 1967 (div. 1982); 1 child, Elizabeth; m. Chiam Peak Yuen, May 21, 1988. BA, Trinity Coll., Cambridge, Eng., 1952, PhD, 1956, ScD, 1989. Lectr. U. Hull, Eng., 1955-65, sr. lectr., 1965-89, prof., chair math. physics, 1989-95; prof. emeritus U. Hull, 1995—; assoc. prof. Middle East U., Ankara, Turkey, 1963. Author: Linear Algebra and Group Representations, 1983; contbr. articles to profl. jours. Fellow Inst. Combinatories and its Applications; mem. London Math. Soc., Am. Math. Soc. Humanist. Avocations: hill walking, contemporary dance, tennis, chess. Office: U Hull Dept of Math, Hull HU6 7RX, England

SHAW, ROSLYN LEE, retired elementary education educator; b. Bklyn., Oct. 1, 1942; d. Benjamin Biltmore and Bessie (Banilower) Deretchin; m. Stephen Allan Shaw, Feb. 1, 1964; children: Laurence, Victoria, Michael. BA, Bklyn. Coll., 1964; MS, SUNY, New Paltz, 1977, cert. advanced study, 1987; cert. gifted edn., Coll. New Rochelle, 1986. Cert. sch. adminstr., supr., sch. dist. adminstr., reading tchr., tchr. N-6. Tchr. Hillel Hebrew Acad., Beverly Hills, Calif., 1965-66, P.S. 177, 77, Bklyn., 1964-65, 66-67; tchr. Middletown (N.Y.) Sch. Dist., 1974-77, reading specialist, 1977-99, compensatory edn. reading tchr., 1977-99, tchr. gifted children, 1984-87, asst. project coord. pre-K, 1988-89, instrnl. leader, 1989-93; ret., 1999; adj. assoc. prof. SUNY, Coll. at New Paltz, 1997-98; newspaper in edn. coord. The Times Herald Record, 1999—. Pres. Middletown H.S. Parents' Club, 1983-86; bd. dirs. Mental Health Assn., Goshen, N.Y., 1980-81; mem. Middletown Interfaith Coun., 1983-85. Mem. Amy Bull Crist Reading Coun. (pres. 1989-91, 93-95), N.Y. State Reading Assn. (Coun. Svc. award 1990, regional dir. 1991-94, bd. dirs. 1991—, chair reading tchrs. spl. interest group 1993-94, pres.-elect 1999—, pres. 2000—, newsletter editor The Empire State Reading Scene), Internat. Reading Assn., Univ. Women's Club, Delta Kappa Gamma. Avocations: photography, walking, reading. Home: 133 Highland Ave Middletown NY 10940-4712 Office: The Times Herald Record 40 Mulberry St Middletown NY 10940-6302

SHAW, TREVOR HENRY MONTAGUE, food company executive; b. London, Sept. 28, 1933; s. Jack and Rose Shaw; m. Paula Deborah Henry, Sept. 6, 1984. B.Law with honors, London U., 1955. Ptnr. A. Kramestle, London, 1961-68; group legal advisor Assoc. Brit. Foods Plc, London, 1969-72, sec., 1972-80, dir., 1980—. Avocations: music, antiques, tennis, opera. Home: 115 North Hill, London N6 4DP, England Office: Associated British Foods Plc, 68 Knightsbridge/Bowater Ho, London SW1X 7LR, England

SHAWCROSS, JOHN THOMAS, English educator; b. Hillside, N.J., Feb. 10, 1924; s. Ernest Edward and Lillian Anderson (Kuncken) S. AM, NYU, 1950, PhD, 1958; DLitt, Montclair State U., 1975, St. Bonaventure U., 1995. Prof. English Rutgers U., New Brunswick, N.J., 1963-67; prof. English U. Wis., Madison, 1967-70, CUNY, 1970-79, U. Ky., Lexington, 1979—. Author: (book) John Milton: The Self and the World, 1992 (Milton Soc. award 1993), With Mortal Voice: The Creation of Paradise Lost, 1984. Lt. (j.g.) U.S. Navy, 1942-46. E-mail: s1674jt@aol.com. Home: 4818 Hartland Pkwy Lexington KY 40515-1106

SHAWDALE, BRIAN JOHN, organization executive; b. Hyde, Cheshire, Eng., Apr. 6, 1943. Cert. engr. Asst. chief draftsman Hawker Siddley, Manchester, Eng., 1979-82; indsl. rels. mgr. Brit. Aerospace, Manchester, 1982-86, pers. mgr., 1986-90; engring. team mgr. Avro Aerospace, Manchester, 1989-91, effectiveness mgr., 1991-93; dir. Manchester Minibus Agy, 1993—. Justice of the Peace, Tameside Magistrates, 1994—. Mem. Chartered Inst. Pers. and Devel., Royal Aero. Soc. (assoc.). Home: 1 Turner Ln, Hyde SK14 4AG, England

SHAWEESH, HAMZEH MOHAMMED, telecommunications engineer; b. Jerusalem, Aug. 10, 1917; came to Jordan, 1949; s. Mohammed Musa and Khadijeh Hussain (Abu-Alkas) S.; m. Subhieh Hamzeh Al-Turk, Apr. 25, 1940; children: Ayda, Wijdan, Hajar, Mohammed, Musa, Radwan, Montaha, Issa, Iman, Khadijeh. Grad. in Secondary Edn., Rashidieh U., Jerusalem, 1935; apprenticeship in Elec. Installations, Wagner Factory, Jaffa, Palestine, 1935-37; grad. in Telecom. Engring., Post, Telephone & Telegraph Inst., Jerusalem, 1940. Cert. radio engr., telecom. engr. Instr. telecom. Palestine Post Office Engring. Inst., 1940-42; chief Internat. Telecom. Ctr., Ramaleh Town Palestine, 1942-46; dir. Post Office Telecom. Inst., Jaffa, 1946-47; dep. divisional engr. West of Palestine, Jaffa, 1947-48; radio dealer, 1948-49; telecom. engr. Jordan Post, Telephone & Telegraph, 1949-55, sr. radio engr., 1955-56; sr. engr. radio, long distance comm., auto exchs. div. Engring. and Internat. Ctrs., 1957-61; chief projects planning div., 1961-64; chief engr. Min. of Comm., 1964-65; asst. under sec. Min. of Comm., Amman, Jordan, 1965-71; appointed exec. dir. telecom. and elec. div. Devel. Office Co. Ltd., 1971-86; mem. mission to U.K. to specialize in Microwave System, September 1956. Author tech. papers published on various confs. Recipient Jordan Star medal His Majesty King Hussain, Jordan, 1965, Commemorative Medal Man of Yr., 1996, Presdl. Seal of Honor Cert. Mem. IEEE, Jordan Inst. Engrs., Brit. Inst. Engring. Tech., Soc. Engrs. Eng. Avocations: tennis, amateur radio, electronic experiments, preparing technical papers. Home and Office: PO Box 394, Amman 11118, Jordan

SHAXSON, THOMAS FRANCIS, land husbandry agronomist; b. Harting, Sussex, Eng., May 25, 1933; s. Thomas Ronald and Helen Louise (Hermes) S.; m. Annabel Louise Hoyle, Sept. 3, 1961; children: Louise Janet, Nicholas Thomas. BSc in Agr. with honors, Wye, Eng., 1955; diploma in tropical

agr., Imperial Coll. Tropical Agr., 1958; MS in Agronomy, Cornell U., 1956. Soil conservation officer Nyasaland/Malawi Govt., Blantyre, Malawi, 1958-61; rsch. agronomist Tea Rsch. Found. Ctrl. Africa, Mulanje, Malawi, 1961-68; prin. land husbandry officer Overseas Devel. Adminstrn. of U.K. Govt. and Govt. Malawi, Lilongwe, Malawi, 1968-76; Brit. team's leader land husbandry Overseas Devel. Adminstrn. U.K. Govt., Indore, India, 1976-80; chief tech. adviser in land husbandry Food and Agr. Orgn. of UN, Brasilia, Brazil, 1981-88; and Food and Agr. Orgn. of UN, Maseru, Lesotho, 1988-91; ind. cons. in land husbandry agronomy Broadstone, U.K., 1991—. Author: A Land Husbandry Manual, 1977, Land Husbandry: A Framework for Soil and Water Conservation, 1989; contbr. articles to profl. jours. Named Officer of Brit. Empire by Her Majesty Queen Elizabeth, 1978; recipient Hugh Hammond Bennett award Soil and Water Conservation Soc., 1995. Mem. Assn. for Better Land Husbandry (chmn. 1993-2000). Avocations: music, ornithology, mountain walking. Home and Office: Greensbridge, Sackville St, Winterborne Kingston, Dorset DT11 9BJ, England

SHAYKH, ABDALLAH MUHAMMED IBRAHIM-AL, federal official. Min. of justice Saudi Arabia. Office: Ministry of Justice, University St Main Ministry, Riyadh 11137, Saudi Arabia*

SHAYNE, LEONARD M(ARVIN), customs broker; b. N.Y., Sept. 29, 1920; s. Martin L. and Estelle (Greenberg) S.; m. Theresa Deerson Shayne, May 14, 1952; children: William Charles, Claydia Shayne Ferguson. BA, Columbia Univ., 1941. Clerk, bank examinations dept. Federal Reserve Bank N.Y., 1941; fighter group 8th Air Force U.S. Army Air Force, 1942-45; pres. Leading Forwarders Inc., N.Y., 1946-99; dir. Am. Assn. Exporters & Importers, N.Y., 1949-99; bd. govs. N.Y. Forwarders & Brokers Assn., 1987-99; lectr. Baruch Sch. Bus. Adminstrn., 1948-60. Contbr. articles to profl. jours. Mem. Nat. Customs Brokers and Forwarders Assn. Am., Inc. (pres., dir., sr-counselor). Avocations: writing, tennis. Office: Leading Forwarders Inc 325 E 79th St New York NY 10021-0954

SHAYO, STEPHEN MASHINDANO, accountant; b. Moshi, Tanzania, Sept. 1, 1954; s. Augustine Tamamu Shayo and Hyasinta Mkarawi Mangoti; m. Maria Elly Nyange, Aug. 9, 1986; children: Stephen, Deodatus, Angela, Amedeus, Consolata. Diploma, Inst. Purchasing and Supply, U.K., 1982. CPA; lic. tax cons. Tutor Dar-es-Salaam (Tanzania) Sch. Accountanty, 1979-82; tax and mgmt. cons. Massawe & Co., Tanzania, 1982-84; fin. cons. Internat. Fin. Adv. Svcs., Tanzania, 1984-85; mng. ptnr. Stephen Shayo & Co., Dar-es-Salaam, 1985—; mng. dir. Fin. & Produrement Cons. Ltd., 1990—; bd. dirs. Afro Med. Supplies Ltd., Metro Agys. Councilor Christian Profls. of Tanzania, 1984, rep. affiliate Tanzania Episcopal Conf., 1987; chmn. Youth Devel. Fund, Tanzania, 1990. Fellow Nat. Bd. Accts. and Auditors, Tanzania Assn. Accts; mem. Tanzania Assn. Cons., Inst. Tng. and Devel. (assoc.). Roman Catholic. Avocations: music, poultry, horticulture, youth movements, health matters. Home: Plot 226 Blk F Mbezi Beach, PO Box 5148, Dar es Salaam Tanzania Office: Stephen Shayo & Co, Plot 416/129 Nkrumah St, POB 5148 Dar es Salaam Tanzania

SHCHENNIKOV, VLADIMIR VICTOROVICH, physicist, researcher; b. Krasnoturinsk, Russia, July 18, 1952; s. Victor Nikolaevich and Georgina Denisova (Anuchina) S.; m. Valentina Nikolaena Ovsyannikova, May 12, 1978; children: Sergey, Vsevolod. Diploma, Ural State U., Sverdlovsk, Russia, 1974, PhD in Physics, 1984. Jr. scientist Inst. Metals Physics, Ekaterinburg, 1974-86, rschr., 1986-88, head patent dept., 1989-91, sr. rschr., head high pressure group, 1992—. Contbr. articles to profl. jours. and conf. and symposium procs.; inventor in field of high pressure physics. Grantee Am. Physics Soc., 1993. Fellow Internat. assn. for Advancement of High Pressure Sci. and Tech.; mem. Inventors Soc. Russia (chair Inst. Metals Physics divsn. 1986-91). Avocations: chess, travel, bard music, literature. Office: Inst Metals Physics, S Kovalevskaya Str 18, 620219 Ekaterinburg GSP-170, Russia

SHCHEPETKIN, IGOR ALEXANDROVICH, biochemist; b. Novosibirsk, Russia, Apr. 16, 1962; s. Alexander and Maria (Zubareva) S.; m. Olga Skrjabina, Oct. 26, 1985 (div. Dec. 1989); m. Lily Kirpotina, Mar. 30, 1990; children: Arthem, Alexander, Veronika. MSc, Med. Inst. Tomsk, Russia, 1985; PhD, Oncology Rsch. Inst. Tomsk, 1992. From sr. laborer to sr. rschr. Oncology Rsch. Inst. Tomsk, 1985—. Mem. N.Y. Acad. Scis. Fax: 007-3822-224097. Home: Pushkina str 48A box 5, 634003 Tomsk Siberia, Russia

SHCHIPANOV, NIKOLAY ALEXANDER, zoologist, researcher; b. Moscow, Mar. 19, 1955; s. Alexander Ivanovitch and Tatiana Michailovna (Mill) S.; m. Marina Vasilievna Kasprook, Jan. 24, 1976; children: Olga, Alexander. Diploma, Moscow State Pedagogical Inst., 1977; PhD, Moscow U., 1986; ScD, Severtzov's Ecology/Evol Inst, Moscow, 1996. Sr. laborant Mowcow State Pedagogical Inst., 1977-81; sr. engr. Desinfection Inst. of Health Min. of USSR, Moscow, 1981-89; sr. rschr. Severtzov's Ecology and Evolution Inst., Russian Acad. Sci., Moscow, 1989—; chief Cathedral of Disinfection in Russian Med. Acad. for Postgrad. Edn., 1997—. Author: White-toothed Shrew, 1993; inventor in field; contbr. articles to profl. jours. Chief Student's Nature Conservation Orgn., Moscow State Pedagogical Inst., 1975-81. Soros Sci. Found. grantee, 1993. Mem. russian thereology Soc. Avocation: painting. Home: Gontcharova 17a 1 47, 127254 Moscow Russia Office: Severtzov's Ecol/Evol Inst, Leninski pr 33, 117071 Moscow Russia

SHCHUKIN, VASILII GEORGIEVICH, literature historian, educator; b. Moscow, USSR, Sept. 4, 1952; arrived in Poland, 1979; s. Georgii Alexandrovich and Nadezhda Vasil'evna (Kunshina) S.; m. Małgorzata Maria Siwek, Feb. 1, 1975; 1 child, Barbara. D in Philology, U. Moscow, 1978; D in Arts Habilitation, Jagiellonian U., Cracow, Poland, 1987. Ednl. diplomate. Lectr. U. Moscow, 1978-79; tchr. primary sch. #13, Cracow, Poland, 1979-81; asst. Jagiellonian U., Cracow, Poland, 1980-89, asst. prof., 1989-97; prof. Pedagogical Acad. Cracow, Cracow, 1997—; cons. Ctr. Soviet Rsch., Łódź, Poland, 1990—. Author: Russkoye Zapadnichestvo, 1987 (Min. of Edn. award 1988); editor: Russkaya Nauka o Literature, 1992 (Jagiellonian U. rector award 1993), Mif Dvoryanskogo Gnezda, 1997 (Pedagogical Acad. Cracow rector award 1998); contbr. articles to profl. jours. Problems of Russian Geoculturology grantee Sci. Rsch. Com., Poland, 1994. Mem. Internat. Comparative Lit. Assn., Polish Soc. Comparative Lit. (v.p. 1994—). Office: Pedagogical Acad Cracow, ul Studencka 5, 31 116 Cracow Poland

SHEA, GERALD PATRICK, engineering executive; b. N.Y.C., May 10, 1935; s. William James and Mary M. (Fitzmaurice) S.; m. Joan Elaine Bergener, Mar. 3, 1938; children: Jerry, Kevin, Kathleen O'Connell, William, Brian. BSCE, U. Notre Dame, 1956; MCE, NYU, 1963. Registered profl. engr., N.Y., N.J., Conn., Pa., Fla., Ark., S.C., Va. Bridge design engr. Parsons Brinckerhoff, N.Y.C., 1956-58; bridge engr. Bur. Pub. Roads, Richmond, Va., 1958-62; assoc. TAMS Consultants, N.Y.C., 1963-78; v.p. Louis Berger Internat. Inc., East Orange, N.J., 1978-97; corp. v.p. Louis Berger Group Inc., East Orange, 1997-98; dir. gen., CEO Internat. Road Fedn., Washington, 1998—; bd. dirs., vice chmn. Internat. Road Fedn.; pres. Internat. Road Ednl. Found. Contbr. numerous articles to profl. jours. Fellow Inst. Transp. Engrs.; mem. ASCE, Soc. Am. Mil. Engrs., MOLES. Roman Catholic. Avocations: golf, walking, travel, sailing. Home: 2 Otranto Ct Hilton Head Island SC 29928-6108 Office: Internat Road Fedn 1010 Massachusetts Ave NW Washington DC 20001-5402

SHEA, MEGAN CARROLL, lawyer, law educator; b. Lake Forest, Ill., Sept. 7, 1967; d. Barry Joseph and Barbara (Pehrson) C.; m. Timothy J. Shea II. Student, Middlebury Coll., Paris, 1987-88; BA in Philosophy, French Lit., Boston Coll., 1989, JD, 1992. Bar: Mass., 1993, Ill. 1994, D.C. 1995. Law clk. Middlesex County Probate & Family Ct., Cambridge, Mass., 1990-91; assoc. Powers & Hall, Boston, 1991; asst. dist. atty. Norfolk County, Mass., 1992; prin., owner Carroll Assocs., Counsel for the Arts, Boston, 1994—; bd. dirs. Carroll Internat. Corp., Des Plaines, Ill.; adj. prof. law New Eng. Sch. Law, 1998—. Arts review writer various publs. Mem. Am. Ireland Fund, Boston, Chgo., 1985—, Phillips Acad. Alumni Coun., Andover, Mass., 1991-95; trustee Regency Pk. Condominiums, Brookline, Mass., 1989-91; sec. Phillips Acad. Alumni Class of 1985, Andover, 1989-95; bd. overseers Boston Ballet, 2000—, French Libr., Boston, 2000—; bd. dirs. Alliance Française, Boston, 1998-2000; mem. exec. com. capital campaign Boston Coll., 1998—. Recipient Golden Key Nat. Honor Soc., Boston Coll., 1989, Order of the Cross and Crown, Scholar of the Coll., 1989. Mem. ABA, Arts and Media Law Assn. of Boston Coll. (pres., founder), Social Register, Woman's Athletic Club Chgo., Order of Malta Aux., DAR (vice regent Wellesley, Mass. 1999—), Jr. Internat. Club Lauterbach (Germany), East Chop Beach Club, East Chop Yacht Club, East Chop Tennis Club, Boston Coll. Club (bd. dirs. 1998—), Phi Delta Phi. Republican. Roman Catholic. Avocations: classical ballet, choreography, scuba diving, flying (lic. pilot). Home: 24 Columbia St Wellesley Hills MA 02481-1603 Office: Carroll Assocs 200 Linden St # 322 Wellesley MA 02482-7964

SHEA, SPENCER CLIVE, polymer physicist; b. Strand, South Africa, Feb. 28, 1945; s. Leonard and Anna (Dillion) S.; m. Joy Birch, Dec. 28, 1968; children: Rory, Andrea. BSc, U. Cape Town, 1966; MSc, U. Manchester, 1976. Devel. chemist Duropenta, Cape Town, 1968-70, Plasbou, Cape Town, 1970-71; sr. chemist Van Leer, Springs, South Africa, 1971-81; tech. mgr. Contronics Cables, Springs, 1981-82; tech./mktg. mgr. Darling & Hodson, Springs, 1982-84; quality mgr. Plastamid, Cape Town, 1984—. Fellow Plastics Inst. So. Africa, Plastics and Rubber Inst. Avocations: caravanning, woodworking, photography, Toastmasters. Home: 12 Conifer Way, 7405 Pinelands South Africa Office: Plastamid Pty Ltd, 43 Coleman St, Elsies River Cape South Africa

SHEA, WILLIAM RENE, historian, science philosopher, educator; b. Gracefield, Que., Can., May 16, 1937; s. Herbert Clement and Jeanne (Lafreniere) S.; m. Evelyn Fischer, May 2, 1970; children: Herbert, Joan-Emma, Louisa, Cecilia, Michael. BA, U. Ottawa, 1958; LPh, Gregorian U., Rome, 1959; LTh, Gregorian U., 1963; PhD, Cambridge U., Eng., 1968. Assoc. prof. U. Ottawa, Ont., Can., 1968-73; fellow Harvard U., Cambridge, Mass., 1973-74; prof. history and philosophy of sci. McGill U., Montreal, 1974—; dir. d'etudes Ecole des Hautes Etudes, Paris, 1981-82; sec.-gen. Internat. Union of History and Philosophy of Sci., 1983-89, pres., 1990-93; mem. gen. com. Internat. Coun. of Sci. Union, Paris, 1983-89; cons. Killam Found., Ottawa, Ont., 1983-85; mem. McGill Centre for Medicine, Ethics and Law, 1990-95; Hydro Que. prof. environ. ethics, 1992—; vis. prof. U. Rome, 1992; dir. Inst. History of Sci., U. Louis Pasteur, Strasbourg, 1995—. Author: Galileo Intellectual Revolution, 1972, The Magic of Numbers and Motion, 1991; co-author: Galileo Florentine Residences, 1979; editor: Nature Mathematized, 1983, Otto Hahn and the Rise of Nuclear Physics, 1983, Revolutions in Science, 1988, Creativity in the Arts and Science, 1990, Persuading Science: The Art of Scientific Rhetoric, 1991, Interpreting the World, Science and Society, 1991, Energy Needs in the Year 2000: Ethical and Environmental Perspectives, 1994, The Scientific Image in the Enlightenment, 2000. Can. Coun. fellow, 1965-68, Can. Cultural Inst. fellow, Rome, 1973, Social Scis. and Humanities Rsch. Coun. Can., 1980-81, Inst. of Advanced Studies in Berlin fellow, 1988-89; recipient The Alexandre Koyre medal Internat. Acad. of History of Sci., 1993, Knight of the Order of Malta, 1993. Fellow Royal Soc. Can.; mem. Royal Swedish Acad. Scis. (fgn.), Acadmie D'Alsace, Academia Europaea, History of Sci. Soc. (coun. 1973-76), European Sci. Found. (standing com. for humanities 1989-95, chmn. 1999—), Can. Nat. Com. of History and Philosophy of Sci. (coun. 1982-93), Can. Philos. Assn., Internat. Acad. History of Sci. (pres. 1997—), Rotary. Fax: 0033-388-52-80-30. Home: 6 Rue Gottfried, 67000 Strasbourg France Office: Inst d'Histoire des Scis, 7 Rue de L'Universite, 67000 Strasbourg France

SHEAFF, RICHARD DANA, communications and graphic designer; b. Winchester, Mass., Apr. 26, 1944; s. Harold Dana and Edna Mae (Mosher) S.; m. Cheryl Ann Barchard Ferguson, July 18, 1970 (div. Oct. 1984); 1 stepchild, Leonard Sean; m. Margaret Jean Reiley, Nov. 11, 1987; 1 child, Dana. AB in Biology, Dartmouth Coll., Hanover, N.H., 1966; MFA in Visual Comm./Design, Syracuse (N.Y.) U., 1977. Asst. media buyer Benton & Bowles Inc., N.Y.C., 1966; account exec. Donald W. Gardner, Inc., Boston, 1966-67; tech. cons. Internat. Pers. Cons., Hanover, N.H., 1968-69; ops. coord. N.H.-Tomorrow, Concord, 1969-71; environtl. cons. Dartmouth Coll., Hanover, 1972-73; design cons. U.S. Postal Svc., Washington, 1983—; sr. designer Gregory Fossella Assocs., Boston, 1977-78; pres., creative dir. Sheaff Design, Inc., Needham, Mass., 1978-89; creative cons. R. Dana Sheaff & Co., Scottsdale, Ariz., 1989—; cons. in field. Author: Formation of Land Trusts, 1971; designer/dir.: (handbook) Varnish Techniques, 1984; contbr. articles to profl. jours.; designer and/or art dir. some 250 issued stamps. Chmn. bd. dirs. Upper Valley Children's Ctr., Lebanon, N.H., 1968-69; project coord. The Upper Valley Project, Hanover, N.H., 1972-73. With USAR, 1966-69. Mem. Soc. Printers (mem. coun. 1986-88), Nat. Early Am. Glass Club, Am. Inst. Graphic Arts, Am. Philatelic Soc., Am. Revenue Assn., Ephemera Soc. Am. (bd. dirs. 1996-99), Soc. for Protection of N.H. Forests. Avocations: collecting early American glass, photography, antiques, postal history, ephemera.

SHEAHAN, ROBERT EMMETT, lawyer, consultant; b. Chgo., May 20, 1942; s. Robert Emmett and Lola Jean (Moore) S.; m. Pati Smith, Mar. 20, 1991. BA, Ill. Wesleyan U., 1964; JD, Duke U., 1967; MBA, U. Chgo., 1970. Bar: Ill. 1967, La. 1975, N.C. 1978. Vol. VISTA, N.Y.C., 1967-68; trial atty. NLRB, Milw. and New Orleans, 1970-75; ptnr. Jones, Walker, Waechter, Poitevent, Carrere & Denegre, New Orleans, 1975-78; pvt. practice, High Point, N.C., 1978—; bd. dirs. Inst. for Effective Mgmt., Bus. Publs. Inst. Author: Employees and Drug Abuse: An Employer's Handbook, 1994, The Encyclopedia of Drugs in the Workplace, Labor and Employment Law in North Carolina, 1991, Personnel and Employment Law in North Carolina, 1992, Desk Book of Labor and Employment Law for Healthcare Employers, 1995, North Carolina's Healthcare Employers' Desk Manual, 1995, North Carolina lawyers' Desk Book; contbg. author: The Developing Labor Law, 1975—; editor: The World of Personnel; contbg. editor: Employee Testing and the Law; contbr. periodic supplements N.C. Gen. Practice Deskbook, 1992—. Bd. dirs. High Point United Way, 1979-83; mem. congressional action com. High Point C. of C., chmn., 1991—, bd. dirs., 1996—. Mem. ABA, N.C. Bar Assn., High Point Bar Assn., Ill. Bar Assn., La. Bar Assn. Republican. Roman Catholic. Clubs: Sedgefield (N.C.) Country, String and Splinter (High Point), Bald Head (N.C.) Island Club. Home: 101 Bellwood Ct Jamestown NC 27282-9446 Office: Eastchester Office Ctr 603 Eastchester Dr Ste B High Point NC 27262-7647

SHEALY, COURTNEY, Olympic athlete; b. Columbia, S.C., Dec. 12, 1977. Student, U. Ga. Recipient Gold medal 4 x 100-meter freestyle Sydney Olympics, 2000; named co-NCAA Swimmer of Yr., 2000. Office: USA Swimming 1 Olympic Plz Colorado Springs CO 80909-5746*

SHEAR, IONE MYLONAS, archaeologist; b. St. Louis, Feb. 19, 1936; d. George Emmanuel and Lella (Papazouglou) Mylonas; m. Theodore Leslie Shear, June 24, 1959; children: Julia Louise, Alexandra. BA, Wellesley Coll., 1958; MA, Bryn Mawr Coll., 1960, PhD, 1968. Rsch. asst. Inst. for Advanced Study, Princeton, N.J., 1963-65; mem. Agora Excavation, Athens, 1967, 72-94; lectr. art and archaeology Princeton U., 1983-84; lectr. Am. Sch. Classical Studies, Athens, summers 1989-98; also excavator various other sites in Greece and Italy. Author: The Panagia Houses at Mycenae, 1987; contbr. articles to profl. jours. Mem. Archaeol. Inst. Am., Greek Archaeol. Soc. (hon.). Address: 87 Library Pl Princeton NJ 08540-3015 also: Deinokratous 30, Athens 106-76, Greece

SHEAR, MERVYN, oral pathologist, educator; b. Johannesburg, South Africa, Nov. 24, 1931; s. Samuel and Minnie Julia (Labè) S.; m. Caryll Frances Posel, June 25, 1961; 1 child, Keith S.T. B Dental Sci., U. Witwatersrand, Johannesburg, 1954, M Dental Sci., 1961, DSc in Dentistry, 1973, LLD (hon.), 1992; DChD (hon.), U. Pretoria, 1999. Jr. lectr. Faculty of Dentistry U. Witwatersrand, 1955-56, lectr., 1958-65; sr. house officer Eastman Dental Hosp., U. London, 1957; CSIR scholar dept. histochemistry Postgrad. Med. Sch., London, 1962; sr. lectr., head joint oral pathology unit U. Witwatersrand and South African Inst. for Med. Rsch., 1965-82; prof. oral pathology U. Witwatersrand, 1968-82, dep. vice chancellor student affairs, 1983-91, prof. emeritus, 1992—; Extraordinary prof. U. We. Cape, Capt Town, South Africa, 1993—; vis. asst. prof. dept. oral pathology U. Ill., Chgo., 1963; vis. prof. Royal Dental Coll., Copenhagen, 1974, 80, U. Adelaide, Australia, 1976; chair bd. Eastern Seaboard Assn. Tertiary Instns., Kwazulu-Natal, 1993-98; mem. coun. U. Durban-Westville, 1992-99, U. Lesotho, 1990-93. Author: Cysts of the Oral Regions, 3d edit., 1992, Wits: A University in the Apartheid Era, 1996, (with IRH Kramer and JJ Pindborg) Histological Typing of Odontogenic Tumours, 2d edit., 1992; contbr. some 100 articles to profl. and sci. jours. Fellow Royal Coll. Pathologists, Royal Soc. South Africa, Coll. Dentistry South Africa (hon.); mem. Internat. Assn. Oral Pathologists (pres. 1981-84), Internat. Assn. Dental Rsch., South African Dental Assn. Mem. African Nat. Congress Party. Avocations: listening to classical music, reading, swimming, walking. Home: 19 Disa Rd Murdock Valley, 7975 Simon's Town South Africa Office: Faculty of Dentistry, U Western Cape, Pvt Bag X08, 7785 Mitchells Plain South Africa

SHEAR, THEODORE LESLIE, JR., archaeologist, educator; b. Athens, Greece, May 1, 1938; s. Theodore Leslie and Josephine (Platner) S.; m. Ione Doris Mylonas, June 24, 1959; children: Julia Louise, Alexandra. AB summa cum laude, Princeton U., 1959, MA, 1963, PhD, 1966. Instr. Greek and Latin Bryn Mawr Coll., 1964-66, asst. prof., 1966-67; asst. prof. art and archaeology Princeton (N.J.) U., 1967-70, assoc. prof., 1970-79, chmn. program in classical archaeology, 1970-85, assoc. chmn. dept. art and archaeology, 1976-78, 82-83, prof. classical archaeology, 1979—; prof. archaeology Am. Sch. Classical Studies, Athens, 1988-94; mem. mng. com. Am. Sch. Classical Studies, Athens, 1972—; mem. archaeol. expdns. to Greece and Italy, including Mycenae, 1953-54, 58, 62-63, 65-66, Eleusis, 1956, Perati, 1956, Corinth, 1960, Morgantina, Sicily, 1962; mem. Ancient Agora of Athens, 1955, 67, field dir., 1968-94; trustee William Alexander Procter Found., 1982-89, Princeton Jr. Sch., 1983—, pres., 1994—. Author: Kallias of Sphettos and the Revolt of Athens in 286 B.C., 1978; contbr. articles to profl. jours. White fellow Am. Sch. Classical Studies, 1959-60. Mem. Archaeol. Inst. Am., Am. Philol. Assn., Coll. Art Assn., Archaeol. Soc. Athens (hon.), Phi Beta Kappa. Republican. Episcopalian. Clubs: Century Assn. (N.Y.C.); Nassau (Princeton); Princeton (N.Y.C.); Hellenic Yacht (Piraeus, Greece). Home: 87 Library Pl Princeton NJ 08540-3015 also: 30 Deinokratous St, Athens Greece

SHEARBURN, DUDLEY DOVEL, retired education educator; b. Birmingham, Ala., Jan. 8, 1929; d. James St. Real and Mary Nelle (Holley) Dovel; m. Everett Brice Shearburn Jr., May 5, 1951 (div. June 1970); children: E. Brice III, James Pickering, Thomas Fitzmaurice, Mary Holley, John Woodley, William Dudley, Martha Ellen. BA, So. Coll., Birmingham, 1951; MEd, St. Louis U., 1971, PhD, 1976. Elem. tchr. St. Louis Pub. Schs., 1964-69; tchr. spl. edn. St. Louis County Spl. Sch. Dist., 1969-71, supr. programs for learning disabled, 1972-77; instr. Fontbonne Coll., St. Louis, 1971-72; assoc. prof. Salem Coll., Winston-Salem, N.C., 1977-95, prof. emerita, 1995—; bd. dirs. Coun. Exceptional Children, Winston-Salem, 1978-80; mem. literacy bd. Literacy Project, Winston-Salem, 1985-88. Author: Get A Good Life, 1995. Democrat. Avocation: travel. Home: PO Box 10277 Winston Salem NC 27108-0277

SHEARD, STEPHEN JOHN, engineering science educator, researcher; b. Slough, Berkshire, Eng., June 23, 1962; s. Lionel John and Anne (Meyrick) S.; m. Jennifer Elaine Sabourin, Nov. 2, 1985; children: Emma Jane, Jessica Helen, Connie May Alison. BS, Univ. Coll., London, 1984, PhD, 1987; MA (hon.), U. Oxford, Eng., 1988. Chartered Engr., Eng. Lectr. Oxford (Eng.) U., 1988—. Author: (with others) Non-Destructive Evaluation, 1994; contbr. articles to profl. jours. Mem. IEE, Optical Soc. Am. Office: Oxford U, Trinity College, Oxford OX1 3BH, England

SHEARER, ALAN, professional soccer player; b. Newcastle upon Tyne, Eng., Aug. 13, 1970. Forward Southampton Football Club, Eng., 1988-92, Blackburn Rovers Football Club, 1992-96, Newcastle United Football Club, 1996—; with Eng. Nat. Team, 1992-2000; forward World Cup, 1994, 98. Named PFA Footballer of Yr., 1994-95. Office: SFX Sports Group (Europe), 35/36 Grosvenor St, London W1X 9FG, England

SHEARER, DEREK NORCROSS, international studies educator, diplomat, administrator; b. L.A., Dec. 5, 1946; s. Lloyd and Marva (Peterson) S.; m. Ruth Y. Goldway, July 8, 1976; 1 child, Casey; stepchildren: Anthony, Julie. BA, Yale U., 1968; PhD, Union Grad. Sch., Yellow Springs, Ohio, 1977. Lectr. U. Calif., L.A., 1979-81; dir. internat. and pub. affairs ctr., prof. of pub. policy Occidental Coll., L.A., 1981-94, 98—; dep. under sec. U.S. Dept. Commerce, Washington, 1993; U.S. ambassador to Finland, U.S. Dept. State, Washington, 1994-97; prof. internat. affairs Occidental Coll., L.A., 1997—; fellow Econ. Strategy Inst., Washington, 1993; policy adv. to Presidential Candidate Bill Clinton, 1990-92; adv. on NATO peace keeping USN, 1997—; pub. policy fellow Woodrow Wilson Internat. Scholars Ctr., 1999-2000. Contbr. articles to profl. publs. Planning commr. City of Santa Monica (Calif.), 1984; bd. mem. Nat. Consumer Bank, Washington, 1991. Recipient Guggenheim Fellowship Guggenheim Found., 1984, U.S.-Japan Leadership fellow Japan Soc., 1991. Democrat. Avocations: basketball, tennis, travel, mysteries. Fax: 323-259-2734. Office: IPAC Occidental Coll Los Angeles CA 90041

SHEARGOLD, RONALD HARRY, engineer, military officer; b. Sydney, NSW, Australia, June 27, 1947; s. Harry Cecil and Merlene Malvine (New) S.; m. Judith Ann Foster, Sept. 27, 1968; children: Andrew, Matthew, Nathan. Enlisted Royal Australian Navy, 1964, advanced through grades to sub-lt., 1985; sr. artificer HMAS Stuart, Sydney, 1977-79; tech. instr. HMAS Nirimba, Sydney, 1980-82; charge artificer HMAS Kimbla, Australia, 1982-84; tech. support engr. Navy Office, Canberra, Australia, 1986-88; ret. Royal Australian Navy, 1988; civilian tech. support engr. Navy Office, Canberra, 1988-95; re-entered Royal Australian Navy, 1995, advanced to lt. comdr.; asst. engr. HMAS Torrens, Australia, 1995-97; engr. HMAS Kanimbla, Australia, 1997—. Recipient Australian Active Svc. medal Australian Govt., Vietnam, Malaya, 1966, Brit. Gen. Svc. medal, Borneo, 1966, Vietnam Logistics Support medal Australian Govt., Vietnam, 1966. Anglican. Avocations: rugby, carpentry.

SHEARLOCK, DAVID JOHN, dean; b. Kingston-upon-Thames, Surrey, Eng., July 1, 1932; s. Arthur John and Honora Frances (Hawkins) S.; m. Jean Margaret Marr, May 30, 1959; children: Ann Margaret, Timothy John. BA in Geography with honors, U. Birmingham, Eng., 1955; postgrad. Cambridge, Eng., 1957. Curate of Guisborough Yorkshire, 1957-60; curate Christchurch Priory, Hampshire, 1960-64; vicar of Kingsclere Hampshire, 1964-71; vicar Romsey Abbey, Hampshire, 1971-82; hon. canon Winchester Cathedral, 1978-82; dean, rector St. Mary's Cathedral, Truro, 1982-97; ret., 1997. Author: The Practice of Preaching, 1990, When Words Fail, 1996. Chaplain Cornwall Fire Brigade, 1990-97; chmn. Truro Victim Support, 1983-95, Truro Diocesan Bd. Ministry, 1985-97, Cathedral Music Working Party, 1992-97. With Royal Arty., 1950-52, Honourable Artillery Co., 1952-56. Fellow Royal Soc. Arts, Royal Geog. Soc. Avocations: music, walking, wine, reading, railways. Home: 3 The Tanyard, Shadrack St, Beaminster Dorset DT8 3BG, England

SHEATH, ROBERT GORDON, botanist; b. Toronto, Ont., Can., Dec. 26, 1950; came to U.S., 1978; s. Harry Gordon and Shirley Irene (Rose) S. BSc, U. Toronto, 1973, PhD, 1977. Nat. Rsch. Coun. Can. postdoctoral fellow U. B.C., 1977-78; asst. prof. aquatic biology U. R.I., Kingston, 1978-82, assoc. prof., 1982-86, chmn. dept. botany, 1986-90, prof., 1987-91; head dept. biology Meml. U., St. Johns, Nfld., Can., 1991-95; dean coll. biol. sci. U. Guelph, Ont., 1995—; mem. evolution and ecology grant selection com NSERC, 1994-97, chair, 1996-97, selection com. life scis., 1996, chair maj. facilities access life scis. subcom., 2000. Editor: (with M.M. Harlin) Freshwater and Marine Plants of Rhode Island, 1988, (with K.M. Cole) Biology of the Red Algae, 1990; contbr. more than 115 articles to profl. jours. Recipient G.A. Cox Gold medal, U. Toronto, 1973, Darbaker prize Bot. Soc. Am., 1997; grantee NSF, 1980-91, NSERC, 1991—. Mem. Internat. Phycological Soc. (editl. bd. 1993-95, nominating com. chair 2000—), Phycological Soc. Am. (editl. bd. 1983-86, 96—, assoc. editor 1984-89, pres. 1991-92, Bold award 1976), Am. Soc. Limnology and Oceanography, Arctic Inst. N.Am., Brit. Phycological Soc. (overseas v.p. 1997-99, freshwater flora com. 1993—, assoc. editor 1999—), Sigma Xi, Phi Kappa Phi. Office: U Guelph, Dean Coll Biol Sci, Guelph, ON Canada NIG 2WI

SHEDRINSKY, ALEXANDER MIKCHAIL, chemistry educator, art conservation consultant; b. Leningrad, USSR, Mar. 27, 1943; arrived in U.S., 1980; s. Mikchail Alexander Shedrinsky and Mussa A. (Gordon) Tsipkina; m. Raissa A. Bekker, Oct. 16, 1965 (div. Apr. 1975); 1 child, Mikchail Alexander; m. Maria G. Kurbatova, June 30, 1982; 1 child, Maria-Antonia. MS (equivalent) in Chemistry, Leningrad U., 1965; MS in Organic Chemistry, NYU, 1983, PhD in Organic Chemistry, 1986. Rsch. asst. State

Sci. Rsch. Inst. Pulp and Paper, Leningrad, 1971-72; asst. prof. chemistry Leningrad NW Poly. Tech., 1972-75; lectr. in organic chemistry Leningrad Pharm. Sch., 1976-79; tchg. fellow NYU, N.Y.C., 1981-83, postdoctoral fellow Conservation Ctr. Inst. Fine Arts, 1986-88; asst. prof. chemistry L.I. U., Bklyn., 1988-92, assoc. prof. chemistry, 1992-97, prof. chemistry, 1997—; adj. assoc. prof. Conservation Ctr. Inst. Fine Arts NYU, 1993-97, adj. prof. conservation Conservation Ctr. Inst. Fine Arts, 1997-98; cons. Met. Mus. Art, N.Y.C., 1994—; vis. scientist Am. Mus. Natural History, N.Y.C., 1995—; vis. prof. Forchheimer, 1997—; adj. prof. conservation Conservation Ctr. Inst. Fine Arts NYU, 1998—. Contbr. chpt. to book, articles to internat. scientific jours.; reviewer Jour. Analytical and Applied Pyrolysis, (jour.) Curator, (jour.) Archeometry, 1989—. Fulbright professor USIA, St. Petersburg (Russia) Acad. Art, 1995, Andrew W. Mellon fellow Met. Mus. Art, Dept. Object Conservation, 1988-90, Charles and Francis Atkins fellow Met. Mus. Art, Dept. Paintings Conservation, 1984-86. Mem. Am. Chem. Soc. (tour spkr. 1992—, Washington), Internat. Inst. Conservation, N.Y. Acad. Scis. Achievements include synthesis of new synthetic varnish for the purpose of painting conservation; introducing analytical pyrolysis in the field of art conservation (first review on the subject in 1989); development of new analytical approach (Py-GC and Py-GC-MS) to analysis of different ambers. Office: NYU Conservation Ctr IFA 14 E 78th St New York NY 10021-1706 also: LIU 1 University Plz Brooklyn NY 11201-5301

SHEDYAKOV, VLADIMIR E., economic theory educator; b. Yaroslavl, Russia, Oct. 7, 1963; s. Eugeni A. and Valentina V. (Peshkina) S. B of Journalism, Internat. Affairs, Kharkov (Ukraine) State U., 1983, B of English and Germanic Letters, 1983, MS in Econs., 1986, PhD in Econs. and Mgmt., 1990, DSc in Sociology, 1997. Lectr. Kharkov State U., 1986-89, 90-91, rschr., 1989-90, sr. lectr., 1991-93, assoc. prof., 1993-96, prof., 1996—; coun. mem. Kharkov Stock of Goods, 1990-92, Renaissance Found., Ukraine, 1995-97. Editor sci. jours. and bus. newspaper, 1995—; author: K. Marx and Actual Problems of Agrarian Theory, 1989, the Solving of Socialization's Economic Contradictions as Create Activiey's Motive Power, 1998, The System of Socialism's Economic Laws, 1989, Economic Reform, 1990, Creative Activity of workers and It's Economic Stimulation, 1990, Man in Society of Alienation's Labour, 1991, Man and Alienation of Labour in Our County, 1991, The System of Economically Active Populations Social Protection, 1993, The Introduction in Economic Theory, 1993, Fundamentals of Market Economy, 1993, Macroeconomics, 1993, Microtransition Period, 1996, Economic Theory and Practice, 1993, The Management in the OSphere of the Investment and the Personnel: Peculiarities Under the Transition Period, 1996, Postmodernization of Labour Relations as an Object of Social Management, 1996, The Economic Theory, 1997; contbr. numerous articles to profl. jours. Chmn. Kharkov dept. NGO Ukrainian Perspectives, 1991—; majority leader Kharkov Regional Soviet, 1991—, vice-chmn. com., 1994—. Lt. Soviet Army, 1985. Lenin's grant Kharkov State U., 1983-86; Salzburg Seminar fellow, 1996, All-Asian Congress of Internat. Indsl. Rels. Assn. fellow, 1996, Nippon Found. fellow, 1996. Mem. Scientists Assn. (pres.), Kharkov Bus. Assn. (bd. dirs. 1994—), Internat. Acad. Cycles (pres. Kharkov dept. 1994—), Internat. Slavonic Acad. (mem. coun. Kharkov dept. 1994—. Christian Orthodox. Avocations: journalism, theater, farming. Home: Apt 370, Korchagintsev St 13, 310178 Kharkov Ukraine Office: Kharkov State U/Econ Theory, Square of Freedom 4, 310077 Kharkov Ukraine

SHEEHAN, LAWRENCE JAMES, lawyer; b. San Francisco, July 23, 1932. AB, Stanford U., 1957, LLB, 1959. Bar: Calif. 1960. Law clk. to chief judge U.S. Ct. Appeals 2d Cir., N.Y.C., 1959-60; assoc. O'Melveny & Myers, L.A., 1960-68, ptnr., 1969-94, of counsel, 1995—; bd. dirs. FPA Mut. Funds, TCW Convertible Securities Fund Inc., Source Capital, Inc. Mem. ABA, Los Angeles County Bar Assn., Calif. Bar Assn., Order of Coif. Office: O Melveny & Myers 1999 Avenue Of The Stars Los Angeles CA 90067-6035 also: 400 S Hope St Los Angeles CA 90071-2801

SHEEHAN, MICHAEL JARBOE, archbishop; b. Wichita, Kans., July 9, 1939; s. John Edward and Mildred (Jarboe) S. MST, Gregorian U., Rome, 1965; D of Canon Law, Lateran U., Rome, 1971. Ordained priest Roman Cath. Ch., 1964. Asst. gen. sec. Nat. Coun. Cath. Bishops, Washington, 1971-76; rector Holy Trinity Sem., Dallas, 1976-82; pastor Immaculate Conception Ch., Grand Prairie, Tex., 1982-83; bishop Diocese of Lubbock, Tex., 1983-93; archbishop Archdiocese of Santa Fe, Albuquerqe, N.Mex., 1993—; past chmn. Am. Bd. Cath. Missions, 1989-91; trustee Cath. Relief Svcs., 1992—. Contbr. articles to New Cath. Ency. Trustee St. Mary Hosp., Lubbock, 1983-89; bd. dirs. Tex. Conf. of Chs. Mem. Serra Club (chaplain 1983-93, chmn. NCCB com. on Evangelization 1996-99, mem. NCCB adminstrv. com. Washington). Avocations: snow skiing, racquetball. Office: Archdiocese Santa Fe 4000 Saint Josephs Pl NW Albuquerque NM 87120-1714*

SHEEHAN, PETER WINSTON, psychology educator, researcher; b. Sydney, Australia, Dec. 8, 1940; s. John Dominic and Frances Mary (Quinn) S.; m. Mary Christina Tutt, Dec. 14, 1963; children: Grania Rachael, Madoc Emmanuel. BA with honours, U. Sydney, 1961, PhD, 1965. Research assoc. Pa. Hosp., Phila., 1965-67; asst. prof. CUNY, 1967-68; from lectr. to sr. lectr. U. New Eng., Armidale, Australia, 1968-73; prof. U. Queensland, Brisbane, Australia, 1973-97; dir. research U. Queensland, 1987-97; vice chancellor Australian Cath. U., 1998—; chmn. Australian Research Grants Scheme, Canberra, 1983-85, 92-93, dep. chair Australian Rsch. Coun., 1993-94; pres. Acad. Social Scis. in Australia, 1991-93; pres. Internat. Congress Psychol., 1988. Co-author: Methodologies of Hypnosis, 1976, Hypnosis and Experience (Arthur Shapiro award 1983), 1982, Hypnosis, Memory, and Behavior in Criminal Investigations, 1995; editor: The Function and Nature of Imagery, 1972, Australian Jour. Psychology, 1986-91; assoc. editor Internat. Jour. Clin. and Exptl. Hypnosis, 1981-92; editorial bd. Jour. Abnormal Psychology, 1979-89. Dep. chmn. Commonwealth Films Bd. Rev., Sydney, 1985, chmn., 1986-87. Decorated Officer Gen. Divsn. Order of Australia; recipient Henry Guze award Soc. Clin. and Exptl. Hypnosis; best Research Publ. in Hypnosis grantee, 1971, 81, 82, 84. Fellow Australian Psychol. Soc. (hon.), Am. Psychol. Assn., Acad. Social Scis. Australia (hon.). Roman Catholic. Avocation: film appreciation and evaluation. Fax: 2 9739 2905. Home: 25 Glenfield St, Hill End QLD 4101, Australia Office: Australian Cath U, MacKillop Campus, North Sydney NSW 2059, Australia

SHEEHY, ALAN JAMES, microbiology researcher, educator; b. Hampton, Australia, June 21, 1951; s. Thomas A. and Enid G. (Chamberlain) S.; m. Tania E. Jacobini, Sept. 26, 1987; children: Jessica Elena, Rachel Grace. B of Applied Sci., U. Canberra, Australia, 1977; M of Applied Sci., U. Tech., Sydney, 1989. Tech. asst. Monash U., Melbourne, 1970-72; rsch. asst. Melbourne U., 1972-74; med. scientist ACT Health Svcs., Canberra, Australia, 1974-79; from lectr. to sr. lectr. U. Canbera, 1979-95; prof. microbiology U. Canberra, 1995-97; dean sci. U. Sunshine Coast, 1996—; exec. dir. microbiology rsch. unit, 1989-97; cons., sr. prin. rsch. scientist CSIRO Divsn. of Exploration Geosci./Water Resources, Perth, 1987-91; conv. Live Oil Svcs., London, 1987-91: cons. Australian Inst. of Med. Scientists, 1983-96. Contbr. articles to profl. jours.; inventor recovery of oil from oil reservoirs, biological oil stimulation. Gen. Tech. grantee Australian Govt. Dept. Industry, Sci. and Tech., 1990-95. Fellow Australian Inst. of Med. Scientists; mem. Australian Soc. for Microbiology, Am. Soc. Microbiology. Avocations: hockey, golf. Fax: 61 7 5430 2889. E-mail: asheehy@usc.edu.au. Office: U Sunshine Coast, Maroochydore DC QLD 4558, Australia

SHEEHY, BRENDAN MATTHEW, systems engineer; b. London, June 21, 1972; s. Daniel and Rosemary Margaret S. Sys. adminstr. King Edwards Hosp. Fund for London, 1990-95; sys. mgr. NHS Exec., London, 1995-97; customer interest mgr. UK Dept. Health, London, 1997—. Roman Catholic. Home: 33 Alan Hocken Way, London England E15 3AT Office: Dept Health, 79 Whitehall, London SW1A 2NS, England

SHEEHY, JEROME JOSEPH, electrical engineer; b. Hartford, Conn., Dec. 3, 1935; s. Jeremiah and Anna (Foley) S.; m. Jean Ann Baldassari, Oct. 13, 1962; children: Caroline, Jerome, Daniel, Carlene. BSEE, U. Conn., 1962, MSEE, 1967. Electronic engr. USN Underwater Sound Lab., New London, Conn., 1962-69; mem. tech. staff Rockwell Internat., Anaheim, Calif., 1969-74; staff engr. Hughes Aircraft Co., Fullerton, Calif., 1974-83; systems engr. Norden Systems, Santa Ana, Calif., 1983-89; advanced engring. specialist Lockheed Martin Aircraft Svc., Ontario, Calif., 1990-97. Contbr. articles to Jour. Acoustical Soc. Am. With USAF, 1954-57. Mem. Acoustical Soc. Am., Tau Beta Pi, Eta Kappa Nu. Achievements include research in detection and estimation theory for non-gaussian noise, non-normal statistics. Home: 8 Sagitta Way Coto De Caza CA 92679-5102

SHEEN, PORTIA YUNN-LING, retired physician; b. Republic of China, Jan. 13, 1919; came to U.S., 1988; d. Y. C. and A. Y. (Chow) Sheen; m. Kuo, 1944 (dec. 1970); children: William, Ida, Alexander, David, Mimi. MD, Nat. Med. Coll. Shanghai, 1943. Intern, then resident Cen. Hosp., Chungking, Szechuan, China, 1943; with Hong Kong Govt. Med. and Health Dept., 1948-76; med. supt. Kowloon (Hong Kong) Hosp., 1948-63, Queen Elizabeth Hosp., Kowloon, 1963-73, Med. and Health Hdqrs. and Health Ctr., Kowloon, 1973-76, Yan Chai Hosp., New Territories, Hong Kong, 1976-87. Fellow Hong Kong Coll. Family Physicians; mem. AAAS, British Med. Assn., Hong Kong Med. Assn., Hong Kong Pediatric Soc., N.Y. Acad. Sci. Methodist. Avocations: reading, music. Home: 1408 Golden Rain Rd Apt 7 Entry 1 Roosmoor Walnut Creek CA 94595-2442

SHEEN, SHYN-SHIN, aquaculture engineer; b. Kaohsiung, Taiwan, Nov. 22, 1956; s. Her-Ruzen and Hui-Mei (Lin) S.; m. Wu-Mei Wei, May 25, 1990; chilren: Sunny, Alice. BS, Nat. Taiwan Ocean U., 1979; MS, U. N.C., 1985; PhD, Miss. State U., 1989. Prof. Nat. Taiwan Ocean U., 1989—; cons. Capson Internat., Inc., 1997—, Hon Soon Marine and Fishery Co., 1995—. Author: (book) CRC Handbook of Mariculture: Crustacean Aquaculture, 1993. Mem. Am. Fishery Soc., World Aquaculture Soc., The Fishery of Taiwan. Avocations: fishing, badminton. Office: Nat Taiwan Ocean Univ, 202 Keelung Taiwan

SHEENA BAILURE, SHERIGARA, chemistry educator, researcher; b. Udupi, Karnataka, India, Dec. 17, 1945; s. Beeranna and Akkamma Bailure S.; m. Jayashree Udupi Sherigara, Mar. 12, 1978; children: Mahima, Chritha. BS, Mahatma Gandhi Meml. Coll., Udupi, India, 1965; LLB, Law Coll., Udupi, India, 1969; MS, Mysore (India) U., 1976; DS, Mangalore (India) U., 1978. Demonstrator in chemistry Mahatma Gandhi Coll., Udupi, India, 1965-69, Govt. Sci. Coll., Tumkur, India, 1969-77, Govt. Coll., Mangalore, India, 1977-78; lectr. in chemistry Govt. Coll., 1978-83; lectr. chemistry Mangalore U., 1983-85, reader in chemistry, 1985-94; prof. indsl. chemistry Kuvempu U., Shankaraghatta, Shimoga, India, 1994—; chmn. indsl. chemistry, rsch. supr. Kuvempu U., 1994—. Contbr. articles to profl. jours. Capt. Nat. Cadet Corps, 1974-83. Grantee Dept. Atomic Energy, 1996; recipient Appreciation award Indian Assn. Analytical Scientists, Mumbai, 1998. Fellow Indian Chem. Soc.; mem. Indian Coun. Chemists, Indian Assn. Nuclear Chemists and Allied Scientists (life), Electrochem. Soc. India. Hindu. Avocations: fiction, biographies, articles. E-mail: root@shikuv.kar.nic.in. Office: Kuvempu U, Shankaraghatta, 577451 Shimoga India

SHEFER, OLGA VLADIMIROVNA, physician, mathematician, researcher; b. Tomsk, Russia, May 26, 1960; d. Vladimir Vasilievich and Elisaveta Ivanovna (Nemoliaeva) Martinenko; m. Vladimir Alexandrovich Shefer, Mar. 31, 1984; 1 child, Evelina. PhD, Inst. Atmospheric Optics, Tomsk, Russia, 1992. Jr. scientist Inst. Atmospheric Optics, Tomsk, 1983-93; sr. lectr. Tomsk State U., 1993-96, assoc. prof., 1996—. Contbr. articles to profl. jours. including Applied Optics and Atmospheric and Oceanic Optics. Grantee Ministry Russian Edn., 1996, Russian Found. Fund Rsch., 1998. Avocations: music, literature, climbing. Home: Bela Kun St 28-4, 634063 Tomsk Russia Office: Tomsk State U, 36 Lenin Ave, 634050 Tomsk Russia

SHEFFIELD, DAVID JOHN, software engineer; b. July 4, 1946; s. Hugh Frederick and Eileen Emily (Sturgess) S.; m. Patricia Roullier, Sept. 12, 1970. Apprentice Standard Range & Foundry, Watford, Herts., Eng., 1963-68; research asst. Unilever Research Lab., Welwyn, Eng., 1968-71; design mgr. TFS Ltd., Welwyn, 1971—; automation cons. D.J.S. Devels., 1978—. Mem. Ch. of Eng. Home: 57 Beverley Gardens, Saint Albans Herts AL4 9BJ, England Office: Avdel Ltd, Mundells, Welwyn Garden City, Herts., TFS Ltd Mundells, Welwyn Garden City, Herts England

SHEFFIELD, LESLIE JON, geneticist, physician; b. Melbourne, Victoria, Australia, Nov. 19, 1944; s. Henry and Ruth Sheffield; m. Edith Rogers, 1977; children: David, Allan. Degree in med. sci., U. Melbourne, 1967, B Medicine B Surgery, 1968; MSc, McMaster U., 1978. Intern St. Vincent's Hosp. Medicine; resident Royal Children's Hosp., Melbourne; dir. genetics dept. Adelaide Children's Hosp., 1978-85; med. geneticist Victorian Clin. Genetic Svc., Melbourne, 1985—, dir. edn. and tng., 1995—. Mem. Human Genetics Soc. Australasia (prenatal diagnosis com.). E-mail: sheffld@cryptic.rch.unimelb.edu.au. Office: Royal Childrens Hosp, Flemington Rd, Parkville VIC 3052, Australia

SHEFTE, DALBERT UHRIG, lawyer; b. Evanston, Ill., Sept. 17, 1927; s. Frederick William and Edna Helena (Uhrig) S.; m. Adelaide Morrison, May 9, 1953; children: William Scarr, Scarlett Ann, Robert Uhrig, John Dalbert. BS in Mech. Engring., Northwestern U., 1949, JD, 1952. Bar: Ill. 1952, N.C. 1960, U.S. Supreme Ct. 1960, U.S. Dist. Ct. N.C., U.S. Ct. Appeals (4th, 7th and fed. cirs.). Assoc. Hofgren, Schroeder et al, Chgo., 1954-56, Ooms & Dominik, Chgo., 1956-58, Parrott & Richards, Charlotte, N.C., 1958-61; ptnr. Shefte, Pinckney & Sawyer, Charlotte, 1961-97, Kennedy, Covington, Lobdell & Hickman, LLP, Charlotte, 1997—; patent expert witness, spl. master in field. Mem. com., bd. dirs. United Way, Charlotte, 1971-95; v.p., chmn., com. mem. Boy Scouts Am., Charlotte, 1963-88. Served to sgt. U.S. Army, 1952-54. Mem. ABA (various coms.), N.C. Bar Assn. (various coms., chmn. intellectual property law sect.), Mecklenburg County Bar Assn. (com. mem., bd. dirs.), Carolina Patent, Trademark and Copyright Law Assn. (pres. 1982-83), Am. Intellectual property Law Assn. (various coms.), Charlotte Eng. Club (pres. 1966-67), Myers Park Country Club (pres. 1985-86), Charlotte Rotary Club (pres. 1984-85). Republican. Presbyterian. Home: 1445 Maryland Ave Charlotte NC 28209-1527 Office: Kennedy Covington Lobdell & Hickman 4200 Bank Am Corp Ctr 100 N Tryon St Charlotte NC 28202-4006

SHEFTMAN, HOWARD STEPHEN, lawyer; b. Columbia, S.C., May 20, 1949; s. Nathan and Rena Mae (Kantor) S.; children from a previous marriage: Amanda Elaine, Emily Catherine; m. Karyn L. Jenkins. BS in Bus. Adminstrn., U. S.C., 1971, JD, 1974. Bar: S.C. 1974, U.S. Dist. Ct. 1975, U.S. Ct. Appeals (4th cir.) 1982. Assoc. Kirkland, Taylor & Wilson, West Columbia, S.C., 1974-75; ptnr. Sheftman, Oswald & Holland, West Columbia, 1975-77, Finkel & Altman, LLC, Columbia, 1977—. Mem. S.C. Bar Assn. (chmn. practice and procedure com. 1999—), S.C. Trial Lawyers Assn. (chmn. domestic rels. sect. 1982-83, bd. govs. 1987-93, 94-98), Richland Bar Assn., Met. Sertoma Club (pres. 1986-87). Jewish. Office: Finkel & Altman LLC PO Box 1799 Columbia SC 29202-1799

SHEHAB, MOUFID, university president. Pres. Cairo U. Office: Cairo U, PO Box 12611, Orman, Giza Cairo Egypt*

SHEHABI, YAHYA, critical care physician; b. Al-Karak, Karak, Jordan, Mar. 1, 1954; arrived in Australia, 1991; s. Mahmoud and Adla Shehabi; m. Samar Khatib, Dec. 26, 1981; children: Faris, Omar, Noor. MB BChir, U. Jordan, 1979. Registrar in tng. anesthesia Prince of Wales Group, Sydney, Australia, 1984-87, registrar in tng. intensive care, 1987-88; sr. fellow intensive care Westmead Hosp., Sydney, 1989; dir. critical care U. Jordan, Amman, 1989-91; dir. intensive care Lidcombe Hosp., U. Sydney, Sydney, 1991-92, Prince Henry Hosp., U. NSW, Sydney, 1992—; gen. mgr. So. Cross Intensive Care Group, Sydney, 1994—; critical care cons. on design and function Health Care Australia, Sydney, 1994—; critical care cons. Jordan Hosp. and Med. Ctr., Amman, 1996-97; established Nat. Capital Intensive Care Group, Canberra, 1998; mgr., dir. critical care svcs. Prince of Wales Hosp., 1998—, Canberra Hosp., 1999—. Recipient Divisional medal Divsn. Anesthesia and Critical Care, 1997. Fellow Faculty Anaesthesia Royal Australian Coll. of Surgeons, Faculty Intensive Care Australian New Zealand Coll. Anasethetists, Australian Coll. Anesthetists; mem. Am. Heart Assn. (critical care coun.), European Soc. Intensive Care (internat. mem.). Avocations: traveling, tennis, chess, music, swimming. E-mail: yshehabi@ozemail.com.au. Home: 11 Harrison Ave, 2035 South Coogee NSW 2034, Australia Office: Prince of Wales Pvt Hosp, Ste 1A Level 7 Barker St, 2031 Randwick NSW, Australia

SHEHAN, GERRY D., nurse, healthcare executive; b. Dallas, Sept. 18, 1949; s. William D. Shehan and Anna Lee Hart; m. Amy Christine Hoffman, Dec. 3, 1988; children: Sean Patrick, Maura Kate. BA in Biology, North Tex. State U., 1977; BSN, Tex. Woman's U., 1979; M of Health Sci., Tex. Wesleyan U., 1989. Cert. nurse anesthetist, Tex., Okla. Nurse Denton (Tex.) State Sch., 1979-80; nurse cons. U. N.Mex. Hosp., Albuquerque, 1980-83; asst. head nurse burn unit King Fahad Mil. Hosp., Jeddah, Saudi Arabia, 1983-84; CEO Preferred Anesthesia Svc., Sheman, Tex., 1989—; nurse cons. for pain mgmt. Grayson County Home Hospice, Sherman, 1997-2000. Bd. dirs. Olde Towne Cmty. Neighborhood Assn., Sherman, Tex., 1993-2000; chairperson Keep Sherman Beautiful commn. City of Sherman, 1998-2000; mem. natural resources adv. com. Texoma Coun. of Govts., Sherman, 1998-2000. Mem. Tex. Assn. Nurse Anesthetists (bd. dirs. 1996-98, sec.-treas. 1998-99). Unitarian. Avocations: backpacking, kayaking, camping, jogging. Home and Office: Preferred Anesthesia Svc 1503 S Travis St Sherman TX 75090-8822

SHEHU, AVNI, judge; b. Burrel, Albania, Feb. 6, 1957; married; 2 children. Student Faculty of Law, U. Tirana (Albania), 1977-81. Lawyer Dist. Ct., Mati, Albania, 1981-83; judge Dist. Ct., Mirdita, Albania, 1983-87; justice civil cases Supreme Ct., Tirana, 1987-92, pres., 1998; chmn. bd. dirs. Sch. Magistrates, 1996—, prof., 1997—; v.p. Ct. Cassation, Tirana, 1992-95, pres., 1995—; chn. bd. office of adminstrn. budget of judiciary, 1998-99; mem. commn. drafting Constitution Republic of Albania, 1994; mem. working group draft of procedures of Civil Code; mem. working group draft of law on orgn. of judiciary, law on Sch. Magistrates, 1993-95; participant internat. confs. including 14th Congress Internat. Assn. Juvenile and Family Ct. Magistrates, Bremen, Germany, 1994, 9th Congress on the Prevention of Crime and the Treatment of Offenders, Cairo, 1995, Internat. Jud. Conf. Ctr. for Democracy, Washington, 1996, Strasbourg, 1997. Contbr. articles to profl. jours.; mem. bd. dirs. The Justice mag., Jurisprudence mag. Founder (with others) Conflict Resolution and Reconciliation of Disputes, Albania. Mem. Jurists Assn. (dep. chmn.). Office: Rruga Vasil Shanto, Tirana Albania*

SHEIKH, ABDEL QADAR, engineering management executive; b. Silwad, Jordan, Jan. 13, 1948; came to U.S., 1967; s. Khalil Ayyad and Tamam Mohammad (Atra) Silwadi Sheik; m. Carmen Elsa Ortiz, June 7, 1973; children: Khalil, Samir, Farid, Samia. BSChE, U. P.R., Mayaguez, 1975; postgrad., Calif. State U., Turlock, 1983. Process engr., process supr. P.R. Olefins, Ponce, 1975-79; chief engr., ops. SWCC, Alkhobar, Saudi Arabia, 1979-80; field supt. Catalytic, Phila., 1980-81; project leader Aramco, Udhailyeh, Saudi Arabia, 1982-83; sr. process engr. Saudi Petrochem. Co., Sadaf/Sabic Jubail, Saudi Arabia, 1983-86; supt. Saudi Yanbu Petrochem. Co., Yanpet/Sabic, Yanbu, Saudi Arabia, 1986-91; utilities and off-sites mgr., engring. constrn. cons. Arabian Indsl. Fibers Co., Ibn Rushd/Sabic, Yanbu/London, 1994-97; cons. water treatment, Ponce, 1978. Mem. AIChE, Nat. Assn. Corrosion Engrs., Am. Chem. Soc. Home: PO Box 187 Chowchilla CA 93610-0187

SHEIKH, AHSAN IMDAD, company executive; b. Lahore, Pakistan, Nov. 3, 1970; s. Imdad and Salma Imdad Hussain. B in Commerce, Govt. Islamia Coll. Commerce, Lahore, 1990. V.p. Imdad Comml. Corp., Lahore, 1985—; gen. mgr. Faisal Thread Wks., Lahore, 1987—; CEO Sheikh & Co., Lahore, 1992—; pres. Mohsin Ahsan & Co., Lahore, 1992—. Avocations: reading, gardening, stamp collecting, pen pals, picture collecting. Home: Multan Rd, 29/C Bank Cly St #3, Lahore 54500, Pakistan Office: 29/C Noor Ullah Colony, Str #72 Multan Rd Zubaida Park, Lahore Punjab 54500, Pakistan

SHEIKH, ASRAR UL HAQ, engineering educator; b. Jullundhar, Punjab, India, Sept. 23, 1942; arrived in Canada, 1981; s. Mohammad Ali and Nawab (Begum) S.; m. Parveen Akhtar Gulzar, Jan. 15, 1970; children: Farhana, Fahim, Samia. BSc in Engring., U. Engring. and Tech., Lahore, Pakistan, 1964; MSc in Info. Engring., U. Birmingham, Eng., 1966, PhD in Electronic and Elec. Engring., 1969. Cert. engr. Assn. of Profl. Engrs., Can., 1986. Postdoctoral fellow U. Birmingham, 1975-78; assoc. prof. Gar Younis U., Benghazi, Libya, 1978-81; assoc. prof. Carleton U., Ottawa, Can., 1981-85, prof., assoc. chair, 1988-91, prof. dir. PCs rsch. lab., 1985-97; prof, assoc. head, dir. Wisrcenter HK Polytech., Hong Kong, 1997—; pres. Radnet Comms., Ottawa, 1985-95; sr. assoc. cons. Lapp-Hancock Assocs., Ottawa, 1985-97. Contbr. articles to profl. jours. Vol. Helping Edn. U. Engring. and Tech., Lahore, 1993, 96. Recipient Rsch. Achievement award Carleton U., 1995. Fellow IEE; mem. IEEE (sr.). Avocations: reading books on religion, hiking, traveling. Office: HK Polytech U, Dept Elecronic/Info Engring, Hong Kong China

SHEIKH, ATIQUE ZAFAR, public information officer; b. Lucknow, India, Nov. 15, 1940; s. Zafar Ahmed and Kishwar Zafar; m. Rukhsana Atique; children: Mubeen-uz, Moeen-uz, Uzma Atique. MA in History, Punjab U., Lahore, Pakistan, 1962; cert., Nat. Inst. Pub. Adminstrn., Lahore, 1970, Royal Inst. Pub. Adminstrn., London, 1986; diploma in archives, U. London, 1976; cert. nat. mgmt. course, Adminstrv. Staff Coll., Lahore, Pakistan, 1996. Lectr. Govt. Coll., Dera Ghazi Khan & Sahiwal Punjab, Pakistan, 1963-65; sect. officer Ministry Edn. Govt. Pakistan, Islamabad, 1965-72, chief conservator Quaid-i-Azam Papers Cell, 1973; dep. dir. Prime Mins. Inspection Team, Islamabad, 1972-73; dep. dir. Dept. Nat. Archives, Islamabad, 1973-74, dir., 1974-87, dir. gen., 1987—. Editor The Pakistan Archives, Guide to the Sources of Asian History; Pakistan, vols. I and II; mem. editorial bd. Quaid-i-Azam Papers Project, vols. I and II; writer books; contbr. articles to profl. jours. Mem. adv. com. Nat. Mus. Pakistan, Karachi, Sind, 1975—; bd. govs. Nat. Inst. Hist. and Cultural Rsch., Islamabad, 1983—; bd. govs., exec. com. Nat. Inst. Folk Heritage, Islamabad, 1981-95, exec. com. Archeol. Assn. Pakistan, Staff Welfare Orgn., Islamabad, 1974—, State's Enterprises Officers' Coop. Housing Soc., Lahore, Pakistan, 1982-95; chmn. Asian-History UNESCO Project, 1982-90; vice chairperson Regional Com. for the Memory of the World Programme (UNESCO) in Asia Pacific, 1998—. Recipient Pres.'s award, 1993. Mem. SWARBICA (chmn. 1986-89, sec. gen. 1989—), Internat. Coun. Archives (Paris), Islamabad Club. Muslim. Avocations: photography, reading and research. Home: House No 105, St No 60, I-8/3 Islamabad Pakistan Office: Dept Nat Archives, Pakistan Secretariat Block N, Islamabad Capital, Pakistan

SHEIKH, KHALID HUSSAIN, mechanical engineer; b. Karachi, Sind, Pakistan, Apr. 16, 1963; s. Hussain and Hamida Sheikh; s. Farah Naz Qureshi, Jan. 18, 1990; children: Sidra Khalid, Saad Mohammad. B Mech. Engring., U. Engring. and Tech., Karachi, Pakistan, 1987; diploma in English lang., Pakistan Am. Cultural Ctr., Karachi, 1981. Mfg. engr. Gen. Tyre & Rubber Co. of Pakistan, Ltd., Karachi, 1987-92; dep. mgr. Philips Elec. Industries of Pakistan, Ltd., Karachi, 1992-95; quality mgr. Abdullah Hashim Indsl. Gases and Equip. Co., Dammam, Saudi Arabia, 1995—. With Pakistan Nat. Cadet Corps, 1979-80. Mem. Am. Soc. Quality, Internal Quality Audit. Office: Abdullah Hashim Indsl Gases, PO Box 5180, Dammam 31422, Saudi Arabia

SHEILS, DENIS FRANCIS, lawyer; b. Ridgewood, N.J., Apr. 7, 1961; s. Denis Francis and Anna Marie (Clifford) S.; m. Harriet A. Bonawitz, Sept. 17, 1988. BA, La Salle Coll., 1983; JD, Fordham U., 1986. Bar: N.Y. 1987, Pa. 1987, U.S. Dist. Ct. (ea. dist.) Pa. 1987, U.S. Ct. Appeals (3d cir.) 1987, U.S. Dist. Ct. (so. and ea. dists.) N.Y. 1992, U.S. Supreme Ct. 1994, U.S. Dist. Ct. (no. dist.) N.Y. 1997, U.S. Ct. Appeals (2d cir.) 1999. Assoc. Kohn, Swift & Graf, P.C., Phila., 1987-97, shareholder, 1997—. Active Lower Makefield Twp. Cable TV Adv. Bd. Mem. ABA, Phila. Bar Assn. Roman Catholic. Home: 2124 Ashley Rd Newtown PA 18940-3737 Office: Kohn Swift & Graf PC 21st Fl One South Broad St Philadelphia PA 19107

SHEILS, WAYNE LESLIE, physicist, engineer; b. Melbourne, Australia, Sept. 23, 1957; s. Norman Robert and Norma Joyce (Murfitt) S.; m. Machiko Hirata, Feb. 2, 1986. BSc, LaTrobe U., Melbourne, 1984, MSc, 1988, PhD, 1996. Lectr. Swinburne Inst. Tech., Melbourne, 1986-88, La Trobe U., Melbourne, 1993-95; tchr. Dept. Edn., Hyogo, 1988-89; engr. Applied Precision Systems, Melbourne, 1996-99, RLM Sys., Melbourne, 1999-2000; physicist ETP Electron Multipliers, Sydney, 2000—. Contbr. articles to profl. jours. Mem. Australian Inst. Physics. Avocation: Aikido.

SHEINBAUM, STANLEY K., economist; b. N.Y.C., June 12, 1920; m. Betty Warner, May 29, 1964; 4 children. AB in Far East History summa cum laude, Stanford U., 1949, postgrad., 1949-53. Mem. faculty dept. econs. Stanford (Calif.) U., 1950-53, Mich. State U., East Lansing, 1955-60, U. Calif., Santa Barbara, 1963; pres. Bd. Police Commr., L.A., 1991-93; Pres. Fairtree Enterprises, 1980-90; cons. in econs. Ency. Brit., 1961-64, Calif. State Commn. Manpower and Tech., 1963-65; cons. fiscal policy Govt. South Vietnam, Saigon, 1957-59; cons. on Vietnam Spl. Ops. Rsch. Office Am. U., Washington, 1958-59; sr. fellow Ctr. for Study Dem. Instns., Santa Barbara, 1960-70; v.p. Warner Ranch, Inc., L.A., 1965-69. Cons. editor: Ramparts, 1965-73; mem. editorial bd. Democracy, 1981-84; pub. New Perspectives Quarterly, 1985—. Dec. candidate Congress, Santa Barbara and Ventura, 1966-68; del. Dem. Nat. Conv., 1968-72; So. Calif. fin. chmn. McGovern presdl. campaign, 1972; exec. dir. Com. to Improve Tchr. Edn., 1961-62; bd. dirs. , Com. for Pub. Justice, 1972-85, Bill of Rights Found., N.Y., 1973—, Ctr. for Law in Pub. Interest, L.A., 1976—, , People for Am. Way, Washington, 1980—; organizer, coord. legal def. team Pentagon Papers Trial, L.A., 1971-73; chmn. bd. dirs. ACLU Found., So. Calif., L.A., 1973-84; founder, bd. dirs. Energy Action Com., Washington, 1975-82; mem. Coun. on Fgn. Rels., 1990—; commr. Calif. Postsecondary Edn. Commn., 1978-80; bd. dirs. Presidio Savs. and Loan Assn. Santa Barbara, 1964-69; Music Ctr. Dance Assn., L.A., 1978-85, chmn. 1979-85, Helsinki Watch and Am. Watch, N.Y., N.Y., L.A., 1981—; chmn. Human Rights Watch, Calif., 1987—; co-chmn., trustee Internat. Ctr. Peace in Mideast, Tel Aviv, 1982—; regent U. Calif., 1977-89, vice-chmn., 1983-84; founder Legal Def. Ctr., Santa Barbara, 1970—. Fulbright fellow, Paris, 1953-55, fellow Hoover Inst., Stanford U., 1955—. Mem. Phi Beta Kappa, Phi Eta Sigma. Home: 345 N Rockingham Ave Los Angeles CA 90049-2635

SHELBY, CHARLES FRANCIS, priest, fundraising executive; b. L.A., Feb. 18, 1941; s. Peter Paul and Ruth (Russell) S. Student, St. John's Sem. Coll., Camarillo, Calif., 1959-62; BA, St. Mary's Sem., Perryville, Mo., 1964; MDiv, De Andreis Sem., Lemont, Ill., 1984; MS, DePaul U., 1972. Ordained priest Roman Cath. Ch., 1968. Adminstr., mem. faculty St. Vincent's Sem., Montebello, Calif., 1971-73; mem. faculty St. Mary's Sem., Perryville, 1973-79; assoc. dir. Assn. of Miraculous Medal, Perryville, 1980-82, dir., pres., 1983—; bd. dirs. Nat. Cath. Devel. Conf., Hempstead, N.Y., 1992—, v.p., 1992-96, pres., 1996-97, chair, 1997-98; bd. trustees DePaul U., Chgo., 1998—. Mem. fin. com. Congregation of the Mission, St. Louis, 1980—; trustee Lazarist Trust, St. Louis, 1990—; treas. Ministerial Alliance, Perryville, 1975—. Mem. AAAS, Post Com, Perryville C. of C. Avocations: computer programming, photography, travel. Office: Assn of Miraculous Medal 1811 W Saint Joseph St Perryville MO 63775-1594

SHELBY, JAMES STANFORD, cardiovascular surgeon; b. Ringgold, La., June 15, 1934; s. Jesse Audrey and Mable (Martin) S.; m. Susan Rainey, July 15, 1967; children: Bryan Christian, Christopher Linden. BS in Liberal Arts, La. Tech. U., 1956; MD, La. State U., 1958. Diplomate Am. Bd. Surgery, Am. Bd. Thoracic Surgery. Intern Charity Hosp. La., New Orleans, 1958-59, resident surgery and thoracic surgery, 1959-65; fellow cardiovascular surgery Baylor U. Coll. Medicine, Houston, 1965-66; practice medicine specializing in cardiovascular surgery Shreveport, La., 1967—; mem. staff Schumpert Med. Ctr., Highland Hosp., Willis-Knighton Med. Ctr.; assoc. prof. surgery La. State U. Sch. Medicine, Shreveport, 1967—. With M.C., AUS, 1961-62. Recipient Woer of Medallion award La. Tech. U., 1982. Mem. AMA, Am. Coll. Cardiology, Soc. Thoracic Surgeons, Am. Heart Assn., Southeastern Surg. Congress, So. Thoracic Surg. Assn. Home: 6003 E Ridge Dr Shreveport LA 71106-2425 Office: 2751 Virginia Ave Ste 2G Shreveport LA 71103-3970

SHELBY, NINA CLAIRE, special education educator; b. Weatherford, Tex., Oct. 23, 1949; d. Bill Hudson and Roselle (Price) S.; m. Richard Dean Powell, May 29, 1971 (div. 1973); 1 child, Stoney Hudson. BA in English, Sul Ross State U., 1974, MEd, 1984; MA in English, U. Tex., 1995. Jr. high lang. arts educator Liberty Hill, Tex., 1974-75; H.S. resource educator Georgetown (Tex.) I. S. D., 1976-77; intermediate resource educator Raymondille (Tex.) I. S. D., 1977-81; educator of severe profound Napper Elem. Pharr (Tex.) San Juan Alamo Ind. Sch. Dist., 1981-90; H. S. life skills educator Pharr (Tex.) San Juan Alamo ISD. North H.S., 1990-93; intermediate inclusion educator Carman Elem. Pharr (Tex.) San Juan Alamo Ind. Sch. Dist., 1993—; coach asst. Tex. Spl. Olympics, Pharr, 1981—, sponsor vocat. adj. club, 1990-93, adaptive asst. device team, Edinburg, Tex., 1993-95. Asst. cub scout leader Boy Scouts Am., 1994-95, sec. parental com. bd. rev., 1997—; parent vol. boy's and girl's Club McAllen, 1992-96. Mem. DAR, Assn. of Tex. Profl. Educators, Alpha Delta Kappa. Democrat. Mem. Ch. of Christ. Avocations: reading, horticulture, piano, opera. Home: PO Box 426 Elgin TX 78621-0426 Office: Pharr San Juan Alamo ISD Carman Elem 100 Ridge Rd San Juan TX 78589

SHELBY, TIM OTTO, secondary education educator; b. Longview, Wash., Mar. 23, 1965; s. William Richard and Ruth (Masser) S. BA in Edn., Eastern Wash. U., 1989. Cert. grades 4-12 English tchr., Wash., Calif. English tchr., head basketball and football coach Kahlotus (Wash.) H.S., 1989-90; tchr. various dists., 1990-92; English tchr., asst. basketball coach Kalama (Wash.) H.S., 1992-95; tchr. English, head basketball coach Frazier Mountain H.S., Lebec, Calif., 1995-97; English tchr., asst. basketball coach Shafter (Calif.) H.S., 1997-98; English tchr., asst. basketball coach, English dept. chmn. Mojave (Calif.) H.S., 1998—. Mem. ASCD, Nat. Coun. Tchrs. Eng., Calif. Edn. Assn. Roman Catholic. Avocations: traveling, reading, coaching sports, theatre, movies. Home: 21321 Santa Maria Dr Tehachapi CA 93561-8715 Office: Mojave Unified Sch Dist Mojave CA 93501

SHELDON, J. MICHAEL, lawyer, educator; b. Mt. Carmel, Pa., Sept. 1, 1951; s. Lloyd Loomis and Helen Roberta (Sosnoski) S. AA, Harrisburg (Pa.) Community Coll., 1978; BS, Pa. State U., 1980; M in Journalism, Temple U., 1991; JD, Widener U. Sch. Law, 1996. News announcer Sta. WNUE-AM, Ft. Walton Beach, Fla., 1974-76, Sta. WFEC-AM, Harrisburg, 1977-78; announcer Sta. WCMB-AM, Wormleysburg, Pa., 1979-80; writer newspaper Pa. Beacon, Harrisburg, 1982-85; media specialist Commonwealth Media Svcs., Harrisburg, 1982-86; dir. communications Pa. Poultry Fedn., Harrisburg, 1986-89; news anchor Sta. WGAL-TV, Lancaster, Pa., 1989-90; dir. pub. rels. Profl. Ins. Agts. - Pa., Md., Del., Mechanicsburg, Pa., 1990-92; v.p. comm. and mktg. United Way of the Capital Region, Harrisburg, Pa., 1992-93, Widener U. Sch. of Law, 1994-96; pres. Open Mike Comm., Harrisburg, 1994—; mem. adj. faculty dept. journalism Temple U., 1992; mem. faculty dept. humanities Pa. State U., 1995-97, 99—. Contbg. author: Pa. 12th Annual Civil Litigation Update, Spoliation of Evidence: Why You Can't Have Your Cake and Eat it Too, 1999; contbg. editor: A Practical Guidebook to Massachusetts Aviation Law, 1999; Contbr. articles to profl. jours. Pub. rels. advisor Cen. Pa. Leukemia Soc., Harrisburg, 1989-90; media advisor Polit. Campaign, Hershey, Pa., 1990. With USAF, 1969-73. Mem. Vets. of Foreign War (life), Am. Legion, Knights of Columbus, Chi Gamma Iota, Delta Tau Kappa. Republican. Roman Catholic. Avocations: motorcycles, music, electronics, martial arts. Office: 6059 Allentown Blvd Harrisburg PA 17112-2672

SHELDON, MICHAEL GRAHAM, physician; b. Evesham, Eng., Mar. 14, 1941; s. Murray Fosbrook and Gladys (Evans) S.; m. Jennifer Christine White, Oct. 1, 1966; children: Matthew, Polly, Barnaby, Toby. MB, BChir, London U., 1964. Surg. registrar Harefield Hosp., Middlesex, Eng., 1966-67; rsch. registrar St. Thomas' Hosp., London, 1967-68; med. asst. Horton Hosp., Banbury, Eng., 1971-73; gen. practice medicine Banbury, 1973-79; sr. lectr. Nottingham U., Eng., 1979-85; med. missionary Youth With a Mission, Nuneaton, Eng., 1985-92; sr. lectr. gen. practice St. Bartholomew's, Royal and London Sch. Medicine, 1993-99; gen. practitioner, 1999—; cons. Trent Regional Health Authority; temporary advisor WHO; past chmn. rsch. com. WONCA. Editor: Decision Making in General Practice, 1985, Trends in General Practice Computing, 1985, To Bind Up The Broken-Hearted, 1999; contbr. articles to profl. jours. Fellow Royal Coll. Gen. Practitioners (coun. 1983-89, Upjohn prize 1975, Stanning fellow 1976, Butterworth medal 1981); mem. Brit. Computer Soc., World Orgn. Nat. Colls. and Acads. Gen. Practice (chmn. rsch. com. 1983-85), Irish Coll. Gen. Practice. Avocations: gardening, whole-person medicine. Office: 23 Lancaster Dr Isle Dogs, London E14 9PT, England

SHELDON, WILLIAM FREDERICK, cultural institute administrator, consultant; b. Salina, Kans., June 22, 1938; s. Richard Robert and Helen Irene (Zerzan) S.; m. Ulrike Waltraud Teschner; children: Barbara Helen, Caroline Susanne. BA, U. Kans., 1960; PhD, U. Mpls., 1967. Asst. prof. U. Pacific, Stockton, Calif., 1967-70, assoc. prof., 1970-75; assoc. prof. U. Marburg, Germany, 1975-78; mem. staff Herzog August Libr., Wolfenbüttel, Germany, 1978-80; dir. German-Am. Inst./America House, Nuremberg, 1981—; cons. on German-Am. affairs. Author: The Intellectual Development of Justus Möser. The Growth of a German Patriot, 1970; editor: (with Ulrike Sheldon) Im Geist der Empfindsamkeit, Freundschaftsbriefe der Mösertochter Jenny von Voigts an die Fürstin Luise von Anhalt-Dessau 1780-1808, 1971, Justus Möser Briefwechsel, 1992; contbr. articles and book revs. to profl. jours. Spkr. to various orgns., Germany, 1995; founder Erlangen-Greater Richmond City Partnership, 1998; co-founder, bd. dirs. Franconian Internat. Sch., Herzogenaurach, Germany, 1998; co-founder Little Friends, kindergarten, Fürth, Germany, 1998. Mem. Am. Hist. Assn. (life), Nürnberger Studienkreis Kommunikation (founding mem., bd. dirs. 1991—), Freunde Sigmund Schuckert Gymnasiums (founding mem.), Freunde Herzog August Bibliothek. Home: Kloster-Ebrach Strasse 33a, 90453 Nuremburg Germany Office: German-Am Inst/Am House, Gleissbühl Strasse 13, 90402 Nuremberg Germany

SHELDRICK, GEORGE MICHAEL, chemistry educator, crystallographer; b. Huddersfield, Great Britain, Nov. 17, 1942; s. George and Elizabeth S.; m. Katherine E. Herford, 1968; 4 children. Student, Huddersfield New Coll., Jesus Coll., Cambridge. Lectr. Cambridge U., Eng., 1966-78; prof. structural chemistry U. Göttingen, Germany, 1978—; with Inst. Anorg Chemie, Göttingen, Germany. Contbr. numerous articles to profl. jours. Recipient Meldola and Corday-Morgan medals Royal Soc. Chemistry, Leibniz prize Deutsche Forschungsgemeinschaft, A.L. Patterson award Am. Crystallographic Assn., 1993, Carl-Hermann medal Deutsche Gesellschaft für Kristallographie, 1999, mineral Sheldrickite named in hon. Achievements include authorship of widely used computer programs for crystal structure determination. Office: Institut für Anorganische Chemie, Tammannstrasse 4, D-37077 Göttingen Germany

SHELDRICK, KATHARYN ELIZABETH, musicologist; b. Boston, Mar. 31, 1948; d. Martin Edward Meakin and Mary (Crago) Herford; m. George Michael Sheldrick, July 13, 1968; children: Abigail June, Nicola Sylvia, Peter Martin, Alexander Noel Dean. MA in Music, Knightsbridge U., 1995; diploma in Russian, Fernschulen, Hamburg, Germany, 1997; Advanced French Diploma, Linguaphone, 2000. Legal sec. Pye of Cambridge, Ltd., UK, 1971-73; solo clarinetist Cambridge Philharm. Orch., 1976-78, Acad. Orch., Gottingen, Germany, 1980-81, Musa Srs. Orch., Gottingen, 1987-92; sales rep. Quelle, Gottingen, 1993—. Author: Blackbird Has Spoken, 1996. Avocations: sailing, gardening, cooking, handrafts. Home: Heinrich Deppe Ring 51, 37120 Bovenden Germany

SHELGREN, RICHARD ERIC (SVEN), JR., film and television producer; b. Buffalo, N.Y., Aug. 11, 1951; s. Richard Eric Sr. and Mary Ann (Veigel) S.; m. Margaret Ballard, Feb. 10, 1973 (div. Jan. 1983); m. Kyra Fetch Shelgren, Oct. 5, 1985 (div. 1998); children: Cody Tyler, Roxanne Leigh. BA with honors, Haverford Coll., 1973; postgrad., Columbia U., 1976. Shop mgr., dispatcher Feature Systems, N.Y.C., 1978-79; freelance prodn. asst. N.Y.C., 1979-80; prodn. mgr. Johnston Films, N.Y.C., 1980-83, producer, exec. producer, 1983-84; exec. producer Stiefel & Co., N.Y.C., 1984-88; producer, exec. producer Jon Francis Films, San Francisco, 1988-94; exec. producer RCR, Inc., L.A., 1994—; exec. prodr. Dektor Film, L.A., 1994—; film researcher Cinematheque Francaise, Paris, 1973-74. Troop leader Boy Scouts Am., 1965-69. Recipient Gold and Silver Lions awards Cannes (France) Film Festival, 1991, 92, 93, Moma Best Commls. award AICP, 1992, 93, 94, Clio award, 1994, Andy award, 1993-94. Mem. Dirs. Guild Am. (unit prodn. mgr. 1992), Nat. Parks and Conservation Assn., World Wildlife Fund, Greenpeace, Sierra Club. Roman Catholic. Avocations: children, writing, reading, sports, camping.

SHELL, ROBERT EDWARD LEE, photographer, writer; b. Roanoke, Va., Dec. 3, 1946; s. James Ralph and Mary (Terry) S.; m. Darlene Bridget. Student, Va. Poly. Inst. and State U., 1965-68, Elkins Inst., 1972, Nat. Camera Inst., 1973. Staff SMithsonian Inst., Washington, 1968-72; photographer Sta. WBRA-Pub. TV, Roanoke, 1972-74; owner Camera, Inc., Salem, Va., 1974-76; photographer, technician Gentry Studios, Blacksburg, Va., 1976-81; tech. editor Shutterbug Mag., Patch Communications, Radford, Va., 1984-91; editor Shutterbug Mag., Patch Communications, Titusville, Fla., 1991-98, Primedia Spl. Interest Mags., 1998—; U.S. corr. Asahi Camera, Tokyo, 1986—, Color Foto, Munich, 1989—, Photo Answers, U.K.; pub. PIC Mag., U.K., 1994-96. Author: Photography with Canon EOS System, 1990, Hasselblad Camera System Guide, 1991, Mamiya Camera System Guide, 1992, Photo Business Careers, 1992, Canon Compendium, 1994, Metz Flash System Handbook, 1994, Olympus IS System Handbook, 1994, Canon Rebel Handbook, 1994, Canon EOS-3 Handbook, 1999, Canon Rebel 2000 Handbook, 1999, The Hand Exposure Meter Book, 1999, Mamiya Camera System Guide, 2000, Canon EOS-3, 2000, Canon Flash System Guide, 2000, Canon EOS-1V, 2000, Canon Compendium, 2d edit., 2000, 12 other books on photography, 1994-99; tech. editor numerous publs; contbr. articles to profl. jours. Smithsonian Inst. grantee, Washington, 1968. Mem. Photo Mktg. Assn. Internat., German Photographers Soc., Megapress, Profl. Photographers of Am. Avocations: painting, drawing, classic automobiles. E mail: bob@bobshell.com. Home and Office: Bob Shell Photography 1601 Grove Ave Radford VA 24141-1624

SHELLENBERGER, GRANT C., lawyer; b. Mpls., Mar. 25, 1969; s. Charles Russell "Shelly" and Linda Kay (Conkright) S.; m. Jennifer S. Flax, Mar. 18, 1995; 1 child, Dylan. BA in Social Studies, Kans. State U., 1992; JD, U. Kans., 1995. Bar: Kans. 1995, Okla. 1996, U.S. Dist. Ct. (we. dist.) Okla. 1996. Ptnr. Gilmore, Shellenberger & Maxwell, P.A., Liberal, Kans., 2000—. Editor Kans. Law Rev., 1993-95. Legal intern U. Kans. Legal Aid Clinic, Lawrence, 1994-95. Recipient Am. Jurisprudence award 1993. Mem. ATLA, NACDL, Kans. Bar Assn., Okla. Bar Assn., Kans. Trial Lawyers Assn. Avocations: golf, softball, basketball, billiards. Office: Gilmore Shellenberger & Maxwell PA 1017 S Kansas Ave Liberal KS 67901-4609

SHELLEY, CLYDE BURTON, artist; b. Murphy, Tex., Mar. 21, 1922; s. Jesse Dewey and Florrie Elizabeth (Eldridge) S.; m. Freddie Lavern Mitchell, Aug. 31, 1946 (dec. Aug. 1978); m. Grace Rosamond Muder, Dec. 24, 1979. Student, Ohio Weslayan U., 1944-45, Art Ctr. Sch., L.A., 1957-58. Artist Interstate Theatres, Inc., Dallas, 1941-42, Oakite Products, N.Y.C., 1946-47; cartoonist Reddy Kilowatt, Inc., N.Y.C., 1947-50; freelance cartoonist, comml. artist N.Y.C., 1950-52, Dallas, 1952-55, L.A., 1955-56, Las Vegas, 1970-75; comml. artist Northrup Corp., Hawthorne, Calif., 1956-59; indsl. illustrator Douglas Aircraft Corp., Long Beac, El Segondo, Calif., 1959-62; comml. artist Nortronics, Palos Verdes, Calif., 1962-64; sr. illustrator Holmes & Narver, Inc., Honolulu, 1964-70, Las Vegas, 1964-70; sr. artist Houston Post Newspaper, 1975-87. One man shows at First City Nat. Bank, 1985, 87; exhibited in group shows at Clampitt Paper Co., Houston, 1985, Sportsman's Gallery, Galleria, Houston, 1986, Marriott Hotel, Houston, 1990, Lone Star Restaurant, Houston, 1991-92, CMR Gallery, Corpus Christi, Tex., 1994, 96; contbr. cartoons Am. Mag., Bluebook Mag., King Features Syndicate, AT&T, Las Vegas Sun, Las Vegas Rev./Jour., others; caricaturist;. Mem. Houston World Affairs Coun., 1996—. With U.S. Navy, 1942-46. Mem. Houston Mus. Fine Arts, Braeburn Valley West Civic Club, Am. Legion. Avocations: running, physical fitness, reading, politics, world affairs. Home and Office: 9443 Portal Dr Houston TX 77031-2212

SHELTON, BESSIE ELIZABETH, school system administrator; b. Lynchburg, Va.; d. Robert and Bessie Ann (Plenty) Shelton; B.A. (scholar), W.Va. State Coll., 1958; student Northwestern U., 1953-55, Ind. U., 1956; M.S., SUNY, 1960; diploma Profl. Career Devel. Inst., 1993. Young adult libr. Bklyn. Pub. Libr., 1960-62; asst. head cen. ref. div. Queens Borough Pub. Libr., Jamaica, N.Y., 1962-65; instructional media specialist Lynchburg (Va.) Bd. Edn., 1966-74; ednl. research specialist, 1974-77; ednl. media assoc. Allegany County Bd. Edn., Cumberland, Md., 1977—. Guest singer Sta. WLVA, 1966—, WLVA-TV Christmas concerts, 1966—;cons. music and market rsch. Mem. YWCA, Lynchburg, 1966—, Fine Arts Ctr., Lynchburg, 1966—; ednl. adv. bd., nat. research bd. Am. Biog. Inst.; mem. U.S. Congl. Adv. Bd., USN Nat. Adv. Coun.; amb. goodwill Lynchburg, Va., 1986. Named to Nat. Women's Hall of Fame. Mem. AAUW, NEA, NAFE, Md. Tchrs. Assn., Allegany County Tchrs. Assn., Va. Edn. Assn., State Dept. Sch. Librarians, Internat. Entertainers Guild, Music City Songwriters Assn., Vocal Artists Am., Internat. Clover Poetry Assn., Internat. Platform Assn., Nat. Assn. Women Deans, Adminstrs. and Counselors, Intercontinental Biog. Assn., World Mail Dealers Assn., N.Am. Mailers Exch., Am. Assn. Creative Artists, Am. Biog. Inst. Research Assn., Tri-State Community Concert Assn. Pi Delta Phi, Sigma Delta Pi. Contbr. poems to various publs. Democrat. Baptist. Clubs: National Travel, Gulf Travel. Home: PO Box 187 Cumberland MD 21501-0187

SHELTON, CHRISTIE MARTINA, writer; b. Richmond, Va., Sept. 19, 1971; d. Gladys Mae Shelton. Student, J Sargeant Reynolds Coll., 1990, 98—. Dietary asst. The Windsor Nursing Home, Richmond, Va., 1992, Richmond Eye & Ear Hosp., 1992-95; security specialist Abacus Security Corp., Richmond, 1995-96, Clemons Security, Richmond, 1996, Admiral Security, Richmond, 1996-97; writer Black Butterfly Prodn. Inc., Richmond, 1996-97, Inspired Creations Prodns., Richmond, 1997—. Author (poetry book) Visions of Inspirations, 1997 (Girl Scouts Recognition award 1998). Field aide, program coordinator for Commonwealth Girl Scouts, 1999—. Avocations: writing, forensics, acting. Home and Office: 2100 N 20th St Richmond VA 23223-3936

SHELTON, JAMES KEITH, journalism educator; b. Altus, Okla., Oct. 28, 1932; s. Willis Oscar and Theodosia Agnes (Rupert) S.; m. Deborah Kennedy Evans, Dec. 26, 1953; children: Leslie Lynn, Lawrence Evans. BA, Midwestern State U., 1954; MA, U. North Tex., 1972. Reporter Lawton (Okla.) Constn., 1954; wire editor Wichita Falls (Tex.) Record-News, 1956-59; city hall reporter, polit. writer Dallas Times Herald, 1959-65; mng. editor, exec. editor Denton (Tex.) Record-Chronicle, 1965-69, 79-88; faculty mem., dir. pub. info. U. North Tex., Denton, 1969-79, journalist-in-residence, 1988—. Author: What Journalists Should Know About Business, 1993. Mem. Supreme Ct. Task Force on Jud. Ethics, Austin, 1992-94. with U.S. Army, 1954-56. Mem. Soc. Profl. Journalists, Freedom on Info. Found. of Tex., Inc. (sec., bd. dirs.). Democrat. Methodist. Home: 621 Grove St Denton TX 76209-7323 Office: Univ North Tex PO Box 305280 Denton TX 76203-5280

SHELTON, KENNETH N., bishop; b. Phila., Jan. 26, 1959. Baccalaureate, Am. Coll., Geneva, Switzerland, 1982, LHD, 1995; MA in Polit. Sci., Human Behavior, Webster U., Geneva, Switzerland, 1984; Alliance Francais, Ecole Schulz, Geneva, Switzerland, 1985. Elder of oversight for nat. youth dept. Ch. of the Lord Jesus Christ of the Apostolic Faith, Phila., 1976-91, elder (adminstrv.) of Pa., 1976-91, bishop (gen. overseer), 1991—. Home: 2401 Pennsylvania Ave Apt 21a4 Philadelphia PA 19130-3007 Office: 701 S 22d St Philadelphia PA 19146

SHELTON, OLGA-JEAN, school counselor; b. Omaha, Aug. 10, 1957; d. Howard Kenton and Doris Jean (Harkness) Z. Student, U. Minn., 1975-77; BA, Adams State U., Alamosa, Colo., 1980; MS, Emporia (Kans.) State U., 1987. Cert. in counseling and lang. arts, Colo. Tchr. speech Upward Bound, Alamosa, 1980; tchr. English Wyandotte High Sch., Kansas City, Kans., 1980-81; tchr. English and speech Bishop Ward High Sch., Kansas City, 1984-86; grad. asst. Emporia State U., 1986-87; counselor Winfield (Kans.) High Sch., 1987-88, Perry (Kans.)-Lecompton High Sch., 1988-91, Clear Creek High Sch., Idaho Springs, Colo., 1991-93, Heritage High Sch., Littleton, Colo., 1993-96, Elbert (Colo.) Schs., 1996-98, Arvada Middle Sch., Jefferson County (Colo.) Schs., 1998—; instr. psychology Highland (Kans.) Community Coll., 1989. Editor newsletter for Kans. Sch. Counselors Assn., 1988-91. Grantee in field. Mem. Am. Sch. Counselors Assn., Rocky Mountain Soc. Adlerian Psychology (pres. 1993), Kans. Assn. Counseling and Devel. (bd. dirs. 1990-91), Kans. Sch. Counselors Assn. (pub. rels. chmn. 1988-89, pres. 1990-91), Colo. Sch. Counselors Assn. (grants chmn. 1994-95), Optimist Club (Arvada). Democrat. Roman Catholic. Avocations: collecting, reading, travel. Home: 8041 Eagleview Dr Littleton CO 80125-9107

SHELTON, THOMAS ALFRED, pastor; b. Kansas City, Mo., Dec. 6, 1951; s. Thomas and Savanna S.; m. Phyllis Annette White, Aug. 18, 1979; children: Thomas, Reginald, Veronica. AA, Penn Valley Community, 1975; BA, U. Mo. Kansas City, 1983; MDiv, Cen. Bapt. Theol. Seminary, 1988. Cert. secondary tchr., social scis., Mo. Dean MidWest Dist. Congress, Kansas City, Mo., 1984-95; pres. Black Student Fellowship, Kansas City, 1985-87; regional v.p. Nat. Conf. Black Seminarians, N.Y.C., 1986-88; asst. pastor Kansas City, 1985-95; resource tchr. Kansas City Sch. Dist., 1988—; pastor Ward Meml. Missionary Bapt. Ch., Sedalia, Mo., 1995—; pres. Mt. Sinai Day Care Bd., Kansas City, 1989-95; tchr. Five State Laymens Meeting, St. Louis, 1989. Bd. dirs. Kansas City Youth Ct., 1989—. Master sgt. USAF Res., 1979-93. Mem. Tchrs. Union, ASCD. Home: 1706 E 60th St Kansas City MO 64110-3550 Office: Ward Meml Bapt Ch 412 N Osage Ave Sedalia MO 65301-2943 also:: Ward Meml Miss Bapt Ch Sedalia MO 65301

SHEMESH, ILANA ELLEN RUTH, nurse, midwife, educator; b. Bklyn., Nov. 22, 1952; arrived in Israel, 1973; d. Harry and Sarah (Weinberg) Riback; m. Asher Shemesh, June 21, 1975; children: Lital, Inbal, Maayan. Diploma in nursing, Sheinbron Sch. Nursing, Tel Aviv, 1976, diploma in midwifery, 1982. Nurse-midwife Assuta Hosp., Tel Aviv, 1983-88, Misgav Ledach Hosp., Jerusalem, 1988—; founder, ptnr. Israel Ctr. for Natural Childbirth, Motherwise, Tel Aviv, 1993—; mem./lectr. Israel Childbirth Edn. Ctr., Haifa, 1983-94; lectr. in field. Activist for progressive childbirth edn. and reform in Israel, for various women's birthing issues. Mem. Internat. Childbirth Edn. Assn., Israel Women's Network, Assn. of Ams. and Canadians in Israel, La Leche League Internat. Meretz Party. Jewish. Avocations: travel, gardening, folkdancing, stainglass. E-mail: shemesha@inter.net.il. Home: Moshav Yeshresh 53, D N Emek Sorek 76838, Israel

SHEMESH, MORDECHAI, biochemist, researcher; b. Bazra, Iraq, Oct. 17, 1937; arrived in Israel, 1949; s. Menashe and Aziza (Karmush) S.; m. Naomi Gafni, Aug. 12, 1945; children: Sharon, Donna, Ido. MSc, Tel-Aviv U., 1964; PhD, Weizmann Inst., Rehovot, 1972. Head lab. steriod biochemistry Kimron Vet. Inst., Bet-Dagan, 1965-72, head dept. hormone rsch., 1975-81, 85—; rsch. assoc. Cornell U., Ithaca, N.Y., 1972-74; vis. prof. Cornell U., Ithaca, 1982-84; prof. Hebrew U., Jerusalem, 1993—. Editor: Maternal Recognition of Pregnancy, 1989; inventor high efficiency methods and composition for integrated exogenous DNA into genomic DNA of sperm. Recipient Outstanding Scientist award Kimron Vet. Inst., 1989, 96, Henry Barron Lectr. U. Fla., 1998, award Assn. Biochemistry and Microbiology, 1971. Mem. Soc. for the Study of Reprodn., Soc. for the Study of Fertility, Endocrine Soc. Jewish. Avocations: swimming, walking, traveling, gym. E-mail: mshem@vs.moag.gov.il. Home: 8 Fishman St, 432710 Raanana Israel Office: Kimron Vet Inst, PO Box 12, 50250 Bet Dagan Israel

SHEN, BINGHUI, molecular biologist, educator; b. Shaoxing, Zhejiang, China, Mar. 18, 1961; s. Baiqi Shen and Aijin Lou; m. Karen Shen, Apr. 5, 1986; children: Sherry, Carolyn. BS in Biology, Zhejiang U., 1983; PhD in Molecular Genetics, Kans. State U., 1991. Rsch. asst. Zhejiang U., Hangzhou, China, 1982-83; tchg./rsch. asst. Zhejiang U., Hangzhou, 1983-86; rsch./tchg. asst. Kans. State U., Manhattan, 1986-91; postdoctoral fellow U. Calif., Irvine, 1991-94, Los Alamos (N.Mex.) Nat. Lab., 1994-96; asst. prof. City of Hope Grad. Sch., Duarte, Calif., 1996—. Contbr. articles to profl. jours. Grantee NIH, 1997—, 99—. Mem. Soc. Chinese Bioscientists in Am., Am. Soc. Microbiology, Am. Soc. Molecular Biology and Biochemistry, Ray Wu Soc., Phi Kappa Phi. E-mail: bshen@coh.org. Fax: 626-301-8972. Office: City of Hope Nat Med Ctr 1500 Duarte Rd Duarte CA 91010-3012

SHEN, CHIA THENG, former steamship company executive, religious institute official; b. Chekiang, China, Dec. 15, 1913; came to U.S., 1952, naturalized, 1964; s. Foo Sheng and Wen Ching (Hsai) S.; m. Woo Ju Chu, Apr. 21, 1940; children: Maria May Shen Jackson, Wilma Way Shen George, David Chuen-Tsing, Freda Foh. BEE, Chiao Tung U., 1937; LittD (hon.), St. John's U., 1973. With Central Elec. Mfg. Works, China, 1937-44; factory mgr. Central Elec. Mfg. Works, 1942-44; dep. coordinating dept. Nat. Resources Commn., Govt. of China, 1945-47; pres. China Trading and Indsl.

Devel. Corp., Shanghai, 1947-49; mng. dir. China Trading & Indsl. Devel. Co. Ltd., Hong Kong, 1949-53; with TransAtlantic Financing Corp., 1954-62, pres., 1958-62; pres. Pan-Atlantic Devel. Corp., N.Y.C., 1955-70; with Marine Transport Lines Inc., N.Y.C., 1958-70; sr. v.p. Marine Transport Lines Inc., 1964-70; with Am. Steamship Co., Buffalo, 1967-80; chmn. bd., chief exec. officer Am. Steamship Co., 1971-80. Trustee Inst. Advanced Studies World Religions, N.Y., 1970—, chmn. bd., chief exec. officer, 1970-92, pres., 1970-84, 90—; trustee China Inst. in Am., N.Y.C., 1963-90, vice chmn., 1970-79, chmn., 1979-80, mem. exec. com., 1963-84; trustee, v.p. Buddhist Assn. U.S., N.Y.C., 1964—. Mem. Chinese Inst. Engring. E-mail: bausny@aol.com. Home and Office: 2020 Route 301 Carmel NY 10512-3426

SHEN, E-CHIN, dentist, periodontist; b. Keelung, Taiwan, June 19, 1955; s., Yuei-Hwa and Huei-Lien (Wang) S.; m. Chi Yang, Jan. 23, 1982; 1 child, John T. B of Dental Surgery, Nat. Def. Med. Ctr., Taipei, Taiwan, 1981; MS, cert. periodontist, Northwestern U., 1995. Resident, chief resident Tri-Svc. Gen. Hosp., Taipei, Taiwan, 1987-90, physician, 1991—; lectr. NAt. Defense Med. Ctr., Taipei, Taiwan, 1991—; physician Air Force Gen. Hosp., Taipei, Taiwan, 1991-93; sect. head dental dept. Hsin Chu Mil. Hosp., Taiwan, 1995-96; dir. dental dept. Tao Yuan Mil. Gen. Hosp., Taiwan, 1996—. Contbr. articles to profl. jours. Col. Taiwan Mil., 1996—. Mem. Am. Acad. Periodontology, Dental Assn. China (sec. 1991-93, 97-99), Acad. Periodontology (bd. dirs. 1989-91, 95—). Avocations: travel, tennis, golf. Office: Tao Yuan Mil Gen Hosp, #168 Chung Shing Rd, Lung Tan 325, Taiwan

SHEN, EDWARD NIN-DA, cardiologist, educator; b. Hong Kong, July 3, 1950; came to U.S., 1979; s. Han-Ting and Yay-Wen (Tsu) S.; m. MaryRose Yung-Yung Wong, June 19, 1983; children: Erin Pey-Juan, Dylan Hua-Juan. BSc in Biochemistry with 1st class honors, McGill U., Montreal, Que., Can., 1972, MD, CM, 1976. Diplomate Am. Bd. Internal Medicine, Am. Bd. Cardiovascular Disease, Am. Bd. Clin. Cardiac Electrophysiology, Am. Bd. Interventional Cardiology. Resident in internal medicine McGill U., 1976-79; cardiology fellow U. Calif., San Francisco, 1979-81, electrophysiology fellow Cardiovascular Rsch. Inst., 1981-82, instr. in medicine Moffitt Hosp., 1982-83; assoc. chief cardiology Santa Clara Valley Med. Ctr., San Jose, Calif., 1983-85; clin. asst. prof. U. Calif., San Francisco, Stanford, 1983-85; dir. clin. electrophysiology Straub Clinic, Honolulu, 1986-93, chief of medicine, 1991-93; assoc. prof. medicine U. Hawaii, Honolulu, 1988-93, chief cardiology, 1993—, prof. medicine, 1994—; attending physician Moffitt-Long Hosps., 1982-83; dir. electrocardiography, co-dir. noninvasive cardiac lab. Santa Clara Valley Med. Ctr., 1983-85; attending cardiologist Queen's Heart Inst., Straub Clinic & Hosp., St. Francis Hosp., Kuakini Hosp., 1993—; fellow Med. Rsch. Coun. Can., 1981-83; presenter in field. Contbr. over 90 articles to profl. jours. Bd. dirs. Am. Heart Assn., 1987-89, mem. peer rev. bd. for grant-in-aid applicants, 1987-89. Univ. scholar, 1968-75; recipient Charles E. Frosst prize and medal, Cushing Meml. prize Montreal Children's Hosp., John C. Milnor Profl. and Grey Champion Activities award Straub Found., 1990; Edward N. Shen scholar award in his honor U. Hawaii. Fellow ACP, Royal Coll. Physicians and Surgeons of Can. (specialist cert.), Am. Coll. Cardiology (gov. 1989-92), Am. Coll. Chest Physicians, Am. Heart Assn. Coun. Clin. Cardiology (Hawaii rep. 1991—); mem. N.Am. Soc. Pacing and Electrophysiology, Assn. Profs. of Cardiology, Mensa. Roman Catholic. Achievements include performance of first percutaneous transaluminal coronary angioplasty in Hong Kong, the first cases of automatic implantable cardiovertor-defibrillator, catheter ablation of arrhythmic circuits, coronary atherectomy, intracoronary stenting in Hawaii. Avocations: golf, classical guitar, Chinese poetry and literature. Office: 1380 Lusitana St Ste 701 Honolulu HI 96813-2443

SHEN, GARY GUIXIONG, electrical engineer educator; b. Shanghai, People Republic China, Dec. 10, 1946; s. Binfang and Aizhu (Ni) S.; m. Chen Shan, Feb. 1, 1972; 1 child, Yi. BS, Tsinghua Univ., Beijing, People Republic China, 1970, MS, 1981; PhD, Univ. Tex., 1990. Chief engr., dir. rsch. devel. Dantong TV Co., Dantong, Peoples Republic China, 1970-78; asst. prof. dept. elec. engr. Shanghai Univ., 1981-84; rsch. asst. dept. EECS Univ. Mich., 1984-86; RF rsch. engr. Univ. Tex., Arlington, 1986-90; sr. engr., dir. RF engring. GE Medical System, Fort Collins, Colo., 1990-93; assoc. prof. dept. elec. engring. Hong Kong Univ., Hong Kong, 1999—; assoc. prof. dept. radiology Univ. Pitts., 1993—; bd. mem. Nat. TV Standard Com., Dantong, 1972-78; pres. N.A. Chinese Soc. Meganetic Resonant in Medicine, Cleveland, 1993—; cons. GE Medical System, Milw., 1993-94. Contbr. articles to profl. jours. Pres. student and scholar assn. Univ. Tex., Arlington, 1988-89. Recipient Robert Leroy award Robert Leroy Found., 1990, Pres. award Otsuka Elec., Inc., Fort Collins, 1991. Mem. Internat. Soc. Magnetic Resonance in Medicine (com. mem. 1988—), IEEE, Eta Kappa Nu, Phi Beta Delta. Avocations: boating, traveling, swimming, hiking. E-mail: gxshen@eee.hku.hk. Fax number: 852 2559-8738. Office: Hong Kong Univ Dept EEE, CYC Building, Hong Kong Hong Kong

SHEN, GENE GIIN-YUAN, organic chemist; b. Taipei, Taiwan, Apr. 12, 1957; came to U.S., 1981; s. Chi and Su-Chin Shen; m. Grace Hsiao-Fen Shen, July 31, 1982; 1 child, Jennifer Iting. BS in Chemistry, Nat. Taiwan U., 1979; PhD in Organic Chemistry, U. Calif., Riverside, 1986; MBA, Calif. State U., Fullerton, 1998. Postdoctoral fellow U. Calif., Riverside, 1986-87; rsch. chemist Nucleic Acid Rsch. Inst. ICN, Costa Mesa, Calif., 1987-88; prin. investigator Pharm-Eco Labs., Inc., Simi Valley, Calif., 1988-91; staff scientist Beckman Instruments, Inc., Brea, Calif., 1991—. Contbr. articles to Jour. Am. Chem. Soc., Jour. Steroid Biochemistry and Molecular Biology, Tetrahetron Letters, Nucleosides and Nucleotides, others. Mem. Am. Chem. Soc., Phi Beta Kappa. Achievements include research in antisense oligonucleotides, near infrared fluorescent dyes and their applications to fluoroimmuno assay and DNA sequencing, dideoxynucleosides and deoxynucleosides as anti-AIDS drugs, highly sulfated cyclodextrins as chiral drugs separators using capillary electrophoresis, avidin-biotin chemistry, turbidimetric and nephelometric immunoinhibition assay, Vitamin A and Vitamin D analogs as cancer chemopreventive and chemotherapeutic agents, sigmatropic rearrangement of vinylallenes. Office: Beckman Instruments Inc 200 S Kraemer Blvd Brea CA 92821-6228

SHEN, HONG, pharmacologist, researcher; b. Kaili, China, May 16, 1971; s. Shen Youzhao and Guizheng Hu; m. Yue Jia, Mar. 22, 1997; 1 child, Brian. BS, Wuhan U., 1992; PhD, Chinese Acad. Scis., Shanghai, 1996. Asst. prof. Shanghai Inst. Planned Parenthood Rsch. WHO, 1996-97; rsch. fellow Coll. Pharmacy U. Mich., Ann Arbor, 1997-2000, investigator Coll. Pharmacy, 2000—. Reviewer Chinese Jour. Cell Biology, 1995-97; co-author book; contbr. articles to profl. jours. Nat. Found. Natural Sci. grantee Chinese Acad. Scis., 1997. Mem. Am. Soc. Nephrology, Am. Assn. Pharm. Scientists, Chinese Soc. Cell Biology. Avocations: fishing, soccer, music, travel. Fax: 734-763-0982. Home: 1634 Murfin Ave Apt 27 Ann Arbor MI 48105 Office: U Mich 4301 Upjohn Ctr Clin Pharm 1310 E Catherine St Ann Arbor MI 48109-0504

SHEN, HUI-SHEN, civil engineering educator; b. Shanghai, Jan. 1, 1947; s. Zhi-Huang and Le-Shui (Pan) S.; m. Xiao-Qing Ding, Jan. 1, 1977; children: Bo, Ding-Yuan. Diploma, Tsinghua U., Beijing, 1970; MS, Shanghai Jiao Tong U., 1982, PhD, 1986. Engr. Henan (China) Transp. Co., 1972-79; lectr. Shanghai Jiao Tong U., 1986-88, assoc. prof., 1988-92, prof., 1992—; vis. lectr. U. Wales, Cardiff, 1991-92, vis. prof., 1995; rsch. fellow U. Liverpool, U.K., 1992, Hong Kong Poly. U., 1998, 99. Author: Buckling of Structures, 1993. Recipient Sci. and Tech. award China State Shipbldg. Corp., 1994, Wu Shao-Lin award Shanghai Jiao Tong U., 1998, Sci. and Tech. award Shanghai Municipality, 1998. Mem. ASCE, Chinese Soc. Theoret. Applied Mechanics, China Civil Engring. Soc. Avocation: stamp collecting. Office: Shanghai Jiao Tong Univ, 1954 Hua Shan Rd, 200 030 Shanghai China

SHEN, JIANFA, geography educator; b. Ningbo, Zhejiang, China, Sept. 30, 1963; s. Gongmiao Shen and Baoqin Li; m. Yefang Huang, Feb. 2, 1989; 1 child, Haobo. BSc, East China Normal U., Shanghai, 1983, MSc, 1986; PhD, London Sch. Econs., 1994. Asst. instr. East China Normal U., 1986-88, lectr., 1988-94, adv. prof. Sch. Resources and Environ., 1997—; sr. rsch. asst. U. Wales, Swansea, 1994-95, lectr., 1995-96; rsch. fellow U. Leeds, Eng., 1996; asst. prof. geography Chinese U. Hong Kong, 1996—. Author: Theory of Regional Scicnce, 1991, Geographical Systems Engineering, 1993, Dynamic Analysis of Spatial Population Systems, 1994, Internal Migration and Regional Population Dynamics in China, 1996; editor: Urban, Rural and Regional Development, China Toward 21st Century, 1999; co-editor: China Review 2000, 2000. Rsch. grantee Rsch. Grant Coun., Hong Kong, 1998. Fellow Royal Geog. Soc., Hong Kong Geog. Assn. Avocations: reading, swimming. Office: Chinese U Hong Kong, Dept Geography, Shatin NT HK, China

SHEN, JING, physicist, educator, researcher, consultant; b. Shanghai, China, Oct. 31, 1935; s. Becan Shen and Xiuyu Zhang; m. Yongjun Wang, Oct. 20, 1962; children: Song, Pu. BS, Nanjing (China) U., 1958. Cert. engr., Chinese Ctrl. Govt. Ministry Electronics Industry; cert. prof., Chinese Acad. Scis. Designer-in-chief, nuc. instruments Chongqing (China) Radio Factory, 1958-66; head R & D Lab. Nuc. Medicine Instruments Jianan Nuc. Instrument Factory, Longchang, China, 1966-80; prof. rsch. electronics Inst. High Energy Physics, Beijing, 1980—; collaborator high energy physics rsch. R. Hofstadter Group Stanford (Calif.) U. and Inst. High Energy Physics, Beijing, 1984-87; officiating coord. 1st Project of China/U.S. Official Sci.-Tech. Cooperation (High Energy Collider) at U.S. Nat. Lab., SLAC at Stanford, 1985-86; specially invited prof., Inst. Power Electronics, Jinan U., Gaungzhou, China, 1993—; cons. Capital Ctr. Nuc. Medicine, Beijing, 1988—; tech. com. mem. Nat. Standardization Com. of Nuc. Instruments and Apparatuses, Beijing, 1991-95; tech. com. mem. IEC TC45 Chinese State Bur. Tech. Supervision, 1991-95; co-founder, com. mem., gen. sec. Chinese Soc. Nuc. Electronics and Nuc. Detection Tech., Beijing, 1979-85; assoc. mem. China Ctr. Advanced Sci. and Tech., 1998—; prof. Instrumentation Tech. and Economy Inst., China, 1998—. Co-founder, co-editor Chinese jour. Nuclear Electronic Instruments and Methods, 1973-85; contbr. to internat. sci. and engring. jours., chpts. to books; contbr. The Chinese Gtr. Encyclopedia, Vol. Electronics and Computer, The Chinese Encyclopedia of Medicine, Vol. Nuclear Medicine; editor procs.; inventor. Recipient Youth medal Chonqing Municipality Govt. Youth Conf., 1961; Nat. Sci. and Tech. Conf. medal, Beijing, 1978, Sci. and Tech. Medal Sichuan Province Govt., 1979; mem. team that won top grade nat. award of advancing scis. and techs., 1991. Mem. IEEE (sr.), N.Y. Acad. Scis. Achievements include research in nuclear physics, electronics, photonics, biomedical information, high energy physics, new idea of collider physics about muon collider, quantum accelerator, standardization of instrumentation and digital communication bus and economy/culture/history of science and technology, research on applying the tech of instrumentation, automation and fieldbus to reform the agriculture and acquaculture in China to make the equilibrium of ecology and economy; applying tech. of instrumentation, automation and field bus to reform the agriculture and acquaculture in China. Avocations: American computer arts and electronic music, Chinese poetry and characters, European classical arts, music. Office: Inst High Energy Physics, 19 Yu Quan Rd/POB 918(38), Beijing 100039, China

SHEN, JINXING, engineer; b. Tongxiang, Zhejiang, Peoples Republic of China, Feb. 25, 1963; s. Fuhong and Wenxian (Wang) S.; m. Pang Li Shen, Sept. 1, 1987; 1 child, Kaili. BS, Zhejiang U., Hangzhou, China, 1982, MS, 1985; PhD, Tech. U. Berlin, Germany, 1994. Devel. engr. Zhejiang Household Motor Co., Huzhou, China, 1982; lectr. Zhejiang U., Hangzhou, China, 1985-88; rsch. assoc. Tech. U. Berlin, Germany, 1988-95; engr. R&D Integrated Engring. Software Inc., Winnipeg, Can., 1995; tech. staff ABB Corp. Rsch., Heidelberg, Germany, 1996—, project mgr. for rotating machines, 1997—, sr. cientist for electromech. systems, 1999—, group leader for electromagnetic systems, 2000—; rsch. asst. Heinrich-Hertz Inst., Berlin, Germany, 1989-91; project leader United Tech. Rsch. Ctr., East Hartford, 1992. Author: Computational Electromagnetics Using Boundary Elements, 1995. Mem. IEEE, Compumag (edtl. bd.). Office: ABB Corporate Rsch, Speyerer Str 4, 69115 Heidelberg Germany

SHEN, JOHN JIANYUE, fuel cell company executive; b. Shanghai, Sept. 21, 1960; arrived in Can., 1988; s. P.Z. and Qiaozin (Xie) S. BS, ECUST, Shanghai, 1982; MS, SRICI, Shanghai, 1985; PhD, Laval U., Que., Can., 1992. Registered profl. engr., Can. Engr. SRICI, 1985-88; vis. rschr. NIMCR, Japan, 1993; rschr. Simon Fraser U., Vancouver, B.C., Can., 1993; v.p. Palcan Envirotech Ltd., Vancouver, 1994-95; chief engr. Nexcel Power Sys. Corp., Richmond, B.C., Can., 1995-98; founder, pres. Palcan Fuel Cell Co. Ltd., Burnaby, B.C., Can., 1998—. Patentee in applied surface sci., applied spectroscopy, others. Mem. AIChE, Am. Chem. Soc., Internat. Ziolite Assn. Christian. Avocations: hockey, fishing, pop music. Office: Palcan Fuel Cell Co Ltd, 8624 Commerce Ct, Burnaby, BC Canada USA 4N6

SHEN, JUN, computer science educator, researcher; b. Taizhou City, Jiangsu, China, Dec. 8, 1946; s. Yu-Cheng and Tong-Zhi (Wu) S.; m. Zhan-Ru Zhao, Jan. 22, 1970; 1 child, Dan-Fei. BS, Tsing Hua U., Peking, China, 1968; MSc, Paul Sabatier U., Toulouse, France, 1981, PhD, 1982, Doctorat d'Etat, 1986. Chief engr. Nanjing (China) Chemistry Ltd., 1968-78; asst. prof. Tsinghua U., Peking, 1978-80; vis. scientist Paul Sabatier U. and Nat. Sci. Rsch. Ctr., Toulouse, 1986-87; prof. Southeast U., Nanjing, 1988-89; vis. prof. Paul Sabatier U., Toulouse, 1989-91; prof. computer sci., image processing and computer vision Bordeaux-3 U., France, 1991—, head of image lab., 1991—; cons. Project Elf Aquitaine, Pau, 1997-99; sci. com. Nat. Lab. in Pattern Recognition, Sinica, China, 1986; sci. com. nat. Lab. in Artificial Intelligence, Peking U., 1987, Lab. in Image Processing, Huazhong U., Wuhan, China, 1996—. Contbr. articles to profl. jours. Mem. IEEE, Soc. Photo-Optical Instrumentation Engrs. (sci. program com. 1995—). Avocations: Chinese chess, chess. Office: U Bordeaux, Image Lab EGID, 33607 Pessac Cedex France

SHEN, KECHENG, reliability and safety engineer; b. Chengde, Hebei, China, Aug. 16, 1957; arrived in Sweden, 1983; s. Guo Shen and Xiuxian Cui; m. Jing Fang, Sept. 6, 1986; 1 child, Winnie Shen. BSc in Engring., Beijing U. Sci. and Tech., 1982; PhD in Engring., Lund (Sweden) U., 1991. Lic. engr., Sweden. Lectr. Lund U., 1985-90; reliability cons. Studsvik EcoSafe, Nykoping, Sweden, 1991-97; reliability and safety mgr. Adtranz Sweden, Vasteras, Sweden, 1998—. Trans.: Abstract Algebra, 1992; contbr. articles to sci. publs., including IEEE Transactions on Reliability, Microelectronics and Reliability, others. Postgrad. scholar Lund U., 1983. Mem. IEEE, Swedish Mfg. Industries (mem. reliability com.), Swedish Assn. Quality (mem. reliability and safety com.). Office: Dept ICT/KS, Adtranz Sweden, S 721 73 Vasteras Sweden

SHEN, KUI, chemist; b. Bengbu, China, May 22, 1966; parents Jinzhang Niu and Hongxian Shen; m. Lixin Qi, Oct. 11, 1991; 1 child, Grace. BS, Beijing U. Aero. & Astronaut., 1987, MS, 1990; MS, Albert Einstein Coll. Medicine, 1999. Asst. engr., then engr. Chinese Acad. Scis. Inst. Photographic Chemistry, Beijing, 1990-95; grad. asst. SUNY, Buffalo, 1995-96; rschr. Albert Einstein Coll. Medicine, Bronx, N.Y., 1996—. Mem. AAAS, Am. Chem. Soc. Avocations: reading, gardening. Office: Albert Einstein Coll Medicine Dept Biochemistry 1300 Morris Park Ave Bronx NY 10461-1926

SHEN, LIYONG, materials scientist, research facility administrator; b. Shanghai, China, Jan. 28, 1956; came to U.S. 1991; s. Zhi-Jie and Gui-Ying (Wang) S.; m. May Min Guo, Dec. 25, 1986; children: Julie, Yan. BS in Mech. and Metall. Engring., Shanghai Jiao Tong U., China, 1983, MS in Materials Sci. and Engring., 1988; MS Solid State Sci., Tech., Syracuse (N.Y.) U., 1993, PhD Solid State Sci., Tech. (Physics), 1997. Sr. engr. Shanghai Paper Machinery Corp., China, 1983-85; rsch. fellow Shanghai Jiao Tong U., China, 1985-88; asst. prof. Shanghai Jiao Tong U., China, 1988-91; rsch. fellow Syracuse (N.Y.) U., 1991-97; mgr. materials rsch. facility, rsch. fellow U. Ala., Tuscaloosa, 1997-99; rsch. scientist, mem. faculty Vanderbilt U., Nashville, 1999—; vis. rschr. Oak Ridge (Tenn.) Nat. Lab., 1998—. Contbr. articles to profl. jours. including Astrophysics Jour., Jour. of Vacuum Sci. and Tech., Jour. Applied Physics. Grantee NASA, 1993-97, NSF, 1997—, Dept. Def., U. Ala., 1997—, Dept of Energy Oak Ridge Nat. Lab., 1997—. Mem. IEEE, Am. Phys. Soc., Materials Rsch. Soc., Am Vacuum Soc. Achievements include: contributed research on nanostructured materials for electrical engineering, semiconductor, optics, MEMS, sensor; leading development of high areal density, low thermal decay, thin film magnetic materials for information data storage; first chemical synthesis of astrophysical interested materials in ultra high vacuum and extreme low temperature circumstances; earliest created computer aided design program for die mould and alloy solidification process simulation; pioneer material design of high temperature, corrosion-resisting, abrasion-proof alloy. Office: Box 1807 Sta B Dept Physics & Astronomy Vanderbilt Univ Nashville TN 37235

SHEN, PEIYAN, scientist, researcher; b. Dezhou, Shandong, China, Aug. 9, 1959; arrived in Australia, 1986; s. Fuming and Zhenying (Liu) S.; m. Nina Ning Kang, July 4, 1984; 1 child, Cary. MB, Shandong Med. U., Jinan, China, 1982, MSc, 1986; PhD, U. Melbourne, Australia, 1991. Rsch. scientist Melbourne U., 1991—. Contbr. articles to profl. jours. V.p. Australian and Chinese Student Assn., 1989. Mem. Internat. Soc. Atherosclerosis, Australian Soc. Atherosclerosis, Australian Soc. Biochemistry and Molecular Biology. Avocations: swimming, tennis, walking. Office: Melbourne U Sch Dental Sci, Biochemistry Molecular Biol, Melbourne VIC 3000, Australia

SHEN, PETER YI, laboratory assistant; b. Xin Jing, China, Nov. 17, 1977; came to U.S., 1989; s. Guoqiu Shen and Lanmin Wang. Student, UCLA, 1996. Rsch. technician Specialty Lab. Inc., Santa Monica, Calif., 1996-98; lab. asst. Lab. of Tomas Ganz dept. medicine UCLA, 1996-98, student rschr., lab. asst., 1998—. Student vol. Dept. Vet. Affairs Med. Ctr., L.A., 1996; clinic asst. Venice (Calif.) Family Clinic, 1998—. Mem. AIChE (chief of staff UCLA 1998-99, co-pres. UCLA 1999—), Tau Beta Pi. E-mail: pyshen@ucla.edu. Home: 3464 Greenwood Ave Los Angeles CA 90066-2257

SHEN, QING, education educator; b. Hangzhou, Zhejiang, China, May 7, 1956; s. Chuan-Yong and Pei-Zhang (Hu) S.; m. Hui-Feng Zhu, 1987; 1 child, Dian. Diploma, Shanghai Chem. Fiber Coll., Shanghai, 1984; D Tech., Abo Acad. U., Turku, Finland, 1998. From engr. to dept. mgr. Shanghai No. 6 Chem. Fiber Mill, 1984-93; rschr. Abo Acad. U., Turku, 1993-99; assoc. prof. Dong Hua U., Shanghai, 2000—. Co-author: Advances in Lignocellu Charact., 1999; contbr. articles to profl. jours; author: Interfacial Characterization of Wood and Cooking Liquor in Relation to Delignification Kinetics, 1998. Recipient New Product award Shanghai Govt., 1992, award for advance in sci. and tech., 1993. Mem. N.Y. Acad. Scis., China Pulp and Paper Assn., China Textile Engring. Soc., China Capital Constrn. (Manuscript award 1989), Optimization Rsch. Soc. Office: Dong Hua U, 1882 Yan An W Rd, Shanghai 200051, China

SHEN, QING, urban planning educator, researcher; b. Jinyun, Zhejiang, China, Apr. 5, 1962; s. Xianxing and Aili (Cheng) S.; m. Yongmei Zhu, Aug. 25, 1989; 1 child, Sophie. BS, Zhejiang U., 1982; MA in Urban Planning, U. of B.C., Canada, 1986; PhD in Urban Planning, U. Calif., Berkeley, 1993. Asst. prof. Urban Studies & Planning MIT, Cambridge, 1993-99; assoc. prof. Urban Studies & Planning MIT, 1999—. Contbr. articles to profl. jours. Emerging Scholar Paper award Assn. Am. Geographers, 1999; Horwood Critique prize Urban and Regional Info. Sys. Assn, 1998. Mem. Assn. Collegiate Schs. Planning, Assn. Am. Geographers, Transp. Rsch. Bd., Urban and Regional Info. Sys. Assn. Avocations: poetry, tennis. E-mail: qshen@mit.edu. Office: MIT Room 9-526 77 Massachusetts Ave Rm 9-526 Cambridge MA 02139-4307

SHEN, RONG-SEN, chemist; b. Tianjin, Hebei, China, Mar. 18, 1938; s. Shun-Zhang Shen and Xiu-Ying Jiang; m. Yun-Hua Chen, Jan. 6, 1968; children: Ming, Bai Shen. Grad. in analytical chemistry, Tianjin U., 1962. Mem. rsch. staff Inst. Radiation Medicine, Beijing, 1963-78, mem. sr. rsch. staff, 1978-90, assoc. prof. chemistry, 1990-95, prof., 1996—, dir. postgrads., 1990—. Author: Radiochemical Manual for Analysis of Fission Nuclides, 1983 (cert. of merit 1986), Antibodies Immobilized on Magnetic Particles for Radioimmunoassay and Immunoradiometric Assay of Hormenes, 1996, Application of Immunomicrospheres to Radioimmunoassay and Cell Identification, 1988 (Nat. award 1989), (with others) Modern Trends in Radiopharmaceuticals for Diagnosis and Therapy, 1998, Immunodiagnostics: A Practical Approach, 1999; contbr. articles to sci. publs., including Bull. Acad. Mil. Med. Scis., Chinese Jour. of Radiol. Medicine and Protection, Chem. Reagents, Kexue Tongbao, Progress in Biochemistry and Biophysics, Jour. Radioanal. Nuclear Chem. Avocations: reading history and biography, Chinese poker, sightseeing, talking, cycling. Home: 27 Taiping Rd 9-B-302, Beijing 100850, China Office: Inst Radiation Medicine, 27 Taiping Rd, Beijing 100850, China

SHEN, SHANXIONG, physicist; b. Shanghai, China, Dec. 13, 1933; s. Changrun and Caidian (Bian) S.; m. Hairon Wang, Aug. 22, 1961 (wid. Mar. 1973); 1 child, Sunny Shen; m. Xiaofeng Yepin, Apr. 4, 1989. B, Fudan U., Shanghai, China, 1958. Asst. prof. East China Normal U., Shanghai, 1958-62, prof., 1962-98. Author: (books) Optics, 1981, Applied Physics, 1982; editor: (jour.) Physics Teaching, 1989. Recipient Excellent Tchg. award, Tech. Coll. E. China Normal U., 1998. Mem. Chinese Physics Soc., Chinese Optics Soc. Avocations: photography, travel, bicycling, TV, cooking. Office: E China Normal U Physics, 3663 Zhongshan Bei Rd, 200062 Shanghai China

SHEN, TIANSHENG, research scientist; b. Mizhi, Shaanxi, People's Republic of China, Mar. 3, 1965; d. Changzhong Shen and Shaoping Ye; m. Shaogang Lu, Feb. 10, 1988; 1 child, Yunhe Lu. MD, Xi'an Med. U., People's Republic of China, 1985, MS, 1988; PhD in molecular and cellular pharmacology, U. Pierre and Marie Curie (Paris VI), 1997. MS candidate Xi'an Med. U., People's Republic of China, 1985-88, rsch. assoc. Rsch. Lab. Keshan Disease, 1988-93; trainee French lang. Beijing Foreign Lang. U., 1993-94; PhD candidate, INSERM U-99 Henri Mondor Hosp., France, 1994-97; postdoctoral rschr. Lankenau Med. Rsch. Ctr., Pa., 1997-98; postdoctoral rschr. dept. oral biology Ohio State U., 1998—. Contbr. numerous articles to profl. jours. Xi'an Med. U. fellow, 1985-88, Chinese Nat. Edn. Com. fellow, 1994-97. Mem. AchemS Assn. Chemoreception Scis., Sigma Xi. E-mail: tianshengs@hotmail.com. Home: 690 Riverview Dr Apt 104 Columbus OH 43202-3240 Office: Ohio State U PO Box 182357 305 W 12th Ave Columbus OH 43218

SHEN, XINGHAI, chemist, educator; b. Wujiang, China, Aug. 6, 1965; parents Fuliang Xu and Hongdi Shen; m. Li Dong, Dec. 29, 1992; 1 child, Jian. BSc, Peking U., 1986, MSc, 1989, DSc, 1993. From lectr. to assoc. prof. tech. physics Peking U., Beijing, 1993—; vis. scholar U. Montreal, 1996-97. Grantee Royal Soc. Chemistry U.K., 1999. Mem. Chinese Materials Rsch. Soc. Avocations: swimming, fishing, music. Office: Peking U, Dept Physics, Beijing China 100871

SHEN, YA-CHING, natural product chemistry educator, researcher; b. Taipei, Taiwan, May 30, 1953; s. Tiao and Ching-Yin Wu S.; m. Show-Ching Dai, Oct. 5, 1986; two children. BS, Taipei Med. Coll., 1976; MS, Nat. Taiwan U., 1980, PhD, 1987. Pharmacy diplomate. Instr. Nat. Taiwan U., Taipei, 1987-89, assoc. prof., 1989; vis. assoc. prof. U. N.C., Chapel Hill, 1989-90; post doctor U. Calif. San Diego, La Jolla, 1990-92; assoc. prof. Nat. Sun Yat-Sen U., Kaohsiung, Taiwan, 1992-97; prof. Nat. Sun Yat-Sen U., Kaohsiung, 1997—; cons. Nat. Rsch. Inst. of Chinese Medicine, Taipei, 1993-97; pharmacist The Pharmacist Assn. of Taipei, 1976-97. Contbr. articles to profl. jours. Lt. U.S. Army, 1976-78, King-Meng. Grantee Nat. Sci. Coun., Taipei, 1993—, Nat. Health Rsch. Inst., Taipei, 1995—, Nat. Sci. Coun., Taipei, 1997—. Mem. Am. Soc. Pharmacognosy, Chinese Pharm. Assn., Chinese Pharmacist Assn. Avocations: gardening, plant identification, nature, book reading, tourism. Office: Inst Marine Resources, Nat Sun Yat-Sen U, 804 Kaohsiung Taiwan

SHEN, YONG, physicist; b. Yang Zhou, Jiangsu, China, Aug. 18, 1962; s. Da-hua and Yu-xuan (Zhou) S.; m. Sue Siyang Zhang, Aug. 22, 1987; children: Carol Y., Eric T. BSc in Physics, Nanjing (China) U., 1982; PhD in Physics, U. Va., Charlottesville, 1988. Rsch. scientist Argonne (Ill.) Nat. Lab., 1989-90; rsch. assoc. Carnegie Mellon U., Pitts., 1990-92; dept. mgr. Read-Rite Corp., Milpitas, Calif., 1996-98; dir. advanced product design SAE Magnetics, TDK Corp., Hong Kong, 1998—. Contbr. articles to profl. jours.; patentee in field. Mem. IEEE, Hong Kong Critical Component Assn. (dir. magnetic chpt. 1998—). Home: 10415 Dempster Ave Cupertino CA 95014-1224 Office: SAE Magnetics, 38-42 Kwai Fung Crescent, Kwai Chung Hong Kong

SHEN, YUANHUA, physics educator; b. Quzhou, Zhejiang, China, Nov. 8, 1939; s. Wen Liang Shen and Shu Ying Zhang; m. Ye Ping Lu, Feb. 28, 1969; childen: Anding, Anqiang. Diploma in physics, Fudan U., Shanghai, 1956. Asst. Fudan U., 1961-78, lectr., 1978-85, assoc. prof., 1985-94, prof. physics, 1994—; vis. scholar Northwestern U., Evanston, Ill., 1982-84, 88-89. Author booklet: Thin Film Optics, 1970; editor: Optics, 1995; patentee diamond optical thin film. Mem. Chinese Optical Soc. (mem. thin-film com.), Shanghai Laser Soc. (chmn. thin-film com.). Office: Fudan U Physics Dept, 220 Handan Rd, Shanghai 200433, China

SHEN, ZHONGXIANG, electrical engineering educator; b. Haiyan, China, July 12, 1966; s. Fulin Shen and Fengbao Zhong; m. Xinman Yang, Nov. 17, 1992. B.S. in Engring., U. Electronic Sci. and Tech., Chengdu, China, 1987; MS, Southeast Univ., Nanjing, China, 1990; PhD, U. Waterloo, Ont., Can., 1997. Asst. prof. aero. and astro. Nanjing U., 1990-94; asst. prof. Nanyang Technol. U., Singapore, 1994—; mem. tech. staff ComDev Ltd., Cambridge, Can., 1997. Recipient award Chinese Aero. Fund, 1993; postdoc. fellow Harvard U., U. Mich., 1998. Mem. IEEE, N.Y. Acad. Scis. Avocations: fishing, bridge. Home: Block # K 03-03, 102 Nanyang Crescent, Singapore 637820, Singapore Office: Nanyang Technol U, Sch EEE, Singapore 639798, Singapore

SHENG, DONGYUAN, software engineer; b. Qidong, China, Jan. 4, 1973; s. YongLiang Sheng and Juying Gao.; BS, Northeastern U., Shenyang, China, 1992, PhD, 1997. Tech. support ATE, Beijing, 1996-97; postdoctoral rschr. Seoul Nat. U., 1997; cons. AID Co., Seoul, 1997; rschr. MEFOS, Lulea, Sweden, 1998—. Avocation: bridge. Office: MEFOS, S-97125 Lulea Sweden

SHENG, GANG (GANG CHEN), engineer; b. Wuhan, Hubei, China, Mar. 26, 1963; arrived in Singapore, 1993; s. Yukuen and Yilan (Chen) Zhang; m. Linda Juan Zhang, May, 1989; 1 child, Hanlu Chen. B Engring., Shanghai (China) Jiao Tong U., 1984, M Engring., 1987; PhD, Nanyang Tech. U., Singapore, 1997. Asst. prof., lectr. Huazhong U. Sci. & Tech., Hubei, China, 1987-92; engr. Magnetic Tech. Ctr., Singapore, 1996; sr. engr. Data Storage Inst., Singapore, 1997-98, prin. engr., 1999-2000; leader HDI group Singapore Rsch. Lab. Sony Electronics, 2000—. Author: Dynamic Modeling of Mechanical Systems, 1991, Mechanical Vibration Systems, Vol. I and II, 1992 (award Nat. Ednl. Coun. 1994); contbr. articles to profl. jours. Recipient grad. scholarship Nanyang Tech. U., Singapore, 1993-96. Mem. ASME, IEEE. Avocations: Qigong, tennis. Home: Block 338 # 19-38, Clementi Ave 2, Singapore 120338, Singapore Office: Singapore Rsch Lab Sony, 10 Science Park Rd #03-08, Singapore 117684, Singapore

SHENG, HWAI-PING, physiology educator, researcher; b. Ayer Hitam, Johore, Malaysia, July 18, 1943; d. Pong-Yuen and Soei-Kok (Chin) Shang; m. Barry Fegan Will, Jan. 4, 1977; 1 child, Ewen. BSc, U. Singapore, 1966, BSc with honors, 1967; PhD, Baylor Coll. Medicine, 1971. Lectr. U. Hong Kong, 1971-74, 91-93, sr. lectr., 1993—; asst. prof. Coll. Medicine Baylor Coll. Medicine, Houston, 1975-88, assoc. prof., 1988-91. Contbr. articles to profl. jours. including Am. Jour. Clin. Nutrition, Jour. Nutrition, Pediat. Rsch., and Jour. Applied Physiology. Fulbright fellow, 1967-71. Mem. Am. Physiol. Soc., Am. Inst. Nutrition. Home: Flat 1A 2 University Dr, Hong Kong Hong Kong Office: U Hong Kong Dept Physiology, 5 Sassoon Rd, Hong Kong Hong Kong

SHENGWU, XIE, academic administrator; b. Shanghai, Nov. 22, 1943; m. Gu Meifeng; 1 son. Grad., Shanghai Jiao Tong U., 1966, MS in Applied Physics, 1981. Mem. faculty Shanghai Jiao Tong U., Shanghai, 1966-70, mem. faculty Inst. of Laser, 1970-78, lectr., 1982-85, assoc. prof., 1985-90, prof., 1990-94, PhD advisor, 1994—, v.p., 1991-97, dean Grad. Sch., 1994-98, pres., 1997—. Editl. bd. Acta Optica Sinica; chmn. editl. bd. The Jour. of Shanghai Jiao Tong U; author numerous books and contbr. articles to jours. in field. Mem. Chinese People's Polit. Consultative Conf.; mem. Shanghai Mcpl. Govt.'s Expert Com. for Sci. and Technology Progress; chmn. Shanghai Laser Soc., others. Recipient Gold prize Shanghai Expo - Sci. and Technology, 1997, Disting. Master Degree Owner's award Chinese State Commn. of Edn. and the Degree awarding com. of the Chinese State Coun., 1991, Excellent Rsch. Achievement award Chinese State Commn. of Edn., 1986, Nat. Sci. Conf. Key Rsch. award, 1978. Avocations: map collecting, bowling. Office: Shanghai Jiao Tong U, 1954 Hua Shan Rd, Shanghai 200030, China*

SHENKIN, ALAN, clinical chemist, educator; b. Glasgow, Scotland, Sept. 3, 1943; s. Louis and Miriam Leah (Epstein) S.; m. Leonna Estelle Delmonte, June 27, 1967; children: Susan Deborah, Trudi Freda, Stephen Andrew. BSc with honors, U. Glasgow, 1965, MB ChB, 1969, PhD, 1974. Lectr. U. Glasgow, 1970-74; sr. registrar Glasgow Royal Infirmary, 1974-78; Royal Soc. European Exch. fellow Karolinska Inst., Stockholm, 1976-77; cons. in clin. chemistry Royal Infirmary, Glasgow, 1978-90; prof. clin. chemistry U. Liverpool, Eng., 1990—; hon. cons. Royal Liverpool U. Hosp., 1990—; examiner U. London, 1990—, Chinese U. Hong Kong, 1990-94. European editor Nutrition Jour., Syracuse, N.Y., 1986—; mem. editl. bd. Clin. Nutrition, JPEN, others; author rsch. papers, book chpts. and rev. articles on micronutrient requirement in nutritional support, and the metabolic and cytokine response to serious illness. Fellow Royal Coll. Pathologists (London) (coun., chmn. of specialty adv. com. on chem. pathology 1995-98), Royal Coll. Physicians (Glasgow), Royal Coll. Physicians (London); mem. Assn. Clin. Biochemists (coun., chair sci. com. 1994-96, pres. 2000—), European Soc. Parenteral and Enteral Nutrition (treas. 1988-92), Brit. Med. Assn., N.Y. Acad. Scis., Am. Soc. Clin. Nutrition, Am. Assn. Clin. Chemistry, Nutrition Soc. (clin. metabolism and nutritional support group sec. 1988-91, com. 1991-94, coun. 1995-98), Brit. Dietetic Assn. (hon. assoc.), Czechoslovakian Med. Soc. (hon.), Czechoslovakian Soc. Parenteral and Enteral Nutrition (hon.), Intercollegiate Group Nutrition (chmn. 1997—). Avocations: golf, word games, travel. Home: 10 Rockbourne Green, Woolton Liverpool L25 4TH, England Office: U Liverpool, Dept Clin Chemistry, Liverpool L69 3GA, England

SHENKMAN, MARK RONALD, investment and finance executive; b. Providence, Aug. 17, 1943; s. George and Florence (Littman) S.; children: Andrew Harris, Gregory Alexander; m. Rosalind Schmidt, Aug. 10, 1997; 1 stepchild, Justin Warren Slatky. BA, U. Conn., 1965; MBA, George Washington U., 1967. bd. dirs. Crown Books Corp. Security analyst New Eng. Mchts. Bank, Boston, 1969-71; fin. analyst Stone & Webster Securities Corp., Boston, 1971-73; portfolio mgr. Fidelity Mgmt. & Research Co., Boston, 1973-79; v.p. Lehman Bros. Kuhn Loeb, N.Y.C., 1979-83; pres. First Investors Asset Mgmt. Co., N.Y.C., 1983-85; pres., chief exec. officer Shenkman Capital Mgmt. Inc., N.Y.C., 1985—. Vice chmn. bd. dirs. Wilbraham (Mass.) and Monson Acad.; trustee U. Conn. Found.; bd. visitors George Washington U. Sch. Bus. 1st lt. U.S. Army, 1967-69. Mem. Am. Bankruptcy Inst., N.Y. Soc. Security Analysts, Boston Security Analysts Soc., Am. Statis. Assn., Assn. Investment Mgmt. and Rsch. Home: Gaston Farm Rd Greenwich CT 06831 Office: 461 Fifth Ave New York NY 10017-6234

SHENKO, WILLIAM EDWARD, JR., lawyer; b. Sioux Falls, S.D., July 1, 1954; s. William Edward and Jeanette Elizabeth Shenko; m. Linda Mulford, Nov. 21, 1981. AA, Edison C.C., Ft. Myers, Fla., 1975; BA, U. South Fla., 1977; JD, Stetson U., 1980. Bar: Fla. 1980, U.S. Dist. Ct. (mid. dist.) Fla. 1980, U.S. Dist. Ct. (so. dist.) Fla. 1982. Legal intern Organized Crime Unit, 6th Cir., Clearwater, Fla., 1980; asst. state atty. 20th Cir. of Fla. Juvenile Divsn., Ft. Myers, 1980, Lee County Commrs., Ft. Myers, 1980, Felony Divsn., 20th Cir., Ft. Myers, 1981; assoc. Alderman and Gerald, Ft. Myers, 1981-85; assoc., ptnr. Echols Cotter & Shenko, Ft. Myers Beach, Fla., 1985-95; pres. William E. Shenko, Jr. P.A., Ft. Myers Beach, 1995—; counsel Ft. Myers Beach Bd. Realtors, 1984, 94, 95, 96, Iona Mcgregor Fire Dist., Ft. Myers, 1984—; spl. master City of Sanibel, Fla., 1995-96; pres. Pink Shell VV Condo Assn., Ft. Myers Beach, 1988-93. Founder Ft. Myers Beach Incorporation Com., 1993; mem. bd. rev. Eagle Scouts, Ft. Myers, 1994-97; bd. dirs. Ft. Myers Beach Voters Assn., 1994-96. Mem. Ft. Myers Beach C. of C., Marathon Yacht Club, Ft. Myers Beach Bd. Realtors, Bonita Springs Bd. Realtors. Republican. Roman Catholic. Avocation: sailing. Office: 2801 Estero Blvd Ste C Fort Myers Beach FL 33931-3530

SHENNAK, MUSTAFA MAHMOUD MUSA, internist, gastroenterologist, medical educator; b. Irbid, Jordan, Sept. 10, 1942; s. Mahmoud M. and Naima (Ahmed) S.; m. Muna Jamil Arif Barakat, Jan. 17, 1974; children: Maha, Meral, Zaina, Dina, Lana, Bana. MD, Istanbul U., Turkey, 1967. Diplomate gen. medicine, internal medicine, 1967-71, gastroenterology, liver disease. Intern Istanbul Faculty of Medicine Hosps., 1966-67; resident in internal medicine Ankara U. Med. Sch. Hosps., 1967-71; intern Istanbul Univ. Hosp., 1966-67; residency in internal med. Ankara Med. Faculty Hosp., 1967-71; fellow in gastroenterology Ankara U. Med. Sch. Hosps., 1971-72; gastroenterology fellow Ankara, Turkey, 1971-72; specialist internal medicine, gastroenterology Amman, Jordan, 1973-75, 77-79; specialist internal medicine, gastroenterolgy Abu Dhabi, United Arab Emirates, 1975-77; chmn. internal medicine dept., gastroenterology unit Amman, Jordan, 1977-90; gen. dir. Al-Bashir Hosp., Amman, Jordan, 1984-86; chief med. staff Jordan Med. Inst., Amman, Jordan, 1987-89; prof. internal medicine, gastroenterology U. Jordan, Amman, Jordan, 1990—, chmn. internal medicine, chief gastroenterology & liver unit, 1996—; mem. exam. com. Arab Bd. Internal Medicine, Damascus, Syria, 1982—, chmn. 1988-92; vice chmn. sci. exam. com. Jordan Med. Coun., Amman, 1982—, chief gastroenterology exam. com., 1982—, vice chmn. internal medicine exam. com., 1982—; mem. acad. & profl. com. Med. Sch. & Univ. Hosp., Amman, 1996—. Author: Essential Drugs In Arabic, 1989; editor Jordan Med. Jour., 1979-94, editor-in-chief, 1997—; mem. editl. bd. Hepato-Gastroenterology and Jour. Amer. Med. Assn. (JAMA) Middle East; mem. editl. bd. sect. hepato-gastroenterology Jour. Internat. Gastro Surg. Club. Fellow Am. Coll. Gastroenterology; mem. Internat. Gastro-Surg. Club. Moslem. Home: Tila-Al-Ali Drs Housing, Ismail Abu-Luli St No 26, Amman Jordan Office: Jordan U Faculty Medicine, PO Box 13389, Amman 11942, Jordan

SHENNAN, IAN, geography educator; b. Spalding, England, Dec. 7, 1954; m. Louise Shennan. BS in Geography, U. Durham, 1976, PhD, 1981. Lectr. in geography U. Durham, 1981-83, 1983-92, sr. lectr. in geography, 1992-95, reader in geography, 1995, prof. in geography, 1995—; chmn. Environ. Rsch. Ctr.-U. Durham, 1995-97. Co-editor: (book) Sea-Level Changes, 1987, Holocene Land-Ocean Interaction and Environmental Change around the North Sea, 2000; contbr. numerous articles to profl. jours. Mem. Quaternary Rsch. Assn., Internat. Union Quaternary Rsch. Avocations: mountaineering, mountain biking. Office: U Durham-Dept Geography, South Road, DH1 3LE Durham England

SHENOUDA, POPE III, patriarch; b. Cairo, Aug. 3, 1923; B.A., Cairo U.; B.D., Coptic Orthodox Theol. Coll. Theol. tchr. and writer; former Bishop and prof. theol. Orthodox Clerical Coll., Cairo; 1st chmn. Assn. of Theol. Colls. in the Near East; 117th Pope of Alexandria and Patriarch of the See of St. Mark of Egypt, the Near East and All Africa (Coptic Orthodox Church), 1971-81, 85—; removed from post by Pres. Sadat;banished to desert monastery Wadi Natroun, Sept. 1981, released Jan. 1985. Office: Coptic Orthodox Ch St Mark Cathedral, POB 9035 Anba Ruess 222 Ramses St, Abbasiya Cairo Egypt*

SHENOY, KAUP BHASKER, science educator, researcher; b. Karwar, Karnataka, India, Dec. 10, 1960; s. Kaup Gopalakrishna and Kaup Shantha (Nayak) S. BS, Canara Coll., Mangalore, India, 1981; MS, Mangalore U., 1984, PhD, 1991. Postgrad. rsch. fellow Mangalore U., 1984-85, univ. grants commn. jr., sr. rsch. fellow, 1985-90, rsch. assoc. coun. scientific and indsl. rsch., 1990-91, lectr. applied zoology, 1991—; co-investigator All India Coun. Tech. Edn., Mangalore, 1997—; mem., organizer Marine Shells Exhibn., Mangalore, 1996; mem. organizing com. Dept. Sci. and Tech., Mangalore, 1995, Wildlife Biology Seminar, Mangalore, 1994. Participant Nat. Social Svc., Mangalore, 1980, Blood Donor Camp, Mangalore, 1994. Mem. Indian Soc. Comparative Animal Physiologists (life), Soc. Biol. Chemists, Philately Club. Hindu. Avocations: gardening, philately. Home: Prabhu Niwas, Mannagudda, 575003 Mangalore India Office: Mangalore U Applied Zoology, Mangalagangothri, 574 199 Mangalore India

SHENTON, MIKE, software consultant; b. Leicester, Eng., May 18, 1954; s. Roy Trevor and Betty (Knight) S.; m. Helen Jane Moore, Sept. 9, 1978; children: Claire, Richard, Nicola. BSc with honours, Nottingham (Eng.) U., 1976. Design engr. Marconi Radar, Leicester, 1977-83, project leader, 1983-85; prin. system engr. Marconi Command and Control, Leicester, 1985-86, bid mgr., 1986-87, software cons., 1987-94; dir. ISAS, Leicester, 1994-97, Cadalec, Blaby, Leicester, 1997—. Author programming lang. PIPAL. Deacon Free Ch., Kirby Muxloe, Eng., 1982-86. Mem. Instn. Elec. Engrs. (com. 1988—), Brit. Computer Soc. Baptist. Avocation: fund raising. Office: Cadalec, Blaby Leicester LE8 4DR, England

SHEPARD, KIRK VAN, SR., physician, researcher; b. Columbus, Ohio, Aug. 17, 1951; s. Ivan Albert and Miriam Adele (Murray) S.; m. Nadine Joyce Martello, Aug. 27, 1983; children: Kirk Van II, Devin, Austin, Pierce. BA, Cornell U., 1973; MD, U. Cin., 1978. Diplomate Am. Bd. Internal Medicine, Am. Bd. Med. Oncology, Am. Bd. Hematology. Intern in medicine Case Western Res. U., Cleve., 1978-79, resident in medicine, 1980-81; fellow in hematology and oncology U. Chgo., 1981-84; staff physician Cleve. Clinic Found., 1984-87; med. dir. Roxane Labs., Inc., Columbus, 1987-88, v.p. med. affairs, 1989-97, sr. v.p. mktg. and med. affairs and product devel., 1997-98; sr. v.p. RX/Hosp. Bus. Unit Strategy, 1998-2000; v.p. mktg. pipeline products Boehringer Ingelheim Pharms., 2000—; asst. clin. prof. Ohio State U. Med. Ctr., 1988—; mem. publ. com. Hospice Update, 1989-95. Author: (with others) Gastroinestinal Malignancies, 1984, Tumors of Upper GI Tract, 1987, Review of Controlled Release Morphine, 1990; editor Palliative Care Letter, 1989—; contbr. over 65 articles to profl. jours. Cornell U. nat. scholar, 1970-73; recipient Disting. Alumni award BVH, 1996. Mem. Northeastern Ohio Soc. Oncologists (mem. at large 1987), Ohio Cancer Pain Inst. (bd. dirs. 1990-91). Office: Boehringer Ingelheim PO Box 368 Ridgefield CT 06877-0368

SHEPHARD, DOUGLAS STUART, chemist, researcher, consultant; b. Harrogate, Yorkshire, Eng., Sept. 2, 1971; s. William Stuart and Pamela Margaret (Tolley) S.; m. Sarah Victoria Hill, June 19, 1999. BSc in Chemistry, Edinburgh (Scotland) U., 1993, PhD in Chemistry, 1997. Cert. chemist. Post-doctoral rsch. asst. Cambridge (Eng.) U., 1997-99; Smithson rsch. fellow Peterhouse Coll., Cambridge, 1999—; cons. Redcastle, Cambridge, 1998-99; cons. in field, 1999—. Patentee novel catalyst preparation; contbr. papers to pee reviewed jours. Smithson Rsch. fellow Peterhouse & Royal Soc., 1998. Mem. AAAS, Royal Soc. Chemists, New York Acad. Scis., Amnesty Internat. Avocations: mountaineering, sailing, surfing, gardening, folk music. Home and Office: Peterhouse, Cambridge CB2 1RD, England

SHEPHERD, ALAN ARTHUR, electronics company executive, consultant; b. Stalybridge, Cheshire, Eng., Sept. 6, 1927; s. Arthur and Hannah Shepherd; m. Edith Hudson, Apr. 2, 1953; children: Gillian Helen, Alison Paula. BSc with 1st class honours, U. Manchester, Eng., 1948; MSc, U. Manchester, 1949, PhD, 1951. Chartered engr., Eng. Lectr. U. Keele, Eng., 1951-54; gen. mgr. Ferranti Instruments plc, Eng., 1966-71; mng. dir. Ferranti Electronics plc., Eng., 1971-87; sr. engr. Ferranti plc, Eng., 1954-60, chief engr., 1960-66, ops. dir., dep. mng. dir., 1987-92, non-exec. dir., 1992-95; ret., 1995; mem. Electronics Rsch. Coun., Eng., 1972-76; chmn. Ferranti Calif. Inc., 1978-90. Author: Theory and Practice of Semiconductors, 1960. Bd. dirs. N.W. Devel. Bd., Eng., 1970-76. Decorated comdr. Order of Brit. Empire; recipient J.J. Thomson medal Instn. Ele. Engrs., 1984; hon. fellow U. Manchester, 1988. Fellow Royal Acad. Engring., Inst. Physics. Avocations: music, golf, sailing, reading, gardening. Home: Ridge Hill, 6 Southern Crescent, Bramhall SK7 3AH, England

SHEPHERD, DONALD RAY, pathologist; b. Pampa, Tex., Sept. 7, 1935; s. Ray Browden and Lillie Lorene (Moore) S.; m. Elizabeth Day Poole, June 6, 1958; children: Lisa, Stephanie, Leslie, Don Poole. BS cum laude, Austin Coll., 1958; MD, U. Tex., Dallas, 1962. Diplomate Am. Bd. Pathology. Intern Univ. Hosp., Little Rock, 1962-63; gen. practice medicine Bay City, Tex., 1965-66; resident in pathology Hermann Hosp., Houston, 1966-68, Baylor U. Med. Ctr., Dallas, 1968-70; asst. pathologist Harris Hosp., Ft. Worth, 1970-71; chief pathology, dir. labs. Leggett meml. Hosp. (name now Cleve. Regional Med. Ctr.), Cleveland, Tex., 1982—, chief of staff, 1989-92; pathologist, pres. Donald R. Shepherd M.D., P.A., Conroe, 1973—; pres. Profl. Labs., Inc., Houston, 1973-82; dir., gen. ptnr. Profl. Pathology Labs., Ltd., 1997—; chief of staff Liberty-Dayton Hosp., Inc., Liberty, Tex., 1998—. Bd. dirs. Am. Cancer Soc. Capt. M.C., U.S. Army, 1963-65. Decorated Army Commendation medal; Am. Cancer Soc. grantee 1970-71. Fellow Coll. Am. Pathologists, Am. Soc. Clin. Pathologists; mem. Tex. Soc. Pathologists (del.), Tex. med. Assn., Montgomery County Med. Soc., Phi Chi. Republican. Presbyterian. Home: 175 Granite Point Rd Tow TX 78672 Office: PO Box 250 Tow TX 78672-0250

SHEPHERD, HENRY (HEPESH SHEPHERD), horticulture educator; b. Sept. 4, 1969. I.C.S.E., St. Joseph's Coll., 1984, I.S.C.E., 1986; BSc in Agr., Allahabad U., India, 1989; internship, Dr. Y.S.P. U., Solan, India, 1991; MSc in Agr., Allahabad U., 1991; PGD in Environ. Sci., Purvanchal U., India, 1992; PGRDM, IERT, Allahabad, India, 1998; PGD in Agr. R&D, Cinadco, Israel, 1999; DBA, NILEM, Chennai, India, 1999, DLL, 2000. Lectr. hort. sci. Non-Formal Ctr., India, 1991; lectr. soil and environ. sci. Allahabad Agrl. Inst., India, 1991-93; vis. prof. environ. sci. Birla Inst. Tech., Ranchi, India, 1998; asst. prof. dept. horticulture Allahabad Agrl. Inst., India, 1993—; field investigator Indian Market Rsch. Bur., New Delhi; field officer Steward's Trust; landscape engr. Royal Guest House GArden of King of Saudi Arabia, 1995-96; cons. Garden Planning and Designing; vis. lectr. in field. Recipient Man of Achievement award Internat. Pub. House, New Delhi, 1999, Young Scientist award Bioved Rsch. Soc., India, 2000. Mem. Uttar Pradesh Land Devel. Corp. (state level core com.). Avocations: gardening, social work, sports, environmental protection. Fax: 91-532-695639. E-mail: hipesh s@hotmail.com. Address: 3 Agricultural Inst, Allahabad 210007, Uttar Pradesh India

SHEPHERD, JOHN GRAHAM, marine scientist; b. Croydon, Surrey, Eng., Aug. 24, 1946; s. Ian Alastair and Eileen Alice Mary (Roe) S.; m. Deborah Mary Powney; children: Ian James, Thomas Edwin. MA, Pembroke Coll., Cambridge, Eng., 1967; PhD, Cavendish Lab., Cambridge, 1971. Rsch. officer CEGB, Eng., 1970-74; rsch. scientist Maff Fisheries Lab., Lowestoft, Eng., 1974-89, dep. dir., 1989-94; dir., prof. marine scis. Southampton Oceanography Ctr. NERC and U. Southampton, Eng., 1994-99; dir. Earth system modelling initiative Sch. of Ocean and Earth Sci./U. Southampton, Eng., 1999—. Contbr. numerous articles to profl. jours. Fellow Inst. Maths. and Applications, Soc. for Underwater Tech., Royal Geographical Soc., Royal Soc.; mem. Challenger Soc. (pres. 2000—). Avocations: rowing, walking, music. Office: Southampton U, European Way, Southampton Hants S014 3ZH, England

SHEPHERD, LEWIS A., JR., educational administrator, minister; b. Shreveport, La., Sept. 19, 1958; s. Lewis A. and Rosie L. Shepherd; m. Joyce Rose Shepherd, May 9, 1986. BA in Religion, Ouachita Bapt. U., Arkadelphia, Ark., 1980, MSEd in History, 1982; EdD in Administrn., U. Ark., Little Rock, 1997; DDiv (hon.), Ark. Bapt. Coll., 1996. Lic. funeral dir., Ark.; ordained to ministry, Bapt. Ch., 1976. Asst. dean students Ouachita U., Arkadelphia, 1980-87, TRIO dir., 1987-97, asst. to pres., 1997—; pastor New Haven Bapt. Ch., Camden, Ark., 1982—; bd. dirs. Summit Bank, Arkadelphia. Sec. Arkadelphia 2025 Commn.; bd. dirs. Ark. Arts Coun., Little Rock, 1991-95, Arkadelphia Housing Resource, 1989-94, Arkadelphia Cmty. Found., 1997—; mem. bioethics com. Bapt. Med. Ctr., Arkadelphia, 1997—. Mem. Ark. Assn. for Student Assistance Programs, S.W. Assn. for Student Assistance Programs, Ouachita Dist. Congress of Christian Edn. (pres. 1988—), Arkadelphia C. of C. (pres.-elect). Democrat. Avocations: reading, movies, fishing. Office: Ouachita Bapt Univ 410 Ouachita St PO Box 3779 Arkadelphia AR 71998-3779

SHEPHERD, SCORESBY ARTHUR, marine biologist, researcher; b. Port Lincoln, Australia, Jan. 22, 1935; s. Geoffrey Lincoln and Olga Adele (Woodman) S.; m. Ruth Ellen Rudman, June 14, 1957 (div. Apr. 1970); children: Louise Janette, Lincoln Scoresby, Christopher John; m. Anna Martha Steingraber, July 16, 1976. LLB, U. Adelaide, 1957; BA, Classics U., Adelaide, Australia, 1958; M of Environ. Sci., U. Adelaide, 1979; PhD, Deakin U., Victoria, Australia, 1988. Judge's assoc. South Australian Govt., Adelaide, 1957-59; pvt. law practice Adelaide, 1960-62, 64-68; lectr. U. South Australia, Adelaide, 1962-63; biologist State Dept. Fisheries, Adelaide, 1968-92, South Australian Rsch. Devel. Inst., Adelaide, 1992—; vis. prof. Sultan Qaboos U., Muscat, Oman, 1991; hon. assoc. South Australian Mus., Adelaide, 1976—. Editor: (books) Marine Invertebrates of Southern Australia, Vols. 1, 1982, Vol. 2, 1989, Vol. 3, 1997, Biology of Seagrasses, 1989, Abalone of the World, 1992; contbr. papers to profl. jours. Fellow Royal Soc. South Australia (pres. 1970-71, treas.); mem. Australian Marine Scis. Assn. (Jubilee award for excellence in marine sci. 1997), New Zealand Marine Scis. Assn. Avocations: canoeing, rock climbing, cycling, bush walking, swimming, diving. Home: 53 Esplanade Henley S, 5022 South Australia Australia Office: South Aust Rsch Devel Inst, PO Box 120 Henley Beach, 5022 South Australia Australia

SHEPHERDSON, DAVID, school caretaker, tutor; b. Ilkley, Eng., June 14, 1955; s. Fred and Lucie (Oliver) S. Shop asst. Maypole Shops Ltd., Ilkley, 1971; gardener Stephen M. Smiths, Otley, 1971-72; shop asst. C.R. Tempests, Otley, 1972-75; asst. mgr. Liptons' Shops Ltd., Ilkley, 1975-76; mgr. Otley Motors, 1976-77; driver Ross Bros., Ilkley, 1977-82; caretaker Moorfield Sch., Ilkley, 1983—; computer tutor, programmer Moorfield Sch., Ilkley, 1984; programmer Database Publs., Cheshire, 1991; columnist for U.K. Citizen's Band Mag., 1984-98, columnist U.K. Radio Active CB mag., 1998—. Mem. Dragonrider QSL Club (founder, pres. 1982—), Brit. Mensa, Stores & Membership Sec. Ilkley Gardeners' Assn. (v.chmn. 1999—). Avocations: computing, gardening, QSL card collecting, reading, writing. Home: Brackley 46 Valley Dr, Ben Rhydding, Ilkley LS29 8NN, England

SHEPHERDSON, JOHN CEDRIC, mathematics educator; b. Huddersfield, Yorkshire, Eng., June 7, 1926; s. Arnold and Elsie (Aspinall) S.; m. Margaret Smith, July 5, 1957; children: David, Jane, Judith. BA, U. Cambridge, Eng., 1946, MA, 1951, ScD, 1981. Asst. experimental officer Nat. Phys. Lab., London, Eng., 1946; asst. lectr. U. Bristol, Eng., 1946-49, lectr., 1949-55, reader, 1955-63, prof. pure math., 1964-77, H.O. Wills prof. math., 1977-91. Contbr. articles to profl. jours.; mem. editorial bd. Zeitschrift für Math. Logik, 1955-75, Jour. Computer and Systems Scis., 1966-91, Archiv für Math Logik, 1972-87. Fellow Inst. Math. and Its Applications; mem. London Math. Soc. (mem. editorial bd., 1970-77), Am. Math. Soc., Assn. for Symbolic Logic, Math. Assn. Mem. Liberal Democratic Party. Clubs: Bristol Corinthian Yacht (Somerset), Fell and Rock Climbing. Avocations: skiing, climbing, walking, cycling, skin diving. Home: Oakhurst North Rd, Leigh Woods, Bristol, Avon BS8 3PN, England Office: Bristol U, Sch Math, Bristol BS8 1TW, England

SHEPPARD, ANNE DEBORAH RAPHAEL, educator; b. Glasgow, Scotland, Nov. 10, 1951; d. David and Sylvia (Daiches) Raphael; m. Anthony Raphael Reeves Sheppard, Aug. 15, 1978; children: Alan, Sarah. BA, Oxford U., England, 1973, DPhil, 1977. Lectr. Jesus & Pembroke Colls., Oxford, England, 1976-78, U. Durham, England, 1978-87; tutor The Open U., London, 1987-89; lectr. Royal Holloway U. London, 1989-91, sr. lectr., 1991—. Author: Studies on the 5th and 6th Essays of Proclus' Commentary on the Republic, 1980, Aesthetics, 1987; contbr. articles to profl. jours., chpts. to books. Derby scholar Craven Com., Oxford U., 1973; rsch. fellow St. Hilda's Coll., Oxford, 1975-76. Mem. Soc. Promotion Hellenic Studies, Joint Assn. Classical Tchrs.

SHEPPARD, AUDLEY WILLIAM, lawyer; b. Hastings, N.Z., Aug. 19, 1960; arrived in Eng., 1985; s. William Searle and Joyce Marion (Audley) S. LLB with honors, Victoria U. of Wellington, N.Z., 1984, B.Commerce, 1985; LLM, U. Cambridge, Eng., 1986. Barrister and solicitor of High Ct. of N.Z., 1985; solicitor Supreme Ct. of Eng. and Wales, 1990. Atty. Bell, Gully, Buddle, Weir, Wellington, 1984-85; atty. Clifford Chance, London, 1986—, ptnr., 1995—; co-rapporteur Internat. Commn. Arbitration. Fellow Chartered Inst. Arbitrators; mem. Internat. Law Assn. (mem. com.). Avocations: theatre, sport, travel. Office: Clifford Chance, 200 Aldersgate St, London EC1A 4JJ, England

SHEPPARD, DAVID FLEETWOOD, patent lawyer; b. Dorking Surrey, Eng., May 13, 1937; arrived in South Africa, 1969; s. Edmund Fleetwood and Marie Theresa (Garstone) S.; m. Joan Boorman Chasmar, June 4, 1960; children: Claire, Paul, Helen. BSc in Chemistry with honors, King's Coll., London, 1958, Assoc., 1958; atty.'s admission diploma, UNISA, South Africa, 1975; Diploma Theology, Theol. Edn. by Extension Coll., Johannesburg, South Africa, 1988. Chartered patent agt., patent atty., South Africa.

Trainee patent agt. Elkington & Fife, London, 1958-65; patent agt. John Wyeth & Brother, Maidenhead, Eng., 1965-69; candidate atty. Adams & Adams, Pretoria, South Africa, 1969-76, ptnr., 1976—. Contbr. articles to profl. publs. Chancellor Anglican Diocese and Orgn., Pretoria, 1986-92, trustee, 1984—; trustee St. Alban's Coll., Pretoria, 1984—; mem. governing body Clapham H.S., Pretoria, 1986-95. Fellow Chartered Inst. Patent Attys., South African Inst. Patent Attys. (mem. com. 1980—, patent attys. examiner 1988—), Royal Inst. Chemistry; mem. Wingate Park Golf Club. Avocation: golf. Office: Adams & Adams, PO Box 1014, Pretoria 0001, South Africa

SHEPPARD, WALTER LEE, JR., chemical engineer, consultant; b. Phila., July 23, 1911; s. Walter Lee and Martha Houston (Evans) S.; m. Dorothy Virginia Cosby Vanderslice, Oct. 17, 1942 (div. Mar. 1947); m. Boudinot Atterbury Oberge Kendall, Mar. 24, 1953 (dec. Feb. 1996); stepchildren: Charles H. Kendall Jr., John Atterbury Kendall. BChem, Cornell U., 1932; MS, U. Pa., 1933. Registered profl. engr., Del., Calif.; diplomate Am. Acad. Environ. Engrs.; ordained deacon Liberal Cath. Ch., 1954, priest, 1955, pastor, 1970. Control chemist various cos., 1933-35; advt. writer N.W. Ayer & Son, 1937-37; asst. to editor The Houghton Line (E.F. Houghton Co.), 1937-38; salesman Atlas Mineral Products, 1938-48; plant mgr., cons. engr. Tanks & Linings, Ltd., Droitwich, Eng., 1948-49; sales engr., dist. mgr. ElectroChem. Engring. & Mfg., and successor cos., 1949-68; asst. pastor St. Paul's Liberal Cath. Ch. Phila., 1965; nat. accounts mgr., field sales mgr. Corrosion Engring. divsn. Pennwalt Corp., Phila., 1968-76; pres. C.C.R.M., Inc.; cons. on chemically resistant masonry, 1976—, profl. genealogist, 1936—. Author: Ancestry and Descendants of Thomas Stickney Evans and Sarah Ann Fifield, His Wife, 1940, Chemically Resistant Masonry, 1977, 2d edit., 1982, Ancestry of Edward Carleton and Ellen Newton, His Wife, 1978, microfilm, 1982; author, editor: Corrision and Chemical Resistant Masonry Materials Handbook, 1986; editor: Passengers and Ships Prior to 1684, 1965; successor editor: Ancestral Roots of 60 New England Colonists, 3d to 7th edits., 1992, Magna Charta Sureties 1215, 2d to 4th edits., 1991; contbg. editor Am. Genealogist, 1941-70, Nat. Geneal. Quar., 1961-98; mem. publs. com. Pa. Geneal. Mag., 1960-76; contbr. articles on corrosion resistant masonry constrn. to profl. jours. Dir. displaced persons camps, Salzburg, Austria, UNRRA, also d.p. specialist, staff Chief of Mission, Vienna, Austria, 1945-46; founding trustee, v.p. Bd. Cert. Genealogists, 1965-82, pres., 1969-78, chmn., 1978-79; asst. to rector, then rector Ch. of St. Paul. Maj. U.S. Army, 1941-45, UNRRA, 1945-46; lt. col., Res., ret., 1960. Named Hon. Mem. Class of 1928, U.S. Naval Acad., 1976. Fellow Am. Soc. Genealogists (sec. 1958-61, 66-67, v.p. 1967-70, pres. 1970-73), Nat. Geneal. Soc., Pa. Geneal. Soc.; mem. ASTM (membership sec. 1975-83, C-3 com.), NSPE, VFW, Am. Acad. Environ. Engrs., Welcome Soc. (pres. 1969-76), Illegitimate Sons and Daus. of Kings and Queens of Britain (founder, sec. 1950-68, pres. 1968-88), Flagon and Trencher Soc. (co-founder, pres. 1967-73), Nat. Assn. Corrosion Engrs. (cert. competence in corrosion engring., chmn. Phila. sect. 1962), New Eng. Hist. Geneal. Soc. (com. on Heraldry 1991—), Nat. Geneal. Soc. Quar. (contbg. editor), Geneal. Soc. Pa., Soc. Genealogists (London), Yorkshire Archaeol. Soc., Savoy Co., Gilbert and Sullivan Soc. (founder, pres. Phila. br. 1957-63), Sovereign Orders St. John of Jerusalem, Mil. Order Fgn. Wars, Mayflower Descs., Order of Three Crusades, Order of the Crown of Charlemagne in Am. (3d v.p. 1989-95), Ret. Officers Assn., Phi Kappa Psi (nat. v.p. 1964-68, pers. 1968-70), Alpha Chi Sigma. Home and Office: 923 Old Manoa Rd Havertown PA 19083-2610

SHEPTULIN, ARKADY ALEXANDROVICH, medical educator; b. Ul'yanovsk, USSR, Aug. 21, 1953; s. Alexander Petrovich and Nina Nikolayevna (Krasnova) S.; m. Larisa Luvsanovna Volod'kina, Jan. 9, 1988; children: Vladimir, Dmitry. Doctorate Degree, First Moscow Med. Inst., 1976, MD, 1982, PhD, 1990. Resident dept. internal disease propedeutics Moscow Med. Acad., 1976-78, doctor clinic internal disease propedeutics, 1978-84, asst. prof. dept. internal disease propedeutics, 1984-91, sr. lectr. dept. internal disease propedeutics, 1991-95, prof. dept. internal disease propedeutics, 1995—. Author: Peptic Ulcer, 1987, Ulcers of Stomach, 1990, Basics of Medical Care, 1991; editor: Manual on Gastroenterology, 1995. Mem. N.Y. Acad. Scis. Home: Shipilovsky proyezd 49/1-64, 115551 Moscow Russia Office: Pogodinskaya St 5, 119881 Moscow Russia

SHER, EMMANUIL MOISEYEVICH, physicist, researcher, consultant; b. Port Khorly, Ukraine, Mar. 29, 1929; s. Moisey Solomonovich and Lisa Abramovna (Kholdin); m. Elena Stepanovna Sher, July 5, 1953; 1 child, Michael. BS in Physics, Moscow State U., 1951; physicist, St. Petersburg State U., Russia, 1952; PhD in Phys. Electronics, Russian Acad. of Scis., St. Petersburg, 1967; DSc in Physics of Semiconductors and Dielectrics, A.F. Ioffe Phys. Tech. Inst., St. Petersburg, 1983. Electron tube engr. Saratov, Russia, 1952-59; leader thermoelec. devices group Inst. of Semiconductors, St. Petersburg, 1959-62; rsch. scientist in emission electronics A.F. Ioffe Phys. Tech. Inst., St. Petersburg, 1962-71, leader rsch. group in physics of thermoelectricity, 1971-86, leader rsch. group in physics of high-temp. superconductors, 1987-94, leader rsch. group. in physics and tech. of thin solid films, 1994—; cons. Phys-Tech. Inst., Sukhumi, Georgia, 1978-80, Leningrad Optical Union, St. Petersburg, 1979-82, Moscow dist. Indsl. Union, 1982-84. Contbr. articles to profl. jours.; editor 2 books; patentee in field. Recipient Bronze medal, 1963, Russian Acad. Scis., Silver medal, 1983; named Honorary Academician Internat. Acad. Refrigeration. Mem. N.Y. Acad. Scis., Internat. Thermoelectric Soc. Judaist. Avocation: the great Russian poets Pushkin and Mandelshtam. E-mail: em@sher.ioffe.rssi.ru. Home: 20 Orbely Str Apt 73, 194223 Saint Petersburg Russia Office: AF Ioffe Phys Tech Inst, 26 Polytechnicheskaya str, 194021 Saint Petersburg Russia

SHER, PHYLLIS KAMMERMAN, pediatric neurology educator; b. N.Y.C., Aug. 13, 1944; d. Seymour K. and Shirley (Parmit) Kammerman; m. Kenneth Swaiman, Oct. 6, 1985. BA, Brandeis U., 1966; MD, U. Miami, 1970. Diplomate Am. Bd. Psychiatry and Neurology. Pediatric intern Montefiore Hosp., Bronx, N.Y., 1970-71; resident in neurology U. Miami (Fla.) Med. Sch., 1971-73, fellow in pediatric neurology, 1973-75, asst. prof. neurology, 1975-80; rsch. assoc. NIH, Bethesda, Md., 1980-83; asst. prof. neurology and pediatrics U. Minn. Med. Sch., Mpls., 1983-86, assoc. prof., 1986-96; mem. Hennepin Faculty Assocs., 1996-99; dir. Ripple program United Cerebral Palsy Found., Miami, 1972-75; chmn. med. svcs. com. 5-yr. action plan State of Fla., 1975; cons. Minn. Epilepsy Program for Children, 1983-85; vis. prof. Japanese Soc. Child Neurology, 1985, Chinese Child Neurology Ctr., 1989, Hong Kong Soc. Child Neurology & Devel. Pediat., 1995. Mem. editl. bd. Pediatric Neurology, 1991—, Brain and Devel., 1994-99; contbr. articles and abstracts to med. jours., chpts. to books. Comdr. USPHS, 1980-83. Fellow United Cerebral Palsy Found., 1972-73; rsch. grantee Gillette Children's Hosp., U. Minn. Grad. Sch., Viking Children's Fund, Minn. Med. Found. Fellow Am. Neurol. Assn., Am. Acad. Neurology; mem. Child Neurology Soc. (exec. com., councillor 1993-95), Upper Midwest Child Neurology Soc., So. Clin. Neurology Soc. Office: Pediatric Neurology 1821 University Ave W Ste N188 Saint Paul MN 55104-2870

SHERALI, HANIF DOSTMAHOMED, engineering educator; b. Bombay, Oct. 15, 1952; came to U.S., 1975; s. Dostmahomed and Zohra S.; m. Semeen Hanif Sherali, Dec. 28, 1953; 1 child, Azeem Hanif. BSEE, Bombay U., 1975; MS in Ops. Rsch., Ga. Inst. Tech., 1977, PhD in Ops. Rsch., 1979. Instr. dept. indsl. mgmt. Ga. Inst. Tech., 1977-79; asst. prof. dept. indsl. and sys. engring. Va. Poly. Inst. and State U., Blacksburg, 1979-83, assoc. prof., 1983-86, prof., 1986-92, Charles O. Gordon endowed prof., 1992-99, W. Thomas Rice prof., 1999—; presenter in field. Author: Disjunctive Programming, 1982, Linear Programming and Network Flows, 1990, Nonlinear Programming: Theory and Algorithms, 1993, A Reformulation-Linearization Technique for Solving Discrete and and Continuous Nonconvex Problems, 1999; contbr. numerous articles to sci. publs.; assoc. editor, mem. editl. bd. Ops. Rsch., Ops. Rsch. Letters, Informatica, others; reviewer tech. jours. Rsch. grantee FBI, NSF, Naval Surface Warfare Ctr., Assn. Am. R.R., numerous others. Fellow Inst. Indsl. Engrs.; mem. NAE, Inst. Ops. Rsch. and Mgmt. Scis., Math. Programming Soc. Islam. Avocations: philosophy, tennis. E-mail: hanifs@vt.edu. Office: Va Poly Inst & State U Dept Indsl Sys Engring 0118 Blacksburg VA 24061

SHERARD, RODNEY MERLE, retired military officer, educator; b. Grand Island, Nebr., Dec. 21, 1942; s. Howard Laverne and Sylvia Gertrude (Hurlbert) S.; m. Kathleen Ann Meis, Oct. 6, 1962 (div. Apr. 1979); children: Jeanette R., Gilbert J., Gregory H., Joanne E., Todd A.; m. Betty Jane Fultz, Nov. 16, 1985. AS, Vincinnes U., 1978; B in Gen. Studies, Ind. U., Indpls., 1993; grad., Armor Officer Candidate Sch., 1967, Command and Gen. Staff Coll., 1982. Commd. 2d lt. U.S. Army, 1967, advanced through grades to maj., 1979, ret., 1990; JROTC instr. Manual H.S., Indpls., 1990—. Author: The Descendants of William Henry Hurlbert and Amy Adeline Austin, 1995, (booklet) The Descendents of Merle Adam Sherard and Ida Eleanor Waddington, 1992, revised, 1997, (newsletter) Hurlbert Family Reunion Annual, 1994—. Decorated Bronze Star. Mem. VFW, Am. Legion, Nat. Guard Assn. Ind., 38th Infantry Divsn. Assn., Nebr. State Hist. Soc. Mem. Ch. of Christ. Avocations: travel, computers. E-mail: Rod-Sherard@aol.com.

SHERBAN, SEMEN DMITRIEVICH, oncology researcher, pathologist; b. Reni, Odessa, Ukraine, Aug. 18, 1939; s. Dumitru Nikitovich and Maria Petrovna (Nedelcu) S.; m. Tamara Petrovna Pererva, 1967 (div. 1975); m. Zhanna Grigorevna Litvinchuk, 1985. Degree, Med. Inst., Kishinev, Moldova, 1962; postgrad., L.V. Gromashevsky Inst., Kiev, Ukraine, 1964-67; DSc, A.a. Bogomolets Med. U., Kiev, 1969. Med. diplomate. Asst. lectr. Med. U., Kishinev, 1967-70; jr. rschr. R.E. Kavetsky Inst. Exptl. Pathology Oncology NAS, Kiev, 1971-85, rschr., 1985—. Contbr. articles to profl. jours. Mem. N.Y. Acad. Scis. Avocations: art, literature, music. Home: Apt 156, 24 Prospekt Glushkova, 03187 Kiev Ukraine Office: RE Kavetsky Inst NAS, 45 Vasylkovska St, 03022 Kiev Ukraine

SHERBET, GAJANAN VENKATRAMANAYA, pathologist, cell biologist, research scientist; b. Bantval, Karnataka, India, Mar. 25, 1935; arrived in Eng., 1964; s. Venkatramanaya and Chandravati (Kalambi) S.; m. Lakshmi Madurai Subramanyam, Sept. 11, 1974. BSc, Poona (India) U., 1956, MSc, 1958, PhD, 1962; MSc, London U., 1967, DSc, 1978. Rsch. scientist Chester Beatty Rsch. Inst., London, 1964-69; rsch. fellow Harvard U., Cambridge, Mass., 1966; rsch. scientist Med. Sch. Univ. Coll. Hosp. U. London, 1970-77; rsch. scientist cancer rsch. unit U. Newcastle upon Tyne (Eng.) Med. Sch., 1977-81, acting dir., 1988-89, dep. dir., 1981-2000, reader in exptl. oncology, 1988-2000; prof. Inst. Molecular Medicine, Huntington Beach, Calif., 1999—; pres. Newcastle Sai Ctr., 1994-97; mem. adminstrv. and sci. coms. Author: The Biophysical and Biochemical Characterization of the Cell Surface, 1977, The Biology of Tumor Malignancy, 1982, The Metastatic Spread of Cancer, 1987, The Genetics of Cancer: Genes Associated with Cancer Invasion, Metastasis and Cell Proliferation, 1997, Calcium Signalling in Cancer, 2000; editor: Neoplasia and Cell Differentiation, 1974, Regulation of Growth in Neoplasia, 1981, Artificial Neural Networks in Cancer Diagnosis, Prognosis and Patient Management, 2000; co-editor: Monographs in Experimental Biology and Medicine, 1975-87; mem. editl. bd. Exptl. Cell Biology, 1977-80, editor, 1981-89; guest editor: Retinoids, their physiological function and therapeutic potential, 1997; mem. editl. bd. Oncology, 1973-77, Anticancer Rsch., Pathobiology, Anticancer Rsch., 1998—; sr. editor Pathobiology, 1990-98; contbr. articles to profl. jours. on growth factors and genes associated with cancer invasion, metastasis and cell cycle regulation, neurl networks in cancer biology and prognosis. Recipient Lord Dowding Fund award London U., 1969-73, Felix Wankel and Ernst Hutzenlaub prize, 1977; Beit Meml. and Williams fellow London U., 1969-73, Cancer Rsch. Campaign fellow U. Newcastle upon Tyne, 1985-2000. Fellow Inst. Biology, Royal Soc. Chemistry, Royal Coll. Pathologists; mem. Am. Assn. for Cancer Rsch., European Assn. for Cancer Rsch., Brit. Assn. for Cancer Rsch., Brit. Neuro-Oncology Group, Indian Assn. for Cancer Rsch. (life), N.Y. Acad. Scis. Avocations: Indian classical music, classical tabla (Delhi Gharana). Office: U Newcastle Upon Tyne, Cancer Rsch Unit Med Sch, Newcastle upon Tyne NE2 4HH, England

SHERBINSKI, LINDA ANNE, nurse anesthetist, nursing educator; b. Rochester, N.Y., Jan. 17, 1956; d. Edward Marion and Helen Marie (Kindzera) S. Student, Genesee Hosp. Sch. Nursing, Rochester, N.Y., 1977; BSN, Alfred U., 1978; grad. in anesthesia, Univ. Health Ctr. Pitts., 1987; MSN, Duqusne U., 1991. RN, Pa. Leader day team CCU The Genesee Hosp., 1978-84, staff nurse operating rm., 1984-85; staff nurse ICU Forbes Met. Hosp., Pitts., 1985-87; staff anesthetist Presbyn. Univ. Hosp., Pitts., 1987-92, preceptor anesthetist, 1991-92; instr. Univ. Health Ctr. Pitts. Sch. Anesthesia, 1987-90, U. Pitts. Grad. Anesthesia Program, 1990-92; staff anesthetist Meml. Med. Ctr., Springfield, Ill., 1992-94; anesthetist Rochester (N.Y.) Gen. Hosp., Highland Hosp., Genesee Hosp., N.Y., 1994-98, Emory U. Hosp., Atlanta, 1998—; item writer Acad. Item Writers AANA, Chgo., 1991—. Contbr. articles to profl. jours., chpt. to book. Med. vol. Pitts. Marathon, 1990, 91. Mem. Am. Assn. Nurse Anesthetists (cert. nurse anesthetist, program dir. internship grant 1990), Nat. League Nursing, Sigma Theta Tau (sec. Delta Sigma chpt. 1978-80, Rsch. scholar Epsilon Phi chpt. 1991). Roman Catholic. Home: 1404 Treelodge Pkwy Atlanta GA 30350-6013 Office: Emory U Hosp 1364 Clifton Rd NE Atlanta GA 30322-1061

SHERBY, KATHLEEN REILLY, lawyer; b. St. Louis, Apr. 5, 1947; d. John Victor and Florian Sylvia (Frederick) Reilly; m. James Wilson Sherby, May 17, 1975; children: Michael R.R., William J.R., David J.R. AB magna cum laude, St. Louis U., 1969, JD magna cum laude, 1976. Bar: Mo. 1976. Assoc. Bryan Cave, St. Louis, 1976-85; ptnr. Bryan Cave LLP, St. Louis, 1985—. Contbr. articles to profl. jours. Bd. dirs Jr. League, St. Louis, 1989-90, St. Louis Forum, 1992-99, pres., 1995-97; chmn. Bequest and Gift Coun. of St. Louis U., 1997-99; jr. warden Ch. of St. Michael and St. George, 1998-2000; bd. dirs. Bistate chpt. ARC, 2000—. Fellow Am. Coll. Trust and Estate Coun. (regent 1997—), Estate Planning Coun. of St. Louis (pres. 1986-87), Bar Assn. Met. St. Louis (chmn. probate sect. 1986-87), Mo. Bar Assn. (chmn. probate and trust com. 1996-98, chmn. probate law revision subcom. 1988-96). Episcopalian. Home: 47 Crestwood Dr Saint Louis MO 63105-3032 Office: Bryan Cave LLP 1 Metropolitan Sq Ste 3600 Saint Louis MO 63102-2733

SHERESKY, NORMAN M., lawyer; b. Detroit, June 22, 1928; s. Harry and Rose (Lieberman) S.; m. Elaine B. Lewis, Oct. 30, 1977; 1 child, from previous marriage, Brooke Hillary. A.B., Syracuse U., 1950; LL.B., Harvard U., 1953. Bar: N.Y. 1953. Assoc. Gold & Pollack, N.Y.C., 1954-60; sole practice, N.Y.C., 1960-72; ptnr. Sheresky & Kalman, N.Y.C., 1972-77; ptnr. Colton, Hartnick, Yamin & Sheresky, N.Y.C., 1977-93; ptnr. Baer, Marks & Upham, N.Y.C., 1993-95; ptnr. Sheresky, Aronson & Mayefsky, 1995—. adj. prof. matrimonial litigation N.Y. Law Sch., 1979-86; mem. judiciary com. N.Y.C. Bar Assn.; pres.-elect Am. Coll. Family Trial Lawyers. Mem. Internat. Acad. Matrimonial Lawyers (past treas., gov. N.Y. chpt.), Am. Acad. Matrimonial Lawyers (gov., past pres. N.Y. chpt., pres. elect.), N.Y. State Bar Assn., Assn. Trial Lawyers Am., Met. Trial Lawyers Assn., Internat. Acad. Matrimonial Lawyers (bd. govs. 1986—, com. to examine lawyer conduct in matrimonial actions 1992-95). Author: (with Marya Mannes) Uncoupling, 1972; On Trial, 1977; contbr. editor: Fairshare mag. Office: Sheresky Aronson & Mayefsky LLP 750 Lexington Ave New York NY 10022-1200

SHERIDAN, DIANE FRANCES, public policy facilitator; b. Wilmington, Del., Mar. 12, 1945; d. Robert Kooch and Eileen Elizabeth (Forrest) Bupp; m. Mark MacDonald Sheridan III, Dec. 7, 1968; 1 child, Elizabeth Anne. BA in English, U. Del., 1967. Tchr. English Newark (Del.) Sch. Dist., 1967-68, Lumberton (Tex.) Ind. Sch. Dist., 1969-71, Crown Point (Ind.) Sch. Dist., 1972-75; sr. assoc. The Keystone (Colo.) Ctr., 1986-98; environ. policy facilitator Taylor Lake Village, Tex., 1986—; chair Keystone Siting Process Local Rev. Com.; mem. pub. adv. panel Chem. Mfrs. Assn. Responsible Care, 1989-97. 1st v.p. LWV, Washington, 1992-94, sec. treas. voters edn. fund, sec. treas. Nat. LWV, 1994-96, bd. dirs. 1996-98; pres. LWV of Tex., 1987-91, chair edn. fund, 1987-91, bd. dirs., 1983-87; pres. LWV of the Bay Area, 1981-83; mem. adv. com. Ctr. for Global Studies of Houston Advanced Rsch. Ctr., The Woodlands, Tex., 1991-97, Ctr. for Conflict Analysis and Mgmt., bd. advisors Environ. Inst.; mem. U. Houston-Clear Lake Devel. Adv. Coun., 1989-95; mem. Bay Area Cmty. Awareness and Emergency Response Local Emergency Planning Com., 1988-92; active Tex. House-Senate Select Com. on Urban Affairs Regional Flooding Task Force, 1979-80, Congressman Mike Andrews Environ. Task Force, 1983-85, Gov.'s Task Force on Hazardous Waste Mgmt., 1984-85; dir. local PTAs, 1981-91; coord. Tex. Roundtable on Hazardous Waste, 1982-87; sec., v.p. Tex. Environ. Coalition, 1983-85; co-chair Tex. Risk Commn. Project, 1986-89; mem. Leadership Tex., Class of 1988; mem. cmty. adv. bd. U. Tex. Med. Br. Ctr. Nat. Inst. Environ. Health Studies, 1998—. Mem. LWV (nat. bd. dirs. 1992-98, trustee nat. edn. fund 1992-98), Soc. for Profls. in Dispute Resolution, Internat. Assn. for Pub. Participation, Mortar Board, East Harris County Mfrs. Assn. (risk mgmt. comm. com. 1994-99), Pi Sigma Alpha, Kappa Delta Pi.

SHERIDAN, JIM, director, screenwriter; b. Dublin, Ireland, 1949. Student, Univ. Coll., Dublin, NYU. Dir., writer Lyric Theatre, Belfast, No. Ireland; artistic dir. Project Arts Theatre, 1976-80, N.Y. Irish Arts Ctr., 1982-87; founder Children's Theatre Co., Dublin, Ireland. Scripts include (plays) Mobile Homes, Spike in the First World War (Edinburgh Festival Fringe Best Play award 1983); (film) Into the West, 1993; screenwriter, dir.: My Left Foot, 1989 (Acad. award nomination best dir. 1989, Acad. award nomination best adapted screenplay 1989), The Field, 1990, In the Name of the Father, 1993 (Acad. award nomination best dir. 1993, Acad. award nomination best adapted screenplay 1993), Same Mother's Son, 1996, The Boxer, 1997; prodr., exec. prodr.: Agnes Browne, 1999, On the Edge, 2000, Bonstal Boy, 2000. E-mail: hellskit@aol.ie. Office: Hells Kitchen Ltd, 21 Mespil Rd, Dublin 4, Ireland also: CAA 9830 Wilshire Blvd Beverly Hills CA 90212-1804

SHERIDAN, MARK WILLIAM, mechanical engineer, strategic planner; b. Bryn Mawr, Pa., July 9, 1959; s. Phillip Frederick and Shirley (Fraser) S. BSME, Lafayette Coll., 1981; MBA, Cornell U., 1987, M. Engring. (Mech.), 1988. Registered profl. engr., Ohio. Project engr. Internat. Paper Co., Mobile, Ala., 1981-83, sr. process engr., 1983-85; assoc. Booz-Allen & Hamilton, Cleve., 1988-90; coord. long range planning appliance motor divsn. Emerson Electric Co., St. Louis, 1990-93, resident engr. Paragould Plant, 1993-96; dir. mfg. Thermodisc, Mansfield, Ohio, 1996—; summer intern Saturn Corp., Troy, Mich., 1986, 87. Patentee in field. Bd. dirs. ABC Condominium Assn., St. Louis, 1992-94; chmn. JGSM Student Faculty Com./Quality of Life Com., Ithaca, N.Y., 1985-87; pres. Mobile Soap Box Derby, 1983-85; v.p. ways and means, bd. dirs. Mobile Jaycees, 1984-85; active YMCA; treas. First Presbyn. Ch. of Mansfield, 1998—. Lester B. Knight scholar Cornell U., 1986-88, J. Stanford Smith scholar Cornell U., 1985-87; named Outstanding Young Man of Am., 1984, 85, 87. Mem. ASME, Inst. Indsl. Engrs., The Planning Forum, Soc. Indsl. Archaeology, World Future Soc., St. Louis Jaycees (bd. dirs. 1992-94), Am. Mensa. Republican. Avocations: biking, golf, reading, tennis, computing. Home: 2403 Ranchwood Dr Mansfield OH 44903-9044 Office: Thermodisc 1320 S Main St Mansfield OH 44907-5500

SHERIDAN, RICHARD BERT, economics educator; b. Emporia, Kans., Feb. 10, 1918; s. Bert and Olive Nancy (Davis) S.; m. Audrey Marion Porter, Oct. 18, 1952; children—Richard David, Margaret Anne. B.S., Emporia Kans. State U., 1940; M.S., U. Kans., 1947; Ph.D., London Sch. Econs. and Polit. Sci., 1951. Instr. to assoc. prof. U. Kans., Lawrence, 1947-62, prof. econs., 1963-88; emeritus prof. econs., 1988—; external examiner U. W.I., Kingston, Jamaica, 1964-74; vis. prof. Coll. V.I., St. Thomas, 1971, U. West Indies, St. Augustine, Trinidad, 1987. Author: Economic History of South Central Kansas, 1956, Chapters in Caribbean History, 1970, Sugar and Slavery, 1974, Doctors and Slaves, 1985; cons. editor: Jour. Caribbean History, 1971—; contbr. articles to profl. jours. Served to lt. USNR, 1942-46. Recipient Article award N.C. Bicentennial Contest, 1976, article award Kans. State Hist. Soc., 1989; honored with a festschrift, 1996; Fulbright scholar U. W.I., 1962-63; grantee NIH, Nat. Libr. Medicine, 1973. Fellow Royal Hist. Soc.; mem. Soc. for Human Econs., Assn. Caribbean History. Democrat. Congregationalist. Home: 1745 Louisiana St Lawrence KS 66044-4055 Office: U Kans Dept Of Econ Lawrence KS 66045-0001

SHERIDAN, SUSAN MARGARET, educator; b. Sydney, NSW, Australia, Nov. 3, 1944; d. Arthur Palgrave and Catherine Mary (Green) Young; m. John Winton Higgins, Dec. 18, 1965 (div. 1978). BA with honors, U. Sydney, Australia, 1967; PhD, U. Adelaide, Australia, 1980. Diploma in TESOL, Royal Soc. Arts, U.K., 1970. Tutor U. Sydney, NSW, 1967-69, U. Adelaide, 1973-77; lectr. South Australia Coll. Advanced Edn., Adelaide, 1978-84, Deakin U., Geelong, Australia, 1985-86; lectr. Flinders U., Adelaide, 1987—, prof., 1999—; gov. Humanities Rsch. Ctr., A.N.U., Canberra, Australia, 1986. Editor: (books) Grafts: Feminist Cultural Criticism, 1988, (with others) Debutante Nation, 1993; author: (books) Christina Stead, 1988 (Walter MacCrae Russell award 1989), Along the Faultlines: Australian Women's Writing, 1995. Office: Flinders U, GPO Box 2100, 5001 Adelaide Australia

SHERIF, MOHAMED SAFWAT, Egyptian government official; b. Garbia, Egypt, Dec. 19, 1933; married; 3 children. BSc in Mil. Scis. Chmn. state info. svc. Govt. of Egypt, Cairo, 1978-83, min. info., 1983—. Author studies and rsch. on comm. and mass media. Decorated various Egyptian and fgn. orders. Office: Ministry of Info Radio & TV, Kournish al-Nile Steet Mespiro, Cairo Egypt*

SHERIF, S. A., mechanical engineering educator; b. Alexandria, Egypt, June 25, 1952; came to U.S., 1978; s. Ahmed and Ietedal H. (Monib) S.; m. Azza A. Shamseldin, Feb. 6, 1977; children: Ahmed S., Mohammad S. BSME (hon.), Alexandria U., 1975, MSME, 1978; PhD in Mech. Engring., Iowa State U., 1985. Tchg. asst. mech. engring. Alexandria U., 1975-78; tchg. asst. mech. and environtl. engring. U. Calif., Santa Barbara, 1978-79; rsch. asst. mech. engring. Iowa State U., Ames, 1979-84; asst. prof. No. Ill. U., Dekalb, 1984-87, mem. grad. faculty, 1985-87; mem. grad. faculty U. Miami, Coral Gables, Fla., 1987-91, asst. prof. civil, archtl. and mech. engring., 1987-91; assoc. prof. mech. engring. U. Fla., Gainesville, 1991—, mem. doctoral rsch. faculty, 1992—; cons. Solar Reactor Techs., Inc., Miami, 1988-91, Dade Power Corp., Miami, 1988-91, Ind. Energy Sys., Miami, 1988-91, Carey Dwyer Eckhart Mason Spring & Beckham, P.A. Law Offices, Miami, 1988-89, Michael G. Widoff, P.A., Attys. at Law, Ft. Lauderdale, Fla., 1989-93, Law Offices Pomeroy and Betts, Ft. Lauderdale, 1991-92, Ctr. for Indoor Air Rsch., 1994—; cons. Fla. Power and Light Co., 1996—; cons. U. Roorkee, 1994-95, 98—; adj. faculty cons. Kennedy Western U., Thousand Oaks, Calif., 1994-97; resident assoc. Argonne (Ill.) Nat. Lab., Tech. Transfer Ctr., summer 1992; faculty fellow NASA Kennedy Space Ctr., Cape Canaveral, Fla., summer 1993; rsch. assoc. summer faculty rsch. program USAF Office Sci. Rsch., Arnold Engring. Devel. Ctr., Arnold AFB, Tenn., summer 1994—; faculty fellow NASA Marshall Space Flight Ctr., Huntsville, Ala., 1996, 97; reviewer over 25 internat. jours., over 100 conf. procs. and several pub. cos. and rsch. svc. orgns. Co-editor: Industrial and Agricultural Applications of Fluid Mechanics, 1989, The Heuristics of Thermal Anemometry, 1990, Heat and Mass Transfer in Frost and Ice, Packed Beds, and Environmental Discharges, 1990, Industrial Applications of Fluid Mechanics, 1990, rev. edit., 1991, Mixed Convection and Environmental Flows, 1990, Measurement and Modeling of Environmental Flows, 1992, Industrial and Environment Applications of Fluid Mechanics, 1992, rev. edit., 1998, Thermal Anemometry-1993, 1993, Developments in Electrorheological Flows and Measurement Uncertainty-1994, 1994, Heat, Mass and Momentum Transfer in Environmental Flows, 1995, Thermal Anemometry, 1996, Fluid Measurement Uncertainty Applications, 1996, Devices for Flow Measurement and Analysis, 1997, Heat and Mass Transfer in Environmental Flows, 1998; contbr. numerous articles to profl. jours. NASA ambassador, 1996—, lab. host student sci. tng. program Ctr. for Precollegiate Edn. and Tng., 1997—; mem. environ. awareness adv. com., Dade County Pub. Schs., 1989-91, lab. dir. cmty. lab. rsch. program, 1989-91, also faculty liaison design svcs. dept.; active Com. for Nat. Inst. for Environ., 1992—; mem. senate U. Fla., 1994-95, mem. OUTREACH Spkrs. program, 1996—. Mem. ASME (mem. coord. group fluid measurements, fluids engring. divsn. 1987—, vice chmn. 1990-92, chmn. 1992-94, fluids engring. divsn. adv. bd. 1994—, honors and awards com. 1995—, mem. fluid mechs. tech. com. 1990—, fluid mech. com. 1987-90, environ. heat transfer com. heat transfer divsn. 1987—, mem. fluid applications and systems tech. com. 1990—, systems analysis tech. com. advanced energy sys. divsn. 1989—, newsletter editor advanced energy sys. divsn. 1995—, fundamentals and theory tech. com. solar energy divsn. 1990—, chmn. CGFM nominating com. 1992-94, mem. 1994—, chmn. profl. devel. com. Rock River Valley sect. 1987, tech. activities operating com. Gator sect. 1994-96, MFFCC subcom. 1 on uncertainties in flow measurements 1995—), ASHRAE (mem. heat transfer fluid flow com. 1988-92, 93-97, corr. mem. 1992-93, 97—, mem.

thermodynamics and psychrometrics com. 1988-92, 96—, corr. mem. 1992-96, vice chmn. 1990-92, mem. liquid to refrigerant heat exchangers com. 1989-93, 96-97, sec. 1990-92, corr. mem. 1993-96, 97—, chmn. stds. project com. on measurement of moist air properties 1989-95), AIAA (sr.), AIChE, Internat. Assn. Hydrogen Energy, Internat. Solar Energy Soc., Am. Solar Energy Soc., Internat. Energy Soc. (mem. sci. coun.), European Assn. Laser Anemometry (ASME/FED rep., mem. steering com.), Internat. Inst. Refrigeration (U.S. nat. com.), ABI (hon. mem. rsch. bd. adv. 1994—), Sigma Xi. Moslem. Avocations: reading, soccer, basketball, history, astronomy. Home: 3544 NW 88th Ter Gainesville FL 32606-3802 Office: U Fla Dept Mech Engrng 228 MEB PO Box 116300 Gainesville FL 32611-6300

SHERIFO, MAHMUD AHMED, Eritrean government official; b. Keren, Apr. 4, 1947; divorced; 1 child. With Eritrean Liberation Front, 1966-70; founding mem. Eritrean People's Liberation Front, 1970, various positions, 1970-77, mem. ctrl. com. and polit. office, 1977, head dept. info., 1977-87, head dept. pub. adminstrn., 1987-92; sec. dept. external affairs Govt. of Eritrea, Asmara, 1992-93, min. fgn. affairs, 1993-94, v.p., 1994—. Office: Office of the Pres, PO Box 257, Asmara Eritrea*

SHERLAW-JOHNSON, ROBERT, music educator; b. Sunderland, Co. Durham, Gt. Britain, May 21, 1932; s. Robert and Helen (Smith) Johnson; m. Rachael Maria Clarke; children: Rebecca, Christopher, Austin, Griselda, Edward. BA with honors, Durham U., 1953, BMus, 1959; DMus, Leeds U., 1971, Oxford U., 1990. Asst. lectr. in music Leeds U., 1961-63; dir. of music Bradford Girls' Grammar Sch., 1963-65; lectr. in music York U., 1965-70; univ. lectr. in music and fellow Worcester Coll., Oxford, 1970-99, reader in music, 1998, fellow emeritus, 1999—. Author: Messiaen, 1971, 89; publisher compositions including operas, piano sonatas, piano concerto, clarinet concerto, chamber works and choral works, and a symphony. Fellow Royal Acad. Music (hon.); mem. Brit. Acad. Composers and Songwriters (vice-chmn. Composers Guild of Great Britain 1979-81). Roman Catholic. Avocations: bell-ringing, wine-making, croquet. Home: Malton Croft Woodlands Rise, Stonesfield, Oxfordshire OX8 8PL, England Office: Worcester Coll Fac Music, St Aldates, Oxford 0X1 1DB, England

SHERLIN, JERRY MICHAEL, retired hydro meteorological technician; b. Chattanooga, Oct. 8, 1938; s. Chester Wallace and Eva Pearl (Scruggs) S; m. Susan Loxie Doenhoefer, July 22, 1993. BGS, U. Nebr., 1971; MA, Ball State U., 1976. Advanced through grades to master sgt. USAF, 1959, ret., 1981; rsch. asst. Sacramento Peak Solar Observatory, Sunspot, N.Mex., 1981-82; meteorological technician Nat. Weather Svc., Sioux City, Iowa, 1982-89; coop. program mgr. Nat. Weather Svc., Denver, 1989-94, hydrometeorological technician, 1994-99; ret. Co-editor: Observe-and Understand the Sun, 1976; contbr. articles to profl. jours. Vol. Denver Mus. of Natural History, Denver, 1990—; chmn. Astronomical League 50th Ann. Nat. Conv., Copper Mountain, Colo., 1997. Recipient G. R. Wright Svc. award Astronomical League, 1992; decorated Air Force Commendation medal with 2 oak leaf clusters, 1974, 79, 81. Fellow Royal Astron. Soc.; mem. AAAS, Am. Astron. Soc., Am. Assn. Variable Star Observers, Astron. Soc. of the Pacific, Astronomical League and Internat. Dark-Sky Assn. Home: 17002 E Prentice Dr Aurora CO 80015-2412

SHERLOCK, ITALO RODRIGUES DE ARAÚJO, parasitologist, researcher; b. Sobral, Ceará, Brazil, Apr. 5, 1936; s. Raymond Araújo and Alda d'Albuquerque Rodrigues de Arújo S.; m. Juracy Machado, Sept. 7, 1953; children: Italo M., Emília M., Ricardo M. MD, Faculty of Medicine, Salvador, Bahia, Brazil, 1963; DSc in Med. Entomology, Inst. Oswaldo Cruz, Rio de Janeiro, 1996. Cert. med. dr., med. entomologist. Entomologist Found. Oswaldo Cruz, Salvador, 1955-63; dir. Centro de Pesquisas Gonçalo Moniz-Found. Oswaldo Cruz, Salvador, 1963-80, rschr., 1963—, pres. ethical com., 1996-98. Author: Vectors of Chagas Disease and Leishmaniases; contbr. over 275 papers and chpts. to profl. publs. Mem. Brazilian Soc. Tropical Medicine, Brazilian Soc. Parasitology (gen. sec. 1997-98), Royal Entomol. Soc. London. Roman Catholic. Avocations: painting, sculpting. Home: Rua Valdemar Falcao 121, 40295001 Salvador Bahia, Brazil Office: Alameda Dos Flamboyants 164, Caminho das Arvores, 40820410 Salvador Bahia, Brazil

SHERLOCK, JOHN MICHAEL, bishop; b. Regina, Sask., Can., Jan. 20, 1926; s. Joseph and Catherine S. Student, St. Augustine's Sem., Toronto, Ont., Can., 1950; student canon law, Catholic U. Am., 1950-52; LLD (hon.), U. Windsor, 1986; DD (hon.), Huron Coll., London, Ont., 1986. Ordained priest Roman Catholic Ch., 1950, bishop, 1974; asst. pastor St. Eugene's, Hamilton, Ont., 1952-59, St. Augustine's, Dundas, Ont., 1959-63, Cathedral Christ the King, Hamilton, also, Guelph and Maryhill, Ont., 1950-52; pastor St. Charles Ch., Hamilton, 1963-74; aux. bishop London, Ont., 1974-78; bishop Diocese of London, 1978—; chaplain Univ. Newman Club, McMaster U., Hamilton, 1963-66; pres. Canadian Conf. Cath. Bishops, 1983-85, liaison with U. Chaplains Can. and Pres. Cath. Coll. and Univs.; chmn. social affairs com. commn. Ont. Conf. Cath. Bishops, edn. commn., family life com.; adv. judge for the Regional Marriage Truban, 1954-72. Mem. Wentworth County Roman Cath. Separate Sch. Bd., 1964-74, chmn., 1972-73; chmn. Nat. Cath. Broadcasting Found., 1995—. Fellow honoris cause U.St. Michael's Coll., Toronto, 1994. Address: Chancery Office, 1070 Waterloo St, London, ON Canada N6A 3Y2

SHERMAN, ALAN THEODORE, computer science educator; b. Cambridge, Mass., Feb. 26, 1957; s. Richard Beatty and Hanni Fey (Fechenbach) S.; m. Tomoko Shimakawa, Aug. 2, 1986. ScB in Math. magna cum laude, Brown U., 1978; SM in Elec. Engring and Computer Sci., MIT, 1981, PhD in Computer Sci., 1987. Instr. Tufts U., Medford, Mass., 1985-86, asst. prof., 1986-89; asst. prof. U. Md. Balt. County, Catonsville, 1989-95, assoc. prof., 1995—; mem. Inst. for Advanced Computer Studies U. Md., College Park, 1989-92, 95-98; rsch. affiliate MIT Lab. for Computer Sci., Cambridge, 1985-88. Author: VLSI Placement and Routing: The PI Project, 1989; co-editor: Advances in Cryptology: Proceedings of Crypto 82, 1983; contbr. articles to profl. jours. Mem. Assn. for Computing Machinery, IEEE, Internat. Assn. for Cryptologic Rsch., AAUP, Soc. for Indsl. and Applied Maths., Phi Beta Kappa, Sigma Xi. Avocations: tennis, Aikido, piano, chess. Home: 5025 Columbia Rd Apt 104 Columbia MD 21044-5547 Office: U Md Baltimore County Dept Comp Sci Elec Engring Baltimore MD 21250-0001

SHERMAN, GARTH LYNDON, counselor administrator, consultant; b. Ipswick, Queensland, Australia, May 8, 1948; s. Albert Oliver and Frances Kathleen (Brown) S.; m. Lesley Dalyell, Dec. 12, 1980; children: Adam, Robin. BA, U. Queensland, Brisbane, Australia, 1976, grad. diploma in counseling, 1987; grad. diploma in tchg., Queensland U., Brisbane, Australia, 1977; grad. diploma in spl. edn., Griffith U., Brisbane, Australia, 1980. Grad. Dip. counselor. Pers. mgr. Pub. Svc. Bd., Australia, 1976; sociologist Commonwealth Employment Svc., Brisbane, Australia, 1976-80; tchr. Queensland Edn., Brisbane, Australia, 1980-86, guidance officer, 1987-95, sr. guidance officer, 1996-97; prin. edn. officer student svcs. Queensland Edn., Brisbane, 1998—. Author: (behavior mgmt. survey) Teacher Perceptions of Behavior, 1996. exec. Warwick Welfare Group, 1990—. Mem. Queensland Guidance and Counseling Assn., Australian Bd. Cert. Counselors, Warwick Welfare Coord. Group. Avocations: music, caligraphy. Office: Warwick Dist Office Edn Qld, 24 Palmerin St, Warwick QLD 4370, Australia

SHERMAN, GERALD, nuclear physicist, financial estate adviser, financial company executive; b. Bklyn., Sept. 7, 1938; s. Saul and Claire S.; m. Annette Ellen Drasin, Aug. 29, 1965; children: Rochelle Heidi, Sondra Nicole. BA in Physics, UCLA, 1960, MS in Nuclear Physics, 1962; PhD in Physics, Columbia Pacific U., 1985. Cert. Nat. Assn. Securities Dealers, Series 6 and 63, Investment Co. Products/Variable Contracts, registered rep.; lic. in securities and health and life ins. Calif.; lic. Fed. Securities Series 7. Physics instr., lower divsn. Lab. UCLA, 1960-62, physics instr. upper divsn. nuclear physics, 1961-62; nuclear ion engine rocket physicist Rocketdyne, Canoga Park, Calif., 1961; sr. scientist Advanced Tech. Co., L.A., 1965-66; physicist, principle superconductivity investigator Northrop Space Sci. Lab., Hawthorne, Calif., 1966-70; pres. Sherman Ins. Agy., Inc., L.A., 1970-84; pres., CEO Sherman Fin. Svcs., Inc., Thousand Oaks, Calif., 1984—; cons. TRW, 1970; spkr. sci. seminars for NASA, U.S. Air Force, Lockheed; speaker fin. seminars, 1972—; developer bus. plan between Bank of China and New USA-China Project; create internet interactive website bus. plan, 1998—. Author: Microwave Phenomenological Theory of Superconductivity, 1965, Superconductive Antennas, 1966, Estate Tax Savings of 90%, 1992, Financial Security for Life, 1993; creater original internet interactive ins. investment website bus. plan, 1998-99. Recipient AEC Time Reduction Analysis award Am. Electronics, 1960, Top Prodr. Nationwide award U.S. Life Ins. Co. Calif., 1978, Leading Disability Prodr. Nationwide award Chubb Life Ins. Co. Am., 1983-85, 90, Leading Combined Life and Disability Prodr. award Chubb, 1987, Leading Combined Disability and Life Ins. Producer award Chubb, 1989, Internat. Life and Health Ins. awards Chubb Corp./Summit Club Calif., 1979, 88, 89, 92, 94, Hawaii, 1982, 92, 94, Italy, 1984, 93, Greece, 1984, Bermuda, 1985, 72, 88, England, 1985, Scotland, 1985, Mex., 1986, Monaco 1987, Switzerland, 1987, Hong Kong, 1988, Thailand, 1988, France, 1989, Africa, 1989, Puerto Rico, 1990, 95, Ariz., 1991, Australia, 1992, Fla., 1993, Austria, 1994, Securities Acad. Award, 1997, Stock Option award Jefferson Pilot Fin., 1999, Locust Street Securities award, Hawaii, 1999, Summit award Jefferson Pilot Fin., Eng./ Scotland, 1999; PhD Rsch. fellow UCLA, 1962-64. Mem. Calif. Assn. Life Underwriters, Westlake Art Guild, UCLA Physics Honor Soc. (v.p. 1959, exec. v.p. 1960), Sigma Pi Sigma. Avocations: seascape/landscape artist, gallery and bank exhibitions, 1991; played trumpet and drums, 1956-58, USAF ROTC marching band; arranger and composer of ballad/symphonic music; planetary astrophotography. One of the first to design the NASA crystal experiment for astronauts; originated and performed first superconductive non-destructive test to determine aircraft titanium alloy strength; created concept and experimentally performed the first superconductive short antenna for very low frequency communication. Office: Sherman Financial Svcs Inc 2158 Calle Riscoso Thousand Oaks CA 91362-1141

SHERMAN, HOWARD D., financial consultant; b. Tuscon, May 25, 1961; s. Donald J. and Elaine (Schwartz) S. BA, George Washington U., 1982; MBA, U. Pa., 1986. Rsch. asst. Fed. Res. Bd., Washington, 1982-84; sr. analyst Investor Responsibility Rsch. Ctr., Washington, 1986-88; sr. v.p., dir. Inst. Shareholder Svcs., Washington, 1988-97, pres., CEO, 1997-99; pres. Thomson Fin. Investor Rels., N.Y.C., 1999—; speaker in field. Contbr. articles to profl. jours. Mem. Phi Beta Kappa. Office: Thomson Fin Investor Rels 75 Wall St Fl 18 New York NY 10005-2833

SHERMAN, JANE, author; b. Beloit, Wis., June 14, 1908; d. Horace Humphrey and Florentine (St. Clair) Sherman; m. Ned Lehac, Feb. 8, 1940 (dec.). Grad., Newtown H.S., Elmhurst, N.Y., 1925. Mem. Far East tour Ruth St. Denis-Ted Shawn Denishawn Dancers, 1925-26, mem. U.S. tour, 1926-27, mem. U.S. Ziegfeld Follies tour, 1927-28; mem. Doris Humphrey-Charles Weidman Co., 1928-29; appeared in Broadway musicals, 1929-31; mem. Radio City Music Hall Rockettes, 1934-35; artistic advisor Denishawn Repertory Dancers, Trenton, N.J., 1981—; adv. bd. Vanaver Caravan, Rosendale, N.Y., 1981—; lectr. in field; re-created dances for the Martha Graham Co., the Vanaver Caravan, the Phila. Dance Co., others. Author: Soaring: The Diary and Letters of a Denishawn Dancer in the Far East, 1976 (de la Torre Bueno prize), The Drama of Denishawn Dance, 1979, Denishawn: The Enduring Influence, 1983; co-author: Barton Mumaw, Dancer, 1986, paperback edit., 2000; contbr. numerous articles on dance to Ballet Rev., Dance Chronicle, Dance Mag., 1976—. Avocation: reading. Home: Actors Fund Residence 155 W Hudson Ave Englewood NJ 07631-1609

SHERMAN, MARY ANGUS, public library administrator; b. Lawton, Okla., Jan. 3, 1937; d. Donald Adelbert and Mabel (Felkner) Angus; m. Donald Neil Sherman, Feb. 8, 1958; children: Elizabeth, Donald Neil II. BS in Home Econs., U. Okla., 1958, MLS, 1969. Br. head Pioneer Libr. System, Purcell, Okla., 1966-76; regional libr. Pioneer Libr. System, Norman, Okla., 1976-78, asst. dir., 1978-80, dir., 1987—; bd. dirs. McClain County Bank, chair audit com., 1997—. Mem. bd. visitors U. Okla. Coll. Arts and Scis., 1998—; bd. dirs. Women's Resource Ctr., Norman, 1998—, v.p., 2000—. Named one of Distinguished Alumni Sch. Home Econs., U. Okla., 1980; recipient award of merit Okla. Sch. Libr. and Info. Sci. Mem. ALA (councilor 1988-96, planning and budget assembly 1990-91, internat. rels. com. 1992-96, internat. rels. round table 1989—, orientation com. 1998-99, mem. com. 1999—, exec. bd. 2000—), Pub. Libr. Assn. (divsn. of ALA, pres. pub. policy for pub. librs. sect. 1995-96), Internat. Fedn. Libr. Assns. (standing com. on pub. librs. 1999—), AAUW (pres. Okla. chpt. 1975-77, nat. bd. dirs. 1983-87, S.W. ctrl. region dir. 1983-85, v.p. nat. membership 1985-87, Woman of the Yr. Purcell chpt. 1982), Okla. Libr. Assn. (pres. 1982-83, interlibr. cooperation com. 1993-95, chair 1994-95, Disting. Svc. award 1986), Norman Soc. Internat. Affairs (v.p. 1998-99, pres. 1999—), Norman C. of C. (bd. dirs. 1988-96, pres. 1994-95), Rotary (program chair 1991-92, 99—, bd. dirs. 1993-97, pres. 1995-96, 99—, Paul Harris fellow, group study exch. leader to Iceland 1998, dist. literacy chair 1998—), Norman Assistance League Club (cmty. assoc.), Norman Sister City Com. 1994—, Delta Gamma Mothers (pres. 1978-79), Kappa Alpha Theta (pres. Alpha Omicron House Corp. 1984-87, nat. dir. house corps. 1987-88), Beta Phi Mu, Phi Beta Kappa. Democrat. Methodist. Office: Pioneer Libr System 225 N Webster Ave Norman OK 73069-7133

SHERMAN, RICHARD ALLEN, lawyer; b. Atlanta, Mar. 16, 1946; s. Robert Hiram and Olivia Mae (Latham) S.; m. Mary Margaret Sawyer, June 23, 1973 (div. June 1994); children: Richard A. Jr., Jill Mary, James Warren; m. Catherine Agnes Oakley, May 4, 1996. BA, Tulane U., 1968, JD, 1972. Bar: Fla. 1974, La. 1973, U.S. Ct. Appeals (5th cir.) 1978, U.S. Ct. Appeals (11th cir.) 1981, U.S. Supreme Ct. 1981. Ptnr., head appellate divsn. Wicker, Smith, Blomqvist, Davant, Tutan, O'Hara, McCoy et al, Miami, 1973-83; pvt. practice Ft. Lauderdale, Fla., 1983—; practice limited to handling appeals in Fla. Active Rep. Nat. Com. Mem. ABA (vice-chmn. U.S. Ct. Appeals 5th cir. com. 1981), Fla. Bar Assn. (appellate rules com. 1979-81), Dade County Bar Assn. (chmn. appellate cts. com. 1982-83), Mensa, Pres. Club, Lauderdale Yacht Club, Upper Keys Sailing Club (bd. dirs.). Avocations: yacht racing, boating, scuba diving, travel, theatre. Office: 1777 S Andrews Ave Ste 302 Fort Lauderdale FL 33316-2517

SHERMAN, ROBERT, broadcaster; b. N.Y.C., July 23, 1932; s. Isaac Jacob and Nadia (Reisenberg) S.; m. Veronica Jean Bravo; children: Steven J., Peter M. BA, NYU, 1952; MA, Columbia U., 1953. Music dir. Sta. WQXR-FM, N.Y.C., 1960-70, program dir., 1970-85, exec. prodr., 1985-93, sr. cons., 1993—; faculty The Julliard Sch., N.Y.C., 1988—, Manhattan Sch. Music, N.Y.C., 1995—; artistic advisor Pulvermann Found., Rye, N.Y., 1993—; narrator West Point Band, Rye, 1994—; bd. dirs. Paul Robeson Found., Naumburg Found., The Mannes Coll. of Music. Co-author: Nadia Reisenberg, 1986, Complete Idiot's Guide to Classical Music, 1997; contbr. reviews and articles The New York Times, 1964—. Bd. dirs. Tisch Ctr. for the Arts, 1996-97. With U.S. Army, 1953-56. Recipient Verdi medal Met. Opera Nat. Coun., 1987, Sanford medal Yale U., 1994, Appreciation award ASCAP, 1993, radio competition prizes N.Y. festivals, 1994. Home: 5 Tavano Rd Ossining NY 10562-3105 Office: WQXR 122 5th Ave New York NY 10011-5605

SHERMAN, ROBERT LEE, JR., chemist, educator; b. Mt. Carmel, Ill., Dec. 24, 1974; s. Robert Lee and Nancy Joan Sherman; m. Crystal Lynn Kirby, July 26, 1997. BS in Chemistry, So. Ill. U., 1997, MS in Chemistry, 2000; postgrad., Okla. State U., 2000—. Lab. technician Ctrl. State Analytical Co., Evansville, Ind., 1996, 97; tchg. asst. dept. chemistry So. Ill. U., Carbondale, 1997-2000; with Okla. State U., Stillwater, 2000—. C. David Schmulbach tchg. scholar So. Ill. U., 1997-98. Mem. Am. Chem. Soc. (assoc.). Baptist. Avocations: U.S. Civil War history, models. E-mail: rlschem@aol.com. Home: 608 Copp Ave Mount Carmel IL 62863-1716 Office: Okla State Univ Chemistry Dept Stillwater OK

SHERMAN, ROGER ANTHONY, air force officer; b. Marrero, La., Dec. 16, 1969; s. Lynn Charles and Barbara Ann Sherman; m. Miranda Eve Distel, Aug. 23, 1997. BA in Psychology, U. New Orleans, 1992; postgrad., Leslie Coll., 1994. Commd. 2d lt. USAF, 1993, advanced through grades to capt., 1997; nuclear missile launch officer USAF, Cheyenne, Wyo., 1994-98; ops. officer 50th Space Wing Command Post USAF, Colorado Springs, Colo., 1994-98; protocol officer USAF, Al Jabber, Kuwait, 1999—; orbital analyst Cheyenne Mountain Air Force Sta., Colorado Springs, 2000—. Officer-in-charge pistol team USAF Acad., Colorado Springs, 1990-2000, host for cadets host family program, 1999-2001. Mem. U.S. Practical Shooters Assn., Porsche Club Am. Republican. Roman Catholic. Avocations: Porsche cars, action pistol shooting. E-mail: Prairiedawgl@juno.com. Home: 7937 Lexington Park Dr Colorado Springs CO 80920-4074 Office: Cheyenne Mt Air Force Sta Colorado Springs CO

SHERMAN, SANDRA BROWN, lawyer; b. Galesburg, Ill., May 14, 1953; d. Charles Lewis and Lois Maria (Nelson) Brown; m. Robert Sherman, June 10, 1979; children: Michael Wesley, Stephen Averill, Alexander Joseph. B of Music Edn., Ind. U., 1975; JD, U. Ill., 1979, LLM, 1981. Bar: Ill. 1979, Tex. 1982, N.J. 1984, U.S. Tax Ct. 1988, N.Y. 1997. Instr. law U. Ill., Champaign, 1979-81; assoc. Law Offices of William E. Remy, San Antonio, 1984; assoc. Gutkin Miller Shapiro & Selesner, Millburn, N.J., 1985-88, ptnr., 1989-91; counsel Riker Danzig Scherer Hyland & Perretti LLP, Morristown, N.J., 1991-95; ptnr. Riker Danzig Scherer Hyland & Perretti, LLP, Morristown, N.J., 1996—. Contbr. articles to profl. jours. Trustee, sec. Found. U. Medicine and Dentistry N.J., 1998—; trustee Jersey Battered Women's Svc., 1999—. Scholar Ind. U., 1971-75, U. Ill., 1977-79. Mem. ABA (probate and trust law divsn.), N.J. Bar Assn., Estate Planning Coun. No. N.J., Estate Planning Coun. N.Y.C., Park Ave. Club. Avocation: music. Home: 15 Hawthorne Dr New Providence NJ 07974-1111 Office: Riker Danzig Scherer Hyland & Perretti LLP Headquarters Plz 1 Speedwell Ave Ste 2 Morristown NJ 07960-6823

SHERMAN, SEMYON IONOVICH, geologist, educator; b. Luginy Village, Zhitomir, Ukraine, Apr. 30, 1934; arrived in Russia, 1953; s. Iona Samoilovich and Malka Mikhelevna Sherman; m. Svetlana Vasilievna Lysak, Dec. 4, 1956; children: Elena, Michail. Grad. in engrng. and geology, Irkutsk State U., Russia, 1958, PhD, 1964; prof., Inst. Geology & Geophysics, Novosibirsk, Russia, 1977. Jr. rschr. Inst. of the Earth's Crust, Irkutsk, Russia, 1958-68, sr. rschr., 1968-79, head lab. tectonophysics, 1979—. Author: Physical Regularities of Crustal Faulting, 1977; co-author: Crustal Stress Fields and Geological and Structural Methods of Studies, 1989, Faulting in the Lithosphere, 3 vols., 1991, 92, 94, Applied Geodynamics Analyssi, 1995. Recipient State award for sci. and techniques Coun. of Mins. of the USSR, 1988; grantee Russian Found. for Sci., 1995, 96, 97, Soros Prof. grantee Soros Found., 1995-96, 97. Mem. Russian Acad. Natural Scis. Office: Inst of the Earths Crust, 128 Lermontov St, 664033 Irkutsk Russia

SHERMAN, SIGNE LIDFELDT, portfolio manager, former research chemist; b. Rochester, N.Y., Nov. 11, 1913; d. Carl Leonard Broström and Herta Elvira Maria (Tern) Lidfeldt; m. Joseph V. Sherman, Nov. 18, 1944 (dec. Oct. 1984). BA, U. Rochester, 1935, MS, 1937. Chief chemist Lab. Indsl. Medicine and Toxicology Eastman Kodak Co., Rochester, 1937-43; chief rsch. chemist Chesebrough-Pond's Inc., Clinton, Conn., 1943-44; ptnr. Joseph V. Sherman Cons., N.Y.C., 1944-84; portfolio strategist Sherman Holdings, Troy, Mont., 1984—. Author: The New Fibers, 1946. Fellow Am. Inst. Chemists; mem. AAAS, AAUW (life), Am. Chem. Soc., Am. Econ. Assn., Am. Assn. Ind. Investors (life), Fedn. Am. Scientists (life), Union Concerned Scientists (life), Earthquake Engrng. Rsch. Inst., Nat. Ctr. for Earthquake Engrng. Rsch., N.Y. Acad. Scis. (life), Cabinet View Country Club. Office: Sherman Holdings Angel Island 648 Halo Dr Troy MT 59935-9415

SHERMAN, SUSAN JEAN, writer, editor, educator; b. N.Y.C., Oct. 30, 1939; d. Monroe and Gertrude Jean (Horn) S. BA, Sarah Lawrence Coll., 1969, MA in Lit., 1971. Tchr. English Dwight-Englewood, 1970-72, Riverdale Country Sch., N.Y., 1972-97; writer Riverdale, N.Y., 1997—. Author: Give Me Myself, 1961 (Amy Loveman award 1960, Huntington Hartford fellow 1961), (rec.) Promises to Be Kept, 1962; editor: Forward Into the Past, 1992, May Sarton: Among the Usual Days, 1993, May Sarton: Selected Letters, 1997, To Bid Still Rejoice, 1998, Dear Juliette: Letters of May Sarton to Juliette Huxley, 1999.

SHERMAN, THOMAS WEBSTER, JR., environmental company executive; b. Newark, Oct. 17, 1929; s. Thomas Webster and Myrtle Agnes (Benson) S.; m. Marilyn Margaret Noss, Nov. 15, 1952; children: Susan, Catherine, Thomas, Janet. BS in Engring., U.S. Naval Acad., 1951; MS in Bus. Adminstrn., George Washington U., 1964. Commd 2d lt. USAF, 1951, advanced through grades to col., 1969, retired, 1981; engring. coord. Systems Mgmt. Am., Washington, 1984-85; dir. govt. mktg. Sullair Corp., Michigan City, Ind., 1985-90; pres. Aquacide LLC, Michigan City, Ind., 1996—, MGS Technology LLC; cons. in field; guest lectr. Purdue U. Contbr. articles to profl. jours. Coord. Round Table, Michigan City, 1997; bd. dirs. Mil. Mus., Michigan City, 1996-97, Civil War Club, Michigan City, 1995-97. Decorated DFC. Mem. AAAS, Air Force Assn., Naval Inst., Air Commd. Assn., Partnership for Sustainability with Russia, Nat. Shipbuilding Rsch. Program, Doctors for Disaster Preparedness. Avocations: conversation, reading, golf. Home: 12255 Clipper Dr Woodbridge VA 22192 Office: Aquacide 2 Devonshire Ct Ste 9 Michigan City IN 46360-1584

SHERMAN, VICTOR, lawyer; b. Indpls., Aug. 28, 1951; s. Marshall and Sara Lee Sherman; m. Claudia Ann Cron, Oct. 8, 1988; children: Mark, Daniel, Miles, Oliver, Luke. BS, UCLA, 1962; LLB, U. Calif., Berkeley, 1965. Bar: Calif. 1966, Conn. 1996, U.S. Ct. Appeals (9th cir.) 1971, U.S. Supreme Ct. 1996. Ptnr. Nasatir, Sherman & Hirsch, L.A., 1970-83, Main St. Law Bldg., Santa Monica, Calif., 1984—; mng. ptnr. Sherman & Sherman, Santa Monica, 1984—; speaker, founder Advanced Criminal Law Seminar, Aspen, Colo., 1981—. Pvt. 1st class U.S. Army, 1960-67. Mem. Nat. Assn. Criminal Def. Lawyers (life). Office: Sherman & Sherman 2115 Main St Santa Monica CA 90405-2215

SHERMAN, WILLIAM FARRAR, lawyer, former state legislator; b. Little Rock, Sept. 12, 1937; s. Lincoln Farrar and Nancy (Lowe) S.; m. Carole Lynn Williams, Sept. 2, 1967; children: John, Anna, Lucy. BA in History, U. Ark.-Fayetteville, 1960; LLB, U. Va., 1964. Bar: Ark. 1964, U.S. Supreme Ct. 1970. Assoc. Smith, Williams, Friday & Bowen, Little Rock, 1964-66; asst. U.S. atty. Ea. Dist. Ark., Little Rock, 1966-69, Ark. Securities Commr., Little Rock, 1969-71; ptnr. Jacoway, Sherman & Pence, Little Rock, 1971—. Legal counsel Voice of the Retarded, BBB Ark., 1971-99; mem. Ark. Ho. of Reps., 1974-84; spl. assoc. justice Supreme Ct., 1991; del. Constnl. Conv. Ark., 1979. With U.S. Army, 1960-61, now brig. gen. U.S. Army ret. Mem. ABA, Ark. Bar Assn., Pulaski County Bar Assn., Ark. Bar Found. Democrat. Methodist. Office: 221 W 2nd St Little Rock AR 72201-2505

SHEROVER, CHARLES M., retired philosophy educator; b. N.Y.C., Jan. 20, 1922; s. Max and Anna Ranov Sherover. BA, Oberlin Coll., 1943; MA, Northwestern U., 1947; PhD, NYU, 1966. Various positions to pres. Linguaphone Inst., N.Y.C., 1948-59; pres., cons. Ednl. Resources Corp., N.Y.C., 1960-93; various positions to prof. grad. faculty New Sch. Hunter Coll./CUNY, N.Y.C., 1987-90; ret., 1994. Author: Heideger, Kant and Time, 1971, Human Experience of Time, 1975, Time, Freedom & the Common Good, 1989, Rousseau & Voltaire, 1996. Chmn. bd. govs. Young Rep. Club, N.Y.C., 1957. Sgt. U.S. Army, 1943-47. Unitarian-Congregational. Office: PO Box 6604 Santa Fe NM 87502-6604

SHERRATT, ALAN FREDERICK CAVE, college director; b. Overseal, Eng.; s. Sidney Arthur and Alice Mary (Cave) S.; m. Pamela Mary Storer, Aug. 1964; children: Jonathan Adam, Emma Ruth, Rachel Mary. BSc (Hons.), U. Nottingham, 1957, PhD, 1960. Chartered engr. ICI rsch. fellow U. Nottingham, U.K., 1960-61; lectr. indsl. heat transfer Nat. Coll. for Heating Ventilating, Refrigeration & Engring., London, 1961-64; sr. lectr. indsl. heat transfer Nat. Coll. for Heating Ventilating, Refrigeration, Engring., London, 1964-66; lectr. in archtl. and bldg. sci. U. Nottingham, Eng., 1966-72; asst. dir. Thames Polytechnic (now U. Greenwich), London, 1972-86; dir. Mid Career Coll., Cambridge, Eng., 1986—, Safety Course Unit, Brighton, Eng., 1986—; v.p. Chartered Inst. Bldg. Svc. Engrs., London, 1994-96, 97-98; vice-chmn. London Energy Group, London, 1992-96. Editor: Build Internat. Jour., 1973-75; coord. editor: Internat. Jour. Ambient Energy, 1980—; editor/joint editor books in field, 1974-00. Gov. South Thames Coll., London. Recipient Silver medal Midland Counties Inst. Engrs., 1961, Instn. Heating and Ventilating Engrs., London, 1973. Fellow Instn. Mech. Engrs., Chartered Inst. Bldg. Svcs. Engrs. (recipient silver medal 1987), Inst. Refrigeration. Office: Mid Career College, PO Box 20, Cambridge CB1 5DG, England

SHERRATT, GERALD ROBERT, retired university president; b. Los Angeles, Nov. 6, 1931; s. Lowell Heyborne and Elva Genevieve (Lamb) S. B.S. in Edn., Utah State U., 1953, M.S. in Edn. Adminstrn., 1954; Ph.D. in Adminstrn. Higher Edn., Mich. State U., 1975. Staff assoc. U. Utah, Salt Lake City, 1961-62; dir. high sch. relations Utah State U., Logan, 1962-64, asst. to pres., 1964-77, v.p. for univ. relations, 1977-81; pres. So. Utah U., Cedar City, 1982-97; dir. Honeyville Grain Inc., Utah; mem. coun. pres. Utah Sys. Higher Edn., 1982-97; chmn. bd. Utah Summer Games, Cedar City, 1984-97; chmn. pres.'s coun. Rocky Mountain Athletic Conf., Denver, 1984-85. Author hist. pageant: The West: America's Odyssey, 1973 (George Washington Honor medal 1973); musical review: How the West Was Won, 1998. Chmn. Festival of Am. West, Logan, Utah, 1972-82; chmn. bd. Utah Shakespearean Festival, Cedar City, 1982-86; chmn. bd. dirs. Salt Lake City Br. of the Fed. Res. Bank of San Francisco, 1996-98; bd. trustees Salt Lake Organizing Com. Winter Olympics 2002. 1st lt. USAF, 1954-57. Recipient Editing award Indsl. Editors Assn., 1962, Robins award Utah State U., 1967, Disting. Alumnus award Utah State U., 1974, So. Utah U., 1991, Total Citizen award Cedar City C. of C., 1993, Minuteman award Utah Nat. Guard, 1997; named to Utah Tourism Hall of Fame, 1989; Centennial medal So. Utah U., 1997; Imperial Order Utah Shakespearean Festival, 1997; named to Hall of Honor Utah Summer Games, 1997, Utah Educators Hall of Fame, 1999. Mem. Am. Assn. State Colls. and Univs., Cache C. of C. (bd. dirs. 1980-82), Cedar City Civic Club, Phi Kappa Phi, Phi Delta Kappa, Sigma Nu (regent 1976-78). Mem. LDS Ch.

SHERREN, ANNE TERRY, chemistry educator; b. Atlanta, July 1, 1936; d. Edward Allison and Annie Ayres (Lewis) Terry; m. William Samuel Sherren, Aug. 13, 1966. BA, Agnes Scott Coll., 1957; PhD, U. Fla., Gainesville, 1961. Grad. tchg. asst. U. Fla., Gainesville, 1957-61; from instr. to asst. prof. Tex. Womans U., Denton, 1961-66; rsch. participant Argonne Nat. Lab., 1973-80, 93-94; assoc. prof. chemistry North Cen. Coll., Naperville, Ill., 1966-76, prof., 1976—. Contbr. articles to profl. jours. Ruling elder Knox Presbyn. Ch., 1971—, clk. of session, 1976-94. Mem. AAAS, AAUP, Am. Chem. Soc., Am. Inst. Chemists, Ill. Acad. Sci., Sigma Xi, Delta Kappa Gamma, Iota Sigma Pi (nat. pres. 1978-81, nat. dir. 1972-78, nat. historian 1989—). Presbyterian. Office: North Ctrl Coll Dept Chemistry Naperville IL 60566

SHERRIFFS, ALEXANDER CARLTON, higher education administrator; b. San Jose, Dec. 14, 1917; s. Alexander and Ruth Irene (Turner) S.; m. Dawn Aloha Hart, Apr. 1, 1966 (div. May 1998); m. Bette Sansome Meredith, July 4, 1998. BA in Econs., Stanford U., 1939, MA in Psychology, 1941, PhD in Psychology, 1946; LLD, Pepperdine U., 1974. Lic. psychologist, Calif. Prof. psychology U. Calif., Berkeley, 1944-67, rsch. assoc. Inst. Human Devel., 1949-50, vice chancellor student affairs, 1958-65; edn. advisor to gov. State of Calif., Sacramento, 1967-73; statewide vice chancellor acad. affairs Calif. State U., Long Beach, 1973-83; cons., writer, 1983—; lectr. in field. Contbr. articles to profl. jours. Democrat. Avocations: fly fishing, photography, gardening, reading, grape growing and wine making. Home and Office: 3607 Windspun Dr Huntington Beach CA 92649-2016

SHERRY, NEIL, advertising executive; b. Chadderton, Eng., May 7, 1947; s. Ronald and Nellie (Warwick) S.; m. Margaret Helen Wolfenden, Dec. 14, 1968; children: Thomas Neil, Elizabeth Margaret, Helen Catherine. Artist Crane Wood, Manchester, Eng., 1966-68; art dir. Farmer Advt., Manchester, 1968-69; group head Brunning Advt. Group, Manchester, 1969-75; creative dir. Stowe & Bowden, Manchester, 1975-79; dir., creative dir. Brockie Haslam, Manchester, 1979-83; dir. Ingham Middleton Dicks Maud Ltd., Manchester, 1983-85, Baglow Harris Sherry, Salford, Eng., 1985-86, Baglow Sherry & Ptnrs. Ltd., Salford, 1986-95; chmn. creative dir. The Crescent Agy., Salford, 1995—. Fellow Inst. of Dirs. Office: Jherry Internat Comm Group, 24 The Cresent, Salford Manchester M54PF, England

SHERSHNEV, VLADIMIR ANDREJEVICH, chemistry educator, researcher; b. Moscow, Apr. 12, 1932; s. Andrei Abramovich and Anna Petrovna (Nikolskaja) S.; m. Galina Zacharovna Krasikova, Sept. 7, 1957 (div. 1985); children: Tatjana, Olga; m. Raisa Aleksejevna Postojeva, July 15, 1994. Grad. in Chem. Engring., Inst. Fine Chem. Tech., Moscow, 1955, Candidate in Chem. Sci., 1959, D of Chem. Sci., 1981. Asst. prof. Inst. Fine Chem. Tech., 1958-62, assoc. prof., 1962-64, prorector, dep. pres., acad. worker, 1964-73, head dept. polymer chemistry and physics, 1974—. Contbr. to jour.: Rubber Chemistry and Technology, 1982; co-author: Principles of Polymer Chemistry and Physics, 1977, Chemistry of Elastomers, 1981, The Chemistry and Physics of Polymers, 1990; mem. editl. bd. Jour. Izvestija Vuzov, 1984, Jour. Plastmassy, 1996. Recipient Honor award Am. Chem. Soc., 1976, Honor award Ministry of Edn., 1971, 97, medal Order of People Friendship, Moscow, 1970, 81, 85, Hon. Prof. award Ministry of Edn., 1997. Mem. Internat. Polymer Network Group, Russian Mendelejev Chem. Soc. Avocations: music, singing, swimming, skiing. Office: State Acad Fine Chem Tech, Vernadskogo Prosp 86, 117571 Moscow Russia

SHERSTYUK, ANDREI, computer programmer; b. Melitopol, Ukrain, Russia, Dec. 20, 1964; s. Victor and Lidia (Bobrova) S.; m. Katerina, Feb. 7, 1989. BS in Physics, Novosibirsk State U., Russia, 1989; MS in Computer Sci., Calif. Inst. Tech., 1994; PhD in Computer Sci., Monash U., Melbourne, Australia, 1999. Programmer Inst. Automation, Acad. Sci., Novosibirsk, 1986-89; cons. NCR Corp., Pasadena, Calif., 1991-94; programmer Square USA, Inc., Honolulu, 1999—. Contbr. articles to profl. jours. Lt. Infantry, Russia, 1984-86. Mem. Assn. Computing Machinery. Avocations: reading, music, traveling. Office: Square USA Inc 55 Merchant St Honolulu HI 96813-4306

SHERWOOD, JAMES ALAN, physician, scientist, educator; b. Oneida County, N.Y., Jan. 4, 1953; s. Robert Merriam and Sally (Trevett-Edgett) S. AB, Hamilton Coll., 1974; MD, Columbia U., 1978. Diplomate Nat. Bd. Med. Examiners, Am. Bd. Internal Medicine. Intern Duke U. Med. Ctr., Durham, N.C., 1978-79; resident physician Strong Meml. Hosp., Rochester, N.Y., 1979-81; fellow U. Rochester Sch. Medicine and Dentistry, 1981-83, NIH, Bethesda, Md., 1983-86; rsch. investigator Walter Reed Army Inst. Rsch., Washington, 1986-92; vis. scientist Clin. Rsch. Ctr. Kenya Med. Rsch. Inst., Nairobi, 1987-92; physician Saradidi Rural Health Programme, Nyilima, Kenya, 1987-92; rsch. cons. Rockville, Md., 1992-93; physician St. Mary's Hosp., Waterbury, Conn., 1993—; clin. instr. Sch. Medicine Yale U., 1994—; founding donor Yale Univ.-Kazan State Medical Univ. fellow exchange program, Russia. Contbr. chpt. to book, articles to profl. jours. Comty. svc. vol. The Door, N.Y.C., 1976-77; vol. physician Washington Free Clinic, 1985-87; charity Sisters of St. Joseph of Chambery. Lt. col. Med. Corps, USAR, 1986-92. Recipient Norton prize in chemistry, 1974, Underwood prize in chemistry, 1974. Fellow Am. Coll. Physicians; mem. Med. Soc. D.C., Am. Fedn. Clin. Rsch., Am. Soc. Tropical Medicine and Hygiene, Muthaiga Club, Phi Beta Kappa, Sigma Xi. Avocations: drawing, book collecting. Office: PO Box 112 Waterbury CT 06720-0112

SHERZER, HARVEY GERALD, lawyer; b. Phila., May 19, 1944; s. Leon and Rose (Levin) S.; m. Susan Bell, Mar. 28, 1971; children: Sheri Ann, David Lloyd. BA, Temple U., 1965; JD with honors, George Washington U., 1968. Bar: D.C. 1970, U.S. Ct. Appeals (D.C. cir.) 1970, U.S. Ct. Fed. Claims 1970, U.S. Ct. Appeals (fed. cir.) 1970, U.S. Supreme Ct. 1974. Law clk. to trial judges U.S. Ct. Fed. Claims, Washington, 1968-69; law clk. to chief judge U.S. Ct. Appeals for Fed. Cir., Washington, 1969-70; assoc. Sellers, Conner & Cuneo, Washington, 1970-75, ptnr., 1975-80; ptnr. McKenna, Conner & Cuneo, Washington, 1980-82, Pettit & Martin, Washington, 1982-85, Howrey & Simon, Washington, 1985-2000, Howrey Simon Arnold & White, Washington, 2000—; adv. bd. The Govt. Contractor, 1996-99. Author: (with others) A Complete Guide to the Department of Defense Voluntary Disclosure Program, 1996; contbr. articles to profl. jours. Office: Howrey Simon Arnold & White 1299 Pennsylvania Ave NW Ste 1 Washington DC 20004-2400

SHESTACK, ALAN, museum administrator; b. N.Y.C., June 23, 1938; s. David and Sylvia P. (Saffran) S.; m. Nancy Jane Davidson, Sept. 24, 1967. BA, Wesleyan U., 1961, DFA (hon.), 1978; MA, Harvard U., 1963. Mus. curator graphic art Nat. Gallery Art, Washington, 1965-67; assoc. curator prints and drawings Yale Art Gallery, New Haven, 1967-68; curator prints and drawings Yale Art Gallery, 1968-71, dir., 1971-85; adj. prof. history of art Yale U., 1971-85; dir. Mpls. Inst. Art, 1985-87, Boston Mus. Fine Arts, 1987-93; dep. dir. Nat. Gallery of Art, Washington, 1994—; mem. adv. com. Art Mus., Princeton, 1972-75; mem. vis. com. Harvard U. Art Mus., 1990-95, Davis Mus. Wellesley Coll., 1997—; mem. mus. panel Nat. Endowment for the Arts, 1974-77; mem. com. prints and illustrated books Mus. Modern Art, N.Y.C., 1972—; mem. Fed. Arts and Artifacts Indemnification Panel, 1979-83. Author: Fifteenth Century Engravings of Northern Europe, 1967, The Engravings of Martin Schongauer, 1968, Master LCZ and Master WB, 1971, Exhibitions Organized and Catalogued: Master E.S, 1967, The Danube School, 1969, Hans Baldung Grien, Prints and Drawings, 1981; contbr. articles to profl. jours. Woodrow Wilson fellow Harvard U., 1963, David E. Finley fellow, 1963-65. Mem. Print Coun. Am. (bd. dirs., v.p. 1970-71), Coll. Art Assn. (bd. dirs. 1972-76), Am. Assn. Mus., Am. Fedn. Arts (trustee 1981-94), Alpha Delta Phi, Phi Beta Kappa. Office: Nat Gallery Of Art Washington DC 20565-0001

SHESTACK, JEROME JOSEPH, lawyer; b. Atlantic City, N.J., Feb. 11, 1925; s. Isidore and Olga (Shankman) S.; m. Marciarose Schleifer, Jan. 28, 1951; children: Jonathan Michael, Jennifer. AB, U. Pa., 1944; LLB, Harvard U., 1949; LLD (hon.), Dickinson Coll. Law, 1997, Stetson Sch. of Law, 1998, Whittier Coll. Law, 1998. Bar: Ill. 1950, Pa. 1952. Teaching fellow Northwestern U. Law Sch., Chgo., 1949-50; asst. prof. law, faculty editor La. State Law Sch., Baton Rouge, 1950-52; dep. city solicitor City of Phila., 1952, 1st dep. solicitor, 1952-55; ptnr. Schnader, Harrison, Segal & Lewis, Phila. and Washington, 1956-91, Wolf, Block, Schorr & Solis-Cohen, Phila., 1991—; adj. prof. law U. Pa., 1956; U.S. amb. to UN Human Rights Commn., 1979-80; U.S. del. to ECOSOC, UN, 1980; sr. U.S. del. to Helsinki Accords Conf., 1979-80; mem. U.S. Commn. on Improving Effectiveness of UN, 1989—; chmn. Internat. League Human Rights, 1973-94, hon. chmn., 1994—, U.S. del. to CSCE Conf., Moscow, 1991; founder, chmn. Lawyers Com. Internat. Human Rights, 1978-80, Jacob Blaustein Inst. Human Rights, 1988-92; mem. nat. adv. com. legal svcs. OEO, 1965-72; bd. dirs., exec. com. Laywers Com. Civil Rights; mem. coun. Holocaust Mus., 1999—, exec. com. Editor: (with others) Rights of Americans, 1971, Human Rights, 1979, International Human Rights, 1985, Bill of Rights: A Bicentennial View, 1991, Understanding Human Rights, 1992, Thomas Jefferson: Lawyer, 1993, Francis Scott Key, 1994, Abraham Lincoln, Circuit Lawyer, 1994, The Holocaust, 1997, Moral Foundations of Human Rights, 1997, The Philosophy of Human Rights, 1997, W.B. Yeats, Poet of Passionate Intensity, 1997. Mem. exec. com. Nat. Legal Aid and Defender Assn., 1970-80; trustee Eleanor and Franklin Roosevelt Inst., 1986—; bd. govs. Tel Aviv U., 1983—, Hebrew U., 1969—; v.p. Am. Jewish Com., 1984-89; chmn. bd. dirs. Am. Poetry Ctr., 1976-91; trustee Free Libr. Phila., vice chmn., 1989-96. With USNR, 1943-46. Rubin fellow Columbia U. Law Sch., 1984; hon. fellow U. Pa. Law Sch., 1980. Mem. ABA (ho. of dels. 1971-73, 77—, mem. jud. com. 1985-90, bd. govs. 1992-95, exec. com. 1994-95, counsellor 1999—, pres. elect 1996, pres. 1997-98, pres. ALI-ABA 1997-98), Internat. Bar Assn. (chmn. com. on human rights 1990-94), Am. Soc. Internat. Law (exec. com. 1993-95, counsellor 1999—, internat. com. jurists exec. com. 1998—), Am. Law Inst., Am. Arbitration Assn. (bd. dirs. 1999—), Am. Coll. Trial Lawyers, Am. Acad. Appellate Lawyers, Internat. Assn. Jewish Lawyers and Jurists (Am. Soc. pres. 2000—), Order of Coif., Am. Soc. Internat. Law, Nat. Conf. Bar Found. (bd. dirs. 1998—). Home: Parkway House 2201 Pennsylvania Ave Philadelphia PA 19130-3513 Office: Wolf Block Schorr & Solis-Cohen 1650 Arch St Fl 20 Philadelphia PA 19103-2029

SHESTAKOV, VITALI ALEXANDROVICH, physiologist; b. Kirov, Medyanski, Russia, Nov. 10, 1940; s. Alexandr Alekseevich and Maria (Nikolaevna) S.; married, Mar. 26, 1973; 1 child, Ekaterina Vitalievna. PhD in Biology, Inst. Hematology & Blood Transfusion, Moscow, 1980. Head dept. physiology sports Rsch. Inst. Phys. Culture, Moscow, 1974-79; prof. human and animal anatomy and physiology Moscow Tchr.'s Tng. Coll., 1979-89; gen. dir. Rsch. Ctr. Vital Human Activity Russian Acad. Scis., Moscow, 1989—. Author: Human Sociobiology: Physiological Aspects, 1997; patentee method to obtain the biologically active serum. Mem. Internat. Acad. Nature and Soc. Scis., N.Y. Acad. Scis. E-mail: mmbc@orc.ru. Office: Russian Acad Scis/Rsch Ctr, Bolshaya Polianka St 50, 109180 Moscow Russia

SHESTOPALOV, IGOR PAVLOVICH, physicist, researcher; b. Moscow, May 1, 1938; s. Pavel Michaylovich and Agrafena Vasilyevna (Osipova) S.; m. Valeria Stepanovna Karpenkova, June 4, 1966; 2 children. Degree in Physics, Moscow State U., 1966, Candidate Phys. and Math. Scis., 1979. Sr. sci. rschr. Inst. Nuclear Physics, Moscow State U., 1966-89, Inst. Biomed. Problems, Moscow, 1989-94; leading sci. rschr. Rsch. Ctr. of Spacecraft Radiation Safety, Moscow, 1994—. Contbr. articles to profl. jours. Mem. AAAS, Nat. Geog Soc.

SHET, RAMAKANT TUKARAM, polymer scientist, consultant; b. Orgao, Goa, India, Aug. 19, 1935; came to U.S., 1984; s. Tukaram Shamba and Jijabai Shablo (Parab) S.; m. Aruna G. Halarnkar, Sept. 3, 1971; children: Kavita, Aditee. BS in Chemistry, U. Bombay, Mumbai, India, 1957, BS in Tech., 1959, MS in Tech., 1961; PhD in Polymers, U. Leeds, U.K., 1964. Lectr. Ahmadu Bello U., Zaria, Nigeria, 1964-68, sr. lectr., 1969-77, reader, 1978-80, prof., 1981-83; vis. scientist Western Regional Res. Lab., Albany, Calif., 1984-88; assoc. rsch. fellow Kimberly-Clark Corp., Neenah, Wis., 1988-95; pres., cons. Tech. Foresight Internat., Neenah, Wis., 1996—; tech. expert Teltech, Mpls., 1998—; vis. prof. Indian Inst. of Tech., New Delhi, 1968; vis. scientist U. Calif, Davis, 1980-81. Contbr. numerous articles to profl. jours. Vol. community svc. Seva, Fox Cities, Wis., 1990—. Recipient Raja Maharaj Singh medal Bombay U., 1959; scholar Govt. of India, New Delhi, 1959-61, U. Leeds, 1962-64; Tata scholar J.N. Tata Endowment, Mumbai, India, 1961-64; Sir Mangaldas scholar Bombay U., 1962-64. Fellow Textile Inst. U.K., Royal Soc. Chemistry U.K.; mem. Am. Chem. Soc. Achievements include patentee hydrogel for absorption of proteinaceous fluids, surface modified cellulose for improved wet strength, curl and absorbent properties, sulfonated cellulose. Avocations: community service, fundraising for charities, cooking, travel, promoting Indo-Am. friendship and goodwill. Office: Tech Foresight Internat 809 Heather Ct Neenah WI 54956-4967

SHETH, JAYESH JAYANTILAL, biochemist, researcher; b. Modasa, Gujarat, India, Feb. 26, 1957; s. Jayantilal Nathalal and Rmilaben Chunilal S.; m. Frenny Jayesh Vin, Feb. 3, 1959; children: Riddhi, Harsh. BS, J&J Sci. Coll., Nadiad, India, 1976; MS, Six Huakisondas Nurrotumdas Ho, Bombay, 1979, PhD, 1983. Jr. rsch. assoc. M.P. Shah Cancer Hosp., Ahmedabad, India, 1983-85; in charge, hon. Hosp. Sheth V.S. Hosp., Ahmedabad, 1989—; asst. prof. endocrinology N.H.L. Mcpl. Medical Coll., Ahmedabad, 1989—; ptnr. Shah Pathology Lab and Endocrine Unit, Ahmedabad, 1985—; dir. Genetics Ctr., Ahmedabad, 1994—; vis. lab. endocrinologist (hon.) Bharatiya Vidya Bhavan's SPARC, Bombay, 1995—; mem. gov. bd. Sheth Rasiklal Shah Sarvjanik Hosp., Modasa, 1996—; mem. adv. bd. Diagnostic Sys. Lab. Inc., Houston, 1997—; scientific mem. Jivraj Mehta & Bakesi Medical Rsch. Hosp., Ahmedabad, 1998—; mem. adv., sec. Hosp. Growth Colloquia Pharmacia Upjohn, Bombay, 1999—. Contbr. articles to profl. jours.; inventor on thyroid. Exec. mem. Maharaja Agrasen Kendriy Vidyalaya, Ahmedabad, 1997—; mng. intern Sheth Neelam Charitable Trust, Ahmedabad, 1991—. Jr. rsch. fellow Indian Coun. Med. Rsch., 1990—, summer fellow med. rsch. Erasmus U., 1991. Mem. Endocrine Soc. India, Endocrine Soc. (we. zone), Endocrine Soc. (U.S.A.), Lions (chmn. health com. 1994-95). Avocations: spiritual discourses, reading, gardening, badminton, yoga. Home: Shree Raj 15 Kapidhwaj Bung, Jodhpur Gam Rd, Satellite, 380015 Ahmedabad India Office: Genetics Ctr 20/1 Bimanagar, Satellite Rd, 380015 Ahmedabad India

SHETTY, MAMBETTU VASANTH KUMAR, consultant radiologist; b. Mambettu, Karnataka, India, May 8, 1924; s. Mulki Chandaya and Mambettu Kamalakshi Hedge S.; m. Marakada Nalini Rai, Jan. 19, 1954; children: Ashwin Kumar, Gitanjali, Snehalatha Rai. BSc, N. Wadia Coll., Pune, India, 1945; MB, BChir, Madras (India) Med. Coll., 1954, diploma med. radiology, 1955. Diplomate Am. Bd. Radiology. Tchg. fellow U. Pitts, 1961-64; prof. pediat. radiology Inst. Child Health and Hosp. for Children, Madras, 1968-80; cons. radiologist Dr. Rai Meml. Med. Ctr., Madras, 1980—. Dir. Child Trust Hosp., Madras, 1980-92, South India Sugars, 1982-94. Mem. Soc. Pediat. Radiology, Indian Radiol. and Imaging Assn. (Dr. Arthur Daniel Meml. Orator award 1960), Madras Gymkhana Club, Madras Club. Avocations: photography, traveling, social work, Hindusthani classical music, cricket. Home: The Manor, P Cemtaph Rud Ln, Chennai 600018, India Office: Dr Rai Med Ctr, 562 Anna Salai, Chennai 600018, India

SHETTY, MANGALORE NAGAPPA, engineering educator, researcher; b. Mangalore, India, Oct. 10, 1937; s. Bail Koraga and Daramma Shetty; m. Sukanya Shetty, Sept. 18, 1947; children: Meghnad, Shubhrata. BS, U. Madras, India, 1956; DIISc, Indian Inst. Sci., Bangalore, 1958; MS, U. Utah, 1960; PhD, U. B.C., 1964; grad., Prayag Music Acad., Allahabad, India, 1977. Chartered engr., India. Asst. prof. IIT Kanpur, India, 1964-66; vis. scientist NRC, Ottawa, Can., 1967-68; vis. faculty Ohio State U., Columbus, 1968-72; vis. prof. IIT Bombay, 1989-90; prof. IIT Kanpur, 1997—; cons. Bharat Heavy Elecs., Hyderabad, India, 1975-77; advisor curriculum devel. to engring. colls., India, 1980—; cultural counsellor IIT Kanpur, 1990-94. Contbr. articles to profl. jours. Mem. ISKCON, Bangalore/Mangalore, 1996—. Recipient Kidar Singh Sadoo award UBC, Vancouver, CAn., 1961, Metallographic award ASM, 1962, Disting. Leadership award ABI, 1986. Fellow Instn. Engrs.; mem. N.Y. Acad. Scis., Internat. Planetary Soc. Janata Dal. Hindu. Avocations: bridge, music, astrology, photography, theatre. Home: Shetty's Cottage Jeppoo, 575002 Mangalore India

SHETTY, MULKI RADHAKRISHNA, oncologist, consultant; b. Hiriadka, Karnataka, India, July 10, 1940; came to U.S., 1974; s. Mulki Sunderram and Kusumavati Shetty. MBBS, Stanley Med. Coll., Madras, 1964; DTM, U. Liverpool, Eng., 1968; LMCC, Med. Coun., Can., 1975. House surgeon and physician Bombay Hosp., 1965-66; sr. house officer Manor Pk. Hosp., Bristol, Eng., 1966-67, Torbay Hosp., 1967-68, St. Lukes Hosp., Huddersfield, 1969-70; sr. resident Gen. Hosp. Meml. U., New Foundland, 1971-72; intern Ottawa Gen. Hosp., 1972-73; fellow in chemotherapy Ont. Cancer Found., Ottawa, Can., 1973-74; fellow in clin. oncology U. Fla., Gainesville, 1974-75; attending oncologist N.W. Community Hosp., Arlington Heights, Ill., 1975-2000; ret., 2000; cons. N.W. Community Hosp., 1975—. uthor: Lung Cancer, 1980, Recent Advances in Chemotherapy, 1985, Wildlife Adven tures, 1997, Chicago, 1997; contbr. numerous articles to profl. jours.; coined new word calcifectomy. Recipient Cert. for Outstanding Svc., Am Cancer Soc., 1982. Hindu.

SHETTY, SHIVARAM NARAYAN, pharmacologist, toxicologist; b. Honavar, Karnataka, India, Apr. 8, 1934; s. Narayan Narnappa and Lakshmi (Narayan) S.; m. Susheela Shivaram Shetty, Apr. 23, 1962 (dec. Jan. 1993); children: Satish, Sharad, Roopa Rani. B Vet. Sci., Bombay Vet. Coll., 1959, cert. exptl. pharmacology, 1964; MS in Pharmacology, U. Fla., Gainesville, 1968, PhD in Pharmacology, 1970. Vet. asst. surgeon Vet. Dept. Karnataka, Bangalore, India, 1959-60; lectr. pharmacology Vet. Coll., Bangalore, 1960-68, asst. prof., 1968-74, assoc. prof., 1974-75, prof., 1987; reader pharmacology U. Nigeria, Nsukka, 1975-87; cons. biochemist Suman Clin. Lab., Bangalore, 1988-94; chief analyst Prerace Dope Testing Lab., Bangalore Turf Club, 1990—. Author: Laboratory Manual of Pharmacology and Toxicology, 1982. Social worker YMCA, Bangalore, 1960. European Econ. Cmty. Rsch. grantee Deutch Agy. Devel. German Agy., U. Nigeria, 1979-80. Mem. Indian Pharmacological Soc. (life), Assn. Ofcl. Racing Chemists (affiliate), N.Y. Acad. Scis., Sr. Vets. Assn. (Kamataka chpt. pres.). Avocations: scientific literature, music, games, developing experimental techniques using simple equipments, setting and organizing analytical/chemical laboratories. Home: 95/4 1st Main Rd, Seshadripuram, Bangalore 560020, India

SHETTY, SHRIDHARA MAHABALA, bank executive; b. Mangalore, Karnataka, India, Mar. 11, 1943; s. Mahabala and Sundari Mahabala S.; m. Sumathi Shridhara, Apr. 17, 1972; children: Ashok S., Ajay S., Vijay S. BA with honors, K.C. Coll., Mumbai, India, 1968; MA, Mumbai U., 1970; diploma in commerce, Indian Merchants Chamber, Mumbai, 1972. Lectr. M.D. Coll. Arts & Scis., Mumbai, 1970-71; sur. supt., asst. gen. mgr. Vijaya Bank, Bangalore, India, 1971-77; asst. gen. mgr. Karnataka Bank Ltd., Mumbai, 1977-88; from dep. gen. mgr. to gen. mgr. Karnataka Bank Ltd., Mangalore, 1988-98, sr. gen. mgr., 1998—. Editor House Mag.; contbr. articles to profl. jours. Mem. Assn. Indian Inst. Bankers (cert.), All India Mgmt. Assn. Avocations: reading, writing, swimming. Home: Devi Kripa Behind Canara Co, 575 003 Mangalore India Office: Karnataka Bank Ltd, Head Office Kodialbail Post, 575 003 Mangalore India

SHETTY, VILASINI THIMMAPPA, science educator; b. Bombay, India, July 8, 1962; d. Thimmappa Jogappa and Shakuntala S.; m. Srinivas Rao Ravanam; 1 child, Angad Srinivas Ravanam. PhD, U. Bombay, 1992. Instr. Rush Presbyn.-St. Lukes Med. Ctr., Chgo., 1994-97, asst. prof., 1997—; lab. mgr. Rush Cancer Inst., Chgo., 1997—. Sr. rsch. fellow Inst. Cancer Rsch. and Royal Marsden Hosp., London, 1989-91, Jaslok Hosp. Rsch. Ctr., Bombay, 1991-92, postdoctoral fellow Rush Presbyn.-St. Lukes Med. Ctr., 1992-94. Mem. Am. Soc. Hematology, Am. Assn. Cancer Rsch., Am. Soc. Clin. Oncology, Internat. Soc. Exptl. Hematology, Women in Cancer Rsch. Avocations: swimming, reading, dancing. Home: 425 S Harvey Ave Apt B Oak Park IL 60302-4118 Office: Rush Presbyn-St Lukes Med Ctr Rush Cancer Inst 2242 W Harrison St Ste 108 Chicago IL 60612-3515

SHEU, JENGTZONG, research scientist; b. Taipei, Taiwan, Jan. 21, 1961; s. Jengcheng and Chai Wang; m. Chia Hui Li, Dec. 27, 1989; children: Sunny, Peter. Phd, Mich. State U., 1994. Engr. Sony, Orangeburge, N.Y., 1992-93; assoc. rschr. Nat. Nanodevice Lab., Hsinchu, Taiwan, 1994-96; rsch. scientist Synchrotron Radiation Rsch. Ctr., Hsinchu, 1996—; mem. program com. SPIE Micromachining and Microfabrication, 1998, 99. Patentee in field. Lt. Taiwanese Navy, 1986-88. Grantee Nat. Sci. Coun., 1997, 98, 99. Mem. Internat. Soc. for Optical Enging. Avocations: tennis, golf, reading. Fax: 886-3-5783890. E-mail: jtsheu@srrc.gov.tw. Office: Synchrotron Radiat Rsch Ctr, # 1 D&D Rd VI, Hsinchu 30077, Taiwan

SHEU, MENG LIEH, electronics engineer; b. Pu-Li, Nan-Tou, Taiwan, July 30, 1962; s. Gin-Dwell Sheu and Hee Lee; m. Sabrina Re-Er Tsai, May 20, 1990; 1 child, Yit-Sen Sheu. Bachelor's, Nat. Chiao Tung U., Hsin-Chu, Taiwan, 1984, Master's, 1986, PhD, 1995. Registered profl. electronics engr. Instr. Chinese Jr. Coll. Tech., Taipei, Taiwan, 1986-89; dep. mgr. Chip Implementation Ctr., Hsin-Chu, Taiwan, 1995—; assoc. prof. Chung-Hwa U., Hsin-Chu, 1997—; cons. Grand Micro Co., Taipei, 1987-90, Global Unichip Corp., Hsin-Chu, 1999—. Patentee in field. Mem. IEEE, Nat. Geographic Soc. Avocations: painting, reading, nature. Home: 5F 27, Ln 145 Po-San Rd, Hsinchu 300, Taiwan Office: Chip Implementation Ctr, 1F # 1 Prosperity Rd I, Hsinchu 300, Taiwan

SHEU, STEVE CHAO-KAE, food products company executive; b. Tainan, Taiwan, Republic of China, Feb. 10, 1960; s. Lian-Buh Sheu and Bih-Shiou Chen; m. Lisa Yeuan-Fang Shen, Nov. 2, 1997. BA, Cheng-Chi U., Taipei, Republic of China, 1983; MBA, Bradley U., 1989. Sales rep. Evergreen Marine Corp., Taipei, 1985-87; sales mgr. Kuang-Chuan Dairy Co. Ltd., Taipei, 1987-88, corp. mgr., 1989-91, country mgr., 1991-93, spl. asst., 1993-94, mktg. dir., 1994—; mktg. cons. Chinese Productinity Ctr., Taipei, 1991-93; mgmt. cons. Elite Music Co., Taipei, 1992-93. Author: The Trend of Conventient Store, 1993, Beverage Industry Aduting, 1995, Annual Marketing Strategy, 1998. Supr. KMT, Taipei, 1983, dir., Kaohsuing, 1985, inspector, Taipei, 1992. 2d lt. U.S. Army, 1983-84. Superior scholarship Cheng-Chi U., 1983. Mem. Common-Wealth, Chinese Mgmt. Assn. Avocations: swimming, jogging, judo, reading, basketball. Home: 3rd Fl No 19 Ln 30, Wan Li St, Taipei 116, Taiwan Office: Kuang-Chuan Dairy Ltd, 18F No Min Chuan E Rd Sec 3, Taipei Taiwan

SHEU, TSANG-LING, electrical engineering educator; b. WinLin, Taiwan, May 27, 1959; s. Chiou and Hwa (Lau) S.; m. Sheuan-Ling Chen, Aug. 15, 1997; children: Christine, Tiffany. BSEE, Nat. Sun Yat-Sen U., Tainan, Taiwan, 1983; MSEE, Va. Poly. Inst & State U., 1985; PhD in Elec. Engring., Pa. State U., 1989. Adv. engr. IBM, Research Triangle Park, N.C., 1989-95; assoc. prof. NSYSU, Kaohsiung, Taiwan, 1995—. Author: International Conference on Information Networking, 1998. Mem. IEEE Computer Soc., IEEE Comm. Soc. Avocations: tennis, golf, swimming. Office: Nat Sun-Yat-Sen Univ, Dept Elec Engring, Kaohsiung Taiwan

SHEU, WAYNE HUEY-HERNG, diabetologist, educator, physician; b. Tainan, Taiwan, Nov. 17, 1957; s. Ker Chin and Shiu King (Lin) S.; m. Terry R. Chen; children: Amy, Victoria. MD, Nat. Def. Med. Ctr., Taipei, 1983, PhD, 1989. Resident Tri-Svc. Gen. Hosp., Taipei, 1983-85, 89-90, chief resident, 1990-91, attending physician, 1991-96; chief dept. endocrinology, prof. medicine Taichung (Taiwan) Vet. Gen. Hosp., 1996—. Contbr. articles to profl. jours. Maj. Taipei Mil. Avocations: reading, basketball, swimming. Office: Taichung Vet Gen Hosp, #160 Sect 3 Chung Kang Rd, 407 Taichung Taiwan

SHEVADE, PRATAP DATTATRAY, bookseller; b. Ahmedabad, India, Jan. 30, 1944; s. Dattatray and Vijaya (Kuwalekar) S.; m. Meena Eknath Jambhekar, May 12, 1967; 2 children. Proprietor Vijaya Prakashan, Ahmedabad, 1965—. Home: 19/220 Parishram Apts, Satellite Rd, Ahmedabad 380 015, India

SHEVARDNADZE, EDUARD AMVROSIYEVICH, Georgian government official, former minister of foreign affairs of Soviet Union; b. Mamati Lanchkhutsky Raion, Georgia, Jan. 25, 1928; m. Nanuli Shevardnadze; children: Manana, Paata. Grad., Republican Party Sch. of Cen. Com., Communist Party of Georgia, 1951, Kutaisi Pedagogical Inst., 1959; hon. degree in polit. sci. and diplomacy, U. Trieste, 1991, Harvard U. Joined Communist Party Soviet Union, 1948, Komsomol work, 1948-61; 2d sec. Cen. Com. Georgian Komsomol, 1956-57; 1st sec. Cen. Com. Georgian Komsomol, 1957-61; party work, 1961-91; mem. Cen. Com. Georgian Communist Party, 1961-91; 1st sec. Mtskheti Raion Com., 1961-63, Pervomaisky Raion Com., Tbilisi City, Communist Party of Georgia, 1963-64; 1st dep. minister for Protection of Pub. Order, 1961-65, minister (renamed Ministry of Internal Affairs 1968), 1965-72; 1st sec. Tbilisi City Com. of Cen. Com., Communist Party of Georgia, 1972; 1st sec. Cen. Com. Georgian Communist Party, 1972-85; min. fgn. affairs USSR, 1985-90, 91; mem. Cen. Com. of Communist Party Soviet Union, 1976-91; candidate mem. Politburo, 1978-85, dep. to USSR Supreme Soviet, 1978-91; mem. Presdl. Coun., 1990-91; chmn. State Coun. Georgia, Tbilisi, 1992-93; Pres. of Parliament, head of state Republic of Georgia, 1992-95, pres., 1995—. Decorated Order of Lenin (5), Order of Red Banner of Labour, Hero of Socialist Labour, (2), others. Office: Chancellery Pres Georgia, Rustaveli Prospect 29, 300002 Tbilisi Georgia*

SHEVCHENKO, PAVEL VLADIMIROVICH, physicist, researcher; b. Donetsk, Ukraine, July 22, 1971; s. Vladimir Pavlovich and Galina Evgenevna (Lavrik) S.; m. Elena Vladimirovna Kanunnikova, Apr. 25, 1992; 1 child, Elena. B, Moscow inst. Physics & Tech, 1992, M, 1994; PhD in Physics, U. New South Wales, Sydney, Australia, 1999. Rschr. Kapitza Inst. Phys. Problems, Moscow, 1992-96; rsch. fellow U New South Wales, U. Sydney, 1996-99; rsch. scientist CSIRO, Sydney, 1999—. Contbr. articles to profl. jours. Landau grantee, Kapitza Inst., Moscow, Germany, 1994, Soros grantee Kapitza Inst., Moscow, 1995, Australian Rsch. Coun. grantee, Sydney, 1996; recipient Gordon Godfrey award in theoretical, physics, Sydney, 1997. Mem. Australian Inst. Physics. Office: CSIRO, North Ryde, Sydney NSW 1670, Australia

SHEVCHENKO, VALERY NIKOLAEVICH, mathematics educator; b. Minsk, Byelorussi, USSR, June 17, 1940; s. Nikolay Kondratyevich and Nadezhda Ivanovna (Karachazova) S.; m. Valentina Ivanovna Bogdanova, Apr. 30, 1964 (div.); m. Irina Struchkova, Dec. 15, 1991 (div.); m. Natalya Shestakova, July 12, 1995. Diploma, State U., Gorki, USSR, 1962, Candidate Phys./Math. Sci., 1966, Doctor Ph&M, 1989. Asst. State Univ., Gorki, 1965, sr. tchr., 1965-67, asst. prof., 1967-70, head of chmn., 1970; rsch. worker Inst. Applied Math. and Cybernetics, Gorki, 1963-85. Author: (books) Qualitative Topics in Integer Programming, 1995; editor: Methods in Discrete Mathematics, 1991. Mem. Am. Math Soc., Math. Programming Assn. (mem. mgmt.), Nizhni Novgorod Math. Soc. (mem. mgmt.). Avocation: tennis. Office: Nizhni Novgorod State Univ, Gagarin Ave 23, 603000 Nizhni Novgorod Russia

SHEVCHUK, IGOR, chemist; b. Suure-Jaani, Estonia, Jan. 20, 1953; s. Nikolai and Ilse (Siimu) S.; m. Evi Parts. BS, Tartu U., 1975; PhD, Inst. Chemistry Tallinn, 1984. Scientist Inst. Chemistry, Tallinn, Estonia, 1978—. Office: Inst Chemistry, Akadeemia Tee 15, 12618 Tallinn Estonia

SHEVEL, VALERY NIKOLAEVICH, nuclear engineer; b. Kirivoi Rog, Ukraine, Sept. 20, 1944; s. Nikolai Gerasimovich and Maria Bernadovna (Kobylyanskaya) S.; m. Nina Ivanovna Skripka, May 17, 1973; children: Andrej, Maria. MS in Physics, Dnepropetrovsk State U., Ukraine, 1968. Electromechanic So. Iron-Ore Processing Corp., Krivoi Rog, 1961-63; engr. Isotope Lab., Dnepropetrovsk, 1968-70; sr. engr., dosimetrist E.O. Paton's Electrowelding Inst., Kiev, Ukraine, 1970-73; sr. engr., dosimetrist Inst. Nuclear Rsch., Kiev, 1973-94, dep. gen. engr. Nuclear Reactor, 1994—. Contbr. numerous articles to profl. jours.; 5 patents in field. Recipient Medal for liquidation of aftermath of Chernobyl accident Verkhovna Rada of Ukraine, 1986. Mem. Nuclear Reactor's Trade Union (chmn. 1989—). Office: Inst Nuclear Rsch, Prospekt Nauki 47, 03680 Kiev Ukraine

SHEVELEV, IGOR ALEXANDER, physiologist; b. Moscow, Sept. 29, 1932; s. Alexander Boris and Mina Solomon (Meller) S.; m. Ludmila Yuryevna Knutova, Sept. 11, 1955 (dec. Jan. 1987); children: Romanova, Olga I., Shevelev Dmitri I.; m. Elena Semyon Mikhailova, Dec. 9, 1989. Dr. of Biol. Scis., I.P. Pavlov Inst. Physiology, 1970. Surgeon Hosp. #30, Moscow, 1956-58; rsch. scientist Inst. of Higher Nervous Activity and Neurophysiology, Moscow, 1958-64, sr. rsch. scientist, 1967-72, head of the sensory physiology dept., 1972-2000, dir., 2000—; prof. Lomonosov State U., Moscow, 2000—; dep. dir. Inst. of Higher Nervous Activity and Neurophysiology, Moscow, 1964-67; lectr. on sensory physiology Lomonosov State U., Moscow, 1976-83. Author: Dynamics of Initial Afferent Inflow in the Visual System, 1971, Neurons of the Visual Cortex: Adaptivity and Dynamics of Receptive Fields, 1984; co-author: Thermoencephaloscopy, 1989; contbr. articles to profl. jours. Mem. Communist Party of Soviet Union, 1959-91. Sci. grantee European Sci. Found., 1992, Russian Found. Basic Rsch., 1993, 96, 97, 99, 2000, Internat. Sci. Found., 1994, 95, Russian Found. Humanitarian Sci., 1997, 2000. Mem. Russian Physiol. Soc., Internat. Brain Rsch. Orgn., N.Y. Acad. of Scis., Russian Acad. Scis. Avocations: travel, fine arts, poetry, reading. Office: Inst Higher Nervous Activity/Neurophysiology, 5-A Butlerova St, 117865 Moscow Russia

SHEVELEV, IGOR VYACHESLAVOVICH, molecular biologist; b. Leningrad, USSR, Jan. 10, 1957; s. Vyacheslav Alexeevich and Julia Petrovna (Yemyasheva) S.; m. Irina Ivanovna Kalitvinova, Sept. 20, 1979; 1 child, Julia Igorevna. Grad., Leningrad Poly. Inst., 1980. Probation mem. staff dept. biology Petersburg Nuclear Physics Inst., Russian Acad. Sci., Gatchina, 1980-81, jr. rschr., 1981-88, rschr., 1988-95, sr. rsch. assoc., 1995—. Contbr. articles to profl. jours.; patentee in field. Officer USSR Army, 1983-85. Home: H 6 93 7 Army St, 188300 Gatchina Russia Office: PNPI BP Konstantinov, Dept Molecular Biology, 188300 Gatchina Russia

SHEVITZ, LAURIE MICHELLE, social services administrator; b. Balt., Oct. 12, 1965; d. Norman Irvin and Natalie Kerxton Yaffe; m. David Lewis Shevitz, Apr. 2, 1989; children: Jessica Carli, Joshua Zachary, Kaylee Gabrielle. BS, Towson U., 1989, postgrad. Cert. chem. dependency counselor; internationally cert. alcohol and drug counselor. Sec. Family Svc. Found., Balt., 1990-91, case mgr. for the deaf, 1991-92, substance abuse therapist for the deaf, 1992-95, program dir. for the deaf substance abuse program, 1997—; cons. Gov.'s Adv. Bd. for Deaf and Hard of Hearing Individuals, Balt. Com. mem. Balt. Substance Abuse Sys., 1997—. Mem. ATAM, Nat. Assn. of the Deaf, Md. Assn. of the Deaf, Cmty. Planning Group, Regional Planning Groups. Avocations: golfing, fishing, photography, kickboxing. E-mail: aniazrie@aol.com. Fax: 410-467-9239. Home: 3811 Tabor Rd Owings Mills MD 21117-1245 Office: Family Svc Found 2310 N Charles St Baltimore MD 21218-5127

SHI, BOLIN, political science educator; b. Changsha, Hunan, China, Sept. 17, 1953; s. Shengwan Shi and Meigu Deng; m. Xiaoping Peng, Oct. 1, 1982; 1 child, Pengyi. B, Xiangtan (China) U., 1982; M, Fundan U., Shanghai, China, 1988. Vice prof. Ctrl. South U. Tech., Changsha, 1982-92, prof., 1992—; legal adviser Dongyong Group, Changsha, 1993-97, Sanjin Corp., Changsha, 1998-99. Author: From Changsha Fire to Hengyang's Failure, 1989 (High rate award History Soc. 1989), The Evolution of Modern Chinese Political System, 1991 (Excellent Works award 1991), The Economy of the Republic of China Under Wretched Circumstances, 1993 (Excellent Works award Hunan Province Govt. 1993), Economic Policy Evolution of Modern China, 1998, The Mode of Rule of Law of the Supervisory Mechanism, 1999, Reform and Revolution, 1999; contbr. articles to profl. jours. Mem. Communist Party China. Sgt. 1st class troops under Guangzhou comd., 1971-77. Recipient Citation Unit 5448 People's Army of China, 1973-76. Mem. Jurisprudence Society of Hunan Province (v.p. 1997-99, 1st prize 1998), Hunan Rule of Law Study Soc. Civil Run Economy (v.p. 1997-99, 1st prize 1998). Avocations: mountain-climbing, tourism, singing, table tennis, badminton. Office: Ctrl South U Tech, 410083 Changsha Hunan, China

SHI, FENG SHENG, mathematician; b. Shanghai, China, Sept. 28, 1935; came to U.S., 1990; s. Jing Long and Xu Wenzheng Shi; m. Dorothy Shi, May 30, 1992. Degree of engr., 1957. Prof. math. and physics U. Industry, Shanghai, 1961-64; ship designer Govt. of China, Shanghai, 1964; rschr., business liaison Hong Kong of U.S.A. Liaison for Bus. Investment; owner, editor Pendulum Math. Jour. in Libr. of Congress; trustee, founder, dir. Chinese Math. Students Orgn., Miami, Fla., 1993—; dir. Chinese Internat. Math. Students Orgn., 1994—; mem. bd. intellectuals, Oxford Internat. Dictionary; trustee Nat. Heritage Found. Author: (math. solutions) Exist, 1991 (Libr. of Congress), Solving the Fermat Problem and Goldbach's Conjecture, 1993. Recipient Son of Yr. award Son's & Daughter's Found., 1990, Internat. award for poetry, Nat. award for Poetry, Gold Star award for knowledge. Mem. All Nations (trustee, bd. dirs. 1990-93, Internat. Man of Yr. 1991). Home and Office: 1000 8th St N Saint Petersburg FL 33701-1510

SHI, GUANG RONG, geology educator, palaeontologist; b. Puqi, Peoples Republic of China, Oct. 23, 1962; arrived in Australia, 1986; s. Ri Xing and Ying Sheng (Ma) S.; m. Rong Zhu Shi, Jan. 16, 1986; children: Robin, Kevin. BS, China U. Geoscis., Peoples Republic of China, 1984; PhD, U. Queensland, Australia, 1991. Rsch. assoc. U. Melbourne, Australia, 1991; rsch. fellow Deakin U., Melbourne, Australia, 1992-94; lectr., 1995-96, sr. lectr., 1997—; sec. Geol. Soc. Australia, Melbourne, 1994-96; guest assoc. rsch. prof. China U. Mining and Tech., Xuzhou, China, 1994—; Australian Official Del. to 30th IGC, Australian Acad. Sci., 1996. Author: Environmental Management in Asia: Training, Education and Research, 1993, Lower Permian brachiopods and mollusca from the Upper Jungle Creek Formation, Yukon Territory, Canada, 1996; contbr. articles to profl. jours. Grantee Australian Rsch. Coun., 1993, 94, 95-99. Avocations: swimming, fossil hunting. Office: Deakin U, 662 Blackburn Rd, Clayton 3168, Australia

SHI, HONG HUI, aeronautical engineer, fluid machinery engineer; b. Fuzhou, Fujian, China, Nov. 11, 1962; s. She Mo and Shu Feng (Li) S.; m. Bin Xu, Oct. 25, 1968. BSc, Xi'an Jiaotong U., Xi'an, China, 1983, MSc, 1986, PhD, 1989; DrEngr, Tohoku U., Sendai, Japan, 1995. Vis. scientist Cambridge (Eng.) U., 1990-91; invited rschr. Tohoku U., Sendai, Japan, 1991-92; asst. prof. Nagoya (Japan) Inst. Tech., 1995-97, lectr., 1997—; expertiment asst. wet steam group Xi'an Jiaotong U., Xi'an, China, 1986-87. Contbr. articles to sci. conf. proceedings and profl. jours. Recipient Tang Zhao-Qian scholarship, Xi'an Jiaotong U., Xi'an, China, 1990, Japanese Govt. scholarship Ministry Edn. Japan, Tokyo, 1992. Mem. AAAS, AIAA, Japan Soc. Mech. Engrs., Japan Soc. for Aeronautical and Space Sci., Japan Explosives Soc., Turbomachinery Soc. Japan, The Gas Turbine Soc. Japan, N.Y. Acad. Scis. Office: Nagoya Inst Tech, Dept Mech Engr Gokiso-cho, Aichi Pr Showa 466-8555, Japan

SHI, JIALAN, pathologist, educator; b. Harbin, China, Feb. 1, 1957; s. Wuyou and Jingzhen (Zhang) S.; m. Yingli Yang, Aug. 1, 1987; 1 child, Yinan. MD, Harbin Med. U., China, 1978-83; MS, Harbin Med. U., 1986-89; PhD, Tokyo Med. and Dental U., 1993-97. Tchg. asst. Harbin Med. U., China, 1983-88, asst. prof., 1988-91; dir. Harbin Med. U., 1989-91; rsch. fellow Tokyo Med. & Dental U., 1991-93, tchg. asst., 1996-98; postdoctoral fellow Harvard Med. Sch., Boston, 1998—. Contbr. articles to profl. jours. Grantee, Japanese Govt., Tokyo, 1991; 3rd prize Acad. Sci., Harbin, China, 1991, 2nd prize Dept. Health, Harbin, 1991. Mem. Japanese Soc. Immunology, N.Y. Acad. Scis., Am. Assn. Advancemsnt Sci., Am. Soc. of Hematology, Am. Chem. Soc. Avocations: swimming, skiing, classical music, travel. Home: 89 Manet Rd Chestnut Hill MA 02467-1167 Office: Brigham and Women's Hosp 75 Francis St Boston MA 02115-6110

SHI, JIUYONG, judge; b. Zhejiang Province, China, Oct. 9, 1926. BA in Govt. and Pub. Law, St. John's U., Shanghai, 1948; MA in Internat. Law, Columbia U., 1951. Rschr. internat. law Columbia U., N.Y.C., 1951-54; asst. rsch. fellow in internat. law Inst. Internat. Rels., Beijing, 1956-58; sr. lectr., assoc. prof. internat. law Fgn. Affairs Coll., Beijing, 1958-64, prof. internat. law, 1984-93; rsch. fellow in internat. law Inst. Internat. Law, Beijing, 1964-73, Inst. Internat. Studies, Beijing, 1973-80; prof. law Fgn. Econ. Law Tng. Ctr. Ministry of Justice, Beijing, 1985-86; judge Internat. Ct. Justice, The Hague, The Netherlands, 1994—, v.p., 2000—; legal advisor Chinese Del. ann. meeting bd. govs. IMF and Internat. Bank for Reconstrn. and Devel., 1980, Office of Chinese Sr. Rep., Sino-Brit. Joint Liaison Group, 1985-93, Ministry Fgn. Affairs, Beijing, 1980-93, numerous other Chinese dels. to UN Gen. Assemblies and other fgn. govts.; mem. fgn. econ. and trade arbitration commn. China Coun. Promotion Internat. Trade, 1984-88; mem. standing com., Beijing com. Chinese People's Polit. Consultative Conf., 1988-93, mem. 8th nat. com., 1993; mem. Internat. Law Commn., 1987-93, rapporteur, 1988, chmn., 1990; expert of China Sr. Legal Expert Meetings on rev. Montevideo Programme, UN Environ. Programme, 1991; tchr. internat. law Dept. Law Peking U., 1980-85, Fgn. Econ. Law Tng. Ctr., Ministry of Justice of China, 1988; lectr. Nat. Bur. Oceanography, China, 1986, Hague Acad. Internat. Law Regional Program, Beijing, 1987, Peking U., China, 1987, 88, 89, 91, Grad. Inst. Internat. Studies, Geneva, 1988, others; mem. steering com. on revision of Hague Conv. of 1907 on Pacific Settlement of Internat. Disputes of Permanent Ct. of Arbitration, 1994—; participant in numerous confs. and meetings. Mem. Chinese Soc. Internat. Law (adviser), Chinese Law Soc. (mem. coun. Inst. Hong Kong Law), Am. Soc. Internat. Law. Office: Peace Palace, Carnegieplein 2, 2517 KJ The Hague The Netherlands

SHI, JONATHAN JINGSHENG, engineering educator; b. Huangmei, Hubei, China, June 19, 1962; arrived in Canada, 1992; s. Haitao and Xingmei (Xiong) S.; m. Junli Bai; children: Sandy, David. BSc, Wahan U. Tech., China, 1982, MSc, 1985; PhD, U. Alta., 1995. Lectr. Wuhan U. Tech., China, 1985-92; rschr. Constrn. Rsch. Inst., China, 1985-92; rsch. assoc. U. Alta., 1992-95; asst. prof. City U. Hong Kong, 1995-98, assoc. prof., 1999; assoc. prof. Ill. Inst. Tech., Chgo., 1999—. Contbr. articles to profl. jours. Province of Alta. Grad. fellow U. Alta., 1995. Mem. Am. Soc. Civil Engrs., Hong Kong Instn. Engrs., Constrn. Mgmt. Assn. Am. Home: 1100 Columbian Ave Oak Park IL 60302-1226

SHI, MEIREN, chemical engineering educator; b. Yuyao, China, Apr. 12, 1934; s. Rugi and Lindi (Ye) S.; m. Juzhen Zhang, Oct. 17, 1934; children: Jin, Lei, Hong. B of Engring., Zhejiang U., Hongzhou, China, 1955; MChemE, Acad. Scis. China, Taiyuan, China, 1964. Rsch. trainee Inst. of Coal Acad. Scis. of China, Dalian, China, 1955-61; asst. rsch. fellow Inst. of Coal Chemistry Acad. Scis. of China, Taiyuan, China, 1961-78, assoc. rsch. fellow Inst. Coal Chemistry, 1978-83; assoc. rsch. fellow Nanjing (China) U. Chem. Tech., 1983-86, prof., 1986—. Contbr. articles to profl. jours. Recipient First award of Shanxi Province for Sci. and Tech. Rsch Report, 1979, First award of Acad. Scis. of China for Sci and Tech. Rsch. Report, 1983, Third award, 1990. Office: Nanjing U Chem Tech, #5 Xinmofan Rd, Jiangsu 210009, China

SHI, MIN, science educator, researcher; b. Shanghai, China, Jan. 5, 1963; s. Zheng Yuan Shi and Mei Li Shen; m. Hong Gao, March 20, 1999. B, Sci. and Tech. U. East China, Shanghai, 1984; M, Gifu U., Japan, 1988; D, Osaka U., Japan, 1991. Engr. Gifu Shellac Co., 1991-93; asst. prof. Gifu Pharm. U., 1993-95; postdoctoral fellow Okla. U., Norman, 1995-96, Inoue Photochirogenesis Project Zrato JST, Osaka, 1996-98; assoc. prof. Shanghai Inst. Organic Chemistry Chinese Acad. Scis., Shanghai, 1998—. Contbr. articles to profl. jours. Mem. ACS, Chinese Chem. Soc., Chem. Soc. Japan. Avocations: tennis, golf. Home: 5 Ln 362 Fenglin Rd 401, 200032 Shanghai China Office: Shanghai Inst Organic Chem, Chinese Acad Scis, 200032 Shanghai China

SHI, MING FENG, engineer; b. Ningbo, Zhejiang, China, Apr. 5, 1960; came to U.S., 1984; s. Benfa and Xuachai S.; m. Haoming Li, July 24, 1986; children: Lucy Z., Jennifer S., Michael S. BS, Hehai U., Nanjing, China, 1982; MS, Mich. Tech. U., 1986, PhD, 1989. Project engr. Nat. Steel Corp., Livonia, Mich., 1989-90, sr. engr., 1991-93, staff specialist, 1994-96; tech. specialist U.S. Steel, Troy, Mich., 1997-99, tech. mgr., 2000—; Presenter in field. Author: (papers) Zinc-Based Steel Coating Systems Metallurgy and Performance, 1990, Automotive Stamping Technology, 1993, 95, 99. Treas. Chinese Sch. of Greater Detroit, 1996-97. Named to Outstanding Young Men of Am., 1996. Mem. Soc. Automotive Engr., Am. Soc. for Metals (Outstanding Young Mem. award 1995-96), The Minerals, Metals, Materials. Avocations: basketball, ping-pong, golf. Home: 5470 White Hall Cir West Bloomfield MI 48323-3459

SHI, PENG, mathematics researcher; b. Harbin, China, Feb. 10, 1958; arrived in Australia, 1989; s. Jin Che Shi and De Yun Zou; m. Feng Mei Sun; children: Bo Lisa, Michael. B in Math., U. Harbin, 1982, M in Engring., 1985; PhD in Elec. Engring., U. Newcastle, Australia, 1994. Postgrad. applied math. diplomate. Assoc. lectr. Heilongjiang U., Harbin, 1985-86, lectr., 1986-89; rsch. assoc. Newcastle U., 1994-95; postdoctoral fellow U. South Australia, Adelaide, 1995-97, lectr., 1998—. Contbr. articles to profl. jours. Recipient 2nd prize Heilongjiang Com. of Sci. Tech., Harbin, 1988. Sr. mem. IEEE, Soc. Indsl. and Applied Math. Avocations: tennis, bridge, cards, swimming. Home: 36 Goodfield Rd, Adelaide 5096, Australia Office: Sch Math, U South Australia, Adelaide 5095, Australia

SHI, XUAN ZHENG, medical physiologist, researcher; b. Susong, Anhui, China, Oct. 18, 1962; came to U.S., 1992; s. Guo Cun Shi and Zhi Yin Zhu; m. Ping Fu, Sept. 14, 1987; 1 child, Bo Shi. MD, Wannan Med. Coll., Wuhu, Anhui, China, 1984; MS in Physiology, Med. Coll. Wis., 1997. Postgrad. fellow Lanzhou (China) Med. Coll., 1984-87, lectr., 1987-92; vis. scholar Med. Coll. Wis., Milw., 1992-94, postdoctoral fellow, 1997-98, rsch. scientist, 1998—. Contbr. articles to profl. jours. Recipient fellowship Internat. Union Physiol. Scis., 1992, Young Investigator award Am. Motility Soc., 1998, Young Investigator award Internat. Motility Soc., Belgium, 1999. Mem. Crohn's and Colitis Found. Am., Chinese Physiol. Assn., Gansu Physiol. Assn. China (sec.-in-chief 1990-92), N.Y. Acad. Scis. E-mail: xshi@mcw.edu. Office: Med Coll Wis Dept Surgery 9200 W Wisconsin Ave Milwaukee WI 53226-3522

SHI, YANGGU, genomics scientist; b. Ninhua, China, Apr. 20, 1964; came to U.S., 1985; BS, Peking U., Beijing, 1984; PhD, NYU, 1992. Postdoctoral rschr. Columbia U., N.Y.C., 1992-95; scientist Human Genome Scis., Rockville, Md., 1996—. Contbr. articles to profl. jours.; patentee in field. Cancer Rsch. Inst. fellow, 1993. Office: Human Genome Scis 9410 Key West Ave Rockville MD 20850-3331

SHI, YAOLIN, geophysics educator; b. Guilin, Guangxi, China, Feb. 10, 1944; s. Yiyong and Rugui (Yu) S.; m. Jia Qi, Apr. 15, 1971; children: Jing, Peng. BS, U. Sci. and Tech. China, 1966; MA, U. Calif., Berkeley, 1982, PhD, 1986. Engr. Inst. Geomechanics, Beijing, 1968-78; assoc. prof. grad. sch. U. Sci. and Tech. China, Beijing, 1988-89, prof. grad. sch., 1989—; chmn. dept. earth scis. Grad. Sch., Academia Sinica, Beijing, 1993-96, dep. pres., 1996—. Contbr. over 100 articles to profl. jours. Mem. Seismol. Soc. China (standing coun. mem. 1992—), Chinese Geophy. Geol. Soc., Am. Geophys. Union. Fax: 86-10-68210501. E-mail: shiyl@sun.ihep.ac.cn. Office: U Sci and Tech China, 19a Yuquan Rd Acad Sinica, 100039 Beijing China

SHI, YONG, information science educator; b. Chengdu, Sichuan, China, Aug. 24, 1956; came to U.S., 1985; s. Yuanqing Shi and Guihua Li; m. Bailing Gong, Aug. 30, 1984; 1 child, Christopher S.B. BS in Math., S.W. Petroleum Inst., Nanchong, China, 1982; PhD in Bus., U. Kans., 1991. Disting. chair, prof. info. tech. U. Nebr., Omaha, 1999—. Contbr. articles to profl. jours. Mem. IEEE (Disting. Visitor Program 1997—). Home: 16024 Wakeley St Omaha NE 68118-2080 Office: Coll Info Sci and Tech U Nebr-Omaha Omaha NE 68182

SHI, ZHAOYUN, engineering educator, statistics educator; b. Cixi, Zhejiang, China, Sept. 9, 1965; s. Xingkun Shi and Meijuan Huang; m. Ying Dai, June 6, 1990; 1 child. B in Engring., S.E. U., Nanjing, China, 1987, M in Engring., 1991, D in Engring., 1997; PhD, Grad. U. Advanced Studies, Tokyo, 1999. Rsch. assoc. S.E. U., Nanjing, 1987-93, lectr., 1993—; vis. sr. rsch. fellow Inst. Statistical Maths., Tokyo, 1997—. Author: Advancement in Research of Chaos, 1999; contbr. articles to profl. jours. Scholar Japan Ministry Edn., 1995-97; recipient Best Paper prize China Soc. Inertial Tech., 1992, Sci. and Tech. Progress prize China Stateship Industry, 1994. Mem. Japan Statistical Soc., Japan Soc. Precision Engring. Avocations: reading, sports, volleyball, classical music. Office: Inst Statistical Maths, 4-6-7 Minami-Azabu, 106-8569 Minato-ku Tokyo, Japan

SHI, ZHONGZHI, computer science researcher; b. Jiangsu, China, Sept. 12, 1941; s. Zelin Shi and Fenpei Jiang; m. Zhihua Yu, Oct. 1, 1970; children: Jing, Jun. BS, U. Sci. & Tech. China, Beijing, 1964; MS, Chinese Acad. Scis., Beijing, 1968. Rschr. assn. Inst. Computing Tech., Chinese Acad. Scis., Beijing, 1968-80, assoc. prof., 1983-89, prof., 1990—; prof., dir. dept. computer sci. U Sci. & Tech. China Grad. Sch., Beijing, 1994—; vis. scholar Ohio State U., Columbus, 1980-82, U. Md., College Park, 1982-83; vis. prof. Erasmus U. Rotterdam, The Netherlands, 1989-90. Authro: Knowledge Engineering, 1988, Principles of Machine Learning, 1991, Neural Computing, 1993, Advanced Artificial Intelligence, 1998. Grantee Multimedia Info. Retrieval Sys., Beijing, 1996, Multiagent Environment, Beijing, 1998. Mem. IEEE (sr.), Internat. Fedn. Info. Processing Tech. Com. 12, Chinese Assn. Artificial Intelligence (v.p. 1991—), Pacific Rim Internat. Conf. on AI (standing com. mem. 1992—). E-mail: shizz@ics.ict.ac.cn. Fax: 86-10-62567724. Home: Rm 107, Zhongguan Village Bldg 952, Beijing 100080, China Office: Inst Computing Tech CAS, Zhongguan Village Kexueyuan, Beijing 100080, China

SHIAU, YUH YUAN, dentist, educator; b. Taipei, Taiwan, Sept. 1, 1942; s. Long Yuh Shiau and Yueh Li Tang; m. Mei Hwei Lee, Dec. 6, 1969; children: Yu-Shuan, Bei-Chen. DDS, Nat. Taiwan U., Taipei, 1967; MS in Dentistry, U. Mich., 1979. Assoc. prof. Sch. Dentistry Nat. Taiwan U., 1981-87, prof., 1987—, dir. Grad. Inst. Oral Biology, Sch. Dentistry, 1997—; cons. Nat. Health Dept., Republic of Taiwan, Taipei, 1998—. Author: (textbook) Medicine and Art, 1999 (Coll. Medicine prize); contbr. articles to profl. jours. 2d lt. Taiwan Army, 1967-68. Recipient Outstanding Rsch. award Nat. Sci. Coun., 1990-99; rsch. grantee Nat. Sci. Coun., 1990-99. Mem. Assn. Dental Scis. Republic of China (pres. 1999—), Internat. Assn. Dental Scis. (pres. S.E. Asia divsn. 1996-98), Alumni Assn. Coll. Medicine Nat. Taiwan U. (pres. 1996—). Home: 159-19-49 Sang-Ming Rd, Shin-Tian 231, Taipei Taiwan Office: Nat Taiwan U Coll Medicine, 1 Chang-Te St, 100 Taipei Taiwan

SHIBASAKI, SOSUKE See CIVASAQUI, JOSE

SHIBASAKI, YOSHIO, chemistry educator, researcher; b. Gyoda, Japan, Mar. 21, 1934; s. Reiji and Shige (Kobayashi) S.; m. Teiko Ishizuka Shibasaki, Apr. 15, 1967; children: Hideaki, Miki. BS, Saitama U., Japan, 1959; DSc, U. Tokyo, 1980. Tech. official U. Tokyo, Japan, 1960-63, asst., 1963-67; lectr. Saitama U., Urawa, Japan, 1967-70, assoc. prof., 1970-92, prof., 1992-99, ret., 1999. Inventor: Kobunshi Kagaku, 1964, J. Polymer Science, 1967, 80, 98, 99. Mem. AAAS, Internat. Conf. Thermal Analysis and Calorimetry, Japan Soc. Calorimetry and Thermal Analysis, N.Y. Acad. Sci. Avocations: appreciation of pictures. Home: 1642 Tsutsumine, Gyoda 361-0035, Japan

SHIBATA, AKENORI, structural engineering educator; b. Shizuoka, Japan, Dec. 4, 1936; s. Kozo and Masa (Sanguu) S.; m. Kishiko Iizumi, May 28, 1967; children: Masahiro, Takahiro. B of Engring., U. Tokyo, 1960, M of Engring, 1962, DEng, 1965. Rsch. assoc. Tohoku U., Sendai, Japan, 1965, assoc. prof., 1966-86, prof., 1986-99; prof. Tohoku Bunka Gakuen U.,

1999—. Author: (book) Earthquake Resistant Analysis and Design, 1981. Com. mem. The Bldg. Ctr. of Japan, Tokyo, 1980; chmn. Nuclear Power Engring. Corp., Tokyo, 1990. Recipient Acad. prize Archtl. Inst. of Japan, Tokyo, 1986. Mem. ASCE, Japan Soc. Natural Disaster Sci. (pres. 1996-99), Japan Soc. Civil Engrs., Am. Concrete Inst., Archtl. Inst. Japan. Home: 14-30 Yagiyama-Kasumicho, Sendai 982-0831, Japan Office: Tohoku Bunka Gakuen U, 6-45-16 Kunimi Aoba-ku, Sendai 981-8551, Japan

SHIBATA, AKIKAZU, engineer, semiconductor scientist; b. Sendai, Japan, Feb. 25, 1935; s. Kitaro and Toshi (Tsushima) S.; m. Saeko Margaret Kurakake (wid. 1994); children: Yasushi, Izumi. BA, Internat. Christian U., Mitaka, Japan, 1957; MA, Cornell U., Ithaca, N.Y., 1959; D in Engring., Nagoya (Japan) U., 1967. Rsch. asst. Cornell U., Ithaca, 1957-59; rsch. sci. Sony Corp., Tokyo, 1959-61, Sony Rsch. Ctr., Yokohama, 1976-84; gen. mgr. engring. Sony Trading Corp., Tokyo, 1980-83; staff sci. Sony Rsch. Ctr., Tokyo, 1984-86; mgr., internat. standardization Sony Corp., Tokyo, 1987-2000; tech. advisor Japan Printed Circuit Assn., Tokyo, 2000—. Contbr. articles to profl. jours.; patentee in field. Recipient Spl. Recognition award Japanese Stds. Assn. for contbns. to internat. standardization, 1996, Recognition award Minister of the Internat. Trade and Industry of the Japanese Govt., 1996, Electronics Industries Assn. Japan, 1998. Mem. IEEE. Home: 914 Serizawa, Chigasaki 253-0008, Japan Office: Japan Printed Circuit Assn, 3-12-2 Nishiogikubokita, Suginami Tokyo 167-0042, Japan

SHIBATA, MITSUHIRO, chemist, educator; b. Higashiosaka, Osaka, Japan, Dec. 30, 1957; s. Yoshihisa and Mikiko (Tomura) S.; m. Yoko Iida, Oct. 1, 1964; children: Naohisa, Saki, Takashi. Bachelor's, Osaka (Japan) U., 1980; MEng, Kyoto (Japan) U., 1982, DEng, 1985. Rsch. assoc. Sumitomo Chem. Co. Ltd, Osaka, 1990-96; asst. prof. Chiba Inst. Tech., Narashino, Japan, 1996—. Patentee in field. Mem. The Soc. of Polymer Sci., Chem. Soc. of Japan. Home: 6-6-6 Kinunodai Yawaramura, Tsukubagun, Ibaraki 300-24, Japan Office: Chiba Inst Tech, 2-17-1 Tsudanuma, Narashino 275-0016, Japan

SHIBATA, MOTOHIRO, pediatrician; b. Nagoya, Japan, Sept. 11, 1952; s. Sadao and Kikuyo (Nishigaki) S.; m. Kumiko Yoshikawa, Oct. 10, 1984; children: Hirofumi, Takenori, Katsuaki. MD, Nagoya U., 1977, PhD, 1983. Vis. fellow NIH, Bethesda, Md., 1986-88; lectr. Nagoya Univ. Sch. Medicine, 1992—; assoc. head Chukyo Hosp., Nagoya, 1992—, chief pediatrician, 1997—. Contbr. articles to profl. jours. Mem. AAAS, N.Y. Acad. Scis., Japan Pediat. Soc., Japanese Hepatic Assn., Japanese Soc. for Virology, Japanese Assn. for Infectious Diseases. Office: Chukyo HospDept Radiology, 1-1-10 Sanjo Minami ku, Nagoya 457-0866, Japan

SHIBATA, SUSUMU, electric company researcher; b. Hiroshima, Japan, May 1, 1942; s. Takashi and Hiroko (Tada) S.; m. Ayako Dobashi, Apr. 1, 1972; children: Tomoko, Fumihiro. BS, Waseda U., Tokyo, 1966, ME, 1968; D Engring., Sci. U. Tokyo, 1988. Cert. cons. engr. Mgr. Oki Electric Industry Co., Ltd., Hachioji City, Japan, 1980-85, gen. mgr., 1985-91; sr. rsch. mgr., 1992-95; rsch. mgr. superconductivity rsch. lab. Internat. Superconductivity Tech. Ctr., 1995—; operating committeeman, chmn., co-chmn. 5th Internat. Microelectronics Conf., Tokyo, 1988, 6th, 1990. Co-author: Electronic Devices and Thin Film, 1991; assoc. editor spl. issue IEICI Trans. on Electronics, 1991; numerous patents in Japan; patentee thermal printing head, thermal head in U.S. Recipient 12th Ichimura award, Japan, 1985, outstanding tech. paper award 5th Internat. Microelectronics Conf., 1988, outstanding paper award 6th Conf., 1990. Mem. IEEE, IEEE Components, Hybrids and Mfg. Tech. Soc. (sec., treas. Tokyo chpt. 1987-91, operating com., chmn. Japan Internat. Electronic Mfg. Tech. Symposium 1989, operating com. 1991, fin. com. 1993), Inst. Electronics Info. and Communication Engrs., Japan Soc. Mech. Engrs. (rsch. com. on thermal and/or mech. problems of micro devices). Avocation: art appreciation. Office: Superconductivity Rsch Lab, 10-13 Shinonome 1-chome, Koto-Ku Tokyo 135, Japan

SHIBATA, TAIRA, construction company executive; b. Jan. 7, 1920. Grad., Seoul U., Korea, 1944. Mng. dir. Nishimatsu Constrn. Corp., Tokyo, 1977, chmn. bd. Office: Nishimatsu Constrn Co Ltd, 20-10 Toranomon 1-Chrome, Minatoku Tokyo Japan*

SHIBATA, TAKANORI, oral and maxillofacial surgeon, researcher; b. Tokyo, Aug. 16, 1951; s. Yoshinori and Kotaka (Tsuru) S.; m. Midori Mashiko, July 7, 1973; children: Schun, Ryoko. DDS, Tokyo Dental Coll., 1977, PhD, 1981. Mem. faculty Tokyo Dental Coll., 1981-89; asst. prof. Yamagata (Japan) U. Sch. Medicine, 1989-93, assoc. prof., 1993—; advisor Japanese Social and Health Ins. Found., Yamagata, 1992—. Editor, author: (books) Fundamentals and Managements of Tempotomandibular Joint Disorders, 1986, Encyclopedia of Temporomandibular Joint, 1990, 93. Mem. Internat. Assn. for Dental Rsch., Internat. Assn. Oral and Maxillofacial Surgeons, Osteoarthritis Rsch. Soc. Avocation: fishing. Fax: 81-23-628-5416. E-mail: tshibata@med.id.yamagata-u.ac.jp. Office: Yamagata U Sch Medicine, 2-2-2 Iidanishi, Yamagata 990-9585, Japan

SHIBAZAKI, AKIRA, veterinary surgery educator; b. Kamakura, Kanagawa, Japan, Oct. 11, 1969; s. Yilchiro and Chikako (Ito) S. DVM, Azabu U., Kanagawa, Japan, 1995; PhD, Gifu (Japan) Prefecture U., 1999. Asst. prof. vet. surgery Osaka (Japan) Prefecture U., 1999—. Contbr. articles to profl. jours. Mem. Japanese Soc. Vet. Sci., Japanese Soc. Small Amimal Vet. Sci., Japanese Soc. Clin. Vet. Medicine. Avocations: driving, fishing, scuba diving. Home: 3-18-3-108 Shirasagi-cho, Sakai, Osaka 599-8107, Japan Office: Osaka Prefecture U Coll Agr, Gakuen-cho 1-1, Sakai, Osaka 599-8531, Japan

SHIBUE, YASUHIRO, geologist, educator; b. Higashi-Osaka, Japan, Sept. 9, 1955; s. Keiichi and Misako (Sugishita) S.; m. Yumiko Yanai, Feb. 28, 1988; children: Mika, Akitoshi. BS, U. Tokyo, 1979, MS, 1981, PhD, 1986. Rsch. asst. Hyogo U. Tchr. Edn., 1987-88, asst. prof., 1988-90, assoc. prof., 1990-99, prof., 1999—. Author: Proceedings Eighth IAGOD Symposium, 1993; contbr. articles to profl. jours including Geochem. jours., 1996, Clays and Clay Minerals, 1981, Am. Mineralogist, 1999. Home: Suehiro Mansion A-3, Oomura 426, Hyogo Miki City 673-0404, Japan Office: Geosci Inst Hyogo U Tchr En, Yashiro-cho Kato-gun, Hyogo 673-1494, Japan

SHIBUYA, AKIRA, immunologist, researcher; b. Yokote, Akita, Japan, July 26, 1955; s. Takeshi and Chie (Saitoh) S.; m. Kazuko Sugita, June 4, 1988; children: Ko, Megumi. MD, Hokkaido U., Sapporo, Japan, 1981; PhD, U. Tsukuba, Japan, 1996. Resident Mitsui Meml. Hosp., Tokyo, 1981-85; chief resident Tsukuba U. Hosp., 1985-87; clin. staff Tokyo Met. Bokuto Hosp., 1987-89; asst. prof. U. Tsukuba, 1989-93, assoc. prof., 1998—; postdoctoral fellow DNAX Rsch. Inst., Palo Alto, Calif., 1993-96; asst. prof. Okayama (Japan) U., 1996-98. Contbr. articles to profl. jours. Recipient award Ohmoni Taro Meml. Found., 1993. Office: Inst Basic Med Scis, U Tsukuba, Tsukuba, Ibaraki 305-8575, Japan

SHIDEHARA, FRANCESCO EICHI, musicologist, educator; b. Kobe, Hyogo, Japan, May 8, 1935; s. Masamichi and Yasuko (Shidehara) Honda; m. Naoko Takagawa, Nov. 20, 1967; children: Sonoko, Kaoru. B in Econs., Osaka (Japan) U., 1958; BA, Tokyo U., 1964, MA, 1967. Lectr. Musashino Acad. Music, Tokyo, 1967-69, assoc. prof., 1969-84; prof. Hiroshima (Japan) U., 1984-94, Doshisha Women's Coll. of Liberal Arts, Kyoto, Japan, 1994—; prof. emeritus Hiroshima U., 1995—. Mem. Japanese Soc. for Aesthetics, Musicological Soc. Japan, Internat. Musicological Soc., Japanese Soc. for 18th Century Studies. Anglican. Avocation: violin playing. Home: 1565 Kishimoto Mikage, Higashinada-ku, Kobe 658-0056, Japan Office: Doshisha Womens Coll, Kohdo Kyotanabe, Kyoto 610-0332, Japan

SHIDHAM, VINOD BABURAO, pathologist, cytopathologist, surgical pathologist; b. Wani, India, Mar. 23, 1954; s. Baburao T. and Sunanda Baburao Shidham; m. Anjani Vinod Shidham, Dec. 31, 1983; children: Sushrut, Anushree. MBBS in Physiology with honors, Govt. Med. Coll., Nagpur, India, 1975, MD in Pathology, 1979. Diplomate Am. Bd. Pathology Cytopathology, Am. Bd. Pathology, Royal Coll. Pathologists. Rotating intern Govt. Med. Coll., 1976, resident in pathology, 1977, lectr., 1977-83; assoc. prof. Grant Med. Coll., Baljurashi, India, 1983-85; dir. pathology, cons. histo/cytopathology Siddham Pathology Lab., Ghamed Nat. Clinic, RST Cancer Ctr., Rsch. Ctr., Nagpur, Saudi Arabia, 1985-92; hematologist Al-Ymamah Specialist Hosp., Riyadh, Saudi Arabia, 1992-94; resident, chief resident, then cytopathology fellow Allegheny U. Helath Scis., Phila., 1994-98; asst. prof., dir. cytopathology tng. program Med. Coll. Wis., Milw., 1998—, also dir. fine needle aspiration biopsy svc., 1998—. Contbr. or co-contbr. articles to profl. jours., including Acta Cytologica, Diagnostic Cytopathology, Am. Jour. Clin. Pathology, Archives of Pathology and Lab. Medicine, Am. Jour. Clin. Oncology, Am. Jour. Ophthalmology, Lab. Medicine. Fellow Internat. Acad. Cytology; mem. Coll. Am. Pathologists (molecular biology workshop stipend 1996), Am. Soc. Clin. Pathologists, U.S. and Can. Acad. Pathologists, Am. Soc. Cytopathology, Am. Assn. for Cancer Rsch., Wis. Soc. Pathologists (program chair in tng. 1998—, Hematology Assn. Ctrl. India (founding, joint sec. 1991-94), Royal Coll. Pathologists (London)(diplomate), Internat. Acad. Cytology. Hindu. Avocations: gardening, photography, painting, crafts. Fax: 414-80584445. E-mail: vshidham@mcw.edu. Office: Med Coll Wis Dept Pathology 9200 W Wisconsin Ave Milwaukee WI 53226-3522

SHIDRAWI, GEORGE ROMANOS, entomologist, consultant; b. Hadeth El-Jobbeh, North, Lebanon, Oct. 27, 1932; s. Romanos Salim and Marie Joseph (El-Khoury Hanna) S.; m. Odile Toufic Chaptini, Feb. 17, 1963; children: Brigitte, Ray, Tatiana. BS, Am. U., Beirut, 1953; MSc, Sch. Hygiene and Tropical Medicine, London, 1955; DSc, Pacific We. U., 1974. Entomologist malaria control bur. Ministry Health, Beirut, 1955-56, dir. divsn. malaria eradication, insects and rodent control, 1956-59; entomologist malaria pre-eradication survey team WHO, Tunis, Tunisia, 1959; entomologist malaria eradication team WHO, Lahore and Dacca, Pakistan, 1959-63; entomologist interregional malaria rsch. team WHO, Masaka, Uganda, 1963-65, Kankiya, Nigeria, 1965-69; sr. entomologist interregional rsch. team epidemiology malaria WHO, Garki, Nigeria, 1969-73; regional entomologist Ea. Mediterranean Regional Office/WHO, Alexandria, Egypt, 1974-79; regional adviser med. entomology WHO, Alexandria, Egypt, 1980-84, regional adviser vector biology and control, 1984-86; scientist, entomologist ecology and control vectors WHO, Geneva, 1986-88, scientist, entomologist vector control tech. vector biology, 1989, scientist/entomologist tng. and devel. of tng. tech., 1990, scientist/entomologist, operational rsch., 1990-92, cons., 1992—; short term cons. WHO, Pakistan, 1992, Egypt, 1992, 94, Saudi Arabia, 1992, 96, Kuwait, 1994, Syria, 1994, Madagaskar, 1994, Sudan, 1995, Iraq, 1995, 98, Sri Lanka, 1996, Indonesia, 1996, Lebanon, 1996, Yemen, 1996, 99. Avocations: horology, philately, numismatics, golf, dancing. Home: 9 Av de Sardaigne, 74160 Saint-Julien-en-Genevois France

SHIEH, JIANN-SHING, mechanical engineering educator; b. Taipei, Taiwan, Feb. 28, 1960; s. Yo-Ming and Lin-cha (Lin) S.; m. I-Yun Hsiao, June 28, 1997; 1 child, Yuan-Lun. BSChemE, Nat. Cheng Kung U., Tainan, Taiwan, 1983, MSChemE, 1986; PhD in Automatic Control & Sys. Engring., Sheffield (Eng.) U., 1995. Tchg. asst. Nat. Cheng Kung U., 1983-86; assoc. engr. FIRDI, Hsin-Chu, Taiwan, 1989-91; rsch. assoc. Sheffield U., 1995-96, Nat. Taiwan U., Taipei, 1996-98; asst. prof. YIMT, Hsin-Chu, 1998-99, Yuan Ze U., Chung-Li, Taiwan, 1999—. Contbr. articles to profl. jours. Avocations: basketball, tennis, golf. Home: No 21 LN2 Yuh-Min 4 Rd, 112 Taipei Taiwan Office: Yuan Ze U, 135 Yuan-Tung Rd, 320 Chung-Li Taoyuan Taiwan

SHIEH, WEI T., senior hardware design engineer; b. Keelung, Taiwan, Jan. 22, 1934; came to U.S., 1961; m. Mei W. Huang, Dec. 30, 1961; children: Karl, Karen, Denise. BASc, U. Toronto, 1961; MS, U. Ill., 1963, PhD, 1968. Rsch. metallurgist Timcen Co. Rsch. Ctr., Canton, Ohio, 1968-69, rsch. specialist, 1969-72, rsch. mission leader, 1972-77; engr. Gen. Electric Co., Utica, N.Y., 1977-87, sr. engr., 1988-91; cons. Ford Electronics, Lansdale, Pa., 1992-93; sr. hardware design engr. Lockheed Martin Corp., Pittsfield, Mass., 1993-96, Gen. Dynamics, Pittsfield, 1997—. Contbg. author: Resistance Welding Manual, 1997; editor: Microelectronic Packaging Technology, 1989; contbr. articles to profl. jours. including Corrosion Jour., Jour. Applied Physics, Internat. Jour. Fracture, Engring. Fracture Mechs., Metallurg. Trans., Internat. Inst. Weld Conf. Mem. ASM Internat. (chmn. electronic packaging and interconnect group of 4 tech. coms. 1987-90, session chmn. microelectronic packaging confs. 1987-88, conf. chmn. electronic packaging conf. 1989), Am. Welding Soc. (chmn. resistance welding/test methods subcom. 1979—). Achievements include development of world's first maximum shear fatigue test method to observe crack initiation and propagation by inclusion in bearing steels. Avocations: swimming, skiing, fishing, concerts, plays. Home: 66 Norwich Dr Dalton MA 01226-1707 Office: Gen Dynamics Corp 100 Plastics Ave Pittsfield MA 01201-3632

SHIEH, WUNG YANG, microbiologist, educator, researcher; b. Taipei County, Taiwan, Sept. 22, 1956. Master, U. Tokyo, 1986, doctor, 1989. Assoc. prof. Inst. of Oceanography, Nat. Taiwan U., Taipei, 1989-94, prof., 1994—. Contbr. articles to profl. jours. Office: Nat Taiwan U, Inst Oceanog, No 1 Sec 4 Roosevelt Rd, Taipei 106, Taiwan

SHIELDS, CAROL ANN, writer, educator; b. Oak Park, Ill., June 2, 1935; came to Can., 1957, naturalized, 1974.; d. Robert Elmer and Inez Adelle (Sellgren) Warner; m. Donald Hugh Shields, July 20, 1957; chldren: John, Anne, Catherine, Margaret, Sara. BA, Hanover Coll., 1957; MA, U. Ottawa, Ont., Can., 1975; hon. degree, U. Ottawa, 1995, Hanover Coll., 1996, Queen's U., 1996, U. Winnipeg, 1996, U.B.C., 1996, U. Western Ont., 1997, U. Toronto, 1998, Concordia U., 1998, Carleton U., 2000. Editl. asst. Can. Slavonic Papers, Ottawa, 1972-74; lectr. U. Ottawa, 1976-77, U.B.C., Vancouver, Can., 1978-80; prof. U. Man., Winnipeg, Can., 1980-2000, prof. emerita, 2000—; chancellor U. Winnipeg, 1996-2000; chancellor emerita, 2000—. Author: (poems) Others, 1972, Intersect, 1974, Coming to Canada, 1991; (novels) Small Ceremonies, 1976, the Box Garden, 1977, Happenstance, 1980, A Fairly Conventional Women, 1982, Various Miracles, 1985, Swann: A Mystery, 1987, The Orange Fish, 1989, The Republic of Love, 1992, the Stone Diaries, 1993 (Nat.Book Critics Circle award for fiction 1995, Pulitzer Prize for fiction 1995), Larry's Party, 1997 (Orange prize for fiction 1998), Dressing Up for the Carnival, 2000; (play) Women Waiting, 1983, Departures and Arrivals, 1984, Thirteen Hands, 1993; (with Catherine Shields) Fashion Power Guilt; (with David Williamson) Aniversary, 1998. Grantee Can. Council, 1973, 76, 78, 86, Man Arts Council, 1984, 85; recipient prize CBC, 1983, 84, Nat. Mag. award, 1985, Arthur Ellis award, 1987, Can. Book Sellers' award 1994, Manitoba Book of the Yr., 1994, Marian Engel award Writers' Devl. Trust, 1990, Gov. Gen's award Can. Coun., 1993, Nat. Book Critics Circle award, 1995, Pulitzer prize, 1999; Order of Can.; Guggenheim Fellowship 1999. Mem. PEN, Writers Union Can., Writers Guild Man., Jane Austen Soc., Royal Soc. Can. Quaker. Home: 990 Terrace Ave, Victoria, BC Canada V8S 3V3 Office: care Bella Pomer Agency Inc, 22 Shallmar Blvd Penthouse 2, Toronto, ON Canada M5N 2Z8

SHIELDS, MARTHA BUCKLEY, middle school educator; b. Ridley Park, Pa., Mar. 4, 1942; d. John Edward and Anne Josephine (Hayes) Buckley; m. James F. Shields, Aug. 22, 1964; children: James F., Martha S. Runzer, Katharine Anne Shields Landaiche, John Edward. BA, Wheeling (W.Va) Jesuit U., 1964; postgrad., Widener U., Chester, Pa., 1975-76. Cert. paralegal. Exec. asst. Economy Engring. and Machine Works, Chester, 1970-77; tchr. gifted program RoseTree-Media S.D., Media, Pa., 1979-80; tchr. grade 5 St. Kevin Sch., Springfield, Pa., 1980-85; tchr. honors math. grades 4-7 St. Thomas the Apostle Sch., Glen Mills, Pa., 1985-97, tchr. 7th grade, 1997—; bd. dirs. Chester County Voices Abroad, 1994—. Bd. dirs. St. Thomas the Apostle CYO, Glen Mills, 1977—, volleyball and track coach, 1977—; mem., sec., vice chair adv. com. Children and Youth Svcs. Delaware County, Media, 1979-99; chmn. adv. com. Children and Youth Svcs. Delaware County, 1999—. Recipient Clifford M. Lewis alumnus award Wheeling Jesuit U., 1976, Coaches award for Christian leadership Archdiocese of Phila.-Cath. Youth Orgn., 1989, Julia Forst award Archdiocese of Phila., 1999, Father Francis Griffin award St. Thomas the Apostle Parish, 1999; named Educator-Vol. of Yr., Leadership Delaware County Alumni Assn., 1992; named to Harry Watson Track Hall of Fame, K.C.,1996. Roman Catholic. Avocations: travel, sewing, reading. Home: 190 Andrien Rd Glen Mills PA 19342-1168 Office: St Thomas the Apostle Sch 430 Valleybrook Rd Glen Mills PA 19342-9440

SHIELDS, ROBERT, surgery educator; b. Paisley, Scotland, Nov. 8, 1930; s. Robert Alexander and Isobel Dougall (Reid) S.; m. Grace Marianne Swinburn, Jan. 19, 1957; children: Gillian, Jennifer, Andrew. MB ChB, U. Glasgow (Scotland), 1953, MD with honors, 1965; DSc, U. Wales, 1990. Intern and resident Western Infirmary, Glasgow, 1953-61; rsch. asst. Mayo Found., Rochester, Minn., 1959-60; lectr. surgery Western Infirmary, Glasgow, 1960-62; reader in surgery Welsh Nat. Sch. Medicine, Cardiff, Wales, 1963-69; prof. surgery U. Liverpool, Eng., 1969-96; vice-chmn. Royal Liverpool U. Hosp. Trust, 1992-95; Zachary Cope lectr. Royal Coll. Surgeons of Eng., 1992; apptd. dep. lord lt., 1991—. Named Knight Bachelor, 1990. Fellow ACS (hon.), Royal Coll. Surgeons (London), Royal Coll. Surgeons (Edinburgh, pres. 1994, 95, 96), Royal Coll. Physicians and Surgeons of Glasgow, South African Coll. Surgeons; mem. Brit. Soc. Gastroenterology (pres. 1990-91), Surg. Rsch. Soc., Royal Australasian Coll. Surgery, Royal Coll. Surgeons Ireland, Hong Kong Coll. Surgeons, Royal Coll. Physicians Edinburgh. Home: 81 Meols Dr, West Kirby, Wirral CH48 5DF, England

SHIELS, PAUL GERARD, molecular biologist; b. Belfast, Ireland, Sept. 14, 1961; s. Edward and Kathleen Shiels; m. Lesley Elizabeth Johnston, Sept. 29, 1990; children: Callan, Eoin. BA, Trinity Coll., Dublin, Ireland, 1984; PhD, U. Glasgow, Scotland, 1990. European molecular biology orgn. longterm fellow Netherlands Cancer Inst., Amsterdam, 1990-91; postdoctoral scientist U. Glasgow, 1991-96; sr. scientist molecular biologist PPL Therapeutics, Edinburgh, Scotland, 1996-2000; sr. lectr. transplant biology U. Glasgow, Scotland, 2000—. Contbr. articles to profl. jours. Scholar Irish Am. Found., 1983. Roman Catholic. Avocations: soccer, Gaelic music, literature. Fax: 44 (0) 141 211 2972. Office: PPL Therapeutics, Roslin, Edinburgh EH25 9PP, Scotland

SHIENTAG, FLORENCE PERLOW, lawyer; b. N.Y.C.; d. David and Ester (Germane) Perlow; m. Bernard L. Shientag, June 8, 1938. BS, NYU, 1940, LLB, 1933, JD, 1940. Bar: Fla. 1976, N.Y. Law aide Thomas E. Dewey, 1937; law sec. Mayor La Guardia, 1939-42; justice Domestic Relations Ct., 1941-42; mem. Tchrs. Retirement Bd., N.Y.C., 1942-46; asst. U.S. atty. So. dist. N.Y., 1943-53; cir. ct. mediator Fla. Supreme Ct., 1992; pvt. practice N.Y.C., 1960—, Palm Beach, Fla., 1976—; lectr. on internat. divorce; mem. Nat. Commn. on Wiretapping and Electronic Surveillance, 1973—, Task Force on Women in Cts., 1985-86. Contbr. articles to profl. jours. Candidate N.Y. State Senate, 1954; bd. dirs. UN Devel. Corp., 1972-95, Franklin and Eleanor Roosevelt Inst., 1985—; bd. dirs., assoc. treas. YM and YWHA; hon. commr. commerce, N.Y.C. Mem. ABA, Fed. Bar Assn. (exec. com.), Internat. Bar Assn., N.Y. Women's Bar Assn. (pres., dir., Life Time Achievement award 1994), N.Y. State Bar Assn., N.Y.C. Bar Assn. (chmn. law and art sect.), N.Y. County Lawyers Assn. (dir.), Nat. Assn. Women LAwyers (sec.). Home: 737 Park Ave New York NY 10021-4256

SHIER, GLORIA BULAN, mathematics educator; b. The Philippines, Apr. 20, 1935; came to U.S., 1966.; d. Melecio Cauilan and Florentina (Cumagun) Bulan; m. Wayne Thomas Shier, May 31, 1969; children: John Thomas, Marie Teresita, Anna Christina. BS, U. Santo Tomas, Manila, Philippines, 1956; MA, U. Ill., 1968; PhD, U. Minn., 1986. Tchr. Cagayan (Philippines) Valley Coll., 1956-58, St. Paul Coll., Manila, 1959-62, Manila Div. City Schs., 1958-64; asst. prof. U. of East, Manila, 1961-66; rsch. asst. U. Ill., Urbana, 1968-69; instr. Miramar Community Coll., San Diego, 1974-75, Mesa Community Coll., San Diego, 1975-80, Lakewood Community Coll., St. Paul, 1984, U. Minn., Mpls., 1986-87, North Hennepin Community Coll., Brooklyn Park, Minn., 1987—; cons. PWS Kent Pub. Co., Boston, 1989—. Chairperson Filipino Am. Edn. Assn., San Diego, 1978-79. Fulbright scholar U.S. State Dept., U. Ill., 1966-70; fellow Nat. Sci. Found., Oberlin Coll., 1967; recipient Excellence in Teaching award UN Edni. Scientific Cultural Organ., U. Philippines, 1960-62, Cert. Commendation award The Gov. of Minn., 1990, Outstanding Filipino in the Midwest Edn. Cat. award 1992, Cavite Assn., 1998, Gintong Pamana Found. Mem. Am. Math. Soc., Math. Assn. Am., Philippine-Am. Acad. Sci. and Engring., Phi Kappa Phi, Sigma Xi Rsch. Honor Soc., Nat. Coun. Tchrs. Math., Am. Math. Assn. for Two Yr. Colleges, Internat. Group for Psychology of Math. Edn., Minn. Coun. of Tchrs. Math., Minn. Math. Assn. of Two Yr. Colleges, Philippine-Am. Acad. Sci. and Engring., Fil-Minnesotan Assn (bd.dirs. 1991—), Am. Statistical Assn. Roman Catholic. Avocation: piano. Home: 210 Wexford Heights Dr New Brighton MN 55112-3144

SHIER, SHELLEY M., production company executive; b. Toronto, Mar. 15, 1957; d. Harry Shier and Rosaline (Cutler) Sonshine; m. Hank O'Neal, May 14, 1985. Student, H.B. Studio, N.Y.C., 1975-76, Stella Adler Conservatory, N.Y.C., 1976-80. Company mem., actor Soho Artists Theater, N.Y.C., 1976-81; casting dir. Lawrence Price Prodns., N.Y.C., 1981-82; pres. Hoss, Inc., N.Y.C., 1983—; v.p. Chiaroscuro Records, N.Y.C., 1987—; pres. Broadway Bound, Inc., N.Y.C., 1998—; cons. Peter Martin Assocs., N.Y.C., 1983, Norwegian Cruise Line, Miami, Fla., 1983-98, Floating Jazz Festival, 1983—, Big Bands At Sea, Rhythm & Blues Cruise, Dixieland At Sea, 1991—, The Blues Cruise, 1991—, Oslo (Norway) Jazz Festival, 1986—, New Sch. for Social Rsch., N.Y.C., 1989—, Beacons In Jazz Awards Ceremony, A Tribute to the Music of Bob Wills and The Texas Playboys, Mardi Gras at Sea. Talent acquisition agt. Save the Children, N.Y.C., 1986, Tomorrow's Children, N.Y.C., 1990, Royal Caribbean Internat., Miami, 1994-96, Ultimate Caribbean Jazz Spectacular, Country Music Festival in the Caribbean, CUNARD N.Y.C., 1994—, Barcelona Olympics, NBC, 1992, Broadway at Sea, 1996, Millennium at Sea, 1999—, Broadway Bound, 1999—, others. Avocations: karate, photography, riding, fishing, weightlifting. Office: HOSS Inc 830 Broadway New York NY 10003-4827

SHIFFERT, SARAH ANNE IDELL, association executive; b. Abington, Pa., Nov. 27, 1957; d. John Albert and Anne Weidner Shiffert; m. John Patrick Cody Fogarty, Jan. 20, 1989; children: Jackson, Conor. AB, Vassar U., 1979. Dir. publs. Enviro Law Inst., Washington, 1985-87; dir. comms. Am. Landscape Archs. Assn., Washington, 1987-88; dir. publs. Internat. Pers. Mgmt. Assn., Alexandria, Va., 1989-95, dir. assn. svcs., 1989-95, sr. dir. assn. svcs., 1995—; exec. secretariat fed. sec. Internat. Pers. Mgmt. Assn., Alexandria, 1995—. Trustee Sch. for Friends, Washington, 1997—. Mem. Am. Soc. Assn. Execs. Quaker. E-mail: sshiffert@ipma-hr.org.

SHIGEMITSU, TOSHIRO, ophthalmologist, researcher, pathologist; b. Kyoto, Japan, Feb. 7, 1953; s. Yoshito and Eiko (Yoshioka) S.; m. Kumiko Nakahori, Oct. 27, 1990. MD, Fujita Health U., Toyoake, 1982, DMSc, 1987. Asst. prof. ophthalmology Fujita Health U., Toyoake, 1988-91, assoc. prof. ophthalmology, 1991—; dir. ophthalmology Hojinkai Med. Found., Kawade Hosp., Toyota, 1984-99. Patentee in field; contbr. articles to profl. jours. Mem. judging com. Fund Med. Security Sys., Aichi, 1996—. Recipient Japan Soc. Clin. Ophthalmology prize, 1998; grantee Eye Bank Assn. Aichi, 1993, 94, 95. Mem. Am. Soc. Cataract and Refractive Surgery, European Soc. Cataract and Refractive Surgeons, Am. Aging Assn., Japanese Ophthalmic Pathology Soc. (councillor 1997—), Asia Pacific Intraocular Implant Assn. (faculty 1997—). Avocations: travel, movies, golf, art. Home: 540-4A Shihongi, Midori-ku Nagoya 458-0039, Japan Office: Fujita Health U Sch Med, Dept Ophthalmology, Toyoake Aichi 470-1192, Japan

SHIGENAGA, SHOJI, plant geneticist, agronomist; b. Otsu, Japan, June 3, 1929; s. Sadasuke and Etsu (Tahara) S.; m. Setsuko Furutani Shigenaga, Apr. 19. 1959 (widowed Mar. 19, 1996); children: Yoko, Sayuri. BA, Kyoto (Japan) U., 1954, PhD, 1967. Rsch. assoc. Hyogo U. Agr., Sasayama, Japan, 1955-65; assoc. prof. Kyoto (Japan) U., 1965-74, prof., 1974-93; project leader JICA, Bangkok, Thailand, 1993-94; adv. Shiga Prefectural Govt., Otsu, Japan, 1994-95; prof. U. Shiga Prefecture, Hikone, Japan, 1995-00; postdoctoral fellow The U. Manitoba, Winnipeg, Can., 1969-71; dir. Experimental Farm, Kyoto U., Takatsuki, Japan, 1987-89, Sub-Tropical Plant Inst., Kyoto U., Kushimoto, Japan, 1987-89; dean student affairs U. Shiga Prefecture, Hikone, Japan, 1995-99. Office: Univ Shiga Prefecture, Hassaka, Hikone 5220057, Japan

SHIGERU, OBARA, trading company executive; b. Esashi, Iwate, Japan, July 10, 1944; s. Kiichi and Michiyo (Fujii) O.; m. Keiko Nishida, Oct. 9, 1970; children, Ichiro, Ayako, Masako. BArch, Waseda U., Tokyo, 1968. Cert. archtl. engr. Mgr. Nippon Light Metal Co., Tokyo, 1968-77; gen. mgr. Shin Nikkei Corp., Tokyo, 1977-89; CEO Blixon Corp., Tokyo, 1990—, All Season Corp., Tokyo, 1995—; cons. Carter Holt Harvey, Auckland, New Zealand, 1992-94. Dir. Human Being and Environment, Tokyo, 1992—.

Avocations: drawing pictures, baseball, golf, traveling, movies. Home: 1-9-1 Minamicho, Kokubunji, Tokyo 185-0021, Japan Office: All Season Corp, Suga Bldg Yotsuya 3-1, Tokyo Shinjuku-ku Japan

SHIGETOMI, KEITH SHIGEO, lawyer; b. Honolulu, Oct. 16, 1956; s. Samson Shigeru and Doris (Ogawa) S.; m. Ann Keiko Furutomo, Oct. 29, 1985; children: Samson Shigeru II, Marisa Mae. BSBA magna cum laude, Drake U., 1978; JD, U. Hawaii, 1983. Bar: Hawaii, 1983, U.S. Dist. Ct. Hawaii 1983, U.S. Ct. Appeals (9th cir.) 1986. Dep. pub. defender Office of Pub. Defender, Honolulu, 1983-88; pvt. practice, Honolulu, 1988-90, 94—; ptnr. Shigetomi & Thompson, Honolulu, 1990-94; ind. grand jury counsel Cir. Ct., State of Hawaii, Honolulu, 1988-89. Finalist Three Outstanding Young Persons Hawaii Jaycees, 1994; named Criminal Def. Lawyer of Yr. Consumer Bus. Rev., 1996, 97, 99. Mem. Hawaii Bar Assn., Nat. Asian Pacific Bar Assn., Beta Gamma Sigma, Beta Alpha Psi, Phi Eta Sigma. Office: 711 Kapiolani Blvd Ste 1440 Honolulu HI 96813-5238

SHIH, JUNG-WEI, chemical engineer, researcher; b. Tainan, Taiwan, Republic of China, Sept. 1, 1931; s. Tian Su and Shing Yuan (Ye) S.; m. Ruay Lian Tsay; children: Chih Horng, Tsin Lin, Chih Loung. B degree, Nat. Taiwan U., Taipei, 1954; M degree, U. Tokyo, 1961, D degree, 1965. Engr. China Petroleum Co., Taipei, 1955-58; rschr. Coal Rsch. Inst., Tokyo, 1967-69; rschr. Coal Mining Rsch. Centre, Tokyo, 1970-73, chief rschr., 1974-90, sr. chief rschr., 1991-97; adv. rschr. Japan Resources Assn., Tokyo, 1972-78, Nippon Kodo Co., Ltd., 2000; mem. com. Indsl. Rsch. Inst., Tokyo, 1974-76, Japan Tech. Assn., Tokyo, 1974-90, New Energy Devel. Orgn., Tokyo, 1981-91. Co-author, editor: Resources and Utilization of Coal, 1977; co-author: Resources Dictionary, 1978, Coal Utilization: Power Generation Technology, 1980; editor Jour. Japan Fuel Soc., 1982-93, Jour. Japan Inst. Energy, 1982-93. Lt. ROTC, 1954-55. Mem. Japan Inst. Energy (New Energy Tech. award 1992), Chinese Inst. Engrs. Japan (dir. gen. 1997—.). Avocations: history, cycling. Office: Ctr for Coal Utilization, 6-2-31 Roppongi, Minato-ku, Tokyo 101, Japan

SHIH, NENG-YAO, molecular cell biologist; b. Taipei City, Taiwan, Dec. 24, 1958; came to U.S., 1991; s. Hwa-Hsun and Mei-Man (Lien) S.; m. Huoy-Hwa Wang, June 9, 1962; children: Wan-Ling, Chia-Ling. PhD, Ariz. State U., Tempe, 1996. Tchg. ast. dept. biology Tunghai U., Taichung, 1982-83, rsch. asst. Biology Instn., 1982-84; rsch. assoc. cardiovascular dept. Chang Gung Hosp., Linchou, Taiwan, 1986-88; assoc. rsch. scientsit Devel. Ctr. fo Biotech., Taipei, 1990-91; rsch. assoc. Ariz. State U., Tempe, 1992-96; molecular cell biologist Washington U. Sch. Medicine, St. Louis, 1996—. Contbr. articles to profl. jours. Recipient scholarships and grants. Mem. Phi Kappa Phi. Avocations: swimming, travel, baseball. Office: Washington U Sch Medicine 4939 Childrens Pl Saint Louis MO 63110-1001

SHIH, SHIN-RU, medical educator; b. Taichung, Taiwan, May 6, 1965; d. I-Fang S. and Chung-Hsing Yeh; m. Guang-Wu Chen; 1 child, Li-Fang. BS, Nat. Taiwan U., 1988, MS, 1991; PhD, Rutgers U., 1996. Asst. prof. Chang Gung U., Tao-Tuan, Taiwan, 1996-97, assoc. prof., 1997—; dir. clin. virology lab. Chang Gung Meml. Hosp., Tao-Yuan, 1999—, mem. com. rsch. faculty, 1997—, mem. com. fin. mgmt., 1997—; cons. Dr. Chip Biotech. Inc., Taichung, 1999—. Contbr. articles to profl. jours. Postdoctoral fellow Rutgers U., N.J., 1995-96. Mem. Am. Soc. Microbiology, Internat. Soc. Antiviral Rsch. Avocations: piano, softball. Office: Chang Gung U, 259 Wen-Hwa 1st Rd, Tao-Yuan 333, Taiwan

SHIH, STAN, electronics manufacturing executive; b. 1944; married; 3 children. With Unitron Indsl. Corp., 1972, Multitech Internat. Corp.; chmn., CEO Acer Inc., Taipei, Taiwan; mem. adv. bd. GE Asia-Pacific. Mem. Asian Inst. Mgmt. (gov.). Fax: 8862-719-8458. Office: 21F 88 Hsin Tai Wu Rd Sec 1, Hsic-Hih Taipei-Hsien 221, Taiwan*

SHIH, TSO MIN, mining engineering educator; b. Ying-Chen, Shantung, China, Apr. 4, 1935; s. Ren Ying and Sun Sum S.; m. Ching Chi Hsia, June 1, 1961; children: Rosa Hung-Chen, Kim Hung-Wei, Sophia Hung-Ren. BS, Nat. Cheng-Kung U., Tainan, Taiwan, 1958; MS, McGill U., Montreal, Can., 1965; postgrad., U. B.C., Vancouver, 1966-68. Rsch. asst. Nova Scotia Tech. Coll., Halifax, N.S., Can., 1965-66; lectr. Nat. Cheng-Kung U., Tainan, Taiwan, 1968-72, assoc. prof., 1972-74, dept. chmn., 1974-80, prof., 1980—; dir. Chinese Inst. Mining and Metal Engring., Taipei, 1976-78. Author: Diamond, 1996, (in Chinese) Graphite, 1999; contbr. over 50 articles to profl. jours. 2d lt. ROTC, 1958-60. Recipient award Pi Epsilon Tao, 1989, award dept. reconstructions Govt. Taiwan, 1993. Mem. Chinese Inst. Mining and Metal. Engring. (award 1972, 91), Mining Assn. Rep. of China (dir. 1988-94, 96—, award 1996), Chinese Inst. Engrs., Assn. of Chinese Kung-Fu (3rd prize Chung-Cheng Cup 1996, 2nd prize Tai-Chung City Mayor Cup). Office: Nat Cheng-Kung U, Ta-Hsueh Rd, 700 Tainan Taiwan

SHIH, WEI, astrophysicist; b. Shanghai, China, May 5, 1943; came to U.S., 1959; s. Frank I. and Emily Kwong S.; m. Yen-Chi Cheng, July 1980; children: Fredrick Yu-Fun Shih, Edwin Shih. BS in Physics, Nat. Taiwan U., 1956; MS in Physics, U. Del., 1963; PhD in Physics, NYU, 1969. Rsch. assoc. Union Indsl. Rsch. Inst., Hsinchu, Taiwan, 1956-59; rsch. microwave physicist Frequency Engring. Lab., Farmingdale, N.J., 1968-71; rsch. physicist Atomic Energy Coun., Taipei, Taiwan, 1972-74; prof. physics Soochow U., Taipei, 1972-78; adj. prof. physics Tam Kang U., Tamsui, Taiwan, 1972-78. Author: Accretion Power and Mechanism for Conversion of Gravitational Potential to Radiative Energy in Active Galactic Nuclei, 1980; co-author: Magnetohydrodynamics of Viscous Gas Accreting on Highly Magnetized Neutron Stars and White Dwarfs, 1974, Dynamics and Accretion Column Structure for Neutron Stars, 1989. Rsch. grantee NASA, Goddard Space Flight Ctr., Greenbelt, Md., 1968. Mem. Am. Assn. for Advancement of Sci., Am. Phys. Soc., Nat. Geographic Soc., N.Y. Acad. Scis. Avocations: piloting, boating, fishing, travel. Office: Fortuna-CRX Inc 50 Bayard St Apt 7K New York NY 10013-4918

SHIHAB, ALWI ABDURAHMAN, minister of foreign affairs; b. Rappang, Indonesia, Aug. 19, 1946; married. BS, Indonesia Islamic Inst., Ujung Pandang, 1968; MA, U. Al-Azhar, Cairo, 1986; PhD, Ain Shams U., Cairo, 1990; MA, Temple U., 1992, PHD, 1995; postgrad., Harvard U., 1995-96. Chief exec. Priangan Glass Factory, 1975-79, PT Prima Advera, Jakarta, Indonesia, 1982-86; pres., dir. Alfa Contracting Co., Jeddah, 1979-82; commr., mem. Darul Qor'an Found., Jakarta, 1982—; chief commr. PT Dhafco Manunggal Sejati, 1996; min. fgn. affairs Indonesia, 1999—; tchr. Averroes U., Jakarta, 1985-88, Temple U., 1993-95, Phila. Coll. Textile and Sci., 1994-95, Hartford (Conn.) Sem., 1996—, Harvard U. Div. Sch., 1998—; mem. adv. bd. Religious Consultation on Population Reproductive Health and Ethics, Washington, 1994—. Trustee Harvard Ctr. for Study of World Religions, Cambridge, Mass., 1998—. Mem. Presidium Internat. Forum Indonesia, Internat. Scholars Annual Trialogue, Am. Acad. Religion (mem. internat. connections com. 1996—). Office: Ministry Fgn Affairs, Taman Pejambon 6, Jakarta 10410, Indonesia*

SHIIKI, KAZUO, engineering educator; b. Tokyo, Jan. 17, 1947; s. Mariko Shiiki; m. Toyoko Ogishima, Apr. 6, 1974; 3 children. BS, Keio U., Tokyo, 1969, M Engring., 1971, D Engring., 1977. Sr. rschr. Hitachi Ltd., Tokyo, 1985-91; sr. engr. Hitachi Ltd., Kanagawa, Japan, 1991-93; assoc. prof. Keio U., Kanagawa, 1993-94, prof., 1994—. Author: (in Japanese) Magnetic Thin Films, 1988. Mem. Phys. Soc. Japan, Magnetics Soc. Japan. Avocations: tennis, music. Office: Keio U, 3-14-1 Hiyoshi Kohoku-ku, Yokohama Kanagawa 223-8522, Japan

SHIINA, ISAMU, chemist, educator; b. Tokyo, Dec. 10, 1967; s. Junsuke and Nobuko (Isoyama) S.; m. Masae Yamada, July 30, 1993; 1 child, Ayano. BS, Sci. U. of Tokyo, 1992; Phd, U. Tokyo, 1997. Rsch. assoc. Sci. U. of Tokyo, 1992-97, asst. prof., 1998—. Inventor and patentee in field. Mem. Chem. Soc. Japan (spl. lectureship 1996, Young Chemist award 1997), Soc. Synthetic Organic Chemistry. Avocations: tennis, skiing, fishing. Office: Science U, 1-3 Kagurazaka Shinjuku-ku, Tokyo 162-8601, Japan

SHIINO, MASATAKA, anatomy educator; b. Sadowara, Miyazaki, Japan, July 31, 1932; s. Denzo Hino and Kin S.; m. Kazuko Izaki, Jan. 8, 1961; 1 child, Yayoi. BS, Miyazaki U., 1955; MS, Kyushu U., 1957, PhD, 1965. Assoc. prof. Miyazaki (Japan) U., 1966-70; sr. rsch. assoc. U. Tex. Med. Sch., San Antonio, 1970-72, assoc. prof., 1972-74, 76-81; assoc. prof. Miyazaki Med. Sch., 1974-76; prof., head dept. anatomy Wakayama (Japan) Med. Coll., 1981-98; assoc. dean acad. affairs Wakayama Med. Coll., 1992-96, dir. of library, 1996-98, prof. emeritus, 1998—; part-time prof. Shinshu U., Japan, 1982, Kagawa U., Japan, 1983, 86, Nagoya City U., Japan, 1993-98, Wakayama Med. Coll., 1998—. Editor Tissue and Cell, 1995-98; contbr. articles to profl. jours. Fellow U. Tex. Med. Br., Galveston, 1965-67; Rsch. grantee NIH, 1979-82, Japanese Govt., 1987-90; recipient Sci. prize Miyazaki News Paper Co., Ltd., 1975. Avocations: painting, gardening, travel. Home: 246-3 Kamitajima, Sadowara, Miyazaki 880-0301, Japan

SHIKATA, YASUSHI, physician; b. Maizuru, Kyoto, Japan, July 21, 1964; s. Akira and Matsuko (Murakami) S.; m. Yuko Yokomura, Oct. 26, 1997; 1 child, Shunsuke. MD, Okayama (Japan) U., 1992, PhD, 1999. Physician Matsuyama (Japan)-Shimin Hosp., 1992-94, Okayama U. Hosp., 1994-99; rsch. fellow Sch. Medicine Okayama U., 1999—; chief physician Fiujitsuna Hosp., Sayo, Japan, 1999—. Contbr. articles to profl. jours. Fellow Japan Soc. Internal Medicine, Japan Soc. Ultrasonics in Medicine; mem. AAAS, Japan Diabetes Soc., Japanese Soc. Nephrology, Japanese Respiratory Soc., Japan Rheumatism Assn., Japan Soc. for Bronchology. Office: Okayama U Sch Medicine, 2-5-1 Shikata-cho, Okayama 700-8558, Japan

SHIKHALIEV, POLAD MAMEDOGLU, physicist, researcher; b. Sheki, Azerbaijan, Jan. 30, 1964; arrived in Russia, 1982; s. Mamed Abdulla oglu and Garanfil Bilal gysy (Gadizova) S.; m. Zumrud Ovchu gysy Arabova, Aug. 19, 1991; 2 children. PhD in Physics, St. Petersburg Tech. U., Russia, 1988. Engr. Electrophysics Corp., St. Petersburg, 1988-91; sr. rschr. A.F. Joffe Inst. Phys.-Tech. Inst.-Russian Acad. Scis., St. Petersburg, 1991—. Contbr. articles to profl. jours.; patentee in field. Mem. IRPS. Home: Bogaychuka 24-40, 189631 Saint Petersburg Russia Office: AF Ioffe Phys Tech Inst RAS, Politechnicheskaya 26, 194021 Saint Petersburg Russia

SHIKHMURZAEV, YULII DAMIR, mathematician, researcher, consultant; b. Ryazan, Russia, Sept. 12, 1957; arrived in U.K., 1996; s. Damir Usmanovich and Agniya Nikolayevna (Melyoshkina) S.; m. Zimfira Gallyamova, June 10, 1980; 1 child, Uliana. MSc in Mechanics, Moscow State U., 1980, PhD in Physics and Math., 1985. Jr. rsch. scientist Moscow State U., 1984-88, rsch. scientist, 1989-92, sr. rsch. scientist, 1992-96; vis. rschr. U. Naples, Italy, 1988-89; lectr. U. Leeds, U.K., 1996-98; sr. lectr. U. Birmingham, U.K., 1999—; cons. Kodak Ltd., Harrow, 1997—; vis. prof. U. Mons-Hainaut, Belgium, 1999. Contbr. articles to profl. jours. Rsch. grantee Internat. Sci. Found., 1993, Min. of Higher Edn. and Rsch. (France), 1995, Eastman Kodak Co., 1996, 97, 99. Mem. Internat. Soc. Coating Sci. and Tech., European Mechanics Soc., German Soc. for Applied Math. and Mechanics, London Math. Soc. Avocations: history, photography, travel. Office: U Birmingham, Dept Math and Stats, Edgbaston Birmingham B15 2TT, United Kingdom

SHIKTOROV, PAVEL NIKOLAEVICH, physicist, researcher; b. Vilnius, Lithuania, June 28, 1954; s. Nikolai Kalinovish and Liubov Michailovna (Yakubovskaya) S.; m. Olga Nikolaevna Prusakova, Feb. 26, 1983; children: Anastasiya, Pavel. MS, U. Vilnius, 1976; PhD in Physics, Semiconductor Physics Inst., Vilnius, 1986. Jr. rschr. Semiconductor Physics Inst., 1976-87, rschr., 1987-89, sr. rschr., 1989—; cons. Info. Ministry, Lithuania, 1994—. Recipient Gold medal in sci., State Govt., USSR, 1987; grantee NATO, 1995, 96, 2000, French Govt., 1998. Home: Gelvony 13-18, LT2000 Vilnius Lithuania Office: Semiconductor Physics Inst, Goshtauto 11, LT 2600 Vilnius Lithuania

SHILEPSKY, ARNOLD CHARLES, mathematics educator, computer consultant; b. Norwalk, Conn., Dec. 10, 1944; s. Morris Jacob and Rose (Pfeffer) S.; m. Carol Irene Carter, June 15, 1968; children: Lisa Ruth, Beth Carter. AB, Wesleyan U., Middletown, Conn., 1966; PhD, U. Wis., 1971. Asst. prof. Ark. State U., Jonesboro, 1971-74; asst. prof. Wells. Coll., Aurora, N.Y., 1974-79, assoc. prof., 1979-85, prof., 1985—, Herbert E. Ives prof. of scis., 1985-91; cons. Digicomp Rsch. Corp., 1992—. Pres. Cmty. Devel. Fedn., S.W. Cayuga County, N.Y., 1987-92. Mem. Am. Math. Soc., Math. Assn. Am., Assn. for Women in Math. Home: Main St 295 Aurora NY 13026 Office: Wells Coll Aurora NY 13026

SHILLER, ROBERT JAMES, economist; b. Detroit, Mar. 29, 1946; s. Benjamin P. and Ruth R. (Radzville) S.; m. Virginia M. Fualstich, June 13, 1976; 2 sons. BA, U. Mich., 1967; SM, MIT, 1968, PhD, 1972. Asst. prof. U. Minn., 1972-74; rsch. fellow Nat. Bur. Econ. Rsch., Cambridge, Mass., 1974-75; vis. scholar dept. econs. MIT, Cambridge, 1974-75, vis. prof., 1981-82; assoc. prof. dept. econs. U. Pa., Phila., 1974-81, prof. econs., 1981-82; prof. fin. Wharton Sch., 1981-82; prof. econs. Yale U., New Haven, 1982—; co-founder Case, Shiller, Weiss Inc., Cambridge, Mass.; vis. scholar dept. econs. Harvard U., Mass., 1980; mem. academic adv. panel Fed. Reserve Bank of N.Y. Fgn. editor Rev. Econ. Studies, 1981-84; assoc. editor Jour. Econometrics, 1980-83; author: Market Volatility, 1989, Macro Markets, 1993, Irrational Exuberance, 2000. Grantee NSF, 1976—; Guggenheim fellow. Fellow Econometric Soc., Am. Acad. Arts and Scis. Office: Yale U Cowles Found New Haven CT 06520-8281

SHILLING, KAY MARLENE, psychiatrist; b. July 1, 1953; d. Harrison Gene and Rose Marie (Allen) Herber. BS, U. Nebr., Lincoln, 1976; MD, U. Nebr., Omaha, 1980. Diplomate Nat. Bd. Med. Examiners. Resident in psychiatry U. Nebr. Med. Ctr., Omaha, 1981-84; pvt. practice Omaha, 1984—; med. dir., chief of staff La Plaza (Nebr.) Cmty. Health Ctr., 1999—, also bd. dirs. Bd. dirs. Indian Chicano Health Ctr., 1983-92; bd. dirs. Omaha Symphony Guild, 1999—, encore chair, 2000—; mem. Henry Doorly Zoo Guild, Opera Omaha Guild, 2000—. Mem. AMA, Royal Soc. Medicine, Ctrl. Neuro Psychiat. Assn. (bd. dirs., pres. 1996-97), Am. Med. Women's Assn. (pres. Omaha chpt. 1986-88, Nebr. State dir. 1988-94, regional gov. 1993-95, bd. dirs. 1993-95, book reviewer for JAMWA, Outstanding Physician award 1989, 90-93, nat. cmty. svc. award 1990), Am. Psychiat. Assn., Met. Omaha Med. Soc., Nebr. Med. Assn., Alpha Xi Delta. Avocations: gardening, travel, gourmet cooking, interior decorating, house renovation. Home: 1103 S 80th St Omaha NE 68124-1419 Office: 7602 Pacific St Ste 302 Omaha NE 68114-5405

SHILLINGBURG, HERBERT THOMPSON, JR., dental educator; b. Mar. 21, 1938; s. Herbert Thompson and Stefi Marie (Schuster) S.; m. Constance Joanne Murphy, June 11, 1960; children: Lisa Grace, Leslie Susan, Lara Stephanie. Student, U. N.Mex., 1955-58, 65-66; DDS, U. So. Calif., 1962. Gen. practice dentistry Albuquerque, 1964-67; asst. prof. fixed prosthodontics sect. UCLA Sch. Dentistry, 1967-70, chmn., 1970-72; chmn. dept. fixed prosthodontics U. Okla. Coll. Dentistry, Oklahoma City, 1972—, David Ross Boyd Disting. prof., 1983; cons. VA Hosp., Muskogee, Okla., 1975-84, Oklahoma City, 1977-93, U.S. Army Dental Activity, Ft. Knox, Ky., 1980-94. Author: (also in Japanese, German, Greek, Spanish, Italian, French, Portuguese, Polish, and Korean) Preparations for Cast Gold Restorations, 1974, Fundamentals of Fixed Prosthodontics, 1976, 2d edit., 1981, 3d edit., 1997, Guide to Occlusal Waxing, 1979, 3d edit., 2000, Restoration of the Endodontically Treated Tooth, 1984, Fundamentals of Tooth Preparations for Cast Metal and Porcelain Restorations, 1987; co-editor: Quintessence of Dental Technology, 1984-88; sect. editor: Quintessence Internat., 1988—; mem. editl. coun. Jour. Prosthetic Dentistry, 1996-99. Capt. U.S. Army, 1962-64. Recipient award for tchg. excellence UCLA Sch. Dentistry, 1969, 72, 73, U. Okla. Coll. Dentistry, 1976, 78, 82, 87, 93, 94, 97, 1st prize Am. Med. Writers Assn., 1988, La Mèdaille de la Ville de Paris (èchelon Argent), 1990; named O U Assocs. Disting. Lectr., 1989. Fellow Am. Coll. Dentists; mem. ADA, Acad. Operative Dentistry, Am. Acad. Fixed Prosthodontics (George H. Moulton award 1998), Am. Acad. Restorative Dentistry, Am. Coll. Prosthodontists (hon.), Okla. State Dental Assn., Internat. Assn. Dental Rsch., Omicron Kappa Upsilon (Stephen H. Leeper award for tchg. excellence 2000), Phi Kappa Phi. Republican. Episcopalian. Avocations: traveling, photography. Home: 1312 Brixton Rd Edmond OK 73034-3314 Office: U Okla Coll Dentistry PO Box 26901 Oklahoma City OK 73190-0001

SHIM, JAE HU, chemist, educator, researcher; b. Milyang-gun, Kyongnam, Korea, Sept. 15, 1927; s. Byung Sup Shim and Dan Chun Lee; m. Myung Sun Park, Feb. 28, 1957. BS, Saitama U., Urawa, Japan, 1953; PhD, Seoul (Korea) Nat. U., 1970. Assoc. prof. Chung-nam U., Taejon, Korea, 1958-65; prof. Hanyang U., Seoul, 1965-69; prof. Dongguk U., Seoul, 1969-93, emeritus prof., 1993—; dean coll. engring. Dongguk U., Seoul, 1973-78, dir. indsl. tech. rsch. inst., 1974-80, head sci. hall, 1980-84, dir. grad. sch. com., 1986-88, head dept. chem. engring. grad. sch., 1991-93. Contbr. articles to Jour. Korean Chem. Soc., Jour. Korean Inst. Chem. Engring., Polymer, Bulletin Korea Chem. Soc. Recipient Order of Nat. Svc. Merit award Pres. Republic Korea, 1993. Mem. Korean Chem. Soc. (life), Korean Inst. Chem. Engring. (life), Polymer Soc. Korea (life). Achievements include research in Tropolones I-III, novel thermostable radial polymellitimides, phase transfer catalyst, Synthesis and catalytic activities of Lariat Azacrown Ethers. Home: Song-In Edn Acad, 484 Kwangjang-dong, Kwangjin-ku, Seoul 143-210, Republic of Korea Office: Dongguk U, 26 Pil dong 3 ga Chung ku, Seoul 100 715, Republic of Korea

SHIM, JUNG-SOON, English educator, theater critic; b. Seoul, Korea, Aug. 30, 1949; d. Kwang-Bin Shim and Young-Ae Choi. BA, Ewha Women's U., 1972, MA, 1974; PhD, U. Hawaii, 1984. Reporter Korea Herald, Seoul, 1973-75; cross-cultural coord. Peace Corps, Korea, 1977; lectr. Korea U., 1982-84; instr. Chungbuk Nat. U., 1979; lectr. Ewha Women's U., 1977-79; prof. Soongsil U., Seoul, 1985—. Author: Megan Terry and Women's Theatre in Asia, 1997, Sexuality and Popular Culture, 1999, Feminism and Korean Theater, 1999, Understanding Women's Literature and Arts, 1999; co-author: Single Women, 1993; translator books. Mem. orgn. com. Theater of Nations, Seoul, 1997; judge Nat. Seoul Theater Festival, 1996-98; organizer Asia-Pacific Women and Theatre Conf., 1995-98; dean of women students, 1995-97; dir. Women's Studies Rsch. Ctr., 1995—. Mem. MLA (exec. mem. East Asian lit. divsn. 2000—), Women Playwrights Internat. (Korean rep., internat. adv. com. 1994—), Korean Assn. of Women in Theater (founder, v.p. 1994-99, pres. 1999—), Korean Theater Studies Assn. (v.p. 1995-97), Ewha Alumni Assn. of Theatre (pres. 1999—).

SHIM, SANG-TAI, theologist, educator; b. Seoul, Korea, July 29, 1940; s. Ri-Taek Shim and Kang-Sin Lee. BA, Catholic U., 1968; ThD, Tubingen U., 1975. Prof., dir. libr. Catholic U., Seoul, 1976-93; prof. Suwon Catholic U., Hwasong, Korea, 1993—; guest prof. Grad. Sch. Sogang U., Seoul, 1995—. Author: Anonymous Christian, 1975, Man: An Introduction to the Theological Anthropology, 1989, Faith in Encounter with the New Millennium, 2000, Korean Church and Theology in the Third Millennium, 2000; editor: Theological New-Series I-XVI, The Just Society and Church, 1992. Office: Korean Christian Thought In, 168 Wangnim-ri Pongdam-myon, 445-890 Hwasong-gun Kyounggi do, South Korea

SHIMA, HIROKI, urology educator; b. Osaka, Japan, Feb. 5, 1944; s. Sumiko Shima; m. Junko Kikuchi, June 22, 1973; children: Yuko, Ryotaro. MD, Osaka U., 1973, PhD, 1981. Resident dept. anesthesia, urology Osaka U. Hosp., 1973-74; resident dept. urology Nat. Osaka Hosp., 1975; asst. dept. urology Hyogo Coll. Medicine, Nishinomiya, Japan, 1976-84, instr. dept. urology, 1984-91; rsch. fellow Harvard Med. Sch., Boston, 1981-84; asst. prof. U. Calif., San Francisco, 1989-90; assoc. prof. dept. urology Hyogo Coll. Medicine, 1991-98, chief prof., 1998—. Recipient Hamilton Thorne outstanding original rsch. award Am. Soc. Andrology, 1996. Avocations: martial arts, tennis, golf, yoga, reading. Fax: 81-798-45-6368. Office: Hyogo Coll Med Dept Urology, 1-1 Mukogawa-cho, Nishinomiya Hyogo 663-8501, Japan

SHIMA, HIROMU, management educator; b. Kyoto, Japan, June 20, 1929; s. Seitaro and Teru Shima; m. Atsuko Onogi, Mar. 26, 1961; children: Katsutoshi, Yukihiro. B in Commerce, Doshisha U., Kyoto, Japan, 1951, M in Commerce, 1953; D in Bus. Adminstrn., Kobe (Japan) U., 1982. Teaching asst. Doshisha U., Kyoto, 1953-55, lectr., 1955-58, assoc. prof., 1958-67, prof., 1967—. Author: The Research of Scientific Management, 1963, Personnel Management, 1981, Big Business and Management, 1991, Management in an International Economy, 1996, Theory of Human Resource Management, 2000. Libr. Doshisha U., 1989-91. Mem. Assn. for Study of Theory of Pers. Mgmt. (pres.), Am. Acad. Mgmt., Assn. for Study of Bus. Adminstrn., Japan Soc. for Pers. and Labor Rsch. (dir.). Home: 26 Hiraki-machi, Uji-shi Kyoto 611-0026, Japan Office: Doshisha U Karasuma, Imadegawa Kamikyo-ku, Kyoto 602-8580, Japan

SHIMABAYASHI, SABURO, science educator; b. Shiga, Japan, Sept. 6, 1943; s. Riei and Shizu (Hayashi) S.; m. Mitsuko Oota, May 1972; children: Eiko, Yuhko. BS, Kyoto (Japan) U., 1966, PhD, 1973. Rsch. asst. Kyoto U., 1967-74, 75-86; rsch. assoc. U. Mich., Ann Arbor, 1974-75; assoc. prof. U. Tokushima, Japan, 1986-92; prof. U. Tokashima, 1992—. Author, editor: (acad. book) Biocolloids, 1992; co-author: (acad. book) Encyclopedia of Polymeric Material, 1996, Formation and Inhibition of Mineral Scale, 1995, Calcium Phosphates in Biological and Industrial Systems, 1997, Water Soluble Polymers, 1998. Recipient Incitement award Pharm. Soc. Japan, 1986. Office: U Tokushima Fac Pharm Sci, Shomachi 1-78-1, Tokushima 770-8505, Japan

SHIMABUKURO, YOSIO EDEMIR, research scientist, educator; b. Santos, Brazil, Apr. 1, 1950; s. Tokumoske and Makata S.; m. Vera Lucia Arashiro, Dec. 11, 1976; children: Alessandro, Vanessa, Fernanda, Leandro. BSc in Forestry Engring., Fed. Rural U. Rio de Janeiro, Brazil, 1972; MSc in Remote Sensing, Inst. Nac. Pesquisas Espaciais, São José dos Campos, Brazil, 1977; PhD in Remote Sensing, Colo. State U., 1987. Asst. rschr. Inst. Nac. Pesquisas Espaciais, São José dos Campos, 1973-88, sr. scientist, 1988—; vis. scientist NASA Goddard Space Flight Ctr., Greenbelt, 1992-94. Contbr. and tech. reviewer for profl. jours. Home: Av Tivoli 233 Apto 32, 12245230 Sao Jose dos Campos Brazil Office: Inst Nac Pesquisas Espacias, Av Dos Astronautas 1758, 12227010 Sao Jose dos Campos Brazil

SHIMADA, AKIHIKO, evolutionary biochemist, educator; b. Nishinomiya, Japan, Nov. 8, 1953; s. Soichi and Sumiko (Chikaraishi) S.; m. Yoshie Suyama, Oct. 30, 1984; children: Hiroko, Kadzuaki, Sakuko, Natsuo. MS, Osaka U., 1980; DSc, U. Tsukuba, 1990. From rsch. assoc. to asst. prof. U. Tsukuba, Japan, 1987—. Author: The Role of Radiation in the Origin and Evolution of Life, 1999. Mem. Internat. Soc. for the Study of the Origin of Life (reg. rep.). Avocations: kitchen garden, Sunday carpentry. Home: Kaname 710, Tsukuba-shi 300-2622, Japan Office: U Tsukuba Inst Appl Biochem, Tennoudai 1-1-1, Tsukuba-shi 305-8572, Japan

SHIMADA, HARUO, physical chemistry educator; b. Himeji, Hyögo, Japan, Mar. 27, 1935; s. Shigeyoshi and Shige (Okamoto) S.; m. Ikuko Tanaka, Sept. 21, 1968; children: Yöko, Kenichiro. Grad., U. Tokyo, 1958, doctorate, 1968. Rschr. Yawata (Japan) Iron & Steel Co., 1958-72; sr. rschr. Nippon Steel Corp., Kawasaki, Japan, 1973-80; chief rschr. Nippon Steel Corp., Kawasaki, 1980-90; prof. Sci. U. Tokyo, Shinjuku, Japan, 1990—. Editorial mem.: (monthly jour.) Chem. Industry, 1972—; contbr. articles to profl. jours. Mem. Nat. Assn. Corrosion Engrs., Internat. Tech. Inst. (life mem.). Avocations: jogging, swimming. Home: Chuö 5-3-5, Tokyo Ota 143-0024, Japan Office: Sci Univ Tokyo, 1-3 Kagurazaka, Shinjuku 1628601, Japan

SHIMADA, KAZUHITO, health facility administrator; b. Asahi, Chiba, Japan, Feb. 18, 1959; s. Tsutomu and Natsumi (Nomura) S.; m. Fumi Matsuyama, Sept. 30, 1990; children: Yumi, Eiji, Mina. MD, U. Tsukuba, Japan, 1983, PhD, 1987; MS in Aerospace Medicine, Wright State U., 1995. Diplomate Am. Bd. Preventive Medicine (del. aerospace medicine 1997); cert. NASA Internat. Flight Surgeon, Internat. Space Station Flight Surgeon, 1999. Otorhinolaryngologist Saku Sogo Hosp., Nagano, Japan, 1987-88; chief otolaryngology Ibaraki (Japan) Kenritsu Chuo Hosp., 1989-93; med. officer Space Sta. Dept., Nat. Space Devel. Agy. of Japan, Ibaraki, 1993—; chief med. ops. Japan Manned Space Sys. Corp., Tsuchiura, 1998-99; founding dir. Kenritsu Rehab. Ctr., Ibaraki, 1989-90; instr. Wright State U., Ohio, 1993-95; resident NASA Johnson Space Ctr., 1995-96. Author: Sailplane Aerobatics, Japanese edit., 1990, Practical Wave Flying (transl.), 1992. Recipient Cert., Ednl. Commn. for Fgn. Med. Grads., 1983. Mem. AMA, Acoustical Soc. Am., Aerospace Med. Assn. of U.S. and Japan, Civil Aviation Med. Assn. (U.S.), Oto-Rhino-Laryngological Soc. of Japan (delegate). Avocations: flying, amateur radio, skiing, amateur astronomy, Judo. Office: Med Ops Tsukuba Space Ctr, 2-1 Sengen, Tsukuba 305-8505, Japan

SHIMADA, NOBUO, mathematician, researcher; b. Tokyo, Oct. 13, 1925; s. Toku and Hisako (Hozumi) S.; m. Setuko Sugiyama, May 20, 1955; children: Kyoko Nanki, Shoichi Shimada. MSc, Nagoya U., Japan, 1947, DSc, 1954. Instr. Nagoya U., 1947-53, lectr., 1953-58, assoc. prof., 1958-60, prof., 1960-64; prof. Kyoto U., Japan, 1964-89, prof. emeritus, 1989—; prof. Okayama U. Sci., Japan, 1989-97; dir. Rsch. Inst. Math. Sci. Kyoto U., 1979-83, 85-87; adv. com. Japan-U.S. Math. Inst. Johns Hopkins U., 1987-92; organizing com. Internat. Cong. Mathematicians, Kyoto, 1989-90. Editl. bd. Jour. Math. Scis., 1964-89. Yukawa fellow Yukawa Found., 1952. Mem. Math. Soc. Japan (councilor 1981-86), Am. Math. Soc. Avocation: playing Go. Home: 702, Sugumo-cho 4-65-1, Mizuho-ku, Nagoya 467-0804, Japan

SHIMADA, SHOICHI, engineering educator; b. Osaka, Japan, Feb. 6, 1945; s. Hajime and Chiyoko (Ueda) S.; m. Yoko Higashitani, Apr. 13, 1974; children: Naoyuki, Takahiro, Yoshitake. B in Engring., Osaka U., 1967, M in Engring., 1969, D of Engring., 1984. Rschr. Sanyo Electric Co., Ltd., Moriguchi, Japan, 1969-73; rsch. assoc., lectr. Osaka U., Suita, Japan, 1973-89; assoc. prof. Osaka U., Suita, 1989—. Author: Machining of Ceramics and others (8 books), 1985—; contbr. articles to profl. jours. Recipient Paper awd., Machine Tool Engrg. Found., 1983, 94, Rsch. awd., Precision Measurement Engrg. Found., 1991. Mem. Internat. Inst. for Prodn. Engring. Rsch., Am. Soc. Precision Engring., Japan Soc. Precision Engring. Avocations: skiing, tennis, gardening. Home: 3-4-20 Nanryo-cho, Sakai Osaka 590-0811, Japan Office: Osaka U Dept Sci and Tech, 2-1 Yamada-oka Suita, Osaka 565-0871, Japan

SHIMAMOTO, KAZUHIRO, radiologist; b. Gamagori, Aich, Japan, Dec. 8, 1958; s. Hirota and Mitsuru (Hirohama) S.; m. Yuka Itoh, May 20, 1984; children: Hironori, Risa. MD, Nagoya U., 1983, PhD, 1992. Cert. radiologist. Resident Okazaki (Japan) Mcpl. Hosp., 1983-84; resident Nagoya (Japan) U. Hosp., 1984-85, instr., 1988-95, lectr., 1995-98; instr. Nagoya U. Sch. Medicine, 1985-86; staff Komaki (Japan) Mcpl. Hosp., 1986-88; assoc. prof. dept. radiol. tech. Nagoya U. Sch. Health Scis., 1998—. Contbr. articles to profl. jours. Fellow Japan Radiol. Soc., Japanese Soc. of Med. Ultrasonics (sr.); mem. Radiol. Soc. N.Am. Avocation: classical music. Office: Nagoya U Sch Health Scis, 1-1-20 Daikominami Higashi, Nagoya 461-8673, Japan

SHIMAMURA, TADAKATSU, microbiology educator; b. Atsugi, Japan, Aug. 16, 1942; s. Umeo and Fuku (Hosoya) S.; m. Yoshiko Sakakibara, Jan. 23, 1969; children: Yuko, Tadao. MD summa cum laude, Showa U., 1968; D of Med. Sci., Keio U., 1973. Instr. Keio U. Sch. Medicine, Tokyo, 1972-74; rsch. assoc. Rutgers U., New Brunswick, N.J., 1972-73; asst. prof. Tokai U. Sch. Medicine, Isehara, Japan, 1974-83, assoc. prof, 1983-87; prof., chmn. Showa U. Sch. Medicine, Tokyo, 1987—; vis. prof. Rutgers U., 1977, vis. investigator, 1983; vis. asst. prof. Harvard Med. Sch., Mass., 1977. Author: Microbiology, 1989, Microbiology and Immunology for Medical Students, 1991, Immunology, 1993; inventor in field. Postdoctoral fellow Yale U. Sch. Medicine, Conn., 1978; recipient Kamijo prize Showa U., 1968, Tea Meritorious award Japan Tea Ctrl. Assn., 1996. Mem. AAAS, Japanese Soc. Bacteriology (councilor 1991—, chmn. bd. dirs. Kanto br. 1991-94, dir. 1997-99), Janapese Assn. Infectious Diseases (councilor 1994—), Japanese Assn. Germfree Life and Gnotobiology (dir. 1994—), Am. Soc. Microbiology. Avocations: tennis, golf, reading. Office: Showa U Sch Med, 1-5-8 Shinagawa-ku, Tokyo 142-8555, Japan

SHIMAMURA, TETSUYA, computer and information sciences educator; b. Kawagoe, Saitama, Japan, Nov. 17, 1963; s. Minoru and Sumiko (Shimamura) S.; m. Masako Sawatari, Feb. 10, 1991; 1 child, Yutaro. BS, Keio U., 1986, MS, 1988, PhD, 1991. Rsch. assoc. Saitama (Japan) U., 1991-98, assoc. prof. computer and info. scis., 1998—. Mem. IEEE, IEICE, EURASIP. Avocations: shopping, baby care, golf, sightseeing. Home: 1-6-32-803 Kamifukuoka, Kamifukuoka-shi, 356-0004 Saitama Japan Office: Saitama U Dept Info Scis, 255 Shimo-Okubo, Urawa 338-8570, Japan

SHIMAMURA, TOTARO, English educator; b. Saitama-ken, Japan, Mar. 1, 1938; m. Reiko Shimamura, June 1978; 1 child, Kentaro. B Agr. in Agrl. Econs., Tokyo U. Edn., 1960, BA in English, 1962, MA in English, 1968. Tchr. Koyamadai Sr. H.S., Tokyo, 1962-66; lectr. Otaru (Japan) U. Commerce, 1968-71; lectr. Utsunomiya (Japan) U., 1971-72, assoc. prof., 1972-86, prof., 1986—; vis. scholar Cambridge, 1977-78; headmaster Utsunomiya U. Sch. for Handicapped Pupils, 1994-97. Author: Notes on the Teaching of English, 1991, A Preface to Bernard Shaw, 1992, Bernard Shaw and the Court Theatre, 1992. Mem. Internat. Assn. Study Irish Lit.-Japan(auditor 1996—), Bernard Shaw Soc. Japan (editor 1971-74, 92-2000, pres. 2000—), Am. Soc. Eighteenth Century Studies. Avocations: art, town walking, gardening. Home: 978-38 Omaki, Urawa-shi 336-0922, Japan Office: Utsunomiya U, Dept English, Utsunomiya-shi 321-8505, Japan

SHIMAO, TADAO, epidemiologist; b. Tokyo, Sept. 17, 1924; s. Hideichi and Yoshie (Hirata) S.; m. Hiroko Tanaka, Nov. 30, 1958; 1 child, Makoto. MD, Tokyo U. Sch. Medicine, 1948. From med. officer to dir. Rsch. Inst. Tuberculosis Japan Anti-Tuberculosis Assn., Kiyose-shi, 1949-84; from standing bd. mem. to pres. Japan Anti-Tuberculosis Assn., Tokyo, 1984—; chmn. bd. dirs. Japanese Found. for AIDS Prevention, Tokyo, 1999—; exec. bd. WHO, 1987-90; chmn. Japanese delegation Japan-U.S.; coop. med. sci. program, 1993—. Author: Public Health Nursing in TB Control, 1991, TB Control in Japan, 1996. Recipient medal WHO, 1988, 97. Mem. Japanese Soc. Tuberculosis, Japan Pub. Health Assn., Japan Assn. Internat. Health. Home: 1-14-9 Kohyama Nerima-ku, Tokyo 176-0022, Japan Office: Japan Anti-Tuberculosis Assn, 1-3-12 Misaki-cho Chiyodaku, Tokyo 101-0061, Japan

SHIMEK, JOHN ANTON, legal investigation business owner, educator; b. Chgo., Sept. 1, 1925; s. John Anton Sr. and Florence Marie (Redman) S.; m. Corinne Gladys Hornburg, Mar. 1, 1947 (div. June 1988); m. Janet Lea Inghram Snyder, Sept. 10, 1988; children: Ronald Wayne, Scott Anthony, Brian Dean Snyder. AA, Phoenix Coll., 1963; BS, Grand Canyon Coll., 1967; M of Phys. Edn., Sussex (Eng.) Coll., 1974. Cert. sch. adminstr. Am. Police Acad.; cert. aquatic dir.; lic. pvt. investigator; lic. ins. agt. Patrolman Chgo. Police Dept., 1946-51; agt. Met. Life Ins., Colorado Springs/Phoenix, 1951-61; owner, head coach Ariz. Swim Devils, Phoenix, 1967-80; phys. dir., assoc. dir. Phoenix YMCA, 1957-67; sch. adminstr. Cartwright Sch. Dist., Phoenix, 1967-88; pres., owner Shimek & Assocs., Inc., Glendale, Ariz., 1988—; adj. prof. Grand Canyon Coll., Phoenix, 1963-83; spl. agt Internat. Intelligence and Organized Crime Investigations Assn., Washington, 1981-83; mem. AAU Regional Swimming Com., 1967-68; mem. coach AAU State Swim Com., chmn., 1966-67. Author: Physical Education Handbook, 1979, 80, Shimek Heritage, 1998, Swimming Today, 1998, revised, 2000, So You Want To Be a P.I., Vols. I, II & III, 1999, IV, 2000; co-author: An Annotated Bibliography of Experimental Research Concerning Competitive Swimming, 1970, (video) Desert Survival, 1983; contbr. articles to mags. Commdr., instr. search and rescue team Maricopa County Sheriff's Office, Ariz., 1980-89; counselor police acad. Ariz. Dept. Pub. Safety, Tucson, 1982. With USN, 1942-47, WWII, USNR, 1965-80, ret., 1980. Named to Swimming Hall of Fame, Internat. Swimming Hall of Fame, 1971-72. Mem. Am. Legion (comdr. 1980—), Americanism citation 1980-81), Fraternal Order of Police (life, trustee 1980—), Arrowhead Country Club. Republican. Methodist. Home: 7101 W Beardsley Rd #1604 Glendale AZ 85308-5691

SHIMIZU, HIROYASU, speed skater, office worker; b. Obihiro, Hokkaido, Japan, Feb. 27, 1974. Student, Nihon U. Speed skater. Recipient Gold medal 500 meter speed skating Olympic Games, Nagano, Japan, 1998, Bronze medal 1000 meters, 1998. Avocations: fishing, cars. Address: Japanese Olympic Com, 1-1-1 Jinnan Shibuya-ku, Tokyo 150-50, Japan*

SHIMIZU, ICHIRO, hepatologist; b. Osaka, Japan, May 7, 1952; m. Harumi Miyamoto, Mar. 15, 1981; children: Shun, Kaori, Yu. MD, U. Ehime, 1980; PhD, U. Tokushima, 1987. Resident Hosp. Tokushima U., Japan, 1980-81; rsch. assoc. U. Tokushima, 1985-87; postdoctoral fellow U. Pa., Phila., 1989-91; from rsch. assoc. to instr. U. Tokushima, 1991—. Mem. Am. Gastroenterol. Soc., Am. Assn. Study of Liver Disease, World Soc. Gastroenterology, Japan Soc. Gastroenterology. Office: Dept Internal Med 2, U Tokushima Kuramoto-cho, Tokushima 770-8503, Japan

SHIMIZU, KATSUJI, orthopaedic surgeon; b. Yokkaichi, Mie, Japan, Apr. 1, 1948; s. Eizo and Hisako (Mizunuma) S.; m. Michiko Sato, Oct. 22, 1972; children: Katsusuke, Ryosuke. MD, Kyoto (Japan) U., 1973, D.M.Sc., 1982. Lic. physician, Japan; diplomate Japanese Bd. Orthopaedic Surgery. Orthopaedic resident Kyoto U./Tamatsukuri Koseinenkin Hosp., 1973-77; chief orthopaedic divsn. Moriyama (Japan) City Hosp., 1981-82; chief dept. orthopaedic surgery Kokura Meml. Hosp., Kitakyusyu, Japan, 1982-84; asst. prof. orthopaedic surgery Kyoto U., 1984-90, sr. lectr. orthopaedic surgery, 1990-95; assoc. prof. orthopaedic surgery, 1995-96; prof., chmn. orthop. surgery Gifu U. Sch. Medicine and Hosp., 1996—; vis. scientist in orthopaedic rsch. Mayo Clinic, Rochester, Minn., 1985-86; vis. prof. orthopaedic surgery U. Pecs, Hungary, 1996. Editor: Orthops. Today, 1997, Clin. Orthop. Tokyo, 1997—; referee Jour. Orthop. Sci., 1998—; mem. editl. bd. Orthopaedics Internat., 1993—. Nihon Ikueikai scholar for postgrad. med. students, Japan, 1977-81; grantee 10th Ann. Fund for Basic Rsch. of Joint Diseases, Japan, 1983; Japan Rheumatism Assn. fellow, 1985. Mem. Japanese Orthopaedic Assn., Japan Spine Rsch. Soc., Internat. Soc. for Orthopaedic Surgery and Traumatology. Office: Gifu U Sch Medicine, 40 Tsukasa-machi, Gifu 500-8705, Japan

SHIMIZU, SAKAE, physicist, educator; b. Tokyo, July 18, 1915; s. Eijiro and Naka (Sakurai) S.; m. Momoe Iwamura, Feb. 1, 1947; children: Toru, Masaru. BSc, Kyoto (Japan) Imperial U., 1940, MSc, 1943; PhD, Kyoto U., 1950. Lectr. physics Kyoto Imperial U., 1943-46, assoc. prof., 1946-52; prof. Kyoto U., 1952-79, prof. emeritus, 1979—, dir. Radioisotope Rsch. Ctr., 1960-79; field surveyor after Hiroshima atomic bomb, 1945; studied fallout from bomb at Bikini atoll, 1954. Author: Nuclear Measurement Instrument, 1949. Mem. Kyoto City Bd. Edn., 1979-93. Recipient Hon. Mention award Min. Edn. Japan, 1995. Mem. Japan Radioisotope Assn. (v.p. 1990—), Roland Eötvös Phys. Soc. (hon.), Hungarian Acad. Scis. (hon.). Home: 35 Naka-Osagicho Iwakura, Sakyo-ku Kyoto 606-0002, Japan

SHIMIZU, SHUN-ICHI, management consultant; b. Bunkyo-ku, Tokyo, Japan, Jan. 1, 1940; s. Saboro and Shizuko (Imamura) S.; m. Haruno Okamoto; children: Daisaku, Kota. Grad., St. Paul's U., Tokyo, 1962; BSBA, NYU, 1976; Program Mgmt. Devel., Harvard U., 1981. Sr. gen. mgr. Nissho-Iwai Corp., 1988-94; mng. dir. C.U.E. Mgmt. Consulting Ltd., 1994—; spl. advisor Toenec Corp., 1994—, Amagasaki City, 1994-95; dir. Trammel Crow Internat., 1994-95; Japanese liaison rep. Occidental of Japan, Inc., 1994—; mem. com. Miti Gas Energy Import Policy, 1992; dir. Ivanhoe Energy Inc., Can., 1999—. Spl. advisor Kobe City, Japan, 1999—. Mem. Tokyo Am. Club, Tokyo North Rotary Club. Avocations: golf, walking, oil painting, photography, old map collecting. Home: # 201 5-24-1 Hakusan, Bunkyo-ku, Tokyo 112-0001, Japan Office: CUE Mgmt Cons Ltd Anwa Bldg, 8F 2-10 Kanda Chukasa-cho, Chiyoda-ku Tokyo 101-0048, Japan

SHIMIZU, WATARU, cardiologist; b. Hiroshima, Japan, Mar. 7, 1961; s. Hiroshi and Miyoko (Okano) S.; m. Hiroko Sato, Feb. 20, 1993. MD, Hiroshima U., 1985, PhD, 1992. Resident in medicine Hiroshima U., 1985-87, rsch. and clin. fellow, 1990-91; resident in cardiology Nat. Cardiovascular Ctr., Suita, Japan, 1987-90; clin. staff Nat. Cardiovascular Ctr., Suita, 1992-96, 98—; rsch. scientist Masonic Med. Rsch. Lab., Utica, 1996-98. Reviewer Jour. Am. Coll. of Cardiology, Annals of Noninvasive Electrocardiology, Jour. of Cardiovascular Electrophysiology, Pacing Clinical Electrophysiology; contbr. articles to profl. jours. Office: Nat Cardiovascular Ctr, 5-7-1 Fujishiro-dai Suita, Osaka 565-8565, Japan

SHIMIZU, YASUTOSHI, research scientist; b. Nagasaki, Japan, Mar. 12, 1957; s. Minoru and Aiko (Matsuo) S.; m. Yuko Yoshida, Jan. 7, 1982; children: Kota, Tsumugi, Kaze. BSc, Kyushu Inst. Tech., Kitakyushu, Japan, 1979; PhD, U. Tokyo, 1990. Rschr. GS Battery Co., Kyoto, Japan, 1979-84; rschr. ToTo Ltd., Kitakyushu, 1984—, chief rschr., 1994-97, gen. mgr., 1998—; guest prof. Kyushu Inst. Tech., Kitakyushu, 1996—; guest rschr. Govt. Indsl. Rsch. Inst. Osaka; environ. counselor Environ. Agy., Japan, 1997—. Contbr. articles to profl. jours. Mem. Japanese Soc. Water Environment (councilor 1996—), Japan Soc. Biosci., Biotech. and Agrichemistry (councilor 1996), Soc. Chem. Engring. Japan. Avocations: sailing, camping. Office: ToTo Ltd Water Environ Engr, 1-1 Nakashima 2 Kokurakita, Kitakyushu City 802-8601, Japan

SHIMODA, KOICHI, physics educator; b. Urawa, Saitama, Japan, Oct. 5, 1920; s. Seishi and Kiyo (Takemasa) S.; m. Kana Fujiwara, Nov. 28, 1947; children: Sachiko, Etsuko, Jun-ichi, Masataka. BS, Tokyo Imperial U., 1943; ScD, U. Tokyo, 1955. Asst. prof. U. Tokyo, 1948-59, prof., 1959-81; chief scientist Inst. Phys. and Chem. Rsch., Wako, Japan, 1960-81; prof. Keio U., Yokohama, Japan, 1981-92; guest prof. Tokyo Met. Inst. Sci. and Tech., 1993-94; cons. Sci. and Tech. Agy., Tokyo, 1981—. Editor/author: High Resolution Laser Spectroscopy, 1976; author: Introduction to Laser Physics, 1984. Recipient 70th Ann. award Japan Acad., Tokyo, 1980; decorated Order of Merit, 2d Class, Emperor of Japan, 1990. Fellow Optical Soc. Am. (C.E.K. Mees medal 1979); mem. Am. Phys. Soc., Phys. Soc. Japan, Laser Soc. Japan, Physics Edn. Soc. Japan. Avocations: piano music, painting. Home: 1-19-15 Kichijoji-Minamicho, Musashino, Tokyo 180-0003, Japan

SHIMODA, MICHIKO, botanist; b. Oasa-cho, Japan, Apr. 3, 1951; d. Hiroshi and Hisako Kihara; m. Eiji Shimoda, Mar. 30, 1974; children: Fuyuki, Yuji. BS, Hiroshima (Japan) U., 1974, MS, 1976, DSc, 1984. Libr. Hiroshima U., 1984-91; mgr. Lab. Biol. Rsch. Towa Kagaku Co. Ltd., Hiroshima, 1991—; advisor Govt. Akashi (Japan) City, 1996-97; part-time lectr. Ehime (Japan) U., 1997—; mem. com. for protection of cultural properties Higashi-Hiroshima City, 1998—. Co-author: River Environment and Riverside Plants, 1996, Nature of Sera Plateau, 2000, Biotopes of Rural Areas, 2000; contbr. articles to profl. jours. Avocations: movies, art appreciation. E-mail: CXE01364@nifty.ne.jp. Home: Tsurumi-cho 14-21, Naka-ku, Hiroshima 730-0045, Japan Office: Towa Kagaku Co Ltd, Funairi-machi 6-5, Naka-ku, Hiroshima 730-0841, Japan

SHIMOJI, KOKI, anesthetist, educator; b. Tarama, Japan, Nov. 21, 1935; s. Kochu and Eiko Shimoji; m. Yoko Sano, Jan. 9, 1972; children: Yuko, Kaoru. MD, Kumamoto U., Japan, 1960; D Med. Sci., Kyoto U., Japan, 1965. Intern Kumamoto U. Hosp., 1960-61; instr. Kyoto U., 1965-66; asst. prof. Kumamoto U., Japan, 1966-68; assoc. prof. Kumamoto U., 1968-73, Tokyo Med. and Dental U., 1973-74; prof., chmn. Niigata U., Japan, 1974—. Author: Neuroanesthesia, 1972; editl. bd. Pain Rev., Jour. Neurosurg. Anesthesiol., Pain Res., Pain Rev.; others; contbr. articles to profl. jours. Fellow Royal Coll. Anaesthetists (Eng., hon.); mem. Japan Soc. Anesthesiology (councillor, pres. 1997; most disting. paper award 1965), Japan Soc. EEG and EMG (councillor, pres. 1996), Japan Soc. Acute Medicine (councillor), Japan Soc. Pain Clinic (pres. 1982-83), Japan Med. Assn. (clin. application of spinal cord potential award 1983), Am. Soc. Anesthesiologists, Assn. Univ. Anesthesiologists, Internat. Brain Rsch. Orgn., Internat. Assn. Study Pain, Assn. Univ. Anesthesiologists (hon.). Buddhist. Home: 2-808 Suido-cho, Niigata 951, Japan Office: Niigata U Sch Medicine, Asahi-Machi, Niigata 951-8510, Japan

SHIMOMURA, YOSHIHARU, biochemist, educator; b. Ishiki-cho, Japan, Apr. 15, 1953; s. Matao and Mitsue (Maki) S.; m. Noriko Kato, Nov. 23, 1982; children: Daisuke, Sayako. BS in Nutritional Sci., Tokyo U. Edn., 1976; MS in Nutritional Sci., U. Tsukuba, Japan, 1978; PhD in Biochemistry, U. Nagoya, Japan, 1983. Asst. prof. U. Nagoya, 1983-87; rsch. assoc. Ind. U., Indpls., 1986-87; asst. prof. U. Tsukuba, 1987-92; assoc. prof. biochemistry Nagoya Inst. Tech., 1992-97, prof., 1997—. Contbr. articles to profl. jours. Grantee Ministry of Edn., Sci., Sports and Culture, 1996-97, 99—. Mem. Japanese Soc. of Phys. Fitness and Sports Medicine (councillor 1995—), Am. Soc. of Nutritional Scis., Japanese Soc. of Nutrition and Food Sci. Home: 1-152-9 Mino-cho, Kasugai 486-0917, Japan Office: Nagoya Inst of Tech, Gokiso-cho Showa-ku, Nagoya 466-8555, Japan

SHIN, DONG-WOO, materials engineering educator, executive; b. Sangju, Republic of Korea, June 16, 1960; s. Won-Shik and Kwan-Yi (Chang) S.; m. Youn-Sun Lim, Dec. 25, 1986; children: Jae-Hyun, Jee-Hun. BA with honors, Hanyang U., Seoul, Republic of Korea, 1983; MSc, Korea Advanced Inst. Sci., Seoul, Republic of Korea, 1985; PhD, Cambridge (Eng.) U., 1993. Rschr. Max-Planck Inst., Stuttgart, Germany, 1985-86; staff rschr. Agy. Def. Devel., Taejon, Republic of Korea, 1987-88; rsch. fellow Nat. Inst. Rsch. in Inorganic Materials, Tsukuba, Japan, 1991-92; rsch. prof. Ceramic Materials Rsch. Inst., Hanyang U., 1993-95; prof. materials engring. Kyongsang Nat. U., Chinju, Republic of Korea, 1995-97, head divsn. materials sci. & engring., 1997-99; exec. mem. industry std. com. Ministry of Industry and Trade, Seoul, 1996—; exec. mem. fine ceramic com. Nat. Inst. Tech. and Quality, Seoul, 1997—; CEO Nano Co., Ltd., Chinju, 1999—. Author: Raw Materials of Ceramics, 1995, Fracture of Ceramics, 1996; contbr. articles to profl. jours. Vol. adviser Small and Medium Bus. Adminstrn., Changwon/Kyungnam, Republic of Korea, 1995. Mem. Korean Assn. Crystal Growth (exec. mem.), Korean Ceramic Soc. Christian. Avocations: mountain climbing, swimming. Office: Kyongsang Nat U Divsn Mat Eng, 900 Gazwadong, Chinju 660-701, Republic of Korea

SHIN, EUI-SOON, economist, educator; b. Seoul, Republic of Korea, June 9, 1950; s. Ki-Suk Shin and Kwi-Bok Kim; m. Sun-Hee Park; children: Sun-Young, Dong-Ho. BA, Yonsei U., Seoul, Republic of Korea, 1972; MA, U. Wash., 1977, PhD, 1980. Postdoctoral rsch. fellow Calif. Inst. Tech., Pasadena, 1980-81; prof. Yonsei U., Seoul, 1981—, assoc. dean Grad. Sch., 1995-96, chmn. dept. econs., 1996-98; vis. assoc. prof. Brown U., Providence, 1988-89; fellow East-West Ctr., Honolulu, 1991; vis. scholar dept. econs. Harvard U., 1999—. Author: Energy Policies in Korea and Japan, 1986, Natural Resource Economics, 1988; contbr. articles to profl. jours. 1st lt. Korean Mil., 1972-74. Recipient 24th Economist award The Mae-Il Daily Econ. Newspaper, 1994. Mem. Korea Resource Econs. Assn. (pres. 1993-95). Avocations: stamp collecting, Kumdo. Office: Yonsei Univ Dept Econs, 134 Shinchon-dong, Seodaemun-gu Seoul 120-749, Republic of Korea

SHIN, EUN JU, chemistry educator; b. Pusan, Republic of Korea, May 14, 1961; s. Kyung Hwan Shin and Og Ran Lee; m. Ho Kwon Kang, May 24, 1987; children: Igojeo, Ironae. BSc, Seoul Nat. U., 1983; PhD, Korea Advanced Inst. Sci. Tech., 1987. Rschr. Korea Advanced Inst. Sci. Tech., Seoul, Republic of Korea, 1987; sr. rschr. Kumho Petrochem. Co., Yeochon, Republic of Korea, 1988-89; from lectr. to assoc. prof. Sunchon (Republic of Korea) Nat. U., 1989-95, assoc. prof., 1995—; vis. prof. Ariz. State U., Tempe, 1991-92. Contbr. articles to profl. jours. Mem. Am. Chem. Soc., Korean Chem. Soc., Korean Soc. Photosci. E-mail: ejs@sunchon.sunchon.ac.kr. Fax: 082-661-750-3608. Office: Sunchon Nat Univ, Maegog 315, Sunchon Chonnam 540-742, Republic of Korea

SHIN, EUNGBAI, engineering educator; b. Heasan, Korea, Apr. 17, 1938; s. SeokTai Shin and HongOk Yeon; m. KyungSook Kim, July 10, 1971; children: MooKyun, HyunAh. BE, Hanyang U., Seoul, 1961; MS, Seoul Nat. U., 1965; PhD, Vanderbilt U., 1973. Registered profl. engr., Tenn., Korea. Dir. environ. engring. Korea Inst. Sci. and Tech., 1974-90; vis. scientist Harvard U., Mass., 1983-84; WHO short-term cons. Instr. for PNG Tng. Course on Water Pollution Control, 1989; mem. Presdl. Adv. Coun. on Sci. and Tech., Seoul, 1999-2001; pres. Korean Fedn. Water Sci. and Engring. Socs., 2000—; vice-chmn. Pacific Rim steering com. Water Environment Fedn., 1986-95, mem. program subcom., joint tech. exch. program, 1998—; chmn. Pacific Basin Consortium for Hazardous Waste Rsch. and Mgmt., 1990-92; chmn. 6th pilot phase guidance group meeting Asia Europe Environ. Tech. Ctr., Asia-Europe Meeting, 2000—; mem. bd. control UNEP Nat. Com. for Republic of Korea, 1996—. Contbr. articles to profl. jours. Cpl. Korean Army, 1961-63. Recipient Presdl. Cert. of Honor for Sci. Day, Korean Gov., 1981, UNEP Global 500 Roll of Honor award, 1992, Arthur Sidney Bedell award Water Environment Fedn., 1992, Order of Merit Dong-Baek medal for World Environment Day, Korean Govt., 1997. Mem. Nat. Acad. Engring. Korea, Korean Acad. Sci. and Tech., N.Y. Acad. Scis. Presbyterian. Achievements include patents for high-rate anaerobic septic tank, high-rate aerobic septic tank. Avocation: Go. Home: 105-202 WooBang Villa, 75 GumiDong, 463-500 SungNamSi Korea Office: Hanyang U Env Eng Rsch Inst, Hangdang Dong, 133-791 Seoul Korea

SHIN, HYUNGCHEOL, electrical engineer, educator; b. Jeonju, CheonPook, Korea, Oct. 29, 1962; s. Hoseon and Malyeo (Kim) S.; m. Heejung Kang, June 1, 1990. BS, Seoul Nat. U., 1985, MS, 1987; PhD, U. Calif., Berkeley, 1993. Sr. device engr. Motorola, Phoenix, 1994-96; asst. prof. Korea Advanced Inst. Sci. and Tech., Taejon, 1996-99, assoc. prof., 1999—. Author: Plasma Charging Damage, 1996; contbr. articles to profl. jours. 2d lt. Korean Army, 1987-88. Recipient 2d Best Paper award Am. Vacuum Soc., 1991. Mem. IEEE, Korean Inst. Telematics and Electronics. Avocations: travel, tennis. Office: Korea Adv Inst Sci and Tech, 373-1 Kusong-dong Yusong-gu, Taejon 305-701, Korea

SHIN, JOHN JOONGSUNG, mechanical nuclear engineer, consultant; b. Keuchang-Gun, Kyongnam, Korea, Feb. 27, 1941; came to U.S., 1966; s. Jong-Hyup and Hyunpoong (Kwak) S.; m. Sooky C. Shin, Apr. 22, 1972; children: Michael P., Eric P. BS, Korea Maritime U., Pusan, 1963, Hanyang U., Seoul, Korea, 1965; MS, Syracuse U., 1968; PhD, U. Del., 1974. Tchg. asst. Korea Maritime U., Pusan, 1965-66; rsch. asst. Syracuse (N.Y.) U., 1966-68; design engr. Sargent, Webster, Crenshaw, Syracuse, 1968-69; rsch. asst. U. Del., Newark, 1969-73; engr., sr. engr., prin. engr. Ebasco Svcs., Inc., N.Y.C., 1973-93; prin. engr., cons., sr. cons. Raytheon Nuclear, Inc., N.Y.C., 1993—; tech. cons. Ebasco/Raytheon Nuclear, Inc., N.Y.C., 1973—; tech. cons., seminar Korea Atomic Energy Rsch. Inst., Taejon, 1993, Korea Power Engring. Co., Yongin, Korea, 1992—; condr. seminar Seoul Nat. U., Korea Advanced Inst. Sci. and Tech., Seoul and Taejon, 1992, 93; mem. adv. bd. Korea Next Generation Reactor Tech. Devel., 1992—. Contbr. articles to profl. jours. 2nd engring. officer on ocean going vessels Korea Maritime Bur. Recipient awards U.S. Dept. Energy, 1988, 93, shining star awards Ebasco Svcs., Inc., Entergy Ops., Inc., 1986, 97. Mem. ASME, Am. Nuclear Soc., Korean Scientists and Engrs. Am., Korea Maritime U. Alumni Assn. (pres. 1990-92, 96-98). Democrat. Achievements include research on passive containment cooling of new production reactor and advaned reactors following loss of coolant accident, advanced reactor analyses including incontainment refueling water storage tank during air bubble oscillation, condensation-oscillation and chugging; hydrogen generation, hydrogen distribution, steam and hydrogen explosion, corium-concrete interaction and recritcality analyses following severe reactor accident of 100% reactor core meltdown, universal passive containment protection analysis for inherently safe advanced light water reactor, advanced neutron source reactor analyses, hydrogen ignitor location analyses inside reactor containments, boiling water reactor suppression pool analyses following loss of coolant accident; avocations: swimming, boating, hiking. Home: 314 Division Ave Hasbrouck Heights NJ 07604-1722 Office: Raytheon Nuclear Inc 2 World Trade Ctr Fl 88 New York NY 10048-0002

SHIN, MYUNG HI, physician; b. Seoul, Republic of Korea, Nov. 2, 1936; d. Suck Ho Shin and Nam Hee Kang; m. Sang Wook Kim, Dec. 2, 1972 (dec. Jan. 1994); 3 children. MD, Seoul Nat. U., 1962. Diplomate Am. Bd. Pediat. Resident in pediat. Albert Einstein Med. Ctr., Phila., 1964-65, 66-67, Jefferson Med. Coll., Phila., 1965-66; fellow in pediat. nephrology Mayo Clin., Rochester, Minn., 1967-68; chief pediat. Korea Hosp., Seoul, 1968-73, Bapt. Hosp., Pusan, Republic of Korea, 1974-84, St. Joseph Hosp., Pusan, 1984—. Roman Catholic. Avocations: stamp collecting, reading. Home: Lucky Apt 15-1205, 707 On-Chun-Dong Dong-Rae-Ku, 607-062 Pusan Republic of Korea

SHIN, SANG CHUL, pharmacist, educator, researcher; b. Kwangju City, South Korea, July 12, 1947; s. Yong Jin and Keum Yi (Lee) S.; m. Ok Hee Kim, Nov. 1, 1973. B degree, Seoul Nat. U., 1969, M degree, 1973, PhD, 1979. Pres. Il-Yang Pharm. Ctrl. Rsch. Inst., Seoul, 1970-85; prof. Chonnam Nat. U., Kwangju City, 1985—, dean Coll. Pharmacy, 2000—; mem. pharm. affairs com. Min. Health and Social Affairs, Seoul, 1992—. Editor-in-chief Jour. Korean Pharm. Scis., 1996-97; editor Archives Pharm. Rsch., 1992-98. Recipient Acad. award Korean Soc. Pharmaceutics, 1995, Excellence Sci. Thesis award Korean Fedn. Sci. and Tech., 1997, 2000 Outstanding Scientists of the 20th Century Internat. Biog. Ctr., Eng., 1000 World Leaders of Influence Am. Biog. Inst. Mem. Korean Soc. Pharmaceutics (v.p. 2000—). Avocations: tennis, golf. Fax: 82-62-530-2949. Home: Hyundai Apt 103-203, Hwajong-1-dong, Kwangju City 502-240, Republic of Korea Office: Chonnam Nat U, Coll Pharm, Kwangju City 500-757, Republic of Korea

SHIN, SUNG-CHUL, physicist, educator; b. Taejon, Republic of Korea, July 19, 1952; s. Hyun-Soo Shin and Jae-Soon Kim; m. Won-Ki Min, Dec. 20, 1980; children: Jessica, Grace. BS, Seoul Nat. U., Republic of Korea,

1975; MS, Korean Advanced Inst. Sci. and Tech., Taejon, 1977; PhD, Northwestern U., 1984. Vis. scientist Nat. Inst. Stds. and Tech., Washington, 1977-78; sr. rsch. scientist Eastman Kodak Rsch. Labs., Rochester, N.Y., 1984-89; prof. physics Korean Advanced Inst. Sci. & Tech., 1989—; tech. cons. Sam Sung LG, Seoul, 1989-94; dir. internat. rels. Korean Advanced Inst. Sci. & Tech., 1993-95, dean of planning, 1995-96, dir. Establishment Corps, Korean Inst. Advanced Studies, 1996, dir. Ctr. Nanospinics of Spintronic Materials, 1998—. Editor: Structure and Properties of Multilayered Thin Films, 1995; contbr. articles to profl. jours. and conf. procs. (Excellent Paper award Korean Fedn. Sci. & Tech. 1998). Recipient Scientist of Month award IPPP. Fellow Korean Phys. Soc. (Best Paper award 1998); mem. Am. Phys. Soc., Materials Rsch. Soc., Korean Magnetic Soc. Christian. Office: KAIST Dept Physics, 373-1 Kusung-dong Yusung-gu, Taejon 305-701, Republic of Korea

SHIN, WON SOP, forestry educator; b. Jinchon, Korea, Sept. 15, 1959; s. Dong In and Yong Kyu (Lee) S.; m. Mi Chong Ha, Dec. 20, 1985; children: Jae Sung, Jae Eun. BS, Chungbuk Nat. U., Cheongju, Korea, 1985; MS, U. New Brunswick, Fredericton, Can., 1988; PhD, U. Toronto, Can., 1992. Grad. asst. U. New Brunswick, Fredericton, Can., 1986-88, U. Toronto, Can., 1988-91; prof. Chungbuk Nat. U., Cheongju, Korea, 1993—. Author: Forest Policy in Korea, 1997, Outdoor Recreation Management, 1998. Korean-Can. Found. scholar, 1990, vis. scholar U. Idaho, Moscow, 1996-97; Connaight fellow U. Toronto, 1988-91, Edward Elsworth Johnson Forestry fellow, 1991, postdoctoral fellow U. Toronto, 1992. Mem. Korean Inst. Plants, People & Environment (v.p. 1988—), Korean Forestry Soc., Korean Forest Econ. Soc. Roman Catholic. Avocations: camping, hiking, bowling, photography. Home: 302-702 Hyundai 3cha, Yongam-dong Sangdang-ku, Cheongju 360-181, Republic of Korea Office: Chungbuk Nat U, 48 Gaesin-Dong, Cheongju 361-763, Republic of Korea

SHIN, YOON SOOK, biochemist, researcher; b. Seoul, Korea, Aug. 5, 1946; arrived in Fed. Republic Germany, 1975; d. Jung Sik and Chung Ja (Kwon) S.; m. Teodor Podskarbi, April 5, 1991. BS, U. Seoul, 1968; Pharmacist, 1968; PhD, U. Calif., Berkeley, 1972; Dr. Med. Habilitation, U. Munich, 1989. Tchg. asst. U. Calif., 1970-72, rsch. asst., 1968-72; rsch. assoc. U. Calif.-Berkeley and U. Rochester, N.Y., 1972-75; Wissenschaft Asst. U. Munich, 1975—, lectr., 1989, full prof., 1995—. Contbr. over 250 articles in field to profl. jours. Deutsche Forschunge Gemeinschaft grantee, 1975-79, 1987-93. Mem. Am. Assn. Advanced Sci., N.Y. Acad. Scis., Curopean Soc. Pediat. Rsch., Soc. Inborn Errors of Metabolism, Sigma Xi. Office: U Munich Kinderklinik, Lindwurmstr 4, 80337 Munich Germany

SHINDLER, COLIN, editor, lecturer; b. London, Sept. 3, 1946; s. Hyman and Rachel (Nathan) S.; m. Jean Pollock, Oct. 27, 1976; children: Sara, Joshua, Ruthie, Miriam. BS with honors, Leicester (Eng.) U., 1968; MS, CNAA, 1981. Editor Jews in the U.S.S.R., 1972-75; fgn. sec. World Union of Jewish Students, 1970-72; editor Jewish Quarterly, 1985-94, Judaism Today, 1994—. Author: Exit Visa: Detente Human Rights The Jewish Emigration Movement in the USSR, 1978, Ploughshares Into Swords? Israelis and Jews in the Shadow of the Intijada, 1991, Israel, Likud and the Zionist Dream: Power, Politics and Ideology from Begun to NEtaryahu, 1995. Fellow Israel Studies, Sch. Oriental and African Studies U. London, 1998—. Mem. European Jewish Pub. Soc. (dir. 1996—). Labour Party. Avocations: numismatics, reading, writing.

SHINDO, KATSUHISA, surgeon; b. Osaka, Japan, Nov. 2, 1939; s. Tomoo and Setsue (Danyasu) S.; m. Takako Inoue, June 15, 1968; children: Masahisa, Tokuhisa. MD, Tokyo Med. and Dental U., 1966; PhD, Osaka U., 1974. Intern U.S. Naval Hosp., Yokosuka, Japan, 1966-67; resident in surgery Osaka U. Hosp., 1967-69, Temple U. Hosp., Phila., 1969-71; rsch. fellow Osaka U. Sch. Medicine, 1971-75, asst. in surgery, 1976-84; asst. pathology Heidelberg (Germany) U., 1975-76; vice adminstr. Kawachi Gen. Hosp., Higashi-Osaka, 1984-86; assoc. prof. Kinki U. Sch. Medicine, Osaka-Sayama, 1987-94, prof. surgery, 1994—, cons. indsl. hygiene, 1993—, chief dept. surgery, 1999—; judge Exam Bd. of Soc. Ins. Fund., Osaka, 1991—; del. of Japan ISO TC173/SC3, Stockholm, 1991—. Author: Stoma Rehabilitation, 1974, Informed Consent Manual, 1995, How To Be Free from Piles, 1994, Clinical Skills and Practical Materials for Informed Consent, 1999; editor-in-chief STOMA, 1982—. Recipient First award Internat. Acad. Proctology, 1972, Hon. award, 1975; Osaka Anticancer Assn. rsch. grantee, 1980. Mem. Internat. Soc. Univ. Colon and Rectal Surgeons (continental sec. 1978-98, continental v.p. 1998—), Japan Soc. Colo-Proctology (v.p. 1991-92), Japanese Soc. Stoma Rehab. (bd. dirs. 1984—, pres. 1998—), Japanese Soc. Gastroent. Surgery (councillor 1989—), Japanese Coll. Surgeons (councillor 1995—), Japanese Soc. Genetics Aspects Human Malignancy (gov. 1986—), Japan Soc. Clin. Oncology (councillor 1995—), Japanese Soc. Hepato, Biliary and Pancreatic Surgery (councillor 1995—), Japanese Soc. Abdominal Emergency Surgery (councillor 1995—), Japanese Soc. Surg. Pathology (councillor 1996—), Japanese Soc. Cancer Colon Rectum (sec. gen. 1992—), Japan Surg. Assn. (councillor 1998—), Asian Fedn. Colo-proctology (founder 1975), Asian Forum Stoma Rehab. (founder 1999). Achievements include research in new histochemical examination of phosphoamidase and its application to the digestive epithelium; diagnostic pattern of DNA-content in the borderline neoplasm of the large intestine. Avocation: personal computers. Home: 13-4 Ohnodai 7-chome, Osaka Sayama 589-0023, Japan Office: Kinki Univ Sch Medicine, Kinki Univ Sch Medicine, Harayamadi 2-cho, Sakai Osaka 590-0132, Japan

SHINDO, MASAOMI, neurologist; b. Kobuchizawa, Yamanashi, Japan, Sept. 28, 1948; s. Masakane and Chihoko (Uchida) S.; m. Yasuko Sekine, Dec. 9, 1973; children: Mizuho, Aya. B of Medicine, Shinshu U., Matsumoto, Japan, 1973, PhD, 1985. Medical diplomate. Jr. resident Shinshu U., Matsumoto, 1973, asst., 1973-79, 80-86, lectr., 1986-93, assoc. prof., 1993-98, prof., 1998—; chief doctor Nat. Nagano Hosp., Kamiyamada, Japan, 1979-80. Avocations: skiing, bicycling, classical music. Home: Omura 1076-1, Matsumoto 390-0304, Japan Office: Shinshu U, Ctr Health Svcs Asahi 3-1-1, Matsumoto 390-8621, Japan

SHINE, DANIEL JOSEPH, JR., management consultant; b. Lawrence, Mass., Feb. 17, 1944; s. Daniel Joseph and Catherine Theresa (Mahoney) S.; Rosanne Marie Pingaro, Sept. 30, 1967; children: Matthew David, Jonathan Marc. BA in History, Merrimack Coll., 1965; MS in Fgn. Svc., Georgetown U., 1968. Mem. staff, intelligence officer CIA, Washington, 1967-76; dir. Sanders Assocs., Nashua, N.H., 1976-85; sr. v.p. Arthur D. Little, Inc., Cambridge, Mass., 1985-94; prin. EDS/Mgmt. Consulting, Plano, Tex., 1994-95; v.p./global practice leader A.T. Kearney, Inc., Chgo., 1995—; bd. advisors Georgetown U. Admissions, Washington, 1976—; mem. pres.'s coun. Merrimack Coll., North Andover, Mass., 1995—. E-mail: dan.shine@atkearney. Home: 11 Granada Way Andover MA 01810-4201 Office: AT Kearney Inc 1 Memorial Dr Ste 14 Cambridge MA 02142-1346

SHINE, KENNETH IRWIN, cardiologist, educator; b. Worcester, Mass., 1935. Grad., Harvard Coll., 1957; MD, Harvard U., 1961. Diplomate Am. Bd. Internal Medicine. Intern Mass. Gen. Hosp., 1961-62, resident, 1962-63, 65-66, fellow in cardiology, 1966-67; surgeon USPHS, 1963-65; instr. Harvard Med. Sch., from 1968; asst. prof. medicine UCLA Sch. Medicine, 1971-73, assoc. prof., 1973-77, prof., 1977-92, prof. emeritus, 1993—, dir. CCU, 1971-75, chief div. cardiology, 1975-79, vice chmn. dept. medicine, 1979-81, exec. chmn., 1981-86, dean, 1986-92; clin. prof. medicine Georgetown U. Med. Ctr., Washington, 1993—; provost for med. scis. UCLA Sch. Medicine, 1991-92; pres. Inst. of Medicine, Washington, 1992—. Mem. Am. Heart Assn. (pres. 1986-87), Assn. Am. Med. Colls. (adminstrv. bd. coun. deans 1989-92, exec. bd. 1990-92, chmn. coun. deans 1991-92). Office: Institute of Medicine 2101 Constitution Ave NW Washington DC 20418-0007

SHINE, MARY TONISSEN, retired advertising executive; b. Jacksonville, Fla., Apr. 16, 1926; d. Otto John and Anna Ruth (Simms) T.; m. James Munnerlyn Shine, Mar.12, 1955; children: James Munnerlyn Jr., Wallace Tonissen. Student, Salem Coll., 1944-45, Greenleaf Bus. Coll., 1945-46. Sec. Morris Plan Bank, Jacksonville, 1945-46, Riverside Bank, Jacksonville, 1947; loan and discount teller Northwestern Bank, Hendersonville, N.C., 1947-48; sec. trust dept. Fla. Nat. Bank, Jacksonville, 1948-50; office mgr., sales asst. Harry E. Cummings Radio/TV Rep., Jacksonville, 1950-62; traffic and billing clk. Sta. WJAX, Jacksonville, 1963-64; media dir. William Cook Advt., Inc., Jacksonville, 1966-90. Bd. dirs. Meth. Regional Hosp. System, Jacksonville, 1986-92, Morning Star Sch., Jacksonville, 1985-92; com. mem. Communications Com., Drug and Substance Abuse Com., Episcopal Diocese Fla., Jacksonville, 1984-88. Recipient Jack Philipps Gold medal 4th Dist. Am. Advt. Fedn., 1984. Mem. Jacksonville Advt. Fedn. (bd. dirs. 1972-81, treas. 1973-74, v.p. 1974-76, pres. 1976-77, 77-78, Silver medal 1988, life). Democrat. Avocations: oil painting, playing piano and organ. Home: 1984 Eventide Rd Switzerland Rte Jacksonville FL 32259

SHINE, NEAL JAMES, journalism educator, former newspaper editor, publisher; b. Grosse Pointe Farms, Mich., Sept. 14, 1930; s. Patrick Joseph and Mary Ellen (Conlon) S.; m. Phyllis Theresa Knowles, Jan. 24, 1953; children: Judith Ann, James Conlon, Susan Brigid, Thomas Patrick, Margaret Mary, Daniel Edward. BS in Journalism, U. Detroit, 1952; PhD (hon.), Cleary Coll., 1989, Siena Heights Coll., 1995, U. Mich., 1995, U. Detroit Mercy, 1996, Ctrl. Mich. U., 1996. Mem. staff Detroit Free Press, 1950-95, asst. city editor, 1963-65, city editor, 1965-71, mng. editor, 1971-82, sr. mng. editor, 1982-89, pub., 1990-95; prof. journalism Oakland U., Rochester, Mich., 1995—. Host, moderator Detroit Week in Rev., Sta. WTVS-TV, 1981-89, host Neal Shine's Detroit, 1989-91. Trustee, vice chmn. bd. trustees Youth for Understanding, 1973-75, chmn., 1975-78; mem. bd. for student publs. U. Mich.; bd. dirs. Children's Hosp., Econ. Club Detroit, Detroit Renaissance, New Detroit, Inc., Detroit Symphony Orch., Detroit Inst. Arts, Detroit Hist. Soc., United Way of Southeastern Mich., Met. Detroit Conv. and Visitors Bur., Operation ABLE, Detroit Press Club Found. With U.S. Army, 1953-55. Inducted Mich. Journalism Hall of Fame, 1990. Mem. Am. Soc. Newspape Editors, Am. Newspapers Pubs. Assn., Mich. Press Assn. (bd. dirs. 1990-95), AP Mng. Editors, Sons of Whiskey Rebellion (comdr.-in-chief 1979—), Inc. Soc. Irish-Am. Lawyers, Detroit Press Club (charter, bd. govs. 1966-89, sec. 1957-68, v.p. 1969-71, pres. 1971-73). Home: 11009 Harbor Place Dr Saint Clair Shores MI 48080-1527 also: Carraig Rinn, 13240 Crystal Beach Rd, Pointe aux Roches, ON Canada N0R 1N0

SHINER, REBECCA LYNN, psychology educator; b. Johnstown, Pa., July 27, 1968; d. Harold Samuel and Bonnie Jean Mitchell; m. Mark Todd Shiner, Sept. 14, 1991; 1 child, Leo Mitchell. BA, Haverford Coll., 1990; PhD, U. Minn., 1998. Case mgr. Cambridge (Mass.) and Sommerville Coop. Apt. Project, 1990-91; rsch. asst. Harvard Med. Sch., Boston, 1991-92; psychology intern U. Rochester (N.Y.) Med. Ctr., 1998-99; asst. prof. Colgate U., Hamilton, N.Y., 1999—. Contbr. articles to profl. jours. Dissertation fellow U. Minn., 1996-97, Eva D. Miller fellow, 1995-96; Nat. Merit scholar Soc. of Engrs., 1986-90. Mem. APA, Soc. for Rsch. in Child Devel. Roman Catholic. Avocations: singing, cooking. E-mail: rshiner@mail.colgate.edu. Office: Colgate U Dept Psychology 13 Oak Dr Hamilton NY 13346-1383

SHINER, STEPHEN LEWIS, anesthesiologist; b. N.Y.C., Sept. 10, 1946; s. Irving Sydney and Shirley Estelle (Wechsler) S.; m. Deborah Aaronnette Tarschis, Aug. 7, 1969; children: David I., Michael Ian, Lara Suzzanne. BS, U. Miami, 1976, MD, 1980. Diplomate Nat. Bd. Med. Examiners, Am. Bd. Pain Mgmt., Am. Bd. Anesthesiology, Am. Bd. Forensic Medicine, Am. Bd. Forensic Examiners; qualified med. examiner, Calif.; lic. physician Fla., Calif., Tex., Tenn., Wyo., N.Y., Mich., Iowa. Resident in internal medicine Mt. Sinai Med. Ctr., Miami Beach, Fla., 1980-81; resident in anesthesiology Jackson Meml. Hosp., Miami, 1981-82, 83-84; chief resident in anesthesiology Miami VA Hosp./Jackson Meml. Hosp., Miami, 1982-84; cardiovascular anesthesiology and critical care mgmt. fellow Miami VA Hosp./Jackson Meml. Hosp., 1982-83; clin. dir. dept. anesthesia, dir. surg. ICU Raleigh Gen. Hosp., Beckley, W.Va., 1984-85; dir. anesthesia Brandon Surg. Group, Humana Hosp. of Brandon, Fla., 1985-86; pvt. practice anesthesia Phoenix, 1986-87; med. dir. anesthesia and pain mgmt. projects Jackson & Coker Physician Svcs., 1988-90; dir. Marina Del Rey Pain and Med. Ctr., 1990-92, Marina Del Rey Surg. Ctr., 1990-92, Pain Ctrs. of Am., 1990-92, Allegiant Physician Svcs., Inc., 1990-92; chief exec. med. dir., cons. Pain Relief Network, Tex. Pain Relief Inst., Dallas; mediator med. legal and med. ins. cases; dir. quality assurance and med. chart rev. Nat. Pain Inst. of Am., Allegiant Physician Svcs., Inc.; expert reviewer med.-legal documentation and cases; chief police physician Hollywood (Fla.) Police Dept.; cons. on mil. affairs Rep. Senatorial Com., Rep. Presdl. Round Table. Contbr. articles to profl. jours. Mem. Rep. Presdl. Round Table, 1990—, campaign advisor, 1992—; ad hoc rep. Rep. Presdl. Nat. Conv., 1992, 96; defensive coord., asst. head coach J.V. football team Coral Springs (Fla.) H.S., 1992-98; mem. Fla. Boxing Commn., 1989-90; physician Fla. State Athletic Commn., 1989-90; ringside physician Tex. State Golden Gloves Assn., 1987-88, for Wichita County, 1987-88, AAU, 1987-88; coach Little League Baseball, Pop Warner Football, Wichita Falls, Tex., 1987-89, Scottsdale, Ariz., 1986-87; mem. Miami Boxing Commn. and ringside physician, 1981-84; others. With Spl. Forces, U.S. Army, 1964-72. Decorated Silver Star (5), Bronze Star medal with V for Valor (6), Purple Heart (6), Air Medal with V for Valor, Vietnam Campaign medal, republic of Vietnam Cross of Honor 1st class, Australian Cross of Valor, others. Fellow Am. Coll. Forensic Medicine, Am. Coll. Forensic Examiners, Am. Coll. Pain Mgmt., Am. Coll. Anesthesiology, Am. Coll. Occupl. Medicine; mem. Am. Soc. Pain Medicine, Am. Soc. Forensic Medicine, Am. Soc. Anesthesiologists, Am. Soc. Regional Anesthesia, Am. Soc. Forensic Examiners, Internat. Soc. Police Surgeons, Internat. Narcotic Enforcement Officers Assn., FOP. Republican. Avocations: hunting, fishing, scuba diving, hiking, horseback riding. Home: 5454 NW 87th Ter Coral Springs FL 33067-2857

SHINGAREVA, INNA KONSTANTINOVNA, mathematician; b. Moscow, Nov. 17, 1964; d. Konstantin Sergeevich and Margarita Ivanovna Shingarev. MSc, Moscow Inst. Electronics/Math., 1988; MA, Moscow State Conservatory, 1989; PhD, Russian Acad. Scis., Moscow, 1995. Programmer Rsch. Inst. Electronic Industry, Moscow, 1988-91; jr. rsch. scientist Inst. for Problems in Math., Russian Acad. Scis., Moscow, 1992-95, rsch. scientist, 1995—; tchr. Physico-Math. Sch., Moscow, 1988-90; asst. prof. Moscow Inst. Radiotechnics, Electronics and Automatics, 1991, Moscow Inst. Food Tech., 1992-95; translator Jour. Mechs. of Solids, Moscow, 1995-98. Contbr. articles to profl. jours. Grantee Russian Found. for Basic Rsch., 1994, 95-98, 97—. Avocations: piano, concerts. Office: Inst Problems in Mechs RAS, Vernadsky Ave 101, 117526 Moscow Russia

SHINI, SHANIKO, veterinarian, researcher; b. Tirana, Albania, July 31, 1960; d. Mamut and Kadrije (Pali) Kadriu; m. Agim Shini, Aug. 10, 1986; children: Indrit, Arlind. BSc in Vet. Medicine, Agrl. U. Tirana, 1983, Cand. Scis., 1991, DSc, 1994. Mem. sci. staff Agrl. U. Tirana, 1983-91, lectr., 1991-97; vis. scientist Vet. Medicine Sch. Hannover, Germany, 1995—. Contbr. article and rev. to sci. jours., including Deutsche Tierärztliche Wissenschaft, Archiv für Geflügelkunde. Roman Catholic. Avocations: research, writing scientific publications, learning foreign languages, painting. Home: 39 Grosser Hillen, 30559 Hannover Germany Office: Vet Medicine Sch Hannover, Poultry Clin Bünteweg 17, 30559 Hannover Germany

SHINKAI, HISASHI, medicinal scientist, researcher; b. Kofu, Japan, Jan. 30, 1958; s. Hisao and Yoshiko (Watanabe) S.; m. Yurika Yoneyama, Apr. 30, 1984; children: Akihilo, Hideaki. BS, Tohoku U., Sendai, Japan, 1980, MS, 1982, PhD, 1989. Pharmaceutical diplomate. Leader diabetic drug group Ctrl. Rsch. Labs., Ajinomoto, Inc., Kanagawa, Japan, 1982-92; leader medicinal chemistry group Ctrl. Pharm. Rsch. inst., JT, Inc., Osaka, Japan, 1992—. Author: New Antidiabetic Drugs, 1990; contbr. articles to profl. jours., including Nature, Jour. Medicinal Chemistry, Jour. Liquid Chromatography, Drug Discovery Today, Drugs of the Future, others. Mem. AAAS, Am. Chem. Soc. (mem. task force on the publ. 1993—), Pharm. Soc. Japan. Home: 90-6 Iwakura-Shimozaichicho, Sakyo-ku Kyoto 606-0013, Japan Office: Ctrl Pharm Rsch Inst/JT Inc, 1-1 Murasaki-cho, Takatsuki Osaka 569-1125, Japan

SHINKI, TOSHIMASA, pharmacologist, educator; b. Ageo, Japan, July 30, 1951; parents Tsunemasa and Haruko S.; m. Kyoue Takasu, May 12, 1978; children: Tomohide, Kenji. BS, Showa U., 1975, PhD, 1985. Faculty pharm. scis. Showa U., 1971-75, asst. prof. dept. biochemistry, 1980—; rsch. assoc. dept. biochemistry U. Rochester, N.Y., 1975-76. Recipient Acad. prize Japanese Soc. for Bone and Mineral Metabolism. Home: 5-11-7-310 Higashiyukigaya, Ohta-ku, Tokyo 145-0065, Japan

SHINKIN, VLADIMIR NIKOLAEVICH, mathematician, educator; b. Kaliningrad, USSR, Mar. 29, 1955; s. Nikolay Yakovlevich and Anna Grigor'evna (Khor'kina) S. MSc in Math., Moscow State U. Lomonosov, 1977, PhD in Math., 1982; sr. rsch. worker degree, Physics and Tech. Prob. Inst., Moscow, 1989; DSc in Math., Moscow State U. Lomonosov, 1995. Jr. rsch. worker Control Problems Inst., Moscow, 1980-83; sr. rsch. worker Physics and Tech. Problem Inst., Moscow, 1984-91; chief expert, Scientific and Orgnl. Mgmt. Dept. Russian Acad. Scis., Moscow, 1993-96; asst. prof. math. Technol. U., Moscow, 1993-96, prof. math., 1996—. Contbr. numerous articles to profl. jours. Mem. N.Y. Acad. Scis., German Assn. Mathematicians and Mechanics, European Astronomy Soc., Moscow Math. Soc. Avocation: watercolor painting. Home: Kantemirovskaya St 22-1-460, 115522 Moscow Russia Office: Technol U (MISiS), Leninskiy Ave 4, 117936 Moscow Russia

SHINN, CLINTON WESLEY, lawyer; b. Haworth, Okla., Mar. 7, 1947; s. Clinton Elmo and Mary Lucille (Dowdy) S.; m. Catherine Borne; children: Laura Kathryn, Clinton Wesley, Timothy Daniel. BS, McNeese State U., 1969; JD, Tulane U., 1972; LLM, Harvard U., 1973. Bar: La. 1972, U.S. Dist. Ct. (ea. dist.) La. 1975, U.S. Dist. Ct. (we. dist.) La. 1980, U.S. Ct. Appeals (5th cir.) 1981, U.S. Ct. Appeals (11th cir.) 1982, U.S. Tax Ct. (1982). Asst. prof. law Tulane U., New Orleans, 1973-75; assoc. Stone, Pigman et al, New Orleans, 1975-78, ptnr., 1979-97; ptnr. Gill & Shinn, LLC, Covington, La., 1998-2000, of counsel, 2000—; assoc. prof. law Appalachian Sch. Law, 1999—; faculty advisor, 1974-75, editor in chief Tulane Law Rev., 1971-72. Editor in chief Tulane Law Rev., 1971-72. Co-founder, bd. dirs. Childhood Cancer Families Network, 1987-90; co-founder Camp Challenge, 1988; team leader Campaign for Caring, Children's Hosp., New Orleans, 1989-91; bd. dirs. Christ Episcopal Sch., Covington, 1988-91, chmn. long-range planning, 1990-91, exec. com., 1989-91, chmn. legal com., 1989-91, chmn. admissions/recruitment com., 1988-90, mem. headmaster search com., 1993; bd. dirs. Greater New Orleans YMCA, 1989-98, 99-2000, exec. com., 1991-98, asst. sec., 1994-95, sec., 1996-98, mem. fin. com., 1994-98, exec. dir. search com., 1996, 2d vice-chair, 1998; mem. Leadership Coun., 1997-98; active Indian Guides/Princesses; bd. dirs. West St. Tammany YMCA, 1987-95, exec. com., 1988-95, bd. chmn., 1989-90, 92-93; bd. dirs. Christwood, 1992-2000, bd. v.p., 1997-99; bd. dirs. La. Air & Waste Mgmt. Assn., 1993-99; chmn. corp. rels. com., 1992-93, vice-chmn., 1996-97, chair, 1997-98, past chair, 1998-99. Co-recipient Pals of the Yr. award Greater New Orleans YMCA Indian Guides/Princesses, 1987-88; named Vol. of Yr. West St. Tammany YMCA, 1990, 92. Fellow Am. Coll. Trust and Estate Counsel, La. Bar Found., Northshore Estate Planning Coun.; mem. ABA, Nat. Assn. Securities Dealers (bd. arbitrators), Nat. Wildlife Fedn. (life), La. Bar Assn., La. Forestry Assn., New Orleans Estate Planning Coun., Air and Waste Mgmt. Assn., Order of Coif, Nat. Commn. for Planning Giving (New Orleans chpt.), Federalist Soc. Avocations: backpacking, gardening. Home: PO Box 694 Grundy VA 24614-0694 Office: Gill & Shinn LLC 109 Northpark Blvd Ste 201 Covington LA 70433-5080 also: Appalachian Sch Law PO Box 2825 Grundy VA 24614-2825

SHINN, DAVID HAMILTON, diplomat; b. Yakima, Wash., June 9, 1940; s. Guy Wilson and Ada Louise (Gelvin) S.; m. Judy Karen Rolfe, Sept. 9, 1961; children: Steven Hamilton, Christopher Rolfe. AA, Yakima Valley Coll., 1960; BA, George Washington U., 1963, MA, 1964, PhD, 1980; cert. African studies, Northwestern U., Evanston, Ill., 1969. With U.S. State Dept., 1964—; rotational officer U.S. Embassy, Beirut, Lebanon, 1964-66; polit. officer Nairobi, Kenya, 1967-68; desk officer East African affairs Washington, 1969-72; polit. officer Dar es Salaam, Tanzania, 1972-74; dep. chief of mission Nouakchott, Mauritania, 1974-76, Office of Mayor, City of Seattle, 1977-78; dep. coord. state and local govt. U.S. Dept. State, Washington, 1978-81; dep. chief of mission Yaounde, Cameroon, 1981-83, Khartoum, Sudan, 1983-86; U.S. ambassador Ouagadougou, Burkina Faso, 1987-90; diplomat-in-residence Southern U., Baton Rouge, La., 1990-91; diplomat State Dept., Washington, 1991-96; U.S. Amb. Addis Ababa, Ethiopia, 1996-99; diplomat-in-residence UCLA, 1999—. Bd. dirs. U.S. Cares for Ethiopia, People to People, Inc.; mem. Pacific Coun. Internat. Policy. Recipient Superior Honor award State Dept., 1980, 85, 94, Alumnus of Yr. award Am. Assn. Cmty. Colls., 1994, Phi Theta Kappa, 1995. Mem. Internat. Studies Assn., Am. Fgn. Service Assn., Am. Philatelic Soc., Rotary Internat. Methodist. Avocations: philately, skiing, softball, tennis, volleyball. Address: 1242 S Barrington Ave Apt 109 Los Angeles CA 90025-1647

SHINOHARA, HARUO, anatomy educator; b. Taisha, Shimane, Japan, Feb. 18, 1956; s. Kuzou and Takako (Hoshino) S.; m. Saeko Namba, May 18, 1985; children: Noriko, Hajime, Atsuko. MD, Shimane Med. U., Izumo, 1982, PhD, 1988. Asst. prof. Shimane Med. U., Izumo, 1986-90; sr. rschr. Inst. for Developmental Rsch., Kasugai, 1990-92; assoc. prof. Sch. Medicine Mie U., Tsu, 1992—. Contbr. articles to profl jours. including European Jour. Neurosci., Jour. Neurosci., Acta Anatomica, Jour. Neurol. Scis., and Anat. Record. Office: Mie U Sch Medicine Dept Anatomy, 2-174, Tsu Mie 514-0001, Japan

SHINOHARA, SHIGENOBU, electrical engineering educator; b. Takase, Kagawa, Japan, Oct. 21, 1942; s. Shigeo and Tamae (Nagamori) S.; m. Sonoi Kato, Oct. 16, 1990. BS of Elec. Engring., U. Tokyo, 1965, MS of Elec. Engring., 1967, PhD of Elec. Engring., 1970. Asst. prof. Shizuoka U., Hamamatsu, Japan, 1970-74, assoc. prof., 1974-89, prof., 1989—. Contbr. articles to profl. jours. Mem. IEEE, Internat. Soc. for Optical Engring., Inst. of Electronics, Info. and Comm. Engrs., Soc. Instrument and Control Engrs., Optical Soc. of Am. Avocations: tennis, golf. Home: 2-2 Anmacho, Hamamatsu 435-0012, Japan Office: Shizuoka U, 3-5-1 Johoku, Hamamatsu 432-8561, Japan

SHINOLT, EILEEN THELMA, artist; b. Washington, May 18, 1919; d. Edward Lee and Blanche Addie (Marsh) Bennett; m. John Francis Shinolt, June 14, 1956 (dec. Aug. 1969). Student, Hans Hoffman Sch Art, 1949, Pa. Acad. Arts, 1950, Corcoran Sch. Art, 1945-51, Am. U., 1973-77. Sect. chief Dept. Army, Washington, 1940-73, retired, 1973. One-woman shows include various locations, 1982, 83, 85, 90, 94, 96; group shows include Perlmutter & Co., 1981, Fitch Fox and Brown, 1986, Foundry Gallery, 1987, Ann. Add Arts, 1986, Westminster Gallery, London, 1995; represented in permanent collections Women's Nat. Mus., Washington, Cameo Gallery, Columbia, S.C., Strathmore Hall Arts Ctr., North Bethesda, Md., 1997, 98, 99. Mem. Woman's Nat. Dem. Club, Washington, 1980—. Mem. Am. Art League (editor newsletter 1985-86, 1st pl. 1987, 2d pl. 1986), Arts Club Washington (exhbn. com. 1985—, admissions com. 1987-88), Miniature Painters, Sculptors & Gravers Soc. (historian 1989—, editor newsletter 1986-89). Roman Catholic. Avocations: reading, studying art periodicals, art galleries. Home: 4119 Davis Pl NW Apt 203 Washington DC 20007-1254

SHINTON, NEVILLE KEITH, retired hematologist, consultant; b. Dudley, W Midlands, Eng., June 28, 1925; s. Arthur Golding and Doris (Billingham) S.; m. Margaret Hyde, Oct. 10, 1953; children: Roger Anthony, John Philip. MB ChB, U. Birmingham, 1947, MD, 1961. Cons. pathologist Health Authority, Coventry, Eng., 1958-72, cons. hematologist, 1972-91; chmn. postgrad. edn. U. Warwick, Coventry, 1983-91, prof. emeritus, 1991—, ret., 1991. Editor: New Technologies in Clinical Laboratory Science, 1985, CRC Desk Reference to Hematology, 1998. Mem. Regional Health Authority, West Midland, 1978-90. With RAF, 1948-50. Mem. Internat. Soc. Hematology (counsellor 1978-86), Brit. Soc. Hematology (pres. 1984-85), European Com. Clin. Lab. Stds. (bd. mem. 1982-86), Assn. Clin. Pathologists (v.p. 1986-88, pres. 1990-91), Internat. Com. Stds. Haematology (bd. mem. 1976-96). Avocations: gardening, mountain walking, music. Home: 22 Winterbourne Rd, Solihull, West Midlands B91 1LU, England Office: U Warwick, Coventry CV4 7AL, England

SHIOIRI, TAKAYUKI, pharmaceutical science educator; b. Yokohama, Kanagawa, Japan, Aug. 15, 1935; s. Hideji and Hisako (Iyoda) S.; m. Haruko Terashima, Mar. 13, 1966; children: Azusa, Akane. BSc, U. Tokyo, 1959, MSc, 1961, PhD, 1967; Diploma, Imperial Coll., London, 1970. Lic. pharmacist. Instr. U. Tokyo, 1962-64, rsch. assoc., 1964-77, assoc. prof., 1977; vis. academics Imperial Coll., London, 1968-70; prof. Sch. Pharm. Scis. Nagoya (Japan) City U., 1977—. Regional editor Tetrahedron, 1990—. Recipient Young Scientists award Pharm. Soc. Japan, 1974, PSJ award, 1993, Abbott award, 1978, Aichi Pharm. award Aichi Pharmacist Soc., 1981,

Award Japanese Peptide Soc., 1999. Mem. Japanese Peptide Soc. (pres. 2000—). Avocations: growing vegetables, travel, walking, reading, bird watching. Home: 1-18-12 Minamigaoka, Nisshin Aichi-Ken 470-0114, Japan Office: Nagoya City U Sch Pharm Sci, 3-1 Tanabe-Dori, Mizuho-Ku, Nagoya 467-8603, Japan

SHIONOIRI, HIDEO, computer technologist; b. Urawa, Saitama, Japan, July 15; came to U.S., 1996; m. Kimiko Sekine; 1 child, Yayoi. MSc in MIS, LaSalle U., La., 1998. Sys. designer Kawasaki Steel Corp., Japan, 1966-68; project mgr. CAC, Tokyo, 1968-71; project leader CSG, Can., 1971-77; IT mgr. Permanent Trust, Toronto, Ont., Can., 1977-83; v.p. info. sys. Barclays Bank of Can., Toronto, 1983-96; sr. tech. advisor, prin. AMS Inc., N.Y.C., 1996—. Achievements include research in international and wholesale banking systems software development and integration. Office: AMS Inc 1 Chase Plz New York NY 10005

SHIOTA, KOHEI, anatomist, embryologist, teratologist, educator; b. Ueno, Mie, Japan, Sept. 1, 1946; s. Kiyoshi Ohya and Fumiko Shiota; m. Mitsuko Maeda, May 19, 1974; children: Hirokatsu, Hirotaka. MD, Kyoto (Japan) U., 1971, PhD, 1976. Lectr. anatomy Kyoto U. Faculty Medicine, 1979, assoc. prof. teratology, 1981-90, prof., chmn. dept. anatomy and devel. biology, 1990—, dir. Congenital Anomalies Rsch. Ctr., 1992—; vis. scientist U. Wash., Seattle, 1980-82; vis. prof. Free U., Berlin, 1988, 89; mem. Adv. Com. Japanese Ministry of Health & Welfare, Tokyo, 1985—; hon. vis. fellow U. Leicester, Eng., 1993. Author (with H. Nishimura and other): Atlas of Human Prenatal Histology, 1983, (with K.L. Moore and T.V. N. Persaud) Color Atlas of Clinical Embryology, 2000; editor Jour. Congenital Anomalies, 1990—, Jour. Reproductive Toxicology, 1995-99. Mem. Japanese Teratology Soc. (pres. 1996-97), Japanese Assn. Anatomists (bd. dirs. 1997-98), Internat. Fedn. Teratology Socs. (coun. 1995—), U.S. Teratology Soc. Fax: 81 75 751 7529. E-mail: kshiota@med.kyoto-u.ac.jp. Home: 38-9 Kitaojicho Kamigamo, Kita-ku, Kyoto 603-8071, Japan Office: Kyoto U Fac Med Anatomy/Dev Bio, Yoshida-Konoecho, Sakyoku Kyoto 606-8501, Japan

SHIOTSU, MASAHIRO, engineering educator; b. Osaka, Japan, June 15, 1942; m. Yoshi Oyama, July 9, 1972. B in Engring., Kyoto U., 1966, D of Engring., 1978. Rsch. assoc. Kyoto U., Uji, 1968-79, assoc. prof., 1979-96, prof., 1996—. Mem. ASME (Best Paper award 1990, Melville medal 1991), Japan Soc. Mech. Engrs., Atomic Energy Soc. of Japan, Cryogenic Energy Soc. Japan, Heat Transfer Soc. Japan. Office: Kyoto U Grad Sch Energy Sci, Dept Energy Scis & Tech, Gokasho Uji Kyoto 611-0011, Japan

SHIPBAUGH, CALVIN LEROY, physicist; b. Huntington, Ind., Aug. 28, 1958; s. Paul and Marguerite (Pinkerton) S. BA, Rice U., 1980; PhD, U. Ill., 1988. Rsch. asst. U. Ill., Champaign-Urbana, 1981-88; analyst RAND Corp., Santa Monica, Calif., 1988—; mem. space and surface power panel RAND support to NASA Project Outreach, Santa Monica, 1990; vis. scientist Fermilab, Batavia, Ill.,1982-85; workshop leader biotech. group RAND; team mem. POET, Arlington, Va., 1989-92; mem. bioscis. panel AAN Workshop, 1997; sr. assoc. Inst. Molecular Manufacturing. Contbr. articles to Phys. Rev. Letters, Physics Letters, RAND Pub. Series, others. Mem. Am. Phys. Soc., Internat. Meteoritical Soc. Achievements include research to measure charm particles' decay and hadronic production properties; evaluation of proposals from the public to the Space Exploration Initiative; policy analysis of nanotechnology; analysis of rotorcraft markets. Office: The RAND Corp 1700 Main St Santa Monica CA 90401-3297

SHIPLEY, D(ONALD) GRAHAM J., historian; b. Tynemouth, Eng., 1956. BA, U. Oxford, Eng., 1978; MA, U. Oxford, 1981, DPhil, 1983. Bowra jr. rsch. fellow Wadham Coll., Oxford, 1982-83; Dyson jr. rsch. fellow in Greek culture Balliol Coll., Oxford, 1983-86; rsch. fellow St. Catharine's Coll., Cambridge, Eng., 1986-87; lectr. ancient history U. Leicester (Eng.), 1987-98, sr. lectr. ancient history, 1998-99, reader ancient history, 1999—; mem. mng. com. Brit. Sch. Athens, London, 1981-83, 90-96, vis. fellow, 1999. Author: A History of Samos, 1987, The Greek World After Alexander, 2000; co-author: The Laconia Survey, 1996—; editor: (jour.) Annual of the Brit. Sch. Athens, 1991-96, (with J. R. Salmon) Human Landscapes in Classical Antiquity, 1996. Fellow Soc. Antiquaries of London; mem. Soc. Promotion Hellenic Studies (mem. coun. 1993-96), Classical Assn. (mem. coun. 1998—).

SHIPLEY, WALTER VINCENT, retired banker; b. Newark, Nov. 2, 1935; s. L. Parks and Emily (Herzog) S.; m. Judith Ann Lyman, Sept. 14, 1957; children: Barbara, Allison, Pamela, Dorothy, John. Student, Williams Coll., 1954-56; BS, NYU, 1961. With Chem. Bank, N.Y.C., 1956-96; chmn., CEO, chmn. bd. dirs. Chase Manhattan Corp., N.Y.C., 1996-99, ret., 2000; Bd. dirs. Exxon Mobil Corp., Verizon Comms. Bd. dirs. Lincoln Ctr. for Performing Arts Inc., Goodwill Industries Greater N.Y. Inc. Mem. The Bus. Coun., Coun. Fgn. Rels., Links, Augusta Nat. Golf Club, Baltusrol Golf Club (Springfield, N.J.). Office: Chase Manhattan Corp 270 Park Ave Fl 12 New York NY 10017-2036

SHIPMAN, HARRY LONGFELLOW, astrophysicist, educator; b. Feb. 20, 1948; s. Arthur Leffingwell and Mary Dana Shipman; children: Alice Elizabeth, Thomas Nathaniel. BA summa cum laude, Harvard U., 1969; MS, Calif. Inst. Tech., 1970, PhD, 1971. Programmer Travelers Ins., 1966; rsch. asst. Smithsonian Astrophys. Obs., summer 1968, 69; tchg. asst. Calif. Inst. Tech., 1969-71; J.W. Gibbs instr. astronomy Yale U., 1971-73; asst. prof. U. Mo., St. Louis; astronomer McDonnell Planetarium, 1973-74; asst. prof. physics U. Del., 1974-77, assoc. prof., 1977-81, prof., 1981-99, prof. Annie Jump Cannon, 1999—; dir. Ctr. Tchg. Effectiveness, 1988-94; vis. fellow sci. edn. U. Ga., 1994; Harlow Shapley vis. lectr. Am. Astron. Soc., 1975—; trustee, Mt. Cuba Obs., 1977—. Author: Black Holes, Quasars and the Universe, 2d edit., 1980, The Restless Universe: An Introduction to Astronomy, 1978, Space 2000-Meeting the Challenge of a New Era, 1987, Humans in Space-21st Century Frontiers, 1988; contbr. articles to profl. jours. NSF fellow, 1960-71, Guggenheim fellow, 1980-81; NASA grantee, 1975-80, 83—, NSF grantee, 1974-92, 96—. Mem. AAUP, AAAS, Internat. Astron. Union, Am. Astron. Soc. (task group on edn. in astronomy 1977-85, edn. officer 1979-85), Am. Assn. Physics Tchrs., Nat. Assn. for Rsch. in Sci. Tchg., Assn. Educators of Tchrs. of Sci., Phi Beta Kappa. Office: U Del Physics Dept Newark DE 19716

SHIPOVSKAYA, ANNA BORISOVNA, chemistry educator; b. Saratov, Russia, May 8, 1968; d. Boris Konstantinovich and Valentina Ivanovna Reshetnikov; m. Andrey Alexandrovich Shipovsky, July 23, 1988; 1 child, Nikita. BS, Saratov State U., Russia, 1990, PhD, 1996. Engr. Rsch & Ednl. Dept. Reflector Inc., Saratov, Russia, 1990; sr. tchr. Saratov State U., 1992-97, assoc. prof., 1997—. Contbr. articles to profl. jours. and books. Russian Acad. Scis. grantee, Moscow, 1992—. Mem. Mendeleyev Chemistry Soc. Office: Saratov State U Chem Dept, 83 Astrakhanskaya St, 410026 Saratov Russia

SHIPTON, SIDNEY LAWRENCE, non-profit association consultant, solicitor; b. London, July 25, 1929; s. Harold and Rose (Horowitz) S.; m. Judith Scott, June 2, 1974; stepchildren: Jonathan Michael, Elana. LLB, U. London, 1951; MBA, Middlesex U., 1985. Pvt. practice law London, 1956-72; gen. sec. Br. Zionist Fedn., 1972-82; dir. Jewish Nat. Fund, 1982-87; exec. dir. Ta'Ali, 1987-96; solicitor Supreme Ct. Judicature; coord. Three Faiths Forum, 1997—; chmn. United Zionists of U.K., hon. v.p., chmn. ZF constn. com. Freeman City of London; former exec. Coun. Christians & Jews; former bd. mem. Middlesex U. Alumni. Fellow Royal Soc. Arts, Inst. Mgmt.; mem. Law Soc., Medico-Legal Soc., Brit. Acad. Forensic Sci., Mensa, B'nai B'rith (pres. Leo Baeck lodge). Jewish. Avocations: collecting books, lecturing, travel, cinema, theatre. Office: The Three Faiths Forum, 104-8 Grafton Rd, London NW5 4BD, England

SHIPWRIGHT, ADRIAN JOHN, lawyer; b. Southampton, Eng., July 2, 1950; s. Jack and Jennie (Eastman) S.; m. Diana Evelyn Treseder, Aug. 17, 1974; children: Henry William James, Fiona Catherine Jane. BA, Oxford (Eng.) U., 1972, BCL, 1973, MA, 1977. Cert. solicitor. Asst. solicitor tax dept. Linklaters & Paines, London, 1974-77; univ. lectr. U. Oxford, 1977-82; tax ptnr. Denton Hall Burgin & Warrens, London, 1982-87, SJ Berwin & Co., London, 1987-92; prof. bus. law King's Coll., London, 1992—; vis. prof. King's Coll., London, 1990-92; cons. S. J. Berwin & Co., London, 1992, Barrister Lincoln's Inn, 1993, Pump Ct. Tax Chambers, London. Editor, author: (wih others) Strategic Tax Planning, 1988; author: VOL 5 CCH British Tax Reporter, 1985, UK Tax and Intellectual Property, 1989, 2d edit., 1996, UK Tax Land Development and Tax Planning, 1990, Capital Gains Tax Strategies, 1990, VAT, Property and the New Rules; contbr. artilces to profl. jours. Mem. Law Soc., Internat. Bar Assn. Avocation: music. Office: Pump Ct Tax Chambers, 16 Bedford Row, London WC1R 4EB, England

SHIRAHATA, SANETAKA, cell biologist; b. Nase City, Japan, Oct. 22, 1950; s. Reio and Miyo (Nakaba) S.; m. Sachiko Yanase; children: Ayano, Nobuhiro, Mitsuhiro, Kimie. B of Agrl., Kyushu U., 1973, M of Agrl, 1975, PhD, 1978. Assoc. prof. Shokei Jr. Coll., Kumamoto, Japan, 1982-89; assoc. prof. Kyushi U., Fukuoka, Japan, 1989-95, prof., 1995—. Contbr. articles to profl. jours. Mem. Japanese Assn. Animal Cell Tech. (v.p. 1999—), Japanese Soc. Agrl. Chemistry (award 1991), Japanese Tissue Culture Assn. Avocations: jogging, swimming, reading. Home: 1-21-9 Mainosato, Koga-city 811-3114, Japan Office: Kyushu U Grad Sch Genetic Resources Tech, Hakozaki Higashi-ku, Fukuoka 812-81, Japan

SHIRAI, HIROSHI, electrical engineering educator; b. Aichi, Japan, Mar. 17, 1958; m. Madoka Ohmi; 1 child, Tomohiro. BSEE, Shizuoka U., Hammatsu, Japan, 1980, MSEE, 1982; PhD in EE, Polytechnic U., N.Y.C., 1986. Rsch. fellow Polytechnic U., N.Y.C., 1982-86, postdoctoral scientist, 1986-87; asst. prof. Chuo U., Tokyo, 1987-88, assoc. prof., 1988-98, prof., 1998—; lectr. Tokyo Denki U., 1988-91. Author: Introduction to Applied Analysis, 1993, Analytical and Numerical Methods in Electromagnetic Wave Theory, 1993. Mem. IEEE (sr., R.W.P. King award 1987), Inst. Electronics, Info. and Comm. Engrs. Japan (Shinohara Kinen award 1988), Inst. Elec. Engrs. Japan (Paper Presentation award 1991), Acoustical Soc. Japan, Acoustical Soc. Am. (assoc.), Sigma Xi. Avocations: swimming. Office: Chuo U Dept Elec & Comm Eng, 1-13-27 Kasuga, Bunkyo-ku Tokyo 112-8551, Japan

SHIRAI, SHUN, law educator, lawyer; b. Tokyo, June 18, 1942; s. Kyo and Tomi Shirai; m. Junko Matsushita, Apr. 10, 1969; children: Akiko, Yuko, Jin. LLB, Hitotsubashi U., Tokyo, 1966, LLM, 1969. Cert. atty. at law. Asst. prof. criminal law Kokugakuin U., Tokyo, 1974-81, prof., 1981—, dean Grad. Sch., 1999—; atty. at law Tokyo 2nd Bar Assn., 1992—. Author: Phenomenology of Crime, 1984, Thought on Criminal Law of Ancient India, 1985, Legal History on Criminal Law of Ancient India, 1990, Philosophy of Criminal Law in Ancient India, 1995, Phenomenology and Indian Philosophy for the Study on Ancient Indian Criminal Law, 1997, Prof. Shirai's Lectures on the Law of Criminal Procedure, 1998, Philosophy of Criminal Law in Bhagavad-gitā at Ancient India, 1998, Crime and Sorrowness of Human Being, 1999, Defence Lawyer's Statements in Criminal Court, 2000, Thoughts on Death Penalty in Ancient India, 2000, The Sanskrit, as a Legal Language, appearing in Judicial Documents of British India and Non-Violent Theory of Punishment, originated in Ancient India, 2000. Mem. Indian History Congress. Buddhist. Home: 17-25 Matsudoshinden, Matsudo-shi Chiba Pref 270-2241, Japan Office: Kokugakuin U, 4-10-28 Higashi Shibuya-Ku, Tokyo 150-8440, Japan

SHIRAI, YASUTO, information science educator, researcher; b. Kooriyama, Fukushima, Japan, Aug. 9, 1961; s. Keiji and Yoko (Ishii) S.; m. Miki Ito, May 15, 1993. BS, U. Toronto, Toronto, Can., 1984, MS, 1987. Rsch. assoc. U. Tokyo, Tokyo, Japan, 1989-90; assoc. prof. Shizuoka (Japan) U., 1990—. Author: Progress in Fuzzy Sets and Systems, 1990. Mem. IEEE, Computer Graphics Soc., Assn. for Computing Machinery, Info. Processing Soc. Japan, Japan Soc. Fuzzy Theory and Systems. Avocations: reading, gardening. Office: Shizuoka U Dept Comp Sci, Faculty Info Johoku 3-5-1, Hamamatsu 432-8011, Japan

SHIRAIWA, YOSHIHIRO, educator; b. Sagae, Japan, Feb. 9, 1951; s. Katsumi and Shimeo (Endou) S.; m. Kumiko Yoshida, May 8, 1980; children: Shuko, Manabu. BS, Niigata U., Japan, 1973; MS, Tokyo Kyoiku U., 1975; PhD, Tokyo U., 1979. Asst. prof. Niigata U., Japan, 1979-89, assoc. prof., 1989-97; prof. U. Tsukuba, Japan, 1997—. Author: Chloroplasts, 1980, Research Methods in Photosynthesis, 1981, Preparation Methods for Biological Materials, 1982. Rsch. grantee Salt Sci. Found., Tokyo, 1992-93, Sumitomo Found., Tokyo, 1994, Marine Biotech. Inst., Tokyo, 1997; rsch. fellow Japanese Soc. Promotion of Sci., Tokyo, 1979, Alexander von Humboldt rsch. fellow, Bonn, Germany, 1984-86, 87, 93, vis. fellow Phillips U. Marburg, Germany, 1980, 93, Bielefeld U., Japan, 1987, Mich. State U., East Lansing, 1989, 90. Avocations: rakugo listening, classical music, walking. Office: U Tsukuba Inst Biol Scis, Tennoudai 1-1-1, Tsukuba 305-8572, Japan Home: Namiki 3-12-1-717, Tsukuba 305-0044, Japan

SHIRAKAWA, HIDEKI, chemist, researcher; b. Tokyo, 1936. Prof. chemistry Inst. Materials Sci. U. Tsukuba, Japan, 2000—. Recipient Nobel prize in chemistry, 2000. Office: U Tsukuba Inst Materials Sci, 1-1-1 Tennodai, Tsukuba Ibaraki 305-8577, Japan*

SHIRAKAWA, SHINGO, electrical engineer; b. Hiroshima, Japan, Mar. 8, 1944; parents Noboru and Kazue S.; m. Taiko Okuda, Nov. 5, 1977; children: Nobuyuki, Sonoko, Tetsuyuki. BS, Yamaguchi U., 1966; MS, Kyushu Inst. Tech., 1968, DSc, 1988. From engr. to dep. mgr. Hitachi, Ltd., Hitachi, Japan, 1972—. Mem. IEEE (sr.). Home: Kanesawacho 6-8-6, Hitachi Ibaraki-ken 316-8501, Japan

SHIRAKAWA, TARO, genetic epidemiologist, researcher; b. Beppu, Oita, Japan, June 18, 1955; arrived in Eng., 1991.; s. Tetsuo Ito and Yoko Shirakawa; m. Xiaoquan Mao, June 18, 1997. MD, Kyoto (Japan) U., 1983; PhD, Osaka (Japan) U., 1994. Med. diplomate. Intern Kyoto Univ. Hosp., Japan, 1983-84; resident Kyoto Univ. Hosp., 1984-87; chest physician Takatsuki Red Cross Hosp., Takatsuki, Japan, 1984-87; asst. prof. Osaka U., 1987-95; sr. rsch. doctor, hon. lectr. Nat. Health Svc. Trust, Oxford, Eng., 1995—; sr. rsch. lectr. dept. exptl. medicine U. Wales, Swansea, Wales, 2000; prof. dept. health promotion and human behavior Kyoto U. Grad. Sch. Pub. Health, 2000—. Contbr. articles to profl. jours.; inventor in field. Recipient Astra Japan award Astra Japan, 1995. Mem. AAAS, N.Y. Acad. Scis. Avocations: traveling, taking spa. Home: 4-12-3-107 Tsukahara, Takatsuki 569, Japan Office: Dept Hlth Promotion and HB, Kyoto U Grad Sch PH, Kyoto 606-8501, Japan

SHIRAKI, KAZUHIRO, engineering educator; b. Kobe, Japan, Jan. 11, 1933; s. Manjiro and Sueyoshi Shiraki; m. Teruko Kuramoto, Mar. 29, 1964; children: Mariko, Chieko. Bachelor, Himeji (Japan) Tech. Coll., 1955; D of Engring., Kyoto (Japan) U., 1964. Engr. Mitsubishi Heavy Industry, Kobe, Japan, 1955-71, mgr. vibration rsch. lab., 1971-83; vice gen. mgr. of Takasago R&D ctr. Mitsubishi Heavy Industry, Takasago, Japan, 1983-86, gen. mgr. Takasago R&D ctr., 1986-89; dir. Mitsubishi Heavy Industry, Tokyo, 1989-93; prof. Kansai U., Suita, Japan, 1994—; corp. adviser Mitsuibishi Heavy Industry, Tokyo, 1993-97. Editor: Design and Simulation for the Noise Prevention, 1987; co-author: Handbook of Vibration Engineering, 1976; contbr. articles to profl. jours. Recipient Purple Decoration prize Japanese Prime Min., 1994, Merit award for Scientific Tech. Min. of Sci. and Tech. of Japan, 1991. Mem. Japan Soc. of Mech. Engring. (hon., vice chmn. 1992, chmn. Kansai br. 1989), Marine Engring. Soc. in Japan. Avocations: golf, tennis, skiing. Home: 4-3 Mikageishimachi 2-chome, Higashinada-ku, Kobe 658-0045, Japan Office: Kansai U, Yamate-machi 3-chome, Suita PO 564, Japan

SHIRANE, KUNIO, publishing executive. Exec. dir. Mainichi Shimbun, Japan. Office: Mainichi Shimbun, 1-1-1- Hitotsubashi, Chiyoda-ku 100, Japan

SHIRASAKA, YUKIYOSHI, pediatric neurologist, pediatrician; b. Shizuoka, Japan, Oct. 7, 1956; s. Kaoru and Kinuyo (Shiratori) S.; m. Kyoko Hashimoto, Jan. 19, 1991; children: Ideya, Kento. MD, Kyoto U., 1982, PhD, 1991. Diplomate in pediatric neurology. Resident Shizaoka (Japan) Prefectural Children's Hosp., 1982-84; med. staff Shimane Prefectural Ctrl. Hosp., Izumo, Japan, 1984-85, Shiga Pediat. Orthopedic Ctr., Moriyama, Japan, 1985-87, Kyoto Nat. Hosp., 1991-92; postdoctoral scholar UCLA Med. Sch., 1992-95; chief pediatric neurology Nat. Utano Hosp., Kyoto, 1995—. Contbr. articles to profl. jours. Internat. fellow Am. Epilepsy Found., 1992, Internat. Epilepsy Congress awardee, 1991; recipient JA Wada award Japan Epilepsy Soc., 1999. Mem. Japanese Soc. Pediatric Neurology (mem. coun. 1999—), Internat. Child Neurology Assn., Soc. Neurosci. Avocations: skiing, golf, travel, wine, driving. Office: Nat Utano Hosp, 8 Narutaki-Ondoyama-cho, Ukyo-ku Kyoto 616-8255, Japan

SHIRASAWA, TAKUJI, molecular biologist, researcher; b. Hatano, Kanagawa, Japan, Mar. 10, 1958; s. Minoru and Chieko (Awano) S.; m. Ikumi Inoue, May 12, 1986; children: Masayuki, Hidiki. MD, Chiba (Japan) U., 1982, PhD, 1990. Med. diplomate, Japan; pathol. diplomate, Japan. Resident Chiba Univ. Hosp., 1982-84; sr. resident Chiba Mcpl. Hosp., 1984-86; rsch. assoc. Tokyo Met. Inst. Gerontology, 1990-96, lab. chief molecular genetics, 1997—. Contbr. articles to profl. jours. Named Hon. Citizen, City of Balt., 1992; The Mochida Meml. Found. grantee, 1994. Mem. Japanese Assn. Molecular Biology, Japanese Assn. for Immunology, Japanese Assn. for Basic Gerontology. Avocations: computers, Internet, travel. Office: Tokyo Met Inst Gerontology, 35-2 Sakae-cho Itabashi-ku, Tokyo 173, Japan

SHIRAYAMA, SADAO, art educator; b. Toyota, Japan, Jan. 25, 1930; s. Kakuichi and Sumi (Nagata) S. Grad., Kyoto U., 1959. Prof. Aichi U. Edn., Kariya, Japan, 1962-93, Tokai Women's Coll., Kagamigahara, Japan, 1993-98. Home: Tatsumi-nishi, Lions Mansions 503, Okazaki 444-0875, Japan

SHIRAYANAGI, PETER SEIICHI, retired archbishop; b. Hachioji, Japan, June 17, 1928. D Canon Law, Universitas Urbaniana, Rome, 1960. Ordained priest Roman Cath. Ch., 1954, consecrated bishop, 1966, created cardinal, 1994. Archbishop of Tokyo Roman Cath. Ch., Tokyo, Japan, 1966-2000; ret., 2000; pres. Japanese Cath. Bishops' Conf., 1983-92; mem. Cardinal's Coll. Home: 301 3-2-11 Shimo-ochiai, Bunkyo-ku Shinjuku-ku Tokyo 161-0033, Japan Office: Archbishops House, 3-16-15 Sekiguchi, Bunkyo-ku Tokyo 112-0014, Japan

SHIRCLIFF, JAMES VANDERBURGH, communications executive; b. Vincennes, Ind., Dec. 11, 1938; s. Thomas Maxwell and Martha Bayard (Somes) S.; m. Sally Anny Hoing, June 20, 1964; children: Thomas, Susan, Anne, Catherine, Caroline. AB, Brown U., 1961; postgrad., U. Va., 1963-64. Asst. gen. mgr. Pepsi Cola Allied Bottlers, Inc., Lynchburg, Va., 1964-65; v.p., divisional coord. Pepsi Cola Allied Bottlers, Inc., Lynchburg, 1966-68, v.p., dir. personnel, 1968-70; gen. mgr. First Colony Canners, Inc., Lynchburg, 1965-66; v.p., gen. mgr. GCC Beverages, Inc., Lynchburg, 1970-74; group v.p. GCC Beverages, Inc., Va., 1974-75; corp. v.p. Gen. Cinema Corp., Beverage Divsn., 1976-77; owner/mgr. WLLL-AM, WGOL-FM, 1977-86; pres. Jamarbo Corp., 1977-88; chmn. bd. SignWaves, Inc., pres., The Shircliff Partnership, Ltd., presdl. interchange exec., 1975-76; exec. dir. Nat. Indsl. Energy Coun., Dept. Commerce, Washington, 1975-76. V.p. JOBS, Lynchburg, 1970; dir. Ctrl. Va. Health Planning Coun., 1974-75; mem. Govs. Indsl. Energy Adv. Coun., 1976—; dir. Piedmont coun., Boy Scouts Am., 1972-73; mem. City of Lynchburg Keep Lynchburg Beautiful Commn., 1974-75, chmn. emergency planning bd., 1974-75, chmn. overall econ. planning coun., 1977-88; bd. dirs. Lynchburg Broadway Theatre, 1973-75, Acad. Music, 1973-74, United Fund, Lynchburg, 1966-67, Ctrl. Va. Industries, 1971-72, VA. Pub. Telecomm. Coun.; former trustee Culver Ednl. Found.; chmn. campaign United Way, 1982, pres., 1983; chmn. Citizens for a Clean Lynchburg; campaign chmn. United Way of Ctrl. Va., Dir., 1996; chmn. Arts Coun. Ctrl. Va., 1990-93; mem. nat. adv. coun. U.S. Small Bus. Adminstrn., 1990-93; past trustee Va. Episc. Sch.; past mem. pres.' coun. Randolph-Macon Women's Coll., Ctrl. Va. C.C. Found. Bd.; past mem. Va-Israel Commn.; dir. Lynchburg Hist. Found., 1996-99. Lt. (j.g.) USN, 1961-63. Recipient Cloyd Meml. award for outstanding svc., Greater Lynchburg C. of C., 1975; Va. Soft Drink Assn. citation, 1970, 73, 74; NCCJ Brotherhood citation; Pub. Svc. award RAdio-TV Commn. of So. Bapt. Conf., NCCJ State Adv. Bd., Exec. Com. Swensen's Owners Coun., 1988, Centurian award for bus. moral and leadership C. of C., 1999. Mem. Va. Soft Drink Assn. (pres. 1973-74), Va. Pepsi Cola Bottlers Assn. (pres. 1970-73), Nat., Va. (dir. 1974, pres. 1985-86) assns. broadcasters, Lynchburg Advt. Club (v.p.), Va. AP Broadcasters Assn. (pres.), Lynchburg Fine Arts Ctr. (pres.), Va. C. of C. (dir. 1976-79), Greater Lynchburg C. of C. (dir., v.p. 1973-74, chmn. cmty. appearance task force 1977-79), Culver Academies Alumni Assn. (pres.), Culver Cum Laude Soc. (award 1996, hon.), Mensa, Commonwealth Club, Oakwood Country Club, Boonsboro Country Club, Piedmont Club, Navy League, The Pavane Club, Lynchburg Sports Club, Knight Sovereign Mil. Order Malta Fedn. Assn., Rotary (past pres., Paul Harris fellow 1982, dist. gov. 1986-87). Roman Catholic. Home: 3525 Otter View Pl Lynchburg VA 24503-3035 Address: PO Box 10486 Lynchburg VA 24506-0486

SHIRES, GEORGE THOMAS, surgeon, educator; b. Waco, Tex., Nov. 22, 1925; s. George Thomas and Donna Mae (Smith) S.; m. Robbie Jo Martin, Nov. 27, 1948; children: Donna Blain, George Thomas III, Jo Ellen. MD, U. Tex., Dallas, 1948. Diplomate Am. Bd. Surgery (dir. 1968-74, chmn. 1972-74). Intern Mass. Meml. Hosp., Boston, 1948-49; resident in surgery Parkland Meml. Hosp., Dallas, 1950-53; faculty U. Tex. Southwestern Med. Sch., Dallas, 1953-60, assoc. prof. surgery, acting chmn. dept., 1960-61, prof., chmn. dept., 1961-74; surgeon in chief surg. svcs. Parkland Meml. Hosp., 1960-74; prof., chmn. dept. surgery U. Wash. Sch. Medicine, Seattle, 1974-75; chief of service Harborview Med. Center, Seattle, Univ. Hosp., Seattle, 1974-75; chmn. dept. surgery N.Y. Hosp.-Cornell U. Med. Coll., 1975-91; dean, provost for med. affairs Cornell U. Med. Coll., 1987-91, prof. emeritus, 1996—, 1996—; prof., chmn. surgery Tex. Tech. U., Lubbock, 1991-95, Canizaro disting. prof. surgery, 1995-97; prof. surgery U. Nev. Sch. Medicine, Las Vegas, 1997—; cons. Surgeon Gen., U.S. Army, 1965-75, Jamaica Hosp., 1978-91, Inst. Medicine Nat. Acad. Scis., 1975—; metabolism and truama com. Nat. Acad. Scis.-NRC, 1964-71, com. trauma, 1964-71; rsch. program evaluation com., reviewer clin. investigation applications career devel. program VA, 1972-76; gen. med. rsch. program projects com. NIH, 1965-69; mem. Surgery A study sect., 1970-74, chmn., 1976-78; mem. Nat. Adv. Gen. Med. Scis. Coun., 1980-84; cons. editl. bd. Jour. Trauma, 1968-88. Mem. editl. bd. Year Book Med. Publs., 1970-92, Annals of Surgery, 1972—, Surg. Techniques Illustrated: An International Comparative Text, 1974-75, Am. Jour. Surgery, 1968—, Contemporary Surgery, 1973-89; assoc. editor-in-chief Infections in Surgery, 1981; mem. editl. coun. Jour. Clin. Surgery, 1980-82; editor Surgery, Gynecology and Obstetrics, 1982-93. Lt. M.C. USNR, 1949-50, 53-55. Life Ins. Med. Rsch. fellow, 1947. Mem. ACS (bd. regents 1971-82, chmn. bd. regents 1978-80, pres. 1981-82), AMA, Dallas Soc. Gen. Surgeons (pres.-elect, pres. 1972-74), Am. Assn. Surgery Trauma, Am. Surg. Assn. (sec. 1969-74, pres. 1980), Digestive Disease Found. (founding mem.), Halsted Soc., Internat. Soc. Burn Injuries, Internat. Surg. Soc. (sec. 1978-81, v.p. 1982-83, pres. U.S. chpt. 1984-85), Pan-Am. Med. Assn. (surgery council 1971—), Pan Pacific Surg. Assn., Soc. Clin. Surgery, Soc. Surgery Alimentary Tract, Soc. Surg. Chairmen (pres. 1972-74), Soc. Univ. Surgeons (chmn. publs. com. 1969-71), So. Surg. Assn., Surg. Biology Club (sec. 1968-70), Western Surg. Assn., Allen O. Whipple Surg. Soc., James IV Assn. Surgeons (bd. dirs. 1980-81, sec. 1981-87, pres. 1987-91), Alpha Omega Alpha, Alpha Pi Alpha, Phi Beta Pi. Office: U Nev Sch Medicine 2040 W Charleston Blvd Ste 501 Las Vegas NV 89102-2207

SHIRLEY, ANN See SAVOURS, ANN MARGARET

SHIRLEY, DONNA, former aerospace engineer, management consultant, speaker; b. Wynnewood, Okla.; 1 child, Laura. BS in Aerospace Engring., U. Okla., BA in Journalism; MS in Aerospace Engring., U. So. Calif. With Jet Propulsion Lab., Pasadena, Calif., 1966—, Cassini project engr., mgr. exploration initiative studies, mgr. automation and robotics, mgr. Space Sta. program, mgr. mission design sect., project engr. for Mariner 10, mgr. Mars Pathfinder microrover Flight Experiment team, mgr. Mars exploration program; ret., 1998; pres. Managing Creativity, Norman, Okla.; leader NASA-wide Sys. Engring. Working Group, 1990-93; leader NASA-wide team on program/project mgmt. NASA, 1991. Author: Managing Martians, 1998. Office: Managing Creativity 1517 Oklahoma Ave Norman OK 73071-0466*

SHIROCHKOV, ALEXANDER VASILIEVITCH, physicist, researcher; b. Kemlja, Russia, Nov. 10, 1934; s. Vasily Sergeevitch and Anna Ivanovna

(Dakina) S.; m. Lidia Alexandrovna Mironova Shirochkova, Aug. 20, 1958; children: Ekaterina, Elizaveta. BE in Electronics, Nautical Coll., Leningrad, Russia, 1958; PhD in Geophysics, Arctic and Antarctic Rsch Inst, Leningrad, Russia, 1973. Jr. rsch. scientist Arctic and Antarctic Rsch Inst., Leningrad, Russia, 1959-73, sr. rsch. scientist, 1974-77; head ionospheric lab. Arctic and Antarctic Rsch Inst., St. Petersburg, Russia, 1977—; station leader Russian Antarctic Expedition, Vostok Station, Antarctica, 1965; soviet exchange scientist USA Antarctic Expedition Byrd Station, Antarctica, 1971. Contbr. papers in field. Mem. N.Y. Acad. Scis. Avocations: gardening, classic jazz music collector. Home: Pobeda St 4 Apt 197, 196070 Saint Petersburg Russia Office: Arctic & Antarctic Rsch Ins, 38 Bering St, 199397 Saint Petersburg Russia

SHIROISHI, YOSHIHIRO, materials scientist; b. Tokyo, Mar. 10, 1951; s. Yoshiji and Teruko (Kobayashi) S.; m. Yasuko Ohshiro, Oct. 3, 1981; children: Takuya, Kenji, Ayako. BS, Tokyo Inst. Tech., 1973, MS, 1975, PhD, 1978. Rschr. Cen. Rsch. Lab., Hitachi Ltd., Tokyo, 1978-87, sr. rschr., 1987-95, dept. mgr., 1995-98; sr. mgr. Data Storage and Retrieval Sys. divsn. Hitachi, Ltd., Tokyo, 1998-99, gen. mgr., 1999—; lectr. Waseda U. Patentee magnetic recording head (local commendtaion for Invention of Kanto 1992); contbr. articles to profl. publs. Dir. town assembly Higashiasakawamachi, Tokyo, 1993-94. David Sarnoff scholar RCA, U.S.A., 1973. Mem. Magnetics Soc. of IEEE (sr. mem.), Magnetic Soc. Japan (mem. planning com. 1991-94), Applied Physics of Japan, Inst. Elec. Engrs. Japan. Avocations: reading, bicycling. Home: 988 Higashiasakawamachi, Hachioji Tokyo 193, Japan Office: Hitachi Ltd, Data Storage & Retrieval Sys Div, Kozu, Odawara Kanagawa 256-8510, Japan

SHIROKOV, FELIX V., electronics executive, researcher; b. St. Peterbourg, Russia, Sept. 12, 1927; s. Vladimir N. and Vera A. (Kuznetrova) S.; m. Nina M. Demukova, Mar. 25, 1969 (div. July 1984); m. Tatiana L. Khotrianova, Oct. 2, 1987. PhD, Moscow U., 1956. Lectr. MEI, Moscow, 1961-71; dept. head Inform-Electro, Moscow, 1971-76; lab. head IFTAN, Moscow, 1976-82; head sector Coun. of Cybervetica, Moscow, 1982-84; dept. head NITS/ASK, Moscow, 1984-91; v.p. Union Electronic of Russia, Moscow, 1991—; mem. Coun. Cybervetics, Moscow, 1958-72, fin. cons. several companies, Moscow, 1990—; mem. coun. State Pub. House of Fgn. Lit., 1962-72. Author: Underway to the Fifth Generation of Computers, 1985; editor (book translation) Automate Studies, 1956; interpretor (book translation) Fourie Transform, 1962, Theorie der Distributiom, 1964. Advisor State Duma, Moscow, 1993—. Recipient several trade union awards, 1960-70. Fellow Soc. Tech. Analysts. Avocations: Tibetan medicine. Home and Office: Profsoyuznaya 16 #306, 117292 Moscow Russia

SHIROKOVA, ELENA, mathematics educator, translator; b. Kazan, Russia, May 14, 1951; d. Aleksandr and Nina (Talantova) S.; m. Nickolai Ivan'shin; children: Alexandra, Piotr. Cand, Kazan U., 1978, Degree, 1986. Asst. Kazan U., 1979-86, dozent, 1986—, chair dept. math., 1989-94, head math. curriculum com.; Contbr. articles to profl. jours. Ministry of Edn. grantee, 1990-93. Avocations: English, sewing, knitting, gardening, cooking. Home: Vishnevsky str 14-31, 420043 Kazan Russia Office: Kazan U, Kremlevskaya str 18, 420008 Kazan Russia

SHIRTUM, EARL EDWARD, retired civil engineer; b. Montague, Mich., Feb. 20, 1927; s. Earl Willard and Elizabeth Caroline (Boelke) S.; m. Martha Louise Wright, June 19, 1953. BS in Civil Engring., Ind. Tech. Coll., Ft. Wayne, 1950. Bridge design squad leader Mich. Dept. Transp., Lansing, 1952-63, transp. planning engr., 1963-96; mem. Bridge Replacement and Rehab. Com., Lansing, 1967-94. With U.S. Army, 1945-46, ETO. Mem. Mich. Profl. Engring. Soc. (rep. engr. in govt. 1974-77), Lansing Engr. Club (bd. mem. 1980-84). Republican. Methodist. Avocations: fishing, bridge. Home: 1617 Victor Ave Lansing MI 48910-6511

SHIRTZ, JOSEPH FRANK, lawyer, consultant; b. Yeadon, PA, June 26, 1959; s. Raymond Loren and Ann Gredel (Lutz) S.; m. Catherine Irene Enright, Sept. 6, 1987; children: Ryan, Erin. BSME, U. Ala., Tuscaloosa, 1981; JD, Villanova, 1984. Bar: Pa. 1984, N.Y. 1985, N.J. 1986, U.S. Dist. Ct. N.J. 1986, U.S. Patent Office 1985, U.S. Ct. Appeals (fed. cir.) 1986. Law clk. Ct. of Common Pleas, Norristown, Pa., 1983; assoc. Pennie & Edmonds, N.Y.C., 1984-87; patent atty. Johnson & Johnson, New Brunswick, N.J., 1987-94, supervisory atty., 1994-98; assoc. patent counsel Johnson & Johnson, New Brunswick, 1998—. Mem. N.J., N.Y. Intellectual Property Law Assn. Office: Johnson & Johnson One Johnson & Johnson Plaza New Brunswick NJ 08933-0001

SHIRYAEV, VLADIMIR MIKHAILOVICH, mathematics educator; b. Pskov, Russia, Mar. 3, 1941; s. Mikhail Pheodorovich and Zoya Mikhailovna (Skokova) S.; m. Ludmila Viktorovna Malishevskaya, June 21, 1968; 1 child, Ivan. Student, Byelorussian State U., Minsk, 1960-65, postgrad., 1966-69; Diploma in Phys. and Math. Scis., Saratov (Russia) State U., 1973. Prin. tchr. math. Vitebsk (Byelorussia) Pedagogical Inst., 1969-71, Byelorussian State U., Minsk, 1971—. Author: Geometry and Algebra, 1987, A Collection of Problems in Geometry and Algebra, 1999; contbr. articles to profl. jours. Home: Frolikova 29A 27, 220037 Minsk Belarus Office: Byelorussian State Univ, Prospect Skorini 4, 220080 Minsk Belarus

SHISEKI, NOBUO, electrical engineer, company executive; b. Ichikawa City, Chiba, Japan, Sept. 10, 1944; s. Hideo and Saki Shiseki; m. Keiko Ishiguro, June 14, 1945; children: Yasuyuki, Yoshinobu, Hideaki. BSEE, Seikei U., Tokyo, 1969, PhD in Engring., 1993. Elec. engr. Fujikura Ltd., Tokyo, 1969-79, sect. mgr., 1982-84, mgr., 1985-90, gen. mgr., 1991—; elec. engr. Saudi Consolidated Elec. Co. Western Region, Jeddah, Saudi Arabia, 1980-81; cons. Sasol II, Secunda, South Africa, 1985; lectr. Seikei U., Tokyo, 1994—. Contbr. articles to profl. jours. Mem. IEEE (sr., treas. DEi-32 Tokyo sect. 1991—, vice chmn. DEi-32 Tokyo sect. 1997-98, chmn. 1998—), Inst. Elec. Engrs. Japan. Avocations: classical music, tennis. Home: 1-5-19 Minami-Ohno, Ichikawa Chiba 272, Japan Office: Fujikura Ltd, 1-5-1 Kiba, Koto Tokyo 135, Japan

SHISHIGINA, OLGA, Olympic athlete. Winner Gold medal 100 meter hurdles Sydney, 2000. Office: Athletic Fedn Rep Kazakhstan, Abai St 48, 480072 Almaty Kazakhstan*

SHISHKOV, ROUSKO IVANOV, materials scientist, educator; b. Pleven, Bulgaria, July 17, 1948; s. Ivan Valchev and Genica Rouskova (Dimitrova) S.; m. Virginia Velkova Petrova, July 2, 1972; 1 child, Vladimir. MSc, U. Rousse, 1973, PhD, 1982. Asst. U. Rousse, Bulgaria, 1973-75, sr. asst., 1975-80, main asst., 1981-85, assoc. prof., 1985—; vice dir. sci. lab. Vacuum Heat Treatment and Metallizing, Rousse, 1977-84, Scientific Ctr. Vacuum Tech., Rousse, 1984-87, dir., 1987, head dept. materials engring., 2000—. Co-author: Vacuum Thermo- and Thermo-chemical Treatment, 1984; copatentee method for plasma vacuum diffusive metallizing. Recipient Honorary Diploma Ministry Edn. Sci. and Tech., 1996. Mem. Union Scientists in Bulgaria (Rousse award for considerable achievements in the field of sci.), Soc. Materials and Heat Treatment, N.Y. Acad. Sci. Avocations: ancient history, philosophy, music, photography, sports. Office: U Rousse, Studentska 8, 7017 Rousse Bulgaria

SHISTLE, PATRICIA ANNE, fine artist; b. Shreveport, La., Apr. 3, 1964; d. James C. and Elleanor H. McCrudden; m. Terrence D. Shistle, Feb. 14, 1996; children: Moriah, Benjamin, Emillie. BFA, Ringling Sch. Art and Design, Sarasota, Fla., 1995. Instr. Maitland (Fla.) Art Ctr., 1993—, Osceola Ctr. for Arts, Kissimee, Fla., 1999—. Exhibited in group shows Longboat Key (Fla.) Ctr. for Arts (1st pl. award), Art League of Willcox, Cochise, Ariz. (1st pl. award), Parkersburg (W.Va.) Art Ctr., Akron (Ohio) Soc. Artist, Longboat Key Art Ctr. (Longboat Key award, 3d pl. award [2], 1st pl. award), Morningside Gallery, Latham, N.Y. (Stewart's Shops Portrait award), Breckenridge (Colo.) Galleries, 1999, Breckenridge Fine Arts Ctr., Tex., 1999 (2d pl. award, Dorothy Mayes Still Life award), Maitland Art Ctr., 1995, 99, Seaside Art Gallery, Nags Head, N.C., Isabel Anderson Comer Mus. and Arts Ctr., Sylacauga, Ala., 1999 (2d pl. award); represented in permanent collections Town of Longboat Key Commn., Maitland Art Ctr. Collection, Longboat Key Ctr. for Arts. Home: 1300 Palmer St Orlando FL 32801-4121

SHIU, MAN HEI, surgeon; b. Hong Kong, Hong Kong, Aug. 10, 1936; s. Po Ku and Mary (Fung) S.; m. Kwai-Har Chau, Jan. 17, 1962; children: Jenifer Mei-Yee, Kenneth Kai-Huen. MD, U. Hong Kong, 1961. Diplomate Am. Bd. Surgery. Lectr. in surgery U. Hong Kong, 1966-68; asst. attending surgeon Meml. Sloan-Kettering Cancer Ctr., N.Y.C., 1973-80, assoc. attending surgeon, 1981-88, attending surgeon, 1989-91; asst. prof. Med. Coll. Cornell U., N.Y.C., 1973-80, assoc. prof., 1981-88, prof. clin. surgery, 1989-91; pvt. practice surgeon Hong Kong, 1991—; cons. in surgery Meml. Sloan-Kettering Cancer Ctr., 1991—, Hong Kong Sanatorium and Hosp., 1993—; assoc. examiner Am. Bd. Surgery, N.Y.C., 1986. Author: (with M.F. Brennan) Surgical Management of Soft Tissue Sarcoma, 1991. Assn. of Commonwealth Univs. scholar, 1964; recipient Digby Meml. Gold medal in surgery U. Hong Kong, 1961. Fellow ACS, Royal Coll. Surgeons Eng., Coll. Surgeons Hong Kong (mem. coun. 1993—, editor-in-chief newsletter 1994-96), Hong Kong Acad. Medicine; mem. Am. Soc. Clin. Oncology, Soc. Surg. Oncology, World Assn. Hepato-Pancreatic Biliary Surgery. Office: Ctrl Bldg 16/F, 1-3 Pedder St, Central District Central Hong Kong China

SHIU, YIU CHEUNG, electrical engineer; b. Hong Kong, China, 1960; s. Hoi Shiu and Kwan Ying Ng; m. Yim Ling Lo, Jan. 5, 2000. BSc, U. Toronto, 1983; MSEE, Purdue U., 1985, PhD, 1989. Asst. prof. Wright State U., Dayton, 1989-94; sr. lectr. VTC, Hong Kong, 1994—. Fellow Hont Kong Assn. Advancement Sci., N.Y. Acad. Sci.; mem. IEEE, Soc. Mech. Engrs.

SHIUE, SHAM-TSONG, materials science educator, researcher; b. Tainan, Taiwan, Feb. 4, 1955; s. Yao-Kuan and So-Din (Kang) S.; m. Su-Chen Lin, Nov. 23, 1980; children: Chiang-Jin, Yu-Jin. PhD, Nat. Tsing-Hua U., Hsinchu, Taiwan, 1988. Rschr. Chung-Hwa Telecom. Co., Taoyuang, Taiwan, 1981-92; assoc. prof. Feng-Chia U., Taichung, Taiwan, 1992-96, prof., 1996—; corp. project exec. Chung-Hwa Telecom. Co., Taoyuang, 1993-99. Contbr. over 50 articles to profl. jours. 2d lt. Army of Taiwan, 1977-79. Recipient Rsch. award Nat. Sci. Coun., Taipei, 1993-94, 96-2000. Mem. IEEE, Soc. Photo-Optical Instrumentation Engrs., Chinese Soc. Materials Sci. (sr.), Phi Tau Phi (hon.). Avocations: travel, exercise, reading, watching TV. E-mail: stshiue@fcu.edu.tw. FAX: 886-4-451-0014. Home: 8 Lane 18, Fu-Chiang St, Taichung 407, Taiwan Office: Feng Chia U Materials Sci, 100 Wenhwa Rd, Taichung 407, Taiwan

SHIVAJI, ARE, geophysicist, researcher; b. Bhongir, India, Nov. 10, 1963; s. Are Shankaraiah and Are Krishna Veni; m. Are Vijaya Laxmi, Feb. 6, 1988; children: A. Mallikharjun, A. Narasimham, A. Hymavathi. BSc, Osmania U., India, 1982; MSc in Tech., Osmania U., 1985, PhD, 1999. Cert. in seismology Sci. & Engring. Rsch. Coun., Govt. of India. Rsch. scholar Osmania U., 1985-90, geophysicist, 1990-97; sr. scientific officer Nat. Ctr. Antarctic and Ocean Rsch. Dept. Ocean Devel., Govt. of India, Vasco-da-Gama, India, 1997—; cons. geophysicist Mineral Exploration Corp., Govt. of India, 1989-93; participant Geophys. Exploration in Antarctica (geomapping 1995-96, part of scientific expdn. to Antarctica 1996). Tree planter Horticulture Divsn., Osmania U., 1986. Recipient Jr. Rsch. fellowship Dept. Sci. & Tech., Govt. of India, 1986-87, Jr. Rsch. fellowship Univ. Grants Commn. India, 1987, Sr. Rsch. fellowship Univ. Grants Commn. India, 1989. Mem. Assn. Exploration Geophysicists (life), Antarctic Club of India (life). Avocations: reading, music, nature watching, exploration of remote and interior places. Office: Nat Ctr Antarctic & Ocean Rsch, Headland Sada, 403804 Goa India

SHIVAKUMAR, KUNIGAL NANJUNDAIAH, aerospace engineer; b. Kunigal, Karnataka, India, Mar. 28, 1951; came to U.S., 1980; s. Kunigal H. Nanjundaiah; m. Netra D. Shivakumar, Nov. 1, 1984; children: Nishkala K., Nirmala K., Dhruva K. BE in Civil Engring., Bangalore (Karnataka) U., 1972; ME in Civil Engring., Indian Inst. Sci., Bangalore, 1974, PhD in Aeronautics, 1979. Rsch. assoc. Indian Inst. Sci., Bangalore, 1979, NRC, NASA Langley Rsch. Ctr., Washington, 1980-82; rsch. asst. prof. Old Dominion U., Norfolk, Va., 1982, rsch. assoc. prof., 1983-84; sr. scientist, group leader Analytical Svcs. & Materials, Hampton, Va., 1985-89, group leader, 1989-91; rsch. prof. N.C. Agrl. and Tech. State U., Greensboro, 1991—; dir. Ctr. Composite Materials Rsch., 1999—; cons. Bharat Heavy Elecs., Hyderbad, 1979, Aerotech, Lockheed Corp., Hampton, 1990, AS&M, NASA Langley Rsch. Ctr., Hampton, 1991. Contbr. over 100 articles to profl. jours. Com. mem. Kannada Sanga, Bangalore, 1978; pres. India Assn. of Peninsula, Hampton, 1984. Recipient 9 tech. awards NASA, I.I. Sc. Assoc. Fellow AIAA (assoc., sr., bd. dirs. 1991, gen. chair 37th SDM Conf., chair long-range planning com. 1996-97, vice chair materials TC, awards); mem. ASTM, ASME, ASC. Hindu. Avocations: tennis, gardening. Home: 5124 Hedrick Dr Greensboro NC 27410-9320 Office: NC A&T State U Fort Irc Bldg Rm 205 Greensboro NC 27411-0001

SHIVAS, MARK, film and television producer; b. London, Apr. 24; s. James Dallas and Winifred Alice (Bristow) S. MA in Law, Oxford (Eng.) U., 1960. Freelance journalist London, 1960-63; rschr., performer, prodr. Granada TV, Manchester, Eng., 1964-69; prodr. BBC, London, 1969-79; freelance prodr. London, 1979-88; head drama and tv BBC, London, 1988-93, head films, 1993-97; ind. prodr. Perpetual Motion Pictures, London, 1997—; coun. mem. BSAC, London, 1995—, BAFTA, London, 1997—. Prodr. TV dramas including The Six Wives of Henry the Eighth, 1970, Casanova, 1971, The Evacuees', 1974, The Glittering Prizes', 1975, Rogue Male, 1976, Professional Foul, 1977, On Giants' Shoulders, 1979, The Price, 1985, What If It's Raining, 1985, Jimensons The Storyteller, 1986, Talking Heads 2, 1998, feature films Moonlighting, 1982, A Private Function, 1984, The Witches, 1988; exec. prodr. feature films Truly, Madly, Deeply, Enchanted April, The Snapper, Small Faces, Regeneration, Hideous Kinky, Jude. Recipient Prodn. award Brit. Acad. Film and TV Arts, London, 1970, Emmy awards, N.Y., 1975, L.A., 1986. Fellow Royal TV Poetry; mem. AMPAS L.A. (prodr.), Atelier Cinematographique Europeen (bd. mem.).

SHIWAKOTI, DINESH RAJ, geotechnical engineer, researcher; b. Kshamawati, Dolakha, Nepal, July 30, 1966; s. Chudamani and Naradevi (Upreti) S.; m. Sandhya Regmi, 1999. M Engring., Asian Inst. Tech., Bangkok, 1994; DEng, Yokohama (Japan) Nat. U., 1997; BSc in Engring., Ranchi U., Jamshedpur, India, 1991. Civil engr. Govt. of Nepal, Kathmandu, 1992; rsch. assoc. Asian Inst. Tech., 1994; rsch. fellow Port and Harbor Rsch. Inst., Yokosuka, Japan, 1997—. Contbr. articles to sci. jours., including Geosynthetic Internat. Jour., also Asian Regional Conf., Internat. Conf. on Offshore Polar Engring. Recipient Mahendra Bidhya Bhusan medal King of Nepal, 1992, 99; scholar Govts. of Japan, Austria, India, 1987-97. Mem. Internat. Soc. Soil Mechanics and Geotech. Engring., Nepal Geotech. Soc. (exec. com., v.p.), Japan Geotech. Soc. Avocations: reading, traveling, swimming. E-mail: dinesh@ipc.phri.go.jp. Office: Port and Harbor Rsch Inst, 3-1-1 Nagase, Yokosuka 239-0826, Japan

SHIYAN, ANATOLIY ANTONOVICH, physicist; b. Gibalovka, Vinnitsa, Ukraine, Mar. 7, 1956; s. Anton Pilipovich and Anna Leontiivna (Kozhykhar) S.; m. Julia Moiseeva Volodimirivna Koreniyk, Aug. 17, 1979 (div. Oct. 1981); 1 child, Anastasia; m. Olga Micolaivna Baeva, Dec. 30, 1988; 1 child, Maksim. M.Physics, State U., Odessa, Ukraine, 1978, Cand. Theoretical and Math. Physics, 1984. Asst. prof. physics Bldg. Engring. Inst., Odessa, 1981-85; sci. rschr. State U., Odessa, 1985-90; self-employed Khmelnik, Ukraine, 1990-94; chief tech. Electrotseh Kilimniyka, Khmelnik, Ukraine, 1995-99; head Interant. SocTech Inst., Khmelnik, 1999—; sci. rschr. Sea Hydrophys. Inst. AS of Ukraine, Sevastopol, 1991-93; head Synergetics of Life Lab., 1995—. Contbr. articles to profl. jours. Mem. N.Y. Acad. Scis. Office: Synergetics of Life Lab, 1st May St 58/23, 22000 Khmelnik Ukraine

SHIYANOVSKII, SERGIJ, physicist; b. Kiev, Ukraine, Dec. 1, 1955; s. Vladislav Ivanovich and Irina Efimovna S.; m. Irina Nestoyanova, Nov. 15, 1975; children: Natalie, Yuriy. MS in Physics/Theoretical Physics, Kiev Nat. U., 1977, PhD in Physics and Math., 1982, DSc, 1994. Lectr. of maths. and physics Lyceum of Natural Scis., Kiev, 1977-79; jr. rschr. Kiev Nat. U., 1977-79; sr. rschr. Inst. for Nuclear Rsch./Ukrainian Acad. of Scis., Kiev, 1979-93, prin. rsch. fellow, 1994—; vis. scientist, adj. assoc. prof. Liquid Crystal Inst./Kent State U., Ohio, 1997—; vis. scientist U. Essen, Germany, 1996, Newton Inst. for Math. Scis., Cambridge, U.K., 1995; mem. rev. panel European INTAS, Brussels, Belgium, 1999, Ukrainian State Coun. for Sci. and Tech., Kiev, 1991—. Contbr. more than 80 articles to profl. publs. Travel grantee in field; grantee Sci. and Tech. Coun. of Ukraine, 1991-94, Cambridge U., 1995, German Rsch. Found., 1996, European INTAS, 1998; recipient award Soros Found., 1994, medal for Best Young Scientist Rsch. Work, Ukrainian Acad. Scis., 1978. Mem. Internat. Liquid Crystal Soc., Soc. for Info. Display. Avocations: tennis, soccer, kayaking. E-mail: svshiyan@lci.kent.edu. Office: Kent State U Liquid Crystal Inst Kent OH 44242-0001

SHI-ZHONG, BAI, mathematics educator; b. Yan'an, Shaanxi, China, Apr. 4, 1954; m. Li Dong-Mei; 1 child, Shi Bai. Bachelor's degree, Yan'an U.; postgrad., Shaanxi Normal U., Xi'an, China. Assoc. prof. Yan'an U., 1976-94; prof. Xiang'ton (China) U., 1994-99, Wu'yi (China) U., 1999—. Contbr. articles to profl. jours. Recipient Sci. and Tech. Advancement award Shaanxi Province, 1994, Outstanding Paper award Hunan Province, 1996, 98. Mem. Math. Assn. (China). Home: Wu'yi U, Math Dept, 529020 Jiangmen Guangdong, China

SHKOLNIKOV, VICTOR ALEXEEVITCH, academic administrator; b. Perm, Russia, May 21, 1940; s. Alexei and Elizabeta (Vinogradova) S.; m. Ludmila Dronova, June 11, 1943; children: Alexei, Andrei. Master's degree, U. Voronezh, Russia, 1962; PhD, Moscow Inst. Physics and Tech., 1970. Cert. in engring. physics. Asst. Moscow Inst. Physics and Tech., 1969-72, asst. prof., 1972-90, prorector, 1975—. Author and editor inventions and periodicals. Mem. Am. Phys. Soc. Avocations: fishing, hunting, painting. Office: Moscow Inst Physics & Tech, Institutsky Pereulok 9, 141700 Dolgoprudnyi Russia

SHKOLNIKOV, VLADIMIR DAVID, civil servant; b. St. Petersburg, Russia, Jan. 24, 1964; s. David Zucia and Ginda S.; m. Elena Bogolioubova, July 19, 1997. BS with honors, Calif. State U., Sacramento, 1987; MS, U. Calif., Irvine, 1989; PhD, Rand Grad. Sch., Santa Monica, 1994. Rsch. cons. Rand Corp., Santa Monica, Calif., 1989-95; adviser OSCE, Warsaw, Poland, 1995—. Contbg. author: (book) Conflicts in the Caucasus; author: (monograph) Scientific Bodies in Motion, 1995. Recipient commendation OSCE Summit, Lisbon, Portugal, 1996. Mem. Internat. Inst. Strategic Studies, Am. Assn. Advancement of Slavic Studies. Avocations: chess, travel. Office: OSCE, Al Ujazdowskie 19, Warsaw Poland

SHLAPUNOV, GENNADY SEMYONOVICH, historian; b. Vladivostok, Primorskiy, Russia, Oct. 20, 1938; s. Semyon Eliseevich and Polina Afanasievna (Vlasova) S.; m. Larisa Vasilievna Razbeiko, May 18, 1944; children: Elena, Tatiana, Natasha. Degree, Far East State U., Vladivostok, 1963; PhD, People's Inst. of Economy, Moscow, 1968. Vice rector Far Ea. Trade Inst., Vladivostok, 1971-82; dir. Advanced Sch. for Trade Unions, Vladivostok, 1982-96; cons. Govt. of Primorskiy Region, Vladivostok, 1996—. Author books; contbr. articles and reports to profl. publs. Co-chmn. Coordinative Coun. Internat. Congress Asia-Pacific Rim Ters., 1996—; pres. Peacemaking Pub. Fund, Vladivostok, 1998—; hon. pres. Asia-Pacific Internat. Investment Corp., Hong Kong, 1998—; hon. rector Fgn. Affairs Inst., Beltin U., Dalian, China, 1999—; chmn. Internat. Com. on Selection and Recommendation of High-Quality Goods, Harbin, China, 1999—. Mem. Internat. Acad. Ecology and Life Protection Scis. (academician), N.Y. Acad. Scis. Avocations: playing guitar, writing poetry, travel, jazz and classical music. Home: Pologaya Str 30/34, 36, 690000 Vladivostok Primorsk, Russia Office: Peacemaking Pub Fund, 6 Petra Velikogo Str, 690000 Vladivostok Primosrk, Russia

SHLAUDEMAN, HARRY WALTER, retired ambassador; b. L.A., May 17, 1926; s. Karl Whitman and Florence (Pixley) S.; m. Carol Jean Dickey, Aug. 7, 1948; children: Karl Frederick, Katherine Estelle, Harry Richard. BA, Stanford U., 1952. Joined U.S. Fgn. Svc., 1955; vice consul Barranquilla, Colombia, 1955-56; polit. officer Bogotá, Colombia, 1956-58; assigned lang. tng. Washington, 1958-59; consul Sofia, Bulgaria, 1960-62; chief polit. sect. Santo Domingo, Dominican Republic, 1962-64; officer charge Dominican Affairs State Dept., 1964-66; asst. dir. Office Caribbean Affairs, 1965-66; sr. seminar fgn. policy State Dept., 1966-67, spl. asst. to sec. state, 1967-69; dep. chief of mission Santiago, Chile, 1969-73; dep. asst. sec. state for Inter-Am. affairs Washington, 1973-75; amb. to Venezuela, 1975-76, asst. sec. state for Inter-Am. affairs, 1976-77, amb. to Peru, 1977-80, amb. to Argentina, 1980-83; exec. dir. Nat. Bipartisan Commn. on Central Am., 1983-84; spl. amb. to Cen. Am., 1984-86; amb. to Brazil Brasilia, 1986-89; amb. to Nicaragua, 1990-92, ret., 1992. Served with USMCR, 1944-46. Recipient Disting. Honor award Dept. State, 1966, Pres. Disting. Svc. award, 1988, Pres. Medal Freedom, 1992. Mem. Am. Acad. Diplomacy, San Luis Obispo Golf and Country Club, Phi Gamma Delta. Home: 7006 Pebble Beach Way San Luis Obispo CA 93401-8916

SHLENSKY, OREST FEDOROVICH, mechanics and thermal physics educator, researcher; b. Moscow, Russia, Nov. 29, 1935; s. Fedor Ivanovich and Ecatherine Ivanovna (Glushkova) S.; m. Nataly Nikolaevna Grevtzeva, Jan. 7, 1964; children: Michael, Maria. Heat and Mech. Engr., N. Bauman Moscow Tech. Sch., 1959, CandSci, 1964; Doctors Degree, Mendeleev U. Chem. Tech., Moscow, 1975. Mech. engr. N. Bauman Inst., Moscow, 1959-65; lectr. Moscow Inst. Chem. Mechanics, 1965-75; prof., head mech. dept. Moscow Mendeleev U. Chem. Tech., 1975-88, prof., 1988—; cons. Inst. Aviation Materials Tech., Moscow, 1975-85, Inst. High Temperature of Russian Acad. Sci., 1986-97. Author: Thermal Properties of Reinforced Plastics, 1973, Thermal Physics of Decomposing Materials, 1985, Thermal Decomposition of Materials, 1991, Thermal Disrapture of Materials, 1996; contbr. articles to profl. jours. Grantee Internat. Sci. Found., 1995-97, Internat. Soros Sci. Edn. Program, 2000, Russian Found. for Fundamental Rsch., 1997-98. Mem. Moscow House of Scientists, N.Y. Acad. Scis. Orthodox Christian. Avocations: international travel, canoeing, skiing. Fax: (095) 2004204. Office: Mendeleev U Chem Tech, Miusskaya Sq 9, 125047 Moscow Russia

SHLYAKHOV, ELIE NAHUM, epidemiologist, researcher; b. Kishinev, Republic of Moldova, Feb. 8, 1920; s. Nahum Khaanany and Elvire Elie (Dimentstein) S.; m. Valentina Andrey Burumov, May 25, 1956 (div. Aug. 1959); 1 child, Andrey; m. Tzila Meyer Steklov, Aug. 30, 1959. MD, Med. High Inst., Tashkent, Uzbekistan, 1942; PhD, Acad. Med. Scis., Moscow, 1966. Prin. epidemiologist Ministry of Health, Nukus, Uzbekistan, 1942-45; dep. chief dept. epidemiology Ministry of Health, Kishinev, Moldova, 1945-50; sci. leader Inst. Epidemiology, Kishinev, Moldova, 1950-67; chief chair State Med. Inst., Kishinev, Moldova, 1967-90; sr. rschr. Sheba Med. Ctr., Tel-Hashomer, Israel, 1990—, prin. investigator; dep. dir. Inst. Epidemiology, 1960-74. Author: Practical Epidemiology, 1974, 5th edit., 1990, Immunology, Immunodiagnosis and Immunoprevention of Infectious Diseases, 1977, Immunology, 1985; patentee in field. People dep. Dist. Mayoralty, Kishinev., 1960-62. Recipient Gold medal All Union Exhbn. of Nat. Economy, Moscow, 1966, Hon. Scientist award Supreme Soviet of Moldova, 1967, Gold medal Internat. Exhbn., Plovdiv, Bulgaria, 1967. Mem. Soc. Epidemiologists (hon., pres. 1964-90), Soc. Immunologists (pres. 1978-90), Sci. Med. Coun. Ministry of Health (Moldova v.p. 1979-90). Avocations: photography, collection of watches and pencils, fountain pens. Home: PO Box 2457, 42124 Netanya Israel Office: Sheba Med Ctr, Infectious Diseases Unit, 52621 Tel Hashomer Israel

SHLYAPNIKOV, YURY ALEXANDROVICH, chemist; b. Moscow, Feb. 27, 1926; s. Alexandr Gavrilovich and Ekaterina Sergeevna (Woscinska) S.; m. Nina Leonidovna Galanina, Apr. 16, 1958 (dec. Mar.); children: Marina, Mikhail. PhD, Inst. Petrochem. Synthesis, 1961; DSc, Inst. Chem. Physics, 1969, Prof. in Phys. Chemistry, 1978. Jr. scientist Gorky State U. Chem. Inst., 1957-58; jr. scientist Inst. Chem. Physics, USSR Acad. Scis., 1958-64, sr. scientist, 1964-73, head lab., 1973-92, main scientist, 1992-96; main scientist Inst. Biochem. Physics, 1996—. Author: Antioxidative Stabilization of Polymers, 1986, rev. edit., 1996; contbr. articles to profl. jours. E-mail: Yurysh30@mailru.com. Home: 43-2-307 Profsoyuznaya St, 117420 Moscow Russia Office: United Inst Chem Physics, 117334 Moscow Russia

SHMERLING, DAVID HAIM, pediatrician, educator, retired; b. Tel Aviv, Aug. 3, 1928; arrived in Switzerland, 1959; s. Moshe and Berta (Shochet) S.; m. Hildegard Becker, Jan. 18, 1955; children: Daniella, Doroh, Uriel. MD, U. Faculty Medicine, Zurich, Switzerland, 1953; MD (hon.), U. Warsaw, Poland, 1990. Resident U. Dept. Pediat., Zurich, 1959-63, rsch. fellow pediat. gastroenterology and nutrition, 1963-69, head divsn. pediat. gas-

troenterology and nutrition, 1969-93. Contbr. over 120 articles to profl. publs. Lt. Israeli Marine Med. Corps., 1956-58. Home: Saumstr 29, CH 8625 Gossau Switzerland

SHMOTKIN, DOV, psychologist; b. Rishon Le-Zion, Israel, Apr. 30, 1949; s. Benjamin and Tova (Landau) S.; m. Malka Katz, Feb. 28, 1974; children: Shimrit, Shirit. BA, Tel-Aviv U., 1971, MA, 1974, PhD, 1985. Clin. psychologist Nes-Ziona Govt. Psychiat. Hosp., 1977-85, Jaffa Mental Health Cmty. Ctr., Israel, 1986-87; sr. lectr. Tel-Aviv U., 1993—; instr. Tel-Aviv U., 1981-86, lectr., 1986-93, chmn. com. psychology undergrad. studies, 1990-96; vis. scholar U. Mich., Ann Arbor, 1988-89; hon. fellow Inst. on Aging, U. Wis., Madison, 1996-97; rsch. coord. Herczeg Inst. on Aging, 1993—, head grad. clin. psychology program, 1999—. Contbr. articles to profl. jours. Sec. Israel Coun. Psychologists, Tel-Aviv, 1987-92. Maj. Israel Naval Def. Forces, 1972-77. Rsch. grantee Israel Found. Trustees, 1982, Sapir Ctr. for Devel., 1986. Mem. Coun. The Israel Gerontol. Soc. (Prochowniek award 1990), Israel Soc. Psychol. Assessment (founding com., rep. 1990-95), Israel Psychol. Assn., Gerontol. Soc. Am. Office: Tel-Aviv Univ, Dept Psychology, 69978 Tel-Aviv Israel

SHMUELI, ALFRED, accountant, educator; b. Bagdad, Iraq, Mar. 27, 1930; arrived in Eng., 1969; s. Oved and Naima (Sofer) S.; m. Rivka Polak, Nov. 27, 1956; children: Ehud, Aviya. LLM, Hebrew U., Jerusalem, 1956; MSc, City U., London, 1972, MPhil, 1973. Fin. analyst Ha'Aretz Newspaper, Tel Aviv, 1960-69; sr. lectr. N.E. London Poly., 1973-84, Southeastern U., London, 1988—. Author: Murder in the Kibbutz, 1993, In the Harem of the Sublime Porte, 1993, Withdrawal, 1994, The Murder of Selim III, 2000. Mem. Assn. Cert. Accts. Jewish. Mem. Labour Party. Avocations: writing, music. Home: 97 Geary Rd Dollis Hill, London NW10 1HS, England

SHNAID, ISAAC, mechanical engineer, researcher, educator; b. Odessa, USSR, Apr. 6, 1937; s. Michael and Riva (Shraiber) S.; m. Galina Belaigorod, Aug. 2, 1963; children: Michael (dec.), Nora. MSc, Odessa Inst. Low Temperature Techniques and Energetics, 1959, PhD, 1965. Rschr. Odessa Inst. Low Temperature Technique and Energetics, 1959-65, teaching and rsch. asst., 1965-67, sr. lectr., sr. rschr., head lab., 1967-90; sr. rsch. engr. R&D div. Israel Elec. Corp. Ltd., Haifa, 1991-96, sr. specialist, 1996—. Contbr. more than 100 articles to sci. and profl. jours. in field of rsch. thermodynamics, heat engines, cryogenics, refrigeration, compressors and expanders; patents, U.S., Israel and Germany; inventions relating to gas turbines, compressed air energy storage plants, cryogenic liquefaction of gases, heat engines with a pulse tube, cryogenic coolers, free-piston compressors and refrigerators. Mem. ASME, Assn. of Engrs. and Architects Israel. Judaism. Achievements include patents in U.S., Israel and Germany. Office: Israel Elec Corp Ltd R&D Divsn, PO Box 10, 31000 Haifa Israel

SHNEERSON, JOHN MICHAEL, medical educator; b. London, Sept. 27, 1946; s. Gregory and Alfreda (Ledger) S.; m. Anne Maclean, Mar. 15, 1975; children: Joanna, Catherine, Robert. MA, Oxford U., 1971, DM, 1977; MD, Cambridge U., 1986. Sr. registrar Brompton and Westminster Hosps., London, 1978-80; cons. physician, dir. respiratory support and sleep ctr. Papworth Hosp., Cambridge, Eng., 1980—; assoc. lectr. U. Cambridge, Eng., 1985—; cons. Addenbrookes Hosp., Cambridge, 1980—. Author: Manual of Chest Medicine, 1986, Disorders of Ventilation, 1988. Bd. dirs. Brit Scoliosis Rsch. Found. Fellow Royal Coll. Physicians, Am. Coll. Chest Physicians. Avocations: tennis, golf. Home: 129 North St, Burwell Cambridge CB5 0BB, England

SHNEIDER, GENNADY LVOVICH, metallurgical engineer; b. Kazan, Tassr, USSR, Aug. 28, 1936; s. Lev Abramovich and Muza Grigorievna Shneider; m. Galina Ivanovna Seliverstova, Aug. 14, 1960; 1 child, Sergey Gennadyevich. Ed., Moscow Inst. Aircraft Tech., 1965; candidate in tech. sci., ALL Union Light Alloys Inst., Moscow, 1975, D in Tech. Sci., 1991. With Works Light Alloys, Moscow, 1958-62; technologist AIL Union Light Alloys Inst., 1962-64, engr., 1964-75, jr. scientist, 1975-80, sr. scientist, 1980-91; prin. scientist All Russis Inst. Light Alloys, 1991—. Contbr. articles to sci. jours.; patentee in field (Bronze and Silver Russian medals 1976, Nat. Econ. Achievement award 1989). Sgt. arty., Russian Mil., 1955-58. Avocation: beekeeping. Home: Kv 145, Ulitsa Marshala Birjzova 28, 143000 Odintsovo Moskovskoi Oblasti, Russia Office: All Russia Inst Light Alloy, Gorbunova 2, 121596 Moscow Russia

SHNEIDMAN, EDWIN S., psychologist, educator, thanatologist, suicidologist; b. York, Pa., May 13, 1918; s. Louis and Manya (Zukin) S.; m. Jeanne E. Keplinger, Oct. 1, 1944; children: David William, Jonathan Aaron, Paul Samuel, Robert James. AB, UCLA, 1938, MA, 1940; MS, U. So. Calif., 1947, PhD, 1948. Diplomate: Am. Bd. Examiners Profl. Psychology (past v.p.). Clin. psychologist VA Center, Los Angeles, 1947-50; chief research VA Center, 1950-53; co-dir. Central Research Unit for Study Unpredicted Deaths, 1953-58; co.-dir. Suicide Prevention Center, Los Angeles, 1958-66; chief Center Studies Suicide Prevention NIMH, Bethesda, Md., 1966-69; vis. prof. Harvard U., 1969; fellow Ctr. Advanced Study in Behavioral Scis., 1969-70; clin. assoc. Mass. Gen. Hosp., 1969, Karolinska Hosp., Stockholm, 1978; prof. med. psychology UCLA, 1970-75, prof. thanatology, 1975-88, emeritus, 1988—; vis. prof. Ben Gurion U. of Negev, Beersheva, 1983. Author: Deaths of Man, 1973, Voices of Death, 1980; Definition of Suicide, 1985, Suicide as Psychache, 1993, The Suicidal Mind, 1996; editor: Thematic Test Analysis, 1951; editor: (with N.L. Farberow) Clues to Suicide, 1957, The Cry for Help, 1961, Essays in Self-Destruction, 1967, (with M. Ortega) Aspects of Depression, 1969, On the Nature of Suicide, 1969, (with N.L. Farberow, L.E. Litman) Psychology of Suicide, 1970, Death and the College Student, 1972, Death: Current Perspectives, 1976, 80, 84, Suicidology: Contemporary Developments, 1976, Endeavors in Psychology: Selections From The Personology of Henry A. Murray, 1981, Suicide Thoughts and Reflections, 1981. Served to capt. USAAF, 1942-45. Recipient Harold M. Hildreth award Psychologists in Pub. Service, 1966; Louis I. Dublin award Am. Assn. Suicidology, 1969. Mem. Am. Assn. Suicidology (founder, past pres.), Am. Psychol. Assn. (past div. pres., Disting. Profl. Contbn. to Pub. Svc. award 1987, Henry A. Murray award 1997), Melville Soc. Address: 11431 Kingsland St Los Angeles CA 90066-1329

SHNYREVA, ALLA VICTOROVNA, biologist, educator; b. Chelyabinsk, Russia, Dec. 20, 1958; d. Victor and Alexandra Mikhailovna (Dreval) Daraga; m. Andrei Pavlovich Shnyrev, Oct. 15, 1988; 1 child, Anastassya. MSc in Biology with honors, Moscow State U., 1982, PhD in Biology, 1986. Rsch. assoc. Moscow State U., 1986-88, rsch. scientist, 1989-93, assoc. prof., 1993—, lectr., 1996—; vis. scientist U. Montreal, Que., Can., 1991; vis. academic King's Coll. London, 1993, 94, 96; cons. Russian Space Agy., Korolev, 1997-98, Fedn. Mushroom Growers, Russia, 1997—. Editor: English-Russian Biological Dictionary, 1999; contbr. articles to profl. jours. Leader ecol. program Support, Care, Initiative. Recipient fellowships Royal Soc., London, 1994-95, European Environ. Rsch. Orgn., 1996, Fedn. European Microbiol. Socs., 1993. Fellow Russian Found. Basic Rsch.; mem. Russian Microbiol. Soc., Russian Mycological Soc. Avocations: music, literature, skiing, swimming, travel. Office: Moscow State U, Dept Mycology & Algology, 119899 Moscow Russia

SHOAFF, THOMAS MITCHELL, lawyer; b. Ft. Wayne, Ind., Aug. 21, 1941; s. John D. and Agnes H. (Hanna) S.; m. Eunice Swedberg, Feb. 7, 1970; children: Andrew, Nathaniel, Matthew-John. BA, Williams Coll., 1964; JD, Vanderbilt U., 1967. Bar: Ind. 1968. Assoc. Isham, Lincoln & Beale, Chgo., 1967-68; ptnr. Baker & Daniels, Ft. Wayne, Ind., 1968—; bd. dirs. Weaver Popcorn Co., Inc., Ft. Wayne, Dreibelbiss Title Co., Inc., Ft. Wayne, Am. Steel Investment Corp., Ft. Wayne. Bd. dirs. McMillen Found., Ft. Wayne, Wilson Found., Ft. Wayne. Mem. ABA, Allen County Bar Assn., Ind. State Bar Assn. Presbyterian. Avocations: golf, sailing. Office: Baker & Daniels 111 E Wayne St Ste 800 Fort Wayne IN 46802-2603

SHOCHAT, AVRAHAM, Israel government official; b. 1936; s. Shochat and Fania (Perel) S.; m. Tama Eskkol; two children. Student, Haita Thacmon. Br. dirs. Solel Boneh, Israel Aircraft Industries; now min. fin. Israeli Ministry Fin., Jerusalem. Founder, mayor Arad, 1967-89, chmn. first citizen's com.; chmn. Devel. Towns Coun.; dep. chmn. Union Local Authorities; mem. Knesset, 1988—; chmn. Com. on Economy, Fin. Com. Paratrooper Israeli Def. Force. Mem. Labour Party. Fax: 972 0 2 675 4157. Office: PO Box 13195, 1 Kaplan, 91008 Jerusalem Israel*

SHODA, EMPRESS MICHIKO, Empress of Japan; b. Tokyo, Oct. 20, 1934; d. Hidesaburo Shoda; m. Emperor Akihito, Apr. 10, 1959; children: Naruhito Hironomiya, Fumihito Ayanomiya, Sayako Norinomiya. BA in English Lit., U. of Sacred Heart, Tokyo, 1957. Hon. pres., former hon. v.p. Japanese Red Cross Soc. Avocations: piano, harp, embroidering, weaving, handicrafts. Office: Imperial Household Agency, Secretariat of Grand Steward, 1-1 Chiyoda, Chiyoda-ku Tokyo 100, Japan*

SHOECRAFT, TIM HENRY, tax minimization strategist; b. Syracuse, N.Y., June 27, 1949; s. Byron Henry and Frances Genevive S.; m. Marianne T. Shoecraft, Aug. 15, 1982; children: Alison, Kellyn, Austin. BA, State U. N.Y., 1973; MBA, Columbia State U., 1997, PhD, 1997. Pres. Shoecraft & Assocs., Oswego, N.Y., 1976-80, Profl. Fin. Svcs., Bedford, N.Y., 1980-98; chmn., CEO Profl. Fin. Svcs., 1998—; spkr. in field; cons. to nat. law firms. Ave. chmn. Rotary, Oswego, N.Y., 1976-80; troop leader Boy Scouts Am., 1970-73. Mem. Internat. Forum, Internat. Assn. Fin. Planners, Top of Table, Million Dollar Round Table, Mensa, Assn. Advanced Life Underwriters. Republican. Office: Profl Fin Svcs LLC 762 N Bedford Rd Bedford NY 10507

SHOEMAKER, CAMERON DAVID JAMES, dean, educator; b. Honolulu, Dec. 15, 1940; s. John James and Belle Bird (Kellogg) S.; m. Catherine LaMoyne Prevost, May 23, 1966 (div. 1969); 1 child, David James; m. Leona Martha Wohlwend, May 18, 1972; 1 child, Jennifer Lee. BA in Polit. Sci., The Citadel, 1963; MA in History, San Jose State U., 1973; EdD, U. San Francisco, 1990. Commd. 2d lt. U.S. Army, 1963, advanced through grades to maj., 1971; fgn. area officer U.S. Army, U.S., Korea, Germany and Vietnam, 1972-84; ret. U.S. Army, 1984; fin. cons. Merrill Lynch, Carmel, Calif., 1984-85; mgmt. analyst Def. Lang. Inst., Monterey, Calif., 1985; ednl. tech. project mgr. Def. Lang. Inst., Monterey, 1985-86, dir. info. resources mgmt., 1986-90; evening coll. adminstr., instnl. researcher Monterey Peninsula Coll., 1990-92; dean of bus. Sacramento (Calif.) City Coll., 1992-98; dean Vista Coll., Berkeley, Calif., 1999-2000; dir. ednl. svcs. Heald Coll., Roseville, Calif., 2000—; instr., Chapman Coll., Monterey, 1982-84, Monterey Inst., 1987; chmn. Asian Employment Program Com., Monterey, 1983-84; guest lectr., Naval Postgrad. Sch., Monterey, 1986-87; mem. Handicapped Individual Program Com., Monterey, 1986-90, treas., 1989-90. Contbr. articles to various publs. Pres., Creekside Community Assn., Salinas, Calif., 1985-86; mem. County Svc. Area Adv. Bd., Salinas, 1985-87, Flood Control Dist. Planning Com., Salinas, 1986-87; active Leadership Monterey Peninsula, grad., 1992. Decorated Silver Star medal; recipient Comdrs. award for Civilian Svc. Dept. of Army, 1990; Carl D. Perkins fellow, 1993. Mem. Chief Instrnl. Officers Calif. Cmty. Colls., Royal Asiatic Soc., Monterey Peninsula Scottish Soc. (treas. 1986-92), Los Rios Mgmt. Assn. (pres. 1995-96), Caledonian Club of Sacramento (treas. 1994-97, chief 1997-99). Republican. Roman Catholic. Home: 11577 Melones Cir Gold River CA 95670-7738 Office: Heald Coll 7 Sierra Gate Plz Roseville CA 95678-6602

SHOEMAKER, FORREST HILTON, JR., marketing and sales executive, consultant; b. Waycross, Ga., Sept. 2, 1953; s. Forrest Hilton Sr. and Flora Kay (Jacobs) S.; married 1974 (div. 1985) children: Thomas, Myriah. BA, Armstrong State Coll., 1975. Pres., mng. ptnr. Shoemaker Cons. Inc., Savannah, Ga., 1981-85; v.p., gen. mgr. Hawaii Juice Co./Island Liquid Sunshine, Honolulu, 1986-88; gen. mgr. Barry Hall Sales/Banana Boat Hawaii, Honolulu, 1988-91; v.p. sales Practice Mgmt. Svcs., Honolulu, 1987-88; dir. mktg. and sales Webco Hawaii Inc.-Schering-Plough Healthcare Divsn., Honolulu, 1991—; pres. The Hilton Group, 1994—; pres., CEO Hawaii Candlelight, 1998—. Avocations: surfing, running, playing tennis, diving, reading. Home: 1142 Auahi St Ste A7 Honolulu HI 96814-4996

SHOEMAKER, HAROLD LLOYD, infosystem specialist; b. Danville, Ky., Jan. 3, 1923; s. Eugene Clay and Amy (Wilson) S.; A.B., Berea Coll., 1944; postgrad. State U. Ia., 1943-44, George Washington U., 1949-50, N.Y. U., 1950-52; m. Dorothy M. Maddox, May 11, 1947 (dec. Feb. 1991). Research physicist State U., Ia., 1944-45, Frankford Arsenal, Pa., 1945-47; research engr. N.Am. Aviation, Los Angeles, 1947-49, Jacobs Instrument Co., Bethesda, 1949-50; asso. head systems devel. group The Teleregister Corp., N.Y.C., 1950-53; mgr. electronic equipment devel. sect., head planning for indsl. systems div. Hughes Aircraft Co., Los Angeles, 1953-58; dir. command and control systems lab. Bunker-Ramo Corp., Los Angeles, 1958-68, v.p. Data Systems, 1968-69, corp. dir. data processing, 1969-75; tech. staff R & D Assocs., Marina Del Rey, Calif., 1975-85; info. systems cons., 1985—. Served with AUS, 1945-46. Mem. IEEE, Ky. Cols. Patentee elec. digital computer. Home: PO Box 3385 Granada Hills CA 91394-0385

SHOEMAKER, HELEN E. MARTIN ACHOR, civic worker; b. Houston, Mar. 24, 1915; d. Earl L. and Blanche L. (Williams) Martin; AB, Anderson (Ind.) Coll., 1960, LLD, 1978; m. Harold E. Achor, Oct. 11, 1935; children: Dianne Achor Johnston, Lana Achor Wolfe; m. Robert N. Shoemaker, May 19, 1972. Resident dir. Anderson Coll., 1967-69, dir. alumni svcs., 1969-72; legis. counsel Ind. Colls. and Univ. Ind., 1970-72; spl. asst. Ctr. Public Svc., Anderson, 1973-77, spl. asst. to dean for acad. devel., 1977-78. Sec.-treas. Ind. State Libr. and Hist. Bldg. Expansion Commn., 1973-78; mem. com. region VII, Girl Scouts U.S.A., 1958-66; adv. coun. fin. aid to students Office Edn. HEW, 1976-78. Mem. Ind. Ho. of Reps. from Madison County, 1968-70; v.p. Ind. Fedn. Women's Republican Clubs, 1945-46; treas. Nat. Fedn. Women's Rep. Clubs, 1947-51; Rep. precinct vice chmn. Madison County, 1946-68, vice chmn., Anderson, 1967-68; bd. dirs. Urban League Madison County, 1969-76; adv. com. Georgetown U. Grad. Sch. Acad. in Public Service, 1976-83; mem. adv. com. on sex discrimination Ind. Civil Rights Commn., 1978-83; bd. dirs. Anderson Symphony Orch.Women's Guild, 1987 trustee Anderson Coll., 1978-85; bd. dirs. Opportunities Industrialization Ctr., Inc., Madison County, 1980-84, Ind. Acad. Public Svc., 1981-83, Women's Alternatives Inc., Anderson, 1982-93 (Elizabeth Howard McMahan award, 1987); mem. exec. com. devel. bd. St. John's Med. Ctr., Anderson, 1981-92; bd. dirs. life enrichment Park Place Ch. God, 1989-94; bd. dirs. Anderson Symphony Womens Guild. Recipient William B. Harper award Urban League Madison County, 1975; named Sagamore of Wabash, State of Ind., 1979. Hon. mem. Anderson Symphony Orch. Guild; mem. LWV (dir. Madison County 1973-76, 78-84, 87), Anderson Council Women, Anderson Fine Arts Center (treas), women's league 1984—, pres. 1987-88). Mem. Ch. of God. Home: 5801 W Bethel Ave Muncie IN 47304-9549

SHOEMAKER, MARK T., minister; b. Kokomo, Ind., Aug. 29, 1947; s. Ithel D. Shoemaker and Delsie L. McQueary; m. Ruth Ann Lennington, Oct. 15, 1977; 1 child, Melissa Marie Shoemaker. BSID, Inst. Design Ill. Inst. Tech., 1969; MDiv, So. Bapt. Theol. Seminary, 1982. Cert. EMT. Tchr. Indpls. Pub. Schs., 1969-73; coord. inner scout camping Ctrl. Ind. Coun. Boy Scouts Am., Indpls., 1970-73; dist. scout exec. Licking County Coun. Boy Scouts Am., Newark, Ohio, 1973-76; edn. exec. Old Ky. Home Coun. Boy Scouts Am., Louisville, 1976-79; chaplain intern Jewish Hosp., Louisville, 1982; dir. retreat ctr. EUMBA Assbmely Ground, Newark, 1983-89; minority recruiter, counselor Ohio State U., Newark, 1985-86; chaplain, dir. Licking County Justice Ctr./Licking County Jail Ministries, Newark, 1989—; assoc. min. Mt. Lebanon Bapt. Ch., Louisville, 1978-83, Shiloh Bapt. Ch., Newark, 1983—. Chaplain, EMT Madison Twp. Vol. Fire Dept., Newark, 1984-90, Hanover (Ohio) Vol. Fire Dept. Inc., 1987—. Eagle Scout Boy Scouts Am., 1962; recipient Bronze Pelican Roman Cath. Diocese Columbus, 1998. Mem. Am. Protestant Correctional Chaplains Assn., Am. Correctional Chaplains Assn., Hon. Order of Ky. Cols., Moundbuilders Kiwanis Club. Avocations: outdoors, photography. Home: 3302 Hickman Rd Newark OH 43055-9157 Office: Licking County Justice Ctr 155 E Main St Newark OH 43055-6245

SHOHIEB, MOUSTAFA MOHAMED, orthopedic surgeon, researcher; b. Alexandria, Egypt, Apr. 28, 1967; s. Mohamed Sabry S. and B. Anwar Rizk. MBChB, Alexandria U., 1990, MD, 1994. Orthopedic surgeon Alexandria (Egypt) U. Hosp., 1990—; resident ortho. traumatology El-Hadra Univ. Hosp., 1991-93; exec. mgr. ICON Co. Avocations: chess, football, fishing, medical mailing. Home: PO Box 130 El-Saray, Alexandria 21411, Egypt Office: ICON Co, 197 Abd El-Salam Aaref St, Alexandria Egypt

SHOHOJI, NOBUMITSU, nuclear engineer; b. Okayama, Japan, July 18, 1949; s. Takehiko and Kiyomi (Kondoh) S.; m. Maria Candida Barrinha Loia, Feb. 28, 1981. B in Engring. Sci., Osaka U., 1972, M in Nuclear Engring., 1974, D in Nuclear Materials, 1977. Vis. researcher Karlsruhe Nuclear Rsch. Ctr., West Germany, 1977-78; post-doctoral rsch. worker metallurgy dept. U. Sheffield, England, 1979-82; researcher Inst. Nat. de Engring. Indsl. Tech., Lisbon, Portugal, 1982-88, prin. researcher, 1988—. Mem. Japan Inst. Metals, Iron & Steel Inst. Japan, Inst. Materials London, Portuguese Metals Soc. Avocation: tennis. Office: INETI/IMP/DM, Estrado de Paso do Lumiar, 1649-038 Lisbon Codex Portugal

SHOHOJI, TAKAO, statistician; b. Kure, Japan, Jan. 1, 1938; s. Mitsuto and Takeko (Ishida) S.; m. Yoshie Nagasawa, May 25, 1967; children: Takashige, Mio. BA, Hiroshima U., 1962, MA, 1965; PhD, NYU, 1972. Analytical statistician Atomic Bomb Casualty Commn., Hiroshima, 1965-72; assoc. rsch. scientist NYU Med. Ctr., 1968-72, acting head computing ctr., 1972-78, head lab computing ctr., 1978-80, assoc. prof., 1974-85, prof., 1985—, chmn. info. engring., 1994-95, head info. processing ctr., 1999—; chmn. info. engring Senogawa Hosp., Hiroshima, 1966-90; mem. organizing com. 12th Internat. Biometric Conf., Tokyo, 1984; mem. exclusive com. 3d Japan and Korea Conf. Stats., 1985, 4th Japan and Korea Conf. Stats., 1986, 46th Internat. Statis. Inst., Tokyo, 1987; mem. organizing and program com. Honolulu Conf. on Computational Stats., 1992; mem. sci. program com. Internat. Biometric Conf., Hamilton, Can., 1994; mem. internat. organizing com. Internat. Conf. Statis. Method and Statis. Computing for Quality and Productivity Improvement, Seioul, 1995; mem. joint sci. program com. 9th Korea and Japan Joint Conf. Stats., 1997. Contbr. articles to profl. jours. Recipient Founders Day award NYU, 1973. Fellow Human Biology Coun.; mem. Japan Math. Soc., Japan Statis. Assn. (coun. 1988-91), Chugoku New Media Assn. (chmn. 1987-90), Higashi-Hiroshima Community Info. Coun. (chmn. 1995—), Japanese Soc. Applied Statis. (coun. 1986-91, 94-99), Internat. Biometric Soc. (coun. 1988-96), Am. Statis. Assn., Internat. Statis. Inst., Japanese Soc. Co. Statis. Assn. (coun. 1987—, assoc. editor Japanese jour. 1986-92, 97—, editor English lang. jour. 1999—, v.p. 1993, pres. 1993-96, bd. dirs. 1987—), Biometric Soc. Japan (sec. 1986-90, treas. 1991-93, coun., bd. dirs. 1982-96), Japanese Classification Soc. (bd. dirs. 1991-93), N.Y. Acad. Scis., Gehnan Tennis Club. Home: 2-10-46 Shimizu, Kure 737-0022, Japan Office: Hiroshima U Integrated Arts Scis, 1-7-1 Kagamiyama, Higashi Hiroshima 739-8521, Japan

SHOICHI, NAKAJIMA, chemistry educator; b. Minato-ku, Tokyo, Dec. 6, 1929; s. Kuraji and Sadae (Konno) N.; m. Keiko Ooki, Nov. 20, 1960; children: Kazunori, Makiko. MS, Tokyo U., 1953, D of Pharmacy, 1964. Lic. pharmacist, English interpreter. Rsch. staff Eizai Co. Ltd., Tokyo, 1953-54; rsch. assoc. Columbia U., N.Y.C., 1965-68; assoc. prof. Hoshi U., Tokyo, 1962-70, prof. organic chemistry, 1970-95; prof. emeritus, 1995—. Contbr. over 90 articles to profl. jours. Mem. Japan Pharm. Soc. (exec. com. Kanto br. 1992—, v.p. Grand Kanto Dist. mtg.). Achievements include Japanese patents for electrochem. mfg. of amides, 1987, electrochem. transesterification, 1987, electrochem. mfg. of barbiturates, 1989, others. Home: Higiriyama 1-33-32, Koonan-ku Yokohama 2330015, Japan Office: Hoshi Univ, Ebara 2-4-41, Shinagawa-ku, Tokyo 142, Japan

SHOJAI, FARANAK, ceramist, researcher; b. Tehran, Iran, Sept. 25, 1959; d. Shokrolah and Mahin (Esna Ashari) S.; m. Aliakbar Shamlou, Feb. 18, 1982; children: Nasim, Siavash. MSc, U. Tehran, 1988; PhD in Materials Sci., U. Tampere, Finland, 1995. Supr. metal-related rsch. projects Ministry of Mines and Metals, Tehran, 1989-91; rsch. engr. Tampere U. Tech., 1992—. Avocations: aerobics, reading, mountaining, cycling, swimming. Home: Orivedenkatu 8C 62, 33720 Tampere Finland Office: Tampere Univ Tech, PO Box 589, FIN33101 Tampere Finland

SHOJI, HIROMU, orthopedic surgeon, educator; b. Chiba-Ken, Japan. Grad., Coll. Gen. Edn., 1959, U. Tokyo, Faculty Medicine, 1964. Diplomate Am. Bd. Orthopedic Surgery (examiner). Intern U. Tokyo Hosp., 1964-65, resident, 1965-67; resident Bklyn. Cumberland Med. Ctr., 1967-68, NYU Med. Ctr., 1968-69, Bowman Gray Med. Sch., Winston-Salem, N.C., 1973-74; orthopedic surgeon pvt. practice, Sacramento, 1974-76, New Orleans, 1976-90, Riverside, Calif., 1990—; mem. staff Parkview Hosp., Riverside Cmty. Hosp., Corona Regional Hosp.; asst. prof. dept. orthopedic surgery U. Calif., Davis, 1974-76; assoc. prof. dept. orthopedic surgery La. State U. Med. Ctr., 1976-80, prof., 1980-90; clin. prof. Loma Linda U., 1990—. Contbr. numerous articles to profl. jours. Bone tumor clin. fellow Meml. Sloan-Kettering Med. Ctr., N.Y.C., 1966-70, orthopedic fellow Hosp. Spl. Surgery, N.Y.C., 1971-72. Mem. AMA, NAS, Am. Acad. Orthopedic Surgeons, Am. Assn. Hip and Knee Surgeons, Japanese Orthopedic Assn., Orthopedic Rsch. Soc., Japanese Soc. Connective Tissue Rsch., Japanese Rehab. Assn., Am. Orthopedic Assn., So. Med. Assn., Am. Rheumatism Assn., Calif. Orthopedic Assn., Internat. Soc. Orthopedics and Traumatology, Knee Soc., Internat. Soc. Knee Surgery. Office: 3838 Sherman Dr Riverside CA 92503-4001

SHOJI, ISAO, statistician, educator; b. Chiyoda, Japan, Jan. 13, 1960; s. Kiyoshi and Kazuko (Suzuki) S. BSc, U. Tokyo, 1983; PhD, Grad. U. for Advanced Studies, Tokyo, 1996. Rschr. NEC, Tokyo, 1983-87, ICOT, Tokyo, 1987-89, Sumitomo Trust & Banking, Tokyo, 1989-90, Sumitomo Life Ins., Tokyo, 1990-96; asst. prof. U. Tsukuba, Japan, 1996-98, assoc. prof., 1998—. Contbr. articles to profl. jours. Avocations: trekking, cycling. Home: 3-25-4-501 Matsushiro, Tsukuba 305-0035, Japan Office: U Tsukuba, Inst Policy/Planning Scis, Tsukuba Ibaraki 305-8573, Japan

SHOJI, SHIN'ICHI, medical educator, neurologist, anthropologist; b. Tokyo, Mar. 5, 1942; s. Yoshiyuki and Miyuki (Nakayama) S.; m. Kimiko Izumi, Nov. 29, 1970; children: Tsubasa, Kai, Yume. MD, U. Tokyo, 1966, PhD, 1974. Med. diplomate in neurology. Intern Tokyo U. Hosp., 1966-68, resident, 1968-72, asst., 1972-74; asst. prof. Shinshu U. Hosp., Matsumoto, Japan, 1974-86; assoc. prof. Shinshu U., Matsumoto, Japan, 1986-92; prof. U. Tsukuba, Japan, 1992—; Rep. Party for Death Learning, Matsumoto; lectr. med. edn., clin. anthropology. Author: Diagnosis and Treatment of Muscle Diseases, 1988. Mem. Ibaraki Neurology Video Forum (bd. dirs. 1993—), Ibaraki Cerebrovascular Disease Soc. (bd. dirs. 1993—), Ibaraki Neurology Soc. (bd. dirs. 1993—), Japanese Soc. Neurology (diploma for neurologist; coun. 1970—), Japanese Soc. Palliative Medicine (coun. 1996—), Japanese Soc. Med. Edn. (mgr. 1997-99, dir. 2000—), Japanese Soc. Internal Medicine (fellows' assn., coun. 1998—), Japanese Soc. Neurol. Therapeutics (coun. 1993—). Avocations: swimming, cycling, cinema, music, art. Home: 3-1-552 Namiki, Tsukuba 305-0044, Japan Office: U Tsukuba Inst Clin Med, 1-1-1 Tennohdai, Tsukuba 305-8575, Japan

SHOKHANOV, STEPAN OLEGOVICH, geneticist; b. Lviv, Ukraine, Nov. 3, 1971; s. Oleg Stepanovich and Anastasia Vasylivna (Betsko) S. Diploma, 1994. Lab. asst. dept. genetics and biotechnology Lviv Franko State U., 1994—, educator biology and chemistry, 1994—; cons. Little Acad. Sci., Lviv, 1996—. Contbr. articles to profl. jours. Mem. Ukrainian Ornithol. Soc., Methodology Ctr. Edn. Avocations: sacred music and penture, ornitology. Home: G Vashington St 11 Apt 84, 790032 Lviv Ukraine Office: Franko State U, Dept Genetics & Biotechnol, 290005 Lviv Ukraine

SHOKIN, YURY ALEXANDROVICH, astronomer; b. Kimry, Russia, Sept. 27, 1939; s. Alexander and Tatiana T. (Komarova) S.; m. Lidia A. Roy, July 4, 1949 (div.); 1 child, Michael; m. Nina M. Evstigneeva, Jan. 30, 1950; children: Roman, Tatiana. Candidate of Sci., Moscow U., 1970, DSc, 1996. Rschr. Sternberg Astron. Inst., Moscow, 1970-75, sr. rschr., 1975-96, leading rschr., 1996—. Contbr. articles to profl. jours. Recipient Silver medal Exhbn. Nat. Econ. Achievement, Moscow, 1986, Tsiolkovsky medal Astronautics Fedn. Bur., Russia, 1987, medal Presidium of Supreme Soviet of USSR, 1987. Home: Prospect Vernadskogo 93I49, 117526 Moscow Russia Office: Sternberg Astron Inst, Universitetskii Prospect 13, 119899 Moscow Russia

SHOKOUHMAND, HOSSEIN, mechanical engineering educator; b. Kashan, Iran, Nov. 22, 1950; married; 2 children. MSc in Mech. Engring., U. Tehran, 1972; DEA, U. Paris VI, 1973; Diploma Docteur Ingenieur, U. Paris, 1977. Prof. U. Tehran, 1978—, head rsch. com. mech. engring. dept., 1989-94, head mech. engring. dept., 1994-97; dir. Iranian Cons. and Engring. svcs. Ministry of Energy Iran, 1982-84; cons. Powerplant Indsl. & Pe-

trochemical Mfg. Co., 1984-98, Azarab Ind Co.; dir. transfer of tech. of rotary gas air pre-heaters for power plants, 1985-87; head Orgn. Transfer of Tech. for Pressure and Heat Exchangers, 1987-89; sr. advisor Oil Industries Investment Corp. Iran. Con5br. articles to profl. publs. Mem. ASME. Home: 2d Alley No 33, Ave Kargar Shomali, Tehran Iran Office: Tehran U Faculty Engring, PO Box 11365-4568, Tehran Iran

SHOL, KIM DURAND, accountant, computer programmer; b. Fergus Falls, Minn., Oct. 19, 1955; s. Robert Walter and Doris Ruby (Wahl) S.; m. Cheryl Renee Casmey, Sept. 18, 1992; children: Heidi Renee and Heather Kay (twins). AAS in Bus. Computer Systems, U. Minn., crookston, 1988. Program asst. Northwestern Apts., Crookston, 1982-86; jr. programmer U. Minn., Crookston, 1988-90; acctg. technician Northwestern Mental Health Ctr., Inc., Crookston, 1991—; mem. computer adv. com. U. Minn., Crookston, 1989-90. Mpls. Tribune scholar, 1970. Mem. N.Y. Acad. Scis. Lutheran. Avocations: studying history and religion, painting still life and landscapes, collecting music. Office: Northwestern Mental Health Ctr 603 Bruce St Crookston MN 56716-2914

SHOLL, JOHN GURNEY, III, physician; b. Phila., Mar. 6, 1915; s. John Gurney Jr. and Helen (Hare) S.; m. Marjorie Louise Hill, June 27, 1942 (dec. July 1999); children: John Douglas, Debora Sholl Humphreys, Robert Roy, David Gurney, Rebecca Sholl Baer. BS, Bucknell U., 1937; MD, Harvard U., 1941. Diplomate Am. Bd. Internal Medicine; cert. Nat. Bd. Med. Examiners. Intern Germantown Hosp., Phila., 1941-42; asst. resident in medicine Univ. Hosp., Cleve., 1942-43; pvt. practice in internal medicine Cleve., 1943-78; from demonstrator to assoc. clin. prof. medicine Case-Western Res. U., Cleve., 1943-78, assoc. prof. principles of medicine Dental Sch., 1965-76; dir. med. edn. U. Suburban Health Ctr., Cleve., 1973-78; chmn. edn. commn. Ohio Med. Assn., 1973-76; clin. prof. medicine U. Calif. San Diego, La Jolla, 1978-88, dir. internal medicine group, 1979-85; med. dir. E.F. Hutton Life Ins. Co., La Jolla, 1978-82; vol. cons. to med. staff Maine Vets. Homes, 1990—. Mem. editoral bd. Consultant mag., Greenwich, Conn., 1980-84, San Diego Physician, 1986-87. Served to capt. U.S. Army, 1944-46, ETO. Fellow ACP; mem. AMA, Calif. Med. Assn., VFW (life), Am. Legion (life), U. Calif. San Diego Emeriti Assn. Republican. Baptist. Club: Rowfant (Cleve.). Avocation: writing, golf, reading. Home: 1 Huntington Common Dr Apt 200 Kennebunk ME 04043-6564

SHOLTO-DOUGLAS, IAN GORDON, manufacturing company executive; b. Durban, Kwazulu, South Africa, Mar. 14, 1959; s. Howe Archibald and Violet Gwenneth (Emery) S.; m. Christine Ann Brownridge, Apr. 6, 1991; children: Samantha, Natasha, Michelle, William, Tanya. BSc, U. Natal, Durban, South Africa, 1982, BSc (hons.), 1983. Sci. officer Uranium Enrichment Corp., Pretoria, South Africa, 1984-85; scientist UCOR, Pretoria, 1985-86; sales engr. S.A. Philips, Pinetown, 1986-87; sales mgr. Philquip Sci., Durban, 1987-89; CEO Fred Emery (Pty) Ltd., Pinetown, 1989—; computer cons. COMUSA (Pty) Ltd., Durban, 1985-89, dir., 1989—; ind. rschr., Durban, 1996—. Editor COMUSA Jour., 1990, 91. With South African Def. Force, 1984-87. Mem. AAAS, South African Chem. Inst., N.Y. Acad. Scis. (cert.), The Planetary Soc. (cert.), Nat. Geog. Soc., Oxfordian, The Oxford Club. Democratic Party of South Africa. Ch. of Eng. Avocations: shooting, space exploration, computers, science fiction, satellite television. Home: 43 Mpushini Ave, 3652 Waterfall Kwazulu, Republic of South Africa Office: Fred Emery (Pty) Ltd, PO Box 1846, 3600 Pinetown Kwazulu, Republic of South Africa

SHOLUKHA, VICTOR ANATOLIEVITCH, applied mathematics and biomechanics educator; b. St. Petersburg, Russia, Jan. 11, 1953; s. Anatoly Grigorievitch and Zinaida Ivanovna (Asauluk) S.; m. Tatjana Mikhailovna Dudnikova; children: Mikhail, Pavel. Diploma, Leningrad Poly. Inst., USSR, 1976; PhD, State Tech. U. St. Petersburg, 1989, DSc, 1997. Engr. Leningrad Poly. Inst., 1973-76, Scientific Rsch. Union Sphere, Leningrad, 1976-79; rschr. Leningrad Poly. Inst., 1979-85, asst. prof., 1985-89; assoc. prof. applied math. and biomechanics State Tech. U. St. Petersburg, 1989-97, prof. applied math. and biomechanics, 1997—; cons. Ctrl. Robototechnics Inst., St. Petersburg, 1980—. Author: Anthropomorphic Mechanisms: Modelling, Motion Analysis and Synthesis, 1994, Mathematical Modelling and Computer Simulation of Biomechanical Systems, 1997. Grantee Project INTAS, Brussels, 1994. Mem. Internat. Soc. Biomechanics, Internat. Baltic Acad. Edn. (elected). Avocations: travel, gardening. Home: Svetlanovsky ave 38-1-104, 195427 St Petersburg Russia Office: State Tech U St Petersburg, Polytechnicheskaya, 29, 195251 St Petersburg Russia

SHONK, ALBERT DAVENPORT, JR., advertising executive; b. L.A., May 23, 1932; s. Albert Davenport and Jean Spence (Stannard) S. BS in Bus. Adminstrn., U. So. Calif., 1954. Field rep. mktg. divsn. L.A. Examiner, 1954-55, asst. mgr. mktg. and field supr. mktg. divsn., 1955-56, mgr. mktg. divsn., 1956-57; account exec. Hearst Advt. Svc., L.A., 1957-59; account exec., mgr. keith H. Evans & Assocs., San Francisco, 1959-65; owner, pres. Albert D. Shonk Co., L.A., 1965-97; gen. ptnr. Shonk Land Co.LTD, Charleston, W.Va., 1989—; pres. Signet Cir. Corp., Inc., 1977-81, dir., 1962-81, hon. life dir., 1981—, treas., 1989—. Bd. dirs. Florence Crittenton Ctr., sec., 1978, 1st v.p., 1978-79, exec. v.p., 1979-81, pres., 1981-83, chmn. bd., 1983-85, hon. life dir.,, 1986—, treas., 1997, pres., 1997—; co-chair centennial com., founding chmn. Crittenton Assocs.; treas. Balboa Island Mus. and Hist. Soc., 1999—. Recipient Medallion of Merit Phi Sigma Kappa, 1976, Founders award, 1961, NIC Interfraternal award, 1989. Mem. Advt. Club L.A., Pubs. Rep. Assn. of So. Calif., Nat. Assn. Pubs. Reps. (past v.p. West Coast 1981-83), Jr. Advt. Club L.A. (hon. life, dir., treas., 1st v.p.), Trojan Club, Skull and Dagger, U. So. Calif. Alumni Assn. (bd. govs. 2000—), U. S.C. Marshall Sch. Bus. Alumni Assn. (nat. bd. 1991-99, treas. 1995-99), U. S.C. Assocs., Marshall Assocs. (bd. dirs. 1999—), Inter-Greek Soc. (co-founder, hon. life mem. and dir., v.p. 1976-79, pres. 1984-86), Rotary (Paul Harris fellow), Phi Sigma Kappa (dir. grand coun. 1962-70, 77-79, grand pres. 1979-83, chancellor 1983-87, 90-91, recorder 1995—, v.p. meml. found. 1979-84, pres. 1984, trustee pres. Phi Sigma Kappa found. 1984-95, trustee emeritus 1995—), World Affairs Coun., Alpha Kappa Psi, Town Hall. Home: 225 Sapphire Ave Newport Beach CA 92662-1148

SHONK, SCOTT LAMAR, architect, educator; b. Ephrata, Pa., July 12, 1967; s. Clyde Eugene and H. Elaine Shonk. BS in Architecture, Pa. State U., 1990, BArch, 1990; MArch, U. Pa., 1993. Registered architect, Pa., N.J., Del. Archtl. intern Althouse, Martin & Assocs., Ephrata, Pa., 1985-91; project mgr. Yan Tilburg & Ptnrs., Santa Monica, Calif., 1993-94; project architect Beers & Schillaci, Ltd., Lancaster, Pa., 1995-97; assoc. Beers, Schillaci & Hoffman Ltd., Lancaster, 1998—; adj. instr. Pa. Sch. of Art and Design, Lancaster, 1997-98. Editor-in-chief Ephrata Mountaineer, 1985; contbr. articles to jours. Mem. James Buchanan Wheatland Found., Hist. Ephrata Cloister Assncs., Friends of Gettysburg Nat. Park; legis. activist Nat. Hemophilia Found., 1987—. Recipient 1st prize facade design, John Wingate Davidson FIBA, London, 1989. Mem. AIA (bd. dirs. cen. Pa., chpt., pres. 2000, v.p., sec.-treas. 1997-99, alternate bd. mem. 2000—), Hist. Preservation Trust of Lancaster, Nat. Trust for Hist. Preservation, American Mensa. Avocations: Beaux-art renderings, water color painting, drawing portraits. Home: 70 Spencer Ave Lancaster PA 17603-4855 Office: Beers Schillaci & Hoffman Ltd 20A E Roseville Rd Lancaster PA 17601-3800

SHONS, ALAN RANCE, plastic surgeon, surgical oncologist, educator; b. Freeport, Ill., Jan. 10, 1938; s. Ferral Caldwell and Margaret (Zimmerman) S.; m. Mary Ella Misamore, Aug. 5, 1961; children: Lesley, Susan. AB, Dartmouth Coll., 1960; PhD in Surgery, U. Minn., 1976. Diplomate Am. Bd. Surgery, Am. Bd. Plastic Surgery. Intern U. Hosp., Cleve., 1965-66, resident in surgery, 1966-67; rsch. fellow transplantation immunology U. Minn., 1969-72; resident surgery U. Minn. Hosp., 1972-74; resident plastic surgery NYU, 1974-76; asst. prof. plastic surgery U. Minn., Mpls., 1976-79, assoc. prof., 1979-84, prof., 1984; dir. divsn. plastic and reconstructive surgery U. Minn. Hosp., St. Paul Ramsey Hosp., Mpls. VA Hosp., 1976-84; cons. plastic surgery St. Louis Park Med. Ctr., 1980-84; prof. surgery Case Western Res. U., Cleve., 1984-93; dir. divsn. plastic and reconstructive surgery Case Western Reserve U., Cleve., 1984-92; prof. surgery H. Lee Moffitt Cancer Ctr. and Rsch. Inst. U. South Fla., Tampa, 1992—; examiner Am. Bd. Plastic Surgery, 1987—. Author: (with G.L. Adams and D. McQuarrie) Head and Neck Cancer, 1986; (with R. Jensen) Plastic Surgery Review, 1993. Capt. USAF, 1967-69. Fellow ACS (chmn. Minn. com. on trauma 1978-84); mem. AMA, Am. Soc. Plastic and Reconstructive Surgeons, Am. Assn. Plastic Surgeons, Minn. Acad. Plastic Surgeons (pres. 1981-82), Soc. Head and Neck Surgeons, Transplantation Soc., Plastic Surgery Rsch. Coun., Am. Soc. Aesthetic Plastic Surgery, Am. Soc. Maxillofacial Surgeons, Am. Assn. Immunologists, Soc. Exptl. Pathology, Am. Cleft Palate Assn., Am. Soc. Craniofacial Surg. Assn., Fla. Soc. Plastic and Reconstructive Surgeons, Tampa Bay Soc. Plastic and Reconstructive Surgeons, Sigma Xi. Office: H Lee Moffitt Cancer Ctr & Rsch Inst 12902 Magnolia Dr Tampa FL 33612-9416

SHOOK, ANN JONES, lawyer; b. Canton, Ohio, Apr. 18, 1925; d. William M. and Lura (Pontius) Jones; m. Gene E. Shook Sr., Nov. 30, 1956; children: Scott, William, Gene Edwin Jr. AB, Wittenberg U., 1947; LLB, William McKinley Law Sch., 1955. Bar: Ohio 1956, U.S. Dist. Ct. (no. dist.) Ohio 1961, U.S. Ct. Appeals (6th cir.) 1981. Cost acct. Hoover Co., North Canton, Ohio, 1947-51; asst. sec. Stark County Prosecutor's Office, Canton, Ohio, 1951-53; ins. adjuster Traveler's Ins. Co., Canton, 1953-56; ptnr. Shook & Shook, Toledo, 1958-62, North Olmsted, Ohio, 1962—. Mem. at large coun. Olmsted Community Ch., Olmsted Falls, Ohio, 1987-90; chmn. ways and means com. North Olmsted PTA, 1968; area chmn. United Way Appeal, North Olmsted, 1963; v.p. LWV, Toledo, 1960-62. Mem. Cleve. Bar Assn. Avocations: reading, boating, dancing, fitness.

SHOOK, GEORGE BREZGER, quality assurance engineer; b. East Cleve., May 20, 1945; s. Robert Leonard and Helen Caroline (Urban) S.; m. Ellen G. Giberson, Feb. 5, 1972; children: Jeffrey George, A. Luis, Philip Brezger, Amy Lynne. BBA, Baldwin-Wallace, 1990. Purchasing agent Union Carbide Corp., Cleve., 1968-70, lab. asst., 1970-72, engring. asst., 1972-82, assoc. engr., 1982-86; quality control engr. Eveready Battery Co., Inc., Westlake, Ohio, 1986-87, graphic design engr., 1987-92, sr. quality assurance engr., 1992-97, staff quality assurance engr., 1998—; bar code coord. Eveready Battery Co., Inc., Cleve., 1984—. Chair ad hoc com. Cleve. Heights (Ohio) Bd. Edn., 1976, housing ins. Heights Community Congress, Cleve. Heights, 1980, chmn. fin. com., 1982-84; seminar facilitator/presenter for Adoption Network, Adoption Advocate, 1990—; pres. bd. mgrs. Villas I at Easton Estate, 1999—. Recipient Pres.'s Creative Mgmt. award Eveready Battery Co., 1987. Mem. VFW. Democrat. Episcopalian. Avocations: vocal music, Cleve. orchestra chorus, Singers Club of Cleve., Eveready Battery Co. choir, country western partner dancing. Office: Eveready Battery Co Inc PO Box 450777 Westlake OH 44145-0616

SHORE, ERIC EUGENE, physician, consultant; b. Phila., Feb. 12, 1948; s. Reuben and Mary (Osinoff) S.; m. Mona Diane Cherry, Oct. 23, 1977 (div. Dec. 1991); children: Brett Ian, Matthew Adam. Student, Temple U., 1965-67; BS in Biology, Widener U., 1969; DO, Phila. Coll. Osteo. Med., 1973; MBA, St. Joseph's U., 1997; postgrad. in law, Widener U., 1999—. Med. diplomate Nat. Bd. Examiners, diplomate Am. Bd. Utilization Rev. and Quality Assurance. Intern Botsford Gen. Hosp., Farmington, Mich., 1973-74; resident Phila. (Pa.) Gen. Hosp., 1974; instr. in medicine Hahnemann Med. Coll., Phila., 1975-78; treas. med. staff West Park Hosp., Phila., 1986-87, chief of geriatrics, 1986-88; sec. of med. staff Jefferson Park Hosp., Phila., 1987-91, chief of family medicine, 1988-96; pres. Gen. Medicine Assocs., Ltd., Phila., 1987—, Bala Clin. Assocs., P.C., 1989—; asst. prof. medicine Phila. Coll. Osteopathic Medicine, Phila., 1987—; clin. asst. prof. medicine Med. Coll. Pa., Phila., 1991—; med. dir. Fairmount Geriatric Ctr., Phila., 1985-88, Bala Nursing & Retirement Ctr., Phila., 1990-95; chmn. bd. UniMed Systems, Inc., Phila., 1989—, Am. Medigroup, Inc., 1997—; CEO, Am. MediGroup, Inc., 1996—; cons. in medicine and geriatrics Phila. Psychiat. Ctr., Phila., 1987—. Med. officer Civil Air Patrol, Phila., 1976-78. Recipient Legion of Honor, Chapel of Four Chaplains, Phila., 1981. Fellow Am. Acad. Family Physicians, Am. Coll. Utilization Rev. Physicians; mem. AMA (physician's recognition award 1990, 94, 97), AAAS, ABA, ATLA, Royal Soc. Medicine, Am. Geriatrics Soc., Am. Coll. Physician Execs., N.Y. Acad. Scis. Avocations: music, flying, computers, sculpting, tennis. Home: 19 W Dartmouth Rd Bala Cynwyd PA 19004-2520 Office: Gen Medicine Assocs Ltd 7516 City Ave # 8 Philadelphia PA 19151-2102

SHORE, LAURENCE STUART, reproductive endocrinologist; b. Phila., Mar. 16, 1944; arrived in Israel July 1977; s. Morris Aaron and Evelyn (Costin) S.; m. Maxine Carole Frank, July 9, 1967; children: Joshua, Yaakov, Simcha, Avichail. BA, Yeshiva U., 1965; PhD, Hahnemann U., 1972. Instr. Temple U. Med. Sch., Phila., 1973-75; investigator Kimron Vet. Inst., Bet Dagan, Israel, 1978—; scientific sec. Internat. Workshop in Maternal Recognition of Pregnancy, 1988. Sr. Smithsonian fellow Smithsonian Inst., 1993-94. Mem. Soc. for Study of Reproduction. Jewish. E-mail: ashor@vs.moag.gov.il. Home: Jacobson 11/5, 76206 Rehovot Israel Office: Kimron Vet Inst, PO Box 12, 50250 Bet Dagan Israel

SHORENSTEIN, WALTER HERBERT, commercial real estate development company executive; b. Glen Cove, N.Y., Feb. 23, 1915; m. Phyllis J. Finley, Aug. 8, 1945 (dec.); children: Joan (Dec.), Carole, Douglas. Student, Pa. State U., 1933-34, U. Pa., 1934-36; D in Econs. (hon.), HanYang U., Seoul, Republic of Korea, 1988. With property sales mgmt. depts. Milton Meyer & Co., San Francisco, 1946-51, ptnr., 1951-60, owner, chmn. bd. dirs., 1960—; owner, chmn. bd. dirs. Shorenstein Group, San Francisco, Shorenstein Co., San Francisco, 1960—. Past chmn. bd. trustees Hastings Law Ctr., U. Calif., San Francisco; founding mem. exec. adv. com. Hubert H. Humphrey Inst. Pub. Affairs, U. Minn.; founder Joan Shorenstein Ctr. on Press, Politics and Pub. Policy, Harvard U. Kennedy Sch. Govt.; past pres., hon. life bd. dirs. San Francisco Park and Recreation Commn.; chmn. Vietnam Orphans Airlift; bd. dirs. San Francisco Performing Arts Ctr.; trustee Asia Found.; fin. chmn. Dem. Nat. Conv., 1984; apptd. by Pres. Clinton to Nat. Svc. Commn., 1994, Bd. of Americorp, founding mem. WWII Nat. Monument com., Nat. Endowment Arts, White House Endowment Fund; apptd. by Pres. Carter chair White House Preservation Fund; apptd. by Mayor Frank Jordon chair Save the San Francisco Giants com.; personal advisor Pres. Johnson, Carter, Clinton; chmn. Pacific Rim Econ. Coun., San Francisco; chmn. San Francisco UN50 nat. com., 1995, also numerous polit. activities. Maj. USAF, 1940-45. Named Leader of Tomorrow, Time mag., 1953, Calif. Dem. of Yr., 1985; recipient Nat. Brotherhood award NCCJ, 1982, Disting. Svc. award Dem. Nat. Com., 1983, Golden Plate award Am. Acad. Achievement, 1991, Lifetime Achievement award Dem. Party, 1997; inducted Real Estate Legends Hall of Fame, 1997, Bay Area Coun. Bay Area Bus. Hall of Fame, 1998. Mem. Calif. C. of C. (bd. dirs.), San Francisco C. of C. (past chmn. bd. dirs., life bd. dirs. Office: Shorenstein Co 555 California St Ste 4900 San Francisco CA 94104-1714

SHORNIKOV, SERGEY IVANOVICH, chemist, researcher; b. Leningrad, Soviet Union, June 23, 1960; s. Ivan Petrovich and Vera Pavlovna (Petrova) S.; m. Olga Yurjevna Shlikova, Oct. 23, 1988; children: Masha, Natasha, Ivan. Diploma of Physicist, Leningrad State U., 1983; PhD, Inst. Silicate Chemistry, Leningrad, 1993. Engr., rschr. State Inst. Applied Chemistry, Leningrad, 1983-84, jr. sci. rschr., 1984-87, sci. rschr., 1987-88; sr. sci. rschr. Sci. Ctr. Applied Chemistry, St. Petersburg, Russia, 1990-96; sci. rschr. Inst. Silicate Chemistry, St. Petersburg, 1996-99, sr. sci. rschr., 1999—. Contbr. articles to Russian and fgn. jours. Home: 55-1, Kondratievskiy prospekt, 195197 Saint Petersburg Russia Office: Inst Silicate Chemistry RAS, Odoevskogo 24/2, 199155 Saint Petersburg Russia

SHORR, BORIS, mechanical engineer, educator; b. Moscow, Apr. 5, 1926; s. Feodor Shorr and Elisabeta Shul'meyster; m. Rosa Kravetzkaya, June 18, 1948 (dec. Nov. 1992; children: Yury, Ol'ga; m. Galina Mel'nikova, Apr. 2, 1994;. Student, Moscow Aviation Inst., 1949; PhD, Ctrl. Inst. Aviation Motors, Moscow, 1955, DSc, 1965. Engr., rsch. scientist, prof. Ctrl. Inst. Aviation Motors, 1949-92, chief dynamics dept., 1955-92, sr. rschr., 1992—, prof., 1970—; prof. Moscow Inst. Physics and Engring., 1958-64, Moscow Inst. Physics and Technics, 1965-78, Moscow Tech. Inst., 1982-89. Co-author, editor: (with I.A. Birger), Strength Calculation of Machine Components, 1959, 4th edit., 1993, Thermal Strength of Machine Components, 1975 (Zhukovsky award), Dynamics of Aircraft Engines, 1981; co-author: (with Y.S. Vorob'ev) Theory of Twisted Rods, 1983, (with G.V. Mel'nikova) Calculation of Mechanical Systems Using Method of Direct Mathematical Modelling, 1988; author: Archive of Applied Mechanics 65, 1995, Mechanics of Time-Dependent Materials 1, 1998, Mechanics Research Communications 26, 1999; contbr. articles to profl. jours. Recipient Ukrainian State award, 1982; named Honored Scientist of Russian Fedn., 1996. Mem. Moscow Scientists House. Home: App 18, Novokhoroshevsky pr 19, 123308 Moscow Russia Office: Ctrl Inst Aviation Motors, Aviamotornaya Str 2, 111250 Moscow Russia

SHORS, CLAYTON MARION, cardiologist; b. Beemer, Nebr., June 10, 1925; s. Joseph Albert and Morva Edith (Clayton) S.; m. Arlene Towle, June 6, 1948; children—Susan Debra, Clayton Robert, Scott Towle. B.S., U. Nebr., 1950, M.D., 1952. Diplomate Am. Bd. Internal Medicine (subspecialty cardiovascular disease). Intern Detroit Receiving Hosp., 1952-53, resident, 1953-56; practice medicine specializing in cardiology Detroit; chief cardiology St. John Hosp., Detroit. Bd. dirs. Sedona Acad.; mem. Sedona 30. Served with U.S. Army, 1943-46. Fellow Am. Coll. Cardiology, Internat. Coll. Angiology, Am. Heart Assn. Council on Clin. Cardiology; mem. Alpha Omega Alpha. Home: 44 Rue De La Rose Sedona AZ 86336-5970 Office: 1785 W Highway 89A Sedona AZ 86336-5567 also: 6562 E Crested Saguaro Ln Scottsdale AZ 85262-7373

SHORT, CLARE, administrator; b. Birmingham, England, Feb. 15, 1946; widowed; 1 child. Student, Keele U., Leeds U. Elected MP Birmingham Ladywood, England, 1983—, opposition spokesman employment, 1985-88, opposition spokesman social security, 1989-91, opposition spokesman women, 1993-95, opposition spokesman transport, 1995-96, shadow min. overseas devel., 1996-97, sec. of state internat. devel., 1997—, min. overseas devel. assistance. Office: Internat Devel Adminstrn, 94 Victoria St, London SW1E 5JL, England*

SHORTAL, TERENCE MICHAEL, systems company executive; b. St. Louis, Oct. 13, 1937; s. Harold Leo and Catherine margaret S.; m. Linda Margaret Elias, May 29, 1965; children: Jennifer (Mrs. Clay Morris Westbrook), Bradley Alexander. BSEE, U. Mo., 1961; MS, U.S. Naval Postgrad. Sch., 1966; grad. program execs., Carnegie Mellon U., 1979. Commd. ensign USN, 1961; advanced through grades to capt., 1980, svc. in Vietnam; asst. officer in charge Engring. Duty Officer Sch. Vallejo, Calif., 1974-77; ship engring. mgr. AEGIS shipbldg. project Naval Ea Sys. Command, Washington, 1977-79; tech. dir. DDGX project, 1979-81; v.p., dir. Kastle Sys., LLC, 1981—. Trustee Cathedral Choral Soc., Washington, 1983-95, 97—, pres., 1986-88, 2000—; mem. vestry St. John's Episcopal Ch., McLean, Va., 1982-85; bd. dirs. Langley Sch., McLean, 1984-94, pres. 1986-88. Decorated Meritorious Svc. medal (2), Navy Commendation medal (2); recipient award of merit Cathedral Choral Soc., 1996. Mem. IEEE (br. award 1961), Am. Soc. Naval Engrs. (Flagship Sect. award 1979), Nat. Press Club (Washington), Tower Club, Gridiron Club (Washington), Sigma Xi, Phi Kappa Theta. Home: 858 Canal Dr Mc Lean VA 22102-1408 Office: 1501 Wilson Blvd Arlington VA 22209-2403

SHORTEN, ROBERT NOEL, engineering educator; b. Dublin, Leinster, Ireland, Dec. 2, 1968; s. Austin and Kathleen S.; m. Jana Haase. B in Engring., U. Coll. Dublin (Ireland), 1990, M in Engring. Sci., 1993, PhD, 1996. Cert. engr. Elec. engr. AEG Westinghouse, Berlin, 1990-92; rsch. asst. U. Coll. Dublin (Ireland), 1992-93, Presdl. fellow, 1997-98; rschr. Daimler-Benz Research, Berlin, 1993-97; lectr. Nat. U. Ireland, Maynooth, 1998—; Vis. fellow Yale U., New Haven, 1996; lectr. Irish Signals and Syss. Conf., 1998, mem. steering com., 1999—; mem. quality control com., dept. computer sci. Nat. U. Ireland, 1999—, mem. rsch. com., 2000—; program rsch. evaluator Nat. Sci. Agy., Dublin, 1998, 99; lectr. in field. Contbr. over 50 articles to profl. jours. Marie Curie fellow European Union, 1993, 96; recipient Presdl. award Irish Govt., 1998. Mem. IEEE, Inst. Engrs. Ireland, Marie Curie Fellowship Assn. (founder, nat. coord. 1997—). Address: 15 Eden Grove, Grange Rd, Rathfarnham Dublin 16, Ireland

SHORTER, JOHN, chemistry educator; b. Redhill, Surrey, England, June 14, 1926; s. Frank Side and Edith Mabel (Doney) S.; m. Mary Patricia Steer, July 28, 1951; children: Christopher John, Stephen James, Caroline Mary. BA, Oxford (England) U., 1947, BSc, 1949, DPhil, 1950. Asst. lectr. in chemistry U. Coll. Hull, England, 1950-52, lectr. in chemistry, 1952-54; lectr. in chemistry U. Hull, 1954-63, sr. lectr. in chemistry, 1963-72, reader in phys. organic chemistry, 1972-82, emeritus reader in chemistry, 1982—; R.T. French vis. prof. U. Rochester, N.Y., 1966-67; sec.-treas. Internat. Group for Correlation Analysis in Chemistry, Whitby, Eng., 1982—. Author: Correlation Analysis in Organic Chemistry, 1973, Correlation Analysis of Organic Reactivity 1982; co-editor: Advances in Linear Free Energy Relationships, 1972, Correlation Analysis in Chemistry, 1978, Similarity Models in Organic Chemistry, Biochemistry, and Related Fields, 1991; contbr. articles to profl. jours. Fellow Royal Soc. Chemistry (sec. then chmn. history of chemistry group 1982-93); mem. Assn. Univ. Tchrs., Internat. Union of Pure and Applied Chemistry. Anglican. Avocations: mountaineering, family history researching, animal welfare. Home and Office: 29 Esk Terrace, Whitby Y021 1PA, England

SHORTER, NICHOLAS ANDREW, pediatric surgeon; b. London, Oct. 14, 1953; came to the U.S., 1961; s. Roy Gerrard and Rhiannon (Morris) S.; m. Sally Jo Trued, Aug. 28, 1982; children: Timothy Anders, Brittain David, Jaime Elizabeth Rhiannon. AB, AM, Harvard U., 1975; MD, Johns Hopkins U., 1979. Bd. cert. in surgery and pediatric surgery. Intern in surgery The Johns Hopkins Hosp., Balt., 1979-80, jr. asst. resident in surgery, 1980-81, sr. asst. resident in surgery, 1981-82, 83-84, chief resident in surgery, 1984-85; rsch. fellow in surgery The Children's Hosp. Med. Ctr., Boston, 1982-83; asst. chief resident in pediatric surgery The Children's Hosp., Phila., 1985-86, chief resident in pediatric surgery, 1986-87; hosp. staff Duke U. Med. Ctr., Durham, N.C., 1987-91; chief pediatric surgery Children's Hosp. at Dartmouth, Dartmouth-Hitchcock Med. Ctr., 1991-99, exec. com., 1991-99; assoc. attending surgeon Meml. Hosp., N.Y.C., 1999—; teaching fellow biology Harvard U., Cambridge, Mass., 1974-75; asst. instr. pediatric surgery U. Pa., Phila., 1985-87, Duke U., Durham, 1987-91, asst. prof. pediatric surgery and pediatrics, 1987-91; asst. prof. pediatrics Dartmouth Med. Sch., Hanover, N.H., 1991-94, asst. prof. surgery, 1991-94, assoc. prof. pediatrics, 1994-99, assoc. prof. surgery, 1994-99; hosp. staff The Children's Hosp., Phila., 1986-87, Dartmouth-Hitchcock Med. Ctr., Lebanon, N.H., 1991-99, Duke U. Med. Ctr., Durham, 1987-91, Meml. Hosp., N.Y., 1999—; dir. Kiwanis Affiliated Pediatric Trauma Ctr., Children's Hosp. at Dartmouth, Lebanon, 1993-99; others. Referee Jour. Pediatric Surgery; contbr. chpts. to books and articles to profl. jours. Recipient Regular Clin. fellowship Am. Cancer Soc., 1985-86. Fellow ACS, Am. Acad. Pediatrics, Southeastern Surg. Congress, Royal Soc. Medicine, Soc. Surg. Oncology; mem. Am. Pediatric Surg. Assn., Brit. Assn. Pediatric Surgeons, Internat. Soc. Pediatric Oncology, Internat. Pediatric Surg. Oncology, Pediatric Oncology Group (assoc.), Am. Assn. for Cancer Rsch., Assn. for Acad. Surgery, N.Y. Acad. Scis., Royal Soc. Medicine, Cum Laude Soc., Phi Beta Kappa, Alpha Omega Alpha. Republican. Episcopalian. Avocation: collecting political memorabilia. Office: Meml Sloan-Kettering Cancer Ctr Dept Surgery 1275 York Ave New York NY 10021-6094

SHORTZ, WILMA WILDES, writer, Arabian horse breeder; b. Kansas City, Mo., Dec. 16, 1910; d. John Henry Jr. and Viola Alberta (Warner) Wildes; m. Lyle Alton Shortz, Sept. 16, 1939 (dec. Nov. 1994); children: April Irene, Richard Alan, William Frederic. Grad. ct. reporter, Gregg Coll., Chgo., 1931. Freelance ct. reporter Chgo., 1930-43; supr. Montgomery County Soil & Water Conservation Dist., 1970-85, chair, 1981-85, assoc. supr., 1986—. Contbg. author: Montgomery County Legend and Lore, 1988; spkr. weekly program on horses Sta. WCVL, 1980-81; contbr. horse articles, stories and humor to mags. Mem. Presbyn. Women's Assn., 1955—, pres., 1963-64; pres. Crawfordsville (Ind.) PTA, 1961-63; mem. organizing com. Montgomery County 4-H Horse and Pony Club, 1960-61, officer, 1961-65; mem. Current Events Club, 1959—, pres., 1966-67. Presbyterian. Avocations: writing, contests.

SHORVON, PHILIP JOHN, radiologist; b. Sutton, England, May 14, 1950. MA, Cambridge U., England, 1972; MBBS, London U., 1976. Cons. radiologist Ctrl. Middlesex Hosp., London, 1988—, clin. dir. radiology dept., 1989—. Deputy editor Brit. Jour. Radiology, 1995-98. Fellow Royal Coll. Radiologists; mem. Royal Coll. Physicians, Brit. Soc. Gastroenterology (chmn. 1995-98), European Soc. Gastrointestinal amd Abdominal Radiology, Soc. Gastrointestinal Radiologists. Office: Ctrl Middlesex Hosp, Action Ln, London NW10 7NS, England

SHOSHINA, ELENA VASILJEVNA, algologist, researcher; b. Onega, Russia, Jan. 2, 1956; d. Vasiliy Alecksandrovich and Klavdia Vasiljevna

(Rasheva) S.; 1 child, Maxim. MS, Leningrad (Russia) U., 1978, D of Biol. Scis., 1989. Jr. rschr. Polar Sci. Inst. of Fisheries and Oceanography, Archangelsk, Russia, 1978-84; sr. rschr. Murmansk (Russia) Marine Biol. Inst. of Russian Acad. Sci., 1984—. Mem. Bot. Soc. St. Petersberg. Home: ul Chalatina 11-71, 183037 Murmansk Russia Office: Murmansk Marine Biol Inst, Vladimirskaya 17, 183010 Murmansk Russia

SHOTWELL, SHEILA MURRAY, medical/surgical nurse; b. Alamance County, Dec. 27, 1963; d. Homer Banks and Betty Jane (Robertson) Murray; m. Tony Allen Shotwell, July 30, 1988; children: Brent Allen, Emily Beth. Diploma, Watt's Sch. Nursing, 1985. RN, N.C. Staff nurse Durham (N.C.) County Gen. Hosp., 1985-91; home health nurse Home Care Providers, Burlington, N.C., 1992-98; utilization rev. case mgr. Jefferson Pilot Fin., Greensboro, N.C., 1998; disease mgr. Accordant Health Svcs., Greensboro, N.C., 1999—. Mem. Watt's Alumni Assn. Office: 4900 Koger Blvd Ste 300 Greensboro NC 27407-2710

SHOU, KEH-JIAN, engineering educator; b. Taipei, Taiwan, Mar. 21, 1962; s. Yi-Kao and Shu-Chen (Tian) S.; m. Chia-Chen Jackie Lee. BS, Nat. Cheng Kung U., Tainan, Taiwan, 1984, MS, 1986; PhD, U. Minn., 1993. Geotechnical engr. Nat. Expressway Engring. Bur., Taiwan, 1993-94; assoc. prof. Nat. Chung-Hsing U., Taichung, Taiwan, 1994-98; rsch. engr. CSIR/Miningtek, S. Africa, 1998-99; assoc. prof. NCHU, Taiwan, 1999—. Contbr. articles to profl. jours. Mem. Internat. Soc. Rock Mechanics. Baptist. Avocation: tennis. Office: Nat Chung-Hsing U Civil Eng, 250 Kuo-Kuang Rd, Tiachung 402, Taiwan

SHOU, MAGANG, pharmacologist; b. ZhengZhou, China, Dec. 17, 1954; s. Hua-Shan Shou and Shu-Jie Ma; m. Ruiping Wang, Jan. 15, 1985; children: Louie, Jeffery X. BS in Pharmacy, Beijing U. Chinese Medicine, 1981; MS in Pharmacology, Henan Med. U., Zheng Zhou, 1985; PhD, Uniformed Svcs. U. Health Sci., Bethesda, Md., 1991. Rsch. assoc. Beijing Inst. Radiation Medicine, China, 1985-86; postdoctoral rschr. U. Pa. Med. Sch., Phila., 1991; vis. assoc. Nat. Cancer Inst., Bethesda, 1991-94, sr. staff fellow, 1994-96; rsch. fellow Merck Rsch. Labs., West Point, Pa., 1996—; hon. prof. Henan Med. U., Zheng Zhou, 1994—. Author: Cytochrom P450 Protocols, 1998; mem. editl. bd. Pharmacogenetics, 1996—; contbr. articles to profl. jours. Mem. Internat. Soc. Study Xenobiotics, Am. Assn. Cancer Rsch., Soc. Chinese Biologists in Am. Fax: 215-652-2410. E-mail: magang shou@merck.com. Office: WP75A-203 Dept Drug Metabolism Merck Rsch Labs 770 Sumneytown Pike West Point PA 19486

SHOUB, EARLE PHELPS, engineer, industrial hygienist, educator; b. Washington, July 19, 1915; m. Elda Robinson; children: Casey Louis, Heather Margaret Shoub Dills. BS in Chemistry, Poly. U., 1938, postgrad. 1938-39. Chemist, Hygrade Food Products Corp., N.Y.C., 1940-41, Nat. Bur. Standards, 1941-43; regional dir. U.S. Bur. Mines, 1943-62, chief divsn. Accident Prevention & Health, 1962-70; dep. dir. Appalachian Lab. Occupational Respiratory Diseases, Nat. Inst. Occupational Safety and Health, Morgantown, W.Va., 1970-77, dep. dir. div. safety research, 1977-79; mgr. occupational safety, indsl. environ. cons., safety products div. Am. Optical Corp., Southbridge, Mass., 1979; cons., 1979—; assoc. clin. prof. dept. anesthesiology W.Va. U. Med. Center, Morgantown, 1977-82, prof. Coll. Mineral and Energy Resources, 1970-79. Recipient Disting. Service award Dept. Interior and Gold medal, 1959. Registered profl. engr.; cert. safety profl. Fellow Am. Inst. Chemists, Royal Soc. Medicine; mem. AIME, ASTM, NSPE, ANSI, Am. Indsl. Hygiene Assn. (emeritus mem.), Vets. of Safety, Am. Soc. Safety Engrs., Nat. Fire Protection Assn. (life), Am. Conf. Govtl. Indsl. Hygienists, Internat. Soc. Respiratory Protection (past pres., William H. Revoir award 1993, emeritus mem.), Am. Nat. Standards Inst., Soc. Mining Engrs., fellow Royal Soc. of Med., Sigma Xi. Methodist. Contbr. articles to profl. jours. and texts. Home: 5850 Meridian Rd Apt 202C Gibsonia PA 15044-9690

SHOUCHE, SHOBHA SANJAY, zoologist, educator; b. Gwalior, India, May 28, 1960; d. Purushottam and Indira Sangamnerkar; m. Sanjay Ramchandra Shouche, Dec. 7, 1985; children: Sudeep, Surabhi. BSc, KRG Coll., 1979; MSC, Jiwaji U., 1981; MPhil, Vikram U., 1994, PhD, 1998. Asst. prof. Govt. P.G. Coll., Shivpuri, India, 1985-86, Mandsur, India, 1986—. Avocations: music, drawing, painting. Home: 23/2 Sudama Nagar Ram Tekri, 458001 Mandsaur India Office: Govt PG Coll, Mhow Neemuch Rd, 458001 Mandsaur India

SHOVELTON, (WALTER) PATRICK, shipping and aviation company adviser; b. London, Aug. 18, 1919; s. Sydney Taverner and May Catherine (Kelly) S.; m. Marjorie Lucy-Joan Manners, Mar. 9, 1942 (div. 1967); 1 child, Clare Nina Frances; m. Helena Richards, Sept. 14, 1968 (div.); m. Dana Helena Shovelton. MA, Oxford (Eng.) U., 1940. From asst. prin. to dep. sec. U.K. Civil Svc., Eng., 1946-78; dir. gen. U.K. Gen. Coun. Brit. Shipping, London, 1978-85; dir. Brit. Airports Authority, London, 1982-86; dir., vice chmn. The Maersk Co., Ltd., London, 1985-95, adviser, 1996—; chmn. Birmingham (Eng.) European Airways, 1988-93; bd. dirs. Maersk Air Ltd., Birmingham; adviser on select coms. on shipping Ho. of Commons and Ho. of Lords, Eng., 1985-87. Founder, chmn. Friends of Tunbridge Wells and Rusthall Commons (Eng.), 1991-98. Maj. Royal Arty., 1940-46. Decorated Comdr. Order of St. Michael and St. George, Companion Order of Bath (U.K.), Officer Order of Orange Nassau (The Netherlands). Fellow Chartered Inst. Transport (Brancker meml. lectr. 1978, Grout meml. lectr. 1986); mem. Sr. Golfers Soc. U.K., Brooks's Royal Ashdown Forest Golf Club (capt.), Hampstead Golf Club (capt.), Rye Golf Club. Anglican. Avocations: golf, reading, opera, music, bridge.

SHOWALTER, DAVID SCOTT, accounting executive; b. Harrisonburg, Va., May 23, 1953; s. Harold Marvin and Martha (Myers) S.; m. Elizabeth Allison, June 1, 1974; children: Braxton, Allison, Mason. AS, Ferrum Coll., 1973; BSBA, U. Richmond, 1975. CPA, Ill., Mo., Wis., Ind.; cert. govt. fin. mgr. Asst. to nat. dir. KPMG, N.Y.C., 1981-84, asst. to vice chmn., 1986-88, ptnr., 1986—; area ptnr. in charge KPMG, Indpls., 1993-96; nat. dir. industry state, local govts., Chgo., 1996-98; nat. mng. ptnr. Assurance and Advisory Svcs. Ctr., Montvale, N.J., 1998—. Editor newsletter Govt. Acctg. and Auditing Update. Bd. dirs. Greater Indpls. Rep. Fin. Com., 1990-94; pres. Indpls. Youth Hockey Assn., 1990-93; pres. coun. Boy Scouts Am., St. Charles, Ill., 1995-97, chmn. bd. dirs., 1997-98, now bd. dirs. Named Ky. Col., State of Ky., 1986, Sagamore of Wabash for svc. to State of Ind., 1990; recipient Silver Beaver award Boy Scouts Am., 1994, Dist. Eagle Scout award, Boy Scouts Am., 1998; D. Scott Showalter Day named in his honor City Indpls., 1994. Mem. AICPA (mem. com.), Govt. Fin. Officers Assn. (mem. com., exec. com. cert. program), Assn. Sch. Bus. Ofcls. (exec. com. cert. program), Am. Acctg. Assn., Ill. CPA Soc., Nat. Intergovtl. Audit Assn. Presbyterian. Avocations: camping, jogging, backpacking, stamps. Home: 26w471 Interlachen Ln Winfield IL 60190-2347 Office: KPMG 3 Chestnut Ridge Rd Montvale NJ 07645-1842

SHOWALTER-KEEFE, JEAN, data processing executive; b. Louisville, Mar. 11, 1938; d. William Joseph and Phyllis Rose (Reis) Showalter; m. James Washburn Keefe, Dec. 6, 1980. BA, Spalding U., 1963, MS in Edn. Adminstrn., 1969. Cert. tchr., Ky. Tchr., asst. prin. Louisville Cath. Schs., 1958-71; cons. and various editorial positions Harcourt Brace Jovanovich Co., Chgo. and N.Y.C., 1972-82; dir. editorial Ednl. Challenges, Alexandria, Va., 1982-83; mgr. project to cons. Xerox Corp., Leesburg, Va., 1983-88, mgr. systems edn., 1988-89; curriculum devel. mgr. corp. edn. and tng. Xerox Corp. Hdqrs., Stamford, Conn., 1989-94; mem. bd. Belcastle Cluster Assocs., Reston, Va., 1994-98, pres. bd., 1995-98, mgmt. and sys. cons., 1995—; pres. JK Cons., Ltd., Reston, Va., 1996; mem. adv. bd. Have a Heart Homes for Abused Children, 1991-93; instr. Sales Exec. Club N.Y., 1974-79; cons., Houston, 1980-83. Moderator Jr. Achievement, Louisville, 1968-70; cons. Future Bus. Leaders Am., Dade County, Fla. 1983. Named Outstanding Young Educator Louisville Jaycees, 1968. Mem. Nat. Assn. Female Execs., Am. Soc. Tng. and Devel., Am. Mgmt. Assn. Avocations: gardening, classical music. Home and Office: 1419 Belcastle Ct Reston VA 20194-1245

SHOWELL, GRAHAM ANDREW, chemistry educator, researcher; b. London, June 15, 1955; s. Herbert Alfred and Dorothy Lilian (Hall) S.; m. Carole Preston, Sept. 13, 1980; children: Benjamin, Jack. BSc with honors, U. Exeter, U.K., 1976. Rsch. chemist Beechams, Harlow, U.K., 1976-80, Smith, Kline & French, Welwyn, U.K., 1980-84; sr. rsch. chemist Merck, Harlow, U.K., 1984-97; dir. chemistry Cambridge (Eng.) Discovery Chemistry, 1997—. Contbr. articles to profl. jours.; over 30 sci. patents. Mem. Royal Soc. Chemistry (chartered chemist), Soc. for Med. Rsch. Avocations: soccer, amateur dramatics, hiking. Home: 9 Kent Rd, Lackford Bury St Edmunds IP28 6HP, United Kingdom Office: Cambridge Discovery Chemist, Merrifield Ctr Rosemary Ln, Cambridge CB1 3LE, United Kingdom

SHOYAMA, ETSUHIKO, electronics executive. CEO Hitachi Ltd., Tokyo. Office: Hitachi Ltd, 4-6 Kandasurugadai, Chiyoda-ku Tokyo 101-8010, Japan*

SHPEK, ROMAN VASSYLYOVICH, Ukrainian government official; b. Broshniv, Ukraine, Nov. 10, 1954; s. Vassyl Oleksiyovich and Katerina Yuriivna (Soop) S.; m. Maria Romanivna Midjak, Nov. 17, 1979; children: Natalia, Yuri. Engr.-Technologist, Lviver Wood Tech. Inst., Lviv, Ukraine, 1976; MBA, Internat. Inst. Mgmt., Kiev, Ukraine, 1991. Dep. min. Ukraine Timber Industry Ministry, Kiev, 1989-91; dep. head Ukraine State Timber Industry Com., Kiev, 1991-92; min. Ministry Privatization & Demonopolization, Kiev, 1992; dep. min. Ministry Economy of Ukraine, Kiev, 1992-93, min., 1993-95, vice prime min. for the economy, 1995-97; chief Nat. Agy. Reconstrn. and Devel., Kiev, 1997—; academician Acad. Economical Scis., Ukraine, 1993. Capt. Ukrainian Army, 1971-76. Mem. Lviv Inst. Timber Industry (head students' trade-union of faculty 1972-75, mem. trade-union). Mem. Orthodox Ch. Avocations: history, literature, painting, tourism, music. Home: Tarasivska St 10 Flat 3, 253167 Kiev Ukraine Office: Nat Agy Recovery-Eur Integr, 19A Bohdan Khmelnytsky St, 01030 Kiev Ukraine*

SHPITALNIK, VLADIMIR, set and costume designer; b. Kursk, Russia, Jan. 8, 1964; s. Boris Abramovich and Dora Alexandrovna Shpilanik; m. Tatiana Evgenevna Strunina, Oct. 15, 1983 (div. 1990); children: Elizaveta, Anna; m. Cornelia Anne Evans, July 10, 1993; 1 child, Alexandra. BA, Abramtsevskoe (Russia) Art Sch, 1984; MFA, Moscow Art Theater Sch., 1990, Yale U., 1992. Prof. So. Conn. State U., New Haven, Paier Coll. Art, Hamden, Conn., 1996—; Resident designer Oakdale Theater, Wallingford, Conn., 1996—, Meadows Theater, Hartford, Conn., 1998—. Illustrator: Uncle Fedya, His Dog and His Cat, 1994, Crocodile Gene and His Friends, 1995; set and costume designer Stage One, Joffrey Ballet, Am. Pl. Theatre, New Harmony Theater, Eugene O'Neill Theatre Ctr. Fellow Nat. Endowment for Arts/Theatre Comms. Group, 1997. Mem. ASSITEJ, Internat. Alliance of Theatrical and Stage Employees, Soc. Illustrators. E-mail: shpitalnik@aol.com. Home: 31 Forest St Branford CT 06405-6212

SHPOLYANSKIY, YURI A., physicist, optics scientist; b. St. Petersburg, Russia, USSR, Sept. 2, 1977; s. Alexander N. and Vera Y. (Lombrozo) S.; m. Ksenia S. Gornostaeva, 2000. BS with 1st class honors, Inst. Fine Mechanics & Optics, St. Petersburg, 1998, MS with 1st class honors, 2000. Cert. ultrafast non-linear optics, numerical simulations. Rschr. Vavilov State Optical Inst., St. Petersburg, 1998—. Contbr. articles to sci. publs. Spl. scholar Russian Fedn. Govt., 1998, Pres. Russian Fedn., 1999; grantee Soros Found., 1997-99, Russian Fund Basic Rsch., 1997-98. Mem. IEEE, Lasers & Electro-Optics Soc. (grad. student fellowship 2000), Soc. Photo-Optical Instrumentation Engrs. (scholar 1999), Optical Soc. Am., Rozhdestvensky Optical Soc., Assn. Young Scientists (pres. 1998—). Avocations: photography, travel, sports. Office: Inst Fine Mechanics Optics, 14 Sablinskaya St, 197101 Saint Petersburg Russia

SHRAGER, ROBERT NEIL, business executive; b. London, May 21, 1948; s. Benjamin and Ruth (Kempner) S.; m. Elizabeth Fiona Bogod, July 4, 1982; children: James, Edward. MA, Oxford (Eng.) U., 1970; MBA, City U., London, 1971. Exec. Barclay Securities Ltd., London, 1971-73; with Morgan Grenfell & Co. Ltd., London, 1973-88, dir., 1985-88; corp. fin. dir. Dixons Group plc, Hemel Hempstead, Eng., 1988-98; chmn. House of Fraser PLC, London, 1999-2000, Tempo Holdings Ltd., London, 1999—; dir. RJB Mining PLC, Matalan PLC. Mem. Royal Automobile Club. Avocations: family, golf, reading, theatre, travel.

SHREINER, CURT, educational technologist, consultant; b. Ephrata, Pa., June 27, 1952; s. Paul H. and Grace B. BS in Edn., Millersville U., 1974; MS in Integrative Edn., Marywood Coll., 1977; MEd in Tech. and Media, Temple U., 1982; EdD in Tech. and Media, Columbia U., 1989. Tchr. Lebanon (Pa.) Sch. Dist., 1974-76; instr., researcher Millersville (Pa.) State U., 1976-77; writer, pub. Instrnl. Design Assocs., Lancaster, Pa., 1977-80; tchr. trainer Mainland (Pa.) Inst., 1980-81; videodisc designer WNET/THIRTEEN, Pub. TV, N.Y.C., 1981-82; computer software designer Academic Tech., Inc., Moorestown, N.J., 1982-86; audio scriptwriter Learn Inc., Mt. Laurel, N.J., 1986-87; CAI curriculum developer Constructive Alternatives, Inc., Phila., 1987-88; GUI designer Resolute, Ltd., Phila., 1988-91; multimedia designer Remtech Svcs. Inc., Newport News, Va., 1991-92; database design and info. mgmt. trainer The Work Group, Pennsauken, N.J., 1992; multimedia project dir. Vocat. Rsch. Inst., Phila., 1993-95; owner Curt Shreiner Prodns., 1995-96; multimedia designer Galaxy Scientific Corp., Warminster, Pa., 1996—; computer cons. Phila. Mayor's Commn. on Literacy, 1987-91; learning cons. for Pub. Health Videos, Phila. Dept. Pub. Health, 1989-90. Co-author: Straight Talk Parenting Series, 1988, Teacher Revitalization, 1982, The Giggle Kids Present, 1978; designer: Ollie and Seymour, 1986 (Media and Materials Portfolio award); prodr., writer Maria's Story, 1995 (Telly award). Mem. Am. Soc. Tng. & Devel., Soc. for Applied Learning Tech., Internat. Soc. Performance Improvement. Avocations: fine art, photography, travel.

SHREM, CHARLES JOSEPH, metals corporation executive; b. Cairo, May 9, 1930; came to U.S., 1959; s. Joseph C. and Paula (Cadranel) S.; m. Vivian L. Chalom, Jan. 30, 1955; children: Jeff, Leslie Allen. Degree in bus. and economy, Coll. Français, Cairo, 1951. Export mgr. Stanton Ironworks U.K., Middle East, 1950-57; comml. mgr. Soc. Sovibor, Paris, 1957-59; purchasing dir. Montanore, Inc., N.Y.C., 1959-65; exec. v.p. Commonwealth Metal Corp., Englewood Cliffs, N.J., 1965-85, pres., CEO, 1985-2000, chmn., 2000—; bd. govs. Coll. Democracy, Arlington, Va. Bd. dirs. Adult Edn., Pequannock, N.J., 1970-80; bd. govs. Nat. Grad. U., Arlington, Va. Mem. U.S. C. of C. (econ. coun., exec. com. U.S. Polish Coun./U.S. C. of C.). Office: 560 Sylvan Ave Englewd Clfs NJ 07632-3104

SHRESTHA, HEMANTA KUMAR, economist, researcher, educator; b. Kathmandu, Nepal, Dec. 2, 1964; came to U.S., 1992; s. Ganesh B. and Mishri D. Shrestha; m. Rashmi Shrestha, June 15, 1991; 1 child, Ravi. BS, Tribhuvan U., Kathmandu, 1988, MBA, 1992; PhD, U. Conn., 2000. Exec. dir. Shyam & Krishna Mills, Narayargarh, Nepal, 1987-89; v.p. Narayargarh Jaycees, 1988; rsch. asst. Conn. Ctr. for Econ. Anaysis, Storrs, 1995—, Conn. Econ. Resource Ctr., Rocky Hill, 1998. Editor Ann. Jour. of Mgmt., 1993 (Svc. award 1992); contbr. articles to profl. jours. Polit. activist Nepal Student Union, 1990. Mem. Am. Econ. Assn., Nepalese Assn. of So. New Eng. (v.p. 1999—), Nepalese Student Assn. of U. Conn. (pres. 1994). Avocations: music, sports, reading. Home: 4A Zygmunt Dr Storrs Mansfield CT 06268 Office: Univ of Connecticut Dept Econs 341 Mansfield Rd Storrs Mansfield CT 06268

SHRESTHA, SANTOSH MAN, hepatologist; b. Kathmandu, Nepal, Nov. 14, 1938; s. Chinia Man and Mangal Maya Shrestha; m. Shobhana Tuladhar, Oct., 1965; 1 child, Soni. M.B.B.S., Osmania Med. Coll., Hyderabad, India, 1961; D.T.M & H., Liverpool Sch. Tropical Med., 1965. MRCP, FRCPE, Royal Coll. Physicians of Edinburgh, U.K. Med. officer Bir Hosp., Kathmandu, 1962-65, physician, 1970-74, cons. physician, 1979-83, sr. cons. physician, 1983-89, chief liver unit, 1989—; nat. coord. Chronic Liver Disease and Liver Cancer Study, WHO/SEAR, 1981-85; advisor WHO/SEARO Intercountry Consultative Meeting on viral hepatitis, Rangoon, Burma, 1984, 85. Contbr. articles to profl. jours.; chief editor Jour. Nepal Med. Assn., 1972-73. Pres. Liver Found. Nepal, 1995—. Recipient Bises Sewa Padak award H.M. The King of Nepal, 1970, Mahendra Vidya Bhusan award, 1971, Gorkha Dakshin Bahu IV award, 1977, Chitra Pahari Sci. Med. Award Med. Assn. Nepal, 1988. Mem. Nepal Med. assn. (life), Internat. Assn. for Study of Liver, N.Y. Acad. Scis. Home: Tripureswar PO Box 3439, Mangal Sadan, Kathmandu Nepal Office: Liver Found Nepal, PO Box 3439, Kathmandu Kathmand, Nepal

SHRESTHRA, SATYENDRA PYARA, banker. Gov. Nepal Rastra Bank, Kathmandu, Nepal, 1996—. Office: Nepal Rastra Bank, PO Box 73, Baluwatar Kathmandu Nepal*

SHREVE, GENE RUSSELL, law educator; b. San Diego, Aug. 6, 1943; s. Ronald D. and Hazel (Shepherd) S.; m. Marguerite Russell, May 26, 1973. AB with honors, U. Okla., 1965; LLB, Harvard U., 1968, LLM, 1975. Bar: Mass. 1969, Vt. 1981. Appellate atty. and state extradition hearing examiner Office of Mass. Atty Gen., 1968-69; law clk. U.S. Dist. Ct., Dallas, 1969-70; staff and supervising atty. Boston Legal Assistance Project, 1970-73; assoc. prof. Vt. Law Sch., Royalton, 1975-81; vis. assoc. prof. George Washington U., Washington, 1981-83; assoc. prof. law N.Y. Law Sch., N.Y.C., 1983-84, prof., 1984-87; vis. prof. law Ind. U., Bloomington, 1986, prof., 1987-94, Ira C. Batman faculty fellow, 1988-89, Charles L. Whistler faculty fellow, dir. grad. studies, 1992-93, Richard S. Melvin Prof. Law, 1994—. Author: A Conflict of Laws Anthology, 1997; co-author: Understanding Civil Procedure, 2d edit., 1994; mem. editl. bd. Am. Jour. Comparative Law, 1994—, Jour. Legal Edn., 1998—; contbr. numerous articles to legal jours. Mem. Am. Law Inst., Am. Soc. for Pol. and Legal Phil., Assn. Am. Law Schs. (civil procedure sect. chair 1997, conflict of laws sect. chair 1998). Democrat. Episcopalian. Office: Ind U Sch Law Bloomington IN 47405

SHRIER, ADAM LOUIS, investment firm executive, consultant; b. Warsaw, Poland, Mar. 26, 1938; came to U.S., 1943, naturalized, 1949; s. Henry Leon and Mathilda June (Czamanska) S.; m. Diane Kesler, June 10, 1961; children: Jonathan, Lydia, Catherine, David. BS, Columbia U., 1959; MS (Whitney fellow), MIT, 1960; D.Engr. and Applied Sci. (NSF fellow), Yale U., 1965; postdoctoral visitor, U. Cambridge, Eng., 1965-66; J.D., Fordham U., 1976. With Esso Research & Engring. Co., Florham Park and Linden, N.J., 1963-65, 66-72; head. environ. scis. research area Esso Research & Engring. Co., 1969-72; coordinator pollution abatement activities, tanker dept. Exxon Internat. Co., N.Y.C., 1972-74; project mgr., energy systems Exxon Enterprises Inc., N.Y.C., 1974-75; gen. mgr. solar energy projects Exxon Enterprises Inc., 1975-77, pres. solar thermal systems div., 1977-81; corp. planning cons., sec. new bus. investments Exxon Corp., N.Y.C., 1981-82; div. mgr. supply and transp. Exxon Internat. Co., N.Y.C., 1983-86, mgr. policy and planning, 1986-88; mng. dir. Splty. Tech. Assocs., Washington, 1988-97; pres. Global Devel. Opportunities, LLC, Washington, 1997—; adj. lectr. chem. egnring. Columbia U., N.Y.C., 1967-69; industry adv. bd. Internat. Energy Agy., 1984-88, Energy and Environ. Policy Ctr., Harvard U., 1986-88, Internat. Energy Program, Johns Hopkins U., 1987-88; sr. assoc. Global Bus. Forum, 1988—, Cambridge Energy Rsch. Assocs., 1988—; adj. prof. internat. bus. Am. U., Washington, 2000—. Patentee in field; contbr. articles to profl. jours. Mem. AIChE, Internat. Assn. Energy Econs., U.S. Energy Assn., Cosmos Club, Sigma Xi, Tau Beta Pi, Phi Lambda Upsilon. Office: 4000 Cathedral Ave NW Washington DC 20016-5249

SHRIMPTON, DAVID, accountant; b. Bromley, Kent, Eng., May 19, 1943; s. George Henry (dec.) and Joyce (Little) S.; m. Rosemary Sarah Fone, Oct. 25, 1969; children: Matthew, Ben, Daniel. Student, Dulwich Coll., 1953-61. Mgr. Deloitte Haskins, London, 1961-75; prin. indsl. devel. unit Dept. of Industry, London, 1975-77; corp. fin. exec. Midland Bank, London, 1975-79; ptnr. BDO Stoy Hayward, London, 1979—; chmn. Broomleigh HA, Bromley, 1998—. Named Freeman City of London, Liveryman Worshipful Co. of Chartered Accts. Mem. Fulham Football Club (dir. 1992-98), Royal Automobile Club. Home: 27 Manor Way, Kent Beckenham BR3 3LH, England Office: BDO Stoy Hayward, 8 Baker St, London W1M 1DA, England

SHRIVASTAVA, ARUN KUMAR, engineering educator, researcher; b. Ballia, India, Mar. 18, 1946; m. Rani Shrivastava, Feb. 17, 1978; children: Juhi Raviraj, Kunal Ravirah. BSc, Tata Coll., 1966; MSc in Math., Ranchi (India) U., 1970; MSc in Physics, Agra U., India, 1974; PhD in Engring., Birla Inst. of Tech., Ranchi, India, 1980. Rsch. scholar Dept. Physics, Patna U., India, 1974-75, Dept. Mech. Engring., BIT, Ranchi, India, 1975-78; sr. rsch. fellow Dept. Space Engring. and Rocketry, BIH, Ranchi, 1978-79, scientist, 1979-84, asst. prof., 1984-91, assoc. prof., 1991—; prin. investigator Govt. of India, 1989-92, 92-96; chief coord. AICTE Project, Govt. of India, 1993-94, 97-99. Author: Rocket, 1995, Antriksha Vigyan Avang Kachiya Gati Vigyan, 1998 (Indira Gandhi award); contbr. numerous articles to profl. publs. Mem. Indian Soc. for Tech. Edn. Avocations: gardening, reading, religious books. Home: Amla Tola, Chairasa, 833201 Birar India Office: Birla Inst Tech, Mesra, 83515 Ranchi India

SHRIVASTAVA, SANJAY, physician, researcher; b. New Delhi, India, July 22, 1969; s. Madhava Prasad and Shashi Shrivasta; m. Anjna Aggarwal, Nov. 16, 1996. MB, U. Coll. Med. Scis., New Delhi, 1993, BChir, 1993; student for pub. health, Med. Coll. Wis. Diplomate Am. Bd. Internal Medicine. Jr. resident U. Coll. Med. Scis., New Delhi, 1993, sr. demonstrator, instr. pharmacology, 1993-94; sr. house physician Dudley (Eng.) Group Hosps., 1994-96; resident physician Med. Coll. Wis., Milw., 1996-99; hospitalist internal medicine Fort Hamilton (Ohio) Hosp., 1999—; mem. Critical Care Com. Contbr. article to profl. jour. Trustee Fairfield/Hamilton divsn. Am. Heart Assn., 2000. Recipient R Vishwanathan prize for securing the highest grade in Internal Medicine U. New Delhi, 1991, cert. of merit for highest grade in Otorhinolaryngology U. New Delhi, 1991, Smt. Ram Pyari and Shri L N Chugh Meml. medal for highest grade in U. New Delhi, 1991, cert. of merit for third position in order of merit U. New Delhi, 1991. Mem. ACP, AMA, Quality Rev. Com., Royal Coll. Physicians, Ohio State Med. Assn., Butler County Med. Soc. Avocations: golf, traveling, biking, reading. Achievements includes original research in cardiovascular medicine having to do with inducibility predicting ventricular tachycardia prognosis in the absence of electrophysiologically guided therapy, the relationship between the inner and outer T-wave shock induction zones and findings at electrophysiologic testing, and efficacy of lisinopril in the treatment of essential hypertension. Fax: 810-454-2042. Home e-mail: sanjanj@hotmail.com. Office e-mail: shrivast@mcw.edu. Home: 1410 Springfield Pike Apt 57D Cincinnati OH 45215-2156 Office: Fort Hamilton Hosp 630 Eaton Ave Hamilton OH 45013-2767

SHRIVER, DONALD WOODS, JR., theology educator; b. Norfolk, Va., Dec. 20, 1927; s. Donald Woods and Gladys (Roberts) S.; m. Peggy Ann Leu, Aug. 9, 1953; children: Gregory Bruce, Lionel, Timothy Donald. B.A., Davidson Coll., 1951; B.D., Union Theol. Sem. Va., 1955; S.T.M., Yale U., 1957; Ph.D. (Rockefeller Doctoral fellow), Harvard U., 1963; L.H.D. (hon.), Central Coll., 1970, Davidson Coll., 1984, Union Medal, Union Theol. Sem. Am., 1991; D.D. (hon.), Wagner Coll., 1978, Southwestern Coll., Memphis, 1983, Colgate U., 1996; LHD (hon.), Jewish Theol. Sem., 1991; DD (hon.), Colgate U., 1996. Ordained to ministry Presbyterian Ch., 1955; pastor Linwood Presbyn. Ch., Gastonia, N.C., 1956-59; u. minister, prof. religion N.C. State U., Raleigh, 1963-72; dir. u. program on sci. and soc. N.C. State U., 1968-72; prof. ethics and soc. Emory U., Atlanta, 1972-75; William E. Dodge prof. applied Christianity Union Theol. Sem., N.Y.C., 1975-96, pres. faculty, 1975-91; adj. prof. bus. ethics Sch. Bus. Adminstrn., Columbia U., prof. ethics Sch. Internat. Affairs, 1995-98; sr. fellow freedom forum Sch. Journalism, Columbia U., 1992-93; adj. prof. ethics, 1994—; lectr. Duke U., Va. State U., Ga. State U., numerous colls. and univs. in Can., Kenya, India, Japan and Korea. Author: How Do You Do and Why: An Introduction of Christian Ethics for Young People, 1966, Rich Man Poor Man: Christian Ethics for Modern Man Series, 1972, (with Dean D. Knudsen and John R. Earle) Spindles and Spires: A Restudy of Religion and Social Change in Gastonia, 1976, (with Karl A. Ostrom) Is There Hope for the City?, 1977, The Social Ethics of the Lord's Prayer, 1980, The Gospel, The Church, and Social Change, 1980, The Lord's Prayer: A Way of Life, 1983, An Ethic for Enemies: Forgiveness in Politics, 1995; co-author: Redeeming the City, 1982, Beyond Success: Corporations and Their Critics in the Nineties, 1991; editor: The Unsilent South, 1965, Medicine and Religion: Strategies of Care, 1979. Dir. Urban Policy Study N.C. State U., 1971-73; precinct chmn. Democratic Party, Raleigh, N.C., del. to nat. conv., 1968; mem. Mayor's Com. on Human Relations, Raleigh, 1967-71; chmn. Urban Policy Seminar, Center for Theology and Public Policy, 1978-82. Served with Signal Corps U.S. Army, 1946-47. Recipient The Union medal, Union Theol. Sem., 1991; Kent fellow in religion, 1959; fellow Am. Acad. in Berlin, 1999. Mem. Am. Soc. Christian Ethics (pres. 1979-80), Soc. for Values in Higher Edn., Soc. for

Health and Human Values, Soc. for Sci. Study of Religion, AAAS, Am. Sociol. Assn., Am. Soc. Engring. Edn. (chmn. liberal arts div. 1972-73), United Christian Youth Movement of Nat. Council of Chs. (nat. chmn. 1951-53), Council on Fgn. Relations. Home and Office: 440 Riverside Dr Apt 58 New York NY 10027-6830

SHRIVER, PAMELA H., retired professional tennis player, sports analyst; b. Balt., July 4, 1962; m. Joseph Shapiro, 1998. Profl. tennis player, 1979—; winner 21 career singles, 112 career doubles titles 21 career singles, 92 career doubles titles; winner 7 Australian Opens (with Martina Navratilova), 4 French Opens (with Navratilova), 5 Wimbledons (with Navratilova), 6 U.S. Opens, French Open mixed doubles (with Emilio Sanchez); analyst, commentator HBO, NBC, CBS, ABC, BBC, ESPN; part-owner Balt. Orioles baseball team; pres. Women's Sports Legends; mem. U.S. Fedn. Cup Team, 1986, 87, 89, U.S. Wightman Cup Team, 1978-81, 83, 85, 87; co-winner 1998 Wimbledon 35 and Over Doubles title; mem. President's Coun. on Phys. Fitness and Sports, 1986-92; mem. Md. Fitness Commn.; v.p. Internat. Tennis Hall of Fame. Active ann. charity tennis exhbn. through Balt. Cmty. Found., also trustee; trustee McDonogh Sch.; hon. chmn. Balt. Tennis Patrons. Recipient Gold medal 1988 Olympic Games in doubles (with Zina Garrison), Palyer Who Makes a Difference award Family Circle mag., 1996. Mem. U.S. Tennis Assn. (bd. dirs. 1997—), Women's Tennis Assn. (pres. 1991-94, Corel Trou David Gray Svc. award 1998), Tour Players Assn. Address: PHS Ltd 401 Washington Ave Ste 902 Towson MD 21204-4835

SHRONTZ, FRANK ANDERSON, airplane manufacturing executive; b. Boise, Idaho, Dec. 14, 1931; s. Thurlyn Howard and Florence Elizabeth (Anderson) S.; m. Harriet Ann Houghton, June 12, 1954; children: Craig Howard, Richard Whitaker, David Anderson. Student, George Washington U., 1953; LLB, U. Idaho, 1954; MBA, Harvard U., 1958; postgrad., Stanford U., 1969-70. Asst. contracts coordinator Boeing Co., Seattle, 1958-65, asst. dir. contract adminstrn., 1965-67, asst. to v.p. comml. airplane group, 1967-69, asst. dir. new airplane program, 1969-70, dir. comml. sales operations, 1970-73, v.p. planning and contracts, 1977-78; asst. sec. Dept. Air Force, Washington, 1973-76, Dept. Def., Washington, 1976-77; v.p., gen. mgr. 707/727/737 div. Boeing Comml. Airplane Co., Seattle, 1978-82, v.p. sales and mktg., 1982-84, pres., 1985-86; pres., chief exec. officer The Boeing Co., Seattle, 1986-96, chmn., 1988-97, chmn. emeritus, 1997—; bd. dirs. Boise Cascade Corp., 3M Co., Chevron; mem. Boeing bd., 1985-97. Regent Smithsonian Instn. 1st lt. AUS, 1954-56. Mem. Phi Alpha Delta, Beta Theta Pi. Clubs: Overlake Golf and Country, Columbia Tower. Office: The Boeing Co PO Box 3707 Seattle WA 98124-2207*

SHROPSHIRE, DONALD GRAY, hospital executive; b. Winston-Salem, N.C., Aug. 6, 1927; s. John Lee and Bess L. (Shouse) S.; m. Mary Ruth Bodenheimer, Aug. 19, 1950; children: Melanie Shropshire David, John Devin. B.S., U. N.C., 1950; Erickson fellow postgrad., U. Chgo., 1958-59; LLD (hon.), U. Ariz., 1992; EdD (hon.), Tucson U., 1994. Personnel asst. Nat. Biscuit Co., Atlanta, 1950-52; asst. personnel mgr. Nat. Biscuit Co., Chgo., 1952-54; adminstr. Eastern State Hosp., Lexington, Ky., 1954-62; assoc. dir. U. Md. Hosp., Balt., 1962-67; adminstr. Tucson Med. Ctr., 1967-82, pres., 1982-92, pres. emeritus, 1992—, bd. dirs., 1995; pres. Tucson Hosps. Med. Edn. Program, 1970-71, sec., 1971-86; pres. So. Ariz. Hosp. Council, 1968-69; bd. dirs. Ariz. Blue Cross, 1967-76, chmn. provider standards com., 1972-76; chmn. Healthways Inc., 1985-92; mem. bd. La Posada at Park Centre, Inc., Green Valley, Ariz., 1996-2000, chmn. bd., 1996-99. Bd. dirs. Health Planning Coun. Tucson, mem. exec. com., 1969-74; chmn. profl. divsn. United Way, Tucson, 1969-70, vice chmn. campaign, 1988, Ariz. Health Faciltities Authority, bd. dirs., 1992—; chmn. dietary svcs. com., vice chmn., 1988, Md. Hosp. Coun., 1966-67; bd. dirs. Ky. Hosp. Assn., 1961-62, chmn. coun. profl. practice, 1960-61; past pres. Blue Grass Hosp. Coun.; trustee Assn. Western Hosps., 1974-81, pres., 1979-80; mem. accreditation Coun. for Continuing Med. Edn., 1982-87, chair, 1986; bd. govs. Pima C.C., 1970-76, sec., 1973-74, chmn., 1975-76, bd. dirs. Found., 1978-82, Ariz. Bd. Regents, 1982-90, sec., 1983-86, pres., 1987-88; mem. Tucson Airport Authority, 1987—, bd. dirs., 1990-95, pres., 1995; v.p. Tucson Econ. Devel. Corp., 1977-82; bd. dirs. Vol. Hosps. Am., 1977-88, treas., 1979-82; mem. Ariz. Adv. Health Coun. Dirs., 1976-78; bd. dirs. Tucson Tomorrow, 1983-87, Tucson Downtown Devel. Corp., 1988-95, Rincon Inst., 1992-97, Sonoran Inst., 1992-97; dir. Mus. No. Ariz., 1988—; nat. bd. advisors Coll. Bus. U. Ariz., 1990—, mem. Dean's Bd. Coll. Fine Arts, 1992—, chmn., 1992-96, pres. Ariz. Coun. Econ. Edn., 1993-95; vis. panel Sch. Health Adminstrn. and Policy Ariz. State U., 1990-92; bd. dirs. Cmty. Found. So. Ariz., 1996—; mem. adv. bd. Steele Meml. Rsch. Ctr., U. Ariz. Coll. Medicine, 1996—. Named to Hon. Order Ky. Cols.; named Tucson Man of Yr. 1987, Tucson Father of Yr. 1997; recipient Disting. Svc. award Anti-Defamation League B'nai B'rith, 1989. Mem. Am. Hosp. Assn. (nominating com. 1983-86, trustee 1975-78, ho. dels. 1972-78, chmn. coun. profl. svc. 1973-74, regional adv. bd. 1969-78, chmn. joint com. with NASW 1963-64, Disting. Svc. award 1989), Ariz. Hosp. Assn. (Salisbury award 1982, bd. dirs. 1967-72, pres. 1970-71), Ariz. C. of C. (bd. dirs. 1988-93), Assn. Am. Med. Colls. (mem. assembly 1974-77), Tucson C. of C. (bd. dirs. 1968-69), United Comml. Travelers, Nat. League for Nursing, Ariz. Town Hall (bd. dirs. 1982-92, chmn. 1990-92, treas. 1985), Pima County Acad. Decathlon Assn. (dir. 1983-85), The Rotary Club of Tucson (pres. 1993-94), U. Ariz. Alumni Assn. Coll. Nursing (hon. alumnus 1998). Baptist (ch. moderator, chmn. finance com., deacon, ch. sch. supt., trustee, bd. dirs. ch. found.). Home: 6734 N Chapultepec Cir Tucson AZ 85750-1001 Office: Tucson Med Ctr 5301 E Grant Rd Tucson AZ 85712-2805

SHRYOCK, VERNA E., artist; b. Hatton, Mo., July 18, 1921; d. Finis W. Boulware and Corynne Ferguson; m. G.H. Shryock, Feb.. 3, 1945 (dec. 1976); children: Dennis, Joe. Student, U. Mo., 1940-41. Art tchr. Grapevine, Tex., 1970—. V.p. Hatton (Mo.) Extension Civic Club, 1999—. Mem. Internat. Porcelain Artists & Tchrs., Showme China Painters (pres. Columbia club 1988-9, sec. 1991-94, 96-98), Mo. China Painters, World China Painters, Fulton (Mo.) Art League. Methodist. Avocations: quilting, investment, fishing, travel. Home and Studio: 3638 State Rd E Auxvasse MO 65231-1107

SHTALENKOV, MIKHAIL, hockey player; b. Moscow, Oct. 20, 1965; married. Goal keeper Coyotes, Phoenix, 1998—; mem. Russian Nat. Ice Hockey Team, 1988—; goal keeper Mighty Ducks, Anaheim, Calif., 1993-98, Oilers/Coyotes, 1998-99, Panthers/Coyotes, 1998-2000; goalie Fla. Panthers, Sunrise, 2000. Recipient Silver medal men's ice hockey, Olympic Games, Nagano, Japan, 1998. Avocation: reading. Office: Fla Panthers 2555 Panther Pkwy Sunrise FL 33323*

SHTAMBURG, VASILIY GEORGIY, chemist, researcher; b. Dnepropetrovsk, Ukraine, July 25, 1955; s. Georgiy Nikifor Shtamburg and Zoya Vladimir Pultrok; m. Inna Ivan Sizon II, Mar. 5, 1983; children: Victor, Katya. Diploma in chem. engring., Inst. Chem. Tech., Dnepropetrovsk, 1977; PhD in Chemistry, Moscow State U., 1982. Engr. Nitrogen Industry Inst., Severodonesk, 1977-78; rschr. Chem. Phys. Inst.-Russian Acad. Scis., 1978-81, Reagents Inst., Dnepropetrosk, 1982-91; leading scientist Nerudstroykomplex, Dnepropetrosk, 1991-97; scientist Dnepzopetrovsk State U., 1998—; asst. prof. State Acad. Bldg. & Architecture, Dnepropetrosk, 1995-96. Contbr. articles to profl. jours; patentee in field. Avocations: mushroom hunting, fishing, history. Home: Mostovaya str 2-6, 49038 Dnepropetrovsk Ukraine Office: Dnepropetzosk State U, 13 Nauchnaya Str, 320625 Dnepropetrovsk Ukraine

SHTIENBERG, DAN, research scientist; b. Safad, Israel, Dec. 28, 1955; s. Shimon and Miriam (Domidiamo) S.; m. Hanna Virtzer, June 29, 1978; 3 children. BA, Hebrew U. Jerusalem, Rehovot, Israel, 1980, MS, 1982, PhD, 1987. Rsch. asst. Hebrew U., Rehovot, Israel, 1984-87; rschr. Cornell U., Ithaca, N.Y., 1988-89, Hebrew U., 1989-91, ARO, The Volcani Ctr., Bat-Dagan, Israel, 1991—; adj. prof. The Hebrew U., 1997; sr. scientist ARO, The Volcani Ctr., 1995. Maj. Israeli Def. Forces, 1994-97. Mem. Israeli Phytopathological Soc. (pres. 1994-96). E-mail: danish@netvision.net.il. Office: ARO Dept Plant Pathology, The Volcani Ctr PO Box 6, 50250 Bet Dagan Israel

SHTOKALO, MIROSLAVA IOSIPHOVNA, chemistry educator, researcher; b. Dneprodzerzhinsk, Ukraine, Aug. 24, 1926; d. Iosiph Zacharovich and Zinaida Evstafievna (Gavrilenko) S.; m. Ivan Eliseevich Debrivnija, Apr. 21, 1952; 1 child, Isaeva Miroslava. Chemic-Analytic, Kiev (Ukraine) State U., 1950; PhD, Nat. Acad. Scis., Kiev, 1958, DSc in Chemistry, 1987. Jr., sr. rsch. worker Nat. Acad. Sci., Kiev, 1959-68; lectr., chief chair, prof. Ukraine State U. Food Tech., Kiev, 1968—, Soros prof., 1996. Recipient 2nd prize for monographie All-Union Chem. Mendeleev Soc., 1969, 2nd degree diploma for best rsch. work. Ministry Higher Edn., Ukraine, 1983. Mem. Acad. Engring. Sci. Ukraine (academician 1991), N.Y. Acad. Scis. Avocations: classical music, travel. Home: Suvorova St 19a f 26, 252010 Kiev Ukraine Office: Ukraine State U Food Tech, Vladimirskaja St 68, 252033 Kiev Ukraine

SHU, CHANGDA, endocrinologist, educator; b. Shanghai, China, Jan. 2, 1930; m. Yanhua Zhu, Oct. 1, 1955. MD, St. Johns U., Shanghai, 1952. Physician Affiliated Hosp., Shanghai Med. Coll., 1952-58; prof. medicine First Affiliated Hosp., Chongqing (China) Med. U., 1958—; rschr. McGill U., Montreal, Can., 1979-80. Contbr. articles to profl. jours. Mem. Internat. Artificial Organs Assn. Home and Office: First Affiliated Hosp, Chongqing U Med Sci, Chongqing 400016, China

SHU, DEGAN, paleobiologist, researcher; b. Ezhou, China, Feb. 17, 1946; s. Dahang and Fengjiao (Hu) S.; m. Ling Chen, Aug. 6, 1970; children: Qiang, Gang. BS, Peking U., Beijing, 1969; Master, Northwest U., Xi'an, China, 1981; PhD, China U. Geoscis., Beijing, 1987. Tchr. Mid. Sch., Bingxian, China, 1970-78; lectr. Northwest U., 1981-84, assoc. prof., 1988-92, prof., 1992—; vis. scholar Smithsonian Instn., Washington, 1988, U. Würzburg, Germany, 1994-95, U. Cambridge; postdoctoral U. Bonn, Germany, 1988-89; chmn. Peleobiogeogr. Symposium 29th Internat. Geol. Congress, Kyoto, Japan, 1992. Author: Cambrian Bradoriida of China, 1991; discoverer of earliest-known crustacean in world, 1995, of earliest-known chordate in world, 1996, of earliest-known hemichordate in world, 1996, of earliest-known vertebrates in the world, 1999. Recipient Prize for advancing sci. and tech. State Ednl. Com. China, 1986, 92, Papeontology and Stratigraphy prize Yin-Zanxun Found., Nanjing, China, 1993, Prize for advancing sci. and tech. Govt. Shaanxi Province, China, 1993. Mem. Paleontol. Soc. China (mem. coun. 1997—), A.V. Humboldt Club (Xi'an br. sec. 1991—), Shaanxi Paleontol. Soc. (sec. gen. 1992-96, chmn. 1997—). Avocations: sports, music. Office: Northwest Univ Dept Geology, Taibai Rd, 710069 Xian China

SHU, WATARU, materials scientist, researcher; b. Yudu, Jiangxi, China, Feb. 14, 1963; arrived in Japan, 1989; s. Huiquan and Haiyu (Zhao) S.; m. Ikue Shu, Apr. 26, 1991; children: Ruri, Hiromi. BSc, Nanjing (China) U. Sci., Tech., 1983, MSc., 1986; postgrad. studies, Tsinghua U., Beijing, China, 1986-89; DSc, Kyushu U., Fukuoka, Japan, 1993. Rsch. assoc. Nanjing U. Sci. & Tech., 1986, Jaeri, Tokai-Mura, Japan, 1991-93; asst. prof. Kyushu U., Fukuoka, Japan, 1993-95; assoc. prof. Toyoma (Japan) U., 1995-98; rsch. scientist Japan Atomic Energy Rsch. Inst., 1998—, sr. scientist, 1999—. Chief editor Jour. Postgrad. Students Tsinghua U., Beijing, China, 1987-88; contbr. articles to profl. jours. including Phys. Rev. B, Jour. Applied Physics, Acta Materiala, Jour. Vacuum Sci. Tech. Recipient Most Excellent Postgrad. Student scholarship, Nanjing U. Sci. and Tech., 1986; grantee Ministry Edn., Sci. and Culture of Japan, 1994, 96, 97. Mem. Japan Inst. Metals, Atomic Energy Soc. Japan, Japan Soc. Plasma Sci. and Nuclear Fusion (specialist com. mem. 1995-97), Chinese Materials Rsch. Soc. (coun. mem. youth br. 1996-98). Avocations: contract bridge, basketball, soccer. Home: Nagahorijutaku C30-1, Tokai-mura, Naka-gun Ibaraki 319-1112, Japan Office: Tritium Engring Lab JAERI, Tokai-mura Naka-gun, Ibaraki 319-1195, Japan

SHUAIBOV, ALEXANDR KAMILOVYCH, physicist; b. Yasinya, Ukraine, USSR, Apr. 19, 1951; s. Kamil Sulymanovych and Maria Afanasivna (Lunhor) S.; m. Nadiya Yosypivna Penyak, May 27, 1978; 1 child, Victoria. First yr., U. Uzhhorod (Ukraine, USSR), 1968, postgrad., 1976, candidate of sci., 1987. Jr. sci. worker U. Uzhhorod (Ukraine, USSR), 1976-78, sr. sci. worker, 1978; sr. sci. worker Prolem Lab., Uzhhorod, 1987-2000. Contbr. articles to profl. jours.; patentee in field. Mem. Ukrainian Phys. Soc., SPIE. Greek Catholic. Avocations: chess, tennis, reading, gardening. Home: 25 Kapushanska St, 294018 Uzhhorod Ukraine Office: Uzhorod State U, 46 Pidhirnd St, 294000 Uzhhorod Ukraine

SHUART, TINA WARD, municipal official; b. Cobleskill, N.Y., Nov. 25, 1958; d. Lewis Adelbert Ward and Thelma Irene Pangburn; m. Theodore Bernard Shuart III, Aug. 11, 1979; 1 child, Nathaniel Ward. A in Occupl. Studies, Albany (N.Y.) Bus. Coll., 1979. Registered mcpl. clk.; cert. mcpl. clk. Acad. Advanced Edn. Office mgr. Daily Editor, Cobleskill; supr. mortgage account Dime Savs. Bank, Albany; sec. Harva Co., Schoharie, N.Y.; office asst. Avis Rent A Car, Albany, 1978—; town clk., collector Town of Cobleskill, 1992—. Fin. mgr. 1st Ref. Ch., Schnectady, N.Y.; mem. com. Cornell Coop. Ext. Home Econs. Program, 1992-98, mem. nominations com., 1995, rep. to bd. dirs., 1997, 98, mem. personnel com., 1997, 98; bd. dirs. Family & Cmty. Svcs., 1993—, mem. fin. com., 1993-96, mem. nominating com., 1994—, mem. fundraising com., 1996—; bd. dirs. Town of Cobleskill Hist. Soc., 1992-98; treas. Town of Cobleskill Bicentennial, 1993-98, mem. com., 1997; treas. Lawyersville/Sharon Ref. Ch. Youth Group, 1995—, Roundhead and Hayseeds, 1997—; trustee, treas. Union Cemetery Lawyersville Ref. Ch., 1993—. Mem. N.Y. State Assn. Tax Receivers and Collectors, N.Y. State Town Clk. Assn. (dir. dist. 3 1996-99, scholarship chair 1998-99, mem. registered mcpl. clk. com. 1998—, membership chair 1999—), Schoharie County Town Clk.'s Assn. (pres. 1993-97, treas. 1998-99, sec. 2000—). Democrat. Avocations: travel, history, antiques. Home: HC 2 Box 92 Cobleskill NY 12043-9403 Office: Town of Cobleskill PO Box 316 Cobleskill NY 12043-0316

SHUBART, DOROTHY LOUISE TEPFER, artist, educator; b. Ft. Collins, Colo., Mar. 1, 1923; d. Adam Christian and Rose Virginia (Ayers) Tepfer; m. Robert Franz Shubart, Apr. 22, 1950; children: Richard, Lorenne. AA, Colo. Women's Coll., 1944; grad., Cleve. Inst. Art, 1946; student, Western Res. U., 1947-48; BA, St. Thomas Aquinas Coll., 1974; MA, Coll. New Rochelle, 1978. Art tchr. Denver Mus., 1942-44; art tchr. adults and children Cleve. Recreation Dept., 1944-50; adult edn. art tchr. Nanuet (N.Y.) Pub. Schs., 1950-65, Pearl River (N.Y.) Adult Edn., 1950-51; rec. sec. Van Houten Fields Assn., West Nyack, N.Y., 1969-74. Exhibited in group shows at Hopper House, Rockland Ctr. for Arts, CWC, Cleve. Inst. Art, Coll. New Rochelle, Rockland County Ann. Art Fair, Gonzalez Sr. Ctr.; co-author, photographer: Windmills & Dreams, 1997, Cover for Eldorado Greenbelt Pathways, 2000. Leader 4-H Club, Nanuet, 1960-80, Girls Scouts U.S., Nanuet, 1961-68; mem. scholarship com., gen. com. PTA, Nanuet, 1964-68; rec. sec. Van Houten Fields assn., West Nyack, N.Y., 1969-74; com. mem. Eldorado (Santa Fe) Cmty. Improvement Assn.-Arterial Rd. Planning Com., 1992-94, Environ. Def. Fund, Union of Concerned Scientists, Nat. Com. to Preserve Social Security and Medicare; capt. Neighborhood Watch, local organizer Eldorado chpt. security com.; mem. Eldorado Conservation Greenbelt Com., 1996-97; campaign vol. Jim Baca for Gov., N.Mex., 1996, Eric Serna for Congress, 1996, Tom Udall for Congress, 1999—; mem. Eldorado Hist. Com., 1995-97, Shakespeare in Santa Fe Guild, 1998, Mil. Hist. Found., 2000—; vol. Santa Fe Libr., 1998-2000, Cerro Grande Food Bank. Gund scholar Cleve. Inst. Art, 1946. Mem. AAUW, NOW, Audubon Soc., Ams. for Dem. Action, Environ. Def. Fund, Union Concerned Scientists, Action on Smoking and Health, Wilderness Club, Delta Tau Kappa, Phi Delta Kappa. Democrat. Avocations: books, gardening, photography, bicycling, writing. Home: 8 Hidalgo Ct Santa Fe NM 87505-8898

SHUBEROFF, OSCAR JULIO, university administrator; b. Buenos Aires, July 17, 1943; s. Pablo Shuberoff and Jaica Malitz; m. Silvia Graciela Quesada; children: Pablo Alfredo, Diego Leandro, Analia Ines. Degree in Ciencias Econs., U. Buenos Aires, 1968. Pres. Empryser Aedes SA, Buenos Aires, 1976-88; assoc. prof. U. Buenos Aires, 1972-82; v.p. Colegio de Graduados de Ciencieas Economicas, 1977-80; dean of the faculty of Ciencias Econs. U. Buenos Aires, 1984-86; chaired prof. U. Lomas de Zamora, Argentina, 1983—; rector U. Buenos Aires, 1986—; v.p. de la O.U.I. para el Cono Sud, 1990-2000. Author: Organizing and Administration, 1972; contbr. articles to profl. jours. Sec.-gen. Argentine Fedn. of Econs. Grads., 1982; del. Com. Radical Civic Union-Capital, 1986. Office: U Buenos Aires, Calle Viamonte 430/444, 1053 Buenos Aires Argentina

SHUBIK, MARTIN, economics educator; b. N.Y.C., Mar. 24, 1926; s. Joseph Louis and Sara S.; m. Julia Kahn, Aug. 11, 1970; 1 child, Claire Louise. B.A., U. Toronto, 1947, M.A., 1949; Ph.D., Princeton U., 1953. Research asst. Princeton U., 1950-53, research asso., 1953-55; fellow Center for Advanced Study in Behavioral Scis., Palo Alto, Calif., 1955-56; cons. mgmt. consultation services Gen. Electric Co., 1956-60; adj. research prof. Pa. State U., 1957-59; vis. prof. econs. Yale U., New Haven, 1960-61; prof. econs. of orgn., dept. adminstrv. sci. Yale U., 1963-75, Seymour H. Knox prof. math. instl. econs., 1975—; bd. dirs. Equity Strategies, Third Avenue Funds; mem. staff T.J. Watson Rsch. Labs., IBM Corp., 1961-63; vis. prof. Escuela de Estudios Económicos U. Chile, Santiago, 1965, Inst. Advanced Studies, Vienna, Austria, 1968, 70, U. Melbourne, Australia, 1973; cons. Rand Corp., Santa Monica, Calif., 1963; dir. Cowles Found. for Rsch. In Econs., Yale U., 1973-76; external faculty Sante Fe Inst., 1994—, sci. bd. 1996—; cons. in field. Author or co-author: numerous books, including The War Game, 1979, (with G. Brewer) The Aggressive Conservative Investor, 1979, (with M.J. Whitman) Market Structure and Behavior, 1980, (with R.E. Levitan) Game Theory in the Social Sciences, vol. 1, 1982, vol. 2, 1984, The Theory of Money and Financial Institutions, vols. 1 and 2, 1999; mem. editorial bd. Conflict Resolution; mem. editl. adv. bd. Internat. Studies Series; assoc. editor Mgmt. Sci, 1965-81; contbr. articles to profl. jours. Served to lt. Royal Can. Navy. Recipient Lanchester prize, 1983, Koopman prize mil. ops. rsch., 1996; named hon. prof. U. Vienna. Fellow Econometric Soc., World Acad. Arts and Scis.; mem. Am. Acad. Arts and Scis., Conn. Acad. Arts and Scis. Home: 140 Edgehill Rd Hamden CT 06517-4011 Office: 30 Hillhouse Ave New Haven CT 06511-3704

SHUBIK, PHILIPPE, academic administrator; b. London, Apr. 28, 1921; m. Valerie Reid , July 22, 1963; children: Anna, Kathryn, Peter. BA, Oxford (Eng.) U., 1941, MA, 1943, PhD, 1949, DM, 1965. Demonstrator Junn Sch. of Pathology, Oxford, 1946-47; instr. in pathology Northwestern U., Chgo., 1947-57; prof., dir. Inst. Med. Rsch. Chgo. Med. Sch., 1957-67; prof., dir. Eppley Inst. Cancer Rsch. U. Nebr., Omaha, 1967-79; vis. prof. German Nat. Cancer Inst., Heidelberg, Fed. Republic of Germany, 1979-80; pers. Toxicology Forum Green Coll., Washington and Oxford, 1980—; expert advisor WHO, Geneva, 1960—; mem. U.S. Nat. Cancer Adv. Bd., Washington, 1962-82. Author: (textbook) International Handbook of Food Toxicology, 1989—; mng. editor Cancer Letters, 1970-99; editor: Teratogenesis, Carcinogenesis and Mutagenesis, 1990—. Maj. M.C., Royal Army, 1944-46. Recipient Merit award Soc. Toxicology, 2000; Green Coll. fellow, 1980. Mem. Athanaeum Club of London. Office: Green Coll Toxicology Forum, 29 Beaumont St, Oxford OX1 2NP, England

SHUBNIKOV, EUGENE IVANOVICH, optical engineering researcher, administrator; b. Omsk, Russia, Dec. 27, 1940; s. Ivan Modestovich and Serafima Nikolaevna (Egorova) S.; m. Ludmila Anisimovna Polyakova, 1963 (div. June 1972); 1 child, Alexander; m. Ludmila Michaylovna Vetrova, July 2, 1976; 1 child, German. BS in Electronics, Electrotech. Inst., St. Petersburg, Russia, 1962, MS in Electronics, 1964; PhD in Optics, Vavilov State Optical Inst., St. Petersburg, 1976. Engr. Vavilov State Optical Inst., 1965-68, jr. rschr., 1968-78, sr. rschr., 1978-90, head lab. optical neural networks, 1990—. Contbr. rsch. articles to sci. publs. Grantee, Russian Fundamental Rsch. Found., Moscow, 1995. Mem. Russian Optical Soc. Achievements include research on photon count for optical location problem of satellites and moon, optical images processing of landscapes for navigation problems, optical neural networks, pattern recognition, image processing, retina, brain. Avocations: music, automobiles. Home: 74/1 Apt 89, Svetlanovskiy Prospect, 195297 Saint Petersburg Russia Office: Vavilov State Optical Inst, Birgevaya Line 12, 199034 Saint Petersburg Russia

SHUBUKSHI, USAMA BIN ABD AL-MAJID, federal official; b. 1943. PhD in Internal Medicine, Germany, 1976. Assoc. prof. King Abd al-Aziz U., dean, 1984-90, pres., 1993; min. Ministry of Health, Riyadh, Saudi Arabia, 1995—. Fellow Royal Coll. Surgeons. Office: Ministry of Health, Airport Rd Main Ministry, Riyadh 11176, Saudi Arabia*

SHUCHENG, WANG, government official. Min. Ministry Water Resources, Beijing, 1998—. Office: Ministry Water Resources, 1 Bai Guang Lu Er Tiao, Beijing 100761, China*

SHUDO, RYUSHI, physician; b. Sapporo, Japan, May 1, 1964; s. Shizuo and Toshiko (Ishihara) S.; m. Minako Sato, June 7, 1994; 1 child, Yurina. MD, Jichi Med. Coll., Minamikawachi, Japan, 1990; PhD in Molecular Oncology, Asahikawa (Japan) Med. Coll., 1998. Med. diplomate in internal medicine, gastroenterology, gastroendoscopy, gen. physician, geriatrics, occupl. medicine. Intern Asahikawa Med. Coll., 1990-91, resident, 1991-92; asst. instr. dept. internal medicine Wakkanai (Japan) City Hosp., 1992-93; divsn. chief dept. internal medicine Shari (Japan) Mcpl. Hosp., 1993-95; clin. and rsch. fellow Asahikawa Med. Coll., 1995-97; divsn. chief dept. internal medicine Shizunai (Japan) Mcpl. Hosp., 1997-99; divsn. chief dept. internal medicine, digestive diseases Kobayashi (Japan) Hosp., 1999—. Contbr. articles to profl. jours. Recipient award Japanese Pancreas Soc., 1998. Mem. ACP, Am. Soc. for Gastrointestinal Endoscopy, Am. Coll. Gastroenterology, Japanese Soc. Internal Medicine (award 2000), Japanese Soc. Gastroendoscopy, Japanese Soc. Gastroenterology, The Japan Geriatrics, Japan Physicians Assn. Avocations: Jeet Kune Do, karate, Sho-Gi, movies, travel. Home: 77-28 Shinsei-cho, Kitami, Hokkaido 090-0815, Japan Offce: Asahikawa Med Coll/Int Med, 1-1 1 St E 2 Midorigaoka, Asahikawa, Hokkaido 078-8510, Japan

SHUEH, JOHN WEI-CHUNG, finance company executive, management educator; b. Kwangtung, China, July 29, 1940; arrived in Taiwan, 1949; s. Chung Shu and Li (Mei) S.; m. Cathy Chen, Sept. 26, 1969; children: Cindy, Teddy. Bachelor's degree, Nat. Taiwan U., Taipei, 1964; Master's degree, U. Sask., Saskatoon, Can., 1968, U. Mass., 1970; exec. degree, MIT, 1978. Cert. engring. mgr. Dep. dir. Ministry of Comms., Taipei, 1972-78; dir. performance evaluation dept. Coun. for Econ. Planning and Devel., Taipei, 1978-81; dir., secretariate Ctrl. Bank of China, Taipei, 1981-88, gen. mgr., 1988-93; chmn. China Bills Fin. Corp., Taipei, 1993—; assoc. prof. Chiao Tung U., Taipei, 1978—; bd. dirs. Taipei Bank; mng. dir. Taipei Found. Fin., 1994—. Author: Taiwan Pricing Structure, 1972, Taiwan Pricing Trends and Directions, 1972, Application of Calculus in the Studies of Economics and Commercial Usage, 1975. 2d lt. Taiwanese Army, 1964-65. Mem. Phi Lambda (gen. secretariate 1980, 83, chmn. 1996), Taipei Found. of Fin. (mng. dir. 1994-97). Roman Catholic. Avocations: golf, tennis, badminton, swimming, hiking. Office: China Bills Fin Corp, 11/F 14 Tun Hua S Rd Sec 2, Taipei Taiwan

SHUGALEI, IRINA VLADIMIROVNA, chemistry educator; b. Leningrad, Russia, Dec. 13, 1950; d. Vladimir Timofeevich and Tamara Konstantinovna (Tolpyugo) S.; m. Michael Alekseevich Ilyushin, Oct. 1, 1983; 1 child, Tatyana. Degree in Chem. Engring., Leningrad Tech. Inst., 1974, PhD, 1978; D Chem. Sci., St. Petersburg Inst. Tech., 1996. Rschr. Leningrad Tech. Inst. USSR, 1974-75, aspirant, 1975-78, rschr., 1978-83, 1990-91, doctorate, 1991-94, asst. prof., 1994-97, prof., 1997—; asst. prof. Leningrad Pediatric Med. Inst. USSR, 1983-90; rschr. spl. constrn. Tech. Bur., Leningrad, 1978-83; tchr. Sch. 533, St. Petersburg, 1993-95. Author: (textbook) Physical Chemistry of Nitrogen Compounds, 1985; contbr. articles to profl. jours. Avocations: travel, gardening. Office: State Inst Tech, Moskovsky Prospect, 198013 Saint Petersburg Russia

SHUHAN, JANICE-LYNN NAZZIOLA, educator; b. Passaic, N.J., Sept. 11, 1959; d. Gabriel Anthony and Camille Mary (Monisera) Nazziola. BS in Math., Montclair State U., 1981, MA in Adminstrn. and Supervision, 1999. Cert. tchr. Substitute tchr. Belleville (N.J.) High Sch., 1977-81, long-term substitute tchr., 1981—, secondary math. tchr., 1986—; sch. choreographer Belleville Mid. and High Schs., 1978—; dir. mus. Belleville H.S., 1991—; performer nat. tour U.S. Coast, 1979-80; performer off-Broadway and dinner theatres, N.Y. and N.J., 1977-86; presenter N.J. Sch. Bds. Curriculum Fair at Conv. Hall, 1989, 90, 91, 92; profl. performer, actress, singer, dancer. Author (poem): Selections of the Heart, 2000, External Songs, 2000, Between Darkness and Light, 2000; co-author: Math Essentials, Selected Strategies of Teaching Math Essentials, 1992, 93; contbr. articles to profl. jours.; appeared in motion pictures Other People's Money, A Fire in the Dark, Carlito's Way, and nat. commls. Campaign mgr. Belleville B.O.E., 1989; judge Bell/Nutley Columbus Day Parade Bella Signorina, 1988-91; dance classes Nutley Italian Am. Club, 1988; bd. dirs. Cranford Dramatic Club Theatre, mem. bd. govs. Recipient Steven's Leadership award Steven's Inst., Hoboken, N.J., 1990,

Outstanding Math Nat. Educator award Tandy Corp., 1991; named Mrs. West Paterson N.J. America, Essex County Tchr. of Yr. 1999-00. Mem. NEA, ASCD, Nat. Coun. Tchrs. Math., Assn. Math. Tchrs. N.J., Belleville Edn. Assn., N.J. Edn. Assn. Republican. Roman Catholic. Avocations: acting, singing, dancing, writing poetry. Office: Belleville High Sch 100 Passaic Ave Belleville NJ 07109-1898

SHUHUAI, WEN, physicist; b. Liao Yang, Lian Ning, China, July 11, '936; s. Chang Jiun and Si Zhang; m. XiuYan Zhang, Mar. 10, 1966; children: Tiansu Wen, Zhi Wen, Haisu Wen. B., U. Jilin, Chang Chun, China, 1963. High sch. researcher nuclear physics and plasma physics. Technician Ninth Inst. Nuclear Industry, XiNing, China, 1963-69, Inst. Nuclear Physics and Chemistry, Mian Yang, China, 1970-82; asst. prof. Inst. Nuclear Physics and Chemistry, Mian Yang, 1983-86, assoc. prof., 1987-90, prof., 1991—, dep. head rsch. lab., 1974-83, head rsch. lab., 1984-89, dep. head engring., 1990-98, cons. sci. and tech., 1999—; chief ICF phys. experiment spls. group Chinese Nat. High Technical Com., 1993-98, cons., 1998—; acad. committeeman. Chinese Nat. Lab for High Temps. and Densities Plasmas, 1993—. Inventor pulse neutron detector, pulse neutron spectra; contbr. articles to profl. jours. Recipient Chinese Nat. Invention award, 1984, 85, Chinese Nat. Sci. and Technique Advancement award Chinese Nat. Sci. and Tech. Com., 1988, 89, 92, award Guan Hua Found., 1992. Office: Inst Nuclear Physics & Chem, PO Box 919-201, Mian Yang Sichuan, China 621900

SHUJA, SHAHZADA ZAMAN, mechanical engineer, researcher; b. Lahore, Punjab, Pakistan, Oct. 19, 1964; s. Shuja-ud-din and Shahzadi (Abdul-Majeed) S.; m. Al-Asifa Abdul-Haq, Mar. 1, 1995; 1 child, Qudsiyah Zaman. BSc in Engring., U. Engring. & Tech., Pakistan, 1988; MSc in Nuclear Engring., Quaid-A-Azam U., Pakistan, 1990; MSc in Mech. Engring., King Fahd U. Petroleum & Min., Saudi Arabia, 1993, PhD, 1998. Trainee engr. Descon Engring. Wks., Pakistan, 1988; fellow Centre for Nuclear Studies, Pakistan, 1988-90; rsch. asst. King Fahd U. Petroleum and Minerals, Dhahran, 1990-93; lectr. dept. mech. engring. King Fahd U. Petroleum and Minerals, Dhahran, 1994-98, asst. prof. dept. mech. engring., 1998—, computer lab. cons. supr., 1993-98. Contbr. articles to profl. jours. Mem. Jamma'a Mosque, Lahore, Pakistan, 1986-88. With Pakistan Nat. Cadet Corp, 1980-81. Ministry of Higher Edn. assistantship, Saudi Arabia, 1990-98; Pakistan Atomic Energy Commn. scholar, 1988-90. Mem. Pakistan Engring. Coun., Pakistan Engring. Forum. Avocations: computer programming and games, gardening. Home: 15-D Block C Samanabad, Lahore 54500, Pakistan Office: King fahd Univ Petroleum, Box 1642, Dhahran 31261, Saudi Arabia

SHUKHAT, BORIS, software development company executive; b. Odessa, Ukraine, Aug. 16, 1957; came to U.S., 1995; s. Arkadiy and Bella Shukhat. MS in Computer Sci. with honors, Odessa Poly. Inst., 1979; PhD in Computer Sci. and Elec. Engring., Ukrainian Acad. Scis., Kiev, 1991. Cert. powerbuilder developer. Rschr., sr. software engr. Inst. Machines and Tools, Odessa, 1979-88; rschr. Inst. Simulation Problems in Power Engring., Kiev, 1989-91; assoc. prof. Odessa Poly. U., 1991-94; project leader Info. Builders Inc., N.Y.C., 1995—. Office: Information Bldrs Inc 2 Penn Plz New York NY 10121-0101

SHUKHMAN, ILYA GRIGOR'EVICH, physicist, researcher; b. Novokuznetzk, USSR, Dec. 18, 1947; s. Grigory Shukhman and Sarah Nemirovskaya; m. Nina Ronzhina, Sept. 20, 1969; children: Grigory, Maria. Diploma, Novosibirsk State U., 1970; CandSci, Leningrad State U., St. Petersburg, Russia, 1973; DSc, Inst. Cosmic Rsch., Moscow, 1987. Jr. rsch. fellow Inst. Solar-Terrestrial Physics, Russian Acad. Sci., Irkutsk, 1973-78, sr. rsch. worker, 1978-80, head of lab., 1980-86, leading rsch. worker, 1986—. Contbr. articles to profl. jours. Grantee Internat. Sci. Found., 1994-95, Russian Found. for Fundamental Rsch., 1995-97. Avocations: fishing, philately, Hebrew language, travel. E-mail: shukhman@iszf.irk.ru. Office: Inst Solar-Terrestrial Phys, Lermontova 126, Irkutsk Russia 664033

SHUKRI, SABIH MAHMOOD, banker, consultant; b. Baghdad, Iraq, Dec. 18, 1928; s. Mahmood Hassan and Latifa; m. Raghda Hassan, Nov. 14, 1969. BSc in Commerce and Econs., U. Baghdad, 1953; postgrad. diploma in politics, LSE, London, 1964. With Rafidain Bank, Baghdad, 1945-55, mgr., head main br., 1956-58, acting gen. mgr., 1958-63; regional mgr. Rafidain Bank, London, 1963-65, Amman, Jordan, 1965-72; dir. chief mgr. ARAB Bank, London, 1972-77; founder, mng. dir., CEO Allied Arab Bank, London, 1977-83; founder, pub. The Internat. Who's Who of the Arab World, London, 1975-97; cons. Supermoney Svcs., London, 1998-99, Continental Exch. Ltd., London, 1997—; founder, mem. Inst. of Bankers, Jordan, 1965; banking lectr. Inst. of Banker, Aman, Jordan, 1965; founder, chmn. World of Islam Ency. Co., London, 1975—. Mem. devel. appeal com. Royal Opera Ho., London, 1980-84; dep. chair New Queen's Hall Orch., London, 1986—. Mem. Philharm. Soc. (life), The Soc. for Music Internat. (founder, chmn.), Inst. of Dirs. (life), Arab Club. Muslim. Avocations: painting collecting, vintage cars, classic music and Arabic classic music, horse riding. Office: Continental Exch Ltd, 77 Baker St, London W1M 1AH, England

SHULCLOPER, JOSÉ RUIZ, mathematician, researcher; b. Havana, Cuba, Oct. 9, 1948; s. Guillermo Raúl Ruiz Medina and Ana Olga Shulcloper-Yatveskaia; m. Matilde Galindo Sánchez, Mar. 9, 1993; children: Dalys Orlaida, Rasiel, Alejandro, Nephtalí. BS, U. Havana, 1972; PhD, State U. Moscow, 1978. Instr. U. Havana, 1971-72; prof. math. logic Havana U., 1972-74, prof. algebra, 1978-80; sr. rschr. Inst. Cybernetics, Math. and Physics, Havana, 1980—, vice-dir., 1985-92; dir. Dept. Math. Logic, Havana, 1972-74; invited prof. Autonomous Nat. U. Mexico, Mexico City, 1992-93, Worthy Autonomous U., Puebla, Mexico, 1993-94, Nat. Poly. Inst., Mexico City, 1996-99, invited rschr., 1994-96. Author: Lógica Polivalente, 1976, Introducción a la Teoría de Testores, 1995, Introducción al Reconocimiento de Patrones, 1995, Enfoque Lógico Combinatorio al Reconocimiento de Patrones. I Selección de Variables y Clasificación Supervisada, 1999. Active Com. for Revolution Def., 1962, Sci. Labor Union, 1971, Cuban Communist Party, 1980. Recipient Nat. Math. prize Cuban Math. and Computer Soc., 1986, Nat. Prize of Rsch., Cuban Acad. Scis., 1998, rsch. prize, Nat. Poly. Inst. Mexico, 1998; named Nat. Rschr. Level I, Nat. Rschrs. Sys. Mexico, 1996. Avocations: movies, sports. E-mail: recpat@cidet.icmf.inf.cu. Fax: 537 33-3373. Office: Inst Cybernetics Math Phys, E #309 e 15 y 13 Vedado, CP 10400 Havana City Cuba

SHULDINER, VICTOR ISRAILEVICH, geologist, researcher; b. St. Petersburg, Russia, May 28, 1931; s. Israil Borisovich and Eugenie Alexandrovna (Arkhipova) S.; m. Iraida Stepanovna Agafontseva, June 2, 1960 (dec. 1981); children: Alexander, Marina; m. Antonina Sergeevna Krichevskaya, Oct. 3, 1986. Grad. in Engring., Inst. Mines, St. Petersburg, 1954; Candidate of Sci., Acad. Sci., Novosibirsk, Russia, 1967; Doctor, Acad. Sci., Moscow, 1981. Sr. geologist Geol. Office, Chita, Russia, 1954-63; sr. sci. worker Far East Geol. Inst., Vladivostok, Russia, 1963-86; chief sci. worker Russian Geol. Inst., St. Petersburg, 1986—. Author: Petrology of Archean of Transbaikalia, 1969, Precambrian of North Pacific Belt, 1973, Precambrian Basement of Pacific Belt, 1982, The Basement of Pacific Active Margins, 1987. Home: Zagorodny 23 f 14, St Petersburg Russia Office: Russian Geol Inst, Sredny pr 74, 199106 St Petersburg Russia

SHULEPOV, SERGEI, physicist, researcher; b. Kiev, Ukraine, Apr. 4, 1965; s. Yurij Vladimirovich and Raisa Filimonovna (Semenichina) S.; m. Elena Vladimirovna Yurchnko, July 9, 1987; 1 child, Alexander. MSc, Kiev State U., 1989; Doctorate, Delft (Netherlands) U. Tech, 1997. Cert. physics and phys. chemistry. Rschr. Inst. Colloid and Water Chemistry, Kiev, 1989-92, Eindhoven (The Netherlands) U. Tech., 1997—. Contbr.: Interfacial; Forces and Fields: Theory and Applications, 1998; contbr. articles to profl. jours. Sgt. Russian Mil., 1984-86. Fax: 31-40-2445619. Office: Eindhoven Univ Tech, Postbus 513, 5600 MB Eindhoven The Netherlands

SHULEPOV, YURIY VLADIMIROVICH, physicist; b. Zaporojie, Ukraine, July 14, 1937; s. Vladimir Dmitrievich and Rajisa Andreevna (Onischenko) S.; m. Rajisa Filimonovna Semenikhina, Oct. 14, 1964; 1 child, Sergei. Diploma in Physics, Nat. U., Kiev, Ukraine, 1959, The Main Geophys. Observatory, St. Peterbourg, 1967, Inst. Theoretical Physics, Kiev, 1987. Engr. Inst. of Physics, Kiev, 1959, Inst. of Gen. and Inorganic Chemistry, Kiev, 1959-63; first rschr. Inst. of Hydrometeorology, Kiev, 1963-68; sr. rschr. Inst. of Collid Chemistry and Chemistry of Water, Kiev, 1968-93, head of lab. of mass transfer in membranes and dispersions, 1993—; leading scientist, cons. Inst. of Oncology Problems, Kiev, 1991-94, Interscientific Scientif and Tech. Ctr., Chernobyl, Ukraine, 1995; prof., cons. Interscientific Dept. Electrochemistry Energetics, Kiev, 1996—. Author: (book) Lattice Gas, 1981, (booklet) Phase transitions in the submonolayer adsorbed films, 1978; contbr. articles to profl. jours. Sgt. Acad. of Aviation Engrs., Kiev, 1954-56. Grantee European Colloid and Interface Soc. Conf., Montpellier, 1994, Barcelona, 1995. Mem. European Colloid and Interface Soc., Interscientific Dept. Electrochemistry of Energetics. Avocations: walking dog, table tennis. Office: Inst Colloid/Water Chem, Acad Sci/ Vernadsky Prospect, 252142 Kiev Ukraine

SHULER, JAMES MANNIE, health physicist; b. Orangeburg, S.C., Oct. 23, 1951; s. Ellie Grier Shuler and Gerdene Rickenbaker Shuler. BS in Botany, Clemson U., 1974; MA in Mgmt. and Supervision, Ctrl. Mich. U., 1977; MS in Radiation Sci., Georgetown U., 1988; MPA in Public Adminstrn., U. So. Calif., 1997, DPA in Public Adminstrn., 1999. Registered radiation protection technologist, environ. profl., environ. mgr.; cert. hazard control mgr., hazardous materials mgr., environ. trainer transp. of hazardous materials and waste occupl. health and safety. Health physics technician Allied-General Nuclear Svcs., Barnwell, S.C., 1975-79; supr. health physics Chem-Nuclear Sys., Inc., Barnwell, 1979, customer and compliance rep., 1979; radioactive materials enforcement specialist U.S. Dept. Transp., Washington, 1979-81, 83-88; radwaste/transp. specialist Applied Tech. of Barnwell, Inc., 1981-83; phys. scientist U.S. Dept. Energy, Germantown, Md., 1988-89; health physicist U.S. Dept. Energy, Aiken, S.C., 1989-93; from sr. health physicist to phys. scientist U.S. Dept. Energy, Washington, 1993-96, health physicist, 1996—; assoc. staff instr. U.S. Dept. Transp./Transp. Safety Inst., Oklahoma City, 1981-89; vis. instr. Georgetown U., Washington, 1988-89. Contbr. over 100 articles to profl. jours. and tech. publs. Mem. ASTM (sect. 6 leader radiation protection methods verification 1993), Nat. Environ. Tng. Assn., Assn. of MBA Execs., Am. Nuclear Soc., Health Physics Soc. (environ. radiation sect., govt. sect. 1993—). E-mail: James.Shuler@hq.doe.gov. Home: 12835 Locbury Cir Apt I Germantown MD 20874-3858 Office: US Dept Energy Em-5 Gtn Washington DC 20585-0001

SHULER, JON EMMETT, securities industry professional; b. Aiken, S.C., Sept. 21, 1946; s. Cyril Ovierre and Elizabeth Carolina (Smith) S.; m. Virginia Rose Harris, Aug. 1, 1981; children: Jon Emmett Jr., Kline Martin. BA in Econs., Clemson U., 1968; MBA, U. S.C., 1970. CFP. Broker J.C. Bradford & Co., Spartanburg, S.C., 1972-81, br. mgr., 1981-88; br. mgr. Raymond James & Assocs., Spartanburg, S.C., 1988-94; owner, pres., reg. investment adv. Wealth Mgmt. Assocs., Inc., 1994—. Co-author: Getting to the Heart of the Matter, 1999. Bd. dirs. Habitat for Humanity, Spartanburg, 1990; mem. ARC State Pub. Support Com., Columbia, S.C., 1993; trustee Spartanburg Day Sch., 1997 . Mem. Rotary (pres. North Spartanburg chpt. 1990, Paul Harris fellow 1989), Soc. Mayflower Descendants. Republican. Presbyterian. Avocations: snow skiing, antique collecting, woodworking.

SHULGA, VLADIMIR IVANOVICH, physicist, researcher; b. Artjomovsk, Krasnojarsky, Kraj, Mar. 9, 1944; s. Ivan Ivanovich Shulga and Serafima Terent'evna (Ershova) Mikhailova; m. Tamara Andreevna Antonjuk, July 29, 1972 (div. Dec. 1989); 1 child, Oksana. MS, Moscow State U., 1968, PhD, 1971. Engr. Inst. Nuc. Physics, Moscow State U., 1971-72, minor sci. rschr., 1972-74, sr. sci. rschr., 1974-93, leading sci. rschr., 1993—. Mem. editl. bd. Internat. Jour. Radiation Effects and Defects in Solids, 1997—; contbr. articles to profl. jours. Mem. Bohmische Phys. Soc. Avocations: travel, photography. Home: Domodedovskaja 38-1-180, 115582 Moscow Russia Office: Inst Nuc Physics Moscow U, Vorob'evi Gori, 119899 Moscow Russia

SHULGINA, GALINA IVANOVNA, neuro physiologist; b. Kerch, Krim, Russia, July 28, 1932; d. Ivan and Anna Konstantinovna (Orlova) Pheodorov; m. Igor Shulgin, May 10, 1956 (div. June 1958); 1 child, Olga; m. Nicolai Nicolaevich Parphenov, Dec. 3, 1958; 1 child, Dmitry. M in Physiology, Moscow State U.; cand. sci., Russian Acad. Scis., 1962, DSc in Physiology, 1978. Sr. asst. Inst. Occupl. Hygiene Acad. Med. Scis., Moscow, 1955-58; from jr. rschr. to sr. rschr. Russian Acad. Scis., Moscow, 1960-88, leading rschr., 1988—. Author: Bioelektrical Activity of Brain and Conditioned Reflex, 1978 (1st prize 1979); co-author: Biologyy of Learning and Memory, 1990 (E.A. Asratyans prize 1991); co-author, editor: Neurocomputer as the Basis of Intellectual Computers, 1993 (1st prize 1994); contbr. articles to profl. jours. IBRO. Avocations: photography, swimming, kayaking. Office: Russian Acad Scis, Butlerova St 5A, 117865 Moscow Russia

SHULL, CLIFFORD G., physicist, educator; b. Pitts., Sept. 23, 1915; s. David H. and Daisy I. (Bistline) S.; m. Martha-Nuel Summer, June 19, 1941; children: John C., Robert D., William F. BS, Carnegie Inst. Tech., 1937; PhD, NYU, 1941. Rsch. physicist Texas Co., 1941-46; chief physicist Oak Ridge Nat. Lab., 1946-55; prof. physics MIT, 1955-86, prof. emeritus, 1986—; Chmn. vis. com. Brookhaven Nat. Lab., 1961-62; chmn. vis. com. Nat. Bur. Standard reactor, 1972-73; chmn. vis. com. solid state div. Oak Ridge Nat. Lab., 1974-75; chmn. policy com. Nat. Small-Angle-Scattering Center, 1978-81. Contbr. articles to profl. jours. Recipient Merit award Alumni Assn. of Carnegie Mellon U., 1968, Humboldt Sr. U.S. Scientist award, 1979, Disting. Scientist award Gov. of Tenn., 1986, Gregori Aminoff prize, 1993, Ilja Frank prize, 1993, Nobel prize in Physics, 1994. Fellow Am. Phys. Soc. (Buckley prize 1956, chmn. solid state physics divsn. 1962-63), AAAS, Am. Acad. Arts and Scis., N.Y. Acad. Scis., Nat. Acad. Scis. (vice chmn. panel on neutron sci. 1977); mem. Am. Crystallographic Assn., Rsch. Soc. Am., Sigma Xi, Tau Beta Pi, Phi Kappa Phi, Phi Beta Kappa. Home: 4 Wingate Rd Lexington MA 02421-4516

SHULL, HARRISON, chemist, educator; b. Princeton, N.J., Aug. 17, 1923; s. George Harrison and Mary (Nicholl) S.; m. Jeanne Louise Johnson, 1948 (div. 1962); children: James Robert (dec.), Kathy, George Harrison, Holly; m. Wil Joyce Bentley Long, 1962; children: Warren Michael Long, Jeffery Mark Long, Stanley Martin, Sarah Ellen. A.B., Princeton U., 1943; Ph.D., U. Calif. at Berkeley, 1948. Assoc. chemist U.S. Naval Research Lab., 1943-45; asst. prof. Iowa State U., 1949-54; mem. faculty Ind. U., 1955-79, research prof., 1961-79, dean Grad. Sch., 1965-72, vice chancellor for research and devel., 1972-76, dir. Research Computing Center, 1959-63, acting chmn. chemistry dept., 1965-66, acting dean arts and scis., 1969-70, acting dean faculties, 1974; mem. faculty, provost, v.p. acad. affairs Rensselaer Poly. Inst., 1979-82; chancellor U. Colo., Boulder, 1982-85; prof. dept. chemistry U. Colo., 1982-88; provost Naval Postgrad. Sch., 1988-95; asst. dir. rsch., quantum chemistry group Uppsala (Sweden) U., 1958-59; vis. prof. Washington U., St. Louis, 1960, U. Colo., 1963; founder, supr. Quantum Chemistry Program Exchange, 1962-79; chmn. subcom. molecular structure and spectroscopy NRC, 1958-63; chmn. Fulbright selection com. chemistry, 1963-67; mem. adv. com. Office Sci. Personnel, 1957-60; chmn. First Gordon Research Conf. Theoretical Chemistry, 1962; mem. com. survey chemistry Nat. Acad. Sci., 1964-65; mem. adv. panel chemistry NSF, 1964-67; mem. adv. panel Office Computer Activities, 1967-70, cons. chem. information program, 1965-71, mem. adv. com. for research, 1974-76; mem. vis. com. chemistry Brookhaven Nat. Lab., 1967-70; mem. adv. com. Chem. Abstracts Service, 1971-74; dir. Storage Tech. Corp., 1983-99; chief of Naval Ops. Exec. Panel, 1984-88. Assoc. editor: Jour. Chem. Physics, 1952-54; editorial adv. bd.: Spectrochimica Acta, 1957-63, Internat. Jour. Quantum Chemistry, 1967—, Proc. NAS, 1976-81; contbr. articles to profl. jours. Trustee Argonne U. Assn., 1970-75, Asso. Univs., Inc., 1973-76, U. Rsch. Assn., 1984-89, Inst. Defense Analysis, 1984-96. Served as ensign USNR, 1945. NRC postdoctoral fellow phys. scis. U. Chgo., 1948-49; Guggenheim fellow U. Uppsala, 1954-55; NSF sr. postdoctoral fellow, 1968-69; Sloan research fellow, 1956-58. Fellow Am. Acad. Arts and Scis. (v.p. 1976-83, chmn. Midwest Ctr. 1976-79), Am. Phys. Soc.; mem. AAAS, Nat. Acad. Scis. (com. on sci. and pub. policy 1969-72, coun., exec. com. 1971-74, chmn. U.S.-USSR sci. policy subgroup for fundamental rsch. 1973-81, naval studies bd. 1974-79, 96—, chmn. Commn. on Human Resources, 1977-81, nominating com. 1978), Am. Chem. Soc., Royal Swedish Acad. Scis. (fgn. mem.), Royal Acad. Arts and Scis. Uppsala (corr. mem.), Cosmos Club (Washington), Old Capitol Club (Monterey), Phi Beta Kappa, Sigma Xi, Phi Lambda Upsilon. Office: Naval Postgrad Sch Monterey CA 93943

SHULMAN, ALON HAMILTON, multimedia entertainment entrepreneur; b. London, Sept. 9, 1970; s. Neville Lionel and Emma (Broide) S. BA with honors, London U., 1993. Dir. Goodfoot Prodns., London, 1991-96; mng. dir. World Famous Ltd., London, 1992—; CEO Universe, 1998—; dir. The Youth Branding Consultancy, 1991—; CEO Universe TV, MD Chris Eubank Inc. Author: The Style Bible—An A-Z Guide to Youth Culture, 1999. Amb. Internat. Fund for Animal Welfare. Mem. Mensa. E-mail: alon@universe.co.uk. Office: 4 George's House, 15 Hanover Square, London W1R 9AJ, England

SHULMAN, MARK RUSSELL, lawyer; b. Morristown, N.J., Aug. 7, 1963; s. Robert Gerson and Sara Lee (Deutsch) S. BA, Yale U., 1985; M in studies, Oxford U., U.K., 1986; PhD, U. Calif. Berkeley, 1990; JD, Columbia U., 1999, Columbia U., 1999. Advanced rsch. fellow U.S. Naval War Coll., Newport, R.I., 1989-99; Olin postdoctoral fellow Yale Internat. Security Program, New Haven, 1990-91; lectr. history dept. Yale U., New Haven, 1991-94; Bradley fellow Georgetown U., Washington, 1994-95; fellow Nat. Strategy Info. Ctr., Washington, 1994-95; prof. conflict and change Air War Coll., Montgomery, Ala., 1995-96; assoc. Debevoise & Plimpton, N.Y.; lectr. in law Columbia U. Sch. Law. Author: Navalism and Emergence of American Sea Powers 1882-1893, 1995; co-editor: Laws of the War, 1994; editor: An Admiral's Yarn, 1999. Recipient MacArthur Faculty grants Yale U., 1991-93, Smith Richardson Found. grant, 1994-95. Democrat. Avocations: jogging, hiking.

SHUL'PIN, GEORGIY BORISOVICH, chemist; b. Moscow, July 22, 1946; s. Boris Ivanovich and Olga Pavlovna (Romanova) S.; m. Lidia Sergeyevna Polkovnikova, Feb. 4, 1978; children: Svyatoslav, Pavel. MS in Chemistry, Moscow State U., 1969; PhD in Organoelement Compounds, Acad. Scis. USSR, 1975. Head of lab. metal complex catalysis Inst. Chem. Physics, Moscow, 1992—. Contbr. articles to profl. jours., books. Home: Ul Znamenskie Sadki, 7-2-173, 113216 Moscow Russia Office: NN Semenov Inst Chem Phys, Russ Acad Sci ul Kosygina 4, 117977 Moscow Russia

SHULTZ, DELRAY FRANKLIN (LUCKY SHULTZ), management consultant; b. South Bend, Ind., Apr. 4, 1948; s. Jack Raymond and Georgina Martha (Johnston) S.; m. Catherine Elizabeth Yontz, June 6, 1970; children: Jeremy Frank, Eric Bruce, Jon Karl. BS, USAF Acad., 1970; MS, Air U., 1978. Commd. 2d lt. USAF, 1970, advanced through grades to capt., 1973; navigator USAF, Anchorage, 1972-77; adminstrv. contracting officer USAF, L.A., 1978-81; mgr. purchasing, contracts supr. BP Exploration, Anchorage, 1981-92; internal cons. BP Exploration, Bogotá, Colombia, 1992-93; mgr. contracts, internal cons. Alaska Petroleum Contractors, Anchorage, 1994-97; mgr. assurance and devel., internal cons. Natchiq Inc., Anchorage, 1997—; owner Pathways Leadership, Alaska, 1999—, Seattle, 2000—; owner Buckley W., Seattle, 2000—; adj. prof. U. Alaska, Anchorage, 1988-96. Bd. mem., vice chair bd. dirs. Family Connection, Inc., Anchorage, 1981-84; dir., bd. elders Bethany Christian Cmty., Anchorage, 1982-93; del. Rep. Party of Alaksa, Anchorage, 1988, 96. Named Outstanding Young Men of Am., U.S. Jr. C. of C., 1978; recipient Silver medal Buckley Sch. Pub. Spkg., 1997. Mem. Nat. Contract Mgmt. Assn., Nat. Assn. Purchasing Mgrs., Am. Soc. for Quality. Avocations: commercial pilot, public speaker, personal development teacher, musician. Home: 13495 Baywind Dr Anchorage AK 99516-3451

SHULTZ, GEORGE PRATT, former government executive, economics educator; b. N.Y.C., Dec. 13, 1920; s. Birl E. and Margaret Lennox (Pratt) S.; children: Margaret Ann Shultz Tilsworth, Kathleen Pratt Shultz Jorgensen, Peter Milton, Barbara Lennox Shultz White, Alexander George; m. Charlotte Mailliard, Aug. 15, 1997. BA in Econs., Princeton U., 1942; PhD in Indsl. Econs., MIT, 1949; Hon. degree, Yeshiva U., U. Tel Aviv, Technion-Israel Inst. Tech., Keio U., Tokyo, Brandeis U., U. Notre Dame, Princeton U., Loyola U., U. Pa., U. Rochester, Carnegie-Mellon U., Baruch Coll., Northwestern U., Tblisi State U. Mem. faculty M.I.T., 1949-57; assoc. prof. indsl. relations MIT, 1955-57; prof. indsl. relations Grad. Sch. Bus., U. Chgo., 1957-68; dean sch. Grad. Sch. Bus. U. Chgo., 1968-69, fellow Ctr. for Advanced Study in Behavioral Scis., 1968-69; U.S. sec. labor, 1969-70; dir. Office Mgmt. and Budget, 1970-72; U.S. sec. treasury, also asst. to Pres., 1972-74; chmn. Council on Econ. Policy, East-West Trade Policy com.; exec. v.p. Bechtel Corp., San Francisco, 1974-75, pres., 1975-77; vice chmn. Bechtel Corp., 1977-81; also dir.; pres. Bechtel Group, Inc., 1981-82; prof. mgmt. and pub. policy Stanford U., 1974-82, prof. internat. econs., 1989-91, prof. emeritus, 1991—; chmn. Pres. Reagan's Econ. Policy Adv. Bd., 1981-82; U.S. sec. of state, 1982-89; disting. fellow Hoover Instn., Stanford, 1989—; bd. dirs. Charles Schwab & Co., Bechtel Group, Inc., Infrastructureworld.com; mem. GM Corp. Adv. Coun., Gilead Scis. Bd., Unext.COM Bd.; chmn. J.P. Morgan Internat. Coun.; chmn. adv. coun. Inst. Internat. Studies, 1990-98, Calif. Gov.'s Econ. Policy Adv. Bd., 1995-98. Author: Pressures on Wage Decisions, 1951, (with Charles A. Myers) The Dynamics of a Labor Market, 1951, (with John R. Coleman) Labor Problems: Cases and Readings, 1953, (with T.L. Whisler) Management Organization and the Computer, 1960, (with Arnold R. Weber) Strategies for the Displaced Worker, 1966, (with Robert Z. Aliber) Guidelines, Informal Controls and the Market Place, 1966, (with Albert Rees) Workers and Wages in the Urban Labor Market, 1970, Leaders and Followers in an Age of Ambiguity, 1975, (with Kenneth W. Dam) Economic Policy Beyond the Headlines, 1977, 2d edition, 1998, Turmoil and Triumph: My Years as Secetary of State, 1993; also articles, chpts. in books, reports, and essays. Served to capt. USMCR, 1942-45. Mem. Am. Econ. Assn., Indsl. Relations Research Assn. (pres. 1968), Nat. Acad. Arbitrators. Office: Stanford U Hoover Instn Stanford CA 94305-6010

SHULTZ, JEANNE MARIE, training director, workforce improvement analyst; b. Detroit, Mich., Oct. 27, 1954; d. Raymond Vincent and Helen Frances (Towne) S. AA, Wayne State U., 1975, BA, 1978. Catering, sales dir. Maxwell's Plum, San Francisco, 1982-84; sales rep. Heath Sign Co., Hayward, Calif., 1984-87; sales assoc. Cornish & Carey Real Estate, San Jose, Calif., 1987-88, Fox & Carskadon/ Better Homes & Gardens, Danville, Calif., 1988-95; sales, telesales and conf. mgr. Coun on Edn. in Mgmt., Walnut Creek, Calif., 1995-98; tng. dir. No. Calif. Tng. Coun., Monterey, Calif., 1998—; workforce improvement analyst Pacific Grove, Calif., 1998—; advisor, cons. Internat. Inst. of Rsch., London, 1995-97; assoc. Calif. Dept. Real Estate, 1987—. Author: (book) Telesales Encyclopedia, 1996, (tng. manual) Complete Sales Successes, 1985, rev. edit. 1990; (short story) in Ladies Home Jour.; contbg. editor Law Update Monthly; publisher, editor: (newsletter) Lines of Fortune, 1995-98; radio talk show host, prodr. Sta. KNRY/KIEZ, Monterey, Calif. Tech. advisor Jr. Achievement U.S., N.Y.C., 1985-88; chair Bay Area Women in Bus., San Francisco, 1986-90; vol. Battered Women's Alternative, Contra Costa County, 1995-98, Monterey County Vols., 1988—, Friends of the Aquarium, Monterey, 1998; comm. coord City of Monterey, 1998; mem. Fairway Ptnrs. Salvation Army, Monterey County, Calif., 1998—. Mem. AAUW, Del Monte Women's Club, Toastmasters Group, Alliance on Aging Monterey County (sec.). Avocations: golf, golf tournament coord., storytelling, martial arts, rsch. Office: No Calif Tng Ctr 651 Cannery Row Monterey CA 93940-1035

SHULTZ, JOHN DAVID, lawyer; b. L.A., Oct. 9, 1939; s. Edward Patterson and Jane Elizabeth (Taylor) S.; m. Joanne Person, June 22, 1968; children: David Taylor, Steven Matthew. Student, Harvard Coll., 1960-61; BA, U. Ariz., 1964; JD, Boalt Hall, U. Calif., Berkeley, 1967. Bar: N.Y. 1968, Calif. 1978. Assoc. Cadwalader, Wickersham & Taft, N.Y.C., 1968-77; ptnr. Lawler, Felix & Hall, L.A., 1977-83, mem. exec. com., chmn. planning com., co-chmn. recruiting and hiring com.; ptnr. Morgan, Lewis & Bockius, L.A., 1983—, chmn. mgmt. com., mem. lateral entry com.; chmn. profl. evaluation com., chmn. bus. plan com., chmn. practice devel. com., chmn. recruiting com. Trustee St. Thomas Ch., N.Y.C., 1969-72, Shore Acres Point Corp., Mamaroneck, N.Y., 1975-77; mem. adv. bd. Internat. and Comparative Law Center, Southwestern Legal Found., 1981—; active Practicing Law Inst. Adv. Bd., Corp. and Securities Law, 1992—. Mem. ABA, Assn. Bar City N.Y., State Bar Calif., N.Y. State Bar Assn., Jonathan Club (L.A.), Phi Delta Phi, Sigma Chi. Episcopalian. Office: Morgan Lewis & Bockius LLP 300 S Grand Ave Ste 22 Los Angeles CA 90071-3109

SHUM, PING, educator; b. Chang Chun, Jilin, China, Sept. 16, 1968; s. Tai Koi Sin and Yim Suen; m. May King Lun Wong, Jan. 17, 1997; 1 child, Leo Chun Wa. B in Engring. with honors, Birmingham (Eng.) U., 1991, PhD,

1995. Hon. postdoctoral rsch. fellow U. Birmingham, 1995; rsch. fellow City U. of Hong Kong, 1997-99; asst. prof. Nanyang Tech. U., Singapore, 1999—; vis. rsch. fellow U. Hong Kong, 1996-97. Recipient India chpt. IEEE EDS/MTTS Best Paper award, 1998. Mem. Internat. Soc. for Optical Engring. (com. mem. Hong Kong chpt. 1998-99). Avocations: basketball, reading. Fax: 65 7920415. E-mail: pshum@technologist.com. Home: Flat 1309 13th Fl, Chun King Hse King Shing Ct, Fanling Hong Kong China Office: Sch Elec & Electronic Eng, Nanyang Tech U, Singapore China

SHUMAKE, JAMES MARTIN, emergency medicine physician; b. St. Louis, Mar. 31, 1957; s. Lindell Paul and Modesta Shumake; m. Denice Ann Craig, Apr. 12, 1986 (div. July 1987); m. Tori Kei, Nov. 5, 1994; 1 child, Elizabeth Mei Rose. BS in Biology, Northeast Mo. Sate U., 1980; DO, Kirksville Coll. Osteo. Med., 1984. Emergency medicine physician NES, 1985—, HMI, 1991—, EmCare, 1999—; dir. emergency medicine St. Joseph's Hosp., Centerville, Iowa, 1995—. Mem. Am. Osteo. Assn., Am. coll. Osteo. Emergency Medicine. Avocations: cycling, tennis, jet skiing. Home: 604 N Florence St Kirksville MO 63501-3019

SHUMAN, EARL STANLEY, songwriter, music publisher; b. Boston, Aug. 2, 1923; s. Benjamin Morris and Mildred Judith (Kaplan) S.; m. Margaret Stein, Nov. 25, 1956; children: Cathy Elizabeth, Daniel James, Steven Lewis. BA, Yale U., 1947. Owner, pres. Earl/Peg Music Cos., N.Y.C., 1957—; pub. BMI, ASCAP, N.Y.C., 1977—. Composer (lyric writer) popular songs including Seven Lonely Days, 1953 (Country and Western award 1970), Hey There Lonely Girl, 1970 (Gold record), Banjo's Back in Town, Caterina, Clinging Vine, Close to Cathy, Hotel Happiness, Left Right Out of Your Heart, Most people Get Married, My Shy Violet, The River, Starry-Eyed, Theme For a Dream, Young New Mexican Puppeteer; composer (musicals) Secret Life of Walter Mitty, 1964 (award 1965), (country song) Leaves are the Tears of Autumn, 1968 (Country and Western award 1969), (TV theme) Confidence/NFL-CBS), 1967-76; pub. Bat Out of Hell album, 1977 (platinum award 1979). Capt. USMCR, 1943-46, 50-51. Mem. ASCAP. Avocations: music, baseball. Home and Office: 111 E 88th St Apt 3B New York NY 10128-1158

SHUMAN, GEOFFREY, aerospace scientist; b. Folkestone, Kent, Eng., Oct. 12, 1952; s. Jack and Kathleen Olive (West) S. BA with honors, Sussex U., 1974. Surveyor Civil Engring., Cambridge, Eng., 1976-79; computer sys. analyst Brit. Aerospace, Eng., 1980-82; attache de direction AECMA, Paris, 1982-85; programme mgr. Brit. Aerospace, Paris, 1985-91; dep. dir. European Assn. Aerospace Industries, Brussels, 1991-94, dep. sec. gen., dir. policy, 1994-97; air safety expert European Commn. Transport Directorate, Brussels, 1997—. Mem. Centre des études Politique et Strategique Paris. Avocations: jazz saxophone and flute, skiing, tennis. Home: 95 Ave des Coccinelles, 1000 Brussels Belgium

SHUMOVSKY, ALEXANDER STANISLAW, physics educator; b. Moscow, Jan. 20, 1945; s. Stanislaw Anton and Tamara Georgia (Haritonenko) S.; m. Natalia Eugenia Kravtsov, Sept. 21, 1970; children: Alexander Boris, Daria Alexandre. MS in Physics, Moscow State U., 1969, PhD in Physics, 1971. Scientific researcher Moscow State U., 1972-81; sr. sci. researcher Joint Inst. Nuclear Rsch., Dubna, Russia, 1981-87, head quantum optics divsn., 1987-95; prof. physics Bilkent U., Ankara, Turkey, 1992—. Author: Lectures on Phase Transactions, 1990, Mathematical Methods on Statistical Mechanics of Model Systems, 1993. Mem. Am. Math. Soc., Am. Phys. Soc., N.Y. Acad. Scis., Russian Optical Soc. Avocations: history, art. Home: Leningrad Ave 69/107, 125057 Moscow Russia Office: Bilkent U, Physics Dept, 06533 Ankara Turkey

SHUNGU, DIKOMA CYRILLE, radiology educator; b. Wembo-Nyama, Congo Republic, Nov. 15, 1958; s. Wembi and Lutshumba Louise S. BA, Southwestern U., Georgetown, Tex., 1981; PhD, U. Ark., 1986. Postdoctoral rsch. fellow Milton S. Hershey Med. Ctr. of Pa. State U., Hershey, 1986-87, U. Fla. Health Sci. Ctr., Gainesville, 1987-89; postdoctoral rsch. fellow Johns Hopkins U. Sch. of Medicine, Balt., 1989-92, rsch. assoc., 1992-93; asst. prof. radiology Columbia U., N.Y.C., 1993—; grant rev. NIH, Bethesda; reviewer Magnetic Resonance in Medicine, Rockville, Md. Rsch. grantee NINDS/NIH, Bethesda, 1986, 1999, 2000. Mem. Internat. Soc. for Magnetic Resonance in Medicine, AAAS. Avocations: classical guitar, Baroque recorder, photography. Office: Columbia U 710 W 168th St New York NY 10032-2603

SHUR, DMITRY, physicist; b. Kiev, Ukraine, Dec. 17, 1970; arrived in Israel, 1993; s. Vladimir and Ana (Krichman) S. MSc, Moscow Inst. Aircraft Tech., 1992; PhD, Tel Aviv U., 1998. Rsch. asst. Tel Aviv U., 1994-98; physicist Applied Materials Israel, 1998—. Home: 10/8 Shenkar st ent 2, 58261 Holon Israel

SHURBAJI, M. SALAH, pathologist; b. Cairo, 1957; came to U.S., 1984; BS with distinction, Am. U. Beirut, 1979, MS, 1981, MD with distinction, 1984. Diplomate Am. Bd. Pathology; cert. cytopathologist, anatomic and clin. pathologist; lic. physician Md., Tenn., Mich. Intern Am. U. Beirut Med. Ctr., 1983-84; resident pathology Johns Hopkins Hosp., Balt., 1984-87, resident dept. lab. medicine, 1987-89; clin. fellow dept. pathology Johns Hopkins U. Sch. Medicine, Balt., 1984-89, rsch. fellow dept. pathology, 1989-90; asst. prof. pathology East Tenn. State U., Johnson City, 1990-94, assoc. prof. pathology, 1994-2000; prof. pathology, 2000—; staff pathologist Univ. Physicians Practice Group, Johnson City, 1990—; staff pathologist Vets. Affairs Med. Ctr., Johnson City, 1990—, acting chief pathology and lab. medicine svc., 1993-94, chief pathology and lab. medicine svc., 1994—. Contbr. articles to profl. jours. Fellow Am. Soc. Clin. Pathologists, Coll. Am. Pathologists; mem. A.P. Stout Soc. Surg. Pathologists, Am. Soc. Cytopathology, U.S. and Can. Acad. Pathology, Papanicolaou Soc. Cytopathology, Internat. Soc. Urologic Pathology, Sigma Xi, Alpha Omega Alpha. Achievements include contribution to understanding of certain factors that affect the prognosis of neoplasms especially prostate cancer. Office: East Tenn State U Coll Med Dept Pathology PO Box 70568 Johnson City TN 37614-1707

SHURIN, AARON BEN-ZION, rabbi, Judaic studies educator; b. Rieteve, Lithuania, Sept. 3, 1914; came to U.S., 1940; s. Moshe and Ruth (Davidowitz) S.; m. Ella Rivkin, July 2, 1944; children: Jacob, Joseph, David. Student, Rabbinical Coll. Telz and Ponvez, Lithuania, 1930-36, Rabbinical Coll. Hebron, Jerusalem, 1936-40, Rabbinical Coll. Lomze, Petach Tikvah, Israel, 1936-40, Yeshivah U., 1940-44. Ordained rabbi, 1939. Rabbi Congregation Anshe Slutzk, N.Y.C., 1942-46, Congregation Toras Moshe, Bklyn., 1946-48; prin. New Hebrew Sch., N.Y.C., 1949-56; prof. Judaic studies Stern Coll. Yeshiva U., 1941-42, 66—. Columnist (bi-weekly) Jewish Daily Forward, 1944—; author: Keshet Giborim, 1964, Bein Yehudai Arzot Habrit, 1981, Keshet Giborim, Book II, 1995; assoc. editor: Edenu, 1942; contbr. numerous articles to various publs. Recipient State of Israel Bonds 25th Anniversary award, 1975, award Alumni Assn. of Lomze, 1975, Chief Rabbi Kook award Religious Zionists of Am., 1980, Ponivez Yeshivah award, 1985, Kether Torah award Ezras Torah, 1994. Mem. Union of Orthodox Rabbis of U.S. and Can. (vice chmn. exec. com. 1960-80), Rabbinical Coun. of Am. (exec. bd. 1985-89, award 1985), Rabbinical Bd. Flatbush (v.p. 1994—), Yiddish Writers Union (v.p. 1970—). Home: 2176 New York Ave Brooklyn NY 11210-5426 Office: 245 Lexington Ave New York NY 10016-4605

SHURKIN, LORNA GREENE, writer, publicist; b. N.Y.C., Mar. 5, 1944; d. Morris and Rita Rose (Cohen) Greene; m. Joel N. Shurkin, July 4, 1966 (div. Nov. 1981); children: Jonathan Greene, Michael Robert. BA, Bklyn. Coll., CUNY, 1964; postgrad., NYU, 1965-66; fundraising cert., U. Pa., 1997. English tchr. N.Y.C. Schs., 1963-64; asst. to articles editor Womans Day mag., N.Y.C., 1964-66; reporter, columnist News-Herald, Willoughby, Ohio, 1966-68; reporter, reviewer Phila. Inquirer, Reuters and others, 1974-76; pub. rels. rep., editor Thomas Jefferson U., Phila., 1976-79; account exec. Sommers/Rosen Pub. Relations, Phila., 1979-81; dir. pub. relations Swarthmore (Pa.) Coll., 1981-94; writer, publicist, fund raiser St. Davids, Pa., 1995-99; corr. Delaware County Daily Times, 1998-2000; dir. media rels. Dickinson (Pa.) Coll., 2000—. Advt. mgr. STAGE: A Theater Monthly, 1997-2000. Pub. rels. coord. Pa. Resources Coun., 1999; dem. cand. Radnor Twp. (Pa.) Sch. Bd., 1987; mem. Radnor Dem. Com., 1988-99, vice chair, 1998-99: v.p. Footlighters Theater, Berwyn, Pa., 1985-88; ofcl. pronouncer Delaware County (Pa.) Spelling Bee, 1986-2000; mem. adv. bd. Ea. Pa. Theater Coun., 1986-2000; twp. rep. Dem. County Coun., 1994, ; bd. dirs. Friends of the Anthony Wayne Theatre, 1995-98, Anti-Violence Partnership Phila., 1989-97. Mem. Del. County Press Club (bd. dirs. 1991-99, program chmn. 1991-93), Nat. Writers Union, Coll. and Univ. Pub. Rels. Assn. Pa., Coun. for Advancement and Support of Edn., Coun. Advancement & Support Edn. Jewish. Home: 604 Devonshire Dr Carlisle PA 17013-3604

SHURTLEFF, AKIKO AOYAGI, artist, consultant; b. Tokyo, Jan. 24, 1950; d. Kinjiro and Fumiyo (Sugata) Aoyagi; m. William Roy Shurtleff, Mar. 10, 1977 (div. 1995); 1 child, Joseph Aoyagi. Grad., Women's Coll. Art, Tokyo, 1971; student, Acad. Art, San Francisco, 1991-92. Fashion designer, illustrator Marimura Co. and Hayakawa Shoji, Inc., Tokyo, 1970-72; co-founder, art dir. Soyfoods Ctr. consulting svcs., Lafayette, Calif., 1976-94; freelance illustrator, graphic designer; lectr. U.S. Internat. Christian U., Tokyo, 1977, Japanese Tofu Mfrs. Conv., Osaka, 1978; presenter cooking demonstrations, tchr. cooking classes. Co-author, illustrator: The Book of Tofu, 1975, The Book of Miso, 1975, The Book of Kudzu, 1977, Tofu and Soymilk Prodduction, 1979, The Book of Tempeh, 1979, Miso Production, 1979, Tempeh Production, 1980; illustrator: Spirulina (L. Switzer), 1982, The Book of Shiatsu-The Healing Art of Finger Pressure (S. Goodman), 1990, Staying Healthy with Nutrition (E. Haas), 1992, Culinary Treasures of Japan (by John and Jan Belleme), 1992, Yookoso, An Invitation to Contemporary Japanese, Vols. 1 and 2 (Hasu-Hiko Tohsaku), 1994-95, Blue Collar and Beyond (Yana Parker), 1995, Damn Good Ready to Go Resumes, 1995, Homework (Peter Jeswald), 1995, Vegetarian's A to Z Guide to Fruits and Vegetables (Kathleen Robinson with Pete Luckett), 1996, Hubert Keller's Cuisine, 1996, Doctor Generic Will See You Now (Oscar London), 1996, Everyday Pediatrics for Parents (Elmer R. Grossman, M.D.), 1996, Angels in My Kitchen-Devine Dessert Recipes (Caryl Westwood), 1997. Avocations: walking, designing greeting cards, running, dancing. Office: PO Box 443 Lafayette CA 94549-0443

SHUSHKEWICH, KENNETH WAYNE, structural engineer; b. Winnipeg, Man., Sept. 22, 1952; m. Valdine Cuffe, Sept. 28, 1980. BSCE, U. Man., Winnipeg, 1974; MS in Structural Engring., U. Calif., Berkeley, 1975; PhD in Structural Engring., U. Alta., Edmonton, Can., 1985. Engr. Wardrop and Assocs., Winnipeg, 1974-78, Preconsult Can., Montreal, Que., 1978-80; prof. U. Alta., 1981-85, U. Man., 1985-87; engr. T.Y. Lin Internat., San Francisco, 1988-90, H.J. Degenkolb Assocs., San Francisco, 1990-92, Ben C. Gerwick, Inc., San Francisco, 1993-94, J. Muller Internat., Chgo., 1994-95, T.Y. Lin Internat., San Francisco, 1995—; mem. bridge design com., prestressed concrete com. ASCE-Am. Concrete Inst. Prin. works include design of prestressed concrete segmental bridges, seismic strengthening of San Francisco Ferry Building damaged in Loma Prieta earthquake, seismic retrofit of Presidio Viaduct in San Francisco; design mgr. for long-span west approach bridge of Northumberland Strait Crossing in Can.; contbr. articles to profl. jours. Recipient award for design of Vierendeel truss bridge, Man. Design Inst., 1977. Mem. ASCE, Am. Concrete Inst., Prestressed Concrete Inst., Internat. Assn. Bridge and Structural Engrs. Office: PO Box 2590 San Francisco CA 94126-2590

SHUSHURIN, GREGORY SERGEEVICH, publishing company executive, consultant; b. Moscow, Nov. 17, 1961; s. Sergey Philippovich Shushurin and Nora Grigorievna Gurvich; m. Alla Yurievna Mankova, Jan. 11, 1992; 1 child, Philip. M, Moscow State U., 1983. Rsch. scientist Inst. Control Scis., Moscow, 1983-91; head internat. dept. Inst. Control Scis., 1991-94; v.p. NFQ, Moscow, 1994-99; dep. gen. dir. SPN-GRANAT, Moscow, 1998—; advt. cons. SPN-GRANAT, 1998—; pub. Where Moscow Mag., 1995—. Home: Pr Vernadskogo 117-94, 117576 Moscow Russia

SHUSTER, SAM, dermatology educator, consultant, researcher; b. London, Aug. 24, 1927; s. Sidney and Anne (Feldman) S.; m. Rosemary Roberts, July 13, 1951; children: David, Gabriel, Saskia. MB, BS, U. Coll. London, 1951, PhD, 1956. Resident various hosps., London, 1951-52, 1955-57; rsch. asst. dept. physiology U. Coll., London, 1952-55; rsch. assoc. Royal Postgrad. Med. Sch., London, 1958-59; lectr. in medicine Welsh Nat. Sch. Medicine, Cardiff, Wales, 1959-61; sr. lectr. U. London Inst. Dermatology, 1961-64; prof. dermatology U. Newcastle upon Tyne, Eng., 1964-92, emeritus prof., 1992—; cons. various pharmacological and chem. industries worldwide, TV and radio programs on med. and gen. topics. Author book on medicine, 1973, book on dermatology, 1981, also 2 books on pharmacology, 1988; contbr. articles to profl. jours. Mem. various govt. coms. Grantee numerous instns. Fellow Royal Coll. Physicians; mem. various dermatol. and sci. assns.; hon. mem. many fgn. acad. socs. Avocations: sport, writing, talking. Office: U Newcastle Upon Tyne, Med Sch, Newcastle upon Tyne NE1 4LP, England

SHUSTERMAN, PETER IVAN MICHAEL, financial advisor; b. L.I., N.Y., June 16, 1959; s. Herman and Ann Shusterman; m. Becki Larae Farris, Dec. 30, 1989 (div. Aug. 1996); 1 child, Alexa Noelle. BS, U. Utah, 1981; MBA, Temple U., 1983. Fin. advisor Shusterman Fin. Svcs., San Diego, 1985—; planned giving chmn. San Diego Am. Diabetes Assn., 1991-97; spl. gifts advisor Planetary Coral Reef Found., San Diego, 1993—. Author: (book) San Diego Retirement Living, 1986. Treas. San Diego Exch. Club, 1988-97; dir. San Diego Boy Scout Explorer Club, 1990-91. Mem. Internat. Assn. for Fin. Planning, Letip Internat. Avocations: spending time with daughter, golf, scuba diving, aquatic art, investing. E-mail: psnoopy@aol.com. Home: Apt 108 11835 Carmel Mountain Rd # 1304-182 San Diego CA 92128-4609 Office: Shusterman Fin 15373 Innovation Dr Ste 390 San Diego CA 92128-3429

SHUSTOV, ANDREY VICTOROVICH, engineering reseacher, mathematics educator; b. Zhukovsky, Moscow Region, Russia, Dec. 6, 1951; s. Victor Ivanovich and Lidia Ivanovna (Simonova) S.; m. Zoya Konstantinovna Khatova, Feb. 1, 1974 (div. Mar. 1983); 1 child, Natalya; m. Eugenia Eduardovna Fedorenko, June 22, 1983; children: Olesya, Anastasiya. Degree in engring. and physics, Moscow Inst. of Physics and Tech., 1975; PhD, Ctrl. Aerohydrodynamic Inst., Zhukovsky, Russia, 1982, sr. scientist degree, 1989. Registered profl. engr., Moscow; cert. physicist, Moscow. Engr. Ctrl. Aerohydrodynamic Inst., Zhukovsky, 1975-80, sr. engr., 1980-81, leading engr., 1981-83, sector chief, 1983—; tchr. math. Lyceum N14, Zhukovsky, 1995-2000, asst. prof. math. Moscow Inst. Physics and Tech., Zhukovsky, 1999-2000. Recipient Project 200 Internat. Sci. and Tech. Ctr., 1995, Project 1018, Internat. Sci. and Tech. Ctr., 1998. Mem. Soc. Automotive Engrs. Avocation: painting. Home: Fedotov St, 140180 Zhukovsky Moscow Russia Office: ISAGI, Zhukovsky St, 140180 Zhukovsky Moscow Russia

SHUTE, STEPHEN CAMERON, law educator; b. Cambridge, Eng., May 13, 1955; s. Charles Cameron Shute and Lydia May (Harwood) Ruthroff; m. Julia Mary Jones, Aug. 17, 1996; 1 child, Miranda Rosemary Alice. LLB with honors, Kingston U., London, 1987; MA, Oxford (Eng.) U., 1989; BCL, Jesus Coll. U. Oxford, 1989; PhD, U. Birmingham, 1999. Fellow and tutor in law Corpus Christi Coll., U. Oxford, 1989-94; sr. lectr. law U. Birmingham, Eng., 1994-2000, reader in criminal law, 2000, prof. criminal law and criminal justice, 2000—; vis. prof. law U. S.C., Columbia, 1997; assoc. Ctr. for Criminol. Rsch., U. Oxford, 1989—. Editor: (with Susan Hurley) On Human Rights, 1993, (with John Gardner and Jeremy Horder) Action and Value in Criminal Law, 1993, (with Roger Hood) The Parole System at Work, 2000; contbr. articles to profl. jours. Organizer, co-founder Oxford Amnesty Lectures, 1991—. Fulbright scholar J. William Fulbright Fgn. Scholarship Bd. and U.S. Info. Agy., 1997, Brit. Acad. Maj. State studentship, 1987-89. Mem. Internat. Assn. Penal Law (sec.-treas. Brit. nat. sect. 1998—). Avocations: gardening, travel. Office: Univ Birmingham Fac of Law, Edgbaston, Birmingham B15 2TT, England

SHUTRUMP, MARY JILL, writer, editor, photographer, educator; b. Youngstown, Ohio, Sept. 24, 1964; d. Albin George and Joanne Donna (Torello) S. BA in Journalism, Ohio State U., 1986; MFA in Creative Writing, Clayton U., 1990, PhD in Communications/English, 1991. Mgr. Riverwatch Tower, Columbus, Ohio, 1987-88; editor, writer UPS, Columbus, 1988-95; freelance writer Columbus, 1990-95, Folly Beach, S.C., 1995—; v.p. publicity Arc Entertainment, Columbus, 1992-94, copywriter, acct. mgmt. advt., 1993, asst. producer videos, 1994; publicist Pet Helpers Orgn., Folly Beach, S.C., 1995; writer The Connection Newspaper, Kiawah Island, S.C., 1995-99; mem. faculty dept. English Trident Tech. Coll., 2000—; cons. Comms. and Advt., 1993-94; tech. writing cons. Mauswerks, Inc., Columbus, 1991; proofreader, Columbus, 1990-95; cons., commn./pub. rels. dir. FAN Engring. (U.S.A.) Inc., 1993-95; owner, freelance cons. Profl. and Acad. Svcs., 1991; instr. dept. English Columbus State C. C., 1991-93; owner Au Natural internat. health and beauty products brokers, 1995-96; owner, publicist Moondog Café and Graphics Internat., 1995; adj. English, comm. and speech instr. Trident Tech. Coll., Charleston, 1996-2000; adj. faculty comm. & speech Johnson & Wales U., Charleston, 1997-99, dept. English. Author: Indians and Alligators, 1997; publicist and pub. rels. (rock band) Eurogression, 1991—; prodr. MD Entertainment, 1994; model and actress in music field, Europe, 1992-93; music editor/writer Atlantic Surfer mag., 1994; asst. publicist Innovative Resources LLC, 1995—; asst. publicist Coyote Enterprises, 1995-97; publicity dir., shareholder Street Records, 1997—. Active Greenpeace, Washington, 1987—, Environ. Def. Fund, Washington, 1988—, World Wildlife Fund, PETA, 1987—. Mem. Humane Soc. of the U.S., ASPCA. Home: PO Box 1356 Folly Beach SC 29439-1356 Office: PO Box 1396 Folly Beach SC 29439-1396 also: 5742 Mill Creek Blvd Youngstown OH 44512-2716

SHUTTLEWORTH, ANNE MARGARET, psychiatrist; b. Detroit, Jan. 17, 1931; d. Cornelius Joseph and Alice Catherine (Rice) S.; m. Joel R. Siegel, Apr. 19, 1959; children: Erika, Peter. AB, Cornell U., 1953, MD, 1956. Intern Lenox Hill Hosp., N.Y.C., 1956-57; resident Payne Whitney Clinic-N.Y. Hosp., 1957-60; practice medicine specializing in psychiatry Maplewood, N.J., 1960—; cons. Maplewood Sch. System, 1960-62; instr. psychiatry Cornell U. Med. Sch., 1960; mem. Com. to Organize New Sch. Psychology, 1970. Mem. AMA (Physicians Recognition award 1975, 78, 81, 84, 87, 90, 93, 96, 99), Am. Psychiat. Assn., Am. Med. Women's Assn., N.Y. Acad. Scis., Acad. Medicine N.J., Phi Beta Kappa, Phi Kappa Phi. Home: 46 Farbrook Dr Short Hills NJ 07078-3007 Office: 2066 Millburn Ave Maplewood NJ 07040-3715

SHVALB, VIL, researcher; b. Odessa, Ukraine, Aug. 4, 1924; arrived in Israel, 1974; s. Michael Baitalsky and Eve Shvalb; m. Nina Guildenblat, Jan. 27, 1960. MSc, U. Moscow, 1952; PhD, Inst. Comm. Acad. Sci. USSR, Moscow, 1966. Rschr. Inst. for Comm. Problems, Acad. Sci. USSR, Moscow, 1959-70; head lab. Ctrl. Statis. Bd., Moscow, 1970-74; sr. rschr. Telecom. Corp., Tel Aviv, 1979-89; freelance rschr. Netanya, Israel, 1989—. Contbr. articles to books and jours. Soldier Russian Army, 1942-45, WWII. Mem. IEEE (affiliate), N.Y. Acad. Scis. Home: 10/13 Hashiva St, 42306 Netanya Israel also: PO Box 2153, 42125 Netanya Israel

SHVARTSMAN, ALEXANDER ALLISTER, computer scientist; b. Chisinau, Moldova, May 11, 1955; came to U.S., 1976; m. Robin Karian, Dec. 28, 1980; children: Ginger Allister, Theodore Allister. BS, Stevens Inst. Tech., Hoboken, N.J., 1979; MS, Cornell U., Ithaca, N.Y., 1981; PhD, Brown U., Providence, 1992. Mem. tech. staff Bell Labs., Andover, Mass., 1981-82; engr. Digital Equipment Corp., Maynard, Mass., 1983-94; sys. architect Logica, Inc., Lexington, Mass., 1994-95; rsch. assoc. MIT, Cambridge, 1995—; prof. U. Conn., Storrs, 1997—; cons. Robin Industries, Inc., Bristol, R.I., 1981-91, Mitre Corp., Eatontown, N.J., 1997-99, GTE, Waltham, Mass., 1997-98. Author: Fault-Tolerant Parallel Computation, 1997; contbr. articles to profl. jours., chpts. to books. Recipient St. Andrew's scholarship Stevens Inst. Tech., 1978, Outstanding Rsch. award Sigma Xi, Brown U., 1991, digital doctoral fellowship Digital Equipment Corp., 1990-92, Career award NSF, 2000. Mem. Assn. Computing Machinery, IEEE Computer Soc. Sigma Xi. E-mail: alex@theory.lcs.mit.edu. Office: MIT Lab for Computer Sci 545 Tech Sq NE 43-371 Cambridge MA 02139

SHVETSOV, ALEXANDER ANATOLIEVICH, biochemist, researcher; b. Orel, Russia, July 25, 1960; s. Anatoly Ivanovich and Anna Yakovlevna (Tsytsarkina) S.; m. Tatiana Vasilevna Orlova, Feb. 26, 1988; 1 child, Oksana. MS in Agronomy, Agrl. Acad., Orel, 1983; PhD in Biochemistry, Inst. Biochemistry, Moscow, 1992, postgrad., 1992-95. Jr. rsch. assoc. Inst. Agrl. Industry, Orel, 1986-88; sr. rschr. Inst. Biochemistry, 1995-98; sr. rsch. investigator Plant Physiology Inst., Moscow, 1998-2000; postdoctoral fellow UCLA, 2000—; reviewer Nat. Rsch. Initiative Grants Program, Washington, 1996-99; sec. Internat. Symposium on Stress and Inorganic Nitrogen Assimilation, Moscow, 1996. Patentee in field; contbr. numerous articles to profl. jours. Lt. USSR Military Svc., 1983-85. Mem. Russian Biochem. Soc., Russian Soc. Plant Physiologists. Russian Orthodox. Avocations: music, philosophy, painting. Home: 48 Pepvomalskaya Str Ap 14, 303120 Orel Russia Office: UCLA/Dept Chemistry 405 Hilgard Ave Los Angeles CA 90024-1569

SHVIDLER, MARK JOSEPH, mathematician; b. Khmelnitsky, Ukraine, USSR, Mar. 25, 1931; s. Joseph Zuss and Lea Gersh (Gleyzer); m. Mariam Moses Mendelson, July 24, 1959; children: Irene, Eugene. MS in Applied Mechanics, Kiev State U., USSR, 1953; PhD, All-Union Rsch. Sci. Oil and Gas Inst., Moscow, 1958, DS, 1964. Scientist Sci. Rsch. Oil Inst., Ufa, USSR, 1953-58, dept. head, 1958-67; scientist All-Union Rsch.-Sci. Natural Gas Inst., Moscow, 1967-70; scientist, prof., dept. head All-Union Rsch.-Sci. Oil and Gas Inst., Moscow, 1970-91; scientist Lawrence Berkeley Nat. Lab., Berkeley, Calif., 1991-92; vis. scientist Atomic Energy of Can. Ltd., Chalk River, Ont., Can., 1993, Lawrence Berkeley Nat. Lab., Berkeley, 1994-2000. Author: (books) Filtration Flow in Heterogeneous Media, 1964, One-Dimensional, Immiscible Flow Through Porous Media, 1970, Statistical Hydrodynamics of Porous Media, 1985; contbr. 160 articles to profl. jours. Mem. Am. Geophys. Union, Internat. Acad. Edn. Science Arts & Industry. Achievements include pioneer rsch. studies on statis. hydrodynamics of porous media and devel. of the theory. Avocations: chess, swimming. Home: 2951 Derby St Apt 228 Berkeley CA 94705-1350

SHWAYDER, ELIZABETH YANISH, sculptor; b. St. Louis, 1922; d. Sam and Fannie May (Weil) Yaffe; m. Nathan Yanish, July 5, 1944 (dec.); children: Ronbald, Marilyn Ginsburg, Mindy; m. M.C. Shwayder, 1988. Student, Washington U., 1941, Denver U., 1961; pvt. studies. One-woman shows include Woodstock Gallery, London, 1973, Internat. House, Denver, 1963, Colo. Women's Coll., Denver, 1975, Contemporaries Gallery, Santa Fe, 1963, So. Colo. State Coll. Pueblo, 1967, others; group shows include Salt Lake City Mus., 1964, 71, Denver Art Mus., 1961-75, Oklahoma City Mus., 1969, Joslyn Mus., Omaha, 1964-68, Lucca (Italy) Invitational, 1971, Denver Art Mus., Mus. Natural History, Mizel Mus., Eden Theatrical Workshop, Rose Hosp. Aux., Nat. Mus. Women in the Arts, Colo. Chpt. 8th Air Force Aux., Women's Art Ctr., others; represented in permanent collections including Colo. State Bank, Bmh Synagogue, Denver., Colo. Women's Coll., Har Ha Shem Congregation, Boulder, Colo., Faith Bible Chapel, Denver, others. Chmn. visual arts Colo. Centennial-Bicentennial, 1974-75; pres. Denver Coun. Arts and Humanities, 1973-75; co-chmn. visual arts spree Denver Pub. Schs., 1975; trustee Denver Ctr. Performing Arts, 1973-75; chmn. Concerned Citizens for the Arts, 1976; pres. Beth Israel Hosp. Aux., 1985-87; organizer Coat Drive for the Needy, Denver, N.Y.C., 1982-87, Common Cents penny drive for homeless, 1991-93; bd. dirs. Mizel Mus., Srs., Inc.; active Mayor's Com. on Cultural Affairs, Denver Art Mus., Mus. Natural History, Freedom Found. at Valley Forge, Hospice of Metro. Denver; bd. dirs. Rainbow Bridge; bd. dirs. Diabetes Found., Asian Arts Assn. Denver Art Museum; historian Childrens Diabetes Found., Univ. Colo. Found. Inc. Humanities scholar Auraria Librs.-U. Colo.; recipient McCormick award Ball State U., Muncie, Ind., 1964, purchase award color Women's Coll., Denver, 1963, Tyler (Tex.) Mus., 1963, 1st prize in sculpture 1st Nat. Space Art Show, 1971, humanitarian award Milehi Denver Sertoma, 1994, The Gleitsman Found., 1994, svc. to mankind awards Freedom Found. at Valley Forge, Mile Hi Sertoma Club, Minoruyasui Found., Gleitsman Found. Home: Unit 503 2400 Cherry Creek South Dr Denver CO 80209-3259

SHWE, TIN, tropical medicine physician; b. Mawlamyine, Burma, Aug. 13, 1936; s. U Pa and Daw Shin Shin; m. Daw Aye Thant, Oct. 23, 1960; children: Ma Tin, Ma Thet, Mg Thet. MBBS, Inst. Medicine, Yangon, Myanmar, 1960; PhD, London Sch. Hygiene Tropical, 1968. From med. officer to twp. med. officer Govt. Myanmar, 1961-68; med. officer in-charge Leprosy Hosp., Myanmar, 1977-84; rsch. scientist Govt. Myanmar, 1984—; cons. WHO, Philippines, 1996. Fellow Australasian Coll. Tropical Medicine, Royal Coll. Physicians (Edinburgh), Indian Assn. Leprologists; mem. My-

anmar Med. Assn. Buddhist. Avocation: writing books. Home: 39 Oo Kywe Hoe St, Kyimyindine Myanmar Office: Dept Med Rsch, 5 Ziwaka Rd Dagon PO, Yangon Myanmar

SHYY, WEI, aerospace and mechanical engineering researcher, educator; b. Tainan, Taiwan, China, July 19, 1955; came to U.S. 1979; s. Chiang-Chen and June-Hua (Chao) S.; m. Yuchen Shih; children: Albert, Alice, Andrew Chang, Kevin Chang. BS, Tsin-Hua U., Taiwan, 1977; MSE, U. Mich., 1981, PhD, 1982. Postdoctoral rsch. scholar U. Mich., Ann Arbor, 1982-83; rsch. scientist GE Corp. Rsch. and Devel. Ctr., Schenectady, N.Y., 1983-88; faculty mem. of aeronautics and astronautics Nat. Cheng-Kung U., Taiwan, 1987; assoc. prof. aerospace engring., mechanics and engring. sci. U. Fla., Gainesville, 1988-92, prof. aerospace engring., mechanics and engring. sci., 1992—, chmn. dept. aerospace engring, mechs. and engring. sci., 1996—; dir. Fla. NASA Space Grant Consortium, 1998-2000; cons. numerous pvt., fed. agencies U.S., Taiwan; lectr. in field. Author: Computational Modeling for Fluid Flow and Interfacial Transport, 1994; co-author: Computational Fluid Dynamics with Moving Boundaries, 1996, Computational Techniques for Complex Transport Phenemona, 1997; editor: Recent Advances in Comoputational Fluid Dynamics, 1989, Fluid Dynamics at Interface, 1999; mng. editor Cambridge U. Press: Aerospace Book Series; mem. editl. adv. bd. Numerical Heat Transfer Jour.; reviewer U.S. govt., other govts., indsl. labs., profl. jours.; contbr. numerous articles to profl. jours. Recipient GE Rsch. and Devel. Ctr. 1986 Pubs. award, Chinese Soc. of Mech. Engrs. 1987 Rsch. Paper award, NASA/ASEE 1991 Cert. of Recognition. Fellow AIAA (assoc.), ASME (Combustion and Fuel Com. 1984 Hon. Paper award); mem. Minerals, Metals and Materials Soc., Am. Phys. Soc., Combustion Inst. Achievements include research in computational fluid dynamics, combustion and propulsion, gravity-induced thermofluid transport processes, materials processing and solidification, microgravity sciences and engring. contributions to gas turbine, hydraulic turbine, high pressure lamp and electronic cooling. Office: U Fla Dept Aerospace Engring 231 Aero Bldg Gainesville FL 32611

SI, YING-JIE, ophthalmologist; b. Jinan, China, Sept. 27, 1962; parents Fulian Si and Min Li; m. You Qing Zhang, Mar. 26, 1963; 1 child, Yong-Jian. MD, Shandong Med. U., 1985; PhD, Gunma U. Sch. Medicine. Resident in ophthalmology Shandong Med. U. Hosp., 1985-92, asst. prof. ophthalmology, 1992-94; vis. scholar, investigator, invited rschr. Depts. Opthalmology, Cell Biology Gunma U., Maebashi, Japan, 1994-99; vis. scholar New Eng. Eye Ctr., Boston, 2000—. Mem. Assn. Rsch. in Vision & Ophthalmology, Japanese Ophthalmol. Soc., Chinese Ophthalmol. Soc. Avocations: stamp collecting, music, travel. Office: Gunma U Lab Mol Genetics, 3-39-15 Showa-machi, Maebashi Gunma, Japan 371

SIA, ALEX TIONG-HENG, anesthesiologist, educator, consultant; b. Muar, Johor, Malaysia, June 5, 1964; arrived in Singapore, 1982; s. Joseph Han-Sze Sia and Maria Geok-Lay Tan; m. Hwee-Lee Yeak, July 7, 1989; children: Sean, Zach, Josh. MB, B Surgery, Nat. U., Singapore, 1989, M Medicine, 1994. Intern Singapore Gen. Hosp., 1989-90; resident in medicine Nat. U. Hosp., Singapore, 1990-91; fellow Tan Tock Seng Hosp., Singapore, 1991-93; staff specialist KK Women's and Children's Hosp., Singapore, 1994-98, cons., jour. sci. reviewer, 1999—; clin. instr. Nat. U., Singapore, 1998—, coord. for final M Medicine course, 1999—; physician liaison officr for Diagnostic Related Group Com., 1998—; lectr. sci. meetings Acad. Medicine, Singapore, 1999—. Contbr. articles to med. jours., cinluding Anesthesia and Analgesia, Internat. Jour. Obstetric Anesthesia, Anaesthesia and Intensive Care, Can. Jour. Anesthesia. Asean scholar Pub. Svc. Commn., Singapore, 1982-83; rsch. grantee for obstet. analgesia Ministry Health, Singapore, 1998. Mem. Soc. for Obstetric Anesthesia and Perinatology, Internat. Anesthesia Rsch. Soc., N.Y. Acad. Scis. Avocation: golf. Office: KK Hosp Dept Anesthesiology, 100 Bukit Timah Rd, Singapore 229 899, Singapore

SIAL, ALCIDES NOBREGA, geologist, educator; b. Recife, Brazil, Dec. 14, 1942; s. Alberico and Maria do Carmo Nobrega Sial; m. Tania Maria Limongi, Dec. 30, 1967 (div. Dec. 1987); children: Erik Limongi Sial, Andrew Limongi Sial; m. Valderez Pinto Ferreira; 1 child, Adrian Ferreira Sial. BSc, Fed. U. Pernambuco, Recife, 1966; PhD in Geology, U. Calif., Davis, 1974. Instr. Fed. U. Pernambuco, 1967-72, asst. prof., 1972-74, assoc. prof., 1976-89, prof. geology, 1989—; founder Stable Isotope Lab., Federal U. of Pernambuco, Recife, Brazil, 1990—; teaching asst. U. Calif., Davis, 1971-72; adj. prof. U. Ga., Athens, 1983, 88, U. Tex., Austin, 1977-78; cons. NRC, Brasilia, Brazil, 1979-82, 96-98, councillor, 1991-93; adj.-coord. geoscis. CAPES Agy., Brasilia, 1993—; councillor FACEPE Agy., Recife, 1990-92. Author: Petrologia Ignea, 1984; editor spl. vol. Earth-Sci. Revs., 1981; editor supplement (annals) Brazilian Acad. Sci., (spl. issues) Lithos, Jour. of S.Am. Earth Scis., Brazilian Geol. Jour., Annals of the Brazilian Acad. Sci., 1999; author more than 100 sci. articles. Served with Brazilian Army, 1960-62. Recipient Silver Hammer award Brazilian Geol. Soc., 1975, One Hundred Yrs. of the Sch. of Engring. medal Fed. U. Pernambuco, 1995, medal of the centennial of the engring. Fed. U. Pernambuco, Brazil, 1995. Fellow Geol. Soc. Am., Geol. Assn. Can.; mem. AAAS, Brazilian Acad. Scis., Mineral Soc. Am., N.Y. Acad. Scis., Mineral Assn. Can., Am. Geophys. Union, Internat. Assn. Valcanology and Chemistry of the Earth's Interior (mem. commn. on granites), Am. Geophys. Union, Sigma Xi Soc. E-mail: ans@npd.ufpe.br. Home: Rua Dr Joao Marques 100/501, 50750-320 Recife Brazil Office: Fed U Pernambuco, PO Box 7852, 50732-970 Recife Brazil

SIALOM, SEDAT SAMI, advertising executive; b. Istanbul, Turkey, Dec. 14, 1940; s. Elie Guy and Sarah (Barzilay) S.; 1 child from previous marriage, Sandy; m. Cana Lakse, Mar. 3, 1985; 1 child, Selin. M in Econs., Istanbul U., 1961. Technicien en Publicite Ecole Superieure Technique de Publicite, Brussels, 1963; account exec. Bodden Et Dechy S.A., Brussels, Belgium, 1962-63, D.T.V., London, 1963-64; account dir., group dir. Client Contact dir. Grafika-Maya A.S., Istanbul, Turkey, 1964-70, vice chmn., 1970-73, chmn., 1973; chmn. Grafika-Lintas A.S., Istanbul, Turkey, 1987—; cons. in field. Served with Turkish Navy, 1960-61. Recipient Rizzoli award, 1972. Mem. Internat. Advt. Assn., Turkish Advt. Assn. Office: Maslak Meydani # 57, 80670 Levent Istanbul Turkey

SIARDOS, GEORGE C., agriculture educator; b. Thessaloniki, Greece, Aug. 6, 1938; s. Constantine G. and Demeter (Pigadas) S.; m. Maria Prodrome Seisoglou, May 12, 1968; children: Constantine, Prodrome. BSc in Agr., Aristotle U. Thessaloniki, 1967, BSc in Econs., 1980, PhD in Agrl. Extension, 1983; MSc in Agrl. Econs., U. London, 1975. Agriculturist Nat. Orgn. Welfare, Kastoria, Greece, 1967-69, dir., 1969-70; asst. Sch. Agr., Aristotle U. Thessaloniki, 1970-83; lectr. Aristotelian U. Thessaloniki, 1983-86, asst. prof., 1986-91; agrl. and socioecon. advisor Nat. Orgn. Welfare, Kastoria, Greece, 1967-70. Author: Mathematical Economics, 1979, Exercises on Mathematical Economics, 1984, Agricultural Extension, 1992, Methodology of Rural Sociological Research, 1997, Methods of Multi-Variable Statistical Analysis, Part I, 1999, Part II, 2000. 2d lt. arty. Greek Army, 1960-62. Ministry Coordination fellow, 1974; Fulbright scholar, Salzburg, Austria, 1981, U.S., 1994, Internat. Agr. Ctr. scholar, Wageningen, The Netherlands, 1985. Mem. Geotech. Chamber Greece, Agr. Assn. Macedonia, Rural Sociol. Soc., Internat. Rural Sociol. Assn. Home: 19 Sarantaporou St, 546 40 Thessaloniki Greece Office: Aristotle U Sch Agr, 540 06 Thessaloniki Greece

SIARRY, PATRICK, educator; b. Pertuis, France, May 28, 1952; s. Julien and Jany (Meskel) S.; m. Laurence Le Marquer, July 4, 1987; children: Caroline, Bruno, Paul. Degree in engring., Grenoble, France, 1975; degree in elec. engring., Paris, 1977; D, U. Paris 6, 1986; postgrad., U. Paris II, 1994. Engr. EDF, Chatou, France, 1978-82; asst. ESPCI, Paris, 1982-88; asst. prof. ECP, Paris, 1988-95; prof. U. Cergy-Pontoise, France, 1995-99, U. Paris 12, 1999—. Mem. IEEE (sr.). Home: 6 rue du Puits de l'Ermite, 75005 Paris France Office: U Paris 12, LERISS, Ave du General de Gaulle, 94010 Créteil France

SIAZON, DOMINGO LIM, JR., Philippine government official; b. Aparri, Cagayan, Philippines, July 9, 1939; s. Domingo and Rafaela (Lim) S.; m. Kazuko Ichikawa, July 29, 1940; children: Dan, Ken. BA, Ateneo de Manil, Philippines, 1959; BS in Physics, Tokyo U. Edn., 1964; MPA, Harvard U., 1979. Amb. ext. and plen. and perm. rep. Philippines Internat. Atomic Energy Agy and UN Indsl. Devel. Orgn., Vienna, 1979-80, amb. ext. and plen. to Austria and permanent rep., 1980-85; dir.-gen. UN Indsl. Devel. Orgn., Vienna, 1985-94; sec. fgn. affairs Govt. of The Philippines, Manila, 1995—. Contbr. articles to profl. jours. Recipient Grofes Goldenes Ehrenzeichen am Bande, Republic of Austria, 1985. Mem. Harvard Club of Austria (v.p. 1984-86). Avocation: tennis. Office: Dept of Fgn Affairs, 2330 Roxas Blvd, Pasay City Manila The Philippines*

SIBAYA, PATRICK THEMBA, psychologist, educator; b. Durban, South Africa, Aug. 8, 1950; s. Aaron Sokela and Petronica Tholi (Maboso) S.; m. Duduzile Christinah Mbata, July 11, 1974; 4 children. BA with hons., U. Zululand, South Africa, 1974; BEd, U. Zululand, 1978; MEd, U. Natal, South Africa, 1987; DEd, U. Stellenbosch, South Africa, 1992. Rschr. U. Zululand, 1974-81, lectr., 1982-83, from sr. lectr. to prof., 1987-95, prof., 1995—; head dept. Umlazi Coll., Durban, 1984-87; Mem. com. Nat. Commn. Spl. Edn., 1996—; v.p. South African Fedn. of Mental Health. Mem. editl. bd. Advance With Guidance, 1994 (Rector's Merit award 1996, 97), other nat. and internat. jours.; contbr. articles to profl. jours. Councillor Kwa Zulu-Natal, Ngwelezane, 1988. Grantee Ernest Oppenheimer Meml. Trust, 1997. Mem. Internat. Union Psychol. Svcs., Psychol. Soc. South Africa (bd. dirs. 1996—), South African Med. & Dental Coun. (bd. dirs.), Assn. Ednl. Psychology South Africa (chairperson), Health Professions Coun. (exec. mem.), Profl. Bd. Psychology South Africa (chairperson edn. com.). Roman Catholic. Avocations: soccer, fishing. Home: B 110 Ngwelezane, Kwazulu Natal South Africa Office: U Zululand, Pvt Bag X 1001, Kwadlangezwa 3886, South Africa

SIBBALD, JOHN RISTOW, management consultant; b. Lincoln, Nebr., June 20, 1936; s. Garth E.W. and Rachel (Wright) S.; BA, U. Nev., 1958; MA, U. Ill., 1964; m. Kathryn J. Costick ; children: Allison, John, Wright. Office mgr. Hewitt Assocs., Libertyville, Ill., 1964-66; coll. rels. mgr. Pfizer Inc., N.Y.C., 1966-69; pres., chief exec. officer Re-Con Systems, N.Y.C., 1969-70; v.p. Booz, Allen & Hamilton, N.Y.C., 1970-73, Chgo., 1973-75; pres., founder John Sibbald Assocs., Inc., Chgo., 1975; mem. Nat. Advisory Coun., Nat. Club Assn. Author: The Career Makers, 1990, 92, The New Career Makers, 1995; pub. Club Leaders Forum; contbr. articles to profl. jours. Served to capt. AUS, 1958-64. Mem. Mid-Day Club Chgo., St. Louis Club. Episcopalian. Office: 7733 Forsyth Blvd Saint Louis MO 63105-1817

SIBEYN, JOP FREDERIK, computer scientist; b. Abcoude, The Netherlands, Dec. 19, 1962; arrived in Germany, 1992; s. Frederik and Maria Jacoba (Boddeke) S.; m. Petra Kless, July 4, 1994. MS in Math., U. Utrecht, Netherlands, 1987; PhD in Computer Sci., 1992. Postdoctorate Max-Planck Inst., Saarbrücken, Germany, 1992; researcher, 1993—. Mem. IEEE. Avocations: French, German, Italian, Arabic, biking around the world. Office: MPI für Informatik, Im Stadtwald, 66123 Saarbrücken Germany

SIBIRTSEV, VLADIMIR STANISLAVOVICH, biochemist, researcher; b. St. Petersburg, Russia, Oct. 26, 1969; s. Stanislav Nikolaevich and Undina Petrovna (Denisova) S.; m. Yulia Lvovna Kavalerchik, May 25, 1991 (div.); 1 child, Sibirtseva, Anastasiya; m. Victoriya Rostislavovna Peshkovskaya, June 6, 1998; children: Malashev Nikita, Peshkovskiy Alesha. MS, St. Petersburg State Tech., 1992, PhD, 1995. Rsch. scientist Ctrl. Rsch. Inst. Roentgenology and Radiology, St. Petersburg, 1992—. Contbr. articles to profl. jours. Recipient Favorsky scholarship St. Petersburg State Tech. Inst., 1990-92, grant, St. Petersburg, 1995, Russia Fond Fundamental Investigations, 1999. Mem. Assn. Writers St. Petersburg, Club Tourists St. Petersburg. Avocations: tourism, photography, writing. Home: St Kluchevaya, House 31 Apt 58, 195221 Saint Petersburg Russia Office: Ctrl Rsch Inst Roent & Rad, St Leningradskaya House 70/4, 189646 Pesochnyi 2, Russia

SIBLEY, ANTHONY ROBERT, retired meter manufacturing company executive; b. Luton, Eng, Sept. 16, 1932; s. Percy Stuart and Winifred Gertrude (Hawks) S.; m. Marjorie Cross, Mar. 20, 1957; children: Claire, Sarah. Cert. in mech. engring., Luton Tech. U., 1958. Apprentice, tech. salesman George Kent Ltd., Luton, 1948-64; mng. dir. Kent Belgium S.A., Brussels, 1964-84, Compteurs Kent, Lyon, France, 1973-84; pres., gen. mgr. Kent Meters Inc., Fla., 1984—, Isabela, P.R., 1984—; mng. dir. Kent Meters Ltd., Luton, l984—; mng. dir. meter div. ABB Kent PLC, Luton, 1984—; ret. Mem. Ch. of England. Avocation: sailing.

SIBLEY, JAMES MALCOLM, retired lawyer; b. Atlanta, Aug. 5, 1919; s. John Adams and Nettie Whitaker (Cone) S.; m. Karen Norris, Apr. 6, 1942; children: Karen Mariea, James Malcolm Jr., Jack Norris, Elsa Alexandria Victoria, Quintus Whitaker. A.B., Princeton U., 1941; student, Woodrow Wilson Sch. Law, 1942, Harvard Law Sch., 1945-46. Bar: Ga. 1942. Assoc. King & Spalding, Atlanta, 1942-47, ptnr., 1947-91; bd. dirs. Summit Industries, Inc.; exec. com., mem. pub. affairs com. Coca-Cola Co., 1979-91; chmn. exec. com. John H. Harland Co., 1963-91; chmn. exec. com., mem. compensation com. Trust Co. of Ga., 1975-92; mem. exec. com., mem. compensation com. SunTrust Banks, Inc., 1985-92. Trustee Joseph B. Whitehead Found., Lettie Pate Evans Found., A.G. Rhodes Home, Inc., Robert W. Woodruff Found., Inc. (formerly Trebor Found.), John H. and Wilhelmina D. Harland Charitable Found., Inc.; trustee emeritus Callaway Gardens Found, Emory U. With USAF, 1942-45. Mem. ABA, Ga. Bar Assn., Atlanta Bar Assn., Am. Coll. Probate Counsel, Am. Bar Found., Am. Law Inst. Episcopalian. Clubs: Piedmont Driving, Commerce. Home: 63 Peachtree Cir NE Atlanta GA 30309-3556 also: King & Spalding 191 Peachtree St NE Ste 40 Atlanta GA 30303-1740

SIBREE, WILLIAM JAMES, solicitor; b. Kuala Lumpur, Malaysia, Mar. 19, 1961; s. John Herbert Douglas and Elizabeth (Miskin) S. BA, Queens' Coll., Cambridge, Eng., 1982, MA, 1987. Bar: Eng. 1984; solicitor Supreme Ct. 1988. Ptnr. Slaughter and May, Brussels. Contbr.: Common Market Law of Competition, 1993. Avocations: opera, skiing, bridge. Office: Slaughter and May, Ave de Cortenberg 118, 1000 Brussels Belgium

SICARD, ANDRÉ, medical administrator; b. Paris, Dec. 1; m. Veuf Sicard; 3 children. Pres. Nat. Acad. Surgery, Nat. Acad. Medicine. Mem. French Soc. Medicine (pres.). Fedn. Acads. of Medicine of the European Union (pres. 1995). Home: 18 ave de Villars, 75007 Paris France

SICHERL, PAVLE, economics educator; b. Ljubljana, Slovenia, Feb. 16, 1935; s. Janko and Ana (Debeljak) S.; m. Jana Milava Primc, Aug. 11, 1962; children: Igor, Borut. Diploma in Econs., U. Ljubljana, 1960; MA, Williams Coll., Williamstown, Mass., 1962; PhD, U. Ljubljana, 1967. Economist Yugoslav Inst. Econ. Rsch., Belgrade, 1962-66; Hallsworth rsch. fellow U. Manchester, Eng., 1966-67; dep. dir. Yugoslav Inst. Econ. Rsch., Belgrade, 1967-68, acting dir., 1968-69; macroecon. advisor Harvard Inst. Internat. Devel., Addis Ababa, Ethiopia, 1970-74; prof. econs. U. Ljubljana Law Sch., 1975—; vis. prof. Williams Coll., Williamstown, 1980; vis. fellow Yale U., New Haven, 1986-87; vis. scholar Ctr. for the Study of Pub. Policy, Strathclyde U., Glasgow, and Ctr. for Econ. Performance, London Sch. Econs., 1992-93, Inst. World Econs., Kiel, 1992-93; vis. prof. Inst. for Advanced Studies, Vienna, 1996, 97; mem. Fed. Coun. Econ. Advisors, Belgrade, 1980-84; cons. UN, World Bank, Washington, 1987, 92, OECD, 1991; chmn. Subcom. Commn. Econ. Reform,1988; dir. Sicenter, Ljubljana, 1993—. Author: Capital as a Factor of Economic Growth, 1971, Personality of Public Enterprise, 1981, Methods of Measuring Disparity Between Men and Women, 1989, Slovenia Now, 1990, Integrating Comparisons Across Time and Space, 1993; A Novel Methodology for Comparisons in Time and Space, 1997, The Time Dimension of Disparities in the World, 1999. Recipient Sr. Fulbright rsch. award Fulbright Commn., 1986. Mem. Internat. Assn. Rsch. Income and Wealth, Am. Econ. Assn., Slovenian Statis. Soc., Slovenian Econ. Assn. Avocation: chess. Home: Brajnikova 19, 1000 Ljubljana Slovenia Office: U Ljubljana Faculty Law, Kongresni trg 12, 1000 Ljubljana Slovenia

SICKEL, WERNER HERMANN REINHARD, physiologist. MD, U. Leipzig, Germany, 1952. Asst. U. Leipzig, 1953-61; rsch. assoc. Johns Hopkins U., Balt., 1961-65; prof. physiology U. Cologne, Germany, 1966—. Contbr. chpts. to Handbook of Sensory Physiology Vol. 7, part 2, articles to sci. publs. Achievements include research on methods to preserve vertebrate, including human retinas in isolations for study of under tissue slice conditions of metabolism and function; on electrophysiological techniques for physiological, toxicological, clin. and classroom purposes. Home: Carl-Schurz Str 18, 50935 Cologne Germany Office: Univ Cologne Dept Physiolgy, Robert-Koch Str 39, 50931 Cologne Germany

SICKER, DIETER, chemist, educator; b. Karl-Marx-Stadt, Saxony, Germany, Oct. 16, 1954; s. Guenter and Irmgard S.; m. Angelika Lohmueller; 1 child, Susanne. Diploma in Chemistry, U. Leipzig, 1980, Dr.rer.nat., 1983, Dr.rer.nat.habil., 1991, Privatdozent, 1995, prof., 1997. Scientist, faculty of chemistry and mineralogy U. Leipzig, 1980—. Patentee in field; contbg. author books in field; contbr. articles to profl. jours. Avocations: history, arts, cooking. Office: Inst Organic Chem/U Leipzig, Johannisallee 29, D-04103 Leipzig Germany

SICKING, LOUIS HENRICUS JOANNES, historian, researcher; b. Nijmegen, The Netherlands, Mar. 11, 1966; s. Jan L.J.M. and Elly Catharina (Van Hofwegen) S. MA, U. Leiden, The Netherlands, 1990, PhD, 1996; diplôme d'études approfondies, U. Provence, Aix-En-Provence, France, 1990; Archivist first class, Nat. Sch. Archives, The Hague, The Netherlands, 1994. Archivist, trainee Nat. Archives of Drenthe Assen, The Netherlands, 1990-92; rschr., translator Musée Maritime de Tatihou, Saint-Vaast-La-Hougue, France, 1992; rschr. Netherlands Orgn. Sci. Rsch., Leiden, 1992-96, Niels Stensen Found., Amsterdam, The Netherlands, 1996-97, U. Leiden, 1997—; vis. scholar Columbia U., N.Y.C., 1997. Fellow Royal Netherlands Acad. Arts and Scis. Office: Leiden U Dept History, Doelensteeg 16, 2300RA Leiden The Netherlands

SIDAMON-ERISTOFF, ANNE PHIPPS, museum official; b. N.Y.C., Sept. 12, 1932; d. Howard and Harriet Dyer (Price) Phipps; m. Constantine Sidamon-Eristoff, June 29, 1957; children—Simon, Elizabeth, Andrew. BA, Bryn Mawr Coll., 1954. Chmn., bd. trustees Am. Mus. Natural History, N.Y.C.; dir.-at-large Black Rock Forest Consortium; trustee God Bless Am. Fund, Hudson River Found. Bd. dirs. Greenacre Found., Highland Falls (N.Y.) Pub. Libr., N.Y. Cmty. Trust, Storm King Art Ctr., Mountainville, N.Y., World Wildlife Fund.; former bd. dirs.Scenic Hudson, St. Bernard's Sch., N.Y.C., Mus. Modern Art, N.Y.C., Mus. Hudson Highlands. Home: 120 E End Ave New York NY 10028-7552

SIDAMON-ERISTOFF, CONSTANTINE, lawyer; b. N.Y.C., June 28, 1930; s. Simon C. and Anne Huntington (Tracy) Sidamon-E.; m. Anne Phipps, June 29, 1957; children: Simon, Elizabeth, Andrew. B.S.E. in Geol. Engring, Princeton U., 1952; LL.B., Columbia U., 1957. Clk., then assoc. firm Kelley Drye Newhall Maginnes & Warren, N.Y.C., 1957-64; individual practice law N.Y.C., 1964-65, 74-77; exec. asst. to Congressman John V. Lindsay, 1964-65; city coordinator Lindsay Mayoral Campaign, N.Y.C., 1965; asst. to mayor City of N.Y., 1966, commr. hwys., 1967-68, transp. adminstr., 1968-73; ptnr. Sidamon-Eristoff, Morrison, Warren, & Ecker, N.Y.C., 1978-83; counsel Morrison & de Roos, 1984-88; pvt. practice N.Y.C., 1988-89; regional adminstr. Region II EPA, N.Y.C., 1989-93; of counsel Patterson, Belknap, Webb & Tyler, N.Y.C., 1993-99, Lacher & Lovell-Taylor P.C., N.Y.C., 1999—; mem. N.Y. State Met. Transp. Authority Bd., 1974-89; commr. N.Y. State Jud. Commn. on Minorities, 1987-91; mem. Gov.'s Coun. on Hudson River Valley Greenway, 1989; trustee United Mut. Savs. Bank, N.Y.C., 1979-82; trustee Phipps Houses, N.Y.C., 1974—, chmn. 1986—. Trustee Allaverdy Found., N.Y.C., 1962—, Am. Farm Sch., Thessaloniki, Greece, 1973-79, Carnegie Hall, N.Y.C., 1967-92, Millbrook (N.Y.) Sch., 1971-89, hon. trustee, 1989—, Orange County (N.Y.) Citizens Found., 1974-81, Am. the Beautiful Fund, Washington, 1985-97; bd. dirs. Caramoor Center for Music and Arts, Katonah, N.Y., 1961-80, Tolstoy Found., Inc., N.Y.C., 1975—, chmn., 1979-89, 94—, Boyce Thompson Inst. for Plant Rsch., Ithaca, N.Y., 1994—; chmn. Nat. Audubon Soc. N.Y., 1999—; mem. Orange County (N.Y.) Planning Bd., 1997—; bd. dirs., mem. exec. com. Mid-Hudson Pattern for Progress, Poughkeepsie, N.Y., 1975-89, chmn., 1981-85; bd. dirs. Coun. on Mcpl. Performance, N.Y.C., 1979-87, chmn., 1979-83, vice chmn., 1986, 87, N.Y. State Republican committeeman, 1980-89. Served to 1st lt. arty. AUS, 1952-54, Korea. Decorated Bronze Star; recipient Honor award Kings County chpt. N.Y. State Soc. Profl. Engrs., 1969, Honor award Greater N.Y. coun. Girl Scouts U.S., 1973, Board Leadership award Coun. Mcpl. Performance, 1984, Transp. Man of Yr. award Greater N.Y. March of Dimes, 1985, Award of Excellence Mid-Hudson Pattern for Progress, 1990, Honor award Nat. and N.Y. Parks and Conservation Assn., 1992, Bronze medal USEPA, 1993, Civic Leadership award (with wife) Citizens Union, 1997, Force for Nature award (with wife) Natural Resources Def. Coun., 1999. Mem. ABA, N.Y. State Bar Assn., Assn. of Bar of City of N.Y., N.Y. County Lawyers Assn., Kent Moot Ct., AIME, Phi Delta Phi, Delta Psi. Eastern Orthodox. Clubs: Century Assn. (N.Y.C.), Knickerbocker (N.Y.C.), Racquet and Tennis (N.Y.C.). Office: Lacher & Lovell-Taylor PC 6th Fl 770 Lexington Ave New York NY 10021-8165

SIDAR, THOMAS WILSON, retail executive; b. New Brunswick, N.J., Nov. 21, 1949; s. Alexander George Jr. and Jean (Wilson) S.; m. Ellen Elizabeth Woods,. BA, Colby Coll., 1972. Sales rep. L.L. Bean, Inc., Freeport, Maine, 1975, retail buyer, 1976-82, asst. product mgr., 1982-85, product mgr., 1985-88, sr. product mgr., 1988-89, dir. product devel., 1990-91; v.p. creative dept. L.L. Bean, Inc., 1991-98, sr. v.p., gen. mgr. of men's, 1998—; with L.L. Bean Inc. Trustee North Yarmouth Acad. Mem. Acadia Nat. Park (bd. advisors, chmn. park use com.), Maine Inland Fisheries and Wildlife (adv. com. non-game), Leadership Maine (Maine Devel. Found.), Appalachian Mountain Club (bd. dirs., chmn. capital campaign com., v.p.), Megantic Club, The Woodlands Club. Democrat. Episcopalian. Avocations: fly fishing, bird hunting, cross-country skiing, mountain climbing, canoeing. Home: 91 Glen Rd Yarmouth ME 04096-8136 Office: LL Bean Inc Casco St Freeport ME 04033-0001

SIDDIQI, JAWED IQBAL AHMED, software engineer, research consultant, educator; b. Karachi, Pakistan, Apr. 4, 1951; arrived in Eng., 1960; s. Iqbal Ahmed and Siddiqa (Khatoon) S.; m. Shahnaz Ali. BSc in Math. with honours, U. London, 1974; MSc in Computer Sci., U. Aston, Birmingham, Eng., 1979, PhD in Computer Sci., 1984. Chartered engr. Rsch. coord. Wolverhampton U. Inst., 1982-88; head software engring. Sheffield (Eng.) Hallam U., 1989-94, prof. software engring., dir. rsch. ctr., 1994—, mem. acad. bd., 1989-94, bd. govs., 1990-93; rsch. cons. Oxford (Eng.) U.,1990-93. Editor Computer Sci., 1989—; also articles. Chmn. Racial Equality Coun., Staffordshire, 1985-88. Mem. IEEE (mem. editorial bd. Software 1992—), Brit. Computer Soc., European Assn. Theoretical Computer Scientists, European Assn. Cognitive Ergonomics. Office: Sheffield Hallam U, Howard St, City Campus Sheffield S11 WB, England

SIDDIQI, SALMAN H., microbiologist, researcher; b. July 1, 1942; came to U.S., 1962; s. Zaheer Uddin and Kaniz Fatima Siddiqi; m. Shahida Baig, Sept. 18, 1970; children: Adila, Fariha, Nauman. BS in Zoology/Microbiology, U. Karachi, Pakistan, 1959, MS in Med. Microbiology, 1961; PhD in Med. Microbiology, U. Okla., 1967. Bacteriologisat Ctrl. Govt. Drug Testing Lab., Karachi, 1961-62; grad. tchg. asst. U. Okla., Norman, 1963-67; rsch. assoc. U. Md., Balt., 1967-68, 68-73; chief microbiology divsn. Pakistan Med. Rsch. Ctr., 1968-73; hon. asst. prof. bacteriology Postgrad. Med. Ctr., King Edward Med. Coll., Lahore, 1975-78; rsch. dir. Pakistan Med. Rsch. Coun. Tuberculosis Rsch. Ctr., Mayo Hosp., Lahore, 1973-78; cons. Johnston Labs., Towson, Md., 1978-79, sr. microbiologist, program mgr., 1979-85; sr. scientist, project mgr. Beckton Dickinson Diagnostic Instrument Sys., Sparks, Md., 1985-89; rsch. fellow Beckton Dickinson & Co., Sparks, 1990-99, bd. of fellows, 1999—; cons. Fatima Meml. Hosp., Lahore, 1977-78, Gulab Devi. Chest Hosp., Lahore, 1976-78, United Christian Hosp., Lahore, 1976-97; guest scientist U. Md., Balt., 1978-79; mem. com. on bacteriology and immunology Internat. Union Against Tuberculosis and Lung Disease, 1988—. Chief editor Progress in Medicine, 1974-78; spl. reviewer Jour. Clin. Microbiology, 1983-84, 87-89, mem. editl. bd., 1985-87, 89-92; reviewer European Jour. Clin. Microbiology, 1988—; mem. NCCLS subcom. on antimycobacterial drug susceptibility testing, 1987—; mem. task group for mycobacterial drug susceptibility testing Internat. Working Group on Mycobacterial Taxonomy, 1989—; contbr. numerous articles to profl. jours., chpts. to books; patentee in field. Fellow Am. Acad. Microbiology; mem. AAAS, Am. Soc. Microbiology (Barnet Cohan award for disting. scientist), Internat. Union Against Tuberculosis, Am. Thoracic Soc., N.Y. Acad. Scis. Achievements include development of Bactec TB system with invention of new tests and culture media. Home: 15 Glencoe Manor Ct Sparks MD

21152-9312 Office: Becton Dickinson Biosciences Sys 7 Loveton Cir Sparks MD 21152-9213

SIDDIQUE, IMAM AMIR, creative consultant, casting director; b. Bombay, India, Oct. 12, 1965; s. Amir Uddin and Afroze Hasiena (Durrani) S. Field supr. Indian Market Rsch. Bur., 1982-87; store mgr. Vama Benetton, India, 1987-88; instr., hon. mem. faculty Sophia Poly., India, 1988-89; creative cons. FCB, Ulka, India, 1989-96; dir. talent and casting Ammirati Puris Lintas India Ltd., 1997—; prin. contemporary dancerm choreographer, fashion stylist, event mgr. Columnist, The Asian Age Newspaper, India, 1997—; TV anchor Channel V, Musia Asia, BBC, India, 1995—; contbr. poetry to mag. Activist, NBA, India, 199-97; activist for various social/cultural orgns. Home: F/6 Sherwood Studio, Sea Beach View Apts Mt Mary Rd, Bandra Bombay 400 050, India Office: Ammirati Puris Lintas India Ltd Ste 131, 13th Fl Exp Towers/Nariman Point, Bombay 400 021, India

SIDDIQUI, ALIMUDDIN A. RASHID, investment company executive, consultant; b. Karachi, Sind, Pakistan, July 26, 1958; s. Abdul Rashid Mohammad Saheem and Samina A. Rashid Khatoon; m. Mahmooda Azeem, June 12, 1988; children: Faseehuddin, Sara, Samra, Saad. B, Karachi U., 1977. Asst. mgr. Atlas Battlay Ltd., Karachi, 1977-89; pricing mgr. Al-Maktaba, Jeddah, Saudi Arabia, 1989-92; mgr. accounts Omar K. Alesami, Jeddah, 1992—; mem. Pakistan Accts. Forum, 1998—. Assoc. Inst. Cost and Mgmt. Accts. Pakistan. Home and Office: PO Box 8361, Hail St, Jeddah 21482, Saudi Arabia

SIDDIQUI, ATHAR, publishing executive, editor; b. Karachi, Pakistan, Jan. 8, 1958; s. Nasim Ahmed and Zaheer Fatima Siddiqui; m. Afshan Jamal, Oct. 5, 1982; 1 child, Ifrah Athar. BA, Karachi Intermediate Sch., 1981. Salesman Sethi Internat., Karachi, 1977-78; bus. rep. Sawasho Trading Co. Ltd., Tokyo, 1980-82, v.p., 1982-85; pres. Showa Tsusho Co. Ltd., Tokyo, 1985—; publ. Oriental Comm. Inc., Tokyo, 1991—; editor Nawaetokyo Publ., Tokyo, 1991—. Editor Urdu mag., 1991, Web mag., 1999, Pakistan mag., 1999. Mem. Pakistan Assn. Japan (media sec. 1997—). Islam. Avocations: reading, cricket, music. Office: Showa Tsusho Co Ltd Ste 702, St Akihabara Bldg 1-33-6 Taito, Taito-ku Tokyo 110-0016, Japan

SIDDIQUI, DILNAWAZ AHMED, communications educator, international communication planning advisor, consultant; b. Amroha, India, July 4, 1937; came to U.S., 1975; s. Aijaz Rosool and Safina (Begum) Khan; m. Narjis Bano Naqvi, May 18, 1963; children: Shajee Raza, Aamera. BEd, MA, Aligarh Muslim U., Aligarh, India, 1960; postgrad., U. London, 1968, CAS, 1977; PhD, Syracuse U., 1980. Asst. prof. MSG Coll., Malegaon, India, 1961-63; edn. officer H.H. The Aga Khan and Ministry of Edn., Dar-es-salaam, Tanzania, Lusaka, Zambia, 1963-71; chmn. Sir Evelyn Hone Coll. Can. Commn. Tech. Edn. and Vocat. Tng. CIDA later under, Ministry of Edn., Lusaka, 1971-75; rsch. asst. tchg. asst. Syracuse U., 1975-80; dir. Human Resource Planning and Devel. Action Programs Internat., Washington, 1980; prof. faculty commn. Clarion U., Pa.; pres. Siddiqui Assocs., Shippenville, Pa.; cons. Can. Commn. for Tech. Edn. and Vocat. Tng., Lusaka, 1971-75, IDD&E Syracuse U., 1977-78; chief U.S. adviser human resource planning and devel. Ctrl. Planning Orgn., Prime Minister's Office, Yemen Arab Republic, Sana'a, 1980-82; adviser Mid-East/Africa API, Sheladia Assocs., 1983—; cons. Ariz. State U., 1983, chief of party U.S. evaluators' team to Hashemite Kingdom of Jordan Adminstrv. Tng. Project IV, 1992; human resource devel. master plan adviser to Govt. of Sudan, 1994-95. Author: Human Resources Development Master Plan for the Government of Sudan, 1995; co-author: A Proposed System of Managing Scholarships, 1983, An Analysis of Comparative Adult Education Methods, 1988, The Gulf War: Implications for Global Business and Media, 1992, Contributions of A.N. Charters To Field of Adult Education, 2000; contbr. articles to profl. jours., chpts. to books; mem. editl. bd. Am. Jour. Islamic Social Scis.; mem. rev. bd. Jour. Internat. Acad. Bus. Disciplines; contbr. to Field of Adult Education, 2000. Active Internat. Congress for Univ. Adult Edn.; mem. U.S./NGO Delegation to World Congress on Adult Edn. UNESCO, Hamburg, Germany, 1997; advisor Interfaith Coun. Syracuse U., 1975-80. Recipient substantive contbn. to lit. for edn. ERIC award, 1977, rsch. and svc. East and Ctrl. Africa Disting. Contbn. to Edn. Adults award ICAE award, 1980, Aligarh Muslim U. improtu lit. writing competition Gold medal award, 1958, 1st prize award Anjuman-e-Taraqqui-Urdu, Amroha, India, 1957, VC award for rsch. in Africa Syracuse U., 1978-79, Profl. Excellence award Am. Fedn. Muslims from India, 1997; named Academician honoris causa Russian Acad. Humanities, 1996. Mem. Am. Assn. Tng. and Devel. (mem. editl. bd. jour.), Assn. Muslim Soc. Scis. (pres. 1993-95), Internat. Comm. Assn. (meml editl. bd. world-wide web jour. 1996—). Home: 510 Ridgewood Rd Marianne Est Shippenville PA 16254 Office: Clarion U Pa Dept Comm Clarion PA 16214

SIDDIQUI, MAQBOOL AHMAD, engineering consultant and executive; b. Sangla Hill, Punjab, Pakistan, Sept. 18, 1941; s. Pir Bakhash and Sahib Nisa Siddiqui; me. Ceyla, Oct. 1964 (div.); m. Robina Anjum, Aug. 22, 1985; children: Sahib Nisa, Ertan Maqbool, Khalid Maqbool. BSc, Punjab U., Lahore, Pakistan, 1961; postgrad. diploma, Bettersea Coll., London, 1964; MPhil, London U., 1976; PhD, Century U., 1994. Registered profl. engr., Pakisan, U.K. Civil svc. Army Tech. Liaison Office Pakistan Embassy, London, 1962-63; project engr. Film Cooling Towers, Ltd., Richmond-London, 1964-66; chem. engr. Atomic Power Constrn., Ltd., Sutton-London, 1966-68; process engr. Badger Ltd./Badger N.V., London and The Hague, 1968-73; cons. process engring. Pritchard Rhodes, Ltd., London, 1973; lead process engr. Lummus Crest Co./Monsanto Co., London and St. Louis, 1973-75; mgr. engring. Alarko A.S., Istanbul, Turkey, 1975-76, dep. mng. dir., 1976-83; chmn. Pirsons Chem. Engring. (Pvt) Ltd., Multan, Pakistan, 1984—. Contbr. articles to profl. jours. Fellow Inst. Chem. Engrs. (Eng.); mem. AIChE, Engring. Coun. London (chartered engr.), Pakistan Engring. Coun., Pakistan-Turkish Soc., Svcs. Club, Pakistan Engring. Coun. Mem. Pakistan Saraiki Party. Muslim. Home: 321A Sher Shah Rd, Multan Punjab, Pakistan Office: Pirsons Chem Engring Ltd, Siddiqui Lodge Sher Shah Rd, Multan Punjab, Pakistan

SIDDIQUI, MOHAMMAD SHAHID, pathologist, consultant, researcher; b. Sukkur, Pakistan, Sept. 21, 1963; s. Mohammad Anwar ul Haque and Bashir Unnisa. MBBS, U. Sindh, 1988. House officer Liaquat Nat. Hosp., Karachi, Pakistan, 1988-89; med. officer Health Dept., Govt. of Sindh, Sukkur, 1990; Taluka health officer Health Dept., Govt. of Sindh, Karachi, 1992; postgrad. tng. in clin. pathology Jinnah Postgrad. Med. Ctr., Karachi, 1992-94; resident in pathology Aga Khan U. Hosp., Karachi, 1994-99; asst. prof. Ziauddin Med. U., Clifton, Karachi, 1999—; cons. histopathologist Karachi Adventist Hosp., 2000. Contbr. articles to profl. jours. Fellow Coll. Physicians and Surgeons Pakistan; mem. Pakistan Assn. Pathologists (Gold medal 1996). Avocation: table tennis (champion 1986). E-mail: mahammadsiddiqui@hotmail.com. Office: Ziauddin Med U Hosp, ST-4/B Block 6 Clifton, Karachi 75600, Pakistan

SIDDIQUI, SALEEM, plant physiologist; b. Delhi, India, May 25, 1959; s. Karim Uddin and Raisa S.; m. Nuzhat Anees; children: Uzma, Sameer. BS, Delhi U., India, 1978; MS, Haryana Agrl. U., India, 1980, PhD, 1984. Asst. scientist Haryana Agrl. U., India, 1984-89, assoc. prof., 1990—. Editor Soc. Nat. Hort. Sci., 1992-94, 94—; contbr. articles to profl. jours. Islam. Avocations: music, badminton, swimming, fishing. Home: Sector 15A, 1097-A Housing Bd Colony, Haryana 125 001, India Office: Haryana Agrl U, Dept Hort, Haryana 125 004, India

SIDEBOTTOM, STEPHEN RICHARD, human resource administrator; b. Ashton under Lyne, Eng., Apr. 12, 1963; s. William Joseph and Barbara (Walker-Catchpole) S.; m. Catherine Margaret Elspeth Walder, July 27, 1991; children: Alexandra Lucy Domenica, Amelia Flora Isobel. MA in Modern History and Econs., St. John's Coll., Oxford, Eng., 1985; MBA, London Bus. Sch., 1991. Various positions Std. Chartered Bank, Edinburgh/London/Persian Gulf, 1986-89; advisor Ministry Fin. and Nat. Economy, Bahrain, 1992-94; sr. cons. Hay Mgmt. Cons., London, 1994-96; human resources dir. investment banking and risk mgmt. divsns. Barclay de Zoete Wedd, London, 1996-97; human resources dir. Commerzbank AG, London, 1998—; part-time lectr. U. Bahrain, 1992-94. Fellow Royal Soc. for Encouragement of Arts, Mfrs. and Commerce; mem. Inst. Pers. and Devel., Assn. MBAs. Anglican. Avocations: Oriental art, textiles, 20th century art.

SIDELSKY, PATRICIA LONEY, science educator; b. Hanover, N.H., Jan. 5, 1945; d. Charles Alexander and Mary (Zurbrugg) Loney; m. Richard W. Lippincott, Apr. 17, 1971 (div. Apr. 1980); 1 child, Richard Ryan; m. Michael G. Sidelsky, May 24, 1980; 1 child, Cory Charles. BS in Biology, Bucknell U., 1967; MS in Biology, Rutgers U., 1987. Cert. in comprehensive sci. tchr., N.J. Tchr. sci. Easton (Md.) Mid. Sch., 1972-79; med. technologist Easton Meml. Hosp., 1974-76; tchr. Easton Middle Sch., 1976-79; tchr. advanced placement biology and genetics Cherokee High Sch., Marlton, N.J., 1979—; med. technologist HIP of N.J., Medford, 1979-87, 90-92; lead tchr. Ctr. for Maths., Sci. and Computer Edn. Rutgers U., New Brunswick, N.J., 1988-93; lead tchr. Douglass Summer Sci. Inst., New Brunswick, 1988-92; mem. Douglass Coll. Bd. for Women in Maths. & Sci., 1988-92. Co-author: Molecular Approaches to the Study of Gene Activity, 1987—. Recipient Outstanding Tchr. award, N.J., Nat. Assn. Biology Tchrs., 1989, Tandy Tchr. Scholar award, 1991; Access Excellence fellow Genentech, 1994; grantee Ptnrs. in Sci. Rsch. Corp., 1994-95; named Tchr. of Yr. Lenape Regional H.S. Dist., 1996. Mem. Biology Tchrs. Assn. N.J. (v.p. 1990, pres. elect 1991-92, pres. 1992—), Nat. Sci. Tchrs. Assn., N.J. Sci. Tchrs. Assn., Nat. Biology Tchrs. Assn., Am. Soc. Clin. Pathologists, Am. Soc. Microbiology. Episcopalian. Home: 8 Rockledge Ct Marlton NJ 08053-9774 Office: Cherokee High Sch Willowbend Rd Marlton NJ 08053

SIDHARTH, BURRA GAUTAM, research scientist; b. Visakhapatnam, India, July 7, 1948; s. Burra Sivarama Sastry and Burra Kameswari; m. Burra Subbalakshmi, May 23, 1975; children: Avinash, Anupam. BSc with honors, St. Xavier's Coll., Calcutta, 1967; MSc, Calcutta U., 1970, PhD, 1977. Coll. prof. St. Xavier's Coll., Calcutta, 1971-80; sci. officer Birla Planetarium, Calcutta, 1980-84; reader Osmania U., Hyderabad, India, 1984-85; dir. B.M. Birla Sci. Ctr., Hyderabad, 1985—; mem. bd. studies in astronomy Osmania U., Hyderabad, 1989—; sr. assoc. Internat. Ctr. for Theoretical Physics, Italy, 1991-96; hon. assoc. Societa Indoloyica L.P. Tessitori, Italy, 1995—; mem. bd. studies math. Jawaharlal Nehru Tech. U., H yderabad, 1996—. Author (short story collection) The Yankee and The Yogi, 1981; co-editor (conf. procs.) Treasures of Indian Astronomy, 1993; contbr. articles to profl. jours. Named Man of the Decade, Indian Express, Hyderabad, 1990. Fellow Royal Astron. Soc., Andhra Pradesh Acad. Scis.; mem. Indian Sci. Congress Assn. (nat. convenor 1997—), Indian Geophys. Union (mem. exec. coun.). Avocations: reading, music. Home and Office: BM Birla Sci Ctr, Adarshnagar, Hyderabad 500063, India

SIDHU, JATINDER SINGH, production and software engineer; b. Sirhind, India, Apr. 15, 1970; s. Harpal and Balbir (Sarwara) S. B in Mech. Engring., Panjab U., 1992. Trainee engr. to sr. engr. GG Engring. Co., Chandigarh, India, 1992-96; gen. mgr. Air Agro Ltd., Chandigarh, 1996—. Mem. ASME, Inst. Engrs. Australia. Avocations: reading, playing basketball. E-Mail: jatinder Sidhu@USA.net. Home: #2078 Sec. 44-C, 160 047 Chandigarh India

SIDIME, LAMINE, judge. Chief justice Supreme Court of Guinea. Office: Supreme Court of Guinea, Conakry Guinea*

SIDIQI, GHIASUDDIN, holding company executive; b. Sibi, Pakistan, Oct. 16, 1953; s. Zaheeruddin Sidiqi and Zakia Khatoon; m. Galina Babaeva, Oct. 25, 1978; children: Naeem, Alia. MSc, journalist diploma, Moscow State U., 1981. Mgr. Fateh Textile Mills, Moscow, 1978-81; gen. mgr. Tabami Corp.-Moscow Office, Moscow, 1982-86; founder, pres. Grid Internat. Holding B.V., Katwijk, Pakistan, 1987—, Katwijk, The Netherlands, 1991—; bd. dirs. Grid Group Cos., No. Shipping Co., Archangilsk, Russia, 1st Shipping Bank, Russia. Bd. dirs. Grid Found., Ctrl. Asian Culture Found. Avocations: reading, travel, social work. Home: Van Bronckhorstlaan 14, PX-2242 Wassenaar The Netherlands Office: Grid Internat Holding BV, Ambachtsweg 5F, 2222 AH Katwijk ZH, The Netherlands

SIDJANSKI, SACHA P., scientist; b. Geneva, Switzerland, Dec. 5, 1964; s. Dusan and Monique (Foex) S.; m. Deirdre A. Perreault, Sept. 11, 1998. Diploma of Biology, Geneva U., 1992; MSc, NYU, 1994, PhD, 1997; postdoctoral study, SUNY, Stony Brook, 1998. Scientist Pasteur Inst., Paris, 1999, W.H.O., Geneva, Switzerland, 2000—. Recipient Young Investigator award Am. Soc. Tropical Medicine and Hygiene, 1997. Office: RPC, World Health Orgn, 1211 Geneva Switzerland

SIDKIN, STEPHEN LEE, lawyer; b. London, Dec. 15, 1956; s. Jack and bertha (Cohen) S.; m. Lynne Juliette Goldman, Apr. 8, 1984; 1 child, Samuel. LLB, King's Coll., London, 1978; MA in Bus. Law, Guildhall, London, 1984. Solicitor, Eng. Asst. solicitor Norton Rose, London, 1981-84; asst. solicitor Oppenheimers, London, 1984-88, assoc. ptnr., 1988; ptnr.-elect Denton Hall, London, 1988-89; founding ptnr. Fox Williams, London, 1989—. Author: Product Tampering in the United Kingdom, 1993, The General Product Safety Regulations, 1996. Chmn. comml. law subcom. City of London Law Soc., 1995-99. Mem. The Chartered Inst. of Mktg., The Law Soc. of Eng. and Wales. Avocations: travel, international affairs, boating. Home: 62 Howards Ln, London SW15 6QD, England Office: Fox Williams City Gate Hse, 39-45 Finsbury Sq, London EC2A 1UU, England

SIDNEY, WILLIAM WRIGHT, retired aerospace company executive; b. Anaconda, Mont., Dec. 31, 1929; s. Paul and Lily Maud (Wright) S.; divorced; children: Kay Elise, Paul Daniel. Student U. Calif., Berkeley, 1953-56. Supr. prodn. Kaiser Aerospace, San Leandro, Calif., 1953-57, project engr., 1957-67, chief engr., 1967-69, gen. mgr., 1969-77; pres. Kaiser Aerotech, San Leandro, Calif., 1977-95, Kaiser Space Products, Pueblo, Colo., 1988-95, ret., 1995. With USN, 1948-52. Recipient NASA Pub. Svc. medal 1981. Home: 6025 Ridgemont Dr Oakland CA 94619-3721

SIDORCZYK, ZYGMUNT, microbiologist; b. Czyzewice, Poland, Apr. 7, 1940; s. Lucjan and Aleksandra (Jarocka) S.; m. Iwona Gajdka, Oct. 17, 1964; 1 child, Michal. Doctorate, U. Lodz, 1964. From asst. to full prof., dir. Inst. Microbiology, Lodz, Poland, 1964—. Recipient golden cross of merit Pres. Poland, 1985, medal Commn. Nat. Edn., 1984. Mem. Polish Soc. Microbiologists, Internat. Endotoxin Soc. Roman Catholic. Avocations: sports, bridge, reading. Home: Klonowa 13 m 32, 91-036 Lodz Poland Office: Inst Microbiology U Lodz, Banacha 12/16, 90-237 Lodz Poland

SIEBBELES, LAURENS DIRK ANDRÉ, physicist, researcher; b. Amsterdam, The Netherlands, Feb. 12, 1963; s. André Thomas Cornelis and Helena Maria (Vangorkum) S. Grad., Free U. Amsterdam, 1986; PhD in Physics, U. Amsterdam, 1991. Rschr. Nat. Ctr. Sci. Rsch., Paris, 1991-94, FOM-Inst. Atomic & Molecular Physics, Amsterdam, 1994; dep. dept. head, rschr. Tech. U., Delft, The Netherlands, 1994—. Contbr. over 50 articles to profl. jours. Mem. Royal Dutch Chem. Soc., Dutch Phys. Soc. Avocations: tennis, drumming, cycling. Office: IRI Tech Univ, Mekelweg 15, 2629 JB Delft The Netherlands

SIEBER, HANS-PETER, orthopedist; b. Visp, Switzerland, Sept. 2, 1949; s. Hans Peter and Heidi (Matti) S.; m. Maya Elsa Schmidt, June 25, 1971; children: Pascal-Jorg, Simone-Eva. MD, U. Basel, 1975. Asst. phys. surg. dept. Cantonal Hosp., Schafhausen, Switzerland, 1975-78; sr. asst. physician dept. orthopedic surgery/traumatology Hosp. St. Gallen, Switzerland, 1978-82; sr. resident orthopedics Regional Hosp., Biel-Bienne, Switzerland, 1983-85; head dept. orthopedics Ctrl. Hosp., Biel-Bienne, 1986—. Mem. Swiss Orthopedic Soc. Office: Ctrl Hosp Ortho Clin, Vogelsang 84, Kanton Bern CH-2500, Switzerland

SIEBER, ULRICH, law educator, consultant; b. Stuttgart, Fed. Republic Germany, Nov. 18, 1950; s. Helmut and Hanna Sieber. D in Law, U. Freiburg, Fed. Republic Germany, 1977, Habilitation, 1987. Rsch. fellow U. Freiburg, 1973-87; pvt. practice Freiburg, 1978-87; full prof. criminal law U. Bayreuth, Fed. Republic of Germany, 1987-91, U. Würzburg, Fed. Republic Germany, 1991-2000, U. München, Fed. Republic Germany, 2000—; cons. German Ministry of Justice, German Ministry of Rsch., Edn. and Tech., U.S. Senate, Can. Ministry of Justice, Commn. European Communities, Coun. Europe, OECD, UN. Author: Computerkriminalität u. Strafrecht, 1977, 2d edit., 1980, Informationstechnologie u. Strafrechtreform, 1985, International Handbook on Computer Crime, 1986, The International Emergence of Criminal Information Law, 1992, Liability for On-Line Data Bank Services in the European Communities, 1992, Logistik der Organisierten Kriminalität, 1993, Europäische Einigung und Europäisches Strafrecht, 1993, Information Technology Crime, 1994, Internat. Organisierte Kriminalitat, 1997, Kinderpornographie, Jugendsruk u. Providerveantwartlichkeit im Internet, 1999, Verantwortlichkeit im Internet, 1999, Handbuch Multimediarecht, 1999; editor: lus Informationis - European Series on Information Law, lus Criminale - Series on European Criminal Law, lus Europaeum - series on European Law, MultiMedia and Recht, Jour. for Multimedia and Law. Mem. German Assn. for European Criminal Law (pres.). Office: U Würzburg, Domerschulstrasse 16, 97070 Würzburg Germany 7

SIEBERICHS, THOMAS, regional government official, lawyer; b. Duisburg, Northrhine-Westphalia, Germany, Jan. 28, 1968; s. Heinrich Gerardus and Gundi Maria (Peikert) S. LLB, U. Liège, 1994. Bar: Liège, Belgium. Lawyer pvt. practice Verviers, Belgium, 1994-96, Roeselare, Belgium, 1996-97; head planning and environ. dept. Evere Municipality, Brussels, 1997-98; adminstr. for external rels. Walloon Region, 1998—. Activist Amnesty Internat.. Krefeld, Germany, 1985-87, Malaysia coord. Aachen, Germany, 1987-89, coord. Malaysia and Indonesia, Liège, 1989-90. 3rd rank Civilian Alternative Svc., 1987-89, Aachen, Germany. Mem. The Planetary Soc. Avocations: space exploration, social and religious history. Office: Région Wallonne DGRE, Pl Sainctelette 2, B-1080 Brussels Belgium

SIEBERT, HORST, economics educator, foundation administrator; b. Neuwied, Germany, Mar. 20, 1938; s. Fritz and Anna (Heini) S.; m. Christa Causemann, Apr. 29, 1965. MA in Econs., U. Cologne, Fed. Republic Germany, 1963; PhD, U. Muenster, Fed. Republic Germany, 1965, habilitation, 1969. Asst. prof. Tex. A&M U., 1967-68; prof. econs. U. Mannheim, Fed. Republic Germany, 1969-84, U. Konstanz, Fed. Republic Germany, 1984-89; prof. theoretical econs. U. Kiel, Fed. Republic Germany, 1989—; pres. Kiel Inst. World Econs., 1989—; mem. Coun. Econ. Advisors, Germany, 1990—. Author: Economics of the Environment, 1987, 5th revised edit., 1998, Aussenwirtschaft, 7th edit., 2000, The New Economic Landscape in Europe, 1991, Geht den Deutschen die Arbeit aus?, 1995, Weltwirtschaft, 1997, The World Economy, 1999. Mem. Am. Econ. Assn., European Econ. Assn., Verein Fuer Socialpolitik. Office: Kiel Inst World Econs, Duesternbrooker Weg 120, 24105 Kiel Germany

SIEBERT, MANFRED, geophysics educator; b. Ribbeck, Templin, Germany, June 2, 1925; s. Walter and Lisbeth (Rosner) S.; m. Barbara Gassmann, Apr. 27, 1962; children: Ina, Anja. Diploma in Physics, U. Göttingen (Germany), 1954, D Natural Sci., 1955, Habilitation, 1965. Rsch. asst. Inst. Geophysics, Göttingen U., 1955-64, acting dir., 1964-68, prof., dir., 1968-90, prof. emeritus, 1990—; mem. sci. adv. com. Deutscher Wetterdienst, Federal Republic of Germany, 1970-90; mem. adv. bd. Max-Planck-Inst. for Aeronomy, Katlenburg-Lindau, 1976-88. Fellow Göttingen Acad. Scis.; mem. Am. Geophys. Union, German Geophys. Soc. (chmn. 1975-77), German Phys. Soc., Gauss Soc. (chmn. 1978-93). Home: Hohler Graben 4, D-37077 Göttingen Germany Office: Inst Geophysik, Herzberger Landstr 180, D-37075 Göttingen Germany

SIEBLER, MARIO, physician; b. Voelklingen, Germany, Apr. 9, 1956; s. Eugen and Giesela (Nackas) S.; m. Ulrike Schwab, Aug. 1991; 1 child, Ariane. MD, U. Hamburg, 1983. Postdoctoral Dept. of Physiology, Homburg, Germany, 1983-85, resident in neurology, 1985-86; fellowship Deutsche Forschungsgemeinschaft, Dusseldorf, Germany, 1987-88; resident U. Dusseldorf, 1980-93, cons., 1994—; cons. in field, 1994—. Doctor Air Force, 1976-77, 84. Mem. Deutsche Physiologische Gesellschaft, Deutsche EEG Gesellschaft, Deutsche Neurologen Gesellschaft. Avocations: music, biking. Office: U Dusseldorf, Moorenstr 5, 40225 Dusseldorf Germany

SIEBOLD, HORST, medical physics executive, research; b. Bad Hersfeld, Germany, June 17, 1950; s. Karl and Elfriede (Fischer) S.; m. Susanne Lasch, July 10, 1992. Physics diploma, TH Darmstadt, Germany, 1973, PhD in Physics, 1979. Sci. asst. TH Darmstadt, 1974-79; group head corp. R&D Siemens AG, Erlangen, Germany, 1979-94; head dept. basic devel. Siemens Med., Erlangen, 1994-98, head group tech. med. engring., 1998—; presenter in field. Contbr. articles to profl. jours. Office: Siemens AG Med Engring, Henkestr 127, D-91052 Erlangen Germany

SIEBZEHNRUEBL, ERNST ROBERT, gynecologist, consultant; b. Passau, Bavaria, Germany, Oct. 4, 1956; s. Franz Xaver and Rosa (Rudolf) S.; m. Christine Oeller, Aug. 4, 1978; 1 child, Florian. Abitur, Adalbert-Stifler Gymnasium, Passau, 1977, MD, 1984, PhD, 1995. Med. diplomate. Rsch. fellow U. Erlangen, Germany, 1983-84; registrar ob-gyn. U. Erlangen, 1984-88, sr. registrar dept. ob-gyn., 1988-90, cons., dir. in-vitro fertilization and asst. reproduction, 1991—. Fellow Am. Fertility Soc., Soc. for Cryobiology, German Fertility Soc. Home: Im Herrnloh 5, 91054 Buckenhof Bavaria, Germany Office: Univ Frauenklinik, Universitaetsstr 21-23, 90154 Erlangen Bavaria, Germany

SIEDE, WERNER HEINRICH, physician; b. Kiel, Germany, Oct. 12, 1949; s. Werner and Ilse (Schuett) S.; m. Martina Kaubruegger, Nov. 18, 1986; children: Dominik, Marisa. MD, U. Frankfurt, 1980, PhD, 1987. Asst. dir. Zentrallabor U., Frankfurt, 1974-89; dir. of lab. Klinikuk Lippe, Germany, 1989—. Co-author: Diabetologie in Klinik und Praxis, 1994; contbr. articles to profl. jours. Mem. German Soc. Clin. Chemistry, Internat. Soc. Clin. Enzymology, Rotary Club. Avocations: carnivorous plants, antique toys, doppelkopf, skiing, golfing. Office: Klinikum Lippe Lemgo, Rintelner Str 85, 32657 Lemgo Germany

SIEDLE, ROBERT DOUGLAS, management consultant; b. Canton, Ohio, Aug. 8; m. Beverly Rose Scholl, Mar. 18, 1972 (div. Oct. 1983). BA in Econs., Hiram Coll., 1956; profl. cert. edn., Kent State/Western Res. Univs., 1963. Tchr., prin. Ohio secondary schs., 1957-65; salesman, area rep. visual products divsn. 3M Co., 1966-68; mgr. market devel. and tng. AV divsn. Bell & Howell, 1968-69; Chgo. br. mgr. info. systems divsn. Am. Std., 1969-72; mgr. edn. systems divsn. Audiotronics Corp., 1972-76; gen. mgr. Niles Entertainment/Wardway Films, 1977-80; pres. The Ultimate Image, Lakeland, Fla., 1985—. Producer: (films) New Dimensions in Learning II, 1969, District 65: The Exceptional Child, 1969, Career Exploration: Health, 1976, The Wide World of Work, 1976; author: Multisensory Learning: A Training Guide, 1973, Alphabet Zoo, 1973, City of Boston Young Adult Alternate Career Program, 1974, The Quick Job Hunt Guide, 1991; author, producer, dir.: (multimedia rd. show) "Rap" With Students, 1975; producer, editor: (film) Stampin' Ground, 1977; author poetry appearing in books and mags., 1991—; appeared on nat. radio and TV programs in U.S. and Can. advocate, heritage assoc. Defenders of Wildlife. Named to Nat. Aviation and Space Exploration Wall of Honor Smithsonian Nat. Air and Space Mus. Dulles Ctr., 2000. Mem. U.S. Naval Aviation Mus. (life), U.S. Naval Inst. (life), Navy League of U.S. (life), Internat. Platform Assn., Sun 'n Fun Air Mus. (life), Am. Air Mus. in Britain (founding mem.), Aircraft Owners and Pilots Assn. (life), Aircraft Owners and Pilots Assn. Safety Found. (life), Exptl. Aircraft Assn., Warbirds of Am., Great Lakes Hist. Soc. (life), Air Force Assn. (life), Steamship Hist. Soc. Am. (life), Marine Hist. Soc. Detroit, Palm Springs Air Mus., Airship Assn. Ltd., World War II Meml. Soc. (charter), Air Force Meml. Found. (charter). Baptist. Office: The Ultimate Image PO Box 91388 Lakeland FL 33804-1388

SIEDLER, GEROLD, physical oceanographer educator; b. Olmutz, Czechoslovakia, Aug. 16, 1933. D Natural Scis., U. Kiel, Germany, 1960, Habilitation, 1966. Rsch. scientist Oceanographic Inst., Kiel, 1960-69; dir. marine physics dept. Oceanographic Inst., 1969-98, dir. Inst., 1976-78; prof. U. Kiel, 1969-98, prof. emeritus, 1998—, dean faculty math. sci., 1991-92; vis. scientist Woods Hole (Mass.) Oceanographic Instn., 1967-68, 71-72, 83, 89, U. Hawaii, Honolulu, 1984, 85, U. Marie et Pierre Curie, Paris, 1989, U. Miami, 1990, Jet Propulsion Lab., Pasadena, Calif., 1990, Ifremer Brest, 1994, U. Concepcion, 1998; v.p. Internat. Assn. Phys. Sci. Ocean, 1975-79; v.p. Sci. Com. on Oceanic Rsch., 1980-83, pres., 1983-88; assoc. investigator Inst. Marine Sci., Telde, Spain, 1998—. Co-author: General Oceanography, 1980, Physical Properties of Sea Water, 1986, The South Atlantic, 1996, Ozeanographie Bergmann-Schaefer, 1997. Mem. AAAS, Am. Geophys. Union, Oceanography Soc., German Phys. Soc., German Meteorol. Soc., German Geophys. Soc., European Geophy. Soc. Office: Inst fü Meereskunde, Dusternbrooker Weg 20, 24105 Kiel Germany

SIEGBAHN, KAI MANNE BÖRJE, physicist, educator; b. Lund, Sweden, Apr. 20, 1918; s. Manne and Karin (Hogbom) S.; m. Anna-Brita Rhedin, May 23, 1944; children: Per, Hans, Nils. B.S., 1939, Licentiate of Philosophy, 1942; Ph.D., U. Uppsala, 1944; D.Sc. honoris causa, U. Durham, 1972, U. Basel, 1980, U. Liege, 1980, Upsala Coll., 1982, U. Sussex, 1983. Research assoc. Nobel Inst. Physics, 1942-51; prof. physics Royal Inst. Tech., Stockholm, 1951-54; prof., head physics dept. U. Uppsala, Sweden, 1954-84, prof. physics; prof. Papal Acad. Sci., 1996—. Author: Beta and Gamma-Ray Spectroscopy, 1955; Alpha, Beta and Gamma-Ray Spectroscopy, 1965; ESCA-Atomic, Molecular and Solid State Structure Studies by Means of Electron Spectroscopy, 1967; ESCA Applied to Free Molecules, 1969. Recipient Lindblom Prize, 1945, Bjorken Prize, 1955, 77, Celsius medal, 1962, Sixten Heyman award, 1971, Harrison Howe award, 1973, Maurice F. Hasler award, 1975, Charles Frederick Chandler medal, 1976, Torbern Bergman medal, 1979, Nobel Prize in Physics, 1981, Pitts. award spectroscopy, 1982, Röntgen medal, 1985, Fiuggi award, 1986, Humboldt award, 1986, Premio Castiglione Di Sicilia, 1990. Mem. Royal Swedish Acad. Sci., Royal Swedish Acad. Engring. Scis., Royal Soc. Sci., Royal Acad. Arts and Sci. Uppsala, European Acad. Arts, Scis. and Humanities, Academia Europaea, Royal Physiograph. Soc. Lund, Societas Scientairum Fennica, Norwegian Acad. Sci., Royal Norwegian Soc. Scis. and Letters, Am. Acad. Arts and Scis. (hon.), Comite des Poids et Mesures, Internat. Union Pure and Applied Physics (pres. 1981-84), Pontifical Acad. Scis., NAS (fgn. assoc.), U.S. NAS, Japan Acad. Scis., Russian Acad. Scis. *

SIEGEL, ABRAHAM J., economics educator, academic administrator; b. N.Y.C., Nov. 6, 1922; s. Samuel J. and Dora (Drach) S.; m. Lillian Wakshull, Dec. 22, 1946; children: Emily Jean Siegel Stangle, Paul Howard, Barbara Ann Pugliese. B.A. summa cum laude, CCNY, 1943; M.A., Columbia U., 1949; Ph.D., U. Calif., Berkeley, 1961. Instr. dept. econs. CCNY, 1947-49; research economist Inst. Indsl. Relations, U. Calif., Berkeley, 1952-54; instr. dept. econs. M.I.T., Cambridge, 1954-56, asst. prof., 1956-59, assoc. prof., 1959-64, prof. dept. econs. Sloan Sch. Mgmt., 1964-93, assoc. dean Sloan Sch. Mgmt., 1967-80, dean, 1980-87, prof. emeritus, sr. lectr., 1993—; spl. lectr. Trade Union Program, Harvard U., 1961-64; vis. prof. Brandeis U., 1956-60; vis. prin. mem. div. Internat. Inst. Labour Studies, Internat. Labour Office, Geneva, 1964-65; asso. staff dir. Com. Econ. Devel., Study Group on Nat. Labor Policy, 1960-61; trustee, chmn. adminstrv. com. M.I.T. Retirement Plan for Staff Mems., 1970-91. Co-author: Industrial Relations in the Pacific Coast Longshore Industry, 1956, The Public Interest in National Labor Policy, 1961, The Impact of Computers on Collective Bargaining, 1969, Unfinished Business: An Agenda for Labor, Management and the Public, 1978. Bd. dirs. Whitehead Inst. Biomed. Rsch., Analysis Group, Inc., Internat. Data Group; mem. adv. group Internat. Inst. for Applied Systems Analysis, Laxenburg, Austria; mem. Framingham Sch. Com., South Middlesex Regional Dist. Vocat. Sch. Com., 1968-71. With USAF, 1943-46. Mem. Am. Econ. Assn., Indsl. Relations Research Assn., Nat. Acad. Arbitrators, Am. Arbitration Assn. (mem. various panels), Inst. Mgmt. Scis. Bus. Roundtable (exec. com.), Phi Beta Kappa. Clubs: Comml, St. Botolph's. Home: 112 Gardner Rd Brookline MA 02445-4537 Office: MIT Sloan Sch Mgmt 50 Memorial Dr Cambridge MA 02142-1347

SIEGEL, BERNARD LOUIS, lawyer; b. Pitts., Sept. 15, 1938; s. Ralph Robert and Frieda Sara (Stein) S.; m. Marcia Margolis, Sept. 3, 1961 (div. Aug. 1983); children: Jonathan, Sharon; m. Susan Erickson, Aug. 31, 1997. BA, Brandeis U., 1960; JD, Harvard U., 1963. Bar: Pa. 1964, U.S. Dist. Ct. (we. dist.) Pa. 1964, U.S. Dist. Ct. (ea. dist.) Pa. 1985, U.S. Ct. Appeals (3d cir.) 1985, U.S. Supreme Ct. 1985. Assoc. Silin, Eckert & Burke, Erie, Pa., 1963-66; ptnr. Silin, Eckert, Burke & Siegel, Erie, Pa., 1966-73; 1st asst. dist. atty. Erie County, 1972-76; dep. atty. gen. Pa. Dept. Justice, Phila., 1976-78; dep. dist. atty. Dist. Atty. of Phila., 1978-86; pvt. practice Phila., 1986—; adj. prof. La Salle U., Phila., 1986-98; lectr. Fed. Law Enforcement Tng. Ctr., Glynco, Ga., 1986-97, Mercyhurst Coll., Erie, 1974-76, Nat. Coll. Dist. Attys., Houston, 1978-85; adj. prof. Temple U. law sch., 1995—; mem. criminal rules com. Pa. Supreme Ct., Phila., 1976-85; commr. Pa. Crime Commn., Harrisburg, 1976-79. Author: (with others) Pennsylvania Grand Jury Practice, 1983, By No Extraordinary Means, 1986. Mem. ABA, Nat. Assn. Criminal Def. Lawyers, Pa. Assn. Criminal Def. Lawyers (bd. dirs. 1988—), Pa. Bar Assn. (chmn. criminal law sect. 1988-91), Phila. Bar Assn. (chmn. criminal justice sect. 1990-91). Democrat. Jewish. Avocations: bicycling, reading, hiking. Office: 1515 Market St Ste 1915 Philadelphia PA 19102-1920

SIEGEL, EBERHARD GOTTFRIED, endocrinologist, gastroenterologist, educator; b. Grötzingen, Germany, Sept. 21, 1950; s. Guenther Joachim and Gisela Siegel; m. Gerlinde Wöhlert; children: Melanie, Christine, Markus. MD, U. Heidelberg, Germany, 1976; Habilitation, U. Göttingen, Germany, 1988. Asst. physician Dept. Medicine, Tübingen, 1977; rsch. fellow Inst. Clin. Biochemistry, Geneva, 1977-80; asst. physician Dept. Medicine, Göttingen, 1980-88, oberarzt, 1988-91, prof. medicine, 1992; head St. Vincentius Hosp., Karlsruhe, Germany, 1991—. Contbr. articles to profl. jours. Mem. City Coun., Wolfschlugen, 1971-77. Sci. grantee Deutsche Forschungsgemeinschaft, Bonn, 1982-91. Mem. German Diabetes Assn. (förderpreis 1977, Bertram prize 1989), European Diabetes Assn., German Gastroenterol. Assn., German Endocrine Soc., Acad. Ethics in Medicine, Rotary, Am. Diabetes Assn. Avocations: music, mountain climbing, skiing. Office: St Vincent Hosp, Südendstr 32, 76137 Karlsruhe Germany

SIEGEL, IRA T., publishing executive; b. N.Y.C., Sept. 23, 1944; s. David Aaron and Rose (Minsky) S.; m. Sharon Ruth Sacks, Sept. 5, 1965. BS, NYU, 1965; MBA, L.I. U., 1968. Bus. mgr. Buttenheim Pub. Co., N.Y.C., 1965-72; corp. v.p. rsch. Cahners Pub. Co. div. Reed Pub. USA, Boston, 1972-86; pres., COO, R.R. Bowker Pub. Co. div. Reed Pub. USA, New Providence, N.J., 1986-91; pres. Martindale-Hubbell div. Reed Pub. USA, New Providence, N.J., 1990-91; pres., CEO Reed Reference Pub. (includes R.R. Bowker Co., Martindale-Hubbell, Nat. Register Pub. Co., The Salesman's Guide, Marquis Who's Who), New Providence, N.J., 1991-95, Lexis-Nexis, Dayton, Ohio, 1995-97; bd. dirs. Edata.Com, Boca Raton, Fla. Address: 16766 Knightsbridge Ln Delray Beach FL 33484-6948

SIEGEL, MARY ANN GARVIN, author; b. Louisville, Apr. 3, 1944; d. Samuel Hughes and Ann Wendell (Smith) Garvin; m. Charles Holladay Siegel, Sept. 2, 1967 (div.); children: Emily Hughes, Charles Holladay, Jr., Margaret Shafer. BA, Conn. Coll., 1966. Photog. rschr. Time Inc., N.Y.C., 1966-67, Nat. Geog. Soc., Washington, 1967-68; content project mgr. FundraisingINFO.com, 2000—; Leadership Atlanta, 1993-94, exec. com., 1995-96. Trustee Conn. Coll., New London, 1985-90; chair Friends of Spelman Coll., Atlanta, 1990-92; active Atlanta/Fulton County adv. bd. United Way Met. Atlanta, 1994-96; Olympic Envoy to Republic of Nauru, Atlanta Com. Olympic Games, 1994-96; formerly active adv. bd. N.C. Outward Bound Sch., Asheville. Recipient Agnes Berkeley Leahy award Conn. Coll. Alumni Assn., 1991.

SIEGEL, MICHAEL ELLIOT, nuclear medicine physician, educator; b. N.Y.C., May 13, 1942; s. Benjamin and Rose (Gilbert) S.; m. Marsha Rose Snower, Mar. 20, 1966; children: Herrick Jove, Meridith Ann. AB, Cornell U., 1964; MD, Chgo. Med. Sch., 1968. Diplomate Nat. Bd. Med. Examiners. Intern Cedars-Sinai Med. Ctr., L.A., 1968-69, resident in radiology, 1969-70; NIH fellow in radiology Temple U. Med. Ctr., Phila., 1970-71; NIH fellow in nuclear medicine Johns Hopkins U. Sch. Medicine, Balt., 1971-73, asst. prof. radiology, 1972-76; assoc. prof. radiology and medicine U. So. Calif., L.A., 1976—, prof. radiology, 1989—, dir. divsn. nuclear medicine, 1982-99; dir. Sch. Nuclear Medicine, Los Angeles County-U. So. Calif. Med. Ctr., 1976-99; dir. divsn. nuclear medicine Kenneth Norris Cancer Hosp. and Rsch. Ctr., L.A., 1983-99; dir. dept. nuclear medicine Orthopaedic Hosp., L.A., 1981—, Intercmty. Hosp., Covina, Calif., 1981—, U. So. Calif. Univ. Hosp., L.A., 1993—; clin. prof. radiology U. Calif., San Diego, 2000—. Author: Textbook of Nuclear Medicine, 1978, Vascular Surgery, 1983, 88, numerous other textbooks; editor: Nuclear Cardiology, 1981, Vascular Disease: Nuclear Medicine, 1983. Mem. Maple Ctr., Beverly Hills. Served as maj. USAF, 1974-76. Recipient Outstanding Alumnus award Chgo. Med. Sch., 1991. Fellow Am. Coll. Nuclear Medicine (sci. investigator 1974, 76, nominations com. 1980, program com. 1983, trustee 1993, disting. fellow, 1993, bd. reps. 1993—, bd. dirs. 1994—, treas. 1996—, chmn. ann. sci. program 1996—, pres.'s award 1997, v.p. 1997-98, pres. 1999—); mem. Soc. Nuclear Medicine (sic. exhbn. com. 1978-79, program com. 1979-80, Silver medal 1975), Calif. Med. Assn. (sci. adv. bd. 1987—), Radiol. Soc. N.Am., Soc. Nuclear Magnetic Resonance Imaging, Friars So. Calif., Alpha Omega Alpha. Achievements include research on development of nuclear medicine techniques to evaluate cardiovascular disease and diagnose and treat cancer; clinical utilization of video digital displays in nuclear medicine development; invention of pneumatic radiologic pressure system. Office: U So Calif Med Ctr PO Box 693 1200 N State St Los Angeles CA 90033-1029

SIEGEL, ROBERT JAMES, communications executive; b. N.Y.C., Feb. 26, 1929; s. Hiram and Regina (Goldstein) S. ; m. Gonnie McClung, Jan. 8, 1953; children: William Laird, Richard Joseph. BS in Econs., Marietta Coll., 1950. With copy desk N.Y. Times, 1951-53; assoc. editor Lorain (Ohio) Jour., 1953-56; reporter Cleve. Press, 1956-61; with IBM, Armonk, N.Y., 1961—, data processing div. press rels. mgr., corp. info. mgr., corp. pub. affairs mgr., 1979—, dir. info., dir. internal communications, 1988-89; mng. dir., mktg. comm. agy. Metaphor, Inc., Atlanta, 1989-90; pres. Siegel Assocs., Communications Cons., Bal Harbour, Fla., 1991—. Mayor Key Colony Beach, Fla., 1995-98; bd. dirs. Fla. Keys Land and Sea Trust. Mem. Nat. Press Club, Overseas Press Club, Deadline Club of N.Y., Sigma Delta Chi. Home: 4427 SW 91st Dr Gainesville FL 32608-7137

SIEGEL, WAYNE PERRY, composer, music studio director; b. L.A., Feb. 14, 1953; s. Samuel Aaron and Geraldine (Levine) S.; m. Elisabeth Kirsten Fraemohs, Mar. 22, 1980; children: Gabriel Jacob, Mira Rebecca. BA, U. Calif., Santa Barbara, 1975; diplomeksamen, Royal Acad. Music, Aarhus, Denmark, 1977. Adminstrv. dir. West Jutland Symphony Orch. and chamber ensemble, Esbjerg, Denmark, 1984-86; dir. Danish Inst. Electroacoustic Music, Aarhus, Denmark, 1986—; chmn. Internat. Computer Music Conf., Aarhus, 1992-94; bd. mem. Internat. Soc. Contemporary Music World Music Days, Copenhagen, 1994-96; chmn. Danish State Arts Found. Music Coms., 1996-98. Composer: (chamber works) Watercolor, Acrylic, Watercolor, 1981, Tracking for string quartet and computer, 1991, (orch. work) Devil's Golf Course, 1986, (opera) Livstegn (Signs of Life), 1994, Jackdaw, 1995, Movement Study, 1997. Grantee for composition Danish State Arts Found., 1978. Office: DIEM Concert Hall Aarhus, Thomas Jensens Alle, DK-8000 Århus C, Denmark

SIEGELMANN, HAVA TOVA, information systems educator; b. Haifa, Israel, Aug. 23, 1964; d. Joseph Elijah and Hanna S. BA, Technion, Haifa, 1988; MSc, Hebrew U., 1992; PhD, Rutgers U., 1993. Prof. Technion, Haifa, 1994—, head info. sys. engring., 1999—; adv. bd. mem. Am. Inst. Physics, 1999. Author: Neural Networks and Analog Computation: Beyond the Turing Limit, 1999. Recipient Artist cert. in piano Rubin Conservatory, Israel, 1982. Office: Fac Indsl Engring & Mgmt, Technion, 32000 Haifa Israel

SIEGENTHALER, WALTER ERNST, internal medicine educator; b. Davos, Switzerland, Dec. 14, 1923; s. Walter and Anna S.; m. Gertrud Siegenthaler, Dec. 31, 1957. MD, U. Zurich (Switzerland), 1948; Dr.h.c., Martin Luther U., Halle, Germany, 1991. Chief resident in internal medicine St. Gallen, Switzerland, 1954-58; prof. internal medicine, chmn. dept. U. Bonn, Fed. Republic Germany, 1969-71; asst. in pathology U. Zurich, 1949-50, asst. in internal medicine, 1950-54, chief resident, 1958-61, lectr., 1961-67, asst. prof., 1967-69, assoc. prof., 1971-91, chmn. dept., dean Med. Sch., 1978-80; pres. Conf. Clinic Dirs., Zurich, 1980-91; pres. 10th Internat. Congress Chemotherapy, 1977, Zurich; pres. Swiss Rsch. Inst. for Climate and Medicine, Davos, 1992—. Author textbooks on differential diagnosis, 18th edit., 2000, on clin. pathophysiology, 8th edit., 2000, on internal medicine, 3d edit., 1992; bd. dirs. numerous nat. and internat. sci. jours.; contbr. articles to profl. jours. Bd. dirs. EMDO Found. Zurich, 1974—, Jung Found., Hamburg, 1982-95, Opo Found., Zurich, 1994—, Swiss Found. for the promotion of young people, 1995—. Col. Swiss Army, 1941-88. Recipient Ernst von Bergmann plaque, 1972, Ludwig Heilmeyer gold medal, 1984, Jung Found. Sci. and rsch. gold medal for medicine, 1997, Crystal of Davos, 1998; Hon. Medal of the Charité U. Berlin, 1999, Walter Siegenthaler prize German Med. Jour., 2000, Gustav von Bergman Gold medal German Soc. Internal Medicine, 2000; named to Acad. Naturforscher Leopoldina, 1981. Fellow Infectious Diseases Soc. Am. (corr. 1983); mem. German Soc. Internal Medicine (pres. 1983-84, bd. dirs., hon. mem. 1992), Swiss Soc. Internal Medicine (bd. dirs., hon. mem. 1993), Soc. for Progress in Internal Medicine (Cologne; bd. dirs., pres. 1992—), Paul Ehrlich Soc. (pres. 1969-71, 73-75, 75-77, hon. mem. 1994), Rotary. Home: Forsterstrasse 6l, CH-8044 Zurich Switzerland Office: Univ Hosp, Rämistrasse 100, CH-8091 Zurich Switzerland

SIEGLE, SVEN, pulp and paper specialist, researcher; b. Waiblingen, Germany, Nov. 15, 1974; s. Erich Karl and Roswitha (Ehmann) S. Abitur, Chemisch-Tech. Asst., U. Stuttgart, Germany, 1995, BS, 1997. Chmn. bd. Natural Pulping AG, Winnenden, Germany, 1996-2000; R & D mgr. Natural Pulping AG, 1998—. Inventor in field. Named Young Scientist, European Union, 1995. Mem. Tech. Assn. of Pulp and Paper Industry, Paper Industry Mgmt. Assn., Zellcheming. Avocations: sports, computers, animals, chemistry, traveling. Home: Silcher St 30, D-71364 Winnenden BW, Germany Office: Natural Pulping AG, Silcherstr 30, D-71364 Winnenden BW, Germany

SIEGLER, NICHOLAS, astrophysicist; b. Tel Aviv, July 29, 1964; s. Marcel and Eveline (Caciularu) S. B of Enging., Stevens Inst. Tech., 1985; MBA, Rotterdam (The Netherlands) Sch. Mgmt., 1993. Project engr. Nat. Starch and Chem., Plainfield, N.J., 1985-86; plant supr. Nat. Starch and Chem., Kansas City, Mo., 1986-89; project engr. Nat. Starch and Chem., Milan, 1990-91; project mgr. Nat. Starch and Chem., Johannesburg, South Africa, 1993; site mgr. Nat. Starch and Chem., Villefranche, France, 1994-96; European ops. mgr. Permabond, Eastleigh, U.K., 1997; concentrator in astrophysics Harvard U., Cambridge, Mass., 1998—. Mem. Boston Jr. Chamber (membership dir. 1998—), Southampton Jr. Chamber (project mgr. 1997), Lyon Jr. Chamber, Milan Jr. Chamber (founder 1990-91), Kansas City Jr. Chamber (project mgr. 1986-89). Avocations: hiking, reading, travelling. Home: 21 Chauncy St Apt 47 Cambridge MA 02138-2454

SIEGMUND-SCHULTZE, REINHARD, historian; b. Halle, Germany, Apr. 2, 1953; s. Walther and Dorothea (Haake) S-S.; m. Ute Romberg, Feb. 13, 1976 (div.); children: Hanna, Ulrike. Diploma in Maths., U. Halle (Germany), 1975, PhD, 1979; Dr. habil., Humboldt U., Berlin, 1987. Asst. Humboldt U., Berlin, 1978-87, assoc. prof., 1987-91, 97-2000, rsch. assoc., 1994-97; vis. prof. U. N.H., Durham, 1991-92, Harvard U., Cambridge, Mass., 1992-94; prof. history Math. Agder Univ. Coll., Kristiansand, Norway, 2000—. Author: Mathematische Berichterstattung in Hitlerdeutschland, 1993, Mathematiker auf der Flucht vor Hitler, 1998; assoc. editor: Historia Mathematica, 1993—; contbr. articles to profl. jours. Mem. Internat. Acad. Sci. History (Paris). Avocations: music, chorus. Home: Bausdorffstr 24, 12621 Berlin Germany Office: Agder Univ Coll, Dept Math, 4630 Kristiansand Norwayy

SIEJKA, GEORGE JOHN, artist; b. Vienna, Austria, June 24, 1946; came to U.S., 1950; Cert. Fine Arts, Sch. Visual Arts, N.Y.C., 1969; BS in Art Edn. cum laude, NYU, 1974, MA in Fine Arts, 1975. represented by Nancy Hoffman Gallery, N.Y.C. Group exhbns. include Fitchburg (Mass.) Art Mus., Anchorage (Alaska) Mus. Art, Rockford (Ill.) Coll. Art Gallery. Recipient Founders Day award NYU, 1974. Mem. N.Y. Artists Equity Assn.

SIEKMANN, DONALD CHARLES, accountant; b. St. Louis, July 2, 1938; s. Elmer Charles and Mabel Louise (Blue) S.; m. Linda Lee Knowles, Sept. 10, 1966; 1 child, Brian Charles. BS, Washington U., St. Louis, 1960. CPA, Ohio, Ga. Regional mng. ptnr. Arthur Andersen & Co., Cin., 1960-98. Columnist Cin. Enquirer, 1983-86, Gannett News Services, 1983-86; editor "Tax Clinic" column Tax Advisor mag., 1974-75. Mem. bd. Cin. Zool. Soc., 1985-88; officer, bd. dirs. Cin. Found. for Pub. TV, 1984-88, Cin. Symphony Orch., 1973-85, Cin. Ballet Co., 1973-88, Atlanta Symphony Orch., 1988-91, The Atlanta Opera, 1988-91, Cin. Theatrical Assn., Jewish Hosp., 1993—, Cin. Assn. for Performing Arts, 1992—, Cin. United Way, 1992-99, Cin. Pk. Bd. Found., 1995-98; pres. Greater Cin. Arts and Edn. Ctr., 1996-99; mem. Friends of Sch. for Creative and Performing Arts, 1996-99, Cin. Arts Festival, 1992-96, Ronald McDonald House, 1998—. Mem. AICPA, Ohio Soc. CPAs, Cin. Country Club (trustee 1983-88), Optimists Club (pres. Queen City chpt. 1986). Lutheran. Club: Cin. Country (trustee 1983-88). Home: 5495 Waring Dr Cincinnati OH 45243-3933 Office: Arthur Andersen & Co 425 Walnut St Ste 1500 Cincinnati OH 45202-3946

SIELEMANN, GERHARD, retired bank clerk; b. Soest, Sourland, Germany, Nov. 3, 1935; s. Herbert Hennig and Magdalene (Selves) S. Grad. vocat. sch., Germany, 1954. Lehrling textiles, 1951-54; clk. textile fabrics, 1954-58, beverage wholesale, 1959-60, adminstrn., 1960-64, bank, 1964-91; ret., 1991; official-in-charge office, 1954-91. Avocation: travel. Home: Füsilierstreet 12, 40476 Düsseldorf Germany

SIEMION, IGNACY ZENON, chemistry educator; b. Krzczonow, Poland, Aug. 8, 1932; s. Mikolaj and Apolonia (Urban) S.; m. Alicja Teresa Szastynska, June 23, 1959; 2 children. MSc in Chemistry, Lomonosov U., Moscow, 1955; PhD in Chemistry, Tech. U., Wroclaw, Poland, 1964, DSc, 1968. Asst. Wroclaw U., 1955-58, docent, 1970-74, prof., 1974—, dir. organic chemistry, 1976—; asst. Med. Acad., Wroclaw, 1958-69; mem. Ctrl. Commn. for Degrees in Scis., Warsaw, 1994—. Author: Biostereochemistry, 1985; editor-in-chief Chem. News, 1983-93; mem. editl. bd. Acta Biochimica Polonica, 1978-84, Polish Jour. Chem., 1990—. Recipient M. Sklodowska-Curie award, 1986, Ministry of Edn. awards, 1972, 76, 78, 80, 84, 87, 94. Mem. Wroclaw Sci. Soc., European Peptide Soc., Am. Peptide Soc. Avocations: history of chemistry, history of sciences in Poland. Home: Krainskiego 3 m 10, 50-153 Wrocław Poland Office: Wrocław U Fac Chemistry, Joliot-Curie 14, 50-383 Wrocław Poland

SIEMON-BURGESON, MARILYN M., education administrator; b. Whittier, Calif., Nov. 15, 1934; d. John Roscoe and Louise Christina (Secoy) Mason; m. Carl J. Siemon, Aug. 18, 1956 (div. Oct. 1984); children: Timothy G., Melanie A. Siemon Imes; Troy M.; m. James K. Burgeson, Jan. 24, 1987. BA, U. Redlands, 1956; MA, Pacific Oaks Coll., 1975; postgrad., Point Loma Coll., 1979-80. Cert. adminstr., elem. and early childhood tchr. Tchr. Sierra Madre (Calif.) Cmty. Nursery Sch., 1970-77; tchr. parent edn. and music Pasadena (Calif.) Unified Schs., 1977-79, project coord., 1980-82, tchr. curriculum resource dept., 1982-83, adminstr. Washington Children's Ctr., 1983-99; endorsed trainer High Scope Found. Register, 1990—; cons. staff devel. and tng. Pasadena; trainer Program for Infant/Toddler Caregivers; instr. Citrus Coll., 1996-98; conf. chair Calif. High Scope Educators, 1995—. Active Arcadia (Calif.) Bicentennial Commn., 1974-76; mem. policy coun. for cmty. housing svcs. Pasadena Head Start, 1992-95; life mem. Sierra Madre Sch. PTA; mem. Child Care Coalition, Pasadena; Altar Guild, lay Eucharistic minister St. Edmunds, San Marino, Calif.; mem. edn. and libr. com. Pasadena Hist. Mus., 2000—. Ednl. Professions Devel. fellow Pacific Oaks Coll., Pasadena, 1969. Mem. AAUW (past pres., co-chair Math.-Sci. Conf. 1983, chair Coll./Univ. Rels. 1988—, v.p. ednl. found. 1996-98, grantee 1982, 83), Nat. Assn. Edn. Young Children (grantee 1970), Child Care Info. Svc. (bd. dirs., chair parent edn. and family affairs 1986—), Women Ednl. Leadership (asst. program v.p.), Calif. Child Devel. Adminstrs. Assn. (bd. dirs. 1994—), Pasadena Coll. Women's Club (pres. 2000-2002), Coun. Women's Clubs (pres. 1995-98), Delta Kappa Gamma (pres. Omicron chpt. 1986-88, 92-94), Pasadena Women's City Club (chmn., dir. membership 2000-2002). Republican. Episcopalian. Avocation: music. Home: 2266 Kinclair Dr Pasadena CA 91107-1022

SIEMON-NETTO, UWE, journalist, theologian; b. Leipzig, Germany, Oct. 25, 1936; s. Karl Heinz and Ruth (Netto) S.; m. Gillian Mary Ackers, Dec. 1, 1962. MA, Luth. Sch. Theology, Chgo., 1988; PhD, Boston U., 1992. Cert. profl. journalist, 1958. Slot editor AP, Frankfurt, Berlin, 1958-61; fgn. corr. Springer Fgn. News, London, 1962, N.Y.C., 1962-64, Vietnam, 1965-69; fgn. corr. Stern Mag., N.Y.C., 1969-73; mng. editor Hamburger Morgenpost, Hamburg, Germany, 1973-75; writer, editl. cons., 1975—; cons. Axel Springer Verlag, Hamburg, Berlin, 1988-92, Der Tagesspiegel, Berlin, 1993-94, Sci. Am., N.Y.C., 1994-95, Idea Protestant Pub. House, Wetzlar, Germany, 1991—; resident scholar Ctr. of Theological Inquiry, Princeton, 1996-97. Author: The Acquittal of God, A Theology for Vietnam Veterans, 1990, Luther als Wegbereiter Hitlers?, 1993, The Fabricated Luther, 1995; contbr. numerous articles to profl. jours.; co-founder, co-pub. CA Lutheran quar. mag., Neuendettelsau, Germany, 1995—. Active Vietnam Vets. Ministers Assn., Washington. Lutheran. Home: Connétable, 16320 Gurat Charente, France Office: 420 E 55th St New York NY 10022-5139

SIEMS, ROLF, theoretical physics educator; b. Bremen, Germany, June 24, 1930; s. Albert Hinrich and Dora (Bohlmann) S.; m. Helgard Renate Sindermann, Aug. 28, 1965. Diploma in Physics, U. Göttingen, Germany, 1956; postgrad., Mich. State Coll., 1950-51; D Natural Sci., Inst. Tech., Aachen, Germany, 1963, Habilitation, 1969. Asst. U. Göttingen, 1955-56; scientist Kernforschungsanlage, Jülich, Germany, 1957-61, C.E.N., Mol, Belgium, 1962-63; asst., asst. prof. Inst. Tech., Aachen, 1963-70; guest prof. U. Giessen, Germany, 1969-70; prof. U. Saarbrücken, Germany, 1970—, chmn. dept. physics, 1975-77, senator, 1985-87. Contbr. articles to profl. jours. Recipient Borchers Plakette Inst. Tech. Aachen, 1963. Mem. German Phys. Soc., Inst. Physics (affiliate). Achievements include contributions to solid state physics and statistical mechanics: properties of dislocations, grain boundaries, point defects, phase transitions, hydrogen in metals, composite materials, domain walls, pseudo spin models, classical and quantum mechanics of chaotic systems. Home: Eulenweg 6, 66125 Saarbrücken Germany Office: U Saarbrücken, Dept Physics Bau 38, 66041 Saarbrücken Germany

SIENNICKI-LANTZ, ARKADIUSZ, physician, researcher; b. Walbrzych, Poland, Oct. 28, 1963; arrived in Sweden, 1991; s. Mieczysław and Jadwiga (Sofinska) S.; m. Violetta Leszczynska, 1990; children: Patrik, Filip, Anna. MD, Jagiellonian U., Krakow, 1990; postgrad., U. Lund (Sweden), 1999—. Med. lic. Sweden, Norway. Physician dept. clin. physiology Malmö (Sweden) Gen. Hosp., 1991-93, physician intern, 1993-95, clin. asst. dept. cmty. medicine, physician resident dept. geriatric medicine, 1998—, physician resident dept. neurology, 1998—. Contbr. articles to profl. jours. ALF grantee Swedish State, 1999. Avocations: family life, books. Office: Malmö U Hosp, Dept Cmty Medicine, SE-20502 Malmö Sweden

SIESLER, HEINZ WILHELM, physical chemistry educator; b. Vienna, Austria, Oct. 4, 1943; arrived in Germany, 1974; s. Anton and Maria (Ponath) S.; m. Monika Maria Feldmann, Oct. 6, 1971; children: Patricia, Tanja. PhD in Chemistry, U. Vienna, 1970, Habilitation, 1988. Postdoctoral fellow dept. phys. chemistry U. Cologne, Germany, 1970-72; rsch. assoc. dept. chemistry U. Witwatersrand, Johannesburg, South Africa, 1972-73, lectr., 1973-74; sect. leader R&D Bayer AG, Dormagen, Germany, 1974-87; prof. dept. phys. chemistry U. Essen, Germany, 1987—; cons. Bran & Luebbe GmbH, Norderstedt, Germany, 1989-94, Wolff-Walsrode (Germany) AG, 1995-96. Author: Infrared and Raman Spectroscopy of Polymers, 1980; editor: Polymer Spectroscopy, 1991, Procs. of the 8th Internat. Conf. on Fourier-Transform Spectroscopy, 1992; patentee in field. Recipient award in near-infrared spectroscopy Eastern Analytical Symposium, Somerset, N.J., 1994, Tomas Hirschfeld award, New Orleans, 2000. Mem. Gesellschaft Deutscher Chemiker, Deutsche Physikalische Gesellschaft, Internat. Com. on Near Infrared Spectroscopy. Roman Catholic. Avocations: skiing, soccer. Home: Hofringstrasse 43, D 45138 Essen Germany Office: U Essen Dept Phys Chemistry, Schützenbahn 70, D 45117 Essen Germany

SIESS, ALFRED ALBERT, JR., engineering executive, management consultant; b. Bklyn., Aug. 16, 1935; s. Alfred Albert and Matilda Helen (Suttmeier) S.; m. Gale Murray Scholes, Dec. 17, 1966; children: Matthew Alan, Daniel Adam. BCE, Ga. Inst. Tech., 1956; postgrad. in bus., Boston Coll., 1968; MBA, Lehigh U., 1972. With fabricated steel constrn. divsn. Bethlehem (Pa.) Steel Corp., 1958-76, project mgr., 1969-76, engr. projects and mining divsn., 1976-86; sr. cons. T.J. Trauner Assocs., Phila., 1986-87; assoc. S.T. Hudson Internat., Phila., 1987-90; dir. mktg. SWIN Resource Sys., Inc., Bloomsburg, Pa., 1989-90; mem. adj. faculty Drexel U., 1976-96. Weekly columnist Economic and Environmental Issues, East Pa. edit. The Free Press, 1981-86; co-patentee suspension bridge erection equipment. Founder S.A.V.E. Inc., Coopersburg, Pa., 1969, pres., 1970, 75, 81, bd. dirs. 1970—. Served with C.E., USN, 1956-58. Recipient Environ. Action award S.A.V.E., Inc., 1975. Mem. ASCE (chmn. environ. tech. com. Lehigh Valley

sect. 1971-83, life), Lions, Chi Epsilon. Republican. Mem. United Church of Christ. E-mail: siess@quixnet.net. Home: 6460 Blue Church Rd Coopersburg PA 18036-9371 Office: C E Resource Group PO Box 39 Coopersburg PA 18036-0039

SIETHOFF, HANS FRIEDRICH, physicist, researcher; b. Unna, Germany, Feb. 17, 1939; s. Johannes Wilhelm and Auguste (Bock) S.; m. Heide Margarete Maria Schmidt, Feb. 20, 1965; children: Johannes, Sebastian, Bernhard. Diploma, U. Göttingen, Germany, 1965, DrRerNat, 1968. Asst. U. Göttingen, 1968-69; asst. U. Würzburg, Germany, 1969-70, lectr., 1970-74, sr. lectr., 1974-90, acad. dir., 1990—. Author: Semiconductors and Semimetals, vol. 37, 1992, Properties of Crystalline Silicon, 1999; contbr. over 75 articles to various internat. jours. Mem. Deutsche Physikalische Gesellschaft, N.Y. Acad. Scis. Roman Catholic. Avocations: music, photography. Office: U Würzburg Phys Inst, Am Hubland, D-97074 Würzburg Germany

SIEVEKING, VINCENT JAN, publishing executive; b. Hamburg, W. Germany, Apr. 5, 1938; s. Wilhelm Georg and Susanne Camilla (Heymann) S.; m. Edda Johanna Kuepper, Apr. 14, 1978; 1 child, Johanna Camilla. MA, U. Hamburg, 1965. Editor, Langenscheidt KG, Berchtesgaden, W. Ger., 1965-66; editor Wilhelm Fink Verlag, Munich, 1966-74; editor Felix Meiner Verlag, Hamburg, 1974-77; bd. dirs. Franz Steiner Verlag, Stuttgart,1977—, medpharm. Sci. Pubs., Stuttgart, 1981—, Wissenschaftliche Verlagsgesellschaft, Stuttgart, Deutscher Apotheker Verlag, Stuttgart, S. Hirzel Verlag, Stuttgart, 1986—. Translator: Book on Tchekhov (P.M. Bicilli), 1966; contrb. translations of articles to profl. jours. Office: F Steiner Verlag Wiesbaden GMBH, Birkenwaldstrasse 44, 70191 Stuttgart Germany

SIEVERS, JOSEPH, Jewish studies educator; b. Recklinghausen, Germany, Jan. 18, 1948; arrived in Italy, 1988; s. Eberhard Ludwig and Irma (Pschorn) S. Dissertantenpruefung, U. Vienna, Austria, 1971; PhD, Columbia U., 1981; BD, Lateran U., Rome, 1991; Lic. Theology, Gregorian U., Rome, 1997. Adj. lectr. CUNY, N.Y.C., 1974-75; adj. lectr., assoc. prof. Seton Hall U., South Orange, N.J., 1975-83; vis. prof. Teresianum, Rome, 1989-93, P. Ateneo S. Anselmo, Rome, 1989-96; vis. prof., prof. Pontifical Bib. Inst., Rome, 1991—; bd. dirs. Svc. Internat. Documentation Judéo-Chrétienne, Rome. Author: The Hasmoneans and Their Supporters, 1990; co-editor: Josephus and the History of the Greco-Roman Period, 1994; editor: (jour.) Svc. Internat. Documentation Judéo-Chrétienne, 1994-2000; mem. editl. bd.: Jour. for Study of Judaism, 1993—. Fellow Studienstiftung Des Deutschen Volkes, 1967-76, pres.'s fellow Columbia U., 1973-74, Summer fellow NEH, 1983. Mem. World Union for Jewish Studies, Soc. of Bib. Lit., Italian Assn. for Jewish Studies (bd. dirs. 1991-94). Roman Catholic. Avocation: jogging. Home: Via XXV Luglio 11/A/2, 00046 Grottaferrata Rome, Italy Office: Pontifical Bib Inst, Via della Pilotta 25, 00187 Rome Italy

SIEVERS, REINHARD, banker, lawyer; b. Kiel, Germany, May 28, 1946; s. Helmut and Asta (Papst) S.; m. Christiane Becker, Aug. 30, 1974; children: Tim, Christian. LLB, U. Kiel, 1970, LLD, 1974. With Landesbank Schleswig-Holstein, Kiel, 1974—; trainee Landesbank Schleswig-Holstein, Luxembourg and London, 1982-85; head of capital markets and derivatives Landesbank Schleswig-Holstein, Kiel, 1985—; trainee Chem. Bank, N.Y.C., 1980. Mem. local parliament, Kiel, 1993—. Mem. Aero Club Kiel (pres.). Avocations: flying, tennis. Office: Landesbank Schleswig-Holstein, Martensdamm 6, 24100 Kiel Germany

SIEVERT, HORST, internist, cardiologist, angiologist; b. Ibbenbüren, Germany, Dec. 24, 1954; s. Manfred and Lore (Schorling) S.; m. Nicola Maly, Oct. 29, 1979; children: Niko, Inga, Eiko, Kolja. MD, U. Frankfurt, Germany, 1979. Cert. specialist in internal medicine, cardiology, angiology Landesarztekammer, Frankfurt. Intern, resident, then staff physician Stadtkrankenhans, Offenbach, Germany, 1978-83; staff physician, postdoctoral fellow U. Frankfurt, 1983-90; sr. cons. Herz-Kreislanfzentrum, Rotenburg, Germany, 1990-93, Bethanien Hosp., Frankfurt, 1993—. Author: Closure of Left to Right Shunts, 1987, Long Term Observations in Mild Forms of Cardiomyopathy, 1988, Calcium Antagonist Treatment in Mild Forms of Cardiomyopathy, 1988, Eine Kardiologische Dokumentation, 1990. Fellow Am. Coll. Cardiology, Internat. Coll. Angiology, Am. Coll. Antiology, Am. Heart Assn.; mem. European Soc. Cardiology, German Soc. Cardiology, German Soc. Angiology, Internat. Soc. Endovascular Surgery. Office: Cardiovasc Ctr Bethanien, Im Prüfling 23, 60389 Frankfurt Germany

SIEVERT, JOHANNES, physicist; b. Luedinghausen, Germany, Oct. 7, 1935. Physicist, Tech. U. Braunschweig, 1963, D of Engring., 1968. Head magn. meas. lab. Physikalisch Tech. Bundesanstalt, Braunschweig, 1974—. Mem. IEC (sec. tech. com. magnetic alloys and steels 1987—). E-mail: johannes.sievert@ptb.de. Office: Phys Tech Bundesanstalt 2, Bundesallee 100, 38116 Braunschweig Germany

SIFF, MARLENE IDA, artist, designer; b. N.Y.C.; d. Irving Louis and Dorothy Gertrude (Lahn) Marmer; m. Elliott Justin Siff, July 11, 1959; children: Bradford Evam, Brian Douglas. BA, Hunter Coll., 1957. Cert. tchr. elem. edn., N.Y., N.J. Tchr. Stewart Manor (N.Y.) Sch. Sys., 1957-59, Teaneck (N.J.) Sch. Sys., 1959-60; freelance interior designer Westport, Conn., 1966-70; designer Varo Inertial Products, Trumbull, Conn., 1970; designer signature collections J.P. Stevens & Co. Inc., N.Y., 1974-78, J.C. Penney Co., N.Y., 1978, C.R. Gibson Co., Norwalk, Conn., 1980; corp. sec., treas., bd. dirs. Belmar Corp., Westport, 1972—; chmn. bd. Marlene Designs Inc., Westport, 1973-77; owner Marlene Siff Design Studio, Westport, 1978—; aesthetic cons. Alcide Corp., Norwalk, 1980-88. One-person shows include David Segal Gallery, N.Y.C., 1987, Conn. Pub. TV Gallery, Hartford, 1987, Paul Mellon Art Ctr., Choate Rosemary Hall, Wallingford, Conn., 1989, Conn. Nat. Bank Hdqs., Norwalk, 1990, Michael Stone Collection, Washington, 1992, Bergdorf Goodman Men, N.Y.C., 1993, Joel Kessler Fine Art, Miami Beach, Fla., 1994, Park Pl., Stamford, Conn., 1995, Westport Arts Ctr., 1995, Mitchells, Westport, 1998, NIH, Bethesda, Md., 1999, Durst Lobby Gallery, N.Y.C., 1999; represented in permanent collections B'nai Brith Klutznick Nat. Jewish Mus., Washington, 1997. Decorator Easter Seal Home Svc. Charity Ball, 1976; bd. dirs. United Jewish Appeal, Westport, 1982-86; com. mem. Levitt Pavillion of the Performing Arts, Westport, 1982-89. Recipient award for creating the most beautiful working environment in an indsl. facility in lower Conn., Lower Conn. Mfrs. Assn., 1970. Mem. LWV, Nat. Coun. Jewish Women, Anti Defamation League, Kappa Pi. Jewish. Avocations: tennis, swimming, race walking, gardening. Home: 15 Broadview Rd Westport CT 06880-2303

ŠIFNER, OLDŘICH, mechanical engineer; b. Prague, Bohemia, Czech Republic, Sept. 11, 1930; s. Oldřich and Marie (Vlachová) S.; m. Eva Bezoušková, Aug. 21, 1965; children: Jan, Hana. ME, Czech Tech. U. Prague, 1954; PhD, Czechoslovak Acad. Scis., 1964. Asst. engr. Mech. Engring. Lab., Prague, 1954-59; sr. engr. Mech. Engring. Rsch. Inst. Czechoslovak Acad. Scis., Prague, 1959-64, rsch. worker Inst. Thermomechanics, 1964-90; cons. Inst. Thermomechanics Acad. Czech Republic, Prague, 1990—. Contbr. articles to profl. jours. Office: Acad Scis Czech Republic, Dolejskova 5, 18200 Prague Czech Republic

SIGALA, ELENI, business consultant; b. Athens, Hellas, Jan. 19, 1972; d. Spyros and Zoe (Koussidou) S. BSc, Deree Coll., 1990-94; MBA, Henley Mgmt. Coll., London, 1995-96. Accountant S. Sigalas S.A., Athens, 1989-95, fin. administrator, 1995—; bus. cons. Athens, 1999—; cons. Sena S.A., Athens/Hellas, 1995—. Contbr. articles to profl. jours. Mem. Greek Assn. Bus. Adminstrn., Alumni Assn. Athens Coll. Christian Orthodox. Avocations: sailing, skiing, gardening. Home: 74 VAs Konstantinou, Athens 16672 Hellas Office: PO Box 65157, 15401 Athens Hellas

SIGAL-IBSEN, ROSE, artist; b. Bucharest, Romania, Aug. 22; came to U.S., 1957; d. Joseph and Tilly (Eckstein) Cohen; m. Albert D. Sigal, Dec. 25, 1941 (dec. May 1970); 1 child, Daniel M.; m. Joseph Ibsen, Oct. 1973. Diploma, Fashion Inst. Technology, N.Y.C., 1978; Parson, Sch. of Design, N.Y.C., 1985-86; student, Koho Sch. of Sumi-E, N.Y.C., 1979-90, Zhejiang Acad. Fine Arts, China, 1990. Curator Metro N.Y. Chpt. of Sumi-E Soc., 1990—, v.p., 1990—. One-woman shows include: Roumanian Cultural Found., Bucharest, 1998, World Fine Art Gallery, N.Y.C., 1998, N.Y. Pub. Libr., 1996, Bankers Fed., N.Y.C., 1996, Rep. Bank for Savs., N.Y.C., 1996, Chem. Bank, N.Y.C., 1993-95, Manhattan Savs. Bank, N.Y.C., 1993-94, China-Gallery Weizhi Schubert, Hanover, Germany, 1991, others; group shows include: Steinhardt Conservatory, Bklyn. Bot. Garden, 1996, Nat. Mus. of Women in the Arts, Washington, 1996, 80 Washington Square East Galleries, N.Y.C., 1996, Seton Hall U., South Orange, N.J., 1996, Fourth World Conf. on Women, Beijing, 1995, China Nat. Acad. of Fine Arts, Hangzhou, 1994, Golden West Coll. Fine Arts Gallery, Huntington Beach, Calif., 1995, Seton Hall Gallery, South Orange, N.J., 1996, Wesleyan U., Middletown, Conn., 1998, Taipei Callery Chinese Info. and Culture Ctr. and the Chinese-Am. Arts Copun., 1998, Cork Gallery/Lincoln Ctr., N.Y.C., 1998, Pen and Brush, (All-sections award), Sumi-e Soc. Am., Inc., 1999, Japanese Am. Cultural & Cmty. Ctr. at Doizaki Gallery, 1999, Broome St. Gallery, 1999, Nat. Mus. of Women in Arts, 1999, Asia Soc. Store, 1999, others; artwork Courage Card design, 1998. Recipient Manhattan Arts award Cover Art Competition, N.Y.C., 1992, 94, 95, 97, King Point award, Fla., 1991, Tenth Japanese Internat. Calligraphy Exhbn. award, N.Y.C., 1996, Manhattan Arts Internat. Showcase award, Emily N. Hatch Meml. award Pen and Brush, Inc., Spring Watercolor Exhbn., 1998. Mem. Nat. Mus. of Women in the Arts, Artist Equity of N.Y., Am. Soc. Contemporary Artists, Art of Ink in Am., The Oriental Brushwork Soc. of Am. Avocations: sculptor in clay, dancing. Home: One Irving Pl #222B New York NY 10003-9741

SIGCAU, STELLA N., South African government official; b. 1938. Tchr. area sch.; chief Mpondo tribe, No. Transkei, South Africa; prime min. Transkei black homeland; min. pub. enterprises Govt. of South Africa, Pretoria, 1994—, min. pub. works; rep. Transkei's traditional chiefs during democracy negotiations. Address: Ctrl Govt Bldg/Pvt Bag x890, Crnr Bosman & Vermeulen Sts, Pretoria 0001, South Africa*

SIGELLE, MARC OLIVIER, telecommunications researcher; b. Paris, Mar. 18, 1954; s. Robert and Anna (Sokol) S. Degree in Engring., Ecole Poly., Paris, 1975, Ecole Nat. Superieure Telecom., Paris, 1977; PhD, Ecole Nat. Superieure Telecom., Paris, 1993; Applied Rsch. Degree in Physics, U. Orsay, France, 1977. Rschr. Centre Nat. d'Etude des Telecom., Bagneux, France, 1977-82, Issy, France, 1983-88; rschr. Ecole Nat. Superieure Telecom., Paris, 1989—; working group leader Groupe de Recherches/Ctr. Nat. de la Rsch. Contbr. articles to profl. jours. Sub-lt. French Air Army, 1972-75. Avocations: classical piano, swimming, randoning. Office: Ecole Nat Sup Telecom, 46 rue Barrault, 75634 Paris France

SIGETY, CHARLES EDWARD, lawyer, family business consultant; b. N.Y.C., Oct. 10, 1922; s. Charles and Anna (Toth) S.; m. Katharine K. Snell, July 17, 1948; children: Charles, Katharine, Robert, Cornelius, Elizabeth. BS, Columbia U., 1944; MBA, Harvard U., 1947; LLB, Yale U., 1951; LHD (hon.), Cazenovia Coll., 1994. Bar: N.Y. 1952, D.C. 1958. With Bankers Trust Co., 1939-42; instr. adminstrv. engring. Pratt Inst., 1948; instr. econs. Yale U., 1948-50; vis. lectr. acctg. Sch. Gen. Studies Columbia U., N.Y.C., 1948-50, 52; rapporteur com. fed. taxation for U.S. coun. Internat. C. of C., 1952-53; asst. to com. fed. taxation Am. Inst. Accts., 1950-53; with Compton Advt. Agy., N.Y.C., 1954; vis. lectr. law Yale U., 1952; pvt. practice law N.Y.C., 1952-67; pres., dir. Video Vittles, Inc., N.Y.C., 1953-67; dep. commr. FHA, 1955-57; of counsel Javits and Javits, 1959-60; 1st asst. atty. gen. N.Y., 1958-59; dir., mem. exec. com. Gotham Bank, N.Y.C., 1961-63; dir. N.Y. State Housing Fin. Agy., 1962-63; chmn. Met. Ski Slopes, Inc., N.Y.C., 1962-65; pres., exec. adminstr. Florence Nightingale Health Ctr., N.Y.C., 1965-85; dir. Schaerer AG, Wabern, Switzerland, 1982-88; chmn. Kenbar Group, N.Y.C., 1997—, Internat. Bioimmune Sys., Inc., Great Neck, N.Y., 1999—; professorial lectr. Sch. Architecture, Pratt Inst., N.Y.C., 1962-66; mem. Sigety Assocs., cons. in housing mortgage financing and urban renewal, 1957-67; ho. cons. Govt. of Peru, 1956; mem. missions to Hungary, Poland, Fed. Republic Germany, Malta, Czechoslovakia, Russia, Israel, Overseas Pvt. Investment Corp., 1990-92; owner, operator Peppermill Farms, Pipersville, Pa., 1956—. Bd. dirs., sec., v.p., treas. Nat. Coun. Health Ctrs., 1969-85; bd. dirs. Am.-Hungarian Found., 1974-76, Pritikin Rsch. Found., 1991—, Stratford Arms Condo Assn., 1992-93, Global Leadership Inst., 1993—; founding mem., bd. dirs., Natl. Assn. for Continence, 1982—, trustee Cazenovia (N.Y.) Coll., 1981—, Delaware Valley Coll. Sci. and Agr., Doylestown, Pa., 1998—; trustee Woodmere Art Mus. Phila., 2000—, Navy Supply Corps Found., Athens, Ga., 2000—; del. White House Conf. on Aging, 1971, White House Conf. on Mgmt. Tng. and Market Econs. Edn. in Ctrl. and Ea. Europe, 1991; bd. visitors Lander Coll., U. S.C., Greenwood, 1982-84; mem. fin. com. World Games, Santa Clara, 1981, London, 1985, Karlsruhe, 1989, The Hague, 1993, Confrerie des Chevaliers du Tastevin, Confrerie de la Chaine des Rotisseurs, Wine and Food Soc., Wednesday 10. Lt. (j.g.) Supply Corps, USNR, 1942-46. Recipient President's medal Cazenovia Coll., 1990, George Washington laureate Am. Hungarian Found., 1996; named Prin. for Day, Townsend Harris H.S. N.Y.C. Bd. Edn., 1997-2000, Disting. Alumnus U.S. Navy Supply Corps Sch., Athens, Ga., 1998; Baker scholar Harvard U., 1947. Mem. DOCA (Defense Orientation Conf. Assn.). Presbyterian. Office: 7155 Old Easton Rd Box 156 Pipersville PA 18947-9701

SIGETY, CORNELIUS EDWARD, family office manager; b. N.Y.C., June 6, 1958; s. Charles Edward and Katharine (Snell) S.; m. Virginia White, Oct. 28, 1995; children: Charles Edgar, Bradford Earle. BA, U. Rochester, N.Y., 1980; MBA, Harvard U., Boston, 1985. Asst. adminstr. Florence Nightingale Health Ctr., N.Y., 1980-83; v.p. Profl. Med. Products, Greenwood, S.C., 1985-88; mng. dir. Kenbar Group, N.Y., 1988—; bd. dirs. Heritage Conservancy. Mem. Union Club, Doylestown Country Club, Mantoloking Yacht Club. Presbyn. Avocations: sailing, golf, skiing. Home: PO Box 369 Pipersville PA 18947-0369 Office: Kenbar Group 1760 3rd Ave New York NY 10029-6810

SIGFUSSON, THORSTEINN INGI, physics educator; b. Westman Islands, Iceland, June 4, 1954; s. Sigfus J. and Kristin (Thorsteinsdottir) Johnsen; m. Bergthora K. Ketilsdottir, Aug. 16, 1975; children: David, Dagrun, Thorkell. Abitur, Hamrahild Coll., Reykjavik, Iceland, 1973; candidate scientist, U. Copenhagen, 1974-78; PhD in Physics, U. Cambridge, Eng., 1983. Rschr. Sci. Inst., Reykjavik, 1983-86, sr. scientist, 1986-89; chair in metals physics Icelandic Alloys, Reykjavik, 1989—; chmn. Icelandic Rsch. Coun., Rannis, 1997-2000, U. Iceland Veshmannayjar Rsch. Ctr., 1994—; chmn. bd. dirs. Sci. Inst., 1991-95, Univ. Libr., Reykjavik, 1992—; dir. Engring. Rsch. Inst., 1995-98; vice chmn. Nat. Libr., 1995-98; chmn. Icelandic New Energy, 2000—; with governing coun. European Sci. Found., 2000—. Editor: I Hlutarins Edli, 1986; mem. editl. bd. Physica Scripta, 1989-95. Bd. mem. Iceland Human Capital Mgmt. Com., Brussels, 1992—, Fulbright Inst. U.S.-Iceland Culture and Edn., 1993-98. Clerk-Maxwell scholar U. Cambridge, 1979; rsch. fellow Darwin Coll. Cambridge, 1982. Fellow Icelandic Acad. Scis., Physics Soc. (pres. 1989-91). Achievements include first studies of the Fermi surface of weak itinerant ferromagnets; establishment of Univ. of Iceland cooperation with the Icelandic metals industry; innovation linked corporations established in Iceland. Home: Austurbrun 17, 104 Reykjavik Iceland Office: Sci Inst, Dunhagi 3, 107 Reykjavik Iceland

SIGGEIRSSON, EINAR INGI, phytopathologist, researcher; b. Eyrarbakki, Arnessysla, Iceland, Aug. 26, 1921; s. Magnus Siggeir Bjarnason and Gudrun Palina Gudjonsdottir; m. Kristin Fridriksdottir, Apr. 13, 1924; children: Gylfi Magnus, Helgi Valgard, Margret Astrun. BS, N.D. State U., Fargo, 1948, MS, 1949; Diploma Ing. agr., Tech. Univ., Hannover, Germany, 1977; Dr.rer.hort, Tech. U., Hannover, Germany, 1977. Instr. Agrl. Sch., Holar, Iceland, 1950-52, Horticultural Sch., Reykjum, Iceland, 1957-58, High Sch., Reykjavik, 1961-89; rschr. Rsch. Inst., Hveragerdi, Iceland, 1963-96; Sci. rsch. fellow NAS, 1959-61. Co-editor Horticultural Jour. Iceland, 1951—, Bull. Rsch. Inst. Nedri-As, 1970—; contbr. articles to profl. jours. Sci. rsch. fellow NATO, 1963; Icelandic Sci. Found. fellow, 1972-73. Mem. Horticultural Soc. Iceland (bd. dirs. 1965-95, Gold medal 1985), Anthropologie Soc. Iceland, Nat. Acad. Scis., N.Y. Acad. of Scis., Icelandic Natural History Soc., Agrl. Soc. Iceland, Alpha Zeta, Phi Kappa Thi. Home: Stangarholt 30, 105 Reykjavik Iceland

SIGINER, DENNIS A., mechanical engineering educator, university dean; b. Ankara, Turkey, July 10, 1943; came to U.S., 1976; s. Kazim Siginer and Emine Turkoz. BS, MS with honors, Tech. U. Istanbul, 1966, ScD, 1971; PhD, U. Minn., 1982. Rsch. assoc. U. Minn., Mpls., 1976-80; asst. prof. U. Ala., Tuscaloosa, 1981-83; assoc. prof. Auburn (Ala.) U., 1984-92, prof. mech. engring., 1992-97; prof., head dept. mech. engring. N.J. Inst. Tech., Newark, 1998-2000; dean Coll. Engring., Wichita (Kans.) State U., 2000—; organizer, chmn. several internat. and nat. confs.; invited speaker to several countries, fgn. and nat. instns., internat. and nat. meetings; reviewer NSF, Internat. Sci. Found., Jour. Non-Newtonian Fluid Mechanics, Jour. Engring. Sci., Rheologica Acta, Jour. Fluids and Structures, Jour. Fluids Engring., Jour. Heat Transfer, Jour. Dynamic Systems Measurement and Ctrl., Jour. Applied Mechanics, Applied Mechanics Revs., Chem. Engring. Comm., Exptl. Thermal and Fluid Sci., Indsl. and Engring. Chemistry Rsch., Applied Mech. Revs., Chem. Engring. Comm., Exptl. Thermal & Fluid Sci., Indsl. Engring. Chem. Rsch., book revs. for pubs. Editor procs. of 1st East-West Conf. on advances in structured and heterogeneous continua, Moscow, 1993; editor numerous books on devels. in non-Newtonian flows, electrorheol. fluids and fluid mechanics phenomena in microgravity; editor-in-chief: Advances in the Flow and Rheology of Non-Newtonian Fluids, 1999; assoc. editor Jour. of Applied Mechanics, 1997—; guest editor Jour. Non-Newtonian Fluid Mechanics, 1999; author books in field; contbr. more than 120 articles to profl. jours. Recipient 3 univ.-wide teaching awards; Summer faculty fellow NASA, 1991, 92. Fellow ASME (organizer, editor procs. Symposia on Applications and Devels. Non- Newtonian Flows 1995, Symposia on Rheology and Fluid Mechanics Nonlinear Materi als 1996, 97, 98, svc. award 1993, 95, 96, 97, fluids engring. divsn. lectr. 2000), Sci. and Tech. Rsch. Coun. Turkey; mem. Am. Soc. Engring. Edn. (rsch. award 1992), Soc. Rheology, Am. Acad. Mechanics, Am. Inst. Physics, Soc. Engring. Sci., N.Y. Acad. Scis., Sigma Xi, Pi Tau Sigma (hon.). Home: 13211 Edgewood Dr Wichita KS 67230 Office: Wichita State U Coll Engring 105 Wallace Hl 1845 Fairmount Wichita KS 67260-0044

SIGMON, ROBERT LELAND, lawyer; b. Roanoke, Va., Apr. 3, 1929; s. Ottis Leland and Aubrey Virginia (Bishop) S.; m. Marianne Rita Gellner, Nov. 28, 1963 (div. 1992); m. Jean Mary Anderson, June 12, 1992. BA, U. Va., 1951, JD, 1954; postgrad., Sorbonne, Paris, 1956, London Sch. Econs., 1956-58. Bar: U.S. Supreme Ct., D.C., Va., U.S. Ct. Appeals (2nd and D.C. cir.). Lawyer Breed, Abbott & Morgan, London, 1958; ptnr. Pearl & Sigmon, London, 1959, Coudert Bros., London, 1960-63; pvt. practice London, 1964—. Contbr. articles to profl. jours. Chmn. The Pilgrims of G.B., London, 1977-94, v.p., 94—; trustee Magna Carta Trust, London, 1984-94, Am. and Internat. Friends of the Victoria and Albert Mus., N.Y.C., 1986—, pres. 1987-95, Gov. English Speaking Union, 1984-90, Am. Sch. in London, 1977-91. Fellow Royal Soc. Arts; mem. Brit. Inst. Internat. and Comparative Law (mem. coun. mgmt. 1982—), Am. Soc. (exec. com. 1970—), Reform Club, Chevalier du Tastevin, Mid-Atlantic Club of London (vice chmn. 1977—), European-Atlantic Group (v.p. 1978-94), Selden Soc. Avocations: collecting antiquarian books, oenology. Office: 2 Plowden Bldgs, Middle Temple, London EC4Y 9AS, England

SIGMON, SCOTT B., psychologist; b. Newark, Dec. 30, 1946; s. Henry and Shirley (Juffe) S. BA, Bloomfield Coll., 1973; MA, Montclair State Coll., 1975; profl. diploma in sch. psychology, Kean Coll., 1977; EdD, Rutgers U., 1985. Sch. psychologist Middlesex Borough Pub. Schs., N.J., 1976-77, Milton Sch., Millburn, N.J., 1977-78; sch. psychologist, chair child study team Irvington Pub. Schs., N.J., 1978-87; psychotherapist Family Svc. Bur. Newark, 1987; supr. child study East Orange (N.J.) Sch. Dist., 1987-88; sch. psychologist Elizabeth (N.J.) Pub. Schs., 1988-89; sch. psychologist, child study team chairperson Carlstadt-East Rutherford Regional H.S. Dist., N.J., 1989—; pvt. practice Union, N.J., 1991—; adj. prof. grad. psychology, Kean Coll. N.J., 1986, adj. prof. grad. psychology and spl. edn. Seton Hall U. (N.J.), 1988-90; asst. prof. coun. svcs. program William Paterson U. of N.J., 1992-95. Author: Radical Socioeducational Analysis, 1985, Radical Analysis of Special Education: Focus on Historical Development and Learning Disabilities, 1987; author, editor: Critical Voices on Special Education: Problems and Progress Concerning the Mildly Handicapped, 1990; editor The N.J. Sch. Psychologist newsletter, 1986-88; contbr. articles to profl. jours. With USMC, 1966-69. Mem. ACA, Internat. Sch. Psychology Assn., N.Am. Soc. Psychology of Sport and Phys. Activity, Assn. for the Advancement of Applied Sport Psychology, Am. Ednl. Rsch. Assn., N.J. Assn. Sch. Psychologists, N.J. Psychol. Assn. Office: 1945 Morris Ave Union NJ 07083-3518

SIGMUND, THUE, corporate lawyer; b. Balestrand, Norway, Dec. 31, 1943; s. Ole and Jensina (Skaasheim) T.; m. Inger-Johanne Tholfsen, June 26, 1971; children: Anders, Katrine. JD, U. Oslo, 1968. Edn. cons. U. Oslo, 1968; assoc. Govt. Oslo, 1969-70, Wikborg & Rein, Oslo, 1970-72; barrister Lillehammer, Norway, 1972-90; from dir. to mng. dir. Lillehammer Olympic Orgn. Com., 1990-96; ptnr. Thue & Selvaag AS, Lillehammer, 1996—; Office phone: 47612-69940. Mem. Norwegian Law Assn. Avocation: sports. Home: Hammersengveg 51, 2600 Lillehammer Norway

SIGNORELLI, CARLO, university educator; b. Milan, July 23, 1962; s. Innocenzo and Mirella (Sironi) S. MD, U. Milan, 1986; MSc in Epidemiology, U. London, 1989; Degree in Law, U. Milan, 1993; PhD, U. London, 1994; degree in polit. scis., U. La Sapienza, 1995, splty. in hygiene & preventive medicine, 1999. Lectr. U. La Sapienza, Rome, 1989-90, univ. rschr., 1992-98; assoc. prof. of environ. hygiene Politechnik of Milan, 1998-2000; dep. med. dir. Policlinico Umberto I Hosp., Rome, 1998; prof. hygiene U. Parma, 2000—; sci. journalist Unica Lombardia TV, Lecco, Italy, 1995—, La Gazzetta di Lecco e Provincia, 1995—; press officer Italian Soc. of Hygiene, 1994—; editor in chief View and Review Hosp., Milan, 1994—. Author: Elementi di Metodologia Epidemiologica, 5th edit., 2000, Caesarean Birth in Italy, 1995, Il Parto e la Legge, 1993, The new Italian Health reform, 1999; contbr. over 250 articles to profl. jours. Mem. Banca Popolare Provincial Lecchese (bd. mem.), Townhouse com. bd. Municipality of Perledo, Lecco, 1988-99; mem. Italian Nat. Commn. for AIDS and other infectious diseases. Mem. Italian Soc. Hygiene, Internat. Epidemiol. Assn., Hosp. Infection Soc., Milano Scala Rotary. Avocations: golf, waterskiing, skiing. Office: Inst. Hygiene, Via Volturno 39, I-43100 Parma Italy

SIGNORILE, VINCENT ANTHONY, lawyer; b. Jersey City, Mar. 22, 1959; s. Ralph R. and Rita (DeRosa) S. BS, St. Peter's Coll., Jersey City, 1981; JD, Seton Hall U., 1985. Bar: N.J. 1985, Pa. 1985. Aide Jersey City Mcpl. Coun., 1980-81, Office of Mayor, City of Jersey City, 1981; law clk. Corp. Counsel Jersey City, 1981-85; law sec. Superior Ct. N.J. for Hudson County, Jersey City, 1985-86; assoc. atty. Jersey City, 1986-89; ptnr. Signorile & Saminski, Jersey City, 1989-97; atty. Jersey City Zoning Bd. Adjustment, 1994-97, Bayonne City Ethics Bd., 1995-97; judge Jersey City Mcpl. Ct., 1996—. Mem. Hudson County Dem. Com., 1977-81, Jersey City Environ. Com., 1989-93, Jersey City Planning Bd. Com., 1991-93, Jersey City Ins. Fund Com., 1989-93; co-chmn. Hudson County Columbus Parade, 1984-85; elected to Mcpl. Coun. Jersey City, 1989-93. Mem. ABA, N.J. Bar Assn., Pa. Bar Assn., Hudson County Bar Assn. (treas. Young Lawyer's Assn. 1987-88, scholar 1984-85), Assn. Trial Lawyers Am. Roman Catholic. Home: 1691 John F Kennedy Blvd Jersey City NJ 07305-1841 Office: Jersey City Municipal Ct 769 Montgomery St Jersey City NJ 07306-4603

SIGNORINO, CURTIS STEPHEN, political science educator, researcher; b. Great Falls, Mont., June 6, 1966. BS in Sys. Engring., Rensselaer, Troy, N.Y., 1988, MS in Ops. Rsch. and Statistics, 1990; AM in History, Harvard U., 1993, AM in Polit. Sci., 1996, PhD in Polit. Sci., 1998. Network security project mgr. USAF, Bedford, Mass., 1989-92, theater and simulator warfare modeling project mgr., 1992-93; teaching fellow dept. govt. Harvard U., Cambridge, Mass., 1995-96, lectr., 1996-97; instr. dept. polit. sci. U. Rochester, 1997-98, asst. prof. dept. polit. sci., 1998—; dir. Watson Ctr. for Conflict and Coop., Rochester, N.Y., 1999—. COntbr. articles to profl. jours. Grantee Nat. Sci. Found., 1999, Mellon; recipient Gosnell Prize Hon. Mention, Polit. Methodology Sect., 1998, Atherton Fellowship in Internat. Rels., Harvard, 1993. Mem. Am. Polit. Sci. Assn., Internat. Studies Assn., Peace Sci. Soc., Am. Statistical Assn., Econometric Soc., Midwest Polit. Sci. Assn. Office: U Rochester 325 Harkness Hall Rochester NY 14627

SIGNOROVITCH, DENNIS J., communications executive; b. Norristown, Pa., July 23, 1945; s. James and Regina S.; m. Susan E. McLaughlin, 1968; children: James Edward, Sarah Elizabeth. BS in Fgn. Svc., Georgetown U., 1967; MA, Old Dominion U., 1972; postgrad., U. Toledo., 1972. Instr. U. Toledo, 1972-77; writer/editor Doehler Jarvis div. NL Industries, Toledo, 1977-78; mgr. pub. rels. Eltra Corp., N.Y.C., 1979, mgr. planning, 1980;

various assignments AlliedSignal Corp., Morristown, N.J., 1980-92; v.p. pub. affairs AlliedSignal Inc., Torrance, Calif., 1992-98; v.p. mktg. and comm. AlliedSignal Aerospace, Torrance, 1998-99; v.p. comms. Honeywell Aerospace, 1999—; mem. Exec. Comm. Forum. With U.S. Army, 1967-70. Decorated Bronze Star with oak leaf cluster. Mem. The Conf. Bd. (corp. comm. coun. 1991), Vol. Ctr. of South Bay (bd. dirs. 1994) Arthur W. Page Soc., San Francisco Acad. (dir.). Office: Honeywell Aerospace 2525 W 190th St Torrance CA 90504-6002

SIGNY, MARK, cardiologist, consultant; b. Chiswick, London, Jan. 22, 1954; s. Aaron Gordon and Vivien Winifred (Imber) S.; m. Helen Mary Stuart, July 19, 1975; children: Katherine, James. BA in Physiol. Sci., Oxford (Eng.) U., 1975, MA, 1980; MBBS, London U., 1978; MA, Oxford (Eng.) U., 1980; MRCP, Royal Coll. of Medicine, England, 1980; FRCP, Royal Coll. of Medicine, London, 1994. Specialist registration cardiology and gen. internal medicine. House physician, sr. house officer St. Thomas Hosp., London, 1978-79; sr. house officer Guys Hosp./Brompton Hosp., London, 1979-80; registrar St. Mary's Hosp., London, 1981-82; registrar, lectr. St. Thomas Hosp., London, 1983-87; sr. registrar St. Thomas' and Medway Hosps., U.K., 1987-88; cons. cardiologist Worthing (Eng.) Hosp., 1988—; hon. cons. cardiologist St. Thomas Hosp., London, 1993—; cons. cardiology Brighton, 1990—; mem. regional specialist tng. com. cardiology, 1996—. Contbr. articles to profl. jours. Fellow Royal Coll. Physicians London; mem. Brit. Cardiac Soc., Jr. Cardiac Club (past pres. 1987-88), Brit. Cardiovascular Intervention Soc. Avocations: cricket, golf, snow skiing, rugby, travel. Office: Worthing Hosp, Lyndhurst Rd, Worthing BN11 2DH, England

SIGORSKY, VITALY PETROVICH, engineer, researcher, educator; b. Village Bubnova Slobidka, Cherkasy, Ukraine, Nov. 19, 1922; s. Petro Ivanovich and Marija Tryfonivna (Lysenko) S. Degree in elec. engring., Lviv Politech. Inst., 1949, PhD, 1952; D in Tech., Kyiv Politech. Inst., 1959. Dep. dir., head dept. Machinery and Automation Inst., Lviv, 1953-59, Auomation and Electrometrical Inst., Novosibirsk, 1959-62; head dept. Math. Inst., Novosibirsk, 1962-64; head chair Novosibirsk U., 1962-64; head chair, prof. Nat. Tech. U. Ukraine, Kyiv, 1964—. Author: Two-Port Theory, 1955, Method of Network Analysis with Multiple Components, 1958, Electronic Network Analysis, 1960, 5th edit., 1966, Mathematics for Engineers, 1975, 2d edit., 1977; contbr. more than 300 articles to profl. jours. Mem. Internat. Acad. Computer Scis. and Sys., Ukraine Acad. Engring. Scis., Internat. Acad. Info., IEEE. Avocations: arts, travel, photography.

SIGRIST, R. MARCEL, religious education educator; b. Bessines-sur-Gartempe, France, Aug. 19, 1940; arrived in Israel, 1969; s. Jean and Marie-Antoinette (Gerber) S. Lector in Theology, Le Saulchoir, France, 1969; Licenciate in Holy Scripture, Rome, 1971; PhD in Assyriology, Yale U., 1976. Joined Dominican Order. Prof. Ecole Biblique Francaise, Israel, 1976—; libr. Ecole Biblique Francaise, 1976-89, dir., 1990-96; lectr. Bir-Zeit U., Palestine, 1978-80; sci. com. Bible Lands Mus., Jerusalem, 1992. Author: Textes économiques néo-sumériens de l'Université de Syracuse, 1983, Les Sattukku dans l'ESUMESA durant la période de Larsa, 1984, The John Frederick Lewis Collection, 1984, Neo-Sumerian Account Texts in the Horn Archaeological Museum, 1984-87, Collaboration in Cuneiform Tests in the Metropolitan Museum of Art, 1988, Concordance of the Isin-Larsa Year Names, 1989, Concordance of the Ur III, 1991, Messenger Texts in the BM, 1992, Drehem, 1992, Texts in the BM, 1992; contbr. articles to profl. jours. Recipient Chevalier de la Légion d'Honneur, Jerusalem, 1996. Roman Catholic. Fax: 172-2-6282567. Home: 6 Nablus Rd PO Box 19053, 91190 Jerusalem Israel

SIGUION-REYNA, LEONARDO, lawyer, business executive; b. Dagupan City, The Philippines, Apr. 18, 1921; s. Lamberto and Felisa (Tiongson) S.; m. Armida Ponce-Enrilie, Nov. 24, 1952; children: Monica, Leonardo, Carlos. LLB, U. Santo Tomas, Manila, 1946-48. Bar: Philippines, 1948. Sr. ptnr. Siguion Reyna, Montecillo, and Ongsiako, Makati Metro Manila; chmn. bd. Phimco Industries, Inc., Manila, Sandvick Philippines, Inc.; pres. Electronic Tele. Systems Industries, Inc., Manila Meml. Park Cemetary, Inc., Valmora Investment & Mgmt. Corp.; dir. ABB (Phils) Inc., Crismida Realty Corp., Dole Philippines, Inc., Filflex Indsl. & Mfg. Corp., Goodyear Philippines, Inc., Indsl. Realties, Inc., Investment & Capital Corp. of the Philippines, Rizal Comml. Banking Corp., Unilever (Phil) Inc., Ionics Circuits., Inc., Petronas (Phil) Inc. Mem. Philippine Bar Assn., Casino Español de Manila. Roman Catholic. CLubs: Manila Yacht, Manila Polo, Rotary. Home: 7 Tangile Rd/North Forbes, Manila The Philippines

SIGURBJORNSSON, EINAR, theology educator; b. Reykajavik, Iceland, May 6, 1944; s. Einarsson and Magnea (Thorkelsdottir) Sigurbjorn; m. Gudrun Edda Gunnarsdottir, Sept. 1, 1946; children: Sigurbjorn, Gudny, Magnea. Candidatus theologie, U. Iceland, 1969; ThD, U. Lund, 1974. Minister Ch. of Icleand, Olafsjordur, 1969-70, Hals, 1974-75, Reynivellir, 1975-78; lectr. Faculty of Theology, U. Iceland, Reykjavik, 1975-77; prof. Christian Doctrine Faculty of Theology, U. Iceland, 1978—; chmn. Liturgical Commn., Ch. of Iceland, Reykjavik, 1979-97, mem. Faith and Order Commn., Geneva, 1985-90. Author: Ministry within the People of God, 1974, Ordid og truin, 1976, Kirkjan jatar, 1980, 2d edit., 1991, Dogmatics, 1989, 2d edit., 1993, Pastoral Theology, 1996, Dogmatics for Laypersons, 1996. Fellow Visindafelag Islendigna, Den norske vitenskaps akademi; mem. Soc. for Study of Theology. Home: Nedstaberg 8, Reykjavik Iceland Office: Haskoli Islands, Reykjavik Iceland IS-101

SIGURDSSON, EINAR, librarian; b. Skógarstrandarhreppur, Iceland, Apr. 10, 1933; s. Sigurdur Einarsson and Gudrún Björnsdóttir; m. Margrét Sigurdardóttir, Nov. 2, 1957; children: Arnthrúdur, Gudrún, Sigurdur. Cand. mag., U. Iceland, Reykjavik, 1963. Rsch. asst. Arnamagnean Inst., Iceland, 1963-64; asst. librarian Univ. Libr., Reykjavik, 1964-74, univ. librarian, 1974-94; Nat. Librarian Nat. and Univ. Libr., Reykjavik, 1994—. Author (bibliographies): Skrá um efni í tímaritum Bókmenntafélagsins, 1966, Bókmenntaskrá Skírnis, 1968-93, Íslensk tímarit í 200 ár, 1991. Recipient Kommandör award, Pres. of Finland, 1995. Home: Kringlan 45, 103 Reykjavik Iceland Office: Nat and Univ Library, Arngrimsgata 3, 107 Reykjavik Iceland

SIGURDSSON, JON, banker; b. Isafjordur, Iceland, Apr. 17, 1941; s. Sigurdur Gudmundsson and Kristin Gudjona (Gudmundsdottir) G.; m. Laufey Thorbjarnardottir, Aug. 26, 1962; children: Thorbjorn, Sigurdur Thor, Anna Kristin, Rebekka. Grad. in econs., stats., U. Stockholm, 1964; MSc Econs., London Sch. Econs. and Polit. Sci., 1967. Economist Econ. Inst. Iceland, 1964-67, chief econ. div., 1967-70, dir. econ. research, 1970-71; chief econ. research div. Econ. Devel. Inst., 1972-74; mng. dir. Nat. Econ. Inst., 1974-80, 83-86; mem. Althing (Parliament), minister Commerce Iceland, 1987-93; min. justice and ecclesiastical affairs, 1987-88, min. industries and energy, 1988-93, min. Nordic co-op, 1987-88; chmn. bd. dirs., gov. Ctrl. Bank of Iceland, 1993-94; pres. and CEO Nordic Investment Banks, 1994—; Iceland rep. to econ. and devel. rev. com. OECD, 1970—; alt. gov. IMF for Iceland, 1980, 83-86, assoc. joint IBRD/IMF devel. com., 1974-80; exec. dir. for Nordic countries in IMF Exec. Bd., 1980-83; adviser to Icelandic govt., 1974-80, 83-86; bd. dirs. Nordic Investment Bank, Helsinki, 1976-87, chmn. bd., 1984-86; chmn. Nordic Council Min., 1989. Contbr. articles to econ. jours. Candidate Social Dem. Party, Reykjavik, Iceland, 1987-93. Lutheran. Home: Selbraut 15, 170 Seltjarnarnes Iceland Office: Nordic Investment Bank, Fabianinkatu 34, 00171 Helsinki Finland also: Ostra Allen 3A4, 00140 Helsinki Finland*

SIGURDSSON, RAGNAR, ophthalmologist; b. Akyreyri, Iceland, July 16, 1942; s. Sigurdur Bjornsson and Kristin Bjarndottir; m. Valgerdur Tomasdottir, Feb. 15, 1969 (dec. Apr. 1995); children: Sigrid, Unnur. MD, U. Iceland, 1972. Am. bd. cert. ophthalmologist. Resident U. B.C., Vancouver, 1975-78; cons. Akureyri, Iceland, 1980—; head dept. ophthalmology Akureyri Ctrl. Hosp., Iceland, 1998—. Fellow Am. Acad. Ophthalmology, Soc. Eye Surgeons; mem. Am. Intraocular Implant Soc. Avocations: golf, skiing, traveling. Home: Alfabyggo 11, 600 Akureyri Iceland Office: Kaupangur v/Myraveg, 600 Akureyri Iceland

SIGURDSSON, THORDUR BALDUR, retired data processing executive; b. Reykjavik, Iceland, July 9, 1929; s. Sigurdur and Olafia (Hjaltested) Thordarson; m. Anna Hjaltested, Nov. 30, 1951; children: Magnus, Bjoern, Sigurdur, Anna, Ingveldur, Olafur, Katrin. Grad., Comml. Coll. Iceland, 1949; postgrad., U. Iceland, 1949-52. Chief acct. Icelandic State Land Reclamation, Reykjavik, 1947-72; mng. dir. Raftaekjaverzlunin Ltd., 1959-65; EDP mgr. Agrl. Bank of Iceland, Raykjavik, 1972-77; br. mgr. Agrl. Bank of Iceland, Stykkisholmur, 1974-75; tchr. math. Vogaskoli, Reykjavik, 1966-71; mng. dir. Icelandic Banks Data Ctr., Reykjavik, 1977-96, mem. adv. bd., 1973-77. Editor Verzlunarskolabladid, 1947, Studentabladid, 1949, Ithrottabladid, 1967-68; maj. acting role Nord-deutsce Rundfunk's TV series Paradise Regained, 1979-80. Vestryman, Langholt Parish, Reykjavik, 1969-76. Recipient Gold Emblem, Athletic Union Iceland, 1968, Iceland Sports Fedn., 1972; Ace-Emblem, Athletic Union Iceland, 1967. Mem. Reykjavik Football Club (Emblem Gold/Laures 1974),. Home: Langholtsvegur 179, 104 Reykjavik Iceland

SIGURJONSSON, THROSTUR OLAF, management consultant; b. Reykjavik, Iceland, July 29, 1969; s. Sigurjon Hannes and Kristin (Briem) Olafsson. BBA, U. Iceland, Reykjavik, 1994, BA, 1996; MBA, IESE, Barcelona, 2000. Project leader Eimskip, Reykjavik, Iceland, 1994-96; with bus. devel. Shell Iceland, Reykjavik, 1996-2000; analyst Henkel AG, 1999; mgmt. cons. Price-WaterhouseCoopers, Denmark, 2000—; pres. Shell Co. Union, 1996—; cons. in field. Author: Business Ethics, 1994; contbr. articles to profl. jours. Mem. Icelandic Economists Orgn. Avocations: golf, fly-fishing, skiing.

SIGWART, ULRICH, cardiologist; b. Mar. 9, 1941; s. Christine Sartorius, Sept. 2, 1967; children: Anne, Philip, Jan, Catherine. MD, U. Münster, 1967; Dr. med. magna cum laude, U. Freiburg, 1967; Dr.med.habil., U. Düsseldorf, 1978; Doctorate (hon.), U. Lausanne, 1999. Intern Cmty. Hosp. Loerrach, 1967-68; resident Framingham Union Hosp., Boston VA Hosp., 1968-71; fellowship in cardiology Baylor Coll. Medicine, 1971-72; chief of cath lab. Gollwitzer Meier Inst., Bad Oeynhausen, 1973-79; chief invasive cardiology U. Hosp., Lausanne, 1979-89; dir. dept. invasive cardiology Royal Brompton Hosp., London, 1989—; cons. Royal Brompton Hosp., London, Heart Hosp., London, Harley St. Clinic, London, Humana Wellington Hosp., London, Cromwell Hosp., London, London Bridge Hosp., Clinique de Genolier, Switzerland, Clinique Cecile, Lausanne, Switzerland, Centre Cardiothoracique de Monaco; prof. medicine U. Düsseldorf; lectr. in field. Author: Automation in Cardiac Diagnosis, 1978; editor: Ventricular Wall Motion, 1984, Coronary Stents, 1992, Endoluminal Stenting, 1996, Handbook of Cardiovascular Interventions, 1996, Intraluminal Stents, 1996; editl. bd. Clin. Cardiology, Cardiac Imagin, Interventional Cardiology, Frontiers in Cardiology, Stents, Latinamer Jour. Hemodyn., Angiogr. & Therap. Cath.; co-editor Handbook on Cardiovascular Interventions; contbr. over 400 articles to profl. jours. Fellow Am. Coll. Cardiology, European Soc. Cardiology (founding fellow, past chmn. working group myocardial function), Am. Coll. Angiology, Royal Coll. Physicians; mem. Swiss Soc. Cardiology (founding chmn. working group PTCA & Lysis), Internat. Stent Investigators Group, Russian Soc. Interventional Cardiology (hon.), Brit. Cardiac Soc., Soc. Vandoise de Médicine, German Soc. Cardiology, Am. Soc. Cardiac Interventionists, Internat. Andreas Grüntzig Soc., Internat. Soc. for Endovascular Surgery, Am. Coll. Angiology, Am. Heart Assn., Brit. Cardiac Interventionist Soc., Royal Soc. Medicine, Med. Pilots Assn., Polish Cardiac Soc. (hon.), Argentinian Soc. Cardiology (corr.). Office: Royal Brompton Hosp, Dept Invasive Cardiol Sydney St, London SW3 6NP, England

SIHAG, R.C., apiculturist, ecologist, educator, researcher; b. Siwani Bolan, Haryana, India, Jan. 5, 1952; s. Sudhan Ram and Birjo Devi (Panghaal) S.; m. Nirmala Boora, Mar. 11, 1962; 1 child, Ravi. BSc, Govt. Coll., Hisar, India, 1973; MSc, Kurukshetra (India) U., 1975; PhD, Haryana Agrl. U., Hisar, 1980. CSIR jr. rsch. fellow Haryana Agrl. U., 1976-79, rsch. assoc., 1979-80, asst. prof., 1980-88, assoc. prof., 1988-95, prof. apiculture, 1995—, rsch. leader bee unit, 1988-96, head dept. zoology and aquaculture, 1997-2000. Author: Apicultural Research in India, 1987; editor: Pollination Biology, Vols. 1-3, 1995, Recent Advances in Biosciences for Sustainable Food Security, 1999; mem. editl. bd. Jeevnati, Kurukshetra, 1990—, Asian Bee Jour., 1999; contbr. over 140 articles to profl. jours. Recipient Rafi Ahmad Kidwai Meml. prize Indian Coun. Agrl. Rsch., 1980-81, group award USDA, 1993, Ambedkar award, 1998, also various awards of merit, appreciation, 1985-95. Fellow Royal Entomol. Soc. (London).; mem. Asian Apicultural Assn. (sect. chairperson 1992—), All India Beekeepers Assn. (bd. mgmt. 1990-94, editor Indian Bee Jour. 1990-94), Internat. Union for Study of Social Insects (exec. mem. 1990—). Avocations: reading newspapers and magazines. Office: Haryana Agrl U, Dept Zoology, Hisar Haryana 125004, India

SIHANOUK, NORODOM, King of Cambodia; b. Phnom Penh, Oct. 31, 1922; s. Norodom Suramarit and Kossamak Nearireath. Studied in, Saigon, Viet-Nam, Paris. Elected King of Cambodia, 1941, abdicated, 1955; prime min., min. fgn. affairs Govt. of Cambodia (now Kampuchea), 1955-57, elected head state, 1960, deposed by Junta of Putschist Lon Nol, 1970, restored as head state when Royal Govt. Nat. Union Cambodia overthrew Khmer Republic, 1975, resigned, 1976; spl. envoy of Khmer Rouge to UN Security Coun., 1979; head of state in exile Govt. Democratic Kampuchea, 1982-87, 88-89, head of state, 1990—; leader Supreme Nat. Coun., 1991-93; pres. Cambodia, 1991-93; crowned King of Cambodia, 1993—; permanent rep. to UN, 1956, spl. envoy of Dem. Kampuchea to UN, 1979; formed Nat. United Front for an Ind. Kampuchea, 1981. Author: (with Jean Lacouture) L'Indochine vue de Pekin, 1972, (with Wilfred Burchett) My War with the C.I.A., 1973, War and Hope: The Case for Cambodia, 1980, Bitter and Sweet Remembrances, 1981, Prisonnier des Khmers Rouges, 1986, Charisme et Leadership, 1990; producer (film) Le Petit Prince, and other films. Head Popular Socialist Community, 1955-70. Office: Khemarindra Palace, Phnom Penh Kampuchea*

SIHVER LILJEGREN, CARL HENRIK, Swedish ambassador; b. Tallinn, Estonia, Apr. 17, 1936; s. Edmund Sihver (Schiffer) and Eva (Kjellberg) Liljegren; m. Nil Nevder (Ilden) Kirectepe, Oct. 4, 1984; 1 child, Nilden. BS in Law, U. Stockholm, 1960. With Swedish Fgn. Svc., 1960—, posted Japan, posted Fed. Republic of Germany; asst. undersec. Ministry Fgn. Affairs, amb. to Turkey, 1982-85, amb. to German Democratic Republic, 1985-89, amb. to Belgium and Luxembourg, 1989-93; amb. to U.S., Ministry Fgn. Affairs, Washington, 1993-97; amb. to Turkey, Ministry Fgn. Affairs, Ankara, 1998—. Office: Swedish Embassy, Ambasada RP Ataturk Bulvari 241, Kavaklidere PK 20 Ankara 06692, Turkey*

SIHVO, PÄIVÄ MARKETTA, voice therapist, voice researcher; b. Lappajärvi, Finland, June 11, 1941; d. Viljo and Päivä (Herttua) Lampola; m. Jouko Sihvo, Dec. 31, 1961; children: Minna, Henrikki, Katariina, Hannu. BA, Turku (Finland) U., 1964; MA, Helsinki (Finland) U., 1990; PhD, Tampere (Finland) U., 1997, docent of voice care, 2000. Cert. speech therapist. Spl. edn. tchr. Ground Sch., Helsinki, 1985-87; speech therapist Tampere (Finland) Hosp., 1989—. Mem. Union of Speech Therapists in Finland, The Finnish Assn. Logopedics and Phoniatrics. Lutheran. Avocations: voice care and research, singing, thinking, outdoor activities. Office: Tampere U Hosp, PL 2000, SF-33521 Tampere Finland

SIHWEIL, ISA SALIBA, nuclear power engineering specialist, corporate planner; b. Ramallah, Palestine, Jan. 27, 1942; d. Saliba Isa and Zahieh Butros (Michael) S.; m. Rudina Asad Habibi, Aug. 23, 1969; children: Ranya, Deema, Omar. BS in Engring., Am. U.-Beirut, 1963. Registered profl. engr., Va. Engring. specialist Bechtel, Washington, 1965-73; chief structural engring. U.S. NRC, Washington, 1973-79; project mgr. Consol. Contractors Co (CCICL), Oman, 1979-81; mgr. corp. planning Consol. Contractors Co (CCICL), Athens, Greece, 1981-88; group v.p., CFO The Morgant Group, Danbury, Conn., 1988-96; asst. v.p. CCICL, Athens, 1996—. Contbr. articles to publs. Mem. Am. Concrete Inst. Greek Orthodox. Office: CCIC,, PO Box 61092,, Amaroussion,, Athens, Greece

SIIGUR, ENE, biochemist, researcher; b. Tallinn, Estonia, Oct. 27, 1944; d. Ellen Rampe; m. Jüri Siigur, May 16, 1968; children: Margus, Katrin. MSc, Tartu (Estonia) U., 1967, PhD, 1975. Rschr. Tartu (Estonia) U., 1968-71, jr. rsch. scientist, 1973-74; jr. rsch. scientist Inst. Cybernetics, Tallinn, Estonia, 1974-80; jr. rsch. scientist Inst. Chem. Physics and Biophysics, Tallinn, 1980-84, sr. rsch. scientist, 1984—; guest rschr. Colo. State U., Fort Collins, 1993. Contbr. articles to profl. jours.; patentee in field. Recipient Estonian State prize for sci. Coun. Mins., Estonia, 1987. Mem. Internat. Soc. Thombosis and Haemostasis, Estonia Biochem. Soc., Estonia Chem. Soc. Avocations: traveling, jogging, theatre. Office: Nat Inst Chem Physics/Bioph, Akadeemia tee 23, 12618 Tallinn Estonia

SIIKONEN, MARJA-LIISA, engineering administrator; b. Seinäjokl, Finland, Apr. 29, 1954; d. Jaakko and Anni (Komsi) Jokela; m. Timo Siikonen, June 19, 1980; 1 child, Hannu. MS in Engring., Helsinki (Finland) U. Tech., 1979, Lic. in Tech., 1989, PhD, 1997. Trainer Tech. Rsch. Ctr. Finland, Espoo, 1979; applications engr. Nokia Co., Helsinki, 1980-84; designer Kone Co., Helsinki, 1985-90, project mgr., 1991-95, mgr., 1996—. Patentee in field. Avocation: singing in a choir. Office: Kone Corp, Munkkiniemen puistotie 25, 00330 Helsinki Finland

SIIMANN, MART, prime minister; b. Kilingi-Nõmme, Pärnu, Estonia, 1946; married; 2 children. Degree in psychology and philology, Tartu (Estonia) State U., 1971. Psychologist, dep. head Lab. Sci. Orgn. of Work and Adminstrn., 1971-75; sr. rsch. asst. Faculty of Philosophy Tartu State U., 1975-82; broadcast journalist, dep. dir. gen. programming, editor-in-chief Estonian TV, 1982-87, dir. gen., 1989-92; dir. Estonian Radio, 1987-89; mng. dir. AS Reklaamitelevisioon, 1991-95; elected to Riigikogu Estonia, 1995, prime min., 1997-99; chmn. coalition party faction, mem. constl. com. Riigikogu, 1995-97. Avocations: sports, literature, fishing, philosophy. Office: Office of Rugikogu, Lossi Plats 1A, 10130 Tallinn Estonia*

SIIMER, ENN, chemistry researcher; b. Tallinn, Estonia, Apr. 25, 1936; s. Hans and Marta (Trei) S.; m. Kadri Erm, July 2, 1960; children: Mare, Mart. PhD, Tallinn Tech. U., 1965. Lectr. Tallinn Tech. U., 1965-86; sr. scientist Inst. Chemistry, Tallinn, 1986-89, 95—, leading scientist, 1989-95. Recipient Nat. Sci. Prize of Estonia, 1978. Mem. N.Y. Acad. Scis. Achievements include research in generalized rate equation for one substrate enzymatic reactions; complex study of thermodynamics of multicomponent systems; co-developed modified group contribution model UNIFAC (3Q). Office: Inst Chemistry at Tallinn Tech U, Akadeemia tee 15, Tallinn 12618, Estonia

SIIRTOLA, HARRI TAPANI, research scientist digital electronics; b. Kittilä, Lapland, Finland, Sept. 25, 1962; s. Leo Mikael and Leena Inkeri (Hytönen) S. MSc, U. Tech., Tampere, Finland, 1991. Rsch. asst. Tampere U. Tech., 1987-91, rsch. scientist, 1991-95; rsch. scientist Tech. Rsch. Ctr. Finland, Tampere, 1995—. Avocations: music, sports.

SIK, TIBOR H., chemical engineer, educator; b. Pecs, Hungary, May 26, 1928; s. Lajos and Stefania (Hameril) S.; m. Györgyi Abrudbanyay, Apr. 9, 1952 (div. 1974); 1 child, Peter; m. Edit Eva Morelli, Mar. 17, 1975; 1 child, Dora. Diploma chemistry, Tech. U. Budapest, Hungary, 1951, DrTech, 1968; CSc, Hungarian Acad. Scis., 1968, DSc, 1983. Rsch. assoc. Inst. of Genetics, Budapest, 1951-70; dep. dir. Inst. of Genetics, Biol. Rsch. Ctr., Hungarian Acad. Scis., Szeged, 1971-80, sr. rschr., 1981-84; prof. U. Agr., Gödöllö, Hungary, 1984-98, prof. emeritus, 1998—. Author several publs.; patentee in field. Recipient Acad. award Hungarian Acad. Scis., 1995, Jour. Szentágothai award, 1999. Mem. Genetic Soc. Hungary (gen. sec. 1989-93), Soc. Hungarian Biochemists (mem. of presidency 1989-95), Microbiol. Soc. Roman Catholic. Avocations: tennis, skiing. E-mail: h12185sik@ella.hu. Home: Primas 2, H-1026 Budapest Hungary Office: U Agrl Scis, Dept Biotech, H-2103 Gödöllö Hungary

SIKES, CYNTHIA LEE, actress, singer; b. Coffeyville, Kans., Jan. 2, 1954; d. Neil and Pat (Scott) S.; m. Alan Bud Yorkin, June 24, 1989. Student, Am. Conservatory Theater, San Francisco, 1977-79. Appeared in TV series St. Elsewhere, 1981-83, L.A. Law, 1989; TV movies include His Mistress, 1990; films include Man Who Loved Women, That's Life, Arthur On The Rocks, Love Hurts, 1988; producer, actress (television) Sins of Silence, 1996; also Broadway musical Into The Woods, 1988-89, Possums, 1998, JAG TV series, 2000. Active Hollywood Women's Polit. Com.; apptd. Pres. Clinton's adv. com. on arts John F. Kennedy Ctr. for Performing Arts, 1999. Recipient Gov.'s Medal of Merit, Kans., 1986. Democrat. Avocations: hiking, writing, reading.

SIKLOSI, GYORGY SZILARD, obstetrician and gynecologist, educator; b. Szombathely, Hungary, June 15, 1942; s. Gyorgy and Eleonora (Habacher) S.; m. Zsuzsanna Hedvig Hiermayer, Mar. 23, 1975. MD, Semmelweis U., Budapest, Hungary, 1967, postgrad., 1971; PhD, Hungarian Acad. Scis., Budapest, 1986, Dsc, 1995. Asst. prof. 2d dept. ob-gyn. Semmelweis U. Med. Sch., Budapest, 1971-86, 1st asst., 1986-91, assoc. prof., 1991-97, prof., 1997—, vice dir. 2d dept. ob-gyn., 1994—. Author more than 100 articles and book chpts. Recipient Sub Auspiciis Rei Publicae Popularis award Pres. of State of Hungary, 1968. Mem. Hungarian Soc. Ob-Gyn. (sec.-gen. 1990—), Hungarian Soc. Endocrinology in Ob-Gyn. (v.p.). E-mail: siklosi@noi2.sote.hu. Office: Semmelweis U Med Sch 2d OG, Ulloi u 78a, Budapest 1082, Hungary

SIKORA, BARBARA JEAN, library director; b. Passaic, N.J., Apr. 12, 1943; d. Stanley Francis and Jean (Sobczyk) S.; m. Richard Bendoritis, July 15, 1970 (div.). BA in Edn., English, William Paterson Coll., 1969, MEd in Learning Disabilities, 1978; MLS, Rutgers U., 1978; Cert. in Fundraising Mgmt., Fairleigh Dickinson U., 1990. Profl. libr. N.J. Tchr. Clifton (N.J.) Pub. Schs., 1969-73; office mgr. Singer/TRW, Fairfield, N.J., 1974-76; prin. libr. Passaic Pub. Libr., 1978-88; asst. libr. dir. Pub. Libr. Livingston, N.J., 1989-90; libr. dir. Pub. Libr. Livingston, 1991—; adj. faculty William Paterson Coll., 1977-90; trustee Wayne Pub. Libr., 1986-88; bd. dirs. Polish and Slavic Fed. Credit Union. Mem. Polish Heritage Festival Com., Holmdel, N.J., 1987—, gen. chmn., 1999; trustee, bd. dirs. Livingston Area C. of C., 1998—; pres. Libr. Pub. Rels. Coun., 1997; trustee N.J. Pops Orch., 1999-2000, West Essex br. YMCA of the Oranges, 1997—, Literacy Vols. Am., Essex County, N.J., 2000—; mem. Polish Children's Heartline, Inc. Grantee U.S. Dept. Edn. libr. literacy program, 1987, N.J. State Libr. Leadership Inst., 1988, Christopher Leadership Inst., 1997; Paul Harris fellow Rotary Internat., 1999. Mem. ALA (ethics com. 1995—), AAUW, N.J. Libr. Assn., Nat. Spkrs.' Assn., Rotary (pres. Livingston chpt. 1994-96, 2000), Rutgers Sch. Comm. and Info. Libr. Studies Alumni Assn. (pres. 1991-94), Beta Phi Mu. Avocations: writing, speaking, adult education, psychology, leadership skills training. Home: The Mill 300 Main St Apt 314 Little Falls NJ 07424-1359 Office: Pub Libr Livingston 10 Robert Harp Dr Livingston NJ 07039

SIKORA, KAROL, radiologist; b. Falkirk, Scotland, June 17, 1948; s. Witold and Thomasina (Browlee) S.; m. Alison Mary Rice, June 7, 1974; children: Simon, Emma, Lucy. BA, Cambridge U., 1969, MS, 1972, PhD, 1978, MB, BChir, 1972. Intern Middlesex Hosp., London, 1973; resident Hammersmith Hosp., London, 1976-78; clin. fellow Stanford U., Calif., 1978-80; cons. Addenbrooks Hosp., Cambridge, Eng., 1980-81; dir. Ludwig Inst. for Cancer Rsch., Cambridge, 1981-86; prof. clin. oncology Royal Postgrad. Med. Sch., London, 1986-99; v.p. global clin. rsch. Pharmacia Corp., 1999—. Author: Molecular Biology and Medicine, 1984, Monoclonal Antibodies, 1984, Endocrine Problems and Cancer, 1984, Clinical Physiology, 1984. Fellow Royal Coll. Radiologists (Twining medal 1983), Royal Coll. Physicians, Athenaeum Club (London). Roman Catholic. Avocations: canoeing, traveling. Office: Royal Imperial Coll Sch Med, Hammersmith Hosp, London W12 ONN, England

SIKORA, LYUBOMYR STEPANOVYCH, research scientist; b. Dashava, Lviv, Ukraine, Nov. 1, 1942; s. Stepan Mykhailovych and Natalia Romanivna (Vashchyshn) S.; m. Iryna Romanivna Porytko, Aug. 9, 1963. Student, Comm. Coll., Lviv, 1963, Poly. U., Lviv, 1975; PhD, Physics and Mech. Inst., Lviv, 1991. Physicist Physics and Mech. Inst., Lviv, 1968-74; elec. engr. Comm. Networks, Lviv, 1974-81; sr. engr. rsch. Automatstrom, Lviv, 1981-93, Ctr. Sci. Rsch., Lviv, 1993-94; pres. Ctr. Strategic Rsch., Lviv, 1994—. Author: Laser Informative Measuring Systems for Control Technological Processes, 1998, Systems Concepts Dicisions Control in Complicated Technological Structures, 1998, Basic Modern Theory Stokhastic Signals, 1999, Information Resources Concept Identification and Synthesis Robust Systems of Control, 1999. Mem. IEEE, Info. Theory Soc. Eng., N.Y. Acad. Scis., Engring. Acad. Ukraine, Intelligent Sys. Lasers Elektro-Optiks Soc., Comm. Computing Control Sys. Soc. Avocation: his-

tory books. Home: Lystopadovogo Chynu Str, 79000 Lviv An2o Ukraine Office: Ctr Strategic Rsch, Sichovyeh Strileiv 21/2, 79000 Lviv Ukraine

SIKORA, SADIQ SALEEM, gastrointestinal surgeon, oncologist, researcher; b. Chandrapur, India, Mar. 20, 1960; s. Hussaini A. and Shirin H. (Hasanali) S.; m. Rehana Abbasi, Mar. 1, 1990; 1 child, Zeba. MB BS, All India Inst. Med. Scis., New Delhi, 1983, MS, 1987; postgrad., U. Pitts., 1996. Registrar in surgery All India Inst. Med. Scis., 1987-89; registrar in gastrointestinal surgery Sanjay Gandhi Postgrad. Inst. Med. Scis., Lucknow, India, 1990-91, assoc. prof., 1991—; fellow in surg. oncology U. Pitts. Med. Ctr., 1994-96. vis. fellow sect. colorectal surgery Singapore Gen. Hosp., 1993; vis. fellow Johns Hopkins U., Balt., 1994. Internat. Cancer Rsch. and Tech. Transfer Program fellow Union Internat. Contré Cancer, 1993-94. Fellow UICC; mem. Am. Assn. Cancer Rsch., Internat. Gastro Surg. Club. Avocations: cricket, tennis, golf. Home: Sanjay Gandhi Postgrad Inst, Med Scis Campus, Type IV/83, Lucknow India Office: Sanjay Gandhi Post Grad Inst Med Scis, Rae Bareli Rd, Lucknow India

SIKORA, SUZANNE MARIE, dentist; b. Kenosha, Wis., Dec. 4, 1952; d. Leo F. and Ida A. (Dupuis) S. BS, U. Wis., Parkside, 1975; DDS, Marquette U., 1981. Assoc. Paul G. Hagemann, DDS, Racine, Wis., 1981-84; pvt. practice dentistry Racine, 1984—; cons. Westview Health Care Ctr., Racine, 1981-89, Lincoln Luth. Home, Racine, 1981—, Becker-Shoop Ctr., Racine, 1981—, Lincoln Village Convalescent Ctr., Racine, 1986—, Lincoln Luth. Cmty. Care Ctr., 1989—. Mem. ad hoc study com. County Health Dept., Racine, 1982-83. Mem. ADA, Wis. Dental Assn. (coun. on access prevention and wellness com. 1984-86, impaired provider program intervenor 1990—, del. 1993—, Dental Care for Older Persons award 2000), Racine County Dental Soc. (pres.-elect). Office: 1900 Lathrop Ave Racine WI 53405-3707

SIKORSKI, ALEKSANDER F., biochemist, educator; b. Sosnowiec, Poland, Feb. 3, 1949; s. Bazyli and Alicja (Bugajska) S.; m. Irena Zeleźniakowicz, Sept. 2, 1971; children: Anna, Paweł. MS, U. Wroclaw, Poland, 1972, PhD, 1977, Dr. Habil., 1988. Tchg. asst. U. Wroclaw, 1972-78, adj. rsch. assoc., asst. prof., 1978-93, assoc. prof./prof. biochemistry, 1993-95, prof., 1995—; co-organizer internat. sci. conf. series, 1995, 98. Contbr. articles to profl. jours.; co-editor Cellular and Molecular Biology Letters 1-5, 1996-2000; co-author: Student's Laboratory Handbook for Biochemistry, Student's Laboratory Handbook of Molecular Organization of the Cell. Recipient Award of the Sec. of Polish Acad. Sci., 1989; Polish Sci. Com. (KBN) grantee, 1991-94, 96-99, 2000—. Mem. Polish Biochem. Soc., Polish Soc. Cell Biology. Home: Rogowska 26/16, 51-148 Wroclaw Poland Office: U Wroclaw Dept Genetic Bioc, ul Przybyszewskiego, 51-148 Wroclaw Poland

SIKORSKI, ZDZISŁAW EDMUND, food chemistry educator; b. Wilno, Poland, Oct. 29, 1930; s. Bernard and Maria (Grzonkowska) S.; m. Krystyna Stołyhwo; children: Ewa, Anna, Grazyna. BS, Poly. Gdansk, Poland, 1954, MS, 1956, PhD, 1960, DSc, 1965. Lic. food technologist, chemist. Asst. Poly. Gdanska, 1954-60, adj., 1960-66, asst. prof., 1966-73, assoc. prof., 1973-80, prof., chmn. dept. food chemistry and tech., 1980—, dean faculty of chemistry, 1973-75, 78-81; asst. prof. Ohio State U., Columbus, 1964-65; sr. rsch. fellow Commonwealth Sci. and Indsl. Rsch. Orgn., Hobart, Tasmania, 1975-76; scientist Dept. Sci. Indsl. Rsch., Auckland, New Zealand, 1981-82; vis. rsch. prof. Nat. Taiwan Ocean U., Keelung, 1990-91; mem. com. food tech. and chem. Polish Acad. Scis., 1969—, chmn. 1996—. Author: Gas Chromatography, 1962, Gas Chromatography in Food Analysis, 1964, Basic Marine Food Technology, 1967, Marine Food Technology, 1971, 3d edit., 1980, Seafood Raw Materials - Resources, Properties, and Refrigeration, 1992, (with others) Preservation of Marine Foods by Refrigeration, 1973; co-author, editor: Food Chemistry, 1988, Seafood: Resources, Nutritional Composition, and Preservation, 1990, Seafood Proteins, 1994, Chemical and Functional Properties of Food Components, 1997, Food Chemistry, 2000. Mem. bd. Main Coun. for Sci. and Tertiary Edn., Warszawa, 1977-88. Mem. Polish Soc. Food Technologists (founder). Roman Catholic. Avocation: outdoor activities. Home: Chrzanowskiego 64D5, 80-278 Gdansk-Wrzeszcz Poland Office: Poly Gdanska, Gabriela Narutowicza 11/12, 80-952 Gdansk Poland

ŠIKUROVA, LIBUŠA, physicist, educator; b. Bratislava, Czech Republic, July 27, 1953; d. Jan and Zdeňka (Černavová) Šulc; m. Vladimir Šikura, Sept. 17, 1977; children: Slávka, Veronika, Zuzana. MSc in Physics, Comenius U., Bratislava, 1976, PhD in Physics and Math., 1984. Asst. Comenius U. Faculty Math. and Physics, Bratislava, 1983-91, assoc. prof. biophysics, 1992—, postgrad. study advisor in biophysics, 1993—; referee Grant Agy. for Sci., Bratislava, 1994—. Referee Gen. Physiology and Biophysics, 1987—, Acta Physica Universitatis Comenianae, 1988—; contbr. articles to profl. jours. Grant Agy. for Sci. grantee, 1996—. Mem. Slovak Phys. Soc., European Phys. Soc. Avocations: hiking, skiing, costume designing and sewing. Home: Pod Rovnicami 41, SK841-04 Bratislava Slovakia Office: Comenius Univ, Mlynská dolina F1, SK84215 Bratislava Slovakia

SIL, ANJAN, materials scientist, educator; b. Chinsurah, India, May 21, 1960; s. Nabakumar and Malinabala S.; m. Nandini; 1 child, Nairitee. BSc, Burdwan U., 1981; MSc, Indian Inst. Techology, Kharagpur, 1984; M in Technology, Banaras Hindu U., 1986, PhD, 1991. Lectr. Thapar Inst., Patiala, India, 1992-96, asst. prof., 1997—. Avocations: playing table tennis, reading books, listening to music. Home: IV/26 Thapar Inst Campus, 147004 Patiala Punjab, India Office: Thapar Inst Engring Tech, 147004 Patiala Punjab, India

SILA, CATHY ANN, neurologist; b. Cleve., Apr. 21, 1955; d. Andrew Lee and Mary Florence (Patrick) S.; m. Gene H. Barnett, Dec. 9, 1990; children: Austin Andrew, Addison Edgar. BA Chemistry, Zoology summa cum laude, Miami U., 1977; MD, Case Western Res. Sch. Med., 1981. Intern, resident in neurology Cleve. Clinic, 1981-83; resident in neurology Mayo Clinic, Rochester, Minn., 1983-85; rsch. fellow in cerebrovascular rsch. studies Cleve. Clinic, 1985-86; assoc. med. dir. cerebrovascular ctr. Cleve. Clin. Found., 1987—; examiner Am. Bd. Psychiatry and Neurology, 1987—; mem. expert panel Agy. for Health Care Policy and Rsch., 1995-96; presenter in field. Mem. editl. bd. Stroke, Jour. Stroke and Cerebrovascular Disease, Jour. Thrombosis and Thrombolysis, Cleve. Clinic Jour. Medicine; contbr. articles to profl. jours., chpts. to books. Fellow Am. Heart Assn. (brain-stroke peer rev. com. 1998-2000, women and minorities com. 1993-95, operaton stroke med. subcom. 1999—, sci. programs com. 1999-2000), Am. Acad. Neurology (editl. panel Brain Matters Stroke Initiative 1997-98, quality stds. subcom. 1989-98); mem. AMA (name bank for divsn. rsch. grants 1995—, cons. file project 1996—), Nat. Stroke Assn., Internat. Stroke Soc., Phi Kappa Phi. Office: Cleve Clinic Found S91 9500 Euclid Ave Cleveland OH 44195-0001

SILAGY, CHRISTOPHER ALLEN, public health physician, educator; b. Melbourne, Australia, Sept. 14, 1960; s. Leslie and Marianne (Kalmar) S.; m. Jane Elizabeth Russell, Sept. 16, 1959; children: Andrew, Michael, Nicholas, Benjamin. MBBS, U. Melbourne, 1983; PhD, Monash U., 1992. Fellow, then lectr., sr. lectr. Monash U., Melbourne, 1987-91; sr. rsch. fellow U. Oxford, England, 1992-93; prof. gen. practice Flinders U., Adelaide, Australia, 1993-99; dir. Inst. Pub. Health & Health Svcs. Rsch., Monash Med. Ctr., Clayton, Australia, 1999—; prof. pub. health Monash U., 1999—; dir. Australasian Cochrane Ctr., 1994—; officer Order of Australia, 2000. Named Officer in the Order of Australia. Avocations: theatre, tennis. Office: Inst Pub Health & Health Svcs Rsch, Monash Med Ctr, 3168 Clayton Victoria, Australia

SILAJDZIĆ, HARIS, former prime minister of Bosnia-Herzegovina; b. 1945. BA, U. Benghazi, MA in Internat. Rels. and Ea. Studies, PhD in Internat. Rels. Prof. U. Prishtina, Kosovo, Serbia; min. fgn. affairs Govt. of Bosnia-Herzegovina, Sarajevo, 1990-93; prime min. Govt. of Boznia-Herzegovina, Sarajevo, 1993-96; co-chmn. coun. mins. Rep. of Bosnia and Herzegovina, Sarajevo, 1996—, co-prime min. Office: Coun Mins, Vojvode Putnika 3, 71000 Sarajevo Bosnia-Herzegovina*

SILAS, CECIL JESSE, retired petroleum company executive; b. Miami, Fla., Apr. 15, 1932; s. David Edward and Hilda Videll (Carver) S.; m. Theodosea Hejda, Nov. 27, 1965; children: Karla, Peter, Michael, James. BSChemE, Ga. Inst. Tech., Atlanta, 1953. With Phillips Petroleum Co., Bartlesville, Okla., 1953-94; pres. Europe-Africa, Brussels and London Phillips Petroleum Co., 1968-74; mng. dir. natural resource group Europe/Africa Phillips Petroleum Co., London, 1974-76; v.p. gas and gas liquids div. natural resources group Phillips Petroleum Co., Bartlesville, 1976-78, sr. v.p. natural resources group, 1978-80, exec. v.p. exploration and prodn., minerals, gas and gas liquids, 1980-82, pres., chief operating officer, 1982-85, chmn., CEO, 1985-94. Bd. dirs. Reader's Digest Assocs., Inc., bd. dirs. of Halliburton Co., Boys/Girls Clubs Am., Atlanta, parton councillor Atlantic Coun. of the U.S.; bd. dirs. Okla. Found. for Excellence, Ga. Tech. Found.; trustee Frank Phillips Found.; active Trilateral Commn. Served to 1st lt. Chem. Corps, AUS, 1954-56. Decorated comdr. Order St. Olaf (Norway); inducted into Ga. Inst. Tech. Athletic Hall of Fame, 1959, recipient Former Scholar-Athlete Total Person award, 1988; inducted into Okla. Bus. Hall of Fame, 1989; named CEO of Yr., Internat. TV Assn., 1987. Mem. Am. Petroleum Inst., U.S. C. of C. (past chmn. bd. dirs.), 25 Yr. Club, Phi Delta Theta. Avocations: fishing, golf, hunting. Office: PO Box 2127 Bartlesville OK 74005-2127

SILBERBERG, REIN, nuclear astrophysicist, researcher; b. Tallinn, Estonia, Jan. 15, 1932; came to U.S., 1950; s. Jüri and Elisabeth (Linkvest) S.; m. Ene Liis Rammul, Aug. 28, 1965; children: Hugo Valter, Ingrid Kaja. MA, U. Calif., Berkeley, 1956, PhD, 1960. Postdoctoral rsch. Naval Rsch. Lab., Washington, 1960-62, rsch. physicist, 1962-81, head cosmic ray sect., 1981-85, dep. br. head cosmic and gamma ray, 1985-90; co-dir., editor, lectr. Internat. Sch. Cosmic Ray Astrophysics, Erice, Italy, 1978-96; cons. Univs. Space Rsch. Assn., Washington, 1990-95; cons. in nuclear astrophysics Roanoke Coll., 1995—. Author: (with others) Albert Einstein 100-Year Memorial Volume, 1979; co-editor: Currents in High Energy Astrophysics, 1993, Cosmic Rays and the Interstellar Medium, 1991, Particle Astrophysics and Cosmology, 1995, Toward the New Millennium in Astrophysics, Problems and Prospects, 1997; contbr. chpts. to Ann. Revs. of Nuclear Sci., articles to Astrophys. Jour., Phys. Revs., and Radiation Rsch. Recipient Meritorious Civil Svc. award U.S. Govt., 1980, Handicapped Employee of Yr. award U.S. Govt., 1985. Fellow Am. Phys. Soc., Am. Astron. Soc., Am. Geophys. Union, Radiation Rsch. Soc., Internat. Astron. Union; mem. AAAS, N.Y. Acad. Scis., Cosmos Club. Achievements include development of Silberberg-Tsao cross section equations; derivation and explanation of cosmic ray source composition; pioneering development of theoretical high-energy neutrino astronomy, gamma-ray astrophysics; energy deposition by nuclear interactions; formulation of radiation protection requirements for lunar base and for manned Mars mission; calculation of single event upsets on shielded spacecraft; evaluation of models of cosmic-ray origin. Home: 7507 Hamilton Spring Rd Bethesda MD 20817-4541

SILBERG, LOUISE BARBARA, physician, anesthesiologist; b. Bklyn., Apr. 13, 1958; m. David J. Lazar. BA, Rutgers U., 1981; MS, Seton Hall U., 1986; DO, U. Health Scis., 1990. Diplomate Am. Bd. Anesthesia. Intern Union (N.J.) Hosp., 1990-91; resident in anesthesiology Albany (N.Y.) Med. Ctr., 1991-94, fellow in obstet. anesthesiology, 1994-95; anesthesiologist Anesthesia Consultants Assocs., El Paso, Tex., 1995—; chair dept. anesthesia, Providence Meml. Hosp., El Paso, 1998—. Bd. dirs. El Paso Symphony Chorale, 1996—; mem. Nat. Coun. Jewish Women, 1996—. Mem. AMA, Am. Soc. Anesthesiologists, Soc. Obstet. Anesthesia and Perinatology. Office: Anesthesia Consultants Assocs 1700 Murchison Dr Ste 104 El Paso TX 79902-2918

SILBERGELD, CAROL A., clinical social worker, psychotherapist; b. Bklyn., July 10, 1948; d. Albert Schwartz and Alice Halperin Sachs; m. Arthur F. Silbergeld, May 1, 1970; children: Diana, Julia. BA cum laude, Goucher Coll., 1969; MSW, Bryn Mawr Coll., 1973. Lic. clin. social worker. Psychiatric social worker Balt. City Hosps., 1969-70; Hahnemann Hosp., Phila., 1970-75; clin. social worker, cons. Jewish Family and Children's Svcs., N.Y.C., 1975-77; pvt. practice, 1975—; supr., therapist Reiss-Davis Child Study Ctr., L.A., 1977-83, dir. children divorce clinic, 1980-98, co-dir. postgrad. tng., 1983-94, dir. clin. social work, 1983-95, mem. faculty, supervising cons., 1995—; dir. children divorce project L.A. Child Devel. Ctr., 1998—, also bd. dirs.; dir. program devel. Safety Zone, Santa Monica, Calif., 1999—. Contbg. author: Social Work in Health Settings, 1993; author: Meeting Children on Their Own Grounds, 1999. Fellow Calif. Soc. Clin. Social Work; mem. Academy Cert. Social Workers, Nat. Assn. Social Workers, Nat. Soc. Clin. Social Work (mem. com. psychoanalysis), Pa. Soc. Clin. Social Work (founding). Office: 2730 Wilshire Blvd Ste 250 Santa Monica CA 90403-4749

SILBERMAN, CURT C., lawyer; b. Wuerzburg, Fed. Republic Germany, May 23, 1908; came to the U.S., 1938, naturalized, 1944; s. Adolf and Ida (Rosenbusch) S.; m. Else Kleemann, 1935. Student, U. Berlin, U. Munich; JD summa cum laude, Wuerzburg U., 1931, Rutgers U., 1947; Dr. (hon.), Middlebury Coll., 1997. Bar: N.J. 1948, U.S. Supreme Ct. 1957. Pvt. practice internat. pvt. law West Orange, N.J., 1948—; lectr. internat. pvt. law, 1954, 81, 82, 87, 91, 95; prin. guest lectr. at Univ.'s 400th anniversary U. Wuerzburg, 1982. Contbr. articles to legal jours. Pres. Am. Fedn. Jews from Ctrl. Europe, N.Y., 1962-86, chmn. bd., 1986—; past pres. Jewish Philanthropic Fund of 1933, Inc., N.Y., 1971-87, chmn. bd., 1987—; trustee Leo Baeck Inst., N.Y., 1962—, N.Y. Found. Nursing Homes, Inc.; hon. trustee Jewish Family Svc. of Metro-West, N.J.; past co-chmn. Coun. Jews from Germany, 1974—; chmn. Rsch. Found. for Jewish Immigration, Inc., N.Y.; past bd. dirs. Conf. on Jewish Material Claims Against Germany. Recipient Golden Doctoral Diploma, U. Wuerzburg Law Faculty, 1982, Festschrift dedicated to him by Am. Fedn. Jews from Ctrl. Europe in N.Y., 1969; recipient Pub. Svc. medal. Mem. N.J. Bar Assn. (chmn. com. comparative jurisprudence 1966-73, chmn. com. internat. trade 1974-78), Essex County Bar Assn., Am. Coun. on Germany, Internat. Biographical Dictionary of Ctrl. European Emigres (adv. bd.).

SILBERMANN, MICHAEL, cell biologist, maxillo-facial surgeon; b. Acre, Israel, Jan. 19, 1935; s. Herbert and Marga-Mirjam (Pick) S.; Gisela Rozanski, Nov. 17, 1960; children: Anat-Nechama, Ronit-Esther. DMD, Hebrew U., Jerusalem, 1961; cert., Boston U., 1968, Boston City Hosp., 1970; PhD, Tufts U., 1973. Cert. oral and maxillo-facial surgery Israel Min. Health. House officer in oral surgery Hadassah Med. Ctr., Jerusalem, 1961-63; chief resident in oral surgery Boston City Hosp., 1969-70; rsch. fellow in anatomy Tufts Med. Sch., Boston, 1970-73; affiliate in oral surgery Harvard U. Sch. Dental Medicine, Boston, 1972-74; sr. rsch. assoc. U. So. Calif., Los Angeles, 1976-77; chmn. dept. anatomy Faculty of Medicine Technion, Haifa, Israel, 1975-94, prof. dept. anatomy and cell biology Faculty of Medicine, 1985; dean Faculty of Medicine Technion, Haifa, 1991-92, chmn. Israel assoc. deans faculties medicine, 1991-92; chief Lab. Musculoskeletal Research Rappaport Inst., Haifa, 1985-95; vis. scientist Max Planck Inst. Biochemistry, Munich, 1984, 85, Japan Soc. Promotion Sci., Osaka, 1987; mem. nat. steering commn. Laser in Medicine, 1987—; chief scientist Min. Health, Jerusalem, 1993-96; Israel del. BIOMED Program European Union, Brussels, 1996-97; mem. sci. com. Medicinal Products and Med. Devices, European Union, Brussels, 1997—. Co-editor (book) Current Advances in Skeletogenesis, 1982, Directory of Medical Research in Israel, 1996; patentee assay for diagnosis of toxemia of pregnancy, 1986; contbr. or co-contbr. numerous articles to profl. jours. Chmn. bd. govs. U.S.-Israel Binational Sci. Found., 1996-97; interim exec. dir. Middle East Cancer Consortium, 1996-98, exec. dir., 1998—; bd. dirs. Haifa U.; mem. Nat. Coun. for R & D Israel. Served to med. officer Israeli Med. Svc., 1953-85. Fogarty Internat. fellow NIH, 1982-83; Irving and Jeanette Benveniste chair in medicine, 1990—. Mem. Israel Acad. Sci. and Numanities, Israel Soc. Anat. Scis., Israel Soc. Calcified Tissue Rsch., European Soc. Calcified Tissues Rsch., Israel Assn. Dental Medicine (chmn. nat. sci. coun. 1982-83), Inst. Advanced Studies in Dentistry (chmn. Haifa chpt. 1982-87, 96-97), Nat. Coun. Higher Edn. (Y. Alon com. 1985-87), Am. Assn. Anatomists, Am. Soc. Bone and Mineral Rsch., Clore Found., Foulkes Found. Avocation: painting. E-mail: mdsilber@tx.technion.ac.il. Home: 45 Yotam St, Haifa 34675, Israel Office: Technion Faculty Medicine, Box 9649 Anatomy Cell Biol, Haifa 31096, Israel

SILBERSTEIN, MORRY, radiologist, educator; b. Melbourne, Victoria, Australia, Aug. 16, 1961; s. Abraham and Rosa (Lehrc) S.; m. Tamara Silberman, Nov. 11, 1995; 1 child, James. MBBS, U. Melbourne, Australia, 1984; MD, U. Melbourne, 1992; diploma, Royal Australasian Coll. Radiologists, 1990. Radiology registrar Austin Hosp., Australia, 1987-90; rsch. fellow Royal Melbourne Hosp., 1990-91; sr. lectr. radiology U. Melbourne, 1991-98; assoc. prof. radiology U. Sydney, 1999—, head dept. radiology, 2000—; sr. radiologist Canberra Hosp., 1999—; hon. adv. Australian Health Tech. Adv. Com., 1993—, Job Guide Victoria, 1992-94; sr. lectr. anatomy U. Melbourne, 1995-99; mem. mgmt. com. Inst. Neurosci., Melbourne, 1996-99. Mem. adv. panel Australasian Radiology, 1993—; contbr. numerous articles to profl. jours. Recipient Sophi Davis Gold medal Monash U., Australia, 1984; O'Rourke Travelling fellow, 1992, U. Pa. fellow, 1992-93; grantee Australian Rsch. Coun., Royal Australasian Coll. Radiologists Rsch. Fund. Fellow Royal Australasian Coll. Radiologists; mem. N.Y. Acad. Scis., Australian New Zealand Soc. Neuroradiology. Jewish. Office: U Sydney Clinical Sch, Canberra 2606, Australia

SILBERSTON, (ZANGWILL) AUBREY, economics educator; b. London, Jan. 26, 1922; s. Louis and Polly (Kern) S.; m. Dorothy Marion Nicholls, May 19, 1945 (div. 1985); 1 child, Richard Jeremy; m. Michele Ledic, May 23, 1985. BA, Cambridge (Eng.) U., 1945, MA, 1950; MA, Oxford (Eng.) U., 1971. Economist Courtaulds Ltd., London, 1946-50; fellow St. Catharine's Coll., Cambridge, 1950-53; lectr. econs. Cambridge U., 1951-71; fellow Nuffield Coll., Oxford, 1971-78; prof. econs. Imperial Coll., London, 1978-87, sr. rsch. fellow, 1987-99; prof. econs. emeritus U. London, 1987—. Author: The Motor Industr, 1959, The Patent System, 1967, The Economic Impact of the Patent System, 1973, The Multi-Fibre Arrangement, 1984, 2d study, 1989, Beyond the Multifibre Arrangement, 1995, Changing Industrial Map of Europe, 1996. Mem. Monopolies Commn., London, 1965-68, Royal Commn. on the Press, London, 1974-77, Royal Commn. Environ. Pollution, 1986-96. Lt. Royal FUS, 1941-45. Recipient Comdr. of British Empire, The Queen, 1987; Cambridge fellow St. Johns Coll., 1958-71. Mem. Royal Econ. Soc. (sec.-gen. 1979-92, v.p. 1992—), Confederation European Econ. Assns. (pres. 1988-90), Travellers Club. Avocations: opera, ballet. Office: Imperial Coll Mgmt Sch, 53 Prince's Gate, London SW7 2PG, England

SILCOX, FRANCES ELEANOR, museum and exhibits planning consultant; b. Orange, Calif., Sept. 26, 1956; d. William Henry and M. Eleanor (Saulpaugh) S.; m. David William Smith, June 21, 1986; children: Lena Celeste, Reid Whitney. BA in English, U. San Francisco, 1979; MA in Mus. Studies, George Washington U., 1984. Intern divsn. performing arts Smithsonian Instn., Washington, 1978; adminstrv. asst. exhibits dept. Calif. Acad. Scis., San Francisco, 1979-81; gallery coord. The George Washington U., Washington, 1981-83; intern art dept. aide Smithsonian Instn., Washington, 1983-84; asst. dir. Torpedo Factory Arts Ctr., Alexandria, Va., 1983-84; accreditation coord. Am. Assn. Mus., Washington, 1984-86; interpretive planner Design and Prodn. Inc., Lorton, Va., 1986-88; mus. planner West Office Exhbn. Design, San Francisco, 1988-91; ind. mus. and exhibits planner, owner Dallas, 1991—. Bd. mem. St. Gerard Circle, St. Rita Cath. Cmty., Dallas, 1995-98; contbr. numerous natural and cultural resources orgns. Scholar Nat. Endowment for the Arts-Am. Law Inst.-ABA, Washington, 1982. Mem. Am. Assn. for State and Local History, Am. Assn. Mus., Archaeol. Inst. Am., Internat. Coun. Mus., Nat. Assn. for Mus. Exhibition, Tex. Assn. Mus. Democrat. Avocations: travel, correspondence, photography, reading, walking. Home and Office: 463 Fernwood Dr Moraga CA 94556-2119

SILÉN, JOHAN VILHELM, physicist, researcher; b. Helsinki, Finland, Nov. 18, 1951; s. Åke and Brita (Eklund) S.; m. Vivica Antell, July 28, 1975; children: Niklas, Kim. MS, U. Helsinki, 1974, PhLic, 1978, Doctorate, 1990. Asst. U. Helsinki, 1972-77; project scientist EISCAT, Sodenkyla, Finland, 1978-84; indsl. rschr. Rosenlew Automation, Pori, Finland, 1984-86; scientist Finnish Meteorol. Inst., Helsinki, 1986—. Premier lt. Finnish Mil., 1977. Mem. AGU, IEEE. Bahai. Avocations: music, sailing, science, religion. Office: Finnish Meteorol Inst, Vuorikatu 24 PO Box 503, 00101 Helsinki Finland

SILENY, JAN, geophysicist, researcher; b. Jilemnice, Czech Republic, Nov. 20, 1952; s. Rudolf and Milena (Madlova) S.; m. Emilie Telecka, Apr. 30, 1983; children: Jana, Lukas, Josef. MSc, Charles U., Prague, 1979; PhD, Czechoslovak Acad. Scis., 1984. Researcher Czechoslovak Acad. Scis. Inst. Geotechnics, Prague, 1982-85, Geophys. Inst. Acad. Scis., Prague, 1986—; vis. scientist Internat. Ctr. for Sci. and High Tech., Trieste, Italy, 1990; Go-West fellow Internat. Ctr. for Theoretical Physics, Trieste, 1993; researcher U. Trieste, 1993; dep. dir. Geophys. Inst. Acad. Scis., 1992, chmn. sci. coun., 1993—; cons. Integrated Seismic Sys., Welkom, S. Africa; titular mem. European Seismol. Commn. Contbr. articles to profl. jours. NATO fellow U. Trieste, 1997. Mem. Assn. Czech Mathematicians and Physicists, Internat. Ctr. for Theoretical Physics (assoc.). Roman Catholic. Avocations: music, gardening. Home: Hekrova 853, 14900 Prague Czech Republic Office: Geophys Inst Acad of Scis, Bocni II/1401, 14131 Prague Czech Republic

SILFWERBRAND, JOHAN LARS, engineering educator; b. Stockholm, May 28, 1958; s. Carl-Helmer Mattias and Margareta Ingrid (Stenson) S.; m. Cecilia Lucie Malmquist, Oct. 22, 1993. MSc, Royal Inst. Tech., Stockholm, 1982, PhD, 1987. Asst. prof. Royal Inst. Tech., Stockholm, 1988-92, assoc. prof., 1995-97, prof. engring., 1997—; rschr. Swedish Cement and Concrete Rsch. Inst., Stockholm, 1991-95. Contbr. articles to profl. jours.; patentee in field. Recipient Thernwall's award for R&D in Civil Engring., 1992. Mem. Swedish Concrete Assn. (sec. 1994-98, v.p. 1998-2000, pres. 2000—), Am. Concrete Inst., Fedn. Internat. du Béton (Lausanne), Internat. Union Testing Rsch. Labs. Materials Structures, Internat. Assn. Bridge & Structural Engring.

SILHANKOVA, LUDMILA, microbiology educator, researcher; b. Cermna, Czech Republic, Nov. 27, 1927; d. Josef and Ruzena (Leitlova) S. MA, Czech Tech. U., Prague, 1950; PhD, Inst. Chem. Tech., Prague, 1958. Rschr. Rsch. Inst. Fermentation Industry, Prague, 1950-53; rschr. mutagenesis rsch. unit Med. Rsch. Coun., Edinburgh, Scotland, 1967-68; asst. prof. microbiology Inst. Chem. Tech., 1953-67, assoc. prof., 1968-91, prof., 1991-98, cons., 1993—; Author: Microbiology for Food Technologists, 1983 (award Creative Premium Lit. Fund 1985), Microbiology for Food Technologists and Biotechnologists, 1996; patentee for method for preparation of vitamin B1, preparation of reduced co-factors, fermentation prodn. of hyaluronic acid. Mem. Czechoslovakian Microbiol. Soc., Czechoslovakian Biochem. Soc., Czechoslovakian Biol. Soc. Roman Catholic. Avocation: symphonic music. Office: Inst Chem Tech, Technická 5, 166 28 Prague 6, Czech Republic

SILIN, VICTOR PAVLOVICH, physicist, researcher; b. Moscow, May 26, 1926; s. Pavel Ivanovich and Valentina Fedorovna (Kolentseva) S.; m. Rozalia Pavlovna Paruntseva, Nov. 3, 1951; children: Pavel, Victor. Candidate of physics, Lebedev Inst., Moscow, 1953; D in physics, Moscow, 1963; diploma, Moscow State Univ., 1949. Jr. scientist Lebedev Physical Inst., Moscow, 1949-56, sr. scientist, 1956-62, head of sect., 1962—; dir. of solid state physics divns. LPI, Moscow, 1989-95; prof. Moscow Engring. Physical Univ., 1963—; deputy editor-in-chief Bulletin of Lebedev Physics, 1970—, Jour. Physical Soc., 1991—; mem. editorial bd. The Physics of Metals, 1994—. Contbr. numerous articles to profl. jours. Coun. mem. Physics of the Highest State Attestasion Commn., Moscow, 1963-99; scientific coun. mem. Plasma Physics of Russian Acad. Sci., 1970—. Recipient State Prize in physics, Moscow, 1970, 1987. Mem. Russian Acad. Sci. (corr. mem.), Acad. Natural Sci. Office: Lebedev Physical Inst, Leninsky Prospekt 53, 117924 Moscow Russia

SILINA, ALLA VLADIMIROVNA, biologist, researcher; b. Vladivostok, Russia, June 21, 1950; d. Vladimir Alekseyevich and Nina Nikolaevna Grishko; m. Nikolay Vitalyevich, Mar. 31, 1973; children: Ekaterina, Natalya. M of Math., U. Vladivostok, Russia, 1972; PhD in Biology, Russian Acad. Scis., Vladivostok, 1979. Cert. mathematician, hydrobiologist. Postgrad. fellow Inst. Marine Biology Russian Acad. Scis., Vladivostok, 1973-77, rsch. scientist Inst. Marine Biology, 1977-90, sr. rsch. scientist Inst. Marine Biology, 1990—. Author: (with others) Japanese Scallop, 1986; contbr. papers to profl. jours. including Aquaculture, Crustaceana, Ophelia

Soviet Jour. Marine Biology. Avocations: playing piano, listening to music, reading books, traveling. E-mail: inmarbio@mail.primorye.ru. Fax: 4232 310900. Home: Kuznetsova str 74 Apt 248, 690013 Vladivostok Russia Office: Inst Marine Biology, Palchevskogo str 17, 690041 Vladivostok Russia

SILLANPDD, JARKKO, financial professional, lawyer; b. Eurajoki, Finland, Nov. 10, 1970; p. Aarne and Aino Sillanpdd. Bus. Degree, Bus. Sch., Rauma, Finland, 1991; LLM, Turku (Finland) Law Faculty, 1996; JOKO Degree, Turku Sch. Econs., 1999. Contract lawyer Orion Co., Helsinki, Finland, 1996-98; fin. mgr., lawyer, sec. bd. divs. Ldnnen Tehtaat plc, Sdkyld, Finland, 1998—. Author of essays. Mem. Finnish Lawyers Assn. Avocations: art painting, glass art. E-mail: jarkko.sillanpaa@lannen.fi. Fax: 358-2-8397 4022. Office: Ldnnen Tehtaat plc, PO Box 100, 27821 Sdkyld Finland

SILLARD, YVES, political organization worker; b. Coutances, France, Feb. 5, 1936. Engr. gen. Flight Test Ctr., 1960-64; head of Concorde program Civil Aviation Gen. Secretariat, 1964; with Guyana Space Ctr., 1965-76; gen. mgr. Nat. Ctr. Space Studies, 1976-82; chmn., mgr. French Inst. Exploration of the Sea, 1982-88; del. gen. for armaments, 1989-93; chmn., gen. mgr. Internat. Def. Coun., 1994-97; ofcl. rep. Min. of Def., 1997; asst. sec. gen. sci. and environ. affairs NATO, Brussels, 1998—. Office: NATO Hdqtrs, Blvd Leopold III, 1110 Brussels Belgium*

SILLER, MAX, literature educator; b. Vipiteno, Italy, Sept. 28, 1946; arrived in Austria, 1966; s. Max and Martha (Sparber) S.; m. Heidi Runggaldier, Feb. 11, 1954; children: Kathrin, Thomas. PhD, U. Innsbruck, 1975. Lectr. U. Aberdeen, Scotland, 1969-71; from asst. to prof. U. Innsbruck, Austria, 1975—; guest prof. U. Szeged, Hungary, 1993. Office: Univ Inst German, Innrain 52, 6020 Innsbruck Tirol, Austria

SILLITOE, ALAN, writer; b. Mar. 4, 1928; s. Christopher and Sabina (Burton) S.; m. Ruth Fainlight, Oct. 19, 1959; 1 child, David Nimrod; 1 adopted child, Susan. Student, Nottingham schs. Radio operator RAF, 1946-50; writer, 1950—. Author: (novels) Saturday Night and Sunday Morning, 1958, The General, 1960, Key to the Door, 1961, The Death of William Posters, 1965, A Tree on Fire, 1967, A Start in Life, 1970, Travels in Nihilon, 1971, Raw Material, 1972, Flame of Life, 1974, The Widower's Son, 1976, The Storyteller, 1979, Her Victory, 1982, The Lost Flying Boat, 1983, Down From the Hill, 1984, Life Goes On, 1985, Out of the Whirlpool, 1988, The Open Door, 1989, Last Loves, 1990, Leonard's War, 1991, Snowstop, 1993, Collected Stories, 1996, The Broken Chariot, 1998, The German Numbers Woman, 1999, (autobiography) Life Without Armour, 1995, Alligator Playground Stories, 1997, (essays) Mountains and Caverns, 1975, (stories) The Loneliness of the Long Distance Runner, 1959, The Ragman's Daughter, 1963, Guzman, Go Home, 1968, Men, Women and Children, 1973, The Second Chance, 1981, (poems) The Rats, 1960, A Falling Out of Love, 1964, Love in the Environs of Voronezh, 1968, Storm and Other Poems, 1974, Snow on the North Side of Lucifer, 1979, Sun Before Departure, 1984, Tides and Stone Walls, 1985, Collected Poems, 1994, (travel) Road to Volgograd, 1964, (with David Sillitoe) Nottinghamshire, 1986, Leading the Blind, 1995, (with Fay Godwin) The Saxon Shore Way, 1983, (juvenile) The City Adventures of Marmalade Jim, 1967, Big John and the Stars, 1977, The Incredible Fencing Fleas, 1978, Marmalade Jim on the Farm, 1979, Marmalade Jim and the Fox, 1984, (plays) (with Ruth Fainlight) All Citizens Are Soldiers, 1969, This Foreign Field, 1970, Three Plays, 1978. Address: 14 Ladbroke Ter, London W11, England

SILLS, NANCY MINTZ, lawyer; b. N.Y.C., Nov. 3, 1941; d. Samuel and Selma (Kahn) Mintz; m. Stephen J. Sills, Apr. 17, 1966; children: Eric Howard, Ronnie Lynne Sills Lindberg. BA, U. Wis., 1962; JD cum laude, Union U., 1976. Bar: N.Y. 1977, U.S. Dist. Ct. (no. dist.) N.Y. 1977, U.S. Tax Ct. 1984. Asst. editor fin. news Newsweek mag., N.Y.C., 1962-65; staff writer, reporter Forbes mag., N.Y.C., 1965; rsch. assoc. pub. rels. Ea. Airlines, N.Y.C., 1965-67; asst. editor Harper & Row, N.Y.C., 1968-69; freelance writer, editor N.Y.C., Albany, 1967-70; confidential law sec. N.Y. State Supreme Ct., Albany, 1976-79; assoc. Whiteman, Osterman & Hanna, Albany, 1979-81, Martin, Noonan, Hislop, Troue & Shudt, Albany, 1981-83; ptnr. Martin, Shudt, Wallace & Sills, Albany, 1984; of counsel Krolick and DeGraff, Albany, 1984-89; ptnr. Hodgson, Russ, Andrews, Woods & Goodyear, Albany, 1990-91; pvt. practice Albany, 1991—; of counsel Lemery & Reid, Albany and Glens Falls, N.Y., 1993-94; asst. counsel N.Y. State Senate, 1983-88; cons. The Ayco Corp., 1975; jud. screening com. Third Jud. Dept., 1997—. Editor: Reforming American Education, 1969, Up From Poverty, 1968; rschr.: The Negro Revolution in America, 1963; contbr. articles to mags. Bd. dirs. Jewish Philanthropies Endowment, 1983-86, United Jewish Fedn. N.E. N.Y. Endowment Fund, 1992-96, Daus. Sarah Found., 1994-97, Albany Jewish Cmty. Ctr., 1984-87; mem. Guilderland (N.Y.) Conservation Adv. Coun., 1993-96; mem. planned giving tech. adv. com. Albany Law Sch., Union U., 1991-95, chmn., 1992-95; mem. regional cabinet State of Israel Bonds Devel. Corp. for Israel, 1991-92. Mem. ABA, N.Y. State Bar Assn., Albany County Bar Assn., N.Y. Criminal and Civil Cts. Bar Assn., Estate Planning Coun. Ea. N.Y., Aux. Albany County Med. Soc., Capital Dist. Trial Lawyers Assn., Capital Dist. Women's Bar Assn., Phi Beta Kappa, Sigma Epsilon Sigma. Republican. Home: 16 Hiawatha Dr Guilderland NY 12084-9526 Office: 126 State St Albany NY 12207-1637

SILLS, RICHARD REYNOLDS, scientist, educator; b. N.Y.C., Sept. 19, 1946; s. Leonard Harold and Carol (Rudin) S. BA, Boston U., 1968. Tchr. N.Y.C. Pub. Schs., 1968-70, 79-81; v.p. Plutronics, Inc., N.Y.C., 1981-85; pvt. practice N.Y.C., 1985—. Author: (children's book) Jonny the Jester, 1977; contbr. articles to profl. jours.; patentee method and apparatus for encoding and decoding signals, method and apparatus for modifying synthesized sound signals, analog processing system. Mem. Rep. Nat. Com., Washington, 1981—, Rep. Presdl. Task Force, Washington, 1982—, Rep. Senatorial Inner Cir., 1987—, Rep. Senatorial Trust, 1999—; founding mem. Chmn.'s Club, Ronald Reagan Presl. Found., 1997—. Named Educator of Decade, Found. for Universal Brotherhood Inc., 1978; recipient Rep. Senatorial Medal of Freedom, 1999. Mem. AAAS, N.Y. Acad. Scis., Union of Concerned Scientists. Avocations: running, weight lifting.

SILTON, RONALD HELMUT, electrical engineer; b. Erfurt, Germany, May 11, 1951; arrived in U.S., 1953; s. William Frederick Siegel and Gerda Alma (Röhrborn) S.; m. Christine Marie Theresa Spinde, Aug. 24, 1985; children: John, James. BSEE, Fairleigh Dickinson U., 1973. Reg. profl. engr., fireman-in-charge (high pressure boilers). Field engr. Fla. Power & Light, West Palm Beach, 1973-77; assoc. engr. Pub. Svc. Elec. & Gas, Linden, N.J., 1977-78; staff engr. Gilbert Assoc., Reading, Pa., 1978-89; sr. engr. Combustion Engring., Aiken, S.C., 1989, Westinghouse Savannah River Co., Aiken, 1989—; cons. Gilbert Assoc., Jackson, Mich., 1983-89, lead auditor, 1983-86, level III elec. inspector, 1987-89. Author, contbr. Jackson Edge, 1979-83; editor Cygnus, 1972. Charter orgn. rep. Boy Scouts Am., Augusta, 1994-98, asst. scoutmaster, Aiken, 1997-99, troop com., 1999—. Recipient Award of Merit, Boy Scouts Am., 1995. mem. IEEE (regional dir. 1982-84), NSPE (chpt. pres. 1997-98, bd. dirs. 1994-99, engr. of yr. 1995), SCSPE (edn. found. vice-chmn. 1998—, state chpt. bd. dirs. 1999—), Jackson Ski Club (pres. 1978-82). Home: 211 Pebble Ln Aiken SC 29801-1200 Office: Westinghouse Savannah River Bldg 706-8C Aiken SC 29808-0001

SILVA, DEONISIO DABOIT DA, literature educator; b. Sideropolis, Brazil, Sept. 24, 1948; s. Cecilio and Leobertina (Daboit) S.; m. Soeli Gasparin Schreiber, July 8, 1972; 1 child, Manuela. MSc, Univ. Fed. Rio Grande Sul, Porto Alegre, Brazil, 1981; PhD, U. Sao Paulo, 1989. Prof. U. de Ijui, Brazil, 1975-81, Univ. Fed. São Carlos, 1981—. Author: The Silent Woman, 1981, Ears for Rent, 1987, Go Back, Soldiers, 1992, City of Priest, Teresa, The Warriors of the Land, 1996. Roman Catholic. Avocation: football. Home: Major Jose Inacio 1844, São Carlos Brazil

SILVA, JOÃO BATISTA C., geophysicist, researcher; b. Novo Horizonte, Brazil, Feb. 5, 1949; s. Ademaro Costa and Amelia (Bruza) S.; m. Hiroko Sido, Feb. 16, 1974; 1 child, Ronald Sido Correa. BS, Fed. U. Rio de Janeiro, 1972; MS, Fed. U. Pará, Belém, Brazil, 1976; PhD, U. Utah, 1982. Prof. Fed. U. Pará, 1974—. Contbr. articles to profl. jours. Mem. Soc. of Exploration Geophysicists, Soc. Brasileira de Geofisica. Office: CG-UFPA, Caixa Postal 1611, 66017-900 Belém Brazil

SILVA, MONICA, gifted education educator; b. Miami, May 13, 1927; d. Arthur E. and Laura E. (Fernandez) S.; m. Alfred Bethel, Apr. 30, 1955 (annulled 1959); 1 child, Leonard James. BA in Edn., Fordham U., 1970, MS in Adminstrn. Supervision, 1976. Cert. tchr. elem. edn., N.Y.; cert. math. tchr. K-8, Va.; cert. social studies tchr. 7-12, N.Y.; cert. adminstr., N.Y. Tchr., adminstrv. asst. Intermediate Sch. 10 Bd. of Edn., N.Y.C., 1970-73, St. Peter's U.F.S.D., Peekskill, N.Y., 1973-76; assoc. dir. Harlem Hosp. Med. Ctr., N.Y.C., 1976-78; tchr. math., K-8 Bd. Edn., N.Y.C., 1980-83; tchr. math. Middle. Sch., Newport News, Va., 1983-86; tchr. talented and gifted Pub. Sch. 31 Bd. Edn., N.Y.C., 1986-91; dir. summer ednl. program Episcopal Diocese, N.Y., 1970-89; dir. Arista Honor Soc., Intermediate Sch. 10, N.Y. Pub. Schs., 1971-73. Co-editor: (handbook) Frederick Douglass Teacher's Handbook, 1971. Counselor/tutor N.Y.C. Pub. Schs., 1970-73, mem. PTA, 1970-76, 80-83; mem. Cancer Support Group, Newport News, Va., 1994; vol. tchr. Queen Street Bapt. Ch., Hampton, Va., 1993-94. Grantee Chase Bank, N.Y.C., 1972. Mem. Libr. Congress, AAUW, Smithsonian Inst. Democrat. Episcopalian. Avocations: reading, playing piano, gardening, sewing and numismatics. Home: 3423 Shell Rd Hampton VA 23661-1441

SILVA, PAUL DOUGLAS, reproductive endocrinologist; b. Durban, Natal, Republic South Africa, Oct. 29, 1956; came to U.S., 1968; s. George Douglas and Georgette Marie (Schedivetz) S.; m. Diane Elisabeth Deterville, June 28, 1980; children: Julie Renee, Jennifer Marie, Dawn Elisabeth. BA in Biology, UCLA, 1976; MD, U. Calif., Davis, 1981. Diplomate Am. Bd. Ob-Gyn, Am. Bd. Reproductive Endocrinology. Resident in ob-gyn U. Calif., Irvine, 1981-85; fellow in reproductive endocrinology U. So. Calif., L.A., 1985-87; reproductive endocrinologist Gundersen/Luth. Med. Ctr., La Crosse, Wis., 1987—; med. researcher Gundersen Med. Found., La Crosse, 1987—; cons. St. Francis Med. Ctr., La Crosse, 1988—. Coontbr. articles to Jour. Am. Acad. Dermatology, Am. Jour. Ob-Gyn, Jour. Clin. Endocrinology and Metabolism, Acta Endocrinology, also others. Lectr. to community orgns. Recipient Geog. Acad. award U. Calif., Irvine, 1984, rsch. award Soc. for Gynecologic Investigation, 1987, svc. award Pacific Coast Fertility Soc., 1987; Gundersen Med. Found. grantee, 1989—. Fellow Am. Coll. Ob-Gyn., Am. Fertility Soc.; mem. Am. Assn. Gynecologic Laparoscopists, Soc. Reproductive Endocrinologists. Roman Catholic. Achievements include development of outpatient methods for surgical treatment of reproductive diseases which were previously treated by inpatient methods; demonstration that androstenedione may be a more important androgen in women than testosterone. Office: Gundersen Clinic 1836 South Ave La Crosse WI 54601-5494

SILVA, ZELMIRA MARIA, economist, consultant, researcher; b. Buenos Aires, Sept. 6, 1967; d. Roberto Emilio Silva and Zelmira Llerena. BA in Econs., Cath. U. Argentina, Buenos Aires, 1991. Intern Citibank NA, Buenos Aires, 1991; jr. economist Alpha Econ. and Bus. Consultants, Buenos Aires, 1991-93, sr. economist, 1994-96; rsch. analyst McKinsey & Co., Buenos Aires, 1997-98; rsch. and info. mgr. McKinsey & Co., Buenos Aires/Santiago, Chile, 1998—. Vol. Caritas Argentina pub. hosp., Buenos Aires, 1990-91. Avocations: travel, languages.

SILVA MARTINS, JOAO FRANCISCO, television company executive; b. Lisbon, Portugal, Apr. 30, 1964; s. Rui Navvel Carmo and Maria Isabel Ribeiro da Silva Martins; m. Catarina Castel-Branco Mota; 1 child, Constança. Degree in chem. engring., IST, Lisbon, 1987; PhD in Engring., UNL, Lisbon, 1993, MBA, 1994. Cert. in engring. Rschr. Houione, Loures, Portugal, 1987-89; exec. dir. IBET, Oeiras, Portugal, 1992-95; CEO TV Cabo Sad, Almada, Portugal, 1995-99, TV Cabo Lisbon, 1999—. Recipient Sci. and Tech. award Gulbenkian Found., 1992. Avocations: sailing, swimming, scuba diving. Office: TV Cabo Lisbon, Rua Soeiro Pereira Gomes 7, 1649-001 Lisbon Portugal

SILVA-PANDO, FRANCISCO JAVIER, biologist; b. Vilagarcia de Arousa, Pontevedra, Spain, Oct. 20, 1955; s. Celestino José and Maria Luisa (Pando Durán) Silva Ruiz; m. Maria Del Carmen Espiña Guldris, Sept. 6, 1955; children: Ero Vinicius, Cristina Ultreia. B.Biology, U. Santiago, Spain, 1978; PhD in Biology, U. Complutense, Madrid, 1990. Rschr. CIFOR Lourizan, Pontevedra, 1981-91, sect., 1991-94; biologist Wildlife Svc., Pontevedra, 1994-98, fishing sect. chief, 1998-99; head dept. ecology CIFORAM Lourizan, 1999—; sec. sch. tchr. Xunta de Galicia, Pontevedra, 1985-86, Vigo, 1986-87; asst. prof. Oreg. State U., Corvallis, 1995; part-time prof. U. Santiago, 1995—; vis. rschr. Forest Rsch. Inst. Malaysia, Kuala Lumpur, 2000. Co-author: Guia das Arboles y Bosques de Galicia, 1992, Mapa Forestal de España: Hojas 2-2, 2-3, 2-4, 1-3, 1-4, 1991-92, Guia das Plantas Medicinais de Galicia, 1996; editor: Proc. of Actas I Congreso Forestal Español Lourizan, 1993. Recipient Forestry Rsch. award Diputacion Provincial de Pontevedra, 1983; Xunta de Galicia Rsch. grantee, 1994, 2000. Mem. Spanish Soc. Forestry Sci. (sec. 1992—), Brit. Ecol. Soc. London, Portuguese Soc. Forestry Sci., Ecol. Soc. Am. Office: Lourizan Forestry Rsch Ctr, PO Box 127, 36080 Pontevedra Spain

SILVA-PEREIRA, ANA PAULA TOMÁS, veterinary surgeon, educator; b. Lisbon, Portugal, Nov. 4, 1959; d. José Silva and Beatriz Martins Tomaás P.; m. José Martins, Sept. 16, 1991 (div. 1995); 1 child, Filipe Tomá Pereira Martins. Cert. vet. surgeon, Higher Vet. Medicine Sch., Lisbon, 1982; DVM, Tierartzliche U., Hannover, Germany, 1986. Vet. diplomate, Portugal. Asst. Escola Superior Agrária de Santarém, Portugal, 1986-89, prof., 1989—; vet. surgeon SCALVET, Santarém, 1989—; mem. vet. groups European Commn., 1998—. Friend Kindernothilfe, Germany, 1986—, Internat. Med. Assitance, Lisbon, 1999—; mem. Quercus, Lisbon, 1993—, Grupo Lobo, Lisbon, 1993—. Mem. Vet. Surgeons Coll., N.Y. Acad. Scis. Avocations: swimming, cardio-fitness. Home: 12-4 Esq, Praceta Augusto Costa, 2000-212 Santarém Portugal Office: ESAS-IPS, Complexo Andaluz, 2000 Santarém Portugal

SILVE, JEAN PAUL, retired shipping and mining company executive; b. Paris, Oct. 18, 1920; s. Paul Jean and Suzanne Andrée (Saurin) S.; m. Hélène Marguerite Ferronnière; children: Jacques, Guillaunee, Caroline, Jean-Yves, Benoit. Diploma in mining engring., Paris Sch. of Mines, Paris, 1944. Chief engr. Cie Miniere, Conakry, France, 1950-57; ops. mgr. Bauxites Midi, Paris, 1957-62; dept. head Pechiney, Paris, 1963-82; chmn. Jebsen France, Paris, 1982-95, Philmar Assurance, Paris, 1987-97; ret. Capt. French Army, 1944-49. Decorated Chevalier (Knight) Legion d'honneur. Mem. SFEN, Australian Pioneers Sydney, ACF Morfontaine Golf Club. Avocations: golf, computers. Home: 15 Paul Doumer, 92400 Courbevoie France

SILVENNOINEN, PEKKA OLAVI, engineering physicist, researcher; b. Hämeenlinna, Finland, Jan. 2, 1945; s. Osmo Olavi Silvennoinen and Helga Siviä Matoniemi; divorced; children: Teemu, Petra, Juri; m. Tarja Ranta-Silvennoinen, Jan. 4, 1980. Diploma Engring., Helsinki U. of Tech., 1968; PhD, Va. Polytechnic Inst./State U., 1971. Prof. Nuclear Engring. Lab., 1975-89; head OECD Nuclear Energy Agy. Nuclear Devel. Div., Paris, 1982-84; rsch. dir. Div. Energy Tech. VTT Tech. Rsch. Ctr. of Finland, Helsinki and Espoo, 1989-92, rsch. dir. Div. Info. and Elec. Tech., 1993-94; rsch. dir. VTT Info. Tech., 1994—; vis. scholar MIT, 1973. Author: (book) Reactor Core Fuel Management, 1976, Nuclear Fuel Cycle Optimization, 1982. Mem. European Nuclear soc. (pres. 1994-95), Finnish Acad. Tech. Home: Kajavatie 1, FIN-00200 Helsinki Finland Office: VTT Info Tech, PO Box 1200, FIN-02044 Espoo Finland

SILVER, ERIC, journalist, writer; b. Leeds, Eng., July 8, 1935; arrived in Israel, 1987; s. Harry Hyman and Fanny Rebecca (Coss) S.; m. Bridget Amy Hale, Aug. 9, 1959; children: Sharon, Rachel, Dinah. BA, St. Catherine's Coll., Oxford, Eng., 1956. Reporter Harrogate (Eng.) Herald, 1957-59; copy editor No. Echo, Darlington, Eng., 1959-60, The Guardian, Manchester, Eng., 1960-64; reporter The Guardian, London, 1964-72; fgn. corr. The Guardian, Israel and India, 1972-87; freelance journalist Jerusalem, 1987—. Author: (biographies) Victor Feather, 1973, Begin, the Haunted Prophet, 1984, (history) The Book of the Just, 1992 (Christopher award 1993), German edit., 1994 (Gustav Heinemann award 1995). Chair Fgn. Press Assn., Israel, 1975; pres. Fgn. Corrs.' Assn., India, 1986. Mem. Savile Club London. Jewish. Home and Office: 64 St of the Prophets, 95141 Jerusalem Israel

SILVER, IAN ADAIR, pathology educator; b. Poona, India, Dec. 28, 1927; s. George James and Nora Adair (Seckham) S.; m. Marian Scrase, June 30, 1950 (dec. June 1994); children: Alison Janet, Fiona Marian, Alastair John, Robin Angus. m. Maria Erecinska, May 6, 1996. BA, Cambridge (Eng.) U., 1948, MA, 1952; DVM, London U., 1952. Demonstrator Cambridge U., 1952-57, lectr., 1957-70; prof. Bristol (Eng.) U., 1970—, chmn. dept. pathology and microbiology, 1980-93, dean of medicine, 1987-90, prof. emeritus pathology, 1993—, sr. rsch. fellow, 1995—; chmn. Southmead Hosp., Bristol, 1992-99; adj. prof. neurology U. Pa., 1976—. Editor numerous sci. books; contbr. articles to profl. jours. Lt. Brit. navy, 1944-46. Fellow Royal Coll. Vet. Surgeons (pres. 1985-87); mem. Internat. Soc. 02 Transport to Tissue (pres. 1977, 86), Brit. Vet. Assn. (Sir Frederick Hobday medal 1981, Dalrymple Champney medal 1985), Anat. Soc. U.K., Path. Soc. U.K., also others. Avocations: farming, mountain climbing, fishing, reading. Office: Bristol U Vet Sch, Southwell St, Bristol BS2 8EJ, England

SILVER, JOHN RUSSELL, spinal injury consultant, researcher, consultant; b. London, Oct. 16, 1931; s. Aron Gideon and Cissie (Silman) S.; m. Marilyn Duke, 1960; children: Kevin, Daniel. MB BS, London U., 1954. House surgeon in orthopedics Luton Dunstable Hosp., 1955-56; house physician in medicine New End Hosp., 1956; spinal injuries registrar Stoke Mandeville Hosp., 1956-57; registrar neurology Middlesex Hosp./Stoke Mandeville Hosp., 1959-61, sr. registrar rsch., 1962-65; cons., lectr. in spinal cord injuries, Liverpool, 1965-70; cons. in spinal injuries Nat. Spinal Injuries Ctr., 1970-92. Author: Renal Failure, Management of Spinal Injuries; contbr. articles to profl. jours. including Brain, Brit. Med. Jour., Brit. Jour. Orthopaedics. Flight lt. RAF, 1956-59. Fellow Royal Coll. Physicians (Edinburgh and London), Inst. Sports Medicine (London), Tissue Viability Soc. (chmn., pres.), Internat. Soc. Paraplegia (coun. 1965-70), Assn. Brit. Neurologists, Internat. Soc. Electrophy and Kinesiology (v.p. 1976). Avocation: sports. Office: 8 High St, Wendover Bucks, England

SILVER, JONATHAN M., physician; b. Paterson, N.J., May 10, 1953; s. Elihu Avigdor and Carol Ann Silver; m. Orli Silver, Mar. 4, 1979; children: Elliot, Benjamin, Leah. BA, Duke U., 1971-75; MD, Albert Einstein U., 1975-79. Diplomate Am. Bd. Psychiatry and Neurology. Intern in psychiatry Overcook Hosp., Summit, N.J., 1979-80; resident in psychiatry N.Y. State Psychiat. Inst., Columbia U., N.Y.C., 1980-83; rsch. fellow NIMH/N.Y. State Psychiat. Inst., Creedmoor, N.Y., 1983-84; dir. psychiatry Allen Pavilion, Columbia-Presbyn. Med. Ctr., N.Y.C., 1988-93, Columbia Presbyn. Psychiat. Assocs., N.Y.C., 1993-99; dir. neuropsychiatry Columbia Presbyn. Med. Ctr., 1989-99; chief Outpatient Ctr. for Mental Health, Lenox Hill Hosp., N.Y.C., 1997—, asst. dir. clin. svcs. and rsch., dept. psychiatry, 1999—; attending psych. inpatient psychiatry svc. Columbia Presbyn., 1987-88; clin. prof. psychiatry NYU Sch. Medicine, 1998—; assoc. prof. clin. psychiatry Columbia U., 1998, lectr., 1998—. Editor: Neuro Psychiatry of Traumatic Brain Injury, 1994; assoc. editor Jour. Neuropsychiatry; contbr. chpts. to books and articles to profl. jours. Recipient Laughlin award Nat. Psychiat. Endowment Fund, 1983. Mem. Am. Neuropsychiat. Assn. (chairperson membership com.), Phi Beta Kappa. Office: Lenox Hill Hosp 100 E 77th St New York NY 10021

SILVER, MARC A., physician; b. Chgo., Oct. 14, 1949; s. Samuel and Ida (Reiter) S.; m. Laureen Dunne, Aug. 5, 1983. AB, U. Ill., Chgo., 1971; MD, Rush Med. Coll., Chgo., 1979. Instr. Rush Med. Coll., Chgo., 1979-82, instr. medicine and pathology, 1984-86; fellow NIH, Bethesda, Md., 1982-84; asst. prof. Loyola U. Med. Ctr., Maywood, Ill., 1986-88; assoc. prof. medicine and pathology Michael Reese Hosp. Med. Ctr., Chgo., 1988—, med. dir. cardiac surveillance unit, 1988—, chief div. cardiology and cardiovascular inst., 1988—, dir. heart failure programs, 1988—; prof. medicine Stritch Sch. Medicine Loyola U., Chgo., 1994-98, dir. Heart Failure Ctr./assoc. dir. heart transplant program, 1994-98; lectr. cardiac pathology Stritch Sch. Medicine; dir. Midwest Ctr. for Heart Failure, 1992-94; clin. prof. medicine U. Ill., 1998—; dir. cardiovascular disease fellowship Heart Failure Inst. Christ Hosp. and Med. Ctr., 1998—, chmn. dept. medicine, 2000—. Author: Success with Heart Failure, 1998; co-editor-in-chief Congestive Heart Failure; assoc. editor Angiogenesis and Myogenesis; contbr. articles to profl. jours.; mem. editl. bd. several jours. Manuscript Review Several Profl. Jours. Fellow ACP, Am. Coll. Cardiology, Am. Coll. Chest Physicians; mem. Internat. Soc. Heart Transplantatino, Am. Heart Assn., Soc. Cardiovasc. Pathology, Ctrl. Soc. Clin. Rsch., Alpha Omega Alpha. E-mail: marc.silver@advocatehealth.com.

SILVER, PAUL ROBERT, marketing executive, consultant; b. Balt., Mar. 15, 1931; s. Harry and Frieda (Rosengarten) S.; m. Natalie Nessa Nechamkin, May 17, 1957; children: Geri Ellen, Steven Marc, Lawrence Alan. BA, U. Md., 1949; BS, U. Balt., 1958; postgrad., Eckerd Coll., 1984. Pres., CEO Sterling Prodns. Inc., Balt., 1950-51; advt. mgr. Hecht Co., Washington, 1951-53; pres., CEO Artists & Models, Inc., Washington and Balt., 1974-76, The Charles Agy. Inc., Washington and Balt., 1955-80, The Golden Triangle Agy., Clearwater, Fla., 1980-82; COO Bridgman Assocs. Inc., Annapolis, Md., 1985-86; dir. promotions Internat. Beverage Expn., Washington, 1986; pres., CEO Prasco Inc., Tampa, Fla., 1982—; cons. Lewis and Ptnrs., Inc., San Francisco, Corp. Vision, Inc., L.A., Computer Response, Inc., Balt., Themes and Schemes, Inc., Dunedin, Fla., San Diego, 1984—, J&B Mgmt. Co., 1991, Alberee Products, Inc., 1992; v.p. Coupon Am., Bel Air, Md., 1987-88; dir. mktg. Miles Homes, Inc., Cheshire, Conn., 1993; CEO Universal Industries, Inc., 1994—; ptnr. Drakeford & Drakeford, PA, 1995-96; v.p. Chapman Security Inc., 1995-98; ptnr. Global Mktg. Internat., 1997, CEO, also chmn. bd. dirs. Stoppit! Corp., New Port Richey, Fl., 1999—. Active in Radio Free Asia, 1972, Pinellas County Heart Savers, Clearwater, 1981; campaign mgr. for candidates for Balt. City Coun., U.S. Senate and U.S. Congress, 1968, 88, Fla. Commr. Agr., 1990. With U.S. Army, 1953-55, 72. Democrat. Jewish. Avocations: writing, art. Office: Prasco Inc PO Box 24461 Tampa FL 33623-4461

SILVER, PETER JOHN, accountant; b. Birmingham, Eng., Sept. 8, 1949; s. John Simeon and Daisy Grace S.; m. Marylyn Anne Smith, June 24, 1972; children: Paul, Christine, John. Cert. in acctg., Coventry U., 1969. From articles clk. to sr. clk. Ernst and Young (formerly Whinney Murray and Co.), Birmingham, 1969-73; sr. clk. B.D.O. Stoy Haywood (formerly W. Vincent Vale & Co.), Wolverhampton, Eng., 1973-74, Tranter Lowe and Co., Telford, Eng., 1974-77; ptnr. Holyoak Southgate and Co., Shrewsbury, Eng., 1977-89; sr. ptnr. Silver and Co., Bridgnorth, Eng., 1989—. Treas. Bridgnorth and Dist. Bus. Assn., 1992-95, Much Wenlock Parochial Ch. Coun., Shropshire, 1977-82, Much Wenlock Ratepayer Assn., Shropshire, 1972-77; chmn. 1st Priorslee and St. George Scout Group, Telford, 1992—. Fellow Royal Soc. Arts (elected), Inst. Chartered Accts.; mem. Saffs Salop and Wolverhampton Soc. Chartered Accts. (v.p. 1996-97, d.p. 1997-98, pres. 1998-99, treas. 1999—), Shropshiry Soc. Chartered Accts. (v.p. 1994-95, pres. 1995-97), Much Wenlock and Dist. C. of C. (chmn., pres. 1978—). Anglican. Avocations: railway history, railway modelling, antiques. Office: Silver & Co, 7 Whitburn St, Bridgnorth WV164QN, England

SILVER, ROBERTA FRANCES (BOBBI SILVER), educator, writer; b. Sedalia, Mo., Oct. 11, 1941; d. Elvin Joshua and Hilda M. (Abrams) Gordon; m. Wayne E. Mason, July 19, 1959 (div. 1974); m. Burton B. Silver, June 3, 1989 (div. 1992); children: Lori Atkins, Philip A., Marc A. Mason. BA in Spl. Edn., Avila Coll., 1972; MA in Counselor Edn., U. Mo., 1974; MA in Spl. Edn., Santa Clara U., 1992. Cert. counselor, tchr., Calif.; specialist learning handicapped credential and multiple subject credential, 1992, C.L.A.D. Tchr. Learning Disabled Shawnee-Mission (Kans.) Sch. Dist., 1972-75; sch. counselor Hickman Mills Consolidated Sch. Dist. #1, Kansas City, Mo., 1975-77; tchr. Behavior Disorders Jefferson County Pub. Schs., Louisville, 1978-80; tchr. West Valley Ctr. for Edn. Therapy, Canoga Park, Calif., 1981-82, Ozanam Home for Boys, Kansas City, 1983-89; instr. in human svcs. and continuing edn. dept. Longview C.C., Lee's Summit, Mo., 1985-89; instr. learning handicapped Franklin-McKinley Sch. Dist., San Jose, Calif., 1990-95; chr. 2d grade Franklin-McKinley Sch. Dist., San Jose, 1990—, Vietnamese bilingual English immersion/lang. devel. tchr.; writing and art mentor Gifted and talented (G.A.T.E.) program, coord. Author (as Roberta Gordon Silver) 3 novels; watercolorist; contbr. articles to pvt. in-house mag., poems to anthologies, short stories and articles to mags. Avocations: photography, painting, reading, hiking.

SILVERA, HUGO F., engineer, consultant; b. Melo, Uruguay, May 15, 1939; s. Santiago and Analia (Almitrán) S.; m. Susana M. Sequeiros, June 17, 1961. Bachelor, Inst. Alfredo Vazquez Acevedo, Montevideo, Uruguay, 1960; diploma in Indsl. Engring., U. La Repúlica, Montevideo, Uruguay, 1970; Postgrad. in Advance Ordnance Course, U. S. Army Ordnance Ctr., Aberdeen Proving Ground, Md., 1973; Grad. in Nat. Security Mgmt., Indsl. Coll. Armed Forces, Washington, D.C., 1976. Chief indsl. dept. Servicio de Material y Armamento, Uruguayan Army, Montevideo, Uruguay, 1970-76, dir. asst., 1976-78; dir. mgr. Hufersil Ltda., Montevideo, Uruguay, 1978-82; pres. Le Mans S.A., Montevideo, Uruguay, 1980-85, Consorcio Le Mans-Bycic, 1982-84; owner, mgr. Estudio Silvera Ind. Consulting Engr., Montevideo, Uruguay, 1978—; tchr. math. Uruguayan-Am. Sch., Montevideo, 1964; prof. calculus Mil. Sch., Montevideo, 1969-70; prof. tech. and devel. Mil. Inst. of Higher Studies, Montevideo, 1974-78; prof. elec. engring. and lighting Facultad de Arquitectura, U. de La Republica, Montevideo, 1977-85; cons. engr. Comipal for Palmar Dam Hydroelectric Project. Engr., project mgr. for various projects including Complete Elec. Engring., Fire Alarms, CCTV, and Comm. Sys. for Victoria Plaza Hotel Complex (now Radisson Montevideo), 1990-96, Punta Carretas Shopping Center, Montevideo, 1992-94, New Hosp. of Armed Forces, Montevideo Urugua, 1981—; Buquebus Port Terminal, Montevi deo, 1994-96, Punta Del Este Internat. Airport, Uruguay, 1995-97, bus terminal and shopping mall Tres Cruces, Montevideo, 1991-93, Maldonado Hosp., Salto Hosp., Maciel Hosp., La Paloma Bus Terminal, 1999, all the McDonald's restaurantes erected in Uruguay, 1991— (34 sites), numerous others. Full col. Army, 1955-78, Montevideo. Mem. The Planetary Soc., Socioactivo de la Assn. de Ingenieros del Uruguay, Socio Fundador de la Sociedad de Arquitectos E Ingenieros Hospitalarios del Uruguay. Avocations: sci. fiction lit., water sports, painting, astronomy. Office: Consultor Profl Ind, PO Box 56054, Punta Del Este 20100, Uruguay

SILVERMAN, ALAN HENRY, lawyer; b. N.Y.C., Feb. 18, 1954; s. Melvin H. and Florence (Green) S.; m. Gretchen E. Freeman, May 25, 1986; children: Willa C.F., Gordon H.F. BA summa cum laude, Hamilton Coll., 1976; MBA, U. Pa., 1980, JD, 1980. Bar: N.Y. 1981, U.S. Dist. Ct. (so. and ea. dist.) N.Y. 1981, U.S. Ct. Internat. Trade 1981, D.C. 1986, U.S. Supreme Ct. 1990. Assoc. Hughes, Hubbard & Reed, N.Y.C., 1980-84; asst. counsel Newsweek, Inc., N.Y.C., 1984-86; v.p., gen. counsel, sec., dir. adminstrn. Cable One, Inc., Phoenix, 1986—. Contbr. articles to profl. jours. Mem. prevention adv. com. Gov. Pa. Justice Commn., 1975-79; bd. dirs. Lawyers' Alliance for N.Y., 1982-85, N.Y. Lawyers Pub. Interest, 1983-85, Nat. Assn. JD-MBA Profls., 1983-85, Bus. Vols. for Arts, Inc., Phoenix, 1989-93, Ariz. Vol. Lawyers for the Arts, Inc., 1994-97, First Amendment Coalition Ariz., Inc., 1991—; mem. Maricopa County Citizens Jud. Adv. Coun., 1990-93; mem. citizens' bond com. City of Phoenix, 2000. Mem. ABA, Assn. of Bar of City of N.Y., D.C. Bar Assn., Phi Beta Kappa. Home: 5833 N 30th St Phoenix AZ 85016-2401 Office: Cable One Inc 1314 N 3d St Phoenix AZ 85004

SILVERMAN, ALBERT A., retired lawyer, manufacturing company executive; b. Copenhagen, Oct. 14, 1908; came to U.S., 1909, naturalized, 1921.; s. Louis and Anna (Mendelsohn) S.; m. Gertrude Adelman, 1929 (div. 1934); 1 child, Violet (Mrs. Robert Blumenthal); m. Florence Cohen, Aug. 5, 1939 (dec. 1966); m. Francie Seifert, Oct. 1, 1975. Student, Northwestern U., 1929-34; AA, Cen. YMCA Coll., Chgo., 1936; JD, Loyola U., Chgo., 1940. Bar: Ill. 1940, Wis. 1959, U.S. Supreme Ct. 1960. With Cen. Republic Bank & Trust Co., Chgo., 1926-32; sec.-treas. Cen.-Ill. Co., 1932-42; corp. atty., sec. Republic Drill & Tool Co., 1942-44; asst. to treas. Hansen Glove Corp., Milw., 1944-45; v.p. Vilter Mfg. Corp., Milw., 1945-49, pres., 1949-88, 89-92, chmn., chief exec. officer, 1970-92, chmn. emeritus, 1992—; bd. dirs., pres. Vilter Found., Inc.; mem. coun. Marquette U. Engring. Sch., 1974-96, assoc., 1995—. Council, Med. Coll. Wis.; bd. dirs. Albert J. and Flora H. Ellinger Found., 1974-96. Named Man of Yr. Milw. chpt. Unico Nat., 1967; recipient Francis J. Rooney-St. Thomas More award Loyola U. Law Sch., Chgo., 1974, Community Relations award Milw. police chief, 1974, Antonio R. Rizzuto Gold Medal award Unico Nat., Community Svc. awad, VFW, 1989, award Wis. Reg. Bd. NCCJ, 1989; honored by VFW for community svc., 1988. Mem. ABA, ASHRAE, Wis. Bar Assn., Milw. Bar Assn., Chgo. Bar Assn., Am. Zool Soc., Loyola U. Alumni Assn. (hon.), Milw. Athletic Club, Wis. Club, Univ. Club of Milw., Tripoli Country Club, Milw. Athletic Club, Milw. Press Club (Knight of Bohemia award 1979, Headliner award 1981, NCJJ award 1989), Masons (past master Milw. Harmony Lodge 1961, 32 deg.), Shriners, Philosopher's Stone Soc., Beta Gamma Sigma (hon.). Jewish. Office: 2405 W Dean Rd River Hills WI 53217-2008

SILVERMAN, ARNOLD BARRY, lawyer; b. Sept. 1, 1937; s. Frank and Lillian Lena (Linder) S.; m. Susan L. Levin, Aug. 7, 1960; children: Michael Eric, Lee Oren. B Engring. Sci., Johns Hopkins U., 1959; LLB cum laude, U. Pitts., 1962. Bar: U.S. Dist. Ct. (we. dist.) Pa. 1963, Pa. 1964, U.S. Patent and Trademark Office 1965, U.S. Supreme Ct. 1967, Can. Patent Office 1968, U.S. Ct. Claims 1975, U.S. Ct. Appeals (3d cir.) 1982, U.S. Ct. Appeals (fed. cir.) 1985. Patent atty. Alcoa, New Kensington, Pa., 1962-67, 68-74, sr. patent atty., 1972-76; ptnr. Price and Silverman, Pitts., 1967-68; v.p., gen. patent counsel Joy Mfg. Co., Pitts., 1976-80; ptnr. Murray Silverman & Keck, Pitts., 1980-81, Buell, Blenko, Ziesenheim & Beck, Pitts., 1984; ptnr. intellectual property dept. Eckert, Seamans, Cherin & Mellott, Pitts., 1984—, chmn., 1992—, chair info. tech. practice group, 1995-97; spl. asst. atty. gen. State of W.Va., 1985—; spl. counsel patents U. Pitts., 1975—; spkr. on patents, trademarks, copyright, computer law; nat. panel of arbiters Am. Arbitration Assn., 1987—. Contbr. articles to profl. jours. Mem. Churchill CSC (Pa.), 1967-90, chmn., 1975-90; mem. Pitts. law com. Anti-Defamation League, 1981—, regional adv. bd., 1982—, ch-chmn. Pitts. region ann. dinner, 1983, mem. chmn. by-laws com., 1983; bd. govs. Slippery Rock U. Found., 1985-91; Pitts. steering com. MIT Enterprise Forum, 1986-87. With U.S. Army, 1963-64. Recipient Am. Spirit Honor medal, Ft. Knox, 1963,. Mem. ABA, ASME, Allegheny County Bar Assn. (chmn. pub. rels. com. 1978-80, vice-chmn. intellectual property sect. 1981-83), Pitts. Patent Law Assn. (chmn. pub. rels. com., 1968-69, chmn. patent laws com., 1970-72, chmn. nominating com., 1973, chmn. legis. action com., 1972-75, bd. mgrs. 1974-88, newsletter editor 1974-88, sec.-treas. 1976-84, v.p. 1984-85, pres. 1985-86, pub. rels. com. 1994-95, program com. 1995-96), Am. Intellectual Property Law Assn. (membership com. 1985-88, mem. pub. rels. com. 1994—), U.S. Trademark Assn. (chmn. task force on advt. agys. 1981, membership com. 1987-89), D.C. Bar Assn., Pa. Bar Assn., Nat. Assn. Coll. and Univ. Attys., Am. Chem. Soc. (chemistry and the law sect.), Licensing Execs. Soc. (co-chmn. Pitts. chpt. 1994-96), Brit. Inst. Chartered Patent Agts. (fgn. mem.), Johns Hopkins U. Alumni Assn. (chmn. publicity com. 1963-66, exec. com. 1966-87, v.p. 1969-70, pres. 1971-72, nat. alumni coun. 1989-92), U. Pitts. Gen. Alumni Assn., U. Pitts. Law Alumni Assn. (bd. dirs. 1992-97, treas. 1997-98, v.p. 1998-99, pres. elect 1999—), Robert Bruce Assn. Law Fellows (life), Golden Panthers, Stratford Cmty. Assn. (v.p. 1966-67, gov. 1966-70, pres. 1967-68), Mensa (fellow, lawyers in Mensa 1978—, nat. assoc. counsel patents and trademarks copyrights 1980-82, inventors' spl. interest group 1980-86), Intertel (treas. Pitts. Forum 1983—), Duquesne Club, Order of Coif, Tau Epsilon Rho, Psi Chi. Republican. Jewish. Home: 2019 High Pointe Ct Murrysville PA 15668-8515 Office: 600 Grant St 44th Fl Pittsburgh PA 15219-2703

SILVERMAN, BERNARD WALTER, statistics educator, priest; b. London, Feb. 22, 1952; s. Elias and Helen (Korn) S.; m. Rowena Fowler, Mar. 9, 1985; 1 child, Matthew. BA, Cambridge (Eng.) U., 1973, PhD, 1978, ScD, 1989; BTh, Southampton U., 2000. Rsch. fellow Jesus Coll., Cambridge U., 1975-77; mgr. calculator dept. Sinclair Radionics Ltd., Eng., 1976-77; jr. lectr. Oxford (Eng.) U., 1977-78; lectr. U. Bath, Eng., 1978-80, reader, 1981-84, prof. stats., 1984-93; prof. stats. U. Bristol, Eng., 1993—; provost Inst. for Advanced Studies, Bristol, 2000—; hon. curate Cotham Parish Ch., Bristol, 1999—; vis. scholar, vis. prof. various univs. and related instns., including Stanford (Calif.) U., Princeton (N.J.) U., U. Wis., Heidelberg (Germany) U., U. Paris, Csiro, Australia, 1977—. Author: Density Estimation, 1986, Nonparametric Regression and Generalized Liner Models, 1994, Functional Data Analysis, 1997; editor Internat. Statis. Rev., 1991-95; contbr. articles to profl. jours. Recipient Pres. award Am. Statis. Assn., 1991, others. Fellow Royal Statis. Soc. (Guy Bronze medal 1984, Guy Silver medal 1995, mem. coun. 1982-90, hon. sec. 1984-90), Inst. Math. Stats. (coun. 1991-94, pres. 2000-01); mem. Internat. Statis. Inst. (chmn. Bernoulli Soc. European com. 1988-90). Jewish Christian. Avocations: music, reading, talking. Office: U Bristol, Sch Math, Bristol BS8 1TW, England

SILVERMAN, CHARLOTTE, epidemiologist, educator; b. N.Y.C., May 21, 1913; d. Harry and Gussie (Goldman) S. BA, Bklyn. Coll., 1933; MD, Woman's Med. Coll. Pa., 1938; MPH, Johns Hopkins U., 1942, DrPH, 1948. Diplomate Am. Bd. Preventive Medicine. Intern Beekman Hosp., N.Y.C., 1939-40; resident Sea View Hosp., Staten Island, N.Y., 1940-41; asst. dir., dir. Bur. Tuberculosis Balt. City Health Dept., 1946-56; chief epidemiology, planning and rsch. Md. State Dept. Health, Balt., 1956-62; med. officer in various programs NIMH, Bethesda, Md., 1962-68; dep. dir. div. biol. effects and other positions Bur. Radiol. Health USPHS, Rockville, Md., 1968-83; assoc. dir. for human studies FDA, Rockville, 1983-92; mem. faculty dept. epidemiology Johns Hopkins U. Sch. Hygiene and Pub. Health, Balt., 1950—. Author: Epidemiology of Depression, 1968; contbr. articles to profl. jours. Sr. Surg. USPHS, 1944-45. Recipient Mary Pemberton Nourse Meml. award AAUW, 1941-42, Merit award FDA, 1974, Alumni Life Achievement award Bklyn. Coll., 1994. Fellow APHA, Am. Coll. Preventive Medicine, Am. Orthopsychiat. Assn., Am. Coll. Epidemiology; mem. Delta Omega. Home: 4977 Battery Ln Apt 1001 Bethesda MD 20814-4929

SILVERMAN, DAVID GARY, physician, anesthesiologist; b. N.Y.C., July 6, 1949; s. Arthur and Henriette Silverman; m. Sally Anne Kniffin, Aug. 31, 1984; children; Tyler Joseph, Charlotte Anne. BA, Hofstra U., 1971; MD, Cornell U., 1975. Lic. MD, N.Y., Conn., Pa. Diplomate Am. Bd. Anesthesiology. Intern in medicine Albert Einstein Coll. Medicine, N.Y.C., 1975-76; resident in anesthesiology U. Pa., Phila., 1977-80, asst. prof. anesthesiology, 1980-84; chmn. of anesthesiology Park City Hosp., Bridgeport, Conn., 1984-86; med. dir. pre-admission testing Yale U. Sch. Medicine, New haven, 1986-99, prof. anesthesiology, dir. clin. rsch., 1986—. Editor: Neuromuscular Block, 1995, Rev. of Clin. Anesthesia, 1996, 1998-2000. Office: Yale U Sch Medicine Dept Anesthesiology 333 Cedar St New Haven CT 06510-3289

SILVERMAN, FRANCES JOY, solicitor; b. Eastbourne, Eng., Sept. 3, 1949; d. John and Peggy (Stewart) Learmouth; m. Harvey Alan Silverman, July 31, 1971; children: Alexander, Richard. Grad., The Coll. of Law, Eng.; LLM, U. Leicester. Articled clk. Booth & Blackwell, Eng., 1967-73; reader in law The Coll. of Law, Eng., 1973-97; solicitor Eng., 1973—; part-time chmn. employment Tribunals, 1992—; external examiner U. Northumbria, 1992-99, U. Hertfordshire, 1994-99. Author: The Law Society's Conveyancing Handbook, 1992-99, Standard Conditions of Sale, 1996; editor: Halsburys Laws, vol. 44, 1994, Encyclopedia of Forms and Precedents, vols. 35-36, 1997; mem. editl. bd. The Conveyancer, 1995—. Mem. The Law Soc., Inst. of Expert Witnesses. Anglican. Avocations: quilting, gardening, golf. Home: Garden Cottage, Rowfold, Billingshurst RH14 9DD, England

SILVERMAN, HUGH J., philosophy educator; b. Boston, Aug. 17, 1945; s. Leslie and Eleanore (Riffin) S.; m. L. Theresa Watkins, June 22, 1968 (div. Apr. 1983); children: Claire Christine, H. Christopher; m. Gertrude Postl, Sept. 1, 1987. BA, Lehigh U., 1966, MA, 1967; postgrad., U. Paris, 1968, 71-72; PhD, Stanford U., 1973. Lectr. Stanford U., Calif., 1973-74; asst. prof. SUNY, Stony Brook, 1974-79, assoc. prof., 1979-83, prof. philosophy and comparative lit., 1983—; vis. sr. lectr. U. Warwick, Coventry, Eng., 1980, U. Nice, France, 1980, 81; vis. prof. Duquesne U., Pitts., 1978, 2000, NYU, 1978-80, 85-86, U. Leeds, Eng., 1988, U. Torino, Italy, 1989, U. Vienna, Austria, 1993, 94, 97, 2000, U. Nice, France, 1994, U. Helsinki, Finland, 1997, 99, U. Sydney, Australia, 1998; co-dir. Internat. Philos. Seminar, Alto Adige, Italy, 1991—; Fulbright Disting. chair on humanities U. Vienna, 2000. Author: Inscriptions: Between Phenomenology and Structuralism, 1987, Textualities: Between Hermeneutics and Deconstruction, 1994 (German translation 1997), Inscriptions: After Phenomenology and Structuralism, 1997; editor: Piaget, Philosophy and the Human Sciences, 1980, 97 (Spanish translation 1989), Philosophy and Non-Philosophy since Merleau-Ponty, 1988, 97, Derrida and Deconstruction, 1989, (Korean translation 1999), Postmodernism - Philosophy and the Arts, 1990 (Korean translation 1990), Gadamer and Hermeneutics, 1991, Writing the Politics of Difference, 1991, Questioning Foundations: Truth/Subjectivity/Culture, 1993, Cultural Semiosis: Training the Signifier, 1997, Philosophy and Desire, 2000; co-editor: Jean-Paul Sartre: Contemporary Approaches to His Philosophy, 1980, Continental Philosophy in America, 1983, Hermeneutics and Deconstruction, 1985, Descriptions, 1985, Critical and Dialectical Phenomenology, 1987, Horizons of Continental Philosophy, 1987, Postmodernism and Continental Philosophy, 1988, The Textual Sublime: Deconstruction and its Differences, 1990, Merleau-Ponty: Texts and Dialogues: On Philosophy, Politics and Culture, 1992, 96, Textualität der Philosophie-Philosophie und Literatur, 1994; series editor: Routledge Continental Philosophy series, 1986—; co-editor: Humanities Press Humanity Books Contemporary Studies in Philosophy and the Human Sciences series, 1989—, assoc. editor, 1979-89; Humanities Press Humanity Books Series in Philosophy and Literary Theory, 1989—, SUNY Press Contemporary Studies in Philosophy and Literature, 1988-96, Northwestern U. Press Series in Philosophy, Literature, and Culture, 1996—; Bull. for Rsch. in Humanities, 1983-84; mem. editorial bd. Rsch. in Phenomenology, 1981—, Rev. of Existential Psychology and Psychiatry, 1979—; translator: Consciousness and the Acquisition of Language, 1973; contbr. numerous articles to profl. jours., and chpts. in books. Fulbright-French Govt. and Alliance Francaise fellow, Paris, 1971-72; faculty rsch. fellow SUNY-Stony Brook, 1977, 78, 81; rsch. fellow Am. Coun. Learned Socs., 1981-82; Experienced Faculty Travel fellowship SUNY, 1985, 88, 93, 99; recipient MLA travel grant (Brazil), 1993, N.Y. Coun. for Humanities grant, 1976-77, SUNY Chancellor's award for excellence in teaching, 1977, medal U. Helsinki, 1997. Mem. Soc. Phenomenology and Existential Philosophy (exec. co-dir. 1980-86), Internat. Assn. Philosophy and Lit. (exec. com. 1976—, exec. sec. 1979-87, exec. dir. 1987—), Brit. Soc. Phenomenology (exec. com. 1980-95), Merleau-Ponty Circle (chmn. publs. com. 1978—), Heidegger Conf., Am. Soc. Aesthetics, Am. Philos. Assn. (program adv. com. 1986-89, lectures publs. and rsch. com. 1991-94). Home: 105 Bleeker St Prt Jefferson NY 11777-1232 Office: SUNY Dept Philosophy Stony Brook NY 11794-0001

SILVERMAN, LESTER PAUL, economist, energy industry consultant; b. N.Y.C., Feb. 28, 1947; s. Eli and Irene B. (Karp) S.; m. Janit Roslyn Smith, June 14, 1969 (dec.); 1 child, Leigh; m. Patty Abramson, Jan. 7, 1995. BS in Adminstrn. and Mgmt. Sci., Carnegie-Mellon U., 1969, MS in Indsl. Adminstrn., 1969, PhD in Econs., 1973. Economist Ctr. for Naval Analyses, Arlington, Va., 1969-74; assoc. exec. dir. NAS, Washington, 1974-78; dir. policy analysis Dept. Interior, Washington, 1978-80; prin. dep. asst. sec. Dept. Energy, Washington, 1980-81; exec. v.p. Dist. Heat & Power, Inc., Washington, 1981-82; dir. McKinsey & Co., Inc., Washington, 1982—; cons. in field, 1966-78. Author (with others) govt. report: Reducing U.S. Oil Vulnerability, 1981; editor: Population Redistribution and Public Policy, 1978; contbr. articles to profl. publs. Mem. exec. coun. Am. Jewish Com., Washington, 1983-84. Recipient Spl. Achievement award Dept. Interior, 1979, Outstanding Svc. award Dept. Energy, 1981. Mem. NAS (panel on natural gas stats., 1983-84, exploratory com. on future of nuclear power, 1984, alternative energy R&D com., 1989), Am. Econ. Assn., Internat. Assn. Energy Economists, Omicron Delta Epsilon, Omicron Delta Kappa. Home: 3005 0 St NW Washington DC 20007 Office: McKinsey & Co Inc 1101 Pennsylvania Ave NW Washington DC 20004-2514

SILVERMAN, MICHAEL, pediatrician, educator; b. Leeds, Eng., Feb. 8, 1943; s. Philip and Beatrice (Wolfe) S.; m. Penelope Mary Baker, Feb. 14, 1970; children: Ben, Tom. MB, BChir, Cambridge (Eng.) U., 1967, MA, 1968, MD, 1972. Rsch. fellow Cardiothoracic Inst., London, 1970-71; lectr. in pediatrics Ahmadu Bello U., Zaria, Nigeria, 1972-74, Bristol (Eng.) U., 1974-77; sr. lectr. pediatrics Royal Postgrad. Med. Sch., London, 1977-88, reader in pediatric respiratory medicine, 1988-94, prof. pediatric respiratory medicine, 1994-95; prof. child health Leicester (Eng.) U., 1995—; pediatric advisor Nat. Asthma Campaign, London, 1992—. Editor: Childhood Asthma, 1995. Fellow Royal Coll. Paediatric Child Health; mem. Brit. Pediatric Assn., Am. Thoracic Soc., Brit. Thoracic Soc. (coun. mem. 1994—), European Respiratory Soc. Avocations: flute music, walking, botany. Office: Child Health Dept, Leicester Royal Infirmary, Leicester LE2 7LX, England

SILVERMAN, MORTON MAYER, psychiatrist, educator; b. Utica, N.Y., Aug. 15, 1947; s. Hirsch Lazaar and Mildred (Friedlander) S.; m. Kineret Shelli Jaffe, July 5, 1970; children: Ariana, Noah, Ethan. BA, U. Pa., 1969; MD, Northwestern U., 1974. Diplomate Am. Bd. Psychiatry and Neurology. Resident in psychiatry U. Chgo., 1975-78, asst. prof., 1978-80, assoc. prof., 1987—; asst. prof. Georgetown U., Washington, 1981-87; dir. Ctr. Prevention Rsch. NIMH, Rockville, Md., 1981-85; assoc. adminstr. prevention Alcohol, Drug Abuse & Mental Health Adminstrn., Washington, 1985-87; temporary advisor WHO, Geneva, 1979-80, cons., 1998—; cons. forensic malpractice, 1992—; cons. U.S. Surgeon Gen., Washington, 1998—. Co-editor 4 books, 1995-2000; co-author: Comprehensive Textbook Suicidology, 2000; contbr. articles to profl. jours. Bd. dirs. U. Chgo. Lab. Schs., 1992—. Recipient Spl. Recognition award USPHS, 1985; fellow Am. Coll. Forensic Examiners, 1997. Mem. Am. Psychiatric Assn. (fellow 1991), Am. Assn. Suicidology (editor-in-chief Suicide Jour. 1997—), Am. Found. Suicide Prevention, Internat. Assn. Suicide Prevention, Group Advancement Psychiatry, Sigma Xi. Jewish. Avocations: contemporary glass art collecting, opera, coin collecting. Home: 4858 S Dorchester Ave Chicago IL 60615-2012 Office: U Chgo 5737 S University Ave Chicago IL 60637-1507

SILVERMAN, SAM MENDEL, physicist, lawyer; b. N.Y.C., Nov. 16, 1925; s. Moshe Aaron and Gitel (Korenbaum) S.; m. Jacqueline Greenberg, Sept. 12, 1948 (div. Apr. 1965); children: Ann, William, Nancy; m. Phyllis Rolfe, June 26, 1966; children: Gila, Aaron. BChE, CCNY, 1945; PhD, Ohio State U., 1952; JD, Suffolk U., 1982. Bar: Mass. 1982, U.S. Dist. Ct. Mass. 1982, U.S. Ct. Appeals (1st cir.) 1982, N.Y. 1983, U.S. Supreme Ct. 1986. Assoc. Ohio State U., Columbus, 1952-55; asst. prof. chem. physics U. Toledo, 1955-57; rsch. physicist Air Force Cambridge Rsch. Labs., Bedford, Mass., 1957-80; chief polar atmospheric processes br. and dir. geopole obs. Air Force Cambridge Rsch. Labs., Bedford, 1963-74, cons., 1980—; vis. rsch. assoc. Queens U., Belfast, 1963-64; vis. prof. Osmania U., Hyderabad, India, 1965-66; mem. adv. bd. Inst. Space and Atmospheric Studies, U. Sask. (Can.), 1965-69; sr. rsch. physicist Boston Coll., 1981-97; co-chmn. interdivisional commn. history Internat. Assn. Geomagnetism and Aeronomy, 1987-91. Contbr. articles to profl. jours. Mem. Town Meeting Lexington, Mass., 1973-79, 84—; elected mem. Lexington Dem. Town Com., 1996—; legal counsel Internat. Work Group. With USAAF, 1945-46. Fellow Am. Phys. Soc., Explorers Club; mem. Am. Geophys. Union (editor History of Geophysics newsletter 1983-91), Internat. Work Group on Death, Dying and Bereavement. Home: 18 Ingleside Rd Lexington MA 02420-2522

SILVERMAN, STANLEY HARRY, surgeon, consultant; b. London, July 21, 1954. MBChB, U. Birmingham, Eng., 1977, MD, 1988. Rsch. fellow Gen. Hosp., Birmingham, 1983-85; sr. surg. registrar W. Midlands Regl. Health Authority, United Kingdom, 1986; lectr. in surgery U. Birmingham, 1986-89; cons. surgeon Dudley Health Authority, United Kingdom, 1989-92, City Hosp. NHS Trust, Birmingham, 1992—; clin. tutor City Hosp. NHS Trust, 1995-2000; external profl. advisor to Health Svc., 2000. Fellow Royal Coll. Surgeons Edinburgh, Royal Coll. Surgeons Eng., Vascular Surg. Soc. of Great Britain, European Soc. Vascular Surgery, Assn. of Surgeons of Great Britain. Office: City Hosp NHS Trust, Dudley Rd, Birmingham B187 QH, England

SILVERMAN, WARREN, physician; b. N.Y.C., Nov. 16, 1954; s. Leon and Ruth S.; m. Jean Marie Ogburn, Apr. 11, 1981 (div. Sept. 1990); 1 child, Arone Yacov; m. Elena Gennadievna Kiyatkina, Oct. 13, 1997; children; Inessa, Danielle Nicole, Samantha Leah. BS in Biology, Rensselaer Polytech Inst., 1978; MD, Albany Med. Coll., 1978. Bd. cert. internal medicine, occupational medicine, forensic medicine. Med. dir. Ocrancoke (N.C.) Health Ctr., 1981-85; asst. prof. Albany Med. Coll., 1985-87; dir. emergency dept. Cmty. Hosp., Cobleskill, N.Y., 1989-91; med. dir. Workplace Health & Safety Assn., Latham, N.Y., 1986-95, dir., 1995-97; dir. Access Case Mgmt. Svcs., Latham, N.Y., 1998—, Access Health Systems, Latham, N.Y., 1999—; profl. adv. bd. Ctr. for Disabled, Albany, 1994—; exec. dir. Northeast N.Y. Fed. Safety & Health Coun., Albany, 1998—; sr. aviation med. examiner FAA, Latham, 1989—; cons. in field. Editor Nat. Safety Data Sheets, 1989-91. Exec. dir. Theater Dance Network, Voorheesville, N.Y., 1998; med. officer Civil Air Patrol, Albany, 1988-91; dir. Voohheesville Cmty. Sch. Found., 1990. Lt. comdr. USPHS, 1981-85. Fellow Am. Coll. Forensic Medicine, Am. Coll. Forensic Examiners; mem. Am. Coll. Occupational & Environ. Medicine, Internat. Soc. Police Surgeons. Jewish. Home: 547 New Salem Rd Voorheesville NY 12186-4829 Office: Access Health Systems 776A Watervliet Shaker Rd Latham NY 12110-2296

SILVERSTEIN, GERSON, retired rehabilitation counselor; b. N.Y.C., Nov. 3, 1918; s. Jacob and Ida Silverstein. BA, CCNY, 1942; MA, NYU, 1970. Cert. rehab. counselor, N.Y. Ptnr. export/import bus. Amesco Corp., N.Y.C., 1946-51; sr. prodn. planner Revlon Corp., N.Y.C., 1951-60; self employed Home Safety Products Corp., Bklyn., 1961-64; with N.Y. State Civil Svc., N.Y.C., 1964-70, N.Y. State Office Vocat. Rehab., N.Y.C., 1970-87; ret., 1987. Author: Choose Life, 1968; contbr. poetry to N.Y. Times, Wis. Poetry Mag. Trustee Village Temple, 1994—. Sgt. U.S. Army, 1942-46. Recipient award Met. chpt. Nat. Rehab. Assn., 1987. Democrat. Jewish. Avocations: writing, fiction. Home: 720 W End Ave New York NY 10025-6299

SILVERSTONE-SOPKIN, PHILIP ARTHUR, biologist, educator; b. Chgo., Oct. 9, 1939; arrived in Colombia, 1981; s. Eugene Henry and Rose (Sopkin) Silverstone; m. Mary Sugayo Hino, Mar. 1969 (div. 1977); 1 child, Barbara Amaterasu Silverstone; m. Albina Alexandrovna Krasnopërova, Aug. 14, 1998. BA, U. Miami, 1961, BS, 1965; PhD, U. So. Calif., 1971; postgrad., Calif. State U., L.A., 1978-79, 80-81. Cert. tchr., Calif. Presdl. intern Smithsonian Instn., Ft. Pierce, 1972-73; instr. Cerritos Coll., Norwalk, Calif., 1973-79, Calif. State U., 1980-81, Bolívar Coll., Cali, Colombia, 1981-82; asst. prof. U. del Valle, Cali, 1979-80, assoc. prof., 1982-84; prof. titular U. del Valle, 1984—; rsch. assoc. Natural History Mus., L.A., 1971—; dir. herbarium CUVC, 1997—. Co-contbr. chpt. to: Biodiversity and Conservation of Neotropical Montane Forests, 1995; contbr. articles to profl. jours. With Fla. Army N.G., 1962. Rsch. grantee COLCIENCAS, Cali, 1987-90, Nat. Geog. Soc., Washington, 1988; recipient Cert. Merit award Nat. Merit Scholarship Test, Coral Gables, Fla., 1957. Mem. Am. Soc. Plant Taxonomists, Internat. Assn. Plant Taxonomy, Assn. Tropical Biology, Soc. Econ. Botany. Office: U del Valle, Dept Biologia, AA25360 Cali Colombia

SILVESTER, FREDERICK JOHN, public affairs consultant; b. London, Sept. 20, 1933; s. William Thomas and Kathleen Gertrude (Jones) S.; m. Victoria Ann Lloyd-Davis, 1971; children: Jessica, Lucy. MA, Sidney Sussex Coll., Cambridge U., Eng., 1954; Degree in Edn., Cambridge U., Eng., 1955. Barrister at law: Gray's Inn, London, 1957. Tchr. Newcastle under Lyme Grammar Sch., Eng., 1955-57; polit. edn. officer Conservative Party No. Eng., 1957-60; sr. assoc. dir. J. Walter Thompson Co., London, 1960-67, 70-74; mem. Parliament, Walthamston West, Eng., 1967-70, Manchester Withington, Eng., 1974-87; chmn. Advocacy Ltd., London, 1987-2000. Author: The North Briton, 1985. Active with Conservative Party, 1955-87; councillor Walthamston Town Coun., London, 1961-66. Mem. Inst. Practitioners in Advt., Carlton Club.

SILVESTRINI, ACHILLE CARDINAL, archbishop, prefect; b. Brisighella, Italy, Oct. 25, 1923. Ordained priest Roman Cath. Ch., 1946. Elected titular archbishop of Novaliciana Mauritania, 1979; consecrated bishop, 1979; sec. Coun. for Pub. Affairs of the Ch., 1979; created cardinal, 1988; prefect Supremal Tribunal of the Apostolic Signatura, 1988, Congregation for the Oriental Chs., Rome, 1991—. Address: 00120 Vatican City State Vatican City State*

SILVONEN, KIMMO JUHANI, electrical engineering educator; b. Koski HL, Finland, Oct. 10, 1957; s. Jorma Juhani and Kerttu Helena (Falt) S.; m. Kirsi Helena Toivanen, June 20, 1982; children: Riku, Toni, Niko. MS, Helsinki U., 1983, Lic. Tech., 1988, DS, 1999. Registered profl. elec. engr. Rsch. asst. Helsinki U. Technology, 1979-80, asst., 1981-83, lectr., 1983-90, acting prof. circuit theory, 1990-91, lectr., 1991—; instr. Helsinki Inst. Tech., 1984—, Mil. Acad., 1985-87, Nokia Corp., Finland, 1989. Contbr. articles to profl. jours. Mem. Assn. Elec. Engrs. in Finland, Soc. Europaea Lepidopterologica. Avocations: insects, photography, sports, music. Office: Helsinki U Tech S TST, PO Box 3000, FIN-02015 Hut Finland

SIM, JAI-HOON, electronics researcher; b. Seoul, Korea, Oct. 20, 1967; s. Kisub Sim and Joonghee Choi; m. Heaseung Oh, April 12, 1999; 1 child,

Janie. BSEE, Nat. Taiwan U., Taipei, 1990, PhD in Elec. Engring., 1993. Assoc. rschr. Samsung Electronics Co., Ltd., Kyungki-Do, Korea, 1993-94, tech. mgr., 1995-98; adv. rschr. IBM, Hopewell Junction, N.Y., 1999—. Contbr. articles to profl. jours. Mem. IEEE. Roman Catholic. Avocations: skiing, swimming, ancient Chinese literature. E-mail: jaihoons@us.ibm.com. Office: IBM Microelectronics 1580 Rt 52 Bldg 630 Zip 33A Hopewell Junction NY 12533

SIM, KWANG MONG, computer scientist; b. Singapore, Sept. 18, 1964; s. See Liak and Siew (Guek) S. BSc in Computer Sci., U. Ottawa, Ont., 1990, MSc in Computer Sci., 1992; PhD in Computer Sci., U. Calgary, Alta., 1995. Programmer/analyst Singapore Computer Sys., 1988; tchg./rsch. asst. U. Ottawa, 1989-90, U. Calgary, 1991-94; rschr. Netherlands Orgn. for Sci. Rsch., Maastricht, Holland, 1996-97, Osaka (Japan) U., 1997-98; lectr. in computing Hong Kong Poly. U., 1998—; asst. prof. info. engring. Chinese U. Hong Kong. Mem. IEEE, Am. Assn. Artificial Intelligence. Avocation: archery. Office: Chinese U of Hong Kong, Dept Info Engring, Shatin NT, Hong Kong

SIM, LEE-LING, government official; b. Penang, Malaysia, Mar. 29, 1949; arrived in Australia, 1991; d. Keng-Hoe Sim and Suat-Eng Lim; (div.); children: Gina, Giuliana. BSc, Kuala Lumpur (Malaysia) U., 1972, BSc with honors, 1973. Sr. rsch. officer for publs. Rubber Rsch. Inst. of Malaysia, 1973-91; rsch. liaison officer for sci. publs. NSW Agr., Orange, Australia, 1991-92; divisional liaison officer NSW Agr., Orange, 1992—. Home: 13 Karimi Way, Orange NSW 2800, Australia Office: NSW Agr, 161 Kite St, Orange NSW 2800, Australia

SIM, PENG CHOON, manufacturing representative; b. Singapore, Dec. 20, 1932; s. Ban Chye and Lian Keow (Koh) S. Sr. Cambridge cert. Anglo Chinese Sch., Ipoh, 1951; m. Alice Chong Swee Kheng, Nov. 21, 1958; children: Rita, Koon Weng, Grace, Su-San. Storekeeper, Barlow & Co., Ltd., Kuala Lumpur, Malaysia, 1952; med. rep. Allen & Hanburys, Ltd., Singapore, 1953-56; mng. dir. H. Rogers & Co., Ltd., Kuala Lumpur, 1957-63; chmn., mng. dir. Polychem (M) Sdn. Bhd., Kuala Lumpur, 1967—, N.P. King Pte., Ltd., Singapore, 1970—, N.P. King (HK), Ltd., Hong Kong, 1970—; bd. dirs. Siah Brothers Corp, SKF Bearing Industries Sdn. Bhd., Malaysia. Vice chmn. Kwan Inn Teng Found., Petaling Jaya, Malaysia, 1980—, Selangor Tung Shin Hosp., Kuala Lumpur, 1981—, Cabot (Malaysia) Sdn Bhd. Port Dickson, Selangor, 1988—; S.E. Asian rep. G.E. Crane Holdings, Ltd., Sydney, 1989—; dir. Pacific Asia Carbon Black Divsn. (Cabot), Kuala Lumpur, Selangor, 1997-98, Cabot Specialty Chems. Inc., Cons., Asia Pacific Region, 1999—. Office: 7500 A Beach Rd, # 10-303/305 The Plaza, Singapore 199591, Singapore

SIM, STEPHEN SZE HIAN, advertising executive; b. Singapore, Jan. 29, 1954; arrived in Eng., 1956.; s. Soon Seng and Siew (Lan) S.; m. Jane Frances Stimson; children: Rachel Li Ming, Theresa Li Hsa, Jonathan Juen Fa, Nicholas Juen Wen. Student, Westminster City Coll., 1965-70. Prodn. control exec. J. Walter Thompson, London, 1972-75; prodn. exec. Golley Slater, London, 1975-78; progress controller Saatchi, Saatchi Garland Compton, London, 1978-81; prodn. mgr. RPG, Gloucester, Eng., 1981-84, Target Advt., Cheltenham, 1984—. Home: 213 Stroud Rd, Gloucester GL1 5JU, England

SIMA, ANDERS ADOLPH FREDRIK, neuropathologist, neurosciences researcher, educator; b. Jönköping, Sweden, Dec. 3, 1943; came to the U.S., 1990; s. Karl Jonas Simon and Svea Gunhild (Nilsson) S.; children: Patricia, Alexander, Vanessa. BS, U. Vienna, Austria, 1967; MD, U. Göteborg, Sweden, 1973, PhD, 1974. Asst. prof. pathology U. Goteborg, Sweden, 1973-83; asst. prof. pathology U. Toronto, Ont., 1978-81, assoc. prof. pathology, 1981-82; assoc. prof. pathology U. Manitoba, Winnipeg, 1982-85, prof. pathology, 1985-90, dir. Diabetes Rsch. Ctr., 1988-90; prof. pathology U. Mich., Ann Arbor, 1990-96, prof. internal medicine, 1991-96; dir. neuropathology core MADRC Mich. Alzheimer Disease Rsch. Ctr., Ann Arbor, 1992—; prof. pathology and neurology Wayne State U., Detroit, 1996—, dir. rsch. Morris Hood Jr. Comprehensive Diabetes Ctr., 1998—; hon. prof. neuroscis. Med. Univ., Shanghai, China, 1988; cons. Pfizer, Inc., N.Y.C., 1987—, FDA, Washington, 1988—, Miles Pharm. Inc., West Haven, Conn. 1990—; mem. internat. adv. bd. Hoffman La Roche, Basel, Switzerland, 1992—. Assoc. editor: Jour. PNS, Internat. Jour. Diab.; editor-in-chief Frontiers in Animal Diabetes Research, Internat. Jour. Exptl. Diabetic Rsch., Internat. Jour. Diabetes Rsch.; assoc. editor Diabetes/Metabolism Rsch. and Revs.; mem. editl. bd. mem. for 8 nat. and internat. jours.; contbr. numerous articles to profl. jours. Recipient Chinese Acad.'s award for Sci. Achievement, 1981, Acad. Achievement award Toku Med. Soc., Sendai, Japan, 1985, Gold medal Consiglio Nat. delle Ricerche, Rome, 1987, Internat. Order of Merit, 1999, Order of Internat. Ambs., 1999; Diabetes Rsch. grantee NIH, Bethesda, Md., 1991, 92, Dementia Related grantee NIH, Bethesda, Md., 1994, Ednl. Tng. grantee Pfizer, Inc., N.Y.C., 1994. Fellow Royal Coll. Physicians and Surgeons Can., Internat. Study Group on Diabetes in Animals, Am. Assn. Pathologists, Juvenile Diabetes Found. (hon. chmn. 1984, Appreciation award 1984, Spl. Achievement award 1989, 97). Achievements include major contributions to the pathogenesis of diabetic neuropathy; description of genetically linked senile dementias. Avocations: international civic history, medical history, visual arts, linguistics. Office: Wayne State U Dept Pathology 540 E Canfield St Detroit MI 48201-1928

ŠÍMA, JIŘÍ, theoretical computer scientist; b. Prague, Czech Republic, Mar. 6, 1968; s. Oldřich and Lydie (Vernerová) Š; m. Kateřina Fiedlerová, Oct. 7, 1995; 1 child, Lucien. MS, Charles U., 1991; PhD, Acad. Scis., 1993. Rschr. Inst. of Computer Sci. Rsch. Acad. Scis., Prague, 1991—; tchr. Tech. U., Prague, 1992-95, Charles U., Prague, 1993—. Author: Theoretical Issues of Neural Networks, 1996, Numerical Processing of Immunochemical Methods, 1985; contbr. articles to profl. jours. Mem. Acad. Scis. Czech Republic (young scientist prize 1998). Mem. Brethren Ch. Achievements include complexity analysis of neural learning and finite neural networks, neural expert system architecture design. Office: ICS CAS, Pod Vodárenskou Vezi 2, 18207 Prague Czech Republic

SIMA, PETR, immunologist; b. Prague, Dec. 23, 1942; Petr and Frantiska (Kandusova) S. Student, Jr. Coll., Prague, 1960; BS, Charles U., Prague, 1965; postgrad., Acad. of Scis. of Czech, Republic, 1970-74. Asst. Lab. of Animal Physiology and Genetics, Libechov, Czech Republic, 1965-67; postdoctoral rsch. assoc. Inst. Microbiology Acad. of Scis. of Czech Republic, Prague, 1975-81, sr. rsch. scientist, 1982—; cons. immunology Hosp. Amerigo Boavida, Luanda, Angola, 1987-88. Co-author: (books) Evolution of immune reactions, 1990, Immune system accessory cells, 1992, Immunology of Annelids, 1994, Annelids, 1994, Evolutionary Mechanisms of Defense Reactions, 1998. Recipient J.E. Purkyne award Czech Acad. of Scis., 1988. Mem. Czech Immunol. Soc., Czech Biol. Soc., Internat. Soc. of Devel. and Comparative Immunology. Avocation: water rescue. Home: Sladkovicova 1242, 142 00 Prague 4 Czech Republic Office: Inst Microbiology, Videnska 1083, 142 20 Prague 4 Czech Republic

SIMA, VASILE, control engineer, researcher, educator; b. Lita, Cluj, Romania, Oct. 21, 1949; s. Vasile and Hortenzia (Deac) S.; m. Nicoleta Ulubeanu, Sept. 20, 1975; children: Diana-Maria, Vlad-Paul. Diploma in Engring., Polytech. Inst., Bucharest, Romania, 1972, D in Engring., 1983; diploma in Math., U. Bucharest, 1978. Sr. rschr. Rsch. Inst. for Info., Bucharest, 1983-90, 1st degree sr. rschr., 1990—; rschr. Rsch. Inst. for Info., Bucharest, Romania, 1972-82; assoc. prof. Polytech. Inst., Bucharest, 1977-92, Inst. Applied Info., Bucharest, 1993-94; sec. sci. coun. Rsch. Inst. for Info., Bucharest, 1990-95, v.p. sci. coun., 1995—,. Author: (books) New Methods in Applied Mathematics (in Romanian), 1992 (Romanian Acad. award 1994), Algorithms for Linear-Quadratic Optimization, 1996 (Gen. Assn. Engrs. in Romania award 1997); also contbr. articles to profl. jours. Grantee: Internat. Rsch. and Exchange Bd., Chgo., 1992, Commn. European Cmtys., Chemnitz, Germany, 1994, Belgian Office for Sci., Tech. and Cultural Affairs, Leuven, 1996-97, Katholieke U. Leuven, Belgium, 1998-99. Mem. IEEE, Internat. Fedn. Automatic Control (nat. com.), Am. Math. Soc. Mem. Ea. Orthodox Ch. Avocations: reading, symphony concerts, skiing, tourism. Office: Nat Inst R&D in Informatics, Maresal Alex Averescu NR 8-10, 71316 Bucharest Romania

ŠIMA, VLADIMÍR, physicist, educator; b. Prague, Czech Republic, Mar. 4, 1952; s. Václav and Jarmila (Lojdová) Š; m. Hana Čechová, July 14, 1978; children: Alice, Sandra. MS, Charles U., 1975, PhD, 1982. Rsch. fellow Charles U., Prague, 1982-85, asst. prof., 1985-92, assoc. prof., 1992—, head dept., 1992—. Contbr. articles to profl. jours. Alexander von Humboldt fellow, Germany, 1989. Home: Komenskeho 495, CZ 253 01 Hostivice Czech Republic Office: Charles U, Ke Karlovu 5, CZ 121 16 Prague Czech Republic

SIMADER, HARALD MAXIMILIAN, physician; b. Linz, Austria, Dec. 5, 1950; s. Max and Hildegard (Kafka) S.; m. Elisabeth Baurecht, Aug. 18, 1979; 1 child, Carina. MD, U. Innsbruck, 1977. Physician Diakonissen-Hosp. Schladming, Austria, 1989—. Avocations: skiing, sailing.

SIMALARIDES, ANASTASIOS, mathematician, educator; b. Constantinople, Turkey, Aug. 27, 1955; s. Demetrios and Theodora (Gregoriadou) S. BSc in Maths., U. Patras, Greece, 1977; PhD in Maths., U. Athens, Greece, 1986. Prof. maths. Tech. Edn. Inst. Chalcis, Greece, 1987—. Contbr. articles to profl. jours. Home: 196 Kifissias St, 14562 Athens Greece

SIMAL-GÁNDARA, JESÚS, nutrition and food science educator; b. Santiago de Compostela, Galicia, Spain, Apr. 5, 1966; s. Jesús Ángel Simal-Lozano and María del Carmen Gándara-López. Grad. First Class Mark, U. of Santiago de Compostela, Spain, 1989; D Apto cum laude, U. Santiago Compostela, Spain, 1991. Trainee, rschr.'s fellow Superior Coun. Sci. Rsch., 1988-89; rschr. U. of Santiago de Compostela, Santiago de Compostela, 1989-91; temporary assoc. prof. nutrition and food sci. U. Vigo, Ourense, Spain, 1991-93, assoc. prof., 1993-99, prof., 1999—; collaborator Gairesa Co., Lago-Valdoviño, Spain, 1988-91, Grafinsa Co., Vigo, Spain, 1994-97, Coren, Ourense, Spain, 1999—; participant in Spanish and internat. confs., 1989—; rsch. projects dir. on food-packaging interactions, European Union, Spanish Govt., Galician Govt., U. Vigo, 1992—; rsch. articles referee Am. Chem. Soc. Jour. Agrl. and Food Chemistry, Washington, 1993—, Internat. Assn. on Water Quality, U.K., 1995—, Jour. of AOAC Internat., Arlington, 1995—, Food Sci. and Tech. (Spanish), Ourense, 1996—, Vibrational Spectroscopy, 1997—, Food Additives and Contanimants, 2000—, Biomauemolecules, 2000—. Author: Infrared Spectrophotometry and Computing in the Quality Control of Food Preservatives, 1989, Contribution to the Quality Control of Epoxy Resins Intended to be Into Contact With Food Stuffs, 1992; editor: Spanish Social Anthropology Jour., 1993—; mem. editl. com. Food Sci. and Tech., 1996—; contbr. articles to nat. and internat. profl. jours. Recipient award for rsch. profl. tng. Pharmacy U. Paris-South, 1990, Chemistry U. Del., Newark, 1991, Comett II European Union award Fraunhofer Inst. Lebensmitteltechnologie und Verpackung, Munich, 1992, Ministry Agr., Fisheries and Food, Norwich, U.K., 1993, TNO-Nutrition and Food Rsch., Zeist, The Netherlands, 1994, U. of Vigo award TNO-Nutrition and Food Rsch., Zeist, 1995, Spanish Ministry of Edn. and Sci. award Pira Internat., Leatherhead, U.K., 1996, SIK-Swedish Inst. Food & Biotech., Goteborg, 1997, Ministry Agr., Fisheries, and Food, Norwich, U.K., 1998, Xunta de Galicia TNO-Nutrition and Food Rsch., Zeist, 2000, 1st prize at nat. level in Spain for pharmacists grads., 1990, Caixa Galicia-Claudio San Martín prize of the Royal Acad. Medicine, A Coruña, Spain, 1991, Eloy Díez prize, ofcl. Assn. Pharmacists, Pontevedra, Spain, 1992, 1st prize for pharmacists doctors U. Santiago de Compostela, 1992. Mem. European Assn. Food Law, Programme d'Échanges Avec Les Anciens Chercheurs, Stagiaires et Étudiants Étrangers (Paris), Spanish Nutrition Soc., Spanish Bromatology Soc., Spanish Food Scientists and Technologists Assn., Galician Nutrition and Dietetics Assn. Avocations: cycling, diving, reading, computer science, languages. Fax: 34-988-387001. E-mail: jsimal@uvigo.es. Home: Rua Paris-7B-2A, 15707 Santiago de Compostel, 15707 Galicia Spain Office: U Vigo Campus of Ourense, U Vigo Campus of Ourense, Faculty Sci, 32004 Ourense Galicia, Spain

SIMANAVIČIUS, LEONAS, chemist, researcher; b. Panevežys, Lithuania, June 28, 1929; s. Eduardas and Zofija (Paeglyte) S.; m. Elena Šinkūnaitė, June 27, 1954 (div. Mar., 1975); 1 child Jolanta; m. Aldona Levinskienė, Jan. 30, 1992. PhD, Leningrad (Russia) U., 1958; DSc (Habil. D.), Inst. of Chemistry, Vilnius, Lithuania, 1988. Lectr. Vilnius U., 1957-60, docent, 1960-65; sr. rsch. fellow Inst. Chemistry, Vilnius, 1965-75, dept. head, 1975-99, chief rsch. fellow, 1999-2000; dean of chemistry faculty, Vilnius U., 1961-64; asst. dir. Inst. Chemistry, Vilnius, 1990-92. Editor-in -chief Jour. Chemija, Vilnius, 1994—; contbr. numerous articles to profl. jours.; patentee several inventions. Mem. Internat. Soc. Electrochemistry, Am. Chem. Soc., Lithuanian Acad. Sci. (corr. mem.). Avocation: travel. Home: Rinktines 21-156, LT 2051 Vilnius Lithuania Office: Inst of Chemistry, A Gostauto Str 9, Lt-2600 Vilnius Lithuania

SIMANDIRI, SIM SIEHONGLIANG, manufacturing engineer, educator; b. Indonesia, Oct. 21, 1941; arrived in Singapore, 1985.; s. John and Elizabeth Sarina (Tan) S.; m. Regina Tanzil, July 14, 1964; children: Abraham Tiongham Sie, Fifi Gwatfie Simandiri. BE, Bandung Inst. Tech., Indonesia, 1964; M Engring. Sci., U. NSW, 1974, PhD, 1979. Head dept. Inst. Tchrs. Tng., Indonesia, 1969; teaching fellow U. NSW, 1974-79; rsch. engr. Ampol Ltd., Australia, 1980-84; PhD external examiner U. Allahabad, India, 1984-85; coord. adv. diploma course Ngee Ann Polytechnic, Singapore, 1987-93, CNC section head, 1989—; chmn. joint organizing com. Hong Kong Study Mission IE, SME, IIE, Hong Kong/Singapore, 1990, Internat. Conf. on Computer Integrated Mfg., Singapore, 1993, Internat. Symposium on Indsl. Robots, 1995, Internat. Conf. on Precision Engring., 1995, Tech. Opportunities and Mfg. Bus. Conf., 1995. Contbr. articles to sci. jours. Recipient Rsch. grants Austrlian Rsch. Grants Com., 1973, Paul Henderson Meml. award Instn. Mechanical Engrs., 1980. Fellow IBA; mem. ASME (chmn., chmn. elect, hon. sec. Singapore chpt. 1994-95, 1995-96, 1996-97), Australian Alumni Singapore, Singapore Indsl. Automation Assn., Soc. Mfrg. Engrs. (edn.-treas. 1986-93, sec., vice chmn., chmn. elct, chmn., Singapore del.), U. NSW Alumni Assn. (life). Home: 100 B Oxley Rise, Singapore 0923, Singapore Office: Ngee Ann Polytechnic, 535 Clementi Rd, Singapore 2159, Singapore

SIMANDL, MIROSLAV, electrical engineer, educator; b. Ledce, Czechoslovakia, Jan. 6, 1954; s. Josef and Milena (Reiprichova) S.; m. Miloslava Simbartlova, Aug. 20, 1977; two children. Grad. in engrin., Inst. Technology Pilsen, Czechoslovakia, 1978, MSc, 1984; CSc, U. West Bohemia, Pilsen. From rsch. worker to lectr. Inst. Technology Pilsen, 1979-93; assoc. prof. U. West Bohemia, 1993—; cons. in field. Office: U West Bohemia, Univerzitni 8, 306 14 Pilsen Czech Republic

SIMAO, LEONARDO, Mozambican government official; b. Manjacaze, Gaza, Mozambique, June 6, 1953; m. M. Fatima, 1977; 2 children. MS. Dist. med. officer, 1981-82; dir. tng. ctr. Village Health Workers, 1981-82; provincial dir.health, 1982-86, provincial med. officer, 1982-86, provincial hosp. dir., 1984-86, provincial assembly, 1986; head Dept. Cmty. Health, 1988; min. health Govt. of Mozambique, Maputo, 1988-94, min. fgn. affairs, 1994—. Office: Min Fgn Affairs and Cooperation, Avda Julius Nyerere 4, Maputo Mozambique

SIMBRUNER, GEORG, pediatrician, educator; b. Grieskirchen, Austria, Aug. 3, 1945; arrived in Germany, 1993; s. Georges Teteart and Elisabeth Simbruner; m. Annette Moira Jackson, Dec. 13, 1972; children: Anja, Gregory, Laurenz, Bernadette, Lilly, Carl. MD, U. Vienna, 1970. Asst. prof. U. Stellenbosch, South Africa, 1970-72, U. Vienna, Munich, Austria, 1972-83; assoc. prof. pediatrics U. Vienna, 1983-93; prof. pediatrics Ludwig-Maximilians- U., Munich, Germany, 1993—; head pediat. intensive care Vienna, 1989-93, head divsn. neonatology, Munich, 1993—; founder, chmn. Internat. Postgrad. Orgn. for Knowledgetransfer, Rsch. and Tchg. Excellent Students, Vienna, 1985-96; chmn. IPOKRaTES Internat., Munich, 1996—. Author: Thermodynamic Models, 1983, Neonatology, 1995, Twins; editor Intensive Care Medicine, 1993; contbr. articles to profl. jours.; patentee in field. Chmn. Cath. Acad. Soc., Vienna, 1986-92. Recipient Clemens V. Pirquet award Pediat. Soc., Austria, 1986, Humboldt/South Africa Rsch. award, 1999. Mem. European Soc. Pediat. Intensive Care, German-Austrian Soc. Neonatal and Pediat. Intensive Care, European Pediat. Rsch. Soc. Roman Catholic.

SIME, JAMES THOMSON, psychologist, consultant; b. Elgin, Moray, Scotland, Aug. 9, 1927; s. James Alexander and Jessie Ann (Scott) S.; divorced; children: James A., Julie-Ann; m. Jaya Rani Sinha, June 3, 1992. MA, U. Edinburgh, Scotland, 1954, diploma in edn., 1955; cert. in teaching, Moray House, Edinburgh, 1955; MEd, U. Glasgow, Scotland, 1957. Psychologist in charge various psychol. svcs., 1960-64, 67-80, pvt. practice as psychotherapist, 1960-84; cons. psychologist brain damage, pain, post-traumatic stress U.K., 1984—; lectr., 1964-67. Served with Royal Air Force, 1945-48. Fellow Brit. Psychol. Soc. (assoc.); mem. Internat. Auster Pilot Club (founder 1973, hon. v.p.). Avocations: flying, hill walking, travel, human behavior, languages. Home and Office: 44 Nicol Rd, Broxburn EH52 6JN, England Office: 8 Lindley St, Rotherham S65 1RT, England

ŠIMEČEK, CYRIL METHODEJ, physician, educator; b. Brno, Morava, Czech Republic, May 13, 1920; s. Cyril Š. and Marie (Korínková) Simecková; m. Blanka Hnátková, May 26, 1951; 1 child, Blanka. M in Pharmacology, Charles U., Prague, 1946, MD, 1950, DSc, 1983; MS, Palacky U., Olomuc, Czechoslovakia, 1963. Physician U. Hosp., Olomuc, Czechoslovakia, 1950-55; lectr., asst. prof. Palacky U., Olomuc, Czechoslovakia, 1956-67; dir. dept. pneumology U. Hosp., Plzeň, Czechoslovakia, 1967-85, researcher, 1986-92; cons. St. George Hosp., Plzeň, Czechoslovakia, 1993—; lectr. Inst. Postgrad. Edn., Bratislava and Prague, Czechoslovakia, Magdeburg, Germany, Novi Sad, Yugoslavia, 1962-82; v.p. Symposium Cancerology, Brussels, 1971. Author: (in Czech) Bronchology, 1978 (Czech Literary Grant Agy. award 1978), (in Czech) Diseases of the Mediastinum, 1981, (in Czech) Differential Diagnosis in Pneumology, 1984 (Czech Literary Grant Agy. award 1984), Cytological Examinations, 1963, (in English) Regional Pulmonary Function Testing, 1991; inventor apparatus for distribn. evaln. regional lung ventilation, among others. Decorated Chévalier d'Honneur Chevalerie du Fourquet, 1971, Medal Pro Merito Assn. Internat. Broncho-pneumologic, 1976. Mem. Czech Med. Assn. (hon.), Cz. Pneumoptisiologic Soc., Soc. Europeen Patho-physiol. Respiration, European Respiratory Soc. Avocations: violin, basketball, volleyball, physics. Home: V koutě 152, 330 08 Zruč Plzen Czech Republic Office: Nemocnice U Sv Jiri, Staniční 74, 312 17 Plzeň Czech Republic

SIMEK, RUDOLF, humanities educator; b. Eisenstadt, Austria, Feb. 21, 1954; arrived in Germany, 1995; s. Rudolf and Maria (Schattauer) S.; m. Angela Hall, July 10, 1982; children: Koloman, Benedict, Rosemarie. Dr.Phil., U. Vienna, Austria, 1980, Mag.theol., 1981, Dozent, 1990. Lectr. U. Edinburgh, Scotland, 1976-79; head libr. U. Vienna, 1980-95, lectr., 1982-90, dozent, 1990-95; lectr. U. Heiligenkreuz, Austria, 1988-95; prof. U. Bonn, Germany, 1995—. Author: Dictionary of Northern Mythology, 1984, 2d edit., 1995, Lexikon der altnordischen Literature, 1987, Altnordische Kosmographie, 1990, Erde und Kosmos im Mittelalter, 1992, Die Wikinger, 1998, 2d edit., 2000. Roman Catholic. Avocation: sailing. Office: U Bonn, Am Hof 1d, D53113 Bonn Germany

ŠIMEK, VLADIMÍR, animal physiologist, educator; b. Brno, Czech Republic, Sept. 6, 1937; s. Vladimír and Ludmila Šimek; m. Edith Revesz, July 1962; children: Edith, Eva. Grad., Masaryk U., Brno, 1964; postgrad., Inst. Clin. Exptl. Medicine, Prague, Czech Republic, 1967. Lab. asst. Inst. of Hygienic, Brno, 1956-59; asst. Masaryk U., 1963-67, asst. prof., 1967-90, assoc. prof., 1990-97, head dept. animal physiology, 1990—, prof. animal physiology, 1997—. Co-author: Animal and Human Physiology, 1995. Mem. Czech Med. Soc., Czech Lab. Animal Sci. Assn. Avocations: traveling, music. Home: Jiraskova #16, 602 00 Brno Czech Republic Office: Faculty of Sci Masaryk U, Kotlarska 2, 611 37 Brno Czech Republic

SIMELANE, MAWENI, Swazi government official. Min. justice and constitutional affairs Govt. of Swaziland, Mbabane. Office: Ministry of Justice, PO Box 924, Mbabane Swaziland*

ŠIMELYTE, EGLE, medical researcher, physician; b. Vilnius, Lithuania, Oct. 10, 1970; arrived in Finland, 1994; d. Ceslovas Šimelis and Regina Nijole (Utkaite) Šimeliene. MD, Vilnius U., 1994. Rsch. assoc. Dept. Med. Microbiology Turku (Finland) U., 1994—. Contbr. articles to profl. jours. Recipient prize for excellent rheumatology rsch. European League Against Rheumatism 19th European Workshop for Rheumatology Rsch., 1999. Mem. Finnish Microbiology Soc., Finnish Med. Soc. Duodecim, Finnish Immunology Soc., Scandinavian Soc. Immunology. Roman Catholic. Avocations: tennis, piano, cooking, reading, travelling. Fax: 358 2 233 0088. E-mail: eglesim@utu.fi.

SIME-NGANDO, TÉLESPHORE, biologist; b. Batchingou, Cameroon, Nov. 26, 1962; parents Dieudonné and Christine Sime; m. Valérie Battut; 1 child, Melanie. MS, U. Yaounde, 1987; PhD, U. Blaise Pascal, 1991. Rsch. asst. U. Quebec, Montreal, 1991-94; rschr. French Nat. Ctr. Scientific Rsch., Clermont-Ferrand, 1994—. Mem. Am. Soc. Limnology & Oceanography, Inc., French Assn. Limnology, Assn. French-Spoken Protistologists. Office: Upres A CNRS 6023, 24 Ave des Landais, 63177 Aubiere cedex France

SIMEÓN NEGRÍN, ROSA ELENA, veterinary educator; b. Havana, June 17, 1943; married; 1 child. M.D., U. Havana, 1973. Chief dept. virology Nat. Ctr. Sci. Rsch., 1970-75, mem. sci. commn., 1970-75, sci. coun., 1971-73, chief microbiol. divsn., 1974-76, pres. agrl. br., 1975-81; pres. sci. coun. Nat. Ctr. Agrl. Health, 1976-81, agrl. br., 1977-81, dir. 1985; mem. Assessor Coun., 1981-83, agrl. br., 1981-85; pres. Acad. Scis., Cuba, 1985—; min. sci., tech. and environment Govt. of Cuba, Havana, 1996—; prof., lectr., cons. in veterinary medicine including Nat. Ctr. Animal Health. Contbr. articles to profl. jours. on animal virology. Mem. Cen. Com. Partido Comunista de Cuba, 1980, mem. Polit. Bur., 1985; disputada to Asamblea Nacional del Poder Popular, 1985; foreign mem. Akademie der Landwirtschaft Wissenchaften, German Dem. Republic, 1986. Recipient Anniversary medal U. Havana, 1980; France medal U. D'Alfort, 1980; medal of merit, Czechoslovakia, 1981; medal Agrl. Syndicat of Czechoslovakia, 1983; Order of Marianna Grajales, 1985. Address: Acad Scis Cuba, Capitolio Nacional, 10200 Havana Cuba*

SIMES, STEPHEN MARK, pharmaceutical products executive; b. N.Y.C., Nov. 23, 1951; s. Herbert H. and Mimi (Maurer) S.; m. Anita H. Herzog, Aug. 23, 1975. BS in Chemistry, Bklyn. Coll., 1973; MBA in Mktg., NYU, 1980. Sales rep. G.D. Searle and Co., N.Y.C., 1974-78; supr. sales tng. G.D. Searle and Co., Chgo., 1978-79; dist. sales mgr. G.D. Searle and Co., N.Y.C., 1979-81; product mgr. G.D. Searle and Co., Chgo., 1981-82, sr. product mgr., 1982-83, dir. pub. affairs and communications, 1983-84; v.p. Gynex Inc., Chgo., 1984-88; dir. Gynex Pharms. Inc., Deerfield, 1985-93; pres., dir. Gynex Labs., Chgo., 1985-88; pres., CEO Contracap Inc., Ill., 1988-89; pres., CEO Gynex Pharms., Inc., Chgo., 1989-93, chmn., 1992-93; sr. v.p., dir. Bio-Technology Gen. Corp., 1993-94; pres., CEO, dir. Unimed Pharms., Inc., 1994-97; bd. dirs., CEO, pres. Simes Pharm. Cons., 1997-98; vice chmn., CEO, pres., BioSante Pharms., Inc., Lincolnshire, Ill., 1998—. Mem. Chgo. Coun. Fgn. Rels., Licensing Exec. Soc. Fax: 847-793-2435. Office: 175 Olde Half Day Rd Lincolnshire IL 60069-3061

SIMHANDL, CHRISTIAN ALOIS, physician; b. Vienna, Sept. 25, 1956; s. Alois and Margareta Philomena (Bauer) S.; m. Martina Souschill, July 28, 1979; children: Thomas, Lukas. Diploma in Medicine, U. Vienna, 1980; Specialization, U. Clinic, Vienna, 1986. Specialisation Univ. Clinic, Vienna, 1980-86, head of ward, 1989-92, head of outpatient dept. for prophylactic treatment, 1990-92, head of rsch. unit, 1990-92; lectr. psychiatry U. Clinic, Vienna, 1989—; sport medicine profl. Austrian Squash Racket Assn., 1986-90; head of CNS dept. Eli Lilly & Co., Vienna, 1992-93; head outpatient dept. U. Vienna, 1994—; chief psychiat. dept. Gen. Hosp., Neunkirchen, Austria; trainer Logotherapy and Existential Psychotherapy, Vienna, 1985—. Chief editor: Klassifikationsprobleme in der Psychiatrie, 1986; creator poster (1st prize Austrian Biol. Psychiat. Assn. 1989). Mem. Austrian Psychiat. Assn., Viennese Soc. for Psychiatry and Neurology (sec. 1995-99), Soc. for Depression and Anxiety Rsch. (pres. 1996—). Roman Catholic. Avocations: riding, squash, tennis, skiing. Home: Wiedner Guertel 12/4, A-1040 Vienna Austria

ŠIMIĆ, DIANA, statistics educator; b. Zagreb, Croatia, Oct. 4, 1958; d. Marko and Dragica (Nalbani) S.; 1 child, Mislav. B in Math. Engring., U. Zagreb, 1982, M in Math., 1994. Applications programmer Radio Industry

Zagreb, 1983-85; rsch. asst. Inst. Med. Rsch. and Occupational Health, Zagreb, 1985—; sec. Commn. on Med. Anthropology and Epidemiology Internat. Union of Anthrop. and Ethnol. Scis., Zagreb, 1989-90; head exec. bd. Inst. for Med. Rsch. and Occupl. Health, Zagreb, 1991-92, mem. exec. bd., 1992-93, head biomath. unit, 1995—; mem. Secretariat of the Exec. Com. of the 12th Internat. Congress of Anthropol. and Ethnol. Scis., Zagreb, Croatia, 1986-88, Organizing Com. of the 12th-15th Internat. Sch. Biol. Anthropology, Zagreb, 1986-89, Commn. on Med. Informatics of the Com. for Human Ecology of the Med. Acad. Croatia, Zagreb, 1988-89, Organizing Com. of the 28th Congress of the Yugoslav Anthropol. Assn., Zadar, Croatia, 1989; dir. Biostat 96 Sch. Biometrics, Pula, Croatia, 1996; mem. organizing com. 23d Internat. Conf. Info. Tech. Interfaces, Puea, Croatia. Author: Anthropological Investigations of the Eastern Adriatic-Book I: Biological and Cultural Microdifferentiation of Rural Populations of Korcula and Peljesac, 1987, Bioanthropological Investigations of the Derdap Region, 1988, Anthropological Practicum, 1989, others; editorial bd.: Collegium Antropologicum, Zagreb, 1986-92; editor: (book of abstracts) Abstracts of the 12th International Congress of Anthropological and Ethnological Sciences, 1988; contbr. articles to profl. jours. Mem. Croatian Math. Soc., Croatian Biometric Soc. (mem. ct. of honor 1989-91, sec. 1996-98, pres. 1998—), Am. Statis. Assn., Croatian Soc. Simulation Modelling. Office: Inst Med Rsch Occpl Health, Ksaverska cesta 2 PO Box 291, HR 10001 Zagreb Croatia

ŠIMIĆ, GORAN, neuroscientist, researcher; b. Zagreb, Croatia, May 8, 1967; s. Ivan and Milka (Vojnović) Š.; m. Durdica ŠeŠo, Oct. 17, 1992; children: Sunćica, Vedran. MD, Med. Sch. Zagreb, 1992, PhD, 1998. Asst. Med. Sch. Zagreb, 1993—. Recipient fellowships Austrian Govt., Vienna, 1992, Karolinska Inst., Stockholm, 1994, 96, 97. Mem. European Neeurosci. Assn. Home: Škorjančeva 18, 10000 Zagreb Croatia Office: Croatian Inst Brain Rsch, Šalata 11, 10000 Zagreb Croatia

SIMICEVIC, VELIMIR NICHOLAS, pharmaceutical executive, research scientist; b. N.Y.C., Oct. 12, 1968; s. Luka and Maria (Persic) S. MSc, Med. Sch. Zagreb (Croatia), 1995; postgrad., Faculty Natural Sci., 1998, MS in Biology, 2000. Rsch. inst. biomed. dept. Pliva Pharm. Co., Zagreb, 1995-98, clin. rsch. physician rsch. inst. med. dept., 1998-99, clin. rsch. physician pharm. ops-med. affairs, 1999—. Contbr. articles to profl. jours. Mem. Am. Acad. Pharm. Physicians, Croatian Pharmacol. Soc., Internat. Union Pharmacology, N.Y. Acad. Scis., Internat. Brain-Gut Soc., Assn. Clin. Rsch. for Pharm. Industry, Croatian Soc. Clin. Pharmacology and Therapeutics, Croatian Med. Assn. Roman Catholic. Office: Pliva Pharm Co Pharm Ops/Med Affairs, Ulica grada Vukovara 49, HR-10000 Zagreb Croatia

SIMINICEANU, ILIE, chemist, educator; b. Corni, Romania, June 12, 1946; s. Costache and Elena S.; m. Lizeta Medaru, Oct. 1, 1970; children: Laura-Elena, Radu-Ionel. M in Chem. Engring., Poly. Inst. Iasi, 1969, PhD, 1980. Asst. prof. Poly. Inst. Iasi, Romania, 1969-89; prof., head dept. Tech. U. Gh.Asachi, Iasi, 1990—; asst. prof. INES, Bougie, Algeria, 1983-84; vis. prof. U. Poitiers, France, 1998. Author: Technology of Mineral Fertilizers, 1984, Fundamentals of Chemical Reaction Engineering, 1987; contbr. articles to profl. jours. Mem. European Fedn. Chem. Engring., European Sci. & Environment Forum, Romanian Soc. Catalysis, Romanian Soc. Chem. Engring. Home: 4 St Lazar Bloc, Penes Curcanul Scara B, RO-6600 Iasi Romania

SIMION, OTILIA MARIA, chemical engineer, researcher; b. Craciunel, Alba, Romania, Aug. 14, 1955; d. Petru and Maria (Popa) Ciontea; m. Nicolae Simion, May 3, 1980; 1 child, Simion Oana. Diploma in Chem. Engring., T.Vuia-Polytech. Inst., Timisoara, Romania, 1979. Chem. engr. Azomures-Photosensitive Divsn., Tg Mures, Romania, 1979-82; chemist, prin. rschr. Azomures-Photosensitive Materials Divsn., Tg Mures, Romania, 1982—. Inventor Silver halide color photographic light sensitive material, 1989, 98; also presented papers at sci. confs. Mem. Royal Photographic Soc. Britain, N.Y. Acad. Scis., and IS & T. Mem. Eastern Orthodox Ch. Avocations: lecture, travel. Office: Azomures SA-Photo sensitive, Materials Divsn 9 Plopilor, 4300 Târgu Mures Mures, Romania

SIMIONESCU, CRISTOFOR, chemistry educator; b. Dumbrăveni, Suceava, Romania, July 17, 1920; s. Ioan and Lucretia (Sireteanu) S.; m. Natalia Voitenco, June 22, 1947; children: Bogdan, Tudor. MSc magna cum laude, Polytech. Inst., 1944, PhD in Chemistry, 1948; doctor honoris causa, Higher Chemico-Tech. Inst., Sofia, Bulgaria, 1987. Prof. organic macromolecular chem. Polytech. Inst. Jassy, Romania, 1951-95, prof. organic macromolecular chem. emeritus, 1995—; dir. P.Poni Inst. Macromolecular Chem., Jassy, Romania, 1970—. Editor-in-chief Cellulose Chemistry and Technology, 1967—, Memoirs of the Scientific Sections of the Romanian Academy, 1977—; author 23 books; contbr. over 700 articles to profl. jours.; patentee in field. Recipient Golden medal Am. Chem. Soc., 1976, diploma of honor Acad. of Cuba, diploma Slovak Superior Tech. Sch. Mem. Hungarian Acad. Scis., Acad. Sci. of Moldavia, Romanian Acad. (pres. Jassy br. 1963-74, 89—, v.p. 1974-89), Acad. of Men of Sci. of Romania (hon. pres.), Romanian Soc. of Chemists (hon. pres.), European Acad. of Scis. and Arts, Internat. Acad. Wood Sci. Avocation: canary birds breeding. Home: Palade str 11, 6600 Iasi Romania Office: Jassy Br Romanian Acad, Bd Copou 8, 6600 Iasi Romania

SIMIONESCU, RADU ION, anesthesiologist, consultant; b. Chilia, Romania, June 19, 1930; s. Ion Ioan And Natalia Victor (Banu) S.; m. Elena Ion Fenichiu, Feb. 7, 1942; children: Ioana Adriana, Ozana Maria. MD, Bucharest Faculty of Medicine, 1955, DSc, 1976. Epidemiologist Rosiori, Romania, 1955-58, family practice physician, 1958; anesthesiologist Suceava, Romania, 1959-63; specialist in anesthesiology Ploiesti, Romania, 1963-66; rschr. in anesthesiology Bucharest, 1966-76, cons. in anesthesiology, 1976—; chief dep. anesthesiology, intensive care Cancer Inst., Bucharest, 1966-76. Patentee in field; contbr. articles to profl. jours. Fellow Royal Coll. Anaesthetists U.K.; mem. Romanian Soc. Anesthesia Intensive Care (sec. 1973-96, senate mem. 1973—, jour. editor 1994—), Found. for Anesthesia Intensive Care (pres. 1995—), European Acad. Anesthesia, N.Y. Acad. Scis. Avocation: hunting. Home: Bul Iuliu Maniu 158 apt 70, 77538 Bucharest Romania Office: Munposan Hosp, Witing 12, 77121 Bucharest Romania

SIMIONESCU-BADEA, CLAUDIA LIDIA, mathematics educator; b. Cluj, Romania, Jan. 12, 1937; d. Ion and Ethel (Santa) Iacob; m. Dan Badea, Aug. 9, 1979; 1 child from previous marriage: Mihnea Alexandru Simionescu. BS in Math., U. Bucharest, Romania, 1958, PhD, 1973; Cert in English Lang., Princeton U., 1973; Irex fellow in System Sci., UCLA, 1973-74; Doktor der Naturwissenschaften, U. Vienna, 1987; Docent in Math., U. Salzburg, 1991. Tchr. high sch., Brasov, Romania, 1958-61; asst. dept. math. Pedagog Inst., Brasov, 1961-62, lectr. dept. math., 1962-75, assoc. prof., 1975-82, prof., 1982—; rschr. Siemens AG, Osterreich, Vienna, 1985; mem. Faculty Council, Math., U. Brasov, 1963—, Univ. Senate, 1970-79, 84—, sci. sec. Faculty of Math., 1985—, head dept. analysis, 1976-85; vis. prof. U. Salzburg, Austria, 1987. Author books in math.; contbr. chpts. to books, articles to profl. jours.; patentee in field; editor seminar and conf. procs. Pres., Red Cross Commn. for U. Brasov, 1945-85. Recipient Medalia Muncii, U. Brasov, 1968. Mem. Romanian Math. Soc. (bd. editors 1977—), Austrian Soc. Cybernetic Studies, Am. Math. Soc., Soc. Indsl. and Applied Math. Avocations: music, violin, history. Home: Quellenplatz 6/3/1/1, A-1100 Vienna Austria

SIMIS, ARON, mathematician, researcher; b. Recife, Brazil, June 20, 1942; s. José and Betty (Schver) S.; m. Raquel Mancovetzky, Feb. 19, 1967 (div. Feb. 1975); children: Shelley, Gabriela, Isabela I., Mariana M. BSC, U. Fed. de Pernambuco, Recife, 1964; MSC, Queen's U., Kingston, Ont., Can., 1969; PhD, Queen's U., 1972; postgrad., Brandeis U., 1973. Prof. Inst. Mat. Pura e Aplicada, Rio de Janeiro, 1972-81, U. Fed. de Pernambuco, Recife, 1982-88; rschr. Conselho Nacional de Pesquisas, Brazil, 1982—; prof. U. Fed. da Bahia, Salvador, Brazil, 1989-97, U. Fed. Pernambuco, Recife, Brazil, 1997—; mem. consulting com. Conselho Nacional de Pesquisas, Brasilia, Brazil, 1985-87, 94-96, 98-2000; head grad. sch. math. U. Fed. de Pernambuco, 1982-84, 98—, U. Fed. da Bahia, Salvador, 1989-93; mem. com. Commn. Devel. and Exch. (Internat. Math. Union), Switzerland, 1986-90, Candidate Selection 3d-World Acad. Scis.,1997— ; spkr. in field. Author: Queen's Papers in Pure and Applied Mathematics, 1969; editor: Commutative Algebra Procs., 1994; contbr. articles to profl. jours. Educator Hashomer Hatzair, Recife, 1958-60; actor student theater orgn., Recife, 1961-62; activitist Brazilian Soc. for Progress of Sci., 1985-87. Fellow J.S. Guggenheim Found., 1976; grantee Japan Soc. for Promotion of Sci., 1990, Max-Planck Inst. Math., 1991. Fellow Brazilian Acad. Scis., 3d World Acad. Scis.; mem. Brazilian Math. Soc. (pres. 1985-87), Am. Math Soc., N.Y. Acad. Scis., Brazilian Excellence Group in Commutative Algebra and Algebraic Geometry (founding mem.). Avocations: writing, painting. Office: Fed U Pernambuco Dept Math CCEN, Av Prof Luis Freire S/M, 50740540 Recife PE Brazil

SIMITIS, CONSTANTINE, prime minister of Greece; b. Athens, Greece, June 23, 1936; s. George and Fani (Christopoulos) S.; m. Daphne Arkadiou; children: Fiona, Marilena. PhD in Law and Econs., U. Marburg, Germany, 1959; grad., London Sch. Econs., 1963. Atty., 1961—; reader U. Konstanz, Germany, 1971; prof. comml. law and civil law Justus Liebig U., Giessen, Germany, 1971-75; prof. comml. law Pantios U. of Polit. Scis., 1977—; min. agr. Govt. of Greece, Athens, 1981-85, min. nat. economy, 1985-87, M.P. for Piraeus dist., 1985—, min. edn., 1989-90, min. industry, energy, tech. and commerce, 1993-95, prime min., 1996—. Author: The Patent Right, 1967, The Fictitious Pledge, 1967, Good Morals and Public Order, 1959, The Protection of the Consumer, 1976, The Structural Opposition, 1979, Politics, Government, Law, 1981, Development and Modernization of the Greek Society, 1988, Policy for Economic Stabilization, 1989, Populism and Politics, 1989, Proposal for a Change in Politics, 1992, Nationalistic Populism or National Strategy?, 1992, Let's Try Together, 1994; contbr. articles to profl. jours. Co-founder Alexandros Papanastasiou Soc., 1965; mem. Nat. Coun. Panhellenic Liberation Movement, 1970; founding mem. Panhellenic Socialist Movement, 1974, mem. ctrl. com., mem. exec. com., 1974—. Office: Office of Prime Min, Megaro Maximou, 106 74 Athens Greece*

SIMITSES, GEORGE JOHN, retired engineering educator, consultant; b. Athens, Greece, July 31, 1932; came to U.S., 1951, naturalized, 1963; s. John G. and Vasilike (Goutoufas) S.; m. Nena Athena Economy, Sept. 11, 1960; children: John G., William G., Alexandra G. BS in Aerospace Engring., Ga. Tech. Inst., 1955, MS in Aerospace Engring., 1956; PhD in Aeronautics and Astronautics, Stanford U., 1965. From instr. to prof. engring. Ga. Tech. Inst., Atlanta, 1956-89; prof., head dept. aerospace engring., interim dean engring. U. Cin., 1989-2000, retired, 2000; cons. Lockheed-Georgia Co., Marietta, Ga., 1965-70, King & Gavaris Engrs., N.Y.C., 1977-79, Ga. Power Co., Atlanta, 1971-72. Author: Stability of Elastic Structures, 1976, Dynamic Stability of Suddenly Loaded Structures, 1989; contbr. chpts. to books, articles to profl. jours. Cmty. rep. Am. Hellenic Inst., Washington, 1976-91; del. Ga. State Dem. Conf., Macon, 1969. Fellow AIAA (various coms. 1974—), ASME (coms. 1976—), Am. Acad. Mechs.; mem. Hellenic Soc. Theoretical and Applied Mechs. (founding hon. mem.), AHEPA (v.p. chpt. 1978-79, coms. 1975-90), Sigma Xi (Sustained Rsch. award 1980, Best Paper award 1985). Office: Ga Inst Technology Aerospace Engring Atlanta GA 30332-0001

SIMKIN, BENJAMIN, retired endocrinologist; b. Phila., Apr. 17, 1921; s. Aaron and Rebecca (Schor) S.; m. Muriel Shapiro, June 1, 1947; children: Barbara Ellen, Jonathan Asher. AB magna cum laude, U. So. Calif., 1941, MD, 1944. Intern L.A. County Gen. Hosp., 1943-44; resident Cedars of Lebanon Hosp., L.A., 1944-46, beaumont rsch. fellow, 1946-47; fellow in metabolism and endocrinology Michael Reese Hosp., Chgo., 1947-48; rsch. fellow in diabetes The May Inst. The Jewish Hosp., Cin., 1948-49; asst. clin. prof. medicine U. So. Calif. Sch. Medicine, L.A., 1949-71; attending physician in medicine and endocrinology Cedars-Sinai Med. Ctr., L.A., 1950-2000, clin. chief endocrinology, 1960-73. Contbr. over 60 articles to profl. jours., over 45 articles to music publs. Concertmaster L.A. Doctors' Symphony Orch., 1960-81. Fellow Am. Coll. Endocrinology, Performing Arts Med. Assn.; mem. AAAS, AMA, Am. Assn. Clin. Endocrinologists, Endocrine Soc., Am. Coll. Nuclear Medicine (charter mem.), Am. Fedn. Clin. Rsch., Am. Assn. History of Medicine, Phi Beta Kappa (hon.), Sigma Xi (hon.), Phi Mu Alpha (hon.), Phi Kappa Phi (hon.). Avocations: amateur violinist, essays on Mozart's personality and music. Home: 701 Amalfi Dr Pacific Palisades CA 90272-4509

SIMKIN, SANDRA JOAN, women's medical rights advocate, public relations; b. London; d. Francis Morris and Irene Lucy (Drake) Hodson; m. Royston Albert Simkin, Dec., 1973. Librarianship diploma, West London Coll., 1971; student, Open U., 1979-81. Libr. Nat. Coal Bd., London, 1974-78; info. officer pub. affairs Shell U.K. Ltd., London, 1978-84; info. officer corp. affairs Brit. Gas, London, 1984-93; cons. Sandra Simkin Pub. Rels., 1993-95; dir. Campaign Against Hysterectomy and Unnecessary Ops. on Women, Woking, Surrey, 1995. Author: The Case Against Hysterectomy Year: 1996. Councillor Woking Borough Coun., 1996-2000, Cmty. Health Coun., North West Surrey, 1996—. Mem. Inst. Pub. Rels. Independent. Avocations: keeping fit, reading, music, cooking. Home and Office: The Maltings, 99 Saunders Ln Mayford, Woking Surrey GU22 ONT, England Office: PO Box 300, Woking Surrey GU22 0NT, England

SIMKISS, KENNETH, biologist, advisor; b. Blackpool, Lancashire, Eng., July 4, 1934; s. Clifford and Edith (Howe) S.; m. Nancy Carolyn McGilvray, Mar. 25, 1961; children: Douglas Eric, Gillian Varina, Gregory Daryl. BS, London U., 1955; PhD, U. Reading, Eng., 1958; DSc, U. London, 1975. Lectr. London U., 1958-65; rsch. fellow Duke U., Durham, N.C., 1962-63; reader U. Reading, 1965-68; prof. London U., 1968-72, Reading U., 1972—; mem. acad. adv. coun. U. Buckingham, Eng., 1988-91; mem. Radioactive Waste Mgmt. Adv. Coun., 1994-99; mem. Soc. Exptl. Biology Coun., 1975-77, Marine Biol. Assn. Coun., 1979-91, Freshwater Biol. Assn. Coun., 1980-84. Author: Bird Flight, 1964, Calcium in Reproductive Biology, 1967; co-author: (with K.M. Wilbur) Biomineralization, 1989. Commonwealth Prestige fellow, New Zealand, 1986. Fellow Inst. Biology. Avocations: music, art. Office: U Reading Sch, Animal and Microbial Sci, Reading RG6 6AJ, England

SIMKO, ROBERT, hematologist, consultant; b. Abaujszanto, Hungary, Aug. 10, 1963; s. Jozsef and Jozsefne Eva (Orosz) S.; m. Csilla Simkone Kesmarki, July 13, 1991; children: Peter, George. MD, Med. Sch., Debrecen, Hungary, 1987; specialty degree in pediat., Imre Haynal Med. Sch., Miskolc, Hungary, 1991; specialty degree in hematology, Imre Haynal Med. Sch., Budapest, Hungary, 1995. Resident in pediat. Imre Haynal Med. Sch., Miskolc, 1987-91, pediatrician, 1991-95, hematol. cons., 1995—. Author: Practical Pediatrics, 1995, Yearbook of Pediatric Radiology, 1995, 96; contbr. articles to profl. jours. Chmn. Achondroplastic Assn., Hungary, 1996—. State scholar French Cmty. of Belgium, Brussels, 1994, scholar Soros Found., 1996. Mem. Hungarian Hemophilia Assn., N.Y. Acad. Sci. (Mary Frank prize 2000). Home: Kapos 14, 3527 Miskolc Hungary Office: Imre Haynal Med Sch, Szentpeteri kapu 72, 3501 Miskolc Hungary

SIMMERMACHER, ROGER KARL, surgeon, educator; b. Heidelberg, Germany, Nov. 13, 1957; arrived in The Netherlands, 1976; s. Volker Horst and Ilse (Broer) S.; m. Ginel van Weering, Dec. 31, 1994; children: Philip, Floris, Isabel. Resident U. Hosp., Groningen, Holland, 1988-91, Sophia Hosp., Zwolle, Holland, 1991-94; trauma fellow U. Hosp., Munich, 1994, Groote Schuur, Capetown, South Africa, 1994; cons. Elisabeth Hosp., Haarlem, Holland, 1994-95; cons., surgeon U. Hosp., Utrecht, Holland, 1995—; lectr. anatomy H.S., Amsterdam, Holland, 1982-88, lectr. kinesiology, 1982-88; dir. anatomy U. Amsterdam, 1980-87; lectr. surgery U. Utrecht, 1996—. Author: Biomaterial Repair of Adbominal Wall Defects, 1994; contbr. articles to profl. jours. Mem. Am. Hernia Soc., European Hernia Soc. Office: U Hosp Utrecht, Postbox 85500, NL35089A Utrecht The Netherlands

SIMMONDS, KENNETH, management educator; b. Christchurch, New Zealand, Feb. 17, 1935; s. Herbert Marshall and Margaret (Trevurza) S.; m. Nancy Miriam Bunai, June 19, 1960; children: John, Jane, Peter. BCom, U. New Zealand, 1956, MCom with 1st class hons., 1960; DBA, Harvard U., 1963; PhD, London Sch. Econs., 1965; MGCE (hon.), U. de Deusto, Spain, 1974. Clk. Guardian Trust Co., Wellington, New Zealand, 1950-53; asst. co. sec. Gordon & Gotch, Ltd., Wellington, 1953-55; chief acct. William Cable Ltd., Wellington, 1955-59; cons. Arthur D. Little, Inc., Cambridge, Mass., 1959-60; cons. Harbridge House, Inc., Boston, 1962-64; asst. prof. internat. bus. Ind. U., Bloomington, 1964-66; prof. mktg. U. Manchester, Eng., 1966-69; Ford Found. prof. internat. bus. U. Chgo., 1974-75; prof. mktg. and internat. bus. London Bus. Sch., 1969—; mktg. advisor Internat. Pub. Corp., 1967-78; dir. Brit. Steel Corp., 1970-72, Redpath Dorman Long Ltd., 1972-74, EMAP Plc., 1981-96; chmn. Planners Collaborative, 1985-88; dir. MIL Rsch. Group Plc., 1986-89, Aerostructures Hamble, 1991-92, Enviros Ltd., 1996-99, M&M Ltd., 1996-97, Diagnology, Ltd., 1997-00, Manor House Grp., Ltd., 1997—, gov. London Bus. Sch., 1980-86; chmn. London Bus. Group, 1988-91; Drapers Co. lectr., 1975. Editor-in-chief Internat. Jour. Advt., 1982-96; John Schram lectr. U. Mo., 1996; author: International Business and Multinational Enterprises, 1973, 4th edit. 1989; Case Problems in Marketing, 1973; Strategy and Marketing, 1982, 2d edit., 1986; Short Cases in Marketing, 1987. Fulbright scholar, 1959; Smith Mundt scholar, 1959; U. New Zealand traveling scholar, 1960; Ford Found. fellow, 1961, Inter-U. Coun. fellow, 1978; Social Sci. Rsch. fellow, 1980; Croucher Found. fellow, 1983. Fellow Inst. Chartered Accts. New Zealand, Inst. Chartered Secs. and Adminstrs., Chartered Inst. Mgmt. Accts., Chartered Inst. Mktg., Acad. Internat. Bus.; mem. The Textile Coun. U.K., 1968-70; com. mem. Social Sci. Rsch. Coun. U.K., 1971-72; com. mem. Confedn. Brit. Industry, 1971-74; mem. Elec. Engring. Econ. Devel. Com. U.K., 1982-86, Chartered Inst. Mktg. Senate, 1994—, vice-dean, 1995—. Office: London Bus Sch, Sussex Pl Regents Park, London NW1 4SA, England

SIMMONDS, RAE NICHOLS, musician, composer, educator; b. Lynn, Mass., Feb. 25, 1919; d. Raymond Edward and Abbie Iola (Spinney) Nichols; m. Carter Fillebrown, Jr., June 27, 1941 (div. May 15, 1971); children: Douglas C. (dec.), Richard A., Mary L., Donald E.; m. Ronald John Simmonds, Oct. 9, 1971 (dec. Nov. 1995). AA, Westbrook Coll., Portland, Maine, 1981; B in Music Performance summa cum laude, U. Maine, 1984; MS in Edn., U. So. Maine, 1989; PhD, Walden U., 1994. Founder, dir. Studio of Music/Children's Studio of Drama, Portsmouth, N.H., 1964-71, Studio of Music, Bromley, Eng., 1971-73, Bromley Children's Theatre, 1971-73, Oughterard Children's Theatre, County Galway, Ireland, 1973-74; founder, dir. Studio of Music, Portland, Maine, 1977-96, West Baldwin, Maine, 1997—; resident playwright Children's Theatre of Maine, Portland, 1979-81; organist, choir dir. Stevens Ave. Congl. Ch., Portland, 1987-95; field faculty advisor Norwich U., Montpelier, Vt., 1995; field advisor grad. program Vt. Coll., Norwich U., 1995; cons./educator mus. tng. for disabled vets. VA, Portsmouth, N.H., 1966-69; show pianist and organist, mainland U.S.A., 1939-59, Hawaii, 1959-62, Rae Nichols Trio, 1962—; mus. dir. Theatre By the Sea, Portsmouth, N.H., 1969-70. Author/composer children's musical: Shamrock Road, 1980 (Blue Stocking award 1980), Glooscap, 1980; author/composer original scripts and music: Cinderella, If I Were a Princess, Beauty and the Beast, Baba Yaga - A Russian Folk Tale, The Journey - Musical Bible Story, The Perfect Gift - A Christmas Legend; original stories set to music include: Heidi, A Little Princess, Tom Sawyer, Jungle Book, Treasure Island; compositions include: London Jazz Suite, Bitter Suite, Jazz Suite for Trio, Sea Dream, Easter (chorale), Rae Simmonds Jazz Trio Songbook Series, (CD) Fascinatin' Gershwin Rae Simmonds Jazz Trio, 2000; contbr. Maine Women Writers Collection. Recipient Am. Theatre Wing Svc. award, 1944, Pease AFB Svc. Club award, 1967, Bumpus award Westbrook Coll., 1980; Nat. Endowment for Arts grantee, 1969-70; Women's Lit. scholar, 1980, Westbrook scholar, 1980-81, Nason scholar, 1983; Kelaniya U. (Colombo, Sri Lanka) rsch. fellow, 1985-86. Mem. ASCAP, Internat. Soc. Poets, Internat. League Women Composers, Music Tchrs. of Maine, Am. Guild of Organists, Music Tchrs. Nat. Assn., Internat. Alliance for Women in Music, Doctorate Assn. N.Y. Educators, Inc., Delta Omicron, Phi Kappa Phi. Democrat. Episcopalian. Avocations: travel, philately. Home: RR 1 Box 950 West Baldwin ME 04091-9715

SIMMONDS, ROBERT MAURER, engineering educator; b. Beaver Falls, Pa., Apr. 16, 1947; s. Harold Maurer and Mary Simmonds; m. Deborah Lynne Carawan, June 25, 1977; children: Stephen Maurer, Kent Hayes. BS, Youngstown State U., 1972, MS, 1975; advanced cert. edn., Coll. William and Mary, 1983, EdD, 1985. Regional planner Southeastern Va. Planning Dist. Commn., Norfolk, 1977-78; statis. rsch. analyst Nat. Ctr. for State Cts., Williamsburg, Va., 1978-82; assoc. prof. St. Leo Coll., Ft. Eustis, Va., 1982-85; ops. rsch. analyst U.S. Army Transp. Sch., Ft. Eustis, 1985-88; assoc. prof. rsch. ops. sys. engring. dept. U.S. Army Logistics Mgmt. Coll., Ft. Lee, Va., 1988—; cons. Dep. Chief of Staff for Tng., Ft. Monroe, Va., 1992, Picatinny Arsenal, N.J., 1994-96, Concepts and Analysis Agy., Washington, 1999—. Contbr. articles to profl. jours. Mem. bus. adv. coun. Chesterfield (Va.) Tech. Ctr., 1999—; faculty advisor U.S. First Regional Robotics Competition, Chesterfield, 1999—. With USN, 1965-68. Recipient Dubach Scholarship award Sigma Phi Epsilon, Youngstown State U., 1972. Mem. IEEE, Mil. Ops. Rsch. Soc. (Coin for Excellence 1998). Avocations: walking, golf. E-mail: simmondr@lee.army.mil. Office: US Army Logistics Mgmt Coll 2401 Quarters Rd Fort Lee VA 23801-1705

SIMMONS, BRIAN EDWIN, computer operator; b. Akron, Ohio, Feb. 17, 1962; s. Charles Edwin and Dorothy Lee Simmons. Cert. electronic tech., Nat. Inst. Tech., 1988. Computer operator Allstate Ins., Hudson, Ohio, 1988-98, Nat. City Bank, Cleve., 1999—; co-founder, dir., chmn., sec., devel. com. chair Akron Area Pride Collective, 1997-99; artist rep. Unhinged, Almost Human & Co., Akron, 1999-2000. Author of poems. Summer Missionary Intern Tng. for Evangelism, Haiti, 1979, Mexico, 1981; co-chair Equality Begins At Home, Akron, 1998-99. Named Vol. of Yr., Cmty. AIDS Network, Akron, 1997. Mem. Stonewall Akron. Avocations: music, poetry, travel. E-mail: orange@rainbow-akron.com and unhinged@akrobiz.com.

SIMMONS, CARL KENNETH, cooperative executive; b. Kingman, Ind., Dec. 5, 1914; s. Claud Elmer and Sylvia Ethyl (Myers) S.; grad. exec. devel. program Ind. U., 1959; m. Allice Lucille Weaver, Dec. 16, 1939; 1 child, Erma Jane (Mrs. Thomas Stephen Barlow). Petroleum dept. mgr. Fountain County Coop., Veedersburg, Ind., 1936-40; dist. mgr. Ind. Farm Bur. Coop., Indpls., 1946-47; treas., mgr. Delaware County Coop., Muncie, 1940-46, 48-86; emeritus gen. mgr., treas. 1986—. Mem. Mayor's Citizens Com. Muncie, 1962; bd. dirs. Delaware County Airport Authority, 1972-84, pres., 1983-84, CEO, 1984—. Mem. Ind. Flying Farmers, Masons (32 degree), Muncie Rifle Club. Home: 225 E Centennial Ave Muncie IN 47303-2903 Office: 1100 W Carl Simmons Dr Muncie IN 47303

SIMMONS, DAVID, government official; b. Apr. 28, 1940; married; 2 children. LLM, London Sch. Econ.; degree, Lincoln's Inn. Lawyer pvt. practice, 1969-94; senator, 1981-85; MP Govt. Barbados, St. Michael, 1976-81, 85—, senator, 1981-85, atty. gen., 1985-86, atty. gen. min. home affairs, pub. safety, postal svcs., 1994—. Office: Office of Atty Gen, Frank Walcott Bldg Culloden Rd, Saint Michael Barbados*

SIMMONS, GEOFFREY STUART, physician; b. Camp Gordon, Ga., July 28, 1943; s. Ted R. and Jane A. (Lavander) S.; m. Sherry Simmons, Sept. 7, 1985; children: Bradley, Anais. BS, U. Ill., 1965, MD, 1969. Intern U. So. Calif., L.A., 1969-70, resident, 1971-74; pvt. practice Astoria, Oreg., 1974-77, Eugene, Oreg., 1977—; chmn. internal medicine dept. Peace Health Med. Group, 1996-98, 2000—; bd. dirs. Lane County Med. Soc.; med. correspondent KUGN Radio, 1993-95. Author: The Z Papers, 1977, The Adam Experiment, 1978, Pandemic, 1980, Murdock, 1982, The Glue Factory, 1995, To Glue Or Not To Glue, 1997; med. commentator KABC Radio, 1970. Avocation: writing.

SIMMONS, JANET BRYANT, writer, publisher; b. Oakland, Calif., Apr. 22, 1925; d. Howard Pelton and Janet Horn (McNab) Bryant; m. William Ellis Simmons, May 17, 1944 (div. 1979); children: William Howard, Janet Margaret Simmons McAlpine. BA, San Jose State U., 1965, MA, U. San Francisco, 1979. Social worker Santa Clara County Social Svcs., San Jose, Calif., 1965-91; editor, pub. Enlightenment Press, Santa Clara, 1994—. Author: The Mystical Child, 1996. Mem. AAUW, Am. Booksellers Assn., Pubs. Mktg. Assn., Bay Area Ind. Pubs. Assn., Audubon Soc., Jacques Cousteau Soc. Avocations: playing piano, swimming, Tai Chi, travel, gardening. Office: Enlightenment Press PO Box 3314 Santa Clara CA 95055-3314

SIMMONS, JOHN DEREK, financial consultant; b. Essex, Eng., July 17, 1931; came to U.S., 1952; s. Simon Leonard and Eve (Smart) S.; m. Rosalind Wellish, Mar. 5, 1961; children: Peter Lawrence, Sharon Leslie. BS, Columbia U., 1956; MBA, Rutgers U., 1959; postgrad., NYU, 1959-62.

Chief cost acct. Airborne Accessories, Hillside, N.J., 1952-57; sr. cost analyst Curtiss-Wright Corp., Wood Ridge, N.J., 1957; sr. fin. analyst internat. group Ford Motor Co., Jersey City, 1958-60; rsch. assoc. Nat. Assn. Accts., N.Y.C., 1960-64; asst. to v.p. fin. Air Reduction Co., Inc., 1965-67; mgr. corp. planning Anaconda Wire & Cable Co., N.Y.C., 1968; ind. fin. cons., 1968-71; assoc. cons. Rogers, Slade & Hill, Inc., N.Y.C., 1969-71; v.p., security analyst, economist Moore & Schley, Cameron & Co. (now Fourteen Rsch. Corp.), 1972-81; v.p., security analyst, corp. fin. specialist Smith Barney, Harris Upham & Co., Inc., N.Y.C., 1989-90; sr. cons. Carl Byoir & Assocs., N.Y.C., 1991-94; assoc. mng. dir. Commonwealth Assocs., N.Y.C., 1994-95; mng. dir. State St. Capital Markets Corp., N.Y.C., 1996; v.p. GKN Securities Corp., N.Y.C., 1996-97; dir. instnl. sales Gabelli & Co., Rye, N.Y., 1997; assoc. Manning, Selvage & Lee, N.Y.C., 1998—; lectr. profl. socs. and confs.; lectr. econs., mgmt., polit. sci. Rutgers U., 1957-64. Contbr. articles on econs. of underdeveloped nations, polit. sic., mgmt., fin. to U.S. and fgn. publs. Served to 1st lt. Brit. Army, 1950-52. Granted personal coat of Arms by Queen Elizabeth II: manorial Lord of Ash., Suffolk, Eng. Mem. N.Y. Soc. Security Analysts, Knight Templar Sovereign Mil. Order Temple of Jerusalem. Home: 360 E 72d St New York NY 10021-4753 Office: Manning Selvage & Lee 79 Madison Ave Fl 3 New York NY 10016-7802

SIMMONS, JOHN FRANKLIN, writer; b. Detroit, Oct. 5, 1945; s. John Edward Simmons and Valeria Octavia (Spiller) Gibson; M. Debra Maxine Powell, Oct., 1962 (div. Jan. 1964); 1 child, Tracey Aileen; m. Laura Alice Jones, Jan. 8, 1965 (div. Oct. 1979); children: John Marque, Carla Valeria; m. Lynda Marie Watkins, Dec. 2, 1979 (div. Sept. 1991); children: Lisa Marie, Joshua Franklin. Student, U. Detroit, 1968-70, U. Hawaii, 1971. Child care worker Wayne County Child Devel. Ctr., Plymouth, Mich., 1967-68, Detroit Psychiat. Inst., 1968-70. Author numerous poems including Journey, 1982, Love of My Life, 1983, Note to a Graceful Lady, 1987, Titles and Atributes of God, 1988, Lotion, 1990, Older Lady, 1990, Greatest General, 1990, Abraham Lincoln, 1990, Love of My Youth, 1990, Worm, 1990. Active Rep. Presdl. Commn. Task Force, 1986, Nat. Rep. Senatorial Inner Circle Inaguration, Washington, 1989, Presdl. Round Table, Washington, 1989; co-founder Battle Normandy Mus., Caen, France, Am. Air Force Mus., Duxford, Eng., Nat. Law Enforcement Meml. Bldg., Washington, Police Hall of Fame, Miami, Fla., U.S. Naval Meml. Bldg., Washington. With U.S. Army, 1964-67. Mem. U.S. Naval Inst., Am. Assn. Advancement Sci., Am. Fedn. of Police, N.Y. Acad. Scis., Internat. Assn. Chiefs of Police (life), Internat. Platform Assn., Order of Michael the Archangel (knight chevalier 1989), Venerable Order of St. Francis of Assisi (Humanitarian award 1989). Mem. Jewish Christian Ch. Avocations: books, music, collecting art, nature, travel. Home: 19131 Lahser Rd Apt 202 Detroit MI 48219-1804

SIMMONS, LAWRENCE WILLIAM, healthcare company executive; b. Omaha, May 7, 1947; s. Albin Pachola and Leella Clarice (Franklin) S.; m. Leanna Carol McGee, Nov. 3, 1968; children: Scott, Anthony. Assoc. Gen. Studies, U. Nebr., 1977, B Gen. Studies, 1978. Pharm. sales rep. 3M Pharms., Omaha, 1972-83; dist. sales mgr. 3M Pharms., Chgo., 1983-89; regional sales mgr. midwest region 3M Pharms., St. Paul, 1989-92; group bus. mgr. pharm. and personal care 3M Pharms., Mexico City, 1992-95; group bus. dir. divsn. V health care 3M Mex., 1995-98; nat. mgr. managed care 3M Pharm., St. Paul, 1998—; cluster mem. Xavier U., New Orleans, 1987—; minority outreach rep. 3M, St. Paul, 1987—. With U.S. Army, 1968-71, Vietnam. Mem. Kappa Alpha Psi (polemarch 1981-83, best chpt. award 1983). Office: 3M Center W-01 Bldg 275-3 Saint Paul MN 55144-0001

SIMMONS, MARSHA THRIFT, science and reading educator, musician; b. Brunswick, Ga., Jan. 18, 1953; d. James Russell II and Ouida (Tyre) Thrift; m. Samuel Leland Simmons, Aug. 2, 1975; 1 child, Natalie Renee. BA, Agnes Scott Coll., 1975; MEd, Coll. of Charleston, 1980; postgrad., Regent U., 1998—. Cert. tchr., Tenn., postgrad. profl. lic., Va. Organist Epworth United Meth. Ch., Atlanta, 1975-76; tchr. 3d grade Hanahan (S.C.) Acad., 1976-77; grad. asst. Coll. of Charleston, S.C., 1977-78, sub. tchr. Early Childhood Devel. Ctr., 1978-79; owner, tchr. Marsha's Music (Studio and Store), S.C., Ga., Tex., Tenn., Va., 1979—; tchr. presch. Sykes Daycare, Lawrenceville, Ga., 1994; sub. tchr. Glynn County Schs., Brunswick, Ga., 1994; tchr. 6th grade sci. and reading Jackson (Tenn.)-Madison County Schs., 1995-97; sub. tchr. Virginia Beach (Va.) City Pub. Schs., 1997—; treas. Kingwood (Tex.) Music Tchrs. Assn., 1985-87; mem. local sch. adv. com. Gwinnett County Bd. Edn., Lawrenceville, Ga., 1993-94; Odyssey of the Mind coord., coach N.E. Mid. Sch., Jackson, 1995-97; lead tchr. sci. stds. implementation Jackson-Madison County Schs., 1996-97. Leader Girl Scouts Am., St. Simons Island, Ga., 1988-89; PTA v.p. and cultural arts chmn. Benefield Elem. Sch., Lawrenceville, 1991-93; chmn. cmty. outreach West Tenn. Music Tchr.'s Assn., Jackson, 1996-97. Recipient Spl. Svc. award Girl Scouts Am., 1989, Outstanding Woman in Bus. and Edn. award Parker Chapel Christian Meth. Episcopal Ch., Tenn., 1996, Lockheed Martin fellow Lockheed Martin Corp., 1997. Mem. ACA, Am. Guild Organists, Music Tchrs. Nat. Assn., Am. Assn. of Christian Counselors. Avocations: reading, cooking, sewing, crafts, drawing, painting. Home: 313 Chase Arbor Ct Virginia Beach VA 23462-7407

SIMMONS, PETER LAWRENCE, lawyer; b. N.Y.C., May 1, 1965; s. John Derek and Rosalind (Wellish) S. AB magna cum laude, Columbia U., 1985, JD, 1987. Bar: N.Y. 1987, U.S. Dist. Ct. (so. and ea. dists.) N.Y. 1988, U.S. Ct. Internat. Trade 1991, U.S. Spreme Ct. 1991, U.S. Ct. Appeals (2d cir.) 1992, U.S. Ct. Appeals (1st cir.) 1993. Law clk. to Hon. Lawrence W. Pierce U.S. Ct. Appeals (2d cir.), N.Y.C., 1987-88; assoc. Fried, Frank, Harris, Shriver & Jacobson, N.Y.C., 1988-94, ptnr., 1994—. Treas., sr. editor Columbia Law Rev., 1985-87. Harlan Fiske Stone scholar, 1985-87. Mem. ABA, Fed. Bar Coun., N.Y. Bar Assn., Assn. of Bar of City of N.Y. (profl. responsibility com. 1998—, civil rights com. 1989-92), Phi Beta Kappa. Home: 203 E 72nd St Apt 20A New York NY 10021-4551 Office: Fried Frank Harris Shriver & Jacobson 1 New York Plz Fl 22 New York NY 10004-1980

SIMMONS, RICHARD CLIVE, American history educator; b. Bristol, Eng., Aug. 21, 1937; s. Geoffrey George and Phyllis May (Sweet) S.; m. Patterson Carr, Mar. 31, 1965; children: Elizabeth, Diana. BA, U. Cambridge, 1958, MA, 1962; PhD, U. Calif., Berkeley, 1965. Exec. dir. Hist. Soc. Del., Wilmington, 1964-65; lectr., sr. lectr. U. Birmingham, Eng., 1964-87, prof. Am. history, 1987—, head history, 1992—. Author: American Colonies, 1976, Studies in Massachusetts Franchise, 1989, British Imprints Relating to North America, 1621-1760, 1996; editor: British parliamentary Debates Relating to America, 1982-87, Midland History, 1971-78, British Records Relating to America, 1991—. Gov. Royal Grammar Sch., Worcester, 1989—. Robert Owen Bishop scholar Christ's Coll. Cambridge, 1955; fellow Am. Coun. Learned Socs., 1968-69, Charles Warren Ctr., Harvard U., 1968-69; vis. fellow Gonville and Caius Coll. Cambridge, 1993. Mem. Brit. Assn. Am. Studies, Oxford and Cambridge Club, Colonial Soc. Mass., Worcestershire Hist. Soc. (hon. chmn. 1984—). Office: U Birmingham, Sch History, Birmingham B15 2TT, England

SIMMONS, ROBERT BURNS, history and political science educator; b. Gadsden, Ala., Dec. 27, 1937; s. Burns Hunter and Grace Barbara (Armstrong) S.; m. Eleanor Conner, Nov. 11, 1959 (dec.); children: Kathleen D., Mary Ellen. BS in Chemistry, U. Ala., 1961; BA in Biology and History, Athens State Coll., 1968, MA in Tchg., 1969; EdS (Coll. Scholar, PhD, George Peabody Coll., 1976; MAS, U. Ala., 1978. Quality control chem. lab. supr. Goodyear Tire & Rubber Co., Gadsden, 1961-65; sect. leader, R&D chem. labs. Thiokel Chem. Corp., Redstone Arsenal, Huntsville, Ala., 1966-69; prof. history, polit. sci. and mgmt. John C. Calhoun State C.C., Decatur, Ala., 1969—; adj. prof. Athes (Ala.) State Coll., 1988—, asst. coord. instnl. devel. grant, 1983-84; asst. acad. dean Vol. State C.C., Gallatin, Tenn., 1974; cons. Ala. govs. office, 1987; attended Internat. Rels. Conf. U.S. State Dept., 1989; program presenter Conf. Tchg. Excellence, U. Tex., 1991, found. grant award; presenter Ala. Geog. Assn., 1998, 99; del. Ala. Edn. Assn. Post Secondary Com. Conf., 1990-98, Ala. Edn. Assn. Del. Assembly, 1997-98. Author: texts on world regional geography and on western civilization. Chmn. coms. Decatur Band Boosters; program com. coord. Congressman James Martin of Ala.; mem. acad. affairs com. Commn. on Instnl. Self Study, chmn. Instnl. Effectiveness, Exec. Com. on Articulation Post Secondary Insts. Ala., Calhoun's Instnl. Effectiveness Com., 1998-2000; chmn. Post Secondary Social Sci. Articulation Com., 1996-99, Faculty Senate, 1989-2000. Woodrow Wilson fellow Athens State Coll., 1968; E. U.S. Office Edn. grantee, 1970-71, grantee, 1985—, Master Tchr. award NISOD U. Tex., 1990. Mem. Am. Hist. Assn., So. Hist. Assn., Ala. Hist. Assn. (mem. post secondary polit. action com. 1990—), Ala. Coll. Assn. (history chmn. 1990-93, coord. 1990-95, mem. curriculum com. 1993-95, instnl. effectiveness 1993-94, mem. Calhoun pres. cabinet 1994—), C.C. Humanity Assn., Am. Assn. Higher Edn., Am. Chem. Soc., Archaeol. Inst. Am., Burningtree Country Club, Decatur C. of C., Beta Beta Beta, Phi Delta Kappa. Achievements include patent for missile propellants. Home: PO Box 2328 Decatur AL 35602-2328 Office: Calhoun C C PO Box 2216 Bldg Decatur AL 35609-2216

SIMMONS, ROBERT MALCOLM, biophysics educator; b. London, Jan. 23, 1938; s. Stanley Laurence and Marjorie Simmons; m. Mary Ann Simmons, July 8, 1967; children: Rebecca, Nicholas. BSc in Physics, King's Coll., London, 1960; PhD, London U., 1965; MSc in Physiology, U. Coll. London, 1967. FRS 1995. Lectr. dept. physiology U. Coll. London, 1967-79, rsch. fellow med. rsch. coun., 1979-81; mem. sci. staff med. rsch. coun. King's Coll., 1981-83, prof., head dept. biophysics, 1983-88, head div. biomolecular scis., 1988-91, hon. dir. med. rsch. coun. muscle and cell motility unit, 1990—; dir. Randall Centre Molecular Mechanisms of Cell Function, King's Coll., London, 1999—. Editor: Muscular Contraction, 1991; contbr. articles to profl. publs. Fellow Royal Soc.; mem. Physiol. Soc., Brit. Biophys. Soc. Avocations: music, fishing. Office: Randall Ctr New Hunts House, King's Coll London Guy's Campus, London SE1 1UL, England

SIMMONS, SCOT DAVIS, engineering company executive; b. New Orleans, May 27, 1969; s. Gaycon F. and Gloria Annette Simmons; m. Lory Denise S., Mar. 6, 1995; 1 child, Reid Davis. BS in Bus. Fin., U. Tex., Dallas, 1993, BSBA, 1996. Gen. mgr. Dallas, 1990-97; bus. mgr. Hunt, Guilot & Assocs., Ruston, La., 1997—; bd. dirs. Loutex, New Orleans. Bd. dirs. Valley Ranch Assn., Dallas, 1995-96, v.p. Cypress Springs Assn., Ruston, 1998-99, pres., 1999—. Republican. Baptist. Avocations: golf, hunting. E-mail: ssimmonss@hga-llc.com. Home: 2904 Lakeview Dr Ruston LA 71270-5253 Office: Hunt Guillot & Assocs 106 W Mississippi Ave Ruston LA 71270-4422

SIMMONS, STEPHEN JUDSON, lawyer; b. Columbus, Ohio, Feb. 19, 1946; s. Samuel A. and Jane A. (McGrath) S.; m. Claire Maxine Schriber, Aug. 15, 1970; children—Darren, Judson. B.A., Ohio State U., 1968; J.D., U. Cin., 1972. Bar: Tex. 1982, Ohio 1973. Sr. law clk. U.S. Dist. Ct. (ea. dist.) Tenn., Knoxville, 1972-74; asst. atty. gen. Office of Atty. of Ohio, Columbus, 1974-75; assoc. McGrath & Shirey, Columbus, 1975; corp. counsel Wendys, Inc., Columbus, 1975-79; sr. v.p., gen. counsel Precision Tune, Inc., Beaumont, Tex., 1979-87, also dir.; sr. v.p. adminstrn., dir. Kwik-Kopy Corp., Cypress, Tex., 1988-90; v.p. Deli Mgmt., Inc., 1990-94; pvt. practice, Houston, 1994—. Bd. editors U. Cin. Law Rev., 1971-72. Mem. Tex. Bar Assn. Roman Catholic. Home: 13603 Balmore Cir Houston TX 77069-2703 Office: 3845 Fm 1960 Rd W Ste 250 Houston TX 77068-3548

SIMMONS, TED CONRAD, writer; b. Seattle, Sept. 1, 1916; s. Conrad and Clara Evelyn (Beaudry) S.; m. Dorothy Pauline Maltese, June 1, 1942; children: Lynn, Juliet. Student, U. Wash., 1938-41, UCLA and L.A. State U., 1952-54, Oxford (Eng.) U., 1980. Drama critic Seattle Daily Times, 1942; indsl. writer, reporter-editor L.A. Daily News, 1948-51; contbr. Steel, Western Metals, Western Industry, 1951—; past poetry dir. Watts Writers Workshop; instr. Westside Poetry Center; asst. dir. Pacific Coast Writers Conf. Calif. State Coll. Los Angeles. Author: (poetry) Deadended, 1966; (novel) Middlearth, 1975; (drama) Greenhouse, 1977, Durable Chaucer, 1978, Rabelais and other plays, 1980, Dickeybird, 1981 (nominated TCG Plays-in-Progress award 1985), Alice and Eve, 1983, Deja Vu, Deja Vu, 1986, The Box, 1987, Ingrid Superstar, 1988, Three Quarks for Mr. Marks, 1989, Ingrid: Skier on the Slopes of Stromboli, 1990, A Midsummer's Hamlet, 1991, Hamlet Nintendo, After Hours, Dueling Banjoes, Viva el Presidente, Climate of the Sun, 1992, Nude Descending Jacob's Ladder, 1993, Almost an Opera, 1994, Landscape with Inverted Tree and Fred Astaire Dancing, 1995, O.J. Othello, Fast Track, Searching for Alice Liddell, Mr. Blue of Freaky Animals, Inc., 1997, Rosenstern & Guildencrantz II, 1997, Rosa/Rosa of the Centuries/Rosa of the Thorns, 1997, Joyce, 1997, Joyce-After Hours, 1997, Amadeus & da Cultchur Club, 1997, Wonderland: Alice's New Adventures, 1998, The Brilliant Life of an Intelligent Orchid-A Play About Ingrid Bergman, 1998, Chekhov Off-Broadway, The Premiere, Good Night Sweet Prince, The Scare, 1999, 18 Mini-Micro Dramas, BloomsDay, The Scream, The Bird, 2000; writer short story, radio verse; book reviewer Los Angeles Times; contbr. poetry to the Am. Poet, Prairie Wings, Antioch Rev., Year Two Anthology; editor: Venice Poetry Company Presents, 1972. Served with USAAF, 1942-46. Grantee Art Commn. King County, 1993.

SIMMONS, WARREN HATHAWAY, JR., retired retail executive; b. Indpls., May 10, 1927; s. Warren Hathaway and Jane (Jillson) S.; m. Nancy Lynn Sullivan; 1 child, Warren Hathaway III. AB in English, Princeton U., 1948. From mgr. tour ops. to supr. employees svcs. NBC, 1949-53; various positions in pers., labor rels. and store ops. Bamberger's, a divsn. of R.H. Macy and Co., Inc., 1953-63; v.p., dir. pers. and labor rels. Bamberger's divsn. R.H. Macy and Co., Inc., 1963-65; sr. v.p., dir. R.H. Macy and Co., Inc., 1965-70, sr. v.p. pers. and indsl. rels., 1970-83, cons., 1983-89; ltd. practice in human resource cons. and project mgmt. Princeton, N.J., 1983-87. Mem. Plainfield Planning Bd. and Traffic/Parking Commn.; mem., former chmn. and life gov. Muhlenberg Regional Med. Ctr.; life trustee Muhlenberg Found.; trustee, former chmn. Huntington Found.; mem., former chmn. bd. Nat. Captioning Inst., Vienna, Va., former co-chmn. bd.; trustee emeritus Wardlaw/Hartridge Sch.; trustee Rider U., Lawrenceville, N.J., Princeton/Blairstown Ctr., Prospect Found., Princeton; past trustee McCarter Theatre Co., Princeton, 1981-88, N.J. Symphony Orch., Symphony Hall, Newark, United Way of Essex and Union County, Mental Health Assn. Essex County, Robert Treat coun. Boys Scouts Am.; trustee, past pres. Friends of Pub. Broadcasting in N.J.; commr. Pub. Broadcasting Authority in N.J; former trustee David Lawrence Found. for Mental Health, Naples; mem. Pub. Employee Rels. Commn., Naples, 1992-98; With USN, 1945-46. Mem. Am. Mgmt. Assn. (human resources coun.), U.S. C. of C., (bus. adv. com. on white collar crime). Home: 508 Terhune Rd Princeton NJ 08540-3656

SIMMROCK, KARL HANS, technical chemistry educator; b. Darmstadt, Germany, Apr. 29, 1930; s. Karl and Erna Maria (Greunig) S.; m. Juliane Ottes, June 21, 1959; children: Hans Ulrich, Andrea Nicole. Dipl.-Chemiker, Tech. U., Darmstadt, 1958; Dr. rer. nat., Tech. U., 1959. Chemist Chemm. Werke Huls A.G., Marl, Fed. Republic Germany, 1959-69; ordentlicher prof. emeritus tech. chemistry U. Dortmund, Fed. Republic Germany, 1968-95. Home: Karoline Zorwald Strasse 4, 44229 Dortmund Germany Office: U Dortmund, Lehrstuhl fur Technische, 44221 Dortmund 50 Chemie A, Germany

SIMMS, BEVERLEY SINGLETON, music educator, musician; b. Charleston, S.C., Sept. 22, 1955; d. Edmund Bellinger Simms and Doris Evelyn Hancock; m. Matthew Cannon Brennan, May 21, 1994. BMus, U. Montevallo, Ala., 1976; MMus, Eastman Sch. Music, 1978; DMA, U. North Tex., 1990. Tchr. Dallas Ind. Sch. Dist., 1982-83; dir. Prepatory Sch. Music, Coker Coll., Hartsville, S.C., 1983-87; instr. music Ind. State U., Terre Haute, 1987-88, asst. prof., 1988-93, assoc. prof., 1993—; concert pianist, chamber musician. Mem. Music Tchr. Nat. Assn. (cert. evaluator 1998—), Nat. Guild Piano Tchrs. (adjudicator 1982—), Ind. Music Tchrs. Assn. (bd. dirs. 1989—), Pi Kappa Lambda, Phi Kappa Phi. Avocations: swimming, reading. E-mail: misimms@ruby.indstate.edu. Home: 1013 Maple Ave Terre Haute IN 47804-2936 Office: Ind State U Dept Of Music Terre Haute IN 47809-0001

SIMMS, JOHN WILLIAM, retired foreign service officer, consultant; b. Upland, Pa., Jan. 2, 1924; s. Earle and Katharyn Hamilton (Van Roden) S.; m. Ronda Jean Motter, Sept. 11, 1965; children: Llewellyn Earle Simms, Eric Marion Simms. Student, U. Pa., 1941-43; BA in Govt., George Washington U., 1948; postgrad., Georgetown U., 1948-50, Am. U., Washington, 1959-60, 63-64. U.S. foreign svc. officer various cities, Germany, 1950-53, 56-58; staff aide to amb. Tokyo, Japan, 1953-55; U.S. foreign svc. officer Bureau Internat. Orgns. Affairs, Washington, 1958-61; consul, prin. officer Kisangani, Zaire, 1962; U.S. fgn. svc. officer Bureau African Affairs, Washington, 1963, Bureau European Affairs, Washington, DC, 1964-65; staff aide to sec. gen. NATO, Paris, 1965-67, Brussels, Belgium, 1967-68; chief polit. sect. U.S. Embassy, Port-au-Prince, Haiti, 1968-71; chief polit. sect. U.S. Embassy Asuncion, Paraguay, 1971-73; U.S. foreign svc. officer Bureau Inter-Am. Affairs, Washington, 1973-74; from dep. chief of mission to charge d'affaires Bridgetown, Barbados, 1974-77; congl. liaison officer Office Congl. Rels., Washington, 1977-78; polit. counselor Bogotá, Colombia, 1978-80; sr. officer Bureau Pers., Washington, 1980-81; v.p. COMEX, Washington, 1981-82; cons. Profl. Mgmt. Assocs., Bethesda, Md., 1986-90; sr. crisis mgmt. assoc. Rsch. Planning, Inc., Arlington, Va., 1990-93. Mem. Fairfax County (Va.) Republican Com., 1983-85. Warrant Officer (j.g.) U.S. Army, 1943-46, ETO, lt. col. res. ret. Recipient Orden de la Democracia, Congress of Rep. Colombia, Bogotá, 1980. Republican. Avocations: drawing, painting, traveling in the U.S. and abroad.

SIMMS, MARIA ESTER, health services administrator; b. Bahia Blanca, Argentina; came to U.S., 1963; d. Jose and Esther (Guays) Barberio Esandi; m. Michael Simms, July 15, 1973 (Aug. 1993); children: Michelle Bonnie Lee Carla, Michael London Valentine, Matthew Brandon. Degree medicine, Facultad del Centenario, Rosario, Argentina, 1962; Physician Asst. Cert. (hon.), U. So. Calif., 1977. Medical diplomate. Pres. Midtown Svcs. Inc., L.A., 1973—; dir. internat. affairs, speaker Gov. of Papua, New Guinea, 1996—; dir., CFO, pres. World Film Inst., 1996—; commr. Inmate Welfare Commn. L.A. County Sheriff's Dept.; dir. internat. affairs, speaker on humanitarian, cultural and econ. matters Govt. of Papua New Guinea; advocate, internat. spkr. for women, children and animal rights. Chmn. bd. Am.'s Film Inst., Washington; chmn. bd. trustees World Film Inst, Dir. Intl. Affairs, speaker-Humanitarian, Economic and Cultural Consulate of Papua New Guinea, Los Angeles, Calif. Nominated chairwoman of bd. trustees World Film Inst., nominated pres. 1997. Fellow Am. Acad. Physicians' Assts.; mem. Bus. for Law Enforcement (northeast divsn.), Physicians for Social Responsibility, Mercy Crusade Inc., Internat. Found. for Survival Rsch., Noetic Scis. Soc., Inst. Noetic Scis., So. Calif. Alliance for Survival, Supreme Emblem Club of U.S., Order Eastern Star, Flying Samaritans, Shriners. Avocations: coin collecting, designing, writing, oil painting, flying.

SIMOES, EDUARDO JARDIM, epidemiologist, educator; b. Recife, Brazil, Mar. 5, 1957; came to U.S., 1989; s. Mauro Simoes Jr. and Maria do Carmo de Almeida Jardim; m. Suyenne Mulatinho; children: Julia, Raisa. MD, U. Pernambuco, Recife, 1981; MSc, London U., 1987; MPH, Emory U., 1991. Primary care physician Secretariat of Health, Recife, 1982-89, med. officer, 1985-86, asst. health planner, 1986-89, cons. health planner, 1989; vis. assoc. Ctrs. Disease Control, Atlanta, 1991-93; asst. rschr. Emory U. Sch. Medicine, Atlanta, 1993-95; med. epidemiologist Mo. Dept. Health, Columbia, 1995—; chief of office epidemiology, state epidemiologist Mo. Dept. Health, Jefferson City, 2000—; asst. prof. epidemiology, St. Louis U. Sch. Pub. Health, 1995—, U. Mo. Sch. Medicine, Columbia, 1998—; cons. Coun. State and Territorial Epidemiologists, 1995—, Mo. Patient Care Rev. Found. Task Force, 1998—. Contbr. articles to profl. jours. Mem. APHA, Am. Coll. Epidemiology, Assn. State and Territorial Chronic Disease Program Dirs. Fax: 573-526-4102. E-mail: simoes@mail.health.state.mo.us. Home: 1800 Muirfield Dr Columbia MO 65203-6280 Office: Mo Dept Health Office of Epidemiology 920 Wildwood Dr Jefferson City MO 65109-5796

SIMOES, ERIC ARUN FRANCIS, pediatrics educator; b. Bombay, India, Sept. 17, 1956. B Medicine B Surgery, Madras U., Vellore, India, 1980, diploma in child health, 1982, MD, 1984. Lectr. gen. pediats. U. Madras, Crishan Medical Coll., Vellore, 1984-86; instr. in pediat. infectious diseases U. Colo. Sch. Medicine, Denver, 1989-90, asst. prof. pediat. infectious diseases, 1991-96, assoc. prof. pediat. infectious diseases, 1997—; med. officer divsn. child and adolescent health WHO, Geneva, 1999; hon. sr. lectr. divsn. pediats., ob-gyn Imperial Coll. Sci. and Tech. and Medicine, St. Mary's Hosp., Eng., 1999—; cons. WHO, 1989—; fellowship dir. infectious diseases program U. Colo. Health Scis. Ctr. Sch. Medicine, Denver, 1995-99. Editor: Manual of Pediatric Emergencies for House Officers, 1987; contbr. chpts. to books in field. Mem. AAAS, Am. Soc. Microbiology, Western Soc. Pediat. Rsch. Fax: (303) 764-8117. E-mail: simoes.eric@tchden.org. Office: Children's Hosp 1056 E 19th Ave # B70 Denver CO 80218-1088

SIMOES, RENE, professional soccer coach; b. Dec. 17, 1952; married; 3 children. Coach Portugal, Aryan Sports Club; winner Nat. Club Title; coach Arabi Sports Club; winner Nat. Club Title; coach Brazil Nat. Squads (under-17, under-20, under-23), Jamaica Nat. Team, 1994—, World Cup, France, 1998. Office: Jamaica Football Fedn, 20 St Lucia Crescent, Kingston 5, Jamaica*

SIMOLA, LIISA KAARINA, educator; b. Helsinki, June 8, 1938; d. Paavo Eevertti and Kerttu Marjatta S. MS in Physiological Botany, U. Helsinki, Finland, 1962, PhD, 1968. Asst. botany U. Helsinki, Finland, 1962, docent plant physiology, 1969, assoc. prof., 1971-74, prof. botany, plant physiology & anatomy, 1974—. Contbr. over 120 articles to profl. jours. Mem. Regia Soc. Sci. Upsaliensis, Finnish Acd. Sci., N.Y. Acad. Scis., Scandinavian Soc. Plant Physiology (bd. dirs. 1979-85), Finnish Biol. Soc. (bd. dirs. 1973-81, pres. 1978-81), Internat. Assn. Plant Tissue Culture (nat. cor. 1970—, bd. dirs. 1981-86), Finnish Soc. Physiology (bd. dirs. 1974-77, 79-96), Finnish Histochem. Soc. (bd. dirs. 1971-76, sec. 1972-73, v.p. 1974-76), Soc. Biochem. Biophys. and Microbiology Fenniae (bd. dirs. 1975-81). Lutheran. Avocations: fine arts, literature, geology, theology, scouting. Office: Helsinki U Dept Biosci, PO Box 56 Viikinkaari 9, FIN00014 Helsinki Finland

SIMON, ALEKSANDER MACIEJ, physicist, consultant; b. Bytom, Katowice, Poland, July 19, 1959; s. Jan Franciszek and Joanna (Antonow) S.; m. Jolanta Kosinska, Feb. 24, 1962; 1 child, Antonia. MSc, Silesian Tech. U., Gliwice, Poland, 1983; PhD, Inst. Fundamental Tech. Rsch., Warsaw, 1990. Tech. asst. Silesian Tech. U., Gliwice, 1986-90, asst. prof., 1990-96; cons. Telcell Telecom, Krakow, 1996—. Contbr. articles to profl. jours. including Internat. Jour. Hydrogen Energy, Polish Jour. Chemistry, among others. Fellow Leverhulme Trust, 1994-95. Roman Catholic. Avocation: classical music. Office: Telcell Telecom, Garncarska 3/11, PL-31115 Cracow Poland

SIMON, ANDRAS, economist; b. Budapest, Hungary, Aug. 17, 1942; s. Lajos and Rozsa (Rausch) S.; m. Zsuzsa Csepregi, 1968 (div. 1992); children: Balazs, Balint; m. Julianna Sebestyen, 1994; 1 child, Andrea. Diploma, Budapest U. Econs., 1964. With Inst. Econ. and Market Rsch., Budapest, 1964-94; prof. Budapest U. Econs., 1986-94; dep. mng. dir. Nat. Bank Hungary, Budapest, 1994—; cons. UN, N.Y.C., 1985, UN, Bangkok, 1989; rsch. fellow Internat. Ctr. Study E. Asian Devel., Kitakyushu, Japan, 1991-92. Author: Markets, Rationing and Shortages, 1989, Open Economy Macroeconomics, 1991, A Guide to Macroeconomics, 1996. Home: Trencsenyi utca 10, 1122 Budapest Hungary Office: Nat Bank Hungary, Szabadsag ter 8/9, 1054 Budapest Hungary

SIMON, CLAUDE EUGÈNE HENRI, writer; b. Tananarive, Madagascar, Oct. 10, 1913; s. Louis and Suzanne (Denamiel) Simon; m. Yvonne Ducuing, 1951 (div.); m. Réa Karavas, 1978, 1978. Ed., Coll. Stanislas, Paris; DLitt, U. East Anglia, Norwich; DHC, U. Bologna. Author: (fiction) Le Tricheur, 1945, Gulliver, 1952, Le Sacre du printemps, 1954, Le Vent: tentative de restitution d'un rétable baroque, 1957 (pub. as The Wind: Attempted Restoration of a Baroque Masterpiece, 1959), L'Herbe, 1958 (pub. as The Grass, 1960), La Route des Flandres, 1960 (pub. as The Flanders Road, 1961; Prix de l'Express 1960), Le Palace, 1962 (pub. as The Palace, 1963), Historie 1967 (Prix Medicis 1967), La Bataille de Pharsale, 1969 (pub. as The Battle of Pharsalus, 1971), Les Corps conducteurs, 1971 (pub. as Conducting Bodies, 1974), Triptyque, 1973 (pub. as Triptych, 1976, Leçon de choses, 1975 (pub. as The World About Us, 1983), Les Géorgiques, 1981 (pub. as The Georgics, 1989); (play) La Séparation, 1963; (other writings) La Corde raide, 1947, Femmes, 1966 (pub. as La Chevelure de Bérénice, 1983), Orion aveugle, 1970, Discours de Stockholm, 1987, L'acacia, 1989, Photographies, 1992, Le Jardin des Plantes, 1997. Recipient Nobel prize for literature, 1985. Office: Editions de Minuit, 7 rue Bernard-Palissy, 75006 Paris France*

SIMON, FRANCOIS MELCHIOR, stockbroker; b. Paris, Mar. 23, 1956; s. Jean and Mary (Shilson) S. IEP, U. Paris; MBA, INSEAD, Fontainebleau, France. Analyst Cheuvreux, Paris, 1980-94, head of sales, 1994-98, dep. mng. dir., 1998-99, pres., 1999—. Office: Cai Cheuvreux, 9 Quai Paul Doumer, 22920 Courbevoie France

SIMON, GARY B., health care manager, investor; b. Honolulu, Oct. 15, 1960; s. Benedict Joseph and Frances (Seno) S.; m. Akemi Hata, July 9, 1993; 1 child, Seth Carlos Hisao. BS in Chemistry, U. Hawaii, 1985. Notary public, Hawaii. Vol. U.S. Peace Corps, Sierra Leone, 1985-87; exec. asst. to pres. Focus Techs., Inc., Washington, 1989-90; office mgr. St. Francis Hospice, Honolulu, 1990-95, bus. mgr., 1995—. Mem. Health Care Info. Sys. Hawaii User Group (pres. 1996—). Republican. Office: St Francis Hospice 24 Puiwa Rd Honolulu HI 96817-1127

SIMON, HELMUT FRANZ, chemist, educator, researcher; b. Würzburg, Bavaria, Germany, Apr. 14, 1927; s. Georg and Emma (Kunz) S.; m. Hildegard Ida Simon, Aug. 7, 1954; 1 child, Karl Michael. D of Natural Scis., U. Heidelberg, Germany, 1954; Habilitation, Tech. U. Berlin, 1959. Sci. asst. U. Heidelberg, 1951-54, U. Tübingen, Germany, 1954-55, Tech. U. Berlin, 1955-59, Tech. U. Munich, 1959-65; prof. chemistry faculty agriculture Tech. U. Munich, Freising-Weihenstephen, 1965-71; prof. chemistry sci. faculty Tech. U. Munich, 1971-97; prof. emeritus Tech. U., Munich, 1997—; bd. dirs. Soc. Biotech. Rsch., Braunschweig, 1977-84; chmn. working party Dechema, Frankfurt, 1972-90. Co-author two books; mem. editorial bd. sci. jours.; contbr. numerous articles to profl. jours; patentee: 12 internat. Mem. Deutscher Chemiker Assn., Assn. Biologische Chemie (pres., v.p. 1988-91). Home: Egilbert 31, D-85354 Freising Bavaria, Germany Office: Inst Organic Chemistry/Bio, D-85747 Garching Bavaria, Germany

SIMON, HERBERT A(LEXANDER), social scientist; b. Milw., June 15, 1916; s. Arthur and Edna (Merkel) S.; m. Dorothea Pye, Dec. 25, 1937; children: Katherine S. Frank, Peter Arthur, Barbara. AB, U. Chgo., 1936, PhD, 1943, LLD (hon.), 1964; DSc (hon.), Case Inst. Tech., 1963, Yale U., 1963, Marquette U., 1981, Columbia U., 1983, Gustavus Adolphus U., 1984, Mich. Tech. U., 1988, Carnegie-Mellon U., 1990; Fil. Dr. (hon.), Lund U., Sweden, 1968; LLD (hon.), McGill U., 1970, U. Mich., 1978, U. Pitts., 1979, U. Paul Valery, France, 1984, Harvard U., 1990; Dr. Econ. Sci. (hon.), Erasmus U. Rotterdam, Netherlands, 1973, Duquesne U., 1988; DSc (hon.), LHD (hon.), Ill. Inst. Tech., 1988; D in Polit. Sci. (hon.), U. Pavia, Italy, 1988; D in Psychology (hon.), U. Rome, 1993; D (hon. causa), U. Buenos Aires, 1999. Rsch. asst. U. Chgo., 1936-38; staff mem. Internat. City Mgrs.' Assn.; also asst. editor Pub. Mgmt. and Municipal Year Book, 1938-39; dir. adminstrv. measurement studies Bur. Pub. Adminstrn., U. Calif., 1939-42; asst. prof. polit. sci. Ill. Inst. Tech., 1942-45, assoc. prof., 1945-47, prof., 1947-49; also chmn. dept. polit. and social sci., 1946-49; prof. adminstrn. and psychology Carnegie Mellon U., Pitts., 1949-65, Richard King Mellon univ. prof. computer scis. and psychology, 1965—; head dept. indsl. mgmt. Carnegie Mellon U., 1949-60; assoc. dean Grad. Sch. Indsl. Adminstrn., 1957-73, trustee, 1972-93; emeritus trustee, 1993—; cons. to Internat. City Mgrs. Assn., 1942-49, U.S. Bur. Budget, 1946-49, U.S. Census Bur., 1947, Cowles Found. for Research in Econs., 1947-60; cons. and acting dir. Mgmt. Engring. br. Econ. Cooperation Adminstrn., 1948; Ford Disting. lectr. NYU, 1959; Vanuxem lectr. Princeton, 1961; William James lectr. Harvard, 1963, Sigma Xi lectr., 1964, 76-78, 86; Harris lectr. Northwestern U., 1967; Karl Taylor Compton lectr. MIT, 1968; Wolfgang Koehler lectr. Dartmouth, 1975; Katz-Newcomb lectr. U. Mich., 1976; Carl Hovland lectr. Yale, 1976; Ueno lectr., Tokyo, 1977; Gaither lectr. U. Calif., Berkeley, 1980; Camp lectr. Stanford U., 1982; Gannon lectr. Fordham U., 1982; Oates vis. fellow Princeton U., 1982; Marschak lectr. UCLA, 1983; Auguste Comte lectr. London Sch. Econs., 1987; Lee Kuan Yew lectr. U. Singapore, 1989, Hitchcock lectr. U. Calif., Berkeley, 1990, lectr. U. Roma Sapienza, 1993, Mattioli lectr. Bocconi U., Milan, 1993; Grunberg lectr. U. Akron, 2000; hon. prof. Tiánjin (China) U., 1980, Beijing (China) U., 1986; hon. rsch. scientist Inst. Psychology, Chinese Acad. Scis., 1985; chmn. bd. dirs. Social Sci. Rsch. Coun., 1961-65; chmn. Pa. Gov.'s Milk Inquiry Com., 1964-65; chmn. div. behavioral scis. NRC, 1968-70; mem. President's Sci. Adv. Com., 1968-72; trustee Carnegie Inst., Pitts., 1987-93, hon. trustee, 1993—; cons. bus. and govtl. orgns. Author or co-author books relating to field, including Administrative Behavior, 1947, 4th edit., 1997, Public Administration, 1950, with new Introduction, 1992, Models of Man, 1956, rev. edit., 1991, Organizations, 1958, with new Introduction, 1993, New Science of Management Decision, 1960, rev. edit., 1977, The Shape of Automation, 1965, The Sciences of the Artificial, 1968, 3d edit., 1996, Human Problem Solving, 1972, Skew Distributions and Business Firm Sizes, 1976, Models of Discovery, 1977, Models of Thought, Vol. I, 1979, Vol. II, 1989, Models of Bounded Rationality, Vols. I and II, 1982, Vol. III, 1997, Reason in Human Affairs, 1983, Protocol Analysis, 1984, with new Introduction, 1993, Scientific Discovery, 1987, Models of My Life, 1991, An Empirically Based Microeconomics, 1997. Recipient Adminstrs. award Am. Coll. Hosp. Adminstrs., 1957, Alfred Nobel Mem. prize in econ. scis., 1978, Dow-Jones award, 1983, scholarly contbns. award Acad. Mgmt., 1983, Nat. Medal Sci., 1986, Pender award U. Pa., 1987, Fiorino d'Oro City of Florence, Italy, 1988, Am. Psychol. Found. Gold medal, 1988, award for excellence in the scis. Gov. of Pa., 1990, rsch. excellence award Internat. Joint Conf. Artificial Intelligence, 1995. Fellow AAAS, APA (disting. sci. contbn. award 1969, lifetime contbn. award 1993), Am. Acad. Arts and Scis., Am. Assn. Artificial Intelligence, Am. Econ. Assn. (disting. Ely lectr. 1977), Econometric Soc., Am. Psychol. Soc. (William James fellow), Am. Sociol. Soc., Inst. Mgmt. Scis. (life, v.p. 1954, Von Neumann theory award 1988), Brit. Psychol. Assn. (hon.); mem. IEEE (hon.), Jewish Acad. Arts and Scis., Am. Polit. Sci. Assn. (James Madison award 1984, John M. Gaus award 2000), Am. Soc. Pub. Adminstrn. (Frederick Mosher award 1974, Dwight Waldo award 1995, Donald C. Stone lectr. 1997), Assn. Computing Machinery (A.M. Turing award 1975), NAS (com. on sci. and pub. policy 1967-69, 82-90, chmn. com. air quality control 1974, chmn. com. behavioral scis. NSF 1975-76, coun., 1978-81, 83-86, chmn. com. scholarly com. with PRC, 1983-87, co-chmn. com. behavioral sci. in prevention of nuclear war 1986-90), Cognitive Sci. Soc., Soc. Exptl. Psychologists, Am. Philos. Soc., Royal Soc. Letters (Lund; fgn. mem.), Orgnl. Sci. Soc. (Japan, hon.), Yugoslav Acad. Scis. (fgn.), Chinese Acad. Sci. (fgn.), Russian Acad. Sci. (fgn.), Indonesian Economists Assn. (hon.), Univ. Club Pitts., Phi Beta Kappa, Sigma Xi (Proctor prize 1980). Democrat. Unitarian. Office: Carnegie Mellon U Dept Psychology Schenley Park Pittsburgh PA 15213

SIMON, HERMANN Y., business executive, business educator; b. Hasborn, Germany, Feb. 10, 1947; m. Cecilia Sossong, July 8, 1949; children: Jeannine, Patrick J. Degree, U. Bonn, 1976. Asst. prof. bus. U. Bonn, 1973-78; visiting fellow MIT, Cambridge, 1978-79; prof. U. Bielefeld, Fed. Republic of Germany, 1980-85; scientific dir. USW German Mgmt. Inst., Cologne, 1985-88; prof. Johannes Gutenberg U., Mainz, 1988-95; chmn., CEO Simon, Kucher & Ptnrs., Bonn, Paris, Vienna, Zurich, Tokyo and Cambridge, 1995—; vis. prof. Inst. Europeen Adminstrn. Affaires, France, Keio U., Tokyo, 1984, Stanford (Calif.) U., 1988, Harvard U. Bus. Sch., 1988-89; mem. London Bus. Sch., 1993—; mem. supervisory bd. Gerling-Konzern AG, Ihr Preisode AG. Author: Price Management, 1982, rev. edits., 1989, 92, Goodwill, 1985, Simon for Managers, 1991, Hidden Champions: Lessons from the 500 World's Best Unknown Companies, 1996, Power Pricing (with R.J. Dolan) 1997, Handbook of Strategy, 2000. With German Air Force, 1967-68. Mem. European Mktg. Acad. (pres. 1984-86), Internat. Acad. Mgmt. Roman Catholic. E-mail: hsimon@simon-kucher.com. Office: Simon Kucher & Ptnrs, Haydnstr 36, D-53115 Bonn Germany also: One Cambridge Center Cambridge MA 02139

SIMON, H(UEY) PAUL, lawyer; b. Lafayette, La., Oct. 19, 1923; s. Jules and Ida (Rogére) S.; m. Carolyn Perkins, Aug. 6, 1949 (dec. Dec. 1999); 1 child, John Clark. B.S., U. Southwestern La., 1943; J.D., Tulane U., 1947. Bar: La. 1947; CPA, La. 1947. Pvt. practice New Orleans, 1947—; asst. prof. advanced acctg. and taxation U. Southwestern La., 1944-45; staff acct. Haskins & Sells (now Deloitte & Touche), New Orleans, 1945-53, prin., 1953-57; ptnr. Deutsch, Kerrigan & Stiles, 1957-79; sr. founding ptnr. Simon, Peragine, Smith & Redfearn, 1979—; mem. New Orleans Bd. Trade. Author: Community Property and Liability for Funeral Expenses of Deceased Spouse, 1946, Income Tax Deductibility of Attorney's Fees in Action in Boundary, 1946, Fair Labor Standards Act and Employee's Waiver of Liquidated Damages, 1946, Louisiana Income Tax Law, 1956, Changes Effected by the Louisiana Trust Code, 1965, Gifts to Minors and the Parent's Obligation of Support, 1968; co-author: Deductions—Business or Hobby, 1975, Role of Attorney in IRS Tax Return Examination, 1978; assoc. editor: The Louisiana CPA, 1956-60; mem. bd. editors Tulane Law Rev., 1945-46, adv. bd. editors, 1992—; estates, gifts and trusts editor The Tax Times, 1986-87. Bd. dirs., mem. fin. com. World Trade Ctr., 1985-86; mem. New Orleans Met. Crime Commn., Coun. for a Better La., New Orleans Met. Area Com., Bur. Govtl. Rsch., Pub. Affairs Rsch. Coun.; co-chmn. NYU Tax Conf., New Orleans, 1976; mem. dean's coun. Tulane U. Law Sch. Fellow Am. Coll. Tax Counsel; mem. ABA (com. ct. procedure tax sect. 1958—), AICPA, La. Bar Assn. (com. on legis. and adminstrv. practice 1966-70, bd. cert. tax atty.), New Orleans Bar Assn., Internat. Bar Assn. (com. on securities issues and trading 1970-88), Am. Judicature Soc., Soc. La. CPAs, New Orleans Assn. Notaries, Tulane U. Alumni Assn., New Orleans C. of C. (coun. 1952-66), Tulane Tax Inst. (program com. 1960-96), Internat. House (bd. dirs. 1976-79, 82-85), Internat. Platform Assn., City Energy Club, Press Club, New Orleans Country Club, Phi Delta Phi (past pres. New Orleans chpt.), Sigma Pi Alpha. Roman Catholic. Home: 6075 Canal Blvd New Orleans LA 70124-2936 Office: 30th Fl Energy Ctr New Orleans LA 70163

SIMON, ISTVÁN, biophysicist, scientific advisor; b. Budapest, Hungary, Jan. 15, 1947; s. Imre and Imréné (Markovics) S.; m. Istvánné Éva Ernst, June 27, 1971; 1 child, Ágnes. MS in Physics, Eotvos Lorand U., Budapest, 1969; PhD in Biology, Hungarian Acad. Sci., 1975, DS in Biology, 1987; D of Habilitation (hon.), Szentgyorgyi Albert Med. Sch., Szeged, Hungary, 1996. Jr. rsch. fellow Inst. Enzymology, Budapest, 1969-74, rsch. fellow, 1974-85, sr. rsch. fellow, 1985-88, sci. advisor, 1988—. Recipient Youth award Hungarian Acad. Scis., 1973, Rsch. award, 1986. Mem. Hungarian Biophys. Soc. (mem. of presidency 1985-94). Achievements include developing new experimental techniques and prediction methods to determine the structure and stability of various proteins and other macromolecules. Home: Dugonics u 40/a, H-1043 Budapest Hungary Office: Inst Enzymology, Karolina ut 29, H-1113 Budapest Hungary

SIMON, JACQUELINE ALBERT, political scientist, journalist; d. Louis and Rose (Axelroad) Albert; m. Pierre Simon; children: Lisette, Orville. BA cum laude, NYU, MA, 1972, PhD, 1977. Adj. assoc. prof. Southampton Coll., 1977-79; mng. editor Point of Contact, N.Y.C., 1975-76; assoc. editor, U.S. bur. chief Politique Internationale, Paris, 1979—; sr. vis. scholar Inst. French Studies, NYU, 1980—, assoc. prof. govt., 1982-83; assoc. Inst. on the Media for War and Peace; frequent appearances French TV and radio. Contbg. editor Harper's, 1984-92; contbr. numerous articles to French mags., revs., books on internat. affairs. Bd. dirs. Fresh Air Fund, 1984—. Mem. Women's Fgn. Policy Group, Women in the Media, Overseas Press Club of Am. (v.p. 1996—), Phi Beta Kappa. Home: 988 5th Ave New York NY 10021-0143

SIMON, JOHN BERN, lawyer; b. Cleve., Aug. 8, 1942; s. Seymour Frank and Roslyn (Schultz) S.; children: Lindsey Helaine, Douglas Banning. BS, U. Wis., 1964; JD, DePaul U., 1967. Bar: Ill. 1967. Asst. U.S. atty. U.S. Justice Dept., Chgo., 1967-70, dep. chief civil div., 1970-71, chief civil div., 1971-74; spl. counsel to dir. Ill. Dept. Pub. Aid, Chgo., 1974-75; legal cons. to Commn. on Rev. of Nat. Policy Toward Gambling, Chgo., 1975-76; ptnr. firm Friedman & Koven, 1975-85, mem. exec. com., 1983-85; ptnr. firm Jenner & Block, 1986—; spl. cons. to adminstr. DEA Dept. Justice, 1976-77; counsel to Gov.'s Revenue Study Commn. on Legalized Gambling, 1977-78; spl. counsel Ill. Racing Bd., 1979-80; lectr. tng. seminars and confs.; instr. U.S. Atty. Gen.'s Advocacy Inst., Washington, 1974; lectr. Nat. Conf. Organized Crime, Washington, 1975, Dade County Inst. Organized Crime, Ft. Lauderdale, Fla., 1976; faculty Cornell Inst. Organized Crime, Ithaca, N.Y., 1976, judge Miner Moot Ct. competition Northwestern U., 1971-73; mem. law coun. DePaul U., 1974-83, mem. alumni assn., 1984-85, chmn., 1975-79; adj. prof. DePaul U. Coll. Law, 1977, 81; faculty Practising Law Inst., Chgo., 1984. Contbr. articles to profl. jours. Bd. dirs. Lawyer's Trust Fund of Ill., 1998—, treas., 2000—, Cmty. Film Workshop of Chgo., 1977-90, Friends of Glencoe Parks, 1977-78, sec., 1978-79; mem. nominating com. Glencoe Sch. Bd., 1978-81, chmn. rules com., 1980-81; pres. Glencoe Hist. Soc., 1979-82; mem. Glencoe Zoning Bd. Appeals, Zoning Commn., Sign Bd. Appeals, 1981-86, chmn., 1984-86; mem. Ill. Inaugural Com., 1979, 83, 87, 95; bd. dirs., mem. exec. com. Chgo. World's Fair 1992 Authority, 1983-85; mem. Chancery divsn. task force Spl. Commn. on Adminstrn. of Justice in Cook County, 1985-87; trustee De Paul U., 1990, chair phys. plant and property com., 1992-94, vice chair, 1995—; commr. Ill. Racing Bd., 1990—; gen. trustee Lincoln Acad. Ill., 1993—, regent, 1999—; mem. Ill. Supreme Ct. Planning and Oversight Com. for Jud. Performance Evaluation Program, 1997-98, 2000—. Recipient Bankcroft-Whitney Am. Jurisprudence award, 1965, 66, Judge Learned Hand Human Rels. award Am. Jewish Com., 1994, award for outstanding svc. to legal profession DePaul U. Coll. Law, 1996, Am. ORT Jurisprudence award, 1999. Mem. ABA (com. on liaison with the judiciary 1983-95), FBA (fed. civil procedure com. 1979-85, chmn. 1985-86, bd. mgrs. 1987-89, chmn. house com. 1989-90, treas. 1990-91, 2d v.p. 1991-92, 1st v.p. 1992-93, pres. 1993-94), Ill. State Bar Assn., Women's Bar Assn., Ill. Police Assn., Ill. Sheriffs Assn., U.S. Treasury Agts. Assn., Chgo. Bar Assn., DePaul U. Alumni Assn. (pres. 1985-87, chmn. spl. gifts com. campaign, chmn. Simon Commn. 1989-91, nat. chair for ann. giving 1991-94), Std. Club. Office: Jenner & Block One IBM Plz Chicago IL 60611

SIMON, KATALIN EDITH, interior architect, designer artist; b. Budapest, Hungary, Oct. 23, 1952; d. Karoly and Edith (Balogh) S.; m. Janos Doczi, Aug. 23, 1996; 1 child, Gryllus Abris. PhD, Coll. Automation & Sys. Engr., Miskolc, Hungary, 1974; Architect, Tech. U. Budapest, 1979; Interior Architect, Acad. Design Arts, Budapest, 1984. Arch. S.B.B.S. Ltd., Budapest, 1985—; tchr. arts and craft Acad. Design Arts, Budapest, 1998. Prin. archtl. works include hqrs. Budapest Bank, 1989, br. office Budapest Bank in Györ Country, 1990, br. office Budapest Bank in Tapolca Country, 1992, Shop in the City Ctr. in Budapest, 1996. Mem. Art Found. of Hungarian Republic, Chamber of Hungarian Architect, 1997. Home: Szepvolgyi 131/B, 1037 Budapest Hungary Office: SBBS Ltd, Frankel Leo 72 V1/28, 1023 Budapest Hungary

SIMON, KATRIN, economist; b. Pamplona, Navarra, Oct. 31, 1964; d. Javier and Angeles Elorz S. Degree in Econs. and Bus. Adminstrn., Zaragoza U., Spain, 1987; PhD in Bus. Adminstrn., U. navarra, Pamplona, 1994. Fin. mgr. Pinhor, Alsasua, Spain, 1987-88; account mgr. AP Arvin/Kayaba, Ororbia, Spain, 1988-90; rschr. info. tech. U. Publica Navarra, Pamplona, 1990—. Contbr. articles to profl. jours. Grantee in field. E-mail: katrin@unavarra.es. Office: Univ Publica de Navarra, Campus de Arrosadia S/N, Pamplona E-31006, Spain

SIMON, LAJOS, pharmaceutical chemistry educator; b. Bágyog, Hungary, Feb. 13, 1936; s. Jenö and Mária (Horváth) S.; m. Gizella Talpas, Dec. 26, 1963; children: Rita, Lajos Jr., Barbara. M in Pharmacy, Med. U., Szeged, Hungary, 1960, PhD in Pharmacy, 1966, Candidate Sci., 1977. Univ. lectr. dept. pharmacognosy Med. U., Szeged, 1961-62, univ. lectr. dept. pharm. chemistry, 1963-70, asst. prof. dept. pharm. chemistry, 1971-77, assoc. prof. pharm. chemistry, 1978—, vice dean Faculty Pharmacy, 1988-90. Mem. Hungarian Pharm. Soc. (v.p. 1996—), Hungarian Chem. Soc., Am. Peptide Soc. Roman Catholic. Avocations: gardening, tennis, music, history of sciences.

SIMON, LAURENT, chemical engineer, researcher; b. Port-au-Prince, Haiti, May 4, 1968; came to U.S., 1988; s. Wiener and Claudie (Bresier) S. BSChemE, N.J. Inst. Tech., Newark, 1996; MS in Chem., Bioresource Engring., Colo. State U., 1998. Rsch. asst. Hoffman-La Roche, Nutley, N.J., 1995; instr. pre-coll. program N.J. Inst. Tech., 1995-96; rsch. asst. Exxon Rsch. & Engring. Co., Florham Park, N.J., 1996. Contbr. articles to profl. jours. Instr. elem. sci. outreach program at N.J. Inst. Tech., 1995; v.p. Biotech. Club at Colo. State U., 1997-98. Recipient Hon. Mention All-USA Coll. Acad. Team USA Today, 1996; UNCF Merck grad., 1998; pres. Omega Chi Epsilon Chem. Engring. Honor Soc. at N.J. Inst. Tech., 1995-96. Home: 1714 Stover St Apt 1A Fort Collins CO 80525-1059 Office: Dept Chem Bioresource Colo State U Fort Collins CO 80523-0001

SIMON, MARTIN LORENZ, internist, hematologist, oncologist; b. Biberach, Riss, Germany, Oct. 15, 1956; s. Franz Josef and Lore Emilie (Gropper) S.; m. Sabine Ingrid Throm, June 16, 1990; children: Hannah Lore, Julian Rudolf. M in Biochemistry, U. Montpellier, France, 1981; MD, U. Freiburg, Germany, 1984. Cert. specialist in internal medicine, hematology and oncology Bd. Coll. Physicians and State Med. Assn. Rsch. asst. pathology U. Ulm, Germany, 1985-89; postdoctoral fellow rsch. and clin. hematology U. Heidelberg, Mannheim, Germany, 1989-96; cons. internal medicine Ehingen, Germany, 1996—. Contbr. articles to sci. publs. Capt. German Mil., 1984-85. Dr. Carl Duisberg Found. scholar U. Montpellier, 1977; award recipient European Philips Contest for Young Scientists, Hamburg, Germany, 1975. Mem. Assn. German Internists, German Soc. Hematology and Oncology. Avocations: skiing, bicycling, tennis, French, Spanish. Office: Kreiskrankenhaus, D-89584 Ehingen Germany

SIMON, NANCY RUTH, lawyer; b. Gary, Ind.. BSEE, Iowa State U., 1985; MBA, U. Dallas, 1988; JD, So. Meth. U., 1991. Bar: Tex. 1991, Calif. 1994; registered to practice before U.S. Patent and Trademark Office 1992; lic. real estate salesperson. Elec. engr. Tex. Instruments, Dallas, 1986-88; law clk. to pvt. law firms Dallas, 1989-91; law clk. U.S. Attys. Office, 1991; assoc. Felsman, Bradley, Gunter & Dillon, LLP, Ft. Worth, 1991-93; patent counsel Apple Computer, Inc., Cupertino, Calif., 1993-2000; ptnr. Simon & Koerner, LLP, Cupertino, 2000—; realtor Coldwell Banker, San Jose, Calif, 1997-98. Co-author: Attorneys' Fees in IPL Cases; mem. So. Meth. U. Law Rev. Jour. of Air Law and Commerce, 1990-91. Mem. ABA, State Bar Tex., State Bar Calif., Nat. Assn. Realtors, Calif. Assn. Realtors, Peninsula West Valley Assn. Realtors, Mensa Iowa State U. Student Alumni Assn. (mem. career awareness com. 1984-85), Sigma Iota Epsilon, Zeta Tau Alpha (social chmn. 1982-83, house mgr. 1983-84, chmn. jud. bd. 1984-85), Phi Delta Phi. Avocations: reading, music, scuba diving. Office: Simon & Koerner LLP 10052 Pasadena Ave Ste B Cupertino CA 95014-5945

SIMON, NEIL, playwright, television writer; b. N.Y.C., July 4, 1927; s. Irving and Mamie Simon; m. Joan Baim, Sept. 30, 1953 (dec.); m. Marsha Mason, 1973 (div.); m. Diane Lander, 1987. Student, NYU, 1946; LLD (hon.), Hofstra U., 1981, Williams Coll., 1984. Author materials for Tamiment (Pa.) revues, 1952-53; author: (with brother Danny) sketches Catch a Star, 1955, (with brother Danny) for New Faces of '56; book for musicals Little Me, 1962, Sweet Charity, 1966 (Evening Standard Drama award 1967), Promises, Promises, 1968 (Tony award nomination 1969), They're Playing Our Song, 1979, Little Me (Tony award nomination 1963 version, rev. version), 1982, The Goodbye Girl, 1993, Rewrites: A Memoir, 1996; plays include Come Blow Your Horn, 1961, Barefoot in the Park, 1963 (Tony award nomination 1963), The Odd Couple, 1965 (Tony award 1965), The Star-Spangled Girl, 1966, Plaza Suite, 1968 (Tony award nomination 1968), Last of the Red Hot Lovers, 1969 (Tony award nomination 1970), The Gingerbread Lady, 1970, The Prisoner of Second Avenue, 1971 (Tony award nomination 1972), The Sunshine Boys, 1972, The Good Doctor, 1973, God's Favorite, 1974, California Suite, 1976, Chapter Two, 1977, I Ought to be in Pictures, 1980, Fools, 1981, Brighton Beach Memoirs, 1983, Biloxi Blues, 1985 (Tony award for Best Playwright 1985, Best Play 1985), The Odd Couple (female version), 1985, Broadway Bound, 1986 (Tony award nomination 1987), Rumors, 1988, Lost in Yonkers, 1991 (Pulitzer Prize for drama 1991, Tony award Best Play 1991), Jake's Women, 1992, Laughter on the 23rd Floor, 1993, London Suite, 1995; wrote screenplays adapted from own plays: Barefoot in the Park, 1967, The Odd Couple, 1968, Plaza Suite, 1971, Last of the Red Hot Lovers, 1972, The Prisoner of Second Avenue, 1975, The Sunshine Boys, 1975, California Suite, 1978, Chapter Two, 1979, Only When I Laugh (adapted from play The Gingerbread Lady), 1981, I Ought to be in Pictures, 1982, Brighton Beach Memoirs, 1986, Biloxi Blues, 1988, Broadway Bound, 1992 (TV motion picture), Lost in Yonkers, 1993, (TV motion picture) Jake's Women, 1996; other screenplays include After the Fox, 1966, The Out-of-Towners, 1970, The Heartbreak Kid, 1973, Murder by Death, 1976, The Goodbye Girl, 1977, The Cheap Detective, 1978, Seems Like Old Times, 1980, Max Dugan Returns, 1983, The Lonely Guy (adaptation), 1984, The Sluggers Wife, 1984, The Marrying Man, 1991; other motion pictures based on his stage plays: Come Blow Your Horn, 1963, Sweet Charity, 1969, The Star-Spangled Girl, 1971; wrote for TV shows: The Phil Silvers Arrow Show, 1958, The Tallulah Bankhead Show, 1951, The Sid Caesar Show, 1956-57 (Emmy award 1956-57), Phil Silvers Show, 1958-59 (Emmy award 1958-59), Garry Moore Show, 1959-60; also NBC spl. The Trouble with People, 1972. Served to cpl. USAAF, 1945-46. Recipient Sam S. Shubert award 1968, Writers Guild screen awards, 1968, 70, 75, Writers Guild Laurel award, 1979. Mem. Dramatists Guild, Writers Guild Am. (Laurel award 1979, screen awards 1968, 70, 75). Address: care Albert DaSilva 502 Park Ave New York NY 10022-1108

SIMON, ROBERT STEPHEN, artist; b. Flushing, N.Y., Nov. 4, 1939; s. Benjamin and Clara (Helsel) S. BA, Ill. Wesleyan U., Bloomington, 1962; degree in Fine Arts, Arts Students League, N.Y.C., 1965. Landscape, portrait artist N.Y.C., 1965-82; sports and portrait artist, 1983—. Sports artist: more than 500 paintings in last 10 yrs.; displayed in Baseball's Hall of Fame, Nat. Acad. Fine Art, Madison Sq. Garden, Downtown Athletic Club, Sports Immortals Mus., as well as in the personal collections of Mickey Mantle, Sylvester Stallone and Joe DiMaggio; The 70 Karat Diamond depicting 70 of baseball's greatest players on a diamond-shaped canvas will be displayed at the entrance of a baseball mus. that will open in Orlando, Fla., in 2001; recent completion of Masters of the Millenium a 50x50 oil painting depicting over 50 of the greatest golfers in history of game proving to be 1st of its kind. Sports Artist of Yr. U.S. Sports Acad. of Art, 1992; People's Choice 1st prize Broward Art Guild, 1997; 1st Prize Oil Norwood U., 1998; nominated for Disting. Alumni award Ill. Wesleyan U., 1999; Color Trend award for Disting. Artwork in Lithography, 1998. Mem. Nat. Soc. of Illustrators, Am. Soc. of Classical Realism, Internat. Soc. Artists, Allied Artists of Am., Salmagundi Club, Norton Mus. Fine Art Guild. Home and Studio: 2700 S Oakland Forest Dr Fort Lauderdale FL 33309-7527

SIMON, ROBIN JOHN HUGHES, magazine editor, publisher, writer; b. Llandaff, Wales, July 23, 1947; s. William Glyn Hughes and Sarah Ellen Sheila (Roberts) S.; m. Jette Margaret Brooke, July 10, 1972 (div. 1979); children: Benet Glyn Hughes, Alice Emily Hughes; m. Joanna Christine Ross, Dec. 7, 1979; 1 child, Poppy Candida Hughes. BA with honours in English, U. Exeter, Eng., 1969; MA in History of European Art, Courtauld Inst. Art, London, 1971. Lectr. history of art and English U. Nottingham, Eng., 1972-78; hist. bldgs. rep. The Nat. Trust, London, 1979-80; dir. Inst. European Studies, London, 1980-90; editor-in-chief Apollo, internat. art and antiques mag., London, 1990-97; head publs., editor Art Quar. and Rev., Nat. Art Collections Fund, London, 1997-98; founding ptnr. Draig Pub., London, 1997—; founding pub., editor-in-chief The Brit. Art Jour., 1999—; arts corr. Daily Mail, London, 1987-90, art critic, 1990—; vis. lectr. history of art U. Warwick, Coventry, Eng., spring 1978; vis. prof. history of art and architecture Westminster Coll., Fulton, Mo., spring 1989; mem. adv. coun. Paul Mellon Ctr. for Studies in Brit. Art, 1993-98; multimedia cons. Courtauld Inst. Art, 1998. Author: (with Alastair Smart) The Art of Cricket, 1983; The Portrait in Britain and America, 1987; editor: Buckingham Palace: A Complete Guide, 1993; contbr. numerous articles to profl. publs., mags. and newspapers. Fellow Delmas Found., Venice, Italy, 1978. Mem. Assn. Art Historians (exec. com. 1993-96), Walpole Soc. (coun. 1991-96, exec. and editl. com. 1993-96), Johnson Club, Garrick Club. Anglican. Avocations: cricket, music. Office: The Brit Art Jour, 46 Grove Ln, London SE5 8ST, England

SIMON, TERU, artist, sculptor, ceramist, educator; b. Paris, Mar. 11, 1949; (parents Am. citizens); d. Sidney and Joan (Crowell) S. Student, Bennington Coll., 1967-70; BS, Skidmore Coll., 1978; MFA, Johnson (Vt.) State Coll., 1998. Tchr. art Mt. Anthony H.S., Bennington, Vt., 1987; artist, participant Showhegan (Maine) Sch., 1978. One-woman shows include Southern Vt. Coll., Bennington, Vt. Johnson (Vt.) State Coll., Artisan Market, Cambridge, N.Y.; exhibited in group shows at Provincetown, Ma., PSA, N.Y, N.Y., Elaine Benson Gallery, Bridgehamton, N.Y., SAkidmore Coll., Saratoga, N.Y., Castle HIll Ctr. for the Arts, Truro, Ma. Bd. dirs. Mt. Anthony Preservation Soc., 1990—. Mem. NEA (union rep. 1997—). Office: Mt Anthony HS Park St Bennington VT 05201

SIMON, WERNER FRANZ HEINZ, theology educator; b. Nieder-Walluf, Hessen, Fed. Republic Germany, Mar. 15, 1950; s. Franz and Margarete (Decku) S.; m. Eva-Maria Herrmann, Apr. 3, 1974. Diploma in Catholic Theology, U. Mainz, Fed. Republic of Germany, 1975; ThD, U. Mainz,

1982. Wiss. mitarbeiter seminar religionspaedagogik fachbereich Kath. Theologie, U. Mainz, Germany, 1977-82; wiss. angestellter seminar religionspaedogogik fachbereich Kath. Theologie U. Mainz, 1982-84, hochschulasst. instr. in religious edn. theory fachbereich, 1984-85; prof. religious edn. theory and didactics Freie U., Berlin, 1985-91; prof. religious edn. theory, catechetics and didactics Gutenberg U., Mainz, 1991—. Author: Didaktik und Fachdidaktik Religion, 1979, Inhaltsstrukturen des Religionsunterrichts, 1983, Kirche in der Stadt, 1990; editor: Zwischen Babylon und Jerusalem, 1988, Spiritualität aus Glaubenserfahrung, 1990, Lernorte des Glaubens, 1991, Weggemeinschaft mit den Menschen, 1992, Bilanz der Religionspädagogik, 1995. Mem. Arbeitsgemeinschaft Katholischer Katechetik-Dozenten, Europäische Arbeitsgemeinschaft für Katechese, European Soc. for Cath. Theology. Office: U Mainz fachbereich Kath Theologie, Saarstrasse 21, D-55099 Mainz Germany

SIMON DIAZ, JOSE, bibliography educator; b. Madrid, July 17, 1920; s. Ezequiel Simon and Carmen Diaz; m. Josefina Palmer, Dec. 12, 1945; children: Maria Del Carmen, Paloma, Jose. Degree in art, Madrid U., 1943, D of Philology, 1957. Libr. aux. Madrid, 1943—; tchr. Spanish lit. Mid. Sch., Logroño and Madrid, 1945-48, 50-70; sci. rschr. CSIC, Madrid, 1954—; prof. bibliography U. Complutense, Madrid, 1955-85; dir. programs in Spanish bibliography CSIC and U. Complutense, Madrid, 1964-90; dir. Cuadernos Bibliograficos, CSIC, Madrid. Author: Bibliografia de la Literatura Hispanica, 1950, Manual de Bibliografia de la Literatura Española, 1971, El libro español antiguo: Analisis de su estructura, 1983, Historia del Colegio Imperial de Madrid, 1952, 92. Recipient Internat. prize on bibliography Syracuse U., 1984, Comendador de la Orden de Isabel la Catolica, Ministry Asuntos Exteriones, 1988, Medalla De Oro de las Bellas Artes, Ministry Culture, 1995. Home: Amado Nervo 13, 28007 Madrid Spain

SIMONDS, MARTHA MUÑOZ, musician, educator; b. Washington, Nov. 26, 1960; d. Roger Tyrell and Peggy (Muñoz) S.; m. David Robert Teeters, May 5, 1996. MusB, Juilliard Sch., 1982; MusM, Eastman Sch. Music, 1984. Tchg. asst. Eastman Sch. Music, Rochester, N.Y., 1984; violinist Santa Fe Opera Orch., 1984; 1st violin San Francisco Ballet Orch., 1984—; assoc. prin. 2nd violin San Francisco Opera Orch., 1985—; assoc. concertmaster New Century Chamber Orch., San Francisco, 1993—; violinist Due Voci Duo, San Francisco, 1993—; pvt. music tchr., Oakland, Calif., 1985—; performer Earplay, San Francisco, 1985—, Berkeley (Calif.) Contemporary Players, 1998—. Cmty. activist Cmty. Action Network, Oakland, 1991—. Touring grantee Calif. Arts Coun., 1992. Mem. Musicians Union Local 6. Democrat. Avocations: gardening, rescues animals, improvisational acting, Qi Gong, salsa dancing. Home: 5464 El Camile Ave Oakland CA 94619-3200

SIMONE, ALBERT JOSEPH, academic administrator; b. Boston, Dec. 16, 1935; s. Edward and Mary (DiGiovanni) S.; m. Carolie Roberta Menko, Nov. 7, 1959; children: Edward, Karen, Debra, Laura. BA, Tufts U., 1957; PhD, MIT, 1962. Lectr. Coll. Bus. Adminstrn., Northeastern U., Boston, 1958-59; instr. econs. MIT and Tufts U., Boston, 1959-60; asst. prof. Northeastern U., Tufts U., 1960-63; assoc. prof. Coll. Bus. Adminstrn. Boston Coll., 1963-66, prof., dir. quantitative mgmt. program Coll. Bus. Adminstrn.,, 1966-68; prof., head dept. quantitative analysis Coll. Bus. Adminstrn. U. Cin., 1968-72, dean Coll. Bus. Adminstrn., 1972-83; v.p. acad. affairs U. Hawaii, Honolulu, 1983-84, acting pres., 1984-85; pres. U. Hawaii System, Honolulu, 1985-92; chancellor U. Hawaii at Manoa, 1985-92; pres. Rochester (N.Y.) Inst. Tech., 1992—; mem., chair numerous univ. coms.; program chmn. 1970 Nat. Conf. of Am. Prodn. and Inventory Control Soc.; mem. accreditation com. Am. Assembly Collegiate Schs. Bus., 1978-83, visits to U. Ky., Carnegie-Mellon U., 1982; session chmn. various profl. confs.; cons. statis. forecasting, prodn. scheduling and sample design models various cos. including Cin. Gas & Electric Co., Cin. Milacron, Kroger Co.; econ. and mgmt. cons. Atty. Gen.'s Office, State of Mass.; mem. coun. econ. advisors to Gov., Commonwealth of Mass.; bd. dirs. Fed. Res. Bank N.Y.; adv. group M&T Bank. Author: Matematica Finita Con Aplicaciones A Las Ciencias Administrativas, 1969, Foundations of Contemporary Mathematics with Applications in the Social and Management Sciences, 1967, Probability: An Introduction with Applications, 1967; (with L. Kattsoff) Finite Mathematics with Applications in the Social and Management Sciences, 1965, (with R. Wessel and E. Willett) Statistics as Applied to Economics and Business, 1965; also articles. Bd. dirs. Greater Rochester Visitors Assn., Inc., Rochester/So. Region, United Way of Greater Rochester, Vis. Nurse Svc. of Rochester and Monroe County, Inc., High Tech. of Rochester, Greater Rochester Metro C. of C., past chair; bd. dirs. Indsl. Mgmt. Coun.; chmn. United Way Vol. Resources Divsn. Steering Com.; trustee George Eastman House; chmn. Commn. Indep. Colls. and Univs.; corp. mem. Hillside Children's Ctr. Fellow of grad. sch. U. Cin.; named Prof. of Yr., Delta Sigma Pi, Alpha Theta chpt., U. Cin., 1972, Citizen of Yr. Henrietta Commerce Network, 2000; recipient Tree of Life award Jewish Nat. Fund. Fellow Am. Inst. Decision Scis. (v.p. publs. 1969-70, v.p. and student liaison 1972, pres. 1974-75, founding editor and editor-in-chief jour. 1970-72, Disting. Svc. award 1972); mem. Acad. Mgmt., Am. Econ. Assn., Am. Inst. Indsl. Engrs., Am. Prodn. and Inventory Control Soc., Am. Statis. Assn., Assn. Computing Machinery, Univs. Rsch. Assn., Assn. of Ind. Tech. Univs., The Conf. Bd. RIT Rsch. Corp. (chmn., bd. dirs.), Nat. Commn. for Coop. Edn., N.Y. Commn. for Ind. Coll. and Univs. (chmn.), Rochester Area Coll. Consortium, Econometric Soc., Fin. Execs. Inst., Inst. Mgmt. Sci., Ops. Rsch. Soc. Am., Phi Beta Kappa, Phi Kappa Phi, Beta Gamma Sigma. Office: RIT George Eastman Bldg 2 Lomb Memorial Dr Rochester NY 14623-5604

SIMONE, LUIZ RICARDO LOPES, biologist, surgeon; b. São Paulo, Brazil, May 1, 1961; s. Egydio Do carmo and Neyde (Lopes) S.; m. Lucia Valeria Ramos, Jan. 24, 1987; children: Ana Beatriz R., Luiz Felipe R., Joao Victor R. MD, U. São Paulo, 1985, M in Zoology, 1995, postgrad., 1995—. Resident in surgery Hosp. Clinic Fac. Medicine Ribeirao Preto, U. São Paulo, Ribeirao Preto, Brazil, 1985-86; clin. dr. Servicos Medicos Assistanciais, São Paulo, 1987-96. Author: (with S. Mezzalira) Fossil Molluscs of Brazil, 1994; contbr. articles to profl. jours. Mem. Brazilian Malacological Soc. (regional rep. 1993-97). Avocation: scuba diving. E-mail: lrsimone@usp.br. Home: Rua Antonio Teixeira 143, 03060020 São Paulo Brazil Office: Museu de Zoologia da USP, Caixa Postal 42694, 04299970 São Paulo Brazil

SIMONEIT, BERND ROLF TATSUO, geochemistry educator; b. Heilbronn, Republic of Germany, Sept. 7, 1937; came to U.S., 1952; s. Kurt Erich and Anna (Dietrich) S.; m. Lynda J. Wells, June 17, 1961 (div. Mar. 1966); m. Doreen Joy Gee, Sept. 7, 1968; 1 adopted child, Amanda Jane Houlding. BS, U. R.I., 1960; postgrad., MIT, 1961, 64; PhD, U. Bristol, Eng., 1975. Chemist A.C. Lawrence Leather Co., Peabody, Mass., 1962-63; spectroscopist space sci. lab. U. Calif., Berkeley, 1965-70, assoc. specialist space sci. lab., 1970-72, specialist space sci. lab., 1972-73; assoc. rsch. geochemist UCLA, 1976-81; assoc. prof. sch. oceanography Oreg. State U., Corvallis, 1981-83, prof. coll. oceanography, 1983-93; prof. coll. oceanic and atmospheric scis. Oreg. State U., 1993—; cons. EG&G Idaho, Inc., Idaho Falls, 1983-92, Refineria de Petroleo, SA, Concon, Chile, 1990—, Chevron Petroleum Tech. Co., La Habra, 1992-97; mem. NASA Exobiology Adv. Panel, Washington, 1980-85; mem., chmn. deep sea drilling project Joint Oceanographic Instns. for Deep Earth Sampling Orgn. Geochemisty Adv. Panel, Washington, 1978-83; vis. faculty assoc. Calif. Inst. of Tech., Pasadena, 1995—; vis. prof. Ctr. d'Investigacio Desenvolupament, Consell Superior d'Investigacions Sci., Barcelona, Spain, 1996-97; adj. prof. U. Utah, Salt Lake City, 1998—. Editor: Organic Geochemistry, 1982-87, 90—, Applied Geochemistry, 1992—; co-editor: Gulf and Peninsular Province of the Californias, 1990; contbr. articles to profl. jours. Recipient Best Paper of Yr. award Geochemical Soc., 1977, 81. Mem. AAAS, Internat. Assn. Geochemistry and Cosmochemistry, Am. Assn. for Aerosol Rsch., Internat. Soc. for the Study of the Origin of Life, Am. Assn. Petroleum Geologists, Am. Chem. Soc., Am. Geophys. Union, Am. Soc. for Mass Spectrometry, European Assn. for Organic Geochemistry. Office: Oreg State U Coll Oceanic and Atmospheric Scis Oceanography Adminstrn Bldg 104 Corvallis OR 97331-5501

SIMONETTI, FRANCESCO, radiologist, Italian navy officer; b. Taranto, Italy, Feb. 7, 1949; s. Giuseppe and Chiara (Leogrande) S.; m. Donatella Failla, Dec. 23, 1989. MD, Pisa Med. Sch., 1975, specialist radiology, 1979; tng. ultrasonography, Med. Sch. Ancona, 1983; hosp. mgmt. cert., Advanced Sch. Med. Studies, Rome, 1988. Cert. radiologist. Commd. sub-lt. Italian Navy, 1975, advanced through grades to rear adm., 1995, chief med. officer, 1976-77; from asst. x-ray dept. to dir. Main Naval Hosp., La Spezia, Italy, 1977-91; dir. Naval Med. Sch., Leghorn, Italy, 1991-93; head studies and planning office Naval Med. Svc., Rome, 1993-94; asst. surgeon gen. Surgeon Gen. Office, Rome, 1994-96; med. advisor Allied Command Europe, SHAPE, Brussels, 1996-99; med. adv. Comdr. In Chief North-West dept. Italian Navy, 1999—; chmn. working group emergency medicine NATO, 1992-96; coord. healthcare projects Ministry of Health, Rome, 1995-96. Contbr. chpts. in books and articles to profl. jours. Mem. Italian Soc. Radiology and Nuclear Medicine, Assn. Mil. Surgeons U.S. (hon.), Rotary Club Rome. Avocations: reading, running. Office: Via Fieschi 16, 19100 La Spezia Italy

SIMONI, ISABELA CRISTINA, microbiologist; b. São Paulo, Brazil, May 17, 1958; d. Milton and Cely (Cintra) S.; m. Marco Antonio Pereira Pasquini; children: Pedro Simoni Pasquini, Julia Simoni Pasquini. Grad., OSEC, São Paulo, 1981; M in Cellular Biology, U. Campinas, Brazil, 1984, postgrad. Biologist Biol. Inst., São Paulo, 1985-88, pesquisador cientifico, 1988—. Contbr. articles to sci. publs. E-mail: simoni@biologico.be. Office: Biol Inst, CP 12898, R Cons Rodrigues Alves 1252, 04010970 São Paulo Brazil

SIMONIĆ, ANTE, pharmacologist, educator, researcher; b. Rijeka, Croatia, Sept. 19, 1949; s. Anton and Iva (Feretić) S.; m. Višnja Bobinac, July 16, 1975; 1 child, Sunčana. MD, Med. Sch., Rijeka, 1973, MSc, 1977, PhD, 1980. Rsch. fellow Med. Sch., 1975-81, asst. prof., 1981-87, assoc. prof., 1987-91, prof., 1991—, head dept. pharmacology, 1985—, dean, 1990-94, dir., 1991-92. Co-author: General Pharmacology, 1987, 2d edit., 1988, 3d edit., 1991; Pharmacology, 1989; contbr. articles to profl. jours. Adviser Min. Health, Zagreb, 1991-92; pres. State Union Med. Schs., Zagreb, 1988-90; mem. State Drug Commn., Zagreb, 1991-92. Mem. Croatian Pharmacol. Soc. (pres. 1994), Panathlon (v.p. 1994), Lions Club, Rowing Club Jadran (pres. 1988-90). Croatian Peasantry Party. Roman Catholic. Avocations: rowing, fishing, football, philosophy, diplomacy. Home: Trg B Mažuranića 8, 51000 Rijeka Croatia Office: Sch Medicine, Braće Branchetta 20, 51000 Rijeka Croatia

SIMONIS, ADRIANUS JOHANNES CARDINAL, archbishop; b. Lisse, Rotterdam, The Netherlands, Nov. 26, 1931. ordained priest Roman Cath. Ch., 1957. Consecrated bishop Rotterdam, 1971; archbishop Utrecht, 1983; proclaimed cardinal, 1985; pres. Dutch Bishop's Conf. Address: Bishop's Conf, PO Box 13049, 3507 LA Utrecht The Netherlands also: Aartsbisdom, Maliebaan PO Box 13049, NL-3507 Utrecht The Netherlands

SIMONIS, UDO E., environmental educator; b. Hilgert, Germany, Oct. 11, 1937; m. Heide M. Steinhardt, July 26, 1967. MA in Econs., U. Freiburg, Germany, 1963; PhD in Econs., U. Kiel, Germany, 1967. Asst. prof. U. Kiel, Germany, 1964-67; advisor to pres. of Zambia, 1967-69; rsch. fellow U. Tokyo, 1970-71; prof. econs Tech. U. Berlin, 1974-88; vis. prof. The Chinese U., Hong Kong, 1976, 89; prof. environ. policy Sci. Ctr., Berlin, 1988—. Author or editor of 55 books; contbr. 700 articles to profl. jours. and books; mem. editorial bd. Internat. Jour. Social Econs. Mem. bd. trustees German Environ. Found., 1988—; chmn. Com. on Devel. Countries, German Econ. Assn., 1981-85; mem. Com. Devel. of the UN, N.Y.C., 1988—. Recipient Book prize German Employment Agy., Nuernberg, Germany, 1984, Environment prize BAUM, 1998. Mem. World Soc. Ekistics (pres.), German Econ. Assn., European Environ. and Resource Econ. Assn. (editorial bd. Environ. Values Jour.), German Global Change Coun. Avocation: cycling. Home: Klosterufer 2, Bordesholm D 24582, Germany Office: Sci Ctr Berlin, Reichpietschufer 50, Berlin D 10785, Germany

SIMONNEAUX, LAURENCE DELALANDE, biotechnology researcher; b. Mayenne, France, June 4, 1955; d. Paul and Helene (Maisonneuve) D.; m. Jean Simonneaux, Aug. 13, 1976; children: Jeremie, Maeva. MS, U. Rennes, Beaulieu, France, 1977; PhD in Sco. Edn. & Museology, U. Lyon, France, 1995. In charge study CEMAGREF, Rennes, France, 1980-81; tchr. CFTA-Montfort, Le Rheu, France, 1981-89; farmer Bais, France, 1983-89; in charge rsch. Inst. Nat. Promotion Agronomique INSPA, Dijon, France, 1989-92; lectr. Ecole Nat. Formation Agronomique ENFA, Toulouse, France, 1992—. Author: Animal Cloning, 1998, Cloning and Transgenesis from Animal to Human?, 1999, Les Biotechnologies a l'école, 2000; contbr. articles to profl. jours. Mem. European Initiative Biotech. Edn., European Sci. Edn. Rsch. Assn., Learned Soc. Edn. & Mus. Avocations: painting, hiking. Home: 135 La Farguette, 31560 Nailloux France Office: Ecole Nat Formation Agron, ENFA BP 87, 31326 Castanet Tolosan France

SIMONOVSKY, FELIX ISAAK, polymer chemist, researcher; b. Klintsy, Bryansk, Russia, July 6, 1949; came to U.S., 1995; s. Isaak Moishe Koukouy and Shifra Ruva Simonovsky; m. Lydia Paula Zakharov, Aug. 29, 1981; 1 child, Maxim. MChemEngring., Poly. Inst., Vladimir, Russia, 1974; PhD in Chemistry, Inst. Chemistry amd Tech., Gorky, Russia, 1985. Registered sr. rschr. scientist, USSR Govt. Rsch. chemist Inst. Synthetic Resins, Vladimir, Russia, 1978-85; sr. rsch. scientist Polymer Synthesis Inc., Vladimir, 1985-90, sr. assoc. rschr., 1990-95; rsch. scientist U. Wash., Seattle, 1995—; exec. mgr., mem. bd. dirs. Vitur Co., Vladimir; mem. coun. Polymersynthesis Inc., Vladimir, 1990-95; mem. bd. dirs. Vniss Tech. Co., Vladimir, 1988-92. Contbr. articles to profl. jours.; patentee in field. Mem. Am. Chem. Soc., Soc. for Biomaterials. Avocations: singing Vladimir Chamber choir, 1981-92, Seattle Peace Chorus, 1995-98, Seattle Pro Musica, 1997—. E-mail: simonovsky@uweb.engr.washington.edu. Office: U Wash PO Box 351720 Seattle WA 98195-1720

ŠIMONOVSKY, VÁCLAV, radiologist, educator; b. Příbram, Czech Republic, Apr. 8, 1957; s. Václav and Marie (Matejkova) S.; m. Dana Jará, Oct. 6, 1984; 1 child, Martin. MD, Charles U., Prague, Czech Republic, 1983, CSc, 1992. Bd. cert. in radiology, Czech Republic. Resident in radiology Dist. Hosp., Příbram, 1984-97, staff radiologist, 1987-92, head radiologist ultrasound unit, 1994—; rsch. asst. Clinic Imaging Methods, Univ. Hosp. Motol, Prague, 1992-94, sr. radiologist, 1994—; assoc. prof. radiology Charles U., Prague, 1998—. Contbr. articles and abstracts to med. jours., including European Radiology, European Jour. Radiology, Clin. Radiology, Brit. Jour. Radiology, Jour. Ultrasound Medicine, Am. Jour. Roentgenology, Pediatric Radiology. Mem. Radiol. Soc. N.Am., Am. Inst. Ultrasound in Medicine, N.Y. Acad. Scis. Home: U Slávie 34, 263 01 Dobříš Czech Republic

SIMONS, BARBARA M., lawyer; b. N.Y.C., Feb. 7, 1929; d. Samuel A. and Minnie (Mankes) Malitz; m. Morton L. Simons, Sept. 2, 1951; 1 child, Claudia. BA, U. Mich., 1950, JD, 1952. Bar: N.Y. 1953, U.S. Supreme Ct. 1963, U.S. Ct. Appeals (D.C. cir.) 1971, (5th cir.) 1992, (1st cir.) 1994. Ptnr. Simons & Simons, Washington, 1962—. Pres. Forest Hills Citizens Assn., Washington, 1998—; past pres. D.C. chpt. U. Mich. Alumnae, Washington. Alumnae scholar U. Mich., 1946-50. Mem. Washington Coun. Lawyers, Nat. Partnership Women & Families, Sierra Club, Nat. Symphony Orch. Assn., Phi Beta Kappa, Phi Kappa Phi, Alpha Lambda Delta. Office: Simons & Simons 5025 Linnean Ave NW Washington DC 20008-2042

SIMONS, BARRY THOMAS, lawyer; b. Lynn, Mass., Dec. 14, 1946; s. Emanuel Isador and Betty (Darish) S.; m. Laurie Jean Louder, May 5, 1985; children: Britton Eugene, Brett Jacob. BS in Govt., Am. Univ., 1968; JD, NYU, 1971. Bar: Calif. 1971, U.S. Dist. Ct. (ctrl. dist.) Calif. 1972, U.S. Ct. Appeals (9th cir.) 1972, U.S. Supreme Ct. 1978, U.S. Dist. Ct. (so. and no. dists.) Calif. 1979. Pvt. practice Laguna Beach, Calif., 1971—. Editor (law rev.) N.Y. Law Forum, 1971. Apptd. mem. gen. plan revision com. and local coastal task force City of Laguna Beach, 1980. Mem. Orange County Bar Assn. (bd. dirs. 1981), Newport/Harbor Bar Assn. (bd. dirs. 1979), South Orange County Bar Assn. (pres. 1986, bd. dirs. 1980-95), Calif. Attys. for Criminal Justice (chair misdemeanor com. 1995), Nat. Assn. Criminal Def. Attys., Nat. Coll. D.U.I. Def. (founding mem., regent), Assn. Calif. D.U.I. Defenders (bd. dirs.), Deuce Defenders Assn. Fax: 949-497-3971. E-mail: simonslaw@aol.com. Office: 260 Saint Anns Dr Laguna Beach CA 92651-2737

SIMONS, CAROL LENORE, magazine editor; b. Bklyn., Feb. 2, 1942; d. Paul and Grace (Rotwein) Seiderman; m. Lewis M. Simons, Feb. 7, 1965; children: Justine, Rebecca, Adam. BA, Tufts U., 1963; MS, Columbia U., 1964. Rschr. Newsweek mag., N.Y.C., 1964-65, CBS News, N.Y.C. and Saigon, Vietnam, 1967-68; reporter Denver Post, 1965-67; editor Pres. Commn. on Marijuana and Drug Abuse, Washington, 1971-72; assoc. editor Smithsonian mag., Washington, 1978-82; dir. publs. Am. C. of C. in Japan, Tokyo, 1991-96; mng. editor Modern Maturity mag., Washington, 1997—. Office: Modern Maturity 601 E St NW Washington DC 20049-0001

SIMONS, G. WILLY, NATO official; b. Eisden, Belgium, Mar. 23, 1941; m. Monique Simons; 2 children. BS in Social and Mil. Scis., Royal Mil. Acad., 1965; grad., War Coll., 1974. Commd. Belgium Armoured Corps, advanced through grades to lt. gen., 1999, various platoon and squadron leadership positions, 1972-76; with Generalstabslehrgang at Funhrungskademie Belgium Armoured Corps, Hamburg; with Belgian Def. staff Belgium Armoured Corps, 1978-82, chief of personal staff of Belgian Def. staff, 1982-85; comdr. 4th Lancers Regiment SOEST Belgium Armoured Corps, Germany, 1985-87; chief disarmament sect., then chief of br. Belgium Armoured Corps, 1987-92, mil. adviser to Head of Permanent Del. of Belgium to NATO, 1992-93, aide to the King, 1993, comdg. officer Royal Def. Coll., 1994-97, comdr. Gen. Intelligence and Security Svc., 1997-99; perm. rep. of Belgium to NATO Mil. Com. Belgium Armoured Corps, Brussels, 1999—. Office: NATO Hdqrs, Blvd Leopold III, 1110 Brussels Belgium*

SIMONS, KAI LENNART, cell biologist; b. Helsinki, Finland, May 24, 1938; s. Lennart Jacob and Rut Gunhild (Waselius) S.; m. Carola Marita Smeds, June 19, 1965; children: Mikael, Katja, Matias. MD, U. Helsinki, 1964. Postdoctoral fellow Rockefeller U., N.Y.C., 1965-67; researcher U. Helsinki, 1967-75, prof., 1976; group leader European Molecular Biology Lab, Heidelberg, Fed. Republic Germany, 1975—, program coordinator, 1982-97; hon. prof. U. Heidelberg, 1984—; exec. dir. Max Planck Inst. Molecular Cell Biology and Genetics, Dresden, Germany, 1998—; Dunham lectr. Harvard U. Med. Sch., Boston, 1996; Li lectr. U. Calif., Berkeley, 1998. Former editor Jour. Cell Biology; editor: Current Opinion of Cell Biology, 1994—; contbr. over 250 articles to profl. jours. Recipient prize Fedn. European Biochem. Socs., 1975, Jahre prize, 1991. Mem. European Molecular Biology Orgn., Soc. Scientiarum Fennica, Heidelberg Acad. Scis., Acad. Europaea, Am. Acad. Arts and Scis., Nat. Acad. Scis. (U.S.), European Life Scientist Orgn. (pres.), Akademie Leopoldina.

SIMONS, KENETH ALDEN, consultant; b. Phila., Mar. 10, 1913; s. Samuel and Gertrude Winifred (Alden) S.; m. Reta Evens (dec. 1973); children: Kurt Alden, Andri Muth, Dona Vigo; m. Mary Kerr Richey (dec. 1986). BSc in Elec. Engring. with distinction, U. Pa., 1938. Radar-TV field engr. RCA, Camden, N.J., 1938-46; gen. engr. WCAU, Phila., 1941; chief TV instr. Ctrl. Radio Sch., Kansas City, Mo., 1946-49; TV advanced devel. Sylvania, Buffalo, 1950; cons., then chief engr., then v.p. R&D Jerrold Electronics, 1951-76; cons. U. Pa., Phila., 1990—. Author U.S. Navy SYNCHRCS, Technical Handbook for CATV; holder Brit., Can. and U.S. patents; author some 20 tech. mag. articles. Chmn. panel 1 CTAC, Washington, 1973-75. Named CATV Engr. of Yr. NCTA, 1965. Fellow Brit. Soc. Cable Engrs.; mem. IEEE (life), Soc. Cable and TV Engrs. Avocation: skin diving. Home: 2935 Sycamore Rd Huntingdon Valley PA 19006-4811

SIMONS, THOMAS W., JR., history educator; b. Crosby, Minn., Sept. 4, 1938; s. Thomas Winston and Mary Jo (Enochs) S.; m. Margaret Eleanor Quinn, Dec. 23, 1963; children: Suzanne Deirdre, Benjamin Thomas. BA, Yale U., 1958; MA, Harvard U., 1959, PhD, 1963. Joined Fgn. Svc., Dept. State, 1963; sec. del., tech. sec. U.S. Del. to 6th round trade negotiation in GATT, 1964-67; consular officer, polit. officer Am. Embassy, Warsaw, Poland, 1968-71; Coun. on Fgn. Rels. fellow Hoover Instn., Stanford, Calif., 1971-72; internat. rels. officer Bur. Politico-Mil. Affairs, 1972-74, mem. policy planning staff, 1974-75; chief external reporting unit, polit. sect. Am. Embassy, Moscow, 1975-77; dep. chief of mission Am. Embassy, Bucharest, Romania, 1977-79; counselor for polit. affairs Am. Embassy, London, 1979-81; dir. for Soviet Union affairs Dept. State, 1981-85; mem. Sr. Seminar in Fgn. Policy, 1985-86; dep. asst. sec. for European and Can. affairs Dept. State, 1986-89; diplomat-in-residence, adj. prof. history Brown U., Providence, 1989-90; amb. extraordinary and plenipotentiary Poland, 1990-93; coord. U.S. assistance to new ind. states of former Soviet Union, Washington, 1993-95; amb. extraordinary and plenipotentiary, Pakistan, 1995-98; cons. prof. history Stanford U., disting. vis. fellow Hoover, 1998—. Author: The End of the Cold War?, 1990, Eastern Europe in the Postwar World, 2d edit., 1993. Office: Dept History Stanford U Stanford CA 94305-2024

SIMONSSON, ERIK, physician, researcher; b. Båstad, Skåne, Sweden, Nov. 15, 1965; s. Ingemar and Elisabet (Eklund) S. MD, Lund (Sweden) U., 1994, PhD in Internal Medicine, 2000. Rsch. student in medicine Lund U., 1994-2000; physician Univ. Hosp. of Malmoe, Lund U., 2000—. Capt. Swedish Air Force, 1988—; pres. Lund Univ. Postgrad. Student's Union, 1996-98. Home: Jörgen Ankersgatan 20, 21145 Malmö Sweden Office: Lund Univ Malmö U Hosp, Dept Medicine, 20502 Malmö Sweden

SIMONSSON, TOMAS, biochemist; b. Molndal, Sweden, Mar. 23, 1965; s. Jan Erik and Barbro Margareta (Meuller) S.; m. Stina Odén, Sept. 17, 1994; children: Linn, Klara. MSc, Chalmers U., Goteborg, Sweden, 1992, MBA, 1992, PhD, 1998. Biochemist Chalmers U., Gothenburg, Sweden, 1998—. Office: Chalmers Univ Dept Biochem, Medicinaregatan 9, SE-41390 Goteborg Sweden

SIMONYAN, ARMEN ARSCHALUYS, biochemist, researcher; b. Gavar, Armenia, Oct. 15, 1932; s. Arschaluys Gegan and Varduhy Armenak S.; m. Ida Hrant Batikyan, Aug. 15, 1958; 2 children. Degree in bio. scis., Armenia State U., Yerevan, 1958, Armenian Nat. Acad. Scis., Yerevan, 1973. Investigator Inst. Biochem. Armenian Nat. Acad. Scis., 1960, prof. bio. scis., 1973, head dept. embryochem., 1978; head dept. bio. Gavar (Armenia) State U., 1993; prof. intern univ. ecology, politology Armenian Nat. Sect., 1996. Contbr. 250 articles to rsch. publs. Recipient State Prize Laureate, 1968. Mem. Scis. Cncl. Inst. Biochem., Nat. Acad. Scis. Armenia, Gavar State U., Internat. Rsch. Organ Brain (IBRO), European Biochem. Soc., Armenian Biochem. Soc., Russian Acad. Ecology. Office: Inst Biochem Armenian Nat Acad, P Sevak Str 5/1, 375014 Yereven Armenia

SIMONYI, ANDRAS, Hungarian diplomat, NATO official; b. Budapest, 1952; m. Nada Simonyi; 2 children: Daniel, Sonja. Grad., Budapest U. of Econs. Various positions internat. youth work, govt. ofcl. in youth exchange programs; with Am. Coun. of Young Polit. Leaders, West Germany and Italy; with Internat. Dept. Socialist Workers' Pary, Budapest, 1984-88, co-ord. Ctrl.-European Initiative, then asst. to State Sec., 1989-90; dep. chief of Mission for Hungary The Hague, 1990-92; dep. chief of mission for polit. and security affairs Hungarian Mission to NATO and European Cmtys., 1992-95; amb., head of liaison office of Hungary NATO and Western European Union, 1995-97, ambs., head of mission of Hungary, 1997—. Office: NATO Hdqrs, Blvd Leopold III, 1110 Brussels Belgium*

SIMONYI, TAMAS SANDER, banker; b. Budapest, Hungary, Aug. 31, 1957; arrivedin Australia, 1992; s. Imre and Klara (Hoffman) S.; m. Andrea Krizsan, Mar. 15, 1986. MBA, U. Econs., Budapest, Hungary, 1980; postgrad., Chiba (Japan) U., 1988. Asst. mgr. Nat. Bank of Hungary, Budapest, 1981-83; fin. journalist Vilaggazdasag, Budapest, 1983-86; mgr. Tokai Bank, Sydney, Australia, 1988-92; joint gen. mgr. Girocredit, Budapest, 1992-96; gen. mgr. Rabobank, Budapest, 1996—; mng. dir. East-West Investment, Chiba, 1986-88. Contbr. articles to profl. jours. Mem. U.S.-Hungarian C. of C., U.K.-Hungarian C. of C. Avocations: tennis, travel, films. Office: Rabobank Hungaria RT, Madach Imre ut 13-14, 1075 Budapest Hungary

SIMOPOULOS, DIONYSIOS P., planetarium director; b. Gryllos, Ilias, Greece, Mar. 8, 1943; s. Panagiotis D. and Eleni (Demetropoulou) S.; m. Karen L. Peterson, Aug. 17, 1968; children: Eleni, Panagiotis, Vassilis. BA, La. State U., 1968, BS, 1972. Asst. edn. curator La. Arts & Sci. Ctr., Baton Rouge, 1968-69, planetarium dir., 1969-73; planetarium dir. Eugenides Found., Athens, 1973—; pres. Inst. Communication and Devel., Athens, 1991-95; lectr. Ctr. Econ. Rsch., Athens, 1987-95; dir. Ctr. Mgmt. Scis.,

Athens; sci. cons. Hellas TV, Athens, 1981-92. Scriptwriter TV sci. shows ET-1 and ET-2, 1982-96; contbr. articles to profl. jours. Councilman Municipality of Papagos, Athens, 1987-90. Recipient Best Orator award So. Speech Assn., 1965, IPS Svc. award, 1996. Fellow Internat. Planetary Soc. (exec. coun. 1978—), Royal Astron. Soc. U.K.; mem. AIAA, N.Y. Acad. Scis., European-Mediterranean Planetraium Assn. (sec.-gen. 1978-96), European Assn. for Astronomy Edn. (pres. 1994—). Greek Orthodox. Home: 28 Vlahava St, 156-69 Papagou Athens Greece Office: Eugenides Found, 387 Sygrou Ave, 175-64 Athens Greece

SIMOPOULOS, SIMOS EUTHIMIOS, nuclear engineer, researcher, educator; b. Athens, Greece, Apr. 17, 1947; s. Euthimios Simos and Mary Thomas (Souli) S. Diploma Mech. & Elec. Engring., Nat. Tech. U. Athens, 1970; PhD, Imperial Coll. Sci. and Tech., London, 1978; Diploma, Imperial Coll., London, 1978. Rsch. asst. Nat. Tech. U. Athens, 1978-79, rsch. fellow, 1979-82, lectr., 1982-84, asst. prof., 1984-87, assoc. prof., 1987-92, prof., 1992—, chmn. dept. mech. engring., 1999—, vice rector, 2000—; deputy chmn. Dept. Mech. Engring., Nat. Tech. U. Athens, 1993-97; vice chmn. Greek Atomic Energy Commn., Athens, 1996-97. Author: Mechanical Measurements, 1992, Nuclear Reactor Thermohydraulics, 1990; contbr. 60 articles to profl. jours. Sub.-lt. Green Air Force, 1970-73, Athens. Mem. Instn. Nuclear Engrs., N.Y. Acad. Scis. Home: 21 Parmenidou St, 11636 Athens Greece Office: Nat Tech Univ Athens, 15780 Athens Greece

SIMOVSKI, CONSTANTIN RUFOVICH, medical educator; b. Leningrad, Russia, July 12, 1957; s. Ruf Anatolievich and Lubov Pavlovna (Yakhontova) S.; m. Olga Leonidovna Nedol, May 17, 1987; children: Stanislav, July. Engr.-rschr., LPI, Leningrad, 1980, PhD, 1986. Engr., sr. engr. Impulse, Leningrad, 1980-89, head rsch. group, 1989-92; asst. prof. State IFMO, St. Petersburg, Russia, 1992-95; assoc. prof. State IFMO, St. Petersburg, 1995—. Contbr. articles to profl. jours. Mgr. Komsomol, Impulse, Leningrad, 1982-85. Capt. Russian Inf. Res., 1986—. Recipient award Komsomol, 1984; named Soros assoc. prof. ISSEP, 1999; grantee Russian Found. for Basic Rsch. and Others, 1996—. Mem. IEEE. Roman Catholic. Avocations: music. Home: Krasnogo Kursanta 8-30, 197110 St Petersburg Russia Office: State Inst Fine Mechanics, Sablinskaya 14, 197101 St Petersburg Russia

SIMPSON, ALLAN BOYD, real estate company executive; b. Lakeland, Fla., Nov. 24, 1948; s. Alfred Forsythe and Ruth Jeanette (Coker) S.; 1 child, Lauren Leigh. B in Indsl. Ingring., Ga. Inst. Tech., 1970; MBA, U. Pa., 1972. Cert. rev. appraiser; lic. realtor, Ga. Dir. mortgage banking Ackerman & Co., Atlanta, 1972-73; v.p. B.F. Saul & Co., Atlanta, 1973-79; pres. L.J. Hooker, Atlanta, 1979-88; also bd. dirs. Hooker/Barnes, Atlanta; bd. dirs. Hooker Holdings (USA), Inc., Century Ins. Co., Hooker Internat. Devels. Ltd., Hooker Internat. Fin. BV, Charter Credit Corp. Ltd., Simpson Spring, Inc., Strategic Land, Inc., Dunwoody Retail, Inc., 750 Park Ave.; bd. dirs., treas. Midtown Bus. Assn., 1979-88; chmn., CEO The Simpson Orgn., Inc., Coker Capital Corp., 1989—. Bd. dirs. YES Atlanta, 1991—, Atlanta Coll. Art, Theatrical Outfit. Mem. Am. Inst. Indsl. Engrs., MBA Execs. Assn., Bldg. Owners and Mgrs. Assn., Nat. Assn. Realtors, U.S. C. of C., Atlanta C. of C., Internat. Coun. of Shopping Ctrs., Urban Land Inst., Nat. Assn. of Office and Indsl. Pks., Ctrl. Atlanta Progress, Cherokee Town and Country Club, Amelia Island Club, Mystic Krewe of Ga. (capt.), Loch Lomond Golf Club, Pinehurst Country Club. Democrat. Methodist. Home: 750 Park Ave NE Atlanta GA 30326-3266 Office: 600 W Peachtree St NW Atlanta GA 30308-3607

SIMPSON, ANDREA LYNN, energy communications executive; b. Altadena, Calif., Feb. 10, 1948; d. Kenneth James and Barbara Faries Simpson; m. John R. Myrdal, Dec. 13, 1986; 1 child, Christopher Ryan Myrdal. BA, U. So. Calif., 1969, MS, 1983; postgrad., U. Colo., Boulder Sch. Bank Mktg., 1977. Mktg. officer United Calif. Bank, L.A., 1969-73; asst. v.p. mktg. 1st Hawaiian Bank, Honolulu, 1973-78; v.p. corp. comms. Pacific Resources Inc., Honolulu, 1978-89, BHP Hawaii, Inc., 1989-98; v.p. corp. rels. Tesoro Petroleum Corp., San Antonio, 1998-2000; v.p. corp. comms. Edison Internat., Rosemead, Calif., 2000—. Bd. dirs. Arts Coun., Hawaii, 1977-81, Hawaii Art Assn., 1978-83, Coun. Pacific Girls Scouts USA, 1982-85, Child and Family Svcs., 1984-86, Honolulu Symphony Soc., 1985-91, Sta. KHPR Hawaii Pub. Radio, 1988-92, Kapiolani Found., 1990-95, Hanahauoli Sch., 1991-98, Hawaii Strategic Devel. Corp., 1991-98, Children's Discovery Ctr., 1994-98, Pacific Asian Affairs Coun., 1994-96, adv. dir. Hawaii Kids at Work, 1991-98, Hawaii MADD, 1992-96; bd. dirs., 2d v.p. Girl Scout Coun. Hawaii, 1994-96, mem. adv. bd., 1996-98; trustee Hawaii Loa Coll., 1984-86, Kapiolani Women's and Children's Hosp., 1988-97, Hawaii Sch. for Girls at LaPietra, 1989-91, Kapiolani Med. Ctr. at Pali Momi, 1994-98; bd. dirs. Aloha coun. Boy Scouts Am., 1998-2000, Alamo coun., Hawaii Pub. TV, 1998, bd. dirs., San Pedro Playhouse, 1999-2000; bd. dirs. Red Cross of San Antonio, 1999-2000; commr. Hawaii State Commn. on Status of Women, 1985-87, State Sesquecentennial of Pub. Schs. Commn., 1990-91. Named Advt. Women of Yr., Honolulu Advt. Fedn., 1982, Pub. Rels. Profl. of Yr., Honolulu Pub. Rels. Soc., 1993, Communicator of Yr., Utilities Communicators Internat., 1983; recipient Silver Anvil award Pub. Rels. Soc. Am., 1983, 97. Mem. Internat. Pub. Rels. Assn. (Golden World award 1997), Am. Mktg. Assn., Pub. Rels. Soc. Am. (bd. dirs. Honolulu chpt. 1984-86, Silver Anvil award 1984, Pub. Rels. Profl. Yr. 1991, Silver Anvil award of excellence 1996), Utilities Communicators Internat. (Communicator of Yr. 1984), Honolulu Advt. Fedn. (Advt. Woman of Yr. 1984), U. So. Calif. Alumni Assn. (bd. dirs. Hawaii 1981-83), Outrigger Canoe Club, Pacific Club, Rotary (pub. rels. chmn. 1988-97, Honolulu chpt., bd. dirs. 1998), Rotary Club of San Antonio, Alpha Phi (past pres., dir. Hawaii), Hawaii Jaycees (Outstanding Young Person of Hawaii 1978). Office: Edison Internat 2244 Walnut Grove Ave Rosemead CA 91770-3714

SIMPSON, DANIEL H., ambassador; b. Wheeling, W.Va., July 9, 1939; married; 4 children. BA, Yale U., 1961; cert. in African studies, Northwestern U., 1973. Joined Fgn. Svc., U.S. Dept. State, Washington, 1966—, staff asst. Bur. Security and Consular Affairs, 1966-67, speech writer for asst. sec. state for African affairs, 1968, desk officer for Rhodesia, Botswana, Lesotho, and Swaziland, 1973-74; tng. officer USIA, Washington, 1967-68; polit., econ. and consular officer Am. Embassy, Bujumbura, Burundi, 1968-70; polit. officer Am. Embassy, Pretoria, Republic South Africa, 1970-72; dep. chief mission Am. Embassy, Beirut, until 1989; amb. to Cen. African Republic, Bangui, 1989-93; dep. comdr. Army War Coll., Carlisle, Pa., 1993-94; ambassador to Somalia Mogadishu, 1994-95; ambassador to Congo Kinshasa, 1995-98; v.p. Nat. Def. U., Washington, 1998—. Bd. mem. U.S. Inst. Peace; chmn. bd. Nat. Security Edn. Program. Address: Nat Def U 300 5th Ave Washington DC 20319-5066

SIMPSON, DIANE JEANNETTE, social welfare administrator; b. Denver, Sept. 20, 1952; d. Arthur Henry and Irma Virginia (Jordan) S.; 1 child, Shantē N. BS, Nebr. Wesleyan U., 1974; MSW, U. Denver, 1977. Asst. Mile Hi coun. Girl Scouts U.S.A., Denver, 1971-77; social worker asst. Denver Pub. Schs., 1974-75, social worker, 1977—; field instr. Grad. Sch. of Soc. Work, U. Denver, 1984—. Tour leader Kenyan Safari to Kenya, East Africa, 1988. V.p. United Meth. Women, Christ United Meth. Ch., Denver, 1989-91; chmn. Christian action com., 1985-88; active Girl Scouts U.S.A., 1959—; mem. collaborative decision making com. Denver Pub. Schs., 1993-95; mem. Shorter A.M.E. Ch., sr. usher bd. and edn. and scholarship com., 1996—. Mem. NASW, Delta Kappa Gamma. Democrat. Avocations: reading, health and fitness, travel, genealogy. Home: 6865 E Arizona Ave # D Denver CO 80224-1829 Office: Denver Pub Schs 900 Grant St Denver CO 80203-2907

SIMPSON, GEORGE, manufacturing executive; b. July 2, 1942; s. William and Elizabeth S.; m. Eva Chalmers, 1964; 2 children. Student, Morgan Acad., Dundee, Dundee Inst. Tech. Sr. acct. Gas Ind., Scotland, 1962-69; ctrl. audit mgr. BLMC, 1969-73; fin. controller Leyland Truck and Bus divsn., 1973-76; dir. acctg. Leyland Cars, 1976-88; dir. fin. and syss. Leyland Trucks, 1978-80; mng. dir. Coventry Climax Ltd., 1980-83, Freight Rover Ltd., 1983-86; ceo Leyland DAF, 1986-88, mng. dir., 1989-91, chmn., 1991-94, ceo, 1992-94; ceo Lucas Industries plc, 1994-96; mng. dir. Gen. Electric Co. plc, London, 1996—, ceo, 1999—; also bd. dirs.; bd. dirs. Pilkington plc, 1992—, No. Venture Capital, 1992—, Pro Share, 1992—, ICI plc,1995—. Fellow CCA, IMI, CIT; mem. SMMT (mem. exec. com. 1986—, v.p. 1986-95, pres. 1995-96, coun.), Royal Birkdale Golf, Leamington and Country Golf, Wisley Golf, Alyth Golf, Kenilworth RFC. Avocations: golf, squash, rugby. Office: GEC plc, 1 Stanhope Gate, W1A 1EH London England*

SIMPSON, H. RICHARD (DICK SIMPSON), retailer; b. Oct. 10, 1930; s. Bert M. and Violet K. (Mathias) S.; m. Joan Rose Marshall, Mar. 22, 1970; children: Carla Sue, Barry Nelson, Richard Drew, Catherine Irene; m. Charlotte S. Fox, Dec. 12, 1999. Student, U. Akron, 1949-50; BS, U. Md., 1955. Mgr. Tex. GMC, Detroit, 1959-62; pres. Friendly Pontiac, Friendly Toyota, Derrick Chrysler, Simpson Oil Corp., Corp. S., Dick Tiger Homes, Austin, 1962-85, Simpson Hill Country Realty and Builders, 1989-98. Served to lt. col. USAF, 1953-75; Korea. Decorated D.F.C., Air Medal. Mem. Soc. Automotive Engrs., Res. Officers Assn., Horseshoe Bay Yacht Club, Horseshoe Bay Country Club, Rotary Internat., Masons. Methodist. Office: PO Box 8186 Marble Falls TX 78657-8186

SIMPSON, JEROME DEAN, librarian; b. Edmond, Okla., Sept. 25, 1934; s. John Butler and Selma Teresa (Bohlken) S.; m. Kathryn Dale Powers Flobeck, Aug. 17, 1956 (div. Aug. 1970); children: Donald Richard, Jason Bateman. BA in Edn., Cen. State Coll., Edmond, 1956; MLS, U. Okla., 1963. Ref. libr. Cen. State Coll., 1963-65; circulation libr. U. N.Mex., Albuquerque, 1965-68; rsch. libr. U. Ill., Champaign/Urbana, 1968-69; southwest history libr. N.Mex. State Libr., Santa Fe, 1969-72; sr. libr. Libr. for the Blind, Oklahoma City, 1977-91. Editor: newsletter/Libr. for the Blind, Oklahoma City, 1987-91; contbr. articles to profl. jours. Bd. dirs. Common Cause, Oklahoma City, 1992-93, Okla. Homeless Network, Oklahoma City, 1993-96, Downtown Outreach Com., Oklahoma City, 1989-91; southwest regional coord. Unitarian-Universalist Svc. Com., Cambridge, Mass., 1994—. With U.S. Army, 1957-59, Korea. Fellow U. Ill., Champaign/Urbana, 1968-69; named Outstanding Mem. of Yr., 1st Unitarian Ch., Oklahoma City, 1994. Mem. Okla. Libr. Assn., N.Mex. Libr. Assn. Democratic Socialists. Avocation: civic vol. Home: 4853 N Blackwelder Ave Apt 136 Oklahoma City OK 73118-2013

SIMPSON, JOHN ANDREW, lexicographer; b. Cheltenham, Eng., Oct. 13, 1953; s. Robert Morris and Joan Margaret (Sersale) S.; m. Hilary Croxford, Sept. 25, 1976; children: Katharine Jane, Eleanor Grace. BA in English, U. York, Eng., 1975; MA in Medieval Studies, U. Reading, Eng., 1976; LittD, Australian Nat. U., 1999. Mem. editl. staff Supplement to Oxford Eng. Dictionary Oxford (Eng.) U. Press, 1976-85, co-editor Oxford English Dictionary, 1986-93, chief editor Oxford Eng. Dictionary, 1993—; vis. prof. dept. English U. Waterloo, Ont., Can., 1985; cons. Australian Nat. Dictionary, Canberra, 1984-88; mem. faculty of English U. Oxford, 1993—. Coeditor: Oxford Dictionary of Modern Slang, 1992, Oxford English Dictionary Additions Series, vols. 1 and 2, 1993; editor: Concise Oxford Dictionary of Proverbs, 1982, 3d edit., 1998; chief editor Oxford English Dictionary 3d edit. online, 2000—; gen. editor: Oxford English Dictionary Additions Series, vol. 3, 1997; contbr. articles to profl. jours. Kellogg Coll. fellow, Oxford, 1991—. Mem. Philological Soc. Avocation: cricket. Office: Oxford English Dictionary Oxford U Press, Great Clarendon St, Oxford OX2 6DP, England

SIMPSON, JOHN BERCHMAN, JR., clergy member, chaplain, retired law enforcement officer, retired newspaper editor, retired military officer; b. Hartford, Conn., July 18, 1938; s. John Berchman Simpson and Gertrude Elizabeth; m. Yvonne Elaine McGruder, July 2, 1958 (div. Dec. 1978); children: John B. III, Joan B. Gupton, Jeffery Brian, James Bryant, Jason Brent; m. Donna Jean Hadra, Dec. 27, 1978; children: Cheri Lynn DeBolt, Byrl Arthur Gibson, Michele Renee Thacker. BA in Journalism, Bklyn. Coll., 1963; BS in Divinity, Houston Divinity Coll., 1984, DD, 1989. Cert. protection profl., Ariz. Editor USAF, 1956-65; mng. editor Enfield (Conn.) Press, 1967; bur. chief, state editor The Hartford (Conn.) Times, 1965-67; publs. editor Aetna Life & Casualty Co., 1968-69, The Hartford Ins. Co., 1969-70; rewrite editor, svcs. editor The New Haven Register, 1970-73; dir. pub. affairs U.S. Coast Guard Res., New London, Conn., 1970-89; pres. Loss Prevention Inst., Houston, 1980-84; asst. pastor Chapel of Prayer, Houston, 1982-84; officer, chaplain Maricopa County Sheriff's Office, Phoenix, 1985-96; pastor Chapel of Divine Faith, Scottsdale, Ariz., 1996-98; sr. chaplain Ariz. State Vets. Home Adv. Bd., Phoenix, 1998-00. Author: Retail Loss Prevention, 1983; editor The Deputy, 1986. Active Ariz. Zoo Soc., Am. Diabetes Assn., Rep. Presdl. Task Force 2000; merit award sponsor U.S. Olympic Shooting Team; bd. dirs. Maricopa County Dep. Sheriff's Assn., Phoenix, 1986-93, Coun. of Chs., Houston, 1984, Phoenix, 1996; chaplain VA Hosp., Houston, 1980-84; chaplain 396th Aircrw Tng. Squadron, Ariz. N.G., 2000—. Comdr. U.S. Coast Guard Res., 1970-89. Named to Hon. Order of Ky. Cols., 1970, Editor of Yr., Sigma Delta Chi, Hartford, 1966; recipient Medal of Valor, New Haven (Conn.) Police Dept., 1972, Disting. Svc. award VA Hosp., Houston, 1984. Mem. NRA, VFW (post 7968), Caledonian Soc. Ariz., Navy League U.S., Phoenix Coun., Res. Officers Assn. (life, chaplain 1993— chpt. 6, sr. vice comdr. 1999—), U.S. Naval Inst. (life), Soc. Profl. Journalists (Pres.'s Club), Elks (Lodge 2656), Fraternal Order of Police Lodge 5, Am. Legion (life, Aviators Post 743), Ret. Officers Assn. (Superstition Springs chpt.), Diabled Am. Vets. (life, chpt. 8, chaplain 1998—), Scottish Am. Mil. Soc. (Phoenix chpt. #48 chaplain 1999—), 396th Air Crew Tng. Soc., USAF Ariz. Air NG (chaplain 2000—, 396th aircrew tng. sq. USAF/Explorers chaplain 2000—). Republican. Avocations: photography, reading. Home: 6226 E Anaheim St Mesa AZ 85205-8333

SIMPSON, LESLIE AINSLEY, physicist; b. Middlebrough, Cleveland, Eng., July 29, 1947; s. Raymond and Ivy (Ainsley) S.; m. Caroline Mary Bate; children: William Raymond, Mark Ainsley, Rowena Jane. BSc with honors, London U., 1969; PhD, Surrey U., Eng., 1972. Powder tech. Plastic Coatings, Guildford, Eng., 1972-73; researcher Tioxide Group PLC, Cleveland, 1973-74, team leader, 1974-78, sect. mgr., 1978-84, dep. tech. svc. mgr., 1984-88, rsch. mgr., 1988-91, bus. mgr., 1991-93, coatings devel. mgr., 1993-98, European tech. svc. mgr., 1998—. Contbr. articles to profl. jours.; patentee in field. Vice chmn. Normanby Primary Sch. Bd. Govs., Cleveland, 1989, 99. Recipient Roon award, Fedn. Soc. of Coating Tech., U.S., 1981, Venables award, Paint Makers Assn., Eng., 1985. Fellow Oil and Colour Assn.; mem. Paint Rsch. Assn. (chmn. working party 1982-87, bd. dirs.). Anglican. Avocations: tennis, gardening. Office: Huntsman Tioxide Specialties Ltd, Haverton Hill Rd, Billingham TS23 1PS, England

SIMPSON, LINDA ANNE, retired protective services official, municipal official; b. Greensburg, Pa., Oct. 23, 1953; d. Henry Theodore and Marceline (Krempasky) S.; m. Gail Montgomery, Jan. 10, 1977 (div. May 1981); m. Jeri Anne Sheely, July 10, 1981; children: Jessica Ann, Alexander Richard, Allison Dawn. BA, Calif. U. Pa., 1976, 78; cert., Pa. Police Acad., 1978. Asst. security supt. Rouse Svc. Co., Greensburg, 1971-77; asst. police chief Ellsworth (Pa.) Borough Police Dept., 1977-78; police officer Fallowfield Twp. Police Dept., Charleroi, Pa., 1978-80; police detective, trainer, instr., coord. field tng., supr. sex crimes unit Rock Springs (Wyo.) Police Dept., 1980-96, ret., 1996; security officer ACSS Microsoft Co., Redmond, Wash., 199799; control rm. supr. Guardsmark at Microsoft, Redmond, 1999-2000; quality assurance analyst, software test engr. Sierra-On-Line, Bellevue, Wash., 2000—; rsch. asst. centennial com. Rock Springs Police Dept.; police instr. State of Wyo., 1982—; instr. Women's Inst., Western Wyo. Coll., Rock Springs, 1996—, actor, cons. tng. film series theater dept., 1987-88. Editor quar. newsletter Blue Knights News Wyo., 1986-92. Asst. basketball coach Spl. Olympics, Rock Springs, 1987; mem. Sweetwater County Child Protection Team, 1995-96; mem. Domestic Violence Coun., 1995-96, Harry Benjamin Internat. Gender Dysphoria Assn., 1997—, City of Seattle Sexual Minorities Commn., 1996—; regional dir. Transgendered Officers Protect and Serve (TOPS), 1999-2000, web mistress on-line internet mag. and website, 1999-2000; bd. dirs. Ingersoll Gender Ctr., 1999—. Recipient numerous commedations Rock Springs Police Dept., 1980-96, Outstanding Law Enforcement Officer award, 1985, Disting. Svc. medal, 1987, Svc. medal 1988. Mem. Internat. Found. for Gender Edn., Nat. Assn. Field Tng. Officers, Police Protective Assn. (v.p. 1984-85, treas. 1990-94), Western Alliance Police Officers (v.p. 1985-87), Svcs. and Comm. Dirs., Calif. U. Pa. Alumni Assn., Intermountain World War II Reenactment Assn., Shooting Stars Motorcycle Club (pres. 1980-84), Blue Knights Internat. Law Enforcement Motorcycle Club (pres. Wyo. chpts. 1985-92, bd. dirs. Wyo. chpt. 1 1992-96), High Desert Riders, Motorcycle Club (legis. officer 1991-94), Salt Lake Gender Consortium (mem. bd. protectors 1995-96). Avocations: camping, reading, gender studies. Home: 4306 156th Ave NE # FF120 Redmond WA 98052 Office: Sierra On Line 3060 139th Ave SE Ste 500 Bellevue WA 98005

SIMPSON, SANDRA KAY, maintenance management administrator; b. Rutland, Vt., Feb. 26, 1949; d. Freeman Edward and Ruth Gail (Smith) Campbell. BA, U. Vt., 1971; M of Pub. Adminstrn., Troy State U., Europe, 1988, MSc in Internat. Rels., 1991. Isntr., trainer U.S. Govt., Ft. McClellan, Ala., 1975-79; asst. logistics officer U.S. Govt., Kitzingen, Germany, 1979-82; property acctg. officer U.S. Govt., Ft. Hood, Tex., 1982-86, Wiesbaden, Germany, 1986-93; exec. mgmt. asst. Sport and Sound, Mainz Kastel, Germany, 1993-94; maintenance mgmt. coord. U.S. Govt., Wiesbaden, 1994—, dep. dir. internal logistics, 1999; cons. U.S. Govt., Heidelberg, Germany, 1994—. Served with U.S. Army, 1973-93. Mem. Women in Mil. Svc. to Am. Found. (charter mem.), USAREUR Retiree Coun., Wiesbaden/Mainz Retiree Coun. (sec. 1994—), Oxford Club. Avocations: photography, ultra-marathons. Home: Cmr 430 Box 1505 APO AE 09096-1505

SIMPSON, SHANE DAVID, lawyer, educator; b. Auckland, New Zealand, Jan. 22, 1951; arrived in Australia, 1974; s. Alan and Cecilia S.; m. Danielle Rose Michel, Mar. 5, 1983. LLB with honors, U. Auckland, 1973, MJur, 1975. Bar: High Ct. New Zealand 1973, Supreme Ct. Victoria 1976, Supreme Ct. New South Wales 1978. Lectr. U. New South Wales, Australia, 1974-80; dir., founder Arts Law Ctr. Australia, 1981-85; prin. ptnr. Simpsons Solicitors, Sydney, Australia, 1986—; vis. prof., dir. Ctr. for New Technologies, Law & Mgmt., U. Wollongong, Australia, 1994-96; cons. to govt. Australia, 1994, apptd. Cultural Grants Adv. Coun., New South Wales State Govt., 1985-87; bd. Music Coun. Australia, Nat. Assn. Visual Arts; chmn. Mus. and Galleries Found., NSW, 1999—, IPR Sys., 2000—, NSW Film and TV Office, 2000—. Author: Visual Artists and the Law, 1982, 2d edit., 1989, Museums and Galleries: Legal Guide, 1989; co-author: Discovery and Interrogatories, 1984, 2d edit., 1990, Music Business, 1994; contbg. editor: Music: The Business and the Law, 1986. Dir. Australian Exhbns. Touring Agy., Ltd., 1993-96, Crafts Coun. Australia, 1987-92, Copyright Agy. Ltd., 1999—, Nat. Assn. for Visual Arts, 1998—, Music Coun. of Australia, 1998—; trustee Peggy Glanville-Hicks Composers Trust, 1991—, Visual Artists Benevolent Trust, 1986-98, Freedman Found.; apptd. Coun. Sydney Coll. Arts, 1984-87; bd. dirs. Arts Law Ctr. Australia, 1992-97. Mem. ABA, Australian Soc. Authors, Law Soc. of New South Wales, Copyright Soc. of Australia, Soc. for Computers and the Law. Avocations: tennis, fishing, music. Office: Simpsons Solicitors, 135 Macquarie St Ste 1202, 2000 Sydney Australia

SIMPSON, WILLIAM GEORGE, university librarian; b. Liverpool, Eng., June 27, 1945; s. William Anion and Sarah Jane S.; m. Margaret Lilian Pollard, Nov. 2, 1968; children: Nicola Margaret, Fiona Sarah. BA with honors, U. Liverpool, Eng., 1967; MA, U. Dublin, Ireland, 1995. Assoc. Libr. Assn. Gilroy scholar U. Aberdeen, Scotland, 1968; asst. libr. U. Durham, Eng., 1969-73; from asst. libr. to sr. sub-libr. John Rylands U. Libr., Manchester, Eng., 1973-85; libr. U. Surrey, Guildford, Eng., 1985-90; univ. libr. U. London, 1990-94; libr., archivist Trinity Coll., Dublin, Ireland, 1994—; dir. Consortium of Univ. Rsch. Librs., Leeds, Eng., 1993—, IRIS, Dublin, Ireland, 1994—. Author: (monograph) Libraries, Languages and the Interpretation of the Past, 1987. Chmn. Guildford (Eng.) Inst., 1987-90; trustee Worth Libr., Dublin, 1997—. Recipient Jubilee medal Charles U. Prague, 1998. Fellow Royal Soc. Arts, Royal Asiatic Soc. Mem. Anglican Ch. Avocations: astronomy, Everton F.C., genealogy, languages, travel. Office: Trinity Coll Libr, College St, Dublin 2, IRELAND

SIMPSON, WILLIAM KELLY, curator, Egyptologist, educator; b. N.Y.C., Jan. 3, 1928; s. Kenneth Farrand and Helen L.K. (Porter) S.; m. Marilyn E. Milton, June 19, 1953; children: Laura Knickerbacker Simpson Thorn, Abby Rockefeller Simpson Mydland. BA, Yale U., 1947, MA, 1948, PhD, 1954. Asst. in Egyptian art Met. Mus. Art, 1948-54; rsch. fellow Center Middle East Studies, Harvard U., 1957-58; mem. faculty Yale U., New Haven, 1958—; prof. Egyptology Yale U., 1965—, chmn. dept. Near Eastern langs., 1966-69; curator Egyptian and ancient Near Eastern art Mus. Fine Arts, Boston, 1970-86; ltd. partner Kin and Co., 1967-69; ltd. ptnr. Venrock, 1970—; dir. editor of papers Penn-Yale Archaeol. Expdn. to Egypt, 1960—; mem. adv. council fgn. currency program Smithsonian Instn., 1966-69. Author: Papyrus Reisner I-Records of a Building Project, 1963, Hekanefer and the Dynastic Material from Toshka, 1963, Papyrus Reisner II-Accounts of the Dockyard Workshop, 1965, Papyrus Reisner III: Records of a Building Project in the Early Twelfth Dynasty, 1969, The Terrace of the Great God at Abydos, 1974, The Mastabas of Qar and Idu, 1976, The Offering Chapel of Sekhem-ankh-ptah, 1976, The Offering Chapel of Kayemnofnet in the Museum of Fine Arts Boston, 1992, The Inscribed Material from the Pennsylvania-Yale Excavations at Abydos, 1995, (with others) The Ancient Near East, A History, 2d edit., 1998, The Literature of Ancient Egypt, 1972, The Mastaba of Queen Mersyankh III, 1994. Trustee Am. Sch. Classical Studies, Athens, Am. U. in Cairo; mem. internat. council Mus. Modern Art, N.Y.C.; pres. Wrexham Found., 1965-67. Fulbright fellow Egypt, 1955-57; Guggenheim fellow, 1965. Mem. Am. Oriental Soc., Am. Philos. Soc., Archaeol. Inst. Am., Internat. Assn. Egyptologists, Egypt Exploration Soc., Soc. française d'egyptologie, German Archaeol. Inst., Foundation egyptologique Reine Elisabeth. Clubs: Century (N.Y.C.), Met. Opera (N.Y.C.), University (N.Y.C.), Union (N.Y.C.), River (N.Y.C.); Bedford (N.Y.); Golf and Tennis. Home: 129 Katonah Woods Rd Katonah NY 10536-3846

SIMS, ANDREW CHARLES PETTER, psychiatry educator; b. Exeter, England, Nov. 5, 1938; s. Charles Henry and Norah Winnifred Kennan (Petter) S.; m. Ruth Marie Harvey, Apr. 25, 1964; children: David, Mary, John, Ann. BA, Cambridge U., 1960, MB BChir, 1963, MA, 1964, MD, 1974. Prof. psychiatry U. Leeds (England), 1979—. Author 11 books including Psychiatry, 6th edit., 1993, Symptoms in the Mind, 2d edit., 1995, Speech and Language Disorders in Psychiatry, 1995; contbr. articles to profl. jours. Fellow Royal Soc. Medicine, Royal Coll. Psychiatrists (pres. 1990-93), Royal Coll. Physicians (Edinburgh and London), Coll. Physicians and Surgeons Pakistan, Coll. Medicine South Africa; mem. Christian Med. Fellowship, Gen. Med. Coun., Athenaeum. Avocations: walking, gardening, music, theatre. Office: St James U Hosp, Divsn Psychiatry, Leeds LS9 7TF, England

SIMS, CALVIN GENE, journalist; b. Compton, Calif., Dec. 17, 1963; s. Lonnie Gene and Calvina Odessa Sims. BA, Yale U., 1985. Reporter dept. sci. The N.Y. Times, N.Y.C., 1985, reporter dept. bus., 1986-90, reporter met., 1990-92, nat. corr. L.A., 1992-94, fgn. corr. Buenos Aires, 1994-98, fgn. corr. Tokyo, 1999—; editor-in-chief Yale Sci. Mag., New Haven, Conn., 1983-84. Contbr. articles to profl. jours. Recipient Mass Media fellowship AAAS, 1984, Poynter fellowship Poynter Inst., St. Petersburg, Fla., 1985. Mem. Nat. Assn. Black Journalists. Avocations: antique collecting, running, soccer, travel. Office: The NY Times Fgn Desk 229 W 43d St New York NY 10036

SIMS, GEORGE EDWARD, electronics company executive; b. London, Oct. 2, 1938; s. Edward Elliott and Mabel Winifred Sims; m. Brenda Margaret Peace, Sept. 9, 1972. BSc with honors, U. London, 1960. Head of VC10 sys. group Elliott Flight Automation, U.K., 1960-65; mgr. Elliott Med. Automation (GEC), U.K., 1965-71; mng. dir. SB Electronic Sys., Harpenden, Eng., 1971—. Author: (book) Automation of a Biochemical Laboratory, 1972; inventor telepen barcode; patentee in field. Methodist. Office: S B Electronic Sys Ltd, Arden Grove, Harpenden AL5 4SL, England

SIMS, MARK RAYNER, astronomer; b. Bristol, Eng., Feb. 10, 1956; s. Norman William and Sheila Florence (Inglis) S. BSc with 1st class honors, U. Leicester, 1977, PhD, 1982. Rsch. fellow European Space Agy., Holland, 1981-84; rsch. assoc. U. Leicester, 1984-91, rsch. fellow, 1991—; cons. Space Applications Svcs., Belgium, 1988-89. Contbr. articles to profl. jours. Recipient European Space Agy. Team Achievement award, 1983, NASA Group Achievement award, 1991. Fellow Royal Astron. Soc., Brit. Interplanetary Soc. Achievements include active role in 8 space missions with roles from data analysis to launch site operations manager; currently project mgr. for the Beagle 2 Mars Lander.

SIMS, RALPH ERNEST HARPER, renewable energy educator, researcher; b. London, Sept. 9, 1947; arrived in New Zealand, 1971; s. Sydney James Harper and Elizabeth Anne (Bausor) S.; m. Catherine Elisabeth Davison, July 31, 1971; children: Adam James Harper, Miranda Charlotte. BSc, Reading (Eng.) U., 1969; MSc, Newcastle U., Newcastle-Upon-Tyne, Eng.,

1971. Chartered engr. Lectr. Massey U., Palmerston North, New Zealand, 1971-77, sr. lectr., 1978-85, 86-92, prof., 1992—, dir. Ctr. for Energy Rsch.; lectr. U. London, 1977-78; programme mgr. Energy Tech. Support Unit, Harwell, Eng., 1985-86; project mgr. Ctr. for Advanced Engring., Christchurch, New Zealand, 1995-96; convenor New Zealand Sustainable Energy Forum. Joint author: (tng. books) Tractor Facts, 1987; joint author/editor seminar and workshop procs.; lead author intergovtl. panel on climate change third assessment report. Counselor New Zealand Outward Bound Trust, Wellington, 1983-89. Fellow Inst. Agrl. Engrs.; mem. New Zealand Solar Action. Anglican. Avocations: jazz, soccer, cycling, marathons. Office: Massey U, Pvt Bag 11021, Palmerston North New Zealand

SIMSER, JUDITH IRWIN, childhood hearing impairment consultant, therapist; b. Montreal, Que., Can., Aug. 17, 1941; d. Selwyn and Gertrude Florence (Sharp) Irwin; m. Graham Ray Simser; children: Scott Irwin, Blair Mitchell. BEd, McGill U., Montreal, 1963; Edn. of Deaf diploma, Manchester (Eng.) U., 1976. Cert. auditory-verbal therapist. Tchr. Ottawa (Ont., Can.) Sch. Bd., 1963-65; auditory-verbal therapist Children's Hosp. Ea. Ont., Ottawa, 1976, supr. aural habilitation, 1982-95; cons., trainer tchrs. in auditory-verbal therapy Children's Hearing Found., Taipei, Taiwan, 1995—; dir. emeritus, cons. Children's Hearing Found., Taipei, 1996—; bd. dirs. Voice for Hearing Impaired Children, Toronto, Ont., 1985-92, Ctrl. Speech and Hearing Ctr., Winnipeg, Man., Can., 1989—; bd. dirs. Auditory-Verbal Internat., Va., 1986-98, pres., 1989-91. Contbr. articles to profl. jours., chpts. to books. Decorated Order of Ont., 125th Commemorative medal (Can.); recipient Tchr. of Yr. award Internat. Orgn. Eductors Hearing Impaired-Alexander Graham Bell Assn. for Deaf, 1982, Outstanding Achievement award City of Kanata, Can., 1989. Avocations: sports, travel. Home: #4 Chung Yang 9th Rd, Wellington Heights Peitou, Taipei 112, Taiwan Office: Children's Hearing Found, 3F 128 Yu Ming 6th Rd, Taipei 111, Taiwan

SIMSON, PEREGRINE ANTHONY LITTON, solicitor; b. Harlow, Essex, England, Apr. 10, 1944; s. Ernest Clive Litton and Daphne Camilla Marion (Todhunter) S.; m. Caroline Basina Hosier, May 4, 1967 (div. 1979); children: Christian Edward Litton, Camilla Basina Litton. BA, Oxford (England) U., 1963-66. Solicitor Supreme Ct. Eng. and Wales. Ptnr. Clifford-Turner, London, 1972-87, Clifford Chance, London, 1987—. Mem. Law Soc. Eng. and Wales, Honourable Solicitors Co., City of London Solicitors, City Club. Office: Clifford Chance, 200 Aldersgate St, London EC1A 4JJ, England

SIMSON, WILHELM, company executive. PhD in Bio-organic Compounds, U. Munich, 1968. Vis. dir. paint sector ICI Lacke-Farben, Slough, Eng., 1984; exec. dir. paints divsn. ICI, London, 1987; with SKW Trostberg AG, 1989-91, chmn. bd. mgmt., pers. dir., 1991-98; chmn. bd. mgmt. VIAG Aktiengesellschaft, Munich, 1998—; co-chmn. bd. mgmt., co-CEO E. ON AG, Dusseldorf; chmn. supvervisory bd. Bayernwerk AG, SKW Trostberg AG, Th. Goldschmidt AG, Essen, Germany; trustee Chem. Industry Fund, 1994. Mem. Assn. Chem. Industry, Fedn. German Chem. Industry (bd. dirs. 1997, chmn. com. for trade policy 1998—), German Paint Makers' Assn. (pres. 1982-86), others. Office: E ON AG, Bennigsenplatz 1, D-40474 Dusseldorf Germany*

ŠIMUNDŽA, DRAGO, Roman Catholic priest, literature educator; b. Bisko, Croatia, Jan. 20, 1935; s. Jure and Agneza Iva (Banić) Š. Diploma, Faculty of Philosophy, 1967; D of Lit., U. Zagreb, 1975. Prof. lit. Grammar Sch., Split, Croatia, 1969-97; prof. Catechetic-Theol. Inst. and Faculty of Theology, Split, 1980—. rschr. Ch. in the World, Split, 1969-92; adviser Sociol. Inst., Split, 1992-94; councillor U. Split, 1993—. Editor Crkva u svijetu, 1969-92, Future of Religion, 1991-96; contbr. articles to profl. jours. Mem. Soc. of Croatian Writers, European Coun. of Priests, Acad. Soc. Home: Mile Budaka 3, 21000 Split Croatia Office: Archbioshopric of Split, Zrinska 19, 21000 Split Croatia

ŠIMUNEK, ANTONÍN, physicist; b. Prague, Czech Republic, Mar. 24, 1944; s. Antonín and Marie (Pleskotová) Š; m. Marie Vackářová, May 30, 1970; children: Marie, Lucie, Veronika. Diploma in physics, Charles U., Prague, Czech Republic, 1967, RNDr, 1972; PhD in Solid State Physics, Acad. Scis., Prague, 1973. Rschr. Inst. Solid State Physics, Prague, 1973-84; head dept. Inst. Physics, Prague, 1984—, vice dir., 1995-97; vis. prof. Deutsche Forschungsgemeinschaft, Ludwig-Maximilians U., Munich, 1991-93; mem. adv. bd. Charles U., 1991, Tech. U., Prague, 1992—. Contbr. more than 80 articles to sci. jours. Mem. Inst. Physics (U.K.), Union Czech Mathematicians and Physicists, European Phys. Soc., Acad. of Sci. (mem. acad. assembly), Mensa. Roman Catholic. Achievements include research on solid state physics, electron states, x-ray spectroscopy, and ab-initio electronic structure and pseudopotentials. Office: Inst Physics AV CR, Cukrovarnická 10, 162 53 Prague Czech Republic

ŠIMUNEK, JAN EDUARD, veterinary pharmacologist; b. Ústí n. Labem, Czechoslovakia, Jan. 27, 1924; s. Eduard and Juliana (Bayerová) Š.; m. Věra Hloušková, July 31, 1948; 1 child, Jan. DVM, U. Sch. Vet. Medicine, Brno, Czechoslovakia, 1950, PhD, 1964; DSc, U. Sch. Vet. Medicine, Košice, Czechoslovakia, 1976. Asst. lectr., sr. lectr. U. Sch. Vet. Medicine, Brno, 1950, 52-66, head dept. pharmacology, 1961-86, asst. prof. vet. pharmacology, 1966-71, prof. vet. pharmacology, 1972-90; rschr. Inst. State Control Vet. Drugs, Brno, 1990—; cons. various state insts. and rsch. ctrs., Czechoslovakia, 1961—; mem. Czech Pharmacopoetic com., Prague, Czechia, 1961—. Author (mimeographed text) General and Special Pharmacology, 8 edits., 1963-89; co-author: Veterinárna Farmakológia, 1980, Veterinärmedizinische Pharmakologie, 1982, Veterinární Receptář, 4 edits., 1970-93, Lehrbuch der Pharmakologie und Toxikologie für Veterinärmedizin, 1996, Antibiotika, sulfonamidy a chinolony ve veterinarni medicine, 1998; contbr. more than 100 articles to profl. jours. Disting. Mil. Courage medal, Pres. of Czechoslovakia, 1945. Avocations: tourism. Home: Huskova 43, CZ 61800 Brno Czech Republic Office: Inst State Control Vet Drug, Hudcova 56A, CZ 62100 Brno Czech Republic

SIN, JAIME LACHICA CARDINAL, archbishop; b. New Washington, Aklan, The Philippines, Aug. 31, 1928; s. Juan C. and Maxima R. (Lachica) S.; B.S. in Edn., Immaculate Conception Coll., 1959; LL.D. (hon.), Adamson U., 1975, Angeles U., 1978; S.T.D. (hon.), U. Santo Tomas, 1977; L.H.D. (hon.), De La Salle U., 1975; LLD (hon.), Adamson U., 1975. Ordained priest Roman Cath. Ch.; missionary priest Diocese of Capiz, Philippines, 1954-57; first rector St. Pius X Sem., Roxas City, 1957-67; domestic prelate of Pope John XXIII, 1960; titular bishop of Obba, from 1967; aux. bishop of Jaro, from 1967; apostolic adminstr. Sede Plena, archdiocese of Jaro, from 1970; titular archbishop of Massa Lubrense; met. archbishop of Jaro, from 1972; met. archbishop of Manila, 1974—; elevated to Sacred Coll. of Cardinals, 1976; pres. Cath. Bishops' Conf. of the Philippines, 1977; mem. Sacred Congregation for Cath. Edn., 1978—, Sacred Congregation for the Evangelization of Peoples, 1978—; participant Conclave, The Vatican, 1978. Recipient numerous awards and citations, latest being: Real Academia de la Lengua Española award, 1978; Ayuntamiento de Palma de Mallorca, España, award, 1978; Disting. and Meritorious Service award Am. Legion Aux., 1979; Outstanding Citizen's award Manila, 1979. Mem. Synod of Bishops. Author: The Revolution of Love, 1972; The Church Above Political Systems, 1973; A Song of Salvation, 1974; Unity in Diversity, 1974; The Future of Catholicism in Asia, 1978; Christian Basis of Human Rights, 1978; Separation, Not Isolation, 1978; Slaughter of the Innocents, 1979. Office: Arzobispado, 121 Arzobispo St Intramuros POB 132, 1099 Manila The Philippines*

SINACHOPOULOS, DIMITRIS, astronomer, researcher; b. Athens, Greece, Apr. 13, 1951; s. Constantine and Dimitra (Kotsiki) S.; m. Antonia Svarna, Oct. 6, 1974. MSc, U. Athens, 1975; PhD, U. Vienna, Austria. Astronomer U. Bonn, Germany, 1984-88, Royal Belgian Observatory, Brussels, 1989-98, Nat. Observatory of Athens, 1998—; guest prof. astronomy, U. Bordeaux, France, 1995. Contbr. numerous articles to profl. jours. and conf. procs. Sub-lt., Greek Army Res., 1977—. Mem. Internat. Astron. Union, Germany Astronomy Soc., Hellenic Astron. Soc. (founding mem.). Mem. Greek Social Democratic Party. Home: Persepoleso 11, GR-15771 Athens Greece Office: 1 metaxa and Vas Pavlou, Palea Peuteli, GR-15236 Attica Greece

SINAI, ALLEN LEO, economist, educator; b. Detroit, Apr. 4, 1939; s. Joseph and Betty Paula (Feinberg) S.; m. Lee Davis Etsten, June 23, 1963; children: Lauren Beth, Todd Michael. AB, U. Mich., 1961; MA, Northwestern U., 1966, PhD, 1969. From asst. prof. to assoc. prof. econs. U. Ill., Chgo., 1966-75; chmn. fin. info. group, chief fin. economist Data Resources, Lexington, Mass., 1971-83; chief economist, mng. dir. Lehman Bros. and Shearson Lehman Bros. Inc., N.Y.C., 1983-87; chief economist, exec. v.p. The Boston Co. Inc., 1988-93; pres., CEO The Boston Co. Econ. Advisors Inc., Boston and N.Y.C., 1988-93, Econ. Advisors, Inc., Boston, 1993-96; mng. dir., chief global economist, dir. global econs. Lehman Bros., N.Y.C., 1993-96; pres., CEO, chief global economist Primark Decision Econs., Boston, N.Y., London, Tokyo, 1996—; chief global economist, vice-chmn. The WEFA Group, 1997—; cons. Laural Cons., Lexington and Evanston, Ill., 1966; vis. assoc. prof. econs. and fin. MIT, Cambridge, 1975-77; adj. prof. econs. Boston U., 1977-78, 81-83, NYU, 1984-88; adj. prof. econs. and fin. Lemberg Sch., Brandeis U., 1988-95; vis. faculty Sloan Sch., MIT, 1989-91. Contbr. articles to profl. jours. and books. Mem. reducing the fed. budget deficit task force Roosevelt Ctr., Washington, 1984; bd. govs. Com. on Developing Am. Capitalism, 1984-96, chmn., 1990-95; bd. economists Time Mag., 1991—. Recipient Alumnus Merit award Northwestern U., 1985. Mem. Am. Econ. Assn., Econometric Soc., Ea. Econs. Assn. (v.p. 1988-89, pres. 1990-91, Otto Eckstein prize 1988, fellow 1994), Western Econ. Assn. (exec. com.), Econometric Soc., Nat. Assn. Bus. Econs. Jewish. Avocations: tennis; skiing. Home: 16 Holmes Rd Lexington MA 02420-1917 Office: Primark Decision Econs 1 World Trade Ctr Lbby 11 New York NY 10048-0202 also: Primark Decision Econs 260 Franklin St Fl 15 Boston MA 02110-3112

SINAI, YAKOV G., theoretical mathematician, educator; b. Moscow, Sept. 21, 1935. BS, Moscow State U., 1957, Ph.D. in Math., 1960, Doctor Degree, 1963; Dr. Honoris Causa (hon.), Warsaw U., 1993. Sci. rschr. lab. probabilistic and statis. methods Moscow State U., 1960-71; sr. rschr. Landau Inst. Theoretical Physics Acad. Scis., Moscow, USSR, 1971—; prof. math. Moscow State U., 1971-93; prof. math. dept. Princeton (N.J.) U., 1993—; Loeb lectr. Harvard U., 1978; plenary speaker Internat. Congresses Math. Physics, Berlin, 1981, Marseille, 1986, Internat. Congress Math., Kyoto, 1990; disting. lectr., Israel, 1989; S. Lefshetz lectr., Mex., 1990. Recipient Boltzman Gold medal, 1986, Heineman prize, 1989, Markov prize, 1990, Paul Adrian Maurice Dirac medal Internat. Centre for Theoretical Physics, 1992, Wolf Found. prize in Math., 1997. Mem. Am. Acad. Arts and Sci. (fgn. hon.), Russian Acad. Scis., Hungarian Acad. Scis. (fgn.), London Math. Soc. (hon.), Nat. Acad. Scis. of USA (fgn. assoc.), Brazilian Acad. Scis. (fgn.). Office: Princeton University Dept of Mathematics Fine Hall Washington Rd Princeton NJ 08544-0001

SINAISKI, EMMANOUIL GENRICHOVITCH, fluid mechanics educator; b. Kcharkov, Ukraine, Oct. 31, 1940; d. Genrich Emmanoulovitch and Isabelle Savelevna (Vekslarskaya) S.; m. Olga Vladimirovna Vainbaum, Apr. 27, 1962; 3 children. B Mechanics and Math., Moscow State U., 1963, Candidate Sci., 1973; DSc, State Acad. Oil and Gas, Moscow, 1989. Rschr. Acad. Sci. USSR Inst. Mechanics, Moscow, 1963-67, Inst. Electronic Industry, Moscow, 1967-70; rschr., head lab., prof. State Acad. Oil and Gas, Moscow, 1970—. Author: Separation of Two Phase Multicomponent Mixtures in Oil and Gas Production Equipment, 1990, Hydromechanics of Oil Technology Processes, 1992, Hydrodynamics of Physico-Chemical Processes, 1997, Stochastic Methods in Microhydrodynamics, 1998, Statistical Microhydrodynamics, 1999, Separation of Multiphase Multicomponent Systems, 2000. Home: Novokosinskaya St 13-3-145, 111673 Moscow Russia Office: Russian State U Oil and Gas, Leninsky Prospect 65, 117917 Moscow Russia

SINAISKY, NICHOLAS ALEKSEEVICH, mechanical engineer, researcher, consultant; b. Volgograd, Russia, Aug. 10, 1924; came to U.S., 1992; s. Aleksey Ivanovich and Klavdja Stepanovna (Krasukova) S.; m. Elizaveta Agapovna Kargina, Mar. 16, 1962 (div. Nov. 1984); children: Natalia, Nadezda, Julia; m. Valentina Alekseevna Pilgasova Pokrovskaya, Jan. 16., 1985. BME, Tomsk Poly. U., Russia, 1958; MME, USSR Acad. of Sci., Moscow, 1968; PhD in ME, USSR Acad. of Sci., Novosibirsk, Russia, 1980. Sr. designer combustion Siberian Sci. Rsch. Inst. for Aviation, Novosibirsk, Russia, 1958-60; lead engr. Inst. Theoretical and Applied Physics Siberian Dept. of USSR Acad. Sci., Novosibirsk, Russia, 1960-62, sci. worker Inst. for Physics and Chem., 1962-68, sr. rsch. assoc. Inst. for Solid Matter, 1968-74; adj. prof., sr. rsc. assoc. Inst. for Constn. & Clinker, Novosibirsk-Krasnoyarsk, 1974-85; top mgr. in environ. protection Sci. Rsch. Inst. for Energy & Cavitator Enterprise, Baku, Azerbaijan, 1985-92; prin. rschr., cons. Cavitator Internat., Portsmouth, N.H., 1992—. Patentee low temperature plasma and cavitation; contbr. numerous articles to Russian and Am. profl. jours. Polit. prisoner, north camps USSR, 1947-50, Kazakhstan, 1950-54. Recipient Vet. of Labour medal Presidium of the Supreme Ct. of the USSR, 1983, Golden medal and diploma 26th Salon Int. of Inventions, Geneva, Switzerland, 1998; named laureate in ecology Georgia Energo USSR, Tbilisi, 1990. Achievements include work in ballistic missile reentry radiation analysis, demonstrating short wave excitomic decay photoeffect in wide-gap insulators; atomization with atoms/molecules excitation/radiation through plural cumulative shock in spray used by means of cavitator to reduce boiler fouling, NOx/CO/carbon emission and improve fossil fuel saving, including orimulsion. Avocations: walking, reading, tourism. Fax: 603-436-9720. Home and Office: Cavitator Internat 140 Court St S302 Portsmouth NH 03801-4448

SINAMENYE, MATHIAS, Burundi government official. Former gov. Bank of Republic of Burundi, Bujumbra; 2d v.p. Republic of Burundi, Bujumbra, 1998—. Office: Office of Vice President, Bujumbura Burundi*

SINCLAIR, BRUCE DAVID, physics educator; b. Edinburgh, Scotland, Apr. 18, 1961; s. William and Muriel Elma (Bruce) S.; m. Marina Elizabeth Blair, Aug. 17, 1991; children: Callum Dennis, Paul Bruce. BS in Physics with honors, U. St. Andrews, Scotland, 1983, PhD, 1987. Rsch. asst. U. St. Andrews, 1986-89, temp. lectr., 1989, lectr., 1989-96, sr. lectr., 1996—; hon. sec. Inst. Physics Quantum Electronics Group, U.K., 1994-98; local organiser Inst. Physics, U.K., 1991—. Co-editor: Advances in Lasers and Applications, 1999; author: (chpt.) Optoelectronic Devices, 1995; contbr. articles to profl. jours. Hon. pres. Student Vol. Svc., St. Andrews, 1993-2000. Recipient Microchip Laser Rsch. grantee Engring. and Phys. Sci. Rsch. Coun., U.K., 1994, Microchip Laser Rsch. grant Sci. and Engring. Rsch. Coun., U.K., 1990, others, 1990—. Achievements include invention of green microchip laser; (with others) discovery of electromagnetically induced focussing; development of computer aided learning packages "Software Teaching of Modular Physics" and Photonic Software Simulations for Teaching. Avocations: family, tandem, garden, walking. Office: Univ St Andrews, Sch Physics and Astronomy, Saint Andrews KY16 9SS, Scotland

SINCLAIR, CLIVE JOHN, writer, literary editor; b. London, England, Feb. 19, 1948; s. David and Betty (Jacobs) S.; m. Frances Ann Redhouse, Nov. 2, 1979 (dec. July 1994); 1 child, Seth Benjamin. BA, U. E. Anglia, Norwich, Eng., 1969, PhD, 1983. Vis. lectr. U. Calif., Santa Cruz, 1980-81; literary editor Jewish Chronicle, London, 1983-87. Author: Bibliosexuality, 1973, Blood Libels, 1985, Hearts of Gold, 1979, Bed Bugs, 1982, Diaspora Blues, 1987, Cosmetic Effects, 1989, Augustus Rex, 1992, The Lady with the Laptop, 1996, A Soap Opera From Hell, 1998. Bicentennial Arts fellow British Council, 1980, Brit. Libr. Penguin Writers fellow, 1996; named Best of Young British Writers Book Mktg. Council, 1983, Brit. Coun. writer-in-residence U. Uppsala, Sweden, 1988; recipient Somerset Maugham award, 1981, Writing Bursary Arts Council, 1984, Jewish Quar./Wingate award for fiction, 1996, the P.E.N. MacMillan Silver Pen for Fiction, 1996. Fellow Royal Soc. of Literature; mem. Pen Internat. (exec. com. 1985-87). Jewish. Home: 22 Church St, Saint Albans AL3 5NQ, England

SINCLAIR, DAVID GRANT, accountant; b. London, Feb. 12, 1948; s. Leslie and Zena Sinclair; m. Susan Carol Merkin, June 7, 1970; children: Alexander, Julian, Olivia. Sr. ptnr. Sinclair Silverman, London, 1972—; chmn. Motivision Worldwide PLC, London, 1993—; dir. Internet Preferential Plc, 2000—, Motivision Am., Inc., North Miami, 1996—, Auditfree Ltd., London, 1991—, Economic Lifestyle, Ltd, 1995—; forensic acct., London, 1978—. Fellow Inst. Chartered Accts. Jewish. Office: Roman House, 296 Golders Green Rd, London NW11 9PT, England

SINCLAIR, LEON R. (PETE), retired literature educator, writer; b. Boston, Aug. 25, 1935; s. Leon R. and Lina Janet (Coffin) S.; m. Connie Poulsen, June 8, 1963; children: Melanie, Kirk, Summer. Student, Dartmouth, 1954-56, 58; BA, U. Wyo., 1964; PhD, U. Wash., 1971. Instr. U. Wash., Seattle, 1967-68; asst. prof. U. Wyo., Laramie, 1969-71; mem. faculty The Evergreen State Coll., Olympia, Wash., 1971-99; emeritus The Evergreen State Coll., Olympia, 1999—; ranger-in charge mountain rescue Grand Teton Nat. Pk., Jackson's Hole, Wyo., 1960-67; founder, chief guide Jackson's Hole Mountain Guides, 1968-71. Author: We Aspired: The Last Innocent Americans, 1993, Thinking Out Loud Through the American West, 1999. With U.S. Army, 1956-58. Recipient Valor award Dept. of Interior, Washington, 1968. Avocations: running, mountaineering, sailing. E-mail: sinclairp@home.com and sinclaip@elwha.evergreen.edu. Home: 3200 Lilly Rd NE Olympia WA 98506-3064 Office: Evergreen State Coll Lab Ii Olympia WA 98505-0001

SINCLAIR, ROBERT, anesthesiologist; b. Göteborg, Sweden, June 17, 1951; s. John Percival and M.S. Sinclair; m. Suzanne Sinclair, Nov. 27, 1987; children: Charles, Jeanne, Caroline. MD, U. Göteborg, 1977, PhD, 1996; Diploma Tropical Medicine & Hygiene, Karolinska Inst., Stockholm, 1984. Anesthesiologist Mölndal (Sweden) Ctrl. Hosp., 1977-96, adminstrv. dir., 1994—; CEO Internat. Health Ctr., Göteborg, 1990-96; head dept. anesthesia, operation and intensive care Sahlgrenska U. Hosp., Mölndal, 1997—. Author: Health Abroad, 1987. Fellow Royal Soc. Tropical Medicine and Hygiene; mem. Royal Bachelor's Club, Internat. Soc. Travel Medicine, Internat. Assn. Physicians for the Overseas Svcs. Avocations: sailing, tennis, skiing. Office: Sahlgrenska U Hosp, Dept Anesthesiology, S-43180 Mölndal Sweden

SINCLAIR, RODNEY DANIEL, dermatologist, educator; b. Melbourne, Australia, Aug. 3, 1964; s. Henry Wolf and Mirte Maja (Craig) S.; m. Ellen Amanda Williamson, Mar. 18, 1994; children: Eliza Robin, Thomas Francis. MB, BS, U. Melbourne, Australia, 1987. Intern St. Vincent's Hosp., Melbourne, 1988-89; registrar Royal Melbourne Hosp., 1990-91, Slade Hosp., Oxford, Eng., 1991-92; sr. registrar John Radcliffe/Churchill Hosp., Oxford, 1992-93; lectr. Monash U., Melbourne, 1996—; sr. lectr. Melbourne U., 1996—; cons. dermatologist Alfred Hosp., Melbourne, 1996—, Skin and Cancer Found., Melbourne, 1996—, Mercy Hosp. for Women, Melbourne, 1996—. Author: Diseases of the Hair and Scalp, 1999; mem. editl. bd. Clinics in Dermatology Med. Jour., 1997-98; contbr. chpts. to books, more than 50 articles to med. jours. Australian Coll. Dermatologists travelling fellow, 1993. Fellow Australasian Coll. Dermatologists (clin. sec. 1996-98), Am. Acad. Dermatology; mem. Brit. Assn. Dermatologists, Royal Soc. Medicine, Australasian Hair and Wool Rsch. Soc. (pres. 1997-99). Avocations: cricket, chess, Australian rules football. Home: 10 Boston Rand Balwyn, Elsternwick, Melbourne, Victoria 3185, Australia Office: St Vincent's Hosp Dept Derm, 41 Victoria Parade, Melbourne, Victoria 3061, Australia

SINCLAIR, ROGER NEVILLE, brand valuator, educator; b. London, Sept. 20, 1938; arrived in South Africa, 1946; s. Maurice Moss and Doris (Dale) S.; m. Stella Ellen Thorn, Oct. 27, 1960; children: Victoria Loise Thorn, Richard PatrickThorn. MCom, U. Witwatersrand, Johannesburg, South Africa, 1991. Trainee London Press Exch., 1958-62; advt. mgr. Gallaher Internat., U.K., 1962-65; accounts dir. Lindsay Smithers, Cape Town, South Africa, 1965-69; dir. FCB Lindsay Smithers, Johannesburg, 1969-75; mng. dir. Jonsson Advt., Johannesburg, 1975-83; lectr. Witwatersrand U., Johannesburg, 1985—; ptnr. Roger Sinclair Comms., Johannesburg, 1984—; mng. dir. Brand Metrics (Pty) Ltd., 1999—. Author: Make the Other Half Work Too, 1982, 4th edit., 1997, Marketing in Practice, 1987. Recipient Young Exec. award Internat. Advt. Assn., 1965. 67. Mem. Inst. Mktg. Mgmt., Comms. Advt. Mktg. Found., INtenrat. Wine and Food Soc. (chair 1994-98). Avocations: studying, squash, exercise. Home: 33A 12th Ave, 2193 Parrton North Gauteng, South Africa

SINCLAIR, WILLIAM ANGUS, retired economics educator; b. Edinburgh, Scotland, May 30, 1929; arrived in Australia, 1930; s. James and Margaret Cockburn (Porteous) S.; m. Jean Dorothy Parker (dec. Sept., 1991). B. Comm. (hons), U. Melbourne, Australia, 1951; M. Comm., U. Melbourne, 1954; PhD in Econs., Oxford U., Eng., 1958. Lectr. U. Melbourne, 1958-61; sr. lectr. Monash U., Melbourne, 1962-67; reader La Trobe U., Melbourne, 1968-72; prof. Flinders U., Adelaide, Australia, 1973-82; dean Monash U., Melbourne, 1983-92, prof., 1992-95. Author: (book) The Process of Economic Development in Australia, 1976; editor: Australia Economic History Review, 1972-82. Named fellow of the Acad. of Social Scis. in Australia, Canberra, 1971. Avocations: tennis, swimming. Home: 186 George St, Victoria East Melbourne 3002, Australia

SINCLAIR, WILLIAM DONALD, state legislator, former church official; b. L.A., Dec. 27, 1924; s. Arthur Livingston and Lillian May (Holt) S.; m. Barbara Jean Hughes, Aug. 9, 1952; children: Paul Scott, Victoria Sharon. BA cum laude, St. Martin's Coll., Olympia, Wash., 1975; postgrad., Emory U., 1978-79. Commd. 2d lt. USAAF, 1944; advanced through grades to col. USAF, 1970; served as pilot and navigator Italy, Korea, Vietnam, Japan; ret., 1975; bus. adminstr. 1st United Mth. Ch., Colorado Springs, Colo., 1976-85, Village Seven Presbyn. Ch., 1985-87, Sunrise United Meth. Ch., 1987-89; vice chmn. coun. fin. and adminstrn. Rocky Mountain Conf., United Meth. Ch. U.S.A., 1979-83; mem. Colo. Ho. of Reps., Denver, 1996—. Bd. dirs. Chins-Up, Colorado Springs, 1983-86; chmn. bd. dirs. Pikes Peak Performing Arts Ctr., 1985-92; pres. Pioneers Mus. Found., 1985—; Rep. candidate for Colo. State Chmn., 1992-93. Decorated Legion of Merit with oak leaf cluster, D.F.C., Air medal with six oak leaf clusters, Dept. Def. Meritorious Svc. medal, Vietnam Cross of Gallantry with palms; named Legislator of Yr., Colo. Assn. Commerce and Industry, 1998, 99; recipient Guardian Small Bus. award Nat. Fedn. Ind. Bus., 1999, 2000, Frying Pan award Colo. Restaurant Assn., 1999. Fellow Nat. Assn. Ch. Bus. Adminstrn. (nat. dir., regional v.p., v.p. 1983-85, pres. 1985-87, Ch. Bus. Adminstr. of Yr. award 1983, inducted into Hall of Fame 1995), Colo. Assn. Ch. Bus. Adminstrs. (past pres.), United Meth. Assn. Ch. Bus. Adminstrs. (nat. sec. 1978-81), Christian Ministries Mgmt. Assn. (dir. 1983-85), USAF Acad. Athletic Assn., Colorado Springs Country Club, Garden of Gods Club, Met. Club (Denver), Winter Night Club, Rotary (pres. Colorado Springs 1985-86), Order of Daedalians. Home: 3007 Chelton Dr Colorado Springs CO 80909-1008

SINDELKA, JOSEF, postal service and telecommunications administrator; b. Vienna, Austria, May 24, 1938; m. Martina Jammernegg; 1 child, Thomas. Student, Technologisches Gewerbemuseum, Vienna; JD, U. Vienna, 1964. Cert. in gen. mgmt. Engr., mem. bd. Post and Telecomm. Adminstrn., 1957-69, dep. gen. dir., 1985, gen. dir., 1985-96; chmn. bd. dirs. Post and Telecomm. Austria, 1996—; gen. dir. Post and Telecom Austria; with telephone law dept. Gen. Post and Telecomm. Directorate, 1969-75; with dept. 02 Gen. Post Directorate, 1975-79, head dept. 02, 1979-85; sec. to Fed. Min. of Transport, 1977-79; bd. dirs. Austrian Postal Savings Bank. Contbr. articles to specialist jours. Avocations: reading, classical music, sports. Office: Post and Telecom Austria, Postgasse 8-10, A-1010 Vienna Austria*

SINDEN, SIR DONALD ALFRED, actor; b. Plymouth, Eng., Oct. 9, 1923; s. Alfred Edward and Mabel Agnes (Fuller) S.; m. Diana Mahony, May 3, 1948; children: Jeremy, Marc. First appeared on stage in 1942, leading roles in prodns. including There's a Girl in My Soup, 1966, The Relapse, 1967, Twelfth Night, 1969, London Assurance, 1970, An Enemy of the People, 1975, King Lear, 1976, Much Ado About Nothing, 1976, Othello, 1979, Present Laughter, 1980, Uncle Vanya, 1982, School for Scandal, 1983, The Scarlet Pimpernel, 1985, Major Barbara, 1988, Oscar Wilde, 1990, She Stoops to Conquer, 1992, Hamlet, 1994, That Good Night, 1996, Ariadne Auf Naxos, 1997, Quartet, 1999; appeared in 28 films including The Cruel Sea, Doctor in the House. Mem. Leicestershire Edn. Arts Com., London Acad. Music and Dramatic Arts, Fedn. Playgoers Socs. (pres.), Royal Theatrical Fund (pres.), London Appreciation Soc. (v.p.), Garrick Club (trustee), Beefsteak Club, MCC. Avocations: theatrical history, London, architecture, ecclesiology. Home: Rats Castle, London TN30 7HX, England

SINDHU, RAGHUBIR SINGH, chemist, educator; b. Patla, India, July 8, 1950; s. Abhey Ram and Ishwa Kaur Singh; m. Manju Singh, Nov. 17, 1978;

children: Nishant Singh, Neha Singh. BSc, Meerut U., 1970, MSc, 1972; PhD, Delhi U., 1977. Lectr. colls. Meerut U., India, 1976-85; from lectr. to reader NCERT, Amjer, Bhopal, India, 1985—. Author: Analytical Aspects of Hydroxypyridines, 1987, Practical Chemistry XI, 1991, Practical Chemistry XII, 1992, Language of Chemistry, 1999, Reflections on and from Periodic Table, 2000; editl. sec. Oriental Jour. Chemistry, 2000; contbr. 100 articles to profl. jours. Fellow Indian Chem. Soc. (assoc. editor Jour. Indian Chem. Soc. 2000—); mem. Indian Thermal Analysis Soc. Office: Regional Inst Edn, 462013 Bhopal India

SINESHCHEKOV, VITALLY ALEKSEEVICH, biologist, researcher; b. Moscow, July 14, 1939; s. Alexey Davydovich Sineshchekov and Zinaida Ivanovna Sheremet; m. Nataliya Konstantinovna Orlyankina, June 13, 1961; children: Alexey, Helena. MD, M.V. Lomonosov U., Moscow, 1962, PhD, 1970, DSc, 1983. Jr. rsch. scientist M.V. Lomonosov U., Moscow, 1962-73, sr. rsch. scientist, 1973-86, leading rsch. scientist, 1986—, mem. sci. coun. biology dept., 1977, dep. head, chair physico-chem. biology, 1980—; vis. rschr. U. Ill., Urbana, 1967-68; sr. rsch. scientist in biophysics M.V. Lomonosov U., Moscow, 1977; vis. prof. U. Marburg, Germany, 1990, 92, U. Munich, Germany, 1991. Contbr. chpts. to books. Recipient D.A. Sabinin prize M.V. Lomonosov Moscow U., 1999; grantee Internat. Sci. Found., Moscow, 1993-95, Russian Found. for Fundamental Investigation, Moscow, 1993—. Mem. Soc. for Photobiology Presidium. E-mail: v.sineshchekov@mtu-net.ru, vitally@vsineshchekov.home.bio.msu.ru. Home: Prospekt Mira 184 1 22, 129301 Moscow Russia Office: Biology Dept, MV Lomonosov Moscow State U, 119899 Moscow Russia

SINEV, SERGUEI YU, biologist, researcher; b. Leningrad, Russia, Sept. 3, 1956; s. Yuri S. and Natalia I. (Kiseleva) S.; m. Swetlana A. Mironovich, Dec. 2, 1982; children: Galina, Ivan. PhD in Biology/Entomology, St. Petersburg State U., 1978; DSci in Biology/Entomology, Zool. Inst./Russian Acad. Sci., St. Petersburg, 1992; Diploma, Internat. Sci. Found., U.S.A., 1993. Sr. asst. Inst. Plant Protection, Pushkin, Russia, 1980-81; asst. Zool. Inst. Russian Acad. Scis., St. Petersburg, 1981-86, sci. rschr., 1986-92, leading sci. rschr., 1992—. Co-author: Problems of Systematics and Evolution of Insects, 1989, Gall-Producing Insects from the Cultural and Wild Plants, 1991, Insects and Mites--Pests of Agricultural Plants, vol. 1, 1994, vol. 2, 1999, Key to the Insects of Russian Far East, vol. 1, 1997, vol. 2, 1999. Grantee Deutsche Forschungsgemeinschaft, 1994, Prof. Hering Meml. Rsch. Fund, 1997. Fellow Zool. Inst./Sci. Coun.; mem. Russian Entomol. Soc. (mem. coun.), Societas Europaea Lepidopterologica, Sociedad Hispano-Luso Americana de Lepidopterologia. Avocations: construction, travel. Office: Zool Inst Russian Acad Scis, Universitetskaya Nab 1, 199034 St Petersburg Russia

SINGAL, SURESH KUMAR, manufacturing executive; b. Ludmiana, India, Jan. 9, 1968; p. SH B.R. Singal; married. BA, Punjab U., Lydhiana; MBA, Kruksheira U., India, 1993. Owner Shezco Bike Industries, Ludhiana; cons. Avocations: sports, drama, reading. Home: 614 Church Rd, Ludhiana 141 001, India Office: Shezco Bike Industries, D-122(B) Phase V, Ludhiana 141 001, India

SINGARAM, PONNAIYAN, bank officer; b. Coimbatore, Madras, India, Feb. 11, 1949; s. Peter Ponnaiyan and Gowli Angappa; m. Nirmala Devi, June 17, 1977; children: Ilayaraja, Kanimozhi. BS in Agr., Agrl. Coll. Coimbatore, 1971. Dep. mgr. State Bank India, 1989—; agrl. tech. advisor State Bank of India, Ooty, 1977-79. Avocations: educating and encouraging tree planting, writing poetry in Tamil language, social service. Home: 7/7 Balajinagar Ex RN Puran, 641045 Coimbatore Madras, India Office: State Bank India, Sankari, 637301 Sankari Madras, India

SINGER, ALAN EVAN, management educator; b. London, Feb. 14, 1954; s. Ivor Isaac and Helena Joyce (Fry) S.; m. Ming Huang, May 10, 1983; 1 child, Alexander. BA with honors, Oxford U., 1975; BSc with honors, London U., 1980; PhD, U. Canterbury, 1994. Lectr. City of London Polytech., 1977, Emile Woolf & Assoc., London, 1978-81, Victoria U., Wellington, 1982-85; sr. lectr. U. Canterbury, 1985-98, assoc. prof., 1998—; vis. fellow U. Western Australia, Perth, 1990-91, U. Hawaii, 1997, London Sch. Econs., 1997. Author: Strategy as Rationality, 1996, (with Prof. Werhane) Business Ethics, 1999; mem. editl. bd. Human Sys. Mgmt., Jour. Bus. Ethics; contbr. over 90 articles to profl. jours. Mem. Internat. Soc. for Bus. Ethics and Econs., New Zealand Strategic Mgmt. Soc. Office: Univ Canterbury, Christchurch New Zealand

SINGER, ANDREW LAWRENCE, export expansion consultant; b. Quy, Cambridge, Eng., May 12, 1942; s. Charles Herbert and Florence May (Clarke) S.; m. Gloria Ann Williams, June 29, 1974; 1 child, Chloe Ann. MA with honours, Cambridge U., 1964; diploma bus. adminstrn., London Sch. Econs., 1965. Cons. P.A. Internat., London, 1965-69; cons. in export expansion Cambridge, Eng., 1969—. Author: (with Donald B. Keesing) Development Assistance Gone Wrong - Why Support Services Have Failed as Expanded Exports, 1990, How Support Services Can Expand Manufactured Exports, 1990, (with Donald B. Keesing and Paul Hogan) The Role of Support Services of Expanding Manufactured Exports in Developing Countries, 1991. Fellow Inst. Mgmt. Cons. Home and Office: 26 Chesterton Hall Crescent, Cambridge CB4 1AP, England

SINGER, ARMAND EDWARDS, foreign language educator; b. Detroit, Nov. 30, 1914; s. Elvin Satori Singer and Fredericka Elizabeth (Edwards) Singer Goetz; m. Mary Rebecca White, Aug. 8, 1940; 1 child, Fredericka Ann Hill. A.B., Amherst Coll., 1935; M.A., Duke U., 1939, Ph.D., 1944; diplôme, U. Paris, 1939; postgrad., Ind. U., summer 1964. Teaching fellow in sci. Amherst Coll., 1935-36; instr. French and Spanish, part-time Duke, 1938-40; teaching fellow Romance langs. W.Va. U., Morgantown, 1940-41, instr., 1941-47, asst. prof., 1947-55, assoc. prof., 1955-60, prof., 1960-80, prof. emeritus, 1980—, chmn. program for humanities, 1963-72, chmn. dept. integrated studies, 1963, acting chmn. dept. religion and program for humanities, 1973; dir. ann. colloquium on modern lit. and film W.Va. U., Morgantown, 1976-80, 85-86, 96-97, 99—. Author: A Bibliography of the Don Juan Theme: Versions and Criticism, 1954, The Don Juan Theme, Versions and Criticism: An Annotated Bibliography, 1965, Paul Bourget, 1975, The Don Juan Theme: A Bibliography of Versions, Analogues, Uses, and Adaptations, 1993, The Armand E. Singer Tibet, 1809-1975, 1995, supplement, 1998, The Armand E. Singer Nepal, 1772-1961 and Beyond, 1997, The Officials of Tibet, 1999, (with J.F. Stasny) Anthology of Readings: Humanities I, 1966, Anthology of Readings: Humanities II, 1967; editor: West Virginia George Sand Conference Papers, 1981, (with Jürgen E. Schlunk) Martin Walser: International Perspectives, 1987, Doctor Faustus: Archetypal Subtext at the Millennium, 1999; editor W.Va. U. Philol. Papers, 1948-50, 53-55, editor-in-chief, 1951-52, 55—; editor: 1001 Horny Limericks by Ward Marden, 1996; editor, contbr. Essays on the Literature of Mountaineering, 1982; contbr. numerous articles to profl. and philatelic jours. Bd. dirs. Community Concert Assn., Morgantown, 1959-60, Humanities Found. W.Va., 1981-87. Recipient 4th Ann. Humanities award W.Va. Humanities Coun., 1990. Mem. MLA (internat. bibliography com. 1956-59, nat. del. assembly 1975-78), So. Atlantic MLA (exec. com. 1971-74), Am. Assn. Tchrs. Spanish and Portuguese, Am. Philatelic Soc., Nepal and Tibet Philatelic Study Circle (pres. 2000—), Nepal Philatelic Soc., Collectors Club of N.Y., Phi Beta Kappa. Republican. Home: 248 Grandview Ave Morgantown WV 26501-6925

SINGER, DAVID MICHAEL, marketing and public relations company executive; b. Bklyn., Feb. 11, 1957; s. Seymour Allen and Ellen Sybil (Pavnick) S.; m. Pamela Rae Silton, July 20, 1986; children, Max!, Bobby. BA in History, NYU, 1978; MA in Comms., Syracuse U., 1979; MA in Media, New Sch. Social Rsch., 1983; JD, Yeshiva U., 1981. Cons. pub. rels. Burson-Marsteller, N.Y.C., 1979-81, The Haas Group, N.Y.C., 1981-84, Braff & Co., N.Y.C., 1987-89; pub., editor-in-chief Lodestone Pub., N.Y.C., 1984-87; chief oper. officer Pentagon Ltd., N.Y.C., 1989-91; v.p. pub. rels. Braff & Co., N.Y.C., 1991-92; v.p. G.S. Schwartz & Co., N.Y.C., 1993-97; v.p. mktg. comm. Imedia, Morristown, N.J., 1998-99; pres. S&S Mktg. Comms. Inc.; lectr. evening div. NYU, 1982-96; dir. media rels. Braff & Co. Contbr. articles and poems to profl. and consumer jours. and mags. Pres. Jewish Cultural Found., N.Y.C., 1976. Named Mem. of Yr., N.Y. State Kiwanis, 1976, Outstanding Young Man of Am., Jaycees, 1977; recipient Cert. Recognition Am. Film Inst., 1982, ANDY Design award Advt. Club N.Y., 1983, Proclamation Bklyn. Borough Pres., 1987. Mem. Alpha Epsilon Pi (Bro. of Yr. 1976). Avocations: baseball, politics, ping-pong, films, theater.

SINGER, DONALD ROBERT JAMES, medical researcher; b. Forres, Morayshire, Scotland, Aug. 20, 1954; s. Dennis L. and Isabel M. (Brown) S.; m. Fiona Elizabeth Carswell, July 2, 1979; children: Emma, Ramsay, Eleanor. BMed, U. Aberdeen, Scotland, 1975, MB,ChB, 1978, MD, 1995. House physician City Hosp., Aberdeen, 1978-79; sur. house officer Aberdeen Royal Infirmary, 1979, sr. house officer, 1979-81; med. registrar Aberdeen Hosp., 1981-82; renal registrar Hammersmith Hosp., London, 1982-85; rsch. registrar Charing Cross & Westminster Med. Sch., London, 1985-89; hon. sr. registrar St. George's Hosp. Med. Sch., London, 1989-95, sr. lectr. in clin. pharmacology, hon. cons. physician, 1996-98, reader in cardiovasc. pharmacology, 1998—; hon. sr. registrar Harefield Hosp., 1994-95, hon. cons. cardiovascular medicine, 1996—; hon. sr. lectr. Imperial Sch. Medicine Nat. Heart and Lung Inst., Heart Sci. Ctr., Harefield, 1996—. Dep. then assoc. editor European Jour. for Internal Medicine, 1989—; contbr. articles on blood pressure, heart and transplantation to profl. jours. British Heart Found. fellow, 1986-88, 89-93. Fellow Royal Coll. Physicians (U.K.), Brit. Cardiac Soc., Brit. Hypertension Soc., Am. Heart Assn., London Hypertension Soc. (organizing com. 1986—), Med. Soc. London, Med. Soc. Finland (hon.). Avocations: family, music, racket sports, golf. Office: St George's Hosp Med Sch, Cranmer Terrace, London SW17 0RE, England

SINGER, EDWARD NATHAN, radio engineer, consultant; b. Phila., Jan. 20, 1917; s. David and Esther (Levy) S.; (widowed Apr. 1965); 1 child, Gary L.; m. Hilda Gofstein, Sept. 7, 1966. BS, CCNY, 1938; MEE, Polytech. Inst. Bklyn., 1959. Registered profl. engr., N.Y. Electronic scientist Watson Labs., Eatontown, N.J., 1946-48; field engr. FCC, N.Y.C., 1948-54; radio engr. Naval Applied Sci. Lab., N.Y.C., 1954-70, N.Y. Fire Dept., N.Y.C., 1970-85; pvt. practice N.Y.C., 1985—. Author: Land Mobile Radio Systems, 1989, 2d edit. 1994, 20th Century Revolutions in Technology, 1998. Pres. Home Owners Assn., S.I., 1987-88. Capt. USAF, 1941-46, CBI. Fellow Radio Club Am.; mem. IEEE, N.Y. Acad. Scis., Sigma Xi. Jewish. Achievements include patents for pulse statistical distribution analyzer, pulse percent indicator, time controlled switching system, adjustable cam, and automatic peak level indicator system; development of broad band antenna for field intensity meters. Home and Office: 68 Claradon Ln Staten Island NY 10305-2809

SINGER, GEORGE MILTON, clinical psychologist; b. Phila., Oct. 13, 1924; s. Benjamin and Bessie (Podlisker) S.; m. Carol Ann Horton, June 15, 1977; children: Elizabeth Carol, Susan Theresa, Sonnet Marie-Anne. BA, Temple U., 1950, AM, 1952, PhD, 1958. Grad. asst. exptl. psychology lab. Temple U., Phila., 1950-51, grad. asst. psychol. clinic, 1951-53, lectr., 1953-54; chief psychologist Phila. State Hosp., 1953-56; dir. psychol. services Pennhurst State Hosp., Spring City, Pa., 1958-61; clin. psychologist Kern County Mental Health Dept., Bakersfield, Calif., 1961-68; project dir., coordinator Kernview Community Mental Health Ctr., Bakersfield, 1968-70; pvt. practice clin. psychology Bakersfield, 1953—; mem. med. staff Kern View Mental Health Ctr. and Hosp., Bakersfield, Calif., 1988-92; mem. med. staff Meml. Ctr. for Behavioral Health, Bakersfield, 1992-97; affiliated med. staff Hoag Meml. Hosp., Newport Beach, Calif., 1972-73; cons. psychologist Pioneer Cmty. Hosp., 1976-83. Cons. editor Dictionary of Psychology, Corsini, 1999. Mem. Kern County Mental Health Adv. Bd., 1976-83, adv. bd. Patton State Hosp., 1979-85; bd. dirs. Orange County Child Guidance Clinic, 1973-74. Served with USAAF, 1943-46, ETO, MTO. Recipient Service award Psi Chi, 1952, Cert. of Achievement Southeast Pa. Mental Health Assn., 1956. Mem. AAAS, APA, Calif. Psychol. Assn., Am. Soc. Clin. Hypnosis, Kern County Soc. Clin. Psychologists (pres. 1993-94), Kern County Psychol. Assn. (pres. 1968-69), Internat. Soc. Hypnosis, Rotary of Spring City (pres. 1960-61). Home: 1805 Ridgewood Dr Bakersfield CA 93306-3829 Office: 1712 19th St Ste 202 Bakersfield CA 93301-4313

SINGER, J. DAVID, political science educator; b. Bklyn., Dec. 7, 1925; s. Morris L. and Anne (Newman) S.; m. C. Diane Macaulay, Apr., 1990; children: Kathryn Louise, Eleanor Anne. BA, Duke U., 1946; LLD (hon.), Northwestern U., 1983; PhD, NYU, 1956. Instr. NYU, 1954-55, Vassar Coll., 1955-57; vis. fellow social relations Harvard U., 1957-58; vis. asst. prof. U. Mich., Ann Arbor, 1958-60; sr. scientist Mental Health Research Inst. U. Mich., 1960-82, assoc. prof., 1964-65, prof. polit. sci., 1965—, coordinator World Politics Program, 1969-75, 81-90; vis. prof. U. Oslo and Inst. Social Research, 1963-64, 90, Carnegie Endowment Internat. Peace and Grd. Inst. Internat. Studies, Geneva, 1967-68, Zuma and U. Mannheim (W. Ger.), 1976, Grad. Inst. Internat. Studies, Geneva, 1983-84; cons. in field; U. Groningen, The Netherlands, 1991, Nat. Chengchi U., Taiwan, 1998. Author: Financing International Organization: The United Nations Budget Process, 1961, Deterrence, Arms Control and Disarmament: Toward a Synthesis in National Security Policy, 1962, rev. 1984, (with Melvin Small) The Wages of War, 1816-1965: A Statistical Handbook, 1972, (with Susan Jones) Beyond Conjecture in International Politics: Abstracts of Data Based Research, 1972, (with Dorothy La Barr) The Study of International Politics: A Guide to Sources for the Student, Teacher and Researcher, 1976, Correlates of War I and II, 1979, 80, (with Melvin Small) Resort to Arms: International and Civil War, 1816-1980, 1982, Models, Methods, and Progress: A Peace Research Odyssey, 1990, (with Paul Diehl) Measuring the Correlates of War, 1998, (with D. Geller) Nations at War, 1998; monographs; contbr. articles to profl. jours.; mem. editorial bd. ABC: Polit. Sci. and Govt., 1968-84, Polit. Sci. Reviewer, 1971—, Conflict Mgmt. and Peace Sci., 1978—, Etudes Polemologiques, 1978—, Internat. Studies Quar., 1989—, Jour. Conflict Resolution, 1989—, Internat. Interactions, 1989—. With USNR, 1943-66. Ford fellow, 1956; Ford grantee, 1957-58; Phoenix Meml. Fund grantee, 1959,, 1981-82; Fulbright scholar, 1963-64; Carnegie Corp. research grantee, 1963-67; NSF grantee, 1967-76, 1986-89, 1992-94; Guggenheim grantee, 1978-79. Mem. Am. Polit. Sci. Assn. (Helen Dwight Reid award com. 1967, 95, chmn. Woodrow Wilson award com., chmn. nominating com. 1970), Internat. Polit. Sci. Assn. (chmn. conflict and peace rsch. com. 1974—), World Assn. Internat. Rels., Internat. Soc. Polit. Psychology, Internat. Soc. Rsch. on Aggression, Social Sci. History Assn., Peace Sci. Soc., Internat. Peace Rsch. Assn. (pres. 1972-73), Consortium on Peace Rsch., Edn. and Devel., AAAS, Fedn. Am. Scientists (nat. coun. 1991-95), Union Concerned Scientists, Arms Control Assn., Internat. Studies Assn. (pres. 1985-86), Com. Nat. Security, Am. Com. on East-West Accord, World Federalist Assn. Office: U Mich Dept Polit Sci Ann Arbor MI 48109

SINGER, JEFFREY ALAN, surgeon; b. Bklyn., Feb. 2, 1952; s. Harold and Hilda (Ginsburg) S.; m. Margaret Sue Gordon, May 23, 1976; children: Deborah Suzanne, Pamela Michele. BA cum laude, Bklyn. Coll., 1973; MD, N.Y. Med. Coll., 1976. Diplomate Am. Bd. Surgery. Intern Maricopa County Gen. Hosp., Phoenix, 1976-77, resident, 1977-81, mem. teaching faculty, 1981-96; trauma cons. John C. Lincoln Hosp., Phoenix, 1981-83; pvt. practice Phoenix, 1981-87; group pvt. practice Valley Surg. Clinics, Ltd., Phoenix, 1987—, S.W. Surg. Clinics, P.C., Phoenix, 1996-97; sec.-treas. med. staff Humana Desert Valley Hosp., Phoenix, 1987-89, chief surgery, 1985-87, 91-93, exec. com., 1993-95; adj. asst. prof. divsn. clin. edn. Ariz. Coll. Osteo. Med., Midwestern U., 1998—; mem. adj. clin. faculty Kirksville (Mo.) Coll. Osteo. Medicine. Assoc. editor Ariz. Medicine, 1994—. Rep. precinct committeeman, Phoenix, 1986—; bd. dirs. Goldwater Inst. for Pub. Policy Rsch. Fellow ACS, Internat. Coll. Surgeons, Southwestern Surg. Congress, Am. Soc. Abdominal Surgeons; mem. Ariz. Med. Assn. (bd. dirs. polit. com. 1985, chmn. bd. dirs. polit. com. 1991-93, legis. com. 1986—), Maricopa County Med. Soc. (v.p. 1998, bd. dirs. 1998—). Avocations: philosophy, politics, history, travel, underwater sports, writing. Office: Valley Surg Clinics Ltd 16601 N 40th St Ste 105 Phoenix AZ 85032-3353

SINGER, JULIA, mathematician; b. Kolozsvár, Romania, Mar. 4, 1955; arrived in Hungary, 1988; d. Ivan Singer and Irén Kántor; m. Gusztáv Molnár; children: Peter Lukács-Singer, Ilka Molnár. Grad., U. Bucharest, Romania, 1978. Biostatician Inst. for Drug Rsch., Budapest, 1988-93, Chinoin RT, Budapest, 1994—. Mem. Hungarian Soc. for Clin. Biostats. (sec. 1998—). Home: Fecske 8, 2141 Csömör Hungary Office: Chinoin Chem & Pharm Works, To 1-5, 1045 Budapest Hungary

SINGER, MARCUS GEORGE, philosopher, educator; b. N.Y.C., Jan. 4, 1926; s. David Emanuel and Esther (Kobre) S.; m. Blanche Ladenson, Aug. 10, 1947; children: Karen Beth, Debra Ann. A.B., U. Ill., 1948; Ph.D. (Susan Linn Sage fellow), Cornell U., 1952. Asst. in philosophy Cornell U., Ithaca, N.Y., 1948-49; instr. philosophy Cornell U., 1951-52; instr. philosophy U. Wis.-Madison, 1952-55, asst. prof., 1955-59, assoc. prof., 1959-63, prof. philosophy, 1963-92, prof. emeritus, 1992—, chmn. dept. philosophy, 1963-68; chmn. philosophy dept. U. Wis. Center System, 1964-66; dir. pub. lectr. series Royal Inst. Philosophy, London, 1984-85; vis. fellow Birkbeck Coll., U. London, 1962-63; research assoc. U. Calif.-Berkeley, 1969; vis. Cowling prof. philosophy Carleton Coll., Northfield, Minn., 1972; vis. prof. humanities U. Fla., Gainesville, 1975; vis. fellow U. Warwick, 1977, 84-85; vis. Francis M. Bernardin disting. prof. humanities U. Mo., Kansas City, 1979; hon. research fellow Birkbeck Coll., U. London, 1984-85; acad. visitor London Sch. Econs., U. London, 1984-85. Author: Generalization in Ethics, 2d edit., 1971, Verallgemeinerung in der Ethik, 1975; editor: Morals and Values, 1977, American Philosophy, 1986, Reason, Reality, and Speculative Philosophy, 1996, Essays on Ethics and Methods, 2000; contbr. Essays in Moral Philosophy, 1958, Ency. of Philosophy, 1967, Law and Philosophy, 1971, Skepticism and Moral Principles, 1973, Morals and Values, 1977, Acad. Am. Ency., 1982, 84, 89, World Book Ency., 1984, 86, Gewirth's Ethical Rationalism, 1984, Morality and Universality, 1985, American Philosophy, 1986, New Directions in Ethics, 1986, The Handbook of Western Philosophy, 1988, Applying Philosophy, 1988, Moral Philosophy: Historical and Contemporary Essays, 1989, Key Themes in Philosophy, 1990, Essays on Henry Sidgwick, 1992, Ency. of Ethics, 1992, A History of Western Ethics, 1992, Ethics, 1993, Consequentialism, 1993, Cambridge Dictionary of Philosophy, 1995, 99, Biographical Dictionary of Twentieth Century Philosophers, 1996, Pragmatism, Reason, and Norms, 1998; co-editor: Introductory Readings in Philosophy, 2d edit., 1974, Reason and the Common Good, 1963, Belief, Knowledge and Truth, 1970, Legislative Intent and other Essays on Law, Politics and Morality, 1993. Served with USAAF, 1944-45. Am. Philos. Assn. Western Div. fellow, 1956-57; Summer Research grant Social Sci. Research Council, 1958; Guggenheim fellow, 1962-63; Inst. for Research in Humanities fellow U. Wis., 1984. Mem. AAUP, Am. Philos. Assn. (v.p. Western divsn. 1984-85, pres. Ctrl. divsn. 1985-86, bd. officers 1991-94), Royal Inst. Philosophy, Wis. Acad. Scis., Arts and Letters, Sidgwick Soc. (exec. dir.), Phi Beta Kappa, Phi Kappa Phi. Home: 5021 Regent St Madison WI 53705-4745

SINGER, MAXINE FRANK, biochemist, scientific institute executive; b. N.Y.C., Feb. 15, 1931; d. Hyman S. and Henrietta (Perlowitz) Frank; m. Daniel Morris Singer, June 15, 1952; children: Amy Elizabeth, Ellen Ruth, David Byrd, Stephanie Frank. AB, Swarthmore Coll., 1952, DSc (hon.), 1978; PhD, Yale U., 1957, DSc (hon.), 1994; DSc (hon.), Wesleyan U., 1977, U. Md.-Baltimore County, 1985, Cedar Crest Coll., 1986, CUNY, 1988, Brandeis U., 1988, Radcliffe Coll., 1990, Williams Coll., 1990, Franklin and Marshall Coll., 1991, George Washington U., 1991, NYU, 1992, Lehigh U., 1992, Dartmouth Coll., 1993, Harvard U., 1994; PhD honoris causa, Weizmann Inst. Sci., 1995. USPHS postdoctoral fellow NIH, Bethesda, Md., 1956-58; rsch. chemist biochemistry NIH, 1958-74; head sect. on nucleic acid enzymology Nat. Cancer Inst., 1974-79; chief Lab. of Biochemistry, Nat. Cancer Inst., 1979-87, rsch. chemist, 1987-88; pres. Carnegie Inst. Washington, 1988—; Regents vis. lectr. U. Calif., Berkeley, 1981; bd. dirs. Johnson & Johnson; mem. sci. coun. Internat. Inst. Genetics and Biophysics, Naples, Italy, 1982-86. Mem. editorial bd. Jour. Biol. Chemistry, 1968-74, Sci. mag., 1972-82; chmn. editorial bd. Procs. of NAS, 1985-88; author (with Paul Berg) 3 books on molecular biology; contbr. articles to scholarly jours. Trustee Wesleyan U., Middletown, Conn., 1972-75, Yale Corp., New Haven, 1975-90; bd. govs. Weizmann Inst. Sci., Rehovot, Israel, 1978—; bd. dirs. Whitehead Inst., 1985-94; chmn. Smithsonian Coun., 1992-93. Recipient award for achievement in biol. scis. Washington Acad. Scis., 1969, award for rsch. in biol. scis. Yale Sci. and Engring. Assn., 1974, Superior Svc. Honor award HEW, 1975, Dirs. award NIH, 1977, Disting. Svc. medal HHS, 1983, Presdl. Disting. Exec. Rank award, 1987, U.S. Disting. Exec. Rank award, 1987, Mory's Cup Bd. Govs. Mory's Assn., 1991, Wilbur Lucius Cross Medal for Honor Yale Grad. Sch. Assn., 1991, Nat. Medal Sci. NSF, 1992, Pub. Svc. award NIH Alumni Assn., 1995, Vannevar Bush award Nat. Sci. Bd., 1999. Fellow Am. Acad. Arts and Scis.; mem. NAS (coun. 1982-85, com. sci., engring and pub. policy 1989-91, chmn. 1999—), AAAS (Sci. Freedom and Responsibility award 1982), Am. Soc. Biol. Chemists, Am. Soc. Microbiologists, Am. Chem. Soc., Am. Philos. Soc., Inst. Medicine of NAS, Pontifical Acad. of Scis, Human Genome Orgn., N.Y. Acad. Scis. (nat. bd. advs. for biolab). Home: 5410 39th St NW Washington DC 20015-2902 Office: Carnegie Inst Washington 1530 P St NW Washington DC 20005-1933

SINGER, MERTON, engineer; b. Superior, Wis., Aug. 21, 1913; s. Samuel N. and Lena H. (Dorf) S.; m. Jean Helen Eidelberg, Oct. 19, 1941; children: Stephen L., Robert E. BS, U.S. Mil. Acad., 1938; MS, U. Pitts., 1947; postgrad., Wharton Sch., U. Pa., 1955. Registered profl. engr. Commd. 2d lt. U.S. Army, 1938, advanced through grades to col., 1951; various comdg. officer positions U.S. Army, worldwide, 1938-65; chief ops. divsn. Army-Navy petroleum bd. Joint Chiefs of Staff, Washington, 1947-48; army mem. Pacific command Petroleum office, comdr.-in-chief Pacific and Pacific Fleet, Pearl Harbor, 1949-53; prof. mil. sci. and tactics U. Pa., Phila., 1953-56; comdg. officer U.S. Army Petroleum Distbn. Command, Fontainebleau, France, 1956-60; commdr. Ft. Jay, Governors Island, N.Y., 1960-64; ret. U.S. Army, 1965; v.p. and asst. to the pres. United Bd. and Carton Corp., N.Y.C., 1964-70; exec. dir. Rsch. and Devel. Assocs. for Mil. Food and Packaging Systems, N.Y.C., 1970-89; CEO Merton Singer Assocs., San Antonio, Tex., 1989; trustee U.S. Mil. Acad., West Point, N.Y., 1961-67, 68-69. Inventor field method of distilling water, 1942, geologic calculator/U.S., 1950, geologic calculator/internat., 1955; contbr. articles to profl. jours. Founding pres. Jewish Cadet Chapel Fund. Decorated Legion of Merit, Bronze Star, Army Commendation medal, French Croix de Guerre with Palm, 1944, French Order of the Black Star Pres. Charles DeGaulle, 1960; recipient Decoration for Disting. Civilian Svc., Sec. of Army, 1989, Royal Jugoslav Commemorative War Cross, King of Yugoslavia, 1945; named to Hall of Fame, Rsch. and Devel. Assocs. for Mil. Food and Packaging Systems, 1996, European Theater of Ops. Campaign medal with one silver svc. star, Army of Occupation medal with Germany clasp. Mem. Assn. Grads. U.S. Mil. Acad., Mil. Order of World Wars (exec. com. 1960-70), Army Athletic Assn., U. Pitts. Alumni Assn., Masons (pres.), West Point Soc. of N.Y. (bd. dirs. emeritus 1968), Am. Logistics Assn. (pres. Phila. chpt. 1951-52, pres. Orleans France chpt. 1954-55, pres. N.Y.C. chpt. 1960-61), West Point Soc. of South Tex. (bd. dirs. 1972-75), R&D Assoc. (exec. dir. 1969-89, exec. dir. emeritus 1989), Navy Art Inst., Club Giraud. Republican. Jewish. Home: 10119 N Manton Ln San Antonio TX 78213-1932 Office: Merton Singer Assocs 2161 NW Military Hwy San Antonio TX 78213-1877

SINGER, NORBERT, health services professional, education consultant; b. Vienna, Austria, May 3, 1931; arrived in Eng., 1939; s. Salomon and Mina (Korn) S.; m. Brenda Margaret Walter, May 23, 1980. BSc in Spl. Chemistry, U. London, 1951, PhD in Phys. Chemistry, 1954; DSc (hon.), U. Greenwich, London, 1993. Project leader Morgan Crucible Co. Ltd., London, 1954-57; lectr., dept. head No. Polytechnic, London, 1958-70; prof., head dept. life scis. Polytechnic of Cen. London, 1971-74; asst., dep. dir. Polytechnic of North London, 1974-78; dir. Thames Polytechnic, London, 1978-92; vice chancellor U. Greenwich, London, 1992-93; chmn. Oxleas NHS Health Trust, Bexley, 1993—; vis. prof. U. Westminster, 1996. Contbr. articles to profl. jours., including Jour. Chem. Soc. Chmn. Rose Bruford Coll., 1994-99. Decorated comdr. Order Brit. Empire; fellow Queen Mary and Westfield Coll., U. Coll., Northampton. Fellow Royal Soc. Chemistry. Home: Croft Lodge, Bayhall Rd, Tunbridge Wells TN2 4TP, England

SINGER, PIERRE, physician; b. Erstein, France, Dec. 23, 1953; arrived in Israel, 1982; s. Robert and Paulette (Dreyfuss) S.; m. Joelle Eliane Attal; children: Raphael, Nathanael, Binjamin. MD, Strasbourg U., France, 1977. Cert. Bd. Gastroenterology, Bd. Intensive Care. Resident St. Jacques Med. Ctr., Besangon, France; dir. ICU Rabin Med. Ctr., Petah Tikva, Israel, 1995—; v.p. Israel Transplant, 1995-98; head nutrition com. KH Israel, 1996—. Recipient award European Coun. Human Rights, 1981. Jewish. Office: Rabin Med Ctr, Kaplan St, 49100 Petah Tikva Israel

SINGH, ABHA LAKSHMI, geography educator and researcher; b. Lucknow, India, July 6, 1946; parents Narendra Vir and Rama Singh; m. Rana Janardan, June 21, 1967; 1 child. BA, Allahabad (India) U., 1967;

MA, Aligarh (India) Muslim U., 1969, MPhil, 1970, PhD, 1976. Lectr. Aligarh Muslim U., 1978-84, reader, 1985-991, prof. geography, 1991—, chmn. dept. geography, 2000. Author: Economics and Geography of Agricultural Land Reclamation, 1978, The Problem of Wasteland in India, 1984, Aligarh Environment Study, 1993, Agriculture and Rural Geography, 1997, Land Resource Management, 1997, Resource Management, 1999. Avocations: gardening, dogs, listening to music, reading. Home: 3.288 Durga Bari, Marris Rd, 202002 Aligarh India Office: Aligarh Muslim U, Dept Geography, 202002 Aligarh India

SINGH, AJIT, economist; b. Lahore, Punjab, Pakistan, Sept. 11, 1940; s. Gurbachan and Pushpa (Bawa) S. BA, Punjab U., Chandigarh, India, 1958; MA, Howard U., 1960; MA (hon.), Cambridge (Eng.) U., 1965; PhD, U. Calif., Berkeley, 1970. Coll. lectr. Queens' Coll., Cambridge U., 1965, dir. of studies in econs., 1975-94, sr. fellow, 1990—, prof. emeritus, 1995—; Dr. William M. Scholl prof. econs. U. Notre Dame, Ind., 1987—; sr. econ. advisor Ministry of Oil and Natural Resources, Govt. of Mex., 1977-82, Ministry of Planning and Econ. Devel., Dar-es-Salaam, Tanzania, 1981-84; cons. various UN orgns., including ILO, UNCTAD, UNIDO, World Bank. Editor Cambridge Jour. Econs., 1975; author: Takeovers, 1971, Corporate Financial Structures in Developing Countries, 1993; co-author: Growth, Profitability and Valuation, 1968, Economic Crisis in Third World Agriculture, 1993; co-editor: (with C. Howes) Competitiveness Matters, 2000; contbr. articles and tech. papers to profl. jours. Mem. Soc. for Internat. Devel. World Hdqrs., Rome, 1987; mem. panel of eminent persons advising sec. gen. UN Conf. on Trade and Devel., Geneva, 1984. Mem. Royal Econ. Soc., Am. Econ. Assn., European Econ. Assn., European Assn. for Rsch. in Indsl. Econs. (chmn. programme com. 1985). Sikh. Avocations: table tennis, hiking. Home: 15 Westberry Ct Grange Rd, Cambridge CB3 9BG, England Office: Cambridge U, Queens Coll, Cambridge CB3 9ET, England

SINGH, AMOOL RANJAN, psychology educator, academic administrator; b. Varanasi, India, June 17, 1965; s. Tej Bahadur and Shail S.;m. Archana Verma, Apr. 23, 1998. BA in Psycholgy and English Lit., Kanpur (India) U., 1984, MA in Psychology, 1986; MPhil in Med. and Social Psychology, Ranchi (India) U., 1989, PhD in Clin. Psychology, 1991, DLitt, 1998. Chief clin. psychologist, cons. Vidia Sagar Hosp., New Delhi, India, 1990-93; sr. clin. psychologist, cons. Samvedna Psychiat. Clinic, New Delhi, 1993-97; assoc. prof., head Ranchi Inst. Neuro-Psychiat. and Allied Scis., 1997—; cons. UNFPA/UNDP, New Delhi, 1997; project coord. psycho-socio-vocat. rehab. program Ministry of Welfare Govt. of Inida, Internat. Labor Orgn. and UN Devel. Program, 1990-93. Editl. cons. SIS Jour. Mental Health and Projective Psychology, 1996; mem. editl. adv. bd. Jour. Personality and Clin. Studies, India, 2000—; contbr. about 36 articles to profl. jours. Scholarship Dir. Gen. Health Svcs., 1987-89. Fellow Somatic Inkblot Soc.; mem. Indian Acad. Applied Psychology, Indian Hosp. Assn. (exec. mem. Ranchi chpt.), Assn. Clin. Psychologists (Delhi, Best Paper award 1989). Avocations: palmistry, swimming, reading, excursions. Home: Rinpas Campus, Kanke, Ranchi 834006, India Office: Ranchi Inst Neuro-Psychiat, s Kanke, Ranchi 834006, India

SINGH, BAJRANG BALI, chemical company executive; b. Koraun Sultanpur, India, July 14, 1943; s. Shamsher Bahadur and Surya Kali Singh; m. Rajeswari Singh, June 6, 1960. BSc, Allahabad (India) U., 1961, MSc, 1964; PhD in Chem. Scis., Indian Inst. Tech., Kanpur, 1970. Devel. chemist Hindustan Insecticides Ltd., New Delhi, 1974-79; R & D mgr. Govt. Opium and Alkaloids Undertaking, Neemuch, India, 1979-80; rsch. mgr., dep. gen. mgr. R & D Reckitt & Colman, Hosur, India, 1981-87, gen. mgr. R & D, 1988-90, gen. mgr., chem. divsn., 1991-95, R & D dir., South Asia, 1996-97; gen. mgr. R & D, internat. ops. Godrej Hi Care, Bombay, India, 1997—; chmn. pollution control com. Hosur Industries Assn., 1991-95; mem. exec. com. Household Insecticide Mfrs. Assn., Bombay, 1996-97. Contbr. articles to profl. jours. Mem. Am. Chem. Soc., N.Y. Acad. Scis. Avocations: reading nonfiction and biographies, TV, international affairs. Home: Godrej Sara Lee Ltd, Bldg # B-4/1&2, Bombay 400079, India Office: Godrej Hi Care Ltd, Eastern Express Hwy, Pirojshanagar Bombay 400079, India

SINGH, CHANDRA JEET, microbiologist, biotechnologist; b. Firozabad, India, Dec. 1, 1970; s. Shetan and Saroj (Devi) S. BSc, St. John's Coll., Agra, India, 1988, MSc, 1990; PhD, Agra U., India, 1994. JRF U. Grants Commn., New Delhi, India, 1992-93; postdoctoral rsch. fellow St. John's Coll., Agra, 1994-96; asst. prof. Govt. (P.G.) Coll., Morena, India, 1996-98; lectr. K.R. (P.G.) Coll., Mathura, India, 1998—; guest lectr. Inst. of Home Sci., Agra, 1993; hon. vis. prof. St. John's Coll., 1996—. Inventor in field; contrbr. rsch. articles to nat. and internat. jours. Vol. Nature Watch, Mathura Agra, 1998—. Fellow Acad. Plant Scis. India; mem. Assn. Microbiologists of India, Botanical Soc. India, N.Y. Acad. Scis. Avocations: reading, writing, playing cricket, loving animals.

SINGH, GAGAN DEEP, engineering software consultant; b. Ambala City, Haryana, India, May 22, 1972; s. Manjit Singh and Jasbir Kaur (Sarna) Duggal. BSc, D.A.V. Coll., Ambala, India, 1991; BE in Mech. Engring., Thapar Inst. Engrs. & Tech., Patiala, India, 1995. Engr. Engrs. India Ltd., New Delhi, 1995—. Mem. N.Y. Acad. Scis. (membership cert. 1999). Avocations: reading automobile magazines, software development, listening to music. Home: 23 Jupiter Apt D-Block, Vikaspuri, New Delhi 110018, India Office: Engr India Ltd, 1 Bhikaji Cama Pl, New Delhi 110066, India

SINGH, GANGARAM, business educator; b. Unity Village, Guyana, Apr. 12, 1966; s. Akbar and Katie Singh; m. Pamela Kumari Thanik, Aug. 4, 1996; 1 child, Anil Kumar. MBA, U. Toronto, Ont., Can., 1990, MIR, 1994, PhD, 1998. CPM, Human Resource Profl. Assn. Ont. Prof. Case Western Res. U., Cleve., 1997-99, San Diego State U., 1999—. Hindu. Avocations: cricket, writing. E-mail: gangaram.singh@sdsu.edu. Fax: 619-594-3272. Office: Coll Bus Adminstrn 5500 Campanile Dr San Diego CA 92182-0001

SINGH, GARNISH BENEDICT, bishop; b. Lusignan, Demerara, Guyana, Dec. 2, 1927; s. Joseph Alexander and Matilda Amanda (Fredericks) S. Licentiate in Philosophy, Urban U., Rome, 1951, STD, 1957. Ordained priest Roman Cath. Ch., 1954, ordained bishop, 1971. Asst. parish priest Diocese of Georgetown, Guyana, 1957-58, parish priest, 1959-71; aux. bishop of Georgetown, 1971-72, bishop, 1972—; mem. Antilles Episcopal Conf., 1971, Caribbean Conf. of Churches, 1971. Recipient Cacique Crown of Honour Govt. of Guyana, 1993. Address: Bishop's House, 27 Brickdam/PO Box 10720, Georgetown Guyana

SINGH, GAUTAM B., computer science researcher, educator, consultant; b. New Delhi, India, May 7, 1961; came to U.S., 1983; s. Narinder and Harsharan (Kaur) S.; d. Harkirat Kaur, June 19, 1995; children: Kabir, Sukhmani. BTech in Electrical & Computer Engring., Indian Inst. Tech., Kanpur, India, 1983; MS in Computer Sci., Wayne State U., 1985, MS in Computer Engring., 1989, PhD in Computer Engring., 1993. Design engr. View Engring., Simi Valley, Calif., 1985-87; CAD sys. engr. Erie Automation, Troy, Mich., 1989-92; asst. rsch. prof. Wayne State U., Detroit, 1993-95; sr. scientist Nat. Ctr. for Genome Resources, Santa Fe, 1995-97; asst. prof. Oakland U., Rochester, Mich., 1998—; database cons. Daimler Chrysler Corp., Auburn Hills, Mich., 1998; software cons. Bioimage, Inc., Ann Arbor, Mich., 1995; vis. scientist Nat. Libr. Medicine, Bethesda, Md., 1994. Contbr. articles to profl. jours. Mem. IEEE (2nd prize in student paper competition 1983), Assn. Computing Machinery, Soc. Mfg. Engrs. Achievements include establishment of world wide web site that analyses DNA sequences. Office: Oakland U Computer Sci and Engring Rochester MI 48309

SINGH, GOPAL S., ecologist, environmentalist; b. Kolna Chunar, Mirzapur, India, June 9, 1963; s. Ram Surat Singh and Shivpatti Devi. BSc in Botany with hons., Banaras Hindu U., Varanasi, India, 1983; MSc in Botany, Banaras Hindu U., 1986; PhD, Sch. Environ. Scis., Jawaharlal Nehru U., New Delhi, 1993. Jr. rsch. fellow dept. sci. & tech. Govt. of India, New Delhi, 1987-88; jr. rsch. fellow Jawaharlal Nehru U.- U. Grant Commn., New Delhi, 1988-89, sr. rsch. fellow, 1989-92; rsch. asst. Norad Gbpihed, Almora, India, 1993-94, rsch. asst. Envis, 1995, rsch. asst. tropical soil biology and fertility, 1995-96; exec. dir. Ctr. Sustainable Environment and Heritage, New Delhi, 1996—; mem. editl. bd. Himalayan Paryavaran, Sikkim, India, 1997—; mem. mountain forum ICIMOD, Nepal, Kathmandu. Contbr. more than 35 articles to profl. jours. Mem. Nat. Inst. Ecology (life), Indian Sci. Congress Assn. (life), Indian Soc. Tree Scientists (life), Range Mgmt. Soc. India (life). Avocations: hiking, gardening, reading, creative writing, social help. Home: Sector-8 N-289, RK Puram New Delhi 110022, India Office: Ctr Sustainable Environ & Heritage, Sector 8 N-289, RK Puram 110022 New Delhi India

SINGH, GULAB, statistician, accountant; b. Kolana, U.P., India, Oct. 23, 1953; s. R.S. and Shivpatti Devi Singh; m. Sheela Singh, Feb. 25, 1982; children: Shweta, Siris G. BSc, Banaras Hindu U., Varanasi, U.P., 1972, MSc, 1974; PhD, Indian Agrl. Rsch. Inst., New Delhi, 1981. Rsch. officer Planning Commn., New Delhi, 1981-83, mgmt. analyst, 1983-88; under sec. dept. co. affairs Ministry Industry, New Delhi, 1988-91; Indian statis. svc. probationer Ctrl. Statis. Orgn., New Delhi, 1979-81, dy dir., 1991-96, joint dir., 1996-97, dir., 1998—; cons. Inst. Cost and Works Acctg., Calcutta, India, 1989; advisor Nat. Coun. for Ednl. Rsch. and Tng., New Delhi, 1999. Contbr. articles to profl. jours., including Statistician, Statistics and Probability Letters, Econ. and Polit. Weekly, Indian Jour. Labour Econs., Indian Jour. Econs., Manpower Jour., Econ. Jour., Biometrical Jour. Nat. scholar Govt. of Uttar Pradesh, 1968; rsch. fellow Indian Coun. Agrl. Rsch., 1977. Mem. Indian Assn. for Rsch. in Nat. Income and Wealth (joint sec. 1998—), Indian Soc. Agrl. Stats. Avocations: reading, writing. Fax: 091-11-3342384. E-mail: post2gulab singh@hotmail.com. Home: N-289, Sector 8, RK Puram, New Delhi 110 022, India Office: Ctrl Statis Orgn, Parliament St, New Delhi India

SINGH, GURMUKH, physicist, educator, researcher; b. Nanagal Kalan, Punjab, India, Mar. 20, 1949; came to the U.S., 1985; s. Nirmal Singh and Karam Kaur; m. Sumanjeet Kaur, Dec. 25, 1983; children: Harkiran, Mankiran. BSc, Panjab U., Chandigarth, India, 1970, MSc, 1971, PhD, 1979. Asst. prof. Govt. Coll. Men, Chandigarth, 1978-81, Shiwalik Coll., Naya Nangal, India, 1981-82, Guru Nanak Dev U., Amritsar, 1982-85; postdoctoral assoc. SUNY, Buffalo, 1985-94, rsch. asst. prof., 1995—; asst. prof. Erie C.C., Williamsville, N.Y., 1997—; dir. SUNY, Fredonia, 1995—, vis. asst. prof., 1999—. Jr. Rsch. fellow Coun. Sci. and Indsl. Rsch., 1971-73, Dept. Atomic Energy, 1973-75; sr. Rsch. fellow Univ. Grants Commn., 1975-78. Mem. United Univ. Profs., N.Y. State United Tchrs., Am. Fedn. Tchrs., Am. Phys. Soc. Fax: 716-645-2507. Home: 184 Princeton Ave Apt 2 Amherst NY 14226-5031 Office: SUNY Buffalo 239 Fronczak Hall Buffalo NY 14260-1500

SINGH, HARBACHAN, solicter, barrister; b. Klang, Malaysia, Mar. 11, 1939; came to U.S., 1969; s. Kishen Singh and Than Kaur; m. Susil Kaur, Jan. 12, 1963; children: Sukhwant, Ramesh, Praveen. Barrister-at-law, Honorable Soc. Lincoln's Inn, London, 1967; MA, St. John's U., 1981. Police interpreter Royal Malaysian Police, Malaysia, 1957-63; advocate, soliciter Allen & Gledhill Law Firm, Kuala Lumpur, Malaysia, 1967-69; chief of travel UN, N.Y.C., 1969-79, chief of transportation, 1979-90, chmn. hdqrs. com. on contracts, 1990-99; team leader Return of Property from Iraq to Kuwait, Baghdad, Kuwait, 1994-95; sr. exec. officer UN Mission East Timor, 1999; chmn. UN Appointments and Promotion Com., 1978-89; mem. UN Panel of Counsel Joint Appeals bd.; pres. Gateway Improvement Task Force. Home: 19312 Foothill Ave Hollis NY 11423-1259

SINGH, HAUSILA, electronic engineer; b. Varanasi, India, Jan. 25, 1934; s. Shambhoo Sharan and Manica Devi Singh; m. Pratibha Singh, July 8, 1955; children: Usha, Sudhir, Sunanda, Anju. BSc, Banaras Hindu U., Varanasi, 1955, MSc, 1957; MTech, Indian Inst. Tech., Kharagpur, 1959; PhD, U. Manchester Inst. Sci. Tech., Eng., 1971. Lectr. Udai Pratap Coll., Varanasi, 1957-58; scientist Ctrl. Elec. Engring. Inst., Pilani, India, 1960-64, sr. scientist, 1965-73, asst. dir., 1974-86, dep. dir., 1987-93, jt. dir., 1994-95, cons. Instrument and Control, 1995—; cons. UNDP/UNHCR, Hanoi, Viet Nam, 1986, Dept. Electronics, New Delhi, 1980-94, Nat. Phys. Lab., New Delhi, 1991-96; advisor Nat. Sugar Inst., Kanpur, India, 1984-94. Contbr. articles to profl. jours. Pres. CEERI Club, Pilani, 1981-83. UNESCO fellow UNDP, Eng., 1968-71; rsch. grantee Dept. Electronics, 1981-92. Mem. IEEE (sr.), Manchester Inst. Sci. and Tech. Hindu. Avocations: table tennis, religious literature. Fax: 0542-366336. Home: Jarkhore (Baburi), Chandauli (Varanasi) 232102, India

SINGH, HERMANT, lawyer; b. Varanasi, India, Oct. 25, 1959; s. Muni and Ragni (Devi) S.; m. Preetika Aggarwal, Apr. 23, 1985; children: Pallavi, Mahima. BA in History with honors, Ramjas Coll., Delhi (India) U., 1979; LLB, Delhi U., 1982. Assoc. lawyer Anand & Anand Law Firm, Delhi, 1984-89, ptnr., 1989-91; ptnr. Intel Advocare, IPR Law Firm, Delhi, 1991—; spkr. in field. Mem. Intenrat. Bar Assn., LawAsia, South Asian Bar Assn. for Regional Cooperation. Avocations: music, sports, tourism, reading, gardening. Home: F-252 Western Ave, Sainik Farms, New Delhi 110062, India Office: Intel Advocare C-27, Greater Kailash Encave-I, 110048 New Delhi India

SINGH, JAGDISH PRASAD, novelist, retired English educator; b. Mirgunj, Bihar, India, Dec. 31, 1934; s. Khobhari and Sanyukta Singh; m. Krishna Kumari Singh, May 19, 1952; children: Ashok Kumar, Sarita, Namita, Mihir Kumar. BA with honors, Patna (India) Coll., 1953; MA, Patna U., 1955, PhD, 1966. Lectr. Maharaja Coll., Arrah, India, 1956-69; assoc. prof. Magadh U., Bodh Gaya, India, 1969-83, prof., 1984-94, head English dept., 1982-94, chmn. bd. moderators in English, 1982-94; ret., 1994. Author: Curfew, Release, Summer Flowers, Honeycomb, Insider, The Sacred Flame, The White Horse, other novels in Hindi, also short stories; author, editor: Maharoja Coll. Jour., 1957-69. Mem. All India English Tchrs.' Conf. (life), Am. Studies Rsch. Ctr. (life), Beast Fable Soc. Am. Hindu. Avocations: photography, music, travel. Home: East of Anurag Hosp, Bailey Rd, Patna Bihar 801503, India

SINGH, JASVIR, engineering educator; b. Murad Nagar, India, Oct. 31, 1958; s. Santok and Chanan (Kaur) S.; m. Mohinder Kaur; 1 child, Ankur. BE in Elec. Engring, Punjab U., Chandgarh, India, 1981; M Tech. in Systems and Control, P.A. U., Ludhiana, India, 1985; PhD in Electronics Tech., Guru Nanak Dev U., Amritsar, India, 1994. R & D engr. Pb Micro Circuit Rsch. Lab., Ledhira; lectr. dept. electronics Guru Nanak Dev U., Amritsar, 1985, sr. lectr., reader, head, 1999—. Contbr. articles to profl. jours. Mem. IEEE, Inst. Elec. Engrs. U.K., Inst. Elecs. India, IETE, ISTE, CSI, NSI. Avocations: teaching and research. Office: Guru Nanak Dev U, Dept Electronics Tech, Amritsar 143005, India

SINGH, JASWANT, federal official; b. Village Jasol, Rajasthan, India, Jan. 3, 1938; s. Thakur Sardar Singhji. Student, Mayo Coll., Ajmer, Nat. Def. Acad., Khadakvasla, Indian Mil. Acad., Premnagar, Dehra Dun. Commd. Ctrl. India Horse, 1957-66; elected Rajya Sabha, 1980, 9th Lok Sabha, 1989; chmn. parliamentary standing com. on energy; mem. exec. com. Indian Parliamentary Group; elected Eleventh Lok Sabha, 1996; min. fin.; elected Rajya Sabha, 1998; dep. chmn. Planning Commn., 1998—; external affairs min. Contbr. articles to mags., newspapers and jours. Avocations: Equestrian sports, books, music, golf, chess. Office: South Block 11, New Delhi 110 111, India*

SINGH, JYOTI SHANKAR, international organization executive; b. Pathalgaon, India, Apr. 15, 1935; came to U.S., 1972; s. Brijnath Kumar and Tirthmani (Singh) S.; m. Maria Luz Molares, 1962; children: Anil, Rajeev, Ajit. BA, Banaras U., India, 1952, MA, 1954, LLB, 1955; MA, NYU, 1979; D (honoris causa), Internat. Inst. Integration, Bolivia, 1980. Assoc. sec. coordinating secretariat Leiden, The Netherlands, 1960-61, sec. gen. coordinating secretariat, 1961-64; programme cons. Internat. Youth Centre, New Delhi, 1965-66; sec. gen. World Assembly of Youth, Brussels, 1966-72; liaison officer Fund for Population Activities UN, N.Y.C., 1972-73, asst. exec. sec. World Population Yr., 1973-74, dep. chief info. and pub. affairs, 1975-80, chief info. and external rels., 1980-85, dir. info. and external rels., 1986-90; dir. tech. and evaluation div. UN Population Fund, N.Y.C., 1990-95; dep. exec. dir. UN Population Fund, 1995-96; spl. adviser to exec. dir. UNFPA, N.Y.C., 1996-99; pres. Population 2005, 1999—; exec. coord. 23rd spl. session UN Gen. Assembly, 2000; hon. prof. Cen. Am. U., Managua, Nicaragua, 1975; exec. coord. UN Internat. Conf. on Population, 1982-84; exec. coord. Internat. Conf. on Population and Devel., 1992-94; chmn. The Earth Times, 1996-98. Author: Creating a New Consensus on Population, 1998; editor-in-chief Populi, 1980-90. Mem. Soc. for Internat. Devel., U.S. Com. for UNFPA, Population Inst. (dir.). Home: 10 Waterside Plz Apt 26D New York NY 10010-2606 Office: 107 2nd St NE Washington DC 20002-7303

SINGH, KAMESHWAR PRASAD, toxicologist, researcher; b. Bihar, India, Nov. 1, 1951; came to U.S., 1993; s. Narain Prasad and Nagina Prasad Singh; m. Madhu Singh, June 9, 1971; children: Rajesh, Nishi, Neetu. DVM, Rajendra Agrl. U., Pusa, India, 1974; MS in Vet. Sci., Ruhelkhand U., Bareilley, India, 1976; postgrad., All India Sch. Med. Scis., New Delhi, 1988. From jr. sci. asst. to head Divsn. of Preventive Toxicology & Environ. Microbiology, Indsl. Toxicology Rsch. Ctr., Lucknow, India, 1977-92; rsch. assoc. Inst. Chem. Toxicology/Wayne State U., Detroit, 1993—; cons. Indsl. Toxicology Rsch. Ctr., Lucknow, 1988-92; mem. hosp. equipment sect. com. Bur. Indian Standard, New Delhi, 1991-92. Author: (books) Advances in Medical Mycology, 1992, Chemical Pollution in Environment, 1995; editl. bd. various scientific jours.; contbr. numerous articles to profl. jours. UCLA postdoctoral fellow, 1988, Raman Rsch. fellow coun. of sci. and indsl. rsch. Govt. India, New Delhi, 1988. Mem. AAAS. Achievements include first to discover n-hexane metabolite hexanediol and hexanedione suppress immune function of the body well before producing neuropathy in exptl. model; used bacterial protein A for protection from toxic and carcinogenic chemicals and cytotoxic anticancer drugs. Home: 11942 Frazho Rd Warren MI 48089-1267 Office: Inst Chem Toxicology Wayne State Univ 2727 2nd Ave Detroit MI 48201-2671

SINGH, KARUN KANT, scientist; b. Hudahudipur, Varanasi, India, July 1, 1946; s. Bikrama and Ramakesha Singh; m. Kamala Singh, June 11, 1973; children: Geeta, Jaya, Jitendra. BSc Ceramic Engring., Banaras Hindu U., Varanasi, India, 1969; MSc Ceramic Engring., B.H.U., Varanasi, India, 1971, PhD Ceramic Engring., 1978. Scientist B Nat. Metall. Lab., Jamshedpur, India, 1972-77; scientist C Nat. Metall. Lab., Jamshedpur, 1977-83, scientist E1, 1983-88, scientist EII, 1988-94, scientist F, 1994—. Contbr. articles to profl. jours. Fellow Indian Inst. Ceramics (life); mem. Indian Ceramic Soc. (life, refractory technologist award 1997), Material Rsch. Soc. India (life), Indian Inst. of Mineral Engrs. Achievements include 6 patents in field. Office: Nat Metallurg Lab, FRP Divsn, Jamshedpur 831007, India

SINGH, KEHAR, physicist, educator; b. Haraula, India, July 3, 1941; s. Harbans and Prahladvati (Tanwar) S.; m. Indira Chaudhary, Apr. 24, 1974; children: Ruchi, Komudi, Mayank. BSc, Meerut (India) Coll., 1962, MSc in Physics, 1964; postgrad. diploma in applied optics, Indian Inst. Tech., Delhi, 1965. Assoc. lectr. Indian Inst. Tech., Delhi, 1965-66, lectr., 1967-73, asst. prof., 1974-83, prof. physics, 1984—, head dept. physics, 1996-99. Contbr. over 300 articles to profl. jours. Fellow Optical Soc. Am., Optical Soc. India (pres. 1991-94), SPIE; mem. Internat. Soc. Optical Engrs. Avocation: reading legal literature. Office: Indian Inst Tech, Hauz Khas, New Delhi 110016, India

SINGH, KRISHAN PAL, horticulturist; b. Hasanpur Kaddim, Meerut, India, July 1, 1960; s. Ram Pal and Jalvatri Devi S.; m. Kamlesh Kumari, Mar. 7, 1988; 1 child, prachi. BS, Meerut U., India, 1980, MS in Hort., 1983, MPhil in Hort., 1984, PhD in Hort., 1990. Scientist Indian Coun. Agrl. Rsch., Indian Inst. Hort. Rsch., Bangalore, 1986-91, sr. scientist, 1991—. Author: Tuberose Cultivation, 2000; contbr. 125 articles to profl. jours. Hindu. Avocations: reading, walking, friends. Office: Divsn Floriculture & Landscaping, Indian Agrl Rsch Inst, New Delhi 110012, India

SINGH, LAIKANGBAM JANMEJAY, botany educator; b. Imphal, Manipur, India, July 1, 1937; s. Laikangbam Parikshit Singh and Irengbam Chandramukhi Devi; m. Laikangbam Rashmani Akham, Nov. 23, 1962; four children. Degree in Intermediate Sci., D.M. Coll., Imphal, India, 1956, BSc, 1958; MSc, Gauhati U., Guwahati, India, 1961, PhD, 1970. Lectr. botany D.M. Coll., Imphal, 1961-72, sr. lectr. botany, 1972-73; asst. prof. Jawaharlal Nehru U. Imphal Campus, New Delhi, 1973-82; assoc. prof. Manipur U., Imphal, 1982-84, prof., 1984-97, ret., 1997, prof., 1997—; coord. nomenclature in botany lang. cell dept. Govt. Manipur, Imphal, 1987—; pres. Internat. Soc. Plant Physiologists for South Asian Assn. for Regional Cooperation Countries, Ahmedabad, India, 1995—. Chief editor Frontier Botanist India. Bd. mem. Manipur Wildlife, Forest Dept. Govt. Manipur, Imphal, 1990—. Fellow Internat. Soc. for Krishna Consiousness (life), Indian Soc. for Plant Physiology (life, pres. 1987-88, 88-89), Indian Bot. Soc. (life, Vishambhar Puri medal 1997), Manipur Bot. Soc. (pres. 1985-86), N.Y. Acad. Sci.; mem. Indian Sci. Congress (life), Manipur Hort. Soc. Avocations: gardening, painting, social service, enjoying TV and radio.

SINGH, MAHARAJ KUMAR MANVIJAI, property, industry and business executive; b. Dumraon, Bihar, India, Dec. 24, 1957; s. Maharaja Bahadur Kamal Singh and Maharani Usha Rani; m. Arunima Jamwal, Nov. 24, 1986; children: Aakriti, Rohini. Higher Secondary in Arts, Mayo Coll., Ajmer, India, 1975; student, Fergusson Coll., Pune, India, 1975-78. Naturalist, tour operator Tiger Tops Pvt. Ltd., Chitawan, Nepal, 1980-82; mgmt. trainee Dumraon (India) Industries Pvt. Ltd., 1983-84, dir., 1984-96, mng. dir., 1996—; mng. dir. Dumraon Properties & Enterprises Pvt. Ltd., 1985—; dir. Dumraon Cold Storage Refrigeration Svcs. Pvt. Ltd., 1986-96, mng. dir., 1996—; ptnr. Qutab Stud & Agr. Farm, Delhi, 1982-96, Dumraon Petrol Sta., 1985—, Buxar Petrol Sta., 1985—; propr. Dumraon Poultry Farm, 1990—, Dumraon Farm, Gadaipur, Delhi. Trustee D.R. Charitable Trust, Dumraon, D.R. Hosp. Trust, Dumraon, D.R. Temples Trust. Mem. NRA India, Lions (charter pres. 1994-95, eye camps 1995—), Bombay Natural History Soc. (life). Avocations: wildlife photography, nature, camping, fishing, travelling. Fax: 91 06185 42747. Home: Bhojpur House, Dumraon Buxar, India 802136

SINGH, MAHENDRA KUMAR, chemist; b. Dibai, India, Jan. 1, 1930; arrived in Germany, 1958; s. Thakur Karan and Jai Devi (Kunwar) S.; m. Ute Bentel, Oct. 7, 1966; children: Manoj, Sanjiv. MSc, Agra (India) Coll., 1949; Dr rer. nat., U. Hamburg, Germany, 1963. Lectr. B.N.S.D. Coll., Kanpur, India, 1951-52; scientific asst. Def. Rsch. Labs., Kanpur, 1952-58, British Petroleum Hamburg, 1958-60; rsch. scholarship U. Hamburg, 1960-63; rsch. asst. Med. Coll., Hamburg, 1963-74; officiating head Dept. of Microbiology and Blood Bank, Gen. Govt. Hosp., 1974-78; product mgr., head Blood Bank, Hamburg, 1978-92; prof. tchg. Hindi, indology dept. U. Kiel, 1997-99. Author: Haemophilia, 1971; contbr. articles to profl. jours. Pres. Deutsch-Indisch Kultur, Hamburg, 1963-66, Kiwani Internat. Club, Hamburg, 1991-92. Nehru scholarship Govt. of India in Delhi for Germany, 1958; scholarship Friedrich-Ebert-Stiftung, Germany, 1960, Coun. of Europe Med. Com., 1976. Mem. Internat. Soc. Blood Transfusion, German Soc. Blood Transfusion and Immunohematology. Achievements include development in blood group serology in practical field; research in relation between F VIII and ATP-ase system thrombocytes, HLA-monospecific rare antiserum, protein analysis for FVIII in hemophilic patients. Home: Brookring 18, 22889 Tangstedt Hamburg, Germany

SINGH, MALVINDER, financial executive; b. Jullundur, Punjab, India, Aug. 28, 1951; arrived in U.K., 1992; s. Dilbagh and Jeeri Dilbagh (Kaliana) S.; m. Sadhana Dutt, July 15, 1972; children: Pavani, Shiv, Bharat. B of Commerce with honors, Delhi (India) U., 1972; MBA, Rutgers U., 1973. Exec. trainee Shri Ram Industries, 1972; acct. Ford Motor Co., Mahwah, N.J., 1973-74; sr. fin. analyst Personal Products Co. Johnson & Johnson, New Brunswick, N.J., 1974-76; gen. mgr. Som Datt Builders, Baghdad, Iraq, 1976-78; mng. dir. Sitac Ltd., London and Baghdad, 1978-92; chmn., mng. dir. Muddy Fox Ltd., London, 1992—; founder 247xtreme.com. Fellow Inst. of Motor Industry. Sikh. Avocations: music, golf, traveling, contemporary art of India. Office: 233-236 Nestles Ave, Middlesex Hayes UB34Y, England

SINGH, MANMOHAN, orthopedic surgeon, educator; b. Patiala, Punjab, India, Oct. 5, 1940; came to U.S., 1969; s. Ajmer and Kartar (Kaur) S.; m. Manjit Anand, Jan. 1, 1974; children: Kirpal, Gurmeet. MB, BS, Govt. Med. Coll., Patiala, 1964; MSurgery, Panjab U., Chandigarh, India, 1968. Diplomate Am. Bd. Orthopaedic Surgery. Mem. vis. faculty Mayo Grad. Sch., Rochester, Minn., 1969; rsch. fellow Inst. Internat. Edn., Chgo., 1969-74; resident in orthopedic surgery Michael Reese Hosp. and Med. Ctr., Chgo., 1974-78; pvt. practice, Chgo., 1979—; mem. attending staff, dir. orthopedic rsch. Michael Reese Hosp. and Med. Ctr., Chgo., 1979-94; fellow

in orthopedic oncology Mayo Clinic and Mayo Found., Rochester, 1979; assoc. prof. U. Ill., Chgo., 1996—; founder Quantum Health Cir./Enterprises for Holistic Medicine. Developer x-ray method (Singh Index) and bone density method (Radius Index) for diagnosis of osteoporosis. Fulbright travel grantee, 1968. Fellow Am. Acad. Orthop. Surgeons, Am. Orthop. Foot and Ankle Soc.; mem. Orthop. Rsch. Soc., Am. Soc. for Bone and Mineral Rsch., Internat. Bone and Mineral Soc. Democrat. Sikh. Avocations: stamp collecting, photography, tennis. Office: 443 E 31st St Chicago IL 60616-4051

SINGH, MAYA SHANKAR, chemistry educator, researcher; b. Varanasi, India, Feb. 6, 1960; s. Raja and Pyari Singh; m. Meera Singh, June 22, 1985; 1 child. BSc, Gorakhpur U., India; MSc, B.H. U., Varanasi, PhD; DSc, Vikram U., Ujjain, India. Jr. rsch. fellow Coun. for Sci. and Indsl. Rsch., New Delhi, 1983-85, sr. rsch. fellow, 1985-86, postdoctoral fellow, 1986-87; lectr. chemistry Vikram U., 1987-92, sr. lectr., 1992-97, assoc. prof., 1997—; assoc. prof. DDU Gorakhpur U., India. Contbr. articles to sci. jours., including Indian Jour. Chemistry. Program officer Nat. Svc. Scheme, Ujjain, 1996. Recipient young scientist award Coun. for Sci. and Indsl. Rsch., 1997; fellow Indian Nat. Sci. Acad., 1998. Fellow Indian Chem. Soc., Indian Coun. Chemists, Indian Sci. Congress. Mem. B.J.P. Party. Hindu. Avocations: reading, research, swimming, photography, writing. Home: 3G New Flats Hirapuri, colony Univ Campus, MP Gorakhpur 273 009, India Office: Dept Chemistry, DDU Gorakhpur U., UP Gorakhpur 273 009, India

SINGH, MONA, engineering consultant, adult education educator; b. Delhi, India; d. S.S. and Mohinder Kaur Narang; m. Munindar Paul Singh. MA, Jawaharlal Nehru U., New Delhi, 1988; PhD, U. Tex., 1990, MA, 1994. Tech. staff mem. Microelectronics and Computer Tech. Corp., Austin, Tex., 1992-95; rsch. scientist Dragon Sys., Newton, Mass., 1995-97; sr. staff engr. Ericsson Inc., RTP, N.C., 1997-99, cons. engr., 1999—; adj. asst. prof. N.C. State U., Raleigh, 1995—. Inventor, patentee in field. E-mail: mona.singh@ericsson.com. Fax: (919) 472-1561.

SINGH, NARINDER KUMAR, management educator, advisor; b. Lahore, India, Aug. 15, 1937; s. Thakur Prakash Chander and Saraswati Devi; m. Raj SIngh, Apr. 13, 1966; children: Apurva, Amit. BA (hons.), New Delhi Univ., 1957, MA in psychology, 1960. Dir. Steel Authority of India Ltd., Bhilai, India, 1960-70; exec. dir. All India Mgmt. Assn., New Delhi, 1983-84; chmn. Internat. Aiports Authority of India, New Delhi, 1986-89; sr. manpower tng. cons. ICAO, Can., 1990-91; mgmt. advisor UN Devel. Programme, 1991-92; chmn. Nat. Shipping Bd., New Delhi, 1991-97; founder, pres. FORE Sch. Mgmt., New Delhi, 1992-97; chmn. Orgnl. Assistance and Restructuring Svcs. and Delhi Sch Bus., New Delhi, 1997—; pres. Agricultural Social Ctr., 1995; hon. prof. Moreton Inst., Brisbane, Australia, 1996. Author: Dimension of Personnel Management, 1996, Dialogues with Yeti, 1990; co-author: Corporate Soul, 1985; editor: Corporate Success, 1994. Founder Tigri Vikas Sangh, Delhi, 1990; mem. Inter Cultural Mgmt. Bd. Brussels Bus. Sch., 1993; chmn. Cross Civil Airports Assn. Asia, 1987. Recipient Nat. Citizenship award, 1989, Plaque of Honor, Asian Airlines Assn., 1990, Gem of India award for instnl. devel., 1992. Fellow Nat. Inst. of Pers. Mgmt.; mem. Soc. for Advancement of Econ., All India Coun. for Tech. Edn., India Internat. Ctr. Avocations: writing, painting, poetry, photography. Home: H 71C Saket, 110 017 New Delhi India

SINGH, NEELOO, research scientist; b. Kanpur, India, Jan. 17, 1961; parents Shailendra Singh and Lata Singh Chauhan. BSc, Lucknow U., India, 1982, MSc, 1984; PhD, Kanpur U., India, 1991. Cert. in molecular biology and biochemistry. Scientist B Cen. Drug Rsch. Inst., Lucknow, 1991-96, scientist C, 1996—. Contbr. articles to rsch. publs.; patentee in field. Recipient B. K. Aikat Oration award Indian Coun. Med. Rsch., 1996. Hindu. Avocations: reading, music, writing, traveling, driving. E-mail: neeloo@scientist.com. Home: B-1/4 Nirala Nagar, Lucknow 226020, India Office: Cen Drug Rsch Inst, Divsn Biochemistry, Lucknow 226001, India

SINGH, NITYANAND KAWALASHANKAR, meteorologist; b. Varanasi, U.P., India, Aug. 14, 1953; s. Kawalashankar Nandgopal Singh and Sanwari Kawalashankar Devi; m. Urmila Nityanand Singh, Mar. 9, 1974; children: Vibha, Vivek Kumar, Vinayak. BSc, Banaras Hindu U., 1973, MSc, 1975, PhD, 1994. Rsch. scholar Cen. Rsch. Inst. for Dryland Agr., Hyderabad, India, 1976-79; jr. hydrometeorologist Ground Water Dept., Jodhpur, India, 1979-82; sr. scientific officer II Indian Inst. of Tropical Meteorology, Pune, India, 1982-89, sr. scientific officer I, 1989-94, asst. dir., 1994-99, dep. dir., 1999—; cons., resource person Ctr. for Advanced Studies in Agrl. Meteorology, Pune, 1988—, resource person India Meteorol. Dept., Pune. Inventor in field; contbr. articles to profl. jours. Recipient Young Scientist award in meteorology and environment South Asian Assn. for Regional Cooperation, 1999. Fellow World Meteorol. Orgn.; mem. Indian Meteorol. Soc. (life), Indian Agrometeorol. Soc., Indian Hydrologists Soc. Hindu. Avocations: reading, tourism, religious fellowship, listening to music. E-mail: nsingh@tropmet.ernet.in. Office: Indian Inst Trop Meteorolog, Dr Homi Bhabha Rd/Pashan, 411008 Pune/Maharashtra India

SINGH, PABAN BAHADUR, federal official; b. Kathmandu, Nepal, Oct. 1920. MA in Philosophy, Banras Hindu U., India, 1950. Pvt. sec. King Tribhuvan as Subba, 1951, King Tribhuva as Mir-Subba, 1955; sec. Regency Coun., 1955; prin. sec. King Mahendra as Sardar, 1956-72; mem. Bibhusan Com., 1960-72; master ceremonies Royal Palace, 1972-79; chief Royal Household, 1980-88, hon. chief. Decorated Grand Cross Order Merit (Germany); Order Million Elephant Parsal Blanc (Laos); Grand Cordon Yogoslav Flag I (Yugoslavia); Grand Officer Legion Honour II (France); Isabel Catolica II (Spain). Address: Bhote Bahal, Kathmandu Nepal

SINGH, PRAKASH RANGILAL, surgeon, educator; b. Nagpur, India, Oct. 5, 1945; s. Rangilal Mewaram and Rupa Singh; m. Vimal Prakash Tijare, Jan. 26, 1994; 1 child, Digvijay. MB BS, Govt. Med. Coll., Nagpur, India, 1969, MS in Gen. Surgery, 1979. Med. officer Health Dept. Aheri, Nagpur, 1971-85; med. supt. Rural Hosp., Aheri, 1985-94; supt. C.R. Das U. Med., Nagpur, 1994-96; civil surgeon Gen. Hosp., Nagpur, 1996—. Grantee Asian Productivity Orgn., 1998. Mem. Indian Med. Assn., Assn. Surgeons India. Home: Sadar, Mangalwari, Nagpur, Maharashtra 440 001, India Office: Indira Gandhi Med Coll, Centra Ave, Nagpur Maharashtra 440 018, India

SINGH, PRATAP, hydrologist; b. Ahera, India, July 15, 1957; s. Ram and Shayama S.; m. Anju Chaudhary, Dec. 4, 1988; children: Arpit, Aman. BSc in Phys. Chemistry and Maths., Bareilly (India) Coll., 1978, MSc in Physics, 1980; PhD in Physics, U. Roorkee, India, 1986. Cert. profl. water resources engr. From sr. rsch. asst. to scientist B Nat. Inst. Hydrology, Roorkee, 1983-93, scientist C, 1993—; prin. project investigator, Nat. Inst. Hydrology, 1993—; vis. scientist U. B.C., Vancouver, 1992; postdoctoral fellow Inst. for Torrent and Avalanche Control, Boku, Vienna, 1995-96. Contbr. articles to jours. hydrology. Mem. Internat. Assn. Hydrological Scis. Hindu. Avocations: mountaineering, badminton. Home: 150/11 New Teachers Hostel, U Roorkee, UP Roorkee 247 667, India Office: Nat Inst Hydrology, Jalvigyan Bhavan, UP Roorkee 247 667, India

SINGH, R. V., chemistry educator; b. Silana, India, July 1, 1953; s. Asha and Sitari (Devi) Malik; m. Krishna Premi, Nov. 28, 1979; two children. BSc, Meerut U., 1973, MSc, 1975; PhD, Rajasthan U., 1979. Rsch. fellow CSIR, Delhi, India, 1976-79; from asst. prof. to assoc. prof. Rajasthan U., Jaipur, India, 1979—. Internat. editl. bd. Main Group Metal Chemistry; authored numerous research publications. Fellow Indian Chem. Soc. (life) (assoc. editor Jour. Indian Chem. Soc.), Am. Biog. Inst., U.S. (rsch.); mem. Indian Sci. Congress Assn. (life), Indian Assn. Nuclear Chemists and Allied Scientists (life), Bhabha Atomic Rsch. Centre (life), Soc. for Advancement Chemistry Edn. and Rsch. (founder), Am. Chem. Soc. Home: 4 Kailash Vihar Janpath, Lalkothi 302015 Jaipur India

SINGH, RAJINDER, chemical company executive; b. Bhondian, Punjab, India, May 15, 1945; s. Mehar and Pritam (Kaur) S.; m. Joginder Kaur, Nov. 17, 1974; children: Sukhdip, Navdip. Diploma in Mech. Engring., State Bd. Tech. Edn., Chandigarh, India, 1965; Degree in Mech. Engring., Instn. Engrs., Calcutta, 1970. Asst. project engr. Projects & Devel. India Ltd., Sindri, 1972-76, project engr., 1976-80, asst. chief engr., 1980-86; dep. chief engr. Projects & Devel. India Ltd., Delhi, 1987-94; addl. chief engr. Projects & Devel. India Ltd., Noida, 1995—. Avocations: reading, gardening, music. Home: C-89 Pocket-B, Mayur Vihar Phase II, Delhi 110091, India Office: Projects & Devel India Ltd, PDIL Bhavan A-14 Sector I, Noida 201 301, India

SINGH, RAKESH PRABHAKAR, chemical engineering educator; b. Bhopal, India, June 27, 1942; s. Harish Chandra and Shanti (Saran) S.; m. Meenakshi Sinha, May 17, 1970; children: Rajit, Mayur. BS, Banaras Hindu U., Varanasi, India, 1959, BSChemE., 1963; PhD, Indian Inst. Tech., Kanpur, 1976. Assoc. lectr. Indian Inst. Tech., Kanpur, 1966-68, lectr., 1969-77, asst. prof., 1977-88, prof., 1988—; vis. scientist Delft U. Tech., The Netherlands, 1987; cons. in field. Postdoctoral fellow U. Canterbury, Christchurch, New Zealand, 1978-79. Mem. Indian Inst. Chem. Engrs. Avocations: bridge, music, reading, travel, sports. Home: 644 IIT Campus, Kanpur 208 016, India Office: Indian Inst Tech, Dept Chem Engring, Kanpur 208 016, India

SINGH, RAM B., cardiologist; b. Auraiya, India, July 1, 1943; s. Raj B. and Kamala D. Singh; m. Sushav Singh; children: Reema, Kartikey. BSc, Agra U., Kanpur, India, 1964; B Medicine B Surgery, Inst. Med. Scis. BHU, Vasanasi, India, 1986, MD, 1973. Resident physician Inst. Med. Sci., Varanasi, 1971-74; cons. physician Railway Hosp., Palghat, India, 1974-75, Med. Clinic, Moradabad, India, 1975-78; cons. cardiologist Med. Hosp. Rsch. Clinic, Moradabad, 1978-83, dir., 1983—; hon. prof. preventive cardiology NKP Salve Inst., 1995—; lectr. in field. Author monographs in field; contbr. over 500 articles to profl. publs., chpts. to books; mem. editl. bd. Jour. Environ. Medicine, Trace elements and Electrolytes, Jour. Internat. Medicine India. Recipient Best paper award 3d Internat. Congress on Preventive Cardiology, 1993, award India Health Mission, 1993, Dr. SubbaRow Meml. Internat. award, 1994, Dr. H. Mori Felicitation award, 1996, Ann. Sci. award U. Exeter, U.K., 1996, Dr. T.K. Basu Felicitation award, Can., 1997, Prof. Raymond Wgmann Oration award, 1997; grantee Sandoz Found. of Gerontologic Rsch., 1993. Mem. Internat. Soc. and Fedn. of Cardiology (mem. coun. on arteriosclerosis). Home: Civil Lines, Moradabad 10 UP, India 244001

SINGH, RAM DAYAL, regional planner, educator; b. Bihar, India, Mar. 29, 1954; s. Awadhesh and Sumitra (Devi) S.; m. Purnima Singh, May 19, 1982; children: Madhulika, Prashant. BSc, G.L.A. Coll., Ranchi U., India, 1974; MA in Geography, Ravishankar U., Raipur, India, 1977; M Regional Planning, India Inst. Tech., Kharagpur, 1979; Postgrad. Diploma in Econ. Planning, Inst. Econ. Planning Problems, Naples, Italy, 1984; PhD, Barkatullah U., Bhopal, India, 1993; postgrad., Indian Inst. Remote Sensing, 1993. Asst. dir. Town and Country Planning Orgn., Bhopal, 1981-82; lectr. dept. regional planning and econ. growth Bhopal U., 1985-93, reader, 1993, dir. Ctr. for Study of Environment and Sustainable Devel., 1995—; organizer nat. workshop on modern concepts of town and country planning Barkatullah Bhopal U., 1989. Author rsch. articles. Organizer Nat. Coun. for Environ. Mgmt. and Sustainable Devel., Bhopal, 1995. Mem. Inst. Town Planners India (life; vice chmn. 1981), Regional Sci. Assn. India (life), Remote Sensing Soc. India (life). Avocations: creative writing, music. Home: Barkatullah U Tchrs Qtrs, Bhopal India Office: Dept Regional Planning/Econ, Hoshangabad Rd Post Box 802, 462026 Bhopal India

SINGH, RAM KUMAR, nuclear/mechanical engineer, researcher; b. Siwan, Bihar, India, May 17, 1953; s. Ram Parekhi Singh and Chandrakala (Sharma) Devi; m. Ranjana Singh, Mar. 9, 1977; children: Sambhavi, Atindra. BSc in Mech. Engring., BIT, Sindri, India, 1977; postgrad. in nuclear/mech. engring., BARC Centre, Mumbai, India, 1978; PhD in Structural Engring., IIT, Mumbai, 1990. Scientific officer-C Bhabha Atomic Rsch. Ctr., Mumbai, 1978-82, scientific officer-D, 1982-86, scientific officer-E, 1986-91, scientific officer-F, 1991-96, scientific officer-G, 1996—; rsch. paper reviewer ISET Jr. of Earthquake Tech., India, 1998-99. Contbr. articles to profl. jours. Mem. Indian Nuclear Soc. (life), Indian Soc. for Heat and Mass Transfer (life). Avocations: literature, photography, music. Office: Bhabha Atomic Rsch Ctr, Trombay Hall 7, Mumbai 400 085, India

SINGH, RAMESH PRATAP, geophysics educator; b. Varanasi, India, Jan. 2, 1954; s. Rama N. and Uma Singh; m. Alka Singh, Apr. 27, 1980; children: Ritesh Gautam, Rachita. BSc with honors, Banaras Hindu U., India, 1974, MSc, 1976, PhD, 1980. Rsch. fellow Nat. Geophys. Rsch. Inst., India, 1976-77, Banaras Hindu U., 1977-81; sr. rsch. officer ISM, India, 1981; postdoctoral fellow U. Alta., Can., 1981-84, AOSTRA fellow, 1984-86; lectr. Indian Inst. Tech., Kanpur, 1986, asst. prof., 1986-91, assoc. prof., 1991-97, prof., 1997—; guest scientist ICTP, Trieste, Italy, 1977, U. Uppsala, Sweden, Inst. Geophysics, Sopron, Hungary, Nat. Sci. Rsch. Ctr., Garchy, France, CNR, Pisa, Italy. Editor: Remote Sensing of the Earth's Surface and Atmosphere, 1992, Observations of Earth from Space, 1994, Natural Hazards: Monitoring and Assessment Using Remote Sensing Technique, 1995. Recipient Nat. Mineral award Govt. of India, 1992, JSPS Rsch. award Govt. of Japan, 1993, Indian Nat. Remote Sensing award, 1997, Hari Om Ashram Prerit Dr. Vikram Sarabhai Rsch. award, 1997, Hari Om Ashram Prerit Vikram Sarabhai Rsch. award, 1997; fellow Alexander von Humboldt Found., 1994. Mem. Indian Soc. Remote Sensing (life, mem. exec. coun. 1998—), Indian Sch. Mines, Internat. Ctr. for Theoretical Physics, Ctr. for Nat. Rsch. France, Alta. Oil Sand Tech. and Rsch. Authority, Japan Soc. Promotion Scheme, Soc. Exploration Geophysicists, Am. Geophys. Union, European Assn. Geoscientists and Engrs. Avocation: reading. Office: Dept Civil Engring, Indian Inst Tech, Kanpur 208 016, India

SINGH, RANA P.B., cultural geographer, educator; b. Majhanpura-Revelganj, Saran, India, Dec. 15, 1950; s. Bharat and Rupamati S.; m. Manju Singh; children: Pratibha, Pravin, Prabha, Prashant. MA, Banaras Hindu U., Varanasi, India, 1971, PhD, 1974; Dip. Computer, Datamation Inst., Varanasi, India, 1976. Landscape surveyor; seminar organizer, eco-tourism and pilgrimage guide. U. Grants Commn. fellow geography Banaras Hindu U., Varanasi, India, 1975-77, lectr. geography, 1977-80, 83-88, sr. lectr. geography, 1988-90, reader, assoc. prof., 1991-2000, prof., 2000—; dir. United Nations Orgn.: Ctr. of Housing, Bldg. and Planning Project, N.Y. and Varanasi, India, 1976-77; Ron Lister lectr. Otago U., Dunedin, New Zealand, 1995; scientist poolship Coun. Sci. and Indsl. Rsch., New Delhi, 1981; vis. prof. U. of Karlstad, Sweden, 1989, 93, 96, U. Groningen, The Netherlands, 1999; vis. scholar lectr. in many Univs. of Australia, Belgium, Denmark, Finland, France, Germany, Iran, Italy, Japan, Korea, The Netherlands, New Zealand, Norway, Spain, Sweden, Switzerland, Thailand, U.S.A., USSR.; dir. India: South Asia Inst. Heidelberg, German Project on Cultural Atlas of Banaras, 1998—, India: Imperial Coll., London project on changing Peri-Urban land use in Banaras, 1999—, India: U. Colo., Boulder project on religious landscape and cosmology of India's holy ctrs., 1998-2000; vis. prof. Va. Tech., Blacksburg, 1980-81. Author, editor of 30 vols. including: Rural Settlement Geography, 1975, Clan Settlement in the Saran Plain, 1977, Rural Habitat Transformation, 1980, Indian Village Ecology: A Village Study, 1981, Where Cultural Symbols Meet, 1989, Sarnath, 1991, Panchakroshi Yatra, Varanasi: Sacred Journey, Ecology of Place, 1993, Varanasi Region-An Insight Guide, 1993; Banaras: Cosmic Order, 1993, The Layout of Sacred Places, 1993, Environmental Studies, 1993, The Spirit and Power of Place, 1994; exec. editor: Nat. Geog. Jour. India, 1990-95; editor: Earth Sci. sect. Jour. Scientific Rsch., 1989-95; founding editor Sacred Earth and Eco-healing, 2000—; contbr. numerous articles on Cosmic Geometry, Sacredspace, Pilgrimage to Geosci. and Man, Geographica Medica, Nat. Geog. Jour. India, GeoJournal, Erdkunde, The Ley Hunter, Place, Vista in Astronomy, Architecture & Behaviour, Geog. Religionum, Religion and Environment. Sec. commn. rural habitat Internat. Geog. Union, Varanasi, India, 1976-84; mem. Commn. on Correcting Indian History, New Delhi, 1989; coord. N.Y. State Ind. Colls. Consortium for Study in India, Varanasi, India, 1995—; coord. Village Lifeworld Project, U. Karlstad, Sweden, 1996-2000. Scientist fellow Japan Found., 1980. Mem. Indian Soc. Environ. and Culture (founding pres. 1994—), Soc. Pilgrimage Studies (pres. 1989—), Soc. Heritage Planning and Environ. Health (pres. 1995—), Environ. Monitoring Soc. (exec.), Nat. Geog. Soc. India, Nat. Assn. Geographers India. Avocations: guiding eco-tours and pilgrimages, wandering, lecturing slide shows. E-mail: ranapbs@rediffmail.com Fax: 091-542-368174. Phone: 091-542-314011. Office: Dept Geog, Banaras Hindu U, Varanasi, UP 221005, India

SINGH, RANJAN, veterinarian; b. Varanasi, India, Oct. 7, 1966; s. Tej Bahadur and Shail Kumari Singh; m. Kanchan X., Apr. 3, 1998; 1 child, Swaraj Ranjan. B Vet. Sci. and Animal Husbandry, Govt. Vet. Coll., Mathura, India, 1988, M Vet. Sci., 1992; postgrad., Inst. Environment and Mgmt., Lucknow, India, 1999. Vet. officer in-charge Govt. of Rajasthan, India, 1994-97; vet. med. officer Govt. of Uttar Pradesh, India, 1997-98; officer in-charge divsnl. animal disease rsch. lab. Govt. of Uttar Pradesh, Kanpur, 1999—; cons. Govt. of Rajasthan, 1994-97; cons. to animal husbandry World Bank projects, 1999—; rschr. in animal disease prevention. Exec. founding mem. Health Care Soc., Kanpur, 1997—; dir. Inst. Environ. Protection, Kanpur, 1999—. Chandra Sekhar Azad Univ. scholar, 1990-92. Mem. Indian Vet. Coun., U.P. Vet. Assn., Soc. for Promotion of Human Devel. (sec. 1988—), Kanpur Vets.' Club (exec. mem.). Avocations: environmental management and wildlife protection, reading, yoga. Home: 120/501 Shiva Ji Nagar, Kanpur 208005, India Office: Divsnl Animal Disease Rsch, Rawatpur, Kanpur India

SINGH, RIPUDAMAN, aerospace structure engineering researcher; b. Ambala, India, July 8, 1964; came to U.S., 1992; s. Manmohan Singh and Kuljit Kaur; m. Anupinder Kaur, Aug. 16, 1967; 1 child, Amanjot Singh. BE in Aero. Engring., Punjab Engring. Coll., Chandigarh, India, 1986; ME in Aerospace Engring., Indian Inst. Sci., Bangalore, 1988, PhD in Engring., 1992. Postdoctoral fellow Ga. Inst. Tech., Atlanta, 1992-94; asst. prof. aerospace engring. Indian Inst. Sci., Bangalore, 1994-98; sr. rsch. engr. Karta Techs., Inc., San Antonio, 1998—. Editor: Life Extension Technologies for Ageing Aircraft, 1998; contbr. over 50 articles to profl. jours. Avocations: music, travel, dance, humor. E-mail: rsingh@karta.com. Home: 11911 Ghostbridge Helotes TX 78023-4456 Office: Karta Techs Inc 5555 Northwest Pkwy San Antonio TX 78249-3339

SINGH, SARVA DAMAN, historian, educator; b. Angai, India, Apr. 15, 1934; arrived in Australia, 1974; s. Jaideo Singh and Kanchan Kunwar; m. Kumud Rani Singh, May 27, 1955; children: Vagish, Rahul. BA with honors, Lucknow (India) U., 1953, MA, 1954; PhD Oriental and African Studies, U. London, 1962; PhD, U. Queensland, Brisbane, Australia, 1975. Lectr. Lucknow U., 1954-63, reader, 1963-65, 67-73; prof. history Nat. Acad. Adminstrn., Mussoorie, India, 1965-67, Vikram U., Ujjain, India, 1973-74; assoc. prof. U. Queensland, 1974-99; prof., dir. Inst. Indian Studies, Brisbane, Australia, 1999—. Author: Ancient Indian Warfare, 1965, Polyandry in Ancient India, 1978, The Archaeology of the Lucknow Region, 1972; author, editor: Culture Through the Ages, 1996; contbr. numerous articles to profl. jours. Pres. Indian Cultural Assn. Queensland, Brisbane, 1982-84, Asian Australian Action Com., Brisbane, 1984. Fellow Royal Asiatic Soc. Gt. Britain and Ireland; mem. Asian Studies Assn., N.Y. Acad. Scis., India Club Queensland (pres. 1974). Avocations: photography, travel, tennis. Home: Jaigarh, 211 Sugars Rd Belllbowrie, Brisbane QLD 4070, Australia Office: Inst Asian Studies, 211 Sugars Road, Anstead QLD 4070, Australia

SINGH, SHASHI PRABHA, library and informations science educator; b. Muzaffarnagar, India, July 8, 1949; d. Raj and Satya (Kapil) Sharma; m. Narendra Pratap, Nov. 17, 1972; two children. MSc, Meerut U., 1971; M in Libr. Sci., U. Delhi, 1976, PhD, 1994. Documentation asst. Govt. India, 1976-78; prof. assist. U. Delhi, 1978-82, serials libr., 1982-87, lectr., 1987-94, reader, 1995—. Mem. Indian Libr. Assn., Indian Assn. Spl. Librs. and Info. Ctrs., Assn. Govt. India Librs. & Info. Sys. Home: F-507 Rashmi Appartments, 110034 Shakti Vihar Delhi, India

SINGH, SHEETLA, journalist; b. Faizabad, U.P., India, Aug. 6, 1932; s. Raj Bahadur and Naina Devi Singh; m. Kanti Devi Singh; children: S.K., S.N., Alok. Sub editor Janmorcha, India, 1958-62, editor, 1963—; pres. RachnatMaks ama, India, 1984-91, U.P. Press Club, India, 1994—, Judo Karates Orgn., India, 1990-93; v.p. IFWJ, India, 1991-94. Gen. sec. U.P. Kisam Sabha Faizabad, India, 1950-61; sec. CPI, Faizabad, India, 1956-63. Recipient Meritorious Svc. award IFSMN, 1991, Patrakar Bhaskar award RasKriti, India, 1996. Mem. ILNA (gen. sec. 1998), U.P. Working Journalists (pres. 1981-88), Hindi Samachar Patra Samellan (pres. 1993—), All India Gram Pradian Saigh (pres. 1986-91), Dewar Club Prisidem, Working Journalist Union (v.p.), Press Coun. India. Avocations: seminars, driving. Home: 8/8197 Beghum Gunj Maqbara, 224001 Faizabad India Office: Janmorcha, Byajor, 224001 Faizabad India

SINGH, SHIV PRATAP, chemist, educator; b. Etawah, U.P., India, Apr. 5, 1938; s. Iqubal Bahadur and Raj Kumari (Singh) S.; m. Prahha Singh, June 23, 1965; children: Hemendu P., Shubhendu P. BSc, Lucknow (India) U., 1959, MSc, 1961, PhD, 1964. Lectr. Kurukshetra (India) U., 1965-76, reader, 1976-85, prof., 1985-98, chmn. chemistry dept., 1989-92, prof. emeritus, 1998—; post-doctoral fellow U. Ill. Chgo., 1968-70; vis. rsch. prof., 1989; Indo-Spanish fellow, Consejo Superior de Investigaciones Cientificas Madrid, 1989; I.N.S.A. Royal Soc. fellow, Eng., 1993; mem. Univ. Exec. Coun., Acad. Coun and Univ. Court; convenor chemistry panel Univ. Grants Commn., New Delhi, 1997-2000; mem. adv. bd. Regional Sophisticated Instruments Ctr., Ctrl. Drug Rsch. Inst., DST Govt. of India, New Delhi, 1997-2000. Author: (books) Reaction Mechanism in Organic Chemistry, 1976, Organic Chemistry Vol. I, II, III, 1985; contbr. more than 130 rsch. papers to profl. jours, sci. confs., etc. Sr. Fulbright scholar, 1979-80. Mem. Indian Chem. Soc. (v.p. 1996-97, 2000—, coun. mem. 1998-2000, Acharya P.C. Ray Meml. award, 1994). Avocations: reading, nature watching, travel, making friends. Home: E-19 Kurukshetra U, Kurukshetra Haryana, India Office: Kurukshetra U, Dept Chemistry, Kurukshetra India

SINGH, SHYAM PRATAP, cardiologist, consultant; b. Padruna, India, Apr. 4, 1932; s. Raisahib Capt. Gur Pratap S.; divorced; children: Kishan, Sanjeev, Sheila. MB, BS, Lucknow U., 1954. Med. registrar United Birmingham (Eng.) Hosps., 1960-62, cardiology fellow, 1964-68; clin. rsch. fellow Mass. Gen. Hosp., 1962-63; hon. asst. tutor in medicine Harvard U., Cambridge, Mass., 1962-63; vis. scientist Mayo Clinic, Rochester, Minn., 1967-68; sr. lectr. pediatrics U. Birmingham, 1968-82; dir. cardiothoracic unit Birmingham Children's Hosp., 1972-83; sr. lectr. clin. cardiology U. Birmingham, 1983—; cons. cardiologist City Hosp. NHS Trust, Birmingham; chmn. session on coronary angiography Asean Congress of Cardiology, Bangkok, 1984. Author: (with others) Coronary Artery Disease in Young Women, 1978; co-editor textbook: Key Points in Cardiovascular Disease, 1998; contbr. over 100 articles to profl. jours. Fellow Royal Coll. Physicians; mem. Brit. Cardiac Soc., Assn. European Pediatric Cardiologists (sr.), Tennis Club, Rotary. Avocations: cricket, traveling, reading. Home: 101 Westfield Rd, B15 3JE Birmingham England Office: Dudley Rd Hosp, Dudley Rd, B18 7QH Birmingham England

SINGH, SUKHCHAIN, agriculturist; b. Ahmed Garh, India, Oct. 13, 1953; s. Mukhtiar and Basant (Kaur) S.; m. Amarjit Kaur, Oct. 5, 1980; 1 child, Gagandeep. BSc in Agrl., COA, Ludhiana, India, 1974; MSc in Plant Breeding, COA, 1978, PhD in Plant Breeding, 1990. Rsch. assoc. Agrl. U., Gurdaspur, 1978-81; asst. cotton breeder Agrl. U., Muktsar, 1981-84; asst. seed specialist PAU, Moga, 1984-90; plant breeder PAU, Ropar, 1990-99; seed prodn. specialist PAU, Ludhiana, 1999—; forage breeder, 1999—. Author: (Book) Mitti Da Mor, 1976, Ghar, 1997; contbr. articles to profl. nat. and internat. jours. Recipient Sauhard Samman award U.P. Hindi Sansthan. Fellow Indian Soc. Genetics and Plant Breeding; mem. Range Mgmt. Soc. India, Indian Soc. Forage Rsch., Indian Soc. Genetics & Plant Breeding. Avocation: poetry. Home: 75 Ashapuri Nr Aggar Nagar, Ludhiana 141004, India Office: Plant Breeding Dept, PAU, 141004 Ludhiana India

SINGH, SURENDRA NIHAL, journalist, writer; b. Rawalpindi, Pakistan, Apr. 30, 1929; s. Gurmukh Nihal and Lachchmi (Devi) S.; m. Geertje Nihal Zuiderweg, Nov. 4, 1957 (wid.). BA with honours, Delhi U., 1948. Resident editor The Statesman, New Delhi, India, 1973-75; cief editor The Statesman, Calcutta, 1975-79; editor-in-chief Indian Express, New Delhi, 1981-82; founding editor The Indian Post, Bombay, 1987-88; dir. Press Inst. of India, New Delhi, 1992-94; editor Khaleej Times, Dubai, United Arab Emirates, 1994—; syndicated columnist, New Delhi, 1980-81, 88-92; sr. assoc. Carnegie Endowment for Internat. Peace, N.Y.C., 1982-84; project dir. Twentieth Century Fund, Paris, 1984-86. Author: The Gang and 900 Million, 1979, The Yogi and the Bear, 1986, The Rise and Fall of UNESCO, 1987, The Rocky Road of Indian Democracy, 1993. Named Internat. Editor of Yr., Atlas World Press, 1978. Mem. India Internat. Ctr., Press Club of

India (pres. 1994). Avocations: reading, travel, Western classical music. Office: Khaleej Times, Shaikh Zayed Rd Box 11243, Dubai United Arab Emirates

SINGH, SURINDER PAL, molecular biologist, researcher; b. Pune, Maharashtra, India, Oct. 25, 1955; arrived in Australia, 1980.; s. Gurcharan Singh and Sukhnandan Kaur; m. Margaret Joan Howard; children: Timothy, Kiran. BS, Khalsa Coll., Amritsar, India, 1976; MS, G.B. Pant U., Pantnagar, India, 1980; PhD, U. Adelaide, India, 1985. Postdoctoral fellow U. Queensland, Brisbane, Australia, 1986-88; rsch. fellow Queensland Inst. Med. Rsch., Brisbane, 1988-90; prin. rsch. scientist Commonwealth Scientific and Indsl. Rsch. Orgn., Canberra, Australia, 1991—. Patentee in field. Recipient Nat. Sci. Talent award Sci. Coun. India, 1973, NIH grant, U.S.A., 1994-96, Grains Corp. grant, Australia, 1997-99. Mem. Australian Soc. Molecular Biology, Australian Oil Chemist Soc. Avocations: tennis, cricket, soccer, movies, travel. Home: 10 Lucas Pl, Canberra 2602, Australia Office: CSIRO Div Plant IND, GPO Box 1600, Canberra 2601, Australia

SINGH, SWARAN, political science researcher; b. Gagret, India, Aug. 9, 1961; s. Permeshwari Dass Jaswal and Ram Rakhi Devi; m. Madhu Malti Malik Jaswal, July 2, 1988; 1 child, Arunhati Jaswal. BA in Polit. Sci. with honors, Delhi U., 1983, MA in Polit. Sci., 1985; MPhil, Jawaharlal Nehru U., New Delhi, 1989, PhD, 1994; postdoctoral diploma conflict resolution, Uppsala (Sweden) U., 1994. Sr. rsch. fellow U. Grants Commn., New Delhi, 1989-94; rschr. Inst. Def. Studies and Analysis, New Delhi, 1992-95, rsch. officer, 1995-97, rsch. fellow, 1997—; staff writer, cons. China, Muzinet, 1996-97. Author: Limited War, 1995; cons. editor Third World Impact, 1994—; editl. adv. SAPRA India, 1995-97. Avocations: Hindustani classical music, nature watching, long drives. Office: Inst Def Studies & Analyses, Blk 1 Old JNU Campus, New Delhi 110067, India

SINGH, THAKUR PRASAD, zoology educator, researcher; b. Jaunpur, India, Jan. 14, 1940; s. Sharda Prasad and Shyama Devi Singh; m. Savitri Singh, May 11, 1954; children: Vijay Kumar, Sanjay Kumar, Dhanajay Kumar. BSc, Udai Pratap Coll., Varanasi, India, 1958; MSc, Banaras Hindu U., Varanasi, India, 1960, PhD, 1969. Lectr. Banaras Hindu U., 1963-66, Udaipur (India) U., 1966-68; lectr. Banaras Hindu U., 1968-79, reader, 1979-87, prof. zoology, 1987—; mem. agriculture scientist recruitment bd., New Delhi, 1981-83, 91-93; chmn. 2d Quinquennial Com. Nat. Bur. Fish Genetic Resource, Lucknow, India, 1985-90; mem. State Pub. Svc. Commn., Allahabad, India, 1997. contbr. over 120 papers to profl. jours. Recipient award Hari Om Ashram Trust, Indian Coun. Agrl. Rsch., Govt. India, New Delhi, 1981, Profl. Devel. award Internat. Devel. Rsch. Ctr., Ottawa, Can., 1982. Mem. Indian Soc. of Gen. and Comparative Endocrinology (gen. sec. 1988—). Avocation: reading. Home: N8 236, R-52, Nevada, Sunderpur, Varanasi 221005, India Office: Banaras Hindu U, Dept Zoology, Varanasi 221005, India

SINGH, VED RAM, biomedical engineer, researcher; b. Ferozepur, Faridabad, India, Feb. 24, 1946; s. Nathi and Devi (Saraswati) S.; m. Chitra Singh, June 5, 1972. BE, Thapar Engring. Coll., Patiala, India, 1968; PhD, Indian Inst. Tech., New Delhi, 1974. Cert. biomed. engr. Rsch. fellow Nat. Phys. Lab., New Delhi, 1968-73, sr. scientist, 1973—, head instrumentation and sensors group, 1985—; engr., tchr. Engring. Tutorial Coll., New Delhi, 1968-69; postdoc. rsch. fellow U. Toronto, Ont., Can., 1974-77, European Commn. postdoc. fellow vis. scientist U. Tech., Delft, The Netherlands, 1991-92; vis. prof. Katholieke Univ, Leuven, Belgium 1998-99; scientist, head Electronics & Tranducers Group, 1973-85; cons. various industries and rsch. insts., 1973—. Author: Directory of Ultrasonic Scientists, 1987; editor: Trends in Tranducers Vols I and II, 1985; contbr. articles to profl. jours.; patentee in field. Preacher Sanskrit Religious Soc., India, 1960—; tchr. Yoga Soc., India, 1961—; meditator Religious Saints Socs., India, 1960—. Recipient Merit award Nat. Phys. Lab., New Delhi, 1973, Young Scientist medal award Indian Nat. Sci. Acad., New Delhi, 1974, Young Scientist award Indian Coun. Med. Rsch., 1983, Afsumb medal Asian Fed. Soc. Ultrasound Medicine and Biology, 1988. Fellow IEEE (Best paper award 1999, chmn., fellowship and awards com., rev. com.), Indian Coll. Ultrasound Radiologists, Instn. Engrs. (India, prizes 1985; Best Paper awards 1989, 91), Instn. Electronics and Telecomm. Engrs. (vice chmn. 1994, chmn. 1996, guest editor, tech. rev. on sensors and transducers, 1991), Ultrasonic Soc. India (gen. sec. 1985—, v.p. 1996—), Indian Fedn. Ultrasound in Med. Biology (v.p. 1996—). Samadhan. Avocations: travel, reading, gardening. Home: NPL Colony, D-II-8, New Delhi 110 060, India Office: Nat Physics Lab I & S Group, Dr K S Krishnan Rd, New Delhi 110 012, India

SINGH, VIJAY, professional golfer; b. Lautoka, Fiji, Feb. 22, 1963; m. Andrena Seth Singh; 1 child, Qass Seth. Winner Buick Classic, 1993, PGA European Tour Scandanavian Masters, 1994, Phoenix Open Buick Classic, 1995, Memorial Tournament Buick Open, 1997, PGA Championship Sprint Internat., 1998, Honda Classic, 1999, Masters Tournament, 2000; mem. Pres. Cup Team, 1994; also won 10 other times worldwide. Set PGA Tour record for earnings in first two seasons. Avocations: snooker, cricket, rugby, soccer. Office: South Fla Sect PGA 10804 W Sample Rd Coral Springs FL 33065-2632

SINGH, VINOD, biochemistry educator and researcher; b. Gola Gokaran Nath, India, July 4, 1956; s. Tahal Behari and Lalli (Devi) S.; m. Manju Singh, Nov. 24, 1986; children: Gunjan, Garima. BSc, Kanpur (India) U., 1974, MSc, 1976, PhD, 1981. Rsch. fellow UGC, New Delhi, India, 1977-79; lectr. Kanpur U., 1980; jr. rsch. officer All India Inst. Med. Scis., New Delhi, 1981-82, rsch. oficer, 1982-86; assoc. prof. North-Eastern Hill U., Shillong, India, 1986—; vis. prof. Washington U., St. Louis, 1989, 90-92; guest prof. U. Heidelberg, 1996-97; faculty dept. biol. and technol. rsch. San-Raffaele Inst., Milan. Author: Neuroendocrine Regulation in Fertility Control, 1989; contbr. some 75 rsch. articles to profl. jours. Recipient UGC-Career award, 1993; Rockefeller Found. fellow, 1987; Alexander von Humboldt Found. fellow, 1995. Avocations: reading, hockey, football, tennis, volleyball, music. Home: House No 57, North-Eastern Hill Univ Campus, 793022 Shillong Meghalaya, India Office: Inst Self-Org Sys & Biophys, North-Eastern Hill U, Shillong 793022, India

SINGH, YADHU NAND, pharmacology educator, researcher; b. Suva, Fiji, Aug. 4, 1944; came to U.S., 1988, naturalized, 1995; s. Shri Ram and Janki Kumari Singh; m. Kamal Kuar, Feb. 14, 1976; children: Yatesh Nand, Kashmir Kaur. BS, U. Otago, Dunedin, New Zealand, 1967; MS, U. Strathclyde, Glasgow, Scotland, 1974, PhD, 1979. H.s. tchr. Marist H.S., Suva, 1967-70; lectr. biol. chemistry U. South Pacific, Suva, 1970-80, sr. lectr. biology, 1980-86; asst. prof. pharmacology S.D. State U., Brookings, 1988-91, assoc. prof., 1991-97, prof., 1997—; lectr. pharmacology U. Alberta, 1986-88; adj. lectr. Fiji Sch. Medicine, 1980-84; Fiji dir. Commonwealth med. plants project, 1981-84; cons. on kava. Author: Kava Bibliography; author 6 book chpts., more than 60 articles to profl. jours. Recipient McCarthy prize, 1974; MRC fellow U. Strathclyde, 1976-79; AHFMR fellow 1984-86; NIH grantee. Mem. Am. Assn. of Colls. of Pharmacy, Am. Soc. Pharmacology and Exptl. Therapeutics, Internat. Soc. Toxinology, Brit. Pharmacol. Soc., Sigma Xi, Rho Chi. Democrat. Hindu. Avocations: soccer, chess, gardening, reading. Office: SDSU Coll Pharmacy Administration Ln Brookings SD 57007-0001

SINGH, YESH PAL, mechanical engineering educator, consultant; b. Muzaffarnagar, India, Jan. 1, 1940; came to U.S., 1970; s. Chhatar and Gyandevi Singh; m. Veera Singh, Feb. 27, 1963; children: Sveta, Vinay. BSME, Roorkee (India) U., 1962; MSME, Youngstown State U., 1974; postgrad., SUNY, Buffalo, 1974-75; DEng, U. Wis., Milw., 1984. Design engr., asst. engr. H.E.C. Ltd., Ranchi, India, 1962-70; design engr. Youjuralmashzavod, Orsk, USSR, 1964-65, Birdsboro (Pa.) Corp., 1970, 72-73; mech. engr. DES-ENG-Corp., Reading, Pa., 1971-72; engr. Allis-Chalmers Corp., Milw., 1975-77, sr. engr. I, 1977-84, sr. engr. II, 1984-85; assoc. prof. mech. engring. U. Tex., San Antonio, 1985—, chmn. mech. engring., 1993-96, chair mech. engring. grad. studies, adv. records, 1998—, dir. machine shop, 1998—; chair mech. design group U. Tex., 1985—, chmn., advisor records ME grad. program, 1998—, dir. machine shop Coll. Scis. and Engring., 1998—. Contbr. articles to profl. jours. Recipient Coll. Engring. and Applied Sci. Outstanding Alumni award U. Wis., Milw., 1996, Charles E. Balleisen Awd., 1999. Fellow ASME (treas. San Antonio sect. 1991-92, sec. 1992-93, vice-chmn. 1993-94, chmn. 1994-95, chair nomination and nat. agenda com. 1995-96, chair coll. rels. 1996-97, chair profl. practice 1997-98, Clifford H. Schumaker award Region X, 1998). Achievements include development of design procedures for very large spur and helical gears; of procedures and design programs for determining natural frequency and mode shapes of centrifugal pump systems; of designs for various units of high speed continuous slab casters; of finite element based design procedures for endodontic root canal instrument; of synthesis procedures for design of planar cam-link mechanisms. Home: 19715 La Sierra Blvd San Antonio TX 78256-2015 Office: U Tex San Antonio 6900 N Loop 1604 W San Antonio TX 78249-1130

SINGH, ZORA, agricultural researcher, educator; b. Aitaiana, Punjab, India, Oct. 10, 1956; s. Balbir Singh and S. Nasib Kaur Khangura; m. Ravjit Kaur Khangura Gill, Jan. 21, 1989. BSc in Agr. with honors, Punjab Agrl. U., Ludhiana, 1980, MSc, 1982, PhD, 1986. Jr. rsch. fellow Indian Coun. Agrl. Rsch., Ludhiana, 1979-81, sr. rsch. fellow, 1981-86; Commonwealth postdoctoral fellow Hort. Rsch. Internat., Kent, Eng., 1986-87; asst. horticulturist, asst. prof. horticulture Punjab Agrl. U., Ludhiana, 1988-91; tchg. and rsch. fellow Murdoch U., Perth, Australia, 1992-96; vis. prof. horticulture U. Bologna, Italy, 1995-96; rsch. fellow Curtin U. Tech., Perth, 1997—; v.p. I. Co-editor procs.; contbr. chpt. to book, articles to profl. jours. Recipient Pran Vohra award, 1991, UNESCO/ROSTSCA Young Scientist award UN, 1989, Young Scientist medal Indian Nat. Acad. Scis., 1988, Jawahar Lal Nehru award Indian Coun. Agrl. Rsch., 1987, Prof. LSS Kumar Meml. award Indian Nat. Acad. Scis., 1988. Mem. Internat. Soc. for Tropical R&D (v.p. 1997—), Internat. Soc. for Horticulture (cert.), Internat. Soc. Hort. Sci. (v.p. 1997), Am. Soc. Hort. Sci. Sikh. Avocations: gardening, reading. Home: 31 Freshwater Dr, Atwell Australia 6164 Office: Curtin U Tech Bentley, Dept Horticulture, Perth Australia 6845

SINGHAL, ATUL, pediatrician, researcher; b. Harpur, India, Dec. 24, 1962; arrived in the Eng., 1968; s. Anjani and Mithlesh Singhal; m. Pamela Christine Shiers, Aug. 19, 1995. MB, BS, U. London, 1986, MD, 1998. Diploma in child health, 1988. Pediat. resident St. Marys Hosp., Hosp. for Sick Children, Univ. Coll. Hosp., London, 1987-89; clin. scientist Med. Rsch. Coun., Sickle Cell Unit U. West Indies, Kingston, Jamaica, 1989-94; sr. registrar North East Thames Region, London, 1994-98; lectr. in pediatric nutrition Inst. Child Health, London, 1998—. Contbr. articles to profl. jours. Mem. Royal Coll. Physicians (London), Royal Coll. Paediatrics and Child Health. Avocations: travel, hill walking, photography.

SINGHAL, DEEPAK, finance executive; b. Aligarh, UP, India, Dec. 17, 1958; s. Ramesh Chandra and Urmila (Gupta) S.; m. Shobha Tiwary, May 14, 1982; children: Nikhil, Shreshth. B in Tech., Birla Inst. of Tech., Ranchi, India, 1981; MBA, Indian Inst. Mgmt., Ahmedabad, India, 1984. CFA. Engr. Telco, Jamshedpur, India, 1981-82; fin. mgr. Max India Ltd., New Delhi, India, 1984-89; gen. mgr. fin. DCM Ltd., New Delhi, India, 1989-94; v.p. fin. Mesco Kalinga Steels Ltd., New Delhi, India, 1994-96; CFO Modi GBC Ltd., New Delhi, India, 1996-2000, Max India Ltd., New Delhi, India, 2000—; dir. Trans-Global Steel Inc., Pitts., 1995-96. Recipient Sr. mention Hovercraft Design, 1981. Mem. Inst. CFAs. Avocations: sports, reading, travel. Home: 99-A Pocket "A", Sukhdev Vihar, New Delhi 110 025, India Office: 20-A Ring Rd, Lajpat Nagar-IV New Delhi 110025, India

SINGHA L., RAKESH KUMAR, molecular biology educator, consultant, researcher; b. Khurja, India, Apr. 24, 1955; came to U.S., 1985; s. Pooran Mal Gupta and Shanti Devi; m. Mohanie Sookram, Sept. 7, 1991; 1 child, Krtin. BSc (hon.), Aligarh (India) Muslim U., 1975, MSc, 1977; PhD, Indian Inst. Tech., New Delhi, 1985. Sr. rsch. asst. Indian Inst. Tech., 1981-85; postdoctoral assoc. Cornell U. Med. Coll., N.Y.C., 1985-87; postdoctoral fellow U. Rochester, N.Y., 1987-91; vis. scientist U. Tex. Med. Br., Galveston, 1991-96; asst. prof. pediat. N.Y.-Presbyn. Hosp.-Cornell U. Weill Med. Coll., N.Y.C., 1996—. Author: DNA Damage and Repair, 1998, Genetic Instability and Hereditary Neurological Diseases, 1998; contbr. articles to sci. jours., including Biochemistry, Jour. Biol. Chemistry, Nature. Rsch. grantee Am. Lung Assn., 1998. Mem. AAAS. Hindu. Avocations: reading, cooking, worshipping, volleyball, hiking. E-mail: rsinghal@med.cornell.edu. Home: 500 Central Park Ave Apt 338 Scarsdale NY 10583-1081 Office: NY-Presbyn Hosp-Cornell U Weill Med Coll 1300 York Ave New York NY 10021-4805

SINGHAL, SAT PAL, aerospace engineer; b. Jagadhri, Punjab, India, Sept. 5, 1941; came to U.S., 1963; s. Chandgi Ram and Sukh Devi (Bansal) Gupta; m. G. Cheryl Harmison, May 6, 1967; 1 child: Mahesh Daniel. BS with honors, Punjab U., Chandigarh, India, 1961, MS with honors, 1962; rsch. diploma, Saha Inst. Nuclear Physics, Calcutta, India, 1963; PhD in Solid State Physics, U. Md., 1971. Rsch. assoc. La. State U., Baton Rouge, 1970-72, vis. asst. prof., 1972-80; mem. tech. staff Computer Scis. Corp, Silver Spring, Md., 1980-83; computer scientist Computer Scis. Corp, Silver Spring, 1983-90, cons. engr., 1990-96, sr. prin. engr., 1996—. Contbr. articles to Phys. Review and others profl. jours. Chmn. troop com. Boys Scouts Am., 1994—, vol., 1984—; vol. PTA, Montgomery County, Md., 1982-95. Named Manned Space Flight Honoree NASA, 1989; recipient of several group achievement awards NASA, 1990-98; U.S. Army grantee, 1972-79. Mem. Am. Phys. Soc., Nat. Mgmt. Assn., U. Md. Alumni Assn. Office: Computer Scis Corp 15245 Shady Grove Rd Rockville MD 20850-3222

SINGHAL, VIVEK KUMAR, management consultant; b. Delhi, India, May 15, 1949; came to the U.S., 1970; s. Om Prakash Saraswati and Kirti Rani; m. Asha Garg; children; Ritu, Vikas. BSEE, Indian Inst. Tech., New Delhi, 1970; MSEE, U. Mich., 1971, MBA, 1973. Cert. mgmt. cons. Inst. Mgmt. Cons. Various positions Rockwell Internat., Troy, Mich., 1973-77; dir. strategic planning Sara Lee Corp., Chgo., 1977-84; v.p. Beatrice Cos., Chgo., 1984-85; founder, pres. Global Outsource Bids, Oakbrook Terrace, Ill., 1986—; treas. Chgo. chpt. Planning Forum, 1981-83. Exec. com. mem. Assn. Indians in Am., Chgo., 1993-95; treas. Midwest Club, Oakbrook, Ill., 1994-96, dir. Inst. Mgmt. Cons., Chgo. Mem. U. Mich. Alumni Assn., World Future Soc. (v.p. Greater Chicagoland Futurists). Avocations: reading, travel, public speaking. E-mail:vsingha1@hotmail.com. Office: Strategic Bus Mgmt Co 2 Mid America Plz Oakbrook Terrace IL 60181-4451

SINGHANIA, LALIT KUMAR, environmental engineer, consultant; b. Lailunga, India, Dec. 8, 1954; s. Nathu Lal and Imarti Devi (Jain) S.; m. Sandhya Gupta, Jan. 27, 1981; children: Swadhaf, Vatsala. BSc in Agr. with honors, G.B. P.U. A & T, Nainital, India, 1974. Farmer Lailunga, 1975-77; sales and import exec. V.V. Rama Rao & Co., Hyderabad, India, 1978-83; propr. Analogic Devices, Raipur, India, 1983-85; propr., cons. Project Consultancy Bur., Raipur, India, 1985-89; mng. dir. Indus Tech. & Fin. Cons. Ltd., Raipur, India, 1990—; cons. RTFC Ltd., Raipur, 1990—; mng. dir. Indus Smelters Ltd., 1993—, Rameshwar Industries Ltd., 1993—; dir. Rameshwar Granite Ltd., 1998—, Rameshwar Agrofarm Ltd., 1997—; convenor Capitol Devel. Forum, 1999—. Editor Paryavaran Urja (Environment Energy) Times, Raipur, 1998—; author: (poetry) Kranti Kavya Kalash (Revolution Poetry), 1999, Samasyaon se Samadhan Tak (Problems to Solutions), 1993. Chmn. Environment Energy Found., Raipur, 1995—. Mem. N.Y. Acad. Scis., Nihon Kensei Kai Internat., Diabetic Rsch. Soc. (treas. Raipur chpt. 1995—), 4-H Club of Kans. Hindu. Avocations: reading, writing, meditation, gardening, music. Home: 28 College Rd, Chaubey Colony, Raipur 492001, India Office: Indus Tech Fin Cons Ltd, 325 Samata Colony, Raipur 49200, India

SINGHATEH, EDWARD, Gambian government official. Vice chmn. Govt. of Gambia, Banjul, sec. of state in Office of Pres. Office: Office of the Vice Chmn/Pres-Sec of State, State House, Banjul The Gambia*

SINGHER, LIVIU, electro-optical engineer; b. Bucharest, Romania, Dec. 17, 1959; s. Aurel and Marta (Gutman) S.; m. Anda Weintraub, July 21, 1983; three children. BSc, Technion U., 1985, MSc, 1988, DSc, 1994. Cons. DPA, Tel Aviv, Israel, 1988-90; vis. prof. Purdue U., Lafayette, Ind., 1994-96; lectr. Technion U., Haifa, Israel, 1996—. Office: Technion U Inst Technology, Agricultural Engring, 32000 Haifa Israel

SINGLA, SHAM LAL, surgeon; b. Kalanwali, India, Aug. 8, 1950; s. Parkash Chand and Ram (Pyari) S.; m. Sunita Aggarwal, Jan. 23, 1977; 1 child, Vitika. MBBS, MEd. Coll., Rohtak, India, 1974, MS, 1979. Lectr. surgery Med. Coll., Rohtak, India, 1980-85, reader surgery, 1985-90; assoc. prof. surgery PGIMS, Rohtak, India, 1990—; cons. in field. Contbr. articles to profl. jours. Fellow Internat. Coll. Surgeons; mem. Assn. Surgeons India, Indian Med. Assn., Assn. Surgery Haryana (hon. sec. 1993—). Avocations: singing, towing. Home: 321 Housing Bd Colony, Rohtak 124001, India

SINGLETARY, ALVIN D., lawyer; b. New Orleans, Sept. 27, 1942; s. Alvin E. and Alice (Pastoret) S.; m. Judy Louise Singletary, Dec. 3, 1983; children: Kimberly Dawn, Shane David, Kelly Diane. B.A., La. State U., 1964; J.D., Loyola U., New Orleans, 1969. Bar: La. 1969, U.S. Dist. Ct. (ea. dist.) La. 1972, U.S. Ct. Appeals (5th cir.) 1972, U.S. Supreme Ct. 1978, U.S. Ct. Appeals (11th cir.) 1981, U.S. Ct. Internat. Trade 1981, U.S. Ct. Customs and Patent Appeals 1982. Instr. Delgado Coll., New Orleans, 1976-77; sole practice, Slidell, La., 1970—; spl. asst. dist. atty. 22d Judicial Dist. Ct. Parish of St. Tammany, State of La.; sec.-treas. St. Tammany Pub. Trust Fin. Authority, Slidell, 1978—; Councilman-at-large City of Slidell, 1978—, interim mayor, 1985; mem. Democratic State Central Com., 1978-82; mem. Rep. State Ctrl. Com. Dist. 76, La., 1996—; del. La. Constl. Conv., 1972-73; chmn. sustaining membership enrollment Cypress dist. Boy Scouts Am., 1989—; chmn. Together We Build Program First Baptist Ch. of Slidell, La.; treas. Slidell Centennial Commn.; bd. dirs. St. Tammany Coun. on Aging. Mem. Delta Theta Phi. Baptist. Lodge: Lions. Office: PO Box 1158 Slidell LA 70459-1158

SINGLETARY, SONJA EVA, surgeon, educator; b. Coward, S.C., Dec. 23, 1952; m. Jim Harkrider; 1 child, Benjamin. BS, Clemson U., 1973. Faculty assoc. U. Tex. M.D. Anderson Cancer Ctr., Houston, 1985-86, assoc. prof. surgery, 1986-91, prof., 1996—. Author: Breast Cancer, 1999, Breast Cancer-M.D. Anderson Solid Tumor Oncology Series, 1999. Recipient Women on the Move award Tex. Exec. Women, 1998, Ptnrs. in Courage award, Houston, 1999, Cancer Fighters Eagle award, Houston, 1999; named to Good Housekeeping's Best Doctors in Am., 1999. E-mail: esinglet@mdanderson.org. Fax: 713-792-0722. Office: U Tex MD Anderson Cancer Ctr Box 106 1515 Holcombe Blvd Houston TX 77030-4009

SINGLETERRY, ROBERT CLAY, JR., aerospace technologist, research scientist; b. Fayetteville, N.C., Jan. 4, 1961; s. Robert Clay and Phyllis Lea (Donovan) S.; m. Maria Star Groshner, May 18, 1984. BS in Nuclear Engring., U. Ariz., 1984, MS, 1990, PhD, 1993; postgrad., U. Idaho, 1986-91, Coll. of William and Mary, 1998—. Software-reactor engr. Ga. Power Co., Baxley, 1984-85; software engr. Energy Inc., Idaho Falls, 1985-89; grad. rsch. asst. U. Ariz., Tucson, 1989-93; rsch. asst. Argonne Nat. Lab., Idaho Falls, summers 1989-93, staff nuclear engr., 1993-97; prin. mem. Quantum Solutions, LLC, Idaho Falls, 1995-97; aerospace technologist, research scientist NASA Langley Rsch. Ctr., Hampton, Va., 1997—; adj. prof. dept. nuclear sci. and engring. Idaho State U., Pocatello, 1994-97; vis. scientist program coord. Idaho Acad. Sci., 1997. Contbr. articles to profl. jours. Vice-chair Young Women's Conf., Idaho Falls, 1993-94, chair, 1994-95. Mem. Am. Nuc. Soc. (leader tech. working group on nuclear space techs.), Va. Acad. Sci. Avocations: golf, volleyball, teaching, community service. Fax: 757-864-8094. E-mail: r.c.singleterry@larc.nasa.gov. Home: 102 Chadwick Ct Yorktown VA 23693-5004 Office: NASA Langley Rsch Ctr Mail Ctr Stop 188B Hampton VA 23681-0001

SINGLETON, ROBERT CULTON, graduate school administrator, Bible educator; b. Amarillo, Tex., Oct. 17, 1950; s. William Madison and Doris (Culton) S.; m. Stephanie Diane Lawrence, May 17, 1975; children: Kristin Michelle, Robert Culton Jr. BSEE, U. Tex., 1973; ThM in Bible Exposition, Dallas Theol. Sem., 1977; PhD in Higher Edn., U. Tex., 1993. Ordained to ministry Cmty. Bible Chapel, 1981. Campus staff Campus Crusade for Christ, Dallas, 1974-77; dean Nairobi (Kenya) Internat. Sch. Theology, 1978-83; grad. studies staff Campus Crusade for Christ, Austin, Tex., 1984-92; dean faculty East Asia Sch. Theology, Singapore, 1993-96; faculty The Orlando (Fla.) Inst., 1997—; bd. dirs. Nairobi Internat. Sch. Theology, 1981-83. Contbr. articles to profl. jours. Mem. Kappa Delta Pi, Phi Kappa Phi. So. Bapt. Avocations: personal computers, tennis.

SINGLETON, ROGER, charitable association executive; b. Sheffield, U.K., Nov. 6, 1942; s. Malcolm and Ethel S.; m. Ann Hasler, July 30, 1966; children: Jane, Katharine. MA, Durham (Eng.) U., 1965; Diploma in Social Studies, London U., 1970; MSc, Bath (Eng.) U., 1980. Various positions in care/edn. disadvantaged young people, 1961-71; profl. advisor Children's Regional Planning Com., Durham, 1971-74; dep. dir. Barnardo's, London, 1974-84, sr. dir./chief exec., 1984—. Contbr. articles to profl. jours. Mem. Inst. of Mgmt. (companion), Reform Club. Avocations: timber-framed buildings, gardening. Office: Barnardo's, Tanner's Ln, Barkingside Ilford IG6 1QG, England

SINGLETON, SOLVEIG M., lawyer; b. Berkeley, Calif., Oct. 2, 1965; d. Marvin and Marilyn (Kolstad) S. BA, Reed Coll., Portland, Oreg., 1987; JD, Cornell U., 1992. Dir. info. studies Cato Inst., Washington, 1996—. Co-editor: Regulators' Revenge, 1998, Economic Casualties, 1999; co-creator web site: y2kculture.com., 1999; editor Telecomm. and Electronic Media News, Federalist Soc., Washington, 1996-99. Avocations: painting, knitting, gardening, raising tropical fish. Office: Cato Inst 1000 Massachusetts Ave NW Washington DC 20001-5400

SINGMASTER, DAVID BREYER, mathematics educator; b. St. Louis, Dec. 14, 1938; s. James Arthur Jr. and Marjorie Love (Breyer) S.; m. Geralda Brighouse, Dec. 20, 1960 (div. 1968); m. Deborah De Vere White, Apr. 15, 1972; 1 child, Jessica. Student Calif. Inst. Tech., 1956-59, Pasadena City Coll., 1959-60; BA, U. Calif.-Berkeley, 1961, MA, 1964, PhD, 1966. Asst. prof. Am. U. Beirut, Lebanon, 1966-68; temporary lectr. Bedford Coll., London, 1970; lectr., sr. lectr., profl. reader math. Poly. of South Bank, London, 1970-96, vis. prof., 1996—; hon. research fellow Univ. Coll., London, 1996—; research fellow U. Pisa, Italy, 1972-73, Open U., Milton Keynes, Eng., 1979; pres. David Singmaster Ltd., London, 1981-82; series editor Oxford U. Press, Eng., 1983-90. Author: Notes on Rubik's Magic Cube, 1980; (with A.D. Frey, Jr.) Handbook of Cubik Math., 1982. Compiler: list of 16mm films on math. subjects, 5 edits., 1979-83, broadcasts of puzzles on Can. radio; mem. Puzzle Panel, BBC Radio 4, 1998-99. Columnist: Enigma column L.A. Times, Braintwister column Daily Telegraph, 1988-2000; contbr. articles to profl. jours. Fellow Inst. Math. and Its Applications; mem. Am. Math. Soc., Math. Assn. Am., Assn. Tchrs. Math., London Math. Soc. (sec. 1976-79, council 1979-80), Brit. Combinatorial Com., Com. of Brit. Math. Colloquium, Brit. Soc. History Math. (council), Univ. Math. Teaching Conf. Avocations: tourism, art, puzzles, games, music, humour. Home: 87 Rodenhurst Rd, London SW4 8AF, England Office: South Bank U, London SE1 0AA, England

SINHA, ABINASH KUMAR, science administrator; b. Dalsingsarai, Bihar, India, Jan. 12, 1940; p. Radha Madhav Prasad and Daya Manjari Sinha; m. Rani Asthana, Jan. 10, 1967; m. Reeta Sinha, Nov. 29, 1970; 1 child, Anupama. BA, Ranchi (Bihar) U., 1959; MA, Bhagalpur U., Bihar, 1961. Auditor Defence Accounts, Gauhat, India, 1963; sub inspector Ministry Home Affairs, New Delhi, 1964; inspector MHA, Patna, India, 1971-84; dep. supt. of police MHA, Patna, 1984-96, joint asst. dir., 1996-97, asst. dir. cabinet secretriat, 1997-98. Avocations: painting, photography, mountaineering, shooting. E-mail: anupama sinha7@yahoo.com. Office: MHA, New Delhi 110022, India

SINHA, BIKASH CHAN, science administrator; b. Calcutta, India, June 16, 1945; s. Kumar Brindaban Chandra and Uma (Sarkar) S.; m. Debjani Bose, Dec. 11, 1967; children: Tanya, Amartya. BSc in Physics with honors, Presidency Coll., Calcutta, 1964; BA in Natural Scis. Tripos, Cambridge, London, 1967, MA in Natural Scis. Tripos, 1968; PhD, London U., 1970, DSc, 1981. Sr. rsch. fellow King's Coll., London, 1970-76; sr. sci. officer Bhabha Atomic Rsch. Ctr., Bombay, 1976-83; head sect. Variable Energy Cyclotron Ctr. Bhabha Atomic Rsch. Ctr., Calcutta, 1983-85, head divsn., 1985-86, dir. Variable Energy Cyclotron Ctr. dept. atomic energy, 1987—; dir. dept. atomic energy Saha Instn. Nuclear Physics, Calcutta, 1992—; mem. coun. Inst. Physics, Bhubaneswar, India, 1988; mem., chmn. adv. com. Atomic Energy Commn., Bombay, 1988. Editor various conf. procs. Mem.

coun. Cancer Ctr. & Welfare Home, Calcutta, 1990; mem. senate Calcutta U., 1992; pres. Kandi Raj Sch., Murshidabad, India, 1994. Recipient Satyendra Nath Bose Birth Centenary award Indian Sci. Congress Assn., 1994. Fellow NAS, Indian Nat. Sci. Acad., N.Y. Acad. Scis.; mem. Indian Phys. Soc. (life), Indian Vacuum Soc. (pres. Calcutta chpt.), Indian Physics Assn. (life), Internat. Soc. Radiation Physics (pres. 1997—), Bengal Club (com. mem.), Calcutta Club, Saturday Club, South Club. Avocations: tennis, literature, folk music, science education, cancer therapy and diagnostics. Home: 2/4B Sarat Bose Rd, Calcutta 700 020, India Office: Variable Energy Cyclotron, Ctr 1/AF Bidhan Nagar, Calcutta 700 064, India

SINHA, BRAJRAMAN PRASAD, civil engineer, educator; b. Hazipur, Bihar, India, Dec. 20, 1936; s. B.N. and S. (Devi) S.; m. N. Sahay, June 2, 1962; children: Sangeeta, Saurabh, Shameek. BSc, Patna (India) U., 1957; postgrad. diploma in bldg. sci., Liverpool (England) U., 1964; PhD, U. Edinburgh, Scotland, 1967, DSc, 1998. Engring. asst. works dept. Patna U., 1957-59; asst. engr. Bihar Electricity Bd., Ranchi, India, 1959-60; asst. engr. dept. pub. works Bihar, 1960-63, design engr. dept. pub. works, 1968-69; demonstrator and rsch. asst. U. Edinburgh, 1966-68, from rsch. fellow to sr. lectr., 1969-95, reader, 1995—, prof., 1999; UNDP cons., Roorkee, Madras, India, 1986; vis. prof. Bihar Coll. Engring., 1984; vis. cons. and advisor dept. civil engring. U. Santa Catarina, Florianopolis, Brazil, 1991—; vis. prof. U. Ancona, Italy, 1999, Indian Inst. Sci., Bangalore, 2000. Co-author: Load-Bearing Brickwork Design, 1987; co-editor: Structural Masonry for Developing Countries, 1992; contbr. chpt.: Reinforced and Prestressed Masonry, 1989; contbr. articles to profl. jours. Active Lothian Racial Equality Coun., Edinburgh, 1984—; mem. senate Edinburgh U., 1984—; chmn. Hindu Temple and Cultural Ctr., Edinburgh, 1985-86; active Boroughmuir Sch. Coun., Edinburgh, 1981; pres. Indian Arts Coun., 1994. Recipient prize Instn. of Engrs. India, 1991-92. Mem. Internat. Masonry Engring. for Developing Countries (exec. dir. 1982), Internat. Coun. Bldg. Rsch. (mem. commn. W23A 1976). Hindu. Avocations: reading, overseas travel, photography, table tennis, writing. Office: U Edinburgh Dept Civil Engr, Kings Bldgs, Edinburgh EH9 3JN, Scotland

SINHA, DIPENDRA NARAYAN, economist, educator; b. Giridih, India, Oct. 29, 1951; s. Dwijendra and Pratima (Ghosh) S.; m. Dorina Sinha, July 23, 1993. BA, U. Calcutta, 1970, MA, 1972; PhD, U. Nebr., 1987. Dep. magistrate Govt. West Bengal, Maldah, India, 1974-76; asst. dir. Govt. India, New Delhi, 1976-81; rsch. & tchg. asst. U. Nebr., Lincoln, 1981-86; asst. prof. Moorhead (Minn.) State U., 1987-88, U. Ctrl. Okla., Edmond, 1988-91; from lectr. to sr. lectr., dir. grad. studies Macquarie U., Sydney, Australia, 1991—. Office: Macquarie U, Dept Econs, Sydney NSW 2109, Australia

SINHA, KAMESHWAR PRASAD, biochemist; b. Kubauli Ram, Bihar, India, May 5, 1929; s. Sanandandan Prasad Sinha and Rajkumari Devi; m. Kusum Pandey, June 4, 1956; children: Jayshree, Rajiv Ranjan. B Medicine B Surgery, Darbhanga Med. Coll., Laheriasarai, India, 1954; MSc in Med. Sci., Patna (India) Med. Coll., 1958; MD, Patna U., 1966; PhD, London U., 1970. Cert. Bihar Coun. Med. Registration. Tutor in biochemistry Patna Med. Coll., 1955-60, lectr., 1961-66, 70-76, prof. biochemistry, 1977-86; sr. rsch. asst. Univ. Coll., London, 1967-70; dir. health svcs. Govt. of Bihar, 1986-87; dir. lab. Biochem.-Lab., Patna, 1987—. Author: Manual of Practical Biochemistry, 1973; editor Indian Jour. Clin. Biochemistry, 1985-90. Fellow Assn. Clin. Biochemists of India (founding sec. 1975-85, v.p. 1986, pres. 1987, sec. 1990-94, sec.-gen. 1995—), Asian-Pacific Fedn. Clin. Biochemistry (treas. 1979-85), Asian-Pacific Congress Clin. Biochemistry (chmn. organizing com. 1996—), Bankipore Club. Home: Budha Colony Main Rd, Neer Shreekunj Apt, Patna Bihar 800001, India Office: Biochem Lab, East Boring Canal Rd, Patna Bihar 800001, India

SINHA, NAKUL, cardiologist; b. Lucknow, India, June 16, 1955; s. Krishna and Shailla (Lal) S.; m. Jyoti Shrivastava, May 8, 1983; two children. MBBS, KG Med. Coll., Lucknow, 1976, DM, 1981, MD, 1985. Lectr. KG Med. Coll., 1985-87; from asst. prof. to prof. Sanjay Ghandi Med. Sch., Lucknow, 1987—, prof., head dept. cardiology, invasive and interventional cardiologist; advisor Forest Hosp., Haldwani, India, 1992—; mem. Internat. Lipid Info. Bur., 1995. Editl. advisor Cardiology Today; mem. editl. bd. Indian Heart Jour. Fellow Soc. Cardiac Angiography; mem. Am. Coll. Cardiology, Cardiol. Soc. India (exec. com. mem. UP chap., founder mem., sec.), Assn. Physicians India. Home: VA-9 Sanjay Ghandi PGI, 226 014 Lucknow India

SINHA, PRABHAS CHANDRA, political geographer, environmentalist, researcher, educator, consultant; b. Punhad Darbhanga, Bihar, India, Dec. 3, 1960; s. Mutki Nath and Sone (Devi) Singh; m. Mamta, July 04, 1991; children: Vidit, Aabhas. MA in Geography/Regional Devel., 1983; MPhil, Jawaharlal Nehru U., New Delhi, 1986, Doctoral Degree, 1988; diploma in conflict resolution, Uppsala (Sweden) U., 1988; participant global studies/IHP program, Peace Studies Around the World, 1989-90. Postdoctoral Environ. and Policy Inst. East West Ctr., Honolulu, 1988-89; Univ. Grants Commn. jr. rsch. fellow Jawaharlal Nehru U., India, 1984-86, Univ. Grants Commn. sr. rsch. fellow, 1986-88, Coun. Sci. and Indsl. Rsch. pool officer, 1990-93, rsch. assoc. Sch. Internat. Studies, 1994-99; sr. program officer World Wide Fund for Nature India, New Delhi, 1993-94; cons. Indian Law Inst., New Delhi, 1991-92, Ministry Environ. and Forests, New Delhi, 1993-94, World Wide Fund for Nature-India, 1997-2000, EQUATIONS, Bangalore; cons., advisor Soc. for Indian Ocean Studies, New Delhi, 1996-99; cons., vis. fellow Nat. Law Sch. of India U., Bangalore, 1998-2000. Author: India's Ocean Policy, 1994; contbr. articles to profl. publs. Mem. Dr. Heniryk Skolimowski Internat. Ctr. for Ecophilosophy, 1995—, Eco Devel. Found. India, New Delhi, 1997—. Bradley Found. fellow Salzburg (Austria) Seminar, 1996. Mem. Soc. Ocean Scientists and Technologists (joint sec. 1996-2000), Pacific Congress on Marine Sci. and Tech. (India chpt. Honolulu), East West Ctr. Alumni Assn., Salzburg Seminar Alumni Assn., Indian Maritime Found., Am. Exch. Alumni Network, Found. for Conflict Resolution (sec. 1998-2000), Aqua Found. (treas. 1998-2000). Avocations: travel, cooking, reading, sight-seeing, photography. Home: B-1/1485 Vasant Kunj, New Delhi 110070, India Office: Jawaharlal Nehru U, Sch Internat Studies, 110067 New Delhi India

SINHA, PRABHAT KUMAR, anesthesiologist, educator, consultant; b. Bodhgaya, Bihar, India, Mar. 30, 1961; s. Ishwari Prasad and Tuneshwari Devi. MB, BS, Darbhanga (India) Med. Coll., 1988, MD in Anesthesiology, 1994; diploma in orthopedics, Patna (Bihar) Med. Coll., 1992; postdoctoral cert. course in neuroanesthesiology, Sanjay Gandhi Postgrad. Inst. of Med. Scis., 1996. Jr. resident Darbhanga Med. Coll., 1989-91, 92-94, Patna Med. Coll., 1991-92; registrar Holy Family Hosp., Patna, 1994-95; sr. resident Sanjay Gandhi Postgrad. Inst. Med. Scis., Lucknow, India, 1998; sr. lectr. anesthesiology Govt. Med. Coll., Chandigarh, India, 1998—. Contbr. articles to med. jours., including Jour. Neurosurg. Anesthesia, Anesthesia Analgesia, Anesthesiology, Brit. Jour. Anaesthesia. Mem. Rasttriya Swayamsewak Sangh, India, 1983-94. Comdg. officer Nat. Cadet Corps, 1982-85. Fellow Nat. Cadet Corps, 1983. Mem. Nat. Medicos Orgn. (life, sec. Darbhanga 1983-88), Indian Soc. Anesthesiology (life, T.N. Jha meml. travel grantee 1993), Indian Soc. Neuroanesthesiology and Critical Care (life). Avocations: creative writing, chess, travel, social and constructive work. Fax: 91-172-600531. E-mail: global@ch1.dot.net.in. Home: 1220C, Sector 32B, UT Chandigarh 160 047, India Office: Govt Med Coll, Sector 32, UT Chandigarh 160 047, India

SINHA, PRADEEP KUMAR, computer scientist, researcher; b. Gaya, India, Nov. 10, 1958; s. Manmohan and Prabhavati Prasad; m. Priti Srivastava, May 13, 1987; 1 child, Deeptansu. B of Engring., U. Allahabad, India, 1980; MS, Indian Inst. Tech., Madras, 1983; DSc, U. Tokyo, 1991. Devel. engr. ORG Systems, Baroda, India, 1983-84; programmer Oil and Ntural Gas commn., Nazira, India, 1984-87; sr. coord. Matsushita Electric Indsl. Co. Ltd., Tokyo, 1991-96; program coord. Ctr. for Devel. of Advanced Computing, Pune, India, 1996—. Author: Distributed Operating Systems: Concepts & Design, 1997, Computer Fundamentals, 1991. Mem. IEEE, Computer Soc. India (life). Avocations: movies, songs, family outings. Office: Ctr Devel Advanced Computin, Pune Univ Campus, Pune 411007, India

SINHA, RAJESHWAR PRASAD, scientist, researcher; b. Darbhanga, Bihar, India, Jan. 2, 1965; s. Maheshwar Prasad and Asha Lata Sinha; m. Alka Sahay, Feb. 5, 1995; 1 child, Prakhar Raj. BS with honors, Lalit Narayan Mithila U., Darbhanga, India, 1988; MS, Lalit Naravan Mithila U., Darbhanga, India, 1990; PhD, Banaras Hindu U., Varanasi, India, 1995; grad. aptitude test in engring., Indian Inst. Tech., Bangalore, India, 1991. Cert. biotechnologist. Jr. rsch. fellow Dept. Biotech., Varanasi, 1990-95; German Acad. Exch. Svc. fellow Inst. Botany I, Erlangen, Germany, 1993-96; rsch. assoc. Inst. Agrl. Scis., Varanasi, 1996-97, 98-99; vis. scientist Inst. Botany I, Erlangen, 1997-98, 99—. Contbr. rsch. articles to profl. jours. Recipient Spl. State Merit award Bihar Govt., 1988, Rsch. Associateship, Coun. Sci. and Indsl. Rsch., 1996. Mem. European Soc. for Photobiology, The Internat. Soc. for Study of Origin of Life (com. on space rsch.). Avocations: reading, writing, music, games and sports, travel. Office: Inst for Botany I, Staudstrasse 5, D-91058 Erlangen Germany

SINHA, RATHINDRANATH, chemical engineering educator, researcher; b. Dakshin Barasat, W. Bengal, India, Jan. 27, 1945; s. Nitya Niranjan and Nirupama (Bose) S.; m. Pratibha Chanda, May 14, 1983; 1 child, Proteeti. B in Tech. (Chem. Engring.), Andhra U., Visakhapatnam, India, 1968, M in Tech. (Chem. Engring.), 1972, PhD in Chem. Engring., 1978. Sr. rsch. fellow Coun Sci. and Indsl. Rsch., Visakhapatnam, 1972-75; rsch. fellow Andhra U., Visakhapatnam, 1975; sr. rsch. fellow U. Grants Commn. Govt. of India, Visakhapatnam, 1975-78; lectr. in chem. engring. Andhra U., Visakhapatnam, 1979-87, reader in energy engring. dept. chem. engring., 1987-94, prof. chem. engring., 1994; co-prin. investigator C.S.I.R. Scheme, Viskhapatnam, 1979-82, MHRD Project, Govt. India, Viskhapatnam, 1988-96; group scientist PL-480 Project, Viskhapatnam, 1984-87; group scientist Univ. Grants Commn. to establish Energy Park, 1999—, co-prin. investigator project on devel. alternate fuel oil from bio-wealth, 2000—. Contbr. articles to profl., internat. jours. Mem. Indian Soc. for Tech. Edn. (life), Indian Inst. Chem. Engrs. (life), AICTE (All India Councl. for Tech. Edn.) (Southern Region, expert com. Polymers & Plastics at the Poly. level, 1997-98). Avocations: fine arts and literature. Office: Andhra U, Dept Chem Engring, AP Visakhapatnam 530 003, India

SINHA, SATYABROTO, electrical engineering educator; b. Calcutta, India, June 3, 1940; s. Prabhat Chandra and Sailabala (Basu) S.; m. Gita Dutta, Dec. 4, 1969; children: Santanu, Sandipan. BSc with honors, Calcutta U., 1957, MSc in Tech., 1960; MTech, Indian Inst. Tech., Kharagpur, 1967, PhD, 1980; MASc, U. Toronto, 1975. Chartered engr., India. Asst. elec. engr. DVC, Calcutta, 1962-63; lectr. elec. engring. Indian Inst. Tech., Kharagpur, 1963-71, asst. prof. elec. engring., 1971-82, prof. curriculum devel. in elec. engring., 1982-84, prof. elec. engring., 1984—, dean campus mgmt., 1998-99; mem. bd. govs. Indian Inst. Tech., Kharagpur, 1986-87; bd. govs. REC Durgapur, India, 1985-88. Co-author: Computer Aided Analysis, Synthesis and Expertise of Active Filters, 1995. Mem. IEEE (sr.; founder mem., chmn. program com. Kharagpur sect.), Inst. Engrs. India. Avocation: reading. Office: Indian Inst Tech, Kharagpur 721302, India

SINHA, SATYAJIT SAHAY, ophthalmologist; b. Colchester, U.K., Apr. 8, 1969; arrived in India, 1972; s. Ajit and Renu (Verma) S. MBBS, Kasturba Med. Coll., Mangalore, India, 1996; postgrad., J.J.M. Med. Coll., Davangere, India, 1996-99. Dep. dir. A.B. Eye Hosp., Patna, India, 1995—. Avocations: social work, traveling, swimming. Office: AB Eye Hosp Rd 12, Rajendra Nagar, Patna 800 016, India

SINHA, SUDIPTA, marketing research company executive; b. Mumbai, India, Sept. 11, 1953; s. Debi Prasad and Sushama Sinha; m. Durga Rani Basu, Feb. 5, 1980; children: Surjo, Siddhartha. BA with honors, K.C. Coll., Mumbai, 1974; MMS, J.S. Bajaj Inst. Mgmt., Mumbai, 1976. Rsch. exec. Indian Market Rsch. Bur., Calcutta, India, 1976-79; sr. rsch. exec. Indian Market Rsch. Bur., Calcutta, 1979-81, mgr. Calcutta office, 1981-85, dep. gen. mgr. Calcutta office, 1985-90, exec. v.p., 1990-94; chmn., mng. dir. Indica Rsch. India Pvt. Ltd., Calcutta, 1994—; former vis. faculty Indian Inst. Mgmt., Calcutta; vis. faculty Nat. Inst. Mgmt., Calcutta. Mem. European Soc. for Opinion and Mktg. Rsch., Market Rsch. Soc. U.K., The Saturday Club Ltd., Tollygunge Club Ltd., Royal Bombay Yacht Club. Hindu. Avocations: current business affairs, scientific developments. Home: 93/3A Bakul Dagen Rd, Calcutta 700025, India Office: Indica Rsch Pvt Ltd, 190/1 Rash Behari Ave 1st, Calcutta 700029, India

SINHA, YASHWANT, Indian government official; b. Patna, Bihar, India, Nov. 6, 1937; s. Shri Bipin Bihari Saran and Dhana Saran Devi; m. Nilima Sinha; children: Sharmila Kantha, Shri Jeyant, Shri Sumant. MA in Polit. Sci., Patna U., 1958. With Indian Adminstrv. Svc., 1960; Dy. commr. Santhal Pargana, 1965-67; consul gen. India Frankfurt, Germany, 1971-74; prin sec. to Chief Min. Bihar, 1977-80; joint sec. Ministry Shipping and Transport, India, from 1980; chmn. Delhi Transport Corp., 1982-83; gen. sec. Samajwadi Janata Party, 1986, elected to Rajya Sabha-Upper Parliament, 1988, mem. high level com., union fin. min.; now pres. Rajya Sabha, New Delhi; min. of finance Govt. of India, New Delhi, 1998S. Chmn., pres. several workers' unions, philanthropic and polit. orgns. Mem. D.G. Club. Home: 4 Teem Murti Marg, New Delhi 110011, India Office: Ministry of Finance, North Block, 110 001 New Delhi India*

SINISGALLI, ROCCO, classicist; b. Gallicchio, Italy, Jan. 26, 1947; s. Paolo and Teresina (Pandolfo) S.; m. Raffaela Vilardo, June 13, 1986; 1 child, Paola. Degree in classical studies, U. Rome, 1968, degree in architecture, 1973. Researcher U. Rome, 1980—; cons. in field, 1986—. Author or co-author, editor: Per la storia della prospettiva 1405-1605, 1978, Borromini a quattro dimensioni, 1981, I sei libri della prospettiva, 1984, Il planisfero di Tolomeo, 1992, L'Analemma di Tolomeo, 1992, La Prospettiva di Federico Commandino, 1993, La Rappresentazione degli Orologi Solari di Federico Commandino, 1994, La Teoria sui Planisferi Universali di Guidobaldo Del Monte, 1994, Leonardo's Conical Sections and Commandino's Editions on Ptolemy's Sphere, 1997. Nat. Gallery of Art fellow, Washington, 1988, 92. Avocations: music, drawing. Home: Lungomare, Paolo Toscanelli 14, 00122 Roma Ostia Lido Italy Office: Dept Rappresentazione e Rilievo, Piazza Borghese 9, 00189 Rome Italy

SINITSYN, IGOR NIKOLAEVICH, information scientist, educator; b. Moscow, Aug. 14, 1940; s. Nikolay Vasilievich and Alexa Gavrilovnandra (Baryshnikova) S.; m. Irina Vladimirovna Pugacheva, Oct. 18, 1963; 1 child, Vladimir Igorevich. Grad., Moscow State U., 1963, PhD, 1966; DSc, Inst. Applied Mechanics, Moscow, 1983. Prof. Air Force Engring. Acad. Zhukovsky, Moscow, 1966-75; head lab. Inst. Applied Mechanics, Moscow, 1975-84; head dept. Inst. for Informatics Problems, Russian Acad. Scis., Moscow, 1984—; prof. Moscow State Tech. Aviation U., 1987—. Authro: Stochastic Differential Systems, Analysis and Filtering, 1985, 90, English edit., 1987, Statistical Simulation of Forward Financial Transactions, 1996, Lectures on Functional Analysis and Applications, 1999. Mem. N.Y. Acad. Scis. E-mail: sinitsin@dol.ru. Fax: 095 310 70 50. Home: Leningradskii Prospect, 125167 Moscow Russia Office: Inst Informatics Problems, Vavilova 30/6, 117900 Moscow Russia

SINKEVICH, OLEG ARSEN'EVICH, physicist, educator, researcher; b. Pskov, Russia, Nov. 24, 1934; s. Arseny Vasil'evich and Zinaida Grigor'evna (Bogdanova) S.; m. Ludmila Petrovna Butchkova, Dec. 22, 1967. BSc in Engring., Power Coll., St. Petersburg, 1955; MSc in Heat Physics and Engring., Power Engring. Inst. Tech. U., Moscow, 1966; PhD in Physics and Math., Acad. Scis. USSR, Moscow, 1970. Technician Power Plant, Tashkent, Uzbekistan, 1955, Power Plant Constrn. Co., Narva, Estonia, 1958-59, Power Plant, Vilnius, Lithuania, 1959-60; asst. prof. Tech. U., Moscow, 1968-74, assoc. prof., reader, lectr., 1974-83, prof., 1983—; jr. rsch. scientist sci. br. Moscow Power Engring. Inst., 1966-70, rsch. scientist, 1970-81, chief rsch. scientist, 1981—, head plasma lab., 1969—; reviewer Inst. Sci. and Tech. Info., Acad. Scis. USSR, Moscow, 1970-92, Zentralblatt Math, Berlin, 1997—; cons. state and pvt. orgns.; mem. organizing com. All Union Sci. Conf. Gas Discharge, 1986, 88, 90, 92, 94, All Union Sci. Conf. Disperse Tech., 1989, Sci. Conf. and Workshops, 82, 85, 89, 90. Author: Physics of Solid Part I Statistic and Thermodynamic Properties of Solids, 1981, Part II The Kinetic Theory of Transfer Processes and Surface Phenomena in Solids, 1983, Part III The Cooperation Phenomena in Solids, 1984 (Moscow Power Engring. Inst. 1986), Plasma Physics, 1991, Instabilities and Turbulence in Low-Temperature Plasmas, 1994, Problems in Solid State Physics for Mechanical Engineers, 1998; contbr. articles to profl. jours.; mem. editl. bd. High Temperature Jour., 1985—; mng. editor Heat Physics of the Energetic Sys., 1983. Sgt. Soviet Mil., 1955-58. Grantee Presdl. Stipend for Prominent Russian Scientists, 1992-96, 96—, Russian Fund of the Fundamental Investigation, 1993-95, 97—. Mem. Russian Acad. Scis. (low temperature plasma sci. coun., vice chmn. glow discharge sect. 1979-90), Moscow Phys. Soc. Fax: (095) 362 89 38. E-mail: oleg.sinkevich@itf.mpei.as.ru. Office: Moscow Power Engring Inst, Krasnokazarmennay St 14, 105835 Moscow Russia

SINKO, CHRISTOPHER MICHAEL, pharmaceutical scientist; b. Englewood, N.J., July 19, 1962; s. Patsy John and Patricia Lou (Anderson) S.; m. Angela Carole Small, Aug. 5, 1984. BS in Chem. Engring., Rutgers U., 1984; MS in Pharmaceutics, U. Mich., 1986, DPhil in Pharmaceutics, 1989. Scientist The Upjohn Co., Kalamazoo, 1989-91; rsch. scientist Pfizer, Inc., Groton, Conn., 1991-93, sr. rsch. scientist, 1993-95, sr. rsch. investigator, 1995-97, mgr., 1997-98, asst. dir., 1998—; lectr. U. Mich. Coll. Pharmacy, Ann Arbor, 1990. Contbr. articles to profl. jours. Pharmaceutical Mfrs. Assn. fellow, 1987; recipient North Jersey Sect. Rsch. award AICE, 1984. Mem. Am. Assn. Pharm. Scientists. Achievements include identification and definition of physical aging mechanisms in glassy polymers, flow testing technique which is now routinely used to characterize the flowability of pharmaceutical formulations during product development. Office: Pfizer Ctrl Rsch Eastern Point Rd Groton CT 06340

SINKO, OTTO, holding company executive; b. Balassagyarmat, Hungary, Jan. 19, 1958; s. Jozsef Sinko and Erzsebet Bugyi; m. Gabriella Hegedüs; children: Szabolcs, Zsolt. BS in Elec. Engring., Tech. U. Budapest, 1982; MBA, Brunnel U., 1995; exec. edn. program, Harvard U., 1997—. Software engr. Medicor RT, Budapest, 1982-84; head of R&D dept. Müszertechnika RT, Budapest, 1984-89; v.p. Procomp USA, Cleve., 1989-91, Müszertechnika RT, Budapest, 1991-92, Videoton Holding RT, Szekesfehervar, Hungary, 1991—; mem. tech. foresight program, Budapest, 1998—. Mem. higher edn. and rsch. coun. Ministry of Edn. and Culture, Budapest, 1998—. Mem. C. of C. and Industry for Fejer County (bd. dirs. 1993—). Avocations: sailing, skiing, swimming. Office: Videoton Holding RT, Berenyi St 72-100, 8000 Szekesfehervar Hungary

SINKOVIC, VJEKOSLAV, electrical engineer; b. Bratkovec, Croatia, June 15, 1938; m. Djurdjica. BS, U. Zagreb, 1962, MSEE, 1966, PhD, 1968. From asst. to prof. electrical engring. U. Zagreb, Croatia, 1963—. Author: Information Networks, 1994, Information Theory, 1984, Information: Symbolic and Semantic, 1997, Fusion of Neural Networks, Fuzzy Sets, & Genetics, 1999. Office: Faculty EE & Computing, Unska 3, Zagreb Croatia 10000

SINNADURAI, NIHAL, electronics technology educator, consultant; b. Colombo, Sri Lanka, Sept. 25, 1941; arrived in Eng., 1958; s. Namasivayam and Hilda Maisie (Heyn) S.; children: Natalie, Paul. BSc in Physics with honors, U. London, 1966, MSc in Semiconductor Physics, 1969; PhD, U. Southampton, Eng., 1978. Head advanced hardware Brit. Telecom Rsch. Ctr., Ipswich, Suffolk, Eng., 1980-85; sr. cons. BPA Tech. and Mgmt., Dorking, Surrey, Eng., 1985-86; from head CAE strategy to divsn. mgr. Brit. Telecomm. Labs., Ipswich, 1986-93; prof. electronics tech., head microelectronics dept. Middlesex U., London, 1994-95; prin. cons. TWI, Cambridge, Eng., 1995-2000; freelance eldctronics tech. and reliability cons., 2000—; dir. edn. Ctr. for Profl. Advancement, East Brunswick, N.J., 1982-94; bd. dirs. Advanced Tech. and Tng. Access Consultancy (ATTAC), U.K., 1987—, Vikas Hybrids and Electronics Ltd., New Delhi, India, 1988-94; expert, sr. expert UN Devel. Program, Geneva, 1982-94; vis. prof. Loughborough (Eng.) U., 1995—. Author: Mechanisms of Failure in Semiconductors, 1970; author, editor: Handbook of Microelectronics Packaging, 1985; inventor, patentee EPIC Microelectronics Package, 1981, Liquid Crystal Temperature Measurement, 1974, HAST Humidity Test Technique, 1968. Fellow IEEE, Inst. Physics, Internat. Microelectronics and Packaging Soc. (chmn. 1986-88, 94-96, Europe chmn. 1987-89, Man of Yr. 1988, Best paper 1982, Tech. Achievement award 1983). Avocations: long distance running, squash, contract bridge, sailing, scuba diving.

SINNING, MARK ALAN, thoracic and vascular surgeon; b. Holton, Kans., Apr. 24, 1953; s. Henry Harold andf Valere Madelene (Davey) S.; m. Kathy Diann Pugh, Sept. 25, 1982; children: Sarah, Emily, Mark, Rachel, Walter. BA, U. Kans., 1975; MD, U. Kans., Kansas City, 1978. Diplomate Am. Bd. Surgery, Am. Bd. Thoracic Surgery. Gen. surgery resident St. Luke's Hosp., Kansas City, Mo., 1978-83, thoracic surgery resident, 1983-85; pvt. practice Coastal Surg. Specialists, PA, New Bern, N.C., 1986—; attending staff Danbury (Conn.) Hosp., 1985-86, Craven Regional Med. Ctr., New Bern, 1986—; asst. clin. prof. East Carolina U., Greenville, 1992—. Fellow ACS, Am. Coll. Chest Physicians; mem. AMA, Soc. Thoracic Surgeons, So. Assn. Thoracic Surgery, N.C. Med. Soc., Phi Beta Kappa, Alpha Omega Alpha. Avocations: golf, snow skiing, music. Office: Coastal Surgical Specialists 800 Hospital Dr Ste 10 New Bern NC 28560-3489

SINNOTT, JAN MARIE DYNDA, psychologist; b. Cleve., June 14, 1942; d. Edward Joseph and Dorothy Mary (Zurek) Dynda; children: James, Gwenn, Kiersten, Gavyn. BS, St. Louis U., 1964; MS, Cath. U., Washington, 1973, PhD, 1975. Lic. psychologist, Md. Rsch. psychologist Human Scis. Rsch. Inc., McLean, Va., 1975; rsch. psychologist, prof. Cath. U. Sch. Social Svcs., Washington, 1975-77; rsch. psychologist, pres. Human Devel. Rsch. Inc., Silver Spring, Md., 1977-80; rsch. psychologist U. Md. Ctr. on Aging, College Park, 1978-81; rsch. psychologist, guest scientist Gerontology Rsch. Ctr., Nat. Inst. Aging, NIH, Balt., 1980-89; prof. psychology Towson U., Balt., 1978—, dir. honors program in human devel. psychology, 1999—; dir. Ctr. for Study of Adult Devel. and Aging Towson State U., Balt., 1989-91; steering com. Soc. for Rsch. in Adult Devel., 1987-91; bd. dirs. Inst. Noetic Scis. Editor: Everyday Problem Solving, 1989, Bridging Paradigms, 1991, Everyday Memory, 1991, Interdisciplinary Handbook of Adult Lifespan Learning, 1993; author: Sex Roles and Aging, 1986, Reinventing the University, 1996, Development of Logic in Adulthood: Postformal Thought & Its Applications, 1998; editl. bd. Jour. Adult Devel., 1992—; contbr. articles to profl. jours. Policy com. U. Md. System Women's Forum, College Park. Grantee NIH, 1980-89, Adminstrn. on Aging, 1979-82. Fellow APA, Gerontol. Soc. Am., Am. Psychology Soc.; mem. NOW, AAUP, Assn. for Women in Psychology, Philosophy of Psychology Study Group, Am. Assn. for Study Mental Imagery, Internat. Soc. Study of Energy Medicine, Ea. Psychol. Assn., Amnesty Internat., Planned Parenthood Internat. Office: Towson U Psychology Dept Baltimore MD 21252-0001

SINOHARA, HYOGO, medical educator; b. Kitaibaraki, Ibaraki, Japan, Jan. 16, 1931; s. Makiko Susuki, May 1, 1961; 2 children. B Medicine, Tohoku U., Sendai, Japan, 1955; MD, Tohok U., 1960. Rsch. assoc. Presbyn.-St. Luke's Hosp., Chgo., 1960-65, U. Ill., Chgo., 1960-65; asst. prof. Iwate Med. Sch., Morioka, Japan, 1965-74; prof. Kinki U., Osaka-Sayama, Japan, 1974-2000; prof. emeritus Kinki U., 2000—; dir. Mikinosono Inst. Elderly Health, Sakai, Japan, 2000—. Author: Life Science in the Living Room (in Japanese), 1973, Forerunners of Life Science (in Japanese), 1983. Mem. N.Y. Acad. Sci. Home: 3-16-7 Onodai, Osaka 589, Japan Office: Mikinosono Inst, 1359-2 Mikitakami, Sakai Osakla 590-0136, Japan

SIOCHI, RAMON ALFREDO CARVALHO, physicist; b. Manila, May 22, 1963; came to the U.S., 1985; s. Andres Eulogio and Loiva (Carvalho) S.; m. Ann Webb, June 15, 1991; children: Jeremiah, Katherine. BS in Physics, Ateneo de Manila, Quezon City, The Philippines, 1985; PhD in Physics, Va. Tech., 1990; MS in Radiol. Physics, U. Cin., 1995. Rsch. asst. Va. Tech., Blacksburg, 1987-90, asst. prof., 1991; asst. prof. Muskingum Coll., New Concord, N.H., 1991-93; rsch. asst U. Cin., 1993-95; med. physicist Siemens Med. Sys., Concord, Calif., 1995—. contbr. articles to profl. jours. Mem. Am. Assn. Physicists Medicine, S.E. chpt. Am. Assn. Physicists Medicine. Republican. Achievements include patents in Optimization of an Intensity Modulated Field, Virtual Compensator. Avocations: music, bird watching, computers, languages. Fax: 919-387-7869. Office: Siemens Med Sys 1103 Smokewood Dr Apex NC 27502-8526

SIODLA, KRZYSZTOF, electrical engineering educator; b. Poznan, Poland, Nov. 16, 1955; s. Benedykt and Bogumila (Krodkiewska) S.; m. Dorota Borowczyk, 1986; children: Elzbieta, Anna. MS, Poznan U., 1980; PhD, Poznan U. Tech., 1989. Constructor Poznan U. Tech., 1980-83, asst., 1983-84, sr. asst., 1984-90, asst. prof., 1990—; chief high voltage lab. Poznan U. Tech., 1991—. Contrb. articles to profl. jours. Mem. Assn. Polish Elec.

Engrs. (expert 1990—). Home: os W Jagielly 5/24, 60-694 Poznan Poland Office: Poznan U Tech, 3A Piotrowo Str, 60-965 Poznan Poland

SION, JEAN-PAUL O.M., physician; b. Sint-Amandsberg, Belgium, Mar. 1, 1960; s. Hubert Sion and Agnes Heynderickx; m. Dominique Roofthooft, Dec. 3, 1988; children: Christophe, Stephanie. MD, UIA, Antwerp, Belgium, 1985. Infection control physician U. Hosp., Antwerp, 1990-97; lab. medicine specialist Monica, Antwerp, 1990—. Mem. Am. Soc. Microbiology, European Soc. Clin. Microbiology Infectious Diseases, Belgische Vereniging voor Klinische Biologie. E-mail: jpsion@monica.be. Fax: 03/238 72 48. Office: Harmoniestraat 68, B-2018 Antwerp Belgium

SIONKOWSKA, ALINA, chemist, researcher; b. Trzemeszno, Poland, June 16, 1963; d. Stanislaw and Boleskawa (Szajda) Manikowski; m. Grzegorz Sionkohski; children: Piotr, Mateusz. D Chemistry, Copernicus U., Torun, Poland, 1997. Primary sch. tchr., 1987-88; asst. Copernicus U., Torun, 1994-97, lectr., 1997—. Author: Metody 8 Techgniki in Spektzedkopie, 1998; contbr. articles to profl. jours. Grantee N. Copernicus U., 1996, 97, 98-99. Mem. Polish Chem. Soc. Home: Sw Jopzefa 11/45, 87-100 Torun Poland Office: Faculty Chemistry, Gagarin 7, 87-100 Torun Poland

SIOPONGCO, JOAQUIN ORODÑEZ, structural engineer, civil engineer; b. Mabalacat, The Philippines, Apr. 11, 1927; s. Jose Lim and Maria Hopolito (Orodoñez) S.; m. Milagros Dela Cruz, Feb. 9, 1954; children: Joaquin Jr., Marilou, Marisa, Joel, Marimil, Miriam, Jojet Niño. BSCE, Mapua Inst. Tech., Manila, 1953; M Applied Sci. in Structural Engring., U. Vancouver, B.C., Can., 1962; PhD, U. of The Philippines, Los Bañas, 1982. Dean engring. dept. Laguna Coll., San Pablo City, The Philippines, 1992—, affiliate professorial lectr. in civil engring., 1997-98; scientist dept. sci. and tech., dep. dir. Forest Products Rsch. and Devel. Inst., The Philippines, chief sci. rsch. specialist, dep. dir., 1953-92; mem. Internat. Com. on Bamboo Stds.; bd. cons. Nat. Structural Code of the Philippines, 1992. Author books, manuals and articles in field. Mem. Lay Ministers of the Holy Eucharist, Bukas Loob Sa Diyos. 2d lt. Philippine Mil. Res. Recipient Outstanding Alumnus in Forest Utilization Rsch. award U. of The Philippines, 1986, Outstanding Rsch. award Nat. Sci. and Devel. Bd., The Philippines, 1980, others. Mem. Assn. Structural Engrs. of The Philippines (bd. cons.), Nat. Rsch. Coun. of The Philippines (Achievement in Forest Utilization Rsch. award 1991), KC. Roman Catholic. Home: 10021 Mt Halcon St, Los Baños Laguna, The Philippines Office: Laguna Coll, San Pablo City Laguna, The Philippines

SIORES, ELIAS, mechanical engineering educator; b. Athens, June 17, 1960; s. Christopher and Panayota (Mahaira) S.; m. Dawn Patricia Moran, Sept. 11, 1988; 1 child, Christopher. BS, Newcastle-on-Tyne U., England, 1983; MS, Brunel U., London, 1985; MBA, U. Wollongong, Australia, 1991; PhD, Brunel U., 1988. Sr. lectr., lectr. U. Wollongong, Australia, 1988-92; assoc. prof. QUT, Brisbane, Australia, 1992-95; head sch. SUT, Melbourne, Australia, 1996-97; exec. dir. IRIS, Melbourne, Australia, 1997—; prof. mech. engr. SUT, Melbourne, Australia, 1997—; hon. prof. Tsinghua U., Beijing, 1998—; dir. Coop. Rsch. Ctr. Microtech., Australia, 1999—, Coop. Rsch. Ctr. IMST, Australia, 1999—, Coop. Rsch. Ctr. CASTmm, Australia, 1999—, Sinewave Tech. Ltd., Australiam 1989—. Contbr. articles to profl. jours.; inventor in field. Mem. SAE, WTIA (Ramsey Moon award 1992), IE Australia (Rsch. Excellence award 1994). Greek Orthodox. Avocations: sports car racing, squash, model building. Office: IRIS Swinbuane U Tech, 533-545 Burwood Rd, Melbourne VIC 3102, Australia

SIOUMIS, ANTHONY ARCHELAOU, chemistry researcher, educator; b. Kolindros, Pieria, Greece, Jan. 3, 1936; arrived in Australia, 1956; s. Archelaos Constantinos and Theopisti Antonios (Karambini) S.; m. Effie Nikolaos Papas, Feb. 16, 1963; children: Ari, Tammy. BSc, U. Melbourne, Australia, 1963, MSc, 1967. Exptl. scientist Commonwealth Sci. and Indsl. Rsch. Orgn., Australia, 1963-74; sr. rsch. scientist Commonwealth Sci. and Indsl. Rsch. Orgn., 1974-81, prin. rsch. scientist, 1981-95, sr. prin. rsch. scientist, 1995-99; ret., 1999; lectr. in postgrad. studies Royal Melbourne Inst. Tech., Australia, 1967-69. Contbr. over 80 articles to profl. jours.; patentee in field. Pres. Benevolent Brotherhood of Kolandros, Australia, 1967-84, Panmacedonian Assn. of Melbourne, Victoria, Australia, 1982-83; mem. citizens com. City of Melbourne, 1983-85. Mem. RACI, Appita. Avocations: golf, table tennis, bridge, music, guitar. Home: 24 Deakin St, East Bentleigh 3165, Australia

SIPAHIOGLU, HATICE ELCIN, diplomat, interpreter/translator; b. Ankara, Turkey, Apr. 8, 1969; came to U.S., 1997; d. Vahdet and Nurten Sipahioglu. BA, Hacettepe U., Ankara, 1990; MA, Hacettepe U., 1995; MBA, U. St. Thomas, 2000. Translator, interpreter Turkish State Rlwys., Ankara, 1990-95; adminstrv. officer Ministry Fgn. Affairs, Ankara, 1995-97; adminstrv. attaché Turkish Consulate Gen., Houston, 1997—. Scholar INst. for PUb. Adminstrn. for Turkey and Mid. East, Ankara, 1996-97. Mem. Houston World Affairs Coun., Houston Masterworks Chorus. Avocations: music, photography, yoga, hiking, travel. Home: 2345 Bering Dr Apt 435 Houston TX 77057-4754 Office: Turkish Consulate Gen 1990 Post Oak Blvd Ste 1300 Houston TX 77056-3833

SIPAROV, SERGEY VICTOROVICH, physics educator; b. Lenningrad, Apr. 18, 1954; s. Victor Sergeyevich and Julia Alexeyevna (Botkina) S.; m. Natalia Alexeyevna Lapteva, May 9, 1978; children: Georgiy, Ivan, Gennadiy. MS, State U., Leningrad, 1977; PhD, Technol. Inst., Leningrad, 1984; prof., Acad. of Civil Aviation, St. Petersburg, Russia, 1994. Rschr.-engr. Arctic Instn., Leningrad, 1977-81; postgrad. Tech. Inst., Leningrad, 1981-84, jr. rschr., 1984-86; asst. Acad. of Civil Aviation, Leningrad, 1986-88, sr. tchr., 1988-91; assoc. prof. Acad. of Civil Aviation, St. Petersburg, 1991-98; prof. Acad. Civil Aviation, St. Petersburg; sr. rschr. Acad. of Civil Aviation, 1988-92; assoc. prof. Inst. Biology and Psychology, St. Petersburg, 1994-97. Author: (book) Mechanics of adsorption in gas-solid systems, 1985; contbr. articles to profl. jours. Mem. ESSSAT (grant 1996). Avocations: literature, mountain climbing, philosophy. E-mail: sergey@siparov.spb.su. Office: Acad of Civil Aviation, 38 Pilotov St, 196210 Saint Petersburg Russia

SIPE, DENNIS LYLE, lawyer, municipal judge; b. Lansing, Mich., Feb. 20, 1948; s. Lyle O. and Lucille B. Sipe; m. Susan Ann, Jan. 5, 1974; children: Rachel Marie, Matthew Joseph. BS, Mich. State U., 1970; JD, Ohio State U., 1973. Bar: Ohio 1973, U.S. Dist. Ct. (so. dist.) Ohio 1974, U.S. Dist. Ct. (no. dist.) Ohio 1977, U.S. Ct. Appeals (6th cir.) 1977, U.S. Supreme Ct. 1980, U.S. Ct. Appeals (4th cir.) 1996. Pub. defender Clinton County Pub. Defender Office, Wilmington, Ohio, 1974-75; asst. prosecuting atty. Greene County Prosecutor's Office, Xenia, Ohio, 1975-76; asst. atty. gen. Atty. Gen. Ohio, Columbus, 1977-82; atty. Buell and Sipe Co. L.P.A., Marietta, Ohio, 1983—; acting judge Marietta Mcpl. Ct., 1985—; atty. Washington County Cmty. Improvement Corp., Marietta, 1983-85; small claims referee Marietta Mcpl. Ct., 1983-85. Bd. dirs. Marietta Youth Soccer, 1985-90; bd. trustees 1st Bapt. Ch., Marietta, 1988-99. Mem. Washington County Bar Assn. (pres. 1997), Lions. Avocations: golf, basketball, singing. Office: Buell and Sipe Co LPA 322 3rd St Marietta OH 45750-2901

ŠÍPEK, MILAN, physical chemist, researcher; b. Brno, Czech Republic, Aug. 12, 1936; s. Ladislav and Anna (Dolezaliková) Š; m. Jiřina Hanusová, July 29, 1962 (div. Sept. 1994); children: Martin, Libor. MSc, Tech. U. St. Petersburg, Russia, 1961; PhD, Inst. Chem. Tech., Prague, Czech Republic, 1973. Instr. Inst. Chem. Tech., Prague, 1961-63, asst. prof. phys. chemistry, 1963-81, assoc. prof. phys. chemistry, 1981—; head dept. photographic chemistry, Inst. Chem. Tech., 1978—. Author: Examples in Chemistry, 1974; co-author: Polymers as Materials for Packaging, 1987; contbr. articles to profl. jours. Mem. Czech Chem. Soc. Avocations: travel, sports, literatūre. Home: Evropská 676/152, 160 00 Prague 6, Czech Republic Office: Inst Chem Technology, Technická 1905, 166 28 Prague 6, Czech Republic

SIPHANDONE, KHAMTAY, Laotian government official; b. Houa Khong, Champassak, Laos, Feb. 8, 1924. Milit. officer Govt. of Laos, Vientiane, 1947-48; rep. Govt. of Laos, Lao Itsala, 1948; staff mem. Pathet Lao, 1955-56; dep. prime min. nat. def. Govt. of Laos, Vientiane, 1975-91, prime min. and supreme comdr. Lao People's Army, 1991-98, pres., 1998—; mem Front Ctrl. Com., 1950-52; chair Control Com. 1952-54; head Ctrl. Com., 1957-59. Mem. Politburo, 1972, Lao People's Revolutionary Party, 1972, leader 1992—. Office: Office of the Pres, Lane Xang Ave, Vientiane Laos*

SIPILÄ, MATTI KALEVI, professional society administrator; b. Hollola, Finland, Dec. 28, 1938; m. Leila Annikki Leskinen, 1967; children: Mikko, Sanna-Mari. BSc in Agrl., U. Helsinki, 1968. Rsch. worker Market Rsch. Inst. of Pellervo Soc., Helsinki, Finland, 1966-68; rsch. worker, dept. mgr. Pellervo Soc., Helsinki, 1969-75; mgr. Ctr. for Finnish Bus. and Policy Studies, Helsinki, 1975-83; orgn. mgr. Sok Co-op., Helsinki, 1983-87, also bd. dirs.; mng. dir. The Finnish Bankers Assn., Helsinki, 1987—. Author: Third Republic, 1983. Office: The Finnish Bankers Assn, Museokatu 8A, 00100 Helsinki Finland

SIPILÄ, TERO SEPPO, biologist; b. Helsinki, Finland, July 22, 1956; s. Seppo Kalervo and Vappu-Maija Irmeli (Valta) S.; Suvi-Päivi Hannele Peltovirta, Aug. 19, 1977; children: Antti Johannes, Tuuli Johanna, Heini Maris. MS in Geography, U. Joensen, Finland, 1987; lic. philosophy and biology, U. Joensen, 1993. Rschr. U. Joensen, 1984-93; conservation biologist WWF, Helsinki, 1994, Forest and Park Svc., Savonlinna, Finland, 1995—; sec. WWF/Seel Specialist Group, Helsinki, 1982-96. Mem., vice-chair coun. U. Joensen, 1981-83, mem. cabinet, 1984-85; cabinet mem. Karelion Rsch. Inst., Finland, 1982-83, The Coalition Party, Finland, 1984. Recipient Pohjois-Karjalan Luanto-Mitch 58 JSC/SCC, Joesen, 1993. Mem. Finnish Assn. Nature Conservatory (specialist 1986—), Soc. for Marine Mammalogy, Kaippascora Komakina, N.Y. Acad. Scis. Lutheran. Avocations: cross-country skiing, badminton, croquet. Home: Rengastie 18 b 3, 57710 Savonlinna Finland Office: Forest and Park Svc, Akselinkatu 8, 57130 Savonlinna Finland

SIPINEN, SEPPO ANTERO, obstetrician, gynecologist; b. Helsinki, Finland, Aug. 11, 1946; s. Uno Emil Rafael and Martta Liisa (Knuuttila) S.; m. Taru Katriina, Oct. 19, 1968; children: Samuel, Suzanne. MD, U. Freiburg, Germany, 1971, U. Helsinki, 1972; cert. specialist ob.-gyn., U. Helsinki, 1979, DMS, 1981, specialist in diving medicine, 1994; completed Nat. Defense Course, 1994, completed sr. officers course, 1998, completed first repetition course, 1999. Cert. diving medicine and hyperbaric oxygen treatment specialist. Resident in ob-gyn. and surgery U. Helsinki, State Maternity Hosp., Helsinki, 1973-80; sr. physician ob-gyn. State Maternity Hosp., Helsinki, 1981-83; commd. capt. Finnish Navy Med. Corps., 1997, surgeon gen., 1983—, rose through grades to capt., 1997; head naval dept. Rsch. Inst. Mil. Medicine, Helsinki, 1983-98, head, 1998—; assoc. prof. diving and hyperbaric medicine U. Turku, 1996; cons. ob-gyn. Finnish Def. Forces, 1983—, Subway in Helsinki, 1976-77; rsch. group Dept. Med. Chemistry, U. Helsinki, 1977-86; lectr. diving and hyperbaric physiology and medicine, 1977-82; cons. devel. group State Dept. Finland, 1984-86; head diving and hyperbaric med. treatment of State Salv. Edn. Inst., Finland, 1985-86; cons. devel. group of Profl. Diving Nat. Bd. Labor Protection, Finland, 1989-90, Compressed Air Work of Subway, 1976-77; mem., rep. for Finland European Diving Tech. Com., 1986—; mem. sci. bd. Diving Alert Network Europe, 1991; mem. European Commn. Hyperbaric Medicine, 1991-99; cons. Ministry Social Affairs and Health, Nat. Rsch. and Devel. Ctr. for Welfare and Health in Finland, 1994—; pres. XXI ann. meeting European Underwater and Baromed. Soc., Helsinki, 1995. Contbr. around 100 articles in endocrinology, bacteriology, serology, diving and hyperbaric medicine to profl. jours. Recipient medal for Mil. Merits, 1988; decorated Knight 1st class, Order of White Rose of Finland, 1995. Mem. Finnish Soc. Ob-Gyn., European Underwater and Baromed. Soc. (at-large exec. com., pres. XXIst ann. meeting, Helsinki 1995), Finnish Med. Assn., Finnish Soc. Perinatal Medicine, Finnish Soc. Diving and Hyperbaric Medicine (pres. 1977-99, exec. bd. 1999—), Undersea and Hyperbaric Med. Soc., Finnish Sport Divers Fedn. (safety com. 1976-79, pres. 1977-79, exec. bd. 1977-79, med. com. pres. 1980, Silver medal 1988, Diver of Yr. 1989, Gold medal 1999), Espoo Gymnastics Team, Finnish Gymnastics Fedn. (Silver medal 1993). Achievements include construction of diving support vessel; development of decompression tables for air diving, of oxygen-nitrogen mixed gas diving. Office: Finnish Naval Hdqrs, Pohjoiskaari 36, FIN00201 Helsinki Finland

SIPORIN, DAVID, human resources specialist; b. Detroit, June 8, 1954; s. Erwin and Ruth (Haase) S.; m. Maureen Lynn Wertheim, Sept. 4, 1977; children: Kaylyn Nellie, Ariana Molly. BA in Anthropology, Mich. State U., 1976, M in Labor and Indsl. Rels., 1978. Orgn. planning splst. Amoco Corp., Chgo., 1979-81; human resources rep. Amoco Prodn. Co., Denver, 1981-84, Chgo., 1984-88; human resources mgr. Amoco Prodn. Co., Chgo., Ga., 1988-92, Amoco Chem.-Polymers, Alpharetta, Ga., 1992-96; mng. dir. orgn. devel. Aristech Chem. Corp., Pitts., 1996-98, v.p. corp. svcs., 1999—. Mem. Soc. Human Resource Mgmt., Indsl. Rels. Rsch. Assn., Coun. Human Resource Execs. (conf. bd. 1997). Avocations: golf, skiing, gardening, excercise. Home: 3090 Henrich Farm Ln Allison Park PA 15101-1519 Office: Aristech Chem Corp 210 6th Ave Pittsburgh PA 15222-2600

SIPOS, BÉLA, educator; b. Sopron, Hungary, Apr. 7, 1945; s. Béla and Dóra (Szakacs) S.; m. Katalin Redey, Sept. 26, 1970; children: Béla, Balazs. Diploma, Univ. Econ., Budapest, 1967; PhD in econ. scis., Acad. Hungary, Budapest, 1980, D in econ. scis., 1988. Asst. prof. Janus Pannonius Univ., Pécs, 1971-74, asst. lectr., 1974-81, assoc. prof., 1981-89, prof., 1989—, supr. tchr., 1982— head econ. team, 1982-89, gen. vice rector, 1997—; co-researcher Univ. Econ. Budapest, 1971; adv. in price prediction, Pécs, 1970-88; editorial com. Janus , 1987—; mem. editorial bd. stats. Author: Forecasting, 1996; contbr. articles to profl. jours. V.p. forecasting com. MTA, 1990—. Avocations: football, chess, computer games. Home: Fagyongy 38 9, H 7636 Pecs Hungary Office: U of Pecs, H 7622 Pecs Hungary

SIPPRELL, GEORGE SIDNEY, engineering professional; b. Buffalo, N.Y., Jan. 10, 1949; s. George Gilbert and Eleanor M. Sipprell; m. Kathleen Ann Meyer, July 22, 1972; children: Jeffrey David, Benjamin Daniel. BS in Aero. Engring., Rensselaer Poly. Inst., 1970, MEng in Aero. Engring., 1972. Joined Sikorsky Aircraft Corp., Stratford, 1972; UH-60A Black Hawk project engr. Sikorsky Aircraft Corp., Stratford, Conn., 1972-76, engring. mgr. USCG SRR/S76, 1976-79; program mgr., engring. mgr. UH60A Black Hawk ESSS Sikorsky Aircraft Corp., Stratford, 1979-83; engring. mgr. LHX Program Sikorsky Aircraft Corp., Stratford, Conn., 1983-90, dep. program mgr. Comanche Helicopter Program, 1990—. Mem. Am. Helicopter Soc., Sikorsky Ski Club (pres. 1980-82, Outstanding Member award 1982). Avocations: model railroading, snow skiing, automotive restoration, toy collecting. E-mail: gsipprell@sikorsky.com. Home: 51 Hannah Ln Monroe CT 06468-1248 Office: Sikorsky Aircraft Z100A 6900 Main St Stratford CT 06614-1385

SIPPRELLE, DUDLEY GENE, investor; b. Compton, Calif., July 6, 1935; s. Foster and Dolores Lee (Dudley) S.; m. Linda Dekum Mills, Feb. 1, 1957; children: Dwight, Keith, Scott, Mark. BA, U. Redlands, 1957; postgrad., UCLA, 1957-59, Stanford U., 1960. Diplomatic & consular officer U.S. Dept. of State, Washington, 1963-93; investor pvt. practice, Santa Barbara, Calif., 1994—; diplomat in residence Lehigh U., Bethlehem, Pa., 1980-81. Recipient Presdl. Meritorious Svc. award U.S. Dept. State, Washington, 1986. Mem. Coun. Fgn. Rels. Avocations: tennis, stamp and coin collecting, travel. Home: 222 Reef Ct Santa Barbara CA 93109-1958

SIPR, KVETOSLAV, medical educator; b. Brno, Czech Republic, June 23, 1934; s. Alois and Stepanka (Krizova) S.; m. Helena Sramkova, July 15, 1958; children: Helena, Ondrej, Jane, Katerina. MD, Masaryk U., Brno, Czech Republic, 1958. House physician Pub. Hosp., Dacice, Czech Republic, 1958-59; resident med. officer NHS, Prerov, Czech Republic, 1960; gen. practitioner NHS, Drevohostice, Czech Republic, 1961-68; asst. prof. Masaryk U., Brno, Czech Republic, 1968-93; assoc. prof. Maseryk U., Brno, Czech Republic, 1993-98, prof., 1998—, dept. head, 1994-99. Chmn. Hippokrates, Brno, 1999—. With Czech Army, 1960. Mem. European Acad. Gen. Practice. Roman Catholic. Avocations: swimming, skiing. Home: Mickova 59, 614 00 Brno Czech Republic Office: Masaryk U Med Faculty, Jostova 10, 602 00 Brno Czech Republic

SIQUEIRA, JOSÉ FREITAS, JR., dentist, researcher; b. Miracema, Brazil, Oct. 2, 1967; s. José Freitas and Léa (De Poli) S.; prior marriage Rosilene Roale, Jan. 19, 1991; children: Thaís Roale, Marcus Vinicius Roale. DDS, Gama Filho U., Rio de Janeiro, 1985; MSc, Fed. U. Rio de Janeiro, 1996, PhD, 1998. Prof. endodontics Gama Filho U., Rio de Janeiro, 1993-96, Br. Arm Endodontic Course, Rio de Janeiro, 1997-99; chmn. microbiology and immunology Veiga de Almeida U., Rio de Janeiro, 1997—; chmn. endodontics Estácio de Sá U., Rio de Janeiro, 1997—. Author: Inflamção (Inflammation), 1996, Tratamento das Infecções Endodonticas (Endodontic Infections), 1997, Endodontia: Biologia e Técnica (Endodontics: Biology and Technique), 1999; mem. editl. bd. Revista Brasileira de Odontologia, 1997—. Grantee CNPQ, Brasilia, Brazil, 1999—. Mem. Brazilian Dental Assn., Brazilian Assn. Endodontics. Avocations: playing guitar, soccer, books. Fax: 55 21 503-7293. Home: Rua Herotides de Oliveira, 61/601, 24230 Rio de Janeiro Brazil Office: Estácio de Sá U, Av. Paulo de Frontin 628, 20261 Rio de Janeiro Brazil

SIQUEIRA CAMPOS, MARCO ANTONIO, computer company executive; b. Rio de Janeiro, Aug. 8, 1957; s. Ehrlich and Sonia (Terezinha) S.C.; m. Carmen Lucia Mallet,Aug. 29, 1981; children: Marcelo, Luciana. Diploma in electronic technician, Coll. Santo Inacio, Porto Alegre, Brazil, 1977; BS in Statistics, U. Fed. Rio Grande Sul, Porto Alegre, 1988. Cert. quality engring. tech., ASQ Am. Soc. for Quality. Tech. asst. Companhia Rio Grandense Telecom., Porto Alegre, 1973-77; customer engr. SIEMENS, Brasília, Brazil, 1978-79; mgr. quality engring. EDISA-Hewlett-Packard Brazil, Gravatai, 1985-92; tech. dir. Siqueira Campos Assocs., Porto Alegre, 1992—; invited prof. Pontificia U. Catolica do Rio Grande do Sul, 1994-95, U. Fed.do Rio Grande do Sul, 1994. Mem. Am. Soc. Quality (cert. quality engr.), Assn. Brazilian Statisticians. Avocation: painting. Fax: 55 51 3330603. E-mail: marco@siqueiracampos.com. Office: Siqueira Campos Assocs, Rua Vieira Castro 285/303, 90040-320 Porto Alegre Brazil

SIRACUSANO, LOUIS H., communications company executive; b. N.Y.C., July 19, 1942; s. Luciano A. and Mafalda (Rossi) S.; m. Theresa Boegle, June 1, 1963; children: Marie, Louis H. Student, Bronx C.C., 1960-62. Electronics technologist Bendix Corp., Teterborough, N.J., 1962-68; broadcast engr. ABC Network, N.Y.C., 1968-70; field engr. AMPEX Corp., Hackensack, N.J., 1970-72; sales engr. AMPEX Corp., Washington, 1972-75; pres., CEO Video Svcs. Corp., Northvale, N.J., 1975—; mem. adv. bd. Key Bank, Westchester, N.Y., 1997; bd. dirs. Internat. Post Ltd., N.Y.C. Trustee Good Samaritan Hosp., Suffern, N.Y., 1988-94; chmn. Dem. Party, Washington Twp., N.J., 1969-75; bd. govs. CYO Youth Ministry, Newark, 1988-96. Recipient Medal of Honor, Good Samaritan Hosp., 1993, Outstanding Achievement awrd Vision Fund Am., 1992, Ellis Island Medal of Honor, 2000. Mem. KC (3d deg.). Roman Catholic. Avocations: golf, skiing. Home: 4 Concklin Ln Rockleigh NJ 07647

SIRAGUSA, MADDALENA, dermatologist, researcher; b. Erice, Trapani, Italy, May 27, 1957; d. Francesco Paolo Siragusa and Rosaria Miceli. MD, U. Palermo, Italy, 1986. Resident in dermatology U. Messina, Italy, 1991-92, resident in dermatological/cosmetology, 1992; dermatologist Oasi Inst., Troina, Italy, 1992—. Scholarship Nat. Grant, 1991. Avocation: stamp collecting. Office: Associazione Oasi Maria SS, Via Conte Ruggero 73, 94018 Troina Italy

SIRAJUDDIN, ABDULLAH MOHAMMAD YAR, engineering educator; b. Makkah, Saudi Arabia, Sept. 9, 1957; s. Mohammad Yar Sirajuddin and Zarefa Mohammad Obeedullah; m. Nawal Abdullah Ahmad; children: Shady, Sarah, Abdulhady, Norah. BS in Engring., King Abdulaziz U., Jeddah, Saudi Arabia, 1980; MS in Engring., Pa. State U., 1983; PhD, U. Nottingham, 1991. Project coord. King Abdulaziz U., Jeddah, 1980-81, lectr., 1985-86, asst. prof., 1991-97, assoc. prof., 1997—, dir. sci. pub. ctr., 1994-96, asst. dir. master plan project, 1997-99; maintenance dir. Engring. Coll., Jeddah, 1992-94. Contbr. articles to profl. jours. Dep. dir. orphan dept. Islamic Relief Orgn., Jeddah, 1993-95. Recipient Fullbright scholarship, 1997. Mem. ASCE. Islam. Avocations: swimming, travel. Home: PO Box 11485, Jeddah 21493, Saudi Arabia Office: King Abdulaziz U, Civil Engring Dept, Jeddah 21493, Saudi Arabia

SIREN, HEIKKI, architect, educator; b. Helsinki, Oct. 5, 1918; s. Prof. J.S. and Sirkka S.; m. Kaija Siren, 1944; 2 sons, 2 daus. With Kaija Siren. D in Tech. (hon.), Tampere Tech. U., Finland, 1982. Works include: Little Stage of Nat. Theatre, Helsinki, 1954, Concert House, Lathi, 1954, Chapel in Otaniemi, 1957; Church in Orivesi, 1960, Office Bldgs., Helsinki, 1965, Housing Area in Boussy St Antoine, Paris, 1970, 'Round Bank' Kop, Helsinki, Bruckherhaus Concert Hall, Linz, Austria, 1974, Golf complex, Karuizawa, Japan, 1974, Golf Club, Onuma, Hokkaido, Japan, 1976, Reichsbrücke, Vienna, Conf. Palace, Baghdad, Iraq, others. Subject of Kaija and Heikki Siren, Architects, 1976. Recipient Hon. Citation and medal Sao Paulo Biennal, 1957; medal, 1961; hon. citation 'Auguste Perret' Union Internat des Architects, 1965; prof h.c., 1970; Officier Ordre nat. du Merite, 1971; SLK (Finland), 1974; Grand Silver Order of Austria, 1977; Camillo Sitte Prize, Vienna, 1979; Grande Medaille d'Or d'Académie d'Architecture, Paris, 1980; Archtl. Prize State of Finland, 1980; Grand Golden Order, City of Vienna, 1982, Grand Golden Order, City of Linz, Austria. Fellow AIA, (hon.); mem. Finnish Acad. Tech., Finnish Architects Assn. (hon.), L'Academie d'Architecture. Home: Tiirasaarentie 35, 00200 Helsinki 20, Finland

SIREN, KAIJA ANNA-MAIJA HELENA, architect; b. Kotka, Finland, Oct. 23, 1920; d. Gottlieb and Alma Lyyli (Maljanen) Tuominen; m. Heikki Siren, Feb. 22, 1944; children: Kirsi Siren Aropaltio, Sara, Jukka, Hannu. Degree in Arch., U. Tech., Helsinki, 1948. Owner Siren Architects, Helsinki, 1949—. Exhbns. of arch. in Finland and abroad; contbr. articles to profl. jours. Bd. dirs. Found. Rsch. Allergic Diseases, Helsinki, 1960—, chmn., 1971-79. Decorated officer Order of Finnish White Rose, Grand Golden Order (Linz, Austria); recipient Hon. mention and medal for theatre bldgs. Sao Paulo IV Biennale, 1957, medal and diploma for ch. bldgs., Sao Paulo VI Biennale, 1961, Auguste Perret hon. mention Union Intwernat. des Architectes, 1965, Grand Silver Order of Austria with star, 1977, Archtl. prize State of Finland, 1980, La Grand Medaille d'Or de l'Academie d'Architecture, Paris, 1980, Finnish Cultural Found. prize, 1984. Fellow AIA (hon.); mem. Finnish Architects Assn. (hon.), L'Acad. d'Architecture. Office: Tiirasaarentie 35, 00200 Helsinki 20, Finland

SIRGY, MACK JOSEPH (MAGDY SIRGY), marketing science educator, consultant; b. Cairo, Egypt, May 31, 1952; came to U.S., 1970, naturalized, 1972; s. Joseph Ibrahim and Odette Mikhail (Hosni) S.; m. Pamela Ann Jackson; children: Melissa Jane, Danielle Odette, Michelle Anna. BA, U. Calif., 1974; MA, Calif. State U., 1977; PhD, U. Mass., 1979. Asst. prof. mktg. Va. Tech. U., 1979-85, assoc. prof., 1985-91, prof., 1991—; Va. real estate rsch. fellow, 1999—; ptnr. Advantage Advt., Mktg. and Design, Blacksburg, Va., 1989-92. Author: Social Cognition and Consumer Behavior, 1983, Marketing as Social Behavior: A General Systems Theory, 1984, Self-Congruity: Toward a Theory of Personality and Cybernetics, 1986, Consumer Behavior: Concepts and Marketing Applications, 1997, Integrated Marketing Communications, 1998. Served with U.S. Army, 1971-73. Pres.-elect Acad. Mktg. Sci.; exec. dir. Internat. Soc. for Quality-of-Life Studies. Home: 3735 Millstone Ridge Rd Blacksburg VA 24060-0681 Office: Va Tech Mktg Dept Blacksburg VA 24061

SIRIGNANO, WILLIAM ALFONSO, aerospace and mechanical engineer, educator; b. Bronx, N.Y., Apr. 14, 1938; s. Anthony P. and Lucy (Caruso) S.; m. Lynn Haisfield, Nov. 26, 1977; children: Monica Ann, Jacqueline Hope, Justin Anthony. B.Aero.Engring., Rensselaer Poly. Inst., 1959; Ph.D., Princeton U., 1964. Mem. research staff Guggenheim Labs., aerospace, mech. scis. dept. Princeton U., 1964-67, asst. prof. aerospace and mech. scis., 1967-69, assoc. prof., 1969-73, prof., 1973-79, dept. dir. grad. studies, 1974-78; George Tallman Ladd prof., head dept. mech. engring. Carnegie-Mellon U., 1979-85; dean Sch. Engring., U. Calif.-Irvine, 1985-94, prof., 1994—; cons. indsutry and govt., 1966—; lectr. and cons. NATO adv. group on aero. rsch. and devel., 1967, 75, 80; chmn. nat. and internat. tech. congs.; chmn. acad. adv. coun. Indsl. Rsch. Inst., 1985-88; mem. space sci. applications adv. com. NASA, 1985-90, chmn. combustion sci. microgravity disciplinary working group, 1987-90; chmn. com. on microgravity rsch. space studies bd. NRC, 1991-94. Assoc. editor: Combustion Sci. and Tech., 1969-70; assoc. tech. editor Jour. Heat Transfer, 1986-92; contbr. articles to nat. and internat. profl. jours., also rsch. monographs. United Aircraft research fellow, 1973-74; Disting. Alumni Rsch. award U. Calif. Irvine, 1992. Fellow AIAA (Pendray Aerospace Lit. award 1991, Propellants and Combustion award 1992), ASME (Freeman scholar 1992), AAAS; mem. Inst. Dynamics

of Explosives and Reactive Systems (v.p. 1991-95, pres. 1995-99, Oppenheim award 1993), Combustion Inst. (treas. internat. orgn., chmn. ea. sect., Alfred C. Egerton Gold medal 1996), Soc. Indsl. and Applied Math., Orange County Engring. Coun. (Excellence award 1994), Am. Electronics Assn. (recognition 1994). Office: U Calif Sch Engring S3202 Engring Gtwy Irvine CA 92697-0001

SIROKY, KAREL, physics educator, researcher; b. Strazny, Czech Republic, Aug. 5, 1937; s. Karel and Anna (Charvatova) S.; m. Vera Kristofova, May 23, 1964; children: Jana, Michal. MSc, Petrochem. Inst., Moscow, 1961; PhD, Inst. Chem. Tech., Prague, Czech Republic, 1965. Lectr. Inst. Chem. Tech., Prague, 1961-64, asst. prof. physics, 1965—; abstractor Chem. Abstracts Svc., Columbus, Ohio, 1971-94. Author: Semiconductor Physics, 1988 (Rector prize 1989), Humidity Measurements, 1983; contbr. articles to profl. jours. Nat. Found. grantee, Prague, 1995-97, Ministry of Edn. grantee, Prague, 1995-96. Office: Inst Chem Tech, Technicka 1905, 166 28 Prague Czech Republic

SIROTA, NICOLAJ NICOLAEVICH, physics researcher, educator; b. Saint Petersburg, Russia, Nov. 2, 1913; s. Nicolaj Yacovlevich and Lina Vasilievna (Obuchova) S.; m. Zoja Dmitrievna Averkina, June 4, 1944 (dec. Apr. 26, 1976); 1 child, George; m. Irina Mironovna Perfilieva, Mar. 3, 1978. Engr., Inst. Steel, Moscow, 1936, D, 1939; DSc, State U., Moscow, 1951, Prof. Physics, 1952; Honor Scientist, Belorussia, 1968. Asst. Physics Faculty State U., Moscow, 1939-40, docent, 1945-50; head of chair Inst. Metallurgy, Mariupol, Ukraine, USSR, 1940-41; sr. rsch. scientist Inst. Inorganic Chemistry Acad. Sci. USSR, Moscow, 1946-54; head chair of physics Inst. Nonferrous Metals, Moscow, 1954-57; dir., sci. leader Inst. Physics of Solids and Semiconductors Acad. Sci. Belorussia, 1957-63, 63-75; pres. sci. counsel physics of solids, 1963-75; head chair of physics State U. Nature Improvement, Moscow, 1978-89, prof., 1989—; head of chair of physics of solids U., Minsk, Belorussia, 1957-62, head of chair theoretical physics of Pedagogical U., Minsk, Belorussia, 1963-75; mem. All Union Counsels Physics of Solids, Physics and Chemistry of Semiconductors, Magnetism and Low Temperature Acad. Sci. USSR, Moscow, 1969-79; mem. internat. commn. on electron and spin density of Internat. Union Crystallography, Eng., 1969-79. Author: Thermodynamics and Statistical Physics, 1969, Physical-Chemical Nature of Chageable Composition Phases, 1970; author, editor: Chemical Bonds in Semiconductors and Solids, 1967; contbr. article to profl. jour. Mem. Belorussian Com. Trade Union Scientists and H.S. Workers, Minsk, 1966-76; mem. presidium All Union Counsle Scientific-Tech. Socs., Moscow, 1954-75; pres. Belorussian Counsel Scientific-Tech. Socs., Minsk, 1959-66. With Soviet Army, 1942-43. Recipient Order of the Labor Red Banner, Presidium of the Supreme Soviet of USSR, 1967, 73. Mem. Nat. Acad. Sci. (academician 1956—), N.Y. Acad. Scis. Home: Leninsky Prosp 123-1-741, 117513 Moscow Russia Office: Moscow State U Nature Impro, Pzyanishnikova 19, 127550 Moscow Russia

SIROVICH, LIVIO, geophysicist, geologist, seismologist; b. Trieste, Italy, July 5, 1949; s. Guido and Ruth (Isaak) S.; m. Federica Scrimin, May 5, 1984; children: Filippo, Cecilia. D Geology, U. Trieste, 1973. Geologist Studio Geotecnico Italiano, Milano, 1975, Sondater SpA, Trieste, 1975-76; rschr. Nat. Coun. Rsch., Trieste, 1977-80; rschr., coord. rsch. group Seismic Risk O.G.S., Trieste, 1981—; prof. U. Udine, 1990, U. Padua, 1991, U. Pisa, 1992; sr. rschr. Istituto Nazionale di Oceanografia e Geofisica Sperimentale-O.G.S., Trieste; sci. advisor Istituto di Ricerca sul Rischio Sismico, Nat. Coun Rsch., Milan, 1994—. Author: Cari, non scrivetemi tutto, 1995, Cime Irredente, 1996 (awards 1997, 98). Mem. Seismological Soc. Am. Avocations: ski-mountaineering, activities with sons. Office: Nat Inst Oceanog & Geo-OGS, Borgo Grotta Gigante 42C, 34010 Sgonico Trieste, Italy

SIRTL, CLEMENS J.H., physician; b. Zwiesel, Bavaria, Germany, Nov. 23, 1953; s. Rudolf F. and Gertraud M. (Rummelein) S.; m. Petra A. Haupt, Apr. 6, 1958. MD, Tech. U. Munich, 1979, PhD, 1982. Trainee physician Tech. U. Munich, 1979-80; trainee physician ADAÇ Pat.-repatriation svc. Ludwig-Maximilians U., 1980-81; trainee physician dept. anesthesiology Ludwig-Maximilians U., Munich, 1981-88; vice chmn. St. Josef Hosp./Ruhr U., Bochum, Germany, 1988—; mem. Arztekammer Westfalen-Lippe Chamber of Physicians, 1993—; staff mgr. of emergency doctors, Bochum, 1993—; specialist for aviation medicine, Bochum, 1995—; EMS med. dir., 1999; lectr. in field. Author: Anaesthesiologisches Notizbuch, edits. 1-4, 1987-95; contbr. 70 articles to profl. jours. Mem. Deutsche Gesellschaft Anaesthesiologie und Intensivmedizin, European Soc. Anesthesiologists, Am. Soc. Anesthesiologists. Roman Catholic. Avocations: pilot, piano, skiing, classic dances, history. Home: Akademiest 42, D-44789 Bochum Germany Office: Ruhr U St Josef Hosp U Klinik Anaesthesi, Gudrunst 56, D-44791 Bochum Germany

SISK, FRED DEAN, retired cartographer; b. Johnson City, Tenn., May 26, 1940; s. Aubrey Mackenzie and Violet Mae (McCartt) S.; m. Martha Lynn Robinson, Aug. 25, 1963. BS, East Tenn. State U., 1962; MS, George Mason U., 1984. Cartographer Def. Mapping Agy., Brookmont, Md., 1965-79; sr. cartographer Def. Mapping Agy., Ft. Belvior, Va., 1979-81, course mgr., 1981-88, dep. div. chief, 1983-88; new employees tng. coord. Def. Mapping Agy., Bethesda, Md., 1988-89; tng. coord. Def. Mapping Agy. Reston (Va.) Ctr., 1989-90, security analyst, 1990-95. Mem. scholarship com. George Mason U. Alumni Assn., Fairfax, 1990, Republican Presdl. Task Force, Washington, 1990—, adv. com. House of Dels., 54th Dist., 1995—; officer of election City of Fredericksburg, 1995—, mem. pub. transit adv. bd., 1996—, chmn. memls. adv. commn., 2000—; notary public, 1996—, security officer, 1996—; pres. Fox Run Homeowners Assn., 1996—. 1st lt. U.S. Army, 1962-64. Baptist. Home: 18 Devonshire Dr Fredericksburg VA 22401-2100

SISLER, HARRY HALL, chemist, educator; b. Ironton, Ohio, Mar. 13, 1917; s. Harry C. and Minta A. (Hall) S.; m. Helen E. Shaver, June 29, 1940; children: Elizabeth A., David F., Raymond K., Susan C.; m. Hannelore L. Wass, Apr. 13, 1978. BSc, Ohio State U., 1936; MSc, U. Ill., 1937, PhD, 1939; Doctorate honoris causa, U. Poznan, Poland, 1977. Instr. Chgo. City Colls., 1939-41; from instr. to assoc. prof. chemistry U. Kans., Lawrence, 1941-46; from asst. prof. to prof. chemistry Ohio State U., Columbus, 1946-56; Arthur and Ruth Sloan vis. prof. chemistry Harvard, fall, 1962-63; prof., chmn. dept. chemistry U. Fla., Gainesville, 1956-68; dean Coll. Arts and Scis. U. Fla., 1968-70, exec. v.p., 1970-73, dean grad. sch., 1973-79, dir. divsn. sponsored rsch., 1976-79, Disting. Svc. prof. chemistry, 1979—; indsl. cons. W.R. Grace & Co., Martin Marietta Aerospace, Naval Ordnance Lab., TVA; chemistry adv. panel, also vis. scientists panel NSF, 1959-62; cons. USAF Acad., Battelle Meml. Inst., chmn. interinstl. com. nuclear research, Fla., 1958-64; mem. Fla. Nuclear Devel. Commn. Teaching Sci. and Math., 1958; chemistry adv. panel Oak Ridge Nat. Lab., 1965-69; dir. sponsored rsch. U. Fla., 1976-79. Author: Electronic Structure, Properties, and the Periodic Law, 2d edit, 1973, Starlight-A Book of Poems, 1976, Of Outer and Inner Space—A Book of Poems, 1981, Earth, Air, Fire and Water-A Book of Poems, 1989, (with others) Gen. Chemistry: A Systematic Approach, 2d edit, 1959, Coll. Chemistry: A Systematic Approach, 4th edit, 1980, Essentials of Chemistry, 2d edit, 1959, A Systematic Laboratory Course in Chemistry, 1950, Essentials of Experimental Chemistry, 2d edit, 1959, Semimicro Qualitative Analysis, 1958, rev. edit., 1965, Comprehensive Inorganic Chemistry, Vol. V, 1956, Chemistry in Non-Aqueous Solvents, 1961, The Chloramination Reaction, 1977, Dying-Facing the Facts, 1988, Inorganic Reactions and Methods, Vol. 7, 1988, Encyclopedia of Inorganic Chemistry, Vol. 5, Nitrogen: Inorganic Chemistry, 1994, Autumn Harvest-A Book of Poems, 1996, Perspective-A Book of Poems, 1999; cons. editor: (with others) Dowden, Hutchinson & Ross, 1971-78; series editor: (with others) Phys. and Inorganic Textbook Series, Reinhold Pub. Corp. 1958-70; contbr. (with others) articles to profl. jours.; patentee in field. Decorated Royal Order North Star(Sweden); Named Outstanding Chemist in South, Am. Chem. Soc., 1969, Outstanding Chemist in Southeast, Am. Chem. Soc., 1960, James Flack Norris award Am. Chem. Soc., 1979; recipient Outstanding Centennial Achievement award Ohio State U., 1970. Mem. Am. Chem. Soc. (nat. chmn. div. chem. edn. 1957-58, exec. com. 1957-60, bd. publ. Jour. Chem. Edn. 1956-58), Phi Beta Kappa, Sigma Xi, Phi Delta Kappa, Phi Lambda Upsilon, Phi Kappa Phi, Alpha Chi Sigma. Methodist. Home: 6014 NW 54th Way Gainesville FL 32653-3265

SISODIA, PRATAP, economist, researcher; b. Hyderabad, India, June 23, 1956; s. Poonamchand and Pratibha (Chouhan) S. BA, Nizam Coll., Hyderabad, 1976; MA, Osmania U., Hyderabad, 1978; PhD, Bangalore (India) U., 1990. Rsch. asst. Ctr. for Econs. and Social Studies, Hyderabad, 1983, Indian Inst. Mgmt., Bangalore, 1988-89; sr. rsch. officer Indian Inst. Health Mgmt. Rsch., Jaipur, 1990-92; rsch. coord. Rajasthan Vol. Health assn., Jaipur, 1992-95; program officer Vol. Health Assn. India, Delhi, 1995-98; social scientist Farm and Rural Sci. Found., Hyderabad, 1998—; cons. Memisa Medicus Mundi, Rotterdam, The Netherlands, 1996-97, Intuit, Delhi, 1997-98. Authro: Status of Health in Rajasthan, 1993; contbr. articles to profl. jours. Mem. exec. com. Arts Coll. Students Union, Hyderabad, 1977-78; mem. econ. forum Osmania U., Hyderabad, 1977-78. Nat. Merit scholar Govt. India, 1976-78. Mem. Nat. Geog. Soc. Avocations: horseback riding, visiting wildlife sanctuaries, wrestling. Home: 236 Mig Colony Bholakpur, Secunderabad 500 080, India

SISSAKIAN, ALEXEI NORAIROVICH, physicist, researcher; b. Moscow, Oct. 14, 1944; s. Norair Martirosovich and Varvara Petrovna (Alexeeva) S.; m. Tatjana Nikolayevna Gusseva, Apr. 30, 1966 (div. Oct. 1987); 1 child, Anna (dec. 1986); m. Natalia Ivanovna Yeltsova, Jan. 16, 1988; 1 child, Anastasia. Diploma, Moscow State U., 1968; candidate scis., JINR, Dubna, Russia, 1970, DSc, 1980; DSc (hon.), Yerevan State U., Armenia, Internat. U. Dubna. Rschr. Joint Inst. Nuclear Rsch., Dubna, 1968-79; chief sci. sec. JINR, Dubna, 1979-89, vice dir., 1989—; prof. Moscow Radioelectronics and Automations Inst., 1982-92, Moscow State U., 1992—; v.p. Internat. Univ. Dubna, 1994—; co-chmn. JINR-CERN Coop. Com., Dubna, Geneva. Contbr. 300 articles to profl. jours. Decorated Order of Friendship (Korea), Order of Friendship (Mongolia), Order of Friendship (Russia), Order of St. Cyril and Methodius (Bulgaria); recipient Lenin Komsomol prize for sci. and tech. Govt. Russia, 1973, P.L. Kapitsa Medal (Russia), 1998. Mem. Russian Acad. Engring. Scis., Russian Acad. Natural Scis., Internat. Acad. Info., Internat. Acad. Creative Work (corr.), Internat. Comm. Future Accelerators, European Com. Future Accelerators, Armenian Physics Soc. (v.p.), N.Y. Acad. Scis. Avocations: writing poems and short stories. Home: Flerov St 5-2, Dubna 141980, Russia Office: Joint Inst Nuclear Rsch, Joliot-Curie St 6, Dubna 141980, Russia

SISSELMAN, MURRAY, educator, union executive; b. N.Y.C., Jan. 10, 1930; B.Ed., U. Miami; M.S., Ed.S., Nova U.; m. Ludmila Sisselman; children: David, Helen, Jagger. Classroom tchr., Dade County, Fla., 1956—; v.p. Fla. Am. Fedn. Tchrs. AFL-CIO, 1974, pres. United Tchrs. Dade local Am. Fedn. Tchrs., 1974, AFL-CIO, 1975—; v.p. Fla. Edn. Assn./United; mem. exec. bd. South Fla., AFL-CIO, 1977-78, 85-86. Mem. Dade Democratic exec. com., 1971-74; patron Hist. Assn. So. Fla.; mem. com. juvenile health needs Mental Health Bd. Dade County; mem. com. on edn. Third Century U.S.A.; mem. nat. exec. bd. Jewish Labor Com., 1977—; mem. rules com. Dem. exec. com. Fla.; committeeman Fla. Dem. State Com., 1985-86; mem. citizens adv. com. Fla. Dept. Health and Rehab. Services; mem. Dade County Bd. Rules and Appeals, 1975-77; mem. Met. Dade County Zoning Appeals Bd., chmn., 1980-90; trustee City of Hope Pilot Med. Center, 1979—; ednl. dir. Temple Sinai of North Dade, 1966-71; religious sch. prin. Temple Emanu-El, Ft. Lauderdale, Fla., 1971-72. Served with U.S. Army, 1954-56. Recipient Personal Service award C. of C. North Miami Beach (Fla.); cert. of appreciation, Nat. Police Officers Assn., Am. Judges Assn., Fla. Edn. Assn./United, award Fla. Dept. Edn. Mem. Nat. Congress Parents and Tchrs. (hon. life), Fla. Congress Parents and Tchrs. (hon. life), VFW (citation), Dade County Classroom Tchrs. Assn. (acting pres.), Fla. Edn. Assn. (dir., chmn. legis. com.), Fla. Commn. on Ednl. Reform, Nat. Hist. Soc. (founding assoc.), Nat. Assn. Temple Educators, USS Constitution Museum Found. (charter), Alpha Phi Omega (past officer), Sigma Alpha Mu (past pres.), Pi Sigma Rho, Phi Delta Kappa, Kappa Delta Pi. Clubs: Elks (Fla. commn. edn. reform and accountability 1990—), Masons. Office: 2929 SW 3rd Ave Miami FL 33129-2757

SISSMANN, PIERRE ALAIN, recreational facility executive; b. Neuilly sur Seine, France, Sept. 28, 1953; s. Robert Alphonse and Huguette Fanny (Baikowski) S.; m. Joelle Betty Sissmann; children: Sarah and Olivier (twins). MBA, Ecole Superieure de Commerce, Paris, 1975, U. Pa., 1977; M of Law, U. Paris, 1978. Bar: Paris, 1978. With IBM Internat., 1976-77, Peat, Marwick, Mitchell Cons., 1977-78; various positions CBS France, 1979-82; dir. mktg., sales and A&R for Columbia Epic and others CBS Internat. Europe, 1982-86; v.p. mktg., promotion and internat. A&R CBS France, 1986-88; v.p., mng. dir. The Walt Disney Co. (France) S.A., 1988-91; pres. dir. gen. Disney Hachette Presse and Hachette Disney Presse, 1991, Disney Hachette Edition, 1992; pres. dir. gen., chmn. bd., pres. Walt Disney Feature Animation (France) S.A., 1989—, The Walt Disney Co. (France) S.A., 1991—; pres. dir. gen., pres. Disney Consumer Products, 1995—; pres. du conseil de surveillance, pres. supr. bd. The Disney Channel France (S.A.), 1997—; exec. v.p. The Walt Disney Co. (Europe) S.A., 1997—; bd. dirs. Euro Disney S.A.; assoc. prof. in mgmt. and internat. bus. Ecole Supérieure de Commcerce de Paris, 1978-84, Am. Coll. in Paris, 1978-84. Named Knight French Nat. Order of Legion d'Honneur, 1998, French Nat. Order of Merit, 1992. Avocations: tennis, philately, reading, music.

SISSON, DOUGLAS LEE, pension fund executive; b. Gallipolis, Ohio, Sept. 6, 1959; s. Charles Elias and Martha Sue Sisson; m. Anne Blair Sisson, Dec. 27, 1980; children: Phillip, Laura, Andrew, Jeffrey. BA, Ohio State U., 1980, MBA, 1984. CPA, Ohio. Banking mgr. State Savs. Bank, Columbus, 1980-86; asset mgmt. officer State Tchrs. Retirement Sys. of Ohio, Columbus, 1986-89, sr. asset mgmt. officer, 1989-96; investment officer Sch. Employees Retirement Sys. of Ohio, Columbus, 1996-98, sr. investment officer, 1998-99, chief investment officer, 1999—. Mem. Columbus Soc. Fin. Analysts. Presbyterian. Avocations: golf, reading. Address: Sch Employees Retirement Sys of Ohio 45 N 4th St Columbus OH 43215-3602

SISSON, JAMES C., medical educator; b. Tecumseh, Mich., May 1, 1929; s. Harold and Freida S.; m. Doris L. Sisson, June 29, 1956; children: Mark, Matthew, Thomas. BA, U. Mich., 1951, MD, 1954. Diplomate Am. Bd. Internal Medicine. Instr. U. Mich. Med. Sch., Ann Arbor, 1960-62; asst. prof. U. Mich. Med. Sch., 1962-67, assoc. prof., 1967-72, prof., 1972—. Contbr. more than 150 articles to profl. jours. Capt. U.S. Army, 1958-60. Recipient various NIH grants. Fellow ACP (Laureate award 1992); mem. AMA, Am. Thyroid Assn., Endocrine Soc., Soc. Nuclear Medicine. E-mail: jsisson@umich.edu.

SISSON, ROSEMARY ANNE, writer; b. London, Oct. 13, 1923; d. Charles Jasper and Vera (Ginn) S. BA with honors, Univ. Coll., London, 1946; MLitt, Cambridge (Eng.) U., 1948. Instr. English U. Wis., Madison, 1949-50; asst. lectr. in Am. lit. Univ. Coll., London, 1950-54; asst. lectr. in English U. Birmingham, Eng., 1954-55; drama critic Stratford-upon-Avon (Eng.) Herald, 1955-57. Writings include: (fiction) The Advantures of Ambrose, 1951, The Impractical Chimney-Sweep, 1956, The Isle of Dogs, 1959, The Young Shakespeare, 1959, The Young Jane Austin, 1962, The Young Shaftesbury, 1964, The Exciseman, 1973, The Killer of Horseman's Flats, 1973, The Stratford Story, 1975, Bury Love Deep, 1985, Beneath the Visiting Moon, 1986, Footsteps on the Stair, 1999; (plays) The Queen and the Welsrman, 1958, Fear Came to Supper, 1959, Bitter Sanctuary, 1964, The Acrobats, 1965, A Ghost on Tiptoe, 1975, The Dark Horse, 1979; (teleplays) The Six Wives of Henry VIII, 1972, Elizabeth R., 1973, The Vagrant Heart, The Man from Brooklyn, Beyond Our Means, Let's Marry Liz, The Irish R.M., The Bretts, 1987, The Young Indiana Jones Chronicles, 1992-95; (poetry) Rosemary for Remembrance, 1995; (teleplay adaptations) The Ordeal of Richard Feveral (George Meredith), The Mill on the Floss (George Eliot), Mistral's Daughter (Judith Krantz); (TV series) Compact, Upstairs, Downstairs, Within These Walls, The Duchess of Duke Street, The Young Indiana Jones; (miniseries) The Manions of America; (screenplays) The Little Horse Thieves, 1976, (with David Swift) Candleshoe, 1978, (with Brian Clemens and Harry Shoalding) The Watcher in the Woods, 1981, Anstice, The Talking Parcel, The Wind in the Willows; (screenplay adaptation) Ride a Wild Pony (James Aldridge), 1975; contbr. short stories, poetry and articles to mags. and newspapers. Trustee Theatre of Comedy. Served Royal Observer Corps, 1943-45. Recipient Repertory Players award, 1964. Mem. Writers Guild Gt. Britain (past pres.), Writers Guild Am., The Dramatists' Club (hon. sec.). Mem. Conservative Party. Mem. Ch. of Eng. Office: care Andrew Mann Ltd, 1 Old Compton St, London W1V 5PH, England

SISULU, SHEILA VIOLET MAKATE, diplomat. Various sr. positions South AFrican Com. for Higher Edn., 1978-88; edn. coord. African Bursary Fund South African Coun. Chs., 1988-91; dir. Joint Enrichment Project, 1991-94; spl. advisor Min. Edn., 1994-97; consul-gen. South African Consulate-Gen., N.Y., 1997-99; amb. extraordinary and plenipotentiary to the U.S. South African Govt., 1999—; organizer, coord. several confs., workshops and seminars on youth and edn.; presenter in field. Mem. ANC Nat. Edn. Com., U.S.A./South Africa Leadership Tng. Program, Cmty. Bank Found.; coun. mem. U. Witwatersrand; trustee Equal Opportunity Found., Women's Devel. Found., Women's Devel. Bank, South African Broadcasting Cooperation. Fax: 202-265-1607. E-mail: safrica@southafrica.net. Office: Embassy of South Africa 3051 Massachusetts Ave NW Washington DC 20008-3631

SIT, HONG CHAN, minister; b. St. Louis, Nov. 25, 1921; s. Gan and Ying Foon (Wong) S.; m. Amy Wang, June 16, 1949; children: David, Daniel, Esteelle Joy, Mary. BS summa cum laude, U. Ill., 1943; BD, Faith Theol Sem., 1950, STM, 1950; ThD, No. Bapt. Theol. Sem., 1957. Ordained to ministry Blue Ch., Springfield, Pa., 1950. Missionary China Inter-Varsity Fellowship, Shanghai, 1947; pastor Chinese Evang. Ch., N.Y.C., 1950-51, Chinese Bapt. Ch., Houston, 1953-56; pastor Grace Chapel, 1956-90, missionary pastor, 1990—; pres. Chinese Fgn. Missionary Union, 1974, Chinese Full Gospel Fellowship Internat., Hong Kong, 1983-98; mem. bd. govs. Network of Christian Ministries, 1990—. Author: Your Next Step With Jesus, 1977, My View From a Bridge: Autobiography of Hong Sit, 1999; contbr. articles to profl. jours. Mem. Phi Bet Kappa, Phi Lambda Upsilon. Office: PO Box 55664 Houston TX 77255-5664

SIT, VICTOR FUNG SHUEN, geography and geology educator; b. Guangzhou, Guangdong, China, Apr. 10, 1947; arrived in Hong Kong, 1950; s. Pui Tak and Suk Yee (Law) S.; m. Jacquelin Kit Ching Kwan; children: Yat Wah, Yat Cheong. BA with honors, U. Hong Kong, 1970, MA, 1974; PhD, U. London, 1977. Asst. lectr. dept. geography and geology U. Hong Kong, 1977-78, lectr., 1978-84, sr. lectr., 1984-87, reader, 1987—, acting head dept., 1990-91, head dept., 1993-98; rsch. fellow Centre Asian Studies, U. Hong Kong, 1987—, Centre Urban Planning & Environ. Mgmt.. 1098&/; adj. prof. and fellow Inst. of Geography, Academia Sinica, PRC, 1997—; hon. prof. Beijing U., PRC, 1996—, Ctr. for Urban & Regional Studies, Zhongshan U., PRC, 1992—, Inst. Hong Kong & Macau Studies, 1992—, Jinan U., PRC, 1995—. Author: Beijing: Development and Nature of A Chinese National Capital, 1995; mem. editl. bd. Jour. Chinese Geography; assoc. editor Asian Geographer, 1994-96, chief editor, 1982-86. Dep. Nat. People's Congress, China, 1993—; mem. preparatory com. for Hong Kong Spl. Adminstrv. Region, mem. election com.; mem. Airport Core Projects Consultative Com., Hong Kong, 1991; organizer Conf. on Hong Kong's Airport Dispute, Study Group on Infrastructure Devel., 1991. Mem. Royal Chartered Inst. Transport, Inst. Brit. Geographers, Hong Kong Econ. Soc., Hong Kong Geog. Assn. (life, chmn. 1980-83), Internat. Geog. Union (chmn. Hong Kong nat. com. 1993—). Avocations: cricket, lawn bowls, tennis. Office: U Hong Kong Dept Geography & Geol, Pokfulam Rd, Hong Kong Hong Kong

SITENKO, ALEX (OLEXIJ) GREGORY, physics educator; b. Baturyn, Chernihiv, Ukraine, Feb. 12, 1927; s. Gregory P. and Praskovia (Spichenko) S.; m. Helen I. Fedorkova, July 23, 1950 (dec. July 1965); 1 child, Jurij A., Alla A.; m. Joanna G. Zhak, Aug. 28, 1968; 1 child, Gregory A. BA in Physics, Kharkiv (Ukraine) U., 1949, D in Physics and Math., 1959. From lectr. to prof. physics Kharkiv U., 1949-61, prof., 1961-63; head nuclear theory dept. Inst. Physics, Kiev, Ukraine, 1961-68; prof. Kiev U., 1963—, Soros prof., 1994—; head nuclear theory dept. Bogolyubov Inst. Theoretical Physics, Kiev, 1968—, dir., 1988—. Author: Electromagnetic Fluctuations in Plasmas, 1967, Lectures in Scattering Theory, 1971, Fluctuations and Non-Linear Wave Interactions in Plasmas, 1982, Theory of Nuclear Reactions, 1990, Scattering Theory, 1991; co-author: Collective Oscillations in a Plasma, 1967, Lectures on the Theory of the Nucleous, 1975, Linear Theory, 1975, Non-Linear Theory and Fluctuations, 1975, Nuclear Electrodynamics, 1994, Plasma Physics Theory, 1995, Theory of Nucleus, 1997; editor-in-chief Ukrainian Jour. Physics, 1988; contbr. articles to profl. pubs. Recipient State prize Govt. of Ukraine, 1992. Mem. Ukranian Phys. Soc., Ukranian Acad. Scis. (Sinelnikov prize 1978, Bogolyubov prize 1993), Kiev Phys. Soc. (chmn. 1989—), Am. Phys. Soc., Ukranian Mohylo-Mazepian Acad. (hon.), Royal Swedish Acad. Scis. (fgn.), N.Y. Acad. Scis., Hungarian Acad. Scis. (hon.). Orthodox Christian. Avocation: Ukranian literature. Home: Apt 55, 51/53 Volodymyrska St, 01034 Kyiv Ukraine Office: Bogolyubov Inst Theor Phys, 14-B Metrolohicna St, 031433 Kyiv Ukraine

SITES, PAULA J., defender; b. Watseka, Ill., Nov. 29, 1955; d. Paul LeRoy and Florine Etta (Miller) S. BA, So. Ill. U., 1977, JD, 1985. Bar: Ind. 1985. Jud. clk. Judge Robert Staton Ind. Ct. Appeals, Indpls., 1985-87; staff atty. Ind. Pub. Defender Coun., Indpls., 1987—. Editor Ind. Death Penalty Def. Manual, 1993, updated annually; contbg. regional editor Nat. Death Penalty Info. Index, 1992-98. Elder N.E. United Ch. of Christ, 1989-91. Mem. Nat. Legal Aid and Defender Assn., Ind. State Bar Assn. (Women in the Law Achievement award 1999), Ind. Civil Liberties, Ind. Citizens Against Capital Punishment. Avocations: birdwatching, hiking, writing. E-mail: psites@iquest.net. Fax: 317-232-5524. Office: Ind Pub Defender Coun 309 W Washington St Ste 401 Indianapolis IN 46204-2721

SITESH, ARUNA, English educator; b. Saharanpur, India, Oct. 31, 1945; d. Jugmander Das and Krishna (Gupta) Jain; m. Aloke Sitesh, Jan. 17, 1967. BA, U. Agra, India, 1962; MA, U. Allahabad, India, 1964, PhD, 1970. Lectr. Allahabad U., 1964-65, Indraprastha Coll., Delhi, India, 1965-86; reader Indraprastha Coll., Delhi, 1986-97, prin., 1997—. Author: D.H. Lawrence: The Crusader as Critic, 1975, Bharatiya Nari: Nyaya Ke Dwar Par Dastak, 1989, Her Testimony: American Women Writers of the 90s in Conversation with Aruna Sitesh, 1994, (fiction) Doobta Hua Sooraj, 1977, Vahi Sapne, 1980, Lakshman Rekha, 1986, Anavaran, 1982, Chand Bhi Akela Hai, 1984, Ek Phool Vasant, 1984, Chhalang, 1997; editor: D.H. Lawrence: An Anthology of Recent Criticism, 1990, Glimpses: The Modern Indian Short Story, 1992, Beyond Gender and Geography: American Women Writers, Modern Short Stories, 1994; co-editor: India in the 1990s: Perspectives & Prospects, 1990; translator: Bhartendu Harishchandra's Andher Nagari (Blasted Borough, Feckless King), 1982, 84, D.H. Lawrence's Snake, 1985, Vishnu Prabhakar's Toteate Parivesh, 1992, Mohan Rakesh's Adhe Adhure, 1992; translator short stories, poems, and conversations for profl. jours.; pub., co-editor Pratibha India lit. quar., 1981—; contbr. articles to profl. jours. Recipient grants Brit. Coun. Divsn., New Delhi, 1981, Univ. Grants Commn., New Delhi, 1992-95; Fulbright fellow, 1991-92, Rockefeller Found. vis. scholar, Bellagio, Italy, 1993. Avocations: travel, reading, interior design. Home: Principal's Residence, Indraprastha Coll, 110054 Delhi India Office: Indraprastha Coll, Shamnath Marg, 11054 Delhi 110054, India

SITKEI, GYÖRGY, engineer, educator; b. Orosháza, Hungary, Feb. 13, 1931; s. Lajos Sitkei and Erzsébet Szabó; m. Emilia Bereczky, Aug. 18, 1959 (dec. 1993); 1 child, Zsuzsanna. MS, Tech. U., Budapest, Hungary, 1954, PhD, 1960; D Engring. Sci., Hungarian Acad. Scis., Budapest, 1964; D (hon.), U. Gödöllo, 1999. Doctorant U. Agr., Moscow, 1954-57; rschr. Tech. U., Budapest, 1957-75; head dept. Agrl. Machinery Trust, Budaörs, Hungary, 1975-80; prof., head U. Sopron, Hungary, 1980-97, prof. emeritus, 1997—; mem. State Sci. Accreditation Com., Budapest, 1993—. Author: Mixture Formation and Combustion in Diesel Engines, 1964, Heat Transfer and Thermal Loading in IC Engines, 1974, Soil Mechanics Problems of Agricultural Machines, 1976, Mechanics of Agricultural Materials, 1986 (Acad. award 1988). Recipient Szent-Györgyi Albert award Ministry of Edn., 1993, Pattantyus Á. Géza award Sci. Soc. Mech. Engring. Budapest, 1994. Mem. N.Y. Acad. Scis., Hungarian Acad. Scis. (mem. com. for agrl. mechanization 1975—, com. for thermal engines 1978—), Internat. Soc. for Terrain Vehicle Sys. Avocation: ornamental trees and shrubs. Home: Széher ut 19, H-1021 Budapest Hungary Office: U Sopron, Ady E u 5, H-9401 Sopron Hungary

SITNIK, IGOR MICHAILOVICH, physicist; b. Kislovodsk, Russia, June 24, 1941; s. Michail Danilovich Sitnik and Anna Fedozovna Zenkina; m. Tatyana Nikolaevna; children: Anna, Michail. Grad., Moscow State U., 1964; PhD, Joint Inst. Nuclear Rsch., Dubna, Russia, 1974. Jr. investigator Joint Inst. Nuclear Rsch., 1964-87, sr. investigator, 1987—; spokeman spec-

trometer ALPHA Joint Inst. Nuc. Rsch., 1991-96, project BES, 1995—, expt. 249 Saturne, Saclay, France, 1991-92, expt. 305, 1996. Grantee Russian Found Fundamental Rsch., 1995-97, 2000-01; recipient 1st prize Joint Inst. for Nuclear Rsch. ann. competition on exptl. work, 1965, 90, 98. Mem. Dem. Choice Russia. Home: Bogolubov Prospect 15 310, 141980 Dubna Russia Office: Joint Inst Nuclear Rsch, 141980 Dubna Russia

SITNOV, MIKHAIL I., research scientist; b. Gorkii, USSR, July 27, 1959; s. Ivan D. and Tmara A. S.; m. Vera A. Vanichkina, Oct. 30, 1983; children: Ivan, Maria. M, Moscow State U., 1982, PhD. Rsch. scientist Skobeltsyn Rsch. Inst. Nuclear Physics Moscow State U., 1985-93, sr. rsch. scientist Skobeltsyn Rsch. Inst. Nuclear Physics, 1993—; rsch. assoc. dept. astronomy U. Md., College Park, 1997, 98—. Contbr. articles to profl. jours. Lenin scholar USSR Dept. Edn., 1980; recipient H/S Gold Medal USSR Dept. Edn., 1976. Mem. Am. Geophys. Union. Office: U Md Dept Astronomy College Park MD 20742-0001

SITNOV, SERGEI AFRICANOVICH, physicist; b. Kamenka, Ivanovo, Russia, Nov. 12, 1956; s. African Andreevich and Vera Maximovna (Dugina) S.; m. W. Larisa Ivanovna Sharko; 1 child, Denis. MS, Moscow State U., 1980; PhD in Physics and Math. Oboukhov's, Inst. of Atmospheric Physics, Moscow, 1994. Rsch. probationer Oboukhov's Inst. of Atmospheric Physics, Moscow, 1980-82, jr. rsch. scientist, 1982-85, rsch. scientist, 1985-96, sr. rsch. scientist, 1996—. Contbr. articles to profl. jours. Grantee Russian Found. Basic Rsch., Moscow, 1995-96, 96-98, 98—, Internat. Sci. Found., Moscow, 1995. Avocations: drawing, volleyball. E-mail: sitnov@ifaran.ru. Office: Oboukhov Inst Atmos Physics, Russian Acad Sci/Pyzhevsky 3, Moscow 109017, Russia

SITNYAKOVSKY, ROMAN EMMANUIL, scientist, writer, inventor, translator; b. Kiev, Ukraine, Jan. 5, 1934; came to U.S., 1988; s. Emmanuil I. and Yevgeniya N. (Glazova) S. MS in Mech. and Heat Engring., Polytech. Inst., Kiev, Ukraine, 1956; PhD in Heat Theory/Engring., USSR Acad. Scis., Minsk, Belarus, 1967. Project engr. Ural Turbomotor, Sverdlovsk, USSR, 1956-58; mech. engr. Engring Factory, Kiev, Ukraine, 1958-61; project engr. Design Inst., Kiev, Ukraine, 1961-63; sr. engr. Heat & Mass Transfer Inst., Minsk, Belarus, 1963-68; prin. engr. Thermophysics Inst., Kiev, Ukraine, 1968-87; project engr. Hirt Combustion Engring., Montebello, Calif., 1989-90; cons. Socio-Econ. Sys., L.A., 1988-93; translator, Kiev, 1979-87, L. A., 1988—. Author: I Disagree with Guberman, 1995, Chernobyl is our Fate, 1999; contbr. numerous articles to jours., newspapers and mags.; patentee in field; over 80 inventions.

SITSKY, LARRY, composer, pianist, musicologist, educator; b. Tianjin, China, Sept. 10, 1934; arrived in Australia, 1951; s. Abraham and Sarah (Toper) S.; m. Magda Wlczek; children: Petra, David. Grad., NSW State Conservatorium Music, Sydney, Australia, 1956; postgrad., NSW State Conservatorium Music, 1956-58, San Francisco Convervatory, 1959-61; DFA, Australian Nat. U., 1997. Chief study piano tchr. Queensland State Conservatorium of Music, 1961-65; guest lectr. Queensland U. on Contemporary Music, 1961-65; head keyboard studies Canberra Sch. of Music, 1966-78, head dept. composition and electronic music, 1978-81, head dept. composition and musicology, 1981-83, head dept. composition, 1983—; guest lectr. dept. extension and continuing studies Australian Nat. U., 1983—; resident composer Australian Acad. of Music, 1998, Internat. String Sch., Melbourne, 1996, 97. Works include numerous compositions from solo instrumental pieces to large orch. works including Violin Concerto, Concerto for Guitar and Orch., Concerto for Orch.; composer (operas) Fall of the House of Usher, 1965, Lenz, 1970, Fiery Tales, 1975, Voices in Limbo, 1977, the Golem, 1980, De Produndis, 1982, Three Scenes from Aboriginal Life, Campfire Scene, Mathina, Legend of the Brolga, 1988, Incidental Music to Faust, 1996; author: Busoni and the Piano, 1986; pianist Anthology of Australian Piano Music; pub. The Classical Reproducing Piano Roll, 1989, Music of the Repressed Russian Avant-Garde, 1900-1929, 1993, Anton Rubinstein, 1998; author 3 CDs Australian Piano Music; works commissioned by Australian and Internat. bodies including ABC, Musica Viva, The Internat. Clarinet Soc., the Sydney Internat. Piano Competition, Flederman and the Internat. Flute Conv. Scholarship San Francisco Conversatory, 1959; grantee Myer Rsch. Found. 1965, Vaccari Found., ARC, 1998; fellowship Music Bd. Australia Coun., 1974, Dept. of Fgn. Affairs, 1977, 83, China fellowship, 1983, Inaugural Australian composer's fellowship Music Bd. of the Australia Coun., 1984, travelling/rsch. fellowship Union of Composers and Ministry of Culture, USSR, 1988, Fulbright Australian-Am. fellowship, 1988-89; recipient Advance Australia award Gov.-Gen. Sir Ninian Stephen, 1989, Critics Circle award 1994, A.H. Maggs awards, 1971, 81, Alfred Hill Meml. prize, 1968, Inaugural prize Fellowship of Composers, 1989, Nat. Critics' award, 1989;. Fellow Australian Acad. of Humanities. Avocations: gardening, psychic research, Russian poetry. Home: 29 Threlfall St, Chifley, Canberra ACT 2601, Australia Office: Sch Music Australian Nat U, GPO Box 804, Canberra ACT 2601, Australia

SITZLER, PAUL JAMES, surgeon; b. Melbourne, Victoria, Australia, Feb. 20, 1962; s. Peter Whilhelm S. and Lorraine (Maher) S.; m. Jenny Margaret Slowan, Feb. 28, 1993; children: Karl, Claire, Grace, Ruby. MBBS, U. Melbourne, 1985; FRACS, Coll. of Surgeons, Australia, 1993. Intern Royal Hosart Hosp., Australia, 1986-87, surg. resident, 1987-88, 88-89, surg. registrar, 1989-90, 95-97; surg. registrar Launceton Gen. Hosp., Launceton, Australia, 1990-91; surgeon Western Hosp., Melbourne, Australia, 1997—, Werribee Mercy Hosp., Melbourne, 1996—. Fellow RACS; mem. AMA. Avocation: skiing. Office: Epworth Hosp, 89 Bridge Rd, Melbourne VIC 3121, Australia

SIU, GUINNESS, marketing executive; b. Hong Kong, Apr. 28, 1965. Gen. mgr. Pico Internat. (HK) Ltd., Hong Kong, 1988-95, TeamRite Internat. Ltd., Hong Kong, 1996—. Mem. Am. Mgmt. Assn. Internat., Hong Kong Exhbn. and Conv. Organizers and Suppliers, Fedn. Hong Kong Industries. Avocations: horseback riding, golfing, sailing. E-mail: guinness@teamrite.com. Fax: 852-2635 3821. Office: TeamRite Internat Ltd, 28 Yuen Shun Cir Unit 311, Shatin Hong Kong

SIU, WANG-NGAI, solicitor; b. Hong Kong, Feb. 14, 1938; s. Man-Wan and Wai-Ying (Cheung) S.; m. Yuen-Ling April Lee. Grad., St. Francis Xavier's Coll., 1959, Coll. Law, London, 1967. Solicitor T.S. Tong & Co., Hong Kong, 1971-73, Chan & Ho, Hong Kong, 1973-77, Gallant Y.T. Ho & Co., Hong Kong, 1977—; vice chmn. Fedn. Hong Kong-Macau Photographic Assns., Hong Kong, 1988-90, v.p., 1991-93, chmn., 1993-95. Author: Chinese Opera: Images and Stories, 1997. Royal Photographic Soc. Gt. Britain fellow, Bath, 1985, 89. Mem. Law Soc. Hong Kong, Soc. Notaries. Avocations: classical music, go. Office: Gallant Y T Ho & Co 4th Fl, Jardine Ho 1 Connaught Pl, Hong Kong China

SIVABHUSHANAM, ANDRA, electrical engineer, retired; b. Sankarapuram, India, June 20, 1941; s. Andra Veeraswamy and Andra Rajamma; m. Andra Selvarani, Sept. 9, 1968; children: Anitha, Srividya. Fellow, Instn. Engrs., India, 1989; MEE, I.E.E.E., 1993. Design and devel. engr. Best & Crompton Engring. Ltd., Chennai, India, 1961-80, sr. engr. engring. projects, 1971-80; project engr. Best & Crompton Engring. Ltd., Bauchi, Nigeria, 1981-85; project mgr. Best & Crompton Engring. Ltd., Maiduguri, Nigeria, 1986-90; mng. dir. Best & Crompton Engring. Ltd., Lagos, Nigeria, 1991-95; dep. gen. mgr. Best & Crompton Engring. Ltd., Chennai, India, 1996-99, ret., 1999. Sec. Welfare Assn., Korattur, Chennai, 1975. Home: Plot No 949, 39th St TNHB Colony, Chennai 600 080, India

SIVADAS, VAYALAKKARA, fluid dynamist, researcher; b. Thalassery, Kerala, India, July 28, 1963; s. Gangadharan Nambiar and Vayalakkara Jayalakshmi; m. Thazheveetil Girijadevi, Nov. 12, 1989; children: Lakshmidas, Anjalidas. BSc, U. Calicut, India, 1983; MSc, Cochin U. Sci. & Tech., India, 1985; PhD in Engring., Indian Inst. Tech., Bombay, India, 1995. Rsch. scholar Indian Inst. Tech., Bombay, 1988-91; vis. scientist German Aerospace Rsch. Establishment, Göttingen, Germany, 1991-93; sr. rsch. fellow Indian Inst. Tech., Bombay, 1993-95; vis. scientist Nat. Aerospace Labs., Bangalore, India, 1995-97; rsch. scientist Thermodynamics divsn. Inst. Superior Tech., Lisbon, Portugal. Contbr. articles to profl. jours. and procs. Coun. Sci. and Indsl. Rsch. fellow, 1987, German Acad. Exch. Svc. fellow, 1991, Portuguese Sci. and Tech. Found. fellow, 2000. Hindu. Avocations: playing cricket, watching sports. E-mail: das@dem.ist.utl.pt. Home: Jyothi Nivas Talap, 670001 Kannur Kerala, India Address: Mech Engring Ctr Innovation, Av Rovisco Pais, 1049-001 Lisbon Portugal

SIVA-JOTHY, MICHAEL TREVOR, zoologist; b. London, Mar. 4, 1960; s. Aramugam and Christina Sophie (Latzke) S.; m. Deborah Gail Greenway, Sept. 22, 1984; children, Jonathon Aramugam, William Karim. BS, U. London, 1982; DPhil, Oxford U., 1985. Lectr. Sheffield U., 1990—. Contbr. articles to profl. jours. Rsch. fellow Royal Soc., Nagoya, Japan, 1986-88, U. London, 1988-90. Mem. AAAS, ASAB, ISBE, ISDCI, ASN, Royal Entomological Soc. Office: Dept Animal & Plant Scis, Western Bank, Sheffield S10 2UQ, England

SIVAKUMAR, KRISHNAMOORTHY, educator. B in Tech., Indian Inst. Tech., Bombay, 1991; MSEE, Johns Hopkins U., 1993, MS in Math. Scis., 1995, PhD, 1997. Vis. prof. Tex. A&M U., College Station, 1997-98; asst. prof. Wash. State U., Pullman, 1998—. Mem. editl. bd. Jour. Math. Imaging and Vision, 1999—; contbr. articles to profl. jours. Abel Wolman fellow Johns Hopkins U., Balt., 1991. Mem. IEEE (reviewer tech. articles 1993—). E-mail: siva@wsu.edu. Office: Sch EECS Wash State Univ Pullman WA 99164-0001

SIVAKUMARAN, KUMARASWAMY, civil engineer, consultant; b. Inuvil, Sri Lanka, May 29, 1952; came to U.S., 1986; s. Thambipillai and Theivanayaki (Selliah) K.; m. Muthumanimoli Pakkirisamy, June 24, 1982; children: Karthikgeyan, Sathiyan. BS in Civil Engring., U. Sri Lanka, Moratuwa, 1976; MS in Civil Engring., U. Newcastle-upon-Tyne, Eng., 1985; PhD in Civil Engring., Colo. State U., 1989. Irrigation engr. Irrigation Dept., Colombo, Sri Lanka, 1977-80; design engr. Group Engring. Consulting, Colombo, 1981; sr. project engr. Samek Constrn. Co. Ltd., Aba, Nigeria, 1981-84; rsch. asst. Colo. State U., Ft. Collins, 1986-89; guest scientist GKSS Rsch. Ctr., Geesthacht, Germany, 1990-91; assoc., sr. water resources engr. TAMS Consultants, Inc., N.Y.C., 1991—; adj. asst. prof. West Va. U., Morgantown, 1998—. Travel grantee Am. Pub. Works Assn., 1986. Mem. ASCE, U.S. Com. on Large Dams. Home: 5L Edgewood Dr Weston WV 26452 Office: TAMS Consultants Inc 655 3d Ave New York NY 10017

SIVANY, ABDUL RAUF HAJI IBRAHIM, investment company executive; b. Karachi, Sind, Pakistan, Sept. 1957; s. Ibrahim Haji Ismail and Zubaida Hajiani (Hashim) Rodawala; m. Seema Haji Rashid Bano, Sept. 15, 1985; children: Mohammad Owais, Abdul Basit. B of Commerce, U. Karachi. Asst. Habib Bank Ltd., Karachi, 1977-79; asst. supr. FX Dept. Middle East Bank, Dubai, United Arab Emirates, 1979-81; agy. head Syndication Unit Al Bank Al Saudi Al Fransi, Saudi Arabia, 1981-85, interbank dealer, 1985-94; mgr. treasury, issue dept. Altawfeek Co. for Investment Funds, Saudi Arabia, 1994—. Avocations: swimming, soccer, squash, scrabble, sight-seeing. Office: Altawfeek Co Invest Funds, Dallah Tower Palestine St, PO 6854 Jeddah 21452, Saudi Arabia

SIVASHANMUGAM, PALANI, chemical engineering educator; b. Jayankondam, India, June 9, 1963; s. Mudaliar and Palani (Dhanapakyam) Palani; m. Arunagiri Sumathy, Sept. 2, 1990; 2 children. B Engring. in Chemistry, Annamalai U., India, 1985; M Tech., Regional Engring. Coll., India, 1988. Plant supr. Madras Pharms., India, 1986-87; sr. engr. British Phys. Lab. Ltd., India, 1989-92; lectr. Regional Engring. Coll., Tiruchy, India, 1992-98, asst. prof., 1998—; cons. in field. Contbr. articles to profl. jours. Recipient Design award Visvesveraya Inst., Bangalore, 1985, Ministry of Human Resource Devel., India, 1987. Fellow Electrochem. Soc. India; mem. India Soc. for Tech. Edn. (life). Avocations: reading magazines, newspapers, astrology, numorology. Home: No 1 12th St, Tiruchy 620015, India Office: Regional Engring Coll, Dept Chem Engring, Tiruchy 620015, India

SIVASHINSKY, GREGORY, mathematics educator; b. Moscow, Oct. 21, 1945; arrived in Israel, 1971; s. Israel and Tatiana (Oshina) S.; m. Terry Rocks, Feb. 12, 1988. MSc, Moscow State U., 1967; DrSc, Technion, Haifa, Israel, 1973. Rsch. asst. Moscow State U., 1967-71; lectr. Technion, Haifa, 1972-74; sr. lectr. Tel-Aviv U., 1974-78, assoc. prof., 1978-82, prof. math., 1982—; rsch. prof. CCNY, 1987—. Contbr. articles to profl. jours. Sgt. Israel Def. Forces, 1974. Named The Gordon Chair in Combustion Sci., Tel-Aviv U., 1997. Mem. Combustion Inst. Office: Tel Aviv Univ, Dept of Math, 69978 Tel Aviv Israel

SIVASUBRAMANIAN, KOLINJAVADI NAGARAJAN, neonatologist, educator; b. Coimbatore, Madras, India, May 9, 1945; came to U.S., 1971; s. Kolinjavadi Ramaswamy and Sukanthi (Subramanian) Nagarajan; m. Kalyani Hariharier, Feb. 5, 1975; children: Ramya, Rajeev, Ranjan. BSc, Madras U., 1964, MD, 1969. Diplomate Am. Bd. Pediatrics and Neonatal-Perinatal Medicine. Intern in pediat. Jewish Hosp. and Med. Ctr., Bklyn., 1971-72; resident in pediat. U. Md. Hosp., Balt., 1972-74; fellow in neonatology Georgetown U. Hosp., Washington, 1974-76, attending neonatologist, 1976—, dir. nurseries, chief neonatology, 1981—, vice chair pediat., 1988-98, prof. pediat. and ob-gyn. Editor: Trace Elements/Mineral Metablolism During Development, 1993; editor pub. SIDS Series, 1985; editor jour. Current Concepts in Neonatology, India, 1990—; internat. editor Indian Jour. Pediat., India, 1988—. Chmn. Siva Vishnu Temple, Lanham, Md., 1981-91; mem. Fetus and New Born Com., Washington, 1988; founder, bd. dirs. Coun. of Hindu Temples U.S.A.; founder, coord. United Hindu Temples of Met. Washington; 1st v.p. Interfaith Conf., Washington; mem. D.C. bd. dirs. Nat. Youth Leadership Forum. Recipient "Preemies" cover article Newsweek, 1988; featured in "Washingtonian" jour., 1996. Fellow Am. Coll. Nutrition, Am. Acad. Pediat.; mem. AAAS, N.Y. Acad. Scis., Internat. Soc. for Trace Element Rsch. in Humans, Soc. for Bioethics Consultation, Am. Soc. Law, Medicine and Ethics. Hindu. Achievements include research in neonatology, trace elements kinetics, reduction in infant mortality, neonatal immunology, and bioethics. Office: Georgetown U Hosp 3 South Hospital 3800 Reservoir Rd NW Washington DC 20007-2113

SIVASUBRAMONIAN, B., aerospace engineer; b. Thiruvananthapuram, Kerala, India, Apr. 1, 1954; s. S. Bhagavatheeswaralyer and H. Jayalakshmiammal; m. P. Seethalakshmi, Oct. 28, 1983; children: Jayalakshmi, Gouripriya. BSc in Engring., Kerala U., India, 1976; M Tech., Indian Inst. of Tech., Madras, 1982, PhD, 1999. Scientist, engr. SLV project VSSC/ISRO, India, 1977-82, 1982-95; head in vehicle engring. VSSC/ISRO, 1995—. Contbr. articles to profl. jours. Mem. Aeronautical Soc. of India (exec. com. 1988-90), Space Engring. Assn. (joint sec. Trivandrum chpt. 1996-98), others. Avocations: playing percussion instruments, cricket, shuttle badminton. Office: Head Vehicle Engring, Design Analysis Divn/LVDG, 695022 Thiruvananthapuram Kerala, India

SIVERD, ROBERT JOSEPH, lawyer; b. July 27, 1948; s. Clifford David and Elizabeth Ann (Klink) S.; m. Bonita Marie Shulock, Jan. 8, 1972; children: Robert J. Jr., Veronica Leigh. AB in French, Georgetown U., 1970, JD, 1973; postgrad., The Sorbonne, Paris, 1969. Bar: N.Y. 1974, U.S. Dist. Ct. (so. and ea. dists.) N.Y. 1974, U.S. Ct. Appeals (2d cir.) 1974, U.S. Supreme Ct. 1980, U.S. Dist. Ct. (ea. dist.) Pa. 1984, U.S. Ct. Appeals (3d cir.) 1984, U.S. Ct. Appeals (6th cir.) 1985, Ohio 1991, Ky. 1992. Assoc. Donovan Leisure Newton & Irvine, N.Y.C., 1973-83; staff v.p., litigation counsel Am. Fin. Group, Inc., Greenwich, Conn., 1983-85, v.p. litigation counsel, 1986-87; v.p. assoc. gen. counsel Am. Fin. Group, Inc., Cin., 1987-92; sr. v.p., gen. counsel and sec. Gen. Cable Corp., 1992-94, exec. v.p., gen. counsel and sec., 1994—. Mem. ABA, Assn. of Bar of City of N.Y., Ky. Bar Assn. Republican. Office: Gen Cable Corp 4 Tesseneer Dr Newport KY 41076-9167

SIVERS, DENNIS WAYNE, physicist, real estate developer; b. Greeley, Colo., Jan. 20, 1944; s. Wendell Clifford and Elizabeth Elvera Sivers; m. Penny Kathleen Welch, June 18, 1966 (div. Aug. 1980); m. E. Anne Crider, June 3, 1985; children: Derek, Heidi. BS in Physics, MIT, 1966; PhD in Theoretical Physics, U. Calif., Berkeley, 1970. Physicist Argonne (Ill.) Nat. Lab., 1976-91; physicist Portland (Oreg.) Physics Inst., 1991—; pres./CEO Sivers Cos., Portland, 1986—; adj. prof. U. Mich., 1997—. Contbr. articles to profl. jours. Fellow Am. Phys. Soc., Nat. Assn. Indsl. & Office Properties (nat. forum 1993—). Achievements include research in seminal calculations in perturbative quantum chromodynamics. E-mail: densivers@sivers.com. Office: Portland Physics Inst 4730 SW Macadam Ave Portland OR 97201-6417

SIWICKI, MICHAEL, cartographer; b. Warsaw, Poland, July 13, 1962; s. Ryszard and Wanda (Trzebunia) S.; m. Anna Rosinska, Feb. 7, 1987; children: Bartlomei, Paulina, Zuzanna. MS, Warsaw U., Poland, 1987. Cartographer Geokart, Warsaw, Poland, 1988-91, pres. bd., 1991-93; pres. bd. Maplan, Warsaw, Poland, 1993; editor in chief Polkart, Warsaw, Poland, 1993—. Author: (maps) Road Map of Poland, 1992, Lodz-Plan of the City, 1993, (atlas) Atlas Swiata Dla Najmlodszych, 1991, The World Geographical Atlas for Secondary Schools, 1995, Atlas of Poland, 1999, Map of the Tatra National Park, 1998. Avocation: hiking. Fax: 48 22 847 15 25. Office: Cartographical Pub House, ul Batuty 1/406, 02-743 Warsaw Poland

SIXDENIER, GUY-DOMINIQUE, orientalist philologist, monk; b. Blandy les Tours, France, Oct. 1, 1917; s. Gaston Sixdenier and Lucienne Grare. Diploma 3d yr. in Oriental Langs., ICP, Paris, 1947; PhD (hon.), N.Y. Acad. Scis., 1995. Prof. oriental langs. Studium, Wisques, France, 1947-49; prof. theology Roman Catholic Seminary, Rabat, Morocco, 1949-51; sec. Pontifical Abbey, Rome, 1951-69; 2d sec. Soc. Samaritan Studies, Paris, 1985—; co-founder, 2d sec. Soc. des Amis des Manuscrits et des Etudes Karaïtes, Paris, 1987, HECTOR, Paris, 1988. Contbr. numerous articles to profl. jours. philology. Lt., French Army Infantry, 1940, Souge. Roman Catholic. Home: 3 rue de la Source, F-75016 Paris France

SIZMANN, ANDREAS FRANZ LUDWIG, physicist; b. Munich, Oct. 16, 1961; s. Rudolf and Ingeborg (Pilz) S.; m. Nicola Hartmann, June 12, 1992. Diploma in physics, Tech. U., Munich, 1989; PhD in Physics, Ludwig-Maximilians U., Munich, 1992. Rsch. asst. Max Planck Inst. for Quantum Optics, Garching, Fed. Rep. of Germany, 1989-90, U. Konstanz, Fed. Rep. of Germany, 1991; rsch. asst. Laboratiore de Spectroscopie Hertzienne de l'Ecole Normale Superieure, U. Pierre et Marie Curie, Paris, 1991-92, IBM Almaden Rsch. Ctr., San Jose, 1992-93; rsch. asst. Univ. Konstanz, 1993-94, Friedrich-Alexander Univ., Erlangen, Germany, 1994—. Contbr. articles to profl. jours. Mem. Am. Phys. Soc., Mensa in Deutschland E.V., Deutsche Physikalische Gesellschaft. Office: U Erlangen-Nurenberg Lehrstuhl Optik, Staudtstr 7/B2, D-91058 Erlangen Germany

SIZONENKO, PIERRE CLAUDE, pediatric endocrinology educator; b. Paris, Apr. 19, 1932; s. Vladimir and Sarah Lea (Prigogine) S.; m. Marie-Thérèse Magnin, Apr. 30, 1960; children: Ivan, Stephane, Alexandre. Med. diplomate, Sch. Medicine, Paris, 1957; BSc, Sch. Scis., Paris, 1964; MD, Sch. Medicine, Paris, 1965; MSc, Sch. Scis., Paris, 1970. Diplomate Bd. Pediatrics, Bd. Pediatric Endocrinology. Intern Paris U. Hosp., 1957-59, resident, 1961-65, fellow, 1965-67; fellow dept. pediatrics U. Calif., San Francisco, 1967-68; sr. rsch. fellow Paris U. Hosp., 1968-69; rsch. assoc. Geneva Med. Sch., 1969-72, asst. prof., 1972-79, assoc. prof., 1979-82, prof. pediatrics, 1982-97, prof. emeritus, 1997—; head Div. Biology Growth and Reproduction, Geneva, 1982-97; cons. WHO, Geneva, 1975—; cons. pediatric endocrinology. Editor, co-author: Pediatric Endocrinology, 1993, Control of the Onset of Puberty II, 1990, Developmental Endocrinology, 1994, Précis de Pediatrie, 1996. 1st lt. French Air Force, 1959-61. Recipient Bernard Dreyfuss prize Acad. Medicine, Paris, 1965, Nessim Habif World prize U. Geneva, 1981. Mem. Endocrine Soc. USA, Swiss Endocrine Soc. (pres. 1983-85), Swiss Assn. Diabetology (coun. mem. 1984-90), European Soc. for Pediatric Endocrinology (treas. 1977-83, pres. 1980-81, Andrea Prader prize 1995), European Soc. for Pediatric Rsch., European Fedn. Endocrine Socs. (hon. treas. 1990-98), Lawson Wilkins Pediatric Endocrine Soc. (corr.), Growth Hormone Rsch. Soc. (com. mem. 1990-98). Russian Orthodox. Avocation: skiing, swimming. E-mail: Pierre.C.Sizonenko@hin.ch. Home: 17 rue Toepffer, 1206 Geneva Switzerland Office: Hopital de la Tour, av JD Maillard, 1217 Meyrin 14, Switzerland

SIZOV, ALEXANDER NIKOLAI, physicist; b. Pospelikha, Russia, Nov. 19, 1944; s. Nikolai Vasilii and Nadezhda Fedot (Meleshko) S.; m. Lyudmila Ivan Tyutyunnikova, July 27, 1968; children: Ann, Maria. M in Nuc. Engring., Moscow Engring. Phys. Inst., 1968; PhD in Theoretical Physics, All Russia Sci. Rsch. Inst. of Experimental Physics, Arzamas, 1977; doctor of sci., 1998. Staff engr. All Russia Sci. RSch. Inst. Exptl. Physics, 1968-70, jr. rsch. scientist, 1970-75, sr. rsch. scientist, 1975-86, head lab., 1986—. Contbr. articles to profl. publs. Avocations: antiquity, ancient history. Office: All Russia Sci Rsch Inst, Exptl Physics, 607190 Sarov Nizhnii, Russia

SJAKSTE, NIKOLAJS, biochemist, researcher; b. Riga, Latvia, May 11, 1955; s. Izidors and Polina (Korolkova) S.; m. Tatjana Getun, Mar. 25, 1977; children: Jelena, Jelizaveta. MD, 2d Moscow Med. Inst., 1978; PhD, Cancer Rsch. Ctr., Moscow, 1984; D of Biology, Inst. Exptl. Medicine, St. Petersburg, Russia, 1992. Rschr. Inst. Exptl. and Clin. Medicine, Riga, Latvia, 1983-90; head of biochemistry group Inst. Organic Synthesis, Riga, 1990—; CNRS associated rschr. Inst. Jacques Monod, Paris, 1995, 98; full prof. Latvian U., 1998—; assoc. prof. Latvian Med. Acad., Riga, 1991-93. Co-author: DNA Damaging Chemical Compounds, 1991; contbr. articles to sci. jours., including Molecular Genetics, Biochem. Pharm. Mem. N.Y. Acad. Scis., Latvian Biocem. Soc., Latvian Soc. Geneticists and Breeders. Avocations: languages, traveling. Home: A Deglava 108/3-8, LV 1082 Riga Latvia Office: Inst Organic Synthesis, Aizkraukles 21, LV 1006 Riga Latvia

SJOBERG, GUNNAR, pediatrician, researcher; b. Nacka, Stockholm, Sweden, May 17, 1960; s. John and Miriam (Stahl) S.; m. Bodil Strom, Aug. 13, 1988; children: David, Ida, Sara. MD, Karolinska Inst., Stockholm, 1988, PhD, 1997. Jr. physician Sachsska Hosp., Stockholm, 1989-91; intern Nacka Hosp., Stockholm, 1991-93; PhD rschr. Karolinska Inst., Stockholm, 1993-97; pediatrician Astrid Lingrens Hosp., Stockholm, 1997—; rschr. Karolinska Inst. Lab. Genetics, Stockholm, 1997—. Contbr. articles to profl. jours. Ensign Swedish Med. Corps, 1993-99. Mem. N.Y. Acad. Scis. Home: Duvnasvagen 31, 131 50 Saltsjo-Duvnas Sweden

SJÖBERG, JAN STEFAN, physician; b. Stockholm, July 31, 1952; s. Sten Olof and Gyrid Ingeborg (Olsson) S.; m. Anna Birgitta Ståhl Christensen, Feb. 15, 1997; 1 child, Sten. BM, Uppsala (Sweden) U., 1974; MD, Karolinska Inst., Stockholm, 1977; PhD, Karolinska Inst., 1990. Intern Danderyds Hosp., Stockholm, 1978-79; resident Huddinge (Sweden) U. Hosp., 1980-85, cons., 1985—, sr. cons. physician Ctr. for Metabolism and Endocrinology, 1994—, asst. head physician Acute Emergency Dept., 1994—; chmn. bd. Serafimer Kliniken AB, 1986—. Capt. med. corps Royal Swedish Life Guards, 1993—. Fellow Arla Coldin, Swedish Soc. Medicine; mem. Swedish Med. Assn., Swedish Soc. Endocrinology. Lutheran. Avocations: hunting, history, traveling. Office: Dept Medicine, Huddinge U Hosp, S-141 86 Huddinge Sweden

SJÖBLAD, HANS STURE BERNHARD, pediatrician, educator, researcher; b. Virserum, Småland, Sweden, Sept. 3, 1940; s. Bertil Theodor and Maud Vilhelmina (Jaensson) S.; m. Christina Eriksdotter Bendz; children: Axel Erland, Sven Aron, Gustav Hannes. MD, U. Lund, Sweden, 1969, PhD in Physiol. Chemistry, 1977. Profl. cert. physician, specialist in children's diseases, Sweden. Intern, fellow various hosps., Lund, Malmoe, Stockholm, Halmstad Nässjo and Lidköping, 1969-77; fellow, asst. physician dept. pediatrics U. Lund, 1977-81, assoc. prof., 1981—, cons., head metabolic dept., 1981—; prof. Coll. Advanced Nursing, Lund-Helsingborg, Sweden, 1979-89; cons. in clin. chemistry, Lund, 1977-79; mem. med. ref. group for diabetes Nat. Bd. of Health and Welfare, Sweden, 1996—, regional ref. groups, 2000—. Author: Studies on Genetic Diseases Involving Abnormal Metabolism of Glycoconjugates, 1977, Diabetes in Children, 1994, 3d edit., 1999; editor: Diabetes in Children and Adolescents. A Comprehensive Medical Care Program, 1996; contbr. articles to profl. jours. Recipient numerous grants for rsch. Mem. Swedish Med. Assn. (bd. commns.), Swedish Pediatric Assn. (diabetology-endocrinology sect., coun. mem.), European Soc. Pediatric Rsch., Soc. Pediatric Rsch. (U.S.), European Assn. Study of Diabetes, Soc. Study Inborn Errors of Metabolism, Internat. Soc. for Pediatric and Adolescent Diabetes. Fax: 46 46 145459. Office: Univ Hosp of Lund, Dept of Pediatrics, S-22185 Lund Sweden

SJODEN, HILDING KARL, university administrator; b. Sater, Sweden, Nov. 15, 1944; s. Ellinor Birgitta Elisabet Holmstad, Nov. 29, 1968; children: Jens - Tord, Bjorn, Rolf. Licentiate in psychology, Uppsala U.,

Sweden, 1973; Diploma in Edn., Goteborg Inst. of Edn., 1974. Instr. in psychology and edn. Norrkoping/Sch. of Pre-Sch. Edn., Sweden, 1974-76; asst. prof. in psychology and edn. Goteborg U., Sweden, 1976-92; head of dept. Goteborg U., 1979-84, sr. faculty adminstr., 1987-90, head of faculty office, 1990-96, prin. adminstrv. office, 1997—; prin. sec., head of adminstrn. Goteborg U. Libr., 1998—. Author: (book) Och Somliga ar Sma, 1978; contbr. articles to profl. jours. Home: Storgatan 5, S-43430 Kungsbacka Sweden Office: Goteborg Univ Libr, Box 222, SE-40530 Göteborg Sweden

SJÖGREN, ERIK, botanist, educator; b. Kalmar, Sweden, Oct. 5, 1933; s. Alex and Elisabeth (Arnström) S.; m. Berit Jacobsson; two children. PhD, U. Uppsala, 1964. Docent Uppsala, Sweden, 1965—. Mem. Macaronesian Botanical Soc. Home: Fältvägen 1 B, 75646 Uppsala Sweden

SJOHOLT, PETER, economic geographer; b. Orskog, Norway, July 8, 1925; s. Olav and Klara (Myhre) S.; m. Ruth Nielsen, Aug. 16, 1955; 1 child, Bjorn. Degree, U. Oslo, 1955; PhD, U. Bergen, 1982. Lectr. secondary schs., Levanger, Trondheim, Norway, 1956-63; mgr. Okoplan, Trondheim, Norway, 1967-74; from assoc. prof. to prof. U. Bergen Norwegian Sch. Econs. & Bus. Adminstrn., Norway, 1974—. Author: The System of Central Places and Hinterlands, 1981, Tropical Colonization: Problems and Achievements, 1988, Internationalization of Services in the Nordic Countries, 1992. Mem. Finnish Geographical Soc., Norwegian Acad. Sci., Norwegian Assn. Geographers, Poly. Soc. Norway, N.Y. Acad. Scis. Home: Breiviksveien 7, 5035 Bergen Sandviken, Norway Office: Norwegian Sch Econs, Adminstrn Breiviksveien 40, 5045 Bergen Sandviken, Norway

SJÖLAND, KARL ANDERS, physicist; b. Landskrona, Sweden, Jan. 27, 1965; s. Karl-Erik and Vera (Hagman) S.; m. Yimin Qian, Aug. 10, 1996. Grad. theoretical philosophy, Lund (Sweden) U., 1990, Teknologic Licentiat, 1994, PhD, 1996; MSc in Engring. Physics, Lund Inst. Tech., 1992. Rsch. asst. Lund U., 1992-97; aux. agt. Inst. for Reference Materials and Measurements, Geel, Belgium, 1997; temporary agt. Inst. for Reference Materials and Measurements, Geel, 1997—; rsch. leader Com. for R&D of the Oresunal Region, Malmö, 2000—; chmn. Lund Nuc. Microprobe Group, 1994-97; coord. for Swedish Aid Project for Mozambique, Lund U., 1994—. Contbr. articles to profl. jours. Scholar Peter og Emma Thompsens Legat, Copenhagen, 1987-90. Avocations: chess, photography, music, art, philosophy. Home: Jordabalksvägen 56, SE-22652 Lund Sweden Office: Com for R&D Oresund Region, Malmo Univ, SE-20506 Malmo Sweden

SJOLANDER, SVERRE, zoologist, educator; b. Gothenburg, Sweden, Mar. 30, 1940; s. Sven and Carna (Tulin) S.; m. Jane Bagge (div. 1985); children: Kare, Egil; m. Angela Hovorka, 1989; 1 child, Judith. BS, U. Stockholm, 1966, MS, 1967, DSc, 1977. Lectr. U. Ibadan, Nigeria, 1965-66, U. Stockholm, 1966-75; assoc. prof. U. Linkoping, Sweden, 1981-99; full prof. U. Linkoping, 1999—; vis. prof. U. Vienna, Austria, 1992, 94, 95, 96. Author: New Thoughts on Old Brains, 1985; contbr. articles to profl. jours. Lt. Royal Swedish Life Guard, 1959-60. Recipient Konrad-Lorenz medal Austria, 1999; Alexander von Humboldt fellowship, 1975, Swedish-Am. fellow, 1974. Mem. Assn. Study of Animal Behaviour. Home: Stora Greby, S-59062 Linghem Sweden Office: Univ Linkoping Dept Biology, S-58183 Linköping Sweden

SJOLIN, CHRISTER K.G., energy executive; b. Karlskoga, Sweden, May 21, 1943; m. Karen Sjolin. Degree in chem. engring., Royal Inst. Tech., Sweden, 1968, lic. in tech., 1970, D in Tech., 1973. Tech. mgr. Kema Nord Plast, 1975-78; divsn. mgr. Kema Nord Industries, 1978-88; pres. Bergvik Kemi, 1988-89; v.p. Stora Kemi, 1989-90; pres. Stora Teknik, 1990-94, Fortum Kraft AB (formerly Stora Kraft and Stor Enso Energy), 1994—. Mem. Acad. Engring. Scis. Office: Fortum Kraft AB, Box 1900, 5-79119 Falun Sweden

SJOLUND, PETER ERIK, lawyer; b. Ornskoldsvik, Sweden, Oct. 12, 1961. LLM, U. Uppsala, Sweden, 1987; JD, U. Minn., 1989. Assoc. Hagglund & Ramm-Ericson, Stockholm, 1989-94, ptnr., 1995—. Mem. ABA, Inter-Pacific Bar Assn., N.Y. State Bar Assn. Office: Hagglund & Ramm-Ericson, Kungsgatan 6, 111 87 Stockholm Sweden

SJÖNELL, GÖRAN, family physician; b. Solna, Sweden, Oct. 24, 1946; s. Bengt P.B. and Marianne I. (Linblad) S.; m. Barbro M. Ståhle, July 11, 1969; chilren: Carl, Per. Med. degree, Uppsala (Sweden) U., 1968, MD, 1972; PhD in Social Medicine, Karolinska Inst., Stockholm, 1984. Cert. in family medicine Swedish Bd. Welfare. Family physician Uppsala Läns Landsting, 1974-78, Stockholm Läns Landsting, 1978—; chief physician family medicine Stockholm, 1979-83, Kvartersakuten Matteus, Stockholm, 1993—; host/family doctor morning TV program TV 4; sr. lectr. dept. social medicine Karolinska Inst., 1984-91; cons. Stockholm County Coun., 1986-93, European Coun., Strasbourg, France, 1986-87, Nordöstra Sjukvärdsområdet, Stockholm, 1999. Author: Husläkarboken, 1987, Husläkarfallet, 1994; patentee, rschr. in field. Mem. exec. com. Wonca, Melbourne, Australia, 1989, editor, 1993, pres. elect, Hong Kong, 1982, pres. 1985. Recipient Servastian award Coll. Family Doctors Singapore, Nidarosstipendiat award Norwegian Coll. Family Physicians Trondheim, 1999. Fellow Royal Coll. Gen. Practitioners U.K. (hon.); mem. Swedish Coll. Family Physicians (chmn. 1985). Avocations: writing, tennis, downhill skiing, amateur theater, inventing. Home: Askrikevägen 11, S-181 46 Lidingö Sweden Office: Kvartersakuten Matteus, Surbrunnsgatan 66 plan 6, 113 27 Stockholm Sweden

SJÖSTRAND, SVEN-ERIK, business administration educator; b. Stockholm, Apr. 3, 1945; s. Stig Göte and Gerd Ingrid (Melander) S.; m. Laila Anita Östlund; 1 child: Dan Erik. MSc, Stockholm Sch. Econs., 1968, PhD, 1973. Asst. prof. Stockholm Sch. Econs., 1973-74, assoc. prof., 1974-78, prof., 1978—; bd. dirs. Stockholm Sch. Econs., Samhall; chmn. Econ. Rsch. Inst., Sweden, 1995—. Author: Organizational Myths, 1979, The Two Faces of Management, 1997; editor: Institutional Change, 1993, On Economic Institutions, 1996, Invisible Management, 2000. Sgt. Sweden, 1964-65. Recipient Best Dissertation in Sweden in Econ. Scis. Assn. Swedish Univs., 1973, Best Book on Leadership Assn. Swedish Mgrs., Stockholm, 1992. Fellow EAEPE (London); mem. SASE (v.p. 1992-95), SCANCOR, AIK, NAFS, Amnesty Internat., WWF. Avocations: sports, outdoor life, art, artistic painting. Office: Stockholm Sch Econs, PO Box 6501, 11383 Stockholm SE, Sweden

SJÖSTRÖM, ANDERS KJELL, ophthalmologist, clinician, researcher; b. Skön, Medelpad, Sweden, Apr. 15, 1951; s. Kjell and Kerstin (Andersson) S.; m. Monica Birgitta Ericson, May 31, 1980; children: Daniel, Susanna. Odont. kand., U. Gothenburg, Sweden, 1971, Med. kand., 1975, MD, 1979, PhD, 1985. Rsch. fellow dept. physiology U. Gothenburg, 1973-85; house officer Sahlgrenska Hosp., Gothenburg, 1985-91, clin. fellow, registrar, 1991-93; clin. fellow, registrar Mölndal (Sweden) Hosp., 1991-93; cons. ophthalmology Frölunda Hosp, Gothenburg, 1993-94, Sahlgrens U. Hosp., 1995—; assoc. prof. U. Gothenburg, 1995. Scholar, 1980-84; rsch. grantee De Blindas Vänner, 1993-97, Kronprinsessan Margareths Arbetsnämd, 1994-97. Mem. Swedish Soc. Electro-Ophthalmology (sec. 1994, pres. 1997—), Internat. Soc. for Clin. Electro-physiology of Vision, Swedish Soc. Medicine, Gothenburg Soc. Medicine, Swedish Med. Assn., Assn. for Rsch. in Vision and Ophthalmology, N.Y. Acad. Scis. Avocations: collecting older detective novels, crossword puzzles, motor boating, skiing, good food. Office: Queen Silvias Hosp Children, Barnklinikerna, S-416 85 Göteborg Sweden

SJOSTROM, EERO VILHELM, chemical educator, consultant, researcher; b. Helsinki, Finland, May 1, 1924; s. Bertil Alfred and Toini Julia (Haapanen) S.; m. Kerstin Stephansson Sjostrom; children: Ritva, Martin, Lena; m. Margarita Wickstrom Sjostrom. MS, Helsinki U., 1949; PhD, 1955. Rsch. fellow Swedish Forest Products Lab, Stockholm, 1950-51, Chalmers U. Tech., Gothenburg, Sweden, 1951-54; rsch. assoc., chief chemist Orion Corp., Helsinki, Finland, 1954-59; dept. head Stora Kopparberg Ctrl. Rsch. Lab., Falun, Sweden, 1959-67; prof. wood chemistry Helsinki U. Tech., Espoo, Finland, 1967-91, cons. prof. emeritus, 1991—; vis. prof. U. Wash., Seattle, 1981-82; cons. for several orgns. in Finland and abroad. Author: Wood Chemistry-Fundamentals and Applications, 1981, 2nd edit., 1993; editor: (wiht R. Alén) Analytical Methods in Wood Chemistry, Pulping, and Papermaking, 1999; 20 patents; approx. 150 scientific pubs. to internat. jours. Named Comdr. of Order of Lion of Finland, 1980. Fellow Internat. Acad. Wood Sci.; mem. The Swedish Assn. of Pulp and Paper Engrs., The Finnish Chem. Soc., The Swedish Chem. Soc., The Finnish Paper Engrs. Assn. Avocation: tennis. Home: Ullankatu 3A5, 00140 Helsinki Finland Office: Helsinki Univ Tech, Vuorimiement 1, 02150 Espoo Finland

SJÖSTRÖM, INGRID CECILIA, curator; b. Stockholm, Sweden, June 17, 1938; d. Georg and Cecilia (Lovèn) Svensson; m. John Sjöström; children: Maria, Martin. PhD, U. Stockholm, Sweden, 1972. Lectr. U. Stockholm, 1972-89; curator Ctrl. Bd. Antiquities, Stockholm, 1989-95, rsch. expert, 1995—. Co-author: Swedish Churches 1760-1860, 1989; co-editor: Bebyggelse Historisk Tidskrift, 1987—. Office: Riksantikvarieämbetet, Box 5405, 114 84 Stockholm Sweden

SKAGGS, MERTON MELVIN, JR., environmental engineer; b. Kerrville, Tex., Nov. 16, 1953; s. Merton Melvin and Peggy LaNell (Dechert) S.; m. Susan Marie Frawley, Aug. 9, 1980; children: Alan, Marie, Bridget. BSChemE, Tex. A&M U., 1976; MS in Biology, U. Houston, Clear Lake City, Tex., 1979. Registered profl. engr., Tex. Process engr. Diamond Shamrock Chems. Co., Pasadena, Tex., 1976-78, environ. engr., 1979-80, sr. environ. engr., 1981-84; ctrl. ops. mgr. Maxus Energy Corp., Dallas, 1985-91, gen. mgr. environ. affairs, 1991-96; pres. Chem. Land Holdings, Inc., Dallas, 1994-99, Maxus Agrl. Chems., Inc., Dallas, 1994-96; prs. InDepth Environ. Assocs., 1999—. Coach Odyssey of the Mind, Southlake, Tex., 1993-97. Mem. AIChE, Soc. Petroleum Engrs. (chmn. environ. study group 1993-96, sect. treas. 1996-97, edn. dir. 1997-98, chmn. edn. 1997-98, program chmn. 1998-88, social dir. 1999—), Water Environ. Federation, Air and Waste Assn. Methodist. Achievements include management of projects to clean up and/or close five major hazardous waste disposal sites and eight related publications. Home: PO Box 92653 Southlake TX 76092-0653 Office: InDepth Environ Assocs 1500 Corporate Cir Ste 11 Southlake TX 76092-5954

SKAL, DEBRA LYNN, lawyer; b. Dayton, Ohio, Oct. 2, 1958; d. Lawrence and Anne Bernice (Cunix) S. BS with high distinction, Ind. U., 1986; JD, Duke U., 1989. Bar: Ga. 1989. Assoc. Powell, Goldstein, Frazer & Murphy, Atlanta, 1989-96. Exec. editor: Alaska Law Rev., 1987-89. Coun. mem. YES! Atlanta, 1990-98; founding mem. Teaching Tolerance So. Poverty Law Ctr., Montgomery, Ala., mem. leadership coun. Klanwatch; mem. Lupus Found. Am., Atlanta, 1992—, Sjogren's Found., Port Washington, N.Y., 1992—, Am. Diabetes Assn., 1996—, Arthritis Found., Atlanta, 1993—. Mem. State Bar Assn. Ga., Beta Gamma Sigma.

SKALA, GARY DENNIS, electric and gas utilities executive management consultant; b. Bay Shore, N.Y, Oct. 15, 1946; s. Harry A. and Emily Skala. BS in Mgmt. Engring., Rensselaer Polytech. Inst., 1969; MA in Psychology, Hofstra U., 1972; postgrad., Chgo. Theol. Sem., 1996—. Engr. L.I. Lighting Co., Hicksville, N.Y., 1969-71; labor rels. coord. L.I. Lighting Co., 1971-73; mgmt. cons. Gilbert/Commonwealth, N.Y.C., 1973-74; sr. mgmt. cons. Booz, Allen & Hamilton, San Francisco, 1974-78; mgr. utility cons. A.T. Kearney, Chgo., 1978-81; mng. cons. Cresap, div. Towers Perrin, Chgo., 1981-85; pres. Gary D. Skala & Assocs. Mgmt. Cons., Chgo., 1985—; lectr. on utility bus. issues Edison Electric Inst., Utility Exec. Mgmt. Com., Internat. Maintenance Conf., Assn. Rural Electric Coops., Inst. Indsl. Engrs.; subcontracting cons. Arthur D. Little Inc., Liberty Cons. Group, Ernst & Young, Cresap, A.T. Kearney, Towers Perrin, Michael Paris Assocs. Ltd., Planmetrics. Contbr. articles to profl. jours. Bd. trustees Samaritan Inst. for Religious Studies, 1995-97, chair instnl. advancement com., 1995; bd. dirs. Bailiwick Repertory Theater, chair mktg./pub. rels. com.; bd. dirs. Good Shepherd Parish Met. Cmty. Ch. of Chgo, 1995-99, vice moderator, 1996-97; mem. bd. Ordained Ministry o Gt. Lakes Dist. of Universal Fellowship Met. Cmty. Chs., 1996-99; vol. The Night Ministry of Chgo. Mem. Inst. Indsl. Engrs. (sr. mem. utility div. 1978—, charter), Am. Inst. Indsl. Engrs. (chmn. Midwest chpt. utility div. 1980-81). Avocations: managing the Jerry Lee Lewis Archives, Jason D. Williams Archives. Office: Gary D Skala & Assocs PO Box 14838 Chicago IL 60614-0838

SKALKO-BASNET, NATAŠA, pharmacist, educator; b. Zagreb, Croatia, Nov. 27, 1963; d. Davorin and Karin (Weithofer) Skalko; m. Purusotam Basnet. BSc in Pharmacy, U. Zagreb, Faculty of Pharm. and Biochem., 1986, MSc, 1990; PhD, Sch. Pharmacy, London, 1995. Registered pharmacist. Pharmacist Health Ctr., Zagreb, 1986-87; sci. asst. Faculty Pharmacy, Zagreb, 1987-90, asst., 1990-95, lectr., 1995-99, asst. prof., 1999—; mem. bd. pharm. tech. HDUK and HFD, Zagreb, 1994—. Recipient Overseas Rsch. Scheme award U. London, 1992; Alexander von Humboldt fellow U. Freiburg, Germany, 1997-98. Roman Catholic. Avocations: film, theatre, travel. Home: Petrekoviceva 3, 10 290 Zapresic Zagreb, Croatia Office: Dept Pharmacology, Toyama Med Pharm Univ, Sugitani 2630 Toyama 9300184, Japan

ŠKALOUD, MIROSLAV, civil engineering educator; b. Turnov, Czech Republic, Oct. 25, 1930; s. Jindřich and Marie Š; m. Marcela Kuhn, July 14, 1955; 1 child, Markéta. Engr., Czech Tech. U., Prague, 1955; PhD in Civil Engring., Czechoslovak Acad. Scis., Prague, 1959; DSc, Czech Tech. U., 1971; DSc (hon.), Tech. U. Budapest, Hungary, 1990, U. Liège, Belgium, 1997. Lectr. Czech Tech. U., 1955; rschr. Czechoslovak Acad. Scis., 1958-62; vis. prof. civil engring. U. Liège, 1962-63, U. Coll. Swansea, Cardiff, Wales, 1966-69; prof. civil engring., head dept. Czech Acad. Scis. Inst. Theoretical and Applied Mechs., Prague, 1973—; lectr. 3 Czech univs. and 23 univs. abroad; coord. 4 internat. advanced schs.; chmn. or mem. of numerous commns. in rsch., sci., and edn. Author or co-author 14 books; contbr. over 300 articles to profl. jours. and conf. procs. Recipient Czechoslovak State prize, 1975, Czechoslovak Acad. Scis. prize, 1982, 89, Golden medal, 1989. Fellow Czech Engring. Acad. (coun. mem., chair nomination com.); mem. N.Y. Acad. Scis., Internat. Assn. Bridge and Structural Engring., Czech Assn. Civil Engrs. Office: CAS Inst Theoret/Appl Mechs, Prosecká 76, 190 00 Prague 9, Czech Republic

SKALSKI, DETLEF, retired library and information science educator; b. Berlin, Jan. 4, 1937; s. Stefan and Hedwig (Kattarius) S.; m. Rosemarie Seidel, May 12, 1967; children: Martina, Daniela. Diploma in Metall. Engring., Tech. U. Berlin, 1963; postgrad., Bibliothekar-Lehrinsitut, Köln, Germany, 1965. Sci. libr. Tech. U. Libr., Berlin, 1965-69, 1969-72; prof. Freie U. Berlin, 1982-94, dir. Inst. Libr. Sci. and Edn., 1994; prof. Humboldt U., Berlin, 1994-2000; ret., 2000. Co-author: Online-Recherchen im Bibliographier-und Signierdienst, 1986, Wie Finde Ich Normen, Patente, Reports?, 2d edit., 1995; contbr. articles to profl. jours. Mem. Verein Deutscher Bibliothekare, Verein Der Diplombibliothekare an Wissenschaftlichen Bibliotheken, Deutsche Gesellschaft fuer Dokumentation. Avocations: tennis, golf. Home: Elmshorner Str 34A, 14167 Berlin Germany Office: Dorotheen Str 26, 10099 Berlin Germany

SKAN, MARTIN, hotelier, consultant; b. Worcester, Eng., Dec. 28, 1934; s. Reginald Norman and Millicent May (Vaughan) S.; m. Sally Elizabeth Margaret Wade (div. 1988); children: Lara Julie, Tilly Matina; m. Brigitte Bertha Joos, May 8, 1989. Student pvt. sch., Hertford, Eng.; student (exchange scholar), Harvard Sch. Calif., 1954. Mng. dir. Skan Taylor & Co. Ltd., 1957-61; dir. J.A. & P. Holland Ltd., 1961-65; chmn., chief exec. officer Chewton Glen Hotels Ltd., New Milton, Eng., 1965—; founder, dir. Walpole Com., 1992—. Contbr. articles on hotel industry to newspapers and mags. Recipient 5 Red Turrets from Michelin and star for cooking, 1989, Hotelier of Yr. award, 1991, Am. Express Best Country House Hotel award, 1991, English Tourist Bd. Best Hotel award, 1991, Master Innholder award, Freedom award of City of London, 1991, 5 Red Stars A.A.; named Dir. of Yr., Price Waterhouse, 1999. Avocations: skiing, tennis, golf, cycling, swimming. Office: Chewton Glen Hotel, New Milton Hampshire BH25 6QS, England

SKÅNLAND, HERMOD, central banker; b. Tromsö, Norway, June 15, 1925; s. Peder and Margit (Maurstad) S.; m. Jorid Henden, Oct. 14, 1972 (dec. 2000); 1 child, Mari Anne. MA in Econ., U. Oslo, 1951. Asst. Bur. Stats., Oslo, 1949-52; cons. to dir. gen. Ministry Fin., Oslo, 1952-71; dep. gov. Bank of Norway, Oslo, 1971-85, gov., 1985-93; prof. Norwegian Sch. of Mgmt., 1994—; bd. dirs. Nordic Investment Bank, chmn., 1976-78, 86-88. Author: Norwegian Credit Market Since 1900, 1967, Dilemma of Incomes Policy, 1981, Central Banks and Political Authorities in Some Industrial Countries, 1984. Active various royal coms., dels. and bds.; chmn. working party Ogn. Econ. Cooperation and Devel. Rockefeller fellow Am. U., 1955; decorated Comdr. St. Olav (Norwegian) and Luxembourg Order of Merit, Comdr. with star Finnish Lion and Icelandic Falcon Order. Home: Solvegen 1 B, 1177 Oslo 11, Norway Office: Norges Bank, Bankplassen 2, 0107 Oslo 1, Norway

ŠKARE, MARINKO, economics educator; b. Pula, Istrian County, Croatia, Feb. 8, 1969; s. Milivoj and Viktorija (Nedveš) Š.; m. Lorena Mošnja, Sept. 30, 1995. BS, Faculty Econs. and Tourism, Pula, 1994; MSc, Faculty Econs., Zagreb, Croatia, 1996, PhD, 1998. Jr. asst. Faculty Econs. and Tourism Dr. Mijo Mirkovic, Pula, 1994-96, asst., 1996-99, asst. prof., 1999—, asst. dean, 1999—; pub. bd. mem. Faculty Econs. and Tourism Dr. Mijo Mirkovic, Pula, 1996-98; analyst various banks, Pula, 1997—; vis. prof. Bus. Sch., Pula, 1998-99; econ. analyst-rschr. Istrian County, Pula, 1998—. Contbr. articles to profl. jours. City scholarship bd. mem. Scholarship Bd. Pula, 1997, 98, 99; bd. mem. Adv. Bd. Aiesec, Pula, 1999—. Recipient award Assn. Accts. Istra, Pula, 1998; grantee Ministry Sci. Croatia, Pula, 1994, Soros Found., Pula, 1996. Mem. N.Y. Acad. Sci. Avocations: computers, tennis, animals, science fiction. Home: Zadarska 8, 52100 Pula Croatia Office: Fac Econs & Tourism, Preradoviceva 1, 52100 Pula Croatia

SKARI, HANS, physician, researcher; b. Gjøvik, Oppland, Norway, Nov. 26, 1963; s. Even H. and Julie Kristine (Ihle) S.; m. Anne-Sofie Letting, Sept. 4, 1993; children: Even, Sofie. MPH, UCLA, 1988; MD, U. Bergen, Norway, 1989. Intern Krishiansund N., 1989-90; mil. physician Sessvollmoen, 1991; gen. practitioner Oslo, 1992-94; resident in surgery The Nat. Hosp., Oslo, 1994-95, 97, rsch. fellow in surgery, 1998—; resident in surgery Barum Hosp., Oslo, 1995-97; prenatal cons. The Nat. Hosp., Oslo, 1998—. Lt. Norwegian Mil., 1990-91. Recipient Royal Audience, King of Norway, U. Bergen, 1990, Dr. Alexander Malthes award, 1996, 97, 98, 99, Calif. scholarship award, 1987. Mem. Norwegian Med. Assn., Norwegian and Scandinavian Assn. Pediat. Surgeons, Norwegian Assn. Pediat. Surgery, Oslo Surg. Soc., Bergen Conservative Students Assn. (coun. 1985-86), Bergen Med. Students Assn. (coun. 1986-87), Young Doctors Assn. (del. surg. dept. B 1994-95), Vrit. Assn. Paediatric Surgeons. Avocations: athletics, cross-country skiing, alpine skiing. Office: The Nat Hosp, Sect Pediat Surg/Dept Surg, N-0027 Oslo Norway

SKARPETIS, MICHAEL GEORGE, research scientist; b. Preveza, Greece, Mar. 31, 1968; s. George Denis and Chariklia Michael (Koveou) S. MS in Elec. and Computer Engring., Nat. Tech. U. of Athens, Greece, 1991, PhD in Elec. and Computer Engring., 1999. Project engr. HITEC, Athens, 1990-91; rsch. assoc. Nat. Tech. U. Athens, 1993-99; elec. engr. Office Data Svc., Athens, 1994-95; rsch. assoc. Democritus U. Thrace, 1996-99; rsch. asst. U. Thessaly, 1996—, lectr., 1999—. Contbr. articles to profl. publs. State Scholarship Found. rsch. scholar, 1999—. Mem. IEEE, Tech. Chamber of Greece. Avocations: chess, sea sports, model airplanes, ancient geometry, chaotic behavior of physical systems, automatic control of cars. Home: 71 Mpoumpoulivas, Dasos Xaidarioy, 12462 Athens Greece

SKARSAUNE, OSKAR, writer; b. Trondheim, Norway, 1946; m. Karin Skarsaune; children: Martin, Elise, Knut Olav. D.Th, U. Oslo, 1982. Prof. ch. history Norwegian Luth. Sch. Theology, Oslo, 1980—; curriculum writer Caspari Ctr., Jerusalem, 1983; chair theol. com. Ch. of Norway Ministry to Israel; guest prof. Luth. Theol. Sem., Hong Kong, 1990-91. Writings include: The Proof from Prophecy: A Study in Justin Martyr's Proof-text Tradition, 1987, Incarnation: Myth or Fact?, 1991; author of books in Norwegian; contbr. articles to profl. jours. Inf. chaplain Norwegian Army, 1972-73. Mem. Norwegian Acad. Sci. and Letters. Office: PO Box 27 Bekkelaget, N-0137 Oslo 1, Norway

SKAUG, REIDAR, engineer; b. Baerum, Norway, July 14, 1949; s. Per and Edith (Bjerklie) S.; m. Karin Haugen, Feb. 25, 1978; children: Kristin, Hanne Kathrine. BSc with honors, Heriot-Watt U., Edinburgh, Scotland, 1972; BA, North European Mgmt. Inst., Oslo, 1973; postgrad., Norwegian Def. Coll., 1993. Scientist Norwegian Def. Rsch. Establishment, Kjeller, Norway, 1974-82, asst. head divsn., 1982-88, chief scientist, 1988-97, dir. rsch., 1997-98; dir. gen. The Nat. Inst. for Consumer Rsch., Lysaker, Norway, 1998—; vis. rsch. scientist Comm. Rsch. Ctr., Can., 1980; mem. adv. group rsch. and devel. NATO, France, 1980-90, nat. rep. sci. com., The Netherlands, 1988—; mem. subgroup on trade politics Norwegian Def. Commn., Norway, 1990; vis. exec. Norsk Hydro, Norway, 1992-93. Author: Spread Spectrum in Communication, 1985, Spread Spectrum in Mobile Communication, 1998; contbr. articles to profl. jours. With Norwegian Navy, 1974. Mem. IEE, Armed Forces Comm. & Electronics Assn. Home: Åsliveien 8 A, 1368 Stabekk Norway Office: Nat Inst Consumer Rsch, PO Box 173, 1324 Lysaker Norway

SKEA, ALAN DAVID, computer scientist; b. Blackburn, Eng., Apr. 15, 1964; s. David Mackenzie and Ann Ethel (Veasey) S. BSc with honors, U. Sydney, Australia, 1986. Assoc. lectr. U. NSW, Sydney, 1992; cons. Credit Suisse Fin. Products, London, 1993-95; head sys. D.E. Shaw Securities Internat., London, $D, 1995-97; dir. EclipZe, Ltd., New World Wines, Ltd. Mem. IEEE, Assn. Computing Machinery. Avocations: travel, sailing, windsrufing, rock climbing, mountaineering.

SKEELS, STEPHEN GLENN, civil engineer; b. Salem, Oreg., Mar. 8, 1951; s. Glenn Arthur and Shirley Belle (Brown) S. BS in Math., Oreg. Coll. Edn., Monmouth, 1974; cert., Computer Career Inst., Portland, Oreg., 1978. Profl. civil engr., 1994. Engring. aide Oreg. State Hwy. Dept., Coquille, 1974-76; programmer, analyst Northwest Area Sys., Inc., Salem, 1978-81, Interstate Fin. Svcs., Salem, 1981; engring. aide Oreg. Dept. Transp., Portland, 1983-84, engring. tech., 1985-86, assoc. transp. engr., 1986—. Active Rep. Presdl. Legion of Merit, 1992. Mem. ASCE, Math. Assn. Am., Am. Math. Soc., U.S. Chess Fedn. Libertarian. Avocations: chess, guitar.

SKEEN, DAVID RAY, systems engineer, manager, consultant; b. Bucklin, Kans., July 12, 1942; s. Claude E. and Velma A. (Birney) S.; m. Carol J. Stimpert, Aug. 23, 1964; children: Jeffrey Kent, Timothy Sean, Kimberly Dawn. BA in Math., Emporia State U., 1964; MS, Am. U., 1972; grad., Fed. Exec. Inst., 1983, Naval War Coll., 1984; DSc in Engring. Mgmt., George Washington U., 1998. Cert. office automation profl. Computer sys. analyst to comdr.-in-chief U.S. Naval Forces-Europe, London, 1967-70; computer sys. analyst Naval Command Sys. Support Activity, Washington, 1970-73; dir. data processing Office Naval Rsch., U.S. Navy Dept., Arlington, Va., 1973-78; dir. mgmt. info. sys. Naval Civilian Pers. Command, Washington, 1978-80; dep. dir. manpower, pers. tng. automated sys. Dept. Naval Mil. Pers. Command, Washington, 1980-85; dir. manpower, pers. tng. info. resource mgmt. Chief Naval Ops., Washington, 1985-91; assoc. dir. Office of IRM, USDA, Washington, 1992-96; dir. modernization of adminstrn. processes program, 1996-98; dep. dir. office of ops. Office of IRM, USDA, Washington, 1998; sr. engring. manager, cons. Lockheed Martin, Washington, 1998—; lectr. Inst. Sci. and Pub. Affairs, 1973-76; cons. Electronic Data Processing Career Devel. Programs, 1975—; detailed to Pres.'s Reorgn. Project for Automated Data Processing, 1978, spl. Navy IRM studies, SECNAV, 1991, USDA/Office of Mgmt. and Budget IRM, 1993, spl. USDA Field Structure Studies, 1997; adj. prof. Sch. Engring. and Applied Sci., George Washington U; with Pres.'s Fed. Automated Data Processing Users Group, Washington, 1978-80. Contbr. articles to profl. jours. Capt. USNR, 1964-91. Recipient Outstanding Performance award Interagy. Com. Data Processing, 1976, Adminstrv. Staff Performance award, 1998, Sec.'s cert. Appreciation, 1998. Mem. IEEE, Internat. Coun. on Sys. Engring., Sr. Exec. Assn., Assn. Fed. IRM, Naval Res. Assn., Pres. Fed. Automated Data Processing Users Group. Home: 707 Forest Park Rd Great Falls VA 22066-2908

SKEES, WILLIAM EDWARD, lawyer; b. Lexington, Ky., Aug. 13, 1966; s. William Daly Skees and Glenda K. (DeSpain) Turrill; m. Jodi Sue Stearman, Sept. 15, 1990. BS in Acctg., U. Ky., 1989, MBA, 1995; JD cum laude, U. Louisville, 1999. Bar: Ind. 1999, Ky. 1999; cert. mgmt. acct. Estimator Atlantic Envelope Co., Shelbyville, Ky., 1990-91; cost acct. YH Am. Inc., Versailles, Ky., 1991-92; acctg. supr. YH Am. Inc., Versailles, 1992-94; cost acct. Johnson Controls, Inc., Shelbyville, Ky., 1995-99; atty. Brown, Todd & Heyburn PLLC, Louisville, Ky., 1999—. Notes editor Brandeis Law Jour., 1998-99; mem. Jour. of Family Law, 1997-98. Mem.

Chesapeake Bay Found. Recipient Profl. Responsiility award Irving R. Kaufman Meml. Securities Law Moot Ct., 1997; Judge F. Gordon Meml. scholarhip Brandeis Hon. Soc. Phi Kappa Phi. Mem. ABA (1st yr. rep. 1996), Ky. Bar Assn., Ind. Bar Assn., Inst. Mgmt. Accts. Roman Catholic. Avocations: sailing, skiing, bicycling, golf, drums. Office: Brown Todd & Heyburn PLLC 400 W Market St Fl 32 Louisville KY 40202-3346 Address: 7104 Coachwood Dr Georgetown IN 47122-8656

SKEGGS, DAVID BARTHOLOMEW LYNDON, radiotherapist, oncologist; b. Stevenage, Herts, Eng., Aug. 26, 1928; s. Basil Lyndon and Gladys Jessie (Tucker) S.; m. Anne Hughes, Nov. 17, 1957; children: Lucinda Anne, Imogen Christina. MA, BM, BChir, Oriel Coll., Oxford (Eng.) U., 1950. Ho. surgeon St. Bartholomew's Hosp., London, 1952-54, sr. registrar, 1964-66; rsch. asst. St. Thomas' Hosp., London, 1962-64; dir. radio-therapy Royal Free Hosp., London, 1966-86; dir. Radiotherapy Ctr. Cromwell Hosp., 1992-98, chmn. practice priviliges com., 1998—; hon. cons. Royal No. Hosp., London, 1966—, Lister Hosp., Stevenage, Eng., 1979—; sr. examiner D.M.R.T., London, 1975-78; chmn. examining bd. F.R.C.R., London, 1982—. Contbr. chpts. to boks and articles to profl. jours. Coun. mem. Wycombe Abbey Sch. for Girls, 1990—. Served to lt. comdr. Royal Navy, 1954-70. Grantee Imperial Cancer Rsch. Found., 1975, Cancer Rsch. Campaign, 1978. Fellow Royal Coll. Radiologists; mem. English Speaking Union (gov. 1999—). Avocations: music, gardening, sports. Office: Cromwell Hosp, London SW5 0TU, England

SKELEMANI, PHANDU T. C., Botswana government official. Atty. gen. Govt. of Botswana, Gaborone. Office: Office of the Attorney General, Private Bag 009, Gaborone Botswana*

SKELLAND, ANTHONY HAROLD PETER, chemical engineering educator; b. Birmingham, Eng., Feb. 21, 1928; came to U.S., 1959; s. Harold and Hilda Skelland. BSChemE, U. Birmingham, 1948, PhD in Chem. Engring., 1952. Mgr. Procter and Gamble, Eng., 1954-56, R&D engr., 1956-59; asst. prof. Ill. Inst. Tech., Chgo., 1959-62; assoc. prof. U. Notre Dame, South Bend, Ind., 1962-66, prof., 1966-69; Ashland prof. U. Ky., Lexington, 1969-79; prof. Ga. Inst. Tech., Atlanta, 1979—; cons. Monsanto, Babcock and Wilcox, Union Carbide, E.I. duPont de Nemours, FMC Corp., Westinghouse and others. Author: Non-Newtonian Flow and Heat Transfer, 1967, Diffusional Mass Transfer, 1974; contbr. over 80 articles to profl. jours. Fellow AIChE, Inst. Petroleum; mem. Royal Soc. Chemistry (Eng.), Inst. Chem. Engrs. (Eng.). Avocations: tennis, theatre, dining out.

SKELLERN, DAVID JAMES, electronics educator; b. Sydney, NSW, Australia, Feb. 26, 1951; s. Albert Henry and Beryl Catherine (Holmes) S.; m. Josephine Ann Clancy, Apr. 6, 1974; children: Matthew James, Anna Louise, Jeremy David. BS, U. Sydney, 1972, BEE, 1974, PhD, 1985. Engr. Australian Dept. Civil Aviation, Sydney, 1972-74; rsch. asst. U. Sydney, 1974-76; engr. Fleurs Radio Observatory/U. Sydney, 1976-83; lectr., sr. lectr. dept. elec. engring. U. Sydney, 1983-89; prof., head dept. Macquarie U., Sydney, 1989—; chmn. nat. Com. for Radio Sci., Australian Acad. of Sci., Canberra, 1991—, Australian Telecomms. and Electronics, Sydney, 1993-95; vis. faculty Hewlett-Packard Labs, Bristol, End., 1988, Palo Alto, Calif., 1993-98; bd. govs. Sapient Coll., Sydney, 1997-98. Contbr. articles to profl. jours. Chmn. Sydney Montessori Soc., Sydney, 1990-92. Fellow Instn. of Engrs., Instn. of Radio and Electronic Engrs.; mem. IEEE. Roman Catholic. Avocations: guitar, choral singing. Home: 33 Dudley Ave Roseville, 2069 Sydney Australia Office: Electronics Dept, Macquarie Univ, 2109 Sydney Australia

SKELLY, JOHN JOSHUA, retired clergyman, fundraiser; b. Central Falls, R.I., Oct. 25, 1932; s. Joshua Essa and Catherine (Hermiz) S.; m. Una C. Meadowcroft, June 21, 1959 (div.); children: Timothy John, Joan Louise, Steven Allan. BSBA, Pepperdine U., 1956; BD, San Francisco Theol. Sem., 1959, DS in Theology, 1981; DD, Tarkio Coll., 1971. Asst. pastor First Presbyn. Ch., Granada Hill, Calif., 1959-61; pastor Port Hueneme (Calif.) Presbyn. Ch., 1961-65; v.p. devel. Pikeville (Ky.) Coll., 1967-69; sr. pastor Westminster Presbyn. Ch., Topeka, 1969-72; v.p. seminary rels. San Francisco Theol. Sem., 1972-83; pres. Pacific Homes Found., Woodland Hills, Calif., 1988-99; ret.; area counselor The Fifty Million Fund, United Presbyn. Ch., Kans.-Mo., 1965-67; mission devel. cons., 1967—; cons. Model Cities Program, Pikeville, 1968; campaign cons. United Way, L.A., 1986-87. V.p. student body Pepperdine U., L.A., 1955-56; pres. Hueneme-Oxnard Ministerial Assn., Port Hueneme, 1962; chmn. law enforcement com. Ventura County Grand Jury, 1964-65; chaplain of the day Ho. of Reps., State of Kans., 1970. Staff sgt. U.S. Army, 1950-52. Named Most Inspirational Player, Pepperdine Rugby Club, L.A., 1955, Outstanding Young Men of Am., U.S. Jr. C. of C., Port Hueneme, 1964. Democrat. Avocations: gardening, cooking Middle Eastern food, swimming, biking, golfing. Home and Office: 850 E Ocean Blvd Unit 206 Long Beach CA 90802-5446

SKELSEY, GEOFFREY BRIAN, academic administrator; b. Liverpool, Eng., Sept. 25, 1943; s. Joseph Deane and Margery (Hope) S. MA, Cambridge (Eng.) U., 1965. Chartered Inst. Transport, U.K. Legal trainee London Transport Bd., 1965-67; asst. registrary Cambridge U., 1967-71, sr. asst. registrary, 1971-92, prin. asst. registrary, asst. to chancellor, 1992—. Contbr. articles to profl. jours. Bd. dirs., vice chmn. Cambridge Festival Assn., 1973-85; bd. dirs. Cambridge Theatre Co., 1974-79; sec. Univ. Theatre Syndicate, 1999—. With Brit. Royal Navy Res., 1960-65. Recipient Comdr. Order of Civil Merit, King of Spain, 1988. Mem. Labour Party. Mem. Ch. of Eng. Avocations: military and social history, railway engineering, politics. Office: U Cambridge Old Schs, Trinity Ln, Cambridge CB2 1TN, England

SKELTON, BRIAN GEOFFREY, sales and marketing professional; b. London, June 21, 1955; s. Geoffrey Bernard and Daphne (Starkey) S.; m. Angelina Louise Dixon (Sept. 9, 1978; children: Anna Louise, Alexander James, Nicholas David. Cardegree, North Staffordshire Poly., Eng., 1976. Analyst Hawker Siddeley, London, 1976-77; programmer, tech. support mgr. Unichem Ltd., London, 1977-83; cons. Memorex Telex, Middlesex, Eng., 1983-84; product mgr. Memorex Telex, Middlesex, Eng., 1985-86; mktg. mgr. Memorex Telex, Middlesex, Eng., 1986-96; bus. dir. Memorex Telex, Middlesex, 1997—; sales dir. 3DFx, Slough, 1997—. Mem. Brit. Computer Soc., Inst. Data Processing Mgmt., F.I.A.P. Fellow. Inst. Analysts and Programmers. Home: 14 Laurel Rd, West Wimbledon, London SW20 0PR, England Office: Memorex Telex, 3DFX 2-4 The Grove, Slough, Berkshire SL1 1QP, England

SKELTON, WINIFRED KARGER (FREDDIE SKELTON), advertising agency executive, painter; b. McKees Rocks, Penn., Jan. 10, 1930; d. Robert Frank and Elfrieda Rose (Allert) Karger; m. Howard C. Skelton, May 19, 1962; 1 child, Susan. BA, Am. Acad. Art, Chgo., 1949; student, Corcoran Sch. Art, Washington, 1950-52. Asst. art dir. Rich's, Inc., Atlanta, 1949-50; art dir. Hecht Co., Washington, 1950-54, Mandel's, Chgo., 1954-55, Loveman's, Birmingham, Ala., 1955-60, Rich's, Inc., Atlanta, 1960-62, Wm. Buckley Design, N.Y.C., 1966-72; creative dir. Howard Skelton Assocs., Atlanta, Sarasota, Fla., 1973-94; pres. Howard Skelton Assocs., Sarasota, Fla., 1994—. Recipient 196 Addy awards from 1976-96. Mem. The Centre Club (Tampa), Tampa Bay Soc., Bradenton C. of C., The Atlanta Ad Club, The Tampa Ad Club, Suncoast Ad Club. Republican. Presbyterian. Achievements include paintings hanging in numerous galleries. Home and Studio: 2512 Birnam Woods Way Gainesville FL 32605-1663

SKENDE, DHIMITRI, university rector, researcher; b. Korca, Albania, May 13, 1957; s. Jani and Ollga (Themel) S.; m. Kozeta Como, June 18, 1990; 1 child, Johan. BSc, Agrl. U. Tirana, Albania, 1982; M, U. Tirana, 1989, Dsc, 1994. Cert. environ./devel./tourism; cert. prof. Asst. pedagogue U. Korca, 1983-86, head dept., 1986-92; rector, chief exec. U. Fan S. Noli, Korca, 1992—; rschr., vis. lectr. U. North London, 1997—; cons. Regional Bus. Agy. Adv. Bd., Albania, 1993—; rep. Coop. Rsch. Network in Mediterranean Region, 1997—; coord. Phare/Tempus Program, 1993-96; adj. prof. Nichols Coll., Dudley, Mass., 2000—; prof., Framingham (Mass.) State Coll. Recipient hon. fellowship Roehampton Inst., London, 1994. Mem. Conf. Rectors. Avocations: jogging, live music, history, travel. Office: U North London, 277-281 Holloway Rd, London N7 8 HN, England

SKEPPSTEDT, JONAS, computer science educator; b. Halmstad, Halland, Sweden, July 19, 1966; m. Chinda Khun-Narong, Oct. 15, 1994. MSc, Lund (Sweden) U., 1992; PhD, Chalmers U. Tech., Gothenburg, Sweden, 1997. Rsch. asst. dept. computer engring. Lund U., 1992-95, Chalmers U. Tech., 1996-97; asst. prof. Halmstad U., 1997-98; asst. prof. dept. computer sci. Lund U., 1999—. Mem. Assn. for Computing Machinery. Roman Catholic. Avocations: European and Asian history, art, culture. Office: Dept Computer Sci, Lund Univ, S-22100 Lund Sweden

SKERRA, ARNE ALFRED, biochemistry educator, protein designer; b. Wiesbaden, Hessen, Germany, July 30, 1961; s. Alfred and Renate (Dietz) S. Diploma in Chemistry, Technische Hochschule, Darmstadt, Germany, 1985; D Natural Sci. in Biochemistry, Ludwig-Maximilians U., Munich, 1989. Vis. scientist MRC Lab. Molecular Biology, Cambridge, Eng., 1990; group leader Max-Planck Inst. Biophysics, Frankfurt, Germany, 1991-94; prof. Inst. Biochemie, Technische Hochschule Darmstadt, 1994-98, Lehrstuhl für Biologische Chemie, Tech. U. Munich, 1998—. Inventor bacterial prodn. of antibodies, 1987, other inventions; contbr. articles to profl. jours. Recipient Scholarship The German Nat. Scholarship Found., Bonn, 1982, Kekulé fellowship Volkswagenwerk Found., Germany, 1986, Young Investigator's Rsch. award Found. Chem. Industry, Germany, 1996. Mem. Gesellschaft Deutscher Chemiker, Gesellschaft Biologische Chemie (initiator study group on protein engring. and design). Office: Technische Univ Munchen, An der Saatzucht 5, D-85350 Freising Weihenstephan

SKERRITT, JOHN HOWARD, agricultural research executive; b. Sydney, Australia, Mar. 8, 1959; s. Howard Stafford (dec.) and Grace Emilie (West) S.; m. Amanda Susanne Hill, Apr. 23, 1988; children: Samantha, Alexandra. BSc, U. Sydney, 1979, PhD, 1983. Postdoctoral fellow U. Mich., Ann Arbor, 1983; rsch. scientist CSIRO, Sydney, 1983-86, sr. rsch. scientist, 1987-90, prin. rsch. scientist, 1991-94; rsch. program leader Quality Wheat CRC Ltd., Sydney, 1996-99; sr. prin. rsch. scientist CSIRO, Canberra, Australia, 1995-99; dep. dir. Australian Ctr. Internat. Agrl. Rsch., 1999—; hon. cons. Coeliac Soc. New South Wales, 1984-94; sci. adv. bd. ImmunoSys., 1990-95; patentee in field. Contbr. articles to profl. jours. Recipient Univ. medal, 1980, Edgeworth David prize Royal Soc. New South Wales, 1993, Murex Diagnostics award Australian Soc. Microbiology. Mem. Soc. Food & Agrl. Immunology (trustee 1991—), Assn. Ofcl. Analytical Chemists (assoc. referee 1988—), Am. Assn. Cereal Chemists (assoc. editor 1991-94, Biotechnology award 1999). Avocations: bushwalking, travel, gardening, equestrian activities. Office: ACIAR, GPO Box 1571, Canberra 2601, Australia

SKIBA, MARK A., computer company executive. BS in Computer Info. Sys., DeVry Inst. Tech., Ohio, 1987. Programmer Columbus (Ohio) Life Ins., 1987-88; pres., chmn. On-Line Sales and Info. Sys., Inc., Columbus, 1988—; assoc. C.W. Costello & Assocs., Columbus, 1989-91; application programmer IV Franklin County Data Ctr., Columbus, 1991—. Mem. Columbus Coun. on World Affairs. Mem. Ch. of God. E-mail: maskiba@aol.com and osis@earthlink.net. Office: OSIS PO Box 32039 Columbus OH 43232-0039

SKIBA, YURI NICKOLAEVICH, geophysicist, mathematician; b. Ust-Nera, USSR, July 27, 1948; s. Nickolai Ivanovich and Yulia Pavlovna S.; m. Galina Vasilievna Strelkova; children: Andrei, Pavel. PhD in Math. and Physics, Computer Ctr., Novosibirsk, USSR, 1979. Sr. sci. rschr. Computer Ctr., 1984-85, Inst. Numerical Math., Moscow, 1987-92; guest sr. sci. rschr. Indian Inst. Tech., Delhi, 1989-90, Inst. Tropical Meteorology, Pune, India, 1989-90, Indian Inst. Scis., Bangalore, 1989-90; investigator, titular prof. U. Nat. Autonoma Mex., Mexico City, 1992—. Author: (in Russian) Mathematical Problems of Dynamics of Viscous Barotropic Fluid on a Rotating Sphere, 1989, in English, 1990, Introducción a los Métodos Numéricas, 2000; contbr. articles to profl. jours. Mem. N.Y. Acad. Scis., Royal Meteorol. Soc., Am. Math. Soc., Mex. Nat. Sys. Investigators. Avocations: books, sports, classical music. Home: Union 68-3 Col Escandon, CP 11800 Mexico City Mexico Office: UNAM, Ctr Atmopheric Sci, CP 04510 Mexico City Mexico

SKIBSTED, LEIF HORSFELT, food chemistry researcher; b. Silkeborg, Denmark, Aug. 28, 1947; s. Arne and Grethe (Sørensen) S.; m. Benedicte Kruse, Dec. 20, 1983; children: Marie, Anders, Peter. PharmM, Royal Sch. of Pharmacy, Copenhagen, 1972; PhD, Royal Sch. of Pharmacy, 1976. From asst. prof. to docent, prof. Royal Vet. and Agrl. U., Frederiksberg, Denmark, 1974-90; rsch. dir. ctr. food rsch. Royal Vet. and Agrl. U., Frederiksberg, 1991-94; rsch. assoc. U. Calif., Santa Barbara, 1978-79. Contbr. articles to profl. jours. Recipient Ole Rømer award Ministry of Edn., Copenhagen, 1981, Bjerrum Gold medal Ellen and Niels Bjerrum Found., Copenhagen, 1986, Ulrik Brinks award Brinks Found., 1993, Food Sci. award Danish Soc. Food Sci. and Tech., 1994, Carlsberg Rsch. award in agrl. sci., 1996. Fellow Danish Acad. Tech. Scis.; mem. Am. Chem. Soc., Danish Chem. Soc. Avocations: railroad history, botany, horse breeding. Home: Ørstedvej 54, DK-4130 Viby Sj Denmark Office: Royal Vet/Agrl U-Food Rsch, 30 Rolighedsvej, DK-1958 Frederiksberg C, Denmark

SKIDMORE, JAY ROBERT, psychologist; b. L.A., Feb. 6, 1954; s. Robert Homer and Lois Jayne (Vyn) S.; m. Susan Leslie Campbell, June 7, 1980; children: Robert Vyn, Nathan Campbell. BA, Azusa Pacific U., 1976; MA, Calif. State U., 1981; PhD, Va. Tech., 1988. Program dir. Youth Guidance, Sacramento, Calif., 1979-82; grad. asst. Va. Tech., Blacksburg, 1983-87; clin. psychology intern W.Va. U. Med. Ctr., Morgantown, 1987-88; asst. prof. Psychology Utah State U., Logan, Utah, 1988-93; assoc. prof. psychiatry and behavioral sci. U. Okla. Coll. Medicine, 1993-95, dir. Health Psychology Program, 1993-95; chief psychologist Unsted Park Rehab. Hosp., Godalming, Surrey, Eng., 1995-98; dir. pain mgmt. and behavioral medicine Unsted Park Rehab. Hosp., Godalming, 1995-98; cons. clin. psychologist, head Pain Mgmt. Programs Princess Royal Hosp., King Edward VII Hosp., West Sussex, Eng., 1998-99; clin. dir. PRA Pain Ctr., Portland, Oreg., 2000—. Contbr. articles to The Health Psychologist, The Behavior Therapist, Jour. Behavioral Medicine, Behavior Modification, Jour. Personality Assessment, Jour. Clin. Psychology. Faculty rsch. grantee Utah State U., 1989-90. Mem. APA, Assn. Advancement of Behavior Therapy, Assn. for Applied Psychophysiology and Biofeedback, Soc. Behavioral Medicine, Soc. for Clin. and Exptl. Hypnosis, Internat. Assn. for Study of Pain, Am. Pain Soc., Brit. Pain Soc., Brit. Psychol. Soc. Avocations: mountain climbing, bicycling, guitar. Office: PRA Pain Ctr 1815 SW Marlow Ave Ste 110 Portland OR 97225-5186

SKIEPKO, TEODOR, mechanical engineer, educator; b. Gruszki, Bialystok, Poland, Aug. 25, 1947; s. Mikolaj and Maria (Saczko) S.; m. Olga Stulgis, July 22, 1972; children: Anna Maria, Grzegorz. MSME, Warsaw Tech. U., 1972; PhD, Lodz Tech. U., 1981; DS, Polish Acad. Scis., 1993. Rsch. engr. Inst. Thermal Tech., Lodz, Poland, 1972-80; asst. prof. Warsaw U., Bialystok, 1980-81; adj. prof. Bialystok Tech. U., 1981-92; vis. prof. U. da Beira Interior, Covilha, Portugal, 1992-95; assoc. prof. Bialystok Tech. U., 1995—; cons. Polish Soc. Mech. Engrs., Bialystok, 1980—; participant R&D Copernicus joint project Commn. of the European Cmtys., 1994. Inventor in field; contbr. articles to profl. jours. Recipient Nat. Edn. Commn. medal Min. Nat. Edn. Poland, 1997; grantee Sci. Affair Divsn. NATO, 1996. Avocations: swimming, forest and mountain wandering. Office: Bialystok Tech Univ, Wiejska 45C, 15-351 Bialystok Poland

SKIERKA, VOLKER H., journalist, author; b. Rheinfelden, Germany, Sept. 21, 1952; s. Heinz G. and Waltraut (Lindt) S.; m. Annette K.M. Meier, 1988; 2 children. Editorial trainee, editor Nürnberger Nachrichten (Newspapers), Nuremberg, 1973-75; editor Press Agy Redepenning/Reuters; Munich, 1975-77; editor, corres. Reuters News Agy., Bonn and Berlin, 1977-79; corres., reporter Suddeutsche Zeitung/Munich, Berlin, 1979-86; bur. chief and corres. No. Germany and No. Europe Suddeutsche Zeitung/Munich, Hamburg, 1986-89; corres. for Latin Am. Suddeutsche Zeitung/Munich, Santiago, Chile, 1989-92; editor-in-chief Merian-Magazine for Culture and Travel, Hamburg, Germany, 1992-97; bd. mem. Friends of the Villa Aurora Berlin/L.A. Cultural Inst., Hanns Joachim Friedrichs-Preist German TV-Journalism award; adv. bd. Institut fur Ibero-Amerika-Kunde, Hamburg. Author: Lion Feutchtwanger-A Biography, 1984; co-author: Macht u. Machenschaften-The Barschel Affair, 1988, N.Y. Vertical, Introduction into the photo-edition by H. Hamann, others. Recipient Egon-Erwin-Kisch prize (Reporter award) Stern Mag., Hamburg, 1981. Avocations: literature, photography, modern art, hiking.

SKILLING, THOMAS ETHELBERT, III, meteorologist, meteorology educator; b. Pitts., Feb. 20, 1952; s. Elizabeth Clarke. Student, U. Wis., 1970-74; Dr. Humanities (hon.), Lewis U., Romeoville, Ill., 1995. Meteorologist Sta. WKKD-AM-FM, Aurora, Ill., 1967-70, Sta. WLXT-TV, Aurora, 1969-70, Sta. WKOW-TV, Madison, Wis., 1970-74, Sta. WTSO, Madison, 1970-74, Sta. WTLV-TV, Jacksonville, Fla., 1974-75, Sta. WITI-TV, Milw., 1975-78, Sta. WAUK, Waukesha, Wis., 1976-77, Sta. WGN-TV, Chgo., 1978—; weather forecaster Wis. Farm Broadcast Network, Madison, 1970-74; weather cons. Piper, Jaffray & Hopwood, Madison, 1972-74; instr. meteorology Columbia Coll., Chgo., 1982-92, Adler Planetarium, Chgo., 1985-86. Prodr. weather page Chgo. Tribune. Vol. Chgo. chpt. Muscular Dystrophy Assn. Recipient Emmy award for "It Sounded Like a Freight Train," 1991, "The Cosmic Challenge," 1994, Peter Lisagor awards for weather spls. aired on WGN, 1991, 93, Pub. Svc. award NOAA-Nat. Weather Svc., 1998. Fellow Am. Meteorol. Soc. (v.p. Chgo. chpt. 1985-86, TV Seal of Approval, Outstanding Svc. award 1997), Nat. Weather Assn., Soc. Profl. Journalists, Chgo. Acad. TV Arts and Scis. Avocations: hiking, cross country skiing. Home: 6033 N Sheridan Rd Apt 31C Chicago IL 60660-3048 Office: Sta WGN-TV 2501 W Bradley Pl Chicago IL 60618-4701

SKILLINGSTAD, CONSTANCE YVONNE, social services administrator, educator; b. Portland, Oreg., Nov. 18, 1944; d. Irving Elmer and Beulah Ruby (Aleckson) Erickson; M. David W. Skillingstad, Jan. 12, 1968 (div. Mar. 1981); children: Michael, Brian. BA in Sociology, U. Minn., 1966; MBA, U. St. Thomas, St. Paul, 1982. Cert. vol. adminstr.; lic. social worker. Social worker Rock County Welfare Dept., Luverne, Minn., 1966-68; social worker Hennepin County Social Svcs., Mpls., 1968-70, vol. coord., 1970-78; vol. coord. St. Joseph's Home for Children, Mpls., 1978-89, mgr. community resources, 1989-94; exec. dir. Mpls. Crisis Nursery, 1994-97; mem. cmty. faculty Met. State U., St. Paul and Mpls., 1980-97; faculty U. St. Thomas Ctr. for Non Profit Mgmt., 1990—; asst. adminstr. St. Joseph's Home Children, Mpls., 1997-98; asst. dir. Cath. Charities of Archdiocese of St. Paul and Mpls., 1998—; trainer, mem. adv. commn. Mpls. Vol. Ctr., 1978-90, cons., 1980—, chmn. Contbr. articles to Jour. Vol. Admintrn. Mem. adv. bd. Mothers Against Drunk Driving, Minn., 1986-88; vice chmn., chmn. adminstrv. coun., lay leader Hobart United Meth. Ch.; lay rep. to Minn. Ann. Conf. of Meth. Chs., 1989-92; mem. social concerns. commn. Park Ave United Meth. Ch., 1992—; bd. dirs. Ctr. for Grief, Loss and Transition. Named one of Oustanding Young Women Am., 1974, Woman of Distinction Mpls. St. Paul Mag./KARE-TV, 1995. Mem. Minn. Assn. Vol. Dirs. (pres. 1975, sec., ethics chmn. 1987—), Assn. for Vol. Adminstrn. (v.p. regional affairs 1985-87, mem. assessment panel 1986-94, coord. nat. tng. team, cert. process for vol. adminstrs. 1988-92, profl. devel. chair 1990-92), Minn. Social Svcs. Assn. (pres. 1981, 98-99, Disting. Svc. award 1987). Mem. Dem.-Farmer-Labor Party. Methodist. Avocations: bridge, volleyball, accordian, travel, reading. Office: St Joseph's Home Children 1121 E 46th St Minneapolis MN 55407-3562

SKILLMAN, ERNEST EDWARD, JR., real estate sales and management executive; b. New Orleans, Oct. 3, 1937; s. Ernest Edward and Helen Cecilia (Klein) S. BA, La. State U., 1960, postgrad. in law, 1960-61; postgrad., Southeastern La. U., 1973. intelligence work for USN, 1960—. Engaged in real estate mgmt. Baton Rouge, 1964—, sales, 1969—. Sustaining mem. Republican Nat. Com., 1976—, life mem., 1980—, mem. congressional com., 1979-82, 1986—; mem. pres.'s club Democratic Nat. Com., 1979—; mem. Rep. Presdl. Task Force; mem. Jackson (La.) Assembly; Served with USN, 1961-64; Vietnam. Mem. La. Mem. Aviation Mus. Assn. (charter life), Feliciana C. of C., Res. Officers Assn. (life), Mil. Order World Wars (life), Am. Contract Bridge League (sr. master), U.S. Naval Inst. (life), Navy League U.S. (life), Am. Legion, Submarine Force Library and Mus. Assn. (life), Amvets (cmdr. 1985-87, pres. Foss-Landry Post #2 1985-87), Grad. Realtors Inst., Army and Navy Club (pres. comdr. USS Kidd DD661 Navy Club 1997-98, cmdr. 1997-98), Rep. Senatorial Club (Washington), Kiwanis, Sigma Chi (life). Roman Catholic. Home: 753 Kenilworth Pky Baton Rouge LA 70808-5716 Office: 4150 Perkins Rd Baton Rouge LA 70808-3027

SKINHOJ, PETER, medical educator; b. Copenhagen, Apr. 17, 1943; s. Erik and Kirsten (Hoy) S.; 1 child, Jacob. MD, U. Copenhagen, 1969, D of Med. Sci., 1981. Registrar Bispebjerg Hosp., Copenhagen, 1969-74; sr. registrar Rigs Hosp., Copenhagen, 1974-87, asst. prof., 1987-89, head dept. infectious disease, 1988—; prof. U. Copenhagen, 1989—. Home: Parkovsvej 25, 2820 Gentofte Denmark Office: Rigs Hosp, Blegoamsvej 9, 2100 Copenhagen Denmark

SKINNER, DELDA SMITH, artist, educator; b. Waco, Tex., Apr. 15, 1929; d. David Wilkes and Edith Arlene (Landrum) Smith; m. John Finley Skinner, May 27, 1948; children: John Lyle, Arlene, Eleanor, Sarah. BBA, Baylor U., 1949; BA, Dominican Coll., 1972; MA in Pastoral Ministry, Episcopal Sem. of S.W., 1999. Sec. LCRA, Austin, Tex., 1948-50; real estate agt. Houston, 1967-69, H.S. tchr., 1973-78, profl. visual artist, 1974-78; profl. visual artist Wimberley, Tex., 1978-89, San Antonio, 1990-93, Austin, 1993—; adj. prof. pastoral ministry Episcopal Theol. Sem. of the S.W., 2000—. Paintings included in In Harmony With Nature, 1990, Sowest Art Mag., 1992, Creative Collage Techniques, 1994, Best of Watercolor 2, 1997, Best of Watercolor in Textures, 1997, Best of Watercolor in Color, 1997. Bd. dirs. Tex. Watercolor, 1987-89, San Antonio Watercolor, 1991-93; lay eucharist min. Diocese of Tex. Episcopal Ch. Grantee McAshen Found., 1974, Nat. Collage Soc., 1988, Tex. Watercolor Soc., 1991. Mem. Nat. Watercolor Soc. (signature mem.), Nat. Collage Soc. (signature mem., regional dir. 1989-96), Soc. Layerists in Multimedia (bd. dirs. 1982—, v.p. 1999—), Internat. Assn. Paper Makers and Paper Artists (bd. dirs., treas. 1996-99), First Frontier Coll. Soc. (pres. 1999-00). Avocations: reading, travel, book making, paper making. Home: 8111 Doe Meadow Dr Austin TX 78749-2866

SKINNER, HELEN CATHERINE WILD, biomineralogist; b. Bklyn., Jan. 25, 1931; d. Edward Herman and Minnie (Bertsch) Wild; m. Brian John Skinner, Oct. 9, 1954; children: Adrienne, Stephanie, Thalassa. BA, Mt. Holyoke Coll., 1952; MA, Radcliffe/Harvard, 1954; PhD, Adelaide (Australia) U., 1959. Mineralogist sect. molecular structure Nat. Inst. Arthritis and Metabolic Diseases, NIH, 1961-65; with sect. crystal chemistry Lab. Histology and Pathology Nat. Inst. Dental Rsch., NIH, 1965-66; lectr. dept. geology and geophysics Yale U., 1967-69, rsch. assoc. dept. surgery, 1967-72, sr. rsch. assoc. dept. surgery Medical Sch., 1972-75; Alexander Agassiz vis. lectr. dept. biology Harvard U., 1976-77; lectr. dept. biology Yale U., 1977-83; assoc. prof. biochemistry in surgery, Medical Sch. Yale U., New Haven, 1978-84, lectr. dept. orthopaedic surgery, 1972—, lectr., rsch. affiliate in geology and geophysics, 1987—; pres. Conn. Acad. Arts and Scis., 1986-94, publs. chair, 1994—; mineralogist AEC, summer 1953; master Jonathan Edwards Coll., Yale U., 1977-82; Alexander Agassiz vis. lectr. dept. biology Harvard U., 1976-77; vis. prof. sect. ecology and systematics dept. biology Cornell U., 1980-83; disting. prof. geology Adelaide U., 1990-91, disting. lectr., 1993; disting. prof. geology U. Wyo., 1996; dental adv. com. Yale-New Haven Hosp., 1973-80; mem. faculty adv. com. Yale-New Haven Tchrs. Inst., 1983-99; chmn. site visit team Nat. Inst. Dental Rsch., 1974-75; mem. pubs. com. Yale U. Press, 1979-84, Am. Geolog. Inst., 1993-96. Author: (with others) Asbestos and Other Fibrous Materials: Mineralogy, Crystal Chemistry and Health Effects, 1988, Dana's New Mineralogy, 1997; co-editor: Biomineralization Processes of Iron and Manganese: Modern and Ancient Environments, 1992; contbr. over 50 articles to profl. jours.; tech. abstractor Geol. Soc. Am., 1961-65; sect. editor Am. Mineralogist, 1978-82. Mem. bd. edn. com. Conn. Fund for Environ., 1983-89, mem. sci. adv. com., 1989-92; founder, pres. Investor's Strategy Inst., New Haven, 1983-85; trustee Miss Porter's Sch., Farmington, Conn., 1984-91, mem. edn. com., 1986-88, mem. salaries and benefits com., 1988-91; treas. YWCA, New Haven, 1983-84; trustee Geol. Soc. Am. Found., 1998—. Fellow AAAS, Geol. Soc. Am., Mineral. Soc. Am. (mem. various coms., councilor 1979-81, Pub. Svc. award 1991); mem. Am. Soc. Bone and Mineral Rsch., Am. Assn. Crystal Growth, Am. Assn. Dental Rsch., Internat. Assn. Dental Rsch., Mineral Soc. Can., Geol. Soc. Am. E-mail: catherine.skinner@yale.edu. Home: 39 Temple Ct New Haven CT 06511-6820 Office: Yale U Dept Geology Geophysics PO Box 208109 New Haven CT 06520-8109

SKINNER, JAMES LISTER, III, English language educator; b. Emory, Ga., Sept. 24, 1938; s. James Lister and Josephine Norvell (Fry) S.; m. Ramona Ann York Skinner, Apr. 2, 1961; 1 child, James Lister Skinner

IV. AB in English, N. Ga. Coll., Dahlonega, 1960; MA in English, U. Ark., Fayetteville, 1962, PhD in English, 1965. Comdr. Headquarters and Headquarters Battery 28th Artillery Group, Selfridge AFB, Mich., 1964-65; assoc. prof. English Presbyterian Coll., Clinton, S.C., 1965-70, prof. English, 1970-92, Charles A. Dana prof. English, 1992—, chmn. The Russell Program, 1986-98; co-chmn. English dept. Presbyn. Coll., Clinton, S.C., 1996—; sr. faculty coun. Presbyn. Coll., 1995-98, chair sr. faculty coun., 1997-98, chair English dept., 1999—; NDEA fellow U. Ark., Fayetteville, 1960-63; NEH summer fellow Yale U., New Haven, Conn., 1976; hon. vis. fellow Leicester (Eng.) U., 1983; sec. Presbyterian Coll. Faculty, Clinton, S.C., 1995-98. Editor: The Autobiography of Henry Merrell: Industrial Missionary to the South, 1991; co-editor: The Death of a Confederate, 1996. 1st lt. U.S. Army, 1963-65. Recipient Commendation medal U.S. Army, 1965; named Presbyterian Prof. of Yr. Presbyterian Coll., Clinton, S.C., 1991, State Prof. of Yr. Coun. for Advancement and Support of Edn., 1991, Gov's. Prof. of Yr., Gov. of S.C., Columbia, 1991, DAR History Award medal, 1998. Mem. Phi Beta Kappa, Omicron Delta Kappa, Alpha Psi Omega, Phi Alpha Theta. Democrat. Presbyterian. Home: 108 E Maple St Clinton SC 29325-2836 Office: Presbyterian Coll Broad St Clinton SC 29325

SKINNER, NEVILLE JOHN, retired physics educator, amateur ornithologist; b. Lowestoft, Eng., June 28, 1929; s. Wallace and Ruby Alice (Spall) S.; m. Gladys Margaret Wright, July 22, 1967. BSc in Physics, U. Nottingham, Eng., 1950; PhD in Physics, U. London, 1956. Chartered physicist. Lectr./sr. lectr. physics U. Ibadan, Nigeria, 1952-62; prof. physics Ahmadu Bello U., Zaria, Nigeria, 1962-69, U. Nairobi, Kenya, 1969-79; head sch. natural resources U. South Pacific, Suva, Fiji, 1979-83; prof. physics U. Botswana, Gaborone, 1983-87; ret., 1987; dean of sci. Ahmadu Bello U., 1963-65. Co-author (with J.H. Elgood, others): The Birds of Nigeria, 1994; contbr. over 60 articles to internat. profl. jours. physics, including Nature, Jour. Atmospheric and Terrestrial Physics, others; contbr. over 20 rsch. papers to profl. jours. ornithology, including Ibis, Scopus, Notornis, Babbler, Brit. Birds, others. Craftsman, Brit. Army, Royal Elec. and Mech. Engrs., 1950-52, U.K., Singapore. Fellow Inst. of Physics, Royal Astron. Soc.; mem. Am. Geophys. Union, Brit. Ornithologists Union. Avocations: ornithology, genealogy. Home: 60 Gunton Dr, Lowestoft NR32 4QB, England

SKINNER, QUENTIN ROBERT DUTHIE, historian, educator; b. Oldham, Eng., Nov. 26, 1940; s. Alexander and Winifred (Duthie) S.; m. Susan Deborah Thorpe James, Aug. 1979; children: Olivia, Marcus. BA, U. Cambridge, Eng., 1962; hon. degree, U. East Anglia, Eng., 1992, U. Chgo., 1992, U. Helsinki, Finland, 1997, U. Oxford, 2000. Lectr. history U. Cambridge, 1965-78, prof. polit. sci., 1978-96, Regius prof. modern history, 1996—, pro-vice chancellor, 1999. Author: The Foundations of Modern Political Thought, 2 vols., 1978, Machiavelli, 1981, Reason and Rhetoric in the Philosophy of Hobbes, 1996, Liberty Before Liberalism, 1998, numerous other books. Fellow British Acad., Am. Acad., Am. Philos. Soc., others. Office: Christs Coll, Cambridge, Cambridge CB2 3BU, England

SKINNER, ROBERT EARLE, librarian, writer; b. Alexandria, Va., June 25, 1948; s. Earl Woodrow and Pearle Labar (Capper) S.; m. Linda Sue Long, June 12, 1970 (div. 1976); children: Christopher William, Kelly Sue; m. Patricia Ann Friedmann, Mar. 17, 1979 (div. 1996); children: Esme F., Werner H. BA in History, Old Dominion U., 1970; MLS, Ind. U., 1977; postgrad. student, U. New Orleans, 1991-93. Search analyst Strughold Aeromed. Libr., Brooks AFB, Tex., 1977-79; from reference libr. to head med. edn. libr. La. State U. Med. Ctr., New Orleans, 1979-85; spl. cons. Robert L. Siegel & Assocs., New Orleans, 1985-87; univ. libr. Xavier U., New Orleans, 1987—; mng. editor Xavier Rev. Press, 1989—. Author: The Hard-Boiled Explicator, 1985, The New Hard-Boiled Dicks, 1987, rev. edit., 1995, Two Guns From Harlem, 1989, (with Michel J. Fabre) Chester Himes: An Annotated Primary and Secondary Bibliography, 1992, Fiction in Ellipsis, 1992, (with Thomas Bonner, Jr.) Above Ground, 1993, Immortelles, 1995, (with Michel J. Fabre) Plan B, 1993, (with Michel J. Fabre) Conversations with Chester Himes, 1995, Fiction in Hard Boiled, 1994, Fiction in Crime Yellow, 1994, Skin Deep, Blood Red, 1997, Cat-Eyed Trouble, 1998, Daddy's Gone-A-Hunting, 1999, Blood to Drink, 2000; guest editor La. Lit., spring 1998; contbr. fiction to Xavier Rev., 2000. With USCG, 1970-74. Grantee Mellon Found., 1987-95, La. Divsn. of the Arts, 1993, 95, NEH, 1991—. Mem. ALA. Avocations: hiking, photography. E-mail: rskinner@xula.edu. Office: Xavier Univ Libr 1 Drexel Dr New Orleans LA 70125-1056

SKINNER-KLEE, JORGE, lawyer, diplomat; b. San Francisco, July 21, 1923; s. Alfredo and Dolores (Cantón Solórzano) S.-K.; m. Concha Arenales, Sept. 24, 1949; children: Cecilia Skinner-Klee, Carolina Skinner-Klee Hempstead, Alfredo, Jorge. Licenciate in Jud. and Social Scis., U. San Carlos, Guatemala, 1951; D of Jud. and Social Scis. (hon.), Rafael Landívar Cath. U., Guatemala, 1980. Prof. sociology U. San Carlos, Guatemala, 1952-55; Minister of Fgn. Affairs Govt. Guatemala, Guatemala City, 1956-57; prof. sociology Rafael Landívar Cath. U., Guatemala, 1960-65, vice rector, 1969-79; councillor of state Govt. Guatemala, 1974-78, Congressman of the Republic, 1986—; dep. mem. Constituent Assembly Guatemala, 1955, 65, 78; mem. Permanent Tribunal for Arbitration, The Hague, The Netherlands, 1968—; amb. in charge of negotiations with G.B. on Belize question, 1959-76; del. several times to gen. assembly U.N.; bd. dirs. Banco Internat. Guatemala, Productos Duralita, Corrugadora Guatemala, others. Author: Indian Laws of Guatemala, 1954, 2d edit. 1995, Considerations on the Emergence of the Middle Class, 1965, Parlamentarismo, Presidencialismo y Otras Reflexiones, 1991; contbr. articles to newspapers. Mem. Central Am. Jud. Commn. Orgn. of Centroam. Countries, 1955-57; seminar dir. Guatemalan Social Integration, 1955; planner Commn. for New Comml. Code, 1964-65. Named Grand Officier Legion of Honor, Govt. of France, 1954; recipient Grand Cross Order Quetzal, Guatemalan Govt., 1977; awarded numerous other internat. and nat. distinctions. Mem. Acad. Geography and History (pres. 1979-81). Mem. Nat. Ctr. Union Party. Clubs: Guatemalan Country, Caza Tiro y Pesca. Avocation: collecting rare travel books. Office: Skinner-Klee & Ruiz, 9-A Calle 3-72 Zona 1, Guatemala City Guatemala

SKIPETROV, VADIM PETROVICH, physiologist, hematologist; b. Alexin, Tula, Russia, Nov. 24, 1937; s. Pyotr Pavlovich and Alexandra Ivanovna (Kasatkina) S.; m. Tatjana Alexandrovna Kozlova; 1 child, Pyotr. Cand.Medicine, Rjazan Med. Inst., Russia, 1962; MD, Voronezh Med. Inst., Russia, 1967. Prof. ob-gyn. Hosp. v. Turuntajevo, Buryatia, Russia, 1957-60; lectr. Chita Med. Inst., 1960-64; head human physiology dept. Ust-Kamenogorsk Med. Inst., 1964-66; head hominal physiology dept. Semipalatinsk Med. Inst., 1966-68; head hominal physiology dept. Mordovian U., Saransk, 1968-90, chief aeroionization lab., 1990—. Author: (monographs) Obstetric Thrombohemorrhagic Syndrom, 1973, Blood Formed Elements, Vascular Wall, Hemostasis and Thrombosis, 1974, Mechanisms of Changes and Breaches of Blood Coagulation During Pregnancy and Childbirth, 1976, Tissue System of Blood Coagulation and Thrombohemorrhagic Syndrom in Surgery, 1978, Aeroions and Life, 1995, 2d edit., 1997, A.L. Chizhevskii and His Philosophy, 1999, Coagulation-Lithium Tissue System and Thrombohemorrhagic Syndrome in Surgery, 2000, Oxygen Aeroions Treatment, 2000, also others; co-author: Human Physiology, 1985; contbr. over 250 articles to profl. jours., 15 monographs. Named Honored Scientist of Russia, 1993. Mem. Physiology Soc., Russian Soc. Hematologists, N.Y. Acad. Scis. Achievements include research in the role of tissues in blood coagulation; proposed the idea of the coagulation-lithium tissue system existence in the human organism. Avocations: tourism, biking, gardening, classical music. Home: Ul Vasenko 2 kv 29, 430003 Saransk Mordovia, Russia

SKIVER, STEPHEN ALLEN, lawyer, physician; b. Toledo, Ohio, Feb. 14, 1949; s. Arnold Leroy and Elizabeth Jane (Boyer) S.; m. Catherine Ann Reynolds, June 26, 1971; children: Tonia, Justin, Ryan, Laura, Elyssa. BS, Ohio U., 1971; MD, Med. Coll. Ohio, 1974; JD, U. Toledo, 1988. Bar: Ohio 1989, U.S. Dist. Ct. (no. dist.) Ohio 1991; Cert. Am. Bd. Internal Medicine. Physician Maumee, Ohio, 1977-89; clin. asst. prof. medicine Med. Coll. Ohio, Toledo, 1983-89; physician Toledo, 1989—; assoc. Jacobson, Maynard, Tuschman, Toledo, 1990-97; ptnr. Buckley, King & Bluso, Toledo, 1997—adr. Home: 30025 E River Rd Perrysburg OH 43551-3430 Office: Buckley King & Bluso 420 Madison Ave Ste 1100 Toledo OH 43604-1209

SKLADAL, ELIZABETH LEE, retired elementary school educator; b. N.Y.C., May 23, 1937; d. Angier Joseph and Julia May (Roberts) Gallo; m. George Wayne Skladal, Dec. 26, 1956; children: George Wayne Jr., Joseph Lee. BA, Sweet Briar Coll., 1958; postgrad., U. Kans., 1966-67; EdM, U. Alaska, 1976. Choir dir. Main Chapel, Camp Zama, Japan, 1958-59, Ft. Lee, Va., 1963-65; choir dir. Main Chapel and Snowhawk, Ft. Richardson, Alaska, 1968-70; tchr. Anchorage (Alaska) Sch. Dist., 1970-98; ret. Active Citizen's Adv. Com. for Gifted and Talented, Anchorage, 1981-83; mem. music com. Anchorage Sch. Dist., 1983-86; soloist Anchorage Opera Chorus, 1969-80, Cmty. Chorus, Anchorage, 1968-80; mem. choir First Presbyn. Ch., Anchorage, 1971—, deacon, 1988—, elder, 1996—, mission com. chair, 1996-99; participant 1st cultural exch. from Anchorage to Magadan, Russia with Alaska Chamber Singers, 1992; participant mission trip to Swaziland, Africa with First Presbyn. Ch., Anchorage, summer 1995. Named Am. Coll. Theater Festival winner Amoco Oil Co., 1974; recipient Cmty. Svc. award Anchorage U. Alaska Alumni Assn., 1994-95. Mem. AAUW, Anchorage Concert Assn. Patron Soc. (assocs. coun. of dirs.), Alaska Chamber Singers, Am. Guild Organists (former dean, former treas., mem.-at-large). Republican. Presbyterian. Avocations: camping, travel, cycling, fishing, cross-country skiing, gardening. Home: 1841 S Salem Dr Anchorage AK 99508-5156

SKLAR, GAIL JANICE, secondary special education educator; b. Phila., Nov. 10, 1949; d. Harold and Irma (Lusky) S.; m. David William Tucker, May 30, 1976 (div. May 1984); 1 child, Benjamin; m. Howard Rod Cohen, Jan. 2, 1997. BS in Edn., Temple U., 1971, MEd, 1974. Tchr. Simon Gratz High Sch., Phila., 1971—; ednl. diagnostician Phila./Ardmore, Pa., 1980—; owner Buster & Kitty's Pet Pals. Mem. AAUW, Phila. Writing Project, Pa. Mid-Atlantic Seminar for Study of Women in Soc. Avocations: reading, researching women in history, orchid growing. E-mail: gailjsklar@erol.com. Home: 402 Marple Rd Broomall PA 19008-2044 Office: Simon Gratz High Sch 18th & Hunting Park Ave Philadelphia PA 19140

SKLAR, RICHARD LAWRENCE, political science educator; b. N.Y.C., Mar. 22, 1930; s. Kalman and Sophie (Laub) S.; m. Eva Molineux, July 14, 1962; children: Judith Anne, Katherine Elizabeth. A.B., U. Utah, 1952; M.A., Princeton U., 1957, Ph.D., 1961. Mem. faculty Brandeis U., U. Ibadan, Nigeria, U. Zambia, SUNY-Stony Brook, UCLA; now prof. emeritus polit. sci. UCLA; mem. fgn. area fellowship program Africa Nat. Com., 1970-73; Simon vis. prof. U. Manchester, Eng., 1975, Fulbright vis. prof. U. Zimbabwe, 1984; Lester Martin fellow Harry S. Truman Rsch. Inst., Hebrew U. Jerusalem, 1979; fellow Africa Inst. of South Africa, 1994—. Author: Nigerian Political Parties: Power in an Emergent African Nation, 1963, Corporate Power in an African State, 1975; co-author: Postimperialism: International Capitalism and Development, 1987, African Politics and Problems in Development, 1991; co-editor: Postimperialism and World Politics, 1999; contbr. articles to profl. jours. Served with U.S. Army, 1952-54. Rockefeller Found. grantee, 1967. Mem. Am. Polit. Sci. Assn., African Studies Assn. (dir. 1976-78, 80-83, v.p. 1980-81, pres. 1981-82), AAUP (pres. Calif. Conf. 1980-81). Home: 1951 Holmby Ave Los Angeles CA 90025-5905

SKLENÁŘ, KAREL, archaeologist; b. Prague, Czech Republic, July 8, 1938; married; 2 children. Degree in history, Charles U., Prague, 1961, PhD, 1970; CSc, Acad. scis., Prague, 1972, ScD, 1995. Sci. worker Regional Mus., Mělník, Czech Republic, 1963-65, Nat. Mus., Prague, 1965-90; dir. Nat. Mus./Hist. Mus., Prague, 1990-97; ret., 1998. Author: Archaeology in Central Europe: The First 500 Years, 1983, others; editor Czech Archaeol. Soc. News. Mem. Czech Archaeol. Soc. (pres. 1990—). Home: Vinohradska 34, 12000 Prague Czech Republic Office: Ceská Archaeol Společnost, Letenská 4, 118 011 Prague Czech Republic

SKLYAROV, VALERY ANATOLJEVICH, electrical engineer, educator, researcher; b. Novosibirsk, Russia, Mar. 7, 1950; arrived in Portugal, 1994; s. Anatoly Vasilievich and Evfalia Alekseevna (Sulinova) S.; m. Tatiana Ivanovna Shuraskina, June 27, 1973; 1 child, Ioulia. BSc, Tech. U., Uljanovsk, Russia, 1972; PhD, Tech. U., Minsk, Belarus, 1978; DSc, Tech. U., St. Petersburg, Russia, 1986. Rschr. Rsch. Inst., Minsk, 1972-79; lectr. U. Minsk, 1979-83, head of dept., 1983-94; prof. U. Aveiro, Portugal, 1994—; vis. prof. U. Byalostok, Poland, 1992-94, U. Kassel, Germany, 1993-94. Author: The Revolutionary Guide to Turbo C , 1992, C and Object-Oriented Programming, 1997, Assembly Language Programming, 1999; contbr. articles to sci. jours. Avocation: travel. Home: Rua Calouste Gulberakian, 3810 Aveiro Portugal Office: Aveiro U, Campo Universitario, 3810 Aveiro Portugal

SKOBELEV, NIKOLAI, physicist, researcher; b. Ustyzhna, Vologda, USSR, Dec. 18, 1935; s. Konstantin Mikhailovich and Anna Ivanovna (Cheremukhina) S.; m. Tatiana Nikolaevna Bykova, May 23, 1981; 1 child, Nikolai. Red Diploma in Physics, Tech. U., St. Petersburg, USSR, 1959; D The Higher Cert., 1970; Sr. Researcher, Com. of USSR, Moscow, 1985. Asst. in physics secondary sch., Pestovo, USSR, 1952-53; jr. researcher Joint Inst. Nuclear Rsch., Dubna, USSR, 1959-69; researcher Joint Inst. Nuclear Rsch., Dubna, 1969-80; sr. researcher Joint Inst. Nuclear Rsch., Dubna, Russia, 1980—; scientific sec. PAC Joint Inst. Nuclear Rsch., Dubna, 1990—. Contbr. articles to profl. jours. Grantee Internat. Soros Sci. Found., 1993. Mem. Internat. Scientific Club. Avocations: skiing, travel, books. Home: 2 Vavilov St 9 Apart, 141980 Dubna Moscow, Russia Office: Joint Inst Nuclear Rsch, 6 Joliot-Curie St, 141980 Dubna Moscow, Russia

SKODLAR, JASNA, physician, researcher; b. Bosniaci, Croatia, Nov. 13, 1954; d. Andrija and Eva (Domacinovic) Vinkovic; m. Zeliko Skodlar, Dec. 21, 1980; 1 child, Petra. MD, Zagreb U., Croatia, 1988, M degree, 1988, PhD, 1996. Postgrad. fellow in pediatric medicine, 1985; resident in transfusion medicine Zagreb, 1988, postgrad. fellow in hematology, 1988; head clin. transfusion dept. Clin. Hosp. Ctr. U. Hosp. Zagreb, 1988-96, Magdalena Hosp. Cardiovasc. Surgery, Croatia, 1997—. Author: Guidelines for Blood Components in Clinical Medicine, Clinical Transfusion Medicine, 1993. Mem. Am. Assn. Blood Bank, Croatian Med. Assn., Croatian Assn. Hematology and Transfusiology. Roman Catholic. Avocations: music, treking. Home: F Bosniakovica 3, 10000 Zagreb Croatia Office: Magdalena Hosp, Gajeva 2, Krapinske Toplice Croatia

SKOE, EVA ELISABETH ASPAAS, psychology educator; b. Oslo, Sept. 13, 1944; d. Jens Aage Dybwad and Evelyn Vera (Samuelsen) A. BA with honors in Psychology, Simon Fraser U., Vancouver, B.C., Can., 1976, MA in Clin. Psychology, 1980, PhD in Clin. Psychology, 1987. Registered psychologist, Norway. Sessional lectr. dept. psychology Trinity Western Coll., Langley, B.C., 1978, Simon Fraser U., 1987; psychologist residential treatment unit Youth Devel. Ctr., Burnaby, B.C., 1980-84, Riverview Hosp., Coquitlam, B.C., 1986-87; vis. scholar Harvard U. Grad. Sch. Edn., Cambridge, Mass., 1987-88; asst. prof. clin. psychology Acadia U., Wolfville, N.S., Can., 1988-92; assoc. prof. dept. psychology U. Tromsø, Norway, 1992-96, prof., 1997-98; prof. dept. child and adolescence psychiatry U. Trondheim, Norway, 1998—; vis. scholar Ariz. State U., Tempe, 1996; conf. presenter in field; condr. workshops and colloquia in field; article reviewer Can. Psychology/Psychologie Canadienne, European Jour. Social Psychology. Contbr. articles to profl. jours., including Psychology and Aging, Merrill-Palmer Quar., Jour. Early Adolescence. Scholar Simon Fraser U., 1979, 85; rsch. grantee Simon Fraser U., 1984, grantee Social Scis. and Humanities Rsch. Coun. Can., 1989-92, Norwegian Rsch. Coun. Medicine and Health, 1995-97; Fulbright fellow, 1996. Mem. APA, Soc. for Rsch. in Child Devel. (recognition award 1993), Am. Ednl. Rsch. Assn. (Human Devel. Rsch. award 1998), Internat. Soc. for Study Behavioral Devel., Norsk Psykologforening, Moral Edn. Assn. (ann. conf. planning com. 1997), European Assn. for Rsch. on Adolescence, Can. Psychol. Assn. (article reviewer). Avocations: skiing, swimming, horseback riding, hiking, squash. Office: U Trondheim, Dept Child/Adolesc Psychiat, N-7005 Trondheim Norway

SKOGEN, HAVEN SHERMAN, investment company executive; b. Rochester, Minn., May 8, 1927; s. Joseph Harold and Elpha (Hemphill) S.; m. Beverly R. Baker, Feb. 19, 1949; 1 child, Scott H. BS, Iowa State U., 1950; MS, Rutgers U., 1954, PhD, 1955; MBA, U. Chgo., 1970. Registered profl. engr., Wis. Devel. engr. E.I. duPont, Wilmington, Del., 1955-57; prof. Elmhurst (Ill.) Coll., 1957-58; chief engr. Stackpole, St. Marys, Pa., 1958-62; plant mgr. Magnatronics, Elizabethtown, Ky., 1962-65; mgr. Allen-Bradley, Milw., 1965-70; v.p. Dill-Clithrow, Chgo., 1970-74; oil co. exec. Occidental Oil Co., Grand Junction, Colo., 1974-92; ptnr. H&B Investment CO., 1992—. Author: Synthetic Fuel Combustion, 1984; inventor radioactive retort doping, locus retorting zone. Naval Rsch. fellow, 1951-55. Fellow Am. Inst. Chemists; mem. Internat. Platform Assn., Masons, Elks, Sigma Xi, Phi Beta Kappa, Phi Lambda Upsilon. Republican. Avocations: fly fishing, travel, reading, teaching. Home: 3152 Primrose Ct Grand Junction CO 81506-4147

SKOGESTAD, SIGURD, chemical engineer; b. Flekkefjord, Norway, Aug. 14, 1955; s. Ingulf M. and Patricia F. (Lowe) S.; m. Anne-Lise Langangen; children: Thomas, Magnus, Hanne, Ingrid. Diploma in Eng., Norwegian U. of Sci. and Tech., 1978; PhD, Calif. Inst. Tech., 1987. Enlisted engr. Norwegian Defencs Rsch. Ctr., Kjeller, Norway, 1979; engr. Norsk Hydro Rsch. Ctr., Porsgrunn, Norway, 1980-83; prof. Norwegian U. Sci. and Tech., Trondheim, Norway, 1987—; dept. head, 1999—; dir. Ctr. for Process Systems Engr., Trondheim, 1994—; examiner in field. Author: Multivariable Feedback Control, 1996; editor Automatica, 1996—; reviewer numerous jours.; contbr. articles to profl. jours. Recipient Innstilling To The King award NTNU, 1979; Fulbright fellow, 1983. Mem. AIChE, IEEE, Norwegian Chem. Soc., Norwegian Soc. Profl. Engrs., Norwegian Petroleum Soc., Norwegian Acad. Tech. Scis., Det Kongelige Norske Vitenskapers Selskab. Avocations: skiing, orienteering, handball. Home: Stokkanhavgen 203, N7048 Trondheim Norway Office: Norwegian U of Sci and Tech, Dept Chem Engring, N7491 Trondheim Norway

SKOGLÖV, ERIK GUNNAR IVAN, astronomer, researcher; b. Uppsala, Sweden, Jan. 21, 1968; s. Gunnar and Gunilla (Jansson) S. BSc, Uppsala U., 1990, MSc, 1993, 96. With Astronomiska Observatoriet, Uppsala, Sweden. Contbr. articles to profl. jours. Served with Swedish Air Force, 1990. Mem. Astronomiska Föreningen. Avocations: reading, stamp collecting. Home: PO Box 32, S-74121 Knivsta Sweden Office: Astronomiska Observatoriet, PO Box 515, S-75120 Uppsala Sweden

SKOGLUNDH, MAGNUS BO, chemist; b. Lund, Sweden, Dec. 18, 1965; s. Bo and Marie Skoglundh; m. Lotta Reinhold, Dec. 14, 1996. MSChemE, Chalmers U. Tech., Göteborg, Sweden, 1989, Licentiate Engring., 1992, PhD in Engring., 1995; docent in Chemistry, Chalmers U. Tech., 1999. Assoc. prof., project leader competence ctr. for catalysis Chalmers U. Tech., Göteborg, 1995—. Author: New Materials in Environmental Catalysis, 1995; contbr. articles to profl. jours. Mem. Swedish Catalysis Soc. (bd. dirs. 1994—). Office: Chalmers U Tech Competence Ctr, Chalmers U Tech Comp Ctr, Kemigården 3-4, SE-41296 Göteborg Sweden

SKOGÖ, INGEMAR, aviation company executive; b. Tranås, Sweden, Jan. 4, 1949; s. Einar John William and Ingeborg Hilma Linnea (Andersson) S.; m. Ingrid Margareta Feldt, Mar. 31, 1973; children: Mårten, Ola, Per. MBA, U. Lund, Sweden, 1971. Examiner Nat. Audit Bur., Sweden, 1972-78; head of sect. Ministry of Fin., Sweden, 1978-84; asst. under-sec. state Ministry for Indsl. Affairs, Sweden, 1984-86; city mgr. City of Södertälje, Sweden, 1986-90; undersec. state Ministry for Transport and Comm., Sweden, 1990-91; dir. gen. Swedish Civil Aviation Adminstrn., 1992—; bd. dirs. Öresund Link Consortium Sweden/Denmark, 1994—, chmn., vice chmn.; bd. dirs. Swedish Agy. for Govt. Employers, 1995—. Author: Myndigheten I Samhället, 1983, Leda Lärande, 1996. Home: Pukslagargatan 63, S-125 58 Alvsjo Sweden Office: Luftfartsverket, S-601 79 Norrkoping Sweden

SKOKANDIC, IVANKA, public relations executive; b. Zagreb, Croatia, June 18, 1943; d. Antun and Kristina (Horvat) Ivanusa; mm. Antun Skokandic, Apr. 17, 1971; children: Natasa-Kristina, Vedrana. BA in French and English Lit., U. Zagreb, 1966. Cert. in tourism and hotel industry. Translator GeneralExport, Zagreb, 1967-71; with congress dept. Yugotours, Zagreb, 1971-91; dir. Adriaturist, Zagreb, 1991-92; in ind. pub. rels. covering hospitality svcs. Hotel Golden Tulip Holiday, Zagreb, 1992—. Mem. Union Oaneuropéene Zagreb. Roman Catholic. Avocations: literature, fine arts, architecture, astrology. Home and Office: V Filakovca 5, 10 000 Zagreb Croatia

SKOKOS, CHARALAMBOS, physicist, researcher; b. Sydney, Australia, Oct. 12, 1968; s. Dimitrios and Androniki (Stathi) S.; m. Irini Intzoglou, Feb. 15, 1992. BSc, U. Athens, 1990, PhD, 1997. Rschr. U. Milan, Italy, 1992, U. Athens, 1993-94, Nat. Obs. Athens, 1994-95, U. Athens, 1996-97, 99—; tchr. Hellenic Ctr. Info. Technology, 1998-99; sci. collaborator Ellinogermanini A gogi S.A., 1999-2000; collaborator Hellenic Open U., 2000—; rschr. Acad. Athens, 1999—. Mem. Hellenic Astronom. Soc. Avocations: music, reading, photography, travel. E-mail: hskokos@cc.uoa.gr.

SKOLER, CELIA REBECCA, art gallery director; b. Sioux City, Iowa, Apr. 7, 1931; d. Jacob and Flora (Gorchow) Stern; m. Louis Skoler, Aug. 24, 1952; children: Elisa Anne, Harry Jay. BFA in Art and Music magna cum laude, Syracuse U., 1976. Fin. planner Architects' Partnership, Syracuse, N.Y., 1969-71; bus. mgr. Skoler & Lee Architects P.C., Syracuse, 1971-89; owner, dir. New Acquisitions Gallery, Syracuse, 1981-95, New Acquisitions, Syracuse, 1995—; ptnr. Gallery Metro, Syracuse, 1991-93, mng. ptnr., 1992-93; contbg. writer Syracuse Herald and Syracuse Newtimes, Syracuse, 1989-91; art cons. IBM, Syracuse, Rochester, Albany, 1983-86, Costello, Cooney & Fearon, Syracuse, 1981-83, Menter, Rudin & Trivelpiece, Syracuse, 1987-88, Blue Cross/Blue Shield Ctrl. N.Y., Syracuse, 1990, Syracuse Newspapers, 1992-94, GTE Svcs. Corp., Syracuse, 1995; with cmty. internship program Syracuse U., 1981-93, directed mayoral portrait City of Syracuse,1983, Gelling Meml. Portrait U. Coll., 1984, Levine Meml. Commn. Temple. Concord, 1984; TV producer Syracuse U. Friends of Art, 1979-80; curated 45 exhibits, 1981-90; panelist for art critique Everson Mus. Art, Syracuse, 1989; lectr. on gallery mgmt. Syracuse U. Sch. Art., 1989; juror Fine Art N.Y. State Fair, 1989. One-man shows include Camillus Plaza, 1972, The Associated Artists Gallery, Syracuse, 1973, Library of Fayetteville, N.Y., 1974; exhibited in juried shows at N.Y. State Fair (1st prize 1974), U. Coll, 1967, 69, 71, Rochester Meml. Gallery, 1969, 70, 71, 72, 74, The Associated Artists, 1971, 72, Cen. N.Y. Art Open, 1970, 71, (Purchase prize 1970, 71), Munson Williams Protor Inst, Utica, N.Y., 1971, 72, Cayuga Mus., Auburn, N.Y., 1972, Oneida (N.Y.) Art Festival, 1969, (1st prize), Jewish Community Ctr., Syracuse, 1968 (1st prize 1969), St. David's Invitational, Dewitt, N.Y., 1970, 71, 72, 73, 74, 75, Cooperstown Art Inst., Nat. Show, 1973, 74, Arena Nat. Show, Binghamton, N.Y., 1975 (Purchase prize 1975); prodr.: (autobiographical CD-ROM) In Rehearsal, 1997; represented in permanent collection at Savannah (Ga.) Coll. Art and Design. Peer counselor Univ. Coll., Syracuse, 1980-85; Tel-auc auctioneer Sta. WCNY-TV, Liverpool, N.Y., 1982; mem. steering and implementation com. Gelling Meml. Lounge U. Coll., 1984-85; exec. bd. Syracuse U. Friends of Art, 1977-80; fine art juror N.Y. State Fair, Syracuse, 1982, Downtown Com., Syracuse, 1982, Oswego (N.Y.) Art Guild, 1984. Recipient Purchase prize Marine Midland Bank, 1974, Crouse-Irving Hosp., 1974; named to Sioux City Ctrl. High Roster Hall of Fame, 1998. Mem. Everson Mus. Art (corp.) mem. Phi Kappa Phi, Alpha Sigma Lambda (pres. 1980-81). Home and Office: New Acquisitions 213 Scottholm Ter Syracuse NY 13224-1737

SKOLER, LOUIS, architect, educator; b. Apr. 5, 1920; s. Harry and Etta (Mitkoff) S.; m. Celia Rebecca Stern, 1952; children: Elisa Anne, Harry Jay. BArch, Cornell U., 1951. Maj. designer Sargent, Webster, Crenshaw & Folley, Syracuse, N.Y., 1951-59; design critic Cornell U., Ithaca, N.Y., 1956-57; pvt. practice arch. Syracuse, 1956-69; faculty Sch. Arch. Syracuse U., 1959-92, prof. emeritus, 1990—; head of MArch I Program, 1980-82, head undergrad. program, 1989-90, arch. programs abroad, London, 1977, Scandinavia, 1985, Japan, 1988; ptnr. Archs. Partnership, Syracuse, 1969-71; pres. Skoler & Lee Archs., P.C., Syracuse, 1971-89; lectr. Nanjing Inst. Tech., China, summer 1986; arbitrator Am. Arbitration Assn., 1980—. Named Best in Residential Design, Design-in-Steel, 1968-69. Mem. AIA. Home: 213 Scottholm Ter Syracuse NY 13224-1737

SKOLNICK, S. HAROLD, lawyer; b. Woonsocket, R.I., June 17, 1915; s. David and Elsie (Silberman) S.; m. Shirley Marshall. AB cum laude, Amherst Coll., 1936; JD, Boston U., 1940. Bar: R.I. 1940, D.C. 1947, Fla. 1952, U.S. Dist. Ct. (so. dist.) Fla. 1953, U.S. Ct. Appeals (5th cir.) 1960, U.S. Ct. Appeals (11th cir.) 1981. Atty. Dept. of War, Washington, 1940-42;

asst. gen. counsel, asst. chief legal dept. Office Chief Ordnance, Dept. of Army, Washington, 1947-50; assoc. Francis I. McCanna, Providence, R.I., 1951-52; ptnr. French & Skolnick, Miami, Fla., 1953-60; sole practice Miami, Fla., 1961—. Served to lt. col. U.S. Army, 1942-47. Mem. ABA, Am. Judicature Soc., Nat. Def. Indsl. Assn. (life), R.I. Bar Assn., D.C. Bar Assn., Dade County Bar Assn., Estate Planning Coun. Greater Miami, Masons, Shriners. Home and Office: 6521 SW 122d St Miami FL 33156-5550

SKOOG, WILLIAM MELVIN, music/voice educator; b. St. Paul, Minn., Apr. 7, 1953; s. John Chester and Mary Edith S.; m. Elaine Ketter, March 1, 1986; children: Miles William, Rebekah Morgan, Jacquelyn Correlle. BA magna cum laude, Gustavus Adolphus Coll., 1975; MA in Music, U. Denver, 1981; ArtsD in Music, U. Northern Colo., 1992. Musical dir., conductor Littleton (Colo.) Chamber Orch., 1985-89, Longmont (Colo.) Chorale, 1989-90; dir. music and fine arts Littleton United Meth. Ch., 1981-85, St. Andrew United Meth. Ch., Littleton, 1985-89; asst. dir. choral and operatic activities U. No. Colo., Dowagiac, Mich., 1988-90; dir. choral activities, dept. chair Southwestern Mich. Coll., Dowagiac, 1990-97; dir. choral activities dept. music Ind. U.-Purdue U., Fort Wayne, Ind., 1997—; mem. Robert Shaw Chorale, 1996, 97, 98. Guest soloist Carmina Burana, Blue Lake Music Camp, Mich., 1996, Ft. Collins Symphony, Colo., Garden City Symphony; guest conductor Elkart Chorale and Symphony, 1995, Northwest Ind. choral Festival, Denver, Ind., 1996, Fort Wayne Philharmonic Orch., 1997, Fort Wayne All City Choir, 1998, First Wayne St. United Meth. Ch., 2000, Ecumenical 2000 Svc., Ft. Wayne, 1999, Bridges Music Ministry, Littleton, 1999—, Northern Ind. Assn. Chs., Bethel Coll., 2000, European Tour of Germany and Prague, Sanctuary Choir, 2000; rsch. and diagnostic, rsch. cons. Voice Care Ctr., Ft. Wayne, 2000. Pres. Ind. Opera North, South Bend, Ind., 1996-97, Fort Wayne Children's Choir, Inc., 1998—; bd. dirs. Encore Dance Co., Decatur and Dowagiac, Mich., 1995-97, Dowagiac Dogwood Fina Arts Festival, 1995-97. Mem. Nat. Assn. Tchrs. Singing, Nat. Otter Soc., Am. Choral Dirs. Assn. (Ind. chpt.), Am. Guild Organists and Choral Dirs., Ind. Music Educators Conf. (grantee 1999). Democrat. Methodist. Avocations: golf, jogging, biking, reading, fishing. E-mail: skoogw@ipfw.edu. Home: 625 Winterset Rd Fort Wayne IN 46819-1541 Office: Ind/Purdue Univ Ft Wayne Campus Dept of Music 2101 E Coliseum Blvd Fort Wayne IN 46805-1445

SKOOR, JOHN BRIAN, art educator, art consultant; b. Mount Vernon, Wash., Dec. 14, 1939; s. George Nephi and Marie Elizabeth (Collins) S.; m. Susan Diane Waugh, June 17, 1972; children: Marie Elizabeth, Christine Elaine. AA in Edn., Graceland Coll., Lamoni, 1960; BA in Art, Cen. Wash. U., 1962, BA in Edn., 1965, MA in Art, 1969. Art instr. Delta (Mich.) Coll., Saginaw, 1977-79; instr. Renton (Wash.) Vocat. Tech. Inst., 1981-83; art instr. Green River (Wash.) Community Coll., Auburn, 1988—; cons. staff and development instr. various Seattle sch. dists., 1988—; art instr. Highline Community Coll., Seattle, 1990—; adj. faculty Cen. Wash. U., 1984—, Seattle Pacific U., 1986—; dir. sr. programs Highline C.C., 1992—, instr. sr.'s making art program, 1998—; guest speaker Wash. Art Educators Assn. Conv., 1990. Illustrator of religious curriculum texts, 1978-80; exhibited acrylic theol. paintings show, Independence, Mo., 1980. Guest speaker Alma (Mich.) Art Dept., 1977, Nat. Camping Assn., Detroit, 1979, Wash. Art Tchrs. Assn., 1990; coord. sr. programs Highline C.C., 1992-99; elder Reorganized Ch. of Jesus Christ of Latter Day Saints, Seattle, 1966—, pastor, 1987—, bd. dirs. creative arts festival, Mich., 1977; art instr. Srs. Making Art, Greater Puget Sound area. Mem. Wash. Alliance for Arts Edn. (commn. chmn. 1987—), Richland Art Tchrs. Assn. (pres. 1965-66), Tri-City Art Tchrs. Assn. (pres. 1966-67), Nat. Art Educators Assn. Avocations: public speaking, graphic design, calligrapher, performing artist, ministry. Home and Studio: 4830 S Morgan St Seattle WA 98118-3346

SKOPINSKY, VADIM NIKOLAEVICH, materials educator; b. Moscow, May 3, 1946; s. Nikolay Vasiliyevich and Maria Ivanovna (Yurina) S.; m. Elena Sergeevna Chusova, Mar. 1, 1971; children: Sergey, Andrey. D of Tech. Scis., Moscow Engr. Constrn. Inst., Moscow, 1989. Rschr. Moscow Higher Tech. Sch., Moscow, 1973-76; assoc. prof., material strength Tech. Sch. Moscow, 1976-89; prof. material strength Moscow Motor-Car Constrn. Inst., 1989-90, head material strength, 1990—, chair. Contbr. articles to profl. jours. Transport Scis. grantee Acad. Transport Scis., Moscow, 1993, 98, Fundamental Rsch. grantee Russian State Com. Higher Edn., Moscow, 1996. Mem. Moscow State Indsl. U. Home: Alleya Zhemchugovoy 1-1-127, 111402 Moscow Russia Office: Moscow State Indsl U, Avtozavodskaya 16, 109280 Moscow Russia

SKORA, WAYNE PHILIP, retired air force officer; b. Chgo., Jan. 16, 1944; s. Felix Anthony Skora and Lillie (Goshko) St. Thomas; m. Dorothy Mae Barrett, June 13, 1966; children: Tanya Christine, Christopher Michael. BS in Engring. Sci., USAF Acad., 1966; MS in Human Resource Mgmt., U. Utah, 1976. Commd. 2d lt. USAF, 1966, advanced through grades to col., 1988; F-4 pilot USAF, various locations, 1967-69, 71-79; flight safety officer Hdqrs. Tactical Air Command, Langley AFB, Va., 1979-82; chief safety, A-10 pilot 23d Tactical Fighter Wing, England AFB, La., 1982-84; chief Office Mil. Cooperation, Am. Embassy, Manama, Bahrain, 1984-87; asst. chief logistics 507th Tactical Air Control Wing, Shaw AFB, S.C., 1987-88; dep. comdr. for ops. So. Air Div., Howard AFB, Panama, 1988-90; dep. for safety Air Force Devel. Test Ctr., Eglin AFB, Fla., 1990-92; pres. Skora Enterprises, Inc., Colorado Springs, Colo., 1994—. Decorated Legion of Merit, DFC with oak leaf cluster, Air medal with 21 oak leaf clusters, Def. Meritorious Svc. medal, AF Meritorious Svc. medal with oak leaf cluster, AF Commendation medal with oak leaf cluster. Mem. Order of Daedalians (sec. 1988-90). Roman Catholic. Home: 24 Luxury Ln Colorado Springs CO 80921-3300

SKORDIS, NICOS, physician; b. Nicosia, Cyprus, Jan. 5, 1953; s. Andreas and Theopisti (Nicola) S.; m. Agni Petridou, May 12, 1990. MD, U. Athens, Greece, 1978. Diplomate in pediat. and endocrinology. Resident internal medicine State Neuropsychiatric Hosp., Athens, 1979-80; pre-registration dr. dept. surgery Nicosia Gen. Hosp., 1980, pre-registration dr. med. dept. internal medicine, 1980-81; resident pediat. first dept. pediat. Athens U., Aghia Sophia Childrens Hosp., 1981-83, sci. assoc. first dept. pediat., 1983-84; fellow pediat. endocrinology dept. N.Y. State U., Childrens Hosp., Buffalo, 1984-86; fellow pediat. endocrinology dept. pathology and pediat. U. Fla. Coll. Medicine, Gainesville, 1986-87; dir. pediat. endocrine unit Makarios Hosp., Nicosia, 1989—; vis. fellow in genetics as Fulbright scholar Divsn. Med. Genetics, Cedars-Sinai Med. Ctr., L.A., vis. fellow embryology-teratology unit Mass. Gen. Hosp., Harvard Med. Sch., Boston, 1993. Contbr. chpts. to books and articles to profl. jours. Mem. Internat. Soc. for Neonatal Screening, Internat. Soc. for Pediat. and Adolescent Diabetes, European Soc. for Pediat. Endocrinology, European Assn. for the Study of Diabetes, The Endocrine Soc. USA, Greek Pediat. Soc., Hellenic Diabetes Assn., Cyprus Soc. of the Study of Diabetes, Cyprus Pediat. Soc. Christian Orthodox. Home: 22 M Parides, 2108 Nicosia Cyprus Office: Makarios Hosp, Nicosia Cyprus

SKORNA, HANS JUERGEN, literature educator; b. Nordhausen, Germany, Sept. 2, 1926; s. Wilhelm and Else Skorna; m. Rita Hermes, May, 1951; 1 child, Anja. PhD, U. Colone, Fed. Republic Germany, 1962. Asst. Pädagogische Hochschule, Dortmund, Fed. Republic Germany, 1962; lectr. Pädagogische Hochschule, Kaiserslautern, Fed. Republic Germany, 1962-68; prof. U. Koblenz-Landau, Fed. Republic Germany, 1968—, dir. Inst. Germanistik, 1984—. Author: German Short Stories for School Instruction, 1964, Modern Poetry and Education, 1965, Political Poetry and School Instruction, 1968, Problems of Literature in Sight of Education, 1978. Avocations: art, painting, writing. Home: Graf-Recke Str 40, 40239 Duesseldorf Germany Office: U Koblenz-Laudau, Rheinau 1, 56075 Koblenz Germany

SKOROKHOD, YEVGENIY, retired construction engineer; b. Kiev, Ukraine, Dec. 21, 1929; came to U.S., 1991, naturalized, 1996; s. Samuil and Anna Skorokhod; m. Klatseta Zaslavskaya, Feb. 12, 1955; 1 child, Tanya. Master's degree, Inst. Tech., Kiev, 1954. Cert. in constrn. engring. Mgr. in constrn. Kiev, 1955-67; asst. dir.-cons. Inst. Energetic Power, Kiev, 1967-90. Author: (autobiographies) Victim of the Holocaust, 1941-44, The Road to Death (Tragedy of Babiy Yar), 1997, Fablus Around Us, 1999; contbr. articles to profl. jours. Leader, vol. Jewish Comty. House of Bensonhurst Club of Holocaust Survivors, Bklyn., 1993—, U.S. Holocaust Meml. Mus. Mem. World Jewish Congress, Acad. Am. Poets. Democrat. Jewish. Achievements include patent for method of construction. Avocation: writing. Home: 2164 78th St Apt 6A Brooklyn NY 11214-1549

SKOSANA, BEN M., federal official; b. Sharpeville, South Africa, May 7, 1947; 3 children. Grad. in social devel., Can.; BSc, MSc in Internat. Affairs. Dir. Zululand Churches Health and Welfare Assn., 1981-86; permanent rep. Inkatha Freedom Party, London, 1987-94; mem. Parliament, 1994—; min. correctional svcs. Dept. Correctional Svcs., Pretoria, 1998—. chmn. com. fgn. rels. Inkatha Freedom Party. Office: Dept Correctional Svcs, Poyntos Bldg W Pvt Bag X 853, cor Schubart-Church St Pretoria 1 South Africa*

SKOU, BENT, diplomat, public information officer; b. Silkeborg, Denmark, Sept. 27, 1931; s. Soren and Marie (Nielsen) S.; m. Martha Christine B. Petersen, Apr. 20, 1957 (wid. 1998); children: Lene Skou Moynihan, Lise Ringland. Degree in journalism, U. Aarhus, Denmark, 1956. Journalist Danish Newspapers, Denmark, 1949-61; press attache Fgn. Ministry, Denmark, 1961-63; press counselor Danish UN Mission, N.Y.C., 1963-69; cultural and press counselor Danish Embassy, Bonn, Germany, 1970-73, Danish Mil. Mission, Berlin, 1970-73; counselor of embassy Danish Embassy, Washington, 1973-79; min. counselor Danish Embassy, London, 1980-83; head of press. dept. Fgn. Ministry, Copenhagen, 1983-86; min. counselor Danish Embassy, Washington, 1986-92; head Internat. Press Ctr., Copenhagen, 1992-98. Home: Solbakkevej 8, 3050 Humlebaek Denmark

SKOU, JENS CHRISTIAN, biophysics educator; b. Lemvig, Denmark, Oct. 8, 1918; s. Magnus Martinus and Ane Margrethe (Knak) S.; m. Ellen-Margrethe Nielsen, May 17, 1947; children: Hanne, Karen. MD, U. Copenhagen, 1944; DrMedSci, U. Aarhus (Denmark), 1954; DrMedSci (hon.), U. Copenhagen, 1986. Intern Hjørring Hosp., 1944-45, resident, 1945-46; orthopaedist Hosp. Aarhus, 1946-47; asst. prof., 1947-54, assoc. prof., 1954-63; prof., chmn. Inst. Physiology, Aarhus U., 1963-73; prof. Inst. Biophysics, Aarhus U., 1973-88. Contbr. articles to profl. jours. Recipient Leo prize Fond, 1954, Novo prize Fond, 1965, Consul Carlsen prize, 1973, A. Retzius gold medal Swedish Med. Assn., 1977, E.K. Fernstroöm Big Nordic prize, 1985, Prakash Datta medal Fedn. European Biochem. Socs.; co-recipient Nobel prize for chemistry, 1997. Mem. AAAS, NAS (fgn. assoc.), Danish Royal Acad. Scis., Deutsche Acad. der Naturforscher Leopoldina, European Molecular Biology Orgn., Japanese Biochem. Soc. (hon.), Am. Acad. Arts and Scis., Am. Physiol. Soc. (hon.), Academia Europaea. Avocations: classical music, yachting, skiing, fishing. Fax: 45 86129599. E-mail: jcs@biophys.au.dk. Home: Rislundvej 9, 8240 Risskov Denmark Office: Inst of Biophysics, Ole Worms Allé 185, 8000C Århus Denmark

SKOU, PEDER NOES, financial executive; b. Aalborg, Denmark, Mar. 12, 1939; s. Carl Emil and Ebba Asta (Jensen) S. Student, Sorø Acad., 1955; merconom, Copenhagen Bus. Coll., 1977. With Selfridges Ltd., London, 1961, Graumann's Fashion House, Berlin, 1962-63; leader dept. mens clothing Magasin du Nord, Copenhagen, 1963-72; pvt. practice fin., 1972—. Mem. Danish Soransk Soc., The Highlander Club, Oxford Club (dir.'s circle). Lutheran. Avocations: golf, horse-racing, football. Office: Internat Fin Growth, Godthaabsvenget 16, DK-2000 Frederiksberg Denmark

SKOULARIDOU, VICTORIA E., software engineer; b. Nikea, Greece, Sept. 19, 1973; d. Emmanuel G. and Evaggelia E. (Krontira) S. BSc, Athens U., 1995, MSc, 1998. Programmer Signon Co., Athens, 1995-96; seminar tchr. IRIDANOS Edn. Ctr., Athens, 1996; sys. adminstr./rschr. Athens U., 1996-98; software engr. INTRACOM S.A., Peania, Greece, 1998—. Office: Intracom SA, 19.5 Km Markopoulou Ave, Peania Attika, Greece 190 02

SKOURAS, THANOS, economics educator; b. Athens, Greece, Dec. 21, 1943; s. Spyros and Ismini (Xanthopoulou) S.; m. Gella Varnava, Aug. 3, 1966 (div. 1986); children: Spyros-Panos, Stavros; m. Savina Ioannides, May 30, 1998. BA, Durham U., Eng., 1965; MSc in Econs., London Sch. Econs., 1967, PhD, 1975. From lectr. to sr. lectr. Middlesex U., Eng., 1967-73; head econs. divsn. U. Greenwich, Eng., 1974-77; head econs. dept. U. East London, 1978-86; vice rector Athens U. Econs. and Bus., 1989-92, prof., 1986—; vis. prof. Cambridge U., 1978-79, 79-80, China Econ. Mgmt. Inst., 1988, Fudan U., 1991, 93, Leuven U., Belgium, 1993-94; advisor Ministry Nat. Econ., Athens, 1983-84, 86-88; cons. Commn. European Coms., Brussels, 1992-94; chmn. bd. dirs. ABAX Stockbroking, Athens, 1991-95; bd. dirs. ERGOSE, Comml. Bank. Author: Land and Its Taxation in Recent Economic Theory, 1977; co-author: Production or Importation of Advanced Technology Manufactures? The Case of Telecommunications Equipment, 1993; editor: The Greek Economy: Economic Policies for the 1990's, 1992; co-editor: Post-Keynesian Economic Theory: A Challenge to Neoclassical Economics, 1985; editor Thames Papers in Polit. Economy, 1974-86, Brit. Rev. Econ. Issues, 1976-85; contbr. over 40 articles to profl. jours. Office: Athens U Econs and Bus, 76 Patission St, 10434 Athens Greece

SKOURIS, VASSILIOS, international justice; b. 1948. Grad., Free U., Berlin, 1970; D in Constnl. and Adminstrv. Law, Hamburg U., 1973. Prof. pub. law Bielefeld U., Germany, 1978, U. Thessaloniki, Greece, 1982; minister of internal affairs Govt. of Greece, 1989, 96; mem. adminstrv. bd. U. of Crete, 1983-87; dir. Ctr. for Internat. and European Econ. Law U. Thessaloniki, 1997—; judge Ct. of Justice of European Cmtys., 1999—. Mem. higher selection bd. Greek Civil Servants, 1994-96; mem. adminstrv. bd. Greek Nat. Judges' Coll.; mem. sci. com. Ministry of Fgn. Affairs, 1997-99. Mem. Greek Assn. for European Law (pres. 1992-94), Greek Nat. Rsch. Com., Acad. Coun. of Acad. European Law (trier 1995—), Greek Econ. and Social Coun. (pres. 1998). Office: Ct Justice European Cmtys, Palais de Cour de justice, Kirchberg L-2925, Luxembourg*

SKOV, FLEMMING KOBBERØE, hematologist, educator, consultant, researcher; b. Frederiksberg, Denmark, Apr. 1, 1938; s. Jens Kobberøe and Astrid Emilie (Nielsen) S.; m. Hanne Fjeldgaard Vangsgaard, Aug. 26, 1961; children: Lars K., Jens K. MD, U. Copenhagen, 1964. Cert. immune hematologist specialist, Abbott Quality Inst. quality cons. Various positions to 1st asst. to prof. State Univ. Hosp., Copenhagen, 1964-68; 1st asst. State Univ. Blood Bank, Copenhagen, 1969-74; 1st asst. to med. dir. blood bank and blood grouping dept. State Serum Inst., Copenhagen, 1976-82, Glostrup Hosp., Copenhagen, 1982-85; Med. Rsch. Coun. rsch. fellow exptl. hematology unit St. Mary's Hosp. Med. Sch., London, 1974-76; med. dir. Transfusion Ctr. Storstrøms Amt, Nykøbing, Denmark, 1985—; med. dir. (on leave) Transfusion Ctr., Stavanger, Norway, 1997; lectr. Poly. Med. Technicians, Copenhagen, 1969-74, 76—, then mem. edn. bd.; lectr. Folk U., Nykøbing, Denmark, 1993, U. Riga, Latvia, 1993; cons., rep. to Latvia on blood transfusion matters, WHO, Copenhagen, 1992-93. Contbr. articles to med. jours., including Clin. Chim. Acta, Ortho Diagnostic Reporter, Am. Jour. Epidemiology, Vox Sang, Scandinavian Jour. Hematology, Jour. Immunogenetics, Blood, Transfusion, European Jour. Hematology. Grantee Danish Med. Rsch. Coun., 1974-76, Brit. Coun., 1974-76, Found. for Promotion Med. Rsch., Denmark, 1981. Mem. Danish Soc. Clin. Immunology (chmn. bd. edn. 1978-85), Internat. Soc. Blood Transfusion, Geneal. Soc. Storstrøms County (bd. dirs. 1997). Achievements include discovery of blood group Jensen and Dane blood group of Miltenberger Class, confirming that silent gene segment transfer and untemplated mutation can be cause of change in gene conformaton also in humans. Avocations: singing, acting. Fax: 45 54 88 57 43. E-mail: flemmingskov@dadlnet.dk. Office: Centralsygehuset, Transfusion Ctr, DK-4800 Nykøbing F, Denmark

SKOVMAND, OLE, researcher; b. Copenhagen, Denmark, Nov. 19, 1947; s. Arne and Ellen (Steensgaard) S.; m. Suzanne Bosselman, 1988 (div. Nov. 1991); children: Rune, Helle, Aske; m. Myhanh Lyong, July 25, 1998. MSc, U. Copenhagen, 1975, PhD, 1978; grad., Copenhagen Bus. Sch., 1993. Asst. prof. U. Odense, Denmark, 1974-75; asst. scientist Danish Pest Infestation Lab., 1978-84; group leader Benzon Ltd., Copenhagen, 1985-88, Novo Nordisk Ltd., Copenhagen, 1988-94; project leader Danish Blilharzia Lab., Montpellier, France, 1994-98; founder Intelligent Insect Control, 1999—; mem. adv. bd. Danish Ministry Agr., Copenhagen, 1996—; cons. Suisse Coop., Zurich, 1996—. Contbr. articles to sci. jours.; patentee ingestible pesticide composition. U. Copenhagen scholar, 1975-78. Mem. Soc. Invertebrate Pathology, Soc. Vector Control, Entomol. Soc. Am. Avocations: jogging, windsurfing, trekking. Home: 80 Rue Pauline Ramart, Montpellier 1, France Office: ORSTOM, 911 Rue Agropolis, F-34042 Montpellier France

SKOVORODA, ANDREI RADIONOVICH, mathematician; b. Uvalski Sovhoz, USSR, June 6, 1953; s. Radion Andreevich and Matriona Dmitrievna (Alekseeva) S.; m. Tatiana Petrovna Glushkova, Jan. 30, 1975; children: Radion, Nikita. MS, Novosibirsk (USSR) State U., 1975; PhD, Moscow State U., 1985. Lectr. theoretical mechanics Coll. Textile Tech., Barnaul, USSR, 1975-77; jr. rsch. assoc. Rsch. Computing Ctr. USSR Acad. Sci., Pushchino, 1981-85, sr. rsch. assoc. Rsch. Computing Ctr., 1986-88, sci. sec. Inst. Rsch. Computing Ctr., 1988-93; head lab. Inst. Math. Problems Biology Russian Acad. Sci., Pushchino, 1993—; cons. U. Mich., Ann Arbor, 1991—. Contbr. articles to profl. jours. NIH grantee U. Mich., 1998—. Avocations: fishing, mushroom hunting. Office: Inst Math Problems Biology, 4 Instituskaya St, 142290 Pushchino Russia

ŠKOVRÁNEK, JAN, pediatric cardiologist; b. Ostrava, Moravia, Czech Republic, Aug. 8, 1947; s. Vilém and Danuše (Bartková) Š; m. Jitka Kalusová, Mar. 20, 1974; 1 child, Jitka. MD, Charles U., Prague, Czech Republic, 1972, PhD, 1986. Cert. in pediat., pediatric cardiology. Houseman Dist. Hosp., Kladno, Czech Republic, 1972; rsch. fellow Czech Acad. Sci., Prague, 1975-80; resident Univ. Hosp. Motol, Prague, 1973-77, resident, cons. Cardiac Ctr., 1977-91, vice dir. Cardiac Ctr., 1991-93, dir., 1993—. Author 4 books; contbr. over 150 articles to med. jours. Mem. Czech Med. Soc., Czech Soc. Cardiology (pres. working group pediatric cardiology 1994-98, mem. coun. 1995-99), European Assn. Pediatric Cardiologists. Avocations: tennis, football, basketball, skiing. Home: Zdíkovská 63, CZ-15000 Prague Czech Republic Office: Univ Hosp Motol Cardiac Ctr, V Uvalu 84, CZ-15006 Prague 5, Czech Republic

SKOWRONEK, KRZYSZTOF JERZY, microbiologist, molecular biologist; b. Warsaw, Poland, June 11, 1961; s. Jerzy and Maria (Cylwik) S.; m. Magdalena Stolarek, Sept. 25, 1982; 1 child, Agnieszka. MS, Warsaw U., Poland, 1985, PhD, 1997. Rsch. asst. Warsaw U., Poland, 1985-88; sr. rsch. asst. Henry Ford Hosp., Detroit, 1989-91; sr. teaching, rsch. asst. Warsaw U., 1991-97, sr. scientist, lectr., 1997-98; postdoct. Nencki Inst. Polish Acad. Sci., Warsaw, 1998—. Contbr. articles to profl. jours. With Polish Nat. Guard, 1986-87. Grantee Scientific Rsch. Com., Warsaw, 1994. Avocations: rock music, soccer, cycling, hiking. Home: Mieszka Starego 3, 02-495 Warsaw Poland Office: Nencki Inst Dept Muscle Bio, Pasteura 3, 02-093 Warsaw Poland

SKRABKA BŁOTNICKA, TERESA, animal food technologist; b. Przemyśl, Poland, Jan. 4, 1933; d. Karol and Stefania (Dubiniewicz) B.; m. Henryk Skrabka, May 30, 1956; children: Tomasz, Małgorzata. MSc in Chemistry, Tech. U., Gliwice, Poland, 1956; PhD, U. Medicine, Wrocław, Poland, 1965; ScD, Agr. U., Poznan, Poland, 1987. Vice dean faculty indsl. engring. and econs. U. Econs. Wrocław, 1973-81, asst. prof., 1974-90, assoc. prof., 1990-95, prof., 1995—, head food tech. dept., 1988-89, head animal food tech. dept., 1989—; cons. Exptl. Sta. of Inst. of Animal Husbandry, Czechnica, 1967-73. Author: Bioengineering, 1981, Gelling and Emulsifying Properties of Proteins and Muscles from Poultry Especially from Water fowls, 1986; co-author: Food Technology, 1978, 2d edit., 1985, Advances in Food Analysis, 1993. Chair organizing com. sci. confs. U. Econs. Wroclaw, 1992, 94, 97, 99. Recipient awards Min. of Sci., Higher Edn. and Technics, 1977, 82, Order of Nat. Edn. Com., 1980; Cavalier's Cross of Polonia Restitute, State Coun., 1987. Mem. Polish Food Technologists Soc. (organizer, chairperson Wrocław br. 1990-97), World's Poultry Sci. Assn., Polish Chem. Soc. Avocations: music, opera, tourism. Home: Sudecka 140/1, 53129 Wrocław Poland Office: Univ of Economics, Komadorska 118/120, 53345 Wrocław Poland

SKRAMSTAD, ROBERT ALLEN, retired oceanographer; b. Montevideo, Minn., Apr. 3, 1937; s. Vernon Donald and Ann May (Tollefsen) S. Student, St. Olaf Coll., 1956, 60-61; BS in Geol. Engring., S.D. Sch. Mines and Tech., 1965. Geologist Naval Oceanographic Office, Washington, 1965-70, oceanographer, 1970-75; oceanographer Naval Oceanographic Office, Bay St. Louis, Miss., 1975-82, phys. scientist, 1982-95; ret., 1995. With U.S. Army, 1957-60. Mem. Am. Soc. Photogrammetry and Remote Sensing, Nat. Geographic Soc. Republican. Avocations: photography, jogging, travel, mineral collecting. Home: 509 E College Dr Marshall MN 56258-1821

SKREB, MARKO, banker. Gov. Croatian Nat. Bank. Office: Croatian Nat Bank, Burze 3 Square, 10000 Zagreb Croatia

SKRETNY, WILLIAM MARION, federal judge; b. Buffalo, Mar. 8, 1945; s. William S. and Rita E. (Wyroski) S.; m. Carol Ann Skretny; 3 children. AB, Canisius Coll., 1966; JD, Howard U., 1969; LLM, Northwestern U., 1972. Bar: Ill. 1969, U.S. Dist. Ct. (no. dist) Ill. 1969, N.Y. 1972, U.S. Ct. Appeals (7th cir.) 1972, U.S. Dist. Ct. (we. dist.) N.Y. 1973, U.S. Ct. Appeals (2d cir.) 1976, U.S. Supreme Ct. 1980. Asst. U.S. atty. Office of U.S. Atty. No. Dist. Ill., Chgo., 1971-73; asst. U.S. atty. Office of U.S. Atty. We. Dist. N.Y., Buffalo, 1973-81, 1st asst., 1975-81; gen. ptnr. Duke, Holzman, Yaeger & Radlin, Buffalo, 1981-83; 1st dep. dist. atty. Office Dist. Atty Erie County, Buffalo, 1983-88; with Gross, Shuman, Brizdle and Gilfillan, PC, Buffalo, 1988, Cox, Barrell, Buffalo, 1989-90; judge U.S. Dist. Ct. (we. dist.) N.Y., Buffalo, 1990—; mem. jud. conf. com. on security and facilities, 1994, chair subcom. on planning and space mgmt., com. liaison for long range planning. Named Citizen of Yr. Am Pol Eagle Newspaper, 1977, 90, Disting. Grad. Nat. Cath. Edn. Assn. Dept. Elem. Sch., 1991, Disting. Alumnus Canisius Coll., 1993; named to Wall of Fame Law Sch. Northwestern U. Mem. ABA, Fed. Judges Assn., Bar Assn. of Erie County, Di Gamma, Phi Alpha Delta. Republican. Roman Catholic. Office: US District Court 68 Court St Rm 507 Buffalo NY 14202-3405

SKŘIVAN, ALEŠ, historian; b. Prague, Czech Republic, Nov. 11, 1944; s. Aleš and Jiřina (Pihanová) S.; m. Hana Rejfířová, Jan. 30, 1965; children: Markéta Krejčová, Aleš. MA, Charles U., Prague, 1967, PhD, 1969; CSc, Charles U., 1987. Sci. aspirant Charles U. Faculty Arts, 1967-72, asst., 1972-91, sr. lectr. history, 1991-96, prof., 1996—. Author: China and the United States 1941-1945, 1974, The Way of Samurai, 1984, The Fall of Nippon, 1991, German Gains in Africa in 1884-1885, 1991, Imperial Policy: Austria-Hungary and Germany in European Policy in the Years 1906-1914, 1996, The Japanese War, 1931-1945, 1997, Austria-Hungary in European Policy 1906-1914, 1999, European Policy 1648-1914, 1999. Office: Charles U Faculty Arts, nám Jana Palacha 2, 116 38 Prague Czech Republic

SKROBELA, KATHERINE CREELMAN, music producer; b. N.Y.C., Jan. 18, 1941; d. George Douglas and Marjorie Ethel (Broer) Creelman; m. Paul John Skrobela, May 23, 1970 (dec. Feb. 1999). AB, Vassar Coll., 1962; MLS, Columbia U., 1964. Music cataloger Bklyn. Coll., 1964-71; music libr. Middlebury (Vt.) Coll., 1971-80; programmer ADT Co., N.Y.C., 1981-83; sr. cons. Marathon Software & Svcs. Inc., 1983-90; sr. programmer analyst Chase Manhattan Bank, 1990-2000; pres. Miranda Music, Inc., 1995—. Editor Music Cataloging bull., 1970-75; prodr. Blame It On My Youth: Berri Blair Sings Ballads, 1999, Karen Oberlin: My Standards, 2000. Treas., bd. dirs. Middlebury Farmers Market, 1979; dir. St. Stephen's Motet Choir, Middlebury, 1975-78. Mem. ALA, Music Libr. Assn. (chmn. com. on cataloging, rep. to ALA catalog code revision com.), Music OCLC Users Group, UFO-Cobol/XE Internat. Users Group (v.p. 1989-91), Country Dance and Song Soc. Am., Manhattan Assn. Cabarets and Clubs. Home and Office: 234 Lincoln Rd Brooklyn NY 11225-3432

SKROCKI, EDMUND STANLEY, II, health fair promoter, executive; b. Schenectady, N.Y., Sept. 6, 1953; s. Edmund Stanley I and Lorraine (Nocian) S.; m. Diane Carolyn Sittig, Sept. 6, 1976 (div. 1992); children: Carolyn, Michelle, Edmund III, Johnathan Edmund; m. Deborrah Anne

Allen, June 4, 1998 (div. Mar. 2000). AA, LaValley Coll., 1981; BA, Sonoma State U., 1982, MA, 1987; postgrad., Am. Inst. Hypnotherapy, 1988. Pres. Skrocki's Philos. Svc., Lakeview Terrace, Calif., 1971-81, Redding, Calif., 1982—; pres., CEO Skrocki's Superior Svc., Lakeview Terrace, 1971-76, Redding, Calif., 1976—; pres., CEO, promoter, prodr. Realife Expositions, 1991—; producer Realife Expo Stars Over Hollywood, 1997. Prodr. Superstars of Excellence, 2000—. Bd. govs., deacon Ch. of Universal Knowledge, 1991—. Named one of Outstanding Young Men Am., 1980. Mem. Shasta Submarine Soc. (pres. 1984—). Avocations: chess, basketball, reading, health, fitness.

SKROMME, ARNOLD BURTON, educational writer, engineering consultant; b. Zearing, Iowa, Apr. 1, 1917; s. Austin and Belle (Holmedal) S.; m. Lois Lucille Fausch, Sept. 14, 1940; children: Roger, Keith, Deborah, Erik. Agrl. Engr., Iowa State U., 1941. Engr. Firestone Tire & Rubber Co., Akron, Ohio, 1941-45, Auto Splty. Mfg., St. Joseph, Mich., 1945-46; rsch. engr. Pineapple Rsch. Inst., Honolulu, 1946-50; asst. chief engr. John Deere, Ottumwa, Iowa, 1950-55; chief engr. John Deer Spreader Works, East Moline, Ill., 1955-70; mgr. value engring. John Deere Harvester Works, East Moline, 1970-84; writer and cons. East Moline, 1984—; cons. to corps., 1984—. Author The 7-Ability Plan, 1989; The Cause and Cure of Dropouts, 1998; holder 44 patents. Chmn. Citizens Adv. Com., Moline, 1964-66. Mem. Am. Soc. Agrl. Engrs. (v.p. 1965-68, Honor Roll 1997). Lutheran. Avocation: research on children's education. Home: 2605 31st St Moline IL 61265-5309

SKROMNE-KADLUBIK, GREGORIO, nuclear medicine physician; b. Mexico City, Apr. 9, 1939; s. Benjamin and Ana (Kadlubik) Skromne; m. Blanca Sofia Castillo, Nov. 15, 1964; 1 child, Jorge David. MD, Nat. U., 1962, MSc, 1972. Prof. physiology Nat. U., Mexico City, 1965—; rschr. Fac. Medicine, Mexico City, 1972—; coord. Nuclear Medicine Nat. Polytech. Inst., 1978-88; head nuclear medicine ISSSTE, Mexico, 1974-88, Health Sec., 1969—; cons. Nat. U., Chiapas, Mex., 1982—, Renal Ctr., Mexico City, 1988—. Recipient G. Soberon medal Health Sec. of Mex., 1994. Mem. AAAS, N.Y. Acad. Scis., Assn. Latino Am. Medicina Nucler. Achievements include invention of first inadiated vaccine against Hepatitis B; patent of visualization in vivo of steroid receptor in homono-dependence tumor. Office: Nat U of Mexico, Faculty Medicine, Mexico City Mexico

SKROTZKI, WERNER, physics educator; b. Hann.-Muenden, Germany, Oct. 21, 1950; s. Heinrich and Grete (Rost) S.; m. Vivian Puschel, Aug. 20, 1981; children: Sophia Maura, Richard Odin. Diploma in physics, U. Goettingen, Germany, 1977, PhD in Physics, 1980. Scientific asst. U. Goettingen, Germany, 1980-82, 85-89; assoc. NYU, Ithaca, N.Y., 1983-84; prof. Tech. U., Dresden, Germany, 1993—. Contbr. articles to profl. jours. Heisenberg fellow, 1990-92. Mem. German Phys. Soc., German Materials Rsch. Soc. Avocation: tennis. Home: Zum Turmberg 24, 01474 Goennsdorf Germany Office: Tech U Dresden, 01062 Dresden Germany

SKROWACZEWSKI, STANISLAW, conductor, composer; b. Lwow, Poland, Oct. 3, 1923; came to U.S., 1960; s. Pawel and Zofia (Karszniewicz) S.; m. Krystyna Jarosz, Sept. 6, 1956; children: Anna, Paul, Nicholas. Diploma faculty philosophy, U. Lwow, 1945; diploma faculties composition and conducting, Acad. Music Lwow, 1945, Conservatory at Krakow, Poland, 1946; L.H.D., Hamline U., 1963, Macalester Coll., 1972; L.H.D. hon. doctorate, U. Minn. Guest condr. in Europe, S.A., U.S., 1947—; Composer, 1931—, pianist, 1928—, violinist, 1934—, condr., 1939—; permanent condr., music dir. Wroclaw (Poland) Philharmonic, 1946-47, Katowice (Poland) Nat. Philharmonic, 1949-54, Krakow Philharmonic, 1955-56, Warsaw Nat. Philharmonic Orch., 1957-59, Minnesota Orch., 1960-79; prin. condr., mus. adviser Halle Orch., Manchester, Eng., 1984-91; musical advisor St. Paul Chamber Orchestra, 1986-87; first symphony and overture for orch. written at age 8, played by Lwow Philharm. Orch., 1931. Composer: 4 symphonies Prelude and Fugue for Orchestra (conducted first performance Paris), 1948, Overture, 1947 (2d prize Szymanowski Concours, Warsaw 1947); Cantiques des Cantiques, 1951, String Quartet, 1953 (2d Prize Internat. Concours Composers, Belgium 1953), Suite Symphonique, 1954 (first prize, gold medal Composers Competition Moscow 1957), Music at Night, 1954, Ricercari Notturni, 1978 (3d prize Kennedy Center Friedheim Competition, Washington), Concerti for Clarinet and Orch., 1980, Violin Concerto, 1985, Concerto for Orch., 1985, Fanfare for Orch., 1987, Sextett for Oboe, Violin, Viola, Orchestra, 1980, String Trio for Violin, Viola, 1990, Triple Concerto for Violin, Clarinet, Piano, Orchestra, 1992, Fantasie per Tre (Flute, Oboe, Cello), 1993, Chamber Concerto, 1993, Passacaglia Immaginaria for Orch., 1995, Musica a Quattro for Clarinet, Violin, Viola, Cello, 1998; also music for theatre, motion pictures, songs and piano sonatas, English horn concerto; rec. by Mercury, Columbia, RCA Victor, Vox, EMI, Angel. Recipient nat. prize for artistic activity Poland, 1953; First prize Santa Cecilia Internat. Concours for Condrs., Rome, 1956, Comdr. Cross, Polonia Restituta, 1999. Mem. Union Polish Composers, Internat. Soc. Modern Music, Nat. Assn. Am. Composers-Condrs., Am. Music Center. Office: Orch Hall 1111 Nicollet Mall Minneapolis MN 55403-2406

SKRUTVOLD, KRIS ALLEN, physics educator; b. L.A., Apr. 7, 1957; s. Curtis Lee and Gloria Jean (Paulson) S.; m. Mary Bernadette Schwarzrock Edward, Feb. 3, 1994; children: Jennifer, Jessica, Jackie, Sammie, Brennan. BS in Physics and Chemistry, Bemidji (Minn.) State U., 1980, MS in Physics and Chemistry, 1988. Cert. Physics tchr., Minn., Mass. Advanced Physics and K-12 Sci. coord. Detroit Lakes (Minn.) Pub. Schs., 1981-94; AP/IB Physics instr. and K-12 Sci. coord. Internat. Sch. of Prague, Czech Republic, 1994-97; IB Physics instr. Cairo Am. Coll., 1997-98; AP & IB Physics instr. Taipei Am. Sch., Taiwan, 1998—; sci. cons. Detroit Lakes Pub. Schs., 1981-94, Moorhead (Minn.) State U., 1989-94. Contbr. articles to profl. jours. Recipient Moorhead State U. Global Ambassador award, 1999, W.K. Kellogg Found. grant, 1994, Creative and Innovative Tchr. award, Minn. Prins. Assn., 1993, Christa McAuliffe Found. Fellowship award, 1992. Mem. NSTA, Am. Assn. Physics Tchrs., Phi Delta Kappa (webmaster, historian Taiwan chpt. 1998—). Republican. Lutheran. Avocations: building Physics apparatus, writing curricula, designing web sites, reading. E-mail: krismary@ficnet.net. Office: Taipei Am Sch, 800 Chung Shan N Rd Sec 6, Taipei 111 ROC, Taiwan

SKRYABINA, ZINA EDUARDOVNA, chemist, researcher; b. Ekaterinburg (Sverdlovsk), Russia, Nov. 23, 1957; came to U.S., 1996; d. Eduard Vladimirovich and Eya Diomidovna (Zapadnova-Lapshakova) Lipova; m. Dmitry Alexandrovich Skryabin, July 13, 1978 (div. Dec. 1985); 1 child, Anna Dmitrievna; m. David Alan Wilkinson, Aug. 15, 1996; 1 child, Jay Alexander. MSc in Chemistry, Ural State Tech. U., Ekaterinburg, 1980, PhD in Chemistry, 1988. Cert. chem. engr. and technologist. Sci. rschr. Ural divsn. Inst. Chemistry, SSSR Acad. Scis., Ekaterinburg, 1980-88; leader rschr. group Ural divsn. Inst. Organic Synthesis, Russian Acad. Scis., Ekaterinburg, 1988—; dir. Alfa-Omega, Ltd., Ekaterinburg, 1994-96. Contbr. over 40 articles to sci. jours., including Jour. Fluorine Chemistry; patentee in field. Recipient young scientist's prize Ural divsn. SSSR Acad. Scis. and Sverdlovsk Regional Union Sci. and Edn., 1988, 89; grantee Internat. Sci. Found., Washington, 1993, Russian Found. Fundamental Rsch., 1995. Avocations: gardening, skiing, symphonic music. Home: 662 Stillwaters Dr SW Marietta GA 30064-2469

SKRYSHEVSKY, VALERI ANTONOVICH, laboratory administrator; b. Kiev, Ukraine, Dec. 8, 1955; s. Anton Francevich and Eugenia Pavlovna (Polianskaya) S.; m. Maria Gavriilovna Gorbatenko; children: Irina, Ruslan. MSc with honours, Shevchenko U., Kiev, Ukraine, 1978, PhD in Physics and Math., 1984. Jr. rsch. worker Shevchenko U., 1981-86, rsch. worker, 1986-88, sr. rsch. worker, 1988-92, chief of lab., radiophysics dept., 1992—; invited rschr. Comenius U., Bratislava, Slovakia, 1989; invited prof. Ecole Centrale, Lyon, France, 1997, INSA de Lyon, 1998; dep. dir. Centre Emocon, Kiev, 1995—; mem. expert coun. Ministry of Sci., Ukraine, 1996—. Author: Infrared Spectroscopy of the Semiconductor Structures, 1991, also articles. NATO Linkage grantee, 1994, 96; Ministry of Sci. grantee, 1992, 96, 97. Mem. Ukrainian Phys. Soc., Sci. Coun. Sensors of Acad. of Sci. Ukraine. Avocations: Internet, soccer, tennis. Office: Shevchenko U/Radiophysics, 64 Volodijmirska, 01033 Kiev Ukraine

SKRZYPCZAK, HENRYK ALFONS, historian; b. Berlin, Brandenburg, Germany, May 3, 1926; s. Johann Joseph and Gertrude (Krawczyk) S.; m. Dagmar Jubitz Skrzypczak, Aug. 4, 1953; 1 child, Michaela. PhD, Free U., Berlin, 1956. Journalist, editor Pub. Otto H. Hess Ullstein, Berlin, 1956-58; sec. Berlin Hist. Commn., 1958-65, sec. gen., 1965-74, section head rsch., 1974-87, pensioner, 1988—; mem. exec. com. Berlin His. Commn., 1961-96; chmn. Circle for Promotion of Berlin: Germany Archives and Libraries Concerning History of Labour, 1991-92; hon. com. Internat. Conf. of Labour Historians, 1997—. Author: (book) Marx, Engels, Revolution, 1968; editor Internationale Wissenschaftliche Korrespondenz Zur Geschichte Der Deutschen Arbeiterbewegung, 1966-99, (with others) Jahrbuch Fuer Die Geschichte Mitted-and Ostdeutschlands, 1968-81. With Military, Italy, 1944. Social Democratic Party. Roman Catholic. Home: Carstennstr 36, 12205 Berlin Germany

SKUBIS, JERZY ZBIGNIEW, electrical engineer, educator; b. Olkusz, Poland, Jan. 6, 1950; s. Antoni and Irena (Glanowska) S.; m. Maria Stanislawa Wawer, June 16, 1974; children: Anna, Grazyna, Wojciech. MSc in Engring., Silesian Tech. U., Gliwice, Poland, 1974; PhD, Silesian Tech. U., 1981, Habilitation, 1987. From asst. to prof. Technical U. Opole, Poland, 1974-97; prof. Technical U. Opole, 1997—, head dept., 1983-84, vice rector rsch., 1990-96, 99—. Author: Acoustic Emission for Insulation Testing of Electrical Equipment, 1993, 2d edit., 1998; co-author 9 books; contbr. articles to profl. jours. Mem. N.Y. Acad. Sci., Soc. Elec. Engrs. Poland, Polish Soc. Theoretical Applied Electrotechnics, Club Cath. Intelligensia. Avocations: traveling, gardening. Home: Hubala 12A 601, 45 263 Opole Poland Office: Tech U Opole, Mikotajczyka 5, 45 233 Opole Poland

SKUBISZEWSKI, KRZYSZTOF, Polish government official, educator, arbitrator; b. Poznań, Poland, Oct. 8, 1926. Dr jur., Adam Mickiewicz U., Poznan, 1950, docent, 1960; diploma in higher European studies, U. Nancy, France, 1957; LLM, Harvard U., 1958; hon. doctor, U. Ghent, U. Mainz, U. Torino, U. Liège, U. Geneva. Vol. asst., jr. asst., adj. faculty Adam Mickiewicz U., 1948-56, asst. prof., docent, 1956-73, pro dean Law Faculty, 1961-63; prof. Inst. Law Polish Acad. Scis., Warsaw, 1973-96; mem. Social Coun. Cath. Primate Poland, 1981-84; mem. consultative coun. at chmn. of Coun. State, Warsaw, 1986-89; min. fgn. affairs Govt. of Poland, Warsaw, 1989-93; pres. Iran-U.S. Claims Tribunal, The Hague, The Netherlands, 1994—; chmn. Coun. Fgn. Policy, Warsaw, 1996—; vis. scholar Sch. Internat. Affairs, Columbia U., N.Y.C., 1963-64; guest prof. U. Geneva, 1971, 79; vis. fellow All Souls Coll., Oxford (Eng.) U., 1971-72; mem. legal scis. com. Polish Acad. Scis., 1981—; hon. prof. Bucarest U., 1993—; judge ad hoc Internat. Ct. Justice, The Hague, 1994—; chmn. France-Netherlands Arbitration Tribunal, 2000—. Co-author: Manual of Public International Law, 1968, Individual Rights and the State in the Foreign Affairs, 1977, also others. Decorated Gold Cross of Merit, Knight's Cross and Grand Cross Order of Polonia Restituta, Order of White Eagle (Poland), Ordine Piano (Vatican), Grand Officer Legion of Honour (France), Gran Cruz Orden al Merito (Chile), Grand Cross Order of Merit (Germany), Order of Diplomatic Merit (South Korea), Cross of Merit, Hungary. Mem. Inst. Internat. Law, Am. Soc. Internat. Law, French Soc. for Internat. Law, German Soc. Internat. Law, Oxford Soc., Codrington Club (U.K.), Gray's Inn (hon. bencher, London), Inst. de France (corr.). Mem. Solidarity Union. Home: Parkweg 3 B, 2585 JG The Hague The Netherlands Office: Iran-US Claims Tribunal, Parkweg 13, 2585 JH Den Haag The Netherlands

SKUDRA, ALBERTS, civil engineer, educator; b. Riga, Latvia, July 12, 1925; s. Martin and Emilia Skudra; m. Maiga Perne, Jan. 12, 1950; children. Cand. tech. scis., Riga Polytech. Inst., 1956; D of Tech. Scis., Inst. Mechanics Moscow, 1967; dr. habil. sci. ing., Riga Tech. U., 1992. Rschr., head lab. Inst. Civil Engring., Riga, Latvia, 1956-63; head lab. Inst. Polymer Mechanics, Riga, 1963-75; dept. head Riga Tech. U., 1975-94, prof., 1994—. Author: Kriechen und Zeitstandverhalten verstärkter Plaste, 1975; author, editor: Handbook of Composites, 1985, Structural Analysis of Composite Beam Systems; mem. editl. bd. Jour. Composite Materials, 1977-84, Mechanics of Composite Materials, 1988—. Home: 18 Birznieka Upisa St Fl 21, LV-1050 Riga Latvia Office: Riga Tech Univ, 1 Kalku St, LV-1658 Riga Latvia

SKULACHEV, VLADIMIR PETROVICH, research biochemist and bioenergeticist; b. Moscow, Feb. 21, 1935; s. Peter and Nadezda Skulachev; m. Ksenia Myasoedova, July 15, 1960 (div. May 1973); 1 child, Tatyana; m. Inna Severina, June 23, 1973; children: Maxim, Innokenty, Konstantin. Grad. in biochemistry, Moscow State U., 1957, postgrad., 1957-60. Jr. scientist Moscow State U., 1960-65, head dept. bioenergetics Inst. Physico-Chem. Biology, 1965—, dir. Inst., 1973—. Author: Respiratory Chain Oxydative Phosphorylation, 1962, Energy Accumulation by the Cell, 1969 (A.N. Bach prize 1970), Membrane Bioenergetics, 1988. Recipient state prize Govt. of USSR, 1975. Mem. USSR Acad. Scis., USSR Biochem. Soc. (pres. 1989—), Acad. Europaea. Avocations: badminton, jogging, skiing. Home: Vorobyevy Gory MGU M-176, 117234 Moscow Russia Office: Moscow State U Belozersky, Inst Physico-Chem Biology, 119899 Moscow Russia

SKULSKI, LECH PIOTR, chemistry educator; b. Warsaw, June 29, 1931; s. Boleslaw and Kazimiera (Stodulska) S.; m. Elżbieta Maria Świerżewska, Dec. 3, 1955; children: Wojciech, Magdalena. MSChE, Poly. U., Warsaw, 1955; D in Tech. Sci., Poly. U., 1960, PhD, 1966. Sr. asst. dept. chemistry Poly. U., 1955-61, adj., 1961-66, asst. prof., 1966-68; asst. prof., head chair applied chemistry Tech. Mil. Acad., Warsaw, 1969-73; asst. prof., head phys. chemistry lab. dept. pharmacy Med. Univ., Warsaw, 1974-85, extraordinary prof., head chair, and lab. organic chemistry, 1985-93, ordinary prof., head chair and lab. organic chemistry, 1993—; vis. prof. U. Egypt, 1993; head Main Polish Com. Chemistry Olympiad, 1974-81. Co-author 4 textbooks; contbr. over 150 articles to profl. jours. Mem. Solidarity, 1980—, Warsaw City Coun., 1990-98. Grantee Ford Found., 1962-63; recipient award Polish Acad. Scis., 1969, Ministerial awards Ministry Edn., Ministry Health and Social Welfare, 1979, 91, 92, Golden Cross of Merit, 1979, Cross of Polonia Restituta, 1984, Medal Nat. Edn., 1976. Mem. Polish Chem. Soc., Forum on Iodine Utilization Japan. Mem. Polish Union of Liberty. Roman Catholic. Avocation: yachting. Fax: (4822) 8226843. E-mail: lskulski@farm.amwaw.edu.pl. Home: Apt 5, 3/5 Zwycięzców St, 03-936 Warsaw Poland Office: Med Univ Warsaw, 1 Banacha St, 02-097 Warsaw Poland

SKURNICK, JOAN HARDY, biostatistician; b. Mount Vernon, N.Y., Dec. 8, 1942; d. Glendon Day and Ethel Marie (Pritchett) Hardy; m. David Skurnick, Dec. 27, 1964; children: Jennifer Frances, Sarah Skurnick Moskovitz. BA, Wellesley Coll., 1964; MA in Math., U. Calif., Berkeley, 1966, PhD in Biosts., 1983; MS in Biometry, Temple U., 1975. Mathematician Lawrence Livermore (Calif.) Lab., 1964-65; statistician SRI Internat., Menlo Park, Calif., 1978-83; biostatistician coop. studies program VA, Menlo Park, 1983-86; instr. biostats. UMD-N.J. Med. Sch., Newark, 1986-89, asst. prof., 1989-96, assoc. prof., 1996—; mem. scientific adv. bd. and institutional rev. bd. Jersey Cmty. Rsch. Initiative, Newark, 1988—. Contbr. 45 articles to profl. jours. Mem. pub. edn. com. Am. Cancer Soc., Brunswick, N.J., 1991-94. mem. Am. Statis. Assn., Am. Pub. Health Assn., Soc. for Clin. Trials, N.J. Wellesley Club. Democrat. Avocations: choral singing, hiking, chamber music. Home: 4 Grimes Ter Montville NJ 07045-9774 Office: UMD-NJ Med Sch 185 S Orange Ave # F14 Newark NJ 07103-2757

SKURNIK, JOAN IRIS, special education evaluator, educator, consultant; b. Bklyn., Apr. 14, 1935; d. Benjamin and Dorothy (Blum) Hessel; m. Maurice Skurnik, Sept. 1, 1955 (div. Jan. 1982); children: Jennifer, Jonathan. BA magna cum laude, CCNY, 1973; MA, Columbia U., 1975. Cert. tchr. nursery to 6th grade, N.Y. Pvt. practice remedial therapist, diagnostician N.Y.C., 1974—; ednl. cons. in learning disabilities The Calhoun Sch., N.Y.C., 1977-85, The Collegiate Sch., N.Y.C., 1984-87, Riverdale (N.Y.) Country Sch., 1989-90, Abraham Joshua Heschel Sch., N.Y.C., 1991—; cons. Holy Rosary Sch., Pitts., 1976; mem. planning com. Ethical Culture Schs., N.Y.C., 1980-82; presenter, conf. and workshop coord. in field. Mem. NOW, Internat. Reading Assn., Internat. Dyslexia Soc. (N.Y. br. bd. mem. 1985-88), Profl. Colleagues Group, Phi Beta Kappa, Planned Parenthood (N.Y.C.), Appalachian Mountain Club (N.Y.C.). Avocations: archaeology, hiking, traveling, reading, theatre.

SKUTNABB-KANGAS, TOVE ANITA, sociolinguistics researcher; b. Helsinki, Finland, July 6, 1940; d. Erik Anders and Aura Kaarina (Voutila) Skutnabb; m. Tero Tapio Kangas, June 25, 1961 (div. 1978); children: Ilka Elina Kangas, Kea Krista Kangas; m. Robert Henry Lawrence Phillipson, Jan. 7, 1983. BA, Helsinki U., 1962, MA, 1965, PhD, 1976; Advanced Doctorate, Roskilde U., Denmark, 1987. Cert. tchr., Finland. Tchr. Swedish lang. arts and social Sci. Espoon Ammattikoulu, Finland, 1964-66; rsch. asst. dept. Nordic langs. Harvard U., 1967-68; tchr. Swedish and German Rudolf Steiner Sch., Helsinki, 1968-69; tchr. Swedish Comprehensive Schs., Helsinki, 1969-70; from asst. to asst. prof. dept. Nordic langs. U. Helsinki, 1970-76; rsch. asst. Finnish Acad., 1978-80; rschr. Danish Social Scis. Rsch. Coun., 1980-81; dir. rsch. project Finnish Acad., 1984-88, Swedish Humanities Rsch. Coun., 1987; assoc. prof. Copenhagen U., 1990-93, Roskilde U., 1995-97; reader in edn. U. Ostrobothnia, Åbo Akademi, Vasa, Finland, 1993—; programme coord. Finnish Radio, Sch. Radio Langs. Sect., 1970-71; guest rschr. U. Lund, Sweden, 1974, 77, 78, Roskilde U., 1979—; mem. World Univ. Svc., Denmark, 1982—; bd. dirs. Inst. Migrations-und Rassismusforschung, Hamburg, Germany; mem. adv. bd. U. Calif. Ednl. Rsch. Ctr., Fresno, 1994-98; mem. internat. adv. com. Lang. Policy Rsch. Ctr., Bar-Ilan U., Israel, 1995—; mem. expert mission to Slovakia and Hungary OSCE High Commr. on Nat. Minorities, 1996; mem. adv. bd. Ctr. Conflict Resolution, 1994—; v.p. Terralingua Partnerships for Linguistic and Biol. Diversity, 1998—; mem. adv. bd. Eur. Ctr. Min. Issues, 1999—; lectr. in field. Mem. editl. bd. Nordic Minority Rsch. Jour., 1973-93, Jour. Multilingual and Multicultural Devel., 1982-96, Discourse and Soc., 1989—, Lang. Problems and Lang. Planning, 1997—; referee jours.; series editor Multilingualism and Linguistic Diversity; author: Bilingualism or Not: the Education of Minorities, 1984, (with Jim Cummins) Minority Education-From Shame to Struggle, 1988, (with Robert Phillipson) Multilingualism for All, 1995, (with Phil Benson and Peter Grundy) Language Rights, 1998, (with Miklós Kontra, Robert Phillipson, Tove Skutnabb-Kangas & Tibor Várady, Linguistic Genocide in Education-Or Worldwide Diversity and Human Rights?, 1999; pub. more than 300 books and sci. articles. Mem. Finnish Assn. Applied Linguistics (sec. 1970-72, bd. dirs. 1970-72, 75-76), Norden Assn. (chair cultural policy com. 1970-72, chair lang. policy com. 1970-79, v.p. Helsinki bd. 1971-79, ctrl. Nordic bd. 1973-79), Nordic Assn. Immigrant and Minority Rschrs. (bd. dirs. 1981-86), Elverum Namibia Assn., Danish Assn. Applied Linguistics (bd. dirs. 1984-86), Internat. Assn. Applied Linguistics (pres. sci. commn. lang. and edn. in multilingual settings 1984-93), Internat. Sociol. Assn. (bd. dirs., v.p. rsch. com. on ethnic, race and monority rels. 1986-93), Internat. Assn. Study of Racism (bd. dirs. 1991-98), Internat. Network Rschs. on Linguistic Human Rights, Danish Com. Human Rights for Kurds (bd. dirs. 1991—), Critical Rsch. into Text/Talk, Info. and Comm. in Soc. Internat. Found. (bd. dirs. 1994—), Assn. Finnish Lit. (corr. mem. 1989—). Avocations: linguistic human rights, linguistic imperialism, multilingual education, ecological farming, links between biodiversity and linguistic and cultural diversity. E-mail: tovesk@babel.ruc.dk. Office: Roskilde Univ, Dept Langs and Culture, DK-4000 Roskilde Denmark

SKUTNIK, BOLESH J., optics scientist, lay worker, lawyer; b. Passaic, N.J., Aug. 19, 1941; s. Boleslaw Stanley and Helen Marie (Dzierzynska) S.; m. Phyllis Victoria Wojciechowski, Sept. 2, 1967 (div. July 1991); children: Pam, Janeen, Todd; m. Anita Marie Bacon, Aug. 2, 1997. BS, Seton Hall U., 1962; MS, Yale U., 1964, PhD, 1967; JD, U. Conn., 1995. Bar: N.Y. 1996, Conn. 1996. Chief scientist Ensign Bickford Coating Co., Simsbury, Conn., 1979-91; prin. B.J. Assocs., New Britain, Conn., 1991-97, West Hartford, Conn., 1997—; patent atty., rsch. scientist Fiberoptic Fabrications, Inc., East Longmeadow, Mass., 1995-97; dir. rsch., dir. patents and licensing Sci. Fiberoptic Fabrications, Inc., East Longmeadow, Mass., 1997—; lector, mem. parish coun. St. Catherine of Siena, West Simsbury, Conn., 1980-85, St. Maurice, New Britain, Conn., 1985-2000, St. Thomas Apostle, West Hartford, 2000—; chmn., del. synod Archdioces of Hartford, Conn., 1990-96; chmn. parish Holy Family Retreat League, New Britain, 1989-2000; pres. Enbic Employees Credit Union, Simsbury, 1988-91; asst. prof. chemistry Fairfield U., Conn., 1973-79. Patentees in field; contbr. articles to profl. jours. Interviewer Yale Alumni Schs. Com., L.I. and Hartford, Conn., 1969—; mem. Yale Assn. of Yale Alumni Rep., New Britain Club, 1997-2000. Mem. ABA (subcom. chair 1993, 94, 96), Conn. Bar Assn., N.Y. State Bar Assn., Conn. Patent Lawyers Assn., Am. Intellectual Property Lawyers Assn., Nat. Coun. Intellectual Property Lawyers Assn., Soc. Photo-optical Engrs., Am. Ceramic Soc., (coord. symposium 1991), Materials Rsch. Soc. (chair symposium 1987-89), Am. Chem. Soc. (alt. coun. 1988-90, sect. chair 1994, vice chair 1993, bd. dirs. 1985—), Porsche Club Am. (various positions Conn. Valley region), Yale Club New Britain (dir. 1994—), Yale Alumni (assoc.). Democrat. Roman Catholic. Home: 51 Banbury Ln West Hartford CT 06107-1102 Office: Fiber Optic Fabrications Inc 515 Shaker Rd East Longmeadow MA 01028-3126

ŠKVOR, ZDENĚK, acoustical engineering educator; b. Pisek, Czech Republic, Aug. 21, 1935; s. František and Ružena (Hrachová) S.; m. Hana Jilková, Dec. 4, 1963; children: Daniela, Jan. Diploma in engring., Czech Tech. U., Prague, 1958, DSc, 1985. Asst. prof. Czech Tech. U., 1958-74, 1974-86, prof. acoustics, 1986—. Author: Vibrating Systems, 1991. Recipient Gold medal French Acoustical Soc., 1995, medal of 1st grade Ministry of Edn. of Czech Republic, 1996, Gold medal Brussels EUREKA, 1997. Mem. Acoustical Soc. Am., Audio Engring. Soc., Czech Acoustical Soc. (pres. 1992-99, v.p. 1999—). Home: Myslikova 22, 12000 Prague 1, Czech Republic Office: Czech Tech U, Technická 2, 16627 Prague 6, Czech Republic

SKVORECKY, JOSEF VACLAV, English literature educator, novelist; b. Nachod, Czechoslovakia, Sept. 27, 1924; arrived Can., 1969; s. Josef Karel and Anna (Kurazova) S.; m. Zdenka Josefa Salivarova, Mar. 30, 1958. Ph.D., Charles U., Czechoslovakia, 1951; LHD (hon.), SUNY, 1986; postgrad., Masaryk U., 1991, U. Calgary, 1992, U. Toronto, 1992. Vis. lectr. U. Toronto, Ont., Can., 1969-70; writer-in-residence U. Toronto, 1970-71, assoc. prof., 1971-75, prof. English, 1975-90; prof. emeritus, 1990—; lectr. on lit. topics Voice of Am., 1973—; adv. to Pres. Vaclav Havel, 1990. Editor: Sixty Eight Publ. Corp., Toronto, 1972—; author: The End of the Nylon Age, 1967, Republic of Whores, 1969, The Miracle Game, 1972, The End of Lieutenant Boruvka, 1975, The Swell Season, 1975, The Bass Saxophone, 1979, The Cowards, 1980, The Return of Lieutenant Boruvka, 1980, The Engineer of Human Souls, 1984, Miss Silver's Past, 1985, Dvorak in Love, 1986, The Bride from Texas, 1992, Headed for the Blues, 1996, The Two Murders in My Double Life, 1996, Narratio Questi, 1998; short story collections: The Menorah, 1964, The Life of High society, 1965, The Mournful Demeanor of Lieutenant Boruvka, 1966, A Babylonian Story, 1967, The Bitter World, 1969, Sins for Father Knox, 1973, Oh, My Papa! 1972, The Edenvale Stories, 1996; plays: The New Men and Women CBC Radio 1977, God in Your House, 1980 (1st prize Multicultural Theatre Festival Hamilton 1980), Two Murders in My Double Life, 1997, Narratio Questi, 1998, (with Z. Salivarova) Brief Encounter, With Murder, 1999; films: The Tank Battalion, 1991, The Swell Season, 1994, Eine kleine Jazzmusik, 1996, Poe and the Death of a Beautiful Girl, 1997, The Legend of Emoke, 1998, The Detective Agency, 2000; essays: Reading Detective Stories, 1965, They-Which Is We, 1968, All the Bright Young Men and Women, 1972, Working Overtime, 1979, Talkin' Moscow Blues, 1989. Decorated Order of the White Lion; apptd. mem. Order of Can., 1992; recipient Neustadt Internat. prize for lit., U. Okla., 1980, Gov. Gen. Can.'s award, 1985, lit. prize Echoing Green Found., 1990, Czech Republic's State Prize for Lit., 1999. Fellow Royal Soc. Can.; mem. Can. Writers' Union, Authors' League Am., Crime Writers Can., Mystery Writers Am., The Internat. PEN Club, Can. br. Czechoslovak Nat. Assn. Can. (mem. Presidium), Coun. Free Czechoslovakia (mem. Presidium), Order of Can. Progressive Conservative. Roman Catholic. Avocation: swing music. Home: 487 Sackville St, Toronto, ON Canada M4X 1T6

SKVORTSOVA, VERONIKA IGOREVNA, health facility administrator, neurologist; b. Moscow, Nov. 1, 1960; d. Igor A. and Svetlana B. (Kudrjavskaja) S.; m. Givi G. Nadarejshvili, Feb. 25, 1984; 1 child, George. PhD, Russian State Med. U., Moscow, 1983; MD, 1988, Dr. Sci., 1994, Prof., 1997. Cert. Ministry of Health of Russian Fedn. Neurologist Russian State Med. U., Moscow, 1983-88; asst. prof. dept. neurology and neurosurgery Russian State Med. U., 1989-94; assoc. prof. dept. neurology and neurosurgery, 1994-97, prof. dept. neurology and neurosurgery, 1997—, head neuro intensive care unit dept. neurology and neurosurgery, 1991-97, head neurology and neurosurgery, 1997—. Grantee Pres. of Russia Health of Russian Population New Neuroprotective Therapy Medicine, 1997, Russian Found. Fundamental scis., 1998, Ministry of Health Russian Fedn., 1999. Fellow Salzburg-Cornell Found.; mem. European Stroke Coun., European Fedn. Neurol. Socs., All-Russian Soc. Neurologists (main sci. sec. bd.), Rus-

sian Stroke Assn. (v.p.), Korsakoff J. Neurology and Psychiatry (main sci. sec.). Avocations: music, opera, poetry. Home: Namiotkina str 29-1-125, 117420 Moscow Russia Office: Russian State Med U Clinic Neurology & Neurosurgery, Ostrovitjanova str 1, 117437 Moscow Russia

SKWARA, ERICH WOLFGANG, novelist, poet, educator, literary critic; b. Salzburg, Austria, Nov. 4, 1948; came to U.S., 1975, naturalized, 1981.; s. Alois Gaigg and Hermine Maria Skwara; m. Victoria Anne Dufresne, July 10, 1974 (div. Mar. 1978); m. Gloria Elaine Winniski, June 8, 1978; children: Gabriella Maria, Alexandra Felicitas. BA, U. Paris VII, 1970; MA, Salzburg U., 1972; PhD, N.Y. State U., Albany, 1985. Instr. U. Md., Balt., 1975-77; freelance author Balt. and Paris, 1977-82; vis. lectr. Georgetown U., Washington, D.C., 1982-84; freelance author Salzburg, 1984-86; prof. humanities, comparative lit. and German San Diego State U., 1986—; dep. editor-in-chief for cultural affairs Die Welt, Berlin, 1993; cultural and lit. corr. for a number of German and Austrian newspapers and media, 1979—; worldwide readings and lecture tours. Author: (novels) Black Sails, 1979, 99, The Cool Million, 1990, Tristan Island, 1992, Die Heimlichen Könige, 1995, Plague in Siena, 1994, 95, Ice on the Bridge, 1997, Versuch einer Heimkehr, 1998, Nach dem Norden, 1998, The Angel of Death, 1998, Anruf aus Rom, 1999, Die Toten der Place Baudoyer, 2000; others; translated (from English and French to German) works by T. Williams, Thomas Wolfe, J.J. Rousseau, Gustave Flaubert, others; own works translated into English, French, Japanese, Arabic, others. Mem. Internat. PEN Club, PEN Ctr. of German Speaking Authors Abroad (bd. dirs. 1985—), PEN Ctr. of Austria, PEN Ctr. of France. Roman Catholic. Avocations: fine wines, travel, walking. Office: San Diego State U Dept Classics Humanities San Diego CA 92182 also: Suhrkamp Verlag, Linden Str 29-35, D60325 Frankfurt am Main Germany also: 264 rue Saint Honore, F75001 Paris France

SKWARCZYNSKI, HENRYK ADAM (HENRYK SKWAR), writer; b. Lodz, Poland, Aug. 13, 1952; came to U.S., 1980; s. Zdzislaw and Stanislawa Ewa (Laszczyk) S.; m. Egle Juodvalkis, Sept. 2, 1989. MA, U. Warsaw, 1977; postgrad., Polish Acad. Sci., 1978-80, Sorbonne U. Free-lance writer N.Y.C., 1980-81, Voice of Am., Washington, 1981-82; instr. Defense Lang. Inst., Monterey, Calif., 1982-84; staff writer Libertas, Paris, 1984-86; free-lance writer Radio Free Europe, Munich, 1987-95; writer Chgo., 1995—. Author: Man in a Cleft, 1979, the Anguish of Becoming American, 1989, Sweeney Among the Nightingales, 2000; editor-in-chief Ephemeron, 1974-75; contbr. short stories to mags. Activist Solidarity Movement, 1980-89. Rotary Club grantee, 1982, Hoover Inst. grantee, 1985. Avocation: travel in Africa.

SKWEYIYA, ZOLA S. T., South African government official. LLD, U. Leipzig, Germany, 1978. Min. of pub. svcs. and adminstrn. Govt. of South Africa, Pretoria, 1994-99, min. of welfare and population devel., 1999—. Mem. nat. exec. com., mem. polit., legis. and governance coms. African Nat. Congrss. Mem. Assn. Pub. Adminstrn. & Mgmt. (elected mem. nat. working com. 1994—, dep. pres. commonwealth 1994-98, pres. commonwealth 1998). Address: Hallmark Bldg, Vermeulen St Private Bag X 885, Pretoria 1 South Africa*

SKWIERSKY, PAUL, accountant; b. N.Y.C., Aug. 14, 1925; s. Abraham and Dora (Rainer) S.; m. Gloria Evelyn Lederman, Dec. 27, 1947; children: Janet S., Denise C. Skwiersky Cohen. BS, NYU, 1948. CPA, N.Y., N.J. Mng. ptnr. Benjamin Nadel & Co., N.Y.C., 1942-87, Skwiersky, Alpert & Bressler, N.Y.C., 1987—; bd. dirs. Philip & Janice Levin Found., North Plainfield, N.J., Darcy Found., Inc., N.Y.C., 1980-87, Levin Mgmt. Corp., North Plainfield, Allstate Constrn. Corp., North Plainfield; panelist, arbitrator Am. Arbitration Assn., N.Y.C. Dir. Birchwood Park Civic Assn., Syosset, N.Y., 1962. Sgt. U.S. Army, 1943-46. Mem. Fiber Producers Credit Assn., Textile Distbrs. Assn., Inc., N.Y. Credit & Fin. Mgmt. Assn., N.Y. State Soc. CPAs, Masons (master 1977-79), Fountains of Palm Beach Country Club. Avocations: reading, travel, golf. Office: Skwiersky Alpert Bressler 462 7th Ave New York NY 10018-7606

SKWIRUT, JOHN LAURENCE, computer company executive; b. Phila., July 27, 1965; s. Bernard Ludwig Skwirut and Lauretta Stella Gonsowski; m. Patricia Gail Sell, Nov. 23, 1991; children: Katie, William, Rachel. Cert. internat. bus., U. Copenhagen, 1986; BA in Econs. with honors, Franklin and Marshall Coll., 1987; cert. in bus., U. Pa., 1990, MS in Engring., 1994. Fin. mgr. mfg. ctr. Computer Scis. Corp., Integrated Sys. Divsn., Moorestown, N.J., 1988-90; sr. pricing specialist Computer Scis. Corp., Integrated Sys. Divsn., Moorestown, 1991-94, pricing mgr., 1995-96, program control mgr., 1997-98; global dir. pricing Computer Scis. Corp., Chem. and Energy Group, Newark, 1998—; bd. dirs., fin. advisor FAMCare, Bridgeton, N.J. Class pres. Danish Internation Study Program, U. Copenhagen, 1986. Mem. Wharton Club Phila. Republican. Avocations: basketball, sailing. E-mail: jskwirut@jaguarsystems.com. Fax: 302-391-7033. Home: 128 Old Kings Hwy Salem NJ 08079-2014 Office: Computer Scis Corp Chem and Energy Group 400 Commerce Dr Newark DE 19713-6802

SKYBAK, JAN OLAF, packaging company executive; b. Barcelona, Spain, June 4, 1954; s. Jens Olaf and Ruth Christine (Schanke) S.; children: Katrina, Helen. BA in Bus. Orgn., Heriot-Watt U., Edinburgh, Scotland, 1977; M in Internat. Mgmt., Am. Grad. Sch. Internat. Mgmt., Phoenix, Ariz., 1978. Asst. divsn. contr. Gerresheimer Glas (divsn. Owens-Ill., USA), Dusseldorf, Germany, 1980-83, mktg. mgr., 1983-86; dir. sales & mktg. BSN Vidrio Espana (divsn. Danone Group), Madrid, 1987-98; v.p. sales & mktg. BSN Glass, Paris, 1999—. Mem. Spain/Norway C. of C. (pres. 1996-99). Avocations: foreign languages, golf, running, tennis, travelling. Home: 15 Ave du President Wilson, 75116 Paris France Office: BSN Glass Pack, 31 Rue Henri Rochefort, 75017 Paris France

SKYLLAS-KAZACOS, MARIA, electrochemical engineer, educator; b. Kalymnos, Greece, Oct. 26, 1951; arrived in Australia, 1954; d. George Michael and Kalliope (Mamakas) S.; m. Michael Nicholas Kazacos, Mar. 7, 1976; children: Nicholas, George, Anthony. BS in Indsl. Chemistry with 1st class honors, U. New South Wales, 1974, PhD in Chem. Tech., 1979. Chartered profl. engr., chartered chemist. Mem. tech. staff Bell Labs., Murray Hill, N.J., 1978-79; Queen Elizabeth fellow U. New South Wales, Sydney, 1980-81, lectr. chem. engring. and indsl. chemistry, 1982-84, sr. lectr., 1985-87, assoc. prof., 1987-92, prof., 1993—; cons. Comalco Aluminum, Australia, 1985-92, Unisearch Ltd., Sydney, 1986—, Pinnacle VRB, 1998—. Patentee All vanadium redox battery, flexible conducting plastic electrodes; contbr. articles to profl. jours.; author 6 books. Patron indsl. chemistry group Royal Australian Chem. Inst., 1993—; mem. electric vehicles adv. com. New South Wales Energy Authority, 1982-85; mem. syllabus adv. com. sci. 7-12 New South Wales Bd. Studies, 1995-98. Rsch. grantee Australian Rsch. Coun., 1985—, Nat. Energy Rsch. Corp., 1992, New South Wales Office Energy, 1989—; recipient Chemeca medal Instn. of Chem. Engrs., 1998, Whiffen medal, 1997. Fellow Royal Australian Chem. Inst., Instn. Engrs. Australia; mem. Order of Australia. Office: U New South Wales, Sch Chem Engring Indsl Chem, Sydney 2052, Australia

SKYLLSTAD, KJELL MÜLLER, musicology educator; b. Hammerfest, Norway, June 30, 1928; s. Rolf Johan and Helene Marie (Müller) S.; m. Turid Solberg, Sept. 26, 1987; 1 child, Ingrid Helene. BA, Emmanuel Missionary Coll., Mich., 1950; MA in Edn., Walla Walla Coll., 1952; MA in Music, Oslo U., 1960. Cert. in edn. and music. From asst. prof. to assoc. prof. musicology Oslo U., 1962-93, prof. musicology, 1994—; music critic Oslo Press, 1966—; rsch. coord. Oslo U.-Kelaniya U., Norway and Sri Lanka, 1992-95; rsch. cons. Rikskonsertene, Oslo, 1989-95; rsch. fellow Music Acad., Graz, Austria, 1972-75. Co-editor: (dictionary) Familieboken, 1972-76, (rsch. series) Edvard Grieg Collected Works, 1977-93. Vice chmn. Soc. Dem. Party Culture Workers Assn., 1967-69; cofounder Assn. for Internat. Forest and Water Studies, 1987. Recipient Rsch. award Kelaniya U., 1998; rsch. fellow Deutsche Akademische Austauschdienst, 1959-60; rsch. grantee Nat. Humanistic Rsch. Found., 1972-75. Mem. Internat. Soc. for Music Edn., Internat. Assn. Intercultural Edn., Internat. Soc. for Study of European Ideas (exec. com.). Office: U Oslo Dept Music & Theater, PB 1017 Blindern, 0315 Oslo Norway

SLAATTÈ, HOWARD ALEXANDER, minister, philosophy educator; b. Evanston, Ill., Oct. 18, 1919; s. Iver T. and Esther (Larsen) S.; m. Mildred Gegenheimer, June 20, 1951; children: Elaine Slaatte Quaddur, Mark, Paul. A.A., Kendall Coll., 1940; B.A. cum laude, U. N.D., 1942; B.D. cum laude, Drew U., 1945, Ph.D., 1956; Drew fellow, Mansfield Coll., Oxford (Eng.) U., 1949-50. Ordained to ministry Meth. Ch. as elder, 1943. Pastor Detroit Conf. United Meth. Ch., 1950-65; assoc. prof. systematic theology Temple U., 1956-60; vis. prof. philosophy and religion McMurry Coll. (now named McMurry U.), 1960-65; prof. dept. philosophy Marshall U., Huntington, W.Va., 1965-89, prof. emeritus, 1989—, chmn. dept., 1966-81, mem. grad. council, 1970-73, mem. research bd., 1974-76, mem. acad. standards and policy com., 1975-77, research grantee, 1976, 77; mem. bd. Campus Christian Center, 1973-75; prof. ethics St. Leo (Fla.) Coll., 1993; lectr. Traverse City (Mich.) State Hosp., 1966-71, Am. Ontoanalytical Assn. internat. conf., Acapulco, Mex., 1970, World Congress Logotherapy, San Diego, 1980, other orgns. Author: Time and Its End, 1962, Fire in the Brand, 1963, The Pertinence of the Paradox, 1968, The Paradox of Existentialist Theology, 1971, Modern Science and the Human Condition, 1974, The Arminian Arm of Theology, 1977, The Dogma of Immaculate Perception, 1979, Discovering Your Real Self, 1980, The Seven Ecumenical Councils, 1980, The Creativity of Consciousness, 1983, Contemporary Philosophies of Religion, 1986, Time, Existence and Destiny, 1988, Critical Survey of Ethics, 1988; co-author: The Philosophy of Martin Heidegger, 1983, Religious Issues in Contemporary Philosophy, 1988, Our Cultural Cancer and Its Cure, 1995, A Re-Appraisal of Kierkegaard, 1995, Plato's Dialogues and Ethics, 1999, A Purview of Wesley's Theology, 2000; contbr. Analecta Frankliana, 1981; gen. editor: (series) Contemporary Existentialism; contbr. to theol. and philos. jours. Mem. W.Va. Conf. United Meth. Ch., 1966-87, ret., 1987; bd. dirs. Inst. for Advanced Philos. Research, 1979-90; chmn. bd. dirs. Salvation Army of Huntington, W. Va.; courtesy prof. U. South Fla., 1993-99. Recipient Outstanding Educators of Am. award, 1975, Profl. Excellence award Faculty Merit Found., State of W.Va., 1986, U. N.D. Found. award, 2000; named to Honorable Order of Ky. Colonels, W.Va. Ambassador of Good Will; named Internat. Man of Yr., 1993; NSF fellow, 1965, Benedum Found. rsch. grantee, 1970, NSF rsch.-grantee, 1965, 71. Mem. W.Va. Philos. Assn. (pres., 1966-67, 83-84), Am. Philos. Assn., AAUP, Am. Acad. Religion. Home: 300 Kildaire Woods Dr Apt 211 Cary NC 27511-7710

SLABY, ADOLF, internal medicine educator; b. Prague, Czech Republic, Apr. 27, 1932; s. Adolf and Marie (Císařová) S.; m. Jana Suchomelová, Jan. 28, 1967; children: Jiří, Jana. MD, Charles U., 1956, PhD, 1965. Physician Dept. Medicine Charles U., 1958-65; rschr. Inst. Cardiology, Mexico City, Mex., 1965-66; asst. prof. Dept. Medicine Charles U., 1966-80, prof. internal medicine, 1984—; prin. rschr. Inst. of Hygiene, Prague, 1980-84; prof. bioethics Charles U., 1990—. Author: Regulation of the Renin Secretion in Hypertension, 1982, Pastoral Medicine and Healthcare Ethics, 1991. Mem. Czech Med. Soc. (Award 1982). Avocation: music, tourism. Office: 4th Dept Medicine Charles U, U Nemocnice 2, 12808 Prague 2, Czech Republic

SLACK, DONALD CARL, agricultural engineer, educator; b. Cody, Wyo., June 25, 1942; s. Clarence Ralbon and Clara May (Beightol) S.; m. Marion Arline Kimball, Dec. 19, 1964; children: Jonel Marie, Jennifer Michelle. BS in Agrl. Engring., U. Wyo., 1965; MS in Agrl. Engring., U. Ky., 1968, PhD in Agrl. Engring., 1975. Registered profl. engr., Ky., Ariz. Asst. civil engr. City of Los Angeles, 1965; research specialist U. Ky., Lexington, 1966-70; agrl. engring. advisor U. Ky., Tha Phra, Thailand, 1970-73; research asst. U. Ky., Lexington, 1973-75; from asst. prof. to assoc. prof. agrl. engring. U. Minn., St. Paul, 1975-84; prof. U. Ariz., Tucson, 1984—, head dept. agrl. and biosystems engring., 1991—; vis. prof. dept. atmospheric scis. Fed. U. Paraiba, Campina Grande, Brazil, 1997; tech. advisor Ariz. Dept. Water Resources, Phoenix, 1985—, Tucson active mgmt. area, 1996—; cons. Winrock Internat., Morrilton, Ark., 1984, Water Mgmt. Synthesis II, Logan, Utah, 1985, Desert Agrl. Tech. Systems, Tucson, 1985—, Portek Hermosillo, Mex., 1989—, World Bank, Washington, 1992—, Malawi Environ. Monitoring Project, 1996, Mex. Inst. for Water Tech., 1997, Nat. Agrl. Rsch. Inst. La Serema, Chile, 1997; dep. program support mgr. Rsch. Irrigation Support Project for Asia and the Near East, Arlington, Va., 1987-94; mem. adv. team Cearan Found. for Meteorology and Hydrology, Fortaleza, Brazil, 1995—; mem. internat. adv. panel Matrou Resources Mgmt. Project, World Bank, Egypt, 1996—. Contbr. articles to profl. jours. Fellow ASCE (Outstanding Jour. Paper award 1988), Am. Soc. Agrl. Engrs. (Ariz. sect. Engr. of Yr. 1993); mem. Am. Geophys. Union, Am. Soc. Agronomy, Soil Sci. Soc. Am., Am. Soc. Engring. Edn., SAR, Brotherhood of Knights of the Vine (master knight), Sigma Xi, Tau Beta Pi, Alpha Epsilon, Gamma Sigma Delta. Democrat. Lutheran. Achievements include 3 patents pending; developer of infrared based irrigation scheduling device. Avocations: hunting, camping, hiking, model railroading. Home: 9230 E Visco Pl Tucson AZ 85710-3167 Office: U Ariz Agrl Biosystems Engring Tucson AZ 85721-0001

SLADE, ADRIAN CARNEGIE, marketing professional; b. London, May 25, 1936; s. George Penkivil and Mary Albinia (Carnegie) S.; m. Susan Elizabeth Forsyth, June 22, 1960; children: Nicola, Rupert. BA in Law, Cambridge U., 1959. Writer J. Walter Thompson Co., London, 1959-64; creative dir. S.H. Benson Ltd., London, 1964-71; mng. dir. Slade Monico Bluff, London, 1971-75, Slade Bluff & Bigg, London, 1975-86, Slade Hamilton Fenech Ltd, London, 1986-91. Candidate Liberal Party, 1966, 74, 87, pres., 1987-88; mem. Gt. London Coun., 1981-86; joint pres. Social and Liberal Dems., 1988, v.p., 1989. Decorated comdr. Order of Brit. Empire. Avocations: theatre, piano playing, songwriting, photography. Home: 28 St Leonards Rd, London SW14 7LK, England

SLADE, TUILOMA NERONI, Western Samoan diplomat; b. Western Samoa, Apr. 8, 1941; m. Jeanne Schoenberger; 1 child, Priscilla Penni. Cert. barrister, solicitor. Pvt. practice as lawyer Wellington, New Zealand, 1967-68; legal counsel atty.-gen.'s office Govt. of Western Samoa, 1969-73, atty. gen., 1976-82; parliamentary counsel, 1973-75; asst. dir. legal divsn. Commonwealth Secretariat, London, 1983-93; amb., permanent rep. of Western Samoa UN, 1993—; leader Western Samoa delegation 3d UN Conf. Law of Sea, 1973-76; chmn. Pacific Forum Shipping Line, 1978-82; acting chief of justice Western Samoa, 1980-82; counsel to Constl. Commn. Inquiry on Banaban People in Republic of Kiribati, 1984; chmn. 1st South Pacific Law Conf., Western Samoa, 1986; legal cons. South Pacific Forum Fisheries Agy., Solomon Islands, 1989. Joint-editor Commonwealth Law Bull.; mem. editorial com. Law Reports Commonwealth; compiler, editor Western Samoa Law Reports; contbr. articles to profl. jours. UNITAR fellow Hague Acad. Internat. Law and UN Legal Office, 1971, CIDA fellow, 1973. Mem. New Zealand Law Soc., Western Samoa Law Soc., Commonwealth Lawyers' Assn. Office: Embassy of Western Samoa 800 2d Ave Ste 400J New York NY 10017*

SLADEK, JAN, mechanical engineer; b. Trencin, Czechoslovakia, Aug. 23, 1952; s. Pavol and Anna (Zatkova) S.; m. Nadia Materna, Nov. 21, 1981. Master's, Tech. U., Zilina, Slovakia, 1976; PhD, Slovak Acad. Sci., Bratislava, 1981, DSc in Engring., 1990. Rschr. Inst. Constrn. and Architecture Slovak Acad. Scis., Bratislava, 1980-84, sr. rschr., 1984-92, vice-dir., 1992-97, dir., 1997—; lectr. Slovak Tech. U., Bratislava, 1992-94, U. Zilina, 1992—. Co-author: Stress Analysis By Boundary Integral Equations, 1985 (Lit. Found. prize 1985), Stress Analysis By Boundary Element Methods, 1989, Singular Integrals in Boundary Element Methods, 1998 (Lit. Found. prize 1998). Mem. ASME, Internat. Soc. Boundary Elements. Home: Na Revine 17, 83101 Bratislava Slovakia Office: Inst Constrn Architecture, Slovak Acad Scis, 84220 Bratislava Slovakia

SLADEK, VLADIMIR, physicist; b. Martin, Czechoslovakia, Jan. 29, 1954; s. Pavel and Anna (Zatkova) S.; m. Olga Dursova, Apr. 26, 1986; 1 child, Vladimir. D of Natural Sci., Comenius U., Bratislava, Slovakia, 1978; PhD, Slovak Acad. Sci., Bratislava, 1984, DSc, 1990. Rschr. Inst. Constrn. and Architecture Slovak Acad. Scis., Bratislava, 1984-87, sr. rschr., 1987-95, dept. head, 1995—; lectr. Slovak Tech. U., Bratislava, 1991-94, U. Zilina, 1992-2000. Co-author: Stress Analysis By Boundary Integral Equations, 1985 (Lit. Found. prize 1985), Stress Analysis By Boundary Element Methods, 1989, Singular Integrals in Boundary Element Methods, 1998 (Lit. Found. prize 1998). Home: Samorinska 33, 82106 Bratislava Slovakia Office: Inst Constrn Architecture, Slovak Acad Scis, 84220 Bratislava Slovakia

SLAFF, ALLAN PAUL, naval officer, university administrator, educator, entrepeneur; b. Mt. Vernon, N.Y., Feb. 2, 1923; s. Frank Alfred and Augusta Raye (Scher) S.; m. Mary Lee Schaeffer; children: Randolph Elliott, Valerie Anne. BS, U.S. Naval Acad., 1944; postgrad., U.S. Naval Post Grad Sch., 1949-50, U.S. Naval War Coll., Newport, R.I., 1959-60, Harvard U. Commd. ensign USN, 1944, advanced through grades to capt., 1965, WWII Battleship Mass. Fast Carrier TF, 1944-46, personal aide to CNO Adm. Arleigh Burke, 1950-51, spl. security officer commd. in Korean War Navy, comdr. USS Lester, Davis, Luce, Albany, 1957-70, sr. naval advisor to Vietnam Navy, 1967-68, ret., 1970; dean, mem. faculty Bus. Sch. Harvard U., Boston, 1970-80; chmn. Luzerne Co. News Co., Wilkes Barre, Pa., 1980-86, LABSPHERE, Inc., N. Sutton, N.H., 1983-94; cons. Harvard Bus. Sch., 1980-84. Contbr. numerous articles to profl. jours. bd. dirs. numerous schs., clubs, civic and polit. orgns. Decorated Legion of Merit, Bronze Star, Nat. Order of Vietnam, numerous other decorations U.S. Navy, 1941-70; recipient Disting. Grad. award Wyoming Sem., Kingston, Pa., 1990. Mem. Port Royal Club (sec. bd. dirs.), The Naples Yacht Club (treas., bd. dirs.), Royal Poinciana Golf Club, Port Royal Property Owners Assn. (bd. dirs.), Lake Sunapee Country Club, Lake Sunapee Yacht Club, Baker Hill Golf Club. Republican. Episcopalian. Avocations: golf, travel, photograprhy, gardening. Home: 4151 Gulf Shore Blvd N # 601 Naples FL 34103-2292 also: PO Box 1836 27 Highland Rdg New London NH 03257-4321

SLAGLE, RICHARD CORBIN, cardiologist; b. Centralia, Ill., Oct. 15, 1939. BSEE, U. Okla., 1962, MD, 1969; MMM, Tulane U., 1998. Diplomate Am. Bd. Internal Medicine, Am. Bd. Cardiovascular Disease. Systems engr., Project Apollo N.Am. Aviation, 1962; intern U. Okla. Hosps., 1969-70; resident in medicine Duke Med. Ctr., Durham, N.C., 1970-71, fellow in cardiology, 1971-73; pres., chmn. Preferred Physician, Inc., 1985-88; med. dir. St. Francis Hosp., Tulsa, Okla., 1993-97; exec. v.p. St. Francis Hosp., Tulsa, 1994-97; pres., mng. physician Cardiology Tulsa, 1992-95; chief med. officer St. Francis Hosp., Tulsa, Okla., 1997-99, sr. v.p., 1997-99; bd. dirs. St. Francis Hosp., Tulsa, 1984-97; clin. asst. prof. U. Okla.; pvt. practice cardiology, Tulsa, 1973—; pres. Tulsa Med. Edn. Found., 1998-2000; bd. dirs. Laureate Psychiat. Clinic and Hosp., 1990-97; pres. bd. dirs. Tulsa Med. Edn. Found., 1998-2000; mem. faculty Horty Springer Seminars, Complete Course for Med. Staff Leaders, 1997—. With U.S. Army, 1962-64. Fellow ACP, Am. Coll. Cardiology (gov. Okla. 1993-96); mem. Am. Coll. Physician Execs., Am. Heart Assn. (fellow clin. coun.), Alpha Omega Alpha. Office: Cardiology Tulsa 6151 S Yale Ave Ste 400 Tulsa OK 74136-1902

SLAIHEM, AMEER ABDULLAH, career officer; b. Madina Munuwara, Saudi Arabia, July 7, 1959; s. Abdullah Ahmed Slaihem; Noaf, Nada, Scarlett, Gazzi. Diploma in Acctg., Valencia C.C., Orlando, Fla., 1981; B in Acctg., U. N. Fla., Jacksonville, 1984, cert. of Merit in Cost, 1984. Cert. computer mgmt. Commd. lt. Royal Saudi Airforce, 1984, advanced through grades to lt. col., 1998, base level contract officer, 1984-85, central level contract officer, 1985-88, contract officer, 1988-90, capt., 1989-94, O&M squadron asst. comdr., 1990-93, O&M squadron comdr., 1993-98; ret., 1998. pres. Soccer Club, U. N. Fla., 1983-84, social dir. Alpha Sigma Pi, 1983-84, pre. govt. students, 1984, pres. Internat. Student Assn., 1984. Decorated Desert Storm Shield, 1992. Avocations: flying scuba diving, marina sport, volleyball, athletics, soccer playing. Office: Royal Saudi Airforce, PO Box 113, Dhahran Airport 31932, Saudi Arabia also: 5815 SE Federal Hwy Stuart FL 34997-7883

SLAIS, KAREL, analytical chemist, researcher; b. Praha, Czech Republic, Dec. 18, 1948; s. Bohumil and Jarmila (Matelova) S.; m. Vlasta Prochazkova, Feb. 28, 1976; 1 child, Karel. MS, Masaryk U., Brno, Czech Republic, 1973; PhD, Inst. Analytical Chemistry, Brno, 1979, DSc, 1992. Rsch. scientist Inst. Analytic Chemistry, Brno, 1979-89, sr. scientist, 1989-93, chief scientist, 1993—, asst. prof., 1998—. Contbr. articles to profl. jours. Home: Hornikova 2, 62800 Brno Czech Republic Office: Inst Analytic Chem Acad Scis, Veveri 97, 611 42 Brno Czech Republic

SLAMET, YOHAN ROBERTUS, communications executive; b. Bogor, Indonesia, Jan. 9, 1950; s. Budi Jakobus Beng Hoey and Elly Magdalena (Gin Nio) S.; m. Maria Magdalena Sin Lian, Jan. 20, 1993. BA, U. Jayabaya, 1976; MA, Sch. Ministry, San Diego, 1980; M in Orgnl. Communications, Inst. PPM, Jakarta, 1985; M in Mgmt., Prasetia Mulia Inst., 1987. Gen. coord. Cath. Student Assn., Jakarta, 1974-77; cons. Archbishop of Jakarta, 1975-78; store mgr. C.V. Toko Buku Tropen, Jakarta, 1982-85; mgr. Tropen, Jakarta, 1985-88; gen. mgr. Panca Sakti Jaya, Jakarta, 1988-92; vice dir. Persatuan Abadi, Jakarta, 1992—; cons. Cath. Charismatic Renewal, Jakarta, 1983-88; mng. distbr. Asian Productivity Orgn., Tokyo, 1985-97; bd. dirs. Tropen Groups. Contbr. articles to profl. jours. Chmn. Cath. Student Movement, Jakarta, 1974; chmn. Ecumenical Cath. Commn., Jakarta, 1988. Avocations: reading, writing, photography, painting, recreation. Home: Jalan Harpa II Blok AA # 12, Jakarta Utara 14250, Indonesia Office: Persatuan Abadi, Jalan Pasar Baru 113, Jakarta Pusat 10710, Indonesia

SLANGAL, LOVELLA JOEANN, artist; b. Tonti, Ill., July 29, 1923; d. Lawrence Henry and Ruth LouVisa (Dudley) Smith; m. Neil Richard Hill, Feb. 2, 1940 (div. Nov. 1947); children: Lawrence L. Hill, Victor P. Hill; m. Harold Jones, Nov. 28, 1947 (dit. 1954); children: Joan Carole Jones, Bruce Olin Jones; m. Frank Jerry Slangal, Jan. 27, 1968 (div. 1981). seamstress, 1965. Pres. Sage Brushersart, Bassett, Nebr., 1973-78, Ainsworth (Nebr.) Art Guild, 1980-81; scout leader Boy Scouts Am., St. Charles, Ill., 1957-61; chaplain Profl. Bus. Women, St. Charles, 1959-60; cert. nurses aid Sr. Ctr. Ainsworth, 1981-85. Named Artist of the Mo. Ainsworth (Nebr.) Art Guild, 1983—. Avocations: gardening, auctions.

SLANINA, ZDENEK, physical and theoretical chemist, educator; b. Policka, Czech Republic, Aug. 21, 1948; s. Zdenek and Bozena Slanina; m. Jirina Vaneckova, Dec. 31, 1975; 1 child, Jan. RNDr, Charles U., Prague, Czech Republic, 1971; CSc, Czech. Acad. Sci., Prague, 1975. Scientist Czechoslovak Acad. Sci., Prague, 1975-80, sr. scientist, vice head dept. chem. reactivity, 1980-86, head dept. quantum chemistry, 1987-90, sr. prin. scientist, 1987-91; prof. Toyohashi U. Tech., Japan, 1996—; vis. scholar Hokkaido U., Sapporo, Japan, 1985-86, MPI fuer Chemie, Mainz, Germany, 1990-91, U. Ariz., Tucson, 1991-92; vis. prof. U. Ulm, Germany, 1987, Limburg U., Diepenbeek, Belgium, 1992-93, Nat. Chung-Cheng U., Chia-Yi, Taiwan, 1993-96. Author: Theoretical Aspects of the Phenomenon of Chemical Isomerism, 1981, Advances in Quantum Chemistry, Vol. 13, 1981, Contemporary Theory of Chemical Isomerism, 1986, Reviews in Computational Chemistry, vol. 8, 1996, Computational Studies of New Materials, 1998, Advances in Strained and Interesting Organic Molecules, Vol. 7, 1999; contbr. revs. and more than 400 articles to profl. jours.; mem. editl. bd. Understanding Chem. Reactivity, 1984—, Fullerene Sci. and Tech., 1992—; editor GardenGate, 1991-96, co-editor Molecular Complexes in Earth's, Planetary and Cometary Atmospheres, 1992—. Japan Soc. for Promotion of Sci. fellow, 1985-86; Alexander von Humboldt Found. fellow, 1990-91; Nat. Sci. Coun. grantee, Taipei, 1993-95; named Young Outstanding scholar Czechoslovakia Acad. Sci., 1980. Fellow World Assn. Theoretically Oriented Chemists; mem. N.Y. Acad. Scis., Internat. Soc. for Mathematical Chemistry, Internat. Soc. for Theoretical Chem. Physics, Materials Rsch. Soc., Electrochemical Soc.

SLAPAL, JOSEF, mathematician, educator, researcher; b. Brno, Czech Republic, Dec. 21, 1955; s. Josef and Marie (Strakova) S.; m. Ivana Rybarova, Feb. 18, 1984; children: Marketa, Klara. MS, Masaryk U., Brno, 1980, RNDr, 1982, PhD, 1992. Asst. prof. math. Tech. U., Ostrava, Czech Republic, 1981-86; assoc. prof. math. Tech. U., Brno, Czech Republic, 1986-2000; prof. math. Tech. U., Brno, 2000—; external tchr. Masaryk U., 1987-89, Free U. Berlin, 1994-95. Contbr. articles to profl. jours. Fellow Deutscher Akademischer Austauschdienst; recipient Dr. Jiri Nehnevajsa Meml. award U. Pitts., 1999; German Acad. Scis. rsch. scholar, 1994-95; Grant Agy. of Czech republic grantee, 1995-97. Mem. Union Czech Mathematicians and Physicists, N.Y. Acad. Scis., Am. Math. Soc., Nat. Geog. Soc. Avocations: sports, nature, literature, theatre. Home: Milady Horakove 36, 60200 Brno Czech Republic Office: Tech U Brno Dept Math, Technicka 2, 616 69 Brno Czech Republic

SLATER, BARRY HARTLEY, philosophy educator; b. Keighley, Eng., Oct. 28, 1936; arrived in Australia, 1976; s. Hartley and Mabel (Simon) S. BA, Cambridge U., Eng., 1958, MA, 1965; MA, U. Kent, Eng., 1974, PhD, 1976. Tchr. math. Barnes & Wallis Pvt. Sch., London, 1961-67,

Highbury & Islington Comprehensive, London, 1967-68, Bradford (Eng.) Grammar Sch., 1968-71; lectr. in philosophy U. Western Australia, Perth, 1976-82, sr. lectr., 1982-97, assoc. prof., 1997—, sr. rsch. fellow, 2000. Author: (books) Prolegomena to Formal Logic, 1989, Intensional Logic, 1994, Against the Realisms of the Age, 1998; contbr. articles to profl. jours. on philosophy and logic. Avocation: playing croquet. Home: 12/18 The Avenue, 6009 Perth Australia Office: U Western Australia, Mounts Bay Rd, 6009 Perth Australia

SLATER, EDWARD CHARLES, biochemist, educator; b. Melbourne, Victoria, Australia, Jan. 16, 1917; s. Edward Brunton and Violet (Podmore) S.; m. Marion Winifred Hutley, Aug. 3, 1940; 1 child, Ann Catherine. Student, Geelong (Victoria) Coll., 1927-34; BSc, Melbourne U., 1938, MSc, 1939; PhD, ScD, Cambridge (Eng.) U., 1948, 60; DS (hon.), Southampton U., 1990; DS in Biology (hon.), Bari U., 1998. Demonstrator U. Melbourne, 1938-39; biochemist Australian Inst. Anatomy, Canberra, Australia, 1939-46; rsch. fellow Molteno Inst. Cambridge U., 1946-55; prof., dir. Lab. Biochemistry, U. Amsterdam (The Netherlands), 1955-85; hon. prof. U. Southampton (Eng.), 1985—; cons. World Bank, 1983-88. Author: BBA, Story of a Biochemical Journal, 1985; mng. editor Biochimica et Biophysica Acta, 1957—; contbr. articles to profl. publs. Named Knight of Netherlands Lion, Queen of The Netherlands, 1984. Fellow Royal Soc. London, Royal Australian Chem. Inst.; mem. Am. Soc. Biochemistry and Molecular Biology (hon.), Netherlands Biochem. Soc. (hon.), Biochem. Soc. (hon.), Japanese Biochem. Soc. (hon.), Royal Netherlands Acad. Sci., Dutch Co. of Scientists, Royal Acad. Med. Belgium (hon. fgn. mem.), Royal Swedish Acad. Sci. (fgn. mem.), Australian Acad. Sci. (corr.), Argentina Acad. Sci. (corr.), Internat. Union Biochemistry (treas. 1971-79, 99-2000, pres. 1988-91), European Molecular Biology Orgn., Royal Lymington Yacht Club. Avocations: sailing, skiing. Home: 9 Oaklands, Lymington Hants SO41 3TH, England

SLATER, JESS EVERETT, artist; b. Westfield, Mass., Dec. 31, 1910; s. Jess G. and Eva M. (Warman) S.; m. Helen E. Kozlowski, Sept. 1956. Grad. H.S., Westfield, Mass.; studied with Marco Zim, N.Y.C. Indsl. artist Hamilton Std., Windsor Locks, Conn., 1954-68. Group shows include Nat. Exhbn., Old Forge, N.Y., 1987, 89, 93, 97, New Eng. Water Color Soc. (Merit award), Water Color USA, Nat. Soc. Acrylic Painters; represented in numerous permanent collections. Mem. Midwest Water Color Soc. (Members award 1989). Democrat. E-mail: bracreto@javanet.com. Home: 42 Pomeroy Meadow Rd Southampton MA 01073-9410

SLATER, SIR JOCK, naval officer; b. Edinburgh, Scotland, Mar. 27, 1938; s. James K. and B. (Branwell) S.; m. Ann Frances Scott, July 29, 1972; children: Charles, Rory. Student, Edinburgh Acad., 1942-50, Sedbegh, 1951-56, Britannia Royal Naval Coll., Dartmouth, England, 1956-58. Commd. sub lt. British Royal Navy, 1958, advanced through grades to admiral, 1991; various to Directorate Naval Ops., Ministry Defence, England, 1974-75; asst. dir. naval warfare British Naval Staff, 1979-82; various to asst. chief defence staff Ministry of Defence, London, 1985-87; flag officer British Royal Navy, Scotland, No. Ireland, 1987-89; naval base comdr. British Royal Navy, Rosyth, England, 1987-89; chief fleet support, mem. admiralty bd. of defence coun. British Royal Navy, 1989-90, comdr.-in-chief fleet NATO Cinco Channel/East Atlantic, 1990-93, vice-chief def. staff, 1993-95, first sealord, chief naval staff, 1995-98; bd. mgmt. Brit. Nat. Space Centre, 1986-87; dir. Vosper Thornycroft Holdings, Lockheed Martin, U.K.; comdr. HM ships Soberton, Jupiter, Illustrious; comdr. Sch. Marine Ops. Contbr. articles to profl. jours. Freeman City of London, 1989; liveryman Shipwrights Co., 1991; elder brother Trinity House, London, 1995; dep. chmn. Imperial War Mus., 2000; gov. Sedbergh Sch., 1997; other civic orgns. Named Lt. of the Victorian Order, 1971, Knight Grand Cross of the Most Honourable Order of the Bath, 1992, Dep. Lt. Hampshire, 1999; comdr. Legion of Merit, U.S., 1997. Mem. Army & Navy Club. Mem. Ch. of Scotland. Avocation: outdoors. Office: Min Def c/o Naval Sec, HM Naval Base Victory Bldg, Portsmouth PO1 3LS, England

SLATER, JOHN NINIS, journalist; b. Blackdown, Surrey, Eng., Apr. 30, 1928; s. John Nuttall and Dorothy Edith Mary (Ninis) S. Grad., Wellington Coll., Crowthorne, Berkshire, 1946. Cert. mech./elec. engr. Spl. apprentice Mather & Platt Ltd., Manchester, Eng., 1946-51, fire protection engr., 1951-53; fire protection engr. Mather & Platt Ltd., London, 1953-64; editorial asst. Railway Gazette Internat., London, 1964-66; asst. editor Railway Mag., London, 1966-70; editor Railway Mag., London, Sutton, Cheam, 1970-89; editorial cons. Railway Mag., Cheam, London, 1990—. Mem. Talyllyn Railway Preservation Soc. (editor Talyllyn News 1963-99). Ch. of England. Avocation: preservation of the Talyllyn Railway. Home: Flat One 25 Gwendolen Ave, Putney/London SW15 6ET, England Office: IPC Media Ltd, Kings Reach Twr/Stamford St, London SEI 9LS, England

SLATER, MICHAEL DAVID, communication educator; b. Mpls., May 11, 1953; s. Paul and Lillian Irene (Pollack) S.; m. Diane Borrman, Nov. 5, 1983; children: Megan Claire, Jesse Paul. BA, Columbia U., 1974; MPA, NYU, 1983; PhD, Stanford U., 1988. Cmty. coord. Ctr. for Ind. Living, N.Y.C., 1974-75; assoc. Roslyn Willett Assoc., N.Y.C., 1976-78; account supr. M.L. Schneider Assoc., N.Y.C., 1979-84; prof. Colo. State U., Fort Collins, 1988—; presenter in field. Contbr. chpts. to books and articles to profl. jours. Recipient First award NIH-Nat. Inst. on Alcohol Abuse and Alcoholism, 1992-96; grantee NIH-Nat. Inst. on Alcohol Abuse and Alcoholism, Nat. Inst. Drug Abuse, 1995—. Mem. Assn. for Edn. in Journalism and Comm., Internat. Comm. Assn. (chair elect health com. divsn.). Office: Dept Journalism & Tech Comm Colo State Univ Fort Collins CO 80523-0001

SLATER, RALPH EVAN, lawyer; b. Bklyn., July 14, 1948; s. Ralph Groff and Silvia Helen (Montanelli) S.; m. Cynthia Elaine Mahn, Aug. 29, 1970; children: Robert Evan, Andrew Montgomery, Steven Edward. AB, Princeton U., 1970; JD, U. Pa., 1973. Bar: Conn. 1973, U.S. Dist. Ct. Conn. 1984, U.S. Tax Ct. 1984, U.S. Supreme Ct. 1987. Assoc. Gregory & Adams, Wilton, Conn., 1973-79, ptnr., 1980-93; prin. Gregory & Adams P.C., 1994—, pres., 1996—; chmn. bd. The Wilton Bank, 1986—; atty. Planning and Zoning Commn., Zoning Bd. Appeals, Ridgefield, Conn., 1979-81. Chmn. bd. edn. 1st Congl. Ch., Ridgefield, Conn., 1982-84, chmn. bd. trustees, 1985-87. Mem. Conn. Bar Assn. (exec. com. estates and probate sect. 1984-86, 93-99), Western Conn. Estate and Tax Planning Coun. Inc. (dir. 1992-96). Republican. Mem. Ch. of Christ. Home: 30 Strawberry Ridge Rd Ridgefield CT 06877-6019 Office: Gregory & Adams 190 Old Ridgefield Rd Wilton CT 06897-4023

SLATER, RODNEY E., federal official; b. Tutwyler, Miss., Feb. 23, 1955; m. Cassandra Wilkins; 1 child. BS, Ea. Mich. U., 1977; JD, U. Ark., 1980. Asst. atty. gen. State of Ark., 1980-82; spl. asst. for community and minority affairs Gov. of Ark., 1983-85, exec. asst. for econ. and community programs, 1985-87; dir. intergovernmental rels. Ark. State U., 1987-93; adminstr. fed. hwy. adminstrn. U.S. Dept. Transp., Washington, 1993-97, sec., 1997—; mem. Ark. State Hwy. and Transp. Commn., 1987-93, chair, 1992-93; dep. campaign mgr., sr. traveling advisor Clinton for Pres. Campaign, 1992; dep. to chair Clinton/Gore Transition Team, 1992-93. Ark. liaison Martin Luther King, Jr. Fed. Holiday Commn., 1983-87; mem. Ark. Sesquicentennial Commn., 1986. Mem. Ark. Bar Assn. (sec.-treas. 1989-93), W. Harold Flowers Law Soc. (pres. 1985-92). Office: Office Sec Dept Transp 400 7th St SW Washington DC 20590-0001*

SLATER, TERENCE RICHARD, geography researcher, educator; b. Bromley, Kent, Eng., Nov. 23, 1946; s. Richard George and Kathleen Primrose (Keylock) S. BA, U. Hull, 1969; PhD, U. Birmingham, 1985. Lectr. in geography U. Birmingham, 1971-92, sr. lectr. in geography, 1992-95, reader in hist. geography, 1995—. Author: A History of Warwickshire, 1981, 2nd edit. 1997; editor: The Making of the Scottish Countryside, 1979, Field and Forest, 1980, The Built Form of Western Cities, 1990, Managing a Conurbation, 1996, Medieval Towns and the Church, 1998, Towns in Decline 100-1600, 2000. Chmn. Anglican Diocesan Synod, Birmingham, 1995—, Moseley Deanery Synod, Birmingham, 1992-95; mem. Anglican Bishop's Coun., Birmingham, 1993—. Fellow Royal Geog. Soc.; mem. Birmingham and Warwickshire Archaeol. Soc. (pres. 1992-95). Avocations: photography, gardening. Office: U Birmingham Sch Geography, Edgbaston, Birmingham B15 2TT, England

SLATER, WILLIAM ADCOCK, retired social services organization executive; b. Kiangsu, People's Republic China, July 26, 1933; (parents U.S. citizens); s. Paul Raymond and Daisy Roberta (Butcher) S.; m. Karen C. Crutchfield, Sept. 4, 1956; children: Kathleen Ann, Bryan Paul. BA in Sociology and History, Wichita State U., 1958; MSW, Denver U., 1960. Juvenile probation officer Hennepin County Dept. Ct. Svcs., Mpls., 1960-63, program dir., 1963-65, dir. social svcs., 1965-67; clin. dir. St. Cloud (Minn.) Children's Home, 1967-70; exec. dir. Gillis Ctr., Women's Christian Assn., Kansas City, Mo., 1970-88, mng. exec. dir., 1988-95; ret., 1995; team leader Coun. on Accreditation Svcs. for Families and Children, Washington, 1975—; presenter various child welfare confs., Okla., Kans., Mo., 1980-88; mem. Mo. Residential Treatment Task Force, Mo. Licensing Standards Task Foprce; mem. levels of care com. Kans. Dept. Social Svcs.; mem. EEO panels Fed. Exec. Bd., 1978, 79; mem. mental health tour People to People, People's Republic China, 1990. Contbr. articles to profl. jours. Mem. spkr.'s bur. United Way Kansas City, 1970—, chmn. agy. rels. com., agys. div., mem. homeless com.; mem. adv. bd. Bingham Jr. High Sch., Kansas City, 1984-86; mem. Kansas City-Xiao Sister City Com. With U.S. Army, 1953-55. Mem. NASW, Acad. Cert. Social Workers, Mo. Assn. Social Welfare, Mo. Child Care Assn. (bd. dirs. 1972-74, 84-88), Kans. Assn. Lic. Pvt. Child Care Agys., Children's Residential Treatment Assn. Kansas City (chmn.), Child Welfare League Am. (steering com. midwest region, nat. adv. coun. to exec. dir. 1976-80), U.S.-China Peoples Friendship Assn. (Kansas City chpt., bd. dirs. Midwest Region), Waldo Bus. Assn. (v.p.), Alpha Kappa Delta. Mem. Christian Ch. (Disciples of Christ). Avocations: history, photography. Home: 9328 Woodson Dr Shawnee Mission KS 66207-2437

SLATOPOLSKY, MARIO, nuclear medicine physician, political scientist; b. Buenos Aires, Apr. 30, 1938; s. Jaime Slatopolsky and Elisa Cantis; m. Eva Susana Waldman, Dec. 26, 1962; children: Viviana, Gustavo, Silvina. MD, U. Buenos Aires, 1960, PhD in Medicine, 1982; B in History, U. of the Salvador, Buenos Aires, 1986; PhD in Polit. Sci., U. Belgrano, Buenos Aires, 1991; B in Am. Geography, Ministry of Edn., Madrid, Spain, 1994, PhD in Polit. Sci. and Bus. Edn., 1995. Chief nuc. medicine Clinica Güemes, Lujan, Argentina, 1975—; dir. drugs, Med. Confederation of the Argentinian Republic, Buenos Aires, 1979-83; coord. food and drugs, Argentine Ministry of Health & Welfare, 1984-89; coord. Technol. Program of Med. Tech., Pan Am. Health Orgn., Argentina, 1987-88. Author: Reference in National Therapeutics, 1980, The Fall of Radical Governments, 1994; contbr. articles to profl. jours. (Med. Integral Cooperative Medicine Yr. award 1979). Mem. Radical Party. Jewish. Avocations: reading, travel, inventing.

SLATTENGREN, LINN, judge; b. Frankfort, Ky., Aug. 24, 1938. BA in Physics and Math., U. Minn., 1960, JD, 1964. Dir. rsch. Senate Minority, Minn., 1963; law clerk Atty. Gen. Walter Mondale, Minn., 1963; atty. pvt. practice, Minneapolis, 1964-68; co. atty. Chisago Co., Minn., 1968-76; judge dist. ct., Minn., 1976—. Writer: (newspaper column) The Law. Mem. dist. com., Boy Scouts Am. Avocations: running, kayaking, skiing, flying. E-mail: lslattengren@hotmail.com. Office: Courthouse Center City MN 55012

SLAUGHTER, DJUANIQUE NATÉ, healthcare analyst, consultant. BS in Criminal Justice, Grambling State U., 1993; MPA, Calif. State U., Dominiguez Hills, 1998. Med. clinic asst. Green Clinic, Ruston, La., 1993; pub. health intern Dept. Health and Human Svcs., Long Beach, Calif., 1997; project mgmt. specialist Scan Health Plan, Long Beach, 1998; adminstrv. asst. Salick Health Care, L.A., 1998-99; managed care report analyst Health Care Ptnrs., Torrance, Calif., 1999-2000; project mgr. Ops. Health Care Ptnrs., Torrance, 2000—; HIV/AIDS peer counselor Campus Awareness Prevention, Grambling, La., 1993. Am. scholar Grambling State U. Mem. ASPA, Am. Coll. Healthcare Execs., Healthcare Fin. Mgmt. Assn., Women in Health Adminstrn., Nat. Assn. Health Svcs. Execs., Gamma Beta Phi, Pi Alpha Alpha. E-mail: dee-dee@pacbell.net.

SLAUGHTER, DOROTHY ELIZABETH, JR., construction and engineering firm executive; b. Knoxville, Tenn., July 4, 1946; d. Elmer and Dorothy Elizabeth (Covington) Slaughter; children: William Curtis Greer, Andrew Joseph Greer, Nathan Alton Greer. BS, U. Tenn., 1969; postgrad., Sonoma State U., 1980, So. Ill. U., 1989-90, Kennedy-Western U., 1991. Vice pres. Greco, Inc., Victorville, Calif., 1975-80; substitute tchr. Fundacion Educativa, Barranquilla, Colombia, 1983-87; owner, mgr. Greer and Assocs., Houston, 1981-83, Carlinville, Ill., 1987-90; prin. Greer and Assocs., Charlotte, N.C., 1990-93; owner MMI Enterprises, Johnson City, Tenn., 1993—; vol. project mgr. design and constrn. of ch. bldg. 9th Ch. Christ Scientist, Houston, 1983. Roundtable commr., mem. tng. staff Houston area Boy Scouts Am., 1982-83, Springfield, Ill. area, 1987-90; mem. tng. staff Scouts de Colombia, 1984-87; del. Nat. Assn. Women in Constrn.; mem. Nat. Wind Tunnel Complex Team; bd. dirs. First Ch. of Christ, Johnson City, Tenn., 1998-2000; 1st v.p. Johnson City Symphony Guild, 2000—. Recipeint Cub Scout Woodbadge, Boy Scouts Am., 1983, named Master Commr. Sci., 1989. Mem. Am. Inst. Constructors, Constrn. Specifications Inst. (sec. 1992-94), Profl. Constrn. Estimators Assn. Am. (historian 1991). Avocations: golf, camping, hiking, music, knitting. Office: MMI Enterprises 129 Poplar Hill Dr Johnson City TN 37604-2324

SLAUGHTER, FREEMAN CLUFF, retired dentist; b. Estes, Miss., Dec. 30, 1926; s. William Cluff and Vay (Fox) S.; m. Genevieve Anne Parks, July 30, 1948; children: Mary Anne, Thomas Freeman, James Hugh. Student, Wake Forest U., 1944, Emory U., 1946-47; DDS, Emory U. Sch. of Dentistry, 1951. Lic. real estate broker. Practice gen. dentistry Kannapolis, N.C., 1951-89; ret.; mem. N.C. State Bd. Dental Examiners, 1966-75, pres., 1968-69, sec.-treas., 1971-74; chief dental staff Cabarrus Meml. Hosp. (now N.E. Med. Ctr.), Concord, N.C., 1965-66, 75; mem. N.C. Adv. Com. for Edn. Dental Aux. Pers.-N.C. State Bd. Edn., 1967-70; advisor dental asst. program Rowan Cabarrus C.C., 1974-76; Duke Med. Ctr. Davison Century Club. Trustee N.C. Symphony Soc., 1962-68, pres. Kannapolis chpt., 1961; mem. Cabarrus County Bd. Health, 1977-83, chmn., 1981-83, acting health dir., 1981; vice chmn. Kannapolis Charter Commn., 1983-84; mem. City Coun. Kannapolis, 1984-85; Mayor protem, Kannapolis, 1984-85; past active Boy Scouts Am., Eagle scout with silver palm. Served with USN, 1944-46, WW II, ETO, MTO. Recipient Kannapolis Citizen of Yr. award, 1982. Fellow Am. Coll. Dentists (life); mem. ADA (life), Am. Legion, Kannapolis Jr. C. of C. (v.p. 1952), Toastmasters Internat. (pres. Kannapolis chpt. 1963-64), Am. Assn. Dental Examiners (Dentist Citizen of Yr. 1975, v.p. 1977-79), So. Conf. Dental Deans and Examiners (v.p. 1969), N.C. Dental Soc. (resolution of commendation 1975), N.C. Dental Soc. Anesthesiology (pres. 1964), Southeastern Acad. Prosthodontics, So. Acad. Oral Surgery, Am. Soc. Dentistry for Children (pres. N.C. unit 1957), Internat. Assn. Dental Rsch., Cabarrus County Dental Soc. (pres. 1953-54, 63-64, 69), N.C. Assn. Professions (dir. 1976-80), Kannapolis Music Club (pres. 1962-63), Masons, Shriners, Rotary (dir. 1977-80), Omicron Kappa Upsilon, Alpha Epsilon Upsilon.

SLAUGHTER, JOHN BROOKS, former university administrator; b. Topeka, Mar. 16, 1934; s. Reuben Brooks and Dora (Reeves) S.; m. Ida Bernice Johnson, Aug. 31, 1956; children: John Brooks, Jacqueline Michelle. Student, Washburn U., 1951-53; BSEE, Kans. State U., 1956, DSc (hon.), 1988; MS in Engring., UCLA, 1961; PhD in Engring. Scis, U. Calif., San Diego, 1971; D Engring. (hon.), Rensselaer Poly. Inst., 1981; DSc (hon.), U. So. Calif., 1981, Tuskegee Inst., 1981, U. Md., 1982, U. Notre Dame, 1982, U. Miami, 1983, U. Mass., 1983, Tex. So. U., 1984, U. Toledo, 1985, U. Ill., 1986, SUNY, 1986; LHD (hon.), Bowie State Coll., 1987; DSc (hon.), Morehouse Coll., 1988, Kans. State U., 1988; LLD (hon.), U. Pacific, 1989; DSc (hon.), Pomona Coll., 1989; LHD (hon.), Alfred U., 1991, Calif. Luth. U., 1991, Washburn U., 1992. Registered profl. engr., Wash. Electronics engr. Gen. Dynamics Convair, San Diego, 1956-60; with Naval Electronics Lab. Center, San Diego, 1960-75, div. head, 1965-71, dept. head, 1971-75; dir. applied physics lab. U. Wash., 1975-77; asst. dir. NSF, Washington, 1977-79; dir. NSF, 1980-82; acad. v.p., provost Wash. State U., 1979-80; chancellor U. Md., College Park, 1982-88; pres. Occidental Coll., Los Angeles, 1988-99; co-chair Calif. Citizns Commn. on Higher Edn., 1996-99; ret., 1999; bd. dirs., vice chmn. San Diego Transit Corp., 1968-75; mem. com. on minorities in engring. Nat. Rsch. Coun., 1976-79; mem. Commn. on Pre-Coll. Edn. in Math., Sci. and Tech. Nat. Sci. Bd., 1982-83; bd. dirs. Solutia, Inc., ARCO, Avery Dennison Corp., IBM, Northrop Grumman Corp.; chmn. advancement com. Music Ctr. of L.A. County, 1989-93. Editor: Jour. Computers and Elec. Engring, 1972—. Bd. dirs. San Diego Urban League, 1962-66, pres., 1964-66; mem. Pres.'s Com. on Nat. Medal Sci., 1979-80; trustee Rensselaer Poly. Inst., 1982; chmn. Pres.'s Com. Nat. Collegiate Athletic Assn., 1986-88; bd. govs. Town Hall of Calif., 1990; bd. dirs. L.A. World Affairs Coun., 1990. Recipient Engring. Disting. Alumnus of Yr. award UCLA, 1978, UCLA medal, 1989, Roger Revelle award U. Calif.-San Diego, 1991, Disting. Svc. award NSF, 1979, Svc. in Engring. award Kans. State U., 1981, Disting. Alumnus of Yr. award U. Calif.-San Diego, 1982, Martin Luther King Jr. Nat. award, 1997; Naval Electronics Lab. Ctr. fellow, 1969-70; elected to Topeka High Sch. Hall of Fame, 1983, Hall of Fame of Am. Soc. Engring. Edn., 1993; named Kansan of Yr. by Kans. Native Sons and Daus., 1994. Fellow IEEE (chmn. com. on minority affairs 1976-80), Am. Acad. Arts and Scis.; mem. NAE, Nat. Collegiate Athletic Assn. (chmn. pres. commn.), Am. Soc. for Engring. Edn. (inducted into Hall of Fame 1993), Phi Beta Kappa (hon.), Tau Beta Pi, Eta Kappa Nu. Office: Occidental Coll 1600 Campus Rd Los Angeles CA 90041-3314

SLAVEN, GEORGINA MARY, psychologist; b. Liverpool, England, Dec. 2, 1960; d. George and Eileen (Wright) Hoggett. MA, U. Aberdeen, 1989; MSc, U. Sheffield, 1990. Chartered occupl. psychologist. Rsch. fellow The Robert Gordon U., Aberdeen, Scotland, 1990-96; higher scientific officer Inst. Naval Medicine, Alverstoke, England, 1996—. Editor: Managing the Offshore Installation Workforce, 1996; contbr. articles to profl. jours. Assoc. fellow Brit. Psychol. Soc. Avocations: visual and performing arts, walking, archaeology. Office: Inst Naval Medicine, Crescent Rd, PO12 2DL Gosport England

SLAVICK, ANN LILLIAN, art educator, arts; b. Chgo., Sept. 29, 1933; d. Irving and Goldie (Bernstein) Friedman; m. Lester Irwin Slavick, Nov. 21, 1954 (div. Mar. 1987); children: Jack, Rachel. BFA, Sch. of Art Inst. of Chgo., 1973, MA in Art History, Theory, Criticism, 1991. Dir. art gallery South Shore Commn., Chgo., 1963-67; tchr. painting, drawing, crafts Halfway House, Chgo., 1972-73; tchr. studio art Conant H.S., Hoffman Estates, Ill., 1973-74; tchr. art history and studio arts New Trier H.S., Winnetka and Northfield, Ill., 1974-80; tchr. 20th century art history New Trier Adult Edn. Program, Winnetka, 1980-81; tchr. art adult edn. program H.S. Dist. 113, Highland Park, Ill., 1980-81; rschr., writer Art History Notes McDougall-Littel Pub., Evanston, Ill., 1984-85; tchr. art and art history Highland Park and Deerfield (Ill.) H.S., 1980—; tchr. art history Coll. of Lake County, Grayslake, Ill., 1986-88; faculty chair for visual arts Focus on the Arts, Highland Park H.S., 1981-85, faculty coord. Focus on the Arts, 1987—. One woman show Bernal Gallery, 1979, U. Ill., Chgo., 1983, Ann Brierly Gallery, Winnetka, 1984; exhibited paintings, drawings, prints and constrns. throughout Chgo. area; work represented by Art Rental and Sales Gallery, Art Inst. Chgo., 1960-87, Bernal Gallery, 1978-82; group shows at Bernal Gallery; work in pvt. collections in Ill., N.Y., Calif., Ariz., Ohio. Recipient Outstanding Svc. in Art Edn. award Ea. Ill. U., 1992, Mayors award for contbn. to the arts, Highland Park, 1995. Mem. Nat. Art Edn. Assn., Ill. Art Edn. Assn. Avocations: cooking, reading, theatre. Home: 5057 N Sheridan Rd Chicago IL 60640-3127 Office: Highland Park High Sch 433 Vine Ave Highland Park IL 60035-2099

SLAVICKOVA, ALENA HANA, hematological oncology researcher; b. Bohumilec, No Bohemia, Czech Republic, Oct. 28, 1944; d. Frantisek Herman and Marie Jacova; m. Peter Thomas Klouda (div. 1970); m. Jan Slavicek; children: Renata, Irena. Magister, Charles U., Prague, Czech Republic, 1968, RNDr, 1975; PhD, Czech Acad. Scis., 1976. Rsch. asst. Czech Acad. Sci., Prague, 1968-76, rschr., 1976-92; rschr., faculty medicine Charles U., Prague, 1992—. Contbr. articles to sci. jours. including Nucleic Acid Rsch., Folia Biologica, Electrophoresis, Hybridoma, Faseb Jour., others. Mem. Czech Soc. Biochem and Molecular Biology, Prague, 1973, Czech Biotech. Soc., 1976, Acad. Women's Assn. Prague, 1993. Mem. Fedn. European Biochem. Socs. Office: Charles U 1st Dept Internal Med, U Nemocnice 2, 128 08 Prague 2, Czech Republic

SLAVIK, BOHUMIL, botanist; b. Turnov, Czech Republic, Jan. 14, 1935; s. Bohumil and Marie (Dlouha) S.; m. Zdenka Krskova, June 27, 1959; children: Renata, Jitka. PhD, Prague Acad. Scis., 1969. Asst. prof. Charles U., Prague, Czechoslovakia, 1960-64; rsch. scientist Acad. Scis., Prague, 1964—. Author: Atlas of Plant Distribution of the Czech Republic, 1986-98; editor: Flora of the Czech Republic, 1988-00; contbr. articles to profl. jours. Mem. Czech Botanical Soc. Avocations: photography, travel. Home: Konselska 25, CZ-18000 Prague 8, Czech Republic Office: Inst Botany, Acad Scis, CZ-25243 Pruhonice by Praha, Czech Republic

SLAVIK, DONALD HARLAN, lawyer; b. Milw., June 17, 1956; s. Donald Jean and Sally Ann (Croy) S.; m. Cynthia Sue Barfknecht, Jan 5, 1980. BS in Nuclear Engring., U. Wis., 1978, JD, 1981. Bar: Wis. 1981, U.S. Dist. Ct. (ea. and we. dists.) Wis. 1981. Mem. Habush, Habush, Davis & Rottier, Milw., 1981—; lectr. engring. extension U. Wis., Madison, 1985-95. Author: (with others) Anatomy of a Roof Crush Case, 1985, Seat Belt Handbook, 1987, Crashworthiness, 1989, 98; contbr. articles to profl. jours. Mem. Assn. Trial Lawyers Am. (co-chair exch. com. 1986-87, 91-93, chmn. computer law office tech. 1993-97, 2000—), Wis. Bar Assn., Attys. Info. Exch. Group (bd. dirs., exec. com. 1987—, lectr. 1987—, pres. elect 2000—), Assn. for Advancement of Automotive Medicine (sci. program com. 1996—). Office: Habush Habush Davis & Rottier Ste 2300 777 E Wisconsin Ave Milwaukee WI 53202-5381

SLAVIN, MORRIS, historian, educator; b. Kiev, Ukraine, Russia, July 11, 1913; s. Lazar and Vera (Hansburg) S.; m. Sophie Shirley Lockshin, May 28, 1913; 1 child, Jeanne Slavin Kaplan. BS, Ohio State U., 1938; MA, U. Pitts., 1952; PhD in History, Western Res. U., 1961; DHL (hon.), Youngstown State U., 1989. Tchr. Wilson H.S., Youngstown, Ohio, 1941-42, 44-61; asst. prof. Youngstown State (Ohio) U., 1961-63, assoc. prof., 1963-68, prof., 1969-81, prof. emeritus, 1981—; adj. prof. Youngstown Coll., 1948-61. Author: The French Revolution in Miniature, 1984 (award Ohio Acad. of History 1985), The Making of an Insurrection, 1986, The Hébertistes to the Guillotine, 1995, The Left and the French Revolution, 1995; contbr. articles and revs. to profl. jours. Sgt. U.S. Army, 1942-43. Fellow Inst. for Advanced Study; mem. ACLU, Am. Hist. Assn., Am. Soc. for French Hist. Studies, Amnesty Internat. Avocations: golf, theater, chess, hiking. Home: 262 Outlook Ave Youngstown OH 44504-1847 Office: Youngstown State U Dept History Youngstown OH 44555-0001

SLAVIN, THOMAS J., mechanical engineer; b. Toledo, Ohio, Oct. 26, 1948; s. Francis James and Leslie Virginia Jean; m. Laura Ann Spencer, Jan. 20, 1968; children: Sean Francis, Collen Mary Sheppard. AS in Marine Diving Tech., Santa Barbara (Calif.) City Coll., 1970; BSET in Air Conditioning and Refrigeration, Calif. Poly. State U., 1975. Registered profl. engr., Wash. Comml. diving technician Flour Ocean Svcs., Houma, La., 1971; HVAC design and svc. engr. Linford Air & Refrigeration, Oakland, Calif., 1975-78; energy mgmt. engr. Boeing Comml. Airplane Co., Seattle, 1978-84; crew systems lead engr. Boeing Def. & Space Group, Seattle, 1984-97; group support equipment engr. Boeing Comml. Space Co., Tukwila, Wash., 1997-98; instr. cost engring. Boeing Phantom Works, Seattle, 1998—; conf. vice chair Internat. Conf. on Environ. Systems, Boston, 1998, conf. gen. chair, Denver, 1999. Contbr. articles to profl. jours. Pres. Norway Meadows Home Owners Assn., Bothell, Wash., 1993. Mem. AIAA, AIChE (chair program planning com. internat. conf. 1994-97), Divers Alert Network. Avocations: scuba diving, white water rafting, sea kayaking. Office: Boeing Phantom Works 20403 68th Ave S Kent WA 98032-2399

SLAVINSKI, ANTONI DIMITROV, telecommunications executive, consultant; b. Sofia, Bulgaria, May 19, 1946; s. Dimitar Antonov and Nadejda Georgieva (Nikolova) S.; m. Andreana Ivanova Ikonomova, June 11, 1980; 1 child, Dimitar Antoniev. Grad. in Radio-electronics Engring., Tech. U., Sofia, 1969. Engr. Telecom Rsch. Inst., Sofia, 1969-72, rsch. assoc., head electromagnetic compatability divsn., 1972-86, head transmission systems dept., 1986-92; v.p., bd. dirs. Bulgarian Telecom. Co., Sofia, 1992-95; sr. cons. Telecomm. and Legal Cons., Sofia, 1995-97; pres. Com. of Posts and Telecom., Sofia, 1997—. Contbr. over 35 articles to profl. jours. Bd. trustees New Bulgarian Univ. With Bulgarian Mil., 1970. Democrat. Home: 12-16 Trakia Str, 1504 Sofia Bulgaria Office: Com Posts and Telecom, 6 Gourko Str, 1000 Sofia Bulgaria

SLAVIT, DAVID HAL, otolaryngologist; b. N.Y.C., Sept. 5, 1960; s. Leonard S. and Barbara H. (Levine) S.; m. Robin E. Feldman, July 31, 1983; children: Danielle, Evan, Roni. BS, Cornell U., 1982; MD, Mt. Sinai U., 1986. Cert. in otolaryngology. Intern Mayo Clinic, Rochester, Minn., 1986-87, resident in otolaryngology, 1987-91; with Lenox Hill Hosp., N.Y.C.; asst. prof. Health Sci. Ctr.-SUNY Downstate; cons. Juilliard Sch. Music, N.Y.C., 1994-99; dir. Ames Vocal Dynamics Lab., N.Y.C., 1998-99. Author, editor: (book) Essentials of Otolaryngology, 1993; author: (books) Voice Disorders, 1995, Rhinologic Diagnosis and Treatment, 1996, Systemic Disease of the Nasal Airway, 1993; contbr. articles to profl. jours. Mem. AMA, Am. Acad. Otolaryngology-Head and Neck Surgery, Am. Acad. Facial Plastic and Reconstructive Surgery, Am. Rhinologic Soc.

SLAVOV, STEFAN VASSILEV, chemistry educator, researcher; b. Shoumen, Bulgaria, Sept. 13, 1942; arrived in Can., 1994; s. Vassil Stefanov and Ivanka Georgieva (Guenova) S.; m. Joulieta Vergilova Abrasheva, Dec. 17, 1978; children: Ivaylo, Vladislav. BSChemE, MSChemE, Sofia (Bulgaria) Tech. U., 1968, PhD in Chem. Engring., 1975. Rsch. engr. Chem. Enamel Plant, Shoumen, Bulgaria, 1968-71; asst. prof. dept. chemistry K. Preslavski U., Shoumen, Bulgaria, 1975-85, assoc. prof. dept. chemistry, 1985-94; vis. prof. dept. chem. engring. U. Alberta, Edmonton, Can., 1994-96, rsch. assoc. dept. chem. engring., 1996—; vice dean dept. sci. and math. K. Preslavski U., 1986-88, dean, 1988-91; prof. chemistry Inst. Chem. Tech. and Biotech., Razgrad, Bulgaria, 1986-94; lectr. chemistry Pedagogical Coll., Silistra, Bulgaria, 1988-92; spkr. in field. Contbr. articles to profl. jours.; patentee in field. Founder anti-communist movement Union of Dem. Forces, Shoumen, 1989-92. 1st lt. Bulgarian Artillery, 1960-62. Recipient DAAD award Max-Plank-Inst., Göttingen, Germany, 1983-84, Indian Coun. Rsch. Visitor award, Delhi, 1985, Greek award Granting Coun., U. Patras, 1991-92. Mem. Bulgarian Catalytic Soc. Mem. Ea. Orthodox Ch. Avocations: stamp collecting, skiing, cycling, swimming. Home: 11121 82 Ave # 526, Edmonton, AB Canada T6G 0T4 Office: Univ Alberta, Dept Chem/Materials Engring, Edmonton, AB Canada T6G 2G6

SLAVOV, VLADIMIR IONOVICH, physician, researcher; b. Cherepovets, Vologda, USSR, Feb. 19, 1941; s. Iona Petrovich and Vera Sergeevna S.; m. Elena Vladimironva Taran; 1 child, Anastasia; m. Alla Ivanovna Dichova, Nov. 20, 1941; 1 child, Eleha Vladimirovna. Engr., Inst. of Steel, Moscow, 1963, PhD in Physics, 1973. Chief x-ray lab. Sevestral Joint Stock, 1964—. Author: Productin of Quality Low-Carbon Sheet Steel, 1982, Texture and Biological Space - Genetic Code, 1994, Texture and Anisotropy of Polycrystals, 1997; inventor in field. Mem. Russian Acad. Scis. (academician), Textures Nongomogenities Structures and Anisotropy of Properties Material and Elements of Construction. Avocations: poetry, journalism. Home: Prospect Pobeda, 162620 Cherepovets Vologda, Russia Office: Joint Stock Co Severstel, Mira St 30, 126600 Cherepovets Vologda, Russia

SLAWINSKI, CHRISTOPHER MARK, sinologist, interpreter; b. Batu Gajah, Perak, Malaya, May 21, 1955; s. Karol and Krystyna Maria (Andrzejowska) S.; m. Anna Louise Parkinson, Aug. 8, 1981 (div. June 1989). MA with honors, Jesus Coll., Cambridge, U.K., 1977; Cert. Advanced Studies in Modern Chinese, Beijing Langs. Inst., 1981-82. Articled clk. Robson Rhodes, London, 1978-79; translator Brit. Petroleum plc., London, 1980-81; interpreter, translator Subsea Internat., China and Hong Kong, 1982-83; rsch. analyst Cazenove and Co., London, 1984-86. Coworker The Blackthorn Trust, Maidstone, Kent, U.K., 1995-97. Roman Catholic. Avocations: langs., music, travel, photography, skiing. Home: 425 London Rd Ditton, Aylesford, Kent ME20 6DB, England

SLAWSKY LEON, DONNA SUSAN, librarian, singer; b. N.Y.C., Jan. 18, 1956; d. Samuel Slawsky and Lillian (Freizer) Alexander; m. Luis Leon. BA, City Coll. N.Y., 1977; M of Infor. Libr. Sci., Pratt Inst., 1998. Coord. NYNEX Market Info. Ctr., White Plains, N.Y., 1985-87; libr. asst. NYNEX Info. Access Ctr., White Plains, N.Y., 1987-88; dir. Info. Ctr./Archives, exhbns. curator HarperCollins Pubs., N.Y.C., 1988-99; singer N.Y.C., 1987—; dir. content devel. BuyerWeb, Inc., N.Y.C., 1999—. Contbr. articles to profl. jours.; co-founder (quartet women's voices) Rose Ensemble debut Weill Recital Hall, Carnegie Hall, 1997. Pres. Assn. HarperCollins Employees, N.Y.C., 1990-94; dir. Tenants Assn., N.Y.C., 1994; mem. exhbns. com. Ctr. for Book Arts. Recipient Schubertiade Lieder Competition award 92d St. Y, N.Y.C., 1990. Mem. Spl. Librs. Assn., Profl. Women Singers Assn. (treas. 1992-96, mem.-at-large 1997—), Beta Phi Mu. Avocations: art, spirituality, hiking, reading. Home: 31 Jane St Apt 16G New York NY 10014-1982 Office: BuyerWeb Inc 111 John St Rm 1210 New York NY 10038-3002

SLAWTER, JOHN DAVID, JR., oil company and manufacturing executive; b. Winston-Salem, N.C., May 11, 1917; s. John David and Carrie Wess (Linville) S.; m. Josephine McCloone, June 15, 1943 (div. Oct. 1959); children: Suzanne Marie, Sheila Margaret; m. Joan Margaret Pirek, July 7, 1966. Student, U. N.C., 1935-37, 38-40. V.p. B&B Gas and Petroleum, Corpus Christi, Tex., 1950-59; exec. v.p. Cal-O-Tex Oil, Columbus, Ohio, 1959-65; pres. Atlantic Internat. Oil, Charleston, W.Va., 1966-73; CEO Interstate Hotels, Inc., 1975, Pacific Internat. Prodn. Holding Co. for Activated Carbon Corp. Am., Dallas, 1989, Mid-Continent Oil, 1974—, OFG Corp., 1995—, EMTEC, 1997—, HTS, 1999—; chmn. adv. bd. Cal-O-Tex, 1966—, Atlantic Internat. Oil, 1974—, Pacific Internat., 1974—, Black Diamond Coal Co., 1978—, Southwest Interstate Support Sys., 1985—, Activated Carbon Corp., 1989—; vice chair AIOC Trust, Slawter Trust (lifetime). Author: (patents and copyrights) purification and desalination sys., 1991, pumping unit tech., 1995, oil field gen., 1996, oil field mobile remote control unit, 1998, heat transfer sys., 1999. Mem. Rep. Nat. Nom. Com., Washington, 1994-2000. Maj. Engrs. 1941-45, WWII, PTO. Decorated Purple Heart, Silver Star, Bronze Star with oak leaf cluster, Presdl. Citation, 4 Battle Stars. Mem. internat. petroleum clubs, Geneva Exec. Club (v.p. 1970-78), Chi Phi. Avocations: aviation, golf. Office: Pacific Internat Prodn/Subs Ste 8108 4350 Trinity Mills Rd Dallas TX 75287-7037 also: PO Box 795273 Dallas TX 75379-5273

SLECHTA, JIRI, theoretical physicist; b. Havlickuv Brod, Bohemia, Czechoslovakia, Apr. 26, 1939; came to Eng., 1969; s. Josef and Marie (Posikova) S.; m. Miriam Vydrarova, July 17, 1971; children: Vera, Martin. Dr. rer. nat., Charles U., Prague, Czechoslovakia, 1962. Sr. lectr. dept. theoretical physics Charles U., Prague, 1964-69; rsch. fellow dept. physics U. Warwick, Conventry, Eng., 1969-71; sr. rsch. assoc. Sch. Math. and Physics U. East Anglia, Norwich, Eng., 1971-74; rsch. fellow dept. physics U. Leeds (Eng.), 1976-77; chair 3 Symposiums 13th Internat. Congress on Cybernetics, Namur, Belgium, 1992; co-chmn. symposium 17th World Congress SVU, Prague, 1994, chair symposium 14th Internat. Congress on Cybernetics, Namur, 1995, Knowledge Transfer 96, London; rschr. in field. Author 67 papers and 42 contbns. at nonpub. confs.; editor Informatica; patentee in field. 2d lt. Czechoslovakia mil., 1962-64. Benevolent Fund IOP ann. grantee, London, 1979—; recipient Gold Coin Am. Biog. Inst., 1995. Assoc. fellow Inst. Math. and Applications; mem. Am. Phys. Soc., Internat. Acad. Scis. San Marino, Inst. Physics, European Phys. Soc., Brit. Cybernetic Soc., Internat. Assn. Cybernetics, Internat. Cybernetics Acad., N.Y. Acad. Scis., Czechoslovak Math. Phys. Union, Czech Soc. Arts and Sci. Mem. Conservative party. Achievements include theory of disordered materials and self-organizing systems (brain, economy, society) and cybernetics.

ŚLEDZIŃSKI, JANUSZ, engineering educator; b. Bobowa, Cracow, Poland, July 29, 1931; s. Stefan and Helena (Wilkosz) Ś; m. Bogustawa Kalinowska, Dec. 17, 1981. Diploma in engring., Warsaw (Poland) U. Tech., 1953, MSc, 1955, DSc, 1964, Dr. habilitation, 1972. Cert. engring. in surveying and geodesy. Asst. Warsaw U. Tech., 1954-64, adj. prof., 1964-72, asst. prof., 1972-83, full prof., 1983—; UN expert in geodesy, UN chief adviser and team leader Afghan Cartographic and Cadastral Survey Inst., Kabul, Afghanistan, 1976-79; tech. and sci. cons. GEOKART Internat. Cons. Engrs., Warsaw, 1975-97; dir. Inst. Geodesy and Geodetic Astronomy, Warsaw, 1985—; chmn., internat. coord. Ctrl. European Initiative WG Sci. & Tech. Com. of Earth Scis. Sect. C "Geodesy". Author: Satellite Geodesy, 1978; editor Reports on Geodesy, 1990—. Recipient Gold Cross of Merit, Govt. of Poland, 1976, Cross Polonia Restituta, Govt. of Poland, 1985. Mem. Royal Inst. Navigation, Internat. Assn. Geodesy (chmn.), Am. Inst. Navigation, Polish Acad. Scis. (v.p. com. on geodesy 1996—), European Geophys. Soc., Am. Geophys. Union, N.Y. Acad. Scis. Roman Catholic. Home: Kiwerska 14/10, 01-682 Warsaw Poland Office: Warsaw Univ Tech, PL Politechniki 1, 00-661 Warsaw Poland

SLEE, OWEN BRUCE, astronomer; b. Adelaide, Australia, Aug. 10, 1924; s. Cwen and Edith (Golding) S.; m. Nan Linnett, Jan. 3, 1948; three children (one dec.). Diploma in physics, Sydney Tech. Coll., 1955; DSc, U. New South Wales, 1971. Rsch. officer CSIRO, Sydney, Australia, 1946-62; sr. rsch. officer RRE, Malvern, England, 1963-65; prin. rsch. offier CSIRO, 1966—. Fellow Astronomical Soc. Australia; mem. Internat. Astronomical Union. Avocations: music, gardening, walking. Office: Australia Telescope Nat Fac, PO Box 76, Epping NSW, Australia

SLEE, PETER H. TH. J., oncologist; b. Rotterdam, The Netherlands, Feb. 26, 1942; s. Peter H. Th. and Sofia M. (Van Bellen) S.; m. Clazina J.W.B. Straathof, Dec. 11, 1969; children: Danielle, Pieter Bas, Barbara. MD, Leiden U., The Netherlands, 1968; MS, Tropical Sch., Liverpool, England, 1970; PhD, Leiden U., 1985. Med. officer in charge Mlambe Hosp., Lunzu, Malawi, Central Africa, 1970-73; registrar Westeinde Hosp., The Hague, The Netherlands, 1973-75, U. Hosp., Leiden, The Netherlands, 1975-78; with St Jozef Ziekenhuis, Gouda, The Netherlands, 1978-87, St. Antonius Hosp., Nieuwegein, The Netherlands, 1987—. Office: St Antonius Hosp, Postbus 2500, Nieuwegein The Netherlands

SLEEMAN, BRIAN DAVID, mathematics educator; b. London, Aug. 4, 1939; s. Richard Kinsman and Gertrude Cecilia (Gamble) S.; m. Juliet Mary Shea, Sept. 7, 1963; children: Elizabeth Anne, Matthew Alexander, David James. BSc, Battersea Coll. Tech., London, 1963; PhD, U. London, 1966; DSc, Dundee (Scotland) U., 1975. Asst. lectr. math. U. Dundee, 1965-67, lectr., 1967-71, reader, 1971-78, prof., 1978-95; prof. U. Leeds, 1995—; vis. asst. prof. math. Courant Inst., N.Y., 1970-71; vis. prof. U. Tenn., Knoxville, 1976-77, Uppsala (Sweden) U., 1984. Author: Multiparameter Spectral Theory In Hilbert Space, 1978; co-author Differential Equations and Mathematical Biology, 1983; editor, assoc. editor math. jours; editor Jour. Theoretical Medicine. Fellow Royal Soc. Edinburgh, Inst. Math. and Its Applications; Am. Math. Soc., Edinburgh Math. Soc., London Math. Soc. Anglican. Avocations: choral music, hill walking. Office: U Leeds, Leeds LS2 9JT, England

SLEETER, JOHN WILLIAM HIGGS, physician, health service administrator; b. Toledo, Iowa, Feb. 16, 1917; s. Charles Elmer and Meta DeLad (Higgs) S.; m. Betti Deming, Aug. 28, 1943 (div. Mar. 1963); m. Patricia C. Parker, July 1963 (dec. Oct. 1986); m. Patricia Catherine Parrillo, July 8, 1989; children: John William, Marilee Ann, Thomas David. BA, Cornell Coll., Mt. Vernon, Iowa, 1942; MD, U. Iowa, 1945. Pres. San Gabriel Primary Care, Arcadia, Calif., 1952-62, L.A. County Acad. GP, Calif., 1965-66; inst. paramedic care St. Terisita Hosp., Duarte, Calif., 1970-75; pres., chief operating officer Profsnl. Rev. Area 21, 1970-75; 1st pres. L.A. County Paramedic Commn., 1974-75; pres., CEO, dir. pvt. practice assn., Arcadia, 1984—. Capt, AUS, 1945-49. Mem. Balboa Bay Club, San Gabriel Country Club, Masons (32d degree). Republican. Avocation: golf.

SLEIGH, MICHAEL ALFRED, biology educator; b. Taunton, Somerset, England, June 11, 1932; s. Cyril Button and Ida Louisa (Horstmann) S.; m. Peggy Mason, Dec. 28, 1957; children: Roger Timothy, Anne Katherine, Peter Richard. BS, U. Bristol, Eng., 1953, PhD, 1957, DSc, 1974. Chartered biologist. Asst. lectr. U. Exeter, Eng., 1958-61, lectr. in zoology, 1961-63; lectr. in zoology U. Bristol, Eng., 1963-72; reader in zoology, 1972-74; prof. biology U. Southampton, Eng., 1975-98; prof. emeritus U. Southampton, 1998—; dept. chmn. U. Southampton, Eng., 1976-83, 90-93; dir. Co. of Biologists, Cambridge, Eng., 1968-72. Author: The Biology of Cilia and Flagella, 1962, The Biology of Protozoa, 1973, Protozoa and Other Protists, 1989; editor: (books) Cilia and Flagella, 1974, Microbes in the Sea, 1987, Evolutionary Relationships Among Protozoa, 1998. Fellow Inst. of Biology; mem. Marine Biological Assn. of U.K. (councillor 1986-89), Freshwater Biol. Assn. (councillor 1982-86), Assn. Univ. Tchrs., Soc. of Protozoologists (v.p. 1987-88), Brit. Sect. Soc. Protozoologists (pres. 1982-85), Soc. for Exptl. Biology (hon. sec. 1966-70). Avocations: natural history, microscopy, travel, genealogy, gardening. Office: U Southampton Sch Biol Sci, Bassett Crescent East, Southampton S016 7PX, England

SLEIGHT, ARTHUR WILLIAM, chemist; b. Ballston Spa, N.Y., Apr. 1, 1939; s. Hollis Decker and Elizabeth (Smith) S.; AB, Hamilton Coll., 1960; PhD, U. Conn., 1963; m. Betty F. Hilberg, Apr. 19, 1963; children: Jeffrey William, Jeannette Anne, Jason Arthur. Faculty, U. Stockholm, Sweden, 1963-64; with E.I. du Pont de Nemours & Co., Inc., Wilmington, Del., 1965-89, rsch. mgr. solid state/catalytic chemistry, 1981-89; Harris Chair prof. materials sci. Oreg. State U., Corvallis, 1989—; dir. Ctr. for Advanced Materials Rsch., 1995—; adj. prof. U. Del., 1978-89. Mem. Presdl. Commn. Superconductivity, 1989. Recipient Phila. chpt. Am. Inst.. Chemists award, 1988, Gold Medal award Nat. Assn. Sci. Tech. and Soc., 1994. Mem. Am. Chem. Soc. (award Del. sect. 1978, Chemistry of Materials award 1997). Editor Materials Rsch. Bull., 1994—; editorial bd. Inorganic Chemistry Rev., 1979—, Jour. Catalysis, 1986—, Applied Catalysis, 1987—, Solid State Scis., 1987—, Chemistry of Materials, 1988—, Materials Chemistry and Physics, 1988—, Jour. of Solid State Chemistry, 1988—; patentee in field; contbr. articles to profl. jours. Home: PO Box 907 Philomath OR 97370-0907 Office: Oreg State U Dept Chemistry 153 Gilbert Hall Corvallis OR 97331-8546

SLEIGHT, GEORGE ROBIN, aeronautical engineer; b. Ayr, Scotland, Nov. 11, 1937; s. George Ernest and Mary Thompson (McIntyre) S.; m. Eileen Isobel Owens, Apr. 28, 1962; children: David Eugene, Fiona Caroline. BSc with honors, U. Glasgow, 1959. Aerodynamicist Vickers Aircraft, Weybridge, 1959-61; sys. engr. Elliott Automation, Boreham Wood, 1961-64; program mgr. Marconi Avionics, Rochester, 1964-72, divsnl. mgr., 1972-84; asst. mng. dir. GEC Avionics, Rochester, 1984-88; strategy dir. BAE Sys., Rochester, 1988—; presenter numerous confs. Co-inventor take-off director system; contbr. articles to profl. jours. High tech. industry rep. Kent County Coun., Chatham, 1998—; exec. mem. Brit. Overseas Trade Group for Israel, London, 1995—; high tech. adviser Dept. Trade and Industry, London, 1996-98. Named to Order of Brit. Empire; recipient Laurel citation Aviation Week, 1981. Fellow Royal Aero. Soc. (chmn. Medway br. 1992—), Brit. Assn. Radio Controlled Soarers. Avocation: radio-controlled model sailplanes. Office: Bae Systems, Airport Works, Rochester, Kent ME1 2XX, England

SLEIMAN, ASAAD ALI, orthopedic surgeon; b. Bietzini, Tartous, Syria, Apr. 1, 1957; s. Ali Sleiman and Aziza Saeed Ahmed; m. Nahla Ismaeel Merhej, Apr. 7, 1983; children: Lyne, Farah, Sally, Mays. MD, Damascus, Syria, 1982; cert. gen. surgery, Dijon, France, 1988, U. Bourgogne, 1988; diploma orthopedic surgery, Dijon, France, 1990. Gen. surg. resident Decize (France) Gen. Hosp., 1983-84, orthopedic resident, 1984-85; orthopedic resident Louis Pasteur Med. Ctr., Dole, France, 1985-87; sr. registrar in orthopedic surgery Tchg. U. Hosp., Besancon, France, 1987-88; specialist in orthopedic surgery Louis Pasteur Hosp., Dole, 1988-91; cons. orthopedic surgeon Jubail (KSA) Gen. Hosp., 1991—, dir. emergency rm., 1995—. Mem. Internat. Orthopedic Soc., French Orthopedic Soc. Avocations: tennis, computer, swimming. Fax: 96633620343. E-mail: asadali@sps.net.sa and asleiman@doctor.com. Office: Jubail Gen Hosp, PO Box 2208, Jubail 31951, Saudi Arabia

SLEMMER, CARL WEBER, JR., retired lawyer; b. Camden, N.J., Mar. 28, 1923; s. Carl and Annetta (Donner) S.; m. Renée Jeannette Kinsey, Oct. 11, 1952; children: Michael, John, Sandra. BS, Muhlenberg Coll., 1948; JD, Temple U., 1963. Bar: N.J. 1972, Pa. 1972, U.S. Dist. Ct. N.J. 1972, Fla. 1974. Various pers. positions RCA, Camden, 1950-55; mgr. labor rels. Allied Chem. Corp., Morristown, N.J., 1955-67; dir. employee rels. Exide Corp., Phila., 1967-82; pvt. practice Cherry Hill, N.J., 1982-83; dir. labor rels. Columbia U., N.Y.C., 1983-89; mgr. tax office H & R Block, Marlton, N.J., 1991-93; ret., 1993. Mem. labor coun. U. Pa., Phila., 1967-82. Lt. (j.g.) USN, 1943-46, PTO. Republican. Presbyterian. Avocations: tennis, reading, travel, legal research. Home: 432 Paul Dr Moorestown NJ 08057-2809

SLENCZKA, WERNER GEORG, virologist; b. Kassel, Germany, Oct. 21, 1934; s. Hans and Renate (Heldmann) S.; m. Brigitta Maria Schulz, Jan. 22, 1962; children: Katharina, Renate, Christian, Johannes. Abitur, Wilhelmsschule, Kassel, 1955; med. staatsexamen, U. Munich, 1961; MD, Philipps U., Marburg, Fed. Republic Germany, 1961, Dr. med. habil, 1971. Asst. Inst. Pathology U. Frankfurt, Fed. Republic Germany, 1963-64; asst. Med. Poliklinik U. Marburg, 1964-65, asst. hygiene and microbiology, 1965-72, prof. virology, dept. hygiene and microbiology, 1972—. Co-author: Deutscher Aerzteverlag, 1997, 2d edit.; contbr. articles to profl. publs. Fellow Am. Soc. Microbiology, German Soc. Hygiene and Microbiology, German Soc. Virology, German Soc. Tropical Medicine and Parasitology. Achievements include (with others) first isolation and discovery of the Marburg virus. Office: Inst Virology, Robert Koch Str 17, 35037 Marburg on der Lahn Hessen, Germany

SLEPUKHINA, TATYANA DMITRIEVNA, hydrobiologist; b. Saki, Krimea, Ukrain, Feb. 27, 1937; d. Dmitri Antonovich and Ksenya Nikolaevna (Korde) Novozhilov; m. Yuri Grigorjevich Slepukhin, June 1, 1965 (div. Oct. 1971); 1 child, Ksenya. MS, Leningrad State U., 1959; PhD, Zool. Inst. Acad. Scis., Baku/USSR, 1967; DS, Zool. Inst. Acad. Scis., Leningrad, 1991. Rsch. asst. Lab. of Limnology/Russian Acad. Sci., Leningrad, 1959-68, jr. rsch. scientist, 1968-76, learned sec., 1976-81, sr. rsch. scientist, 1981-86; leading rsch. scientist Lab. of Limnology/Russian Acad. Sci., St. Petersburg, Russia, 1986—; mem. scientific coun. Inst. Limnology, 1970—, spl. scientific coun. for acad. degrees, 1991—, spl. scientific coun. for acad. degrees, Fishery Inst., St. Petersburg, 1992—. Co-author: (book) Proc. Russia Hydrobiological Congress, 1996, Role of Wave Action in Biocenoses Formation in Lakes, 1990; contbr. articles to profl. jours. Recipient Bronze medal Exhbn. of Achievements of Nat. Economy, Moscow, 1977, Diploma of Laureate for Best Report, Congress of Scientific and Engring. Socs., St. Petersburg, 1995; state grantee Presidium of Russian Acad. Sci., Moscow, 1994-96. Mem. St. Petersburg Bu. of Hydrobiol. Soc., Russian Acad. Sci. Avocations: homeless animals, flowers. Office: Inst Limnology/Russian Acad, Sevastyanova str 9, 196105 Saint Petersburg Russia

SLESARENKO, VLADIMIR NIKOLAEVICH, mechanic engineer; b. Vladivostok, Russia, Dec. 16, 1930; s. Nikolay and Anna (Tarasovna) S.; m. Genrietta Alekseevna, 1952; two children. Cand. of Tech. Sci., Leningrad Poly. Inst., 1966; PhD Tech. Sci., Moscow Energetic Inst., 1983. Asst. docent Far Eastern Poly. Inst., Vladivostok, 1954-89; prof. Far Eastern Maritime Acad., Vladivostok, 1989—. Author: Desalination of Sea and Salt Waters, 1973, Desalination Plants, 1980, Desalinization of Salt Water, 1992; contbr. articles to profl. jours. Office: Far Eastern Maritime Acad, Verhneportovaya st 50 a, 690059 Vladivostok Russia

SLETTEN, EINAR, chemist, educator; b. Hordaland, Norway, Jan. 19, 1939; s. Olav Andreas Sletten; m. Jorunn Ambjorg Sundsfiord, Aug. 21, 1965. PhD, U. Bergen, Norway, 1965. Prof. chemistry U. Norway, 1969—. Mem. Norwegian Chem. Soc. (bd. dirs. 1976-79), Am. Chem. Soc. E-mail: einar.sletten@kj.uib.no. Office: U Norway, Allegt 41, N-5007 Bergen Norway

SLICKER, FREDERICK KENT, lawyer; b. Tulsa, Aug. 21, 1943; s. James Floyd and Lucille Geneva (Nordling) S.; children: Laura, Kipp. BA, U. Kans., 1965, JD with highest distinction, 1968; LLM, Harvard U., 1973. Bar: Kans. 1968, U.S. Ct. Mil. Appeals 1968, U.S. Supreme Ct. 1972, Tex. 1973, Okla. 1980. Assoc. Jackson, Walker, Winstead, Cantwell & Miller, Dallas, 1973-76; assoc. Worsham, Forsythe & Sampels, 1977-80, ptnr., 1980; assoc. Hall, Estill, Hardwick, Gable, Collingsworth & Nelson, Tulsa, 1980-81, mem., 1982-86; ptnr. Baker, Hoster, McSpadden, Clark, Rasure & Slicker, Tulsa, 1986-91; pvt. practice, Tulsa, 1991-92; shareholder Sneed Lang Adams & Barnett, Tulsa, 1992-96; pvt. practice law Tulsa, 1996-2000; prin. shareholder Slicker & Alberty PC, 2000—. Author: A Practical Guide to Church Bond Financing, 1985, Angels All Around, 1999. Vice chmn. bd. trustees, chmn. admnstrv. bd., chmn. fin. com., treas., trustee 1st United Meth. Ch., Tulsa; mem. task force Tulsa area Promise Keepers; founder Tulsa Men's Ministries Inc. Capt. U.S. Army, 1965-72. Mem. ABA, Okla. Bar Assn., Order of Coif. Democrat. Avocation: Christian men's ministries. E-mail: Fslicker@swbell.com. Fax: 918-496-9024. Office: 4444 E 66th Ste #201 Tulsa OK 74136-4206

SLIGER, BERNARD FRANCIS, academic administrator, economist, educator; b. Chassell, Mich., Sept. 30, 1924; s. Paul and Hazel (MacLauchlin) S.; m. Greta Taube, Sept. 1, 1945; children: Nan, Paul, Greta Lee, Sten. BA in Econs. with high hons., Mich. State U., 1949, MA, 1950, PhD, 1955; postgrad., U. Minn., 1961-62. Mem. faculty La. State U., 1953-61, prof. econs., 1961, head dept., 1961-65, vice chancellor, dean academic affairs, 1965-68; sec. adminstrn., chief budget officer State of La., 1968-69; sec.-treas. La. Office Bldg. Corp., 1969-72; organizer, exec. dir. La. Coordinating Council Higher Edn., 1969-72; prof. econs. Fla. State U., Tallahassee, 1973—, exec. v.p., 1972-76, chief acad. officer, 1973-76, pres., 1977-91, interim pres., 1993, dir. univ.'s London Study Ctr., 1975, pres. emeritus, dir., 1992—; mem. staff sci. and tech. com. Fla. Ho. of Reps., 1979; mem. V.P. Mondale's Select Com. on Sci. and Tech., 1980; mem. bd. dirs. Fed. Res Bank of Atlanta, 1983-88; cons. econ. theory and pub. fin. to pvt. and pub. commns., orgns.; mem., chief cons. Gov. La.'s tax study com., 1968; formerly La. commr. adminstrn. and chief budget officer; mem. NCAA pres.'s commn., 1987-91. Author: (text) Public Finance, 1964, rev. edit., 1970, (with others) Municipal Finance Administration, 1976, rev.; contbr. to profl. publs. Vol. economist Tallahassee C. of C. and La. C. of C.; mem. Acad. Task Force for Review of the Ins. and Tort Systems, 1986-88; trustee The Nature Conservancy, 1986—; trustee Am. Coll. Testing Corp., 1981-87, chmn. 1985-87; ex-officio mem. Fla. Coun. 100. With C.E., U.S. Army, 1943-46. Named Dir. Practical Politics La. Ho. of Reps., 1969; Bernard F. Sliger Eminent scholar Chair in Econ. Edn. created in his name by Fla. State U., 1987, Bernard F. Sliger Bldg. dedicated at univ.-related rsch. park. Mem. Kiwanis, Phi Beta Kappa, Omicron Delta Kappa, Phi Kappa Phi, Omicron Delta Epsilon, Alpha Kappa Psi, Beta Gamma Sigma, Phi Eta Sigma. Presbyterian. Office fax: 850-644-9866. E-mail: sliger@mailer.fsu.edu/sliger@garnet.acns.fsu.edu. Home: 3341 E Lakeshore Dr Tallahassee FL 32312-1440 Office: Gus A Stavros Ctr Adv Free Enterprise & Economic Edu 250 S Woodward Ave Tallahassee FL 32304-8052

SLIGER, HERBERT JACQUEMIN, JR., lawyer; b. Urbana, Ill., Nov. 21, 1948; s. Herbert Jacquemin and Marina (Mantia) S.; m. Sandra Ann Ratti, May 3, 1996; children: Lauren Christine, Matthew Ryan, Nicholas Adam, Claire Nicole, Adam Gregory. BS in Fin., U. Ill., 1970; JD, U. Ariz., 1974. Bar: Ariz. 1974, Ill. 1975, U.S. Supreme Ct. 1983, Okla. 1984, U.S. Ct. Appeals (7th cir.) 1980, U.S. Tax Ct. 1980; CPA, Okla. Lawyer Charles W. Phillips Law Offices, Harrisburg, Ill., 1974-75; trust counsel Magna Trust Co., F/K/A Millikin Nat. Bank, Decatur, Ill., 1976-80, First of America Trust Co., Springfield, Ill., 1980-83; trust counsel personal fin. svcs. group First Interstate Bank Okla. NA, Oklahoma City, 1983-86; mgr. employee benefits trust dept. First Interstate Bank of Okla., NA, Oklahoma City, 1986-89; v.p., pension counsel Star Bank, NA, Cin., Cin., 1989-90; asst. gen. counsel Bank One Ariz. Corp., Phoenix, 1990-95; asst. gen. counsel, nat. practice group head Banc One Corp., Columbus, Ohio, 1995-98; state gen. counsel Banc One Corp., Phoenix, 1996-97; sec. of bd. and cashier Bank One, Ariz. NA, 1996-97; sec. of bd. and statutory agt. Banc One Ariz. Corp., 1996-97; sec. bd. Bank One Trust Co. N.A., Columbus, 1996—; asst. gen. counsel, trust counsel practice group head law dept. Bank One Corp., Chgo., 1999—; co-chmn. Nat. Conf. Lawyers and Corp. Fiduciaries, 1992-94; instr. Chaminade U. Hawaii, Hawaii Tax Inst., 1999. Contbr. articles to profl. jours. Mem. ABA (sect. bus. law, banking law com., trust and investment svcs. subcom. 1991-99, sect. real property, probate and trust law 1974—, fiduciary income taxation subcom. 1994—, fiduciary environ. problems com. 1993-99, sect. of taxation, employee benefits com. 1991—), State Bar of Ariz., Okla. Bar Assn., Am. Bankers Assn. (chmn. trust counsel com. 1992-94, mem. and head of fiduciary law dept. Nat./Grad. Trust Sch. Bd. of Faculty Advisors 1994-95, faculty mem. teaching "fiduciary duties under ERISA" Nat. Employee Benefit Trust Sch. 1994-96, spokesman Environ. Risk Task Force 1994-95, mem. trust and investment divsn. exec. com. 1992-94, mini-adv. bd. chairperson trusts and estates 1995-99), Nat. Conf. Lawyers and Corp. Fiduciaries (co-chmn. 1992-94). Roman Catholic. Avocations: phys. fitness, original print collecting.

SLIM HELÚ, CARLOS, communications executive; b. Mexico City, 1943; m. Sumaya Domit Gemayel. Degree in civil engring., UNAM. Various

constrn. and real estate positions; owner (with others) Galas de Mex., 1976—, Citagem, 1981—; founder Grupo Carso, 1983; owner Segumex, 1984—; owner (with others), pres. bd. dirs. Sanborn's, 1992; owner (with others) Condumex, 1992—; pres. bd. dirs. Teléfonos de Mex., Mexico City, 1990—, chmn. bd., 1990—; owner Tabacos Mexicanos, Nayarit, 1990—; sr. chmn. bd. Sanborn Hermanos; dir. gen. Sanborn Hermanos, Mexico City; pres. bd. dirs. Cigarrera la Tabaclera Mexicana, 1992, Inversora Bursátil, Loreta y Peña Pobre, Seguros de Mex.; shareholder various cos.; mem. fin. com. PRI. Office: Telefonos Mex SA de CV, Parque Via 198 Edifc 701, Mexico City 06500, Mexico Address: Av San Fernando 649, Col Pena Pobre, 14060 Mexico DF Mexico*

SLINN, ERROL WARWICK, language educator; b. Whangarei, New Zealand, Oct. 4, 1943; s. Eric and Alice Vera (Gaddis) S.; m. Eunice Fisher, 1970 (div. 1978); 1 child, Gareth Robert; m. Suzann Clair Olsson, 1979 (div. 1999); 1 child, Vaughan Richard. BA, U. Canterbury, New Zealand, 1964, MA, 1966; MA, U. Hawaii, 1967; PhD, U. B.C., Can., 1971. Tchg. asst. U. B.C., Vancouver, Can., 1967-69; lectr. Massey U., Palmerston North, New Zealand, 1972-90; assoc. prof. Massey U., Palmerston North, 1991—. Author: Browning and the Fictions of Identity, 1982, The Discourse of Self in Victorian Poetry, 1991; contbr. articles to profl. jours. Fellow Can. Coun., 1969-71; Travel award CIES Fulbright, 1989; Massey U. rsch. fellow, 1994, 2000. Mem. Australasian Victorian Studies Assn. (pres. 1992-96), Australasian Lang. and Lit. Assn. (v.p. 1987-91). Avocations: music, cricket. Office: English Dept, Sch English/Media Studies, Massey Univ, Palmerston North New Zealand

SLÍPKA, JAROSLAV, histology and embryology educator; b. Loket, Czech Republic, June 10, 1926; s. Jaroslav and Ludmila (Dvořáková) S.; m. Hana Pabudová, Apr. 8, 1950; children: Jaroslav, Zuzana. PhD in Natural Scis., Charles U., Prague, Czech Republic, 1949, MF, 1953, DSc, 1979. Asst. med. faculty Charles U., 1949-62, docent, 1962-79, prof., dept. head, 1979-93, part-time prof., 1993—; prof. med. faculty Baghdad, Iraq, 1962-66. Mem. 3 editl. bds.; contbr. over 200 articles to sci. jours. Mem. Med. Assn. Pilsen (hon., pres. 1989—), 4 anat. socs. (hon.), Lions (gov. 1995-96). Avocation: entomology. Home: Zahradní 6, 30153 Pilsen Czech Republic Office: Charles U Faculty Medicine, Karlovarská 48, 30166 Pilsen Czech Republic

ŚLIWIŃSKA-BARTKOWIAK, MALGORZATA MARIA, physics educator; b. Chetmno, Bydgoszcz, Poland, Aug. 5, 1947; d. Romuald Edmund and Maria (Szudzinska) Śliwinski; m. Stawomir Leon Bartkowiak, Oct. 25, 1970; 1 child, Marek. MSc in Physics, A. Mickiewicz U., Poznan, Poland, 1970, PhD in Physics, 1977, habilitation, 1991. Sr. asst. A. Mickiewicz U., Poznan, 1970-77, asst. prof., 1978-91, assoc. prof., 1992-94, prof., 1995—; coord. Coop. Rsch. Program, NSF, Cornell U., U.S., 1995-98, Belgium Ministry Edn., Liege U., 1997-98, Polish Com. Sci. Rsch. Grant, 1996-98. Mem. Polish Phys. Soc. (vice chmn. Poznan br. 1992—), Thermophys. Properties Awareness Club, Nat. Phys. Lab., Eng. Avocations: literature, travel. Home: Osiedle Przyjaźni 13, 38, 61-687 Poznan Poland Office: A Mickiewicz U Inst Physics, Umultowska 85, 61-614 Poznan Poland

SLOAN, DANIEL KAY, electrical engineer; b. Walla Walla, Wash., Oct. 20, 1944; s. James Lester and Bertha Louise (Ulstrup) S.; m. Janice Kay Christensen, Jan. 31, 1965 (dec.). BSEE, Wash. State U., 1967. Product line controls engr. Beloit (Wis.) Corp., 1967-72, product line mgr.-controls, 1972-79; elec. engr. U & I Inc., Kennewick, Wash., 1979-81; elec. project engr. Boise-Cascade, Wallula, Wash., 1981-86; sr. elec. project engr. Simpson Tacoma (Wash.) Kraft Co., 1986—. Staff sgt. U.S. Air Guard, 1967-73. Mem. IEEE, Internat. Soc. for Measurement and Control, Elks. Office: Simpson Tacoma Kraft Co 801 Portland Ave Tacoma WA 98421-3098

SLOAN, DONNIE ROBERT, JR., lawyer; b. Nashville, July 24, 1946; s. Donnie R. Sr. and Mary Catharine (Willis) S. BS in Indsl. Engring., Ga. Inst. Tech, 1968; JD cum laude, U. Ga., 1971; LLM, Harvard U., 1975. Bar: Ga. 1971, U.S. Dist. Ct. (no. dist.) Ga. 1971, U.S. Ct. Appeals (11th cir.). Atty. Southwire Co., Carrollton, Ga., 1971-74; assoc., ptnr. Hyatt & Rhoads, P.C., Atlanta, 1975-89; pvt. practice, 1989-96; ptnr. Davidson, Fuller & Sloan, LLP, 1996—; instr. legal rsch. U. Ga., Athens, 1970-71; instr. music law Ga. State U., Atlanta, 1976. Mem. editl. bd. Ga. Law Rev., 1969-71. Treas. Ga. Wheelchair Athletic Assn., Atlanta, 1981-84; pres., treas. Dixie Wheelchair Athletic Assn., Atlanta, 1984-87. Recipient Appreciation award Ga. Wheelchair Sports and Recreation Assn., 1979; named one of Outstanding Young Men of Am., 1981; named to Dixie Wheelchair Athletic Assn. Hall of Fame, 1990. Mem. Am. Judicature Soc., Phi Kappa Phi, Alpha Phi Mu, Ga. Tech. Club, Harvard Club. Presbyterian. Avocations: skiing, jogging, swimming. Home: 735 Brookfield Pkwy Roswell GA 30075-1313 Office: 11330 Lakefield Dr Ste 250 Duluth GA 30097-1578

SLOAN, F(RANK) BLAINE, law educator; b. Geneva, Nebr., Jan. 3, 1920; s. Charles Porter and Lillian Josephine (Stiefer) S.; m. Patricia Sand, Sept. 2, 1944; children—DeAnne Sloan Riddle, Michael Blaine, Charles Porter. AB with high distinction, U. Nebr., 1942, LLB cum laude, 1946; LLM in Internat. Law, Columbia U., 1947. Bar: Nebr. 1946, N.Y. 1947. Asst. to spl. counsel Intergovtl. Com. for Refugees, 1947; mem. Office Legal Affairs UN Secretariat, N.Y.C., 1948-78; gen. counsel Relief and Works Agy. Palestine Refugees, Beirut, 1958-60; dir. gen. legal divsn., dep. to the legal counsel UN Legal Office, N.Y.C., 1966-78, rep. of Sec. Gen. to UN Commn. Internat. Trade Law, 1969-78, rep. to Legal Sub-com. on Outer Space, 1966-78; rep. UN Del. Vietnam Conf., Paris, 1973; rep. UN Conf. on Carriage of Goods by Sea Hamburg, 1978; prof. internat. law orgn. and water law Pace U., 1978-87, prof. emeritus, 1987—; law lectr. Blaine Sloan Internat., 1988—. Author: United Nations General Assembly Resolutions in Our Changing World, 1991; contbr. articles to legal jours. Cons. UN Office of Legal Affairs, 1983-84, UN Water Resources Br., 1983; supervisory com., Pace Peace Ctr.; legal advisor Korean Missions, 1951, 53, UNTSO, Jerusalem, 1952, UNEF I, Gaza, 1957-58; prin. sec.UN Commn. to investigate Sec.-Gen. Hammarskjold's crash, 1961-62. Navigator AC, U.S. Army, 1943-46. Decorated Air medal. Mem. Am. Soc. Internat. Law, Am. Acad. Polit. and Social Sci., Am. Arbitration Assn. (panel of arbitrators), Order of Coif, Phi Beta Kappa, Phi Alpha Delta (hon.). Republican. Roman Catholic. Home: HCR-68 Box 72 Foxwind-Forbes Park Fort Garland CO 81133 Office: 78 N Broadway White Plains NY 10603-3710 also: 375 Soubry Pl Forbes Park Ft Garland CO 81133

SLOAN, HAROLD DAVID, chemical engineering consultant; b. Olney, Tex., Jan. 4, 1949; s. James Robert Jr. and Laura Faye (Riddle) S.; m. Barbara Ellen Wilson, Dec. 17, 1970 (div. 1982); m. Maureen Ann Moriarity, Mar. 17, 1983; children: Christa Lauren, Elizabeth Michele. BSChemE, Tex. Tech U., 1972. Registered profl. engr., Tex. Field engr. Halliburton Svcs., Corpus Christi, Tex., 1972-73; mgr. tech. svc. Engelhard Corp., Houston, 1987-90; systems engr., process engr., then process mgr. M.W. Kellogg Co., Houston, 1973-87, sr. product tech. cons., 1990-94, refining product tech. mgr., 1994-95, product dir. ROSE, 1995-97, product dir. resid upgrading, 1997-98; mgr. refining bus. segment Kellogg Brown & Root Inc., Houston, 1998-99, dir. refining tech. bus. devel., 1999—. Contbr. articles to tech. jours. and mags.; patentee for coke drum unheading system. Pres. Sagemeadow Civic Club, Houston, 1978; v.p. West Harris County Mcpl. Utility Dist. 10, Houston, 1985; Sunday sch. tchr. Met. Bapt. Ch., Houston, 1992—. Mem. AIChE, Tex. Soc. Profl. Engrs. (pres. Sam Houston chpt. 1980, Outstanding Young Engr. award 1978), NRA (life), Tex. State Rifle Assn., Nat. Petroleum Refiners Assn. (co. rep.), Am. Petroleum Inst. (co. rep.), Sigma Xi. Achievements include research on role of delayed coking in a clean fuels environment, economic options for heavy crude upgrading, processing heavier crude blends, process integration for optimizing distillate production, akylation: the ideal process for the reformulated gasoline era; resid upgrading optimization using the ROSE Process, advances in resid upgrading technology optimizing resid upgrading with ROSE and IGCC; conversion of MTBE units to produce isooctane clean gasoline blending component. Home: 17115 North Eldridge Pky Tomball TX 77375-8001 Office: Kellogg Brown & Root 601 Jefferson St Houston TX 77002-7900

SLOAN, HERBERT ELIAS, physician, surgeon; b. Clarksburg, W.Va., Oct. 10, 1914; s. Herbert Elias and Luella (Dye) S.; m. Doris Edwards, May 3, 1943; children: Herbert, Ann, Elizabeth, John, Robert. A.B., Washington and Lee U., 1936; M.D., Johns Hopkins U., 1940. Diplomate Am. Bd. Surgery, Am. Bd. Thoracic Surgery (bd. dirs. 1966-86, v.p. 1971-73, sec.-treas. 1973-86). Resident in surgery Johns Hopkins Hosp., 1941-44; instr. dept. surgery Johns Hopkins U., 1943-44; resident in thoracic surgery U. Mich. Hosp., Ann Arbor, 1947-49, instr. thoracic surgery, 1949-50; asst. prof. U. Mich., Ann Arbor, 1950-53, assoc. prof., 1953-62, prof. surgery, 1962-87, head sect. thoracic surgery, 1970-85; chief clin. affairs U. Mich. Hosps., Ann Arbor, 1982-86, med. dir. operating room, 1986-87, prof. emeritus surgery, 1987—; med. dir. managed health care U. Mich., Ann Arbor, 1989-96; mem. staff VA Hosp., Ann Arbor, 1953—, cons., 1968—. Author: The American Board of Thoracic Surgery: A Fifty Year Perspective, 1998, (with Marvin M. Kirsh) Blunt Chest Trauma, General Principles of Management, 1977; editor Annals of Thoracic Surgery, 1969-85; contbr. (with Marvin M. Kirsh) chpts. to books, articles to profl. jours. Served to maj. M.C. U.S. Army, 1944-47. Recipient Bruce Douglas award in thoracic diseases, 1974, Med. Alumni Svc. award Johns Hopkins Sch. Medicine, 1973, Disting. Svc. award Johns Hopkins U. Sch. Medicine, 1983, Disting. Svc. award Mich. Med. Ctr. Alumni Soc., 1988. Mem. ACS, Am. Surg. Assn., Am. Heart Assn., Am. Assn. Thoracic Surgery (pres. 1979-80), Soc. Thoracic Surgeons (pres. 1974-75, Disting. Svc. award 1981), Central Surg. Assn., Soc. Univ. Surgeons, So. Thoracic Surgery Assn. (hon.), Thoracic Soc. Gt. Britain (hon.), John Alexander Soc., Western Thoracic Surg. Assn. (hon.), Cardiovascular Surgeons Club, Detroit Heart Club, Am. Trudeau Soc., Mich. Heart Assn., Mich. Trudeau Soc., Am. Acad. Pediatrics, Soc. Vascular Surgery, Frederick A. Coller Surg. Soc., U. Mich. Med. Alumni Soc. (Disting. Svc. award 1988), Rsch. Club, Phi Beta Kappa, Alpha Omega Alpha, Omicron Delta Kappa, Sigma Xi. Club: Ann Arbor Figure Skating (pres. 1965-66). E-mail: hsloan@umich.edu. Home: 471 Barton North Dr Ann Arbor MI 48105-1017 Office: Taubman Health Care Ctr Sect Thoracic Surgery PO Box 344 Ann Arbor MI 48106-0344

SLOAN, KAREN LESLIE, journalist; b. Bronx, N.Y., Jan. 31, 1956; d. Nathan and Harriet (Block) S.; m. Jeffrey C. Baron, Jan. 22, 1978 (div. Dec. 1988). BA, Middlebury (Vt.) Coll., 1976; MA, U. Mo., 1982. Newscaster Sta. WBUD, Trenton, N.J., 1976-77, Sta. WJRZ, Manahawkin, N.J., 1977-78; newscaster, reporter St. WOBM, Toms River, N.J., 1978-79; news dir. Sta. WBIO, Parsippany, N.J., 1979-80; newscaster, reporter Sta. WMTR, Morristown, N.J., 1980-81; state house reporter Sta. KBIA, Columbia, Mo., 1981-82; newswoman AP Broadcast, Washington, 1982-85, news editor, 1986-89; European coord. AP Broadcast, London, 1989—. Avocation: bridge. E-mail: ksloan@ap.org. Office: AP Broadcast Radioch, The Interchange/Oval Rd, Camden Lock London NW1 7DZ, England

SLOAN, MICHAEL DANA, information systems specialist; b. Santa Monica, Calif., Sept. 30, 1960; s. Avery and Beverly Rae (Krantz) S.; m. Barbara Rogers; 1 child, Ashley Harrison. BS in Bus. Adminstrn., Calif. State U., Northridge, 1983; MBA, Pepperdine U., 1987. Programmer/analyst TICOR, Inc., L.A., 1979-80; data processing analyst Deluxe Check Printers, Inc., Chatsworth, Calif., 1980-83; fin. systems analyst Wismer & Assocs., Inc., Canoga Park, Calif., 1983-84; sr. systems analyst Coast Savs. & Loan, Granada Hills, Calif., 1984-86; microcomputer systems specialist Litton Industries, Woodland Hills, Calif., 1986-87; systems mgr., info. resources mgr. TRW, Inc.- Space and Def., Redondo Beach, Calif., 1987-93; project mgr. Health Net, Woodland Hills, 1993-95; mgr. fin. and sales systems Merisel Ams. Inc., El Segundo, Calif., 1995-97; sr. mgr. web tech. & devel. Ingram Micro Inc., Santa Ana, Calif., 2000—; cons. Data Most, Inc., Chatsworth, 1982-83, Home Savs. & Loan, North Hollywood, Calif., 1987, Micro Tech., L.A., 1987, TRW, Inc.-Space and Def., Redondo Beach, Calif., 1993—, Pacificare Health Systems, Inc., 1997, Nissan North America (formerly Nissan Motor Corp., USA.), 1998-99, Prosum info. Techs., Inc., 2000—, Am. Honda Motors, Inc., 1999-2000. Mem. IEEE Computer Soc., Salle Gascon Fencing Club, U.S. Fencing Assn., Delta Sigma Pi. Republican. Avocations: fencing, softball, tennis, volleyball, travel, sailing. Office: 1610 E St Andrews Pl PO Box 25125 Santa Ana CA 92799-5125

SLOANE, ANDY, computer scientist, educator; b. Wolverhampton, U.K., Apr. 21, 1954; s. James and Joan (Griffiths) S.; m. Delia Llewellyn, Apr. 26, 1986; children: Peter, Niall. BSc, U. Wales, 1976, PhD, 1979. Computer scientist GCHQ, Cheltenham, U.K., 1979-80; rsch. fellow U. Birmingham, U.K., 1980-81; lectr. West Bromwich (U.K.) Coll., 1982-84, U. Wolverhampton, U.K., 1985—. Author: Computer Communications, 1994, 2d edit., 1999, Multimedia Communications, 1996; spkr. in field; contbr. articles to profl. jours. Mem. IEEE (chair IFIP Working Group 9.3.). Avocations: swimming, motor caravaning, cycling, walking, horse racing. Office: Univ Wolverhampton Sch Computing and IT, Lichfield St, Wolverhampton WV1 1SB, England

SLOANE, BEVERLY LEBOV, writer, consultant; b. N.Y.C., May 26, 1936; d. Benjamin S. and Anne (Weinberg) LeBov; m. Robert Malcolm Sloane, Sept. 27, 1959; 1 child, Alison Lori Sloane Gaylin. AB, Vassar Coll., 1958; MA, Claremont Grad. U., 1975, doctoral study, 1975-76; cert. in exec. mgmt., UCLA Grad. Sch. Mgmt., 1982, grad. exec. mgmt. program, 1982; grad. intensive bioethics course Kennedy Inst. Ethics, Georgetown U., 1987, advanced bioethics course, 1988; grad. sem. in Health Care Ethics, U. Wash. Sch. Medicine, Seattle, summer 1988-90, 94; grad. Summer Bioethics Inst., Loyola Marymount U., summer 1990; grad. Annual Summer Inst. on Teaching of Writing, Columbia U. Tchrs. Coll., summer 1990; grad. Annual Summer Inst. on Advanced Teaching of Writing, Columbia Tchrs. Coll., summer 1993; grad. Annual Inst. Pub. Health and Human Rights, Harvard U. Sch. Pub. Health, 1994; grad. pub. course profl. pub., Stanford U., 1982; cert. clin. intensive biomedical ethics, Loma Linda U. Med. Ctr., 1989, cert. Ethics Fellow, 1989, cert. clin. intensive biomedical ethics, 1989; grad. exec. refresher course profl. pub., Stanford U., 1994; cert Exec. Mgmt. Inst. in Health Care, U. So. Calif., 1995; cert. in ethics corps tng. program, Josephson Inst. of Ethics, 1991; cert. advanced exec. program Grad. Sch. Mgmt., UCLA, 1995; grad. Women's Campaign Sch., Yale U., 1998. Circulation libr. Harvard Med. Libr., Boston, 1958-59; social worker Conn. State Welfare, New Haven, 1960-61; tchr. English Hebrew Day Sch., New Haven, 1961-64; instr. creative writing and English lit. Monmouth Coll., West Long Branch, N.J., 1967-69; writer, cons., 1970—; v.p. council grad. students, Claremont Grad. U., 1971-72, adj. dir. Writing Ctr. Speaker Series, 1993—, spkr., 1996, 97, 98; mem. adv. coun. tech. and profl. writing Dept. English, Calif. State U., Long Beach, 1980-82; mem. adv. bd. Calif. Health Rev., 1982-83; mem. Foothill Health Dist. Adv. Coun. L.A. County Dept. Health Svcs., 1987-93, pres., 1989-91, immediate past pres., 1991-92; vis. scholar Hastings Ctr., 1996; spkr. N.Y. State Task Force on Life and the Law, 1996; panel spkr. ann. conf. Am. Assn. Suicidology, 1998. Author: From Vassar to Kitchen, 1967, A Guide to Health Facilities: Personnel and Management, 1971, 2nd edit., 1977, 3d edit., 1992, Introduction to Healthcare Delivery Organization: Functions and Management, 4th edit., 1999. Mem. pub. relations bd. Monmouth County Mental Health Assn., 1968-69; chmn. creative writing group Calif. Inst. Tech. Woman's Club, 1975-79; mem. ethics com., human subjects protection com. Jewish Home for the Aging, Reseda, Calif., 1994-97; mem. task force edn. and cultural activities, City of Duarte, 1987-88; mem. strategic planning task force com., campaign com. for pre-eminence Claremont Grad. U., 1986-87, mem. alumni coun., bd. dirs. alumni assn., 1993-96, mem. vol. devel. com., 1994-96, alumnae awards com. 1993-96; Vassar Coll. Class rep. to Alumnae Assn. Fall Coun. Meeting, 1989, class corr. Vassar Coll. Quarterly Alumnae Mag., 1993-98; mem. gift com. class of 1958 40th reunion program chmn., 1998, class v.p., 1998-2000, class co-pres., 2000—; co-chmn. Vassar Christmas Showcase New Haven Vassar Club, 1965-66, rep. to Vassar Coll. Alumnae Assn. Fall Coun. Meeting, 1965-66; co-chmn. Vassar Club So. Calif. Annual Book Fair, 1970-71; chmn. creative writing group Yale U. Newcomers, 1965-66; dir. creative writing group Yale U. Women's Orgn., 1966-67; grad. AMA Ann. Health Reporting Conf., 1992, 93; mem. exec. program network UCLA Grad. Sch. Mgmt., 1987—; trustee Ctr. for Improvement of Child Caring, 1981-83; mem. League Crippled Children, 1982—, bd. dirs., 1988-91, treas. for gen. meetings., 1990-91, chair hostesses com., 1988-89, pub. rels. com., 1990-91; bd. dirs. L.A. Commn. on Assaults Against Women, 1983-84; chmn. 1st ann. Rabbi Camillus Angel Interfaith Svc. Temple Beth David, 1978, v.p., 1983-86, spkr., 1997; mem. cmty. rels. com. Jewish Fedn. Council Greater L.A., 1985-87; del. Task Force on Minorities in Newspaper Bus., 1987-89; cmty. rep. County Health Ctrs. Network Tobacco Control Program, 1991; mem. N.Y. Citizens Com. Health Care Decisions; bd. dirs. Coro Nat. Alumni Assn., 1999—. Recipient cert. of appreciation City of Duarte, 1988, County of L.A., 1988, Ann. Key Mem. award L.A. Dept. Health Svcs., 1990; recipient cert. of appreciation Alumni Coun. Claremont Grad Sch., 1996; Coro Found. fellow, 1979; named Calif. Communicator of Achievement, Woman of Yr. Calif. Press Women, 1992. Fellow Am. Med. Writers Assn. (pres. Pacific Southwest chpt. 1987-89, dir. 1980-93, Pacific S.W. del to nat. bd. 1980-87, 89-91, chmn. various conv. coms., chmn . nat. book awards trade category 1982-83, chmn. Nat. Conv. Networking Luncheon 1983-, 84, nat. chmn. freelance sect. 1984-85, gen. chmn. Asilomar Western Regional Conf., 1985, workshop leader 1985, program co-chmn. 1987, speaker 1985, 88-89, program co-chmn. 1989, nat. exec. bd. dirs. 1985-86, nat. adminstr. sects. 1985-86, pres.-elect Pacific S.W. chpt. 1985-87, pres. 1987-89, immediate past pres. 1989-91, bd. dirs. 1991-93, moderator gen. session nat. conf. 1987, chair gen. session nat. conf. 1986-87, workshop leader Nat. Ann. Conf. 1984-89, 90-92, 95, chair Walter C. Alvarez Meml. Found. award 1986-87, appreciation award for outstanding leadership 1989, named to Workshop Leaders Honor Roll 1991); mem. Women in Comm. (dir. 1980-82, 89-90, v.p. cmty. affairs 1981-82, N.E. area rep. 1980-81, chmn. awards banquet 1982, sem. leader, speaker ann. nat. profl. conf., 1985, program adv. com. L.A. chpt. 1987, v.p. activities 1989-90, chmn. L.A. chpt. 1st ann. Agnes Underwood Freedom of Info. Awards Banquet 1982, recognition award 1983, nominating com. 1982, 83, com. Women of the Press Awards luncheon 1988, Women in comm. awards luncheon 1988), Am. Assn. for Higher Edn., AAUW (legis. chmn. Arcadia Br. 1976-77, books and plays chmn. Arcadia Br. 1973-74, creative writing chmn. 1969-70, 1st v.p. program dir. 1975-76, networking chmn. 1981-82, speaker 1987, Cert. of appreciation 1987, chmn task force promoting individual liberties 1987-88, named Woman of Yr., Woman of Achievement award 1986, cert. of appreciation 1987, pres.-elect 1998-99, pres. Arcadia Br. 1999-2000, edn. equity chmn. 1998-99, chmn. delegation to nat. convention 1999, chmn. Tech Trek Sci. Camp Scholarship for Girls 1999, Career Day 1999, writer in residence Calif. State Comm. Com. 1999-2000), Coro Nat. Alumni Assn. (bd. dirs. 1999—), AAUW Calif. State Comms. Com. (writer in residence 1999—), AAUW (program vice chmn. L.A. County Interbranch coun. 2000—, diversity chmn. Arcadia Br. 2000—, interbranch coun. Arcadia br. rep. 2000—), Coll. English Assn., APHA, Am. Soc. Law, Medicine and Ethics, Calif. Press Women (v.p. programs L.A. chpt. 1982-85, pres. 1985-87, state pres. 1987-89, past immediate past state pres. 1989-91, chmn. state speakers bur. 1989-95, del nat. bd. 1989-95, moderator ann. spring conv., 1990, 92, chmn. nominating com. 1990-91, Calif. lit. dir. 1990-92, dir. state lit. com. 1990-92, dir. family literacy day Calif., 1990, Cert. of Appreciation, 1991, named Calif. Communicator of Achievement 1992, named Woman of Millenium Calif. Media Profls. 2000), AAUP, N.Y. Acad. Scis., Ind. Writers So. Calif. (bd. dirs. 1989-90, dir. Specialized Groups 1989-90, dir. at large 1989-90, bd. dirs. corp. 1988-89, dir. Speech Writing Group 1991-92), Hastings Ctr. (vis. scholar 1996), Nat. Fedn. Press Women (bd. dirs. 1987-93, nat. co-chmn. task force recruitment of minorities 1987-89, del. 1987-89, nat. dir. of speakers bur. 1989-93, editor of speakers bur. directory 1991, cert. of appreciation, 1991, 93, Plenary of Past Pres. state 1989—, workshop leader-speaker ann. nat. conf. 1990, chair state women of achievement com. 1986-87, editor Speakers Bur. Addendum Directory, 1992, editor Speakers Bur. Directory, 1991, 92, named 1st runner up Nat. Communicator of Achievement 1992), Soc. for Tech. Comm. (workshop leader 1985, 86), Kennedy Inst. Ethics, Soc. Health and Human Values, N.Y. Acad. Medicine (met. N.Y. Ethics Network), Assoc. Writing Programs, Authors Guild, Nat. Writers Union, Women's City (Pasadena), Claremont Colls. Faculty House, Pasadena Athletic, Town Hall of Calif. (vice chair cmty. affairs sect. 1982-87, speaker 1986, faculty-instr. Exec. Breakfast Inst. 1985-86, mem. study sect. coun. 1986-88), Rotary (chair Duarte Rotary mag. 1988-89, mem. internat. svc. com. 1989-90, info. svc. com. 1989-90), AAUW Calif. State Diversity Com., 2000— (vice chmn. program L.A. County Interbranch Coun. 2000—, rep. Arcadia br. 2000—, diversity chmn. Arcadia br. 2000—). Home and Office: 1301 N Santa Anita Ave Arcadia CA 91006-2419

SLOANE, JAMES ROBERT, chemical engineer; b. Pitts., June 14, 1942; s. Paul Guyer Sloan and Mildred Catherine Reuter; m. Susan Richards, Sept. 18, 1995 (div. May 1992); children: Michelle Karin, James Robert Jr., Jonathan Westby; m. Judy Southerland, Dec. 6, 1997. BSChemE, Pa. State U., 1994; postgrad., U. Ctrl. Fla. Registered profl. engr., Fla. Engr. Westinghouse Electric Corp., 1964, Graver Water Cond. Co., 1967; sales engr. Datum Co., Houston, 1971; charter pilot, aircraft sales mgr. W. Houston Airport, 1972; flight supr. Embry-Riddle Aero. U., Daytona Beach, Fla., 1973; project mgr. Russell and Axon Engrs., Daytona Beach, 1974; sr. project mgr. Briley, Wild and Assocs. Inc., Ormond Beach, Fla., 1986, McKim and Creed Engrs., Daytona Beach, 1994; dep. pub. works dir., city engr. City Daytona Beach, 1998. Mem. AOPA, ASPA, Am. Pub. Works Assn., Fla. Engr. Soc. Methodist. Avocations: flying, aircraft, water skiing. E-mail: JRSloane@aol.com. Home: 635 Lake Winnemissett Dr Deland FL 32724-4817 Office: The City Daytona Beach PO Box 2451 Daytona Beach FL 32115-2451

SLOANE, J.P., television producer, writer, entertainer, theologian; b. Hollywood, Calif., Sept. 6, 1942; s. Jimmy Jackson and Anita (Thibodeaux) Barrios. Grad., Oral Roberts U., Inst. Charismatic Studies, Moody Bible Inst., Chgo.; diploma, Inst. Jewish-Christian Studies, Dallas; cert. in TV prodn., Purdue U., 1981; student, Masters Coll., 1997—. biblical scholar and lectr.; appeared on all major Christian networks worldwide. Guest Art Linkletter's House Party (age 5), CBS Radio Network; played Billy Kettle in Ma and Pa Kettle movie series; appeared on Memory Lane TV show, Hollywood; recorded High on a Mountain, 1960, Linda Darling, 1960; lead singer The Brothers Grim, 1965-68; featured act with Charlie Rich; mem. J.P. Sloane & Co. group, 1973-78; albums include Solid Gold; tv and radio prodr. Recipient Excellence in Media Angel awards for Outstanding TV Prodr., Outstanding Male Vocalist and Outstanding Music Video, Medal of Merit, Pres. Ronald Reagan; named Hon. Sheriff, L.A. County, Hon. Ky. Col., Hon. Lt. Gov. State of Ind., Hon. Citizen, Tulsa, Met. Nashville, 22d Internat. Angel award best multiple character voices, 1999, numerous others; nominee Cleo award, 1980; key to cities Nashville and New Orleans, others.

SLOANE, PETER JAMES, economics educator; b. Cheadle Hulme, Cheshire, Eng., June 8, 1942; s. John Joseph and Elizabeth (Clarke) S.; m. Avril Mary Urquhart, July 30, 1969; 1 child, Christopher Peter. BA in Econs., Sheffield U., U.K., 1964; PhD, Strathclyde U., Scotland, 1968. Asst. lectr./lectr. U. Aberdeen, Scotland, 1966-69; lectr. U. Nottingham, Eng., 1969-75; econ. advisor Dept. of Employment, London, 1973-74; prof. econs. U. Paisley, Scotland, 1975-84; Jaffrey prof. polit. economy U. Aberdeen, 1984—, vice-prin., dean faculty social scis. and law, 1996—; mem. coun. Econ. and Social Rsch. Coun., U.K., 1979-85; mem. Sec. of State's Panel of Econ. Cons., Scotland, 1981-91; mem. mergers com. Scottish Higher Edn. Funding Coun., 1994-97. Co-author: Sex Discrimination in the Labour Market, 1976, Tackling Discrimination at the Workplace, 1982, Labour Economics, 1985; editor: Women and Low Pay, 1980; co-editor: Low Pay and Earnings Mobility in Europe, 1998; contbr. articles to profl. jours. Trustee Robert Nicol Trust, Aberdeen, 1984—. Can. Commonwealth Fund fellow, 1978. Fellow Royal Soc. Arts, Royal Soc. Edinburgh; mem. Royal Econ. Soc., Scottish Econ. Soc. (mem. coun. 1983—), Brit. Indsl. Rels. Assn., European Assn. Labour Economists. Avocation: sport. Home: Hillcrest, 45 Friarsfield Rd, Aberdeen Scotland Office: U Aberdeen Dept Econs, Edward Wright Bl, Dunbar St, Old Aberdeen AB24 3QY, Scotland

SLOBOZHANIN, LEV ARKADIEVICH, fluid mechanics researcher; b. Nylga, Russia, Sept. 1, 1941; s. Arkadii Alexandrovich and Iraida Stepanovna (Vlasova) S.; divorced; children: Andrei L., Darya L. Degree in mech. engring. with honors, Kharkov (Ukraine) Aviation Inst., 1963; PhD in Physics and Math., Inst. for Low Temperature Physics and Engring., Kharkov, 1968; cert. sr. rsch. scientist, Acad. of Scis. of Ukraine, 1975; DSc in Physics and Math., Lavrentyev Inst. Hydrodynamics, Novosibirsk, Russia, 1989. Engr. B. Verkin Inst. Low Temperature Physics and Engring. Nat. Acad. Scis. of Ukraine, Kharkov, 1963-66, sr. engr., 1966-69, jr. scientist, 1969-71, sr. scientist, 1971-89, leading scientist, 1989-98; sr. tchr. Kharkov Aviation Inst., 1969-71, prof., 1989-90; vis. prof. Madrid Poly. U., 1993-94; vis. scholar U. Ala., Huntsville, 1995—; vis. rschr. Case Western Res. U., Cleve., 1999—. Co-author: Fluid Mechanics of Weightlessness, 1976, Low-Gravity Fluid Mechanics, 1987, Solution Methods for Fluid Mechanics Problems Under Weightlessness Conditions, 1992; contbr. articles to profl. jours. Chmn. trade union com. B. Verkin Inst. for Low Temperature Physics and Engring., 1986-89. Mem. Am. Phys. Soc. Office: U Ala Huntsville Rsch Inst D 29 Cmmr Huntsville AL 35899-0001

SLOCUM, DONALD WARREN, chemist; m. Laurel Hopper, 1990 (dec. May 1997); children from previous marriage: Warren, Matthew. BS in

Chemistry, BA in English, U. Rochester; PhD in Chemistry, NYU, 1963. Postdoctoral rsch. assoc. Duke U., Durham, N.C., 1963-64; asst. prof. chemistry Carnegie Inst. Tech., Pitts., 1964-65; from asst. to assoc. prof. chemistry So. Ill. U., Carbondale, 1965-72; prof. So. Ill. U., 1972-81, adj. prof., 1981-84; program dir. chem. dynamics sect., chemistry div. NSF, Washington, 1984-85; program leader div. ednl. programs, sr. scientist chem. tech. div. Argonne (Ill.) Nat. Lab., 1985-90; head dept. chemistry Western Ky. U., Bowling Green, 1990-95, prof. chemistry, 1995—; sr. scientist Gulf Rsch. and Devel. Co., Pitts., 1980-82; vis. prof. U. Ill., 1970, U. Bristol, Eng., 1973, U. Cin., 1976; vis. fellow U. Bristol, 1972; vis. lectr. Carnegie-Mellon U., 1983-84, U. Pitts., 1983-84; organizer symposia on organometallic chemistry and catalysis; bd. dirs. Ctrl. States Univs., Inc., 1986-88, Arts at Argonne, 1988-90; cons. in field; mem. nat. organizing com. XVth Internat. Conf. on Organometallic Chemistry Wayne State U., Detroit, 1990; mem. internat. adv. bd. XVith Internat. Conf. on Organometallic Chemistry, Warsaw, 1992; mem. NSF/EPSCoR subcom., Ky., 1993-94; mem. coun. on undergrad. rsch. Instnl. Liaison Rep. to Western Ky. U., 1995—. Co-editor: Advances in Chemistry Series of Am. Chem. Soc., Vol. 230, 1992, Methane and Alkane Activation (Plenum), 1995; contbr. over 70 articles to profl. jours., chpts. to books. Recipient Rsch./Creativity award Ogden Coll. of Sci., Technology and Health, Western Ky. U., 1996, Sci. award honoring Brian Andreen, Cottrell Coll. Sci., 1999. Mem. Am. Chem. Soc. (sec. gen. elect catalysis and surface sci. secretariat 1992, sec. gen. 1993, organic divsn. rep. to catalysis and surface sci. secretariat, 1993-98, co-chmn. symposium, San Diego, 1994), Chem. Soc. Gt. Britain, Catalysis Soc., Sigma Xi. Avocations: music, literature, sports. Office: Western Ky U Dept Chemistry Bowling Green KY 42101

SLOCUM, ROBERT BOAK, minister, educator; b. Macon, Ga., May 21, 1952; s. James Robert and Sara Lila (Bell) S.; m. Sheryl Stephanie Walter, May 15, 11982; children: Claire Marie, Rebecca Bell, Jacob Robert. BA, Vanderbilt U., 1974, JD, 1977; MDiv, Nashotah House Sem., 1986; DMin, U. of the South, 1992; PhD, Marquette U., 1997. Ordained priest Episcopal Ch., 1987; bar: Tenn. 1978; cert. trial counsel, cert. def. counsel. Deacon-in-tng. Trinity Episcopal Ch., New Orleans, 1986-87; vicar St. Patrick's Episcopal Ch., Zachary, La., 1987-91, St. Andrew's Episcopal Ch., Clinton, La., 1991-92; rector St. Philip's Episcopal Ch., Waukesha, Wis., 1991-92; priest-in-charge Ch. of the Holy Communion, Lake Geneva, Wis., 1993, rector, 1994—; chaplain VA, Milw., 1993-98; lectr. theology Marquette U., Milw., 1997—; chair convention planning com. Episcopal Diocese of Milw., 1996-97. Co-editor: Documents of Witness, A History of the Episcopal Churchy, 1782-1985, 1994, An Episcopal Dictionary of the Church, A User-Friendly Reference for Episcopalians, 2000; editor: Prophet of Justice, Prophet of Life, 2000, Essays on William Stringfellow, 1997, A New Conversation, Essays on the Future of Theology and the Episcopal Church, 1999, A New Conversation, Essays on the Future of Theology and the Episcopal Church, 1999; author: The Theology of William Porcher DuBose, Life, Movement, and Being, 2000. Pres. Lake Geneva Libr. Bd., 1995—, Geneva Lakes Area United Way, 1998-2000. Capt. USAF, 1978-83. Decorated Meritorious Svc. medal. Mem. Am. Acad. Religion, Soc. for Study Christian Spirituality, Soc. Anglican and Luth. Theologians. Avocation: distance running. Home: 1325 Madison St Lake Geneva WI 53147-1136 Office: Ch of the Holy Communion 320 Broad St Lake Geneva WI 53147-1812

SLOMAN, AARON, computer science educator, philosopher, cognitive scientist; b. Que Que, Zimbabwe, Oct. 30, 1936; arrived in Eng., 1957; s. Reuben and Hannah (Rest) S.; m. Alison Mary Dresser, May 29, 1965; children: Benjamin, Jonathan. BSc, U. Cape Town, S. Africa, 1956; DPhil, Oxford (Eng.) U., 1962. Lectr. in philosophy U. Hull, Eng., 1962-64; lectr. in philosophy U. Sussex, Brighton, Eng., 1964-72, 72-75, reader in philosophy and artificial intelligence, 1976-84, prof. cognitive sci. and artificial intelligence, 1984-91; prof. cognitive sci. and artificial intelligence U. Birmingham, Eng., 1991-94; head Sch. Computer Sci. U. Birmingham, Eng., 1991-94; rsch. prof. in cognitive sci. and artificial intelligence U. Birmingham, Eng., 1994—; sr. vis. fellow Edinburgh (Scotland) U., 1972-73; cons. Integral Solutions Ltd., Bramley, England, 1989—. Author: The Computer Revolution in Philosophy, 1978; co-author: Pop II: A Practical Language for Artificial Intelligence, 1985; contbr. articles to profl. jours. Fellow AISB, ECCAI, Am. Assn. Artificial Intelligence. Avocations: playing flute, learning to play violin, listening to music.

SLOMAN, ALBERT EDWARD, retired university administrator, consultant; b. Launceston, Cornwall, Eng., Feb. 14, 1921; s. Albert and Lillie (Brewer) S.; m. Marie Bernadette Bergeron, Aug. 4, 1948; children: Anne Veronique, Isabelle Patricia, Bernadette Jeanne. MA, U. Oxford, 1946, DPhil, 1948; hon. doctor, U. Nice, 1968, U. Essex, 1988, U. Liverpool, 1989. Lectr. Spanish U. Calif., Berkeley, 1946-47; reader Spanish U. Dublin, Ireland, 1947-53; prof. Spanish U. Liverpool, Eng., 1953-62; vice chancellor U. Essex, Colchester, Eng., 1962-87; chmn. internat. bd. United World Coll.s, 1988-92; chmn. Com. Vice Chancellors, U.K., 1981-83; pres. Conf. European Rectors, 1969-74. Flight lt. RAF, 1941-45, ETO. Decorated CBE, KT by Her Majest the Queen. Mem. Internat. Assn. Univs. (v.p. 1970-75), Savile Club. Avocations: travel, walking.

SLOMAN, MARVIN SHERK, lawyer; b. Fort Worth, Apr. 17, 1925; s. Richard Jack and Lucy Janette (Sherk) S.; m. Margaret Jane Dinwiddie, Apr. 11, 1953; children: Lucy Carter, Richard Dinwiddie. BA, U. Tex., 1948; LLB with honors, 1950. Bar: Tex. 1950, N.Y. 1951. Assoc. Sullivan & Cromwell, N.Y.C., 1950-56; assoc. Carrington, Coleman, Sloman & Blumenthal LLP and predecessor, Dallas, 1956-60, ptnr., 1960-97; sr. counsel, 1998—. Office: Carrington Coleman Sloman & Blumenthal LLP 200 Crescent Ct Ste 1500 Dallas TX 75201-1848

SLOMOVITZ, DANIEL, electrical engineer, researcher; b. Montevideo, Uruguay, May 25, 1952; s. bernardo and ana (Steimetz) S.; m. Esther Joskowicz; children: Ruth, Gabriel. Elec. Engr., U. de la Republica, Uruguay, 1978, D in Engring., 2000. Engring. asst. UTE-Lab., Montevideo, 1977-78, dep. head, 1978-79, head of lab., 1979—. Contbr. more than 50 articles to profl. jours. Mem. IEEE (chpt. chmn. 1989—, named Eminent Engr. 1994), CIER (internat. coord.), CIGRE. Home: PO Box 19934, E Lopez 4716/904, Montevideo Uruguay Office: UTE-Laboratory, Paraguay 2385, 11900 Montevideo Uruguay

SLONEM, HUNT, artist; b. Kittery, Maine, July 18, 1951; s. Charles and Louise W. Slonem. Student, Skowhegan Sch. Painting and Sculpture, 1972; BA, Tulane U., 1973. Numerous one-man shows, 1977—, including Tilden-Foley Gallery, New Orleans, 1991, Helander Gallery, N.Y.C., 1991, Charlotte Milburn Fine Art Mus., Oslo, 1991, Pulitzer Gallery, Amsterdam, 1991, Witteveen Gallery, Amsterdam, 1991, numerous others; exhibited in numerous group shows, 1977—, including Laguna Gloria Mus., Austin, Tex., 1990, Bergen Mus. Art & Sci., Paramus, N.J., 1990, Meredith Long Gallery, Houston, 1990, Marlborough Gallery, N.Y.C., Solomon R. Guggenheim Mus., N.Y.C., Centro Cultural Recoleta, Buenos Aires, 2000, Heriard Cimino Gallery, New Orleans, 2000, Vanier Gallery, Scottsdale, Ariz., 2000, Harmon Meek Gallery, Naples, Fla., numerous others; represented in numerous permanent collections including Met. Mus. Art, N.Y.C., Contemporary Mus., Honolulu, Chrysler Mus., Norfolk, Va., Columbus (Ohio) Mus. Art, Oklahoma Art Ctr., Oklahoma City, Portland (Maine) Mus. Art, Wichita (Kans.) Art Mus., many others. McDowell fellow, 1983, 84, 86, Ragsdale Found. fellow, 1983; Elizabeth T. Greenshields Found. grantee, 1976, NEA grantee, 1991; recipient award Millay Colony, 1982. Avocation: aviculture. Home and Studio: 87 E Houston St New York NY 10012-2805

SLONSKA, ZOFIA ANTONINA, sociologist; b. Poznan, Poland, May 16, 1950; d. Mieczyslaw and Emilia (Stalmach) Granat; m. Dariusz Leszek Slonski, Dec. 28, 1971; 1 child, Katarzyna. MA, Inst. Sociology, Warsaw U., Poland, 1973; D of Sociology, Polish Acad. Scis., Warsaw, 1987. Sociologist, asst. prof. dept. epidemiology Nat. Inst. Hygiene, Warsaw, Poland, 1973-91, head unit socio-epidemiology, 1983-91; advisor min. health Ministry of Health, Warsaw, Poland, 1991; cons. health promotion World Health Orgn., Regional Office Europe, Copenhagen, 1991; asst. prof., deputy head dept. health promotion Nat. Inst. Cardiology, Warsaw, 1991—. Co-author: Epidemiological Situation and Control of Infectious Diseases in Poland, 1970-1979, 1984, The Encyclopedia of Sociology, 1998; contbr. articles to profl. jours. Mem. European Soc. Health & Med. Sociology, Internat. Union Health Promotion & Edn., Internat. Soc. & Fedn. Cardiology (scientific sect. epidemiology & prevention). Roman Catholic. Avocation: gymnastics. Office: Inst Cardiology, Dept Health Promotion, 04-628 Warsaw Poland

SLOUTSKI, ILYA LEONIOLOVICH, advertising executive; b. Chelyabinsk, Russia, June 19, 1968; s. Leonia Iosefovich and Lyudmila Alexeema (Kuznetsova) S.; 1 child, Arseny. Moscow Technol. U., 1992; Media Rsch. and Planning Cert., DMC Group, Helsinki, 1995; Med. Mgmt. Certificate, USTA Tng. Ctr., Washington, 1996. Dir. Informatika Mktg. Svc., Moscow, 1990-92; gen. mgr. SFT Advt. Agy., Moscow, 1992-94; pres., CEO Media Arts Mktg. Comm., Moscow, 1994—. Mem. Russian Advt. Agys. Assn. (bd. dirs., head check-up com.), Nat. Broadcasters Assn. Avocations: car racing, music, poetry, downhill skiing. Office: Media Arts Mktg Comm, 55/1 Lesnaya St, 103005 Moscow Russia

SLOVETSKY, DMITRY IPPOLITOVICH, physicist-chemist, researcher; b. Beljachevo, Vologda, Russia, July 1, 1937; s. Ippolit Nicolaevich Slovetsky and Varvara Dmitrievna Voronina; m. Olga Alexandrovna Filippova, Nov. 21, 1964; 1 child, Sergei Dmitrievich. Grad. in physics, M.V. Lomonosov Moscow State U., 1960; PhD, Ctrl. Inst. Machine Bldg., Kaliningrad, Russia, 1967, D Physics and Math., 1978. Dir. lab. Acad. Scis. USSR (now Russia), Moscow, 1988—; jr. rschr. Ctrl. Inst. Machine Bldg., 1960-67; sr. rschr. A.V. Tochiev Inst. Petrochem. Syntheses, Acad. Scis. USSR (now Russia), Moscow, 1967-86, lieder rschr., 1986-88; rschr. in physics and phys. chemistry; chmn. expert Sci. and Tech. Ministry, Moscow, 1988—; chmn. sect. plasma chemistry High Energy Chemistry Coun., Moscow, 1988—. Author: Mechanisms of Chemical Reactions in Nonequilibrium Plasma, 1981; co-author: Chemistry of Plasma, 1991; mem. editl. bd. High Energy Chemistry, 1988—; contbr. over 300 articles to sci. jours., including Jour. Membrane Sci., Applied Physics, Pure and Applied Chemistry. Recipient State prize of USSR, 1989; grantee Soros Internat. Sci. Found., 1993-95. Mem. Russian Membrane Soc., European Membrane Soc. (collective), Russian Acad. Scis. (sci. couns.). Home: Domodedovskay 24/1 Apt 107, 115582 Moscow Russia Office: AV Topchiev Inst Petrochem, Syntheses, Leninsky Pr 29, 117071 Moscow Russia

SLOWIK, RICHARD ANDREW, air force officer; b. Detroit, Sept. 9, 1939; s. Louis Stanley and Mary Jean (Zaucha) S.; 1 step-child, Amber Dawn Evans. BS, USAF Acad., 1963; BS in Bus. Adminstrn., No. Mich. U., 1967; LLB, LaSalle Extension U., 1969; MBA, Fla. Tech. U., 1972; MS in Adminstrn., Ga. Coll., 1979; MA, Georgetown U., 1983; postgrad. cert., Va. Polytech. Inst. and State U., 1986. Commd. 1st lt. U.S. Air Force, 1963, advanced through grades to lt. col.; pilot Craig AFB, Ala., 1963-64, Sawyer AFB, Mich., 1964-68; forward air contr. Pacific Air Forces, South Vietnam, 1968-69; pilot SAC, McCoy AFB, Fla., 1969-71; asst. prof. aerospace studies Va. Poly. Inst. and State U., Blacksburg, 1972-76; br. chief current ops. br. Robins AFB, Ga., 1976-80; asst. dep. chief ops. group Hdqrs. Air Force, Pentagon, Washington, 1980-82; Western Hemisphere and Pacific Area desk officer Nat. Mil. Command Center, Pentagon, Washington, 1982-83; mil. rep. Ops. Ctr., Dept. State, Washington, 1983-85; ops. officer 97th Bombardment Wing, Blytheville AFB, Ark., 1985-87, chief base ops. and trg. div., 97th Combat Support Group, Blythville AFB, 1987-88, chief airfield mgmt. div. Eaker AFB, Ark., 1988-91, free-lance writer, 1991—. Group ops. officer CAP, Marquette, Mich., 1967-68, Orlando, Fla., 1970-72, sr. programs officer, Blacksburg, 1972-76, Warner Robins, Ga., 1976-80, wing plans and programs officer, Washington, 1980—. Contbr. articles profl. jours. Decorated Defense Meritorious Service Medal, 10 Air medals, 3 Air Force Meritorious Service medals, 2 Commendation medals, Cross of Gallantry with Palm, Presdl. Legion of Merit, others; recipient Presdl. Legion of Merit, Presdl. Medal of Merit (3), Presdl. Achievement award (3), Bill Baker Short Story award Miss. County Writers Guild, 1995. Mem. Acad. of Mgmt., Air Force Assn., Cato Inst., Heritage Found., Mil. Order World Wars, Am. Def. Preparedness Assn., Am. Security Council, Order of Daedalians. Roman Catholic. Home and Office: 1708 N Broadway St Blytheville AR 72315-1320

SLUIMAN, HANS JAN, biologist, researcher; b. Goes, The Netherlands, Apr. 5, 1953; arrived in Scotland, 1992; m. Flora A.J. Den Hertog, June 28, 1978; 1 child, Anniek. Diploma, U. Leiden (The Netherlands), 1975, Doctorate, 1978; PhD, Free U., Amsterdam, 1985. Tchg. asst. U. Leiden, 1976-78; rsch. fellow Miami U., Oxford, Ohio, 1979-80; sci. officer Free U., Amsterdam, 1980-84; postdoctoral rsch. fellow U. Leiden, 1985-91; prin. sci. officer Royal Botanic Garden, Edinburgh, Scotland, 1992—; cons. Eden Valley Mineral Water Co., Cumbria, Scotland, 1995—. Editorial advisor (jours.) Archiv Fuer Protisten Kunde, 1990-97, Plant Systematics and Evolution, 1990-95. Miami U. Fulbright fellow, 1979, Huygens fellow Netherlands Orgn. for Sci. Rsch., 1985. Mem. Phycological Soc. Am., Internat. Phycological Soc., British Phycological Soc., German Botanical Soc. Office: Royal Botanic Garden, Inverleith Row, Edinburgh EH3 5LR, Scotland

SLUMAN, JEFF (JEFFREY GEORGE SLUMAN), professional golfer; b. Rochester, New York, Sept. 11, 1957; m. Linda; 1 child, Kathryn Doreen. BA in Fin., Fla. State U., 1980. Professional golfer, 1980-. professional golfer, mem. PGA, winner PGA Championship, 1988; Tucson Chrysler Classic, 1997; Greater Milwaukee Open, 1998; Sony Open in Hawaii, 1999. Office: c/o PGA Tour 112 Tpc Blvd Ponte Vedra Beach FL 32082-3046

SLUSANSCHI, ANCA EUGENIA, computer scientist, researcher; b. Sibiu, Romania, June 10, 1968; d. Iancu and Eufrosina (Pastiu) Voica; m. Horia Cristian Slusanschi, July 7, 1995. MS in Computer Sci., U. Sibiu, 1992. Cert. engr. Analyst Indepenta S.A., Sibiu, 1992-95; rsch. fellow U. Surrey, Guildford, Eng., 1995-96; analyst programmer Anchor Trust, 1996-97; devel. cons. Team Comtex, 1997-98; cons. Glazier Systems (now Advantage Group Ltd.), Wellington, New Zealand, 1998—; sr. team leader e-commerce Advantage Group Ltd., Wellington, New Zealand, 1999-2000; sr. team leader AMP Asset Mgmt., Wellington, New Zealand, 2000—. Mem. AAAS, IEEE, Computer Soc., N.Y. Acad. Sci., Assn. for Computing Machinery, Nat. Geog. Soc. E-mail: anca@acm.org. Home: 117 Realm Dr Lev 5 City Tower, PO Box 3764, Wellington New Zealand Office: New Kelvin Chambers, 44-52 The Terrace POB 5428, Wellington New Zealand

SLUSANSCHI, HORIA CRISTIAN, computer scientist, researcher; b. Bucharest, Romania, Dec. 19, 1970; arrived in N.Z., 1997; s. Dan Mihaiu and Daniela Valeria (Mihaescu) S.; m. Anca Eugenia Voica, July 7, 1995. MSc, Politechna U., Bucharest, 1995. Asst. Politechnica U., Bucharest, 1994-95; rsch. fellow Surrey U., Guildford, Eng., 1995-97; rsch. officer Massey U., Palmerston North, N.Z., 1997—; cons. Advantage Group Ltd., 1998-2000; software devel. cons. The New Zealand Totalisator Agy Bd., Wellington, 2000—. Mem. IEEE, IEEE Computer Soc., Assn. for Computing Machinery. E-mail: horia@computer.org. Office: New Zealand Totalisator, Agy Bd PO Box 38-899, The Terrace POB 5428 Wellington Mail Ctr New Zealand

SLUSSER, EUGENE ALVIN, electronics manufacturing executive; b. Denver, Mar. 13, 1922; s. Jesse Alvin and Grace (Carter) S.; m. Anne L. Longley, Oct. 2, 1943; children: Robert, Jon, Carolyn. BS in Physics, U. Denver, 1947. Registered profl. engr., N.H. Mem. staff MIT Radiation Lab., Cambridge, 1942-45; project engr. Heiland Rsch. Co., Denver, 1945-47; cons. Gen. Telephone Sys., N.Y.C., 1947-51; project engr. Airborne Inst. Lab., Mineola, N.Y., 1951-53; v.p. N.E. Electronics Corp., Concord, N.H., 1953-58; pres. Aerotronic Assocs., Inc., Contoocook, N.H., 1958-84, N.H. Automatic Equipment Corp., Concord, N.H., 1962-90, N.H. Realty Corp., Concord, N.H., 1990-96, E.A. Slusser & Assocs., Concord, N.H. Patentee electronics field. Chmn. Hopkinton (N.H.) Water Bd., 1962-69, Hopkinton Planning Bd., 1971-77, Hopkinton Precinct Bd. Adjustment, 1977. Mem. Aircraft Owners and Pilots Assn., Captiva Island (Fla.) Yacht Club (past commodore), Wharf Rat Club, Anglers Club, Pacific Club (Nantucket, Mass.), Masons (32 degree). Office: 232 Putney Hill Rd Concord NH 03301

SLYNKO, BASIL, technology education educator; b. Brisbane, Australia, Aug. 19, 1951; s. Ivan and Maria (Kolibaba) S.; m. Susan Margaret Sherwell, May 9, 1998. MA, Ohio State U., 1984; B of Ednl. Studies, U. Queensland, Australia, 1977; diploma in tchg., Mt. Gravatt CAE, Brisbane, 1972. Lectr. Mt. Gravatt CAE, 1976; tchr. Dept. Edn., Queensland, 1973-75, 77-80, head dept., 1981-82, 84-89, 91-92, 98-2000, edn. officer, 1990-91, 94-96; cons. Griffith U., Australia, 1991-94, Board Secondary Sch. Studies, 1986-2000. Author: Graphics 8, 1983, Introducing Technology, 1991; co-author: Technology Activity Book 1, 1986, 2d edit. 1994, Technology Activity Book 2, 1992, 2d edit., 1994, Senior Graphics--booklets and work sheets, 1994-96; contbg. author: QCL Queensland Cement-Project and Activity folder, 1995. Active Australian Coun. Edn. Through Tech., 1992-2000. Postgrad. scholar Dept. Edn., Queensland, 1983-84. Mem. Design in Edn. Coun. Australia, Internat. Tech. Edn. Assn., Epsilon Pi Tau. Mem. Genesis Christian Ministries. Fax: 61 7 3848 9089. Home: 37 Fairy St, Moorooka Queensland 4105, Australia

SLYSH, VIACHESLAV IVANOVICH, astronomer; b. Kharkov, Ukraine, Nov. 19, 1935; s. Ivan Mikhailovich and Natalia Kondratievna Slysh; m. Elvira Sergeevna Slysh, Sept. 12, 1959; 1 child, Olga. Electronics Engr., Power Engring. Inst., Moscow, 1959; CandSci in Physics and Math., Moscow State U., 1966, DSc in Physics and Math., 1976. Electronics engr. Lebedev Phys. Inst., Moscow, 1959-61; rsch. assoc. Sternberg Astron. Inst., Moscow, 1965-69; head of lab. Space Rsch. Inst., Moscow, 1969-89; dep. dir. Astro Space Ctr., Moscow, 1989—. Author: Radioastronomia, 1965, Astronomy on the Threshold of the 21st Century, 1992; contbr. articles to profl. jours. Mem. Russian Acad. Sci. (corr.; Bredikhin prize 1996), Sci. Coun. on Astronomy, Internat. Astron. Union, European Astron. Union. Home: 44 Michurin Prospect, Moscow Russia 117192 Office: Astro Space Ctr, 84/32 Profsoyuznaya, Moscow Russia 117810

SMAGIN, ALEXANDER GERASIM, physicist, researcher; b. Staro-Juryevo, Russia, May 30, 1930; s. Gerasim Ksenofont and Polina Demid (Levina) S.; m. Emiliya Arkadiy Bogdanova, Feb. 6, 1954; 1 child, Marina. Student, Moscow State Lomonosov U., 1949-54; PhD, Moscow State Bauman U., 1965; DSc in Physics and Math., Inst. Electronics and Math. Moscow, 1988. Scientist Rsch. Inst. Mendeleevo, Moscow, 1955, sr. scientist, 1955-60, chief of lab., 1960-63; chief of lab. Fonon Co., Moscow, 1963-67, Rsch. Inst. of Mashinbilding, Moscow, 1968-71; prof. physics Engring. Inst., Moscow, 1972-93; chief Crystal Co., Moscow, 1994-98; prof. physics Engring Inst., Moscow, 1999—; mem. sci. tech. com. Piezoelectricity and Stabilization Frequency of State Com., Moscow, 1961-75, Tsunami Commn. of State Com., Moscow, 1975-82, Ocean Commn., 1982-93. Author: (monographs) Precision Quartz Resonators: Physical Grounds, 1964, Piezoelectric Resonators and Their Application, 1967, Methods of Elimination Dissipation Energy in Subsurface Layers of Crystals, 1959, Higher-High-Q-quality and Highstability Resonators for State Frequency and Time Standards, 1962, Higher-High-Stability Low Temperature (Helium) Oscillator, 1975, Fundamental Energetic Losses in Crystals, 1988, Fundamentals of Crystalochemical Physics, 1991, General Methods and Principles of Designing higher-High-Q-quality Crystals Vibrational Systems, 1994; co-author Piezoelectricity of Quartz and Quartz Resonators, 1969, Creation, Industry and Application of Quartz Resonators, 1971, Atomic Energy, 1968; contbr. over 250 articles to profl. jours.; patentee in field. Recipient Diploma of Presidium USSR Acad. Scis., 1957, 60, Internat. Laureate of prize, 1979, Hon. Diploma Gosstandart of USSR, 1963, medal Internat. Order of Merit, USSR, 2000, also 12 medals of USSR. Mem. IEEE, Physical Acoustics, Sci.-Tech. Soc. Radioengring. and Electronics, N.Y. Acad. Scis., Internat. Info. Acad., Russian Acad. Scis. Avocations: hiking, alpinism, music. Home: 9 Park St 47-1-29, 105425 Moscow Russia

SMAGIN, VALERY, mathematician; b. Kobrin, USSR, Nov. 6, 1946; s. Ivan Mihailovich and Valentina Ivanovna (Kazakova) S.; m. Elena Mihailovna Berkovich, June 27, 1970 (div. Apr. 1981); 1 child, Irina; m. Mariya Ivanovna Naidenova, Mar. 30, 1983; children: Sergey, Natalia. Degree in math. engring., Poly. Inst., Barnaul, USSR, 1970; Candidate Tech. Sci., State U., Tomsk, USSR, 1975, D Tech. Sci., 1998. Asst. Poly. Inst., Barnaul, 1970-71, 1974-79; rsch. scientist State U., Tomsk, 1971-74, 79-82, asst. prof., 1982-99, prof., 1999—. Author: (with Y.I. Paraev): Synthesis Tracking Systems by Square Criterions with Incomplete Information, 1996; contbr. articles to profl. jours. Home: Prosp Mira 39 Apts 92, 656027 Tomsk Russia Office: State U, Prosp Lenina 36, 634050 Tomsk Russia

SMAGORINSKY, PETER, education educator; b. Princeton, N.J., Oct. 24, 1952; s. Joseph and Margaret (Knoepfel) S.; m. Anne O'Gorman, July 10, 1982 (dec. Aug. 1982); m. Jane E. Farrell, Oct. 12, 1985; children: Alysha, David. BA, Kenyon Coll., 1974; MA in Tchg., U. Chgo., 1977, PhD, 1989. English tchr. Westmont (Ill.) H.S., 1977-78, Barrington (Ill.) H.S., 1978-85, Oak Park (Ill.) and River Forest H.S., 1985-90; asst. prof. U. Okla., Norman, 1990-98; assoc. prof. U. Ga., Athens, 1998—. Author: Standards in Practice, 1996; co-author: How English Teachers Get Taught, 1995, The Language of Interpretation, 1995; co-editor Rsch. in the Tchg. of English, 1996—; mem. editl. bd. Rev. Ednl. Rsch., Am. Jour. Edn., Written Comm., Reading and Writing Quarterly. Recipient Steve Cahir award for rsch. in writing Am. Ednl. Rsch. Assn., 1991, Raymond B. Cattell award for disting. programmatic rsch. Am. Ednl. Rsch. Assn., 1999. Mem. Nat. Coun. Tchrs. English (chair standing com. on rsch. 1995-96, co-chair assembly for rsch. 1996, trustee rsch. found. 1997—, chair 2000—, pres. nat. conf. rsch. in lang. and literacy, 2001, English Jour. Writing award 1989). Home: 175 Emerald Dr Athens GA 30605-4106 Office: U Ga 125 Aderhold Hall Athens GA 30602

SMAIL, DEREK JAMES RICHARDSON, publishing executive; b. Berwick-Upon-Tweed, Eng., June 26, 1949; s. James Ingram Miles and Dorothy Margaret (Reese) S.; m. Anne Sutherland, Feb. 8, 1974; m. Julia Anne, Henry James Richardson. Dir. Tweeddale Press Ltd., Berwick-Upon-Tweed, 1973-85, mng. dir., 1985—, chmn., 1995—; chmn. Commonwealth Pub. Ltd., 1998—. Bd. dirs. Tyne and Wear Found., Newcastle-Upon-Tyne, 1995; col. The Royal Regiment of Fusiliers, Northumberland, Eng., 1967-95. With Army, 1968-71. Mem. Scottish Newspaper Publs. Assn. (pres. 1987-88), New Zealand Soc. (v.p.). Mem. Ch. of Eng. Avocations: tennis, cricket, rugby, physical fitness. Office: The Tweeddale Press Group, 90 Marygate, Berwick-Upon-Tweed TD15 1BW, England

SMALL, CLARENCE MERILTON, JR., lawyer; b. Birmingham, Ala., July 24, 1934; s. Clarence Merilton and Elva (Roberts) S.; m. Jean Russell, Nov. 18, 1935; children—William Stephen, Elizabeth Ann, Laura Carol. B.S., Auburn U., 1956; LL.B., U. Ala., 1961. Assoc., pres. Rives & Peterson, Birmingham, Ala., 1961—. Served to 1st lt. arty., AUS, to capt. JAGC. Fellow Am. Bar Found., Internat. Acad. Trial Lawyers, Am. Coll. Trial Lawyers, Ala. Law Found.; mem. Birmingham Bar Assn. (pres. 1979), Ala. Def. Lawyers Assn., ABA (ho. of dels. 1984-86), Ala. Bar Assn. (pres. 1992-93), Internat. Assn. Defense Counsel. Office: 1700 Financial Ctr Birmingham AL 35203-4611*

SMALL, DAVID HENRY, biochemist; b. Hobart, Australia, Apr. 12, 1956; s. Angus and Elizabeth Margaret (Parker) S.; m. Agnès Marie Fournier, Oct. 19, 1991; children: Christopher, Caroline. BSc with honors, U. Saskatchewan (Can.), 1977; PhD, U. Melbourne (Australia), 1982. Head lab. molecular neurobiology U. Melbourne, 1993—, rsch. fellow, 1993-95, sr. rsch. fellow, 1995-98, rsch. assoc. in biochemistry, 1994-98; Editor Jour. Neurochemistry, 1995—. Author (web site) Alzheimer WEB; editor Jour. Neurochemistry, 1995—, Jour. Alzheimers Disease, 1999—; contbr. numerous articles to profl. jours. Mem. Internat. Soc. Neurochemistry (internet com. 1995-98, web site designer). Avocations: chess, computers. Office: Dept Pathology, U Melbourne, Parkville VIC 3052, Australia

SMALL, JONATHAN ANDREW, lawyer; b. N.Y.C., Dec. 26, 1942; s. Milton and Teresa Markell (Joseph) S.; m. Cornelia Mendenhall, June 8, 1969; children: Anne, Katherine. BA, Brown U., 1964; student, U. Paris, 1962-63; LLB, Harvard U., 1967; MA, Fletcher Sch. of Law and Diplomacy, 1968; LLM, NYU, 1974. Bar: N.Y. 1967. VISTA vol. Washington and Cambridge, Mass., 1968; law clk. to judge U.S. Ct. Appeals (2d cir.), 1968-69; assoc. Debevoise & Plimpton, N.Y.C., 1969-75, ptnr., 1976-99; pres. Nonprofit Coord. Com. N.Y., 2000—; cons. Spl. Task Force of N.Y. State Taxation, 1976. Trustee Brearley Sch., 1985-95; bd. dirs. Nonprofit Coordinating Com. of N.Y., 1985—, Muscular Dystrophy Assn., 1986-88. Mem. ABA, N.Y. State Bar Assn. (chmn. tax sect. com. exempt orgns. 1980-82, co-chmn., 1995), Assn. Bar City N.Y., Nonprofit Forum, Phi Beta Kappa. Home: 60 E End Ave New York NY 10028-7907 Office: Nonprofit Coord Com of NY 1350 Broadway Rm 1801 New York NY 10018-7718

SMALL, KENNETH ALAN, economics educator; b. Sodus, N.Y., Feb. 9, 1945; s. Cyril Galloway and Gertrude Estelle (Andrews) S.; m. Adair Bowman, June 8, 1968; 1 child, Gretchen Lenore. BA, BS, U. Rochester, 1968; MA, U. Calif., Berkeley, 1972, PhD, 1976. Asst. prof. Princeton (N.J.) U., 1976-83; rsch. assoc. Brookings Inst., Washington, 1978-79; assoc. prof. U. Calif., Irvine, 1983-86, prof. econs., 1986—, assoc. dean social sci., 1986-92, chmn. econs., 1992-95; vis. prof. Harvard U., Cambridge, Mass., 1991-92; cons. N.Y. State Legislature, Albany, 1982-83, Rand Corp., Santa Monica, Calif., 1985-86, ECO N.W., Eugene, Oreg., 1987—, World Bank, Washington, 1990—, Port Authority of N.Y. and N.J., 1994, Nat. Coop. Highway Rsch. Program, 1992-94; mem. study com. on urban transp. congestion pricing NRC, 1992-94, mem. highway cost allocation rev. com., 1995-96, mem. com. for evaluation of CMAQ program, 1999—. Co-author: Futures for a Declining City, 1981, Urban Decline, 1982, Road Work, 1989; author: Urban Transportation Economics, 1992; co-editor: Urban Studies, Glasgow, Scotland, 1992-97, Kluwer Acad. Publs. book series, Dordrecht, The Netherlands, 1993—, Transport Economics: Selected Readings, 1995, Environment and Transport in Economic Modelling, 1998; assoc. editor Regional Sci. and Urban Econs., Amsterdam, The Netherlands, 1987—; editl. bd. mem. Jour. Urban Econs., San Diego, 1989—, Urban Studies, Glasgow, 1992—, Transportation, Dordrecht, 1993—, Jour. Transport Econs. and Policy, Bath, U.K., 1995—, Jour. Econ. Geography, 1999—; guest editor Regional Sci. and Urban Econs., 1992, Transp., 1992, Jour. Transp. Econs. and Policy, 2000. Grantee NSF, 1977-87, Inst. Transp. Studies U. Calif., 1984-89, Haynes Found., 1987-88, U.S. and Calif. Depts. Transp., 1988-94, 97—, Nat. Coop. Highway Rsch. Program, 1995-96, Daimler-Benz, 1996-99; Gilbert White fellow Resources for the Future, Washington, 1999-2000. Mem. Am. Econ. Assn. (com. on status of women in econs. profession 1995-97, Disting. Mem. award, transp. and pub. utilities group 1999), Econometric Soc., Transp. Rsch. Bd., Royal Econ. Soc., Regional Sci. Assn., Am. Real Estate and Urban Econs. Assn. Office: Dept Econs Univ Calif Irvine CA 92697-0001

SMALL, LAWRENCE M., museum executive; b. 1941. BA, Brown U., 1963; JD (hon.), Morehouse Coll. Vice chmn. bd., chmn. exec. com., dir. Citicorp, N.Y.C., 1964-91; pres., COO Fannie Mae, Washington, 1991-2000; sec. Smithsonian Instn., Washington, 2000—; bd. dirs. Chubb Corp., Marriott Internat. Trustee emeritus Brown U., Morehouse Coll., Atlanta, 1973-99, Morehouse Coll., 1998—, Mt. Sinai-NYU Med. Ctr., Nat. Bldg. Mus.; bd. dirs. Spanish Repertory Theatre, Fannie Mae Found. Office: Smithsonian Instn 1000 Jefferson Dr SW Washington DC 20560-0009

SMALL, MICHAEL RONALD, English educator, writer; b. Croydon, Surrey, Eng., Jan. 3, 1943; s. Ronald Herbert and Rose Edith (Leighs) S.; m. Lindsey Mary Westmore, Aug. 4, 1972 (div. 1977). BA, London U., 1966; BEd, Latrobe U., Melbourne, Victoria, 1977; MA, U. Windsor, Ontario, Can., 1980. Cert. tchr. of English as a fgn. lang. Royal Soc. Arts. Tchr. English Carey Bapt. Grammar Sch., Melbourne, Victoria, 1974-98, learning area coord., 1996-98; ret., 1998. Author: Her Natural Life and Other Stories, 1988, Urangeline: Voices of Carey 1928-1997, 1997; co-author: Films: A Resource Book for Studying Film as Text, 1994, Unleashed: The History of Footscray Football Club, 1996. Mem. Victorian Fellowship of Australian Writers (com. mem. 1975-85). Avocations: writing, reading, travel, classical music. Office: Carey Bapt Grammar, 349 Barkers Rd, Kew VIC, Australia

SMALL, MICHELE GESLIN, English studies and modern languages educator; b. Port-Vila, Vanuatu, South Pacific, June 16, 1944; 1 child, Jonathan Michael. Licence d'anglais, U. Nice, 1967; MA in English, SUNY, Albany, 1969; PhD in Social, Psychol. and Philos. Edn., U. Minn., Mpls., 1983. French instr. SUNY, Albany, 1969-72; asst. prof. English and French Northland Coll., Ashland, Wis., 1975-81, assoc. prof. English and French, 1981-85, prof. English and modern langs., 1985—. Recipient Tchg. Excellence award Sears Roebuck Found., 1991. Office: Northland Coll 1411 Ellis Ave Ashland WI 54806-3925

SMALL, PARKER ADAMS, III, investment banker; b. Phila., Feb. 1, 1958; s. Parker Adams Jr. and Natalie (Settimelli) S.; m. Katherine Currier, Aug. 24, 1985; children: Margaret Edmea, Elizabeth Parker. BA, Dartmouth Coll., 1980; MBA, Harvard U., 1985. Account exec. Leo Burnett Advt., Chgo., 1980-83; assoc. Merrill Lynch-Becker Paribas, N.Y.C., 1984; product mgmt. The Gillette Co., Boston, 1985-86; mgmt. cons. Arthur D. Little Inc., Cambridge, Mass., 1986-89; v.p. Butler Capital Corp., N.Y.C., 1989-92; pres. S.R.S. Sera Co., Gainesville, Fla., 1976-91; bd. dirs. Julius Koch USA Inc., Strine Printing Co., Lancaster Press Inc. Author: Understanding Immunology, 1976; producer Dartmouth Coll. video, 1980. Reunion chmn. Dartmouth Coll., 1990, mem. alumni coun., 1999; bd. dirs. Wellesley Edn. Found. Avocations: skiing, tennis, scuba diving. Home: 11 Westwood Rd Wellesley MA 02482-7015

SMALL, ROGER STEVEN, middle school educator; b. Hawthorne, Calif., Mar. 19, 1947; s. Roger Joseph and Mary Alice (Lilly) S.; m. Lois Jean Davis, June 9, 1966 (div. June 1975); m. Janet K. Raber, July 4, 1975; children: Steven Joseph, Jennifer Lynn, Erik Jason. BA, Mich. State U., 1969, MA, 1975. Cert. tchr., Mich. Tchr. Hoover Jr. H.S., Montgomery County, Md., 1969-70; tchr. Gardner Mid. Sch., Lansing, Mich., 1971—, chair dept. social studies, 1985-98; retired, 1998; field instr. for intern tchr.s Mich. State U., 1998—; chair curriculum dept. Lansing Schs., 1992-95; coord. Gardner Earth Expo, Lansing, 1990-91. Editor, author: Playoffs for Officials, 1984-1999; creator course guide Creative World History, 1990, creator course guide World Literature/World History block, 1991, Gardner Enrichment Plan Social Studies, 1996. Active Advent House, Lansing, 1994-95; coord. Sch. Improvement, Gardner-Lansing, 1990-92; Gardner coord. Japanese Exch., Lansing, 1988—; state finals football ofcl., 1986, 90, 96. Everett H.S.-Advanced Placement European history tchr., 1996-98. Mem. NEA, Mich. Edn. Assn., Lansing Edn. Assn., Capital Area Ofcls. Assn. (sec. 1990—, Ofcl. of Yr. 1994, 95), Mich. H.S. Athletic Assn. Presbyterian. Avocations: officiating high school football, sailing, softball, bowling, camping, reading. Home: 338 Chanticleer Trl Lansing MI 48917-3009

SMALL, THOMAS MILTON, lawyer; b. Sullivan, Ind., Mar. 4, 1933; s. Marion Creston and Ruby Bernice (Thomas) S.; m. Tanya Loy, May 12, 1979; children: Sheree Lynne, Angela Rae. BS in Engring. Law, Purdue U., 1957; JD, Ind. U., 1957. Bar: Ill. 1960, Calif. 1970. Assoc. ptnr. Wolf Hubbard Voit and Osann, Rockford, Ill., 1960-68, Fulwider-Patton Rieber Lee & Utecht, L.A., 1968-87; ptnr. Baker & McKenzie, L.A., 1987-92, Small Larkin, LLP, L.A., 1992—. 1st Lt. U.S. Army, 1957-59. Mem. L.A. Patent Law Assn. (pres. 1975-76), Calif. Bar Assn. (pres. intelectual property section 1979-80), Licensing Execs. Soc. (pres. 1997-98). Avocations: tennis, flyfishing, ballroom dance. E-mail: tms@sliplaw.com. Office: Small Larkin LLP 10940 Wilshire Blvd Los Angeles CA 90024-3915

SMALLEY, RICHARD ERRETT, chemistry and physics educator, researcher; b. Akron, Ohio, June 6, 1943; s. Frank Dudley and Virginia (Rhoads) S.; m. Judith Grace Sampierj, May 4, 1968; (div. July, 1979); 1 child, Chad; m. Mary Lynn Chapieski, July 10, 1980 (div. Nov. 1994); m. JoNell Marie Chauvin, Mar. 1, 1997 (div. June 1998); 1 child, Preston. BS in Chemistry, U. Mich., 1965; MA in Chemistry, Princeton U., 1971, PhD in Chemistry, 1973; PhD (hon.), U. Liege, Belgium, 1991; DSc (hon.), U. Chgo., 1995. Assoc. The James Franck Inst., Chgo., 1973-76; from asst. prof. to prof. William Marsh Rice U., Houston, 1976-82, Gene & Norman Hackerman prof. chemistry, 1982—; prof. dept. physics Rice U., Houston, 1990—; chmn. Rice Quantum Inst., Houston, 1986-96; dir. Rice Ctr. for Nanoscale Sci. and Tech., 1996—. Contbr. numerous articles to profl. jours. Recipient Franklin medal Franklin Inst., Phila., 1996, Nobel prize in chemistry, 1996. Fellow Am. Phys. Soc. (divsn. chem. physics, Irving Langmuir prize 1991, Internat. New Materials prize 1992); mem. AAAS, NAS, Am. Chem. Soc. (divsn. phys. chemistry, William H. Nichols medal 1993, S.W. regional award 1992, Harrison Howe award Rochester sect. 1994, Madison Marshall award North Ala. sect. 1995), Materials Rsch. Soc., Am. Acad. Arts and Scis., Sigma Xi. Office: Rice Univ Ctr Nanoscale Sci and Tech 6100 Main St # Ms100 Houston TX 77005-1892

SMALLEY, STEPHEN STEWART, dean; b. London, May 11, 1931; s. Arthur Thomas and May Elizabeth (Kimm) S.; m. Susan Jane Paterson, July 13, 1974 (dec. Nov. 1995); children: Jovian, Evelyn. BA, Cambridge (Eng.) U., 1955, MA, 1958, PhD, 1979. Curate St. Paul's Portman Sq, London, 1958-60; chaplain, dean Peterhouse, Cambridge, 1960-63; lectr. in new testament U. Ibadan, Nigeria, 1963-67; sr. lectr. in new testament U. Ibadan, 1967-69; lectr. in new testament U. Manchester, 1970-77, sr. lectr., 1977; canon precentor Cathedral, Coventry, 1977-86, vice provost, 1986; dean Cathedral, Chester, 1987—; select preacher Univ., Cambridge, 1963-64; mem. Archbishops' doctrine, Commn. of the Ch. of Eng., 1981-86; manson meml. lectr. Univ., Manchester, 1986. Author: John: Evangelist and Interpeter, 1978, 2d edit., 1998, 1, 2, 3 John, 1984, Thunder and Love, 1994; editor: Christ and Spirit, 1973. Mem. Chester City Club. Anglican. Avocations: travel, music, drama, literature. Home: 7 Abbey St, Chester CH1 2JF, England Office: Cathedral Office, 12 Abbey Sq, Chester CH1 2HU, England

SMALLHOOVER, JOSEPH JOHN, lawyer; b. Pitts., Dec. 3, 1953; arrived in France, 1985; s. Joseph Thomas and Dorothy Carmelita (Kane) S. AB magna cum laude, Duke U., 1975; MA, U. Va., 1976; JD, U. Pitts., 1980. Bar: Pa. 1980, Calif. 1983, France 1987. Fulbright exch. tchg. fellow Vienna, Austria, 1976-77; law clk. Superior Ct. Pa., Pitts., 1980-82; assoc. Farnborough & Ptnr., Düsseldorf, Germany, 1983, Rosen, Wachtell & Gilbert, L.A., 1984; assoc. S.G. Archibald, Paris, 1985-95, ptnr., 1995-98; ptnr. Dechert Price & Rhoads, Paris, 1998—. Pres. Rheinischer Internat. Juristen-Verein, Düsseldorf, 1985-89, 97-99; counsel Dem. Party Com. Abroad, 1991-95, vice-chmn., 1995—, chmn., 1999—; active Dem. Nat. Com., 1995—. German Acad. Exch. Svc. fellow, Düsseldorf, 1982-83. Mem. Am. Counsel on Germany, Am. C. of C. France (pres. young execs. program 1992-93), Am. Club Paris. Roman Catholic. Avocations: opera, skiing, theatre, cuisine. Office: Dechert Price & Rhoads, 55 Ave Kléber, 75116 Paris France

SMALLMAN, RAYMOND EDWARD, metallurgist and materials science educator; b. Wolverhampton, W. Midland, Eng., Aug. 4, 1929; s. David and Edith (French) S.; m. Joan Doreen Faulkner, Sept. 6, 1952; children: Lesley Ann Smallman Grimer, Robert Ian. BS, U. Birmingham, 1950, PhD, 1953, DS, 1968; DS (hon.), U. Wales, U.K., 1990, U. Novi Sad, Yugoslavia, 1990. Chartered engr. Scientific officer Atomic Energy Rsch. Est., Harwell, Eng., 1953-55, sr. scientific officer, 1955-58; lectr. Univ. Birmingham, 1958-63, sr. lectr., 1963-64, prof. phys. metallurgy, 1964-69, Feeney prof. metallurgy and materials sci., head dept., 1969-93, dean of faculty of sci. and engring., dean of engring., 1984-85, 85-87, vice prin., 1987-92, prof. metallurgy and materials sci., 1993—; mem. coun. Sci. and Engring. Rsch. Coun., 1992-93; mem. Materials Commn., 1988-92; mem. coun. Inst. Materials, 1993-99, chmn. internat. affairs com., 1992, v.p., 1995-99; mem. Warden Assay Office, Birmingham, 1994-99. Author: Modern Physical Metallurgy, 1962, 4th edit., 1985; Modern Metallography, 1966, Structure of Metals and Alloys, 1969, Defect Analysis in Electron Microscopy, 1975, Vacancies 76, Metals and Materials: Science, Processes, Applications, 1995, Modern Physical Metallurgy and Materials Engineering, 1999; contbr. articles to profl. jours. Decorated Commdr. of Brit. Empire, HM The Queen, 1992; recipient George Beilby Gold medal Inst. of Metals and Inst. of Chemistry, London, 1969. Fellow Inst. Materials (Platinum medal, 1989, Rosenhain medal, 1972), Royal Soc., Royal Acad. Engring., China Ordinance Soc.; mem. Fedn. of European Materials Socs. (v.p. 1992-94, pres. 1994-96), Birmingham Metall. Soc. (pres. 1972-73), Czech. Soc. Metal Sci. (hon. fgn.). Avocations: writing, travel, golf, bridge. Home: 59 Woodthorne Rd South, Wolverhampton WV6 8SN Tettenhall England Office: Univ Birmingham, B15 2TT Birmingham England

SMALLRIDGE, ROBERT CHRISTIAN, endocrinologist; b. Charleston, W.Va., Dec. 28, 1944; s. Horace Hamilton Jr. and Isabel White Smallridge; m. Elizabeth Cone; children: Amy Brewster, Laura Fontaine. BA, Yale Coll., 1966; MD, Med. Coll. Va., 1970. Chief dept. clin. physiology Walter Reed Army Inst. Rsch., Washington, 1978-91, dir. divsn. medicine, 1991-95; chair endocrinology divsn. Mayo Clinic Jacksonville, Fla., 1996—; mem. endocrinology study sect. NIH, Bethesda, Md.; cons. Assessment Techs., Inc., Lexington, Ky., 1998—. Author book chpts.; contbr. numerous articles to profl. jours. Col. U.S. Army, 1973-96. Recipient Peter Forsham Endocrinology award Soc. Uniformed Endocrinologists. Fellow ACP, Am. Coll. Endocrinology; mem. Endocrine Soc., Am. Thyroid Assn. (treas. 1988-93, chair fin./audit com. 1993-99). Avocations: golf, family, travel. Office: Mayo Clinic Jacksonville 4500 San Pablo Rd S Jacksonville FL 32224-1865

SMARANDACHE, FLORENTIN, mathematics researcher, writer; b. Balcesti-Vilcea, Romania, Dec. 10, 1954; came to U.S., 1990; s. Gheorghe and Maria (Mitroiescu) S.; m. Eleonora Niculescu; children: Mihai-Liviu, Silviu-Gabriel. MS in Computer Sci., U. Craiova, 1979; postgrad., Ariz. State U., 1991, U. Phoenix, 1996; PhD in Math., Kishinev U., 1997. Mathematician I.U.G., Craiova, Romania, 1979-81; math. prof. Romanian Coll., 1981-82, 1984-86, 1988; math. tchr. Coop. Ministry, Morocco, 1982-84; French tutor pvt. practice, Turkey, 1988-90; software engr. Honeywell, Phoenix, 1990-95; prof. math. Pima C.C., Tucson, 1995-97; asst. prof. U. N.Mex., 1997—. Author: Nonpoems, 1990, Only Problems, Not Solutions, 1991, numerous other books; contbr. articles to profl. jours. Mem. U.S. Math. Assn., Romania Math. Assn., Zentralblatt fur Math. (reviewer). Achievements include development of Smarandache function, numbers, quotients, double factorials, consecutive sequence, reverse sequence, mirror sequence, destructive sequence, symmetric sequence, permutable sequence, consecutive sieve, prime base, cubic base, square base, class of paradoxes, multi-structure and multi-space, paradoxist geometry, anti-geometry, inconsistent systems of axioms. Office: U NMex Dept Math Gallup NM 87301

ŠMARDA, JAN JIŘÍ, biology educator; b. Brno, Moravia, Czech Republic, Aug. 29, 1930; s. Jan and Hedvika (Blatná) S.; m. Helena Vanda Roháčková; children: Zdenka Adamová, Jan. MD, Masaryk U., Brno, Czech Republic, 1955, PhD, 1963; DSc, Charles U., Prague, Czech Republic, 1989. Asst. lectr. Masaryk U., Brno, 1954-55, asst. prof., 1955-67; assoc. prof. Purkyně U., Brno, 1968-90, Charles U., Prague, 1973-75; prof. biology Masaryk U., Brno, 1990-99, prof. emeritus, rsch. scientist, 1999—; assoc. dean faculty medicine Masaryk U., Brno, 1989-97, sci. bd. mem., 1990-98, sci. bd. mem. faculty medicine, 1989-97. Co-author: Bacteriocine und bacteriocinähnliche Substanzen, 1971; author: The Effects of Colicins, 1978 (prize Czechoslovak Med. Soc. 1979), Man in a Stream of Heredity, 1999; mem. editl. bd. Biologické listy, 1968—. Mem. adv. coun. Internat. Biog. Ctr., Cambridge, 1995—. Recipient Purkyně Meml. medal Czechoslovak Acad. Sci., Prague, 1988, 90, Gold Meml. medals Faculty Medicine and Masaryk U., Brno, 1990, 95, prize and medal Min. of Edn., Prague, 1996, 97. Mem. Internat. Assn. for Cyanophyte Rsch., Czechoslovak Soc. Microbiology (hon., vice-chmn. 1992-95), Czechoslovak Soc. Biology (hon., vice chmn. 1973-75). Avocations: poetry, arts, music, photography, forest weekend-house. Home: Grohova 30, CZ 602 00 Brno Czech Republic Office: Masaryk U Faculty Medicine, Dept Biology Joštova 10, CZ 662 44 Brno Moravia, Czech Republic

SMART, JOHN JAMIESON CARSWELL, retired philosopher, educator; b. Cambridge, Eng., Sept. 16, 1920; s. William and Isabel (Carswell) S.; m. Janet Paine (dec. 1967); m. Elizabeth Margaret Warner; children: Helen, William. MA, Glasgow U., 1946; BPhil, Oxford U., 1948; LittD (hon.), St. Andrews U., 1983, La Trobe U., 1992. Jr. rsch. fellow Corpus Christi Coll., Oxford, England, 1948-50; Hughes prof. philosophy U. Adelaide, Australia, 1950-72; reader in philosophy La Trobe U., Australia, 1972-76; prof. Inst. Advanced Studies Australian Nat. U., 1976-85, prof. emeritus, 1986—; vis. prof. Princeton (N.J.) U., 1957, Harvard U., Cambridge, Mass., 1963, Yale Univ., New Haven, 1964, Stanford (Calif.) U., 1982, U. Ala., Birmingham, 1990. Author: Philosophy and Scientific Realism, 1963, Between Science and Philosophy, 1968, Ethics, Persuasion & Truth, 1984, Our Place in the Universe, 1989, Essays Metaphysical and Moral, 1987; co-author: Atheism and Theism, 1996, Utilitarianism, For and Against, 1973. Decorated companion Order of Australia; hon. fellow Corpus Christi Coll., Oxford (Eng.) U., 1991—. Fellow Australian Acad. Humanities. Avocation: walking. Home: 159 Cumberland View, Whalley Dr, Wheelers Hill Victoria 3150, Australia

SMART, MARY-LEIGH CALL (MRS. J. SCOTT SMART), civic worker; b. Springfield, Ill., Feb. 27, 1917; d. S(amuel) Leigh and Mary (Bradish) Call; m. J. Scott Smart, Sept. 11, 1951 (dec. 1960). Diploma, Monticello Coll., 1934; student, Oxford U., 1935; BA, Wellesley Coll., 1937; MA, Columbia U., 1939, postgrad., 1940-41; postgrad., NYU, 1940-41; painting student, with Bernard Karfiol, 1937-38. Dir. mgmt. Cen. Ill. Grain Farms, Logan County, 1939—; owner Lowtrek Kennel, Ogunquit, Maine, 1957-73, Cove Studio Art Gallery, Ogunquit, 1961-68; art collector, patron, publicist, 1954—; cons. in field. Editor: Hamilton Easter Field Art Found. Collection Catalog, 1966; originator, dir. show, compiler of catalog Art: Ogunquit, 1967; Peggy Bacon-A Celebration, Barn Gallery, Ogunquit, 1979. Program dir., sec. bd. Barn Gallery Assocs., Inc., 1958-69, pres., 1969-70, 82-87, asst. treas., 1987-92, hon. dir., 1970-78, adv. trustee, 1992-94, v.p., 1994—; curator Hamilton Easter Field Art Found. Collection, 1978-79, curator exhbns., 1979-86, chair exhbn. com., 1987-94; mem. acquisition com. DeCordova Mus., Lincoln, Mass., 1966-78; mem. chancellor's coun. U. Tex., 1972—; mem. pres.'s coun. U. N.H., 1978—; bd. dirs. Ogunquit C. of C., 1966, treas., 1966-67, hon. life mem., 1968—; bd. overseers Strawbery Banke, Inc., Portsmouth, N.H., 1972-75, 3d vice chmn., 1973, 2d vice chmn., 1974; bd. advisors U. Art Galleries, U. N.H., 1973-89; pres., 1981-89; bd. dirs. Old York Hist. and Improvement Soc., York, Maine, 1979-81, v.p., 1981-82; adv. com. Bowdoin Coll. Mus. Art Invitational exhibit, 1975, '76 Maine Artists Invitational Exhbn., Maine State Mus., Maine Coast Artists, Rockport, 1975-78, All Maine Biennial '79, Bowdoin Coll. Mus. Art juried exhbn.; mem. jury for scholarship awards Maine com. Skowhegan Sch. Painting & Sculpture, 1982-84; nat. com. Wellesley Coll. Friends of Art, 1983—; adv. trustee Portland Mus. Art, 1983-85, fellow, 1985—; mem. mus. panel Maine State Commn. on Arts and Humanities, 1983-86; adv. com. Maine Biennial, Colby Coll. Mus. Art, 1983; coun. advisors Farnsworth Art Mus., Rockland, Maine, 1986-98; collections com. Payson Gallery, Westbrook Coll., Portland, 1987-91; dir. Greater Piscataqua Cmty. Found., N.H. Charitable Fund, 1991-97; mem. corp. Ogunquit Mus. Am. Art, 1988-90, 95-2000; mem. Maine Women's Forum, 1993—. Lt. (j.g.) WAVES, 1942-45. Recipient Deborah Morton award Westbrook Coll., 1988, Friend of the Arts award Maine Art Dealers Assn., 1993. Mem. Springfield Art Assn., Jr. League Springfield Ill., Western Maine Wellesley Club. Episcopalian. Address: 30 Surf Point Rd York ME 03909-5053

SMART, PETER, civil engineer; b. Louth, Eng., Oct. 7, 1931; s. James Douglas and Maud Muriel (Darlow) S.; m. Leonora D. Burton, July 16, 1955. BA, Oxford U., Eng., 1955, MA, 1959; PhD, Cambridge U., Eng., 1967. Surveyor Royal Artillery, Eng., 1950-52; trainee Ransomes, Sims and Jeffries, Ltd., Eng., 1955-57; demonstrator engring. dept. Oxford U., Eng., 1957-63, lectr. Lincoln Coll., 1961-63; rsch. engr. Eng., 1967; asst. lectr. civil engring. dept. Nottingham U., Eng., 1967-68; lectr. dept. civil engring. U. Glasgow, Scotland, 1968-97, hon. sr. rsch. fellow dept. civil engring., 1997—. Co-author: (books) Electron Microscopy of Soils and Sediments: Examples, 1981, Electron Microscopy of Soils and Sediments: Techniques, 1982; co-editor: Drainage Design, 1992. Mem. Brit. Geotech. Soc., Brit. Soc. for Soil Sci., Clay Minerals Soc., Royal Horticultural Soc., Wadham Coll. Boat Club Soc., Guild of Freemen of the City of London, Inst. Civil Engrs., Inst. Mech. Engrs. Avocation: photography. E-mail: geofun@gla.ac.uk. Office: Civil Engring Dept, Univ Glasgow, Glasgow G12 8QQ, Scotland

SMART, PETER CHARLES, solicitor; b. London, Sept. 5, 1950; s. Charles Reuben and Eileen Ellen (Williams) S.; Glenys Margaret Ogden, Sept. 15, 1973; children: Lauren Naomi Elizabeth, Tamsin Catherine Lucy, Benjamin Toby Edward. BA with honors, Leeds Met. U., 1976. Solicitor Walker Morris & Coles, Leeds, 1979-81, solicitor, ptnr., 1981-84, head of corp. dept., 1984—; mng. ptnr. Walker Morris, Leeds, 1993-98; dir. Yorkshire Housing Trust Plc, Leeds, 1988-94, Airedale & Wharfedale Coll., Leeds, 1993-94, dir. Allied Textile Co. 1999—, dir BWD Air VCT, 1999. Mem. Law Soc., Confederation of British Industry. Avocation: rugby. Office: Walker Morris, Kings Court 12 King Street, Leeds LS1 2HL, England

SMEDLEY, ELIZABETH, researcher, codifier, consultant, historian, writer; b. Phila., Jan. 5, 1915; d. Elwood Quimby and Hazel deRemer (Ward) S. BA cum laude, Bryn Mawr Coll., 1936. Editor, rechr., writer Hist. Records Survey, Phila., 1939-43; rechr., writer U.S. Army Chief of Ordnance, Phila., 1943-45; local govt. specialist Bur. Mcpl. Affairs, Harrisburg, Pa., 1945-51; local govt. codifier, writer Penns Valley Pubs., State College, Pa., 1951-75; rschr., writer Pa. State Assn. Boroughs, Harrisburg, 1975-82; dir. codification, co-owner Century IV Codes, Inc., Hershey, Pa., 1982-95; owner, rechr. Century IV Codes, Inc., Hummelstown, Pa., 1995—; cons., writer Pa. State Assn. Boroughs, Harrisburg, 1962-65, Pa. Dept. Transp., Harrisburg, 1979-81. Author: Zion's Path of History, 1987, 1936: A 50 Year Perspective, 1986. Chmn. State College Govt. Study Commn., 1971-73. Mem. DAR, Daus. Am. Colonists. Republican. LDS. Avocations: collecting postcards and books, gardening, cooking, cats. Home and Office: 54 Ridgeview Rd Hummelstown PA 17036-9721

SMEDSLUND, GEIR, psychologist; b. Boulder, Colo., May 1, 1962; arrived in Norway, 1962; s. Jan Smedslund and Åsebrit Sundquist; 1 child, David. Cand.Psychol., U. Oslo, 1991; PhD, Norwegian U. for Sci. and, Technology, 1996. Clin. psychologist Nordland Psychiat. Hosp., Bodø, Norway, 1992-93; rsch. fellow Norwegian Rsch. Coun., Trondheim, Norway, 1993-96, postdoctoral fellow, 1999—. Author: (with others) Nordic Medical Yearbook, 1995; contbr. articles to profl. jours., chpt. to book. Mem. Norwegian Soc. for Behavioral Medicine. Avocations: music, running. Office: Dept Psych NTNU, PO Box 3008 LADE, Trondheim N-7002, Norway

SMEE, ANTHONY EDWARD JOHN, advertising executive; b. London; s. J. and D. (Mallandaw) S.; m. S.V. Smee, July 22, 1978; children: Alexander, Matthew. Grad., Ardingly Coll. Mng. dir. Smee's Advt. Ltd., London. Trustee The Bible Soc., England. Mem. Inst. Practitioners in Advt., Internat. Christian C. of C. Office: Smee's Advt Ltd, 3-5 Duke St, London W1M 6BA, England

SMEETS, JOEP L.R.M., cardiologist, electrophysiologist; b. Heerlen, Netherlands, Mar. 30, 1952; s. R. H.L.M. and I. F.M. (Damoiseaux) S.; m. Nella P. Van Duuren, Dec. 5, 1991; children: Wouter, Reinier, Michiel. MD, U. Groningen, Netherlands, 1978; PhD, U. Limburg, Maastricht, Netherlands, 1983. Physiologist U. Limburg, 1978-83; resident in cardiology Acad. Hosp., Maastricht, 1983-87, cardiologist, 1987—, electrophysiologist, 1988—, dir. electrophysiology lab., 1991—; sec. Dutch Working Group on Arrhythmias, 1991-96, chmn., 1996-98. Contbr. articles to profl. jours.; patentee linear lesion RF catheter. Fellow European Soc. Cardiology; mem. N.Am. Soc. Pacing and Electrophysiology, Dutch Soc. Cardiology. Avocations: tennis, cycling, cooking. Office: Univ Hosp of Maastricht, P De Byelaan 25 PO Box 5800, 6202 AZ Maastricht Limburg, Netherlands

SMÉKAL, PETR, physicist, researcher; b. Olomouc, Moravia, Czech Republic, May 15, 1949; s. Alois and Marie (Kucerová) S.; m. Darina Lazoriková, Aug. 9, 1975; chldren: Petra, Blazena. Dr. rer. nat., U. Olomouc, 1978; PhD, U. Charles, Prague, Czech Republic, 1987. Faculty dept. physics U. Ostrava, Czech Republic, 1972-89; faculty of sci. dept. physics U. Ostrava, 1989-91, faculty dept. biophysics, 1991—; founder Pvt. Coll. Further Edn., Ostrava, 1996; vice dean, U. Ostrava, 1990-91, vice rector, 1991-95. Author: Electricity and Magnetism, 1983 (best book of pedagogical faculty, 1983); patentee in field. Mem. Czech Sci. Tech. Assn., Com. of Acad. of Sci. of Czech Republic (Terminology in Physics). Avocations: tennis, skiing, photography. Home: Na Jizdarne 12, 70200 Ostrava Czech Republic Office: Pvt Coll Further Edn, 29 dubna 33, 70030 Ostrava Czech Republic

SMELLIE, JEAN MCILDOWIE, pediatrician; b. Liverpool, Eng., May 14, 1927; d. John McIldowie Hope and Mary Wilson (Clarkson) S.; m. Ian Colin Stuart Normand, June 30, 1961; children: Alison, Christopher, Caroline. BA, Oxford U., 1947, MA, 1957, BM BCh, 1950, DM, 1981. First asst. paediatrics U. Coll. Hosp., London, 1957-60, rsch. asst. cons., sr. lectr., 1961-92; lectr. paediatrics Radcliffe Infirmary, Oxford, 1960-61; fellow in pathology Johns Hopkins U., Balt., 1964-65; hon. sr. lectr. Cmty. Child Health, Southampton, U.K., 1978-92; hon. cons. paediatric nephrologist Guy's and Great Ormond St. Hosp., London, 1980—; emeritus cons. U. Coll. Hosp., 1992—; mem. med. adv. com. Sir Jules Thorn Charitable Trust, London, 1975-97; chmn. Cmty. Child Health Group, 1980-85; scientific adviser Internat. Reflux Study in Children, Essen, Germany, Albert Einstein, N.Y. Contbr., co-contbr. chapters in med. textbooks, contbr. numerous articles to profl. jours. Fellow Royal Coll. of Physicians, Royal Coll.

Paediat. and Child Health (hon.); mem. Internat. Pediatric Nephrol. Assn., European Soc. for Pediatric Nephrology, British Assn. for Paediatric Nephrology (hon. 1995), Am. Urol. Assn. (hon.), British Paediatric Assn. (hon.), European Soc. for Paediatric Urology (hon.). Mem. Ch. of Eng. Avocations: music, photography, grandchildren, travel, gardening. Fax: 0-1962-852550. Home and Office: 23 St Thomas St, Winchester SO23 9HJ, England

SMELTZER, STEVEN A., manufacturing executive; b. York, Pa., Oct. 28, 1953; s. Bernard L. and Helen A. (Farry) S.; m. Carol L., Aug. 14, 1976; children: Ross, Colleen. BA in Geography, U. Ariz., 1976; MA in Regional Plannign, Pa. State U., 1980; MBA, SUNY, Albany. V.p. Montgomery County Econ. Devel. Corp., Amsterdam, N.Y., 1985-89, Noteworthy Industries, Amsterdam, 1989—. V.p., N.Y. State Mil. Battle Flags Commn., Albany, 1999. Home: 145 Percy Hill Rd Old Chatham NY 12136-3205 Office: Noteworthy Industries 100 Church St Amsterdam NY 12010-4290

SMEND, RUDOLF, theologian; b. Berlin, Oct. 17, 1932; s. Rudolf and Gisela (Hübner) S.; m. Dagmar Erlbruch, May 24, 1969. Student, U. Tübingen, Fed. Republic of Germany, 1951-52, Göttingen U., Fed. Republic of Germany, 1952-54, U. Basel, Switzerland, 1954-55; DTheol, U. Basel, Switzerland, 1958; DivD (hon.), St. Andrews U., Scotland, 1979. Privat dozent U. Bonn, 1962-63; prof. theology Kirchliche Hochschule, Berlin, 1963-65, U. Münster, Fed. Republic of Germany, 1965-71, U. Göttingen, 1971—. Author: Die Entstehung des Alten Testaments, 1978, Die Mitte des Alten Testaments, 1986, Zur ältesten Geschichte Israels, 1987, Deutsche Alttestamentler in drei Jahrhunderten, 1989, Epochen der Bibelkritik, 1991, Bibel, Theologie, Universitet, 1997, Altes Testament Christlich gepredigt, 2000. Mem. Acad. der Wissenschaften (v.p. 1994-96, 98-2000, pres. 1996-98, 2000—), Brit., Danish, Finish and Norwegian Acad. (corr. fellow), Soc. for Study of Old Testament (hon.), German Forschungsgemeinschaft (v.p. 1986-92, Alfried Krupp-Preis 1998). Home: 6 Thomas Dehler Weg, 37075 Göttingen Germany Office: Theologicum, Platz der Göttinger Sieben 2, 37073 Göttingen Germany

SMETANA, KAREL, JR., anatomist, cell biologist, researcher; b. Prague, Czech Republic, May 6, 1958; s. Karel and Vlasta (Kroužková) S.; m. Markéta Židková, Mar. 11, 1988. MD, Charles U., Prague, 1983, PhD, 1990, DSc, 1997. Asst. prof. Charles U., Prague, 1981-95, assoc. prof. anatomy, 1995—; mem. com. for polymers Czech Ministry Health, Prague, 1993-96. Contbr. articles to profl. jours. Mem. Czech Anatomical Soc. (Ann. award 1991), Czech Soc. Histochem. Cytochem, Anat. Gesellschaft, Soc. Leukocyte Biology, German Soc. for Cell Biology.

SMETANA, PAVEL AMOS, religious organization administrator; s. Jan K. and Věra (Kozáková) S.; m. Zdeňka Adámková, July 2, 1960; children: Ester, Magdalena, Pavla. MgrTh, Theol. Faculty, Prague, Czechoslovakia, 1956-61; postgrad., New Coll., Edinburgh, Scotland, 1969-70. Min., pastor Ch. of Czech Brethren, Hoštálková, 1964-79; min., pastor Ch. of Czech Brethren, Prague-Libeň, 1979-90, dep. moderator, 1987-91, moderator, 1991—; mem. evang. com. Ch. of Czech Brethren, Prague, 1970—; chmn. ecumenical coun. Czech Republic Ch. of Czech Brethren, Prague-Libeň, 1990-91; pres. Ecumenical Coun. of Chs. in Czech Republic, 1990—, Evangel. Ch. of Czech Brethren, 1990—; chmn. E.C. Czech Republic, 1991-95; pres. Ec. Com. Czech Republic, 1995—. Translator (from Hebrew) Old Testament, 1961-89. Avocations: poetry, music, swimming. Office: Evang Ch of Czech Brethren, POB 466 Jungmannova 9, 111 21 Prague Czech Republic*

SMETANA, SHMUEL SANE, nephrologist, researcher; b. Bamberg, Germany, Dec. 1, 1946; arrived in Israel, 1956; s. Hirsh and Gitel (Wachnachter) S.; m. Zahava Migdalovitch, Sept. 9, 1971; children: Lilit, Noam. MD, Tel Aviv U., 1976. Med. diplomate. Intern Ichikov Hosp., Tel Aviv, 1974-75, resident, 1975-76; resident Mt. Sinai Hosp., Chgo., 1977; resident Kaplan Hosp., Rehovot, Israel, 1978-81, sr. resident, 1982-88; dir. nephrology Wolfson Hosp., Holun, Israel, 1988—. Contbr. articles to profl. jours., chpt. to book. Capt. Israeli Def. Force Active Res., 1993—. Levinstein Found. grantee, Tel Aviv U., 1996; recipient Chief Scientist's award, Jerusalem, 1996. Mem. Israeli Soc. Nephrology (sec. 1990-93), Am. Soc. Nephrology. Avocation: chess. Office: Wolfson Med Ctr Nephrology, PO Box 5, 58100 Holon Israel

SMICK, SUSAN SCHNEE, tile designer and manufacturer, airline strategic, marketing planner; b. Bklyn., July 12, 1947; d. Henry and Rhoda (Noskin) Schnee; m. Edward Lewis Smick, Feb. 5, 1972 (separated 1994); 1 child, Joshua Henry. BA with honors, C.W. Post Coll., 1970; postgrad., NYU, 1970-71. Cert. tchr., N.Y. Customer svc. and campus rep. Trans World Airlines, N.Y.C., 1966-71, strategic airline mktg. planner, 1971-72, fleet planning analyst, 1972-73; propr. Sailor's Valentine, Chatham, Mass., 1974-76; ednl. and corp. tour developer Crimson Travel, Cambridge, Mass., 1977-80; propr., tile designer, mfr. Cape Cod Tile Co., 1986-97; founding ptnr. TileGraphics, Weston, Mass., 1994-97; founding ptnr., tile designer, mfr. Great Am. Tile Works, Weston, Mass., 1997—; cons. U.S. Dept. Transp., 1975. Author (ednl. tours) The Flying Classroom, 1977-80; ceramic artist; author mktg. software. Friends of McLean, McLean Hosp., Belmont, Mass., 1997; mem. Mass. Horticulture Soc., 1995—; bd. dirs. Women's Cmty. League of Weston, 1999, chmn. ways and means com., 2000; chmn. of events Pub. Action for the Arts, 1999, adv. bd. mem., 2000. Recipient Howard Gold Polit. Sci. scholarship Howard Gold Meml. Fund, 1965, acad. scholarship C.W. Post Coll., 1967-70, Nat. Profl. Devel. Act fellowship NYU Grad. Sch. Edn. and History, 1970. Mem. Soc. Glass and Ceramic Decorators, Pi Gamma Mu, Phi Beta Kappa. Avocations: fundraising, Am. folk art, interior design, fashion design, horticulture. Home: 89 Ash St Weston MA 02493-1940 Office: Great Am Tile Works PO Box 363 Weston MA 02493-0002

SMIDDY, F(RANCIS) PAUL, stockbroker; b. Leeds, Eng., Nov. 13, 1953; s. Francis Geoffrey and Thelma Vivienne (Penfold) S.; m. Katy Watson, Sept. 2, 1978; children: Oliver, Alexander. BA in Econs., Manchester (Eng.) U., 1975. Mgr. Price Waterhouse, Leeds and London, 1975-82; fin. analyst J. Sainsbury, London, 1982-84; mgr. Capel Cure Myers & Co., London, 1984-85; assoc. dir. Wood MacKenzie & Co., London, 1985-86, County Natwest Securities, London, 1986-88; dir. Kleinwort Benson Securities, London, 1988-93, Nomura Rsch. Inst.-Europe Ltd., London, 1993-95, Credit L. Securities Europe, London, 1995—. Freeman, Guild of Air Pilots and Navigators. Fellow Inst. Chartered Accts. in Eng. and Wales; mem. Securities Inst. Avocations: aviation, France, fresh air. Office: Nomura Rsch Inst-Europe Inc, Credit Lyonnais Securities, 5 Appold St, London EC2A 2DA, England

SMIECINSKI-SALKOWSKI, ALICIA, genetic counselor; b. Detroit, Sept. 1, 1961; d. Theodore Benedict and Marian (Stefanka) S.; m. Daniel Joseph Salkowski, Dec. 30, 1988. Assoc. of gen. studies, Macomb Cmty. Coll., Warren, Mich., 1991; BS, Wayne State Univ., 1994, MS in genetic counseling, 1999. Relocation cons. Bekins, Graebel, Godfrey Moving and Storage Co., Detroit, 1982-87; student rsch. asst. dept. pyhsiology Wayne State Univ., Detroit, 1993, student rsch. asst. dept. radiation oncology and cancer, 1993-94; rsch. asst. dept. pathology Detroit Medical Ctr. Univ. Labs., Detroit, 1996-97; clinical cancer genetic counseling asst. Karmanos Cancer Inst., Detroit, 1997-98; genetic counselor/study coord. Wayne State Univ., Detroit, 1997—, Karmanos Cancer Inst., Detroit, 1999—; adj. faculty Wayne State U. Sch. Medicine and March of Dimes Genetics. Contbr. articles to profl. jours. Recipient Presdl. Scholarship award Wayne State UNiv., 1992-94. Mem. Nat. Soc. Genetic Counselors, Am. Soc. Human Genetics, Phi Beta Kappa, Golden Key Honor Soc. E-mail: salkowsk@karmanos.org. Fax: 313-831-7806. Office: Karmanos Cancer Inst 110 E Warren Ave Detroit MI 48201-1312

SMIETANA, WALTER, educational research director; b. New Bedford, Mass., Nov. 8, 1922; s. Stanislaw and Frances (Wojtal) S. AB in Edn., U. Mich., 1948; MS, Boston U., 1956, EdD, 1965; ScD (hon.), U. Mass., Dartmouth, 1975. Cert. tchr., Mich. Tchr. sci. and math. Somerset (Mass.) Pub. Schs., 1948-65; prof. edn. Elmhurst (Ill.) Coll., 1965-69; prof. edn. Alliance Coll., Cambridge Springs, Pa., 1969-87, chmn. divsn. social sci., pres., 1971-72; dir. rsch. SYLLAGENES, New Bedford, 1987—; liaison Study of Undergrad. Experience in Am., Carnegie Found. for Advancement of Teaching, Alliance Coll., 1984; participant Pa. Dept. Edn. ETS, Tchr. Cert. Test Devel., 1986-87; develop and accredite new tchr. edn. programs, state, regional and nat. levels, 1965-87; develop and evaluate year abroad and exch. programs Alliance Coll./Jagiellonian U., Cracow, Poland in coop. with U.S. Office Edn., 1969-85. Chmn. city com. Rep. Party, New Bedford, 1953-58; mem. citizens adv. com. Heritage State Park, New Bedford, 1989-93; chmn. bd. trustees Inst. Tech., New Bedford, 1963-64; chmn. adv. com. The Rsch. Found., New Bedford, 1962-64. Recipient Cert. of Merit for non-English Lang. Resources Rsch., Yeshiva U., 1981; U.S. Office Edn./ERIC grantee, 1969. Mem. World Future Soc., Inst. for Global Ethics, Nat. Space Soc., Inst. Noetic Scis., Libr. of Congress Assocs. (charter mem.). Republican. Roman Catholic. Avocations: astronomy, photography. Home and Office: 84 Ellen St New Bedford MA 02744-1521

SMIETON, MARY GUILLAN, retired civil service professional; b. London, Dec. 5, 1902; d. John Guillan and Maria Judith (Toop) S. BA/MA, Oxford U., 1925. Asst. keeper Pub. Record Office, London, 1925-28; asst. prin., dep. sec. Ministry of Labour, London, 1925-57; permanent sec. Ministry of Edn., London, 1957-62; gen. sec. W.V.S., London, 1938-40; dir. personnel UN, N.Y.C., 1946-48. Hon. fellow Lady Margaret Hall, 1957, Bedford Coll., London. Mem. Oxford and Cambridge United Univs. Avocation: gardening.

SMILAUER, PAVEL, physicist; b. Praha, Czechoslovakia, Oct. 17, 1961; s. Jan and Eva (Blažková) S; m. Renata Pechanová; children: Zuzana, Michal, Kristyna. RNDr, Charles U., Praha, 1985, PhD, 1990. Rsch. asst. Inst. Physics, Praha, 1989-92; postdoctoral rsch. assoc. Imperial Coll., London, 1992-95; vis. sci. Forschungszentrum, Jülich, Germany, 1995-96. Mem. editl. bd. Czechoslovak Jour. Physics, 1990-93; contbr. articles to profl. publs. Mem. Materials Rsch. Soc., Czech Phys. Soc. Avocations: walking, music. Home: Prusíkova 2399, 15500 Prague 5, Czech Republic Office: Inst Physics, 16200 Prague 6, Czech Republic

SMILEY, FREDERICK MELVIN, education educator, consultant; b. Yuba City, Calif., Apr. 13, 1943; s. Lester Boomer and Claire Leone (DeChesne) S. AA, Yuba Coll., 1963; BA, Chico State U., 1966; MA in Edn., Chapman Coll., 1973, MA in English, 1978, MA in Spl. Edn., 1982; PhD, U. Santa Barbara, 1982; EdD, Okla. State U., 1992. Tchr., coach, v.p. McDermitt (Nev.) High Sch., 1978-80; resource specialist Eagle Mt. (Calif.) High Sch., 1980-81; instr. spl. edn. Mary Stone Sch., San Mateo, Calif., 1981-86; dept. leader Quaezar Corp., Bridgeport, Conn., 1986-87; cons., researcher Multi-functional Resource Ctr., Stillwater and Norman, Okla., 1988-91; assoc. prof. edn. Cameron U., Lawton, Okla., 1991—. Contbr. articles to profl. jours.; contbg. editor Think!, The Writing Teacher, O.A.T.E. Jour., ATE Jour. Mem. AAUP, Am. Assn. for Teaching and Curriculum, Am. Soc. Curriculum Devel., Am. Coun. Rural Spl. Edn., Am. Assn. Colls. for Tchr. Edn., Coun. for Exceptional Children, Okla. Assn. Tchr. Educators, Soc. Educators and Scholars, Kappa Delta Pi, Phi Delta Kappa, Phi Kappa Phi. Democrat. Lutheran. Avocations: reading, writing, racing, tennis, golf. E-mail: freds@cameron.edu. Office: Cameron U 2800 W Gore Blvd Lawton OK 73505-6377

SMILEY, XAN DE CRESPIGNY, journalist; b. Hanover, Germany, May 1, 1949; s. David de Crespigny and Moyra Eileen (Montagu-Douglas-Scott) S.; m. Jane Acton, Aug. 26, 1983; stepchildren: Charlotte, Rebecca Pugh; children: Ben, Adam Smiley. BA, MA, New Coll., Oxford U., Eng., 1970. Editor Africa Confidential (newsletter), London, 1977-81; editorial writer The Times of London, 1981-82; Russia corr. The Daily Telegraph, Moscow, 1986-89; Am. corr. The Sunday Telegraph, Washington, 1989-92; Middle East editor The Economist, London, 1983-86, polit. editor, writer Bagehot column, 1992-94, Europe corr., 1994-96, Europe editor, 1996—; co-proprietor and dir. Africa Confidential, London, 1981-93, dir. 1993—; co-publisher The Soviet Analyst, 1989-90. Avocations: food, genealogy, travel, shooting, skiing (downhill champ Oxford & Cambridge, 1969, mem. Brit. Ski Team, 1969). E-mail: xansmiley@economist.com. Office: The Economist, 25 St James St., London SW1A 1HG, England

SMILGA, ANDREI VOLDEMAROVICH, physicist, researcher; b. Moscow, Aug. 24, 1954; s. Voldemar Petrovich and Irina Semenovna (Zhiguleva) S.; m. Elena Nikolaevna Savvina, May 18, 1985; children: Boris, Ilya. MS in Engring. and Physics, Moscow Inst. Physics & Tech., 1976; PhD, Inst. Theoretical Physics, Moscow, 1980; DSc, Moscow, 1996. Engr. Inst. Oceanology, Acad. Scis. USSR, Moscow, 1979-81; jr. rschr. Inst. Theoretical and Exptl. Physics, Moscow, 1981-85, sr. rschr., 1985-96, leading rschr., 1996-98; prof. U. Nantes, France, 1998—; postdoctorant U. Bern, Switzerland, 1990-93; vis. prof. U. Minn., 1996-97. Editor: Continuous Advances in QCD, 1994; contbr. to over 100 scientific pubs. in profl. jours. Grantee Internat. Sci. Found., 1994-95, INTAS, Brussels, 1994-97, CRDF, 1996-97. Avocations: chess, mountaineering. Office: Dept Math U Nautes, 2 rue de la Houssiniere, 44322 Nantes France

SMILGIES, DETLEF-MATTHIAS FRIEDRICH, physicist; b. Celle, Germany, May 28, 1960; s. Arno and Edith (Stottmeister) Z.; m. Melanie Stein; 1 child, Maximilian. D in Physics, U. Göttingen and Max-Planck-Inst. fur Stromungsforschung, Germany, 1986; Dr.rer.nat, U. Göttingen, Germany, 1991. Postdoctoral AT&T Bell Labs., Brookhaven, 1991-92, Rutgers Univ., New Brunswick, 1992-94, Riso Nat. Lab., Roskilde, Denmark, 1994-96; scientist European Synchrotron Radiation Facility, 1996-2000; with Cornell High Energy Synchrotran Source, 2000—. Recipient Otto Hahn medal Max Planck Gesellschaft, 1991, Feodor Lynen fellowship Alexander von Humboldt Stiftung, 1992. Mem. Deutsche Physikalische Gesellschaft, Am. Physical Soc. Office: Cornell High Energy Synchrotron Source Cornell U Ithaca NY 14853

SMIRNOV, ALEXANDER NIKOLAEVICH, endocrinologist; b. Moscow, Oct. 19, 1946; s. Nikolay Nikiforovich and Antonina Alexeevna (Kolosova) S.; m. Olga Vyacheslavovna Matanova, Jan. 26, 1968; 1 child, Vsevolod. PhD, Moscow State U., 1975, DS, 1986. Jr. rschr. Moscow State U., 1974-76, sr. rsch., 1976-86, leading rschr., 1987-92, head lab., 1993—; v.p. Russian Acad. Coun. Endocrinology Scis., Moscow, 1994—; mem. scientific coun. physiology Moscow State U., 1987—. Co-author: Receptors and Steroid Hormones, 1981, Sex Differentiation of Liver Functions, 1991. With Soviet Army, 1970-71. Rsch. grantee Russian Found. Fundamental Investigation, 1993-95, 96—. Mem. Russian Acad. Scis. (biochem. soc.). Avocations: biking, water travel. Home: Ukhtomskaya st 15 apt 34, 111 020 Moscow Russia Office: Moscow State U Sch Biol, Labn Endocrinology Lenin Hills 1/12, 119 899 Moscow Russia

SMIRNOV, GENNADII VICTOROVICH, physicist; b. Saratov, Russia, Aug. 30, 1937; s. Victor Sergeevich Smirnov and Nina Feodorovna Voloboeva; m. Tatjana Mikhailovna Kuznetsova, June 3, 1966; children: Maxim, Elena. Diploma, Phys. Engring. Inst., Moscow, 1961; Cand. Phys./Math. Sci., Kurchatov Inst. of Atomic, Energy, Moscow, 1970, D of Physics/Math. Sci., 1980. Engr. Kurchatov Inst. of Atomic Energy, Moscow, 1961-64, aspirant, 1965-68, rsch. scientist, 1969-73, sr. rsch. scientist, 1974-87, head of lab., 1987-91; head of lab. Russian Rsch. Ctr., Moscow, 1997—; invited rschr. Stanford U. Brookhaven Nat. Lab., 1991; vis. prof. Kath. U. Leuven, Belgium, 1993, 98, Hamburg U., Germany, 1996, Munich Tech. U., Germany, 1996, 99. Contbr. articles to profl. jours. Recipient Kuzchatov award Kuzchatov Inst. Atomic Energy 1974, 82, State award in sci. USSR Govt. Acad. of Sci., 1976. Avocations: mountains, water skiing, travel. Office: RRC Kurchatov Inst, Kurchatov Square 1, 123182 Moscow Russia

SMIRNOV, NIKOLAI NIKOLAEVICH, research scientist; b. Moscow, Jan. 7, 1928; s. Nikolai Nikolaevich Smirnov and Zinoviya Mikhailovna (Kopylova) Smirnova; m. Lidiya Ivanovna Sheptalina, May 22, 1954 (dec. 1976); 1 child, Nikolai; m. Larisa Andreevna Lokahnina, June 2, 1978; 1 child, Aleksei. Grad., Moscow Tech. Inst. Fisheries, 1950, Moscow State Pedagogical Inst., 1955; DSc in Biology, Russian Acad. Scis., Saint Petersburg, 1969. Postgrad. fellow, asst. prof. Moscow Tech. Inst. Fisheries, 1950-59; sr. scientist Inst. Biology of Inland Waters Russian Acad. Scis., 1959-66, Pondfishculture Inst., Rybnoe, Russia, 1966-68, Inst. Ecology and Evolution Russian Acad. Scis., Moscow, 1968—; mem. initial com. ecological monitoring, Stockholm, 1971; exec. sec. Nat. Com. Internat. Biological Program, 1968-79; expert on ecology SIPRI, Stockholm, 1977-78. Contbr. articles to profl. jours. Avocation: English philology. Office: Inst Ecology & EvolutionRAS, Leninskii prospekt 33, 117071 Moscow Russia

SMIRNOV, VYACHESLAV PAVLOVICH, physicist, educator, researcher; b. Leningrad, Russia, Feb. 25, 1936; s. Pavel Alekseevich and Anna Fedorovna (Balashova) S.; m. Valentina Vasil'evna Kraskova, Mar. 11, 1962. Physicist, U. Leningrad, 1958. Jr. rschr. U. Leningrad, 1961-67, asst., 1967-76, asst. prof. physics, 1976-83; asst. prof. physics Inst. Fine Mechanics and Optics, Leningrad, 1983-90; prof. physics Inst. Fine Mechanics and Optics, St. Petersburg, 1990—, head dept. physics, 1989-96; cons. Phys.-Tech. Inst., St. Petersburg, 1995—. Author: Site Symmetry in Crystals, 1993, 2d edit., 1997, Group Methods in Quantum Chemistry of Solids, 1987, Site Symmetry in Molecules and Crystals, 1997. Grantee Soros Found., 1993, Min. of Higher Edn. of Russia, 1996-97, 98—. Home: Svetlanovskii Ave, 194223 Saint Petersburg Russia Office: Inst Fine Mechanics/Optics, Sablinskaya St, 197101 Saint Petersburg Russia

SMIRNOV, YURI ALEXANDROVICH, virologist; b. Kostroma, Russia, Jan. 14, 1940; s. Alexandr Grigorievich and Klaudija Vasilievna Smirnov; m. Tatiana Alexandrovna Simonova, Dec. 4, 1961; 1 child, Michael Yurievich. Student, 1st Moscow Med. Inst., 1957-63; PhD, Cand. Med. Scis., Ivanovsky Inst. Virology, Moscow, 1966, Dr. Med. Sci., 1993, prof., 1994. Jr. rsch. scientist The Ivanovsky Inst. of Virology, Moscow, 1966-76, sr. rsch. scientist, 1976-87, head of lab. of subviral structures, 1987—, prof., 1994—. Inventor in field; contbr. articles to profl. jours. Mem. steering com. on influenza St. Petersburg, Russia, 1993. Recipient Medal of Excellence, Pub. Health Svc., 1979, medal Vet. of Labor, 1984; Internat. Sci. Found. grantee, 1993. Mem. Moscow Regional Sci. Med. Knowledge Soc. (chmn. 1968-73), Russian Soc. Microbiologists and Epidemiologists (mem. presidium 1983-97), Med. Primatology Found. (v.p. 1995). Avocations: travel, chess, cards. Office: Ivanovsky Inst of Virology, Gamaleya St 16, 123098 Moscow Russia

SMIRNOVA, MARINA SERGEEVNA, physicist; b. Kharkov, Ukraine, Jan. 1, 1955; d. Sergey Alexandrovich and Alexandra Vasil'evna (Solomko) S. M of Math., Kharkov U., Ukraine, 1977, DPhil, 1993. Engr., programmer Khartron, Kharkov, Ukraine, 1977-89; engr., programmer KhIPhT, Kharkov, Ukraine, 1989-90, jr. rsch. assoc., 1990-93, rsch. assoc., 1993-97, maj. rsch. assoc., 1997—. Contbr. articles to profl. jours. Mem. Young Communist League, Kharkov, 1969-83. Avocations: dog breeding, fishing, philosophy, classic music, badminton. Home: Kurchatov ave 10 ap 322, 61108 Kharkov Ukraine Office: Kharkov Inst Phys & Tech, Akademicheskaya Str 1, 61108 Kharkov Ukraine

SMIRNOVA, NATALIA, chemistry educator, researcher; b. Leningrad, Russia, Jan. 4, 1933; d. Alexandr and Olga (Kolpakova) S.; m. Valentin Nazarov, Aug. 15, 1958; 1 child, Ekaterina. M, Leningrad State U., 1955, D of Chem. Sci., 1973; PhD, Moscow State U., 1961. Jr. rschr. Leningrad State U., 1959-65, sr. rschr., 1965-75; prof. St. Petersburg State U., 1976-97, head phys. chemistry chair, 1997—. Author: Methods of Statistical Thermodynamics in Physical Chemistry, 2d edit., 1982, Polish edit., 1980, Japanese edit., 1989, Molecular Theories of Solutions, 1987; co-author: (with A.G. Morachevsky, others) Thermodynamics of Diluted Nonelectrolyte Solutions, 1982, Thermodynamics of Liquid-Vapour Equilibrium (editor A.G. Morachevsky), 1989; mem. editl. bd. Fluid Phase Equilibria, 1977-92, Russian Jour. Phys. Chemistry, 1993—, Russian Jour. Applied Chemistry, 1998—. Recipient State prize Coun. of Ministers of USSR, 1987. Mem. Russian Acad. Scis. (corr.), Russian Acad. Natural Scis., Mendeleev Chem. Soc. (bd. dirs. St. Petersburg divsn. 1978—). Avocation: aerobics. Home: Apt 29, Kamennoostrovsky prosp 9/2, 197046 St Petersburg Russia Office: St Petersburg State U, Universitetsky prosp 2, 198904 St Petersburg Russia

SMIRNOVA, OLGA VYACHESLAVOVNA, biologist, researcher; b. Moscow, Sept. 15, 1947; d. Matanov Vyacheslav Petrovich. Diploma in Human Physiology, Moscow State U., 1970, PhD, 1977, DSc, 1990. Sr. laborant Moscow State U., 1970-71, union rschr., 1971-87, rschr., 1987-90, sr. rschr., 1990-93, leading rschr., 1993—. Author: (book) Sex Differentiation of Liver Functions, 1991; contbr. articles to profl. jours. Grantee Russian Found. Fundamental Rschs., 1995-96. Mem. European Assn. for Study of the Liver, Internat. Assn. for the Study of Liver, Internat. Soc. Andrology. Avocations: travel, painting. Office: Moscow State U/Biol Dept, Lab Endocrinology/Vorobev Hills, 119899 Moscow Russia

SMIT, GERTRUDE NICOLET, psychologist; b. Rotterdam, The Netherlands, Apr. 2, 1968; d. Willem Reinder Smit and Anje Jantiena Helder. MA, U. Groningen, 1991, PhD, 1995. Cons. GITP Internat., Nijmegen, The Netherlands, 1997—. Author: The Assessment of Professional Communication Skills, 1995; contbr. articles to profl. jours. Mem. APA Internat. Affiliate. Office: GITP Internat, Westerstraat 42, Rotterdam Zuid, The Netherlands 3016 DH

SMIT, JAN JACOB ANTONIE, science educator; b. Wolmaransstad, South Africa, Feb. 22, 1942; s. Daniel Stephanus and Annie Elizabeth (Van Vuuren) S.; m. René Estelle Nel, Dec. 18, 1965; children: Jaco, Reinette, Janet. BS, PU for CHE, Potchefstroom, South Africa, 1964, BS with honors, 1965, MS, 1970, DSc, 1977. Tchr. Transvaal Edn. Dept., Potchefstroom, 1966-72; lectr. Potchefstroom U. Christian Higher Edn., 1973-83, asst. prof., 1984-93, prof., 1994—; dir. Sch. for Sci., Math. and Tech. Edn., Potchefstroom, 1986—; advisor Orgn. Ednl. Resources and Technol. Tng: Sci. and Technology Edn. Project Inst., South Africa, 1993—. Author: Supplementary Exercises Physical Science, 1986; contbr. articles to profl. jours. Mem. South African Inst. Physics, South African Assn. Rsch. in Maths. and Sci. Edn., South African Acad. for Sci. Mem. Dutch Reformed Ch. Avocations: rugby, shooting. Office: PU for CHE, Venterstraat, 2520 Potchefstroom South Africa

SMIT, L. J.M., editor, career officer. Capt. Navy, The Netherlands, 1964-94; editor MarineBlad, The Hague, The Netherlands, 1994—; cons. Koninklijke Vereniging van Marineofficierem, The Hague, 1994—. Fax: 3170 383 5911. E-mail: info@kumo.nl. Office: MarineBlad, Wassenaarseweg 2 B, 2596 CH The Hague The Netherlands

SMIT, WILLEM ADRIAAN, plant pathologist, microbiologist, researcher; b. Virginia, South Africa, Oct. 27, 1960; s. Johannes Petrus and Hester (Schreüder) S.; m. Louise Carstens, Dec. 24, 1988; 1 child, Werner Antonio. BSc, Stellenbosch (South Africa) U., 1981, BSc with honors, 1982, MSc in Plant Pathology, 1988; PhD in Microbiology, U. Free State, Bloemfontein, South Africa, 1995. Rsch. technologist Algams Ctr. Limnology, Windhoek, Namibia, 1984-85; agrl. rschr. Fruit Tech. Rsch. Inst., Stellenbosch, 1986-88, sr. agrl. rschr., 1989-91; sr. agrl. rschr. U. Free State, 1992-93; rsch. coord. Fruit, Vine and Wine Rsch. Inst., Stellenbosch, 1994-98, rsch. mgr., 1999—; initiator Mushroom Rsch. Ctr., Stellenbosch, 2000; cons. Eon Corp. (Pty.) Ltd., Paarl, South Africa, 1997-00; chmn. organizing com. Mont Fleur Biotech. Symposium, Fruit Tech. Rsch. Inst., Stellenbosch, 1991, organizing com. Gourmet/Medicinal Mushroom Conf., Franschhoek, South Africa, 2001. Contbr. articles to profl. jours., chpt. to book; patentee in field of mushroom growth medium. With Namibian (South West African) Territory Force, 1985; initiator, pioneer 1st South African Mushroom Rsch. Ctr., Stellenbosch, 2000—. Innovation grantee (consortium ptnr.) Dept. Arts, Culture, Sci. and Tech., Pretoria, South Africa, 2000; recipient Langkloof trophy for rsch. excellence, Agrl. Rsch. Coun., Stellenbosch, 1997; travel grantee Agrl. Rsch. Coun., Pretoria, 1994, 96, 97, 98, 99. Mem. AAAS, Am. Phytopathol. Soc., N.Y. Acad. Scis., Internat. Soc. Plant Pathology, Internat. Soc. Mushroom Sci, So. African Soc. Plant Pathology (regional chmn. 1988). Mem. Dutch Reformed Ch. Achievements include initiating 1st South African Mushroom Rsch. Ctr. Avocations: photography, trail hiking, medium-long-distance running. Fax: 27-21-809-3491. E-mail: adriaan@infruit.agric.za. Office: Fruit Vine and Wine Rsch, Pvt Bag X5013 Helshoogte Rd, Stellenbosch 7599, South Africa

SMITH, ABBIE OLIVER, college administrator, educator; b. Augusta, Ga., Jan. 31, 1931; d. Rowland Sheppard and Abigail Seabrook (Hanahan) Oliver; m. William Parkhurst Smith, Jr., July 2, 1953; children: William Parkhurst Smith, III, Oliver Hamilton. BS, George Washington U., 1953, MEd, 1958, EdDin Higher Edn., 1986. Tchr. St. Mary's Acad., Monroe, Mich., 1954-55; tchr., coach Washington-Lee H.S., Arlington, Va., 1955-58; homemaker, cmty. vol. Bethesda, Md., 1959-64; asst. professorial lectr. Ge-

orge Washington U., Washington, 1965-69, adminstr. continuing edn., 1969-80, asst. dean, dir., 1981-89, acting dean divsn. continuing edn., 1989-93, asst. v.p., asst. to dean institutional advancement, 1993—; panelist t.v. series WETA, Washington; newsletter editor Tng. Officers Conf., 1989—, chair charter expansion 1992—. co-author: (workbook) Developing New Horizons for Women, 1975, Manual for Counselors for Developing New Horizons for Women, 1975. Mem. adv. bd. Washington Bd. Trade, 1975-77, women's branch adv. bd. State Nat. Bank, Bethesda, Md., 1978-81; collegiate adv. bd. Episcopal Diocese of Washington, 1977-79. Recipient Leadership in Adult Edn. award, 1976, GW award for outstanding contbn. to univ. life Office of GW Pres., 1991, Washington Women of Achievement, Washington Edn. TV Assn., 1980. Mem. Nat. U. Continuing Edn. Assn. (awards chair divsn. women's edn. 1977-78, nat. chair 1977-78, chair-elect divsn. part-time students program 1984-86, nat. chair 1984-86, chair coun. human resources 1985-86, nat. spl. com. on couns. and divsn. 1984-86, nat. exec. bd. 1984-86, nat. bd. dirs. 1984-98, nat. charters and bylaws coms. 1987-89, sec.-elect divsn. cert. and nontraditional degree programs 1987-89, chair-elect 1989-90, nat. chair 1990-91, nat. ann. planning coms. 1987, 92, sec. region II 1989-90, chair-elect, ann. conf. chair, single host instn. ann. conf. region II 1990-91, chair region II 1991-92, awards com. chair 1992, Walton S. Bittner Svc. Citation 1994, hon. mention for program catalog nat. divsn. mktg. 1988), Phi Delta Kappa Internat. (G.W. chpt., v.p. for programs 1995-96, pres. 1996-97). Democrat. Episcopalian. Avocations: writing, painting, swimming, dancing, traveling. Home: 3751 Jocelyn St NW Washington DC 20015-1836 Office: George Washington U 2134 G St NW Washington DC 20037-2797

SMITH, ALAN HOWARD, investment banker; b. Dartford, England, Dec. 2, 1943; s. James Sydney and Else (Robinson) S.; m. Penelope Diane Trego, Aug. 13, 1966; children: Benedict James, Oliver Charles. LLB, U. Bristol, 1964. Legal adviser Smiths Industries Ltd., England, 1966-67; lectr. U. East Africa, Nairobi, 1968-69, U. Hong Kong, 1970-72; from dir. to chmn. Jardine Fleming, Hong Kong, 1972-96; vice chmn. Pacific region Credit Suisse First Boston, Hong Kong, 1997—; mem. coun. Stock Exch., Hong Kong, 1988-89, 95-96; mem. govt. adv. com. Govt. Hong Kong, 1994. Justice of peace, Hong Kong, 1994. Mem. Shek O Country Club, Hong Kong Club. Avocations: scuba diving, skiing, bridge. Office: 22 F Three Exchange Sq, 8 Connaught Pl, Hong Kong Hong Kong

SMITH, ALBERT CROMWELL, JR., investments consultant; b. Norfolk, Va., Dec. 6, 1925; s. Albert Cromwell and Georgie (Foreman) S.; m. Laura Thaxton, Oct. 25, 1952; children: Albert, Elizabeth, Laura. BSCE, Va. Mil. Inst., 1949; MS in Govtl. Adminstrn., George Washington U., 1965; MBA, Pepperdine U., 1975; PhD in Bus. Adminstrn., LaSalle U., 1994. Enlisted man USMC, 1944, advanced through grades to col., 1970, comdr. inf. platoons, cos., landing force; assigned to staffs, U.K. Joint Force, U.S. Sec. Navy, Brit. Staff Coll., Marine Staff Coll., U.K. Staff Coll. and Latimer Staff Coll.; advisor, analyst amphibious sys. USMC; ret., 1974; pres. A. Cromwell-Smith, Ltd., Charlottesville, Va., 1973; head broker, cons. A. Cromwell Smith, Investments, La Jolla and Coronado, Calif., 1975—. Author: The Individual Investor in Tomorrow's Stock Market, 1977, The Little Guy's Stock Market Survival Guide, 1979, Wake Up Detroit@ The EVs Are Coming, 1982, The Little Guy's Tax Survival Guide, 1984, Little Guy's Real Estate Success Guide, 1990, Little Guy's Stock Market Success Guide, 1992, Little Guy's Stock Market Future Effectiveness, 1994, The Little Guy's Sailboat Success, 1996, The Little Guy's Business Success, 1997, Business Success, 1997, Stock Market Success, 1998, Semper Fidelis in Peace and War, 1999, Sailboat Success, 1999, Tax Survival Guide, 1999, The EV's Are Coming, 1999, Real Estate Success, 2000; contbr. articles to civilian and mil. publs. Bd. dirs. La Jolla Reps., 1975-76; vestryman St. Martin's Episcopal Ch., 1971-73. Decorated Legion of Merit with oak leaf cluster with V device, Bronze Star with V device with oak leaf cluster, Air medal with two oak leaf clusters, Purple Heart; Vietnamese Galantry Cross with gold star. Mem. ASCE, SAR, Nat. Assn. Realtors, Calif. Assn. Realtors, San Diego Bd. Realtors, Coronado Bd. Realtors, Stockbrokers Soc., So. Calif. Options Soc., Mil. Order Purple Heart. Office: PO Box 180192 Coronado CA 92178-0192

SMITH, ALEXANDER ALAN GEORGE, publishing executive; b. Grimsby, England, Feb. 26, 1970; s. Alan George Edward and Dorothy (Barnbrook) S. Grad., U. Coll., 1992. Tchr. Internat. House, 1994; mktg. export mgr. VNA Santa Ines, Chile, 1995-96; mktg. mgr. Time Life, Inc., London, 1996—. Avocation: mountain sports. Office: Time Like UK, Brettenham House Lancaster, London WC2E 7TL, England

SMITH, ALEXANDER GOUDY, physics and astronomy educator; b. Clarksburg, W.Va., Aug. 12, 1919; s. Edgell Ohr and Helen (Reitz) S.; m. Mary Elizabeth Ellsworth, Apr. 19, 1942; children: Alexander G. III, Sally Jean. B.S., Mass. Inst. Tech., 1943; Ph.D., Duke U., 1949. Physicist Mass. Inst. Tech., Radiation Lab., Cambridge, 1943-46; research asst. Duke U., Durham, 1946-48; asst. prof. to prof. physics U. Fla., Gainesville, 1948-61; asst. dean grad. sch. U. Fla., 1961-69, acting dean grad. sch., 1971-73, chmn. dept. astronomy, 1962-71, prof. physics and astronomy, 1956—, Disting. prof., 1981—; dir. U. Fla. Radio Obs., 1956-85, Rosemary Hill Obs., 1989—. Author: (with others) Microwave Magnetrons, 1958, (with T.D. Carr) Radio Exploration of the Planetary System, 1964 (also Swedish, Spanish and Polish edits), Radio Exploration of the Sun, 1966; also numerous articles in field. Fellow AAAS, Optical Soc. Am., Am. Phys. Soc., Royal Micros. Soc.; mem. Am. Astron. Soc. (editor Photo-Bull. 1975-87), Astron. Soc. Pacific, Internat. Astron. Union, Internat. Sci. Radio Union, Fla. Acad. Scis. (treas. 1957-62, pres. 1963-64, medal 1965), Assn. Univs. for Rsch. in Astronomy (dir., cons.), S.E. Univs. Rsch. Assn. (trustee 1981-91), Soc. Photog. Scientists and Engrs., Athenaeum Club (past pres.), Db Racquet Club, Gainesville Country Club, Sigma Xi (nat. lectr. 1968, past pres. Fla. chpt.), Phi Kappa Phi, Sigma Pi Sigma. Republican. Christian Scientist. Home: 1417 NW 17th St Gainesville FL 32605-4014 Office: U Fla Dept Astronomy 211 Space Scis Bldg Gainesville FL 32611

SMITH, ANDREW, federal official; m. Val Smith. Councillor Oxford U.; mem. Dept. for Edn. and Employment; shadow transport sec., 1996; chief sec. to the treasury U.K., 1999—. Office: Her Majesty's Treasury, Parliament St, London SW1P 3AG, England*

SMITH, ANDREW DAVID, member of parliament; b. Wokingham, Berkshire, Eng., Feb. 21, 1951; s. David Eric and Georgina Harriet (Lowe) S.; m. Val Lambert, Mar. 26, 1976; 1 child, Luke. BA, Oxford U., 1972, BPhil, 1974; ArtsD (hon.), Oxford Brookes U., 1994. M.P. Ho. of Commons, London, 1987—. Mem. econs. affairs and treasury team Labour Party, 1992-94, shadow chief sec., 1994-96, shadow transport sec., 1996-97, employment and welfare to work min., 1997-99, chief sec. to the treasury, 1999. Home and Office: 4 Flaxfield Rd, Blackbird Leys Oxford OX4 5QD, England

SMITH, ANDREW L., electronic design engineer; b. Wayland, Mass., Mar. 8, 1968; s. Arthur Leopold and Margaretha (Van As) S.; m. Janet Flores Cheng. BSEE, Ariz. State U., 1990. Registered profl. electronic engr. CAE designer MJS Designs, Phoenix, 1986-88; CAE/CAD designer MJS Designs, Phoenix-Tempe, 1988-91, electronic design engr., 1991-94; sr. design engr. MJS Designs, Phoenix, 1994-96; pres., sr. design engr., owner Concept Solutions & Engring., Rochester, Minn., 1996—. Inventor High Resolution Asynchronous Video Combiner for Large Screen Display, 1994, Triple Channel VGA Display, 1993, RF Satellite Transmitter, 1995, others. Mem. Etta Kappa Nu. Achievements include finding novel video processing and generation techniques, electroluminescent inverter techniques, low power PDA design techniques, automatic earth watering regulator; custom embedded processor/system design. Office: Concept Solutions & Engring 830-13 AIA N #332 Ponte Vedra Beach FL 32082 Address: 232 N Mill View Way Ponte Vedra Beach FL 32082-4389

SMITH, ARLAN ROBERT, plastic and reconstructive surgeon; b. Surabaja, Indonesia, Aug. 3, 1948; arrived in Holland, 1954; m. Paulina Jacoba de Jong, May 25, 1990; children: Arlana Dominque, Darryl Nathaniël, Beau Aurora Fabiana, Chloé Aphrodite Zoë. Student, St. Ignatius Coll., Amsterdam, The Netherlands, 1961-66; PhD, U. Amsterdam, The Netherlands, 1972, MD, 1974. Cert. plastic and reconstructive surgeon. Gen. surgery tng. dept gen. surgery U. Maastricht, The Netherlands, 1975-79; clin. and rsch. fellow Mass. Gen. Hosp., Harvard Med. Sch., Boston, 1977-79; specialist in plastic and reconstructive surgery dept. plastic surgery U. Hosp. Dijkzigt Rotterdam, The Netherlands, 1979-82, chef de clinique in microsurgery and hand surgery dept. plastic and reconstructive surgery, 1979-86; head dept. plastic and reconstructive surgery Holy Hosp. Vlaardingen, The Netherlands, 1985-96; vis. prof. plastic and reconstructive surgery U. Kristen Idonesia Jakarta, Indonesia, 1989-91; dir., owner Clinic Holystaete Vlaardingen, The Netherlands, 1991—. Contbr. articles to profl. jours. Mem. Dutch Soc. for Hand Surgery, Dutch Soc. Esthetic Surgery, Dutch Soc. Plastic and Reconstructive Surgery, Internat. Microsurg. Soc., Found. Noshe Yemin (chmn.). Avocations: gardening, pre-Columbian art, modern, Egyptian and African art. Office: Clinic Holystaete, Churchillsingel 480, 3137XB Vlaardingen The Netherlands

SMITH, ARTHUR JOHN STEWART, physicist, educator; b. Victoria, B.C., Can., June 28, 1938; s. James Stewart and Lillian May (Geernaert) S.; m. Norma Ruth Askeland, May 20, 1966; children: Peter James, Ian Alexander. B.A., U. B.C., 1959, M.Sc., 1961; Ph.D., Princeton U., 1966. Postdoctoral fellow Deutsches Electronen-Synchrotron, Hamburg, W. Germany, 1966-67; mem. faculty dept. physics Princeton U., 1967—, prof., 1978—, Class of 1909 prof., 1992—, assoc. chmn. dept., 1979-83, chmn. dept. physics, 1990—; vis. scientist Brookhaven Nat. Lab., 1967—, Fermilab, 1974—, Stanford Linear Accelerator Ctr., 1996—; chair sci. and technology steering com. Brookhaven Sci. Assocs. Brookhaven Nat. Lab. Assoc. editor Phys. Rev. Letters, 1986-89; contbr. articles to profl. jours. Fellow Am. Phys. Soc. (chmn. divsn. of particles and fields 1991). Achievements include research on experimental high-energy particle physics; kaon decays, physics of the B particles and quark structure of hadrons. Home: 4 Ober Rd Princeton NJ 08540-4918 Office: PO Box 708 Princeton NJ 08544-0001

SMITH, ARTHUR LEE, lawyer; b. Davenport, Iowa, Dec. 19, 1941; s. Harry Arthur Smith (dec.) and Ethel (Hoffman) Duerre; m. Georgia Mills, June 12, 1965 (dec. Jan. 1984); m. Jean Bowler, Aug. 4, 1984; children: Juliana, Christopher, Andrew. BA, Augustana Coll., Rock Island, Ill., 1964; MA, Am. U., 1968; JD, Washington U., St. Louis, 1971. Bar: Mo. 1971, D.C. 1983. Telegraph editor Davenport Morning Democrat, 1962-64; ptnr. Peper Martin Jensen Maichel & Hetlage, 1971-95, Husch & Eppenberger, St. Louis, 1995—; arbitrator Nat. Assn. Security Dealers, 1980—, Am. Arbitration Assn., 1980—. Columnist St. Louis Lawyer. Lt. USN, 1964-68. Mem. ABA, D.C. Bar Assn. (chmn. law practice mgmt. 1990-91), Mo. Bar Assn. (chair adminstrv. law com. 1995-97, vice-chair ins. programs com. 1981-83, vice-chair antitrust com. 1981-83), P. Buckley Moss Soc. (dir. 1994—, v.p. 1998—), Bar Assn. Met. St. Louis (chmn. law mgmt. com. 1993—, chair tech. com. 1996—, Pres.'s award for Exceptional Svc. 1995), Order of Coif. Home: 1320 Chesterfield Estate Dr Chesterfield MO 63005-4400 Office: Husch & Eppenberger 100 N Broadway Ste 1300 Saint Louis MO 63102-2789

SMITH, AXEL, retired theology and social ethics educator; b. Grimstad, Norway, Mar. 19, 1924; s. Nils Jörgen and Solveig (Tangevald) S.; m. Liv Helena Bö, July 12, 1952; children: Gunvor, Solveig, Anders, Liv Helene. Candidate in theology, Norwegian Luth. Sch. Theology, Oslo, 1950; M Religious Edn., Princeton Theol. Sem., 1952; degree in gen. edn., intermediate subj., U. Oslo, 1954. Tchr. Primary Sch., Holla, Norway, 1952-54; lectr. Coll. Edn., Volda, Norway, 1954-61, Bergen, Norway, 1961-68; rsch. scholar State Rsch. Bd., Oslo, 1968-71; lectr. Norwegian Luth. Sch. Theology, 1971-85, prof. theology and social ethics, 1985-90, prof. emeritus, 1990—. Author: Anton Fridrichsens kristendomsforstaaelse, 1976, Rett fordeling, 1982; editor: På skaperens jord, 1984, Praekener i Aarene 1772-1821, 1997; contbr. articles to profl. jours. Home: Bleikerfaret 81, 1387 Asker Norway

SMITH, BARBARA ANNE (BOBBIE SMITH), book seller, researcher; b. Crayford, Kent, U.K., Oct. 14, 1948; d. Eric Barnaby and Joyce Mary (Williams) S. Asst. seismologist Seismograph Svc. Ltd., Keston, Kent, U.K., 1969-73; group leader Seiscom Ltd., Sevenoaks, Kent, U.K., 1973-77; seismic analyst Digital Resources Corp., Algiers, Algeria, 1977-79; party chief Digital Exploration Ltd., East Grinstead, Sussex, U.K., 1982-86; proprietor Geophysical Books, Sevenoaks, 1986—. Mem. Petroleum Exploration Soc. Great Britain. Mem. Church of England. Avocations: animal welfare, mental health, stress counseling. Home and Office: Geophysical Books, 82 Granville Rd, Sevenoaks Kent, England TN13 1HA

SMITH, BARBARA BARNARD, music educator; b. Ventura, Calif., June 10, 1920; d. Fred W. and Grace (Hobson) S. B.A., Pomona Coll., 1942; Mus.M., U. Rochester, 1943, performer's cert., 1945. Mem. faculty piano and theory Eastman Sch. Music, U. Rochester, 1943-49; mem. faculty U. Hawaii, Honolulu, 1949—; assoc. prof. music U. Hawaii, 1953-62, prof., 1962-82, prof. emeritus, 1982—; sr. fellow East-West Center, 1973; lectr., recitals in Hawaiian and Asian music, U.S., Europe and Asia, 1956—; field researcher Asia, 1956, 60, 66, 71, 80, Micronesia, 1963, 70, 87, 88, 90, 91, Solomon Islands, 1976. Author publs. on ethnomusicology. Mem. Internat. Soc. Music Edn., Internat. Musicol. Soc., Am. Musicol. Soc., Soc. Ethnomusicology, Internat. Coun. for Traditional Music, Am. Mus. Instrument Soc., Coll. Music Soc., Soc. for Asian Music, Music Educators Nat. Conf., Pacific Sci. Assn., Assn. for Chinese Music Rsch., Phi Beta Kappa, Mu Phi Epsilon. Home: 1314 Kalakaua Ave Apt 1403 Honolulu HI 96826-1929

SMITH, BARBARA MARY DIMOND, retired urban and regional studies educator; b. Birmingham, U.K., July 9, 1929; d. Charles Dimond Conway and Edith (Smith) Braine; m. David Arthur Chivers Smith, Sept. 24, 1952. B of Comm., U. Birmingham, 1950. From lectr. to sr. lectr. Ctr. for Urban and Regional Studies, U. Birmingham, 1950-67, acting dir., 1993-94. Mem. Indsl. Tribunal, Birmingham, 1970-99; chair 5 Wages Coun., U.K., 1970-93. Recipient Order British Empire award Her Majesty the Queen, U.K., 1994. Mem. Regional Studies Assn. Home: 72 Chadbrook Crest Brook Rd, Edgbaston Birmingham B15 3RN, England

SMITH, BARRY, organist, conductor, former music educator; b. Port Elizabeth, South Africa, May 13, 1939; s. Eric Smith and Sibyl Lavender. MA, Rhodes U., Grahamstown, South Africa, 1969, PhD, 1991; MusD, U. Cape Town, South Africa, 1996. Dir. St. George's Singers, Cape Town, 1964—; organist, master choristers St. George's Cathedral, Cape Town, 1964—; assoc. prof. music. U. Cape Town, 1966-99; chorus master Cape Town Symphony Choir, 1973-88; city organist City of Cape Town, 1983—. Author: Peter Warlock: The Life of Philip Heseltine, 1994, The Occasional Writings of Philip Heseltine (Peter Warlock) 1997-99, 4 vols., 1999, Frederick Delius and Peter Warlock: A Friendship Revealed, 2000. Bd. dirs. Cape Town Symphony Orch., 1996-97. Recipient Order of Simon of Cyrene, Anglican Ch., 1989. Fellow Guild Ch. Musicians (hon.), Royal Sch. Ch. Music; mem. Owl Club. Anglican. Avocations: films, travel. Home: 15 Belvedere Ave, Oranjezicht, Cape Town 8001, South Africa

SMITH, BARRY HAMILTON, foundation administrator, physician; b. Orange, N.J., Oct. 6, 1943; s. Kenneth Wright and Harriet (Barr) S.; m. Carley Eldredge, Dec. 13, 1969; children: Christopher, Sara. BA, Harvard U., 1965; PhD, MIT, 1968; MD, Cornell U., 1972. Intern, resident N.Y. Hosp., N.Y.C., 1971-75; resident Mass. Gen. Hosp., Boston, 1975-78; program dir. neurosci. rsch. program MIT, Boston, 1975-78; dep. dir. surg. neurology br. NIH, Bethesda, Md., 1978-83; sci. & med. dir. Dreyfus Med. Found., N.Y.C., 1983-88; dir. Dreyfus Health Found., N.Y.C., 1988—; sr. v.p. Rogosin Inst. Bd., 1998—; prof. surgery Cornell U.. Editor Ency. Neurosci.; contbr. articles to profl. jours. Comdr. USPHS, 1978-83. Recipient Commendation medal award USPHS, 1982, EEO award, 1983. Mem. AMA, AAAS, Soc. Neurosci., Am. Pain Soc. (audit com. 1983-85), Nat. Coun. Internat. Health (governing bd. 1990-95, chair 1993-95), Phi Beta Kappa, Sigma Xi. Avocations: sailing, writing. Home: 1192 Park Ave Apt 10B New York NY 10128-1314 Office: Dreyfus Health Found 205 E 64th St Rm 404 New York NY 10021-6635

SMITH, BETTY, writer, nonprofit foundation executive; b. Bonham, Tex., Sept. 16; d. Sim and Gertrude (Dearing) S. Student, Stephens Coll.; BJ, U. Tex. Women's editor Daily Texan; pres. Hope Assocs. Corp., N.Y.C.; pres., owner Betty Smith Assocs., N.Y.C. Author: A Matter of Heart, 1969. Bd. dirs. Melchior Heldentenor Found., N.Y.C., 1987—; pres. Gerda Lissner Found., 1994—; v.p. Herman Lissner Found., 1990—. Mem. Author's Guild. Home: 322 E 55th St New York NY 10022-4157 Office: care Lissner Found 135 E 55th St 8th Fl New York NY 10022-4049

SMITH, BETTY DENNY, county official, administrator, fashion executive; b. Centralia, Ill., Nov. 12, 1932; d. Otto and Ferne Elizabeth (Beier) Hasenfuss; m. Peter S. Smith, Dec. 5, 1964; children: Carla Kip, Bruce Kimball. Student, U. Ill., 1950-52; student, L.A. City Coll., 1953-57, UCLA, 1965, U. San Francisco, 1982-84. Freelance fashion coordinator L.A., N.Y.C., 1953-58; tchr. fashion Rita LeRoy Internat. Studios, 1959-60; mgr. Mo Nadler Fashion, L.A., 1961-64; showroom dir. Jean of Calif. Fashions, L.A., 1965—; freelance polit. book reviewer for community newspapers, 1961-62; staff writer Valley Citizen News, 1963. Bd. dirs. Pet Assistance Found., 1969-76; founder, pres., dir. Vol. Services to Animals L.A., 1972-76; mem. County Com. To Discuss Animals in Rsch., 1973-74; mem. blue ribbon com. on animal control L.A. County, 1973-74; dir. L.A. County Animal Care and Control, 1976-82; mem. Calif. Animal Health Technician Exam. Com., 1975-82, chmn., 1979; bd. dirs. L.A. Soc. for Prevention Cruelty to Animals, 1984-94, Calif. Coun. Companion Animal Advocates, 1993-97; dir. West Coast Regional Office, Am. Humane Assn., 1988-97; CFO Coalition for Pet Population Control, 1987-92; trustee Gladys W. Sargent Found., 1997—, Coalition to End Pet Overpopulation, 1998—; cons. Jungle Book II, Disney Studios, 1997; mem. Coalition to Protect Calif. Wildlife, 1996-97, Spl. Comm. Spay/Neuter City L.A., 1998-99; adv. com. La. Dept. of Animal Reg. 2000; mem. Calif. Rep. Cen. Com., 1964-72, mem. exec. com., 1971-73; mem. L.A. County Rep. Cen. Com., 1964-70, mem. exec. com., 1966-70; chmn. 29th Congl. Cen. Com., 1969-70; sec. 28th Senatorial Cen. Com., 1967-68, 45th Assembly Dist. Cen. Com., 1965-68; mem. speakers bur. George Murphy for U.S. Senate, 1970; campaign mgr. Los Angeles County for Spencer Williams for Atty. Gen., 1966; mem. adv. com. Moorpark Coll., 1988-97; mem. adv. bd. Wishbone Prodn., 1995—; mem. L.A. County Art Mus., L.A. Libr. Assn. Mem. Internat. Platform Assn., Mannequins Assn. (bd. dirs. 1967-68), Motion Picture and TV Industry Assn. (govt. rels. and pub. affairs com. 1992-97), Lawyer's Wives San Gabriel Valley (bd. dirs. 1971-74, pres. 1972-73), L.A. Athletic Club, Town Hall. Home: 1766 Bluffhill Dr Monterey Park CA 91754-4533

SMITH, BETTY L., personal life coach; b. Trinidad, Colo., Oct. 17, 1932; d. Howard Melvin and Annabelle (Eastwood) Wade; m. Earl Gilbert Smith, Nov. 26, 1950; children: Wayne David, Christine E. Thomann, Clifford Todd. Student, Santa Rosa (Calif.) Coll., 1961-63. Owner, founder Gilbert's Gallery Frame Shop, Santa Rosa, 1964-84; ind. rep., regional sales dir. Simplex, Santa Rosa, 1984-91; owner, personal life coach Betty Smith Effectiveness Tng., Santa Rosa, 1992—. Author: Secrets of Living Life Abundantly, 1995, (poetry biography) Here I Am, There I Went, 1968; contbr. articles to profl. jours. Art commr. City of Santa Rosa, 1967-68; mem. steering coun. Earth Elders, treas., 1999—; active Sustainable Sonoma County. Democrat. Democrat. Avocation: environmental education. Home and Office: 2319 Olympia Dr Santa Rosa CA 95405-8119

SMITH, BETTY PAULINE, television producer; b. Benton, Ill., Nov. 27, 1926; d. Roy Herman and Goldie Ada (Rodgers) Keen; m. Richard Caldwell Smith, Jan. 11, 1946; children: Constance Raelene, Elana Gayle, Jill Christina. AA in Mgmt., U. Nev., 1982; cert., Ikenbo Sch. Floral Art, 1985; student, Hawaii Pacific U., 1994. Lic. real estate broker, Nev.; cert. real estate salesperson, Hawaii. TV producer Old Plantation Prodns., Inc.; active Coalition of Women-Legis., Domestic Violence Divsn., State of Hawaii, 1994-96; pres. NaKupuna U. Hawaii, 1999. Exec. prodr. Hawaiin Music, 1985; prodr. (TV) The Open Door, 1992, 95, 96, Health Issues: Issues for Women over 55 Years Old, 1992, Honolulu Police Dept., 1995, There's No Excuse for Abuse, 1995, Gang Violence in the Schools, 1995, Women Against Violence, 1996. Recipient Comm. Svc. award Aloha State Assn. of the Deaf, 1993, scholarship Americorps, 1996, cert. Hope Domestic Violence Counselor, 1996, Internat. Poet merit Internat. Soc. Poets, 1999, Mayor's Proclomation award City of Honolulu, 1999, seal City and County Honolulu, 1999, Pres. award Nat. Authors Registry, 1999, Oahu Unsung Angel award, 1998. Mem. Ind. TV Producers Assn., Hometown Media Alliance TV Producers, Elks, LWV, OES, Mason/White Shrine of Jerusalem, Toastmasters (Hall of Fame), others. Avocations: swimming, bicycling, walking, kayaking, Hawaiian music. Home: PO Box 15853-5853 Honolulu HI 96830

SMITH, BOB, lawyer, assemblyman, educator; b. Scranton, Pa., Mar. 25, 1947; s. Philip and Ruth (Delmar) S.; m. Ellen Theresa Foster, 1968; children: Karen Elizabeth, Lisa. BA in History, U. Scranton, 1969, MS in Chemistry, 1970; MS in Environ. Sci., Rutgers U., 1973; JD, Seton Hall U., 1981. Bar: N.J. 1981. Sci. tchr. Lourdesmont High Sch., Clark Summit, Pa., 1968-70; environ. health sci. curriculum coordinator Middlesex County Coll., Edison, N.J., 1972-73, adminstrv. asst. to dean sci., 1974-77, instr., 1970-74, asst. prof., 1974-76, assoc. prof., 1976-79, prof. chemistry and environmental sci., 1979-86; law clk. N.J. Dept. Environ. Protection, Trenton, 1980; prin., pvt. practice law Bob Smith and Assocs., Piscataway, N.J., 1981—; zoning bd. atty. City of New Brunswick, N.J., 1993—, prosecutor East Brunswick, 1997—, South Brunswick, 1998—. Mayor of Piscataway Twp., 1981-86; N.J. assemblyman N.J. 17th Legis. Dist., 1986—, mem. appropriations com. and environ. quality com., assembly select com. on ocean pollution, 1988, assembly energy and hazardous waste com. policy and rules, 1994; parliamentarian Assembly Dem. caucus, 1988-90, chmn. task force on environment, 1987; chmn. Piscataway Dem. Orgn., 1981-90; counsel N.J. State Dem. Platform Com., 1987, 89; chmn. Middlesex County Dem. Orgn., 1991-92; Assembly Dem. Dep. Minority Leader, 1993-95; councilman-at-large Piscataway Twp., 1977-80, pres. council, 1979, v.p., 1978; mem. Middlesex County Transp. Coordinating Com., 1980-86; chmn. Piscataway Environ. Commn., 1971-75; mem. Piscataway Planning Bd., 1981-86, sec., 1975, chmn., 1976; bd. dirs. N.J. Conf. Mayors, 1984-86; mem. tech. adv. com. air pollution Middlesex County Planning Bd., 1973-74; mem. Greenbrook Basin com. Area 208 Mgmt. Planning Program, 1975-76; mem. commr.'s adv. com. N.J. Dept. Environ. Protection, 1972-86; mem. Joyce Kilmer dist. Thomas A. Edison council Boy Scouts Am., 1983-86. Recipient Disting. Citizen award Piscataway Jewish Congregation B'nai Shalom, 1982; named Legis. of Yr. Eden Inst., 1990, N.J. State VFW, 1998, Environ Legislator of Yr., N.J. Environ. Fedn.; U. Scranton Presdl. scholar, 1965-69. Mem. Middlesex County Bar Assn. Roman Catholic. Contbg. author Jour. of Air Pollution Control Assn., 1976; contbg. author: Environmental Health Science, 1975; co-editor: New Jersey State Wastewater Treatment Operations Manual, 1979. Office: 216 Stelton Rd Piscataway NJ 08854-3284 also: 44 Stelton Rd Piscataway NJ 08854-2600

SMITH, BONNIE GENE, historian, educator; b. Bridgeport, Conn.; d. William Wallace and Harriet Amanda (Howard) Sullivan; m. Donald R. Kelley, June 30, 1979; children: Patrick W., Patience H.; 1 stepchild, John R. Kelley. AB, Smith Coll., 1962; PhD, U. Rochester, 1976. Asst. prof. history U. Wis.-Parkside, Racine, 1977-81; from asst. to full prof. U. Rochester, 1981-90; prof. history Rutgers U., New Brunswick, N.J., 1990—; dir. Inst. Rsch. Women Rutgers U., New Brunswick, 1998—; dir. Susan B. Anthony Ctr. U. Rochester, 1988-90; chair advanced placement com. Coll. Bd./Educational Testing Service, N.Y.C. and Princeton, 1988-94; vis. prof. history U. Calif., Irvine, 1984, Ecole des Hautes Etudes, Paris, 1993-94, U. Bielefeld, Germany, 1993, Princeton U., 1995, 98. Author: Ladies of the Leisure Class, 1981, Confessions of a Concierge, 1985, Changing Lives: Women in European History, 1989, Gender of History, 1998, Imperialism, 2000, Women in Postwar Europe, 2000, Global Feminisms Since 1945, 2000; co-author: What is Property, 1994, Challenge of the West, 1995; gen. editor (book series) Women's and Gender History in Global Perspective, Am. Hist. Assn., 1996—; contbr. articles to profl. jours. Fellow Am. Coun. Learned Socs., N.Y., 1979-80, 84-85, Nat. Humanities Ctr., N.C., 1984, Shelby Cullom Davis Ctr., Princeton U., 1992-93, John Simon Guggenheim Found., N.Y., 1992-93. Mem. Am. Hist. Assn., Soc. for French Hist. Studies (bd. editors 1986-89, William Koren Jr. award 1997). Office: Rutgers Univ Dept History 16 Seminary Pl Dept History New Brunswick NJ 08901-1108

SMITH, BRONA NAOMI, educator; b. Seagrove, N.C., July 1, 1946; d. Vernell James and Ethel Green Caveness; m. General Mac Smith, Aug. 16, 1969. BS, A&T State U., Greensboro, N.C., 1968; MS, Ala. A&M U., 1982. Tchr. Leipheim (Germany) Am. Sch., 1975-76; dir. child devel. ctr. Ala. A&M U., Huntsville, 1978-84; tchr. Orange County Schs., Orlando, Fla., 1984—; exchange tchr. Ednl. Exchange Program, Cairo, 1982-83, G.B., 1991-92. Illustrator: (book) Toys that Teach, 1983. Named tchr. of the Yr., Orange County Pub. Schs., 1987, 89, 97, Instr. of the Yr., Ala. A&M U., 1982. Mem. PTA (life), Orange County Reading Coun. (Outstanding Promoter of Reading 1997), Phi Delta Kappa, Kappa Omicron Phi, Zeta Phi

Beta, Eta Phi Beta. Methodist. Avocations: reading, folk art. Home: 8648 Hill Pin Rd Orlando FL 32825

SMITH, BRUCE WILLIAM, safety engineer; b. Louisville, Ky., July 23, 1932; s. Roy Sylvester and Anna Lois (Levine) S.; m. Barbara Ruth Lischin, Oct. 13, 1951; children: Carl Wayne, Joyce Leslie, Nancy Florence. Student, U. Cin., 1953-58, Miami U., Oxford, Ohio, 1950-52. Registered profl. engr., Ohio. Materials testing spec. Gen. Electric AE, Cin., 1952-56, systems engr., 1956-79, facilities engr., 1979-83, safety engr., 1983-91; ret. Gen. Electric AE, 1991; consulting engr. Exec. Resource Assocs., Inc., Cape Coral, Fla., 1991—. Paramedic, Community Medic Res., No. Hamilton County, 1975-84; asst. fire chief Springdale (Ohio) Vol. Fire Dept., 1956-84; councilman, Springdale, 1960-62; mem. Springdale Charter Comm., 1962. Recipient physics scholarship, Ohio Acad. Sci., 1950. Mem. Am. Soc. Safety Engrs., Nat. Fire Protection Assn. Avocations: sailing, photography. Home: 919 SE 26th Ter Cape Coral FL 33904-2919

SMITH, CARL DEAN, JR., counselor, young adult advocate; b. Denver, Sept. 12, 1949; m. Patricia Ann O'Donnell, Aug. 18, 1973; children: Amanda Paige, Grant Carlton. BA, Springfield Coll., 1972; postgrad., Goethe Inst., Munich, 1972-73, Gordon Conwell Theol. Sem., Hamilton, Mass., 1986-88; MEd, Cambridge Coll., 1993. Bus. analyst Dun & Bradstreet, Inc., Boston, 1974-77; Western U.S. credit mgr. Salomon/N.Am., Inc., Peabody, Mass., 1977-81; regional credit mgr. Stride Rite Corp., Cambridge, Mass., 1981-82; sales mgr., franchisee V.R. Bus. Brokers of Chestnut Hill, Mass., 1982-85; pres. C.D. Smith Assocs., Wakefield, Mass., 1985-90; ind. cons. Swampscott, 1990-94; crisis clinician Ctr. for Mental Health, Lexington, Mass., 1994-97; counselor HRI Counseling, Woburn, Mass., 1994-97, The Salvation Army Boston Adult Rehab. Ctr., Saugus, Mass., 1997—. Class agt. Brewster Acad., 1968-96; asst. basketball coach Nth Shore C.C., Danvers, Mass., 1997—; mem. Park St. Ch., Boston Common, Mass. Avocation: basketball coaching. Home and Office: 314 Forest Ave Swampscott MA 01907-2109

SMITH, CAROL ESTES, retired city councilman; b. Phoenix, Nov. 13, 1934; d. John William and Kathleen (Poynter) Estes; m. David Liles Smith, Jan. 8, 1954 (div. Oct. 1981); children: Kelly Liles, Kevin Estes, Kathleen Marie. BS in Edn., Tex. Christian U., 1957. Ptnr. Waste Control of Ariz., N.Mex., Tex., variouslocations, 1964-81; mem. city coun. City of Tempe, Ariz., 1986-98; ret.; bd. dirs., chmn. Ariz. Recycling Bd., State of Ariz., Phoenix, 1991-96; bd. dirs., pres. S.W. Ctr. for Edn. and Environment, Tempe, 1988—, Papago/Salado Assocs., Tempe, 1990—. Pres. Gen. Fedn. Women's Clubs of Ariz., 1986-88; Tempe gov.'s pres.-elect Ariz. Town Hall. Recipient Silver medallion Boys and Girls Clubs Am., 1991; named Woman of Distinction, Tempe St. Lukes Aux., 1985, Jr. Advisor of Yr. Mem. Zonta of East Valley (pres. 1998—, Don Carlos Humanitarian award), Tempe Rotary. Republican. Presbyterian. Avocations: reading, theatre. Home: 6411 S River Dr Unit 60 Tempe AZ 85283-3336

SMITH, CAROLE DIANNE, lawyer, editor, writer, product developer; b. Seattle, June 12, 1945; d. Glaude Francis and Elaine Claire (Finkenstein) S.; m. Stephen Bruce Presser, June 18, 1968 (div. June 1987); children: David Carter, Elisabeth Catherine. AB cum laude, Harvard U., Radcliffe Coll., 1968; JD, Georgetown U., 1974. Bar: Pa. 1974. Law clk. Hon. Judith Jamison, Phila., 1974-75; assoc. Gratz, Tate, Spiegel, Ervin & Ruthrouff, Phila., 1975-76; freelance editor, writer Evanston, Ill., 1983-87; editor Ill. Inst. Tech., Chgo., 1987-88; mng. editor LawLetters, Inc., Chgo., 1988-89; editor ABA, Chgo., 1989-95; product devel. dir. Gt. Lakes divsn. Lawyers Coop. Pub., Deerfield, Ill., 1995-96; product devel. mgr. Midwest Market Ctr. West Group, Deerfield, Ill., 1996-97; mgr acquisitions, bus. and fin. group CCH, Inc., Riverwoods, Ill., 1997—. Author Jour. of Legal Medicine, 1975, Selling and the Law: Advertising and Promotion, 1987; (under pseudonym Sarah Toast) 71 children's books, 1994-2000; editor The Brief, 1990-95, Criminal Justice, 1989-90, 92-95 (Gen. Excellence award Soc. Nat. Assn. Pubs. 1990, Feature Article award-bronze Soc. Nat. Assn. Pubs. 1994), Franchise Law Jour., 1995; editor-in-chief The Brief, ABA Tort and Ins. Practice Sect., 1998—; mem. editl. bd. The Brief, ABA Tort and Ins. Practice Sect., 1995-98. Dir. Radcliffe Club of Chgo., 1990-93; mem. parents council Latin Sch. Chgo., 1995-96. Mem. ABA, ATLA, Def. Rsch. Inst. Office: CCH Inc Bus and Fin Group 2700 Lake Cook Rd Riverwoods IL 60015-3867

SMITH, CARSTEN, judge; b. Oslo, July 13, 1932; m. Lucy Dahl, 1958; children: Merete, Carine, Terese. Law Degree, U. Oslo, 1956. Atty., 1956; asst. prof. U. Oslo, 1957-60; dep. judge, 1960; assoc. prof. U. Oslo, 1960-64, prof. law, 1964-91, dir. Inst. Pvt. Law, 1972-73, dean faculty of law, 1977-79; temporary judge Supreme Ct., Norway, 1987, 89-90, chief justice, 1991—; mem. Norwegian Bd. of Nordic Law Confs., 1975-99, chmn., 1979-94; chmn. of Commn. for Pub. Appeal in Banking Matters, 1988-90; lectr. various univs. and other instns.; chmn. Law Commn. on Agy., 1966-70; mem. Ctrl. Bank Law Commn., 1968-83, Commn. Law Pvt. Banks, 1975-76; chmn. Law Commn. on Interest on Payments, 1970-74, Saami Rights Commn., 1980-85, Commn. on Human Rights in Norwegian Legislation, 1989-91; spl. advisor Commn. for Gen. Revision of Banking and Monetary Law, 1990-92; chmn. Commn. for Reviewing Norwegian Ct. Sys., 1996-99. Contbr. numerous articles to profl. jours.; author books in internat. law, constn. law, adminstrv. law, pvt. law, including: Law of Guarantees, vols. I-III, 1963-81, State Practice and Legal Theory, 1978, Banking Law and State Regulations, 1980, Contemporary Legal Reasoning, 1992, The Law and the Life, 1996; editor-in-chief Nordic Jour. Legal Sci., 1963-73. Mem. Norwegian Acad. Sci. and Letters (pres. 1991), European Acad. Arts, Scis. and Humanities. Office: Supreme Ct, PO Box 8016 Dep, 0030 Oslo Norway

SMITH, CECE, venture capitalist; b. Washington, Nov. 16, 1944; d. Linn Charles and Grace Inez (Walker) S.; m. John Ford Lacy, Apr. 22, 1978. BBA, U. Mich., 1966; MLA, So. Meth. U., 1974. CPA, Tex. Staff acct. Arthur Young & Co. (CPAs), Boston, 1966-68; staff acct., then asst. to contr. Wyly Corp., Dallas, 1969-72; contr., treas. subs. Univ. Computing Co., Dallas, 1972-74; contr. Steak and Ale Restaurants Am., Inc., Dallas, 1974-76, v.p. fin., 1976-80, exec. v.p., 1980-81; exec. v.p. Pearle Health Services, Inc.,, 1981-84, pres. Primacare div., 1984-86; gen. ptnr. Phillips-Smith Specialty Retail Group, 1986—; pres. Le Sportsac Dallas, Inc., 1981-87; bd. dirs. Cheap Tickets, Inc., Beautyco, Inc.; bd. dirs. Fed. Res. Bank of Dallas, 1992-97, chmn., 1994-96; past v.p., dir. The Dallas Forum. Former co-chmn. pres.'s rsch. coun. U. Tex. S.W. Med. Ctr. Dallas; former mem. vis. com. U. Mich. Grad. Sch. Bus.; former exec. bd. So. Meth. U. Cox Sch. Bus.; former v.p., bd. dirs. Jr. Achievement Dallas, The Dallas Forum (IWF); past pres. Charter 100; past treas. Dallas Assembly. Mem. Tex. Soc. CPAs (mem. com. of 200). Home: 3710 Shenandoah St Dallas TX 75205-2121 Office: 5080 Spectrum Dr Ste 805 Addison TX 75001-4648

SMITH, CHARLES ANTHONY, business executive; b. Santa Fe, Sept. 16, 1939; s. Frances (Mier) Vigil; student various adminstrv. and law courses; m. Paula Ann Thomas, June 26, 1965; 1 child, Charlene Danielle. Circulation mgr. Daily Alaska Empire, 1960-63; agt. Mut. of N.Y. Life Ins. Co., Juneau, Alaska, 1964-65; mng. partner Future Investors in Alaska and Cinema Alaska, Juneau, 1961-62; SE Alaska rep. K & L Distbrs., 1966-68; mgr. Alaska Airlines Newspapers, SE Alaska, 1969; dep. Alaska Retirement System, Juneau, 1970-71; apptd. dir. hwy. safety, gov.'s hwy. safety rep., Juneau, 1971-83; pres. Valley Service Ctr., Inc., 1984-94; chmn. S.E. Alaska Employee Support of the Guard and Reserve, 1992—; pres. 3-S Corp., 1995—; apptd. chmn. S.E. Alaska for ESGR, 1995; apptd. Alaska state dir. Selective Svc., 1996—. Alaska pres. Muscular Dystrophy Assn. Am.; pres. SE Alaska Emergency Med. Services Council, 1965-72; state dir. Selective Svc., 1996. Served to major Army N.G., 1964-88. Named Alaska Safety Man of Yr., 1977. Mem. Am. Assn. Motor Vehicle Adminstrs., Alaska Peace Officers Assn., Nat. Assn. Gov.s' Hwy. Safety Reps., N.G. Assn., Internat. Platform Assn. Roman Catholic. Club: Elks (Juneau). Author various hwy. safety manuals and plans. Home: PO Box 32856 Juneau AK 99803-2856

SMITH, CHARLES IAN, fire engineer, consultant; b. Jan. 27, 1948; s. Charles Henry and Freda Margaret (Scott) S.; m. Bradley Beryl, Feb. 17, 1973; children: Mark Bradley, Sara Carolyn. BS in Metallurgy, U. Manchester, U.K., 1969, MS in Metallurgy, 1970, PhD in Metallurgy, 1972. Chartered engr. Rsch. scientist Turners Asbestos Cement, Manchester, 1972-73; prin. rsch. engr. Brit. Steel Corp., Lanarks and Teesside, 1973-82; dir. Ian Smith Cons Ltd., North Yorkshire, 1982—, Fire Safety Engring. Cons. Ltd., North Yorkshire, 1989—. Contbr. articles to profl. jours. Chmn. Ainderby Steeple Parish Meeting, North Yorkshire, 1994-97. Mem. Inst. Materials, Inst. Fire Safety (treas. N.E. br. 1993-94, membership com. 1992—), Nat. Fire Protection Assn., Soc. Fire Safety Engrs. (treas. 1988-92), Instn. Metallurgists (chmn. young metallurgists 1977-79), Bedale Golf Club (capt. 1999). Anglican. Avocations: golfing, walking, gardening, food. Office: Fire Safety Engring Cons, Warlaby Ln, Ainberby Steeple DL7 9JX, England

SMITH, CHESTER, broadcasting executive; b. Mar. 29, 1930; s. Louis L. and Effie (Brown) S.; m. Naomi L. Crenshaw, July 19, 1959; children: Lauri, Lorna, Roxanne. Country western performer Capitol Records, TV, Radio, 1947-61, Sta. KLOC, Ceres-Modesto, Calif., 1963-81, Sta. KCBA-TV, Salinas-Monterey, Calif., 1963-81; owner, gen. ptnr. Sta. KCSO-TV, Modesto-Stockton-Sacramen, Calif., 1966-97, Sta. KCVU-TV, Paradise-Chico-Redding, Calif., 1986—, Sta. KBVU-TV, Eureka, Calif., 1990—, KNSO-TV, Merced-Fresno, Calif., 1996—, KCSO-TV, Sacramento, Calif., 1996—; owner, gen. ptnr. KFWU-TV, Sacramento, Calif., 1996-97, Fort Bragg, Calif., 1996-97; owner, gen. ptnr. KRVU-TV, Redding, Calif., 1997—, Univision 28, Chico, Calif. Original rec. Wait A Little Longer Please Jesus in Country Music Hall of Fame, Nashville, 1955. Inductee Western Swing Hall of Fame, Sacramento, 1988; recipient cert. of recognition for 50 years of cmty. svc. Calif. Assembly, 1997. Mem. Calif. Broadcasters Assn. Republican. Mem. Christian Ch. Address: Sainte Partners II L P PO Box 4159 Modesto CA 95352-4159

SMITH, CHRISTOPHER HUGHES, minister; b. Nottingham, United Kingdom, Nov. 30, 1929; s. Bernard Hughes and Dorothy Lucy (Parker) S.; m. Margaret Jean Smith, Aug. 20, 1956; children: Jeremy, Philip, Robert, Ernest. BA in Modern Langs., U. Cambridge, 1953, BA in Theology, 1955, MA, 1958; MA (hon.), Birmingham U., 1985. Ordained min. Meth. ch., 1958. Intercollegiate sec. Student Christian Movement, East Midlands, United Kingdom, 1955-58; circuit min. Leicester (Eng.) South Circuit Meth. Ch., 1958-65, Birmingham (Eng.) S.W. Circuit Meth. Ch., 1965-74; dist. chmn. Birmingham Meth. Dist., 1974-87; circuit min. Lancaster (Eng.) Circuit, 1987-88; gen. sec. Divsn. Edn. and Youth, Eng., 1988-95; bd. dirs. Meth. Newspaper Co., London, 1973—; gov. Southlands, Westminster and Westhill Colls. Higher Edn.; mem. coun. Roehampton Inst., London, 1988-95; mem. bd. mgmt. Meth. Residential Schs., 1972-95. Author: Music of the Heart, 1991. Pres. Birmingham Coun. Christian Chs., 1976-87, Meth. Conf., 1985-86, Nat. Christian Edn. Coun., 1995-99. Hon. fellow U. Surrey, Roehampton, London. Fellow Selly Oak Colls. Avocations: gardening, walking, music, theatre, reading.

SMITH, CHRISTOPHER NORMAN, French language and literature educator; b. Norwich, Norfolk, Eng., May 19, 1936; s. Reginald Edward and Monica Alice (Quinton) S.; m. Margaret Isabella Brown, Dec. 28, 1961; 1 child, Helen Frances Isabella. BA, Cambridge U., 1957, MA, 1960, PhD, 1969; diploma in edn., Oxford U., 1961. Asst. lectr. French U. Aberdeen, Scotland, 1966-68; lectr. Sch. Modern Langs. and European History, U. East Anglia, Norwich, 1968-74, sr. lectr., 1974—; reader, 1991, sr. fellow, 1996; mng. editor Norwich Papers Reviews. Author: Alabaster, Bikinis and Calvados: an ABC of Toponymous Works, 1985, Jean Anouilh: Life, Work and Criticism, 1985 and editions of French Renaissance plays and emblem books; mem. editorial bd. New Companion, Cahiers du 17; contbr. articles and revs. to profl. jours. Mem. Soc. for Seventeenth Century French Studies (treas., editor jour. 1978-92). Anglican. Avocations: theatre, music. Office: U East Anglia, Sch Modern Langs, Norwich NR4 7TJ, England

SMITH, CHRISTOPHER UPHAM MURRAY, biology educator, philosopher, writer; b. Brixham, Eng., Dec. 27, 1930; s. Murray James and Gladys Mary (Upham) S.; m. Rosemary Carol Edmonds, Apr. 25, 1961. BS, Birmingham (Eng.) U., 1954, London U., 1959; diploma in biophysics, Edinburgh (Scotland) U., 1963; PhD, Aston U., 1997. Lectr. Aston U., Birmingham, 1959-73, sr. lectr., 1973-84, sr. tutor biology, 1984—, sub-dean Faculty Scis., 1987-90, dean, 1990-94. Author: Molecular Biology, 1968, The Brain, 1970, The Problem of Life, 1976, Elements of Molecular Neurobiology, 1989, 2nd edit., 1996, Biology of Sensory Systems, 2000; contbr. articles to profl. jours. Fellow Inst. Biology, Royal Soc. Arts, Royal Soc. Medicine; mem. Brain Rsch. Assn., Brit. Assn. Advancement Sci. (sec. anthropology 1983-93), Brit. Biophys. Soc., Royal Micros. Soc., Internat. Soc. History Neuroscis. (pres. 1998-99). Home: 104 Moorcroft Rd, Birmingham B13 8LU, England Office: Vision Scis Aston U, Aston Triangle, Birmingham B4 7ET, England

SMITH, CLIVE JOHN, minister; b. Baralaba, Australia, Sept. 19, 1940; s. Harold Edward Elliott and Mavis Harriet (Smith) Humberdross; children: Leticia, Bernadette, Paul. BA, Theol. U. Am., 1990, MA, 1994. Missionary, evangelist Youth With a Mission, Morocco, 1988, Bangkok Inst. Theology, Christ of Thailand Bible Inst., Srirca, 1990; preacher, tchr. Far East Broadcasting Commn., Seoul, South Korea, 1990, New Life League, Tokyo, 1990; internat. evangelist, tchr. Christian Med. Coll., Ludhiana, India, 1990, Philadelphia Mission Hosp., Ambala, India, 1990; tchr., preacher, evangelist Lahore Cathedral, Pakistan, 1989-92, United Christian Conv., Lahore, 1988-89, Full Gospel Assemblies Bible Col., Lahore, Evang. Bible Inst., Faisalabad, Pakistan, 1994-95; chair Faith Ministries Mission Internat., Toowoomba, Australia, 1988—; Australian rep. United Presbyn. Ch. Pakistan, Faisalabad, 1990—; Australian rep. St. Peters Evang. Ednl. Found., 1990—. Mem. Toowoomba Chess Club. Avocations: chess, fitness training, study, prayer. E-mail: solu@dingoblue.net.au. Office: Faith Min Mission Internat, Box 3141 Village Fair, 4350 Toowoomba QL, Australia

SMITH, CLODUS RAY, retired academic administrator; b. Blanchard, Okla., May 15, 1928; s. William Thomas and Rachel (Hale) S.; m. Pauline R. Chaat; children: Martha Lynn, William Paul, Paula Diane. Assoc. degree, Cameron State Coll., 1948; BS in Agrl. Edn., Okla. A & M Coll., 1950; MS in Vocat. Edn., Okla. State U., 1955; EdD in Vocat. Edn., Cornell U., 1960. Grad. asst. Cornell U., 1957-59; asst. prof. U. Md., 1959-62, assoc. prof., 1962-63, dir. Summer Sch., 1963-72, adminstrv. dean, 1972-73; spl. asst. to pres. Cleve. State U., 1973-74, v.p. for univ. rels., 1974-83; pres. Rio Grande Coll. and Rio Grande Community Coll., Ohio, 1983-86, Lake Erie Coll., Painesville, Ohio, 1986-92, Okla. Ind. Coll. Found., Oklahoma City, 1993-96, Okla. Assn. Ind. Colls. and Univs., 1993-96; cons. NEA, Naval Weapons Lab., Dehlgren, Va.; researcher Personal and Profl. Satisfactions; contract investigator Nat. Endowment for Humanities; dir. Human Resources and Community Devel., Prince George's County, Md. Author: Planning and Paying for College, 1958, Rural Recreation for Profit, 1971, A Strategy for University Relations, 1975, State Relations for the 1980 Decade, 1982. Amb. Natural Resources, Ohio, 1984, chmn. dept.; founder N.Am. Assn. of Summer Schs., 1979. Recipient Rsch. award Nat. Project in Agrl. Communications, 1959, Edn. award Prince George's C. of C., 1971, Disting. Alumni award Cameron U. Mem. Am. Assn. U. Adminstrs., Am. Assn. for Higher Edn., Nat. Soc. for Study Edn., Coun. for Support and Advancement Edn., Am. Alumni Coun., Al Koran Hunter's Club, Shriners. Methodist. Avocations: hunting, fishing, volunteering.

SMITH, CORNELIUS A., government official; b. North End, L.I., N.Y., Apr. 7, 1937; married; 3 children. Grad., Bahamas Tchrs. Coll., 1955; MA in Bus. Adminstrn., U. Miami, 1959. Tchr. various schs.; sr. customs officer Freeport, 1959-65; divsn. mgr. E.H. Muncy & Co., 1964-67; adminstrv. svcs. dir. Syntex Corp., 1967-82; owner, mng. dir. Smith & Assocs., 1982—; mem. for Marco City Ho. of Assembly, 1982, re-elected for Pineridge, 1987-92; min. of edn. Govt. Bahamas, Nassau, 1992-95, min. pub. safety and immigration, 1995-97, min. tourism and civil aviation, 1997—. Mem. C. of C. (v.p.). Mem. Free Nat. Movement. Office: Ministry Tourism, Market Plz Bay St Box N3701, Nassau Bahamas

SMITH, CRAIG BRENTON, plastic surgeon; b. Perth, Australia, May 16, 1958; s. Ronald John and Beryle Ellen (Darch) S.; m. Cathrine Gail Baird, May 5, 1984; children: Rachael, Natalie. MB BS, U. Western Australia, Perth, 1982. Resident Royal Perth Hosp., Australia, 1982-83, registrar, 1984-85; plastic surgery Sir Charles Gardner Hosp., Perth, Australia, 1986, Royal Perth Hosp., 1987-88; plastic surgeon St. Vincents Hosp., Melbourne, Australia, 1989; plastic surgeon, hand surgeon pvt. practice, Perth, 1991—; vis. plastic surgeon Sir Charles Gardner Hosp., 1991—; dir. Carana Crest Vineyard, 1997—. Fellow Jewish Hosp., Louisville, 1990. Fellow Royal Australian Coll. Surgeons; mem. Australian Med. Assn., Australian Hand Surgery Soc., We. Australia Soc. Plastic Surgery (sec. 1999—). Baptist. Avocations: wine, motor cars, reading, music, travel. Office: 123 B Colin St, West Perth 6005, Australia

SMITH, CROSBIE WIMPERIS, science historian; b. Belfast, Northern Ireland, Oct. 19, 1949; s. Jack Crosbie and Doreen Esther (Wimperis) S. BA, U. Cambridge, Eng., 1972; MA, U. Cambridge, 1975, PhD, 1975. Rsch. fellow U. Kent, Canterbury, Eng., 1975-77; lectr. U. Kent, Canterbury, 1977-91, sr. lectr., 1991-94, reader, 1994-99, prof., 1999—. Authro: The Science of Energy, 1998; co-author: Energy and Empire, 1989 (Pfizer award 1990); co-editor: Making Space for Science, 1998. Mem. Brit. Soc. for the History of Sci. (hon. sec. 1989-96, hon. editor 1999—), History of Sci. Soc. Avocations: lobster fishing, coastal navigation. Office: Univ Kent, Canterbury Kent CT2 7NX, England

SMITH, D(AISY) MULLETT, publisher; b. Washington, Aug. 17, 1948; d. Gordon Hunt and Suzanne Myrick (Mullett) Smith. BA, Am. U., 1970; cert. computer programming, U. So. Calif., Arlington, Va., 1986; cert. in records mgmt., Assn. Records Mgrs. Am., Prairie Village, Kans., 1987. Christian Sci. practitioner The First Ch. of Christ, Scientist, Boston, 1970-86; clk. Fifth Ch. of Christ, Scientist, Washington, 1971-74; Christian Sci. campus counsellor The Am. U., Washington, 1976-81; editor, computer specialist, desktop pub. Mullett-Smith Press, Washington, 1984-89, owner, pub., author, 1989—, music copyist, pub. on computer, 1990—, web weaver, 1996—; computer cons. and pub. spkr. in field; guest participant divsn. children in trouble White House Conf. on Children, 1970. Author, editor, pub.: AB Mullett, His Relevance in American Architecture, 1990 (Printers award 1990); editor: AB Mullett, Architect Engineer 1862-90, 1985; contbr. articles to profl. jours.; desktop pub. musical scores by Richard Henry Lee, 1991-99; art pamphlets by Suzanne M. Smith, 1999—. Participant White House Conf. on Children, 1970; active Save Pioneer Post Office, Portland, Oreg., 1996—; mem. fund raiser com. U.S. Treasury Bill Restoration Fund, 1998-2000; libr. Christian Sci. Reading Rm., 1999—. Recipient Key to the City, Mayor Lincoln, Nebr., 1989. Mem. Nat. Soc. Arts and Letters (editor/pub. directory 1971-88, 89-91, 92—, treas. 1988-90, web weaver 1996—), Nat. Trust for Hist. Preservation, Assn. Records Mgrs. and Adminstrs., Assn. for Info. and Image Mgmt. Internat., U.S. Treasury Hist. Assn. (spkr. 1992-96), U.S. Capitol Hist. Soc. Avocations: art, design, teaching and playing classical guitar, windsurfing, computers. E-mail: mspress@mullett-smithpress.com. Office: Mullett-Smith Press 4450 Dexter St NW Washington DC 20007-1113

SMITH, DALE CARY, medical historian, educator; b. Orlando, Fla., July 2, 1951; s. D. Carl and Margaret Lee; m. Margaret Gatlin Smith, Aug. 18, 1973; 1 child, Darion Christopher. BA, Duke U., 1973; PhD, U. Minn., 1979. Asst. prof. U. Minn., Mpls., 1979-82; with dept. med. history Uniformed Svcs. U., Bethesda, Md., 1982-97, prof., chmn. dept. med. history, 1997—; historian Mil. Medicine, Bethesda, 1999—; hist. cons. Am. Gastroenterol. Assn., Bethesda, 1995-99. Author: Am. Gastroenterological Assn. (1897-1997) a Centennial History, 1999; editor: William Budd's Essay on Fever, 1984; book rev. editor Jour. History of Medicine, 1979-82, assoc. editor, 1982-87, editl. bd., 1988-91; mem. editl. bd. Bull. History of Medicine, 1996-99. Moderator Redland Bapt. Ch., Rockville, 1997—. Recipient The Laurance D Redway award N.Y. State Med. Soc., 1987. Mem. Am. Assn. for History of Medicine (coun. mem. 1985-87, newsletter editor 1998—). Baptist. E-mail: dcsmith@usuhs.mil. Office: Uniformed Svcs U Dept Med History 4301 Jones Bridge Rd Bethesda MD 20814-4712

SMITH, DAVID ELVIN, physician; b. Bakersfield, Calif., Feb. 7, 1939; s. Elvin W. and Dorothy (McGinnis) S.; m. Millicent Buxton; children: Julia, Suzanne, Christopher Buxton-Smith, Sabree Hill-Smith. Intern San Francisco Gen. Hosp., 1965; fellow pharmacology and toxicology U. Calif., San Francisco, 1965-67, assoc. clin. prof. occupl. medicine, clin. toxicology, 1967—, dir. psychopharmacology study group, dir. Inst. of Health, 1966-70, assoc. clin. prof., rsch. physician Med. Sch.; practice specializing in toxicology/addiction medicine San Francisco, 1965—; physician Presbyn. Alcoholic Clinic, 1965-67, Contra Cost Alcoholic Clinic, 1965-67; dir. alcohol and drug abuse screening unit San Francisco Gen. Hosp., 1967-68; co-dir. Calif. drug abuse info. project U. Calif. Med. Ctr., 1967-72; founder, pres., med. dir. Haight-Ashbury Free Med. Clinic, San Francisco, 1967—; rsch. dir. Merritt Peralta Chem. Dependency Hosp., Oakland, Calif., 1984—; med. dir., bd. dirs. Drug Abuse Scis., 1999; med. dir. Calif. Alcohol and Drug Programs, U. Calif. San Francisco Substance Abuse Policy Ctr., 1999; chmn. Nat. Drug Abuse Conf., 1977; mem. Calif. Gov.'s Commn. on Narcotics and Drug Abuse, 1977—; nat. health adviser to former U.S. Pres. Jimmy Carter; mem. Pres. Clinton's Health Care Task Force on Addiction and Nat. Health Reform, 1993; with Office Drug Abuse Policy, White House Task Force Physicians for Drug Abuse Prevention; dir. Benzodiazepine Rsch. and Tng. Project, Substance Abuse and Sexual Concerns Project, PCP Rsch. and Tng. Project; vis. assoc. prof. U. Nev. Med. Sch., 1975—; bd. dirs., med. dir. Drug Abuse Sci. Inc.; cons. numerous fed. drug abuse agys. Author: Love Needs Care, 1970, The New Social Drug: Cultural, Medical and Legal Perspectives on Marijuana, 1971, The Free Clnic: Community Approaches to Health Care and Drug Abuse, 1971, Treating the Cocaine Abuser, 1985, The Benzodiazepines: Current Standard Medical Practice, 1986, Physicians' Guide to Drug Abuse, 1987; co-author: It's So Good, Don't Even Try it Once: Heroin in Perspective, 1972, Uppers and Downers, 1973, Drugs in the Classroom, 1973, Barbiturate Use and Abuse, 1977, A Multicultural View of Drug Abuse, 1978, Amphetamine Use, Misuse and Abuse, 1979, PCP: Problems and Prevention, 1981, Sexological Aspects of Substance Use and Abuse, Treatment of the Cocaine Abuser, 1985, The Haight Ashbury Free Medical Clinic: Still Free After All These Years, Drug Free: Alternatives to Drug Abuse, 1987, Treatment of Opiate Dependence, Designer Drugs, 1988, Treatment of Cocaine Dependence, 1988, Treatment of Opiate Dependence, 1988, The New Drugs, 1989, Crack and Ice in the Era of Smokeable Drugs, 1992, others; also drug edn. films; founder, editor Jour. Psychedelic Drugs (now Jour. Psychoactive Drugs), 1967—; contbr. over 300 articles to profl. jours.; med. editor Alcohol MD website. Mem. Physicians for Prevention White House Office Drug Abuse Policy, 1995; pres. Youth Projects, Inc.; founder, chmn. bd., pres. Nat. Free Clin. Coun., 1968-72; med. dir. Calif. Alcohol and Drug Programs, 1998, U. Calif. Drug Policy Ctr., San Francisco, 1998—, Drug Abuse Scis., 1998—. Recipient Rsch. award Borden Found., 1964, AMA Rsch. award, 1977, Cmty. Svc. award U. Calif., San Francisco, 1974, Calif. State Drug Abuse Treatment award, 1984, Vernelle Fox Drug Abuse Treatment award, 1985, UCLA Sidney Cohen Addiction Medicine award, 1989, U. Calif. San Francisco medal of honor, 1995; named one of Best Doctors in U.S., 1995, 96, 97. Mem. AMA (alt. del.), CMA (alt. del.), Am. Soc. on Addiction Medicine (bd. dirs., pres. 1995), San Francisco Med. Soc., Am. Pub. Health Assn., Calif. Soc. on Addiction Medicine (pres., bd. dirs.), Am. Soc. Addiction Medicine, Sigma Xi, Phi Beta Kappa. Methodist. Home: 289 Frederick St San Francisco CA 94117-4051 Office: Haight Ashbury Free Clinics 612 Clayton St San Francisco CA 94117-2927

SMITH, DAVID HAROLD, communication educator; b. Wooster, Ohio, Dec. 2, 1936; s. Harold Alexander and Edna Mae (Snyder) S.; m. Sarah Jeanne Ware; children: Catherine, Karen, Kevin, Colleen, Andrew. BS, Ohio State U., 1957, PhD, 1966; MA, Northwestern U., 1963. Assoc. prof. speech communication U. Minn., 1966-72; assoc. dean social and behavioral scis., prof. communication Ohio State U., 1972-76; dean arts and letters, prof. communication U. South Fla., 1976-81, prof. internal medicine and communication, 1981-94; chair prof. applied communication studies Hong Kong Bapt. U., 1994-97, fellow ctr. for applied ethics, 1994-97; vis. fellow The East West Ctr., 1998. Co-author: The Silicone Breast Implant Story, 1996; editor: Health Communication and China, 1997; contbr. articles to profl. jours. Mem. Nat. Communication Assn., Internat. Communication Assn. (chair orgn. communication divsn. 1970-71), Chinese Communication Assn., Pacific and Asian Communication. Avocation: choral singing. Home: 758 Kapahulu Ave Ste 317 Honolulu HI 96816-1196

SMITH, DAVID HORTON, social sciences educator; b. L.A., May 2, 1939; s. Paul Roosevelt Smith and Helen Ethel (Frechem) Mitchell; divorced; children: Gregory David, Laura Ghislaine. AB magna cum laude, U. So. Calif., 1960; MA, Harvard U., 1962, PhD, 1965. Asst. prof. U. So. Calif., L.A., 1966-68; assoc. prof. Boston Coll., Chestnut Hill, Mass., 1968-76; prof.

Boston Coll., Chestnut Hill, 1976—; rsch. fellow, lectr. Harvard U., 1965-66; cons. to govt. agys. and nonprofit orgns., including Nat. Ctr. for Voluntary Action, Brit. Nat. Vol. Ctr., Ctr. for Voluntary Soc., Filer Commn. on Pvt. Philanthropy and Pub. Needs, Union of Internat. Assns. Author: Latin American Student Activism, 1973, Grassroots Associations, 2000; co-author: Becoming Modern, 1974 (award 1975), Voluntary Sector Policy Research Needs, 1974, Participation in Social and Political Activities, 1980, Why People Recreate, 1987; editor: Voluntary Action Research, 1972, 73, 74, Volunteerism, Voluntary Assns. and Devel., 1981, Internat. Perspectives on Voluntary Action Rsch., 1983; contbr. numerous articles to profl. jours., chpts. to books; founding editor-in-chief Jour. Voluntary Action Rsch. (now Nonprofit and Voluntary Sector Quar.), 1971-76. Founding bd. dirs. Nat. Com. for Responsive Philanthropy, 1976-78, Alliance for Volunteerism; dir. rsch. Ctr. for Voluntary Soc., Washington, 1970-74. NSF grad. fellow, 1960-63; Woodrow Wilson Hon. fellow, 1960. Mem. Assn. Rsch. on Non-Profit Orgns. and Voluntary Action (founder, pres. 1971-73, Lifetime Achievement award 1993), Nat. Assn. Pub. Svc. Orgn. Execs. (co-founder, past bd. dirs.), Internat. Soc. for Third Sector Rsch., Authors Guild, Sarasota Fiction Writers, Phi Beta Kappa, Phi Kappa Phi. Avocations: reading, photography, fiction writing, jazz, foreign travel. Office: Boston Coll Sociol Dept 140 Commonwealth Ave Chestnut Hill MA 02467-3800

SMITH, DAVID KINGMAN, retired oil company executive, consultant; b. Malone, N.Y., June 5, 1928; s. Ernest DeAlton and Louisa Kingman (Bolster) S.; m. Lois Louise Wing, June 13, 1959; children: Mara Louise, David Andrew. BS in Engring., Princeton U., 1952. Registered profl. engr., Tex. Civil engr., supt. Raymont Internat. Inc., N.Y.C., 1952-55, asst. v.p., 1970-71, v.p., 1971-74; group v.p. Raymont Internat. Inc., Houston, 1974-80; mgr. Raymond-Brown and Root, Maracaibo, Venezuela, 1955-70; sr. engring. assoc. Exxon Prodn. Rsch. Co., Houston, 1980-81, supr., 1982-95; cons. project mgmt., 1995—. Pres. Yorkshire Civic Assn., Houston, 1979-80, trustee, 1985-97. With U.S. Army, 1946-48, PTO. Mem. ASCE, NSPE, Soc. Petroleum Engrs. (continuing edn. com. Gulf Coast chmn. 1989-93, treas. 1987-88, nat. continuing edn. com. 1991-93, dir. Gulf Coast sect. 1994-95), Tex. Soc. Profl. Engrs., Men's Garden Club Houston, Am. Legion, Princeton Alumni Assn. (dir. Houston sect.), Cen Ners In Square Dance Club (pres. 1996-97). Republican. Methodist. Avocations: photography, gardening, tennis, golf, square dancing. Home: 611 W Forest Dr Houston TX 77079-6915

SMITH, DAVID LANGLEY, education educator, consultant; b. Sydney, Jan. 14, 1944; s. Robert Gordon and Enid Ada (Simms) S.; m. Carolyn Anne Gill, Aug. 22, 1964 (div. 1978); m. Robyn Ann Ewing, Mar. 29, 1998; children: Brendan Mark, Meredith Rehle. BA, Armidale U., 1970; BA with honors, Maequarie U., 1973; MEd, U. Sydney, 1983, D of Philosophy, 1983. Tchr. Tumbarumba H.S., Australia, 1963-69, Muswellbrook H.S., Australia, 1970-72; lectr. social sci. edn. Macquarie U., Sydney, 1972—; faculty head Ryde H.S., Sydney, 1974; lectr. U. Sydney, 1974-81, sr. lectr., 1982, assoc. prof., 1993, assoc. dean, 1987-98; cons. Swedish Nat. Sch. Agy., 1993; vis. prof. dep. edn. Uppsala U., Sweden, 1993, 95; vis. prof. Stockholm U., 1996, 99; cons., evaluator Sunderland Local Education Authority, 1993; evaluator Australian Govt., Participation and Faculty Program, Canberra, 1985, Australian Curriculum Devel. Ctr., H.S. Edn. Law Project, 1978—; cons. Curriculum Devel. Ctr.; prodr. videotapes for social edn. materials; rschr. innovative and best practice project Australian Govt., 1999. Author: Curriculum: Action on Reflection, 1991, 2d edit., 1993, 3rd edit., 1995, The Health Professional As Researcher, 1992, The Role of Principal as Leader: Report of the Sydney Slan Project, 1994; editor: Australian Curriculum Reform: Action and Reaction, 1993; contbr. chpts. to books and articles to profl. jours. Pres. Jumbarumba Jaycees, 1966-68, Muswellbrook Rostrum, 1971-72; ednl. adviser Coll. of Paralegal Studies, Australia, 1995—. Mem. Australian Curriculum Studies Assn. (life), Australian Assn. for Rsch. in En., Spirit of Learning Australia. Avocations: reading, writing, gardening, canoeing, walking. Office: Faculty of Edn, U Sydney, Sydney NSW 2026, Australia

SMITH, DAVID LYLE, art educator, artist; b. Harpersfield, N.Y., June 6, 1926; s. Thomas Howard and Grace Louisa Smith; m. Alyce Louise Oosterhouse, June 6, 1952; children: C Matthew, Markalan, Elizabeth, Leigh, Stuart. BD in Design, U. Mich., 1951, MA in Edn., 1953; DPhil, Mich. State U., 1966. Graphic artist Ednl. TV Program U. Mich., Ann Arbor, 1952-53; tchr. art C.W. Otto Jr. H.S., Lansing, Mich., 1955-63; tchr. elem. art. Lansing Pub. Schs., 1963-67; assoc. prof. Dept. Art and Design U. Wis., Stevens Point, 1967-96, assoc. prof. emeritus, 1996—; CEO Scarabocchio Art, Stevens Point; founder, mem. Scarabocchio Art Found., Stevens Point; dir. Stevens Point Program, 1975-86; site adminstr., semester abroad tchr., Poland, 1978, 83; chmn. State Art Edn. Cert. Stds., 1981-83. Exhbns. include U. Wis. Stevens Point Faculty Show, 1974-76, 87, 90-93, 95, 97, Packages-Carlsten Art Gallery, 1978, 79, New Visions Gallery, Marshfield, Wis., 1989, 92, 95, Milw. Art Mus., 1992, U. Colo. Mountainside Art Guild & Fiske Planetarium, 1992-96, N.Mex., Art League, 1993, 94, 96, Alexander House, Port Edwards, Wis., 1993, 95, Sacramento FAC, 1993, 94, 97, 98, Laredo Art League, Tex., 1994, 95, 96, L.I. Arts Coun., Freeport, N.Y., 1994, Green Bay Neville Pub. Mus., 1995, 96, 97, 98, An Art Pl., Chgo., 1995, 97, Akron Soc. Artists, 1994, 96, 98, Mable (Ga.) Cultural Ctr., 1994, 95, 96, 98, Wis. Painters-Sculptors, 1996, 97, 98, 99, Mac Rostie Art Ctr., 1996, 97, 98, Coastal Ctr. Arts, Ga., 1996, 97, 98, Ridgewood Art Inst., N.J., 1997, 98, 99, Salmagundi Club, 1999, Period Gallery, 1998, 99, Glen Eure's Ghost Fleet Gallery, 1998, 99, Eleven East Ashland, 1997, 98, Wis. Edn. Assn. Art Showcase, 1996, 98, Internat. Registry of Artists and Art calendar, 1998, Studio 107, Ridge Art Assn., 1998, 99, others; accepted in nat. juried art competitions, 15 in 1993, 49 in 1994, 22 in 1995, 26 in 1996, 21 in 1997, 20 in 1998, 25 in 1999; one-man shows include Lincoln Ctr., Stevens Point, Wis., 1989, 93, 95, Charles M. White Libr., Stevens Point, Northeast C.C., Whiteville, N.C., 1998, others.; two-man shows (with Richard Schneider) Alexander House 1993; also Ctr. for Visual Arts 1996, Wausau, Wis.; three person show Brown County Libr., Green Bay, Wis., 1996. Style judge State Odyssey of the Mind, 1990-99; dist. dir. ctrl. divsn. Very Spl. Arts Wis., 1985-88. Mem. Nat. Art Edn. Assn., Wis. Art Edn. Assn. (bd. dirs., higher edn. rep. 1978-82), NEA (life), Wis. Edn. Assn. Coun., Assn. U. Wis. Profls. (sec. 1993-96), Wis. Alliance for Arts Edn., Res. Officers Assn. U.S., Ret. Officers, Nat. Assn. Uniformed Svcs., Air Force Assn., Consumers Union. Republican. Presbyterian. Avocations: sketching, gardening, travel. Fax: (715) 342-5688. E-mail d3smith@uswp.edu. Home: 4242 Janick Cir N Stevens Point WI 54481-2511

SMITH, DAVID MITCHELL, fire and explosion consultant; b. San Bernardino, Calif., Feb. 2, 1947; s. Harry Arnold and Norma Deanne (Miles) S.; m. Linda Sue McCormick, Apr. 9, 1994; children: Sean David Kimble, Jennifer Laura Thacker. Cert. fire investigator Internat. Assn. of Arson Investigators. Patrolman Tucson (Ariz.) Police Dept., 1968-70, detective, 1970-81; president Associated Fire Consultants, Tucson, 1981—. Co-author: (manual) National Fire Protection Association 921, 1995; contbr. articles to profl. jours. Chair Catalina Village Coun., Tucson, 1995—; bd. dirs. Catalina Family Med. Ctr., Tucson, 1996—, Pima Youth Partnership, 1996—. Sgt E-5, USMCR, 1966-72. Recipient Appreciation award Bur. Alcohol, Tobbaco and Fireamrs, Dearborn, Mich., 1990. Mem. Internat. Assn. Arson Investigators (bd. dirs. St. Louis sect. 1982-87, pres. 1989-90, Disting. Svc. award 1993, life mem.), Nat. Fire Protection Assn. (com. mem. 1991—), Congl. Fire Svcs. Inst. (bd. dirs. 1989-90), Internat. Fire Svc. Tng. Assn. (com. mem.). Office: Associated Fire Cons Inc 4257 W Ina Rd Ste 101 Tucson AZ 85741-2233

SMITH, DAVID ROBERT, university administrator; b. Quanah, Tex., Apr. 17, 1952; s. William Ingram and Genevieve (Gushee) S.; m. Jacalyn Ann Rainwater, June 8, 1974; children: Timothy, Alida. BA, Hardin-Simmons U., 1974; MDiv, Southwestern Bapt. Theol. Sem., 1978; EdD, Vanderbilt U., 1993. Ordained to ministry Bapt. Ch., 1978. Youth dir. First Bapt. Ch., Paducah, Tex., 1971-73; pastor First Bapt. Ch., Flora Vista, N.Mex., 1978-81; evangelist So. Bapt. Conv., Southwestern U.S., 1973-74; pastor Thornberry Bapt. Ch., Wichita Falls, Tex., 1975-78; admissions counselor Hardin-Simmons U., Abilene, Tex., 1974-75, dir. admissions, 1981-85; dean admissions Belmont Coll., Nashville, 1985-92, dir. devel./denom. support, 1992-94; bapt. student union dir. San Juan Coll., Farmington, N.Mex., 1978-81; sem. extension dir. San Juan Bapt. Assn., Farmington, 1978-81; cons. Together We Build fund raising program, Abilene, 1982-85; v.p. for institutional advancement Wayland Bapt. U., Plainview, Tex., 1994-98; pres. Brewton-Parker Coll., Mt. Vernon, Ga., 1998—. Coach T-Ball, Abilene, 1985, Western Am. Little League Baseball, Nashville, 1987; den leader Boy Scouts of Am., Nashville, 1986-89; tchr. Harpeth Hts. Bapt. Ch., 1985-94. Mem. Tenn. Assn. Coll. Admissions Counselors, Am. Assn. Higher Edn., Am. Assn. Coll. Registrars and Admissions Officers, Nat. Assn. Foreign Student Advisors, Hardin-Simmons U. Alumni Assn. (NM chpt. pres. 1980), Southwestern Bapt. Theol. Sem. Alumni Assn. (N.Mex. chpt. pres. 1981). Democrat. Avocations: tennis, outdoor sports, reading. Home: BPC Box 2001 Mount Vernon GA 30445 Office: Belmont Coll 1900 Belmont Blvd Nashville TN 37212-3758

SMITH, DIANE, investment manager; b. Spokane, Wash., Aug. 22, 1955; d. Darnell Dean and Lois Louise S. BA in Comms., Wash. State U., 1978; M in Internat. Mgmt., Am. Grad. Sch. Internat. Mgmt., 1984. Asst. v.p. Manufacturers Hanover Trust Co., N.Y.C., 1985-88; v.p. Lincoln Ventures Group, N.Y.C., 1988-90; ptnr. Electra Inc., N.Y.C., 1991-97; mng. dir., ptnr. Pactual Electra Capital Ptnrs., N.Y.C., 1997—; dir. various companies, 1991—. Mem. Phi Beta Kappa. Avocations: high altitude trekking, skiing, travel. E-mail: dsmith4047@hotmail.com. Home: 43 W 61st St Apt 12D New York NY 10023-7609 Office: Pactual Electra Capital Ptnrs 320 Park Ave Fl 28 New York NY 10022-6815

SMITH, DONALD E., broadcast engineer, manager; b. Salt Lake City, Sept. 10, 1930; s. Thurman A. and Louise (Cardall) S.; B.A. Columbia, 1955; B.S.; U. Utah, 1970; postgrad. U. So. Calif., U. Utah, Harvard, PhD (hon.), Columbia, 1985; m. Helen B. Lacy, 1978. Engr., Iowa State U., (WOI-TV), 1955-56; asst. chief engr. KLRJ-TV, Las Vegas, 1956-60; studio field engr. ABC, Hollywood, Cal., 1960; chief engr. Teletape, Inc., Salt Lake City, 1961; engring. supr. KUER, U. Utah, Salt Lake City, 1962-74, gen. mgr., 1975-85. Freelance cinematographer, 1950—; cons. radio TV (mgmt. engr. and prodn.), 1965—. Mem. Soc. Motion Pictures and TV Engrs., Lambda Chi Alpha. Home: 963 Hollywood Ave Salt Lake City UT 84105-3347

SMITH, DONALD FREDERICK, research psychologist, neuropsychopharmacologist; b. Chgo., Jan. 30, 1945; s. Leonard and Gertrude (Sankstone) S.; m. Helle Birgitte Knudsen, Dec. 1, 1972; children: Martin Smith, Stefan Bo Smith. BSc in Psychology, Duke U., Durham, N.C., 1967; MA in Physiological Psychology, McMaster U., Ontario, Canada, 1968; PhD in Biopsychology, U. Chgo., 1971; Lic. Medicine, Aarhus U., Denmark, 1974; DSc in Med. Sci., Copenhagen U., 1980. E-mail: dfsmith@inet.uni2.dk. Office: Psychiat Hosp Aarhus U, Skovagervej 2, 8240 Risskov Denmark

SMITH, DORIS CORINNE KEMP, retired nurse; b. Bogalusa, La., Nov. 22, 1919; d. Milton Jones and Maude Maria (Fortenberry) Kemp; m. Joseph William Smith, Oct. 13, 1940 (dec.). BSN, U. Colo., 1957, MS in Nursing Adminstrn., 1958. RN, Colo. Head nurse Chgo. Bridge & Iron Co., Morgan City, La., 1941-45, Shannon Hosp., San Angelo, Tex., 1945-50; dir. nursing Yoakum County Hosp., Denver City, Tex., 1951-52; hosp. supr. Med. Arts Hosp., Odessa, Tex., 1952-55; dir. insvc. edn. St. Anthony Hosp., Denver, 1961-66; coord. Kiamichi Area Vocat.-Tech. Nursing Sch., Wilburton, Okla., 1969-77; supr. non-ambulatory unit Lubbock (Tex.) State Sch., 1978-85, ret., 1985; steering com. Western Interstate Commn. on Higher Edn. for Nurses, Denver, 1963-65; curriculum and materials com. Okla. Bd. Vocat.-Tech. Edn., Stillwater, 1971-76; mem. Invitational Conf. To Plan Nursing for Future, Oklahoma City, 1976-77; survey team to appraise Sch. of Vocat.-Tech. Edn. Schs. for Okla. Dept. Vocat.-Tech. Edn., 1975-76. Author, editor: Survey of Functions Expected of the General Duty Nurse, State of Colorado, 1958; co-editor: Curriculum Guides; contbr. articles to profl. jours. Recipient citation of merit Okla. State U., 1976. Mem. AAAS, ANA, AAUW (life), Nat. League for Nursing, Tex. League for Nursing, Tex. Nurses Assn., Dist. 18 Nurses Assn., Tex. Employees Assn. (v.p. 1984-85), U. Colo. Alumni Assn., Am. Bus. Women's Assn. (pres. Lubbock chpt. 1986-87, rec. sec. 1989-90, edn. chair 1994-95, hospitality chair 1995-96), Am. Bus. Women's Assn. (program co-chair 1996-97, co-chair Am. Bus. Women's Assn. Day, 1997-98, membership com. 1999-2000, fin. com. 1997-98, Woman of Yr. Sunrise chpt. 1994-95), Bus. and Profl. Women's Assn. (sec. 1992-95), Chancellor's Club U. Colo., Pi Lambda Theta (sec. local chpt. 1957-58). Republican. Avocations: gardening, swimming, walking, travel, reading. Home: 2103 55th St Lubbock TX 79412-2612

SMITH, DOROTHY, artist, actress; b. Ft. Belvoir, Va., Sept. 4, 1963; d. Albert Cowper and Laura (Cary) Smith. BFA with high distinction, George Mason U., 1990; student, Folger Shakespearean Conservat, N.C. Sch. Dramatic Arts, Am. Acad. Dramatic Arts, Royal Acad. Dramatic Arts, Corcoran Sch. of Art. Security escort CIA, McLean, Va., 1982-83; with Kube Constrn., Warrenton, Va., 1984; vet. asst. Manhattan (N.Y.) Vet. Group, 1984-85; waitress Wellington's, Warrenton, 1986. Author: (book) The Phoenix, 1999; author poetry. Mem. U.S. Tae Kwon Do Orgn. (3d degree black belt), U.S. Combined Tng. Orgn., Screen Actors Guild, Am. Fedn. TV and Radio Artists, Commonwealth Dressage and Combined Tng. Assn. Avocations: horseback riding, Tae Kwon Do, swing dancing.

SMITH, DOROTHY OTTINGER, jewelry designer, civic worker; b. Indpls., 1922; d. Albert Ellsworth and Leona Aurelia (Waller) Ottinger; m. James Emory Smith, June 25, 1943 (div. 1984); children: Michael Ottinger, Sarah Anne, Theodore Arnold, Lisa Marie. Student, Herron Art Sch. of Purdue U. and Ind. U., 1941-42. Comml. artist William H. Block Co., Indpls., 1942-43, H.P. Wasson Co., 1943-44; dir. Riverside (Calif.) Art Ctr., 1963-64; jewelry designer Riverside, 1970—; numerous design commns. Adviser Riverside chpt. Freedom's Found. of Valley Forge; co-chmn. fund raising com. Riverside Art Ctr. and Mus., 1966-67, bd. dirs. Art Alliance, 1980-81; mem. Riverside City Hall sculpture selection panel Nat. Endowment for the Arts, 1974-75; chmn. fundraising benefit Riverside Art Ctr. and Mus., 1973-74, trustee, 1980-84, chmn. permanent collection, 1981-84, co-chmn. fund drive, 1982-84, trustee, 1998—; chmn. Riverside Mcpl. Arts Commn., 1974-76, Silver Anniversary Gala, 1992; juror Riverside Civic Ctr. Purchase Prize Art Show, 1975; mem. pub. bldgs. and grounds subcom., gen. plan citizens com. City of Riverside, 1965-66; mem. Mayor's Commn. on Civic Beauty, Mayor's Commn. on Sister City Sendai, 1965-66; bd. dirs., chmn. spl. events Children's League of Riverside Community Hosp., 1952-53; bd. dirs. Crippled Children's Soc. of Riverside, spl. events. chmn., 1952-53; bd. dirs. Nat. Charity League, pres. Riverside chpt., 1965-66; mem. exec. com. bd. trustees Riverside Arts Found., 1977-91, fund drive chmn., 1978-79, project rev. chmn., 1978-79, advisor Eveing for the Arts, 1998, juror Gemco Charitable and Scholarship Found., 1977-85; mem. bd. women deacons Calvary Presbyn. Ch., 1978-80, elder, 1989-92; mem. incorporating bd. Inland Empire United Fund for the Arts, 1980-81; bd dirs. Hospice Orgn. Riverside County, 1982-84; trustee Riverside Art Mus., 1998—; mem. Calif. Coun. Humanities, 1982-86. Recipient cert. Riverside City Coun., 1977, plaque Mayor of Riverside, 1977, Spl. Recognition Riverside Cultural Arts Coun., 1981, Disting. Svc. plaque Riverside Art Ctr. and Mus., Jr. League Silver Raincross Community Svc. award, 1989, Cert Appreciation Outstanding Svc. to the Arts Community Riverside Arts Found., 1990, Top Dog award Riverside Art Mus., 1999. Mem. Riverside Art Assn. (pres. 1961-63, 1st. v.p. 1964-65, 67-68, trustee 1959-70, 80-84, 87-92), Art Alliance of Riverside Art Ctr. and Museum (founder 1964, pres. 1969-70). Address: 3979 Chapman Pl Riverside CA 92506-1150

SMITH, DOUGLAS MAXWELL, author, consultant; b. Cambridge, Mass., July 28, 1964; s. William Hamilton III and Paula Mae (Tagan) S.; m. Tiina Hannelle Ikonen, Aug. 16, 1998. Grad. cum laude, Suffield (Conn.) Acad., 1982; BA, U. Del., Wilmington, 1986; Diploma in Internat. Advt. D. Comml. prodr./dir. Avset Oy, Helsinki, 1989-90; founder DMS Direct & Mtkg. Svcs. Oy, Helsinki, 1991-95; account planner, copywriter BBDO Helsinki, 1995-97; freelance creative cons., writer Helsinki, 1997-99; chief creative officer, co-founder Moving Entertainment, Helsinki, 1999—. Author, co-creator world's first WAP comic series Flip & Mick, 1999, Connected World comic series, 1999; concept co-creator, content cons. customer loyalty sites. Recipient Gold award Finnish AV Festival, 1991, Silver and Honorable Mention awards Graphia Festival, 1997, others.

SMITH, DWIGHT MORRELL, chemistry educator; b. Hudson, N.Y., Oct. 10, 1931; s. Elliott Monroe and Edith Helen (Hall) S.; m. Alice Beverly Bond, Aug. 27, 1955 (dec. 1990); children—Karen Elizabeth, Susan Allison, Jonathan Aaron; m. Elfi Nelson, Dec. 28, 1991. BA, Ctrl. Coll., Pella, Iowa, 1953; PhD, Pa. State U., 1957; ScD (hon.), Cen. Coll., 1986; LittD (hon.), U. Denver, 1990. Postdoctoral fellow, instr. Calif. Inst. Tech., 1957-59; sr. chemist Texaco Rsch. Ctr., Beacon, N.Y., 1959-61; asst. prof. chemistry Wesleyan U., Middletown, Conn., 1961-66; assoc. prof. Hope Coll., Holland, Mich., 1966-69, prof., 1969-72; prof. chemistry U. Denver, 1972—, chmn. dept., 1972-83, vice chancellor for acad. affairs, 1983-84, chancellor, 1984-89; pres., bd. trustees Hawaii Loa Coll., Kaneohe, 1990-92; bd. dirs. Aina Inst., Hawaii; mem. Registry for Interim Coll. and Univ. Pres.; mem. adv. bd. Solar Energy Rsch. Inst., 1989-91; mem. vis. com. Zettlemoyer Ctr. for Surface Studies Lehigh U., 1990-96, dept. chemistry and geochemistry Colo. Sch. Mines; mem. sci. adv. bd. Denver Rsch. Inst. Editor Revs. on Petroleum Chemistry, 1975-78; editl. adv. bd. Recent Rsch. Devels. in Applied Spectroscopy, 1998—; contbr. articles to profl. jours.; patentee selective hydrogenation. Chmn. Chs. United for Social Action, Holland, 1968-69; mem. adv. com. Holland Sch. Bd., 1969-70; bd. commrs. Colo. Adv. Tech. Inst., 1984-88, Univ. Senate, United Meth. Ch., Nashville, 1987-88, 91-93; mem. adv. bd. United Way, Inst. Internat. Edn., Japan Am. Soc. Colo., Denver Winter Games Olympics Com.; mem. ch. bds. or consistories Ref. Ch. Am., N.Y., Conn., Mich., United Meth. Ch., Colo. DuPont fellow, 1956-57, NSF fellow Scripps Inst., 1971-72; recipient grants Research Corp., Petroleum Research Fund, NSF, Solar Energy Research Inst. Mem. AAAS, Am. Assn. Aerosol Rsch., Am. Chem. Soc. (chmn. Colo. 1976, sec. western Mich. 1970-71, joint coun. and bd. com. on sci. 1997-98, award Colo. sect. 1986), Soc. Applied Spectroscopy, Mile High Club, Sigma Xi. Home: 1931 W Sanibel Ct Littleton CO 80120-8133 Office: U Denver Dept Chem & Biochem Denver CO 80208-0001

SMITH, DWYANE, university administrator; b. St. Louis, Feb. 16, 1961; s. Magnolia Smith. BS in Psychology, N.E. Mo. State U., 1983, MA in Edn. Adminstrn., 1991; postgrad., U. Mo., Columbia, 1993 , Harvard U., 1995. Intern IRS, St. Louis, 1983; minority counselor N.E. Mo. State U., Kirksville, 1983-88, dir. minority svcs., 1988-91, asst. dir. admissions, asst. dean multicultural affairs, 1991—, assoc. dean multicultural affairs. Mem. Alpha Phi Alpha (chair statewide conv. 1990, Mo. Man of Yr. 1985), Alpha Phi Omega, Phi Kappa Phi, Habitat for Humanity. Avocations: reading, writing. Home: 837 SE 11th Ter Lees Summit MO 64081-2153

SMITH, EARL CHARLES, nephrologist, educator; b. Pitts., Mar. 1, 1936; s. Mose and Irene (Surloff) S. BS, Tufts U., 1957; MD, U. Pitts., 1961. Diplomate in internal medicine and nephrology Am. Bd. Internal Medicine. Intern Montefiore Hosp., Pitts., 1961-62; resident, fellow Cleve. Clinic, 1964-68; physician Cook County Hosp., Chgo., 1968-71; chief nephrology divsn. Mt. Sinai Hosp., Chgo., 1971—, vice chair medicine, 1987—; chief nephrology divsn. Chgo. Med. Sch., 1994—, prof. medicine, 1995—; pres. med. staff, 1985-87; cons. Internat. Jour. Artificial Organs, Milan, 1986—; med. adv. bd. Kidney Found. Ill., Chgo., 1980—. Co-author: Medical Exam Book-Nephrology, 1976, Self Assessment in Internal Medicine, 1980; assoc. editor Kidney jour., 1991—; contbr. articles to profl. jours. Chair hypertension com. Chgo. Heart Assn., 1973-75. Capt. USAF, 1962-64. Recipient Meritorious Svc. award Chgo. Heart Assn., 1975. Fellow Am. Coll. Physicians; mem. Am. Soc. Artificial Internal Organs, Am. Soc. Nephrology, Am. Soc. Hypertension Specialist in Clin. Hypertension, Internat. Soc. Nephrology, Phi Beta Kappa, Alpha Omega Alpha, Sigma Xi. Achievements include research in described cause and pathophysiology of dialysis dementia; hematological problems in patients with renal disease. Office: Mount Sinai Hosp 15th and California Ave Chicago IL 60608

SMITH, EDWARD MARTIN, III, football player; b. Trenton, N.J., June 5, 1969; s. Edward Martin Jr. and Patricia Marie Smith; 1 child, Edward Martin IV. Baseball player Chgo. White Sox, 1987-91, Milw. Brewers, 1991-93; football players Atlanta Falcons, 1997-98, Detroit Lions, 1999—. Democrat. Baptist. E-mail:ezluv87@aol.com.

SMITH, ELISE BECKET, arts administrator; b. N.Y.C., Aug. 23, 1941; arrived in Eng., 1971; d. George Campbell and Elise Barr (Granbery) Becket; m. Martin Gregory Smith, Oct. 2, 1971; children: Jeremy James, Katherine Elise. BA in History, Stanford U., 1964, MA in Audiology, 1965, JD, 1971. Clin. audiologist San Francisco Hearing and Speech Ctr., 1965-67, Mass. Eye & Ear Hosp., Boston, 1967-68; researcher and writer Amnesty Internat., London, 1972-73; mng. dir. Needle Art House, Ltd., Basingstoke, Eng., 1978-80; cons. Social Dem. Party, London, 1980-83; mng. dir. Becket Publs. Ltd., London, 1983-90; dir. Becket Publs. Ltd., London, 1983-90. Co-author: Hang Your Hat in London, 1974; co-editor: Becket's Directory of the City of London, 1985, rev. eds., 1987, 89. Mem. devel. com. Bodleian Libr., Oxford U., Eng., 1987—; bd. dirs. Orch. of the Age of Enlightment, London, 1989—; chmn. The Becket Collection; bd. govs. Royual Acad. Music; advisor Performing Arts Labs.; mem. devel. com. Cheltenham Internat. Festivals. Avocations: music, skiing, needlework, English history.

SMITH, EMMITT J., III, professional football player; b. Pensacola, Fla., May 15, 1969; s. Emmitt Jr. and Mary Smith. Student, U. Fla. With Dallas Cowboys, 1990—; player Pro-Bowl, 1990-92, NFC Championship game, 1992, 93, Super Bowl XXVII, 1992, Super Bowl XXVIII, 1993; owner Emmitt Inc. Recipient MVP award for season, 1993, MVP award for Super Bowl, 1993; named Running Back, Sporting News Coll. All-Am. team, 1989, Offensive Rookie of Yr., 1990, Running Back, Sporting News NFL All-Pro team, 1992, 93, NFL Player of Yr., Sporting News, 1993; named to Pro-Bowl, 1993, 95. Achievements include leading NFL in rushing, 1991-93, 95; Led NFL running backs in scoring, 1992, 95. Office: Dallas Cowboys One Cowboys Pky Irving TX 75063

SMITH, ERIC MORGAN, virology educator; b. Lafayette, Ind., Feb. 13, 1953; s. James E. and Betty Carolyn (Hanlin) S.; m. Janice Marie Kelly, May 26, 1979; children: David Kendall, Ben Pham. BS cum laude, Syracuse U., 1975; PhD, Baylor Coll. of Medicine, 1980. Postdoctoral fellow Dept. Microbiology, U. Tex. Med. Br., Galveston, Tex., 1979-81, asst. prof., 1982-85, assoc. prof., 1985-90, prof., 1990—; editl. bd. Progress in Neuro-Endocrin Immunology, Washington, 1988-92, Behavior and Immunity, 1993—, Cellular and Molecular Neurobiology, 1994—; mem. mental health AIDS and immunity rev. com. NIMH, 1992-96. Founding co-editor Advances in Neuroimmunology, 1991; contbr. over 140 articles to profl. jours. Mem. Galveston Hist. Found., 1980—. Mem. AAAS, Am. Soc. for Microbiology, Am. Assn. Immunologists, Internat. Soc. Immunopharmacology, Internat. Working Group on Neuroimmunomodulation, Assn. Immuno-Neurobiologists (co-founding pres.), Galveston Yacht Club, Syracuse Scuba Soc. (v.p. 1975). Avocations: sailing, photography, scuba diving. Office: U Tex Med Br Dept Psychiatry Galveston TX 77555-0001

SMITH, ERLINDA FAY, occupational therapist; b. Kansas City, Mo., July 4, 1963; d. Neathy Woods and Lillie Mae (Morgan) Woods-Beatty; m. Tommy Lee Smith, Sept. 19, 1992 (div. Sept. 95). BS in Occupl. Therapy, U. Kans., 1989; grad., Kansas City Coll. of Med. and Dental Assts., 1982. Clin. occupl. therapist Truman Med. Ctr., Kansas City, Mo., 1989-92; indsl. rehab. specialist St. Mary's Hosp., Blue Springs, Mo., 1992-96, occupl. therapist, 1996-98; occupl. therapist Bay Med. Ctr., Panama City, Fla., 1998-2000; Registered Occupl. Therapist. Mem. Am. Occupl. Therapy Assn., Am. Soc. Hand Therapists, Nat. Black Occupl. Therapy Caucus, Met. Kansas City Black Occupl. Therapy Caucus (v.p. 1995—), Mo. Occupl. Therapy Assn., Fla. Occupl. Therapy Assn., Kansas City Hand Study Group. Bapt. Avocations: sewing, travelling, crafts. Home: 2315 Jackson Bluff Rd Apt 302A Tallahassee FL 32304-4570

SMITH, ETHEL FARRINGTON, retired social worker, genealogist, writer; b. Arlington, Mass., Mar. 26, 1910; d. Leander Morton and Blanche Emeline (Clough) Farrington; m. Harland Willard Hawes, Mar. 27, 1951 (dec. 1958); m. John Eldredge Smith, 1959 (dec. 1973); four stepchildren. AB, Smith Coll., 1931; MS, Columbia U., 1942. Cert. genealogist. Case worker N.H. State Dept. Pub. Welfare, Manchester, 1934-35; welfare worker City Dept. Welfare, Rochester, N.Y., 1935-36; placement interviewer N.H. State Employment Svc., Nashua, 1936-37; med. social worker Columbia Presbyn. Med. Ctr., N.Y.C., 1938-47; med. social worker March of Dimes, Asheville, N.C., 1948-49, Boise, Idaho, 1948-49; med. social worker Easter Seal Soc., Billings, Mont., 1949-50. Author: Adam Hawkes, 1980; rschr.: Colonial Doctors and Doctresses 1975-2001; editor: Colonial Tavernkeepers, Vols. 10-12; editor Hawkes Talks, 1969-93; contbr. articles to New Eng. Historic and Genealog. Register vol. 142, 143, 149, 150. Active Girl Scouts U.S., past

vol. tng. dir. Palm Glades coun., bd. dirs.; nat. bd. dirs. Daus. of Founders and Patriots of Am., 1973-90, bd. dirs. local chpt. Mem. Nat. League Am. Pen Women, Nat. Soc. Genealogists, New England Hist. Geneal. Soc. (trustee 1986-89, life, named trustees room the Ethel Farrington Smith Trustees Room 1993), Smith Coll. Club (past pres.), Ancient and Hon. Artillery Co. of Mass. (past state officer women's divsn.), Soc. Mayflower Descendants (past state officer Fla.), Hull Mass. Hist. Soc. (hon. life). Avocations: travel, writing, lecturing, photography, music.

SMITH, EUGENIA SEWELL, funeral home executive; b. Albany, Ky., Oct. 24, 1922; d. Leo Matheny and Marjorie (Warinner) Sewell; m. James Frederick Smith, June 25, 1948; 1 child, Bryson Sewell (dec.). Student Berea Coll., 1937-41, Bowling Green Coll. Commerce, 1944-45. Owner, operator Sewell Funeral Home, Albany, 1977—; bd. dir. Citizens Bank of Albany, Ky., 1989—. Sec. Albany Woman's Club, 1950-54; den mother Cub Scouts, Boy Scouts Am., 1958-62; pres. Clinton County Homemakers, Albany, 1968-70, Modern Homemakers, 1992-98; mission action chmn. Missionary Baptist Ch., 1965-91; v.p. Modern Homemakers Club of Albany, 1990-92, pres., 1994-98. Democrat. Lodge: Demolay Mother's (pres. Albany club 1966-67), Order Eastern Star (former assoc. conductress, former Martha and Esther). Home: RR 5 Box 104 Burkesville Rd Albany KY 42602-9310 Office: Sewell Funeral Home 115 Cross St Albany KY 42602

SMITH, FREDERICK ORVILLE, II, wood products manufacturer, retired naval officer; b. Cambridge, Mass., July 17, 1934; s. Harry Francis and Dorothy Spaulding (Zeller) S.; m. Mabel Roxy Moore, June 6, 1965; children: Sarah Zeller, Jennifer Joy, Erika Hildred. BA, Bowdoin Coll., 1956; MA in Polit. Sci., U. Vt., 2000. Deck officer, 1st lt. USN, 1957-59; officer US Naval Sta., Adak, Alaska, 1959-60; clk. & exec. Fred O. Smith Mfg. Co., New Vineyard, Maine, 1960-71, pres., treas., 1971—; res. officer Naval Res. Tng. Ctr., Augusta, Maine, 1960-69, Bangor, Maine, 1970-79 (ret.). Chair, mem. nat. com. Young Reps., Maine, 1960-68; pres. New Eng. Coun. Young Reps., 1962-64; chmn. Franklin County (Maine) Rep. Com., 1976-80, v.p. state conv., 1994; mem. Maine Rep. State Com., 1980-86, 92-94, 98—; mem. state com. ACSO, 1998—; town chmn. Rep. Com., New Vineyard, 1972-86, Farmington, Maine, 1992—; notary public, 1978—. Paul Harris fellow Farmington Rotary Club, 1996. Master Davis Lodge; mem. Am. Legion, Up Country Artists (bd. dirs. 1996—, v.p. 1997, pres. 1998—). Conglist. Avocations: photography, cabinet making & design, skiing, hiking, writing. E-mail: fosmith@somtel.com. Fax: 207-779-0716. Home: 127 Anson St Farmington ME 04938-5734 Office: Fred O Smith Mfg Co PO Box 248 New Vineyard ME 04956-0248

SMITH, FREDERICK WALLACE, transportation company executive; b. Marks, Miss., Aug. 11, 1944; s. Frederick Smith; m. Diane Avis. Grad., Yale U., 1966. Cert. comml. pilot. Owner Ark Aviation, 1969-71; founder, pres. Fed. Express Corp., Memphis, 1971—, chmn. bd., pres, CEO, 1975—. Served with USMC, 1966-70. Office: FEDEX Corp 2005 Corporate Ave Memphis TN 38132-1796

SMITH, GEOFFREY LILLEY, scientist; b. Leeds, England, July 23, 1955; s. Irvine Battinson and Kathleen Lilley (Turner) S.; m. Tessa Marie Trico, July 14, 1979; children: Ralph, Alexandra, Nicholas, Philippa. BSc in Biochem./Microbiology with honors, U. Leeds, 1977; PhD in Virology, Coun. for Nat. Acad. Awards, 1981; MA, U. Cambridge, Eng., 1988, U. Oxford, Eng., 1989. Postdoctoral rsch. assoc. NIH, Bethesda, Md., 1981-84; lectr. virology U. Cambridge, 1985-89; reader bacteriology U. Oxford, Eng., 1989-96; prof. virology U. Oxford, 1996-2000; prof. virology Imperial Coll. Sch. Medicine, London, 2000—, Wellcome Trust prin. rsch. fellow Wright-Fleming Inst., 2000—; Almroth Wright lectr. St. Mary's Hosp. Med. Sch., 1992. Fellow Wadham Coll., 1989-2000. Mem. Brit. Soc. for Immunology, Soc. for Gen. Microbiology (Fleming lectr. 1992), Am. Soc. for Virology, Christ's Coll. Cambridge Lister Inst. of Preventive Medicine (Jenner fellow 1988). Office: Imperial Coll Sch Medicine, St Mary's Campus Norfolk Pl, London W2 1PG, England

SMITH, GEORGE LARRY, analytical and environmental chemist; b. Beloit, Kans., Oct. 11, 1951; s. Richard Bailey and Vonda Ellene (Cox) S.; m. Charlene Janell Musgrove, Sept. 4, 1973; 1 child, Brian Lawrence. BA, Augustana Coll., 1973. Cert. grade 3 water treatment operator, Calif. Lab. technician Sanitary Dist. of Hammond, Ind., 1973; chemist Federated Metals Corp., Whiting, Ind., 1973-77; rsch. technician Air Pollution Technology, Inc., San Diego, 1978-80, environ. chemist, 1980-81, sr. tech. asst., 1981; staff chemist I Occidental Research Corp., Irvine, Calif., 1981-82, receiving chemist, 1982-84; processing chemist Chem. Waste Mgmt., Inc., Kettleman City, Calif., 1984-87, analytical chemist, 1987-89, wet analytical chemistry group leader, 1989-90, inorganic lab. supr., 1990-94, quality assurance/quality control specialist, 1994-96; lab. mgr. Bolsa Rsch. Assocs., Inc., Hollister, Calif., 1996—; lab. mgr., chemist Tri Cal-Bolsa Rsch. Assocs., Inc., Hollister, Calif., 1999—; lab. analyst for published article in environ. sci. and tech., 1981. bd. dirs. Apostolic Christian Missions, Inc., San Diego, 1978-82. Mem. Am. Chem. Soc., Nat. Geog. Soc., Assn. Ofcl. Analytical Chemists Internat., Planetary Soc., Sierra Club. Avocations: coin collecting, drawing, photography, reading about science, history and religion. Home: 991 Meridian St Hollister CA 95023-4130 Office: Bolsa Rsch Assocs Inc 8770 Hwy 25 Hollister CA 95024

SMITH, GERRIT BRUCE, foreign language educator; b. Munich, Bavaria, Germany, Oct. 17, 1971; came to the U.S., 1988; s. Bruce Alan Smith and Gerlinde Karolina Ward. AA magna cum laude, Coll. William and Mary, 1993, BA magna cum laude, 1995; MA in German, U. Hawaii, 1999; postgrad., U. Okla., 1996—. Cert. sales assoc. Army Air Force Exch. Svc., Ft. Lee, Va., 1991-96; tchg. asst. German U. Hawaii at Manoa, Honolulu, 1997-99; German tchr. Kaimuki Cmty. Sch. for Adults, 2000—. Campaign/poll worker Re-election Campaign Stacy Stafford Clk. of Cir. Ct., Colonial Heights, Va., 1990; part-time vol. adminstrv. and rsch. asst. Judiciary of the State of Hawaii, Honolulu, 1997-99. Presdl. scholar Richard Bland Coll., Petersburg, Va., 1992-93. Mem. ASPA, Dem. Nat. Com., Hawaii Kai Opera Guild, German Nat. Honor Soc. (U. Hawaii chpt. treas. 1997-99), Phi Theta Kappa. Avocations: chess, stamp collecting, opera, reading, weight training. E-mail: gerrit@hawaii.edu.

SMITH, GORDON EUGENE, pilot; b. Corpus Christi, Tex., Nov. 22, 1953; s. Orvis Alvin and Helen Lucille (Lockhart) A.; m. Crisanta Lacson Oqueriza, Jan. 5, 1979; children: Pia Marie, Helena Irita. AAS in Electronics, Riverside City Coll., 1985; BSEE, Calif. Polytech., 1987. Electronics technician Lear Siegler, Inc., Ontario, Calif., 1981-86, Rockwell Internat., Palmdale, Calif., 1986-87; pilot Orion Air Inc., Raleigh, N.C., 1987-90; pilot, dir. maintenance, asst. dir. ops. Nat. Air, Riverside, Calif., 1990-93; pilot MGM Grand Air, 1993-96, San Pacific Internat., Tucson, 1996-99, Sunworld Internat., Cin., 1999—. With USAF, 1972-79, with Res. 1979—. Mem. Aircraft Owners and Pilots Assn., Team One (v.p. 1980—). Republican. Dunkard Brethren. Avocations: flying, golf, bowling, baseball, computers. Office: Sunworld Internat 207 Grandview Dr Fort Mitchell KY 41017-2758

SMITH, GORDON PAUL, management consulting company executive; b. Salem, Mass., Dec. 25, 1916; s. Gordon and May (Vaughan) S.; m. Daphne Miller, Nov. 23, 1943 (div. 1968); m. Ramona Chamberlain, Sept. 27, 1969; children: Randall B., Roderick F. B.S. in Econs, U. Mass., 1947; M.S. in Govt. Mgmt, U. Denver (Sloan fellow), 1948; postgrad. in polit. sci, NYU, 1948-50; DHL (hon.), Monterey Inst. Internat. Studies, 1994. Economist Tax Found., Inc., N.Y.C., 1948-50; with Booz, Allen & Hamilton, 1951-70; partner Booz, Allen & Hamilton, San Francisco, 1959-62, v.p., 1962-67, mng. pntr. Western U.S., 1968-70; partner Harrod, Williams and Smith (real estate devel.), San Francisco, 1962-69; state dir. fin. State of Calif., 1967-68; pres. Gordon Paul Smith & Co., Mgmt. Cons., 1968—; pres., chief exec. officer Golconda Corp., 1972-74, chmn. bd., 1974-85; pres. Cermetek Corp., 1978-80; bd. dirs., exec. com. First Calif. Co., 1970-72, Groman Corp., 1976-85; bd. dirs. Madison Venture Capital Corp.; adviser task force def. procurement and contracting Hoover Commn., 1954-55; spl. asst. to pres. Republic Aviation Corp., 1954-55; cons., Hawaii, 1960-61, Alaska, 1963; cons. Wash. Hwy. Adminstrn., 1964, also 10 states and fed. agys., 1951-70, Am. Baseball League and Calif. Angels, 1960-62; bd. dirs. Monterey Coll. Law; chmn. Ft. Ord Econ. Devel. Adv. Group, 1991; chmn. Coalition on Rsch. and Edn., 1993—; bd. dirs. Monterey Bay Futures Project; adv. bd. Ctr. for Non-Proliferation Studies, 1997—; over 750 TV, radio and speaking appearances on econs., mgmt. and public issues. Author articles on govt., econs. and edn. Mem. 24 bds. and commns. State of Calif., 1967-72, sr. advisor to pres., 1998—; mem. Calif. Select Com. on Master Plan for Edn., 1971-73; mem. alumni council U. Mass., 1950-54, bd. dirs. alumni assn., 1964-70; bd. dirs. Alumni Assn. Mt. Hermon Prep. Sch., 1963; bd. dirs. Stanford Med. Ctr., 1960-62, pres., chmn., 1962-66; chmn. West Coast Cancer Found., 1976-87, Coalition Rsch. and Edn., 1993—, Jim Tunney Youth Fund, 1994—; trustee, chmn. Monterey Inst. Internat. Studies, 1978-92, trustee emeritus, 1995—; trustee Northfield Mt. Hermon Sch., 1983-93, Robert Louis Stevenson Sch., 1993—; mem. devel. council Community Hosp. of Monterey Peninsula, 1983-84; bd. dirs. Friends of the Performing Arts, 1985—; bd. dirs. Monterey County Symphony Orch., 1991-96, Monterey Bay Futures Project, 1992—. Recipient spl. commendation Hoover Commn., 1955, Alumni of Yr. award U. Mass., 1963, Trustee of Yr. award Monterey-Peninsula, 1991, Monterey-Peninsula Outstanding Citizen of Yr. award, 1992, Laura Bride Powers Heritage award, 1991, U.S. Congl. award, 1992, Calif. Senate and Assembly Outstanding Citizen award, 1992, Wisdom award of honor Wisdom Soc., 1992; permanent Gordon Paul Smith Disting. Chair for Internat. Studies established at Monterey Inst. Internat. Studies; Gordon Paul Smith Scholarship Fund named in his honor Northfield Mt. Hermon Sch.; named to Honorable Order of Ky. Cols. Mem. Monterey History and Art Assn. (bd. dirs. 1987-92, pres. 1985-87, chmn. 1987-92, hon. lifetime dir. 1992—), The Stanton Heritage Ctr. (chmn. 1987-92, chmn. emeritus 1992—), Salvation Army (bd. dirs., chmn. hon. cabinet), Monterey Peninsula Mus. Art, Carmel Valley (Calif.) Country Club, Monterey Peninsula Country Club, Old Capitol Club. Home: 253 Del Mesa Carmel CA 93923

SMITH, GRANT WILLIAM, English language educator, civic fundraiser; b. Bellingham, Wash., July 26, 1937; s. George Whitfield and Hazel (Speirs) S.; m. Lelia Dickinson, June 9, 1961; children: Kathryn, Gavin. BA, Reed Coll., 1964; MA, U. Nev., 1966; PhD, U. Del., 1975. Asst. prof. Eastern Wash. U., Cheney, 1968-76, assoc. prof., 1976-79, prof., 1979—; faculty pres. Eastern Wash. U., Cheney, 1976-77, chair English dept., 1978-84, acting vice provost, 1987-88, coord. humanities, 1979—, dir. cultural outreach, 1995-97; host Pub. TV, Here's Shakespeare, 1980, 81. Editor Proceedings of the Am. Name Soc., 1997, 98, 99; contbr. articles to profl. jours. and conf. procs. Moderator Cheney United Ch. Christ, 1982-84; trustee Spokane Symphony, 1996—, chair devel. 2000—; program chair Coun. Geo. Names Authorities, 1999. With U.S. Army, 1957-60. Grantee U.S. Geol. Survey, State Humanities Commn., NEH, others. Mem. MLA, AAUP, Placename Survey U.S. (chair 1990—), Connoisseur Concerts Assn. (pres. 1992-95), Am. Dialect Soc. (regional sec. 1982-98), Rocky Mountain MLA (program chair 1987, 95), Internat. Coun. Onomastic Scientists (exec. bd. dirs. 1999—, editl. bd. ONOMA 2000—), Internat. Soc. Dialectology and Geolinguistics, Am. Name Soc. (v.p. 1996-98, pres. 1999—), Wash. Bd. Geo. Names, others. Avocations: jogging, reading, singing. Home: 905 Gary St Cheney WA 99004-1341 Address: Eastern Wash Univ Dept of English MS-25 Cheney WA 99004

SMITH, HAMILTON OTHANEL, molecular biologist, educator; b. N.Y.C., N.Y., Aug. 23, 1931; s. Bunnie Othanel and Tommie Harkey S.; m. Elizabeth Anne Bolton, May 25, 1957; children: Joel, Barry, Dirk, Bryan, Kirsten. Student, U. Ill., 1948-50; A.B. in Math, U. Calif., Berkeley, 1952; M.D., Johns Hopkins U., 1956. Intern Barnes Hosp., St. Louis, 1956-57; resident in medicine Henry Ford Hosp., Detroit, 1959-62; USPHS fellow dept. human genetics U. Mich., Ann Arbor, 1962-64; rsch. assoc. U. Mich., 1964-67; asst. prof. molecular biology and genetics Sch. Medicine Johns Hopkins U., Balt., 1967-69, assoc. prof., 1969-73, prof., 1973—, emeritus prof. molecular biology and genetics; assoc. Inst. für Molekularbologie der U. Zurich, Switzerland, 1975-76; assoc. Rsch. Inst. Molecular Pathology, Vienna, 1990-91. Contbr. articles to profl. jours. Served to lt. M.C. USNR, 1957-59. Recipient Nobel Prize in medicine, 1978; Guggenheim fellow, 1975-76. Mem. Am. Soc. Microbiology, AAAS, Am. Soc. Biol. Chemists, Nat. Acad. Sci.

SMITH, HANS JURIE, minerals and metals company executive; b. Jan. 15, 1941; married 1969. BSc, U. Pretoria, South Africa, 1963, U. Witwatersrand, South Africa, 1965. Tech. asst. to chief cons. engring. Gold Fields, 1969-70; sr. investment analyst Buffalo Fluorspar Mine, 1970-72, asst. gen. mgr., 72-73; gen. mgr. Masauli Asbestos, 1973-74; ops. mgr. chrome divsn. Gencor, 1974-78; mng. dir. Zululand Titanium, 1978-85; tech. dir. Octha Diamonds, 1978-85; mgr. strategic planning corp. mining divsn. Safety & Health Svcs., Gencor, 1985, sr. mgr. mktg. coal divsn., 1985-88, chief cons., 1988; mng. dir. Trans-Natal Coal Corp. Ltd., 1988, Samancor Ltd., Johannesburg, South Africa, 1989-93; mng. dir. Iscor Ltd., Pretoria, South Africa, 1993—, chmn. bd., 1993-95, exec. chmn., 1995—. Avocations: tennis, golf, jogging, scuba diving, underwater photography. Office: ISCOR Ltd, PO Box 450, Pretoria 01 South Africa

SMITH, HAROLD CHARLES, private pension fund executive; b. N.Y.C., Jan. 11, 1934; s. Harold Elmore and Hedwig Agnes (Gronke) S. BA cum laude with honors, Ursinus Coll., 1955; DD (hon.), 1993; MBA, NYU, 1958; M in Div., Union Theol. Sem., N.Y.C., 1958; DHum (hon.), Springfield Coll., 1998. CFA; ordained minister United Ch. Christ, 1959. V.p. YMCA Retirement Fund, Inc., N.Y.C., 1958-69, portfolio mgr., 1960—, assoc. sec., 1969-77, v.p., 1977-80, exec. v.p., 1980-82, pres. elect, 1982-83, pres., 1983-2000; assoc. prof. bus. and fin. L.I. U., 1969-71; trustee Bank Mart, Bridgeport, Conn., 1983-91; bd. dirs. Y Mut. Ins. Co., treas. 1988—. Author: Getting It All Together in Retirement, 1977. pastor 1st E&R Ch., Bridgeport, Conn., 1958-88, Unity Hill United Ch. of Christ, 1988-2000, treas., 1988—; bd. dirs. United Ch. Residencies, 1962-65, YMCA Greater N.Y., 1983-97, Bridgeport Area Found., 1989-2000, Ursinus Coll., Pa., 1994—, Coun. of Chs. Greater Bridgeport, 1995-96, Silver Bay Christian Conf. Ctr., 1997; trustee YWCA Greater Bridgeport, 1975-79, Pension Funds United Ch. of Christ, 1968—, Springfield Coll. (Mass.), 1983—; trustee United Ch. Found., 1968-95, vice chmn., 1995-98, chmn., 1998. Mem. Am. Econs. Assn., N.Y. Soc. Security Analysts, Fin. Analysts Fedn., World and Trade Club, Masons, Order Ea. Star. Office: YMCA Retirement 140 Broadway Fl 28 New York NY 10005-1101

SMITH, H(AROLD) LAWRENCE, lawyer; b. Evergreen Park, Ill., June 27, 1932; s. Harold Lawrence and Lorna Catherine (White) S.; m. Madonna Jeanne Koehl, June 9, 1956 (div. 1968); children: Lawrence Kirby, Sandra Michele, Madonna Clare Galloway; m. Nancy Leigh Baum, May 2, 1970 (dec. 1983); m. Louise Fredericka Jeffrey, Nov. 2, 1984 (div. 1994); m. Marianne Lorraine Laug, Apr. 19, 1997. BS, U.S. Naval Acad., 1956; JD, John Marshall Law Sch., 1965. Bar: Ill. 1965, Mich. 1986,U.S. Dist. Ct. (no. dist.) Ill. 1965, U.S. Ct. Appeals (7th cir.) 1967, U.S. Ct. of Customs and Patent Appeals, 1976, U.S. Ct. Appeals (fed. cir.) 1982, U.S. Patent and Trademark Office 1968. Asst. prof. naval sci. U. Notre Dame, 1960-61; tech. asst. Langner, Parry, Card & Langner, Chgo., 1961-65, assoc., 1965-69; patent atty. Borg-Warner Corp., Chgo., 1970-74; sr. patent atty. Continental Can Co., Inc., Chgo. and Oak Brook, Ill., 1974-82, asst. gen. counsel, Stamford and Norwalk, Conn., 1982-86; ptnr. Varnum, Riddering, Schmidt & Howlett, Grand Rapids, Mich., 1986-96, counsel, 1996-97; ptnr. Rader, Fishman, Grauer & McGarry, Grand Rapids, Mich., 1997—; adj. prof. patent law Cooley Law Sch., 1991—. Served to lt. USN, 1956-61. Fellow Mich. State Bar Found.; mem. Intellectual Property Law Assn. Chgo., Chartered Inst. Patent Agts. (London), World Affairs Coun. of Western Mich. (dir. 1996—, treas. 1998—), Internat. Platform Assn., Peninsular Club. Office: Rader Fishman Grauer & McGarry 171 Monroe Ave NW Ste 600 Grand Rapids MI 49503-2634

SMITH, IRVING, gerontologist; b. Washington, June 4, 1948; s. Alfonso Marcellus and Nannie (Hunter) S.; children: Bryan, Rashard, Irving, Nevada, Ryan. M Human Svcs., Lincoln U., Pa., 1995, grad. cert. advanced gerontology, 1995. Lic. profl. counselor, Washington. Dir. Sr. Ctr. Md.-Nat. Capital Park & Planning Commn., Prince George's County, Md., 1969-71, 89—; internat., nat. forum spkr. on leisure and aging issues; sport sci. instr. Am. Sports Edn. Program; CPR, first aid instr. ARC; defensive driving instr. Nat. Safety Coun. Fellow Washington Area Geriatric Edn. Ctr. Consortium; mem. Nat. Recreation and Park Assn. (state rep. leisure and aging), Pi Gamma Mu. Democrat. Baptist. Home: 503 Pacer Dr Hyattsville MD 20785-4639

SMITH, IVOR RAMSAY, engineering educator; b. Birmingham, U.K., Oct. 8, 1929; s. Howard and Elsie Emily (Underhill) S.; m. Pamela Mary Voake, Jan. 3, 1962; children: Laurence David, Andrew Paul, Michael Jonathan. BSc, U. Bristol, U.K., 1954, PhD, 1957, DSc, 1973. Design/devel. engr. GE Co., Birmingham, U.K., 1956-59; from lectr. to reader U. Birmingham, 1959-74; prof. elec. power engring. Loughborough (U.K.) U., 1974—, head dept. electronic and elec. engring., 1980-90, dean engring., 1983-86, pro-vice chancellor, 1987-91. Contbr. some 250 articles to profl. jours. Fellow Instn. of Elec. Engrs., Royal Acad. Engring. Avocations: walking, reading, gardening. Home: 83 Nanpantan Rd, Loughborough Leicestershire LE11 3ST, United Kingdom Office: Loughborough U, Dept Electronic & Elec Engring, Loughborough Leicestershire LE11 3TU, England

SMITH, JACK, artist; b. Sheffield, Eng., June 18, 1928; s. John Edward Smith; m. Susan Halkett, June 23, 1956. Hon. degree, Royal Coll. Art, London, 1953. One-man shows include Beaux Arts Gallery, London, 1952, 53, 54, 56, 58, Catherine Viviano Gallery, N.Y.C., 1958, 62, 63, Retrospective Whitechapel Gallery, London, 1959, Mattiesen Gallery, London, 1960, 68, Grosvenor Gallery, London, 1965, Marlborough Gallery, London, 1968, Gothenburg Mus., Sweden, 1968, Whitechapel Gallery, London, 1971, Redfern Gallery, London, 1974, 76, Serpentine Gallery, London, 1978, Fischer Fine Art, London, 1981, 83, Studio 5, 1988, Flowers East Gallery, London, 1990, 91, 92, 96, Brit. Abstract Art Flower East, 1994, Flowers East, 2000; represented in pub. and pvt. collections. Home: 29 Seafield Rd, Hove Sussex BN3 2TP, England

SMITH, JACK CARL, foreign trade consultant; b. Cleve., Sept. 11, 1928; s. John Carl and Florence Agnes (O'Rourke) S.; m. Nannette June Boyd, Dec. 1, 1962; 1 dau., Colleen Wentworth. Student, Baldwin Wallace Coll., 1948-51, postgrad., 1958; BA, Ohio U., 1954. Rep. Flying Tiger Line, Inc., Los Angeles, 1958-61; prin. Pub. Rep. bus., Cleve., 1961-64; pub. Penton Pub., Cleve., 1964-90; spl. advisor Am. Fgn. Policy Coun., Washington, 1990—; dir. Central Cleve. Corp., Nat. Distbn. Terminals; graduated Air Tng. Command Intelligence Officer Sch., served from 1958-62 AFR. Trustee Presdl. task force, Rep. Senatorial Inner Circle, Coun. of Logistics Mgmt., U.S. Bus. and Indsl. Coun. With USAF, 1954-58. Mem. Am. Mgmt. Assn., Material Handling Inst., Am. Trucking Assn., Nat. Council Phys. Distbn. Mgmt., Family Motor Coach Assn., Recreation Vehicle Industry Assn., Am. Bus. Press, Mag. Pubs. Assn., Sci. Research Soc., Internat. Platform Assn., Sigma Xi, Sigma Chi. Club: Wings (N.Y.C.). Home: 457 Devonshire Ct Bay Village OH 44140-3009 Office: Am Fgn Policy Coun 1521 16th St NW Washington DC 20036-1463

SMITH, JAMES BARRY, lawyer; b. N.Y.C., Feb. 28, 1947; s. Irving and Vera (Donaghy) S.; m. Kathleen O'Connor, May 28, 1977; childen: Jennifer, Kelly. BA in Econs., Colgate U., 1968; JD, Boston U., 1974. Assoc. McDermott, Will & Emery, Chgo., 1974-78; assoc. Ungaretti & Harris, Chgo., 1978-80, ptnr., 198OO, head real estate dept., 1988O. Lt. U.S. Navy, 1968-70. Mem. Chgo. Bar Assn., Chgo. Mortgage Atty. Assn. Avocations: sports, reading, travel. Office: Ungaretti & Harris 3500 Three First Nat Pla Chicago IL 60602

SMITH, JAMES EARL, astronautical engineer; b. Aurora, Colo., Jan. 10, 1973; s. James Raymond and Gaylene Joy (Green) S.; m. Kristine Cromar, May 31, 1997; 1 child: James Nathan. BS in Astronautical Engring., USAF Acad., 1997; SM in Aeronautics and Astronautics, MIT, 1999. Draper fellow Charles Stark Draper Lab., Cambridge, Mass., 1997-99; Spacecraft system analyst 2d Space Ops. Squadron, Schriever AFB, Colo., 1999—. 1st lt. USAF, 1997—. Mem. AIAA, Sigma Xi (assoc.), Tau Beta Pi (chpt. pres. 1996-97), Sigma Gamma Tau. Mem. LDS Ch. Avocations: computers, playing piano, family. Home: 7124 Bonnie Brae Ln Colorado Springs CO 80922-3141 Office: 2SOPS/DOAS 300 Omalley Ave Ste 41 Schriever AFB CO 80912-3001

SMITH, JAMES EDWARD, music educator, jazz guitarist; b. San Diego, Aug. 2, 1952; s. Jaems E. and Dorothy A. (Worden) S.; m. Gloria Curtis; children: Shelley, Bryan, Aaron, Rachel. BA, U. N.Mex., 1974; MM, Wis. Conservatory of Music, Milw., 1980. Assoc. prof. music Ctrl. State U., Wilberforce, Ohio, 1980—, chmn. dept. fine and performing arts, 2000—; adj. asst. prof. music Coll. Conservatory of Music, U. Cin., 1984—; chmn. Dept. Fine & Performing Arts Ctrl. State U., 1998—; pub. Jazz from The Conservatory Press, Bellbrook, Ohio, 1985—. Author: Jazz Guitar: Theory and Technique, 1981, Chord Thesaurus for Jazz Guitar, 1986, Guitarist's Guide to Technique, 1989; musician (CD) Cin. Seven, 1987. NEH grantee, 1984. Office: Central State U Dept Music Wilberforce OH 45384

SMITH, JAMES HERBERT, bank executive; b. Nassau, The Bahamas, Oct. 26, 1947; s. Bertram James and Rosalie Blanche (White) S.; m. Portia Marie Campbell, Oct. 13, 1973; children: Kimani, Jason, Nicola. Diploma, Ryerson Poly. Inst., Toronto, Ont., Can., 1970; BA, U. Windsor, Ont., 1972; MA, U. Alta., Edmonton, Can., 1977. Dep. permanent sec. Ministry Econ. Affairs Govt. of the Bahamas, Nassau, 1977-79, undersec. cabinet office, 1979-83, sec. for revenue Ministry of Fin., 1983-85, permanent sec. Ministry of Fin., 1985-86; gov. Ctrl. Bank of the Bahamas, Nassau, 1987-97; amb. for trade and investments Bahamas Govt., 1997—; dep. chmn. Bahamas Mortgage Corp., Nassau, 1990—; bd. dirs. Bahamasair Ltd., Nassau; chmn. Bahamas Bridge Authority, Nassau, 1988-97, Bahamas Maritime Authority, 1995—. Chair Paradise Island Bridge Authority, 1991—. Anglican. Avocations: reading, swimming, golf. Office: Bahamas Maritime Authority, Bahamas House 10 Chesterfield St, London WIX 8AH, England*

SMITH, JAMES RANDOLPH, JR., lawyer; b. Martinsville, Va., Mar. 7, 1945; s. James Randolph and Ruth (Boykin) S. BA, Randolph-Macon Coll., 1967; LLB, U. Va., 1970. Bar: Va. 1970, U.S. Dist. Ct. (we. dist.) Va. 1972, U.S. Supreme Ct. 1973, U.S. Ct. Appeals (4th cir.) 1976. Law clk. to judge U.S. Dist. Ct., Wilmington, Del., 1970-71; asst. commonwealth atty. City of Martinsville, 1971-81; ptnr. Smith & Penn, P.C., Martinsville, 1981-86; commonwealth atty. City of Martinsville, 1981-98; pvt. practice Martinsville, 1998-99; exec. sec. Va. Charitable Gaming Commn., Richmond, 1999-2000; dep. dir. Va. Dept. of Rail and Pub. Transp., Richmond, 2000—; instr. New River Criminal Justice Acad., 1980-97. Vice chmn. Martinsville Rep. Com., 1986-90, chmn., 1990-94; chmn. bd. dirs. Broad Street Christian Ch., 1996. Mem. Martinsville-Henry County Bar Assn. (v.p. 1983-84, pres. 1984-85), Am. Judicature Soc., Va. Assn. Commn. Attys. (bd. dirs. 1992-96, coun. 1996-97), Rotary (pres. 1993-94), Phi Delta Phi. Mem. Disciples of Christ Ch. Home: 817 Mulberry Rd Martinsville VA 24112-4414 Office: Va Dept Rail and Pub Transp 14th Fl 1401 E Broad St Fl 14 Richmond VA 23219-2052

SMITH, JAMES W., JR., state supreme court justice; b. Louisville, Miss., Oct. 28, 1943. BS, U. So. Miss., 1965; JD, Jackson Sch. Law, 1972; MEd with honors, Miss. Coll., 1973. Bar: Miss. 1972, U.S. Dist. Ct. (no. and so. dists.) Miss. 1973, U.S. Ct. Appeals (5th cir.) 1974. Pvt. practice Pearl, 1972-78, Brandon, 1979-80; prosecuting atty. City of Pearl, 1973-80; prosecutor Rankin County, 1976; dist. atty. 20th Jud. Dist., 1977-82; judge Rankin County, 1982-92; Supreme Ct. justice Cen. Dist., 1993—; instr. courtroom procedure and testifying Miss. Law Enforcement Tng. Acad., 1980-91. With U.S. Army, 1966-69. Named Wildlife Conservationist of Yr. Rankin County, 1988; recipient Outstanding Positive Role Model for Today's Youth award, 1991, Child Forever award Miss. Voices of Children and Youth, 1992, You've Made a Difference award, 1995, Alumnus of Yr. award Hinds C.C., 1996. Fellow Miss. Bar Found. (bd. dirs. 1998); mem. VFW, Miss. State Bar Assn., Rankin County Bar Assn., Nat. Wildlife Fedn., Nat. Wild Turkey Fedn., Ducks Unltd., Jackson Downtown Rotary Club. Office: Carroll Gartin Justice Bldg PO Box 117 Jackson MS 39205-0117

SMITH, JANE SCHNEBERGER, retired city administrator; b. Chgo., Aug. 9, 1928; d. Frank R. and Marion (Durante) Schneberger; m. Z. Erol Smith Jr., Oct. 28, 1950 (div. 1974); children: Suzan Mac Kenzie Smith, Tracy Smith Cawley, Cameron Farley, Z. Erol III, Kimberly Van Den Elzen, Scott. BA in Chemistry, U. Colo., 1950; MA in Comm., Mich. State U., 1978, PhD in Ednl. Adminstrn., 1987. Chemist Kellogg Switchboard, Chgo., 1950-51; v.p. South Cook County Girl Scouts, Harvey, Ill., 1967-69; staff advisor South Cook County Girl Scouts, 1970-72; tchr. Crab Orchard Sch., Palos Heights, Ill., 1969-70; program and tng. dir. Mich. Capitol. Coun. Girl Scouts, Lansing, Mich., 1972-75; dir. svc. learning ctr. Mich.

State U., East Lansing, 1975-81; city clk. City of Ashland, Wis., 1981-89; interim city adminstr. City of Ashland, 1989-90; ret., 1990; cons. vol. adminstrn., Mich., Wis., 1975—. Co-editor: Looking Backward Moving Forward; contbr. articles to profl. jours. V.p. Mich. Capitol Girl Scout Coun., Lansing, 1976-78; bd. dirs. Lansing RSVP, 1976-81, Ashland Mus., 1985-87, Ptnrs. in Recovery, 1985-87; v.p. Friends of the Libr., 1992-97, pres., 1997-99; sec. New Horizons, 1985-90, New Day Shelter, 1990-99, v.p., 1993-95, pres., 1995-97, sec., 1997-99; pres. LWV of Ashland Bayfield County, 1992-93, 96-98; sec. No. Wis. History Ctr., 1992-94; commr. Ashland Water and Wastewater Utility, 1993-96; mem. Ashland Beautification Com., 1993—, Big Top Chautauqua, 1996—, vice chair Alliance for Sustainability, 1994-99; v.p. GFWC/Ashland Monday Club, 1994-98, pres., 1998-2000; mem. Ashland County Human Svcs. Bd., 1998—. Recipient cert. appreciation Mich. Capitol Girl Scout Coun., 1975, Thanks Badge, 1972, Tribute to Excellence award LWV of Wis., 1999. Mem. Internat. Assn. Mcpl. Clks., Wis. Mcpl. Clks. Assn. (dist. dir. 1984-86), Am. Bus. Women's Assn. (scholarship chmn. 1985), Zonta (pres. 1979-81). Roman Catholic. Avocations: stained glass, gardening, stamp collecting, genealogy. Home: 700 Macarthur Ave Ashland WI 54806-2903

SMITH, JANET SUE, systems specialist; b. Chgo., Jan. 15, 1945; d. Curtis Edwin and Margaret Louise (Yost) Smith. B.A., Ind. U., 1967. Sales mgr. Marshall Field & Co., Chgo., 1968-70, programmer, 1970-72; sr. programmer, analyst Trailer Train Co., Chgo., 1972-75; mgr. data base and systems devel. Railinc-Assn. Am. R.R., Washington, 1975-85; asst. v.p., corp. sec. Railinc-Assn. Am. R.R., 1985-93, asst. v.p. strategic systems, 1994-98; exec. dir. Interline Svcs., 1998-99, asst. v.p. bus. svcs., 1999—. Nat. student v.p. YWCA, 1966-67; bd. dirs., v.p. planning and fin. Guide Internat.; advisor Jr. Achievement. Mem. Am. Council R.R. Women, Ind. U. Alumni Assn. (life), Women's Transp. Seminar. Home: 903 N Columbia St Chapel Hill NC 27516-1824 Office: 7001 Weston Pkwy Ste 200 Cary NC 27513-2125

SMITH, JARED RUSSELL WILLIAM, research executive; b. Cleve., Mar. 24, 1950; s. Russell Floyd William Smith and Mary Wiltrude Lee; m. Deborah Jane Parriott; children: Russell Jared Webster, Heather Frances. BA cum laude, NYU, 1973, MA, 1976. V.p. The Energy Bur., Inc., N.Y.C., 1976-86; assoc. dir. Inst. Gas Tech., Des Plaines, Ill., 1986-99; spl. appointee Argonee (Ill.) Nat. Lab., 1999—; adj. faculty NYU, N.Y.C., 1974-76; mem. adv. bd. La State U., Baton Rouge, 1999—; adviser to Pres.'s Commn. on Critical Infrastructure Protection, Washington, 1997—; bd. dirs., adviser N.Y. Quar. Literary Found., N.Y.C., 1986. Author: (poetry books) Song of the Blood, 1983, Dark Wing, 1986, Keeping the Outlaw Alive, 1988, Walking the Perimeter of the Plate Glass Window Factory, 2000; editor: (books) Integrating Microelectronics into Gas Distribution, 1987, Gas, Oil and Coal Biotechnology, 1990. Election dist. leader Dem. Party, White Plains, N.Y., 1972; chmn. nominating com. Sch. Dist. 181, Hinsdale, Ill., 1993. Mem. Chgo. Poets Club, Poets and Patrons, Ill. State Poetry Soc. Democrat. Avocations: literature, fishing, hiking, painting, music. E-mail: smithjrw@aol.com. Home: 409 N Vine St Hinsdale IL 60521-3321

SMITH, JEAN WEBB (MRS. WILLIAM FRENCH SMITH), civic worker; b. L.A.; d. James Ellwood and Violet (Hughes) Webb; B.A. summa cum laude, Stanford U., 1940; m. George William Vaughan, Mar. 14, 1942 (dec. Sept. 1963); children: George William, Merry; m. William French Smith, Nov. 6, 1964. Mem. Nat. Vol. Svc. Adv. Coun. (ACTION), 1973-76, vice chmn., 1974-76; dir. Beneficial Standard Corp., 1976-85. bd. dirs. Cmty. TV So. Calif., 1979-93; mem. Calif. Arts Commn., 1971-74, vice chmn., 1973-74; bd. dirs. The Founders, Music Ctr., L.A., 1971-74; bd. dirs. costume coun. L.A. County Mus. Art, 1971-73; bd. dirs. United Way, Inc., 1973-80, Hosp. Good Samaritan, 1973-80, L.A. chpt. NCCJ, 1977-80, Nat. Symphony Orch., 1980-85, L.A. World Affairs Coun., 1990, L.A. chpt. ARC, 1994-95; bd. fellows Claremont Univ. Ctr. and Grad. Sch., 1987—; bd. dirs. Hosp. Good Samaritan, 1973-80; mem. exec. com., 1975-80; mem. nat. bd. dirs. Boys' Clubs Am., 1977-80; mem. adv. bd. Salvation Army, 1979—; bd. overseers The Hoover Instn. on War, Revolution and Peace, 1989-94; mem. President's Commn. on White House Fellowships, 1980-90, Nat. Coun. on the Humanities, 1987-90; bd. govs. Calif. Cmty. Found., 1990—; bd. regents Children's Hosp. L.A., 1993—. Named Woman of Yr. for cmty. svc. L.A. Times, 1958; recipient Citizens of Yr. award Boys Clubs Greater L.A., 1982, Life Achievement award Boy Scouts Am., L.A. coun., 1985. Mem. Jr. League of L.A. (pres. 1954-55, Spirit of Volunteerism award 1996). Assn. Jr. Leagues of Am. (dir. Region XII, 1956-58, pres. 1958-60), Phi Beta Kappa, Kappa Kappa Gamma. Home: 11718 Wetherby Ln Los Angeles CA 90077-1348

SMITH, JEFFREY MICHAEL, lawyer; b. Mpls., July 9, 1947; s. Philip and Gertrude E. (Miller) S.; 1 son, Brandon Michael. Student, U. Malaya, 1967-68; BA cum laude, U. Minn., 1970, JD magna cum laude, 1973. Bar: Ga. 1973. Assoc. Powell, Goldstein, Frazier & Murphy, 1973-76; ptnr. Rogers & Hardin, 1976-79, Bondurant, Stephenson & Smith, 1979-85, Arnall, Golden & Gregory, 1985-92, Katz, Smith & Cohen, 1992-98; shareholder Greenberg Traurig, 1998—; vis. lectr. Duke U., 1976-77, 79-80, 89-93; adj. prof. Emory U., 1976-79, 81-82; lectr. Vanderbilt U., 1977-82. Co-author: Preventing Legal Malpractice, 1999, Legal Malpractice, 1999. Bd. visitors Law Sch. U. Minn., 1976-82. Mem. ABA (vice-chmn. com. profl. liability 1980-82, mem. standing com. lawyer's profl. liability 1981-85, chmn. 1985-87, standing com. lawyer competency 1993-95), State Bar Ga. (chmn. profl. liability and ins. com. 1978-89, trustee Inst. Cont. Legal Edn. in Ga. 1979-80), Order of the Coif, Phi Beta Kappa. Home: 145 15th St NE Apt 811 Atlanta GA 30309-3559 Office: Greenberg Traurig Ivy Place 2d Fl 3423 Piedmont Rd NE Atlanta GA 30305-1754

SMITH, JEFFRY ALAN, health administrator, physician, consultant; b. L.A., Dec. 8, 1943; s. Stanley W. and Marjorie E. S.; m. Jo Anne Hague. BA in Philosophy, UCLA, 1967, MPH, 1972; BA in Biology, Calif. State U., Northridge, 1971; MD, UACJ, 1977. Diplomate Am. Bd. Family Practice. Resident in family practice WAH, Takoma Park, Md., NIH, Bethesda, Md., Walter Reed Army Hosp., Washington, Children's Hosp. Nat. Med. Ctr., Washington, 1977-80; occupational physician Nev. Test Site, U.S. Dept. Energy, Las Vegas, 1981-82; dir. occupational medicine and environ. health Pacific Missile Test Ctr., Point Mugu, Calif., 1982-84; dist. health officer State Hawaii Dept. Health, Kauai, 1984-86; asst. dir. health County of Riverside (Calif.) Dept. Health, 1986-87; regional med. dir. Calif. Forensic Med. Group, Monterey, Calif., 1987-94; med. dir. Cmty. Human Svcs., Monterey, Calif., 1987-94, Colstrip (Mont.) Med. Ctr., 1994-97; cons. San Bernadino County, Riverside County, Riverside, Calif., 1998—; regional med. dir. Point Loma Healthcare Med. Group, Inc., San Diego, 1997-99; med. dir., CEO So. Calif. Mobile Physician Svcs., Riverside, Calif., 1997—. Fellow Am. Acad. Family Physicians; mem. AMA, Am. Occupational Medicine Assn., Flying Physicians, Am. Pub. Health Assn. Avocations: pvt. pilot. Office: Ste 71-448 5225 Canyon Crest Dr Riverside CA 92507-6301

SMITH, JERRY LEON, lawyer; b. Tulsa, Oct. 18, 1938; s. William Ernest and Von Ceil S.; m. Ann Clay, June 17, 1961; children: Grant, Reed. BA, U. Okla., 1960; LLB, Cornell U., 1963. Assoc. White & Case, N.Y.C., Brussels, 1964-71; from assoc. to ptnr. Fried, Frank, Harris et al, N.Y.C., London, 1971-99, ret., of counsel, 1999—. Fulbright scholar, U. Aix-en-Provence-Marseilles, France, 1963-64. Mem. ABA, Assn. Bar City of N.Y. Avocations: literature, theater, music, visual arts, food and wine. Office: Fried Frank et al, 4 Chiswell St, London EC1 4UP, England

SMITH, JERRY WAYNE, pediatric dentist; b. Atlanta, Tex., Nov. 17, 1936; s. Auren Marion and Alma Pearl (Christian) S.; m. Lila Louis Hall, Aug. 22, 1959; children: Leigh Ainsley, Ashley Lynn. BS, Stephen F. Austin Coll., 1958; MS, U. Tex., 1961; DDS, Baylor U., 1966, MS in Dentistry, 1968. Sci. tchr. Texas City (Tex.) High Sch., 1958-59; rsch. assoc. Southwestern Med. Sch., Dallas, 1961-62; pvt. practice Tulsa, 1968—; sr. staff St. Francis Hosp., Tulsa, 1978—. Bd. mem. Okla. Health Systems Agy., Tulsa, 1974-79; mem. exec. com., bd. Delta Dental Plans of Okla., Oklahoma City, 1980-87; youth soccer coach Green County Soccer Assn., Tulsa, 1978-83. Mem. ADA, Okla. Dental Assn. (del. 1979-90, Pres. award 1986, Dentist of the Yr. 1988, Oustanding Clinic award 1971, 84), Tulsa County Dental Soc. (mem. exec. com., Rush award 1970, McBride award 1983)), S.W. Soc. Pediatric Dentists (treas. v.p. 1988-91), Paul P. Taylor Pediatric Soc. (pres. 1977), Am. Acad. Pediatric Dentistry. Republican. Presbyterian. Avocations: tennis, running, soccer. Home: 4011 E 76th St Tulsa OK 74136-8022 Office: 6565 S Yale Ave Ste 401 Tulsa OK 74136-8305

SMITH, JO ANN COSTA, comptroller; b. Houston, Dec. 19, 1937; d. Joseph Anthony and Anna Lois (Grice) Costa; m. Alton Paul Smith, Mar. 3, 1957; children: Robert Carlton, Rex Alan. Grad. high sch., Navasota, Tex. Bookkeeper Our Lady of Victory Ch., Paris, Tex., 1968-69; asst. office mgr. Ayres Dept. Store, Paris, 1969-71; cashier, clk. Mid South Electric Co-op, Navasota, 1971-77; owner, mgr. The Gift Shop, Navasota, 1977-97; v.p., comptroller Smith Bros. Impl. Co. Inc., Navasota, Tex., 1998—. Pack mother Cub Scouts, Paris, 1965-67; v.p. Grimes County United Way, 1988-89, pres., 1989-90, bd. dirs., 1987—. Mem. Grimes County C. of C. (2d v.p. 1986, pres. 1987-88), Ciara Study Club (pres. 1969-70), Brazos Valley Bus. and Profl. Womens Club (charter, chmn. pub. rels. com. 1989-90). Democrat. Roman Catholic. Home: PO Box 70 Navasota TX 77868-0070 Office: Smith Bros Impl Co Inc PO Box 112 Navasota TX 77868-0112

SMITH, JOHN ARTHUR, biochemist, lecturer; b. Bath, Eng., Oct. 3, 1948; s. Arthur Thomas and Doris (Collins) S.; m. Margaret Elizabeth Tansey, July 24, 1971; children: Andrew, Miriam, Thomas. BA in Biochemistry, U. Oxford, Eng., 1971, DPhil, 1974. Rsch. asst. dept. agrl. sci. U. Oxford, 1974-78; group leader Union Internat. Rsch. Centre, St. Albans, Eng., 1978-79; non-clin. scientist Ludwig Inst. for Cancer Rsch., Sutton, Eng., 1979-86; lectr. dept. biochemistry U. Liverpool, Eng., 1987—; vis. prof. PGIMER, Chandigarh, India, 1985; UNESCO lectr. Dhaka (Bangladesh) U., 1991; chmn. Pepsyn Ltd., 1996. Contbr. articles to profl. jours. Mem. Biochem. Soc. Baptist. Office: U Liverpool Dept Biochemistry, PO Box 147, Liverpool L69 7ZB, England

SMITH, JOHN FRANCIS, JR., automobile company executive; b. Worcester, Mass., Apr. 6, 1938; s. John Francis and Eleanor C. (Sullivan) S.; children: Brian, Kevin; m. Lydia G. Sigrist, Aug. 27, 1988; 1 stepchild, Nicola. B.B.A., U. Mass., 1960; M.B.A., Boston U., 1965. Fisher Body div. mgr. Gen. Motors Corp., Framingham, Mass., 1961-73; asst. treas Gen. Motors Corp., N.Y.C., 1973-80; comptroller Gen. Motors Corp., Detroit, 1980-81, dir. worldwide product planning, 1981-84; pres., gen. mgr. Gen. Motors Can., Oshawa, Ont., Can., 1984-85; exec. v.p. Gen. Motors Europe, Glattbrugg, Switzerland, 1986-87, pres., 1987-88; exec. v.p. internat. ops. Gen. Motors Corp., Detroit, 1988-90; vice chmn. internat. ops. Gen. Motors Corp., 1990, bd. dirs., mem. fin. com., 1990—, pres., COO, 1992—; CEO, pres., 1992—; chmn. bd., CEO, pres. Gen. Motors Corp., Detroit, 1996-98; chmn. bd., CEO Gen Motors Corp., Detroit, 1998-2000; chmn bd General Motors Corp., Detroit, 1996—; pres.'s coun. Global Strategy Bd.; bd. dirs. EDS, Hughes Electronics Corp., Gen. Motors Acceptance Corp.; mem. Bus. Roundtable Policy Com.; mem. U.S. Japan Bus. Coun., Am. Soc. Corp. Execs.; mem. Bd. of Detroit Renaissance; bus. coun. Meml. Sloan-Kettering Cancer Ctr.; bd. dirs. Procter & Gamble Co. Mem. chancellor's exec. com. U. Mass., dir.; trustee United Way S.E. Mich., New Am. Revolution, Boston U. Mem. Am. Soc. Corp. Execs., Am. Auto Mfrs. Assn. (bd. dirs.), Econ. Club Detroit (bd. dirs.), Beta Gamma Sigma (pres.), Dirs. Table. Roman Catholic. Office: GM 100 Renaissance Ctr Detroit MI 48265-0001 also: Globe Hdqs at Renaissance PO Box 100 100 Renaissance Ctr Detroit MI 48243-1001

SMITH, JOHN KERWIN, lawyer; b. Oct. 18, 1926; 1 child, Cynthia. BA, Stanford U.; LLB, Hastings Coll. Law. Ptnr. Haley, Purchio, Sakai & Smith, Hayward, Calif.; bd. dirs. Berkeley Asphalt, Mission Valley Ready-Mix, Coliseum Found., Mission Valley Rock, Rowell Ranch Rodeo, Hastings Coll. Law (alumnus of yr. award 1989). Gen. ptnr. Oak Hills Apts., City Ctr. Commercial, Creekwood I and II Apts.; Road Parks commn. 1957; city coun. 1959-66, mayor 1966-70; chmn. Alameda County Mayors conf. 1968, revenue taxation com. League Calif. Cities, 1968; vice chmn. Oakland-Alameda County Coliseum; vol. Hastings 1066 Found. (pres., vol. svc. award 1990), Martin Kauffman 100 Club; bd. dirs. Hastings Coll. of Law, 1999—. Mem. ABA, Calif. Bar Assn., Alameda County Bar Assn., Am. Judicature Soc., Rotary. Office: Haley Purchio Sakai & Smith 22320 Foothill Blvd Ste 620 Hayward CA 94541-2700

SMITH, JOHN LEROY, mathematics educator; b. Cooper, Tex., July 15, 1944; s. John Jr. and Annie (West) S.; m. Barbara Ann Frazier, Dec. 27, 1965 (div. Apr. 1972); m. Mary Anne Anthony, June 17, 1978; children: Alexander Anthony, Annastasia Marie, Jeannette Joy. BS in Math., U. Wash., 1966; MA in Math., San Diego State U., 1971; BS in Info. & Computer Sci., U. Calif., Irvine, 1986. Computer operator U. Wash., Seattle, 1964-66; tchr. math., sci., English, 1966-70; tchr. math., sci. Highline, Wash., 1971-73; tchr. math. & computer scis. Kwajalein (Marshall Islands) Jr./Sr. H.S., 1973-75; instr. scuba diving Santa Ana (Calif.) Coll., 1978-91; prof. math., computer sci. Rancho Santiago C.C. Dist., Santa Ana, 1975—; math dept. chair Santiago Canyon Coll., Orange, Calif., 1998—; mem. adv. bd. govs. Faculty Assn. Calif. C.C., Sacramento, 1991-99; treas. Faculty Assn. Rancho Santiago C.C., 1988—; v.p. Santiago Canyon Coll. Acad. Senate, 1999—. Editor (newsletter) FARSIGHT, 1989—; editor Dive Boat Calender, 1987-91. Choir mem. St. Paul's Greek Orthodox Ch., Irvine, 1993—, mem. parish coun., 1987-89, 99—; asst. scoutmaster Boy Scouts Am., Irvine, 1994—. Mem. NEA, Nat. Assn. Underwater Instrs., Nat. Coun. Tchrs. Math., Am. Math Assn. Two Yr. Colls., Profl. Assn. Diving Instrs. Avocations: scuba diving, camping, hiking, running. Home: 1 Caraway Irvine CA 92604-3217 Office: Santiago Canyon Coll Orange CA 92869

SMITH, JOHN RICHARD, analytical chemist; b. Balt., Jan. 26, 1954; s. William Wallace Smith and Barbara Ann Larson; m. Rosalie Elizabeth Parker, Aug. 1, 1987; children: Jeremy Richard, Emily Elizabeth. BA in Biology, U. Md., 1977. Lab. scientist Md. Inst. Emergency Medicine, Balt., 1980-83; analytical chemist U.S. Army Med. Rsch. Inst. Chem. Def., Aberdeen Proving Ground, Md., 1984—. Contbr. articles to sci. jours. Mem. Arbutus (Md.) Edn. Enrichment Com., 1997—. Mem. Am. Soc. for Mass Spectrometry, Md. Geol. Soc., Sigma Xi. (Chesapeake chpt., pres. 1999-00, Edn. award 1998). Avocation: paleontology. E-mail: john.smith@amedd.army.mil. Home: 1253 Brewster St Arbutus MD 21227-2719 Office: US Army Med Rsch Inst Chem Def 3100 Ricketts Point Rd Aberdeen Proving Ground MD 21010-5400

SMITH, JOHN W(ESLEY), JR., data processing executive, consultant; b. Bklyn., Jan. 6, 1946; s. John Wesley and Eunice (Davis) S.; m. Carolyn Ferrebbee, Aug. 19, 1971 (div. 1980); children: John Wesley III, Janine Carol. Student, NYU, 1989—. Computer ops. supr. Shearson Lehman Stone, Inc., N.Y.C., 1967-70; sr. ops. analyst Fin. Data Svcs., Inc., N.Y.C., 1970-77; tng. program coord. Chem. Bank, N.Y.C., 1977-78; sr. hardware analyst ADP, Clifton, N.J., 1978-79; data base adminstr. Depository Trust Co., N.Y.C., 1979-81; mgr. data ctr. ops. Leviton Mfg. Co., Littleneck, N.Y., 1981-83; dir. corp. info. svcs. Reed Robers Assocs., Inc., Uniondale, N.Y., 1983-86; dir. prodn. planning and control Human Resource Adminstrn., N.Y.C., 1986-87; mgmt. cons. Asbach/Sci., Inc., N.Y.C., 1987—. Mem. Data Processing Mgmt. Assn., Am. Soc. Notaries, Am. Mgmt. Assn., Am. Arbitration Assn. (comml. panel 1983—), Inst. Certification Computer Profls. (cert systems profl.). Office: Smith Wesley Assocs Inc 1072 Barbey St Brooklyn NY 11207-9202

SMITH, JOSEPH COLIN, urological surgeon; b. Lancaster, Eng., Feb. 9, 1931; s. Francis Brian and Kathleen Mary S.; m. Mafalda Anna Cavalieri, Oct. 5, 1957; children: Alexandra, Christopher, Gabriella. MB BS, U. London, 1954, MS, 1966; MA, Oxford U., 1988. Resident surg. officer St. Peter's Hosp., London, 1963; chief asst. St. Bartholomew's Hosp., London, 1964; resident, dept. urology UCLA, 1965; cons. Oxford Health Authority, Eng., 1966-96. Named prof. urology honoris cause, U. Pernambulo, Brazil, 1989; named to Order Brit. Empire, 1996. Fellow Royal Coll. Surgeons Eng.; mem. Royal Soc. Medicine (pres. urology sect. 1987), Brit. Assn. Urol. Surgeons (pres. 1992-94), Med. Def. Union (pres., chmn. bd. dirs.). Avocations: farming, tennis. Home: East End Farm, North Leigh OX8 6PX, England Office: 23 Banbury Rd, Oxford OX8 6PX, England

SMITH, JOSEPH PHELAN, film company executive; b. N.Y.C., 1911; s. John William and Margaret Mary (Phelan) S.; m. Madelyn Eleanor Davis, Jan. 17, 1942; children: Kevin, Karen, Margaret, Lisa. BS, Columbia U. Former salesman Van Alstyne Noel & Co., N.Y.C.; former salesman RKO Radio Pictures, Inc., Boston, Omaha, div. mgr., Los Angeles, Portland, Oreg., San Francisco, 1938-47; former exec. v.p. Lippert Prodns., Hollywood, Calif.; former v.p., gen. mgr. sales Telepictures, N.Y.C.; founding pres. Cinema Vue Corp.; now chmn. Pathe News Inc., N.Y.C., 1995—, Pathe Pictures Inc., N.Y.C., 1995—. Served with U.S. Army. Mem. Motion Picture Pioneers, Am. Film Inst., Elks. Republican. Office: Pathe News Inc 630 9th Ave Ste 305 New York NY 10036-3708

SMITH, JOSEPH PHILIP, lawyer; b. Jackson, Tenn., June 14, 1944; s. William Benjamin and Virginia Marie (Carey) S.; m. Deborah J. Smith, Dec. 22, 1972; 1 child, Virginia Louise. BA, U. Miss., 1967, JD, 1975; MEd, U. So. Miss., 1977; EdD, U. Memphis, 1998. Bar: Miss. 1975, Tex. 1979, Tenn. 1995, U.S. Dist. Ct. (no. dist.) Miss. 1975, U.S. Dist. Ct. (no. dist.) Tex. 1982, N.Mex. 1991, Colo. 1991, U.S. Dist. Ct. N.Mex. 1993, U.S. Dist. Ct. Colo. 1993, U.S. Ct. Appeals (10th cir.) 1993. Tchr. math. Marks (Miss.) Jr. H.S., 1971-73; tchr., then asst. prin. Biloxi (Miss.) City Schs., 1975-78; oil and gas landman Modling & Assocs., 1978-79; assoc., then ptnr. Byrnes, Myers, Adair, Campbell & Sinex, Houston, 1979-85; farmer Quitman County, Miss., 1988-90; pvt. practice Marks, Miss., Memphis, Raton, N.Mex., 1985—. Mem. Archdiocese of Santa Fe Sch. Bd., 1991-92. Capt. USAF, 1967-71. Mem. ABA, Tenn. Bar Assn., Memphis Bar Assn., Miss. Pub. Defender Assn. (treas. 1988-90), Rotary (pres., sec. Marks club 1985-90, mem. Raton club 1990-91). Republican. Roman Catholic. Home: 674 Saint Augustine Sq Memphis TN 38104-5054

SMITH, JULIA A., internist, oncologist, educator; b. N.Y.C., July 18, 1951; d. Carl A. and Ruth G. Smith; children: Matthew Smith Ryan, Rachel Smith Ryan. BA, NYU, 1974, MS in Cell Biology, 1979, PhD in Cell Biology, MD, 1980. Bd. cert. in oncology and hematology Am. Bd. Internal Medicine; lic. physician, N.Y., Mass. Intern, resident dept. internal medicine Peter Bent Brigham Hosp., Boston, 1980-83; fellow divsn. hematology-oncology dept. internal medicine Meml. Hosp. Sloan-Kettering Cancer Ctr., N.Y.C., 1983-86; postdoctoral fellow molecular genetics Rockefeller U., N.Y.C., 1984-86; rsch. fellow Sloan-Kettering Inst. for Cancer Rsch., N.Y.C., 1984-86; clin. fellow dept. internal medicine Harvard U. Med. Sch., 1980-83; acting fellow blood banking N.Y. Blood Ctr., N.Y.C., 1983; clin. fellow dept. internal medicine N.Y. Hosp.-Cornell Med. Ctr., 1983-86; asst. attending Bellevue Hosp. Ctr., 1986—; asst. prof. medicine NYU Med. Ctr., 1986-88, clin. asst. prof. medicine, 1988—; pvt. practice, 1986-95, 98—; acting fellow blood banking N.Y. Blood Ctr., N.Y.C., 1983; clin. fellow dept. internal medicine Harvard U. Med. Sch., 1980-83. Contbr. articles to profl. jours. Mem. med. adv. bd. Laurie Straus Leukemia Found., Avon Breast Cancer Rsch. Grants. Recipient Citation for outstanding acad. achievement Am. Med. Women's Assn.; Am. Cancer Soc. clin. rsch. fellow, NIH Med. Scientist Tng. Program fellow. Mem. Alpha Omega Alpha. Home: 141 E 88th St Apt 8D New York NY 10128-2248 Office: NYU Med Ctr Faculty Practice Office 530 1st Ave Ste 4G New York NY 10016-6402

SMITH, KARLA SALGE JORDAN, early childhood education educator; b. Berlin, July 4, 1943; came to U.S. 1965; d. Hubert Ernst Richard and Irmgard Klara (Alter) Salge; m. William Jackson Jordan, May 28, 1963 (div. 1980); 1 child, Michael Bond; m. Linwood Talmadge Smith, Nov. 17, 1990. BA, Berlin Tchrs. Coll., 1964, Meth. Coll., Fayetteville, N.C., 1974; MA, Fayetteville State U., 1986. Cert. tchr., N.C., ednl. supr., 1995. Tchr. Eastover Elem. Sch., Fayetteville, 1974-75, Montclair Elem. Sch., Fayetteville, 1975—; workshop presenter Cumberland County Sch., Fayetteville, spring 1983,, 1992-95; mem. bldg. leadership team Montclair Elem. Sch., 1992-93, chairperson, 1994-95, grade chairperson, 1980-90,1999—, sch. improvement team chairperson 1995-98. Treas. Montclair PTA, 1987-88, sec., 1988-90, pres. 1985, 86; youth choir dir. Eureka Bapt. Ch., Fayetteville, 1990—, adult choir dir., 1995—; mem., bible study leader for German fellowship Walstone Bapt. Ch., Fayetteville, coord., 1999. Fayetteville Jr. League mini grantee, 1991; named Tchr. of the Yr. Montclair Elem. Sch., 1987-88; recipient Fayetteville Tchr. of the Week Jr. League and the Huntington Learning Ctr., 1997. Mem. ASCD, Cross Creek Reading Coun. (rec. sec. 1990), Fayetteville Assn. for Edn. of Young Children, N.C. Assn. of Edn. (bldg. rep. 1981-83). Republican. Baptist. Avocations: sewing, crafts, gardening, travel, reading. Home: 845 Mary Jordan Ln Fayetteville NC 28311-7075 Office: Montclair Elem Sch 555 Glensford Dr Fayetteville NC 28314-2326

SMITH, KATHLEEN TENER, bank executive; b. Pitts., Oct. 19, 1943; d. Edward Harrison Jr. and Barbara Elizabeth (McCormick) Tener; m. Roger Davis Smith, May 30, 1970 (dec.); children: Silas Wheelock, Jocelyn Tener, Luke Ewing Taft. BA summa cum laude, Vassar Coll., 1965; MA in Econs., Harvard U., 1968. Rsch. assoc. Harvard U. Grad. Sch. Bus., Cambridge, Mass., 1967-69; assoc. economist Chase Manhattan Bank, N.Y.C., 1969-70, asst. treas., 1971, 2d v.p., 1972, v.p., 1973—, sec. asset liability mgmt. com., 1985-90, treas. Global Bank, 1990-91, divsn. exec. structured investment products, 1991-93, global mktg. and comms. exec. Global Risk Mgmt. Sect., 1993-94, global mktg. and comms. product devel. exec., 1994-96, global asset mgmt. and pvt. bank mktg., 1996-98; network ptnr. The Sullivan Group, Salomon Smith Barney, 1999—. Editor: Commodity Derivatives and Finance, 1996. Trustee Vassar Coll., Poughkeepsie, N.Y., 1979-91, mem. exec. com., 1987-91, class pres. 2000—; mem. subcom. on edn. Chase Manhattan Found., N.Y.C., 1985-90; trustee Huguenot Hist. Soc. New Paltz, 1999—, chair fin. com., 1999—; trustee Eleanor Roosevelt Ctr. Val-Kill, 2000—; mem. working com. Huguenot Heritage, 1999—. NSF fellow, 1965-67. Mem. AAAS, N.Y. Acad. Sci., Am. Fin. Assn., Nat. Assn. Corp. Dirs. (steering com. Met. N.Y.), Yale Club, Phi Beta Kappa. Republican. Episcopalian. Home: PO Box 129 New Paltz NY 12561-0129

SMITH, KATIE, basketball player; b. June 4, 1974. Grad., Ohio State U., 1996. With Columbus Quest, 1996—. Recipient Gold medal Jones Cup, 1996; Jr. World Championship, 1993, Kodak All-American, 1993, 96. Avocations: music, being outside, being with friends. Office: Columbus Quest 230 California St Ste 510 San Francisco CA 94111-4331

SMITH, KENNETH GEORGE VALENTINE, retired entomologist, magazine editor; b. Birmingham, Eng., Mar. 11, 1929; s. Robert George Valentine and Eva Doris (Richards) S.; m. Alma Vera Thompson, Sept. 22, 1956; children: Julian Mark Edwin, Adrian Paul Lindsay. Student, U. Acton, Birmingham, 1944-48, U. Keele, Newcastle-under-Lyme, Eng., 1952-54. Chartered biologist. Field asst. Nat. Agrl. Adv. Svc., Ministry Agr., Wolverhampton, Eng., 1950-52; sr. technician Hope dept. entomology Oxford (Eng.) U., 1954-62; prin. sci. officer, head med. insects sect. Brit. Mus. (Natural History), London, 1962-89; ret., 1989; editor-in-chief Entomologist's Monthly Mag., Wallingford, Eng., 1982—; frequent broadcaster on Living World, also other programs natural history unit BBC, Bristol, Eng., 1977-81, also occasionally, 1981—; prin. investigator identification of insects in med. rsch. WHO, 1979-81. Author: (with Vera Smith) Bibliography of the Entomology of the Smaller British Offshore Islands, 1983; A Manual of Forensic Entomology, 1986, An Introduction to the Immature Stages of British Flies, 1989; editor, co-author: Insects and Other Arthropods of Medical Importance, 1976; mem. editl. bd. Entomologist's Gazette, 1969—; contbr. over 300 articles to sci. jours. Fellow Royal Entomol. Soc. (editl. officer 1969-73, libr. com. 1987--96, del. to European Assn. Biol. Editors 1969-73), Linnean Soc., Inst. Biology; mem. Ray Soc. (councillor 1984—, v.p. 1992-95, 97-99). Anglican. Avocations: book collecting, Darwiniana, opera, history of science, natural history. Home: 70 Hollickwood Ave, London N12 0LT, England Office: Entomologist's Monthly Mag, Bell Ln, Brightwell, Wallingford OX10 0QD, England

SMITH, KERRY CLARK, lawyer; b. Phoenix, July 12, 1935; s. Clark and Fay (Jackson) S.; m. Michael Waterman, 1958; children: Kevin, Ian. AB, Stanford U., 1957, JD, 1962. Bar: Calif. 1963, U.S. Supreme Ct. 1980. Assoc. Chickering & Gregory, San Francisco, 1962-70, ptnr., 1970-81; ptnr. Pettit & Martin, San Francisco, 1981-95, Hovis, Smith, San Francisco, 1995-99; pvt. practice San Francisco, 1999—. Mem. editl. bd. Stanford Law Rev., 1961-62. Lt. USN, 1957-60. Mem. ABA (bus. law sect.), Calif. Bar Assn., San Francisco Bar Assn., Orinda Country Club, Palms Golf Club, La Quinta Citrus Golf Club, San Francisco World Trade Club. Office: Smith Law Offices 601 California St Ste 1600 San Francisco CA 94108-2821

SMITH, LAWRENCE BARRETT, IV, art gallery director, curator; b. Cleve., Aug. 29, 1952; s. Lawrence Barrett III and Mary Andrew (Prinios)

S. BA, Baldwin Wallace Coll., 1974. Program dir. Nat. Pub. Radio, Cleve., 1974-77; producer, dir. CitiCorp Ctr.-Treatre at Noon, N.Y.C., 1977-81; dir., curator La Ma Ma La Galleria, N.Y.C., 1981-97, also trustee; owner, curator Marlen Galleries, Ltd., N.Y.C., 1998—; curator poetry and fiction Fordham U., N.Y.C., 1991; producer N.Y. Meets Cleve., Cleve. Performance Arts Festival, 1990, Monday Nights Comedy Series Levitt Pavillion, Westport, Conn., 1988; curator Ken Burgess-A Retrospective, Springfield (Mass.) Coll. Gallery, 1989; cons. grant com. Merrill G. Emita E. Hastings Found., 1987-89. Producer, creator radio series Portraits of Eve, 1978 (Twyla M. Conway Radio/TV Excellence award). Mem. community bd. N.Y.C. Div. Neighborhood Improvement. Grantee Hastings Found., 1988. Mem. SAG, Rhythm Club (acting curator 1997-98), Theta Alpha Phi (life). Democrat. Avocations: theatre, language, jewelry design. Home: 3226 54th St Woodside NY 11377-1928 Office: Marlen Gallery 674 9th Ave New York NY 10036-3602

SMITH, LINCOLN CAIN, banking executive; b. Taree, NSW, Australia, Oct. 8, 1971; s. Raby James and Kathleen May (Worth) S.; m. Helen Grace Richardson, Oct. 12, 1996. Comml. analyst for lenders, Commonwealth Bank Sydney, 1996. Cert. Australian Banking. Corp. banking liaison Commonwealth Bank Australia, Sydney, 1989-90, customer assistance profl., 1990-92, customer svc. mgr., 1992-93, relieving br. mgr., 1993-94, mgr. personal lending, 1994-97, relationship mgr. mascot region, 1997-99, br. mgr. Beaconsfield br., 1999—, mgr. sales and svc., 1999—; mgr. exec. relationship banking Oantas Office Ste., 2000—. Songwriter, performer (bands) Necrophilia, 1990-95, Boxy Smith, 1995—. Mem. Australian Inst. Bankers. Home: PO Box 917, Maroubra NSW 2035, Australia

SMITH, LINDA ZIMBALIST, investment research executive; b. St. Louis, Jan. 27, 1953; d. Sidney Eli and Blanka M. (Wassermann) Zimbalist; m. William Martin Smith, May 27, 1979; children: Brian Alexander, Tyler Scott. BA, Pitzer Coll., Claremont, Calif., 1975; MBA, U. Chgo., 1978. Research asst. Stein Roe & Farnham, Chgo., 1975-76, Chgo. Bd. Options Exchange, 1976-79; arbitrage analyst First Boston, N.Y.C., 1980-82; gen. ptnr. Zimbalist Smith Investments, Bend, Oreg., 1982—. Avocation: tennis. Office: Zimbalist Smith 2955 N Highway 97 Bend OR 97701-7509

SMITH, LOUISE ELLEN, editor-in-chief, publisher; b. Bromley, U.K., Dec. 28, 1964; d. Ronald Edward and Margaret Anne (Maguire) Smith; m. Matthew Salmon, May 5, 2000. BA in Media Studies with honors, U. Westminster, 1986. Dep. editor Cable and Satellite Yearbook, London, 1986-87, editor, 1987-89; reporter Cable and Satellite Mag., London, 1986-87; reporter Satellite TV Europe Mag., London, 1987-89, editor, 1987-93, editor-in-chief, pub., 1993—; mng. editor Satellite and Video mag., London, 1993-94; editor-in-chief Home Cinema Mag., London, 1994—; dir. Millennium Consumer Mags. (formerly 21st Century Pub.), London, 1991—. Avocation: cinema. Office: Satellite TV Europe, 531-533 Kings Rd, London SW10 0TZ, England

SMITH, DAME MAGGIE, actress; b. Ilford, Eng., Dec. 28, 1934; d. Nathaniel and Margaret (Hutton) S.; m. Robert Stephens, 1967 (div. 1974); m. Beverley Cross, 1974. Grad., Oxford High Sch. Girls; D.Litt. (hon.), St. Andrews, 1971; DLitt (hon.), Oxford U., 1994. dir. United British Artists, 1982—. Stage and film actress, 1952—; stage appearances include: New Faces, debut N.Y.C., 1956, Share My Lettuce, 1957, The Stepmother, 1958, Rhinoceros, 1960, Strip the Willow, 1960, The Rehearsal, 1961, The Private Ear and the Public Eye, 1962, Mary, Mary, 1961; appearances at Old Vic, 1959-60, Nat. Theatre, London, 1963—; productions at Nat. Theatre include Private Lives, 1972, Othello, Hay Fever, Master Builder, Hedda Gabbler, Much Ado About Nothing, Miss Julie, Black Comedy, Stratford Festival, Ont., Can., 1976, 77, 78, 80, Antony and Cleopatra, Macbeth, Three Sisters, Richard III, Night and Day, London and N.Y.C., 1979-80, Virginia, London, 1981, Way of the World, Chichester Festival, London, 1984-85, Interpreters, London, 1985-86, Lettice and Lovage, 1988, also in N.Y., 1990, The Importance of Being Earnest, 1993, Three Tall Women, 1994, 95, Talking Heads, 1996, 97, A Delicate Balance, 1997, 98, Curtain Call, 1998; films include Othello, 1966, The Honey Pot, 1967, Oh What a Lovely War, 1968, Hot Millions, 1968, The Prime of Miss Jean Brodie, 1968 (Acad. award for best actress), Love and Pain and the Whole Damn Thing, 1971, Travels with My Aunt, 1972, Murder by Death, 1976, Death on the Nile, 1977, California Suite, 1978 (Acad. award for best supporting actress), Quartet, 1978, Clash of the Titans, 1981, Evil under the Sun, 1981, The Missionary, 1982, A Private Function, 1984 (Brit. Acad. of Film & TV Arts best actress award 1985), Lily in Love, 1985, A Room with a View, 1985, The Lonely Passion of Judith Hearn, 1987 (Brit. Acad. of Film & TV Arts award 1989), Paris by Night, 1988, Hook, 1991, Sister Act, 1992, The Secret Garden, 1993, Richard III, 1995, The First Wives Club, 1996, Washington Square, 1998, Tea with Mussolini, 1999, The Last September, 1999; TV films include Memento Mori, 1992, Suddenly Last Summer, 1993 (Lead Actress-Miniseries Emmy nominee 1993); BBC-TV appearance Bed Among the Lentils, 1988. Recipient Best Actress award Eve. Std., 1962, 70, 82, 85, 94, Best Film Actress award Soc. Film and TV Arts U.K., 1968, Film Critics Guild, 1968, Taomina Gold award, 1985, Antoinette Perry award (Tony), 1990, Hanbury Shakespeare prize, 1991; decorated Dame Brit. Empire, 1989; named Actress of Yr., Variety Club, 1963, 72, Brit. Acad. Best Screen Actress, 1985; Brit. Film Inst. fellow, 1992, Theater Hall of Fame, 1994. Fellow British Acad. Film & Television Arts. Office: Write on Cue, 29 Whitcomb St, London WC2H7EP, England

SMITH, MARGHERITA, writer, editor; b. Chgo., May 24, 1922; d. Henry Christian and Alicia (Koke) Steinhoff; m. Rufus Zartman Smith, June 26, 1943; children: Matthew Benjamin, Timothy Rufus. AB, Ill. Coll., 1943. Proofreader Editorial Experts, Inc., Alexandria, Va., 1974; mgr. proofreading div. Editorial Experts, Inc., Alexandria, 1978-79, mgr. publs. div., 1979-81, asst. to pres., 1980-81; freelance editor, cons. Annandale, Va., 1981-97; instr. proofreading and copy editing, George Washington U., Washington, 1978-82; presenter workshops on proofreading for various profl. orgns., 1981-95. Author: (as Peggy Smith) Simplified Proofreading, 1980, Proofreading Manual and Reference Guide, 1981, Proofreading Workbook, 1981, The Proof Is In the Reading: A Comprehensive Guide to Staffing and Management of Typographic Proofreading, 1986, Mark My Words: Instructions and Practice in Proofreading, 1987, rev. edit., 1993, 98, Letter Perfect: A Guide to Practical Proofreading, 1995; contbr. articles to revs. to various publs. Recipient Best Instrnl. Reporting award Newsletter Assn. Am., 1980, Disting. Achievement award for excellence in ednl. journalism Ednl. Press Assn. Am., 1981, Disting. Citizen award Ill. Coll., 1992. Avocation: writing verse. Home and Office: 9120 Belvoir Woods Pkwy Apt 110 Fort Belvoir VA 22060-2722

SMITH, MARIE EDMONDS, real estate agent, property manager; b. Quapaw, Okla., Oct. 5, 1927; d. Thomas Joseph and Maud Ethel Edmonds; m. Robert Lee Smith, Aug. 14, 1966 (dec. 1983). Grad. vocat. nurse, Hoag Hosp., Costa Mesa, Calif., 1953; BA, Vanguard U., 1955; MS, U. Alaska, 1963. Lic. vocat. nurse, Calif.; cert. sci. tchr., Alaska. Nurse Calif. Dept. Nurses, Costa Mesa, 1952-60; tchr. Alaska Dept. Edn., Aniak and Anchorage, 1955-60; tchr. sci. Garden Grove (Calif.) Sch. Dist., 1960-87; property mgr. Huntington Beach, Calif., 1970—; agent Sterling Realtors, Huntington Beach, 1988—. Author: Ocean Biology, 1969. Bd. dirs., tchr. Harbor Christian Fellowship, Costa Mesa, 1966-83; com. chmn. Garden Grove Unified Sch. Dist. PTA, 1977. NSF grantee, 1960-62. Mem. AAUW, So. Calif. Coll. Alumnae Assn. Republican. Avocations: skin diving, travel. Home: 83ll Reilly Dr Huntington Beach CA 92646 Office: L8153 Brookhurst St Fountain Valley CA 92708

SMITH, MARK WARREN, lawyer, law educator; b. Cheverly, Md., Sept. 4, 1968; s. Warren Bryant and Joan (Hargrave) S. BA, U. S.C., 1992; JD, NYU, 1995. Bar: N.Y. 1996, U.S. Court of Appeals (2d cir.), U.S. Supreme Ct. 2000. Law clk. to Hon. D. Brook Bartlett, Chief Judge US Dist. Ct., Kansas City, Mo., 1995-96; atty. Skadden, Arps, Slate, Meagher & Flom LLP, N.Y.C., 1996-98, Kasowitz, Benson, Torres & Friedman LLP, N.Y.C., 1998-2000; adj. prof. law U. (Lawrence) Kans. Sch. Law, 1999-2000; active Heritage Founds. Guide to Pub. Policy Experts, Journalists Guide to Legal Experts. Contbr. articles to profl. jours. Mem. Federalist Soc. Fax: 212-506-1800. E-mail: msmith@kasowitz.com. Home: 333 E 45th St Apt 20F New York NY 10017-3419 Office: Kasowitz Benson Torres & Friedman LLP 1633 Broadway Ste 2101 New York NY 10019-6799

SMITH, MARTHA VIRGINIA BARNES, retired elementary school educator; b. Camden, Ark., Oct. 12, 1940; d. William Victor and Lillian Louise (Givens) Barnes; m. Basil Loren Smith, Oct. 11, 1975; children: Jennifer Frost, Sean Barnes. BS in Edn., Ouachita Bapt. U., 1963; postgrad., Auburn U., 1974, Henderson State U., 1975. Cert. tchr., Mo. 2d and 1st grade tchr. Brevard County Schs., Titusville and Cocoa, Fla., 1963-65, 69-70; 1st grade tchr. Lakeside Sch. Dist., Hot Springs, Ark., 1965-66, Harmony Grove Sch., Camden, 1972-76; 1st and 5th grade tchr. Cumberland County Schs., Fayetteville, N.C., 1966-69; kindergarten tchr. Pulaski County Schs., Ft. Leonard Wood, Mo., 1970-72; 3d grade tchr. Mountain Grove (Mo.) Schs., 1976-99; ret., 1999; chmn. career ladder com. Mountain Grove Dist., 1991-99. Children's pastor 1st Bapt. Ch., Vanzant, Mo., 1984-88. Mem. NEA (pres.-elect Mountain Grove chpt. 1995-97, pres. Mountain Grove chpt. 1997-99), Kappa Kappa Iota. Avocation: antique and classic cars.

SMITH, MARTIN CHRISTOPHER, electrical engineering educator; b. London. BSc, South Bank U., London, 1978; MSc, King's Coll., London U., 1981. Chartered engr., chartered physicist; European engr. Rsch. asst. U. London, 1971-75; contract engr. Chubb Alarms, 1975-80; prin. engr. Plessey Avionics, 1980-88; prin. lectr. U. East London, 1989—, dep. head dept., 1993—; chair Engring. Coun. London Region, 1993-97; IEE touring lectr., 1996-98; spkr. in field. Author more than 20 articles on robotics and elec. engring.; appeared on 50 TV programs; main exhibitor Robot Olympics, Glasgow, 1996. Trustee Sci. and Tech. Regional Orgn., London, 1998. Freeman, City of London; freeman Worshipful Co. Engrs., 1999. Fellow IEE (coun. 1992-95), Royal Soc. Arts, Royal Astron. Soc.; mem. IEEE (sr.), Cybernetics Soc. (chair 1999—). Avocations: motor racing, collecting antique scientific instruments, reading, going to theatre. Office: U East London/Elec Engring, University Way, London E16 2RD, England

SMITH, MARTIN JAY, physician, biomedical research scientist; b. Bklyn., May 21, 1934; s. I. Richard and Marilyn (Bernard) S.; m. Joyce Ellen Gleason, June 26, 1960 (div. Nov. 1968); children: Danielle, Robert, Alexander; m. Ruby Helen Rhodes, Apr. 7, 1972. BA, Hofstra Coll., 1955; MD, Columbia U., 1959. Diplomate Am. Bd. Internal Medicine, Am. Bd. Internal Medicine in Hematology, Am. Bd. Pathology in Clin. Pathology, Am. Bd. Pathology in Immunopathology. Intern Meth. Hosp., N.Y.C., 1959-60, resident in medicine, 1960-61; resident in medicine Montefiore Hosp., N.Y.C., 1963-64; rsch. fellow in medicine Harvard Coll., Cambridge, Mass., 1964-66; clin. and rsch. fellow in medicine Mass. Gen. Hosp., Boston, 1964-66; physician Gundersen Clinic and Luth. Hosp., La Crosse, Wis., 1966-99, chmn. dept. internal medicine, 1971-73; dir. spl. hematology lab. Gundersen Clinic, La Crosse, 1967-99, chmn. dept. lab. medicine, 1973-96; dir. lab. medicine Luth. Hosp., La Crosse, 1973-96; dir. rsch. Gundersen Med. Found., 1975-88; med. dir. Med. Lab. Tech. Program Western Wis. Tech. Inst., 1978-99. Contbr. articles to New Eng. Jour Medicine, Jour. Lab. Clin. Medicine, Blood, Ann. Internal Medicine, Biochim, Biophys. Acta, Jour. Infectious Diseases, Clin. Chemistry. Capt. USNR, ret. Fellow ACP, Coll. Am. Pathologists (inspector labs. 1983-99); mem. Am. Assn. for Cancer Rsch., Am. Soc. Hematology, Internat. Soc. Hematology, Assn. Med. Lab. Immunologists, Phi Beta Kappa. Home: 1428 Main St La Crosse WI 54601-4225 Office: Gundersen Clinic Ltd 1836 South Ave La Crosse WI 54601-5494

SMITH, MICHAEL, biochemistry educator; b. Blackpool, Eng., Apr. 26, 1932. BSc, U. Manchester, Eng., 1953, PhD, 1956. Fellow B.C. Rsch. Coun., 1956-60; rsch. assoc. Inst. Enzyme Rsch., U. Wis., 1960-61; head chem. sect. Vancouver Lab. Fisheries Rsch. Bd. Can., 1961-66; med. rsch. assoc. Med. Rsch. Coun. Can., 1966-71, career investigator, 1971—; assoc. prof. biochem. U. B.C., Vancouver, 1966-70, prof. biochem., 1970-97; dir. biotech. lab. U. B.C., 1987-96; Peter Wall disting. prof. biotech. U. B.C., Vancouver, 1994—. Recipient Gairdner Found. Internat. award, 1986, Nobel Prize in Chemistry, 1993. Fellow Chem Inst. Can., Royal Soc. (London), Royal Soc. Can., Royal Soc. Chemistry; mem. NAS (fgn. assoc.), Sigma Xi, Order of British Columbia, Companion of the Order of Can. Achievements include research in nucleic acid and nucleotide chemistry and biochemistry using in-vitro mutagenesis gene expression. Office: U BC Biotech Lab, 6331 Crescent Rd Rm 323, Vancouver, BC Canada V6T 1Z3

SMITH, MICHAEL, government official; b. Roscrea, Tipperary, Ireland, 1940; m. Mary T. Ryan; 7 children. Student, U. Coll. Cork. Min. State Dept. Agr., 1980-81; sen. Agrl. Panel, 1982-83, Cultural and Edn. Panel, 1983-87; Min. State Dept. Energy, 1987-88, Min. Energy, 1988-89; Min. State Dept. Industry and Commerce, 1989-91, Min. Environment, 1992-94; Min. Defense Govt. Ireland; Mem. Dáil 1969-73, 77-82. Mem. Tipperary North Riding County Coun. 1967-88, chmn. 1986-87. Mem. Irish Farmers' Assn. Home: Lismackin, County Tipperary Roscrea Ireland Office: Dept Defense Cola'iste Caolmhin, Mobhi Rd, Glasnevin Dublin 9, Ireland*

SMITH, MICHAEL ALAN, insurance industry analyst; b. Schenectady, N.Y., Mar. 5, 1947; s. Norman Leslie and Margaret (Gleeson) S.; m. Denise Pagliaro, July 27, 1972 (separated Dec. 1989); children: James Michael, Dawn Susan. BS in Agrl. Econs., Cornell U., 1970; MBA in Fin., Fairleigh Dickinson U., 1978. Methods analyst Liberty Mut. Ins. Co., Boston, 1970-71; mktg. rep. Texaco Inc., Washington, 1972-74; sec. underwriting div. Palisades Life Ins. Co., Orangeburg, N.Y., 1974-76; sr. planning officer Home Ins. Group, N.Y.C., 1976-83; v.p. planning Ideal Mut. Ins. Co., N.Y.C., 1983-85; sr. v.p., ins. industry analyst Lehman Bros. Inc., N.Y.C., 1985-96; dir., sr. ins. analyst Salomon Bros., N.Y.C., 1996-97; mng. dir. Bear Stearns & Co., 1998—. Contbr. articles to profl. jours. Mem. Assn. Ins. and Fin. Analysts. Avocations: youth coach, skiing, go-kart racing. Office: Bear Stearns & Co Inc 245 Park Ave New York NY 10167-0002

SMITH, MICHAEL ALLEN, mechanical engineer; b. Chgo., Mar. 22, 1948; s. Warren H. and Joan M. Smith; m. Mary N. Sjolund, Sept. 8, 1973; children: Diana, David, Mariel. BSME, U. South Fla., 1972; MS in Bus. Mgmt., SUNY, Utica, 1992. Lic. profl. engr., N.Y. Devel. engr. photo products equipment divsn. DuPont, Wilmington, Del., 1972-75; mech. engr. Remington Arms Co., Ilion, N.Y., 1975-86; sr. facilities engr. GE Co., Utica, 1987-91; with Buckbee-Mears, Cortland, N.Y., 1993-98, Bergman Assocs., Rochester, N.Y., 1999, St. John Engrs., Binghampton, N.Y., 2000—. Mem. ASME, ASHRAE, NSPE, Mohawk Valley Personal Computer Soc. (pres. 1990-91). Home: 273 S 3rd Ave Ilion NY 13357-2401 Office: St John Engrs 1115 Front St Binghamton NY 13905-1115

SMITH, MICHAEL ALLEN, rangeland management educator; b. Georgetown, Tex., Sept. 9, 1944; s. Carl and Hazel (Reagor) S.; m. Diane Marie Fiedler, May 31, 1980; 1 child, Emily Marie. BS, Tex. Tech. U., 1967, MS, 1971; PhD, Utah State U., 1977. Asst. prof. Angelo State U., San Angelo, Tex., 1976-78; from asst. prof. to prof. rangeland mgmt. U. Wyo., Laramie, 1978—; owner Rangeland Mgmt. Specialist Cons., Laramie, 1987—. Contbr. articles, abstracts to profl. jours. Pres. coun. Trinity Luth. Ch., Laramie, 1996-99. Capt. U.S. Army, 1967-70. Recipient Range Stewardship award USDA-Forestry Svc., Wyo. Range Svc. Team, 1996. Mem. Soc. of Range Mgmt. (life, com. chair 1983, Achievement award 1993). Lutheran. Office: Renewable Resources Dept/U Wyo University Sta PO Box 3354 Laramie WY 82071-3354

SMITH, MICHAEL KEVIN, plant biotechnologist, researcher; b. Portsmouth, Ohio, Nov. 8, 1955; arrived in Australia, 1970; s. Forest Denzil and Peggy Louise (Gunter) S.; m. Judith Valma Hillhouse, Dec. 11, 1976; children: Aaron Craig, Zachary Alan, Daniel Lee. BSc, James Cook U., 1977, BSc with honors, 1978; PhD, Murdoch U., 1982. Postdoctoral rsch. assoc. ARCO-Plant Cell Rsch. Inst., Calif., 1982-83; biotechnologist ARCO Seed Co., Oreg., 1983-84; rsch. fellow U. Queensland, Australia, 1984-85; biotechnologist Queensland Dept. of Primary Industries, Redlands, Australia, 1985-90; sr. biotechnologist Queensland Dept. of Primary Industries, Maroochy, Australia, 1990-97, prin. biotechnologist, 1997—; chief sci. investigator Food and Agrl. Orgn. of the UN/Internat. Atomic Energy Agy., Australia, 1989-93; tech. advisor Nat. Banana Plant Health Com., Australia, 1996-98. Mem. editl. bd. Plant Cell, Tissue and Organ Culture, 1998—; contbr. articles to profl. jours. Recipient Eagle Scout Boy Scouts Assn. of Am., 1971, Queen's Scout Boy Scouts Assn. of Australia, 1974, Commonwealth Postgrad. Rsch. award Australian Govt., 1978-81. Mem. Internat. Assn. for Plant Tissue Culture (nat. corr. 1990-94), Internat. Soc. for Horticultural Sci., Australian Soc. of Plant Physiologists, Australian Soc. of Horticultural Sci. Avocations: bushwalking, camping, bird-watching. Office: Queensland Horticulture Int, Maroochy Rsch Station, Nambour 4560, Australia

SMITH, MICHAEL RICHARD, finance director; b. Bushey Heath, Eng., May 10, 1945; s. Richard John and Winifred Vera (Cove) S.; m. Patricia Margaret Colenso Wright, Oct. 30, 1971 (div. Jan. 1989); children: Abigail Jill, Olivia Jane. Audit mgr. Lord, Foster, London, 1969-71; fin. dir. Holt Products, Croydon, Eng., 1971-74; gen. mgr., adminstr. Hanimex, Swindon, Eng., 1974-76; fin. dir. Vacu-Blast, Slough, Eng., 1976-78, Ansafone, Camberley, Eng., 1978-86, Macro 4 PLC, Crawley, Eng., 1986—. Fellow Inst. Chartered Accts. in Eng. and Wales. Office: Macro 4 PLC, The Orangery, Turners Hill Rd, Crawley RH10 4SS, England

SMITH, MICHAEL ROBERT, electro-optical engineer, physicist; b. Tela, Honduras, Aug. 24, 1937; s. Ike Morgan and Edith Helen (Hudson) S.; m. Suzanne Ruth Hudgins, Aug. 20, 1960; children: Stephen, Monica, Meryl. BME, Ga. Inst. Tech., 1959, MS in Nuclear Engring., 1961; PhD, Case Inst. Tech., 1965. Mem. tech. staff Hughes Rsch. Labs., Malibu, Calif., 1965-68; v.p., dir. rsch. Britt Corp., L.A., 1968-73; sr. staff engr. Singer/Librascope divsn., Glendale, Calif., 1973-78; pres. Exocor Tech., Newbury Park, Calif., 1978-95; asst. prof., head physics program Calif. Luth. U., Thousand Oaks, 1990-96; design leader LIGO project Calif. Inst. Tech., Pasadena, 1996—. Contbr. articles to profl. jours.; inventor emergency vehicle warning and traffic control sys., emergency vehicle warning sign, flat electro-optic display panel, high power mirror, laser recording film with opaque coating, pulsed gas laser with radiation cooling, infrared laser photocautery device; 8 U.S. patents; 9 fgn. patents. Greek folk dance tchr. Arts Coun., Thousand Oaks, Calif., 1991-97. Mem. IEEE, Laser Electro-Optic Soc. (chair 1995-97), Sigma Xi, Pi Tau Sigma. Republican. Home: 680 S Marengo Ave Apt 9 Pasadena CA 91106-3659

SMITH, MYRON GEORGE, former government official, consultant; b. Terrebonne, Minn., June 9, 1920; s. Adrian G. and Marie E. (Crompe) S.; m. Louise J. Hennessey, May 22, 1944 (div. 1973); children: Michael, Thomas, John, Patricia, Dennis; m. Nguyen Anh My, Aug. 30, 1975; children: Yvette, Bryan. BS in Agrl. Econs. and Soil Sci., U. Minn., 1946. Soil scientist USDA, 1946-50, agrl. ext. advisor, 1950-58; owner No. Ill. Agrl. Svc., 1958-62; with USAID, Dept. State, 1962-84; agrl. sales advisor USAID, Dept. State, India, 1962-66; asst. dir. crop prodn. Vietnam USAID, Dept. State, 1966-70, chief agrl. divsn. Indonesia, 1970-73; assoc. dir. USAID, Dept. State, Vietnam, 1974-75; chief agrl. divsn. Mali USAID, Dept. State, 1976-81; chief agrl. project mgr. West Africa USAID, Dept. State, Washington, 1981-84; agrl. cons. USAID, Dept. State, Zaire, 1988-90, Indonesia, 1993-94; assoc. prof. U. Ark., 1985. 1st lt. USAAF, 1941-45. Decorated Purple Heart, Air medal with 6 oak leaf clusters, DFC; Agr. medal 2d class, Vietnam, 1969, Agr. medal 1st class, Vietnam, 1970, Labor medal 1st class, Vietnam, 1970, Economy medal 2d class, Vietnam, 1970. Mem. Am. Fgn. Service Assn. Home and Office: 309 N Manchester St Arlington VA 22203-1118

SMITH, NEIL COLIN, military historian; b. Perth, Australia, Sept. 5, 1948; s. Horace George and Margery Alice (Evans) S.; m. Margaret Grace Smales, May 11, 1974 (div. 1987); children: Benjamin James, Kate Alison; m. Noelle Sylvie Bonnet, Dec. 5, 1992. Grad. diploma in strategic studies, Aust. Joint Svcs. Staff Coll., 1989. 2d lt. Australian Army, Australia, 1967-69, South Vietnam, 1970; capt. Australian Army, Australia, 1971-80; maj. Australian Army, U.K., 1981-82, Australia and South Pacific, 1983-85; lt. col. Australian Army, Australia and S.E. Asia, 1986-91; mil. historian Mostly Unsung, Gardenvale, Victoria, Australia, 1992—; cons. various orgns. and instns. including Australian Army, ABC TV, vets.' orgns., 1992—. Author: (books) Mostly Unsung, 1989, Home by Xmas, 1990, Tid-Apa, 1992, Men of Beersheba, 1994, The Red and Black Diamond, 1997, others. Sec. Mil. Hist. Soc. Australia, 1983-89; aide de camp to Pres. of Italy, Australia, 1988. Decorated Mem. of Order of Australia, Brit. Monarchy, 1984, Unit Cross of Gallantry, 1970; recipient Insignia award City and Guilds of London, 1981. Mem. Orders and Medals Rsch. Soc. Anglican. Avocation: squash. Office: Mostly Unsung Mil History, PO Box 20, Gardenvale VIC 3186, Australia

SMITH, NEVILLE IAN, management company executive; b. Sydney, Australia, June 3, 1940; s. Robert Charles and Renee Georgina (Fry) S.; m. Jacqueline Magdalene Lennon, May 12, 1962; children: Brett Neville, Audette Renee Capel, Kimberley Ralph. BA, U. New Eng., 1972. Cert. tchr. H.s. tchr. NSW Dept. of Edn., 1959-64; various mgmt. positions Pfizer Internat., Australia, Hong Kong, N.Y., 1971-79; mgmt. cons. NIS Australia Pty. Ltd., 1980—; dir. Health Explorers, Australia, 1997—, Asia Pacific Mgmt. Edn. Ctr., Australia, 1996—; dir., vice chair Langton Clinic, Sydney, 1980-86; v.p. Lions Club of Greater Sydney, 1995; dir. Campbelltown RSL Club, 1970. Co-author: Idens Unlimited, 1985, Sales Force Incentives, 1987, Managing for Innovation, 1989, Making It Happen, Managing for Performance, 1993; author: Down-to Earth Strategic Planning, 1996. Officer Australian Army, 1964-70. Fellow Australian Inst. of Mgmt.; mem. Inst. of Mgmt. Cons. (chartered mgmt. cons.), United Svc. Club, Returned Svc. Club. Avocations: classic sports cars, reading, golf. Office: NIS Australia Pty Ltd, PO Box 430, Avalon NSW 2107, Australia

SMITH, OLE DA SILVA, systems administrator, engineer; b. Copenhagen; s. Majken I.R. Smith; m. Eunice Pereira Da Silva, Aug. 1988 (dec. July 1995); 1 child, Ole Fernando P. Da Silva. MS in Engring., Tech. U. Denmark, 1990, PhD in Computational Math./Physics, 1996. Tchr. dept. math. Tech. U. Denmark, Lyngby, 1991-92, Unix and NT systems adminstr., 1996—. Avocations: soccer, bicycling, languages (Danish, English, Portuguese, Spanish). Home: Ewaldsgade 8IIIth, DK-2200N Copenhagen Denmark Office: Tch Univ Denmark, Dept Math Bldg 303, DK-2800 Lyngby Denmark

SMITH, ORIN ROBERT, chemical company executive; b. Newark, Aug. 13, 1935; s. Sydney R. and Gladys Emmett (DeGroff) S.; m. Stephanie M. Bennett-Smith; children: Lindsay, Robin; 1 stepchild, Brendan. BA in Econometrics, Brown U., 1957; MBA in Mgmt., Seton Hall U., 1964; PhD in Econs. (hon.), Centenary Coll., 1991; LLD (hon.), Monmouth Coll., 1994. Various sales and mktg. mgmt. positions Allied Chem. Corp., Morristown, N.J., 1959-69; dir. sales and mktg. Richardson-Merrell Co., Phillipsburg, N.J., 1969-72; with M&T Chems., Greenwich, Conn., 1972-77, pres., 1975-77; with Engelhard Minerals & Chems. Corp., Menlo Park, Edison, N.J., 1977-81, corp. sr. v.p., 1978-81, pres. div. minerals and chems., 1978-81, also bd. dirs., 1979-81, pres., dir. various U.S. subs., 1979-81; exec. v.p., pres. div. minerals and chems. Engelhard Corp., Menlo Park, Edison, 1981-84, bd. dirs., 1981—; pres., CEO, Engelhard Corp., Iselin, N.J., 1984-95, chmn., CEO, 1995—; also bd. dirs.; bd. dirs. Summit Bank Co., The Summit Bancorp, Vulcan Materials Co., PE Corp., Ingersoll-Rand Corp., Engelhard Corp., Mfrs. Alliance. Trustee N.J. State C. of C., Inst. for Tech. Advancement; mem. bd. overseers N.J. Inst. Tech.; trustee Plimoth Plantation; 1st vice chmn. bd. trustees Centenary Coll.; past dir. Minorco, La. Land and Exploration Co.; past trustee Henry R. Kessler Found., Inc.; past chmn. Ind. Coll. Fund N.J.; past dir.-at-large U. Maine Pulp and Paper Found. Lt. (j.g.) USN, 1957-59. Mem. Chem. Mfrs. Assn. (past bd. dirs.), Econ. Club (N.Y.C.), Union League Club (N.Y.C.), Duxbury Yacht Club, New Bedford Yacht Club, N.Y. Yacht Club. Office: Engelhard Corp 101 Wood Ave S Iselin NJ 08830-2703

SMITH, OSCAR WILLIAM, nursing home administrator; b. Odem, Tex., Sept. 21, 1933; s. Christopher Columbus, Jr. and Myrtle (Younts) Smith; m. Peggy June Hoefar, June 2, 1962 (wid. Mar. 1994); children: Rhonda, Mike, Billy (dec.). Student, Del Mar Coll., 1970-71, San Jacinto Coll., 1974-75. Lic. nursing home administr., Tex. Enlisted U.S. Army, 1950, advanced through grades to sgt., 1952-62; artillery assignment Tex. Army Nat. Guard, 1978-80; office mgr. Manhattan Constrn. Co., Houston, 1975-80; adminstr. Houston Water Purification Plant and Tranquillity Park, Houston, 1975-80. Patentee in field; poet, country music songwriter: (poetry transcribed to country music recordings) Loving Memories, 1995, The Key to My Heart, 1996, Eternity, 1996, An Angel in Heaven, 1996, I Won't Forget You, 1996, Visions of Him, 1996, Two-Timing Woman, 1996, I Can't Get You Off of My Mind, 1996, others. Master sgt. U.S. Army res. Mem. Disabled Am. Vets. (comdr. Pasadena chpt. 1994—), Am. Security Coun. (nat. adv. bd.

1984-97), N.Y. Acad. Scis., Internat. Soc. of Poets (disting. mem.), Internat. Platform Assn. Democrat. Baptist. Avocations: writing poetry and country music, assisting the blind/disabled and sr. citizens of Tex., Mex. Home: 2716 Sweetgum St Pasadena TX 77502-5754

SMITH, PAUL BRIERLEY, fashion designer; b. July 5, 1946; s. Harold and Marjorie S. Hon. M.Des, Nottingham Trent U, 1991. Mgr. boutique, Nottingham, England, 1966-70; shop owner Nottingham, England, 1970-76; chmn. Paul Smith Ltd. Created knight, 2000; recipient Brit. Knitting and Clothing Export Coun. award, 1991, Queens award for industry-export achievement C.B.E. Svcs. to Fashion Industry, 1994; named Brit. Mgr. Designer of Yr., 1997. Office: 40-44 Floral St. London WC2E 9DG, England also: Riverside Bldg, Riverside Way, Nottingham NG2 1DP, England*

SMITH, PAUL MAPLESTON, physician; b. Harrow, Eng., May 4, 1936; s. Cecil Daniel and Winifred Emily (Mapleston) S.; m. Ragnheidur Olafsdottir, Feb. 28, 1978; children: Asta Gudrun, Karl Mapleston. MB BS, St. Thomas's Hosp., London, 1959; MD, U. London, 1969. Fellow Royal Coll. Physicians, London; full med. registration, Eng. House physician St. Thomas's Hosp., 1960, med. registrar, 1963-65; lectr. in medicine Kings Coll. Hosp., London, 1966-68; rsch. fellow Boston U., 1968-69; sr. registrar U. Coll. Hosp., London, 1970-72; sr. lectr. Welsh Nat. Sch. Medicine, Cardiff, 1972-78; cons. physician Llandough Hosp., Cardiff, 1979—. Author med. papers, rsch. in field. Recipient Lord Riddell Med. Scholarship St. Thomas's Hosp., 1958, State Scholarship, Eng., 1954. Mem. British Soc. Gastroenterology (pres. 1996), MCC, Jesters. Avocation: cricket. Home: Woodside Park Rd, Dinas Powis, S Glamorgan CF6 4HJ, Great Britain Office: Llandough Hosp, Cardiff CF64 2XX, Wales

SMITH, PEGGY O'DONIEL, physicist, educator; b. Lakeland, Fla., Nov. 27, 1920; d. John Arthur and Carrie Mattie (Jackson) O'Doniel; m. Fenton Frederick Smith, Oct. 11, 1943; children: James Scott, Stephen Arthur, Melody Ann, Candy Lou. Aviation Pilot Lic., Stetson U., Deland, Fla., 1941; BS in Sci. and Math., Fla. So. Coll., 1942; MA in Edn., U.S. Internat. U., San Diego, 1968. Physicist degausser U.S. Navy, Key West, Fla., 1942; physicist compass compensator U.S. Navy, Charleston, S.C., 1943; physicist magnetic signature analyst U.S. Navy, Washington, 1944; tchr. Chula Vista (Calif.) Sch. Dist., 1963-73, math specialist, 1974-77; owner Mineral Store, Chula Vista, 1977-82; ret.; leader math. workshops for girls, 1992-96. Author: Laz Goes to New Zealand; contbr. articles to profl. jours. Del. White House Conf. on Edn., 1956; sec. Chula Vista Rep. Women, 1995-97; chmn. Orphans of Italy, 1957-58. Recipient Kazanjian award, Joint Coun. Econ. Edn., Chula Vista, 1972, Fla. So. Coll. Alumni Achievement citation, 1999; Chula Vista Sch. Dist. math grantee, 1975. Mem. AAUW (v.p. 1989), Inner Circle, Calif. Ret. Tchrs. Assn. (v.p. 1998-00), San Diego Gem and Mineral Soc. Avocations: golf, mineral collecting, coin collecting, bridge, travel. Home: 87 K St Chula Vista CA 91911-1409

SMITH, PETER, computer sciences educator; b. Sunderland, Tyne/Wear, Eng., Sept. 19, 1956; s. Thomas and Joyce (Frecker) S.; m. Marie Potts, Mar. 14, 1981; children: Ashleigh, David, Laura. BSc with honors, U. Sunderland, 1978, PhD, 1981. Chartered engr. Rsch. asst. U. Sunderland, 1978-81, lectr., 1981-86, prin. lectr., 1986-89, reader, 1989-92, prof., 1992—. Author: Expert System Development in PROLOG, 1988, Introduction to Knowledge Engineering, 1994, Managing CASE Technology, 1994, Professional Knowledge Engineering, 1994; contbr. numerous articles to sci. jours. Recipient Acclones Integrades award Brit. Coun., 1991. Fellow Inst. Math. and Its Applications, Brit. Computer Soc. (sec. N.E. br. 1990—); mem. Internat. As40AMSDWWA6WP25DAT. Office: U Sunderland, Ryhope Rd, Sunderland Tyne and Wear SR2 7EE, England

SMITH, PETER EDWARD, sculptor, artist; b. Yonkers, N.Y., Jan. 1, 1946; s. Elwin Earl Smith and Mary Ellen Kirchmaier; m. Maria M. Smith, May 23, 1968. BA, Hobart Coll., 1967; MBA, Rutgers U., 1971. Light weapons infantryman U.S. Army, Ft. Carson, Colo., 1968-69; 2d v.p. ins. dept. N.Y. Life Inst. Co., N.Y.C., 1971-86; sculptor, painter Pietro Designs Studio, Princeton Junction, N.J., 1986—. Designer, sculptor West Windsor (N.J.) Vets.' Monument, 1986-89 (citation Am. Legion 1990); designer, sculptor, painter Altar, Ambo, Baptistery, Tabernacle, Tympanum, St. David the King Ch., Princeton Junction, 1990-92 (Visual Art award 1992); designer, mosaicist Stations of the Cross, 1995-96; sculptor limestone stele U.S. Forest Svc., Fredericksburg, Va., 1993; author: Cherubim of Gold, 1993; contbr. Art and Environment Letter, 1994—. With U.S. Army, 1967-69. Recipient artistic contbns. to cmty. award Nat. Art Honor Soc., Princeton Junction, 1993. Office: Pietro Designs Studio 962 Alexander Rd Princeton Junction NJ 08550-1024

SMITH, PETER JAY, insurance company executive, consultant; b. Englewood, N.J., Oct. 9, 1947; s. Seymour A. and Marjorie (Heft) S.; children: Michael J., Douglas A., Brian D. BA, Syracuse U., 1970. CLU; chartered fin. cons. Ins. agt. N.Y.L.C., 1970—; prin. Peter J. Smith, CLU, ChFC & Assocs., 1970—; pres. No. N.J. chpt. CLU, 1980-81. Pres. Dwight Englewood Sch. Alumni Assn., 1979-81, trustee 1978-81; exec. com. Young Men's div. Albert Einstein Coll. of Medicine, Bronx, N.Y., 1986. Recipient Vanguard award New Eng. Life, Boston, 1979, Flagship award New Eng. Life, 1983; named life mem. Hall of Fame, New Eng. Life, 1976. Mem. Assn. Advanced Life Underwriters, Million Dollar Round Table (qualifying, life mem.), Top of the Table, The Forum, The Am. Soc., Life Underwriters Assn. of N.Y.C., Passaic Bergen Life Underwriters Assn., Bergen County Estate Planners Assn. (bd. dirs.). Jewish. Clubs: Preakness Hills (bd. govs. 1985—); Wayne (N.J.) Country. Lodge: B'nai B'rith. Avocations: golf, music, family activities, the arts. Office: One Harmon Plaza Secaucus NJ 07094

SMITH, PETER KENELM, psychology educator; b. Chichester, Sussex, Eng., Sept. 23, 1943; s. Kenelm B.S. Smith and Ruth E.B. (Warner) Smith Farrance; m. Christine Clark; children: James, Samuel Robert; m. Helen Alexander Cowie; 1 child, Benjamin Thomas Finlayson. BA, Oxford (Eng.) U., 1964; PhD, Sheffield (Eng.) U., 1970. Lectr. dept. psychology U. Sheffield, 1974-83, sr. lectr., 1983-85, reader, 1985-91, prof., 1991-95; prof. dept. psychology Goldsmith's Coll., U. London, 1995—; vis. lectr. Inst. Child Devel., U. Minn., Mpls., 1981, vis. rsch. fellow Sch. Edn. Flinders U., Australia, 1994, Sch. Edn. Chuo U., Tokyo, 1995; vis. rsch. fellow dept. psychology Keio U., Tokyo, 1999. Author: The Ecology of Preschool Behaviour, 1980, The Psychology of Grandparenthood, 1991, Practical Approaches to Bullying, 1991, School Bullying: Insights and Perspectives, 1994; editor: Play in Animals and Humans, 1984, Children's Play, 1986, Theories of Theories of Mind, 1996, The Nature of School Bullying, 1999; mem. editl. bd. Brit. Jour. Psychology, 1986-90, Social Devel., 1991—, Children and Society, 1996—, Evolution and Human Behavior, 1997—; assoc. editor Internat. Jour. Behavioral Devel., 1990-95; European editor Ethology and Sociobiology, 1992-96; contbr. chpts. to books and articles to profl. jours. Fellow Brit. Psychol. Soc.; mem. Assn. Child Psychologists and Psychiatrists, Assn. for Study Animal Behavior, Soc. for Rsch. in Child Devel., Soc. for Reproductive and Infant Psychology. Avocations: walking, chess, photography. Office: Goldmiths Coll Dept Psych, U London, New Cross London SE14 6NW, England

SMITH, PETER WOLFGANG, physicist, artist; b. Rostock, Germany, May 16, 1929; U.S. citizen, 1983; s. Hans Schmidt-Isserstedt and Gertrude Calo; m. Marie Smith, Sept. 8, 1954; children: Nicholas, Lydia, Caroline. Student, Cambridge (Eng.) Art Coll., 1950; BS, St. Andrews (Scotland) U., 1952; postgrad., Edinburgh U., 1952-54. Sci. officer Admiralty Signal and Radar Establishment, Portsmouth, Eng., 1954-60; scientist Plessey Co., Hampshire, Eng., 1960-67; supr. Norden Systems, Norwalk, Conn., 1967-89; cons. Peter Smith, Westport, Conn., 1989—; artist Pierre Cochon, Westport, 1993—. Patentee in field; contbr. articles to profl. jours.; artist exhibiting in Wessex shows, U.K., 1956-60, various Conn. shows, 1996-99. Mem. Inst. of Physics of London. Avocations: music, art history, golf. Home and Office: 7 Darbrook Rd Westport CT 06880-3611

SMITH, PHYLLIS MAE, healthcare consultant, educator; b. Coeur d'Alene, Idaho, May 2, 1935; d. Elmer Lee Smith and Kathryn Alice (Newell) Wilson. Diploma, Lutheran Bible Inst., Seattle, 1956, Emanuel Hosp. Sch. Nursing, Portland, Oreg., 1959; student Coll. San Mateo, Calif., 1971. Staff nurse in surgery Emanuel Hosp., Portland, 1959-61, St. Vincent's Hosp., Portland, 1962-63; head nurse central service Sacred Heart Hosp., Eugene, Oreg., 1964-69; dir. central services Peninsula Hosp., Burlingame, Calif., 1969-74; pres. Phyllis Smith Assocs., Inc., Lewiston, Idaho, 1975-88; sr. tech. advisor, dir. ednl. programs, Parkside Material Mgmt. Services, Park Ridge, Ill., 1988-90; AIDS coord. Asotin County Health Dist., 1989-2000; lectr., cons. in field in over 11 countries. Contbr. to manuals, profl. jours. Mem. Internat. Assn. Hosp. Central Service Mgmt. (dir. edn. 1973-88, chmn. technician edn. and affairs com. 1978-88, John Perkins award, 1977, Chesire award 1977), Assn. for Advancement Med. Instrumentation, Nat. Assn. Female Execs. Episcopalian. Lodge: Eagles Aux. Avocations: fishing, walking, photography, chess, reading. Home and Office: 1415 Chestnut St Clarkston WA 99403-2429

SMITH, RALPH, artist; b. San Francisco, July 12, 1919; s. Joseph Jacob and Anna (Holecek) S.; m. Francis Ferne Sierth, Aug. 15, 1942; children: Peter Joseph, Beverly Christine. Student, Art Ctr. L.A., 1940, Oakland Arts/Crafts, 1946, Am. U., 1962-67. Aircraft mechanic Naval Repair Stas., Alameda, Calif., 1945-56; aircraft engrng. technician Dept. Navy, Washington, 1956-74; artist, tchr. Ralph Smith Workshops, Annandale, Va., 1974—; juror awards 100th Ann. Art Exhbn., Nat. League of Am. Pen Women, Washington, 1996. With USN, 1941-43. Mem. Am. Soc. Marine Artists (elected artist mem. 1999), Midwest Watercolor Soc., Va. Watercolor Soc. Republican. Roman Catholic. Avocations: fishing, travel, visiting museums and galleries. Home and Office: 7114 Cindy Ln Annandale VA 22003-5812

SMITH, RALPH WESLEY, JR., federal judge; b. Ghent, N.Y., July 16, 1936; s. Ralph Wesley and Kathleen S. (Callahan) S.; m. Nancy Ann Fetzer, Dec. 30, 1961 (div. 1981); children: Mark Owen, Tara Denise, Todd Kendall; m. Barbara Anne Milian, Nov. 8, 1982; stepchildren: Kim Highter, Jeffrey Highter, Eric Highter. Student, Sorbonne, U. Paris, Paris, 1954-55; BA, Yale U., 1956; LLB, Albany Law Sch., 1966. Bar: N.Y. 1966, U.S. Dist. Ct. (no. dist.) N.Y. 1966. Assoc. Hinman, Straub Law Firm, Albany, N.Y., 1966-69; chief asst. dist. atty. Albany County, N.Y., 1969-73, dist. atty., 1974; regional dir. state nursing home investigation Asst. Atty. Gen., Albany, 1975-77; dir. State Organized Crime Task Force, 1978-82; U.S. magistrate judge U.S. Dist. Ct. (no. dist.) N.Y., Albany, 1982—; judge moot ct. Albany Law Sch., 1983—; lectr. N.Y. State Bar Assn., 1985—, Am. Inns of Ct., 1994-99. Capt. (ret.) USNR, 1957-82. Mem. Fed. Magistrate Judges Assn. (dir. 2d cir. 1992-99), Columbia County Bar Assn., Columbia County Magistrates Assn. Republican. Roman Catholic. Avocations: fishing, bicycling, skiing, sailing, camping. Home: 2375 State Route 66 Chatham NY 12037-1801 Office: US Dist Ct 445 Broadway Ste 314 Albany NY 12207-2925

SMITH, RANDOLPH RELIHAN, plastic surgeon; b. Augusta, Ga., Aug. 13, 1944; s. Lester Vernon and Maxine (Relihan) S.; m. Becky Jo Hardy; children: Katherine, Randolph, Rebecca, Michael. BS, Clemson U., 1966; MD, Coll. Ga., 1970; LLD (hon.), Clemson U., 1997. Diplomate Am. Bd. Otolaryngology, Am. Bd. Plastic Surgery. Intern Bowman Gray Sch. Medicine Wake Forest U., Winston-Salem, N.C., 1970-71; resident in surgery and otolaryngology Duke U., Durham, N.C., 1971-75; resident in plastic and reconstructive surgery Med. Coll. Ga., 1975-77; Christine Kleinert fellow in hand surg. U. Louisville, 1977; attending physician U. Hosp., Augusta, Ga., 1977—; asst. clin. prof. plastic surgery Med. Coll. Ga., 1978—; pres. med. staff Univ. Hosp., Augusta, mem. exec. coun. health care sys.; vol. surgeon in developing countries, 1982—. Contbr. articles to profl. jours. Vol. surgeon in developing countries, 1982—; bd. dirs. United Way, Ga. Bank and Trust Co. of Augusta, Richmond County Hosp. Authority; vestryman, sr. warden St. Paul's Episcopal Ch.; trustee Univ. Health, Inc., Clemson U. Found.; mem. bd. visitors Clemson U. Recipient Book of Golden Deeds award Exch. Club of Augusta, 1997, Civic Endeavor award Richmond County Med. Soc., 1998, Jack A. Raines Humanitarian award Med. Assn. Ga., 1999; Paul Harris fellow Rotary, 1998. Fellow ACS, Am. Acad. Otolaryngology; mem. Am. Soc. Plastic and Reconstructive Surgeons, Am. Soc. Aesthetic Plastic Surgery, Ga. Soc. Plastic and Reconstructive Surgeons, Southeastern Soc. Plastic and Reconstructive Surgeons, Exch. Club of Augusta (bd. dirs., pres.), Augusta Symphony League. Office: Univ Hosp Med Ctr 811 13th St Ste 28 Augusta GA 30901-2772

SMITH, RAOUL NORMAND, computer science educator; b. West Warwick, R.I., May 15, 1938; s. Luke Joseph and Lucienne (Anchambault) S.; m. Mary Frances Hand, Nov. 12, 1966; children: Stephen Edward, Timothy Luke. AB, Brown U., 1963, AM, 1964, PhD, 1968. Instr. Northwestern U., Evanston, Ill., 1967-68, asst. prof., 1968-73, assoc. prof., 1973-80; sr. mem. of tech. staff GTE Labs., Waltham, Mass., 1981-83, prin. mem. of tech. staff, 1983; prof. Northeastern U., Boston, 1983—, dir. grad. schs., 1984-85, dir. rsch., 1985-86; vis. prof. Jilin U. of Tech., Changchun, People's Republic of China, summer 1985; chmn. bd. dirs. Cognitive Computers, Newton, Mass., 1985-87; prin. Raoul N. Smith and Assocs., Cons. Author: Dictionary of Artificial Intelligence, 1989, The Language of Jonathan Fisher, 1985, Probabilistic Performance Models of Language, 1973; co-author: Lexical-Semantic Relations, 1980. Trustee Acton (Mass.) Hist. Soc., 1988-90; mem. AIDS action com., 1985-88. With USAF, 1957-61. Grantee NSF, 1966, 66-67, 71, Am. Philos. Soc., 1974, Am. Coun. of Learned Socs., 1974, Nat. Endowment for the Humanities, 1975, 76-79. Mem. Assn. for Computing Machinery (co-chair spl. interest group on computer and human interaction 1981-85), Union Club. Avocations: antique porcelain, silver and jewelry. Home: 206 Nagog Hill Rd Acton MA 01720-3228 Office: Northeastern Univ MS 161 CN Boston MA 02115

SMITH, RAYMOND LEIGH, plastic surgeon; b. Norristown, Pa., Sept. 27, 1940; s. Walter Joseph and Pauline C. (Wolfskill) S.; m. Coralynn Elder, Jan. 8, 1966; children: Susan, Elizabeth, Christine. BS, Ursinus Coll., 1962; MD, Temple U., 1966. Diplomate Nat. Bd. Med. Examiners, Am. Bd. Plastic Surgery. Active staff Reading Hosp., Pa., 1976—, chief sect. of plastic surgery, 1994—. Mem. ACS, AMA, Republican Majority Found., Washington Legal Found. Mem. Am. Soc. Plastic Surgeons, Robert H. Ivy Soc., Am. Assn. Hand Surgery, Northeastern Soc. Plastic Surgeons, Pa. Med. Soc., Lipoplasty Soc. N.Am., Berks County Med. Soc. Lutheran. Office: 926 Penn Ave Wyomissing PA 19610-3017

SMITH, RAYMOND W., investment banking executive; b. Pitts., 1937. B.S., Carnegie-Mellon U., 1959; M.B.A., U. Pitts., 1969. Budget dir. AT&T, 1976-77; v.p.-regulatory Bell of Pa. and Diamond State Tel., Phila., 1981-83, pres., chief exec. officer, 1983-85; vice chmn., chief fin. officer, dir. parent co. Bell Atlantic Corp., Phila., 1985-88; pres., chief oper. officer Bell Atlantic Corp., 1988; chmn., CEO Bell Atlantic Corp., Phila., 1989-98, Rothschild North America, Inc., N.Y.C., 1999—; bd. dirs., founder Arlington Capital Ptnrs., 1999, U.S. Airways, CBS Corp.; mem. Bus. Roundtable, 1990—; mem. nat. adv. bd. Pvt. Sector Coun., 1990—; mem. James Madison nat. coun. Libr. of Congress, 1990—. Pub. playwright. Mem. Lincoln Ctr., Pres. Commn.-Arts and Humanities, WETA, Carnegie Corp., Carnegie Mellon, Rockham Ventures. With Signal Corps, U.S. Army, 1959-60. Office: Rothschild North Am Inc 1251 Avenue Of The Americas New York NY 10020-1104

SMITH, RICHARD EMERSON (DICK SMITH), make-up artist; b. Larchmont, N.Y., June 26, 1922; s. Richard Roy and Coral (Brown) S.; m. Jocelyn De Rosa, Jan. 10, 1949; children: Douglas Todd, David Emerson. BA, Yale U., 1944. Pioneer dir. first TV make-up dept. NBC-TV, N.Y.C., 1945-59; make-up dir. David Susskind Prodns., N.Y.C., 1959-61; freelance make-up artist, cons., 1961—; lectr. Yoyogi Animation Sch., Tokyo, 1992—, Polytek Devel. seminar, 1996; key spkr. Internat. Make-up and Effects Trade Show, 1997-99; featured make-up expert in Movie Magic tv documentaries, Monster Effects, 1994, Aging Effects, 1995; columnist Make-up Artist mag.; lectr. on spl. make-up effects. Credits include Requiem for a Heavyweight, 1962, The World of Henry Orient, 1963, Mark Twain, Tonight!, 1967 (Emmy award 1967), Midnight Cowboy, 1968, Little Big Man, 1969, The Godfather, 1971, The Exorcist, 1973, The Godfather, Part II, 1974, The Sunshine Boys, 1975, Taxi Driver, 1975, Altered States, 1979, Scanners, 1980, Ghost Story, 1981, The Hunger, 1982, Amadeus, 1983 (U.S. Acad. award 1984, Brit. Acad. award 1985), Starman, 1984, Poltergeist III, 1987, Everybody's All-American, 1988, Sweet Home (Japanese film), 1988, Dad, 1989, Death Becomes Her, 1991, Forever Young, 1992; author: The Advanced Professional Make-Up Course; permanent exhbn. of make-up work from Little Big Man, The Exorcist, Amadeus, others, at N.Y. Mus. of the Moving Image, 1992—. Honored on his 50th ann. in make-up by Am. Film Inst., Visionary Cinema, Cinefex mag., 1995. Home and Office: 27 Wilford Ave Branford CT 06405-3822

SMITH, RICHARD MARK, mortgage company executive; b. Detroit, Jan. 10, 1956; s. James Harold and Viola Emma (Priggee)S.; m. Beverlee Ellen McCreary, June 16, 1977; children: Richard Jr., Christopher, Jillian. Student, U. Cin., 1976-77. Sales/originations mgr. Reliance Mortgage, Brighton, Mich., 1986-90; v.p. Prime Fin., Brighton, 1990-93; pres. Premiere Mortgage Corp., Brighton, 1994—. Auction organizer Women's Resource Ctr., Brighton, 1999. Coach 1st pl. area hockey team Mich. Nat. Hockey League, Detroit, 1998, 1999; recipient diploma as master coach highest level U.S.A. Hockey, 1999. Mem. Livingston Assn. Realtors, Brighton C. of C., Kensington Valley Hockey Assn. (pres. 1999—). Republican. Presbyterian. Avocation: hockey. E-mail: Rikk@ismi.net. Office: Premiere Mortage Corp 218 E Grand River Ave Brighton MI 48116-1512

SMITH, RICK EARL, law enforcement officer; b. Gastonia, N.C., Dec. 28, 1951; s. Harold Parks and Minnie (Forbes) S.; m. Faye Taylor, July 25, 1986 (div. July 6, 1996); 1 child, Christopher Taylor Smith. Cert. forensic examiner, Inst. Applied Sci., Chgo., 1970; cert. basic law enforcement instr., N.C. Justice Acad., Salemburg, 1980; cert. fingerprint examiner, N.C. State Bur. Investigation, Raleigh, 1988. Cert. forensic examiner Inst. Applied Sci., Chgo., 1970, fingerprint comparison expert N.C. Dept. Justice. Dispatcher/chief cadet Chapel Hill (N.C.) Police Dept., 1967-70, chief identification bur., 1970-72, police/pub. safety officer, 1972-87; investigator/major crime mgr. Orange County Sheriff's Office, Hillsborough, N.C., 1987-97; ret. Orange County Sheriff's Office, 1997; spl. dep. U.S. marshal U.S. Martial Svc. Ct. Security, Durham, N.C., 1998—; instr. law enforcement tng. N.C. Justice Acad., Salemburg, N.C., 1980-94; breathalyzer operator/supr. N.C. Dept. Human Resources, Raleigh, 1981-95; expert witness fingerprint evidence, 1991—; res. investigator/cons. Orange County Sheriff's Office, 1997—. Author: (book of poetry) Poetic Pig, 1973. Mem. Gov.'s Crime Commn., Raleigh, 1977-80; co-chmn./advisor Edmiston N.C. Gov. Campaign Orange County/Raleigh, 1980; co-chmn. Orange County Jim Hunt for Gov. campaign, 1978; campaign mgr./speechwriter Orange County Pendergrass for Sheriff campaign, 1982-99. Fellow Fingerprint Soc. of London, Eng.; mem./co-founder N.C. Forensic Assn. (pres. 1991-92); founder/mem. Orange County Fraternal Order of Police (pres. 1989-90); mem. Masons. Democrat. Baptist. Avocations: politics, govt., reading, writing. E-mail: rsmithe1@aol.com. Home: 110 Duchess Ln Chapel Hill NC 27514-7937 Office: US Marshals Office 323 E Chapel Hill St Durham NC 27701-3351

SMITH, ROBERT BLAKEMAN, lawyer; b. Mt. Vernon, N.Y., June 18, 1949; s. William Blakeman and Helen Theresa (Curley) S.; m. Laura Lindley Brock, July 18, 1987; children: Morgan Lindley, Justin Pierce. BS, Rensselaer Poly. Inst., 1971, ME, 1973; JD, Boston U., 1976. Bar: N.Y. 1977, U.S. Dist. Ct. (so. and ea. dists.) N.Y. 1977, U.S. Dist. Ct. (no. dist.) N.Y. 1981, U.S. Dist. Ct. Ariz. 1992, U.S. Patent and Trademark Office 1977, U.S. Ct. Appeals (7th cir.) 1979, U.S. Ct. Appeals (fed. cir.) 1982, U.S. Supreme Ct. 1981. Assoc. Brumbaugh, Graves, Donohue & Raymond, N.Y.C., 1976-84, ptnr., 1984-89; of counsel White & Case, N.Y.C., 1989-99, Skadden, Arps, Slate, Meagher & Flom, N.Y.C., 1999—; lectr. IEEE, N.Y.C., 1983-88, Practising Law Inst., 1990-99. Trustee Delta Phi Found., Ithaca, N.Y., 1978-86, St. Elmo Found., Pearl River, N.Y., 1986—. Mem. N.Y. Intellectual Property Law Assn., Am. Intellectual Property Law Assn. Home: 100 Riverside Dr New York NY 10024-4822 Office: Skadden Arps Slate Meagher & Flom Four Times Sq New York NY 10036-6522

SMITH, ROBERT CONNON, astronomy educator; b. Carlisle, England, Sept. 15, 1941; s. James Walter Dickson and Christian Brown (Connon) S.; m. Eleanor Mary Graham, Sept. 12, 1966; children: Rachel Alison, Deborah Jane, Rebecca Mary. BSc, Univ. Glasgow, Scotland, 1963, PhD, 1968. Asst. Univ. Glasgow, 1966-68; rsch. fellow Univ. Sussex, Brighton, 1968-72, lectr., 1972-90, sr. lectr., 1990-96, reader, 1996—, chmn. physics and astronomy, 1996—; mem. various coms. of sci. and engrng. rsch. coun., 1987-93. Author: Observational Astrophysics, 1995; editor: The Observatory Mag., 1977-83, Quar. Jour. of Royal Astron. Soc., 1984-96; contbr. over 90 articles to profl.jours.; over 100 book reviews. Recipient numerous rsch. grants. Fellow Royal Astronomical Soc. (coun. mem. 1976-79, 87-90). Avocations: reading, hill-walking, skiing. Office: Univ Sussex Astronomy Ctr, CPES Falmer, BN1 9QJ Brighton United Kingdom

SMITH, ROBERT GRANT, JR., public official, retired hotel executive; b. Harrisburg, Pa., July 22, 1932; s. Robert Grant Sr. and Helen C. (Reitz) S.; m. Pamela Ann Pasquariello-Epstein, June 8, 1978 (dec. 1985); stepchildren: Rosalind Ann Giest, Tara Helene Epstein. Attended, U.S. Army Officer's Candidate Sch., 1950-53. Owner Bob Smith Luncheonette, Harrisburg, Pa., 1953-54; pres., chmn. Hook's Diner, Inc., Allentown, Pa., 1954-67, Top of the Mall, Inc., Whitehall, Pa., 1967-71, Sheraton Inn, Inc., Allentown, 1971-83. Chmn. Allentown Housing Rev. Bd., 1964-78, Pa. Ho. of Reps. Workman Compensation Com., 1995—, Allentown Housing Authority; v.p. Allentown City Coun., 1976-77; treas. City of Allentown, 1978-81, Rep. nominee for mayor, 1981, Pa. senate, 1994, city controller, 1999; commr., chmn. Allentown Housing Authority, 1994—; active Mayor's Advancement Team, Allentown, 1993—; bd. dirs. Pa. Econ. Devel. Fin. Authority, commr., 1998—; mem. Lehigh County Small Bus. Loan Rev. Commn.; mem. pres. coun. Luth. Theol. Sem., Phila. Mem. Pa. Soc. (life), Rotary Club od Allentown, West Bethlehem Club, Sertoma Club, Zembo Temple, Harrisburg Consistory, Robert Burns Lodge, Jordan Lodge, Tall Cedars of Lebanon, No. Rep. Club, Bethlehem Club, Northend Rep. Club, Union League Phila., Ye Host's Square Club, Royal Order Jester Ct. # 128, Mercantile Club, Alepha Club. Lutheran. Address: 427 N 29th St Allentown PA 18104-4842

SMITH, ROBERT LUTHER, management educator; b. Kutztown, Pa., Feb. 18, 1927; s. Paul Luther and Esther Florence (Schwoyer) S.; m. Canda Eure Banks, Aug. 18, 1951; children: Kimberley Smith Kidd, Valerie Smith Eudy, Alexandra. BS, U.S. Naval Acad., 1949; MSA, George Washington U., 1975, DBA, 1984. Commd. USN, 1949-72, advanced through grades to comdr.; commanding officer USS Grouper, 1962-65; engr. and repair officer U.S. Submarine Base, Groton, Conn., 1965-67; supt. of test Portsmouth Naval Shipyard, Portsmouth, N.H., 1967-70; asst. project mgr. Naval Systems Submarine Acquisition, Washington, 1970-72; project mgr. EG&G, Washington Analytical, Rockville, Md., 1972-80; pres. Interface Resources Ltd., Alexandria, Va., 1980—; lectr. George Mason U., Fairfax, Va., 1981-84; prof. Coll. of Notre Dame of Md., Balt., 1984-98; faculty Dealer Mgmt. Inst., Columbus, Ohio, 1981-83; cons. in field of human resource mgmt. Contbr. articles to bus. publs. Sr. warden St. Paul's Episcopal Ch., Alexandria, 1980-81; mem. Alexandria Health Svcs., 1983—. Mem. ASQ, Assn. Quality and Participation, Acad. Mgmt., World Future Soc., Kiwanis Alexandria (pres. 1985-86, del. to internat. 1985), Tablet of Hon., 1999, Masons, Beta Gamma Sigma. Republican. Home: 1102 Bayliss Dr Alexandria VA 22302-3506

SMITH, ROBERT MYRON, investment company executive; b. Hartford, Conn., Jan. 10, 1930; s. Sterling Bishop and Harriet (Chamberlain) S.; m. Ellen Prouty, March 31, 1956 (div. 1982); m. Mary Peterson, Dec. 26, 1982; children: Catherine, Allison, Deborah, Elizabeth, Melissa. BA, Wesleyan U., Middletown, Conn., 1951; MBA, U. Pa., 1957. Underwriter Travelers Ins. Co., Hartford, 1951-56; asst. sec. Investors Mgmt. Co., Elizabeth, N.J., 1957-62; asst. v.p. Security Trust Co., Rochester, N.Y., 1962-64; exec. v.p. Keystone Custodian Funds, Inc., Boston, 1964-74; sr. v.p. Reliance Ins. Co., Phila., 1974-80; pres. Intervest Capital Mgmt., N.Y.C., 1980-81, J. Rothschild Capital Mgmt. Corp., N.Y.C., 1981-83, Ansbacher (Dublin) Asset Mgmt. Ltd., N.Y.C., 1983-95; pres. Smith Adv. Ltd., Annapolis, MD, 1995—, also bd. dirs.; bd. dirs. Gabelli Comstock Strategy Fund, Gabelli Comstock Capital Value Fund, Rye., N.Y. Mem. fin. com. Town of Cohasset, Mass., 1973-74; treas. First Parish in Cohasset, 1969-73, trustee, Severn Sch., Severna Park, MD. Served to 1st lt. USAF, 1951-53. Mem. Inst. CFA's, Balt. Security Analysts Soc., Assn. for Investment Mgmt. and Rsch., Annapolis Yacht Club, Ocean Reef Club. Avocations: sailing, gardening, bridge. Home: 812 Coach Way Annapolis MD 21401-6417

SMITH, ROBIN WYNCLYFFE, physics educator, consultant; b. Bristol, U.K., Sept. 23, 1942; s. Clifford John and Winnie May (Morgan) S.; m. Angela Mary Charters, July 18, 1964; children: James Gordon Charters, Peter George Robin, Rosalind Lucy Angela. BA, Trinity Coll., Cambridge, U.K., 1964; PhD, Imperial Coll., London, 1968. Rsch. asst. physics dept. Imperial Coll., London, 1967-68, lectr. physics, 1968-78, sr. lectr., 1978-96, prof. physics, 1996—, head applied optics group, 1987-92, dir. undergrad. studies, 1992-98, assoc. head dept. undergrad. studies, 1998—. Author papers on sci. optics. Mem. Inst. Physics, Optical Soc. Am. Office: Imperial Coll Blackett Lab, Prince Consort Rd, London England SW7 2BZ

SMITH, ROGER GRAHAM, company executive; b. Cambridge, Eng., Jan. 20, 1945; s. Albert Victor and Kathleen Florence (Goodman) S.; m. Rita Anne Rookes, Apr. 4, 1963 (div. 1973); children: Loraine Mary, Steven Graham. Student, Cambridge Coll. Arts & Tech., 1961. Rsch. engr. Cambridge U. Low-Temperature Rsch. Sta., 1961-63; project engr. Metals Rsch. Ltd., Cambridge, 1964-73, product mgr., 1974-78; product/sales mgr. Cambridge Instruments Ltd., 1979-82; dir. joint mng. Sightworth Ltd., Cambridge/York, 1983-90; mng. dir. R.G. Smith M&R Ltd., Cambridge, 1983—; dir. R.G. Smith Mgmt. & Rsch. Ltd. Contbr. articles to profl. jours.; copatentee in laser field, med. electronics. Recipient Queens Award in industry Tech. Award of U.K., 1973, IR-100 award, 1974. Home: 3 Ashcroft Ct, Cambridge England CB4 2SN

SMITH, ROGER KEITH, meteorology educator; b. Nottingham, Eng., May 22, 1943; s. George Henry and Marjorie (Insley) S.; m. Kathlyn O'Neill, Nov. 25, 1965; children: Elena (dec.), Caitlin. BS with honors, Manchester U., Eng., 1964; PhD, Manchester U., 1968. Asst. lectr. in math. U. Manchester, 1966-68; lectr. in applied math. Monash U., Australia, 1968-71, sr. lectr. in applied math., 1973-84, reader in applied math., 1984-88; lectr. in applied math. U. Edinburgh, Scotland, 1971-72; prof. meteorology U. Munich, 1988—. Recipient Dalton Math. prize U. Manchester, 1962. Fellow Royal Meteorol. Soc.; mem. Australian Meteorol. and Ocean Soc. (Priestley medal 1994), Am. Meteorol. Soc. Avocations: squash, photography, travel. Office: Univ Munich, Theresienstrasse 37, 80333 Munich Germany

SMITH, ROLAND BLAIR, JR., university administrator; b. Washington, Mar. 21, 1946; s. Roland Blair and Annie Louise S.; m. Valerie Peyton, June 16, 1969; children: Rovelle Louise, Roland Blair III. BA, Bowie State U., 1969; MPA, Ind. U., 1976; EdD, Harvard U., 1988. Dir. upward bound Notre Dame (Ind.) U., 1973-83, 86-88, dir. Ctr. for Edn. Opportunity, 1980-83, assoc. prof., 1991-96, dir. urban inst., 1992-96; assoc. provost Rice U., Houston, 1996—; tchg. fellow and grad. asst. Harvard U., 1983-86; exec. asst. to pres. U. Notre Dame, Notre Dame, Ind., 1988-96; 1st v.p., treas. Pvt. Industry Coun., St. Joseph Coun., Ind., 1987-91; cons. Lilly Endowment, Indpls., 1990-91; outside reviewer Nat. Ctr. Ednl. Stats, Washington, 1991-92; chmn. bd. dirs. Nat. Assn. Presidential Assts. in Higher Edn., Washington, 1993-94. Contbg. author: (ency.) African- American Education, 1996. Commr. Martin Luther King Fed. Holiday Commn., Washington, 1993-94; trustee YMCA of Michiana, St. Joseph County, Ind.; bd. dirs. NRTS Corp., City of South Bend, Ind., 1993-96, Harvard Alumni Assn. Bd., Cambridge, Mass., 1995—, LifeGift Organ Donation Ctr., 2000—; bd. visitors Bowie State U., 1998—; mem. South Bend Elkhart camp United Negro Coll. Fund. Recipient Outstanding Achievement award Bowie (Md.) State U., 1985; Named Disting. Alumnus Ind. U., South Bend, Ind., 1983, Nat. Assn. for Equal Opportunity in Higher Edn. (Bowie State U.), 1998. Mem. Am. Assn. Higher Edn. (Black caucus vice chair 1995-97, chair 1997-99, Service award 1998), Phi Delta Kappa, Kappa Alpha Psi (Achievement award 1986). Democrat. Methodist. Office: Rice U PO Box 1892 Houston TX 77251-1892

SMITH, RONALD EHLBERT, lawyer, educator, referral-based distributor, public speaker, writer and motivator, real estate developer; b. Atlanta, Apr. 30, 1947; s. Frank Marion and Frances Jane (Canida) S.; m. Annemarie Krumholz, Dec. 26, 1969; children: Michele, Erika, Damian. BME, Stetson U., 1970; postgrad., Hochschule Fuer Musik, Frankfurt, Fed. Republic Germany, 1971-74; Masters in German Lit., Germany & Middlebury Coll., 1975; JD, Nova U., 1981. Bar: Fla. 1982, U.S. Dist. Ct. (mid. dist.) Fla. 1983, U.S. Ct. Appeals (11th cir.) 1990, Ga. 1994, U.S. Dist. Ct. (no. dist.) Ga. 1994. Asst. state atty. 10th Jud. Cir. Ct., Bartow, Fla., 1982-85; pvt. practice Lakeland, Fla., 1985-94, Atlanta, 1994—; of counsel Mark Boychuk & Assocs. and Law Offices of Lori Lero, 1998—; rsch. asst. 10th Jud. Cir. Ct., Bartow, 1981-82; instr. Broward County C.C., Ft. Lauderdale, Fla., 1976-79, 91-94, pub. and pvt. schs., Broward County, Atlanta Schs., 1998—, Offenbach, Germany, 1971-78; instr. Polk C.C. and Police Acad., Winter Haven, Fla., 1981-94; adj. prof. English, Ga. State U., 1996—; adj. prof. law DeKalb Coll., 1997—; reader ETS GMAT, 1997—; part-time police instr. Police Acad., Forsyth, Ga., 1996—; counselor Jr. Achievement, 1997—, music instr. Atl. Pub. Schs., 1999—. Tchr., drama dir. Disciples I and II, United Meth. Ch., Lakeland, 1980-94, Glenn Meml. United Meth. Ch., Atlanta, 1994—, cand. to ministry, 2000—; Billy Graham counseling supr., 1994—;promoter Promise Keepers, 1995—; spkr., promoter ProNet, 1996—; min. music Scott Blvd. Bapt. Ch., Decatur, Ga., 1998, Gideon Internat., 1999—; candidate Ordained Ministry United Meth. Ch. Freedom Bridge fellow German Acad. Exch. Svc., Mainz, 1974-75. Mem. ABA, Christian Legal Soc., Lakeland Bar Assn., Atlanta Bar Assn.

SMITH, R(ONALD) SCOTT, lawyer; b. Washington, June 30, 1947; s. Joseph Peter Smith and Aurelia Ann (Bailey) George; m. Cheryle Rae Coffman, Nov. 15, 1974 (div. July 1977); m. Gloria Jean Haralson, Nov. 30, 1985. BJ, U. Mo., 1970, JD, 1973. Bar: Mo. 1973, U.S. Dist. Ct. (we. dist.) Mo. 1973, U.S. Ct. Appeals (10th cir.) 1990, U.S. Ct. Appeals (8th cir.) 1992, U.S. Dist. Ct. (ea. dist.) Mo. 1996. Field dir. The Mo. Bar, Jefferson City, 1973-75; law clk. to judge Mo. Ct. Appeals (we. dist.), 1975-76; ptnr. Shirkey, Norton & Smith, Kansas City, 1976-77, Jackson & Sherman, P.C. and predecessors, Kansas City, 1977-84, Birmingham & Furry, Kansas City, 1984, Birmingham, Furry & Smith, 1985-92, Birmingham, Furry, Smith & Stubbs, 1992-95, Furry & Smith, Kansas City, 1996—. Author: (with others) Automobile Accident Handbook, 1984, rev., 1986, Vexatious Refusal and Bad Faith, 1990, Insurance Claims, 1993; editor: The Rights & Responsibilies of Citizenship in a Free Society, 1974, Due Process of Law, 1974, News Headnotes, 1976-84, Young Lawyer, 1977-80; mem. editorial bd. Mo. Bar Jour., 1978-81; (TV series) legal script advisor Lex Singularis, 1973-75; (multimedia) producer, author Freedoms Lost, 1976; producer, playwright (musical-comedy play) Silly in Philly, 1987. Mem. ABA (mem. various coms.), Mo. Bar Assn. (dist. 12 chmn. 1979—, mem. various coms., Disting. Svc. award young lawyers sect. 1978, 79, 80), West Mo. Def. Lawyers Assn., Kansas City Met. Bar Assn. (pres. young lawyers sect. 1981-82, mem. various coms., Disting. Svc. award young lawyers sect. 1982, Leadership award sr. sect. 1985, First Ann. Pres. award sr. sect. 1987), Kansas City Claim Assn., Phi Delta Phi. Democrat. Roman Catholic. Fax: (816) 842-5600. E-mail: scottsmith@furrysmithlaw.com. Home: 3411 Shady Bend Dr Independence MO 64052-2816 Office: 1600 Bryant Bldg 1102 Grand Blvd Kansas City MO 64106-2316

SMITH, RONALD THOMAS, environmental scientist; b. Palmerton, Pa., Feb. 17, 1952; s. Albert Hubert and Jeanne Alice (Kemmerle) S.; m. Jeri Lee Hammond, June 21, 1997; 1 child, Clara Lucy. BA in English, U. Notre Dame, 1974; MS in Environ. Sci., Ind. U., 1983. Chemist City of Bloomington (Ind.), 1984-91; rsch. sci. Ind. Geol. Survey, Bloomington, 1994—; sci. advisor and activist McRae & McRae Attys., Bloomington, 1987, People Against the Incinerator, 1988-92, Thousands of People, 1983-87. Author: The Blind Eagle Blues: Power and Poison in the Heartland, 2000. Environ. activist Citizens Clearinghouse on Hazardous Waste, Arlington, Va., 1987; founder Ind. Voters Party, 1991; pro se litigant Schalk & Smith vs. Lee Thomas, U.S. Ct. Appeals (7th cir.), 1990. Notre Dame scholar, 1970-74; Pi Alpha Alpha Hon. Soc., 1982; recipient Giraffe Award for Pub. Svc., Giraffe Soc. Am., Everett, Wash., 1992. Mem. Nat. Coalition Against Mass Burn Incineration. Independent. Avocations: writing, music, politics, outdoors activities. Office: Ind U Ind Geol Survey 611 N Walnut Grv # S427 Bloomington IN 47405-2208

SMITH, ROSS EDWARD WILLIAM, environmental scientist; b. Toowoomba, Australia, July 31, 1961; s. Ian Kieth and Patricia Mary (Robson-Petch) S.; m. Deborah Helen Pinsker, Dec. 20, 1986; children: Timothy William, Eleanor Meg. BSc, James Cook U., Townsville, Australia, 1982, BSc with honors, 1983, PhD, 1988. From sr. biologist to acting mgr. environ. OK TEDI Mining Ltd., Tabubil, Papua, New Guinea, 1987-92, chief scientist, 1994-96; sr. environ. scientist BHP Engring., Sydney, Australia, 1992-94; dir. R & D Environ. Pty. Ltd., Brisbane, Australia, 1996—; rsch. asst. James Cook U., Townsville, 1982-87; damage assessment coord. Broken Hill Proprietary Oil Spill Response Group, Melbourne, Australian, 1993-96. Contbr. articles to profl. jours. Recipient Rsch. award Commonwealth of Australia, 1986-87. Mem. AAAS, Australian Inst. Biology, Australian Soc. for Limnology (Papua New Guinea rep. 1991-92), Australian Soc. for Fish Biology, Soc. Environ. Toxicology and Chemistry, Australian Soc. for Ecotoxicology (PNG rep. 1994-95, 97-2000). Avocations: angling, aquarist, children. Home: 41 Goldieslie Rd, 4068 Indooroopilly Australia Office: R & D Environ Pty Ltd, 49 Station Rd, 4068 Indooroopilly Australia

SMITH, ROSS LAMONT, clinical psychologist, consultant, researcher; b. Fremantle, Australia, May 11, 1922; s. James Lamont and Fanny (Barker) S.; m.Elsie Edith Lee, June 26, 1941; children: Wendy, Dianna, Julie. BA, U. Western Australia, 1951, postgrad. diploma in clin. psychology, 1956. Diploma, Internat. Acad. Behavioural Medicine, Counselling and Psychotherapy. Psychologist Edn. Dept. Western Australia, 1951-52; psychologist Health Dept. Western Australia, 1953-66, prin. clin. psychologist, 1966-82; pvt. practice clin. psychologist Western Australia, 1982—, pvt. practice forensic psychologist, 1982—; permanent vis. lectr. U. Western Australia, 1960-83; vis. lectr. Edith Cowan U., Western Australia, 1991-96; chmn. psychologists registration bd., Western Australia, 1977-83; hon. assoc. in applied psychology, Murdock U., Western australia, 1978-82; mem. Nat. Health and Med. Rsch. Coun., 1973-82.. Sgt. Australian Imperial Forces, 1941-46. Fellow Australian Psychol. Soc. Avocations: golf, photography, writing. Home: 52 A The Avenue, Nedlands 6009, Australia

SMITH, SELWYN M., psychiatrist; b. Sydney, NSW, Australia, Dec. 8, 1942; s. Abraham and Gertrude Lillian (Greenwood) S.; m. May Tsang, June 1, 1968; children: Benjamin Mark, Michelle Anne. MB, BChir, U. Sydney, 1966; MD with honors, U. Birmingham, 1974. Diplomate Am. Bd. Psychiatry and Neurology, Am. Bd. Forensic Psychiatry; cert. addiction specialist. Ho. physician Sydney Hosp., 1967, ho. surgeon, 1967; locum med. officer Royal Australian Army Med. Corps., 1967-68; sr. ho. officer psychiatry All Saints Hosp., 1968, registrar psychiatry, 1968-70; hon. sr. registrar psychiatry United Birmingham Hosps., 1971-75, lectr. psychiatry, 1973-75; dir. dept. forensic psychiatry Royal Ottawa Hosp., 1975-80, psychiatrist-in-chief, 1978-86; pvt. practice psychiatry Ottawa, 1986-96; con. psychiatrist, vis. med. officer St. John of God Hosp., Burwood, NSW, Australia, 1996—; clin. dir. post traumatic stress disorder program St. John of God Hosp., Burwood, 1997—; assoc. prof. psychiatry Sch. Medicine, U. Ottawa, 1975-81, prof. psychiatry, 1981-86; cons. psychiatrist Ottawa Gen. Hosp., 1976-87, Brockville Psychiat. Hosp., Brockville, Ont., 1976-96, Cmty. Care Sys., Inc., Wellesley, Mass., Can. Post Corp., 1986-96, Nat. Life Assurance Co., 1986-96, Can. Pension Plan, Health Can., 1990-96, Edgecliff Med. Ctr., 1997—, Gary Scarf and Assocs., 1997—, Ind. Med. Opinion, Sydney, 1997—, NSW Pvt. Hosp., Ashfield, 1997—; cons. psychiatrist, vis. med. officer Sydney Pvt. Clinic, Waverley, 1998—, Wandene Pvt. Psychiat. Hosp., Kogarah, 1999—, Wesley Pvt. Hosp., Ashfield, 1999—, Alpha Health Care Group and St. Edmund's Pvt. Hosp., 1999—; hon. rsch. fellow psychiatry U. Birmingham; presenter in field. Author: The Battered Child Syndrome, 1975; co-author: Self-Assessment of Current Knowledge in Forensic and Organic Psychiatry, 1978; co-editor: The Maltreatment of Children - A Comprehensive Guide to the Battered Baby Syndrome, 1978; assoc. editor Bull. Am. Acad. Psychiatry and the Law, 1978-91; mem. editl. adv. bd. Psychiat. Jour. U. Ottawa, 1975-87; mem. editl. bd. Behavioural Scis. and the Law, 1979-83, Am. Jour. Forensic Psychiatry, 1983, 85; contbr. chpts. to books and articles to profl. jours. State scholar, 1956-60, Commonwealth scholar, 1961-66; rsch. grantee United Birmingham Hosps., 1970-72. Fellow APA, Royal Coll. Physicians and Surgeons Can., Royal Coll. Psychiatrists U.K. (Bronze medal and rsch. prize 1974), Royal Australian and New Zealand Coll. Psychiatrists; mem. Am. Coll. Psychiatrists, Australian Acad. Forensic Scis., Am. Acad. Psychiatry and the Law (councillor, pres. 1985), Medico-Legal Soc. NSW, Australian Med. Assn., Ea. Suburbs Med. Assn. (coun. mem. 1997—). Avocations: sports, tennis, running, sailing. Fax: 97445879, 0295261145. Office: St John God Med Ctr, 20-24 Gibbs St Ste 4, Miranda NSW 2228, Australia

SMITH, SHEILA MARIE, lawyer; b. Chgo.; d. Donald Thomas and Catherine Ellen (Mariga) Morrison; m. Melvin Smith, Nov. 11, 1989. BSEE, Purdue U., 1981; JD, U. Cin., 1995. Bar: Ohio 1995, U.S. Dist. Ct. (so. dist.) Ohio 1996, U.S. Ct. Appeals (6th cir.) 1996, U.S. Supreme Ct., 1999. Mfg. engr., 1981-92; assoc. Freking & Betz, Cin., 1995-99, ptnr., 2000—; spkr. in field. Named to Order of Coif U. Cin., 1995. Mem. ABA, Am. Trial Lawyers Assn., Nat. Employment Lawyers Assn., Ohio Employment Lawyers Assn., Cin. Employment Lawyers Assn., Ohio Bar Assn., Cin. Bar Assn. Avocations: golf, traveling, cooking. Home: 3345 Legendary Trails Dr Cincinnati OH 45245-3074 Office: Freking & Betz 215 E 9th St Fl 5 Cincinnati OH 45202-2139

SMITH, SHELAGH ALISON, public health educator; b. Oak Ridge, Tenn., June 3, 1949; d. Nicholas Monroe and Elizabeth (Kimbrough) S.; m. Milton John Axley, 1991; 1 child, Elizabeth Claire. BS in Edn., U. Tenn., 1971, AS in Dental Hygiene, 1974; MPH in Health Svcs. Adminstrn., Johns Hopkins, 1979. Lic., cert. health edn. specialist, 1989. Social sci. rsch. analyst Dept. Health and Human Svcs., Health Care Fin. Adminstrn., Balt., 1980-85; pub. health educator, evaluator Nat. Cancer Inst.-NIH, Bethesda, Md., 1985-90; sr. policy analyst NIMH, Rockville, Md., 1990-92; pub. health advisor Ctr. Mental Health Svcs., Rockville, Md., 1992-96; sr. pub. health advisor Office Managed Care Ctr. Mental Health Svcs., Rockville, 1997—. Recipient adminstr.'s citation Health Care Fin. Adminstrn., 1981, dir.'s award Nat. Cancer Inst., 1989, Spl. Act Svc. award, 1997, 99, 2000, Sophe Honor award Nat. Capital Area, Soc. for Pub. Health Edn., 1999; Gen. Alumni scholar U. Tenn., 1973. Mem. APHA (pub. health edn. sect., governing coun. 1996-98, chmn. fin. and reimbursement for prevention svcs. com. 1987-89, 96, resolutions chair 1999, del. coalition nat. health edn. orgn. 1999—), Soc. Pub. Health Edn. (governing bd. and ho. of dels. 1993-95, legis. co-chmn. 1990-91, nat. capital area exec. bd., profl. devel. chair 1996, chpt. pres. 1996-97, treas. 1998-00), Washington Ethical Soc. (family coun.), Phi Kappa Phi. Democrat. Avocations: swimming, cooking, reading, animal activist, sailing. Home: 14106 Heathfield Ct Rockville MD 20853-2760 Office: SAMHSA Ctr Mental Health Svc Office of Managed Care 5600 Fishers Ln Rockville MD 20857-0001

SMITH, SIMON JOHN, physicist; b. Al Khobar, Dahran, Saudi Arabia, Feb. 24, 1969; arrived in U.K., 1977; s. George Arthur and Pauline Anne (White) S. BSc with honors, Nottingham U., Eng., 1990. Sci. officer Def. Rsch. Agy., Farnborough, Eng., 1991-92; higher sci. officer Def. Rsch. Agy. Eglin AFB, Fla., 1992-93, Farnborough, 1993-96; sr. sci. officer Def. Evaluation and Rsch. Agy., Farnborough, 1996—. Mem. AIAA, Inst. Physics (chartered physicist. Mem. Ch. of England. E-mail: sj.smith@physics.org. Home: 28 Beta Rd Cove Farnborough, Hampshire GU14 8PG, England Office: DERA Air Def Weapons Bldg A2, Ively Rd, Farnborough Hants GU14 0LX, England

SMITH, SIR ROLAND, company executive; b. Oct. 1, 1928; s. Joshua and Hannah Smith; m. Joan Shaw, 1954. BA, U. Birmingham, Eng.; MSc, U. Manchester, PhD in Econs. Lectr. econs. U. Liverpool, 1960, dir. Bus. Sch., 1963; prof. mktg. U. Manchester, 1966-88, hon. vis. prof., 1988—, chancellor, 1996—, prof. emeritus mgmt. sci., 1988—; non-exec. chmn. Sr. Engring. Ltd., 1973-92; chmn. Temple Bar Investment Trust Ltd., 1980—, House of Fraser, 1981-86, Readicut Internat., 1984-96, Hepworth plc, 1986-97, Brit. Aerospace, 1987-91, P & P plc, 1988—, Manchester United Plc, 1991—; dir., cons. various pub. cos. Flying officer RAF, 1953. Avocation: walking. Office: care Bank of Eng, Threadneedle, London EC2R 8AH, England*

SMITH, STEPHEN DEWITT, finance educator; b. Jacksonville, Fla., Apr. 30, 1956; s. Lawrence DeWitt and Ruth Virginia (Miller) S. BA in Bus. Adminstrn., U. South Fla., 1977; PhD in Fin., U. Fla., 1980. Asst. prof. U. Tex., Austin, 1981-85; assoc. prof. Ga. Inst. Tech., Atlanta, 1986-90, Mills B. Lane prof. banking and fin., 1990-91; H. Talmage Dobbs Jr. prof. fin. Ga. State U., Atlanta, 1992—; vis. scholar 4th dist. Fed. Home Loan Bank Atlanta, 1988-90, 6th dist. Fed. Res. Bank Atlanta, 1991—. Author: Principles of Interest Rates, 1993; contbr. articles to profl. jours. Mem. Am. Fin. Assn., Fin. Mgmt. Assn., Commerce Club. Democrat. Avocations: squash, whitewater rafting, fishing. Office: Ga State U 35 Broad St Fl 12 Atlanta GA 30303-2302

SMITH, STEPHEN KEVIN, obstetrician, gynecologist; b. Wallasey, Eng., Mar. 8; s. Albert and Drusilla (Hills) S.; m. Catriona Maclean Smith, July 8; children: Lucie Jane, Richard Alan, Alice Charlotte. MBBS, U. London, 1974, MD, 1982; MA, U. Cambridge, 1993. Head dept. ob-gyn. U. Cambridge, Eng., mem. staff dept. pathology; head women's svcs. Addenbrooke's Hosp., Cambridge. Editor Reproductive Medicine Revs., 1992—. Grantee Med. Rsch. Coun., Assn. Med. Rsch. Charities Industry, Cambridge, 1988; fellow Fitzwilliam Coll. Cambridge, 1992. Fellow Royal Coll. Obstetricians and Gynecologists (edn. com., sci. com. 1990-98), Inst. Biology, Acad. Med. Scis.; mem. Royal Coll. Physicians, Royal Coll. Surgeons. Mem. Labour party. Avocations: family, politics, literature, music. Home: 14 Hertford St, Cambridge CB4 3AG, England Office: Robinson Way, Cambridge CB2 2SW, England

SMITH, STEPHEN MARK, lawyer; b. Newport News, Va., July 1, 1948; s. Joseph and Marian (Sturman) S.; m. Dawn Lee Williams, Dec. 10, 1978; children: Ryan David, Miles Stephen. BA in Psychology, William & Mary, 1971, JD, 1974. Bar: Va. 1974, N.Y. 1975, D.C. 1975, U.S. Supreme Ct., U.S. Ct. Appeals (2d, D.C., 4th cirs.). Lawyer Rothblatt, Rothblatt, et al., N.Y.C., 1974-76, Joseph Smith Ltd., Hampton, Va., 1976-99; bd. dirs. Enrenfried Techs. Mem. com. Va. Beach Dems., 1990—. With USN, 1968-70. Included in Best Lawyers in Am., 1997-2000. Mem. ATLA, Am. Bd. Trial Lawyers (diplomate), Am. Bd. Trial Advocates, Va. Trial Lawyers Assn. (bd. dirs. 1978—), Brain Injury Assn. Va. (bd. dirs. 1997—). Avocations: fishing, reading, boating, jogging, golf. Office: Joseph Smith Ltd 2100 Kecoughtan Rd Hampton VA 23661-3215

SMITH, STEVEN DELANO, professional basketball player; b. Highland Park, Mich., Mar. 31, 1969. Student, Mich. State U. Guard Miami Heat, 1991-94, Atlanta Hawks, 1994-99, Portland Trailblazers, 1999—. Named Sporting News All-Am. First Team, 1990, 91, NBA All-Rookie Team, 1992, Dream Team II, 1994. Office: Portland Trailblazer One Center Ct Ste 200 Portland OR 97227

SMITH, STEWART MCMILLAN, software engineer; b. Huddersfield, Eng., Apr. 15, 1957; m. Wendy Carol Knight, Apr. 4, 1992. BS with honors, U. East Anglia, Norwich, Eng., 1978. Trainee programmer Data 100 Sys. Ltd., 1978-79; sr. designer Internat. Computers Ltd., 1979-86; sr. cons. Carnell Computer Tech. Ltd., 1986-90; project leader Unisys Europe-Africa Ltd., Eng., 1990-91; dir. Pentagon Computer Cons. Ltd., Reading, Eng., 1991—. Mem. IEEE, Fedn. Européene d' Assns. Nats. d'Ingénieurs, Brit. Computer Soc., The Engring. Coun. (chartered).

SMITH, SUSAN PORTER, artist, environmentalist; b. Weston, W.Va., Aug. 11, 1934; d. Edward Conrad and Eugenia Porter (Arnold) S. BA, Vassar Coll., 1956; postgrad., Inst. Allende, San Miguel de Allende, Mex., 1975-76, Bellas Artes, San Miguel de Allende, Mex., 1977-79, Nat. Acad. Design, N.Y.C., 1981. Editorial asst. Spl. Libraries Jour., N.Y.C., 1958-59; edn. advisor Sci. Am., N.Y.C., 1962-63; sci. rsch. editor Readers Digest, N.Y.C., 1964-74; freelance artist, painter, photographer East Quogue, N.Y., 1978—. Exhibited in group shows at Bellas Artes, Mex., 1981, San Miguel de Allende, 1987, East End Arts Coun., Riverhead, N.Y., 1988, 93; contbr. to book: Rooms with No View, 1974. Adviser, supporter Ctr. for Adolescents, San Miguel de Allende, 1986—; organizer San Miguel Artists for the Environment; assoc. dir. for environ. Letitia Echlin Meml. Fund, 1997-99; v.p. San Miguel Audubon Soc., 1984-93; pres. Sociedad Audubon de Mex., 1993-96; assoc. dir. Rio Laja project Fundacion Ecologica de Guanajuato, 1997-99; pres., founder Salvemos al Rio Laja, A.C., 1999—.

SMITH, TERENCE EDWIN, art historian; b. Geelong, Australia, Aug. 14, 1944; s. Allan George and Gwennyth Mary (Dunkley) S.; m. Christina Marion White Smith, Dec. 18, 1971; children: Keir, Blake. BA (hon.), U. Melbourne, Australia, 1966; MA (hon.), U. Sydney, Australia, 1976, PhD, 1986. Head dept. fine arts U. Sydney, Australia, 1987-91; vis. prof. U. Calif., San Diego, 1991, U. Chgo., 1994-95; Power prof. contemporary art U. Sydney, 1995—, dir. Power Inst., 1994—; vis. prof. Duke U., 1997; dir. Mus. Contrmporary Art, Sydney, Australia, 1988-94, 96-2000, Australian Ctr. for Photography, Sydney, 1996—; com. mem. Australian Ctr. for Am. Studies, Sydney, 1994-98, Rsch. Inst. for Humanities and Social Scis., U. Sydney, 1996—. Editor: Ideas of the University, 1996, In Visible Touch: Modernism and Masculinity, 1997, Impossible Presence: Surface and Screen in the Photogenic Era, 2000; author: Making the Modern America: Industry, Art and Design, 1993; co-author: Australian Painting 1788-1990, 1991. Chmn. Australian Internat. Sch., Sydney, 1994-99; dir. Union Media Svcs., Sydney, 1976-96. Harkness fellow Commonwealth Rund, N.Y.C., 1972-74, H.V. duPont fellow Hagley Mus., Wilmington, Del., 1993, Rockefeller fellow Rockefeller Found., U. Chgo., 1994-95. Mem. Australian Acad. Humanities, Comite' Internat. de L'Histoire de L'art, Art Assn. Australia (v.p. 1995-96). Avocations: tennis, soccer. Office: Power Inst A26, University of Sydney, Sydney 2006, Australia

SMITH, THOMAS KENT, radiologist, viticulturist; b. Bowling Green, Ohio, Aug. 21, 1934; s. Robert O. and Roslyn Smith; m. Jaleh Saidi, Feb. 1, 1974; children: Jeffrey, Todd, Mark, Blake, Tyler. BS with high honors, U. Cin., 1957; MD, Case Western Res. U., 1961. Intern Nat. Naval Med. Ctr., Bethesda, Md., 1961-62; resident in radiology VA Med. Ctr., Long Beach, Calif., 1965-69; dir. radiology Harriman Jones Med. Group, Long Beach, 1969-88; fellow in MRI/CT U. Calif., San Francisco, 1988-89; dir. MRI Orange County MRI, Fountain Valley, Calif., 1989-90; chmn. dept. diagnostic imaging Kaiser Permanente Med. Ctr., Honolulu, 1990-2000, dir. MRI, 1994-2000; fellow in radiologic pathology Armed Forces Inst. of Pathology, Washington, 1968; mem. adv. bd. Hawaii Permanente Med. Group, Honolulu, 1990-2000; bd. dirs. Harriman Jones Med. Group (chmn. 1978-79), Harriman Jones Assocs. (chmn. 1981-86); assoc. clin. prof. radiology U. Hawaii, Honolulu, 1990—; asst. clin. prof. U. Calif., Irvine, 1970-88; clin. instr. U. Calif., San Francisco, 1988-89, asst. clin. prof., 1989-99; cons. in radiologic devel. Kaiser Permanente Internat., 1996-98; owner Rubaiyat Vineyard, Sonoma County, Calif. Lt. (MC) nulear submarine svcs. USN, 1961-65. Fellow Am. Coll. Radiology; mem. Hawaii Radiol. Soc. (pres. 1992-93), Radiol. Soc. N.Am., Internat. Soc. Magnetic Resonance in Medicine, Margulis Soc., Alpha Omega Alpha. Avocations: fishing, travel, viticulture. E-mail: TKJALEH@aol.com. Fax: (808) 247-6472. Home: 5409 Sonoma Mountain Rd Santa Rosa CA 95404-8884 Office: Kaiser Permanente Med Ctr 3288 Moanalua Rd Honolulu HI 96819-1495

SMITH, THOMAS RAYMOND, III, software engineer; b. Phila., Dec. 6, 1946; s. Thomas Raymond and Naomi (Hart) S.; m. Marguerite Anne LeMoyne de Martigny, Sept. 6, 1969; children: Michelle Renée, Heather Anne, Thomas Raymond IV. Student, MIT, 1964-68. Sr. analyst Dabcovich and Co., Lexington, Mass., 1969-71; sr. analyst, prin. Multi-Logic Corp., Burlington, Mass., 1970-73; sr. mem. tech. staff Digital Equip. Corp. (now Compaq Computer Corp.), Houston, 1974—. Co-editor: IEEE Dictionary, 1993; author, co-editor numerous stds. books for Internat. Electrotech. Commn. and IEEE, 1984-93. Mem. IEEE (chmn. various stds. coms., 1980—). Home: 36 Toppans Ln Newburyport MA 01950-3843 Office: Compaq Computer Corp ZK01-3/H42 110 Spit Brook Rd Nashua NH 03062-2711

SMITH, TROY ALVIN, aerospace research engineer; b. Sylvatus, Va., July 4, 1922; s. Wade Hampton and Augusta Mabel (Lindsey) S.; m. Grace Marie Peacock, Nov. 24, 1990. BCE, U. Va., 1948; MS in Engring., U. Mich., 1952, PhD, 1970. Registered profl. engr., Va., Ala. Structural engr. U.S. Army C.E., Norfolk, Va., Wilmington, N.C., Washington, 1948-59; chief structural engr. Brown Engring. Co., Inc., Huntsville, Ala., 1959-60; structural rsch. engr. U.S. Army Missile Command, Redstone Arsenal, Ala., 1960-63, aerospace engr., 1963-80, aerospace rsch. engr., 1980-96, ind. profl. engr., 1996—. Contbr. articles to AIAA Jour., Jour. Sound and Vibration. With USNR, 1942-46, PTO. Fellow Dept. Army, 1969. Mem. N.Y. Acad. Scis., Assn. U.S. Army, Elks, Sigma Xi. Achievements include research on procedures for analysis of structures. Home: 2202 Yorkshire SE Decatur AL 35601-3470 Office: US Army Aviation & Missile Command Redstone Arsenal AL 35898

SMITH, VAN P., holding company executive; b. Oneida, N.Y., Sept. 8, 1928; m. Margaret Ann Kennedy, Nov. 19, 1960; children: Lynn Ann Smith Walters, Mark Charles, Paul Gregory, Susan Colleen Smith Newell, Victor Patrick. AB in Pub. Adminstrn. and Econs., Colgate U., 1950; JD, Georgetown U., 1955; LLD (hon.), Ball State U., 1980; D of Bus. (hon.), Vincennes U., 1985; LLD (hon.), Ind. State U., 1986. Bar: D.C., Ind. Assoc. Warner, Clark & Warner, Muncie, Ind., 1955-56; co-founder, dir. Ontario Corp. of Muncie, 1956-63, sec. then v.p. sales, 1956-63, pres., CEO, 1963—, also chmn. bd., 1978—; chmn. bd. Sherry Labs. Inc., Ontario Devel. Corp., Ontario Systems Corp., Ontario Corp. Found., all in Muncie, Ontario Techs., Calif., CDS Engring., Calif., Tex., and other subs. Ontario Corp.; bd. dirs. Hoosier Motor Club, Indpls., subs. Ontario Corp.; ptnr. Smittie's Men's Store, Village Developers, all in Muncie. Rep. mem. Ind. Ho. of Reps., 1960-62; del. Ind. and Nat. Rep. Conv.; pres. Muncie Police & Fire Commn., 1963-66; mem. parochial sch. bd. St. Mary's Sch., Muncie, 1968-70; mem. Ind. Employment Security Bd., 1969-71, Ind. Commn. Higher Edn., 1971—, Nat. Adv. Council SBA, 1982—, Gov.'s Fiscal Policy Adv. Council, 1982—, Ind. Labor & Mgmt. Council, 1983—, Ind. Econ. Devel. Council, 1985—, Presdl. Observation Team Phillipine Nat. election, 1986, Presdl. Trade Mission to several Far Eastern countries, 1984; bd. dirs. Bus.-Industry Polit. Action Com., 1984—; trustee Colgate U., 1985—, La Lumiere Sch., 1983—, Acad. for Community Leadership, 1975—; bd. dirs. Muncie Symphony Assn., 1980-88, pres. 1986-87; pres. Del. County United Way, 1969-70; bd. dirs. Newman Found. Ind., 1969—, Religious Heritage Am. 1986-88; active St. Mary's Cath. Parish, Muncie; mem. Diocese of Lafayette Bishop's Com. 100, 1969-80, pres. 1969-70; bd. regents Cath. U. Am., Washington, 1986-90, trustee 1990—; trustee Interlochen (Mich.) Ctr. for Arts, 1991—. Served 1st lt. USAF, 1951-53. Named one of Outstanding Young Men of Am., Jaycees, 1960; recipient Bus. and Layman award, Religious Heritage Am., 1984, Ind. Cath. Layman award, Faith, Family & Football of Ind., Inc. 1985, Civic Service award, Ind. Assn. Cities and Towns, 1985; invested Knight of Equestrian Order of Holy Sepulchre of Jerusalem, 1986. Mem. ABA, Ind. Bar Assn., Ind. Mfrs. Assn. (chmn. 1978-80, bd. dirs. 1978—), Forging Industry Assn. (pres. 1976-77), Alliance of Metalworking Industries (chmn. 1978-80), U.S. C. of C. (chmn. numerous coms., active panels and councils 1977—), Ind. State C. of C. (exec. com. 1982—), Rotary (past pres.), Elks, K.C., Meridian Hills Country Club, Theta Chi (pres. Iota chpt. 1950), Delta Theta Phi, Beta Gamma Sigma (hon.), Delta Sigma Pi (hon.). Clubs: Columbia, Skyline (Indpls.); Ind. Soc. of Chgo. Office: 123 E Adams St Muncie IN 47305-2402

SMITH, VIRGIL BAKER, retired electrical engineer; b. Bastrop, La., Oct. 13, 1916; s. George and Virginia (Mallette) S.; m. Phyllis Patterson, Nov. 10, 1945; children: Nancy E., Patricia A., Randall T.. BSEE, La. State U., Baton Rouge, 1935-39. Supr., elec. engr. USN, Washington, 1941-77, ret., 1977; sr. elec. engr. George G. Sharp Inc., Arlington, Va., 1981-82, Systems & Applied Sci. Corp., Arlington, 1982-85, Designers & Planners, Arlington, 1985-91; ret., 1991. Contbr. article to profl. jour. com. chmn. Boy Scouts Am. Indian guides, Four Corners, Md., 1949; trustee elem. sch., Four Corners, Md., 1950. Recipient Superior Civilian Svc. award USN, 1978, Spl. Achievement award USN, 1975.

SMITH, VIVIAN BRIAN, English literature educator, poet; b. Hobart, Tasmania, Australia, June 3, 1933; s. Vivian S. and Sybil Olive Daniels; m. Sybille Maria Gottwald; children: Vanessa, Gabrielle, Nicholas. BA, U. Tasmania, Hobart, 1954, MA, 1955; PhD, U. Sydney, Australia, 1970. Lectr. in French U. Tasmania, 1955-66; lectr. to sr. lectr. in English U. Sydney, 1970-82, reader in English, 1982-96. Lit. editor (jour.) Quadrant, Sydney, 1975-90; author: (collected poems) Tide Country, 1982, Selected Poems, 1985, New Selected Poems, 1995, Late News, 2000, (criticism) The Poetry of Robert Lowell, 1974, Vance and Nettie Palmer, 1975. Recipient Grace Leven prize for poetry, 1983, NSW Premier's prize (Kenneth Slessor prize) for poetry, 1985, Patrick White Literary award, 1997. Fellow Acad. of Humanities of Australia. Home: 19 McLeod St, NSW Mosman 2088, Australia

SMITH, W. PRESTON, publishing executive, educator, real estate broker; b. Little Rock, Oct. 30, 1938; s. Arthur W. (dec.) and Syble M. (Love) S. (dec.); children: Cynthia Ann Smith Jones, Carey R. BS, Little Rock U., 1959; postgrad., Henderson State U., Arkadelphia, Ark., 1968-69, Ark. State U., 1969, Texarkana Coll., 1981-82, U. Ark., Pine Bluff, 1983, Tulane U., Miss. County Community Coll., 1985; MEd, U. Ark., 1984. Cert. sch. adminstr., social studies tchr., Laubach reading instr. Tchr. math. and social studies 4th St. Jr. High Sch., North Little Rock, 1959-61; owner Walker Enterprises, Little Rock, 1964—; tchr. Malvern (Ark.) Pub. Schs., 1967-68, Prattsville (Ark.) High Sch., 1968-69, Poyen (Ark.) High Sch., 1969-70, Horatio (Ark.) High Sch., 1981-82, Bingham Rd. Acad., Little Rock, 1982-83, Luxora (Ark.) High Sch., 1985, Stanton Rd. Sch., Little Rock, 1986; tchr., prin. Dept. Correction Sch. Dist., Tucker Penitentiary Unit, Ark., 1989-95; mem. sci. textbook selection com., Prattsville High SCh., 1968-69; mem. math. standards com. Ark. Coun. Tchrs. Math., Little Rock, 1983; lectr. Zero Down seminars on creative real estate financing; owner Silver Dollar Press. Author, pub.: Jokebook of the Century, 1989; author: Jokebook of the Century, vol. II, 1990, Jokebook of the Century, vol. III, 1991, How To Start Your Own Business, 1992, Forms For Business, vol. I and II, 1995, Consumers Should Know, vol. I-vol. IV, 1996, Consumers Should Know, vol. V-vol. IX, 1997. Past pres., song leader Sunday Sch. class; former mem. Ch. choir. Mem. AARP (immediate past pres. England, Ark. chpt., chpt. specialist), Ark. Assn. Ednl. Adminstrn. (assoc.), Ark. Ret. Tchr. Assn. (state membership chmn. 1998—), Lonoke County Ret. Tchr. Assn. (pres. 1997-2000). Lodge: Order of DeMolay (master councillor). Avocations: candlemaking, refinishing furniture, tape recording classical music. E-mail: wpsmith 98@yahoo.com. Home and Office: PO Box 1167 Fairfield Bay AR 72088-1167

SMITH, WALDO GREGORIUS, former federal agency administrator; b. Bklyn., July 29, 1911; s. John Henry and Margaret (Gregorius) S.; m. Mildred Pearl Prescott, July 30, 1935 (dec. Jan. 1992); 1 child, Carole Elizabeth Smith Levin. Student, CCNY, 1928-29; BS in Forestry, Cornell U., 1933. Registered profl. engr., Colo. Forester Forest Svc., U.S. Dept. Agr., Atlanta, 1933-41, Ala. Divsn. Forestry, Brewton, 1941-42; engr., civil engring. technician Geol. Survey, U.S. Dept. Interior, 1942-71, cartographic technician, 1972-75; chmn. Public Transp. Council, 1975-89; legislator aide to individuals Colo. State Legis. Internship Program, 1987-95. Contbr. articles to profl. jours. Recipient 40 Yr. Civil Svc. award pin and scroll; 42 Yr. Govt. Svc. award plaque. Fellow Am. Congress Surveying and Mapping (life, sect.-treas. Colo. chpt. 1961, program chmn. 1962, reporter 1969, mem. nat. membership devel. com 1973-74, rep. to Colo. Engring. Council 1976-77); mem. AAAS (emeritus), Denver Fedn. Center Profl. Engrs. Group (U.S. Geol. Survey rep. 1973-76, Engr. of Yr. award 1975), Nat. Soc. Profl. Engrs. (pre-coll. guidance com. 1986-91, life 92—), Profl. Engrs. Colo. (chpt. scholarship chmn. 1979-96, advt. corr., svc. award 1983), Cornell U. Alumni Assn. (alumni secondary schs. com. Quadrangle Club), Common Cause, Colo. Engring. Council (chmn. library com. 1970-99, spl. rep. Regional Transp. Dist., 1974-75; mem. sci. fair com. 1970-71; rep. ex officio Denver Pub. Libr. Found. Bd. Trustees 1975-80, mem. historic agreement with Denver Pub. Libr. 1993, Pres.'s Outstanding Svc. award 1987), Environ. Concerns (chmn. com. 1988—, treas. 1989-91, Rocky Mountain Arsenal Cleanup, 1994—, mem. site specific adv. bd., restoration adv. bd.), Fedn. Am. Scientists, Am. Soc. Engring. Edn., People for Am. Way, Sr. Scientists and Engrs. Home: 3821 W 25th Ave Denver CO 80211-4417

SMITH, WARREN ALLEN, writer; b. Minburn, Iowa, Oct. 27, 1921; s. Harry Clark and Ruth Marion (Miles) S. BA, U. No. Iowa, 1948; MA, Columbia U., 1949. Chmn. dept. Eng. Bentley Sch., N.Y.C., 1949-54, New Canaan (Conn.) H.S., 1954-86; founder, pres., chmn. bd. Variety Sound Corp., N.Y.C., 1961-90; pres. Afro-Carib Records, 1971-90, Talent Mgmt., 1982-90, AAA Rec. Studio, 1985-90; founder, pres. Variety Rec. Studio, 1961-96; instr. Columbia U., 1961-62. Author: Who's Who in Hell, 2000; book rev. editor The Humanist, 1953-58; editor (jour.) Taking Stock, 1967-93, Pique, 1990-93, Van Rijn's Pad, 1991, Janestreeter, 1997-98; contbr. book revs. Libr. Jour.; editl. assoc. Free Inquiry, 1992—; contbg. editor GALHA, Eng., 1996—; syndicated columnist Manhattan Scene in W.I. newspapers; columnist, Humanist Potpourri in Free Inquiry, 1994-98; drama critic Brontë Newsletter, 1995-2000; book reviewer New Humanist, London, 1997—; CD producer: Manuel Salazar. Pres. Taursa Fund, 1971-73; bd. dirs. Jane Street Corp. Treas. Secular Humanist Soc. N.Y., 1988-93; sec. Jane St. Corp., 1995-97, 98-99. With ACT UP, Hume Soc.; founding mem. Voltaire Soc. Am. With AUS, 1942-46. Recipient Leavey award Freedoms Found. at Valley Forge, 1985. Mem. ASCAP, Coun. Secular Humanism, Mensa, N.Y. Skeptics Soc. (bd. dirs. 1990-94), Internat. Press Inst., Am. Unitarian Assn., Rationalist Press Assn., Conn. Edn. Assn., Asociación Iberoamericana Ético Humanista (hon.), Brit. Humanist Assn., Humanist Book Club (pres. 1957-62), Bertrand Russell Soc. (v.p. 1977-80, bd. dirs. 1973—), Omaha Beach Veterans Assn., Stonewall Veterans Orgn. (treas. 1998-99), Mensa Investment Club (chmn. 1967—) Signer Humanist Manifesto II, 1973, Signer Humanist Manifesto 2000. Avocation: teratology. E-mail: wasm@idt.net. Home and Office: 31 Jane St Apt 10 D New York NY 10014-1980

SMITH, WARREN MORRISON, cardiologist; b. Hamilton, New Zealand, Mar. 10, 1945; s. Maurice Hendry and Doreen Ailsa (Brown) S.; m. Josephine Clare Ricketts, Mar. 2, 1974; children: Benjamin, Rachel, Joseph. MBChB, Otago, New Zealand, 1968. Resident Auckland Hosp. Bd., New Zealand, 1969-70, 72-73; vol. physician Vol. Svc. Abroad, Malaysia, 1971; med. tutor specialist Auckland Hosp., 1974-75; rsch. assoc. Duke U., 1978-81; cardiologist Green Lane Hosp., Auckland, 1981—, chmn. dept., 1998—; clin. tchr. Auckland Med. Sch., 1982-96; mem. scientific com. Nat. Heart Found., New Zealand, 1993-96. Co-author: (chpts.) The Heart, 1982, 86, 89; cons. editor Adis Internat., New Zealand, 1983-96. Physician Christian World Svc., Beirut, 1982; mem. Palestinian Human Rights Com., Auckland, 1982-96, Physicians Against Nuclear War, Auckland, 1984-95; personal physician to prime minister, UN, 1988. Rsch. grantee Nat. Heart Found., 1987; cardiology fellow Green Lane Hosp., 1975-77. Mem. N.Am. Soc. Pacing/Electrophysiology, Cardiac Soc. Australia/New Zealand, Soc. Cardiopulmonary Tech. (pres. 1994-96), Electrophysiology Working Group (chmn. 1992). Presbyterian. Home: 1A Lurline Ave EPSOM, Auckland New Zealand Office: Green Lane Hosp, Green Lane W, Auckland New Zealand

SMITH, WAYLAND RUFUS, retired county official; b. Sterling, Colo., Dec. 11, 1936; s. Eldon Emerson and Edith Marie Smith; m. Barbara Hartshorne, Dec. 27, 1959; children: Gregory T., Douglas S., Kristen M. BA, U. Denver, 1958. Project mgr. Denver Housing Authority, 1958-60; housing rehab. specialist Redevel. Land Agy., Washington, 1961-62, asst. chief rehab. divsn., 1963-64; asst. exec. dir. Cumberland (Md.) Urban Renewal Agy., 1965-66; exec. dir. Parkersburg (W.Va.) Urban Renewal Authority, 1967-71, Fayette County Redevel. Authority, Uniontown, Pa., 1971-98; ret. Facilities chmn. State Theater Ctr. for the Arts, Uniontown, 1999. Mem. Nat. Assn. of Housing and Redevel. Ofcls. (v.p. profl. devel. 1985-87, pres. Pitts. chpt. 1983-85, pres. Middle Atlantic Regional Coun. 1995-97, bd. govs. 1985-87, 95-99). Democrat. Avocations: cookie baking, woodworking. Home: 12 Kimberly Dr Uniontown PA 15401-6580

SMITH, WAYNE ANDREW CHRISTOPHER, project engineer; b. Kingston, Jamaica, Aug. 16, 1970; s. Basil Vassel and Nina Dorothy (McDonald) S.; m. Michele Sandra Thomas, June 24, 2000. BSc, U. the West Indies, Port-of-Spain, Trinidad, 1993. Project engr. Grace Kennedy, Kingston, Jamaica, 1993-96; Bulk ops. mgr. Grace Food Processors, Kingston, Jamaica, 1995, plant engr., 1996-97, project/planning engr., 1997—; v.p. exec. com. Venezuelan Inst. Mem. Ch. Dayton. Jamaica Govt. Exhbn. scholar, Kingston, 1990. Avocations: philately, numismatism, collecting gospel music. E-mail: wayne.smith@gkco.com.

SMITH, WAYNE LARUE, lawyer, consultant; b. Marietta, Ohio, June 15, 1955; s. Benjamin LeCompte and Bettigene (Jerman) S. BS, Ariz. State U., 1980, MBA, 1987; JD, U. Ariz., 1986. Bar: Fla. 1994, D.C. 1998, U.S. Dist. Ct. (so. dist.) Fla. 1995. Pres. D,B&H Staffing Svcs., Phoenix, 1984-87; v.p. Alan LaRue & Assocs., Phoenix, 1987-88; pres. The Proview Group, Boca Raton, Fla., 1988-93; lawyer Morgan & Hendrick, Key West, Fla., 1993-99, The Smith Law Firm, Key West, Fla., 1999—; bd. dirs. Fla. Lawyers Assistance, Inc., Ft. Lauderdale. Pres. Stop AIDS Project of South Fla., Inc., West Palm Beach, 1988-91; bd. dirs., treas. Comprehensive AIDS Program of Palm Beach County, 1989-93; mem. adv. bd. The Red Barn Theatre, Key West, 1995—, The Met. Musical Theatre Co., Phoenix, 1996-99; pres. The Experience, Inc., Santa Fe, 1990-95. Recipient New Mem. award, Excellence award Fla. Atlantic Builders Assn., 1989; Up and Comer awards Price Waterhouse/South Fla. Bus. Jour., 1991-92. Mem. ABA, Fla. Bar Assn. (computer law com. 1998-99), Monroe County Bar Assn. (pres. 1995-96), D.C. Bar Assn. Democrat. Office: The Smith Law Firm 330 Whitehead St Key West FL 33040-6543

SMITH, WILLARD GRANT, psychologist; b. Sidney, N.Y., June 29, 1934; s. Frank Charles and Myrtle Belle (Empet) S.; m. Ruth Ann Dissly, Sept. 14, 1957; children: Deborah Sue Henri, Cynthia Lynn Koster, Andrea Kay Richards, John Charles. BS, U. Md., 1976; MS, U. Utah, 1978, PhD, 1981. Lic. psychologist, Utah; cert. sch. psychologist, sch. adminstr., tchr., Utah; nat. cert. sch. psychologist; diplomate Am. Bd. Forensic Examiners, Am. Bd. Psychol. Specialities, Am. Bd. Disability Analysts. Tchg. asst. dept. ednl. psychology U. Utah; rsch. asst. U. Utah Med. Ctr., 1976-78; rsch. cons. Utah Dept. Edn., 1977; program evaluator Salt Lake City Sch. Dist.; program evaluator, auditor Utah State Bd. Edn., 1978; sch. psychologist Jordan Sch. Dist., Sandy, Utah, 1978-82; tchr. Jordan Sch. Dist., Sandy, 1979-80; exec. dir. Utah Ind. Living Ctr., Salt Lake City, 1982-83; spl. edn. cons. Southeastern Edn. Svc. Ctr., 1983-85; sch. psychologist Jordan Sch. Dist., Sandy, 1985-96; assoc. psychologist Don W. McBride & Assocs., Bountiful, Utah, 1989-91; pvt. practice Sandy, 1991—. Master sgt. USAF, 1953-76. Decorated Air Force Commendation medal with 2 clusters. Fellow Am. Coll. Forensic Examiners; mem. APA, Nat. Assn. Sch. Psychologists, Air Force Sgts. Assn., Ret. Enlisted Assn., Phi Kappa Phi, Alpha Sigma Lambda. Home: 8955 Quail Hollow Dr Sandy UT 84093-1903

SMITH, WILLIAM FRENCH, environmental safety adminstrator; b. Bay City, Tex., Nov. 30, 1941; s. William and Willie Mae (Perry) S.; m. Sylvia Knight, Feb. 4, 1977; children: William III, Maurice. BS, Tuskegee U., 1964; postgrad., Washington U., 1968-70. Equipment engr. Boeing Co., Huntsville, Ala., 1964-67; plant design engr. McDonnell Douglas Corp., St. Louis, 1967-69; project engr. St. Louis County Govt., 1969-72; divsn. engr. E.I. duPont de Nemours &Co., Inc., Wilmington, Del., 1972-74, Victoria, Tex., 1972-74; engring. mgr. Westinghouse Corp., Millburn, N.J., 1974-76; bldg. safety engr. Denver Pub. Schs., 1976—, project adminstr., 1977—, energy conservationist, 1978—; dir. hazardous materials Tuskegee U., Denver, 1985-88, environ. safety dir., 1988—; reservist Fed. Emergency Mgmt. Agy. Bd. dirs. Denver Opportunities Industrialization Ctr., 1979-80, Nat. Commn. on Future of Regis Coll.; mem. Mayor's Citizens Adv. Com. on Energy, 1980—, City of Lakewood Sr. Citizens Adv. Coun., Lakewood Bd. Appeals, Lakewood Code Enforcement Com.; past bd. dirs. Colo. Alliance Environ. Edn., Colo. Emergency Planning Commn. Served with USNR, 1979—. Recipient Pres.'s Nat. award for energy conservation, 1980. Mem. Am. Soc. Safety Engrs., Colo. Assn. Sch. Energy Coords., Am. Assn. Blacks in Energy, Denver Pub. Schs. Black Adminstrs. and Suprs. Assn. (treas.), Colo. Environ. Health Assn., Nat. Asbestos Coun., Colo. Hazardous Waste Mgmt. Soc., Colo. Hazardous Materials Assn. (past treas.), Denver Emergency Planning Commn., Civil Air Patrol, Colo. Renewable Energy Soc., Colo. Energy Network, Nat. Assn. Minority Contractors, Internat. Hazardous Materials Assn., Tuskegee U. Alumni Assn. Republican. Home: 102 S Balsam St Lakewood CO 80226-1344 Office: Denver Public Schs 900 Grant St Denver CO 80203-2907

SMITH, WILLIAM RAYMOND, farmer, thoroughbred owner, breeder and trainer, retired history educator, philosophy educator; b. Bowling Green, Ky., June 5, 1932; s. William Raymond and Rose Velta (Biggerstaff) S.; m. Robin Sommers, July 12, 1954 (div. Sept. 1977); children: Dana Leslie Henning, Lauren Reneé Imgrund; m. Lee Ann McClathchey, Dec. 31, 1994. BA in Liberal Arts, U. Chgo., 1953, MA in English, 1959, PhD in History of Culture, 1961. Lic. thoroughbred trainer. Asst. prof. English Pa. State U., Univ. Park, 1961-63, Haverford (Pa.) Coll., 1963-66; asst. prof. English Scripps Coll., Claremont, Calif., 1966-67, exec. officer literature divsn., 1966-67; chmn. integrative studies Shimer Coll., Mt. Carroll, Ill., 1967-70; asst. prof. humanities Reed Coll., Portland, 1970-71; prof. history and philosophy U. Pitts., Johnstown, Pa., 1971-98, acad. dean, 1971-72; ret., 1998; Fulbright prof. Am. studies U. Utrecht, Netherlands, 1969-70. Author: History as Argument, 1966, The Rhetoric of American Politics, 1969; contbr. chpts. to books The Colonial Legacy, 1971, Nineteenth Century Literary Criticism, 1986. Cpl. U.S. Army, 1955-57. Recipient fellow Union for Rsch. in Higher Edn., Kenneybunkport, Maine, 1968. Mem. Va. Thoroughbred Assn., Va. Horseman's Assn., Casanova Hunt. Avocations: fox hunting rider, steeplechase rider. Home: Paradigm Farm 8699 Green Rd Warrenton VA 20187-7732

SMITH, WILLIAM STEVEN, university financial administrator, consultant; b. Waynesboro, Tenn., Dec. 8, 1949; s. William Charles and Betty (Martin) S.; m. Ann Morene Smith, July 19, 1974; children: Tonya Leanne, Christopher Steven. BS, Austin Day State U., Clarksville, Tenn., 1976; MBA, U. N. Ala., 1983; DEd, U. Ala., 1998. Asst. coord. ext. program Ala. Christian Coll., Montgomery, Ala., 1970-78; assoc. comptr. U. North Ala., Florence, 1978-98, dir. bus. affairs, 1998—; fin. cons. Nelson Svc. Group Inc., Florence, 1996—. Bd. dirs. Shoals Econ. Devel. Auth., Florence, 1995—. Named Exec. of Yr. local chpt. Profl. Secs. Internat., Florence, 1987. Mem. Ala. Assn. Coll. and Univ. Bus. Officers (pres. 1997-98), So. Assn. Coll. and Univ. Bus. Officers., Florence Optimist Club (pres. 1992). Baptist. Avocations: boating, amateur radio. Home: 7404 Benji Rd Florence AL 35634-2868 Office: U N Ala PO Box 5001 Florence AL 35632-0001

SMITH, WINSTON EVANS, JR., social worker, writer,; b. Kingston, Jamaica, Sept. 17, 1956; came to U.S., 1974; s. Winston Evans Smith and Monica Montrose Brown-Smith; m. Jan. 1, 1981 (div. Sept. 1984); children: LaToya, Evan. BA, CUNY, 1984. Rsch. analyst Tanzer Econ. Assocs., N.Y.C., 1981-83; dir. Legal Aid Ctr., CCNY, 1984-85; rsch. assoc. National Mus. History, N.Y.C., 1986-88, Smithsonian Instn., Washington, 1986-88; asst. dir. ARC, N.Y.C., 1993-95; paralegal Sobelshon Sch., N.Y.C.; tchr. N.Y.C. Pub. Schs. Mem. Caribbean Media Assn. Avocation: music. Home: PO Box 310912 Jamaica NY 11431-0912

SMITH, WOOLLCOTT, statistician, educator; b. Balt., June 9, 1941; s. Henry Clay and Nancy Woollcott S.; m. Leah Johnson, Feb. 3, 1968; children: Amelia, Keston. BS, Mich. State U., 1962, MS, 1964; PhD, Johns Hopkins U., 1969. Asst. prof. U. N.C., Chapel Hill, 1969-72; sr. statis. Woods Hole (Mass.) Oceanographic Instn., 1972-81; prof. Temple U., Phila., 1981—; dir. Data Analysis Lab., Temple U., 1982-89; sr. rsch. fellow Woods Hole Oceanographic Instn., 1996-98. Author: (book) The Cartoon Guide to Statistics, 1993; editor: (book) Ecological Diversity in Theory and Practice, 1979. Mem. Am. Statis. Assn. (pres. Phila. chpt. 1988-89). Office: Stats Dept/Temple Univ N Broad & Cecil D Moore Philadelphia PA 19122

SMITH, ZACHARY TAYLOR, II, retired tobacco company executive; b. Mt. Airy, N.C., June 15, 1923; s. Eugene Gray and Leonita (Yates) S. AB in Econs., U. N.C., 1947; LLD (hon.), Wake Forest U., 1989. With R.J. Reynolds Tobacco Co., 1947-85, treas., dir., 1970-85. Trustee, past pres. Z. Smith Reynolds Found.; life trustee Wake Forest U.; bd. dirs., past pres. Mary Reynolds Babcock Found., past bd. dirs. Arts and Scis. Found., U. N.C.; past mem. nat. devel. coun. U. N.C.-CH; past bd. dirs. Med. Found. N.C.; past bd. dirs. Leadership Winston-Salem; past mem. adv. coun. The Carolina Challenge; past chmn. bd. visitors U. N.C. Chapel Hill; past mem. Reynolds Scholarship Com., past mem. bd. visitors Wake Forest U.; mem. adv. coun. to hosp., past mem. bd. visitors inst. policy studies and pub. affairs Duke U.; past mem. adv. bd. Duke U. Hosp.; past bd. dirs., N.C. Sch. Arts Found., Devotion Found., N.C. Outward Bound Sch., Small Bus. Devel. Com., Winston-Salem Symphony, Citizens Planning Coun.; past trustee Forsyth Hosp. Authority; past pres., dir. Child Guidance Clinic Forsyth County, YMCA, Red Shield Boy's Clubs; past chmn. indsl. divsn. Arts Coun. fund drive; past v.p., dir. Arts Coun.; past v.p., dir. Amos Cottage; past bd. visitors Meredith Coll.; past trustee St. Augustine Coll.; past bd. dirs. alumni assn. U. N.C.; vice chmn., dir. Friends of U. N.C.-Greensboro Libr. Mem. Old Town Club, Rotary. Democrat. Episcopalian. Home: 2548 Forest Dr Winston Salem NC 27104-2030

SMITH-CARROLL, MYRTLE, civic worker, former journalist; b. N.Y.C., July 16, 1926; d. John Leo and Violet Jane (Robertson) Reilly; m. Charles Jackson Smith Jr., Sept. 21, 1946 (div. Aug. 1962); children: Charles Jackson III, Lynda Maureen Smith Necker (dec.), Robert William, Raymond Gerard, Rosemary Rita, Walter Alfred, Virginia Anne Werly; m. Charles F. Carroll, Mar. 17, 1979. BA in English, Hunter Coll., 1947. Columnist Midland News, S.I., N.Y., 1960-63, Amsterdam News, N.Y.C., 1963-66; editor religious sect. St. Petersburg (Fla.) Times, St. Petersburg, Fla., 1972-73; diocesan reporter, photographer Fla. Cath., St. Petersburg, 1973-76; columnist, photographer Pinellas Dem., St. Petersburg, 1974-76; reporter Sta. WTSP-TV, St. Petersburg, 1975-76; talk show host Sta. WTSP, St. Petersburg, 1977-90; media specialist St. Petersburg Fire Dept., 1983-88; cons. Pinellas County Emergency Med. Svc., Clearwater, Fla., 1987-88, St. Petersburg Jr. Coll., 1992. Asst. prodr.: (TV show) Link to a Lifeline, 1986; prodr.: (child's puppet show) Fire Station 911, 1989; author, prodr.: (theatrical prodn.) Book of Newteronomy, 1995. St. Petersburg rep. on trip to China, 1983; cons. Juvenile Welfare Bd., St. Petersburg, 1992, bd. dirs., 1994—, sec., 1997—; bd. dirs. Brookwood, St. Petersburg, 1992-94, ACLU, St. Petersburg, 1994—; state committeewoman Fla. Dem. Party, 1992—; sec. Women's Caucus, Dem. Nat. Com., 1994—; coord. women's network Fla. Dem. Party, 1995—; del. Women's Initiative on Race, 1998. Recipient Susan B. Anthony award NOW, Pinellas County, 1980. Mem. Suncoast Tiger Bay Club (bd. dirs.). Democrat. Avocations: gardening, creative writing, domestic violence victims' advocate, community redevelopment. Home: 330 Belleair Dr NE Saint Petersburg FL 33704-2437

SMITH-EPSTEIN, MARY KATHLEEN, dancer; b. Austin, Tex., Sept. 12, 1940; d. Walter Bentley Jr. and Kathleen Beatrice (Lancaster) Smith; m. Witaly Osins, June 6, 1967 (div. 1975); m. Howard Irwin Epstein, June 20, 1987. Grad. high sch., Dallas. Demi soloist Am. Festival Ballet, European Tour, 1961; prin. dancer HET Nat. Ballet, Amsterdam, Holland, 1962-67; guest artist Berliner Ballet, Berlin, 1964, Ballet De L'Atlantique, Nantes, France, 1967-68, Cologne, Fed. Republic Germany, 1968-70, Ballet Spectacular, Miami, Fla., 1973-74; prin. dancer Opernhaus, Hannover, Fed. Republic Germany, 1968-70, Musiktheater, Gelsenkirchen, Fed. Republic Germany, 1968-71, Ballet Van Vlaanderen, Antwerp, Belgium, 1971-73, Ballet De Wallonie, Charleroi, Belgium, 1973-74, Irish Nat. Ballet, Cork, Ireland, 1975-85, Chgo. Ballet, 1977-78, Ballet Met., Columbus, Ohio, 1978-79; founder, co-dir. Conservatory Classical Dance, Eugene, Oreg., 1989—; founder N.W. Chamber Ballet, 1988—; artistic dir. 8 Dance Ensemble. Choreographer: (ballets) Opus 1, 1978, For Him From Her, 1982, The Catalyst, 1983 (Bursary Irish Arts Council award 1985), Pas De Deux, 1985

(Bursary Irish Arts Council 1985), Logic of the Heart, 1988, Masquerade Suite, 1988; choreographer Ballet N.W., Performing Ensemble Conservatory Classical Dance, 1989—. Treas. Neighborhood Watch, Vida, Oreg., 1988-89, bd. mem. (sec. to pres.) of Lane Arts Coun., 1993-96; dir. bldg. fund, pres. bd. dirs. Kaygu Dakshana Chuling, 1995—. Alexandra Danilova scholar, Dallas, 1958. Buddhist.

SMITHER-KOPPERL, MARGARET LYDIA, plant pathologist; b. Woking, England, July 8, 1955; d. Derry C. and Lydia (Grugeon) Smither; m. H. Benjamin Kipperl, Sept. 30, 1980; children: Aaron D., Hannah L. BSc in Botany, Royal Holloway U., London, 1976; MSc in Plant Scis., Wye London U., Wye, Kent, London, 1977; PhD in Plant Pathology, Mich. State U., 1988. Rsch. asst. Mich. State U., East Lansing, 1981-88, rsch. assoc., 1988-90; plant physiologist Inst. of Offshore Engring., Orkney, Edinburgh, Scotland, 1991-94; postdoctoral U. Fla., Gainesville, 1995-98; sr. scientist Prediation Inc., Gainesville, 1998-99; dir. of rsch. Entomos LLC, Gainesville, 1999—. Contbr. articles to profl. jours. Mem. Am. Phytopathological Soc. (com. women 1997-2000, soil 1998—), Am. Assn. Advancement of Sci. Avocations: cooking, swimming, reading. E-mail: mlsk@entomos.com. Office: Entomos LLC 4445 SW 35th Ter Gainesville FL 32608-6559

SMITHERMAN, DAVID CONRAD, medical marketing professional; b. Tuscaloosa, Ala., July 27, 1953; s. Lowell Conrad and Ruth (Patton) S.; m. Anne Torrey Van Antwerp, Oct. 13, 1979; children: David Van Antwerp, Garet Patton. BA, U. Ala., 1976. Adminstrv. dir. U. Ala. Mgmt. Inst., Tuscaloosa, 1976-80; mktg. mgr. Gulf States Paper Corp., Tuscaloosa, 1980-86, Advantage Med. Inc., Birmingham, Ala., 1986-90; dir. mktg. Carraway Meth. Health Sys., Birmingham, 1990-99; exec dir. Carraway Hosps. Found., Birmingham, 1993-97; asst. adminstr. for corp. comm. and devel. Carraway Meth. Med. Ctr., 1999—; advisor Jr. League Birmingham, 1999—. Editor: Culture of Excellence: A History of Carraway Methodist Medical Center Vols. 1-2, 1995. Team capt. Boy Scouts Am., Birmingham, 1993-96, Met. Devel. Bd., Birmingham, 1994-95; mem. comm. com. United Way of Ctrl. Ala., Birmingham, 1996; bd. dirs. Jefferson County Task Force on Infant Immunization, Birmingham, 1996—; bd. dirs., trustee Episcopal Found. of Jefferson County, 1995-2000. Mem. Am. Heart Assn. (bd. dirs. Ala. chpt. 1998—), Am. Cancer Soc. (bd. dirs. Ala. chpt. 1992-96, 98—), Am. Hosp. Assn., Soc. Healthcare Strategy and Devel., Assn. for Healthcare Philanthropy (bd. dirs., treas. Ala. chpt. 1992—), Ala. Hosp. Assn. Mktg. Soc. (bd. dirs., treas. 1991-98, pres-elect 1998-99, pres. 1999-2000, chmn. bd. 2000—), Mountain Brook Swim and Tennis Club, Pi Kappa Phi. Episcopalian. Avocations: tennis, travel, skiing. Home: 752 Montgomery Dr Birmingham AL 35213-2504 Office: Carraway Meth Health Sys 1600 Carraway Blvd Birmingham AL 35234-1913

SMITHERS, ALAN GEORGE, educator, researcher; b. London, May 20, 1938; s. Alfred Edward and Queenie Lillian (Carmichael) S.; m. Angela Grace Wykes, Aug. 27, 1962; children: Vaila Helen, Rachel Hilary. BSc in Botany, U. London, 1959, PhD in Plant Physiology, 1966; MSc in Edn., Bradford U., Eng., 1973, PhD in Edn., 1974; MEd, Manchester (Eng.) U., 1981. Chartered psychologist, Eng. Lectr. biology Coll. of St. Mark and St. John, London, 1962-64; lectr. botany Birkbeck Coll., U. London, 1964-67; rsch. fellow in edn. Bradford U., 1967-69, sr. lectr. edn., 1969-76; prof. edn. Manchester U., 1977-96; prof. edn. (policy rsch.) Brunel U., London, 1996-98; Sydney Jones prof. edn. Liverpool (Eng.) U., 1998—; dir. Ctr. for Edn. and Employment Rsch., Liverpool, 1998—; seconded to Brit. Petroleum, London, 1991-92; cons. New Zealand Bus. Roundtable, Wellington, 1997—. Author: Sandwich Courses: An Integrated Education?, 1976, The Progress of Mature Students, 1986, What Employers Want of Higher Education, 1988, The Shortage of Maths and Physics Teachers, 1988, The Growth of Mixed A-Levels, 1988, Increasing Participation in Higher Education, 1989, Teacher Loss, 1990, Trends in Science and Technology Manpower Demands and Mobilities, 1990, Graduates in the Police Service, 1990, Teacher Provision in the Sciences, 1991, Gender, Primary Schools and the National Curriculum, 1991, The Vocational Route into Higher Education, 1991, Teacher Provision: Trends and Perceptions, 1991, Staffing Secondary Schools in the Nineties, 1991, Every Child in Britain, 1991, Beyond Compulsory Schooling, 1991, Teacher Turnover, 1991, Technology in the National Curriculum, 1992, Technology at A-Level, 1992, Assessing the Value, 1992, General Studies: Breadth at A-Level?, 1993, Changing Colleges: Further Education in the Market Place, 1993, All Our Futures: Britain's Education Revolution, 1993, Technology Teachers, 1994, The Impact of Double Science, 1994, Post-18 Education: Growth, Change, Prospect, 1995, Affording Teachers, 1995, Co-educational and Single Sex Schooling, 1995, Trends in Higher Education, 1996, Technology in Secondary Schools, 1997, Staffing Our Schools, 1997, The New Zealand Qualifications Framework, 1997, Coeducational and Single-Sex Schooling Revisited, 1997, Degrees of Choice, 1998, National Student Assessment Policies in Primary Schools in England, 1998, Teacher Supply 1998: Passing Problem or Impending Crisis?, 1998, Teacher Supply 1999: Old Story or New Chapter?, 1999, Further Education Re-Formed, 2000, Coping with Teacher, 2000, Shortages, 2000, Talking, 2000, Heads, 2000; contbr. over 100 articles to profl. jours.; broadcaster and newspaper columnist. Mem. Royal Soc. Com. on Tchr. Supply, 1990-94, Nat. Curriculum Coun., 1992-93, Beaumont Com. on Vocat. Edn., 1995-96; spl. adviser edn. and employment com. Ho. of Commons, 1997—. Fellow Soc. for rsch. into Higher Edn. (coun. mem. 1976-82), Brit. Psychol. Soc. (assoc.). Avocations: walking, theater. Office: CEER Dept Edn U Liverpool, 19 Abercromby Sq, Liverpool L69 7ZG, England

SMITH-LOMBARDINI, MARYELIZABETH ANNE, opera singer, artistic director; b. Norfolk, Va., Sept. 1, 1957; d. John George and Alma Mary (Ross) Smith; m. Danilo Piero Luigi Lombardini, Oct. 30, 1987. MusB, U. Mich., 1979, MusM, 1980; student, Conservatory G. Verdi, Milan, Italy, 1980-83; diploma, La Scala Opera Studio, Milan, Italy, 1982-84. Apprentice Vienna (Austria) State Opera Studio, 1984-86; artistic dir. Laboratorio Lirico-Chamber Music Soc., Palermo, Italy, 1994-96; prof. State Music Conservatory A. Scontrino, Trapani, Italy, 1995-96; artistic dir. Operalaboratorio-City of Palermo Opera, 1997—; tchr. Ars Nova Schola Cantorum, Palermo, 1991-97, The Brass Group, Palermo, 1995-98; dir. Palermo-Detroit Cultural Exch., City of Palermo, 1998—. Singing debut Turin Opera Theatere, 1984, Vienna State Opera, 1985, La Scala Theater, Milan, 1991; recordings include La Griselda (Vivaldi), Stabat Mater (Boccherini). Participant Med. Rsch. Benefits, M.D. Cancer Rsch. Benefits for UNICEF, Palermo, 1994—. Winner internat. singing competition, Turin Opera Theater, 1984; scholar Kosciuszko Found., N.Y., 1978; postgrad. fellow Rotary Internat., Detroit, 1980. Mem. Sicilian Chamber Music Soc., Friends of the Teatro Massimo, Coll. Music Soc., Accademia Siculo-Normanna, Mu Phi Epsilon, Pi Kappa Lambda. Roman Catholic. Avocations: house plants, reading, cats, embroidery, horseback riding. Office: Ars Nova, Via Dante 12, 90141 Palermo Italy

SMITHSON, PETER DENHAM, architect; b. Stockton-on-Tees, Eng., Sept. 18, 1923; s. William Blenkiron and Elizabeth (Denham) S.; m. Alison Margaret Gill, 1949 (dec. Aug. 1993); 3 children. Ed., Stockton-on-Tees Grammar Sch., U. Durham, Royal Acad. Schs., London. Asst. L.C.C., 1949-50; pvt. practice architect with Alison Smithson, 1950-93. Prin. works include Hunstanton Sch., Economist Bldg., London, Robin Hood Gardens, G.L.C. Housing in Tower Hamlets, Garden Bldg. St. Hilda's Coll., Oxford, Amenity Bldg., U. Bath, Second Arts Bldg. 6 East, U. Bath. Arts Barn, U. Bath, 1978-90, Porch at Ansty Plum, Porches at Tecta, Lauenforde, 1992-99, Hexenbesenraum, Karlshafen, 1991-96, Hexenhaus Bridge and Pier, 1997, Hexenhaus Tea-House, Panorama Porch, Tecta, Lauenforde, 1997-98; exhbns. include House of the Future, 1956, Milan Triennale, 1968, Venice Biennale, 1976, On the Floor-Off the Floor, Cologne, 1998, Tichleindeckdich, Cologne and Berlin, 1993, The Lattice Idea, Cologne, 1999, 2000, Madrid, 2000; author: Ordinariness and Light, 1970, Urban Structuring Studies, 1971, Without Rhetoric, 1973, The Heroic Period of Modern Architecture, 1981, The Shift, 1982, Monographs, The 1930's, 1985, Italian Thoughts, 1993, Changing the Art of Inhabitation, 1994, Bath Walks Within Walls: Oxford and Cambridge Walks, (all with A. Smithson) Book Work, 1995, Italienische Gedanken, 1996, The Charged Void: Architecture, 2000, (with K. Unglaub) Flying Furniture, 1999. Address: Cato Lodge, 24 Gilston Rd, London SW10 9SR, England

SMITH-THOMPSON, PATRICIA ANN, public relations consultant, educator; b. Chgo., June 7, 1933; d. Clarence Richard and Ruth Margaret (Jacobson) Nowack; children: Deborah, Kurt, Nancy, Janna, Gail, Lori; m. Tyler Thompson, Aug. 1, 1992. Student, Cornell U., 1951-52; BA, Centenary Coll., Hackettstown, N.J., 1983. Prodn. asst. Your Hit Parade Batten, Barton, Durstine & Osborne, 1953-54; pvt. practice polit. cons., 1954-66; legal sec., asst. Atty. John C. Cushman, 1966-68; field dep. L.A. County Assessor Office, 1968-69; pub. info. officer L.A. County Probation Dept., 1969-73; dir. consumer rels. Fireman's Fund, San Francisco, 1973-76; spl. projects officer L.A. County Transp. Commn., 1977-78; tchr. Calif. State U., Dominguez Hills, 1979-86; editor, writer Jet Propulsion Lab., 1979-80; pub. info. dir. L.A. Bd. Pub. Works, 1980-82; pub. info. cons. City of Pasadena, Calif., 1982-84; pub. rels. cons., 1983-90; cmty. affairs cons. Worldport L.A., 1990-92. contbr. articles to profl. jours. Mem. First United Meth. Ch. Commn. on Missions and Social Concerns, 1983-89; bd. dirs. Depot, 1983-87; mem. devel. com. Pasadena Guidance Clinics, 1984-85; pres. Cultural Arts Assn., Bear Valley Springs, 1999-2000. Recipient Pro award L.A. Publicity Club, 1978, Outstanding Achievement award Soc. Consumer Affairs Profls. in Bus., 1976, Disting. Alumni award Centenary Coll., 1992. Mem. Pub. Rels. Soc. Am. (accredited mem., award for consumer program, 1977, 2 awards, 1984, Joseph Roos Cmty. Svc. award 1985), Nat. Press Women (pub. rels. award 1986), Calif. Press Women (awards 1974, 78, 83, 84, 85, cmty. rels. 1st place winner 1986, 87, 88, 89), Nat. Assn. Mental Health Info. Officers (3 regional awards 1986). Republican. Home and Office: 24145 Jacaranda Dr Tehachapi CA 93561-8309

SMITS, HANS N.J., bank executive. Degree in civil engring., U. Delft, 1973, degree in econs., bus. adminstrn., 1975. Numerous positions Delta Svcs. Min. Pub. Works, 1975-86; head govtl. com. Dutch Telecom. Industry, 1985-86; dep. dir. Min. Econ. Affairs, 1986-88; dir. gen. transp. Min. Transp. & Pub. Works, 1988-89, sec. gen., 1989-92; CEO Amsterdam Schiphol Airport, 1992-98; dep. chmn. exec. bd. Rabobank Group, Utrecht, The Netherlands, 1998; chmn. eec. bd. Rabobank Nederland, Utrecht, The Netherlands. Office: Rabobank Group, PO Box 17100, 3500 HG Utrecht The Netherlands*

SMITS, HELEN LIDA, physician, administrator, educator; b. Long Beach, Calif., Dec. 3, 1936; d. Theodore Richard Smits and Anna Mary Wells; m. Roger LeCompte, Aug. 28, 1976; 1 child, Theodore. BA with honors, Swarthmore Coll., 1958; MA, Yale U., 1961, MD cum laude, 1967. Intern, asst. resident Hosp. U. Pa., 1967-68; fellow Beth Israel Hosp., Boston, 1969-70; chief resident Hosp. U. Pa., 1970-71; chief med. clinic U. Pa., 1971-75; assoc. adminstr. for patient care svcs. U. Pa. Hosp., 1975-77; v.p. med. affairs Community Health Plan Georgetown U., Washington, 1977; dir. health standards and quality bur. Health Care Financing Adminstrn., HHS, Washington, 1977-80; sr. rsch. assoc. The Urban Inst., Washington, 1980-81; assoc. prof. Yale U. Med. Sch., New Haven, 1981-85; assoc. v.p. for health affairs U. Conn. Health Ctr., Farmington, 1985-87; prof. community medicine U. Conn. Sch. Medicine, Farmington, 1985-93; hosp. dir. John Dempsey Hosp., Farmington, 1987-93; dep. administr. Health Care Financing Adminstrn., Washington, 1993-96; pres., chmn. Health Right, Inc., Meriden, Conn., 1996-99; vis. prof. Robert F. Wagner Grad. Sch. Pyb. Svc., NYU, 1999—; commr. Joint Com. on Accreditation Hosps., Chgo., 1989-93, chair, 1991-92. Contbr. numerous articles to profl. jours. Bd. dirs. The Ivoryton Playhouse Fedn., Inc., 1990-92, The Connecticut River Mus., 1990-93, Hartford Stage, 1990-93; mem. Dem. Town Com., Essex, Conn., 1982-89. Recipient Superior Svc. award HHS, Washington, 1982; Royal Soc. Medicine Found. fellow, London, 1973; Fulbright scholar, 1959-60. Mem. ACP (master, regent 1984-90), Inst. Medicine, Nat. Acad. Scis., Phi Beta Kappa, Alpha Omega Alpha. Episcopalian. Avocations: sailing, cooking, gardening. Office: Tisch Hall 40 W 4th St Rm 600 New York NY 10012-1106

SMITS, JOZEF FRANCISCUS MARIA, pharmacology educator; b. Tilburg, The Netherlands, Apr. 7, 1953; s. Johan and Lenie (Tummers) S.; m. Theodora Veronique van Woerkum, Feb. 18, 1975; children: Anke Maria, Tom Joep. MSc, Catholic U., Nijmegen, The Netherlands, 1976; PhD, U. Maastricht, The Netherlands, 1980. Rsch. fellow U. Maastricht, The Netherlands, 1976-80; asst. prof. U. Maastricht, 1980-84, assoc. prof., 1984-92, prof., 1992—; rsch. fellow U. Iowa, Iowa City, 1982; vis. scientist U. Va., Charlottesville, 1989-90; assoc. dean for rsch. Med. Faculty, U. Maastricht, 1991, 93-96, vice dean, 1993-96. Established investigator Netherlands Heart Found., 1986; recipient Organon award Dutch Pharm. Soc., 1992. E-mail: j.smits@farmaco.unimaas.nl. Office: U Maastricht Dept Pharmacol, PO Box 616, Maastricht 6200MD, The Netherlands

SMITS, PAUL H.M., biologist; b. Roosendaal, The Netherlands, Oct. 21, 1962; s. Marinus Smits and Joke Koolen; m. Maria Gigenback. PhD, U. Amsterdam, The Netherlands, 1992. Postdoctoral fellow U. Amsterdam, 1993-94, Leiden (The Netherlands) U., 1994-97; head molecular biology dept. Slotervaart Hosp., Amsterdam, 1997—. Office: Slotervaart Hosp, Louwesweg 6, 1066 EC Amsterdam The Netherlands

SMITS, RONALD FRANCIS, English educator, poet; b. Bayonne, N.J., Dec. 22, 1943; s. Edwin Joseph and Florence Ann Smits; m. Bonnie Lee Brown, June 10, 1970 (div. Mar. 1976); 1 child, Ronald Thomas. AB, Rutgers U., 1966; MS, Ind. State U., 1969; PhD, Ball State U., 1978. Instr. English, Kaskaskia Coll., Centralia, Ill., 1969-74; instr. Ball State U., Muncie, Ind., 1976-78; asst. prof. English, Indiana U. Pa., 1979-92, assoc. prof., 1992-96, prof., 1996—; dir. faculty forum br. campus Indiana U. Pa., Kittanning, 1998—. Contbr. poetry to various publs., including So. Rev., Wildsong, Poetry East, Jour. AMA, Pa. English, The Tex. Observer. 1st lt. U.S. Army, 1966-68, Vietnam. Doctoral fellow Ball State U., 1974-78. Avocations: walking, nature hikes, walks through city neighborhoods, nature study, reading. Home: PO Box 466 Ford City PA 16226-0466 Office: Ind U of Pa Armstrong County Campus Kittanning PA 16201

SMITTLE, NELSON DEAN, artist; b. Peebles, Ohio, Sept. 19, 1934; s. Nelson John and Alma Katherine (Green) S.; m. Claire Wiggins, May 5, 1973. BS, BFA, U. Cin., 1962, MA, 1971. Commd. 2d lt. U.S. Army, 1962; staff officer U.S. Army Photo Agy. Pentagon, Washington, 1966; detachment comdr. tactical comms. Republic South Vietnam, 1967-68; comdr. 907th communications squadron Rickenbacker AFB, Ohio, 1972; dir. ops. fixed communications Air Combat Command Langley AFB, Va., 1982; dir. info. systems AWACS Saudi Arabia, 1984-85; dep. chief of staff standard systems Air Material Command Wright-Patterson AFB, Ohio, 1985; comdr. engring. installation divsn. Tinker AFB, Okla., 1988; commn. transferred to USAF, 1970, commd. col., 1988; ret. USAF, Cin., 1991; pres. Falcon Techs., Cin., 1991-98, Thumbs Up Aerospace Art, Cin., 1998—; tchr. Princeton City Sch. Dist., Cin., 1992-94; cons. Air War Coll., Air Univ., Maxwell AFB, Ala., 1987—, Defense Systems Mgmt. Coll., Ft. Belvior, Va., 1988—. Author: Army Visual Presentation, 1966 (medal 1966), Famous Moments in Aviation History, 1997; exhibited in group shows Mus. of Flight, Seattle, 1997, Midland (Mich.) Arts Ctr., 1997, Wichita Ctr Arts, 1998, Ralice Studio, Cin., 1998, Master Works Exhibit, Cin., 1999, Cin. Mus. Ctr., 1998, Mus. Aviation, Warner Robbins, Ga., 1999, Pub. Libr. Cin., Hamilton County, Ohio, 1999; author cover art Jour of League of World War I Aviation Historians, Jour. WWI Aviation Historians, 1999. Mem. Batavia (Ohio) City Coun., 1972; pres. Ohio Buckeye Wing Assn., Columbus, 1973; mem. Air Force Policy Coun., Washington, 1978; congl. campaign mgr., 1993; bd. dirs. Cin. Art Club, 1995-96. Decorated Commendation medal; recipient Meritorious Svc. medal Dept. Def., 1986, 91. Mem. DAV, Air Force Assn., Res. Officers Assn., Am. Soc. Aviation Artists. Avocations: freelance writer, walking, science fiction, lecturer. Home and Office: Thumbs Up Aerospace Art 198 Palisades Pointe Cincinnati OH 45238-5653

SMOCK, TIMOTHY ROBERT, lawyer; b. Richmond, Ind., June 24, 1951; s. Robert Martin and Thelma Elizabeth (Cozad) S.; m. Martha Carolene Middleton, Apr. 4, 1992; children: Andrew Zoller, Alison Pierce. BA, Wittenberg U., 1973; JD cum laude, Ind. U., 1977. Bar: Ind. 1977, Ariz. 1979, U.S. Dist. Ct. (so. dist.) Ind. 1977, U.S. Dist. Ct. Ariz. 1979, U.S. Ct. Apeals (7th cir.) 1977, U.S. Ct. Appeals (9th cir.) 1979. Jud. clk. Ct. of Appeals of Ind., Indpls., 1977-79; assoc. Lewis and Roca, Phoenix, 1979-82; assoc./shareholder Gallagher & Kennedy, Phoenix, 1982-89; ptnr. Scult, French, Zwillinger & Smock, Phoenix, 1989-94, Smock and Weinberger, Phoenix, 1994-99, Richards and Smock, Phoenix, 1999—; judge, pro tempore Maricopa County Superior Ct., Phoenix, 1989—; faculty, State Bar Course on Professionalism, Ariz. Supreme Ct./State Bar, Phoenix, 1992—; speaker, Continuing Legal Edn., Maricopa County and Ariz. State Bar, 1988—. Mem. Ariz. Bar Assn., Maricopa Bar Assn., Def. Rsch. Inst. Office: Richards and Smock 1202 E Missouri Ave Ste 150 Phoenix AZ 85014-2900

SMOCZYNSKI, LECH JOZEF, chemist, scientist; b. Grudziadz, Poland, Apr. 24, 1951; s. Jozef and Janina (Szwałkiewicz) S.; children: Rafał, Dariusz. M in Chemistry, Nicolaus Copernicus Univ., 1973; D in Agr., ART Univ., Olsztyn, Poland, 1980, Habilitation, 1989. From asst. to prof. dept. chemistry ART U., Olsztyn, 1973-97, prof., head dept. chemistry, 1997—; cons. A/S Polymer, 1990—, Norsk Hydro, Oslo, 1997—; gen. dir. Polclar, Warsaw, Poland, 1990-91; vis. prof. Dekaban Fund, 1996. Author: Water Research, 1985, Jour. Colloid and Interface Sci., 1996; editl. bd. Pollutants in Environ., 1991—; contbr. articles to profl. jours. Grantee EC Brussels, 1993. Mem. Polish Chem. Soc., Polish Soc. Environ. Engring. Avocations: ground tennis, sports bridge, computer science. E-mail: lechs@uwm.edu.pl. Office: Dept Chemistry, Plac Łodzki 4, 10957 Olsztyn Poland

SMOJVER, DUBRAVKA, pharmacist, quality assurance professional; b. Leprovica, Croatia, Aug. 1, 1948; d. Vladimir and Marija (Krznaric) Ivančic; m. Davor Smojver, July 1, 1972; 1 child, Ljubomir. BS, Faculty of Pharmacy, Zagreb, Croatia, 1973. Specialist drug control and release. Technologist prodn. Pliva, Zagreb, Croatia, 1974-76, analyst, group leader quality control, 1976-83, quality coord. quality assurance, 1983-88, mgr. quality assurance, 1988-90, dir. quality assurance, 1990—. Mem. profl. team, mgr.: Guide Book Quality Assurance, 1995; contbr. articles to profl. jours. Mem. Croatian Soc. Quality (pres. 1994-96, v.p. 1996—), European Orgn. for Quality (rep. 1993—), Am. Soc. Quality. Avocations: music, poetry, swimming. Home: Hrvatskih Iseljenika 1, 10000 Zagreb Croatia Office: Pliva Quality Assurance Dept, Prilaz Baruna Filipovica 25, 10000 Zagreb Croatia

SMOKE, RICHARD EDWIN, lawyer, investment adviser; b. Detroit, Sept. 16, 1945; s. Bruno Donald and Else Marie (Reinvaldt) S.; m. Evelyn Panagsagan Navarro, Jan. 24, 1986. BA, Kalamazoo (Mich.) Coll., 1967; JD, Wayne State U., 1970. Bar: Mich. 1970, Calif. 1975, U.S. Supreme Ct. 1980. Gen. counsel Grosse Ile (Mich.) Bridge Co., 1975-78, pres., 1980-83, v.p., 1989—; gen. counsel Campbell-Ewald Co., Warren, Mich., 1978-80; pvt. practice law, investment adviser Grand Rapids, Mich., 1985—; dir. Kent County Cmty. Mental Health, 1996; adj. faculty Davenport Coll., 1993-95; trustee Grand Rapids Charter Twp., 1991-96; commr. County of Kent, 1996—. Bd. dirs. World Affairs Coun. Western Mich., Grand Rapids, 1988-93, pres., 1991-92; mem. exec. com. Kent County Rep. Party, Grand Rapids, 1989-92, 95—; trustee Kalamazoo Coll., 1970-79. London-Sloan fellow, 1983. Mem. State Bar Mich., State Bar Calif., Investment Analysts Chgo., Peninsular Club.

SMOLANSKY, BETTIE MORETZ, sociology educator; b. Columbia, S.C., June 4; d. Walter Jennings Sr. and Opal (Ledford) Moretz; m. Oles M. Smolansky, Dec. 29, 1966; children: Alexandra Smolansky Zentmeyer, Nicholas Jennings. AB in Sociology, Lenoir-Rhyne Coll., 1962; MA in Sociology, Duke U., 1964; PhD in Sociology, Pa. State U., 1984. Instr. sociology Moravian Coll., Bethlehem, Pa., 1964-68, asst. prof., 1968-82, asst. dean, 1980-82, assoc. prof., 1982-88, prof., 1988—, chair dept. sociology, 1991-97, interim dean faculty, 1998-99; mem. bd. trustees Moravian Coll., 1977-81, 91-95, NEH visitor core curriculum workshop, 1985, sec. presdl. search com., 1996-97; mem. curriculum evaluation conf. Bklyn. Coll., 1988. Co-author: The USSR and Iraq, 1991 (AAAS Marshall Schulman prize 1992). Mem. bd. dirs. Northampton County Area on Aging, Bethlehem, 1984-90; vice chair United Way Allocations Panel, Bethlehem, 1984-90; chair YWCA Commn. on Status of Women, Bethlehem, 1992-94; bd. dirs. YWCA of Bethlehem, 1993-97, 98—, 1st v.p., 1998-2000. Recipient NDEA fellow, 1962-64, Disting. Alumnus award Lenoir-Rhyne Coll., 1995. Mem. Am. Sociol. Assn., Ea. Sociol. Assn., Lehigh Valley Assn. Acad. Women (pres. 1988-89, Woman of Yr. 1995-96), ODK (advisor 1987-90), AKD (advisor 1991-97). E-mail: bms01@moravian.edu. Fax: 610-861-3980. Home: 3665 Walt Whitman Ln Bethlehem PA 18017-1553 Office: Moravian Coll Dept Sociology 1200 Main St Bethlehem PA 18018-6614

SMOLEV, TERENCE ELLIOT, lawyer, educator; b. Bklyn., Oct. 5, 1944; s. Lawrence and Shirley (Lebowitz) S.; m. Sherry Gale Rosen, Nov. 24, 1968 (div.); children: Cindy, Scott; m. Phyllis C. Rudko, Oct. 8, 1995. BBA, Hofstra U., 1966; JD, American U., 1969; LLM, NYU, 1974. Bar: N.Y. 1970. Acct. Peat Marwick & Mitchell, N.Y.C., 1969-70; dir. deferred giving Hofstra U., Hempstead, N.Y., 1971-74; editor Panel Publishers, Greenvale, N.Y., 1970-71; ptnr. Naidich & Smolev, P.C., Bellmore, N.Y., 1972-92; mem. bd. trustees Hofstra U., 1992—; adj. prof. Hofstra U., Hempstead, N.Y., 1971—; dist. counsel North Merrick (N.Y.) UFSD, 1975-99. Author of book chpt. Mem. Nassau County, N.Y. Dem. Com., 1972-80, mem. judicial screening com., 1992—; mem. IRS Small Bus. Adv. Com., Washington D.C., 1975-77; bd. dirs. Arthritis Found. L.I., 1995-97, mem Israeli Bond Cabinet Long Island, 1996—. Recipient George M. Estabrook award Hofstra U., 1991, Alumni Achievement award Hofstra U., 1993, Cmty. Svc. award Hebrew Acad. Nassau County, 1997; named Senator of Yr., Hofstra U., 1985, Alumnus of Yr., 1996. Mem. ABA, N.Y. State Bar Assn., Nassau County Bar Assn., N.Y. State Assn. Sch. Attys. (pres. 1984), Hofstra U. Alumni Senate (pres. 1987-89), Hofstra U. Club (bd. dirs. 1981-95). Avocations: photography, golf. Office: One Old Country Rd Carle Place NY 11514

SMOLEWSKI, PIOTR PAWEL, hematologist, educator; b. Lodz, Poland, Dec. 25, 1960; s. Marian and Agata (Golebiewska) S.; m. Elzbieta Miatkowska, Oct. 11, 1986; 1 child, Pavel. MD, Med. U. Lodz, 1985, DSc, 1991. From asst. to assoc. prof. hematology Med. U. Lodz, Poland, 1985—; cons. Dept. Family Medicine, Lodz, 1995—. Office: Copernicus Hosp, Dept Hematology, 93513 Lodz Poland

SMOLKER, GARY STEVEN, lawyer; b. L.A., Nov. 5, 1945; s. Paul and Shayndy Charolette (Sirott) S.; m. Alice Graham; children: Terra, Judy, Leah. BS, U. Calif., Berkeley, 1967; MS, Cornell U., 1968; JD cum laude, Loyola U., L.A., 1973. Bar: Calif. 1973, U.S. Dist. Ct. (ctrl. dist.) Calif. 1973, U.S. Tax Ct. 1973, U.S. Ct. Appeals (9th cir.) 1973, U.S. Supreme Ct. 1978, U.S. Dist. Ct. (so., ea. and no. dists.) Calif. 1981. Guest rschr. Lawrence Radiation Lab., U. Calif., 1967; tchg. fellow Sch. Chem. Engring., Cornell U.; mem. tech. staff Hughes Aircraft Co., Culver City, Calif., 1968-70; in advanced mktg. and tech. TRW, Redondo Beach, Calif., 1970-72; sole practice Beverly Hills, Calif., 1973-89, L.A., 1989—; guest lectr. UCLA Extension, 1973-74, Loyola U. Law Sch., 1979; speaker, panelist in field; adv. Loyola U. Law Sch., 1973—. Columnist Heating Piping Air Conditioning Engrng. Mag., 1999—; contbr. articles to profl. jours. Mem. Nat. Assn. Real Estate Editors, Calif. State Bar Assn., L.A. County Bar Assn., Beverly Hills Bar Assn. (sr. editor jour. 1978-79, contbg. editor jour. 1980-82, 86-90, editor-in-chief 1984-86, pub. Smolker Letter 1985—), B'nai B'rith (anti-defamation league). Jewish. Achievements include inventor self-destruct aluminium tungstic oxide films, electrolytic anticompromise process. Office: 4720 Lincoln Blvd Ste 280 Marina Dl Rey CA 90292-6977

SMOLYAKOV, NIKOLAY VASILIEVICH, physicist, educator; b. Mogilev, Belarussia, USSR, Feb. 18, 1955; s. Vasiliy Nikolaevich and Lyubov Ivanovna (Shirchenko) S.; m. Valentina Michailovna Arutyunova, Jan. 31, 1979; 1 child, Michail. Diploma, Moscow State U., 1978; postgrad., Inst. High Energy Physics, Protvino, USSR, 1978-81; candidate of sci., P.N. Lebedev Phys. Inst., Moscow, 1993. Sci. rschr. Inst. High Energy Physics, Protvino, 1981-88; sci. rschr. Russian Rsch. Ctr. Kurchatov Inst., Moscow, 1988-92, head rsch. group, 1993-94, sr. sci. rschr., 1994-97; assoc. prof. Hiroshima (Japan) U., 1997—; mem. young scientist coun. Inst. High Energy Physics, Protvino, 1980-82. Contbr. articles to profl. jours. Mem. Phys. Soc. Russia, N.Y. Acad. Scis. Mem. Russian Orthodox Ch. Avocations: canoe trips, chess, photography. Office: Grad Sch Sci Hiroshima U, 1-3-1 Kagamiyama, Higashi Hiroshima 739-8526, Japan

SMOOT, DAVID PAUL, finance company executive; b. Guthrie, Okla., Jan. 9, 1947; s. Jerry Edward and Katherine Ann (Doyle) S.; m. Marie Kathleen Stokes, Aug. 6, 1971; children: Aimee, Melissa. Student, Cumberland Coll., 1965-67, Glassboro State Coll., 1967, U. Cin., 1968-69. Regional

mgr. Dennison Mfg., Chgo., 1969-77, Wordstream, Chgo., 1978-79; dist. mgr. AM Jacquard, San Francisco, 1979-82; co-founder, v.p. sales Phaser Systems Pub. Co., San Francisco, 1980-82; dir. cen. ops. Digital Research, Schaumburg, Ill., 1982-85; founder, chmn. bd., chief exec. officer Software Funding Internat., Deerfield, Ill., 1985-89; Software Funding Internat. (acquired by The Meridian Group), Deerfield, Ill., 1989; pres. Meridian Software Funding, 1989-92, Am. Indian Svcs. Inc., 1992-95; pres., founder Airborne Remote Mapping, 1995-98, Am. Indian Fin. Svcs. LLC, 1998—; mem. Native Vision program Johns Hopkins U. Hosp., NFL Players Assn. and Nick Lowery Found. Bd. of Consult Little City Home for Retarded, Palatine, Ill., 1986. Served with U.S. Army, 1969-75. Mem. Assn. Data Processing Services Orgns., Software Pubs. Assn., Syntopicaon XII, IBM PC User's Group (speaker). Avocations: basketball, sailing, camping, fishing, tennis. Home and Office: 6831 E Sunset Sky Cir Scottsdale AZ 85262-7161 also: 111 S Pfingsten Rd Ste 115 Deerfield IL 60015-4994

SMOOT, SKIPI LUNDQUIST, psychologist; b. Aberdeen, Wash., Apr. 10, 1934; d. Warren Duncan and Miriam Stephen (Bishop) Dobbins; m. Harold Richard Lundquist, June 2, 1951 (div. Mar. 1973); children: Kurt Richard, Mark David, Ted Douglas, Blake Donald; m. Edward Lee Smoot, June 14, 1975. BA in Psychology, Coll. of William and Mary, 1978; MA, Pepperdine U., 1980; PhD, Calif. Sch. of Profl., Psychology, San Diego, 1985. Lic. clin. psychologist, Calif.; lic. marriage and family therapist, Calif. Owner, operator McDonald's Restaurants, San Pedro and Torrance, Calif., 1965-76, Williamsburg, Va., 1965-76; psychotherapist Coll. Hosp., Cerritos, Calif., 1979-81, Orange County Child Guidance, Laguna Hills, Calif., 1981-82; psychotherapist Calif. State Police, Costa Mesa, 1982-83, Anaheim, 1983-84; psychologist Orange County Mental Health, Santa Ana, Calif., 1984-85, Psychol. Ctr., Orange and El Toro, Calif., 1985-91; clin. dir. Career Ambitions, Lake Forest, Calif., 1991-98, Psychol. Decisions, Irvine-Laguna Hills, Calif., 1991-94; psychol. cons. seminars and workshops for bus., Irvine and Laguna Hills, 1991-98. Mem. APA, Calif. Psychol. Assn. Democrat. Avocations: Music, travel, rsch. Office: Psychol Decisions Career Ambitions Unltd 23161 Lake Center Dr Ste 124 Lake Forest CA 92630-6822

SMORGON, SAM, academic administrator. Chancellor Royal Melbourne Inst. Tech. Office: Royal Melbourne Inst Tech, GPO Box 2476 V, Melbourne VIC 3001, Australia*

SMRECKI, VILKO, chemist, researcher; b. Zagreb, Croatia, Sept. 7, 1966; s. Ivan and Emilija (Mirkovic) S. BSc in Chemistry, U. Zagreb, 1990, MSc, 1994, PhD in Chemistry, 1998. Rsch. asst. Ruder Boskovic Inst., Zagreb, 1991—. Austrian Ministry of Sci. fellow, 1994; Hungarian Ministry Culture and Edn. fellow, 1996. Mem. Croatian Chem. Soc. Office: Rudjer Boskovic Inst, PO Box 180 Bijenicka 54, HR-10002 Zagreb Croatia

SMULDERS, BEN, retired historian; b. Tilburg, The Netherlands, Sept. 23, 1932; m. Felten Smulders; children: Germaine, Frédérique. Degree in history, U. Tilburg, 1968. Tchr. Secondary Sch., 1961-68, Pedagog. Acad., Bosch, 1968-75; historian, tchr. didactics of history Tchrs. Tng. Coll., Tilburg, 1976-89; ret., 1989; v.p. Mollerinstitut U. Coun., Tilburg, 1971-88; pres. Didactics Commn., Bosch, 1970-80; mem. Nat. Devel. Orgn., Amsterdam, 1970-80. Author: History of Europe, 1989; editor Kwartet, 1984; contbr. articles to profl. jours. Mem. Commn. Health Care Thuiszorg, Bosch, 1992—; pres. Fugit. Found. Bosch, 1991-98; mem. Town Coun., St. Mich. Gestel, 1968-75. Mem. Internat. Soc. for Hist. Didactics, Probus Bosch, Gastr. Club Bosch (past pres.). Avocations: writing, cooking, reading. Home: Pettelaarseweg 1829, 5216 BW s-Hertogenbosch The Netherlands

SMULLENS, SARAKAY COHEN, psychotherapist; b. Balt.; m. Stanton N. Smullens; children: Elizabeth R. Smullens, Douglas R. Smullens, Elisabeth J. Cohen, Kathyanne S. Cohen. Student, Skidmore Coll., 1958-60, Goucher Coll., 1960-62, Cath. U., 1963-64, U. pa., 1964-65. Cert. social worker, group therapist, family life educator; diplomate Am. Bd. Examiners in Clin. Social Work. Regional coord. for Young Dems. Dem. Nat. Com., Washington, 1962-63; protective svc. counselor Soc. to Protect Children from Cruelty, Phila., 1965-66; family therapist Phila. Psychiat. Hosp., 1966-68; marriage and family counselor Jewish Family Svc. of Phila., 1968-73, dir. family life edn., 1971-73; pvt. practice marital, couple, family, group psychotherapy Phila., 1973—; instr. mental health tech. Hahnemann Med. U., 1974-78, sr. instr., 1978-90, clin. asst. prof., 1990-97; presenter, lectr. in field; appearances on local and nat. TV and radio programs. Author: Whoever Said Life is Fair?, 1982, 2d edit., 1988, Japanese edit., 1985; columnist Phila. Inquirer, 1976-81, Phila. Bull., 1981-82. Mem. Goucher Com. for Towson Integration, 1960-62; 8th ward committeewoman Dem. Party, 1967-71; co-founder Women's Way, 1971; mem. cmty. edn. and pub. rels. com. Jewish Family and Children's Agy., 1977-86; bd. dirs. Family Svc. Phila., 1987-92; mem. women's bd. Thomas Jefferson U. Hosp., 1984—, sec., 1989-95; bd. overseers Sch. Social Work, originator of Crystal Stair award U. Pa., 1990—; bd. dirs. Center City Resident's Assn., 1990-94, Phila. chpt. Am. Jewish Congress, 1994—; vice chair Child Welfare Adv. Bd. Phila., 1994, chair, 1994-97; mem. Interdisciplinary Task Force of Child Welfare Sys., 1997; founding co-chair Sabbath of Domestic Peace, 1995. Recipient Peace medal Women's Internat. League for Peace and Freedom, 1962, Louise Waterman Wise award Am. Jewish Congress, 1996.. Mem. NASW, Acad. Cert. Social Workers, Am. Assn. Marriage and Family Therapy, Nat. Coun. Family Rels., Am. Group Therapy Assn., Pa. Assn. marriage and Family Therapy, Authors' Guild. Fax: 215-732-4603. Home and Office: 1710 Pine St Philadelphia PA 19103-6702

SMUNT, TIMOTHY LAWRENCE, management educator, business researcher, consultant; m. Marsha Smunt. BS in Indsl. Mgmt., Purdue U., 1976; MBA, U. Mo., 1978; DBA, Ind. U., 1981. Assoc. instr. Ind. U., Bloomington, 1978-81, vis. asst. prof., 1981-82; asst. prof. Wash. U., St. Louis, 1982-86, assoc. prof., 1986-90; assoc. prof. U. Ill., Urbana-Champaign, 1990-95; Babcock Rsch. prof., assoc. prof. Wake Forest U., Winston-Salem, N.C., 1995-99, prof., 1999—; cost estimator, price analyst McDonnell Douglas Astronautics Co., St. Louis, 1976-81; vis. assoc. prof. Purdue U., 1991; spkr. in field. Mem. editl. bd. Prodn. Ops. Mgmt., Jour. Ops. Mgmt.; referee Mgmt. Sci., Decision Scis., Jour. Ops. Mgmt., others; contbr. numerous articles to profl. jours. Fellow APICS; mem. Inst. Indsl. Engrs. (sr.), Decision Scis. Inst. (v.p. planning devel. 1992-94, treas. 1994-96), Inst. Ops. Rsch. Mgmt. Sci., Prond. Ops. Mgmt. Soc. Fax: 336-758-4514. Home: 1061 W Kent Rd Winston Salem NC 27104-1131 Office: Babcock Grad Sch Mgmt Wake Forest U Winston Salem NC 27109

SMUTKUPT, SUMIN, plant breeder, educator, legume researcher; b. Phrae, Thailand, Sept. 19, 1934; s. Som and Tongin Smutkupt; m. Ubol Ungsriswadi, Nov. 10, 1972; 2 children. BS with honors, Kasetsart U., Bangkok, 1957; MS, Cornell U., 1961; DrScAgr, Göttingen (Germany) U., 1968. Head dept. plant sci. Faculty of Agr. Chiang Mai U., Thailand, 1971-72; dep. dean Faculty of Sci. Kasetsart U., Bangkok, 1981-83, head dept. aplied radiation, 1981-86, dean Faculty of Sci., 1990-94; biotech. program coord. Office of Sci., Technology Devel. Bd., Bangkok, 1987-90; highland legume program coord. Royal Project Found., Chiang Mai, 1982—; sec.-gen. Soc. for Advancement of Breeding Rschs. in Asia and Oceania, 1994-97. Recipient Nat. award for peace Office of Atomic Energy, Bangkok, 1996. Home: 270/30, Dispong Ramkhamhaeng 65, Bangkok 10310, Thailand

SMYTH, CORNELIUS EDMONSTON, retired hotel executive; b. N.Y.C., Aug. 20, 1926; s. Cornelius Joseph and Roberta Ernestine (Anderson) S.; m. Jeanne Laura Dillingham, Nov. 25, 1950 (dec. Oct. 1996); m. Jeanette M. Hubbard, Apr. 18, 1998; children: Cornelius E. Jr., Loretta M., William D., James B., Laura I., Robert B. BS in Econs., U. Pa., Phila., 1946. Cert. Hospitality Acct. Exec. Contr. Caesars Palace Hotel and Casino, Las Vegas, Nev., 1970-73, fin. v.p., 1974, adminstrv. v.p., 1975-77, exec. v.p., 1977-81; pres. Sands Hotel and Casino, Las Vegas, Nev., 1981-83; exec. v.p. Latin Am. ops. Caesars World Internat., L.A., 1983-89, pres. Mexican ops., 1989-90; bd. dirs. Venture Catalyst, Inc., San Diego, 1994—; cons., Coronado, Calif., 1994-2000. Co-author: A Uniform System of Accounts for Hotels, 7th rev. edit., 1977. Comdr. USNR, 1944-70. Named to U.S. Table Tennis Hall of Fame, 1996. Mem. Pi Gamma Mu, Sigma Chi. Republican. Roman Catholic. Avocations: table tennis, body surfing.

SMYTH, CRAIG HUGH, fine arts educator; b. N.Y.C., July 28, 1915; s. George Hugh and Lucy Salome (Humeston) S.; m. Barbara Linforth, June 24, 1941; children: Alexandra, Edward Linforth (Ned). BA, Princeton U., 1938, MFA, 1941, PhD, 1956; MA (hon.), Harvard U., 1975. Sr. mus. aid, rsch. asst. Nat. Gallery Art, Washington, 1941-42; officer-in-charge, dir. Cen. Art Collecting Point, Munich, 1945-46; lectr. Frick Collection, N.Y.C., 1946-50; asst. prof. Inst. Fine Arts NYU, 1950-53, assoc. prof. Inst. Fine Arts, 1953-57, prof. Inst. Fine Arts, 1957-73, acting dir. Inst. Fine Arts, acting head dept. fine arts Grad. Sch. Arts and Scis., 1951-53, dir. inst., head dept. fine arts Grad. Sch., 1953-73; prof. fine arts Harvard U., 1973-85, prof. emeritus, 1985—; Samuel Kress prof. Ctr. for Advanced Study in Visual Arts Nat. Gallery Art, Washington, 1987-88; dir. Villa I Tatti Harvard U. Ctr. Italian Renaissance Studies, Florence, 1973-85; art historian in residence Am. Acad. in Rome, 1959-60; mem. U.S. Nat. Com. History Art, 1955-85; alt. U.S. mem. Comité Internat. d'Histoire de l'Art, 1970-83, U.S. mem., 1983-85; chmn. adv. com. J. Paul Getty Rsch. Inst. History of Art and Humanities, 1982-99; mem. architect selection com. J. Paul Getty Trust, 1983-84; mem. organizing com., keynote speaker 400th Anniversary of Uffizi Gallery, 1981-82; vis. scholar Inst. Advanced Study, Princeton, N.J., 1971, mem., 1978, visitor, 1983, 85-86; vis. scholar Bibliotheca Hertziana, Max Planck Soc., Rome, 1972, 73; mem. vis. com. dept. art and archaeology Princeton U., 1956-73, 85-89; mem. adv. com. Villa I Tatti, 1985-92; trustee Hyde Collection, Glens Falls, N.Y., 1985-87, The Burlington mag., 1987—; mem. commn. Ednl. & Cultural Exch. between Italy and U.S., 1979-83. Author: Mannerism and Maniera, 1963, rev. edit. with introduction by E. Cropper, 1992, Bronzino as Draughtsman, 1971, Michelangelo Architetto (with H.M. Millon), 1988, English edit., 1988, Repatriation of Art from the Collecting Point in Munich After World War II, 1988; editor: Michelangelo Drawings (Nat. Gallery of Art), 1992; editor (with Peter M. Lukehart), contbr.: The Early Years of Art History in the United States, 1993; founding chmn. (periodical) I Tatti Studies: Essays in the Renaissance, 1984-85; contbr. to profl. jours. Hon. trustee Met. Mus. Art, N.Y.C., 1968—; trustee Inst. Fine Arts, NYU, 1973—; mem. mayor's com. Piazza Della Signoria, Florence, 1975-78. Lt. USNR, 1942-46. Decorated Chevalier Legion of Honor France, U.S. Army Commendation medal, Netherlands Medal for Svc. to the States; sr. Fulbright Rsch. fellow, 1949-50, honored by establishment of CHS professorship, Inst. of Fine Arts NYU, 1999. Mem. Am. Acad. Arts and Scis., Am. Philos. Soc., Coll. Art Assn. Am. (bd. dirs. 1953-57, sec. 1956), Accademia Fiorentina delle Arti del Disegno (academician, assoc.), Accademia di San Luca (hon. 1995), Harvard Club (N.Y.C.), Century Assn. (N.Y.C.), Phi Beta Kappa. Address: PO Box 39 Cresskill NJ 07626-0039

SMYTH, DACRE HENRY DEUDRAETH, retired naval officer; b. London, May 5, 1923; s. Nevill Maskelyne and Evelyn Olwen (Williams) S.; m. Jennifer Haggard, Jan. 11, 1952; children: Benita, Bronwen, Belinda, Bambi, Osmond. Commd. naval officer Royal Australian Navy, 1940-78; commanding officer HMA Ships, Latrobe, 1947-48, Hawkesbury, 1953-54, Supply, 1968-70, Cerberus, 1971-72; capt. Royal Australian Naval Coll., Jervis Bay, 1964-65; commodore Australian Naval Rep., London, 1966-68; commodore Naval Officer in-charge, Victoria, 1971-78, ret., 1978; dir. The Age Newspaper, Melbourne, 1982-93; trustee Shrine of Remembrance, Melbourne, 1978—, Overseas Students Assistance Fund, Melbourne, 1979—, Polly Woodside Maritime Mus., 1990—. Author, artist: The Bridges of the Yarra, 1979, The Lighthouses of Victoria, 1980, Historic Ships of Australia, 1982, Old Riverboats of the Murray, 1982, Views of Victoria, 1984, The Bridges of Kananook Creek, 1986, Waterfalls of Victoria, 1988, Gallipoli Pilgrimage, 1990, Immigrant Ships to Australia, 1992, Pictures in my Life, 1994, Images of Melbourne, 1998; exhibited in 23 one-man shows. Gov. Corps. of Commrs., Melbourne, 1989—; pres. Naval and Mil. Club, Melbourne, 1984; councillor Scout Assn. of Australia, Melbourne, 1978-83, Australian Maritime Trust, 1978—; patron N Class Destroyer Assn., 1971—. Named Officer of the Order of Australia, 1977, Order of Merit of France, 1994, Internat. Order of Merit, 1991. Fellow Australian Inst. of Co. Dirs.; mem. Melbourne Club and Naval and Mil. Club, Victorian com. for the ANZAC Awards. Avocations: painting, writing, designing and crafting stained glass windows. Home: 22 Douglas St, Toorak VIC 3142, Australia

SMYTH, DAVID, editor, author; b. Buenos Aires, Feb. 7, 1929; came to U.S. 1962, naturalized 1970; s. Currell Hutchinson and Jessie Rodger (Dodds) S.; m. Elli Helene Dusterhoft, Nov. 9, 1968; 1 child, Clifford Dieter. BA, Cambridge (Eng.) U., 1951, MA, 1967. Tech. writer, copywriter, 1953-55, movie promotion writer, 1956; owner Ace Translation Agy., Buenos Aires, 1957-58; sec. Found. Econ. Edn., 1959; cables editor Buenos Aires Herald, 1960; lexicographer Simon & Schuster English-Spanish Dictionary, 1961; Latin Am. desk editor UPI, N.Y.C., 1962-63; Latin Am. desk editor AP, N.Y.C., 1963-73, world svcs. fin. editor, 1973-96; freelance writer, translator, editor, 1997—. Author: You Can Survive Any Financial Disaster, 1977, Worldly Wise Investor, 1988; co-author: The Speculator's Handbook, 1974, Unusual Investments That could Make You Rich, 1978, No Cost/Low Cost Investing, 1987. Served with Argentine Army, 1952. Mem. N.Y. Fin. Writers Assn. Home: 8 Beechwood Ave Metuchen NJ 08840-2107

SMYTH, DIANE PATRICIA LESLEY, pediatric neurologist; b. Oxford, Eng., Feb. 26, 1943; d. Reginald Victor and Lilian Margaret (Stringer) Gorvette; m. Christopher Smyth, Sept. 23, 1973; children: Nicholas, Katharine, Rebecca. MB, BS, London U., 1966, MD, 1980. Diploma in Child Health, Royal Coll. Physicians Glasgow, FRCP, FRCPCH. Team leader Save the Children Fund, Biafra, Africa, 1969-70; sr. registrar in pediatric neurology Hosp. for Sick Children, London, 1973-75; lectr. in child health Queen Elizabeth Hosp. for Children, London, 1975-77; cons. pediatrician St. Mary's Hosp., London, 1985—; hon. sr. lectr. Imperial Coll. Sch. of Medicine, London, 1985—; med. advisor adoption Parents and Children Together Oxford Diocese, 1987—. Author: The Health and Social Needs of Physically Handicapped Adults, 1984; co-author: New Parents, 1989; editor: Community Child Health and Pediatrics, 1995; contbr. articles to profl. jours. Fellow Royal Coll. Physicians (London); mem. Brit. Pediat. Neurology Assn., Royal Coll. Pediatrics and Child Health, Child Devel. and Disability Group (treas. 1993—), Royal Coll. of Pediatrics and Child Health, Brit. Adoption and Fostering Assn. Anglican. Avocations: horse riding, gardening, travel, music, collecting early English porcelain.

SMYTH, MALACHY, missionary priest, magazine editor; b. Ireland, Jan. 29, 1941. Degree, De La Salle, Ireland, 1959, Columbian U., Ireland, 1966. Pastor Cmty. Care, Korea, 1970-72, Korea, 1972-75; minister to youth Ireland, 1976-80; minister Eucharistic Cmty. Bldg., Korea, 1981-84; producer video documentaries Korea, 1984-85, Rural Cmty. Bldg., Korea, 1985-90; founding editor Mag., Korea, 1991—. Editor The Martyr of Yang Yang, 1984, Pilgrims of the South Han, 1989, Frontier Mission, 1991. Active in helping to devel. rural communities, Korea, 1972-90. Mem. N.Y. Acad. Scis. Roman Cath. Avocations: reading, photography, music, golf, sports. Fax: 2295-6713. Home and Office: CPO Box 1167, Seoul 100-611, Korea

SMYTH, STUART JOHN, history educator; b. Mar. 11, 1939. MA, U. Albany, 1990, PhD, 1998. Vis. asst. prof. Marist Coll., Poughkeepsie, N.Y., 1997; asst. prof. Fordham U., Bronx, N.Y., 1998—, SUNY, New Paltz, 1998—. Contbr. articles to profl. publs. Home: 35 Harlemville Rd Hillsdale NY 12529-6104 Office: Marist Coll 290 North Rd Poughkeepsie NY 12601-1326

SMYTH, THOMAS RAYMOND, psychologist, educator; b. Coleraine, Northern Ireland, Jan. 22, 1942; s. Thomas and Kathleen (Maguire) S.; m. Patricia Veronica Reavley (dec.); children: Elizabeth, Thomas. BA, Flinders U., 1979, BA (with honors), 1980, MA, 1985; PhD, U. Adelaide, 1992. Lectr. U. Adelaide, Australia, 1987-91, Flinders U., Adelaide, 1992-93, Charles Sturt U., Wagga Wagga, N.S.W., Australia, 1994—. Author: Writing in Psychology: A Student Guide, 1994, 2d edit., 1996; contbr. articles to profl. jours. Mem. Australian Psychol. Soc. Presbyn. Avocation: sailing. Home: 6 Churchill Ave, Wagga Wagga NSW 2650, Australia

SMYTHE, COLIN PETER, publisher; b. Maidenhead, England, Mar. 2, 1942; s. Cyril and Jean (Murdoch) S. BA, Dublin U., 1963, MA, 1966, LLD (hon.), 1998—. Mng. dir. Colin Smythe Ltd., England, 1966—; mng. dir. Vista Records Ltd., England, 1979-83, Van Duren Publishers, Ltd., England, 1987-92; vis. prof. U. Moderna, Lisbon, Portugal, 1990—, U. Ulster, No. Ireland, 1993—. Named Officer of the Venerable Order St. John of Jerusalem, Knight of the Order of Our Lady of the Conception of Vila Viçosa. Fellow Royal Soc. of Arts.

SMYTHE, THOMAS IRA, JR., finance educator, researcher; b. Biloxi, Miss., Aug. 16, 1963; s. Thomas Ira and Mary Elizabeth S.; m. Sally Scarbrough, Aug. 16, 1986; children: Meagan Elizabeth, Erica Suzanne. BS in Math., Furman U., 1985; MBA, George Mason U., 1993; PhD, U. S. C., 1999. Commd. ensign U.S. Army, Fort Benning, Ga., 1985-89; analyst Mobil Oil Corp., Fairfax, Va., 1989-95; graduate asst. U. S.C., Columbia, S.C., 1996-76; mem. staff U.S. Army, Fort Benning, Ga., 1985-89. Mem. Financial Mgmt. Assn., So. Finance Assn., Am. Finance Assn. Methodist. E-mail: tom-smythe@utc.edu. Home: 6504 Lake Shadows Cir Hixson TN 37343-3525 Office: Univ Tenn Chattanooga 65 McCallie Ave Chattanooga TN 37403

SMYTHE-GENOVESE, ELIZABETH DEETTE, environmental engineering investigator. Prin. investigator Smythe & Assocs. Mem. cmty. adv. bds. in environ. areas. E-mail: deettes@i-55.com.

SMYTHE-WRIGHT, DENISE, chemical oceanographer, researcher; b. Liverpool, Eng., Dec. 19, 1951; d. Thomas Wilbur and Marjorie Olive (Fleming) Wright; m. Arthur Edward Smythe, June 30, 1979; 1 child, Thomas Edward. BSc in Chemistry, Liverpool U., 1973, BSc in Oceanography, 1974, PhD, 1978. Chartered chemist. Rsch. fellow Southampton (Eng.) U., 1978-80; higher sci. officer Inst. Oceanographic Scis., Wormley, Eng., 1980-84; sr. sci. officer Inst. Oceanographic Studies, Wormley, Eng., 1984-89; head tracer chemistry James Rennell Ctr. for Ocean Circulation, Southampton, 1989-95, Southampton Oceanography Ctr., 1995—; project mgr. U.K. World Ocean Circulation Experiment, 1992-97; sec. Internat. Woce Sci. Steering Com., 1983-86. Editor: Ocean Circulation and Climate, 1991, Understanding Ocean Circulation, 1996. Office: Southampton Oceanography, Ctr Empress Dock, Southampton SO14 3ZH, England

SNAITH, RICHARD PHILIP, psychiatrist, educator; b. Darlington, Durham, Eng., Jan. 5, 1933; s. Herbert Longridge and Katherine Elizabeth (Smith) S.; children: Douglas, Julian, Polly. MB BS, London U., 1957, MD, 1966. Cons. psychiatrist Wakefield, Eng., 1967-76; sr. lectr. St. James Hosp., Leeds, Eng., 1976—. Author: Clinical Neurosis, 1981; co-author: Anxiety in Clinical Practice, 1988. Fellow Royal Coll. Psychiatry. Home: 30 Gledhold Wood Rd, Leeds LS8 4B2, England

SNAKENBERG, SHARON ANN, special education educator; b. Plum City, Wis., Feb. 6, 1952; d. Warren Adolf and Renee Ann (Thibodeau) Meyer; m. William John Hetherington, May 6, 1972 (div. Dec. 1976); 1 child, William John II; m. David F. Snakenberg, July 6, 1985; children: Emma, Jessica Amelia, Elba Francelia. BA, Dominguez Hills, 1984. Substitute tchr. Templeton (Calif.) Sch. Dist., 1987-88; tchr. Calif. Youth Authority, Paso Robles, Calif., 1991-92, St. Rose Sch., Paso Robles, Calif., 1988-92; spl. edn. tchr. L.A. Unified Sch. Dist., 1992-98, tech. coord., 1992-99, assistive tech. specialist, 1998-2000, assistive tech. practitioner, 2000—. Mem. Calif. Assn. Phys. & Health Impairments (treas. 1996-99), Coun. Exceptional Children (treas. 1998—), Computer Using Educators (ATP cert. 2000). Roman Catholic. Avocations: quilting, horseback riding, archery. Home: 260 Juniper Ridge Ln Palmdale CA 93550-9709 Office: 2302 S Gramercy Pl Los Angeles CA 90018-1323

SNÄLL, MITTI MARIA, management consultant; b. Helsinki, Finland, July 1, 1971; d. Jukka Sakari and Seija Mirjami (Peltola) S. MSc in Social Sci., U. Helsinki, 1995. Corp. comms. officer, editor Statistics Finland, Helsinki, 1993-95; prodr. Trainers' House, Helsinki, 1995-97; cons. McKinsey & Co., Helsinki, 1997—. Contbr. articles to profl. jours. Mem., sponsor Save the Children, Helsinki, 1995—. Avocations: exercise, fine arts, movies, roller skating, backpacking. Office: McKinsey & Co, Mannerheimintie 14A, 00100 Helsinki Finland

SNAPP, ELIZABETH, librarian, educator; b. Lubbock, Tex., Mar. 31, 1937; d. William James and Louise (Lanham) Mitchell; m. Harry Franklin Snapp, June 1, 1956. BA magna cum laude, North Tex. State U., Denton, 1968, MLS, 1969, MA, 1977. Asst. to archivist Archive of New Orleans Jazz Tulane U., 1960-63; catalog libr. Tex. Woman's U., Denton, 1969-71, head acquisitions dept., 1971-74, coord. readers svcs., 1974-77, asst. to dean Grad. Sch., 1977-79, instr. libr. sci., 1977-88, acting Univ. libr., 1979-82, dir. librs., 1982—, univ. historian, 1995—; chair-elect Tex. Coun. State U. Librs., 1988-90, chmn., 1990-92; mem. adv. com. on libr. formula Coord. Bd. Tex. Coll. and Univ. Sys., 1981-92; mem. Libr. Sys. Act adv. bd. Tex. State Libr. and Archives Commn., 1999—; del. OCLC Nat. Users Coun., 1985-87, mem. by-laws com., 1985-86, com. on less-than-full-svcs. networks, 1986-87; trustee AMIGOS Libr. Svcs., 1994-00, sec. bd. trustees, 1996-97, vice-chmn. bd. trustees, 1997-99, chair bd. trustees, 1999-00; project dir. NEH consultancy grant on devel. core curriculum for women's studies, 1981-82; chmn. Blue Ribbon com. 1986 Gov.'s Commn. for Women to select 150 outstanding women in Tex. history; project dir. math./sci. anthology project Tex. Found. Women's Resources; co-sponsor Irish Lecture Series, Denton, 1968, 70, 73, 78. Asst. editor: Tex. Academe, 1973-76; co-editor: Read All About Her! Texas Women's History: A Working Bibliography, 1995, enlarged deluxe edit., 1997; contbg. author: Women in Special Collections, 1984, Special Collections, 1986; book reviewer Library Resources and Tech. Services, 1973—; contbr. articles to profl. jours. Sec. Denton County Dem. Caucus, 1970. Recipient Ann. Pioneer award Tex. Woman's U., 1986, Women's Studies Vision award Tex. Woman's U., 1998. Mem. AAUP, ALA (stds. com. 1983-85), AAUW (legis. br. chmn. 1973-74, br. v.p. 1975-76, br. pres. 1979-80, state historian 1986-88, treas. 1998-99), AAUW Ednl. Found. (rsch. and awards panel 1990-94), Tex. Libr. Assn. (program com. 1978, Dist. VII chmn. 1985-86, archives and oral history com. 1990-92, co-chair program com. Tex. Libr. Assn. Ann. Conf. 1994, mem. Tall Texan selection com. 1995-96, treas. exec. bd. 1996-99), Tex. Hist. Commn. (judge for Farenbach History prize 1990-93), Women's Collecting Group (chmn. ad hoc com. 1984-86), So. Conf. Brit. Studies, Tex. Assn. Coll. Tchrs. (pres. Tex. Woman's U. chpt. 1976-77), Alliance Higher Edn. (chair coun. libr. dirs. 1993-95), Woman's Shakespeare Club (pres. 1967-69), Beta Phi Mu (pres. chpt. 1976-78, sec. nat. adv. assembly 1978-79, pres. 1979-80, nat. dir. 1981-83), Alpha Chi, Alpha Lambda Sigma (pres. 1970-71), Pi Delta Phi, Soroptimist Internat. (Denton) (pres. 1986-88), Rotary Internat. (local chpt. sec. 1999—). Methodist. Home: 1904 N Lake Trail Denton TX 76201-0602 Office: TWU Sta PO Box 424093 Denton TX 76204-4093

SNAPP, ROY BAKER, lawyer; b. Strang, Okla., May 9, 1916; s. Harry Moore and Verda Mildred (Austin) S.; m. Dorothy Faye Loftis, Jan. 27, 1942; children: Deborah, Bryan Austin, Martha Lynn, Barbara, James. Lawyer. B.S. in Pub. Adminstrn, U. Mo., 1936; LL.B., Georgetown U., 1941, LL.M., 1942. With U.S. State Dept., 1941; spl. adviser comdg. gen. (Manhattan (Atomic Bomb) Project), 1946; dir. internat. affairs U.S. AEC, 1947, 1st sec., 1948-54, asst. to chmn., 1954-55, sr. staff mem. nat. security coun., 1953-55; v.p. atomic div. (Am. Machine & Foundry), 1957; v.p. Am. Machine & Foundry Co., Washington office, 1961; bd. dirs. Electro-Nucleonics, Inc.; ptnr. Bechhoefer, Snapp and Trippe, 1966. Commd. ensign USNR 1942; assigned secretariat of U.S. Joint Chiefs of Staff and Combined (U.S.-Brit), Chiefs of Staff; naval mem. 1945; Intelligence Staff of Joint Cheifs Staff and Combined Chiefs Staff promoted to lt. comdr. 1945. Recipient D.S.M. AEC, 1955. Mem. SVC, Nat. Assn. Mgrs. (chmn. atomic energy com. 1963-64, dir. 1964-65), Phi Gamma Mu, Delta Theta Phi. Baptist. Clubs: Univ. (Washington), Columbia Country (Washington). Home: 11446 Savannah Dr Fredericksburg VA 22407-9108

SNARE, CARL LAWRENCE, JR., business executive; b. Oct. 25, 1936; s. Carl Lawrence and Lillian Marie (Luoma) S. BBA, Northwestern U., 1968; postgrad. in econs., San Francisco State U., 1976-77; BS, SUNY, 1995; postgrad., Roosevelt U. CPA, cert. fin. planner, Calif. Asst. sec., controller Bache Halsey Stuart & Shields Inc. (now Prudential Securities), Chgo., 1968-73; controller Innisfree Corp. div. Hyatt Corp., Burlingame, Calif., 1973-76; cash mgr. Portland (Oreg.) Gen. Electric Co., Calif., 1976-79; chief fin. officer, controller Vistar Fin. Inc., Marina del Rey, Calif., 1979-82; pres. Snare Properties Co., Long Beach, Calif., 1984-96, Snare Fin. Svcs. Corp., Rialto, Calif., 1985-89, Carl Snare & Assocs., Long Beach; v.p., treas. Carson Estate Co., Rancho Dominguez, Calif., 1988-96; pres., ceo Glenshire Homes, Inc., Phoenix, 1996-98, Glenshire Tech., Boulder, Colo., 1997-99; acct., fin.

planner Calif. Mem. AICPA. Founder Cash Mgmt. Assn., Portland, Oreg. Home: Santa Elena 2543 Alta, Guadalajara JAL 44220, Mexico Office: 11024 N 28th Dr Ste 200 Phoenix AZ 85029-4336

SNAREY, JOHN ROBERT, psychologist, researcher, educator; b. Jan. 12, 1948; s. John Herbert and Esther Snarey; m. Carol Dunn Snarey, June 11, 1970; children: Johnny, Elizabeth. BS, Geneva Coll., 1969; MA, Wheaton (Ill.) Coll., 1973; EdD, Harvard U., 1982. Postdoctoral rsch. fellow dept. psychiatry Harvard U., Cambridge, Mass., 1982-84; assoc. rsch. psychologist Wellesley (Mass.) Coll., 1984-85; assoc. prof. human devel. Northwestern U., Evanston, Ill., 1985-87; prof. human devel. Emory U., Atlanta, 1987—. Author: How Fathers Care for the Next Generation, 1993; mem. editl. bd. Harvard Ednl. Rev., 1979-81, Jour. Psychology and Theology, 1986-89, Society and Animals, 1993—, Jour. Moral Edn., 1998—; mem. editl. adv. bd. Lawrence Erlbaum Assocs., 1988-90; editor: Conflict and Continuity: A History of Ideas on Social Equality and Human Development, 1981; contbr. numerous articles to profl. jours. Recipient Exemplary Dissertation award Nat. Coun. for the Social Studies, 1982, Kuhmerker Dissertation award Assn. for Moral Edn., 1983, Outstanding Human Devel. Rsch. award Am. Ednl. Rsch., 1988, James D. Moran Book award Assn. Family and Consumer Scis., 1994. Mem. APA, Am. Ednl. Rsch. Assn. (div. E exec. bd. 1990—, sec. div. E 1997-99, moral devel. and edn. spl. interest group co-chair 1994-96), Assn. for Moral Edn. (exec. bd. 1986—, program chair 1997), Soc. for Rsch. in Child Devel., Nat. Coun. on Family Rels. Home: 2165 Pine Forest Dr NE Atlanta GA 30345-4184 Office: Emory U Pitts Libr # 3 Atlanta GA 30322-0001

SNÁŠEL, VÁCLAV, computer scientist, educator; b. Tábor, Czech Republic, Aug. 2, 1957; s. Václav Snášel and Libuše (Ižovská) Snášelová; m. Božena Rycová, Nov. 14, 1986; children: Irena Snášelová, Ivana Snášelová, Zuzana Snášelová. M, Palacky U., Olomouc, Czech Republic, 1981; PhD, Masaryk U., Brno, Czech Republic, 1991. Programmer Farmakon, Olomouc, 1983-88; asst. prof. Palacky U., Olomouc, 1988—. Co-author: Spectroscopy in Material Science, 1999. Mem. AMS, N.Y. Acad. Scis., Union Czech Mathematicians and Physicists. Office: Palacky U Tomkova 40, Dept Computer Sci. 779 00 Olomouc Czech Republic

SNASHALL, DAVID CHARLES, physician; b. Buckhurst Hill, England, Feb. 3, 1943; s. Cyril Francis and Phyllis Mary (Hibbitt) S.; children: Lesley, Rebecca, Corinna. MB ChB, U. Edinburgh, 1968; MSc, U. London, 1979; LLM, U. Cardiff, 1996. Resident various hosps., England, Can., France, 1968-75; chief med. officer Majes Project, Peru, 1975-77, Mufindi Project, Tanzania, 1981-82; sr. lectr. United Med. Schs., London, 1982—; clin. dir. Guy's and St. Thomas Hosp. Trust, 1993—; chief med. advisor Fgn. & Commonwealth Office, England, 1989-98, U.K. Health and Safety Exec., 1998—; mem. Internat. Comm. Occupational Health, 1980, Gen. Med. Coun., England, 1989-96, 99—, Ct. of Govs., London Sch. Hygiene, 1995-99; chmn. Internat. Com. Andean Aid, England, 1992-2000. Fellow Royal Coll. Physicians. Office: St Thomas Hosp, Dept Occupational Health, London SE1 7EH, England

SNEATH, PETER HENRY ANDREWS, microbiologist, researcher; b. Galle, Sri Lanka, Nov. 17, 1923; arrived in Great Britian, 1930; s. Alec and Elizabeth Maud (Adcock) Sneath; m. Joan Sylvia Thompson, July 18, 1953; children: Barbara Joan, Catherine Darnley, David Andrews. BA, Cambridge U., Eng., 1944; MA, 1947, MB BChir, 1948, MD, 1959. House physician Kings Coll. Hosp., London, 1948-49, house pathologist, 1949-50; lt., capt., maj. Royal Army Med. Corps., 1950-52; scientist Med. Rsch. Coun., Eng., 1953-64; dir. Microbial Systematics Unit Med. Rsch. Coun., Leicester, Eng., 1964-75; prof. Clin. Microbiology Leicester (Eng.) U., 1975-89, prof. emeritus of microbiology, 1989; Rockefeller Rsch. fellow, 1958-59; vis. prof. U. Kans., Lawrence, 1967-68; Garvin vis. prof. Va. Poly. Inst. and State U., Blacksburg, Va., 1990-91. Co-author: Principles of Numerical Taxonomy, 1963; Numerical Taxonomy, 1973; author: Planets and Life, 1970; contbr. articles to profl. jours. Pres. Leicester Lit. and Philos. Soc., Eng., 1989-90. Maj. Royal Army Med. Corps., 1950-52. Recipient Van Niel prize in Bacterial Systematics, U. Queensland, 1990. Fellow The Royal Soc.; mem. Soc. Systematic Biologists, Am. Soc. Microbiology, Soc. Gen. Microbiology, Am. Acad. Microbiology. Democrat. Methodist. Avocations: gardening, reading, computing. Home: 15 Southmeads Rd, Leicester LE2 2 LR, England Office: U Leicester, Microbiology Dept, Leicester LE1 7RH, England

SNEHALATHA, CHAMUKUTTAN, biochemist; b. Palakkad, Kerala, India, Oct. 14, 1943; d. K.P.K. and K.V. (Saraswathi) Menon; m. Porayath Chamukuttan, May 29, 1966 (dec. Dec. 1988); children: Sreelatha Padmakumar, Sreekumar. BSc, Womens Christian Coll., Madras, India, 1963; MSc, Madras Med. Coll., 1966; DPhil, Calcutta (India) U., 1970; DSc, Madras U., 1988. Asst. rsch. officer neurochemistry Madras Med. Coll., 1970-75; head dept. biochemistry Diabetes Rsch. Ctr., Madras, 1975—; adv. Diabetes Rsch. Ctr. Madras U., 1985, tchr., 1976. Contbr. articles to profl. jours. Mem. Diabetic Assn. India (Hodgkin-Sanger Oration award 1986), Am. Assn. for Clin. Chemistry, Rsch. Soc. for Study Diabetes in India. Avocation: reading. Home: No 9 Damodara Rd, 600 010 Madras India Office: Diabetes Rsch Ctr, No 4 Main Rd, 600 013 Madras India

SNELL, KEITH, biochemistry educator and researcher; b. Chester, Eng., May 10, 1946; s. George Henry and Audrey (Harry) S.; m. Monisha Chaudhuri (dec.); children: Louise Karen, Sushila Carolyn, Timothy Rabindra. BSc in Biochemistry, U. Manchester (Eng.), 1967, PhD in Biochemistry, 1971. Clin. biochemist Salford (Eng.) Royal Hosp., 1967-68; rsch. fellow U. Birmingham (Eng.), 1970-73; lectr. biochem. toxicology U. Surrey, Guildford, Eng., 1974-78, reader in biochemistry, 1978-92; sci. sec. Inst. of Cancer Rsch., London, 1992—; vis. lectr. Harvard Med. Sch., Boston, 1976; vis. prof. Ind. U. Sch. Medicine, Indpls., 1984-88. Editor: Developmental Toxicology, 1982, Biochemical Toxicology, 1987, Understanding Control of Metabolism, 1997, Biochem. Soc. Transactions, 1993—. Fellow Royal Soc. Arts; mem. Biochem. Soc. (coun. 1989—), Brit. Toxicology Soc., Brit. Assn. for Cancer Rsch., Am. Assn. Cancer Rsch. Home: 4 High View Rd, Guildford GU2 7RS, England Office: Inst Cancer Rsch, London SW7 3RP, England

SNELL, NOEL JAMES CREAGH, physician, researcher; b. London, Dec. 17, 1947; s. William Edward and Yvonne Creagh (Brown) S.; m. Barbara Jean Appleby, Oct. 30, 1971; children: Lindsey, Rowan, Roderick. B Medicine, B Surgery, U. London, 1972. Physician London and Berkshire, Eng., 1972-78; clinician scientist Med. Rsch. Coun., London, 1978-81; dir. clin. rsch. Boehringer Ingelheim Ltd., Bracknell, U.K., 1983-87; European med. dir. I.C.N. Pharms. Inc., U.S., 1987-92; assoc. med. dir. Glaxo Pharms., Stockley Park, U.K., 1992-95; European therapeutic area head Bayer p.l.c., Stoke Poges, U.K., 1995—; hon. clinician Royal Brompton Hosp., London, 1978—; vis. fellow Ctr. for Environ. Toxicology, U. Ctrl. Lancashire, 1999—. Editor Jour. of Pharm. Medicine, 1994-96; co-editor procs. Internat. Workshop on Respiratory Tract Secretions, 1987, Internat. Jour. Pharm. Medicine, 1997—; contbr. articles to profl. publs. Councillor Town Coun., Henley-on-Thames, Oxon, Eng., 1977-87, mayor, 1982-83, dep. mayor, 1983-84; dir. Nat. Rowing Mus. Found., 1989-93; trustee UK Tuberculosis Charity "T.B. Alert", 1998—. History of Medicine Rsch. fellow Wellcome Trust, 1995, hon. sr. fellow Nat. Heart and Lung Inst., 1994—. Fellow Faculty Pharm. Medicine, Inst. Biology (chartered biologist), Royal Coll. Physicians (Medicine-Gilliland traveling fellow 1981), Royal Inst. Pub. Health and Hygiene, Royal Soc. Medicine (v.p. sect. respiratory medicine), Soc. Pharm. Medicine (mem. com.), Brit. Assn. Lung Rsch. (chmn. 1995-97), Brit. Pharmacol. Soc., Brit. Thoracic Soc. (rsch. com.), Nat. Liberal Club, Keyhaven Yacht Club, Thames and Henley Rowing Clubs. Liberal Democrat. Avocations: rowing, badminton, sailing, bridge, history of respiratory medicine. Office: Nat Heart and Lung Inst, Host Def Unit Manresa Rd, London SW3 6LR, England

SNELLEN, DEBORAH SUE, training consulting company executive; b. Columbia, Mo., Oct. 23, 1956; d. Howard Earl and Jessie Jewel (Johnson) Durk; m. Steven Wayne Snellen, Jan. 17, 1987; 1 child, Ashlen Dolores. BS in Edn. cum laude, U. Mo., 1979, MA in Speech Communication, 1980. Provider rels. rep. EDS Fed., Columbia, 1981-83; dir. human resources MBS Textbook Exch., Inc., Columbia, 1983-88; pres., owner Business Class, Columbia, 1988—; chmn. adv. bd. for bus. edn. Columbia Adult Edn., 1990-92. Bd. dirs. U. Mo. Arts and Sci. Alumni Exec. Bd., Advent Enterprises, Inc., Columbia, 1990-92; inaugural participant Greater Mo. Focus on Leadership Program, 1990; participant Tiger Scholarship Fund, Jr. League of Springfield, 1994-97; cert. Herrmann Brain Dominance Instrument Adminstr. and Interpretation, 1994; treasurer U. Mo. Alumni Assoc., 2000—. Honors scholar U. Mo. Mem. ASTD (past pres. Cen. Mo. chpt.), Columbia C. of C. (bd. dirs. 1991-92), Leawood C. of C. (charter, bd. dirs. 1997), Women's Network (pres. 1988-89, amb. 1989-92), U. Mo. Alumni Assn. (treas. 2000—). Republican. Presbyterian. Avocations: tailoring, snow skiing, horseback riding.

SNELL-HORNBY, MARY ADAMS CARRUTHERS, translation studies educator, researcher, consultant; b. Mirfield, Yorkshire, Eng., Apr. 2, 1940; arrived in Austria, 1989; d. Arthur and Florence Mary (Adams) Snell; m. Anthony Gage Hornby, Apr. 6, 1973; 1 child, Astrid. MA with honors, U. St. Andrews, Scotland, 1962, BPhil, 1966; PhD, U. Zürich, Switzerland, 1987. Lectr. U. Munich, Germany, 1964-69, U. Pietermaritzburg, South Africa, 1971-72, U. Zürich, 1977-89; acting prof. U. Heidelberg, Germany, 1981-83; prof. U. Vienna, Austria, 1989—; dir. Inst. Translation and Interpretation, U. Vienna, 1990-94; guest linguist Rsch. Ctr. Lit. Translation, U. Göttingen, Germany, 1986-87; on. prof. Ctr. for Comparative Brit. and Cultural Studies, U. Warwick, Eng., 1997—. Author: Translation Studies-An Integrated Approach, Translation und Text, Handbuch Translation; editor: Übersetzungswissenschaft-Eine Neuorientierung, Translation Studies: An Interdiscipline; editor-in-chief Studies in Translation, Tübingen, Germany, 1995—. Recipient medal U. Helsinki, Finland, 1997. Mem. European Soc. Translation Studies (pres. 1992-98), Vienna Lang. Soc. (pres. 1992-94), European Assn. Lexicography (bd. dirs. 1986-92). Anglican. Avocations: theater, opera, travel, hiking, music. Office: U Vienna, Gymnasiumstr 50, A-1190 Vienna Austria

SNETKOV, VLADIMIR, physiologist, researcher; b. St. Petersburg, Russia, Apr. 24, 1950; arrived in Eng., 1993; s. Alexander Shur and Galina Snetkov; m. Elena Blinov, 1972 (div. 1976); 1 child, Dmitri; m. Goutta Vainiounskaia; children: Aglaya, Xenia. MSc, St. Petersburg U., 1973; PhD, Sechenov Inst., St. Petersburg, 1977. Jr. scientist Sechenov Inst., 1976-86, scientist, 1986-87, sr. scientist, 1987-90; rsch. fellow Louis Pasteur U., Strasbourg, France, 1990-93; rsch. asst. St. Thomas' Hosp., London, 1993—. Contbr. over 50 articles to sci. jours. Recipient State Prize in sci. USSR, 1989. Mem. Physiol. Soc. Avocations: reading, classical music. Home: 7 Lewesdon Close, London SW19 6DP, England Office: Guy's Hosp Dept Resp Med, & Allergy Thomas Guy House, London SE1 9RT, England

SNIBBE, PATRICIA MISCALL, advertising executive; b. Hackensack, N.J., June 1, 1932; d. Jack and Margaret Lois (Drake) Miscall; m. Richard Wilson Snibbe, Sept. 8, 1962; stepchildren: John Robinson, Paul Clor. BFA, R.I. Sch. Design, 1954; postgrad., New Sch. for Social Rsch., 1975-80, U. London, 1989. Art dir., film prodr. Peckham Prodns., N.Y.C., 1960-64; dir. art, ptnr. Stallman and Snibbe, N.Y.C., 1964-66; dir. art Shevlo Advt., N.Y.C., 1966-72, Bernard Hodes Advt., N.Y.C., 1972-77; owner, creative dir. Archtl. Film Libr., N.Y.C., 1978-88, creative dir., 1980—; pres. Cromelin and Bliss, Parfumier, N.Y.C., 1988—. Author and artist: Feminist Funnies, 181—; author: (with Richard W. Snibbe) The New Modernist in World Architecture, 1999. Recipient Golden Cir. award Affiliated Advt. Agys. Internat., 1975-77, Creativity award of distinction, 1978. Mem. NOW (bd. dirs. N.Y.C. 1983-84), Graphic Artists Guild (steering com. Cartoonists Guild divsn. 1984-85), NATAS, Archeol. Inst. Am. Avocation: abstract modern painting. Home: 139 E 18th St New York NY 10003-2470

SNIBSON, KENNETH JOHN, cell biologist; b. Hamilton, Australia, Aug. 10, 1955; s. Ronald John and Lois Isabel (Lempriere) S.; m. Mary Mylonas, Feb. 7, 1981; children: Stella, Tom, Natasha. BS, U. Melbourne, Australia, 1976, MS, 1992, PhD, 1999. Tech. asst. Melbourne U., Australia, 1978-82, tech. officer, 1982-88, sr. tech. officer, 1988—; lectr. Melbourne U., 1995—. Author: Transgenic Animals, Gereration and Use, 1997; contbr. articles to profl. jours. Sch. councillor Sherbourne Primary Sch., Melbourne, 1997. Avocations: gardening, beer brewing, table tennis, tennis. Office: Melbourne U, Melbourne U, Grattan St, Parkville 3010, Australia

SNIDER, STEPHEN WILLIAM, art director, graphic designer; b. Boston, July 21, 1943; s. Louis Oscar and Etta Zelda (Rosenberg) S.; m. Marlene Sandra Shuman, Sept. 2, 1973; children: Emily Allison, Jill Tracy. Grad., Sch. Mus. Fine Arts, Boston, 1961-65. Asst. art dir. Arthur D. Little, Inc., Cambridge, Mass., 1965-70; creative dir. Snider Design, Boston, 1970-78; art dir. The Atlantic Monthly, Boston, 1978-81; design dir. Arnold & Co. Advt., Boston, 1981-85; creative dir. Snider Design, Wellesley, Mass., 1985-87; art dir. Little, Brown & Co., Boston, 1987-96; v.p., creative dir. St. Martin's Press, N.Y.C., 1996—. Recipient 1st place and Silver medal New Eng. Hatch awards, Boston, 1974, Gold medal N.Y. Art Dirs. Club, 1984, Best of Category Design, New Eng. Book Show, Boston, 1994, N.Y. Art Dirs. Club, 1997, Lit. Market Pl. award, named Graphic Design Person of Yr., 1998. Mem. Am. Inst. Graphic Artists, Boston Athaneum. Avocations: tennis, theatre, film, photography, antique collecting. Home: 99 Brook St Wellesley MA 02482-6644 also: 226 E 25th St New York NY 10010-3150 Office: St Martin's Press 175 5th Ave Frnt 4 New York NY 10010-7703

ŚNIEŻYŃSKA-STOLOT, EWA MARIA, art historian, educator; b. Łódź, Poland, Jan. 23, 1939; d. Jan Śnieżyński and Marta Leokadia Paj—k; m. Franciszek Michał Stolot, Oct. 7, 1961; 1 child, Kinga. MA, Jagiellonian U., Kraków, Poland, 1961, D, 1969, prof., 1998. Editor Catalogue of Monuments of Polish Art Inst. Art Polish Acad. Sci., Kraków, 1965-92; prof. dept. history of ideas Inst. Ethnology Jagiellonian U., Kraków, 1986—; Author: The Mystery of the Decoration of the Florian Psalter, 1992, Iconography of the Signs of the Zodiac and Constellations in the Middle Ages, 1994, The Iconography of the Signs of the Zodiac and Constellations in Albumasar Manuscripts, 1997, The Iconography of the Signs of the Zodiac and Constellation in the Munich Manuscript of Abraham Jbn Ezra, 1998; editor: Catalogues of Monuments of Polish Art, 1974-91. Recipient Team State award Ministry of Culture, Warsaw, Poland, 1978; grantee Getty Found., Santa Monica, Calif., 1992; mem. editl. adv. bd. Majestas, 1993—; contbr. articles to profl. jours. Home: Na Błonie 3B/99, 30-147 Cracow Poland Office: Inst of Ethnology, Jagiellonian U, 31-044 Cracow Poland

SNIP, JERINA CARLA, periodical editor; b. Groningen, The Netherlands, Apr. 25, 1946. Chief editor De Wereld Van Het Jonge Kind; editor, pub. Dykstra BV Baarn. Office: Bekadidact Pub, PO Box 122, 3740 AC Baarn Netherlands

SNITKER, SOREN, biomedical researcher, educator, physician; b. Copenhagen, July 2, 1961; came to U.S., 1993; s. Hans Emil Valdemar and Gerda Florian (Sorensen) S. MD, U. Copenhagen, 1988, PhD in Human Physiology, 1998. Lic. physician, Denmark, permission to practice independently as physician, Nat. Bd. Health, Denmark. Intern depts. orthopedic surgery/internal medicine & gastro. U. Copenhagen, U. Herlev (Denmark) Hosp., 1988-90; resident dept. internal medicine and endocrinology U. Copenhagen, Herlev (Denmark) Hosp., 1990-93; vis. assoc. clin. diabetes and nutrition sect. NIH, Nat. Inst. Diabetes and Digestive and Kidney Diseases, Phoenix, Ariz., 1993-98; asst. prof. divsn. endocrinology, diabetes, and nutrition U. Md. Med. Sch., Balt., 1999—; mem. resident's coun. U. Copenhagen, Herlev Hosp., 1992-93; lectr. in field. Manuscript reviewer: Clin. Sci., Am. Jour. Physiology, Internat. Jour. Obesity; contbr. articles and abstracts to profl. jours. Recipient salary support NIH, 1993-98. Fellow N.Am. Soc. for Study of Obesity; mem. Am. Diabetes Assn. (travel grantee 1998), Am. Soc. Bariatric Physicians, Danish Assn. Sports Medicine, Danish Assn. for Study of Obesity, Danish Endocrine Soc., Danish Med. Assn., Danish Med. Soc., European Assn. for Study of Diabetes, European Assn. for Study of Obesity, Sigma Xi. Office: U Md Med Sch Divsn Endocrinology Rm S413 725 W Lombard St Baltimore MD 21201-1009

SNITOW, VIRGINIA LEVITT, educator; b. N.Y.C., Apr. 9, 1911; d. Louis and Tania (Rosenberg) Levitt; m. Charles Snitow; children: Ann, Alan. BA in English, Hunter Coll., 1931; postgrad., Columbia U., 1932-35. Cert. secondary English tchr. English tchr. Wadligh H.S., N.Y.C., 1932-44, Seward Park H.S., N.Y.C., 1944-46; v.p. U.S. World Trade Fair, 1956-66; nat. pres. Nat. A. J. Congress Women's Divsn., 1964-70; chair leadership conf. Nat. Jewish Women's Orgn., N.Y.C., 1970-73, Hunter Hall of Fame, 1977; bd. dirs. Hunter Coll. Found., 1991—; founder Virginia L. Snitow Lecture Series at Haifa, Hebrew and Tel Aviv univs., 1986—. Contbr. articles to profl. jours. NGO rep. UN, N.Y.C., 1960-62; del. Dem. Nat. Convention, Chgo., 1968, Miami, 1972; mem. N.Y. State Coord. com. Internat. Women's Yr., 1977-78; founder, hon. chair U.S./Israel Women to Women, 1978—; founding mem. Legal Awareness Women, 1979—. Recipient Woman for Our Time award Am. Jewish Congress, 1971, Louise Waterman Wise Laureate, 1979, Pres. Merit award Haifa U., 1991, Susan B. Anthony award NOW, 1992, Women Whod Made a Difference, The Knesset, 2000. Avocation: gardening. Office: 4 Sniffen Ct New York NY 10016-3505

SNOOK, QUINTON, construction company executive; b. Atlanta, July 15, 1925; s. John Wilson and Charlotte Louise (Clayson) S.; student U. Idaho, 1949-51; m. Lois Mullen, Jan. 19, 1947; children: Lois Ann Snook Matteson, Quinton A., Edward M., Clayson S., Charlotte T. Rancher, Lemhi Valley, Idaho, 1942—; owner, mgr. Snook Constrn., Salmon, Idaho, 1952—; owner Snook Trucking, 1967—, Lemhi Posts and Poles, 1980—. Mem. Lemhi County Commn., Dist. 2, 1980-93. Named to Idaho Agrl. Hall of Fame, 1996. Mem. Am. Quarter Horse Assn., Farm Bur., Nat. Riflemen's Assn., Idaho Assn. Commrs. and Clerks (sec. 1986, v.p. 1987, pres. 1988), Am. Hereford Assn., Idaho Cattlemen's Assn., Elks. Republican. Episcopalian. Home: RR 1 Box 49 Salmon ID 83467-9701

SNOOKS, GRAEME DONALD, political economist; b. Perth, Australia, July 22, 1944; s. William Donald and Eleanor Violet (Williams) S.; m. Loma Rae Graham, Jan. 24, 1970; children: Adrian Graham, Roland William. BS in Econs., U. Western Australia, 1966, MS in Econs., 1968; PhD, Australian Nat. U., 1972. Tutor U. Western Australia, 1966-68; lectr. U. Queensland, Australia, 1971-72; lectr. Flinders U., Australia, 1972-74, sr. lectr., 1975-83, reader, 1984-89; Coghlan rsch. prof. Inst. Advanced Studies Australian Nat. U., Canberra, 1989—; cons. visual arts bd. Australia Council, Sydney, 1974, S. Australian Premiers Dept., Adelaide, 1974-77, Arts Council Great Brit., London, 1978, British Pub. Record Office, London, 1984-86, BBC, London, 1986. Author: Depression and Recovery, 1974, Domesday Economy, 1986, Exploring S.E. Asia's Economic Past, 1991, Land and Sea, 1992, Economic Policy in Australia since the Great Depression, 1993, Historical Analysis in Economics, 1993, Economics Without Time, 1993, Portrait of the Family within the Total Economy, 1994, Was the Industrial Revolution Necessary?, 1994, Wealth and Wellbeing in Australasia, 1996, The Dynamic Society, 1996, The Ephemeral Civilization, 1997, The Laws of History, 1998, Longrun Dynamics, 1998, Global Transition, 1999, The Global Crisis Makers, 2000; editor: Australian Econ. History Rev., 1988-96; gen. editor Macmillan Econ. History of S.E. Asia, 1989—; cons. editor Cambridge Econ. History of Australia, 1990-96; contbr. articles to profl. jours. Australia Coun. grantee, 1974, Australian Rsch. Coun. grantee, 1974-89. Fellow Royal Hist. Soc., Acad. Social Scis. in Australia; mem. Econ. History Assn., Econ. History Soc., Econ. History Soc. Australia and New Zealand, Cliometric Soc. Avocations: bonsai, literature, art, fly-fishing. Office: Australian Nat U, Inst Advanced Studies, Canberra ACT 0200, Australia

SNOUSSI, AHMED, ambassador. Permanent rep. Morocco UN, N.Y.C. Office: Permanent Mission Morocco to UN 866 2d Ave New York NY 10017

SNOW, JOHN WILLIAM, railroad executive; b. Toledo, Aug. 2, 1939; s. William Dean and Catharine (Howard) S.; m. Fredrica Wheeler, June 11, 1964 (div. 1973); children: Bradley, Ian; m. Carolyn Kalk, Aug. 31, 1973; 1 child, Christopher. BA, Kenyon Coll./U. Toledo, 1962; PhD, U. Va., 1965; LLB, George Washington U., 1967. Asst. prof. econs. U. Md., College Park, 1965-67; assoc. Wheeler & Wheeler, Washington, 1967-72; asst. gen. counsel Dept. Transp., Washington, 1972-73, dep. asst. sec. for policy, plans and internat. affairs, 1973-74, asst. sec. for govtl. affairs, 1974-75, dep. under sec., 1975-76; adminstr. Nat. Hwy. Traffic Safety Adminstrn., Washington, 1976-77; v.p. govt. affairs Chessie System Inc., Washington, 1977-80; sr. v.p. corp. services CSX Corp., Richmond, Va., 1980-84, exec. v.p., 1984-85; pres., chief exec. officer Chessie System R.R.s, Balt., 1985-86, CSX Rail Transport, Jacksonville, Fla., 1986-87, CSX Transp., Jacksonville, Va., 1987-88; pres., chief operating officer CSX Corp., Richmond, Va., 1988-89, pres., chief exec. officer, 1989-91, chmn., pres., chief exec. officer, 1991—, also bd. dirs.; adj. prof. law George Washington U., 1972-75; vis. prof. econs. U. Va., Charlottesville, spring 1977; vis. fellow Am. Enterprises Inst., Washington, spring 1977; bd. dirs. USX Corp., Circuit City Stores, Inc., Johnson & Johnson, Verizon. Bd. trustees Johns Hopkins U. Mem. Va. State Bar. Episcopalian. Clubs: Chevy Chase, Metropolitan (Washington); Commonwealth, Country of Va. (Richmond).

SNOW, PAMELA CLAIRE, researcher; b. Melbourne, Victoria, Australia, Apr. 16, 1960; d. Donald William and Nancy Claire (Harris) James; m. Stuart John Snow, Apr. 6, 1984; children: Alexandra Claire, Katherine Isabel. BS in Speech Pathology, Lincoln Inst. Health Scis., Melbourne, 1981, Grad. Diploma in Comm. Disorders, 1986; PhD, La Trobe U., Melbourne, 1997. Speech pathologist Mont Park Psychiat. Hosp., Melbourne, 1982-83; dep. mgr. speech pathology dept. Bethesda Hosp., Melbourne, 1983-84, mgr. speech pathology dept., 1984-94; sessional lectr., clin. supr. La Trobe Univ., Melbourne, 1994-97, lectr., 1998; rsch. fellow Ctr. for Youth Drug Studies Australian Drug Found. and Deakin U. Co-author: (book) Traumatic Brain Injury, 1994; contbg. author: Communication and Traumatic Brain Injury, 1998; contbr. articles to profl. jours. Recipient Australian Postgrad. Rsch. award Fed. Govt. of Australia, 1994. Mem. Australian Soc. for Study of Brain Impairment (pres. 1994-95), Australian Psychol. Soc., Speech Pathology Assn. Australia, Australian Profl. Soc. on Alcohol and Other Drugs. Avocations: playing and listening to music, reading. Office: Sch Psychology Deakin U, 221 Burwood Hwy, 3125 Burwood Victoria, Australia

SNOWDEN, ALAN, editor, consultant; b. London, Dec. 14, 1920; s. Frederick Albert and Verna (Withers) S.; m. Kathleen Ellen Baxter; children: Rosemary Kay, Martin Alan. Photographer The Daily Sketch, London, 1947; dep. mgr. The Daily Telegraph, London; cons. editor The Magic Circular, London, 1972-2000. Magic entertainer sr. citizens clubs. N.C.O. Royal Air Force, 1939-46, India, Burma. Decorated Burma Star, RAF, 1939-45, Medal, Victory medal, Def. medal; recipient bronze medal Royal Life Saving Soc., silver medal London Acad. Music and Dramatic Art, 1947. Mem. United Wards Club City of London (life), Royal Automobile Club (coun. 1966-98), Nat. Press Automobile Club (chmn. 1951-2000), Assn. Brit. Motor Clubs (chmn. south area 1956-2000), League of Safe Drivers (press officer), Magic Circle (hon. v.p.). Avocations: magic, motoring, photography. Home: 5 Folkington Corner, Woodside Park, Finchley London N12 7BH, England

SNOWDEN, CHRISTOPHER MAXWELL, engineering educator; b. Hull, Eng., Mar. 5, 1956; s. William Arthur and Barbara Jeanne (Locking) S.; m. Irena Margaret Lewandowska, Jan. 8, 1993; children: James Christopher, William Matthew. BSc with honors, U. Leeds, Eng., 1977, MSc, 1979, PhD, 1982. Chartered engr. Applications engr. Mullards, London, 1977-78; lectr. U. York, Eng., 1982-83; lectr. U. Leeds, Eng., 1983-88, sr. lectr., 1988-92, prof. microwave engring., personal chair, 1992—, dir. rsch., 1991-95, head Sch. Electronic and Elec. Engring., 1995-97, 1997-98, dir. Inst. of Microwaves and Photonics, 1997-98; exec. dir. tech. Filtronic Plc, Leeds, 1998-99; CEO Filtronic Plc, Leeds, Eng., 1999—; vis. rschr. Calif. Inst. Tech., Pasadena, 1987; sr. staff scientist M/A-Com. Inc., Burlington, 1990-91; cons. M/A-Com. Inc., Lowell, 1991-98, Lucas-Varity plc, U.K.; chmn. Internat. Microwaves & RF Conf., 1995. Author: Introduction to Semiconductor Device Modelling, 1986, Semiconductor Device Modelling, 1988, INCA Interactive Circuit Analysis, 1988, Compound Semiconductor Device Modelling, 1993; editor: Wiley Electronic and Electrical Engineering Book Series, 1989-99; contbr. articles to profl. jours. Warden Bodington Hall, Leeds, 1983-90. Grantee EPSRC; apptd. Top Scientist Internat. Rsch. Ctr. Telecomms.-Transmission and Radar Delft (Netherlands) U. Tech. Fellow Inst. Elec. Engrs. (profl. group 1988-94), IEEE (chmn. terahertz electronics conf. 1998, co-chair microwave theory and techniques com. on CAD, mem. microwave theory and techniques tech. program com., compound semicondr. integrated cir. tech. com.), IEEE Electron Devices Soc. (Disting. lectr. 1996—, Microwave prize 1999), Royal Acad. Engring., Royal Soc. Arts,

MIT Electromagnetics Acad. Avocations: oil painting, photography, music, gardening. Office: U Leeds, Sch Electronic-Elec Engring, Leeds LS2 9JT, England

SNOWER, DENNIS JAMES, economics educator; b. Vienna, Austria, Oct. 14, 1950; arrived in England, 1980.; s. Bernard and Kitty Doris S.; m. Judith Bristow, June 7, 1987; children: David Bernard, Rebecca Yemina. BA, MA, Oxford (Eng.) U., 1971; MA, PhD, Princeton U., 1975. Asst. prof. U. Md., College Park, 1975-79, Inst. Advanced Studies, Vienna, 1979-80; lectr. U. London, 1970-83, reader, 1983-88, prof., 1989—; vis. prof. Columbia U., N.Y.C., 1991, Dartmouth Coll., Hanover, N.H., 1992; rsch. dir. Ctrl. Econ. Policy Rsch., London, 1991—; rsch. dir. welfare state program Inst. for the Future of Work; adv. Dept. Employment, London, 1992—; dir. Labour Mkt. Imperfections Group, London, 1991—, European Network on Labor and Product Mkts., London, 1993; adv. Spanish govt., Madrid, 1993, U.K. govt., Vienna, 1993. Author: The Insider-Outsider Theory, 1989. Royal Soc. Arts fellow, 1993. Mem. European Econ. Assn., Am. Economic Assn., Royal Economic Soc., Econometric Soc. Avocations: skiing, karate, running, painting, poetry. Home: 21 Western Rd, N2 9JB London England Office: Dept Econs Birbeck Coll, 7 Gresse St, W1P 1PA London England

SNOWISS, ALVIN L., lawyer; b. Lock Haven, Pa., June 16, 1930; s. Benjamin and Lillian (Kalin) S.; m. Jean Yarnell, Mar. 16, 1973. BA, U. Pa., Phila., 1952, JD, 1955; hon. alumnus, Pa. State U., 1998. Bar: Pa. 1956, U.S. Dist. Ct. (mid. dist.) Pa. 1958, U.S. Supreme Ct. 1972. Pvt. practice Lock Haven, 1955-61; ptnr. Lugg & Snowiss, Lock Haven, 1961-74, Lugg, Snowiss, Steinberg, Faulkner & Hall, Lock Haven, 1974-86, Snowiss, Steinberg Faulkner, and Hall LLP, Lock Haven, 1987—; solicitor Clinton County, Lock Haven, 1964-72. Chmn. bd. Lock Haven Hosp. Found., 1986-92; pres. Lock Haven Hosp., 1982-86; bd. govs. Clinton County Cmty. Found., Lock Haven, 1970-97; chmn. adv. bd. Palmer Mus. Art, State College; v.p. bd. trustees Ross Libr., Lock Haven, 1963-86; mem. exec. com. Pa. Rep. Com., Harrisburg, 1974-80; state committeeman Clinton County Rep. Com., 1967-80. Fellow Am. Coll. Trust and Estate Counsel, Am. Bar Found., Pa. Bar Found. (founding, bd. dirs. 1984-95); mem. Pa. Bar Assn. (zone del. 1976-82, zone gov. 1983-86, treas. 1987-90), Clinton County Bar Assn. (pres. 1975-76), Kiwanis (pres. Lock Haven 1966-67). Republican. Avocations: art history, golf, historical research. Home: 414 W Main St Lock Haven PA 17745-1107 Office: 333 N Vesper St Lock Haven PA 17745-1342

SNOW-SMITH, JOANNE INLOES, art history educator; b. Balt.; d. Henry Williams and Elsie Orrick (Bagley) Snow; m. Robert Porter Smith (dec.); children: Joanne Tyndale Darby, Henry Webster Smith, III (dec.), Constance Elizabeth Bagley, Cynthia Porter Bloom, Robert Porter Smith, Jr.; m. Robert Edward Willstadter. BA, Goucher Coll.; MA, U. Ariz., 1968; PhD, UCLA, 1976. Prof. Italian Rennaissance art history U. Wash., Seattle, 1981—; program dir. of art history U. Wash. Rome Ctr. in Palazzo Pio, Rome, 1998, 2000. Author: (book) The Salvator Mundi of Leonardo da Vinci, 1982 (Internat. award 1983), The Primavera of Sandro Botticelli: A Neoplatonic Interpretaion, 1993; contbr. numerous articles to profl. jours. Recipient Rsch. Professorship to study in Oxford and London, U. Wash. Grad. Sch., 1986. Mem. Nat. Soc. Colonial Dames of Am., Seattle Symphony Assn., Renaissance Soc. of Am., Leonardo Soc./U. London, Coll. Art Assn., Seattle Art Mus., Met. Mus. Art, Ashmolean Mus. (Oxford, Eng.). Home: 1414 Shenandoah Dr E Seattle WA 98112-3730 Office: Univ Wash PO Box 353440 Seattle WA 98195-3440

SNYDER, ARNOLD LEE, JR., retired air force officer, research director; b. Washington, Oct. 12, 1937; s. Arnold Lee and Frances May (Humbert) S; m. Patricia Dorine Ward, July 6, 1963; children: Heinrick Jason, Sonya Doreen, Ross Nansen. BCE, George Washington U., 1960; MS, U. Colo., 1966; PhD, U. Alaska, 1972. Commd. 2d lt. USAF, 1960; advanced through grades to col., 1981; chief space environ. support sys. devel. sect. Air Force Global Weather Central, Offutt AFB, Nebr., 1972-76; chief ionospheric dynamics br. Geophysics Lab., Hanscom AFB, Mass., 1976-80; test dir. CONUS OTH-B radar system, Columbia Falls AFB, Maine, 1980-81; program dir. CONUS OTH-B radar system, Hanscom AFB, 1981-85; dir. Office of Tech. Support, 1985-87; tech. dir. U. Lowell Ctr. Atmospheric Rsch., 1987-89; with The Mitre Corp., 1989-96; pvt. practice, 1996—; adj. prof. U. Lowell, 1987-89. Contbr. articles to sci. jours. Recipient Legion of Merit, Meritorious Svc. medal with one oak leaf cluster, Commendation medal USAF, R&D award, 1981; Def. Value Engring. award, 1984; Henry Harding scholar, 1955-56. Mem. Am. Geophys. Union, Am. Meteorol. Soc., Air Force Assn., Sigma Xi. Home and Office: 22 Blake Rd Orrington ME 04474-3637

SNYDER, ARTHUR, publishing company executive; b. Valley Stream, N.Y., Feb. 6, 1925; s. Arthur and Kathryn (Staubitzer) S.; m. Betty Lain Harper, July 8, 1950; children: Susan, Arthur, Betsy, Jack, Heidi, Bonnie. B in Metall. Engring., Cornell U., 1950, MBA, 1952. Mfg. engr. Norton Co., Worcester, Mass., 1952-56; chief accountant Norton Co., 1956-58, asst. controller, 1958-59, mgr. data processing, 1959-61, controller, 1961-65; exec. v.p. A.M. Best Co., Oldwick, N.J., 1965-67; pres. A.M. Best Co., 1968—, chmn., 1971—. Author: Principles of Inventory Control and Managing Capital Expenditures. 1st lt. AUS, 1942-45. Decorated Battlefield Commn., Bronze Star with oak leaf cluster, Purple Heart. Mem. Fin. Execs. Inst., Cornell Soc. Engrs., Roxiticus Golf Club (Mendham, N.J.), Baltusrol Golf Club (Springfield, N.J.), U.S. Srs. Golf Assn., Lyford Cay Club (Nassau, Bahamas), Loch Lomond Golf Club (Scotland). Presbyterian. Home: Lloyd Rd Bernardsville NJ 07924-1710 Office: A M Best Company Inc Ambest Rd Oldwick NJ 08858

SNYDER, ARTHUR KRESS, lawyer; b. L.A., Nov. 10, 1932; s. Arthur and Ella Ruth (Keck) S.; m. Mary Frances Neely, Mar. 5, 1953; children: Neely Arthur, Miles John; m. Michele Maggie Noval, May 14, 1973; 1 child, Erin-Marisol Michele; m. Delia Wu, Apr. 18, 1981. BA, Pepperdine U., 1953; JD, U. So. Calif., 1958; LLD, Union U., 1980. Bar: Calif. 1960, U.S. Supreme Ct. 1982. Sole practice L.A., 1960-67; founder, pres. Arthur K. Snyder Law Corp., L.A., 1981-94; pres. Snyder & Assocs., Attys., L.A., 1994—; pres. Marisol Corp., real estate and fgn. trade, 1978—; pres. real estate holdings Keck Investment Properties, 1990—; past instr. L.A. City Schs. Mem. City Coun. L.A., 1967-85. Served to capt. USMC. Decorated La Tizona de El Cid Compeador (Spain), medal Legion of Honor (Mex.), Hwa Chao Zee You medal (Republic of China), numerous other commendations, medals, awards. Mem. ABA, ATLA, Los Angeles County Bar Assn., World Film Inst. (chmn. bd. dirs. 1997—), Am.-Vietnamese Cultural Exch. Assn. (pres. 1998—), Calif. Bar Assn., L.A. County Bar Assn., Am. Judicature Soc., Masons. Baptist. Office: 1000 W Sunset Blvd Ste 200 Los Angeles CA 90012-2105

SNYDER, CAROLYN ANN, university dean, librarian; b. Elgin, Nebr., Nov. 5, 1942; d. Ralph and Florence Wagner; m. Barry Snyder, Apr. 24, 1969. Student, Nebr. Wesleyan U., 1960-61; BS cum laude, Kearney State Coll., 1964; MS in Librarianship, U. Denver, 1965. Asst. libr. sci. and tech. U. Nebr., Lincoln, 1965-67, asst. pub. svc. libr., 1967-68, 70-73; pers. libr. Ind. U. Librs., Bloomington, 1973-76, acting dean of univ. librs., 1980, 88-89, assoc. dean for pub. svcs., 1977-88, 89-91, interim devel. officer, 1989-91; adminstrv. army libr. Spl. Svcs. Agy., Europe, 1968-70; dean libr. affairs So. Ill. U., Carbondale, 1991-2000, prof., 2000—; team leader Midwest Univs. Consortium for Internat. Activities-World Bank IX project to develop libr. system and implement automation U. Indonesia, Jakarta, 1984-86; libr. devel. cons. Inst. Tech. MARA/Midwest Univs. Consortium for Internat. Activities Program in Malaysia, 1985; ofcl. rep. EDUCAUSE, 1996—; mem. working group on scholarly comm. Nat. Commn. on Librs. and Info. Sci., 1998—. Editor Library and Other Academic Support Services for Distance Learning, 1997; contbr. chpt. to book and articles to profl. jours. Mem. Humane Assn. Jackson County, 1991—, Carbondale Pub. Libr. Friends, 1991—. Recipient Cooperative Rsch. grant Coun. on Libr. Resources, Washington, 1984. Mem. ALA (councilor 1985-89, Bogle Internat. Travel award 1988, H.W. Wilson Libr. Staff devel. grantee 1981), Libr. Adminstrn./Mgmt. Assn. (pres. 1981-82), Com. on Instnl. Coop./Resource Sharing (chair 1987-91), Coalition for Networked Info. (So. Ill. U. at Carbondale rep. 1991—), Coun. Dirs. State Univ. Librs. in Ill. (chair 1992-93, 99-00), Coun. on Libr. and Info. Resources Digital Leadership Inst. Steering Com. (Assn. Rsch. Librs. rep. 1998—), Ill. Assn. Coll. and Rsch. Librs. (chair Ill. Bd. Higher Edn. liaison com. 1993-94), Ill. Network (bd. dirs.), Ind. Libr. Assn. (chair coll./univ. divsn. 1982-83), U.S. Grant Assn. (bd. dirs. 1992—), Ill. Libr. Computer Sys. Orgn. (policy coun. 1992-95, 96—), Nat. Assn. State Univs. and Land-Grant Colls. (commn. on info. tech. and its distance learning and libr. bds. 1994-96), NetIllinois (bd. dirs. 1994-96), OCLC Users Coun. (elected rep. 1995-98), Big 12 Plus Libr. Consortium (chair 1997-98), Nat. Commn. on Librs. and Info. Sci. Working Group on Scholarly Comms. Avocations: antiques, theater, movies. Office: So Ill U Morris Libr Carbondale IL 62901-6632

SNYDER, CURT, aerospace engineer; b. Salem, Va., Jan. 30, 1935; s. Talmadge D. and Stella Hughes S.; m. Alice Jane Roach Snyder, Sept. 3, 1954 (div. Dec. 29, 1983); children: Samuel Steven, Mary, Dan; m. Eleanor Overman Snyder, June 15, 1985; children: Kendall, Mason. BS in Aeronautical Engring., Va. Tech., Blacksburg, 1961, MS in Aerospace Engring., 1966. Pfc U.S. Army, Germany, 1954-57; rsch. engr. NASA, Langley, Va., 1961-66; lead engr. Boeing, Seattle, 1966-72; deputy prog. mgr. McAir, St. Louis, 1972-78; prof. mgr. Navy, Washington, 1978—; advisor Nat. Aerospace Plane Joint Program Office, WPAFB, Ohio, 1985-92. Contbr. technical reports to profl. jours. Pres. PTA, St. Charles, 1975-76; mgr. Little League, 1967-77; task leader PTRCA, Port Tobacco, 1996-97. Recipient Nat. Aerospace Plane Program Office commendation, WPAFB, Ohio, 1992. Avocations: golf, gardening, grandchildren. E-mail address: syndercd@navair.navy.mil. Fax: 301-757-0534. Home: 7489 Shirley Blvd Port Tobacco MD 20677-3113

SNYDER, DAVID L., film production designer; b. Buffalo, Sept. 22, 1944; s. Albert R. and Louise M. (Passero) S.; m. Terry Finn, Aug. 1, 1990; children: David Michael, Amy Lynne, Finn Henry. Grad. high sch., Niagara Falls, N.Y. Ind. film prodn. designer Hollywood, Calif.; pres. Snyder Bros. Prodns., Inc., Hollywood; guest speaker Tokyo Internat. Film Festival, 1985. Art dir. (films) In God We Trust, 1980, The Idolmaker, 1980, Blade Runner, 1982 (Academy award nomination best art direction 1982), Brainstorm, 1983; prodn. designer (films) Strange Brew, 1983, Racing With the Moon, 1984, The Woman In Red, 1984, My Science Project, 1985, Armed and Dangerous, 1986, Back to School, 1986, Summer School, 1987, Moving, 1988, She's Out of Control, 1989, Bill & Ted's Bogus Journey, 1991, Class Act, 1992, Super Mario Brothers, 1993, Demolition Man, 1993, Terminal Velocity, 1994, Rainbow, 1995, Vegas Vacation, 1997, Burn, Hollywood, Burn, 1997, Soldier, 1998, The Whole Nine Yards, 1999; assoc. prodr.: (film) Cold Dog Soup, 1990; exec. prodr. (film) Rainbow, 1995. Mem. NATAS, Motion Picture Art Dirs. Guild, Acad. Motion Picture Arts and Scis., Dirs. Guild Am. Democrat. Avocation: researching history of the film industry in America. Address: 3500 W Olive Ave Ste 1470 Burbank CA 91505-5514

SNYDER, FRANCIS GREGORY, law educator, consultant; b. Madison, Wis., June 26, 1942; s. Francis George and Margaret Alpha (Lundberg) S.; divorced; 1 child, Jasper Thomas Francis Snyder. BA, Yale U., 1964; JD, Harvard U., 1968, cert. in economics, 1969; PhD, U. Paris, 1973. Rsch. fellow Yale Law Sch., New Haven, 1970-71; from asst. prof. to assoc. prof. Osgoode Hall Law Sch. York U., Toronto, Can., 1971-78; from sr. lectr. to reader in law U. Warwick, Coventry, Eng., 1979-86; reader to prof. European law U. London, 1986-93; hon. vis. prof. law, 1992—; prof. European cmty. law European U. Inst., Florence, Italy, 1992-2000; prof. law Coll. of Europe, Bruges, Belgium, 1992—; centennial prof. London Sch. Economics, 2000—; prof. associé U. d'Aix-Marseille III, France, 2000—; founding editor European Law Jour., 1994—, vis. prof. U. Internat. des Eaux-de-Vie, 1991-99; cons. on European Union Law and Internat. Trade Law; mem. editl. bd. Modern Law Review, London, 1988—; co-dir. Acad. of European Law, Florence. Author: One-Party Government in Mali, 1965; (with M.A. Savane) Law and Population in Senegal, 1977, Capitalism and Legal Change, 1981, law of the Common Agricultural Policy, 1985, The Common Agricultural Policy of the European Community, 1990, Study Guide on EEC Law, 1st edit. 1988, 2d edit. 1990, 3d edit. 1992, Introduction to European Union Law, (in Chinese) 1996, International Trade and Customs Law of the European Union, 1998. Named Officer Ordre des Palmes Academiques French Republic, 1988; vis. fellow Wissenschaftskolleg zu Berlin, 2000—; fellow in Internat. Devel. Rsch. Ctr., Ottawa, Can., 1974-75, Personal Rsch. fellow Nuffield Found., London, 1985-86, Fgn. Area fellow Ford Found., Paris, 1968-70, Rsch. fellow Wenner-Gren Found. for Anthropological Rsch., 1969-70. Mem. Internat. Bar Assn., Mass. Bar Assn., Soc. Pub. Tchr's. Law, Assn. des Juristes Franco-Britanniques, Rsch. Com. on the Sociology of Law, The Athenaeum, Yale Club of N.Y.C. Avocations: travel, cooking, walking. Office: London Sch Econs Dept Law, Houghton St, F-13090 London WC2A 2AE, England also: CERIC U d' Aix Marseille III, 38 avenue de l'Europe, F-13090 Aix-en-Provence France

SNYDER, GEORGE MORRIS, JR., adult education educator, writer, consultant; b. Upper Chichester, Pa., Aug. 27, 1917; s. George Morris and Mary Alice (McGuirk) Snyder; m. Roberta Rose Riggs, Dec. 21, 1962 (div. Dec. 1973); children: Kent, Rhea; m. Anita Lince Green, Dec. 21, 1948 (dec.). BA in Edn., West Chester (Pa.) State U., 1940; MA in Sociology, Temple U., 1948; postgrad., U. So. Calif., Calif. State U., Long Beach. Cert. secondary edn. social studies, English. Tchr. West Phila. H.S., 1945-46, Redondo Union Dist. H.S., Redondo Beach, Calif., 1946-71, So. Bay Adult Sch., 1977—; asst. prof. Northrop U., Inglewood, Calif., 1972-78. Author: Freshly Remember'd, 1978. Chmn. Dem. Party Club, 1960. Mem. So. Bay United Tchrs. (field staff), South Bay Calif. Ret. Tchrs. Assn. Avocations: writing, reading. Address: 345 E Carson St # 255 Carson CA 90745-2709

SNYDER, JAMES P., audio and digital television engineer, videographer, editor; b. Oct. 20, 1964; s. John Henry Jr. and Anne Snyder. Student, George Washington U., 1982-84; cert. AM broadcast tech., No. Va. Community Coll., 1986; BA in Comm. and Visual Media, Am. U., 1993; BA in CLEG, 1993. Prodn. asst. Sta. WIPB-TV, Muncie, Ind., 1980-84; prodn./engring. asst., bd. operator Sta. WBST-FM, Muncie, 1982-83; chief engr. Sta. WRGW, Washington, 1982-84; technician George Washington U., Marvin Ctr., Washington, 1982-87; engring. asst. Sta. WPFW-FM, Washington, 1984-85; ops. dir. Stas. WAMU/WVAU-FM, Washington, 1985-86; founder, dir. Sta. WRGW Radio/TV, Washington, 1984-87; mng. dir. Sta. WRGW-AM-FM, Washington, 1986-87; news/tech. dir. Sta. WVAU-AM/FM, Washington, 1990; adminstrv. asst. Sullivan & Cromwell, Washington, 1985-92; libr. asst. Paul, Weiss, Rifkind, Wharton & Garrison, Washington, 1989; asst. to the acad. counselor Sch. Communication, Am. U., Washington, 1990-91; sr. asst. to the acad. counselor Sch. Communication, Am. U., 1991; technician, projectionist CAS Media Ctr., 1989-96; chief engr. Am. TV & WVAU Radio, 1990-98; ops. coord. internat. program sales Discovery Channel Inc., 1994; engr. and HDTV editor Advanced Television Test Ctr., 1995-96; engr. Fox News Washington Bureau, 1996-98; ops. dir. Unity Motion High Definition System, 1998; Digital TV engring. specialist, studio course lectr. Harris/PBS DTV Express, 1998-99; freelance engr., TV/HDTV prodn. specialist, ops. specialist, videographer, editor, 1991—; founding mem. Am. U. CATV/Fiber Optic Systems Com., 1991; engring. cons. digital and high definition TV David Sarnoff Rsch. Ctr., Model HDTV Sta. WHD TV Inc., PBS Adv. TV Field Test Project, Turner Engring., Unity Motion HDTV Satellite Svc., PBS Digital TV Strategies Svcs. Group, Advanced TV Tech. Ctr., FedNet-Fed. Network, Inc., ABC Radio Network, Caribiner Internat, News Corp., 1995—; freelance engr. Reuters Television, 1996—. Audio-visual dir. Planned Parenthood of East-Cen. Ind., Muncie, 1982-83; George Washington U. coord. D.C. Spl. Olympics Superdance, 1984-85; bd. dirs. Vol. Clearinghouse of D.C. Student Network, Rosslyn, Va., 1985. Recipient Cert. Appreciation Planned Parenthood of East-Cen. Ind., 1982, Cert. Appreciation D.C. Spl. Olympics, 1984, Cert. Appreciation Ea. Ind. Community Television, 1980. Mem. IEEE, Soc. Motion Picture and TV Engrs., Soc. Broadcast Engrs., Audio Engring. Soc. Avocations: broadcast history, educational advancement, collecting stamps and coins, bicycling, electronics. Office: Apt 210 2700 Wisconsin Ave NW Washington DC 20007-4605

SNYDER, JEAN MACLEAN, lawyer; b. Chgo., Jan. 26, 1942; d. Norman Fitzroy and Jessie (Burns) Maclean; m. Joel Martin Snyder, Sept. 4, 1964; children: Jacob Samuel, Noah Scot. BA, U. Chgo., 1963, JD, 1979. Bar: Ill. 1979, U.S. Dist. Ct. (no. dist.) Ill. 1979, U.S. Ct. Appeals (7th cir.) 1981. Ptnr. D'Ancona & Pflaum, Chgo., 1979-92; prin. Law Office of Jean Maclean Snyder, Chgo., 1993-97; trial counsel The MacArthur Justice Ctr. U. Chgo. Law Sch., 1997—. Contbr. articles to profl. jours. Mem. ABA (mem. coun. on litigation sect. 1989-92, editor-in-chief Litigation mag. 1987-88, co-chair First Amendment and media litigation com. 1995-96, co-chair the woman advocate com. 1996-98, co-chair sect. litigation task force on gender, racial and ethnic bias in the cts. 1998—, standing com. on strategic communications, 1996—), ACLU of Ill. (bd. dirs. 1996-99), Lawyers for the Creative Arts (bd. dirs. 1995-97). Office: The MacArthur Justice Ctr Univ of Chgo Law Sch 1111 E 60th St Chicago IL 60637-2776

SNYDER, JED C., foreign affairs specialist; b. Phila., Mar. 24, 1955; s. David and Lynn S. BA, Colby Coll., 1976; MA, U. Chgo., 1978, postgrad., 1978-79. Rsch. asst. U. Chgo., 1979; asst. rschr. Pan Heuristics div. R&D Assocs., Marina del Rey, Calif., 1979-80, assoc. rschr., asst. div. mgr., 1980-81, cons., 1982-83; cons. Sci. Applications, Inc., 1979-81, Rand Corp., Santa Monica, Calif., 1979-81, Los Alamos Nat. Lab., 1984; sr. spl. asst. to dir. Bur. of Politico-Mil. Affairs, Dept. State, Washington, 1981-82; rsch. assoc. Internat. Security Studies Program, Woodrow Wilson Internat. Ctr. for Scholars, Smithsonian Instn., Washington, 1982-84; founder, chmn. Washington Strategy Seminar, 1984-90, pres., 1984-93, corp. dir., 1984-93; dep. dir. nat. security studies Hudson Inst., 1984-87; sr. rsch. fellow Nat. Strategy Info. Ctr., 1988-90; mgr. internat. strategic planing MPRI, Inc., 1997—; appointee v.p. Bush's Adv. Task Force on Mid. East, 1987-88; appointee sr. fellow Inst. for Nat. Strategic Studies, Nat. Def. U., 1992-97, supr. rsch. prof., team leader; cons. Office of Sec. of Def., 1988-92, Rand Corp., 1983-88. Contbr. articles on U.S. fgn. policy and mil. def. to profl. publs. Trustee Kents Hill (Maine) Sch., 1987-92. Guest scholar Sch. Advanced Internat. Studies, Johns Hopkins U., 1982-83; fellow U. Chgo., 1979, Inter-Univ. Seminar on Armed Forces and Soc., 1980, MacArthur Sr., 1985-86, Herman Kahn, 1985-86, Smith Richardson, 1987-88, John M. Olin, 1987-88; selected as a Young Am. Leader, Am. Coun. on Fed. Republic of Germany, 1984. Mem. Internat. Inst. for Strategic Studies, Internat. Studies Assn., Royal United Svcs. Inst., U.S. Naval Inst., Fgn. Policy Rsch. Inst., Coun. on Fgn. Rels. Home: 1718 M St NW # 197 Washington DC 20036-4504 Office: Mil Profl Resources Inc 1201 E Abingdon Dr Ste 425 Alexandria VA 22314-1420

SNYDER, JOHN MICHAEL, lobbyist, public relations director; b. Kingston, N.Y., Dec. 18, 1939; s. John Ignace and Agatha (Flick) S.; m. Ling-Ling Woo, Jan. 1, 1996. BA, Georgetown U., 1961, MA, 1968. Legis. sec. U.S. Ho. of Reps., Washington, 1964-65; assoc. editor The Am. Rifleman, Washington, 1966-74; chief lobbyist, dir. publs. and pub. affairs Citizens Com. for Right to Keep and Bear Arms, Washington, 1975—. Editor (newsletter) Point Blank, 1974—; Capitol Hill editor (newspaper) Gun Week, 1986—. Active Arlington County Rep. Com., 1994—. Recipient Grand Knighthood award Order of Michael the Archangel, 1988, Cicero award Nat. Assn. Federally Licensed Firearms Dealers, 1996. Mem. Am. Fedn. Police (nat. v.p. pub. rels. 1989—), Nat. Assn. Chiefs of Police (v.p. pub. affairs 1995—), Second Amendment Found. (treas. 1986—), St. Gabriel Possenti Soc. Inc. (pres. 1989—), Internat. Platform Assn., The Asia Soc., Kiwanis Internat., Capitol Hill Club. Republican. Roman Catholic. Avocations: swimming, cycling, reading, movies, theater. Home: 401 12th St S Apt 2218 Arlington VA 22202-4240 Office: Citizens Com Right to Keep and Bear Arms 1090 Vermont Ave NW Ste 800 Washington DC 20005-4961

SNYDER, JOHN MILLARD, recreation resources executive, educator; b. Chelsea, Mass., Apr. 3, 1946; s. John Henry and Grace (Eby) S.; m. Barbara Ripple, Nov. 8, 1969 (div. 1979); 1 child, Logan; m. Glenda Allene Snyder, Sept. 10, 1983; children: Erika, Kimberly. BA, Franklin & Marshall Coll., 1968; MS, Colo. State U., 1974, PhD, 1982; cert., Harvard Sch. Design, 1987. Econ. rsch. asso. Coll. Natural Resources, Ft. Collins, Colo., 1972-76; econ devel. City Devel. Dept., Kansas City, Mo., 1976-77; v.p. Oblinger Smith Corp., Denver, 1977-79; sr. resource analyst Abt Assocs., Denver, 1979-80; dr. devel. analysis URS Engrs., Denver, 1980-83; pres. Strategic Studies, Inc., Littleton, Colo., 1983—; pres. Glacier Bay Outfitters, 1990—; co-founder Ecotourism Internat., 1994—; faculty environ. policy and mgmt. U. Denver, 1990—, dir. environ. policy and mgmt., 1997-2000; econ. faculty Regis U., 1984—; spl. projects dir. Ctr. Sustainable Tourism, U. Colo. Author: (poems) A Far Off Place, 1995, Best Poems of 1995, 1995; contbr. articles to profl. jours. Econ. advisor Treas. and Gov. Colo., Denver, 1979-84; officer YMCA Guides Program, LIttleton, 1984-85; sr. advisor Spl. Family Recreation, Denver, 1985-90; benefactor Le Bal de Ballet, Denver, 1989—. 1st lt. U.S. Army military intelligence, 1968-72. Fellow The Explorers Club, N.Y. Mem. Ctr. for Whale Studies, Stanford Libr. (assoc.), Denver Zoological Found., Nat. Parks and Conservation Assn., several environ. orgns., Phi Kappa Phi, Xi Sigma Pi. Office: Strategic Studies Inc PO Box 3460 Littleton CO 80161-3460

SNYDER, JOSEPH JOHN, editor, historian, author, lecturer, consultant; b. Aug. 27, 1946; s. Joseph John and Amy Josephine (Hamilton) S.; m. Sally Hale Walker, July 4, 1973; children: Lauren Elizabeth, Brian Joseph Seth. BA in Anthropology, George Washington U., 1968; MA in Anthropology, U. N.Mex., 1973. With U.S. CSC, Washington, 1974-77; editor, writer U.S. Nat. Pk. Svc., Harpers Ferry, W.Va., 1977-81; cons. editor Early Man mag., Evanston, Ill., 1978-83; spl. project editor Sea Power Mag., 1986-87, cons. editor, 1987—; cons. editor Jour. Archaeoastronomy, 1987—; freelance writer, 1981—; pres. Sta. at Shepherdstown Inc., 1992-2000; pres., chmn. bd. dirs., Atlantic & Pacific High Speed Railway, Inc., 1993—; lectr. Maya archaeology Norwegian-Caribbean Lines, Miami, Fla., 1982; cons. mus. design. Author: Kenneth Westcott Jones Transport Menu Collection, 1998, A.D. 2025: Transportation in America, 1999, Musings from a New Manse, 1999, The Phaistos Disc, A Commentary, 1999, Fragments of my Fleece, 2000; editor: The Only Fight the Cops Count Not Stop, 1998; contbr. articles to popular mags. Chmn. pks. com. Neighborhood Planning Adv. Group, Croydon Park, Rockville, Md., 1980-81; bd. dirs. Agrl. R&D Orgn., 1985—; v.p., bd. dirs. Hagerstown (Md.) Roundhouse Mus., 1989-91; v.p. bd. dirs. Hagerstown-Washington County Conv. and Visitors Bur., 1993-96, sec., 1993-96; pres. Tourism Found., Inc., 1996-99. With U.S. Army, 1969-71, Vietnam. Decorated Bronze Star. Mem. Coun. Md. Archaeology, Hakluyt Soc., Am. Com. to Advance Study of Petroglyphs and Pictographs (editor), Nat. Geog. Soc. (cons. 1987—), Nat. Ry. Hist. Soc., James Bumsey Torch Club (pres. 1997-99), Internat. Assn. Torch Clubs. Democrat. E-mail: sws@intrepid.net. Home: 2008 Ashley Dr Shepherdstown WV 25443-9767

SNYDER, KARMA KRISTIN, design engineer; b. Wiesbaden, Germany, Oct. 19, 1971; d. Robert Charles and Elaine Marie Schmidt; m. Donal MacLean Snyder, Dec. 16, 1995. BSME, Auburn U., 1995. Cert. engr. intern, Ala. Fed. jr. fellowship student trainee NASA, Stennis Space Ctr., Miss., 1990-95; sr. design engr. liquid space propulsion Pratt and Whitney, West Palm Beach, Fla., 1995—. Vol. Habitat for Humanity, Jupiter, Fla., 1999. Recipient Bausch and Lomb Hon. Sci. award, 1990; Ala. Space grantee, 1995. Mem. ASME (chair, vice-chair, minority and women com. chair 1995—), Miss. Acad. Sci., Tau Beta Pi, Pi Tau Sigma. Roman Catholic. Avocations: ballet, painting, scuba diving, singing in church choir. Fax: (561) 796-7007. E-mail: snyderkk@pwfl.com. Office: Pratt and Whitney Liquid Space Propulsion PO Box 19600 West Palm Beach FL 33416-9600

SNYDER, TERESA ANN, medical/surgical nurse; b. Evansville, Ind., Mar. 4, 1946; d. Stephen Michael and Fredricka Otilia (Memmer) Kurtz; m. James Howard Snyder, June 12, 1976; children: Katrina Michelle, Jacqueline Sue. Diploma, Lakewood (Ohio) Sch. Practical Nursing, 1965; BSN, U. Akron, 1989. Emergency room nurse Parma (Ohio) Community Hosp.; cardiac nurse Cleve. Clinic Found.; neuro-sci. and med.-surg. nurse Akron (Ohio) City Hosp.; acting mem., corr. sec., pres. Summa Nursing Senate, Summa Health Care, Akron City Hosp. V.p. Chatham Vol. Fire and Rescue Assn. Mem. Acad. Med. Surg. Nurses (bd. dirs. N.E. chpt.), N.E. Ohio chpt. Acad. Med. Surg. Nursing (gen. bd. mem., exec. bd. dirs., recording sec.), Sigma Theta Tau. Home: 10145 Shaw Rd Spencer OH 44275-9306

SNYDER, THOMAS DANIEL, retired electronics engineer, consultant; b. Phila., Aug. 30, 1925; s. Thomas Daniel and Edith May (Lees) S.; Asso. in Applied Sci. in Radio and TV Tech., Milw. Sch. Engring., 1951; m. Mary Ann Wilson, Aug. 28, 1954; children: Thomas Daniel, Ellen Mary, John W. Foreman Prime Mfg. Co., Milw., 1951; with engring. dept. No. Light Co., Milw., 1951-52; communications clk. fgn. service U.S. Dept. State, 1952-55; electronics engr. U.S. Dept. Def., Warrenton, Va., 1955-85; staff cons. Am. Elect. Labs. Cons. accoustics and magnetics govt. agys., 1964—; lectr. metric

conversion; participant Solid States Application Conf., Fla. Atlanta U., 1971; participant profl. seminars Mass. Inst. Tech., 1962, 64, 66, Columbia, 1963, Pa. State U., 1967, U. Wis., 1969. Pres., PTA, Fairfax, Va., 1971, county rep., 1972. Served with USNR, 1943-46; PTO. Recipient Meritorious award for outstanding design in electronics equipment, U.S. Govt., 1969. Mem. AAAS, IEEE, Optical Soc. Am., Metric Assn., Am. Nat. Metric Coun., Am. Legion, Cath. War Vets. (adj. 1964-67). Roman Catholic. Contbr. articles to profl. jours. Patentee in field. Home: 4246 Worcester Dr Fairfax VA 22032-1140

SNYDER, TRAVIS CARROLL, evangelist; b. Apr. 9, 1942; s. L.B. and Eula Jean Snyder; children: Trevor Arnoult, Syndy Susanne. Student, Bethany Nazarene Coll., Bethany, Okla., 1960-62; BS, U. Ark., 1964; MS, La. State U., Baton Rouge, 1970. Rschr., tchr. La. State U., Baton Rouge, 1965-67; indsl. chemist Dowell, Arco, Union, Tulsa, 1970-82; owner SEE, Inc., Tulsa, 1982-83; quality control mgr. Bama Pie Inc., Tulsa, 1983-84; prophet of God Tahlequah, Okla., 1969—. Patentee in field of chemistry. With USMC, 1967-69, USAR, 1979-91. Avocations: biking, weight lifting, swimming, walking. Home: 325 S College Ave # C Tahlequah OK 74464-4417

SNYMAN, FREDERIK, engineer; b. Pretoria, South Africa, June 4, 1950; s. Louis Phillupus and Carolina Johanna M. (Augustine) S.; m. Johanna Wilhelmina Brockman, June 3, 1972; 1 child, Louis. Quality inspector Armacov, Pretoria, South Africa, 1976, quality tech., sr. tech., 1978, sect. leader, 1980, tech. engr., 1983. Sgt. South African Mil., 1968-79. Mem. Inst. Civil Svc. Engring. Techs., Chamber Engring. Tech., Engring. Coun. South Africa. Avocation: farming. Home: 114 Charles Jal St, Pretoria 0184, South Africa Office: Vektor, 368 Selbonn Ave, Pretoria 0001, South Africa

SO, RONALD MING CHO, engineering educator; b. Hong Kong, Nov. 26, 1939; came to U.S., 1966; s. Tsang Yee and Grace W.K. (Chan) S.; m. Mabel Yuen May Wu, Aug. 17, 1968; children: Winnie Wing Ning, Nelson Sing Keen. BS with honors, U. Hong Kong, 1962; M in Engring., McGill U., Montreal, Que., Can., 1966; MA, Princeton U., 1968, PhD, 1971; DSc, U. Hong Kong, 1993. Engr. Shell Co., Hong Kong, 1962-63; instr. U. Hong Kong, 1963-64; rsch. scientist Union Camp Corp., Princeton, N.J., 1970-72; asst. prof. Rutgers U., New Brunswick, N.J., 1972-76; rsch. engr. GE R & D Ctr., Schenectady, N.Y., 1976-81; prof. engring. Ariz. State U., Tempe, 1981-98; chair prof., head mech. engring. The Hong Kong Polytech U., 1996—; cons. Research Cotrell, Piscataway, N.J., 1974-76, Garrett Pneumatic, Phoenix, 1982—; adj. prof. Fairleigh Dickenson U., Teaneck, N.J., 1975-76, Union Coll., Schenectady, 1977-80. Contbr. articles to profl. jours. Commonwealth scholar Can. Govt., Montreal, 1964-66; recipient Publ. award Gen. Electric Co., Schenectady, 1981. Fellow ASME (Lewis F. Moody award), AIAA (assoc.), Inst. Mech. Eng. (Dugald Clerk prize 1991), HKIE; mem. Am. Phys. Soc., N.Y. Acad. Sci., Nev. Acad. Sci., Ariz. Acad. Sci. E-mail: mmmcso@polyu.edu.hk. Home: Block 18 Baguio Villa 2/F, 555 Pokfulam Rd Flat 2A, Hong Kong Hong Kong Office: Hong Kong Polytech U, Dept Mech Engring, Hong Kong China

SO, SAMUEL CHO YEE, therapeutic radiological physicist. BA, St. Louis U., 1975; M Med. Sci., Emory U. Sch. Med., 1980; MD, Ross U. Sch. Med., 1986. Diplomate Am. Bd. Radiology, Am. Bd. Therapeutic Radiol. Physics, Am. Bd. Sci. in Nuclear Medicine, State Calif. cons. Radiological Physics. Lab. technolotist hemostasis lab. Barnes Hosp., St. Louis, 1975-77; nuclear medicine tech. trainee nuclear medicine dept. Mallinkrodt Inst. Radiology, St. Louis, 1977-78; resident med. physicist dept. radiation oncology Emory U. Sch. Medicine, Atlanta, 1980-81; chief med. physicist dept. radiation oncology Grady Meml. Hosp., Atlanta, 1981; sr. radiol. physicist West Coast Cancer Round., San Francisco, 1987-97, assoc. dir., 1997—; cons. dept. radiation oncology St. Francis Med. Hosp., San Francisco, St. Mary's Hosp., San Francisco. Mem. AAAS, Am. Coll. Radiology, Am. Assn. Physicists in Medicine, Am. Soc. Clin. Pathologists, Am. Bd. Med. Specialties, N.Y. Acad. Sci. Roman Catholic. Avocations: medicine, computers and technology. Fax: (415) 351-2530. E-mail: wccf@slip.net. Office: West Coast Cancer Found 1488 Pine St Ste 205 San Francisco CA 94109-4720

SO, YING-HUNG, chemistry researcher; b. Hong Kong, Apr. 8, 1948; came to U.S., 1973; s. Wah and Yuen-Yan (Siu) So; m. Dora Tsui Dang, Apr. 22, 1978; children: Albert J., Lisa M. BS with honors, Chinese U. of Hong Kong, 1971; PhD in Organic Chemistry, Colo. State U., 1977; postdoctoral appointment, U. B.C., 1977-79, U. Minn., 1979-81. Sr. rsch. chemist. Ctrl. Rsch. Polymers Dow Chem. Co., Midland, Mich., 1981-84; project leader Ctrl. Rsch.-Polymeric Materials Dow Chem. Co., Midland, 1984-89, rsch. leader CR&D-Advanced Composites Lab., 1989-93, rsch. assoc. CR&D-Advanced Composites Lab., 1993-94, tech. leader CR&D/New Businesses-Electronics, 1995—; vis. assoc. prof. U. Hong Kong, 1997—; H.S. sci. tchr. Sacred Heart Cannosian Coll., Hong Kong, 1971-73; sec. Chinese-Am. Chem. Soc., 1990-94. Contbr. more than 40 articles to profl. jours.; holder 16 U.S. and world patents. Mem. Am. Chem. Soc. (com. mem. regional meeting 1990), Materials Rsch. Soc. Avocations: tennis, travel. Home: 1524 Dilloway Dr Midland MI 48640-2786 Office: The Dow Chem Co Bldg 1712 Midland MI 48674-0001

SOARES, CARL LIONEL, quality control engineer, metrologist; b. New Bedford, Mass., Sept. 14, 1944; s. Lionel Francis and Sarah Vincent (Flor) S.; m. Jean Rosalee Bettencourt, Nov. 11, 1965 (div. Oct. 1974); children: Kevin Carl, Keith Christopher, Kenneth Craig. Student in Indsl. Tech., Fitchburg State Coll., 1980—. Quality assurance specialist Cornell-Dubilier Electronics, Inc., New Bedford, Mass., 1965-66; computer controlled test equipment technician Raytheon Co., Waltham, Quincy, North Dighton, Mass., 1966-79; quality control supt. Raytheon Co., Waltham, 1982-85, metrologist, dept. quality dir., 1979-96; pres., treas., mgr. S.&O. Cleaning Corp. d/b/a The MAIDS, New Bedford, 1995—. Choir mem. St. James Ch., chair Booster Club Com.; pres. bd. dirs. New Bedford Coun. on Substance Abuse; sec. New Bedford First Night Com. With USN, 1963-65. Mem. Buttonwood Park Zool. Soc. (bd. dirs., first night com., events chmn.), Friends of Dartmouth Librs., New Bedford C. of C., Am. Legion. Roman Catholic. Avocations: gardening, bicycling, records and CDs, home computing, music. Home: 205 Maple St New Bedford MA 02740-3513

SOARES, EDUARDO M.R., civil engineer; b. Belo Horizonte, Brazil, July 20, 1960; s. Marcilio and Maria (Mauricio da Rocha) S. BS, UFMG, Brazil, 1983; MA, Ohio U., 1985. Dir. Petromix, Brazil, 1992—. Roman Catholic. Avocation: sports. Home: Rua Espirito Santo 1594/202, Belo Horizonte 30160031, Brazil

SOARES, MÁRIO ALBERTO NOBRE LOPES, political party official, lawyer, historian; b. Lisbon, Portugal, Dec. 7, 1924; s. João Lopes and Elisa Nobre Soares; m. Maria Barroso, 1949; 2 children. B.A. in History and Philosophy, U. Lisbon, 1951, J.D., 1957; D honorus causa, Libre de Bruxelles, Belgium, Sao Paulo U., Rio de Janeiro U., Gama Filho U., Brazil, U. Rennes, U. Sorbonne, France, U. Osnabruck, Germany, U. Dublin, Ireland, U. Bologna, U. Turin, U. Genoa, Italy, U. Malta, Philippines U., U. Coimbra, U. Porto, U. Nova Lisboa, U. Évora, U. Open Internat., U. Ásia-Macau, Portugal, U. Santiago, Compostela, U. Complutense, U. Coruña, U. Vigo, Spain, U. Hankuk, Republic of Korea, U. Oxford, Eng., Brown U., Princeton U., U. South Africa. Founder Movement for Democratic Unity (MUD), Lisbon, 1946; leader MUD Juvenil, 1946; mem. MUD Cen. Com., 1945-48; sec. presdl. candidacy of Gen. Norton da Mattos, 1949; mem. exec. Social Dem. Action, 1952-60; mem. campaign com. for Humberto Delgado in presdl. elections, 1958; candidate as dep. for dem. opposition Lisbon, 1965, 69; exiled to Sao Tome, 1968; in exile Paris, 1970-74; tchr. U. Paris, 1970-74; assoc. U. Rennes, 1970-74; co-founder, sec.-gen. Portuguese Socialist Party, 1973-86; in charge of negotiations leading to independence of Guinea-Bissau, Mozambique, Angola Govt. of Portugal, 1974, min fgn. affairs, 1974-75, minister without portfolio, 1975; dep. Constituent Assembly, 1975, Legis. Assembly, 1976; participant all major Socialist internat. summits, 1973—; v.p. Socialist Internat., 1976; mem. Coun. of State; prime minister Govt. of Portugal, 1976-78, 83-85, pres., 1986-91, 91-96; rep. Portuguese Socialist at various European Socialist Congresses, 11th Congress of Socialist Internat. Eastbourne, 1969; negotiated Portugal's entry into European Com.; Portugese rep. Internat. League Human Rights; mem. Coordination and Solidarity between Europe and Latin Am.; head Socialist Int. Com. Latin Am., Middle East; hon. pres. Socialist Internat. 1986—; imprisoned 12 times on political grounds. Author: Teófilo Braga, 1950, Escritos Políticos, 1969, Portugal Struggle for Liberty, 1972, Destruir o Sistema, Construir uma Vida Nova, 1973, Caminho Difícil, do Salazarismo ao Caetanismo, 1973, Escritos no Exílio, 1975, Portugal, quelle Révolution?, 1976, O Futuro será o Socialismo Democrático, 1979, Resposta Socialista para o Mundo em Crise, 1983, Persistir, 1983, A Arvore e a Floresta, 1985, Intervenções I-VIII, 1987-97; author (with Willy Brandt and Bruno Kreisky) Liberdade para Portugal, 1975; corr. various newspapers. Pres. Mário Soares Found., Ind. World Commn. on Oceans, Portugal/Africa Found., European Movement, Com. of Wies Person of Counsel of Europe. Recipient Joseph Lemaire prize, 1975, Internat. Human Rights prize, 1977, Robert Schuman prize, Strasbourg, 1987, Pricipe das Astúrias prize, Spain, 1995, Carmen Garcia Bloise prize, Spain, 1996, Silver Seagull prize, Italy, 1996, Portugal, 1997, Louise Weiss prize, France, 1997, Adolphe Bentinck prize, Belgium, 1997, numerous Grand Crosses Portuguese and foreign. Mem. Acad. Brasileira de Letras (corres.), Acad. Kingdom Morocco, Acad. Scis. Lisbon. Avocations: collecting books and contemporary Portuguese paintings. Office: Fundacão Mario Soares, Rua de Sao Bento 176, 1200 Lisbon Portugal*

SOARES-COSTA, MANUEL JOSÉ DIAS, animal science educator; b. Lisbon, Portugal, Mar. 19, 1933; s. Antonio Monteiro Soares-Costa and Maria do Patrocinio Dias Costa; m. Maria Helena Rodrigues Goncalves Costa, Sept. 2, 1954; children: Luis Manuel, Maria Teresa, Maria Helena. Lic., Lisbon Tech. U., 1957, DS, 1963. Asst. prof. animal sci. Agrl. Coll. Lisbon Tech. U., 1958-63, assoc. prof., 1969-75, full prof., 1980—; head tech. svcs. dept. Shaver Poultry Breeding Farms, Cambridge, Ont., Can., 1975-80; min. agrl. Portuguese Govt., Lisbon, 1983-84; mem. Parliament, Lisbon, 1987-91; chmn. Portuguese del. Coun. Europe Parliamentary Assembly, Strasbourg, France, 1988-92; v.p. Western European Union Parliamentary Assembly, Paris, 1990-91; chmn. FAO Nat. Com., Lisbon, 1993; chmn. Vetlima Ltd., Lisbon, chmn. dept. animal and crop sci. Agrl. Coll., Lisbon Tech. U., 1996. Contbr. articles to profl. and sci. jours. Auditor Nat. Def., Inst. of Nat. Def., Lisbon, 1993-94; active Social Dem. Party. Recipient Merit medal Coun. of Europe, 1992. Mem. Am. Soc. Agrl. Engrs., Am. Poultry Sci. Assn., Coun. Europe Parliamentary Assembly (hon.), Ordem dos Engenheiros, N.Y. Acad. Scis. Roman Catholic. Home: Av Gen Firmino Miguel, Green Park N-12-7-C, 1600-100 Lisbon Portugal Office: Vetlima Ltd, Av 5 Outubro 35-3rd E, 1050/047 Lisbon Portugal

SOB, MOJMIR, physicist; b. Jihlava, Czech Republic, Aug. 5, 1951; s. Leopold and Milada (Holanova) S.; m. Marie Kanova, Jan. 11, 1975; children: Jana, Eva. Dr.rer.nat., Charles U., Prague, Czech Republic, 1974; PhD, Czech Acad. Scis., Prague, 1980; DS, Acad. Sci. Czech Republic, Prague, 1997. Rsch. asst. Inst. Phys. Metallurgy, Czech Acad. Scis., Brno, 1974-76, rsch. scientist, 1980-87; sr. rsch. assoc. U. Pa., Phila., 1990-92; sr. rsch. scientist Inst. Physics of Materials, Czech Acad. Scis., Brno, 1987—; assoc. prof. Tech. Univ. Brno, 1999. Co-author: Electronic Structure of Disordered Alloys, Surfaces and Interfaces, 1997. Vis. rsch. fellow Inst. Low Temperatures & Structural Rsch., Polish Acad. Scis., 1976-77, Alexander von Humboldt fellow Max-Planck Inst. Solid State Rsch., Stuttgart, Germany, 1985-87. Mem. Materials Rsch. Soc., Am. Phys. Soc., Union Czech Math. & Physicists. Avocations: hiking, travel. Office: Inst Phys Materials, Zizkova 22, CZ-61662 Brno Czech Republic

SOBACI, GÜNGÖR, medical educator, consultant; b. Samsun, Turkey, May 14, 1960; s. Hidayet and Necla (Ergün) S.; m. Emine Eyidemir, Sept. 3, 1983; children: Eren, Erdem. MD, U. Ankara, 1983. Commd. officer Turkish Mil., 1984, advanced through grades to col., 1999; 1st lt. Army hdqrs. Turkish Mil., Diyarbakir, Turkey, 1984-86; resident Gülhane Mil. Med. Acad. Turkish Mil., Ankara, 1986-89, eye surgeon Mevki Mil. Hosp., 1989-90, asst. prof. Gülhane Mil. Med. Acad. and Med. Sch., 1990-92, assoc. prof., 1992—; mem. Turkey Klinikleri Jour. Med. Rsch., 1998—; cons. vitreoretinal surgeon Bayindir Hosp., Ankara, 1999—. Mem. Vitreous Soc., Retina Soc., N.Y. Acad. Scis. Avocations: music, swimming, soccer, tennis, wrestling. Office: Konur Sokak 31/4 Kizilay, 06640 Ankara Turkey

SOBEL, MARK ESAR, physician, researcher; b. N.Y.C., Apr. 14, 1949; s. Abraham David and Selma Etta (Spitzer) S. BA, Brandeis U., 1970; MD, Mt. Sinai Sch. Medicine, N.Y.C., 1975; PhD in Biomed. Scis., CUNY, 1975. Diplomate Nat. Bd. Med. Examiners. Med. intern, clin. fellow in pediatrics Children's Hosp. Med. Ctr./Harvard U. Med. Sch., Boston, 1975-76; rsch. assoc. NIH, Bethesda, Md., 1976-79, 80-83; sr. investigator Nat. Cancer Inst., Bethesda, 1983-92, chief molecular pathology sect., 1992—; vis. scientist Max Planck Inst. for Biochemistry, Martinsried bei Munchen, Germany, 1979-80; dir. Concepts in Molecular Biology course Am. Soc. Investigative Pathology, Rockville, Md., 1987-99. Contbr. more than 100 articles to profl. jours.; patentee in field. Capt. USPHS, 1975—. Recipient Commendation medal USPHS, 1989, other awards. Mem. Am. Soc. for Biochemistry and Molecular Biology, Am. Soc. Investigative Pathology (councilor 1995-97, vice pres.-elect 1997-98, v.p. 1998-99, pres. 1999-2000), Am. Soc. for Cell Biology, Am. Assn. for Cancer Rsch., Assn. for Molecular Pathology (sec.-treas. 1995-97, pres.-elect 1998, pres. 1999), Phi Beta Kappa, Alpha Omega Alpha. Jewish. Avocations: Classical music, English history (Plantagenet and Tudor periods). Office: Nat Cancer Inst Bldg 10 Rm 2A33 NIH Bethesda MD 20892-1500

SOBEL, RICHARD JAY, physician; b. N.Y.C., Oct. 15, 1932; s. Benjamin and Celia Doris (Salzberg) S.; m. Enid Sheila Braker, June 14, 1953; children: Lori, Amy, Steven, Kate. BA, NYU, 1953, MD, 1957. Diplomate Am. Bd. Internal Medicine, Israel Bds. of Internal Medicine and Endocrinology. Physician Hitchcock Clinic, Hanover, N.H., 1967-74; sr. physician Soroka Hosp., Beersheba, Israel, 1974-97, chief endocrinology unit, 1982-97; clin. asst. prof. medicine Dartmouth Med. Sch., Hanover, 1973-74; assoc. prof. Ben Gurion U. Sch. Applied Health Scis., Beersheva, 1985—. Capt. U.S. Army Med. Corp., 1958-60. Fellow Am. Coll. Physicians; mem. Am. Thyroid Assn., Phi Beta Kappa. Mem. Labour Party. Jewish.

SOBELL, NINA R., artist; b. Patchogue, N.Y., May 4, 1947; d. Jack and Helen Ruth (Rosenberg) S.; m. Christopher Rogers Shearer, Sept. 8, 1982 (div. Mar. 1987); 1 child, Jacqueline Corianne. BFA, Temple U., 1969; MFA, Cornell U., 1971. Cert. educator N.Y. Vis. artist Calif. Inst. of the Arts, Valencia, 1975, Sch. of Architecture, London, 1976; vis. lectr. dept. art Reading (Eng.) U., 1976-77; vis. lectr. dept. design & sculpture UCLA, 1979, assoc. prof. electronic imagery, 1984-85; artist-in-residence interactive telecomm. program NYU, N.Y.C., 1991-92, artist-in-residence Ctr. Digital Multimedia, 1994—; instr. video prodn. Sch. Visual Arts, N.Y.C., 1992-93; dir. tech. integration Aux. Svc. High Schs., N.Y.C. Bd. Edn., 1994—; artist-lectr. Documenta VII, Kassel, Germany, 1977; juror U.S. Film and Video Festival, L.A., 1984; juror media arts divsn. N.Y. State Coun. on the Arts, N.Y.C., 1994; artist-presenter Siggraph, New Orleans, 1996; resident Banff Ctr. for the Arts, 1998-99. Prin. works include installation Interactive Brainwave Drawings, 1974—, interactive installation Videophone Relay, 1977-79; artist/dir. HIV-INFO Interactive Call-In TV Show, Manhattan Pub.-Access Cable, 1992, ParkBench Pub-Access Web Kiosks, 1994—; curriculum designer Online Art Network for At-Risk Youth, N.Y.C. Bd. Edn., 1996; represented in permanent collection Mus. Modern Art, N.Y.C., Whitney Mus. Art Whitney Web Site. Installation/Lecture grantee Found. Art Resources, 1981; Installation grantee N.Y. State Coun. Arts, 1981. Mem. Art and Sci. Collaborations, Inc., Coll. Art Assn., Assn. Ind. Video and Filmmakers, United Fedn. of Tchrs. Democrat. Jewish. Avocations: swimming, cooking, biking, birdwatching, skating. Home: 128 E Broadway # 506 New York NY 10002-6373 Office: NYU Ctr Digital Multimedia 719 Broadway Fl 12 New York NY 10003-6860

SOBEN, ROBERT SIDNEY, systems scientist; b. Corpus Christi, Tex., Feb. 7, 1947; s. Sydney Robert and Rose Mary S.; 1 child, Dena Dianne. BSEE, La. Tech. U., 1973; MA in Comm., U. Okla., 1982; MS in Mgmt. Scis., Troy (Ala.) State U., 1988; PhD in Engring. Mgmt. Sci., U. Fla. and LaSalle U., 1990. Digital computer sci. USAF Air Training Command, Keesler AFB, Miss., 1966-71; command pilot USAF, worldwide, 1971-82; NATO instr. pilot 80th Fighter Training Wing, Sheppard AFB, Tex., 1978-82; electro-optics br. chief Electronics Sys. Test Divsn., Eglin AFB, Fla., 1982-84; mission ops. officer Deputate for Testing Engring., Eglin AFB, Fla., 1984-85, test support divsn. chief, 1985-93; sr. TQ analyst 46TW/OG-1 TQM in 46 OG, 1993-94; CEO ORCOM, Nicerille, Fla., 1984—; adj. asst. prof. Troy State U., Ft. Walton Beach, Fla., 1987-94, St. Leo's Coll., Eglin AFB, 1988-94; sys. analyst PACE Group, Orlando, Fla., 1994-98, Fidelio Techs., Naples, Fla., 1998-99, ECI Telecom, Petach Tekva, Israel. Author: Digital Computer Basics, 1970, Application of Expert Systems to Scientific and Technical Information Command, Control and Communication Management, 1990, Score Strategic Business Planning Document, 1999; author USAF tech. report Video Augmentation, 1984, tng. manual and system test engring., 1988, POGI for Quality Results, a mil. pub., 1995. Avocations: sailing, scuba diving, writing, racing cars. E-mail: drsoben@hotmail.com. Home: 2347 Holly Leaf Ln Orange Park FL 32073-5430

SOBER, SIDNEY, retired diplomat, educator; b. N.Y.C., Nov. 12, 1919; s. Isaac and Mary (Krug) S.; m. Elizabeth Holmes Sober, Apr. 2, 1947; children: Stephen, Elizabeth (dec.). BA magna cum laude, CCNY, 1939; MA, George Washington U., 1964. Fgn. svc. officer Dept. of State, Tananarive, Prague, Reykjavik, Ankara, Bombay, 1947-63; econ. affairs South Asia, dir. regional affairs Bur. Near Ea. and So. Asian Affairs, Dept. of State, Washington, 1964-69; staff dir. Interdepartmental Regional Group for Near East and So. Asia, 1967-69; min. counselor, dep. chief of mission Am. Embassy, Islamabad, Pakistan, 1969-73, chargé d'affaires, 1972-73; sr. dep. asst. sec. state N.E. & S. Asia, acting sec. state Dept. of State, 1974-78; chair South Asia Seminar Fgn. Svc. Inst., Dept. of State, Washington, 1982-96; vis. prof., adj. prof. Am. U., Washington, 1978-87; cons. Sisco Assocs., Washington, 1984-93; declassification specialist Dept. of State, Washington, 1981—. Lt. (j.g.) USN, 1944-46. Mem. Am. Fgn. Svc. Assn., Diplomatic and Consular Officers Ret., Asia Soc., Phi Beta Kappa. Home: 4928 Sentinel Dr Apt 106 Bethesda MD 20816-3543

SOBERMAN, DAVID ALLAN, marketing educator; b. Kingston, Ont, Can., Jan. 16, 1960; arrived in France, 1996; s. Daniel Allan and Patricia Margaret (Burrage) S.; m. Shelley Allyson Theresa Steiner, Sept. 22, 1991; children: Mark Joseph, Ellen Rebecca. BSc in Chem. Engring., Queen's U., Kingston, Can., 1981, MBA, 1983; PhD, U. Toronto, 1996. Registered profl. engr. Sys. analyst Imperial Oil Ltd., Toronto, 1982; asst. to v.p. mfg. Nabisco Brands Ltd., Toronto, 1983-84, mktg. mgr., 1984-87; mktg. mgr. Molson Breweries, Toronto, 1987-91; instr., rschr. U. Toronto, 1991-96; prof. Insead, Fontainebleau, France, 1996—; design engr. Imperial Oil Ltd., Toronto, 1980. Author: (with others) Mastering Marketing, 1999; contbr. articles to profl. jours. mem. race com. and rules enforcement Can. Olympic Organizing Com., Kingston, 1976, Can. Olympic Tng. Regatta Kingston, 1974, 75. Seaman Canadian Armed Forces Naval Reserve, 1978. Fellow Social Sci. and Humanities Rsch. Coun. of Can., 1993-95; DI McLeod scholar Queen's U., Kingston, 1981-83, Connaught scholar U. Toronto, 1991-94. Mem. Inst. Mgmt. Sci., Assn. Profl. Engrs., Am. Mktg. Assn. Avocations: sailing, downhill skiing, ice hockey, photography, piano. Office: Insead, Blvd de Constance, 77305 Fontainebleau France

SOBERON, PRESENTACION ZABLAN, state bar administrator; b. Cabambangan, Bacolor, Pampanga, Philippines, Feb. 23, 1935; came to U.S., 1977; naturalized, 1984; d. Pioquinto Yalung and Lourdes (David) Zabian; m. Damaso Reyes Soberon, Apr. 2, 1961; children: Shirley, Sherman, Sidney, Sedwin. Office mgmt., stenography, typing cert., East Cen. Colls., Philippies, 1953; profl. sec. diploma, Internat. Corr. Schs., 1971; A in Mgmt. Supervision, Skyline and Diablo Coll., 1979, LaSalle Ext. U., 1980-82; AA, cert. in Mgmt. and Supervision, Diablo Valley Coll. With U.S. Fed. Svc. Naval Base, Subic Bay, Philippines, 22 yrs; clerical, stenography and secretarial postitions U.S. Fed. Svc. Naval Base, 1955-73, adminstrv. asst., 1973-77; secretarial positions Mt. Zion Hosp. and Med. Ctr., San Francisco, 1977, City Hall, Oakland, Calif., 1978; with State Bar Calif., San Francisco, 1978-79; secretarial positions gen. counsel divsn. and state bar ct. divsn., adminstrv. asst. fin. and ops. divsn., 1979-81, office mgr. sects. and coms. dept., profl. and pub. svcs., 1981-83, appointment adminstr. office of bar rels., 1983-86, adminstr. state bar sects. bus. law sect., estate planning, trust and probate law sect., labor and employment law sect., office of bar rels., 1986-89, adminstr. antitrust and trade regulation law sect., labor and employment law sect., workers' compensation sect., edn. and meeting svcs., 1989-96, adminstr. criminal law sect., 1996—, labor and law employment law sect., 1996—, internat. law sect., 1996—, workers' compensation sect., 1996—, edn. and meeting svcs., 1996-98, ret., 1998; disc jockey/announcer Philippine radio stas. DZYZ, DZOR and DWHL, 1966-77. Organizer Neighborhood Alert Program, South Catamaran Circle, Pittsburg, Calif., 1979-80. Recipient 13 commendation certs. and outstanding pers. monetary awards U.S. Fed. Svc., 1964-77, 20 Yr. U.S. Fed. Svc. pin and cert., 1975; Nat. 1st prize award for cmty. svc. and achievements Nat. Inner Wheel Clubs Philippines, 1975; several plaques and award certs. for cmty. and sch. activities and contbns. Olongapo City, Philippines. Mem. NAFE, Am. Soc. Assn. Execs., N.Y.C. Olongapo-Subic Bay Assn. No Calif. (Pittsburg rep. 1982-87, bus. mgr. 1988-89, 97-98, 99-2000, pub. rels. officer 1993-94), Castillejos Assn. of No. Calif., SRF Tigers No. Calif. Roman Catholic. Home: 207 South Catamaran Circle Pittsburg PA 94565 Office: State Bar of Calif 180 Howard St San Francisco CA 94105-1639

SOBERON VALDEZ, FRANCISCO, federal official. Min. pres. Banco Nacional de Cuba, Havana. Office: Banco Nacional de Cuba, PO Box 736 Aguilar 411, Havana 1, Cuba*

SOBEY, DONALD RAE, industrialist; b. Stellarton, N.S., Can., Oct. 23, 1934; s. Frank H. and Irene (MacDonald) S.; m. Elizabeth Purvis, Sept. 7, 1963; children: Robert George Creighton, Irene Elizabeth, Kent Richard. B in Commerce, Queen's U.; LLD (hon.), Dalhousie U., 1989. Chmn., bd. dirs. Empire Co. Ltd.; bd. dirs. Atlantic Shopping Ctrs. Ltd., Crombie Ins. Ltd., Eng., Highliner Foods Inc., Paribas Participations Ltd., PPL, Sobey Leased Properties Ltd., Sobey's Inc., Toronto-Dominion Bank, Wajax Ltd.; underwriting mem. Lloyd's of London; dir. Alliance Atlantis Comm. Inc., Aliant Telecom., Can. Tennis Assn., Nat. Gallery Can. Gov. Olympic Trust of Can.; mem. AIESEC, The Conf. Bd. of Can., Burns Commn., Privy Counsel, Club de Rels. d'affaires Can.-France; patron World Congress on Edn. and Tech., 1986; mem. bd. govs. Dalhousie U.; mem. Task Force on the Future of the Port of Halifax; found. chmn. Camp Hill Med. Ctr. Mem. Toronto Club, Saraguay Club (Halifax, N.S.), Halifax Club, Abercrombie Golf and Country Club (trustee). Avocations: skiing, squash, tennis, music, art. Office: Empire Co Ltd, 115 King St, Stellarton, NS Canada BOK 1SO

SOBHI, FATMA SALEH, microbiologist, educator; b. Cairo, Shobra, May 18, 1940; d. Saleh Tawfik Sobhi and Abla Rifaat Sami; m. Nihad Abdel Hameed Moharram, July 22, 1969; children: Ashraf, Ayman. MB Chir, Cairo U., 1963, M in Med. Microbiology and Immunology, 1967, PhD in Med. Microbiology and Immunology, 1970; diploma in ednl. tech., Dundee (Scotland) Coll. Tech., 1980; med. edn. cert., Boston U., 1982. From instr. to asst. prof. to assoc. prof. Med. Sch., Cairo U., 1965-80, prof., 1980—, chmn. med. microbiology and immunology dept., 1999—; vis. assoc. prof. Sch. Medicine, U. Wis., 1976-77; owner, dir. pvt. diagnostic lab., Cairo, 1984—; chief, dir. tuberculosis unit Med. Sch., Cairo U., 1990—; cons. Sci. Rsch. Coun., King Abdel Aziz U., Saudi Arabia, 1990—; mem. regional adv. group Ea. Mediterranean in tuberculosis WHO, Cairo, 1990. Author: (books) Microbiology for Nurses, 1975, 80, Microbiology for Dental Students, 1986, Medical Microbiology and Immunology, 1992. Mem. Nongovernmental Orgn. to Care for Tuberculosis Patients and Families, Cairo, 1978—. Mem. Egyptian Soc. for Microbiology (founder, mem. adminstrv. bd., mem. adv. bd. of jour. 1990-93), Egyptian Soc. for Immunology (founder), Am. Soc. for Microbiology, Egyptian Shooting and Sports Club. Muslim. Avocations: reading, music, painting, knitting, embroidery. Home: El Allam City Bldg 63, 12411 Cairo Agoza, Egypt Office: Kasr El Aini Hosp, Sch of Medicine, Cairo Egypt

SOBIESTIANSKAS, RICHARDAS, physicist, educator; b. Druskininkai, Lithuania, Oct. 9, 1962; s. Edmundas and Julija (Balciute) S. MS, Vilnius (Lithuania) U., 1985, D in Natural Scis., 1993. Computer engr. Computing Ctr., Vilnius, 1985-87; lab. asst. Vilnius U., 1987-89, rsch. assoc., 1989-99, rsch. scientist, 1999—; rsch. assoc. U. Electro-Comm., Tokyo, 1995-96. Scholar Sci. and Tech. Com., Vilnius, Lithuania, 1993. Mem. N.Y. Acad. Scis., Lithuanian Math. Rsch. Soc. Avocation: photography. Office: Vilnius U Faculty Physics, SaulETEKIO 9, 2040 Vilnius Lithuania

SOBIESZCZUK, PETER (PIOTR SOBIESZCZUK), molecular biologist; b. Lodz, Poland, Sept. 25, 1953; arrived in Australia, 1981; s. Witold and

Michalina Helena (Kapa) S.; m. Dorothy F. Ciesielska, Nov. 4, 1978; children: Ada, Bartek. MS, U. Lodz, 1978; PhD, U. Melbourne, 1989. Rsch. asst. Med. Acad. Lodz, 1978-81, Ludwig Inst. Cancer Rsch., Melbourne, Australia, 1982-83; rsch. fellow Monash Med. ctr., Melbourne, 1989-91, Melbourne U., 1991-92, IGBMC, Strasbourg, France, 1992-95; mouse transgenic group leader Imperial Coll. Sch. Medicine at St. Mary's, London, 1996-99, U. Manchester Sch. Biol. Sci., 2000—. Contbr. articles to profl. jours. Mem. Australian Soc. Biochemistry and Molecular Biology. Roman Catholic. Avocations: swimming, cycling, horseback riding, film/video editing. Home: 1 Nevern Rd, London SW5 9PG, England Office: Univ Manchester BSU, Inweator Bldg Grafton St, Manchester M13 9XX, England

SOBIN, GUSTAF PETER, poet; b. Boston, Nov. 15, 1935; arrived in France, 1962; s. Newton Harrison and Rena (Pearl) S.; m. Susanna Estelle Bott Sobin, Mar. 2, 1968; children: Esther Renee, Gabriel Olivier. BA, Brown U., Providence, R.I., 1958. Prof. creative writing Sarah Lawrence Coll., Lacoste, France, 1974-80, Cleve. Inst. Art, Lacoste, France, 1981-96, Bard Coll., Lacoste, France, 1997-98. Author: The Earth as Air, 1984, Voyaging Portraits, 1988, Breaths' Burials, 1995, Venus Blue, 1991, The Fly-Truffler, 1999, Luminous Debris (Reflecting on Vestige in Provence & Languedoc), 1999.

SOBISCH, TITUS, chemist; b. Neubrandenburg, Germany, Oct. 7, 1955; s. Kurt and Ursula (Rackow) S.; m. Jutta Hanke, Sept. 10, 1983; children: Christoph, Simon, Martin, Marie. Chem. engr., Tech. U. Budapest, 1978, BSc, 1980; PhD, Acad. Wissenschaften, 1989. Sci. co-worker Acad. Wissenschaften, Berlin, 1980-92; scientist AUFmbH, Berlin, 1992-94; tech. mgr. AERES GmbH, Berlin, 1995-97; project leader LUM GmbH, Berlin, 1998—. Inventor in field; contbr. articles to profl. jours. Mem. Kolloid-Gesellschaft, Unabhängiges Inst. Umweltfragen, Deutsche Friedensgesellschaft, Interdisciplinary Environ. Alternatives Inst. Avocations: hiking, mushrooming, music, reading, fairy tales. Home: Apollostrasse 20A, D-12526 Berlin Germany Office: LUM GmbH, Rudower Chaussee 29 (OWZ), D-12489 Berlin Germany

SOBKÓW, BRONISŁAW, engineering company executive; b. Husiatyn, Poland, May 14, 1944; s. Staniskaw and Eugenia (Szewczuk) S.; m. Jolanta Elzbieta Szaj, Apr. 13, 1973 (div. Mar. 1979). MEngring in Civil Engring., Tech. U., Wroclaw, Poland, 1972; bldg. engr., Tech. Coll. of Bldg., Wroclaw, Poland, 1964; postgrad., U. Toronto (Can.), 1983-84, U. Wroclaw. Registered profl. engr. Poland. Project engr. Project Rsch. Office of Indsl. Bldg., Wrocław, Poland, 1969-75; sr. project engr. Project Rsch. Office of Indsl. Bldg., Wrocław, 1978-80; dir. bldg. group, sr. project engr., sr. constrn. inspector Inwest Project, Wrocław, 1975-76; resident engr., constrn. supervision inspector West Dist. Power Plants, Wrocław, 1977; sr. specialist in charge of project work Fedn. of Scientific Tech. Assns., Wroclaw, 1981; pres. Bronisklaw Sobokow Polcan Bldg. and Civil Engring. Ltd., Poland, London, Toronto, 1983—; pres., project mgr., project engr., designer, cons. Sci. Rsch. Ctr. of Moon, 1999—; prin. project engr. Dist. Adminstn. of Agrl. Investments in Wroclaw, Trzebnica, Poland, 1975-77, Dist. Adminstrn. of Agrl. Investments in Wroclaw, Wokow, Poland, 1977-78; pres., lector Sch. of English Lang., Broniskaw Sobkow Polcan Bldg. nd Civil Engring. Ltd., Oborniki, Slaskie, Poland, 1992—; pres., lectr. Univ. of Grad. Studies, Bronislaw Sobkow Polcan Bldg and Civil Engring. Ltd., Oborniki Slaskie, Poland, London, Toronto, Can., 1987—, Sch. Spanish Language, Bronislaw, Sobkow Polcan Bldg. and Civil Engring. Ltd., Oborniki Slaskie, Poland, 1999—. Soldier Mil., 1964-66. Mem. Polish Assn. of Bldg. Engrs. and Technicians, Assn. of Polish Engrs. in Can., European Pultrusion Tech. Assn., Internat. Assn. for Bridge and Structural Engring., Polish-Israel Chamber of Econ. (dep. mem. coun. 1992—), Am. Inst. Steel Constrn., Polish Private Investors Chamber of trade and Ind., Warsaw, 1991—. Roman Catholic. Avocations: art, gemstones, philately, music, sports. Home: Parkowa 2, 55-035 Oborniki Slaskie Poland Office: Broniskaw Sobkow Polcan, Bldg & Civil Engring Ltd, 55-035 Oborniki Slaskie Poland

SOBKOWIAK, ANDRZEJ, chemist, educator, researcher; b. Rzeszow, Poland, Nov. 8, 1951; s. Leon and Agnieszka (Musielak) S.; m. Krystyna Dzielak, Feb. 5, 1977; children: Alicja, Barbara. BS, Rzeszow U. Tech., 1973; MS, U. Lodz, Poland, 1975, PhD, 1981, DSc, 1994. Rsch. asst. Rzeszow U. Tech., 1973-79, tchg. assoc., 1978-81, sr. rsch. assoc., 1982-93, prof. chemistry, 1994—; fellow U. Vienna, 1986, U. Bonn, Germany, 1992, 93, 94; postdoctoral fellow Tex. A&M U., College Station, 1988-91, 92, 93, 94, 95. Author: General Chemistry, 1986, 91; co-author: Electrochemistry for Chemists, 1995; contbr. articles to profl. jours.; patentee in field. Recipient Sci. award Polish Ministry of Edn., 1982, Polish Chem. Soc., 1992; NATO Linkage grantee, 1996. Mem. Polish Chem. Soc., Am. Chem. Soc., Soc. for Electroanalytical Chemistry. Roman Catholic. Avocations: classical music. Office: Rzeszow U Tech, 35-959 Rzeszów Poland

SOBOL, CONSTANTIN VLADIMIROVICH, biophysicist, researcher; b. St. Petersburg, Russia, Nov. 24, 1961; s. Vladimir Karpovich and Yuzefa Tsezarevna (Gankevich) S. BSc in Radiophysics, State Tech. U., St. Petersburg, 1983, MS in Biophysics, 1987; PhD in Roentgenology and Radiology, Russian Ministry of Health, St. Petersburg, 1997. Jr. rschr. Sechenov Inst. Evolutionary Physiology Russian Acad. Scis., St. Petersburg, 1987—, sr. rschr., 1997—; biophysicist Kirov Mil. Med. Acad., 1985-92, Inst. Influenza, 1989-90, Inst. Cytology Russian Acad. Scis., 1991-95, Ctrl. Sci. Rsch. Inst. Roentgenology and Radiology Russian Ministry of Health, St. Petersburg, 1990-97; tchg. asst. dept. biophysics State Tech. U., St. Petersburg, 1996-98. Contbr. articles to profl. jours. State U. postdoctoral rsch. grantee, 1997, Internat. Soros Sci. Edn. Program Postgrad. grantee, 1995, 97, postdoctoral rsch. grantee Tulane U., New Orleans, 1998-99. Mem. N.Y. Acad. Scis. Roman Catholic. Avocations: religious canticles, flamenco guitar, badminton. Home: Planovaya 24-100, 189631 Saint Petersburg Russia Office: Evolutionary Physiol RAS, 44 Thorez pr, 194223 Saint Petersburg Russia

SOBOL, ILYA M., mathematician, educator; b. Panevežys, Lithuania, Aug. 15, 1926; arrived in USSR (now Russia), 1940; s. Meyer D. and Rachel (Ya) S.; m. Galina P. Portnova, Apr. 15, 1945; 1 child, Alexander. Degree in math. with honors, Moscow State U., 1948; candidate in phys.-math. scis., USSR (now Russian) Acad. Sci., Moscow, 1959, D in Phys.-Math. Scis., 1977. Sr. engr. Geophys. Inst. Russian Acad. Sci., 1949-53, rschr. Inst. Applied Math., 1953-61, sr. rschr., 1961-86, leading rschr., 1986-90, prin. rschr. Inst. Math. Modelling, 1990—; lectr. Moscow Engring. Physics Inst., Tech. U., 1969-80, prof., 1980—; lectr. U. Kaiserslautern, Germany, 1990, State U. Ulyanovsk, Russia, 1993; guest prof. Tech. U. Graz, Austria, 1996. Author: Multidimensional Quadrature Formulas and Haar Functions, 1969, A Primer For the Monte Carlo Method, 1994; contbr. numerous articles to sci. publs.; mem. editl. bd. jour. Monte Carlo Methods and Applications, 1995—. Recipient medal for Valiant Labour, Govt. of USSR, 1954, Badge of Honor, 1956. Mem. Moscow Math. Soc., N.Y. Acad. Scis. Avocations: music, tennis, travel. Home: 48-4-6 Profsoyuznaya St, 117335 Moscow Russia Office: RAS Inst for Math Modelling, 4 Miusskaya Sq, 125047 Moscow Russia

SOBOLEV, ALEXANDRE ANDREEVICH, physicist; b. Ramenskoye, Russia, June 18, 1952; s. Andrew Puzirev and Anna (Soboleva) Terekhova; m. Yaroslava Stepanovna Schumliakovskaya, Nov. 5, 1975 (div. 1980); 1 child, Yegor; m. Tatiana Arkadievna Silitch, Dec. 19, 1992; 1 child, Maria. MSc, Moscow Inst. Engring. Physics, 1978, PhD, 1990. Rschr. Inst. Physics & Power Engring., Obninsk, Russia. Dep. Obninsk City Coun., 1989-93. Jr. sgr. Soviet Army, 1971-73. Mem. Moscow Phys. Soc., Obninsk Phys. Soc. Mem. Orthodox Ch. E-mail: agor@sprint.ca.

SOBOLEV, VICTOR VENIAMINOVICH, physicist, researcher; b. Odessa, Ukraine, USSR, Oct. 2, 1946; m. Natlaia Tatikyan; 1 child, Alice. MSc, U. Novosibirsk, USSR, 1968; PhD in Physics, Siberian Br. Acad. Sci., Novosibirsk, 1973; DSc, Rsch. Ctr. Machine Bldg., Moscow, 1991. Chartered Engr., Engring. Coun. London. Jr. rschr. Inst. Nuclear Physics, Novosibirsk, 1968-69; postgrad. computer ctr. Siberian Br. Acad. Sci., Novosibirsk, 1969-72, rschr. computer ctr., 1972-75, head rsch. group computer ctr., 1975-76, head rsch. lab. dept. physics tech. problems metallurgy, 1988-92; head rsch. lab. Electrosteel Ctr., Krasnoyarsk, USSR, 1976-88; vis. prof., head rsch. group U. Barcelona, Spain, 1992—. Author 5 books; contbr. more than 300 articles to profl. jours. Fellow Inst. Materials London; mem. Am. Soc. Metallurgy. Achievements include 21 patents on methods and installations of continuous casting of steel, on methods of continuous casting of alumunum alloys, on utilization of metallurgical slags (granulation and use of their heat), on non-ferrous metallurgy (copper-nickel matte, lead, bismuth), development of models of thermal spraying and formation of solidified structure. Home: Valencia 29 6 1, 08015 Barcelona Spain Office: U Barcelona, Marti i Franques 1, 08028 Barcelona Spain

SOBOLEVSKY, ROMAN IOSIFOVICH, network marketing professional; b. Lvov, The Ukraine, Oct. 6, 1951; arrived in Israel, 1990; s. Iosif Markovich and Rikul Shleybovna (Kristal) S.; m. Nataliya Igorevna Zabeglovsky, July 28, 1972 (div. 1993); children: Olga, Maksim. B of Chemistry, Lviv Poly. U., 1973. Dep. sr. technologist, chemist, engr. various cos., Ukraine, 1973-81; mgr. restaurant Lviv, 1981-88, owner video co., 1988-90; founder, distbr., network marketer Neways Internat., Lviv, 1993—, mem. nat. adv. bd., 1996-99. Contbr. articles to profl. jours. Mem. All-Ukrainian Assn. Neways Distbrs. (pres. 1994-99). Avocations: music, reading, sports, travel.

SOBOLEWSKI, JÓZEF STANISŁAW, information technology executive, physicist; b. Strzyżów, Poland, Oct. 1, 1953; s. Stanisław and Bernadetta Maria (Kazalska) S. MS in Physics, U. Warsaw, Poland, 1978; DSc, J. Gutenberg U., Mainz, Germany, 1990. Rsch. assoc. Inst. Nuc. Rsch., Świerk, Poland, 1980-82; owner small pvt. bus. Warsaw, 1983-85; rschr. Max-Planck-Inst. for Nuc. Chemie, Mainz, 1985-90; rsch. assoc. J. Gutenberg U., Mainz, 1990-93; bus. analyst EDS, Warsaw, 1993-97, regional mgr. energy, 1997—; Pub. union mag. NSZZ Solidarnose, Warsaw, 1982-85. Contbr. articles to profl. jours. Activist NSZZ Solidarnose, Warsaw, 1982-85; adviser ANS-Polish Parliament, Warsaw, 1997-98. Lt. res. Mil. Acad., 1979. Grantee Max Planck Soc., Mainz, 1985-90. Home: Goscieradowska 19/35, 03-535 Warsaw Poland

SOBOLEWSKI, LUDWIK, company executive; b. Wrocław, Poland, Sept. 13, 1965; s. Stanisław and Sofia Sobolewski; m. Renata Sobolewska; children: Anna, Jakub. LLD, Jagiellonian U., Cracow, Poland, 1989; Judge, Jagiellonian U., Cracow, 1992; PhD, Pantheon-Assas, Cracow, 1992. With Inst. Co. Law and Fgn. Investments, Cracow, 1992-93; adviser to min. Office Coun. Mins., Warsaw, Poland, 1992-93; adviser to bd. Warsaw Stock Exch., 1994; asst. Jagiellonian U., Cracow, 1988-96; v.p. Nat. Depository Securities, Warsaw, 1994—; mem. bd. supervisory Centrum Gieldowe S.A., Warsaw, 1995—; judge ct. arbitration Nat. Depository Securities, Warsaw, 1996—; judge Exch. Ct. Warsaw Stock Exch., 1998—. Author: System of the National Depository for Securities, Legal Issues, 1996, Act on Bonds Commentary, 1997, The Law on the Investment Funds Commentary, 1999, The Law on the Public Trading of Securities Commentary, 1999; mem. editl. bd. The Capital Market, 1998—. Avocations: finance and economics, travel, sports. Office: Nat Depository Securities, 132/134 Chmielna St, 00-805 Warsaw Poland

SOBOTA, PIOTR, chemistry educator, researcher; b. Przyszowice, Katowice, Poland, Jan. 17, 1942; s. Wilhelm and Erna (Widuch) S.; m. Grażyna Żuławińska, May 29, 1971; children: Anna, Maria. MSc, U. Wrocław, Poland, 1966, PhD, 1973, DSc, 1978. Tchr. h.s. Głogów, Poland, 1966-68; postdoctoral fellow U. Sussex, Brighton, Eng., 1978-79; assoc. prof. U. Wrocław, 1978-89, prof., 1989, full prof., 1992—; cons. Union Carbide, Bound Brook, 1992-97. Mem. editl. bd. New Jour. Chemistry, 1997, guest editor, 1997; contbr. articles to profl. jours. Grantee Polish State Com., 1991-93, 95-96, RSC Jour., 1997, Brit.-Polish Joint Collaboration, 1994-96. Mem. Polish Chem. Soc., Polish Catalyst Club, Rotary Club. Avocations: books, music, gardening, skiing. Home: Żwirowa 22A, 54-029 Wrocław Poland Office: U Wrocław, 14 F Joliot-Curie, 50-383 Wrocław Poland

SOBOTKA, WERNER KARL, dean, communication consultant; b. Kasten, Austria, Feb. 18, 1945; s. Karl Josef and Cäcilia Maria (Schnaitt) S.; m. Edeltraud Franziska Tessar, Sept. 5, 1972; 1 child, Barbara. Degree in Engring., Printing Sch., Vienna, 1966; MS, Tech. U., Vienna, 1976, PhD in Tech. Sci., 1985. Engring. diploma; consulting diploma; state cert. expert for ct. affairs in hand writing. Prof. Rochester Inst. Tech., 1976-77; prof. Graphische Lehr und Versuchsanstalt, Vienna, 1976-96, rsch. dir., 1990—; prof. Tech. U., Vienna, 1992; dean Telecom. Media, St. Poelten, 1996; chmn. Std. Orgn., Vienna, 1994—. Author: Umweltschutz im Graphischen Gewerbe, 1993, Fehler bei der Papierezeugung, 1994; editor Print and Pub. V.p. Fedn. Internat. e Physique e Catolique, Brussels, 1992-99. Recipient Olympia Honour medal Austria State, Innsbruck, 1976, Sportehrenzeichen No-Landesregierung, St. Poelten, 1988. Mem. Internat. Assn. Rsch. in Graphic Arts (v.p. 1992—), Austrian Standard Orgn. (chmn.), Rsch. Fedn. for Comm. and Media (exec. pres. 1995—). Avocations: skiing, tennis, book restoration. Home: Austrasse 18, A-3200 Obergrafendorf Austria Office: Inst Telecom Media, Herzogenburgerstrasse 68, A-3100 Saint Poelten Austria

SOBOTKOVÁ, EVA, scientist; b. Dvur Králové, Bohemia, Czech Republic, Dec. 27, 1934; d. Josef and Ludmila (Prausová) Hoffman; m. Zdeněk Sobotka, Aug. 13, 1966; 1 child, Andrea. MS, Charles U., Prague, Czech Republic, 1958; PhD, Acad. Scis., Prague, Czech Republic, 1969. Diplomate phys. chemistry; diplomate theoretical and applied mechanics. Rschr. Inst. Exptl. Medicine, Prague, 1958-60; rschr. Inst. Theoretical Applied Mechanics, Prague, 1960-69, sci. fellow, 1969-92; pvt. rschr. biomechanics, 1993—. Com. mem. Club of Non Partys, Prague, 1990. Avocations: scientific literature, philosophy, politics, economy, gardening. Home: Švédská 10, 150 00 Prague 5 Czech Republic

SOBOVITZ, IACOV ERNEST, physical education administrator; b. Bucharest, Romania, Aug. 12, 1935; arrived in Israel, 1951; s. ITzhak Ignatz and Amalia Golda (Steinberger) S.; m. Nitza Stiebel, Mar. 31, 1963; children: Talila, Harel, Michal. BA, U. Haifa, Israel, 1977, MA, 1982; PhD, U. Budapest, 1994. Tchr. Wingate Inst., 1962; from tchr. phys. edn. to sr. tchr. H.S., Haifa, 1962-74; volleyball coach Nat. Team, Israel, 1969-72; tchr. Univ., Haifa, 1972-76; dir. Sport Orgn., Haifa, 1974-76; tech. adviser Ministry Edn., Israel, 1970-76; supr. phys. edn. Ministry Edn., Israel, 1977-99, acad. advisor, program dir., 1999—. Author: How to Teach Volleyball, 1964, Volleyball Curicculum in School, 1976. 1st sgt. Israel mil, 1956-72. Recipient Award Life Enterprise in Phys. Edn. and Sport, Haifa Municipality, 1998. Avocations: stamp collecting, fishing, swimming, fitness room, movies. Home: Shomron N-4, Haifa 34526, Israel

SOBOYEJO, WINSTON OLUWOLE, materials engineering educator, researcher; b. Palo Alto, Calif., Oct. 13, 1964; s. Alfred Babatunde Olalya and Anthonia Adesiyan (Aileru) S. BSc in Mech. Engring., London U., 1985; PhD in Materials Sci and Metallurgy, Cambridge (Eng.) U., 1988. Rsch. scientist McDonnell Douglas, St. Louis, 1988-92; prin. rsch. engr. Edison Welding Inst., Columbus, Ohio, 1992; prof. Ohio State U., Columbus, 1992-99, Princeton (N.J.) U., 1999—; cons. McDonnel Douglas, St. Louis, 1992—, Allison Gas Turbines, Indpls., 1993, Ohio Dept. Transp., 1996; bd. dirs. Mateng, Inc., Columbus, Ohio; vis. Martin Luther King assoc. prof. MIT, 1997-98. Editor Conf. Proceedings, 1994, 95, 96. Recipient Rsch. Initiation award NSF, 1993, Nat. Young Investigator award, NSF, 1994, Young Investigator award Office of Naval Rsch., 1994. Mem. ASME, ASM Internat. (local chpt. chair 1995-96, Bradley Stoughton award 1998), Materials Rsch. Soc., Minerals, Metals and Materials Soc. (local chpt. chair 1995-96). Democrat. Achievements include Oxidation resistant niobium aluminide intermetallic with comparable toughness to steels; contributions to understanding of toughening and cyclic plasticity in materials. Avocations: piano, current affairs, keeping fit. Office: Princeton U Olden St Princeton NJ 08544-0001

SOBRAL, JOSE TORRES, hydrographer; b. Lisbon, Oct. 6, 1942; s. Florencio Sobral Portela and Ilda Conceicao Torres Sobral; m. Maria Celeste Castilha; children: Alexandre, Sofia. Degree in naval mil. scis., Naval Acad., Lisbon, 1962; MSc in Oceanography, French Nat. Sch. Adv. Tech., Paris, 1975; postgrad., Navy's Grad. Sch., Lisbon, 1989. Sci. and tech. dir., vice dir., acting dir. Hydrographic Inst., Lisbon, 1975-92; comdr. 1st group of naval schs. Portuguese Armed Forces Staff, Portugal; dir. tng. Navy, Portugal, 1993; nat. rep. to NATO Command Control & Comms. Bd. NATO, Lisbon, 1993-94; planning asst. to chief gen. staff Portuguese Armed Forces, Lisbon, 1994-97; gen. dir. Hydrographic Inst., Lisbon, 1997—; mem. improvement com. Oceanographic Inst. of Found. Albert 1st, Prince of Monaco, 1999—. Recipient 5 medals of disting. svc., medal with palm of disting. svc., Mil. Order of Avis Degree of Officer. Mem. Engrs. Order Geographer, Naval Acad., Internat. Maritime Law (v.p. 1996). E-mail: mail@hidrografico.pt. Office: Hydrographic Inst, Rua Das Trinas no 49, 1249-093 Lisbon Portugal

SOBRALSKE, BARBARA NILA, educator; b. Wild Rose, Wis., May 10, 1949; d. Kenneth John and Beverly Janice Graydon; m. Michael John Sobralske Jr., Oct. 17, 1970; 1 child, Mark Michael. Cert., Waushara County (Wis.) Tchrs. Coll., 1969; BS, U. Wis., Oshkosh, 1974; MA, Marian Coll., 1991. Cert. elem. tchr., Wis. Tchr. elem. schs. Waupun (Wis.) Sch. Dist., 1969-72; title I aide Wild Rose Sch. Dist., 1975, tchr. elem. schs., 1975-95, elem. prin., 1995—. Mem. ASCD, Wis. Edn. Assn., Wis. Assn. Environ. Edn., Wis. Sch. Adminstrs., Nat. Assn. Elem. Sch. Prins. Home: N5268 17th Dr Wild Rose WI 54984-6220 Office: Wild Rose Sch Dist PO Box 276 Wild Rose WI 54984-0276

SOBUE, ITSURO, internist, neurologist, educator; b. Konan, Aichi, Japan, Mar. 19, 1921; s. Tei-itsu and Sute Sobue; m. Shigeko, May 17, 1949; children: Gen, Kyoko Fukuzumi. MD, Nagoya U., 1943, PhD, 1951. Asst. prof. internal medicine Nagoya U. Sch. Medicine, 1952-67, assoc. prof., 1967-75, prof., 1975-84, prof. emeritus, 1984—; pres. Nat Chubu Hosp., 1984-87, Aichi Med. U., 1991-2000; chmn. rsch. com. spinocerebellar degeneration Ministery of Health and Welfare, 1975-80, chmn. rsch. com. muscular dystrophy, 1978-84, chmn. rsch. com. new drug for spinocerebellar degeneration, 1979-85, chmn. rsch. com. neuropeptide for neuropsychiat. disorders, 1985-91; chmn. SMON, 1976-82. Author, editor: Spinocerebellar Degenerations, 1980, Peripheral Neuropathy, 1984, TRH and Spinocerebellar Degeneration, 1986; editor Clin. Neurology Jour., 1960-76. Chmn. Com. on Welfare in Nagoya, 1998—; chmn. Com. on Intractable Disease, Aichi-Ken, 1973—. Served with Japanese Navy, 1943-45. Mem. Japanese Soc. Neurology (emeritus), Japanese Soc. Psychosomatic Medicine (emeritus), Japanese Soc. Internal Medicine (emeritus), Japanese Soc. Rehab. Medicine (emeritus). Home: 2-211 Nishi Umemorizoka, Meito-ku Aichi-ken, Nagoya 465-0066, Japan Office: Aichi Med U, 21 Karimata Yasago Nagakute, 65 Tsurumai-cho Aichi-gun 480-1195, Japan

SOCHACKI, ANDRZEJ, mechanical engineer, researcher, tourism educator; b. Warsaw, Poland, July 26, 1948; came to U.S., 1973; s. Jerzy and Halina (Błażejczyk) S.; married. MS, Warsaw U., 1969; AAS, Maricopa Tech. Coll., Phoenix, 1983; postgrad., Ariz. State U., 1985. Sr. mech. engr. Roger Bus. Products div. Rogers Corp., Mesa, Ariz., 1986-87; sr. mech. design engr. Parker Aerospace Co., Phoenix, 1987-88; sr. project engr. Micro-Rel Inc., Tempe, Ariz., 1988-90; cons., project engr., pres., owner Design & Fabricating Co., Phoenix, 1985-96; founder, pres., chmn. The Vagabond Ctr., Phoenix, 1992; tool engr. Boeing Co., Mesa, Ariz., 1996-98; tchr., lectr. traveling Tourism and Hotels Mgmt. Coll., Warsaw, 1998—. Contbr. ednl. articles to publs. Recipient award Medtronic Corp., Phoenix, 1989. Mem. Soc. Mfg. Engrs. (sr.). Roman Catholic. Avocations: travel, piano, research, 6 times travel around the world. Home and Office: The Vagabond Ctr 3715 E Taylor St Phoenix AZ 85008-6316

SOCHAVA, LEV SERGEEVICH, physicist, editor; b. Saint Petersburg, Russia, Sept. 13, 1930; s. Sergej L'vovich and Faina Ivanovna (Belova) Gaukhman; m. Inna Viktorovna Sochava, Feb. 12, 1953; children: Ekaterina, Sergej. PhD, Inst. Semiconductors, St. Petersburg, 1966; DSc in Physics, Ioffe Phys.-Tech. Inst., St. Petersburg, 1990. Engr. Factory of Med. Equipment, St. Petersburg, 1953-55; rsch. scientist Inst. Semiconductors, St. Petersburg, 1955-72; rsch. scientist Ioffe Phys.-Tech. Inst., St. Petersburg, 1972-80, sr. rsch. scientist, 1980-91, leading rsch. scientist, 1991—, team leader for solid state radiospectroscopy, 1980. Sci. editor Jour. Physics of the Solid State, 1960—; contbr. articles to profl. jours. Grantee Internat. Sci. Found., 1994, 95, NATO Sci. Affairs Divsn., 1996, Russian Found. for Basic Rsch., 1996, 99. Home: Sytninskaja Str 12 Apt 11, 197101 Saint Petersburg Russia Office: Ioffe Phys Tech Inst, Polytekhnicheskaja Str 26, 194021 Saint Petersburg Russia

SOCHER, KARL FRIEDRICH, economics educator; b. Berlin, Germany, July 19, 1928; s. Hermann and Emilie (Fick) S.; m. Renate Gertrud Gries, Nov. 7, 1970; children: Michael, Christian, Katrin. Dr.rer.pol., U. Vienna, 1953. Economist Inst. for Econ. Research, Vienna, 1953-60, Deutsche Bundesbank, Frankfurt, 1961-64, Ministry of Fin., Vienna, 1964-70, C. of C. of Austria, Vienna, 1970-73; prof. econs. U. Innsbruck, 1973-96, prof. emeritus, 1996—; cons. in field. Author books on monetary and fiscal policies, economics of tourism, 1972—. With German Army, 1943-45. Mem. Am. Econ. Assn., Verein fur Socialpolitik, Mont-Pelerin Soc. Home: Haus Heimkehr, A-6072 Lans Austria Office: U Innsbruck, Universitaetsstr 15, A-6020 Innsbruck Austria

ŠOCHMAN, JAN, cardiologist, researcher; b. Prague, Czech Republic, June 6, 1956; s. Jan Šochman and Ludmila (Hantáková) Šochmanová; m. Martina Vondrak, Oct. 19, 1991; children: Jan, Barbora. MD, Charles U., Prague, 1981, PhD, 1991. Intern Kolin Hosp., 1981-83; cardiologist, head coronary care unit Inst. Clin. and Exptl. Medicine, Prague, 1983—. Inventor catheterization techniques, 1986. Mem. Czech Cardiologic Soc. (com. mem. sect. invasive cardioangiology), N.Y. Acad. Sci. Avocation: tech. works.

SOCZKIEWICZ, EUGENIUSZ STANISŁAW, physicist, educator; b. Inowrocław, Poland, Oct. 26, 1934; s. Stefan and Anna (Miętkiewicz) S. MS, U. Toruń, Poland, 1956; D in Tech. Scis., Polish Acad. Scis., Warsaw, Poland, 1973; DSc in Physics, U. Poznań, Poland, 1984. Lectr. physics Secondary Sch., Tuchola, Bydgoszcz, Poland, 1956-64, High Pedagogical Sch., Katowice, Poland, 1964-67; lectr. physics Silesian Tech. U., Gliwice/Katowice, 1967-86, asst. prof., 1986-93, assoc. prof., 1993—. Contbr. articles to profl. jours. Mem. IEEE, Polish Phys. Soc., Polish Acoustical Soc., European Phys. Soc., European Acoustics Assn., N.Y. Acad. Scis. Roman Catholic. Achievements include propagation of ultrasonic waves in liquids and randomly inhomogeneous media. Avocation: tourism. Fax: 48-32-2372216. E-mail: soczkiewicz@tytan.matfiz.polsl.gliwice.pl. Home: Derkacza 6/25, 44-100 Gliwice Katowice, Poland Office: Silesian Tech U Inst Physic, Krywoustego 2, 44-100 Gliwice Katowice, Poland

SODANO, ANGELO CARDINAL, cardinal, Vatican official; b. Nov. 23, 1927. Ordained priest Roman Cath. Ch., 1950; consecrated archbishop Roman Cath. Ch., 1978. Sec. of state Holy See, 1990—; created cardinal Roman Cath. Ch., 1991—. Office: Secretary of State, Palazzo Apostolico Vaticano, 00 120 Vatican City Vatican City

SODEI, RINJIRO, historian, educator; b. Kogotamachi, Miyagi, Japan, Mar. 9, 1932; s. Hiraku and Un (Hamada) Sodei; m. Takako Kato, June 27, 1962. B in Polit. Sci., Wased U., Tokyo, 1954, M in Polit. Sci., 1956; MA in Polit. Sci., UCLA, 1964. Exec. asst. to hon. Sugiyama Dep. Spkr. of Lower House, 1956-59; prof. politics and history Hosei U., Tokyo, 1974-99, prof. emeritus, 1999—. Author: Two Thousand Days of MacArthur, 1975 (Best non-fiction book of yr. 1976, Mainichi award for disting. pub. 1976), Were We the Enemy? American Survivors of Hiroshima, 1998; rsch. fellow Jour. Social and Polit. Ideas in Japan, Tokyo, 1963-68; freelance writer, Tokyo, 1968-74. Bd. dirs. Maruki Gallery for Hiroshima Panels, Saitama-ken, 1976—. Mem. Japanese Polit. Sci. Assn., Peace Studies Assn. Japan, Japan PEN. Avocations: collecting books and art, gardening, swimming. Home: 6 Ichigaya-daimachi, Shinjuku Tokyo 1620066, Japan

SODEN, RICHARD ALLAN, lawyer; b. Feb. 16, 1945; s. Hamilton David and Clara Elaine (Seale) S.; m. Marcia LaMonte Mitchell, June 7, 1969; children: Matthew Hamilton, Mark Mitchell. AB, Hamilton Coll., 1967; JD, Boston U., 1970. Bar: Mass. 1970. Law clk. to judge U.S. Ct. Appeals (6th cir.), 1970-71; assoc. firm Goodwin, Procter & Hoar LLP, Boston, 1971-79, ptnr., 1979—; instr. Law Sch. Boston Coll., Chestnut Hill, Mass., 1973-74. Mem. South End Project Area Com.; hon. dir. United South End Settlements, pres., 1977-79; chmn. Boston Mcpl. Rsch. Bur.; pres. Boston Minuteman coun. Boy Scouts Am.; trustee Judge Baker Children's Ctr., chmn., 1994-96, pres., 1992-94; trustee New Eng. Aquarium, Boston U.; bd.

visitors Boston U. Goldman Sch. Grad. Dentistry; mem. bd. overseers WGBH; mem. Mass. Minority Bus. Devel. Commn.; mem. Adv. Task Force on Securities Regulation; mem. Adv. Com. on Legal Edn.; steering com. Lawyers Com. for Civil Rights under Law, chmn., 1992-94. Mem. ABA (chmn. standing com. on bar svcs. and activities), Nat. Bar Assn., Mass. Bar Assn. (past vice chmn. bus. law coun. 1990-91), Boston Bar Assn. (pres. 1994-95), Mass. Black Lawyers Assn. (pres. 1980-81). Home: 42 Gray St Boston MA 02116-6210 Office: Goodwin Procter & Hoar LLP Exchange Pl Boston MA 02109-2803

SODER-ALDERFER, KAY CHRISTIE, counseling administrator; b. Evanston, Ill., Oct. 25, 1949; d. Earl Eugene and Alice Kathryn (Lien) Soder; m. David Luther Alderfer, May 15, 1976. BSE, No. Ill. U., 1972; postgrad., Luth. Sch. Theology, Phila., 1973; MA, Gov.'s State U., University Park, Ill., 1978; PhD, Walden U., 1985. Consecrated deaconess Luth. Ch., 1974. News reporter Suburban Life Newspaper, La Grange Park, Ill., 1972; counselor various orgns. Ill. & Pa., 1973—; parish worker Luth. Ch., De Kalb, Ill., 1973-74; pub. rels. asst. Luth. Ch. Women, Phila., 1974-76; editor Luth. Ch., Chgo., 1979—; spiritual dir. Gentle Pathways, Downers Grove, Ill., 1988—, psychotherapist, 1990—, also bd. dirs.; cons. Evang. Luth. Ch. in Am., Chgo., 1988—, Lehigh Valley Hosp. Assn., Allentown, Pa., 1986, Luth. Social Ministry Orgns. of Pa. and N.J., 1997. Author: Gentle Journeys, 1993, With Those Who Grieve, 1995, Help! There's a Monster in My Head, 1998; editor Entree, 1988-93, Multicultural Jour., 1992-99, project mgr., 1996-98; graphic designs exhbn. Franklin Mus., Phila., 1981. Spokeswoman Progressive Epilepsy Network, Phila., 1980-85; chair spiritual life com. Luth. Deaconess Cmty., Gladwyne, Pa., 1990-92; founder Teens with Epilepsy and Motivation, 1995; vol. March of Dimes, Ill., 1991-93; amb. of goodwill Good Bears of the World, 1993-94; spiritual dir. Evang. Luth. Ch. in Am. Recipient Silver award Delaware Valley Neographics Soc., 1981; 50th anniversary scholar Luth. Deaconess Community, 1983. Mem. AAUW, APA (div. women and psychology, div. psychology and the arts, div. psychology and religion). Avocations: painting, mixed media, story telling, traveling, Native American studies. Office: Gentle Pathways 1207 55th St Downers Grove IL 60515-4810

SÖDERBERG, BO S., marketing executive; b. Avesta, Sweden, Mar. 22, 1939; came to U.S., 1979; s. John Sigfrid and Elisabet A. (Bjorkvall) S.; m. Kerstin Linnea Nordling; children: Monica, Mikael, Bogge, Margareta. BS in Engring., TGO, Orebro, Sweden, 1960; MBA, Fla. Inst. Tech., 1985. Mng. dir. Scandinavian Computer Systems, Stockholm, 1967-69; pres. Bror Andersson AB (BRA), Stockholm, 1969-78; exec. dir. Cap Gemini Sogeti, Paris, 1978-80, Cap Gemini Inc., Washington, 1980-82; pres. DMA Marketing Inc., Palm Bay, Fla., 1982-86; pres. Prisma Am. Inc., Vero Beach, Fla., 1986-87, also bd. dirs.; pres. Scandinavian USA Bus. Ctr., Inc., Clearwater, Fla., 1988-92; pres. DMA Mktg. Inc., St. Petersburg, Fla., 1993-98, Atlanta, 1998—; seminar instr. Swedish Computer Soc., Stockholm, 1970-78; instr., lectr. Swedish Soc. for Info. Processing, Stockholm, 1972-78; lectr. Fla. Outdoor Advt. Assn.,Orlando, Fla., 1986-87. Served as specialist Sweden Air Force, 1960-61. Home: 630 W Northway Ln NE Atlanta GA 30342-2419 Office: 3475 Lenox Rd NE Ste 400 Atlanta GA 30326-3229

SODERBERG, DALE LEROY, English language educator, drama director, producer; b. Warren, Pa., Apr. 24, 1929; s. Leroy Wilbur and Olive Hazel (Conboy) S.; m. Marjorie Ann Hamm, Aug. 19, 1951; children: David J., Valli K., W. Mark, Lisa T., Kathi L. BA, Gettysburg Coll., 1951; BD, Luth. Theol. Sem., Gettysburg, Pa., 1954. Cert. secondary English tchr., N.Y.; ordained mins. Luth. Ch., 1954. Pastor Grace Luth. Ch., Clarion, Pa., 1954-57; mission developer, 1st pastor Our Saviour's Luth. Ch., Horseheads, N.Y., 1957-60; dir. Ecclesia Tours (Luth. Fgn. Tours), Horseheads and North Syracuse, N.Y., 1958-67; mgr. Soderberg Travel Svc., Corning, N.Y., 1960-62; pastor St. John's Luth. Ch., Syracuse, N.Y., 1962-66; guest chapel preacher Wittenberg U., Ohio, 1966; tchr. English Ft. Myers (Fla.) High Sch., 1967-68; tchr. English, dir. drama Hamilton (N.Y.) Cen. Sch., 1968-92; retired, 1992; sermon and story writer Ecclesia Svcs., Hamilton, 1984-96; lay preacher Upstate N.Y. Synod Evang. Luth. Ch. Am., Syracuse, 1968—; advisor student tchrs. Colgate U., Hamilton, 1975-92; clk. Hamilton Stores, Yellowstone Nat. Park, summer 1948, 93. Author: (novels) Pawns, 1980, The Amsterdam Connection, 1999. Dir. tours to Europe, Holy Land and Luth. mission fields in Brit. Guiana, East and West Africa, and India; bd. dirs. Luth. Homes Found., 1993-96; vol. missionary religious edn. tchr. U. of Papua New Guinea, Goroka, spring 1996; mem. Global Missions Team, Upstate N.Y. Synod Evang. Luth. Ch., Syracuse, 1999—; organizer Bishop's tour to Zimbabwe, 2000. Mem. N.Y. State United Tchrs., Hamilton Tchrs. Assn., N.Y. State Ret. Tchrs. Assn. Republican. Avocations: travel, photography, home video, creative writing, Hemingway specialization. Home: 1907 Preston Hill Rd Hamilton NY 13346-9522

SODERBERGH, STEVEN ANDREW, filmmaker; b. Atlanta, Jan. 14, 1963; s. Peter Andrew and Mary Ann (Bernard) S.; m. Elizabeth Jeanne Brantley, Dec. 1, 1989 (div. Oct. 1994). Writer, dir., editor: (films) sex, lies, and videotape, 1989 (Palme d'Or award Cannes Film Festival 1989), King of the Hill, 1993, Schizopolis, 1996; dir., editor: (film) Kafka, 1991; exec. prodr.: (films) Suture, 1994; prodr.: The Daytrippers, 1997, Pleasantville, 1998; dir.: (films) The Underneath, 1995, Gray's Anatomy, 1996, Out of Sight, 1998, The Limey, 1999, Erin Brokovich, 2000, Traffic, 2000; writer: (film) Nightwatch, 1998. Mem. AMPAS, Dirs. Guild Am. Democrat.

SODERGARD, CAJ GUSTAV, information technology scientist; b. Larsmo, Finland, Mar. 2, 1954; s. William Anders and Bergine Katarina (Holm) S.; m. Ulla Irmeli Pekkala; children: Kristian, Thomas, Staffan. MS with honors, Helsinki U. Tech., Finland, 1980, Lic. Tech., 1990; DTech, Helsinki U. Tech., 1994. Asst. Helsinki Sch. of Engring., Finland, 1976-79; system designer, project leader Oy Decon, Finland, 1979-81; rsch. scientist Tech. Rsch. Ctr. of Finland, 1982-83, sr. rsch. scientist, group leader, 1984-96; rsch. prof. VTT Info. Tech., Finland, 1997—; evaluator EU Fourth Rsch. Program, Luxemburg, 1995, EU Fifth Rsch. Program, 2000; mem. tech. bd. Internat. World Wide Web Conf., 1996-97; cons. European Media Cos., 1985—. Inventor in field; patentee in field; numerous papers. Bd. dirs. Orgn. of Finnish-Swedish Parents, 1998—. Mem. Phys. Engring. Soc. (chmn. 1988), Finnish Academies of Tech., Tech. Assn. of Graphic Arts, Soc. of Pattern Recognition. Avocations: skiing, bicycling, boat, lit. Office: VTT Info Tech, Tekniikantie 4 B, 02044 VTT Espoo Finland

SÖDERHOLM, ANNA LISA, maxillofacial surgeon; b. Stockholm, Sweden, Aug. 22, 1941; Finnish citizen; d. Hjalmar and Astrid (Larsson) Stenström; m. Harry Söderholm, Aug. 26, 1961; children: Fredrik, Sonja. DDS, Helsinki U., 1964, MD, 1985, PhD, 1991. Pvt. practice Helsinki, Finland, 1964-88; resident dept. maxillofacial surgery Helsinki U. Ctrl. Hosp., 1985-90, cons. dept. maxillofacial surgery, 1990-96, head dept. maxillofacial surgery, 1996—; expert oral surgeon Nat. Bd. Mediolegal Affaires, Finland, 1996—; del. elimination of violence against women sect. Ministry Social Affaires and Health, Coun. Equality, 1996-98, dept. R&D expert in oral and maxillofacial surgery; chairperson sect. for devel. of svcs. Nationwide Project for Elimination of Violence Against Women; mem. Oral Health Sci. Group, Finland, 2000; mem. Evidence Based Practice Oral Cancer Project Group, 1999—. Contbr. articles to profl. jours. Grantee Found. Swedish Culture in Finland, 1996, Finnish Med. Assn., 1997. Mem. Scandinavian Assn. Oral and Maxillofacial Surgeons (treas. 1996—), Finnish Dental Assn. (vice chmn. Coun. 1992-98, edn. com. 1994-98, grantee 1997), Finnish Assn. Oral and Maxillofacial Surgeons (treas. 1995-2000, bd. dirs. 2000—), Dental Sci. Soc. Finland (bd. mem. 1977-80, 1985, chair, 1986-88; Badge for merit in gold 1993, Per Gadds award 1995, Pervi Bonsdorffs medal for outstanding work for the profession 2000), European Assn. Craniomaxillofacial Surgeons (councillor Finland 1998—). Avocations: boating, hiking, travel. E-mail: anna-lisa.soderholm@huch.fi. Fax: 358-9-47188353. Home: Lars Soncks vag 10, 00570 Helsinki Finland Office: Helsinki U Hosp, PB 263 Dept Oral & Maxillo Dis, FIN-0029 Hus Finland

SODERLIND, JOHANNES, literature educator; b. Skelleftea, Sweden, Sept. 1, 1918; s. Johan and Valborg Maria (Lindberg) S.; m. Ann-Marie Viktoria Andreasson, Apr. 4, 1953; children: Gunnar, Bengt, Staffan, Gudrun. BA, Uppsala U., 1939, MA, 1946, PhD, 1952. Attache Fgn. Dept., Sweden, 1946-51; lectr. Uppsala U., Sweden, 1951-55, 61-64; head tchr. Tchr.'s Tng. Coll., Gothenburg, Sweden, 1955-61; prof. Uppsala U., 1965-85; acting prof. U. Munich, 1963-64, 67, U. Würzburg, 1972; vis. prof. U. Erlangen, 1963-64; vice dean faculty of langs. Uppsala U., 1971-77; mem. Swedish Rsch. Coun. Humanities, 1970-77. Author: Verb Syntax in John Dryden's Prose I-II, 1951, 58, Zero-form v. The-Form, 1962, Infinitive Analysis, 1973, A Novel by Dickens Linguistically Analyzed, 1976, James Joyce and the Linguistic Theories of His Time, 1986, The Interior Monologue: A Linguistic Approach, 1989, Immediate Phrase Repetition in Language and in Music, 1989, The Old English Homiliary BL Cotton Vitellius D XVII, 1995, Finnegans Wake and Other "Circular" Novels, 1998; contbr. articles to profl. jours. Named Knight of Order of Northern Star. Mem. Royal Soc. Humanities Uppsala, Swedish Red Cross. Lutheran. Avocations: music, traveling. Home: Granitvägen 14 A, S-75243 Uppsala Sweden

SÖDERMAN, JACOB-MAGNUS, European ombudsman; b. Helsinki, Finland, Mar. 19, 1938; s. John and Rakel Kezia (Roos) S.; m. Raija Kaarina Immonen, Apr. 13, 1958; children: Päivi, Disa, Peter. M Laws, U. Helsinki, Finland, 1967. Min. of justice Govt. of Finland, Helsinki, 1971, head labour safety dept. Ministry Social Affairs and Health, 1971-82, province gov., 1982-89, parliamentary ombudsman, 1989-95; ombudsman European Union, 1995—; Finnish rep. Governing Body of Internat. Labour Orgn., 1972-75. Chmn. Internat. Chile Commn., 1974-88; bd. dirs. Internat. Ombudsman Inst., 1991-92. Address: BP 403, 67001 Strasbourg France

SÖDERSTRÖM, HANS TSON, economist; b. Stockholm, Feb. 25, 1945; s. Torkel A.R. and Elisabeth (Zielfelt) S.; m. Caroline Fleetwood, June3, 1995; children: Christofer, Ebba, Marie. PhD, Stockholm Sch. Econs., 1974. Sr. fellow Inst. Internat. Econ. Studies, U. Stockholm, 1977-84, assoc. dir., 1979-84; pres., CEO SNS Ctr. Bus. and Policy Studies, Stockholm, 1985—; adj. prof. macroecons. Stockholm Sch. Econs., 1992—; bd. dirs. Investment AB Öresund, Observer AB; vice chmn. Jan Wallander and Tom Hedelius Found. for Social Sci. Rsch., 1993—. Editor: Ekonomisk Debatt, 1977-78, mem. editl. bd. 1979—; author: Microdynamics of Production, 1974, Finland's Economic Crisis: Causes, Present Nature, and Policy Options, 1993, Normer och Ekonomisk Politik, 1996; editor: Sweden-the Road to Stability, 1985, Getting Sweden Back to Work, 1986, One Global Market, 1989, The Swedish Economy at the Turning Point, 1991, Disinflation, Adjustment and Growth: The Swedish Economy 1992 and Beyond, 1992, Sweden's Economic Crisis: Diagnosis and Cure, 1993, The Crisis of the Swedish Welfare State, 1994, Creating an Environment for Growth, 1999; contbr. articles to profl. jours. Mem. Royal Swedish Acad. Engring. Scis., Swedish Econ. Assn. (dir. 1990-94), Am. Econ. Assn., Finnish Soc. Scis. & Letters, Liberal Econ. Club (chmn. 1983-85). Home: Valhallavägen 77, SE-11427 Stockholm Sweden Office: SNS, Box 5629, SE-11486 Stockholm Sweden

SODEUR, WOLFGANG R., educator; b. Hannover, Germany, Sept. 27, 1938; s. Kurt and Milda (Mueller) S.; m. Helga Effmann, 1967; children: Andreas, Stephan. DrRerPol, U. Cologne, 1972. Prof. U. Wuppertal, Germany, 1973-87, U. Essen, Germany, 1987—. Author: Leadership Effects in Small Groups, 1970, Classification Analysis, 1974; co-editor Jour. Mathematical Sociology. Office: U Essen, Universitattsstr 12, D-45117 Essen Germany

SODHI, NIRMAL SINGH, social work educator; b. Ludhiana, Punjab, India, Dec. 15, 1937; s. Sadhu Singh and Basant Kaur Sodhi; m. Prem Kaur Kaur, Dec. 26, 1963; children: Amardeep, Amandeep. BA, Punjab U., Chandigarh, India, 1957; MA, Agra U., 1960; PhD, Punjabi U., Patiala, 1980. Lectr. Govt. Women Coll., Chandigarh, India, 1961-62, Mahendra Coll., Patiala, India, 1962-84; reader Punjabi U., Patiala, 1984-88, prof., 1988—; vis. prof. dept. sociology U. Lethbridge, Can., summer 1983; mem. faculty selection panel of social work Lucknow U., India, 1996—, Kashi Vidyapeth, Varanasi, India, 1996—; dir. Sch. for Deaf/Blind, Patiala, 1970-72, 88—; dir. cons., Sch. for Mentally Retarded, Patiala, 1982—, Family Counseling Ctr., Patiala, 1990-92, 96—, Drug Abuse Ctr., Patiala, 1987—; cons. Punjab State Panel on Drug Abuse, Chandigarh, India, 1996—, Juvenile Remand Home, Patiala, 1996—. Author: Indian Navy and Marine Warfare, 1980, Social Control (adaptation of book in Punjabi lang.), 1980, Caste, Class and Occupation, 1968; chief editor Jour. Mental Health, 1981-84; contbr. articles to profl. jours. Pres. Citizens for Social Action, Patiala, 1983-84. Lt. comdr. Ministry of Def., Govt. India, 1963-84. Recipient Cmty. Svc. award State Red Cross, India, 1975. Mem. Univ. Tchrs. Assn., Indian Assn. Social Work, Tchrs. Local Assn. (sec. 1962-84), Rotary (pres. 1982-83, sec. 1996—), Freemasons (pres. 1991-92). Democrat/Socialist. Sikhism. Home: B-61 Model Town, Patiala 147001, India Office: Punjabi Univ, Dept Social Work, Patiala 147002, India

SODHI, RAMINDER PAUL SINGH, systems engineer; b. New Delhi, Nov. 25, 1973; s. Jotinder Pal Singh and Paminder Sodhi. B in Engring., Delhi Coll. Engring., 1996. Mgr. Pamela Sales Corp., New Delhi, 1990-92; asst. sys. analyst computer consultancy divsn. Tata Consultancy Svcs., Gurgaon, Haryana, India, 1996-98; sys. engr. computer consultancy divsn. Tata Consultancy Svcs., Gurgaon, 1998—. Vol. Helpage India, New Delhi, 1987. Merit scholar Delhi Coll. Engring., 1992, 93, 94, 95. Mem. Planetary Soc., Amateur Astronomers Assn., Nat. Svc. Scheme (pres. coll. working team 1995-96). Avocations: astro-photography, construction of zoom lenses/grinding and polishing spherical mirrors, reading fiction, animal care, trekking. Home: F-70 Lajpat Nagar I, New Delhi 110024, India Address: 23 Lampton Ave, Hounslow, Hounslow Middlesex London TW3 4EW, England

SOE, H.S. SUNNY, painter; b. Kwang Ju, South Korea, Oct. 4, 1951. BFA, Acad. of Art Coll., San Francisco, 1985; MFA, Pratt Inst., N.Y.c., 1993. Exhibited in solo shows at Grow Rich Gallery, Seoul, Korea, 1979, C&A Gallery, N.Y.C., 1992, The Alberti Gallery, London, 1992, St. Peter's Ch. Gallery, N.Y.C., 1997; group shows include Whu-Ni Gallery, Kwang-Ju, Korea, Nat. Mus. Modern Art, Seoul, Ge-Myung U. Gallery, De-Gu, Korea, Sim Gallery, Seoul, Nat. Cultural Ctr., Seoul, Unipas Gallery, N.Y.C., Manhattan Borough Pres. Gallery, N.Y.C., Bus. Design Ctr., London, London Contemporary Art Gallery, Richard Anderson Gallery, N.Y.C., World Wide Art Gallery, N.Y.C., Waterside Art Gallery, West Stockbridge, Mass., Steuben Hall Gallery/Pratt Inst., Bklyn., Fifth Ave Art and Antique Show, N.Y.C.; subject of articles, broadcasts.

SOEDARTO, H., academic administrator. Head dept. parasitology Airlangga U., Jawa Timur, Indonesia, 1974-90, vice rector acad. affairs, 1993-97, rector, 1997—; vice chmn. Admission U. Nat. Bd.; mem. coord. bd. East Indonesian State U. Mem. Indonesian Parasite Control Assn. (advisor), East Java State U. Assn. (chmn.), Indonesian Pub. Health Assn., Soc. Indonesian Med. Drs. Office: Airlangga U, Airlangga 4-6 Surabaya, Jawa Timur 60286, Indonesia

SOEDERMARK, TORE, cardiologist; b. Stockholm, Sweden, Oct. 3, 1936; s. Olof and Ingrid (Bernstrom) S.; m. Elisabeth Westring, Aug. 31, 1962 (div. Nov. 1975); children: Filippa, Johanna, Gustav; m. Monica Riby, Oct. 20, 1978. Degree, Ostra Real, Stockholm, 1957; MD, Karolinska Inst., Stockholm, 1965. Resident in internal medicine Serafimer Hosp., Stockholm, 1965-68; resident in cardiology Karolinska Hosp., Stockholm, 1968-70; chief physician med. clinic Danderyds Hosp., 1970-78; pvt. practice internal medicine and cardiology, 1979—. Fellow Swedish Soc. Medicine; mem. Swedish Soc. Clin. Exptl. Hypnosis (chmn. Stockholm Cir. 1987-90), Swedish Soc. Hypnosis. Avocations: sailing, skating. Home and Office: Krokvagen 9, 182 73 Stocksund Sweden

SOEDERSTROM, ELISABETH ANNA, opera singer; b. Stockholm, May 7, 1927; d. Emanuel Albert and Anna (Palasova) S.; m. Sverker Olow, Mar. 29, 1950; children: Malcolm, Peter, Jens. Student, Opera Sch., Stockholm; also pupil of Andrejewa Skilondz. Appearances include Stockholm Opera, 1950, Salzburg Festival, 1955, Glyndebourne Opera, 1957, 59, 61, 63, 64, Met. Opera, 1959, 60, 62, 63, 83, 86-87, 99; sang three leading roles in Rosencavalier within one year, 1959; toured USSR, 1966; others roles include Fiordiligi in Cosi Fan Tutte, Susanna and Countess in Figaro, Countess in Capriccio, Countess in Queen of Spades; radio, TV and concert appearances in U.S. and Europe; artistic dir., Drottningholm Ct. Theatre, 1993-97; author: I Min Tonart, 1978, Sjung ut, Elisabeth!, 1986. Decorated Order of Vasa, Sweden, 1997, Stelle Della Solidarieta Dell'Italia; recipient King Olav's reward, Norway, prize for best acting Royal Swedish Acad., 1965, Literis et Artibus award, 1969; named comdr. Most Disting. Order Brit. Empire, CBE, comdr. des Arts et des Lettres, Singer of the Ct., Sweden, prof. Swedish Govt. Mem. Royal Acad. Music Gt. Britain (hon.). Office: Drottningholms Theatre Mus, Box 27050, S-10251 Stockholm Sweden also: care Columbia Artists Mgmt 165 W 57th St New York NY 10019-2201

SOEJIMA, DAISUKE, international trade engineer, economist; b. Tokyo, Jan. 17, 1959; s. Aritoshi and Hiroko Soejima; m. Kiyomi Soejima, Sept. 26, 1987; children: Sayuri, Taiga, Chiaki. BS in Econs., Tokyo U., 1983; MBA, Georgetown U., 1991. Assoc. cons., mgr. coord. Mitsubishi Corp., Tokyo, 1991-95; mgr. Mitsubishi Internat. Corp., Washington, 1995-97; mgr. project and planning Mitsubishi Internat. Corp., N.Y.C., 1997-98, mgr. chem. groups M&A divestitures, 1998—; dir. E-Commerce Devel., 1999—; sr. rschr. Japan Inst. for Econ. Rsch., Tokyo, 1981-83. Mem. grad. adv. bd. Georgetown U. Mem. Asian Chem. Mgmt. and Rsch. Assn., Met. Club, Beta Gamma Sigma, Alpha Mu Alpha. Home: 71 Hoyt St Darien CT 06820-3116 Office: Mitsubishi Internat Corp 520 Madison Ave New York NY 10022-4213

SOEPARWATA, RASJID, cardiovascular and thoracic surgeon; b. Yogyakarta, Indonesia, Jan. 1, 1946; arrived in Germany, 1970; s. Raden Ngabei and Raden Nganten (Supardilah) Kartisudarmo; m. Barbara Kleemann; children: Julian, Andi, Jens. MD, Justus Liebig U., Giessen, Germany, 1975. Cert. gen. surgeon, vascular surgeon, cardiovasc. surgeon of cardiothoracic and vascular surgery, thoracic-cardiovasc. surgeon, sr. cardiothoracic surgeon; cert. assoc. prof. Avocations: swimming, badminton, golf. E-mail: soeparw@uni-muenster.de. Office: Univ Hosp Cardiac Surgery, Albert Schweitzer Str 33, D-48129 Muenster Germany

SOERGEL-AHOVI, MARIANNE, pediatrician; b. Freiburg, Ba-Wü, Germany, Aug. 11, 1960; d. Volker and Charlotte (Fabricius) S. Student, Med. Sch., Geneva, 1978-80; MD, U. Basel, Switzerland, 1985. Resident U. Childrens Hosp., Heidelberg, Germany, 1985-92; pediatric nephrology cons. U. Childrens Hosp., Marburg, Germany, 1992-2000; cons. in pediats. Ctr. Hospitalier du Luxembourg, 2000—; rsch. fellow Hosp. Robert Debré, Paris, 1991; coord. Arbeitsgruppe Pädiatrische Hypertonie, Germany, 1993—. Mem. Internat. Soc. Nephrology, Internat. Pediatric Nephrology Assn., Deutsche Tropenmedizinische Gesellschaft. Avocation: musician. E-mail: soergel.marianne@chl.lu. Office: Ctr Hosp Luxembourg, 4 rue Barblé, L-1210 Luxembourg Luxembourg

SOESILO, DAUD H., translation coordinator; b. Surabaya, Indonesia, Aug. 27, 1952; s. Henoch H. Soesilo and Marjam Soesiloningsih; m. Vivian Andriani, Feb. 23, 1980; children: Davi Rafael, Daniel Andi. BA, Inst. Tchr. Tng., Malang, Indonesia, 1973, M. Ed., 1976; MDiv, Asbury Theol. Sem., Wilmore, Ky., 1980; D of Ministry, Vanderbilt U., 1981; PhD, Union Theol. Seminary, Richmond, Va., 1988. Tchr. Holy Word Christian H.S., Malang, 1974-77; lectr. Southeast Asia Bible Seminary, Malang, 1975-77; rsch. asst. Asbury Seminary, 1979; translation advisor Indonesian Bible Soc., Bogor, 1981-83; tchg. asst. Union Theol. Sem., 1985-87; translation cons. United Bible Socs. Asia-Pacific, 1988—; translation coord. Asia-Pacific, 1999—; vice prin. Holy Word Christian H.S., 1976-77; translation sec. Indonesian Bible Soc., 1982-83; vis. prof. Sabah Theol. Seminary, Kota Kinabalu, Malaysia, 1991—. Author/editor: Mengenal Alkitab Anda, 1994, Mengenal Visi & Misi LAI, 1999; contbr. articles and revs. to profl. jours. Chmn. bd. dirs., East Java Christian U., Malang, 1994. Recipient Pres.' award for excellence in preaching, Asbury Seminary, 1980, J.D. Owen prize Vanderbilt U., 1981. Mem. Soc. Bibl. Lit., Indonesian Linguistic Soc., Theta Phi. Indonesian Evangelical. Office: United Bible Soc Indo-Pacific Reg Svc Ctr, GPO Box 1445, Brisbane QLD 4001, Australia

SOETANTO, KAWAN, biomedical-electrical engineering educator, researcher, scientist, inventor, clinical psychologist; b. Surabaya, Jawa, Indonesia, Mar. 10, 1951; came to U.S., 1987; s. Khelim and Suin S.; m. Jennie Herman, Aug. 31, 1976; children: Nerrie, Jun, Ainie. M Engring., Tokyo U. of A&T, 1982; DEng, Tokyo Inst. Tech., 1984; D in Medicine, Tohoku U., Sendai, Japan, 1987. Mgr. fgn. div. R&D Pacific Electronic Co., Surabaya and Tokyo, 1972-80; rsch. asst. surgery dept. Nissei Hosp., Osaka, Japan, 1979-82; rsch. engr./cons. Tokin, Ricoh, Aloka, Tokyo, 1979-88; rsch. fellow diagnostic imaging dept. Kanto Cen. Hosp., Tokyo, 1982-87; sr. rsch. scientist Med. Engring. Lab. Toshiba Corp., Nasu, Japan, 1985-87; rsch. scholar Inst. Chest Diseases & Cancer, Tohoku U., Sendai, 1984-88; vis. prof. Univ. Sci. and Tech. of China, Beijing, 1987, Indonesia U., 1988, Tokyo Inst. Tech., 1989, 90, Calif. Inst. Tech., 1990, Duke U., 1991, U. Calif., 1992; assoc. prof. biomed. engring. Drexel U., Phila., 1987-93; prof. dept. control and system engring. Toin Univ. Yokohama, Japan, 1993—; core prof., dir. med. ultrasound, head med. engring. program Toin Univ., Yokohama, Japan, 1995-98; interim chmn. dept. biomed. engring. Toin Univ. Yokohama, Japan, 1998-99; prof., chmn. dept. biomed. engring. Toin Univ., Yokohama, Japan, 1999—, exec. com. mem. Internat. Interchange Ctr., 1997—, interim chmn. Dept. Biomed. Engring., 1998—, trustee, 1999—; exec. mem. steering com. Human Sci. & Tech. Ctr. (HUSTEC), Yokohama, Japan, 1993—; assoc. dir. Toin Univ., Yokohama, 1996—; dir. Ctr. for Advanced Rsch. of Biomed. Engring. Toin Univ. Yokahama, Yokohama, Japan, 1998—; rsch. dir., assoc. dir. Ctr. Advanced Research for Biomed. Engring., 1998—; adj. assoc. prof. dept. radiology Thomas Jefferson U., Phila., 1989—; mem. U.S.-Japan Collaborating on Sci. Project, Sendai, 1984-86; liaison, exec. mem. AFSUMB, Tokyo, Bali, 1985-88; adj. fellow, tech. cons. Electronic Industries Assn. Japan, 1994—; apptd. indsl. structure coun. Japanese Min. MITI, 1999—. Author: (with others) Medical Ultrasonic Measurement Technique, 1984, Invasive/Noninvasive Technique, 1988, Ultrasound Imaging and Signal Processing, 1986, Ultrasound Speckle Analysis, 1992, Ultrasound Contrast Agent, 1994—, Safety of Ultrasound, 1995, Education Technology, 1994—, Clinical Psychology, 1994—, The Fascination of Science and Engineering, 1996; contbr. articles to EMCJ, Elec. Engring. Japan, Inst. Electronic Com. Japan U.S., Bull. PME, Japan Jour. Med. Ultrasound, Japanese Jour. Applied Physics, Jour. Acoustics Japan, Jour. Acoustic Soc. Am., Jour. Ultrasound in Medicine and Biology, Ultrasonics, IEEE Trans. on Ultrasonics, Ferroelectrics and Frequency Control, The Med. and Test Jour. Adv. mem. Pan Asian Assn. of Greater Phila., 1989-91, bd. dirs. 1991—; Mayor's Asian Adv. Bd., Phila., 1990; v.p. Indonesian Communities of Delaware Valley, 1990—; sch. affair mem. Japanese Assn. Greater Phila., 1989—; mem. Pa. Heritage Affairs Commn., 1993—; guest speaker radio Japan Edn. in Japan, 1994, TVK Talk Show With State Eminent Person, 1996. Recipient Best Tchg. Prof. of the Yr. 1994, 95, 96, 97, 98, 99, The Favorite Educator, 1993, Best Rsch. Prof. Yr., 1995, 96, 97, 98, 99, Best Lectr. Adult Edn. Program, 1994, 96, 98, Toin U. of Yokohama, Outstanding Achievement awards Pan Asian Assn. Greater Phila., 1990, medals Asian Fedn. Socs. of Ultrasound in Medicine and Biology, 1987, 89, rsch. awards Toshiba Corp. Med. Engring. Lab., Japan, 1986-88, Outstanding Rsch. award Tokyu Found., 1985-88, Best Rsch. award Computer and Comm. Found. NEC, 1986-87, Best Lecturer of the Year, Japan Liberal Party, 1997, 98, 99, Best Spkr. Dir. of the Policy and Strategy Office MITI, 1998, Best Paper award Jour. of Med. Ultrasonics, 1998, Best Paper award, Material Tech., 1998, 99, Poster award 1999, Cert. of Honor, Japan and Indonesian Soc. Ultrasound in Medicine, 1985, 87; Fellow award on the Contbn. on Edn. and Microbubbles Acoustics, The Acoustical Soc. of Amer., 1998, Tokyu Found. fellow, 1985-88, Japan Ministry Edn. predoctoral fellow, 1980-82, doctoral fellow, 1982-85; Japan Ministry Edn. Undergrad. scholar, 1978-80; Nat. Cancer Inst. grantee NIH, 1990-93, Japanese Ministry Edn. grantee 1993, 94, 95, 96, 97, 98, 99, 2000; Pvt. U. Grad. Sch. Priority Funding grantee 1995, 96, 97, 98, 99, 2000; High Tech. Ctr. grantee Japan Ministry Edn., 1998—; Best Achievement award Asahi News, 1999, others. Fellow Am. Inst. Ultrasound in Medicine (ethics and profl. stds. com. 1993-95), Acoustical Soc. Am., Japan Soc. Med. Electronics and Biol. Engring.; mem. IEEE/EMBS (co-chmn. Phila. chpt. 1990-92, chmn. 1992—, internat. program com. 1991—), IEEE (sr.), Acoustical Soc. Japan, N.Y. Acad. Scis., Japan Soc. Mech. Engring., Japan Soc. Ultrasound in Medicine (exec. sec. basic tech. rsch. sect. 1994—, mem. Internet com. 1995, ultrasonics and microbubbles sect. 1996—, councilor 1996—, sci. adv. bd. 1997—, bd. dirs. Japan Rsch. Inst. Material Tech. 1997—, exec. dir. Biomed. Tech. Sect. Material Tech. 1998—). Achievements include development of pocket noise simulator, image signal processing technique, medical imaging, ultrasonic medical equipment, contrast agent, ultrasound exposure microscopy, tissue mimicking phamtoms, education technology, education psychology. Office: Toin U Yokohama Human Sci & Tech Ctr, 1614 Kurogane-Cho, Aoba-ku Yokohama 225, Japan

SOFFAIR, KEDDY JOSEPH, travel related services company executive; b. Baghdad, Iraq, Nov. 11, 1927; naturalized Brit. citizen; s. Joseph and Helloi Soffair; m. Bertine Dangoor, Oct. 14, 1948; children: Golda, Bernard, Elizabeth. BA in Econs., Am. U., Beirut, 1952. Dep. mgr. Am. Express Co., Tel Aviv, 1952-56; asst. mgr. Am. Express Co., London, 1956-63, sales mgr., 1963-70, tours devel. mgr., 1970-75; group sales mgr. Am. Express Co., U.K. and Ireland, 1975-80, dir. sales and mktg., 1980-86; dir. promotions Am. Express Co., U.K., 1986-89; pres. Soffair Assocs., London, 1989—; mng. dir. London House Travel Plc, 1990—; mem. Internat. Council Mus., 1980-83. Recipient U.K. incentive award Incentive and Exhbn. Assn., London, 1984. Fellow Inst. Travel Agts., European Travel Orgn. (council 1980—), Nat. Assn. Exhibitors (vice chmn. London 1965-80). Mem. Conservative Party, Jewish. Clubs: Annabel's, Les Ambassadors, Skal (London). Avocations: reading, travel, various sports. Home: 44 Windermere Ave, London N3 3RA, England Office: London House Travel Plc, 150 Southampton Row, London WC1B 5AL, England

SOFONIO, MARK VINCENT, plastic and reconstructive surgeon; b. L.A., May 14, 1963; s. Lawrence and Hendrika Sofonio. BS in Biomed. Sci. magna cum laude, U. Calif., Riverside, 1984; MD, UCLA, 1988. Diplomate Am. Bd. Plastic Surgery; lic. physician, Calif., Ohio, Mich., Hawaii, N.Y. Intern gen. surgery integrated surg. residency program U. Hawaii, Honolulu, 1988-89, resident, 1989-91; fellow burn surgery N.Y. Med. Coll., Westchester County Med. Ctr., Valhalla, 1991-92; resident plastic and reconstructive surgery Med. Coll. Ohio, Toledo, 1992-94; fellow cosmetic surgery Bruce Connell, MD, Santa Ana, Calif., 1994-95; pvt. practice plastic and reconstructive surgery Rancho Mirage, Calif., 1996—. Author: (with others) Plastic, Maxillofacial and Reconstructive Surgery, 3rd edt., 1997, Grabb and Smith's Plastic Surgery, 5th edt., 1997; contbr. to profl. jours. Named Palm Springs Teenager of the Year 1981; recipient Rsch. Presentation award Am. Coll. Surgeons Ann. Hawaiian Conf., 1990. Mem. ACS, AMA, Am. Soc. Laser Medicine and Surgery, Am. Soc. Plastic and Reconstructive Surgery, Calif. Med. Assn., Am. Burn Assn. Republican. Avocations: exercising, tennis, golf, weight lifting, biking. Office: Kiewit Bldg 39000 Bob Hope Dr Ste 407 Rancho Mirage CA 92270-7040

SOGA, HIDEO, mathematics educator; b. Kameoka, Kyoto, Japan, May 1948. BSc, Kyoto (Japan) U., 1972; MSc, Osaka (Japan) U., 1974, DSc, 1979. Asst. prof. Ibaraki U., Mito, Japan, 1979-84; assoc. prof. Ibaraki U., Mito, 1985-92, prof., 1992—. Contbr. chpts. to books, articles to profl. jours. Mem. Math. Soc. Japan. Office: Ibaraki U Faculty Edn, Bunkyo, Ibaraki Mito 310-8512, Japan

SOGHOMONIAN, ZAREH SALMASI, physicist, magnetics engineer; b. Tehran, Iran, June 21, 1967; arrived in Eng., 1984; s. Simon Soghomonian Salmasi and Shooshik (Der Hakopian) S. 'O' level, Hull (Eng.) Coll. Further Edn., 1986; 'A' level, Rumney Coll. Tech., Cardiff, South Wales, 1988; BEng with honors, U. Wales, Cardiff, 1991, PhD in Elec. and Electronics Engring., 1995. Tchg. co. assoc. U. Wales-European Elec. Steels-Orb Elec. Steels, 1991-93; rsch. fellow European Elec. Steels-Orb Elec. Steels, 1994-95; magnetic design engr., physicist Asea Brown Boveri, Luton, Eng., 1995-96, sr. magnetics engr., 1996-2000, cons., 1995—; with ABB Corp. Rsch. Ctr., Heidelberg, Germany, 2000—; sr. software engr. Media Bright Ltd., 2000—. Contbr. rsch. articles to profl. jours. and confs. Ednl. grantee Gulbenkian Armenian Found., Portugal, 1988, Armenian Gen. Benevolent Union, U.S., 1989, Benlian Armenian Trust, U.K., 1990. Mem. IEEE, Inst. Elec. Engrs. (assoc.), Inst. Physics U.K. (assoc.), U.K. Magnetic Soc., Pan Armenian Acad. and Sci. Soc., Am. Physics Soc. Achievements include international, European and U.K. patents in field of non-destructive (real-time) hardness testing of steel and invention of design of power efficient bi-directional magnetic circuit for low power Solid State electromagnetic flow meter, using Vanadium Cobalt Iron bi-table permanent magnets, patent on Solid State battery-powered electromagnetic flow meter for domestic applications, patents pending include Solid State electromagnetic sensors using barkhausen effect in pulse wire material, design of a multi-purpose quasi-stable electromagnetic transducer using soft magnetic metal injected moulded/sintered materials, for dc and low frequency magnetisation, utilizing micro power pulsed width modulated excitation techniques. Home: 20 Downlands Ct, Browning Rd, Luton Bedfordshire LU4-0LW, England Office: Media Bright Ltd, 11-49 Station Rd, Langley Berkshire SL3-84T, United Kingdom also: PO Box 101332, D-63003 Heidelberg Germany

SOH, BYUNG HEE, economist, educator; b. Korea, June 27, 1951; s. Sang Yung and Ock Yun (Choi) S. AB, U. Calif., Berkeley, 1974; PhD, Northwestern U., 1985. Asst. prof. Okla. State U., Stillwater, 1985-86, No. Ill. U., DeKalb, 1986-88; assoc. prof. Pohang (Korea) U. Sci. and Tech., Postech,, 1988-95; prof. econs. Kookmin U., Seoul, Korea, 1995—, dir. Kookmin Inst. Econ. Rsch., 1996—, chmn. dept. econs., 1997-99; chmn. Bd. Cultural Programs, Postech, 1988-91; mem. search com. for Univ. pres., Postech., 1994; dir. UNESCO-Kyungbuk Province, Pohang, 1990-95; cons. Pohang C. of C., 1991-95; mem. Govt. Adv. Group on Internat. Econ. Affairs, 1994-97; adv. bd. Korea Inst. Pub. Fin., 1996-98. Author: Political Economics of Public Choice, 1993; contbr. articles to profl. jours.; editl. bd. Korean Econ. Assn., 1993-97. Capt. Korean Air Force, 1979-83. Recipient Citation, Dept. Prime Minister, Econ. Planning Bd., 1983. Mem. Korean Assn. for Tech. Innovation (bd. dirs. 1993-95), Korean Internat. Econ. Assn. (bd. dirs. 1994), Korea Assn. for Telecomm. Policies (bd. dirs. 1994-95), Korean Soc. Pub. Fin. (bd. dirs. 1995-97), Korea Assn. Negotiation Studies (pres. 1998-99). Avocation: painting. Office: Kookmin Univ Dept Econs, 861-1 Jungreung Sungbuk-Gu, Seoul 136-702, Republic of Korea

SOHIE, GUY ROSE LOUIS, electrical engineer, researcher; b. Antwerp, Belgium, Nov. 8, 1956; came to U.S., 1978; s. Andre and Lydia (Boussery) S.; m. Angela M. Sloman, Apr. 9, 1987; children: Oliver A., Harry N., Dylan A., Annie R. Ind. Ingenieur, Industriele Hogeschool Antwerpen Mechelen, Antwerp, 1978; PhD, Pa. State U., 1983. Asst. prof. Ariz. State U., Tempe, 1985-87; applications engr. Motorola Inc., Austin, Tex., 1988-89; tech. staff GE, Schenectady, 1989-95; mgr. image detection subsystems Global X-Ray Engring. GE Med Sys. Europe, Buc, France, 1995-97; pres. Global Insite, Austin, 1997—. Co-author: The Elements of System Design, 1993; contbr. articles to profl. jours.; pub. 2 newsletters, 3 spl. reports on globalized tech. Ensign Belgian Navy, 1983-84. Fulbright fellow, Brussels, 1978. Mem. IEEE, Sigma Xi, Phi Kappa Phi, Eta Kappa Nu. Achievements include 3 patents in emergency signal warning systems, patent in image processing system for detection and tracking. Home: 6408 Wareham Ln Austin TX 78739-1565 Office: Global Insite 701 Brazos St Ste 500 Austin TX 78701-3232

SOHLENIUS, GUNNAR H., academic administrator, manufacturing educator and researcher; b. Saltsjobaden, Sweden, May 11, 1935; s. Holter R.H. and Catharina E. (Kjellberg) S.; m. R.K. Margareta Östberg, Nov. 3, 1961; children: Eva M., Ulrika K., H. Ragnar. MSc in Mech. Engring., Royal Inst. Tech., KTH, Stockholm, 1960; tech.lic., Royal Inst. Tech., Stockholm, 1964. Rsch. engr. machine tools Royal Inst. Tech. KTH, Stockholm, 1960-64; prin. machine designer Arenco Electronic AB, Stockholm, 1964-65; mgr. rsch. Swedish Inst. Prod. Engring. Rsch. IVF, Stockholm, 1965-68, sect. mgr., 1968-81, sr. sci. advisor, 1981-2000; prof. Linköping (Sweden) U., 1971-76; prof. Royal Inst. Tech. KTH, 1977—, v.p., 1981-93, chmn. ctrl. faculty, 1994—; bd. dirs. Seco Tools AB, Fagersta, Sweden, 1989-99, SMT Machine AB, 1994—; chmn. prod. engring. adv. bd. Incentive AB, Stockholm, 1972-93; mem. Ericsson AB Sci. Couns., 1988-93; mem. bd. Västmanland's Rsch. Coun. Västeras, 1988-96; mem. internat. adv. bd. Tech. U. Madrid, 1991-93; chmn. Nat. Rsch. Programme CADCAM, 1980-90, Nat. Rsch. FMS, 1985-96. Res. officer Swedish Coast Guard, 1957-85. Recipient disting. leadership award ABI, Raleigh, N.C., 1985, 89, George Washington award George Washington U., Washington, 1989. Fellow World Acad. Productivity Sci., 1997; mem. CIRP Internat. Acad. Prod. Engring. Rsch. (pres. 1989-90), Royal Swedish Acad. Engring. Scis., IVA, Soc. Mfg. Engrs. (Gold medal 1993), Swedish Engring. Acad. Finland, NAE (fgn. assoc.). Home: Österskärsvägen 84, 18451 Österskär Sweden Office: Royal Inst Tech KTH, S-100 44 Stockholm Sweden

SOHLMAN, MICHAEL, foundation administrator; b. Stockholm, Sweden, 1944; s. Rolf R. and Zinaida (Yarotskaya) S. BA, U. Uppsala, Sweden, 1964, postgrad. in econs. and polit. sci., 1968; postgrad. in econs. and polit. sci., U. Stockholm, 1968. Asst. sec. to Commn. Environ. Problems, 1969; with Ministry of Industry, 1972-74; with internat. divsn. Ministry of Fin., 1974-76, with budget dept., 1976, head of planning econ. dept., 1982-84, dir. of budget, 1985-87; fin. counsellor, permanent Swedish del. OECD, 1977-80; with rsch. dept. Social-Dem. Parliamentary Group, 1981-82; under-sec. of state Ministry of Agriculture, 1987-89; under-sec. of state for fgn. affairs Ministry for Fgn. Affairs, 1989-91; exec. dir. Nobel Found., Stockholm, 1992—. Chmn. bd. dirs. Royal Dramatic Theatre, Stockholm, 1993-96; active Swedish Internt. Devel. Agy., Internat. Crisis Group. Mem. Royal Swedish Acad. Scuis., Acad. of Engring. Scis. Office: Nobel Foundation, PO Box 5232, 102 45 Stockholm Sweden*

SOHMER, BERNARD, mathematics educator, administrator; b. N.Y.C., July 16, 1929; s. Sol and Florence (Schonfeld) S.; m. Margot Rosette, July 27, 1952; children: Emily Sohmer Tai, Olivia Sohmer Rosenbaum. BA, NYU, 1949, MS, 1951, PhD, 1958. Lectr. CCNY, 1952-57, faculty, 1958—, prof. math., 1969—, dean students, 1969-72, v.p. student affairs, 1972-75, chmn. faculty senate, 1977-79, 85-91, ombudsman, 1991-98, chmn. liberal arts and sci. faculty council, 1979-85, pres. Hillel, 1988—; asst. prof. N.Y. U., 1957-58; trustee PSC-CUNY Welfare Fund, 1982-97. Sec. Univ. Faculty Senate, CUNY, 1992-94, vice chair, 1994-98, chair, 1998—, ex-officio bd. trustees, 1998—. Mem. AAAS, AAUP (pres. CCNY chpt. 1966-67, sec. 1977-78), Am. Math. Soc., Math. Assn. Am. (pres. elect N.Y. Met. sect. 1989-90, pres. 1992-93, past pres. 1993-94, gov. 1996-98), Profl. Staff Congress (chair CCNY chpt. 1993-96, exec. coun. 1997-2000). Home: 3345 92nd St Jackson Hts NY 11372-1851 Office: CCNY 139th & Convent Ave New York NY 10031

SOHN, CHANG WOOK, energy systems researcher, educator; b. Seoul, Jan. 10, 1947; parents Kye Taek and Young Bo (Koh) S.; m. Chung Hae Han Sohn, Aug. 24, 1974; children: Douglas Jemin, Sammy Sungmin. BS in Engring., Seoul Nat. U., 1969; MS in Mech. Engring., Tex. Tech. U., 1975; PhD in Mech. Engring., U. Ill., Urbana, 1980. Registered profl. engr., Ill. 1st lt. Korean Army, 1969-71; tchr. KyungGi H.S., Seoul, 1971-72; rsch. asst. Tex. Tech. U., Lubbock, 1973-74; rsch. asst. U. Ill., Urbana, 1974-79, rsch. assoc., 1979-80; rsch. engr. U.S. Army Constrn. Engring. Rsch. Lab., Champaign, Ill., 1980-84, acting. team leader, 1992, prin. investigator, 1984—, project leader, 1995—; adj. assoc. prof. U. Ill., Urbana, 1992-97; vis. rsch. fellow Korea Inst. Energy Rsch., 1995-96. Contbr. articles on fluid mechanics, heat transfer to profl. jours, ASHRAE transactions. Recipient Tech. Transfer award U.S. Army Corps of Engrs., Washington, 1991, Spl. Act award U.S. Army Yuma (Ariz.) Proving Ground, 1988; Korea Inst. Energy Rsch. fellow, 1995-96. Mem. ASME (K-19 com. 1993—), ASHRAE (com. chair Cool Storage Design Guide 1992, air conditioning rsch. ctr. industry adv. bd. mem. 1991-96). Home: 2910 Robeson Park Dr Champaign IL 61822-7609 Office: US Army ERDC-CERL PO Box 9005 Champaign IL 61826-9005

SOHN, CHAN-JOON, diplomat; b. Sachun, Korea, Sept. 25, 1949; m. Gum-Sook Park, Oct. 22, 1977; children: Seuk-Min, Woo-Seung. BSc, Gyungsang Nat. U., Jinju-Si, Korea, 1973; MPA, Busan (Korea) Nat. U., 1975; MA in Econs., SUNY, Bimghamton, 1983; diploma in Policy Studies, Seoul (Korea) Nat. U., 1995. Dep. dir. Ministry of Agr. and Forestry, Seoul, 1975-80, dir. for internat. coop. and trade, 1980-89, dir. gen for agrl. coop. and trade, 1994-95, dir. gen. food grain policy, 1996; sec. to pres. Blue House, Seoul, 1989-91; spl. program officer UN Internat. Fund, Rome, 1992-93; counselor Embassy of Korea in U.S.A., Washington, 1997—. Avocations: playing tennis, golf, listening to music, calligraphy. E-mail: chanjoon99@hotmail.com. Home: 1007-504 Gwa Chun, Gyung-gi 427-010, Republic of Korea Office: Embassy of Korea 2450 Massachusetts Ave NW Washington DC 20008-2881

SOHN, DONG HUN, pharmacist, educator; b. Bukcheong, Ham Nam, Korea, Apr. 8, 1930; s. Sung Hoo and Keum Sun (Lee) S.; m. Myo Hee Kim, Mar. 30, 1958; children: Soo Young Sohn Kim, Soo Jung Sohn Song. B in Pharmacy, Chung-Ang U., 1957, M in Pharmacy, 1959, PhD, 1970; diploma, Inst. Pub. Health, Tokyo, 1974. Rschr. Warner-Lambert Rsch., N.J., 1959-60; prof. Chung-Ang U., Seoul, 1960-95, prof. emeritus, 1995—, dean coll. pharmacy, 1980-82, dir. Pharm. Rsch. Inst., 1991-93, dir. cen. libr., 1993-95; head environ. hygiene dept. Pharmacal Rsch. Inst., Seoul, 1987—; cons. Ministry of Health and Social Affairs, Seoul, 1976—, Ministry of Environ., Seoul, 1980—. Author: Modern Hygienic Pharmacy, 1993; contbr. articles to profl. jours. Commr. Ctrl. Coun. Pharmacal Affairs, Seoul, 1986—, Environ. Ctr. Han River, Seoul, 1994—. Recipient Pharmacy award The Yak-up-Shin-Moon, Seoul, 1991, Nat. Decoration of Dong-Baek award the Pres., Korea, 1991. Mem. Pharm. Soc. Korea (sec. gen., Acad. award 1971), Pharm. Soc. Kapan, Japanese Soc. Air Pollution, Korea Air Pollution Rsch. Assn. (chmn.), Internat. Union Air Pollution Prevention and Environ. Protection Assns. (exec. mem., v.p., 1995-98). Avocations: golf, mountain climbing, game of Go. Home: 1327-1403 Mokdong Apt, Sinjungdong Yongchun-ku Seoul 158-076, Republic of Korea

SOHN, DONG-RYUL, clinical pharmacology educator; b. Taegu, Republic of Korea, Feb. 26, 1956; s. Gye-Hyun and Jung-Hee (Huh) S.; m. Ji-Sook Shin, Jan. 26, 1983; children: Jung-Hoon, Yeh-Hoon. MD, Kyungpook Nat. U., Taegu, 1980; MS, Hanyang U., Seoul, 1982, PhD, 1986. Asst. Hanyang U. Sch. Medicine, 1980-83, instr., 1983-86; asst. prof. clin. pharmacology Gyeongsang Nat. U. Coll. Medicine, Chinju, Republic of Korea, 1989—; postdoctoral fellow Nat. Med. Ctr., Tokyo, 1991-92. Maj. M.C., Republic of Korea Army, 1987-89. Mem. Korean Toxicology Soc., Soc. Pharmacology Reps. Korea, Am. Soc. Clin. Pharmacology and Therapeutics, Korean Soc. Clin. Pharmacology and Therapeutics. Roman Catholic. Avocations: baseball, volleyball, collecting classical music records. Office: Soonchunhyang U Coll Medicine, Dept Clin Pharmacology, Chonan 330-090, Republic of Korea

SOHN, JAE-KEUN, agronomist, educator; b. Taegu, Korea, Aug. 6, 1948; s. Jong-Man and Jun-Gee (Chae) S.; m. Myeong-Hee Suh, Apr. 25, 1976; children: Hae-Jin, Hee-Jin. BS, Kyungpook Nat. U., Taegu, 1971, MS, 1976, PhD, 1981. Jr. rschr. Rural Devel. Adminstrn., Suweon, Korea, 1975-78; sr. rschr. Rural Devel. Adminstrn., Milyang, Korea, 1978-87, assoc. rschr., 1987-91; post doctor Internat. Rice Rsch. Inst., Losbanos, The Philippines, 1982-83; prof. agronomy dept. Kyungpook Nat. U., Taegu, 1987—, vice-dir. student affairs, 1993-94. Author: Haploid and Plant Breeding, 1992, Plant Biotechnology, 1992, Rice Management Biotechnology, 1994. With Korean Mil. Svc., 1971-74. Recipient Rsch. award Ministry of Agr., Forestry and Fishery, Korean Govt., 1983. Mem. Korean Soc. Plant Tissue Culture, Korean Breeding Soc., Soc. for Advancement of Breeding Researchers in Asia and Oceania, Rice Genetics Coop. Achievements include development of 14 rice cultivars in Korea. Office: Kyungpook Nat Univ Dept Agronomy, Sankeogdong, Taegu 702-701, Republic of Korea

SOHN, KEE-SUN, materials scientist; b. Seoul, Korea, Jan. 7, 1968; s. Heemyoung and Seungja (Park) S. BS, Yonsei U., Seoul, 1990; MS, Pohang U. Sci. and Tech., 1992, PhD, 1996. Postdoctoral fellow U. London, 1996-97, Pohang U. Sci. and Tech., 1997-98; sr. rschr. Korea Rsch. Inst. Chem. Tech., Taejon, 1998—. Contbr. articles to profl. jours. including Jour. Am. Ceramic Soc., Jour. Electrochem. Soc., Metall. Transactions, and Acta Materiallia. Recipient postech. Chevening scholarship Brit. Coun., 1996. Methodist. Avocation: writing. Home: 8-501 Eusonggu, Doryongdong 431, Taejon 305-340, Korea Office: Korea Rsch Inst Chem Tech, Eusonggu Jandong 100, Taejon 305-600, Korea

SOHN, KWANGHOON, electrical engineering educator; b. Seoul, Republic of Korea, Jan. 13, 1961; s. Chung-Sam and Myung-Hee (Hong) S.; m. Chungyeun Ko, May 25, 1987; children: Minsung, Minyoung. B in Engring., Yonsei U., Seoul, 1983; MSEE, U. Minn., 1985; PhD, N.C. State U., 1992. Sr. rschr. Elec. Telecom. Rsch. Inst., Daejeon, Republic of Korea, 1992-93; postdoctoral fellow Georgetown U., Washington, 1994; prof. elec. engring. Yonsei U., 1995—; cons. Dong-A Pharm. Co., Seoul, 1995—, MonAmi Co., Seoul, 1995—. 2d lt., Army of Republic of Korea, 1985-86, Youngchun. Mem. IEEE, Seoul Jr. C. of C. Avocations: soccer, racquetball, golf, piano, astronomy. Home: Bangbae-dong 725 Bangbae, Samho-Apt Ladong # 1103, Seodaemun-ku Seoul 120-749, Republic of Korea Office: Yonsei U Dept Elec Comp Eng, 134 Shinchon, Seodaemun-ku Seoul 120-749, Republic of Korea

SOHN, SO YOUNG, industrial engineer, educator; b. Raju, Korea; d. Jung Tae Sohn and Park Yong Hyun. BS in Maths., Yonsei U., 1981; MS in Indsl. Engring., Korea Advanced Inst. Sci., 1983; MSc in Mgmt. Sci., U. London, 1986; MA, U. Pitts., 1989, PhD in Indsl. Engring., 1989. Ops. rsch. analyst Korea Inst. Def. Analysis, Seoul, 1983-85; rsch. assoc. Bur. Labor Stats., Dept. Labor, Washington, 1990; asst. prof. ops. rsch. Naval Postgrad. Sch., Monterey, Calif., 1990-95; asst. prof. decision scis. and engring. sys. Rensselaer Poly. Inst., Troy, N.Y., 1995-96; assoc. prof. indsl. sys. engring. Yonsei U., Seoul, 1996-99, prof., 1999—. Editl. bd. Internat. Jour. IE Applications & Practice, 1997—, Korean Jour. Engring. Edn., 1997—, Jour. Korean Soc. Maintenance Engrs., 1997—, Jour. Korean Soc. Quality Mgmt., 1998—. Mem. Am. Statis. Assn., Inst. Ops. Rsch. & Mgmt. Scis., Inst. Indsl. Engring., Am. Soc. Quality Control. Office: Yonsei U Dept Indsl Sys Eng, Shinchondong 134, Seoul Republic of Korea

SOHTAOGLU, NAZIF HULAGU, electrical engineer, educator, consultant; b. Istanbul, Turkey, Nov. 11, 1963; s. Tahsin and Ayhan Sohtaoglu. MSc in Elec. Engring., Istanbul Tech. U., 1988; MBA, Istanbul U., 1990; PhD in Elec. Engring., Istanbul Tech. U., 1994. Assoc. prof. elec. engring. Istanbul Tech. U., 1998—. Contbr. articles to profl. and academic jours. Mem. IEEE Power Engring. Soc., IEEE Engring. Mgmt. Soc., Chamber Elec. Engrs., Bus. Adminstrn. Alumni Assn. E-mail: nazif@elk.itu.edu.tr. Office: Istanbul Tech U, Dept Elec Engring, Maslak Istanbul TR-80626, Turkey

SOIFER, JACK, educational consulting company executive, engineer; b. Rio de Janeiro, May 5, 1940; arrived in Sweden, 1959; s. Izidor and Nina (Paskowsky) S.; m. Valkiria Frahya Freitas, Apr. 11, 1973. Cert. in bldg. engr., Esc. Tecnica Nacional, 1958; BA, U. Stockholm, Sweden, 1965; cert. ednl. media mgmt., Konrad Adenauer Stiftung, 1972; cert. in internat. trade, Inst. Cultura Juridica, 1973. Registered profl. engr., Brazil. Mng. dir. Radio & TV Educativa Amazonas, Manaus, Brazil, 1971-72; sr. rsch. officer Inst. Planejamento Econ. & Social, Rio de Janeiro, 1969-73; prof., instr. tech. Pont Universidade Catolica, Rio de Janeiro, 1971-73; trainer ednl. media producers Assn. Brazil Teleducacao, 1974; tng. dep. mgr. Mind do Brazil, 1975-76; ednl. media cons. UNESCO, Philippine and Cape Verde, 1976-79; tng. and indsl. cons. FIDE AB, Varnamo, Sweden, 1978-83; chief exec. officer, mng. dir. Swedish Ednl. Cons. & Mgmt., Varnamo, 1984—, Scandasia, Ltd. Furniture & Wooden Products, Jersey, Eng., 1988-93; pres., bd. dirs. Swedish Ednl. Cons. and Mgmt. HB, Varnamo, 1984—, Scandasia, Ltd., Jersey, 1988-93; bd. dirs. Liscan AB, Varnamo, Reftele Klammer, Varnamo, Scantrop Scandinavia AB, Gothemburg, 1988-93, Liscan Port Invest Lda, Lisbon, 1988-93, Sweduc Brasil, Brasilia, 1997—. Author: Manual De Teleducacao, 1974, (with others) Educacion Y Cambio Social, 1976, Training Personnel for ETV, 1970; contbr. articles to profl. jours. Mem. Rio State Commn. Instruct Broadcast, Rio de Janeiro, 1971; mem. jury 1st Ednl. Film Festival, Rio de Janeiro, 1971; del. ministry planning Ednl. Planning Confs., 1970-73; chief Brazilian del. UNESCO Meeting on Communications, Paris, 1969. Mem. Svenska Naturskyddsforening, Svenska Turistforening.

SOININEN, HILKKA SIRKKU, neurology educator; b. Kuopio, Finland, Aug. 28, 1950; d. Veikko Sulo and Aino Elina (Varinen) Koponen;m. Heikki Kalevi Soininen, Apr. 30, 1971; children: Katja, Petro, Ville-Veikko. MD, U. Helsinki, Finland, 1975; PhD, U. Kuopio, 1981. Specialist in neurology. Pvt. practice City of Hamina, Finland, 1975-77; acting dept. physician Kuopio U. Ctrl. Hosp., 1978-81, chief physician, 1987—; tchg. asst. neurol. dept. Kuopio U., 1981-87, acting assoc. prof. neurology med. faculty, 1987-88, acting prof. neurology, 1989-90, 95-99, acting prof. geriatrics, 1992, prof. neurology, 2000—; jr. rschr. Acad. Finland, 1988-91, 92-95; vis. prof. depts. psychiatry and pharmacology So. Ill. U. Sch. Medicine, Springfield, 1988-89. Reviewer jours. Duodecim, Neurobiology of Aging, Biol. Psychiatry; contbr. articles to profl. jours., chpts. to books. Mem. Finnish Med. Assn., Finnish Med. Soc. Duodecim, Brain Rsch. Soc. Finland, Finnish Neurol. Soc., Soc. Neurosci., Am. Acad. Neurology. Office: U Kuopio Dept Neurology, PO Box 1627, 70211 Kuopio Finland

SOKAL, ETIENNE MARC, pediatrician, consultant; b. Uccle, Bruxelles Capitale, Belgium, Oct. 2, 1959; s. Gerhardt and Anne Marie (Verboomen) S.; m. Anne Marie Hubert, Sept. 23, 1983; children: Perrine, Guillaume, Louis, Yves. MD, U. Louvain, Brussels, 1983, lic. in pediat., 1988, PhD, 1993. Hon. registrar in pediat. King's Coll. Hosp., London, 1986-88; cons. pediat. hepatologist Cliniques St. Luc, U. Louvain, Brussels, 1989—; assoc. prof. U. Louvain, 1993-1998, prof., 1998—. Editor: Management of Digestive and Liver Disorders in Infants and Children, 1993; assoc. editor: European Jour. Pediats., Acta Gastroenterologica Belgia; mem. editl. bd. Archives of Pediats., Pediat. Transplantation. Brit. Coun. fellow, 1987-88; recipient Nutricia Rsch. prize, 1991. Mem. Am. Assn. for the Study of the Liver, European Soc. Pediat., Gastroenterology and Nutrition (chair liver com.), Groupe Francophone Gastroenterology, Nutrition and Pediat. (v.p. 1992—), European Soc. Study of Liver, Belgian Royal Soc. Gastroenterology, Pediat. Rsch. Soc. (London), Soc. Francophone Recherche Pediat., Belgian Pediat. Soc. Avocations: bee keeping, mountain bike. E-mail: sokal@pedi.ucl.ac.be. Office: Cliniques St Luc U Louvain, 10/1301 ave Hippocrate, B-1200 Brussels Belgium

SOKARI, TOKUIBIYE GRAEME, science educator; b. Okrika, Rivers, Nigeria, July 1, 1946; s. Graeme Inichinbia and Janet Okoseimiema (Damieari) S.; m. Ayo Gabriel Oputibeya, Oct. 9, 1976; children: Orinasam Tokoni, Miabiye, Janet, Ikarama, Ipekere, Gabriel. BSc in Microbiology with honors, Ahmadu Bello U., Zaria, Nigeria, 1975; MSc in Food Tech., U. Reading, Eng., 1979; PhD, U. Strathclyde, Glasgow, Scotland, 1984. Tchr. chemistry and biology Okrika (Nigeria) Grammar Sch., 1969; tchr. chemistry and math. Archdeacon Crowther Meml. Girls' Sch., Elelenwo, Nigeria, 1970-71; microbiologist Gen. Hosp., Yola, 1975-76; health tutor Sch. Health Tech., Pt. Harcourt, Nigeria, 1976-84; lectr. U. Sci. & Tech., Pt. Harcourt, 1984—; consulting environ. scientist Shell Petroleum Devel. Co., Pt. Harcourt, 2000—. Contbr. articles to sci. jours. Choirmaster Protestant Chaplaincy, Abu, Zaria, 1973-75, Chapel of Redemption, U. Sci. and Tech., Pt. Harcourt, 1986-94, Glorious Covenant Ch., Pt. Harcourt, 1994-97. Grantee Internat. Found. for Sci., Sweden, 1987-91, Brit. Coun., 1988. Mem. Inst. Food Sci. and Tech., Internat. Soc. for Tropical Root Crops. Mem. Ch. of Nigeria. Home: Rd G U Sci/Tech Main Campus, Port Harcourt Rivers, Nigeria Office: U Sci and Tech, PMB 5080 Dept Biol Scis, Port Harcourt Rivers, Nigeria

SOKMEN, ATALAY, biologist, educator, researcher; b. Ankara, Turkey, Dec. 8, 1960; s. Halil Vehbi and Fadime (Balci) S.; m. Munevver Taskoparan, Sept. 20, 1986; children: Fatma Irem, Mehmet Celik. BSc, Hacettepe U., Ankara, 1984; MSc, Cumhuriyet U., Sivas, Turkey, 1988; PhD, Sheffield (Eng.) U., 1997. Rsch. asst. Cumhuriyet U., Sivas, 1985-99, asst. prof., 1999—. Avocations: sports, swimming, travel, reading. Office: Cumhuriyet U, Dept Biology, 58140 Sivas Turkey

SOKOL, ADOLF, endocrinologist, researcher; b. Vinnitza, Ukraine, USSR, June 9, 1930; arrived in Israel, 1991; s. Efraim and Necha (Zilberstein) S.; m. Klara Tzingiser, Mar. 5, 1960; children: Alla, Vitaliy. MD, Med. Inst. Vinnitza, 1954, PhD, 1968. Med. diplomate in endocrinology, Kharkov, Ukraine, 1963. Physician health svcs. Ukraine, 1954-57; head dept. therapeutics Dist. Hosp., Vinnitza, 1957-63; head dept. endocrinology Regional Endocrinology Prophylactic Ctr., Vinnitza, 1963-70; assoc. prof. Archangelsk, Russia, 1970-85, Med. Inst. Vinnitza, 1985-90; head Pub. Prophylactic Med. Ctr., Dimona, Israel, 1993—; Contbr. numerous articles to profl. publs. Author: Method of Increase of Pronstic and Diagnostic Efficacy in Addison's Disease, 1981, (monograph) Diagnostic Algorithms in Endocrinology, 1981, (monograph) The State of Hemodynamics in Chronic Adrenal Failure, 1967; contbr. articles to profl. jours., including Problems in Endocrinology, Ter Arkh, Vrach Delo, Pediatricia, others. Mem. Partisan Brigade, Ukraine, 1943-44. Mem. N.Y. Acad. Scis. Avocation: reading. Home: Golda Meir str 1034/43, 86058 Dimona Israel

SOKOL, BARNETT JEROME, electronics educator, consultant; b. N.Y.C., Feb. 9, 1942; arrived in Eng., 1971; s. Benjamin and Fanny (Frank) S.; m. Sibyl Ann Grundberg, Dec. 1973 (div.); m. Mary Isobel French, May. 29, 1987. BS, Columbia U., 1963, MA, 1967, MPhil, 1968, PhD, 1975. Tutor St. John's Coll., Santa Fe, 1968-71; temporary lectr. U. London, 1974-75, sr. lectr. lit., 1976—; cons. in electronics and computing., U.S., Eng., France,

Japan. Author: The Undiscover'd Country, 1993, Art and Illusion in The Winter's Tale, 1994, (with Mory Sokol) Shakespeare's Legal Language, 2000, (software program) Promotor, 1986; contbr. over 40 articles to profl. jours. Office: U London Goldsmiths' Coll, New Cross, London SE14 6NW, England

SOKOL, ROBERT JOSEF, haematologist consultant; b. Exeter, Eng., Apr. 13, 1944; s. Josef and Olive (Hobbs) S.; children: Nicola Elisabeth, Emma Katherine. MBChB, Sheffield (Eng.) U., 1968; MD, 1979, PhD, 1985, DSc, 1992. Cons. in Haematology Nat. Blood Svc., Eng., 1976—. Fellow Royal Coll. Pathologists, Royal Coll. Physicians; mem. Assn. Clin. Pathology, Brit. Soc. for Haematology, Brit. Blood Transfusion Soc., Brit. Med. Assn. Avocation: immuno and molecular archaeology. Office: Nat Blood Svc, Longley Ln, South Yorkshire Sheffield S57JN, England

SOKOLICHIN, ALEXANDER ALEXANDROVICH, statistician, fluid dynamics researcher; b. Moscow, Jan. 22, 1965; arrived in Fed. Republic Germany, 1991; s. Alexander Nikolayevich and Marina Sergueyevna (Muravyova) S. Diploma in Math., Karl Marx U., Leipzig, German Dem. Republic, 1985; diploma in Applied Math., Lomonosov U., Moscow, USSR, 1985, PhD in Math., 1988. Dep. dir. labor for identification controlled objects Moscow Steel and Alloys Inst., 1988-90; chief specialist State Assn. Mfrs. Fire Alarm Systems, Moscow, 1990-91; sci. researcher U. Stuttgart, Fed. Republic Germany, 1991—; reviewer Math. Reviews Am. Math. Soc., Providence, R.I., 1989—. Contbr. articles to profl. jours. Office: U Stuttgart ICVT, Böblingerstr 72, 70199 Stuttgart Germany

SOKOLOFF, DMITRY DMITRIEVICH, physicist; b. Moscow, Jan. 28, 1949; s. Dmitry Dmitrievich and Irina Grigorievna Korobanova) S.; m. Margarita Ingo Bujakaite, Sept. 10, 1970; children: Dmitry, Anna. MA, Moscow State U., 1972, PhD, 1974, DS, 1984. Leading rschr. computer ctr. Moscow State U., 1972-93, prof. maths., 1993—; astronomer Observatoire Paris, 1993-94; vis. prof. U. Exeter, England, 1996, Inst. Astronomy, Catania, Italy, 1997, U. Newcastle, Eng., 1998, Ben Gurion U. Negev, Beer-Sheva, Israel, 1999. Contbr. articles to profl. jours. Grantee Internat. Sci. Found., 1994, Civilian Rsch. & Devel. Found., Arlington, Va., 1996; vis. scholar I. Newton Inst., Cambridge, England, 1992. Mem. Russian Found. Basic Rsch. Avocations: ancient history, skiing. Home: 26-139 Litovsky Blvd, 117588 Moscow Russia Office: Moscow State U, Dept Physics, 119899 Moscow Russia

SOKOLOFF, DMITRY DMITRIEVICH, biologist, researcher, educator; b. Vilnius, USSR, Sept. 15, 1973; s. Dmitry Dmitrievich Sokoloff and Margarita Igno Bujakaite. MS, Moscow State U., 1995, PhD, 1998. Lectr. Moscow State U., 1997—; vis. rschr. Royal Bot. Gardens, Richmond, Eng., 1999. Co-author: Manual of Flowering Plants in Neighborhoods of White Sea Biological Station of Moscow Univeristy, 1996; co-editor: Spring Botanical Field Works on the Shores of Black Sea of Russia, 1998. Recipient award Premier Min. Russian Fedn., 1998; grantee Soros Found., 1992-93. Fellow Russian Bot. Soc., Moscow Soc. Naturalists (mem. editl. bd. Bul. Moscow Soc. Naturalists 1997—), Linnaean Soc. Avocation: travelling. Home: 26, Litovsky boul., 117588 Moscow Russia Office: Moscow U, Higher Plants Dept, 119899 Moscow Russia

SOKOLOV, ALEKSANDR IVANOVICH, physical sciences educator; b. Leningrad, U.S.S.R., Sept. 5, 1945; s. Ivan Alekseevich and Olga Ivanovna (Yakovleva) S.; m. Nadezhda Arkad'evna Lobanova, Feb. 26, 1969; children: Elena, Dmitrii. Grad., Leningrad Elec. Engring. Inst., 1969, PhD, 1972; DSc, A.F. Ioffe Physico-Tech. Inst., St. Petersburg, 1984. Jr. rschr. St. Petersburg State Electrotechnical U., 1972-74, sr. rshcr., 1974-79, assoc. prof., 1979-86; prof. St. Petersburg State Electrotechnical U., Russia, 1986—; lectr. State Optical Inst., St. Petersburg, 1988-89; mem. sci. coun. physics of ferroelectrics and dielectrics Russian Acad. Scis., Moscow, 1990—. Author: Ferroelectrics and Related Materials, 1984, Physics of Ferroelectrics Phenomena, 1985; editl. adv. bd. Fullerence Sci. and Tech., 1997-98; contbr. articles to profl. jours. Grantee Internat. Sci. Found., 1993, 98, 99, Ministry Higher Edn., 1993-95, 98—, Found. Intellectural Collaboration, 1993-97. Mem. St. Petersburg Union Scientists. Avocations: playing piano and guitar. Home: Basseinaya St 25 Apt 59, 196191 St Petersburg Russia Office: Electrotechnical Univ, Professor Popov St 5, 197376 St Petersburg Russia

SOKOLOV, BORIS ALEXANDROVICH, geologist, educator; b. Moscow, Dec. 30, 1930; s. Alexandr Ivanovich and Eugenia Alexandrovna Sokolov; m. Julia Nicolaevna Boutenko, Mar. 30, 1957; children: Sergey, Ekaterina. PhD, Moscow State U., 1963, D of Geology, 1978. Prof. geology Moscow State U., 1980—, dean geology dept., head fossil fuel geology chair, 1992—. Author: Evolutional Dynamic Criteria of Oil Potential of the Earth Interiors, 1985, numerous other books; contbr. over 600 articles to profl. jours. Mem. Internat. Acad. High Edn., Russian Acad. Scis. (corr.), Russian Acad. Natural Scis., Moscow Soc. Nat. Investigators. Office: Moscow State U, Vorobijevy Gory, 119899 Moscow Russia

SOKOLOV, PJOTR ALEXEJEVITCH, agricultural studies educator; b. Votkinsk, USSR, Sept. 20, 1933; s. Alexej Nikolajevitch and Antonina Nikolajevna (Belonogova) S.; m. Dina Vasiljevna Yarantzeva, Feb. 1, 1957; 1 child, Irina Petrovna. Cert. engr. forest economy, Povolzhsky Forest Engr. Inst., USSR, 1958; Candidate of Agrl. Scis., Uralsky Forest Engr. Inst., Sverdlovsk, USSR, 1969; D Agrl. Scis., Leningrad Forest Engr. Acad., 1981. Mem. Russian Acad. Natural Scis. (corr.), Internat. Acad. Scis. and Ecology and Life Activity (academician 1996). Engr., taxator Novosibirskaya Office of Forest Raw Materials Investigations, USSR, 1958-59; forest protection inspector Votkinsky (USSR) Forest Arrangement, 1959-62; tchr., docent, prof. Mari Polytechnic, Yoskar-Ola, USSR, 1962-82, dep. dean forest economy faculty, 1975-81, rector, prof., 1982-87, prof., head forest-taxation and forest arrangement dept., 1987—, sci. supr., 1998—; docent Higher Attestation Commn., Moscow, 1971, prof., 1983. Contbr. articles to profl. jours. Dep. Supreme Soviet of the Mari ASSR, Yoshkar-Ola, 1980, 85. Named Honored Man of Sci. Adminstrn. of Pres. of Russian Fedn., 1999, Supreme Soviet of the Mari Autonomous Soviet Socialist Republic. Mem. Europe Forest Inst. Russian Orthodox. Home: 155 Komsomolskaya Str 5, 424000 Yoshkar-Ola Russia

SOKOLOV, RICHARD SAUL, real estate company executive; b. Phila., Dec. 7, 1949; s. Morris and Estelle Rita (Steinberg) S.; m. Susan Barbara Saltzman, Aug. 13, 1972; children: Lisa, Anne, Kate. BA, Pa. State U., 1971; JD, Georgetown U., 1974. Assoc. Weinberg & Green, Balt., 1974-80, ptnr., 1980-82; v.p., gen. counsel The Edward J. DeBartolo Corp., Youngstown, Ohio, 1982-86, sr. v.p. devel., gen. coun., 1986-94; pres., CEO DeBartolo Realty Corp., Youngstown, Ohio, 1994-96; pres., COO Simon DeBartolo Group, Indpls., 1996-98; pres, COO Simon Property Group, Indpls., 1998—. Mem. investment com. Jewish Fedn., Youngstown, 1992—; trustee U. Wis.-Madison Ctr. for Urban Land Econs. Rsch., Youngstown/Mahoning Valley United Way. Mem. Internat. Coun. Shopping Ctrs. (trustee 1994—, chmn. 1998-99), Urban Land Inst. (assoc.). Office: Simon Property Group 115 W Washington St Ste 1465 Indianapolis IN 46204-3464

SOKOLOV, STANISLAV VLADIMIROVICH, geologist, researcher; b. Moscow, Nov. 15, 1936; s. Vladimir Ivanovich Sokolov and Nadezda Ivanovna Veneva; m. Nelja Evdokimovna Shestakova, Nov. 1, 1963; children: Olga, Olesja. Diploma, Moscow State U., 1961, diploma in geology and mineral scis., 1972. Sci. researcher VIMS, Moscow, 1964-72, sr. sci. researcher, 1972—. Co-author: Thermobarometry of Ultrabasic Parageneses, 1988; contbr. articles to profl. jours. Avocations: jazz, sports. Fax: 7-095-959-3447. E-mail: vims@df.ru. Home: Akademik Iljushin 5 Fl 10, 125319 Moscow Russia Office: VIMS, Staromonetnyi per 31, 109017 Moscow Russia

SOKOLOV, SVIATOSLAV SERGEEVICH, physicist; b. Odessa, Ukraine, Aug. 31, 1953; s. Sergey Konstantinovich and Svetlana Savvovna (Plaxienko) S.; m. Anna Ivanovna Tchetchina, July 22, 1978; children: Helene, Sergey. Master's, State U., Kharkov, Ukraine, 1975; PhD, Inst. Low Temp. Physics, Kharkov, Ukraine, 1984. Engr. Inst. Low Temp. Physics, 1975-83, sci. rschr., 1983-89, sr. sci. rschr., 1989—; vis. prof. Fed. U., São Carlos, Brazil, 1994, 96-97, 98—. Author: Introduction to Physics of Helium, 1993. Avocations: classical musics, scientific fiction. Home: Apt 52 1/3 Armianskii per, 310003 Kharkov Ukraine Office: B Verkin Inst Low Temp Phys, Engring 47 Lenin Ave, 310164 Kharkov Ukraine also: Dept de Fisica, Depart de Fisica UFSCar, 13565-905 São Carlos SP, Brazil

SOKOLOV, VICTOR FEDOROVICH, mathematics and control theory educator, researcher; b. Syktyvkar, Russia, Aug. 28, 1952; s. Klavdiya Petrovna Sokolova; m. Elena Vladilenovna Ziskindovich, Sept. 19, 1972. Diploma in Math. and Mechanics, St. Ptersburg State U., Russia, 1974, PhD in Math. and Mechanics, 1979, DSc, 1999. Asst. prof. Syktykvar State U., 1977-81, sr. lectr., 1981-89, assoc. prof., 1989-99, prof., 1999—; sr. rschr. Komi Rsch. Ctr. Russian Acad. Scis., Russia, 1993—. Recipient rsch. grant Russian Ministry of Edn., 1993-95, 98—, rsch. grant Russian Fund of Basic Rsch., 1996—. Office: Syktyvkar State Univ, 55 Oktyabrsky Prospekt, 167001 Syktyvkar Russia

SOKOLOV, VICTOR IVANOVICH, physicist; b. Nev'yansk, Russia, Feb. 2, 1941; s. Ivan Jakovlevich Kharchevnikov and Pelageya Aleksandrovna Sokolova; m. Tatyana Georgievna Kryukova, July 29, 1976; children: Aleksei, Kseniya. BS, Ural State U., Sverdlovsk, Russia, 1964; postgrad. Inst. Semiconductors, Russian Acad. Scis., Leningrad, 1967-71; PhD Inst. Metal Physics, Russian Acad. Scis., Sverdlovsk, 1973, DSc, 1988. Asst. Ural State U., 1965-67; from jr. to sr. scientist Inst. Metal Physics-Russian Acad. Scis., 1971-90, head scientist, 1990-98, prin. scientist, 1999—; mem. specialized sci. coun. Ural State Tech. U., 2000. Contbr. articles to profl. jours. Grantee Am. Phys. Soc., 1993, Internat. Sci. Found.-Russian Govt., 1994-95. Mem. D.S. Rozhdestvensky Optical Soc. Avocation: Pushkin poetry. Home: Khrustalnaya str 35-67, 620138 Ekaterinburg Russia Office: Inst Metal Physics UB RAS, S Kovalevskaya str 18, 620219 Ekaterinburg GSP 170, Russia

SOKOLOV, VLADYSLAV MIKHAILOVICH, metallurgist, researcher; b. Zhitomir, Ukraine, July 6, 1954; s. Mihail Alekseevich and Eleonora Leontevna (Koliakova) S. PhD, Moscow Inst. Steels and Alloys, 1983; DS, State Metall. Acad. Ukraine, Dnepropetrovsk, 1994. Engr. Vladimir Poly. Inst., Russia, 1977-80; sci. worker, leading sci. worker Physico-Tech. Inst. Metals and Alloys, Nat. Acad. Sci., Kiev, Ukraine, 1983—. author: (with L.A. Kovalchuk) Thermodynamics of Metalloids Activity in Casting Melts, 1988, Thermodynamics of Metalloids and Non-metallic Inclusions in Liquid and Solidificating Steel, 1992; patentee method of ALNICO alloy melting. Grantee Sci. and Tech. Ctr. Ukraine, 1997. Mem. ASM Internat. Materials. Home: 73 A Vernadsky Ave Apt 21, 252142 Kiev Ukraine Office: Physico-Tech Inst Metals, 34/1 Vernadsky Ave, 03 680 Kiev 142, Ukraine

SOKOLOVA, EKATERINA PETROVNA, physical chemist, researcher; b. Dushanbe, Russia, Oct. 7, 1941; d. Piotr N. Sokolov and Ekaterina D. Karpova; m. Anatoly N. Marinichev, June 12, 1965; 1 child, Alexey. PhD in Sci., Leningrad State U., 1968; DSc, St. Petersburg State U., Russia, 1990, cert. prof., 1992. Jr. rschr. Leningrad State U., 1967-79, sr. rschr., 1979-90; leading rschr. dept. chemistry St. Petersburg State U., 1990—; invited lectr. Leipzig (Germany) U., 1993-97. Contbr. articles to sci. jours. Grantee Internat. Sci. Found., 1994-95. Avocation: gymnastics. E-mail: esok@evergreen.spb.tu Fax: 7-812-4286939. Office: St Petersburg State U, Universitetski pr 2, 198904 Saint Petersburg Russia

SOKOLOW, ALAN EUGENE, health facility administrator; b. Pasadena, Calif., Dec. 6, 1950; s. William and Mildred Plows S.; m. Robin Hutchison Barnum, Nov. 6, 1977; children: Morgan Millicent, Schuyler Constance, Calder Barnum, Wendy Campbell. BA cum laude, Pomona Coll., 1972; MD, UCLA, 1976. Diplomate Am. Bd. Internal Medicine. Resident in internal medicine U. Utah, Salt Lake City, 1976-79; oncology fellow U. Rochester, N.Y., 1980; attending physician Stamford (Conn.) Hosp., 1980-81; from attending physician to chmn. emergency dept. Norwalk (Conn.) Hosp., 1981-95; v.p. med. programs Oxford Health, Norwalk, 1995-99; chief med. officer Intelliclaim, Norwalk, 1999-2000, Empire Blue Cross Blue Shield, N.Y.C., 2000—; med. adv. bd. Intelliclaim, Norwalk, 2000—, Innovative Clin. Solutions, Syosset, N.Y., 2000—. Fellow Am. Coll. Emergency Physicians. E-mail: asokolow@optonline.net. Office: Empire Blue Cross Blue Shield One World Trade Ctr New York NY 10048

SOKOVNIN, OLEG MICKAILOVICH, electrical engineer, educator; b. Slobodskoy, Russia, Nov. 6, 1958; s. Mickail Semyonovih Sokovnin and Esfira Naumovna Brik; m. Tatyana Nikolayevna Sokovnina, Dec. 10, 1983 (div. Oct. 1996); 1 child, Artem Sokovnin. Degree in Elec. Engring., Vyatka State Tech. U., Kirov, 1981; Degree Candidate Tech. Sci., Kazan State Tech. U., 1989; D in Tech. Scis., Arkhangelst State Tech. U., 1998. Engr. Vyatka State Tech. U., Kirov, 1983-87, jr. rschr., 1987-89, rschr., 1990-91, sr. rschr., 1992-95, doctoral rschr., 1995-98, asst. prof., chair electrical engring. and electronics, 1998-2000, prof., chair elec. engring./electronics, head environ. sci., 1999—; cons. Biochemical Plant, Kirov, 1987-90, Selash Plant, Kirov, 1989-96, Maragrine Plant, 1994-97, Alcohol-Wine Plant, 1994-98, Refrigerating Machinery Plant, 1995-99, Power Sta. N#4, Kirov, 1997—. Contbr. numerous articles to profl. jours. Sr. lt. Armed Forces, 1981-83. Rsch. grantee Ministry Higher Edn., 1997. Mem. N.Y. Acad. Sci. Avocations: chess, swimming, skiing. Home: UL Komosomolskaya 113 KV183, 610014 Kirov Russia Office: Vyatka State Tech. U., UL Moskovskaya 36, 610000 Kirov Russia

SOLAN, ALEXANDER, mechanical engineering educator; b. Warsaw, Poland, Dec. 2, 1934; arrived in Israel, 1945; s. Eljasz and Margot (Slotowski) Solowiejczyk; m. Gabriella Gutkowski, Aug. 18, 1957; children: Alona, Yoram. BSME, Technion, Haifa, Israel, 1957, Engr., 1959, MS, 1963; PhD, Brown U., 1966. Dean faculty mech. engring. Technion, Haifa, 1973-75, prof., 1977—, dean grad. sch., 1978-80, v.p. for rsch., 1983-86, Y. Winograd chair fluid mechanics and heat transfer, 1983—, v.p. for acad. affairs, 1991-94, sr. v.p., 1995-96; mem. Israeli Nat. Coun. for Rsch. and Devel., 1980-82, Israel Coun. for Higher Edn., 1987. Contbr. numerous sci. articles on fluid mechanics and heat and mass transfer to profl. jours. Fellow ASME; mem. Am. Phys. Soc. Hom: 101 Einstein St, 34601 Haifa Israel Office: Technion, 32000 Haifa Israel

SOLANKI, MANISHKUMAR MEGHAJIBHAI, textile technologist; b. Ahmedabad, Gujarat, India, Oct. 14, 1944; s. Meghajibhai Ramajibhai and Maniben Hakubhai (Chauhan) S.; divorced, May, 1971. Third Yr. BS in Physics, Gujarat U., Ahmedabad, 1966. trainer textile personnel, 1998. Lab. asst. Ahmedabad Textile Industry's Rsch. Assn., 1966—, sr. scientific asst., 1983—, in-charge physical testing, 1990-94, textile calibrator, 1996-99. Mem. Textile Assn. India (assoc.), Camera Club Karnavati (life). Hindu. Avocations: photography, swimming, excercising, reading, writing. Home: 207 Umiya Apt, 380 061 Ahmedabad Gujarat, India Office: ATIRA, Po-Ambawadi Vistar, 380015 Ahmedabad Gujarat, India

SOLARI, GIAOVANNI, engineering educator; b. Benova, Liguria, Italy, Jan. 9, 1953; s. Renato and Emilia S.; m. Simonetta Santus, Dec. 6, 1986; children: Davide, Matteo. Degree in engring., U. Genova, Italy, 1977. Asst. prof. U. Genova, 1983-88, assoc. prof., 1988-90, prof., 1991—, head dept. DISEG, 1997—, also bd. dirs.; prof. U. Calabria, Italy, 1990-91. Editor: (books) Proc. 2nd Eur. and AfR. Conf. Wind Engng, 1997, Wind Energy and Landscape, 1997, (jours.) Nonlinear & Stochastic Dyn. in Wind Engng., 1998, Hyundai Industry Forum on Wind Engng, 1999; editor in chief: Wind & Strutures, 1998—. Mem. ASCE (mem. probablistic methods com. 1999—), Italian Assn. Wind Engng. (pres. 1999—), Internat. Assn. Wind Engng. (chmn. European and African Group 1995—, mem. adv. bd. 1997—). Office: Diseg U Genova, Via Montallegro 1, 16145 Genova Italy

SOLARI, LUCA, educator, consultant; b. Trento, Italy, Apr. 21, 1966; s. Attilio and Giuliana (Furlani) S.; m. Ornella Cappabianca, Oct. 2, 1993; 1 child, Enrico. Grad., Bocconi U., Milan, Italy, 1991, PhD in Bus., 1997; Internat. Tchrs. Program, London Bus. Sch., 1997. Asst. rschr. Bocconi U., 1991-96, asst. prof., 1996-98; asst. prof. U. Trento, Italy, 1998—; cons. EOS, Milan, 1996-99; mem. faculty MBA Bocconi, Milan, 1998—. Author: Organization Design for Insurance Companies, (in Italian) 1999, Social Labor, 1999; co-author: Lean Organization, 1999. Elected mem. Green Party, Trento, 1990. Office: Univ Trento, Via Inama 5, 38100 Trento Italy

SOLBRIG, INGEBORG HILDEGARD, German literature educator, writer; b. Weissenfels, Germany, July 31, 1923; came to U.S., 1961, naturalized, 1966; d. Reinhold J. and Hildegard M.A. (Ferchland) S. Grad. in chemistry, U. Halle, Germany, 1948; BA summa cum laude, San Francisco State U., 1964; postgrad., U. Calif., Berkeley, 1964-65; MA, Stanford U., 1966, PhD in Humanities and German, 1969. Asst. prof. U. R.I., 1969-70, U. Tenn., Chattanooga, 1970-72, U. Ky., Lexington, 1972-75; assoc. prof. German U. Iowa, 1975-81, prof., 1981-93, prof. emerita, 1993—. Author: Hammer-Purgtall und Goethe, 1973; main editor Rilke Heute, Beziehungen und Wirkungen, 1975; translator, editor; (bilingual edit.) Reinhard Goering: Seeschlacht/Seabattle, 1977, Orient-Rezeption, 1996; author: Modulationen von Gold und Licht in Goethes Kunstmärchen, 1997; mem. editl. bd. Kairoer Germanistische Studien, Vol. 9 and Vol. 10, 1998, Multiculturalism in Literary Criticism: A German-American Perspective, 1998, J.G. Herder: Echo of the Cultural Philospher's Ideas in Early African-American Intellectual Writing, 2000; contbr. numerous articles, revs. and transls. to profl. jours., chpts. to books. Mem. Iowa Gov.'s Com. on 300th Anniversary German-Am. Rels. 1683-1983, 1983. Recipient Hammer-Purgstall Gold medal Austria, 1974; named Ky. col., 1975; fellow Austrian Ministry Edn., 1968-69, Stanford U., 1965-66, 68-69; Old Gold fellow Iowa, 1977; Am. Coun. Learned Socs. grantee; German Acad. Exch. Svc. grantee, 1980; sr. faculty rsch. fellow in the humanities, 1983; NEH grantee, 1985; May Brodbeck fellow in the humanities, 1989; numerous summer faculty rsch. grants. Mem. MLA (life), Internat. Verein fur Germanische Sprach und Lit. Wiss., Goethe Gesellschaft, Deutsche Schiller Gesellschaft, Am. Soc. for 18th Century Studies, Can. Soc. for 18th Century Studies, Goethe Soc. N.Am., Inc. (founding mem.), Egyptian Soc. Lit. Criticism. Prin. Rsch. Interest: transcultural, interdisciplinary studies. Avocations: horseback riding, photography, writing, travel. Home: 1126 Pine St Iowa City IA 52240-5711

SOLDATENKOV, VIATCHESLAV ALEXANDROVICH, cell and molecular biologist, researcher; b. Moscow, Feb. 17, 1956; came to U.S., 1992; s. Alexander A. and Nina G. (Rodionov) S.; m. Elena I. Bogrash, Dec. 25, 1979; children: Darya, Maria. MD, Pirogov Med. Sch., Moscow, 1979; PhD, Inst. Biophys., Moscow, 1983. Rschr. Inst. Biophys., Moscow, 1983-86, sr. rschr., 1986-90; leading sr. rschr. Inst. Geochem. Analytical Chemistry, Moscow, 1990-92; acad. rsch. assoc. Georgetown U. Med. Ctr., Washington, 1993-96, asst. prof., 1996-99, assoc. prof., 1999—. Contbr. articles and reviews to sci. jours. Postdoctoral fellow Georgetown U. MEd. Ctr., 1992-93; recipient Investigator award Inst. Biophys., 1983, 85, Rsch. award Georgetown U., 1997; Rsch. grantee U.S. Army, 1999. Mem. AAAS, Am. Assn. Cancer Rsch., Radiation Rsch. Soc. (travel award 1999), N.Y. Acad. Sci. Achievements include development of novel anti-cancer therapies. Avocations: travel, fencing, tennis. Office: Georgetown U Med Ctr TRB E204 3970 Reservoir Rd NW Washington DC 20007-2126

SOLDATOS, GERASIMOS THEODORE, economics educator; b. Athens, Greece, July 14, 1956; s. Theodore Gerasimos and Stavroula Spyros (Troumbeta) S.; m. Maria Vasilios S., Aug. 31, 1978; children: Stavroula, Theodore, Eleni, Vasiliki, Anastasios. BSc in Econs., U. Athens, Greece, 1979; MA in Econs., Clark U., Worcester, Mass., 1983, PhD in Econs., 1985. Lectr. in econs. U. Macedonia, Thessaloniki, Greece, 1991-94, asst. prof. econs., 1994—. Contbr. numerous articles to profl. jours. Served with Greek Army, 1985-86. Mem. Am. Econ. Assn. Christian Orthodox. Avocations: outdoors, music, history, philosophy. Home: Anakreondos 8, 54250 Thessaloniki Greece Office: Dept Econs, U Macedonia-Egnatia 156, 54006 Thessaloniki Greece

SOLDO, IVAN, epidemiologist, educator; b. Novska, Slavonia, Croatia, July 15, 1943; s. Rudolf and Kata (Šaravanja) S.; m. Marinka Krmpotic, Dec. 29, 1973; children: Maja, Ivana. MD, U. Zagreb, Croatia, 1968; diploma, U. Zagreb, 1974, Dr. Sci. Medicine, 1981. Clin. asst. Sch. Medicine, Zagreb, 1974-83; head dept. U. Hosp. Infectology, Zagreb, 1984-95; asst. prof. U. Zagreb, Zagreb, 1984-89, prof., 1989—; head dept. Infectology U. Hosp., Osijek, Croatia, 1995—; chmn. dept. Infectology U. Osijek, 1998—; cons. Kidney Transplant program, Croatia, 1978-95, Bone Marrow Transplant program, Croatia, 1986-91, Infectious Diseases, Croatian Olympic Com., 1994-98. Author: Infections in Immunocompromised Patients, 1986, Viral Dieseases- Protection and Treatment, 1990, Health Consults for Sailors, 1990, Croatia Hospitals on Target, 1992. Mem. Croation Red Cross, 1980. Mem. Infectious Disease Soc. Croation Med. Assn. , Internat. Immunocomrpromised Host. Soc., Internat. Assn. Infectious Diseases. Roman Catholic. Avocations: tennis, skiing, fishing. Office: U Hosp, Dept Infectious Diseases, HR-31000 Osijek Croatia

SOLECKI, DIETER, mathematician, consultant; b. Gelsenkirchen, NRW, Germany, Apr. 10, 1959; s. Bruno and Anni (Bröse) S. Diploma in Math., U. Dortmund, Germany, 1983, PhD in Math., 1986. Sci. asst. dept. computer sci. Tech. U., Munich, Germany, 1986-90; cons. Creative Views EDV-Beratung, Munich, 1990—. Grantee: Fritz ter Meer-Stiftung, Leverkusen, 1983, Begabtenförderung des Landes NRW, 1983-86. Mem. Am. Assn. for Artificial Intelligence, Gesellschaft für Informatik, Mensa. Avocations: dancing, folk dancing, contact improvisation. Home and Office: Creative Views EDV-Beratung, Zentnerstr 15, D-80798 Munich Germany

SOLGA, HEIKE, sociologist, researcher; b. Berlin, July 28, 1964; d. Horst and Jutta (Jendroczek) S. Diploma, Humboldt U., Berlin, 1988; MA, Stanford U., 1991; PhD, Free U., Berlin, 1994. Rschr. WZB-Wissenschaftszentrum Berlin for Social Forschung, 1991; fellow Max Planck Inst. for Human Devel., Berlin, 1992-95, sci. rschr., 1995-99, head rsch. group, 1999—; rep. sci. staff sci. bd. Max Planck Soc., Munich, 1996—, senator, 1999—; vis. scholar Harvard U., Cambridge, Mass., 1997. Author: Auf dem Weg in eine klassenlose Gesellschaft?, 1995 (Otto Hohn prize Max Planck Soc. 1996); contbr. articles to profl. jours. Fulbright scholar Stanford U., 1990-91. Mem. ISA (rsch. com.), German Am. Acad. Coun. (orgn. com. German-Am. frontiers of the social and behavioral scis. 1998-2000), German Sociol. Assn. (social inequality sect.). Avocations: classical music, dance, reading, travel. Home: Niebuhrstr 76, 10629 Berlin Germany Office: Max Planck Inst Human Devel, Lentzeallee 94, 14195 Berlin Germany

SOLHEIM, BJARTE GEES, transfusion medicine physician, educator; b. Galati, Romania, May 4, 1941; arrived in Norway, 1947; s. Magne and Cilgia (Gees) S.; m. Karin Owren, Sept. 11, 1962; children: Sigurd, Eivind, Ingar, Sturla. MD, U. Bergen, Norway, 1965; PhD, U. Oslo, 1972, MHA, 1997. Rsch. fellow Norwegian Def. Inst., 1967; rsch. fellow sect. immunology Inst. Exptl. Med. Rsch. U. Oslo, 1968-71; chief resident Inst. Transplantation Immunology Rikshospitalet, The Nat. Hosp., Oslo, 1972-78, chief physician blood bank and immunohematol. lab., 1979-87; med. dir. Red Cross and Nat. Hosp. Blood Ctr., Oslo, 1988-95; chief physician unit for advanced transfusion medicine Inst. of Immunology, Rikshospitalet, The Nat. Hosp., Oslo, 1996—; prof. transfusion medicine dept. group for lab. medicine U. Oslo, The Nat. Hosp., 1991—; mem. expert com. on quality assurance in transfusion medicine The Coun. of Europe, 1995—; chmn. Norwegian reference com. for standardization in med. informatics The Norwegian Gen. Standardizing Body, 1996—; head Norwegian del. Internat. Standardization Orgn., TC215, 1998—; mem. Norwegian Bd. Transfusion Medicine, 1996-99; head Electronic Data Processing bd. The Nat. Hosp., Oslo, 1980-82; prin. lectr. immunohematology H.S. for Biomed. Engrs., Nat. Hosp., 1973—; prin. lectr. in transfusion medicine Faculty of Medicine, U. Oslo, 1988—; tech. auditor European Cmtys. preparatory Advanced Informatics in Medicine Program, 1990; mem. steering group Nordic rsch. program Sys. Devel. Environments and Profession Oriented Langs., 1982-89, Nordic devel. program Nordic Advanced Informatics in Medicine, 1991-96; spkr. in field. Author 10 books; contbr. numerous articles to profl. jours. Lt. Norwegian Navy, 1966. Mem. AAAS, The Transplantation Soc., Internat. Med. Informatics Assn. (bd. dirs. 1990-97, sec. 1991-97), Internat. Soc. for Blood Transfusion (program. com. XXV Congress 1998), Internat. Union Immunol. Socs., Am. Assn. Blood Banks, Internat. Soc. for Hematotherapy and Graft Engring., Norwegian Med. Assn. (head informatics com. 1984-00, head specialty bd. for immunology and transfusion medicine 1990—), Norwegian Med. Informatics Soc. (pres. 1984-90, v.p. 1990-94), N.Y. Acad. Scis., European Fedn. Med. Informatics, Norwegian Wine Acad. Avocations: skiing, tracking, sailing, gardening, wine tasting. Fax: 23073510. Office: Inst Immunology, Rikshospitalet, N-0027 Oslo Norway

SOLIDUM, JAMES, finance and insurance executive; b. Honolulu, Mar. 12, 1925; s. Narciso and Sergia (Yabo) S.; student U. Hawaii, 1949-50; m. Vickie Mayo, Aug. 14, 1954; children: Arlin James, Nathan Francis, Tobi John, Kamomi Teresa. BA, U. Oreg., 1953. Promotional salesman Tongg Pub. Co., 1953-54; editor Fil-Am. Tribune, 1954-55; master planning technician Fed. Civil Svc., 1955-57; publs. editor Hawaii Sugar Planters Assn., 1957; field agt. Grand Pacific Life Ins. Co., 1957-59, home office asst., 1959-60, supr., 1960-62, asst. v.p., 1962-64; propr. J. Solidum & Assos., Honolulu, 1964—; pres. Fin. Devel. Inst., 1967—; contbg. writer Paradise of Pacific Mag., 1957-58, Hawaii Agrl. Mag., 1957-58; gen. ptnr. R.Z. Limited Partnership, 1981—; v.p. Grand Pacific Life Ins. Co., 1983-90; bd. dirs. Hawaii Econ. Devel. Corp., 1982-89. Mem. adv. com. Honolulu dist. SBA, 1971-77; bd. advisors Philippine Consulate of Hawaii, 1959. Pres., Keolu Elem. P.T.A., 1960-62; mem. satisfaction com. Hawaii Visitors Bur., 1963-66; chmn. budget and rev. panel IV, Aloha United Fund, 1966-72, bd. dirs., 1971-77, 82-88, chmn. bd., 1984; mem. mgmt. svcs. com., 1977, mem. cen. com., 1977-82, chmn. budget and allocations com., 1982-84; chmn. Kamehameha Dist. fin. com. Aloha coun. Boy Scouts Am., 1966; vice chmn. Businessmen's Cancer Crusade, 1965; chmn. Operation Bayanihan, Hawaii Immigration Task Force, 1970; participant Oahu Housing Workshop, State of Hawaii, Hawaii chpt. HUD, 1970; mem. task force on housing and transp. Alternative Econ. Futures for Hawaii, 1973; chmn. Bicentennial Filipiniana, 1976; chmn. SBA Bicentennial Com., 1976; campaign chmn. State Rep. Rudolph Pacarro, 1964-68; mem. exec. com. Campaign for Reelection U.S. Senator Hiram L. Fong, 1970, Gov. William Quinn for U.S. Senate, 1976; Rep. candidate for Hawaii Ho. of Reps., 1972; mem. Rep. Citizens Task Force on Housing, 1973; trustee St. Louis Alumni Found., 1970—, Kuakini Med. Ctr., 1984-86, Palama Settlement, 1975-82, v.p., 1976, treas., 1980-82; bd. mgrs. Windward YMCA, 1964-67; bd. advisers St. Louis H.S., 1963-64; bd. govs. Goodwill Industries, 1964; bd. dirs. Children's Ctr., Inc., 1975-77, Hawaii Multi-Cultural Arts Ctr., 1977-81, treas., 1979; fin. fin. chmn. St. Stephen's Parish Coun., 1974—; bd. dirs. St. Louis Fine Arts Ctr., 1985-88. With U.S. Army, 1945-47. C.L.U. Recipient Man of Year award Filipino C. of C., 1965; cert. of merit Aloha United Fund, 1971; Wisdom mag. honor award, 1974; Outstanding Alumnus honor medal St. Louis High Sch., 1976. Mem. Hawaii State C. of C. (bd. dirs. 1964-67, chmn. legis. com. 1966-67, v.p. 1970, chmn. election judges 1971, mem. ad hoc com. bus.-youth rels. 1970), Filipino C. of C. (past pres. 1965, com. chmn.), Am. Soc. CLU, Honolulu Assn. Life Underwriters (bd. dirs. 1963-66, del. nat. conv. 1967, chmn. life underwriters tng. coun. 1962-67), Hawaii Estate Planning Coun., Hawaii Plantation Indsl. Editors Assn. (sec.-treas. 1957), St. Louis Alumni Assn. (bd. dirs. 1964—, chmn. fin. 1969-75, pres. 1976, treas. 1977—), Phi Kappa Sigma. Republican. Roman Catholic. Home: 2622 Waolani Ave Honolulu HI 96817-1362 Office: 225 Queen St Apt 12-a Honolulu HI 96813-4603

SOLIMAN, ABDALLA MAHMOUD, psychology educator, researcher; b. Edfou, Egypt, Jan. 19, 1933; s. Mahmoud Mohammad Soliman and Amna Aly Mahmoud; m. Nagat Ahmad Awad; 1 child, Amel Abdalla. BA, Cairo U., 1955; MA, U. Minn., 1964, PhD, 1967. Counseling psychologist, cons. Am. U., Cairo, 1969-74; asst. to assoc. prof. psychology Cairo U., 1973-78; assoc. prof. to prof. psychology Kuwait U., Kuwait City, 1974-91; prof. psychology United Arab Emirates U., Al-Ain, 1991—, chmn. dept. psychology, 1992-96; vis. scholar Torrance Ctr., U. Ga., Atlanta, 1985-86; acad. coord. faculty humanities and social sci., United Arab Emirates U., 1994-95; counselor Psychology Edn. Clinic, Ain Shams U., Egypt, 1959-61. Mem. editl. bd., adviser Internat. Jour. Advnacement of Counseling, 1978—, Jour. Edn., United Arab Emirates, 1992-94, Jour. Humanities and Social Scis., 1995-97; contbr. articles to profl. jours. Mem. APA, ACA, Internat. Assn. Counseling (exec. coun. 1974-85), Maadi Club (Cairo). Avocation: writing for cultural media on psychological topics. Office: UAE Univ Dept Psychology, PO Box 17771, Al-Ain United Arab Emirates

SOLIMAN, ATEF SHAFIK, geneticist, educator; b. Kewisna, Egypt, Dec. 5, 1937; s. Shafik and Hanouna Hanna (Atia) S.; m. Marie Takla Soliman, Sept. 5, 1965; children: Edward, Emad, Michael. BS, Alexandria (Egypt) U., 1958; MS, Kans. State U., 1962, PhD, 1963. Rsch. asst. Kans. State U., Manhattan, 1960-63; asst. prof. Faculty Agr.-Alexandria U., 1963-72, assoc. prof., 1972-83, prof., 1983-85, prof., head dept. botany, 1985—; Established rsch. unit on microtechnique and cytogenetics Ministry Edn., Iraq, 1977. Co-author: Teaching and Counseling Gifted and Talented Adolescents, 1993. Fellow Fulbright Commn., Egypt, 1987, fellow St. John's U. Ctr. for Study of Learning and Tchg. Styles, N.Y., 1990; scholar NASA, Houston, 1990. Mem. Genetics Soc. Egypt, Genetics Soc. Am., Am. Soc. Agronomy, Sigma Xi, Gamma Sigma Delta. Avocations: hockey, volleyball, basketball, swimming. Home: 38 El-Morsleen Al-American, 21411 Alexandria Schutz, Egypt Office: Alexandria Univ Faculty Agr, Saba-Pacha, 21531 Alexandria Egypt

SOLIMAN, KARAM FARAH ATTIA, pharmacy educator; b. Cairo, Oct. 15, 1944; came to the U.S., 1968; s. Farah Attia and Elaine (Kellini) S.; m. Samia Gorgy Sidhom, Aug. 2, 1973; children: John, Gina, Mark, Mary. BS, Cairo U., 1964; MS, U. Ga., 1971, PhD, 1972. Asst. prof. Sch. Vet. Medicine Tuskegee (Ala.) U., 1972-75; assoc. prof. Fla. A&M U.-Coll. Pharmacy, Tallahassee, 1975-79, prof., 1979—, chmn. divsn. basic pharm. sci., 1981—, asst. dean, 1993—, disting. prof., 1997—. Author: (with others) Practical Clinical Pharmacy, 1977, Chronopharmacology and Chronotherapeutics, 1981; contbr. articles to profl. jours. Rsch. grantee NIH. Mem. Am. Assn. Coll. Pharmacy, Am. Soc. Pharmacology and Exptl. Therapeutics, Am. Physiol. Soc., Neurosci. Soc., Endocrine Soc. Democrat. Avocations: reading, gardening. Fax: 850-599-3667. E-mail: ksoliman@famu.edu. Home: 5358 Pembridge Pl Tallahassee FL 32308-6800 Office: Coll Pharmacy Fla A&M Univ Tallahassee FL 32307

SOLIMAN, MOHAMMAD IBRAHIM, government official; b. Cairo, June 6, 1946; married; 3 children. BSc in civil engring. (hon.), Ain Shams U., Cairo, 1969, MSCE, 1972; M in Structural Engring., McGill U., Can., 1975, PhD in Structural Engring., 1979. Min. State Ministry New Urban Cmtys., 1993-96; prof. civil engring. dept. Ain Shams U., Cairo, 1989—; min. Ministry Housing, Utilities & Urban Cmtys., Cairo, 1996—; rsch. asst. civil engring. dept. Ain SHams U., Cairo, 1970-93.; rsch. asst. civil engring. dept. McGill U., Montreal, Canada, 1973-79; lectr., cons. Ain Shams U. civil engring. dept. structural divsn., 1979-84; mgr. pvt. consulting engring. office, design, supervision engring. projects in fields, 1979-93; asst. prof., consulting engr. Ain Shams U., Cairo, 1984-89; pres. McGill U. alumni Egypt. Contbr. to internat. sci. periodicals, mags. and local, internat. sci. confs. from 150 rschs. in different structural engring. fields. Mem. Internat. Assn. Major Metropolises, Egyptian Soc. Civil Engrs. (bd. dirs.), Canadian Soc. Civil Engrs. in Egypt (sec.), Canadian-Egyptian Freindship Soc. Office: Ministry Housing Utilities, 1 Sharia Ismail Abaza, Cairo Egypt

SOLIN, HEIKKI, Latin educator; b. Helsinki, Finland, Sept. 12, 1938; s. Lauri and Martta (Pitkänen) S.; m. Anneli Meurman, June 15, 1968; children: Otto, Anna. Lauri. MA, U. Helsinki, 1963, PhD, 1971. Tchr. Greek and Latin Normal Lyceum Helsinki, 1957, 1958-59; tchr. various posts U. Helsinki and Abo Akademi, 1965-85; prof. Latin U. Helsinki, 1985—; vis. prof. Hamburg, 1990, Oxford, 1994; docent classical philology U. Helsinki, 1971-85, U. Turku, 1972—; dir. Finnish Inst., Rome, 1976-79; pres. Classical Assn. Finland, 1991—; sec. gen. Del. Finnish Adads. Sci. and Letters, 1999—; lectr., organizer meetings and confs. in field. Mem. editl com. Acta Instituti Romani Finlandiae, Arctos, Hippokrates, Annales Societatis Historiae Medicinae Fennicae (Helsinki), Année philologique (Paris), Orbis terrarum (Stuttgart), Philologus (Berlin), Puteoli (Naples); contbr. articles to profl. jours. Mem. Societas Scientiarum Fennica, 1976, Coun. Assn. Internationale d'épigraphie grecque et latine, 1982-92,sec. gen. 1997—, Academia Scientiarum Fennica, 1983, pres. 1997-98, Academia Europaea, 1989, mem. coun., 1994—, Pontificia Accademia Romana di Archeologia, 1993, Accademia di Archeologia, Lettere e Belle Arti, Naples, 1997, Reial Academia de Bones Lletres de Barcelona, 1998, Heidelberger Akademie der Wissenschaften, 1998, Bayerische Akademie der Wissenschaften, 1999; hon. mem. Societas Philologa Polonorum, Warsaw, 1997; del. Finland to Union Académique Internationale, 1992—, Coun. of ALLEA, 1998—; chmn. Humanities I Academia Europaea, 2000—. With Coastal Arty. Res., 1965. Recipient Commendatore nell'Ordine al Merito della Republica Italiana, 1993. Mem. German Archeol. Inst., Internationale Thesaurus-Kommission. Home: Temppelikatu 6, 00100 Helsinki Finland Office: U Helsinki, Inst Classics, Helsingin yliopisto 00014, Finland

SOLINGER, UWE WOLFGANG, Thailand government official; b. Lich, Hessen, Germany, Mar. 24, 1959; s. Hans and Elsbeth (Loessner) S.; m. Bettina Theresa Schmiederer, Aug. 26, 1986; children: Daniel, Felix. BA in Adminstrv. Sci. and Law, U. Konstanz, Germany, 1983; MA in Pub. and Bus. Adminstrn., U. Konstanz, 1987. Civil servant Fed. Employment Agy., Giessen, Germany, 1978-81; pers. advisor Min. for Social Affairs of State of Hesse, Germany, 1987-91; divsn. dir. Ministry for Youth, Family and Health of State of Hesse, 1991; resident rep. Konrad-Adenauer-Found., Thailand, 1992-96; advisor Secretariat of Ho. of Reps., Bangkok, Thailand, 1997—; adult edn. trainer Ctrs. for Employee Edn., 1982-87; county counselor, Bischofsheim, Germany, 1989-92. Elected ofcl. Christian Dem. Union, 1982-92; dir. Thailand Innovative Adminstrn. consultance Inst., Bangkok, 1992-96. Mem. Thai-German Soc., Fgn. Correspondence Club of Thailand. Avocations: swimming, dancing, social activities, volunteer work. Home: 999/194 Kesinee Ville, Pracha Uthit Huay Khwang, Bangkok 10320, Thailand Office: Secretariat Ho of Reps, Uthong Nai Rd, Bangkok 10300, Thailand

SOLIONOVA, LIYA GENNADIEVNA, epidemiologist; b. Vologda, Russia, Feb. 18, 1942; d. Gennady and Antonina (Kalinina) Roshkov; m. Yury Georgievich Volodin, Feb. 10, 1962 (div. 1966); m. Valery Nikolaevich Solionov, Sept. 26, 1970; three children. Diploma, Pharm. Coll., Moscow, 1962, Med. Inst., Moscow, 1970; PhD, Russian Acad. Med. Scis., 1977, DSc, 1995. From pharmacist to head lab. Cancer Rsch. Ctr., Moscow, 1962—. Home: Eletskaya str 19 2 ap 183, 115583 Moscow Russia

SOLJAČIĆ, IVO, textile chemical engineer, researcher; b. Zagreb, Croatia, Oct. 28, 1935; s. Marko and Zlata (Mihaljević) S.; m. Marija Horvat; children: Ivana, Hrvojka, Marin. BS, Faculty Tech., Zagreb, 1954, PhD, 1971; MS, Pharm. Faculty, Zagreb, 1966. Cert. engr. Technologist Textile Finishing, Zagreb, 1959-63; asst. Faculty Tech., Zagreb, 1963-71, from asst. prof. to assoc. prof., 1971-78, prof., 1978-91, head textile dept., 1974-78, dean, 1983-85, 90-91; prof. Faculty Textile Tech., Zagreb, 1991—, dean, 1995-98. Contbr. articles to profl. jours. Recipient Nikola Tesla award Parliament Croatia, 1989, Rudjer Boskovic award Pres. Rep. Croatia, 1996. Mem. Croatian Assn. Textile Engrs. (Gold medal 1999), Cath. Soc. Novelists, Am. Assn., Textile Chemists and Colourists. Roman Catholic. Office: Faculty Textile Tech, Pierottijeva 6, 10 000 Zagreb Croatia

ŠOLJIĆ, ZVONIMIR, chemistry educator, researcher; b. Tribiševo, Bosnia-Herzegovina, Apr. 6, 1935; s. Mirko and Ana (Lovrić) Š; m. Ina Vidović, Feb. 6, 1993; children: Mirena, Vedrana. BSChemE, U. Zagreb, Croatia, 1961, MSc, 1968, PhD in Chemistry, 1973. Asst. Faculty Tech., U. Zagreb, 1961-71, lectr. chemistry, 1971-75, docent, 1975-79, assoc. prof., 1979-85, prof. Faculty Chem. Engring. and Tech., 1985—. Author: Qualitative Inorganic Chemical Analysis, 1984, 2d edit., 1992, Analytical Chemistry, 1985, 2d edit., 1991, Calculations in Analytical Chemistry, 1987, 2d edit., 1997; contbr. articles to sci. jours., including Chromatographia, Jour. Analytical Chemistry, Chimie Analytique, Jour. Chromatography, Mikrochimica Acta, Jour. Liquid Chromatography, Internat. Jour. Environ. Analytical Chemistry, Acta Pharmaceutica. Mem. Croatian Chem. Soc., Croatian Soc. Chem. Engrs. and Technologists, N.Y. Acad. Scis. Roman Catholic. Office: U Zagreb Fac Chem Eng-Tech, Marulićev trg 20, 10000 Zagreb Croatia

SOLLEVELD, RENÉ JACQUES, film producer; b. Rotterdam, Switzerland, Sept. 22, 1947; s. Abraham Jan Solleveld and Johanna Van Den Bosch-Uittenbroek. Student, Higher Sch. Econs., Rotterdam, The Netherlands, 1969. Theater mgr. Haagsche Comedie, The Hague, The Netherlands, 1970-71; exec. Arvo-TV, Hyilversom, The Netherlands, 1971-75; head drama and arts dept., dir. Rene Solleveld Prodns., Rotterdam, 1975-86; dir. VHS-Prodns., Rotterdam, 1976-78, Praxino Pictures, Rotterdam, 1986—. Prodr. (TV dramas) Tyl Vilenspiegel, The Heritage of Edgar Allan Poe, Amsterdam 700, The Silent Force, (stage prodns.) The Rocky Horror Show, Dusa, Fish, Stas & Vi, The Club, I Jan Cremer, Dracule, They're Playing Our Song, (feature films) The Debut, The Mark of the Beast, Permeke, Mascara, Taxandria, Evenings, Just Friends, Prime Time. Recipient Golden Calf award for Best Feature Film, Dutch Film Festival, 1981, 90, Golden Calf award for Best Short Film, Dutch Film Festival, 1981. Mem. NBF (bd. dirs. 1989-99), SFO (bd. dirs. 1982-99), Dutch Audiovisual Platform (bd. dirs. 1993-99). Democrat. Home: Onstein 190, 1082 KN Amsterdam The Netherlands

SOLODOVNIKOV, SERGEI FEDOROVICH, crystal chemist, educator; b. Smolensk, Russia, July 8, 1954; s. Fedor Ivanovich and Yulia Mikhailovna (Slavina) S.; m. Zoya Aleksandrovna Vasilieva, Sept. 17, 1976; children: Dmitri, Andrei. BSc in Chemistry, Novosibirsk State U., 1976; PhD in Chemistry, Russian Acad. Scis., Novosibirsk, 1989. Probationer Crystal Chemistry Lab. Inst. Inorganic Chemistry Russian Acad. Scis., Novosibirsk, 1976-79, jr. rsch. assoc., 1979-89, rsch. assoc., 1990-92, dept. head, 1991—, sr. rsch. assoc., 1992—; crystal chemistry lectr. Novosibirsk State U., 1997. Contbr. articles to profl. jours. Home: Molodezhi Blvd 28 Apt 11, 630055 Novosibirsk Russia Office: Russian Acad Scis Inst Inor, Acad Lavrentiev Ave 3, 630090 Novosibirsk Russia

SOLODUKHA, ALEXANDER MAYOROVICH, physicist; b. Berdsk, Russia, Nov. 26, 1947; s. Mayor Yakovlevich and Mariya Yakovlevna (Nerobina) S.; m. Eugeniya Mikhaylovna Nepomnyashchaya, June 25, 1971; children: Roman, Inna. Math., Voronezh, Russia, 1966; student, Voronezh State Univ., 1966-71; degree of candidate of physics & math., 1986. Scientific staff mem. Voronezh State Univ., 1973-88, lectr., 1988—. Contbr. articles to profl. jours. Active Com. of Trade Union Orgn. Voronezh State Univ., 1994—. With South Group of Troops, 1971-73. Avocations: music, working in the orchard. Home: Putilovskaya ul 5-72, 394062 Voronezh Russia Office: Voronezh State Univ, University Sq 1, 394693 Voronez Russia

SOLOGOUB, ELENA BORISOVNA, physiology educator, researcher, consultant; b. St. Petersburg, Russia, Sept. 11, 1929; d. Boris Leopoldovich and Shushanika Lazarevna (Saatchian) Shturmer; m. Mikhail Ivanovich Sologoub, Dec. 7, 1958; children: Natalia, Dmitry. MSs in Biology-Physiology summa cum laud, State U., St. Petersburg, 1952, PhD in Human and Animal Physiology, 1955; DSc in Biology, Lesgaft State Acad. Phys. Culture, St. Petersburg, 1967; prof. in physiology, St. Petersburg, 1976. Tutor physiology State U., 1955-56; tutor physiology Lesgaft Acad. Phys. Culture, 1956-62, rschr., 1962-64, asst. prof., 1964-74, prof., 1974—, acting head dept. physiology, 1983-86. Author: Electrical Activity of Human Brain in Course of Movement, 1973, Elektroenzephalografie im Sport, 1976, Cortical Regulation of Human Movement, 1981 (hon. award State Sport Com., Moscow 1982); editor Medicine, 1966-70; mem. editl. coun. Jour. Human Physiology, 1975-87; contbr. over 250 articles to sci. jours., chpts. to books. Recipient medal in memory of 250 years of St. Petersburg, 1958; medal for brave labor Supreme Coun. USSR, Moscow, 1970, medal as Veteran of Labor, 1985; recipient laureate's diploma St. Petersburg Union Sci. and Engring. Socs., 1995; named Hon. Educator Highest Edn., State Com. Highest Edn., Moscow, 1996, hon. academician Baltic Acad. Edn., St. Petersburg, 1997. Mem. Acad. Med. Tech. Scis. of Russian Fedn., Physiol. Soc. Russia (presidium 1970—), Med.-Tech. Soc. Russia (presidium 1980—). Avocations: sport activities, dancing. Home: O Forsh St 13 Apt 211, 195269 Saint Petersburg Russia Office: Lesgaft State Acad Phys Cul, Decabristov St 35, 190121 Saint Petersburg Russia

SOLOGOUB, MIKHAIL IVANOVICH, physiology educator, researcher, consultant; b. Veliko-Mikhailovka, Kursk, Russia, Nov. 17, 1928; s. Ivan Dmitrievich and Elena Stephanovna (Omelchenko) S.; m. Valentina Sergeevna Demakina, 1951 (div. Nov. 1958); 1 child, Sergey; m. Elena Borisovna Shturmer, Dec. 7, 1958; children: Natalia, Dmitry. Grad. engr.-mechanic, Poly. Inst., Donetsk, Ukraine, 1950; MSc in Biology and Physiology, State U., St. Petersburg, Russia, 1953, PhD in Biology and Physics, 1958, DSc in Biology, 1970, prof. in physiology, 1979. Lab. technician, rschr., lectr. State U., 1956-77, dir. rsch. lab., 1971-77, mem. acad. bds. in physiology and biophysics, 1970—; prof., head dept. anatomy and physiology State Pedagogical U., St. Petersburg, 1977-94, dir. rsch. lab., 1977-82; prof. State Tech. U., St. Petersburg, 1995-96; prof. physiology Lesgaft State Acad. Phys. Culture, St. Petersburg, 1996—; rschr. Monash U., Melbourne, Australia, 1968, U. Wash., Seattle, 1991; vis. prof. Ain-Shams U., Cairo, 1964-65. Author: Course of Lectures on General Electrophysiology, 1965; editor, author: Motor Activity Control in Crayfish, 1981, Neurophysiological Mechanisms of Motor Activity in Crayfish, 1983; contbr. over 100 articles to sci. jours. Decorated Medal of Brave Labor, Supreme Coun. USSR, Moscow, 1970. Mem. Physiol. Soc. Russia. Avocations: radio, electronics amateur. Home: O Forsh St 13 Apt 211, 195269 Saint Petersburg Russia Office: Lesgaft State Acad Phys Cul, Dekabristov St 35, 190121 Saint Petersburg Russia

SOLOMON, ALLAN I., mathematical physicist, educator; b. Glasgow, Dec. 11, 1936; s. Louis and Dolly (Brown) S.; m. Paulette S. Baroukh, July 7, 1963; children: Nathalie, Annabel. BA in Math., BSc in Physics, Trinity Coll., Dublin, 1958; PhD, U. Paris, 1963. Chartered physicist. Prin. physicist Republic Aviation, Farmingdale, N.Y., 1963-65; asst. prof. Poly. Inst. Bklyn., 1965-69, D.I.A.S., Dublin, 1969-71; rsch. assoc. Dublin Inst. for Advanced Studies, 1973—; prof. math. physics Open U., Milton Keynes, 1971—; mem. Internat. Com. on Group Theory Methods, 1985—; chmn. Math. Physics Group, Inst. Physics, U.K., 1992-99; presenter BBC TV programmes, 1972—, BBC Radio series, 1980—. Editor 3 books on math. physics, 1985—; contbr. over 150 articles to profl. jours. Pres. Watford & Dist. Jewish Cmty., 1996—. Fellow Inst. Physics U.K.; mem. Irish Math. Soc., London Math. Soc. Jewish. Office: Open Univ, Dept Applied Math, Milton Keynes MK7 6AA, England

SOLOMON, ANDREW WALLACE, author; b. N.Y.C., Oct. 30, 1963; s. Howard and Carolyn Ruth (Bower) S. BA in English magna cum laude, Yale U., 1985; BA, MA in English, Jesus Coll., Cambridge U., Cambridge, Eng., 1987. Editl. intern Met. Mus. Art, N.Y.C., 1981, editl. asst., 1982, asst. editor, 1983, editor, 1986; intern dept. old master paintings Sotheby's N.Y., 1984; galleries corr., contbg. editor Harpers and Queen, London, 1987-91; contbg. editor HG, 1991-93; contbg. writer The N.Y. Times Mag., 1993—. Author: The Irony Tower: Soviet Artists in a Time of Glasnost, 1991, A Stone Boat, 1994; contbr. articles to profl. jours. Bd. dirs. World Monuments Fund, CEC Internat. Partnership, Alliance for the Arts, The Shakespeare Project, The Moscow ICA. Jesus Coll. Travel grantee, Cambridge U., 1986; Yale Conservation Project fellow for travel, 1985; Brit.-Am. Project fellow; Bogliasco fellow, 1998. Mem. Groucho Club, Oxford & Cambridge Club, Chelsea Arts Club, Century Assn., Nat. Arts Club, Coun. on Fgn. Rels., Conservators Coun. of N.Y. Pub. Libr. Democrat. Address: 18 W 10th St New York NY 10011-8702 also: 154 Kensington Park Rd, London W11 2ER, England

SOLOMON, DOROTHY JEANNE ALLRED, writer, communications executive; b. Salt Lake City, June 24, 1949; d. Rulon Clark and Mabel (Finlayson) Allred; m. Bruce Craig Solomon, Jan. 8, 1968; children: Denise, Layla, Jeffrey, Laurie. BA in Lit., Theater and Speech, U. Utah, 1971, MA in Lit. and Creative Writing, 1981. Cert. secondary edn. educator, Utah. Storyteller, libr. Salt Lake City Libr., 1971; tchr. Salt Lake Sch. Dist., 1971-74; instr. U. Utah/Columbia Coll., Salt Lake City, 1974-80; writer-in-residence Utah Arts Coun., Salt Lake City, 1980-93; human devel. trainer Lifespring, San Rafael, Calif., 1983-87; media specialist Rivendell Psychiat. Hosps., West Jordan, Utah, 1987-90; curriculum writer Positive Action Pub., Twin Falls, Idaho, 1990-96; co-founder, v.p. Rising Star Comm. and Team Resource Assocs., Salt Lake City, 1994—; bd. dirs. Rising Star Comm. Author: In My Father's House, 1984 (1st prize Biography, 1981, Pub. prize 1982), Inside Out: Creative Writing, 1989, Of Predators, Prey and Other Kin, 1996 (1st prize Non-fiction 1996); contbr. stories to anthologies Stories That Shape Us, What There Is, The Best of Writers at Work, A New Genesis, Great and Peculiar Beauty, In Our Lovely Deseret, Mormon Fictions, 1998; screenwriter: In My Father's House, 1986-87. Bd. dirs. The Children's Ctr., Salt Lake City, 1982-85, Writers at Work, Park City, Utah, 1986-89, Lifespring Found., San Rafael, Calif., 1985-89; mem. curriculum com. Salt Lake Sch. Dist., 1971-74; coord. (with Bruce Solomon) lit. arts Utah Arts Festival "Performing Word", Salt Lake City, 1982; vol. Big Sisters, Salt Lake City, 1970-71; coord. cmty. edn. Rivendell Conf., West Jordan, Utah, 1987-89. Recipient Disting. Journalism 1st prize Am. Acad. Pediat., San Francisco, 1979, 1st prize feature writing Sigma Delta Chi, Salt Lake City, 1979, 1st prize essay Utah Original Writing Contest, Salt Lake City, 1995, 1st prize Biography, 1981, 96, award of excellence Gov.'s Media Awards, Utah, 1990, Utah State Pub. prize, 1982. Mem. Associated Writing Programs, Acad. Am. Poets. Mem. LDS Ch. Avocations: golf, reading, movies, environmental protection, child/family advocacy projects. Home: 6521 Snowview Dr Park City UT 84098-6167

SOLOMON, ELINOR HARRIS, economics educator; b. Boston, Feb. 26, 1923; d. Ralph and Linna Harris; m. Richard A. Solomon, Mar. 30, 1957; children: Joan S. Griffin, Robert H., Thomas H. AB, Mt. Holyoke Coll., 1944; MA, Radcliffe U., 1945; PhD, Harvard U., 1948. Jr. economist Fed. Res. Bank Boston, 1945-48; economist Fed. Res. Bd. Govs., Washington, 1949-56; internat. economist U.S. State Dept., Washington, 1957-58; professorial lectr. Am. U., Washington, 1964-66; sr. economist antitrust div. U.S. Dept. Justice, Washington, 1966-82; prof. econs. George Washington U., Washington, 1982—; econ. cons., Washington, 1982—; expert witness antitrust, fin. networks, electronic funds transfer cases, Washington, 1988—. Author: Virtual Money, 1997; author, editor: Electronic Funds Transfers and Payments, 1987, Electronic Money Flows, 1991; contbr. articles on econs., banking and law to profl. jours. Mem. Am. Econs. Assn., Nat. Economists Club (bd. govs. 1997—), The Cosmos Club (chair Digital Age series 1999—). Home: 6805 Delaware St Chevy Chase MD 20815-4164 Office: George Washington U Dept Econs Washington DC 20052-0001

SOLOMON, HILDA PEARL, wholesale executive; b. Conway, S.C., Dec. 15, 1948; d. Ezel and Dorothy (Gottlieb) S. BFA, U. S.C., 1968. Buyer Solomon Bros. Dept. Store, Conway, 1969-73; coutourier sales Julius Lewis, Memphis, 1973-75; buyer Helen of Memphis, 1975-78, George M. Muse Clothing Co., Atlanta, 1978-83; sales rep. Whiting & Davis Co. Inc., Plainville, Mass., 1983-84, exec. sales mgr. southeast dist., 1984-92; owner Solomon, Atlanta, 1992—; sec. bd. dirs. Bur. Wholesale Accessory Reps., Atlanta, 1983-87, Accessories On 6 Atlanta Apparel Mart, 1986-87; dir. trade shows, key accounts, export mgr., 1994-98; nat. key account mgr. Westminster, Inc., 1999—. Prin. works include Posh Petals, Atlanta, 1986—. Mem. Atlanta Hist. Soc., Young Careers High Mus. Art. Jewish. Avocations: design, travel, writing. Home: 2917 Hamilton Sq Decatur GA 30033-1140

SOLOMON, ISHAN SAMJEVA DANIEL, research and development engineer; b. Colombo, Sri Lanka, May 27, 1971; arrived in Australia, 1984; s. Samsingh Kelvin and Padmavathy Jevamalar (Devasagayam) S. BEng., U. Adelaide, Australia, 1993, BS, 1994, PhD, 1998. Profl. officer Def. Sci. and Tech. Orgn., Australia, 1994-98, R & D engr., 1999—. Contbr. articles to profl. jours. Mem. IEEE (Oliver Lodge premium 1999), Inst. Engrs. Australia. Mem. Pentecostal Ch. Avocations: golf, cricket, chess. Office: Def Sci & Tech Orgn, PO Box 1500, Salisbury 5108 South Australia, Australia

SOLOMON, JONATHAN, telecommunications executive; b. London, Mar. 3, 1939; s. Samuel and Moselle S.; m. Hester McFarland; June 10, 1966; 1 child, Gabriel. MA, U. Cambridge, Eng., 1963. Asst. prin. Board of Trade, London, 1963-67; prin. London Bd. of Trade, 1967-72, H.M. Treasury, London, 1973-80; asst. sec. Dept. Prices and Consumer Protection, London, 1980-85; undersec. Dept. Trade and Industry, London, 1980-85; dir. corp. strategy Cable & Wireless PLC, London, 1987-96; dir. Millicom Internat. Cellular and Soc. European Comms., 1999—, THUS, 1999—, Flag Telecomms., 1999—; supr. Sidney Sussex Coll., Cambridge, 1960-72, extra mural dept., U. London, 1963-72. Contbr. articles to tech. jours. Leader U.K. Delegation to Internat. Telecommunications Union Plenipotentiary Conf., Nairobi, Kenya, 1982. Mem. English Speaking Union. Jewish. Office: Cable & Wireless PLC, Theobalds Rd, London WC1, England

SOLOMON, NEAL EDWARD, management consultant, executive recruiter, social theorist, author; b. San Diego, Mar. 9, 1960; s. Donald Jay and Roberta Yvonne (Recht) S. BA in Philosophy, Reed Coll., Portland, Oreg., 1981; AM in Philosophy, U. Chgo, 1982. Founder Calif. Legal Search, 1983—; chmn., CEO Am. e-Svcs., Inc., 1999—. Author: A Turning Point in World History?, 1992, High Performance Venture Characteristics, 1992, Dilemmas of Democracy (3 vols.: A Critique of Liberalism, A Critique of Political Ideology, and The Limits of Social Theory), 1992, The Problem of Modernity, 1993, Theoretical Foundations of Dynamic Macroeconomics, 1993, The Evolution of Philosophy, 1995, Legal Management Theory, 2d edit., 1997, Transformation of the Corporate Law Firm, 1998, and others. Democrat. Avocations: fine arts nature photography, high end audio and

book and art collecting. Address: 388 Market St Ste 500 San Francisco CA 94111-5313

SOLOMON, PAUL WAYNE, medical association administrator; b. Kalgoorlie, Australia, Nov. 26, 1956; s. William Ernest and Margaret Isobel (Edgar) S.; m. Ellen Norma Baron-Hay, Feb. 6, 1989; children: Scott, Cassandra, David, Kristen. B in Commerce, U. Western Australia, Australia, 1976. Commr. for declarations Health Dept. Western Australia, 1989-91, mgn. dir., 1991-95; gen. mgr. Austin and Repatriation Med. Ctr., Melbourne, Australia, 1995-98; nat. gen. mgr. SSL Healthcare, Australia, 1998—; cons. World Health Orgn., assoc. prof. U. Woollongong, N.S. Wales, 1995. Fellow Australian Soc. Cert. Practicing Accts., Australian Inst. Mgmt. Office: Spotless Svcs, 350 Queen St, 3000 Melbourne Australia

SOLOMON, PETROS, Eritrean government official; b. May 5, 1951. Student, U. Addis Ababa, 1971-72. Chief mil. intelligence and dep. comdr. Armed Forces, EPLF, 1987-91; min. defense State of Eritrea, 1992-94, min. fgn. affairs, 1994-97, min. fisheries, 1997—, min. marine resources; mem. politbureau Eritrean People's Liberation Front Military Com., 1977, chief military intelligence, dep. comdr. armed forces, 1987-91. Mem. People's Front for Democracy and Justice. Office: care Min Fgn Affairs & Min Marine Resources, Min Fisheries PO Box 923, Asmara Eritrea*

SOLOMON, ROBERT DOUGLAS, pathology educator; b. Delavan, Wis., Aug. 28, 1917; s. Lewis Jacob and Sara (Ludgin) S.; m. Helen Fisher, Apr. 4, 1943; children: Susan, Wendy, James, William. Student, MIT, 1934-36; BS in Biochemistry, U. Chgo., 1938; MD, Johns Hopkins U., 1942. Intern John's Hopkins Hosp., 1942-43; resident in pathology Michael Reese Hosp., 1947-49; lectr. U. Ill., Chgo., 1947-50; fellow NIH pathology U. Ill., 1949-50; asst. prof. U. Md., Balt., 1955-60; assoc. prof. U. So. Calif., L.A., 1960-70; chief of staff City of Hope Nat. Med. Ctr., 1966-67; prof. U. Mo., Kansas City, 1977-78, SUNY, Syracuse, 1968-78; chief of staff The Hosp., Sidney, N.Y., 1985-86; adj. prof. biology U. N.C., Wilmington, 1989—; cons. VA Hosp., Balt., 1955-60, Med. Svc. Lab., Wilmington, 1989-93; active in field of bariatrics, 1997—. Co-author: Progress in Gerontological Research, 1967; contbr. papers and profl. jours. and rsch. in biochemistry, revascular of heart, carcinogenesis, cancer chemotherapy, atherogenesis, discovery of reversibility of atherosclerosis, chemistry of urochrome pigments. V.p. Roty, Duarte, Calif., 1967; v.p. and pres. Force for an Informed Electorate. Capt. Med. Corps, AUS, 1943-46, PTO. Grantee NIH, Fleischmann Found., Am. Heart Assn., Nat. Cancer Inst., 1958-70. Fellow ACP (pres. Md. chpt.), Western Geriatrics Soc. (founding); mem. Coll. Am. Pathologists (past pres. Md. chpt.), Am. Soc. Clin. Pathologists, Assn. Clin. Scientists, Am. Chem. Soc., Royal Soc. Medicine (London), Phi Beta Kappa, Sigma Xi. Achievements include development of fiber-optic arterial catheter for visualization and making movies of aortic endothelium in vivo. Avocations: cruising, astronomy, mathematics, fishing, stamps. Home: 113 S Belvedere Dr Hampstead NC 28443-2504

SOLOMONOW, MOSHE, biomedical engineer, scientist, educator; b. Tel Aviv, Oct. 24, 1944; came to U.S., 1965; s. Jonathan and Eva (Efraim) S.; m. Susanne Elisbeth Nickerson, May 31, 1981; children: Deborah Leigh, Esther Monique. BSc, Calif. State U., L.A., 1970, MSc, 1972; PhD, UCLA, 1976; MD (hon.), Brussels, 1997. Rsch. engr. UCLA, 1976-80; assoc. prof. La. State U. Med. Ctr., New Orleans, 1980-87, prof., 1987—, dir. bioengring., 1983—; I. Cahen M.D. professor La. State U., 1997; dir. occupational med. Rsch. Ctr. La. State U., 2000—; assoc. prof. Tulane U., New Orleans, 1980-83; dir. paraplegic clinic Rehab. Inst., New Orleans, 1991—; cons. Nat. Acad. of Scis., 1998, NIH, 1978—, NSF, 1985, VA, 1978—, also others; reviewer 16 sci. jours. Editor-in-chief Jour. EMG and Kinesiology, 1991—; contbr. over 100 articles to sci. jours.; patentee in field. Pres. Lakeshore Day Sch., New Orleans, 1990. Recipient Crump award UCLA, 1977, Mayor's medal City of Rennes, France, 1992, Disting. Merit award Delta 7 Assn., Paris, 1991, Volvo award for low back pain rsch., 1999. Avocation: sailing. Office: Dept Orthopedic Surgery 2025 Gravier St Ste 400 New Orleans LA 70112-2289

SOLONTSOV, ALEXANDER ZINOVIEVICH, physicist; b. Moscow, Jan. 11, 1951; s. Zinovii Matveevich and Ludmila Pavlovna (Vinogradova) S.; m. Ludmila Victorovna Mimrikova, Dec. 4, 1974; 1 child, Vladimir. BS, Moscow Engring. Phys. Inst., 1974, PhD, 1977; DS, Russian Acad. Scis., 1991. Rschr. P.N. Lebedev Phys. Inst., Moscow, 1977-81; rschr. A.A. Bochvar Inst. Inorganic Materials, Moscow, 1981-91, head theoretical lab., 1991—; dir. State Ctr. Condensed Matter Physics, Moscow, 1995—. Editor: Itinerant Electron Magnetism: Fluctuation Effects, 1998; contbr. articles to profl. jours. Grantee Japan-FSU Scientist Collaboration, 1993, NATO, 1993-95, Minatom-BMFT, 1995-98, State Support for Leading Sci. Schs. Russia, 1997, RFBR, 1996-98, 2000. Avocations: biking, skiing. Fax: (095)196-6389. E-mail: solv.@theor.viinm.msk.su. Home: Paustovskogo str 3-523, 117463 Moscow Russia Office: AA Bochvar Inst, 123060 Moscow Russia

SOLOVIEV, IGOR ALEXEEVITCH, mathematician, educator; b. Moscow, Mar. 4, 1949; s. Alexey Sergeevitch and Zoia Alexandrovna (Fiodorova) S.; m. Vera Vladimirovna Dvoyashova, Apr. 24, 1976; children: Vladimir, Alexey, Dariya. MSc in Physics and Applied Math., Moscow State U., 1972; PhD in Physics and Math., A.V. Luikov Heat and Mass Transfer Inst., Minsk, Belorussia, 1981, Candidate of Sci. in Physics and Math., 1981. Diplomate specialist in physics and math., diplomate prof. math. Instr., chair math. All-Union Food Industry Inst., Moscow, 1974, asst. prof. math., 1974-78, sr. lectr., chair math., 1978-82, prof. math., 1982-86, vice-dean faculty tech., 1983-85; prof. applied math. Moscow Power Engring. Inst., Tech. U., 1986-98, Moscow N.E. Bauman Higher Tech. U., 1996—; prof. math. State U. Land Tenure, Moscow, 1998—. Author: (with V.I. Luisenko and M.S. Smirnov) Express-Information #26, 1979, (with V.I. Luisenko and M.S. Smirnov) Current State and Development Prospects of Agricultural Products Drying Theory, Technology and Techniques, 1979, (with O.G. Martinenko) Methods of Research and Optimization of Transfer Processes, 1979, Vector Algebra, Analytical Geometry, Elements of Linear Algebra, 1979, Heat/Mass Transfer-6, 1980, Algebra, Trigonometry, Elements of Calculus, 1983, (with V.I. Piontkovskaya) Geometry, 1983, (with V.I. Luisenko and M.S. Smirnov) Perfection of Agricultural Products Drying Technology and Techniques, 1984, Methods of Mathematical Modeling in CAD/CAM Systems, 1985, (with V.I. Luisenko and M.S. Smirnov) Analitical Methods of Heat and Mass Transfer Processes, 1986, Linear and Non-Linear Models of Transfer, 1987, (with E.A. Samsonova) Computational Algorythms, 1989, (with E.A. Samsonova) Foundations of Mathematical Modeling, 1990, New Information and Electronic Technologies in National Economy and Education, 1990, Foundations of Mathematical Modeling: Development of Mathematical Models, 1992, Heat-Physical Problems of Industry, 1992, (with V.I. Miroshnichenko, V.V. Mahrow and M.V. Rebrov) Heat/Mass Transfer MMF-92, 1992, Methods and Algorythms of Parametrical Analysis of Linear and Non-Linear Models of Transfer, 1995, New Methods and Means of Power Resources Economy and Ecological Problems in Energetics, 1995, Heat/Mass Transfer MMF-96, 1996, Third Siberian Congress on Applied and Industrial Mathematics, 1998; contbr. articles to profl. jours. Sr. lt. Soviet Army, 1972-74. Avocations: poetry, mushrooms. Home: 54-2-27 Tretya Parkovaya, 105425 Moscow Russia Office: State Univ Land Tenure, 15 Kazakova, 103064 Moscow Russia

SOLOV'YOV, ANDREY VLADIMIROVICH, physicist; b. St. Petersburg, Russia, Nov. 15, 1960; s. Vladimir Georgievich and Aza Ivanovna (BednIagina) S.; m. Irina Michailovna Kichkina, Oct. 16, 1982; children: Ilia, Alena. MS, St. Petersburg State Tech. U., 1984; PhD, A.F.Ioffe Phys.-Tech. Inst., St. Petersburg, 1988, D in Phys. and Math. Scis., 1999. Jr. rsch. fellow A.F. Ioffe Phys.-Tech. Inst., St. Petersburg, 1988-90, rsch. fellow, 1990-96, sr. rsch. fellow, 1996—; assoc. prof. St. Petersburg State Tech. U., 1996—; Alexander von Humboldt fellow Inst. for Theoretical Physics, Frankfurt, Germany, 1990-92, 99, vis. prof., 1994; ex-quota visit of the Royal Soc., Imperial Coll. of Sci., Technology and Medicine U.K., London, 1994-95; prin. investigator Project for Internat. Sci. Found., 1995, grant 1995, NATO Collaborative Grant, 1995-99, Volkswagen Found. Joint Project, 1995-98, 99—, Royal Soc. of London Joint Project, 1996-98, 2000—; Deutche Forschungsgemeinschaft, 1994, 97-98, 98-2000, INTAS project, 1999—; prin. investigator Project for Russian Found. of Basic Rsch., 1996-98, 99—; Deutsche Forschungsgemeinschaft vis. prof. Inst. for Theoretical Physics, Frankfurt, 2000—. Contbr. articles to profl. jours. Sr. lt. Russian Army Res., 1984—. Recipient stipends Alexander von Humboldt Found., Bonn, Germany, 1990, 99, Deutsche Forschungsgemeinschaft, Bonn, 1994, 2000, Royal Soc., London, 1994. Mem. Internat. Ctr. for Sci. and Tech. (leader project rsch. team 1994-97, grant 1994). Russian Orthodox Ch. Avocations: hiking, jogging, poetry. Office: AF Ioffe Phys-Tech Inst, Politechnicheskaja 26, 194021 Saint Petersburg Russia

SOLOW, ROBERT MERTON, economist, educator; b. Bklyn., Aug. 23, 1924; s. Milton Henry and Hannah Gertrude (Sarney) S.; m. Barbara Lewis, Aug. 19, 1945; children: John Lewis, Andrew Robert, Katherine. BA, Harvard U., 1947, MA, 1949, PhD, 1951, DLitt (hon.), 1992; LLD (hon.), U. Chgo., 1967, Brown U., 1972, U. Warwick, 1976, Tulane U., 1983, Dartmouth Coll., 1990; DLitt (hon.), Williams Coll., 1974, Lehigh U., 1977, Wesleyan U., 1982, Boston Coll., 1986, Harvard U., 1992, Colgate U., 1990; DSc (hon.), U. Paris, 1975, U. Geneva, 1982, Bryant Coll., 1988; D of Social Sci. (hon.), Yale U., 1976, U. Mass., Boston, 1989; D Social Sci. (hon.), U. Helsinki, 1990, SUNY, Albany, 1991, U. Glasgow, 1992, Rutgers U., 1994; D honoris causa, U. Chile, 1992; Conservatoire, Nat. des Arts et Métiers, Paris, 1994; D in Engring., Colo. Sch. Mines, 1996; postgrad, U. Buenos Aires, 1999; D Lt. Humanities, New York U., 2000. Mem. faculty MIT, 1949-95, prof. econs., 1958-95, inst. prof., 1973-95, prof. emeritus, 1995—; W. Edwards Deming prof. NYU, 1996-97; sr. economist Coun. Econ. Advisers, 1961-62, cons., 1962-68; cons. RAND Corp., 1952-64; Marshall lectr., fellow commoner Peterhouse, Cambridge (Eng.) U., 1963-64; Eastman vis. prof. Oxford U., 1968-69; overseas fellow Churchill Coll., Cambridge; sr. fellow Soc. Fellows, Harvard U., 1975-89; bd. dirs. Boston Fed. Res. Bank, 1975-80, chmn., 1979-80; active President's Commn. on Income Maintenance, 1968-70, President's Com. on Tech., Automation and Econ. Progress, 1964-65, Carnegie Commn. Sci., Tech. and Govts., 1988-93, Nat. Sci. Bd., 1994—. Author: Linear Programming and Economic Analysis, 1958, (with R. Dortman, P. Samuelson) Capital Theory and the Rate of Return, 1963, The Sources of Unemployment in the United States, 1964, Growth Theory, 1970, Price Expectations and the Behavior of the Price Level, 1970, (with M. Dertouzos, R. Lester) Made in America, 1989, The Labor Market as a Social Institution, 1990, (with F. Hahn) A Critical Essay on Modern Macroeconomic Theory, 1995, Learning from "Learning by Doing", 1997, (with J. Taylor) Inflation, Unemployment and Monetary Policy, 1998, Monopolistic Competition and Macroeconomic Theory, 1998, Work and Welfare, 1998. Bd. dirs., mem. exec. com. Nat. Bur. Econ. Rsch.; trustee Inst. for Advanced Study, Princeton U., 1972-78, Woods Hole Oceanographic Inst., 1988—, Alfred P. Sloan Found., 1992—, Resources for the Future, 1994—, Urban Inst., 1994—, German Marshall Fund of U.S., 1994—. With AUS, 1942-45. Recipient David A. Wells prize Harvard U., 1951, Seidman award in polit. economy, 1983, Nobel prize in Econs., 1987, Nat. Medal of Sci., 2000; fellow Ctr. Advanced Study Behavioral Scis., 1957-58, trustee, 1982-95, chmn., 1987-95. Fellow Am. Acad. Arts and Scis., Brit. Acad. (corr.); mem. AAAS (v.p. 1970), Am. Philos. Soc., Nat. Acad. Scis. (coun. 1977-80, 95), Acad. dei Lincei, Order Pour le merite (Germany), Am. Econ. Soc. (exec. com. 1964-66, John Bates Clark medal 1961, v.p. 1968, pres. 1979), Econometric Soc. (pres. 1964, mem. exec. com.), Internat. Econ. Assn. (pres. 1999—), Royal Irish Acad. (hon.). Home: 528 Lewis Wharf Boston MA 02110-3920 Office: MIT Dept Econs Cambridge MA 02139

SOLT, PÁL, judge. Judge Supreme Ct., Hungary, 1980-87, chmn. chamber civil law cases, 1987-89; judge Constl. Ct., Hungary, 1989-90; pres. Supreme Ct., Hungary, Nat. Coun. Justice, Hungary.

SOLTANOFF, JACK, nutritionist, chiropractor; b. Newark, Apr. 24, 1915; s. Louis and Rose (Yomteff) S.; m. Esther Katcher, Sept. 29, 1939; children: Howard, Ruth C. Soltanoff Jacobs, Hillory Soltanoff Seaton. N.M.D. Mecca Coll. Chiropractic Medicine, 1938, U.S. Sch. Naturopathy and Allied Scis., 1951; D.Chiropractic, Chiropractic Inst. N.Y., 1956; postgrad. Atlantic States Chiropractic Inst., 1962-63, Nat. Coll. Chiropractic, 1964-65; PhD, diplomate in nutrition Fla. Natural Health Coll., 1982. Gen. practice chiropractic medicine, cons. in nutrition, N.Y.C., 1956-75, West Hurley, N.Y. and Singer Island, Fla., 1975—; lectr., cons. in field. Author: Natural Healing; pub. Warner Books; contbr. articles to profl. jours. Syndicated newspaper columnist. Fellow Internat. Coll. Naturopathic Physicians; mem. Am. Chiropractic Assn., Internat. Chiropractic Assn., Brit. Chiropractic Assn., N.Y. Acad. Scis., Am. Council on Diagnosis and Internal Disorders, Council on Nutrition, Ethical Culture Soc. Unitarian. Instrumental in instituting chiropractic care in union contracts for mems. of Teamsters Union. Home: 25 Holiday Dr West Hurley NY 12491 Office: PO Box 239 West Hurley NY 12491-0239

SOLVEY, PABLO, psychiatrist; b. Montevideo, Uruguay, Mar. 27, 1939; s. Mecislao and Judith Ida (Hochenberg) S.; m. Raquel Carmen Ferrazzano, Jan. 20, 1967; children: Sergio, Natalia. MD, Buenos Aires U., 1970; psychoanalyst, Argentine Psychoanalytic Assn., 1973. Assoc. prof. Argentine Psychoanalytic Assn., Buenos Aires, 1976-77, prof., 1979-82, 84-88, mem. dept. further edn., 1980-85; pvt. practice, 1990—. Bd. dirs. Psychoanalist's Guild, Buenos Aires, 1975-77, treas.; bd. dirs. E.M.D.R. Humanitarian Assistance Programs Inc., Calif. Mem. Eye Movement Desensitization and Reprocessing Internat. Assn. (pres. 1998—). Jewish. Avocation: golf. Office: Emdria Latinoamerica, Federico Lacroze 1820 7B, 1426 Buenos Aires Argentina

SOLYMAR, LASZLO, engineering educator; b. Budapest, Hungary, Jan. 24, 1930; arrived in U.K., 1956; m. Marianne Klopfer, Oct. 29, 1955; children: Gillian Kathy, Lucy Suzanne. Diploma in Engring., Tech. U. Budapest, 1952; PhD, Hungarian Acad., Budapest, 1956. Lectr. Tech. U., Budapest, 1952-53; rsch. engr. Rsch. Inst. for Telecom., Budapest, 1953-56, Standard Telecomm. Labs., Harlow, Essex, Eng., 1965-66; lectr. dept. engring. Oxford (Eng.) U., 1966-86, reader dept. engring., 1986-91, prof. dept. engring., 1991-97; vis. prof. U. Paris, 1965-66, Tech. U. Denmark, Lyngby, 1972-73, Tech. U., Berlin, 1990, U. Autonoma, Madrid, 1993, 95; topical editor Applied Optics, 1991-95. Author: Lectures on the Electrical Properties of Materials, 1970, Superconductive Tunnelling and Applications, 1972, Lectures on Electromagnetic Theory, 1976, Volume Holography and Volume Gratings, 1981, Lectures on Fourier Series, 1988, The Physics and Applications of Photorefractive Materials, 1996, Getting the Message: A History of Communications, 1999. Fellow Instn. Elec. Engring. (London; Faraday medal 1992), The Royal Soc. Avocations: swimming, chess, history. Office: Oxford U Dept Engring Sci, Parks Rd, Oxford OX1 3PJ, England

SOLYMOSI, TAMÁS ISTVÁN, mathematics educator; b. Gyoma, Hungary, Jan. 7, 1960; s. János and Jánosné (Laurinyecz Mária) S.; m. Judit Ildikó Halász, Aug. 4, 1990; 1 child, Gergely Tamás. MSc, József Attila U., Szeged, Hungary, 1984, univ. dr., 1990; PhD in Math., U. Ill., Chgo., 1993. Sci. co-worker Szeged Med. U., 1984-87; rsch. fellow Rsch. Group on Automata Theory, Szeged, 1994-95; asst. prof. Dept. Ops. Rsch. Budapest (Hungary) U. Econ., 1995-97, assoc. prof., 1997—. Contbr. articles to sci. publs., including Math. of Ops. Rsch., Internat. Jour. Game Theory, others. Mem. Hungarian Ops. Rsch. Soc., Bolyai János Math. Soc. (Farkas Gyula Meml. prize 1995), Game Theory Soc. Office: Dept Ops Rsch PF 489, Budapest U Econ, H 1828 Budapest Hungary

SOLYOM, JANOS PAUL, concert pianist, conductor, consultant; b. Budapest, Hungary, Oct. 26, 1938; s. Istvan Steiner and Magda (Weill) S.; m. Camilla Maria Lundberg, Jan. 17, 1987. Student, Béla Bartók Conservatory, Budapest, 1955, Franz Liszt Acad. Music, Budapest, 1956; studied with Ilona Kabos, London, 1957-64, with Norman Del Mar, 1970-75; with Nadia Boulanger, Paris, 1963-65. Debut in Stockholm, 1958; extensive internat. career, 1958—; cons. preventive health care. Fellow Royal Swedish Acad. Music, 1995. Avocations: languages, architecture. Home: NORR Maelarstrand 54, S-112-20 Stockholm Sweden

SÓLYOM, JENŐ, physicist, educator; b. Kolozsvár, Hungary, Nov. 27, 1940; s. Jenő and Ilona (Hantos) S.; m. Márta Tóth, July 13, 1973; children: Gyöngyvér, Tünde, Iringó. Cand. .Sci., Hungarian Acad. Sci., 1970, ScD, 1978. Rsch. fellow Ctrl. Rsch. Inst. for Physics, Budapest, Hungary, 1964-70, sci. co-worker, 1972-78, sr. scientist, 1980-84, rsch. prof. solid state programs, 1988—; rsch. fellow Institut Laue-Langevin, Grenoble, France, 1970-71, sci. co-worker, 1985-88; prof. Eötvös U., Budapest, 1992—; vis. prof. U. Ill., Urbana, 1978-80, U. Lausanne, Switzerland, 1984-85. Contbr. 100 articles to profl. jours. Lay chmn. So. Diocese of Hungarian Luth. Ch., 1990—. Recipient State prize State Coun. Hungary, 1980. Mem. Hungarian Acad. Sci., Hungarian Phys. Soc. (vice-chmn. 1993-96). Home: Pelsöc u 1, 1121 Budapest Hungary Office: Rsch Inst Solid State Phys, PO Box 49, 1525 Budapest Hungary

SOLZHENITSYN, ALEKSANDR ISAYEVICH, writer; b. Kislovodsk, Russia, Dec. 11, 1918; imprisoned under Joseph Stalin for critical comments, 1945-53; exiled to Soviet Cen. Asia, 1953; freed from exile, 1956; expelled from USSR, 1974; arrived back in Russia, 1994; m. Natalya Reshetovskaya, 1940 (div.), remarried, 1956 (div.); m. Natalia Svetlova, 1970; children: Yermolai, Ignat, Stephan. Corr. student in philology, Moscow Inst. History, Philosophy and Lit., 1939-41; degree in math. and physics, U. Rostov, 1941; LittD, Harvard U., 1978. Author: Odin den' Ivana Denisovicha, 1962 (pub. as One Day in the Life of Ivan Denisovich, 1963), Dlia pol'zy dela, 1963 (pub. as For the Good of the Cause, 1964), Sluchai na stantsii Krechetovka/Matrenin dvor, 1963 (pub. as We Never Make Mistakes, 1963), Etudy i krokhotnye rasskazy, 1964 (pub. as Stories and Prose Poems, 1971, as Prose Poems, 1971, as Matryona's House and Other Stories, 1975), V kruge pervom, 1968 (pub. as The First Circle, 1968; Prix du Meilleur Livre Etranger France 1969), Rakovyi korpus, 1968 (pub. as Cancer Ward, 1968; Prix du Meilleur Livre Etranger France 1969), Le Droits de l'écrivain, 1969, Sobranie sochinenii (6 vols.), 1969-70, Six Etudes, 1971, Avgust chetyrnadtsatogo, 1971 (pub. as August 1914, 1972), Nobelevskaia lektsiia po literature, 1972 (pub. as Nobel Lecture, 1972, as One Word of Truth, 1972), Arkhipelag Gulag (3 vols.), 1973-76 (pub. as The Gulag Archipelago, 1974-78), Prusskie nochi: poema napisannaia v lagere v 1950, 1974 (pub. as Prussian Nights, 1977), Iz-pod glyb, 1974 (pub. as From Under the Rubble, 1975), Mir i nasilie, 1974, Pis'mo vozhdiam Sovetskogo soiuza, 1974 (pub. as Letter to the Soviet Leaders, 1974), A Pictorial Autobiography, 1974, Solzhenitsyn, the Voice of Freedom, 1975, Bodalsia telenok s dubom, 1975 (pub. as The Oak and the Calf, 1980), Lenin v Tsiurikhe, 1975 (pub. as Lenin in Zurich, 1976), Detente: Prospects for democracy and Dictatorship, 1975, America, We Beg You to Interfere, 1975, Amerikanskie rechi, 1975, Warning to the Western World, 1976, A World Split Apart, 1978, Alexander Solzhenitsyn Speaks to the West, 1978, Sobranie sochinenii, 1978, The Mortal Danger, 1980, East and West, 1980, Issledovaniia noveishei russkoi istorii, 1980, Publitsistika: stat'i i rechi, 1981, Krasnoe koleso: povestvovan'e v otmerennykh srokakh Uzel I: Avgust chetyrnadtsatogo, 1983 (pub. as The Red Wheel: A Narrative in Discrete Periods of Time, 1989), Krasnoe koleso: povestvovan'e v otmerennykh srokakh Uzel II: Oktiabr'shestnadtsatogo, 1984, Krasnoe koleso: povestvovan'e v otmerennykh srokakh Uzel III: Mart semnadtsatogo, 1986, Rasskazy, 1990, Kak nam obustroit' Rossiiu, 1990, Krasnoe koleso: povestvovan'e v otmerennykh srokakh Uzel IV: Aprel'semnadtsatogo, 1991, Rebuilding Russia: Toward Some Formulations, 1991, Les Invisibles, 1992, Nashi pliuralisty: otryvok iz vtorogo toma "Ocherkov literaturnoi zhizni", 1992, The Russian Question At the End of the Twentieth Century, 1995; (plays) Olen' i shalashovka, 1968 (pub. The Love-Girl and the Innocent, 1969), Svecha na vetru, 1968 (pub. Candle in the Wind, 1973), Pir podebitelei, 1981 (pub. as Victory Celebrations, 1983), Plenniki, 1981 (pub. as Prisoners, 1983), P'esy i kinostsenarii, 1981; editor: Russkii slovar' iazykovogo rasshireniia, 1990. Arty. officer Russian Army, World War II. Recipient Lenin prize nomination, 1964, Nobel prize for lit., 1970, Freedoms Found. award Stanford U., 1976, Templeton Found. prize, 1983. Mem. Am. Acad. Arts and Scis., Hoover Inst. War, Revolution and Peace (hon.), Russian Acad. of Scis. (field of lang.). Address: Ul Tverskaya 12 kv 169, 119 121 Moscow Russia

SOMA, JOHANNES, cardiologist; b. Stavanger, Norway, Oct. 1, 1953; s. Johannes and Elin (Dahl) S.; m. Vibeke Warland; children: Cecilie, Johannes, Charlotte. PhD, U. Trondheim, Norway, 1999. Intern Bethesda Hosp., Duisburg, Germany, 1980-81; served in Norwegian mil. svc., 1982-83; asst. physician Ctrl. Hosp., Stavanger, 1983-92; from rsch. fellow to asst. physician U. Hosp. Trondheim, 1992—, cardiologist, 1996—. Mem. Am. Soc. Hypertension, Den norske Laegeforening, N.Y. Acad. Scis., Norwegian Soc. Hypertension, Norwegian Soc. Cardiology. Home: Breisynveien 24 B, 7021 Trondheim Norway Office: Univ Hosp Trondheim, 7006 Trondheim Norway

SOMA, MASAYOSHI, endocrinologist, educator; b. Ootsuki, Yamanashi, Japan, Aug. 30, 1952; s. Kazuo and Kiyoko (Kobayashi) S.; m. Yoko Suda, Nov. 4, 1979; children: Kazuhiro, Sachiho, Keishi. MD, Nihon U., Tokyo, 1979, PhD, 1983. Med. diplomate. Resident Nihon U. Hosp., Tokyo, 1979-83; postdoctoral fellow Efamol Rsch. Inst., Can., 1983-85; chief cardiovascular divsn. Kofu Nat. Hosp., 1986-87; instr. endocrinology Sch. Medicine Nihon U., Tokyo, 1987-92, asst. prof., 1993-98. Mem. editl. bd. Nutrition, 1992—; editor: Advances in Polyunsaturated Fatty Acid Rsch., 1992; contbr. articles to profl. jours. Dir. Heisei Welfare Assn., Japan, 1990—; med. dir. Unum Japan Ins. Co. Ozawa's grantee Nihon U., Japan, 1995. Mem. Soc. for Rsch. Polyunsaturated Fatty Acid India (sec. 1989—), Japan Endocrine Soc. (councilor 1990—), Japan Hypertension Soc. (councilor 1998—), SHR Soc. (councilor 1999—), Japan Cardiovasc. Endocrinology and Metabolism Soc. (councilor 1999—), Japan Soc. Adult Disease (councilor 2000—). Avocation: Japanese chess. Home: 2-10-16 Tagara, 179-0073 Nerima Tokyo, Japan Office: Nihon U Sch Medicine, 30-1 Ooyaguchi Kamimachi, 173-8610 Itabashi Tokyo, Japan

SOMAYAJI, BANTVAL VENKATRAMANA, dental surgeon, periodontics educator; b. Bantval, Karnataka, India, Jan. 25, 1938; s. Bantval Narayana and Bhagirathi Somayaji; m. Varalakshmi Mayya, Feb. 21, 1968; children: Manjunath, Ganesha. B Dental Surgery, U. Bombay, 1965; M Dental Surgery, U. Bangalore, 1973. Registered dental surgeon Dental Coun. India. With Karnataka State Govt. Svc., various locations, 1966-90; dental surgeon on depuattion from Karnataka State Govt., Lusaka, Zambia, 1975-77; assoc. prof. Al-Arab Med. U., Benghazi, Libya, 1991-92; prof., head dept. periodontics A.B.S.M. Inst. Dental Scis., Mangalore, 1992—; cons. practice Splty. Dental Clinic, Mangalore, India, 1972—. Contbr. articles to profl. jours. Fellow Internat. Coll. Dentists, Pierre Fouchard Acad.; mem. Internat. Congress Oral Implantology, Indian Dental Assn. (pres. South Canara Dist. br. 1982-83), Indian Soc. Periodontology (v.p. 1997-98), N.Y. Acad. Scis. E-mail: bvs@bgl.vsnl.net.in. Office: ABSM Inst Dental Scis, Periodontics, Deralakatte, Mangalore, Karnataka 574160, India

SOMBATSOMPOP, NARONGRIT, polymer engineering educator, researcher; b. Bangkok, Thailand, Jan. 12, 1970; s. Wittachai and Kemthong Saetang. BSc in Indsl. Chemistry, King Mongkut's U. Tech., Bangkok, 1992; MSc in Polymer Sci. and Tech., King Mongkut's U. Tech., Eng., 1994, PhD in Polymer Sci. & Tech., 1997. Chem. engr. Thai-Suzuki Co. Ltd., Bangkok, 1992-93; rschr. Caligen Foam Co. Ltd., Manchester, 1995-97; lectr., rschr. in materials tech. King Mongkut's Inst. Tech., Bangkok, 1997-98, asst. prof. materials tech., rschr., 1998—, chmn. for quality mgmt. reassurance, Sch. Energy & Materials, 1999—. Co-author: (with A.K. Wood) Polymer Processing, 2000; mng. editor Asian Jour. Energy & Environ.; contbr. over 45 articles to internat. profl. jours. and conf. procs.; patentee in field; reviewer Polymer Testing and Polymer Recycling, 1999—. Classical guitar tchr. Yamaha Music Sch., 1990-92; Young Scientist's Mentor, Jr. Sci. Talent Project, Nat. Sci. and Tech. Devel. Agy., Thailand, 1998—. Rsch. grantee Thailand Rsch. Fund, 1997, recipient TRF Rsch. Scholar award, 1999, Thailand Young Scientist award, 2000. Mem. Polymer Processing Soc., Polymer Soc. Thailand. Avocations: playing guitar, reading, football. Fax: (662) 427 9062. E-mail: narongrit.som@kmutt.ac.th. Office: King Mongkut's U Tech Thonb, Pracha U-Thit Thungkru, Bangkok 10140, Thailand

SOMER, GÜLER, chemistry educator; b. Ankara, Turkey, Aug. 5, 1937; d. Aziz and Ayten (Stein) Alpaut; m. Tarik Galip Somer, Oct. 26, 1959; 1 child, Deniz. MS, Ankara U., 1960; PhD, Mid. East Tech. U., Ankara, 1971. Tchg. asst. Mid. East Tech. U., Ankara, 1965-71; instr. chemistry dept. Hacettepe U., Ankara, 1971-78, assoc. prof., 1978-85; prof. chemistry Gazi U., Ankara, 1985—, chemistry dept., 1986-98; rep. of Turkey Divsn. Analytical Chemistry, Fedn. European Chem. Socs. Contbr. articles to profl. jours., chpts. to books. Home: Esat Caddesi, 06660 Ankara Turkey Office: Gazi U Fen-Edebiyat Fakulte, Kimya Bolumu, 06500 Ankara Turkey

SOMERS COCKS, ANNA GWENLLIAN, publishing executive, editor; b. Rome, Apr. 18, 1950; d. John Sebastian Somers Cocks and Marjorie Olive

Weller; m. John Julian Hardy, 1978 (div. 1990); children: Maximilian, Katherine; m. Umberto Allemandi, Nov. 30, 1991. MA, Oxford U., 1971, Courtauld Inst. London, 1973. Asst.-keeper Victoria & Albert Mus., London, 1973-86; editor in chief Apollo Mag., London, 1986-90, The Art Newspaper, London, 1990—; mem. conservative parliamentary adv. com. Arts and Heritage, 1988—; expert on export of works of art U.K. Govt.; expert advisor to Nat. Heritage Lottery Fund. Author: The Victoria and Albert Museum: The Making of the Collection, 1980; co-author: (with C. Truman) Renaissance Jewels, Gold Boxes and Objects de Vertu in the Thyssen Collection, 1985; editor, author: (exhbn. catalogue) Princely Magnificence: Court Jewels of the Renaissance, 1980; contbr. articles to profl. jours. Trustee Gilbert Collection, Attingham Summer Sch.; exec. chmn. Venice in Peril. Recipient Award Nat. Art Collections Fund, 1992. Fellow Soc. Antiquaries. Roman Catholic. Avocations: skiing, walking, art. Office: The Art Newspaper, 27-29 Vauxhall Grove, London SW8 1SY, England

SOMERVILLE, JAMES MIDDLETON, III, retired philosophy educator, writer; b. Sept. 21, 1915; s. James Middleton II and Helen (Hannigan) S.; m. Beatrice Bruteau, Jan. 26, 1971. BA in French, Fordham U., 1937, MA in Psychology, 1939; Licentiate in Philosophy, U. St. Louis, 1944; Licentiate in Sacred Theology, Woodstock Coll., 1951; PhD in Philosophy, Fordham U., 1954. Instr. philosophy Fordham U., Bronx, N.Y., 1954-56, asst. prof. philosophy, 1956-61, assoc. prof. philosophy, 1961-70, chair philosophy dept., 1957-66; prof. philosophy Xavier U., Cin., 1971-82; ret., 1982; co-founder, exec. editor Internat. Philos. Quar., 1961—; editor, pub. Schola, Quar. Jour. Philosophy, Religion and Scripture in an East-West Context, 1982-00. Author: The Mystical Sense of the Gospels, 1997, Total Commitment, 1965; translator: Blondel and Christianity, 1966; contbr. over 30 articles to profl. jours. (Best Scholarly Article 1961 Cath. Press Assn.). Democrat. Roman Catholic. Avocation: contemporary scripture scholarship.

SOMÉUS, GEORGE EDWARD, environmental engineer, researcher; b. Budapest, Hungary, Apr. 28, 1951; arrived in Sweden, 1970; s. Desiderio and Martha (Löfler) Somay; m. Erika Biczo, May 13, 1989; children: Laurence Edward, Christopher Daniel. MSc, U. Lund (Sweden), 1978. Dir. Geoteknik AB, Malmö, Sweden, 1979-86, Product Control Ltd., St. Peter Port, Eng., 1987-96, Thermal Desorption Tech. Group LLC N.Am., 1999—, Terra Humana Ltd., 1090—; bd. dirs. United European Environment Controls Ltd., U.K. Achievements include invention of method and apparatus thermal desorption technology and applications, low temperature carbonization and applications, off gas treatment, clean coal, hazardous waste treatment, ceramic-activated carbon, Edward's Aqua Humana filter manufacturer, soil decontamination. E-mail: edward@tdt-3r.com.

SOMJEE, SHEHNAZ, otorhinolaryngologist, surgeon, poet, writer; b. Karachi, Pakistan, Mar. 18, 1953; arrived in Eng., 1980; d. Rahim Jusabhoy Aladin S. and Khairunissa (Aladin) Hasham. MB, BChir, Dow Med. Coll., Karachi, Pakistan, 1979; Diploma in Laryngology, Otology, Royal Coll. Surgeons Eng., 1986; LLB (hon.), Liverpool John Moores U., 1998. House officer Civil Hosp., Karachi, Pakistan, 1978-80; sr. house officer Queen's Med. Ctr., Nottingham, Eng., 1983, Leicester Royal Infirmary, Eng., 1983-84, King's Lynn, Norfolk, Eng., 1984-86; registrar Walton Hosp., Liverpool, 1986-89; sr. registrar Leicester Hosp., 1992; pvt. practice Eng., 1995—; cons. Kirkcaldy and Tameside, Eng., 1994-95. Author numerous poems; contbr. articles to profl. jours. and chpts. to books; inventor somjee-crabtree temporal bone support clamp. Recipient First prize classical solo singing Radio Pakistan, 1972, Internat. Poet of Merit award, 1997-98, 2000; named Honoured Poet 1998. Fellow Royal Coll. Surgeons Eng.; mem. Brit. Med. Assn. (treas. (hon.) 1989-91, bd. sci. and edn. 1998—), Brit. Assn. Otorhinolaryngologists/Head and Neck Surgeons, Liverpool Med. Instn., Pakistan Med. Assn. (mem. coun. 1997—), Internat. Soc. Poetry (disting.), Med. Women's Fedn. (mem. coun. 1997—), Locum Doctors' Assn. (founder, chair 1997—, editor newsletter. Achievements include being first female surgeon to invent and market a surgical instrument in Europe. Home and Office: 8 Martine Close, L31 1DJ Melling England

ŠOMLO, PETER, internist, consultant; b. Šahy, Czechoslovakia, Apr. 24, 1948; s. Stefan and Priska (Vermes) S.; m. Beata Drobna, Nov. 6, 1981; children: Zuzana, Peter. MD, Komensky U., Bratislava, Czechoslovakia, 1972. Intern Gen. Hosp., Sahy, 1972-80, sub-chief med. officer internal med., 1980-85, chief med. officer internal med., 1985—, dir., 1994—. Contbr. articles to profl. jours. Mem. Czechoslovak Soc. Internal Med., Czechoslovak Soc. Cardiology, Czechoslovak Soc. Endocrinology, Slovak Med. Chamber (mem. Cen. Com.), N.Y. Acad. Sci., Assn. Small Hosps. (chmn. 1996—). Home: 936 01, Sahy Slovakia Office: 93601, Gen Hosp, Sahy Slovakia

SOMMARUGA, CORNELIO, humanitarian services organization administrator, diplomat; b. Rome, Dec. 29, 1932; s. Carlo and Anna Maria (Valagussa) S.; m. Ornella Marzorati; 6 children. LLD, U. Zurich, Switzerland, 1957; D of Polit. Affairs (hon.), U. Fribourg, Switzerland, 1985; D in Internat. Rels. (hon.), U. Minho, Portugal, 1989; D of Medicine (hon.), U. Bologna, Italy, 1991; D in Law (hon.), U. Nice-Sophia, Antipolis, France, 1992, Seoul Nat. U., Rep. of Korea, 1992; PhD in Law (hon.), Geneva U., 1997; LHD (hon.), Webster U., 1998. Various diplomatic positions Swiss Confedn.'s Svc., 1960-73; dep. sec. gen. European Free Trade Assn., Geneva, 1973-75; minister plenipotentiary Dept. Pub. Economy, Berne, Switzerland, 1976-77, amb. plenipotentiary, 1977-80, del. Swiss Govt. for Trade Agreements, 1980-83, state sec. external econ. affairs, 1984-86; pres. Internat. Com. Red Cross, Geneva, 1987-99, Found. Moral Rearmament, Caux, Switzerland, 2000—; chmn. bd. J.P. Morgan (Suisse) Geneva, 2000—; pres. Geneva Internat. Ctr. for Humanitarian Demining, 2000—; chmn. bd. Karl PopperFound., Zug, 2000—. Recipient Presdl. award Tel-Aviv U., 1995. E-mail: cornelio.sommaruga@bluewin.ch. Home: 16 chemin Crets-de-Champnel, CF-1206 Geneva Switzerland Office: GICHD, BP 1300, CH-1211 Geneva Switzerland

SOMMER, ANDREAS PETER, physicist, researcher; b. Temesvar, Romania, Feb. 22, 1954; arrived in Germany, 1969.; Diploma in physics, Philipps U., Marburg, Germany, 1992, PhD, 1998. Prin. investigator, co-sponsored by Am. Chem. Soc. European Nearfield Scanning Optical Microscopy Lab. patentee in field; contbr. articles to sci. jours., including Biomed. Engring. Achievements include pioneer work in fields of pulsed ion sources in colinear laser-ion-beam-spectroscopy, low intensity laser activated biostimulation, generation of homogeneously distributed high photon density laser light fields for medical applications, energy density standards for clinical applications of lasers, biostimulatory windows in low intensity laser activation, biological standards for near field microscopy, dielectric optical elements for near field optical analysis, hydrophobic optical elements for near field optical analysis in liquid environments, diamond-coated prostheses for lifelong implantation, gap reduction around light-curing dental fillings by application of light inserts, modelling the polymerisation shrinking of dental composites by selective photo-curing, prevention of ice-accumulation on airplanes by application of perfluorcarbons, free energy reduction by molecular interface crossing for application in nanoscopic blood substitutes and explanation of thundercloud electrification. Avocation: ancient cultures. Home: Weinbergweg 279, 89075 Ulm Germany

SOMMER, ANDREAS URS, philosopher, historian; b. Aarburg, Aargau, Switzerland, July 14, 1972; s. Werner André and Annemarie Sophie (Wehrli) S. MLitt, U. Basel, Switzerland, 1995; PhD, U. Basel, 1998. Sci. collaborator dept. philosophy U. Basel, 1995-97; rsch. fellow Swiss Nat. Found., 1997—; vis. fellow Princeton U., N.J., 1998-99; lectr. Ernst-Moritz-Arndt-U., Greifswald, Germany, 1999—; rschr. Frey-Grynaeum Inst., Basel, 1996-97; sci. collaborator Swiss Mil. Libr., Bern, 1997—. Author: Der Geist der Historie, 1997, Im Spannungsfeld von Gott und Welt, 1997, Friedrich Nietzsches Der Antichrist, 2000, Die Hortung, Basel; editor letters of A. Schweitzer and F. Buri, Internat. Fritz Buri Soc.; co-editor letters of Franz Overbeck, 1994—; contbr. articles to profl. jours. Recipient Eligius prize German Numismatic Assn., 1992. Mem. Schweizer Numismatic Assn., French Numismatic Soc. Presbyterian. E-mail: aestas@gmx.net.

SOMMER, EMMANUEL, civil engineering consultant; b. Paris, July 1, 1937; arrived in Israel, 1963; s. Hélène Chécinski, Aug. 30, 1959; children: Hillel, Yael, Eldad. Degree in engring., ETP Spl. Sch. of Pub. Works, Paris, 1961. Registered and lic. engr., Israel. Planning engr. Metrikin, Efrony & Schoenberg, Architects, Jerusalem, 1964-68; ind. cons. engr. Jerusalem, 1968—; arbitrator, provider expert testimony various ct. procs., Jerusalem, 1985—. Mem. Internat. Assn. for Bridge and Structural Engring., Assn. Civil Engring. (mem. Jerusalem com. 1993). Jewish. Office: E Sommer Cons Engr, Ben-Yehuda St 36, IL-94583 Jerusalem Israel

SOMMER, GERT, psychology educator; b. Dortmund, Germany, Feb. 2, 1941; s. Fritz Wilhelm and Luise (Middelmann) S.; m. Sabine Liselotte Rehahn, Aug. 30, 1986; 1 child, Anna Sonja. Diploma in psychology, Bonn, Germany, 1966, PhD, 1969. Rsch. asst. U. Heidelberg, Germany, 1966-70, asst. prof., 1970-77; prof. U. Marburg, Germany, 1977—. Author: Community Psychology, 1977, Enemy Images, 1987, 3d edit., 1993, Nonviolent Conflict Resolution, 1993, Prevention and Health Promotion, 1999, Human Rights and Peace, 1999. Dir. Peace Psychology, Marburg, 1987—, Rsch. Group on Peace and Conflict Resolution, Marburg U., 1993-95, 97—. Office: Fachbereich Psychol, Gutenbergstr 18, 35032 Marburg Germany

SOMMER, HARALD LEO, physician, researcher; b. Jena, Germany, July 12, 1944; s. Leo Harald and Ebba Marianne von Seidlitz S.; m. Elke Brunhilde Starke, April 4, 1970. Arzt U. Jena, Germany, 1978-93, oberarzt, 1993—; prof. München, 1993—. Office: Univ Fraüenklinik, Maistr 11, D-80337 München Germany

SOMMER, HARTMUT, physician; b. Bad Nauheim, Hessen, Germany, Nov. 21, 1941; s. Wilhelm August and Minni (Haasenstrauch) S.; m. Maria Schreiber, Oct. 10, 1969 (div. 1983); children: Matthias, Miriam, Christoph. MD, U. Giessen, Fed. Rep. Germany, 1969; D in Med. Habil., U. Wurzburg, Fed. Rep. Germany, 1981. Med. diplomate, 1969. Resident in internal medicine U. Wurzburg (Fed. Rep. Germany) Med. Dept., 1970-81, cons., 1981-86; chief of staff, chief of lab. Regional Hosp. Med. Dept., Heidenheim, Fed. Republic Germany, 1986—; prof. internal medicine U. Wurzburg, 1987—. Author: (with others) Pancreatic Diseases, 1974, Hormonal Stimulation of the Pancreas, 1981; co-author (jour.) Crohn's Disease, 1984. Mem. German Soc. Physicians, German Gastroenterological Assn. Avocations: reading, mountaineering. Office: Kreiskrankenhaus Hosp, Schlosshaustr 100, D-89522 Heidenheim German Democratic Republic

SOMMER, JENS-UWE, physicist; b. Bad Saarow, Germany, Apr. 24, 1963; s. Heinz-Lutz Hauenschild and Eva (Annemarie) S.; m. Katrin Maren Sickel, Aug. 11, 1988; 1 child, Carolin. Diploma, Tech. U., Mersebury, 1987, PhD, 1991. Rschr. U. Regensburg, Germany, 1991-93, CEN Saclay, France, 1993-95, U. Freiburg, Germany, 1995—. Contbr. articles to profl. jours. Recipient Scientific award Tech. U. of Mersebury, 1991. Office: Theoretical Polymer Physics, Rheinstr 12, D-79104 Freiburg Germany

SOMMER, LUMIR, chemistry educator; b. Opava, Moravia, Czechoslovakia, Jan. 19, 1929; s. Ervin and Elisabeth Linke S.; m. Eva Shtentsel, Sept. 24, 1955; children: Ludmila, Vit. Rer.Nat.Dr., Masaryk U., Brno, Czechoslovakia, 1952; DS in Chemistry, Tech. U., Prague, 1964. Lectr. Masaryk U., Brno, 1952, sr. lectr., 1955-58, asst. prof., 1958-64, prof., 1964-97, prof. emeritus, 1997—; prof. Chem. Technol. Protection Environment, Brno, 1995—; chmn. dept. analytical chemistry, Masaryk U., 1952-97, dean faculty of sci., 1962-65, 89-91; coord. of state rsch. projects, 1970-80; mem. adv. bd. Internat. Jour. Talanta, 1988-98; mem. Analytical Commn. of IUPAC, Oxford, 1969-74, 77-89; mem. Working Party Chemistry, Commn. for Accreditation of Czech. Govt., 1990-97, 99—; mem. Sci. Couns. of Faculty Sci., Masaryk U. 1989-96, and Faculty Chemistry, Tech. U. Brno, 1995—. Author: (book) Analytical Absorption Spectrophotometry, 1989; co-author: Emission Spectrometry in ICP and HT-Flames, 1992, Handbook of Chemistry and Physics, 74th edit., 1994; contbr. articles to profl. jours. Recipient Gregor Mendel award for sci., Brno, 1968, Memory medal Tech. U. Mines, Ostrava, 1975, Palacky U., Olomouc, 1979, Gold medals Masaryk U., 1990, 94. Avocations: chemistry, world history, travel. Home: Tech U Chem Prot Environ, Purkynova 118, CZ-61200 Brno Czech Republic

SOMMER, MANFRED, philosophy educator, writer; b. Thalmaessing, Germany, Aug. 14, 1945. DPhil, U. Münster, Germany, 1974, Habilitation, 1982. Asst. prof. philosophy U. Münster, Germany, 1974-83, assoc. prof., 1983-88; vis. prof. U. Duisburg, Germany, 1986, U. Würzburg, Germany, 1992-93; vis. prof. U. Kiel, Germany, 1989-92, prof., 1993—. Author: Husserl und der fruehe Positivismus, 1985, Evidenz im Augenblick, 1987, Identitaet im Uebergang: Kant, 1988, Lebenswelt und Zeitbewusstsein, 1990, Sammeln Ein philosophischer Versuch, 1999. Office: Suhrkamp Verlag, Lindenstrasse, 60019 Frankfurt am Main Germany

SOMMER, MARK F., lawyer; b. Portsmouth, Ohio, Nov. 8, 1962; s. Ralph B. and Joan J. Sommer; m. Bridget Downey, Oct. 29, 1988; children: Victoria, Daniel, Thomas, Therese, Bernadette. BSBA, Xavier U., 1985; JD, U. Cin., 1988. Bar: Ky., U.S. Dist. Ct. (we. dist.) Ky. 1988, U.S. Tax. Ct. 1988, U.S. Dist. Ct. (ea. dist.) Ky. 1989, U.S. Ct. Fed. Claims 1989, U.S. Ct. Appeals (6th cir.) 1989, U.S. Dist. Ct. (no. dist.) Ill. 1990; Supreme Ct. Ky., 1988; Supreme Ct. U.S., 1995. Assoc. Greenebaum Doll & McDonald, Louisville, 1988-94, mem., 1995—; presenter in field. Contbr. numerous articles to profl. jours. Recipient Am. Jurisprudence Advanced Tax award. Mem. ABA (mem. environ. taxes subcom., mem. sects. tax, mem. state and local taxation com.), Fed. Bar Assn. (mem. sect. of tax), Ky. Bar Assn. (mem. sects. of tax, sec. tax sect. 1994-95, chair elect, chair tax sect. 1995—), Louisville Bar Assn. (mem. sects. tax, chair tax sect. 1995—), Xavier U. Alumni Assn., Glen Oaks Country Club, Legal Aid Soc. Louisville (vol. lawyer program), Downtown Louisville Rotary Club. Fax: 502-587-3695. E-mail: mfs@gdm.com. Home: 8507 Running Spring Dr Louisville KY 40241-5515 Office: Greenebaum Doll & McDonald PLLC 3300 National City Tower 101 S 5th St Louisville KY 40202-3103

SOMMER, RICK JOSEPH, lawyer, nursing home administrator; b. Troy, Ohio, Aug. 4, 1957; s. William Francis and Carole Ann Sommer; m. Cindy Lee Collins, Aug. 25, 1979 (div. Nov. 1984); m. Judith Bea Cohen, Aug. 2, 1986; children: Joseph (dec.). BS, Rochester Inst. Tech., 1980; M of Gerontol. Studies, Miami U., Oxford, Ohio, 1988; JD cum laude, Salmon P. Chase Coll. Law, Highland Heights, Ky., 1998. Cert. nursing home administr., assisted living administr., subacute care administr. Coord. audiovisual svcs. Mt. Carmel Health, Columbus, Ohio, 1980-81, dir. media svcs., 1981-86; grad. asst. Scripps Gerontology Ctr., Oxford, 1986-88; project mgr., administr. CommuniCare, Inc., Cin., 1988-90; administr. Kettering (Ohio) Convalescent Ctr., 1990-91, Mt. Pleasant Retirement Village, Monroe, Ohio, 1991-98; law clk. The Lawrence Firm, LPA, Cin., 1998-99, atty., 9199—. Recipient scholarship and awards. Avocations: travel, hot air balloons. E-mail: rsommer@cinci.rr.com. Office: The Lawrence Firm LPA 425 Walnut St Ste 2100 Cincinnati OH 45202-3924

SOMMER, RON, telecommunications executive; b. 1949. D in Math., Vienna, Austria, 1971. With Nixdorf, N.Y.C. and Paderborn, Paris, 1980; mng. dir. German subs. Sony Deutschland, 1986-90, chmn. bd. mgmt., 1990-93; pres., COO Sony USA, 1993-95; CEO Deutsche Telekom AG, Bonn, Germany, 1995—; chmn. bd. mgmt. Deutsche Telekom AG, Bonn. Office: Deutsche Telekom AG, Friedrich-Elbert-Allee 140, 53113 Bonn Germany*

SOMMERFELD, DAVID WILLIAM, lawyer, educator; b. Detroit, Jan. 21, 1942; s. Henry Anthony and Hilda (Diffley) S.; m. Anne Marlaine Toth, June 27, 1964; children: Catherine, David Jr., Michael, Caroline. BS, U. Detroit, 1963; JD, Detroit Coll., 1967. Trust officer Nat. Bank Detroit, 1963-68; tax supr. Ernst & Ernst, Detroit, 1968-73; ptnr. Monaghan, Campbell, LoPrete & McDonald, Detroit, 1973-77; prof. Detroit Coll., 1977-86; ptnr. Butzel Long, Detroit, 1987—; lectr. Ind. Soc. CPAs, Indpls., 1980-93, Ohio Soc. CPAs, Columbus, 1987, W.Va. Soc. CPAs, Charleston, 1983-86, 91. Editor Mich. Probate and Trust Law Jour., 1981-83. Named one of Best Lawyers in Am. Woodward/White Inc., 1999-2000. Fellow Am. Coll. of Trust and Estate Counsel; mem. Mich. Bar Assn., Detroit Bar Assn., Am. Inst. CPA's, Mich. Assn. CPA's, Forest Lake Country Club, Detroit Athletic Club. Roman Catholic. Avocations: bowling, spectator sports, gardening. Office: Butzel Long 32270 Telegraph Rd Ste 200 Bingham Farms MI 48025-2457

SOMMERS, GEORGE R., lawyer; b. N.Y.C., Jan. 27, 1955. BA, U. So. Fla., 1975; JD, NYU, 1987. Bar: N.J. 1987, U.S. Dist. Ct. N.J. 1987, N.Y. 1988, U.S. Dist. Ct. (all dists.) N.Y. 1988, U.S. Ct. Appeals (3d cir.) 1988, U.S. Ct. Appeals (2d cir.) 1989, U.S. Supreme Ct. 1992. Assoc. Sullivan & Cromwell, N.Y.C., 1987-90; pvt. practice lawyer N.Y.C., 1990—; pres. Bill of Rights Found., N.Y.C., 1994—. Seidler scholar NYU Sch. Law, N.Y.C., 1985. Mem. Hoboken Bar Assn. (pres. 1994). Jewish. Avocations: sailing, chess. Office: Ste 2211 67 Wall St New York NY 10005-3101

SOMOGYI, JANOS, biochemistry educator; b. Jaszbereny, Hungary, Sept. 19, 1929; s. Janos and Iren (Bodor) S.; m. Antonia Mohacsi Somogyi, Sept. 30, 1953; children: Lilla, Attila. MD, U. Medicine Sch. Budapest, Hungary, 1954; PhD, Hungary Acad. Scis., Budapest, 1963; DSc, Hungary Acad. Acis., Budapest, 1972. Asst. prof. Inst. Biochemistry U. Med. Sch. Budapest, Hungary, 1954-68; first asst. exptl. rsch. dept. U. Med. Sch. Budapest, 1968-70; assoc. prof. exptl. rsch. dept. Semmelweis U. Med. Sch., 1970-75; prof. Inst. Biochemistry Semmelweis U. Med. Sch., 1975—; head membrane unit Inst. Biochemistry Semmelweis U., Budapest, 1975—. Author, editor: Membrane Dynamics and Transport of Normal and Tumor Cells, 1984; Structure and Functions of Biomembranes I-III, 1989-90. Recipient Jendrassik medal and prize Semmelweis U. Med. Sch., Budapest, 1972, Acad. award Hungarian Acad. Scis., Budapest, 1978, Kisfaludy medal City of Sumeg, Hungary, 1997, Romhanyi award Hungarian Soc. Membrane Transport, 1997, Apáczai Csere János medal and price Minister for public edn., Hungary, 1999. Mem. The Biochemistry Soc., European Soc. Neurochemistry (exec. com. 1983-85), N.Y. Acad. Scis. Office: Inst Medcal Chemnistry, Puskin u 9 PO Box 260, 1444 Budapest Hungary

SOMOGYI, KÁROLY, engineer, physicist; b. Kézdivásárhely, Hungary, June 12, 1944; s. Gyula and Gizella (Ettig) S.; m. Károlyné Marianna Havlik, May 11, 1974. MSc, Kiev (USSR) U., 1967; PhD, Budapest (Hungary) Tech. U., 1993. Rsch. co-worker Rsch. Inst. for Tech. Physics, Hungarian Acad. Scis., Budapest, 1967-92; sr. rschr. Rsch. Inst. for tech. Physics of Hungarian Acad. Scis., Budapest, 1992—; mem. gen. assembly Hungarian Acad. Scis., Budapest, 1995—; mem. organizing com. 3 internat. confs. Contbr. numerous articles to profl. jours. Decorated Order of Labour of Republic, Coun. of Ministers, Budapest, 1977, Gold Ring of Pres. of Republic, Hungary, 1993; recipient award for young scientists Hungarian Acad. Scis., 1974. Mem. IEEE, R. Eötvös Phys. Soc. Avocations: gardening, stamp collecting, music. Office: Hungarian Acad Sci, Konkoly Thege M u 29-33, H-1125 Budapest Hungary

SOMOZA, MANUEL JESÚS, physician; b. Buenos Aires, June 13, 1929; s. Manuel and Elisa (Noguerol) S.; m. Nilda Rosa Colombo, May 23, 1956; children: Gustavo Manuel, Patricia Nilda, Cecilia Claudia. MD, Buenos Aires U., 1955. Chief of neurology Mcpl. Hosp., Buenos Aires, 1980—; prof. neurology Buenos Aires U., 1986—, physician, 1971—; vis. fellow Queen Sq. London, 1985; coord. task group Prevention and Control of Neurol. Diseases, Buenos Aires, 1991—; coord. med. residences in neurology, Buenos Aires, 1983—; dir. fellowship Nat. Acad. Medicine, Buenos Aires, 1983-84. Author: Toxoplasmosis, 1975, Semiology (Neurology), 1974, Neurology, 1983, Medicine, 1991. Recipient Mariano R. Castex award Nat. Acad. Medicine, 1975. Mem. Soc. Francaise Neurologie (hon.), Argentine Soc. Neurology (treas. 1972-74, sec. 1974-78, pres. 1984-86, Josè M. Ramos Mejia award 1976), Pan Am. Soc. Neuro-epidemiology (pres. 1999—). Home: Ave Libertador 2254 6 D, 1425 Buenos Aires Argentina

SOMSÁK, LÁSZLÓ, chemist, educator; b. Miskolc, Hungary, Mar. 18, 1954; s. Béla and Ilona (Varró) S.; m. Ildikó Zsupán, July 7, 1984; children: Zsuzsa, Tamás. Dipl. chemistry, Lajos Kossuth U., Hungary, 1978, PhD, 1983. Rsch. fellow Rsch. Group for Antibiotics Hungarian Acad. Scis., Debrecen, 1978-81; asst. lectr. dept. organic chemistry Lajos Kossuth U., Debrecen, 1981-93, assoc. prof. dept. organic chemistry, 1993—, Szechenyi prof. organic chemistry, 1999—. Contbr. chpt. in book and articles to profl. jours. Fellow Alexander von Humboldt Found., 1992-93; recipient poste rouge Ctr. Nat. de la Sci. Rsch., 1990-91. Mem. Hungarian Acad. Scis. (Carbohydrate com. 1991—, cand. sci. 1991, G.A. Olah prize 1999). Office: U Debrecen Dept Org Chem, Egyetem tér 1, H-4010 Debrecen Hungary

SOMSAVAT LENGSAVAD, Lao government official; b. Luang Prabang, June 15, 1945. PhD (hon.), Ramkhamhaeng U., Thailand, 2000. Amb. to Bulgaria, 1989-91; chief Coun. of Ministers, LPRPCC, 1991-93; min. fgn. affairs Govt. of Laos, Vientiane, 1993—, chmn. external rels. commn., dep. prime min., dep. chmn. com. investment and coop.; officer Cabinet of the Lao People's Revolutionary Party Ctrl. Com., 1964-75, head secretariat, 1975-82, dept. chief, 1982-88, mem., 1991, dep. min., 1st vice-chmn. Pres., vice chmn. investment cooperation Nat. Commn. for Mothers and Children. E-mail: cabmofa@pan-laos.net.la. Office: Ministry Fgn Affairs, That Luang Rd, Vientiane Laos

SOMSEN, HENRY NORTHROP, retired lawyer; b. New Ulm, Minn., Aug. 12, 1909; s. Henry N. and Meta (Koch) S.; m. Anne Elizabeth Duncan, Sept. 12, 1936 (dec.); children: Pennell Anne, Stephen Duncan. BA, U. Minn., 1932, JD, 1934. Bar: Minn. 1934. Practice law New Ulm, 1934-85; ptnr. Somsen, Dempsey, Johnson & Somsen, 1934-40, Somen Dempsey & Somsen, 1940-46, Somsen & Somsen, 1946-55; sole practice, 1955-64; ptnr. Somsen & Dempsey, 1965-71; ptnr. Somsen Dempsey & Schade, 1971-85, of counsel, 1985—. Bd. editors U. Minn. Law Rev., 1932-33. Trustee Minn. State Parks Found., 1967-77; bd. dirs. Minn. Council State Parks, 1956—, pres., 1974-75; bd. dirs., pres. New Ulm Community Concert Assn., 1947-85; bd. dirs. Union Hosp., New Ulm, 1959-77, Highland Homes, Inc., 1970-79, New Ulm Meml. Found., 1958-79; bd. dirs. New Ulm Industries Inc., 1952-85, pres., 1968-77; bd. dirs. New Ulm Industries Found., Inc., 1953-85, pres., 1968-77, bd. dirs. 1953-83, chmn., 1978-83 Farmers and Mchts. Bank, New Ulm, Minn.; bd. dirs. Klossner State Bank, Minn., 1947-84, State Bond and Mortgage Co., 1950-80, Am. Artstoone Co., 1955-84; mem. City Charter Commns., 1940, 51, 66, pres., 1966. Served from pvt. to capt. JAGC, AUS, 1943-46. Mem. ABA, Minn. Bar Assn., Am. Judicature Soc., Am. Arbitration Assn. (panel of arbitrators 1967-85), Mpls. Club, Masons, Rotary, Shriners. Episcopalian. Home: 211 2d St NW Apt 1907 Rochester MN 55901-3101

SOMUNCU, MELEK TÜLIN, artist; b. Karabük, Turkey, May 22, 1951; d. Osman Cihat and Sidika (Gümülcüneli) Onbulak; m. Üm9t Somuncu, Feb. 16, 1972; children: Umot, Gaye. Grad., Mimar Sinan Acad., Istanbul, Turkey, 1972. mem. Art Exbhn., Istanbul, 1965—, coord. Habitat II, 1996; dir. Art Programme-Channel 7, Istanbul, 1996, art program SVT, 1994. One-man shows include La Galerie d'Art de l'Abbaye de Forest, Brussels, 1989, Kuzguncuk, Akbank Art Gallery, Istanbul, 1991, Kapadokyo Dedeman Hotel, Nigde, Turkey, 1991, Bebek, Akbank Art Gallery, 1992, The Gallery, Istanbul, 1994, Taksim Art Gallery, Istanbul, Beyoglu Municipality Art Gallery, Istanbul, 1996, Cumali Art Gallery, Istanbul, 1998, Feshane Art Gallery, Istanbul, 1999; group exhbns. include The Galery Galeria, Istanbul, 1988, 89, Kadiköy Kültür Merkezi, Istanbul, 1990, Yildiz Palace, Istanbul, 1990, Marmara Soroptimist Group Exhbn., Istanbul, 1991, Turkish Women Coun., Vakif Bank Exhbn., Istanbul, 1993, Cumali Art Gallery, Istanbul, 1995, Habitat 2, Istanbul, 1996, Altunizade Kültür Merkezi, Istanbul, 1997, Beyoglu Art Gallery, Istanbul, 2000. Home: Altintepe Sirmakes sok No42, Istanbul 81570, Turkey Office: Kazova Trikotaj, Siraceuizler 1 lyiniyet #17, Istanbul 80260, Turkey

SON, HOANG VAN, biochemist, medical educator; b. Hanoi, Vietnam, June 16, 1938; s. Hoang Thuy Ba and Dang Thi Cuc Suong; m. Duong Thi Nguyet Minh, Dec. 20, 1969; children: Hoang Thu Ha, Hoang Duc Dung. MD, Med. U., Hanoi, 1962, specialist doctor grade 2, 1982, PhD, 1985. Cert. med. educator and rschr. Head dept. Proviancial Hosp., Nghe An, Vietnam, 1962-68, Ctrl. Hosp. Viet-Xo, Hanoi, 1968-71; head lab. Ctrl. Hosp. Viet-Duc, Hanoi, 1971-77; from vice-head to head dept. Inst. Pediats., Hanoi, 1977—; postgrad. trainee Erasmus U., Rotterdam, The Netherlands, 1982-83; assoc. prof. U. Blida, Algeria, 1989-94; specialist in biochemistry Ministry of Health, Hanoi, 1987-89. Author: Screening Test of Transaminase, 1976 (highest award Ministry of Health 1976); contbr. articles to profl. jours. Chief children monitor Youth Orgn., Hanoi, 1955-62, vice-sec. Youth Orgn., Nghe An, 1966-68. Recipient medal Ctrl. Youth Union Vietnam, 1962, Order of Resistance Grade 3, Pres. Vietnam, 1987, medal for health care svcs. Ministry of Health, Vietnam, 1996. Mem. Am. Assn. for

Clin. Chemistry (mem. quality assurance com. Asia-Pacific Fedn. of Clin. Biochemistry), Internat. Fedn. Clin. Chemistry (nat. rep. 1989-90, 97—), Vietnamese Assn. Clin. Biochemists (gen. sec. 1985—), Assn. Pediats. Vietnam, Internat. Soc. Clin. Enzymology, Nat. Geog. Soc., Internat. Assn. Therapeutic Drug Monitoring and Clin. Toxicology, N.Y. Acad. Scis., Australian Assn. Clin. Biochemists, Vietnam Assn. Preventive Medicine. Avocations: tourism, languages, collecting stamps, post cards, books. Home: 14 Duong Thanh, Hanoi Vietnam Office: Inst Pediatrics, PO Box 604, Hanoi Vietnam

SON, HYON KU, mechanical engineer; b. Unju, Chonpuk, Korea, May 6, 1944; s. Young Pil and Hwan Sik (Kim) S.; m. Jae Yon Joo, Apr. 26, 1970; children: Won Chun, Minkyung, Mina. BS, Chonbuk Nat. U., Korea, 1967. Registered profl. engr. Dep. mgr. Korea Fertilizer Co., Ulsan, Korea, 1966-76; dep. asst. gen. mgr. Keang Nam Enterprise, Seoul, Korea, 1976-78; gen. mgr. Doosan Devel. Co., Seoul, 1978-79, Doosan Constrn. Co., Seoul, 1980-89; dir. Hanyang Corp., Seoul, 1989-94; mng. dir. Halla Engring. & Constrn. Corp., Seoul, 1994-97; rep. GlobalTech Profl. Engrs. Office, Seoul, 1997—. Author: Pipeline Cleaning by Pig-Launching, 1982; editor: Rehabilitation of Hadisolb Rolling Mill, 1986. Corp. Korean Army, 1970-73. Mem. Korean Profl. Engrs. Assn., Korea Constrn. Engrs. Assn., Korea Solid Waste Engring. Soc., Korea Gas Union. Avocations: reading, fine arts, travel. Home: 409-181 Sillim Dong, Kwan ak-gu, Seoul 151-029, Republic of Korea Office: Globaltech Profl Engrs 409, 181 Sillim Dong Kwanak-gu, Seoul 151-029, Republic of Korea

SONDÉN, ERIK LARS NILS, investment banker; b. Stockholm, Feb. 25, 1960; arrived in france, 1994; s. Lars I. and Karin E. (Ström) S.; m. Marianne B. Préau, June 9, 1990 (div.); children: Gustav, Carl-Philip; m. Eva Cecilia Wolff, Feb. 4, 1998. Grad. in Econs. and Bus. Adminstrn., Stockholm Sch. Econs., 1985. Mgr. PK Banken, Frankfurt, Germany, 1985-87, Luxembourg, 1987-89; mng. dir. Swedish Internat. Property Assn., Stockholm and Brussels, 1989-93, Stockholm and Paris, 1993—; mng. dir. West German Properties B.V., Amsterdam, 1993-95, Nordic Property Brussels S.A., 1990-96; sr. adviser, bd. dirs. Paris Devel. Properties, S.A., Paris, 1994-95; European dir. Jones Lang LaSalle, France, 1996-2000; mng. dir. Deutsche Bank, Real Estate Investment Banking, Paris, 2000—. Co-author: EEC and the Property Markets, 1992; contbr. articles to profl. jours. Mem. Sällskapet Stockholm, Cercle Suedois-Norvegien Paris, Club de L'Immobilier, Ile-de-France. Avocations: family, riding, tennis, travel, languages. Home: Le Petit Chateau, 14810 Gonneville-en-Auge France Office: Deutsche Bank, 3 Ave de Friedland, 75008 Paris France

SONDEREGGER, MARCEL, medical engineering company executive; b. Blumenfeld, Switzerland, Mar. 1, 1968; s. K. Heinz and Maya Widder. Diploma in engring., Swiss Fed. Inst. Tech., Lausanne, Switzerland, 1994; PhD, U. Tokyo, 1998. Co-founder, pres. Sonderegger Engring. AG, Schaffhausen, Switzerland, 1994—; cons. in field. Contbr. articles to profl. jours.; patentee in field. Avocations: climbing, hiking, swimming. Office: Sonderegger Engring AG, Fasenstaubstrasse 43, 8200 Schaffhausen Switzerland

SONDERMANN, DIETER FRIEDRICH WILHELM, economic educator; b. Duisberg, Fed. Republic Germany, May 10, 1937; s. Fritz and Elfriede (Buettgenbach) S.; m. Annemarie Roeters, Mar. 10, 1967; children: Johannes, Matthias. BS, U. Bonn, 1962; MS, U. Hamburg, Fed. Republic Germany, 1966; PhD, U. Erlangen, Fed. Republic Germany, 1968; Dr.habil., U. Saarbrücken, Fed. Republic Germany, 1973. Lectr. U. Saarbrücken, 1969; vis. rsch. prof. U. Leuven, Belgium, 1970-72; vis. prof. U. Calif., Berkeley, 1973-74, 77-78; prof. econs. U. Hamburg, 1974-79; prof. econs. and statistics U. Bonn, 1979—; cons. Swiss Bank Corp., Zurich, 1984—, Deutsche Bank, Frankfurt. Editor: Fin. and Stochastics; contbr. articles to profl. jours. Ford fellow, 1978. Fellow Econometric Soc.; mem. Verein fur Socialpolitik, Gesellschaft fur Mathematik, Okonomie and Ops. Rsch. Home: Weidenweg 2, 53639 Konigswinter Germany Office: U Bonn Dept Econs, Adenauerallee 24-42, 53113 Bonn Federal Republic of Germany

SONE, CHANG SOO, telecommunication engineering consultant; b. Seoul, Korea, June 25, 1956; s. Chae Han and Ye Kyun (Shin) S.; m. Kyung Youn Cho, Nov. 27, 1982; children: Sae Il, Sae Young, Sae Hyun. BS, Yonsei U., Seoul, 1979, MS, 1982. Cert. 1st class electronics engr., Republic of Korea. Mem. rsch. staff Korea Electric and Telecomms. Rsch. Inst., Taejon, Korea, 1982-84; sr. mem. rsch. staff Electronics and Telecomms. Rsch. Inst., Taejon, 1984-92, prin. mem. rsch. staff, 1992-96, sect. head, 1992-96; mng. dir. World Tower Co., Ltd., Seoul, 1997—; cons. mem. Ministry of Info. and Comms., Rep. of Korea, 1995-96. Co-author: Introduction to TDX-10 System, 1994; patentee in field. With Korean Army, 1979-80. Recipient Minister award Ministry of Comm., Republic of Korea, 1991, Ministry of Info. and Comm., Republic of Korea, 1996. Mem. IEEE, IEEE Computer Soc., IEEE Comms. Soc., The Inst. of Electronics Engrs. of Korea (life), Korean Inst. Comm. Scis. Avocations: travel, walking. Office: World Tower Co Ltd, 7-25 Shinchon-Dong, Songpa-Gu Seoul 138-731, Republic of Korea

SONE, SATORU, electrical engineer; b. Tokyo, Apr. 23, 1939; s. Tamotsu and Yoshiko (Shibuya) S.; m. Sachiko (Mugibayashi) Sone, May 20 1965; children: Hiroshi, Toshiko, Loco. BS in Engring., U. Tokyo, 1962, MS in Engring., 1964, PhD in Engring, 1967. Lectr. Dept. Elec. Engring. U. Tokyo, 1967-68, assoc. prof. Dept. Elec. Engring., 1968-78, 83-84; rsch. fellow Dept. Elec. Engring. U. Birmingham, England, 1974-75; assoc. prof. Engring. Rsch. Inst. U. Tokyo, 1978-83, prof. Dept. Elec. Engring., 1984-95, 96-00, prof. Dept. Information & Comm. Engring., 1995-96, prof. emeritus, 2000—; prof. dept. elec. engring. Kogakuin U., 2000—; lectr. Tokushima (Japan) U., 1985-99, Nagoya (Japan) U., 1991-99; council bd. mem. Ministry Transport, Tokyo, 1988—; referee Nat. Inst. Acad. Degrees, Tokyo, Japan, 1996—. Author: New Railway System, 1987 (Divsn. Tech. prize, 1988); contbr. articles to profl. jours. Recipient Special Prize Japan Railway Engrs. Assn., Tokyo, 1988. Mem. Japan Railway Elec. Engring. Assn., Inst. Elec. Engrs. Japan (acad. award, 1996). Avocations: travel, trekking. Home: 1 1 40 Arakino, Abiko Chiba 270 1114, Japan Office: Dept Elec Engr Kogakuin U, 1-24-2 Nishi-shinjuku, Tokyo 163 8677, Japan

SONE, TOSHIO, acoustical engineering educator; b. Furukawa, Japan, May 14, 1935; s. Kikichi and Michio (Haga) S.; m. Noriko Tanaka, Sept. 5, 1964; children: Yasutomo, Atsushi, Susumu. B of Engring., Tohoku U., Sendai, Japan, 1958, M of Engring., 1960, PhD, 1963. Rsch. assoc. engring. faculty Tohoku U., 1963-64, assoc. prof. elec. engring., 1964-79, prof. elec. communications engring., 1979-81, prof. Rsch. Inst. Elec. Comm., 1981-99, dir. computer ctr., 1994-98; prof. Akita Prefectural U., 1999—; vice chmn. Western Pacific Commn. for Acoustics, 1994—; gen. chmn. INTER-NOISE 94, Yokohama, 1994; dir. libr. and info. ctr. Akita Prefectural U., 1999—. Author: Electroacoustic Engineering, 1963, Practice in Electromagnetics, 1973, Foundations of Acoustics, 1990, Life and Sound, 1991. Active Sendai Mcpl. Coun. Environ. Pollution Control, 1978—, Miyagi Prefectural Coun. Environ. Pollution Control, Sendai, Japan, 1982—, Iwate Prefectural Coun. Environ. Pollution Control, Morioka, Japan, 1982—. Rsch. grantee Kajima Sci. Promotion Found., Tokyo, 1984, Sound Tech. Promotion Found., Tokyo, 1987, Hoso-Bunka Found., Tokyo, 1991, Telecomm. Advancement Found., Tokyo, 1994; recipient Kahoku Culture award, 1998. Fellow Acoustical Soc. Am.; mem. Inst. Electronics, Info. and Comm. Engrs. Japan, Acoustical Soc. Japan (bd. dirs. 1989—, v.p. 1991-93, pres. 1993-95, Sato prize 1992, 94), Inst. Noise Control Engring. Japan (bd. dirs. 1980—, v.p. 1990-92), Inst. Noise Control Engring. U.S.A. (corr.), Japan Soc. Mech. Engrs., Japan Audiological Soc. Avocation: calligraphy. Home: 4-9-5 Midorigaoka, Taihaku-ku, Sendai 982-0021, Japan Office: Akita Prefectural U, 84-4 Ebinokuchi Tsuchiya, Honjo City 015-0055, Japan

SONG, CHUNSHAN, chemist, chemical engineer, educator; b. Shijiazhuang, Hebei, China, Feb. 11, 1961; came to U.S., 1989; s. Jingsheng Song and Fengxian He; m. Lu Sun, Jan. 10, 1985; children: Lucy J., James J. BS in Chem. Engring., Dalian (China) U. Tech., 1982; diploma in Japanese, N.E. Shifan U., Changchun, China, 1983; MS in Applied Chemistry, Osaka (Japan) U., 1986, PhD in Applied Chemistry, 1989. Postdoc. rsch. assoc. Osaka Gas Co., 1989; rsch. assoc. Pa. State U., University Park, 1989-94, asst. prof. fuel sci., 1994-97, assoc. prof., 1997—, assoc. dir. lab. hydrocarbon process chemistry, 1995-98, dir. applied catalysis in energy lab., 1998—. Editor: Catalytic Conversion of Polycyclic Aromatic Hydrocarbons, 1996, Advances in Catalysis and Processes for Heavy Oil Conversion, 1998, Shape-Selective Catalysis-Chemicals Synthesis and Hydrocarbon Processing, 1999, Catalysis in Fuel Processing and Environmental Protection, 1999, Chemistry of Diesel Fuels, 2000; contbr. articles to Catalysis Today, Energy Fuels, Catalysis Letters, Fuel, Fuel Processing Tech., Ind. Engring. Chem. Rsch., Applied Catalysis, Studies in Surface Sci. and Catalysis, Chemtech. Agy. Ind. Sci. Tech. fellow, Japan, 1995; NEDO fellow, Japan, 1998. Mem. AAAS, AIChE, Am. Chem. Soc. (co-chair several symposia 1995—, mem. program com. petroleum chemistry divsn. 1996—, exec. com. 1997—, chmn. website com. 1997-2000, chmn. program for fuel chem. divsn., exec. com. of fuel chem. divsn. 2000—). Achievements include development of a novel concept for designing sulfur-resistane noble-metal catalysts; discovery of new method for preparing highly active molybdenum sulfide catalysts by using water and Mo precursor; established several new shape-selective catalytic reactions of polycyclic hydrocarons, including ring-shift isomerization, conformational isomerization, shape-selective alkylation, and shape-selective hydrogenation; established the features and reaction pathways of thermal degradation and stabilization of coal-derived and petroleum-derived aviation jet fuels in pyrolytic regime. Office: Pa State U Energy and Geo-Environ Engring Dept Fuel Sci Program 206 Hosler Bldg University Park PA 16802-5001

SONG, DEFU, Chinese government official; b. Yanshan County, Hubei, China, 1946. Served in polit. dept. PLA Air Force, 1965-72, dep. head youth divsn., 1973-82; sec. CYL Standing Com., 1982; first sec. CYL CC, 1985-93; dir. China Youth Polit. Sci. Inst., 1985, Youth Ideological Edn. Rsch. Ctr., 1987; mem. Commn. for Comprehensive Mgmt. for Social Security, 1991-93; min. personnel Govt. China, 1993—. Office: Ministry of Personnel, 12 He Ping Li Zhong Jie, East Dist Beijing 100716, China*

SONG, GANGBING, engineering educator, researcher; came to US, 1989; BS, Zhejiag U., Hangzhou, China, 1989; MS, Columbia U., 1991, PhD, 1995. Rsch. assoc. Naval Postgrad. Sch., Monterey, Calif., 1995-96; asst. rsch. prof. Naval Postgrad. Sch., Monterey, 1996-98; asst. prof. mech. engring. U. Akron (Ohio), 1998—. Recipient USN Spl. Act award, 1998. Mem. AIAA, ASME. Achievements include patent for articulated mini-manipulator for minimally invasive surgery, 1998; invention of sliding mode based smooth adovpive robust, spacecraft vibration reduction , new approach to robust position/force control. Fax: (330) 972-6027. E-mail: gsong@uakron.edu. Home: 750 Mull Ave Apt 8D Akron OH 44313-7560 Office: U Akron Dept Mech Engring Rm 107D Auburn Sci & Engring Ctr Akron OH 44325-0001

SONG, GWAN GYU, rheumatologist, educator; b. Kyungki Do, Korea; parents ByungKi and JaeSoon Lee; m. Song Mi Lim, Mar. 25, 1987; children: Suk Ha, Sheen Young, Suk Hyun. MD, Korea U. Coll. Medicine, 1985; PhD, Korea U., 1994. Assoc. prof. Korea U. Coll. Medicine, Seoul, 1995-99; rheumatologist Korea U. Med. Ctr., Seoul, 1999—. Mem. Am. Coll. Rheumatology, Korea Rheumatism Assn., Korean Assn. Internal Medicine, Korean Soc. Immunology. Office: Korea U Med Ctr, 126-1 Anam-Dong Sungbuk Ku, Seoul Korea 136-705

SONG, IICKHO, electrical engineer; b. Seoul, Feb. 20, 1960; s. Jaehyun and Moonsoon (Seo) S.; m. Taeyoung S. Seong, May 18, 1988; children: Youngwha, Yeonwha. BS magna cum laude, Seoul Nat. U., 1982, MSE, 1984; MSEE, U. Pa., 1985, PhD, 1987. Chartered elec. engr., engr. Mem. tech. staff Bell Comms. Rsch., Morristown, N.J., 1987-88; asst. prof. Korea Advanced Inst. Sci. Tech., Daejeon, Korea, 1988-91, assoc. prof., 1991-98, prof., 1998—. Assoc. editor: Jour. Acoustical Soc. Korea, 1996—, Jour. Korean Inst. Comm. Scis., 1995—, Jour. Comm. Networks, 1998—; contbr. articles to profl. jours. Korean Honor scholar Korean Embassy in U.S., Washington, 1985-86; recipient Acad. award Korean Inst. Comm. Scis., Seoul, 1991, 96, Best Rsch. award Acoust. Soc. Korea, 1993, LG Acad. award Korean Inst. Comm. Scis., 1998, Haedong paper award, 1999, CEng, Young Scientists award Min. Science and Tech. Korea, 2000. Fellow Inst. Elec. Engrs.; mem. IEEE (sr.), Korea, Korean Inst. Comm. Scis., Acoustical Soc. Korea. Office: KAIST Dept Elec Engring, 373-1 Guseong Dong, 305-701 Daejeon Republic of Korea

SONG, IN KYU, chemical engineering educator; b. Keojin, Rep. of Korea, Aug. 20, 1964; s. Ki Seop Song and Chang Ja Hwang; m. Kyung Hwa Hong, Apr. 20, 1991; children: Ji Hwan Song, Ji Yoon Song. BS, Seoul (Rep. of Korea) Nat. U., 1987, MS, 1989, PhD in Chem. Engring., 1993. Sr. rschr. Samsung Gen. Chems., Seoul, 1993-94; postdoctoral rschr. U. Del., 1995-96; prof. Kangnung (Rep. of Korea) Nat. U., 1996—. Contbr. articles to profl. jours.; patentee in field. Lt. Korean Army, 1989. Postdoctoral fellow Korea Sci. and Engring. Found., 1995. Mem. AIChE, Am. Chem. Soc., Korean Inst. Chem. Engrs, Catalysis Soc. Seoul (mem. com. 1998—). Roman Catholic. Avocations: golf, tennis, fishing, travel, skiing. Office: Kangnung Nat U, Jibyun-dong, Kangnung 210-702, Republic of Korea

SONG, JIAN, scientist, science administrator; b. Rongcheng County, Shandong, China, Dec. 29, 1931; s. Zengjin Song and Yuxian Jiang; m. Yusheng Wang, July 1, 1961; children: Mumin, Muhua. Student, Harbin Tech. U., 1951-53; degree in engring., Moscow Bauman Poly. Inst., 1958, PhD, 1960; DSc, Moscow Nat. Tech. U., 1990; LHD (hon.), Houston U., 1996. Head lab cybernetics Inst. Math., Acad. Sci., Beijing, 1960-70; head dept. space sci. Acad. Space Tech. Min. Machine Bldg. Industry, 1971-78, v.p. Acad. Space Tech., 1978-81; vice min., chief engr.-scientist Ministry Astronautics, Beijing, 1981-84; min. State Sci. and Tech. Commn., Beijing, 1984-98; state councilor State Coun., Beijing, 1986-98; chmn. State Environ. Protection Com., Beijing, 1986-98; vice chmn. Chinese People's Polit. Consultative conf., 1998—; pres. Chinese Acad. Engring. Sci., 1998—; prof. Quinhua U., Beijing, Fudan U., Shanghai; disting. vis. prof. Washington U., St. Louis. Author: Engineering Cybernetics, 1980, China's Population: Problem & Prospect, 1981, Recent Developments in Control Theory and its Applications, 1984, Population Control in China, Theory and Application, 1985, Population System Control, 1988; contbr. 60 articles on sys. control theory and population theory to profl. jours. Recipient Albert Einstein award Internat. Assn. Math. Modeling, 1987, Sci. and Tech. Advancement Nat. award, 1987. Mem. China Automation Soc. (pres. 1980—, coun.), China Systems Engring. Soc. (v.p. 1985-87), Chinese Acad. Scis., Chinese Acad. Engring., Population Sci. Soc. (v.p. 1984—), Internat. Fedn. Automatic Control (coun.), Russian Acad. Sci. (fgn.), Royal Swedish Acad. Engring. Scis. (fgn.), Nat. Acad. Engring. Mex. (corr.), NAE (U.S., fgn. mem.). Achievements include research in space science and technology, system control theory and population theory. Office: Chinese Acad Engring, 3 Fuxing Rd China Hall Sci, Beijing 100038, China*

SONG, JIANLIN, engineer; b. Shanghai, China, Oct. 24, 1969; came to the U.S., 1993; s. Baoren Song and Fangzhong Yao; m. Yong Lin, Apr. 20, 1999. B in Engring., Shanghai Jiao Tong U., 1992; MS, Johns Hopkins U., 1997, PhD, 1999. Engr.-in-tng., Md. Structural engr. Shanghai Modern Arts Design, Inc., 1992-93; rsch. asst. Johns Hopkins U., Balt., 1993-98; sr. rsch. engr. Applied Ins. Rsch., Boston, 1998—; tech. paper reviewer Jour. Structural Engring., ASCE, Reston, Va.; steering com. Big On Asbestos Project/Nat. Inst. Bldg. Sci., Washington. Chmn. Chinese Student and Scholar Assn., Johns Hopkins U., Balt., 1996-97. Scholar Shanghai Jiao Tong U., 1989, 90, Johns Hopkins U., Balt., 1993. Mem. ASCE, Nat. Inst. Bldg. Sci., Earthquake Engring. Rsch. Inst. Avocations: swimming, volleyball, reading. E-mail: rich ellen@yahoo.com and rsong@airworldwidecom. Fax: 617-267-8284. Home: 1408 Commonwealth Ave Apt 8 Brighton MA 02135-3720 Office: Applied Ins Rsch 101 Huntington Ave Boston MA 02199-7603

SONG, JINSOO, electrical engineer, researcher; b. Pusan, Korea, Sept. 5, 1949; m. Youngyee Kang, Mar. 15, 1955; children: Wonsuk, Yurim. BS, Korea U., Seoul, 1971, MS, 1976, PhD, 1986. Vis. rschr. Argonne (Ill.) Nat. Lab., 1979-80; postdoctoral fellow U. Minn., Mpls., 1986-87; dep. dir. Korea Inst. Energy Rsch., Taejon, Korea, 1979—; exec. com. mem. Internat. Energy Agy./Photovoltaic Power Sys., 1995—; mem. World Energy Coun. Solar Power Com., 1987-89; chmn. Cons. Co. Korean Min. Commerce, Industry and Energy, 1988—. Contbr. articles to profl. jours. Lance cpl. Korea Army, 1971-74. Recipient Acad. award Korean Inst. Elec. Engring., 1986, commendation Korean Min. of Sci. and Tech., 1992, PVSEC Paper award Internat. PVSEC-11, 1999. Mem. IEEE, Internat. Solar Energy Soc., Korean Photovoltaic Assn. (chmn. 1995—), N.Y. Acad. scis. Home: 397-42 Doryong-Dong, Yusong-Gu, 305-340 Taejon Republic of Korea Office: Korea Inst Energy Rsch, 71-2 Jang-Dong Yusong-Gu, 305-343 Taejon Republic of Korea

SONG, MICHAEL, marketing educator; b. Putian, China, Aug. 24, 1961; came to U.S., 1983; s. Qing Jiao and Guang Zha Song; m. Lisa Song, April 18, 1986; children: Roger, Katherine. BS, Jinan U., 1982; MS, Cornell U., 1986; MBA, U. Va., 1990, PhD, 1991. Asst. prof. U. Tenn., Knoxville, 1991-95; prof. Mich. State U., East Lansing, 1996-2000, Univ. Washington, 2000—; vis. prof. Internat. U. Japan, 1997—, Eindhoven U. of Tech.; chair mktg. tech. Mich. State U., 1999; cons. Gen. Motors, EXXON Chems., Monsanto, Motorola, Eastman Chem. Co., Citicorp, Boeing, IBM, Sony, Toyota, CATIC, Samsung Elecs., Philips, and Matsushita Elec. Indsl. Co.; keynote spkr. in field. Editl. bd. Advances in Internat. Mktg., 1998—, Jour. Product Innovation, 1999—; contbr. articles to profl. jours. Recipient Wachovia award for Excellence The Darden Found., Va., 1994; Math. Graduate fellow Cornell U., 1984, Consortium fellow The 1991 Acad. Mgmt. TIM Doctoral Consortium, Doctoral Merit fellow The Darden Sch., 1988-91, Doctoral fellow DuPont, 1989-91; grantee Mktg. Sci. Inst., The Darden Found., Citibank Rsch. Funds, The China Nat. Aero-Tech. Import and Export Corp., Hitachi Rsch. Funds, Hewlett Packard Co., NSF, Citicorp Global Scholar Programs, Am. Chem. Mfg. Assn., others. Fellow Acad. Mktg. Sci.; mem. Inst. Mgmt. Sci. (conf. chair 1996), Am. Mktg. Assn. Avocations: music, stamp collecting, travel. E-mail: song@u.washington.edu. Office: Univ Washington Business School PO Box 353200 Seattle WA 98195-3200

SONG, SANG JAE, manufacturing engineering educator, researcher; b. Taegu, Kyungsang, Republic of Korea, Feb. 20, 1959; arrived in Japan, 1984; s. Ji Hong Song and Su Ok Kim; m. Jung Hee Choi, Feb. 23, 1991; 1 child. BS, Yeungnam U., Taegu, Korea, 1982; MS, Kyoto U., 1988, D Engring., 1992. Sr. lectr. Hiroshima Inst. Tech., Japan, 1992-96; postdoctoral fellow Aachen U. Tech., Germany, 1995, Denmark Tech. U., Lyngby, Denmark, 1995-96; assoc. prof. indsl. engring. Hiroshima Inst. Tech., Japan, 1996—; creator flexible integrated mfg., socially responsible mfg. Mem. editl. bd. product and process devel. Internat. Jour. Robotics, 1999—; contbr. chpts. to books, articles to profl. publs. Served with Korean mil., 1982-83. Grantee Sumitomo Found., Tokyo, 1995, Japanese Govt., Tokyo, 1994, 97-98, 99. Mem. Inst. of Indsl. Engrs. (sr./Atlanta), Japan Soc. Mech. Engrs., Japan Indsl. Mgmt. Assn. (v.p. Chushigoku region 1997—). Home: Saeki-ku, 4-14-2-404 Itsukaichi-chuo, Hiroshima 731-5128, Japan Office: Hiroshima Inst Tech, 2-1-1 Miyake Saeki-ku, Hiroshima 731-5193, Japan

SONG, SANG-HYUN, law educator, consultant; b. Seoul, Korea, Dec. 21, 1941; s. Youngsoo and Hyunsoo (Kim) S.; m. Myungshin Kim Song, Nov. 4, 1971; children: Jay, Yoo-Jean. JD, Seoul Nat. U., 1963, LLM, 1965; LLM, Tulane Law Sch., New Orleans, 1968; diploma, U. Cambridge, Eng., 1969; JSD, Cornell Law Sch., Ithaca, N.Y., 1970. Fgn. atty. Haight, Gardner, Poor & Havens, N.Y.C., 1970-71; vis. prof. law U. Melbourne, Australia, 1990, 92, 94, Harvard Law Sch., Cambridge, Mass., 1991, 95, 99; disting. prof. law N.Y.U Law Sch., 1994—; dean of law sch. Seoul Nat. U., 1996-98, prof. law, 1972—; pres. Koreal Intellectual Property Rsch. Soc., Inc., Seoul, Korea, 1986-96, Korean Internat. Trade Law Assn., Seoul, Korea, 1991-94; mem arbitrator Internat. Ctr. for Settlement of Investment Disputes, World Bank, Washington, 1986—; mem. arbitration consultative com., World Intellectual Property Orgn., Geneva, Switzerland, 1994—. Author: A Comparative Study on Maritime Cargo Carrier's Liability Under Anglo-American and French laws, 1970, Introduction to the Law and Legal System of Korea, 1983, Korean Law in the Global Economy, 1996, The Korean Civil Procedure, 1999. Auditor Korea-US Ednl. and Cultural Found., 1991—; pres; Children's Leukemia Found., Korea, 1998; mem., bd. dirs. UNICEF, Korea, 1998; pres. Korean Law Profs. Assn., Seoul, Korea, 1999. Recipient Disting. Alumni award Cornell U., Ithaca, N.Y., 1994, Decoration of Moran, Korean Govt., Seoul, Korea, 1998, The Legal Culture award Korean Fed. Bar Assn., 1998. Mem. Korean Fed. Bar Assn., Seoul-Hangang Rotary Club. Avocations: golf, gardening, hiking. Office: Seoul Nat Univ Law Sch, Seoul 151-742, Korea

SONG, SHENHUA, materials engineer, researcher; b. Peixian, Jiangsu, China, Oct. 13, 1958; s. Siying Song and Daolan Ni; m. Xiaoling Xie, Nov. 8, 1986; 1 child, Dixi. BSc, Northeast U., Shenyang, China, 1983; MSc, Wuhan Water Transport U., China, 1988; PhD, Loughborough (Eng.) U., 1995. Tchg. asst. Wuhan Iron and Steel U., 1983-85, lectr., 1988-92; rschr. Inst. Polymer Tech. and Materials Engring., Loughborough U., 1995—. Contbr. articles to profl. jours. Recipient progress award in sci. and tech. Chinese Ministry Edn., 1991. Office: Loughborough U IPTME, Ashby Rd, Loughborough LE11 3TU, England

SONG, SHUNFENG, economist, researcher; b. Jinhua, China, July 6, 1962; came to U.S., 1986; s. Lin Fu Song and Xiaoying He; m. Jian Ling Feng, July 9, 1985; children: Sisi, Conan A. BS in Mechanics, Beijing U., 1983; MA in Econ., U. Calif., Irvine, 1991, PhD in Econ., 1992. Instr. Xiamen (China) U., 1983-86; asst. prof. dept. econ. U. Nev., Reno, 1992-96, assoc. prof., 1996—. Author, editor: Raising International Competitiveness, 1998; contbr. articles to profl. jours. Mem. Am. Econ. Assn., Am. Real Estate Soc., Chinese Economists Soc. (dir. 1996-98, v.p. 1997-98), Western Regional Sci. Assn., Western Econ. Assn. Internat., Regional Sci. Assn. Internat. Avocations: travel, table tennis, playing cards. Office: U Nev Dept Econ 030 Reno NV 89557-0001

SONG, SIHONG, science educator; b. Chao-Yang-Zhen, Jilin, China, Mar. 29, 1959; came to U.S., 1990; s. Xingbang Song and Qiu Mi; m. Yufei Tang, May 17, 1986; children: Xujia (Annie), Alexander T. BS, Jilin Agrl. U., Changchun, China, 1982, MS, 1990, PhD, U. Fla., 1996. Tchg. and rsch. asst. Jilin Agrl. U., Changchun, 1982-86, lectr., 1987-91; grad. asst. U. Fla., Gainesville, 1992-96, postdoctoral assoc., 1996-99, rsch. asst. prof., 1999— . Recipient Young Investigaator award Alpha One Found., 1999. Mem. AAAS, Am. Soc. Gene Therapy, Sigma Xi, Gamma Sigma Delta. Avocations: sports, pinting, travel. E-mail: shsong@ufl.edu. Fax: 352-846-2738.

SONG, XIN-QI, chemistry educator, researcher; b. Changshu, China, Aug. 7, 1928; s. Zhuan-Ming Song and Bing-Ru Wu; m. Qi-Ai Chen; children: Song Cheng, Song He, Song You. BS, Tsinghua U., Beijing, 1951. Lectr. Tsinghua U., 1956-78, assoc. prof. chemistry, 1978-83, prof. chemistry, 1983—; part-time prof. chemistry, Beijing U. Chem. Tech., 1994—, Zhengzhou (China) U., 1995—, Inst. Chemistry (Academia Sinica), Beijing, 1995-99; sr. rsch. fellow Hong Kong Poly. U., 1995, 96, 97, 2000; sec.-gen. 34th Congress Internat. Union Pure and Applied Chemistry, Beijing, 1993. Author: The Tomorrow of Chemistry, 1995 (2d rank award superior books), Photochemistry-Principles, Techniques and Applications, 2000; inventor in field; chief editor, author popular sci. series Close to Chemistry; contbr. articles to profl. jours. Mem. Chinese Chem. Soc. (pres. 1999—), Beijing Chem. Soc. (pres. 1991-99). Avocations: travel, chess, novels, writing Chinese ancient poems. Office: Tsing Hua U Dept Chemistry, Hai Dian Qinghua Yuan, Beijing 100084, China

SONG, YANG-HEON, chemistry educator; b. Taejon, Republic of Korea, Nov. 19, 1959; s. Seokjae and Sungrim (Kil) S.; m. Hye-Sung Kim, Nov. 9, 1986; 1 child, Da-Eun. MS, Yonsei U., Seoul, Republic of Korea, 1982, PhD, 1987. Asst. prof. Mokwon U., Taejon, 1987-90; assoc. prof. chemistry Mokwon U., 1991-95, chmn. dept. chemistry, 1994—, prof., 1996—; postdoctoral fellow Harvard U., Cambridge, Mass., 1990-91; vis. prof. U. Oreg., Eugene, 1997-98. Contbr. articles to profl. publs.; patentee in field. Mem. Am. Chem. Soc., Korean Chem. Soc. Avocation: mountain climbing. Office: Mokwon U Dept Chemistry, Doan-dong, Taejon 302-729, Republic of Korea

SONG, YEONG WOOK, physician, researcher; b. Taejon, Korea, Feb. 13, 1956; s. Ju Ho and Hyun Shin (Lim) S.; m. Hee Jeong Kwon, Dec. 20, 1982; children: Laura, Klara, Jinwoo. MD, Seoul (Korea) Nat. U., 1980. Intern Seoul Nat. U. Hosp., 1980-81, resident, 1981-84; clin. fellow UCLA Med. Ctr., 1990-92; asst. prof. medicine Seoul Nat. U., 1992-95, assoc. prof. medicine, 1995-2000, prof. medicine, 2000—. Contbr. articles to profl. jours. Capt. Korean Army, 1984-87. Recipient Ellis Dressner award So. Calif.

chpt. Arthritis Found., 1992, Young Investigator award Seoul Nat. U. Hosp., 2000. Fellow Am. Coll. Rheumatology; mem. Korean Assn. Internal Medicine, Korean Rheumatism Assn. Avocations: golf, tennis, hiking. Office: Seoul Nat Univ Hosp, 28 Yun Gun-Dong, Seoul 110-744, Republic of Korea

SONG, YONG-HUA, electronics engineer; b. Baozhong, China, Jan. 1, 1964; s. Zhongwen Song and Xinliang Xio; m. Qing Yun Xuan, July 27, 1964; children: Alice, James. B in Engring., Chengdu U. Sci. and Tech., 1984; MSc, Elec. Power Rsch. Inst., Beijing, China, 1986, PhD, 1989. Vis. fellow Bristol U., Eng., 1991-92; rsch. officer, lectr. Bath U., Eng., 1992-96; prof. elec. energy sys. Brunel U., London, 1997—; head energy sys. and engring. intelligence group Brunel U.; vis. prof. Chongqing U. Author: Progress in System Science, 1991, Computational Intelligence Applications in Power Systems, 1996, Modern Optimisation Techniques in Power Systems, 1999, Flexible AC Transmission Systems, 1999; contbr. articles to profl. jours. Royal Soc. vis. fellow, 1991; grantee Nat. Grid Co., 1995—, U.K. Rsch. Coun., 1997—, Nat. Sci. Found., China, 1988—. Mem. IEEE (sr.), Inst. Elec. Engrs. U.K., Chinese Soc. Elec. Engring., Royal Acad. Engring. (nuclear/electric/Siemens chair of power sys.). Home: 7 Mallard Way, Reading RG7 4UT, England Office: Brunel U, Uxbridge, London UB8 3PH, England

SONG, YU ZHE, chemical engineer, consultant, printing educator; b. Yuncheng, Shangdong, China, Nov. 4, 1936; s. Xing Min and Xian Mei (Meng) Song; m. Shang Bang-Yi, Nov. 16, 1966; children: Shang-Qing, Xiang-Hui. Bachelors degree, Tsinghua U., Beijing, 1964. Asst. engr. dept. organics Beijing Chem. Engring. Rsch. Inst., 1964-69; dir. projects Beijing Zhiben Printing Factory, 1969-73; chief dir. dept. rsch. Beijing Pub. Bur., 1973-78; vice-dir. Beijing Printing Tech. Rsch. Inst., 1978-84, dir., 1984-94; cons. Tech. Consultative Com. Beijing Govt., 1986-97; commissary Printing Standard Tech. Com. China, Beijing, 1990—. Author sect. spl. printing China Encyclopedia, 1985; rschr. (inventions) holographic printing, 1989 (Silver award 1991), glue materials for printing, 1987 (Bronze award 1987). Mem. Screen Printing Assn. China (chmn. 1981—), China Printing Tech. Assn. (dir. of standing com. 1984—), Beijing Printing Assn. (vice chmn. 1985—, Printing Progress award 1988). Avocations: reading history books, Chinese calligraphy and painting, chess, Chinese Qigong. Office: Screen Printing Assn China, A36 Qianliang Hutong, Beijing 100010, China

SONG, ZHIYAN, chemistry educator; b. Hangzhou, Zhejiang, China, Aug. 14, 1953; s. Youlai Wanfeng (Sun) S.; m. Xueping Zhang, Oct. 17, 1981; 1 child, Yun. Undergrad. degree, Nankai U., Tiantsin, China, 1980; PhD, Stockholm U., 1996. Lectr. Sch. of Chem. Tech., Hangzhou, China, 1980-89; postdoctoral rschr. Nat. High Magnetic Field Lab., Tallahassee, 1997-99, U. N.C., Chapel Hill, 1999; asst. prof. Savannah (Ga.) State U., 2000—. Author publs. in field. Mem. AAAS. Avocations: music, reading, travel. Office: Savannah State U Dept Chem Savannah GA 31404

SONGOK, DANIEL KIPSANG, bank executive; b. Eldoret, Kenya, Oct. 10; s. Simeon Kipsongok and Jane Chemwolo (Simatwo) Mengich; m. Rebecca Jelagat Talam Tarakwa Sept. 1, 1982; children: Maureen, Beatrice, Perpetua, Robert, Charity. B of Commerce with honors, U. Nairobi, Kenya, 1983; MBA, U.S. Internat. U., Nairobi, 1999. CPA, Kenya. From acct. to internal auditor Kenya Farmers Assn., Nakuru, 1985-94; from mgr., internal auditor to asst. gen. mgr. Postbank, Nairobi, 1994-98, gen. mgr. fin., 1999—; trustee Postbank Pension Fund, Nairobi, 1995—. chmn. KFA Savs. & Credit Soc., Nakuru, 1993, PTA St. Joseph Primary Sch., Nakuru, 1987-88; chmn. bd. govs. Tulwet Secondary Sch., Eldoret, Kenya, 1992—. Mem. Inst. Cert. Pub. Accts. of Kenya. Avocations: music, reading, travel, socializing, farming. Office: Kenya Post Office Savs Bank, PO Box 30313, Nairobi Kenya

SONGSORE, JACOB, geographer, educator; b. Loho, Ghana, Aug. 30, 1947; s. Sylvinus Danaah Songsore and Magdalene Tene Bagarazie; m. Gertrude Sungliedong Kogo; children: Pascaline Kuunzungla, Evelyn Sumanko, Emmanuel Tifigra. BA, U. Ghana, 1971, PhD, 1975; MSS, Inst. Social Studies, The Netherlands, 1978. Lectr., sr. lect., assoc. prof. U. Ghana, Legon, 1975-96, head geography dept., 1996-99, prof., 1997; guest rschr. dept. geography U. Trondheim, Norway, 1993. Co-editor: Urban Health Research in Developing Countries: Implications for Policy, 1996; contbr. chpts. in books and articles to profl. jours.; author tech. reports. Bd. dirs. Ghana Nat. Atlas Project, Accra, 1987-92, 93, chmn. mgmt. bd., 1994-96. Mem. N.Y. Acad. Scis., Ghana Geog. Assn., Stockholm Environment Inst. (vis. rsch. fellow 1992-93, assoc. scientist 1995-99). Roman Catholic. Achievements include contributions in urban environmental health, inequalities and development, gender and environmental care. Office: Univ Ghana Dept Geography, PO Box 59, Legon Accra Ghana

SONI, INDER MOHAN, retired communications educator; b. Sialkof, India, July 13, 1935; d. Lal Chand and Kamslaya Devi S.; m. Krishna Bhatia, Apr. 20, 1962; children: Sangeeta, Sumita, Ritu. BA, Shimla, India, 1954; MA, Patiala, India, 1959; B Journ., U. Chandigarh, India, 1972. Lectr. S.A. Jain Coll., Ambala City, 1959-62; reporter Sriganganyar, 1965-69, 72; lectr. Panjab U., Charhigash, 1972-95, reader, 1995-98; media cons. DD Found., Charhigash, 1995—; editl. writer, 1994—; polit. corrs., Caravan, New Delhi, 1981-82. Editor: PU News, India, 1977-83; editl. cons. Modern Practical Psychology, 1978-99; vice-chmn. Bharat Sewak Samaj, 1999—; film critic The Tribune, Chandigarh, 1977-83; book reviewer in field. Avocations: reading, social work with orphanages, music, photography.

SONI, RAMESH KUMAR, publisher, journalist; b. Bajwara, Punjab, India, Feb. 1, 1938; arrived in Eng., 1964; s. Tek Chand and Satya Wati (Ohri) S.; m. Shanta Chandhok, Mar. 24, 1970; children: Neeru, Seema, Navin. Student, D.A.V. Coll., Hashiarpur, India, 1954, Dyal Singh Coll., New Delhi, 1963. Clerical officer Ministry of Def., New Delhi, 1958-64; editor, pub. Milap Weekly, London, 1965—, Navin Weekly, London, 1970—. Chmn. Hindi Parents Group. Mem. Indian Journalist Assn. London. Hindu. Home: 30 Stafford Cripps House, Clem Attlee, London SW6 7RX, England Office: Masbro Center, 87 Masbro Rd, London W-140LR, England

SONI, SHANKARLAL, editor in chief, consultant; b. Udaipur Dehra, Madhya Pradesh, India, June 2, 1944; s. Ganesh Prasad S.; m. Malti Verma, Aug. 15, 1947; children: Hemant K., Nitin K., Nisha. MA in English Lit., Holkar Coll., Indore, India. Exec. sec. A.I.M.P., Indore, Madhya Pradesh, India, 1968-81; pres. T.A.O., Indore, 1985-88; hon. sec. S.S.I.O., Indore, 1995-99; chief editor Industrial M.P.; advisor Cement India, 1998—. Editor: Tender Market, 1981—, Mat-Equip India, 1999. Mem. Bhartiya Janta Party. Avocations: social upliftment, travelling, music. Home: 320 M G Rd, 452 002 Indore Madhya Pradesh, India Office: Indsl MP, 12 Dhenu Market GSTI Rd, 452 003 Indore Madhya Pradesh, India

SONNEKSON, ROBERT EDWARD, business counselor; b. Colo. Springs, Colo., July 23, 1916; s. Robert Frederick and Nellie (Martin) S.; m. Claire Schuyler Moffett; children: Robert, Mary. BS in Bus., U. Colo., 1937. With Gen. Electric Co., Schenectady, N.Y., 1937-48; mgr. materials Gen. Electric Co., Utica, N.Y., 1948-56; v.p. mfg. Bell Aircraft Co., Buffalo, N.Y., 1956-59; v.p., gen. mgr. Raytheon Corp., Lexington, Mass., 1959-65; v.p. mfg. Philco Corp., Phila., 1965-67, Amerline Corp., Chgo., 1967-69; group v.p. Lehigh Valley Industries, N.Y.C., 1969-72; bus. counselor Gen. Bus. Services, Germantown, Md., 1972—. Club: Darien Country. Home and Office: 122 Palmers Hill Rd Apt 2107 Stamford CT 06902-2151

SONNEMANS, JOHANNES WILHELMUS, chemical engineer; b. Haarlem, The Netherlands, May 12, 1940; s. Johannes Franciscus and Maria (Klein) S.; m. Rosalia Maria van Ballegoy, Dec. 29, 1965; children: Frank, Jeroen. Degree in chem. engring., Tech. U., Delft, The Netherlands, 1965, PhD, 1973. Rschr. Tech. U. Enschede, The Netherlands, 1965-73; rschr. Akzo Nobel, Amsterdam, The Netherlands, 1974-78, application engr., 1978-80, mgr. application rsch., 1980-83, rsch. mgr. chem. process catalysts, 1983-88, devel. mgr., 1988-91, rsch. mgr. hydroprocessing catalysts, 1991-94, worldwide devel. mgr., 1994-98, mktg. mgr. new bus., 1998—. Contbr. articles to profl. publs.; patentee in field. Chmn. Tennisclub, Losser, The Netherlands, 1970-73, Bridge Club, Losser, 1970-71; mem. mgmt. com. Catalysis Soc., 1985-89; mem. sci. bd. Conf. preparation of Catalysts, Brussels, 1985. Mem. Chem. Soc. Netherlands. Roman Catholic. Avocations: travel, tennis, bridge, walking, reading. Home: de Colignylaan 9, 3761 DD Soest The Netherlands Office: Akzo Nobel, Stationsplein 4, 3800 AE Amersfoort The Netherlands

SONNENBICHLER, JOHANN, biochemist; b. Munich, Nov. 4, 1932; s. Josef and Johanna (Müller) S.; m. Isolde Maurus; children: Andreas, Bernadette. Degree in chemistry, U. Munich, 1957, D in Chemistry, 1961, MD, 1971. Applied prof. U. Munich Faculty Medicine, 1961-71; leader dept. biochemistry Max Planck Inst. for Biochemistry, Martinsried, 1961-97. Contbr. numerous articles to sci. and profl. jours.

SONNENSCHEIN, HUGO FREUND, academic administrator, economics educator; b. N.Y.C., Nov. 14, 1940; s. Leo William and Lillian Silver S.; m. Elizabeth Gunn, Aug. 26, 1962; children: Leah, Amy, Rachel. AB, U. Rochester, 1961; MS, Purdue U., 1963, PhD, 1964, PhD (hon.), 1996; PhD (hon.), Tel Aviv U., 1993; D (hon.), U. Autonoma Barcelona, Spain, 1994; PhD (hon.), Lake Forest Coll., 1995. Faculty dept. econs. U. Minn., 1964-70, prof., 1968-70; prof. econs. U. Mass., Amherst, 1970-73, Northwestern U., 1973-76; prof. econs. Princeton (N.J.) U., 1976-87, Class of 1926 prof., 1987-88, provost, 1991-93; dean and Thomas S. Gates prof. Sch. Arts & Scis., U. Pa., Phila., 1988-91; pres. U. Chgo., 1993-2000, Hutchinson disting. prof., pres. emeritus, 2000—; vis. prof. U. Andes, Colombia, 1965, Tel Aviv U., 1972, Hebrew U., 1973, U. Paris, 1978, U. Aix-en-Provence, France, 1978, Stanford U., 1984-85; bd. dirs. Van Kampen Mutual Funds. Editor Econometrica, 1977-84; mem. editl. bd. Jour. Econ. Theory, 1972-75, Jour. Math. Econs, 1974—, SIAM Jour, 1976-80; contbr. articles to profl. jours. Trustee U. Rochester, 1992, U. Chgo., 1993—. Fellow Social Sci. Rsch. Coun., 1967-68, NSF, 1970—, Ford Found., 1970-71, Guggenheim Found., 1976-77. Fellow Am. Acad. Arts and Scis., Econometric Soc. (pres. 1988-89); mem. NAS.

SONNIER, PATRICIA BENNETT, business management educator; b. Park River, N.D., Mar. 25, 1935; d. Benjamin Beekman Bennett and Alice Catherine (Peerboom) Bennett Brenckinridge; m. William McGregor Castellini (dec.); children: Bruce Bennett Wells (Nabil Subhani), Barbara Lea Ragland; m. Cecil S. Sonnier. AA, Allan Hancok Coll., Santa Maria, Calif., 1964; BS magna cum laude, Coll. Great Falls, 1966; MS, U. N.D., 1967, PhD, 1971. Fiscal acct. USIA, Washington, 1954-56; pub. acct. Bremerton, Wash., 1956; statistician USN, Bremerton, Wash., 1957-59; med. svcs. accounts officer USAF, Vandenberg AFB, Calif., 1962-64; instr. bus. adminstrn. Western New Eng. Coll., 1967-69; vis. prof. econs. Chapman Coll., 1970; vis. prof. U. So. Calif. Sys., Griffith AFB, N.Y., 1971-72; assoc. prof., dir. adminstrv. mgmt. program Va. State U., 1973-74; assoc. prof. bus. adminstrn. Oreg. State U., Corvallis, 1974-81, prof. mgmt., 1982-90, emeritus prof. mgmt., 1990—, univ. curriculum coord., 1984-86, dir. adminstrv. mgmt. program, 1974-81, pres. Faculty Senate, 1981; mem. Interinstl. Faculty Senate, 1986-90, pres., 1989-90; exec. dir. Bus. Enterprise Ctr., 1990-92, Enterprise Ctr. L.A., Inc., 1992-95, Castellini Co., 1995—; commr. Lafayette Econ. Devel. Authority, 1994—, treas., 1995-96, vice chmn., 1996-97, chmn., 1997-98, past chmn., 1998-99, sec., 1999-00, chmn. bldg. com., 1999-00; cons. process tech. devel. Digital Equipment Corp., 1982. Pres., chmn. bd. dirs. Adminstrv. Orgnl. Svcs., Inc., Corvallis, 1976-83, Dynamic Achievement, Inc., 1983-92; bd. dirs. Oreg. State U. Bookstores, Inc., 1987-90, Internat. Trade Devel. Group, 1992-97; cons. Oregonians in Action, 1990-91, sec., 1999, 2000; cert. adminstrv. mng. pres. TYEE Mobil Home Park, Inc., 1987-92. Fellow Assn. Bus. Comm. (internat. bd. 1980-86, v.p. Northwest 1981, 2nd v.p. 1982-83, 1st v.p. 1983-84, pres. 1984-85); mem. Am. Bus. Women's Assn. (chpt. v.p. 1979, pres. 1980, named Top Businesswoman in Nation 1980, Bus. Assoc. Yr. 1986), Assn. Info. Sys. Profls. (chpt. v.p. 1977, chpt. pres. 1978-81), Adminstrv. Mgmt. Soc., AAUP (chpt. sec. 1973, chpt. bd. dirs. 1982, 84-89, pres. Oreg. conf. 1983-85, pres. chpt. 1985-86), Am. Vocat. Assn. (nominating com. 1976), Associated Oreg. Faculties, Nat. Bus. Edn. Assn., Better Bus. Bur. (sec. 1994, 99, treas. 1995, vice-chair 1996, chmn. 1997, past chair 1998, chmn. nominating com. 1999, blue ribbon edn. com. 1999—, chmn. pub. rels.), Nat. Assn. Tchr. Edn. for Bus. Office Edn. (pres. 1976-77, chmn. pub. rels. com. 1978-81), La. Bus. Incubation Assn. (sec.-treas. 1993-95), Corvallis Area C. of C. (v.p. chamber devel. 1987-88, pres. 1988-89, chmn. bd. 1989-90, Pres.' award 1986), Boys and Girls Club of Corvallis (pres. 1991-92), Sigma Kappa, Rotary Corvallis (bd. dirs. 1990-92, dir. voc. svcs. 1991-92, pres.-elect 1992), Rotary Lafayette (bd. dirs. 1993—, cmty. svc. dir. 1993-94, treas. 1995-96, sec. 1996-97, v.p. 1997-98, pres. 1998-99, immediate past pres. 1999-2000, Dist. 6200 award 2000), Acadiana Rep. Women (first v.p. 1997, 98, pres. 1998-2000, gen. chmn. La. Fedn. Rep. Women's Clubs State Conv. 1997, Leadership La. 1998, asst. state CAP chmn. 1999—).

SONNTAG, OSWALD WOLFGANG, clinical chemist; b. Celle, Lower Saxonia, Niedersachsen, Germany, Apr. 24, 1955; s. Waldemar and Margarete (Litke) S. Diploma in chem. engring., Fresenius, Wiesbaden, Germany, 1979. Lab. supr. Med. Hochschule, Inst. Clin. Chemistry, Hannover, Germany, 1979-92; dept. supr. Kodak, Illkirch, France, 1992-94, Johnson & Johnson, Illkirch, France, 1994-96, Ortho-Clin. Diagnostics GmbH, Neckargemünd, Germany, 1997—. Author: Arzneimittel-Interferenzen, 1985, Trockenchemie, 1988, Dry-Chemistry, 1993; co-author sci. books, U.S., Sweden, Germany. Mem. Am. Assn. Clin. Chemistry, Deutsche Gesellschaft Klinische Chemie (cons. 1990—, mem. working group on evaluation 1988—), Deutsche Gesellschaft Laboratoriumsmedizin, Oesterreichische Gesellschaft Klinische Chemie, Svensk Forening Klinisk Kemi, Inst. Standardisierung und Dokumentation Medizinischen Laboratorium. Office: Ortho Clin Diag Sci Tech Dept, Karl-Landsteiner Str, D-69151 Neckargemünd Germany

SONODA, SHIGERU, physiatrist; b. Tokyo, Japan, Nov. 17, 1960; s. Yoshio and Tomoko (Nishimoto) S.; m. Satomi Takemura, Apr. 28, 1985; children: Naomi, Hiroto. MD, Keio U., Tokyo, 1985, DMSc, 1995. Resident in rehab. medicine Keio U. Sch. Med., Tokyo, 1985-91, instr., 1991-93; asst. prof., dir. Keio U. Tsukigase Rehab. Ctr., Shizuoka, 1997—; dir. Tokyo Met. Rehab. Hosp., 1993-97. Author: Functional Evaluation of Stroke Patients, 1996; contbr. articles to profl. jours. Office: Keio U Tsukigase Rehab Ctr, 380-2 Tsukigase, Tagata-gun, Shizuoka 410-3293, Japan

SONODA, TAKAO, urologist, educator; b. Osaka, Japan, July 29, 1931. MD, Osaka U., 1956, PhD, 1961. Asst. urologist Osaka (Japan) U., 1961-63; clin. and rsch. fellow MGH, Boston, 1963-65; asst. prof. urology, prof. Osaka U., 1965-89, prof. organ transplant surgery, 1989-91; pres. Osaka Prefect Gen. Hosp., 1991-99; prof. Takarazuka U. Art and Design, 2000—; rsch. fellow Harvard Med. Sch., Boston, 1963-64; dir. Osaka U. Hosp., 1988-90. Author: Therapeutics in Urology, 1970, X-Ray Diagnostics in Genito-urinary Surgery, 1979, Clinical Kidney Transplantation, 1985, Overview on Treatment of Renal Cell Cancer, 1988; mem. editl. bd. Urologia Internat., 1987—, Clin. Transplantation, 1986-96. Recipient Suzuki Med. prize Suzuki Meml. Med. Found., 1992, Purple Ribbon medal Japanese Govt., 1999. Mem. Japanese Soc. Transplantation (v.p. 1996-99), Japanese Urol. Assn. (hon., Sakaguchi prize 1959), Osaka Kidney Found. (pres. 1980—), Japan Kidney Rsch. Found.(First prize 1995). Avocations: music, golf. Office: Os Pref Gen Ho Sumiyoshi-ku, Bandai-Higashi 3-1-56, Osaka 558 8558, Japan Office: Takarazuka Univ, Hanayashiki Tsutsujigaoka 7-27, Takarazuka City Hyogo 665-0803, Japan

SONOHARA, TOYOJI, research company executive; b. Tokyo, Apr. 25, 1940; s. Shinmatsu and Ritsuyo (Itô) S.; m. Yosiko Nakgawa, Mar. 10, 1969; 2 children. BS, Waseda U., Tokyo, 1963, MS, 1967. Head sect. Mktg. Rsch. Svc., Tokyo, 1967-71; dir. Mktg. Study, 1971-77; pres. Comm. Sci. Inst., 1977—. Mem. AMA, JMRA (mng. dir. 1990-92). Avocations: mountain climbing, walking. Home: 1-18-4 Simiyoshi-cho, Hoya-shi Tokyo 202-0005, Japan Office: Comm Sci Inst, 20-40-1 Hongo, Bunkyo-ku Tokyo 113-0033, Japan

SONOIKE, KINTAKE, biologist, educator; b. Tokyo, Feb. 9, 1961; s. Sanemi and Sumiko (Yamada) S.; m. Yukako Hihara, Apr. 14, 1995. B.Gen.Edn., U. Tokyo, 1983, MS, 1985, ScD, 1988. Rschr. U. Tokyo, 1988-89, rsch. asst., 1990-99; assoc. prof., 1999—; postdoctoral fellow Inst. Phys. and Chem. Rsch., Wako, Japan, 1989-90; outside staff Imperial Household Agy., Tokyo, 1983—. Contbr. articles to profl. jours. Mem. Bot. Soc. Japan (dir., Award of Young Scientists 1996), Japanese Soc. Plant Physiologists. Home: 29 Shinanomachi Shinjukuku, Tokyo 160-0016, Japan Office: U Tokyo Dept Inter Bioscis, 7-3-1 Bunkyoku Hongo, Tokyo 113-0033, Japan

SONOIKE, SANEMI, physics educator; b. Tokyo, Mar. 16, 1922; s. Kinyuki and Shigeko (Takeo) S.; m. Sumiko Yamada, May 25, 1960; children: Kintake, Saeko (Kabuto). B in Engring., U. Tokyo, 1945, postgrad., 1946-48, 48-51, D in Engring. (hon.)., 1959. Lectr. applied physics U. Tokyo, 1952-82; asst. prof. physics Chuo U., Tokyo, 1953-60, prof., 1960-62, prof. dept. physicis, 1962-94, prof. emeritus, 1994—, councillor, 1970-82. Contbr. articles to profl. jours. Recipient tech. award Soc. Photographic Sci. and Tech. of Japan, 1968, Meritorious award, 1994, The Third Order of Merit, 1998. Fellow AAAS; mem. Japan Soc. Applied Physics (dir. 1964-68, councillor 1968-92, meritorious mem. 1994). Avocations: Igo, music, gardening. Home: 29 Shinanomachi, Shinjuku-ku, Tokyo 160, Japan

SONTACCHI, BORIS, radiologist; b. Pakrac, Croatia, June 25, 1959; s. Zdravko and Bojana (Vidović) S.; m. Elma Stanišić, June 25, 1982; 1 child, Bojan. MD, Med. Sch. of Zagreb, 1985, specialist in radiologist, 1993. Radiologist Osijek (Croatia) Clin. Hosp., 1987—. Capt. Croatian Army, 1991-92. Mem. Croatian Radiol. Soc. Avocations: fly fishing, photography, kite making. Home: Trg Slobode 8, Osijek 31000, Croatia Office: Osijek Clin Hosp, Huttlerova 4, Osijek 31000, Croatia

SONTAG, DAVID B., producer, writer, communications executive; b. N.Y.C., Aug. 17, 1934; s. Samuel John and Lily (Gumple) S.; m. Colleen Rae. BS in Textile Engring., N.C. State U., 1955. Dir., cameraman Sta. UNC-TV, 1954-55; program exec. NBC, 1955-59; dir. devel. CBS Films, 1959-61; owner, operator David Sontag Enterprises, 1961-63; exec. producer, head of spls. ABC, 1963-67; pres. David Sontag Prodns. Inc., 1968-76, 80—; sr. v.p. creative affairs 20th Century Fox, 1976-81; pres. Western Slope Comms., Ltd., 1973-87; Wesley Wallace vis. prof. U. N.C., Chapel Hill, 1999—; lectr. Aspen Inst. Humanistic Study, Action for Children's TV, Washington, Colo. Mountain Coll., U. So. Calif., U. Colo., Coll. Santa Fe, Aspen Film Festival; faculty mem. Am. Film Inst., The Ctr. for Advanced Film and TV Studies, 1987-89; cons. U. Calif., Riverside. Producer, writer: (feature films) Break A Leg Mr. President, 1979, Mission: MIA, 1981, Outlaws: A Legend, 1982, Changes, 1987, Threat Case, 1993, Dancer in Madrid, 1998; producer: (feature films) I'll be Down to Get You in a Taxi, Honey, 1979 (also co-author of original story), Mila 18, 1985; creator: (TV programs) What's A Nice Girl Like You Doing In A Place Like This?, 1964, The Las Vegas Show, 1968 (also exec. producer), James At Fifteen, 1976, Central High, 1987—, The Knife and Gun Club, 1990, Kennedy for the Defense, 1990, (also exec. producer, writer); developer (TV show) Shindig, 1963, The Paper Chase, 1979; exec. producer In Concert, 1971-72; exec. producer, writer My Father's House, 1972, Abandoned Child. Past trustee, mem. exec. com. Aspen Music Festival; past bd. dirs. Inst. Preservation of the Original Lang. of Ams., Ctr. for Contemporary Art, Santa Fe; bd. dirs. Doubletake Documentary Film Festival; founder Native Ams. Internat. Film Expn., Santa Fe, N.C. Jewish Film Festival; trustee, vice chmn., bd. trustees Carolina Theater, Durham. Mem. Writers Guild Am.

SONTAG, EDUARDO D., mathematics educator, director; b. Buenos Aires, Argentina, Apr. 16, 1951. Licenciado, U. Buenos Aires, Argentina, 1972; PhD, U. Fla., Gainesville, 1977. Asst. prof. math. Rutgers, 1977-82, assoc. prof. math., 1982-87, prof. math., 1987—; dir. Rutgers Ctr. Sys. and Control Rutgers, New Brunswick, N.J., 1988—. Author: (book) Mathematical Control Theory, 1990; contbr. articles to profl. jours. Fellow IEEE. E-mail: sontag@gauss.rutgers.edu. Office: Rutgers U/Hill Ctr New Brunswick NJ 08854

SONTAKKE, NEELIMA ASHWINIKUMAR, climatologist, researcher; b. Pune, India, Apr. 4, 1949; d. Gopal Pandurang and Veena Gopal (Korde) Potnis; m. Ashwinikumar Purushottam Sontakke, July 5, 1972; children: Dhanashree, Madhavi, Soniya. BSc in Statistics, U. Pune, 1969, MSc in Physics, 1990, PhD in Physics, 1997. Sci. officer Indian Inst. Tropical Meteorology, Pune, 1985-98, sr. sci. officer I, 1999—; guest lectr. in geography U. Pune, 1992; sr. assoc. Abdus Salam Internat. Ctr. for Theoretical Physics, Italy, 2000—. Contbr. articles to profl. jours., chpts. to books. UNDP fellow World Meteorol. Orgn., 1993. Mem. Indian Meteorol. Soc. (life). Avocations: reading, travel, table tennis, cooking, drama. Home: Shahu Coll Rd, 12-B Saurabha Soc, Pune 411009, India Office: Indian Inst Tropical Meteorology, Dr Homi Bhabha Rd, Pune 411008, India

SONU, JONG-HO, academic administrator; b. Nov. 28, 1940. BS, Seoul Nat. U., 1963; MS, U. Saskatchewan, Can., 1968; PhD, Colo. State U., 1973, D (hon.), 1997. Prof. civil engring Seoul Nat. U., 1974—, dean coll. engring., 1994-95, v.p., 1995-96, pres., 1996-98. Chmn. ctrl. bd. coord. between local govts., Korea, 2000—. Fellow Korean Assn. Water Resources (pres. 1997-99), Korean Soc. Civil Engrs. (pres. 1999-2000); mem. ASCE, Am. Geophys. Union, Nat. Acad. Engrs. (Korea), Korea Acad. Sci. & Tech. Office: Seoul U Sch Civil Engring, 56-1 Shillimdong, Seoul 151-742, Korea

SONWANE, CHANDRASHEKHAR GANPATRAO, chemical engineering scientist, educator; b. Nanded, Maharshtra, India, May 2, 1972; s. Ganpatrao Shankarrao and Kamalbai Ganpatrao (Limkar) S. B in Chem. Engring., Bombay U. Matunga, 1994; M Tech. in Chem. Engring., Indian Inst. Tech., Bombay, 1996; PhD in Chem. Engring., U. Queensland, Brisbane, Australia, 2000. Summer trainee Alkyl Amines Chem. Ltd., Patalganga, India, 1993; tutor Indian Inst. Tech., Bombay, 1994-96; turor dept. chem. engring. U. Queensland, Brisbane, 1996-99, rsch. scholar, 1996-2000; rsch. officer Rsch. Sch. Chemistry Australian Nat. U., Canberra, 2000—. Contbr. articles to profl. jours. and books. Student cadet Nat. Cadet Corps, 1985-86. Recipient Sir Dorabji Tata travel award, overseas postgrad. award OPRS, rsch. award U. Queensland Grad. Sch., travel award U. Queensland Grad. Sch., Hindustan Lever rsch. scholarship. Mem. AIChE, ACS, Inst. Engrs. Australia (webmaster 1999-2000), Internat. Assn. Colloid and Interface Scientists, Australian Assn. Engring. Edn., Internat. Absorption Soc. Avocations: classical music, surfing on the web, reading religious, fiction and classical books. Office: Rsch Sch Chemistry, Australian Nat Univ, Canberra ACT 0200, Australia

SOOD, ASHOK KUMAR, pathologist, hematologist, microbiologist; b. Hoshiarpur City, Punjab, India, Sept. 28, 1948; s. Om Parkash and Anusuya (Devi) S. BSc, DAV Coll., Jallandhar, India, 1964; MBBS, Med. Coll. Amritsar, 1972, DCP&M, 1989, MD in Pathology, 1994. Med. officer State Health Dept., India, 1978-88, Pathology Dept., Amritsar, India, 1988-89; sr. med. officer Civil Hosp., Gurdaspur, 1989-90, Nawanshahar, India, 1990-91; sr. med. officer Med. Coll., Amritasr, 1991-95; sr. med. officer, blood transfusion officer Civil Hosp., Hoshiarpur, India, 1995—. Mem. N.Y. Acad. Sci., Internat. Soc. on Thrombosis Hemostasis, Internat. Soc. for Fibrinolysis and Thrombolysis, Soc. for the Study of Inborn Errors of Metabolism, Internat. Soc. for Anaerobic Bacteria, Internat. Soc. for Cutaneous Lymphomas, Internat. Fedn. of Placental Assn. Avocations: reading, letter writing, medical research, photography, pen friendship. Home: Hoshiarpur Sham St, Bahadurpur Rd, Punjab India Office: Civil Hosp, Jallandhar Rd, Hoshiarpur 146001, India

SOOD, DAVINDER NATH, import/export executive; b. New Delhi, India, Nov. 2, 1941; s. Mangat R. and Parma (Vati) S.; m. Margaret Anne Mchale, Oct. 1, 1968; children: Aditya, Abhinav. BA, Indian Mil. Acad., Dehradun, 1961; MSc, Def. Svcs. Staff Coll., Wellington, India, 1972. Commd. officer Indian Army, 1961-75; apparel mfr. AIE Garment Divsn., New Delhi, 1975-87; mng. dir. AIE, New Delhi, 1987—; chmn. Assoc. Label Industries, 1995—; bd. dirs. Legend Watches, Bangalore, India; mng. dir. Universal Buying Office, New Delhi, 1995—. Mem. Indian Am. C. of C., Indian German C. of C., Delhi Gymkhana Club. Avocations: golf, cricket, collecting art and antiques. Home: B-12 West End, 110021 New Delhi India Office: Associated Indian Exports, 501 Internat Trade Tower, 110 019 New Delhi India

SOOD, KAMAL KISHOR, forestry educator; b. India, Feb. 8, 1968. BS in Forestry, YS Parmar U. Horticulture and Forestry, Himachal Pradesh, India, 1989, MS in Forestry, 1991; Diploma in Environment/Pollution Con-

trol, Nat. Inst. of Labour Edn./Mgmt, Chennai, Tamil Nadu, 1995; PG Diploma in Rural Devel., Indira Gandhi Nat. Open U., New Delhi, 1999. Jr. rsch. fellow YS Parmar U. of Horticulture and Forestry, 1989-91, rsch. fellow, 1991-92; environ. scientist Environment Divsn./Gujarat Ambuja Cements Ltd., Himachal, 1992-96; lectr. in forestry Northeastern Regional Inst. Sci. and Tech., Nirjuli/Arunachal Pradesh, 1996—. Contbr. articles to profl. jours. Recipient Indira Gandhi Gold medal, Univ. Gold medal, Univ. Merit scholarship, others. Mem. Indian Soc. Tree Scientists (life), Indian Soc. Conservation Biology (mem.), others. Office: Northeastern Regl Inst Sci, and Tech/Dist Papumpare, Arunachal Pradesh 791 109, India

SOOD, SEEMA, microbiologist; b. Delhi, India, Oct. 30, 1964; m. Anshumalee Sood, Mar. 24, 1985. MB, BS, Lady Hardinge Med. Coll., New Delhi, 1987, MD in Microbiology, 1991. Jr. resident in microbiology Lady Hardinge Med. Coll., 1988-91, sr. resident, 1991-92, microbiology Salmonella Phage Typing Ctr., 1992-93; sr. resident All India Inst. Med. Scis., New Delhi, 1993-96, pool officer, 1996—; spkr., presenter papers, poster presenter in field to congresses, confs., workshops. Contbr. articles and abstracts to med. jours., including Trends in Med. Edn., Indian Jour. Med. Microbiology, Tropical Gastroenterology, Nat. Med. Jour. India, Indian Pratitioner, Emerging Infectious Diseases, Mycoses, Jour. Clin. Microbiology, Lancet, Jour. Assn. Physicians India, Indian Pediat. Mem. Am. Soc. Microbiology, Hosp. Infection Soc. India, Indian Assn. Med. Microbiologists, Delhi Med. Assn. Achievements include research on enteric fever, rabies, female genital trace infections, and molecular biology. Home: M-17 Green Park Main, New Delhi 110 016, India Office: All India Inst Med Scis, Ansari Nagar, New Delhi 110 029, India

SOON, ING YANN, engineering educator; b. Singapore, Dec. 3, 1962; s. Kah Yik Soon and Poh Chun Ting; m. Chai Kiat Yeo, May 31, 1988; children: Shu Ning, Jin Ning. B of Engring. with 1st class honors, Nat. U. of Singapore, 1987, MSc, 1991. Sr. engr. Chartered Industries of Singapore, 1987-91; asst. prof. Nanyany Technol. U., Singapore, 1991—; cons. Motorola Electronics, Singapore, 1993, Compacific Engring., Singapore, 1993, TMI Materials Trading Pte Ltd., Singapore, 1994, IME, Singapore, 1996-99. Contbr. articles to profl. publs. 3SG People Def. Force, 1979-99. Mem. IEEE, Char Yong (Dabu) Assn. Avocations: fish keeping, swimming, martial arts. Home: 63 Jalan Terubok, Singapore 576663, Singapore Office: Nanyang Technol U, Sch EEE Blk S2 Nanyang Ave, Singapore 639798, Singapore

SOONG, JAMES CHU YUL, government official; b. Hsiangtan, Hunan, China, Mar. 16, 1942; s. Ta and Tiao-jung (Hu) S.; m. Viola Chen, Dec. 26, 1966; children: Chen-yuan, Chen-mai. LLB, Nat. Chengchi U., 1964; MA, U. Calif., Berkeley, 1967; MSLS, Cath. U., Washington, 1971; PhD, Georgetown U., 1974; D in Law and Govt. (hon.), Cath. U., 1995; D (hon.), U. South Australia, 1995. Personal sec. to premier Exec. Yuan, Taipei, 1974-77; assoc. prof. Nat. Taiwan U., Taipei, 1975-79; dep. dir. gen. Govt. info. Office, Taipei, 1977-79; dir. gen., govt. spokesman Govt. info. Office, 1979-84; dir. gen. Dept. Cultural Affairs, Kuomintang, 1984-87; dep. sec. gen. Ctrl. Com., 1987-89; sec. gen. Ctrl. Com. Kuomintang, 1989-93; gov. Taiwan Provincial Govt., 1993-94, elected gov., 1994-98; personal sec. to pres. Presdl. Office, Taipei, 1978-79; mem. ctrl. standing com. Kuomintang, 1988—; mng. dir. China TV Co., 1984—, Taiwan TV Enterprise, 1984—. Author: A Manuel for Academic Writers, 1977, Politics and Public Opinion in the United States, 1978 (Dr. Sun Yat-sen Acad. and Cultural award 1978), How to Write Academic Papers, 1979, Keep Free China Free, 1982. Chmn. Motion Picture Devel. Found. of Republic of China, 1979-84; chmn. Huahsia Investment Corp.; bd. dirs. Chinese Inst. Pub. Opinion, 1980—, Nat. Fund for Lit. and Arts, 1982—. Decorated Order of Brilliant Star, Order of Cape of Good Hope, Order of Diplomatic Svc. of Merit, Order of Cloud and Banner; rsch. fellow instn. Internat. Rels., Taipei, 1974—, Eisenhower exch. fellow, Phila., 1982, Ellsworth Bunker fellow Asia Found., 1999, Disting. vis. fellow Inst. East Asian Studies, U. Calif., 1999; recipient Hass Internat. award U. Calif, Berkeley, 1996. Mem. Delta Phi Epsilon, Pi Sigma Alpha. Office: Chung-hsing New Village, No 1 Lane 314 Sect 1 Chein, Taipei Taiwan

SOOPRAYEN, PAUL HENRY, archives director; b. Port Louis, Mauritius, Apr. 21, 1941; s. Henry and Suzanne (Rougeot) S. BA, U. London, 1966; diploma, Paris, 1970; PHD, Aix en Provence, 1974; higher cert., Napier U., 1996. Secondary tchr. Bhujoharry Coll., Port Louis, 1961; clerical officer Registrar Gen.'s Dept., Port Louis, 1961-64; sr. archives asst. Mauritius Archives, Port Louis, 1964-73, dep. chief archivist, 1973-77, chief archivist, 1977—; chmn. com. of mgmt. Mauritius Archives Publ. Fund, 1977—, pub. archives records com. Mauritius Archives, 1977—. Author: (pamphlet) The Mauritius Archives, 1992; editor: Le Reduit 1748-1978, 1978, Histoire Politique de l'ile de France 1791-94, 1982, Histoire Politique de'ile de France 1795-1803, 1989, Témoignages des survivants du Saint-Géran, 199 (pamphlet Brief Guide to the Mauritius Archives, 1984); contbr. articles to profl. jours. Mem. Sr. Civil Servants Assn., Internat. Coun. Archives, Assn. Commonwealth Archivists & Records Mgrs., Assn. Internat. des Archives Francophones, Internat. Coun. Museums. Office: Mauritius Archives, Devel Bnk Mauritius Complex, Petite Riviere Maurice, Mauritius

SOORY, MENA, periodontology educator; b. Sri Lanka, Nov. 10; arrived in England, 1977; d. Ambalavaner and Jegatheseway (Vaitilingam) Nagendran; m. Thangarajah Soory, May 16, 1976; 1 child, DiLeep. BDS, U. Sri Lanka, 1975; PhD, King's Coll. Dental Sch., 1989. Fellow dental surgery Royal Coll. Surgeons, 1978; sr. house officer Barnet Gen. Hosp., England, 1979-80; registrar in restorative dentistry U. Coll. Hosp., London, 1980-81, lectr. periodontology, 1981-92, sr. lectr., 1992-97, sr. lectr., hon. cons., 1997—. Contbr. articles to profl. jours. Rsch. grantee Joint Rsch. Coun., King's Coll., 1991-94, Proctor & Gamble, 1993, 94, 95, 96. Mem. Brit. Dental Assn., Soc. Endocrinology, British Soc. Periodontology, Internat. Assn. Dental Rsch., Internat. Acad. Periodontology. Achievements include cell biology and hormone research: inflammatory repair in response to cytokines and growth factors, hormone mediated periodontol healing in response to adjunctive therapeutic agents, hormone mediated mechanisms of pathogenesis, medication-induced gingival overgrowth; experimental model: cultured human gingival fibroblasts and oral periosteal fibroblasts; research in oestrogen and progesterone in relation to pregnancy and usage of oral contraceptives (population studies and in vitro cell culture investigators); research in effects of nicotine on hormone mediated pathways in human oral periosteal fibroblasts, alkaline phosphatase inhibition by levamisole, implications on periodontal disease presentation and healing in smokers; hormone mediated methods to prevent medication-induced gingival overgrowth; research in effects of steroidal (dexamethasone) and non-steroidal anti-inflammatory agents (indomethacin) on the modulation of androgen metabolism in human gingiral and oral periosteal fibroblasts; research in implications on healing in the inflamed periodontium: a model comparable to that of arthritis, associated with persistent inflammatory cycles. Avocations: swimming, badminton, mountain climbing, travel, art. E-mail: menasoory@netscapeonline.co.uk. Office: GKT Dental Inst Kings Campus, Caldecot Rd, London SE5 9RW, England

SOOS, SANDOR, museum director; b. Tiszaeszlar, Hungary, Mar. 14, 1955; s. Sandor and Borbala (Lubiczki) S.; m. Rozsa Veres, Aug. 8, 1981; children: Eszter, Sandor. Degree, Theol. Coll., 1978; MA in Ethnography and History, Eotvos Lorand U., 1979-84. Rschr. ethnography Pest Megyei Muzeumok/Directorate Mus. Pest County, Szentendre, 1984-90; dir. Mus. Pest County, Szentendre, 1991—; mem. rsch. group Eotvos Lorand U., 1984—; mem. Hungarian Ethnographic Soc., Budapest, 1984—; mem. rsch. group Hungarian Acad. Scis., Budapest, 1992—. Author: (book) Csiksomlyo, 1996, (with Rozsa Soos) The Iconographic Program of the Saint Francis Basilica of Assissi, 1998, The Life of Saint Francis, 1999, The Crucifix of San Damiano, 1999; editor: (book) Studia Comitatensia, 1992, (periodicals) Pest Megyei Muzeumi Fuzetek, 1992—, Szentendrei Muzeumi Fuzetek, 1994—; dir., prodr., scriptwriter, editor (with Rozsa Soos) video films Il Poveretto-Saint Francis of Assissi, 1999, The Poor Mistress-Saint Clara of Assissi, 1999. Local chmn. Christian Democratic People's Party, Szentendre, 1993; vice chmn. Pest County, 1992-94; faction leader Gen. Assembly Pest County, 1994—; mem., councillor Szentendre Self Govt., 1990—; mem. Saint George Order Knighthood, 1996—. Mem. Christian Dem. People's Party. Greek Catholic. Avocations: pilgrimage research, taking photos, gardening. Home: 8 Deak Ferenc utca, 2000 Szentendre Hungary Office: Pest Megyei Muzeumok Igazgatosaga, 6 Fo ter, 2000 Szentendre Hungary

SOOTHILL, JOHN FARRAR, immunologist, educator; b. London, Aug. 20, 1925; s. Victor Farrar and Kathleen Helena (Bradfield) S.; m. Brenda Thornton, May 7, 1951; children: Mary Eileen, Peter William, Charles David, James Stephen. MB, B of Surgery, Cambridge (Eng.) U., 1949, MA, 1950. House officer Guy's Hosp., London, 1949-50; registrar Lewisham Gen. Hosp. and Guy's Hosp., London, 1952-55; rsch. fellow U. Ill. Rsch. and Ednl. Hosp., Presbyn. Hosp., Chgo., 1955-56; lectr., sr. lectr. U. Birmingham (Eng.) Med. Sch., 1956-65; cons. United Birmingham Hosps., 1956-65; sr. lectr., prof. London U. Inst. Child Health, 1965-85; cons. Hosp. for Sick Children, London, 1965-85; mem. WHO Working Parties on Immunology, 1967-87. Editor, contbg. author: (textbook) Paediatric Immunology, 1983; contbr. chpts. to books and articles to profl. jours. Mem. MRC Working Party on Hypogamoglobulinaemia, 1957-70. Capt. Royal Army Med. Corps Germany, 1950-52. Recipient numerous rsch. grants MRC, Wellcome Trust, Action Rsch., others. Fellow Royal Coll. Physicians Eng., Royal Coll. Pathologists, Royal Coll. Pediatrics and Child Health Eng. (hon.); mem. Renal Assn. Eng. (sec. 1966-74), Brit. Soc. Immunolgy (com. chmn. 1980-85), Royal Soc. Medicine (pres. immunology sect. 1990). Avocations: music, swimming, gardening, sailing. Home: Pensylvania Lodge Ln, Axminster, Devon EX13 5RT, England

SOOTHILL, PETER WILLIAM, fetal medicine educator; b. Droitwich, Worcester, Eng., Oct. 30, 1957; s. John Farrar and Brenda (Thornton) S.; m. Caroline Jane Mackenzie, Aug. 4, 1984; children: Emily, Germander, Bryony. BSc, U. London, 1979, PhD, 1987; MB BS, Guys Hosp., London, 1982. Sr. house officer John Radcliffe Hosp., Oxford, Eng., 1987-88; registrar St. Michael's Hosp., Bristol, Eng., 1988-89; lectr. King's Coll. Hosp., London, 1989-92; sr. lectr., cons. Univ. Coll., London, 1992-95; prof. fetal medicine U. Bristol, Eng., 1995—; hon. cons. Univ. Coll. Hosp., London, 1992-95, Gt. Ormond St. Children's Hosp., 1992-95, St. Michael's Hosp., Bristol, 1995—; head dept. ob-gyn. U. Bristol, 2000. Contbr. numerous articles to profl. jours. Mem. genetic approach to human health com. Med. Rsch. Coun., London, 1994—. Rsch. grantee various orgns., 1991—. Mem. Royal Coll. Ob-Gyn. (mem. subspecialty com. 1995—, chmn. joint com. obstetric ultrasound, joint com. med. genetics). Avocation: cello. Office: St Michael's Hosp/U Bristol, Southwell St, Bristol England

SOPENTA QUESADA, ANGEL, physician, veterinary resarcher; b. Madrid, Spain, June 28, 1943; arrived in Paraguay, 1997; s. Angel Sopena Ibanez and Aurelia Quesada Martinez; m. Maria Eugenia Blanco Cachafeiro, Dec. 14, 1972 (div. 1981); children: Elsa, Aixa, Vera, Angel, Beatriz; m. Dolores Spa Rodriguez to Rivera, Dec. 21, 1983; children: Laia, Cecilia, Mariano, Pedro. MD, U. Madrid, 1966, Vet. Diplomate, 1972. Resident physician Hosp. Clinico, Madrid, 1966-68, titular physician, 1970-74; asst. physician Karolinska Sjukhuset, Stockholm, 1968-69; titular prof. genetics Faculty Vet. Medicine, Madrid, 1974-76; dir. assited reprodn. clinic Clinica 2200, Madrid, 1974-93; head Fundacion Arbor, Luque, Paraguay, 1993—. Patentee intrauterine devices. Mem. Spanish Genetic Soc., Spanish Fertility Soc. Avocation: underwater fishing. Office: Fundacion Arbor, Leonismo Luqueno 719, Luque Km12, Paraguay

SOPHUSSON, FRIDRIK KLEMENZ, Icelandic power company executive; b. Reykjavik, Iceland, Oct. 18, 1943; s. Sophus A. Gudmundsson and Áslaug Maria Fridriksdóttir, 1990; m. Sigridur Duna Kristmundsdottir; children: Stefán, Áslaug, Gabriela, Helga, Sigridur. Candidate juris, U. Iceland, 1972. Tchr. Hlidaskoli Lower Secondary Sch., Reykjavik, 1963-67; mgr. Icelandic Mgmt. Assn., Reykjavik, 1972-78; mem. Icelandic Parliament, Reykjavik, 1978-98, minister of industry, 1987-88, minister of fin., 1991-98; pres., CEO Nat. Power Co., Reykjavik, 1999—; mem. radio coun. Icelandic Broadcasting Svc., Reykjavik, 1975-78, NRC, Reykjavik, 1979-83; bd. dirs. The Nat. Bank of Iceland, 1990-92. Chmn. exec. com. State Hosp., Reykjavik, 1984-87; pres. Ind. Party Youth Fedn., Reykjavik, 1973-77; vice chmn. Ind. Party, 1981-89, 91-99, mem. ctrl. com., 1969-77, 81-99. Mem. Assn. Icelandic Lawyers. Lutheran. Office: Landsvirkjun Nat Power Co, Haaleitisbraut 68, 103 Reykjavik Iceland

SOPKO, MICHAEL D., mining company executive; b. Montreal, Jan. 22, 1939; s. John and Mary Sopko; m. Mary Raatikainen, Dec. 28, 1979; children: David, Stuart, Andrew. B Metall. Engring., McGill U., 1960, M Metall. Engring., 1961, PhD, 1964. Jr. engr., mgr. Ont. divsn. Inco Ltd., Copper Cliff, 1964-73; mgr. Iron Ore Recovery Plant, Inco, Copper Cliff, Ont., 1973; ops. mgr. Exmibal (Inco), Guatemala, 1973-78; from mgr. copper refinery to pres. Inco Ltd.-Ont. Div., Copper Cliff, 1978-89; from v.p. human resources to pres. Inco Ltd., Toronto, Ont., 1989-92; chmn., CEO Inco Ltd., Toronto, 1992—, also bd. dirs.; bd. dirs. Inco Ltd., The Toronto Dominion Bank, Voisey's Bay Nickel Co., Co-Steel, Inc. Mem. Mining Assn. Can. (bd. dirs. 1991—, chmn. 1995-97), Nickel Devel. Inst. (bd. dirs. 1991—), Credit Valley Golf and Country Club. Office: Inco Ltd, 145 King St W Ste 1500, Toronto, ON Canada M5H 4B7

SORA, SEBASTIAN ANTONY, business machines manufacturing executive, educator; b. N.Y.C., June 29, 1943; s. Joseph Louis and Angelina Maria (Maletta) S.; m. Janet Lee Dietz, Apr. 11, 1970 (dec. July 1972); 1 child, Joseph Walter; m. Mary Frances Elizabeth Boscketti, Oct. 12, 1974; children: Joseph Walter, Sebastian Nicholas, Frances Ann, Jenny Concetta. BS, Bklyn. Coll., 1964; MBA, Iona Coll., 1974, PMC, 1976; DPS, Pace U., 1989. Math. modeller Assoc. Univs. Inc., 1964-66; with U.S. Coast and Geodetic Survey, Washington, 1967-70; mgr. programming IBM, Yorktown, N.Y., 1966-67, 70-75, programmer, modeller, 1970-72; mgr. program system and design IBM, Fishkill, N.Y., 1971-77; analyst on market models IBM, Harrison, N.Y., 1977-81; sr. programmer IBM, Boeblingen, Fed. Republic Germany, 1981-82; mgr. rsch. staff 1st Josephson system IBM, Yorktown, 1982-84; program dir. Systems Rsch. Inst. IBM, N.Y.C., 1984-87; mgr. edn. program World Trade Corp. IBM, North Tarrytown, N.Y., 1989-90; mgr. promotional-artificial intelligence systems IBM, White Plains, N.Y., 1990—; assoc. prof. MIS Montclair State Coll., Upper Montclair, N.J., 1992-95; pres. Bus. Edn. Systems Tech., 1992-95; assoc. prof. info. sci. Pace U., White Plains, N.Y., 1977-96; asst. prof. telecomm. Iona Coll., New Rochelle, N.Y., 1986; asst. prof. mgmt. Manhattan Coll., Bronx, N.Y., 1988; cons. AID, Washington, 1989; vis. prof. L.I. U., 1997; assoc. prof. computer sci. Marymount Coll., Tarrytown, 1999; spkr. in field. Editor Jour. Value Based Mgmt., 1987—, Jour. Cross Cultural Mgmt., Jour. of Am. Mgmt., 1994-99; pub. Paradegon Shifts in Edn: Paradise Lost or Regained, U. Press of Am.; contbr. articles to profl. jours.; patentee fluxless solder. Mem. IEEE (technol. leadership com. 1986—, info. policy com. 1986-95), Data Processing Mgmt. Assn., Assn. Computing Machinery. Roman Catholic. Home and Office: Internat Bus Edn Sys Techs 1 Christie Ct Somers NY 10589-2430

SORAI, MICHIO, chemistry educator; b. Ryojun, Kanto-shu, Japan, Aug. 4, 1939; s. Toshimichi and Sadako (Maeda) S.; m. Noriko Kida, Jan. 15, 1966; children: Tomoko, Kazuo, Masao. BSc, Osaka U., 1962, MSc, 1964, DSc, 1968. From rsch. assoc. to prof. Osaka U., 1964—, dir. Rsch. Ctr. Molecular Thermodynamics. Mem. Chem. Soc. Japan, Phys. Soc. Japan, Japan Soc. Calorimetry and Thermal Analysis (pres. 1999—), Japanese Liquid Crystal Soc. Office: Osaka U Grad Sch Sci, Rsch Ctr Mol Thermodyn, Toyonaka Osaka 560-0043, Japan

SORCE, RICHARD, music educator, composer, writer; b. Passaic, N.J., July 29, 1943; s. Salvatore and Bridget (Corrubia) S.; m. Barbara Norris, June 6, 1983. BS, NYU, 1969, MA, 1971, PhD, 1991. Cert. educator, N.J., N.Y. Prof. music NYU, N.Y.C., 1980-96; prof. music, program dir. Passaic County Coll., Paterson, N.J., 1996-99; prof. music William Paterson U., Ramapo Coll.; prodr., engr., arranger in field. Author: Music Theory for the Music Professional, 1995; composer in field; works pub. by Boston Music, G. Schirmer, T. Presser, others; works recorded on Arista, Vanguard, CBS Records. Mem. ASCAP (Songwriter award 1982-99), Soc. Composers, Am. Music Ctr., Pi Kappa Lambda. Home: 322 Sicomac Ave Wyckoff NJ 07481-2127

SORDI, MARTA, historian, educator; b. Livorno, Italy, Nov. 18, 1925; d. Mario and Anna (Bernardini) S. Degree with honors, U. Milan, 1948; LLB, Univ. Rome, 1958. Prof. Roman history U. Messina, Italy, 1963-67, U. Bologna, Italy, 1968-70; prof. Greek and Roman history U. Milan, Italy, 1970-96; prof. Greek history Catholic U. Milan, 1996—. Home: Viale E Caldara 22, 20122 Milan Italy

SORDYLOWA, BARBARA LUCJA, librarian; b. Cracow, Poland, Oct. 8, 1934; d. Pawel and Bronislawa (Kowalska) Martysiuk; m. Sordyl Wladyslaw, Dec. 31, 1960; 1 child, Sordyl Danuta. Master of Philology, The Jagiellonian U., Cracow, 1956; Doctor of Arts, U. Lodz, Poland, 1969. Cert. state librarian, 1962. Librarian The Jagiellonian Libr., Cracow, 1957-66, tutor, custodian, sr. custodian, 1966-76, asst. dir., 1974-76; asst. dir. The Libr. of the Polish Acad. Scis., Warsaw, 1976-81, dir., 1981—, asst. prof., 1988—; prof. U. Lodz, 1993-96. Author: Literatura Polska Gabriela Korbuta: z dziejow polskiej bibliografii literackiej, 1971, Podstawowe zagadnienia informacji naukowej, 1977, Gabriel Korbut: zycie i dzielo, 1978, Informacja naukowa w Polsce: problemy teoretyczne, zrodla, organizacja, 1987, Z problematyki bibliotek i informacji naukowej, 1997; editor-in-chief Przeglad Biblioteczny, 1978—. Recipient Gold Cross Merit State Coun. Polish Republic, 1980, Cross Polonia Restitute, 1988. Mem. Libr. Coun. Poland, Polish Librarian Assn., Polish Acad. Scis. (com. sci.), Internat. Assn. Bibliology, Internat. Asns. Futuribles. Roman Catholic. Avocations: reading, theater, cooking. Home: Melsztynska 4-10/6, 02-537 Warsaw Poland Office: Biblioteka PAN, Palac Kultury i Nauki 6p, 00-901 Warsaw Poland

SOREMI, SODIPO OLUGBEMIGA, mycologist, biologist, researcher; b. Abeokuta, Ogun, Nigeria, June 10, 1954; s. Michael Oyebola and Omolola Akawke (Ojo) S. BSc, U. Patras, Greece, 1981; PhD, Athens Med. Sch., 1998. Tutor Oyo State Contlai, Nigeria, 1983-89; lectr. Atanda Inst. Continuing Edn., Ibadan, 1985-88; asst. examiner West African Exam Coun., Nigeria, 1985-88. Contbr. articles to profl. jours. Mem. Am. Soc. Microbiology, Canadian Inst. Environ. Biologist. Avocations: reading, walking, photography. Home: 31 Iyala St, Mushin Lagos Nigeria Office: Athens Med Sch, 75 M Asiae, 11527 Athens Greece Address: Athens Med Sch Dept Microbi, M Asias 75-77, 115 27 Athens Greece

SØRENSEN, FLEMMING BRANDT, pathologist; b. Copenhagen, Apr. 12, 1956; s. Vagn and Vibeke Brandt (Lassen) S. MD, U. Aarhus, 1983, pathologist cert., 1994. Resident Aarhus (Denmark) U. Hosp., 1986-87, 94-95, Randers (Denmark) Hosp., 1983-86; tng. resident pathology Aarhus U. Hosp., 1990-92, sr. resident pathology, 1992-95, chief pathologist, 1997—, prof. pathology, 1999—; chief pathologist Odense (Denmark) U. Hosp., 1995-97. Rsch. fellow Aarhus, 1987-90; Rsch. scholar Danish Cancer Soc., 1987-90. Mem. Danish Soc. Pathological Anatomy and Clin. Cytology (sec., bd. dirs. 1993-97, pres. 1997-2000). Avocations: fishing, hunting, travel. Office: U Inst Path Odense Århus, U Hosp Tage Hausens Gade 2, DK-8000 Århus C, Denmark

SØRENSEN, HILMER, biochemistry educator; b. Skader-Randers, Jutland, Denmark, Mar. 24, 1937; s. Jens Christian and Anne Sørensen; m. Karen Elin Rasmussen, July 11, 1964; children: Susanne, Jens Christian, Anne Dorthe. MSc in Agr., Royal Vet. and Agrl. U., Copenhagen, 1964, PhD in Organic Chemistry, 1967. Instr. chemistry Royal Vet. and Agrl. U., 1962-67, lectr., then asst. prof. organic chemistry, 1967-73, lectr. biochemistry, 1972—, lectr. exptl. biochemistry, 1982—, lectr., then assoc. prof. biochemistry-exptl. biochemistry; rsch. group leader dept. chemistry Royal Vet. and Agrl. U., 1972—, coord. project for biorefining of oilseed crops and bioraf Vet. and Agrl. U., Copenhagen-Aakirkeby, 1995—; Danish rep. Group Consultatif Internat. Rsch. sur le Colza, Paris, 1985—, Assn. Européenne Rsch. sur les Protéagineaux, Paris, 1992—. Author: Chromatography and Capillary Electrophoresis in Food Analysis, 1999; editor: Advances in the Production and Utilization of Cruciferous Crops, 1985; mem. editl. bd. Polish Jour. Food Chemistry, 1994—. Recipient Royal Danish Acad. medal for rsch., 1986. Mem. Am. Oil Chemist Soc., Assn. Ofcl. Analytical Chemists, Union Pure and Applied Chemistry, Fedn. European Chem. Soc. (divsn. food chemistry). Office: Royal Vet Agrl U Dept Chem, Thorvaldsensvej 40, Fredrks, DK-1871 Copenhagen Denmark

SORENSEN, JENS ADSER, parliamentary service administrator; b. Logumkloster, Denmark, July 9, 1948; s. Knud Laurits and Metha Christine (Hansen) S.; m. Anne Birgitte Kristensen, Jan. 5, 1956; children: Soren, Anders. M of Polit. Sci., Aarhus (Denmark) U., 1975; diploma of Internat. Studies, U. Nice, France, 1976. Head sect. Ministry of Interior, Denmark, 1977-78; com. sec. Parliament of Denmark, 1978-85, head com. dept., 1985-90, head internat. dept., 1990-96, dir. internat. dept., 1997—. Co-author: Nordic Parliaments and the European Union, 1997. Recipient Knight's Cross 1st class Her Majest the Queen of Denmark, 1998. Office: Danish Parliament, Christiansborg Palace, 1240 Copenhagen Denmark

SØRENSEN, KAJ HARRY, orthopaedic surgeon; b. Skellebjerg, Sealand, Denmark, Apr. 16, 1924; s. Thorvald Ferdy and Agnete (Petersen) S.; m. Mette Marie Ødum, Feb. 8, 1947; children: Anne, Birgit. MD, U. Copenhagen, 1951. Registrar Randers County Hosps., Sønderborg, Aarhus, Denmark, 1951-58; sr. registrar Bispebjerg Hosp., Copenhagen, 1958-60, registrar in neurosurgery, 1960-61; sr. registrar Orthopaedic Hosp., Aarhus, 1961-65; head orthopaedic dept. Odense (Denmark) Hosp., 1965-93; lectr. U. Odense, 1976-93; cons. orthopaedic dept. County Hosp., Aabenraa, Denmark, 1992-97; cons. in pensions and rehab. five communes, Støvring, North Jutland, 1997—; advisor NIH, Copenhagen, 1976-92; cons. orthopaedic dept. Esbjerg Ctrl. Hosp., 1992-94, Pvt. Hosp., Skørping, Denmark, 1995-96; sch. physician commune at Vojens, 1997. Author: Scheuermann's Juvenile Kyphosis, Munksgaard, 1964; co-author: Danish Orthopaedic Society 1945-1995, 1995; mem. editl. bd. Acta Orthopaedica Scandinavica, 1970-80; contbr. numerous articles to profl. jours. Mem. hygiene com. County of Funen, 1977-92. Lt. Danish Army, 1953-54. Named One of Barons 500 Leaders for New Century, 2000. Mem. Danish Orthopaedic Soc. (v.p. 1976-78, pres. 1978-80, hon. mem. 2000), Scandinavian Orthopaedic Assn. (pres. 1976-78). Home: Hulvejen 110, DK 9530 Støvring Denmark

SORENSEN, KELD, biochemist; b. Copenhagen, June 5, 1953; came to U.S. 1987; s. Alf and Karin S.; m. Susan Linda Hom, June 3, 1980; 1 child, Kasper. PhD, U. Copenhagen, 1980. Research assoc. U. Bern, Switzerland, 1980-82; postdoctoral researcher Tex. A&M U., Temple, 1982-83; asst. prof. U. Bern, 1983-87; dir. biochemistry and immunology NTD Labs., Carle Place, N.Y., 1987-89; lab. dir. Equichem. Rsch. Inst., Carle Place, N.Y., 1989-91; sr. rsch. scientist Pierce Chem. Co., Rockford, Ill., 1991-97; asst. prof. Coll. Medicine, U. Ill., 1993-98; mgr. tech. transfer rsch. & devel. Sigma Chem. Co. (now Sigma-Aldrich), St. Louis, 1997-98, dir. R&D, 1998—. Editorial bd. Clinica Chemica Acta, Glasgow, 1987-89; referee several sci. jours.; contbr. articles to profl. jours.; patentee in field. Unitarian Universalist. Avocations: skiing, scuba diving, hiking. Fax: 314-286-7617. E-mail: ksorensen@sial.com. Home: PO Box 14508 Saint Louis MO 63178-4508 Office: Sigma Aldrich PO Box 14508 3050 Spruce St Saint Louis MO 63103-2530

SORENSEN, PER MORCH, oil company executive; b. Hjorring, Jylland, Denmark, May 20, 1951; s. Carl Johan and Edith Sorensen; m. Lene Dago; 1 child, Kasper Dago. BSc in Structural Engring., Ålborg U., Denmark, 1974; BSc in Comm., Copenhagen Bus. Sch., 1982. Project engr. Monberg & Thorsen, Iraq, 1975-79; project mgr. Monberg & Thorsen, Denmark, 1979-81; contract mgr. Dansk Olie & Naturgar (DONG), Denmark, 1981-83, gen. dep. project mgr., 1983-86, v.p., 1986-91, sr. v.p., 1991-96; pres. Dansk Operatorselskab (DANOP), Hørsholm, Denmark, 1996—; exec. v.p. Don ZEZP, Hørsholm, 2000—. Office: Dong EZP, Agem Alle 24-26, 2970 Hørsholm Denmark

SØRENSEN, TORBEN SMITH, physical chemist; b. Copenhagen, Denmark, June 8, 1945; s. Tage and Nini (Smith) S.; m. Bente B. Knudsen, June 12, 1976; children: Pelle B., Mikkel B. MSc in Chem. Engring., Danmarks Tekniske Højskole, Copenhagen, 1969, PhD in Phys. Chemistry, 1973. From assoc. prof. to prof. Inst. Phys. Chemistry Danmarks Tekniske Højskole, 1973-95; ind. rsch. scientist and cons., 1995—; sr. scientist Nat. Mus. of Denmark, 1998-2000; vis. prof. in Belgium, Germany, Bulgaria, Spain, Chile, and Norway. Author: Dynamics and Instability of Fluid Interfaces, 1979, Textbook on Electrochemistry, 1983, Reaction Kinetics-Systems Theory for Chemists, 1984, Surface Chemistry and Electrochemistry of Membranes, 1999; contbr. articles to profl. jours.; adv. bd. Jour. Colloid & Interface Sci. Recipient P. Gorm Petersen's Memory award, 1977. Mem.

AAAS, N.Y. Acad. Sci. Achievements include work in irreversible and statistical thermodynamics, electrochemistry, membrane science, surface and colloid science, polymer science, chemical reaction kinetics, aluminum reduction, in situ conservation of archaeological artifacts. Home and Office: Phys Chemistry Model/Thermo, dynamics Norager Plads 3, DK2720 Vanlose Denmark

SORENSON, ROGER A., international relations consultant; b. Salina, Utah, May 4, 1928; s. Elmo S. Sorenson and Nellie Jensen; m. Shirley Rae Sorenson, Sept. 15, 1930; children: Erik Roger, David E., Karl W., Laurie. BA, Brigham Young U., 1955, MA, 1958; postgrad., Johns Hopkins U., 1965-66. Internat. economist Dept. State, Washington, 1966-69, mem. policy planning staff, 1975-77; deputy chief of mission U.S. Embassy, Dublin, Ireland, 1969-74; minister U.S. Mission, Geneva, 1977-79; permanent rep. UN Agys., Rome, 1979-82; dir. N.Am. office Food and Agr. Orgn. UN, Washington, 1983-90; internat. rels. cons. Sorenson Consulting Co., Chevy Chase, Md., 1991—; head of U.S. delegation to renegotiation of Nice Agreement, State Dept. Geneva, 1977; signatory Nice Treaty, 1977. Patentee in field. Recipient Meritorious Svc. award Dept. State, Washington, 1966, Superior Honor award Dept. State, Washington, 1969, 74, 80. Mem. DACOR House. Avocations: music, literature. E-mail: ras28@erols.com. Home: 6707 Connecticut Ave Chevy Chase MD 20815-4939

SORENSON, ROXANN, artist; b. Glenwood, Minn., June 22, 1947; d. Robert Burnell Sorenson and Marian Lucille Myers; m. Bruce Lee Kakac, June 25, 1977 (div. 1985). BA, Met. State U., St. Paul, 1976. Cert. fine arts tchr. K-12, Minn. Curator Macalester Coll., St. Paul, 1972-75; dairy farmer kakac Bros. Farm, Alexandria, Minn., 1974-80; founder The Feet of Clay Inst., Alexandria, Minn., 1990—; workshop art tchr. Art of the Lakes, Battle Lake, Minn., 1996-98; self-employed artist Moonfire Porcelain (previously Hudson Prairie Pottery), Alexandria, 1972—; mem. Art of the Lakes Gallery; mem. N.Y. Mills Regional Cultural Ctr.; chair, bd. dirs. Lake Region Arts Coun., Fergus Falls, Minn., 1976-84; bd. dirs. Pope Art, Terrace, Minn., 1999—; cons. Minn. Rural Arts Initiative, St. Paul, 1994-99; vis. artist, exhibitor Arts Alive 2000, Dorking, Mole Valley, Surrey, U.K., 2000. Sculptor, potter, ceramist (Oreg. Invitation). Min., Universal Life Ch., 1997. E-mail: roxann@mymailstation.com. Home and Studio: 7858 Childs Lake Rd SE Alexandria MN 56308-5371

SORENSTAM, ANNIKA, professional golfer; b. Stockholm, Sweden, Oct. 9, 1970; m. David Esch. Student, U. Ariz. With Women's Profl. Golf European Tour, 1992—, LPGA, 1993—, Swedish Nat. Team, 1987-92, Solheim Cup Team, 1994, 96, 98. Recipient Vare Trophy award, 1998; named Rolex Player of Yr., 1995, 97, 98. Achievements in Tournaments won include: Australian Ladies Open, 1994, U.S. Women's Open, 1995, 96, Australian Ladies Masters, 1995, GHP Heartland Classic, 1995, Betsy King LPGA Classic, 1996, Samsung World Championship of Women's Golf, 1995, 96, Michelob Light Classic, 1997, 98, Chrysler-Plymouth Tournament of Champions, 1997, Shop Rite LPGA Classic, 1998, JAL Big Apple Classic, 1998, SAFECO Classic, 1998, Michelob Light Classic, 1999, Welch's/Circle K Championships, 2000, Firstar LPGA Classic, 2000. Office: LPGA 100 International Golf Dr Daytona Beach FL 32124-1092

SOREY, THOMAS LESTER, JR., architect, educator; b. Wichita Falls, Tex., Jan. 26, 1927; s. Thomas Lester and Katherine (Peak) S.; m. Carolyn Drake, Dec. 24, 1959 (div. 1973); 1 child, Drake. Student, U. Okla., 1944-47; BArch, Okla. State U., 1952; MArch, Harvard U., 1954. Registered architect, Okla. Designer McKim Mead & White, Architects, N.Y.C., summer 1954; ptnr. Sorey Hill & Sorey Architects, Oklahoma City, 1958-70; pvt. practice Oklahoma City, 1971-95; vis. prof. arch. U. Okla., Norman, 1972-74, prof. arch., 1975-90, prof. emeritus arch., sculptor, 1991—. Work included in books: Oklahoma Landmarks, 1967, Houses Architects Design for Themselves, 1974, Architecture in Oklahoma: Landmark and Vernacular, 1978, Affordable Houses Designed by Architects, 1979, Oklahoma Homes Past and Present, 1980; sculptor in one-man and group exhbns. Oklahoma City, Norman, Tulsa, 1977—. Mem. prof. adv. com. Okla. State U. Sch. Arch., Stillwater, 1967-69, Neighborhood Alliance, Inc., Oklahoma City, 1971-73; founding dir. CAF, Contemporary Arts Found., Oklahoma City, 1965-67; dir. Sunbeam Family Svcs., Oklahoma City, 1967-75; trustee Oklahoma City Art Mus., 1968-77, v.p., 1975; mem. Citizens League of Ctrl. Okla., Interfaith Alliance . With U.S. Army, 1954-56. Recipient Award of Excellence for House Design, Archtl. Record, 1968, Assocs. Disting. Lectr. award U. Okla., 1984-86. Mem. AIA (pres. Oklahoma City sect. 1965, bd. dirs. Okla. chpt. 1968-69, 75-77), Men's Dinner Club. Democrat. Avocations: photography, travel, reading non-fiction, racket sports. Home and Office: 3801 Ives Way Norman OK 73072-4009

SORGDRAGER, ALBERT JOHAN, educator; b. Djakarta, Indonesia, Mar. 26, 1923; arrived in South Africa; s. Preter Sorgdrager and Jeanette (Paulen) Halbisch; m. Isabella Cornelia Minnaar, Dec. 15, 1945; children: Pieter, Albert Minnaar. D'Econ. diploma, Amsterdam U., The Netherlands, 1961; BComm, UNISA, South Africa, 1952, BComm (hon.), 1953; MComm cum laude, Pokchefskod U., South Africa, 1955; BA, BA (hon.), 1955. Store clk. South Africa, 1945-47, asst. accountant, 1947-49, credit controller, 1949-52, prodn. mgr., 1952-55, prof., 1955-83, cost and mgmt. cons., 1966—; dean, mem. faculty U. Venda, 1983-89; hon. prof. Vista U., South Africa, 1989—; accredited health cons., South Africa, 1999. Contbr. articles to profl. jours. Active South Africa Coun. Edn., Pretoria, 1978; chmn., hon. treas. Suoimimg, 1964-78. Comdr. South African Navy, 1969-80. Fellow CMA; mem. German South African Culture Orgn. Mem. Reformed Ch. South Africa. Avocations: soccer coach, football, philately. Home: House S-3, 73 Van Riebeeck St, Pokhestroom 2531, South Africa Office: PO Box 368, Pokhefshroom 2520, South Africa

SORGE, KAREN LEE, commercial printing company executive, consultant; b. Warwick, N.Y., May 27, 1958; d. Wesley Thomas and Margaret Anne (Storms) Kervatt; m. David W. Farquhar, July 16, 1982 (div. Feb. 1990); 1 child: Lauren Nicole; m. Thomas E. Sorge, May 16, 1997; children: Natalie MaKalen Sorge, Ryan Thomas. AS, Roger Williams Coll., 1978, BS cum laude, 1980. Office mgr. Price-Rite Printing Co., Dover, N.J., summer 1975-76; cons. SBA, Bristol, R.I., 1978-80; account exec. P.M. Press Inc., Dallas, 1980-90, sales trainer, 1984-85; v.p. KDF Bus. Forms Inc., Dallas, 1984-90; account exec. Jarvis Press, Dallas, 1990—; pres. Print Trends, Dallas, 1990—. Printer, Tex. Aux. Charity Auction Orgn., Dallas., 1985, Crescent Gala, Dallas, 1986, Cystic Fibrosis, Dallas, 1989-93, Life Enhancement Assn. Programs Found., 1992—, Dallas Soc. Visual Comm., 1992, AIDS Resources Com., Dallas chpt. Cerebral Palsy, 1994, Lloyd-Paxton AIDS Benefit, 1994, Lloyd-Paxton AIDS Charity, Cerebral Palsy Charity, Yellow Rose Gala for Multiple Sclerosis, 1996. Recipient various awards Clampitt Paper Co., Dallas., 1982, P.M. Press Inc., 1983-89, Mead Paper Co., 1985-89. Mem. Printing Industry in Am. (recipient Judges Favorite award 1992, Best of Show Hon. Mention award 1994, gold award Best of Tex. 1996), Internat. Assn. Bus. Communicators, Nat. Bus. Forms Assn. Republican. Baptist. Avocations: piano, aerobics. Home: 2600 Raintree Dr Southlake TX 76092-5536

SORGEN, HERBERT J., international education educator; b. Bklyn., July 29, 1938; s. Milton Sidney and Frances (Glass) S.; m. Nancy Lee, June 22, 1963; children: David, Laurie. AB, Syracuse U., 1960; MS, SUNY, Oswego, 1964; MLS, U. Mich., 1969. Tchr. English Paul V. Moore Ctrl. Sch., Central Square, N.Y., 1960-65; from asst. prof. to coord. internat. edn. SUNY Coll. Technology, Delhi, 1965—; libr. cons. Northwest Inst. Light Industry, Xianyang, Shaanxi, China, 1998. Mem. Appalachian Mtn. Club, Rotary. Avocations: hiking, travel, photography, cross-country skiing. E-mail: Sorgenhj@delhi.edu. Home: HC 74 Box 230A Delhi NY 13753-9503 Office: SUNY Coll Technology Bush Hall Delhi NY 13753

SORGER, KARIN, pathologist; b. Magdeburg, Germany, June 14, 1939; d. Walter and Aenne (Vollrath) Papendieck; m. Helmut Sorger, 1963 (div. 1972); 1 child, Natalie Karin. MD, U. Leipzig, Germany, 1963; Dr.med.habil., U. Mainz, Germany1984. Med. asst. Cmty. Hosp., Suhl, Germany, 1963-65; fellow Inst. Pathology U. Leipzig, 1965-77; fellow Inst. Pathology U. Mainz, Germany, 1978-87, cons. prof. Inst. Pathology, 1987-88; dir. Inst. Pathology, Göppingen, Germany, 1989—. Author: Postinfectious Glomerulonephritis, 1986; contbr. articles to profl. publs. Mem. German Soc. Pathology, Internat. Soc. Pathology, German Soc. Cytology, Internat. Soc. Cytology, German Soc. Nephrology. Avocations: music, literature, bicycling. Office: Inst Pathology, Eichert Str 3, 73035 Göppingen Germany

SORHAINDO, CRISPIN ANSELM, former president of Dominica; b. Vieille Case, Dominica, May 23, 1931; s. Clive and Rosa (Fredrick) S.; m. Ruby Etheldreda Allport, Apr. 2, 1956; children: Anthony, Elizabeth, Kathleen, Josephine, Christopher, Brenda. Attended, Oxford (Eng.) Trinity Coll., 1957. Former fin. sec. Commonwealth of Dominica, 1966-73; former sec. Caribbean Devel. Bank, Barbados, 1973-88, former v.p., 1985-88; speaker Ho. of Assembly, Dominica, 1989-93; pres. Commonwealth of Dominica, 1993-98; chmn. Nat. Comml. Bank, Dominica, 1988-93. Named Officer Order of Brit. Empire, 1969, Knight Comdr. Order of St. Sylvester, Pope John Paul II, 1993. Roman Catholic. Avocations: gardening, reading. Home: Office of the President, PO Box 572, Roseau Dominica*

SORIA, BERNAT ESCOMS, physiology educator; b. Carlet, Valencia, Spain, May 7, 1951; s. Bernardo and Vicenta (Escoms) S.; m. Rosa Ferrer, Nov. 5, 1978 (div. 1987); m. Veronica Juan, Dec. 18, 1992; children: Aitana, Barbara. MD, U. Valencia, Spain, 1974, PhD, 1978. Med. diplomate. Rsch. assoc. Sch. Biol. Scis., Norwich, Eng., 1980-82; adj. prof. Sch. Medicine, Valencia, 1981-84, vice dean, 1982-84; prof. titular Sch. Medicine, Alicante, Spain, 1984-86, vice dean, acting dean, 1986; head SIBID U. Alicante, 1991-92, chmn. dept. physiology, 1990-97; coord. Nat. Agy. Evaluation, Madrid, 1990-93; dean Sch. Exptl. Sci., U. Miguel Hernandez, Alicante, 1997-98, dir. Inst. Bioengring., 1998—; consultor European Parliament, Strasbourgh, France, 1992-97, Biomatrix, N.J., 1993-95; advisor Pres. Generalitat, Valencia, 1992-95; bd. dirs. U. Miguel Hernandez. Editor: Biophysics of the Pancreatic B-Cell, 1986, Physiology and Pathophysiology of the Islets of Langerhans, 1997, Ion Channel Pharmacology, 1998; editl. asst.: Pflugers Archive-European Jour. Physiology; contbr. articles to profl. jours. Leader Students Union, 1968-74; mem. Partit Socialista Del Pais Valencia, 1972-77; Lt. Health, 1977-78, Valencia. Recipient Can. Blanch, Found. Can. Blanch, Valencia, 1975, La Mata De Jonc, Ateneo Mercantil, Valencia, 1975, Gold medal Real Academia Nacional de Medicine, Madrid, 1989, Alberto Sols prize Generalitat Valenciana, 1997, Diabetes Nat. prize, 1998, Fundacion Salud 2000 prize, 2000. Mem. European Assn. for Study Diabetes, Cell Transplant Soc. (founder), Biophys. Soc., Pancreatic Islet Study Group (coun. 1992), Found. Valenciana Investigaciones Biomedicas (sec. 1993-95), Soc. Biofisica Spain (pres.), Soc. Spanish Sci. Fisiologicas (pres.), Spanish Diabetes Soc. (pres. 2000—). Avocations: reading, contemporary art, music. Office: U Miguel Hernandez, Aptdo 18, San Juan, 03540 Alicante Spain

SORIAL, NAGUI NAGUIB, electrical engineering educator; b. Alexandria, Egypt, Dec. 2, 1946; s. Naguib Sorial Michael and Linda Riad (Georges) Naguib; m. Mona Adly Antoneos Sorial, Aug. 27, 1977; 1 child, Samar. BSc, Alexandria (Egypt) U., 1968, MSc, 1971; PhD, Exeter U., U.K., 1975. Postdoctoral fellow Exeter U., U.K., 1975-76; asst. prof. Basra (Iraq) U., 1980-81; sr. lectr. Macurdi U., Nigeria, 1981-83; prof. Alexandria (Egypt) U., 1983—; cons. Bank of Alexandria, Egypt, 1983—, Petrochem. Industries, Egypt, 1983—, Alexandria Maritime, Egypt, 1983—, Saudi Pulp & Paper, Saudi Arabia, 1992—, others. Contbr. articles to profl. jours. Recipient Govtl. award for rsch., 1985. Fellow Sporting Club Alexandria. Avocations: designing and building computer operated systems. Home: 14 Khalil Khiat St Roushdy, Alexandria Egypt Office: Alexandria U Faculty Engr, El-Hadra, Alexandria Egypt

SORIANO-SANTOS, JORGE, science educator; b. Mexico City, Mar. 28, 1959; s. Justino Soriano-Lopez and Dolores Santos de Soriano Santos. Bachelor's degree, Faculty Chemistry, Mex., 1981; MS, UNAM, Mex., 1987; Doctorate, Tohoku U., Sendai, Miyagi, Japan, 1991. Cert. in chemistry. Head food rsch. U. Autonoma Metropolitana, Mexico City, 1992-94, head dept. biotech., 1994-98, prof., 1986—; cons. Sci. and Tech. Mex. Coun., 1992—. Mem. Mex. Soc. Biotech. and Bioengring., Asociacion de Tecnologos de Alimentos. PRI. Roman Catholic. Avocations: painting, singing, reading. Fax: 58044712. E-mail: jss@xanum.uam.mx. Home: Trugon M 16 L 81, Rinconada de Aragon, 55140 Mexico City Mexico Office: U Autonoma Metropolitana, Av Michoacan y Purisima S/N, 09340 Mexico City Mexico

SORKIN, BORIS, physicist, researcher; b. Kasan, Tataria, USSR, May 9, 1945; s. Smerel-Aleksander Sorkin and Sonja Levitina; m. Riima Raichmann, July 5, 1975; children: Leon, Rita, Edith. Cert., State U., Tartu, Estonia, 1971, PhD, 1984. Cert. in exptl. physics. Jr. rsch. assoc. Inst. Physics, Tartu, 1972-86, rsch. assoc., 1986—. Contbr. articles to profl. jours. Avocations: history of physics, gardening, sports. Office: Inst Physics, U Tartu Inst Physics, Riia 142, 51014 Tartu Estonia

SOROKIN, VICTOR ALEXANDROVICH, biophysicist; b. Kharkov, Ukraine, Apr. 17, 1940; s. Alexander Artyomovich and Tamara Davydovna (Kanter) S.; m. Ninel Ivanovna Goncharenkova, Oct. 8, 1971; 1 child, Andrey Victorovich. Diploma in mech. engring., Technol. Inst. Food & Refrig., Odessa, Ukraine, 1962; postgrad., Inst. Low Temp. Phys. Engring., Kharkov, Ukraine, 1964-67, PhD, 1971; DSc in Biophysics, State U., Moscow, 1992. Engr. Inst. Low Temp. Physics and Engring. Nat. Acad. Scis., Kharkov, 1962-63, sr. engr., 1963-64, engr., 1967-70, jr. sci. worker, 1970-74, sr. sci. worker, 1974-93, leading sci. worker, 1994—; sr. tchr. State U., Kharkov, 1994-95; prof. Acad. Food Tech. and Orgn., Kharkov, 1995-96. Contbr. numerous articles to profl. jours. Grantee Soros Internat. Sci. Found., 1993, 94-96, U.S. Civilian Rsch. and Devel. Found., 1997-99. Mem. Ukrainian Biophys. Soc. Avocations: traveling, collecting ceramics, minerals and shells. Home: Apt 416, 250A Saltovskoye Shosse, 310178 Kharkov Ukraine Office: Inst Low Temp Phys Engring, Nat Acad Sci 47 Lenin Ave, 310164 Kharkov Ukraine

SOROKIN, YURI IVANOVICH, aquatic microbial ecologist; b. Donetsk, Russia, Sept. 24, 1927; s. Ivan and Rachil (Semenovna) S.; m. Inga Josifovna Andreeva, Jan. 5, 1954; children: Michael, Olga, Dimitri, Veronica, Paul, Konstantin, Arcadii. MS, Moscow U., 1950; DSc, Oceanology Inst. USSR, Moscow, 1964. From rsch. fellow to chief microbiol. lab. Freshwater Biology Inst., Borok, Russia, 1953-76; chief microplankton lab. Oceanology Inst., Gelendzhik, Russia, 1976—. Author: The Black Sea, 1982, Coral Reef Ecology, 1993, 2d edit., 1995, Aquatic Microbial Ecology, 1999, Radioisotopic methods in Hydorbiology, 1999, Black Sea Ecology and Oceanography, 2000. Avocation: jogging. Phone: 7-86141-23261. Home and Office: Oceanology Dept Golubaya Bukhta, Gelendzhik, Krasnodar Russia 353470

SOROKINA, ELENA MIKHAYLOVNA, research scientist; b. Moscow, Mar. 12, 1972; d. Mikhail Victorovich Lyamin and Alla Dmitrievna Sorokina. BSc, M.V. Lomonosov Moscow State U., 1994; PhD, Russian Acad. Scis., Moscow, 1999. Cert. biochemistry and enzymology. Sci. rschr. A.N. Bach Inst. Biochemistry, Russian Acad. Scis., Moscow, 1994—; postdoctoral fellow Temple U., Phila., 2000—. Univ. scholar M.V. Lomonosov Moscow State U., 1989-94; grantee Russian Found. for Basic Rsch., 1996-98. Achievements include Russian patent in field. Fax: 7-095 954-4007. E-mail: esorokin@astro.temple.edu. Office: AN Bach Inst Biochemistry, 33 Leninsky Prospekt, 117071 Moscow Russia

SOROS, GEORGE, fund management executive; b. Budapest, Hungary, Aug. 12, 1930; came to U.S., 1956; s. Tivadar and Elisabeth (Szucs) S.; m. Annaliese Witschak, Sept. 17, 1960 (div. June 1983); children: Robert, Andrea, Jonathan; m. Susan Weber, June 19, 1983; children: Alexander, Gregory. BS, London Sch. Econs., 1952; LLD (hon.), New Sch. for Social Rsch., 1990; D. Civil Law, U. Oxford, Eng., 1990; LHD (hon.), Yale U., 1991. Arbitrage trader F.M. Mayer, N.Y.C., 1956-59; analyst Wertheim & Co., N.Y.C., 1959-63; v.p. Arnhold and S. Bleichroeder, N.Y.C., 1963-73; sole proprietor Soros Fund Mgmt., N.Y.C., 1973—; chmn. Soros Fund Mgmt., LLC, N.Y.C., 1996—. Author: The Alchemy of Finance, 1987, 2nd edit., 1994, Opening the Soviet System, 1990, Underwriting Democracy, 1991. Mem. Coun. on Fgn. Rels., N.Y.C., 1988—, Royal Inst. Internat. Affairs, London, 1990—, Bretton Woods Com., Washington, 1989; mem. exec. com. Helsinki Watch, N.Y.C., 1982—; mem. com. Americas Watch, N.Y.C., 1982—; chmn., founding pres. Ctrl. European U., Prague, Budapest, 1991; chmn. Open Soc. Fund, 1981, Open Soc. Inst., 1993, founds. in Albania, Belarus, Bosnia and Herzegovina, Bulgaria, Croatia, Czech Republic, Estonia, Georgia, Hungary, Kazakhstan, Kyrgyestan, Latvia, Lithuania, Macedonia, Moldova, Poland, Romania, Russia, Slovakia, Slovenia, South Africa, Rroma, Ukraine, Yugoslavia. Recipient honor Lawyers Co. for Human Rights, N.Y.C., 1990. Mem. Brooks' London, Queens Club (London), N.Y. Athletic Club, Town Tennis, Meadow Club (Southampton, N.Y.). Avocations: tennis, skiing, chess, backgammon. Office: Soros Fund Mgmt 888 7th Ave Ste 3300 New York NY 10106-0001

SOROSKY, JERI RUTH, academic administrator; b. Chgo.; d. Hans S. and Florence J. (Hurwitz) Pakula; m. Gene E. Sorosky; children: Cindi, Dana, Lesli. BA, Roosevelt U., Chgo., 1952; MEd, Fla. Atlantic U., Boca Raton, 1967; EdS, Nova Southeastern U., Ft. Lauderdale, Fla., 1972; EdD, MS, Nova Southeastern U., 1981. Cert. adminstr., supr., media specialist, gifted and elem. educator, Fla. Chairperson Elem. Highland Oaks, North Miami Beach, Fla., 1967-75; mem. faculty gifted program Highland Oaks Gifted Ctr., North Miami Beach, 1975-85; chairperson gifted program Miami (Fla.) Dade C.C., 1985-2000; site adminstr. grad. tchr. edn. program Nova. Southeastern U., Ft. Lauderdale, 1992—; adj. prof. Nova Southeastern U., Ft. Lauderdale, 1979-87, adv. doctoral practicums, 1985-2000, cluster coord., 1987—, admissions com. doctoral programs Tech. & Distance Edn. and Child & Youth Studies, 1996—; chairperson gifted edn. Dade County Schs., Miami, 1990-93; mem. com. State Gifted Task Force, Tallahassee, 1992; presenter in field. Author: GEM Major Module in Gifted Education, 1981, Ideas Unlimited, 1985, Guide for Elementary Educators, 1995, Technology in the Curriculum, 1998; editor: Readings: Gifted Education, 1991, Early Childhood Education, 1982. Project chairperson Kids in Distress, Ft. Lauderdale, 1989. Named Woman of Yr. Bus. Profl. Women, 1985. Mem. Fla. Assn. Gifted (charter, v.p. 1975-97), Nova Southeastern U. Alumni (bd. dirs. 1981-97), AAUW, Phi Delta Kappa (chairperson newsletter 1985-97). Avocations: dancing, technology. Office: Nova Southeastern U 1750 NE 167th St N Miami Beach FL 33162-3017

SORREL, WILLIAM EDWIN, psychiatrist, educator, psychoanalyst; b. N.Y.C., May 27, 1913; s. Simon and Lee (Lesenger) S.; m. Rita Marcus, July 1, 1950; children: Ellyn Gail, Joy Shelley, Beth Mara. BS, NYU, 1932; MA, Columbia U., 1934, MD, 1939; PhD, NYU, 1963. Diplomate Am. Bd. Med. Psychotherapists (profl. adv. coun. 1992—); qualified psychiatrist, also cert.examiner N.Y. State Dept. Mental Hygiene. Intern Madison (Tenn.) Sanitarium and Hosp., 1939; resident physician Alexian Bros. Hosp., St. Louis, 1940; officer instrn. St. Louis U. Sch. Medicine, 1940-41; asst. psychiatrist Central State Hosp., Nashville, 1941; assoc. psychiatrist Eastern State Hosp., Knoxville, 1942-44; assoc. attending neuropsychiatrist, chief clin. psychiatry Jewish Meml. Hosp., N.Y.C., 1946-59; assoc. attending neuropsychiatrist, chief clin. child psychiatry Lebanon Hosp., Bronx, N.Y., 1947-65; psychiatrist-in-chief Psychiatry Clinic, Yeshiva U., 1950-66, asst. prof. psychiatry, 1952-54, assoc. prof., 1954-58, prof., 1959-62, psychiatrist-in-chief, assoc. dir. Psychol. Center,, 1957-67; prof. emeritus human behavior Touro Coll., 1974—; attending psychiatrist St. Clare's Hosp., N.Y.C., 1983—; asst. prof. clin. psychiatry Albert Einstein Coll. Medicine, 1986—; psychiat. cons. SSS, 1951, N.Y. State Workmens Compensation Bd., 1951—, Bronx-Lebanon Med. Ctr., 1985—; vis. psychiatrist Fordham Hosp., N.Y.C., 1951; attending neuropsychiatrist, chief mental hygiene svc. Beth-David Hosp., 1950-60; attending neuropsychiatrist Grand Central Hosp., 1958-66, Morrisania Hosp., 1959-72; psychiatrist-in-chief Beth Abraham Hosp., 1954-60; psychiat. cons. L.I. U. Guidance Ctr., 1955-60, Daytop Village, 1970-71; assoc. psychiatrist Seton City Hosp., 1955; guest lectr. U. London, 1947; vis. prof. Jerusalem, Israel Acad. Med., 1960, Hebrew U., 1960; mem. psychiat. staff Gracie Sq. Hosp., 1960—; chief psychiatry Trafalgar Hosp., 1962-72; vis. prof. psychiatry Tokyo U. Sch. Medicine, 1964; adj. prof. N.Y. Inst. Tech., 1968; vis. lectr. in psychiatry N.Y. U., 1971-73; Am. del. Internat. Conf. Mental Health, London, 1948; mem. Am. Psychiat. Commn. to USSR, Poland and Finland, 1963, Empire State Med., Sci. and Ednl. Found. Author: (booklets) Neurosis in a Child, 1949, A Psychiatric Viewpoint on Child Adoption, 1954, Shock Therapy in Psychiatric Practice, 1957, The Genesis of Neurosis, 1958, The Prejudiced Personality, 1962, The Schizophrenic Process, 1962, The Prognosis of Electroshock Therapy Success, 1963, Psychodynamic Effects of Abortion, 1967, Violence Towards Self, 1971, Basic Concepts of Transference in Psychoanalysis, 1973, A Study in Suicide, 1972, Masochism, 1973, Emotional Factors Involved in Skeletal Deformities, 1977, Cults and Cult Suicide, 1979, Further Viewpoints on the Genesis of Neurosis, 1996; assoc. editor Jour. Pan Am. Med. Assn., 1992—; contbr. articles on the psychoses. Vice pres. Golden Years Found.; N.Y.C. chmn. Com. Med. Standards in Psychiatry, 1952-54. Recipient Sir William Osler Internat. Honor Med. Soc. Gold Key; 3d prize oil paintings N.Y. State Med. Art Exhibit, 1954; NYU Founders Day award, 1963; Presdl. Achievement award, 1984, medal for med. excellence Pan Am. Med. Assn., 1997, others. Fellow Am. Psychiat. Assn. (life, pres. Bronx dist. 1960-61, other offices, Gold medal 1974, 94), Am. Assn. Psychoananlytic Physicians (pres. 1971-72, bd. govs. 1972—); mem. AMA, Ea. Psychiat. Assn., N.Y. State Soc. Med. Rsch., Am. Med. Writers Assn., N.Y. Med. Soc., N.Y. County Med. Soc., N.Y. Soc. for Clin. Psychiatry, Pan Am. Med. Assn. (various offices including pres. 1989—, assoc. editor jour. 1992—, Disting. Med. Svc. award 1997), Assn. for Advancement Psychotherapy, Bronx Soc. Neurology and Psychotherapy (pres. 1960-61, Silver medal 1970), Mensa. Home: 23 Meadow Rd Scarsdale NY 10583-7642 Office: 263 West End Ave New York NY 10023-2612

SORRELL, ROZLYN, singer, recording artist, actress, educator, entrepreneur; b. Bklyn.; d. Nathaniel Otis and Cupid Viola (Logan) S. BA in Theatre, CUNY, 1976, MS Edn., 1985. Cert. tchr., Calif., N.Y. Tchr. L.A. Unified Sch. Dist., 1997, Sylvan Learning Ctr., L.A., 1998; mem. Albert McNeil Jubilee Singers, L.A., 1994—; voice tchr., L.A., 1992—; bus. cons., L.A., 1989—. Actress various TV programs, comml.s., stage prodns. and films, 1986—; soloist Hour of Power, Glory of Christmas, Glory of Easter, Garden Grove, Calif., 1994—, Anaheim Pond, Calif., 1997, Honolulu Symphony, 1998, Hollywood Bowl, 1998, Gospel Recording Artist, 2000. Mem. AFTRA, SAG, Actors Equity Assn. Avocations: dancing, walking, working out, theatre. Office: Double E Enterprises PO Box 2089 Hollywood CA 90078-2089

SORRELL, STEPHEN A., principal; b. Covington, Ky., June 27, 1952; s. Orville G. and Audrey W. Sorrell; m. Margaret McIntire, June 30, 1990; children: Stephanie, Meaghan. BMus, Carson-Newman Coll., Jefferson City, Tenn., 1974; MA in Edn., No. Ky. U., 1981, postgrad., 1985. Band dir. Cocke County H.S., Newport, Tenn., 1974-76, Union County H.S., Lake Butler, Fla., 1977-81; instr. math. Boone County H.S., Florence, Ky., 1986-92; instr. math. Ryle H.S., Union, Ky., 1992-93, vice prin., 1993-97; prin. Campbell County H.S., Alexandria, Ky., 1997—. Recipient Carnegie Hero medal Carnegie Hero Found., 1994. Home: 6161 Ridgewood Ct Florence KY 41042-9777 Office: Campbell County High Sch 25 W Lickert Rd Alexandria KY 41001-9115

SORRELLS, DOUGLAS EDWARD, court clerk; b. Cumming, Ga., Jan. 22, 1941; s. Garland William and Jeanette (Clyde) S.; children: Rhonda Jane Payne; Scott Douglas, Russ Walker. Grad. h.s., Cumming, Ga., 1961. Clerk Sears, Atlanta, 1962-63; material estimator Lockheed Ga. Co., Marietta, 1963-73; mem. mgmt. Lockheed Ga. Co., 1979-96; tax assessor Forsyth County, Cumming, 1973-79, clerk sup. ct., 1997—. Mem. civil svc. bd. Forsyth County; chmn. deacon bd. Brookwood Ch., Cumming; mem. libr. bd. Forsyth Co. Law, Cumming. Mem. Masons, Oddfellows (Nobel Grand prize 1998), Ga. Sec. Assn. (pres. 1970). Republican. Baptist. Avocations: old cars, woodwork. Home: 3530 Matt Hwy Cumming GA 30040-3204 Office: Forsyth County 100 W Courthouse Sq Cumming GA 30040-2695

SORRELLS, FRANK DOUGLAS, retired mechanical engineer, consultant; b. Toccoa, Ga., May 14, 1931; s. Ralph Price and Ila B. (Freeman) S.; m. Alma M. West, June 19, 1954; 1 child, Desiree G. BSME, U. Tenn., 1957, MS, 1968. Chief engr. Formex Co., Greeneville, Tenn., 1960-67; exec. v.p. Charles Lee Assoc., Knoxville, Tenn., 1967-76; pvt. practice consulting engr. Knoxville, Tenn., 1976-78, 83-88; dir. engring. Cole Nat. Corp., Knoxville, Tenn., 1978-83; mgr. tech. transfer Valmet Paper Machinery div. Valmet-Enerdry, Knoxville, Tenn., 1988-93; pres. PEPE Software LLC, Knoxville, Tenn., 1996-98; ind. cons. Knoxville, 1976—; cons., Knoxville, 1976—; mem. Advanced Toroidal Facility Design Team, cons. Oak Ridge (Tenn.) Nat.

Lab., 1984-85. Inventor, patentee of 8 patents and co-inventor, patentee of 14 patents in fields of filtration, web processing, plastic forming and lens processing; developer and author copyrighted technical software. Staff sgt. USAF, 1950-54. Mem. ASME (Energy Resources Rsch. award 1987), Tenn. Soc. Profl. Engrs. Avocations: fishing, boating. Home and Office: 5516 Timbercrest Trl Knoxville TN 37909-1837

SORRELS, RANDALL OWEN, lawyer; b. Va., Dec. 11, 1962; s. Charles Vernon and Marjorie Elaine (Jones) S.; m. Cheryl Ann Casas, June 29, 1985; children: Ashley Michelle, Stephanie Leigh, Darby Nicole, Garrett Ryan. BA in Polit. Sci.and Speech Comm. magna cum laude, Houston Bapt. U., 1984; JD magna cum laude, South Tex. Coll. Law, 1987. Bar: Tex. 1987, U.S. Dist. Ct. (so. dist.) Tex.; bd. cert. in civil trial law and personal injury trial law tex. Bd. Legal Specialization. Assoc. Fulbright & Jaworski, Houston, 1987-90; ptnr. Abraham, Watkins, Nichols, Sorrels, Matthews & Friend, Houston, 1990—. Contbr. articles to profl. jours. Fellow Houston Bar Found. (bd. trustees 1997—), Tex. Bar Found., Am. Bd. Trial Advocates; mem. ABA, ATLA, State Bar Tex. (bd. dirs. 1994-97, bd. advisor pattern jury charge comm. Vol. 1 1994-97, Vol. 4, 1995-97, chmn. profl. devel. com. 1996-97, vice chair legis. com. 1996-97, Tex. patton jury charge Vol. 1 1998-00), Tex. Trial Lawyers Assn. (sustaining life mem., bd. dirs.), Houston Bar Assn. (bd. dirs. 1998-00), Houston Trial Lawyers Assn. (bd. dirs., v.p., pres.-elect, pres., chmn. CLE com. 1993—), Houston Young Lawyers Assn. (Outstanding Young Lawyer of Houston 1999), Tex. Young Lawyers Assn., Coll. of the State Bar of Tex., Assn. of Civil Trial and Appellate Specialists, Am. Inns of Ct., Million Dollar Adv. Forum. Home: 311 Terrace Dr Houston TX 77007-5046 Office: Abraham Watkins Nichols Sorrels Matthews & Friend 800 Commerce St Houston TX 77002-1776

SORRIN, MARY LOUISE, artist, nurse; b. Woodward, Okla., Mar. 9, 1946; d. Harland Ralph and Mary Elizabeth McCurdy; m. Bruce Michael Sorrin, Oct. 31, 1969; children: Aimee Lynn, Sean David, Keri Leigh. Diploma in nursing, St. John's Hosp., 1967; AA, Ulster County C.C., 1979. Exhbns. include Women Creating-A Celebration of Cape Cod Women, 96, 96, 97, 98, Leo Diehl Exhbn., 1996, 97, 98, Midwest Pastel Soc. Nat., 1996, Cape Cod Art Assn., 1997, 99 (1st pl. 1999), Newport Art Mus., 1998, Northwest Pastel Soc. Open Juried Internat., 1998, Conn. Pastel Soc. 5th and 6th Annual Nat., Creative Arts Ctr., 1998, Internat. Assn. Pastel Soc., 1999, Northern Colo. Artist Assn. 8th Nat. Art Exbhn., 1999, La Fond Galleries, 1999, Pastel Soc. West Coast 12th Annual Internat. Exhibit, Hudson Valley Art Assn. 67th Annual Juried Exhbn., Pastel Soc. No. Fla. 5th Biennial Nat., Pastel Painters Soc. Cape Cod 1st, 2d, 3d and 4th Nat., Pastel Soc. Southwest 18th Annual Juried (merit award). Pres. chpt. Vietnam Veterans Am., 1985; treas. West Hurley (N.Y.) Libr. Assn. 1st lt. Army Nurse Corps, 1967-69. Mem. Pastel Painters Soc. Cape Cod (treas. 1994-98), Pastel Soc. West Coast, Pastel Soc. Southwest, Pastel Soc. Conn. Democrat. Roman Catholic. Avocations: reading, movies, gardening. E-mail: mlousorr@swbell.net. Home and Studio: 2721 N Meridian Pl Oklahoma City OK 73127-1917

SORSA, KALEVI, government representative; b. Keuruu, Finland, Dec. 21, 1930; s. Kaarlo O. and Elsa S. (Leinonen) S.; m. Elli Irene Laakari, July 23, 1953. Ed., U. Tampere. Chief editor Vihuri, 1954-56; bd. dirs. Bank of Finland, Helsinki, 1987-96 (ret.); lit. editor Tammi Pub. House, 1956-59; program asst. specialist UNESCO, 1959-65; sec.-gen. Finnish UNESCO Com., 1965-69; dep. dir. Ministry Edn., Govt. of Finland, 1967-69, mem. Parliament, 1970-91, minister for fgn. affairs, 1972, 75-76, 87-89, prime minister, 1972-75, 77-79, 82-83, 83-87, spkr. Parliament, 1989-91; chmn. fgn. affairs com., 1970-72, 77, 79-82; chmn. bd. adminstrn. Finnair, 1981-94, chmn. bd., 1994-97. Author books; contbr. articles to profl. jours. Sec.-gen. Social Democratic Party Finland, 1969-75, pres., 1975-87; chmn. study group on disarmament Socialist Internat., 1978-80, v.p., 1980—; v.p., chmn. adv. coun. on disarmament, 1980-96, Socialist Internat., 1980-96. Decorated Grand Decoration of Honor (Austria), Grand Cross Order of Dannebrog (Denmark), Grand Star Order of Star of Friendship Between Peoples of German Dem. Republic; Grand Cross Order Icelandic Falcon; Order of Banner (Hungarian People's Republic); 1st class Grand Cross Order St. Michael and St. George, Eng.; Grand Cross Order Merit (Fed. Republic Germany); comdr. Grand Cross Order of White Rose Finland; Grand Cross Order of Orange-Nassau (Netherlands), Grand Cross Order of Merit of Polish People's Republic, Grand Cross Order of St. Marinus / San Marino, Grand Cross Order of Merit of Senegal, Grand Cross Royal Order of No. Star (Sweden), Grand Cross Order of So. Cross (Brazil), Grand Cross Order of Star (Jordan), Grand Cross Order of Isabella the Cath. (Spain), Order of Trishakti-Patta (Nepal). Fax: 358-0-753-6118. Office: Hakaniemenr 16, 00530 Helsinki Finland

SORSCHER, MARVIN LOEB, religious studies educator, rabbi; b. Bklyn., Apr. 29, 1924; s. Abraham and Miriam (Cohen) S.; m. Sylvia London, Feb. 7, 1954; children: Esther S. Rister, Abraham M., Sroya S. BA, Yeshiva Coll., 1946; MA, Hunter Coll., 1950; MHL, Yeshiva U., 1950, MS, 1958, DHL, 1968. Cert. sch. adminstr. and supr., N.Y.; cert. guidance counselor, N.Y. Pres. Yeshiva Haichel Ha Torah, Bklyn., 1969—; guidance counselor John D. Wells Jr. H.S., Bklyn., 1970-74, Franklin D. Roosevelt H.S., Bklyn., 1975-89; chmn. fgn. lang. dept. Washington Irving Evening H.S., Bklyn., 1973-80; rabbi Beth Aaron Synagogue, Bklyn., 1990—; chmn. Hebrew regents testing com. N.Y. State Edn. Dept., 1976—; instr. Yeshiva Tores Emes H.S., Bklyn., 1997—; mem. edn. adv. bd. Yeshiva Gedolah Acad., Bklyn., 1990—; exam. scorer (in Hebrew and Yiddish) oral and written tchr. cert. lics. Nat. Evaluations Systems, N.Y.; translator Hebrew and Yiddish langs. N.Y.C. Bd. Edn., Hard of Hearing-Visually Impaired Bur., 1997—. Author: Havah Nasocheach, Part I, 1969, Part 2, 1972; Manual of Tape Scripts, 1970, Lashon V'Dibbur, 1971, The Laws of Shabbos Erev Pesach, 1974, Blessings and Prayers for the Sabbath Holidays and Special Occasions, 1974, Hakshaiv Va Anai, 1976, I Can Learn Hebrew, 1986. Recipient 1st prize (trip to Israel) Torah Quiz Contest, Jewish Press, 1989. Mem. Am. Assn. Tchrs. Hebrew (pres. 1970—), Assn. Orthodox Jewish Tchrs. (life mem.; former v.p., mem. exec. bd. 1972—). Home: 1375 57th St Brooklyn NY 11219-4637 Office: Beth Aaron Synagogue 2261 Bragg St Brooklyn NY 11229-5401

SORSTOKKE, SUSAN EILEEN, systems engineer; b. Seattle, May 2, 1955; d. Harold William and Carrol Jean (Russ) S. BS in Systems Engring., U. Ariz., 1976; MBA, U. Wash., Richland, 1983. Warehouse team mgr. Procter and Gamble Paper Products, Modesto, Calif., 1976-78; quality assurance engr. Westinghouse Hanford Co., Richland, Wash., 1978-80; supr. engring. document ctr. Westinghouse Hanford Co., Richland, 1980-81; mgr. data control and adminstrn. Westinghouse Electric Corp., Madison, Pa., 1981-82, mgr. data control and records mgmt., 1982-84; prin. engr. Westinghouse Elevator Co., Morristown, N.J., 1984-87; region adminstrn. mgr. Westinghouse Elevator Co., Arleta, Calif., 1987-90; ops. rsch. analyst Am. Honda Motor Co. Inc., Torrance, Calif., 1990-95; project leader parts sys. Am. Honda Motor Co., Inc., Torrance, Calif., 1995-96, mgr. parts systems and part number adminstrn., 1996-97, mgr. parts systems, 1997-2000, mgr. supply chain mgmt., 2000—; adj. prof. U. LaVerne, Calif., 1991-92. Advisor Jr. Achievement, 1982-83; literacy tutor Westmoreland Literacy Coun., 1983-84, host parent EF Found., Saugus, Calif., 1987-88, Am. Edn. Connection, Saugus, 1988-89, 91; instr. Excell, L.A., 1991-92; mem. Calif. Acad. Math. and Sci., 1996-97. Mem. Soc. Women Engrs., Am. Inst. Indsl. Engrs., Optimists Charities, Inc. (bd. dirs. Acton, Calif. 1991-94). Republican. Methodist. Home: 2567 Plaza Del Amo Unit 205 Torrance CA 90503-8962 Office: Am Honda Motor Co Inc Dept Parts 100-5C-2B 1919 Torrance Blvd Torrance CA 90501-2722

SORTE, JOHN FOLLETT, investment firm executive; b. Boston, June 30, 1947; s. Martin Eugene and Elizabeth Foster (Bradley) S.; m. Colleen Sarah Costello, July 28, 1979; children: Bradley Follett, Laura Elizabeth, Kathryn Clare. BAChemE, Rice U., 1969, M in Chem. Engring., 1970; MBA, Harvard U., 1972. Assoc. Shearson Hammill & Co., Inc., N.Y.C., 1972-74; v.p. Shearson Hayden Stone, Inc., N.Y.C., 1974-79; 1st v.p. Shearson Loeb Rhoades, Inc., N.Y.C., 1979-80; 1st v.p. Drexel Burnham Lambert, Inc., N.Y.C., 1980-82, mng. dir., 1982-88, exec. v.p., 1989-90, pres., CEO, dir., 1990-92; pres., CEO New Street Capital Corp., N.Y.C., 1992-94; pres. New Street Advisors L.P., N.Y.C., 1994—; chmn. N.Y. Media Group, Inc., 1995—; bd. dirs. Vail Resorts, Inc., WestPoint Stevens, Inc. V.p., bd. dirs. DBL Found., Inc., N.Y.C., 1991-95; bd. trustees Rippowam Cisqua Sch. Office: New Street Advisors LP 99 Park Ave Rm 17 New York NY 10016-1601

SORTEBERG, ANGELIKA GABRIELE, physician, researcher; b. Munich, Bavaria, Germany, June 29, 1965; arrived in Norway, 1992; d. Dieter and Marliese (Lannert) Walter; m. Gerd Knoke, July 11, 1986 (dec. Dec. 11, 1990); m. Wilhelm Sorteberg, Dec. 28, 1992; children: Wilhelm Eduard, Agnes Luise. MD, U. Munich, 1991; PhD in Neurosurgery, U. Oslo, 1999. Rsch. fellow neurol. dept. Munich, 1987-90; rschr. neurol. dept. U. Munich, 1992-99; neurosurg. fellow, rschr. Nat. Hosp., Oslo, 1993, neurosurg. resident, 1999—. Contbr. articles to profl. jours. Mem. Norwegian Med. Assn. Avocations: painting, antiques. Office: The Nat Hosp, Neurosurg Dept Rikshospital, 0027 Oslo Norway

SORTER, BRUCE WILBUR, federal program administrator, educator, consultant; b. Willoughby, Ohio, Sept. 1, 1931; s. Wilbur David and Margaret Louise (Palmer) S.; m. Martha Ann Weirich, Sept. 2,1960 (div. 1967); 1 child, David Robert. BA, U. Md., 1967; MCP, Howard U., 1969; PhD, U. Md., 1972. Cert. community developer. Commd. USAFR, 1967, advanced through grades to lt. col., 1964; sr. planner, cons. Md. Nat. Capital Park and Planning Com., 1968-71; instr. psychology, sociology Howard and P.G. C.C., Columbia and Largo, Md., 1971-72; cmty. resource devel. dept. Md. Coop. Extension Svc., U. Md., College Park, Md., 1972-92; coord. rural info. ctr. Md. Coop. Ext. Svc., U. Md., College Park, 1989-92; affiliate prof. U. Md., 1985-92, ret., 1996; ext. advisor USDA Internat. Programs, Washington, 1991-96; co-author, co-dir. Dept. Edn. Coun. Effectiveness Tng. Program, 1979-81; author First County Energy Conservation Plan, Prince George's County, 1978-85. Author, co-author 12 books; contbr. articles to profl. publs., chpts. to books. Developer, dir. teamwork tng. programs U.S. Dept. Edn., U.S. Dept. Agriculture, Brazil, Poland, Nat. Grange, 1972-92; cons. Fed. Power Commn. U.S., 1973-75, State Dept. Natural Resources, Md., 1978-79, Dept. Edn., Brazil, 1981-82, Nat. Grange, 1987, Edn. Ext. Svcs., Poland, 1991-92. Urban Planning fellow Howard U., 1968, Human Devel. fellow U. Md., 1970; recipient Meritorious Svc. award Dept. Def., 1983, Disting. Community Svc. award Md. Community Resource Devel. Assn., 1983, Citation for Outstanding Svc., Ptnrs. of Am., 1983, Excellence in Ednl. Programs award Am. Express, 1984, Project of Yr. award Am. Psychol. Assn., 1976, Award of Yr. Am. Vol. Assn., 1976, Achievement award Nat. Assn. of Counties, 1980. Mem. Internat. Cmty. Devel. Soc. (bd. dirs., Achievement award for outstanding contbn. to cmty. devel. 1985, Disting. Svc. award 1990), Md. Cmty. Resource Devel. Assn. (sec.-treas. 1979, pres. 1980, 88-89). Republican. Methodist. Avocations: volunteer work, tennis, sailing, skiing.

SORTLAND, PAUL ALLAN, lawyer; b. Powers Lake, N.D., July 30, 1953; s. Allan Berdette and Eunice Elizabeth (Nystuen) S.; m. Carolyn Faye Anderson, June 23, 1979; children: Joseph Paul, Martha Marie, Nicholas John, Benjamin David. BA, St. Olaf Coll., 1975; JD, U. Minn., 1978. Bar: Minn. 1978, N.D. 1981, U.S. Dist. Ct. Minn. 1979, U.S. Dist. Ct. N.D. 1980, U.S. Ct. Appeals (8th cir.) 1987, U.S. Supreme Ct. 1991. Assoc. Alderson & Ondov, Austin, Minn., 1978-80, Qualley, Larson & Jones, Fargo, N.D., 1980-83; ptnr. Holand, Lochow & Sortland, Fargo, 1983-85; pres. Sortland Law Office, Fargo, 1985-88; ptnr. Messerli & Kramer, Mpls., 1988-92; Sortland Law Office, Mpls., 1993—; adj. prof. bus. law Moorhead State U., 1987. Mem. ATLA, N.D. Bar Assn., Minn. Bar Assn. (cert. civil trial specialist), Kiwanis, Million Dollar Advocates Forum, Gamma Eta Gamma. Lutheran. Home: 120 Quebec Ave S Minneapolis MN 55426-1509 Office: 33 S 6th St Ste 4100 Minneapolis MN 55402-3729

SOSA, SAMUEL (SAMMY SOSA), professional baseball player; b. San Pedro de Macoris, Dominican Republic, Nov. 12, 1968. With Tex. Rangers, 1989; outfield Chgo. Cubs, 1989—. Selected to N.L All-Star Team, 1995, 98; 66 Homeruns in 1998 2nd only to Mark McGwire all time homeruns; lead major leagues in RBI, runs and total bases (416), 1998; RBI total 4th highest in NL history, 1998; record for new major league baseball record for homeruns in a single month (21), 1998; single season club record of 35 homeruns at Wrigley Field, 1998; named Player of Month of June, 1998; winner Roberto Clemente award for outstanding svc. to cmty. Major League Baseball, 1998. Office: Chgo Cubs 1060 W Addison St Chicago IL 60613-4383

SOSKIN, STANISLAV MARATOVICH, physicist; b. Kiev, Ukraine, Sept. 4, 1960; s. Marat Samuilovich and Elena Grigorievna (Lozinskaya) S.; m. Larisa Isaakovna Sudak, Dec. 3, 1993; 1 child, Daniel. BSc in Radiophysics with honors, U. Kiev, 1982, PhD, 1988. Engr. Inst. Semiconductor Physics, Kiev, 1982-86; jr. sci. rschr. Inst. Semiconductor Physics, 1986-88, sci. rschr., 1988-96, sr. sci. rschr., 1996—. Author: Noise in Nonlinear Dynamical Systems, 3 vols., 1989; contbr. articles to profl. jours. Grantee Royal Soc., Eng., 1990, 92, 94, Ukrainian Sci. Coun., 1993-94, Internat. Sci. Found./Soros Found., 1995-96, Engring. and Phys. Scis. Rsch. Coun., Eng., 1995, 97, INTAS, 1998—. Avocations: mountaineering, photography. Home: Flat 77, Rusanovskaya Naberezhnaya 12, 253147 Kiev Ukraine Office: Inst Semiconductor Physics, Prospekt Nauki 45, 252028 Kiev Ukraine

SOSSA, JOSE ANTONIO, Panamanian government official, lawyer; m. Gina Luciani, Dec. 26, 1974; children: Melissa, Manuel Antonio, José Raúl. LLB, U. Panama, 1971. In practice of law, 1971-90; senator Govt. of Panama, 1990-94; atty. gen. Govt. of Panama, Panama City; prof. labor law; pres. Inter-Am. Commn. on Drug Abuse OAS; chmn. justice and constl. affairs commn. Govt. of Panama, 1990-94. Office: Procurador Gen de la Nacion/Min of Justice, Apdo 1080, Panama City 1, Panama*

SOTAMAA, YRJÖ KALERVO, university president, design educator; b. Helsinki, Finland, Sept. 25, 1942; s. Aksel Gunnar and Siiri Tellervo (Johansson) S.; m. Pirkko Tuulikki Tiainen, June 14, 1966; children: Kivi, Tuuli. MA, U. Art and Design Helsinki, 1969. Lic. interior arch. Head dept. interior architecture U. Art and Design Helsinki, 1975-86, pres., 1986—, prof., 1987—; vis. asst. prof. Purdue U., Lafayette, Ind., 1969-70; CEO Design Studio Sotamaa, Finland, 1970—; pres. Retretti Art Ctr., Finland, 1987-97; dir. Nordic Design Programme Varde, Scandinavia, 1992-96; mem. supr. bd. Design Acad., Eindhoven, The Netherlands, 1995—; vice chmn. Finnish Coun. Univ. Rectors, 1997—; chmn. The Found. for the Finnish Inst. in Japan, 1997—; chmn. exec. bd. Japan Finland Design Assn. (JFDA) 2000—; bd. dirs. To the Point, Inc.; adv. bd. Suomi Coll. Internat. (hon. vice chmn. 1999—), The Finnish Ibero-Am. Found. (supr. bd. 1999—). Editor: Industry-Environment-Design, 1969, Plätze Zum Spielen, 1987, Design As Corporate Strategy, 1990, Managing the Corporate Image, 1990, Product Development and Design Practice, 1991. Mem. supr. bd. Finnish Cultural Found., Helsinki, 1995-99; mem. Finnish UNESCO Commn., Helsinki, 1996—; mem. supervisory bd. Valamo Monastery, 1995—; bd. dirs. Asko Found., 1996—; mem. supervisory bd. Tanner Found. Decorated comdr. in de Orde van Oranje-Nassau, 1995, knight First Class of the Order of the White Rose of Finland, 1991, Order of the Lion of Finland, 1999; MTV3 Finland Culture prize, 1999. Fellow Royal Coll. Art (hon.), Finnish Assn. Designers Ornamo (hon.), Finnish Assn. Graphic Designers (hon.); mem. Internat. Assn. Art and Design Sch. AIAS (bd. dirs. 1990-98), Soc. of Sci. of Design in Japan, Finnish Assn. Interior Arch., Info. Soc. Forum of European Commn., Finnish Nat. Info Soc. Forum (chmn. 1996-99). Lutheran. Avocations: contemporary arts, gardening wild flowers. Office: U Art and Design Helsinki, Hämeentie 135 C, 00560 Helsinki Finland

SOTO, GERARDO JAVIER, geologist; b. San José, Costa Rica, Dec. 26, 1963; s. Álvaro and María-Eugenia (Bonilla) S.; m. Tamami Maemura, July 26, 1992. BSc, U. Costa Rica, San José, 1985. Cert. geologist with specialty in volcanology. Instr., rschr. U. Costa Rica, San José, 1985-90; geologist Instituto Costarricense de Electricidad, San José, 1990-98; freelance geologist Kagoshima, Japan, 1998—; sec. nat. com. Internat. Geol. Correlation Program, Costa Rica, 1987-96; v.p. Colegio de Geólogos de Costa Rica, 1989-90; nat. mem. Internat. Commn. on History of Geol. Scis., 1990—; cons. geologist TC&A, San José, 1997. Contbr. articles to profl. jours., chpts. to books; translator (English and Spanish) booklet: Explanatory Notes for the Energy Resources Map of the Circum-Pacific Region, Northeast Quadrant, 1986. Mem. Am. Geophys. Union, Volcanological Soc. of Japan, Internat. Assn. of Volcanology and Chemistry of the Earth's Interior. Avocations: reading, hiking, history of geology. Home: Kotokuji-dai 5-1-16-24, Kagoshima 891-0103, Japan

SOTO, ROBERTO FERNANDO EDUARDO, journalist; b. Oct. 12, 1950; s. Antonio J. and Margarita (Bonachea) S.; children: Natasha, Sabrina. BFA in Speech/Theater, Fla. Internat. U., Miami; MA in Comm./Broadcasting, Paterson State U., 1987. News prodr. NBC-TV, 1979-87; exec. prodr. Univision, L.A., 1987-89; News dir. Telemundo, L.A., N.Y.C., 1989-91; divsn. chief USIA, Washington, 1991-92; prodn. mgr. WJAN-TV, Miami, 1992-93; sta. mgr. KTRG-TV, San Antonio, 1994-95; dir. news svcs. Telemundo, L.A., 1996; sta. mgr. Cablevision, N.Y.C., 1997-98; bur. chief AP Television News, N.Y.C., 1999—. Mem. AFTRA, Soc. Broadcast Engrs., Soc. Profl. Journalists. E-mail: robertosoto ub@yahoo.com. Office: AP Television News 1995 Broadway New York NY 10023-5882

SOTOMATSU, TOMOKO, computational chemist; b. Kyoto, Japan, July 30, 1955; s. Shigetaro and Namiko (Hata) S.; m. Atsushi Niwa, Nov. 11, 1992. BS, Kyoto (Japan) U., 1979, MS, 1981, PHD, 1989. Mgr. Nippon Zoki Pharm. Co., Ltd., Osaka, Japan, 1981-82; auditor Kyoto U., 1982-83, lectr., 1987; rschr. Nippon Shinyaku Co., Lt., Kyoto, 1988. Contbr. articles to profl. jours. Mem. Am. Chem. Soc., Chem. Soc. Japan, N.Y. Acad. Scis. Home: 104 Granferty Kyoto Umekoji, 23 Nishikubocho Nishishichijyo, Shimogyouku Kyoto 600-8874, Japan Office: Nippon Shinyaku Co Ltd, 14 Nishinosho-Monguchi-cho, Kisshoin, Kyoto 601-8550, Japan

SOTOMORA-VON AHN, RICARDO FEDERICO, pediatrician, educator; b. Guatemala City, Guatemala, Oct. 22, 1947; s. Ricardo and Evelyn (von Ahn) S.; m. Eileen Marie Holcomb, May 9, 1990; m. Victoria Monzon, Nov. 26, 1971; children: Marisol, Clarisa, Ricardo III, Charlotte Marie. MD, San Carlos U., 1972; MS in Physiology, U. Minn., 1978. Diplomate Am. Bd. Pediats., Am. Bd. Pediat. Cardiology, Am. Bd. Neonatology-Perinatal Medicine. Rotating intern Gen. Hosp., Guatemala, 1971-72; pediat. intern U. Ark., 1972-73, resident, 1973-75; fellow in pediat. cardiology U. Minn., 1975-78; rsch. assoc. in cardiovasc. pathology United Hosps., St. Paul, 1976; fellow in neonatal-perinatal medicine St. Paul's Children's Hosp., 1977-78, U. Ark., 1981-82; instr. pediats. U. Minn., 1978-79; pediat. cardiologist, unit cardiovasc. surg. Roosevelt Hosp., Guatemala City, 1979-81; asst. prof. pediats. cardiology and neonatology U. Ark., Little Rock, 1981-83; pvt. practice Little Rock, 1983—. Fellow Am. Acad. Pediats., Am. Coll. Cardiology, Am. Coll. Chest Physicians, Am. Coll. Angiology; mem. ABA, AAAS, Ark. Med. Soc., N.Y. Acad. Scis., Am. Heart Assn., Soc. Pediat. Echocardiology, Guatemala Coll. Physicians and Surgeons, Ctrl. Ark. Pediat. Soc., So. Soc. Pediat. Rsch., Soc. Critical Care Medicine, Guatemala Acad. Genealogy, Heraldry and Hist. Studies (corr.), Soc. Genealogists London, Pleasant Valley Country Club (Little Rock), The Little Rock Club. Home: 25 River Ridge Cir Little Rock AR 72227-1523 Office: 280 Doctors Park Bldg Little Rock AR 72205

SOUBARAS, ROBERT, geophysicist; b. Athens, Greece, Dec. 26, 1961; arrived in France, 1978; s. Antoine and Ivane (Hardouin) S.; m. Hélène van den Broek d'Obrenan, Sept. 23, 1989; children: Marie-Sophie, Antoine, François-Xavier, Jean-Baptiste. Engring. degree, Ecole Nat. Sup. Telecomm., Paris, 1984, D in Signal Processing, 1987. Engr. Thomson-CSF, Paris, 1987-89; rsch. scientist Co. Gen. Géophysique, Paris, 1989-98, sci. advisor, 1998—. Contbr. articles to profl. jours.; patents for wavefield propagation method, noise attenuation method, pressure and velocity measurements processing method. Mem. Soc. Exploration Geophysicists, European Assn. of Geoscientists and Engrs., Assn. Française des Techniciens et Professionnels du Pétrole. Avocation: piano playing. Home: 12 rue Prairie des Iles, 91400 Orsay France Office: Co Gen Géophysique, 1 rue Léon Migaux, 91341 Massy France

SOUBRA, YEHIA MUHIEDDINE, economist; b. Beirut, Lebanon, Jan. 1, 1949; s. Souheil and Jeannane (Kadi) S.; m. Suzanne Bishtawi, Mar. 30, 1981; children: Souheil, Lama. BA, Internat. Coll., Beirut, 1967; BA in Econs., Am. U. of Beirut, 1970; MSc in Econs., London U., 1972. Rsch. asst. UN Econ. and Social Office, Beirut, 1974-76; asst. econ. affairs officer Econ. Commn. for Western Asia, Beirut, 1976-78, assoc. econ. affairs officer, 1978-79, econ. affairs officer, 1980-83; econ. affairs officer UN Conf. on Trade and Devel., Geneva, 1984-87, 1st econ. affairs officer, 1987—, spl. asst. to divsn. dir. and head, 1987-91; spl. asst. to divsn. chief Econ. Commn. for Western Asia, 1976-82. Contbr. articles to profl. publs. Fellow Am. U. of Beirut Alumni Assn. Avocations: reading, swimming. Home: 52 chemin de Montfleury, 1290 Versoix Geneva Switzerland Office: UN Conf Trade/Devel Palais des Nations, 8-14 Ave de la Paix, 1211 Geneva 10, Switzerland

SOUBRANE, GISÈLE, ophthalmologist, researcher; b. Juterbog, Germany, Oct. 21, 1942; d. Jacques Lucien and Jeanne Marie (Fix) Daguet; m. Dominique Marie Soubrane, June 24, 1965; children: Claire Marie Josèphe, Marie Augustin, Claire Marie Dominique, Marie Jean Benoit, Pierre. MD, U. Paris, 1968; resident, U. Paris VI, 1970-73, degree in ophthalmology, 1973; PhD, U. Paris, 1986. Clin. assoc. prof. ophthalmology U. Paris XII, Créteil, France, 1986-93, prof. ophthalmology, 1993—, chair dept. ophthalmology, 1996—; rsch. dir. INSERM, Paris, 1995—. Author, editor: Acquired Diseases of the Retinal Pigment Epithelium, 1995; contbr. articles to profl. jours. Rsch. grantee Prevention of Blindness, Balt., 1982, Inst. de Produits de Synthese et d'Extraction Naturelle, Paris, 1984; recipient Bietty medal, Soc. ofOphthalmology of Europa, Milan, 1990. Mem. European Soc. for Vision and Eye Rsch. (pres. 1996-99), European Bd. Ophthalmology (sec. gen. 1996—), Club Jules Gonin (bd. dirs. 1992-98). Roman Catholic. Avocations: swimming, walking, tapestry. Office: Eye Univ Clinic, 40 Ave de Verdun, F-94010 Creteil France

SOUBRENIE, ELISABETH MARIE, English literature educator, translator; b. Rouen, France, Nov. 18, 1965; d. Raymond Georges and Françoise Berthe (Darcy) S. Grad., Ecole Normale Supérieure, Paris; advanced tchg. degree in English Lit., U. Paris, 1988; PhD in English Lit., U. Paris III-Sorbonne Nouvelle, 1994. French lectrice St. Hilda's Coll., Oxford, Eng., 1986-87; tchg. fellow U. Paris III, 1990-94; assoc. prof. English Lit. U. Rouen, 1994-98; assoc. prof. English lit. U. Paris IV-Sorbonne, 1998—; vis. prof. Inst. Catholique, Paris, 1994—; mem. Nat. Tchg. Qualification Com., Paris, 1997—. Author: Présence de la Solitude: La Poésie Anglaise Entre Néoclassicisme et Préromantisme 1725-1785, 1999; translator: L'Empire du Droit, by Ronald Dworkin, 1994; translator articles: Interprétation et Droit, edited by Paul Amselek, 1995; contbr. articles to profl. jours. Mem. Conseil Nat. Univs., Soc. Anglo-Am. Studies in the XVIIth and XVIIIth Centuries, French Soc. of Univ. Specialists in English, European Soc. for Study of English, various French and European acad. assns. Home: 52 ave de la Motte-Picquet, F-75015 Paris France

SOUCEK, BRANKO, research scientist; b. Bjelovar, Croatia, Apr. 25, 1930; s. Frantisek and Marija (Lazic) S.; m. Katarina Skuric, 1959 (div. 1990); 1 child, Marina; m. Snjeska Kulesevic, May 12, 1990; children: Branko, Amalia. Engr., U. Zagreb, 1955, PhD, 1963. Rschr. Inst. Boskovic, Zagreb, Croatia, 1955-64, 70-72; scientist Brookhaven Nat. Lab., Upton, N.Y., 1964-70; prof. SUNY, Stony Brook, 1973-76, U. Zagreb, 1977-84, 88-93, U. Ariz., Tucson, 1984-87; expert UN agencies, Vienna, 1977—. Author: Minicomputers, 1972 (First Choice award 1973), Microprocessors and Microcomputers, 1976 (First Choice award 1976), Neural and Massively Parallel Computers, 1988, Neural and Concurrent Real Time Computers, 1989, Dynamic, Genetic and Chaotic Programming, 1992, Quantum Mind Networks, 1997. Recipient Nikola Tesla award Inst. Electronic Engrs. of Croatia, 1970, 75. Mem. Croatia Acad. of Sci.

SOUCEK, SAVA OLGA FRANTISKA, audiological physician; b. Brno, Moravia, Czech Republic, Apr. 24, 1935; arrived in the U.K., 1980; s. Sava Sedlacek and Edita (Cechova) Sedlackova; 1 child, Magdalena. MD, Charles U., Prague, 1959; specialist in ENT, surgery 1st degree, Inst. Postgrad. Edn., Prague, 1963, specialist in ENT, surgery 2nd degree, 1970; PHD, U. London, 1987. Accreditation in audiol. medicine Joint Com. on Higher Med. Tng., U.K., 1983; registered Gen. Med. Coun., 1983. Resident house officer ENT Gen. Hosp., Nachod, Czechoslovakia, 1960-61; sr. house officer ENT Clinic, Charles U., Prague, 1962-66, Greenock Royal Infirmary, Renfrew, Scotland, 1966, ENT Hosp., Glasgow, Scotland, 1966; registrar ENT Hosp., Glasgow, 1967-68, ENT Clinic, Charles U., Prague, 1968-76; ENT specialist Thomayer's Hosp., Prague, 1976-77, Inst. Occupl. Medicine, 1978-79, Health Ctr. for State Rlwy. Employees, 1979-80; locum sr. registrar in audiol. medicine Royal Nat. Throat, Nose & Ear Hosp., London, 1980-81, sr. registrar audiol. medicine, 1981-88; cons. audiol. medicine St. Mary's and

Ctrl. Middlesex Hosps., Northwick Park Hosp., Royal Nat. Throat Nose & Ear Hosp., 1988-89, St. Mary's and Ctrl. Middlesex Hosps., London, 1989—. Author: Hearing Loss in the Elderly, 1990; contbr. chpts. to books and articles to profl. jours. Fellow Royal Soc. Medicine; mem. Convocation Univ. London, Brit. Med. Assn., Brit. Soc. Audiology, Brit. Assn. Audiol. Physicians, Otorhinolaryngological Rsch. Soc., Assn. for Rsch. in Otolaryngology, Internat. Assn. Physicians in Audiology, Internat. Soc. Audiology, Med. Def. Union, Brit. Med. Acupuncture Soc., Brit. Cochlear Implantation Group, Brit. Tinnitus Assn. Office: ENT Dept Audiol Medicine, St Mary's Hosp, London W2, England

SOUČET, PAVEL, toxicologist; b. Praha, Czechoslovakia, May 9, 1965; s. Zdeněk and Ružena (Starostova') S. RNDr, Charles U., Praha, 1988, PhD, 1996. Postgrad. fellow Oncol. Inst., Praha, 1988-90; staff scientist Nat. Inst. Pub. Health, Praha, 1990-93, sr. scientist, 1995—; rsch. assoc. Ctr. Molecular Toxicology Vanderbilt U., Nashville, 1993-94. Contbr. articles to profl. jours. Recipient Best Poster award Eurotex, 1995; rsch. grantee Agy. Czech Republic, 1996, Czech Ministry of Health, 1996. Mem. Internat. Soc. for Study of Xenobiotics, Czech Biotech. Soc. Avocations: soccer, bonsai. Office: Nat Inst Pub Health, Šroba'rova 48, 10042 Praha 10, Czech Republic

SOUCHAL, FRANCOIS CHARLES, editor; b. Saint-Dié, Vosges, France, July 4, 1927; s. Gilbert Souchal and Marguerite Lemoine; m. Geneviève Boucher (dec. 1988); 1 child, Isabelle. Lic., Sorbonne, Paris, 1950, PhD, 1968; diploma, Ecole Du Louvre, Paris, 1951. Curator Archives Départementales, Corrèze, France, 1951-54, Archives Nationales, Paris, 1954-59, Nat. Mus., Paris, 1959-69; prof. U. Lille, France, 1969-87, U. Paris, 1987-92; editor Gazette Des Beaux-Arts, Paris, 1987—; mem. Commn. Monuments Historiques, Paris, 1969-94, Commn. Inventaire, Paris, 1989-94, Commn. Vieux Paris, 1995; adminstr. Grand Louvre, Paris, 1994. Author: Les Slodtz Sculpteurs et Décorateurs, 1968, French Sculptors of the 17th and 18th Centuries, Vols. I-IV, 1977-93, Les Frères Coustou, 1980; contbr. articles to profl. jours. Mem. Soc. Art History France. Home: 6 Ter Rue D'Auteuil, 75016 Paris France Office: Gazette Des Beaux-Arts, 140 rue Faubourg St Honore, 75008 Paris France

SOUCKOVA-SIEGELOVA, JANA, museum director; b. Tabor, Czech Republic, Sept. 11, 1944; d. Frantisek Siegel and Anna (Horejsi) Siegelova; m. Vladimir Soucek, July 9, 1971 (wid. June 1990). PhD, Philos. Faculty U.K., Prague, 1968; CSc, Philos. Faculty Charles U., Prague, 1971; DSc, Acad. Rsch., Prague, 1988. Asst. for documentation Naprstek Mus. of the Nat. Mus., Prague, 1967-68, rsch. fellow, 1968-71, keeper, 1971-79, dir., 1979—. Author: Appu-Marchen und Hedammu-Mythus, 1971, Staroveky Predni vychod, 1979, Hethitische Verwaltungspraxis im Lichte der Wirtschafts- und Inventardokumente, 1986; editor: Systematische Bibliographie der Hethitologie 1915-1995, 1996. Mem. Czech Soc. for Archaeology, Soc. for Religionistics (sec. Prague br. 1990-92), Czech Com. of Internat. Coun. of Museums (chair 1990-2000). Avocations: music, theatre, art, hiking, gardening. Office: Naprstek Mus of Nat Mus, Prague/Betlemske nam.1, 110 00 Praha 1 Czech Republic

SOUDIJN, KAREL ADRIANUS, psychologist; b. Doetinchem, The Netherlands, Jan. 11, 1944; s. Pieter J.W. Soudijn and Hermina Van Toledo; m. Ilse H. Cox, July 14, 1967; 1 child, Melvin. MA, U. Amsterdam, The Netherlands, 1969, PhD, 1982. Lectr. U. Amsterdam, 1969-75; assoc. prof. Tilburg (The Netherlands) U., 1975—. Author books in field; editor jours. in field. Fellow Netherlands Inst. Advanced Study, 1980-81. Mem. Dutch Psychol. Assn. (bd. dirs. 1986-89, ethics com. 1997—). Avocation: numismatics. Office: Tilburg U Dept Psychology, PO Box 90153, 5000 LE Tilburg The Netherlands

SOUFLIS, JOHN LEONIDAS, electrical engineer, management consultant; b. Athens, Greece, Mar. 5, 1961; s. Leonidas I. and Antonia I. (Roussou) S.; m. Ourania M. Nomicos, Nov. 17, 1994; 1 child, Leonidas. Diploma, Nat. Tech. U., Athens, 1984, PhD, 1990. Chartered elec. engr., Greece; cert. quality ins. mgmt. sys. assessor; cert. environ. quality auditor. Freelance cons. engr. Athens, 1986-97; supervising sr. cons. KPMG Peat Marwick Kyriacou, Athens, 1997-99, mgr., 1999—; head support unit Hellenic Accreditation Sys., Greek Ministry of Devel., 1999-2000. Author: The Cotton Ginning Industry in Greece, 1996, The Textiles Dyeing and Finishing Industry in Greece, 1997, (chpt. in book) Business Consultants, 1997; co-author: The Impacts of the European Environment/Energy Tax on the Greek industry and Economy, 1995, (chpt. in book) Taxes and Environment, 1997, Reliability and Fault Diagnosis Methods of Power System Components, 1987, also textbooks on environ. protection, occupl. safety and indsl. hazard analysis; translation top books in mgmt. issues, in Greek, in cooperation with leading Greek pub. houses; contbr. numerous articles to profl. jours. Internat. bd. dirs. Network for Environ. Tech. Transfer, Brussels, 1990-92. Nat. Tech. U. Athens scholar, 1984-89; elected rapporteur UN Environment Program, Split, Croatia, 1987. Mem. Tech. Chamber Greece, Assn. Greek Elec. and Mech. Engrs., Assn. Greek REgional devel. and Urban Planners (assoc.), Hellenic Quality Forum, Rotary Club. Avocations: foreign policy matters, reading, playing music. Fax: 301-6062111. Office: KPMG Peat Marwick Kyriacou, 3 Stratigou Tombra St, 153 42 Aghia Paraskevi Greece

SOUHAMI, LUIS, physician, radiation oncology; b. Vitoria, Brazil, Feb. 22, 1949; arrived in Can., 1987; s. Luis and Carolina R. (Serra) S.; m. Julia Maria Lopes, Oct. 22, 1974; children: Marcelo, Daniel. MD, Escola Medicina Cirurgia, Rio de Janeiro, 1972. Diplomate Am. Bd. Radiology. Chmn. dept. radiotherapy Instituto Nacional Cancer, Rio de Janeiro, 1981-85, chief med. divsn., 1986-87; prof. McGill U., Montreal, Que., Can., 1987-95; prof. McGill U., Montreal, Ont., Can., 1995 , assoc. dir. dept. radio-oncology, 1991—; advisor WHO, Geneva, Switzerland, 1991; cons. Govt. Que., Montreal, Can., 1994-95; mem. Union Internat. Contre le Cancer, Internat. Sci. Adv. Com., 1995; vis. prof. Instituto Nacional Can cer, Rio de Janeiro, 1992, Queen's U., Kingston, Can., 1993. Editor: Revista Brasileira Cancerologia, 1982 ; mem. editl. bd. Internat. Jour. Radiation Oncology Biology Physics, Current Oncology; contbr. papers to profl. jours., chpts. to books. Mem. Internat. Stereotactic Radiosurgery Soc. (bd. dirs. 1995), Am. Soc. Therapeutic Radiology and Oncology, Can. Assn. Radiation Oncologists (dir. Que. 1995-97). Avocation: sports. Office: McGill U Radiation Oncology, 1650 Cedar Ave, Montreal, PQ Canada H3G 1A4

SOUILHAC, DOMINIQUE JACQUES, optical engineering researcher; b. Paris, France, Mar. 26, 1944; s. Henri Eugene and Yvonne (Blin) S. Lic., U. Paris, 1967; grad. in engring., Ecole Sup. d'Optique, Orsay, France, 1969; MS, Case Western Res. U., 1971; PhD, McGill U., Montreal, Que., Can., 1987. Prof. Sch. Tech., Montreal, 1975-77; rsch. asst. McGill U., 1979-87; asst. prof. Ecole Nat. Sup. d'Elec. et Mech., Nancy, France, 1989-91; rsch. scientist Lab. d'Elec. et Mech. Theorique Appliquée Nat. Ctr. Sci. Rsch., Vandoeuvre les Nancy, France, 1991—. Natural Scis. and Engring. Rsch. Coun. grantee McGill U., 1979-87. Mem. Soc. Optical Engring. and Optical Soc. Am. Home: 35 Rue des Fosses, 58120 Chateau Chinon France Office: LEMTA-CNRS, 2 Ave de la Foret de Haye, 54504 Vandoeuvre Les Nancy France

SOUKIOUROGLOU, IOANNIS EFSTATHIOS, marketing and sales manager, purchasing consultant; b. Thessaloniki, Greece, July 26, 1954; s. Efstathios Ioannis and Persefoni (Votika) S.; m. 91 (div. Apr. 1995). BSME, Engring. Coll., Thessaloniki, 1977; MS in Exec. Mgmt., Free European Sch. Econs. Mech. piping engr. Petrola Internat. S.A., Jeddah, Saudi Arabia, 1981-90; purchasing mgr. Petrola Internat. S.A., Athens, Greece, 1990-93; purchasing cons. SETE Tech. Svcs. S.A., Athens, 1993-96; mktg. and sales mgr. SETE Procurement & Trading S.A., Athens, 1997—, Sete Procurement Trading, Athens, 1997—; mng. dir., bd. dirs. CosmoMarble S.A., 1999—; bd. dirs. Cosmos Bldg. Materials Shanghai Co. Ltd. 2d lt., Greek Army, 1977-80. Mem. Internat. Soc. Logistics (chmn. Athena chpt. 1996-98, dist. dir. Greece 1998-99, v.p. internat., voting mem. exec. bd. 1999—), Hellenic Purchasing Inst., Inst. Logistics Mgmt. Greek Orthodox. Avocations: music, concerts, cooking, reading. Home: 85 Levidou St, 14563 Athens Greece Office: SETE Procurement Trading, 59 Diligianni St, 145 62 Athens Greece

SOUKUP, TOMAS, neurophysiologist; b. Prague, Jan. 4, 1948; s. Mojmir and Zdena (Pokorna) S.; m. Helena Barcalova, July 6, 1972; children: Peter, Tereza. MS, Charles U., Prague, 1971, RNDr, 1972; PhD, Czechoslovak Acad. Scis., Prague, 1980. Rsch. assoc. Inst. Physiol. Acad. Scis., Prague, 1973-74, rsch. fellow, 1979-80, scientific worker, 1980-85, head of the dept., 1985—; main organizer of a satellite symposium of the 2nd IBRO World Congress of Neurosci., Prague, 1987. Contbr. numerous articles to profl. jours. and abstracts; co-editor: Symposial Proceedings Mechanoreceptors. Head of Coord. Ctr. of Internat. Biology Olympiad, Ministry of Edn., Prague, 1994—. Mem. Czech Physiol. Soc., Czechoslovak Electron Microscopical Soc., Nature Conservation. Office: Inst Physiology Acad Sci, Videnska 1083, 142 20 Prague Czech Republic

SOULAGES, PIERRE, painter; b. Rodez, France, Dec. 24, 1919; s. Amans and Aglae (Corp) S.; m. Colette Llaurens, Oct. 24, 1942. Baccalauriat Philosophie Etudes secondaires au, Lycee de Rodez, 1938. Paintings exhibited Lydia Conti Gallery, Paris, 1948-49, Louis Carre Gallery, Paris-N.Y.C., 1950-53, Galerie de France, Paris, 1956, 60-63, 67-72, Kootz Gallery, N.Y., 1954-65, Knoedler Gallery, N.Y.C., 1968; designer for ballet, theater, 1949, 51, for Louis Jouvet, Athenee, Paris, 1951; paintings in permanent collections Mus. Modern Art, N.Y.C., Musée d'Art Moderne, Paris, Museo de Arte Moderna, Rio de Janeiro, Tate Gallery of London, S.R. Guggenheim Mus., N.Y.C., Phillips Gallery, Washington, Mus. of Hamburg, Köln, Germany, Torino, Italy, Zurich, Switzerland, others; expositions retrospective in museums in Hanover, Essen, Den Haag, Zurich, 1960-61, Copenhagen, 1963, Paris, 1967, Pitts., Musée de Quebec, 1968, Buffalo, Montreal, Dakar, Lisboa, Madrid, Mexico, Caracas, São Paulo, Rio de Janeiro, 1974-76; M.I.T., 1962, Fine Arts Mus. Houston, 1966, Centre Georges Pompidou, Paris, 1979, Musée du Parc de la Boverie, Liège, Belgium, 1980, Arhus, Esbjerg, Copenhague, 1982, Colmar (France), 1983, Seibu Mus. Art, Tokyo, 1984, Pulchristudio, Den Haag (Netherland), 1985, Mus. St. Pierre, Lyon, 1987, Fridericianum Mus., Kassel (Germany)-Ivam, Valencia (Spain), Nantes, France, 1989, Moderner Kunst Mus., Vienna, 1991, Nat. Contemporary Art Mus., Seoul, 1993, Fine Arts Mus., Montreal, Taipei, 1994, Meschuguan, Peking, 1996, Musée D'Art Moderne, Paris, Fine Arts Mus., Museu de Arte, Sao Paolo, 1996, Deichtorhallen, Hamburg, 1997, Kunstmuseum, Bern, Switzerland, 1999, others; 109 stained glass windows in Church of Conques, France. Recipient Prix biennale de Tokyo, 1957, Prix de la Biennale de gravure de Ljubljana, Yougoslavie, 1959, Prix Carnegie, 1963, Prix des Arts de Paris, 1975, Prix Rembrandt, 1976, Grand Prix des Arts de la Ville de Paris, 1986, Prix Nat. des Arts, France, 1986, Proemium Imperiale, Tokyo, 1992, 94.

SOULE, MARIS ANNE, writer; b. Oakland, Calif., June 19, 1939; d. Mario and Thelma (Wood) Chirone; m. William L. Soule, May 11, 1968; children: Deryk, Mia. BA, U. Calif., 1961. Tchr. Rio Americano H.S., Sacramento, Calif., 1963-67, La Cumbre Jr. High, Santa Barbara, 1968-70, Galesburg (Mich.)-Augusta H.S., 1970-72; instr. Kellogg C.C., Battle Creek, Mich., 1990—; Pres. Climax-Scotts Sch. Mothers Club, 1981. Author: First Impressions, 1983, No Room for Love, 1984, Lost and Found, 1985, Sounds Like Love, 1986, A Winning Combination, 1987, The Best of Everything, 1988, The Law of Nature, 1988, Storybook Hero, 1989, Jared's Lady, Missy's Proposition, 1992, Lyon's Pride, 1993, Con Man, 1993, No Strings Attached, 1993, No Promises Made, 1994, Stop the Wedding!, 1994, Dark Temptation, 1995, Thrill of the Chase, 1995, Substitute Mom, 1996, Destiny Strikes Twice, 1996, Heiress Seeking Perfect Husband, 1997, Destiny Unknown, 1997, Shelter From the Storm, 1997, Chase the Dream, others. Mem. Mid-Mich. Romance Writers Am., Romance Writers Am., Greater Detroit Romance Writers Am., Novelists Inc. Avocations: horses, gardening, reading. Home: PO Box 250 Climax MI 49034-0250

SOULIS, ATHINA, medical research scientist; b. Melbourne, Victoria, Australia, Nov. 29, 1966; d. Dennis and Vasiliki (Michalopoulos) S. BS, U. Australia, 1988; PhD, U. Melbourne, 1997. Rsch. fellow U. Melbourne, 1988-99; clin. project leader Synermedica Pty. Ltd., 1999—. Grantee Australian Kidney Found., 1994-95, Hoechst Found., 1994-95, Diabetes Australia Rsch. Trust, Melbourne, 1995-96, Sir Edward Dunlop Rsch. Trust, 1996-97; Internat. fellow Juvenille Diabetes Found., 1998. Mem. European Assn. for Study of Diabetes, Australian Diabetes Assn. Greek Orthodox. Avocations: swimming, traveling, reading. Office: ARMC-Repatriation Campus, Synermedica Pty Ltd Level 1, 245 Glenferrie Rd Malvern, 3081 Victoria 3144, Australia

SOULIS, JOHANNES VASSILIOU, fluid mechanics educator; b. Drama, Macedonia, Greece, Jan. 20, 1951; s. Vassilios Johannes and Anastasia (Michael) S.; m. Tzima Constandina, July 27, 1986; children: Vassilios, Anaastasia-Paraskevi, Achilles. BS in Applied Math., Aristotelion U., Thessaloniki, Greece, 1972; MS in Mech. Engring., Strathclyde U., Glasgow, Scotland, 1978; PhD in Engring., Cambridge (Eng.) U., 1982. Lectr. civil engring. Democrition U. of Thrace, Xanthi, Greece, 1982-86, asst. prof. civil engring., 1986-92; assoc. prof. Democrition U. of Thrace, Xanthi, 1993—; rschr. in fluid mechanics and hydraulics engring. Author: Computational Fluid Dynamics, 1986, Solved Problems in Computational Fluid Dynamics, 1989, An Introduction to Open Channel Flow, 1989, Hydraulic Turbomachines vol. I, 1993, vol. II, 1994, vol. III, 1995, Closed Pipe Flow, 1999, Open Channel Flow, 1999; contbr. more than 90 articles to profl. jours. Mem. ASME, AIAA, Internat. Assn. Hydraulic Rsch. Orthodox Christian. Avocation: motoring. Home: 33 Agelaki Str, Thessaloniki 54621, Greece

SOULTOUKIS, DONNA ZOCCOLA, library director; b. Princeton, N.J., July 28, 1949; d. Peter Joseph and Josephine (Taraschi) Zoccola; m. Dimitrios Athanasios Soultoukis, July 26, 1980. AB, Georgian Ct. Coll., Lakewood, N.J., 1971; MS, Drexel U., 1976; Cert., Italian U. for Foreigners, Perugia, 1974. Libr. asst. Geology Libr. Princeton U., 1971-73; libr. Friends Hosp., Phila., 1976-86, dir. libr. svcs., 1986-98; head libr. Temple U., Sch. Podiatric, 1998-99; ref. libr. MCP/Hahnemann U., Phila., 1999-2000; sr. info. scientist Bristol-Myers Squibb Pharm. Rsch. Inst., Hopewell, N.J., N.J., 2000—; cons. Lower Bucks Hosp., Bristol, Pa., 1991-95. Vol. outreach program Old St. Joseph's Ch., Phila., 1992-95, sanctuary min., 1993—, mem. pastoral coun., 1995-98, bd. ministers 1999—, mem. outreach program, bd. dirs., 1997—. Mem. Med. Libr. Assn. (chair mental librs. divsn. 1991-93, chair rsch. com. 1996—), Spl. Librs. Assn. (Phila. chpt. bd. dirs. 1985-88, pres. 1982-84, chmn. long-range planning 1993, mem. adv. bd. 1995—, mem. strategic planning com. solo divsn., chair profl. devel. com. 1995—). Avocations: travel, cooking. Home: 290 Cinnabar Ln Yardley PA 19067-5717

SOUMOY, VINCENT ALBERT, physicist; b. Charleroi, Belgium, Feb. 20, 1964; s. Rene Camille and Monique Maria (Gravy) S.; m. Virginie Micheline Cambon, Sept. 29, 1990. Master, U. Nanur, Belgium, 1986, PhD, 1992; Diploma, Von Karman Inst., Brussels, 1987. Rsch. assoc. Nat. Inst. for Rsch. and Safety, Nancy, France, 1987-91; rsch. engr. French Steel and Iron Rsch. Inst., Metz, France, 1990—; market engr./east agy. mgr. Transoft Internat. S.A., Epinay Sur Seine, France, 1992—. Mem. Belgium Phys. Soc., European Phys. Soc., Am. Phys. Soc. Roman Catholic. Avocations: music, chord song and direction, stamp collecting, flying. Home and Office: 1 Hameau du Parc, 95630 Meriel France

SOUNDARARAJAN, KANNAN, material scientist; b. Chennai, Tamil Nadu, India; m. Anupama Prasad. BE in Metallurg. Engring., Pune U., Maharashtra, India, ME in Material Sci. and Metallurg. Engr.; postgrad., Cotton and Textile Rsch. Inst., 1999—. Sandwich trainee transmissins and foundry divsns. Tata Engring and Locomotive Co. (TELCO), Pune, India, 1976-77; mgmt. trainee fertilizer divsn., part sandwich tng. Imperial Chem. Industries, Kanpur, India, 1978-80; materials engr. Imperial Chem. Industries, Gomia, Bihar, India, 1980-82; engr. mech. svc. explosives divsn. Imperial Chem. Industries, Gomia, 1982-84, sr. maint. supt. acids complex explosive divsn., 1984-86; project design engr. splty. chems./ethoxylated chems. Imperial Chem. Industries, Bombay, 1986, bus. devel. mg. All India heat treatment chems., 1986-90, engring. purchase mgr. fibres divsn./polyester staple fibers, 1990-93; engring. purchase mgr. fibres divsn./polyester staple fibers Terene Fibres India Ltd. (joint venture ICI/Reliance), Bombay, 1993-97; mgr. engring. devel. Terene Fibres India Pvt. Ltd., Thane, 1997—. Author: Crimping of Polyester Staple Fibre, 1993. Fellow Instn. Engrs. (life; India), Indian Instn. Plant Engrs. (life); mem. Am. Chem. Soc., Indian Fibre Soc. E-mail: niriksha@bom4.vsnl.net.in.

SOUNEY, PAUL FREDERICK, pharmacist; b. Bristol, Conn., Mar. 29, 1947; s. Frederick Raymond and Julia Yvonne (Weeks) S.; m. Billie Lorraine Petersen, Apr. 7, 1972; children: Jared Paul, Jeremy Christian. BS, Northeastern U., 1971, MS, 1984. Drug info. pharmacist Hartford (Conn.) Hosp., 1971-77; pharmacy supervisor Boston Hosp. for Women, 1977-81; clin. rsch. pharmacist Channing Labs./Harvard Med. Sch., Boston, 1981-92; med. info. scientist Astra Merck Inc., Providence, 1992-97; field sci. ptnr. N.E. Customer Ctr. Astra Pharms., L.P., Providence, 1997-99; med. mktg. scientific leader AstraZeneca Pharms., Wayne, Pa., 1999-2000, group dir. med. mktg., 2000—; dir. drug info. Brigham and Women's Hosp., Boston, 1981-90, dir. clin. pharmacy, 1985-92; cons. in field. Editor: Comprehensive Pharmacy Review, 4th edit., 2000; contbr. articles to profl. jours.; editl. adv. panelist Internat. Pharm. Abstracts, Pharmacy Practice News, Am. Jour. Gastroenterology. Treas. men's club First Congl. Ch., 1993—; vol. Mansfield (Mass.) Animal Shelter, 1990-94. Mem. Am. Coll. Clin. Pharmacy, Am. Soc. Health Sys. Pharmacists, Am. Pharmaceutical Assn., Acad. Managed Case Pharmacy, New Eng. Coun. Hosp. Pharmacists, Northeastern Univ. Alumnae Assn. Office: AstraZeneca Pharms 725 Chesterbrook Blvd Wayne PA 19087-5677

SOUNKUR, SALHA, Syrian government official, education educator; b. Damascus, Syria, June 27, 1939; d. Muhhy El-Din and Khadija Sounkur; m. Mahmoud Bridi; children: Ahmad, Samer, Lama, Chadi. Mag. in Edn., Damascus U., 1975; PhD in Ednl. Supervision, Ein Shams U., Egypt, 1978. H.s. mgmt. and gen. supervision Damascus, 1966-76; instr. in edn. faculty Damascus U., 1976-77, dep. dean edn. faculty, 1979-81, dean edn. faculty, 1981-86, prof. edn., 1987-90, head curricula and methodology dept., 1991-92; min. high edn. Govt. of Syria, Damascus, 1992-2000; pres. Supreme Coun. of Scis., Syria, Supreme Coun. Lit. and Arts, Syria, Higher Edn. Coun.; active Higher Cultural Com. Author: National Education, 1971, Philosophical Culture, 1981, Developing the Educational Counselling in Syrin, 1980, Pre-Primary School Education, 1982, Special Methods in Primary Education, 1983, Educational Curricula, 1983, General Education, 1990, Educational Aspects in the Thought of Mr. President Hafez Assad, 1992. Mem. Tchrs. Syndicate, Union Arab Authors. Address: PO Box 8004, Rawda St, Damascus Syria

SOUPLET, PHILIPPE PIERRE, mathematician; b. Paris, Mar. 12, 1967. Student, Ecole Poly., France, 1988; Engring. Degree, Ecole Nat. Ponts et Chaussees, Paris, 1990; PhD, U. Paris VI, 1994; Habilitation, U. Paris XIII, 1998. Asst. prof. math. U. Paris XIII, 1994-98; prof. math. U. Amiens, 1998—. Author numerous articles on the theory of nonlinear differential equations. E-mail: souplet@math.uvsq.fr. Office: U Versailles Lab Math Appl, 45 av Etats-Unis, 78035 Versailles France

SOURIS, JOHN NICKOLAS, economist, accountant; b. Athens, Greece, Oct. 5, 1966; s. Nickolas Johns and Mary Georges (Rozakis) S.; m. Mary Tzimopoulou. B of Econs., Athens U., 1991. Lic. accountant. Acct. asst. Acct. Ctr., Patra, Ahaïas, Greece, 1987-88; researcher Focus Ltd., Athens, 1990; acct. asst. Serca Hellas S.A., Mandra, Greece, 1992, Plastino S.A., N. Ionia, Greece, 1993—; chief acct. Nat. Labour Inst., 1995-99; civil servant Labour Affairs Orgn., Patra, Ahias, Greece, 1999—. With Greek Infantry, 1990-92. Democrat. Avocations: reading, music, arts, occultism. Home: 15 Kavalas St, 14342 New Filadelfia Greece

SOUSA, FATIMA APARECIDA EMM FALEIROS, nursing educator, consultant; b. Ribeirão Preto, São Paulo, Brazil, Feb. 12, 1956; d. Carlos and Amalim (Emm Faleiros) S.; div. Aug. 1991; children: Renato Luiz de Paula Jr., Felipe Faleiros. M in Nursing, U. São Paulo, 1989, D in Nursing, 1993. RN, São Paulo. Assoc. prof. Coll. Nursing U. São Paulo, Ribeirão Preto, 1998, vice head dept. gen. and specialized nursing, 1999—. Author: Fechner Day 93, 1993, Fundação dé Pesquisas Cientificas de Ribeirão Preto SP, 2000. Clin. Psychophysics Lab. rsch. scholar State of São Paulo, 1996. Internat. Assn. (effective mem. study pain 1997—). Avocations: walking, swimming, reading, studying. Home: Rui Barbosa 500 Apt 74, 14015-120 Ribeirão Preto São Paulo, Brazil Office: U São Paulo, Av Bandeirantes, 3900 Ribeirão Preto São Paulo, Brazil

SOUSA, MÁRIO, cell biology educator. Student, U. Porto, Portugal, 1979-85, MD, 1988, MSc in Molecular Cell Biology, 1990, PhD in Molecular Cell Biology, 1995; postgrad., Am. Hosp. Paris, 1993-95. Resident St. Antánio Gen. Hosp., Inst. Biomed. Scis., 1986-88; assoc. prof. cell biology Inst. Biomed. Scis., U. Porto, v.p. sci. com., 1998-99; sci. cons. for reproductive biology and genetics Ctr. for Reproductive Genetics; presenter, rschr. in field. Contbr. numerous articles to profl. jours. Grantee UMIB-FCT, ICBAS, U. Porto, 1994, Praxis XII, 1996-99, Engring. António de Almeida Found., Serono-Portugal, Organon-Portugal. Mem. am. Fertility Soc., European Soc. Human Reproduction and Embryology, Soc. for Study of Reproduction, Portuguese Gynecology and Obstetrics Soc., Portuguese Soc. Reproduction Medicine, Portuguese Andrology Soc., Portuguese Soc. Electron Microscopy and Cell Biology, Portuguese Anatomical Soc. Office: U Porto Cell Biology Lab, Lg Prof Abel Salazar 2, 4050 Oporto Portugal

SOUSA, PAULO GANDRA, computer engineering educator, researcher; b. Porto, Portugal, May 22, 1972; s. Lindoro Sousa and Marilia Sousa Gandra; m. Teresa Jesus Carreiro, July 5, 1997. BSc, Higher Sch. Engring., Porto, 1995; postgrad., U. Minho, Braga, Portugal, 1998—. Cert. Microsoft profl. Software developer, Porto, 1992-94, 12S, Porto, 1993-95; instr. dept. info. engring., rschr. Higher Sch. Engring., 1996—. Contbr. articles to sci. jours., including Jour. Intelligent Mfg., Computers in Industry. Mem. Am. Assn. for Artificial Intelligence, Computer Soc. of IEEE. Avocations: cinema, reading, walking. Office: Higher Inst Engring, Rua Dr Antonio B Almeida431, 4200-072 Porto Portugal

SOUSA-NETO, MANDEL DAMAIO, dental educator; b. Sao Paulo, Brazil, May 8, 1965; s. Alfredo Damiao and Severina Ferreira (Silva) Sousa; m. Yara Correa Silva; 1 child, Alice Correa. BDS, FORP-USP, Ribeirao Preto, Brazil, 1988, MSc, 1994, PhD, 1997. Asst. prof. UNAERT, Brazil, 1990-94, adj. prof., 1994-98, full prof., 1999—; head of clinics UNAERP, Brazil, 1996—, postgraduation coord., 1998—. Author: Clareamento Dental, 1996; editor: Brazilian Dental Jour., 1989—, Rev. Odont. UNAERP, 1998; contbr. chpt. to book. Active PFL, Ribeirao Preto, 1998. Recipient Alexander Fleming award ABO-MG, 1990. Mem. APCD. Roman Catholic. Avocation: soccer. E-mail: sousanet@unaerp.edin.br. Home: R Vicente De Carvalho 546, 14020040 Ribeirao Preto Brazil Address: Rua Vicente Carvalho 546, Via Seixas, 14020040 Ribeirao Preto Brazil

SOUSSIGNAN, ROBERT, neuroscience and ethology educator; b. Marseille, France, Sept. 20, 1956; s. Joseph and Marie (Sogoyan) S.; m. Rita Compatangelo, Nov. 3, 1990. Degree, U. Aix-Marseille, 1979; MSc, U. Provence, France, 1980; PhD in Life Scis., U. Franche-Comté, 1985. Assoc. prof. behavioral neurosci. and ethology U. Reims, France, 1989—. Contbr. chpt. to: Hyperactivity Disorders of Childhood, 1996; contbr. articles to profl. publs. Grantee, Que. (Can.) Coun. Social Rsch., Montreal, 1985, 86, French Dept. Agr., 1995—. Mem. French Soc. for Study of Animal Behavior. Avocations: photography, music, cross-country skiing, hiking. Office: U Reims Champagne Ardenne, 57 Rue P Taittinger, 51100 Reims France

SOUTELLO-ALVES, LAURO EDUARDO, diplomat; b. Rio de Janeiro, R.J., Brazil, May 10, 1958; s. Lauro and Maria Eugenia (Ribeiro) Soutello-A.; m. Maria de Fatima Faria, Aug. 31, 1994. BA, NYU, 1981; diploma, Fgn. Svc. Inst., Brazil, 1984; Brevet d'Administrn. Pub., Nat. Sch. Adminstrn., France, 1999. Chief of staff dept. spl. affairs Brazilian Fgn. Ministry, 1986-89, mem. permanent mission to UN, 1989-92, chief of staff dept. UN and disarmament affairs, 1995-98; head econ. sect. Brazilian Embassy, Mex., 1992-95; head sect. multilateral affairs Brazilian Embassy, Paris, 1999—; lectr. Brazilian Naval Acad., 1988, Brazilian Army Staff Coll., 1998, Brazilian War Coll., 1998. Contbr. articles to profl. jours. Recipient Order of Merit, Brazilian Armed Svcs., 1998.

SOUTHAM, G(ORDON) HAMILTON, former Canadian government official; b. Ottawa, Ont., Can., Dec. 19, 1916; s. Wilson Mills and Henrietta Alberta (Cargill) S.; m. Jacqueline Lambert-David, Apr. 15, 1940 (div. Mar. 1969); children: Peter, Christopher, Jennifer, Michael; m. Gro Mortensen,

May 17, 1969 (div. Jan. 1978); children: Henrietta, Gordon; m. Marion Charpentier, June 26, 1981. B.A. with Honors, Trinity Coll., Toronto, Ont., 1939; postgrad., Christ Ch. Coll., Oxford, Eng., 1939; LL.D. (hon.), Trent and Carleton univs.; D.C.L. (hon.), King's Coll. Univ.; D.U. (hon.), Ottawa U. Reporter The Times, London, Eng., 1945-46; editorial writer Ottawa Citizen, 1946-47; with Dept. External Affairs Can., 1948-64; ambassador Warsaw, Poland, 1960-62; head information div. Dept. External Affairs Can., Ottawa, 1962-64; coordinator Nat. Arts Centre, Ottawa, 1964-67; dir. gen. Nat. Arts Centre, 1967-77; spl. advisor to sec. state, 1977-79. Chmn. Ofcl. Residences Coun., 1985-93, Rideau Canal Mus., 1983; pres. Can. Mediterranean Inst., 1980-86, chmn., 1987; gov. Archaeol. Archaeol. Inst. Am., 1982-88; hon. pres. Can. Classical Assn., 1982-87; chancellor King's Coll. Univ., 1988-95; co-chmn. Task Force on Mil. History Mus., 1990-91; bd. dirs. Can. Battle of Normandy Found., 1992, v.p., 1998. Served with Brit. Army, 1939-40; served to capt. Royal Can. Arty., 1940-45. Decorated officer Order of Can.; award of cultural merit (Poland); Opera of Nat. Arts Ctr. renamed Southam Hall in his honor, 2000. Clubs: Rideau (Ottawa). Home: 280 Thorold Rd, Ottawa, ON Canada K1M 0K2

SOUTHARD-BORNYASZ, MARJORIE, special education educator, consultant; b. Fremont, Mich., Jan. 24, 1939; d. Milo R. Southard and Margaret E. Totten; m. Matthew Bornyasz, Aug. 20, 1960 (div. Oct. 1985); children: Megan Sue, Mitchel Stephen, Mikaela Southard. BA in Edn., Ctrl. Mich. U., 1961; MA in Spl. Edn., Calif. State U., 1985. Cert. resource specialist. High sch. phys. edn. tchr. Carlton (Mich.) Unified, 1961, Southfield (Mich.) Unified, 1961-62; adult edn. tchr. Dearborn (Mich.) Unified, 1963-65; phys. edn. specialist Palos Verdes (Calif.) Unified, 1972-83; spl. edn. tchr. San Pedro (Calif.) High, 1983-89; resource specialist Temecula (Calif.) Mid. Sch., 1989-95; spl. edn. tchr. Temecula Valley High, 1995—; instr. Calif. State U. Riverside Ext., 1997; contbg. mem. monograph Problems Facing Tchr. Edn. in 21st Century, Calif. State U., Long Beach, 2000. Site rep. Temecula Valley Educators Assn., 1994-2000; sch. site coun. Temecula Valley High Sch., 1996-2000. Named Outstanding Alumni Tchr., Calif. State U. Dominguez Hills, Carson, 1999; recipient Resolution for Outstanding Tchg., Calif. State Senate, 2000, Calif. House of Reps., 2000. Mem. AAUW (charter, v.p. Temecula Valley chpt. 1992—), Temecula Valley Edn. Assn. (rep.), Alpha Gamma Delta. Methodist. Avocations: traveling, antiquing, skiing, reading, camping. E-mail: yornyasz@hotmail.com. Home: 31520 Corte Pacheco Temecula CA 92592-6401

SOUTHERN, ANN GAYLE, nurse, educator; b. Radford, Va., Oct. 1, 1950; d. William Gale and Harless (Rogers) Farmer. Degree in nursing cum laude, Wytheville (Va.) C.C., 1985; BS, Radford (Va.) U., 1988, MS, 1995. RN. Nurse Pulaski (Va.) Cmty. Hosp., 1985-88, St. Alban's Psychiat. Hosp., Radford, 1988-98; clin. instr. Wytheville RN Program, 1996-98; nurse Sunbridge of New River Valley, Dublin, 1999—, Columbia Pulaski Cmty. Hosp., Pulaski, Va., 1999—. Counselor AIDS/hepatitis disease process cmty. support groups, Radford, 1992—; lectr. breast cancer and self-exam., Radford, 1995. Mem. ANA, Sigma Theta Tau. Methodist. Avocations: old movies, gardening. Home: 6746 Dudley Ferry Rd Radford VA 24141-8876

SOUTHERN, LARRY GILMER, explosive safety specialist; b. Mt. Airy, N.C., Feb. 10, 1959; s. Ed Southern and Gladys Viola Woodruff Payne; m. Donna Hartley Turner, Feb. 14, 1981 (div. Apr. 1986); 1 child, Victor Ross; m. Robin Michele Spicer, Dec. 26, 1996. Explosive Ordnance Disposal Technician, Naval Sch., Indian Head, Md., 1978. Foreman, tank cleaning Caldwell Indsl. Svcs., Lenoir, N.C., 1983-84; dir. ops., indsl. svc. Petroleum Mgmt. Inc., Davie, Fla., 1984-85; dir. ops., indsl. svc. Integrated Resource Recovery, Davie, 1985-87, dir. safety and hazardous ops., 1988-89; project mgr. HAZMAT response Four Seasons Environ., Greensboro, N.C., 1987-88, spl. ops. safety coord., 1993-95; ordnance mechanic Johnson Controls World Svcs., Inc., Cocoa Beach, Fla., 1989-93; safety specialist HASP Inc., Knoxville, Tenn., 1996-97; safety mgr. Molten Metal Tech. Inc., Oak Ridge, 1997-98; health and safety specialist EET Corp., Knoxville, Tenn., 1998-2000, WESK EM LLC, Knoxville, 2000—. Served with USAF, 1978-82. Mem. Internat. Assn. Bomb Technicians and Investigators (assoc.), Am. Soc. Safety Engrs. (assoc.).

SOUTHERN, LONNIE STEVEN, minister; b. San Diego, Sept. 6, 1947; s. Henry Benjamin and Juanita Hilda (Fishburn-Bandy) S.; m. Vicki Leona Musgrave, Aug. 18, 1968; children: Katherine Michelle, Jesse Ryan. BTh, N.W. Christian Coll., Eugene, Oreg., 1970; D of Ministry, Sch. Theology, Claremont, Calif., 1977. Ordained to ministry Christian Ch., 1974. Min. to youth Hillsboro (Oreg.) Christian Ch., 1967-69; assoc. min. Lebanon (Oreg.) Christian Ch., 1969-70; min. in tng. 1st Christian Ch., Pomona, Calif., 1970-74; assoc. min., pastor Sullivan (Ill.)-Allenville Christian Chs., 1974-76; sr. pastor South Bay Christian Ch., Redondo Beach, Calif., 1976-80; pastor Allenville (Ill.) Christian Ch., 1980-86; sr. min. 1st Christian Ch., Selma, Calif., 1986-88, Bethany Park Christian Ch., Rantoul, Ill., 1988-93, Fairfax (Va.) Christian Ch., 1993—; v.p. Sullivan Ministerial Assn., 1975, pres., 1982-83; chmn. Regional Christian Edn. Commn., Sullivan, 1983-86, Lakeland Cluster of Christian Chs., Sullivan, 1983-86, South San Joaquin Cluster of Christian Chs., Fresno, Calif., 1986-88; bd. dirs., mem. exec. com. So. Calif. Coun. of Chs., L.A., 1976-78; v.p., bd. dirs. All Peoples Cmty. Ctr., L.A., 1977-79, Coll. Christian Profl. Mins., Ill., Wis., 1988-90; pres. South Bay Interfaith Coun., Redondo Beach, 1979-80, Selma (Calif.) Ministerial Assn., 1987-88; regional bd. dirs. Christian Chs. of Ill. and Wis., 1983-86; dean East Prairie Cluster, Rantoul, 1989-91; v.p. Christian Ch. Capital Area Ministers Assn., 1994-95, pres. 1996-98; cons. Pilgrimage Christian Ch. Inner City Ministry, 1993; religious/human svcs. coalition Fairfax County Faith in Action, 1998—. Mem. Redondo Beach Coord. Coun., 1976-79, Redondo Beach Mayor's Roundtable, 1977-80, Moultrie County Adult Youth Awareness Coun., Sullivan, 1981-86, Base Reuse adn Devel. Exec. Com., Rantoul, 1990-93; mem. exec. com. Save Chanute AFB, Rantoul, 1990. Maj. U.S. Army D.C. N.G. Decorated Army Achievement medal with oak leaf, Commendation medal with oak leaf, Nat. Def. medal, Res. Officer Achievement medal, Meritorious Svc. medal with oak leaf, 1993; named Best Sr. Officer, 1990; recipient Calif. Medal of Merit, D.C. N.G. Impact award, 1994. Mem. Rotary (Paul Harris fellow 1990). Avocations: photography, golfing. Home: 4903 Carriagepark Rd Fairfax VA 22032-2368 Office: Fairfax Christian Ch 10185 Main St Fairfax VA 22031-3492

SOUTHERN, ROBERT ALLEN, lawyer; b. Independence, Mo., July 17, 1930; s. James Allen and Josephine (Ragland) S.; m. Cynthia Agnes Drews, May 17, 1952; children: David D., William A., James M., Kathryn S. O'Brien. B.S. in Polit. Sci., Northwestern U., 1952, LL.B., 1954. Bar: Ill. 1955. Assoc. Mayer, Brown & Platt, Chgo., 1954-64, ptnr., 1965-96, mng. ptnr., 1978-91; mng. ptnr. Mayer, Brown & Platt, L.A., 1991-96; CEO So. Assocs., Gurnee, Ill., 1997—. Editor in chief Northwestern U. Law Rev., 1953-54. Trustee, v.p., gen. counsel LaRabida Children's Hosp. and Rsch. Ctr., Chgo., 1974-89; trustee Kenilworth (Ill.) Union Ch., 1980-88; pres. Joseph Sears Sch. Bd., 1977-79; trustee Rush-Presbyn.-St. Luke's Med. Ctr., 1983-91, life trustee, 1991—; bd. dirs. Boys and Girls Clubs Chgo., 1986-91; governing mem. Orchestral Assn. Chgo., 1988-93. With U.S. Army, 1955-57. Mem. ABA, Chgo. Bar Assn., Lawyers Club Chgo., Order of Coif, Indian Hill Club, Chgo. Club. E-mail: southern@wwa.com. Office: 7600 Bittersweet Dr Gurnee IL 60031-5110

SOUTHERN, RONALD D., diversified corporation executive; b. Calgary, Alta., Can., July 25, 1930; s. Samuel Donald and Alexandra (Cuthill) S.; m. Margaret Visser, July 30, 1954; children: Nancy, Linda. BSc, U. Alta., Edmonton, 1953; LLD (hon.), U. Calgary, 1976, U. Alberta, 1991. Chmn., CEO ATCO Ltd. and Can. Utilities Ltd., Calgary, 1994-99, ATCO Ltd., Calgary, 1994-99; chmn., CEO Can. Utilities Ltd., Calgary, 1994-99, co-chmn., CEO, 1999—; chmn. Akita Drilling Ltd.; bd. dirs. Fletcher Challenge Ltd., Can. Pacific Ltd., Chrysler Can. Ltd., LaFarge, Royal & Sun Alliance Ins. Ltd., Southam Inc., Atco Ltd., Can. Utilities Ltd.; co-chmn., CEO Spruce Meadows Tournaments, 1999—; chmn. Spruce Meadows Round Table. Decorated Order of Can., comdr. Brit. Empire; recipient Disting. Entrepreneur award U. Man. Faculty Mgmt., 1990; inducted into Can. Bus. Hall, 1995; named Businessman of Yr. U. Alta., 1986, CEO of the Yr. Fin. Post, 1996. Mem. Ranchmen's Club, Calgary Golf and Country Club. Office: ATCO Ltd & Can Utilities, 1600 909-11 Ave SW, Calgary, AB Canada T2R 1N6

SOUTHGATE, VAUGHAN ROBERT, parasitologist; b. Kempston, Eng., May 13, 1944; s. Stanley Robert and Hilda Louisa Peggy (Dean) S.; m. Marilyn Kühn, Aug. 13, 1966; children: Antonia Claire, Crispin Robert William. BSc with honors, Univ. Coll. Wales, 1965; PhD, Christ's Coll., Cambridge, Eng., 1969. Rsch. fellow Natural History Mus., 1968-71; sr. sci. officer Natural History Mus., London, 1971-76, prin. sci. officer, 1976-83, head exptl. taxonomy divsn., 1983-92, sr. prin. sci. officer, head biomed. parasitology divsn., 1992—; dir. WHO Collaborating Ctr., London, 1982—. Editor Jour. Natural History, 1972-83; contbr. rsch. articles to profl. jours. Recipient C.A. Wright Meml. medal Brit. Soc. Parasitology, 1990. Fellow Royal Soc. Tropical Medicine and Hygiene (v.p. 1993-95), Linnean Soc. London (v.p. 1991-92, 98—), Zool. Soc. London (pubs. com. 1975-80, 81-85, sec. 1998—), Brit. Soc. Parasitology (coun. 1979-82, chmn. meetings com. 1984-88), Inst. Biology. Mem. Ch. of England. Avocations: fly fishing, photography, skiing, travel. Home: The Coach House, Woodlands Close, Cople, Bedford MK44 3UE, England Office: Natural History Mus, Cromwell Rd, London SW7 5BD, England

SOUTHWELL, JOHN PHILIP, financial consultant; b. London; m. Susan Sherriff, 1996. Student, Winchester Coll., 1951, Oxford U., 1956. Ptnr. Laing, 1967; dir. Credit Lynnais Laing Corp. Fin., London, 1987-92, cons., 1992—; chmn. Helical Bar Plc., 1987—, Lochain Patrick Holdings, Ltd., 1998—; dir. James Cropper Plc., 1984. Comdr. Order St. John; master Worshipful Co. Ironmongers, 1984. Office: Credit Lyonnais Securities, Broadwalk House 5 Appold St, EC2A 2DA London England

SOUTHWOOD, THOMAS RICHARD EDMUND, zoologist, educator; b. Gravesend, Kent, U.K., June 20, 1931; s. Edmund William and Ada Mary (Regg) S.; m. Alison Langley Harden, Sept. 10, 1955; children: Richard Mark, Charles William. BSc 1st class, U. London, 1952, PhD, 1955, DSc, 1963; DSc, U. Oxford, 1987; DSc (hon.), Griffith U., Australia, 1983; Fil.Doc., U. Lund, Sweden, 1986; ScD (hon.), U. East Anglia, 1987; DSc (hon.), McGill U., Montreal, Que., 1988, U. Warwick, 1989, U. Durham, 1994, U. Sussex, 1994, U. Victoria, B.C., Can., 1994; LLD (hon.), U. London, 1991, Brookes U., Oxford, 1993, U. Bristol, 1994. Rsch. asst., lectr. Imperial Coll. U. London, 1955-64, reader in insect ecology, 1964-67, prof. zoology and applied entomology, 1967-79; Linacre prof. zoology U. Oxford, 1979-93, vice chancellor, 1989-93, pro-vice chancellor, 1987-89, prof., 1993—; apptd. fellow Merton Coll., 1979—, Eton Coll., 1993—, hon. fellow Westminster Coll., 1995; dir. Glaxo-Wellcome p.l.c., 1992-99; vis. prof. Collegio de Postgraduados, Escuela Nacional de Agricultura, Chapingo, Mex., 1964, N.C. State U., 1970-71, Fla. State U., 1971, U. Dar-es-Salaam, Tanzania, 1972-73, U. Tex., Austin, 1977, Rhodes U., South Africa, 1979; vis. assoc. prof. dept. entomology U. Calif., Berkeley, 1964-65; Spencer lectr. U. B.C., 1978; vis. disting. prof. ecology U. Wyo., 1984, Colo. State U., 1984; A.D. White prof.-at-large Cornell U., 1985-91; cons. WHO, FAO, 1966-74; del. Oxford U. Press, 1980-94; adv. coun. biology dept. Princeton U., 1982-86; pres. Coimbra Group of European Univs., 1992-93; chmn., head environ. scis. and policy dept., mem. senate Ctrl. European U., Budapest Coll., 1991-95. Co-author: Land and Water Bugs of the British Isles, 1959, Ecological Methods, 1966, 2d edit. 1978; co-author (with D. Strong and J.H. Lawton): Insects on Plants, 1984; editor: Insect Abundance, 1968; co-editor: Insects and Plant Surfaces, 1986, Radiation and Health: The Biological Effects of Low-Level Exposure to Ionizing Radiation, 1987, The Treatment and Handling of Wastes, 1992; editl. bd. Entomologists Mo. Mag., Entomologist's Gazette, Brit. Jour. Entomology and Natural History, Biol. Jour. of Linnean Soc., Jour. Environ. Law, Polish Jour. Environ. Scis.; contbr. articles to profl. jours. Chmn. trustees Brit. Mus. Natural History, London, 1980-83; dep. lt. Oxfordshire, 1993—; mem. coun. Royal Holloway and Bedford Colls., London U., 1983-85; mem. Hebdomadal coun. Oxford U., 1981-94; chmn. Royal Commn. on Environ. Pollution, 1981-86, Nat. Radiol. Protection Bd., 1985-94; trustee Rhodes, 1986—, chmn., 1999—; trustee Lawes, 1987—, chmn., 1991—; trustee East Malling, 1987—, Lloyds Tricentennial Trust, 1992-94, Habitat Trust, 1991—, Rank Prize Fund, 1993—, World Resources Found., 1995—; gov. Glasshouse Crops Rsch. Inst., 1969-81; mem. Agrl. Rsch. Coun. Adv. Com./Rsch. Grands Bd., 1970-83, JCO Arable & Forage Crops Bd., 1972-79; mem. tropical medicine panel Welcome Trust, 1977-79; co-chmn. U.K. Roundtable on Sustainable Devel., 1994-97, chmn., 1997-99; chmn. Inter-Agy. Com. on Global Environ. Change, 1997—, many others. Decorated Knight Bachelor, 1984, Order of Merit, Republic of Italy, 1991, Ordem de merito II, Republic of Portugal, 1993; recipient Forbes medal Imperial Coll., 1952, Huxley medal, 1962, Sci. medal Zool. Soc., 1969, Gold medal in zoology Linnean Soc., 1988, Marie Theresa medal Pavia U., 1997. Fellow Inst. Biology, Royal Soc., Royal Coll. Physicians London (hon.), Royal Coll. Radiologists (hon.); mem. Am. Acad. Arts and Scis. (hon. fgn. mem.), Norwegian Acad. Sci. and Letters (hon. fgn. mem.), U.S. Nat. Acad. Scis. (fgn. assoc.), Academia Europaea, Pontifical Acad. Scis., Royal Netherlands Acad. Arts and Scis. (fgn. mem.), Hungarian Acad. Sci. (hon. mem.), Royal Soc. London (v.p. 1982-84), Royal Entomol. Soc. (pres. 1983-85), Brit. Ecol. Soc. (pres. 1976-78), Linnean Soc. London (v.p. 1982-84), Zool. Soc. London (coun. 1984, v.p. 1985-88), Ecol. Soc. Am. (hon.), Am. Soc. Naturalists, Japanese Soc. Population Ecology, Australian Ecol. Soc., Brit. Naturalists Assn. (hon. v.p. 1984—), Game Conservancy (hon. life, v.p. 1985—), Earthwatch (Europe) (chmn. sci. panel 1990-98), European Environ. Rsch. Orgn., Field Studies Coun. (exec. com. 1957-61, 65-68, hon. treas. 1961-64, hon. v.p. 1992—), Club of Earth. Office: Oxford Univ Dept Zoology, South Parks Rd, Oxford OX1 3PS, England

SOUTHWORTH, LINDA JEAN, artist, critic, educator, poet; b. Milw., May 11, 1951; d. William Dixon and Violet Elsie (Kuehn) S.; m. David Joseph Roger, Nov. 16, 1985 (div. July 1989). BFA, St. John's U., Queens, N.Y., 1974; MFA, Pratt Inst., Bklyn., 1978. Pvt. practice self-employed, N.Y.C., 1974—; art critic Resident Publs., N.Y.C., 1993-95; adj. prof. art history St. Francis Coll., Bklyn., 1985-94; artist-in-residence Our Saviour's Atonement Luth. Ch., N.Y.C., 1993-95. One-woman shows include Galimaufry, Croton-on-Hudson, N.Y., 1977, Kristen Richards Gallery, N.Y.C., 1982, Gallery 84, N.Y.C., 1990, The Bernhardt Collection, Washington, 1991, The Netherland Club, N.Y.C., 1992, Chuck Levitan Gallery, Soho, 1996, Seventh and Second Photo Gallery, 1998; exhibited in group shows at Union St. Graphics, San Francisco, 1974, Nuance Gallery, Tampa, 1987, 88, Soc. Illustrators Ann. Drawing Show, N.Y.C., 1989-90, Salmagundi Club, N.Y.C., 1991, 92, Henry Howells Gallery, N.Y.C., 1992-93, Mus. Gallery, N.Y.C., 1994, Cavalier Gallery, Greenwich, Conn., 1995, Carib Gallery, N.Y.C., 1995, Chuck Levitan Gallery, N.Y.C., 1996, N.Y. State Mus., 1997, Knickerbocker Gallery, N.Y.C., 1999; artist Christmas card/UNICEF, 1992; represented in permanent collections at Peltz, Walker & Dubinsky, Valois of Am. Recipient first prize award annual watercolor exhibit, Pen and Brush, 2000. Mem. Pen and Brush, Poetry Soc. Am. Mem. Collegiate Ch. Avocations: ballroom dancing, old inns and architecture. Home: 106 Cabrini Blvd Apt 5D New York NY 10033-3422

SOUTHWORTH, WILLIAM DIXON, retired education educator; b. Union City, Tenn., Dec. 28, 1918; s. Thomas and Gertrude (Dyer) S.; m. Violet Kuehn, July 22, 1944; children: Geoffrey Scott, Linda Jean. PhB, Marquette U., 1948, MEd, 1950; PhD, NYU, 1961. Tchr., coach La Follette Sch., Milwaukee County, Wis., 1948-51; teaching dist. prin. Grand View Sch., Milwaukee County, 1951-56; supervising dist. prin. Maple Dale Sch., Milwaukee County, 1956-58; bldg. prin. Main St. Sch., Port Washington, N.Y., 1958-65; asst. supt. for elem. edn. Huntington (N.Y.) pub. schs., 1965-67; assoc. prof., acting head dept. adminstrn. and supervision St. John's U., Jamaica, N.Y., 1967, chmn. dept., 1968-73, prof., 1968-84; parliamentarian for 35 internat., nat. regional orgns., expert witness, pub. moderator, and workshop leader. Author: Care and Nurture of the Doctoral Candidate, 1968, 74, Q The Story of Captain Quimby Scott, U.S. Navy WWII, 1997, The Art of Successful Meetings, 1997, Murder on the Flagship, 1998, Corpsman!, 1998; contbr. over 260 articles to ednl. jours., condominium and parliamentary publs. Served with USN, 1938-44. Lutheran. Home: Apt 608 7100 Sunshine Skyway Ln Saint Petersburg FL 33711-4926

SOUTO, RICARDO MANUEL, chemistry educator, researcher; b. A Coruña, Spain, June 25, 1960; s. Ricardo Souto and Maria Luisa Suarez; m. Veronica Hernandez, July 28, 1984; children: Ricardo Samuel, Natalia Sarai, Alejandro David. B in Music, High Music Conservatory, Tenerife, Spain; Licentiate (MSc) in Chemistry, U. La Laguna, Tenerife, 1983, PhD in Chemistry, 1987; PhD in Sci., U. Utrecht, Netherlands, 1987. Doctoral asst. U. La Laguna, 1982-84, lectr. physics and chemistry, 1988-92, reader, 1992—; doctoral asst. U. Utrecht, 1984-87; vis. scholar Cambridge (Eng.) U., 1993-97; referee sci. papers Acta Cientifica Venezolana, 1994—, Electrochimica Acta, 1997—, Corrosion Sci., 1998—, Material Sci. Forum, 1997—. Contbr. over 40 articles to profl. jours. Chmn. Union Bapt. Chs. Canary Islands, Tenerife, 1992-99; councillor Union Bapt. Chs. Spain, Valencia, 1993-99. Recipient Young Scientist in Electrochemistry award Spanish Electrochem. Soc., 1991. Mem. Internat. Soc. Electrochemistry, Iberoam. Soc. Electrochemistry, Spanish Chem. Soc. (Young Scientist award 1991). Achievements include research in electrochemistry, corrosion science, electrocatalysis. Avocations: music, playing piano, choir activities, church activities. E-mail: rsouto@ull.es. Home: Cl Los Silos 56, E-38008 Santa Cruz Tenerife Spain Office: U La Laguna, Dept Phys Chemistry, E-38205 La Laguna Tenerife, Spain

SOUTOS, NICOLAOS, ship owner, industrialist; b. Samos Island, Greece, June 6, 1932; s. Alexandros and Chrissa (Krassopoulos) S.; m. Maria Fisseris, July 15, 1964; 1 child, Alexandros. Grad., St. John's Coll., London, 1950. Cert. Master Yachts 500 GRT, Master Navigator on Instruments. Master marinier ocean going vessels, 1955-58; officer Chandris Group Vessels, Greece, 1950-60, captain, 1960-65; owner, founder Soutos Maritime Corp., Greece, 1970—; prin., founder Technopyr Fire Fighting Equipment Mfg., 1975—, Soutos Maritime Agys., Greece, 1976—; founder, owner Soutos Marine Ins. Corp., Greece, 1976—, Greek Container Svcs. Co., Ltd., Greece, 1977—; founder, prin. Soutos Ferry Svcs. Co., Ltd. Consul general Rep. Liberia in Greece, 1970—; v.p. Corps Consulaire, 1975-77, pres. 1977-80, exec. bd., 1980—; mem. Greek Congress for Econ. Devel., 1977 (pres. com. for shipping and tourism); founder, mem. exec. bd. Hellenic Marine Environ. Protective Assn.; active in Athenian and Samos Island charity orgns.; mem. exec. bd. Greek Champer of Shipping. Officer Greek Royal Navy. Decorated with Great Band Liberian Humane Order of African Redemption, Pres. Liberia, Knight Grand Commander of the Liberian Humane Order of African Redemption; named National Donor by Govt. of Greece, Honorary Citizen of City of Pithagorion; recipient Gold medal of City of Athens, Gold medal Samos Island; holds Greek Nat. Cup for sailing, 1950-51. Mem. Samos Island Ship Owners and Mgrs. Vessels (founder), Greek Ship Owners Assn. (exec. bd. Greek chpt.), Germanishcer Lloyd Hellenic Com. (bd. dirs.), African Hellenic C. of C., Greek Yachting Club. Office: 2 Efplias & Agiou Nikolaou, 185 37 Piraeus Greece

SOUZA, PAULO RENATO, Brazilian government official; b. Rio Grande do Sul, Brazil, 1964; married; 3 children. Cons. to UN Chile, 1970-79; rector Campinas State U., 1978-82; edn. sec. São Paulo, Brazil, 1982-86; v.p. ops. Inter-Am. Devel. Bank, 1989-94; min. edn., 1994—. coord. Cardoso electoral platform, 1994. Office: Ministry of Education, Esplanada Ministerios Bloco L, 70047900 Brasilia Brazil*

SOUZA DOS SANTOS, PAULO AFONSO, Brazilian diplomat; b. Rio de Janeiro, Sept. 4, 1943; s. Paulino dos Santos and Emilia Souza. Grad., Instituto Rio Branco, Rio de Janeiro, 1967. 3d sec., 2d sec. Ministry of External Rels., Brazil, 1967-75, amb., 1975—; amb. to Abidjan, 1969-71, Sweden, 1972-74, Finland, 1972, Norway, 1972, Iran, 1974-75. Author: (novels) Os Tempos de Mim (premio walmap 1968), 1968, Le Récit de la Difficile Presence, 1975, (poetry) Le Soleil Carré, 1971, 3 fois l'airain, 1973, Années de Gypse, 1980, others. Decorated knight Order of Polar Star (Sweden). Avocations: writing, composing music. Home: Rua Maia de Lacerda 393/201, Rio de Janeiro 20250, Brazil

SOUZA FARIA, ROMARIO, professional soccer player; b. Jacarenzinho, Rio de Janeiro, Jan. 29, 1966. Soccer player Vasco da Gama, Holland, Barcelona, Spain; mem. Brazil Soccer team, Vasco da Gama. Recipient Champs of Dutch League, 1988-89, 91-92, 92-93, Two Holland Cup 1989-90, 90-91; named Best Player in Europe, 1991. Office: Clube de Regatas Vasco da Gama, Rua Gen Almerico Moura 131, 20921060 São Cristóvao Rio de Janeiro, Brazil*

SOUZA NETO, EDMUNDO PEREIRA, anesthesiologist; b. Fortaleza, Ceará, Brazil, Oct. 26, 1966; arrived in France, 1994; s. Elton Nogueira and Rita Necy Bezerra Souza; m. Ana Célia Cachefo, June 3, 1995. MD, Fed. U., Ceará, 1990; degree in anesthesiology, U. São Paulo, Brazil, 1994; BSc, U. Lyon, France, 1996, MSc, 1997, degree in physiology (hon.), 1995, degree in pharmacology (hon.), 1995. Resident U. São Paulo, 1992-94; staff anesthesiologist Amparo Maternal Hosp., São Paulo, 1994, Croix-Rousse Hosp., Lyon, 1994-96, Edouard Herriot Hosp., Lyon, 1994—, Louis Pradel Hosp., Lyon, 1995—; rsch. asst. U. Lyon, 1997—; co-investigator Baxter, Lyon, 1996, Hosp. Lyon, 1998—. Contbr. articles to profl. jours. Investigator Fundação Rondon, Amazonas, Brazil, 1998. Fellow U. Claude Bernard, 1994. Mem. French Soc. Anesthesie-Réanimation, Brazilian Soc. Anesthesiology. Avocations: reading, music, surfing, hurdle races, traveling. Home: 83A Rue Laennec, 69008 Lyon France Office: Lab Physiolol/Environment, 8 Ave Rockefeller, 69373 Lyon France

SOUZA-SANTOS, MARCIO LUIZ DE, engineering educator; b. Sao Paulo, Brazil, Apr. 2, 1949; s. Americo dos Santos and Margarida Maria Souza; m. Marinalva Fraia, May 28, 1974; children: Daniel, Laura. Chem. engr., U. Sao Paulo, 1973, MS, 1980; PhD, U. Sheffield, Eng., 1987. Cert. Regional Coun. for Engring. Brazil. Design engr. C. Greco, Engring., Sao Paulo, 1974-75; process engr. Uniao Petrochemical, Sao Paulo, 1975-76; lectr. U. Sao Paulo, 1976-81; rschr. Inst. for Technol. Rsch., Sao Paulo, 1981-90, rsch. mgr., 1994-98; sci. sr. rschr. Inst. Gas Tech., Chgo., 1991-93; prof. U. Campinas, Brazil, 1995—; paper reviewer ASME, 1987—; sci. advisor Internat. Conf. on Technologies and Combustion for a Clean Environment, Lisbon, Portugal, 1991—. Contbr. articles to profl. jours.; patentee in field. Recipient Overseas Rsch. Students award Com. of Vice-Chancellors and Prins. of the Univs. of U.K., Sheffield, 1985, 86, Thring prize U. Sheffield, 1997. Mem. Brazilian Chem. Engring. Soc. (dir. 1981-82). Avocation: chess. E-mail: souzasan@fem.unicamp.br. Fax: 55-11-30644394. Home: Rua Dr Miguel Pierro 419, 013083 Campinas Brazil Office: UNICAMP U Campinas, Cidade Univ Zeferino Vaz, Campinas 6122, Brazil

SOUZDALTSEV, IGOR NIKOLAYEVICH, economist; b. Krasnousolsky, Bashkiria, Russia, Nov. 30, 1962; came to U.S., 1995; s. Vladimir Egorovich Baev and Tamara Georgievna Souzdaltseva; m. Elena Alfredovna Ratner, June 22, 1985; 1 child, Svyatoslav. BA in History, Krasnodar (Russia) State U., 1985. Social scis. tchr. H.S., Krasnodar, 1985-90; market analyst E.V.A. Co., Krasnodar, 1990-95, Marlin Trading Co., Inc., Ballston Spa, N.Y., 1995-97, Coriander LLC, Ft. Lee, N.J., 1997—. Author: Natiology: Social Science for the Third Millennium, 1999. Mem. Am. Polit. Sci. Assn., Fin. Markets Assn., N.Y. Acad. Scis. E-mail: igor.souzdaltsev@natiology.com. Fax: 877-855-1050.

SÓVÁGÓ, IMRE, chemistry educator; b. Debrecen, Hungary, June 17, 1946; s. Imre and Margit (Győrösi; m. Judit Nagy, Aug. 28, 1971; children: Judit, Krisztina. MS in Chemistry, U. Debrecen, Hungary, 1969, PhD in Chemistry, 1972; DSc in Chemistry, Hungarian Acad. Scis., 1991. Rsch. fellow U. Debrecen, 1970-78, assoc. prof., 1978-92, prof., 1992—, head dept inorganic chemistry, 1994—; mem. steering com. European Sci. Found., 1991—. Contbr. chpt to books Metal Ions in Biological Systems, vol. 9, 1978, Biocoordination Chemistry, 1991, Handbook of Metal Ligand Interactions, 1995. Postdoctoral fellow U. Va., Charlottesville, 1978-79. Mem. Hungarian Chem. Soc. (chmn. divsn. coordination chemistry 1985-95). Office: L Kossuth U, Dept Inorganic Chemistry, 4010 Debrecen Hungary

SOVANI, SANDEEP DINKAR, mechanical engineering educator; b. Nagpur, India, Dec. 1, 1971; s. Dinkar Gangadhar and Shailaja Dinkar Sovani; m. Meghana Vijaykumar Divekar, Dec. 10, 1999. BSME, U. Pune, 1993; M Tech. in Mech. Engring., Indian Inst. Tech., Madras, 1995; PhD in Mech. Engring., Purdue U., 2000. Sr. rsch. engr. Tata Engring. and Locomotive Co., Ltd., Pune, India, 1995-96; grad. rsch. asst. Purdue U., West Lafayette, Ind., 1996-99. Author rsch. in field. Recipient Nat. Talent Search scholarship Nat. Coun. for Ednl. Rsch. and Tng., Govt. of India, New Delhi, 1987. Mem. ASME, Am. Phys. Soc., Am. Soc. Engring. Edn., Inst. Liquid Atomization and Spray Systems. Avocations: travel, photography, painting, writing. Office: Purdue U/Maurice Zucrow Lab 1003 Chaffee Hall West Lafayette IN 47907-1003

SÖVEGJARTO, ANDRAS, mathematics educator, researcher; b. Szombathely, Vas, Hungary, Feb. 4, 1948; s. Jozsef and Iren (Takats) S.; m. Eva Seper, June 18, 1975 (div. 19—); 1 child, Vera; m. Natalia Medvedeva, July 29, 1989; 1 child, Andras. Grad., Eötvös Lorand U., Budapest, 1973; PhD, Moscow State U., 1988. Tchr. Berzsenyi Sec. Sch., Szombathely, 1973-82; instr. Eötvös U., Budapest, 1982-86, asst. prof., 1986-89, assoc. prof., 1989—. Mem. Janos Bolyai Math. Soc., Lorand Eötvös Phys. Soc., Am. Math. Soc. Avocations: music, films. Home: Krudy Gy U 20 I 7A, 1088 Budapest Hungary Office: Eötvös Lorand U, Pazmany Peter Setany 1/D, 1117 Budapest Hungary

SOVERN, MICHAEL IRA, law educator; b. N.Y.C., Dec. 1, 1931; s. Julius and Lillian (Arnstein) S.; m. Lenore Goodman, Feb. 21, 1952 (div. Apr. 1963); children: Jeffrey Austin, Elizabeth Ann, Douglas Todd; m. Eleanor Leen, Aug. 25, 1963 (div. Feb. 1974); 1 child, Julie Danielle; m. Joan Wit, Mar. 9, 1974 (dec. Sept. 1993); m. Patricia Walsh, Nov. 12, 1995. AB summa cum laude, Columbia U., 1953, LLB (James Ordronaux prize), 1955, LLD (hon.), 1980; PhD (hon.), Tel Aviv U., 1982; LLD (hon.), U. So. Calif., 1989. Bar: N.Y. 1956, U.S. Supreme Ct. 1976. Asst. prof., then assoc. prof. law U. Minn. Law Sch., 1955-58; mem. faculty Columbia Law Sch., 1957—, prof. law, 1960—, Chancellor Kent prof., 1977—, dean Law Sch., 1970-79; chmn. exec. com. faculty Columbia U., 1968-69, provost, exec. v.p., 1979-80, univ. pres., 1980-93, pres. emeritus, 1993; rsch. dir. Legal Restraints on Racial Discrimination in Employment, Twentieth Century Fund, 1962-66; spl. counsel to gov. N.J., 1974-77; cons. Time Mag., 1965-80; bd. dirs. AT&T, Pfizer, Sequa; mem. panel of arbitrators N.J. Bd. Mediation, Fed. Mediation and Conciliation Svc.; bd. dirs. Asian Cultural Coun., Shubert Orgn., Sta. WNET-TV, NAACP Legal Def. Fund, 1976-97, Freedom Forum Newseum; chmn. N.Y.C. Charter Revision Commn., 1982-83; co-chmn. 2d Cir. Commn. on Reduction of Burdens and Costs in Civil Litigation, 1977-80; chmn. Commn. on Integrity in Govt., 1986; pres. Italian Acad. Advanced Studies in Am., 1991-93, Shubert Found., 1996—; chmn. Japan Soc., 1993—, Am. Acad. Rome, 1993—; chmn. nat. adv. coun. Freedom Forum Media Studies Ctr., 1993—; chmn. Sotheby's, 2000—. Author: Legal Restraints on Racial Discrimination in Employment, 1966, Law and Poverty, 1969, Of Boundless Domains, 1994; host Sta. WNET-TV series Leading Questions. Mem. Pulitzer Prize Bd., 1980-93, chmn. pro tem, 1986-87; trustee Kaiser Family Found., Presdl. Legal Expense Trust, 1994-98; chmn. Sotheby's, 2000. Commendatore in the Order of Merit of the Republic of Italy, 1991; recipient Alexander Hamilton medal Columbia Coll., 1993, Citizens Union Civic Leadership award, 1993. Fellow Am. Acad. Arts and Scis.; mem. ABA, Coun. Fgn. Rels., Assn. Bar City N.Y., Am. Philos. Soc., Am. Arbitration Assn. (panel arbitrators), Am. Law Inst., Econ. Club, Nat. Acad. Arbitrators. Office: Columbia U Sch Law 435 W 116th St New York NY 10027-7297

SØVIK, NILS, education educator; b. Os in Hordaland, Norway, June 18, 1928; s. Bertin and Nilsina (Lekven) S.; m. Gerd Margrethe Sørhuus; children: Edmund, Øyvind. MA, U. Oslo, 1960, PhD, 1972. Asst. prof. U. Trondheim, Norway, 1963-67; rsch. scholarship U. Wis., Madison, 1968-70; assoc. prof. U. Trondheim, 1971-77, dir. rsch. social sci., 1977-80, prof. edn., 1981. Author: Developmental Cybernetics of Handwriting and Motor Coordination, 1975. Mem. Royal Norwegian Soc. Scis. and Letters (leader humanities 1988-89, sec. gen. 1990-96). Avocation: music. Home: Tyholtveien 16, N-7052 Trondheim Norway Office: Dept Edn NTNU, N-7491 Trondheim Norway

SOW, SY KADIATOU, Malian government official. Min. fgn. affairs Govt. Mali, Bamako, 1994-95, min. urban devel. and housing, 1995—. Office: Ministry Urban Devel and Housing, Koulouba, Bamako Mali*

SOWA, ARTUR, mathematician, researcher; b. Poland, Oct. 27, 1965; came to U.S., 1992; s. Witold and Lucyna Sowa; m. Jolanta Sowa, Aug. 15, 1987; children: Izaak, Oliver. MS, Warsaw U., 1990; PhD, CUNY, 1995. Postdoctoral asst. CUNY, N.Y.C., 1995-97; postdoctoral rsch. assoc. Yale U., New Haven, 1997-2000, lectr., 2000—; cons., rsch. scientist Pegasus Imaging Corp., Tampa, Fla., 2000—; cons. Fast Mathematical Algorithms and Hardware, Hamden, Conn., 1997-2000. Cotnbr. articles to profl. jours. Recipient 1st prize The Marcinkiweicz Competition, Poland, 1990. Mem. IEEE, Am. Math. Soc. Avocations: philosophy, hiking, music. Achievements include proposing a field theory for the mesoscopic description of correlated systems of electrons. E-mail: sowa@math.yale.edu. Office: Yale U Dept Math 10 Hillhouse Ave New Haven CT 06511-6814

SOWDER, KATHLEEN ADAMS, marketing executive; b. Person County, N.C., Feb. 9, 1951; d. George W. and Mary W. (Woody) A.; BS, Radford Coll., 1976; MBA, Va. Poly. Inst., 1978; m. Angelo R. LoMascolo, Apr. 11, 1980 (div.); 1 child, Mary Jennifer. Asst. product mgr. GTE Sylvania, Waltham, Mass., 1978-79, product mgr. video products, 1979-80; comml. mktg. mgr. Am. Dist. Telegraph, N.Y.C., 1980-87; v.p. mktg. ESL, Hingham, Mass., 1987-91; exec. v.p. Falcon Detection Techs., Inc., Plymouth, Mass., 1991-94; gen. mgr. Westec Bus. Security, Irvine, Calif., 1995—. Mem. Am. Mktg. Assn., Am. Soc. Indsl. Security (past chair standing com. on phys. security). Republican. Home: 1851 Royal Oak Rd Tustin CA 92780-6667 Office: Westec 16662 Hale Ave Irvine CA 92606-5031

SOWINSKI, KEVIN MICHAEL, pharmacist, educator; b. Buffalo, N.Y., Mar. 31, 1966; s. Gerard Thomas and Marilyn Louise (Gilbert) S.; m. Elizabeth Marks, July 16, 1994; children: Benjamin, Patrick, Nicholas. BS in Pharmacy, SUNY, Buffalo, 1990, PharmD, 1992. Lic. N.Y., Ind.; bd. cert. pharmacotherapy. Pharmacist The Health Care Plan, Inc., West Seneca, N.Y., 1990-92; grad. asst. SUNY, Buffalo, 1990-92; rsch. fellow, clin. instr. U. Tenn., Memphis, 1992-95; asst. prof. Purdue U. Sch. Pharmacy, Indpls., 1995—; adj. asst. prof. Ind. U. Sch. Medicine, Indpls., 1987-97. Contbr. articles to profl. jours. Recipient Wyeth-Ayerst Labs. Women's Health Care Rsch. award Am. Coll. Clin. Pharmacy Rsch. Inst., Kansas City, Mo., 1998; postdoctoral fellow Am. Heart Assn. Tenn. Affiliate, 1993, Am. Coll. Clin. Pharmacy fellow Am. Coll. Clin. Pharmacy Rsch. Inst., Kansas City, Mo., 2000. Mem. Am. Coll. Clin. Pharmacy, Am. Soc. Clin. Pharmacology and Therapeutics, Am. Heart Assn. Republican. Roman Catholic. Avocations: golf, woodworking. E-mail: ksowinsk@iupui.edu. Fax: 317-613-2316. Home: 5618 Haverford Ave Indianapolis IN 46220-3333 Office: Purdue Univ Sch Pharmacy D711 Myers Bldg WHS 1001 W 10th St Indianapolis IN 46202-2859

SOYFER, VALERY NIKOLAYEVICH, molecular geneticist and biophysicist; b. Gorky, RSFSR, USSR, Oct. 16, 1936; came to U.S., 1988; s. Nikolay Ilya Soyfer and Anna A. Kuznetsova; m. Nina I. Yakovleva, Aug. 12, 1961; children: Marina, Vladimir. BS in Agronomy, Timiryazev Agrl. Acad., Moscow, 1957; MS in Biophysics, Lomonosov State U., Moscow, 1961; PhD in Molecular Genetics, Kurchatov Inst. Atomic Energy, Moscow, 1964; D Phys. and Math. Scis., Moscow, 1994. Head Group Inst. Gen. Genetics, Moscow, 1966-70; dir. Lab. Molecular Genetics, Moscow, 1970-79; sci. dir. USSR Inst. Applied Molecular Biology and Genetics, Moscow, 1974-76; pres. Moscow Ind. U., 1985-88; disting. prof. Ohio State U., Columbus, 1988-90; Robinson prof. George Mason U., Fairfax, Va., 1990-93, disting. prof. molecular genetics, 1993—; sci. sec. Coun. on Molecular Biology and Genetics, Moscow, 1972-80; mem. USSR Govtl. Coun. on Molecular Biology and Molecular Genetics, 1974-80; invited lectr. Halle-Wittenburg U., German Democratic Republic, 1975; prin. investigator USSR State Com. on Sci., 1972, 74, 78, NIH, 1990, Dept. of Energy, 1992, Open Soc. Inst., 1995-98. Author: Molecular Mechanisms of Mutagenesis, 1969, History of Molecular Genetics, 1970, Molekulare Mechanismen der Mutagenese und Reparatur, 1976, Power and Science, History of the Crushing of Soviet Genetics, 1989, Lysenko and the Tragedy of Soviet Science, 1994, Triple Helical Nuclec Acids, 1995; contbr. more than 200 articles on molecular genetics, biophysics and history of sci. to Nature, Science Mutation Rsch., Nucleic Acids Rsch., others. Chmn. bd. Friends of St. Petersburg Ind. U., N.Y., 1990—; pres. USSR Amnesty Internat. Group, Moscow, 1983-88. Recipient Gregor Mendel medals of Czech Nat. Acad. Scis. and Czech Soc. History Scis., 1995, 96. Mem. USSR Soc. Geneticists and Breeders (founding), Gt. Britain Genetical Soc., USSR Biochem. and Microbiol. Soc., Internat. Soc. for History, Philosophy and Social Studies of Biology (charter), European Culture Club (charter), Internat. Sci. Fedn. (bd. dirs. 1992-95, chmn. bd. Internat. Soros Sci. Edn. program), Nat. Acad. Scis. Ukraine (fgn. mem.), Russian Acad. Natural Sci. (fgn. mem.), Am. Soc. of Biochemistry and Molecular Biology, others. Achievements include discovery of DNA Repair in higher plants; establishment of correlation between structural damages in DNA and mitagenesis rate in higher plants; codevelopment of the method of photofootprinting of DNA triplexes, the role of environmental contamination in mutagenesis of organisms. Office: George Mason U Ste 3024 D King Hall Fairfax VA 22030

SOYINKA, WOLE, writer; b. Abeokuta, Nigeria, July 13, 1934; s. Ayo and Eniola S.; married; 4 children. Student, U. Ibadan, U. Leeds, Eng. Msm. staff Royal Ct. Theater, London; Woodruff prof. arts and African Am. studies Emory U., Atlanta; research fellow in drama U. Ibadan, 1960-61; lectr. in English U. Ife, 1962-63, research prof. dramatic lit., 1972, prof. comparative lit., head dept. dramatic arts, 1977-85; Goldwin Smith prof. Africaca studies and theatre arts Cornell U., 1988—; artistic dir. Orisun Theater, 1960; chmn. Internat. Theatre Orgn., UNESCO. Author: (plays) The Lion and the Jewel, 1959, The Swamp Dweller, 1959, A Dance of the Forests, 1960, The Trials of Brother Jero, 1961, The Strong Breed, 1962, The Road, 1964, Kongi's Harvest, 1965, Madmen and Specialists, 1961, Before the Blackout, 1971, Jero's Metamorphosis, 1974, Camwood on the Leaves, 1973, The Bacchae of Euripides, 1974, Death and the King's Horsemen, 1975, Opera Wonyosi, 1978, A Play of Giants, 1984, From Zia With Love, 1994; (novels) The Interpreters, 1964, The Forest of a Thousand Demons, Season of Anomy, 1973; (non-fiction) The Man Died, 1972, Aké: The Years of Childhood, 1982, Isarà: A Voyage Round Essay, 1989, IBADAN: The Penkelemes Years, 1994, The Open Sore of a Continent, A Personal Narrative of the Nigerian Crisis, 1996; (poetry) Idanre and Other Poems, 1967, Poems of Black Africa, 1975, Ogun Abibiman, 1977, A Shuttle in the Crypt, 1972, Mandela's Earth and Other Poems, 1988; (film) Blues for a Prodigal, 1985; (radio play) A Scourge of Hyacinths, 1993; (essay collection) Art, Dialogue and Outrage, 1992. Recipient Prisoner of Conscience prize Amnesty Internat., Jock Campbell-New Statesman Lit. award, 1969, John Whiting Drama prize, 1966, Dakar Negro Arts Festival award, 1966, Nobel Prize in Literature, 1986, Leopold Sedan Senghor award, 1986, Enrico Mattei award for humanities, 1986; Rockefeller Found. grantee, 1969; named Comdr. French Legion of Honor, 1989, Comdr. Fed. Republic Nigeria, 1986, Oomdr. of Order of Italian Republic, 1990. Fellow African Acad. Scis.; mem. AAAL. Office: Emory U Candler Libr Atlanta GA 30322*

SOYLAK, MUSTAFA, chemistry educator, researcher; b. Kayseri, Melikgazi, Turkey, Feb. 13, 1967; s. Mehmet and Lebus (Elmaagacli) S.; m. Isil Candir, Dec. 17, 1993; 1 child, Mehmet. Grad. in Chemistry, Erciyes U., Kayseri, 1988, MS in Chemistry, 1990, PhD, 1993; postgrad., Cordoba (Spain) U., 1997. Rsch. scientist Erciyes U., 1989-95, asst. prof., 1995-97, assoc. prof., 1997—. Author: Kayseri Civarindaki Sifali Kaplica ve icmece Sulari, 1997, Su Kimyasi, 2000. With Turkish Mil., 1994. Muslim. Avocations: football, basketball, computer. Home: Gultepe Mah Destek St, Cicek AP KAT: 9 No 28, 38030 Melikgari-Kayseri Turkey Office: Erciyes Univ, Dept Chemist, 38039 Kayseri Turkey

SOYLU, ARIF, agricultural engineer, educator; b. Konya, Turkey, May 16, 1945; s. Mehmet Ali and Behiye (Öndes) S.; m. Aliye Kibaroğlu, Aug. 1, 1969. Univ., Faculty of Agriculture, Erzurum, Turkey, 1969; PhD, Agrl. Faculty, Ankara, Turkey, 1981. Engineer Tech. Agrl. Svc., Konya, Turkey, 1970-71; rschr. Rsch. Inst., Yalova, Turkey, 1972-84; assoc. prof. Agrl. Faculty, Bursa, Turkey, 1984-93; prof. 5, Bursa, Turkey, 1993—. Author: Pruning Technique, 1984, Principles of Fruit Growing, 1986, Temperate Fruit Species II, 1997. Mem. Internat. Soc. Hort. Sci.(Turkish div.), Agrl. Faculty Hort. Dept. (vice head 1989-91, vice dean 1994-2000). Office: Uladağ U Faculty Agricul, 16384 Bursa Turkey

SOYMAN, ASIM MÜBIN, dental educator; b. Bursa, Turkey, Aug. 25, 1947; s. Mehmet Cemal and Fatma Süreyya) Tamer; m. Engin Esen, Oct. 31, 1977; 1 child, Süreyya Selen. DDS, U. Istanbul, 1973, DMD, 1977, Dozent degree, 1982. Asst. prof. faculty dentistry U. Istanbul, 1974-82, assoc. prof., 1982-88, prof., 1988-99, mem. exec. com. Inst. Health Scis., 1994-99; vis. prof. faculty dentistry U. Yeditepe, Istanbul, 1997—. Mem Turkish Soc. Restorative Dentistry, Turkish Soc. Pedodontics. Avocations: music, reading. Home: C4 blok Daire 30, 5 Gazeteciler sitesi, 80630 Istanbul Levent, Turkey Office: Haciemin Sok #46/4, 80200 Istanbul Turkey

SOZZANI, LAURENT STEVEN GEORGE, art restorer, conservator; b. N.Y.C., May 8, 1949; arrived in The Netherlands, 1990; s. Lawrence and Vincenza (DeGeatano) S.; m. Eneida da Cuhna Parreira, Dec. 29, 1992. BA, San Diego State U., 1977; MS, U. Del., 1984. Assoc. painting conservator Perry C. Huston & Assocs., Ft. Worth, 1984-86; paintings conservator Met. Mus., N.Y.C., 1988-89, consulting conservator, 1990; pvt. practice as paintings conservator N.Y.C., 1988-90; consulting conservator São Paulo (Brazil) Mus. Art, 1991, 93, 95; paintings restorer Rijksmuseum, Amsterdam, The Netherlands, 1990—. Contbr. articles to profl. jours. Recipient Best of Show award Humbolt State U., 1973, Rijksdieeëorganisatie award Ministry of Culture, 1993; internship grantee Samuel H. Kress Found., 1983, 86-88; fellow in painting conservation Met. Mus. Art, 1986-88. Mem. Internat. Inst. Conservation, Internat. Com. on Mus., Western Assn. Conservators, Am. Inst. Conservation. Avocations: collecting Iberian colonial art, Afro Brazilian art, European and American "tramp" art, body surfing. E-mail: l.sozzani@rijksmuseum.nl. Office: Rijksmuseum, Hobbemastraat 21, 1070 DN Amsterdam The Netherlands

SPAAR, FRIEDRICH WILHELM, retired physician, neuropathology educator; b. Dresden, Germany, Mar. 19, 1921; s. Richard and Selma Spaar; m. Ursula Karheiding, Aug. 31, 1963. MD, U. Marburg, Germany, 1951. Med. asst. U. Marburg Clinics-Pathology Inst., Stuttgart, Germany, 1953-54, Psychiatric-Neurol. Clinic, Munich, Germany, 1954-62, Max-Planck-Inst Brain Rsch., Giessen, Germany, 1962-75; lectr. U. Gottingen, Germany, 1964-86, prof., 1978; with Max Planck Inst., 1954-62; physician Clinic Neurol. Psychiatry Neuropathology Göttingen, 1962-86. Author: Die Menschliche Herpes-Simplex-Encephalitis u. Meningitis, 1976; contbr. articles to profl. jours. Lt. German War Marine, 1939-45. Mem. Deutsche Neurologische Assn. Deutsche Assn. Neuropathology & Neuroanatomy, Med. Assn. Göttingen, N.Y. Acad. Scis. Office: Dept Neuropathology, Robert Kochstr 40, D-37075 Göttingen Germany

SPACEK, JOSEF VACLAV, physician, neurobiologist, pathologist, educator; b. Hradec Kralove, Czech Republic, Jan. 15, 1941; s. Josef and Ruzena (Shanelova) S.; m. Eliska Marklova, Aug. 13, 1966; children: David, Petr. MD, DSc, Charles U. Med. Faculty, Prague, Czech Republic, 1964. Lectr. Charles U. Med. Faculty, Hradec Kralove, Czech Republic, 1964-67, sr. lectr., 1967-92, asst. prof., 1992-96, prof. pathology, 1996—. Contbr. articles to profl. jours. 1st lt. Czech Army Med. Svc., 1965. Grantee U. Coll. London, 1969-80, Harvard Med. Sch., Boston, 1994-97. Roman Catholic. Avocations: photography, videomicroscopy, astronomy. E-mail: spacek@lfhk.cuni.cz. Office: Charles U Med Faculty Hosp, Dept Pathology, CZ-50005 Hradec Kralové Czech Republic

SPACEY, KEVIN, actor; b. South Orange, N.J., July 26, 1959. Student, Juilliard Sch., 1979-81. Stage appearances include Henry IV, part I, 1981, Barbarians, 1982, Hurlyburly, 1985, Long Days Journey into Night, 1986, National Anthems, 1988, Lost in Yonkers, 1991 (Tony award for Best Featured Actor, 1991, Drama Desk award, 1991), Playland, 1993, The Iceman Cometh, 1997 (Tony award Best Male Performance/Drama 1999); TV appearances include (series) Wiseguy, 1987-88, (films) The Murder of Mary Phagan, 1988, Will You Remember Me, 1990, Fall From Grace, 1990, Darrow, 1991; films include Heartburn, 1986, Working Girl, 1988, Rocket Gibraltar, 1988, Dad, 1989, See No Evil, Hear No Evil, 1989, A Show of Force, 1990, Henry and June, 1990, Glengarry Glen Ross, 1991, Consenting Adults, 1992, The Ref, 1994, Outbreak, 1995, Swimming With Sharks, 1995, The Usual Suspects, 1995 (Acad. award for best supporting actor 1996), Seven, 1995, A Time to Kill, 1996, Looking for Richard, 1996, Midnight in the Garden of Good and Evil, 1997, L.A. Confidential, 1997, Hurlyburly, 1998, The Negotiator, 1998, A Bug's Life (voice), 1998, American Beauty, 1999 (Best Actor Oscar). Office: Altman Greenfield & Salvaje 36th Fl 120 W 45th St Fl 36 New York NY 10036-4041 also: William Morris Agy 151 S El Camino Dr Beverly Hills CA 90212-2704

SPACHMANN, HOLGER, electrical engineer, researcher; b. Wertheim, Baden-W., Germany, Feb. 5, 1969; s. Edwin and Eleonore (Eckert) S. Grad., Econs. H.S., Wertheim, 1991; diploma in elec. engring., U. Tech., Darmstadt, Germany, 1998. Mng. dir. Elektro Spachmann, Wertheim, 1991-98; elec. engring. rschr. U. Tech., 1998—. With tank bn. German Army, 1991-92. Fellow Studienstiftung deutschen Volkes, 1992-98. Roman Catholic. Avocations: triathlons, theatre, museums, computers. Home: Unterer Sand 5, D-97877 Wertheim B-W, Germany Office: U Darmstadt TEMF, Schlossgartenstrasse 8, D-64287 Darmstadt Hessen, Germany

SPADA, DOMINICK, pharmacist; b. Bklyn., Oct. 21, 1969; s. Vito and Maria A. (Palazzo) S. BS in pharmacy, L.I. U., 1992; postgrad., NYU. Registered pharmacist, N.Y.; cert. orthotic fitter. Staff pharmacist Cobble Court Pharmacy, Bklyn., 1992-94; dir. pharmacy/supervising pharmacist Ocean Breeze Infusion Care, Staten Island, 1994-98; dir. pharmacy svcs. NYU Hosp., N.Y.C., 1998—; cons. pharmacist, 1999—. Bd. dirs. Cmty. Bd. #3, Staten Island, 1996-97, 99—; mem. Rocco Laurie Patrolmen's Scholarship Fund, Staten Island, 1995—. Recipient Anderson gold medal L.I. U. Schwartz Coll. Pharmacy, 1992. Mem. Nat. Assn. Retail Druggists, Am. Pharm. Assn., Pharm. Soc. State of N.Y., Am. Soc. Health Sys. Pharmacists, Nat. Hospice Orgn. Roman Catholic. Avocations: travel, computers, career-oriented activities, fishing. Home: 193 Connecticut St Staten Island NY 10307-1521 Office: NYU Hospital 726 Broadway Fl 4 New York NY 10003-9502

SPADER, JAMES, actor; b. Mass., Feb. 7, 1960. Student, Phillips Acad., Michael Chekhov Studio. Appeared in pictures Endless Love (debut 1981), The New Kids, 1985, Tuff Turf, 1985, Pretty in Pink, 1986, Mannequin, 1987, Wall Street, 1987, Less Than Zero, 1987, Baby Boom, 1987, Jack's Back, 1988, The Rachel Papers, 1989, sex, lies and videotape (Best actor award Cannes Festival 1989), 1989, Bad Influence, 1990, White Palace, 1990, True Colors, 1991, Storyville, 1992, Bob Roberts, 1992, Music of Chance, 1993, Dream Lover, 1994, Wolf, 1994, Stargate, 1994, Two Days in the Valley, 1996, Crash, 1997, Keys to Tulsa, 1997, Critical Care, 1997, Curtain Call, 1998, Supernova, 1998, Slow Burn, 1999, Curtain Call, 1999; TV movies, Cocaine: One Man's Seduction, 1983, A Killer in the Family, 1983, Family Secrets, 1984, Starcrossed, 1985; TV series The Family Tree, 1983. Office: care Toni Howard/ICM 8942 Wilshire Blvd Beverly Hills CA 90211-1934

SPADORA, HOPE GEORGEANNE, real estate company executive; b. Long Branch, N.J., May 13, 1965; d. Joseph Vincent and Gladys Beatrice (Clayton) S.; life ptnr. Rebecca Elise DeAnda; 1 child, Clayton Vincent Spadora. Cert. in Mktg. Comm., San Jose State U., 1988; AA in Biology with hons., Cabrillo Coll., Aptos, Calif., 1991; BA in Sociology with hons., U. Calif., Santa Cruz, 1993; M in Corp. Real Estate, Inst. Corp. Real Estate, 1998. Lic. real estate broker, Calif. Fin. analyst Lam Rsch., Fremont, Calif., 1993-94; portfolio mgr. Lam Rsch., Fremont, 1994-96; v.p. internat. svcs. Cawley Internat., San Jose, Calif., 1996-97; v.p. real estate facilities Sybase Corp., Emeryville, Calif., 1997—; bd. dirs. Emeryville (Calif.) Industries Assn., 1997-98. Mem. editl. bd. Jour. of Corporate Real Estate. Mem. Human Rights Campaign, San Francisco, 1997, The Commonwealth Club of Calif., San Francisco, 1998, Calif. Elected Womens Assn. for Edn. and Rsch., Sacramento, 1998; bd. dirs. Emeryville Cmty. Action Program. Mem. Internat. Assn. Corp. Real Estate Executives, Nat. Assn. Corp. Real Estate Execs., Bldg. Owners and Mgrs. Assn. Democrat. Avocations: golf, fishing, sailing, boating. Office: Sybase 6475 Christie Ave Emeryville CA 94608-1010

SPAGNOLO, SAMUEL VINCENT, internist, pulmonary specialist, educator; b. Pitts., Sept. 3, 1939; s. Vincent Anthony and Mary Grace (Culotta) S.; m. Lucy Aleta Weyandt, June 20, 1961 (div. Feb., 1992); children: Samuel, Brad, Gregg; m. Dorcas R. Hardy, Sept. 29, 1996. BA, Washington & Jefferson Coll., 1961; MD, Temple U., 1965. Diplomate Am. Bd. Internal Medicine, Bd. of Pulmonary Disease; active lic. physician in Fla., Calif., Md., D.C., Va.; inactive Pa., Mass. Sr. resident in medicine VA Med. Ctr., Boston, 1969-70, chief resident in medicine, 1970-71; Harvard Clin. and Rsch. fellow in pulmonary diseases Mass. Gen. Hosp., Boston, 1971-72; asst. chief med. svc. VA Med. Ctr., Washington, 1972-75, acting chief med. svc., 1975-76, chief pulmonary disease sect., 1976-94, chief of staff, 1998-99, dir. respiratory care & sr. attending in pulmonary diseases, 1999—; instr. in medicine Boston U. Sch. of Medicine, Tufts U. Sch. Medicine, Boston, 1970-71; clin. and rsch. fellow in pulmonary diseases Harvard U. Sch. of Medicine, Mass. Gen. Hosp., Boston, 1971-72; clin. asst. prof. medicine Georgetown U., Washington, 1975-77; asst. prof. medicine George Washington U. Sch. of Medicine and Health Scis., Washington, 1972-75, assoc. prof., 1975-81, prof. medicine, 1981—, dir. divsn. pulmonary diseases and allergy, 1978-93; assoc. chmn. dept. medicine George Washington U. Med. Ctr., Washington, 1986-89; cons. in pulmonary diseases The Washington Hosp. Ctr., Washington, D.C., 1977—, Will Rogers Inst., White Plains, N.Y., 1980—, U.S. Dept. Labor, Washington, 1980—, Walter Reed Army Med. Ctr., Washington, 1987; rep. Am. Coll. Chest Physicians to Am. Registry Pathology, Washington, 1981-92; numerous radio tv appearances on Health Oriented Programs; invited lectr. in U.S., Russia, Jordan; chmn., mem. many coms. George Washington U. Sch. of Medicine, George Washington Med. Ctr., VA Med. Ctr., Washington; med. chest cons. in attempted assasination of former Pres. Regan. Author: (books): Clinical Assessment of Patients with Pulmonary Disease, 1986; co-author: (with A.E. Medinger) Handbook of Pulmonary Emergencies, 1986, (with others) Handbook of Pulmonary Drug Therapy, 1993, (with Witorsch, P.) Air Pollution and Lung Disease in Adults, 1994; contbr. numerous articles to profl jours. including Med. Clin. N. Am., Chest, So. Med. Jour., Am. Jour. Cardiology, Jour. Am. Med. Assn., Clin. Rsch., Am. Rev. Respiratory Disease, Am. Lung Assn. Bull., Clin. Notes on Respiratory Diseases, Jour. Nuclear Medicine, Drug Therapy; presented abstracts at over 13 profl. meetings; reviewer for Chest, Am. Review Respiratory Diseases. Pres., chmn. Found. Vets. Health Care, 1998—. Lt. cmmdr. U.S. Pub. Health Svc., 1966-68; founder, chmn. bd. Found. Vets. Health Care, 1998—. Decorated Cavaliere in Order of Merit, Republic of Italy, 1983; nominated for Golden Apple award by med. students Geo. Washington Sch. of Medicine, Phila., 1977; recipient cert. appreciation D.C. Lung Assn., 1983. Fellow Am. Coll. Physicians (coun. critical care 1983-85), Am. Coll. Chest Physicians (gov. D.C., coun. of govs. 1989-96); mem. Am. Thoracic Soc. (exec. com. D.C. chpt. 1978, 85, 89, mem. adv. com. tuberculosis control, 1978-84, pres. D.C. chpt. 19‘‘-83), Nat. Assn. VA Physicians (sec. 1987-89, v.p. 1989-91, pres. 1992-98), Internat. Lung Found. (pres. 1991—). Achievements include first major review of patient outcome during early history of intensive care units; an analysis of mechanisms of hypoxemia in patients with chronic liver disease; first report of Pneumocystis Carinii Pneumonitis in patients with lung cancer; first prospective evaluation of short course therapy reported in U.S. using Isoniazid and Rifampin; first American report using laser through fiberoptic bronchoscope to treat lung cancer; first report to evaluate continuous intravenous morphine to control pain in cancer patients; description of a simple technique to measure the total lung volume non-invasively using the routing chest x-ray. Avocations: reading, swimming, stamp collecting, gardening, chess. Office: Geo Washington U 5-411 2150 Pennsylvania Ave NW Washington DC 20037-3201

SPAHR, CLINTON S., JR., retired elementary education educator; b. Bayshore, N.Y., Feb. 3, 1942; s. Clinton Smith and Averil Witona (Courier) S. BS, Hofstra U., 1967, MA, 1972. Tchr. Brentwood (N.Y.) Pub. Schs., 1966-97. Mem. Am. Philatelic Soc., Brentwood Tchrs. Assn. Avocations: collecting stamps, tapes, cds, books. Home: 62 Clarendon Rd Lk Ronkonkoma NY 11779-1651

SPAHR, ELIZABETH, business executive; b. Warren, Ohio, Nov. 12, 1930; d. Sullivan and Elizabeth (St. Clair) Spahr; children: Gretchen, Carolyn. BS, Case Western Res. U., 1952, MS, 1954, PhD, 1957, MBA, 1973. Sr. rsch. scientist Nat. Aeronautics & Space Adminstrn., Clevel., 1956-71; mgr. internat. ops., mgr. spl. projects The Standard Oil Co., Clevel., 1973-86; v.p. strategic planning Ameritrust Corp., Clevel., 1987-92; dir. fin. & adminstrn. AAUW, Washington, 1993-98; CEO Technol. Exec. Inst., 1998—; pres. AcromaTech Group, Inc., 1999—; dir. supply emergency team Internat. Energy Agy., Paris, 1984-86; chair fed. women's program Fed. Exec. Bd., Cleve., 1969-71. trustee Case Western Res. U., Cleve., 1988-92, chair ann. fund, 1989-93; pres. bd. dirs. Cuyahoga City Hosp. Found., Cleve., 1983-85. Grantee USPHS, 1952-56. Mem. Women in Tech., Arlington C. of C.,

Strategic Alliance Va. Employers, Strategic Alliance Md. Employer. Office: Tech Exec Inst 1700 N Moore St Ste 1650 Arlington VA 22209-1928

SPALDING, JULIAN, museum director; b. Eng., June 15, 1947; s. Eric and Margaret Grace (Savager) S.; m. Frances Spalding, 1974 (div. 1991); 1 child; m. Gillian Tait, Sept. 21, 1991. BA in Fine Arts honors, U. Nottingham. Art. asst. Leicester (Eng.) Mus. Art Gallery, 1970-71, Durham (Eng.) Light Infantry Mus. and Arts Gallery, 1971-72; keeper Mappin Art Gallery, Sheffield, Eng., 1972-76; dep. dir. arts Sheffield City Coun., 1976-82, dir. arts, 1982-85; dir. Manchester (Eng.) City Art Galleries, 1985-89; acting dir. Nat. Mus. Labour History, Manchester, 1987-88; dir. Glasgow (Scotland) Mus., 1989-98; rsch. fellow Nat. Mus., Denmark, 1999-2000; dir. Niki De Saint Phalle Found., 1994—. Author books; contbr. articles to profl. jours. Dir. Scottish Football Assn. Mus. Trust, 1995. Fellow Mus. Assn.; mem. Crafts Coun., Brit. Coun., Guild St. George (bd. dir. 1983—, master 1996—). E-mail: julian.spalding@ukgateway.net.

SPALEK, DARIUSZ ALEKSANDER, engineering educator; b. Swietochlowice, Poland, Oct. 23, 1963; s. Edgar Edward and Elzbieta Bernadeta (Renka) S.; m. Beata Jolanta Jonca, Nov. 23, 1991; 1 child, Adrianna. MS in Engring., Tech. U. Silesia, Gliwice, Poland, 1988; PhD, Tech. U. Silesia, 1994. Asst. prof. Tech. U. Silesia, Gliwice, 1994—. Contbr. articles to profl. jours. Office: Tech U Silesia, Akademicka Str 10, 44 100 Silesia Poland

SPALLEK, ROSWITHA HILDEGARD, pediatrician, psychotherapist; b. Heilbronn/Neckar, Germany, Sept. 26, 1942; d. Nikolai and Anastasia (Skapars) Kirsch; m. Werner Max Spallek, Dec. 23, 1965; children: Axel, Kim, Raoul. MD, U Tubingen, 1969. Intern U. Tubingen, 1967-68, 70, Krieskrankenhaus Munsingen, 1968, 70, Naturheilklinik Odeborn/Berle, 1969; pvt. practice pediatrics Bad Wurzach, Germany, 1977—. Author: A Book for Better Education and Understanding Children, Mommy, Do You Like Me. Mem. dist. assembly, Ravensburg, 1979-84; dist. councillor, Bad Wurzach, 1979-94. Mem. Christian Democrats. Achievements include special activities in treating people get rid of allergies. Home and Office: Albers Weiherweg 18-22, 88410 Bad Wurzach Germany

SPALTON, DAVID JOHN, ophthalmologic surgeon; b. Derby, Eng., Mar. 2, 1947; s. John Roland and Gertrude Edna (Massey) S.; m. Catherine Bompas; children: George, James, Ben. Student, Buxton Coll., Derbyshire, Eng., 1958-65; MB, BS, Westminster Med. Sch., London, 1970. Resident surgeon officer Moorfields Hosp., London; cons. ophthalmic surgeon Charing Cross Hosp., London, St. Thomas Hosp., London, 1983—; hon. ophthomologic surgeon Royal Hosp., Chelsea; surgeon King Edward VII Hosp. for Officers; examiner Royal Coll. Surgeons, London. Author: Atlas of Clinical Ophthalmology, 1985 (Best Med. Textbook of Yr.); contbr. articles to profl. publs. Civil adviser Metropolita Police. Fellow Royal Coll. Surgeons, Royal Coll. Physicians, Royal Coll. Opthalmologists. Avocation: fly fishing. Office: St Thomas Hosp, 59 Harley St, London WIN 1DD, England

SPANDIDOS, DEMETRIOS, virologist, educator; b. Agios Constantinos, Sparta, Greece, May 13, 1947; s. Anastasios and Athanasia (Tourna) S.; m. Panayota D. Kpempeniou, Sept. 4, 1976; children: Athanasia, Nikiforos-Anastasios. BSc in Chemistry, Aristotelian Univ., 1971; PhD in Biochemistry, McGill U., 1976; DSc in Genetics, U. Glasgow, 1989. Sr. scientist Beatson Inst., Glasgow, Scotland, UK, 1981-88; prof. virology Med. Sch. U. Crete, Greece, 1989—; dir. rsch. Nat. Hellenic Rsch. Found., Athens, Greece, 1988—; dir. clin. virology lab. Univ. Hosp., Crete, 1990—; vis. scientist dept. pediatrics U. Calif., San Diego, 1985-87; dir. biochemistry lab. Med. Ctr. Athens Hosp., 1979; adv. bd. Inst. Devel. Neurosci. and Aging, 1986—; founder, pres. Internat. Ctr. for Cancer Rsch., Athens, 1988—. Editor: Ras Oncogenes, 1989, Virology, 1991, Safety Manual for Universities and Research Centers, 1991, Current Perspectives on Molecular and Cellular Oncology, 1992, Molecular and Cellular Oncology, 1992, The Super-Family of Ras Related Genes, 1992; editl. bd. Anticancer Rsch., 1985-93, In vivo, 1988-93, European Jour. Cancer-Oral Oncology, 1993—, Cancer Molecular Biology, 1994—, Pathology Oncology Rsch., 1995, Internat. Jour. Biol. Markers, 1995—, Minerva Biotechnologica, 1996—, Internat. Jour. Oncology, 1992—, Oncology Reports, 1994—, Anticancer Rsch., 1985-90. Fellow Royal Soc. Health (London); mem. Royal Coll. Pathologists (UK), Internat. Assn. Breast Cancer Rsch. (bd. govs. 1991—, nomination com. 1991—), Hellenic Soc. Breast (hon.), Hellenic Soc. Lung Cancer (hon.). Home: 1 S Merkouri St, Athens 11635, Greece

SPANDOW, ODD, physician, educator; b. Oslo, Jan. 7, 1938; s. Helmuth Ivan and Else Johanne (Wideröe) S.; m. Anita Inga Willstrand, Dec. 28, 1964 (div. 1986); children: Jarl, Erik, Mårten (dec.); m. Britt-Marie Nerpin, Mar. 11, 1988; 1 child, Fredrik. MD, Karolinska Inst., Stockholm, 1967; PhD, UMEå U., Sweden, 1989. ENT Östersund Hosp., Linköping U., Halmstad Hosp., 1975-82; with Eye and Ear Clinic U. Pitts., 1982-83, U. Umeå, 1986-97; prof. ear nose and throat Ullevål U. Hosp., Oslo, 1998—. Contbr. articles to profl. jours. Avocations: winter and summer sports. Office: ENT Dept, Ulleval U Hosp, N 0407 Oslo Norway

SPANGLER, DAVID ROBERT, college administrator, engineer; b. Flint, Mich., Aug. 17, 1940; s. John Solomon and Margaret Inger (McKinley) S.; m. Sally Jeanne Henry, Aug. 28, 1965; children: Timothy David, Megan Marie. BS, U.S. Mil. Acad., 1962; MS in Engring., U. Ill., 1966, PhD in Structural Dynamics, 1977. Registered profl. engr. Commd. 2d lt. U.S. Army, 1962, advanced through grades to lt. col., 1979; prof. math. U.S. Mil. Acad. U.S. Army, West Point, N.Y., 1968-71; engr. Korea Support Command U.S. Army, 1972-73; dep. dist. engr. C.E. U.S. Army, Walla Walla, Wash., 1973-74; research coordinator Def. Nuclear Agy. U.S. Army, Washington, 1976-79; bn. comdr. U.S. Army, Hawaii, 1979-81; inspector C.E. U.S. Army, San Francisco, 1981-82; ret. U.S. Army, 1982; prof. engring. St. Martin's Coll., Lacey, Wash., 1982-84, pres., 1984—; mem. Nat. Com. for Tunnelling Tech., Washington, 1977-79; cons. Thurston County, Olympia, Wash., 1982-84. Contbr. articles to profl. jours. Bd. dirs. Econ. Devel. Coun., Thurston County, 1985-88, Wash. State Capitol Mus., 1988-91. Decorated Bronze Star with 2 oak leaf clusters, Meritorious Service medal, Def. Nuclear Agy. Joint Service medal. Mem. Soc. Mil. Engrs. (v.p. 1980-81, pres. 1973-74), Nat. Assn. Ind. Colls. and Univs. (bd. dirs. 1992-95, treas. 1994), Ind. Colls. Wash. (bd. dirs.), Assn. Benedictine Colls. and Univs. (pres. 1994-95), Rotary (mem. gov.'s oversight com. on tech. 1996—). Roman Catholic. Avocation: running. Office: St Martins Coll Office of Pres Lacey WA 98503

SPANGLER, DAVID SHERIDAN, composer, director, creative arts educator, writer; b. Belleville, Kans., June 3, 1948; s. Robert Richard Spangler and Marjorie Claire (Forman) Barrett; m. Cynthia Adler (div. 1981); m. Martha Helen Obrecht; children: Marjorie Anne, Catherine Helen, Isadora Maxine, Sheridan Rose. BFA, Carnegie-Mellon U., 1970. Instr. jazz U. Pitts., 1971-72; pres. Spangler Prodns., Inc., Ft. Lauderdale, Fla., 1974—; music dir., producer AC & R Advt., Inc., N.Y.C., 1975-77; assoc. music dir. Grey Advt., Inc., N.Y.C., 1977-79; producer, writer MZH & F Music Prodns., Inc., N.Y.C., 1980-85; founder, dir. Lovewell Inst. for the Creative Arts, Ft. Lauderdale, Kans., 1987—; artistic dir. The Drama Ctr., Deerfield Beach, Fla., 1992; conducted seminars in creative edn., 1990-00. Composer, lyricist: (film) So Fine, 1981, (TV series, records, videos) Romper Room, 1982—; composer (Broadway show) Elizabeth 1, 1974, Nefertiti, 1977; soloist (original live tour) Bernstein's Mass, 1974; co-writer, dir. Dancing Animals, 1988, Children of the Sun, 1989; dir. The Cover of Life, 1992. Onsite evaluator, panelist Fla. Dept. State divsn. Cultural Affairs - Theatre & Arts Instns., 1998-00; bd. dirs. Miami City Ballet, 2000; v.p. Theatre League S. Fla. Recipient Merit award Awards for Creative Excellence in Communications, 1971, Big Apple Radio award N.Y. Market Radio Broadcasters Assn., 1983. Mem. Nat. Acad. Rec. Arts and Scis., Dramatist Guild. Libertarian. Club: N.Y. Athletic (N.Y.C.). Home and Office: 1600 NE 18th Ave Fort Lauderdale FL 33305-3446

SPANGLER, EDRA MILDRED, clinical psychologist; b. Webbville, Ky., Sept. 6, 1941; d. Chester A. and Laura B. (Webb) Sawyer; m. Robert Noel Spangler, Sept. 6, 1959; children: Robert Mark Spangler, Kendra Lynn Lovett. AS in Bus. Adminstrn., Franklin U., 1975; BA in Social Psychology, Park Coll., 1979; MA in Mgmt. and Supervision, Ctrl. Mich. U., 1980; D in Psychology, Wright State U., 1989. Lic. psychologist Ohio, Fla.; diplomate clin. hypnotherapy; diplomate Am. Bd. Psychol. Specialties in Med. Psychology, Forensic Clin. Psychology and Neuropsychology. With adminstrn., mgmt., fin. and computer sys. design various pvt. and govt. orgns., 1958-85; psychology assoc. Stonegate Psychol. Assocs., Columbus, Ohio, 1989-91; dir. pain & stress program The Rehab. Ctr., Columbus, 1991-94; pvt. practice, 1991—; mem. med. staff Riverside Meth. Hosps., Columbus, 1992—, health psychologist, 1993-95; health psychologist Mind/Body Med. Inst., 1993-95; mem. med. staff Grady Meml. Hosp., Delaware, Ohio, 1997—. Fellow Biofeedback Cert. Inst. of Am. (assoc.); mem. APA, Am. Pain Soc., Am. Coll. Forensic Examiners, Ohio Psychol. Assn., Fla. Psychol. Assn., Assn. Applied Psychophysiology and Biofeedback. Avocations: reading, travel, hiking, family, research in mind/body. Office: Wedgewood Behavioral Health 4141 N Hampton Dr Powell OH 43065-7550

SPANGLER, NITA REIFSCHNEIDER, volunteer; b. Ukiah, Calif., Apr. 17, 1923; d. John Charles and Olga Augusta (Wuertz) Reifschneider; m. Raymond Luper Spangler, Sept. 22, 1946 (dec.); children: Jon Martin, Mary Raymond, Thor Raymond. BA, Univ. Nev., 1944. News reporter Redwood (Calif.) City Tribune, 1944-46, Country Almanac, Woodside, Calif., 1969-77. Mem. bd. dirs. San Mateo (Calif.) County Hist. Assn., 1961-68, pres., 1964-66; founder, 1st pres. Portolá Expedition Bicentennial Found., 1966-70; chmn. San Mateo County Scenic Rds. Com., 1967-76; mem. San Mateo County Hist. Resource Adv.; mem. commn. San Mateo County Parks and Recreation, 1983-97, past chmn.; cons. hwy. aesthetics Cal Trans., 1981-83; mem. sch. coms. Recipient Commendation, County Bd. Suprs., 1968, 1977, 92. Mem. Sierra Club, Western History Assn., Mormon History Assn., Nev. State Hist. Soc. (life), San Mateo County Hist. Assn. (life, Resolution of Thanks 1968, 76, 94), Friends Redwood City, Kappa Alpha Theta. Democrat. Episcopalian. Avocations: historic preservation. Home: 970 Edgewood Rd Redwood City CA 94062-1818

SPANGLER, RONALD LEROY, retired television executive, aircraft executive, automobile collector; b. York, Pa., Mar. 5, 1937; s. Ivan L. and Sevilla (Senft) S.; children: Kathleen, Ronald Jr., Beth Anne. Student U. Miami (Fla.), 1955-59. Radio announcer Sta. WSBA, York, 1955-59; TV producer Sta. WBAL-TV, Balt. and NBC TV, 1958-65; pres., chmn. bd. LewRon Television, N.Y.C., Hollywood, Calif., 1965-78; pres., chmn. bd. Spanair Inc., distbr. Rockwell bus. aircraft, 1975-85; owner Prancing Horse Farm; collector, dealer, racer vintage and modern Ferrari automobiles; racer numerous cources including LeMans, Daytona, Sebring. Mem. Video Tape Producers Assn. N.Y.C., Rolls Royce Owners Club, Ferrari Clubs Am. and Italia, Mercedes Benz Club Am., Porsche Club Am. Home: Prancing Horse Farm 3710 Ady Rd Street MD 21154-1432

SPANGLER, STANLEY EUGENE, international relations educator; b. Billings, Mont., Apr. 7, 1929; s. John Harold Spangler and Winifred Watt; m. Addie Belle Moore, Sept. 21, 1968; children: John Wayland Spangler, Julia Watt Spangler Garlatz. BA, U. Mont., 1952; MA, Columbia U., 1958; PhD, U. N.C., 1978. Program officer Asia Found., San Francisco, 1960-65; assoc. regional dir. Fgn. Policy Assn., Atlanta, 1965-69; dir. Office Pub. and Internat. Affairs U. N.C. Extension Divsn., Chapel Hill, 1969-73; exec. dir. World Affairs Coun. Boston, 1973-81; internat. program advisor Fletcher Sch. Law and Diplomacy, Medford, Mass., 1983-84; sr. fellow Air Univ. USAF, 1984-89; Sec. of Navy sr. fellow U.S. Naval War Coll., Newport, R.I., 1989-92, sr. fellow, prof. strategy, 1993—; prof. govt. and fgn. affairs Bentley Coll., Waltham, Mass., 1993—; commr. U.S. Nat. Commn. for UNESCO, Washington, 1976-81; pres. Nat. Coun. World Affairs Orgns., Washington, 1977-80; mem. editl. adv. bd. Fgn. Policy Assn., N.Y.c., 1975-78; exec. mem. Nat. Def. Exec. Res., Washington, 1980-97. Author: Force and Accommodation in World Politics, 1991; contbr. articles to profl. jours. Dir. Curtis-Saval Internat. Ctr., Boston, 1976-81; mem. exec. com., bd. dirs. Ala. World Affairs Coun., Montgomery, 1986-89; bd. dirs. Ctr. for Internat. Visitors, Boston, 1978-81; mem. African studies adv. com. Boston U., 1978-80. Capt. USAF, 1954-56. Johns Hopkins U. fellow, 1952-53; Columbia U. scholar, 1957-58. Mem. AAUP, Am. Polit. Sci. Assn., Boston Com. on Fgn. Rels. Democrat. Methodist. Avocations: hiking, writing fiction, travel, reading. Home: 17 Kings Way Scituate MA 02066-2609

SPANJER, PATRICIA LAWRENCE, health consultant; b. San Francisco, Sept. 29, 1949; d. Earl Eugene and Lillian King Lawrence; m. Richard Franklin Spanjer, Dec. 31, 1971; children: Michael, Timothy, Genevieve, Alexander, Andrew. Grad., Grady Sch. Nursing, Atlanta, 1970. Cert. Internat. Bd. Lactation Cons. Staff nurse Grady Meml. Hosp., Atlanta, 1970-73, Navajo Sch. for Disabled Children, Chinle, Ariz., 1973-74; breastfeeding counselor La Leche League, Dalton, Ga., 1978—, area coord. leaders, 1986-90, conf. supr., 1994-97. Mem. Internat. Lactation Cons. Assn. Methodist.

SPANN, JAMES WILLIAM, II, minister; b. Birmingham, Ala., May 20, 1934; s. James and Elverta (King) S.; m. Wilma N. Plummer, Aug. 2, 1958; children: James III, Timothy, Terrance, Kemberly, Kelby, Elverta, Peter, Margo. B of Theology, Detroit, 1995. Asst. dir. Medger Sch., Milw.; pastor Corinth Missionary Bapt. Ch., Milw., 1996—. Pres. P.T.A., no. divsn. Milw., 1994-95; pres. Mins. Union, Milw., 1994; chaplain Franklin, Wis., Ho. of Correction, 1989-90. Mem. Lions (pres. North Ctrl. Milw. chpt. 1993-94). Baptist. Office: Corinth MBC 1874 N 24th Pl Milwaukee WI 53205-1404

SPANNAGEL, ALAN WAYNE, physiologist; b. Harlingen, Tex., May 9, 1958; s. Billy Wayne and Ersel Lou (Jones) S.; m. Kathy Lynn Lang, 1980 (div. 1982); m. Maristella Partin, 1987 (div. 1988). BS in Marine Biology, Tex. A&M U., 1980; MS in Biology, U. Houston, Clear Lake City, 1985; PhD in Physiology, U. Tex. Health Sci. Ctr., San Antonio, 1999. Rsch. technician dept. surgery U. Tex. Med. Br., Galveston, 1981-85, rsch. assoc., 1985-87; grad. rsch. asst. dept. physiology U. Tex. Health Sci. Ctr., San Antonio, 1987-99; instr., lectr. Physiology for Occupl. Therapy Students, 1990-93; reviewer and cons. on Physiol. Studies. Contbr. articles to profl. sci. jours. Mem. Am. Pancreatic Assn. Achievements include isolation, purification and physiological studies on a novel gastrointestinal peptide, the luminal CCK-releasing factor; demonstration that adapted changes in pancreatic juice composition have physiological effects on gastrointestinal hormone secretion and gastrointestinal function; showed that dietary peptides, not intact protein, stimulated pancreatic secretion during a meal. Home: 154 Barbara Bnd Universal City TX 78148-3602 Office: Univ Tex Health Sci Ctr Dept of Physiology 7703 Floyd Curl Dr San Antonio TX 78284-6200

SPANÒ, MARCELLO, cytologist, toxicologist; b. Rome, Dec. 11, 1954; s. Michele and Elisabetta (Tortolano) S. BS in Biol. Scis., U. Rome, 1977. Cytochemist of tumor cells Inst. Med. and Sci. Rsch., Rome, 1978-80; exptl. radiobiologist Nat. Com. Nuclear Energy, Rome, 1981-83; vis. scientist Life Scis. div. Los Alamos (N.Mex.) Nat. Lab., 1984; cytology rschr. Lab. Dosimetry & Biophysics, Rome, 1985-90; cytology, reproductive and genetic toxicology rschr. Nat. Agy. for New Tech., Energy and Environ., Rome, 1991—, dir. divsn. molecular biology, biophysics and bioelectronics, 1991-93, dir. divsn. environ. toxicology, 1994-95, dep. dir. sect. of toxicology and biomed. scis., 1996—. Mem. editl. bd. jour. Cytometry; contbr. over 110 articles to nat. and internat. sci. jours., 1979—. Mem. Internat. Soc. Analytical Cytology, Italian Soc. Radiation Rsch., Italian Soc. Cytometry, European Environ. Mutagenesis Soc. Avocations: painting, ancient and medieval history, skiing, reading, photography.

SPANSKY, ROBERT ALAN, computer systems analyst, retired; b. Hamtramck, Mich., July 29, 1942; s. Harry Joseph and Alicia Eileen (Kossak) S. BS, U. Detroit, 1964, MBA, 1967. Asst. br. mgr. Nat. Bank Detroit, 1965-67, sr. asst. br. mgr., 1969-71; computer programmer Ford Motor Co., Dearborn, Mich., 1972-76; sys. analyst, project leader Ford Motor Co., Dearborn, 1976-99; ret., 1999. Active Food Delivery to Elderly, Focus Hope, Detroit, 1990—. Sgt. U.S. Army, 1967-69, Vietnam. Recipient Disting. Svc. award Alpha Kappa Psi, 1967, 83, 91, 25-Yr. Svc. award Alpha Kappa Psi/Ford Motor Co., 1987, 97. Mem. Assn. MBA's, Econ. Club Detroit, Am. Legion. Roman Catholic. Avocations: coin collecting, stamp collecting, landscaping. Home: 5574 Haverhill St Detroit MI 48224-3245

SPARBER, DALE PAUL, banker; b. Erie, Pa., Aug. 21, 1948; s. John Russel and Wilma Jean (Grettler) S. BSBA, Thiel Coll., Greenville, Pa., 1971. Supr. Cleve. Trust Co., 1972-73, ops. officer, 1973-75; exec. dir. MidAm. Automated Payments System, Cleve., 1975-77; asst. v.p. AmeriTrust Co. of Franklin City, Columbus, Ohio, 1977-79; v.p. AmeriTrust Co., Cleve., 1980-85, Security Pacific Mcht. Bank, Chgo., 1985-88, Barclays Bank Pub. Ltd. Corp., Cleve., 1988-93; v.p. new bus. devel. Provident Bank, Cleve., 1996—; arbitrator Nat. Future Assn., Chgo.; bd. dirs. Cheboygan (Mich) Tap & Tool; pres. Shorn Enterprises Inc., 1995—. Fundraiser Chgo. area March of Dimes, 1987, Sta. WQLN Ednl. TV, Erie, 1990. Mem. Cleve. Art Mus., Hunting and Fishing Club of Crawford County (sec.-treas. 1980-87, bd. dirs. 1980-87), Cleve. Athletic Club, Iroquois Club of Conneaut Lake. Republican. Methodist. Avocations: downhill and water skiing, hunting, fishing. Home: 3020 Woodbury Rd Cleveland OH 44120-2441

SPARELL, GUNILLA KERSTIN ANITA, laboratory technologist; b. Stockholm, Nov. 11, 1938; d. Gottfrid H. and Gun L. (Ekdal) S.; children: Saunet, Peder. Head dept. ALERT leprosy hosp. Save the Children, Africa, 1969-88; cons. SIDA, Vientiane, Laos, 1991; tchr. Piteå Uong Bi Assn., Uong Bi, Vietnam, 1995; cons. leprosy Sweden, 1989—; with NORAD, Norway, 1976-77; tchr. tropical medicine, 1988—, Ethiopia and Ghana; cons. Bulawayo, Zimbabwe, 1996. Author: Skin Smears for Leprosy, 1987; contbr. articles to profl. jours. Mem. Local Edn. Authority, Ethiopia, 1986-88, Inst. Edn., Stockholm, 1984. Mem. Inst. Biomed. Sci., Nordic Assn. Parasitology. Avocations: foreign cultures, travel, photography, environmental issues, reading. Home and Office: Jungfruvagen 5, 182 35 Danderyd Sweden

SPARER, MALCOLM MARTIN, rabbi; b. N.Y.C.; m. Erna Reichl (dec. Sept. 1990); children: Ruth, Arthur (dec.), Jennifer, Shoshana. AB, M in Hebrew Lit., Yeshiva U.; MA in Sociology, CCNY; cert. in pastoral counseling, Des Moines Coll. Osteopathic Medicine; PhD in Sociology, NYU. Ordained rabbi, 1953. Pres. Menorah Inst., San Francisco, 1981—; exec. dir. Rabbinical Coun. Calif., L.A., 1957-66; chaplain VA; adminstr. Tchr's. Coll. of West Coast, Torah U. (now Yeshiva U.), 1957-66; rabbi Beth El Jacob, Des Moines, 1966-69, Chevra Thilim, San Francisco, 1969-72; pres. No. Calif. Bd. Rabbis, 1977-96, pres. emeritus, 1996—; sr. lectr. San Francisco C.C.; liason Union of Orthodox Jewish Congregations Am., 1957-66, moderator radio series Lest We Forget, 1962, moderator TV spls. Sta. KNXT, L.A., 1964-65, Des Moines, 1967-69; instr. dept. philosophy Drake U., 1966-69; pres. San Francisco dist. Zionist Orgn. Am., 1969-82, also bd. dirs.; chmn., mem. nat. bd. San Francisco Bay Area Zionist Fedn., 1971-84; co-chmn. Jerusalem Fair, 25th Ann. State of Israel, 1973; chmn. Commn. on Soviet Jewry, Jewish Cmty. Rels. Coun., 1974-81; cons. internat. leaders, founder Menorah Inst.; cons. Commn. on Christian-Jewish and Moslem Rels. to European Parliament Nations; cons. in field; writer, lectr. colls., ch. groups on Judaica and world affairs; chmn. dept. world affairs/internat. politics C.C. San Francisco; former chaplain Letterman Army VA Hosp., San Francisco Presidio; co-founder Black and Jewish Clergy; mem. San Francisco Coun. Chs., bd. dirs. food bank program, United Jewish Appeal, chmn. rabbinic cabinet of western region; invited mem. del. bishops and ch. leaders various denominations conducting meml. svc. at Dachau on 50th ann. Reich's Kristallnacht, Fed. Republic Germany, 1988. Hon. chmn. Mayor's Commn. on Holocaust Meml., San Francisco; mem. Mayor's Task Force for Homeless; co-chmn. Gov.'s Family Task Force, San Francisco. With USN, WWII, Korean War, chaplain USAF. Annual Jerusalem Lectr. Series named in his honor, 1998. Address: PO Box 15055 San Francisco CA 94115-0055

SPARHOLT, HENRIK, fishery biologist, researcher; b. Copenhagen, June 19, 1953; s. Søren Johannes and Esther Sparholt (Rasmussen) Jørgensen; m. Susanne Hauschildt Jensen, Mar. 26, 1983; 2 children. B in Math., U. Copenhagen, 1974, B in Biology, 1977, MSc in Biology, 1981, DSc, 1996. Tchr. Gammel Hellerup Gymnasium, Copenhagen, 1981-82; lectr. Danish Pedagogic U., Copenhagen, 1982-83; scientist Greenlands Fishery Investigations, Copenhagen, 1982-83; scientist Danish Inst. Fishery Rsch., Copenhagen, 1982-88, sr. scientist, 1988-92, dept. head, 1991-92; fishery assessment scientist Internat. Coun. for the Exploration of the Seas, Copenhagen, 1992-97, 98—, interim fisheries advisor, 1997-98; lectr.U. Copenhagen, 1988-92, U. Accra, Ghana, 1991, U. Lagos, Nigeria, 1992. Author: Interactions Between Cod, Herring and Sprat in the Baltic Sea, 1996; contbr. articles to profl. jours. Mem. bur. AB Tennis Club, Copenhagen, 1984-88, 99—. Avocations: family, tennis, gardening, fly fishing, nature. Home: Fredsvej 8A, 2840 Holte Denmark Office: ICES, Palaegade 2-4, DK-1261 Copenhagen Denmark

SPARK, ANDRE VAROUGE, investment banker; b. Washington, June 4, 1966; s. Herbert and Janette (Hacopian) S.; m. Kamilla Baranowska, 1993; children: Krystyna, Klara. BA, Cornell U., 1987; MA, Harvard U., 1989; JD magna cum laude, U. Mich., 1994. Bar: N.Y. 1994. Adv. Min. Privatisation, Warsaw, Poland, 1989-91; cons. Polish Antimonopoly Office, Warsaw, 1992; assoc. Cravath, Swaine & Moore, N.Y.C., 1994-95; portfolio mgr. Alliance Capital Mgmt., N.Y.C., 1995-96; v.p. Credit Suisse First Boston, Warsaw, London, 1996-98; dir. Credit Suisse First Boston Tech. Group, London, 1998—. Office: Credit Suisse First Boston, 1 Cabot Sq, London E14 4QJ, England

SPARKE, PENNY ANNE, history of design educator, writer, researcher; b. London, Nov. 6, 1948; d. Kenneth Stanley and Jacqueline Anne (Castell) Sparke; m. John William Small, Nov. 22, 1986; children: Molly Anne, Nancy Louise and Celia Jane (twins). BA with honours, U. Sussex, Eng., 1971; PhD, U. Brighton, Eng., 1975. Lectr. Brighton (Eng.) Poly., 1975-81, Royal Coll. Art, London, 1981-99; dean design faculty Kingston Univ., 1999—. Author: Japanese Design, 1984, Design and Culture in the Twentieth Century, 1986, Italian Design, 1987, As Long As It's Pink: The Sexual Politics of Taste, 1995, A Century of Design, 1999. Avocations: cinema, theatre. Office: Royal Coll Art, Kensington Gore, London SW7 2EV, England

SPARKS, BENNETT SHER, retired military officer; b. Pitts., Oct. 10, 1925; s. Julius and Anna K. Sparks; m. Elizabeth Regina Sparks, May 8, 1943; children: Bennett Sher Jr., James Robert, Richard T. (dec.), John N., Julieann, Donna Beth (dec.). Diploma, Navy War Coll., 1973, Army War Coll., 1988, Nat. War Coll., 1978; PhD in Philosophy (hon.), Sampson U., Oxford, Eng., 1986. Lic. aircraft pilot. Commd. ensign USCG, 1957, advanced through grades to rear admiral, 1985, reserve inspector 11th Coast Guard Dist.; sr. res. officer Pacific Area USCG, San Francisco; sr. res. officer Atlantic Area USCG, N.Y.C.; comdr. Navy's No. Calif. Maritime Def. Zone USCG, San Francisco; comdr. Navy's Maritime Def. Zone USCG, sector 6, Charleston, S.C.; ret. USCG, 1993; nat. dep. exec. dir. Res. Officers assn. U.S., Washington, 1987-91, dir. adminstrn. and dir. fin., 1987-91; civilian aviator Coast and Geodetic Survey, Alaska; bd. dirs. Bank of Hollywood; chief U.S. Delegation to CIOR, NATO Hdqrs., Belgium, 1985-86; internat. sec.-gen. Inter-Allied Confedn. of Res. Officers, Brussels, 1992-94. Chmn. bd. trustees ROA/US, Washington; mem. Calif. Vets. Bd., 1995-99, chmn., 1998-99. Decorated Legion of Merit, Coast Guard Commendation medals (2), Coast Guard Achievement medal, Humanitarian Svc. medal, Arctic Svc. medal, Coast Guard Combat Air Crew Wings, others; recipient Navy Disting. Pub. Svc. medal Sec. of Navy, 1983, Coast Guard Disting. Pub. Svc. medal Commandant of Coast Guard, 1983, 93. Mem. Res. Officers Assn. U.S. (pres. 1982-83). Home: 573 Pistachio Pl Windsor CA 95492-8168

SPARKS, CHARLES EDWARD, pathologist, educator; b. Peoria, Ill., July 29, 1940; s. William Joseph and Meredith (Pleasants) S.; m. Janet Lindsay Dehoff, Aug. 18, 1977; children: William, Debra, Robert. BS in Biology, MIT, 1963; MD, Thomas Jefferson U., 1968. Diplomate Am. Bd. Pathology, Am. Bd. Clin. Chemistry. Rsch. asst. Mass. Gen. Hosp., Boston, 1963; intern N.Y. Hosp., Cornell Naval Hosp., St. Albans, 1968-69; resident in clin. pathology Hosp. of U. Pa., 1972-75; fellow in cardiopulmonary medicine U. Pa., Phila., 1975-76; fellow in biochemistry Med. Coll. Pa., Phila., 1976-77; asst. instr. U. Pa., Phila., 1972-75; instr. Med. Coll. Pa., Phila., 1976-77, asst. to assoc. prof. biochemistry and physiology, 1977-82; assoc. prof. pathology U. Rochester (N.Y.), 1982-88, prof. pathology, 1988—; advisor med. scientist tng. program U. Rochester (N.Y.), 1984-92; attending pathologist, dir. clin. chemistry unit Strong Meml. Hosp., 1982—, chair rsc. adv. com., assoc. chair pathology, 1994—, dir. grad. studies in Integrative Biomed. Scis., 1998—. Contbr. articles to profl. jours.; patentee in field. Lt. comdr. USN, 1969-72. Postdoctoral fellow NIH, 1975-77. Mem. AAAS, Am. Diabetes Assn. (co-chmn. nat. symposium meeting 1988),

The Acad. Clin. lab. Physicians and Scientists, Am. heart Assn. (fellow coun. on arteriosclerosis, mem. nominating com.). Office: Dept Pathology U Rochester 601 Elmwood Ave Rochester NY 14642-0001

SPARKS, JACK NORMAN, college dean; b. Lebanon, Ind., Dec. 3, 1928; s. Oakley and Geraldine Ruth (Edrington) S.; m. Esther Lois Bowen, Apr. 11, 1953; children: Stephen Michael, Robert Norman, Ruth Ann, Jonathan Russell. BS, Purdue U., 1950; MA, U. Iowa, 1951, PhD, 1960. Tchr. math. Leyden Community High Sch., Franklin Park, Ill., 1954-58; rsch. asst. U. Iowa, Iowa City, 1958-60; assoc. prof. applied stats., dir. bur. of rsch. U. No. Colo., Greeley, 1960-65; assoc. prof. ednl. psychology Pa. State U., State Coll., 1965-68; dir. corr. Campus Crusade for Christ, San Bernardino, Calif., 1968-69; dir. Christian World Liberation Front, Berkeley, Calif., 1969-75; pastor, ch. overseer New Covenant Apostolic Order, Berkeley, 1975-77; dean St. Athanasius Acad. Orthodox Theology, Santa Barbara, Calif., 1977-87, St. Athanasius Coll., Santa Barbara, 1987-93, St. Athanasius Acad. of Orthodox Theology, Elk Grove, Calif., 1996—; cons. Measurement Rsch. Ctr., Iowa City, 1959-60, Western States Small Schs. Project, Greeley, 1962-65, Colo. Coun. on Edn. Rsch., Denver, 1963-65; project dir. Orthodox Study Bible Old Testament Project, 1998—. Author: Letters to Street Christians, 1971, The Mind Benders, 1977, 79, The Resurrection Letters, 1978, The Preaching of the Apostles, 1987, Victory in the Unseen Warfare, 1993; editor: Apostolic Fathers, 1978, 88; gen. editor: The Orthodox Study Bible, 1993, Virtue in the Unseen Warfare, 1995, Prayer in the Unseen Warfare, 1996, Christ Is Our Holiness, 1996, The Coming of the Prince, 1997, Tradition in the Early Church, 1997, The Letters of St. Ignatius, 1998, Faith and Godlines, 1999, Pentecost: A Homily of St. John Chrysostom, 2000, No Graven Image, 2000. Trustee Rock Mont Coll., Denver, 1962-77, Thomas Nelson Co., Nashville, 1977-78. 1st lt. U.S. Army, 1952-54. Mem. Am. Sci. Affiliation, Assn. Orthodox Theologians, Conf. on Faith and History, Phi Delta Kappa (pres. Epsilon chpt. 1959-60). Republican. Orthodox Christian. Home: 8758 Williamson Dr Elk Grove CA 95624-1829 Office: St Athanasius Acad Orthodox Theology 10519 E Stockton Blvd Ste 170 Elk Grove CA 95624-9704

SPARKS, JANET LINDSAY DEHOFF, pathology educator; b. Lawrence, Mass., Sept. 13, 1950; d. Ronald Lee and Barbara Isabelle (Platt) DeHoff; m. Charles Edward Sparks, Aug. 18, 1977; 1 child, Robert. BA in Biology, BS in Med. Tech., U. Pa., 1972, PhD in Pathology, 1980. Cert. med. technologist Am. Soc. Clin. Pathologists. Instr. clin. chemistry U. Pa., Phila., 1974-76; fellow Wistar Inst. Anatomy and Biology, Phila., 1975-80; postdoctoral fellow U. Rochester (N.Y.), 1983-85, scientist, 1985-94, asst. prof. pathology and lab. medicine, 1994-96, assoc. prof. pathology and lab. medicine, 1996—; cons. NIH, Indpls., 1994-96. Contbr. numerous articles to profl. jours.; patentee in field. Nat. NIDDK RO1 grantee, 1995—. Fellow Coun. on Arteriosclerosis Thrombosis and Vascular Biology; mem. AAAS, Am. Soc. Clin. Pathologists, Am. Diabetes Assn., Am. Heart Assn. (coun. on arteriosclerosis, coun. on clin. cardiology), N.Y. Lipid Club, N.Y. Acad. Scis. Office: U Rochester Dept Pathology 601 Elmwood Ave # 626 Rochester NY 14642-0001

SPARKS, JON NICKOLAS, executive; b. Adelaide, Australia, Sept. 11, 1960; s. Stanley George and Evelyn Jeanette (Carlick) S.; m. Jenni Susan Walker, Oct. 9, 1982; children: Peta Jeanette, Andrew Jon. BA, U. Queensland, Australia, 1990, MBA, 1994; MS, U. New South Wales, Australia, 1996; PhD, U. Ala., 1999. Head devel. The Movement Group, Australia, 1996-97; mng. dir. I Will Not Complain, Japan, 1998—, Corcovado, Hong Kong, 1999—; dir. Moriata Pty. Ltd., Australia, 1994-97. Author: Soft Operational Research Techniques, 1997; contbr. articles to profl. jours. Comdr. Australian Navy, 1978-95. Recipient Australian Govt. Svc. medal, 1984, Defense Force Svc. medal, 1993; U. New South Wales fellow, 1995-96. Fellow Royal Geographical Soc. (sec. 1997—); mem. Australian Alpine Assn. (sec. 1995-97). Avocation: mountaineering. Office: 108 Kamiyama Ambassador, 18-6 Kamiyana-cho, Tokyo 150-0047, Japan

SPARKS, KENNETH R., association executive; b. Mar. 26, 1934. BS, Syracuse U., 1956, MS, 1961, PhD, 1964; JD, George Washington U., 1967. Dir. rsch. Voice of Am. USIA, Washington, 1964-67; dep. dir. pub. affairs U.S. Office Econ. Opportunity, Washington, 1967-68, dir., 1968-69; pres. U.S. Cultural and Trade Ctr. Commn., Washington, 1988-90; dep. dir. Fed. City Coun., Washington, 1970-72, exec. v.p., 1972—. Office: 1155 15th St NW Ste 301 Washington DC 20005-2706

SPARKS, WILFRED, plastics company executive, consultant; b. Manchester, Eng., Nov. 13, 1937; s. Wilfred and Jane Sparks; m. Christine Margaret I'Anson, Nov. 9, 1969; children: Chantelle, Justin, Jason. Diploma in textiles, Manchester U., 1962; postgrad. in tech., Brunel U., 1970. Sales mgr. R. Pickles Ltd., Todmorden, Eng., 1958-68, Guthrie Corp.Ferguson Shiers, Manchester, 1968-76; chmn. C.M.I. (Plastics) Ltd., Blackburn, Eng., 1976—; cons. Somic Plc, Prestonn, Lancashire, Eng., 1979—. Mem. Halifax Rugby League Football Club (bd. dirs. 1982-85). Mem. Conservative Party. Anglican. Avocations: tennis, chess. Office: CMI (Plastics) Ltd, Wood St, Burnley BB10 1QH, England

SPARR, MARIE-BRIGITTE, surgeon; b. Colmar, France, Feb. 2, 1958; d. René and Bernadette (Ziegler) S. MD, Louis Pasteur U., Strasbourg, France, 1984. Intern, resident Hosps. of Strasbourg, France, 1983-87; clin. chief asst. Paris VI, Bordeaux, France, 1987-91, sr. registrar surgeon in cardiac surgery, 1991, sr. registrar surgeon in digestive surgery, 1994; fellow in surgery Montreal, 1986, Houston, 1988; fellow Mayo Clinic, Rochester, Minn., 1991; fellow in surgery Washington Medstar Ctr., 1992, Cleve. Clinic, 1993. Contbr. articles to profl. jours. Commandant French Armed Forces, 1991. Grantee N.Y. Acad. Scis., 1985, GMC of London, 1990, Assn. Surgeons Paris, 1991. Mem. Centrale Info. Electronique, ESSEC-SANTE, MBA in Real Time Informatic: Computer System. Roman Catholic. Avocations: skiing, swimming, karate. Home: 31 Ave de Brunerie, 77330 Ozoir la Ferriere France

SPARTZ, ALICE ANNE LENORE, retired retail executive; b. N.Y.C., May 14, 1925; d. John Francis and Alice Philomena (Murray) Rattenbury; m. George Eugene Spartz, Oct. 29, 1949; children: Mary Elizabeth, James, Barbara, Anne, Thomas, William, Michael, John, Matthew, Clare, Robert, Richard. Student, Wright Coll., 1945-47, No. Ill. U., 1950; AA, Triton Coll., 1987. Svc. rep. Ill. Bell Tel., Chgo., 1945-46; stewardess United Airlines, Denver, 1947-49; ret. mgr. Family Life League Resale Shop, Oak Park, Ill., 1987-95; retired, 1995. Mem. Cicero (Ill.) Cmty. Coun., 1967-69; mem. Park Dist. Oak Park Com., 1973-74; active Ill. Right to Life Com., Chgo., 1971—, Com. Pro-Life Caths., Chgo., 1992—; former bd. dirs. Ill. Pro-Life Coalition, Family Life League; vol. canteen workers ARC, Chgo., 1942-45. Mem. St. Edmunds Womens Club. Democrat. Roman Catholic. Avocations: travel, sewing, reading, swimming, pro-life activist. Office: 226 N Ridgeland Ave Oak Park IL 60302-2323

SPASH, CLIVE LAURENCE, environmental economist; b. Reading, U.K., Mar. 10, 1962; s. David Isaac and Patricia (Fitzgerald) S. BA in Econs. with honors, U. Stirling, Scotland, 1984; MS in Resource Mgmt., U. B.C., 1987; PhD in Econs., U. Wyo., 1993. Asst. prof. U. Stirling, 1990-96, asst. warden, 1991-94, dep. warden, 1994-95, warden, 1995-96; dir. Cambridge rsch. for the environment Cambridge U., Eng., 1996—, assoc. prof., 1996—; asst. dir. Environ. Econ. Rsch. Group, 1991-95; mem. com. for interdisciplinary studies Cambridge U., 1998—. Author: CBA and the Environment, 1993, Valuation and the Environment, 1999, Environ. Policy and Societal Aims, 1999; contbr. chpts. to books; contbr. articles to profl. jours. Mem. Green Task Force, Stirling U., 1990-91, Waste Mgmt. Com., Wyo. U., 1989-90. Mem. Scotish Environ. Econs. Discussion Group (coord. 1990-95), European Soc. Ecol. Econs. (v.p. 1996-2000, pres. 2000—). Avocations: sailing, skiing, photography, book collecting. Office: Dept Land Econ, Cambridge U, Cambridge CB3 9EP, England

SPASIC, ALEKSANDAR MIODRAG, chemical engineer, researcher; b. Belgrade, Serbia, Yugoslavia, Dec. 28, 1945; s. Miodrag Aleksandar and Milena Milan (Vukovic) S.; m. Dusica Jovan Popovic, Mar. 25, 1976; 1 child, Pavle Popovic-Spasic. BSc, U. Belgrade, 1977, MSc, 1989, PhD, 1992. IAEA fellow OUN/IAEA/CNRS, Odeillo, France, 1982-83; R&D engr. Inst. Tech. Nuclear Materials, Belgrade, Yugoslavia, 1978-81, rschr., 1984-86, rsch. asst., 1987-89, rsch. assoc., 1990-92, rsch. fellow, 1993—. Editor: Multiphase Dispersed Systems, 1997; contbr. articles to profl. jours. and chpts. to profl. books. Mem. Radioamateur Soc. Yugoslavia, 1959, Am. Radio Relay League, Newington, Conn., 1964. Mem. Serbian Chem. Soc., Soc. Phys. Chemists Serbia, Electrochem. Soc. Avocations: amateur radio, ice skating, skiing. Home: 60 Dalmatinska, 11000 Belgrade, Serbia Yugoslavia Office: Inst Tech Nuc Mat Box 390, 86 Franchet d'Esperey, 11000 Belgrade, Serbia Yugoslavia

SPATHIS, GERASSIMOS SPYROS, physician; b. Sami, Greece, Apr. 20, 1935; s. Spyros Andreas and Olga (Georgopoulos) S.; m. Maria Demetrius Messinezy, June 3, 1967; children: Anna Olga, Sonia Alexandra. MA, Oxford U., Eng., 1958, B. Medicine, 1960, DM, 1970. House officer Guys Hosp., London, 1961-62; house officer Addenbrookes Hosp., Cambridge, 1961-62, registrar, 1965-68; house officer Osler Hosp., Oxford, 1961-62; registrar St. Thomas' Hosp., London, 1965-68; sr. registrar Middlesex Hosp., London, 1968-72, Ctrl. Middlesex Hosp., London, 1968-72; physician St. Helier Hosp., 1972-98; hon. cons. physician Royal Marsden Hosp., 1975-98; hon. sr. lectr. St. Georges Hosp. Med. Sch., 1986—, subdean, 1980-92; physician St. Anthony's Hosp., London; vice chmn. S.W. Thames Regional Health Authority, 1986-93. Contbr. numerous reports on health and rsch. Justice of Peace, Inner London Youth Cts., 1995—. Fellow Royal Coll. Physicians (examiner 1986-99), Royal Soc. Medicine, Med. Soc. London, Soc. Endocrinology; mem. Nat. Assn. Health Authorities and Trusts (mem. coun. 1988-94), Brit. Diabetes Assn. (sec. med. adv. com. 1980). Avocations: photography, hill walking, theatre. Office: Saint Anthonys Hosp, London Rd, North Cheam SW3 9AA, England

SPATOLA, ARNO F., chemist, educator; b. Albany, N.Y., May 9, 1944; s. Salvatore and Liberty (Tobia) S.; m. Jacqulyn Browning, Jan. 5, 1982; 1 child: Kimberly Elysia. AB in Chemistry, Cornell U., 1966; MS, U. Mich., 1969, PhD in Organic Chemistry, 1971. Prof. chemistry U. Louisville, 1983—, prof. biochemistry, 1991—; vis. prof. U. Padua, Italy, 1982; pres. Peptides Internat., Louisville, 1983—; co-chmn. Gordon Conf. Peptides, Ventura, Calif., 1990. Patentee in field; contbr. numerous profl. jours. Co-chmn. United Way campaign, U. Louisville, 1993. Mem. AAAS, Am. Chem. Soc. (publs. chmn. 1966—), Am. Peptide Soc. (publs. chmn. 1990—), U. Louisville Athletic Assn. (bd. dirs. 1991—), U. Club (bd. dirs. 1994—), APS Sec., 1999-00 (Athletic Assn.) 1991-94, (U. Club), 1994-00. Avocations: cooking, jogging, video photography. Home: 808 Oxmoor Woods Pky Louisville KY 40222-5589 Office: Univ Louisville Dept Chemistry Louisville KY 40292-0001

SPATTA, CAROLYN DAVIS, mediator, consultant; b. Gauhati, Assam, India, Jan. 20, 1935; d. Alfred Charles and Lola Mildred (Anderson) Davis; m. John Robert Spatta, June 2, 1957 (div. Feb. 1964); children: Robert Alan, Jennifer Lynn Spatta-Harris; m. S. Peter Karlow, July 25, 1981. AB, U. Calif., Berkeley, 1964; MA, U. Mich., 1968, PhD, 1974. Rsch. asst. U. Calif., Berkeley, 1963-65; instr. Schoolcraft Coll., Livonia, Mich., 1968-74; corp. sec. Oberlin (Ohio) Coll., 1974-78; pres. Damavand Coll., Tehran, Iran, 1978-79; cons. pvt. practice, Washington, 1979-80; v.p., adminstr. E. Mich. U., Ypsilanti, Mich., 1980-81; Dir. Inst. grants programs and adv. svc. Assn. Am. Colls., Washington, 1982-84; v.p., adminstrn. and bus. affairs Calif. State U., Hayward, 1984-92, prof. geography and environ. studies, 1992-94; ind. mediator, cons. higher edn., 1995—; vis. lectr. Eastern Mich. U., Ypsilanti, 1969, 1970; mem. accreditation team Western Assn. Schs. Colls.; bd. dirs. Ada Mabel, Inc., 1995—. Contbr. articles to profl. jours. Bd. dirs. Wellness, Inc.; mem. Oberlin Open Space Com., Tenaya Guild, John Muir Hosp., Walnut Creek, Calif.; pres. steering com. Ann Arbor Citizens for Good Schs.; trustee Pacific Sch. of Religion, 1992-98, Sch. for Deacons, 1998—. Nat. Def. Fgn. Lang. fellow, 1966-68; Fulbright scholar, Malaysia, 1994—. Mem. Asian Studies on Pacific Coast, Assn. Asian Studies, Assn. Am. Geographers, Soc. Profls. in Dispute Resolutions, No. Calif. Mediation Assn., Acad. Family Mediators, U. Mich. Alumni Assn. Episcopalian. Avocations: travel, reading, walking, cooking and entertaining, golf, art, music.

SPAULDING, JOHN PIERSON, public relations executive, marine consultant; b. N.Y.C., June 25, 1917; s. Forrest Brisbine and Genevieve Anderson (Pierson) S.; m. Eleanor Rita Bonner, Aug. 18, 1947; children: Anne Spaulding Balzhiser, John F., Mary T. Spaulding Calvert; m. 2d, Donna Alene Abrescia, May 15, 1966. Student Iowa State Coll., 1935-36, Grinnell Coll., 1936-38, U. Chgo., 1938-39. Reporter, Chgo. City News Bur., UPI, 1939-40; editor Cedar Falls (Iowa) Daily Record, 1940-41; picture editor Des Moines Register & Tribune, 1941-42, 47-50; pub. relations dir. Motor Club Iowa, Davenport, 1950-51; commd. 2d. lt. USAF, 1942, advanced through grades to maj., 1947, recalled, 1951, advanced through grades to lt. col.; ret., 1968; v.p. Vacations Hawaii, Honolulu, 1969-70; dir. pub. relations, mgr. pub. relations services Alexander & Baldwin, Inc., Honolulu, 1970-76; mgr. community relations Matson Navigation Co., Honolulu, 1976-81. Pres., Econ. Devel. Assn., Skagit County, Wash., 1983-85; pres., chmn. Fidalgo Island Ednl. Youth Found.; mem. Anacortes (Wash.) Sch. Bd., 1982-88; mem. Gov.'s Tourism Devel. Council, 1983-85; mem. adv. com. State Ferry System, 1982—, productivity coun., 1990—; chmn. Everett chpt. S.C.O.R.E., 1984-86, Bellingham chpt., 1991—; mem. citizens adv. com. Skagit County Transit, 1995—. Decorated Air medal. Mem. Pub. Relations Soc. Am. (pres. Hawaii chpt. 1974), Hawaii Communicators (pres. 1973), Nat. Def. Transp. Assn. (pres. Aloha chpt. 1980-81, Disting. Service award 1978-79), Air Force Assn., Can. Inst. Internat. Affairs, Anacortes C. of C., Sigma Delta Chi (life). Clubs: Propeller (pres. Port of Honolulu 1979-80), Honolulu Press, Fidelgo Yacht, Hawaii Yacht, Royal Hawaiian 400 Yacht (comdr. 1977-81), Rotary (sec. 1996-98). Home: 6002 Sands Way Anacortes WA 98221-4015

SPAULDING, KARLA RAE, lawyer; b. Breckenridge, Mich., Feb. 22, 1954; d. Donald Hugh and Shirley Ann (Federspiel) S. BA magna cum laude, Western Mich. U., 1975; JD, Northwestern U., 1980. Bar: Ohio 1980, Fla. 1987. Vis. prof. Grand Valley State Colls., Allendale, Mich., 1975-76; assoc. Baker & Hostetler, Cleve., 1980-83; asst. U.S. atty. U.S. Atty. Office, Tampa, Fla., 1983-88, Grand Rapids, Mich., 1988-89; chief maj. drug trafficking sect. Mid. Dist. Fla. U.S. Atty. Office, Tampa, 1989-90, chief appellate div. Mid. Dist. Fla., 1990-92; asst. U.S. atty. Organized Crime and Drug Enforcement Task Force, Tampa, 1992; chief fraud and econ. crime sect. So. Dist. Tex. U.S. Atty. Office, Houston, 1992-93; ptnr. Holland & Knight, Tampa, Fla., 1994; pvt. practice Tampa, 1994-97; U.S. magistrate judge U.S. Dist. Ct. (mid. dist.) Fla., Orlando, 1997—. Bd. editors, dep. editor-in-chief Fed. Bar Jour., 1992-95; contbr. articles to profl. publs. Recipient Dir.'s award IRS, 1988. Mem. ABA, FBA, Orange County Bar Assn. Office: George C Young US Courthouse 80 N Hughey Ave Orlando FL 32801-2231

SPAULDING, WALLACE HOLMES, retired federal agency professional; b. Oakland, Calif., Sept. 3, 1928; s. Wallace Holmes and May Gibbons (Alves) S.; m. Dorothy Anne Wollon, Jan. 30, 1960; children: James Wallace, Anne Catherine Bridger. AB, U. Calif., Berkeley, 1950; MA, Johns Hopkins U., 1951; PhD, U. Pa., 1969. Rschr. CIA, McLean, Va., 1952-91; ret., 1991. Author: Is the Comintern Coming Back?, 1998; contbr. chpts. to books and articles to profl. jours. V.p. Fellowship of Concerned Churchmen, San Beernardino, Calif., Found. for Christian Theology, Washington; Am. regional sec. Soc. of Mary, McLean. Col. USAR, 1950-81, ret. Decorated Meritorious Svc. medal U.S. Army; Fulbright scholar, The Philippines, 1951-52. Mem. Phi Beta Kappa, Alpha Delta Phi, Pan Xenia. Avocations: hiking, cycling, domestic and foreign travel. Home: 1206 Buchanan St Mc Lean VA 22101-2943

SPAULDING, WILLIAM ROWE, investment consultant; b. Cambridge, Mass., Nov. 26, 1915; s. William Rowe and Jennie Jane (Gillam) S.; m. Gertrude Ellen Mowry, June 7, 1947; children: Edward Albert, William Mathews. BS, U. N.H., 1938; MBA, Harvard U., 1940. Trader Kidder Peabody & Co., N.Y.C., 1940-41; asst. exec. v.p. Mut. Savs. Cen. Fund, Inc., Boston, 1946-58; v.p. Vance Sanders & Co., Boston, 1959-63; trustee Century Shares Trust, Boston, 1963-71, mng. trustee, chmn., 1969-71; chmn. bd., chief exec. officer Wakefield Savs. Bank (Mass.), 1971-81, trustee, 1959-84, hon. trustee, 1994—; ind. non-affiliated dir., trustee Fidelity Group of Mut. Funds, Boston, 1972-87, active emeritus, 1988-89; ret., 1989; dir. Mass. Congl. Fund, 1970-96; spkr. Investment Analyst Soc. of South Africa, Johannesburg Stock Exch. Auditorium, 1995; mem. Initiative for Edn. Sci. and Tech. South Africa Investment Mgmt. and Rsch. Assn., 1995. Trustee Melrose-Wakefield Hosp., 1973-84, Lakeside Cemetery Corp., Wakefield, 1973—; dir., fin. v.p. Citizens Scholarship Found., Wakefield, 1962—; mem. nat. adv. bd. Citizens' Scholarship Found. Am., 1989-92; mem. fin. com., mem. ho. of dels. Mass. Easter Seal Soc., 1972-97, v.i.p. telethon, 1990—; trustee Laudholm Farm Trust, Wells Nat. Estuarine Rsch. Res., 1982-94, hon. trustee, 1994—; exec. vol. Internat. Exec. Svc. Corps., Kingston, Jamaica, 1989, shirtsleeve amb., 1994—; citizen amb. People to People, 1994—; with Securities Industry Delegation to China, 1994; mem. Wakefield Hist. Commn., 1984-86; co-chmn. bd. advisors U. New Eng., Biddeford, Maine/Westbrook Coll., Portland, Maine, 1996-98. With AUS, 1942-45, MTO, ETO, lt. col. Decorated Bronze Star; Croix de Guerre (Belgium); named to Eagle Scout Boy Scouts Am., 1928; named Grand Marshall, Independence Day Parade, Wakefield, Mass., 1994. Mem. Pres.'s Coun. U. N.H., Boston Security Analyst Soc. Inc., Phi Kappa Phi. Congregationalist. Home and Office: 35 Yale Ave Wakefield MA 01880-2337 also: Drakes Island Box 1999 Wells ME 04090

SPAZIER, REINFRIED WILHELM, sporting goods executive; b. Salzburg, Austria, May 8, 1945; s. Wilhelm Walter and Herma (Huber) S.; m. Ingrid Wayand, Oct. 8, 1976; children: Martin, Georg, Thomas, Stephan, Lena. Dr. of Law, U. Vienna, 1967; MBA, INSEAD, Fontainebleau, France, 1969. Mktg. mgr. L'Oreal, Paris, 1969-71; mng. dir. L'Oreal, Vienna, Austria, 1971-81, London, 1981-86, Karisrvhe, Germany, 1986-89; mng. dir., ptnr. Kneissl, Kufstein, Austrial, 1989-92; CEO Kueissl Dachstein Ag, Molln, 1992—. Mem. Top Team, Austria, 1989—, chmn. 1994—; mem., Austria Racing Team, 1989—. Pvt. Guard, 1964-65. Mem. Rotary Club. Home: 12 Pienzenauer Str, 6330 Kufstein Austria Office: Kneissl Dachstein Ag, Postfach 17, A-4591 Molln Austria

SPEAR, SCOTT LAWRENCE, plastic surgeon; b. Chgo., Aug. 25, 1948; s. Louis and Esther S.; m. Cynthia Staley Spear; children: ALexandra, Geri, Louis. BA (hon.), U. Mich., Ann Arbor, 1968; MD, U. Chgo., 1972. Cert. Mass., 1986, Calif., 1992, Fla., 1990, Washington, 1981—, Md., 1982—, Va., 1982—. Intern Beth Israel Hosp., Boston, 1972-73; jr. residency San Francisco Gen. Hosp., 1973-74; jr. residency Beth Israel Hosp., Boston, 1974-75, sr. residency, 1976-78; plastic surgery residency U. Miami, 1978-80; asst. prof. plastic surgery U. Fla., Gainesville, 1980-81; asst. prof. plastic surgery Georgetown U. Sch. Medicine, Washington, 1981-86, assoc. prof. plastic surgery, 1988-90, prof. plastic surgery, 1990—; dir. Nat. Capitol Tng. program, Washington, 1992—, Divsn. of Plastic and Reconstructive Surgery, Georgetown U. Sch. Medicine, Washington, 1992—; vis. prof. U., Tex., 1982, U. Fla., 1982, 84, 85, 86, 87, Nat. Naval Med. Ctr., 1983, 85. Contbr. articles to profl. jours. Mem. ACS, Med. Soc. of D.C., Plastic Surgery Ednl. Found., Am. Cleft Palata Assn., Nat. Capital Soc. of Plastic Surgeons, Am. Soc. of Maxillofacial Surgeons, Am. Soc. of Plastic and Reconstructive Surgeons, Northeastern Soc. of Plastic and Reconstructive Surgeons, Am. Assn. Plastic Surgeons, Am. Soc. for Aesthetic Plastic Surgery. E-mail: spears@gunet.georgetown.edu. Fax: 202-687-2804. Office: Georgetown U Med Ctr 3800 Reservoir Rd NW Washington DC 20007-2113

SPEARING, ANTHONY JOHN SPENCER, engineering consultant; b. Harare, Mashon., Zimbabwe, Oct. 31, 1956; arrived in S. Africa, 1979; s. Michael John Spencer Spearing and Bridget Elizabeth Everett Bewick; m. Mary-Ann Saunders, May 7, 1983; children: Kerren, Taryn. BS in Mining/Engring., Witwatersrand U., Johannesburg, S. Africa, 1978, MS in Civil Engring., 1989; PhD in Engring., Tech. U. of Silesia, Gliwice, Poland, 1993. Chartered engr., registered profl. engr. Tech. works mgr. Fosroc Ltd., Alberton, S. Africa, 1982-85; chief rock mechanics engr. Randfontein Estates Gold Mining Co., S. Africa, 1985-88; sr. divsnl. mining engr. gold divsn. Anglo Am. Corp., Johannesburg, 1988-95; dir. various pvt. cos., Johannesburg, 1997—; head internat. mining, tech. dir. Master Builders Inc., Cleve., 1995-97; with Welprop Mining Svcs., Johannesburg, 1995-97; owner Rock Mechanics and Backfilling Cons., 1995-97. Author: (book) Handbook on Hard Rock Strata Control, 1995; inventor in field; co-author: Support Catalogue/Mining. Mem. PTA, Johannesburg, 1995-97, Witwatersrand U. Mining Engrs. Assn. Fellow South African Inst. of Mining and Metallurgy, South African Nat. Inst. Rock Engring.; mem. Am. Inst. Mining Engrs., Instn. Mining and Metallurgy, Geol. Soc. of S. Africa, N.Y. Acad. Sci. Anglican. Avocations: chess, hockey. Office: Master Builders Inc 23700 Chagrin Blvd Cleveland OH 44122-5554

SPEARING, RUTH LILIAN, hematologist; b. Walthamstow, Essex, Eng., Jan. 7, 1952; arrived in New Zealand, 1977; d. John Kenneth and Joan Kathleen (Choat) S.; m. Leslie Snape; children: Philip, Michelle. MB ChB, Bristol (Eng.) U., 1977. Registrar in internal medicine Canterbury Area Health Bd., Christchurch, New Zealand, 1978-81, Dunedin (New Zealand) Hosp. Bd., 1981-83; registrar in hematology Plymouth (U.K.) Hosp., 1983-84; sr. registrar in hematology Liverpool (Eng.) Regional Health Authority, 1984-87; acting dir. regional blood transfusion svc. Canterbury Area Health Bd., Christchurch, 1987-89; cons. hematologist, sr. clin. lectr. Canterbury Health, Otago Med. Sch., Christchurch, 1989—; clin. dir. dept. hematology Canterbury Health, 1999—; trustee Blood and Leukemia Found., Auckland, New Zealand, 1995—; pres. Regional Blood Donor Orgn., 1989-94, chmn. ceredase treatment panel, 1996-99; chmn. Leukemia and Blood Found., 1998-2000. Contbr. articles to profl. jours. V.p. View Hill br. North Canterbury Pony Club, 1994-96, pres., 1997—. Rsch. grantee (3) U. Liverpool, 1980. Fellow Royal Coll. Pathologists Australia, Royal Australasian Coll. Physicians; mem. Hematology Assn. Australia and New Zealand, Australian and New Zealand Childrens Cancer Group (conf. organizer 1995). Office: Dept Hematology, PO Box 151, Christchurch New Zealand

SPEARS, DIANE SHIELDS, artist, retired art academy administrator; b. Seattle, May 21, 1942; d. Richard Keene McKinney and Dorothy Jean (Shields) Thacker; m. Howard Truman Spears, Sept. 3, 1977; 1 child, Truman Eugene. BA in Art, English, Edn., Trinity U., 1964; MA in Christian Counseling, San Antonio Theol. Sem., 1986, D of Christian Edn., 1988. Cert. tchr. secondary edn., elem. edn., ednl. supervision, Tex. Instr. ESL Dliel-Geb (Def. Lang. Inst.), San Antonio, 1973-74, Ceta/Ace Bexar County Sch. Bd., San Antonio, 1975-78; tchr. elem. edn., art, music New Covenant Faith Acad., San Antonio, 1983-89; instr. ESL Jewish Family Svc., San Antonio, 1991; tchr. elem. art Edgewood Ind. Sch. Dist., San Antonio, 1992-93, dist. art specialist, 1993-95, fine arts coord., 1995-98, dir. visual arts, 1998-99; owner, operator Art for Kings, San Antonio, 1985—; adv. bd. Zion Arts Inst., San Antonio, 1995—. Illustrator teacher-created materials-lit. activities for young children, 1989-90; author: (art curriculum) Art for Kings, 1987; editor: (art curriculum) Edgewood Ind. Sch. Dist. Elem. Art Curriculum, 1993; exhibited in group shows at Charles and Emma Frye Mus., Seattle, 1966, 68, Centro Cultural Aztlan Galerie Expression, 1998 (Best of Show 1998). Dir. intercessory prayer New Covenant Fellowship, San Antonio, 1980-90. Recipient awards for painting and graphics, San Antonio, 1996-98. Mem. NEA, Nat. Mus. for Women in Arts (charter), Colored Pencil Soc. Am. (charter), Tex. Art Edn. Assn. (1st pl. graphics divsn. 1995), San Antonio Art Edn. Assn. (1st pl. 1995), Hill Country Arts Found. Republican. Avocations: water skiing, motorcycle riding, sewing, writing. Home: 264 Mountain Dr Lakehills TX 78063-6725

SPEARS, DORIS ANN HACHMUTH, entrepreneur, writer, publisher, real estate and management consultant; b. Jersey City, July 6, 1951; d. Arthur Charles Hachmuth and Diana Sofia Moroz; m. Richard Alan Spears, May 13, 1969; children: Andrew, Mark, Daniel. B, Barry U., 1993, MS, 1997. Broker, owner Doris Spears Realty, Inc., Port Jervis, 1981-86, Spears & Spears, INc., Stuart, Fla., 1987-97; owner, pub. Arrow Pub., Inc., Palm City, Fla., 1988—; editor, pub. Today's Fla. Woman, Inc., Palm City, 1994-96; owner, broker, sr. cons. D.H. Spears & Assocs., Inc., Palm City, 1997—; adj. instr. Indian River C.C., Ft. Pierce, Fla., 1994—; founder-owner Sunny Lifestyles TM, 1996. Author: Living Better for Less, 2000; (annual seminar) Building Wealth/Buying Property. Bd. dirs. Hibiscus Children's Ctr., Jensen Beach, Fla., 1993-96; sec. bd. dirs. Hibiscus Children's Found., Jensen Beach, 1996-99; mem. bus. adv. bd. Indian River C.C. Mem. Internat. Assn. Female Execs., Women's Coun. of Realtors, Real Estate Brokerage Mgrs. Coun., Martin County Bd. Realtors (bd. dirs. 1988-90), Realtor Assn. of Martin County, Nat. Spkrs. Assn., Sierra Club, Martin County C. of C., Nature Conservancy, Fla. Spkrs. Assn. Avocations: tennis, reading, travel. Office: Arrow Pub Inc 46 SW Riverway Blvd Palm City FL 34990-4238

SPECHLER, MARTIN CHARLES, economist; b. N.Y.C., Jan. 25, 1943; s. Sidney and Dorothy (Gelber) S.; m. Dina Rome, Aug. 30, 1964; children: Avraham Ravit, Michal Ya'arit. AB, Harvard Coll., 1964; MA, Harvard U., 1967, PhD, 1971. Teaching fellow in econs., social studies Harvard U., Cambridge, Mass., 1965-71, asst. prof., head tutor in econs., 1971-74; lectr. Hebrew U., Jerusalem, 1974-80; sr. lectr. Tel Aviv U., 1980-82; vis. assoc. U. Wash., Seattle, 1982-83, U. Iowa, Iowa City, 1983-84; assoc. prof. econs. Ind. U., Indpls., 1984-90, prof. econs., 1990—; mem. faculty coun. Ind. U., 1993-97, 99—. Author: Perspectives in Economic Thought; mem. editorial bd. Comparative Econ. Studies; contbr. articles to profl. jours. Active Dem. Cen. Com., Monroe County, Ind., 1988—; pres. Beth Shalom, Bloomington, Ind. Jewish Community, 1999—; mem. exec. com. Assn. for Comparative Econ. Studies. With Israel Def. Forces, 1980-82. Mem. Am. Econ. Assn., Phi Beta Kappa, Hasty Pudding Club. Avocations: golf, tennis. Home: 4418 E Sheffield Dr Bloomington IN 47408-3135 Office: 542 Ballantine Rd Bloomington IN 47401-5018 also: Cavanaugh 519 425 University Blvd Indianapolis IN 46202-5148

SPECHT-JARVIS, ROLAND HUBERT, fine arts and humanities educator, dean; b. Dortmund, Germany, Oct. 31, 1954; came to U.S., 1982; s. Otto and Waltraud Specht; m. Shawn Cecilia Jarvis, June 15, 1982; children: Alex Jarvis, Elly Jarvis. Staatsexamen in German and pedagogy, Ruhr U. Bochum, Germany, 1982, Staatsexamen in Law and German, 1982, PhD, 1988. Instr. German St. Cloud (Minn.) State U., 1982-87, asst. prof. German, 1987-89, assoc. prof. German, 1989-92, prof. German, 1992—, dir. Ingolstadt program dept. fgn. langs. and lit., 1984—, chmn. and dir. dept. fgn. langs., 1988-94, dir. quality enhancement programs State Minn., 1994-97, dean Coll. Fine Arts & Humanities, 1997—. Author: (with H. Walbruck) Deutsch Gestern und Heute, 1986, tchrs. annotated edit., 1986, audio tape program and manual, 1987, workbook, 1987, test series, 1988, Deutsch Aktuell 3 tchrs. edit., 1993, 4th edit. workbook, 1999, Compendium College of Fine Arts and Humanities, 1998, 2000, student edit., 1993, workbook, 1993, tape program manual, 1993, Microsoft Word. Textverarbeitung mit dem Macintosh, 1990, Die Ausbildung des Literarischen Diskurses Friedrich Schlegels zur Zeit der Herausgabe des Athenaeums, 1994, (with Shawn C. Jarvis and Isolde Mueller) Deutsch Aktuell 3, 1998. V.p., founder Förderverein Ingolstadt-St. Cloud, 1985; bd. dirs. Alexandria-St. Cloud Performing Arts Found., 1997, St. Cloud State U. Alumni Asn., 1995, Theatre L'Homme Dieu, 1997; mem. coun. Coll. of Arts and Scis., 1997. Mem. St. Cloud Rotary (v.p. 2000), Amnesty Internat. Avocations: kids, outdoors, chess, racquetball, motorcycles. E-mail: roland@stcloudstate.edu. Home: 1922 9th Ave SE Saint Cloud MN 56304-2118 Office: St Cloud State Univ 720 4th Ave S Saint Cloud MN 56301-4498

SPECK, CATHERINE MARGARET, art historian; b. Adelaide, Australia, Feb. 6, 1950; d. Gerald Anthony and Margaret Mary (Keany) S.; m. Christian Edward Mortensen; children: Edith Jennnifer, Alexander Jesse. Diploma of Teaching, Western Tchrs. Coll., Adelaide, Australia, 1971; BA (hons.), Flinders U., 1977; MEd, U. Canberra, Australia, 1985; PhD, Monash U., Australia, 1996. Tchr. South Australia Edn. Dept., 1971-79, 83; tutor Hartley Coll. Advanced Edn., 1979; lectr. South Australian Coll. Advanced Edn., 1983, 84-90; lectr. U. South Australia, 1990-92, sr. lectr., 1993—; convenor Art and Design Rsch. Group, 1996—. Mem. editol. bd. Australian Art Edn., 1988—, book rev. editor, 1988-91; mem. editol. bd. Australian Jour. of Art, 1996—; contbr. numerous articles to profl. art jours. Recipient John Treloar Grant-in-Aid, Australian War Meml., Canberra, 1992-93. Mem. Contemporary Art Ctr. of South Australia, Exptl. Art Found., Art Assn. Australia, Rsch. Ctr. for Gender Studies. Office: U S Australia City West, South Australia Sch of Art, Adelaide 5000, Australia

SPECK, KURT GEORG, publisher; b. Schaffhausen, Switzerland, Sept. 1, 1945; s. Franz and Emma (Hofmann) S.; m. Francoise Viguet, June 28, 1975; children: Dominique, Bertrand, Fabienne. D degree, U. Zurich, 1974. Editor econ. desk Tages Anzeiger, Zurich, 1978-80; fgn. corr. Washington, 1981-85; pub. Handelszeitung Fachverlag, Küsnacht, 1986-88; editor-in-chief Handelszeitung, Zurich, 1988—; co-owner, 1992—. Home: Schwalbenbodenstr 20, Wollerau, 8832 L. Switzerland Office: HandelsZeitung, Seestr 37, 8027 Zurich Switzerland

SPECK, MATTHIAS, orthopedic surgeon; b. Karlsruhe, Germany, Dec. 20, 1961; s. Klaus and Helga (Seufert) S.; m. Kristina Kroha, Dec. 04, 1992; children: Lucca, Siobhan, Florentin. Student, U. Medicine, Rome, 1983-84, U. Medicine, Ulm, Germany, 1984-88, U. Medicine, Heidelberg, Germany, 1989-90; MD, U. Medicine, Heidelberg, Germany, 1990. Resident dept. surgery St. Gallen, Switzerland, 1990-91, resident dept. orthop. surgery, 1991-92; resident dept. orthop. surgery U. Basel, Switzerland, 1992-94, U. Berne, Switzerland, 1994-97; cons./asst. prof. dept. orthop. surgery Klinikum Karlsbad, Germany; cons./asst. prof. dept. orthop. surgery U. Heidelberg, Germany, 1997—, Klinikum Karlsbad, Germany, 1997—. Contbr. articles to profl. jours. Mem. European Soc. Foot and Ankle, German Soc. Orthop. Surgery, German Foot and Ankle Surgery. Office: Klinikum Karlsbad Dept Orth, U Heidelberg, 76307 Karlsbad Germany

SPECTOR, LARRY WAYNE, osteopath; b. Elkins Park, Pa., Sept. 1, 1968; s. Harvey M. and Rochelle M. (Fleishman) S. BA, U. Del., 1990; DO, Phila. Coll. Osteo. Medicine, 1994. Chief intern Grad. Hosp. Phila. Coll. Osteopathic Medicine, 1994-95; resident in internal medicine Med. Ctr. of Del., Newark, 1995-98. St. George's soc. grant, 1991. Mem. AMA (del. resident sect.), Am. Osteo. Assn., Pa. Osteo. Med. Assn. (del.), Delaware Med. Soc. (pres. resident sect.). Avocations: weight lifting, sports, movie watching, reading, sports fan. Home: 1851 Foothill Dr Huntingdon Valley PA 19006-7919

SPECTOR, MICHAEL JOSEPH, agribusiness executive; b. N.Y.C., Feb. 13, 1947; s. Martin Wilson and Dorothy (Miller) S.; m. Margaret Dickson, Sept. 14, 1977. BS in Chemistry, Washington and Lee U., 1968. Rsch. chemist Am. Viscose, Phila., 1968-69; pres. MJS Entertainment Corp., Miami, Fla., 1970-84; also MJS Internat., Inc.; ptnr. Old Town Key West Devel. Ltd., Fla., 1977—; pres. MJS Entertainment o Can. Inc., Toronto, Ont., Margo Farms, MJS Prodns., Inc., N.Y.C.; chmn., pres., CEO, Margo Caribe, Inc., Dorado, P.R., 1981—, also bd. dirs.; pres. Costa Del Norte Devel., Inc., Dorado, 1998—; bd. dirs. Goodwill Industries So. Fla., v.p. fin., 1980, bd. dirs. Plz. Bank of Miami; hon. consul for Belgium in P.R. and U.S. Virgin Islands. Internat. judge The Floralies Exhbn., Gent, Belgium, 2000. With AUS, 1969-70. Robert E. Lee rsch. grantee Washington and Lee U., 1967-68; named Agri-bus. Exec. of Yr., Govt. of P.R., 1999. Mem. Nat. Assn. Record Merchandisers (dir. Nova divsn., chmn. one-stop distbn. com. 1982-83), Country Music Assn., Dorado Beach Golf and Tennis Club, Bankers Club P.R., Ocean Reef Club (Key Largo, Fla.), Grove Isle Club (Coconut Grove, Fla.). Achievements include patent for synthetic stretching process. Home: PO Box 706 Dorado PR 00646-0706

SPECTOR, PHILLIP LOUIS, lawyer; b. L.A., July 15, 1950; s. Everett L. Spector and Rebecca (Horn) Newman; m. Carole Sue Lebbin, May 11, 1980; children: Adam, David. Student, U. Birmingham, Eng., 1970-71; BA with highest honors, U. Calif., Santa Barbara, 1972; M in Pub. Policy, Harvard U., 1976, JD magna cum laude, 1976. Bar: Calif. 1976, D.C. 1978, U.S. Ct. Appeals (D.C. cir.) 1983, U.S. Supreme Ct. 1983, U.S. Dist. Ct. D.C. 1985. Law clk. U.S. Ct. Appeals (2d cir.), Brattleboro, Vt., 1976-77; law clk. to U.S. Supreme Ct., Washington, 1977-78; assoc. asst. to Pres. U.S., Washington, 1978-80; assoc. Verner, Liipfert, Bernhard & McPherson, Washington, 1980-83; ptnr. Goldberg & Spector, Washington, 1983-92, Paul, Weiss, Rifkind, Wharton & Garrison, Washington, 1992—; cons. U.S. exec. br. Close-Up Found., Alexandria, Va., 1980—. Co-author: Communications Law and Practice, 1995, Communications and Techology Alliances: Business and Legal Issues, 1996; mem. bd. editors Multimedia & Internet Strategist; contbr. articles to profl. jours. Mem. Coun. on Fgn. Rels., N.Y.C., 1980-85; moot ct. judge Nat. Assn. Attys. Gen., Washington, 1987—; adviser Dem. caucus U.S. Ho. Reps., Washington, 1981-83; speechwriter, podium prodr. Dem. Nat. Convs., N.Y.C., 1980, Phila., 1982, San Francisco, 1984, Atlanta, 1988, N.Y.C., 1992, Chgo., 1996, L.A., 2000. Recipient Disting. Achievement in Pub. Svc. Medal U. Calif., Santa Barbara, 1981, Close-Up Found. awards Via Satellite Mag., Vol. Recognition award Nat. Assn. Attys. Gen., 1993; named Leading Satellite Specialist in Washington, European Counsel, 1998. Mem. ABA (chair internat. comm. law com.), Fed. Communications Bar Assn., Bethesda Country Club, Wintergreen Ptnrs., Phi Beta Kappa. Jewish. Office: Paul Weiss Rifkind Wharton & Garrison 1615 L St NW Ste 1300 Washington DC 20036-5694

SPECULAND, BERNARD, oral and maxillofacial surgeon; b. Norwich, Norfolk, Eng., Aug. 26, 1949; s. Cyril Hannah (Shelower) S.; m. Christine Turner, Dec. 19, 1975; children: Caroline, Mary, Alex. BDS with honors, Bristol (Eng.) U., 1971, MDS, 1982. Sr. registrar accreditation cert., Eng. House surgeon Birmingham (Eng.) Dental Hosp., 1972; sr. house officer Bristol Royal Infirmary, 1973; registrar Royal United Hosp., Bath, Eng., 1973-75; sr. registrar Royal Adelaide (Australia) Hosp., 1976-77; sr. registrar in oral and maxillofacial surgery Bristol, 1978-85; cons. oral and maxillofacial surgeon City Hosp., Birmingham, 1985—; hon. sr. clin. lectr. U. Birmingham, 1985—; examiner final FDS exams Royal Coll. Surgeons Eng. Contbr. articles to profl. jours., chpt. to book. Fellow Brit. Assn. Oral and Maxillofacial Surgeons, Royal Coll. Surgeons Eng., Royal Coll. Surgeons Ireland, Royal Australasian Coll. Dental Surgeons; mem. Craniofacial Soc. Gt. Britain, Birmingham Medico-Legal Soc. (pres. 1993-95). Avocations: squash, running, windsurfing, skiing. Home: 30 Reddings Rd, Moseley, Birmingham B13 8LN, England Office: City Hosp Dept Oral and, Maxillofacial Surgery, Birmingham B18 7QH, England

SPEEDY, ERIC DAWSON, biologist; b. York, Pa., July 11, 1969; s. Harry Wilson and Janet Patricia (Roney) S.; m. Melissa Ann Rao, May 13, 1995. BS, Allegheny Coll., 1991. Biology technician Allegheny Coll., Meadville, Pa., 1991-93; spl. project mgr. Hilltop Lab. Animals, Inc., Scottdale, Pa., 1994-95. Bd. dirs. Greater Latrobe Recreation Soccer Assn, Latrobe, Pa., 1995. Mem. Am. Assn. Lab. Animal Sci., Nat. Ski Patrol Systems. Avocations: skiing, golf, outdoor activities, reading. Home: 2955 Seminary Dr Greensburg PA 15601-3736 Office: Hilltop Lab Animals Inc Hilltop Dr Scottdale PA 15683

SPEER, JOHN ELMER, paralegal, reporter, counselor; b. Conrad, Mont., Mar. 19, 1956; s. Elmer Constant and Mildred Saphronia (LaBelle) S.; m. Sharron D. Knotts, May 23, 1982 (div. Mar. 1986); 1 child, Jeremy Keith; 1 foster child, Casey; m. Adah C. Corbett, May 10, 2000; 1 stepchild, Jessica. Paralegal assoc., Coll. of Great Falls, Mont., 1994; BS in paralegal studies, U. of Great Falls, Mont., 1999. Bar: Mont. 1996; cert. scuba diver. Farmer Valier, Mont., 1956-73; janitor Shelby (Mont.) pub. schs., 1974-75; freelance news reporter Sta. KSEN, Shelby, 1980—, various TV stas., newspapers, Great Falls, 1980-90; office cleaner Parkdale Housing Authority, Great Falls, 1990-95; freelance paralegal Great Falls, 1993—; law clk., paralegal Mont. State Dist. Judge Thomas McKittrick, Great Falls, 1993; rschr. line-up identification appeal binder to U.S. Supreme Ct., 1993; trial assistance atty. Chas. Joslyn, spring 1996. Contbr. victim-witness assistance program operating manual, 1992. Counselor and adv. Victim-Witness Assistance Svcs., Great Falls, 1991-93. Mem. Mont. Big Sky Paralegal Assn., Am. Counseling Assn., Brain Injury Assn. of Mont. (chpt. v.p. 1997). Jehovah's Witness. Avocations: hiking, fishing, cooking, travel, swimming. Address: PO Box 206 Great Falls MT 59403-0206

SPEER, NANCY GIROUARD, educational administrator; b. Mankato, Minn., Sept. 14, 1941; d. Jared and Katherine (Schmitt) How; m. Robert L. Girouard, Aug. 29, 1964 (dec. Mar. 1983); children: Robert James Girouard, Mark Jared Girouard; m. David J. Speer, Dec. 21, 1985 (dec. Aug. 1999). BA, Wellesley Coll., 1963; MA in Tchg., Wesleyan U., 1965; cert. mgmt., Smith Coll., 1985. Tchr. secondary sch. Bunnell H.S., Stratford, Conn., 1964-65; tchr., class advisor Lincoln Sch., Providence, 1965-69; substitute tchr. Mankato, 1972-74; pub. info. dir. City of Mankato, 1974-78; univ. editor, dir. pub. affairs forum Mankato State U., 1978-79; comms. mgr. Humphrey Inst., U. Minn., Mpls., 1980-83, dir. external rels., 1983-87, dir. devel. and external rels., 1987-95; dir. devel. Breck Sch., Mpls., 1996-2000; v.p. Abbott Northwestern Hosp., Mpls., 2000—; mem. steering com. Minn. Meeting, Mpls., 1990-96. Contbr. articles to mags. and periodicals; photographer for publs. and newspapers. Bd. dirs. Minn. Newspaper Found., St. Paul, 1985-91, chairperson, 1990-91, bd. dirs., vice-chairperson Cabrini House, Mpls., 1993-97; bd. dirs., sec. Minn. Ctr. for Book Arts, Mpls., 1990-97; bd. dirs. Minn. Landmark Ctr., St. Paul, 1994-2000; dir. Minn. Women's Campaign Fund, Mpls., 1994—, co-pres. bd., 1997; commr. Metropolitan Airport Commn., 1999—; mem. Leadership Mpls., Mpls. C. of C., 1982. Bush Leader fellow, 1985-87. Avocations: horseback pack trips, appreciation of nature, books. Home: 23235 Saint Croix Trl N Scandia MN 55073-9725 Office: Breck Sch 123 Ottawa Ave N Minneapolis MN 55422-5189

SPEHR, CHRISTOPHER, clergyman; b. Bad Oeynhausen, Germany, Oct. 9, 1971; s. Dieter and Renate (Engau) S. Grad., Evangelische Kirche Westfalen, Bielefeld, Germany, 1999; postgrad., U. Tübingen, Germany, 1999, U. Munster, Germany, 1999—. Asst. to Prof. Dr. Petra von Gemünden, Geneva, 1994—; asst. U. Zurich, Switzerland, 1996-97. Scholar Konrad Adenauer Stiftung, 1994-99. Mem. Wingolf. Avocations: leading a youth club, playing the horn, gardening. Home: Volmerdingsener Strasse 156, 32549 Bad Oeynhausen Germany

SPEKULJAK, ZVONKO, chemical engineer; b. Ludina, Croatia, Sept. 15, 1948; s. Francisco and Antonia (Luksic) S.; m. Alicia Martina Irazoqui, Feb. 14, 1975 (dec. Aug. 1991); children: Andrea, Gabriela, Pablo Jose; m. Alicia Estela Guadalupe Pascual, June 21, 1993. Degree in chem. engring., Faculty Engring., Sante Fe, Argentina, 1975, DSc, 1986. From asst. prof. to prof. Chem. Engring. Faculty, Stafe, Argentina, 1973—; fellow, tech. researcher Conicet, Argentina, 1976—; mgr. SIT Engring., Santa Fe, 1995—. Roman Catholic. Avocations: languages, cycling, rowing. Home: Hernandaria's 771, 3000 Santa Fe Argentina Office: SIT Engring, San Jose 2832, 3000 Santa Fe Argentina

SPELFOGEL, EVAN J., lawyer; b. Boston, Jan. 28, 1936; s. Morris R. and Helen S. (Steinberg) S.; m. Beverly Kolenberg; children: Scott, Douglas, Karen. AB, Harvard U., 1956; JD, Columbia U., 1959. Bar: Mass. 1959, N.Y. 1964, U.S. Supreme Ct. 1969. Atty. Office of Solicitor, U.S. Dept. Labor, Washington, Boston, 1959-60, NLRB, Boston, N.Y.C., 1960-64; assoc. Simpson, Thacher & Bartlett, N.Y.C., 1964-69, Dewey, Ballantine, N.Y.C., 1969-77; ptnr. Fellner, Rovins & Gallay, N.Y.C., 1977-80, Summit, Rovins & Feldesman, N.Y.C., 1981-91, Epstein Becker and Green, P.C., N.Y.C., 1991—; adj. prof. law Baruch Coll., CCNY. Bd. editors Developing Labor Law: The Board, The Courts and the National Labor Relations Act, also co-editor-in-chief Supplements; bd. sr. editors Employee Benefits Law; contbr. articles to profl. jours. Fellow Coll. Labor and Employment Lawyers; mem. ABA (sect. on labor and employment law, exec. coun. 1978-86, coeditor sect. newsletter 1976-92, editl. bd. The Labor Lawyer 1986—, mem. ho. dels. 1987-90, sect. dispute resolution 1992—), FBA (coun. on labor law), N.Y. State Bar Assn. (chmn. labor and employment law sect. 1977-78, exec. coun. 1975—, ho. dels. 1978-79, com. on profl. discipline 1987-90), Assn. of Bar of City of N.Y. (labor com. 1968-71, 87-90, employee benefits com. 1992-96), Am. Arbitration Assn. (nat. panel labor arbitrators), Harvard Varsity Club, Phi Alpha Delta. Home: 17 Parkside Dr Great Neck NY 11021-1042 Office: 250 Park Ave New York NY 10177-0001

SPELLER, ROBERT ERNEST BLAKEFIELD, publishing executive; b. Chgo., Jan. 19, 1908; s. John Ernest and Florence (Larson) S.; m. Flora Maxine Elliott Watkins (dec. May 5 1997); children: Robert Ernest Blakefield, Jon Patterson. Student, Columbia U., 1929. Mag. editor Fgn. Press Svc., 1930-31; pres. Mohawk Press, 1931-32, Robert Speller Pub. Corp., 1934-52, Record Concerts Corp., 1940-53, Robert Speller & Sons, Pubs., inc., 1955—, Norellyn Press, Inc., 1960-83, Transglobal News Svc., Inc., 1960—; corresp. Raleigh News & Observer, 1949-53; pub. Hough's Ency. Am. Woods, 1957—, mng. editor 1964-75; chmn. bd., pres., chief exec. officer Nat. Resources Publs., Inc., 1968-84; pres., dir. Transglobal Resources Devel. Corp., 1983—; owner, operator, prodr. Concert Theatre, N.Y.C., 1939-43, mgr. Otto Klemperer, Leon Barzin, Margaret Speaks, others; pub. East Europe Mag., 1970—; sec., dir. Encoder Research & Devel. Corp., 1971—, Pecos Internat., Inc., 1974-77; v.p., dir. Pecos Western Corp. of Del., 1973-83; dir. Gen. Research Corp., Fashion Form Mfg. Corp. Mem. founding bd. USO. Trustee Philippa Schyler Meml. Found. With Signal Corps, AUS, 1944-45. Mem. Gourmet Soc. (founder), Am. Legion, Columbia U. Club (N.Y.C.), Delta Chi. Office: 115 E 9th St New York NY 10003-5414

SPELLER, ROBERT ERNEST BLAKEFIELD, JR., choreographer; b. N.Y.C., Feb. 5, 1936; s. Robert E.B. and Flora Maxine Elliott (Watkins) S. Student, Duke U., 1954-56, NYU, 1958-59, New Sch. for Social Rsch., 1967-68. V.p. Robert Speller & Sons, Publishers, N.Y.C., 1963—; coordinator models New School Soc. Rsch., Parsons, N.Y.C., 1972—; instr. Baruch Col., N.Y.C., 1980-83. Choreographer many shows including Toulouse, 1981, The Ritz, 1983, Let's Misbehave, 1985-86; translator: The Mime (by Jean Dorcy), 1961; dir. I Died Yesterday, 1983. Mem. AFTRA, Actors' Equity Assn. (councillor, 1967-73), Screen Actors' Guild, Am. Guild Variety Artists, Soc. Stage Dirs. & Choreographers. Episcopal. Office: Robert Speller and Sons 115 E 9th St New York NY 10003-5414

SPELLMAN, MITCHELL WRIGHT, surgeon, academic administrator; b. Alexandria, La., Dec. 1, 1919; s. Frank Jackson and Altonette Beulah (Mitchell) S.; m. Billie Rita Rhodes, June 27, 1947 (dec.); children: Frank A., Michael A., Mitchell A., Maria S. Weaver, Melva A., Mark A., Manly A. (dec.), Rita S. Parks. A.B. magna cum laude, Dillard U., 1940, LL.D. (hon.), 1983; M.D., Howard U., 1944; Ph.D. in Surgery (Commonwealth Fund fellow), U. Minn., Mpls., 1955; D.Sc. (hon.), Georgetown U., 1974, U. Fla., 1977. Intern Cleve. Met. Gen. Hosp., 1944-45, asst. resident in surgery, 1945-46; asst. resident in surgery Howard U. and Freedmen's Hosp., Washington, 1946-47; chief resident in thoracic surgery Howard U. and Freedmen's Hosp., 1947-48, teaching asst. in physiology, 1948-49, chief resident in surgery, 1949-50, teaching asst. in surgery, 1950-51; asst. prof. surgery Howard U., 1954-56, assoc. prof., 1956-60, prof., 1960-68; dir. Howard surgery service at D.C. Gen. Hosp., 1961-68; fellow in surgery U. Minn., 1951-54; sr. resident in surgery U. Minn. Med. Sch. and Hosp., 1953-54; dean Charles R. Drew Postgrad. Med. Sch., Los Angeles, 1969-77; prof. surgery Charles R. Drew Postgrad. Med. Sch., 1969-78; asst. dean, prof. surgery Sch. Medicine, U. Calif. at Los Angeles, 1969-78; clin. prof. surgery Sch. Med., U. So. Calif., 1969-78; dean for med. svcs., prof. surgery Harvard Med. Sch., Boston, 1978-90, dean emeritus for med. svcs., 1990—, dean emeritus for internat. projects, 1990—, prof. surgery emeritus, 1990—; dir. internat. exch. programs Harvard Med. Internat., 1995—; exec. v.p. Harvard Med. Ctr., 1978-90; fellow Ctr. for Advanced Study in Behavioral Scis.; vis. prof. Stanford, 1975-76; bd. dirs. Kaiser Found. Hosps., Kaiser Found. Health Plan, 1971-89; mem. D.C. Bd. Examiners in Medicine and Osteopathy, 1955-68; mem. Nat. Rev. Com. for Regional Med. Programs, 1968-70; mem. spl. med. adv. group, nat. surg. cons. VA, 1969-73; mem. Commn. for Study Accreditation of Selected Health Ednl. Programs, 1970-72; chmn. adv. com. br. med. devices Nat. Heart and Lung Inst., 1972; Am. health del. to visit People's Republic of China, 1973; hon. dir. State Mut. Cos., 1990—; mem. com. mandatory retirement in higher edn. NAS/NRC, 1989-91; mem. panel on internat. programs Nat. Libr. Medcine, 1996, 97. Mem. editorial bd.: Jour. Medicine and Philosophy, 1977-90; Contbr. articles on cardiovascular physiology and surgery, measurement of blood volume, and radiation biology to profl. jours. Past bd. dirs. Sun Valley Forum on Nat. Health; mem. ethics adv. bd. HEW, 1977-81; bd. dirs. Harvard Comty. Health Plan, 1979-84; former trustee Occidental Coll.; former bd. overseers com. to visit univ. health svc. Harvard, bd. overseers Harvard Comty. Health Plan, 1984-95; former regent Georgetown U., bd. dirs., 1986-92; former vis. com. U. Mass. Med. Ctr.; mem. bd. visitors UCLA Sch. Medicine; mem. corp. MIT; adv. bd. PEW Scholars Program in Biomed. Scis., 1984-86; bd. dirs. Med. Edn. for South African Blacks, 1985—. Markle scholar in med. scis., 1954-59; recipient Distinguished Alumnus award Dillard U., 1963; Distinguished Postgrad. Achievement award Howard U., 1974; Outstanding Achievement award U. Minn., 1979. Mem. AMA, AAAS, AAUP, ACS, Nat. Med. Assn. (William A. Sinkler Surgery award 1968), Soc. Univ. Surgeons, Am. Coll. Cardiology, Am. Surg. Assn., Inst. of Medicine of Nat. Acad. Scis. (chmn. program com. 1977-79, governing coun. 1978-80), Nat. Acad. Practice in Medicine, Am. Assn. Sovereign Mil. Order of Malta (Knights and Dames of Malta), MIT Corp. (life mem. emeritus), Cosmos Club. Roman Catholic. Address: One Renaissance Park 1135 Tremont St 9th Fl Ste 900 Boston MA 02120

SPELLMAN, THOMAS JOSEPH, JR., lawyer; b. Glen Cove, N.Y., Nov. 11, 1938; s. Thomas J. and Martha H. (Erwin) S.; m. Margaret Mary Barth, June 23, 1962; children: Thomas Joseph, Kevin M., Maura N. BS, Fordham U., 1960, JD, 1965. Bar: N.Y. 1966, U.S. Dist. Ct. (so. and ea. dist.) N.Y. 1968, U.S. Ct. Appeals (2nd cir.) 1980, U.S. Supreme Ct. 1981. Staff atty. Allstate Ins. Co., N.Y.C., 1966-69; trial atty. Hartford Ins. Co., Hauppauge, N.Y., 1969-71; ptnr. Wheller & Spellman, Farmingville, N.Y., 1971-76, Devitt Spellman Barrett Callahan Leyden & Kenney LLP and predecessors, Smithtown, N.Y., 1976—; mem. grievance com. 10th Jud. Dist., Westbury, N.Y., 1984-92. Trustee Acad. St. Joseph, Brentwood, N.Y., 2000—. Capt. USAR, 1960-68. Fellow Am. Bar Found., N.Y. Bar Found.; mem. Suffolk County Bar Assn. (bd. dirs., sec.-treas., v.p. 1982, pres. 1992-93), N.Y. State Bar Assn. (Ho. of Dels. 1989—, nominating com. 1992-93, v.p. 1996-98), Swordfish Club (bd. dirs., sec. 2000—, Westhampton Beach, N.Y.). Home: 8 Highwoods Ct Saint James NY 11780-9610 Office: Devitt Spellman et al 50 Route 111 Ste 314 Smithtown NY 11787-3700

SPENCE, FRANCIS JOHN, archbishop; b. Perth, Ont., Can., June 3, 1926; s. William John and Rose Anna (Jordan) S. BA, St. Michael's Coll., Toronto, 1946; postgrad., St. Augustine's Sem., Toronto, 1946-50; JCD, St. Thomas U., Rome, 1955. Ordained to priest Roman Cath. Ch., 1950. Consecrated bishop, 1967; diocesan sec. Kingston, Ont., 1950-52; parish asst., 1955-61; mem. Marriage Tribunal, 1961-66; diocesan dir. hosp. and charities, 1961-66; pastor Sacred Heart Ch., Marmora, Ont., 1966-67; aux. bishop Mil. Vicar Canadian Forces, 1967-82; bishop of Charlottetown P.E.I., 1970-82; archbishop of Kingston Ont., 1982—; mil. vicar of Can., 1982-88; pres. Can. Conf. Cath. Bishops, 1995-97. Office: Catholic Diocesan Centre, 390 Palace Rd, Kingston, ON Canada K7L 4T3

SPENCE, JANET BLAKE CONLEY (MRS. ALEXANDER PYOTT SPENCE), civic worker; b. Upper Montclair, N.J., Aug. 17, 1915; d. Walter Abbott and Ethel Maud (Blake) Conley; m. Alexander Pyott Spence, June 10, 1939; children: Janet Spence Kerr, Robert Moray, Richard Taylor. Student, Vassar Coll., 1933-35; cert., Katharine Gibbs Sch., 1936. Active various community drives; chmn. Darien (Conn.) Assembly, 1955-56; sec., chmn. Wilton Jr. Assembly, 1961-63; subscription chmn. Candlelight Concerts Wilton, Conn., 1963-65; rec. sec. Pub. Health Nursing Assn. Wilton Bd., 1964-67; corr., rec. sec. Royle Sch. Bd., Darien, 1952-55; fund raiser Vassar Class of 1937; mem. Washington Valley Community Assn.; mem. N.J. Symphony Orch. League, treas. Morris County br. 1978-83, corr. sec. 1982-83, pres. 1985-89, acting pres. 1989—, state coun. mem. 1985-89, acting pres. Morris br. 1989-90; docent Macculloch Hall Historica Mus., Morristown, N.J., 1992—. Mem. Vassar Alumni Assn., Dobbs Alumni Assn., Jersey Hills Vassar Club Morristown (ann. fund raiser), Woman's Club, Wilton Garden Club (life), Washington Valley Cmty. Assn. (life corr. sec. 1977-82, pres. 1982-84, v.p. 1984-85, co-pres. 1985-86, chmn. membership com. 1987-89, archives com. 1988—, treas. 1990—), Washington Valley Home Econs. Club. Congregationalist. Home: 168 Washington Valley Rd Morristown NJ 07960-3333

SPENCE, NICOL, language educator; b. Harare, Zimbabwe, July 29, 1924; s. William and Marie Rose (Tockert) S.; m. Andrée Henriette Friedrich, July 11, 1959; children: Robert Paul, Anita Rosemary. BA in Modern Langs., U. Leeds, Eng., 1948; PhD in Romance Philology, U. London, 1955. Asst. lectr. Queen's U., Belfast, Ireland, 1951-54, lectr., 1955-61, reader, 1961-66; asst. lectr. U. Coll. North Staffordshire, Keele, Eng., 1954-55; reader U. London Bedford Coll., 1966-79, prof. French linguistics, 1979-84. Author: A Glossary of Jersey French, 1960, Narcissus: poéme du 12e siecle, 1964, Essays in Linguistics, 1976, Le Francais Contemporain, 1976, A Brief History of Jèrriais, 1993, The Structures of French, 1996; contbr. numerous articles to profl. jours. Mem. Soc. of Romance Linguistics, Soc. French Studies. Anglican. Avocations: travel, walking. Home: Le Cresson, Grande Route de Rozel, Saint Martin Jersey, Channel Islands, Great Britain

SPENCER, CHARLES SAMUEL, art historian, educator; b. London, Aug. 26, 1920; s. Samuel and Henrietta (Cohen) Sabaroff. Student, Caurtauld Inst., London, 1945-46, Rome U., 1947-48; 1976, freelance lectr., exhbn. organizer. Sec. Anglo-Jewish Assn., London, 1954-64; art critic N.Y. Times (Paris edit.), London Daily Mail, 1965-69; cons. Grosvenor Gallery, London, 1965-69; editor Art & Artists, London, 1970-73, Editions Alecto, London, 1973-75; prin. lectr. Croydon Coll., Eng., 1976-79; freelance lectr., exhbn.

organizer, 1979—. Author: Erté, 1970, Leon Bakst, 1973, Alecto Monographs, 1974, Cecil Beaton, 1975, rev. edit., 1994, The World of Serge Diaghilev, 1974, Leon Bakst and the Ballets Russes, 1995; editor: The Aesthetic Movement, 1973, A Decade of Print Making, 1973, The World of Flo Ziegfeld, 1974. Mem. Internat. Assn. Art Critics, Arts Club London. Avocations: travel, cooking. Home and Office: 24a Ashworth Rd, London W9 1JY, England

SPENCER, DAVID ANTHONY, geologist, researcher; b. London, Nov. 7, 1963; s. Henry William George and Veronica Clair (Bonanno) S.; m. Cinzia Spencer-Cervato, Mar. 10, 1990. BSc in Geology with honors, U. Exeter, Eng., 1986; Diploma, U. London, 1988, MSc in Structural Geology, 1988; Dr Natural Sci., Swiss Fed. Inst. Tech., Zurich, 1993. Chartered geologist, European geologist. Ins. claims broker Winchester Bowring Ltd., London, 1982-83; platinum exploration geologist Eastern Bushveld Complex, South Africa, 1986-87; rsch. fellow Swiss Fed. Inst. Tech., Zürich, 1988-89, rsch. and tchr. asst., 1989-92, vis. ETH rsch. fellow, 1992-93, vis. rsch. fellow, 1993-94; rsch. fellow in tectonics Swiss Fed. Inst. Tech., Zurich, 1994-97; vis. lectr. U. of the Punjab, Lahore, Pakistan, 1995; vis. scientist Tokyo Inst. Tech., Zurich, 1996; rsch. asst. prof., lectr. in structural geology U. Maine, Orono, 1997-98; vis. scientist U. Beijing, 1986; vis. prof. U. of the Punjab, Lahore, 1997—; Himalayan regional coordinating com. Internat. Lithosphere Program, 1992-96, com. tectonic map of Himalaya, 1995; organizer confs. in field; founder, moderator, coord. HimNet, 1994-96; presenter, cons., lectr. in field. Contbr. numerous articles to profl. jours.; European regional editor Himalayan Notes, 1994-97; reviewer numerous internat. jours. in field. Sir John Cass Found. scholar, 1987-88, travel award, 1988; recipient travel award Swiss Geol. Soc., 1991, 93, Huber-Kudlich Found., 1992, Swiss Acad. Natural Scis., 1992, Pub. award Staub Fund, 1992; rsch. fellow Swiss Nat. Sci. Found., 1994-97; recipient Duke of Edinburgh Gold award, 1987. Fellow Geol. Soc., Royal Geog. Soc., Royal Soc. Arts, Am. Geog. Soc., Geol. Assn. of Can.; mem. AAAS, Inst. Petroleum, Royal Instn. of Gt. Britain, Royal Scottish Geog. Soc. (profl. assoc.), Order of Internat. Fellowship, Internat. Assn. Structural/Tectonic Geologists, Mineral. Soc., European Assn. Geoscientists and Engrs., Soc. for Sedimentary Geology, Geosci. Info. Soc., Computer Oriented Geol. Soc., European Union Geoscis., Am. Geophys. Union, Assn. Geoscientists for Internat. Devel., Geol. Soc Am., Geol. Soc. Switzerland, Geol. Soc. Pakistan, Geol. Soc. Punjab, Geol. Soc. Nepal, Swiss Mineral. and Petrological Soc., Soc. for Mining, Metallurgy and Exploration, Geochem. Soc., Am. Chem. Soc., Petroleum Exploration Soc. of Gt. Britain, Am. Assn. Petroleum Geologists, Nat. Geog. Soc., Assn. Am. Geographers, Can. Assn. Geographers, Brit. Assn. for Advancement of Sci., Sci. Exploration Soc., N.Y. Acad. Scis., Nat. Earth Sci. Tchrs. Assn., Nat. Assn. Geosci. Tchrs., Assn. for Sci. Edn., Himalayan Found., Himalayan Club, Himalayan Explorers Club, Nepal Studies Assn., Internat. Assn. for Ladakh Studies, Integrated Mountain Rsch. Soc., Internat. Mountain Soc., Brit. Mountaineering Coun., Sigma Xi. Avocations: mountaineering, guitar, long distance walking, sports.

SPENCER, FRANCIS MONTGOMERY JAMES, pharmacist; b. St. John's, Antigua, Mar. 11, 1943; came to U.S., 1974; s. Stanley M. and Sarah Jane Elizabeth (Spencer) James; m. Jean V. Cole, May 9, 1981; children: David, Frances, Weslie. BS in Pharmacy, Northeastern U., Boston, 1982. Registered pharmacist, Mass., N.H., Fla.; registered cons. pharmacist, pharmacy preceptor, Fla. Sr. dispensing druggist Holberton Hosp., Antigua, 1968-73, lectr. in pharmacy, 1970-73; pharmacist, intern Mount Auburn Hosp., Cambridge, Mass., 1978-82; staff pharmacist Centro-Asturiano Hosp., Tampa, Fla., 1986-90, Dr.'s Hosp., Tampa, Fla., 1991-97; pharmacy mgr. Eckerd Drug Co., Tampa, Fla., 1983—; co-founder, pres., chief exec. officer Spenscott, Inc., Bronx, N.Y., 1989—; assoc. mem. Delta Search, Inc., Tampa, 1987-97. Mem. profl. adv. panel Drug Topics mag., Oradell, N.J., 1987—. Fellow Am. Soc. Cons. Pharmacists (registered cons. Fla.), Internat. Biog. Assn. (life, dept. dir. gen.); mem. AAAS, Fla. Pharmacy Assn., Am. Biog. Inst. Inc. (dep. gov., hon. mem. rsch. bd. advisors), N.Y. Acad. Scis., Am. Soc. Pharmacy Law, Mass. State Pharmacy Assn., N.H. Pharmacy Assn., Am. Coll. Heatlh Care Adminstrs. Methodist. Avocations: reading, travel, classical music. Home: PO Box 245 Mango FL 33550-0245

SPENCER, FRANK THOMAS, executive search firm executive; b. N.Y.C., Oct. 1, 1950; s. Frank and Dorothy Evelyn (Shinick) S.; m. Francine Falzone, Feb. 8, 1975; 1 child, Jenna Kate. BBA in Mktg., Hofstra U., 1973. Cert. profl. trainer. Store mgr. The Gap, Inc., N.Y.C., 1973-76, dist. mgr., 1976-81, regional mgr., 1981-84, zone ops. and human resource dir., 1984-85; exec. recruiter Kenzer Corp., N.Y.C., 1985-92, sr. assoc., 1992-97; exec. v.p. DHR Internat., N.Y.C., 1997-98, regional mng. dir., 1998-99, vice chmn., 1999—. Mem. U.S. Tennis Assn. (capt. 1996-99). Avocations: tennis, basketball, reading, piano, electronics. Office: DHR Internat 280 Park Ave New York NY 10017-1216

SPENCER, HEIDI HONNOLD, psychotherapist, writer, educator; b. Washington, June 30, 1943; d. John Otis and Annamarie (Kunz) Honnold; m. Charles David Spencer, Dec. 28, 1962; children: Hans Steven, Jason John, Tanya Anna. BA, U. Pa., 1965; MA, Columbia U., 1966; MSW, Cath. U., 1982; PhD in Adult and Family Psychology, Union Inst., Cin., 1990. Cert. clin. social worker, cert. nat. bd. addictions examiners; lic. social worker, D.C., Md., W.Va. Tchr. h.s. Peace Corps, Yap Island, 1966-68; faculty instr. Ctrl. Wash. State Coll., Ellensburg, 1972-75; parent group facilitator Individual Psychology Assocs., Chevy Chase, Md., 1975-79; group facilitator Georgetown U. Med. Sch., Washington, 1977-80; staff clinician D.C. Inst. Mental Health, 1980-86; pvt. practice in adult psychotherapy Bethesda, Md., 1985—; faculty Cath. U. Wa. Psychoanalytic Found., 1989-91; bd. dirs., cons., faculty, supr. Clin. Social Work Inst.; mem. bd. doctoral program for clin. social workers; counselor, tchr. The Spl. Sch. for Pregnant Teenagers, Seattle, 1969-71; crisis intervention counselor Montgomery County (Md.) Hotline, 1975-79; mental health intern No. Va. Mental Health Inst., Falls Ch., 1979-80; mem. part-time faculty Cath. U., Washington, 1991; cons., counselor Christ Child Soc., Rockville, Md., 1985-86; cons. Jewish Cmty. Ctr., Rockville, 1992, Brooklane Psychiat. Ctr., Hagerstown, Md., 1992, AmeriCorps, Washington, 1996, Affiliated Cmty. Counselors, Inc., Rockville, 1996—; insvc. instr. psychol. and learning ctr. Am. U., Washington, 1990—; chair, Conf. Washington Psychoanalytic Found., 1989-90; cons. The Bilingual Project/Project BUILD, Yakima, Wash., 1973-75; mem. curriculum com. Clin. Social Work Inst., 1991-94; spkr. and presenter in field. Author: (2 vols. book and record) Our Valley-Our Song, 1974, (book) Did I Do Something Wrong: A Supportive Guide for Parents and Loved Ones or People in Psychotherapy, 1995; columnist Family Therapy Acad., 1996-97. Trainer, cons. cmty.-based overflow shelters for homeless, Bethesda, 1989-94; vice chair bd. social concerns Cedar Ln. Unitarian Ch., 1986-87; active dr.-lawyer anti-drug program Fairfax Bar Assn., 1997. Mem. Greater Washington Soc. Clin. Social Work (v.p. for edn. 1992-94, at-large 1994-96, membership task force 1995-96). Baha'i. Avocations: violin, piano, accordion, gardening, writing.

SPENCER, HERBERT HARRY, structural engineering researcher, computer analyst; b. Vienna, Austria, Jan. 2, 1928; came to U.S., 1953; s. Ingenieur Oskar and Bronia (Steinberger) Schnabel; m. Margot Goldrei (div.); m. Sara Slomka, July 24, 1992; 1 child, Gil Oskar. BSc in Engring., U. London, 1948, PhD, 1976; MS, Poly. Inst. Bklyn., 1955. Jr. engr. asst. Tarmac Ltd., Coventry, England, 1944-45, George Wimpey & Co., Coventry, 1945-46, Kershaw & Kaufman, London, 1946-48; engr. William Halcrow & Ptnrs., London, 1948-49, Hydraulic Dept., Nazareth, Israel, 1949-50, Quibuts Eyn Hashofet, Galilee, Israel, 1950-51, Rendel Palmer & Tritton, London, 1951-53; rsch. asst. Poly. Inst. Bklyn., 1953-55; instr. Yale U., New Haven, Conn., 1955-56; rsch. asst., lectr. Columbia U., N.Y.C., 1956-59; asst. prof. San Diego (Calif.) State Coll., 1959-61; rsch. assoc. Caltech, Pasedena, Calif., 1961-62; asst. prof. U. So. Calif., L.A., 1961-65; sr. scientist Ford Instrument Co. Sperry Gyro, L.I.C., N.Y., 1965-66, Tech. Rsch. Group, Melville, N.Y., 1966-67; engr. cons. Spencer Rsch., N.Y.C. and London, 1967-77; sr. lectr. Hatfield (Eng.) Poly., 1970-77; vis. assoc. prof. U. Pitts., 1976-77; assoc. prof. La. State U., Baton Rouge, 1977-79; vis. rsch. cons. Columbia U., N.Y.C., 1979; asst. prof. Rutgers U., New Brunswick, N.J., 1979-82; pres. Spencer Sci. Computing, New Brunswick, 1982—; vis. prof. Aero Lab., Technion, Haifa, Israel, 1988, Rutgers U., Piscataway, N.J., 1998—. Contbr. articles to rsch. publs. Mem. ASCE, ASME, Israeli Soc. Engrs. and Architects, Gesellschaft für Angewandte Mathematik und Mechanik, Structural Rsch. Coun., Mensa, Intertel. Home: 10-8M Landing Ln New Brunswick NJ 08901-1070 Office: Spencer Scientific Comp PO Box 4191 Highland Park NJ 08904-4191

SPENCER, IVOR, company executive; b. London, Nov. 20, 1928; m. Estella Spencer; children: Nigel, Phillipa. Chmn., mng. dir. Ivor Spencer Enterprises, London, 1959—; prin. Ivor Spencer Sch. for Butler Adminstrn., London, 1981—; owner sch. for butlers, U.S.A.; dep. lt. of Her Majesty; master of ceremonies for over 1,000 royal events. Author: Speeches and Toasts, 1984. Active various charitable orgns. Mem. Guild Internat. Profl. Toastmasters (founder, life pres.), Guild Brit. Butlers (pres. 1981-89), Inst. Dirs. London, Guild of Profl. After-Dinner Speakers (pres.), Toastmastres for Royal Occasions (pres.), Euro Profl. Toastmasters and Bulter Adminstrs. Authority (pres.), Guild Internat. Butler Adminstrs./Personal Asst. (bd. dirs.). Address: 12 Little Bornes, London SE21 8SE, England

SPENCER, JACK B., management consultant; b. Tucson, Jan. 10, 1945; s. Clyde Edwin and Elizabeth (Burns) S.; m. Elizabeth Day, Dec. 1970 (div. 1975); children: Kimberly A. Fitzgerald, Matthew J. Spencer; m. Letitia Collura, Jan. 9, 1980; children: Sean Fairburn, Rodger Fairburn, Robin Spencer. BS, DePaul U., 1967; M in Bus. Adminstrn., Washington U., 1969. Chief acctg. officer General Terminal Corp., Tustin, Calif., 1980-83, CFO, 1983-85; chief acctg. officer PDA Engring., Santa Ana, Calif., 1985-88; CFO Resdel Industries, Irvine, Calif., 1988-90; owner Sunrise Cons., Ltd., Hammond, La., 1990—; mem. fin. adv. bd. Resdel Industries, 1989-90. With USAR, 1972-77. Mem. Hammond C. of C. Avocations: reading, playing, bridge. E-mail: MRMOGUL1@i-55.COM. Office: Sunrise Cons Ltd 3 Edwards Pl Hammond LA 70401-1007

SPENCER, JANE, literary critic, educator; b. Penwortham, Lancashire, England, Sept. 15, 1957; d. Philip and Margaret Amelia (Tomlinson) S.; m. Edward Hugh Glover, April 17, 1979; children: Kate, Eleanor. BA (hons), U. Hull, 1978; DPhil, U. Oxford, 1982. Jr. rsch. fellow Trinity Coll., Oxford, 1981-84; lectr. U. Edinburgh, 1984-87; lectr. U. Exeter, 1988-96, sr. lectr., 1996—; co-dir. Ctr. Women's Studies U. Exeter, 1993-95. Author: The Rise of the Woman Novelist, 1986, Elizabeth Gaskell, 1993; co-editor: Political Gender, 1994; editor: Aphra Behn, The Rover and Other Plays, 1995. Recipient fellowship Huntington Libr., 1994; major rsch. grant Brit. Acad., 1994. Fellow Royal Soc. Arts. Avocations: birdwatching, drawing, painting. Office: U Exeter Sch English, Queen's Bldg Queens Dr, Exeter EX4 4QH, England

SPENCER, JOHN BURTON, III, state agency administrator; b. Jennings, La., Mar. 24, 1963; s. John Burton Jr. and Betty Joe S. B in Acctg., U. Miss., 1985, MBA, 1989. Property tax agt. Tex. Ea. Corp., Houston, 1986-87; budget officer Miss. Dept. Corrections, Parchman, Miss., 1990-92; staff acct. Entergy Sys. and Svc., Inc., Memphis, 1992-93; acct. auditor III, Miss. Dept. Transp., Jackson, 1994-97; CFO, Dept. Fin. and Adminstrn., Jackson, 1997-99, dir. adminstrn. and fin., 1999—. Activist World Wildlife Fund, Nat. Arbor Day Found. Chancellor's scholar U. Miss., 1982-83. Mem. Golden Key, Beta Alpha Psi, Sigma Nu. Avocations: world travel, fishing, music, sports. Home: 580 S Pear Orchard Rd Apt 405 Ridgeland MS 39157-4211 Office: Miss Dept Fin and Adminstrn 1501 Walter Sillers Bldg Jackson MS 39201-1100

SPENCER, JOHN FRANCIS THEODORE, microbiologist, consultant; b. Magrath, Alta., Can., Jan. 18, 1922; s. John Arthur and Olga Annie Thérèse (Soderman) S.; m. Dorothy Mary Higgins, Apr. 6, 1973 (dec. July 1995); m. Alicia Leonor Ragout, Nov. 4, 1996. BSc, U. Alta., 1949, MSc, 1951; PhD, U. Sask., Can., 1955. Sr. rsch. officer NRC of Can., Saskatoon, Sask., 1951-73; hon. rsch. officer Thames Poly., London, 1973-75, Goldsmiths' Coll., London, 1975-87; vis. scientist PROIMI, Tucuman, Argentina, 1988-94; vis. prof. U. Nacional de Tucuman, 1995—; cons. Kroger Corp., Cin., 1984-86, Fleischman Colombiana, Cali, Colombia, 1993. Co-author: Methods in Yeast Genetics, 1989; editor, author: Yeast Technology, 1990, Yeasts, 1997; editor: Yeast Genetics: Fundamental and Applied Aspects; author abour 200 book chpts. and monographs. Officer RCAF, 1942-45. Recipient various travel and study grants Royal Soc. London. Mem. AAAS, Am. Soc. Microbiology, Internat. Commn. on Yeasts (governing com. 1969—), Sigma Xi. Achievements include patents for discovery of production of polyhydroxy alcohols by yeasts and production of glycolipids by yeasts. Home: Avda 25 de Mayo 577 8B, 4000 San Miguel Tucuman Argentina Office: PROIMI, Avda Belgrano y Pje Caseros, 4000 San Miguel de Tucuman Argentina

SPENCER, JOHN LORAINE, retired headmaster; b. Woodford Green, Essex, U.K., Jan. 19, 1923; s. Arthur Loraine and Emily Maude (Hagger) S.; m. Brenda Elizabeth Loft, Apr. 4, 1954; children: Christopher, Elizabeth, Nicholas. MA with 1st class honors, Cambridge (Eng.) U., 1947. Asst. master Haileybury Coll., Hertford, U.K., 1947-61; headmaster Lancaster (U.K.) Royal Grammar Sch., 1961-72, Berkhamsted Sch., Herts, U.K., 1972-83; asst. dir. Gap Activity Projects, Reading, U.K., 1984-94; ret., 1994. Capt. Brit. Army, 1942-45, ETO. Recipient Territorial decoration Ministry of Def., 1960. Mem. Ch. of England. Avocations: walking, travel, volunteer work. Home: Crofts Close Aston Rd, Haddenham Aylesbury HP17 8AF, England

SPENCER, MARY GOLDACRE, real estate executive; b. Bradford, Yorkshire, Eng., June 7, 1950; d. Raymond and Jean (Williams) Goldacre; divorced; children: Damian, Zoë. Cert. acctg., math., and French, Lincoln Tech. Coll., 1969. Exec. sec. Dormy House Conf. Centre, Ascot, 1970-72, George Hotel, Reading, 1972-75, Both World Hotel, Gibraltar, 1977-80, D.W.S. Ins. Brokers, Gibraltar, 1980-84; mgr. Sunway Properties S.L., Tenerife, Spain, 1987-94; dir., owner Tenerife Property Shop S.L., Tenerife, Spain, 1994—. Recipient numerous awards Internat. Property Awards, 1996—. Mem. Nat. Assn. Estate Agts. (overseas mem.), Internat. Real Estate Inst. (U.S.). Avocations: travel, reading. Office: Tenerife Property Shop SL, 117 Puerto Colon, Adeji, Tenerife Canary Islands Spain

SPENCER, MARY MILLER, civic worker; b. Comanche, Tex., May 25, 1924; d. Aaron Gaynor and Alma (Grissom) Miller; 1 child, Mara Lynn. BS, U. North Tex., 1943. Cafeteria dir. Mercedes (Tex.) Pub. Schs., 1943-46; home economist cood. All-Orange Dessert Contest Fla. Citrus Commn., Lakeland, 1959-62, 64; tchr. purchasing sch. lunch dept. Fla. Dept. Edn., 1960. Clothing judge Polk County (Fla.) Youth Fair, 1951-68, Polk County Federated Women's Clubs, 1964-66; pres. Dixieland Elem. Sch. PTA, 1955-57, Polk County Coun. PTA's, 1958-60; chmn. pub. edn. com. Polk County unit Am. Cancer Soc., 1959-60, bd. dirs., 1962-70; charter mem., bd. dirs. Lakeland YMCA, 1962-72; sec. Greater Lakeland Cmty. Nursing Coun., 1965-72; trustee, vice-chmn. Polk County Eye Clinic, Inc., 1962-64, pres., 1964-82; bd. dirs. Polk County Scholarship and Loan Fund, 1962-70; mem. exec. com. West Polk County (Fla.) Cmty. Welfare Coun., 1960-62, 65-68; mem. budget and audit com. Greater Lakeland United Fund, 1960-62, bd. dirs., 1967-70, residential chmn. fund drive, 1968; mem. adv. bd. Polk County Juvenile and Domestic Rels. Ct., 1960-69; sec. bd. dirs. Fla. West Coast Ednl. TV, 1960-81; mem. Polk County Home Econs. Adv. Com., 1965-71; mem. exec. com. Suncoast Health Coun., 1968-71; worker children's svcs. divsn. family svcs. Dept. Health and Rehab. Svcs., State of Fla., 1969-70, social worker, 1970-72, 74-82, social worker Overpayment Fraud Recoupment unit, 1977-81, with other pers. svcs., 1981-82, supr. Overpayment Fraud Recoupment unit, 1982-83, pub. assistance specialist IV, 1984-89; bd. dirs. Lake Region United Way, Winter Haven, 1976-81; mem. Polk County Cmty. Svcs. Coun., 1978-88; with other pers. svcs. Emergency Fin. Assistance Housing Program, 1990-96. Mem. AAUW (pres. Lakeland br. 1960-61), Nat. Welfare Fraud Assn., Fla. Congress Parents and Tchrs. (hon. life, pres. dist. 7 1961-63, chmn. pub. rels. 1962-66), Fla. Health and Welfare Coun., Fla. Health and Social Svc. Coun., Polk County Mental Health Assn., U. North Tex. Alumni Assn., Order Ea. Star. Democrat. Methodist. Home and Office: PO Box 2161 Lakeland FL 33806-2161

SPENCER, RACHEL MARY ASHLEY, barrister, solicitor; b. Bradford, Eng., Mar. 10, 1964; arrived in Australia, 1965; d. Derrick Atkinson and Marie Caroline Spencer; m. Andrew Cameron Dunncliff, Aug. 3, 1994; 2 children. BA, U. Adelaide, 1985, LLB, 1986, LLM, 1994; grad. diploma in legal practice, South Australian Inst. Tech., 1990. Tchr. Lycée Paul Langevin, Paris, 1986-87; legal officer AMP Soc., Adelaide, 1987-90; pvt. practice Adelaide, 1990-96; corp. solicitor Austereo Pty Ltd., Adelaide, 1996-98; dir. practical legal tng. Flinders U. of South Australia, Bedford Park, 1998—; lectr., tutor U. South Australia, 1989-94; cons., lectr. Radio 5UV, 1997-98. Dir. Intellectual Disability Svcs. Coun., Adelaide, 1994-97; dir., deputy chair So. Youth Theatre Ensemble, Noarlunga, South Australia, 1997-98; trustee Australian Fedn. of Univ. Women, Adelaide, 1995—. Mem. Law Soc. of So. Australia. Avocations: literature, French language and culture, horticulture, theatre, cinema. Office: Sch of Law Flinders U, Sturt Rd, Bedford Park SA, Australia

SPENCER, THOMAS MELVIN, III, soft drink company executive; b. Richmond, Va., Feb. 16, 1949; s. Thos Melvin Jr. and Frances (Lawson) S.; m. Leslie Graham Murray, Sept. 14, 1984. AB, U. N.C., 1972. With fountain sales dept. Coca-Cola U.S.A., Atlanta, 1973-80; with Russell Pierce and Assocs., Richmond, Va., 1980-81; mgr. fountain sales div. Allegheny Pepsi, Richmond, Va., 1982; corp. mktg. equipment mgr. Pepsi Bottling Ventures, LLC, Raleigh, N.C., 1983—. Mem. Nat. Soft Drink Assn. Democrat. Presbyn. Home: 1115 Lakeside Dr NW Wilson NC 27896-2015 Office: Pepsi Bottling Ventures LLC 1800 Pepsi Way Garner NC 27529-7231

SPENCER-PHILLIPS, PETER TYRELL NELSON, mycologist, plant pathologist; b. London, June 13, 1956; s. Anthony Tyrell and Hazel Audrey (Reid) Spencer-Phillips; m. Pamela Elizabeth Doughty, Aug. 11, 1979; children: Robert, Edward, Matthew. BSc, ARCS, Imperial Coll., London, 1977, PhD, DIC, 1984. Rsch. fellow U. Liverpool, Eng., 1981-82; lectr. Bristol (Eng.) Polytechnic, 1982-89; from sr. lectr. to prin. lectr. U. of West of Eng., Bristol, 1989—. Contbr. articles to profl. jours. and books. Ch. warden St. John the Bapt. Ch., Farrington Gurney, Somerset, Eng., 1990-94, 95-96, covenant sec., 1995—; chmn. Farrington Gurney Village Day, Avon, 1991, Farrington Gurney Cmty. Questionnaire, 1992; county gov. Chewton Mendip Sch., Somerset, 1997—; founder, dir. Rush Hill Wood Nature Res., 2000—. Mem. Internat. Soc. for Plant Pathology (convenor Downy Mildews working group), Brit. Mycol. Soc., Brit. Soc. Plant Pathology. Mem. Ch. of Eng. Avocations: gardening, woodland management, food, travel. Office: U West of Eng, Coldharbour Ln, Bristol BS16 1QY, England

SPENCKER, FRIEDRICH-BERNHARD, physician, medical institute executive; b. Quedlinburg, Germany, Jan. 30, 1941; s. Hermann and Gertrud (Papenfuss) S.; m. Irmgard Feifer, May 8, 1970. Abitur, Oberschule, Quedlinburg, 1959. Asst. physician U. Leipzig, Germany, 1965-70; head dept. med. bacteriology Dist. Inst. Hygiene, Leipzig, 1970-78; head bacteriology lab. dept. pediatrics U. Leipzig, Germany, 1978-95, vice dir. Inst. Med. Microbiology, 1995—; cons. bd. mem. Deutsche Gesellschaft für Pediatric Infektiologie, Munich, 1993-95. Author: Fetale und Neonatale Infektionen, 1990. Ltd. Med. Svc. Mem. Am. Soc. for Microbiology. Lutheran. Avocation: classical music. Home: Scheffelstr 31a, 04277 Leipzig Germany Office: Inst Med Microbiology, Liebigstr 24, 04103 Leipzig Saxony, Germany

SPENER, FRIEDRICH, biochemist, educator; b. Berlin, Sept. 10, 1939; s. Gustav and Gerda (Kaessmann) S.; m. Reingard Gauby, June 26, 1966 (div. 1976); children: Arno, Maja; m. Ulrike Kruse. PhD, U. Graz, 1968. Fellow U. Minn., Mpls., 1968-70; sect. leader Fed. Ctr. Lipid Rsch., Munster, Germany, 1970-74; asst., dozent U. Munster, 1974-82, prof., 1982—; bd. dirs. Spener & Spener Consulting, Munster; guest prof. U. Paris, 1986, Graz U. Tech., 1996, 98. Exec. editor Biochim. Biophys. Acta; editor Biocatal Biotransform; adv. editor biochem Jour.; editor-in-chief Europeoan Jour. Lipid Sci. Tech., 2000—; contbr. chpts. in books. Advisor BioGenTec NRW, Cologne, 1994—. With Austrian Pioneer Corps, 1957-58. Recipient Chevreul medal AFECG, 2000; fellow Japanese Soc. Promotion of Sci., 1995. Mem. Internat. Soc. Fat Rsch. (bd. dirs., pres. 1999—), Internat. Conf. Biosci. of Lipids (steering com., pres. 1998—), German Soc. Fat Sci. (pres. 1998-2000). Avocations: mountaineering, music. Office: Univ Munster Dept Biochem, Wilhelm-Klemm-Str 2, D-48149 Münster Germany

SPENNEMANN, DIRK HEINRICH RUDOLPH, archeologist, cultural heritage administrator; b. Bonn, Germany, Jan. 28, 1958; arrived in Australia, 1993, citizen, 1996; MA, Johann Wolfgang Goethe U., Frankfurt, Germany, 1982; PhD, Australian Nat. U., 1990. Archaeologist Alele Mus., Majuro, Marshall Islands, 1989-90; chief archaeologist Govt. of Marshall Islands, 1990-92; lectr. Charles Sturt U., Albury, Australia, 1993-95, sr. lectr., 1996—; cons. and lectr. in field. Author 11 books; contbr. 1117articles to profl. jours. NCP grantee, 1993, 95-96, CAUT Gmat, 1993, recipient Tchg. Excellence award Charles Sturt U., 1995, AVCC Electron Public Grant, 1995-96, Rsch. Excellence award, 1996, Riverina Acad. Scis., 1996. Office: Charles Sturt U., Off Old Sydney Rd NSW, 2640 Albury Australia

SPERANZA, LINDA M., art educator, artist; b. Hoboken, N.J., May 31, 1953; d. Hubert A. and Emma L. Speranza; m. James Hourihan, Apr. 10, 1987 (dec. Apr. 20, 1987). BFA, SUNY, Alfred, 1975; MFA, Ariz. State U., 1983. Faculty Mesa (Ariz.) Cmty. Coll., 1984—; faculty assoc. Ariz. State U., Tempe, 1988, 90; pres. Solid Concepts, An Ariz. Corp., Tempe, 1997—, DBC Equipment, Inc., Tempe, 1997—. Works published in Working with Clay, Smashing Glazes. Project dir. The Many Faces of HIV/AIDS, Mesa, 1999-2000; organizer Empty Bowl Charity to Feed the Homeless, Mesa, 1996-2000. Recipient Gov.'s award for the arts Ariz. Commn. on the Arts, 1984. Mem. Nat. Coun. on Edn. in the Ceramic Arts, Am. Driving Soc., Am. Morgan Horse Club, Ariz. Driving and Carriage Soc. (pres. 1994-97, 2000—). Avocations: raising Morgan horses, carriage driving. E-mail: linda.speranza@mcmail.maricopa.edu. Office: Mesa CC 1833 W Southern Ave Mesa AZ 85202-4822

SPERBER, DANIEL, physicist; b. Vienna, Austria, May 8, 1930; came to U.S., 1955, naturalized, 1967; s. Emanuel and Nelly (Lieberman) S.; m. Ora Yuval, Nov. 29, 1963; 1 son, Ron Emanuel. M.Sc., Hebrew U., 1954; Ph.D., Princeton U., 1960. Tng. and rsch. asst. Israel Inst. Tech., Haifa, 1954-55, Princeton U., 1955-60; sr. scientist, rsch. adviser Ill. Inst. Tech. Rsch. Inst., Chgo., 1960-67; assoc. prof. physics Ill. Inst. Tech., 1964-67, Rensselaer Poly. Inst., Troy, N.Y., 1967-72; prof. Rensselaer Poly. Inst., 1972—; Nordita prof. Niels Bohr Inst., Copenhagen, 1973-74, NATO research fellow, vis., prof., 1974-77; vis. prof. G.S.I., Darmstadt, Fed. Republic Germany, 1983; sr. Fulbright research scholar, Saha Inst. Nuclear Physics, Calcutta, India, 1987-88. Contbr. over 100 sci. papers to profl. jours. Served to capt. Israeli Army, 1948-51. Fellow Am. Phys. Soc.; mem. Israel Phys. Soc., N.Y. Acad. Scis., Sigma Xi. Jewish. Home: 1 Taylor Ln Troy NY 12180-7162 Office: Rensselaer Poly Inst 110 8th St Dept Physics Troy NY 12180-3522

SPERBER, HELMUT, museum director; b. Munich, Nov. 22, 1937; s. Michael and Franziska (Doering) S.; m. Gerlinde Guerlich, June 1, 1962; children: Wolfgang, Reinhard, Monika. Diploma in econ. adminstrn., Bayerische Verwaltungsschule, Munich, 1961; grad. in european ethnology, U. Munich, 1977. Insp. Cmty. of Munich, 1961-65, chief insp., 1965-71; verwaltungsamtmann Bavarian Adminstrn. Acad., Munich, 1971-79; sci. employee Open Air Mus. Upper Bavaria, Grossweil, Fed. Republic Germany, 1979-82; cultural councillor, mus. referent Bezirk Schwaben, Augsburg, Fed. Republic Germany, 1982-86; cultural councillor, mus. referent, lectr., reader U. Munich, 1986—; mus. dir. Schwaebisches Volkskundemuseum Oberschoenenfeld; chief rsch. work Volkswagenwerk Found., Hannover, Fed. Republic Germany, 1979-82; lectr., reader Bavarian Adminstrn. Acad., 1969-79. Author books in field; contbr. articles to profl. jours. Roman Catholic. Avocations: ethnology, folklore, ergology, etymology. Home: Vinzenz-Schuepfer-Str 21, D-81475 Munich Germany Office: U Munich, Ludwigstr 25, D-80539 Munich Germany

SPERDUTO, HECTOR M., communication executive, consultant; b. Montevideo, Uruguay, Apr. 19, 1935; s. Pedro D. and Maria Teresa (Melillo) S.; m. Nilsa Valdez, Dec. 11, 1971; 1 child, Maria Laura. Diploma in engring., U. Montevideo, 1971; diploma, E.S.C.E.S., Ahmedabad, India, 1972, Kokusai Denshin Denwa, Tokyo, 1977. Asst. engr. Usinas y Telefonos del Estado, Montevideo, 1963-71; sect. chief Usinas y Telefonos del Estado/Antel, Montevideo, 1971-73; 2d chief transmission dept. Nat. Telecoms. Adminstrn., Montevideo, 1973-80, transmission dept. chief, 1980-84, transmission mgr., 1984-87, area mgr., 1987—; cons. TV sta., Montevideo, 1992-97. Author: Communications Via Satellite, 1986. Mem. IEEE (sr.), Uruguayan Assn. Engrs., CIDAE (collaborator engr.). Avocations: classical

and jazz music, travel, WWII, geometry. Home: Dr Alejandro Gallinal 1552, 11400 Montevideo Uruguay Office: Antel # 1534 5o Piso, Ave De Fernandez Crespo, 11200 Montevideo Uruguay

SPERELAKIS, NICHOLAS, SR., physiology and biophysics educator, researcher; b. Joliet, Ill., Mar. 3, 1930; s. James and Arestia (Kayadakis) S.; m. Dolores Martinis, Jan. 28, 1960; children: Nicholas Jr., Mark, Christine, Sophia, Thomas, Anthony. BS in Chemistry, U. Ill., 1951, MS in Physiology, 1955, PhD in Physiology, 1957. Teaching asst. U. Ill., Urbana, 1954-57; instr. Case Western Res. U., Cleve., 1957-59, asst. prof., 1959-66, assoc. prof., 1966; prof. U. Va., Charlottesville, 1966-83; Joseph Eichberg prof. physiology Coll. Medicine U. Cin., 1983-96, chmn. dept., 1983-93, Eichberg prof. emeritus, 1996—; cons. NPS Pharm., Inc., Salt Lake City, 1988-95, Carter Wallace, Inc. Cranbury, N.J., 1988-91; vis. prof. U. St. Andrews, Scotland, 1972-73, U. San Luis Potosi, Mex., 1986, U. Athens, Greece, 1994; Rosenblueth prof. Centro de Investigacion y Avanzades, Mex., 1972; mem. sci. adv. com. several internat. meetings, editorial bd. numerous sci. jours. Co-editor: Handbook of Physiology: Heart, 1979; editor: Physiology and Pathophysiology of the Heart, 1984, 2d edit., 1988, 3rd edit., 1994, 4th edit., 2000, Calcium Antagonists: Mechanisms of Action on Cardiac Muscle and Vascular Smooth Muscle, 1984, Cell Interactions and Gap Junctions, vols. I and II, 1989, Frontiers in Smooth Muscle Research, 1990, Ion Channels in Vascular Smooth Muscle and Endothelial Cells, 1991, Essentials of Physiology, 1993, 2d edit., 1996, Cell Physiology Source Book, 1995 (Outstanding Acad. Book, Choice Am. Libr. Assn. 1996, 98), 3d edit., 2000, Electrogenesis of Biopotentials, 1995; assoc. editor Circulation Rsch., 1970-75, Molecular Cellular Cardiology; contbr. articles to profl. jours. Lectr. Project Hope, Peru, 1962. Sgt. USMC, 1951-53, Res., 1953-59. Recipient Disting. Alumnus award Rockdale (Ill.) Pub. Schs., 1958; U. Cin. Grad. fellow, 1989; NIH grantee, 1959-99. Mem. Am. Physiol. Soc. (chair steering com. sect. 1981-82), Biophys. Soc. (coun. 1990-93), Am. Soc. Pharmacology and Exptl. Therapeutics, Internat. Soc. Heart Rsch. (coun. 1980-89, 92-98), Am. Hellenic Ednl. Progressive Assn. (pres. Charlottesville chpt. 1980-82), Ohio Physiol. Soc. (pres. 1990-91), Phi Kappa Phi. Independent. Greek Orthodox. Avocations: ancient coins, stamp collecting. Office: U Cin Coll Medicine 231 Bethesda Ave Cincinnati OH 45229-2827

SPERLICH, DIETHER, biology educator; b. Vienna, Jan. 15, 1929; s. Karl and Maria (Sperlich) S.; m. Eva Sebek, June 26, 1957; children: Guenther, Monika, Martin, Klaus. PhD, U. Vienna, 1952; Hon. Doctoral Degree, U. Oulu, Finland, 1994. Asst. prof. biology U. Vienna, 1955-63; guest investigator The Rockefeller Inst., N.Y.C., 1964; assoc. prof. biology U. Tuebingen, Germany, 1971-75, prof., head dept. population genetics, 1976-97; hon. prof. U. Salzburg, Austria, 1982—. Author: Populationsgenetik, 1973, 2d edit., 1988; co-author: Beiträge zur Evolutionstheorie, 1980, Biologie fuer Medizinen, 1995; editor Jour. Zool. Sys. Evol. Rsch. Recipient Th. Koerner award Koerner Found., 1960-64, Kardinal Initzer Preis, Archdiocese of Vienna, 1967. Fellow Deutsche Zoologische Gesellschaft, Gesellschaft für Genetik, European Soc. Evolutionary Biology; mem. Finnish Acad. Sci. (corr. mem.). Roman Catholic. Avocations: music, mountains. Home: Goesstrasse 82, Tuebingen D72070, Germany Office: Biologisches Inst U Tuebingen, Auf der Morgenstelle 28, Tuebingen D72076, Germany

SPERLICH, THOMAS, journalist, consultant; b. Deggendorf, Bavaria, Germany, Aug. 16, 1956; s. Rudolf S. and Anita (Patzke) Lueras. Producer, author Die Tageszeitung, Berlin, 1979-88; mgr. Biofeedback Studio Relax, Berlin, 1988-90; pub. rels. mgr. Megabrain, Hamburg, Germany, 1990-92; freelance journalist, cons. Gruenwald, 1992—; mem. consultancy group for the virtual reality demonstration ctrs., Fraunhofer Soc., 1994—. Co-author: (book) The Virtual Reality Casebook, 1994, Virtual Reality-Scheinwelten der dritten Dimension. Avocations: body exercises, reading, cinema, travel. Home and Office: Auf Der Eierwiese 14, Gruenwald 82031, Germany

SPERLING, MICHAEL, chemist; b. Hamburg, Germany, Mar. 5, 1954; s. Walter and Emmy (Grimm) S.; m. Jocelyne Diolez, Sept. 3, 1988. Diploma, U. Hamburg, 1982, PhD of Chemistry, 1986. Postdoctoral fellow U. Hamburg, 1986-87; rschr. Bodenseewerk Perkin-Elmer, Ueberlingen, Germany, 1987—. Inventor in field; co-author: Atomic Absorption Spectrometry, 1997. Mem. Soc. Applied Spectroscopy. Office: Bodenseewerk Perkin-Elmer, PO Box 101761, Überlingen D-88647, Germany

SPERLING, SCOTT EDWARD, software consultant, Bible expositor; b. Tucson, Jan. 11, 1961; s. Fritz Eric and Ruth Ann S.; m. Moon Hee, March 16, 1985; children: Scott Edward, Charlotte Moon. BSc in Applied Physics, Calif. Inst. Tech., Pasadena, 1983; BSc in Info. Computer Sci., U. Calif., Irvine, 1985. Software engr. Interstate Electronics, Anaheim, Calif., 1985-87, Hughes Aircraft, Fullerton, Calif., 1987-88; software cons. Hughes Aircraft, Azusa, Calif., 1991-92; software engr. Librascope Corp., Glendale, Calif., 1988-91; software cons. Litton Guidance & Control Sys., Woodland Hills, Calif., 1993—; prin., owner Scripture Studies Inc., SSper Inc., Foothill Ranch, Calif., 1994—, 1997—. Author, editor Scripture Studies, 1994—. Avocations: music, literature. E-mail: ssper@aol.com. Home and Office: Scripture Studies Inc 20 Pastora Foothill Rnch CA 92610-1730

SPEROS, MARTHA CHRIS, mathematics and science educator; b. Kolindros, Greece, Apr. 18, 1936; came to U.S., 1956; d. Costas Elia and Zachary Elia and Zachary Eleni (Glekos) Siopaulos; m. Spyro William Speros, Oct. 30, 1960 (dec. Nov. 1974); children: Polyxena Chrysanthy, William Spyro. BA in Math., Villa Maria Coll., Erie, Pa., 1960; MEd, Gannon U., Erie, 1977. Tchr. chemistry Villa Maria Coll., Erie, 1960-65; tchr. math. Wattsburg (Pa.) H.S., 1963-65, Millcreek Sch. Dist. Westlake, Erie, 1965—; dept. chairperson math. dept. Westlake Sch., Erie, 1968-74, student coun. advisor, 1974-99; dist. 1 dir. 6 counties, Erie, 1974-96; PASC workshop dir. Grove City (Pa.) Coll., 1985-99. Sustaining mem. Rep. Nat. Com., Erie, 1996-99; mem. Erie Play House, 1984-99; pres. St. Nicholas Orthodox Ch., Erie, 1990-99; mem. state exec. bd. Pa. Assn. Student Coun., 1976—. Mem. AAUW, Delta Sigma. Avocations: golf, travel, mathematics coach, stock market game coach. E-Mail: Speros@trojan.MMTSD.org. Home: 840 Donation Rd Erie PA 16509-5305 Office: Millcreek Twp Sch Dist 3740 W 26th St Erie PA 16506-2039

SPERRIN, MALCOLM WILLIAM, medical physicist, researcher; b. Havana, Cuba, Feb. 4, 1963; parents Brit. citizens; s. Roy William and Joan Mary (Bates) S. BSc with honors, U. Reading, Eng., 1984, MPhil, 1994; PhD, U. Cranfield, Eng., 2000. Software engr. Marconi, Camberly, Eng., 1984-85; reactor engr. Ukaea, Warrington, Eng., 1985-86; spectroscopist V.G. Sci., East Grinstead, Eng., 1986-88; sr. physicist Churchill Hosp., Oxford, Eng., 1990-94; prin. physicist Princess Margaret Hosp., Swindon, Eng., 1995—; cons. Open U., Milton Keynes, 1997—; chmn. Emerging Tech. Spl. Interest Group, 1997—; mem. Brit. Standards Com. on Labor Safety, 1996—; mem. Brit. Standards Com. on Med. Device Risk Mgmt., 1996—. Contbr. articles to profl. jours.; inventor in field. Anglican. Avocations: mountain sports, caving, canoeing. Office: Princess Margaret Hosp, Dept Med Physics, Swindon SN1 4JU, England

SPERRY, LEN THOMAS, psychiatrist and preventive medicine educator; b. Milw., Dec. 1, 1943; s. Leonard V. and Wanda R. (Sadowski) S.; m. Patricia L. Garcia, June 11, 1977; children: Tracey, Christen, L. Timothy, Steven, Jonathon. BA, St. Mary's U. Minn., Winona, Minn., 1966; PhD, Northwestern U., 1970; MD, U. Cen. Technol. Studies, Dominican Republic, 1981. Diplomate Am. Bd. Profl. Psychology, Am. Bd. Psychiatry and Neurology, Am. Bd. Preventive Medicine. Asst. prof. Marquette U., Milw., 1971-74; assoc. prof. U. Wis., Milw., 1974-75, U.S. Internat. U., San Diego, 1976-78; resident in psychiatry and preventive medicine Med. Coll. Wis., Milw., 1982-85; fellow in behavioral medicine U. Wis. Med. Sch., Milw., 1984-85; assoc. prof. psychiatry, preventive medicine Med. Coll. Wis., Milw., 1986-92, prof., 1992-2000, prof. cmty. and family medicine, 1998-2000, vice chair dept. psychiatry, 1997-2000; prof. health adminstrn. Barry Univ., Miami Shores, Fla., 2000—; cons.. dir. Staff Devel. Am. Appraisal Assn., Milw., 1972-76. Author: Learning Performance and Individual Differences, 1972, Contract Counseling, 1974, You Can Make It Happen: Self-Actualization and Organization, 1977, Together Experience, 1978, Aderian Counseling and Psychotherapy, 1987, Psychiatric Case Formulations, 1992, Psychopathology and Psychotherapy, 1993, 2nd edit., 1996, Psychiatric Consultation in the Workplace, 1993, Handbook of Diagnosis and Treatment of DSM-IV Personality Disorders, 1995, Psychopharmacology and Psychotherapy, 1995, Treatment Outcomes in Psychotherapy and Psychiatric Interventions, 1996, Aging in the 21st Century, 1996, Family Therapy: Ensuring Treatment Efficacy, 1997, The Disordered Couple, 1997, The Intimate Couple, 1998, Brief Therapy Strategies with Individuals and Couples, 2000, Ministry and Community, 2000, Integrative and Biopsychosocial Therapies, 2000 ; contbr. articles to profl. jours. Bd. dirs. Am. Coun. on Sci. and Health, Nat. Acad. for Certified Family Therapists, St. Camillus Health Ctr., 1996—. Northwestern U. fellow, 1969, Med. Coll. Wis. grantee, 1981. Fellow APA (Harry Levinson award 1998), Am. Psychiat. Assn. (chair com. on psychiatry in workplace 1998—), Am. Coll. Preventive Medicine, Am. Coll. Psychiatrists, Am. Bd. Profl. Psychology, Am. Bd. Psychiatry and Neurology, Acad. Orgnl. and Occupational Psychiatry (v.p. 1993-96, Alan McLean lifetime achievement award 2000), Group for Advancement of Psychiatry, Coalition for Family Diagnosis. Avocations: reading, racquet sports, music. Office: Barry Univ 11300 NE Second Ave Miami FL 33161

SPETH, GERALD LENNUS, education and business consultant; b. Logan, Utah, July 14, 1934; s. Fredrick William and Elizabeth LaVern (Nuttall) S.; m. Dora Goff, Aug. 11, 1955; children: Camille, Michael Gerald, Mark Alan, Janell, Doreen. BS, Utah State U., 1956; MBA, Ind. U., 1969; EdD, Ball State U., 1988. Auditor Ernst & Ernst, Salt Lake City, 1956, 58-59; officer 1st and 2d lt. U.S. Army, 1956-58, officer capt. to col., 1959-82; controller Columbia Club, Indpls., 1982-83; sr. v.p. Allied Fidelity Corp., Indpls., 1983-85; adj. faculty Ind. Cen. U., Indpls., 1982-85; prof., dir. grad. bus. progs. U. Indpls., 1985—; cons. in mgmt. and strategic planning. Counselor in stake presidency, bishop, welfare dir., mission pres., high councilor LDS Ch., 1965—. Recipient Legion of Merit, 1971-80, Bronze Star medal, 1966. Mem. Am. Soc. Mil. Comptrollers, U.S. Govt. Accts. Assn., Beta Gamma Sigma, Sigma Iota Epsilon, Alpha Kappa Psi, Kappa Delta Psi, Delta Mu Delta. Home: 8337 Goldfinch Cir Indianapolis IN 46256-1629 Office: U Indpls 1400 E Hanna Ave Indianapolis IN 46227-3630

SPETH, JAMES GUSTAVE, dean, environmental studies educator, lawyer; b. Orangeburg, S.C., Mar. 4, 1942; s. James Gustave and Amelia St. Clair (Albergotti) S.; m. Caroline Cameron Council, July 3, 1965; children: Catherine Council, James Gustave, Charles Council. BA summa cum laude, Yale U., 1964, LLB, 1969; MLitt, Oxford U., 1966; LLD (hon.), Clark U., 1995. Bar: D.C. 1969. Law clk. to Justice Hugo L. Black U.S. Supreme Ct., 1969-70; sr. staff atty. Natural Resources Def. Council, Washington, 1970-77; mem. Council Environ. Quality, Washington, 1977-79, chmn., 1979-81; prof. law Georgetown U. Law Ctr., Washington, 1981-82; pres. World Resources Inst., Washington, 1982-93; adminstr. UN Devel. Program, N.Y.C., 1993-99; dean, prof. Yale Sch. Forestry and Environ. Studies Yale U., 1999—; founded World Resources Inst.; organized Western Hemisphere Dialogue environ. and devel., 1990; chaired U.S. Task Force internat. devel. and environ. security. Contbr. articles to profl. jours.; speaker in field. Bd. dirs. World Resources Inst., Nat. Resources Def. Coun., Woods Hole Rsch. Ctr., Keystone Ctr., Leadership award 1994. Recipient Resources Def. award Nat. Wildlife Fedn., 1976, Barbara Swain award of honor Nat. Resources Coun. Am., 1992, Environ. Law Inst. Lifetime Achievement award, 1999; named to Global 500 Honor Role United Nations Environ. Program, 1988; Rhodes scholar, 1964-66. Mem. Coun. on Fgn. Rels. (N.Y.C.). Episcopalian. Home: 88 Mulberry Farms Rd Guilford CT 06437-3215

SPETH, JOSEF, physicist; b. Kisslegg, Germany, May 16, 1938; s. Josef and Maria (Binzer) S.; m. Irmgard Edel, 1965; children: Gabriele, Michael, Christoph. PhD, Tech. U., Munich, 1968; prof. honoris causa, Inst. Nuc. Physics, Krakow, Poland, 1998. Rsch. assoc. Tech. U. Munich, 1965-69, asst. prof., 1969-72; assoc. prof. U. Bonn, Germany, 1972-82, prof. physics, 1982—; acting dir. KFA, Jülich, Germany, 1979-82; dir. Forschungszentrum Julich/Inst. for Kernphysik, Jülich, 1982—; vis. prof. SUNY at Stony Brook, 1975; vis. staff mem. Jefferson Lab., Newport News, 1996. Editor: Physics at Kaon, 1990, Electric and Magnetic Giant Resonances in Nuclei, 1991; contbr. articles to profl. jours. Ablett fellow U. Johannesburg, 1991, Murdock fellow U. Wash., 1991, Disting. fellow Found. for Rsch. Devel. South Africa, 1995; named prof. honoris causa, Inst. Nuclear Physics, Krakow, Poland, 1998. Mem. Lions Club Internat. (pres. 1993-94). Achievements include research on nuclear, particle and theoretical physics. Home: Fliederweg 4, 52428 Jülich Germany Office: KFA Inst for Kernphysik, 52425 Jülich Germany

SPETZGER, UWE, neurosurgeon; b. Karlsruhe, Germany, June 9, 1962; m. Hans and Elisabeth (Richter) S.; m. Martina Karoline Scheurer, Aug. 26, 1994. Medical examination, U. Heidelberg, 1989; FMGEMS, ECFMG, 1990. Intern Dept. Neurosurgery, Aachen, Germany, 1990-94, sr., 1994-96, asst. prof., 1996-99; prof., vice chmn. Dept. Neurosurgery U. Freiburg, Germany, 1999—; examination of neurosurgery, Düsseldorf, 1997, European exam of neurosurgery, 1999. Editor (book): Navigated Brain Surgery; contbr. articles to profl. jours. Mem. German Soc. of Neurosurgery, European Spine Soc., Congress of Neurosurgeons. Roman Catholic. Office: Dept of Neurosurgery, Breisacher Str 64, D-79106 Freiburg Germany

SPEVACEK, JIRI, physicist, chemist; b. Benesov u Prahy, Czech Republic, Sept. 4, 1946; s. Josef and Marie (Schneiderova) S.; m. Gabriela Lamosova, June 21, 1975. MSc, Charles U., Prague, 1968, Rerum Naturalium Doctoris, 1974, PhD, 1974; DSc, Czechoslovak Acad. Sci., Prague, 1990. Rsch. worker Inst. Macromolecular Chemistry, Czechoslovak Acad. Sci., Prague, 1974-79, sr. rsch. worker, 1979-84, chief rsch. worker, 1985—, head dept. vibrational and NMR spectroscopy, 1984-97, head Ctrl. Lab. of Solid State NMR, 1987—; postdoctoral rsch. assoc. Carnegie-Mellon U., Pitts., 1979-80; mem. bd. for math. and phys. scis. Grant Agy. of Acad. of Scis. of the Czech Republic, 1996-99. Contbr. articles to profl. jours. Recipient prize Czechoslovak Acad. Scis., 1991; grantee Agy. of Czech Republic, 1996-98, Acad. Scis. of Czech Republic, 1991-93, 96-98, Czech Republic Ministry of Edn. Youth and Sports, 1997—. Mem. Groupement AMPERE, Soc. Czech Mathematicians and Physicists, Czech Chem. Soc. Avocations: travel, recreational activities, music. Home: Egyptska 648, 160 00 Prague 6, Czech Republic Office: Acad Scis of Czech Rep Inst Macromolecular Chem, Heyrovsky sq 2, 162 06 Prague 6, Czech Republic

SPEYRER, JUDE, bishop; b. Leonville, La., Apr. 14, 1929. Ed., St. Joseph Sem., Covington, La., Notre Dame Sem., New Orleans, Gregorian U., Rome. Ordained priest Roman Cath. Ch., 1953. Consecrated bishop Lake Charles, La., 1980—. Office: PO Box 3223 414 Iris St Lake Charles LA 70602-5234

SPICER, HAROLD OTIS, retired English educator, communications educator; b. Gosport, Ind., Dec. 10, 1921; s. Otis R. and Hattie Grace (Wampler) S.; m. Hilda Jane Templeton, June 12, 1946 (dec. Nov. 1994); children: Sherry Lynne (dec. May 1987), Sylvia Jean, Stephen Michael, Zachary Ian. BA, DePauw U., 1947, MA, 1949; PhD, Ind. U., 1962. Instr. English DePauw U., Greencastle, Ind., 1947-49, asst. prof. English, 1957-63; from instr. to prof. English We. Ill. U., Macomb, 1949-57; adj. prof. English Ind. U., Indpls., 1960-63; assoc. prof. to prof. English Ind. State U., Terre Haute, 1963-85; ret., 1985; sec. Main Street, Greencastle, 1983-95. Author: Covered Bridges of Putnam County, 1989, Organizational Handbook for Council on Aging, 1989 (Ameritech Tchr. Vol. award 1989), James Whitcomb Riley: Hoosier Poet, 1993; co-author: DePauw: Pictorial History, 1987. Pres. Ret. Tchrs. Putnam County, Greencastle, 1988-90, Putnam County Coun. on Aging, 1990-96 (Man of Yr. award 1994); bd. dirs. Heritage Preservation Soc., Greencastle, 1993—, Putnam County Found., 1995—; pres. West Ctrl. Ind. Area Agy. on Aging, 2000. Recipient Man of Yr. award Area 7 Agy. on Aging West Ctrl. Ind. Econ. Devel. Dist., Terre Haute, 1994; named Older Hoosier of Yr. Ind. Gov.'s Conf., Indpls., 1994, RSVP Vol. of Yr., 1995, Ameritech Vol. Tchr. of Yr., 1989, Martin H. Miller Vol. of Yr. award Ind. Family and Social Svcs. Adminstrn., 1999, Outstanding Leadership award in area/agy. on aging Ind. Assn. Area Agys. on Aging, 2000. Life mem. VFW; mem. Am. Legion, Am. Assn. Retired Persons (pres. Putnam County chpt. 1995-96, 99—), Greencastle C. of C. (Putnam County Citizen of Yr. 1996, bd. dirs. 1995-99), West Ctrl. Ind. Civil War Roundtable (v.p. 1998-99), Kiwanis Club Greencastle. Avocations: music, writing, travel. Home: 706 Highwood Ave Greencastle IN 46135-1420

SPICER, LANCE STANLEY KEITH, writer; b. Sydney, NSW, Australia, June 29, 1960; s. Keith Samuel Spicer and Yvonne Olga (Hudson) Williamson; m. Valeria Ellen Gorczynski, June 5, 1982; 1 child, Andrew Lance Stanley. Commerce (acctg.) cert., Sydney Tech. Coll., 1982. Chief acct. Hooker Corp., Sydney, 1980-84; co. sec. Austral, Sydney, 1984-85; gen. mgr. Security Mailing, Sydney, 1985-87; cons. Sydney, 1988-91; fin. contr. Mirvac Ltd., Sydney, 1991-94; author Sydney, 1994—; dir. Trident Press Pty. Ltd., Sydney, 1995—; spkr. in field. Author: The Invisible World, 1995 (Best Seller 1998), Invisible Banking, 1997, Going Out On Your Own, 1998, High Yield Investments, 1998 (Best Seller 1999), For We Are Young and Free, 1998, Investing to Win, 1999, High Yield Investments 2, 1999, Underground Knowledge, 1999, Future Wealth, 2000. Anglican. Avocations: traveling, reading, political debate, economics. Office: Trident Press Pty Ltd, PO Box 68, Bangor NSW 2234, Australia

SPICER, RONALD L., financial services educator; b. Louisville, Jan. 21, 1949; s. Robert Joseph and Ann (Stafford) S.; m. Joan E. Vining, Dec. 20, 1969 (div. June 1988); children: Jennifer Joan Spicer McMullen, Ronald Geoffrey; m. JoAnn F. Snyder, Feb. 18, 1989; 1 child, Veronica Michelle. BS in Psychology and Sociology, Carroll Coll., 1971; MA in Orgn. Mgmt., U. Phoenix, 1997; MBA in Bus., Regis U., 1999; postgrad., Capella Univ. CPCU, CLU, CHFC, ARM. V.p. sales Alexander & Alexander, Atlanta, 1982-88; exec. v.p. Powell and Co., Atlanta, 1988-89; v.p. sales Corroon and Black, Balt., 1989-90; broker, owner Profl. Ins. Brokers, York, Pa., 1990-93; sr. account exec. Hilb, Rogal and Hamilton, Denver, 1993-95; ins. program coord. Pikes Peak C.C., Colorado Springs, 1995-97; pres., CEO Peak Profl. Svcs., Inc., Colorado Springs, 1997—, owner, 1997—; adv. com. Ins. Inst. of Am., Malvern, Pa., 1995—; mem. next generation com., Life and Health Ins. Edn. Assn., N.Y.C., 1996-97. Author: (book) Colorado P&C PreLicense Course, 1998, Colorado Life and Health Pre-License Course, 1999; contbr. articles to profl. jours. Mem. Soc. CPCU (pres. 1998-99), Soc. CLU/CHFC (v.p. 1998-99, pres. 2000—), Optimist (pres. Uptown Club 1979-81), Masons. Republican. Episcopal. Avocations: skiing, camping, scuba diving. Office: Peak Profl Svcs Inc PO Box 2013 Colorado Springs CO 80901-2013

SPICER, TIM SIMON, broadcasting executive, retired military officer; b. U.K., Dec. 10, 1952; s. James and Wendy (Matthews) S.; m. Carline Merton, Oct., 1995; 1 child, Sam. Lt. col., Scots Guards Brit. Army, 1976-94; ret., 1994; CEO Sandline Internat., London, 1996—. Author: Unorthodox Soldier; contbr. articles to newspapers, including the London Times, the Spectator. Recipient Order of the Brit. Empire. Mem. Cavalry and Guards Club. Avocations: art and antique collecting, skiing, boating, martial arts. Office: c/o Plaza 107, 535 Kings Rd, London SW10 0SZ, England

SPICHAK, VJACHESLAV VALENTINOVICH, science administrator; b. Tbilisi, Georgia, USSR, Sept. 10, 1950; s. Valentin Michailovich and Varvara Aleksandrovna (Zamitskaya) S.; m. Tatiana Vladimirovna Zhuk, July 17, 1971; 1 child, Alex. BSc in Computer Sci., Inst. Mgmt., Moscow, 1971; MSc in Physics, Inst. Physics & Technics, Moscow, 1973; Candidate Sci. in Geophysics, Inst. Earth Magnetism, Ionosphere and Radio Wave Propagation, Troitsk, Russia, 1983; DSc in Geophysics, Inst. Physics of the Earth, Moscow, 1997. Engbr. United Energy Sys. of the USSR, Moscow, 1973-79; rschr. Inst. Earth Magnetism, Ionosphere and Radio Wave Propagation, Troitsk, 1979-89, sr. rschr., 1989-92; chief lab. Geoelectromagnetic Rsch. Inst., Troitsk, 1992-98, vice dir., 1998-99, dir., 1999—; vice-dir. Geophys. Rsch. Ctr., Moscow, 1989-92, dir., 1992—; vis. prof. U. Paris Sud, Orsay, France, 1994-96, U. Federico II, Napoli, Italy, 1998. Author: Magnetotelluric Fields in 3D Geoelectrical Models, 1999; co-author: Mathematical Modeling of EM-Fields in 3D Inhomogeneous Media, 1992; guest editor A Multi-Disciplinary Study of Volcanoes, 2000. Commn. mem. Supreme Coun. Russia, Moscow, 1991-92. Named winner sci. competition Acad. Scis. of the USSR, Moscow, 1989; grantee Russian Basic rsch. Found., Moscow, 1994, 99, Oyo Co., Japan, 1995. Mem. Internat. Assn. Volcanology, Chemistry of the Earth Interior, Russian Acad. Nat. Scis., N.Y. Acad. Scis. Achievements include inventor of method of electroprospecting. Avocations: playing piano, chess, photography, musical records, collecting teaspoons. E-mail: v.spichak@g23.relcom.ru. Office: Geoelectromagnetic Rsch, PO Box 30, 142190 Troitsk Moscow Region, Russia

SPIEGEL, ELWYN, advertising agency executive, creative director; b. N.Y.C., Apr. 26, 1926; s. Morris and Rose Ann (Nemetzky) S.; m. Doris Kay, Apr. 25, 1954 (dec.); children: Elizabeth Ann Simendinger, Susan Gail Ambrose, Laura Faith Ciecierski. BSEE, N.C. State U., 1945; BS in Econs., Columbia U., 1950. Pres. Ad Infinitum, Inc., Hackensack, N.J., 1954-63; exec. v.p. Alden Advt. Agy., N.Y.C., 1964-81; pres. Spiegel/Labatt-Simon, Inc., N.Y.C., 1981-88, Compris, Inc., N.Y.C., 1989-96, Elwyn Spiegel & Ptnrs., N.Y.C., 1996—; cons. in field. creative dir. TV commls. including Colorforms, 1976 (Clio award 1976); mag. Russell Fabrics, 1981. Judge, Clio Awards, N.Y.C., 1975. Recipient Silver award, Neographics 1977, Addy (4), Am. Advt. Fedn., 1977-80, Desi (8), Graphics Design USA, 1981-82, Clio (3), Clio Adv. Bd., 1981. Mem. Nat. Trust for Hist. Preservation, Kiwanis (pres. 1954-55), Alpha Delta Sigma. Avocations: photography, music, sports cars, literature, writing. Office: Elwyn Spiegel & Ptnrs 325 E 41st St New York NY 10017-5955

SPIEGEL, GERALD MARTIN, electrical engineer, computer scientist; b. Kehl, Baden, Germany, Apr. 29, 1966; s. Heinz and Lucie (Bartsch) S.; m. Beate Höger, June 11, 1993; children: Nina Simone, Annika Kristin. Diploma, U. Karlsruhe, Germany, 1991, PhD, 1995. Rsch. asst. Inst. Computer Sci. and Fault Tolerance, U. Karlsruhe, 1992-95; project mgr. Digitaltest GmbH, Stutensee, Germany, 1995-97; develop. engr. Siemens AG, Karlsruhe, Germany, 1997-98; info. tech. cons. SerCon GmbH, Frankfurt, Germany, 1998—. Author: Bestimmung möglicher Fabrikationsfehler aus dem Schaltungslayout, 1995. Mem. Social Democratic Party. Avocations: sports, art, literature.

SPIEGEL, WOLFGANG, mathematics educator; b. Berlin, Jan. 15, 1944; s. Kurt Ernst and Elfriede (Schmitz) S.; m. Sigrid Paul, July 24, 1969; children: Marcus, Ulrike. Dipl. Math., Free U. Berlin, Fed. Republic Germany, 1968. Dr. rer. nat., 1970, Habilitation, 1975. Asst., Free U. Berlin, 1968-71, asst. prof., 1971-75; dozent Bergische Universitä t GHS Wuppertal, Fed. Republic Germany, 1976-79, apl. prof., 1979-80, prof. math., 1980—. Co-author: Schülerduden Mathematik II, 1982. Contbr. articles to math. jours. Mem. Berliner Mathematische Gesellschaft, Deutsche Mathematiker Vereinigung, Am. Math. Soc. Mem. Evangelical Ch. Office: Bergische U GHS Wuppertal M, Gauss Str 20, 42097 Wuppertal Germany

SPIEKHOUT, JAN, head corporate inspection and material expertise; b. Wieuwerd, The Netherlands, Dec. 15, 1954. B, Tech. Coll., Groningen, The Netherlands, 1976; M, Tech. U., Delft, The Netherlands, 1981. Civil engr. SIPM, The Hague, The Netherlands, 1981-83; material and construction cons. Gasunie, Groningen, The Netherlands, 1983-86, rsch. mgr., 1986-89, head pipeline and mech. engring., 1989-94, head corp. inspection and material expertise, 1994—; mem. nat. and internat. standardization and legis. instns. on pipelines; active Commn. Pipelines Dutch Transp. Safety Bd. Contbr. articles to profl. jours. Mem. European Pipeline Rsch. Group (asst. sec. gen.), Royal Inst. Engrs., Royal Inst. Gas Frbricators. Avocations: history, trains, skating. Home: Hoofdweg 115 C, 9761 ED Eelde-Paterswolde The Netherlands Office: NV Nederlandse Gasunie, PO Box 19 Concourslaan 17, 9700 MA 9700 MA Groningen The Netherlands

SPIELBERG, STEVEN, motion picture director, producer; b. Cin., Dec. 18, 1946; m. Amy Irving, Nov. 27, 1985 (div.); 2 children: Max Samuel, Sasha; m. Kate Capshaw; 1 dau. BA, Calif. State Coll., Long Beach; Hon. Doctorate in Creative Arts, Brandeis U., 1986. Founder Amblin Entertainment (Universal Studios), Dreamworks SKG (with Jeffrey Katzenberg and David Geffen); directed segments of TV series Columbo; dir. TV movies Night Gallery, 1969, Duel, 1971, Savage, 1972, Something Evil, 1972; exec prodr. series: Steven Spielberg's Amazing Stories, Tiny Toon Adventures, Family Dog, seaQuest DSV; films include (dir.): The Sugarland Express, 1974 (also story), Jaws, 1975, Close Encounters of the Third Kind, 1977 (also co-writer), 1941, 1979, Raiders of the Lost Ark, 1981, Indiana Jones and the Temple of Doom, 1984, Indiana Jones and the Last Crusade, 1989, Hook, 1991, Jurassic Park, 1993, Men in Black, 1996; (dir., prodr.): E.T. The Extra-Terrestrial, 1982, The Color Purple, 1985, Empire of the Sun, 1987, Always, 1989, Schindler's List, 1993 (Best Drama & Best Dir. Golden Globe awards, Best Picture & Best Dir. Acad. awards), Saving Private Ryan (Golden Clobe award for Best Dir. 1999, Best Director Academy Award

1998, nominee Best Picture Academy award 1999); (dir., exec. prodr.): Twilight Zone: The Movie, 1983; (prodr.): Poltergeist, 1982 (also co-writer), An American Tail: Fievel Goes West, 1991, Casper, 1995; (exec. prodr.): I Wanna Hold Your Hand, 1978, Used Cars, 1980, Continental Divide, 1981, Gremlins, 1984, The Goonies, 1985, Back to the Future, 1985, Young Sherlock Holmes, 1985, The Money Pit, 1986, An American Tail, 1986, Innerspace, 1987, *batteries not included, 1987, Who Framed Roger Rabbit?, 1988, The Land Before Time, 1988, Dad, 1989, Back to the Future Part II, 1989, Joe Verses the Volcano, 1990, Back to the Future Part III, 1990, Gremlins 2: The New Batch, 1990, Arachnophobia, 1990, Cape Fear, 1991, We're Back!: A Dinosaur's Story, 1993, The Flintstones, 1994, The Little Rascals, 1994, Balto, 1995, Twister, 1996, The Lost World, 1997, Amistad, 1997, Deep Impact, 1998, The Mask of Zorro, 1998, The Last Days, 1998; (T.V. series) Steven Spielberg Presents Toonsylvania, 1998; (actor): The Blues Brothers, 1980; exec. prodr.: Flintstones in Viva Rock Vegas, 1999, Band of Brothers, 1999, (TV series) The Unfinished Journey, 1999, Semper Fi, 2000. Recipient Man of Yr. award Hasty Pudding Theater, Harvard U., 1983, Outstanding Directorial Achievement award for feature films Dirs. Guild Am., 1985, Film award Brit. Acad. Film and TV Arts, 1986, Irving Thalberg Mem. award Acad. Motion Picture Arts and Scis., 1987, Golden Lion award for career achievement Venice Film Festival, 1993, Life Achievement award Am. Film Inst., 1995. Fellow Brit. Acad. Film and TV Arts. Achievements include winning film contest with 40-minute war movie, Escape to Nowhere, at age 13; made film Firelight at age 16, and made 5 films while in coll.; became TV dir. at Universal Pictures at age 20. Office: CAA 9830 Wilshire Blvd Beverly Hills CA 90212-1804

SPIELBÜCHLER, KARL, law educator; b. Bad Ischl, Upper-Austria, Sept. 27, 1939; s. Karl and Elfriede (Schäffer) S.; m. Michaela Pilz, Aug. 15, 1963; children: Julia, Hanna, Jörg. D in Law, U. Vienna, Austria, 1962; Venia Legendi, U. Linz, Austria, 1970. Cert. judge, 1966. Preparation for judge Upper Austria, 1963-66; judge Mühlviertel, 1966; asst. to law prof. Linz, 1967-70; prof. U. Linz, 1971-73, prof. civil law, labor law, 1973—; mem. constl. ct. Vienna, 1976—. Author: Der Dritte im Schuldverhältnis, 1973, Individualarbeitsrecht, 1976, 4th edit., 1998; co-author: Kommentar zum ABGB, 1983, 3d edit., 2000. Mem. Internat. Soc. Labour Law and Social Security (v.p. Austrian sect.); Internat. Commn. Juristes (Austrian sect.). Social-Democrat. Lutheran. Avocations: music, history. Home: Wolfauerstrasse 86, 4040 Linz Austria Office: U Linz, Altenbergerstrasse 69, 4040 Linz Austria

SPIELMAN, ANDREW IAN, biochemist; b. Tirgu Mures, Romania, June 23, 1950; arrived in Can., 1982; s. Joseph and Rachel S.; m. Kathy Szabó, Dec. 15, 1977; 1 child, Robert-Dan. DMD, U. Medicine and Pharmacy, Tirgu Mures, 1974; cert. specialist in oral surgery, Technion, Haifa, Israel, 1982; MSc, U. Toronto (Can.), 1985, PhD in Oral Biology and Biochemistry, 1988. Asst. mem. Monell Chem. Senses Ctr., Phila., 1988-89; clin. assoc. U. Pa. Sch. Dental Medicine, Phila., 1989-92; affiliate mem. Monell Chem. Senses Ctr., Phila., 1989—; prof. oral medicine and pathology NYU Coll. Dentistry, N.Y.C., 1996; assoc. dir. rsch. NYC Coll. Dentistry, N.Y.C., 1992-00, acting head basic sci. divsn., 1999—; presenter in field. Author: (with others) Encyclopedia of Human Biology, 1991; editor: Experimental Cell Biology of Taste and Olfaction, 1995; contbr. articles to Brain Rsch., Chem. Senses, Jour. Dental Rsch., Archives Oral Biology, Experientia, Physiology and Behavior, Am. Jour. Physiology, Jour. Chem. Ecology, Jour. Neurophysiology, Critical Rev. in Oral Medicine and Biology, Jour. of Biol. Chemistry, Biochemistry, Nature (Neurosci.), also procs. Republican fellow Univ. of Medicine and Pharmacy, Tirgu-Mures, 1972, U. Toronto Open fellow, 1983, Med. Rsch. fellow Med. Rsch. Coun. can., 1983-88. Mem. AAAS, Internat. Assn. for Dental Rsch., N.Y. Acad. Sci., Assn. for Chemoreception Scis., Am. Assn. Oral Biologists (bd. dirs. 1996-99, pres.-elect 1999—), Sigma Xi. Jewish. Achievements include research on the molecular basis of bitter taste mechanisms; on the interaction of saliva and taste; on identification of sweat-odor binding proteins in human axillary secretion. Office: NYU Coll of Dentistry 345 E 24th St New York NY 10010-4020

SPIES, HEINZ-JOACHIM, metallurgical engineer, educator; b. Frankfurt/Oder, Germany, June 25, 1934; s. Heinrich and Katharina (Duy) S.; m. Siegrun Eleonore Schnerrer, May 2, 1959; children: Cordula, Olaf-Torsten. Dipl.-Ing., Bergakademie, Freiberg, Germany, 1958, Dr.Ing., 1966, Dr.Ing.-habil., 1972. Engr. High Grade Steel Works, Freital, Germany, 1958-61, mgr. for quality control, 1961-65, mgr. rsch., 1965-74; prof. materials engring. Tech. U. Bergakademie, Freiberg, 1974—. Author: Behaviour of Non-Metallic Inclusions During Solidification and Deformation, 1968, 2d edit. 1971, Microsegregation During Solidification of Steel, 1972; co-author: Theory and Technology of Nitriding, 1990, Theory and Technology of Quenching, 1991, Testing of Materials, 1994; editor: Stories Above Steel, 1982, Production and Behaviour of Components, 1983, Mechanical Behaviour of High Strength Low Alloy Steels, 1984, Uncommon Properties of Common Metals, 1987; contbr. more than 230 articles to profl. jours. Trustee Fedn. Britannique des Alliances Francaises. Recipient Agricola medal Bergakademie Freiberg, 1959, Nat. award German Govt., Berlin, 1968. Mem. Verein Deutscher Eisenhüttenleute, Verein Deutscher Ingenieure, Deutsche Gesellschaft für Materialkunde, Deutscher Verband für Materialprüfung, Arbeitsgemeinschaft Wärmebehandlung und Werkstofftechnik. Avocations: gardening, wandering. Home: Bertolt-Brecht-Str 19, 09599 Freiberg Germany Office: Tech Univ Bergakademie, Gustav-Zeuner-Str 5, 09596 Freiberg Germany

SPIESS, HANS WOLFGANG, physical chemist; b. Frankfurt, Germany, Oct. 14, 1942. Diploma, U. Frankfurt, Fed. Republic Germany, 1966, PhD, 1968. Cert. phys. chemistry. Rsch. assoc. Fla. State U., Tallahassee, 1968-70, Max-Planck-Inst., Heidelberg, Fed. Republic Germany, 1970-75; rsch. assoc. U. Mainz, Fed. Republic Germany, 1975-78, prof. chemistry, 1978-80; prof. U. Münster, Fed. Republic Germany, 1981-82, U. Bayreuth, Fed. Republic Germany, 1983-84; dir. Max-Planck Inst. Polymer, Mainz, 1984—; pres. European Polymer Fedn., Strasbourg, France, 1991-92; mem. Sci. Coun. Germany. Contbr. over 300 rsch. articles to profl. publs. Recipient Leibniz award, Deutsche Forschungs-Gemeinschaft, Bonn, Fed. Republic Germany, 1988. Office: Max-Planck-Inst Polymer, PO Box 31 48, Mainz D-55021, Germany

SPIETH, MARTHA MAXWELL, writer; b. Washington, Apr. 30, 1923; d. Thomas F. and Jessie (Anderson) Orr; m. George A. Maxwell; children: Christine, George A., Barbara; m. Walter Spieth. BA, U. Md., 1946, MA, 1948, PhD, 1960. Dir. reading & study skills program, assoc. prof. edn. U. Md., College Park, 1958-66; acad. advisor, dir., mem. grad. faculty U. Calif. Student Learning Ctr., Berkeley, 1968-79. Author: Skimming and Scanning Skills, 1968, Improving Student Learning Skills, 1978, rev. edit., 1997, Evaluating Academic Skills Programs: A Sourcebook, 1991, 2d edit., 1996; editor: When Tutor Meets Student, 1994, From Access to Success: A Book of Readings on College Development Education and Learning Assistance Programs, 1994. Recipient Nat. Assn. of Developmental Educators Pub. awards, 1979, 97; NSF grantee, 1979. Fellow Am. Coun. Devel. Edn. Assn., Am. Psychol. Assn. Counseling; mem. Am. Men. Sci., Women of the South, Coll. Reading & Learning Assn. Avocations: biology, writing. Home: 322-4 Collington 10450 Lottsford Rd Mitchellville MD 20721-2734

SPIGA, MARCO, mechanical engineering educator; b. Bologna, Italy, Feb. 7, 1952; s. Alberto and Anna (Lazzari) S.; m. Alessandra Gualandi, June 27, 1981; 1 child, Federico. Degree in nuclear engring., U. Bologna, Italy, 1976. Rschr. U. Bologna, 1976-87, assoc. prof. mech. engring., 1987-99, prof. mech. engring., 1999—; cons. CEE, Brussels, 1986-90; mem. Eurotherm Com., 1986-96; mem. Tech. Com., Rome, 1988-95. Assoc. editor Internat. Jour. Heat and Tech, 1983; contbr. articles to sci. jours., including ASME Jour. Heat Transfer, Internat. Jour. Heat and Mass Transfer, Internat. Comm. in Heat and Mass Transfer, Internat. Jour. Heat and Fluid Flow. Office: Dienca, Viale Risorgimento 2, 40136 Bologna Italy also: U Parma, Dept Indsl Engring, Parma 43100, Italy

SPILIOTOPOULOS, EPAMINONAS, law educator; b. Thessaloniki, Greece, Dec. 23, 1925; s. Panayotis and Maria (Voutsina) S.; m. Sophia Koukoulis, Oct. 19, 1957; children: Maria, Iphigenia. Law degree, U. Athens, Greece, 1950, degree in polit. and econ. scis., 1952, D, 1963; D, U. Paris, 1955; D honoris causa, U. Aix-en-Provence, France, 1981, U. Paris II, 1986, U. Louvain, Belgium, 1991, Lille II, 1996, Temple U., 1996. Bar: Athens 1952. Assoc. prof. U. Athens, 1972-74, prof. pub. law, 1974-93; vis. prof. U. Aix-en-Provence, 1986, U. Paris I, 1982, Temple U., Phila., 1982, U. Paris II, 1990; mem. sci. com. Greek Parliament, Athens, 1987—. Group leader resistance orgns., 1942-44. Recipient Mil. medal of disting. action during occupation Greek Govt., 1945, Mil. medal of resistance during occupation Greek Govt., 1952; hon. fellow UCL, 1999. Mem. Adminstrv. Law Soc., Greek Inst. Adminstrv. Sci., Assn. Internationale de la Fonction Publique, CIRIEC, Athens Club, Spl. Forces Club (London). Christian Orthodox. Home and Office: 51 Omirou Str, 106 72 Athens Greece

SPILLANE, DENNIS KEVIN, lawyer; b. N.Y.C., Sept. 15, 1953; s. Denis Joseph and Mary Kate (Sullivan) S. BA magna cum laude, Manhattan Coll., 1974; JD, N.Y. Law Sch., 1978; MS in Taxation, Pace U., 1986, post-masters cert. in bus., 1992. Bar: N.Y. 1979, U.S. Dist. Ct. (ea. and so. dists.) N.Y. 1979, U.S. Tax Ct. 1986, D.C. 1988, U.S. Ct. Appeals (2d cir.) 1988, U.S. Supreme Ct. 1988, Conn. 1989. Asst. dist. atty. Borough of Bronx, N.Y.C., 1978-85; prin. atty. N.Y. State Tax Dept., N.Y.C., 1985-87; supervising atty. Office of Profl. Discipline, N.Y. State Edn. Dept., 1987—; prof. law and taxation Pace U., 1987—. Contbr. articles to profl. jours. Mem. Conn. Bar Assn, N.Y. State Bar Assn., D.C. Bar Assn. Conservative. Roman Catholic. Office: NY State Edn Dept 475 Park Ave S Frnt 3 New York NY 10016-6901

SPILLER, GENE ALAN, nutritionist, health facility administrator; b. Milan, Feb. 19, 1927; came to U.S., 1950, naturalized, 1962; s. Silvio and Beatrice (Galli) S. D of Chemistry, U. Milan, 1949; MS, U. Calif., Berkeley, 1968, PhD in Nutrition, 1972. Cons. nutrition rsch. and edn. L.A., 1952-65; rsch. chemist U. Calif., Berkeley, 1966-67, assoc. specialist physiology dept., 1968-72; prin. scientist, head nutritional physiology Syntex Rsch., Palo Alto, Calif., 1972-80; cons. clin. nutrition rsch. Los Altos, Calif., 1981—; head Health Rsch. and Studies Ctr., 1988—; lectr. Mills Coll., Oakland, Calif., 1971-81, Foothill Coll., Los Altos, 1974—. Co-author: The Last Puff, 1990; editor: Fiber in Human Nutrition, 1976, Topics in Dietary Fiber, 1978, Medical aspects of Dietary Fiber, 1980, Nutritional Pharmacology, 1981, The Methylxanthine Beverages and Foods, 1984, CRC Handbook of Dietary Fiber in Human Nutrition, 1986, 2d edit., 1992, New Protective Roles for Selected Nutrients, 1989, The Mediterranean Diets in Health and Disease, 1991, The Superpyramid Eating Program, 1993, CRC Handbook of Lipids, 1995, Nutrition Secrets of the Ancients, 1996, Cancer Survivor's Nutrition & Health Guide, 1996—, Caffeine, 1997, Healthy Nuts, 2000, Calcium Power, 2000, Diagnosis Heart Disease, 2000; rev. Jour. Am. Coll. Nutrition, 1976-95. Pres. SPHERA Found., 1990—. Mem. Am. Inst. Nutrition, Am. Soc. Clin. Nutrition, Brit. Nutrition Soc., Am. Assn. Cereal Chemists, Am. Diabetes Assn., Am. Coll. Nutrition, Alpine Hills Club.. Achievements include research on human nutrition; prin. investigator in human nutrition studies; dietary fibers, lipids, and carbohydrates effect on humna health; role of lesser known food components in nutrition; effect of whole foods vs. single nutrients; food antioxidants. Office: Health Rsch and Studies Ctr 340 2nd St Los Altos CA 94022-3624

SPILLER, JOAN MARILYN, company executive; b. Melbourne, Victoria, Australia, Aug. 23, 1946; d. Michael and Phyllis (Croughan) S. BA, U. Melbourne, 1978, B.Commerce, 1982. Gen. mgr. ops. Australia Post, 1984-86; regional dir. Health Dept. Victoria, 1986-92; dir. psychiat. svcs. Victorian Health and Cmty. Svcs., 1992-93; bd. dir. Health and Arts, 1993—; dir. Monash IVF, Australia, Victorian Rehab. Ctr., 1994-97. Bd. dirs. Melbourne Symphony Orch., 1986-97, Australian Art Orch., 1995—; mem. Victorial Health Partnerships with Industry steering com., 1996—; chmn. Women in Mgmt., Melbourne. Fellow Australian Inst. Co. Dirs.; mem. Melbourne Cricket Club. Avocations: opera, dance, classical music, theatre, art.

SPILLER, ROBIN CHARLES, gastroenterologist educator; b. Limpsfield, U.K., Apr. 3, 1950; s. Reginald Harvey and Margaret (Percy) S.; m. Susan Angela Smith, Feb. 11, 1978; children: Katherine, Rachel, Thomas. MB BChir, Cambridge U., 1975, MD, 1985; MSc, London Sch. of Econs., 1973. Sr. registrar Ctrl. Middlesex Hosp., London, 1985-87; cons. physician Queen Med. Ctr., Nottingham, 1988-98; reader in gastroenterology Nottingham Med. Sch. Contbr. articles to profl. jours. Fellow Royal Coll. Physicians; mem. British Soc. of Gastroenterology, Am. Gastroenterolog. Assn., European Neurogastroenterology and Motility. Office: Nottingham U Hosp, Derby Rd, Nottingham NG7 2UH, England

SPILLER, SUSAN COATES, plant physiologist-biologist; b. New Orleans, June 18, 1945; d. Elisha Balssingaime and Caroline Pennock (Coates) S.; m. James Sidney Acquistapace, Oct. 21, 1978; children: Anna Maurin, Marian Elliot, Caroline Canniff. BA in English, U. Calif., Berkeley, 1967, BA in Biology, 1973, PhD in Plant Physiology, 1979. Postdoct. rsch. asst. U. Calif., Davis, 1979-82; postdoct. rsch. asst. plant molecular biology U. Calif., Berkeley, 1985-88; fellow dept. plant biology Carnegie Instn. Washington, Stanford, Calif., 1982-85; prof. biology Mills Coll., Oakland, 1988—; mem. adv. panel Exploratorium, Traits of Life, San Francisco, 1997—. Contbr. articlrs to profl. jours. Bd. trustees Jr. Ctr. Arts and Scis., Oakland, Calif., 1997—; bd. dirs. Coll. Prep. Sch., Oakland, 1995—. Mem. AAAS, Sigma Xi. Office: Mills Coll Dept Biology 5000 Macarthur Blvd Oakland CA 94613-1301

SPILLMAN, MARJORIE ROSE, producer, dancer; b. Norfolk, Va., Jan. 5; d. William Bert and Rose Marjorie (Naperski) S.; m. David E. Marks, Apr. 4, 1985 (dec. July 1997); children: F. Oscar Marks, Miranda Rose. AS, Mt. Ida Jr. Coll., 1974; CT, Northeastern U., 1975; BS in Nursing, U. Mass., 1977. RN, Mass. Charge nurse VA Med. Ctr., Northampton, Mass., 1977-82; dancer N.E. Am. Ballet, Northampton, 1982, Ballet Theater Sch., Springfield, Mass., 1982-84, Smith Coll., Northampton, 1984-96; sales rep. Winthrop Pharm., N.Y.C., 1982-94, Nycomed, N.Y.C., 1994-96; dir. mktg. and devel. The Northampton Ctr. for the Arts, 1997; prin. dancer Project Opera, Northampton, 1984-86; dancer Polobulus East St. Dance, Hadley, Mass., 1985; dance and theatre reviewer Holyoke T. Telegram, 1991, 92; theater critic Daily Hampshire Gazette, 1993-96; dance panelist Mass. C.C., 1998; curator The Refrigerator Door art exhibit Smith Coll., 1999, 2000; dance anelist Mass. Cultural Coun., 1998; prodr. Pioneer Valley Performing Arts H.S., 1998; founder Open Door Prodns., 1999; cons. Organic Trade Assn., 1999; cons. New Eng. Artist Trust, 1999—. Dancer, creator part of Carmen in Carmen, 1985, Ruth St. Denis in the House of Ruth Ted and Martha, 1994; dancer, choreographer A Victorian Evening, 1986; dancer Nutcracker Ballet, Pioneer Valley Ballet, 1988; creator, prodr. The Halloween House at Sunnyside, 1990, producing dir., 1991, 92; actor, author play Mary P. Wells Smith Narrates, 1987; founder, prodr., dir. Northampton Children's Theater, 1993—; prodr. Northampton's First Night Children's Parade, 1996, dir. First Night Northampton, 1997-98, Saturday As a Work of Art—Summer Series, 1997; contbg. writer Healthy & Natural Mag. Theater panelist Mass. Cultural Coun., 1997, 2000; mem. devel. com. Cooley Dickerson Hosp., 1999. Democrat. Lutheran.

SPINA, ANTHONY FERDINAND, lawyer; b. Chgo., Aug. 15, 1937; s. John Dominic and Nancy Maria (Ponzio) S.; m. Anita Phyllis De Orio, Jan. 28, 1961; children: Nancy M. Spina Okal, John D., Catherine M. Spina Samatas, Maria J. Spina Samatas, Felicia M. BS in Social Sci., Loyola U., Chgo., 1959; JD, DePaul U., 1962. Bar: Ill. 1962. Assoc. Epton, Scott, McCarthy & Bohling, Chgo., 1962-64; pvt. practice Elmwood Park, Ill., 1964-71; pres. Anthony & Spina, PC, 1971-84, Spina, McGuire & Okal, PC, Elmwood Park, 1985—. Author Rosemont Village Ordinances, 1971, Elmwood Park Bldg. Code, 1975, Leyden Twp. Codified Ordinances, 1987. Atty. Leyden Twp., Ill., 1969=89, Village of Rosemont, Ill., 1971; counsel for Pres. and dir. Cook County Twp. Ofcls. Ill., 1975-96; counsel for exec. dir. Ill. State Assn. Twp. Ofcls., 1975-96; counsel Elmwood Park Village Bd., 1967-89, Norwood Park St. Lighting Dist., 1988—, various Cook County Twps. including DuPage, 1980-82, Maine, 1981-97, Norwood Park, 1982—, Wayne, 1982-84, Berwyn Twp., 1997—, Hanover Twp., 1997, Cook county Hwy. Commrs. Traffic Fine Litigation, 1974-96, 1999—, Hanover Twp. Mental Health Bd., 1991—, Glen Edens Assn., 1994—, Berwyn Twp. Mental Health Bd., 1997—; active Elmwood Pak Bldg. Code Planning Commn. Bd. Appeals; bd. dirs. Sheridan Carrol Charitable Works Fund, 1996—. Recipient Lacodaire medal, Deans Key Loyola U., Loyola U. Housing awards, 1965, 71, 76; Appreciation award Cook County Twp. Ofcls., av rating Martindale-Hubbel. Mem. ABA, Ill. Bar Assn., Chgo. Bar Assn., West Suburban Bar Assn. Cook County (past chmn. unauthorized practice law sect.), Am. Judicature Soc., Justinian Soc. Lawyers, Ill. State Twp. Attys. Assn. (past v.p., pres. 1982-86, dir. 1996-99, dir. emeritus 1999—), Nat. Inst. Town and Twp. Attys. (past v.p., pres. 1993-95, Ill. del.), Montclare/Leyden C. of C., Edgebrook C. of C. (past bd. dirs.), Nat. Assn. Italian Am. Lawyers, Joint Civic Com. Chgo. (exec. com.), World Bocce Assn. (dir.), St. Rocco Soc. Simbario, KC (scribe, trustee, past Grand Knight, bldg. corp. dir. (1967-99), Calabresi in Am. Orgn. (bd. dirs. 1991—), Fra Noi Ethnic Publ. (dir. 1995—), Blue Key, Delta Theta Phi, Tau Kappa Epsilon, Pi Gamma Mu. Roman Catholic. Office: 7610 W North Ave Elmwood Park IL 60707-4100

SPINADEL, VERA WINITZKY DE, mathematics educator; b. Buenos Aires, Aug. 22, 1929; d. Alejandro and Rosa (Schajnovidze) Winitzky; m. Erico Spinadel, June 30, 1955; children: Laura Patricia, Pablo, Irene, Andrea Gisela. PhD in Math., U. Buenos Aires, 1955. Prof. faculty architecture U. Buenos Aires, 1957—, coord. math. area, 1986—, prof. faculty econ. scis., 1993—; chmn. 1st Internat. Congress Math. and Design, Buenos Aires, 1995; dir. 2d Internat. Conf. Math. and Design, San Sebastian, Spain, 1998. Author: Ordinary Differential Equations, 1976; Calculo 1 - Suplemento, 1983, Calculo 2 - Suplemento, 1984, Geometria Fractal, 1993, Notas de Matemática, 1994, From the Golden Mean to Chaos, 1998; contbr. articles to internat. jours. V.p. Ericmar S.A., Fla., Buenos Aires, 1970—. Scholar Orgn. Estados Am., Trieste, Italy, 1972, Consejo de Investigaciones Científicas y Técnicas, Buenos Aires, Berkeley, Calif., 1986, Internat. Ctr. for Theoretical Physics, Trieste, Cuzco, Peru, 1989. Mem. Unión Math. Argentina, Argentine Sci. Soc., Assn. Math. and Design (pres.). Avocations: piano playing, sailing, rowing. Home: Jose Maria Paz 1131, 1602 Florida Argentina Office: U Buenos Aires, Dept Math, 1428 Buenos Aires Argentina

SPINDLER, JUDITH TARLETON, elementary school educator; b. Dayton, Tenn., Mar. 4, 1932; d. Frank Willson and Julia Elizabeth (Venable) S. BS in Edn., Longwood Coll., 1953; MA in Edn., Va. Commonwealth U., 1976. Tchr. Oceana, King's Grant Sch., Virginia Beach, Va., 1953-66, Ginter Park Elem. Sch., Richmond, Va., 1966-67, Bon Air Elem. Sch., Chesterfield County, Va., 1967-87; ret., 1987. Charter mem. Web of Hope sponsored by ARC (Humanitarian award). Recipient 66 ribbons for 1st, 2nd and 3rd pl. awards various knitting competitions, 5 Best in Show awards rosette competition, including blue ribbons State Fair Va., 1998, 6 ribbons Best in Show rosette Chesterfield County Fair, 1998, 2 Best in Show Chesterfield County Fair, 1 Best in Show State Fair of Va., among others. Mem. NEA, Va. Edn. Assn., Knitting Guild Am. (qualified tchr.), Knit Wit Guild. Avocation: knitting. Home: 4103 Hyde Park Dr Chester VA 23831-4826

SPINDLER, KONRAD, archaeologist; b. Leipzig, Germany, June 20, 1939; arrived in Austria, 1988; s. Erwin and Madgard (Beyer) S.; m. Dorothee Heinze, Feb. 26, 1988; children: Richard, Robert, Lea, Raimund. PhD, U. Freiburg, 1970. Asst. U. Regensburg, Germany, 1974-77; prof. U. Erlangen, Germany, 1977-88, U. Innsbruck, Austria, 1988—. Office: U Innsbruck, Inst Pre & Proto History, A-6020 Innsbruck Austria

SPINETTA, JEAN-CYRIL, airline executive; b. Paris, Oct. 4, 1943; s. Adrien Spinetta and Antoinette Brignoli; m. Nicole Ricquebourg, Nov. 22, 1969; children: Eric, Isabelle, Cécile, Adrien. Student, Paris Law Sch.; diploma, Inst. Internat. Politics, Paris. Assoc. tchr., 1961-69, ctrl. adminstrv. attache, 1969-70; nat. adminstr. Paris Higher Edn. Secondary Schs., 1970-72; bur. chief dept. investments and planing Nat. Edn. Ministry, 1972-76; spl. prosecutor State Coun. Govt., 1976-78; sec. gen. French Govt., 1978-81; info. svc. chief Prime Min. of France, 1981-83; dir. colls. Ministry Nat. Edn., 1983-84; cabinet dir. Min. Labour, Employment and Profl. Devel., 1984-86; inspector gen. Nat. Edn. Adminstrn., 1986-88; cabinet dir. Min. Social Affairs and Employment, Min. Overseas Transport, 1988-90; pres., dir. gen. Air Internat., 1990-93; indsl. advisor Presidency of the Republic, 1994-95; adminstr. to 1st mission pub. svc. relevant to govt., 1995; CEO Air France, 1996—. Recipient Chevalier Medal of Honor to Order of Nat. Merit. Avocations: tennis, skiing. Office: Air France 125 W 55th St New York NY 10019-5369 also: 45 Rue de Paris, 95747 Roissy France*

SPINETTO, MARCO, sales executive; b. Caracas, Venezuela, Apr. 17, 1962; s. Giovanni and Guiseppina (Boggiano) S.; m. Natascha Swoboda, Jan. 10, 1993. D, Politenico, Milan, 1988. Asst. mgr. Pirelli Group, Milan, 1988-91; acct. mgr. Pirelli K.K., Tokyo, 1993, tech. dir., 1993-97, rep. dir., 1994-97; benchmarking and planning dir. product divsn. Pirelli Group, Milan, 1997—. Mem. Italian C. of C. (bd. dirs. 1996-97), ETP Assn., Soc. Competitive Intelligence Profl., European Rsch. Indsl. Mgmt. Assn., Am. Mgmt. Assn. Avocations: sports, photography. Office: Pirelli Group Tyre Sector, Viale Sarca 222, 20126 Milan Italy

SPINKS, JEFFREY THOMAS, bank officer; b. Birmingham, Eng., Sept. 4, 1950; arrived in South Africa, 1975; s. William and Elsie (Coleyshaw) S.; m. Irene Roth; children: Peter, Michael, Andrew. CFP; chartered mgmt. acct. Gen. mgr. So. Life, Johannesburg, South Africa, 1989-98; dir. momentum employee benefits Std. Bank South Africa, Johannesburg, 1998, dir. employer benefits and life assurance products, 1998—. Fellow Inst. Chartered Accts. Eng. and Wales, Inst. Chartered Accts. South Africa. Avocations: rubgy, cricket, military history, opera. Office: Standard Bank South Africa, 5 Simmonds St 5th Fl, Johannesburg 2001, South Africa

SPINNER, KASPAR HEINRICH, educator; b. Biel, Switzerland, Mar. 6, 1941; s. Wilhelm Heinrich and Marianne (Wyss) S.; m. Elisabeth Scheerer, July 11, 1973; children: Selina, Veronika. Matura, Gymnasium, Biel, 1960; MD, U. Zurich, Switzerland, 1969. Asst. in Germanic philology U. Geneva, 1968-72; asst. prof. U. Kassel, Fed. Republic of Germany, 1972-75, prof., 1975-79; prof. U. Tech., Aachen, Fed. Republic of Germany, 1980-88, U. Augsburg, Fed. Republic of Germany, 1988—. Author: Zur Struktur des Lyrischen Ich, 1975, Zeichen Text Sinn, 1977, Identiät und Deutschunterricht, 1980, Moderne Kurzprosa, 1984, Vorschläge für einen Kreativen Literaturunterricht, 1990. Imaginative und emotionale Lern-prozesse in Deutschunterricht, 1995. Home: Leonhardstr. 78, 86415 Mering Germany Office: U Phil Fac II, U Phil Fac II, Universitatsstr 10, D-86135 Augsburg Germany

SPINNER, LEE LOUIS, accountant; b. Hillsboro, Ill., Nov. 9, 1948; s. John Louis and Clara Mae (Brown) S. BS in Acctg., U. Ill., 1971, MAS in Acctg., 1972; MS in Taxation, DePaul U., 1983. CPA, Ill. Sr. tax acct. Ernst & Young, Chgo., 1972-78; dir. tax returns and audits Sunbeam Corp., Chgo., 1978-82; dir. tax compliance Sara Lee Corp., Chgo., 1982-83; mgr. tax compliance AM Internat., Inc., Chgo., 1983-85; mgr. taxes Household Mfg., Inc., Prospect Heights, Ill., 1985-89; mgr. internat. taxes Pittway Corp., Chgo., 1990-2000; dir. taxes Methode Electronics, Inc., Harwood Heights, Ill., 2000—; instr. tax tng. program Ernst & Young, 1975-78; tax advisor Sta. WIND, Call Your Acct., Chgo., 1977-78. Sec. Grant Park Accts. Softball League, Chgo., 1976-77. Mem. AICPA, Ill. CPA Soc., U. Ill. Alumni Assn. (bd. assoc., audit com. 1997—), Top Social Athletic Club, Moose, KC. Democrat. Roman Catholic. Home: 923 Stonehedge Ln Palatine IL 60067-7114

SPINNER, ROBERT JAY, orthopedic surgeon; b. N.Y.C., Dec. 8, 1961; s. Morton and Paula (Lerner) S. SB, MIT, 1984; M of Studies, Oxford (Eng.) U., 1985; MD, Mayo Clinic, 1989. Rsch. fellow, Luce scholar Prince of Wales Hosp., Hong Kong, 1989-90; intern in surgery Duke Univ., Durham, N.C., 1990-91, jr. resident in surgery, 1991-92, resident in orthopaedic surgery, 1992-96; resident in neurosurgery Mayo Clinic, Rochester, Minn., 1996—; fellow in peripheral nerve surgery David Kline M.D., New Orleans, 1998-99. Recipient Davison Teaching award Duke U. Med. Sch., 1993, Goldner Rsch. award in Orthopaedic Surgery Duke U. Med. Ctr., 1996, Mayo Bros. Disting. Fellowship award, 2000; Schilling scholar Mayo Found., 1985-87. Mem. Phi Beta Kappa, Sigma Xi, Alpha Chi Sigma. Avocations: travel, reading.

SPIOTTO, JAMES ERNEST, lawyer; b. Chgo., Nov. 25, 1946; s. Michael Angelo and Vinnetta Catherine (Henninger) S.; m. Ann Elizabeth Humphreys, Dec. 23, 1972; children: Michael Thomas, Mary Catherine, Joan Elizabeth, Kathryn Ann. AB, St. Mary's of the Lake, 1968; JD, U. Chgo.,

1972. Bar: Ill. 1972, U.S. Dist. Ct. (no. dist.) Ill. 1973, U.S. Ct. Appeals (3rd and 7th cir.) 1974, U.S. Supreme Ct. 1978, U.S. Ct. Appeals (9th cir.) 1984, U.S. Dist. Ct. (so. dist.) Calif. 1984. Exclusionary rule study-project dir. Law Enforcement Assistance Agy. Grant, Chgo., 1972; law clk. to presiding justice U.S. Dist. Ct., Chgo., 1972-74; assoc. Chapman and Cutler, Chgo., 1974-80, ptnr., 1980—; chmn. program on defaulted bonds and bankruptcy Practising Law Inst., 1982—, chmn program on troubled debt financing, 1987—. Author: Defaulted Securities, 1990; contbr. numerous articles to profl. jours. With USAR, 1969-75. Mem. Assn. Bond Lawyers, Soc. Mcpl. Analysts, Law Club of City of Chgo., Union League, Econs. Club Chgo. Roman Catholic. Office: Chapman and Cutler 111 W Monroe St Ste 1700 Chicago IL 60603-4006

SPIRES, ROBERT CECIL, foreign language educator; b. Missouri Valley, Iowa, Dec. 1, 1936; s. Roy C. and Ellen M. (Epperson) S.; m. Roberta A. Hyde, Feb. 2, 1963; children: Jeffrey R., Leslie Ann. BA, U. Iowa, 1959, MA, 1963, PhD, 1968. Asst. prof. Ohio U., Athens, 1967-69; asst. prof. dept. Spanish and Portuguese U. Kans., Lawrence, 1969-72, assoc. prof., 1972-78, prof., 1978—, chmn. dept., 1983-92. Author: La novela española, 1978, Beyond the Metafictional Mode, 1984, Transparent Simulacra, 1988, Post-Totalitarian Spanish Fiction, 1996; contbg. editor SigloXX/20th Century; editl. bd. Jour. of Interdisciplinary Literary Studies, 1993—, Ind. Jour. of Hispanic Lit., 1992—. Served with U.S. Army, 1959-61. NEH fellow, 1981-82, U.S.-Spain Joint Com. fellow, 1985-86, Hall Ctr. for Humanities fellow, 1992, Program Cultural Coop. fellow, 1993. Mem. Revista de Estudios Hispánicos (editorial bd. 1985—), Anales de Literatura Contemporánea (editorial bd. 1981—), Letras Peninsulares (editorial bd. 1987—), MLA (del. assembly 1989-91), MLA 20th Century Spain (exec. com. 1983-89), 20th Century Spanish Assn. Am. (v.p. 1989-92). Home: 2420 Orchard Ln Lawrence KS 66049-2710 Office: U Kans Dept Spanish & Portuguese Lawrence KS 66045-0001

SPIRIN, NIKOLAI NIKOLAEVITCH, medical educator; b. Tumen, Russia, Sept. 19, 1956; s. Nikolai Vasilyevitch and Raisa Nikolaevna (Vasina) S.; m. Elena Alexandrovna Klockova; children: Alexei, Natalia. Student, Yaroslavl (Russia) Med. U., 1973-79, postgrad., 1981-84, Doctorate, 1992. Resident Yaroslavl Med. U., 1979-81, asst. dept. nervous disorders, 1984-92, asst. prof., 1992-95, prof., 1995—, head of dept., 1996—; med. dir. Spine Correction Ctr., Yaroslavl, 1997—, Neuro-Endocrinology Disorders Ctr., Yaroslavl, 1998—; cons. hosps., Yaroslavl, Kostroma, Vologda, 1981—. Editor-in-chief: (collection of articles) Diagnostics and Treatment of Neuritis and Polyradiculoneuritis, 1991, Diagnosis and Treatment of Demyelinating Diseases, 1998; author: (monograph) Nervous System Disorders in Systemic Rheumatic Diseases, 1999; mem. editl. bd. News of Pharmacy and Medicine, 1992—. Mem. Regional Soc. Neurologists, N.Y. Acad. Sci., Russian Soc. Neurologists (bd. dirs.). Avocations: boating, photography, drawing, woodworking, poetry. E-mail: spir@nw.uniyar.ac.ru. Home: 27 Ribinskaya St Apt 54, 150014 Yaroslavl Russia Office: Yaroslavl Med U, 5 Revolutsionnaya St, 150000 Yaroslavl Russia

SPIRLEA, IRINA, tennis player; b. Bucharest, Mar. 26, 1974. Profl. tennis player, 1994—. Named WTA Most Impressive Newcomer, 1994. Office: c/o WTA tour 133 1st St NE Saint Petersburg FL 33701-3352*

SPIRNAK, JOHN PATRICK, urologist, educator; b. Cleve., Mar. 17, 1951; s. John Joseph and Mary Barbara (Mancos) S.; m. Diane Lynne Miller, Sept. 15, 1979; children: Jennifer, Patrick, Christopher. BS in Zoology, Ohio U., 1973; MD, Emory U., 1977; degree in Urology, Case Western Reserve U., 1983. Diplomate Am. Bd. Urology. Intern, gen. surg. resident Univ. Hosp., Cleve., 1977-79, urology resident, 1980-83; nephrology rsch. resident Metro Health Med. Ctr., Cleve., 1979-80, dir. urology, 1987—; sr. instr. divns. urology Case Western Reserve U., Cleve., 1983-85, asst. prof. urology, 1985-91, assoc. prof. urology, 1991-2000, prof., 2000—; adv. panel mem. U.S. Pharmacopeia Urology, Washington, 1986—. Editor Urologic Decision Making, 1991, New Diagnostic Tests, 1996; manuscript reviewer Jour. Endourology, 1989—, Urology, 1993—, Jour. Urology, 1994—; contbr. articles to profl. jours. and chpts. to books. Named One of Top Doctors Cleve. Mag., 1996, 99. Fellow ACS; mem. AMA, Am. Assn. Surgery Trauma, Am. Urol. Assn., Cleve. Urol. Soc. (sec./treas. 1986-88, pres. 1988-89). Avocations: sports, gardening. Home: 2178 Silveridge Trl Westlake OH 44145-1797 Office: Metro Health Med Ctr 2500 Metrohealth Dr Cleveland OH 44109-1900

SPIRO, THEODORE ERICH, physician, researcher, pharmaceutical executive; b. Columbus, Ohio, July 28, 1946; arrived in France, 1994; s. Erich and Pauline (Konecny) S. BA, Columbia Coll., 1968, postgrad., 1968-69; MD, U. Cinn., 1973. Diplomate Am. Bd. Internal Medicine, Am. Bd. Pathology, Nat. Bd. Med. Examiners; cert. ACLS, ATLS. Intern in internal medicine NYU Tchg. Hosp., Manhattan VAMC, Bellevue Med. Ctr., N.Y.C., 1973-74, resident in anatomic pathology, 1974-76; resident fellow in clin. pathology NIH, Bethesda, Md., 1976-77; postdoctoral rsch. fellow, USPHS commd. officer Nat. Cancer Inst., L'Inst. Jules Border, Brussels, Belgium, 1977-80; resident fellow in blood bank dept. and clin. pathology NIH, Bethesda, Md., 1980; lab. dir., clin. pathologist Clin. Rsch. Lab. The Upjohn Co., Kalamazoo, 1980-85; resident in internal medicine Kalamazoo campus Mich. State U. Coll. Human Medicine, 1986-88; assoc. dir. clin. rsch. Rhone-Poulenc Pharms., Inc., Princeton, N.J., 1988-90; assoc. dir. clin. rsch. Cardiovasc. Diseases R&D Rhone-Poulenc Rorer Pharms., Inc., Collegeville, Pa., 1990-93; dir. clin. rsch., clin. project leader cardiovasc. diseases Rhone-Poulenc Rorer S.A., Antony, Hauts-de-Seine, France, 1993-99; dir. clin. rsch., clin. project leader Aventis Pharma S.A., Antony, Hauts-de-Seine, France, 1999—; med. officer Battle Creek (Mich.) VAMC, 1988-89; lab. asst. biol. scis. Columbia U., N.Y.C., 1968-69; mem. faculty pathology NYU Med. Ctr., N.Y.C., 1975-76; lectr. Found. for Advanced Edn. in the Scis., NIH, Bethesda, Md., 1977; mem. faculty medicine Mich. State U., Coll. Human Medicine, Kalamazoo, 1987-88; clin. asst. prof. U. Medicine and Dentistry N.J., R.W. Johnson Med. Sch., New Brunswick, N.J., 1989-94; cons. clinician l'Universite Libre de Bruxelles, l'Inst. Jules Bordet, Brussels, 1995-98; lectr. in field; participant numerous symposia, confs., seminars. Contbr. more than 40 articles to profl. jours. including Drug Alcohol Dependence, Am. Jour. Medicine, Biomedicine, Brit. Jour. Haematology, among others. Lt. comdr. USPHS, 1976-80, lt., 1980—. Biochemistry fellow U. Cin. Coll. Medicine, 1970; fellow Damon Runyan-Walter Winchell Cancer Found., 1977-79, Jean et Marie Hoguet Found. for Cancer Rsch., 1978-79. Fellow Am. Soc. Clin. Pathologists, Coll. Am. Pathologists; mem. ACP, Internat. Soc. for Exptl. Hematology, Internat. Soc. Thrombosis and Haemostatis, Am. Soc. Hematology. Achievements include research in hematology, pharmaceutical produce research and development, clinical research, management, internal medicine, and anatomic and clinical pathology. Office: 20 avenue Raymond Aron, 92165 Antony Cedex, France

SPIRTOS, ANDREA C., columnist, muralist, office manager; b. Freeport, Ill., May 23, 1952; d. Carl E. H. and Eldora E. (Baker) DeFrane; m. Nicholas George Spirtos, Aug. 19, 1979. BA in Psych., BA in Edn. cum laude, U. Dubuque, 1973; MA in Guidance Counseling cum laude, U. Iowa, 1974; JD, Loyola U., L.A., 1983; EdD in Instl. Mgmt., Pepperdine U., 1994. Cert. rape crisis counselor, Calif. Tchr., counselor Kennedy H.S., Cedar Rapids, Iowa, 1973-74; counselor UCLA, 1974-77; youth cons. Am. Red Cross, 1977-79; dir. donor svcs. and shelter svcs. United Way, 1979-80; dir. youth svcs. Am. Heart Assn., 1980-82; pres. Comprehensive Office Sys. Technology, 1982; co-founder, corp. officer Pacific Multiple Sclerosis Rsch. Found., 1982-99; devel. dir. Junipero Serra H.S., 1987-88; v.p. Compensation Strategies, 1988; office mgr. Law Office of Nicholas G. Spirtos, 1982—; pres. Tekni-query Cons., 1990—; account rep. Met. Life, 1996; contbr. The Desert Woman Monthly, Palm Springs, Calif., 1997-99; columnist Charity Check The Desert Sun Gannet Pub., 1997-99; columnist Random Acts of Kindness Profile mag., 1999—. Author: Not in My Wildest Dreams, 1995; co-editor, author: Cutting Edge Technologies: The Future of Community Colleges, 1993; columnist: Seventeen Mag., 1969-70, Freeport Jour. Standard, 1968-70, Freeport H.S. Gazette, 1967-70, Trumpeter, 1990-92; columnist, editor, layout Youth News, 1977-82. Recipient Danworth fellow, 1973-74, medallion of recognition Joint Chiefs of Staff U.S., 1993, Presdl. Order of Merit, 1991, Presdl. Legion of Merit, 1992. Mem. ACLU, Am. Pen Women, Internat. Platform Assn. (gov. 1994—, author poetry newsletter 1995-96, coeditor poetry anthology 1992, 93, 94, 95), Amnesty Internat., Soroptimist Internat. La Quinta, Kappa Delta Pi. Republican. Greek Orthodox. Avocations: painting, knitting, hot rodding, organic gardening, gourment cooking. E-mail: rydnhdl@aol.com. Office: Law Office of Nicholas G Spirtos 44489 Town Center Way Ste D404 Palm Desert CA 92260-2723

SPIRY, JEAN LOUIS, oral surgeon; b. Paris, Nov. 24, 1949; married July 7, 1980; 1 child, Christelle. DDS, U. Paris, 1973. Chief of unity orthodontics Hosp. St. Louis, Paris, 1976—. Patentee in field. Laureat Indsl. Found. Avocations: skiing, golf, sailing, tennis, classical music.

SPITALNIK, JORGE, engineering executive; b. Montevideo, Uruguay, Sept. 20, 1933; s. Herman and Dina (Orlovich) S.; m. Susana Nathan, June 19, 1958; children: Monica, Daniel. Indsl. Engr., U. Republic, Montevideo, 1958; Atomic Energy Engr., U. Paris, Saclay, France, 1959; Diploma in Nuclear Power, London U., 1960; Mech. Engr., Fed. U. Rio de Janeiro, 1976. Chartered engr., U.K., Brazil, Uruguay. Sci. sec. Mex.-U.S. study group nuclear power and desalination Internat. Atomic Energy Agy., Vienna, 1965-68; dir. C.I.N., Montevideo, 1969-73; project mgr. Nuclebras, Rio de Janeiro, 1973-77, dept. head, 1978-85; nat. dir. UNDP/NUCLEBRAS, Rio de Janeiro, 1977-82; dir. asst./dir. advisor NUCLEN, Rio de Janeiro, 1985-96, supt., 1996-97; tech. advisor to dir. Electronuclear, Rio de Janeiro, 1997-98, mgr. nuclear safety culture, 1999—; vice chmn. Internat. Nuclear Energy Acad., Seoul, 1997—. Mem. nuclear safeguards com. Internat. Atomic Energy Agy., Vienna, 1969-71, govt. rep., 1970-71, bd. govs.; vice chmn. Inter-Am. Nuclear Energy Commn., Washington, 1964-66. Fellow Am. Nuclear Soc. (dir. 1994-98, 2000—, chmn. internat. com. 1997-99, L.Am. sect. chmn. 1975-77, 81-82, chmn. nuclear socs. coop. com. 1999-2000); mem. World Fedn. Engring. Orgns. (vice chair com. on transfer, sharing and assessment of tech., 2000—), Internat. Nuclear Socs. Coun. (sec.-treas. 1990-98, vice-chair 1999—), Brazilian Fedn. Engring. Socs. (dir. 1998—), Brazilian Assn. Nuclear Energy, Instn. Mech. Engrs. London, Uruguayan Club of Rio de Janeiro (pres. 1992). Avocations: photography, walking, soccer, reading, classical music. Home: ap 1001, Av Epitacio Pessoa 2900, 22471000 Rio de Janeiro Brazil Office: Electronuclear - CT T, Rua da Candelaria 65 8th Fl, 20091020 Rio de Janeiro Brazil

SPITERI, JOSEPH FRANCIS, corporate executive; b. Sliema, Malta, Feb. 22, 1912; m. Blanche Ellul, May 11, 1944; children: Hubert, Oswald, Liliana Spiteri de Korte, Martin, Gloria Spiteri Vella, Elizabeth Spiteri Vella, Joseph Francis, Jr. Student, Stella Maris Coll., 1920-26, His Majesty's Dockyard Tech. Sch., 1926-29; engring. studies, Prof. Nixon, 1929-31; diploma in sci. taxidermy, The Northwestern Sch. of Taxidermy, Omaha, 1933; Cultural Doctorate in Fin. and Banking, World U., 1988; BA in Mgmt., Calif. U. for Advanced Studies, Novato, 1989. Engring. apprentice His Majesty's Dockyard, 1926-32; founder Joseph F. Spiteri & Co., 1927, chmn., 1948-77; founder Chemists & Druggists Supplies Co., 1949; founder, dir. Bank of Valletta Ltd., 1974-79; chmn. Portelli Internat., Ltd., 1976-79; vice chmn. Marsa Flour Mills, Ltd., 1976-79; chmn. Moeninnghoff Metals (Malta), Ltd., 1977-79; Mqabba Marbles, Ltd., 1977-79. Mem. Bd. Prison Visitors, 1972-79, Wine Adv. Bd., 1977-79; candidate Parliament of the Progressive Constl. Party, 1962, Malta Labour Party, 1971; mem. The Confraternity of St. Barbara Ch., Valletta, 1978, procurator, 1981-91; senate mem. High Chamber of the Internat. Parliament for Safety and Peace, 1989; envoy at large Republic of Malta, 1989; hon. appointment to the Rsch. Bd. of Advisors Am .Biog. Inst., Raleigh, N.C., 1986; hon. mem. Internat. Biog. Ctr. Adv. Coun., Cambridge, Eng., 1986. Created Knight of Grace, Sovereign Order St. John of Jerusalem, Prior of Malta, knight comdr. of Justice; diplomate in sci. taxidermy. Fellow Royal Commonwealth Soc., Royal Hort. Soc., Internat. Inst. Community Svc. (founder, diploma of honour); mem. Soc. Study and Conservation of Nature, Malta Soc. Arts, Mfrs. and Commerce, Malta Agrarian Soc., World U. Roundtable, Calif. U. for Advanced Studies Alumni Assn. (lifetime), Royal Commonwealth Club (London). Home: 30 Gilda Court, Triq L-Gharbiel Saint Andrew's STJ 04, Malta Office: 120/122 Marina St, Pieta Malta

SPITERI, JOSEPH FRANCIS, JR., psychiatrist, educator; b. Sliema, Malta, July 22, 1962; s. Joseph Francis and Blanche (Ellul) S.; m. Carmen Calafato, Sept. 29, 1988; children: Daniel, Simon. MD, U. Malta, 1986. Cert. in psychiatry. Psychiatrist Oxford (Eng.) Health Region, 1991-95; policy psychiatrist Old Age Psychiatry Dept. of Health, Malta, 1995—; chmn. Mt. Carmel Hosp., Attard, Malta, 1997-98; chief exec. Sedqa-Agy. Against Drugs and Alcohol, Malta, 1998, cons. psychiatrist, 1995—; cons. psychiatrist Corradino Correctional Facilities, Malta, 1996—, Dept. of Health, Malta, 1997-98; bd. govs. Richmond Fellowship Found., Malta, 1997-98; mem. Bd. Coun. of Health, Malta, 1998, Bd. of Rehab. in Civil Prison, 1996—, Mental Health Commn., Malta, 1997-98; lectr. dept. gerontology U. Malta, 1995—. Mem. med. bd. Electoral Commn., Malta, 1995—. Mem. Royal Coll. Psychiatrists (U.K.), Agrarian Soc. Malta, Schizophrenia Soc., Maltese Psychiat. Assn., Alzheimer's Assn. (founder in Malta). Roman Catholic. Avocations: gardening, reading, modeling. Office: Mt Carmel Hosp, Attard Malta

SPITTLE, MARGARET FLORA, consultant clinical oncologist, radiotherapist; b. London, Nov. 10, 1939; d. Edwin William and Ada Florence (Axam) S.; m. Clive Lucas Harmer (div. 1977); children: Kasha Harmer-Hirst, Victoria Harmer; m. David John Hare. MB BChir, U. London, 1963, MS, 1971. House physician Westminster Children's Hosp., London, 1964; registrar Westminster Hosp., London, 1965; lectr. St. Bartholomew's, London, 1968; sr. registrar Westminster Hosp., London, 1969; instr. radiation divsn. Stanford (Calif.) U., 1970; cons. The Middlesex Hosp., London, 1971—, St. Thomas' Hosp., London. Contbr. numerous chpts. to books and articles to profl. jours. Fellow Royal Coll. Radiologists (dean), Royal Coll. Physicians, Royal Soc. Medicine (v.p.). Avocations: family, golf, flying, skiing, gardening. Office: Middlesex Hosp Meyerstein Inst Oncology, Mortimer St, WIN 8AA London England

SPITZ, HUGO MAX, lawyer; b. Richmond, VA, Aug. 17, 1927; s. Jacob Gustav and Clara (Herzfeld) S.; m. Barbara Steinberg, June 22, 1952; children: Jack Gray, Jill Ann Levy, Sally Spitz. AA, U. Fla., 1948, BLaws, 1951, JD, 1967. Bar: Fla. 1951, S.C. 1955, U.S. Dist. Ct. (so. dist.) Fla. 1951, U.S. Dist. Ct. (ea. dist.) S.C. 1956, U.S. Ct. Appeals (4th cir.) 1957. Asst. atty. gen. State of Fla., Tallahassee, 1951; assoc. Williams, Salomon & Katz, Miami, Fla., 1951-54, Steinberg & Levkoff, Charleston, S.C., 1954-57; sr. ptnr. The Steinberg Law Firm L.L.P., Charleston, 1957—; lectr. S.C. Trial Lawyers Assn., Columbia, 1958—, S.C. U. Sch. Law, Columbia, 1975, S.C. Bar Assn., 1955—; assoc. mcpl. judge Charleston, 1972-74, mcpl. judge, 1974-76; commr. Charleston County Substance Abuse Commn., 1976-79; bd. govs. S.C. Patient's Compensation Fund, Columbia, 1978-97; adv. mem., atty. S.C. Legis. Coun. for Worker's Compensation; chmn. bd. dirs. Franklin C. Fetter Health Ctr., Charleston, 1977-78; mem. S.C. Appellate Def. Commn., 1985-86; founding sponsor Civil Justice Found., 1986—; bd. pres. Charleston Jewish Fedn., 1990-91, pres., 1991-92. Pres. Synagogue Emanu-El, 1969-71. With USN, 1945-46. Fellow S.C. Bar Assn., U. S.C. Ednl. Found.; mem. ABA, Civil Justice Found., S.C. Law Inst., S.C. Trial Lawyers Assn. (founder and pres. 1985-86), S.C. Claimants' Attys. for Worker's Compensation (exec. com. 1986), S.C. Worker's Compensation Ednl. Assn. (bd. dirs. 1978-98), S.C. Law Inst., Am. Judicature Soc., Assn. Trial Lawyers Am. (mem. pres. council 1986-87), Nat. Rehab. Assn., Nat. Orgn. Social Security Claimants' Reps. S.C. Bar (chmn. trial and appellate sect. 1982-83, ho. of dels. 1984-85), So. Assn. Workmen's Compensation Adminstrs., Nat. Inst. for Trial Advocacy (com. chmn. 1985). Democrat. Clubs: Hebrew Benevolent Soc. (pres. 1974-75, life), Jewish Community Ctr. (Charleston, v.p. 1972-74), Hebrew Orphan Soc. (life, v.p. 1999—), B'nai B'rith, Elks (life). Home: 337 Confederate Cir Charleston SC 29407-7430 Office: PO Box 9 Charleston SC 29402-0009

SPITZ, JANET, business educator, consultant; b. Columbus, Ohio, Feb. 24, 1952; d. David and Ruth (Sachere) S.; m. Gerard J. Macdonald, Aug. 10, 1974 (div. 1980); children: Leo S., Orion S. BA, Cornell U., 1973, MBA, 1985; PhD, Stanford U., 1991. Owner Rainbow Distbuting, Ithaca, N.Y., 1978-83; lectr. Swedish Sch. Econs., Helsinki, Finland, 1990; asst. prof. Rensselaer Polytechnic Inst., Troy, N.Y., 1990-94; assoc. prof. bus. Coll. Saint Rose, Albany, N.Y., 1994—; cons. Dept. Justice, Bur. Immigration, Washington, 1998-99; cons., expert witness Miner Barnhill & Galland, Chgo., 1997-98; reviewer Jour. Applied Mgmt. Studies, 1995—, Internat. Soc. for the Study of Work and Orgnl. Values, 1997—, Jour. Human Resources, 1995-96. Mem. editl. bd. Collegiate Press, 1995-96; contbr. articles to profl. jours. Bd. dirs. Rensselaer Taconic Land Conservancy, Troy, N.Y., 1993—; mem. leadership coun. So. Poverty Land Ctr., Atlanta, 1995—. Grantee Russian rsch. Dept. State, Internat. Rsch. and Exch. Bd., 1994-98, World Bank, 1993, Stanford U., 1989-90. Mem. Assn. for Comparative Econ. Sys., Internat. Indsl. Rels. Assn., Indsl. Rels. Rsch. Assn., Com. on Status of Women in the Econs. Profession. Democrat. Mem. Soc. Friends. Avocations: gardening, reading, raising sheep and golden retrievers. Home: 386 Potter Hill Rd Petersburgh NY 12138-3213 Office: Coll of Saint Rose Bus Sch 432 Western Ave Albany NY 12203-1419

SPITZE, GLENYS SMITH, retired educator; b. Rozel, Kans., May 20, 1919; d. Harry H. and Mary Louisa (Mishler) Smith; m. LeRoy A. Spitze, Dec. 31, 1942 (dec. Nov. 1995); children: Randall LeRoy, Kevin Lance, Kimett Alvin, Terril Christian, Shawn Smith; 1 fosterchild, Theo Ritz-Spitze. Cert. tchg., U. Kans., 1939; AA, San Jose (Calif.) City Coll., 1963; BA in Psychology, San Jose State U., 1965, MA in Child Devel., 1968. Cert. tchr., counselor, Calif. Elem. sch. tchr. Topeka County Schs., Richland, Kans., 1939-40, Kinsley (Kans.) Pub. Schs., 1940-42; presch. substitute tchr. AAUW Kindergarten, Newark, Ohio, 1945-46; presch. tchr. Meth. Ch. Facility, Campbell, Calif., 1956-58; guest lectr. Govt. Sch. Social Work, Colombo, Sri Lanka, 1965-66; instr. man-woman relationship San Jose State Free U., 1966-67; child devel. lab. psychol. examiner Child Labs San Jose State U., 1967-68; pvt. informal practice tchr., counselor, cons. Kailua, Hawaii; vocal music dir. grades 1-3 Southside Sch., 1940-41; 6th dist. Calif. Congress Parent-Tchrs. Social Welfare dir., officer 6th dist. com. Calif. Coun. on Crime and Delinquency, San Jose, 1956-62; mem. kindergarten com. AAUW, Newark, 1945-46; coord. Sangha Symposium, Asian Philosophy Club, San Jose State U., 1964-65; lectr. in field. Contbr. articles, poems to profl. publs. Hon. del. Gov. Brown's Conf. on Prevention of Juvenile Delinquency, Sacramento, 1963; co-organizer Post Polio Support Group, Kailua-Kona, HI, 2000. Mem. Psi Chi. Avocations: writing, reading, swimming, snorkeling, anthropology and archeology travel. Home: 78-6800 Alii Dr Apt 5-103 Kailua Kona HI 96740-4421 Home (summer): care Gen Delivery Woodland Park CO 80863

SPITZER, KAREL, entomologist; b. Jindřichuv Hradec, Czech Republic, Oct. 13, 1939; s. Leo and Anna (Prušová) S. M in Agrl. Sci., U. Agr., Brno, Czech Republic, 1963; PhD, Czech Acad. Scis., Praha, 1970. Cert. biologist. Agrl. engr. Jindřichuv Hradec, 1963-64; lectr. in entomology U. Agr., České Budějovice, Czech Republic, 1965-76; entomologist scientist Inst. Entomology, České Budějovice, 1977-88, entomologist, head dept., sr. scientist, 1989—; entomologist, rschr. Massey U., Palmerston North, New Zealand, 1969-70; cons. State Nature Conservation, Czech Republic, 1990—; lectr. ecology and entomology U. South Bohemia, České Budějovice, 1992—. Author: Endangered World of Insects, 1982 (Academia award 1982), Life of Wetlands, 1984 (Pubs. award 1984); contbr. articles to profl. jours. Avocations: traveling, art, history. Home: Radounka 58, CZ377 01 Jindřichuv Hradec Czech Republic Office: Czech Acad Sci Inst Entomol, Branišovská 31, CZ370 05 Ceske Budejovice Czech Republic

SPITZER, MATTHEW, retired retail store executive; b. Pitts., June 20, 1929; s. Martin and Ruth G. S.; children: Mark, Edward, Eric, Joseph. Student, U. Buffalo, 1948-50. Lic. airline transport pilot. Product line mgr. Gen. Dynamics, Rochester, N.Y., 1962-67; dir. contracts Friden divsn. Singer, San Leandro, Calif., 1968-69; asst. v.p. Talcott Computer Leasing, San Francisco, 1970-71; pres. Spitzer Music Mgmt. Co., Hayward, Calif., 1972-95, Spitzer Helicopter Leasing Co., Hayward; chmn. bd. Leo's Audio and Music Techs., Oakland, Calif. Mem. Masons, Mensa.

SPITZER, VLAD GERARD, lawyer; b. Bucharest, Romania, Mar. 3, 1956; came to U.S., 1963; s. Adrian and Carole Spitzer; m. Denise J. Borenstein, July 9, 1989; 1 child, Max Oliver. BA with honors, NYU, 1978; JD, Yeshiva U., 1981. Bar: N.Y. 1988, Conn. 1995, U.S. Dist. Ct. (so. and ea. dists.) N.Y. 1988, U.S. Dist. Ct. Conn. 1996, U.S. Ct. Appeals (2d cir.) 1994, U.S. Supreme Ct. 1995. Asst. dist. atty. Dist. Atty.'s Office of King's County, Bklyn., 1981-83; ptnr. Goldbergh & Spitzer LLC, N.Y.C., 1988-95, Stamford, Conn., 1995—; adv. bd. Nat. Employee Rights Inst., Cin., 1997—; founding mem. Conn. Employee Rights Inst., Stamford, Conn., 1997; coop. atty. ACLU, N.Y. Civil Liberties Union; judge Wagner Nat. Lab. and Employment Law Moot Ct., N.Y. Law Sch., 1996-98. Belkin scholar, 1981. Mem. ATLA (labor and employment sect. 1996—), Assn. of the Bar of the City of N.Y., Nat. Employment Lawyers Assn., Conn. Bar Assn. (labor and employment sect. 1996—, employee benefits com. 1996—), Nat. Employee Rights Inst., Stamford-Norwalk Regional Bar Assn., Stamford Rotary Club. Office: Spitzer Sundheim & Brey LLC 350 Bedford St Stamford CT 06901-1741

SPITZLI, DONALD HAWKES, JR., lawyer; b. Newark, Mar. 19, 1934; s. Donald Hawkes and Beatrice (Banister) S.; children: Donald Hawkes III, Peter Gilbert, Seth Armstrong. A.B., Dartmouth Coll., 1956; LL.B., U. Va., 1963. Bar: Va. 1963. Assoc. Willcox, Savage, Lawrence, Dickson & Spindle, Norfolk, Va., 1964-67, 68-70; ptnr. Willcox, Savage, Lawrence, Dickson & Spindle, Norfolk, 1971-77; atty. Eastman Kodak Co., Rochester, N.Y., 1967-68; pres. Marine Hydraulics Internat., Inc., Chesapeake, Va., 1978-80; sole practice Virginia Beach, Va., 1980—; owner Chieftain Motor Inn, Hanover, N.H., 1980-87. Comdr. USNR, 1956-70. Episcopalian. Office: 281 Independence Blvd Ste 605 Virginia Beach VA 23462-2975

SPIVACK, HENRY ARCHER, life insurance company executive; b. Bklyn., Apr. 15, 1919; s. Jacob and Pauline (Schwartz) S.; m. Sadie Babe Meiseles, Jan. 1, 1941; children: Ian Jeffrey, Paula Janis. Student, CCNY, 1936-42; BBA, Am. Coll., Bryn Mawr, Pa., 1965. CLU. Comptr. Daniel Jones, Inc., N.Y.C., 1947-59; field underwriter Union Ctr. Life Ins. Co., N.Y.C., 1959-79, mgr. programming dept., 1966-69, assoc. agy. mgr., 1977-79; pension dir. Bleichroeder, Bing & Co., N.Y.C., 1975-77; sr. v.p. NCA Agy., Inc. (formerly New Confidence Agy.), N.Y.C., 1979-90, Luxco & Assocs., Jericho, NY., 1990—; pension dir., employee benefit plan cons., estate and fin. planning, pres. Profl. Benefit Planners Inc. N.J.; instr. N.Y. State Ins. Dept., C.W. Post Coll., L.I. U., N.Y. Ctr. for Fin. Studies; coord. Ins. Dept. Yeshiva U., N.Y.; ins. courses instr.; also lectr., moderator. Contbr. articles to publs. With USN, 1943-46. Mem. Life Underwriters Assn. N.Y. (past chmn. blood bank), Am. Soc. CLUs (past chmn. N.Y. chpt. pension sect., past chmn. profl. liaison com.), Am. Soc. Pension Actuaries, Pensioneers at C.W. Post Coll., C.W. Post Coll. Tax Inst. and Fin. Planning Inst., Practising Law Inst., Internat. Assn. Fin. Planners, Internat. Assn. Registered Fin. Cons., Greater N.Y. Brokers Assn., KP (life, past dep. grand chancellor N.Y. State). Office: 500 N Broadway Jericho NY 11753-2127

SPIVAK, DMITRI, linguistic and psychological studies scientist; b. St. Petersburg, Russia, Nov. 25, 1954; s. Leonid and Nonna (Yastrebova) S.; m. Irina Martynova, Aug. 23, 1985. MA in Econs., State U. St. Petersburg, 1976, PhD in Econs., 1980, DrSc in Linguistics and Psychology, 1999. Sr. rschr. Inst. Adult Edn., St. Petersburg, 1980-89; sr. rsch. assoc. Inst. of the Human Brain, St. Petersburg, 1989—. Author: Language Under Altered States of Consciousness, 1989, Altered States of Mass Consciousness, 1996, The Northern Capital: Metaphysics of St. Petersburg, 1998; mem. editl. bd. The Transpersonal Inst. Pub. House, Moscow, 1998—. Grantee Russian Found. for Fundamental Rsch., 1997, 2000, Russian Found. for Humanitarian Rsch., 1998; State Sci. grantee, 2000. Mem. APA, Russian Acad. Natural Scis. (corr.), Sci. and Med. Network Gt. Britain, European Assn. Sci. and Theology. Russian Orthodox. Avocation: learning languages. Home: Po Box 19, 191186 Saint Petersburg Russia Office: Inst of Human Brain, Pavlova St 12, 197 376 Saint Petersburg Russia

SPIVAK, JACQUE R., bank executive; b. San Francisco, Nov. 5, 1929; d. Robert Morris and Sadonia Clardine Breitstein; m. Herbert Spivak, Aug. 26, 1960; children: Susan, Donald, Joel, Sheri. BS, U. So. Calif., 1949, MS, 1950, MBA, 1959. Mgr. Internat. Escrow, Inc., L.A., 1960-65, Greater L.A. Investment Co., 1965-75; mgr. escrow Transam. Title Ins. Co., L.A., 1975-78; mgr. escrow, asst. v.p. Wells Fargo Bank, Beverly Hills, Calif., 1979-80; adminstr. escrow, v.p. 1st Pacific Bank, Beverly Hills, 1980-85; escrow adminstr. Century City Savs. & Loan Assn., L.A., 1986-87; pres. Prodrs. Escrow Corp., Beverly Hills, 1987—. Recipient awards PTA, Girl Scouts U.S.A., Jewish Fedn. L.A., Hadassah. Mem. Nat. Assn. Bank Women, Calif. Escrow Assn., Inst. Trustees Sales Officers, Hadassah (nat. bd., pres.

L.A. chpt.). Republican. Jewish. Office: Producers Escrow Corp PO Box 5771 Beverly Hills CA 90209-5771

SPIVAK, KENIN MATHEW, executive; b. N.Y.C., May 14, 1957; s. Edwin Howard and Charlotte S. AB, Columbia U., 1977, MBA, 1980, JD, 1980. V.p. Merrill Lynch Capital Markets, 1985-88; COO, MGM/UA Comm. Co., 1988-90; pres. Island World Group, 1991-94; co-chmn., exec. com. Premiere Radio Network, L.A., 1995-97; chmn. Knowledge Exch., L.A., 1995-97; pres., CEO, Archon Comm., Inc., L.A., 1995-97; vice chmn. John Paul Mitchell Systems, Beverly Hills, Calif., 1994—; chmn., CEO, Spivak Sports, L.A., 1997-99; chmn. Aquarius Holdings, Inc., L.A., 1997-2000; chmn., CEO, Telemac Corp., 1998—; chmn. Savage Mountain Sports Corp., 2000—. Editor: Knowledge Exchange Business Encyclopedia. Office: 6701 Center Dr W Ste 700 Los Angeles CA 90045-1565

SPIVAKOV, VLADIMIR TEODOROVICH, conductor; b. Ufa, Russia, Sept. 12, 1944; m. Satinik Saakyants; two children. Student, Moscow State Conservatory. Conductor Chamber Orch. Virtuosi, Moscow, 1979—. Office: Columbia Artists Mgmt Inc c/o Mary Joe Connealy 165 W 57th St New York NY 10019*

SPÍZEK, JAROSLAV PAVEL, microbiologist, institute executive; b. Prague, Czech Republic, Aug. 11, 1935; s. Karel and Bozena Ruzena (Moravkova) S.; m. Jana Ruzena Behounkova; children: Moravcova Barbora, Ceralova, Katerina. MSc, Charles U., 1958; PhD in Biology, Czech. Acad. Sci., Prague, 1963. Postdoctoral rsch. fellow Case Western Res. U., Cleve., 1964-65; sr. rsch. scientist Inst. of Microbiology, Acad. of Sci. of Czech Republic, Prague, 1970-89; dep. dir. Inst. of Microbiology, Acad. of Scis. of Czech Republic, Prague, 1990-91, dir., 1992—; vis. prof. U. Wis., Madison, 1991; mem. sci. counsel U. of Chem. Tech., Prague, 1994—, Internat. Com. on Genetics of Indsl. Microorganisms, 1996—, NATO Adv. Panel on Security-Related Civil Svc. and Tech., Brussels, 1998—. Editor: Gene Manipulation and Expression, 1984; co-author: Selected Methods in Microbiology, 1981; guest editor Overproduction of Microbial Products, 1990. Mem. Czech Assn. of Club of Rome (bd. dirs. 1992—), Czechoslovak Soc. for Microbiology (pres. 1997—), Czech and Slovak Soc. for Biochemistry and Molecular Biology. Avocations: music, literature, tennis. Home: U smaltovny 20F, 17000 Prague 7 Czech Republic Office: Inst of Microbiology, Videnska 1083, 14220 Prague 4 Czech Republic

SPLETT, JOCHEN, Germanic philology educator; b. Magdeburg, Germany, June 9, 1938; s. Bruno Emil and Elisabeth (Schieb) S.; m. Eva Maria Dlugi, May 12, 1966; children: Tatjana Splett Weiland, Marcel Splett. DPhil, U. Bonn, Germany, 1967; Habil., U. Münster, Germany, 1972. Asst. U. Bonn, 1965-69; asst. U. Münster, 1969-72, docent, 1972-77, asst. prof., 1977-79, prof. Germanic philology, 1980—, dean sect. Germanic philology, 1991-93. Author: Rüdiger von Bechelaren, 1968, Abrogans-Studien, 1976, Samanunga-Studien, 1979, Althochdeutsches Wörterbuch, 3 vols., 1993, (with Franz Hundsnurscher) Semantik der Adjektive des Deutschen, 1982, others; editor: Das Bremer Evangelistar, 1996. Recipient Louis Braille prize German Soc. of the Blind, 1984. Roman Catholic. Home: Dettenstrasse 1, Münster D-48147, Germany Office: Westf Wilhelms-Univ, Johannisstrasse 1-4, Münster D-48143, Germany

SPLETT, JÖRG, philosophy educator; b. Magdeburg, Germany, Aug. 29, 1936; s. Bruno Emil and Elisabeth (Schieb) S.; m. Ingrid Maria Margulies, Sept. 10, 1964; children: Martin, Thomas. Dr.phil., U. Munich, 1965, Dr.phil.habil., 1971. Sci. asst. U. Munich, 1964-71; prof. St. Georgen U., Frankfurt, Germany, 1971—; mem. staff Theologie u. Philosophie, Frankfurt, 1980—, Il Nuovo Areopago, Rome, 1982—. Author: Die Trinitätslehre G.W.F. Hegels, 1965, 3d edit., 1984, Italian edit., 1993, Gotteserfahrung im Denken, 1973, 4th edit., 1995, Freiheits-Erfahrung, 1986, Leben als Mit-Sein, 1990, Spiel-Ernst, 1993, Denken vor Gott, 1996, and others on Hegel, man and religion, 1964—; editor: Wie frei ist der Mensch?, 1980, Italian edit., 1984, Höllenkreise-Himmelsrose, 1994; contbr. more than 500 articles to profl. jours. Mem. European Acad. Sci. and Art. Roman Catholic. Home: Isenburgring 7, 63069 Offenbach Germany

SPOEHEL, RONALD ROSS, communications company executive; b. L.A., Oct. 28, 1957; s. Edwin Henry and Geraldine Jean (Hoskins) S.; m. Deborah Elizabeth Bell, Jan. 29, 1994; children: Elizabeth Schuyler, James Henry. BS in Econ., U. Pa., 1979, MS in Engring., 1980, MBA, 1980. V.p. Bank Am., San Francisco, N.Y.C., L.A., 1980-85, Lehman Bros., N.Y.C., 1985-90; sr. v.p., chief fin. officer ICF Kaiser Internat., Washington, 1990-94; v.p. corp. devel. Harris Corp, Melbourne, Fla., 1994—. Mem. Metro. Club Washington, Eau Gallie Yacht Club.

SPOELDERS, MARC HUBERT PAUL, education educator; b. Antwerp, Belgium, Mar. 14, 1947; m. Anne-Marie Cotton; children: Seth, Sara, Simon. Tchg. Cert. in Lower Secondary Edn., Pius X Tchr. Tng. Coll., Antwerp, 1966, lic. in psychol. and ednl. scis., 1970; PhD, U. Ghent, Belgium, 1975. Rschr. Belgian Sci. Rsch. Fund, 1970-80; asst. prof. U. Ghent, 1981-91, prof., 1991—. Editor-in-chief Scientia Paedagogica Experimentalis jour., 1988—. Mem. Internat. Assn. Applied Linguistics (sec. gen. 1987-93, pres. 1993-96). Office: Univ Ghent Dept Edn, 1 Henri Dunantlaan, B-9000 Gent Belgium

SPOERI, RANDALL KEITH, healthcare company executive; b. Cleve., June 12, 1946; s. Theodore Warren and Marion (Barrick) S.; m. Kathleen Loma Bryden Hayes, Aug. 31, 1968 (div. Mar. 1981); 1 child, Jennifer Anne; m. Deborah Jean Hammett, June 20, 1981 (div. Nov. 1998); 1 child, Jason Randall; m. Laura Joan Lenhardt, Apr. 24, 1999. BS, Calif. Polytech. State U., 1968; MS, Tex. A&M U., 1970, PhD, 1976. Math. statistician U.S. Bur. of the Census, Suitland, Md., 1976-80; assoc. prof. U.S. Naval Acad., Annapolis, 1980-83; assoc. exec. dir. Am. Statis. Assn., Alexandria, Va., 1983-88; sr. corp. statistician Humana, Inc., Louisville, Ky., 1988-92; chief program coord., info. branch Health Care Fin. Adminstrn., Balt., 1993; asst. v.p. Nat. Com. for Quality Assurance, Washington, 1994-95; adminstrv. v.p. health care analysis NYLCare Health Plans, Inc., N.Y.C., 1995-98; v.p. med. and quality informatics HIP Health Plans, N.Y.C., 1998—. Author: Quantitative Methods In Quality Management, 1991; contbr. articles to profl. jours. Mem. adv. com. Health Care Fin. Adminstrn., Balt., 1990-92, bur. dir. citation, 1993, adv. bd. Juran Inst., Wilton, Conn., 1995-98. 1st lt. U.S. Army, 1970-72. Recipient Svc. award Am. Statis. Assoc., Alexandria, 1994. Fellow AAAS, Am. Soc. for Quality (health care divsn. chair 1995-96); mem. Am. Statis Assn., Inst. Indsl. Engring., Inst. for Ops. Rsch. and the Mgmt. Scis., Am. Med. Informatics Assn., Assn. for Health Svcs. Rsch. Avocations: sports, music. Home: 148 Top Of The World Way Green Brook NJ 08812-1839

SPOHN, BRYAN GORDON, entomologist; b. Plainfield, N.J., Sept. 13, 1970; s. Ralph Joseph and Veronica Mary (Gordon) S.; m. Veronica Mary Gordon, 1967 (dec. 1988); m. Marina Spohn. BS in Biology, Villanova U., 1992; MS in Biology, U. Ky., 1995, PhD in Entomology, 2000. Rsch. asst. dept. entomology U. Ky., 1995—. Contbr. articles to profl. jours. including Biosystems, Jour. of Insect Beh., Ethology. Lobbyist, advocate, vol. Ky. Breast Cancer Coalition, Lexington, 1996-97, sec., 1999—; vol. Cancer Support Network, Lexington, 1998, God's Party, Lexington, 1993; vol., cantor Newman Ctr., Lexington, 1993—. BEACON tng. grant NIMH, 1995. Mem. Am. Mus. of Natural History (assoc.), Phi Kappa Phi, Sigma Xi (assoc.). Democrat. Roman Catholic. Avocations: choir singing, Kiyojute Ryu Kempo Bugei. Home: 1313 Nancy Hanks Rd Apt 1 Lexington KY 40504-1223 Office: U Ky S-225 Ab Sci Bld N Dept Entomology Lexington KY 40546-0091

SPOHN, WILLIAM GIDEON, JR., mathematician, musician; b. Lancaster, Pa., Mar. 8, 1923; s. William Gideon and Inza Mae (Huber) S.; m. Alice Liane Bailey, Sept. 13, 1946 (div.); children: Susan Jeannine Grochowina (dec.), William Gideon III (dec.), Peter Jonathan, Kathleen Anne Precht, Mary Louise; m. Evelyn Walsh Moreland, June 15, 1963 (div. Oct. 1978); m. Claire Louise Burgstahler, Dec. 19, 1987 (div. Sept. 1999). BA, St. Johns Coll., 1947; MA, U. Calif., Berkeley, 1950; PhD, U. Pa., 1962. Instr. math. Temple U., Phila., 1952-54, U. Del., Newark, 1954-56; mathematician Aberdeen Proving Ground, Md., 1954-55; instr. math. Bowling Green State U., 1956-59; mathematician, sr. staff Johns Hopkins U. Applied Physics Lab., Laurel, Md., 1959-84; singer, prodr. Spohn Music Co., Columbia, Md., 1981-99. Contbr. articles to profl. jours. Served to lt. USNR, 1943-46, PTO. Johns Hopkins U. Applied Physics Lab. fellow, 1966-67. Mem. Math. Assn. Am. Home: 943C Marimich Ct Eldersburg MD 21784-4909

SPONA, JURGEN, scientist, educator; b. Vienna, Austria, May 4, 1940; s. Raimund and Stephanie (Brauner) S.; m. Bdrbel Hassmann, Feb. 14, 1967 (div. Oct. 1986); children: Martin, Christian; m. Ingrid Heckel, Mar. 3, 1988; children: Clara, Philipp. PhD, Vienna U., 1967. Rsch. assoc. Princeton (N.J.) U., 1966, Cornell U. Med. Ctr., N.Y.C., 1969-70; asst. prof. Vienna U., 1970-75, assoc. prof., 1975-81, prof., 1981—; dir. Ludwig Boltzmann Inst., Vienna, 1987—; dir. LAB 19, Vienna, 1990—. Author more than 400 sci. publs. Mem. N.Y. Acad. Scis., Soc. for Advancement of Contraception (bd. dirs. 1990—). Avocations: skiing, horse dressage. Home: Adolfstorgasse 11, A-1130 Vienna Austria Office: Billrothstrasse 78, A-1190 Vienna Austria

SPOONER, DAVID ERIC, military officer; b. Norwhich, N.Y., Apr. 10, 1973; s. Mark Irving Spooner and Alexa Lynn Cook. BS in English and Religion, Liberty U., 1997; postgrad., Regis U., 1999—. Enlisted U.S. Army, West Monroe, N.Y., 1997—; squad leader U.S. Army, Ft. Jackson, Ala., 1998—. Youth pastor Protestant Youth, Ft. Rucker, Ala., 1998-2000. Republican. Charismatic. E-mail: dspoonerb@aol.com. Home: 31 Northway Manor West Monroe NY 13167 Office: Bldg 8945 Red Cloud Fort Rucker AL 36362

SPOONER, DONNA, public administrator; b. Deland, Fla., May 18, 1948; d. Michael and Ruth Elizabeth (Hauser) Linkovich. BS in Housing and Interior Design, Fla. State U., 1971, MPA, 1993, postgrad. owner Spooner Energy Assocs., Tallahassee, 1996—. Budget analyst Dept. Adminstrn./Exec. Office of Gov. State of Fla., Tallahassee, 1977-80, spl. projects adminstr./acting chief, Bur. of Employee Cert., 1980-81, sr. govtl. analyst Exec. Office of Gov., 1981-85, pub. and legis. affairs dir. Dept. Adminstrn., 1985-87, asst. dir. Gov.'s Drug and Crime Policy Office, 1987-90; statewide planning coord. alcohol, drug abuse, mental health Fla. Dept. Health and Rehab. Svcs., Tallahassee, 1990-95. Mem. Am. Soc. Pub. Adminstrn., S.E. Evaluation Assn., Capital Women's Network, Pi Alpha Alpha. Avocations: reading, hiking. Home: PO Box 14595 Tallahassee FL 32317-4595

SPOONER, FRANK CLYFFURDE, economic history educator; b. Cleveland, Australia, Mar. 5, 1924; s. Harry Gordon Morrison and Ethel Beatrice (Walden) S. BA, U. Cambridge, Eng., 1947, MA, 1949, PhD, 1953, LittD, 1985. Commonwealth Fund fellow U. Chgo., NYU, Columbia U., Harvard U., 1955-57, U. Paris, 1957-63; lectr. advanced studies U. Oxford, Eng., 1958-59; vis. lectr. econs. Harvard U., Cambridge, Mass., 1961-62; Irving Fisher rsch. prof. econs. Yale U., New Haven, 1962-63; mem. faculty U. Durham, Eng., 1963—, dir. Inst. European Studies, 1969-76, prof. econ. history, 1966-85, prof. emeritus, 1985—. Author: The International Economy and Monetary Movements in France, 1493-1680, 1956, English lang. edit., 1972, The International Economy and Monetary Movements in France, 1493-1725, 1972, Risks at Sea, 1983. Sub-lt. Royal Navy, 1943-46, ETO. Recipient Prix Limantour Acad. Scis. Morales et Politiques, 1957; Leverhulme Fund fellow, 1976-78, 85-86. Fellow Royal Hist. Soc., Royal Numismatic Soc., Soc. Antiquaries London; mem. Econ. History Soc., Econ. History Assn., Vereniging Economisch-Historisch Archief, Royal Econ. Soc., Am. Econ. Assn., Cliometric Soc., Assn. Marc Bloch, Hakluyt Soc., Soc. Francaise Numismatique, Mark Twain Soc., Friends Nat. Librs., United Oxford and Cambridge U. Club. Home: 31 Chatsworth Ave, Bromley Kent BR1 5DP, England Office: U Durham Dept Econs, 23-26 Old Elvet, Durham DH1 3HY, England

SPOONER, SIR JAMES (DOUGLAS), business executive; b. July 11, 1932; s. E.J. and Megal (Foster) S.; m. Jane Alyson, 1958; 3 children. Ed., Eton Coll. Chartered acct. Ptnr. Dixon Wilson & Co., Chartered Accts., 1963-72; chmn. Coats Viyella (formerly Vantona Viyella), 1969-89; chmn. bd. dirs. Morgan Crucible Co., Berkshire, Eng.; now with Swire & Sons, London. Bd. dirs. Royal Opera Ho., Covent Garden, 1987—, dep. chmn., 1992—; chmn. trustees Brit. Telecom. Pension Scheme, 1992—; chmn. coun. King's Coll. London, 1986—. Mem. NAAFI (bd. dirs. 1968-86, chmn. bd. dirs. 1973-86). Avocations: music, history, shooting. Office: Swire House, 59 Buckingham Gate, London England*

SPOONLEY, PAUL, sociologist, educator, researcher; b. Upper Hutt, Wellington, New Zealand, Aug. 26, 1951; s. John and Maire (Hill) S.; m. Jennifer Crowley, Jan. 10, 1975; children: Jacob, Nathan. BA, Victoria U., Wellington, 1973; MA, U. Otago, New Zealand, 1976; MSc, U. Bristol, Eng., 1978; PhD, Massey U., New Zealand, 1986. Tchr. fellow U. Auckland, New Zealand, 1974-75, 78; lectr. Massey U., New Zealand, 1979, assoc. prof., 1992-95, prof., 1995—; vis. fellow U. Bristol, 1985, 92-93; vis. prof. U. Calif., Irvine, 1985; pres. Fedn. Social Sci. Orgns., New Zealand, 1990-91, 93-96. Author: The Politics of Nostalgia, 1987, Racism and Ethnicity, 1988, 2d edit., 1993; editor: New Zealand Society, 1994, Racism and Ethnic Relations in Aoteaoro/New Zealand, 1996. Mem. Nat. Coun., Barnados, New Zealand, 1990-96. Recipient New Zealand Commemoration medal Govt. of New Zealand, 1990. Avocations: soccer, apple growing, collecting Chinese porcelain. Office: Massey U-Albany, Pvt Bag 102-904, Auckland New Zealand

SPOOR, JAMES EDWARD, human resources executive, entrepreneur; b. Rockford, Ill., Feb. 19, 1936; s. Frank Kendall and Genevieve Eileen (Johnson) S.; m. Nancy E. Carlson, Sept. 8, 1962; children: Sybll K., Kendall P., Andrea K., Marcie K. BS in Psychology, U. Ill., 1958. Pers. mgr. Nat. Sugar Refining Co., N.Y.C., 1960-64; Pepsico, Inc., N.Y.C., Auburn, N.Y., 1964-67; mgr. internat. pers. Control Data Corp., Mpls., 1967-75; v.p. pers. and employee rels. Vetco, Inc., Ventura, Calif., 1975-79; v.p. employee rels. Hamilton Bros. Oil Co., Denver, 1979-84; pres., founder, pres., CEO Spectrum Human Resource Systems Corp., Denver, 1984—; cons., author, spkr. on human resources and entrepreneurism. Mem. adv. bd. Salvation Army, 1978-79; chmn. Spl. Commn. for Ventura County Bd. Suprs., 1978; mem. task force on human resources Colo. Sch. Mines, 1983; state chair Coun. Growing Cos., 1991-92, nat. pres., 1992-94; bd. dirs. Breckenridge Outdoor Edn. Ctr., 1994-98, chmn., 1996-98. Mem. Internat. Human Resources Mgmt. Assn. (nat. bd. dirs. 1997—).

SPOOREN, PIETER, internist; b. Maarheeze, The Netherlands, Mar. 10, 1951; s. Harrie and Annie (Van Dongen) S.; m. Henny Schaart; children: Jaap, Thijs, Henke, Bart. MD, U. Nijmegen, The Netherlands, 1979; PhD, Free U., Amsterdam, 1995. Sr. house officer Med. Spectrum, Enschede, The Netherlands, 1979-84, rschr./specialist for internal medicine, 1987-92; rschr. U. Leiden, The Netherlands, 1985-87; specialist for internal medicine Twee Steden Ziekenhuis, Tilburg, The Netherlands, 1992—. Author: Diabetic Nephropathy, 1995. Mem. Am. Diabetes Assn. Office: Twee Steden Ziekenhuis, Dr Deelenlaan 5 Box 90107, 5000LA Tilburg The Netherlands

SPOORS, GERALD, chemist; b. Shiney Row, Durham, U.K., Aug. 16, 1948; s. Leslie and Kathleen (Oliver) S.; m. Elaine Maughan; children: Julie Lavinia, Geoffrey Hardin, Kenneth Martin. BSc, Teesside U., 1972. Process devel. chemist Steetl.y Refractories, Hartlepool, U.K., 1972; sr. tech. officer Streetley Minerals, Hartlepool, 1978; head product devel. sect. Steetley Minerals, Hartlepool, 1984-88; mgr. devel. Steetley Magnesia, Hartlepool, 1988-91; mgr. sales Redland Magnesia, Hartlepool, 1991-94; mgr. tech. svcs. Redland Minerals, Hartlepool, 1994-96; mgr. tech. Britmag Ltd., Hartlepool, 1996—. Contbr. articles to profl. jours. Chmn. gov.'s North Blunts Sch., Peterlee, 1985—. Fellow Royal Soc. Chemistry, Inst. Materials. Avocations: researching family history, early British history, playing piano. Home: 10 Bewley Grove, Durham Peterlee SR8 1PP, England Office: Britmag Ltd, PO Box 8, Hartlepool TS24 0B4, England

SPORNITZ, UDO MEINHARD, anatomist, researcher; b. Reinach, Switzerland, May 20, 1943; s. Willy Franz Paul and Liselotte Helène Sophie (Schnurr) S.; m. Renate Cathy Schilling, Apr. 15, 1966; children: Patrick Oliver, Vanessa Aglaia. PhD, U. Basel, Switzerland, 1978, Prof. in Medicine, 1997. Head dept. electron microscopy Technische Hochschule Aachen, Germany, 1967-72, Inst. Anatomy, Basel, 1980—. Author: The Functional Morphology of the Human Endometrium and Decidua, 1992, Anatomy and Physiology for Nursing Profession, 1993, Anatomy and Physiology, Textbook and Atlas, 1996; contbr. chpts. to books and 60 articles to profl. publs. Pres. Liberal Dem. Party, Canton Baselland, Switzerland, 1995-2000, Pfeffingen, 1989-96. Recipient CDS award Soc. for Advancement of Contraception, Nairobi, 1985. Mem. Deutsche Anatomische Gesellschaft, Schweizer. Gesellschaft für Histologie Embryologie und Anatomie, Schweizer. Gesellschaft für Optik und Elektronenmikroskopie, Kiwanis. Avocation: photography. Home: Bergmattenweg 46, CH-4148 Pfeffingen Switzerland Office: Inst Anatomy, Pestalozzistrasse 20, CH-4056 Basel Switzerland

SPOSITO, JAMES ANTHONY, lawyer, consultant; b. Carbondale, Pa., Jan. 11, 1943; s. Anthony James and Hortense (Talarico) S.; m. Karen Mascelli, Nov. 25, 1966 (div. Nov. 1976); children: James A. Jr., Angela. BS in History, U. Scranton, 1964; MS, Marywood Coll., Scranton, 1969; JD, George Mason U., 1980; LLD, Strasburg (France) U., 1980. Bar: Pa. 1980, U.S. Dist. Ct. (mid. dist.) Pa. 1980, U.S. Ct. Appeals (3rd cir.) 1983; cert. tchr., Pa. Tchr. elem. and secondary schs., Pa., 1966-76; aide to Congressman Phil Sharp U.S. Ho. of Reps., Washington, 1977-78; pres. James A. Sposito & Assocs., Scranton, 1980—; pres. Spo-Jac Enterprises, Carbondale, 1964—; pres., owner, broker Sposito Realty Co., Carbondale, 1965—. Advisor 114th legis. dist. State Rep.'s Office, Pa., 1978—. Acting 2d lt. U.S. Army N.G., 1964-71. Mem. ATLA, Pa. Bar Assn., Pa. Trial Assn., Susquehanna County Bar Assn., Lackawanna Bar Assn., Thunderbird Investment Club (pres. 1966-70), Elkview Country Club. (sr. golf mem.), Lions. Roman Catholic. Avocations: golf, hunting, fishing. Home: RR 1 Box 1155 Carbondale PA 18407-9016 Office: 547 Hickory St Scranton PA 18505-1322

SPRAGENS, WILLIAM CLARK, public policy educator, consultant; b. Lebanon, Ky., Oct. 1, 1925; s. Thomas Eugene and Edna Grace (Clark) S.; m. Elaine Jean Dunham, June 14, 1964. AB in Journalism, U. Ky., 1947, MA, 1953; PhD, Mich. State U., 1966. Instr. U. Tenn., Knoxville, 1962-64; part-time instr. Mich. State U., East Lansing, 1964-65; asst. prof. Millikin U., Decatur, Ill., 1965-67, Wis. State U., Oshkosh, 1967-69; assoc. prof. Bowling Green (Ohio) State U., 1969-82, prof., 1982-86, prof. emeritus, 1986—; chmn. Spragens and Skinner Assocs., Reston, Va., 1996—. Author: Electronic Magazines, 1995, New Media for the New Millenium, 2001; editor-in-chief: Popular Images of American Presidents, 1988. Del. candidate McGovern for pres. campaign, Bowling Green, 1972; co-dir. Nat. Convs. Program, 1972, 76, 80, 84. Lyndon Baines Johnson Found. grantee, 1977, 78. Mem. AAAS, World Affairs Coun. Washington, Am. Polit. Sci. Assn., Internat. Soc. for Polit. Psychology, Am. Soc. for Pub. Adminstrn. Democrat. Presbyterian. Avocations: collectibles, psychology. Home and Office: PO Box 410 Herndon VA 20172-0410

SPRAINGS, VIOLET EVELYN, psychologist; b. Omaha, Aug. 1; d. Henry Elbert and Straunella (Hunter) S. AB, U. Calif., Berkeley, MA, postgrad., 1982; PhD, U. Calif., San Francisco, 1982. Tchr. Oakland (Calif.) Pub. Schs.; psychologist Med. Edn. Diagnostic Ctr., San Francisco, 1959-62; dir. psychol. edn. and lang. svcs. Calif. Dept. Edn., 1963-71; asst. prof. San Francisco State U., 1964-71; assoc. prof. ednl. psychology Calif. State U., Hayward, 1971-79; dir. Spraings Acad. and Diagnostic Clinic, Orinda and Walnut Creek, Calif., 1967—; pvt. practice, 1962—; bd. dirs. Western Women's Bank; adv. bd. Bay Area Health Systems Agy.; instr. U. Calif., Berkeley extension, 1964—; mem. oral bd. for Ednl. Psychologists, 1972—; mem. Calif. Dept. Task Force on Psychol. Assessment, 1987—; mem. adv. bd. Educators Pub. Co., 2000—. Contbr. articles to profl. jours. Mem. adv. com. Foothill Jr. Coll. Dist.; cons. psychologist Casey Family Program, 1986—. Recipient Phoebe Apperson Heart award San Francisco Examiner, 1968. Mem. AAUW, APA, Internat. Neuropsychol. Assn. (charter), Calif. Psychol. Assn., Calif. Assn. Sch. Psychologists and Psychometrists, Western Psychol. Assn., Nat. Coun. Negro Women, Delta Sigma Theta, Psi Chi, Pi Lambda Theta. Home: 170 Glorietta Blvd Orinda CA 94563-3543 Office: 89 Moraga Way Orinda CA 94563-3023

SPRANDEL, ULRICH V., physician, educator; b. Krumbach, Bavaria, Germany, Oct. 31, 1946; s. Viktor K. and Erika (Karlinger) S.; m. Anna Maria Grabowski, Sept. 18, 1970; children: Claudia Anne, Julia Susanne, Martin Ulrich. Degree in physician, U. Munich, Germany, 1972, MD, 1972; Dr. med. habil., Privatdozent U. Munich, Germany, 1984. Sci. asst. U. Munich, 1973-78; rsch. officer Royal Soc. Clin. Rsch. Ctr., London, 1978-80; sci. asst., internist Polyclinic U. Munich, 1980-84; lectr., apl. prof. internal medicine U. Munich, 1984—; head internal medicine Krankenhaus Marktoberdorf, 1984—; med. dir. Kreiskliniken Ostallgaeu Marktoberdorf, 1997. Author: Kompendium der Inneren Medizin, 1987, 90; author, editor: Red Blood Cells as Carrier for Drugs, 1985; co-author: Pharmakologie und Toxikologie, 1980, 87; editor: Erythrocytes as Drug Carriers in Medicine, 1995. Chmn. Child Spacing Family Health and AIDS Edn. in Northern Nigeria, 1999; vice chmn. Intercounty Com. Egypt-Germany, 1995—; active Parents Coun. for All Schs. of Munich, 1980-94. Mem. Anglo-Germany Med. Soc. (pres. 1996—), Internat. Soc. Resealed Erthrocytes (pres. 1995—), Rotary Internat. (chmn. German vol. drs. 1998—, Paul Harris fellow 1999, gov. dist. 1840 1998-99), Med. Coun. Bavaria (chmn. examination bds. 1991—), Deutsche Gesellschaft fur Innere Medizin, Deutsche Diabetes Gesellschaft. Avocations: family, history, futurology, classic music, geography. Home: Kriss St 11, D-87616 Marktoberdorf Bavaria, Germany Office: Kreiskliniken Ostallgaeu, Saliterstr 96, D-87616 Marktoberdorf Bavaria, Germany Address: Krankenhaus Innere Abteilun, Saliterstr 60, D-87613 Marktoberdorf Bavaria, Germany

SPRANGER, JOERG, veterinarian, researcher; b. Homberg, Germany, June 3, 1950; arrived in Switzerland, 1997; s. Werner Spranger and Dagmar (Olowson) Seiwert; m. Christiane Doering Spranger-Paul, Mar. 24, 1972 (div. Jan. 1982); m. Jutta Erbsloeh, Feb. 25, 1983; children: Ronja, Jana. Student, U. Cologne and U. Munich, Germany, 1968-74; M in Agr., Marburg, Germany, 1976; veterinarian, Vet. U., Hannover, Germany, 1983; Doctorate (hon.), U. Kassel, Germany, 1989; specialist in homeopathics (hon.), U. Duesseldorf, Germany, 1992. Cert. in vet. medicine rsch. Farm mgr. monastery Bursfelde, Germany, 1976-78; asst. vet. various practices Germany, 1984-85; pvt. practice Coppenbruegge, Germany, 1985-88; pvt. practice as vet. advisor Wuppertal, Germany, 1988-97; head of animal health divsn. Rsch. Inst. Organic Agr., Frick, Switzerland, 1997—; lectr. in agr. and vet. medicine various univs., including U. Utrecht, The Netherlands, U. Helsinki, Finland, U. Zurich, Switzerland, U. Munich, U. Kassel, U. Hannover, U. Berlin, U. Ljubljana, Slovania, 1988—; cons. various pharm. orgns., Germany and Switzerland, 1988—. Co-author: (books) Organic Farming, 1995, Handbuch fuer die Tiergesundheit, 1998; contbr. sci. papers to profl. jours. Mem. Internat. Anthroposcopic Vet. Soc. (pres. 1999—), Rsch. Soc. Biol.-Dynamic Agr. Avocations: literature, traveling. Office: Rsch Inst Organic Agr, Ackerstrasse, CH-5070 Frick Aargau, Switzerland

SPRAOS, JOHN, economics educator; b. Athens, Greece, Nov. 4, 1926; arrived in Eng., 1946; s. Menelaus and Penelope (Voudouroglu) S.; m. Mary Constance Whitwill, Sept. 26, 1956; children: Paul, Helen. MA, U. Edinburgh, Scotland, 1950. Research scholar U. Manchester, Eng., 1950-53; research fellow U. Sheffield, Eng., 1953-57; lectr. econs. U. London, 1957-64, reader econs., 1964-65, prof. econs., 1965-82, prof. emeritus, 1982—; prof., hon. rsch. fellow Univ. Coll., London, 1982—; chmn. Coun. Econ. Advisers, Greece, 1985-88; mem. Econ. Com. of European Community, 1986-87; cons. UN Conf. Trade and Devel., Geneva, 1974-75; mem. com. indexation experts UN, 1975; editorial adviser Penguin Books, 1967-77; adv. macroecons. to prime min. Kazakhstan, 1995; chmn. Prime Min.'s Com. Long Term Econ. Policy, Greece, 1996-97; alternate exec. dir. Internat. Monetary Fund, 1998-2000. Author: The Decline of the Cinema, 1962, Inequalising Trade?, 1983; mem. editorial bd. Review of Econ. Studies, 1955-65; contbr. articles to profl. jours. Chmn. Greek Com. Against Dictatorship, London, 1967-74. Mem. Am. Econ. Assn., Royal Econ. Soc., European Econ. Assn. Office: University Coll, Gower St, London WC1E 6BT, England

SPRAUVE, MARGARET E., physician; b. L.A., Jan. 3, 1965; d. Gilbert A. and Alvara E. Ritter S.; m. Michael J. Margin, June 1, 1999; children: Mitchell, Michelle, Braeanna. BS, Univ. Detroit, 1985; MD, Harvard Univ., 1990, M in pub. health, 1991. Diplomate Am. Bd. Am. Coll. of Obstetrics and Gynecology. Asst. prof. obstetrics and gynecology Emory Univ., Atlanta, 1997; dir. women's health Virgin Island Dept. Health, USVI, 1997—; territorrial perinatologist Virgin Island Gov., 1997—, acting commr

of health, 1998; treas. Roy L. Schneider Hosp. Medical staff, 1999—. Contbr. articles to profl. jours. Mem. Virgin Island Inter-Agy. Coun., 1999—, chairperson Virgin Island Health Start Consortia, 1999—; testifier on health realted bills Virgin Island Leg., 1998, 99; co-chair Third World Caucus of Harvard Medical Sch.,1989, participant in Health Fair Lions Club, 1998, 99. Recipient Outstaning Women of Yr. award Alpha Kappa Alpha, 1999, Wilinsky Award for Academic Excellence, 1991. Fellow Am. Coll. Obstetrics and Gynecology, Nat. Medical Assn., Alpha Kappa Alpha. Avocations: travel, softball. E-mail: mesm3@hotmail.com. Fax number: 340 779 7300. Home and Office: PO Box 7312 Saint Thomas VI 00801-0312

SPRAY, PAUL ELLSWORTH, retired surgeon; b. Wilkinsburg, Pa., Apr. 9, 1921; s. Lester E. and Phoebe Gertrude (Hull) S.; m. Mary Louise Conover, Nov. 28, 1943; children: David C., Thomas L., Mary Lynn (Mrs. Thomas Branham). BS, U. Pitts., 1942; MD, George Washington U., 1944; MS, U. Minn., 1950. Diplomate Am. Bd. Orthopedic Surgery. Intern U.S. Marine Hosp., S.I., 1944-45; resident Mayo Found., Rochester, Minn., 1945-46, 48-50; practice medicine specializing in orthopedic surgery Oak Ridge, Tenn., 1950-98; retired, 1998; vol. physician Knoxville Interfaith Clinic, 1998—; mem. active staff Oak Ridge Hosp., 1950-98, hon. staff, 98-2000, mem. staff, 2000—; courtesy staff Harriman Hosp., Tenn., ret., 1998; vol. vis. cons. CARE Medico, Jordan, 1959, Nigeria, 1962, 65, Algeria, 1963, Afghanistan, 1970, Bangladesh, 1975, 77, 79, Peru, 1980, U. Ghana, 1982; AMA vol. physician, Vietnam, 1967, 72; vis. assoc. prof. U. Nairobi, 1973; mem. tchg. team Internat. Coll. Surgeons to Peru, 1979, 84 ; vis. prof. orthop. surgery U. Khartoum, 1976; hon. prof. San Luis Gonzaga U., Ica, Peru, 1979; AmDoc vol. cons. U. Biafra Tchg. Hosp., 1969; vis. prof. Mayo Clinic, 1988; sec. orthops. overseas divsn. CARE Medico, 1971-76, sec. Medico adv. bd., 1974-76, vice chmn., 1976, chmn., 1977-79, v.p. CARE, Inc., 1977-79, pub. mem. CARE bd. dirs., 1980-90, mem. bd. overseers, 1991-99; chmn. Orthops. Overseas, Inc., 1982-86, treas., 1986-88, emeritus mem., 1994; mem. U.S. organizing com. 1st Internat. Acad. Symposium on Orthops., Tianjin, China, 1983; mem. CUPP Internat. Adv. Coun., 1986-99; invited guest spkr. Japan Orthop. Assn., 1994. Mem. editorial bd. Contemporary Orthopedics, 1984-96. V.p. Anderson County Health Coun., 1975, pres., 1976-77, hon. bd. dirs.; pres. health commn. Coun. So. Mountains, 1958-65, sec., bd. dirs., 1965-66; Tenn. pres. UN Assn., 1966-67; vice-chmn. bd. Camelot Care Ctr., Tenn., 1979-82, chmn., 1982-86; bd. dirs. Camelot Found., 1986—, chmn., 1986-87; hon. mem. World Orthopedic Concern, 1990; with del. to Vietnam People to People, citizen amb. to Vietnam, 1993; del. to Oak Ridge's Sister City, Obinsk, Russia, 1993; trustee Vietnam Am. Scholarship Fund, 1992-95; Rotary vol. orthopaedic surgeon Kikuyu Hosp. Rehab. Ctr. of East Africa Presbyn. Ch., Nov. 1998. Recipient Svc. to Mankind award Sertoma, 1967, Humanitarian award Lions Club, 1968, Freedom Citation Sertoma, 1978, Amb. Goodwill Lions Club, award 1979, Medico Disting. Svc. award, 1990, 1st Ann. Vocat. Svc. award Oak Ridge Rotary, 1979, Tech. Communication award East Tenn. chpt. Soc. for Tech. Communication, 1983, Individual Achievement award Meth. Med. Ctr. of Oak Ridge, 1991, Humanitarian award Orthopaedics Overseas, 1992; Melvin Jones fellow Lions Club, 1993. Fellow ACS, Internat. Coll. Surgeons (Tenn. regent 1976-80, bd. councillors 1980-84, hon. chmn. bd. trustees 1981-83, trustee 1983-84, v.p. U.S. sect. 1982-83, mem. surg. teams com. 1983-90, Humanitarian award 1992); mem. AMA (Humanitarian Svc. award 1967, 72), Sociètè International Chirugie Orthopèdique et de Traumatologie, So. Orthopedic Assn., Western Pacific Orthopedic Assn., Am. Fracture Assn., Am. Acad. Orthopedic Surgeons (mem. com. on injuries 1980-86), Tenn. Med. Assn. (com. on emergency med. svcs. 1978-97), Peru Acad. Surgery (corr.), Peruvian Soc. Orthopedic Surgery and Traumatology (corr.), Clin. Orthopedic Soc., Mid-Am. Orthopaedic Soc., Rotary Club (Oak Ridge chpt., Paul Harris fellow). Fax: 423-483-8657. Home: 507 Delaware Ave Oak Ridge TN 37830-3902

SPRECHER, DREXEL ANDREAS, retired lawyer, writer; b. Independence, Wis., Mar. 25, 1913; s. Walter Edmund Sprecher and Florence LaVerne Maloy; m. Eleanor Rust Peirce, 1941 (div. 1946); m. Virginia Lee Sprecher, Sept. 24, 1949; children: Drexel A. Jr., Jenna Garman, Karen Maloy. Student, North Ctrl. Coll., Naperville, Ill., 1930-31; BA, U. Wis., 1934; JD, Harvard U., 1938. Bar: Wis. 1938, U.S. Supreme Ct. 1957. Trial atty. Nat. Labor Rels. Bd., Washington, 1938-42; from sgt. to capt. U.S. Army., 1942-46; asst. prosecutor Chief of Counsel for War Crimes, Nuremberg, Germany, 1945-49; asst. adminstr. Small Def. Plants Adminstrn., Washington, 1950-51; writer Chevy Chase, Md., 1972—; pres. Potomac Constrn. Co., Chevy Chase, 1957-59; co-owner Ridgeland Farm Estates, Potomac, Md., 1957-65; pres., v.p. Leadership Resources, Inc., Washington, 1960-72. Author: Inside the Nuremberg Trial, 1998 (Ann. List Acad. Titles, Choice Mag. 1999); chief editor: Trials of War Criminals Before the Nuremberg Military Tribunals, 15 vols., 1948-51. Pres. Potomac Dem. Club, 1955-56; dep. chmn. Nat. Dem. Com., Washington, 1957-60. Unitarian. Avocations: gymnasium exercise, walking.

SPRECHER, GUSTAV EWALD, pharmacy educator; b. Kupferzell, Germany, Nov. 17, 1922; s. Emil and Emma (Küstner) S.; m. Helga Mohr, Aug. 28, 1955; 1 child, Wolfram. BS in Pharmacy, Tech. U. Karlsruhe, 1953, Dr. rer. nat., 1956, Dr. Habil., 1960. Asst. prof. Tech. U. Karlsruhe, Fed. Republic Germany, 1955-64; assoc. prof. Tech. U. Karlsruhe, 1964-69; prof. U. Hamburg, Fed. Republic Germany, from 1969; now prof. emeritus U. Hamburg. Author: Arzneistoffproduktion, 1983, (with F. Deutschmann and B. Hohmann) Drogenanalyse I: Morph. Anatomie, 3d edit., 1992; contbr. articles to profl. jours. Mem. German Pharm. Soc. (Hermann-Thoms medal), Soc. Medicinal Plant Rsch. (hon. mem., pres. 1988-89). Home: Sandmoorweg 31, D 22559 Hamburg Germany

SPRECHER, BARON WILLIAM GUNTHER, pianist, composer, conductor, diplomat; b. Saarbrucken, Germany, Jan. 20, 1924; came to U.S., 1952.; s. Wolf and Karoline (Jung) Sprecher; m. Blossom Tag, Aug. 6, 1952. Studied piano with Prof. Wittels, Tel Aviv; studied piano with Madame Vengerova, N.Y.C.; studied composition with Paul Ben-Haim, Tel Aviv, studied conducting with Georg Singer; hon. degree, Inst. of Vocal Arts, 1957; Dr. honoris causa in Philosophy of Music, World Univ. Roundtable, 1988; MusD (hon.), London Inst. Applied Rsch., 1991, DFA (hon.), 1993, HHD, 1993; MusD (hon.), Australian Inst. Coord. Rsch., 1991; diploma, Gran Premio Am., 1990, Paladino del Tricolore, 1990; D Musicology, Somerset U.; D Music (hon.), Atlantic Southeastern U.; Diploma, Acad. Argentina de Diplomacia; Assoc. (hon.), Inst. Affairs Internat., Paris, 1993; DD (hon.), The Christian Congregation; D rerum politicarum (hon.), LittD, U. Aeterna Lucina Vitama, 1991; DD (hon.), LittD, Eng., 1994; PhD (hon.), Germany, 1994. Korrepetitor Israel Folk Opera, Tel-Aviv, 1940-43; piano soloist Israel Philharm. Orch., Tel-Aviv, 1946-48; pres., music dir. Bronx Philharm., N.Y.C., 1971-83; music dir. Sta. WEVD, N.Y.C., 1969-85; asst. pianist accompanying Lotte Lenya, Richard Tucker, Jan Peerce, Itzhak Perlman, Jan Kiepura, Ilona Massey; prof. Inst. Hautes Etudes Economiques et Sociales; rsch. prof. Alliance Universelle Paix Connaissance, Paris, 1991; prof. Haute Ecole de Recherche, Inst. des Hautes Etudes Economiques et Sociales; mem. coun. Inst. de Documentation et D'Etudes Europeennes; dep. mem., diplomat Internat. State Parliament; dep. mem. assembly Internat. Parliament for Safety and Peace. Composer: (Song Book) Yinglish, piano soloist 1st performance of Gershwin's Concerto in F in Israel; composer Piano Sonata, 1945, Jerusalem Concerto for Piano and Orch., 1967, (TV spl.) Great is Thy Faith, 1970; pianist-condr. 24 record albums; mem. The First Piano Quartet (Acad. award nomination, Peabody award). Consul Sovereign State Aeterna Lucina for State and City of N.Y.; comdr. fgn. rels. Island Du Caricom, 1995; diplomat World Jewish Congress; senator Coun. of States for Protection of Life and Human Rights, Palermo, Italy; del. at large Rep. Presdl. Task Force; active Nat. Rep. Senatorial Com., Nat. Com. to Preserve Social Security and Medicare, Ctr. for Am. Values, Sr. Coalition, Common Cause. Decorated noble knight Noble House of Amena, knight order Knight Templars of Jerusalem, knight comdr. Lofsensis Ursinius Order, baron Order of Bohemian Crown, comdr. Order of Golden Lance (Australia), Capt. Légion de L'Aigle Mer, Baron of Montsalvat, knight Holy Grail, count San Ciriaco, comdr. fgn. rels. Island du Caricom, 1995, Sen Maison Internationale Des Intellectuels, Sen European Parliament, Internat. Parliament for Safety and Peace, diplomat World Jewish Congress, Laird-Lord of Camster, Caithness, Scotland, 1995; recipient Diplomatic medal Internat. Parliament for Safety and Peace, 1995, Gold Cross of Honour, Albert Schweitzer Soc. Austria, Albert Einstein medal, Circulo Nobiliario Caballeros Universales, 1992, Swan Knight (Chevalier du Cygne), Order of the Swan, Knight of Yr. award Internat. Writers and Artists Assn., 1995, Medal of Merit, Rep. Presdl. Task Force, 1998, Noble Conquistador, Internat. Chivalric Order of the Knights of Justice, and other. Fellow United Writers' Assn. India; mem. ASCAP, Maison Internat. des Intellectuels, Internat. Parliament for Safety and Peace, World Parliament Confedn. of Chivalry (Grand Coun.), World Acad. Assn. of the Universe (life), Bronx Philharm. Symphony Soc., Inc. (founder, pres.), Internat. Platform Assn., Am. Fedn. Musicians, Robert Stolz Soc. Gt. Britain, World Univ. Roundtable (trustee, founder), Internat. Cultural Corr. Inst., Circulo Nobiliario de los Caballeros Universales (grandmaster U.S.), Royal Order Bohemian Crown (baron), Lègion de L'Aigle de Mer (capt.), USA United Srs. Assn. Inc. Avocations: walking, chivalry and heraldry, cats, collecting rare musical books and recordings, collecting rare medieval coins and antique Coptic Ethiopian Crosses. Home and Office: Res Montsalvat 1D 2235 Cruger Ave Bronx NY 10467-9411

ŚPRECKELSEN, KAY, physics education educator; b. Kiel, Germany, Feb. 14, 1934. Prof. Dr.rer.nat., U. Kassel, Germany, 1971—. Contbr. articles to profl. jours. Office: U Kassel, FB18-Physik, 34109 Kassel Germany

SPRENG, MANFRED PETER, neurophysiologist, researcher; b. Mannheim, Baden, Germany, May 28, 1936; s. Hermann Hugo and Luise Anna (Nonnenmacher) S.; m. Sieglinde Marie Roth, Mar. 24, 1962; children: Martin, Dorothea, Peter. Diploma in engrng., Tech. U., Karlsruhe, Germany, 1961; D in Engrng., Tech. U., Stuttgart, Germany, 1967. Asst. Univ. Erlangen, Germany, 1961-66, asst. prof., 1967-70, lectr., 1970-78, prof., 1978—; asst. Tech. U., Stuttgart, 1967. Author: (book) Physiology of Hearing, 1994; editor: (book) Articulation/Perception, 1980; co-editor: Cybernetics and Bionics, 1974; patentee recruitment hearing aid. Mem. German Soc. Physiology, German Soc. Elec. Engring., German Soc. Cybernetics (chmn. 1978-87), Soc. Info. Tech. (chmn. 1988-97), Assn. Med. Tech. (chmn. 1993-99). Avocation: genealogy. Office: U Erlangen/Nuremberg, Universitaetsstr 17, D-91054 Erlangen Germany

SPRENGARD, ULRICH, chemist; b. Mainz, Germany, Dec. 21, 1967; s. Karl Anton and Ortrun (Mueller) S.; m. Cornelia Sprengard-Eichel, June 21, 1997. Diploma in chemistry, U. Mainz, 1993, PhD, 1996. Rsch. asst. U. Mainz, Germany, 1993; rschr. CRT/Hoechst, Frankfurt, Germany, 1993-96; process devel. project mgr. Process Devel./Hoechst, Frankfurt, 1996-98, reporting and project coord., 1998-99; global process defel. project coord. Process Devel./Aventis Pharma AG, Frankfurt, 1999—. Patentee in field. Officer German mil. police, 1987-88. Fellow DAAD, 1991. Office: Aventis Pharma AG, D-65926 Frankfurt Germany

SPRENGER, ERNEST HENRY, pastor, translator; b. Elgin, N.D., Apr. 7, 1924; s. Christian and Martha (Schaible) S.; m. Elizabeth May Strobel, June 20, 1947 (dec. Apr. 1973); children: Elizabeth Ann, Mark Randall, Scott Anderw, Cynthia Adele; m. Thelma Jean Koch McCormick, July 28, 1973; stepchildren: David Charles McCormick, Darlene Mae McCormick Hoefel. BA, Yankton Coll., 1946, B in Theology, 1947; B in Divinity, Hartford Sem., 1959; M in Sacred Theology, Pacific Sch. Religion, Berkeley, Calif., 1965. Pastor German Congl. Conf., S.D. and Colo., 1947-52; frat. worker in Germany world Coun. Chs., 1952-55; student pastor 2d Congl. Ch., Middle Haddam, Conn., 1955-59; prof. practical theology Sch. Theology Yankton (S.D.) Coll., 1959-62; pastor Phila. Congl. Ch., Ritzville, Wash., 1965-77, Zion Congl. Ch., Ritzville, Wash., 1977-86; ret. Author: Roots and Relatives, 1995. Bd. dirs. H.E. Gritman Sr. Ctr., Ritzville, 1970-86; mem. book com. Adams County Hist. Soc., 1968-90. Mem. Masons. Republican. Avocations: fishing, woodworking, traveling, translating German script.

SPRENGER, MARILEE BROMS, educational consultant; b. Peoria, Ill., Sept. 20, 1949; d. Lee and Mollie Broms; m. William Scott Sprenger, Aug. 12, 1972; children: Joshua Daniel, Marnie Anne. BS, Bradley U., Peoria, Ill., 1971, MA, 1997. Cert. tchr., Ill. Tchr. Pearce Middle sch., Chillicothe, Ill., 1971-75, I.V.C. H.S., Chillicothe, 1982-83, Chillicothe Jr. H.S., 1983-84, Cath. Diocese of Peoria, 1989-94, Peoria Dist. #150, 1994-99; trainer, cons. Posmer/Sprenger Tngs., Peoria, 1992—; ednl. cons. Two Rivers Profl. Devel. Ctr., Peoria, 1999—; adj. prof. Aurora (Ill.) U., 1992—; conf. spkr. Author: Learning and Memory: The Brain in Action, 1999, Powerfully Simple Techniques, 1994, 2d edit., 1997. Mem. ASCD, Am. Acad. Neurology (assoc.), The Brain Based Ednl. Learning Styles Network, Phi Delta Kappa. Home: 5820 N Briarwood Ln Peoria IL 61614-4231

SPRENGLER-RÜPPENTHAL, ANNELIESE BRÜNHILDE, retired ecclesiatical history and law educator; b. Hamburg, Germany, Sept. 13, 1923; d. Karl Philipp Johannes and Helene Betty (Jebens) Ruppenthal; m. Gerhard Sprengler, Sept. 30, 1946 (dec. Dec. 1966). ThD, U. Göttingen, Germany, 1950, Habilitation, 1965. Rsch. asst. Inst. for Evang. Ecclesiastical Law, Göttingen, 1952-65; lectr. ecclesiastical history and law U. Göttingen, 1965-70, prof., 1970-85, prof. emeritus, 1985—; vis. prof. U. Hamburg, 1988-89, 92-95; mem. Hist. Commn. for Lower Saxony, Hannover, Germany, 1984—; mem. working group on canon law U. Chgo., 1987—. Author: Kirchenordnungen, 3 vols., 1963-94, Mysterium und Riten, 1967, Canon Law in Church Orders: Comparative Studies in Continental and Anglo-Am. Legal History, vol. 11, 1992, Bremer Kirchenordnung von 1534: Zeitschrift d. Savigny-Stiftung, 1996-97, Biography and Bibliography: Kirchengeschichte als Autobiographie-Schriftenreihe des Vereins f. Rhein. Kirchengeschichte, 1999; also articles and essays. Recipient Bugenhagen medal Evang. Ch. Greifswald, 1985. Lutheran. Avocations: psychology, philosophy, biographical books. Home: Basselweg 63A, 22527 Hamburg Germany

SPRENT, JOHN FREDERICK ADRIAN, retired parasitology educator, researcher; b. London, July 23, 1915; s. Frederick Pullar S. and Violet Agnes (Clay) Rees; m. Muriel Florence Hines; children: Jonathan, Anthony, Elizabeth. BS in Zoology first class honors, U. London, 1943, PhD, 1945, DSc, 1953. Vet. rsch. officer Nigeria, 1942-44; rsch. fellow vet. labs. Ministry Agr., Eng., 1945-46; Cooper Centenary rsch. fellow U. Chgo., 1946-47, Seymour Coman rsch. fellow in preventive medicine, 1947-48; sr. rsch. fellow Ontario Rsch. Found., 1948-52; sr. lectr. vet. parasitology U. Queensland (Australia), 1952-54, rsch. prof. parasitology, 1954-56, prof. parasitology, 1956-84, prof. emeritus, 1984, dean faculty vet. sci., 1960-63, rsch. cons. (hon.), 1984; cons. WHO, Geneva and Rio de Janeiro, 1963—, mem. expert panel on parasitic disease, 1963—; cons. first regional seminar on parasitic diseases, helminthic infections, Manila, Philippines, 1965, seminar on helminthiases, eosophilic meningitis S. Pacific Commn., Noumea, New Caledonia, 1967; chmn. Colloquium on Life Cycles of Helminths II Internat. Congress Parasitology, Washington, 1970, Symposium on Ascaroid Infections III Internat. Congress for Parasitology, Munich, 1974, chmn. organizing com. Sixth Internat. Congress Parasitology, 1982-85; external examiner faculty medicine U. Malaya, Kuala Lumpur, Malaysia, 1981, 89; participant Deuxième Symposium Spécificité parasitaire des parasites des Vertébrés Mus. Nat. d'Histoire Naturelle, Paris, 1981, Internat. Symposium and Discussion Systematics Assn./Assn. Applied Biologists U. Cambridge (Eng.), 1981. Editor-in-chief: Internat. Jour. Parasitology, 1974-93, organizer, chmn. editl. meeting to mark 21st anniversary, 1991, retiring editor, 1994. Mem. postgrad. studentship selection com. Commonwealth Sci. and Rsch. Orgn., 1971-72. Travelling fellow Australian Wool Bd., 1964; rsch. grantee Australian Biol. Resources Study, 1995. Fellow Australian Acad. Scis., Australian Coll. Vet. Scientists, Australian Soc. Parasitology (pres. 1964-65, chmn. organizing com. for preparation for ICOPA VI 1981, spkr.), Queensland Inst. Med. Rsch., Royal Coll. Vet. Surgeons, N.Y. Acad. Scis.; mem. Australian Acad. Scis. (mem. coun. 1974-77), Australian Vet. Assn. (life), Australian/New Zealand Assn. Advancement Sci. (pres. sect. L vet. sci. 1962, sect. 16 1972, Mueller award 1981), Helminthol. Soc. Washington (hon.), Am. Soc. Parasitologists (Henry Baldwin Ward award 1962, 4th R.B. McGhee Meml. lectr. 1987), Brit. Soc. Parasitology. Avocations: gardening. Office: U Queensland, St Lucia, 4072 Brisbane Australia

SPRIGGINS, ANTHONY JOHN, orthopedic surgeon; b. Melbourne, Victoria, Australia, Sept. 10, 1954; s. George Leo and Monica Patricia (O'Connor) S.; m. Carmen Alexandra Bruce, Mar. 3, 1985; children: Ryan, James, Connor. B Medicine B Surgery, U. Melbourne, 1978, MS, 1990. Registrar East Birmingham (U.K.) Hosp., 1980-82, Univ. Coll. Hosp., London, 1982-84, Nuffield Orthopedic Ctr., Oxford, Eng., 1984-88, Royal Adelaide (Australia) Hosp., 1988-91; fellow Hosp. for Sick Children, Toronto, Ont., Can., 1992; cons. SMSA, Australia, 1993; dir. Sportsmed SA, Adelaide, 1993—, Sportsmed SA Hosps., Adelaide, 1993—. Fellow Royal Australian Coll. Surgeons, Royal Coll. Physicians and Surgeons of Glasgow, Girdlestone Soc. Avocations: snow skiing, fishing, climbing, sailing, camping. Office: Sportsmed SA, 32 Payneham Rd, Stepney SA 5069, Australia

SPRING, DICK, Irish government official and diplomat; b. Tralee, County Kerry, Ireland, Aug. 29, 1950; s. Dan and Anne S.; life partner, Kristi Hutcheson; 3 children. Student, Trinity Coll., Dublin, Ireland, Kings Inns, Dublin. Former barrister, min. state, justice, 1981-82; leader Irish Labour Party, 1982-97; dep. prime min., 1982-87, min. environ., 1982-83, min. energy, 1983-87, party spokesman on No. Ireland, 1987-97, on women's affairs, 1989-91, dep. prime min., min. for fgn. affairs, 1993-97; leader Labor Party Del., New Ireland Forum, 1984-85; negotiator Anglo-Irish Agreement, 1985; leader Irish Del. at Stormont Talks, 1996-97; mem. steering com. Brit. Irish Parliamentary Body, 1989-92; mem. Kerry County Coun., 1979-83, 87-91, 91-92; assoc. fellow Kennedy Sch. Govt. Harvard U., 1998; non-exec. dir., chmn. various pub. and pvt. cos. Mem. Gaelic Athletic Assn., Tralee Rugby Football Club, Lansdowne Football Club, Tralee Golf Club, Ballybunion Golf Club. Labor Party. Home: Cloonanorig, Tralee, County Kerry Ireland

SPRING, KATHLEEN, writer; d. Edward and Mary Broilo; m. Samuel Taylor (div. 1984); 1 child, Justin; m. Paul Riethmeier (div. 1991). AD summa cum laude, Oakland C.C., 1990; BA cum laude, Wayne State U., 1993. Adminstr. comm. dept. Wayne State U., Detroit, 1990-95; stringer The Daily Tribune, Royal Oak, Mich., 1992-98; writer, photographer Spring Times, Detroit, 1992-98; pub. rels. mktg., editor Fanclub Found. for Arts, Southfield, Mich., 1993-98; writer, tchr. Spring Times, Lyons, Colo., 1998—; travel cons. Rocky Mt. Retreats, 1998—. Author: Small Towns, Detroits Crown, 1997. Vol. PBS-Detroit, 1982-95. Named Journalist of Yr., Wayne State U., 1992, Howard Dubin Outstanding Pro Chpt. Mem., Soc. Profl. Journalists, 1996, Cir. of Excellence-Newsletter Soc. Profl. Journalists, 1996. Mem. Soc. Profl. Journalists (1st v.p. 1993-98), Women in Comm., U. Film & Video Assn., Colo. Author's League, Denver Film Soc. Avocations: travel, books, films, photography. Office: Spring Times PO Box 512 Lyons CO 80540-0512

SPRING, STEFAN, microbiologist, researcher; b. Munich, July 31, 1964; s. Max and Theresia (Müller) S. Diploma in biology, Tech. U. Munich, 1990, PhD in Biology, 1993. Postdoctoral in biology Tech. U. Munich, 1993-95, rsch. asst. in biology, 1995-2000; rsch. asst. in biology Deutsche Sammlung von Microorganismen und Zellhulturen Gublt, Braunschweig, Germany, 2000—. Mem. Vereinigung für Allgemeine und Angewandte Mikrobiologie (PhD prize 1994, Hannover, Germany). Avocations: literature, photography, skiing, hiking.

SPRINGENSCHMID, RUPERT OTTO LUGWIG, engineering educator; b. Salzburg, Austria, Dec. 21, 1929; arrived in Germany, 1973; s. Karl and Hermine (Radinger) S.; children: Gundula, Rainer, Hartwig, Wolfram, Barbara. Diploma in Civil Engrng., Tech. U., Vienna, Austria, 1955, D Tech., 1959, D (hon.), 1997; postgrad., Princeton U., 1955-56. Cert. engrng. cons. Rsch. asst. Princeton U., 1955-56; head materials lab. Svietelsky Road Constrn., Linz, Austria, 1956-58; rsch. asst. German Cement Rsch. Inst., Düsseldorf, Germany, 1958-62; dir. Austrian Cement Rsch. Inst., Vienna, 1969-73; prof. Tech. U. Munich, 1973-98, dean faculty civil engring., 1977-79; pres. Permanent Internat. Assn. Rd. Congresses Com. Concrete Rds., 1970-79; dir. Inst. Structural Materials, 1973-98; chmn. RILEM TC 119, 1989-96. Contbr. articles to profl. jours. Cons. mem. Austrian Concrete Soc., German Conrete Soc. Home: Seinsheimstrasse 4, 81245 München Germany Office: Tech U, Baumbachstrasse 7, 81245 München Germany

SPRINGER, ASHTON, JR., theatrical producer; b. N.Y.C., Nov. 1, 1930; s. Ashton and Julia Euphemia (Horsham) S.; m. Myra Louise Burns, Nov. 5, 1956; children: Mark, Chesley Anne. B.S., Ohio State U., 1953, postgrad., 1953-54. Dir. Richard Lawrence Youth Center, Bronx, N.Y., 1955-57; ptnr. A&M Laundromats and Coin Equipment Maintenance, N.Y.C., 1956-60; pres. Motor Car Assos., Inc., New Rochelle, N.Y., 1960-67, Chesmark Prodns., Inc., N.Y.C., 1967-70, Theatre Mgmt. Assos., Inc., N.Y.C., 1970—; mng. ptnr. Helen Hayes Theatre, N.Y.C., 1979-87. Producer Broadway shows No Place to Be Somebody, 1970 (Pulitzer prize 1970), My Sister, My Sister, 1974, Bubbling Brown Sugar, 1975, Going Up, 1976, Cold Storage, 1977, Eubie!, 1978, Whoopee, 1978, A Lesson From Aloes, 1980 (Drama Critics award 1981), Inacent Black, 1981, The Apollo--Just Like Magic, 1981, revival of No Place to Be Somebody, 1993, Lotto, Experience the Dream, 1992. Bd. dirs. Goodspeed Opera House, 1978-86. Mem. League Am. Theatres and Producers (dir.). Office: Theatre Mgmt Assocs 1600 Broadway Ste 410 New York NY 10019-7413

SPRINGER, FLOYD LADEAN, architect; b. Goodrich, N.D., Feb. 1, 1922; s. George Roy Springer and Louise Baumbach; m. Dorothy Mae Shepard (dec. Sept. 1995); children: Debra Louise, Tami June. Student, U. Denver, 1948-51; BS in Archtl. Engrng., U. Colo., 1952; postgrad., U. Wash., 1953-54, U. Utah, Portland, Oreg., 1980. Apprentice to arch. Gilbert R. Horton AIA, 1946-48; job capt. Robert Hall and Ira Cummings, Archs., 1956-57; mem. archtl. staff Austin Co., 1964, Naramore, Bain, Brady and Johanson, 1965, Roland Terry and Assocs., 1967, John Graham & Co., 1967-68; mem. various archtl. firms Wash. and Alaska, 1952-69; prin. Floyd Springer/Arch., Seattle, 1969—; arch. numerous pvt. comml. and residential projects, 1969—. Contbr. articles to profl. jours. Cpl. inf. U.S. Army, 1941-44, PTO. Decorated Silver Star. Mem. Masons. Presbyterian. Avocations: photography, ballroom dancing, leaded art glass, oil painting, writing. Home and Office: 18548 60th Ave NE Kenmore WA 98028-8725

SPRINGER, LEONARD, musician, educator; b. Evanston, Ill., Mar. 11, 1953; s. George and Annemarie (Keiner) S.; m. Jennifer Susan Litz, Dec. 16, 1977 (div. Nov. 1993); 1 child, Benjamin Joseph. BA, Ind. U., 1987; MEd, Vanderbilt U., 1991; PhD, Pa. State U., 1996. Co-owner Ribbon Rail Recording, Bloomington, Ind., 1976-81; musician Donna Fargo, Nashville, 1981, Brenda Lee, Nashville, 1981-85, Ronnie Reno, Hendersonville, Tenn., 1985-90, Highwater, Junction City, Wis., 1998—; rsch. asst. Ctr. for Study of Higher Edn., University Park, Pa., 1992-96; rschr. Wis. Ctr. for Edn. Rsch., Madison, 1996-98; dir. Southern Wis. Bluegrass in the Schs., Verona, Wis., 2000—; edn. and rsch. cons., Verona, Wis., 1998—. Contbr. articles to ednl. jours. Bd. dirs. coord. com. Shaarei Shamayim, Madison, 1998. Fellow Am. Edn. Rsch. Assn./Spencer Found., 1994, Nat. Inst. Sci. Edn., 1997. Democrat. Jewish. Avocations: horseback riding, sailing. E-mail: lspring@chorus.net.

SPRINGETT, PETER ANTONY, financial consultant; b. Ealing Ws. Middlesex, Eng., Dec. 12; arrived in South Africa, 1956; s. Frederick William and Dorothy Rhoda Blache (Sage) S.; m. Kathleen Lorraine Myers, Aug. 19, 1966; children: Michel, Mark William. Exec. dir. First Nat. Bank of South Africa, Johannesburg, 1956-89; chmn. Global Tech. LTD, Johannesburg, 1989—, Regal treasury Pvt. Bank Ltd., Johannesburg, 1995-97, Arcay Group Ltd., Johannesburg, 1999—. Mem. River Club, Dainfern Golf and Country club. Avocations: golf, reading history, gardening. Home: Stand 780 Gateside Ave, Dainfern Republic of South Africa Office: PO Box 70269, Bryanston 2021, Republic of South Africa

SPRINGFELDT, BENGT DANIEL, health researcher, engineer; b. Stockholm, Oct. 17, 1919; s. Sven Ivar Gullek and Iris Helen (Lönborg) S.; m. Gulli Augusta Linnea Melin; children: Gunnar, Per Erik. Grad. engr., Royal Inst. Tech., 1944; PhD, Royal Inst. Tech., Stockholm, 1993. Cert. in engring. Supr. Gillwell Scout Edn. Gatukontoret, Stockholm, 1945-46; supr. Svenska Väg AB, Stockholm, 1946-49, Nat. Bd. Safety & Health, Stockholm, 1953—; labor inspector Labor Inspectorate, Stockholm, Linköping, Umeå, Jönköping, 1950-53, 56-61, 61-66, 67-68; chief Labor Inspectorate, Stockholm, 1968-82; chief machine sect. Nat. Bd. Safety and Health, Stockholm, 1982-85; rschr. Karolinska Inst., Stockholm, 1993—. Author: (books) Technical Safety Work, 1975, Technical Safety Work-Rooms and Machines, 1987, (chpts.) Graphic Professions, 1956, Fifteen Years of Occupational Accident Research in Sweden, 1996, Rollover, 1997, Safety Promotion Research, 1999, others. Chief Sanct Stefan's Scoutcorps, Linkoping, 1957-61, Umebro Scoutcorps, Umeå, 1962-66; chief scout Sweden's Meth. Scout Assn., Stockholm, 1969-71. Mem. Swedish Workers Protection Assn. (bd. dirs. 1968-82), Sweden's Mech. Standardization (bd.

dirs. 1982-85). Methodist. Avocations: outdoor life, music. Home: Palmfeltsvägen 43, 12048 Enskede Gård Sweden Office: Karolinska Inst, Norrbacka, 17176 Stockholm Sweden

SPRINGFELDT, BJORN ERIC, Swedish cultural official; b. Malmo, Sweden, Apr. 30, 1941; s. Eric Walter and Marta Ingegerd (Ljungberg) S.; m. Kerstin Eriksson (div. 1968); 1 child, Pernilla Elisabeth; m. Milla Tragardh, Jan. 14, 1983; children: Lina Maria, Eric Gustav Tobias. BA, U. Lund, Sweden, 1973. Asst. curator Moderna Museet, Stockholm, 1968-72, curator, 1973-78, sr. curator, 1979-85, mus. dir., 1990-95; dir. Malmo Konsthall, 1986-89; counsellor for cultural affairs Swedish Embassy, Bonn, Germany, 1996—. Home: Knobelsdorffstrasse 39, 14059 Berlin Germany Office: Swedish Embassy, Ranchstrasse 1, 10787 Berlin Germany

SPRINGFORD, MICHAEL, physics educator; b. Chalfont St. Giles, Bucks, Eng., Jan. 10, 1936; s. Stanley Walter and Lillian (Tyler) S.; m. Kathleen Elizabeth Wyatt, Apr. 11, 1958 (div. 1986) children: Sarah, Simon, Matthew; m. Maria Sergeevna Morosova, Apr. 4, 1991. BSc, U. Durham, 1957; PhD, U. Hull, 1962. Rsch. fellow NRC, Can., 1962-64; lectr. physics U. Sussex, Eng., 1964-79, reader physics, 1979-84, prof. physics, 1984-89; prof. physics U. Bristol, Eng., 1989—, head dept. and dir. H.H. Wills Physics Lab., 1996—; Henry Overton Wills prof. physics U. Bristol, 1996—. Author, editor: Electrons at the Fermi Surface, 1980, Electron-A Centenary Volume, 1997. Fellow Inst. Physics (Charles Vernon Boys award 1995, Mott prize, lectr. 1995). Avocations: music, walking, cooking, pursuit of quietness. Office: U Bristol HH Wills Physics Lab, Tyndall Ave, Bristol BS8 1TL, England

SPRINGGATE, CLARK FRANKLIN, physician, researcher; b. Champaign, Ill., Nov. 14, 1946; s. William F. and Marjorie E. (Fitch) S.; children from a previous marriage: Elizabeth, Benjamin; m. Diane Louise Rotnem, Oct. 19, 1991. AB in Biology, Boston U., 1967; PhD in Biochemistry, Boston Coll., 1972; MD, U. Miami, 1983. Diplomate Nat. Bd. Med. Examiners, Am. Bd. Pathology. Med. dir. Richardson Vicks Pharm., Shelton, Conn., 1989-91; v.p., med. dir. TSI Biomed. Rsch. Group, Medford, Mass., 1992-94; v.p. Scicor, Indpls., 1988-89; pres. Springgate Biotech, Guilford, Conn., 1991—, Biotech Regular Cons., Guilford, 1994—; designer/executor Phase I, Phase II, Phase III and Phase IV clin. trials in oncology, cardiology, rheumatology, endocrinology, infectious diseases, neurology. Contbr. articles to jours. Heart Transplant, Am. Soc. Hist. Immunogey. Bd. dirs. AIDS Protect New Haven, 1994-95; funding bd. Leap Youth Program, New Haven, 1991-92. Leukemia Soc. Am. fellow, 1972-74. Mem. AAAS, ACP Execs., Conn. State Med. Soc. Achievements include research in immune monitoring of heart transplant patients to prevent rejection and infection, diagnostic flow cytometry-oncology, gene therapy for cancer, heart disease, autoimmune disease and infectious disease. Home: 1320 Little Meadow Rd Guilford CT 06437-1659

SPRINKLE, ROBERT LEE, JR., podiatrist; b. Winston-Salem, N.C., July 13, 1932; s. Robert Lee and Elton Elizabeth Sprinkle; children: Robert III, Karen, Ralph, Richard, Roy, Randy, Drouin; m. Nancy House Dixon. Student, Salem Coll., 1952; BS, Ohio Coll. Podiatry, 1956; DPM, Pa. Coll. Podiatry, 1970. Diplomate Am. Bd. Disability Analysts, Am. Coun. Cert. Podiatric Phys. and Surgeons, Sr. Acad. Ambulatory Podiatric Surgeons. Pvt. practice Winston-Salem, 1957—; chmn. N.C. Bd. Podiatry Examiners, 1968-74; clin. assoc. prof. Dr. William M. School Coll. Podiatric Medicine; researcher reconstructive surgery human foot and ankle; bd. dirs. Cmty. Gen. Hosp. Found., Thomasville, N.C. Chmn. Mayor's Com. on Hiring the Handicapped, 1963-64; commr. Old Hickory Coun., Boy Scouts Am., 1970-71, v.p., 1973-74, Silver Beaver award, 1969, mem. adv. bd. Old North State Coun.; pres. St. Leo's Parochial Sch. PTA, 1969-70; dir. Halfway House, 1965-66; chmn. Bishop McGuiness PTA, 1976. Grantee Schering, Inc., 1972-74; recipient St. George medal, Charlotte Diocese, Roman Catholic Ch., 1971. Mem. APHA, Am. Podiatry Assn., N.C. Podiatry Assn. (past pres.), Piedmont Podiatry Assn., Internat. Analgesia Soc., Forsyth Country Club, Colonial Country Club, Twin City Club, KC (4th degree), SAR, SCV, Rotary (Paul Harris fellow, dist. gov. 1976-77), Sons of Am. Revolution, Sons of Confederate Vets., Sons of the Revolution. Democrat. Roman Catholic. Home: 10 Mock St Thomasville NC 27360-4622 Office: ABC Family Foot and Ankle Clinic PO Box 336 17 W Main St Thomasville NC 27360-3934 Also: ABC Family Foot & Ankle Clinic PO Box 5442 2057 Kerensky St Winston-Salem NC 27103-3657

SPRINTZEN, DAVID A., educator, community activist; b. N.Y.C., Dec. 16, 1939; s. Irving Sprintzen and Theresa Ruth lefkowitz; m. Alice Carol Hochman, Nov. 20, 1946; 1 child, Daniel Dylan. BA, Queens Coll., 1961; MA, Pa. State U., 1963, PhD, 1968. Asst. prof. philosophy Denison U., Granville, Ohio, 1966-68; prof. philosophy C.W. Post Coll., Brookvill, N.Y., 1968—; Co-dir., founder Inst. for Sustainable Devel. at L.I. Univ., Brookville, 1997—. Author: The Drama of Thought, 1978, Camus: A Critical Examination, 1988. Founder, co-chair L.I. Progressive Coalition, Massapeava, N.Y., 1979-99; founder, dir. Rsch. and Edn. Projects of L.I., Syosset, 1984—; bd. mem. Syossett's Concern About its Neighborhood, Syosset, 1976-94. Recipient Leadership Civic award Newsday, L.I., 1994. E-mail: dsprintz@liv.edu. Home and Office: 16 Southwoods Rd Syosset NY 11791-2901

SPRINZ, DETLEF FRIEDRICH, environmental social scientist, educator; b. Saarbruecken, Germany, Dec. 2, 1960; s. Gerhard and Annemarie (Krueger) S. Diploma in polit. econs., U. Saarland, Saarbruecken, 1986; MA, U. Mich., 1986, PhD, 1992. Sr. fellow Potsdam (Germany) Inst. for Climate Impact Rsch., 1992—; ptnr. Ecologic Ctr. for Internat. and European Environ. Rsch., Berlin, 1995—; adj. asst. prof. U. Potsdam, 1997—; reviewer European Union, Brussels; mem. adv. bd. Jour. Environ. and Devel.; mem. task force VI European Sci. Found., 1990-92. Editor spl. issue Internat. Studies Note,s 1994; contbr. articles to profl. jours. Mem. coll. European Acad., Bad Neuenahr-Ahrweiler, Germany, 1999—. Rsch. grantee European Commn., 1993-96, NATO, 1997-99. Mem. Internat. Polit. Sci. Assn. (exec. com. study group on global environ. change 1994-97), Internat. Studies Assn. (exec. com. environ. studies sect. 1996-98), Am. Polit. Sci. Assn. Avocations: sailing, wine, stock market. Fax: 49 (30) 345 31 95. E-mail: sprinz@sprint.org. Home: Suarezstrasse 57, 14057 Berlin Germany Office: Potsdam Inst for Climate, Impact Rsch, Telegrafenberg, 14473 Potsdam Germany

SPROAT, JOHN GERALD, historian; b. L.A., Apr. 1, 1921; s. John Gerald and Grace (Elwell) Drummond S.; m. Ruth Christensen, Mar. 18, 1967; 1 child by previous marriage, Barbara. B.A., San Jose State Coll., 1950; M.A., U. Calif.-Berkeley, 1952, Ph.D., 1959. Instr. Mich. State U., 1956-57; asst. prof. Williams Coll., 1957-63; prof. Lake Forest Coll., Ill., 1963-74; prof. history U. S.C., Columbia, 1974-92, chmn. dept., 1974-83; dist. prof. emeritus, 1992—; sr. fellow Inst. for So. Studies, 1992—; Fulbright prof. Hamburg U., Fed. Republic Germany, 1961-62; vis. fellow Cambridge U., Eng., 1970; vis. prof. U. Calif.-Berkeley, 1972; Fulbright prof. U. Munich, Fed. Republic Germany, 1982, Indonesia, 1993-94; Am. participant lectr. USIA, India, Pakistan, 1987; mem. S.C. Commn. Archives and History, 1974-83, chmn., 1979-83; mem. S.C. Bd. Rev. Hist. Places, 1974-86, chmn., 1978-83; del. Am. Council Learned Socs. Author: The Best Men: Liberal Reformers in the Gilded Age, 1988; (with others) The Shaping of America, 1972, Making Change: South Carolina Banking in the 20th Century, 1990; contbr. chpts. to books; exec. producer A Bond of Iron, S.C. ETV, 1979; gen. editor So. Classics Series. Past pres., trustee Columbia Mus. Art; pres. Historic Columbia Found., 1997-99. Served with USAAF, 1941-45. NEH grantee, 1976, 77, 79, 85; Shell Found. grantee, 1967, 70, 73; Lilly Endowment grantee, 1966-67. Mem. Am. Hist. Assn., Orgn. Am. Historians, So. Hist. Assn. Episcopalian. Clubs: Capital City (Columbia). Home: 1686 Woodlake Dr Columbia SC 29206-4647 Office: U SC Inst For So Studies Columbia SC 29208-0001

SPROSTY, JOSEPH PATRICK, producer, writer, weapons specialist; b. Cleve., Aug. 25, 1947; s. Joseph Patrick and Anna Margret (Louchka) S. Grad., Midpark H.S., Middleburgh, Ohio, 1965; student, San Diego City Coll., 1972-73. Class 2 firearms lic. Prop builder The Goulardi Show WJW-TV8, Cleve., 1962-65; sub-agent Internat. Artists Agy., San Diego and L.A., 1982-83; casting dir. Cinemode Films, 1982; operator, owner Actors Artists Agy., L.A., 1983-87; founder, prodr., dir. Magnum Prodns., 1985; founder Sprosty Prodns., 1990; demonstrator weapons and handling of weapons, Propmaster TV Co., Van Nuys, Calif., 1992; expert witness Laser Weapon Scam, 1984; vis. lectr. firearms safety, handling, rules and regulations governing use of firearms in motion picture, TV prodn. U. So. Calif., 1996—; animal wrangler specializing in opossums. Scripwriter: (films) Vanishing Point II, The Apartment Manager, The Big House, Rambo III (optioned), Rambo IV (revised), Boneyard, Mister Ed - Talking Again, Mister Ed - Radio Talk, Brick, Life Plus One, Gun Slave, Fixation, Last Chance (renamed Terminal Virus), You're So Beautiful, Home Dead Home, Kung Fu Cop, The Fisherman, numerous others; prodr., dir. (video) Break Disc, 1985; location mgr., armorer, weapons splst.: (film) Heat from Another Sun (retitled Maladiction), 1988; armorer, 2nd asst. dir., assoc. prodr., weapons splst.: (film) Provoked, 1989; weapons splst., armorer: (film) Big City, 1990; co-prodr., animal wrangler, weapons splst.: (film) Opossum de Oro, 1996; weapons splst.: (tv shows) Jake and the Fat Man, Black's Magic, Hill Street Blues, Murder, She Wrote, On the Edge of Death, Emerald Point N.A.S., (7 episodes) America's Most Wanted, (3 episodes) FBI: The Untold Stories, numerous others, (films) Revolt, Rocky IV, Streets of Fire, Walk in the Sun, Cloak & Dagger, One Man's Poison, Killing Zoe, Desert Storm, The Movie, Live Shot, Outer Heat, Zipperhead, Four Minute Warning, The Robbery, Spirit, Texas Payback, High Adventure, The Waterfront, The Philadelphia Experiment II, Opossum de Oro, Harlem Nights, Tango & Cash, Die Hard, Provoked, Beverly Hills Cop II, Big City, numerous others. Spkr. Veterans Day Calif. State U., Dominguez Hills, 1993. Served with USN, 1965-67 (hon. discharge). Mem. AFTRA, SAG (charter mem. San Diego br.). Home: 337 W Maple St Glendale CA 91204-2014

SPRUIELL, VANN, psychoanalyst, educator, editor, researcher; b. Leeds, Ala., Oct. 16, 1926; s. Vann Lindley and Zada (Morton) S.; m. Iris Taylor, Sept. 20, 1951 (div. Oct. 1966); children: Graham, Fain, Garth; m. Joyce Ellis, Feb. 11, 1967; stepchildren: Sidney Reavey, Catherine Ellis, Matson Ellis. BS, U. Ala., Tuscaloosa, 1948; MD, Harvard U., 1952. Resident Bellevue Hosp., N.Y.C., 1952-53, N.Y. Hosp., N.Y.C., 1953-55; fellow Tulane Sch. Medicine, New Orleans, 1955-57; pvt. practice New Orleans, 1957—; vis. rschr. Anna Freud Ctr., London, 1972-73; co-pub. JOURLIT and BOOKREV; pres. and founding mem. Psychoanalytic Archives CD-ROM Texts (PACT), New Orleans, 1993—; clin. prof. psychiatry La. State U. Sch. Medicine, Tulane U. Sch. Medicine; sec. Ctr. for Advanced Studies in Psychoanalysis, 1989—. Editl. bd. Psychoanalytic Quarterly, 1973—; N.Am. editor Internat. Jour. Psychoanalysis, London, 1988-93; editor Psychoanalysis South, 1996—; mem. various other editl. bds.; contbr. articles to profl. jours. and books. Sgt. U.S. Army, 1944-46. Mem. Am. Psychoanalytic Assn. (sec. bd. on profl. stds. 1979-92), Wyvern Club. Avocations: interdisciplinary studies, sailing. Home: 215 Iona St Metairie LA 70005-4137

SPRUŠIL, BORIS, physics educator; b. Břeclav, Czech Republic, Feb. 6, 1938; s. František and Anna (Weis) S.; m. Olga Kovarnikova, Feb. 1, 1938 (wid. 1995); children: Robert, Tamara. MS, Charles U., Prague, Czech Republic, 1966, PhD, 1967. Asst. Charles U., 1960-64, sr. asst., 1964-82, docent, 1982-92, prof., 1992—; sr. lectr., asst. prof. various tech. univs., Germany, 1970-77, others. Author: (textbooks) Point Defects in Metals and Alloys, 1973, Solid State Thermodynamics, 1982; co-author: (textbooks) Introduction to Metal Physics, 1984, Mechanics, 1989; contbr. articles to profl. jours. Avocations: history, arts. E-mail: sprusil@met.mff.cuni.cz. Office: Charles Univ/Fac Math/Phys, Ke Karlovu 5, CZ 12116 Praha Czech Republic

SPRY, DONALD FRANCIS, II, lawyer; b. Bethlehem, Pa., Nov. 17, 1947; s. Donald Francis and Carol Annette (Bolger) S.; m. Mary Frances, June 20, 1981; stepchildren: Michael Matlaga, Michelle Fehnel. BA, Moravian Coll., 1969; JD, U. Pitts., 1972. Bar: Pa. 1972, U.S. Dist. Ct. (ea. dist.) Pa. 1975. Assoc. Law Offices of Edmund P. Turtzo, Bangor, Pa., 1973-76; ptnr. Turtzo, Spry, Powlette & Sbrocchi, P.C., Bangor, 1976-83, Turtzo, Spry, Powlette, Sbrocchi & Faul, P.C., Bangor and Stroudsburg, Pa., 1983-90, Turtzo, Spry, Sbrocchi, Faul & LaBarre, P.C., Bangor & Stroudsburg, Pa., 1990—. Capt. USAR 1979-80. Mem. ABA (family law sect.), Pa. Bar Assn. (family law sect. edn. law com., zone del. Ho. of Dels.), Northampton County Bar Assn. (family law com.), North County Bar Assn. (pres.-elect 1989, pres. 1990), Pa. Sch. Bds. Assn., Nat Sch. Bds. Assn., ACLU, Edn. Law Assn., Pomfret Club. Republican. Methodist. Office: Turtzo Spry Sbrocchi Faul & LaBarre PC 109 Broadway Bangor PA 18013-2505 also: 930 N 9th St Stroudsburg PA 18360-1208

SPUNT, SHEPARD ARMIN, real estate executive, management and financial consultant; b. Cambridge, Mass., Feb. 3, 1931; s. Harry and Naomi (Drooker) S.; m. Joan Murray Fooshee, Aug. 6, 1961 (dec. June 1969); children: Erica Frieda and Andrew Murray (twins). BS, U. Pa., 1952, MBA, 1956. Owner Colonial Realty Co., Brookline, Mass., 1953—, Cambridge, 1960—; sr. assoc. Gen. Solids Assocs., 1956—; chmn. bd. Gen. Solids Sys. Corp., 1971-74; trustee Union Capital Trust, Boston; incorporator Liberty Bank & Trust Co., Boston; dir., clk. The Computer Co., Inc., Cambridge, 1986—, treas., 1997—; author, sponsor consumer protection, election law and pub. safety legislation Mass. Gen. Ct., 1969—, pub. safety U.S. Congress, 1998. Co-author: A Business Data Processing Service for Small Business Practitioners, 1956, A Business Data Processing Service for Medical Practitioners, 1956, rev. edit., 1959; patentee in field of automation, lasers, dieelectric bonding. Chmn. Com. for Fair Urban Renewal Laws, Mass., 1965—; treas. Ten Men of Mass., 1980; pres. New Eng. Coun. Young Reps., 1964-67, 69-71; vice chmn. Young Rep. Nat. Fedn., 1967-69, dir. region I, 1964-67, 69-71; mem. Brookline Rep. Town Com., 1960—, treas., 1996—; del. Atlantic Conf. Young Polit. Leaders, Brussels, 1973; bd. dirs. Brookline Taxpayers Assn., 1964—, v.p., 1971-72, pres., 1972—; dep. sheriff Norfolk County, 1998. Mem. Nat. Soc. Profl. Engrs., Rental Housing Assn., Greater Boston Real Estate Bd., Navy League, Boston Athenaeum, Copley Soc. Boston, Collector's Club N.Y., Masons, Shriners. Home: 177 Reservoir Rd Chestnut Hill MA 02467-1426 Office: 21 Elmer St Cambridge MA 02138-6107

SPUR, INGA BIRGITTA, museum director, educator; b. Fyn, Denmark, Dec. 28, 1931; d. Erik Hoyrup Spur and Asta (Munck) S.; m. Sigurjón Olafsson, Jan. 5, 1956 (dec. Dec. 1982); children: Olafur Spur Sigurjónsson, Hlif Sigurjónsdóttir, Freyr Sigurjónsson, Dagur Sigurjónsson. BA, U. Iceland, Reykjavik, 1980. Tchr. Danish Icelandic Tech. Coll., Reykjavik, 1980-81, Sund Gymnasium, Reykjavik, 1981-85; mus. dir. The Sigurjón Olafsson Mus., Reykjavik, 1984—, curator, pub., 1985—. Editor: Sculptor Sigurjón Olafsson, 1985, Sigurjón Olafsson's Works in Metal, 1989, (catalogue) Sigurjón Olafsson Totem's and Columns, 1994, The Biography of Sigurjón Olafsson, Vol. I, 1998, Vol. II, 1999, others. Recipient Silver Medal U.S. Internat. Film & Video Festival, Chgo., 1994; named Order of Falcon, Pres. Iceland, 1989. Mem. ICOM, Scandinavian Assn. Mus. Avocations: music, literature, fine arts, swimming, cooking. Fax no.: 354-581-4553; e-mail: lso@vortex.is. Home: Laugarnestangi 70, 105 Reykjavik Iceland Office: Sigurjon Olafsson Mus, Laugarnestangi, 105 Reykjavik Iceland

SPURNY, FRANTIŠEK, physicist, educator; b. Letonice, Czech Republic, Oct. 14, 1942; s. František and Anežka (Polackova) S.; m. Marta Lysá, July 8, 1968; children: Marta, Markéta, František. Diploma in engring., Czech Tech. U., Prague, 1965, PhD, 1970; DSc, Acad. Sci. Czech Republic, Prague, 1987. Asst. prof. Czech Tech. U., Prague, 1965-71; assoc. prof. physics, 1995; head of rsch. Inst. Rad. Dos. Acad. Sci. Czech Republic, Prague, 1971-75, dept. dir. Inst. Rad. Dos., 1975-87, dir. Inst. Rad. Dos., 1987-94, head dept. Nuclear Physics Inst., 1994—; rsch. fellow Inst. Physics, Sukhumi USSR, 1966, 68-69, French Atomic Energy Commn., Fontenay-aux-Roses, France, 1973-74, 84-85, 96-99. Co-author (chpts. in book) Progress of Ionizing Radiation Dosimetry, 1984; mem. editl. bd. Radiation Protection Dosimetry, Radiation Measurements, Radio-protection; contbr. over 180 articles to profl. jours. Mem. European Radiation Dosimetry Group (assoc.). Office: Nuclear Physics Inst AS CR, Na Truhlářce 39/64, 180 86 Prague Czech Republic

SPURRELL, ROWORTH ADRIAN, consultant cardiologist; b. Eng., May 27, 1942; s. Ivor Pritchard and Marjorie (Cheyney) S.; m. Susan Jane Kemp, Apr. 28, 1973; children: Emma Louise, Clare Alexandra. MB, BS, U. London, 1966, MD, 1974. Registrar St. George's Hosp., London, 1969-70, Nat. Heart Hosp., London, 1970-71; sr. registrar Guy's Hosp., London, 1971-74; cons. St. Bartholomews Hosp., London, 1974—, cons. in charge cardiology, 1976—; pvt. practice London, 1974—. Fellow Royal Coll. Physicians, Am. Coll. Cardiology; mem. Brit. Cardiac Soc., Royal Yacht Squadron (Cowes, Eng.), RAF Club. Mem. Ch. of England. Office: 10 Upper Wimpole St, London W1 7TD, England

SPYER, KENNETH MICHAEL, physiology educator, university dean; b. Woodford, Essex, Eng., Sept. 15, 1943; s. Harris and Rebecca (Jacobs) S.; m. Christine Spalton; children: Simon, Nicholas. BSc with honors, U. Sheffield, Eng., 1966; PhD, U. Birmingham, Eng., 1969, DSc, 1979; MD (hon.), U. Lisbon, 1991. Rsch. fellow U. Birmingham, Eng., 1969-72; Royal Soc. program fellow Inst. di Fisiologia, Pisa, Italy, 1972-73; rsch. fellow U. Birmingham, Eng., 1973-78, sr. rsch. fellow, 1978-80; prof. physiology Royal Free Hosp., London, 1980—; dir. Brit. Heart Found. Neural Control Group, London, 1985—; head dept. Univ. Coll. London and Royal Free Hosp. Sch. Medicine, London, 1994-99, dean, 1999—; chmn. Wellcome Trust Phy/Pharm Panel, London, 1993-96; adv. panel Brain Rsch. Trust, London, 1993—; reviewer and lectr. in field. Editor Jour. Physiology, 1977-85, chmn. editl. bd., 1982-85; editor Jour. Applied Physiology, 1988-90; assoc. editor Jour. Autonomic Nervous Sys., 1991—; editl. adv. bd. Clin. Autonomic Sci., 1991—; field editor News in Physiol. Sci., 1992-95. Grantee in field. Fellow Acad. Med. Scis. (founder); mem. Harveian Soc., European Neurosci. Assn., European Biomed. Rsch. Soc. (chmn. 1996—), Internat. Brain Rsch. Orgn., Clin. Autonomic soc., Physiol. Soc. (chmn. 1987-91), Rsch. Def. Soc., Brain Rsch. Assn., Clin. Autonomic Soc., German Physiol. Soc., Soc. for Neurosci. Avocations: traveling, reading, gardening, fly fishing. Office: Royal Free U Coll Med Sch, Rowland Hill St, London NW3 2PF, England

SPYERS-DURAN, PETER, librarian, educator; b. Budapest, Hungary, Jan. 26, 1932; came to U.S., 1956, naturalized, 1964; s. Alfred and Maria (Almasi-Balogh) S-D; m. Jane F. Cumber, Mar. 21, 1964; children: Kimberly, Hilary, Peter. Certificate, Free U. Budapest, 1955; M.A. in L.S, U. Chgo., 1960; Ed.D., Nova U., 1975. Profl. asst. libr. adminstrn. div. ALA, Chgo., 1961-62; assoc. dir. librs., assoc. prof. U. Wis., 1962-67; dir. librs., prof. Western Mich. U., 1967-70; dir. librs., prof. libr. sci. Fla. Atlantic U., 1970-76; dir. libr. Calif. State U., Long Beach, 1976-83; prof. libr. and info. sci., dir. libr. Wayne State U., Detroit, 1983-86, dean, prof. libr. and info. sci. program, 1986-95, dean and prof. emeritus, 1995—; cons. Spyers-Duran Assocs., 1995—; acting univ. libr. Nova Southeastern U., Ft. Lauderdale, Fla., 1996-97; vis. prof. State U. N.Y. at Geneseo, summers 1969-70; cons. publs., libr. and info. scis.-related enterprises; chmn. bd. internat. confs., 1970—. Author: Moving Library Materials, 1965, Public Libraries - A Comparative Survey of Basic Fringe Benefits, 1967; editor: Approval and Gathering Plans in Academic Libraries, 1969, Advances in Understanding Approval Plans in Academic Libraries, 1970, Economics of Approval Plans in Research Libraries, 1972, Management Problems in Serials Work, 1973, Prediction of Resource Needs, 1975, Requiem for the Card Catalog: Management Issues in Automated Cataloging, 1979, Shaping Library Collections for the 1980's, 1981, Austerity Management in Academic Libraries, 1984, Financing Information Systems, 1985, Issues in Academic Libraries, 1985; mem. editorial bd. Jour. of Library Adminstration, 1989-95. Mem. Kalamazoo County Library Bd., 1969-70; Bd. dirs. United Fund. Reciient G. Flint Purdy award for outstanding contbns. Wayne State U., 1999. Mem. ALA, Mich. Libr. Assn., Internat. Fed. Libr. Assns., Assn. Info. Sci., Fla. Libr. Assn., Calif. Libr. Assn., Fla. Assn. Community Colls., Boca Raton C. of C., U. Chgo. Grad. Libr. Sch. Alumni Club (pres. 1973-75), Solinet Mich. Libr. Consortium (founder charter bd. mem. 1973—, bd. dirs. 1973-76), Detroit Area Libr. Network (pres. bd. dirs. 1985-95), Mich. Ctr. for Book (pres. 1988-89), Am. Soc. Info. Sci., Assn. Libr. and Info. Sci. Edn. Republican. Methodist. Home: 7295 Maidencane Ct Largo FL 33777-4900 Office: Wayne State Univ Librs Detroit MI 48202

SPYROPOULOS, GEORGE NICHOLAS, physician; b. Westwood, N.J., July 24, 1965; s. Nicholas George and Asimina Vasilios (Tassini) S.; m. Maria Evangelia Stavropoulos, May 3, 1968. BA in Biology, Franklin and Marshall, 1987; DO, Phila. Coll. Osteo. Medicine, 1992. Diplomate Am. Acad. Family Practice. Intern Crozer-Chester Med. Ctr., Springfield, Pa., 1992-93; resident family and community medicine Med. Ctr. Delaware, Wilmington, 1993-95; attending family physician Chadds Ford, Pa., 1995—; team physician West Chester (Pa.) U., 1998—; active staff Christian Hosp., Wilmington, 1995, So. Chester County Med. Ctr., Jennersville, Pa., 1996, Chester County Hosp., West Chester, 1996—; courtesy staff A.I. DuPont Children's Hosp., Wilmington, 1996; medical dir. Pepperridge Farm Downington, PA Plant. Vice pres. The Peloponnesian Soc. of Greater Delaware Valley, 1996-97. Recipient Ahepa Dist. scholarship, 1984-85. Mem. AMA. Am. Osteo. Assn., Am. Acad. Family Physicians, Am. Acad. Osteo. Family Physicians, Soc. Tchrs. of Family Medicine, Pa. Med. Soc., Delaware Med. Soc., Del. State Osteo. Med. Soc., Chester County Med. Soc., Hellenic U. Club of Phila., Hellenic Med. Soc. of Greater Delaware Valley. Avocations: travel, photography, sports, music. Home: 1104 Radley Dr West Chester PA 19382-8074 Office: Christiana Care Chadds Ford Ctr 101 Points Edge Dr Chadds Ford PA 19317-7307

SPYROU, NICHOLAS, astronomy educator; b. Lemnos-Lesvos, Greece, June 20, 1944; s. Constantinos and Triantafyllio (Kazakou) S.; m. Euphemia Mavrommatis, Apr. 26, 1970; children: Constantina, Anastassia. BSc in Physics, U. Thessaloniki, Greece, 1967; PhD in Physics, U. Thessaloniki, 1973, habilitation degree in astronomy, 1979. Asst. U. Thessaloniki, Greece, 1970; chief asst. U. Thessaloniki, 1974, dozent with assignment, 1980, asst. prof. astronomy, 1982, assoc. prof. astronomy, 1983, full prof. astronomy, 1986—; assoc. Com. on Space Rsch.; lectr. in field. Author: Introduction to the Theory of General Relativity, 1985, 2d edit., 1989, Principles of Stellar Evolution: White Dwarfs, Neutron Stars and Black Holes, 1986, Problem Book in Astronomy, Astrophysics, Relativity and Cosmology, 1995, others; editor: Procs. of the Fourth Greek Relativity Workshop Recent Developments in Gravitation-IV, 1990, Jour. Balkan Physics Letters, 1993—, Procs. of the IV European Predoctoral Astrophysics School, 1993; contbr. articles to profl. jours. Recipient Cultural Diploma of Honour, Hellenic Club of Writers; grantee Greek State Found., 1962-67, Nat. Hellenic Rsch. Found., 1970, Brit. Coun., 1975, 87, Fulbright-Hays, 1977, Cornell U., 1977, 94, U. Grete, 1984, U. Cardiff, 1987, 91, Max-Planck Gesellschaft, 1979, 91, 94, Deutsche Akademische Austauschdienst, 1983, Max-Planck Inst. für Astrophysik, 1991, 94, Max-Planck Inst. für Radioastronomie, 1994 Astronomische Inst. der U. Bonn, 1994. Fellow Royal Astron. Soc.; mem. Internat. Astron. Union (commn. on cosmology), Am. Astron. Soc., Internat. Soc. on Gen. Relativity and Gravitation, Planetary Soc., European Astron. Soc. (founding mem.), N.Y. Acad. Scis., Union Greek Physicists, Union Greek Astronomers (founding mem.), Assn. Greek Fulbright Scholars, Hellenic Astronomical Soc. (founding mem.), Hellenic Scientific Soc. Office: Astronomy Dept, Univ Thessaloniki, 540 06 Thessaloniki Macedonia, Greece

SQUAZZO, MILDRED KATHERINE (MILDRED KATHERINE OETTING), corporate executive; b. Bklyn., Dec. 22; d. William John and Marie M. (Fromm) Oetting; student L.I. U. Sec.-treas., Stanley Engring., Inc. and v.p. Stanley Chems., Inc., 1960-68; founder, pres. Chem-Dynamics Corp., Scotch Plains, N.J., 1964-68; gen. adminstr., purchasing dir., Richardson Chem. Co., Metuchen, N.J., 1968-69; owner Berkeley Employment Agy. and Berkeley Temp. Help Service, Berkeley Heights, N.J., 1969-91, Berkeley Employment Agy., Morristown, N.J., 1982-91, Bridgewater, N.J., 1987-91; pres. M.K.S. Bus. Group, Inc., Berkeley Heights, 1980-91; mgmt. cons.; personnel fin.; lectr. Served with Nurse Corps, U.S. Army, 1946-47. Mem. Nat. Bus. and Profl. Women's Club. Home and Office: 16 Heather Ln Warren NJ 07059-5258

SQUIRE, VERNON ARTHUR, mathematics educator, researcher; b. Wembley, Middlesex, England, July 2, 1952; s. Vernon Fritz and Elsie Elizabeth (Sale) S.; m. Patricia Jean Langhorne, Feb. 13, 1987; children: Jonathan, Dougal. BSc in Applied Math. with honors, U. Coll. Wales, Aberystwyth, Wales, 1974; PhD, Cambridge U., England, 1978; DSc, U. Wales, 1997. Rsch. assoc. Cambridge U., Scott Polar Rsch. Inst., 1978-84, sr. asst. in rsch., 1984-87; chair applied math. U. Otago, Dunedin, New Zealand, 1987—, chmn., 1996—; convenor environ. assessment and review panel Ministry Fgn. Affairs and Trade, Wellington, New Zealand, 1996-98. Author: Moving Loads on Ice Plates, 1996; contbr. numerous articles to profl. jours. Mem. sea ice commn. IAPSO, USA, 1987—, chair working group, 1991-96; mem. antarctic sci. standing com. RSNZ, Wellington,

1995—. Recipient Polar medal HM Queen Elizabeth II, 1988, Rsch. award Inst. New Zealand Math. Soc., 1984. Fellow Royal Soc. New Zealand, Inst. Math. and Applications, New Zealand Math. Soc.; mem. The Arctic Club, Antarctic Club. Avocations: music, hiking, children. Office: U Otago, Cumberland St, Dunedin Otago, New Zealand

SQUIRES, DIGBY PETER LEIGHTON, economist; b. Wolverhampton, U.K., Nov. 9, 1953; s. Raymond Arthur and June (Summerhill) S.; m. Delfina Maria Entrecanales, Sept. 9, 1973. Student, U. Dundee, 1973; BSc in Econs., Queen Mary Coll., 1978. Articled clk. KPMG Peat Marwick, London, 1978-81, insolvency mgr., 1981-83; divsnl. fin. exec. Mitsubishi Electric U.K., London, 1983-85; dir. Leighton Properties Ltd., London, 1985-97; prin. Squires Cons., London and Madrid, 1989-99; trustee The Delfina Studio Trust, London, 1988—; cons. Haynes and Trias, Marbella, Spain, 1989-99; dir. Millwall Prodns. Ltd., D.S. Café Ltd. Bd. dirs. Manilva Opera Festival, Spain, 1992-94. Mem. Chelsea Arts Club (hon.). Mem. Labour Party. Avocations: visual arts, sailing, reading, salmon fishing, stepgrandchildren. Office: The Delfina Studio Trust, 50 Bermondsey St, London SE1 3UD, England

SQUIRES, RICHARD FELT, research scientist; b. Sparta, Mich., Jan. 15, 1933; s. Monas Nathan and Dorothy Lois (Felt) S.; m. Else Saederup, 1 child, Iben. BS, Mich. State U., 1958; postgrad., Calif. Inst. Tech., 1958-61. Rsch. biochemist Pasadena Found. for Med. Rsch., 1961-62; chief biochemistry sect. rsch. dept. A/S Ferrosan, Soeborg, Denmark, 1963-78; neurochemistry group leader CNS Biology sect. Lederle Labs. div. Am. Cyanamid Co., Pearl River, N.Y., 1978-79; prin. rsch. scientist The Nathan S. Kline Inst. for Psychiat. Rsch., Orangeburg, N.Y., 1979-2000, ret., 2000. Contbr. over 85 articles to profl. jours.; patentee in field. Nat. Inst. Neurol. and Communication Disorders and Stroke grantee, 1981-84. Mem. Soc. Neurosci., Collegium Internat. Neuro-Psychopharmacologicum, Internat. Soc. Neurochemistry, European Neurosci. Assn., Am. Soc. Neurochemistry, Am. Soc. Biochemistry and Molecular Biology, Am. Soc. Pharmacology and Exptl. Therapeutics. Home: 861 Laugenour Ct Woodland CA 95776-4911

SQUIRRELL, MAURICE DENTON, retired real estate valuation educator; b. Melbourne, Australia, Dec. 29, 1939; s. Percy and Grace (Clarke) S.; m. Jane Randell, Feb. 8, 1966; children: Carolyn, Mark, Alison. B in Bus., Royal Melbourne Inst. Tech., Australia, 1977; MS, U. Wis., 1979. Land valuer State River & Water Supply, Victoria, Australia, 1959-68; from lectr. in valuation to assoc. prof. property Royal Melbourne Inst. Technology, 1968-97; sr. cons. Rogers Milne & Asocs., Melbourne, 1985—. Author: Readings in Property Economics, 1997; contbr. articles to profl. jours. Avocation: raising beef cattle. Home: 565 Ridge Rd, 3757 Whittlesea Victoria, Australia

SRB, VLADIMÍR, biologist, hygienist; b. Hradec Králové, E. Bohemia, Czech Republic, Feb. 23, 1931; s. František and Marie (Srbová) S.; m. Eva Havelková, July 28, 1956; 1 child, Daniela. MSc, Masaryk U., Brno, Czechoslovakia, 1956, PhD, 1965, Docent, 1967; DSc, prof., Charles U., Hradec Králové, 1992. Lectr. asst. Mil. Med. Acad., Hradec Králové, 1957; lectr. asst. faculty of pharmacy Masaryk U., Brno, 1957-58; lectr. asst. med. faculty Charles U., Hradec Kralové, 1958-69, scientist, 1969-74; hygienist Region Hygiene Sta., Pardubice, Czechoslovakia, 1975-79, Dist. Hygiene Sta., Hradec Králové, 1979-90; assoc. prof. med. faculty Charles U., Hradec Králové, 1990-92, prof., 1992—. 5o-author: Atlas of Chromosome Abberrations, 1982, Cytogenetics of Birds, 1986; editor-in-chief: In vitro v ČSR jour., 1964-72; contbr. articles to profl. jours. Mem. European Environ. Mutagen Soc., Czech Biol. Soc. (hon. mem., Gold medal 1996), Czech Med. Soc., Soc. for Sustainable Devel. (hon.). Avocations: lit., music, tennis, swimming. Office: Charles Univ Med Faculty, Šimkova Str No 870, 500 01 Hradec Králové Czech Republic

SREBOTNIK, EWALD, research scientist; b. Maennedorf, Switzerland, July 31, 1961; s. Franz and Amelia (Mores) S. M, Tech. U. Vienna, 1985, PhD, 1988. Applied Microbiology prof. Tech. U. Vienna (Austria), 1988—; vis. scientist FPL, Madison, Wis., 1992-94; researcher in field. Editor: Biotechnol in the Pulp and Paper Industry, 1996. Avocations: sailing, nature, jazz, photography. Home: RNurejew Prom 1/6/12, A-1220 Vienna Austria Office: Inst Biochem Tech, Getreidemarkt 9, A-1060 Vienna Austria

ŚREDNIAWA, BRONISŁAW EDWARD, physicist, retired educator; b. Ciężkowice, Tarnów, Poland, June 17, 1917; s. Edward and Bronisława (Skabowska) Ś; m. Olga Solarz, Feb. 6, 1927; children: Maria, Bronisława. Magister in Physics, Jagellonian U., Cracow, Poland, 1945, Magister in Math., 1945, PhD in Physics, 1947. Asst. Jagellonian U., Cracow, 1945-52, lectr., 1952-56, asst. prof., docent, 1956-62, assoc. prof., 1962-69, full prof., 1969-87, pro-dean math and natural scis. faculty, 1952-56, dean math and physics faculty, 1969. Author: Hydrodynamics and Elasticity, 1977, Quantum Mechanics, 1988; contbr. articles to profl. jours. Recipient awards Ministry Higher Edn., Warsaw, 1969, 77, 87, 89. Mem. Polish Phys. Soc., Com. of History of Sci., Centro Superiore di Logica. Roman Catholic. Avocations: methodology of science, sea-sailing, traveling. Home: Bałuckiego 21, 30-318 Cracow Poland Office: Jagellonian Univ, Reymonta 4, 30-059 Cracow Poland

SREE, USHA, research fellow; b. Hyderabad, India, Nov. 8, 1972; d. Ramesh and Anasuya Babu. BSc, Osmania U., Hyderabad, India, 1992; MSc in Tech., JNTU, Hyderabad, 1995. Cert. environ. chemist. Rsch. fellow JTNU, Hyderabad, 1995-97, Vienna U. Tech., 1997—. Contbr. articles to profl. jours. North-South Dialogue scholar Austrian Acad. Exch. Svc., 1997-98. Avocations: reading, badminton, crossword puzzles. Home: House # 3-6-700 1A St # 11, Himayatnagar, Hyderabad 500029, India Office: Vienna U Tech, Uetreidemarkt 9/151, A-1060 Vienna Austria

SREENIVASAN, KUNNATHEERY, scientist; b. Trichur, Kerala, India, Jan. 19, 1952; s. Nair Sankunny and Amma Narayani; m. Retnamony Manjusha; children: Nandini, Gautham. BSc, Calicut U., India, 1973, MSc, 1975; PhD, Sree Chitra Inst., India, 1991. Sci. asst. Indian Inst. Sci., 1977-79; scientist B Sree Chitra Inst., Trivandrum, India, 1979-85, scientist C, 1985-89, scientist D, 1989-93, scientist E, 1993—. Contbr. rsch. papers to profl. jours.; patentee in field. Nat. Merit scholar Govt. of India, 1973-75. Fellow Indian Chem. Soc.; mem. Material Rsch. Soc. India (Best Paper award 1995, Medal of Yr. 1999), Soc. Biomaterials and Artificial Organisms (life). Avocations: reading, writing. Office: Sree Chitra Tribunal Inst, BMT Wing Poojapura, 695012 Trivandrum Kerala, India

SREEPADA, BHANOJEE RAO, chemist, researcher; b. Ponnamanda, India, July 15, 1941; s. Satyanarayana and Suryalakshmi (Musti) S.; m. Varalakshmi Mamidipalli, June 4, 1964; children: Srinivas, Suvarna. BSc with honors, Visakhapatnam (India) U., 1960, MSc, 1961; cert. in Russian, Bhubaneswar (India) U., 1966, PhD, 1985. Demonstrator Andhra U., India, 1961-62, jr. rsch. fellow, 1962-64; sr. sci. asst. Regional Rsch. Lab., Bhubaneswar, 1964-68, scientist, 1968-81, asst. dir., head inorganic chems. divsn., 1981-91, dep. dir., head inorganic chems. divsn., 1991—; organizer seminar Internat. Geosphere Biosphere Program, 1998. Contbr. numerous rsch. papers to profl. jours.; patentee in field. Mem. Catalysis Soc. India (life), Indian Inst. Metals (life), Indian Thermal Analysis Soc. (life), Indian Coun. Chemists (life), Indian Inst. Mineral Engrs. (life), Orissa Environ. Soc. (life). Hindu. Office: Regional Rsch Lab, Bhubaneswar 75103, India

SRIDHARAN, VARADACHARI, mathematician, educator; b. Chennai, Tamil Nadu, India, July 2, 1960; s. Josiar Srilakshmi Narasimhar Varadachari and Vasantha V.; m. Sudha Sridharan, June 18, 1992; 1 child, Sindhuja. BSc, Presidency Coll., Chennai, 1982; MSc, U. Madras, 1984; PhD, Indian Inst. Tech., Chennai, 1989; P.D.F., Inst. Math. Scis., 1990. Lectr. Internat. Inst. for Population Scis., Mumbai, India, 1990-91; lectr. Vellore Engring. Coll., Chennai, 1991-92; lectr. Anna U., Chennai, 1992-98, asst. prof., 1998—. Contbr. articles to profl. jours. Recipient Directorate of Tech. Edn. cash award, 1982. Life mem. Indian Soc. for Probability and Statistics, Indian Soc. for Tech. Edn., Bulletin Pure & Applied Scis. Avocations: reading books, listening to carnatic music, playing chess, cricket, tennis. Office: Dept Math, Anna U, 600025 Chennai India

SRIKIATKHACHORN, ANAN, neurologist, researcher; b. Bangkok, Jan. 29, 1961; s. Sutee and Siriporn Srikiatkhachorn; m. Siripat Gosinjit. BSc, Mahidol U., Bangkok, 1982, MD with honors, 1984; diploma in neurology, Chulalongkorn U., Bangkok, 1990. Diplomate Bd. Neurology, Thailand. Intern Chonburi (Thailand) Hosp., 1984-85; gen. practitioner Haadyai Hosp., Songkhla, Thailand, 1985-87; resident in neurology Chulalongkorn U., 1987-90; asst. prof. faculty of medicine Chulalongkorn U., Bangkok, 1995-97, assoc. prof. neurosci., 1997—; instr. Inst. Sci. Tech. for R&D, Nakornpathom, Thailand, 1990-92; asst. prof. Inst. Sci. Tech. for R&D, Nakornpathom, 1992-94; dir. grad. study in physiology, Bangkok, 1997—, headache clinic Chulalongkorn Hosp., 1996—; assoc. prof. neuroscis. Mahidol U. 1990-94. Author: (CD-ROM) Neurobase, 1995—; contbr. articles to profl. jours. Grantee Nat. Rsch. Coun., 1993, Overseas Rsch. grant Asahi Glass Foudn., 1996, Thailand Rsch. Fund, 1997. Mem. Am. Assn. for Study of Headache (Kaplan award 1997), Thai Neurosci. Soc. (exec. 1996—), Med. Coun. Thailand, Med. Assn. Thailand, Neurol. Soc. Thailand, Asia-Pacific Soc. Neurochemistry, Internat. Headache Soc. (fellowship award 1994, Best Basic Rsch. Poster award 1999), Internat. Assn. for Study of Pain, Internat. Brain Rsch. Orgn., N.Am. Cervicogenic Headache Soc., N.Y. Acad. Sci. Home: 34/19 Petchburi Rd, Rajthewee Bangkok 10400, Thailand Office: Dept Physiology, Chulalongkorn U, 10330 Bangkok Thailand

SRIMANI, PRADIP K., computer science educator. BSc in Physics with honors, U. Calcutta, India, 1970, B.Tech. in Radiophysics and Electronics, 1973, M.Sc. in Radiophysics and Electronics, 1975, PhD in Computer Sci., 1978. Asst. divsnl. engr. dept. post and telegraph Govt. India, 1976; lectr., computer engr. Indian Statis. Inst., Calcutta, 1976-80; Alexander von Humboldt post doctoral fellow computer sci. Informatik Kolleg, Bonn, West Germany; asst. prof. computer sci., chair computer ctr. Indian Inst. Mgmt., Calcutta, 1981-84; vis. assoc. prof. computer sci. So. Ill. U., Carbondale, 1984-85, assoc. prof., 1985-87, prof., 1987-89; prof. Colo. State U., Fort Collins, 1990—, interim chair dept. computer sci., 1994-96; keynote spkr. computing confs. and workshops, 1993, 98. Editor IEEE Computer Soc. Press, 1990-92, assoc. editor-in-chief, 1993-96, editor-in-chief, 1997—; editor Internat. Jour. Computer Simulation, 1991-96, IEEE Software, 1993—, IEEE Transaction on Knowledge and Data Engring., 1998—; guest editor numerous jours.; contbr. articles to profl. jours. Grantee Hewlett-Packard, 1996, NSF, 1999-2000. Fellow IEEE, IEEE Computer Soc. (planning com. 1991, 97, 99, mag. adv. com. 1990-91, edn. activities bd. 1004-00, conf. and tutorial bd. 1993, 97-99, press activities bd. 1997-99, awards com. 1995-97, task force on year 2001 model curricula for computing). Fax: 970-49102466. E-mail: srimani@cs.colostate.edu. Office: Colo State U Dept Computer Sci Fort Collins CO 80523-0001

SRINATH, LATHA, physician; b. Bangalore, India, Jan. 1, 1958; came to U.S., 1985; d. Krishna and Shamanthaka (Ananthachar) Iyengar; m. Sampath Holevanahalli Srinath, Jan. 22, 1984; children: Shilpa, Preetha. BS, Bangalore U., 1978; MBBS, Bangalore Med. Coll., 1984; MD, Georgetown U., 1990. Diplomate Am. Bd. Internal Medicine. Fellow in infectious diseases U. Louisville, 1992-94; pvt. practice infectious diseases Boynton Beach, Fla., 1994—; mem. staff Bethesda Meml. Hosp., Boynton Beach, 1994—, JFK Med. Ctr., Boynton Beach, 1994—; cons. HIV Adv. Bd., Fla., 1997—. Contbr. articles to profl. jours. Nat. Merit scholar, India, 1975. Mem. Am. Assn. Physicians from India, Fla. Med. Assn., Palm Beach Med. Soc. Hindu. Avocations: travel, yoga, tennis, oil painting, athletics. Home: 473 N Country Club Dr Lake Worth FL 33462-1003 Office: ID Cons Inc 2623 S Seacrest Blvd Boynton Beach FL 33435-7501

SRINIVAS, KRISHNAMOORTHY, neurologist; b. Calicut, Kerala, India, Feb. 15, 1933; s. Sunderam and Janaki Krishnamoorthy; m. Padma, July 14, 1965; two children. MBBS, Madras Med. Coll., 1957, DM in neurology, 1968. Postgrad. tng. Safdarjang Hosp., New Delhi, 1957-59; resident Queen Elizabeth Hosp., Montreal, 1959-60; resident in neurology U. Hosp. Saskatoon, Can., 1960-61; registrar in neurology Atkinson Morley Hosp., London, 1961-62; registrar in internal medicine Royal Hosp. Richmond, London, 1962-63; rsch. fellow in neurology Atkinson Morley Hosp., 1963; registrar in medicine Wimbledon Hosp., London, 1963-64; registrar in neurology U. Newcastle-upon-Tyne, England, 1964-65; hon. prof. Inst. Neurology Madras Med. Coll., 1965-91; hon. cons. neurology Armed Forces of India, 1978—; chmn. neurology depts., comty. ctrs., Madras. Contbr. over 50 articles to various publs. Recipient several nat. awards, and internat. fellowships. Fellow Am. Coll. Physicians, Royal Coll. Physicians (Edinburgh and London), Acad. Med. Scis., Indian Coll. Physicians; founder fellow Indian Acad. Neurology. Avocations: Indian music, collecting photographs, history of neurology. Home: Srinagar Colony, 3 S Mada St, 600 015 Madras India

SRINIVAS, LEELA, biochemist, researcher; b. Coimbatore, Tamil Nadu, India, June 1, 1941; d. Ramaswamy Pankajam; m. Srinivas, Jan. 28, 1970; 1 child. BSc, Madras U., India, 1961; MSc, Madras U., 1964, PhD, 1977. Rsch. fellow C.F.T.R.I., Mysore, India, 1965-70; sr. rsch. asst. C.F.T.R.I., 1970-79, scientist, 1984—; rsch. assoc. St. Louis U. Med. Sch., 1979-84; vis. fellow NIH, 1980-84; officer-dir. Adicuchana Giri Cancer Rsch. Ctr.; vis. scientist NIH, 1998. Contbr. articles on antioxidants to profl. jours. Mem. project adv. com. Dept. of Sci. and Tech. Life Scis. Govt. of India. Recipient various nat. and internat. awards. Mem. Indian Assn. Career Rschrs. (exec.), Nutrition Soc. India (exec.), Soc. Biol. Chemists. Avocations: Indian classical music, nature study. Office: Adichunchana Giri Cancer, BG Nagara Nagamangala Taluk, 571448 Mandya Dis Karnataka India

SRINIVASA, AREHALLI MUNISWARLAH, emergency physician; b. Bangalore, India, Nov. 17, 1946. Rotating intern Bangalore Med. Coll., 1969-70; sr. house officer surgery Victoria Hosp., Bangalore, 1970-71; lectr. in anatomy Bellary Med. Coll., India, 1971; sr. house officer trauma and orthopedics Neath (U.K.) Gen. Hosp., 1971-72, registrar gen. surgery, 1974-77; rotating sr. house officer surgery Lewisham Hosp., London, 1972-74; specialist med. officer surgery Papua, New Guinea, 1978-90, Mt. Hagen Hosp., 1978-80, Wewak Gen. Hosp., 1980-88; sr. specialist med. officer Goroka Base Hosp., 1989-90; med. officer, family medicine practice rotation Queen Elizabeth II Jubilee Hosp., Brisbane, Australia, 1991; sr. med. officer accident and emergeny Logan Hosp., Meadowbank, Australia, 1991—. Fellow ACS, Royal Coll. Surgeons (Edinburgh), Royal Australian Coll. Gen. Practitioners; mem. Internat. Fedn. of Surg. Colls. (assoc.), Surg. Soc. of P.N.G. (v.p. 1983, pres. 1984), Rotary Club of Wewak (treas. 1987-88). Avocations: music, reading, photography, cricket. Home: 38 Vaughan Dr, Ormeau QLD 4208, Australia Office: Ormeau Med Ctr, 3 Vaughan Dr, Ormean QLD 4208, Australia

SRINIVASA, VENKATARAMANIAH, engineer; b. Mysore, India, Aug. 30, 1941; came to U.S., 1968; s. Venkataramaniah and Gowramma S.; m. Janakimala Muthiah, June 1972; children: Supreeth, Suman. BSc, Mysore U., 1962, MSc, 1964; MS, Rutgers U., 1972, PhD, 1975. Rsch. fellow CFTRI, Mysore, 1964-67; tech. officer Indian Inst. Packaging, Bombay, 1967; rsch. intern, rsch. tching. asst. Rutgers U., New Brunswick, N.J., 1972-75, fellow Bur. Engring. Rsch., 1972-75; sr. packaging engr. Abbott Labs., Abbott Park, Ill., 1975-78, sr. project engr., 1978-83, mgr., 1983—. Mem. Inst. Packaging Profls., Soc. Plastics Engrs., Am. Chem. Soc., Am. Soc. Engring. Mgmt., N.Y. Acad. Sci., Sigma Xi. Home: 2729 Sallmon Ave Waukegan IL 60087-3514

SRINIVASAN, DURAIRAJ, microbiology educator; b. Nallamaicken Patty, Tamil Nadu, India, June 5, 1967; s. Raj Durai and Rathamani. BSc, V.H.N.S.N. Coll., Virudhunagar, India, 1988; MSc, Annamalai U., Chidambaram, India, 1990; MPhil, Bharathiar U., Coimbatore, India, 1991, PhD, 1997. Head dept. microbiology Sree Narayana Guru Coll., Coimbatore, 1996—; cons. IVC Labs. and Environ. Svcs., Chennai, India, 1999—. Contbr. articles to profl. jours. Mem. Am. Soc. Microbiology, Assn. Microbiologists India, Acad. Plant Scis. India. Avocations: trucking, photography, music. Home: 1/2 IInd Cross, Periyar Nagar, Coimbatore Tamilnadu 641 041, India Office: Sree Narayana Guru Coll, Dept Microbiology, Coimbatore Tamilnadu 641 105, India

SRINIVASAN, PARTHIBAN, atmospheric scientist, researcher; b. Malligarai, Tamil Nadu, India, July 2, 1967; came to U.S., 1997; s. Venkatachalam and Chandravathanam (Rajulu0 S.; m. Anan Thalakshmi Meenakshisondaram, Aug. 29, 1997; 1 child, Sowmya Parthiban. BSc in Chemistry, U. Madras, 1987, MSc in Polymer Sci., 1989; MSc in Aerospace Engring., Indian Inst. Sci., Bangalore, 1991, PhD in Aerospce Engring., 1996. Project assoc. Supercomputer Edn. and Rsch. Ctr., Indian Inst. Sci., Bangalore, 1996-97; NRC rsch. assoc. NASA Ames Rsch. Ctr., Moffett Field, Calif., 1997—; coord. in-house symposium aerospace engring. Indian Inst. Sci., Bangalore, 19996, convenor seminar dept. aerospace engring., 1990-91; sr. rsch. fellow Coun. Sci. and Indsl. Rsch. India, New Delhi, 1993-96. Contbr. articles to profl. jours. Mem. Geophys. Union. Home: 450 N Mathilda Ave Apt L101 Sunnyvale CA 94085-4247 Office: NASA Ames Rsch Ctr MS 230-3 Moffett Field CA 94035

SRINIVASAN, SUNDARAM, engineering educator, academic administrator; b. Trichy, Madras, India, Oct. 24, 1944; s. Nagiaratnam Srinivasan and Subbiah Suseela; m. Chandra Subbiah, Apr. 27, 1945; 1 child. B in Engring., Annamalai, India, 1967; M in Tech., Indian Inst. Sci., Bangalore, India, 1969, PhD, 1976. Cert. engr. Assoc. lectr. Regional Engring. Coll., Trichy, India, 1969-70, lectr., 1970-82, assoc. prof., 1982-94, prof., chmn., 1996—; student advisor Regional Engring. Coll. Trichy, 1976-92, 98—, warden hostels, 1976-86, cultural advisor, 1976-94, chmn. coll. day com., 1980-90; mem. All India Coun. Tech. Edn., New Delhi, 1996—. Author: Chemical Engineering Thermodynamics, 1998; contbr. articles to profl. jours. Mem. Am. Chem. Soc., N.Y. Acad. Scis. Avocations: music, social service. Home: No. 5 1st St REC Qrs, Trichy 620015, India Office: Regional Engring Coll, Dept Chem Engring, Trichy 620015, India

SRISKANTHAN, NADARAJAH, engineeering educator; b. Nallur, Jaffna, Sri Lanka; s. Vallipuram and Thillaipillai Nadarajah; m. Meera Sachithanandam; children: Ragulan, Gayathri, Veena. BSc in Elec. Engring., U. London, 1972; MSc in Elec. Equipment Design, Cranfield Inst. Tech., Eng., 1978. Sr. test engr. Plessey Radar Ltd., Surrey, U.K., 1973-76; design engr. Philips, Croydon, U.K., 1979-82; rsch. officer Cranfield Inst. Tech., U.K., 1982-84; sr. lectr. Nanyang Tech. U., Singapore, 1995-98, assoc. prof., 1999—. Rschr., designer devel. teletext access system for P.C., 1995, devel. P.C. based IIC protocol-analyser, 1999. Recipient scholarship Sci. and Engring. Rsch. Coun., U.K., 1976-78. Mem. IEEE (sec. C.E. chpt. Singapore 1998-99, chmn. 1999—). Achievements include research in multimedia, parallel processor, com. interfacing Internet. Avocations: sports, photography, stamp collecting, social-welfare, travel. Home: 33 Nanyang View, Singapore 639635, Singapore Office: Nanyang Tech U SAS, Nanyang Ave, 639798 Singapore Singapore

SRIVASTAA, ANAND BEHARI, dentistry educator; b. Jaunpur, India, July 9, 1933; s. Banke Behari and Sushila Devi; m. Shila, June 22, 1959. B in Dental Sci., King George's Med. Coll., Lucknow, India, 1959; M in Dental Sci., Nair Hosp. Dental Coll., Bombay, 1962. From lectr. to prof., head dept. Inst. Med. Scis. Bananas Hindu U., Varanas, India, 1962—; prin. Santosh Dental Coll. and Hosp., Ghaliabad, India; prof. emeritus Subhavati Inst. Med. Scis., Meerut, India; mem. Dental Coun. India, 1979-89. Mem. Indian Dental Assn. (founder sec. 1982-86), Fedn. Operative Dentistry of India. Avocations: hockey, badminton, gardening, photography, sight seeing. Home: 21B Juhi Colony Muir Rd, 211002 Allahabad India

SRIVASTAVA, BRIJNANDAN, physician, consultant; b. Gwalior, India, Aug. 10, 1930; s. Shivnandan and Kaushilya Srivastava; m. Sharan Dulari Srivastava, June 10, 1951. MBBS, Gwalior Agra U.(India), 1951, MD, 1954. Lectr. in medicine Agra U., Gwalior, 1954-58; Rockefeller fellow G.S. Med. Coll., Bombay, 1956-57; reader Med. Coll., Bhopal, Indore, India, 1958-65, prof., head medicine, 1965-90, emeritus prof. medicine, 1995—, dean, 1988-90; hon. cons. Ctrl. Railway Hosp., Jabalpur, 1990-95; coord. ICMR, Jaalpur, India, 1985-90. Recipient Nat. Unity award Gov. M.P., 1990, Charak award Indian Med. Assn., 1995; Rsch. fellow WHO, 1979. Fellow Nat. Acad. Med. Scis., India Coll. Physicians (founder, mem. A.P.I. faculty coun. 1999); mem. Internat. Diabetes Fedn., Isim, N.Y. Acad. Scis., Am. Coll. Chest Physicians, Am. Coll. Angiology, Am. Geriatric Soc. Home: 1139/Prem Nagar, Jabalpur 482001, India Office: Med Coll, Jabalpur 482003, India

SRIVASTAVA, KAUSHAL KISHORE, biochemist; b. Lucknow, India, Feb. 4, 1940; s. Nawal Kishore and Shail Kumari S.; m. Sushma Srivastava, Feb. 25, 1963; children: Kishore, Sanjeev, Srivastava, Shikhar. BSc, U. Lucknow, 1958, MSc, 1960; PhD, U. Delhi, 1969; M in Pub. Adminstrn., Indian Inst. Pub. Adminstrn., Delhi, 1983. Scientist Def. Rsch. Devel. Orgn., Delhi, 1963-74; asst. prof. sch. medicine U. Basrah, Iraq, 1974-75, 75-77; under sec. Union Pub. Svc. Commn., Delhi, 1977-78; scientist, head dept. biochemistry, dir. projects Def. Inst. Physiology Allied Sci., Delhi, 1978-99; dir. biomed. scis. DRDOHQ, 1999-2000, emeritus scientist, 2000—. Author: (monographs) Stay in High Mountains and Panax Ginseng, 1994, management of environmental Stress With Composite Indian Herbal Preparation, 1995, Combat Stress: Management with CIHP-I, 1998; contbr. numerous articles to profl. jours. Univ. Grants Commn. fellow, merit rsch. scholar, 1960-63; recipient Talented Scientists award 35th World Congress Natural Medicine, 1995, Scientist of Yr. Life Scis. DRDO, Min. of Def. award, India, 1997, Subhash Mukherjee Meml. award Endocrine Soc. India, 1997, C.L. Nepali Meml. Delhi State award, Def. Scientist, 1999. Fellow Assn. Clin. Biochemists India (Seth G.S. and Kem Hosp. Oration award 1995), Indian Acad. Neurosci., Assn. Biomed. Scientists India. Avocations: music, visiting remote areas, films. Office: Def Inst Physiology, Lucknow Rd Timarpur, New Delhi 110054, India

SRIVASTAVA, LALIT MOHAN, biochemistry educator, researcher; b. Gonda, India, July 1, 1938; s. Govind Saran and G.S. Srivastava; m. Renu Srivastava, Jan. 22, 1969; children: Anant Mohan, Tapasya. BSc, Lucknow (India) U., 1957, MSc, 1959; PhD in Med. Biochemistry, U. Birmingham, Eng., 1967. Rsch. assoc. U. Birmingham, 1965-68; rsch. officer All India Inst. Med. Scis., New Delhi, 1968-70, lectr. biochemistry, 1970-77, asst. prof., 1977-83, prof., 1983—, head dept., 1995-98; sr. cons., head dept. biochemistry Sir Ganga Ram Hosp., New Delhi, 1999—. Editor: Textbook of Biochemistry and Human Biology, 1989; contbr. over 125 articles on immunology, cardiac biochemistry and metabolism to sci. jours. and popular publs. Recipient Dr. B.C. Roy natl award for spltys. devel. Med. Coun. India, 1995, gold medal for biomed. scis. Dr. Vishwanath Found., 1995, Sr. Scientist Oration award Nat. Inst. Immunology and Indian Immunology Soc., 1998; Alexander von Humboldt Found. fellow Inst. Human Genetics, Hamburg, Germany, 1974-75, 81, 92, 2000. Mem. Indian Immunology Soc. (sec. 1984-95, pres. 1992-93), Assn. Clin. Biochemists India (King Edward Med. Hosp. and G.S. Med. Coll. oration award 1994). Hindu. Home: 91 Charak Sadan Vikaspuri, New Delhi 110018, India Office: Dept Biochemistry, Sir Ganga Ram Hosp, New Delhi 110060, India

SRIVASTAVA, NARESH CHANDRA, scientist; b. Hardoi, India, June 30, 1940; s. Uma Shankar and Kamla Devi Srivastava; m. Madhu Lata Srivastava, Jan. 28, 1965; two children. B in Vet. Sci. and Animal Husbandry, Vet. Coll., Mathura, India, 1964; M in Vet. Sci., Post Grad. Coll., Indian Vet. Rsch. Inst. Izatnagar, Bareilly, India, 1970, PhD in Vet. Bacteriology, 1984. Rsch. asst. Indian Vet. Rsch. Inst. Izatnagar, Bareilly, 1964-70, sr. rsch. asst., 1971-72, asst. bacteriologist, 1972-75, jr. bacteriologist, 1975-80, sr. scientist, 1980-85, prin. scientist, 1986—. Assoc. editor Indian Jour. Vet. Microbiology Immunology Infectious Diseases. Mem. Indian Assn. Vet. Microbiologist Immunologist Specialist Infectoius Diseases (life), Indian Assn. Vet. Rsch. (life), Rohilkhand Vets. Club (life, gen. sec. 1996). Avocation: music. Home: 149 Janak Puri Izatnagar, Bareilly 243122, India Office: Divsn Bact & Mycol, Indian Vet Res Inst, Izatngar Uttar Pradesh 243 122, India

SRIVASTAVA, P. N., research scientist, educator; b. Basti, India, July 1, 1927; s. R. S. Srivastava and Chandrawati Devi; m. Rani Gaur (dec.); children: Anil, Anita, Archana, Aparna. MSc, U. Allahabad, India, 1949, PhD, 1951; DSc (hon.), Kanpur (India) U., 1995. Asst. prof. U. Allahabad, 1951-61; assoc. prof. U. Rajasthan, Jaipor, India, 1961-66, prof., 1966-75; prof. Jawaharlal Nehru U., New Delhi, 1975-87, rector, 1977-79, 81-82, vice chancellor, 1980-82, prof. emeritus; mem. planning commn. Min. of State, India; vis. prof. Thomas Jefferson Med. U., Phila., 1979, Inst. Nuclear Medicine, Julich, Germany, 1992, Kyoto (Japan) U., 1975-76, Pasteur Inst. Med. Rsch., Kyoto, 1997; rsch. assoc., vis. scientist Dalhousie U., Halifax, N.S., Can., 1958-60, Bingham Oceanographic Lab., Yale U., New Haven, 1961, Nat. Inst. Radiol. Scis., Chiba, Japan, 1963, Cornell U., Ithaca, N.Y.,

Paterson Labs. and Holt Radium Inst., Manchester, U.K., 1965, Italian Atomic Energy Agy., Casaccia, 1969, Kyoto U.; pres. sect. zoology, entomology and fisheries Indian Sci. Congress, 1977; pres. Internat. Coun. Sci. Devel., Heidelberg, Germany, 1989-94; gen. pres. Indian Sci. Congress, 1993-94; mem. steering com. for establishment of Indira Gandhi Nat. Open U., New Delhi, All India Coun. for Tech. Edn.; chmn. com. for development of Nat. Sci. U.; mem. steering com. for establishment of Asian Assn. Univs. UNESCO, mem. adminstrv. bd. Internat. Assn. Univs., Paris, 1985-90, 90-95, planning bd., 1990-95. Contbr. over 170 articles to profl. jours. Recipient award Fedn. Indian C. of C. and Industry, Atma Ram award Ministry of Human Resources Devel., K. N. Bahl Meml. Gold medal Indian Soc. Bioscis., J. C. Bose award Univ. Grants Commn., Scholarly award Inst. Oriental Philosophy, award Goyal Found. Fellow Indian Nat. Sci. Acad. (exec. com., treas., Arybhata Gold medal), Nat. Acad. Scis. (exec. com., v.p., pres. sect. biol. scis. 1978), Nat. Acad. Med. Scis., Royal Microscopical Soc., Linnean Soc. U.K.; mem. N.Y. Acad. Scis. (fgn.), Indian Soc. Radiation Biology (founding pres. 1988-90), Indian Soc. Sci. Values (pres. 1992-95, 95-98), Internat. Assn. Hyperthermic Oncology. Avocations: gardening, photography. Home: 163 Nat Media Ctr, Nat Hwy # 8, Gurgaon Haryana 122002, India Office: Jawaharlal Nehru U, New Delhi 110067, India

SRIVASTAVA, RADHEY SHYAM, scientist, researcher; b. Bahadurganj, India, June 7, 1931; s. Umeshwar Prasad and Ganesha Devi; m. Vijay Laxmi, Feb. 12, 1959; children: Suneeta, Sanjay, Sangita. BSc, Lucknow (India) U., 1951, MSc, 1953, PhD, 1963, cert. in French, 1957. Rsch. fellow, lectr. Lucknow U., 1954-56, 56-57; jr. sci. officer Def. Sci. Lab., New Delhi, 1958-61, sr. sci. officer, 1961-71, prin. sci. officer, 1971-80; dep. chief sci. officer Def. Sci. Ctr., New Delhi, 1980-91; pvt. rschr., 1991—; postdoctoral rsch. fellow Royal Soc. London, Imperial Coll. Sci. and Tech., 1965; vis. scientist MRL, Melbourne, Australia, 1983, Inst. Aerospace Studies, Toronto, Can., 1980, Chiba U., 1991; vis. prof. Ernst Mach Inst., Freiburg, Germany, 1995; mem. organizing com. winter sch. in physiol. fluid dynamics, 1975. Author: Turbulence (Pipe Flows), 1977, Interaction of Shock Waves, 1994; contbr. to profl. publs. Mem. gen. body Welfare Assn., New Delhi, 1985—. Grantee Def. Rsch. Can., 1980, USAF, 1980, Min. Def., New Delhi, 1983, Min. Edn. Japan, Chiba, 1991. Fellow Nat. Acad. Scis.; mem. Bharat Ganita Parishad (life), Indian Sci. Congress, Sci. Officer's Assn. Hindu. Achievements include development of Srivastava's Theory. Avocations: music, movies, sports. Home and Office: A-3/260 Janakpuri, New Delhi 110058, India

SRIVASTAVA, RAJENDRA NATH, pediatrician, educator; b. Barabanki, India, July 10, 1937; s. Triloki Nath and Sarojini Srivastava; m. Manju Srivastava, July 21, 1961; 1 child, Ruma. MD, U. Lucknow (India), 1959; diploma in child health, U. London, 1962. Diplomate Am. Bd. Pediatrics. Lectr. All India Inst. Med. Scis., New Delhi, 1970-73, asst. prof. pediatrics, 1973-79, assoc. prof., 1979-88, prof. pediatrics, 1988-97; pediatric nephrologist cons. Apollo Hosp., New Delhi, 1997—; dir. Inst. Child Health, Kabul, Afghanistan, 1974-79; vis. prof. med. br. U. Tex., Galveston, 1990-91. Author: Pediatrics, 1989, Pediatric and Neonatal Emergencies, 1990, Pediatric Nephrology, 1997; contbr. over 100 articles to profl. jours. Recipient K. Menon award Indian Coun. Med. Rsch., 1993; named World Leader in Pediatrics award Internat. Soc. of Tropical Pediatrics, 1999. Fellow Royal Coll. Physicians, Nat. Acad. Med. Scis.; mem. Indian Soc. Nephrology (R. Khullar award 1988), Indian Acad. Pediatrics (pres. 1996, S.T. Achar award 1972). Hindu. Avocations: serious reading, semi-classical music, bird watching. E-mail: rns2@vsnl.com. Home and Office: 487 Mandakini Enclave, Alaknanda, New Delhi 110019, India

SRIVASTAVA, RATNA KUMAR, environmental scientist, educator, researcher; b. Rewa, M.P., India, June 4, 1961; s. Vimlendu and Sushila (Devi) Srivastava; m. Sangita Srivastava, Nov. 29, 1987; children: Abhiram, Abhishruti. BSc, Apsu-Awadhesh Pratap Singh U., Rewa, 1979, MSc in Environ. Sci., 1981, MPhil, 1982, PhD, 1985. Jr. rsch. fellow APSU-Awadhesh Pratap Singh U., Rewa, 1981-84, sr. rsch. fellow, 1984-86; chemist Madhya Pradesh Pradushan-Niwaran Mandal, Bhopal, India, 1986; asst. prof. Govt. Coll., Amarpatan, India, 1987; asst. prof. dept. botany and environ. sci. Govt. Autonomous Sci. Coll., Jabalpur, India, 1987—; project dir. Min./Dept. Environment, New Delhi, 1997—; co-investigator Madhya Pradesh Coun. of Sci. and Tech., Bhopal, 1997—; prin. investigator Univ. Grants Commn., New Delhi, 1993-94. Contbr. articles to profl. jours. Presenter state level tchrs. tournament in table tennis, R.D. U. Mem. Tchrs. Union (treas. 1995-96), Environ. Biology Soc. (life), ISES (life). Avocations: games, acting, music, stamp collecting, research. Home: P-4 Professors Colony, Pachpedhi South Civil Lines, Jabalpur 482001, India Office: Govt Autonomous Sci Coll, Dept Environ Sci, Jabalpur 482001, India

S. RÓZSA, KATALIN, neurobiologist, scientific adviser; b. Jászszentandás, Szolnok, Hungary, Nov. 29, 1930; d. Sándor R. and Ilona Jezsoviczki; m. János Salánki, Dec. 29, 1960; children: Zsuzsanna, Katalin. PhD, Moscow State U., 1958; DSc, Hungarian Acad. Scis., Budapest, 1975; prof. (hon.), Eötvös Lóránd U., Budapest, 1982. Lectr., prof. Kossuth L. U., Debrecen, Hungary, 1961-63; rsch. fellow, scientific adviser Balaton Limnol. Rsch. Inst., Tihany, Hungary, 1963-97. Editor: (book series) Annales of Biology, 1966-77, Neurotransmitters in invertebrates, 1981, Neurobiology of Invetebrates, 1988, Signal molecules, network and behavior in Invertebrates, 1992-95. Mem. Internat. Brain Rsch. Orgn., Internat. Soc. Invertebrate Neurobiology, European Neuroscience Assn., Internat. Union Biol. Scis., Biol. Soc. (bd. dirs. 1980-90), Biophysics Sco. 9bd. dirs. 1971-85), Physiol. Soc. (bd. dirs. 1990-97). Avocations: mollusk shell collection. Office: Limnol Rsch Inst, Fürdötelepi u 3, H-8237 Tihany Veszprem, Hungary

SSENYONGA, GUSTAVUS STEPHEN ZZIRIDDAMU, veterinarian; b. Kibaale Dist., Uganda, Oct. 2, 1944; s. Samuel Ndebede and Tereza (Babirye) Zziriddamu; m. Mary Antoinette Nankya, June 28, 1980; 8 children. BVM, Nairobi U., 1970; Diploma in Tropical Vet. Medicine, Edinburgh (Scotland) U., 1972, PhD, 1974. Vet. officer Uganda Govt., Kampala, 1970-71; lectr. Makerere U., Uganda, 1974-76, sr. lectr., 1976-80, assoc. prof., 1980-86, prof., 1987—, head dept. vet. parasitology, 1975-80, head dept. vet. pathobiology, 1980-85, head dept. parasitology and microbiology, 1985-91, dean faculty of vet. medicine, 1987-89; vis. prof. U. Zambia, Lusaka, 1986-87; permanent sec. Min. Agr., Uganda, 1991-96; chmn. subcom. Nat. Coun. Sci. and Tech., 1989-92. Author: A Manual of Veterinary Protozoology and Protozoan Diseases, 1987, A Handbook of Tropical Veterinary and Medical Entomology, 1988; contbr. articles to profl. jours. Recipient Gandhi Smarak Trust prize Nairobi U., 1968, 69, Commonwealth Bur. of Animal Health prize, Edinburgh U., 1972; Fulbright fellow, 1988-89. Mem. Uganda Vet. Assn., World Assn. for Advancement of Vet. Parasitology. Mem. Anglican Ch. Avocations: soccer, gardening, poultry farming, writing. Fax: (256-41) 321305. Home: PO Box 880, Entebbe Uganda Office: Mukono Farmers Shop, PO Box 588, Mukono Uganda

S. SILVA, ANTONIO VICENTE, electrical engineer; b. Belem, Brazil, Mar. 23, 1939; s. Lucullo Vicente and Alzira (Albuquerque) S.; children: Luis Andre, Luis Roberto. BS in Electonic Engring. suma cum laude, Inst. Tech. Aeronautica, Brazil, 1961; MS in Electrical Engring., SUNY at Buffalo, 1966. Mgr. industry and defense Westinghouse Electrical Corp., Brazil, 1970-76, sr. engr., 1964-70; pres. Tetronic, Brazil, 1976-86; dir. S.S. Engring., Brazil, 1986-99; cons. Avibras Aeroespacial, 1990-99, Acesita, Westinghouse Electric Corp., 1990-94. Holder 11 patents in field. Mem. N.Y. Acad. Scis., Interplanetary Soc. Avocations: sailing, building sail boats. Office: V ABC, Av Dr Jose Fornari, 164 San Bernardo Campo Brazil

STAAB, HEINZ A., chemist; b. Darmstadt, Germany, Mar. 26, 1926; m. Ruth Mueller, Aug. 22, 1953; children: Doris, Volker. BSc, U. Marburg, Fed. Republic Germany, 1949; Diploma in Chemistry, U. Tuebingen, Fed. Republic Germany, 1951; PhD, U. Frankfurt, Fed. Republic Germany, 1953; MD, U. Heidelberg, Fed. Republic Germany, 1960; PhD (hon.), Weizmann Inst., Rehovot, Israel, 1983. Research assoc. Max Planck Inst., Heidelberg, 1953-59; successively asst. prof., assoc. prof., prof. chemistry U. Heidelberg, 1959—, dir. Inst. Organic Chemistry, 1964-76; head dept. organic chemistry Max Planck Inst. Med. Rsch., Heidelberg, Germany, 1976—, also bd. dirs.; pres. bd. dirs. Bayer AG Leverkusen, Degussa AG, Frankfurt. Author: Azolides in Organic Syntheses and Biochemistry, 1998; contbr. numerous articles to profl. jours. Decorated Order of Merit (Govt. Baden-Wuerttenberg, Germany); recipient Weizmann Award in Scis. and Humanities, 1989, Grosses Bundesverdienstkreuz mit Stern, Govt. Fed. Republic Germany, 1990. Mem. German Chem. Soc. (pres. 1984-85, Adolf v. Baeyer medal 1979, hon. mem. 99), Gesellschaft Deutscher Naturforscher und Aerzte (pres. 1980, 81), Deutsche Forschungsgemeinschaft (senator 1976-82, 84-90), Internat. Union Pure and Applied Chemistry (v.p., pres.-elect 1991-93), Heidelberg Acad. Wissenschaften (nat. sci. sect. sec. 1970-77, pres. 1994-96), Austrian Acad. Scis., Acad. Leopoldina (chmn. chem. com. 1974-90), Bavarian Acad. Scis., Indian Acad. Scis. (hon.), Academia Sinica (hon. prof.), Academia Europaea London (found. mem., exec. coun. 1988-89), Russian Acad. Scis. (fgn. mem.), Max-Planck Soc. (hon., pres. 1984-90, Adolf von Harnack medal 1996), Rotary. Avocations: music, travel. Home: Schloss-Wolfsbrunnenweg 43, 69118 Heidelberg Germany Office: Max Planck Inst Med Rsch, Jahnstr 29, 69118 Heidelberg Germany

STAATS, THOMAS ELWYN, neuropsychologist; s. Percy Anderson and Julia (Bourmorck) S.; m. Debra R.; children: Lauren Malu, Kara Kristyn, Stacy Rhnea, Ronald Derek. BA cum laude, Emory U., 1970; MA, U. Ala., 1972, PhD, 1974; postgrad., U. Tex., Tyler, 1992. Diplomate Am. Bd. Profl. Disability Cons.; lic. psychologist. Dir., chief psychologist Caddo Parish Diagnostic Ctr., Shreveport, La., 1974-81; exec. dir. Doctors Psychol. Ctr., Shreveport, 1979-91, Comprehensive Assessments, 1991—; cons. to Charter Forest Hosp., Shreveport Impairment and Disability Evaluation Ctr.; neuropsychol. cons. dept. neurosurgery and psychiatry La. State U. Med. Ctr.; clin. assoc. prof. psychology La. State U., Shreveport, 1977—, clin. assoc. prof. psychiatry Sch. Medicine, 1980—; mem. faculty Am. Acad. Disability Evaluating Physicians, Health South Impairment Evaluation Lectr. Series, 1998—. Author: Manual for the Stress Vector Analysis Test Series, 1983, The Doctors Guide to Instant Stress Relief, 1987, Stress Management and Relaxation Training System Handbook; contbr. articles to profl. jours. and popular mags. Mem. Gov.'s Com. of 1000, La., 1979. Recipient AADEP award, 1991; Grad. Rsch. Coun. fellow, 1974. Fellow Am. Inst. Stress; mem. APA, Nat. Acad. Neuropsychology, Nat. Register of Health Svc. Providers. Episcopalian. Avocations: scuba diving, gun collecting, camping, boating, paintball competition. Home: 10816 Sunrise Pt Shreveport LA 71106-9357 Office: Comprehensive Assessments Inc 1801 Fairfield Ave Ste 201 Shreveport LA 71101-4460

STABELL, ULF, psychologist, researcher; b. Ålesund, Norway, July 31, 1938; s. Rolf and Reidun (Christensen) S.; m. Kari Berg, June 21, 1963; children: Sindre, Njål. Psychology, Univ. Oslo, Oslo, Norway, 1966. Rsch. scholar Norwegian Coun. for Social Sci. and the Humanities, Oslo, 1967-75; researcher Nansen Found., Oslo, 1975-86; govt. scholarship Norway, 1986—. Contbr. articles to profl. jours. Recipient Rsch. grant Norwegian Coun. Social Sci. and Humanities, 1967-75, Nansen Found., 1975-86. Avocations: skiing, mountain climbing, philosophy study. Office: U Oslo Inst Psychology, PO Box 1094, N-0317 Blindern Norway

STABLER, LEWIS VASTINE, JR., lawyer; b. Greenville, Ala., Nov. 5, 1936; s. Lewis Vastine and Dorothy Daisy Stabler; m. Monteray Scott, Sept. 5, 1958; children: Dorothy Monteray Scott, Andrew Vastine, Monteray Scott Smith, Margaret Langston. BA, Vanderbilt U., 1958; JD with distinction, U. Mich., 1961. Bar: Ala. 1961. Assoc. Cabaniss & Johnston, Birmingham, Ala., 1961-67; assoc. prof. law U. Ala., 1967-70; ptnr. Cabaniss, Johnston, Gardner, Dumas & O'Neal (and predecessor firms), Birmingham, 1970-91, Walston, Stabler, Wells, Anderson and Bains, Birmingham, 1991-97; pvt. practice, Birmingham, 1997—; Mem. com. of 100 Candler Sch. Theology, Emory U. Bd. editors: Mich. Law Rev, 1960-61. Fellow Am. Bar Found. (life); mem. Am. Law Inst., Ala. Law Inst. (mem. council, dir. 1968-70), ABA, Ala. Bar Assn., Birmingham Bar Assn., Am. Judicature Soc., Am. Assn. Railroad Trial Counsel, Order of Coif. Methodist (cert. lay speaker). Clubs: Country of Birmingham, Rotary. Home: 3538 Victoria Rd Birmingham AL 35223-1404 Office: PO Box 53-1161 Birmingham AL 35253-1161

STABREIT, IMMO FRIEDRICH HELMUT, diplomat; b. Rathenow, Germany, Jan. 24, 1933; s. Kurt and Johanna Maria (Groeger) S.; m. Barbara Philippi, Aug. 1, 1962; children: Eberhard, Felix, Sophie Charlotte. BA, Princeton U., 1953; First Law Exam., Free U. Berlin, Germany, 1957; Second Law Exam., U. Heidelberg, Germany, 1961, LLD, 1963. With Fgn. Ministry, Bonn, Germany, 1962, German Embassy, Moscow, 1962-63; with divsn. Russian affairs Fgn. Ministry, Bonn, 1964-66; first and second sec. German Embassy, Moscow, 1966-71; dep. dir. divsn. Russian affairs Fgn. Ministry, Bonn, 1971-74; with Ctr. Internat. Affairs, Harvard U., 1974-75; head divsn. fgn. rels. Internat. Energy Agy., Paris, 1975-78; head divsn. European polit. affairs Fgn. Ministry, Bonn, 1978-83; head directorate fgn. and devel. policy Fed. Chancellery, Bonn, 1983-87; amb. German Embassy, Pretoria, Cape Town, South Africa, 1987-92, Washington, 1992-95, Paris, 1995-98; exec. v.p. German Soc. Fgn. Affairs, Berlin, 1998—. Recipient Commendatore del Orden de merito de la Republica Italiana, 1978, Commendeur de l'Ordre de Merite de la République Francaise, 1987, Ehrenritterkreuz of the Order of St. John, 1988, Grand Officer of the Order of Good Hope Republic of South Africa, 1992, Comdr. de la Légion d'Honneur de la République Française, 1996, Comdrs. Cross of the Order of Merit of the Fed. Republic of Germany, 1997; named Diplomat of Yr., World Affairs Coun., 1994. Mem. Phi Beta Kappa. Avocations: tennis, squash. Home: Budapester Str 13, 10787 Berlin Germany Office: German Soc Fgn Affairs, Rauchstr 18, 10787 Berlin Germany

STACEWICZ, TADEUSZ EDWARD, physicist, researcher, educator; b. Warsaw, Poland, May 17, 1952; s. Witalis and Zofia (Zebrowska) S.; m. Zanine Staneva, Dec. 11, 1975; children: Marta, Maria, Irena. MS, Warsaw U., 1976, PhD, 1982, Habilitation, 1994. Asst. dept. physics Warsaw U., 1976-82, adj. dept. physics, 1982—. Author: (with A. Kotlicki) Electronics in Scientific Laboratory, 1994; contbr. articles to profl. jours. Roman Catholic. Avocations: tourism, sailing, books-memoirs. E-mail: tadstac@fuw.edu.pl. Office: Warsaw U Inst Exptl Physics, Hoza 69, 00-681 Warsaw Poland

STACEY, GLYN NIGEL, clinical scientist; b. Bishop's Stortford, Eng., Oct. 16, 1958; m. Geoffrey Collingwood and Valery Anne (Bedwell) S.; m. Alison Rose Gosney, July 1986; children: Emily Charlotte, Victoria Anne. BSc, U. Coventry, Eng., 1982; MPhil, U. Southampton, Eng., 1991; PhD, Open U., 1995. Med. sci. officer Pub. Health Lab. Svc., Coventry, 1980-81, Southampton, 1982-87; clin. scientist Ctr. for Applied Microbiology and Rsch., Porton Down, Eng., 1989-97; sr. scientist Nat. Inst. for Biol. Stds. and Control, South Mimms, Eng., 1998—; co-organizer, initiator sci. interactions with U. Nottingham, 1991, Marasyk U., Brno, Czech Republic, 1992, 96, Oeiras, Portugal, 1996, U. Derby, 1997, Brescia, Italy, 1997. Editor: Safety in Cell and Tissue Culture, 1998. Rsch. grantee European Commn., 1996, Dept. Health, 1996. Fellow Inst. Biomed. Scis.; mem. Brit. Soc. Immunology, Soc. for Low Temperature Biology (treas. 1993-96), European Soc. for Animal Cell Tech. U.K., European Tissue Culture Soc., Biochem. Soc., Internat. Assn. Plant Tissue Culture, European Soc. for Animal Cell Tech.-UK (com. mem.), Soc. for In Vitro Biology (biosafety com. 1997), European Culture Collection Orgn. (sci. officer 1999—), Low Temp Biology (mtgs. sec. 1998-2000). Mem. Ch. of England. Achievements include standardization in cell culture and biosafety. Office: Nat Inst Biol Stds and Control (NIBSC), South Mimms EN6 3QG, England

STACEY, MARGARET, retired sociology educator; b. London, Mar. 27, 1922; d. Conrad Eugene and Grace Priscilla (Boyce) Petrie; m. Frank Arthur Stacey, May 20, 1945 (dec. Oct. 1977); children: Patricia Milligan, Richard John, Catherine Margaret, Peter Frank, Michael Read. BSc of Econs., London Sch. Econs., 1943. Labour officer Royal Ordnance Factory, Glasgow, Scotland, 1943-44; tutor Oxford (U.K.) U., 1944-51; lectr., sr. lectr., dir. Univ. Coll. of Swansea, U.K., 1959-74; prof. sociology U. Warwick, Coventry, Eng., 1974-89, emeritus prof., 1989—; Lucille Petry Leone Disting. vis. prof. U. Calif., San Francisco, 1988, Hon. LL.D. (Keele) 1998. Author: Tradition and Change: A Study of Banbury, 1960, (with Marion Price) Women Power and Politics, 1982 (Fawcett Book prize), The Sociology of Health and Healing, 1988, Regulating British Medicine: The General Medical Council, 1992; editor, author: Hospitals, Children and Their Families, 1970. Mem. Gen. Med. Coun., 1976-83, Welsh Hosp. Bd., Cardiff, Wales, 1970-74; mem. Cmty. Health Coun., South Warwickshire, 1972-94; chairperson South Warwickshire Maternity Svcs. Liaison Com., 1994—. Hon. fellow Univ. Coll. of Swansea, 1987—. Fellow Royal Soc. Medicine; mem. Brit. Sociol. Assn. (chair 1977-79, pres. 1981-83). Buddhist. Avocations: gardening, walking. Office: U Warwick, Dept Sociology, Coventry CV7 4A2, England

STACH, ALEX G., retired sociology educator, social worker; b. Letcher, S.D., Aug. 2, 1918; s. Jozef F. and Maria (Machova) S.; divorced; 1 child, Jeanette Stach Lynch. Student, U. Minn., 1939-41, MA in Polit. Sci., 1954, PhD, 1973; student, Charles U., Prague, 1948-50, Sch. Social Work, Brno, Czechoslovakia, 1949. Caseworker I Beltrami County Welfare Dept., Bemidji, Minn., 1953-56; social worker II Willmar State Hosp., Hastings State Hosp. Minn. Dept. Pub. Welfare, 1956-65; social worker White Earth (Minn.) Indian Reservation Office of Econ. Opportunity, 1965-67, dir. social svcs. Nett Lake (Minn.) Indian Res., 1965-67; counselor chem. dependency Shoreview (Minn.) Treatment Ctr., 1971-72; pvt. practice, ret., 1980; mem. field work com., curriculum com. Resource Ctr. Social Work Edn., 1969. Author: numerous poems; author, illustrator: Ax Not the Tao, 1985; contbr. poems, artwork, editor, rev. Sharing; editor: We. Sun Publs., 1984; rev. poems Que Pasa, Yuma Daily Sun, Yma Supershopper; contbr. poems to Diaspora, Valhalla, Studio One, others; dancer with 4 dance troupes including Ballet Arts Minn. Mem. Welfare Forum, St. Cloud, Minn. Mem. AAUP, Faculty Assn. St. Cloud State Coll. and Inter-Faculty Orgn. Mem. Soc. of Friends. Avocations: tennis, chess, dancing, yoga, drama. Home: Ap 1910 2523 Portland Ave Apt 1910 Minneapolis MN 55404-4456

STACHEL, GÜNTER MAX ALBERT, religious studies educator; b. Leipzig, Saxonia, Germany, June 25, 1922; s. Paul and Theresia S.; m. Elisabeth Mayr; children: Johanna, Maria, Paul, Thomas. B in Fine Arts, U. Leipzig, Germany, 1941; Lic. in Theology, U. Munich, Fed. Republic Germany, 1949, PhD in Philospy, Theology, 1951. Lectorate Kösel (publisher), Munich, Fed. Republic Germany, 1949-52, Echter (publisher), Würzburg, Fed. Republic Germany, 1952-67, Benzinger (publisher), Zürich, Switzerland, 1967-80; paedagogics and theology prof. Pädagogische Hochschule, Weingarten, Fed. Republic Germany, 1967-70, U. Frankfurt au Main, Fed. Republic Germany, 1970-72, U. Mainz, Fed. Republic Germany, 1972-90; bd. dirs. Deutscher Katecheten-Verein, Munich, 1970-90; chmn. Arbeitsgemeinschaft Katholischer Katechetik-Dozenten, Fed. Republic of Germany, 1973-90. Author: Der Bibelunerricht, 1967, Unterricht Über Lebensfragen, 1969, Curriculum und Religionsunterricht, 1971, Erfahrung Interpretieren, 1982, Gebet-Meditation-Schweigen, 1989, 2d edit., 1993, Meister Eckhart Alles Lassen-Einswerden, 1992, Metodi e Proposte didatiche per l'Insegnamento della Religione, 1992, Gebet-Meditation-Schweigen.Schritte Spiritueller Praxis, 1993, Meister Eckhart Beiträge zur Diskussion seiner Mystik, 1998, Meister Eckhart Gottesgeburt Mystisohe Predigten, 1999, Erzähl mir aus der Bibel, 1992, vol. 2, 1994; editor: (11 vols.) Unterweisen und Verkünden, 1968-76, (42 vols.) Studien zur Praktischen Theologie, 1972-92; contbr. 332 essays and articles to books and jours. in field of religious edn. and spirituality. Sgt. German Army, 1941-45. Recipient 1st prize Die schönsten Bücher Deutschlands; grantee DFG, Bonn, Fed. Republic of Germany. Roman Catholic. Avocations: classical music, literature, linguistic aspects of translation, ornitology, astronomy. Home: Carl-Orff Strasse 12, 55127 Mainz Germany

STACHEL, HANS DIETRICH, chemist, educator; b. Tapiau, Germany, June 9, 1928; s. Fritz and Gertrud (Ragnit) S.; m. Anneliese Hummel, 1957; children: Klaus Daniel, Carolin, Claudia. PhD, U. Marburg, 1956. T. asst. U. Marburg, 1957-60, dozent, 1960-63; rsch. assoc. Princeton (N.J.) U., 1963-64; prof. medicinal chemistry U. Munich, 1965—, dean, 1971-72, prorektor, 1975, v.p., 1976-86, prof., head Inst. Pharmacy and Food Chemistry. Home: 149 Ammerseestr, D-82061 Neuried Germany Office: Ctr Pharm Rsch, Butenandstr 11, D 81377 Munich Germany

STACHOWICZ-RICHARD, MARGARETHA, pharmacist; b. Bydgoszcz, Poland, Sept. 19, 1961; arrived in France, 1988; d. Jan and Kristina (Guzman) Stachowicz; m. Stephane Richard, June 27, 1997; 1 child, Eva. D in Pharmacy, U. Karol Marcinkowski, Poznan, Poland, 1987. Physics and chem. analyst Cen. Hosps. Pharm. Lab., Paris, 1989-98; boss lab. control Pierre Fabre Lab., Gien, France, 1999—. Contbr. articles to profl. jours. Mem. N.Y. Acad. Sci. Home: 41 Bd Saint Germain, 75005 Paris France Office: Labs Pierre-Fabre, 140 Route de Paris, 45500 Gien France

STAČIOKAS, STASYS, lawyer, educator; b. Alytus, Lithuania, Aug. 25, 1937; s. Juozas and Marija (Zukauskaite) S.; m. Irena Vaitkevic, Dec. 26, 1959; childrren: Donatas, Rimantas. MSci, Vilnius (Lithuania) U., 1960; D in Social Scis., Moscow U., 1967. Cert. lawyer. Tchr., assoc. prof., dean Vilnius U. Faculty Law, 1968-70, assoc. prof., 1991-93; dir. Inst. Forensic Scis., Vilnius, 1971-90; assoc. prof. Inst. Internat. Rels. and Polit. Sci., Vilnius U., 1993-99; judge Constnl. Ct. of the Republic of Lithuania, Vilnius, 1993-96; chmn. legal com. Seimas of the Republic of Lithuania, Vilnius, 1996-99; mem. com. legal affairs and human rights Parlimentary Assembly/Coun. of Europe, 1996-99. Contbr. articles to profl. jours. Bd. dirs. Lithuania Open Soc. Fund, Vilnius, 1992-96. Recipient Order of Grand Duke Gediminas III Degree, Pres. of the Republic of Lithuania, Vilnius, 1996. Mem. European Legislation Assn., Assn. Lithuanian Lawyers. Avocations: football, sailing, gardening. E-mail: s.staciokas@lrkt.omnitel.net. Fax: 370 2 227975. Home: Zirmunu 129-52, 2012 Vilnius Lithuania Office: Constnl Ct Republic Lithuania, Gedimino Ave 36, 2600 Vilnius Lithuania

STACK, DANIEL, lawyer, financial consultant; b. Bklyn., July 29, 1928; s. Charles and Gertrude (Heller) S.; m. Jane Marcia Gordon, Apr. 18, 1953; children: Joan, Gordon. BA cum laude, Bklyn. Coll., 1949; LLB, Columbia U., 1952; LLM, Georgetown U., 1955. Bar: N.Y. 1956. Project Adminstr. Am. Overseas Finance Corp., 1957-58; Asst. counsel ABC-TV, N.Y.C., 1959-60; gen. counsel IFC Securities Corp., N.Y.C., 1961-63; exec. asst. to sr. v.p. N.Y. Stock Exch., 1963-64; sec. pension com. Consol. Foods Corp., Chgo., 1967-69; v.p. legal Seaway Multi Corp. Ltd., Toronto, Ont., Can., 1969-72; v.p. mergers and acquisitions Acklands Ltd., Toronto, 1972-74; sr. v.p., sec., counsel Greenwich Savs. Bank, N.Y.C., 1978-81; sole practice, N.Y.C., 1982-85; ptnr. Brennen and Stack, N.Y.C., 1986-96; cons. venture capital, corp. fin., med. edn., health care, mining, and oil, N.Y.C., 1982—; pres. Bus. and Fin. Resources, Inc., 1982-84; adj. faculty NYU; officer and dir. various public cos.; bd. advisors, Sch. of Bus., St. John's Univ., chmn. sect. on mergers and acquisitions, North Amer. Soc. for Corp. Planning, lectr., guest speaker on mergers and acquisitions, Fac. of Mgmt. Studies, Univ. Toronto, 1974, State Univ. of New York at Buffalo, 1976; gen. counsel Greater N.Y. Safety Council, 1980—. Mem. Congl. mil. service acads. nominations com. and Civil Service intern selection com., 1978—; info. officer U.S. Naval Acad., 1972—. Served to lt. j.g. USNR, 1952-55, capt. Res. ret. 1983. Decorated Joint Service Commendation medal, 1981. Naval Order of US, 1984, N.Y. State Regents scholar, 1945-49. Mem. N.Y. State Bar Assn., N.Y. County Lawyer's Assn., chmn. , Law Com., Ramapo Republican Org., ABA. Republican. Home: 8 Linda Dr Suffern NY 10901-3004

STACK, JANE MARCIA, lawyer; b. Bklyn., Aug. 11, 1928; m. Daniel Stack, Apr. 18, 1953; children: Joan, Gordon. Student, Ohio U., 1945-47; BA, NYU, 1949; JD, N.Y. Law Sch., 1983. Bar: N.Y., 1984; U.S. Dist. Ct. (ea. and so. dists.) N.Y. 1988. Assoc. Shannon, Flaherty, Purchase, N.Y., 1984-85, Schwall & Becker, New City, N.Y., 1985-87; pvt. practice Suffern, N.Y., 1987-90; sr. atty. N.Y. State Div. Human Rights, N.Y.C., 1990—. Vice-pres. Montebello (N.Y.) Civic Assn., 1988—. Republican. Home: 8 Linda Dr Suffern NY 10901-3004 Office: NY State Div Human Rights 1 Fordham Plz Bronx NY 10458-5871

STACK, MAURICE NEVILLE, journalist, consultant; b. U.K., Feb. 9, 1932; m. Molly Rowe, Oct. 1955; children: Portia, Jonathan. MA, Leicester (Eng.) U., 1986. Reporter Fleet Street Newspapers, 1960, news editor, 1972-74; editor Stockport Advertiser, 1974-89; editor-in-chief Leicester Daily, Mercury, 1989-91; Press fellow Wolfson Coll., Cambridge, 1991—; cons. Straits Times, Singapore, 1991—; freelance polit. commentator, columnist and cons., 1991—; cons. Commonwealth Press Union, London; cons. 13 countries; mem. Wolfson Coll., Cambridge U.; freelance polit. commentator, columnist The Peak, Singapore, The Hindu, Madras, Indian Bus. Barons, Life Unltd., South Africa, Daily Express, Trinidad. Author: (novel) The Empty Palace, 1974, (textbook) Editing for the 90's, 1989. Avocations: writing, traveling, generating ideas. E-mail: nstack@esatclear.ie. Home and Office: Cois Farragher, The Glebe, Donegal Town Ireland

STACK, PAUL FRANCIS, lawyer; b. Chgo., July 21, 1946; s. Frank Louis and Dorothy Louise Stack; m. Nea Waterman, July 8, 1972; children: Nea Elizabeth, Sera Waterman. BS, U. Ariz., 1968; JD, Georgetown U., 1971. Bar: Ill. 1971, U.S. Ct. Claims 1975, U.S. Tax Ct. 1974, U.S. Ct. Internat. Trade 1977, U.S. Supreme Ct. 1975. Law clk. U.S. Dist. Ct., Chgo., 1971-72; asst. U.S. atty. No. Dist. Ill., Chgo., 1972-75; mng. dir. Stack & Filpi, Chgo., 1976—. Bd. dirs. Riverside (Ill.) Pub. Libr., 1977-83, Suburban Libr. Sys., Burr Ridge, Ill., 1979-82; mem. Mayor's ad hoc adv. com. on Ctrl. Libr., Chgo., Ill., 1987-88; mem. bd. edn. Twp. H.S. Dist. 208, Riverside, Ill., 1989-97; pres. Village of Riverside, Ill., 1997—; mem. exec. com. Chgo. Area Transp. Study, 1999. Mem. Chgo. Zool. Soc. (gov. 1980—, planned giving adv. com. 1996-99), Chgo. Bar Assn., Union League Club of Chgo. (bd. dirs. 1986-89). Home: 238 N Delaplaine Rd Riverside IL 60546-2035 Office: 140 S Dearborn St Ste 411 Chicago IL 60603-5201

STACKABLE, FREDERICK LAWRENCE, lawyer; b. Howell, Mich., Dec. 4, 1935; s. Lawrence Peter and Dorothea R. (Kiney) S. BA, Mich. State U., 1959; JD, Wayne State U., 1962. Bar: Mich. 1962, U.S. Dist. Ct. (ea. and we. dists.) Mich. 1964; U.S. Supreme Ct. 1968. Lawyer Ingham County Cir. Ct. Commnr.; v.p. Mich. Assn. Cir. Ct. Commrs., 1963, pres., 1967-70; 18th dist. rep. Ingham County Bd. Suprs.; mem. Com. on Mich. Law Revision Commn.; state rep. 58th House Dist., 1971, 72, 73, 74. County del. Rep. Party, Ingham County, Mich., 1969-70, state del., Mich., 1971-74; Lansing city atty., 1975. Recipient Disting. Alumni award Wayne State U. Sch. Law, Detroit, 1987. Mem. Mich. Bar Assn., Ingham County Bar Assn., Nat. Conf. Commrs. Uniform State Laws, Mich. Trail Riders Assn. (dir., past pres.), Mich. Internat. Snowmobile Assn., Sportsman's Alliance Mich., Cycle Conservation Club, Am. Judicature Soc. Avocations: horseback riding, snowmobiling, skiing, traveling. Office: 300 N Grand Ave Lansing MI 48933-1214

STACKELBERG, JOHN RODERICK, history educator; b. Munich, May 8, 1935; came to U.S., 1946; s. Curt Freiherr and Ellen (Biddle) von Stackelberg; m. Steffi Heuss, Oct. 10, 1965 (div. Apr. 1983); m. Sally Winkle, Mar. 30, 1991; children: Katherine Ellen, Nicholas Olaf, Emmet Winkle. AB, Harvard U., 1956; MA, U. Vt., 1972; PhD, U. Mass., 1974. Reading instr. Baldridge Reading Svcs., Greenwich, Conn., 1957-62; lang. tchr. Hartnackschule, Berlin, 1963-67; English and social studies tchr. Lake Region Union High Sch., Orleans, Vt., 1967-70; lectr. history San Diego State U., 1974-76; asst. prof. history U. Oreg., Eugene, 1976-77, U. S.D., Vermillion, 1977-78; asst. prof. history Gonzaga U., Spokane, Wash., 1978-81, assoc. prof. history, 1981-88, prof. history, 1988—; Powers prof. of humanities Gonzaga U., Spokane, 1997—. Author: Idealism Debased, 1981, Hitler's Germany: Origins, Interpretations, Legacies, 1999; contbr. articles to profl. jours. Pres. Spokane chpt. UN Assn., 1986-90. With U.S. Army, 1958-60. Leadership Devel. fellow Ford Found., 1969-70. Avocations: chess, tennis. Home: 9708 E Maringo Dr Spokane WA 99206-4429 Office: Gonzaga U Dept History Spokane WA 99258-0001

STACKPOLE, KERRY CLIFFORD, association executive; b. Putnam, Conn., Feb. 24, 1955; s. Howard Thompson Stackpole and Shyrlee Gladys (Leazer) Burr; m. Miriam Weisberg, July 29, 1984. MEd, Cambridge Coll., 1983. Gen. mgr. E.J. Ardon Co., Boston, 1978-82; ops. mgr. Fotobeam/Brookside, Waltham, Mass., 1982-83; assoc. dir. Printing Industries of New Eng., Natick, Mass., 1983—; v.p. Printing Industries of New Eng., 1989-91; exec. dir. Smaller Bus. Assn. New Eng., Waltham, Mass., 1991-93; pres., CEO The Assn. for Work Process Improvement, Inc., 1993-97, EMA-The E-Bus. Forum, 1997-2000, Data Interchange Stds. Assn., 2000—; bd. dirs. Mass. Cert. Devel. Corp. Recipient HIRE Trust Fund award Graphic Arts Employers of Am., 1987. Fellow Am. Soc. Assn. Execs. (cert., mem. ann. meeting adv. com. 1996-97, mem. edn. com., 1996-99, chmn., exec. mgmt. sect. coun., 1997-98, bd. dirs., 1997-98); mem. Assocs. Advance Am. Com. (chmn. 1999—), New Eng. Soc. Assn. Execs. (committeeman 1983-84, membership devel. com. 1989-91, chmn. edn. com. 1991-93, bd. dirs. 1991—, treas.-sec. 1994-95, chmn.-elect 1995, chmn. bd. dirs. 1996—, immediate past chmn, 1997-98, Ralph Louis Towne award 1986). Avocations: reading, cross country skiing, ocean kayaking, jazz music buff. Office: DISA 333 John Carlyle St Ste 600 Alexandria VA 22314-5745

STADEL, MANFRED PETER, information systems administrator; b. Landau, Palatinate, Germany, Mar. 18, 1950; s. Bernhard and Margot (Schmitt) S. Baccalureate, Otto-Hahn Gymnasium, Landau, 1969; MA, U. Saarbrucken, Fed. Republic of Germany, 1975, D in Natural Sci., 1976. Computer scientist U. Saarbrucken, 1975-78; computer scientist rsch. dept. Siemens, Munich, 1978-90; mgr. compiler devel. Siemens Nixdorf Info. Systems, A.G., Munich, 1991-99; mgr. migration tools devel. Fujitsu Siemens Computers, Munich, 2000—; lectr. in field. Contbr. articles to profl. jours. Mem. Assn. Computing Machinery U.S., Gesellschaft Informatik GI. Achievements include patents in information technology. Office: Fujitsu Siemens Computers, Otto-Hahn-Ring 6, 81730 Munich Germany

STADJE, WOLFGANG, mathematician, educator; b. Braunschweig, Germany, Nov. 21, 1952; s. Walter and Elvira (Kemper) S.; m. Monika Ress, Apr. 23, 1979; children: Mitja, Rebekka. Diploma in Math., U. Göttingen, Germany, 1976, PhD in Math., 1978, Habilitation, 1981. Prof. U. Osnabrück, Germany, 1982—. Contbr. more than 120 articles to profl. jours. Office: Univ Osnabrück, Fachbereich Math/Informatik, D-49069 Osnabrück Germany

STADNICK, CYRIL, obstetrician, gynecologist; b. Tientsin, Republic of China, Nov. 15, 1946; s. Wladimir and Eugenia Stadnick; m. Célia Maria Pedrosa, July 25, 1974 (div. Mar. 1986); children: Alexandre Pedrosa, Ricardo Pedrosa. Student, Alliance Française, 1971, Goethe Inst., 1972; MD, U. Rio de Janeiro, 1972. Diplomate in Ob-Gyn. 1st asst. Fernando Pedrosa Clinic, Rio de Janeiro, 1973-88; mem. staff Miguel Couto Mcpl. Hosp., Rio de Janeiro, 1974—, Silvestre Adventist Hosp., Rio de Janeiro, 1973—, Vassouras U., Rio de Janeiro, 1972-73, Snata Casa da Misericordia, Rio de Janeiro, 1973-74, São Lucas, Rio de Janeiro, 1986—, Samaritano Hosp., Rio de Janeiro, 1973—, Sã Vicente Hosp., Rio de Janeiro, 1987—, São Marcelo Hosp., Rio de Janeiro, 1973—; cons. Plastic Surgery Clinic, Rio de Janeiro, 1986—; laparoscopy cons. São Lucas, Rio de Janeiro, 1986—; chief Miguel Couto Maternity, Rio de Janeiro, 1977—; organizer Internat. Congress on Endoscopy, Rio de Janeiro, 1987. Author: (film) Laparoscopy, 1975; contbr. papers and articles to profl. publs. Dir. Med. Study Hall, Hosp. Silvestre, 1975-78, Hosp. Miguel Couto, 1977-79, Hosp. São Lucas, 1986—. Fellow Mastology Soc.; mem. Ibero Am. Endoscopy (founder 1985), Obstetrics and Gynecol. Soc., Human Reproduction Soc. Clubs: Caiçaras, Flamengo Soccer (Rio de Janeiro). Avocations: gymnastics, jogging. Home: Visconde de Albuquerque 1324, Apt 302, 22450 Rio de Janeiro Brazil Office: Med Clinic, Alaulfo de Paiva 135/409, 22440 Rio de Janeiro Brazil

STADTMILLER, MARGUERITA W., advertising executive; b. Liverpool, Eng., June 14, 1942; came to U.S., 1963; d. William Melville and Ada Lillian (Baker) Melville; m. Gerald Carl Stadtmiller, Oct. 8, 1968. Grad., Ellergreen Coll., Liverpool, 1960; diploma, Liverpool Sch. Journalism, 1962. Cert. state gen. contractor, real estate salesperson, Fla. Editl. asst. Nat. Assn. Elec. Distbn., N.Y.C., 1963-65; asst. editor Nassau (Bahamas) Guardian, 1965-68; exec. sec. Ft. Lauderdale (Fla.) News, 1969-73, sales exec., 1973-78; suburban sales mgr. West, Lauderhill, Fla., 1978-80; retail advt. mgr. Sun Sentinel, Pompano Beach, Fla., 1980-83; retail sales mgr. Ft. Lauderdale News/Sun Sentinel, 1983-90; nat. travel sales mgr. Sun Sentinel Co., Ft. Lauderdale, 1990-96, diversity trainer, 1995-99; sr. sales mgr. Leisure Group, 1997-2000; owner/operator internet svc. provider, 2000—. Mem. leadership in giving United Way, Broward County, 1996-99. Mem. Newspaper Advt. Sales Assn. (sec., bd. dirs. 1993-99), Fla. Hotel Motel Assn., Bon Vivants, Am. Bus. Women's Assn. (pres. 1985, Woman of Yr. award 1986), Internat. Soc. Poets. Avocations: writing, golf, collectibles, travel. Office: Sun Sentinel Co 200 E Las Olas Blvd Ste 1000 Fort Lauderdale FL 33301-2293

STAEHLER, THOMAS PAUL, legal assistant, consultant; b. Limburg/Lahn, Hessen, Germany, Apr. 26, 1962; m. Marie-Joëlle, Sept. 20, 1996. Jr. barrister, Dept. of Justice, Giessen, Germany, 1988-90; LLD, U. Frankfurt, Germany, 2000. Assessor Dept. Justice, Wiesbaden, Germany, 1991; asst. U. Frankfurt, Germany, 1991; cons./asst. Verband Deutscher Rentenversicherungsträger, Frankfurt, 1992—; atty. Frankfurt, 1991—; staff mem./collaborator in a pub. house Nordkirchen, 1996—; contbr. online svc. IWW Nordkirchen, 1997—. Author: Schwerbehindertengesetz, 1994; contbr. articles profl. jours. Mem. DAJV (Bonn), ERA (Trier), Frankfurter Juristische Gesellschaft, Verein zur Förderung d. Sozialrechts (dep.), German Assn. for Rehab. of Disabled People (mem. com.), Nat. Geographic Soc. Avocations: reading, writing, piano, travel, concerts. Office: Verband Deutscher Rentenversicherungstra, Eysseneckstrasse 55, D 60322 Frankfurt Germany

STAEMPFLI, RUDOLF SAMUEL, publisher; b. Berne, Switzerland, Aug. 3, 1955; s. Samuel Carl and Anna Louise)Lang) S.; m. Maria Elisabeth Lehmann, Sept. 21, 1990. Dr.oec.HSG, U. St. Gallen, 1985. CEO Staempfli Holding Ltd., Berne, Switzerland, 1988—, Staempfli Pub. Ltd., Berne, Switzerland, 1991—. Bd. Swiss Chamber Industry, Zurich, 1998—. Mem. Rotary. Office: Staempfli Pub Ltd, Hallerstrasse 7, 3001 Bern Switzerland

STAFAST, HERBERT, physical chemist, educator; b. Wiesbaden, Hessen, Germany, Feb. 10, 1947; s. Herbert and Hilde (Bach) S. Diploma in chemistry, U. Frankfurt, Germany, 1971, PhD, 1974. Asst. inorganic chemistry dept. U. Frankfurt, 1971-75, 76-77; rschr. U. Franfurt, 1985-87; scientist Max Planck Inst. of Plasma Physics, Garching, Germany, 1975-76; asst. phys. chemistry U. Konstanz, Germany, 1977-79; asst. phys. chemistry U. Zurich, Switzerland, 1979-85, lectr., 1985; scientist Battelle Inst., Frankfurt, 1987-93; prof. U. Jena, Germany, 1993—; head divsn. laser tech. Institut fuer Physikalische Hochtechnologie, Jena, 1993—. Author: State and Perspectives of Laser Applications in Advanced Chemistry, 1988, Angewandte Laserchemie-Verfahren und Anwendungen, 1993. Mem. Am. Phys. Soc. (life), Deutsche Bunsengesellschaft, Gesellschaft Deutscher Chemiker, Deutsche Olympische Gesellschaft. Avocation: gymnastics. Office: Inst Physikalische Hochtech, POB 100239, D-07702 Jena Germany

STAFFELBACH, BRUNO, business economist; b. Lucerne, Switzerland, July 13, 1957; s. Otto and Margrith (Gasser) S. MBA, U. Zurich, Switzerland, 1981, D Econs., 1984, PhD, 1991. Lectr. U. Zurich, 1982-90, rsch. asst., 1981-91, prof., 1992—; lectr. U. Fribourg, Switzerland, 1989. Col. Swiss Army, 1999—. Office: U Zurich Inst Rsch Bus Adm, Plattenstrasse 14, CH-8032 Zurich Switzerland

STAFFEN, ALFRED, surgeon, educator, medical educator; b. Vienna, Austria, July 23, 1935; s. Alfred and Martha (Skorianetc) S.; m. Gudrun Heisz, May 2, 1959; 1 child, Wolfgang. MD, U. Vienna, Austria, 1955. Tng. Physiol. Unit, U. Vienna, 1959-60; tng. Wilheminer Hosp., Vienna, 1960; gen. surgeon Clin. U. Vienna, 1960-94; prof. dept. thoracic surgery U. Vienna, 1994—. Contbr. over 125 articles to sci. publs. and books. Pres. Nat. Motor Sporting Authority on Motorsport, Austria. Mem. Austrian Soc. Surgery, Soc. Gastroenterology Vienna, Soc. Surgeons Vienna, Austrian Soc. Senology (bd. dirs.), German Soc. Senology (bd. dirs.). Avocations: motorsports, golf, skiing. Office: U Vienna Dept Surgery, Wahringer Gurtel 18-20, 1090 Vienna Austria

STAFFORD, ARTHUR CHARLES, medical association administrator; b. Cleve., May 10, 1947; s. Charles Arthur and Florence Mildred (Hovey) S.; m. Patricia Anne Cz, Dec. 20, 1991. BS, Kent State U., 1977; MBA, Lake Erie Coll., 1984. Med. tech. VA, Cleve., 1977-81, supr. med. tech., 1981-97; lab. mgr. Univ. Hosps. Health System Meml. Hosp. of Geneva, Ohio, 1998-99; instr. Lake Erie Coll., Painesville, Ohio, 1980-82, Cuyahoga C.C., Cleve., 1988-91; pres. Kent State U. Veterans Assn., 1974, mem. Kent State U Budget Review Com., 1975. Contbr. articles to profl. jour. Mem. Am. Legion, 1974, VFW, 1973. With USN, 1968-72. Mem. Am. Soc. Clin. Pathologists, Clin. Lab. Mgmt. Assn. (treas. Cleve. chpt. 1990-96), Founders Club, Rock and Roll Hall of Fame. Republican. Avocations: stereo, computers, antiques, chess, cooking. Home: 2193 Chimney Ridge Dr Madison OH 44057-2588

STAFFORD, GODFREY HARRY, physicist; b. Sheffield, Apr. 15, 1920; s. Henry and Sarah Stafford; m. Helen Goldthorp, 1950; 3 children. MSc, U. CapeTown, 1941; PhD, Cambridge U., 1950; MA, Oxford U., 1971; DSc (hon.), U. Birmingham, 1980. Head biophysics subdivsn. Coun. for Sci. and Indsl. Rsch., Pretoria, South Africa, 1951-54, Cyclotron Group, AERE, Eng., 1954-57; head proton linear accelerator group Rutherford Lab., 1957; head high energy physics divsn., 1963, dep. dir., 1966, dir., 1969-79; dir. Atlas and Rutherford Lab., 1975-79, dir. gen., 1979-81; hon. scientist CLRC Rutherford Appleton Lab.; U.K. del. IUPAP Com. on Particles and Fields, 1975-80; v.p. Inst. Physics Meetings Com., 1976-79; chmn. sci. policy com. CERN, 1978-81; master St. Cross Coll., Oxford, 1979-87, hon. fellow, 1987. Contbr. articles to profl. jours. Decorated comdr. Order Brit. Empire; Ebden scholar U. Cape Town. Fellow Inst. Physics (Glazebrook prize and medal 1981, pres. 1986-88), Royal Soc. London; mem. European Phys. Soc. (pres. 1984-86), others. Office: U Oxford, Saint Cross Coll, Oxford OX1 3LZ, England also: Ferry Cottage, N Hinksey Vill, Oxford OX2 0NA, England*

STAFFORD, JAMES EDWIN HARRY, pharmaceutical information management consultant; b. Bude, Cornwall, Eng., July 14, 1946; s. Harry and Barbara Louise Ruth (Johns) S. BS with honors, Reading U., Berks, Eng., 1967, PhD, 1971. Rsch. fellow King Edward VII Hosp., Windsor, Eng., 1971-73; rsch. biochemist G.D. Searle & Co. Ltd., High Wycombe, Eng., 1973-81, group leader, 1981-86; head pharmacokinetics dept. Tech. Servier, Orleans, France, 1986-87; cons. Sci. Info. Svcs., Sherborne, Eng., 1987-90; pharm. cons. Fisons Instruments LIMS, Altrincham, Eng., 1990-96; sr. cons. MI Svcs. Group Ltd., Northwich, Eng., 1996—; lectr. European Continuing Edn. Coll., Liverpool, Eng., 1993—. Editor: Advanced LIMS Technology, 1995; contbr. articles to profl. jours. County scholar Dorset Edn. Authority, 1964-67, postgrad. scholar Brit. Egg Mktg. Bd., 1967-70; rsch. grantee N.W. Thames Health Authority, 1971-73. Mem. Brit. Computer Soc. Avocations: hockey, sailing, genealogy, local history, arts.

STAFFORD, JAMES FRANCIS, archbishop. Former archibishop of Denver; pres. Pontifical Coun. for Laity, Vatican, 1998—. Office: Pontifico Consiglio peri, Palazzo San Calisto, 00120 Vatican City Vatican City

STAFFORD, JEFFREY S., small business owner; b. Ridgewood, N.J., 1954; s. William Warren and June Elizabeth Stafford; m. Pamela Marguerite Stafford, Apr. 1, 1984; children: Gary, Mark. Student, Fairleigh Dickinson, 1973. Owner, pres. Stafford Tire Ctr., Inc., Red Bank, N.J., 1975—; cmty. advisor Tinton Falls (N.J.) State Bank, 1999. Sponsor Men's Major Modified Ditch Wiring Champs, 1993. Named Oustanding Citizen of the Yr. VFW, 1993. Republican. Avocations: softball, travel. Office: Stafford Tire Ctr Inc 400 Rte 35 Red Bank NJ 07701-5916

STAFFORD, JOHN ROGERS, pharmaceutical and household products company executive; b. Harrisburg, Pa., Oct. 24, 1937; s. Paul Henry and Gladys Lee (Sharp) S.; m. Inge Paul, Aug. 22, 1959; children: Carolyn, Jennifer, Christina, Charlotte. AB, Dickinson Coll., 1959; LLB with distinction, George Washington U., 1962, Degree (hon.), 1994. Bar: D.C. 1962. Assoc. Steptoe & Johnson, Washington, 1962-66; gen. atty. Hoffman-LaRoche, Nutley, N.J., 1966-67, group atty., 1967-70; gen. counsel Am. Home Products Corp., N.Y.C., 1970-74, v.p., 1972-77, sr. v.p., 1977-80, exec. v.p., 1980-81, pres., 1981—, chmn., chief exec. officer, 1986—; bd. dirs. The Chase Manhattan Corp., Honeywell Internat. Inc., Deere & Co., Inc., Bell Atlantic Corp.; trustee Thirteen/WNET. Bd. dirs. Project Hope, Christopher Reeve Paralysis Found. Recipient John Bell Larner 1st Scholar award George Washington U. Law Sch., 1962, Outstanding Achievement Alumnus award, 1981. Mem. ABA, D.C. Bar Assn., Nat. Assn. Mfrs. (bd. dirs.), Essex Fells (N.J.) Country Club, Baltusrol Club (N.J.), Robert Trent Jones Club. (Va.). Office: American Home Products Corp 5 Giralda Farms Madison NJ 07940-1021

STAFFORD, MATTHEW JACKSON, newspaper writer; b. San Francisco, Aug. 4, 1960; s. Lyle Russell and Julia Anne (Gray) S. BA, San Francisco State, 1982. Writer, editor Mill Valley Record, Mill Valley, Calif., 1982-91, Pacific Sun, Mill Valley, 1987—; writer Film/Tape World, San Francisco, 1988—; writer, editor Mill Valley Mag., Mill Valley, 1991-94; writer SF Weekly, San Francisco, 1999—. Avocations: astonomy, poker, cooking, Am. History, hiking. Home: 2235 Larkin St Apt 21 San Francisco CA 94109-1983

STAFFORD, REBECCA, academic administrator, sociologist; b. Topeka, July 9, 1936; d. Frank C. and Anne Elizabeth (Larrick) S.; m. Willard Van Hazel. AB magna cum laude, Radcliffe Coll., 1958, MA, 1961; PhD, Harvard U., 1964. Sociology lectr., dept. social rels. Sch. Edn., Harvard U., Cambridge, Mass., 1964-70, mem. vis. com. bd. overseers, 1973-79; assoc. prof. sociology U. Nev., Reno, 1970-74, prof., 1973-80, chmn. dept. sociology, 1974-77, dean Coll. Arts and Scis., 1977-80; pres. Bemidji (Minn.) State U., 1980-82; exec. v.p., prof. sociology Colo. State U., Ft. Collins, 1982-83; pres. Chatham Coll., Pitts., 1983-91; prof. sociology Chatham Coll., Pitts., N.J., 1992-93; pres. Monmouth U., West Long Branch, N.J., 1993—; cons. higher edn., 1992—, U.S. Internat. U. on Acad. Planning, 1992-94, USDA, 1992-93, Integra Bank, 1992-93, Millsaps Coll, Jackson, Miss., 1991, U. Pitts. Med. Sch., 1992-93; co-dir. acad. leadership inst. Carnegie Mellon U., 1991-93, U. Tenn., Knoxville, 1992-93; vis. scholar dept. sociology Harvard U., 1991; mem. faculty coll. mgmt. program. Carnegie Mellon U., Pitts., 1984-93; cons. adult devel. grant Harvard U. Health Svcs., Cambridge, 1979, rsch. sociologist, 1964-69; dir. ednl. enrichment project Harvard Sch. Edn., 1966-67, 69-70. Mem. editl. bd. Sociometry, 1974-77, Sociol. Focus., 1974-77; contbr. articles to profl. jours.; presenter papers at profl. confs. Trustee Monmouth Med. Ctr., 1993—, Winchester-Thurston Sch., Pitts., 1986-91, Montefiore Hosp., Pitts., 1990-93; trustee Presbyn.-Univ. Hosp., Pitts., 1984-93, exec. planning com., 1986-89, fin. com., 1989-93; pres. Pitts. Coun. Higher Edn., 1990; mem. Found. Ind. Colls. Inc. Pa., 1984-91, sec., 1986; mem. Colo. Commn. Higher Edn. Task Force on Quality, 1981; mem. adv. bd. Animal Rescue League, Pitts., 1989-93; founder Bemidji Area Women's Network, Minn., 1980-82; mem. intergovtl. planning steering com. Bemidji, 1980-82; mem. cmty. rels. com. Girl Scouts Southwestern Pa., 1983-86; mem. brotherhood dinner coun. Nat. Conf. Christians and Jews, 1985; mem. hon. centennial com. Pa. Sch. Blind Children, Pitts., 1986; mem. citizens sponsoring com. Allegheny Conf. Cmty. Devel., Pitts., 1983-91; mem. five state regional bd. First Union Nat. Bank, 1996—; bd. dirs. Pitts. Symphony, 1984-93, First Fidelity Bank, N.A., N.J., 1993-95, Integra Bank, Pitts., 1987-97, Urban League, Pitts., 1984-87, Women's Ctr., Ft. Collins, Colo., 1982-83, Coun. Colls. Arts and Scis., 1978-81; chmn. Harvard U. Grad. Soc. Coun., 1987-93. Recipient McCurdy-Rinkle prize for rsch. Eastern Psychiat. Assn., 1970; named Woman of Yr. in Edn., City of Pitts., 1986, Vectors/Pitts., 1987, Woman of Yr. in Edn., YWCA Tribute to Women, 1989, Women of Distinction award Muscular Dystrophy Assn., 1999, Women of Leadership award Monmouth County Girl Scouts Am., 1995, Woman of Achievement in Edn. award Monmouth County Adv. Commn. on Status of Women, 1994, Salute to Policymakers award Exec. Women in N.J., 1994; grantee Am. Coun. Edn. Inst. Acad. Deans, 1979, Inst. Ednl. Mgmt., Harvard U., 1984. Mem. Assn. Ind. Colls. and Univs. of N.J. (v.p. 1999—, sec. 1998-99, treas. 1994-98, pres. northeastern conf. 1995-99, bd. dirs. 1993—), Am. Coun. on Edn., Assn. Am. Colls., Soc. for Coll. and Univ. Planning (mem. instl. decision making and resource planning acad. 1994—), Ind. Coll. Fund (treas. 1995-96, bd. dirs. 1993—), Nat. Coun. Family Rels., Harvard U. Alumni Assn. (bd. dirs. 1985-87), Phi Beta Kappa, Phi Kappa Phi. Office: Monmouth University West Long Branch NJ 07764

STAFFORD, SHANE LUDWIG, lawyer; b. Camden, N.J., Mar. 10, 1955; s. Joseph and Victoria Stafford; m. Connie, Jan. 19, 1980; children: Courtney, Ashley and Shaun (twins). BS, Calif. State U., 1977; JD, Southwestern U., L.A., 1980; LLD, U. Miami, 1980. Bar: Fla. 1980, U.S. Dist. Ct. (so. dist.) Fla. 1981. Intern Ins. Co. North Am., Miami, Fla., 1980-81; assoc. Miami, Fla., 1981-83; ptnr. Varner & Stafford, Lake Worth, Fla., 1983-85, Varner, Stafford & Seaman, Lake Worth, 1985—. Mem. Assn. Trial Lawyers Am., Acad. Trial Lawyers Fla., Palm Beach County Bar Assn., Phi Delta Phi. Avocations: golf, family. Office: Varner Stafford & Seaman 2328 10th Ave N Ste 2B Lake Worth FL 33461-6606

STAGE, KEY HUTCHINSON, urologist; b. Washington, June 12, 1947; s. Anson H. and Lucie T. Stage; m. Jo-Ellen Arpin; children: Jennifer, Amanda. BA, Linfield Coll., 1969; MD, U. Oreg., 1973. Diplomate Am. Bd. Urology. Intern U.S. Naval Regional Med. Ctr., Oakland, Calif., 1973-74; resident in urology U. Tex. Southwestern Med. Sch., Dallas, 1977-81; pvt. practice Dallas, 1981—; assoc. prof. U. Tex. Southwestern Med. Sch.; chief urology Parkland Mem. HOsp., Dallas. Lt. comdr. USNR, 1973-77. Fellow ACS; mem. Am. Urol. Assn. Episcopalian. Office: U Tex Southwestern Med Sch Dept Urology 5323 Harry Hines Blvd Dallas TX 75390-7208

STAGE, RICHARD LEE, consultant, retired utilities executive; b. Byesville, Ohio, Nov. 5, 1936; s. Clifford Earl Stage and Evelyn Virginia (Nunley) Rolston; m. Joan Eleanor Bednarz, Feb. 1, 1958; 1 child, Julie Marie. B in Mgmt., Malone Coll., 1987. Fleet office supr. Ohio Power Co., Canton, 1954-77; supr. automotive acctg. and leasing Am. Electric Power, Canton, 1977-83; dir. fleet mgmt. Am. Electric Power, Columbus, 1983-95; fleet mgmt. cons., Canton, 1995—. Mem. Soc. Automotive Engrs. (chmn. utilities com. 1988-89, exec. com.), Edison Electric Inst. (fleet mgmt. com. 1983-95), Masons. Republican. Avocations: golf, woodworking. Home and Office: 1329 Davis St SW Canton OH 44706-4503

STAGLIANO, VITO ALEXANDER, former government official, company executive, energy policy analyst; b. Catanzaro, Calabria, Italy, May 13, 1942; came to U.S., 1956; s. Filippo and Maria Stagliano; m. Julie Ann Werth, Sept. 30, 1967; children: Jason Vito, Carlos Otobed. Program analyst U.S. Office Econ. Opportunity, Washington, 1968-69; exec. dir. Palau Community Devel. Agy., Micronesia, 1969-71; program officer U.S. Peace Corps, Ghana, Africa, 1971-73; dir. U.S. Peace Corps, Mauritania, Africa, 1973-74; dir. West Africa U.S. Peace Corps, Washington, 1974-77; counselor Interstate Commn. on Drought Control, Ouagadougou, Bourkina Faso, 1977-79; staff asst. Sec. of Energy, Washington, 1979-81; dir. River Basins Devel. Office, Dakar, Senegal, Africa, 1981-85; dir. Office of Energy Demand Policy, U.S. Dept. Energy, Washington, 1986-89, assoc. dep. undersec. of energy, 1990-91, dep. asst. sec. energy for policy planning, 1991-93; vis. scholar Resources for Future, 1993-95; dir. Energy Security Analysis, Inc., Washington, 1996-98; v.p. Commonwealth Edison Co., Chgo., 1998—; mem. adv. bd. Sch. Advanced Internat. Studies, Johns Hopkins U., GAO, U.S. Office Tech. Assessment. Co-author: A Shock to the System: Restructuring America's Electricity Industry, 1996, Energy and National Security in the 21st Century, 1995; contbr. articles to profl. jours. Peace corps vol., Mauritania, 1966-67; founder Micronesia Legal Svcs. Program, 1971; mem. foster care review bd. State of Md. Ampart fellow USIA, 1981; recipient Silver Medal for Meritorious Svc., U.S. Dept. Energy, Bronze medal for exceptional svc., awarded rank of meritorious sr. exec. by Pres. George Bush. Mem. NAACP (legal def. fund), Amnesty Internat. Avocations: Roman and medieval history, 20th century poetry. Home: 30 E Division St Apt 8E Chicago IL 60610-5292

STAGNER, ROBERT DEAN, lawyer; b. Simi, Calif., May 23, 1950; s. Cecil William and Mary Jane (Davis) S.; children: Rebecca Lyn, Brenda Deann. BA in History and Polit. Sci., Pasadena Coll., 1972; JD, Western State U., Fullerton, Calif., 1977; student, Civil Engring Tech. Ctr. Degree Studies. Bar: Calif. 1977, U.S. Dist. Ct. (cen. dist.) Calif. 1979. Ptnr. Stagner & Gregg, Orange, Calif., 1978-86, sr. ptnr., 1994—; project mgr. Carolina Gold, Inc., Mex., 1991; officer, cons. Richard Walker Inc., Anaheim, Calif., 1976-86, sec. 1978-81, bd. dirs., Seafood Dimensions ACAL Corp.; gen. counsel Greater Am. Produce, Anaheim, 1978-84, acting pres. 1984; pres. Orion Constrn., Tustin, Calif., 1980-82; counsel Whittier Police Officers Assn., 1982-85; cons. ballistics Kraemer Industries, Anaheim, 1985—, Exodus One Mktg., Placentia, Calif., 1985—, A.W. Schnitger, Encinada, Mexico, 1985—; mem. Nat. Edn. Corp.; instr. Navigation & Coastal Piloting; cons. Gower Industries, Ltd., 1994; co-founder Aegis Security and Exec. Protection, 1996; gen. counsel Lunches, Etc., Inc.; dir., corp. sec. Gower Industries Internat., 1998. Trainer USN Sea Cadet Corps, El Toro, Calif., 1984-94; adult edn. Nazarene Ch., Chino, Calif., 1982-85, bd. dirs. Ont. Nazarene Ch.; lifetime dep. gov. Am. Biog. Inst. Rsch. Assn., 1989; founding mem. Am. Air Mus., Eng., 1997; co-founder Round Tree Inst. for Pub. Svc., 1997, Barnabas Found., 1997. Named one of Outstanding Young Men Am., 1981. Avocations: hunting, fishing, woodworking, scuba diving, sky diving. Office: 630 N Tustin St # 179 Orange CA 92867-7127

STAHEL, ALBERT ALEXANDER, political scientist, educator; b. Zurich, Switzerland, Mar. 3, 1943; s. Albert and Georgette Clovis (Boimond) S.; m. Claudia Mathilda Fetz, 1968; children: Sandra, Andreas. MA in Econs., U.

Zurich, 1970, PhD in Econs., 1973, Habilitation, 1979. Rschr. Total Def. Strategy and Warfare, Switzerland, 1973-80; outside lectr. U. Zurich, 1979—, prof., 1987; prof. Swiss Mil. Coll., Zurich, 1980—. Author: Air Defence-Strategy & Reality, 1993, Army 95-A Chance for the Army of Conscripts, 1994, The Classics in Strategy, 2d edit., 1996, Strategic Thinking, 1997, Organized Crime and Security Policy, 1998, Conflicts and Wars, 1999. Lt. col. Swiss Air Force, 1994—. Mem. Guild Kämbel Zurich (sec.), Internat. Inst. Strategic Studies, U.S. Naval Inst. Freisinnig-Demokratische. Avocations: photography, mountain biking, collecting model trains. Home: Drusbergstr 5, 8820 Waedenswil Switzerland Office: Swiss Mil Coll, Steinacherstr 101 b, 8804 Au Zurich Switzerland

STAHEL, WALTER RUDOLF, industrial analyst, consultant; b. Zurich, Switzerland, June 5, 1946; s. Walter Max and Frida (Abrecht) S.; m. Christiane Andrée Collaud, Feb. 9, 1970; children: Dominique Halim, Thomas Baylon. Diploma, Swiss Fed. Inst. Tech., 1970. Architect Bicknell & Hamilton, London, 1967-68, 71-72, Aebli & Sochalski, Zurich, 1970-71; design architect Obrist & Ptnr., St. Moritz, Switzerland, 1972-73; project mgr. Battelle INst., Geneva, 1973-79; personal asst. to CEO, Phymec Luxembourg S.A., Geneva, 1980-82; ind. rschr., cons. Geneva, 1982—; founder, dir. Product-Life Inst., Geneva, 1983—; sec. gen. European chpt. Internat. Sci. Policy Found., Geneva, 1986-98; treas. European Group Local Employment Initiatives, Brussels, 1985-95; dep. sec. gen. Geneva Assn., Geneva, 1988—; mem. Environ. Coun. of the German Rys., 1996—; mem. jury Safety Health Environment Excellence awards DuPont de Nemours Co., 1996, 98, 99. Author: Handbuch Abfall 1, 1995, Langlebigkeit und Material-Recycling, 1991, The Limits to Certainty, 1989, 93, Jobs for Tomorrow, 1981, Unemployment-Occupation-Profession, 1980; assoc. editor Geneva Papers on Risk and Ins.; mem. editl. bd. Jour. Indsl. Ecology/Yale U., Internat. Jour. for Disaster Prevention and Mgmt.; contbr. articles to profl. jours. Recipient 1st prize Deutsche Gesellschaft für Zukunftsfragen, West Berlin, 1978, 3d prize Mitchell Prize Competition, Houston, 1982. Mem. Assn. Mitchell Prize Winners, Internat. Sci. Policy Found., Assn. Former Students of Swiss Fed. Inst. Tech., European Sci. and Tech. Obs. (assoc.). Home: 7 chemin des Vignettes, Conches, CH-1231 Geneva Switzerland Office: Product Life Inst, PO Box 3632, CH-1211 Geneva 3, Switzerland

STAHL, FRANCIS, automobile manufacturing company executive; b. Thann, Haut-Rhim, France, Dec. 25, 1939; s. Jules Stahl and Marie Garber; m. Mireille Delpech, May 26, 1947. Grad., Ecole Poly., France, 1960; postgrad., Nat. Sch. Stats. and Econ. Adminstrn. With Renault, Paris, 1966-72; dir. Renault Austria, 1972-76; program dir. Renault, 1976-78; dir. Deutsch Renault, Germany, 1978-82; v.p. internat. ops. Renault, 1982-86; dir. Fasa Renault, Spain, 1986-92; sr. v.p., contr. Renault, 1992-97; sr. v.p. iight comml. divsn. Renault, Boulogne, France, 1997—. Home: 15 Blvd de Montmonarcy, 75016 Paris France Office: Renault, 34 Quai du Point du Jour, 92109 Boulogne Billanc, France

STAHL, GÜNTER, publisher, editor, writer; b. Weilburg, Germany, June 25, 1935; s. Wilhelm and Erna (Diehl) S.; m. Irmgard Jutta Döhler, 1962; children: Andreas, Armin Seyer. Diploma in engring. Cert. constrn. asst., 1968. Masonry tchr. Giessen, Germany, 1952-55, Darmstadt, Germany, 1955-62; subway constrn. worker Berlin, 1962-65; constrn. cons. Hessian St. Constrn. Office, 1973-99; editor, pub. Freundenberger Gegegnung, Wiesbaden-Freundenberg, Termany, 1990—. Recipient Svc. Cross of Order of Merit, Fed. Republic Germany, 1992. Mem. Rsch. Soc. for Sts. and Traffic, Soc. European Culture. Home: Freudenberger Begegnung, Veilchenweg 93, D-65201 Wiesbaden-Venedig Freundenberg, Germany

STAHL, HANS JOACHIM ALEXANDER, youth organization administrator; b. Netzschkau, Sachsen, Germany, Apr. 27, 1938; s. Rudolf and Gertraud Hilma (Frenzel) S.; m. Bärbel Schultheis, Feb. 13, 1943; children: Jesco, Tibor. Diploma in politics, Free U., Berlin, 1965. Adviser on informal edn. for the young Arbeitskreis deutscher Bildungsstätten, Bonn, Germany, 1964-66; lectr. polit. edn. Jugendhof Vlotho, Germany, 1966-69; specialist officer Landesjugendamt, Münster, Germany, 1969-72; youth officer Land Youth Office, Westfalen-Lippe, Münster, 1972—; lectr. polit. sci. Police Acad., Münster-Hiltrup, Germany, 1968-70; dep.-in-chief bd. film censors Freiwillige Selbstkontrolle der Filmwirtschaft, Wiesbaden, Germany, 1989—. Councillor, Stadt Münster, 1975-79. Mem. Christian Democratic Union. Avocations: books, film, music. Home: Von-Humboldt-Str 33, 48159 Münster Germany Office: Landesjugendamt, Westfalen-Lippe Landeshaus, 48133 Münster Germany

STAHL, HERBERT ROBERT, mathematics educator, consultant; b. Fehl-Ritzhausen, Germany, Aug. 3, 1942; s. Alfred and Helene (Schuster) S. PhD, Tech. U. Berlin, 1974, degree in statistics and informatics, 1983, degree in math., 1984. Electrician AEG, Frankfurt, Germany, 1958-64; tchg. asst. Tech. U. Berlin, 1974-78, asst. prof., 1978-83, assoc. prof., 1984-86; prof. Technische Fachhochschule, Berlin, 1986—; cons. GEOMET, Berlin, 1984. Author: Harri Deutsch Verlag, 1985; co-author: (with V. Totih) General Orthogonal Polynomials, 1992. Avocation: long distance running. E-mail: stahl@tfh-berlin.de. Office: TFH-Berlin/FB2, Luxemburger Str 10, 13353 Berlin Germany

STAHL, LARRY ENOS, social welfare specialist; b. Bloomville, Ohio, Nov. 29, 1941; s. Enos Joseph and Esther Louise (Weber) S. A Applied Bus., North Ctrl. Tech. Coll., Mansfield, Ohio, 1992, postgrad., 1992—. Co-owner, ptnr. God's Squad Upholstery, Galion, Ohio, 1971-89, God's Squad Ministries, Galion, 1971—, God's Squad Politica, Galion, 1971—. Mem. NRA (life, Legion of Honor 1996, Defender of Second Amendment award 1998), AARP, Med. Alert Found., People for Ethical Treatment of Animals, Cat Lovers Am., Cats, Cats and More Cats. Republican. Avocations: wild and domestic activism and advocacy. Home and Office: 5935 State Route 19 Galion OH 44833-8930

STAHL, NORMAN A., educator; b. San Francisco, Apr. 21, 1949. AA, City Coll. San Francisco, 1969; BA, San Francisco State U., 1971, MA, 1976; PhD, U. Pitts., 1983. Rsch. assoc. U. Pitts., 1980-82; asst. prof. divsn. devel. studies Ga. State U., Atlanta, 1982-87; assoc. prof. dept. curriculum & instrn. No. Ill. U., DeKalb, 1987-93, prof., chair dept. curriculum & instrn., 1994-99, chair dept. literacy edn., 1999—. Contbr. articles to profl. jours. Pres. DeKalb Edn. Found., 1999—. Recipient Disting. Rsch. award Coll. Reading & Learning Assn., 1990, N.Y. Coll. Learning Skills Assn., 1996. Mem. Coll. Reading Assn. (pres. 1991-92, treas. 1985-88), Internat. Reading Assn. (pres. history reading spl. interest group 1992-94), Am. Reading Forum (chair bd. dirs. 1996-97), Nat. Reading conf. (historian 1998—). Office: No Ill U Dept Literacy Edn Dekalb IL 60115

STAHLE, AGNETA ELISABETH, physiotherapist; b. Stockholm, Dec. 11, 1951; d. Rolf Eugen and Sylvia Margareta (Person) Wirne; m. Anders Nils Åke Stahle, Mar. 25, 1978; children: Ulrika, Niklas. BSc, Karolinska Inst., Stockholm, 1993, MSc, 1996, PhD, 1999. Cert. physiotherapist. Master phys. edn. pub. sch. Stockholm, 1972-73; physiotherapist Karolinska Hosp., Stockholm, 1976-77, Serafimerlasarettet, Stockholm, 1978-79, Skelleftea Hosp., 1980-82; master phys. edn Swedish sch., Paris, 1982-86; lectr., tchg. mem. Karolinska Hosp., Stockholm, 1986—, head clin. tng. ctr., 1999—. Author: Physical Fitness and Quality of Life in Elderly Patients Recovering from an Acute Coronary Event: A Randomised Controlled Study on the Effects of Aerobic Group Training, 1999. Avocations: sports, aerobics. Home: Gripsholmsvagen 6, SE-12571 Älvsjö Sweden Office: Karolinska Inst, Karolinska Hospital, SE-17176 Stockholm Sweden

STAHLE, JAN, retired medical educator, researcher; b. Eksjö, Småland, Sweden, Sept. 28, 1924; s. John Erik and Helfrid Josefina (Berdén) S.; m. Ulla Ingegerd Hillman, June 12, 1948; children: Oscar, Charlotte, Fredrik. MD, Uppsala U., Sweden, 1950, PhD, Uppsala U., 1958. Assoc. prof. Uppsala U., 1960-78, prof., 1979-90; chmn. dept. otolaryngology Uppsala U. Hosp., 1978-90; ret., 1990; pres. Bárány Soc. (internat. orgn. for neuro-otol. rsch.), 1978-90; pres. Swedish Otolaryn. Soc., 1987-88. Editor: (book) Vestibular Function on Earth and in Space, 1970, Frontiers in Vestibular and Oculomotor Research, 1979, The Vestibular System, Fundamental and Clinical Observations, 1984, The Vestibular and Oculomotor Systems, 1989. Capt. Med. Corps Res. Swedish Navy, 1948-84. Fellow Royal Soc. Scis.; mem. (hon.) Japan Soc. Otolaryngology, Östgöta Student's Club, Uppsala; mem. Lyckorna Golf Club, Ljungskile. Avocations: history of medicine, horticulture, golf. Home: Villa Roma Pilvagen 4, S 459 31 Ljungskile Sweden

STAHLSCHMIDT, PER, landscape architect, educator; b. Naestved, Denmark, Apr. 19, 1943; s. Mogens and Grethe (Kristiansen) S.; m. Ulla Larsen, Nov. 14, 1987; children: Morten, Juliett, Marie. Candidate Hort., Royal Vet. and Agrl. U., Copenhagen, 1969. Landscape architect Copenhagen, 1973—; asst. prof. dept. econs. and natural resources Royal Vet. and Agrl. U., Copenhagen, 1974—. Designer parks and green spaces; contbr. articles to profl. jours. Mem. Assn. Danish Landscape Architects. Office: KVL Unit Landscape, Rolighedsvej 23, DK-1958 Frederiksberg Denmark

STAHR, CURTIS BRENT, photographer, art association administrator, educator; b. West Union, Iowa; s. Freman H. and Lucile M. (Schreiner) S. AA, Ellsworth Coll., 1966; BFA, Peru (Nebr.) State U., 1968. Cert. tchr., Iowa, Colo., Ariz. Art dir. Iowa Falls (Iowa) High Sch., 1968-70, Wiley (Colo.) Schs., 1971-72, Judson Sch., Scottsdale, Ariz., 1973-79; freelance graphic artist, photographer and mktg. dir., 1979-88; prof. photography, photography dir. Des Moines Area C.C., 1988—; art dir. Homestead Assn., Des Moines, 1993-98; bd. dirs. Homestead Corp., Alpha Inst., Unoged Corp., v.p., 1999; v.p. Young Masters Photographic Art Collection, 1998—; pres. Interpretive Photography, 1999; art dir. Starland Design Band Group, 1979-86, graphic effects dept. Bischoff's, 1987-88; photographic dir. ednl. exchange trip to China. Exhibited in 16 one-man art shows, in 34 invited/juried art shows; represented in numerous pvt. collections; photographer numerous field trips including migration of Am. eagle from Alaska to Fla., all 99 Iowa County Courthouses, Yellowstone Nat. Park, Grand Teton Nat. Park, Waterton-Glacier Internat. Peace Park (U.S. and Can.), Isle Royale Nat. Park, Grand Canyon Nat. Park, Denali Nat. Park, Arctic Nat. Park & Preserve, Canyon de Chelly Nat. Monument, Rainbow Bridge Nat. Monument, Devils Tower Nat. Monument, Effigy Mounts Nat. Monument, Yosemite Nat. Park, Sequoia Nat. Park, Kings Canyon Nat. Park, Japser Nat. Park (Can.), Glacier Nat. Park (Can.), Banff (Can.) Nat. Park, Terra Nova Nat. Park (Newfoundland), Boundary Waters Canoe Area Wilderness, Quetico Provincial Park, Can., North Magnetic Pole, Can., Canyonlands (Utah), Auyuittuq Nat. Park Res., Can., Ellesmere Island Nat. Park Res, Can. Yoho Nat. Park, Can., Kootenay Nat. Park, Can., Angel Falls, Venezuela, Machu Picchu, Peru; numerous cross coutnry trips to U.S., Can., Mex., Cen. Am., S.Am., Yukon Territory and Arctic Cir. Speaker Ariz.-Calif. Lecture Series, 1982-84; chairperson art evaluation com. State of Iowa, 1970; bd. dirs. Ariz. Arts Festival, 1974-79, Muscular Dystrophy Assn. Fund Drive, Ariz., 1982-85. Recipient 8 purchase awards. Democrat. Office: Des Moines Area CC 2006 S Ankeny Blvd Ankeny IA 50021-8995

STAICU, STEFAN, engineering educator; b. Goicea, Dolj, Romania, Apr. 29, 1940; s. Nicolae and Stana (Fira) Staicu; m. Maria-Ana Dragoescu, Apr. 30, 1966; children: Laurian, Daniela. Engr., Polytech. U., Bucharest, Romania, 1963; PhD, Inst. Fluid Mechanics, Bucharest, 1969. Asst. lectr. Polytech. U., Bucharest, 1963-74, lectr., 1974-90, assoc. prof., 1990-91, prof., 1991—; rsch. bd. advisors ABI, 1999. Author: Applications of the Matriceal Calculus to the Mechanics of Rigid Bodies, 1986, Theoretical Mechanics, 1998, (with E. Carafoli) Theoretical Model Concerning a Thin Delta Wing with Separation at the Leading Edges, 1967, The Study of Supersonic Flow Around Delta with Forced Antisymmetry Taking into Consideration the Falling Off of Flow at the Leading Edges, 1978, (with A. Marinescu) Elements of Space Flight Mechanics, 1997; mem. editl. adv. bd. Sci. Bull. Polytech. U., Bucharest, 1990; contbr. numerous papers to profl. jours. Mem. Commn. Aeronautics and Astronautics, Romanian Acad. Home: Rosia Montana Nr 4 Bloc O5, ScD Ap 184 Sector 6, Bucharest Romania Office: U Politehnica, Splaiul Independentei 313, 77206 Bucharest Romania

STAIR, WILSON ALFRED, JR., urban planner, landscape architect; b. St. Louis, Feb. 9, 1946; s. Wilson Alfred Stair and Teresa Kathleen Donahoe; m. Jan Hanson, Nov. 1, 1968. BS in Environ. Design, U. Okla., 1973, BArch, 1974, MArch, 1974. Registered landscape arch., Ariz., N.Mex., Fla., S.C. Urban designer divsn. urban redevelopment City of St. Petersburg, Fla., 1976-81; design dir., project mgr. D.V. Preiser Designs, Inc., Tampa, Fla., 1982-83; project mgr. H.L. Yoh Co., Inc., Tampa, 1983-86; urban design mgr. dept. planning and mgmt. City of Tampa, 1986—; mem. Livable Roadways Com., Tampa, 1992—; design rev. com. Fla. Dept. Transp., Tampa, 1992—; bd. dirs. Mayor's Beautification Program, Tampa. Project designer Janus Landing, 1981, Tampa Downtown Riverwalk, 1989, CBD Streetscape. Staff sgt. USAF, 1966-70. Recipient Recognition award for ednl. contbn. to dept. landscape arch. U. Fla., 1992. Mem. Am. Soc. Landscape Archs., Tau Sigma Delta. Democrat. Methodist. Avocations: martial arts, motorcycling, hiking, watercolor painting. Home: Unit 206 782 Village Lake Ter N Saint Petersburg FL 33716-3146 Office: City of Tampa Dept Planning and Mgmt 306 E Jackson St Tampa FL 33602-5223

STÁJER, GÉZA, pharmacist, educator; b. Szeged, Hungary, Mar. 26, 1936; s. Géza and Gézáné Dinnyés (Eszter) S.; m. Gézáné Szabó Angela, July 12, 1958; children: Anette, Ildikó. Tchr., Tchrs. Tng. Coll., Szeged, 1954; Pharmacist, Med. U. Szeged, 1959, PhD, 1975; DSc in Chem. Scis., Hungarian Acad. Scis., Budapest, 1989. Cert. pharmacist, Hungary. Pharmacist Pharm. Ctr. of Somogy County, Kaposvár, Hungary, 1959-60; lectr. Med. U. Szeged, 1960-90; prof. pharm. chemistry Univ. Szeged, Szeged, 1990—, dean faculty of pharmacy, 1991-97; lectr. in field. Contbr. over 150 articles to profl. jours. Recipient Lo Little Cross of medal Hungarian Republic, 1997. Mem. Hungarian Pharm. Soc. (nat. bd. 1992—, v.p. 1996—). Home: Fésü u 3/A, H-6726 Szeged Hungary Office: Inst of Pharm Chemistry, PO Box 121 Eötvös u 6, H-6701 Szeged Hungary

STALAND, (JOHAN GUSTAF) BERTIL, retired gynecologist; b. Dalsland, Sweden, May 24, 1913; s. Olof Gustaf and Selma Kristina (Johansson) Magnuson; m. Britt Frick, June 8, 1946; children: Gustaf Peter, John Gunnar. MM, U. Uppsala, Stockholm, 1941. Authorized physician, specialist in gynecology and gen. surgery. Asst. physician various hosps., Sweden, 1942-53; head gynecology Samariterhemmet, Uppsala, Sweden, 1953-79, ret., 1979; sci. advisor Pharmacia AB, Uppsala, 1952-65; sci. worker Novo-Nordisk, Inc., Malmoe and Copenhagen, 1970—. Contbr. articles to profl. jours. Physician Red Cross Hosp., Norway, 1945. Capt. Swedish mi., WWII. Mem. Internat. Menopause Soc., Swedish Assn. Ob-Gyn., Scandinavian Assn. Ob-Gyn., Scandinavian Oncologic Soc. Avocations: nature and environment. Home: Hästeskovägen 22, SE-31137 Falkenberg Sweden

STÅLBERG, ERIK VALDEMAR, clinical neurophysiologist, educator; b. Skellefteå, Sweden, Apr. 21, 1936; s. Frans Valdemar and Amanda Karolina (Vikström) S.; m. Eva Birgit Maria Lögdberg, June 23, 1961; children: Stefan, Peter, Annika. MD, Uppsala (Sweden) U., 1963, PhD, 1966. Resident in internal medicine Uppsala U., asst. prof. clin. neurophysiology, 1967-77, assoc. prof. clin. neurophysiology, 1977-91, prof., chmn. dept. clin. neurophysiology, 1991—. Author: Single Fibre Electromyography, 1979, 94; editor: Clinical Neurophysiology, Neurology, 1981. Recipient Mangberg's award Umea (Sweden) U., 1994. Fellow Royal Coll. Physicians; mem. Swedish Soc. Clin. Neurophysiology (pres. 1982-83), Am. Assn. Electrodiagnostic Medicine (bd. dirs. 1988-90, Disting. Rsch. award 1994, Lifetime Achievement award 1999), Royal Swedish Soc. Sci., Swedish Med. Assn. (Thureus' award 1994, Ingvar award 1996), Lions Club (charter pres. 1972), Slovene Acad. of Scis. and Art (corr. mem.). Lutheran. Avocations: sailing, travel. Home: Rörbäcksvägen 40, S 757 57 Uppsala Sweden Office: Dept Clin Neurophysiology, U Hosp, S 751 85 Uppsala Sweden

ŠTALC, ANTON, physiologist, researcher; b. Kropa, Slovenia, Nov. 4, 1940; s. Janez and Helena (Šifrar) Š.; m. Bernarda Rihar, Aug. 15, 1970; children: Monika, Jurij. BSc in Pharmacy, U. Ljubljana, Slovenia, 1965, M in Physiology, 1972, DSc, 1974. Rsch. staff Inst. Pharmacy, Ljubljana, 1965-70; instr. pharmacy U. Ljubljana, 1970-76; head rsch. projects Lek Pharm. and Chem. Co., Ljubljana, 1976—; scientific worker U. Ljubljana Med. Faculty, 1970-95; pres. Yugoslav Biophys. Soc., Ljubljana, 1978-80. Contbr. chpt. to: Synaptic Constituents in Health and Disease, 1980; contbr. articles to Pharmacology and Toxicology, Biochem. Pharmacology; co-inventor and patentee in field. Recipient Boris Kidrič Found. award Rsch. Cmty. Slovenia, 1983, and diploma Rsch. Cmty. Ljubljana, 1989. Mem. N.Y. Acad. Scis., Physiol. Soc. Slovenia, European Cytokine Soc. Roman Catholic. Achievements include contributions to the description of the microgeography of acetylcholinesterase active site and its allosteric properties, including the relation to membrane lipid organization; contributions to the development of new immunomodulating agents. Home: Rašiška 5, 1000 Ljubljana Slovenia Office: Lek dd R&D, Celovška 135, 1526 Ljubljana Slovenia

STALDER, HANS, medical educator; b. Basel, Switzerland, Feb. 26, 1941; s. Hans and Elisabeth (Suter) S.; m. Anne Guisan, May 12, 1966; children: Nicole, Laurent. MD, Med. Sch. Basel, 1965. Intern La Chaux-De-Fonds (Switzerland) Hosp., 1966-68; resident and chief resident Hosp. Cantonal U., Geneva, 1968-71, assoc. physician in infectious disease, 1974-78; fellow in infectious disease Children's Hosp., Boston, 1971-74; chief physician internal medicine Hosp. Cantonal, Liestal, Switzerland, 1978-86; chief physician Policlinique de Médecine Hosp., Cantonal U., Geneva, 1986—; head dept. cmty. medicine Hosp. Cantonal U. Geneva, Geneva, 1995—; assoc. prof. Med. Sch. Basel, 1985; prof. Med. Sch. Geneva, 1986. Mem. Swiss Acad. Med. Scis. (com. 1988), Swiss Soc. Internal Medicine (com.), Found for Fellowships in Med. and Biol. Scis. (com.). Avocations: hiking, photography. Home: 9A Ch Castan, 1224 Chêne-Bougeries Switzerland Office: Hosp Cantonal U, 24 Rue Micheli-Du-Crest, 1211 Geneva 14, Switzerland

STALEY, DAWN, basketball player; b. Phila., May 4, 1970. Grad., U. Va., 1992. Basketball player US Nat. Women's Basketball Team, Olympics 2000, 1999—; basketball player, guard Charlotte Sting, 1997—. Scholar U. Va.; named 1994 USA Basketball Female Athlete of Yr. Avocations: played professional basketball Italy, Brazil, Spain and France. Office: Charlotte Sting 3308 Oak Lake Blvd Ste B Charlotte NC 28208-7707

STALFELT, SVEN OLOV, publishing executive, writer; b. Karlskoga, Orebrolan, Sweden, May 14, 1928; s. Sven Mauritz and Hulda (Ringdal) E.; m. Ann Marie Salander, June 4, 1957; children: Annika, Pernilla, Jan. MA, U. Uppsala, Sweden, 1955, PhD, 1963. Sr. master Nikolai Sr., Orebro, Sweden, 1964-68; studies dir. high sch., Orebro, Sweden, 1968-69, tchr. tng. coll., Uppsala, Sweden, 1969-75; pub. Samspraak, Orebro, Sweden, 1975—. Author: (textbook) Skrivet och Klart, 1990, Engagera Päverka, 1992, (novel) The Wasp's Nest, 1992, Literary Ways, 1999, Murder at School, 1999. Mem. Rotary. Home: Karlsgatan 32M, 70341 Orebro Sweden Office: Sampråk Förlags AB, Box 247, 70144 Orebro Sweden

STÅLHAMMAR, NILS-OLOV, health economist; b. Torsby, Sweden, Sept. 25, 1953; s. Holger and Margit Stålhammar; m. Reija Sarianne Rapo, July 19, 1986; children: Anja, Sanna, Madeleine. BSc, U. Karlstad, Sweden, 1977; PhD in Econs., U. Gothenburg, Sweden, 1987, assoc. prof. econs., 1996. Lectr. econs. U. Karlstad, 1977-78; rsch. asst. U. Gothenburg, 1985-87, asst. prof., 1987-90; dir. health econs. Astra Hässle AB, 1990-99; global dir. health econs. AstraZeneca R&D, Wilmington, Del., 1999—. Contbr. articles to profl. jours., book chpts. Capt. Swedish Army Res., 1977—. Rsch. grantee Savings Bank Found. Rsch., 1983, Jan Wallander's Found. Social Rsch., 1987, Bank Rsch. Inst., Royal Swedish Acad. Scis., Swedish Inst., Sweden-Am. Found., 1988. Office: AstraZeneca PO Box 15437 Wilmington DE 19850-5437

STALIKAS, ANASTASSIOS, psychotherpist, educator; b. Thessaloniki, Makedonia, Greece, Aug. 22, 1960; s. Grigerios and Athina (Platamona) S. BA, Concordia U., Montreal, Can., 1985; PhD, Ottawa (Can.) U., 1991. Cert. psychologist. Lectr. U. Ottawa, 1986-90; prof. Heritage Coll., Hull, Can., 1987-91; instr. Algonquin Coll., Ottawa, 1988-90; dir. Hellenic Sch. Ottawa, 1986-91; assoc. prof. McGill U., Montreal, 1991—; pvt. practice Montreal, Athens, Greece, 1991—; assoc. prof. Panteion U., Athens, Greece, 1998—; dir. Psychoeducational Clinic, Montreal, 1995—. Co-author: Current Psychotherapies, 1999, Evaluations of Mental Health Professionals, 2000; contbr. articles to profl. jours.; host (TV series) Psychology Speaking, 2000. Mem. com. edn. Ministry Health, Athens; mem. Polit. Amnesty, AIDS Soc. Thessaloniki. Mem. APA, Order Psychologists Que., Hellenic Psychol. Soc. Avocations: music, saxophone playing, theater, squash, cinema. Home: Psychari 46A, 11141 Athens Greece Office: McGill U, 3700 McTauish St, Montreal, PQ Canada H3A 1Y3

STALL, ALAN DAVID, packaging company executive; b. Moose Jaw, Sask., Can., June 14, 1951; came to U.S., 1982; s. Joel and Evelyn (Schwartz) S.; m. Carol I. Johnston; children: Jeffrey, Jennifer, Michael, Timothy. BSME, U. Sask., 1973; MBA, Lewis U., 1986. Registered profl. engr., Ont. Devel. engr. DuPont Can., North Bay, Ont., 1973-76; project engr. Union Carbide Corp. Can., Lindsay, Ont., 1976-79, engring. mgr., 1979-82; mgr. shirring rsch. Union Carbide Corp., Chgo., 1982-85; dir. engring. tech. Viskase Corp., Chgo., 1985-90, v.p. engring., 1990-95; gen. mgr. Kuko Corp., Gross-Gerau, Germany, 1995-98; pres. Films Casings Tech. Inc., Woodridge, Ill., 1996—; gen. mgr. Alfacel Inc., Woodridge, Ill., 1998—. Patentee breathable plastic, shirring apparatus, sausage stuffing machine, cellulose casings, cellulose regeneration. Rotary bus. exchange fellow, London, 1982. Mem. Engring. Inst. Can., Can. Soc. Mech. Engrs., Soc. Plastics Engrs., Assn. Profl. Engrs., Ont., Am. Mensa, Can. Club Chgo. Home: 23W540 James Way Naperville IL 60540-9552 Office: Alfacel Inc PO Box 5415 Woodridge IL 60517-0415

STALLARD, GEORGE THOMAS (DUKE STALLARD), retired retail store owner; b. Lakin, Kans., Oct. 1, 1937; s. George Aubry and Gladys Agnes (Prather) S.; m. Carolyn Diane Flower, Mar. 18, 1967. Student, Colo. State U., 1955-56; cert. of agriculture, Lamar (Colo.) Community Coll., 1958-60; student, Adams State Coll., Alamosa, Colo., 1963, 67. Parts mgr. Irrigation and Power Co., Greeley, Colo., 1965-67; owner, mgr. Shelpers, Inc., Roswell, N.M., 1967-87; bd. dirs. Tabosa Devel. and Tng. Ctr., Roswell; cons. numerous establishments in N.M. including N.M. Rehab. Ctr. and Ea. N.M. Med. Ctr. Vice chmn. Gov.'s Com. Concerns of Handicapped, Sante Fe, 1981-87; past pres. Roswell Area Com. Concerns of Handicapped, 1978-79; rep. Nat. Conf. for Coalition of Handicapped, Houston, 1978; life mem. Disabled Am. Vets., Roswell, Paralized Vets. Am.; mem. Agrl. Council Chaves County, Roswell. Served with U.S. Army, 1961-66. Recipient Outstanding Handicapped New Mexican N.M. Gov.'s Com. Concerns of Handicapped, 1983; agrl. scholarship Lamar Coll., 1958. Republican. Methodist. Clubs: Roswell Sertoma, Paralized Vets. Am., Disabled Am. Vets. Lodges: Elks, York Rite, Scottish Rite, Masons, Shriners. Avocations: writing poetry, breeding horses. Home: 227 Peaceful Valley Rd Roswell NM 88201-9791

STALLINS, ELLEN RAE, trade development executive; b. Farrell, Pa., Feb. 12, 1969; d. Raymond and Loretta Jane Mudrak; m. William Edward Stallins. BA in Pub. Adminstrn., Internat. Rels., U. Ctrl. Fla., 1995, MA in Applied Econs., 1997. Asst. dir. trade EDC of Mid-Fla., Inc., Orlando, 1997, dir. metro. Orlando internat. affairs, 1997-98; dir. S.E. U.S. Scottish Trade Internat., Orlando, 1998-99, sr. dir. U.S., 1999—. Mem. Scottish Am. Soc. (sec. 1999—), German Am. Heritage Soc. (bd. dirs. 1998), Horizon Investment Club (sec. 1999-2000). Home: 1408 S Oak Ave Sanford FL 32771-3450 Office: Scottish Tech & Rsch Ctr 12565 Research Pkwy Ste 300 Orlando FL 32826-3283

STALLMAN, DAVID ALLEN, retired computer company executive, researcher; b. Holmesville, Ohio, Nov. 23, 1933; s. Roy Allen and Dorothy Rebecca (Patterson) S.; m. Wanda L. Long, Jan. 22, 1957 (div. July 1976); children: Gregory, Susan; m. Peggy Ann Langworthy, Oct. 2, 1976 (div. Oct. 1994); children: Jamie, Rebecca, Emily; m. Carol P. Hovey, July 15, 1996. BA in Acctg. and Bus. Adminstrn., Ohio Inst. Bus., 1953; postgrad., Pace U., 1980. Customer engr.-svc. IBM, Akron, Ohio, 1955-62; field mgr. br. office IBM, Akron, 1962-69; field support mgr. IBM, Endicott, N.Y., 1969-74; program mgr. cost estimating IBM, Armonk, N.Y., 1974-89; pvt. practice rschr./writer Ridgefield, Conn., 1989—. Author: A History of Camp Davis, 1990, Operation Bumblebee, 1992, ECHOES of Topsail, 1996. Rschr., writer Pub. Edn. Reform, Ridgefield, Conn., 1992—; key leader Nat. Right to Work Found., Va., 1995-99; mem. Nat. Right to Work Com., Washington, 1994—, Cato Inst., Washington, 1996—. With U.S. Army, 1953-55. Rsch. grantee Nat. Trust for Historic Preservation, Topsail Island, 1992. Mem. Junto N.Y.C., Topsail Is. (N.C.) Hist. Soc. Republican. Avocations: motorcycle touring, writing. E-mail: StallmanD@aol.com. Home:

205 Mountain Rd Ridgefield CT 06877-1613 Office: PO Box 1171 Ridgefield CT 06877-9171

STALLONE, SYLVESTER ENZIO, actor, writer, director; b. N.Y.C., July 6, 1946; s. Frank and Jacquline (Labofish) S.; m. Sasha Czack, Dec. 28, 1974 (div.); children: Sage, Seth; m. Brigitte Nielsen, Dec. 15, 1985 (div. 1987). Student, Am. Coll. of Switzerland, 1965-67, U. Miami, 1967-69. Formerly, usher, fish salesman, horse trainer, delicatessen worker, truck driver, bouncer, zoo attendant, short order cook, pizza demonstrator, phys. edn. tchr., motel supt., bookstore detective. Appeared in motion pictures Lords of Flatbush, 1973, Capone, 1974, Rocky, 1976, (Oscar for Best Picture 1976, Golden Globe award for best picture 1976, Donatello award for best actor in Europe 1976, Christopher Religious award 1976, Bell Ringer award Scholastic Mag. 1976, Nat. Theatre Owners award 1976) F.I.S.T, 1978, Paradise Alley, 1978, Rocky II, 1979, Nighthawks, 1981, Victory, 1981, Rocky III, 1982, First Blood, 1982, Rhinestone, 1984, Rambo: First Blood Part II, 1985, Rocky IV, 1985, Cobra, 1986, Over the Top, 1987, Rambo III, 1988, Lock Up, 1989, Tango and Cash, 1989, Rocky V, 1990, Cliffhanger, 1993, Demolition Man, 1993, The Specialist, 1994, Judge Dredd, 1995, Assassins, 1995, Firestorm, 1996, Daylight, 1996, Copland, 1997, An Alan Smithee Film: Burn Hollywood Burn, 1998; producer, dir. film Staying Alive, 1983; author: Paradise Alley, 1977, The Rocky Scrapbook, 1977, Rocky II, 1979. Recipient Star of the Year award 1977, named Show West actor of the year 1979, Artistic Achievement award Nat. Italian Am. Found., 1991, Order of Arts and Letters, French Ministry, 1992, Caesar award for Career Achievement, 1992. Mem. Screen Actors Guild, Writers Guild, Stuntmans Assn. (hon.), Dirs. Guild. Achievements include being nominated for two Oscars (acting and writing) in same year (1976); occurred for only 3d time in history.

STALLWORTH, CHARLES DEROTHA, JR., psychologist; b. Riderwood, Ala., July 4, 1940; s. Charles D. and Annie (Horn) S. BS, Tenn. StateU., Nashville, 1963; MS, Tenn. StateU., 1966; postgrad., Calif. Sch. Profl. Psychology, 1977-79, U. South Ala., 1967, Tuskegee Inst., 1968, U. Ky., 1980; PhD in Psychology, Internat. Coll., 1983. Diplomate Am. Bd. Psychotherapy. Psychiat. asst. Hubbard Hsop., Nashville, 1964-66; counselor, tchr. North Ctrl. H.S., Chatom, Ala., 1966-68; tchr. Washington County H.S., 1969-70; supr. adult edn. Washington County Bd. Edn., Chatom, 1968-70; dir. counseling ctr. Albany State Coll., Ga., 1970-92; pvt. practice, 1993—; staff assistance Auburn U., 1969; cons. Peace Corps, 1979-82; cons. Peace Corps., 1979-82. Bd. dirs. Dougherty County CODAC, Inc., Albany, 1973-77. Recipient Eagle Scout award, 1955; Grantee HEW, 1970-77, U.S. Office Edn., 1972. Mem. Am. Psychol. Assn. (assoc.), Am. Psychotherapy Assn. (diplomate, Acad. Cert. Neurotherapists, Alpha Phi Alpha. Democrat. Baptist. Achievements include research on impact of affective domain on learning outcomes and on application of cognitive therapies as a means of controlling negative effects. Home: 805 E 4th Ave Albany GA 31705-1203

STALS, CHRISTIAN LODEWYK, retired bank executive; b. Mar. 13, 1935; s. Petrus J. and Lilian (Barnard) S.; m. Hester Barnard; 4 children. Student, U. Pretoria, South Africa. With South African Reserve Bank, Pretoria, 1955-99, gen. mgr., 1975-76, dep. gov., 1976-81, sr. dep. gov., 1981-85, dir.- gen. dept. fin., 1985-89; spl. econ. advisor Min. of Fin., 1989; gov. South African Res. Bank, Pretoria, 1989-99; ret., 1999; chancellor U. Pretoria, 1997—. Recipient State Pres.'s Decoration for Disting. Svc.; named Grand Officer in Order of Crown, Kingdom of Belgium. Office: PO Box 66071, Woodhill 0076, South Africa*

STA MARIA, FELIXBERTO CANGCO, retired university president; b. Mexico, Pampanga, Philippines, Aug. 22, 1922; s. Graciano and Cayetana (Cangco) Sta Maria; m. Teresita Pronove, June 7, 1953; children: Cynthia, Thelma, Sonia. BS cum laude, U. Philippines, 1948; MA, Stanford U., 1952; PhD, Mich. State U., 1962. Chmn. dept. English and lit. U. Philippines, 1962-63; dean coll. U. Philippines, Baguio, 1963-67, dean Coll. Edn., 1967-70; prof., dir. Ateneo U. Press, 1970-77; pres. Far Eastern U., Manila, 1989-95; pres. Philippine Accrediting Assn. Schs., Colls. and Univs. of Philippines, 1957-82, Fedn. Accrediting Agys. of Philippines, 1977-82; cons. Commn. on Higher Edn., Philippines, 1993-95. Author: The Philippines in Song and Ballad, 1976, Communication Strategies in Management, 1996; author, editor: Higher Education Reform: Now or Never, 1994. Recipient Professiorial award in edn. U. Philippines Alumni Assn., 1993; named internat. Man of Yr. Internat. Biog. Ctr., Cambridge, Eng., 1992. Avocations: watercolor, acrylic painting. Home: 37 Maginhawa St UP Village, Quezon City 1101, Philippines

STAMATESCU, ION-OLIMPIU, physicist, researcher; b. Ploiesti, Romania, Feb. 1, 1941; arrived in Germany, 1971; s. Theodor Marius and Floarea (Florescu) S.; m. Elsbeth Brombacher Stamatescu, Jan. 23, 1989; children: Lilly Pia, Ariane Leonie. Diploma, U. Bukarest, Romania, 1962; PhD, U. Heidelberg, Germany, 1972. Cert. in physics. Jr. rsch. fellow Inst. Physics, Bukarest, Romania, 1963-71; post doctorate U. Heidelberg, Germany, 1972-79, U. Wuppertal, Germany, 1979-80; rsch. fellow MPI-Physik, Munchen, Germany, 1980-84; asst. prof. Freie U., Berlin, Germany, 1984-87; sr. scientific fellow FEST - Protestant Inst. for Interdisciplinary Rsch., Heidelberg, Germany, 1988—; scientific assoc. CERN, Geneve, Switzerland, 1982-83, 1992. Co-editor: Philosophy, Mathematics and modern Physics, 1994, Intelligence and Artificial Intelligence, 1998, Decoherence, 2000; co-author: Decoherence and Classical World, 1996; contbr. articles to profl. jours. Mem. Deutsche Physikalische Gesellschaft, Vereinigung Deutscher Wissenschaftler, Académie Internationale Philosophie des Sciences, European Soc. for Study of Sci. and Theology, Union of Concerned Scientists, Protestant Inst. for Interdisciplinary Rsch. Avocations: painting, dancing. Office: FEST, Schmeilweg 5, D-69118 Heidelberg Germany

STAMATI, ALEKSI, oil industry executive; b. Saranda, Albania, July 29, 1951; s. Jorgji and Anastasia (Mulos) S.; m. Lindita Dema, Sept. 10, 1982; children: Nastiola, Krisaldi. Degree in physics, Tirana U., Albania, 1974, degree in geophysics, 1976, PhD, 1985. Analyst Data Processing Ctr., Albania, 1976-82; mgr. data acquisition ALBSEIS, Albania, 1982-87; exploration mgr. ALBSEIS, 1987-92; dep. dir. New Venture, Albania, 1992-94; exploration mgr. Anglo-Albanian Petroleum, Fier, Albania, 1994-98; dir. of geology and geophysics, 1998—; Bd. dirs., cons. Nat. Petroleum Agy., 1994—. Contbr. articles to profl. jours. Fellow Geophys. Soc. Albania. Greek Orthodox. Avocations: sports. Office: Anglo Albanian Petroleum, Vila Lagja 29 Nentori, Fier Albania

STAMBAUGH, JOHN EDGAR, oncologist, hematologist, pharmacologist, educator; b. Everett, Pa., Apr. 30, 1940; s. John Edgar and Rhoda Irene (Becker) S.; m. Shirley Louise Fultz, June 24, 1961; 4 children. BS in Chemistry cum laude, Dickinson Coll., 1962; MD, Jefferson Med. Coll., 1966, PhD, 1968. Intern Thomas Jefferson U. Hosp., Phila., 1968-69, resident, 1968-69; oncology fellow Jefferson Med. Coll., 1970-72, instr. pharmacology, 1969-70, asst. prof., 1970-74, assoc. prof., 1974-82, prof., 1982—; pvt. practice med. oncology, hematology and cancer pain, Woodbury, N.J.; staff physician Cooper Med. Ctr., Camden, N.J., 1972—, Underwood Meml. Hosp., Woodbury, 1972—, West Jersey Hosp., 1973—, J.F. Kennedy Hosp., 1978—, Our Lady of Lourdes Hosp., 1990—. Contbr. articles to profl. jours. Fellow Am. Coll. Clin. Pharmacology, Am. Acad. Pain Mgmt., Am. Soc. Pain Mgmt.; mem. ABA, AMA, Am. Soc. Clin. Pharmacology, N.J. Med. Soc., Gloucester County Med. Soc., Camden County Med. Soc., Am. Soc. for Pharmacology and Exptl. Therapeutics, Am. Soc. Clin. Oncology, Am. Assn. for Cancer Rsch., Internat. Assn. for Study of Pain, Am. Pain Soc., Am. Assn. Clin. Rsch., Sigma Xi. Office: 17 W Red Bank Ave Ste 101 Woodbury NJ 08096-1630 also: 100 Carnie Blvd Ste 3 Voorhees NJ 08043-4512

ŠTAMBERG, KAREL, nuclear chemical engineering educator; b. Dubno, Czech Republic, Apr. 3, 1932; s. Karel and Anna (Jonáková) Š.; m. Jitka Štědronská, July 6, 1957; children: Hana, Iva, Roman. MSc, Inst. Chem. Tech., Prague, Czech Republic, 1957, PhD in Nuclear Chem. Engring., 1972. Rsch. asst. Rsch. Inst. Inorganic Chemistry, Usti, Czech Republic, 1957-62; prin. rsch. asst. Czech Uranium Industry, Mydlovary, Czech Republic, 1962-70, Nuclear Fuels Inst., Zbraslav, 1970-76; sr. rsch. worker dept. nuclear chemistry Czech Tech. U., Prague, 1977-85, prin. rsch. worker dept. nuclear chemistry, 1985-91, chief rsch. worker dept. nuclear chemistry, 1991—; lectr. Tech. U., Ostrava, Czech Republic, 1966-69; asst. prof. Czech Tech. U., Prague, 1978-92, assoc. prof., 1992—. Author (textbooks) Nuclear Fuels Technology, 1994, vol. 2, 1998, Modelling of Migration Processes in Environment, 1996. Modelling and Simulation of Migration Processes grantee, 1997-99. Mem. Czech Chem. Soc. Roman Catholic. Avocations: music, singing in chorus, hiking. Home: Novodvorská 1119, 14200 Prague 4, Czech Republic Office: Czech Tech U Dept Nucl Chem, Brehová 7, 115 19 Prague 1, Czech Republic

ŠTAMBUK, NIKOLA, research scientist; b. Varaždin, Croatia, Mar. 25, 1959; s. Ranko and Vjera (Mrakovčić) Š.; m. Ana Lazić, Nov. 12, 1988; 1 child, Albert. MD, Zagreb (Croatia) U., 1984, MS, 1988; PhD, Inst. Med. Rsch. Occup. Health, Zagreb, 1991. Intern Sisters of Mercy Clin. Hosp., Zagreb, 1984-85; resident Railway Health Ctr., Zagreb, 1986-88; postdoctoral fellow Mc Gill U., Montreal, Can., 1991-92; rschr. Rugjer Bošković Inst., Zagreb, 1994—; sci. com. Internat. Conf. on Math. and Computer Modelling and Sci. Computing, Berkeley, Calif., 1993, Boston, 1995, Washington, 1997. Contbr. articles to profl. jours. Mem. Internat. Assn. for Math. and Computer Modelling, Internat. Ocular Inflammation Soc., Internat. Soc. for Thymology and Immunotherapy. Achievements include the discovery of necklace model and horseshoe map representation of the genetic code (SCA procedure), rsch. in models of artificial barriers constrn., protein transfer and molecular recognition, computer-aided drug design, compartmental volume-pressure relationships. Home: Šubićeva 16, HR-10000 Zagreb Croatia Office: Rugjer Bošković Inst, Bijenička 54, HR-10000 Zagreb Croatia

STAMM, MANFRED, physicist, polymer materials scientist, educator; b. Frankfurt/Main, Germany, 1949; married, 2 children. PhD, U. Mainz, 1979, habilitation, 1993. Rsch. scientist KFA, Jülich, 1979-85, Brookhaven Nat. Labs., Upton, N.Y., 1984-85, Max Planck Inst. Polymerforschung, Mainz, 1985-99; rsch. scientist, prof. phys. chem. polymeric materials, head inst. phys. chem. and phys. polymers Inst. Polymer Rsch., Dresden, Germany, 1999—. Office: Inst Polymer Rsch Dresden, Hohe str 6, 01069 Dresden Germany

STAMMINGER, GUDRUN KATHARINA, physician, laboratory consultant; b. Schneeberg, Germany, May 3, 1958; d. Martin and Johanna (Gendolla) Roessler; m. Jochen Horst Stamminger, (dec. June 30, 1992); 1 child, Simone. MD, Humboldt U., Berlin, 1983, lab. cons., 1987. Asst. Humboldt U., Berlin, 1983-87, lab. scientist, 1987-95; dep. lab. chief Klinikum Chemnitz, Germany, 1995—. Contbr. articles to prof. jours. Sponsorship, World Vision, India, 1997—. Mem. Deutsche Gesellschaft Lab. Medicine, Deutsche Gesellschaft Hamatologie & Inkologie, Inst. Standadisierung Eingetvagener Verein. Avocations: swimming, gymnastics, literature. Office: Klinikum Chemnitz GmbH, Flemmingstr, D-09116 Chemnitz Germany

STAMMINGER, GUDRUN MATHILDE, microbiologist; b. Frankfurt, Fed. Republic Germany, Nov. 22, 1943; d. Emil Stephan and Li Katharina (Abé) S. PhD, U. Frankfurt, 1970. Research asst. U. Med. Sch. Frankfurt, 1970-72; postdoctoral fellow NIH, Lab. Molecular Biology, Bethesda, Md., 1972-75; sr. research scientist U. Frankfurt, 1975-83; microbiologist New England Biolabs GmbH, Frankfurt, 1983—. Contbr. articles to profl. jours. Mem. Am. Soc. Microbiology, Vereinigte Allgemeine und Angewandte Mikrobiologie, Deutsche Gesellschaft fuer Hygiene und Mikrobiologie, N.Y. Acad. Sci. Roman Catholic. Avocations: languages, tennis, music. Office: New Eng Biolabs GmbH, Brüningstr 50, 65926 Frankfurt Germany

STAMMLER, MICHAEL HANS, portfolio manager, financial research executive; b. Dossenheim, Germany, July 4, 1955. Diploma in engring., Berufsakademie Mannheim, Germany, 1977; diploma, Kaufmann U., Mannheim, 1982. Engr. Siemens AG, 1979-82; cons. Roland Berger, 1987-90; CEO FERI Trust GmbH, 1991—. Mem. Rotary. Office: FERI Trust GmbH, Haus Park Rathausplatz 8-10, 61348 Bad Homburg Germany

STAMOU, SPYROS DIMITRIOS, chemical engineer, researcher; b. Athens, Attiki, Greece, Dec. 21, 1970; s. Dimitrios Spyros and Maria Aristides (Forti) S. PhD in Chem. Engring., U. Patras, 1999. Rschr. Lab. Plasma Chemistry U. Patras, 1994—. Contbr. articles to profl. jours. including Chem. Physics, Jour. Physics D., Applied Physics. Recipient Best First Appearing Poster Presentation 4th European Conf. on Thermal Plasma Processes, Athens, 1996. E-mail: spyros@chemeng.upatras.gr. Office: U Patras Dept Chem Engring, PO Box 1407, Patras Achaia, Greece

STAMOULAS-KARLAS, NICK, social welfare, recreation administrator; b. Melbourne, Victoria, Australia, Nov. 21, 1968; s. John and Penny (Mavrigiannis) S.-K. BA in Youth Affairs, Phillip Inst. Tech., Melbourne, Australia, 1990; advanced cert. in sales mgmt. (mktg.), Holmesglen Inst. Tech. Edn., Melbourne, 1996. Day ctr. aide Spastic Soc. Victoria, Melbourne, Australia, 1988-93; relief worker City of Nunawading, Melbourne, 1990-91; youth leisure officer City of Waverley, Melbourne, 1991-93; sr. youth project officer Youth Adult Bur. Inc., Melbourne, 1991-95; sr. youth activities svc. officer City of Greater Dandenong, Melbourne, 1995—. Co-founder Cmty. Youth Radio Svc., 1992-97; founder Infexious Entertainment Inc. Youth Com., Melbourne, 1997; creator numerous youth recreation programs. Mem. Camberwell Youth Participation Inc., Leo's Svc. Club, Camberwell, Melbourne, 1989; com. mem. Sta. HITZ-FM Broadcasters Inc., Melbourne, 1992-97. Grantee: City of Nunawading, 1992-94, Dept. Justice, 1997, Vic Health, 1998, Fed. Dept. Family and Cmty. Svcs., 1996-99. Mem. Australian Inst. Mgmt., Australian Coun. Health, Phys. Edn. and Recreation, Melbourne Sports Network, Camping Assn. Victoria (orgnl.), Youth Rsch. Ctr. U. Melbourne (orgnl.). Avocations: travel, sport, professional reading, internet research, jogging. E-mail: nkarla@cgd.vic.gov.au. Home: 31 Silvertop Cr, Franklin North 3200, Australia

STAMP, ROBERT COLIN, media company executive; b. Johannesburg, South Africa, Sept. 28, 1960; s. Josiah C. and Gillian P. (Tatham) S.; m. Susan Caroline Lester, June 4, 1988; children: Samuel, Robert, Josiah, Olivia, Joscelyne, Isabel. BA in History, Cambridge (Eng.) U., 1982. Rschr. Ctrl. TV, London and Birmingham, Eng., 1984-88; prodr. Ctrl. TV, London and Birmingham, 1988-93; mem. editl. bd. Context, London, 1993-94; non-exec. dir. Chord, London, 1990—. Co-author: Trojan Horses, 1989, The Day War Broke Out, 1989, Top Guns and Toxic Whales, 1991. Avocations: flying kites, Aikido, family activities. E-mail: robbie@h2g2.com. Office: h2g2 Ltd, 11 Maiden Ln, Covent Garden, London WC2E 7NA, England

STAMPER, EWA SZUMOTALSKA, psychologist; b. Warsaw, Poland, Sept. 8, 1954; came to U.S., 1984; d. Tadeusz and Regina (Sobczak) S.; m. Ryszard Zwierowicz, Dec. 30, 1980 (div. Jan. 13, 1986); m. Allen Malcolm Stamper, Oct. 23, 1992. MA in Clin. Psychology, U. Warsaw, Poland, 1978; PhD in Psychology, New Sch. for Social Rsch., N.Y.C., 1992. Staff therapist Marital Therapy Counseling Ctr., Warsaw, 1978-79, Ctr. for Psychotherapy and Personality Growth, Warsaw, 1978-80; sr. staff therapist Lab. for Psychoedn. Polish Psychol. Assn., Warsaw, Poland, 1981-85; postgrad. affiliate Washington Square Inst. for Psychotherapy, N.Y.C., 1990-92; police psychologist Honolulu Police Dept., 1993-98; pvt. practice, Honolulu, 1994—; with Tng. Ctr. for Family Therapy, Warsaw, 1976-78, Bridges Ctr. for Adolescent Treatment, Malibu, Calif., 1985-86, Stuyvesant Poly., N.Y.C., 1988-89, North Ctrl. Bronx (N.Y.) Hosp., 1988-89, Yale Psychiat. Inst., 1989-90, Castle Med. Ctr., Kailua, Hawaii, 1993-94; co-chmn. Crystal Methampetamine Forum, Honolulu, 1996—. Mem. APA, Am. Acad. Experts in Traumatic Stress, Internat. Critical Incident Stress Found., Hawaii Psychol. Assn. (clin. divsn. rep. 1998-99). Avocations: horseback riding, raising German Shorthaired Pointers and Siamese cats, gardening, fiction writing, running. Office: 1188 Bishop St Ste 3212 Honolulu HI 96813-3313

STAMPER, MALCOLM THEODORE, publishing company executive; b. Detroit, Apr. 4, 1925; s. Fred Theodore and Lucille (Cayce) S.; m. Marion Philbin Guinan, Feb. 25, 1946; children: Geoffrey, Kevin, Jamie, David, Mary, Anne. Student, U. Richmond, Va., 1943-44; BEE, Ga. Inst. Tech., 1946; postgrad., U. Mich., 1946-49; DHumanities, Seattle U., 1994. With Gen. Motors Corp., 1949-62; with Boeing Co., Seattle, 1962-90; mgr. electronics ops., v.p., gen. mgr. turbine div. Boeing Co., 1964-66; v.p., gen. mgr. Boeing Co. (747 Airplane program), 1966-69, v.p., gen. mgr. comml. airplane group, 1969-71, corp. sr. v.p. ops., 1971-72; pres. Boeing Co., 1972-85, vice chmn., 1985-90; CEO, Storytellers Ink Pub., Seattle, 1990—, also chmn. bd. dirs.; bd. dirs. Esterline Co., Pro-Air Inc.; trustee The Conf. Bd., 1988—. Candidate for U.S. Ho. of Reps., Detroit, 1952; trustee, chmn. Seattle Art Mus.; nat. bd. dirs. Smithsonian Assocs. With USNR, 1943-46. Named Industrialist of Year, 1967; recipient Educator's Golden Key award, 1970, Elmer A. Sperry award, 1982, AIEE award, Ga. Inst. Tech. award, Sec. Dept. Health and Human Services award, Silver Beaver award Boy Scouts Am., 1989, Literary Lions award, 1995; named to Engring. Hall of Fame. Mem. Nat. Alliance Businessmen, Phi Gamma Delta.

STAMPKE, STUART REH, physicist, researcher; b. Burbank, Calif., Apr. 20, 1950. BS in Physics summa cum laude, Calif. State U., Northridge, 1973; PhD in Physics, Calif. Inst. Tech., Pasadena, 1982. Rsch. fellow in physics Calif. Inst. Tech., Pasadena, 1982; rsch. assoc. Mich. State U., East Lansing, 1982-86; scientist I Superconducting Super Collider Lab., Waxahachie, Tex., 1989-94; sr. scientist Aura Sys., Inc., El Segundo, Calif., 1996—; from vis. asst. prof. to vis. assoc. prof. U. Notre Dame, Ind., 1986-88; mem. part-time faculty Calif. State U., Northridge, 1994-96. Contbr. articles to profl. jours. on particle physics, detectors, and accelerator physics. Mem. IEEE, Am. Phys. Soc., Internat. Solar Energy Soc., Am. Solar Energy Soc. E-mail: srstampke@earthlink.net. Home: 17803 Superior St Apt 215 Northridge CA 91325-4795 Office: Aura Sys Inc 2335 Alaska Ave El Segundo CA 90245-4822

STAMPS, GEORGE MORELAND, communications consultant, facsimile pioneer; b. Kuling, Jiangxi, China, June 15, 1924; came to U.S., 1926 (parents Am. citizens); s. Drew Fletcher and Elizabeth Camilla (Belk) S.; m. Helen Leone Paty, Nov. 29, 1946; children: Margaret Evalyn, Robert Fletcher, Thomas Paty, John Belk. BS magna cum laude, Wake Forest U., 1947; MA in Physics, Columbia U., 1949; postgrad., Poly. Inst. Bklyn., 1950-52. Instr. physics and math. SUNY Maritime Coll., Bronx, 1949-51; asst. chief engr., dir. tech. sales Hogan Labs. Inc., N.Y.C., 1951-59; chief engr., asst. to pres. mktg. Telautograph Corp., Los Angeles, 1960-62; program mgr. Magnafax Program Magnavox Co., Torrance, Calif., 1963-65; mgr indsl. mktg. Magnavox Co., Urbana, Ill., 1965-71, mgr. bus. devel., 1971-73; corp. mgr. bus. devel. Xerox Corp., Stamford, Conn., 1973-76; pres. GMS Consulting, Westport, Conn., 1976-86, Oxford, Ga., 1986—; expert witness on facsimile-visual scis. N.Y. Supreme Ct., 1982; chmn. numerous sci. and profl. confs. Contbr. over 35 articles on facsimile and telecommunication scis. to profl. jours. and govt. coms. Patentee in field. Del. Conn. Dem. Conv., Hartford, 1980; bd. dirs. Champaign-Urbana (Ill.) Symphony Orch., 1968-72, Newton County Red Cross, 1988-94; sec. Newton County Hist. Soc., 1991-93, v.p., 1993-95, pres., 1995-96; v.p. Friends of Newton County Porter Meml. Libr., 1988-91, pres., 1991-93; pres. Newton County Facilities Bd., 1997—; chmn. Newton County Facilities Bd., 1997—; co-chair Newton County Impact Fee Adv. Com., 1999—. Decorated Air medal with two oak leaf clusters; named Friend of Newton County Libr., 1994; named Wake Forest U. Alumnus of Yr., 1997, recipient Disting. Svc. citation for sci. and tech., 1997. Mem. IEEE, Computer Soc. of IEEE, Comm. Soc. of IEEE (officer Ft. Wayne chpt. 1972-73), Geosci. and Remote Sensing Soc. of IEEE, Electronics Industries Assn. (chmn. comm. terminals and interfaces sect. 1963-73, founder TR-29 facsimile systems and equipment engring. com. 1961), Armed Forces Comm. and Electronics Assn., Am. Phys. Soc., Kiwanis (pres. Covington club 1993-94, lt. gov. 21st divsn. 1996-97), Phi Beta Kappa, Omicron Delta Kappa. Presbyterian. Home: 1280 Lake Stone Lea Dr PO Box 1299 Oxford GA 30054-1299

STAMPS, PETER DAVID, manufacturing administrator; b. Dearborn, Mich., June 4, 1963; s. David William and Alice Janette (Travis) S. BSME, USN Acad., 1985; MBA in Global Mgmt., U. Phoenix, 1999. Registered engr.-in-tng. Commd. ensign USN, 1985, advanced through grades to lt., 1992, commd. officer Operation Desert Storm, 1990-91; lt. commander USNR, San Diego, 1992—, CO NR DESRON 24, 1998-00; prodn. supr., quality steering com., quality edn. trainer Cargill Inc., Lynwood, Calif., 1992-93, plant engr., 1993-94; site mgr. McWhorter Techs., Inc. (formerly Resin Products divsn., Cargill Inc.), Lynwood, 1994; western regional quality mgr. McWhorter Techs., Inc. (formerly Resin Products divsn., Cargill Inc.), 1994-96; divsn. engr. Cargill Energy Divsn., Beverly, Mass., 1996-97; EHS engr. Cargill Inc., Mpls., 1997-99; maint. mgr. Cargill N.Am. Grain Divsn., Savage, Minn., 1999—. Mem. budget and fin. com. Arcada Cmty. Assn., 1993-96; econ. devel. com. and scholarship com. Lynwood (Calif.) C. of C., 1994-96, mem. bd. dirs. 1995-96; mem. VITA Taxpayer Asst. Program, 1998—. Mem. ASME, Am. Soc. for Quality, USN Inst., Am. Assn. Individual Investors, Sur face Navy Assn., Naval Res. Assn., USN Acad. Alumni Assn., Rotary Internat. (bd. dirs. Lynwood, Calif. chpt. 1995-96), Lynwood C. of C. (bd. dirs.-treas. 1995-96), Lions Internat. Avocations: water sports, racquet sports, investments, coin collecting, skiing. Office: N Am Grain Divsn 12101 Lynn Ave Savage MN 55378-1475

STAN, SORIN GHEORGHE, electrical engineer; b. Brasov, Romania, Apr. 16, 1964; s. Gheorghe and Viorica (Muscan) S.; m. Daniela Luca, Oct. 14, 1989; 1 child, Robert George. MSc, Transilvania U., Brasov, Romania, 1988; MEE, Eindhoven Internat. Inst., The Netherlands, 1992; PhD, Eindhoven U. of Tech., 1999. Devel. engr. Tohan Mech. Co., Romania, 1988-90; system architect Philips Optical Storage, Eindhoven, 1992—. Author: The CD-ROM Book--A Brief System Description, 1998; contbr. articles to profl. jours.; inventor in field. Recipient Gold Medal in Elec. Enring. at Traian Lalescu contest, Ministry of Edn., Romania, 1986. Mem. IEEE (sr., 2d Place Chester Sall Meml. Paper award IEEE Transactions on Consumer Elecs. 1998, mem. tech. com. internat. conf. consumer electronics). Avocations: gardening, table tennis, books on physics and history. Office: Philips Optical Storage, PO Box 80 002 Bldg SFJ-1, 5600 JB Eindhoven The Netherlands

STANBERRY, D(OSI) ELAINE, English literature educator, writer; b. Elk Park, N.C.; m. Earl Stanberry; 1 child, Anita St. Lawrence. Student in Bus. Edn., Steed Coll. Tech., 1956; BS in Bus. and English, East Tenn. State U., 1961, MA in Shakespearean Lit., 1962; PhD, Tex. A&M U., 1975; postgrad., North Tex. State U., U. South Fla., NYU, Duke U., U. N.C. Prof. Manatee Jr. Coll., Bradenton, Fla., 1964-67; Disting. prof. English Dickinson State U., N.D., 1967-81; retired, 1981. Author: Poetic Heartstrings, Mountain Echoes, Love's Perplexing Obsession Experienced by Heinrich Heine and Percy Bysshe Shelley, Poetry from the Ancients to Moderns: A Critical Anthology, Finley Forest, Chapel Hill's Tree-lined Tuck, (plays) The Big Toe, The Funeral Factory; contbr. articles, poetry to jours., mags. Recipient Editor's Choice award Nat. Libr. Poetry, 1988, 95, Distinguished Professor of English Award, Dickinson State U., 1981; included in Best Poems of 1995. Mem. Acad. Am. Poets, N.C. Writers Network, N.C. Poetry Soc. (Carl Sandburg Poetry award 1988), Poetic Page, Writers Jour., Poets and Writers, Friday-Noon Poets, Delta Kappa Gamma. Home: Finley Forest 193 Summerwalk Cir Chapel Hill NC 27514-8642

STANBERRY, LAWRENCE RAYMOND, virologist, vaccinologist, pediatrician, educator; b. Detroit, Aug. 27, 1948; s. Raymond Tilford and Susan (Cobb) S.; m. Elizabeth Ann Thompson, Aug. 16, 1969; children: Lindsey Elizabeth, David Martin. BS in Chemistry, Southwestern U., Georgetown, Tex., 1970; MD, U. Ill., Chgo., 1977, PhD in Pharmacology, 1979. Intern in pediatrics Children's Med. Ctr., Dallas, 1977-78; fellow in oncology and exptl. therapeutics U. Ill. Med. Ctr., Chgo., 1978-79; resident in pediatrics Primary Children's Hosp., Salt Lake City, 1979-80; fellow in pediatric infectious diseases U. Utah, Salt Lake City, 1980-82; asst. prof. pediatrics U. Cin. Coll. Medicine, 1982-87, assoc. prof., 1987-91, prof., 1991-2000; dir. divsn. infectious diseases Children's Hosp. Rsch. Found., Cin., 1995-2000; chair vaccine study sect. NIH, Bethesda, Md., 1998—; prof., chmn. pediat. U. Tex. Med. Br., Galveston, 2000—, dir. Sealy Ctr. for Vaccine Rsch., 2000—; mem. study sect. NIH, Bethesda, 1988—; cons. Smith Kline Biologicals, Rixensart, Belgium, 1992—; sci. advisor Am. Social Health Assn., Research Triangle Park, N.C., 1994—; Albert B. Sabin prof. pediats., U. Cin. Coll. of Medicine, 1996—. Author: Understanding Herpes, 1998; editor: Perinatal and Genital Herpes, 1996; editor: Sexually Transmitted Diseases: Vaccines Prevention and Control, 2000; editl. bd. Jour. Med. Virology, 1994—. James scholar U. Ill., Chgo., 1974-77; Hartford Found. fellow, N.Y.C., 1984-87; grantee NIH, Bethesda, 1985—. Fellow Infectious Diseases Soc. Am., Am.

Acad. Pediatrics; mem. Internat. Soc. Antiviral Rsch. (fin. com. 1988—). Office: U Tex Med Br Galveston Dept Pediat 301 University Blvd Galveston TX 77555-0351

STANCHEV, WALTER MIKLOSH, computer science educator; b. Dobrich, Bulgaria, Apr. 26, 1940; s. Miklosh Nikolov and Ganka Raynova S.; m. Valentina Ivanovna Diachenko, Apr. 24, 1970; 1 child, Irena Walter. Grad., Higher Inst. Elec. Engring., 1966, PhD, 1970. Assoc. prof. dept. computer engring. Tech. U., Varna, Bulgaria, 1976—, dean, 1993—. Author: Programming and Use of Computer Systems, 1990, Microprocessor System CM600 Description, Programming, Application, 1984, 86, Excel Know How, 1994, Application Software Systems, 1995, Microprocessor Techniques, 1996, MC68HC12 One chip Microcontoller, 1999; contbr. articles in profl. jours.; patentee in field. Mem. Assn. Computing Machinery, Assn. Computing Machinery Bulgaria. Avocations: music, travel. Home: Tchaika bl 59 wh A app 31, 9005 Varna Bulgaria Office: Tech U, 9010 Varna Bulgaria

STANCHI, NESTOR OSCAR, microbiology educator; b. La Plata, Argentina, Feb. 22, 1957; s. Nestor Oscar and Amanda Carmen (Gardella) S.; m. Nora Beatriz Vázquez, Mar. 16, 1990; 1 child, Oscar Agustin. Degree in vet. medicine, Nat. U. La Plata, Buenos Aires, 1981, D in Vet. Sci., 1985, clin. bacteriologist, 1992. Rsch. scientist Leptospirosis Lab. Instituto Nacional Tecnologia Agropecuaria, La Plata, Argentina, 1981-83; sr. scientist Commn. Sci. Rsch., La Plata, Argentina, 1984-88; asst. prof. microbiology Nat. U. La Plata, 1983-91, prof., 1992—, dir. distance edn. Faculty Vet. Sci., 1998—, dir. Lab. Rsch. and Diagnostical Bacteriology Fac. Vet. Sci., 1998; head lab. leptospirosis Nat. U. La Plata, 1988-94; lead lab. human virology La Plata Hosp., 1988-94; founder. ref. human virology lab. Ministry of Health, Argentina, 1992. Author, editor: Veterinary Microbiology Handbook, (in Spanish), 1995, Diseases of the Female Genital Tract (in Spanish), 1999, Introduction to Immunology, 2000 (in Spanish); editor in chief Jour Revista de Enfermedades Infecciosas Emergentes, 1996—, scientific editor: jour. Avances en Medicina Veterinaria, 1997; dir. Analecta Vet. jour. Faculty of Vet. Sci. Nat. U. La Plata, 1998—; contbr. more thann 55 articles to nat. and internat. sci. jours. Pres. Assn. Chiron, 1994-2000. Mem. AAAS, Am. Soc. Microbiology, N.Y. Acad. Sci., Argentina Assn. Microbiology, Argentina Assn. Zoonosis (founder). Achievements include research on animal toxins and photography. Home: C.C. 741, B1900AVW Buenos Aires Argentina Office: Nat Univ La Plata, Nat Univ La Plata, CC 296, Faculty Vet Sci, B1900AVW Buenos Aires Argentina

STANČIĆ, MARIN FRANE, neurosurgeon, educator; b. Rijeka, Croatia, Sept. 22, 1956; s. Frane Marin and Nada (Orlić) S.; m. Giuliana Superina, Jan. 22, 1983; children: Ivana, Frane, Katarina. MD, Med. Sch., Rijeka, Croatia, 1981; MA, Med. U. Rijeka, Rijeka, Croatia, 1994, PhD, 1996. Diplomate neurosurg., Croatia. Intern Gen. Hosp., Banja Luka, Bosnia, 1981-82; physician Nat. Army, Knin, Croatia, 1982-83; intern Clin. Hosp., Rijeka, 1983-86, resident, 1986-93, neurosurgeon, 1993—; assoc. prof. Med. Sch., Rijeka, 1990-98; lectr. Med. Sch., Rijeka, 1990—. Home: Sisplac 5, HR-52100 Pula Croatia Office: Pula Gen Hosp Negrijeva 6, HR-52100 Pula Croatia

STANCIKOVA, PAVLA, information technology executive; b. Prostejov, Czechoslovakia, July 12, 1943; d. Rudolf and Pavla (Kaniova) Cuda; m. Jan Stancik, July 13, 1963; children: Jana, Martin. Degree, Slovak Tech. U., Bratislava, Slovakia, 1966; PhD, Comenius U., 1977; cert., Georgetown U., 1991. Designer Vahostav, Bratislava, 1966-72; head info. sys. dept. WHO project Czechoslovak Ctr. Environ. Pollution Control, Bratislava, 1972-77; head info. sys. dept. Water Rsch. Inst., Bratislava, 1978-90, Slovak Commn. on Environment, Bratislava, 1991-92; dir. Ctr. Eco-Info. and Terminology, Bratislava, 1992—; trainer Asian Inst. Tech., Bangkok, 1992; cons. divsn. water sci. UNESCO, Paris, 1995—, Danube Program Coord. Unit, Vienna, Austria, 1995—. Editor: (with I. Dahlberg) Environmental Knowledge Organization, 1994; (with S. Krizikova) English-Slovak and Slovak-English Dictionary of Water Terms, 1984; (with M. Smihla) Multilingual Vocabulary of Water Terms, 2000; editor CD ROM: (with M. Smihla) Multilingual Vocabulary of Water Terms. English-Slovak-Hungarian-Russian 8172 terms, 1997; prodr. (with M. Smihla and J. Smihlova) PROFLIB - Software for Libraries and Terminology, 1995—; (with J. Smihlova) Water Standards, 19983, 99, 2000. Fellow WHO, 1972, mgmt. study fellow Georgetown U., 1991. Mem. Internat. Soc. Knowledge Orgn. (exec. bd. 1994-98), Internat. Orgn. Info. Specialists (exec. bd. 1995—). E-mail: pavla@ceit.sk. Home: Bodrocka 40, 82107 Bratislava Slovakia Office: Ceit Ltd, Biskupicka 1, 82106 Bratislava Slovakia

STANCIULESCU, FLORIN S., information scientist, educator; b. Pitesti, Arges, Romania, Aug. 28, 1929; s. Stratilat I. and Florica M. (Motoescu) S.; m. Natalia-Maria D. Slaniceanu, Dec. 31, 1956; 1 child, Oana-Alina. Electrical engr. degree, U. Polytechnica, Bucharest, 1954, D, 1970. Electrical engr. Electrical Rsch. Inst., Bucharest, 1954-60, rsch. worker, 1960-65; chief rsch. worker Rsch. Inst. Informatics, Bucharest, 1965-82, head rsch. lab., 1982—; assoc. prof. Postgrad. Sch. Advanced Informatics, Bucharest, 1982—. Author: Analysis and Simulation of Nonlinear Systems, 1974, Large Scale Systems Dynamics, 1982; co-author: Computational Systems Analysis, 1992; editor in chief: Jour. Informatics and Control, 1990—; contbr. articles to profl. jours. Mem. Scientists Assn., Univ. Solidarity, N.Y. Acad. Scis., European Simulation Soc. Avocations: classical music, art collector, mountain tourism, ecology. E-mail: sflorin@u3.ici.ro. Home: Pictor Stahi 20, 70764 Bucharest Romania Office: Rsch Inst Informatics, Averescu Ave 8-10, 71316 Bucharest Romania

STĂNCULESCU, VICTOR ATANASIE, former Romanian government official, executive; b. May 10, 1928; m. Elena Popa, 1952; 1 child, Alina Monica. Min. nat. economy Govt. of Romania, Bucharest, 1989-90, min. of nat. def., 1990-91, min. of industry, 1991; country del. from Romania Balli-Group Ltd., London, Bucharest, 1992-94, sr. advisor to chmn., 1994-97; v.p. Robank, 1995. Gen. Four Stars Romanian army, 1991. Recipient Man of Yr. award for outstanding comm. and profl. achievement Am. Biog. Inst., 1995, Man of Yr. award Internat. Biog. Ctr., Cambridge, Eng., 1994-95. Office: Balli Trading Ltd, 4 Romulus St, Bucharest Romania also: Balli Group plc, 5 Stanhope Gate, Park Lane London England*

STANDISH, RUSSELL KIM, computational scientist; b. Esperance, Australia; s. Peter Miles and Mardi Louise (Mosely) S.; m. Kim Gail Crichton, Apr. 24, 1992; 1 child, Hal. BSc with honors, U. Western Australia, 1985; PhD, Australian Nat. U., 1990. Scientific programmer supercomputer facility Australian Nat. U., Canberra, 1990-91; wissenschaftliche angestellte Rechenzentrum, U. Karlsruhe, 1992; programming cons. computer svcs. dept. U. NSW, Sydney, 1993-94, distributed systems mgr. acad. computing support unit, 1995-97, dir. high performance computing support unit, 1997—. Author: (with others) The Role of Innovation within Economics, 1999. Treas., sec. Scientists Against Nuclear Arms, Canberra, 1988-92; mem. Cmty. Aid Abroad, Canberra, 1989-95. Mem. Australian Inst. of Physics. Fax: 612-9385-6965. E-mail: r.standish@unsw.edu.au. Office: U NSW High Performance, Computing Support Unit, Sydney NSW 2051, Australia

STANDISH, WILLIAM LLOYD, judge; b. Pitts., Feb. 16, 1930; s. William Lloyd and Eleanor (McCargo) S.; m. Marguerite Oliver, June 12, 1963; children: Baird M., N. Graham, James H., Constance S. BA, Yale U., 1953; LLB, U. Va., 1956. Bar: Pa. 1957, U.S. Supreme Ct. 1967. Assoc. Reed, Smith, Shaw & McClay, Pitts., 1957-63; ptnr., 1963-80; judge Ct. Common Pleas Allegheny County (Pa.), 1980-87, U.S. Dist. Ct. (we. dist.) Pa., 1987—; solicitor Edgeworth Borough Sch. Dist., 1963-66. Bd. dirs. Sewickley (Pa.) Cmty. Ctr., 1981-83, Staunton Farms Found., mem., 1984—, trustee, 1984-92; corporator Sewickley Cemetery, 1971-87; trustee Mary and Alexander Laughlin Children's Ctr., 1972-90, Leukemia Soc. Am., 1978-80, we. Pa. chpt., 1972-80, We. Pa. Sch. Deaf, 1983—, YMCA of Sewickley, 1996—. Recipient Pres. award Leukemia Soc. Am., 1980. Mem. ABA, Pa. Bar Assn., Allegheny County Bar Assn., Am. Judicature Soc., Acad. Trial Lawyers Allegheny County (treas. 1977-78, bd. dirs. 1979-80), Am. Inn of Ct. (Pitts. chpt. 1993—). Office: US Dist Ct 605 US Post Office Ct House 700 Grant St Pittsburgh PA 15219-1906

STANEK, BRUNO L., software developer, author, commentator; b. Rorschach, Switzerland, Nov. 9, 1943; s. Leopold A. and Gertrud (Siebert) S.; m. Erika E. Schraner, Nov. 28, 1979; children: Ganymed, Oliver. Diploma in math., Swiss Fed. Inst. Tech., Zurich, 1968, DSc in Math., 1971. Asst. Inst. Applied Math., Swiss Fed. Inst. Tech., 1968-70; freelance book and TV author, Switzerland, 1971-75; prof. math., physics and computer sci. Engring. Coll., Brugg, Switzerland, 1976-79; founder, CEO, Ärztesoftware, Arth, Switzerland, 1980—, Astrosoftware, Arth, 1994—; space commentator Swiss Nat. TV and other stas., 1968—; over 1000 pub. lectures on space and astronomy, Switzerland, Germany, 1968—; med. emergency software planner for Swiss cities, 1991-96. Author: Der Weg ins All, 1969, Kursbuch für das Sonnensystem, 1971, Bildatlas des Sonnensystems, 1974, Space Shuttle, 1975, Neuland Mars, 1976, Hallwag-Taschenbuch 111, 1977, Space Art-Weltraumkunst, 1980, Raumfahrtlexikon, 1983 (CD-ROM ed. 1997, 98, 99, 2000), Planetenlexikon, 1979 (last edit. 1992, also CD-ROM ed. 1995, 98, 99, 2000), Sparer leben gefährlich, 1987, Tragbare Opfer, 1988, (software) Air Traffic Control Simulator, 1996, (med. software) Ganymed; contbr. numerous articles on space and astronomy to Swiss and fgn. publs. Mem. supervising bd. high sch. graduation KKS Schwyz, 1996—. Mem. Swiss Frieds U.S.A., Lions (pres. Zurich 1977-78). Avocations: studying United States culture, travel. E-mail: Bruno@Stanek.ch. Home and Office: Wybergliweg 62, CH-6415 Arth Switzerland

STANEK, STEVEN ROBERT, optometrist, military officer; b. San Antonio, Feb. 7, 1957; s. Robert Gunderson and Ellinor (Engelstad) S. AA, U. Md., 1977, BS in Zoology, 1979, BS in Optometry, Pa. Coll. Optometry, 1981, OD, 1984; MA, Webster U., 1995. Asst. chief optometry, capt. Evans Army Hosp., Ft. Carson, Colo., 1984-88; div. optometrist 7th Infantry Div., Ft. Ord, Calif., 1988-89; optometrist pvt. practice San Jose, Calif., 1989-90; dep. chief, clin. optometry Wilford Hall USAF Med. Ctr., Lackland AFB, Tex., 1990-96; flight comdr., lt. col. 96th aerospace medicine squadron, Elgin AFB, 1996—; adj. faculty So. Coll. Optometry, 1998—; adj. asst. prof. U. Houston Coll. of Optometry, 1984-88. Decorated Army Commendation medal, Meritorious Svc. medal, 1996; recipient Biol. Sci. award U. Md., 1977, Optometric Recognition award, 1993; Health Professions scholar U.S. Army, 1980-84. Fellow Am. Acad. Optometry; mem. Air Force Assn., Am. Optometric Assn., Alamo Tri-Svc. Optometric Soc. (treas. 1990-91, sec. 1991-92, pres. 1992-93), Am. Coll. Healthcare Execs. (diplomate), Armed Forces Optometric Assn. (sec. treas.), Assn. Mil. Surgeons U.S., Classic Chevy Club Internat., Am. Nat. Sojourners, Masons (Hero of '76), Interant. Brotherhood Magicians, Soc. Am. Magicians, Beta Sigma Kappa. Avocations: classic car restoration, woodworking. Home: 449 Crownpointe Cir Vacaville CA 95687-5545 Office: 96 AMDS/SGPFE 302 N 1st St Bldg 200 Eglin AFB FL 32542-5448

STANFORD, JANE HERRING, management consultant, retired business educator, writer; b. Lockhart, Tex., Dec. 17, 1939; d. John William and Frances Argyra (Cheatham) H. Jr.; m. Rube Valton Stanford, Sept. 17, 1966; children: (Steven) Scott, Lisa Ann. BS in Secondary Edn., Texas A&M U., Kingsville, 1965; MS in Counseling, Texas A&M U., Corpus Christi, 1982; MBA, Texas A&M U., Kingsville, 1988; PhD in Orgn. Theory and Strategic Mgmt., U. North Tex., 1992. Cert. secondary sch. tchr., coun., Tex. English tchr. Robstown (Tex.) H.S., 1965-67; Bus. tchr. Miller H.S., Corpus Christi, 1967-78; owner, mgr. The Cottage, Portland, Tex., 1978-81; instr. Del Mar Coll., Corpus Christi, 1981-83, Bee County Coll., Beeville, Tex., 1984-88; tching. fellow U. North Tex., Denton, 1988-90; assoc. prof. bus. policy and internat. mgmt. Texas A&M U., Kingsville, 1990-98, full mem. grad. faculty, 1992-99, grad. rsch. advisor, MBA program, Coll. Bus., 1992-98, chair dept. mgmt. and mktg., 1994-98, head, asst. v.p. acad. affairs, 1998-99, ret., 1999; mgmt. cons. Strategic Mgmt. Solutions, Inc., 1999—, pres., primary cons., 2000—; grad. faculty Tex. A&M U., Kingsville, pres. faculty senate, 1995-96, exec. com. of senate, 1993-98, chair dept. mgmt. and mktg., 1994-98, chair univ. assessment, budgeting and planning com., 1997-98, chair univ. cmty. devel. com., 1998-99, co-chair univ. distance learning com., 1998, co-chair sys. distance learning task force subcom., 1998; internat. lectr. on strategic mgmt. within internat. context; workshop leader and participant in acad. issues, including S.W. Fedn. Adminstrv. Disciplines, Houston, 1992-95; paper presenter internat. conf. Soc. for the Advancement of Mgmt., 1998; sec. S.W. New Millennium, Inc., 1998—; session presenter annual meeting SACS, Atlanta, 1998. Author: Building Competitiveness: U.S. Expatriate Management Strategies in Mexico, 1995; co-editor Tex. A&M U. System Internat. Bus. Newsletter, 1993; contbr. articles to profl. jours. and conf. procs. Co-author Best Conf. Paper, Richard d. Irwin, Inc., Houston, 1991; grantee SBA for Women in Bus. Conf., 1993; finalist Disting. Svc. award Tex. A&M U., 1997, 98, 99; Tex. A&M U. Sys. Chancellor's fellow in leadership in higher edn. program, 1997. Mem. AAUW, Inst. Mgmt. Cons., Am. Assn. Higher Edn., Acad. Internat. Bus. (track chair 1994-95), Acad. Mgmt., Soc. Advancement of Mgmt., Kappa Delta Pi (life), Delta Sigma Pi. Presbyterian. Avocations: book collecting, photography, art, travel. E-mail: jhstanford@aol.com. Home and Office: 13526 Carlos Fifth Ct Corpus Christi TX 78418-6913

STANFORD, KATHLEEN THERESA, secondary school educator; b. Belize City, Belize, Sept. 28, 1933; d. Frederick Gill and Ila Mae (Cherrington) Hyde; m. Herman Emanuel Stanford, Oct. 3, 1970 (dec. Feb., 1989). Student (summer), S. We. La. U., Lafayette, 1958; BA, Seton Hill Coll., 1962; student (summer), Xavier U., New Orleans, 1956, 68; postgrad., Southern U. and A&M Coll., 1962, 67, Adelphi U., 1988, C.W. Post, N.Y., 1988. Cert. sci. tchr., La. (life). Tchr. Mem. Sisters of Holy Family Order, various cities, U.S. & Belize, 1953-69; sci. tchr., moderator Sisters of Holy Family, Grand Coteau, La., 1967-68, Lafayette, La., 1968-70; laicized, 1970; sci. tchr., sponsor of sci. fair N.Y.C. Bd. of Edn., Bklyn., 1981—; sci. coord. La. Sci. Acad., Lafayette, 1968-70; mem. U.F.T. /IHS sci. com., N.Y.C., 1984-85. Contbr. poetry to Poetry Mags., 1974—. Hon. mem. Pres. Clinton's 2d Term Com., Washington, 1997; sci. sponsor Ford Future Scientists of Am., 1968, Dist. Sci. Fair, Bklyn., 1984; sec. Belize Parkfest of N.Y., Inc., 1990-92. Recipient Commendation for pupils 20th Internat. Sci. Fair, 1969, poetry awards Am. Poetry Assn., 1989, 90, cert. for leadership, Dem. Nat. Com., Washington, 1997. Mem. Belize Cosmopolitan Benevolent Assn. (v.p.). Democrat. Avocations: writing poetry, photography, bird watching, swimming, walking, singing.

STANGE, GERD, electrical engineering educator; b. Borgdorf-Seedorf, Rendsburg, Germany, Mar. 8, 1941; s. Wilhelm and Charlotte (Brügmann) S.; m. Renate Ursula Sauerberg, July 3, 1970; children: Leif Christian, Marion, Jan-Erik. Dipl.-Ing., Tech. U., Braunschweig, Germany, 1967, PhD, 1980; Prof., U. Applied Scis., Kiel, Germany, 1982. Rschr. DESY, Hamburg, 1968-72, sr. scientist, 1972-76, Linac group leader, 1976-82; prof. elec. engring. U. Applied Scis., Kiel, 1982—, dean, 1998—; cons. KfK, Karlsruhe, 1984-87, Sincrotrone Trieste, Italy, 1988-89; project leader Min. of Economy, Kiel, 1990-96; founder Nutech GmbH, Neumünster, 1996. Patentee in field. Vice pres. VDI, Schleswig-Holstein, Germany, 1992-94; communal cons. City Coun., Nortorf, Germany, 1996—. Mem. FDI, FDE. Avocations: painting, history, philosophy, sports. Office: Inst Tech Info Sys Tech, Legienstr 35, 24103 Kiel Germany

STANGE, LUISE MAGDALENE CHRISTINE, plant physiology educator; b. Göttingen, Germany, May 6, 1926; d. Carl Gustav and Marie Friederike Luise (Dunkel) S. Student natural scis., U. Göttingen, 1943-44; Dr.rer.nat., U. Freiburg, 1950; Habilitation, U. Cologne, 1957. Sci. asst. Inst. Sugar Beet Rsch., U. Göttingen, 1950-52; sci. asst. Inst. Devel. Physiology, U. Cologne (Fed. Republic Germany), 1952-57, lectr., 1957-63, prof., 1963; prof. Tech. U. Hannover (Fed. Republic Germany), 1964-73; prof. plant physiology U. Kassel (Fed. Republic Germany), 1973—. Contbr. articles and revs. on genetics, biochemistry and plant physiology to sci. jours. Mem. German Bot. Soc., Gesellschaft Deutscher Naturforscher und Ärzte, Fedn. European Soc. Plant Physiology, Internat. Plant Growth Substances Assn. Office: U Kassel, Heinrich Plett-Strasse 40, D-34132 Kassel Germany

STANGER, ROBERT HENRY, psychiatrist, educator; b. N.Y.C., N.Y., May 19, 1937; s. Sidney and Mary (Strassner) S.; m. Andrea Rogin, Aug. 28, 1960; children: Lee Ann, David Neal. AB, Guilford Coll., 1959; MD, Emory U., 1964. Intern in internal medicine Wake Forest U., 1964-65; resident in gen. psychiatry U. Pitts., Western Psychiat. Inst. and Clinic, 1967-70; pvt. practice gen. psychiatry Monroeville, Pa., 1970—; med. dir. Allegheny Valley Mental Health-Mental Retardation Ctr., New Kensington, Pa., 1970-76; dir. psychiat. svcs. Allegheny Valley Hosp., Natrona Heights, Pa., 1983-96, chmn. dept. psychiatry and behavioral medicine, 1983-96; pvt. practice Natrona Heights, 1984-97; clin. instr. psychiatry U. Pitts. Sch. Medicine, 1970-79, clin. asst. prof., 1980—; cons. Westinghouse Elec. Corp., East Pitts., 1977-87; mem. ethics com. human rsch. Allegheny Valley Hosp., 1976-97; chmn. dept. psychiatry Citizens Gen. Hosp., 1978-88. Capt. M.C., U.S. Army, 1965-67, Vietnam. Mem. AMA, Am. Psychiat. Assn. (del. 1986-88), Pa. Psychiat. Soc. (councilor 1976-79, treas. 1979-80, sec. 1980-81, v.p. 1981-82, pres.-elect 1982-83, pres. 1983-84), Pitts. Psychiat. Soc. (councilor 1974-76, sec. 1977-78, pres.-elect 1978-79, pres. 1979-80), Allegheny County Med. Soc. Home: 3910 Old William Penn Hwy Pittsburgh PA 15235-4837

STANGLER, FERDINAND, natural sciences educator, dean of faculty; b. Vienna, Austria, May 11, 1928; s. Ferdinand and Aloisia (Biczowsky) S.; m. Helga Mag. Reichel, Oct. 9, 1944; 1 child, Eva. PhD, U. Vienna, 1952. U. asst. U. Vienna, 1951-62, u. docent, 1962-71, full prof., 1971-96, dean of faculty nat. scis., 1982-86, 87-90, prof. emeritus, 1996—; dir. Inst. Solid State Physics U. Vienna, 1979-92. Contbr. articles to profl. jours. Recipient Felix Kuschenitz award Acad. Sci. Austria, 1961. Mem. Öster. Physikal. Ges., Chem. Physikal. Ges., Dt. Ges. f.Materialkde. Roman Catholic. Avocations: music, old watches and clocks. Home: Bruneckerg 16/9, Mödling Austria A 2340 Office: Univ Vienna, Strudlhofg 4, Boltzmanngasse 5, Vienna Austria A 1090

STANGO, JULIETTE MARY, composer, music publisher, educator; b. Phila., Aug. 15, 1962; d. Dominick A. and Rita F. Stango. Diploma in arts, Sessione Senese Musica l'Arte, Siena, Italy, 1990. Music copyist Music Art Co., N.Y.C., 1987-88; music therapist Golden Slipper Uptown Home, Phila., 1988-90, HCR-Manor Care, Huntingdon Valley, Pa., 1997-99; composer, pub. Juliette Stango Pub., Phila., 1990—; staff condr., composer Sessione Senese per La Musica e L'Arte, 1987, 90; MMC rec. artist Slovak Radio and TV Orch. Composer: (aria) Hopeless, 1990, (solo piano work) Nice Weather for a War, 1992; commd. composer (orchestral composition) Sol Per Dirti Adio, 1994; commd. composer and lyricist (aria) Heathcliff's Lament, 1998; commd. by Alberto Barbetti Pub., Siena, 1987, 93, Millennial Arts Prodn., N.Y.C., 1998; live TV performance Siena Palio, RAI, 1986. Mem. World Affairs Coun. Phila. Democrat. Roman Catholic. Avocations: swimming, travel, languages and cultural studies. E-mail: posercom@aol.com. Office: 9747 Susan Rd Philadelphia PA 19115-2918

STANGOS, NICOLAS, publishing executive; b. Athens, Greece, Nov. 21, 1936; arrived in U.K., 1965; s. Constantine and Natalia (Syvrides) S. BA with honors, Denison U., 1958; postgrad., Harvard U., 1958-60; Fulbright scholar, Wesleyan U., Middletown, Conn., 1955-56. Edn. dir. Sch. Ekistics Doxiadis Assocs., Athens, 1962-65; press attaché Greek Embassy, London, 1965-67; sr. commissioning editor Penguin Books Ltd., London, 1967-74; editl. dir. Thames and Hudson Ltd., London, 1974—; mem. cons. bd. Inst. Contemporary Arts, London, 1967-72, Arts Coun. Gt. Britain, 1976-81. Author: Selected Poems, 1975, The Familiar Surrounding of Words, 1981; editor: John Berger Sel Essays, 1972, Concepts of Modern Art, 1974, Hockney by Hockney, 1976, David Hockney: That's the Way I See It, 1993; translator numerous books. Mem. Cranium Club, Groucho Club. Avocation: music. Home: 38 Montagu Sq, London W1H 1TL, England Office: Thames and Hudson Ltd, 181A High Holborn, London WC1V 7QX, England

STANHILL, GERALD, agricultural climatologist, researcher; b. London, Apr. 28, 1929; arrived in Israel, 1958; s. David Bernard and Minnie (Priel) S.; m. Rachel Bechler, Jan. 15, 1963; children: David, Michal, Ariel. BS, Reading (Eng.) U., 1953, PhD, 1956; MA (hon.), Cambridge (Eng.) U., 1975. Sci. officer Agrl. Rsch. Coun., U.K., 1954-58; rsch. officer Agrl. Rsch. Orgn., Israel, 1958-67; vis. scientist Oak Ridge (Tenn.) Nat. Lab., Tenn., 1968-69; rsch. prof. Agrl. Rsch. Orgn., Israel, 1970; overseas fellow St. John's Coll. U. Cambridge, 1975-76; dir., rsch. worker Inst. Soils and Water Agrl. Rsch. Orgn., Israel, 1977-80; vis. prof. soil and water sci. dept. U. Ariz., Tucson, 1986-87; Sir Fredereck Masters fellow Commonwealth Sci. and Indsl. Rsch. Orgn., Canberra, Australia, 1992-93; rsch. worker Agrl. Rsch. Orgn, Israel, 1988-92, 94—. Editor-in-chief: (sci. rev. book series) Advances in Bioclimatology, 1992—, (sci. jour.) Irrigation Sci., 1978-96; contbr. 150 sci. articles to profl. publs. Fellow Royal Meteorol. Soc. U.K.; mem. Israel Meteorol. Assn. Office: Agrl Rsch Orgn, Volcani Center, 50 250 Bet Dagan Israel

STANHOPE, RICHARD GRAHAM, pediatric endocrinologist, consultant, pilot; b. London, June 12, 1950; s. Richard Frank and Marion Logan (Broad) S.; m. Carol Every, May 8, 1976; children: Oliver Every, Sophie Caroline. BSc in Biochemistry with honors, London U., 1971, MD, 1989; MB BS, St. Bartholomew's Hosp., London, 1974. Lic. comml. pilot, 1978, airline transport pilot, 1985. Flying instr., 1973—; pre-registration house physician St. Bartholomew's Hosp., 1974; registrar various hosps., 1976-82; registrar in pediats. Ctrl. Middlesex Hosp./Middlesex Hosp., 1982-84; rsch. fellow Middlesex Hosp., 1984-86; lectr. pediat. endocrinology Gt. Ormond St./Inst. Child Health, London, 1986-89, cons., 1989—; airline pilot capt. Dan Air Lines, London, 1980-85, Air Europe Ltd., London, 1987-91. European editor Jour. Pediat. Endocrinology and Metabolism, 2000—; contbr. more than 100 articles to profl. jours. Freedom City London, Guildhall, 1985—. Fellow Royal Coll. Physicians, Royal Soc. Medicine; mem. Royal Coll. Obs., Royal Aero. Soc., Soc. Endocrinology (joint program sec. 1994-98). Office: Gt Ormond St Hosp Children, Dept Endocrinology, London WC1N 3JH, England

STANIA, PETER RICHARD, lawyer; b. Salzburg, Austria, Nov. 8, 1943; s. Rudolf and Margarethe (Mayer) S.; m. Alcira Josefina Gomez Ramos, Feb. 27, 1976; children: Kai, Ainaru, Larissa. MA, U. Vienna, Austria, 1968, Inst. Alcide de Gasperi, Rome, 1982, Webster Coll., 1983. Editor, sec. gen. Internat. Inst. for Peace, Vienna, dep. dir., 1988—; guest prof. U. Vienna, Bari, Italy, del Salvador, Buenos Aires; bd. dirs. Instituto de Relaciones Internacionales y de Investigaciones papa la Paz, Guatemala; hon. consul Domenican Republic in Vienna, Austria. Editor: Der Kalte Tod, 1982, (series) Peace and Security, 1997—, The IIP Monitor, 1989; contbr. articles to profl. jours. Bd. dirs. Osterreichisches Nord-SudInst. Entwicklungskooperation, Vienna, 1991, Osterreichisch Kubanische Gesellschaft, Vienna, 1989—. Mem. Internat. Peace Rsch. Assn. (coun. mem. 1988-92, exec. bd. dirs. 1990—), Latin Am. Assn. of Internat. Rels. (hon. pres. 1997—). Roman Catholic. Avocations: sports, mountain climbing. Office: Internat Inst for Peace, Mollwaldpl 5, 1040 Vienna Austria

STANIC, GORDANA, pharmacist, researcher, educator; b. Karlovac, Croatia, Jan. 27, 1952; d. Dusan and Ivanka (Benkovic) Savatovic; m. Nenad Stanic, Nov. 27, 1976; children: Ivana, Drazen. BSc, Faculty Pharmacy & Biochem., Zagreb, Croatia, 1974, PhD, 1984; MSc, U. Zagreb, 1979. Asst. Faculty Pharmacy & Biochemistry, Zagreb, 1974-90, asst. prof., 1990—. Contbr. articles to profl. jours. Mem. Croatian Pharm. Soc. Avocations: fitness, jogging, concerts, theatre. Home: J Pupacica 3, 10000 Zagreb Croatia Office: Faculty Pharm & Biochem, A Kovacica 1, 10000 Zagreb Croatia

STANISLAVSKI, VLODZIMIERZ STANISLAV, computer engineering educator; b. Nieborow, Poland, June 11, 1949; s. Stefan and Helena (Kolankiewicz) S.; m. Danuta Dobrzanska, Feb. 23, 1974; children: Urszula, Rafal. MSc, U. Opole, 1973; BSc in Engring., Silesian Tech. U., Gliwice, Poland, 1978, PhD, 1983. Asst. U. Opole, 1973-84, lectr., 1986-91; prin. Secondary Sch. Elec. Engring., Opole, 1984-86; edn. coord. computer engring. Provincial Coun., Opole, 1990-94; lectr. Tech U., Opole, 1990-94; lectr., rector cons. Tech. U., Opole, 1991—; prin. Pvt. Tech. Coll., Opole, 1995—; lectr. Tech. U., Czestochowa, Poland, 1997—; software cons. Machine Tools Factory, Opole, 1986-89; chief advisor Prin. Counsil, Opole, 1990-94; reviewer computer edn. books Ministry of Edn., Warsaw, 1995—. Author: Automatic Control Labolatory, 1980, Fundamentals of Microprocesor Technology, 1996; patentee in field. Fellow Polish Acad. Sci. (electronics com.). Avocations: hiking, climbing, guide in Tatra Mountains. Home: Borkowice 13, 49-125 Skorogoszcz Opole, Poland Office: Tech U Opole, 31 Sosnkowski Str, 45-233 Opole Poland

STANISLAW, TKOCZ, priest, editor; b. Jastrzebie, Poland, July 28, 1931; s. Józef and Wicktoria (Mazur) S. Diploma in theology, journalism, Jagiel-

logian U., Krackow, 1957. Curate Wodzislaw, Poland, 1957-60; notary Episcopal Curia, Katowice, 1960-68, chancellor, 1968-74; editor-in-chief Gosc Niedzielny, Katowice, 1974—. Contbr. articles to profl. jours. Named Prelate Honor Holiness, 1985. Home: ul.Gen Zajaczka 1, Katowice Poland Office: Editl Office, ul.Wita Stwosza 11, Katowice Poland

STANISTREET, JAMES HUDSON, sales and marketing executive; b. Sydney, Australia, July 29, 1953; s. Robert Woolcott and Helen Alison (Savage) S.; m. Gina Lenore Buckle, Aug. 20, 1977; children: Georgina, James, Angus, Julia. Cert. in Acctg., U. Tech., Sydney, 1975-78; Dertrr in Mktg., U. NSW, Sydney, 1983. Acct. W.D. & H.O. Wills, Sydney, 1972-74; sales and mktg. mgr. 3M Australia, Sydney, 1974-90; dir. sales and mktg. Bard Australia, Sydney, 1990-99, Vascular Medtronic Australasia, 1999—. V.p. Shore Found., Sydney. Mem. Inst. Affiliate Accts, Palm Beach Surf Club. Church of England. Avocations: swimming, rugby, golf. Home: 1A Orana Ave, Pymble NSW 2073, Australia Office: Medtronic Australasia, Unit 4/446 Victoria Rd, Gladesville NSW 2111, Australia

STANKIEWICZ, ANDRZEJ, telecommunications company executive; b. Gdańsk, Poland, Nov. 21, 1947; s. Bolesław and Helena (Muszyńska) S.; m. Barbara Zofia Szydłowska, Sept. 22, 1973; children: Filip, Paulina. MSc, Tech. U. Gdańsk, 1970, PhD, 1979. Asst. Ctrl. Shipbuilding Office, Gdańsk, 1970-71; rsch. scientist Tech. U. Gdańsk, 1971-79, asst. prof., 1979-92; sr. specialist Polish Telecom-Gdańsk, 1992-93, contract mgr., 1993—. Recipient Rsch. award Min. of Telecomms., 1975, Min. of Sci., Higher Edn. and Tech., 1982. Mem. IEE, Assn. of Polish Elec. Engrs. Avocations: bridge, chess, scrabble, literature. Home: ul Dzielna 73/1, 80-404 Gdańsk Poland

STAňKOVÁ, MARTA, nursing educator; b. Boskovice, Blansko, Czech Republic, Feb. 12, 1938; d. Karel and Josefa (Fučíková) Bašná; m. Rostislav Staňek, June 26, 1971 (dec. July 1990); children: Lucie, Zuzana. Degree in Nursing, Higher Nursing Sch., Praha, Czech Republic, 1960; M Philosophy, Charles U., Praha, 1964; D, Charles U., Prague, 1981, PhD in Pedagogy, 1988. Lic. nursing educator. Gen. nurse surg. dept. Regional Hosp., Svitavy, Czech Republic, 1956-60; tchr. nursing nursing schs., Svitavy and Prague, 1960-68; tchr. asst. nursing Charles U., Prague, 1968-90, asst. prof. Inst. Nursing Theory and Practice, Faculty Med., 1993—; dir. Dept. Edn. and Sci. Ministry Health, Praha, 1990-93; mem. steering group Workgroup of European Nurse Rschrs., Copenhagen, 1985-95, chairperson, 1992-93; temporary adviser WHO/Euro, Copenhagen, 1980-85; nursing adviser Ministry of Health, Praha, 1993-95; mem. adv. group WHO/EURO/NURS, Copenhagen, 1993—; mem. supervisory coun. Czech Acad. Sci., Prague, 1994—. Author: (workbooks) Ošetřovatelství I, 1980 (Ministry of Education award 1984), Základy Teorie Ošetřovatelství, 1996; chief editl. bd. Sestra, pres. editl. bd., 1991—; pres. editl. bd. Zdravotnická pracovnice, 1987-91; contbr. articles to profl. jours. Mem. Czech Soc. Nursing (hon., mem. com., pres. nurses sect. 1972-94), Sigma Theta Tau. Roman Catholic. Avocations: collection of porcelain, books, tourism. Home: Mirovická 1088/42, 18200 Prague 8, Czech Republic Office: Inst Nursing Theory & Pract, Studnickova 5, 12000 Praha 2, Czech Republic

STANLEY, ANDREW PHILIP, scientist, chemistry researcher; b. Adelaide, Australia, July 16, 1971; s. Philip Gordon and Joan Lynette (Paulson) S.; m. Lyndal Peta Hill, Apr. 12, 1997. BSc with honors, Flinders U., South Australia, 1994; PhD, U. South Australia, 1999. Tutor Univ. Hall, Adelaide, Australia, 1994; rsch. fellow Murdoch U., Perth, Australia, 1999—. Contbr. articles to profl. jours. Mem. Royal Australian Chem. Inst. Avocations: golf, cycling, sailing. Office: Chemistry/MPS, Murdoch U South St, Murdoch 6150, Australia

STANLEY, BRIAN JORDAN, corporate lawyer; b. Duncan, Okla., Sept. 10, 1954; s. Elmer E. and Betty Sue Stanley; m. Ruth Anne Lynn Stanley, Apr. 6, 1979 (div. Mar. 1989); children: Lindsey Jordan, Brent Alan; m. Francine Michelle La Valle, Oct. 18, 1996. BA in Polit. Sci., U. Okla., 1979; JD with honors, Oklahoma City U., 1985. Bar: Okla. 1985, U.S. Dist. Ct. (we. dist.) Okla. 1985. Sports writer The Norman (Okla.) Transcript, 1979-80; oil and gas landman Milt McCullough, Oklahoma City, 1980-81; trust officer Liberty Nat. Bank & Trust, Oklahoma City, 1981-83; atty. Michael P. Rogalin, Oklahoma City, 1985-86, William H. Mattoon, Norman, 1986-87, Fed. Deposit Ins. Corp., Oklahoma City, 1987, Reed, Shadid & Pipes, Oklahoma City, 1987-88, Mosburg, Sears, Kunzman & Bollinger, Oklahoma City, 1988; v.p., corp. gen. counsel The Hefner Co., Inc., Oklahoma City, 1989—; bd. dirs. The Hefner Co., Inc.; trustee Dr. Brent Hisey Irrevocable Trust, Oklahoma City, 1998—. Contbr. articles to profl. jours. Mem. ABA, Okla. Bar Assn. Republican. Episcopalian. Avocations: golf, Italian and German language, theology. Office: The Hefner Co Inc PO Box 2177 Oklahoma City OK 73101-2177

STANLEY, DANIEL JEAN, geological oceanographer; b. Metz, France, Apr. 14, 1934; came to U.S., 1941, naturalized, 1946; s. Paul Emile and Madeleine (Simon) Streisguth; m. Adrienne N. Ellis, Mar. 5, 1988; children: Marc Michel, Eric Paul, Brian Northrop, Natalie Anne, Susan N. B.Sc., Cornell U., 1956; M.Sc., Brown U., 1958; D.Sc., U. Grenoble, France, 1961. Rsch. geologist French Petroleum Inst., Paris, 1958-61; asst. to dir. U.S. Waterways Expt. Sta., Vicksburg, Miss., 1961-63; asst. prof. geology Ottawa U., Ont., Can., 1963-64; rsch. assoc. prof. Dalhousie U., Halifax, N.S., Can., 1964-66; sr. scientist, oceanographer, dir. Deltas-Global Change Program div. sedimentology Smithsonian Instn., Washington, 1966—; adj. prof. U. Québec, 1992—; cons. to govts. Mediterranean countries; sci. expert Internat. Ct. Justice, 1981—. Editor: New Concepts of Continental Margin Sedimentation, 1969, Mediterranean Sea: A Natural Sedimentation Laboratory, 1972, Marine Sediment Transport and Environmental Management, 1976, Sedimentation in Submarine Canyons, Fans and Trenches, 1978, The Shelfbreak: A Critical Interface on Continental Margins, 1983, Geological Evolution of the Mediterranean Basin, 1985, Nile Delta, A Geological Excursion, 1997; contbr. chpts to books, articles to profl. jours. Bd. dirs. Mediterranean Basin and Deltas Programs. Served to capt. C.E., U.S. Army, 1961-63. Recipient médaille Alpes Maritimes, France, 1976, F.P. Shepard medal Soc. for Sedimentary Geology, 1990, Gold Trident medal Italian Acad., 1998; named Hon. Prof., East China U., 1995; grantee in field. Fellow Geol. Soc. Am., AAAS, Geol. Soc. Belgium; mem. Internat. Assn. Sedimentologists, Am. Assn. Petroleum Geologists, Soc. Econ. Paleontologists and Mineralogists, Geol. Soc. Washington, Sigma Xi. Republican. Club: Cosmos (Washington). Office: Smithsonian Instn Sedimentology Dv Washington DC 20560-0001

STANLEY, DUFFY B., architect; b. Midland, Tex., Feb. 14, 1923; s. Benjamin M. and Mary L. (White) S.; m. Irene M. Muller, July 31, 1948; children: Sheila, Lars, Brock, Sonya, Sharon. BArch, Tex. A&M U., 1948; hon. diploma, U. Autonoma de Cd. Juarez, Mex., 1977. Registered architect, Tex., N.Mex. Draftsman, designer J.J. Black, Architect, Midland, 1948-51; job capt. Carroll & Daeuble Architects, El Paso, Tex., 1951-57; pvt. practice El Paso, 1957—. Author: Open Space in the El Paso Region, 1970. Vice chmn. Citizen's Environ. Coun. of El Paso, 1972-73; dir. Mission Heritage Assn. of El Paso, 1977-84; chmn. GARC com. of West Tex. Coun. Govts., El Paso, 1977; chmn. El Paso County Hist. Commn., 1978, Zoning Bd. of Adjustment, El Paso, 1970; mem. Open Space Com., El Paso, 1970-71. Capt. U.S. Army, 1943-46; ETO. Recipient Caudill award Tex. Assn. Sch. Bd. and AIA Tex., 1996. Mem. AIA (chpt. pres. 1964, Design award 1995, Service to Profession award 1991), FAIA. Avocations: tennis, reading, travel, family activities. Office: 303 Texas Ave Ste 402 El Paso TX 79901-1452

STANLEY, HELEN CAMILLE, composer, musician; b. Tampa, Fla.; d. Edward and Lucy Gage (Crehore) S.; widowed; 1 child, Helen Marjorie. MusB, Cin. Conservatory Music, 1951; MusM, Fla. State U., 1954; BS, Muskingum Coll., 1961. Instr. music and fine arts Jacksonville (Fla.) U., 1962-67; instr. music in communications Jones Coll., Jacksonville, 1965-66; composer, condr. St. Paul's by-the-Sea, Jacksonville Beach, Fla., 1976; composer-in-residence, pianist Fla. Contemporary Ensemble, Jacksonville, 1986; ind. composer, lectr., pianist, 1963—; cons. Beaches Fine Arts Series, Neptune Beach, Fla., 1973—. Composer Rhapsody for Electronic Tape and Orchestra, 1972 (Composition Commn. award), Allegro, Passacaglia, Sonata for trombone and piano, various instrumental and vocal works, Evocation I for piano; orchestral works on CD include: Fanfare for Orchestra (Warsaw Nat. Philharmonic Orch. and Owensboro Symphony), 1994, Passacaglia (St. Petersburg Philharmonic), Concerto Romantico, Prague, 1997, Fanfare for Orchestra (All American Celebration by Owensboro Symphony). Mem. Nat. Soc. Arts and Letters, Soc. Mayflower Descs., 1987—. Recipient Pogner Music Composition award, Cin., 1950, C. Hugo Ensemble Composition award, Cin., 1951, Anthem Descant award St. Paul's by-the-Sea, 1980, Art Ventures Fund award, 1992, Jacksonville Cmty. Found. award, 1994; named Outstanding Achievements Classical Music, Jacksonville, 1997. Mem. ASCAP, Am. Music Ctr., Am. Keyboard Artists, Performing Arts Directory, Pi Kappa Lambda. Avocations: art, walking, dancing. Home: 1768 Emory Cir S Jacksonville FL 32207-7707 Studio: Aladdin Farm 12047 Aladdin Rd Jacksonville FL 32223-3201

STANLEY, JOHN, educational administrator, financial consultant; b. Trivandrum, Kerala, India, May 5, 1953; s. John Peter and Joyce (Joshua) Lazarus. B in Commerce, U. Kerala, 1974; A, Inst. Co. Secs. of India, New Delhi, 1986; LLB, U. Pune, India, 1987; diploma in taxation, U. Pune, 1992; diploma in fin. mgmt., Indira Gandhi Nat. Open U., New Delhi, 1997. Asst. auditor Servsda Pvt. Ltd., Madras, India, 1980-82; sec. India Fin. Assn. of SDA, Madras, 1982-84; fin. cons. Gen. Conf. 7th Day Adventists, Pune, 1985-87, asst. treas., 1987-89, 89-90; assoc. treas. Gen. Conf. 7th Day Adventists, Hosur, India, 1990-93; dir. fin. Manipal (India) Acad. Higher Edn., 1993-99; CFO Mahe Consultancy Svcs., Manipal, 1998—; advisor fin. Manipal Acad. Higher Edn., 1999—; fin. cons. Manipal Edn. and Med. Group, Ltd., 1995—, Manipal Pas Found., 1995—, Healthcare and Wellness Found., Ltd., Bangalore, India, 1998—, Med. Relief Soc., 1996—, Manipal Edn. Network, 1997—, Manipal Heart Found. Pvt. Ltd., Bangalore, 1997—, JVMC Corp. Sdn Bhd, Malaysia, 1998—; mgmt. cons. Christian Med. Coll., Ludhiana, India, 1989-92; mem. hon. faculty dept. bus. Spice Meml. Coll., Pune, 1984-93; fin. advisor Sikkim-Manipal U. Health, Med. and technol. Scis., 1998—; fin. cons. Manipal Health System Ltd., 1999—, Valley View Travels Pvt. Ltd., 1999—; dir. MNE Technologies Pvt. Ltd., 2000—. Advisor British Med. Jour. (S.E. Asia Edit.) 1997—, Jour. of the Am. Acad. Pediats. (Indian Edit.), 1997—, British Jour. Ophthalmology (S. Asia Edit.), 1998—. Chmn. Found. for Integrated Voluntary Outreach, Bangalore, 1992—, SN David Found., Trivandrum, 1993—; bd. dirs. Teach Internat., Inc., Md., 1990—; treas. Manipal Inst. for Devel. of Human Resources, 1996—; mem. high power com. on savs. and efficiency Univ. Grants Commn., New Delhi, 1998—. Recipient Cmty. Svc. award Kares, Inc., Md., 1992, Dr. TMA Pai Centennial Rsch. award, 1998, Rising Personalities of India award, 1999; rsch. fellow Ctr. for Policy Rsch., New Delhi. Fellow United Writers Assn. of India; mem. Am. Acctg. Assn., Internat. Soc. for Strategic Mgmt. and Planning (Strategic Leadership Forum), Inst. Co. Secs. of India (assoc.), Inst. Internal Auditors, Inc. (assoc.). Seventh Day Adventist. Avocations: reading, nature walks, gardening. Office: Manipal Acad Higher Edn, University Bldg, Manipal 576 119, India

STANLEY, JOHN RICHARD, virologist, research scientist; b. Hemel Hempstead, Hertfordshire, Eng., Apr. 17, 1950; s. Reginald Edgar Allan and Margaret Laura (Erskine) S.; m. Judith Rosemary Haseler; children: Alison Kate, Thomas James, Eleanor Rose. BS, U. East Anglia, Norwich, Eng., 1971; PhD, U. East Anglia, 1975. Rsch. scientist Inst. de Biologie Moleculaire/Celluaire U. Louis Pasteur, Strasbourg, France, 1975-78; rsch. scientist IBMC Agrl. U., Wageningen, The Netherlands, 1978-80, John Innes Ctr., Norwich, Eng., 1980—. Sr. editor: Virology, 1995—; contbr. articles to profl. jours. Avocations: carp fishing, football, gardening, bird watching. Home: South Cottage, Victoria Ln Deopham, NR18 9DU Wymondham Norfolk, England Office: John Innes Ctr, Colney Ln, Norwich NR4 7UH, England

STANLEY, MARGARET KING, performing arts administrator; b. San Antonio, Dec. 11, 1929; d. Creston Alexander and Margaret (Haymore) King; children: Torrey Margaret, Jean Cullen. Student, Mary Baldwin Coll., 1948-50; BA, U. Tex., Austin, 1952; MA, U. Incarnate Word, 1959. Tchg. cert. 1953. Elem. tchr. San Antonio Ind. Sch. Dist., 1953-54, 55-56, Arlington County Schs., Va., 1954-55, Ft. Sam Houston Schs., San Antonio, 1955-57; art and art history tchr. St. Pius X Sch., San Antonio, 1959-60; English tchr. Trinity U., 1963-65; designer-mfr., owner CrisStan Clothes, Inc., San Antonio, 1967-73; founder, exec. dir. San Antonio Performing Arts Assn., 1976-92; founder Arts Coun. of San Antonio, 1962; founding chmn. Joffrey Workshop, San Antonio, 1979; originator, founding chairwoman Student Music Fair, San Antonio, 1963; host On Stage with Margaret Stanley Sta. KTRU-FM, San Antonio, 1983-98; mem. Met. Opera Nat. Coun., 1969-80; pres. San Antonio Symphony League, 1971-74; v.p. Arts Coun. San Antonio, 1975; bd. govts. Artists Alliance San Antonio, 1982; founding organizer Musica San Antonio, 1997-98; v.p., founder San Antonio Opera Guild, 1974-76, founder Early Music Festival, San Antonio, 1990-92; mem. adv. bd. Hertzberg Circus Mus., San Antonio Dance Umbrella, Houston Early Music, Morgan-Scott Ballet. Originator of the idea for a new ballet created for the City of San Antonio, "Jamboree," commd. from the Joffrey Ballet, world premiere in San Antonio, 1984. Recipient Outstanding Tchr. award Arlington County Sch. Dist., 1954, Today's Woman award San Antonio Light Newspaper, 1980, Woman of Yr. in Arts award San Antonio Express News, 1983, Emily Smith award for outstanding alumni Mary Baldwin Coll., 1973, Erasmus medal The Dutch Consulate, 1992, Mary Baldwin Sesquicentennial medallion, 1992; named to Women's Hall of Fame, San Antonio, 1984, Disting. Alumnae, St. Mary's Hall, 1995, Opera Guild award 2000; tchg. fellow Trinity U., San Antonio, 1964-66. Mem. Internat. Soc. for the Performing Arts (regional rep. 1982-85, bd. dirs. 1991-97), Assn. Performing Arts Presenters, Women in Comm. (Headliner award 1982, San Antonio chpt.), Jr. League of San Antonio, Battle of Flowers Assn., S.W. Performing Arts Presenters (chmn. 1988-92). Avocations: traveling, reading, cooking, music, dance.

STANLEY, MARLYSE REED, horse breeder; b. Fairmont, Minn., Sept. 19, 1934; d. Glenn Orson and Lura Mabel (Ross) Reed; m. James Arthur Stapleton, 1956 (div. 1976); 1 child, Elisabeth Katharene; m. John David Stanley, Oct. 22, 1982. BA, U. Minn., 1957. Registered breeder Arabian horses in Spain, 1976-94. Chmn. bd. dirs. Sitting Rock Spanish Arabians, Inc., Greensboro, N.C., 1978-81; pres. Sitting Rock Spanish Arabians, Inc., Hollister, Calif., 1981-91, Stanley Ranch, Yerington, Nev., 1991—; bd. dirs. Glenn Reed Tire Co., Fairmont, Minn. Author Arabian hunter/jumper rules Am. Horse Shows Assn.; contbr. articles to horse jours. Named Palomino Queen of Minn., 1951, Miss Fairmont, 1954, Miss Minn., 1955. Mem. AAUW, Arabian Horse Registry Am., Internat. Arabian Assn. (bd. dirs. region 10, Minn. and Wis. 1973-76, nat. chmn. hunter-jumper com. 1976-81, chair IAHA sport horse rules com. 1998—), Minn. Arabian Assn. (bd. dirs. 1972-75), Am. Paint Horse Assn. (nat. bd. dirs. 1967-70), Assn. Española de Criadores de Caballos Arabes (Spain), World Arabian Horse Assn., Alpha Xi Delta. Republican. Episcopalian. Avocations: fox hunting, fishing, breeding and importing Arabian horses.

STANLEY, RICHARD HOLT, consulting engineer; b. Muscatine, Iowa, Oct. 20, 1932; s. Claude Maxwell and Elizabeth Mabel (Holthues) S.; m. Mary Jo Kennedy, Dec. 20, 1953; children: Lynne Elizabeth, Sarah Catherine, Joseph Holt. BSEE, BSME, Iowa State U., 1955; MS in Sanitary Engring., U. Iowa, 1963. Lic. profl. engr., Iowa. With Stanley Cons. Inc., Muscatine, Iowa, 1955—, pres., 1971-87, chmn., 1984—; also bd. dirs. Stanley Cons. Inc.; bd. dirs. Dover Resources, Inc.; bd. dirs. HON Industries, Inc., vice-chmn., 1979—; chmn Nat. Constrn. Industry Coun., 1978, Com. Fed. Procurement Archtl.-Engring. Svcs., 1979; pres. Ea. Iowa C.C., Bettendorf, 1966-68; mem. indsl. adv. coun. Iowa State U. Coll. Engring., Ames, 1969-97, chmn., 1979-81. Contbr. articles to profl. jours. Bd. dirs. N.E.-Midwest Inst., 1989-95, treas., 1991-93, chmn., 1993-95; bd. dirs. Stanley Found., 1956—, pres., 1984—, chmn., 1995—; bd. dirs. Muscatine Health Support Found., pres., 1984—; bd. dirs. Muscatine United Way, 1969-75, Iowa State U. Meml. Union, 1968-83, U. Dubuque, Iowa, 1977-93, Inst. Social and Econ. Devel., 1992—, Unity Health Sys., 1999—, chmn. 1999—; bd. govs. Iowa State U. Achievement Found., 1982-96. Recipient Young Alumnus award Iowa State U. Alumni Assn., 1966, Disting. Svc. award Muscatine Jaycees, 1967, Profl. Achievement citation Coll. Engring., Iowa State U., 1977, Anson Marston medal Iowa State U., 1991, Harry S. Truman disting. svc. award Am. Assn. C.C., 1998; Disting. Alumni Achievement award U. Iowa Alumni Assn., 1999, award for Citizen Diplomacy, Nat. Coun. for Internat. Visitors, 2000; named Sr. Engr. of Yr., Joint Engring. Com. Quint Cities, 1973; named to Disting. Engring. Alumni Acad., U. Iowa, 1998; inducted into Muscatine H.S. Hall of Honor, 2000. Fellow ASCE, Am. Cons. Engrs. Coun. (pres. 1976-77, Cmty. Svc. award 1997, Disting. Award of Merit 1998), Iowa Acad. Sci.; mem. IEEE (sr.), ASME, Am. Soc. Engring. Edn., Nat. Soc. Profl. Engrs., Cons. Engrs. Coun. Iowa (pres. 1967), Iowa Engring. Soc. (pres. 1973-74, John Dunlap-Sherman Woodward award 1967, Disting. Svc. award 1980, Voice of Engr. award 1987, Herbert Hoover Centennial award 1989), Muscatine C. of C. (pres. 1972-73), C. of C. of U.S. (constrn. action coun. 1976-91), Rotary, Tau Beta Pi, Phi Kappa Phi, Pi Tau Sigma, Eta Kappa Nu. Presbyterian (elder). Home: 601 W 3rd St Muscatine IA 52761-3119 Office: Stanley Cons Inc Stanley Bldg Muscatine IA 52761

STANNARD, FRANK RUSSELL, physics educator; b. London, Dec. 24, 1931; s. Frank Samuel and Lillie (Birkin) S.; m. Ann Heath, Jan. 25, 1958 (div. 1978); children: Adrian, Tracy, Peter, Carolyn; m. Glenys Margaret Hawkins, May 26, 1984. BS in Physics, U. Coll., London, 1953, PhD, 1956. Rsch. asst. U. Coll., London, 1956-59, lectr., 1960-69, hon. rsch. fellow, 1969-82; physicist Lawrence Radiation Lab., Berkeley, Calif., 1959-60; reader Open Univ., Milton Keynes, Eng., 1969-71; prof. physics Open U., Milton Keynes, Eng., 1971-97, pro vice chancellor, 1975-77; prof. emeritus, 1999—; vis. fellow Ctr. Theol. Inquiry, Princeton, N.J., 1987-88; v.p. Inst. Physics, Eng., 1987-91. Author: Science and the Renewal of Belief, 1982, Grounds for Reasonable Belief, 1989, The Time and Space of Uncle Albert, 1989, Black Holes and Uncle Albert, 1991, Here I Am!, 1992, World of 1001 Mysteries, 1993, Doing Away with God?, 1993, Uncle Albert and the Quantum Quest, 1994, Science and Wonders, 1996, The God Experiment, 1999, The New World of Mr. Tompkins, 1999; contbr. over 60 articles to profl. jours. Recipient U.K. project award Templeton Trust, 1986; U. Coll. London fellow, 2000—. Fellow Inst. Physics. Anglican. Avocations: sculpture, gardening, music. Home: 21 Alwins Field, Linslade Bedfordshire LU7 7UF, England Office: Open U, Milton Keynes MK7 6AA, England

STANSBERY, DAVID HONOR, biology diversity educator, malacologist; b. Upper Sandusky, Ohio, May 5, 1926; s. Honor Gerald and Daisy Elizabeth (Kirby) S.; m. Mary Lois Pease, June 16, 1948; children: Michael David, Mark Andrew, Kathleen Mary, Linda Carol. BS, Ohio State U., 1950, MS, 1953, PhD, 1960. Instr. Ohio State U., Columbus, 1956-62, asst. prof., 1962-66, assoc. prof., 1966-71; state curator of natural history Ohio State Mus., Columbus, 1962-72; vis. scientist Smithsonian Instn., Washington, 1973-74; sr. rsch. assoc. The Ohio State Mus., Columbus, 1972—; dir. mus. of zoology Ohio State U., Columbus, 1970-92, prof. zoology, 1971-91, curator of mollusks Mus. of Biol. Diversity, 1962-2000, prof. emeritus, 1991—; adv. bd. Ohio Biol. Survey, 1961-72; exec. com. Ohio Acad. of Sci., 1961-69; chair collection stds. Coun. of Systematic Malacologists, 1977-81; bd. govs. The Nature Conservancy, 1979-86; rsch. adv., guest lectr. Huazhong Agrl. U., Wuhan, Hubei, China, 1992; mem. faculty Upper Cumberland Biol. Sta. Tenn. Tech. U., 1987-91; presenter in field. assoc. editor: Ohio Jour. Sci., 1960-61, editor, 1961-64; contbr. articles to profl. jours. Bd. trustees Columbus Audubon Soc., 1969-73; bd. dirs. Am. Rivers Cons. Coun., 1973-88. Recipient Oak Leaf award Nature Conservancy, 1977, Ohio Conservation Achievement award Ohio Dept. Natural Resouces, 1974, Lifetime Achievement award Freshwater Mollusk Conservation Soc., 1999, Herbert Osborn award Ohio Biol. Survey, 1999; grantees U.S. Dept. Interior, U.S. Dept. Commerce, U.S. Army Corps of Engrs., Battelle, Am. Electric Power, and others. Fellow AAAS, Ohio Acad. of Sci., Acad. of Zoology; mem. Am. Malacol. Union (pres. 1970-71), Sigma Xi (pres. 1974-75). Achievements include building the world's largest freshwater bivalve mollusk collection at the Ohio State University Museum of Zoology. Avocations: geology, history of science, evolution of ethics linguistics. E-mail: stansbury.1@osu.edu. Fax: 614-292-7774. Home: 32 Amazon Pl Columbus OH 43214-3502 Office: Mus of Biol Diversity Ohio State Univ 1315 Kinnear Rd Columbus OH 43212-1157

STANSELL, LELAND EDWIN, JR., lawyer, educator; b. Central, S.C., July 13, 1934; s. Leland Edwin and Hettie Katherine (Hollis) S.; children: James Leland, Susan. BS, Fla. So. Coll., 1957; LLB, U. Miami, Fla., 1961, JD, 1968. Bar: Fla. 1961; cert. civil mediator Fla. Supreme Ct., U.S. Dist. Ct. Fla. Assoc. Wicker & Smith, Miami, 1961-62, ptnr., 1962-75; pvt. practice, Miami, 1975-99, Leland E. Stansell, Jr., P.A., Miami, 1995—; chmn. Appellate Jud. Nominating Com., Dade County (Fla.), 1983-87; mem. adv. com. Am. Arbitration Assn., 1975-90. Served with U.S. Army, 1957. Mem. ABA (ho. of dels. 1982-86), Fla. Bar (bd. govs. 1966-70, 70-80), Dade County Bar Assn. (dir. 1969-72, exec. com. 1974-75, pres. 1975-76), U. Miami Law Alumni Assn. (dir., officer, pres. 1968-69), Fla. Criminal Def. Attys. Assn. (treas. 1964-66), Am. Judicature Soc., Am. Bd. Trial Advs., Internat. Assn. Def. Counsel, Fla. Acad. Profl. Mediators, Fedn. Ins. Counsel, Miami Beach Rod and Reel Club (pres.), Coral Reef Yacht Club, Bankers Club, Ocean Reef Yacht Club, Delta Theta Phi (pres. Miami alumni chpt. 1966, regional dir. 1968. Office: 19 W Flagler St Miami FL 33130-4400

STANSELL, RONALD BRUCE, investment banker; b. Hammond, Ind., Apr. 9, 1945; s. Herman Bruce and Helen Rose Stansell; m. Kathie Van Atta, Oct. 2, 1976; children: Kelsey, Kymberlie. BA, Wittenberg U., 1967; MA, Miami U., Oxford, Ohio, 1969. Investment officer First Nat. Bank, Chgo., 1969-73; mgr. investments Chrysler Corp., Detroit, 1973; asst. v.p. A.G. Becker, Chgol, 1973-76; v.p. Blyth Eastman Dillon, Chgo., 1976-79, Dean Witter Reynolds Inc., Chgo., 1979-82, First Boston Corp., 1982-88; sr. v.p. Prudential-Bache Securities, Chgo., 1988-90; ptnr. William Blair & Co., 1991-99; pres. Oakmont of Carolina, 1999—. Mem. Mettawa (Ill.) Zoning Bd., 1978-80; trustee Village of Mettawa, 1980-91, village treas., 1977-78. With USMCR, 1968-74. Mem. Bond Club Chgo., Investment Analyst Soc., Fixed Income Group, Bob O'Link Golf Club, Grandfather Golf Club, LaSalle Club, Forest Creek Golf Club, Belfair Golf Club, Berkeley Hall Club.

STANTON, ELIZABETH MCCOOL, lawyer; b. Lansdale, Pa., Apr. 12, 1947; d. Leo J. and Helen M. (Gillooly) McCool; m. Robert J. Stanton, June 13, 1970; children: Jonathan R., James Alfred. BBA, Drexel U., 1969; JD magna cum laude, U. Houston, 1979. Bar: Tex. 1979, U.S. Dist. Ct. (so. dist.) Tex. 1980, Ohio 1982, U.S. Dist. Ct. (so. dist.) Ohio 1983, U.S. Ct. Appeals (6th cir.) 1986, (3d cir.) 1992, U.S. Supreme Ct. 1990. Assoc. Friedman & Chaffin, Houston, 1979-80, Law Offices of Elaine Brady, Houston, 1980-81, Moots, Cope & Weinberger Co., L.P.A., Columbus, Ohio, 1981-86; prin. Moots, Cope and Kizer Co. L.P.A., Columbus, 1986-89, Moots, Cope, Stanton and Kizer, P.A., Columbus, 1989-91, Moots, Cope & Stanton Co., L.P.A., Columbus, 1991-98, Moots, Cope, Stanton & Carter, Co., L.P.A., Columbus, 1998-2000; sole practice Columbus, 2000—; mem. Ohio Supreme Ct./Ohio State Bar Assn. Task Force on Gender Fairness in the Legal Profession, 1991-93. Drexel Bd. Trustees scholar, 1965-67, Internat. Ladies Garment Workers Union scholar, 1965-69. Mem. ABA, State Bar Tex., Ohio Bar Assn., Columbus Bar Assn. (chair Labor Law Com. 1996-98), Nat. Assn. Women Lawyers (Ohio Reps. 1995—), Ohio Women's Bar Assn. (founding mem., bd. trustees 1994-97), Women Lawyers Franklin County (treas. 1989-90, bd. dirs. 1990-92), St. Thomas More Soc., Phi Kappa Phi, Beta Gamma Sigma. Democrat. Roman Catholic. Office: PO Box 12545 Columbus OH 43212-0545

STANTON, JEANNE FRANCES, retired lawyer; b. Vicksburg, Miss., Jan. 22, 1920; d. John Francis and Hazel (Mitchell) S. Student, George Washington U., 1938-39; BA, U. Cin., 1940; JD, Salmon P. Chase Coll. Law, 1954. Bar: Ohio 1954. Chief clk. Selective Svc. Bd., Cin., 1940-43; instr. USAAF Tech. Schs., Biloxi, Miss., 1943-44; with Procter & Gamble, Cin., 1945-84, legal asst., 1952-54, head advt. svcs. sect. legal divsn., trade practice dept., 1954-73, mgr. advt. svcs., legal divsn., 1973-84, ret., 1984. Team capt. Cmty. Chest Cin., 1983; mem. ann. meeting com. Archaeol. Inst. Am., 1983; trustee, asst. corr. sec., statutory agt. Friends of Bronze Age Archaeology in the Aegean area, 1987—. Mem. ABA (chmn. subcom. D of com. 307 copyright sect. 1987-88, 89, 90), Ohio Bar Assn. (chmn. uniform state laws com. 1968-70), Cin. Bar Assn. (sec. law day com. 1965-66, chmn. com. on preservation hist. documents 1968-71), Vicksburg and Warren County Hist. Soc., Cin. Hist. Soc., Intercontinental Biog. Assn., Lawyers Club Cin. (exec. com. Home: 3580 Shaw Ave Apt 323 Cincinnati OH 45208-1454

STANTON, JOHN JEFFREY, editor, broadcast journalist, government programs director, analyst, professional society administrator; b. Wichita Falls, Tex., July 19, 1956; s. John Joseph Jr. and Joan (Marley) S.; m. Scylla Maria Silva, Jan. 6, 1981; 1 child, Damien Kristian. BS in Pub. Adminstrn.

and Bus. Adminstrn., Nichols Coll., 1978; M in Pub. Adminstrn., U. Detroit, 1980. Rsch. asst. Am. Enterprise Inst., Washington, 1977; rep. aide R.I. Ho. of Reps., Providence, 1977-78; mng. editor Am. Politics, Washington, 1982, assoc. editor, 1983, corp. advisor, 1984, sr. editor, 1985-87; editor, govt. programs mgr. ENTEK, Alexandria, Va., 1988-90; govt. programs dir., cons. Tuckerman Group, Springfield, Va., 1991; comm. industry writer Arlington, Va., 1991—; program dir. TeleStrategies, McLean, Va., 1991-93; Washington corr., mem. editl. bd. Tech. Transfer Jour., 1994-98; editor Tech. Transfer Newsletter; asst. to pres., info. transfer specialist Am. Def. Preparedness Assn., Arlington, 1994-97; contbg. writer Nat. Def. Mag., 1996—; adminstrn. dir. Nat. Def. Indsl. Assn., Arlington, 1997—; Washington corr. Australian Def. Mag., 1998-99; creator, co-host (radio programs) Power Breakfast, Sta. WNTR, Washington, 1987, Am. Politics Radio, 1987; frequent guest broadcast journalist Stas. WNTR, WAMU-NPR, Washington, WBAL, Balt. and Washington areas. Polit. campaign cons. to Glenn Tenney, 1992—; commr. Arlington Little League Baseball, 1993, coach 1997—; mentor Arlington County Ct. Sys., 1997; varsity football coach Wakefield H.S., Arlington, Va., 1998—. Recipient Doers Honoree The Washington Times, 1988. Avocations: coaching youth sports programs. E-mail: jstanton@ndia.org.

STANTON, ROGER D., lawyer; b. Oct. 4, 1938; s. George W. and Helen V. (Peterson) S.; m. Judith L. Duncan, Jan. 27, 1962; children: Jeffrey B., Brady D., Todd A. AB, U. Kans., 1960, JD, 1963. Bar: Kans. 1963, U.S. Dist. Ct. Kans. 1963, U.S. Ct. Appeals (10th cir.) 1972, U.S. Supreme Ct. 1973. Assoc. Stanley, Schroeder, Weeks, Thomas & Lysaught, Kansas City, 1968-72; Assoc. Weeks, Thomas & Lysaught, Kansas City, 1969-80, also bd. dirs., chmn. exec. com., 1981-82; also bd. dirs., chmn. exec. com. Stinson, Mag & Fizzell, Kansas City, 1983-96, chmn. products practice group, also bd. dirs., 1993-95; ptnr. Berkowitz, Feldmiller, Stanton, Brandt, Williams & Stueve, Prairie Village, Kans., 1997—. Chmn. bd. editors Jour. Kans. Bar Assn., 1975-83; contbr. articles to profl. jours. Active Boy Scouts Am., 1973-79; pres. YMCA Youth Football Club, 1980-82; co-chmn. Civil Justice Reform Act com. Dist. of Kans., 1991-95; bd. dirs. Kans. Appleseed Found., 2000—. Fellow Am. Coll. Trial Lawyers (state chmn. 1984-86); mem. Internat. Assn. Def. Counsel, Exec. com., 1994-99 East Kansas/West Miss. Chpt., Am. Bd. Trial Adv., Def. Rsch. Inst. (state co-chmn. 1979-90, Exceptionl Performance award 1979), Kans. Bar Assn. (Pres.'s award 1982), Johnson County Bar Found. (pres., trustee), Chmn. Bench/Bar Com. of Johnson Co. Bar Assn., Kans. Assn. Def. Counsel (pres. 1977-78), Kans. Inn. Ct., U. Kans. Sch. Law Alumni Assn. (bd. dirs. 1972-75). Office: Berkowitz Feldmiller Stanton Brandt Williams & Stueve 4121 W 83rd St Ste 227 Prairie Vlg KS 66208-5323

STANTON, SARA BAUMGARDNER, retired secondary school educator; b. Johnstown, Pa., Sept. 11, 1930; d. Emmanuel Boyd and Ethel Leora (Shaffer) Baumgardner; m. George Welles Stanton, June 20, 1953; children: David Mark, Frederick George. BS in Edn., Bucknell U., 1952. Tchr. Adams-Summerhill High Sch., Sidman, Pa., 1952-53, Waymart (Pa.) High Sch., 1953-55, Honesdale (Pa.) High Sch., 1955-57; substitute tchr. Wayne County Sch. Dist., 1957-77; tchr. Honesdale High Sch., 1977-90; ret., 1990; leadership instr. Pa. Assn. Hosp. Auxs., Harrisburg, Pa., 1976-97. Den mother Cub Pack 104, 1965-69; bd. dirs. Health Systems Agy., Wilkes-Barre, Pa., 1983-86; adv. bd. Pa. State U.-Scranton Campus, 1977-85; trustee Wayne County Meml. Hosp., Honesdale, 1974-86. Recipient Leader's Fellowship award Nat. Bd. YMCA, 1964, B'nai B'rith Citizenship Citation, 1974 (co-recipient with husband). Mem. AAUW (br. pres. 1980-81), Pa. Assn. Hosp. Auxs. (mem. leadership tng. team 1975-80, 91-97, chmn. state ann. conv. 1985, pres. 1986-88), Pa. Assn. Sch. Retirees, Hosp. Assn. Pa. (mem. cmty. concerns com. 1974-75, ex officio 1986-88), Wayne County Hist. Soc. (bd. dirs. 1991-92, 95-98, sec. 1995-97), Woman's Club Honesdale (pres. 1958-60), Pa. Fedn. of Women's Clubs (edn. chmn. 1962-66), Wayne County Fedn. of Women's Clubs (pres. 1960-62). Republican. Methodist. Avocations: travel, grandchildren. Home: 1512 West St Honesdale PA 18431-1764

STANTON, STUART LAWRENCE, obstetrician/gynecologist; b. London, Oct. 24, 1938; s. Michael and Sarah (Joseph) S.; m. Julia Heller, Feb. 17, 1991; children: Claire, Talia, Joanna Tamara, Noah. Mb BS, City of London Sch., 1956. Cons. ob/gyn St. Helier Hosp., Carshalton, Surrey, Eng., 1974-84; cons. gynecologist Dept. Ob/Gyn., St. George's Hosp., London, 1984—; prof. pelvic reconstruction; mem. sci. bd. Urologia Internationalis, Switzerland, 1983. Asst. editor Brit. Jour. Obstetrics and Gynecology, 1981-85, editorial bd., 1981; editorial bd. Neurology and Urodynamics, 1982; contbr. articles to profl. jours.; editor: Principles of Gynaecological Surgery, Gynaecology, 3d edition; co-editor: Clin. Urogynaecology, 2nd edition. Recipient Victor and Bonney prize, Royal Coll. Surgeons, Eng., 1984. Mem. Brit. Assn. Urol. Surgeons, Internat. Continence Soc., Soc. Gynecologic Surgeons, Royal Coll. Obstetricians and Gynecologists (council 1980-86). Avocations: photography, travel, music, literture, ceramics. Home: 1 Church Hill, London SW19 7BN, England Office: Dept Ob/Gyn, Saint Georges Hosp, London SW17, England also: Flat 10 43 Wimpole St, London W1M 7AF, England

STANTON, WILLIAM ANTHONY, diplomat; b. Jersey City, N.J., Jan. 17, 1947; s. Harold Arthur Stanton and Armen Katherine Kharajian; m. Karen Clark Stanton, Sept. 14, 1984; children: Katherine Ruth, Elizabeth Armen. BA, Fordham U., 1968; MA, U. N.C., 1970, PhD, 1978. Fgn. svc. officer, 1978—; polit. officer U.S. Embassy, Beijing, 1987-90; sr. tng. Hoover Instn., Stanford, Calif., 1990-91; polit.-mil. affairs officer U.S. Embassy, Islamabad, Pakistan, 1991-93; spl. asst. for East Asian affairs Office Under Sec. for Polit. Affairs, U.S. Dept. State, Washington, 1993-94; dep. dir. office Chinese and Mongolian affairs U.S. Dept. State, Washington, 1994-95; min. counselor for polit. affairs U.S. Embassy, Beijing, 1995-98; sr. seminar U.S. Dept. State, Washington, 1998-99, dir. office of UN polit. affairs, 1999—. Mem. Am. Fgn. Svc. Assn., Phi Beta Kappa. E-mail: stantonwa@state.gov. Office: US Dept State IO/UNP Rm 6334 Washington DC 20520-0001

STANTON, WILLIAM JOHN, JR., marketing educator, author; b. Chgo., Dec. 15, 1919; s. William John and Winifred (McGann) S.; m. Imma Mair, Sept. 14, 1978; children by previous marriage: Kathleen Louise, William John III. BS, Ill. Inst. Tech., 1940; MBA, Northwestern U., 1941, PhD, 1948. Mgmt. trainee Sears Roebuck & Co., 1940-41; instr. U. Ala., 1941-44; auditor Olan Mills Portrait Studios, Chattanooga, 1944-46; asst. prof., asso. prof. U. Wash., 1948-55; prof. U. Colo., Boulder, 1955-90; prof. emeritus, 1990—; head mktg. dept. U. Colo., 1955-71, acting dean, 1963-64; assoc. dean U. Colo. (Sch. Bus.), 1964-67. Author: Economic Aspects of Recreation in Alaska, 1953; (with Rosann Spiro) Management of a Sales Force, 10th edit., 1999 (also Spanish and Protuguese transl.), (with others) Challenge of Business, 1975, (with M. Etzel and B. Walker) Marketing, 12th edit., 2000 (also Spanish, Portuguese and Indonesian transls.), (with M.S. Sommers and J.G. Barnes) Can. edit. Fundamentals of Marketing, 8th edit., 1998, (with K. Miller and R. Layton) Australian edit., 3d edit., 1994, (with R. Varaldo) Italian edit., 2d edit., 1990, (with others) South African edit., 1992; monographs on Alaska Tourist Industry, 1953-54; contbr. articles to profl. jours. Mem. Am. Mktg. Assn., Western Mktg. Assn., Beta Gamma Sigma. Roman Catholic. Home: 1445 Sierra Dr Boulder CO 80302-7846

STANUCH, HELENA, biostatician; b. Tarnow, Jastrzebia, Poland, Aug. 3, 1943; d. Jan and Anna Stanuch. MSc, Jagiellonian U., Poland, 1972; DSc, Med. Sch., 1988. Tchr. dept. biostats. and med. informatics Coll. Medicine/Jagiellonian Univ., Cracow, Poland. Office: Dept Biostats & Med Info, Kopernika 17, Cracow Poland

STAPF, KARL R.G., editor, researcher; b. Mannheim, Germany, July 25, 1937; m. Anneliese Hussong, Apr. 11, 1939; 2 children. Diploma, Johannes Gutenberg U., Mainz, Germany, 1964, DrRerNat, 1970, habilitation, 1999. Asst. Johannes Gutenberg U., 1964-70, lectr., 1970-82, sr. lectr., 1982—. Author: The Lithology of the Altenglan Formation, 1970 (Gutenberg U. prize 1970); editor: The Natural Preserve Region of Donnersberg/Palatinate, 1983; editor Mitteilungen Pollichia, 1975—, book series Pollichia, 1980—; contbr. articles to profl. jours. Mem. Geol. Soc., German Geol. Assn., Soc. Econ. Paleontologists Minerologists, Internat. Assn. Sedimentologists, Am. Assn. Petroleum Geologists, Soc. Geol. France. Fax: 6131-3924769. E-mail: stapf@mail.uni.mainz.de. Office: Johannes Gutenberg U, Johannes J Becher-Weg 21, D-55099 Mainz Germany

STAPLETON, NIGEL JOHN, financial executive; b. London, Nov. 1, 1946; s. Frederick Ernest John and Katie Margaret (Tyson) S.; m. Johanna Augusta Molhoek, Dec. 20, 1982; children: Henry James, Elizabeth Jane, Cornelia. BA with honors, Cambridge U., Eng., 1968; MA, Cambridge U., 1971. Internal auditor Unilever, Ltd., London, 1968-70; group mgr. internal audit Unilever, Ltd., 1970-73, sr. auditor, 1973-75; corp. planning mgr. Bocm Silcock, Hampshire, Eng., 1975-77; devel. dir. Bocm Silcock, 1977-80; comml. mem. N.Am. office Unilever PLC, London, 1980-82; v.p. fin. Unilever U.S., Inc., N.Y.C., 1982-86; fin. dir. Reed Internat. P.L.C., London, 1986-96; dep. chmn. Reed Internat., London, 1994-96; CFO Reed Elsevier PLC, London, 1993-96, chmn., 1996-98, co-chief exec., 1998-99; with Veronis Suhler, London, 2000—; chmn., co-head London Office Veronis Suhler Internat. Ltd., London; hon. fellow Fitzwilliam Coll., Cambridge, 1998—; non exec. dir. Allied Domecq Plc, GEC Co. Plc., Sun Life and Provincial Plc. Fellow Chartered Inst. Mgmt. Accts.; mem. United Oxford and Cambridge Club. Avocations: tennis, opera, classical music. Office: Veronis Suhler Internat Ltd, 3 St James Sq 8th Fl, London SW1Y 4JU, England*

STAPLETON, THOMAS, pediatrician, educator, advisor; b. Lynton, Devon, Eng., Feb. 1, 1920; s. Bryan and Ruth Jane (Friel) S. BM, BCh, Oxford U., 1943, DM, 1951; MD (hon.), Sydney (Australia) U., 1996. Radcliffe travelling fellow Oxford (Eng.) U., 1949-51; asst. dir. pediatric unit St. Mary's Hosp. Med. Sch., London, 1951-60; prof. child health U. Sydney, 1960-83, prof. emeritus, 1983; overseas fellow Churchill Coll., Cambridge, Eng., 1983; mem. protein-calorie adv. group UN System; chmn. child welfare adv. coun. New South Wales, Australia, 1964-83. Contbr. numerous articles to profl. jours. Capt. Royal Army Med. Corps, 194-46. Fellow Royal Coll. Physicians, Royal Australasian Coll. Physicians, Royal Coll. Pediatrics and Child Health (hon.), Am. Acad. Pediatrics (hon.); mem. Royal Soc. Medicine (pres. pediatric sect. 1986, hon. sec. internat. affairs pediatric sect. 1987-99, hon. fellow pediat. sect. 1999), Internat. Pediatric Assn. (sec.-gen. 1965-74), Australian Inst. Internat. Affairs (hon., life, pres. 1969-72), The Athenaeum. Avocations: travel, military colleges, gardening. E-mail: tom.stapleton@talk21.com. Home: Foundry Cottage Lane End, High Wycombe HP14 3JS, England

STARCEVIC, ALEKSANDER BRACO, civil engineer, researcher; b. Gospic, Croatia, Nov. 20, 1941; s. Ivan Nikola and Smiljka (Vojvodic) S.; m. Danica Maricic, Sept. 8, 1970; 1 child, Igor. BS, U. Zagreb, Croatia, 1970; cert. in bus. engring., U. Econ. and C. of C. Zagreb. Site agt. Hidroelektra, Zagreb, 1970-73, chief engr., 1976-80; mng. dir. Hidroelektra, Algeria, 1981-84; chief engr. INGRA, Nairobi, Kenya, 1974-75; fgn. works mgr. INGRA Group, Zagreb, 1985-88; mgr. SAB Ltd., Zagreb, 1989—; cons. engr. Coning Group, Tel Aviv, 1991-93. Mem. European Mouvement Croatia, 1991. Mem. Assn. Civil Engrs. Avocations: astronomy, tennis. Home: Jordanovac 113, 10000 Zagreb Croatia Office: SAB Ltd, Kelekova 2, 10000 Zagreb Croatia

STARCHER-DELL'AQUILA, JUDY LYNN, special education educator; b. Cuyahoga Falls, Ohio, Sept. 20, 1956; d. James Calvin and Jane Yvonne (Hart) Starcher; m. Richard Paul Dell'Aquila, July 16, 1983; 1 child, Jessica Lynn Dell'Aquila. BS in Hearing & Speech Scis., Ohio U., 1978; MEd in Deaf Edn., U. Cin., 1980; PhD in Spl. Edn., Kent State U., 1996. Cert. supr. and tchr., Ohio. Tchr. deaf Parma (Ohio) City Schs., 1978-79, Mayfield (Ohio) City Schs., 1980-81; tchr. deaf, low incidence work study coord. Trumbull County Ednl. Svc. Ctr., Warren, Ohio, 1981-84; work study coord. Cuyahoga Ednl. Svc. Ctr., Valley View, Ohio, 1984-88; instr., student tchg. supr. Kent (Ohio) State U., 1993-95; project dir. Children's Hosp. Med. Ctr./Family Child Learning Ctr., Tallmadge, Ohio, 1995-2000; coord. spl. edn. Cleveland Heights/University Heights (Ohio) City Sch. System, 2000—; Am. Sign Lang. instr. Cuyahoga C.C., Cleve., 1993-2000; dir. adv. bd. Hearing Impaired Toddler Infant & Families Program, Tallmadge, 1995-2000; mem. County Collaborative Group, Medina, Summit counties, Ohio, 1995-2000; state trainer SKI*HI, Logan, Utah, 1997—. Mem. Coun. Exceptional Children. Grantee Job Tng. & Partnership Act, Cleve., 1982, 86-88; Univ. fellow Kent State U., 1991. Democrat. Avocations: antique collector, exercise, reading. Home: 151 E Pleasant Valley Rd Seven Hills OH 44131-5601 Office: Cleveland Heights/University Heights Bd Edn 2155 Miramar Blvd University Ht OH 44118-3301

STARCHMAN, DALE EDWARD, medical radiation biophysics educator; b. Wallace, Idaho, Apr. 16, 1941; s. Hubert V. and Lottie M. (Alford) S.; m. Erlinda Socrates, Dec. 13, 1969; children: Ann, Cindy, Julie, Mark. Student, Rockhurst Coll., 1959-61; BS in Physics, Pitts. (Kans.) State U., 1963; MS in Radiation Biophysics, U. Kans., 1965, PhD in Radiation Biophysics, 1968. Cert. Radiol. Physicist, Health Physicist, Med. Physicist. Chief health physicist IIT Rsch. Inst., Chgo., 1968-71; radiol. physicist Mercy Hosp. Inst. of Radiation Therapy, Chgo., 1968-71; prof., head radiation biophysics Northeast Ohio U. Coll. of Medicine, Rootstown, Ohio, 1971—; pres. Med. Physics Svcs., Inc., Canton, Ohio, 1971—. Author: (with Wayne R. Hedrick and David L. Hykes) Ultrasound Physics and Instrumentation, 3rd edit., 1995; contbr. numerous articles in profl. jours., chpts. in books, monographs. Fellow Am. Coll. Radiology; mem. Am. Assn. Physicists in Medicine (bd. mem. at large 1984-86, pres. Penn-Ohio chpt. 1975-76, rec. sec. midwest chpt. 1970, mem. edn. coun. 1980-83, chmn. Am. assn. med. dosimetrists task group 1976-78, mem. diagnostic radiology task group on quality control 1975—, mem. numerous other coms. 1975-83), Health Physics Soc. (chmn. summer sch. sub. com. 1977-78), Radiol. Soc. N.Am. (assoc. scis. com. 1976-86, task force chmn. 1983-86, mem. 1975-86), Sigma Xi, Kappa Mu Epsilon. Achievements include research areas including selection, quality assurance and acceptance testing of diagnostic x-ray units, design of radiology facilities; effects of tissue inhomogeneities on electron therapy, radiation atrophy in bone, large field therapy swing technique, polymer dosimetry, photon spectra through thick shields, fetal effects, ultrasound, mammography. Home and Office: 5942 Easy Pace Cir NW Canton OH 44718-2216

STARCK, JUKKA PEKKA, physicist; b. Kuusankoski, Finland, May 26, 1943; s. Aksel Frans and Elli Esther (Grönroos) S.; m. Marjo Sinikka Suikkari, May 28, 1966; children: Kikka, Anjti, Jumani, Johanna, Marjukka. BS, U. Helsinki, 1968; PhD, U. Kuopio, Finland, 1984; docent, U. Kuopio, 1985. Math. tchr. Vammalan Yhteislyseo, Finland, 1969; indsl. hygienist Inst. Occupl. Health, Finland, 1970-73; supr. phys. sec. Inst. Occupl. Health, 1974, supr. phys. lab., 1975-88, asst. dept. dir., 1988-90, rsch. prof., 1991-92, dir. dept. physics, 1993—; 2nd lt. Finnish Mil., 1963-64. Home: Ruuvikuja 2B, 01650 Vantaa Finland Office: Finnish Inst Occupl Health, Laajaniityntie 1, 01620 Vantaa Finland

STAREVA, LILIA PETROVA, publisher; b. Sofia, Bulgaria, Aug. 29, 1954; d. Petar Todorov Ignatov and Gina Valova (Komitska) Ignatova; m. Plamen Lubenov Starev, Mar. 29, 1980; children: Mina, Dejana, Plamen. Grad., Univ. Sofia, 1977; PhD, Philosophy Inst., Sofia, 1991. Expert Rsch. Inst. of Culture, Sofia, 1978-92; editor Rsch. Inst. of Culture's Periodical, Sofia, 1980-92; owner, dir. Lista, Sofia, 1992—. Author: Annunciation, 1989 (Best Novel award 1989); compiler, editor Bulgarian Folk Tales, 1993, Bulgarian Folk Tales, Songs and Legends, 1995, Bulgarian Folk Proverbs, Sayings and Riddles, 1996, Children's Folklore Encyclopaedia vol. 1 Astronomy Meteorology Animals Plants, 1996, Children's Folklore Encyclopaedia vol. II—Devil Dragon Fates Sorceresses Elfs Vampires, 1998, Peter Wattles a Fence, Bulgarian Folk Tongue-Twisters, Playthings and Counts, 2000; compiler, interpretation, The Gods and People of Hellas, 1995. Recipient The Best Story award Balkah Airlines, 1988. Avocation: international tourism. Office: Publishing House Lista, Lulin Planina #4, 1606 Sofia Bulgaria

STARIKOV, VADIM VLADIMIROVICH, physicist, researcher, educator; b. Kharkov, Ukraine, Apr. 19, 1966; s. Vladimir Pavlovich and Nadegda Vasilyevna (Shcherbak) S.; m. Svetlana Leonidovna Manukian, Apr. 27, 1990; 1 child, Vladislav. Diploma with hons., Poly. U., Kharkov, 1989, PhD in Physics, 1994. Jr. rschr. Poly. U., Kharkov, 1989-94, rschr., 1995—, lectr., 1997—. Contbr. articles to profl. jours.; patentee in field. Mem. Soc. Young Scientists. Avocations: sports, traveling, fishing. E-mail: star@kpi.kharkov.ua. Home: Metrostroiteley St 22 #47, 61183 Kharkov Ukraine Office: Kharkov State Poly U, 21 Frunze St, 61002 Kharkov Ukraine

STARINK, DIRK, career officer; b. Soest, The Netherlands, Apr. 8, 1950; s. Hendrik and Hendrika Christina (Van Etten) S.; m. Henrietta Antoinette Boot, Sept. 1971; children: Peter, Marco, Christiaan. Student, Royal Mil. Acad., Breda, The Netherlands, 1967-71, Staff Coll., Ypenburg, The Netherlands, 1980-82. Commd. Royal Netherlands Air Force, 1967; advanced through grades to maj.-gen., 1999; 1st sec. Netherlands mission NATO Brussels, 1984-87; with plans and policy DMKLU, The Hague, The Netherlands, 1987-90; dir. materials DMKLU, The Hague, 1999—; nuclear staff officer Def. Staff, The Hague, 1990-93; comdr. Royal Netherlands Air Force Depot Woensdrecht, The Netherlands, 1993-95; dep. nat. armaments dir. MOD, The Hague, 1996-99. Avocation: military history. Office: DMKLU Binckhorstlaan 135, PO Box 20703, 2900 ES The Hague The Netherlands

STARITSKY, YURI GRIGORYEVICH, geologist, researcher; b. St. Petersburg, Russia, Oct. 28, 1913; s. Grigori A. and Lydia V. (Pogozheva) S.; m. Militsa Yevlampievna Morozova, Sept. 9, 1941; children: Natalia, Irina. Engr. Geologist, Mining Inst., St. Petersburg, 1947, Cand. Scis., 1951, ScD, 1969. Sr. rschr. All-Russian Geol. Rsch. Inst., St. Petersburg, 1946-51, head dept., 1955-73, leading rschr., 1973—; asst. prof. Mining Inst., Krivoi Rog, Ukraine, 1951-53; rschr. Acad. Scis., St. Petersburg, 1953-55; lectr. Mining Inst. St. Petersburg, 1967, U. Petrozavodsk, 1968. Author/editor: Minerageny of the Siberian Platform, 1970, Evolution and Minerageny of the Russian Platform Cover, 1981, Metallogenic Map of the Russian Platform Cover, 1985, Metallogenic Map of the West-Siberian Platform Cover, 1985, Life of the Expanding Earth, 1998; mem. editl. bds. all metallogennic maps of former USSR, Russian Fedn. Sr. sgt. Russian Mil., 1942. Recipient Order of Great Patriotic War, Pres. of Supreme Soviet of Russian Fedn., 1990, Scholar Emeritus of the Russian Fedn., 1990. Mem. Russian Mineralogy Soc., St. Petersburg Scientists' Club. Russian Orthodox. Avocations: philately, floriculture. Home: Apt 54 82 Moika Emb, 190000 Saint Petersburg Russia Office: All Russian Geol Rsch Inst, 74 Srednii Prospect, 199106 Saint Petersburg Russia

STARK, EVELYN BRILL, poet, musician; b. N.Y.C., Sept. 12, 1913; d. Henry Brill and Rae Hessberg; m. Morton W. Stark, Apr. 27, 1933; 1 child, Henry. BA, Barnard Coll., 1933; artist student of Edouard Dethier, Juilliard Sch. Music, 1933-40. Bd. dirs., violinist Nat. Found. Mus. Therapy, N.Y.C., 1940-50; violinist ARC Hosp. Music Unit, N.Y.C., 1950-70, Hosp. Music Unit, Protestant Coun. Chs., N.Y.C., 1950-70; bd. dirs., violinist Music Therapy Ctr., N.Y.C., 1960-80; founder, sponsor Nora Hellen Music Friends, N.Y.C., 1970-80; ret., 1980. Mem. editl. bd., contbr. Music Jour., 1969-70; contbr. articles and poetry to Sci. of Thought Rev., Eng., 1982—, Beyond (jour.), Eng., 1982-94; recorded tapes with original programs distbd. internationally to librs., hosps., and homes for the aged; author: (book of poetry) Never Apart, 1992, (autobiography) Life is a Poem, 1999; dramatic presentations of Life is a Poem, Hartford, Conn., 2000, Essex, Conn., 2000; performer (record) All About the Violin, 1969. Donated 3 violins (Amati, Carcassi, Gragnani) to the Met. Mus. Art, N.Y.C., 1974, 80, 97. Recipient 1st prize poetry contest award Altrusa Internat. of Middletown, Conn., 1997, 98, Editors' Choice awards for poetry Nat. Libr. of Poetry, 1996, 97, 98; named Poet Laureate of Conn. Gilbert and Sullivan Soc., 1998; inductee Internat. Poetry Hall of Fame, 1998. Mem. Internat. Soc. Poets. Address: 317 W Main St Chester CT 06412-1057

STARK, HEATHER ALEXANDRA, electronic commerce industry analyst; b. Montreal, Que., May 6, 1960; arrived in Eng., 1986; d. Basil Millan Stark and Inez Muriel (Pearce) Stark Gebert; m. D. Ian Woods. AB, Vassar Coll., 1980; PhD, Stanford U., 1986; MA, U. Cambridge, Eng., 1990. Postdoctoral rschr. dept. exptl. psychology U. Cambridge, 1986-88; rsch. fellow Darwin Coll., Cambridge, 1987-90, assoc. dean, fellow, 1990-92; scientist applied psychology unit Med. Rsch. Coun., Cambridge, 1989-92; with Ovum Ltd., London, 1993—, prin. cons., 1996-2000; cons. A.T. Kearney, 2000—. Contbr. reports to profl. jours. Postdoctoral fellow Nat. Scis. and Engring. Rsch. Coun. of Can., 1986-88, grad fellow Ctr. for Study of Lang. and Info., Stanford U., 1985-86. Mem. Wimbledon Ladies Book Club, Phi Beta Kappa. Avocations: eating and drinking, hiking, gardening, speculative fiction. Office: AT Kearney Ltd Lansdowne Ho, Berkeley Sq, London W1X 5DH, England

STARK, NORMAN, secondary school educator; b. Bronx, N.Y., Sept. 15, 1940; s. Martin and Margaret (Neuman) S.; m. Betty Joanne Kelton, Sept. 4, 1994 (dec. May 1998); 1 child, Michelle Allison. Student, Newark State Coll., Union, 1963-69. Creative writing tchr., acting tchr., singles forum tchr., film tchr. Plantation (Fla.) High Sch., 1988; Hoover Mid. Sch. and Palm Bay H.S., Melbourne, Fla., 1995. Editor West Palm Beach News, 1979; screenplay writer, actor. With U.S. Army, 1963-69. Avocations: reading, puzzles, movies. Home: 2732 Locksley Rd Melbourne FL 32935-2433

STARKEY, RICHARD See STARR, RINGO

STARKEY, RUSSELL BRUCE, JR., utilities executive; b. Lumberport, W. Va., July 20, 1942; s. Russell Bruce and Dorotha Mable (Field) S.; m. Joan McClellan, May 27, 1966; children: Christine, Pamela, Joanne. BS, Miami U., Oxford, Ohio, 1964; grad. student, U. New Haven, 1972-73, N.C. State U., 1974-75; U.S. Navy Schs., 1964-66, 68. Sr. engr., nuclear generation sect. Carolina Power & Light Co., Raleigh, N.C., 1973-74, sr. engr. ops. quality assurance, 1974, prin. engr., 1974-75; quality assurance supr. Brunswick Steam Electric Plant, Southport, N.C., 1975-76, supt. tech. and adminstrn., 1976, supt. ops. and maintenance, 1976-77, supt. tech. and adminstrn., 1976-77; plant mgr. H. B. Robinson Steam Electric Plant, Hartsvile, S.C., 1977-83; mgr. environ. services Raleigh, 1984-85; mgr. nuclear safety and environ services dept., 1985-88; exec. dir. nuc. prodn. Pub. Svc. ind., Jeffersonville, 1983-84; mgr. Brunswick Nuclear Project Dept., 1988-89; v.p., 1989-92, v.p. Nuclear Svcs. Dept., 1992-93, cons., 1993-94; exec. v.p. energy mgmt. divsn. Hesco, Inc., 1994; dir. Indsl. Electrotech. Lab. Advanced Energy Corp., 1994-97, v.p. gen. tech. mgr., 1997; cons. U.S. Enrichment Corp., 1997—. With USN, 1964-73. Mem. Am. Nuclear Soc. Home: 1227 Beresford Way Paducah KY 42001-6552 Office: Bldg C-743T12 PO Box 1410 Paducah KY 42002-1410

STARKOV, RINAT ANVEROVICH, pharmaceutical company executive; b. Moscow, June 28, 1969; s. Anver Achmedovich and Nuria Schlaginiazolianovna (Absaliomova) S.; m. Inesse Mansurovna Bourbaeva, June 29, 1991; 1 child, Victoria. BS, Moscow State U., Russia, 1993; MBA, Clemson U., 1994. Sr. mgr. KPMG, Moscow, 1994-95; CFO Martin Bauer Mgmt., Moscow, 1995—. Office: Martin Bauer Mgmt, ul Lenina ol 25, 143414 Krasnogorsk Dist Moscow, Russia

STARKS, FLORENCE ELIZABETH, retired special education educator; b. Summit, N.J., Dec. 6, 1932; d. Edward and Winnie (Morris) S. BA, Morgan State U., 1956; MS in Edn., CUNY, 1962; postgrad., Fairleigh Dickinson U., 1962-63, Seton Hall U., 1963, Newark State Coll. Cert. blind and visually handicapped and social studies tchr., N.J. Tchr. adult edn. Newark Bd. of Edn.; ret., 1995; tchr. N.Y. Inst. for Edn. of the Blind, Bronx; developer first class for multiple handicapped blind children in pub. sch. system, Newark, 1960; ptnr. World Vision Internat. Mem. ASCD, AFL-CIO, AAUW, Coun. Exceptional Children, Nat. Assn. Negro Bus. and Profl. Women's Club Inc., N.J. Edn. Assn., Newark Tchrs. Assn., Newark Tchrs. Union-Am. Fedn. Tchrs., World Vision Internat. (ptnr.). Home: 4 Park Ave Summit NJ 07901-3942

STARNES, JAMES WRIGHT, lawyer; b. East St. Louis, Ill., Apr. 3, 1933; s. James Adron and Nell (Short) S.; m. Helen Woods Mitchell, Mar. 29, 1958 (div. 1978); children: James Wright, Mitchell A., William B. II; m. Kathleen Israel, Jan. 26, 1985. Student, St. Louis U., 1951-53; LLB, Washington U., St. Louis, 1957. Bar: Mo. 1957, Ill. 1957, Fla. 1992. Assoc. Stinson, Mag & Fizzell, Kansas City, Mo., 1957-60; ptnr. Stinson, Mag & Fizzell, Kansas City, 1960-90, Mid-Continent Properties Co., 1959-90, Fairview Investment Co., Kansas City, 1971-76, Monticello Land Co., 1973-99; of counsel Yates, Mauck, Bohrer, Elliff, Croessmann & Wieland, P.C., Springfield, Mo., 1995—; sec. Packaging Products Corp., Mission, Kans., 1972-89; chmn., treas. Galerie of Naples (Fla.), Inc., 1990-92. Mem. adv. bd. Washington U. Law Quar., 1957-90. Bd. dirs. Mo. Assn. Mental Health, 1968-69, Kansas City Assn. Mental Health, 1966-78, pres., 1969-70; bd. dirs. Heed, 1965-73, 78-82, pres., 1966-67, fin. chmn., 1967-68; bd. dirs. Kansas City Halfway House Found., exec. com., 1966-69, pres., 1966; bd. dirs. Joan Davis Sch. for Spl. Edn., 1972-88, v.p., 1972-73, 79-80, pres., 1980-82; bd.

dirs. Sherwood Ctr. for Exceptional Child, 1977-79, v.p., 1978-79. Served with AUS, 1957. Mem. ABA, Mo. Bar, Fla. Bar, Springfield Bar Assn., Kansas City Bar Assn., Washington U. Law Alumni Assn. (bd. govs. 1990-92). Presbyterian (deacon). Home: 2657 E Wildwood Rd Springfield MO 65804-5271 Office: Yates Mauck Bohrer Elliff Croessmann & Wieland 3333 E Battlefield St Ste 1000 Springfield MO 65804-4048

STARODUB, NICKOLAJ FEDOROVICH, biophysicist; b. Ivanovka, Dnipropetrovsk, Ukraine, Oct. 15, 1941; s. Fedir Vasilovich Starodub and Fedosija Ivanivna (Janghula) S.; m. Marija Ivanivna Dibko, Sept. 4, 1970; children: Olexander, Valentyna. Asst. of Vet. Doctor, Coll. Novomoskovsk, Ukraine, 1960; Biophysicist, U. Dhipropetrovsk, Ukraine, 1965; Cand. Biol. Sci., Inst. Biochemistry, Kiev, Ukraine, 1969; D Biol. Sci., Moscow U., 1982; Docent, Inst. Molecular Biol. and, Genetics, Kiev, 1974; Prof., Inst. Biochemistry, Kiev, 1994. Investigator Inst. Physiology, Kiev, 1965-67; jr. rsch. worker Inst. Molecular Biology and Genetics, Kiev, 1967-69, sr. rsch. worker, 1969-86, leader scientist, 1986-88, chief scientific worker, 1988-93; chief scientific worker Inst. Biochemistry, Kiev, 1993-98, head dept. biochemistry of sensoric and regulatoric sys., 1998—. Editl. bd. Ukrainian Biochem. Zhurnal, 1990—; contbr. articles to profl. jours. Mem. scientific bd. Inst. of Biochemistry, Kiev, 1985—, Ukraine Scientific Ctr. of Gygiene, Kiev, 1994—, Ukrainian Med. Inst. of Non-Traditional Medicine, Kiev, 1993-99; mem. com. New Med. Techniques, Ukraine Ministry of Pub. Health, Kiev, 1992-98; mem. Anti-AIDS com. at Pres. of Ukraine, 1992-97. Recipient A.V. Palladin's prize laureate Ukraine Nat. Acad. Sci., 1988; grantee NATO, Brussels, 1996, 97, 99, others. Mem. N.Y. Acad. Scis., Ukrainian Acad. of Scis. of Nat. Progress, Ukrainian Biochem. Soc., Internat. Electrochem. Soc., Ukrainian Biochem. Soc., Soc. Nexus. Avocations: chess, gardening. E-mail: prof@progress.freenet.kiev.ua and Starodub@paladin.biochem.kiev.ua. Home: Apt 7, 7 Erevanskaya Str, 03087 Kyiv Ukraine Office: AV Palladin Inst Biochemist, 9 Leontovicha Str, 01030 Kyiv Ukraine

STARODUBOV, KIRILL FEDOROVICH, metallurgist, educator; b. Moscow, Apr. 19, 1904. Diploma in engring. and metallurgy, Dnepropetrovsk Metall. Inst., 1928, Candidate of Scis., 1938; DSc, Moscow Metall. Inst., 1946. Engr. Dnepropetrovsk Metall. Plant, 1925-37, docent, 1937-41; docent Magnitogorsk Mining Metall. Inst., 1941-44; head dept. thermal treatment in metals, dep. dir. Dnepropetrovsk Metall. Inst., 1944-53, head dept. thermal treatment metals, 1974—; head dept. thermal treatment of steel Dnepropetrovsk Inst. Iron Metallurgy, 1948-74. Author: Equipment of Thermal Treatment Shop of Metallurgical Plants, 1948; co-author: (with I. Uzlov and V.Y. Savenkov) Thermal Shengthening of Rolling, 1970, (V.I. Bolshakov and M.A. Tilkin) Thermal Treatment of Strengthened Construction Steel, 1977. Recipient prize USSR Coun. Mins., 1987; named hon. worker of sci. and tech., Ukraine, 1962. Avocations: photography, poetry. Home: 5/11 Acad Lazarian St, 49010 Dnepropetrovsk Ukraine

STAROSOLSZKY, ÖDÖN, civil engineer; b. Veszprèm, Hungary, Dec. 26, 1931; s. Sándor and Irma (Benkö) S.; m. Erzsébet Zilahi-Kiss, Apr. 1, 1961. Dipl.Ing., T.U., Budapest, 1954, DEng, 1968; DSc, Hungarian Acad. Sci., 1995. Engring. diplomate. Rsch. engr. Rsch. Inst. Water Rsch., Budapest, 1954-60, head sect., dept., 1960-71; head dept. Nat. Water Authority, Budapest, 1971-76; dir. Inst. of Hydraulics, Budapest, 1976-89; dep. gen. dir. Water Res. Rsch. Ctr., Budapest, 1989-91, gen. dir., 1991-98; expert UN, India, Srilanka, Nigeria, Egypt; chmn. com. on water scis. Hungarian Acad. Scis., Budapest, 1990-97; pres. Commn. for Hydrology, WMO, Geneva, 1984-92. Author: Civil Engineering Hydraulics, 1971; co-author/editor: Hydraulic Engineering, 1973, Applied Surface Hydrology, 1987; co-editor: Hydrology of Disaster, 1989. Recipient Széchenyi prize, 2000. Mem. Hungarian Hydrol. Soc. (chmn. com. internat. affairs 1990-96, pres., 1996—, Vásárhelyi prize 1986, 92), Internat. Assn. Hydraulic Rsch. (v.p. 1988-91), Hungarian Soc. Environment. Roman Catholic. Achievements include rsch. results in the field of hydrology, hydraulics, hydraulic engineering and water managment. Office: Water Resources Rsch Ctr, Kvassay Jenöut 1 PO Box 27, H-1453 Budapest Hungary

STAROV, VICTOR MIKHILOVICH, mathematics educator; b. Temruk, Russia, June 14, 1946; s. Mikhile Vasilievich and Ludmila Iosiphovna (Oleynikova) S.; m. Nadegda Vladimirovna Kulikova, Aug. 22, 1951; 1 child. B, Moscow State U., 1969; PhD, Russian Acad. Scis., 1973; DSc, Leningrad (Russia) U., 1980; Academician, Internat. Info. Acad., 1995. Jr. rschr. Moscow Inst. Physics for Constrn., 1974-75, sr. rschr., 1975-76; asst. prof. Moscow Textile U., 1976-78; head dept. pure and applied math. Moscow State U. Food Industry, 1981-99; prof. dept. chem. engring. Loughborough U., Leicestershire, U.K., 1999—; vis. prof. dept. chem. engring. U. Tex., Austin, 1992-94, 95, chem. dept. Sofia (Bulgaria) U., 1987, 88, 89, 90, Catedratico de Universidad, Instituto Pluridisciplinar, Universidad Complutense, Madrid, 1996; lectr. Coll. de France, Paris, 1989, Weisman Inst. Sci., Rehovot, Israel, 1991, Technion, Haifa, Israel, 1991, Carnegie Mellon U., Pitts., 1992, Rensselaer Poly. Inst., Troy, 1992, SUNY, Buffalo, 1992, Rice U., Houston, 1993, Ill. Inst. Tech., Chgo., 1994, U. Minn., Mpls., 1994. Mem. adv. bd. Jour. Colloid and Interface Sci., 1996-98; mem. editl. bd. Colloid Jour., 1987—, Ukrainian Jour. Water Chemistry, 1985—. Grantee NSF, 1993, Russian Fund for Basic Rsch., Russia, 1994-97; named Soros Prof., Moscow, 1997, 98. Mem. Coun. on Colloid Chemistry and Physico-chem. Mechanics, European Membrane Soc. Achievements include research in wetting phenomena, surface forces, membrane separation. Avocations: classical music, literature. Home: 52 Langdale Ave, Loughborough LE11 3RP, United Kingdom Office: Loughborough U, Dept Engring, Leicestershire LE11 3TU, United Kingdom

STAROVA, GALINA LEONIDOVNA, crystallographer; b. Gavrilov Yam, Russia, Dec. 14, 1946; d. Leonid Alexandr and Elizabete Paul (Crjimova) S.; m. Vladimir Gerasim Krivovitchev, Mar. 20, 1970; children: Sergej, Gerasim. Grad., State U., St. Petersburg, Russia, 1971, PhD, 1981. Engr. Inst. Method & Tech., St. Petersburg, Russia, 1971-78; postgrad. rschr. State U., St. Petersburg, Russia, 1978-81, jr. rschr., 1982-85, rschr., 1985-91, sr. rschr., 1992-95, assoc. prof., 1995—. Contbr. articles to profl. jours. Mem. Russian Chem. Soc., Russian Naturalist Soc. Avocations: reading, walking in forest. Home: Chebishevskaja 14-1-97, 198904 Saint Petersburg Russia Office: State U Chem Dept, Universitetskiy pr 2, 198904 Saint Petersburg Russia

STAROVOYTOV, ALEXANDER FYODOROVICH, library director; b. Jan. 27, 1948; s. Fyodor Georgievich and Nina Mikhailovna (Petukhova) S.; m. Angelina Mikhailovna Konyaeva, Apr. 17, 1970; children: Anton, Mikhail, Polina. Cert. of degree, Tchrs. Tng. Inst., Perm, Russia, 1970. Head Serafimovskaya Sch., Siva/Perm, 1971-74, secondary sch., Siva/Perm, 1974-76, Maisky Secondary Sch., Krasnokamsk/Perm, 1986-89; sr. insp. Regional Dept. Pub. Edn., Perm, 1976-86; dir. Regional Pub. Libr., Perm, 1989—; mktg. cons. to librs., Perm region 1989—. Author: (children's poems) Olyapka N 7, 1987, My Happy Calendar, 1996, From January till January: Poems, 1996, Postscript to September: Poems, 1996, The Poet Has Got a Wife, 1999, I Love You. . .Almanac, 1999; editor: Great Tellers of Fairy Tales, 1993, Lady's novel series, 1993-94, The Directory, Vsya Perm, 1993, Chronicle of Prikamye 1324-1917, 1997; contbr. articles and poems to profl. publs. Mem. Soc. Regional Studies (chmn. 1991—), Writers Union Russia. Avocations: painting, book collecting, travel. E-mail: foreign@lib.raid.ru. Home: Bolshevistskaya St 135-86, 614068 Perm Russia Office: Oblastnaja biblioteka M Gor'kogo, ul Lenina 70, 614600 Perm Russia

STARR, CHARLES CHRISTOPHER, foundation executive, priest; b. Atlanta, Jan. 15, 1952; s. David Homer and Margaret Mary (Bussey) S.; m. C. Kathy Wright, Dec. 15, 1984; 1 child, Anna Katherine. BA in Philosophy, St. Mary's Coll., 1975; MDiv, St. Vincent de Paul, 1980. Ordained to ministry Roman Cath. Ch., 1980; received into ministry Episcopal Ch., 1993. Assoc. pastor Sacred Heart Ch., Atlanta, 1980-82, Immaculate Heart of Mary, Atlanta, 1983, Cathedral Christ the King, Atlanta, 1983-84; vice chancellor Archdiocese of Atlanta, 1982-84; v.p. Lehfeldt and Assocs., 1985-89; dir. devel. Winship Cancer Ctr., 1989-91; exec. dir. Henry W. Grady Found., 1992-95; assoc. rector Ch. of Atonement, Atlanta, 1993—; exec. dir. Nat. Kidney Found. of Ga., Atlanta, 1995—. Pres. Transition House, Atlanta, 1988-92. Mem. Nat. Soc. Fund Raising Execs. (cert., bd. dirs. Ga. chpt. 1992—). Home: 1726 Coventry Pl Decatur GA 30030-1005 Office: Nat Kidney Found of Ga 2951 Flowers Rd S Ste 211 Atlanta GA 30341-5533

STARR, JOSEPH BARTON, history educator; b. Pensacola, Fla., Dec. 24, 1945; s. George B. and Estelle P. (Price) S.; m. Rebekah E. Everage, 1966; children: Christopher Barton, Lance Edward. AB with honors, Samford U., Birmingham, 1966; MA, Fla. State U., 1967, PhD, 1971. Asst. then assoc. prof. Troy State U., Dothan/Ft. Rucker, Ala., 1970-80; Fulbright-Hays sr. lectr. Hong Kong Bapt. U., Kowloon, 1978-79, chair prof. history, 1993-99, head dept., 1994-95, course leaer BA in Arts and Social Scis., 1988-92; assoc. v.p., acad. dean humanities & social studies, chair Lingnan U., Hong Kong, 1999—; subject specialist Hong Kong Coun. for Acad. Accreditation, 1988—. Author: Tories, Dons and Rebels: The American Revolution in British West Florida, 1976; editor: The United States Constitution: Its Birth, Growth and Influence in Asia, 1988; collaborator: Alabama: A Place, A People, A Point of View, 1977; contbr. articles and revs. to profl. publs. Chair Enterprise Bicentennial Commn., Enterprise, Ala., 1973-76; mem. religious edn. and sacred music bds. Hong Kong Bapt. Conv., 1985-92; mem. adv. com. Hong Kong-Am. Ctr., Hong Kong, 1992—; mem. exec. com. Ala. Hist. Commn., 1977-81. Recipient Award of Merit, Ala. Hist. Commn., 1976, Disting. Svc. award City of Enterprise, 1976; rsch. grantee. Mem. So. Hist. Assn. U.S. (chair membership com. 1977-78, 80-81, other offices), Am. Hist. Assn., Orgn. Am. Historians. Avocation: stamp collecting. Office: Lingnan U, Tuen Mun Hong Kong

STARR, RINGO (RICHARD STARKEY), musician, actor; b. Liverpool, Eng., July 7, 1940; s. Richard and Elsie (Gleave) Starkey; m. Maureen Cox, Feb. 11, 1965 (div. 1975); children: Zak, Jason, Lee; m. Barbara Bach, Apr. 27, 1981. Drummer, vocalist mus. group, The Beatles, 1962-69; musician with Rory Storme's Hurricanes, 1959-62; solo performer, 1970-77; toured with All-Starr Band, 1992; recs. include Sentimental Journey, 1970, Beaucoups of Blues, 1970, Ringo, 1973, Goodnight Vienna, 1974, Blast From Your Past, 1975, Starrstruck: Ringo's Best, 1989, Ringo's Rotogravure, 1976, Ringo the Fourth, 1977, Bad Boy, 1978, Stop and Smell the Roses, 1981, Time takes Time, 1992, Live from Montreux, vol. 2, 1994, Vertical Man, 1998, VH1 Storytellers, 1998, I Wanna Be Santa Claus, 1999; solo albumn It Don't Come Easy, 1971, Only You, 1975, No No Song, 1975, (with the Beatles) A Hard Day's Night, 1964, Rubber Soul, 1965, Sgt. Pepper's Lonely Hearts Club Band, 1967, Magical Mystery Tour, Yellow Submarine, 1969, The Beatles, Abbey Road, Let It Be, 1969, Hey Jude, 1970, Reel Music, 1982, numerous others; film appearances with the Beatles include A Hard Day's Night, 1964, Help!, 1965, Yellow Submarine, 1968, Let It Be, 1970, TV film Magical Mystery Tour, 1967; individual film appearances include Candy, 1968, The Magic Christian, 1969, 200 Motels, 1971, Blindman, 1971, Tommy, 1972, That'll Be the Day, 1973, Born to Boogie, also dir., producer, 1974, Son of Dracula, also producer, 1975, Lisztomania, 1975, Ringo Starrs, 1976, Caveman, 1981, The Cooler, 1982, Give My Regards to Broad Street, 1984; appeared in TV miniseries Princess Daisy, 1983; star TV series Shining Time Station, PBS, 1989-91. Decorated Order Brit. Empire; recipient numerous Grammy awards with The Beatles; inducted with The Beatles into Rock and Roll Hall of Fame, 1988. Office: 2 Glynde Mews, London SW3 1SB, England also: care Mercury Records 825 8th Ave New York NY 10019-7416

STARRATT, PATRICIA ELIZABETH, writer, actress, composer, pianist; b. Boston, Nov. 7, 1943; d. Alfred Byron and Anna (Mazur) S. AB, Smith Coll., 1965; grad. prep. dept., Peabody Conservatory Music, 1961; postgrad., Saybrook Grad. Sch./Rsch. Ctr., San Francisco, 1999. Tchg. asst. Harvard U. Grad. Sch. Bus. Adminstrn., 1965-67; mng. dir. INS Assocs., Washington, 1967-68; adminstrv. asst. George Washington U. Hosp., 1970-71; legal asst. Morgan, Lewis & Bockius, Washington, 1971-72; profl. staff energy analyst Nat. Fuels & Energy Policy Study U.S. Senate Interior Com., 1972-74; cons., exec. asst. energy resource devel. Fed. Energy Adminstrn., Washington, 1974-75; sr. cons. energy policy Atlantic Richfield Co., 1975-76; energy cons. Alaska, 1977-78; govt. affairs assoc. Sohio Alaska Petroleum Co., Anchorage, 1978-85; legal asst. Hughes, Thorsness, Gantz, Powell and Brudin, Anchorage, 1989-90; writer, media specialist corp. affairs Alyeska Pipeline Svc. Co., 1990-95; legal asst. Hughes Thorsness Powell Huddleston & Bauman LLC, 1996-97; sr. paralegal Brit. Petroleum, 1997-98; writer, editor Inst. Circumpolar Health Studies U. Alaska, Anchorage, 1998—; exec. dir. Anchorage Cmty. Theatre, 1999—; mem. econ. devel. commn. Municipality of Anchorage, 1981. Actress, asst. dir. Brattle St. Players, Boston, 1966-67, Washington Theater Club, 1967-68, Gene Frankel, Broadway, 1968-69; actress Aspen Resident Theater, Colo., 1985-86, Ranyevskya (The Cherry Orchard), Anchorage, 1994, Bonfila (SLAVS!), Frau Schmidt (The Sound of Music), Anchorage, 1995, Maria (Moonlight), Anchorage, 1997, Olga (Three Sisters), Eccentric Theatre Co., Anchorage, 1998, Mrs. Barker (The American Dream), 7th Ann. Edward Albee Theatre Conf., Valdez, Alaska, 1999, Ethel (Moon Over Buffalo), Eccentric Theatre Co., Anchorage, 1999; writer, assoc. prodr.: Then One Night I Hit Her, 1983; screenwriter, prodr., actress, composer, pianist: A Call to Live, 1995, Marmee (Little Women), 1997; appeared off-Broadway in to Be Young, Gifted and Black; performed as Mary in Tennessee, Blanche in A Streetcar Named Desire, Stephanie Dickinson in Cactus Flower, Angela in Papa's Wine, Elizabeth Procter in The Crucible, Candida in Candida, Zeuss in J.B., Martha in Who's Afraid of Virginia Woolf, Amy in Dinny and the Witches, as Columbina in Servant of Two Masters, as Singer in Death of Morris Biederman, as Joan in Joan of Lorraine, as Mado in Amadee, as Mrs. Rowlands in Before Breakfast, as the girl in Hello Out There, as Angela in Bedtime Story, as Hannah in Night of the Iguana, as Lavinia in Androcles and the Lion, as Catherine in Great Catherine, as Julie in Lilliom, as First Nurse in Death of Bessie Smith, as Laura in Tea and Sympathy, as Amelia Earhart in Chamber Music; appeared at Detroit Summer Theatre in Oklahoma, Guys and Dolls, Carousel, Brigadoon, Kiss Me Kate, Finnian's Rainbow; asst. to dir. Broadway plays A Cry of Players, A Way of Life, Off-Broadway play To Be Young, Gifted and Black; screenwriter Challenge in Alaska, 1986, Martin Poll Films; asst. dir. Dustin Hoffman, 1974; contbr. articles on natural gas and Alaskan econ. and environ. to profl. jours. Bd. dirs. Anchorage Comty. Theatre, Alaska Assn. Legal Assts., 1996-98; industry rep. Alaska Eskimo Whaling Commn.; mem. Alaska New Music Forum. Mem. Actors' Equity. Episcopalian. Avocations: skiing, horseback riding, biking, hiking. Home: 1054 W 20th Ave Apt 4 Anchorage AK 99503-1749

STARR-GLASS, DAVID BARUCH, management education educator, consultant; b. Bellshill, Scotland, May 12, 1948; s. William A. and Barbara H. (Hamilton) Glass; m. Nina Ann Starr, Sept. 27, 1974; children: Aaron, Sarah, Miriam, Moshe, Yisrael, Avraham, Leah, Rachel, Esther. BS with hons., U. Glasgow, Scotland, 1970; BA, Regents Coll., N.Y., 1978, BSBA, 1980; MBA, Coll. of Notre Dame, Belmont, Calif., 1982; postgrad., U. London. Assoc. prof. SUNY-Empire State, Jerusalem, 1984—, Touro Coll., Jerusalem, 1985—, The Zaidner Inst., Jerusalem, 1984—; assoc. registrar Neve Yerushalayim, Jerusalem, 1995—. Author: (books) Gathered Stones, 1995, Simple Guide to Israeli Ettiquette, 1997, Simple Guide to Judaism, 1998; contbr. articles to profl. jours. Alumni advisor Regent's Coll., N.Y., 1993-96. Recipient sci./religion course prize Templeton Found., 1998, Dobbie-Smith medal U. Glasgow, 1970. Fellow Linnean Soc. of London; mem. Chartered Inst. of Marketers, Inst. Mgrs. Avocations: botany, music, poetry. Office: Empire State Coll, PO Box 1154, 91000 Jerusalem Israel

STARTUP, WILLIAM HARRY, chemist; b. Port Jervis, N.Y., Oct. 24, 1945; s. William George and Robina Victoria S.; m. Frances Williams, Nov. 6, 1976; 1 child, Elizabeth. BS in Chemistry, SUNY, Cortland, 1974. Sr. flavor analyst PFW-Hercules, Middletown, N.Y., 1975-91; analytical supr. Tastemaker, Cin., 1991-96; analytical chemistry mgr. Alex Fries and Bros., 1996—. Bd. dirs. Humane Soc. Middletown N.Y., 1985-91. Sgt. USAF, 1966-70. Mem. Am. Chem. Soc., Assn. of Ofcl. Analytical Chemists. Home: 892 Sabino Ct Cincinnati OH 45231-4905 Office: Alex Fries & Bros 10311 Chester Rd Cincinnati OH 45215-1224

STARZEC, PETER PIOTR, geologist, researcher; b. Tarnøw, Poland, Sept. 29, 1965; arrived in Sweden, 1992; s. Stanisław and Stanilława (Duż) S.; m. Katarina Katarzyna Malaga, May 25, 1993; 1 child, Oskar. MSc in Geophysics, U. Mining and Metallurgy, Cracow, Poland, 1991; MSc in Petroleum Exploration, Chalmer U., Göteborg, Sweden, 1994, MSc in Civil Engring., 1996, licentiate in tech. geology, 1999. Tchg. asst. dept. geology Chalmers U. Mem. Internat. Soc. Rock Mechanics. Office: Chalmers U, Sven Hutinsgatan 8, 412 96 Göteborg Sweden

STASH, SUSAN MICHELE, critical care nurse; b. Inglewood, Calif., Mar. 28, 1965; d. Michael Paul and JoAnn Patricia (Margan) S. BSN, Westminster Coll., Salt Lake City, 1987. RN, Calif.; cert. med.-surg. nurse ANCC. Staff nurse gen. surg. unit St. Joseph Hosp., Orange, Calif., 1987-91; staff nurse gen. med. surg. unit Castle Med. Ctr., Kailua, Hawaii, 1992-94; staff nurse renal/pulmonary/telemetry unit Mary Washington Hosp., Fredericksburg, Va., 1994-95; intermediate med. care unit staff nurse Onslow Meml. Hosp., Jacksonville, N.C., 1995-97; staff nurse progressive care unit Swedish Med. Ctr., Englewood, Colo., 1998—; staff nurse subacute ICU Hoag Meml. Hosp. Presbyn., Newport Beach, Calif., 1999—. Mem. ANA, AACN, Am. Assn. Cert. Nurses, Sigma Theta Tau.

STASHANS, ARVIDS, physicist; b. Kraslava, Latvia, Dec. 29, 1965; s. Jazeps and Longina (Prilucka) S.; m. Maria Margarita Cajas, Apr. 8, 1995. MS in Physics, U. Latvia, 1991, PhD in Physics, 1993. Rsch. asst., Inst. Solid State Physics U. Latvia, Riga, 1987-91; rsch. assoc., Inst. Solid State Physics U. Latvia, 1991-93, scientist, Inst. Solid State Physics, 1994-95; guest rschr., Dept. Quantum Chemistry Uppsala (Sweden) U., 1994-95, postdoctoral fellow, Dept. Quantum Chemistry, 1995-97; assoc. prof. dept. phys. Escuela Politecnica Nacional, Quito, Ecuador, 1998-2000; head Rsch. Ctr. of Condensed Matter Physics, Quito, Ecuador, 1998—; vis. scientist Faculty Engring., Utsunomiya (Japan) U., 1995. Co-contbr. articles to profl. jours. Recipient Swedish Inst. scholarship, 1993-94, Matsumae Internat. Found. fellowship, 1995, Uppsala U. fellowship, 1996-97. Mem. N.Y. Acad. Scis. Roman Catholic. Avocation: football (soccer) statistics.

STASIAK, HALINA, language educator; b. Poznań, Poland, July 1, 1934; d. Wiktor and Izabella (Trajtler) Dębicki; m. Jan Horbulewicz, Feb. 10, 1953 (div. 1960); 1 child, Dariusz Horbulewicz; m. Stefan Stasiak, Mar. 14, 1963; 1 child, Wojciech. Magister, Adam-Mickiewicz-U., Poznań, 1956; Doctorate, U. Gdansk, Poland, 1973, Dr. Habil., 1992, prof., 1993. Cert. in philology, linguistics, fgn. lang. educator. Dir. Inst. Lang. Method, Poland, 1966-78; dir. Fgn. Lang. Inst. U. Gdansk, 1979-88, dir. Coll. Fgn. Lang., 1990—; cons. Acad. Adult Learners, Poland, 1990—, Ministry Edn., Warsaw, Poland, 1984—; vis. prof. U. Dresden, Germany, 1985-86, U. Rostock, Germany, 1987-88; vis. prof., dir. German as Fgn. Lang., U. Saarbrücken, Germany, 1988-91. Author: (books) Psychological and Pedagogical Aspects of Foreign Language, 1992 (Gdansk Ministry of Edn. award 1993), Scanning and Teaching, 1988, Curriculum for a Modern Teacher Education, 1995 (Warsaw Ministry of Edn. award 1996). Recipient medal Pres. Poland, 1988, Pres. German Republic, 1993. Mem. Internat. Orgn. German Tchrs., Polish Philology Orgn. Avocations: music, painting, collecting owls and watches. Home phone: 0048 58 3435 993. Home: E Plater 10/10, 80-522 Gdansk Poland Office: U Gdansk, Chodkiewicza 14, 80-506 Gdansk Poland

STASKON, FRANCIS C., research scientist; b. Chgo., Feb. 7, 1960; s. Kenneth C. and Shirley A. S. BS, Loyola U., Chgo., 1982; MS in Psychology, Rutgers U., New Brunswick, N.J., 1985, PhD in Psychology, 1991. Statistician CRC Info., N.Y.C., 1993; sr. statistician Metomail, Lombard, Ill., 1993-95; regular cons. Trilogy Cons. Corp., Waukegan, Ill., 1996-98; vis. rsch. scientist U. Ill. of Springfield, 1998—; adj. faculty various colls./univs. in Ill., N.J., 1992—. Author book in field; contbr. articles to profl. jours. Mem. APA, Am. Statis. Assn., Am. Sociol. Assn.

STASSEN, HENDRIK GERARD, machine systems educator; b. Goes, The Netherlands, Sept. 29, 1935; s. Johannes Wilhelm and Elisabeth (Palm) S.; m. Maria W. Petronella van Zutphen, Apr. 7, 1964; children: Nico-Jan, Eric-Jan, Carolien. BS, Coll. Prodn., Utrecht, The Netherlands, 1956, Delft U. Tech., The Netherlands, 1961; MS, Delft U. Tech., The Netherlands, 1967, DR, 1967; Dr (hon.), U. Craoiva, Romania. Asst. prof. Delft U. Tech., 1964-68, assoc. prof., 1968-77, prof., 1977—, dean, 1990-95; cons. in field. Contbr. chpts. to books, articles to profl. jours. Chmn. Oskar Found., Leersum, The Netherlands, 1972—. With RAF, 1957-58. Mem. IEEE (sr.), Dutch Royal Acad. Scis., Acad. Tech. and Scis., Royal Inst. Engrs., Rlwy. Safety Coun. Avocations: furniture design, stamp collecting, travel, train models. Office: Delft U Tech, Mekelweg 21, 2628 CD Delft The Netherlands

STASSEN, JACQUES MARCEL (KNIGHT STASSEN), emeritus political science educator, legal administration consultant, university director; b. Liège, Belgium, Oct. 15, 1911; s. Marcel and Celestine (Bruwier) S.; m. Madeleine-Emilie Roba, July 5, 1937; children: Jean-Marie, Luc-Jacqueline, Marc, Pierre, Monique, Eric. LLD, State U., Liège, 193, Lic. in Polit. Sci., 1935. Barrister State Coun. Ct. of Liège, Brussels, 1933-68; prof. Social High Sch. Liège, 1953-68, Sch. High Studies Liège, 1958-68; prof. State U. Liège, 1968-81, emeritus prof., 1981—; chmn. bus. sch. and law faculty U. Liège, 1970-77; gen. dir. Internat. Inst. Adminstrv. Scis., Brussels, 1970-79, hon. dir., 1979—; cons. adminstrv. law Liège, 1948—; surrogate tribunal judge City of Liège, 1947-81; adminstr. Univ. Ctr. Pub. Law, 1979—; com. mem. Pub. Adminstrn. Rev., 1973. Author and editor: The Permit Building, 1973; author and editor various articles on legal adminstrn. Chmn. Maison de L'Europe, Liège, 1973-88, Ligne de Vie, Liège, 1984-98; administr. Le Grande Liège, 1979-87. Lt. col. artillery Belgian Mil. Svc. Decorated Grand Officer Order of the Crown, Order of Leopold II, Officer Order of Leopold I, Groix Civique 1st Class. Mem. Prince Albert Club, Lit. Soc. (adminstr.), Nobility's Assn. Kingdom of Belgium, Probvs-Liege. Mem. Christian Social Party. Home: Rue Louvrex 51/0 81, B 4000 Liège Belgium

STASSEN, WILLY, photographer, educator; b. Brussels, Apr. 13, 1948; s. Jean and Maria (Manteleers) S.; m. Monique Coppola, Mar. 7, 1970; children: Frederique, Vincent. Diploma in visual arts A1 superior, St. Lukas Inst. Brussels, 1967. Focus puller various projects, Brussels, 1969-84; instr. St. Lukas High Inst. Visual Arts, Brussels, 1983—; dir. photography various projects, Brussels, 1984—. Dir. photography Love Is A Dog From Hell, Los Angeles, 1987. Recipient Kodak Cristal award for photography of Istanbul, 1986, Oscar for Best Fgn. Movie, 1996. Avocations: music, film. Home and Office: Rue J Lambotte #19, B 1150 Brussels Belgium

STASTNY, MIROSLAV, research scientist; b. Bela pod Bezdezem, Czech Republic, Apr. 5, 1932; s. Frantisek and Helena (Doskarova) S.; m. Vlasta Vesela, Nov. 18, 1954; children: Miroslav, Petr. MS, Czech Tech. U., Prague, 1956; PhD, West Bohemia U., Pilsen, Czech Republic, 1967, DSc, 1990. Designer Skoda Turbines, Pilsen, Czech Republic, 1956-64, rschr., 1964-70, head rsch. divsn., 1970-93, sr. scientist cons., 1993—; prof. Czech Tech. U., Prague, 1998—; mem. European Com. for Conferences Turbomachinery, 1994—. Author: Combined Cycles for Power Plants and Cogeneration, 1993; contbr. 110 articles to profl. jours. Mem. Internat. Assn. for Properties of Water and Steam (nat. com. 1993—), Internat. Gas Turbine Inst. (mem. com. coal, biomass and alt. fuels 1994—), Czech Soc. Mechanics (main com. 1995-99), Assn. Czech. Mech. Engrs. (main com. 1999—). Roman Catholic. Avocations: photography, cycling. Home: Francouzska 38, 30706 Plzeň Czech Republic

STATA, RAYMIE, computer science researcher, investor; b. Woburn, Mass., Mar. 27, 1968; s. Ray and Maria Stata; m. Kimberly R. Sweidy, July 4, 1997. BS, MS in Computer Sci., MIT, 1991, PhD in Computer Sci., 1996. Rschr. Digital Equipment Corp., Palo Alto, Calif., 1996-97; ptnr. Fundamental Capital, Palo Alto, 1996—; v.p. engr. Deploy Solutions, Inc., Mountain View, Calif., 1998; rschr. Compaq Computer Corp., Palo Alto, 1999—; dir. Deploy Solutions, Westwood, Mass., 1997—, iGroove.com, Burlington, Calif., 1999—. Mem. Am. Computing Machinery. Libertarian. Achievements include 2 patents. Office: Compaq Sys Rsch Ctr 130 Lytton Ave Palo Alto CA 94301-1044

STATHIS, NICHOLAS JOHN, lawyer; b. Calchi, Greece, Feb. 27, 1924; s. John and Sylvia (Koutsonouris) S. Student, Columbia U., 1942-43, 44-48, AB, 1946, JD, 1948. Bar: N.Y. 1949. Assoc. James Maxwell Fassett, N.Y.C., 1948-50; asst. counsel to spl. com. to investigate organized crime in interstate commerce U.S. Senate, Washington, 1951; trial atty. Fidelity & Casualty Co., N.Y.C., 1952; law sec. to Harold R. Medina Judge U.S. Ct. Appeals (2d cir.), N.Y.C., 1952-54; spl. dep. atty. gen. N.Y. State Election

Frauds Bur., Dept. Law, 1956; assoc. Watson, Leavenworth, Kelton & Taggart, N.Y.C., 1954-60, ptnr., 1961-81; ptnr. Hopgood, Calimafde, Kalil, Blaustein & Judlowe, N.Y.C., 1981-84, Botein, Hays & Sklar, N.Y.C., 1984-89; of counsel White & Case, N.Y.C., 1989-93; corp. coun., dir. intellectual property Aphton Corp., N.Y.C., 1993—; lectr. Practising Law Inst., 1968-69. Contbr. articles to profl. jours. on trademarks. Pres., exec. dir., chmn., bd. dirs. Found. Classic Theatre and Acad., 1973—; bd. dirs. Concert Artists Guild, 1974-91, Pirandello Soc., 1976—, Bklyn. Philharm. Orch., 1986-91, Orpheon, Inc., 1986-98, Friends of Young Musicians, 1998—. With AUS, 1943-44. Mem. ABA, Assn. of Bar of City of N.Y., N.Y. State Bar Assn., Fed. Bar Coun., Am. Intellectual Property Law Assn., N.Y. Intellectual Property Law Assn. Democrat. Greek Orthodox. Home: 1885 John F Kennedy Blvd Jersey City NJ 07305-2113 Office: 515 Madison Ave Ste 725 New York NY 10022-5403

STATKUS, JEROME FRANCIS, lawyer; b. Hammond, Ind., June 13, 1942; s. Albert William and Helen Ann (Vaicunas) S.; children: Wesley Albert, Nicholas Jerome. BA, So. Ill. U., 1964; JD, U. Louisville, 1968; MA, U. Wyo., 1974. Bar: Wyo. 1971, U.S. Dist. Ct. Wyo. 1971, Wis. 1989, D.C. 1977, U.S. Ct. Claims 1973, U.S. Supreme Ct. 1974, U.S. Ct. Appeals (10th cir.) 1973, U.S. Ct. Appeals (7th cir.) 1992. Law clk. U.S. Dist. Ct., So. Dist. Ill., Peoria, 1968-69; asst. atty. gen. State of Wyo., Cheyenne, 1971-75; legis. asst. to U.S. Senator Clifford Hansen Washington, 1975-76; asst. U.S. atty. U.S. Dept. Justice, Dist. of Wyo., 1976-77; sole practice Cheyenne, 1978-79; assoc. Horisky, Bagley & Hickey, Cheyenne, 1979-81; ptnr. Rooney, Bagley, Hickey Evans & Stratkus, Cheyenne, 1981-88; exec. dir. Wyo. State Bar, 1988-89; trustee Village of Germantown, Wis., 1991-93; office share Ladewig and Rechlicz, 1990-93; pvt. practice Douglas, Wyo., 1993-96; asst. pub. defender State of Wyo., Douglas, 1993-96. Pres. Ret. Sr. Vol. Program, Cheyenne, 1982-83; treas. Pathfinder (drug rehab.), Cheyenne, 1982-85; bar commr. 1st Jud. Dist., 1985-87; mem. Future Milw., 1991; chair Waukesha County Devel. Disability Adv. Coun., 1996—; mem. Washington County Econ. Devel. Com. Served with USNR, 1969-70. Mem. Wyo. Bar Assn., D.C. Bar Assn., Wis. State Bar Assn., Wyo. Trial Lawyers Assn. (bd. dirs. 1984-85), KC, VFW. Republican. Roman Catholic. Home: PO Box 14 Germantown WI 53022-0014 Office: W156N 11340 Pilgrim Rd Germantown WI 53022

STAUB, MARTHA LOU, retired elementary education educator; b. Cumberland, Md., May 29, 1939; d. Walter W. and Velma Grace (Darr) McCoy; m. Paul L. Staub, Apr. 11, 1964; children: Desiree, Paul, Sharon, Lucy, Charles. BS, Frostburg State U., 1961; postgrad., We. Md. State U., 1983; MS, Towson State Coll., 1983; student, Loyola Coll., 1988. Cert. tchr. 1st-mid. sch., Md. Elem. tchr. Cumberland Valley, Bedord, Pa., Garrett County, Oakland, Md., Carroll County, Westminster, Balt. County Bd. Edn., Towson, Md.; with peer coaching, 1990-93, master learning, 1989-91. Recipient Excellence in Edn. award Baltimore County, 1990-91; honored by Randallstown Elem. PTA, 1989; donation made in her honor Christa McAuliffe scholarship fund, 1990. Mem. ASCD, NEA (Excellence in Teaching honor 1992), Md. State Tchrs. Assn., Tchr.'s Assn. of Balt. County Orgn., PTA, Md. Coun. Tchrs. Math., Women Educators of Balt. County Orgn., Delta Kappa Gamma. Home: 710 Melendez Way Lady Lake FL 32159-9265

STAUBERT, RÜDIGER PAUL, astronomer, educator; b. Burg, Magdeburg, Germany, Mar. 25, 1939; s. Paul and Elisabeth (Minck) S.; m. Ursula Will, Oct. 5, 1964; children: Astrid, Andreas. Physicist, U. Kiel, 1965, PhD, 1969; dr. rer. nat. habil., U. Tübingen, 1983. Rschr. U. Kiel, Germany, 1965-69; postdoctoral fellow NASA-MSC, Houston, 1969-71; rschr., asst. U. Tübingen, Germany, 1971-85; prof. U. Tübingen, 1985—. Contbr. articles to profl. jours. Grantee DFG, DARA, DAAD, VW-Stiftung. Mem. Com. on Space Rsch., Internat. Astron. Union, European Astron. Soc., Astronomische Gesellschaft, Deutsche Physikalische Gesellschaft. Avocations: tennis, sailing, skiing, gardening. Office: Univ Tübingen Dept Astron, Waldhäuserstr 64, D-72076 Tübingen Germany

STAUDER, GERHARD M., biochemist; b. Munich, Germany, Oct. 29, 1949; m. Ursula Buch, Apr. 1, 1980; 1 child, Ralf. Diploma in Biology, U. Munich, 1977, PhD, 1980. Clin. rsch. asst. Lederle Pharma/Cyanamid, Wolfratshausen, Germany, 1980-82, head med. info., 1982-84, head clin. rsch. for chemotherapeutics, 1984-85; dir. clin. rsch. Mucos Pharma Group Worldwide, Geretsried, Germany, 1986-87, dir. R&D, 1987—, v.p., 1993—. Contbr. more than 50 articles to profl. jours.; holder 12 patents on enzyme therapy. Mem. N.Y. Acad. Scis., Med. Enzyme Rsch. Soc. (adv. bd.), European Soc. Infectious Diseases in Ob-Gyn. (mem. adv. bd., chmn., group BRM). Home: Primelweg 2, D-82538 Geretsried Germany Office: Mucos Pharma Group, Malvenweg 2, D-82538 Geretsried Germany

STAUDT, ERICH ERWIN, labor economics educator; b. Miltenberg, Germany, Nov. 18, 1941. Diploma physics, U. Mainz, Germany, 1970; Dr. Rer. Pol., U. Erlangen/Nuernberg, 1973, Dr. Habil., 1978. Prof. U. Duisburg, 1978-86; prof. labor econs. U. Bochum, 1986—; chmn. Inst. for Angewandte Innovations Forschung, Bochum, 1982—. Office: Univ Bochum, Universitaetsstrasse 150, D-44780 Bochum Germany

STAUFFER, DIETRICH HERMANN, physicist; b. Bonn, Fed. Republic Germany, Feb. 6, 1943; s. Ethelbert and Hanna (Tummeley) S. PhD, Tech. U., Munich, 1970; Habilitation, Saar State U., Fed. Republic of Germany, 1975. James Chair prof. physics St. Francis Xavier U., Antigonish, Can., 1987; group leader Julich (Fed. Republic of Germany) Super Computer Ctr., 1988-90; assoc. prof. Cologne (Fed. Republic of Germany) U., 1977-88, 90—. Author 4 books; contbr. articles to profl. jours. Univ. rep. GEW Tchr.'s Union, Essen, Fed. Republic of Germany, 1979-81. Recipient Humboldt prize French-German Collaboration, Paris, 1986, Can.-Germany Rsch. award, 1993, Kastler-Gentner prize, 1999, prize Polish Edn. Min., 1999. Mem. German Phys. Soc., European Phys. Soc. Mem. Green Party. Avocation: movies. Home: Unicenter 2111, Luxemberger Str 124, D 50939 Cologne Germany

STAUFFER, JOHN WILLIAM, cultural historian; b. Lincoln, Nebr.; s. William Albert and Jean Stanley Stauffer. MALS in Humanities, Wesleyan U., 1991; MA in Am. Studies, Purdue U., 1993; PhD in Am. Studies, Yale U., 1999. Asst. prof. Harvard U., Cambridge, Mass., 1999—. Contbr. articles to profl. jours. Rec. clk. New Haven Friends, 1997. Newhouse fellow in Writing Yale U., 1996-97, Rsch. fellow, 1994-95, History and Am. Studies Rsch. fellow, 1996, Marcia Brady Tucker fellow, 1994-95, New Britain Mus. of Am. Art fellow New Britain Mus., 1994, Charlotte Newcombe fellowship Woodrow Wilson Nat. Fellowship Found., 1997-98; grantee NEH, 1999; recipient Ralph Henry Gabriel prize, 1999; summer grantee NEH, 1999. Mem. Soc. for Values in Higher Edn., Orgn. of Am. Historians (presenter ann. mtg. 1998), Am. Studies Assn. (Ralph Henry Gabriel prize 1999), Daguerreian Soc. (spkr. ann. mtg.), Phi Kappa Phi. Avocation: dance (jazz, ballet), photography. E-mail: stauffer@fas.harvard.edu. Home: 13 Ware St Apt 14 Cambridge MA 02138-4010 Office: Harvard U Dept English Barker Ctr 12 Quincy St Cambridge MA 02138-3804

STAUSKIS, VYTAUTAS JONAS, acoustical engineer, educator; b. Palanga, Lithuania, May 9, 1942. Degree in engring., Kaunas Politech. Inst., 1968; DSc, Moscow Inst. Comm., 1974, Vilnius Gediminas Tech. U., 1997. Asst. prof. Vilnius Gediminas Tech. U., 1974-80, assoc. prof., 1980-97, prof., 1998—. Contbr. articles to profl. jours. Mem. Audio Engring. Soc. (chmn. Lithuanian sect.). Avocations: symphony music, opera music. Home: Rinktines 21-26, LT-2051 Vilnius Lithuania Office: Vilnius Gediminas Tech U, Sauletekio al 11, LT-2040 Vilnius Lithuania

STAV, ANATOLI OVSEI, anesthesiologist; b. Tchernoviz, Ukraine, USSR, Sept. 23, 1952; arrived in Israel, 1978; s. Ovsei Isaak and Zilia Aba (Zibenberg) Podstavkin; m. Inna Leon Schmulevitz, Aug. 10, 1974; children: Alexandra, Ilana, Anat, Michael. MD, Med. Inst. No. 1, Leningrad, USSR, 1976. Jr. anesthesiologist Rovno, USSR, 1976-78, Hillel Jaffe Meml. Hosp., Hadera, Israel, 1978-80, 81-83, Beilinson Med. Ctr., Petah Tiqva, Israel, 1983-86; sr. anesthesiologist Hillel Jaffe Med. Ctr., 1986-94, work in Pain Clinic, 1987-91, chief postoperative care unit, 1994—; anesthesiologist Hertzlia (Israel) Med. Ctr., 1989-93, Ramat Marpe Hosp., Ramat Gan, Israel, 1989-93, Elisha Hosp., Haifa, 1990—, Am. Med. Ctr., Rishon Lezion, Israel, 1989-94; lectr. postgrad. anesthesiology U. Tel-Aviv, 1986, 89, 90, 94—, anesthesiology immigrant physicians Hillel Jaffe Med. Ctr., 1991, 92, 95, 96, Nursing Med. Sch., 1991, 92, 94; presenter papers in field. Contbr. articles to profl. jours. Maj. Israeli Med. Force, 1980-81. Mem. Israel Med. Assn., Israel Soc. Anesthesiologists, Internat. Soc. Study of Pain, Israelian Soc. Study of Pain, Internat. Soc. Study of Lumbar Spine, World Soc. Pain Clinicians, European Soc. Regional Anesthesia. Home: Scheschet Ayamim str 20/11, Hadera 38100, Israel Office: Hillel Jaffe Med Ctr, Dept Anesthesiology, Hadera 38100, Israel

STAVANS, ISAAC, artist; b. Tampico, Mexico, Aug. 25, 1931; s. Salvador and Bella (Altschuler) S.; m. Malvina Fischer, Mar. 18, 1956; children: Joel, Tamar, Iliana. BA, Mexico City Coll., 1952; MA, CUNY, 1953. Mem. Mex. Soc. Visual Artists. Home: Bosque de Minas, 55B Apt 1104, 53920 Bosque Herradura Mexico

STAVELEY, HENRY SCOWCROFT, building consultant, surveyor; b. Bolton, Lancashire, Eng., Sept. 1, 1920; s. Thomas William and Frances (Scowcroft) S.; m. Margaret Taylor, July 1, 1944; children: Jane Margaret, David Alan. Student, Manchester Coll. Tech., 1938-39. Chartered surveyor; chartered builder, chartered arbitrator. Bldg. surveyor Dist. Bank Ltd., Manchester, Lancashire, Eng., 1948-52; area surveyor H. & G. Simonds Ltd., Plymouth, Devon, Eng., 1952-63; sr. surveyor Courage (Western) Ltd., Bristol, Avon, Eng., 1963-68; sr. ptnr. Martin Staveley & Ptnrs., Clevedon, Avon, Eng., 1968-77; sole prin. Staveley, Budleigh Salterton, Devon, Eng., 1977-88; cons. Staveley & Kelly, Budleigh Salterton, 1988-93; cons. surveyor D.H.S.S. and S.W. Health Authorities, London, Avon and Devon, 1970-88; diocesan surveyor Exeter (Devon) Diocese, 1980-90; chmn. Bldg. Asset Mgmt. Group, 1975-80. Co-author: Surveying Buildings, 1983, Building Surveys, 1990; joint author: Rebuild, 1982; editor: Maintenance Management, 1990. Mem. Govt. Com. on Hosp. Bldg. Maintenance, London, 1968-70; chmn. Bldg. Asset Mgmt. Group, London, 1975-80; mem. Govt. Com. on Tech., London, 1974-80; chmn. local rev. com. Channings Wood Prison, 1986-89. Lt. Royal Arty., Brit. Army, 1939-46. Fellow Royal Instn. Chartered Surveyors (external examiner 1970-80), Chartered Inst. Bldg., Royal Soc. Health, Chartered Inst. Arbitrators, Faculty of Bldg.; mem. Exmouth Probus Club (founder, pres.), Budleigh Salterton Probus Club, East Exe Probus Club, Raleigh Probus Club. Mem. Conservative party. Mem. Ch. of Eng. Avocations: music, croquet, drawing, writing, travel. Home: 1 Sherbrook Close, EX 96DB Budleigh Salterton Devon, England

STAVINSKAYA, OKSANA NIKOLAYEVNA, chemist; b. Samara, Russia, Feb. 1, 1960; d. Nikolay Gavrilovich and Elena Yakovlevna (Melnik) Pastushenko; m.Vladimir Borisovich Stavinskiy, Jan. 27, 1989; 1 child, Irina Vladimirovna. M, Phys.-Tech. Inst., Moscow, 1983; PhD, Inst. Surface Chemistry, Kiev, Ukraine, 1998. Engr. Inst. Phys. Chemistry/Nat. Acad. Scis. Ukraine, Kiev, 1983-86; rsch. scientist Inst. Surface Chemistry/Nat. Acad. Scis. Ukraine, Kiev, 1989-93, 95—. Contbr. articles to profl. jours. Office: Inst Surface Chemistry/NAS, Gen Naumov St 17, 03164 Kiev Ukraine

STAVRINOS, PANAYIOTIS, mathematics educator; b. Athens, Greece, Oct. 19, 1950; s. Charalambos Stavrinos and Crhystalo Hatzipanagi; m. Maria Varela, Dec. 19, 1976; 1 child, Harris. BA in Math., U. Athens, 1975, PhD in Math., 1990. Tchg. asst. math. U. Athens, 1978-89, lectr. math., 1990-99, asst. prof. math., 1999—. Founding mem. editl. bd. Balkan Soc. Geometry, 1995; co-author: Introduction to Physical Principles of Differential Geometry, 1995; contbr. articles to profl. publs. Mem. rsch. bd. advisors Am. Biographical Inst., 1996. Recipient Internat. Cultural Diploma of Honor Am. Biographical Inst., 1995. Mem. Tensor Soc. Tsukuba U. Japan, Balkan Soc. Geometers (v.p. 2000). Avocations: chess, swimming, climbing. E-mail: pstavrin@cc.uoa.gr. Office: U Athens Dept Math, Panepistemiopolis, 15784 Athens Greece

STAVROPOULOS, WILLIAM S., chemical executive; b. Bridgehampton, N.Y., May 12, 1939; m. Linda Stavropoulos; children: S. William, Angela D. BA in Pharm. Chemistry, Fordham U.; PhD in Medicinal Chemistry, U. Washington. Rsch. chemist in pharm. rsch. Dow Chem. Co., Midland, Mich., 1967, rsch. chemist for diagnostics product rsch., 1970, rsch. mgr. diagnostics product rsch., 1973, bus. mgr. diagnostics product rsch., 1976, bus. mgr. polyolefins, 1977, dir. mktg. plastics dept., 1979; comml. v.p. Dow Chem. Co. Latin Am., Coral Gables, Fla., 1980; pres. Dow Latin Am., 1984; comml. v.p., basics and hydrocarbons Dow Chem. Co. U.S.A., Midland, 1985-87; group v.p. Dow Chem. Co. U.S.A., 1987-90; pres. Dow U.S.A., 1990—; v.p. The Dow Chemical Co., 1990; sr. v.p. The Dow Chem. Co., 1991, pres., 1992; pres., CEO, bd. dirs. The Dow Chem. Co., Midland, 1993—; bd. dirs. Dow Corning Corp., The Dow Chem. Co., Marion Merrel Dow Inc.; CEO Essex Chem Corp, 1988-92. Office: Dow Chem Co 2030 Dow Ctr Midland MI 48674-0001

STAVROUDIS, ORESTES NICHOLAS, mathematician, educator; b. N.Y.C., Feb. 22, 1923; arrived in Mex., 1992; s. Nicholas Andreas Stavroudis and Marguerite (Mizner) Fox; m. Dorothea Franziska Allina, Sept. 2, 1949; children: Christopher, Gregory. AB, Columbia U., 1948, MA, 1949; PhD, U. London, Eng., 1959; diploma, Imperial Coll., London, 1959. Mathematician Patuxtent River (Md.) Naval Air Sta., 1951, Nat. Bur. Standards, Washington, 1951-54, 57-67; prof. optical scis. U. Ariz., Tucson, 1967-88, prof. emeritus, 1988—; sr. staff scientist Fairchild Space Co., Greenbelt, Md., 1988-90; sr. staff engr. Lockheed Missile and Space Co., Sunnyvale, Calif., 1990-91; investigator titular Centro de Investigaciones en Optica, León, Mexico, 1992—; vis. prof. Nat. Chiao Tung U., Hsinchu, Taiwan, 1982. Author: Optics of Rays Wavefronts and Caustics, 1972, Modular Optical Design, 1982; patentee in field. Cpl. USAAF, 1943-46, ATO. Fellow AAAS, Optical Soc. Am. (v.p. Nat. Capitol sect. 1966-67, chmn./chmn. elect Tucson sect. 1971-73, assoc. editor jour. 1972-76, topical editor jour. 1986-88); mem. Internat. Soc. Optical Engring., Am. Math. Soc., Math. Assn. Am., Soc. Indsl. and Applied Math., Sistema Nacional de Investigadores. Democrat. Avocation: history. Office: Centro Investigacion Optica, Loma del Bosque 115, 37150 León GTO, Mexico

STAVROULAKIS, ANTHEA MERRIE, biology educator; b. Bklyn., Nov. 9, 1959; d. Zachary Stavroulakis and Evangeline Stella Spirakis. AA, CUNY, 1978; BA, NYU, 1981, MS, 1984, PhD, 1992. Grad. rsch. asst. in biology NYU, N.Y.C., 1981-92, adj. instr., 1984-89; adj. instr. sci. Borough of Manhattan C.C.-CUNY, 1986-92; asst. prof. CUNY, 1992; adj. instr. natural sci. York Coll.-CUNY, 1989-90; assoc. prof. biol. sci. Kingsborough C.C.-CUNY, 1992—; adj. instr. biology Suffolk County C.C., 1991-92; jr. rsch. asst. in biology Brookhaven Nat. Lab., 1991-92. Author: Laboratory Manual-General Biology II, 1996, Laboratory Manual: General Biology I, 1999; contbr. articles to profl. jours.; judge N.Y.C. Sci. and Tech. Fairs, 1996-99. Grantee N.Y. State Edn. Dept., 1995-96, C.C. Sci. and Tech. Equipment Fund, N.Y.C., 1995, Eelgrass Remediation in Jamaica Bay, 1996, 98-99, Eppley Found., 1999-2000, 2000—. Mem. AAAS, Am. Soc. for Microbiology, Nat. Assn. Biology Tchrs., N.Y. Acad. Scis., Profl. and Staff Congress CUNY. Democrat. Greek Orthodox. Avocations: gourmet cooking, aviculture, gardening, travel.

STAZHEVSKIY, STANISLAV BORISOVICH, research laboratory administrator; b. Perm, USSR, May 24, 1940; s. Boris Yakovlevich and Olga Sergeyevna (Koretnyuk) S.; m. Svetlana Pavlovna Vybornova, Dec. 30, 1962; 1 child, Andrey. MSc, Novosibirsk Inst. Rwy. Engrs., Russia, 1962; PhD, Inst. Mining, Novosibirsk, 1975, DSc, 1988. Cert. in engring. (mechanics of rock and soil, bridge and tunnel constrn.). Jr. rschr. Inst. Mining, Novosibirsk, Rusia, 1965-78; sr. rschr. Inst. Mining, Novosibirsk, 1978-80, head of lab., 1980-90, 93—, dep. dir. sci., 1990-93; bd. chmn. Siberian Rsch. and Technol. Lab., Novosibirsk, 1992-97; prof. Novosibirsk U. Arch. and Constrn., 1996—. Author: (books) Ring Structures in Evolution of Solar System's Celestial Bodies, 1998, Genesis of Moon's and Earth's Irregular Ring Structures, 1999; contbr. articles to profl. jours.; patentee in field. Mem. Russian Acad. Sci. (sci. coun. on problem of underground space usage 1997—), Peter Acad. Sci. and Art (corr. mem.). Avocations: fishing, traveling. Office: Inst Mining, 54 Krasny Prospect, RU630091 Novosibirsk Russia

STEAD, (GEORGE) CHRISTOPHER, retired divinity educator; b. Wimbledon, Eng., Apr. 9, 1913; s. Francis Bernard and Rachel Elizabeth (Bell) S.; m. Doris Elizabeth Odom, Apr. 15, 1958; children: William John, Martin Patrick, Catherine Rachel. Student, Marlborough Coll., 1926-31; BA, King's Coll., Cambridge, Eng., 1935; MA, King's Coll., 1938, LittD, 1978; BA, New Coll., Oxford, Eng., 1935, MA, 1949. Ordained priest Ch. of Eng., 1941. Curate St. John's Ch., Newcastle on Tyne, Eng., 1939; asst. master Eton Coll., 1941-44; fellow, lectr. in divinity King's Coll., Cambridge, 1938-40, 45-48; fellow, tutor, chaplain Keble Coll., Oxford, 1949-71; Ely prof. divinity U. Cambridge, 1971-80, emeritus prof., 1980—; canon residentiary Ely Cathedral, 1971-80; professorial fellow King's Coll., 1971-80, fellow 80-85. Author: Divine Substance, 1977, Substance and Illusion in the Christian Fathers, 1985, Philosophie und Theologie I: Die Zeit der Alten Kirche, 1990, Philosophy in Christian Antiquity, 1994, A Filosofia na Antiquidade Christa, 1999, Doctrine and Philosophy in Early Christianity, 2000; also numerous articles in English, German and Italian theol. jours. and dictionaries. Fellow Brit. Acad. Avocations: walking, sailing, music. Home: 13 Station Rd, Haddenham, Ely CB6 3XD, England

STEAD, JAMES JOSEPH, JR., securities company executive; b. Chgo., Sept. 13, 1930; s. James Joseph and Irene (Jennings) S.; m. Edith Pearson, Feb. 13, 1954; children: James, Diane, Robert, Caroline. BS, DePaul U., 1957, MBA, 1959. Asst. sec. C. F. Childs & Co., Chgo., 1957-62; exec. v.p., sec. Koenig, Keating & Stead, Inc., Chgo., 1962-66; 2d v.p., mgr. midwest mcpl. bond dept. Hayden, Stone Inc., Chgo., 1966-69; sr. v.p., nat. sales mgr. Ill. Co. Inc., 1969-70; mgr. instl. sales dept. Reynolds and Co., Chgo., 1970-72; partner Edwards & Hanly, 1972-74; v.p., instnl. sales mgr. Paine, Webber, Jackson & Curtis, 1974-76; v.p., regional instl. sales mgr. Reynolds Securities, Inc., 1976-78; sr. v.p., regional mgr. Oppenheimer & Co., Inc., 1978-88; sr. v.p., regional mgr. fixed income Tucker Anthony, 1988—; instr. Mcpl. Bond Sch., Chgo., 1967—. With AUS, 1951-53. Mem. Security Traders Assn. Chgo., Nat. Security Traders Assn., Am. Mgmt. Assn., Mcpl. Fin. Forum Washington. Clubs: Execs., Union League, Mcpl. Bond, Bond (Chgo.); Olympia Fields Country (Ill.); Wall Street (N.Y.C.). Home: 1005 Hickory Ridge Ct Frankfort IL 60423-2114 Office: 1 S Wacker Dr Chicago IL 60606-4614

STEAD, JERRE L., telecommunications company executive; b. Maquoketa, Iowa, Jan. 8, 1943; s. H. Victor and Anna Catherine (Grindrod) S.; m. Mary Joy Kloppenburg, Dec. 26, 1961; children: Joel A., Jay A. BBA, U. Iowa, 1965; grad. advanced mgmt. program, Harvard U., 1982. Mgr. regional sales Honeywell Corp., Phila., 1971-73; dir. prodn. Honeywell Corp., Mpls., 1974-75, dir. distbn., 1975-76, v.p. fin. and adminstrn., Brussels, 1979-82; v.p., gen. mgr. Honeywell-Phillips Med. Electronics, Brussels, 1981-82; v.p., gen. mgr. Honeywell Corp., Mpls., 1982-85, v.p., group exec., 1986; pres., COO Sq. D Co., Palatine, Ill., 1987-88, pres., CEO, chmn. bd., 1989-91, also bd. dirs.; chmn., CEO Global Info. Solutions AT&T, N.Y.C., 1991-95; CEO Legent Corp., Vienna, Va., 1995-96; chmn., CEO Ingram Micro, Inc., Santa Ana, Calif., 1996-2000; bd. dirs. Eljer Industries, Plano, Tex., Ameritech, Chgo., USG, Chgo., TJ Internat., Inc. Mem. Pres.' coun. Am. Lung Assn., N.Y.C., 1986—, The Wash. Ctr. Nat. Campaign Com.; bus. adv. com. N.C. A&T U.; trustee Coe Coll., Cedar Rapids, Iowa, 1987; mem. coun. on competitiveness Ill. Bus. Roundtable; bd. visitors U. Iowa, Iowa City. Mem. Nat. Elec. Mfrs. Assn. (bd. govs. 1984—), Nat. Assn. Elec. Distbrs. (edn. com.), Chgo. Com., Elec. Mfrs. Club. Republican. Methodist. Office: Ingram Micro Inc PO Box 25125 1600 E Saint Andrew Pl Santa Ana CA 92705-4926

STEAD, RONALD, energy industry executive; b. South Shields, Durham, Eng., Dec. 28, 1935; s. Samuel and Mary (Whittington) S.; m. Irene Parker, Sept. 24, 1966; children: Karen, Jonathan. BS in Mech. Engring. with honors, Durham U., Eng., 1959. Chartered engr., Européen Ingénieur. Office boy to apprentice engr.'s fitter Clarke, Chapman & Co., Ltd., Gateshead, Eng., 1951-56; rsch. engr. Clarke, Chapman & Co., Ltd., Gateshead, 1959-66, chief design engr. to mgr., 1966-71, mgr. strategic planning, 1971-72, mgr. tech. svcs., 1972-73, mgr. contract engring., 1973-76; mgr. boiler dept. M. Dedini S.A. Metalurgica, Piracicaba, Sao Paulo, Brazil, 1976-79; mgr. tech. svcs. NEI Internat. Combustion, Ltd., Derby, Eng., 1980-82; dir., gen. mgr. Cochran Unit NEI Internat. Combustion, Ltd., Annan, Scotland, 1982-91; proprietor, prin. cons. engring. Engring. Plus, Carlisle/Cumbria, 1991—. Inventor: Spl. Boiler, 1989; contbr. articles to profl. jours., 1960-83. Fellow Instn. Mech. Engrs.; mem. Scottish Engring. Employers Assn. (coun.), Power Generation Contractors Assn. (bd. dirs.), Assn. Shell Boilermakers (chmn.), ASME, N.E. Coast Inst. Engrs. and Shipbuilders (assoc.). Conservative. Anglican. Avocations: jogging, squash, tennis, gardening. Office: Engineering Plus Ashdown 5, Brunstock Close/Lowry Hill, Carlisle Cumbria CA3 0HL, England

STEADMAN, DAVID ROSSLYN AYTON, business executive, corporate director; b. Wembley, Eng., June 7, 1937; came to U.S., 1980; s. Eric and Iris Sina (Smith) S.; m. Beryl Ellen Giles, Jan. 5, 1963 (div.); children: Michael, Christopher, Timothy. B.Sc. in Engring. with honors, City U., London, 1960. Mng. dir. Cossor Electronics, Harlow, Eng., 1974-78; chmn. EMI med. Electronics, London, 1978-80; pres. Raytheon Data Systems, Norwood Mass., 1980-84, Raytheon Ventures, Lexington, 1985-87; chmn., chief exec. officer GCA Corp., Andover, Mass., 1987-88; pres. Atlantic Mgmt. Assocs., Inc., Bedford, N.H., 1988—; chmn., CEO Integra-Hotel & Restaurant Co., 1990-94; chmn. Brookwood Cos., Inc., 1989—, Tech. Svc. Group, Inc., 1994-97; chmn. Visibility, Inc., 1996—, CEO, 1999—; bd. dirs. Tech/Ops-Sevcon, Inc., Aavid Thermal Techs., Inc., Telequip Corp.; chmn. Torrent Systems, Inc., 1998—. Fellow Instn. Elec. Engrs. (U.K.); mem. Inst. Mgmt. (U.K.; companion), Inst. Mech. Engrs. (U.K.). Avocations: music; sailing. Office: Atlantic Mgmt Assocs Inc PO Box 10670 Bedford NH 03110-0670

STEADMAN, ROBERT KEMPTON, oral and maxillofacial surgeon; b. Mpls., July 8, 1943; s. Henry Kempton and Helen Vivian (Berg) S.; m. Susan E. Hoffman; children: Andrea Helene, Darcy Joanne, Richard Kempton, Michael Dean. BS, U. Wash., Seattle, 1969, DDS, 1974. Diplomate Am. Bd. Oral and Maxillofacial Surgery. Residency USAF, Elgin AFB, Fla., 1974-75; resident oral and maxillofacial surgery U. Okla., 1977-80, La. State U., Shreveport, 1980-81; pvt. practice Spokane, Wash., 1981—; cons. Group Health Coop., 1989—; mem. adv. bd. Osteoporosis Awareness Resource, 1988—. Select recruiting ptnr. U. Wash. Sch. Dentistry, 1990. Fellow Am. Acad. Cosmetic Surgery, Internat. Assn. Oral and Maxillofacial Surgery, Am. Coll. Oral and Maxillofacial Surgery, Am. Soc. Oral and Maxillofacial Surgery, Acad. Gen. Dentistry; mem. Internat. Soc. Plastic, Aesthetic and Reconstructive Surgery, Am. Acad. Cosmetic Surgery, Delta Sigma Delta (pres. 1987-88). Office: 801 W 5th Ave Ste 212 Spokane WA 99204-2800

STEADMAN, STEPHEN GEOFFREY, physicist; b. Rochester, N.Y., June 28, 1942; s. Luville T. and Elizabeth (Genung) S.; m. Brigitte M. Kreuzer, Aug. 1, 1975; children: Claudia, Mark, William. BS, U. Rochester, 1964; MS, Rutgers U., 1966, PhD, 1969. Vis. scientist Univ. Erlangen-Nurnberg, Erlangen, Germany, 1969-71; asst. Univ. Freiburg, Germany, 1971-72; sr. rsch. assoc. MIT, Cambridge, Mass., 1972-74; asst. prof. MIT, Cambridge, 1975-79, assoc. prof., 1979-82, sr. rsch. scientist, 1982-98; guest scientist Max Planck Inst., Heidelberg, Germany, 1974-75; program mgr. for heavy ion nuclear physics U.S. Dept. Energy, Germantown, Md., 1998—; program dir. nuclear physics NSF, Arlington, Va., 1994-97; E866 co-spokesman Brookhaven Nat. Lab., Upton, N.Y., 1992-98. Contbr. articles to profl. jours. Mem. Arsenal Reuse Com., Watertown, Mass., 1992-97. Mem. AAAS, Am. Phys. Soc. Episcopalian. Avocations: piano, jogging. Office: US Dept Energy SC-23 19901 Germantown Rd Germantown MD 20874-1207

STEAR, CHARLES ANTHONY, author; b. Kingsbridge, Devon, U.K., Apr. 26, 1934; s. Victor Roy and Bessie Emily (Distin) S.; m. Margarete Helene Meltzer, May 25, 1963; children: Suzanne, Peter. Diploma in Bakery and Confectionery Tech., Plymouth Coll. Tech., 1954; diploma in Food Sci. and Tech., Poly. of South Bank, London, 1956. Trainee supr. J. Lyons & Co. Baking Corp., London, 1958-60; rschs. in proteins London, 1960-62; R&D project leader Haco A.G., Bern, Switzerland, 1962-64, Unilever Ltd., London, 1964-66; lab. mgr. COOP Milling, Zürich, Switzerland, 1966-70; R&D mgr. cereals RHM Rsch. Ctr., High Wycombe, U.K., 1970-73; lab. mgr. Auermühlenwerke K.G., Cologne, Germany, 1973-76; ind. author and cons. grain sci. Stear Consult, Salcombe, Devon, Eng., 1976—. Author: Handbook of Breakmaking Technology, 1990; contbr. articles to profl. jours. With U.K. Army, 1956-58. Fellow Inst. Brit. Bakers. Avocations: hor-

ticulture, languages, walking, travel, auto mechanics. Home and Office: Platt Close 9, Beadon Pk, Salcombe TQ8 8NZ, England

STEARNS, SUSAN TRACEY, lighting design company executive, lawyer; b. Seattle, Oct. 28, 1957; d. Arthur Thomas and Roberta Jane (Arrowood) S.; m. Ross Alan De Alessi, Aug. 11, 1990; 1 child, Chase Arthur. AA, Stephens Coll., 1977, BA, 1979; JD, U. Wash., Seattle, 1990. Bar: Calif. 1990, U.S. Ct. Appeals (9th cir.) 1990, U.S. Dist. Ct. (no. dist.) Calif 1990, U.S. Dist. Ct. (we. dist.) Wash. 1991, Wash. 1991. TV news prodr. KOMO, Seattle, 1980-86; atty. Brobeck, Phleger & Harrison, San Francisco, 1990-92; pres. Ross De Alessi Lighting Design, Seattle, 1993—. Author periodicals in field. Alumnae Assn. Coun. Stephens Coll., Columbia, Mo., 1995—. Named Nat. Order of Barristers U. Washington, Seattle, 1990. Mem. ABA (mem. state labor and employment law subcom.), Wash. State Bar Assn. (mem. bench-bar-press com.), State Bar Calif., King County Bar Assn., Bar Assn.San Francisco, Wash. Athletic Club. Avocations: travel, dance. Office: Ross De Alessi Lighting Design 2815 2nd Ave Ste 280 Seattle WA 98121-3217

STEBBINS, GREGORY KELLOGG, foundation executive; b. Lafayette, Ind., Jan. 10, 1951; s. Albert Kellogg and Nancy Ruth (Osborn) S. BS in Data Processing, Calif. Poly., Pomona, 1974; MBA, U. So. Calif., 1976; EdD, Pepperdine U., 1985. Account exec. ADP, Long Beach, Calif., 1977-78; salesman Grubb & Ellis, L.A., 1978-81; v.p. Grubb & Ellis, Beverly Hills, Calif., 1981-83; regional mgr. Hanes Co., Beverly Hills, 1983-85; treas. U. Santa Monica, L.A., 1983—; pres. Stebbins Consulting Group, Santa Monica, 1989—; chair Santa Monica Inst., 1994—. Mem. ASTD, Sigma Xi. Avocations: flying, scuba diving, photography. Home: 445 Washington Blvd Apt 15 Marina Del Rey CA 90292 Office: Santa Monica Inst 4553 Glencoe Ave Ste 355 Marina Del Rey CA 90292

STEC, WOJCIECH JACEK, chemist, educator; b. Warsaw, Poland, Oct. 15, 1940; s. Czeslaw and Helene (Trzaskacz) S.; m. Karola Bozenna Hille, Apr. 10, 1966; children: Magdalena Maria, Malgorzata Anna, Wojciech Julian. MSc, Tech. U., Łódź, Poland, 1963, PhD, 1968; DSc in Organic Chemistry, Polish Acad. Sci., Warsaw, 1973. Rsch. asst. Polish Acad. Scis., Łódź, 1963-68, rsch. adjunct, 1968-70, rsch. assoc. Ctr. Molecular-Macromolecular Studies, 1971-74, docent, 1974-78, prof., head lab., 1978—; postdoctoral fellow Vanderbilt U., Nashville, 1970-71; vis. scientist Bur. Biologics, FDA, Bethesda, Md., 1983-84; co-chmn. Nat Com. Biotech., Warsaw, 1987-90, chmn., 1990— mem. editorial bd. Polish Jour. Chemistry, 1978-91, Heteroatom Chemistry, 1988-96, Antisense Rsch. Devel., 1995—; lectr. for internat. confs., symposia and univs. Editor: Phosphorus Chemistry Directed Towards Biology, 1980; co-editor: Biophosphates and Their Analogues, 1987; contbr. sci. papers to profl. publs. Scholar-in-Residence, Fogarty Internat. Ctr., 1991. Fellow Warsaw Sci. Soc.; mem. Polish Acad. Scis. (corr.), Polish Chem. Soc. (Kostanecki medal 1990), Polish Biochem. Soc. (Marchlewski medal 1995), Am. Chem. Soc. Office: Polish Acad Scis, Sienkiewicza 112, 90363 Łódź Poland

STECICH, JOHN PATRICK, structural engineer; b. Chgo., Nov. 1, 1949; s. William Frank and Margaret Mary (Hanrahan) S.; m. Rita Louise Fahey, July 1, 1972; children: Eric John, Thomas John. BSCE, Ill. Inst. Tech., 1971, MSCE, 1972. Lic. profl. engr., Ill., Ind., Pa., Fla.; lic. structural engr., Ill. Design engr. Chgo. Bridge and Iron Co., Oak Brook, Ill., 1971-79; adjunct prof. Midwest Coll. Engring., 1976-77; sr. cons. Wiss, Janney, Elstner Assocs., INc., Chgo., 1979—; speaker in field. Contbr. papers to prof. publs. Recipient Repair Project of Yr. award Internat. Concrete Repair Inst., 1993, McGraw Hill/CSI Boston Advanced Constrn. Tech. First Place award, 1994, Driehaus Preservation Project of Yr. award, 1994, Ill. Ind. Masonry Coun. 1993 Honorable Mention award, Amoco Bldg. Facade Recladding. Best Publ. award Nat. Coun. Structural Engrs. assn., 1998. Fellow ASCE (design of steel bldg. structures com.); mem. ASTM (dimension stone com.), Am. Inst. Steel Constrn., Am. Concrete Inst. (steel reinforcement com.), Am. Soc. for Metals, Chgo. Com. on High Rise Bldgs., Structural Engrs. Assn. Ill. (1st prize award 1988, Meritorious Publ. award 1991, 96, award of merit for Amoco Bldg. facade 1993, award of merit for Bahai House of Worship restoration 1994, Best Publ. award 1998). Home: 11306 S Central Park Ave Chicago IL 60655-3416 Office: Wiss Janney Elstner Assocs 120 N Lasalle St Chicago IL 60602-2424

STECK, BRIAN JASON, brokerage house executive; b. Montreal, Que., Can., Dec. 26, 1946; s. Edward and Lottie (Potofsky) S.; married; 1 child, Stephen Mitchell. B in Commerce, Sir George Williams U., 1968; MBA, U. Pa., 1969. Cert. fin. analyst. Research analyst Nesbitt Thomson, Inc., Montreal, 1969-72, assoc. mem. corp. fin., 1972-73, dir., v.p. research and instl. sales, 1974-77; pres., chief operating officer Nesbitt Thomson Deacon Inc., Toronto, Ont., Can., 1978-86; pres., chief exec. officer Nesbitt Thomson Deacon Inc., Toronto, Ont., 1986; chmn., chief exec. officer, bd. dirs. Nesbitt Thomson Deacon Inc., Toronto, Ont., Can, 1990—; pres., chief exec. officer Fahnstock and Co. Inc., Toronto, 1985-87; pres., chief exec. officer Nesbitt Thomson Deacon Ltee, Toronto, 1987, chmn., chief exec. officer, bd. dirs., 1990—; chmn., chief exec. officer, bd. dirs. Nesbitt Thomson Inc., Toronto, 1990—, Nesbitt Thomson Securities Ltd., Toronto, 1990—; vice chair Bank of Montreal; bd. dirs. Can. Post Corp.; chmn. N. Y. Gen. Hosp. Bd. dirs. North York Gen. Hosp. Fellow Can. Securities Inst.; mem. Investment Dealers Assn. Can. (chmn. 1990-91), Toronto Soc. Fin. Analysts, Fin. Rsch. Inst., Oakdale Golf and Country Club, Cambridge Club, St. Andrews Golf Club. Avocations: golf, reading. Office: Bank of Montreal, 119 St Jacques, Montreal, PQ Canada H2Y 1L6*

STECKI, JAN, physical chemist; b. Warsaw, Poland, Oct. 1, 1930; s. Jozef and Maria (Mikulska) S.; m. Irena Michałowska, Dec. 30, 1964; children: Maria, Artur, Andrzej. MSc, U. Warsaw, 1952, PhD in Chemistry, 1959; DSc, Polish Acad. Sci., Warsaw, 1962. Tchg. asst. U. Warsaw, 1952-59; postdoctoral fellow Free U. Brussels, 1959-60; docent Polish Acad. Sci., Warsaw, 1960-72; sr. rsch. fellow U. So. Calif., L.A., 1962-64; prof., head dept. phys. chemistry Polish Acad. Sci., 1972—; vis. prof. Trondheim U., 1973, Oxford (Eng.) U., 1982, 87, U. Bristol (Eng.), 1992, U. Copenhagen, 1995, Cornell U., Ithaca, N.Y., 1996. Author: Statystyczna Termodynamika, 1971; contbr. over 125 articles to profl. jours. Recipient Cross Polonia Restituta Pres. Poland, 1995. Mem. Polish Chem. Soc., Soc. Advancement of Sci. Office: Polish Acad Sci Inst Phys Chem, Kasprzaka 44/52, 01-224 Warsaw Poland

STEDGE-FOWLER, JOYCE, retired clergywoman; b. Spring Valley, N.Y., Mar. 2, 1926; d. Sidney and Lila Mae (Joyce) Kearsing; m. Leland Stedge, Sept. 4, 1948 (div. Apr. 1978); children: Leland Jr., Deborah Stedge-Stroud, David, Donald, Claudia, Douglas; m. Joseph Charles Fowler, June 23, 1985. BA in Liberal Arts, U. Iowa, 1947; MDiv, Union Theol. Sem., N.Y.C., 1973. Ordained to ministry Ref. Ch. in Am., 1973; cert. elem. tchr., N.Y. Elem. tchr. Ramapo I Sch. Dist., Suffern, N.Y., 1966-68, Ramapo II Sch. Dist., Spring Valley, 1968-69; pastor Rochester Ref. Ch., Accord, N.Y., 1973-76; NIMH clin. pastoral intern in mental health St. Elizabeths Hosp., Washington, D.C., 1976-77, clin. pastoral resident in supervision and consultation, 1977-79; pastor-at-large New Castle Presbytery, Wilmington, Del., 1979-82; interim pastor Coop. Parish St. George's, Port Penn, Del. City, Pencader Presbyn. chs., 1980; interim pastor 1st and Olivet Presbyn. Ch., Wilmington, 1980, Hanover Presbyn. Ch., Wilmington, 1981, Ocean City (Md.) Presbyn. Ch., 1982; pastor Christ Presbyn. Ch., Martinsville, N.J., 1982-85; min. to elderly United Presbyn. Ch., Plainfield, N.J., 1985-91; ret., 1991; chaplain Robert Wood Johnson Health Care Ctr., Plainfield, 1985-91; cons., clin. pastoral educator and therapist, 1975-95; mem. task force on abortion Nat. Coun. Chs., 1970-73, mem. Commn. on Women in Ministry, 1973-80, mem. women's ecumenical coordinating group, 1973-79; mem. justice for women com. Elizabeth Presbytery, 1982—, mem. social issues com., 1986-91, moderator, 1991-92, mem. gen. coun., 1990-91, mem. pers. com., 1991-95; del. to Gen. Assembly, Presbyn. Ch. (U.S.A.), 1985, 91. Former leader Rockland County coun. Girl Scouts U.S.A.; former treas., fin. chmn., bd. dirs.. LWV; com. mem. Water, Sewer and Fgn. Policy Rockland County Study, 1955-73; former program chmn. Women's Assn., former adult edn. chmn. Spring Valley Ref. Ch.; former mem. coun. and edn. chmn. Ctrl. Rockland Ecumenical Witness, Spring Valley; bd. dirs. Somerset Chaplaincy to Elderly, 1985-91, Somerset Chaplaincy to Ex-Offenders, 1982-86. Democrat. Achievements include becoming the 1st woman ordained in the Reformed Church in America by Rockland-Westchester Classis. Avocations: reading, swimming, walking, children and grandchildren. Home: 10 Summit Park Rd Spring Valley NY 10977-1510

STEDING, GERD, embryologist, educator; b. Hannover, Germany, Feb. 24, 1936. MD, U. Goettingen, Germany, 1963. Prof. dept. embryology U. Gottingen, Germany; vis. prof. Guangxi Med. U., China, 1985. Office: U Goettingen Dept Embryol, Kreuzbergring 36, D 3400 Goettingen Germany

STEDMAN, GEOFFREY ERNEST, physicist, educator; b. Christchurch, Canterbury, New Zealand, Apr. 1, 1943; s. Silas Ingle and Eleanor Maude (Lewthwaite) S.; m. Rachel Ann Dodd, June 7, 1969; 1 child, Timothy James. BSc with honors, U. Canterbury, Christchurch, 1965; PhD, U. London, 1969. Lectr. physics U. Canterbury, 1971-74, sr. lectr., 1974-78, reader, 1978-90, prof., 1990—. Author: Diagram Techniques in Group Theory, 1990; contbr. numerous articles to sci. publs. Fellow Royal Soc. New Zealand (Hector medal 1994), New Zealand Inst. Physics, Inst. Physics U.K. Avocations: music, church activities. Home: 67A Bowenvale Ave, 8002 Christchurch New Zealand Office: U Canterbury, Pvt Bag 4800, Dept Physics and Astronomy, Christchurch New Zealand

STEED, ADRIAN, planning and strategy administrator; b. Crayford, Kent, Eng., Feb. 18, 1948; s. Ronald and Barbara (Guthrie) S.; m. Mercédès de Hults, July 9, 1989; children: Cameron, Kimberly, Elliot. BA in Econs., U. B.C., Can., 1969. Cert. gen. acct., Can. Various positions Procter & Gamble Can., 1969-79, Procter & Gamble USA, 1979-80, Procter & Gamble European Hdqrs., Brussels, 1980-84; fin. dir. Procter & Gamble Benelux, Brussels, 1984-87, Procter & Gamble France, Paris, 1987-89, Cerestar, Brussels, 1990-98; dir. planning and strategy Eridania Beghin Say, Paris, 1999—. Mem. Strategic Planning Assn. Avocations: tennis, bridge, music. Office: Eridania Beghin Say, 14 Blvd General Leclerc, 92572 Neuilly-sur-Seine France

STEED, MICHELLE ELNORA, special education educator, counselor; b. Raleigh, N.C., Sept. 23, 1967; d. Johnnie Wilbert and Ednell (Thornton) S. BA, N.C. State U., 1989, MEd, 1990. Cert. spl. edn. Tchr. Franklin County Schs., Youngsville, N.C., 1999—. N.C. State U. fellow, 1989-90, All Am. scholar N.C. State U. Democrat. Baptist. Avocations: pianist, organist. Home: 5512 Thornton Rd Raleigh NC 27616-5728

STEEDS, JOHN WICKHAM, physics educator; b. London, Feb. 9, 1940; s. John Henry William and Ethel Amelia (Tyler) S.; m. Diane Mary Kettlewell, 1969; children: Emma Charlotte, Lucy Francesca. BSc in Physics with spl. honors, Univ. Coll. London, 1961; PhD, Cambridge (Eng.) U., 1965. Mullard/SRC/IBM rsch. fellow Selwyn Coll., Cambridge, 1964-67; lectr. dept. physics U. Bristol, Eng., 1967-77, reader dept. physics, 1977-85, prof. physics, 1985—; vis. prof. U. Santiago, Chile, 1971, U. Calif., Berkeley, 1981; dir. Interface Analysis Ctr., Bristol, 1990—; chmn. Sci. Rsch. Found., Bristol, 1989-99; chmn. Emerson Innovations Ltd., 1999—. Author: Anistropic Elasticity Theory of Dislocations, 1973, Convergent Beam Electgron Diffraction of Alloy Ph., 1984; editor: Charles Frank 80th Birthday Tribute, 1990, Thin Film Diamond, 1993. Recipient Medaglia Teresiana, U. Pavia, Italy, 1993, Disting. Scientist award Nat. Sci. Coun., Taiwan, 1994, Holweck medal and prize, French Phys. Soc., 1996. Fellow Royal Soc., Inst. Physics; mem. Inst. Materials. Mem. Ch. of England. Avocations: tennis, cycling, overseas travel. Home: 21 Canynge Sq Clifton, Bristol BS8 3LA, England Office: U Bristol HH Wills Physics, Royal Fort Tyndall Ave, Bristol BS8 1TL, England

STEEL, KUNIKO JUNE, retired artist; b. San Francisco, June 3, 1929; d. Jirohei and Moriyo (Shiraishi) Nakamura; m. John Schulein-Steel, Jan. 26, 1963 (dec. May 1978). Student, U. Calif., 1948-49; diploma, Am. Acad. Art, Chgo., 1951; student, Academic Julian, Paris, 1952-53, Art Inst. Chgo., 1954-55, Art Students League, N.Y.C., 1959-62, 79-85. Exhibited in group shows at Rafilson Gallery, Chgo., 1954, Arts of N.E., Silvermine, Conn., 1966, 79, 90, 92, Modern Maturity Traveling Exhibit, 1990-92, Schoharie Exhibit, Cobleskill, N.Y., 1993-94, Mus. of Modern Art, Miami, Coral Gables, Fla., 1993, 37th Chautaqua Nat. Exhibit of Am. Art, 1994, Montclair State U., 1994, 95. Vol., crafts tchr. Hosp. for Spl. Surgery, N.Y.C., 1967-84; vol. Japanese Gallery Met. Mus., 1994; past vol. costume conservation Met. Mus., N.Y.C., 1979-94. Recipient scholarship Palo Alto Quota Club, 1948, Art Students League, 1960. Avocations: designing arts and crafts, painting.

STEEL, PHILIP S., architect, artist; b. Phila., Nov. 1, 1934; s. Robert Wenzing and Beryl (Vanhorn) S.; m. Joan Crawford, June 1, 1979; children: Philip, Amy, Eric, Robert. BArch, Pa. State U., 1957; MArch, U. Calif., Berkeley, 1963. Registered architect, Fla., Maine, Pa., N.J.; Nat. Coun. Archs. Registration Bd. cert. Prin. Philip Steel & Assoc., AIA, West Chester, Pa., 1964-75, Palm Beach, Fla., 1975-88, Ft. Pierce, Fla., 1988—; past mem. Fla. State Bd. Bldg. Codes and Stds. Works exhibited in group shows McBridge Gallery, Annapolis, Md., Patricia Cloutier Art Gallery, Tequesta, Fla., Arnold Art Store, Newport, R.I., Admiralty Gallery, Vero Beach, Fla., Geary Gallery, Darien, Conn. Chmn. Landmark Commn. for Palm Beach, Fla.; chmn. Under Oaks Show and Fla. Competitive, Ctr. for the Arts, Vero Beach; bd. mem. Cultural Affairs Coun. St. Lucie County; mem. St. Lucie County Seaport Adv. Commn., St. Lucie County U. Task Force. Lt. comdr. USNR, 1957-59. Recipient Disting. Bldg. award Pa. Soc. Architects, 1969, 1st honor award, 1971, Internat. Torchburner award Am. Hotel and Motel Assn., 1985, 2nd place watercolor Backus Gallery, Ft. Pierce, Fla., 1994, 1st place watercolor Backus Gallery, Ft. Pierce, 1995, 96, Sanford Studio award N.E. Water Color Soc.'s Ann. Nat. Exbhn., Kent Art Assn., 1996, 2d place award St. Lucie County Profl. Arts League Regional Exhbn., 1997, Silver Brush award Fla. Watercolor Soc., Melvin Gallery, Lakeland, Fla., 1997. Mem. AIA (pres. Palm Beach chpt., state dir. Indian River chpt.), Pa. Soc. AIA (past state dir., past pres.), Rotary Club Palm Beach. Avocations: sailing, music, tennis. Office: 2030 Harbortown Dr Fort Pierce FL 34946-1438

STEELANT, JOHAN, fluid mechanics engineer, researcher; b. Waregem, Belgium, June 30, 1966. MSME, U. Gent, Belgium, 1989, DME, 1995; MS in Aero. Engring., U. Brussels, 1990. Cert. engr. Rsch. asst. U. Gent, 1989-90, rschr., 1991-95; rschr. Royal Mil. Sch., Brussels, 1990-91; sr. rschr. U. Gent, 1995-98, European Space Rsch. and Tech. Ctr./European Space Agy., The Netherlands, 1998—. Contbr. articles to profl. jours. Recipient Internat. Iwan Åkerman award in Mech. Engring., 1998. Fax: 33-71-565-5421. E-mail: jsteelan@estec.esa.nl. Office: Euro Space Rsch Tech Ctr/Euro Space Agy, Keperlaan 1, 2200 AG Noordwijk The Netherlands

STEELE, ARTHUR DAVID MCGOWAN, ophthalmic surgeon; b. Pyramid Hill, Victoria, Australia, Dec. 16, 1935; s. David McGowan and Agnes Claire (Turner) S.; M.B., B.S., U. Melbourne, 1960; D.O. Royal Coll. Surgeons, 1970. Sr. house officer Croyden Eye Unit, Surrey, Eng., 1969-71; resident surg. officer, sr. resident officer Moorfields Eye Hosp., London, 1971-74; lectr. dept. clin. ophthalmology Moorfields Eye Hosp., 1974-76, cons. ophthalmologist, 1976—, dir. Eye Bank, 1980—. Co-editor: Cataract Surgery, 1984. Served with RAAMC to capt., 1955-60. Fellow Royal Coll. Surgeons, Ophthal. Soc. of U.K. (treas. 1979—), Royal Soc. Medicine (v.p. 1983-85). Mem. Ch. of Scotland. Home: 62 Wimpole St, London W1M 7DE, England Office: Moorfields Eye Hosp, City Rd, London EC1V 2PD, England

STEELE, DWIGHT CLEVELAND, lawyer; b. Alameda, Calif., Jan. 23, 1914; s. Isaac Celveland Steele and Mirah Dinsmore Jackson; m. Alberta Evelyn Hill, Oct. 19, 1940; children: Diane Smith, Marilyn Steele. AB, U. Calif., Berkeley, 1935, LLB, JSD, 1939. Bar: Calif. 1939. V.p., mgr. Distributors Assn. of San Francisco, 1941-46; pres. Hawaii Employers Coun., Honolulu, 1946-59; pres., gen. counsel Lumber and Mill Employers Assn., Oakland, Calif., 1961-76, League to Save Lake Tahoe, 1976-78, 89—; chmn. citizens adv. com. Bay Conservation and Devel. Co., San Francisco, 1997—; chmn. Citizens for Eastshore State Park, Calif., 1986—; v.p. Save San Francisco Bay Assn., Berkeley, 1988-91. Dir. Spirit of Stockholm Found., Nairobi, Kenya, 1975-89, Planning and Conversation Found., Sacramento, 1975-91, Eugene O'Neill Found., Walnut Creek, Calif., 1976-81, Tahoe Baikal Inst., 1991—; chmn. Heart Fund Drive, Hawaii, 1959; advisor Legis. Land Use Task Force, Sacramento, 1975-77. Mem. ABA, Hawaii Bar Assn. Democrat. Avocations: skiing, travel. Home: PO Box 696 Tahoe City CA 96145-0696 Office: 1212 Rossmoor Pkwy Walnut Creek CA 94595-2501

STEELE, ELIZABETH MEYER, lawyer; b. San Mateo, Calif., Jan. 12, 1952; d. Bailey Robert and Kathryn Steele (Horrigan) Meyer; 1 child, Steele Sternberg. BA, Kirkland Coll., 1974; JD, U. N.Mex., 1977. Counsel U.S. Dept. Energy, Los Alamos, N.Mex., 1977-78; law clk. to judge Howard C. Bratton U.S. Dist. Ct., Albuquerque, 1978-80; assoc. Davis, Graham & Stubbs, Denver, 1980-84, ptnr., 1985-87; v.p., gen. counsel Jones Internat., Ltd., Englewood, Colo., 1987—. Office: Jones Internat Ltd 9697 E Mineral Ave Englewood CO 80112-3408

STEELE, HENRY CHARLES, marketing professional; b. Birmingham, Eng., Dec. 21, 1944; s. Bunyen Khotbunma, Nov. 9, 1994. BSc in Econs. with honors, London Sch. of Econs., 1966; MA in Mktg., U. Lancaster, 1968. Various positions Stats (MR) Ltd., Birmingham, 1968-72; dir. DPA Rsch. Assocs., 1975-82; chmn. dept. mktg. Lingnan Coll., Hong Kong, 1983-84; subject leader mktg. HK Polytechnic, Hong Kong, 1984-87; head dept. mktg. and internat. bus., prof. Lingnan U., Hong Kong, 1987—, dir. Ctr. for Internat. Bus. Studies, 1991-96; co-organizer, co-chmn. confs.; chmn. bd. of studies and external examiner various courses and instns. Contbr. articles to profl. jours. Fellowship HK Inst. of Mktg., Hong Kong, 1987. Fellow Royal Geograph. Soc.; mem. Hong Kong Inst. of Mktg. (pres. 1991—, chmn. 1989-91, dir. edn. 1986-88, 90-94, 96-97), Chartered Inst. of Mktg., Inst. of Logistics. Avocations: travel, photography, natural history. Office: Lingnan U, Castle Peak Rd Fu Tei Tuen Mun, Tuen Mun NT, Hong Kong

STEELE, HOWARD L., psychology educator; b. Vancouver, B.C., Can., Oct. 16, 1959; arrived in Eng., 1986;; s. Arnold J. and Goldie R. (Karsh) S.; m. Miriam N. Blum, Sept. 2, 1984; children: Gabriella, Joseph, Michael. BA, U. B.C., 1981, MA, 1983; MA, Columbia U., 1986; PhD, U. Coll., London, 1991. Lectr. U. Coll., London, 1991-99, sr. lectr., 1999—. Editor: (jour.) Attachment and Human Devel., 1999; cons. editor: Infant Mental Health Jour., 1998. Recipient Overseas Rsch. Scholar award Com. of Vice-Chancellors and Prins. of Univs. of U.K., 1986-87; Commonwealth scholar, Brit. Coun., 1987-90; rsch. grantee Econ. and Social Rsch. Coun., 1992-94, 98-99. Mem. Soc. for Rsch. in Child Devel. Office: Sub-Dept Clin Health Psy, Univ Coll London/Gower St, London WCIE 6BT, England

STEELE, HOWARD LOUCKS, economic development consultant, author; b. Pitts., Jan. 27, 1929; s. Howard Bennington and Ruby Alberta (Loucks) S.; m. Sally E. Funk, June 6, 1952 (div. 1977); children: John F., David A., Patricia A.; m. Jane R. Cornelius, July 30, 1977 (div. 1996); 1 child, Jennifer L.; m. Elaine Haddock, Aug. 23, 1997. BS, Washington and Lee U., 1950; MS, Pa. State U., 1952; PhD, U. Ky., 1962. Sales mgr. Greenville (Pa.) Dairy Co., 1952-56; owner H.L. Steele Bulk Milk Hauling, Greenville, 1955-60; asst. prof. Clemson (S.C.) U., 1956-57, assoc. prof., 1957-64; assoc. prof. Ohio State U., Columbus, 1964-71; with Fgn. Agrl. Svc./Internat. Coop. and Devel. U.S., Dept. Agr., Washington, 1971-97; ret., econ. devel. cons., 1997—; project mgr. AID, Guatemala, 1976-77, Bolivia, 1977-80, Honduras, 1980-82, Sri Lanka, 1982-84, Bur. L.Am. and Caribbean USAID, Washington, 1984-88, office of the dir. tech. assistance divsn., 1988-90, with office of dep. adminstr., 1990-97; USDA liaison officer Inter-Am. Inst. Coop. in Agr., 1993-97; instr. U. Md., College Park, 1974-76; vis. prof. U. Sao Paulo, Piracicaba, Brazil, 1964-66; ptnr. Kingwood Acres Farm, Rockwood, Pa., 1966-98. Author: Comercializacao Agricola, 1971, A 200 Year History of Some Descendents of the Pioneer James Steel of Castleblaney, Ireland and Mt. Pleasant, Pennsylvania, 1994, Your Tax Dollars at Work (I'd Rather Have Gone Business Class!), 1998, Food Soldier, 2000; contbr. articles to profl. jours. Recipient Nat. Forensic Union award; named One of Outstanding Young Men U.S., U.S. Jaycees, 1965; cert. of merit Dept. Agr., 1975, 92. Mem. Am. Agrl. Econs. Assn., Internat. Assn. Agrl. Economists, SAR, Masons, Shriners, Gamma Sigma Delta, Sigma Nu. Home: 5204 Holden St Fairfax VA 22032-3418

STEELE, RICHARD DONALD, physicist, linguist, rehabilitation researcher; b. Modesto, Calif., Jan. 12, 1943; s. Warren Nelson, Jr. and Fern Marjorie (Thompson) S.; m. Karen Moxness Dorn, July 4, 1983; children: Trilby Dorn, Blythe Dorn. BS in Physics, Stanford U., 1964; MA, Harvard U., 1966, PhD in Slavic Langs., Linguistics, 1973. Asst. prof. Cornell U., Ithaca, N.Y., 1973-74; lectr. Harvard U., Cambridge, Mass., 1974-75, MIT, Cambridge, 1975-76; asst. prof. Grinnell (Iowa) Coll., 1976-80; rsch. health scientist Rehab. Rsch. Devel. Ctr., VA Med. Ctr., Palo Alto, Calif., 1982-90; mgr. comm. products Tolfa Corp., Palo Alto, Calif., 1990-96; chief scientist LingraphiCARE Am., Oakland, Calif., 1996—; rev. rehab. proposals NIH, Washington, 1991-94. Mem. editl. bd. Assistive Tech., 1988-91; contbr. articles to Neuropsychologia, Aphasiology, Brain Lang., Archives Phys. Med. Rehab., Stroke, others. Organizing com., official Clean Air Car Race, MIT, Calif. Inst. Tech., 1970; co-organizer aphasia spkrs. series Stanford U., 1988-89. Recipient Info. Resources Mgmt. award U.S. Govt. Interagy. com., 1987, Excellence in Tech. Transfer award Tech. Utilization Found., 1993; grantee World Rehab. Fund, 1987. Mem. IEEE, Phi Beta Kappa. Democrat. Achievements include research in computer aided visual communication for aphasics, dissemination of rehabilitation technologies; 3 patents for a method of communicating using graphical elements, a method of communication using sized icons. Home: 1325 E 20th Ave Spokane WA 99203-3437 Office: LingraphiCARE Am 425 Jackson St Oakland CA 94607-4329

STEELE, ROBERT DENNIS, radio producer, announcer, actor; b. Cin., Feb. 27, 1956; s. John Robert and Martha Adelaide (Friedmann) S.; m. Denise Elizabeth Rinear, Sept. 1, 1979; children: John Rinear, Benjamn Rinear, Allison Rinear, Emily Rinear. BFA in Radio, TV, Film, U. Cin., 1978. Announcer WSAI-AM, Cin., 1977; prodn. asst. WEBN-FM, Cin., 1977-78; prodn. dir. KGGO-FM, Des Moines, 1978-79, WWCK-FM, Flint, Mich., 1979-80; prodn. dir., then prodn. dir. and morning co-host WYSP-FM, Phila., 1980-81, 83-85; freelance producer, announcer Steele Creative Svcs., Phila., 1981-83, 87—; TV and radio writer, dir. programming Denny Somach Prodns., Havertown, Pa., 1984-87; cons. Olympia Networks, St. Louis, 1988—. Producer, writer radio spls. including Billy Crystal's Countdown to Christmas, 1985, Nat. Rock Test, 1986, 20th Ann. Salute to the Doors, 1987, Am. Comedy Network Awards, 1990, Led Zeppelin, 1993, The World Premiere Broadcast of The Beatles Anthology II, 1996; radio series include: Psychedelic Psnack, 1985-87, John Madden's Sports Calendar, 1988-99; co-producer series Continuous History of Rock and Roll, 1981-83; producer, writer numerous commls. Recipient Addy award Des Moines Advt. Profls., 1979, Flint Advt. Fedn., 1979, 80, Phila. Advt. Club, 1982, 87, Silver Microphone Finalist award, 1986. Roman Catholic. Avocations: tennis, music, reading, cinema, theater. Home and Office: 215 Comrie Dr Villanova PA 19085-1402

STEELE, STUART JAMES, obstetrician-gynecologist, consultant; b. London, Jan. 13, 1930; s. James Richard and Margaret Glass (Leonard) S.; m. Jill Westgate Smith, Oct. 23, 1965; children: Andrew James, Alasdair Malcolm. BA, U. Cambridge, Eng., 1953, MA, MB, BChr, 1956; postgrad. specialty studies, Middlesex Hosp. Med. Sch., London, 1953-56. Cert. specialist Ob-Gyn., Gen. Med. Coun. Reader emeritus in Ob-Gyn. London U., 1974-95; dir. dept. Ob-Gyn. Middlesex Hosp. Med. Sch., London, 1974-87; assoc. dir. dept. Ob-Gyn. Univ. Coll., London, 1987-95; hon. cons. Margaret Pyke Ctr. for Family Planning, London, 1972—, Univ. Coll. London Hosps. Trust, 1972—, Great Ormond St. Hosp. for Children NHS Trust, London, 1995—; chmn. Bd. of Studies Ob.-Gyn. U. London, 1985-88. Author (book) Gynaecology and the Neonate, 1985. Elder Ch. of Scotland, 1959—; v.p. Royal Scottish Corp., 1994—. 2d lt. Royal Artillery Brit., 1948-50. Named Fellow WHO, 1969. Fellow Royal Coll. Surgeons, Royal Coll Obstetricians and Gynecologists (bd. examiners), Royal Soc. Medicine. Avocations: theatre, opera, ballet, gardening. Home: 35 Tring Ave, London W5 3QD, England Office: London Women's Clinic, 113/115 Harley St, London W1N 1DG, England

STEELHAMMER, PAGE MILLER, dairy farmer; b. Chehalis, Wash., Jan. 28, 1924; s. Fritz Harold and Clara Henrietta Steelhammer; m. Margaret Lee Mears, Jan. 4, 1946; children: Normal L., Greg P., Christine S., Gail Diane. Student, Centralia Coll., 1941-42. Dairy farmer, Centralia, Wash., 1947—. Mem. Elks, Lions. Home and Office: 2007 Gallagher Rd Centralia WA 98531-9310

STEEMAN, JOHAN A., nursing administrator; b. Bruges, Belgium, June 20, 1952; m. Lieve Ghyssaert, Sept. 20, 1974; children: Frauke, Ward, Bieke, Wim. RN, St. Jan, Bruges, Belgium, 1973, Pedagogic degree, 1974, Nursing Mgmt., 1980; M Human Ecology, Free U., Brussels, 1991. Psychiat. nurse St. Jan, Bruges, 1973-74; responsible nurse psychiat. wards SFX Ziekenhuis, Bruges, 1974-85, nursing coord.-supr. psychiatry-psychosomatics, 1985-99; nursing coord. dept. neurology and surgery AZ St. Jan Ziekenhuis, 2000—. Author: Psychofarmacotherapie, 1991; co-author books concerning affective disorders and psychopharmacology; author, co-author abstracts on psychopharmacological rsch.; contbr. articles to profl. jours. Mem. Belgian Coll. Neuropsychopharmacology and Biol. Psychiatry, Soc. Royale Medecine Mentale Belgique. E-mail: Johan.Steeman@azbrugge.be. Office: SFX Ziekenhuis, Spaanse Loskaai 1, B-8000 Brugge Belgium also: AV St Jan AZ, B-8000 Ruddershove Belgium

STEENBERG, BÖRJE KARL, forester; b. Stockholm, Aug. 6, 1912; s. Karl and Maja (Ohrstrom) S.; B.Sc., U. Stockholm, 1936, M.Sc., 1938, Ph.D., 1944, D.Sc., 1945; D.Forestry Sci., Royal Inst. Forestry, Stockholm, 1969; m. Elisa Hald, Oct. 15, 1940; children: Kjell, Ann. Mem. faculty Royal Inst. Tech., Stockholm, 1937—, prof., 1949—, emeritus, 1979—, head dept. paper tech., 1949—; asst. dir. gen. FAO, Rome, 1968-74; rsch. dir. Swedish Forest Products Rsch. Lab., 1944-68; cons. in field, del. internat. meetings. Recipient German Mitscherlich medal, 1960, Swedish Ekman Gold medal, 1961, Gold medal TAPPI, 1970, Royal medal of Merit, 1991; named Comdr. Royal Order North Star. Mem. Royal Swedish Acad. Engring. Scis., Finnish Acad. Tech. Scis., Internat. Acad. Wood Sci., Royal Swedish Acad. Agr., Italian Acad. Forestry, N.Y. Acad. Sci. Clubs: Rotary, Travellers. Author papers in field. Home: 19 Ynglingagatan, 113 47 Stockholm Sweden Office: 53 Kristinas Väg, 100 44 Stockholm Sweden

STEEN CRAWFORD, ANDREA, village manager; b. Chgo., July 20, 1963; d. John G. III and Susan M. Crawford; m. Stephen L. Steen; children: Collin, Julia, Gabrielle. BA, Kalamazoo Coll., 1985; MPA, U. Wis., 1987. Budget and planning analyst I State of Wis., Madison, summer 1986; adminstrv. intern City of Madison, 1986-87; adminstrv. asst. Village of Wilmette, Ill., 1987-89, asst. fin. dir., 1989-90; village adminstr. Village of Maple Bluff, Wis., 1990-97; village mgr. Village of Elm Grove, Wis., 1997—. Bd. dirs. Wis. Ctr. for State and Local Govt., Madison, 1995-96; pres. LaFollette Inst. Alumni Bd., Madison, 1992-94; trustee State of Wis. Investment Bd., 2000—. Mem. Internat. City Mgmt. Assn., Wis. City Mgmt. Assn. (pres. 1996-97), Ill. City Mgmt. Assn., Rotary. Office: Village of Elm Grove 13600 Juneau Blvd Elm Grove WI 53122-1679

STEEN-HINDERLIE, DIANE EVELYN, social worker, musician; b. Duluth, Minn., June 13, 1947; d. Julian Sem and Evelyn Synnove (Helgaas) Steen; m. John Peter Hinderlie, June 27, 1971 (div. Sept. 1987); children: Peder Donald, Erik Steen; m. John Richard Olson, July 21, 1989. BA in Asian Studies/Social Psychology cum laude, St. Olaf Coll., 1969; MusB equivalency, U. Minn. and other instns., 1970-91; postgrad., Hamline U., 1989-91. Lic. social worker, Minn.; cert. music tchr. Music Tchrs. Nat. Assn. Social worker child care licensing Hennepin County Welfare Dept., Mpls., 1970-73; mem. clergy team exch. program Luth. World Fedn., Göppingen, Germany, 1973-77; mem. clergy team, music dir. Jubilation Singers Bethel Luth. Ch., Rochester, Minn., 1978-83; mem. clergy team, music dir. youth choir First Luth. Ch., St. Louis Park, Minn., 1983-86; adminstr. Family Child Care facility, St. Louis Park, 1986-90; mem. faculty, tchr. Stenson Suzuki Studios and Home Studio, St. Louis Park, 1988-92; small group leader, tchr. vol. Mt. Olive Ch., Children's Hosp., Mpls., 1993, 96-98; mem. workshop and children's ministry Augsburg Coll. Youth and Family Inst. and Trinity Congregation, 1998—; founding dir. Fair Pay Inst., Mpls., 1995—; trainer United for a Fair Economy, 1997—; founder orgn. and curriculum Early Childhood Orgn. for Edn. with Singing, 1993—, co-leader German-Am. youth group exch., 1979-82; co-founder Family DayCare Cert. Program and Babygarten (B-12 edn.) classes, 1970-73; bd. dirs. Midwest Coun., Nat. Peace Inst. Found., Grinnell, Iowa, 1991; presenter in field.; mem. root causes of violence action team Initiative for Violence-Free Families, 4th Jud. Dist. Minn., 1997—. Author: (tng. manual) Mother Tongue Singing/Voice Method, 1988, (study packet) School Start Time/Teen Sleep Deprivation, 1996-97; rec. artist, mem. ensemble record/cassettes Nowell Sing We, 1986; performer Nordic Am. Psalmodikon Forbundet, 1997—. Vol. People of Faith Peacemakers, Feminists in Faith/ReImagining, Jewish Cmty. Rels. Coun., Muslim-Christian Rels. Coun., Joint Religious Legis. Coalition, Bread for the World; founder People for Reforming Early Start Time for Teens Orgn., Mpls., 1993—; mem. steering com. Progressive Cmty. and FairVote, Minn., 1994—; local host youth com. NAACP Conv., Mpls., 1995; vol. Common Cause, St. Paul and Washington. Recipient appreciation plaque Christian Boy/Girl Scouts Germany; Svc. pin Am. Luth. Ch. Women; listed in Minn. Profiles, Minn. Hist. Soc.; named Asset Builder of Month, St. Louis Park Children First Initiative, 1997; named to Honor Roll, Mendota Mdewakanton Dakota Cmty., 1999. Mem. MADD, UN Assn., Amnesty Internat., Nat. Assn. Tchrs. Singing and VoiceCare Network, Internat. Suzuki Assn., Am. Mensa, Ltd., Sons of Norway (lodge trustee 1991—), Harriet Tubman Ctr., Minn. Parenting Assn., Suzuki Assn. Americas (study area co-organizer, editl. adviser), U.S. Holocaust Mus., Nat. Peace Found., Nat. Luth. Choir Acad., Ctr. for Victims of Torture, Interfaith Alliance Minn., Soc. for Psychol. Studies of Social Issues, Early Childhood Music and Movement Assn., Germanic-Am. Inst., World Wildlife Fund, Wash. Nat. Cathedral, Assn. Pre- and Perinatal Psychology and Health, Am.'s Jr. Miss Coun., Phi Beta Kappa. Green. Lutheran. Avocations: reading, political activism, concerts, travel, memory albums. Office: Fair Pay Inst PO Box 16031 Minneapolis MN 55416-0031

STEENLAND, JAMES PETER, electronics systems engineer; b. Corvallis, Oreg., Aug. 29, 1951; s. Adin Peter and Doris Elizabeth (Stanton) S.; m. Deborah Denise Durkee, July 12, 1975; children: Rebecca, John, Christina, Michael, Sarah, Victoria. BS in Engring. Tech., Le Tourneau Coll., 1983. Adminstr. Christian Mission Farms, Hernandarias, Paraguay, 1983-84; electronics design engr. Teccor Electronics, Inc., Irving, Tex., 1984-88; electronic systems engr. Teccor Electronics, Inc., Brownsville, Tex., 1988-93; engring. svcs. mgr. Eaton Corp., Brownsville, Tex., 1993-96; engring. mgr. ITT Automotive, Laredo, Tex., 1996-98; dir. tech. Datacom Custom Mfg., McAllen, Tex., 1998-2000; pres. EIM, Brownsville, 2000—; chmn. Team Concepts for High Achievement, Matamoros, Mexico, 1991-93. Deacon 1st Bapt. Ch., Brownsville, Tex. With USAF, 1971-79. Recipient Joint Svc. commendation USAF, Mali, Africa, 1974. Mem. Assn. for Computing Machinery, Am. Soc. for Quality. Republican. Avocation: computer programming. Office: EIM 23 E Maple Cir Brownsville TX 78521-2604

STEENSGAARD, ANTHONY HARVEY, federal agency administrator; b. Rapid City, S.D., Mar. 21, 1963; s. Harvey Hans and Dorothy Lorraine (Hansen) S. Student, Anchorage C.C., 1983-84; BSCE, U. Alaska, 1985; AAS in Indsl. Security, C.C. Air Force, 1989; BS in Criminal Justice, Wayland U., 1989; MS in Computer Systems Engring., U. Calif., San Diego, 1996. Lic. pilot, radio operator; cert. hostage negotiator FBI; cert. in-flight security specialist FAA; cert. instr. Am. Soc. Protection Profls.; cert. fed. emergency mgmt. agy. level III incident comdr. Bookseller B. Dalton Bookseller, Rapid City, S.D., 1978-81, Anchorage, Alaska, 1981-83; warehouseman Sears, Roebuck & Co., Anchorage, 1983-85; security specialist Alaska Air N.G., Anchorage, 1985-88; agt., draftsman, engring. cons., asst. itelligence officer U.S. Border Patrol, El Centro, Calif., 1988—; pvt. computer cons., 1994-98, pvt. computer security cons., 1998—; cert. instr. Am. Soc. of Protection Profls., 2000—. Author: Unit Security Manager's Guide Book, 1988; contbg. writer Combatsim.com. Mag., 1998—, simCombat.com mag., 1999—, Combatsim.com Webzine, 1999-2000; editor Simcombat.com Webzine, 1999—. Vol. U.S. Senator George McGovern's Campaign, Rapid City, 1980, Congressman Tom Daschle's Campaign, Rapid City, 1980, Spl. Olympics, Rapid City, 1981; observer CAP, Anchorage, 1981; sr. pilot Civil Air Patrol, Rapid City, 1996; pub. affairs officer CAP, Rapid City, S.D., 1996-98, aerospace edn. officer, 1998-2000, wing dir. of aerospace edn., civil air patrol, S.D., 2000—. With USNR, 1980-81, USMC, 1981-85, USAFR, 1985-95. Recipient hon. sci. award Bausch and Lomb, 1984, commendation State of Alaska, 1987, 2d commendation, 1988, Brigadier Gen. Charles E. Yeager Aerospace Achievement award, 2000. Mem. U.S. Cavalry Assn. (heritage mem.), HTML Writer's Guild, Am. Legion, Air Force Assn., VFW, Fraternal Order Eagles, S.D. Sheriff's Assn., Fraternal Order of Police, Virtual Geog. League, WWII Meml. Soc. (charter mem.), Nat. D-Day Mus. Found. Avocations: reading, computers, aviation, history, wargaming. Office: US Border Patrol 1111 N Imperial Ave El Centro CA 92243-1795

STEENSLAND, ODD, corrosion engineer, consultant, retired; b. Stavanger, Norway, Oct. 17, 1931; s. Gustav and Tomine (Espedal) S.; m. Martina Zwainz, Aug. 13, 1960; children: Siri, Morten. MSc, Tech. U. Graz, Austria, 1961. Rsch. engr. Uddeholms AB, Hagfors, Sweden, 1962-64, head corrosion lab., 1965-69; rsch. engr. Det Norske Veritas, Oslo, 1969-72, head sect. for corrosion, plastic and chem. svcs., 1972-85; prin. engr. Veritas Offshore Tech. and Svcs. A/S, Oslo, 1986-92, Det Norske Veritas A/S, Oslo, 1992-96; retired, 1996. Mem. Norwegian Corrosion Soc., Nat. Assn. Corrosion Engrs., Corrosion Engring. Assn. Avocations: skiing, fishing.

STEENSMA, MICHAEL ERIC, controller; b. Logan, Utah, Sept. 18, 1965; s. Robert Charles and Sharon Carol (Hogge) S.; m. Ginger Hunsaker, June 30, 1989; children: Ryan Michael, Cameron Lewis. BS in Fin., U. Utah, 1989, MBA, 1993. Office asst. Triad Am. Corp., Salt Lake City, 1985-87; acct. Resolution Trust Corp., Salt Lake City, 1987-89; auditor Salt Lake County, Salt Lake City, 1989-90; plant acct. Becton Dickinson & Co., Sandy, Utah, 1991-96, plant contr., 1996—. Youth league coach Sandy City Recreation, 1998. Mem. Inst. Mgmt. Accts., U. Utah Alumni Assn. Avocations: skiing, basketball, golf, softball, reading. Office: Becton Dickinson & Co 9450 State St Sandy UT 84070-3234

STEENTOFT, ANNI, forensic toxicologist; b. Slagelse, Denmark, Apr. 24, 1938; d. Valdemar Carl, Georg and Ellen Marie (Nielsen) Hansen; m. Gunnar Steentoft, Apr. 24, 1964; children: Christian, Peter. MSc in Pharmacy, Royal Danish Sch. Pharmacy, Copenhagen, Denmark, 1961. Toxicologist Inst. Pharmacology U. Copenhagen, Denmark, 1961-73, assoc. prof. Inst. Forensic Medicine, 1973-86; head of lab. Pharmaceutical Manufacturer, Denmark, 1987; assoc. prof. Inst. Forensic Medicine U. Copenhagen, Denmark, 1988—; head of Nordic task force on drug addict deaths, 1986—; mem. Nat. Bd. Health's Com. on narcotic drugs, 1992—, Commr.'s Police task force on drug addict deaths, Copenhagen, 1992—; Nordic task force on drugs other than alcohol in traffic, 1995—. Contbr. numerous articles to profl., internat. jours. Fellow Internat. Assn. Forensic Toxicologists, Internat. Coun. on Alcohol, Drugs, and Traffic Safety, Danish Assn. Forensic Medicine. Avocation: music, flute, mem. several orchs. Office: Inst Forensic Med U Copenhagen, Frederik V's Vej 11, DK-2100 Copenhagen Denmark

STEERE, ANNE BULLIVANT, retired student advisor; b. Phila., July 27, 1921; d. Stuart Lodge and Elizabeth MacCuen (Smith) B.; m. Richard M. H. Harper Jr., Nov. 14, 1942 (div. Oct. 1967); children: Virginia Harper Kliever, Richard M. H. Harper III, Patricia Harper Flint, Stuart Lodge Harper, Lucy Steere, Grace Steere; m. Bruce Middleton Steere, July 5, 1968. BS in Sociology, So. Meth. U., 1978, M in Liberal Arts, 1985. Asst. to dir. Harvard Law Sch. Fund, Cambridge, Mass., 1958-68; advisor to older students So. Meth. U., Dallas, 1976-85. Contbr. articles to profl. jours. Trustee Pine Manor Coll., Chestnut Hill, Mass., 1983—; bd. dirs. Planned Parenthood, Dallas, 1975-85. Mem. New Eng. Hist. and Geneal. Soc., Alpha Kappa Delta, Chilton Club (Boston), Jr. League Club. Episcoplian. Avocations: reading, needlepoint, sailing. Home (winter): 369 S Lake Dr # 5D Palm Beach FL 33480-6509 Home (summer): 59 Snow Inn Rd Harwich Port MA 02646-2413

STEERNEMAN, PIM, child psychologist, researcher; b. Maastricht, Limburg, Holland, Apr. 13, 1961. Degree in child psychology, R.U. Leiden U., 1986, PhD, 1998. Psychologist Youth Care Inst., 1985-86; psychologist Ctr. of Autism of S. Limburg, 1986—, dir., 1989. Author: Social Cognition Training and Theory-of-Mind-Test, 1994, 2d edit., 2000; contbr. articles to profl. jours. Mem. Dutch Assn. for Child Psychology. Office: Ctr Autism S-Limburg, PO Box 165, 6400 AD Heerlen Holland, The Netherlands

STEFAN, CHARLES GORDON, retired foreign service officer and educator; b. Omaha, July 21, 1920; m. Gabrielle M. Patry, May 17, 1952; children: Adrienne, Susan. AA, Salinas (Calif.) Jr. Coll., 1940; BA, U. Calif., Berkeley, 1942; Indsl. Adminstr., Harvard Bus. Sch., 1943. Fgn. svc. officer U.S. Dept. State, 1947-75; part-time instr. Santa Fe C.C., Gainesville, Fla., 1979-90; ret., 1990; participant Santa Fe C.C-VISTA Project, 1977-78; acad. assignments U.S. Dept. State Russian Inst., Columbia U., 1951-52, Nat. War Coll., 1963-64. Contbr. articles to profl. jours. Mem. citizens participation com. North Ctrl. Fla. Regional Planning Coun., Gainesville, 1976-86; mem. Alachua County Citizen Adv. Com. on Variable Rates for Solid Waste Collection, Gainesville, 1993-94. Capt. Counter Intelligence Corps., U.S. Army, 1942-47, Germany. Recipient Meritorious Svc. Increase award Dept. State, Am. Embassy, Asuncion, Paraguay, 1969. Mem. U. Calif. Berkeley Alumni Assn. (life), Harvard Bus. Sch. Alumni Assn., Diplomatic and Consular Officers Ret., Nat. War Coll. Alumni Assn., Am. Legion, Nat. CIC Assn., Phi Beta Kappa. Episcopalian. Avocations: swimming, walking, reading. Home: 8012 SW 5th Ave Gainesville FL 32607-1544

STEFAN, VLADISLAV, research scientist; b. Feb. 5, 1948; s. Bozhidar and Rosanda (Popovich) Stefan; m. Svetlana Milutinovich, 1975 (dec. 1988); 1 child, Andrej. BEE, U. Belgrade, 1972, MS, 1975; DSc, Russian Acad. Scis., 1978. Rsch. scientist Inst. Nuclear Scis., Belgrade, 1973-81; assoc. prof. U. Belgrade, 1979-81; vis. prof. MIT, Cambridge, 1981-82; rsch. scientist UCLA, 1982-83, U. Calif., San Diego, 1984-89; pres. Inst. for Advanced Physics Studies, La Jolla, Calif., 1989-96, The Stefan U., La Jolla, Calif., 1996—; vis. rsch. physicist P.N. Lebedev Physics Inst., Russian Acad. Scis., Moscow, 1977-81; referee Physics of Fluids, Princeton, N.J., 1983—; cons. Maxwell Labs., Inc., San Diego, 1985-89; proposal referee NSF, Washington, 1987-90, NASA, Washington, 1988-90. Author: Physics and Society, 1997, Einstein's Wisdom, 1998; editor: Nonlinear and Relativistic Effects, 1992; series editor: Research Trends in Physics, 1990—. Recipient award Inst. Boris Kidrich, Belgrade, 1978, award Internat. Rsch. Exch., 1980. Mem. AAAS, Am. Phys. Soc., Am. Optical Soc., Am. Acoustical Soc. Avocations: painting, music, rock climbing. Home: 3246 Camihito Ameca La Jolla CA 92038-2946 Office: 7596 Eads Ave La Jolla CA 92037-4851

STEFANELLI, GIUSEPPE, retired agricultural engineering educator, researcher; b. Florence, Italy, June 11, 1905; s. Carlo and Emilia (Albizzi) S.; m. Anna Paola Marchetti, Sept. 18, 1933; children: Stefania, Paolina (dec.), Virginia, Giovanna, Maria-Gemma. Full prof. mech. and agrl. machinery U. Pisa, Bologna, Firenze, 1939-75, prof. emeritus, 1982—; dir. soil tillage experiment Italian Ministry of Agr., 1940-79; experiment agrl. machinery Italian Rsch. Coun., 1966-80; mem. Italian Higher Coun. of Experimentation of Agrl. Ministry, Rome, 1975-78, USDA tasks for tillage experiment in Italian clay soils, 1963-67. Author: Meccanica agraria University Lessons, 1949-66, La trattrice agricola: Shell italiana, 1969, Costruzioni rurali, Edizioni agricole, 1956; contbr. articles to sci. and profl. jours. Mem. Am. Soc. Engring. Agrl. Food and Biol. Sys., Acad. Georgofili (pres. 1977-87, coun. 1987-2000), Italian Assn. Genio Rurale (pres. 1967-76, hon. pres. 1976-2000), Agrl. Sci. Acad. Bologna, Agrl. Sci. Acad. Turin, Agrl. Sci. Acad. Pesaro, Agrl. Forestry Acad. Florence, Acad. Agr. France. Home: 61 Borgo Pinti, 50121 Florence Italy

STEFĂNESCU, DAN MIHAI, electronics engineer; b. Bucharest, Romania, Apr. 6, 1946; s. Dumitru and Viorica (Tomescu) S.; m. Veronica Bratu, June 22, 1974; children: Alexandru, Florian. Diploma, Poly. Inst., Bucharest, 1969, MScEE, 1983, PhD in Elec. Engring. cum laude, 1999. Rsch. scientist Aerospace Inst., Bucharest, 1969-79, head instrumentation, 1992—; asst. prof. and sr. engr. testing lab. Poly. Inst., Bucharest, 1979-92; Romanian rep. IMEKO-Force Com., 1988—; cons. A.M. Erichsen, Germany, 1992—. Author: Strain Gage Measurement of Mechanical Quantities, 1989 (Romanian Acad. prize 1991); co-author: English-Romanian Dictionary for Aeronautics, 1997; contbr. over 150 articles to profl. confs., profl. jours. With Romanian Army Reserve, 1996. Mem. Soc. Exptl. Mechanics, Verband Deutscher Elektrotechniker, Romanian Soc. Measurement, Romanian Assn. Tensometry. Romanian Orthodox. Avocations: travel, literature, sports. Fax: 401-413-0690. E-mail: dstef@aero.incas.ro. Home: CP 76-154, Bucharest Romania Office: Nat Inst Aerospace Rsch, Bd Iuliu Maniu 220, 77538 Bucharest Romania

STEFANIAK, JAROSLAW ERYK, mathematician; b. Poznan, Poland, May 17, 1929; s. Jozef and Jozefa (Krol) S.; m. Miroslawa Krystyna Stolbiak, Apr. 12, 1955. MS, A. Mickiweicz U., Poznan, Poland, 1952; DS, Poznan U. Tech., 1965, Dr.habil, 1969. Vice dean mechanics Poznan U. Tech., 1969-71, deputy dir. Inst. Applied Mechanics, 1970-72, dir. Inst. Applied Mechanics, 1973-81, 84-87, prorector, 1981-84, rector, 1990-93, head sect. applied mechanics, 1972—. Editor: The Influence of Electromagnetic Field on Thermodiffusion in an Isotropic Body, 1982; mem. editl. bd. Jour. Tech. Physics, 1993. Mem. Polish Acad. Sci. (bd. dirs. 1993, mem. com. mechanics), Gesellschaft Angewandte Mathematik und Mechanik, Am. Math. Soc., European Mechanics Soc. Roman Catholic. Avocations: reading, poetry, philosophy. Home: sw Rocha 6A/6, 61-142 Poznan Poland Office: Poznan U Tech, Piotrowo 3, 60-965 Poznan Poland

STEFANICS, BARBARA ZUMBRUN, computer educator, information technology consultant; b. Hanover, Pa., Nov. 23, 1946; arrived in Austria, 1979; d. John David and Anna Virginia (Owings) Z.; m. Karl Stefanics, Jan. 4, 1979; children: Sonja Anna, Robert John. BA, Towson State U., 1968; MA, We. Md. Coll., 1975. Instr. Towson (Md.) State U., 1975-79; tchr. computing, math. Dulaney Sr. High Sch., Timonium, Md., 1969-77, asst. prin., 1977-79; head computing Vienna Internat. Sch., Austria, 1982—; mem. computer com. European Coun. of Internat. Schs., 1986-94, chair, 1989-92, mem. accreditation team; mem. subject com. computer sci. Internat. Baccalaureate, Cardiff, Wales, 1989-93, mem. subject com. info. tech. in a global soc., 1992—, dep. chief examiner ITAS, 2000—. Author, editor periodical European Coun. Internat. Schs. Macintosh Interest Group Newsletter, 1980-96. Recipient Internat. Edn. fellow European Coun. Internat. Schs., 1989, Apple Disting. Educator award, 2000. Mem. IEEE Computer Soc., Austrian Computer Soc., Internat. Soc. for Computers in Edn., Assn. for Computing Machinery. Avocations: computer graphics, web publishing, multimedia, travel. Office: Vienna Internat Sch, Strasse der Menschenrechte 1, A-1220 Vienna Austria

STEFANICS, CHARLOTTE LOUISE, retired mental health nurse; b. Leechburg, Pa., Dec. 30, 1927; d. George J. and Mary Magadelene (Boronyak) S. Dipoma Sch. Nursing, St. Elizabeth Hosp., 1948; BSN, Seton Hall U., 1968; MS, Ohio State U., 1971; EdD, U. Sarasota, 1982. Diplomate Logotherapy. Various nursing positions, 1952-69; staff nurse Med. Ctr. NYU, N.Y.C., 1969-70; pvt. practice, 1971-73; instr. Sch. Nursing Duke U., Durham, N.C., 1974-77; clin. nurse specialist VA Med. Ctr., Bay Pines, Fla., 1977-93; ret., 1993; instr., pvt. practice Community Hosp. Springfield, Ohio; cons. in field; part-time chaplain Miami Valley Hosp., Dayton, Ohio; lectr. U. South Fla. Coll. Nursing, 1978-92. Author: (with G. Niklas) Ministry to the Sick, 1982; (with R. Peck) Learning to Say Good-bye, 1987. Vol. community classes and workshops; vol. Habitat for Humanity Internat. Hungary, nursing exchange with Chinese Nurses Assn. Mem. Inst. Logo Therapy, Assn. Death Educators and Counselors (cert.), Assn. Christian Therapists, Nurses Orgn. Vet. Affairs. Home: 1342 Rosehaven Cir Dayton OH 45429-5744

STEFANIDIS, ALEXANDER, physician, researcher; b. Athens, Attiki, Greece, Jan. 14, 1969; s. Savas and Helen (Sidiropoulos) S. Musik diplomate, Hellenic Conservatory, Athens, Greece, 1986; MD, Athens U., 1993. Resident Tzanio Hosp., Piraeus, Greece, 1996—. Contbr. articles to profl. publs. Greek Orthodox. Avocation: study of Greek philosophy. Home: Socratus 203, Kallithea, 176-73 Athens Attica, Greece Office: Tzanio Hosp, Afentouli and Zanni, 185-36 Piraeus Attica, Greece

STEFANIS, NICO GEORGE, research physicist; b. Larissa, Greece, June 18, 1951; arrived in Fed. Republic Germany, 1969; s. Georgios and Eleni (Athanassopoulou) S. Vordiplom in physics, Heidelberg U., Fed. Republic Germany, 1972, diploma in physics, 1979; Dr.rer.nat. in Theoretical Physics, Heidelberg U., 1983; DSc in Physics and Mathematics, Joint Insts. for Nuclear Rsch., Dubna, Russia, 1997. Teaching asst. Inst. for Theoretical Physics, Heidelberg, 1975-81; staff mem. Inst. for Theoretical Physics, Bochum, Fed. Republic Germany, 1984-88, sr. rsch. assoc., 1988—. Contbr. articles to profl. jours. Mem. Greek Soc. for Study of High Energy Physics. Orthodox. Avocations: diving, oil painting. Office: Inst Theoretical Physics II, Universitaetsstrasse 150, D-44780 Bochum Germany

STEFANO, JOSEPH WILLIAM, film and television producer, writer; b. Phila., May 5, 1922; s. Dominic and Josephine (Vottima) S.; m. Marilyn Epstein, Dec. 5, 1953; 1 son, Andrew Dominic. Ed. pub. schs. Pres. Villa di Stefano Prodns., 1962—. Toured as song and dance man in Student Prince, 1945, Merry Widow, 1946; composer music and lyrics popular songs, night club revues, indsl. shows, others, 1946-57; author screenplays The Black Orchid, 1958, The Naked Edge, 1960, Psycho, 1960, Anna di Brooklyn, 1962, Eye of the Cat, 1969, Futz, 1970, The Kindred, 1986, Blackout, 1989, Psycho IV: The Beginning, 1990, Two Bits, 1995, Psycho, 1998; TV drama Made in Japan, 1959, movies for TV, 1970-78; prodr., author TV series The Outer Limits, 1963-64, Swamp Thing, 1990; exec. con. The Outer Limits, 1995—. Recipient Robert E. Sherwood award for Made in Japan, Fund for Republic, 1959, Edgar Allen Poe award for Psycho, Mystery Writers Am., 1960, Columbia award Federated Italo-Ams. Calif., 1964, Pres.'s award Acad. Sci.-Fiction Fantasy and Horror Films, 1987, Movieguide commendation for Two Bits, One of Ten Best Films of 1995; inducted into Cultural Hall of Fame, South Phila. H.S. Mem. ASCAP, Writers Guild Am., Dirs. Guild Am., Producers Guild Am., Acad. Motion Pictures Arts and Scis., Mystery Writers Am. Home: 10216 Cielo Dr Beverly Hills CA 90210-2035

STEFANOV, STEFAN MINEV, mathematics educator, researcher; b. Sevlievo, Bulgaria, Aug. 8, 1964; s. Minio Stefanov and Nedka Marinova (Kadieva) Minevi. BS, Sofia U., Bulgaria, 1988, MEd, 1989, MS, 1989, PhD in Ops. Rsch., 1991, DSc in Math., 1996. Asst. prof. Neofit Rilski U., Blagoevgrad, Bulgaria, 1991-96, assoc. prof., 1996-97, prof., 1997—; extraordinary prof. and rsch. fellow U. Limerick, Ireland, spring 1998; mem. rsch. group in math. inequalities and applications, Melbourne, Aus. Contbr. numerous articles on math. programming and numerical analysis to profl. jours., textbooks and monographs. Mem. Nat. Acad. Syndicate, Bulgaria, 1992—. Recipient medal Ministry of Edn., Bulgaria, 1982. Fellow Internat. Biographical Assn. (Eng. chpt.), The Natl. Acad. of Scis.; mem. Royal London Math Soc., European Math Soc., Am. Math. Soc. (reviewer, editor Math. Revs. Jour. 1997—), Math. Programming Soc. Phila., Soc. Indsl. and Applied Math., Union Bulgarian Mathematicians, Union Bulgarian Scientists (contbn. award 1996, 98), Activity Group on Optimization Phila., Ops. Rsch. Soc. Bulgaria, Can. Math. Soc., Can. Applied and Indsl. Math. Soc., ABI's Rsch. Bd. of Advs. (Raleigh chpt.), Nat. Geographic Soc. (Wash. chpt.). Avocations: philately, jogging, history, philosophy, fiction, fine arts. Home: 4 Ilio Vlaev Str, 5400 Sevlievo Bulgaria Office: Neofit Rilski U, 66 Ivan Mihailov Str, 2700 Blagoevgrad Bulgaria

STEFANOVICH, VLADIMIR DJORDJE, retired biochemist, educator; b. Novi Sad, Yugoslavia, Nov. 7, 1924; s. Djordje and Olga (Jankelic) S.; m. Inge Helga Zothe, July 21, 1960; children: Michael, Peter, Robert. DiplChem, U. Beograd, Yugoslavia, 1953, PhD, 1960. Asst. prof. faculty of sci. U. Beograd, 1053-60; rsch. fellow Worcester Found. Exptl. Biology, Shrewsbury, Mass., 1960-62; sr. pharmacologist Hoffman LaRoche, Nutley, N.J., 1960-65; assoc. prof. Boston U. Med. Ctr., 1965-71; head dept. biochemistry Hoechst AG Werk Albert, Wiesbaden, W.Ger., 1971-89; tchr. J. Gutenberg U. Med. Sch., Mainz, W.Ger., 1977-90; disting. vis. prof. U. Belgrade (Yugoslavia) Med. Sch. Editor: Animal Models and Hypoxia, 1981, Stroke: Animal Models, 1983, Adenosine: Receptors and Modulation of Cell Function, 1985; assoc. editor Artery, 1976—. NIH grantee, 1966-70; Am. Heart Assn. grantee, 1968-69. Fellow N.Y. Acad. Scis.; mem. Am. Chem. Soc. Methodist. Home: 38 Irenenstrasse, 65791 Wiesbaden Germany

STEFÁNSSON, EINAR, ophthalmology educator; b. Reykjavík, Iceland, May 19, 1952; s. Stefán Pétursson and Bryndís Alda Einarsdóttir; m. Bryndís Thóröardóttir; children: Arnar, Margrét, Stefán, Katrín Ólöf, Anna Bryndís. MD, U. Iceland, Reykjavík, 1978; PhD, Duke U., 1981. Diplomate Am. Bd. Ophthalmology; splst. in ophthalmology Govt. Iceland, 1985. Rsch. assoc. Duke U., Durham, N.C., 1979-81; resident in ophthalmology Duke U. Med. Ctr., Durham, 1982-85; asst. prof. ophthalmology Duke U. Med. Ctr., Durham, Md., 1986-89; vis. scientist Nat. Eye Inst., Bethesda, Md., 1985-86; prof. ophthalmology U. Iceland, Reykjavík, 1987—, dean Sch. Medicine, 1996-98; dir. Icelandic Pharmaceuticals, Reykjavík, 1994-97,

Cyclops ehf, Reykjavík. Author: Ocular Oxygenation and Neovascularization, 1981; co-editor: Icelandic Med. Jour., 1991-94, Acta Ophthalmologica Scandinavica, 1996—, Diabetes Mellitus in Iceland, 1992; contbr. numerous articles and abstracts to profl. jours. Melvin Jones fellow Lions Internat. Found.,d 1994. Mem. Am. Acad. Ophthalmology, Assn. Rsch. and Vision in Ophthalmology, Club Jules Gonin. Avocations: contract bridge, volleyball, fishing. E-mail: einarste@rsp.is. Home: Fjaráarás 13, 110 Reykjavík Iceland Office: U Iceland Dept Ophthalmolog, Landspítalinn, 101 Reykjavík Iceland

STEFÁNSSON, JÓN GRÉTAR, psychiatrist; b. Reykjavík, Iceland, Jan. 10, 1939; s. Stefán Dorsteinn SigurJónsson and Adalbjörg Jónsdóttir; m. Helga Hannesdóttir, Oct. 31, 1964; children: Adalbjörg, Hannes, Stefán, Valgerdur. Candidatus Medicinae Et Chirurgiae, U. Iceland, 1966. Cert. to practice medicine, 1969, cert. to practice psychiatry, 1975, Iceland. Intern U. Hosp., Reykjavik, 1966-67; rural practitioner Ministry of Health, Iceland, 1967-68; resident in psychiatry U. Hosp., Reykjavík, 1968-69, U. Rochester, N.Y., 1969-74; psychiatrist U. Hosp., Reykjavík, 1975-83, chief psychiatrist, 1983—; dir. med. curriculum U. Iceland, Reykjavík, 1974-80, asst. prof. psychiatry, 1975-79, assoc. prof. psychiatry, 1979—, chmn. med. curriculum com., 1981-83. Contbr. articles to profl. jours. Chmn. Icelandic Med. Studies Assn., 1964-65, Icelandic Psychiat. Assn., 1978-80, Icelandic Assn. Mental Health, 1990-96; bd. dirs. Nordic Fedn. Med. Edn.-The Nordic Countries, 1980-92. Fellow Royal Soc. Medicine; mem. Am. Psychiat. Assn. (corr. mem.). Avocations: salmon fishing, hunting, skiing, Golden Retrievers. Home: Trönuhólar 18, 111 Reykjavík Iceland Office: Dept Psychiatry Univ Hosp, Eiríksgata, 101 Reykjavík Iceland

STEFÁNSSON, VALGARDUR, geothermal engineer, consultant; b. Reykjavik, Iceland, June 2, 1939; s. Stefan Gislason and Lara Gudnadottir; m. Ingibjorg Rannveig Gudlaugsdottir, Aug. 7, 1964. FilKand, U. Stockholm, 1965, FilLic, 1969, FilDr, 1973. Lectr. U. Stockholm, 1963-73; staff geophysicist Orkustofnun, Reykjavik, 1973-76, sect. leader, 1976-85, dep. dir. geothermal divsn., 1979-85; interregional adviser UN, N.Y.C., 1985-90; sect. leader Orkustofnun, 1990-96, chief project mgr., 1997—; spl. cons. Virkir-Orkint, Reykjavik, 1980-85, 90—. Author/co-author more than 80 articles in internat. sci. publs. Mem. Internat. Geothermal Assn. (bd. dirs.). Office: Orkustofnun, Grensasvegur 9, 108 Reykjavik Iceland

STEFANUTTI, LEOPOLDO, atmospheric scientist; b. Rome, Apr. 19, 1943; s. Pietro Stefanutti and Adriana Mussafia; m. Jo Ann Schonthal (div. 1985); m. Anna Broggian; 1 child, Sarah. Diploma in Elec. Engring., U. Rome, 1968; PhD (hon.), U. Lyon, 1998. Chief scientist Consiglio Nazionale delle Ric, Florence, 1982—; with Italo-French Coop. in Antarctica, 1987-97; coord. EU Airborne Platform for Earth observation THESEO, 1997-99; with PNRA-APE, 1991-97, APE-Theseo, 1997-99; v.p. Inst. Study Applications of Acronaut and Space Scis., 1999—; cons. European Space Agy., 1986-95, Sesame Core Group mem., CEC, Brussels, 1993-94, European Stratospheric Ozone Panel, 1997—, others; coord. Measurement and Modelling of Ozone and Aerosols in No. Atmosphere, 1993-95; project leader Italian Nat. Programme for Antarctic Rsch.-Airborne Polar Experiment, 1991-97; chmn. European Sci. Found.-Airborne Platform for Earth observation, 1995-99; founder APE Mgmt. Com., 1995, APE Ltd., 1999. Editor six vols. of proceedings of Italian Atmospheric Rsch. in Antarctica, 1988-95; contbr. articles to profl. jours. Recipient Eminent Scientist award Nat. Inst. Water and Atmospheric Sci. New Zealand, 1994. Mem. Party of Dem. Left. Avocations: skiing, travel, reading. E-mail: lidar@iroe.fi.cnr.it. Home: S Martino alla Palma, via di Carcheri 295, 50010 Florence Italy Office: Consiglio Nazionale Delle R, Via Pancaldo 21, 50127 Florence Italy

STEFENELLI, GEORGE EDWARD, physician; b. Bklyn., Sept. 27, 1948; s. George Edward and Ann Marie (Mandel) S.; m. Rosemary Elizebeth Stefenelli, June 16, 1973; children: Stephanie, Rory, George, Samantha. BSN, SUNY, Stony Brook, 1975; DO, Phila. Sch. Osteo. Medicine, 1986. Diplomate Am. Bd. Ob-Gyn.; lic. physician, N.J., Pa., Md. Intern Interfaith Med. Ctr., Bklyn., 1986-87; resident U. Medicine and Dentistry of N.J., Stratford, 1987-91; asst. prof. clin. ob-gyn. U. Medicine and Dentistry N.J., Stratford, 1992-93; ptnr. Potomac Ob-Gyn., Waynesboro, Pa., 1993-2000; chief svc. ob-gyn. dept. Waynesboro Hosp., 1998-2000, v.p. med. staff, 1999-2000; pvt. practice Women's Health Clarion, Pa., 2000—. Capt. U.S. Army, 1976-82. Mem. Am. Osteo. Assn., Am. Coll. Osteo. Ob-Gyn., Am. Coll. Ob-Gyn., Pa. Med. Soc., Franklin County Med. Soc., Pa. Osteo. Med. Soc., Am. Soc. Colposcopy and Cervical Pathology, Am. Assn. Gynecologic Laparoscopists, Am. Soc. for Reproductive Medicine. Home and Office: 113 Oakridge Dr Clarion PA 16214

STEFENS, PAUL EDOUARD, defense electronics company executive, consultant; b. Antwerp, Belgium, July 15, 1929; s. Fernand Marie Stefens and Yvonne Rosalie Frateur; m. Diane Pharaïde Camerman, Sept. 4, 1971; children: Serge, Laurence. Cert., Athenaeum of Koekelberg, Brussels, 1946, Advt. Sch., Antwerp, 1965; postgrad., Harvard U., 1973. Head advt. prodn. GM, Antwerp, Belgium, 1951-62; mktg. asst. Procter & Gamble Geneva s.a., Geneva, Switzerland, 1962-63; pub. affairs dir. GM Continental, Antwerp, 1964-91; pub. affairs rep. Hughes Europe s.a., Brussels, 1991-97; mgr. corp. affairs and comms. Raytheon Internat. Inc., Brussels, 1997—; dir. Tech/Comms. bvba, Brasschaat, Belgium, 1991—. Named Officer in the Order of the Crown Kingdom of Belgium, 1991. Mem. World Orgn. of the Periodical Press, Assn. of Journalists of the Periodical Press (Internat. Info. prize 1973), Rotary Club Antwerp North. Avocations: long distance running, skiing. Home: Mishaegen 132, B2930 Brasschaat Belgium Office: Raytheon Internat Europe, Avenue Ariane 5, B1200 Brussels Belgium

STEFFAN, ILSE MARGARETHE, chemistry educator; b. Vienna, Austria, May 16, 1942; d. Franz and Maria (Tejc) Tauscher; m. Ludwig Maria Steffan, Sept. 5, 1970; 1 child, Isabella. PhD, U. Vienna, 1973. Contract asst. U. Vienna, 1973-79, univ. asst., 1979-89, asst. prof., 1989-98, univ. prof., 1998—. Referee jours. in field. Recipient Fritz Habig award Österreichische Gesellschaft Kinderheilkunde, 1981. Mem. Austrian Soc. Analytical Chemistry, Schweiterische Anbeitsgemeinshaft Spektrometry Elementanalytik. Roman Catholic. Office: Inst Analytical Chemistry, Währingerstr 38, 1090 Vienna Austria

STEFFEN, JAMES RICHARD, science educator, optometrist; b. Parsons, Kans., Mar. 28, 1962; s. James Cecil and Shirley Marie (Johnston) S. BS summa cum laude, Southwestern Okla. State U., 1984, Northeastern State U., 1986; OD magna cum laude, Northeastern State U., 1988. Lic. optometrist, Okla. Assoc. optometrist pvt. practice Derby, Kans., 1988-90, Weatherford, Okla., 1990, Tulsa, 1990-91; optometrist pvt. practice Lawton, Okla., 1991-95; coach Cimarron H.S. Acad. Team, 1996-2000; Sci. Club sponsor, 1996-2000. Mem. C. of C., Lawton, 1991, Elgin (Okla.) United Meth. Ch., 1991. Named Alumni Judge for Chester Pheiffer Optometry Rsch. award, 1990, Outstanding 3rd Yr. Optometry student, 1986-87, Outstanding Sr. Biology student, 1983-84, Outstanding Genetics student, 1982-83, Outstanding Freshman Biology student, 1981-82; recipient Am. Optometric Found. Harold Kohn award, 1988, Heart of Am. Contact Lens Soc. award, 1988, Nikon award, 1984-85, Corning scholarship Am. Optometric Foun., 1986-87, Activity award for Outstanding Contbn. to Beta Sigma Kappa, 1987-88. Mem. Am. Optometric Assn., Okla. Optometric Assn., Okla. Nat. Edn. Assn., Okla. Sci. Tchrs. Assn., Cimarron Edn. Assn., Lions, Gold Key Internat. Optometric Honor Soc. (chpt. sec. 1987-88), Beta Sigma Kappa (chpt. pres. 1987-88), Beta Beta Beta (chpt. pres. 1983-84, chpt. treas. 1982-83). Republican. Avocations: bowling, hiking, computer programming. Office: Cimarron HS PO Box 8 Lahoma OK 73754-0008

STEFFEN, MAXINE LYNN, small business owner; b. Geneva, Nebr., Aug. 14, 1955; d. Edwin and Leta Lucille Dameier. BS, U. Nebr., 1976. Owner Landry & Assocs., Oklahoma City, 1983-86; regional sales mgr. Staley Foodservice, Chgo., 1986-87; sales Marvene Fischer Sales, Northbrook, Ill., 1987-88; owner Am. Food Brokers, Inc., Chgo., 1988—, Flagworks, Lincoln, Nebr., 1997—, Stars & Stripes Antiques, Lincoln, 1999—. Mem. Women Bus. Owners Network, Univ. Pl. Bus. Orgn., Soroptomist (pres. 1997—). Republican. Avocations: piano, tennis, golf, theatre, reading. Office: 2776 N 39th St Lincoln NE 68504-2426

STEFFENS, JOHN LAUNDON, brokerage house executive; b. Cleve., July 7, 1941; m. Louise Cullen, Nov. 25, 1967; children: Drew, Julie, Wesley. B in Econs., Dartmouth Coll., 1963. Various positions Merrill Lynch, 1963—; exec. v.p. U.S. Pvt. Client Group, 1990—, vice-chmn. bd., 1997—. Office: Merrill Lynch & Co Inc World Fin Ctr N Tower 250 Vesey St Fl 32 New York NY 10080-0002

STEFFENS, WERNER LUDWIG, fishery scientist; b. Bautzen, Germany, Apr. 20, 1931; s. Wilhelm and Marie-Luise (Senger) S.; m. Andrea Eleonore Keienburg, May 4, 1963; children: Dirk, Ulf. Diplomfischwirt, Humboldt U., Berlin, 1954, Dr. agr., 1958, Dr. agr. habil., 1964. Scientist Inst. of Inland Fishery, Berlin, 1954-66, head dept. pond culture and fish diseases, 1966-91; head dept. fish culture and fish pathology Inst. Freshwater Ecology and Inland Fisheries, Berlin, 1992-96; prof. fish culture and fish nutrition Humboldt U., Berlin, 1984-99; mem. adv. bd. Internat. Rev. of Hydrobiology, Berlin, 1994-2000, Aquaculture Nutrition, 1995—; vis. prof. fish nutrition U. Philippines Miag-ao, Iloilo, 1997. Author: Der Karpfen, 1958, 62, 69, 75, 80, Principles of Fish Nutrition, 1989, Fischereiforschung am Müggelsee, 2000; editor Moderne Fischwirtschaft, 1981, Binnenfischerei-Produktionsverfahren, 1986. Mem. Inland Fisheries Assn. of East Germany (pres. 1990-94), German Fisheries Assn. (com. mem.), Internat. Assn. of Theoretical and Applied Limnology, German Anglers Assn. (v.p.). Achievements include rsch. in fish nutrition and fish culture. Home: Eitelsdorfer Str 32, D-12555 Berlin Germany Office: German Anglers Assn, Weissenseer Weg 110, D-10369 Berlin Germany

STEFL, STANISLAV, astronomer; b. Pocatky, Czechoslovakia, Nov. 13, 1955; s. Stanislav and Bozena (Strakova) S.; m. Jana Bartonova, Mar. 22, 1979 (div. May 1991); children: Martin, Marketa. MS, Charles U., 1979, PhD, 1987. Rschr. Astronomical Inst., Ondrejov, Czechoslovakia, 1980-91; rsch. assoc. European So. Obs., Garching, Germany, 1991-93; staff Astronomical Inst., 1993—; vis. astronomer Lunar and Planetary Lab., Tucson, Ariz., 1988, U. Toronto, 1988, U. Trieste, Italy, 1989, 91, European So. Obs., La Silla, Chile, 1991-97. Mem. Internat. Astronomical Union, European Astronomical Soc., Nat. Geographic Soc. Avocations: mountaineering, nature, philosophy, music. Home: Dr Frice 60, CZ 25165 Ondřejov Czech Republic Office: Astronomical Inst Acad Scis, CZ-25165 Ondřejov Czech Republic

STEFOS, THEODOR, obstetrics-gynecology educator; b. Ioannina, Greece, Sept. 18, 1955; s. Ioannis and Marina (Sozou) S.; m. Ioanna Litou, Jan. 1, 1980; children: Marina, Spyros. Diploma, U. Athens, 1979; MD, U. Joannina, Greece, 1984. Fellowship on obstetrics Baylor Coll. of Medicine, Tex., 1987-88; ob-gyn. tng. U. Joannina, 1979-84, lectr. of ob-gyn., 1986-89, asst. prof., 1989-99, assoc. prof., 1999—; dir. maternal-fetal medicine U. Joannina, 1989—. Author: Perinatal Care, 1994; contbr. articles to profl. jours. Mem. Am. Inst. Ultrasound in Medicine, Hellenic Ob-Gyn. Inst., Perinatal Soc. of Greece. Avocations: table tennis, football. Home: N Papadopouldu 3, 45444 Joannina Greece Office: U Joannina, Panepistimiou, 45000 Joannina Greece

STEGAROIU, ROXANA, dentistry educator; b. Bucharest, Dec. 17, 1967; d. Mihail and Irina Leontina (Codrea) S.; m. Yasunori Katagiri, July 6, 1998. DDS, U. Medicine and Pharmacy, Bucharest, 1991; PhD, Niigata U., 1998. Dental surgeon Univ. Hosp., Bucharest, 1991-92; asst. prof. Niigata (Japan) U. Sch. Dentistry, 1998—. Contbr. articles to profl. jours. Mem. Internat. Assn. for Dental Rsch., Japan Prosthodontic Soc., Niigata Dental Soc. Avocations: reading, hiking, classical music, skiing. Office: Niigata U Sch Dentistry, Gakkocho Dori 2-5274, 951-8514 Niigata Japan

STEGEMANN, BURCKART, surgeon; b. Werningerode, Germany, Jan. 6, 1941; s. Karl and Dora (Temming) S.; m. Gisela Grothe; children: Heike, Geesche. Staatsexamen, U. M nster, Germany, 1971, Habil, 1981, AplProf, 1986. Asst. surgeon U. M nster, 1971, asst. Pathol. Inst., 1971-72, asst. surgeon, 1972-80, oberarzt surgeon, 1980-81; oberarzt surgeon Allgemeines Krankenhaus Hagen, U. Bochum, Germany, 1982-83, chief surgeon, 1983—, med. dir., 1992—. Mng. editor Klinickarzt Demeter im Thieme-Verlag, Vorstand, Deutsche Gesellschaft fur Interdisziplinäre KLinische Medizin. With German armed forces, 1962-64. Mem. Lions Club Hagen Mark. Avocations: flying, biking, golf. Office: Allgemeines Krankenhaus, Hagen gen GmbH, 58095 Hagen Germany

STEGEMANN, HERMANN, chemistry educator; b. Konigsberg, Ger., June 23, 1923; s. Hermann and Kathe (Robbers) S.; m. Gisela Hagemann, Sept. 7, 1946; children: Monika, Gudula. Dipl.Chemiker, U. Tubingen, 1946, Dr.rer.nat., 1951; Dr.habil. U. Gottingen, 1968, prof.apl., 1970. Group leader research Max Planck Ges., Med. Forsch Anst., Gottingen, 1951-53; research scholar Cancer Research Inst., Fox Chase, Phila., 1954-55; group leader Max Planck Inst., 1956-60; head biochem. Inst., Biol. Bundesanstalt, Hann.Munden, Germany, 1960-68, Braunschweig, 1969-88. Contbr. over 200 articles to profl. jours. Served with German Army, 1940-44. Fulbright fellow, 1954-55; recipient Sci. Merit medal World Cultural Council, 1987, others. Home: Am Sandkamp 15, D 38104 Braunschweig Germany Office: Institut fur Biochemie, Messeweg 11-12, D 38104 Braunschweig Germany

STEGENGA, JAMES ALAN, political scientist, ethicist, author, educator; b. Highland Park, Mich., Mar. 5, 1937; s. Delos Stegenga and Eleanore (Pederson) Gnecco; m. Ann Louise Watzel, Mar. 28, 1959 (div. 1971); three children; m. Michelle Roth, 1974 (dec. 1984); m. Mary Jo Bartolacci, 1984 (div. 1991); m. Vera Lucia de Almeida, 1998. AS, Grand Rapids (Mich.) C.C., 1956; BA, U. Mich., 1959; MA, UCLA, 1963, PhD, 1966. Asst. prof., postdoctoral fellow Ohio State U., Columbus, 1966-68; from assoc. prof. to prof. Purdue U., Lafayette, Ind., 1968-94, prof. emeritus, 1994—; vis. prof., scholar UCLA, 1967, U. Mass., 1979, MIT, 1985, U. Chgo. Divinity Sch., 1991. Author: The United Nations Force in Cyprus, 1968; co-author: The Global Community, 2d edit., 1982, (morality drama) Dunbar's Bremen, 1981; contbr. articles to profl. jours; book rev. editor Armed Forces and Society, 1977-91, Society mag., 1972-76. Home: 639 Ney Cardoso-Costazul, Rio das Ostras RJ, Brazil 28890

STEGER, EDWARD HERMAN, chemist; b. New Orleans, Dec. 11, 1936; s. Herman Christoph and Katherine (Walther) S.; m. Amy Patricia Duvall, July 29, 1960; children: David B., Sandra E. BS, Tulane U., 1958. Analytical chemist Atlantic Rsch. Corp., Gainesville, Va., 1960-64, head control lab., 1964—; presenter at profl. confs. Contbr. articles to Fine Particle Soc. Jour. Lt. USNR, 1958-60. Mem. Am. Chem. Soc., N.Y. Acad. Scis., Phi Beta Kappa, Phi Eta Sigma, Alpha Chi Sigma. Baptist. Home: 4311 Alta Vista Dr Fairfax VA 22030-5302 Office: Atlantic Rsch Corp 5945 Wellington Rd Gainesville VA 20155-1633

STEGER, KLAUS, biologist, researcher; b. Sulzbach-Rosenberg, Bavaria, Germany, Mar. 24, 1963; s. Johann and Emilie Jlselore (Zahn) S.; m. Andrea Christa Hummel, June 13, 1997. BS in Biology and Chemistry, U. Regensburg, Germany, 1989, D of Natural Scis., 1994. Cert. biology, anatomy (male reproduction) tchr. Tchr. biology and chemistry secondary sch., Regensburg, Eichstaett, Germany, 1989-91; scientist Inst. Anatomy, Regensburg, Germany, 1991-94; asst. prof. Inst. Anatomy and Cell Biology, Halle, Germany, 1994-99, Inst. Vet. Anatomy, Giessen, Germany, 1999—. Author: (with T. Klonisch, S. Klonisch, F. Tetens) Neuroanatomy Transparent, 1997; contbr. articles to profl. jours. Rsch. grantee Deutsche Forschungs Gemeinschaft, 1997—. Mem. German Anatomy Soc., German Soc. Andrology. Avocations: jogging, dancing, baking, indoor plants. Office: Inst Vet Anatomy, Frankfurter Strasse 98, 35392 Giessen Germany

STEGGALS, BILL, business executive, educator; b. Fareham, Hampshire, Eng., Apr. 3, 1948; s. Henry William and Daphne (Hawkins) S.; m. Susan Sylvia Ball, Aug. 17, 1972; children: Lucy Kate, William Henry. Sales tng. mgr. Upjohn Ltd., 1977-80; mktg. mgr. Upjohn Ltd., Asia, Turkey, 1980-90; regional mgr. Eastern Europe Upjohn Ltd., 1990-93; spl. projects mgr. Smithkline Beecham Internat., 1994-96; sr. cons. Talentmark, 1996-99; v.p. Ingenix Pharm. Svcs., 1999—; cons. Internat. Bus. and Human Resources Devel. Consultancy, 1992-93; lectr. Aston Univ. Bus. Sch., Birmingham, 1995—. Avocations: sports, cricket. Office: Ingenix Pharm Svcs, St Ives Rd, Maidenhead SL6 1QT, England

STEGMANN, HARTMUT BERNHARD, chemistry educator; b. Weissenfels/Saale, Germany, Oct. 16, 1931; s. Walter and Gertrud (Vahl) S.; m. Margret Ott, 1957; children: Petra, Ekhard. Chem.-techn. asst., Naturalscis. Acad., Isny/Allgäu, Fed. Republic Germany, 1953; diploma in chemistry, U. Tübingen, Fed. Republic Germany, 1959, PhD, 1962. Postdoctoral fellow Harvard U., Cambridge, Mass., 1963-64; asst. U. Tübingen, 1964-69, extraordinary prof. chemistry, 1969—, ordinary prof., 1990—, also dean of faculty chemistry and pharmacy; vis. prof. NIH, Research Triangle Park, N.C., 1982; vice-dir. Chemisches ZentralInst, Tubingen. Author: Elektronenspinresonanz, 1970; contbr. numerous articles to sci. jours., also monographs. Mem. German Chem. Soc. (chmn. 1987-89), Fachgruppe Magnetische Resonanz, Am. Soc. Photobiology, Tennis Club, Yacht Club. Avocations: tennis, alpine skiing, canoeing, sailing. Office: U Tubingen Inst Org Chem, Auf der Morgenstelle 18, D-72076 Tübingen Germany

STEHLE, RICHARD EUGEN, finance educator; b. Stuttgart, Germany, Nov. 7, 1946; s. Eugen and Luise Stehle; m. Ingrid S. Nast, Nov. 7, 1969; children: Jan Oliver, Jörg Andreas. Diploma, U. Mannheim, 1970, habilitation, 1982; PhD, Stanford U., 1977. Vis. asst. prof. fin. U. Chgo., 1982-84; prof. U. Siegen, Germany, 1984-87, U. Augsburg, Germany, 1987-92, Humboldt-Univ. zu Berlin, Berlin, 1992; chmn. fin. dept. Humboldt-Univ. zu Berlin, 1992—; cons. to numerous banks and bus. firms. Contbr. articles to profl. jours. Scholar Am. Field Svc., 1963-64; fellow Ford Found., 1971-74. Mem. Am. Fin. Assn., European Fin. Assn., Hochschullehrerverband, Hochschullehrer für Betriebswirtschaft. Home: Krefelder Str 12, 10555 Berlin Germany Office: Humboldt U Zu Berlin, Spandauer Str 1, 10178 Berlin Germany

STEIER, MICHAEL EDWARD, cardiac surgeon; b. N.Y.C., Mar. 22, 1942; s. Philip (deceased) and Gertrude S.; m. Sheila Elaine Finkelstein, June 9, 1963; children: Douglas, James, Lauren. BA, Long Island U., 1964; MD, Univ. Health Scis., Chgo., 1968. Diplomate Am. Bd. Surgery, Am. Bd. Thoracic Surgery. Resident in gen. surgery St. Vincent's Hosp., N.Y.C., 1969-73; resident in thoracic surgery Mayo Clinic, Rochester, Minn., 1973-75; cardiac surgeon S.W. Fla. Regional Med. Ctr., Ft. Myers, Fla., 1975—, Lee Meml. Hosp., Ft. Myers, 1975—, Cape Coral (Fla.) Hosp., 1977—, Naples (Fla.) Cmty. Hosp., 1996—; pres. Cardiac Surg. Assocs. West Fla., Ft. Myers; ret.; chief surgery, S.W. Fla. Regional Med. Ctr., Ft. Myers, 1980-82, pres. med. staff, 1982; cons. Naples Cmty. Hosp., 1996—. Capt., USAR, 1969-78. Fellow ACS, Am. Coll. Chest Physicians, Am. Coll. Cardiology; mem. Soc. for Thoracic Surgeons, N.Y. Acad. Scis., Cardiac Surg. Assn. S.W. Fla. (pres. 1993-99), Explorers Club. Office: Cardiac Surgical Assocs SW Fla 2675 Winkler Ave Fort Myers FL 33901-9342

STEIGER, OTTO MARTIN KARL, economics educator; b. Dresden, Sachsen, Germany, Dec. 12, 1938; s. Hans and Gertrud (Richter) S.; m. Karin Bendt Schulenberg, 1981; children: Martin Matti, Ferdinand, Tineke, Stephan. MA in Econs. (Diplom-Volkswirt), Freie U., Berlin, 1968; PhD in Econ. History, U. Uppsala, Sweden, 1971. Rsch. asst., reader in econ. history U. Uppsala, 1971-72; lectr. econ. history U. Stockholm, 1971-72, U. Umeaa, Sweden, 1972-73; prof. econs. U. Bremen, Germany, 1973—; invited qualified person to nominate candidates for Nobel prize in econs. Swedish Acad. Scis., 1989-92. Author: Studien zur Entstehung der Neuen Wirtschaftslehre in Schweden, 1971, (with G. Heinsohn and R. Knieper) Menschenproduktion, 1979 (Danish transl. 1981, Swedish transl. 1982), (with G. Heinsohn) Die Vernichtung der weisen Frauen, 1985, 3d edit., 1989 (Swedish transl. 1989), Eigentum, Zins und Geld, 1996, Allgemeine Theorieder Wirtschaft I: Kritik der Schuloekonomie, 2000, (with H.-J. Stadermann) Der Stand und die naechste Zukunft der Geldforschung, 1993, Herausfordetung der Geldwirtschaft, 1999, (with G. Heinsohn) Das Eurosystem und die Verletzung der Zentralbankregeln, 2000; editor: (with H. Hagemann) Keynes' General Theory nach fuenfzig Jahren, 1988; contbr. numerous articles to profl. jours., anthologies, encys. Mem. Am. Econ. Assn., Royal Econ. Soc., European Econ. Assn., History of Econs. Soc., Arbeitskreis Politsche Oekonomie. Home: Fesenfeld 32, D-28203 Bremen Germany Office: U Bremen FB 7 Oekonomie, Postfach 33 04 40, D-28359 Bremen Germany

STEIGLEDER, GERD KLAUS, dermatologist, dermatohistopathologist; b. Fulda, Hessia, Germany, Jan. 25, 1925; s. Phil Klaus and Katharina (Heckenbach) S.; m. Inge Helene Krebs Steigleder, Aug. 12, 1955; children: Stephanie Karbe, Klaus, Jochen. MD, U. Frankfurt, 1949; MD honoris causa, U. Szeged, 1989. Cert. dermatologist, allergologist. Resident U. Frankfurt, Germany, 1948-52, asst. prof., 1952-59, prof., 1959-64; asst. prof. Columbia U., N.Y.C., 1959-61; ordentlicher prof., dept. head Dermatology U. Cologne, Germany, 1964-90; prof. emeritus Dermatology pvt. practice, 1990—; former editor Zeitschrift für Hautkrankheiten, 1981-92. Author: Pocketbook Dermatology and Venerology; several books on Dermatology, Dermatopathology, and allergy; also more than 600 publs. Recipient Kaposi Medaille of Hungarian Dermatological Soc., 1985, Herxheimer Medaille German Dermatological Soc., 1988. Mem. Lions Club Köln-Agrippina. Avocations: contemporary history, walking.

STEILING, DANIEL PAUL, retired railroad conductor, writer; b. San Jose, Calif., June 28, 1944; s. Paul Henry and Lois Kathryn (Barton) S.; m. Dorothy Elise Chaplin, Nov. 6, 1976 (div. July 1978). Right of way agt. Caltrans - Calif. State Dept. Transp., San Francisco, 1969-70; owner Dan's Bicycle Shop, Santa Cruz, Calif., 1970-83; soil inspector Soil Svcs. Inc. divsn. Applied Soil Mechanics, Inc., San Jose, 1983-84; sr. mfg. specialist disk products divsn. IBM, San Jose, 1984-92; R.R. condr. Amtrak, San Jose, 1993-97; ret., 1997; substitute tchr. history, geography, sci. Murrieta Valley Unified Sch. Dist., 1999—. Author: Operation and Maintenance of TRACOR Thickness Measuring Guage (Liquid Nitrogen Cooled), 1987. With USAF, 1966-68. Mem. Assn. Am. Geographers, Antique Auto Club Am., Fallbrook Vintage Car Club, Ford Falcon Club Am. Avocations: bicycle touring, photography, antique auto restoration. Home: 25060 Hancock Ave # 103-219 Murrieta CA 92562-5959

STEIN, BERNHARD OTTO, anesthesiologist; b. Braunschweig, Germany, June 23, 1956; arrived in Luxembourg, 1992; s. Dietrich and Lore (Quost) W.;m. Monika Riehl, Sept. 7, 1984; children: André, Sandra, Svenja. MD, Medizinische Hochschule, Hannover, Germany, 1982; diploma in health econs., European Bus. Sch., Oestrich, Germany, 1998. Diplomate European Acad. Anesthesiology. Cons. anesthesiology chronic pain U. Hosp., Ulm, Germany, 1987, rschr. scientist dept. exptl. anesthesia, 1988; cons. intensive care medicine U. Hosp., Ulm, 1989-91; cons. anesthesiology U. Hosp., Nancy, France, 1991-92; pvt. practice Esch-sur-Alzette, Luxembourg, 1992—; head dept. intensive care medicine Hosp. de la Ville, Esch-sur-Alzette, Luxembourg. Contbr. articles to profl. jours. and books. Mem. European Acad. Anesthesiology, European Soc. Intensive Care Medicine, Coll. Français des Anesthésistes Réanimateurs. Home: 10 rue de l'Hôpital, 4137 Esch-sur-Alzette Luxembourg Office: Hôpital de la Ville, Rue Emile Mayrisch, 4240 Esch-sur-Alzette Luxembourg

STEIN, DALE FRANKLIN, retired university president; b. Kingston, Minn., Dec. 24, 1935; s. David Frank and Zelda Jane S.; m. Audrey Dean Bloemke, June 7, 1958; children—Pam, Derek. B.S. in Metallurgy, U. Minn., 1958; Ph.D., Rensselaer Poly. Inst., Troy, N.Y., 1963. Metallurgist rsch. lab. GE, Schnectady, N.Y., 1958-67; assoc. prof. U. Minn., 1967-71; prof. metall. engring., head dept. Mich. Technol. U., Houghton, 1971-77; head mining engring. Mich. Technol. U., 1974-77, v.p. acad. affairs, 1977-79, pres., 1979-91; pres. emeritus, 1991—; cons. NSF, Dept. of Energy, 1972-90; trustee Rensselaer Poly. Inst., 1989-95; chmn. com. on decontamination and decommissioning uranium enrichment facilities NRC, 1993-96; active Nat. Materials Adv. Bd., 1987-93; chmn. adv. com. Ctr. for Nuclear Waste Regulatory Analyses. Contbr. articles to profl. jours. Paul Harris fellow. Fellow Metall. Soc. (pres. 1979, inst. Hardy Gold medal 1965), Am. Soc. Metals (Geisler award Eastern N.Y. chpt. 1967); mem. AIME, AAAS, NAE, Sigma Xi, Phi Kappa Phi, Tau Beta Pi, Alpha Sigma Nu. *

STEIN, DANIEL ALAN, public interest lawyer; b. Washington, Mar. 9, 1955; s. Edward Seymour and Ann Rose Stein; m. Sharon McCloe, Oct. 18, 1986; children: Claire, Corrieanne. BA, Ind. U., 1977; JD, Cath. U. Am., 1984. Bar: D.C. 1984, U.S. Dist. Ct. D.C. 1985, U.S. Ct. Appeals (D.C. cir.) 1987, U.S. Tax Ct. 1987. Profl. staff mem. select com. on narcotics abuse and control U.S. Ho. of Reps., Washington, 1977-81; pvt. practice Washington, 1984-89; exec. dir. Immigration Reform Law Inst., Washington, 1986-88, Fedn. for Am. Immigration Reform, Washington, 1982-86, 89—.

mem. adv. bd. Social Contract periodical, Petosky, Mich., 1990—. Mem. Capitol Hill Club, Nat. Press Club. Republican. Avocations: trombone, American history, western civilization, jazz, antique books. Office: Fedn for Am Immigration Reform 1666 Connecticut Ave NW Ste 400 Washington DC 20009-1039

STEIN, DAVID ERIC, physicist, defense analyst; b. Jacksonville, Fla., Jan. 13, 1950; s. Stanley Wolfe and Dorothy Jean (Lilley) S. BS with high honors (J. Hillis Miller Me, U. Fla., 1971, postgrad. (Ford Found. fellow), 1971-72, MS in Physics, 1977; grad., Air Command and Staff Coll., 1982, Naval War Coll., 1995, Air War Coll., 1996. Instr. dept. physics U. Fla., Gainesville, 1971-74, NSF rsch. asst., 1974-76; commd. 1st lt. U.S. Army, 1977, advanced through grades to lt. col., 1994; maj. USAF HQ Air Force Systems Command, Andrews AFB, Md., 1992; lt. col. Air Force Sci. adv. bd., 1994-95; project engr. advanced surveillance concepts Rome Air Devel. Ctr., 1979-81; field engr. radar systems test and evaluation Rome Air Devel. Ctr. and MIT Lincoln Lab., 1981-83; radar data and imagery analyst 6585th Test Group, Holloman AFB, N.Mex., 1983-87; elec. engr. specialist LTV Aircraft Products Group, 1987-90; fellow engr. Westinghouse Electric Corp., 1990-91; ops. rsch. analyst CSCI, 1992-94, Office of Asst. Sec. of Air Force, 1995, 96-97, Joint Staff, 1996, 98-99, Army Digitization Office, 1999-2000, CACI, 2000—; part-time coll. faculty, 1982-84; short course instr. radar techs. George Washington U., 1991-97; adv. assoc. editor NATO Advanced Rsch. Workshop, Bad Windsheim, Germany, 1988; cons., 1994—. Editor-in-chief Applied Computational Electromagnetics Soc. Jour., 1987-93; assoc. editor: Frontier Perspectives, 2000—; contbr. articles to profl. jours.; patentee in field. With USAF Res., 1992, 94-99. Recipient Disting. Svc. award Applied Computational Electromagnetics Soc., 1994. Mem. Am. Phys. Soc., Am. Assn. Physics Tchrs., U.S. Strategic Inst., World Affairs Coun., Army-Navy Club, Fla. Blue Key, Phi Beta Kappa, Sigma Pi Sigma, Omicron Delta Kappa, Phi Kappa Phi. Achievements include identification of new atmospheric refractivity effects on low-altitude radar propagation, extended quantum-mech. computational technique to electromagnetic scattering, copioneered new acquisition sizing methodology for next-generation fighter aircraft; co-authored section of Defense Critical Technologies Plan for the Executive Office of the President; key advisor to Air Force Requirements Oversight Council; identified systems acquisition implications of future generic geopolitical scenarios, new concepts in warfare, futuristic techs. Home: PO Box 169 Linthicum Heights MD 21090-0169

STEIN, ELLEN GAIL, executive manager; b. N.Y.C., May 19, 1951; d. Manuel W. and Bella (Skutel) Stein. BA, SUNY, Stony Brook, 1972; M of Urban Planning, Hunter Coll., 1976; cert. program execs. state/local govt., Harvard U., 1985. Sr. rsch. assoc. Nassau Suffolk (N.Y.) Regional Med. Program, 1976-77; sr. planner N.Y.C. Dept. Correction, 1977-79; group leader criminal justice Mayor's Office, Dept. Ops., N.Y.C., 1979-81, dep. asst. dir. citywide spl. projects, 1981, dir. citywide audit implementation, 1981-84; adminstr. Bur. Supplied N.Y.C. Bd. Edn., 1984-90; mgmt. cons. Project Provide Hope, Russia, Citizen's Budget Commn., 1990-94; pres., CEO FEDVentures Inc., 1994-99; assoc. commnr. N.Y.C. Dept. Tech. and Telecomm., 1999—. Mem. Nat. Assn. Purchasing Mgmt., Am. Women Econ. Devel., Ctrl. Women's Focus, Gov.'s Procurement Coun. (N.Y.), Human Svcs. Coun. (contracting com.). Home: 67 Park Ter E New York NY 10034-1445 Office: 75 Park Pl Fl 7 New York NY 10007-2146

STEIN, ELLIOT, JR., media executive; b. St. Louis, Jan. 31, 1949; s. Elliot and Mary Ann (Bleiweiss) S.; m. Pamela Sztybel, Oct. 4, 1997. BA, Claremont McKenna Coll., 1971. Assoc. Lehman Bros., N.Y.C., 1972-79; chmn. Caribbean Internat. News Corp., San Juan, P.R., 1985—; ptnr. Commonwealth Capital Ptnrs., N.Y.C., 1988—; Bd. dirs. ACX Pacific, Inc., Playpower, Inc., VTG Holdings, Inc., Landau Boats, LLC, Cloud Corp., LLC; mem. adv. bd. Investigative Group Internat., 1998—. Trustee Claremont Grad. U., 1980—, New Sch. U., 1990—; dir. non-profit policy and leadership program John F. Kennedy Sch. of Govt., Harvard U., 1995—; bd. dirs. Annenberg Sch. Comm., U. So. Calif., 1998—, NYU, 1998—, Inst. for Edn. and Govt., Columbia U., 1997—, Remarque Inst., NYU, 1997—. Democrat. Office: Commonwealth Capital Ptnrs 444 Madison Ave New York NY 10022-6903

STEIN, GERALD HERBERT, medical educator; b. Phila., Oct. 11, 1936; s. Harry N. and Rose (Miller) S.; Lona Livingston, May 30, 1962 (div.); children: Alexander, Lauren; m. Sara Morton, Jan. 4, 1990; children: Katherine, Frances. BA, U. Pa., 1958, MD, 1962. Asst. prof. U. Fla. Coll. Medicine, Gainesville, 1972-95; staff physician VA Med. Ctr., Gainesville, 1972-92; dir. med. edn., prof.-in-residence Kameda Med. Ctr., Kamogawa, Japan, 1992-99; assoc. clin. prof. dept. medicine U. Hawaii, Honolulu, 1996—; commd. cons. USN, Yokosuka, Japan, 1993-99; teaching cons. Shonan Kamakura Hosp., Japan, 1994—; dir. Mammatech Corp., Gainesville, 1979-84; pres. Corp. Pub. Medicine, Gainesville, 1981-95. Patentee in field. Mem. sch. adv. com. Alachua County Sch. Bd., Gainesville, 1982-90, Capt. U.S. Army Res., 1964-66. Fellow ACP, Am. Coll. Rheumatology; mem. Am. Soc. Hypertension, Phi Beta Kappa, Alpha Omega Alpha. Democrat. Jewish. Avocations: classical music, jogging, windsurfing, computers. Office: 4700 SW Archer Rd #90 Gainesville FL 32608

STEIN, JOHN JOSEPH, sales executive; b. Phila., July 9, 1938; s. John Joseph and Margaret Anna (Kirkpatrick) S.; m. Elizabeth Marie Stein, Jan. 20, 1962; Elizabeth Ann, John Christopher, Douglas James, Brian Stephen. BS, LaSalle U., 1960. Dist. sales mgr. W.B. Driver Co., Chgo., 1968-73, Pfizer HPM, Chgo., 1973-79; v.p. sales and mktg. Kamhal Corp., Bethel, Conn., 1979-86, Molecu Wire, Farmingdale, N.J., 1986—. With U.S. Army, 1961-66. Mem. N.J. Bus. and Industry, N.J. Mfrs., Wire Assn. Internat. Avocations: reading, history, sports, tennis. Office: Molecu Wire Corp PO Box 495 Farmingdale NJ 07727-0495

STEIN, JULIE ESTHER, piano instructor; b. Kingman, Ariz., June 23, 1975; d. John Michael and Eloise Margaret Cook; m. Scott Anthony Stein, Sept. 27, 1997; 1 child, Anthony John. BS in Music Performance, U. Wis., Superior, 1998. Pianist Superior Sch. Dist., 1995-97; pvt. piano instr. Julie Stein's Studio, Duluth, Minn., 1994—; piano instr. John Duss Music Conservatory, Duluth, 1997—. Contbr. musical revs. Daily Telegram and Budgeteer, 1998—. organist Our Saviors Luth. Ch., Superior, 1997; choir dir. Faith United Meth. Ch., Superior, 1998—. Avocations: reading, writing, crafts, dollhouses. E-mail: scolie@juno.com.

STEIN, MICHAEL ALAN, cardiologist, medical educator; b. Chgo., May 31, 1958; s. Harold Marc and Carlyne Mae (Skirow) S.; m. Ann Palmer Coe, June 9, 1984; children: Sarah Elizabeth, David Benjamin, Kathryn Marie. BA magna cum laude, Lawrence U., 1980; MD, U. Ill., 1984. Diplomate in internal medicine and cardiovascular diseases Am. Bd. Internal Medicine. Intern, resident in medicine U. Ill., Chgo., 1984-87; fellow in cardiology, then interventional cardiology U. Iowa, Iowa City, 1987-91; asst. prof. Emory U., Atlanta, 1991-95; dir. cardiology dept. Lower Fla. Keys Health Sys., 1997-98; clin. asst. prof. U. Wis., Madison, 1998—; med. dir. CCU Atlanta VA Med. Ctr., Decatur, Ga., 1991-95; med. dir. cardiac catheterization lab., Dunwoody Med. Ctr., Atlanta, 1994-95; staff cardiologist Cardiology Cons., Pensacola, Fla., 1995-96; staff cardiologist So. Med. Group, Key West, Fla., 1996-98, Fond du Lac Regional Clinic, 1998—; v.p. Fond du Lac (Wis.) City Coun., 2000—. Mem. Fond du Lac City Coun., 2000—, v.p. 2000—. Recipient clin. investigator award NIH, 1990-95. Fellow Am. Coll. Cardiology, Am. Heart Assn. (coun. clin. cardiology, Clin. Scientist award 1990-95); mem. AAAS, Soc. for Cardiac Angiography & Interventions. Avocations: sailing, sailboat racing, hiking, scuba diving, fishing. E-mail: mas@medicine.wisc.edu. Home: 235 S Peters Ave Fond Du Lac WI 54935-3852 Office: 420 E Division St Fond Du Lac WI 54935-4560

STEIN, MILTON MICHAEL, lawyer; b. N.Y.C., Sept. 18, 1936; s. Isidore and Sadie (Lefkowitz) S.; m. Jacqueline Martin, June 17, 1962; children: April, Alicia. AB, Columbia U., 1958, LLB, 1961. Bar: N.Y. 1962, Pa. 1971, U.S. Supreme Ct. 1971. Asst. dist. atty. N.Y. County, 1962-67; sr. counsel Nat. Commn. for Reform of Fed. Criminal Law, Washington, 1967-70; asst. dist. atty., chief of appeals City of Phila., 1970-73; asst. dir. Nat. Wire Tapping Commn., Washington, 1973-75; dir. D.C. Law Revision, Washington, 1975-77; spl. asst. HUD, Washington, 1977-79; asst. gen. counsel U.S. Commodity Futures Trading Commn., Washington, 1979-83; v.p. N.Y. Futures Exch., N.Y.C., 1983-89, N.Y. Stock Exch., N.Y.C., 1989—. Mem. ABA, N.Y. State Bar Assn., Assn. of Bar of City of N.Y. Democrat. Jewish. Home: Hudson House PO Box 286 Ardsley On Hudson NY 10503-0286

STEIN, NORBERT KURT, engineering executive; b. Dettingen/Main, Germany, Jan. 14, 1952. Abitur, Hohe Landesschule, Hanau, Germany, 1972; diploma in engring., Hohe Landesschule, Darmstadt, Germany, 1980, DEng, 1984. Rschr. GFF an der DKD, Wiesbaden, Germany, 1980-84; owner, dir. Vitronic GmbH, Wiesbaden, 1984—; presenter profl. confs., 1980—. Contbr. many articles to sci. jours.; 5 patents pending. Mem. German Soc. Machinery and Plant Mfrs. (bd. dirs. sect. machine vision and robotics and automation 1994—), German Soc. Pattern Recognition (bd. dirs. 1995—), Vision Club (bd. dirs. 1990-94). Fax: 06 11 715233. Office: Vitronic GmbH, Hasengartenstr 14A, 65189 Wiesbaden Germany

STEIN, PAUL CLINTON, financial planner; b. Mpls., Feb. 27, 1960; s. Clinton W. and Pauline Stein; m. Jann Marie Matheis, Mar. 23, 1983; children: Michelle, Andrew. BS in Math. Edn., U. Minn., 1983. Registered investment advisor, series 7 rep.; lic. life, health and variable ins. rep., CFP. Orgnl. mgr. Southwestern Co., Nashville, 1980-85; sr. acct. rep. Gt. Am. Opportunities, Nashville, 1985-90; assoc. gen. agt. Luth. Brotherhood, Balt., 1990-92; sr. advisor Swenson Anderson Assocs., Mpls., 1992 , mem. adv. bd., 1996-98; spkr. on money and fin. to various schs., colls., banks and pvt. corps, and radio, Ill. and Minn., 1985 . Singer, songwriter, performer various ch. and comty. concerts, corp. banquets, 1980 . Mem. Minn. Soc. Inst. CFPs (bd. dirs. 1996-98),Minn. Planned Giving Coun., Fin. Planning Assn. Republican. Office: Swenson Anderson Assocs 1221 Nicollet Ave Ste 400 Minneapolis MN 55403-4499

STEIN, ROBERT A., writer, educator; b. Duluth, Minn., Aug. 5, 1933; s. Abe A. and Grace (Wichterman) S.; m. Betty Lou Pavlik, Nov. 5, 1955; children: Robert Jr., David K., Steven J. BS in Commerce, U. Iowa, 1956, MA in Counselor Edn., 1968, MA in Writing, 1986. Cert. tchr. Iowa; cert. profl. counselor. Commd. 2d lt. USAF, 1956, advanced through grades to col., ret., 1977; asst. prof. aerospace studies U. Iowa, Iowa City, 1964-66; assoc. prof. U. Iowa, 1966-68, prof., 1975-77; dir., safety and security U. Iowa Hosps./Clinics, Iowa City, 1977-85; ret., 1985; mem. faculty divsn. writing Kirkwood C.C., Iowa City & Cedar Rapids, Iowa, 1984-89; writer, tchr. Iowa City, 1985—; writer, tchr. Iowa City/Johnson County Sr. Citizens Ctr., Iowa City, 1994—. Author: (novels) Apollyon: A Novel, 1985, The Chase, 1988, The Black Samaritan, 1997, 2d edit., 2000, The Vengeance Equation, 2000, (fiction) Death Defied, 1988 (Internat. Literary award 1988). Decorated Bronze Star, 1969. Mem. Authors Guild, Authors League Am., Air Force Assn. (life), Military Affairs Assn. (charter), Daedalians, Nat. Iowa Lettermen's Club (past pres.), Nat. Iowa Varsity Club (exec. bd., lifetime achievement award 1999), Rotary (Paul Harris fellow), Phi Delta Kappa. Avocations: flying, international travel, reading, sports announcer U. Iowa, swimming. Home and Office: 2020 Ridgeway Dr Iowa City IA 52245-3238

STEIN, RONALD MAX, advertising executive, consultant; b. London, Nov. 24, 1927; s. Harry and Frances (Flexser) S.; m. Rosalie Landau, Sept. 21, 1958; children: Val, Viv. Student, St. Martins's Sch. Art, London, 1945-47. Jr., staff Leon Goodman Displays, London, 1944; asst. to art dir. Royds Advt. Agy., London, 1945-55; studio mgr. Stowe & Bowden Advt., London, 1955-59; prin. Ronald Stein Advt. Cons., London, 1959—; publicity cons. Guild of Glass Engravers, London, 1979-89. Illustrator (book): The Diabetic Cook Book, 1956; designer: Eve Club Souvenir Brochure, 1959, Guild of Glass Engravers catalogue, St. Lawrence Jewry Exhibition catalogue, 1986. With RAF, 1946-48, Italy, Austria. Mem. Publicity Club of London, Advt. Assn. (investigator 1980-87), Audit Bur. Circulation, Creative Circle, Inst. Dirs. (assoc. mem.), Periodical Proprietors Assn. (with indsl. intelligence). Conservative. Jewish. Avocations: opera, current and internat. affairs, photography, sketching. Office: Ronald Stein Advt Cons, West Hampstead 11 Cleve Rd, London NW6 3RH, England

STEIN, THEODORE ANTHONY, biochemist, educator; b. St. Louis, Aug. 30, 1938; s. Leonard A. and Mathilda M. S.; m. Virginai M. Loos, 1994. BS, St. Louis U., 1960; MS, So. Ill. U., 1970; PhD, CUNY, 1987. Rsch. instr. surgery Washington U. Sch. Medicine, St. Louis, 1972-75; rsch. supr. surgery L.I. Jewish-Hillside Med. Ctr., New Hyde Park, N.Y., 1975-76; rsch. coord. surgery L.I. Jewish-Hillside Med. Ctr., New Hyde Park, 1977-93; asst. prof. surgery SUNY, Stony Brook, 1978-89, Albert Einstein Sch. Medicine, Bronx, N.Y., 1989—; dir. rsch. and dir. vascular lab. L.I. Vascular Ctr., Roslyn, N.Y., 1994—; biostats. cons. NIH grantee, 1962; Am. Liver Found. grantee, 1984. Contbr. articles to profl. jours., chpts. to books. Mem. AAAS, N.Y. Acad. Scis., Am. Fedn. Clin. Rsch., Am. Pub. Health Assn., Am. Gastroenterol. Assn., Sigma Xi. Republican. Roman Catholic. Achievements include development of chromatographic methods to determine prostaglandin and leukotriene content in tissues using fluorescent agents to increase sensitivity, elastase activity in the aorta with disease, and active anabolites of 5-fluoracil in tumors; improvement of regulation of liver growth after surgery by diet; demonstration of diagnostic value of liver function tests, surgery on obese patients interferes with sugar metabolism and intestinal function; research in etiology of pancreatitis and pharmacological modification of pancreatic function; effect of stress on the stomach and colon; investigation of the mediators of inflammatory bowel disease, the long-term reduction of stroke after carotid endarterectomy, the benefit of composite grafts for distal limb salvage, the value of completion angiography for distal bypass, risk factors which may be related to rapid growth of abdominal aortic aneurysms, the value of axillo-axillary bypass grafts. Home: 10 Glamford Rd Port Washington NY 11050-2437 Office: LI Vascular Ctr 1050 Northern Blvd Roslyn NY 11576-1503

STEINBACH, BERND HEINZ, electrical engineer, educator; b. Chemnitz, Germany, Mar. 5, 1952; s. Heinz and Irma (Beu) S.; m. Andrea Hoehne, Aug. 3, 1973; 1 child, Anett. Diploma in engring., U. Tech. Karl-Marx-Stadt, 1977, D in Engring., 1981, PhD, 1984. Electrician Niles, Karl-Marx-Stadt, Germany, 1971-73; scientific asst. U. Tech. Karl-Marx-Stadt, 1977-83; rsch. engr. Robotron, Karl-Marx-Stadt, 1983-85; asst. prof. U. Tech., Chemnitz, Germany, 1985-92; prof. U. Mining and Technology, Freiberg, Germany, 1992—; head XBOOLE Rsch. Group, Chemnitz, 1985—, Steinbeis-TZ Logical Sys., Chemnitz, 1992—; dir. Inst. Computer Sci., 1998—. Author: Logic Design Using XBOOLE, 1991; contbr. articles to profl. jours. Avocations: photography, music, walk, swim, electronic. Home: Nelkentor 7, D-09126 Chemnitz Germany Office: U Mining & Tech Inst Computer Sci, Bernhard-von-Cotta-Str 1, D-09596 Freiberg Germany

STEINBACK, MICHAEL A., electronic component company executive; b. Chgo., Jan. 7, 1954; s. Morton Samual and Rita Hope Steinback; m. Nancy Steinback, July 24, 1976 (div. Dec. 1979); m. Cathy M. Steinback, Sept. 10, 1983; children: Matthew, Zachary, Ryan, Megan. BA in Econs., Ind. U., 1976; postgrad. in Elec. Engring., Devry Inst., Chgo., 1978. V.p. ops., COO Magnecraft Electric Co., Northbook, Ill., 1976-89; v.p. sales and mktg. C.P. Clare, Chgo., 1990-93; v.p. ops. Cii Techs. Inc., Asheville, N.C., 1994-96, COO, 1996-98, pres., 1998-99, CEO, 2000—. Bd. dirs United Way, Asheville, 1999. Republican. Jewish. Avocations: golf, tennis, baseball. Office: Cii Techs 1200 Ridgefield Blvd Ste 200 Asheville NC 28806-2280

STEINBERG, HARRY WILLIAM, data processing executive, consultant; b. Brookline, Mass., Dec. 31, 1948; s. Solomon and Bernice (Klein) S.; m. Ellen Carrie Freund, Oct. 31, 1981 (div. 1987); m. Laura Leigh Ferguson, Aug. 13, 1994. BA, Ohio Wesleyan U., 1971; MBA, Columbia U., 1973. Cons. Wescol, Inc., Ashland, Mass., 1973-74; systems engr. IBM Corp., Armonk, N.Y., 1974-81; systems mgr. Merrill Lynch, N.Y.C, 1982-84; sr. tech. officer Manufacturers Hanover Trust, N.Y.C, 1984-87; mgr. Goldman Sachs & Co., N.Y.C, 1987-89; v.p. Alliance Advt., Inc., Union, N.J., 1986-96; project mgr. IBM Corp., Cranford, N.J., 1997-98; project exec. CTA Inc., Bethesda, Md., 1998—; v.p. tech. Mercer Computer Systems, N.Y.C., 1989-94. Mem. steering com. Concerned Residents WEO, Edgewater, N.J., 1987—; pres. Eleven Eleven River Plz., Inc., Edgewater, 1990—. Jewish. Avocations: recreational flying, skiing, bowling, tennis. Home: 1111 River Rd Edgewater NJ 07020-1335 Office: CTA Inc 6903 Rockledge Dr Bethesda MD 20817-1818

STEINBERG, RUDOLF KARL, law educator, judge; b. Cochem/Mosel, Germany, June 23, 1943; s. Rudolf and Luise (Kistner) S.; m. Marita Schmitz, Feb. 16, 1968; children: Philipp M., Matthias F.; m. Angelika Schriever, Mar. 1, 1985; children: Julia, Felix. Referendar jur, U. Freiburg, Germany, 1967, JD, 1970. Asst. prof. U. Freiburg, 1970-77; prof. U. Hannover, Germany, 1977-80, U. Frankfurt, Germany, 1980-2000; former judge Contstl. Ct., Thuringia; pres. Goethe-U., Frankfurt, Germany, 2000—. Author: Politik und Verwaltungsorganisation, 1979, Fachplanung, 3rd edit., 2000, Der oekologische Verfassungsstaat, 1998; co-author: Aufopferung-Enteignung und Staatshaftung, 1991, Der Energieliefer-und-Erzeuger-Markt nach nationalem und Europaischem Recht, 1995; editor: Staat und Verbände, 1985, Reform des Atomrechts, 1994. Avocations: music, opera, concerts, reading, skiing, hiking. Office: U Frankfurt, Senckenberganlage 31, D-60054 Frankfurt Germany

STEINBERG, STEPHEN PHILLIP, university administrator, philosopher; b. Chgo., Mar. 9, 1949; s. David Louis and Dena Sudow Steinberg. AB in Philosophy with distinction, U. Mich., 1971; MS in Journalism, Columbia U., 1972; MA in Philosophy, New Sch. for Social Rsch., 1982; PhD in Philosophy, U. Pa., 1989. News writer WGN-TV and Radio, Chgo., summer 1970; writer U.S. Info. Agy., Washington, summer 1971; staff writer Med. Tribune, Inc., N.Y.C., 1972-73; account exec. Joseph Dermer and Assoc., Inc., N.Y.C., 1974-75; account assoc. Bruce Porter Co., Inc., N.Y.C., 1975-76; adj. instr. humanities, devel. officer Pratt Inst., N.Y.C., 1977-78; asst. dean Sch. Arts and Scis., U. Pa., Phila., 1978-87, adminstrv. fellow Offices of Pres. and Provost, 1987-90, lectr. dept. philosophy Sch. Arts and Scis., 1981—, asst. to pres., 1990—, interim dir. 21st Century Project for Undergrad. Experience, 1997-98, exec. dir. Penn Nat. Commn. on Society, Culture and Cmty., 1996—; dir. Master of Arts and Profl. Studies program U. Pa., 1985-87, coord. Faculty Coun. on Undergrad. Edn., 1986-87, asst. dir. Grad. Programs and Adminstr., Coll. of Gen. Studies, 1982-87, acad. and career advisor Coll. Gen. Studies, 1978-87, coord. Provost's Coun. on Undergrad. Edn., 1987-92, coord. Provost's Coun. on Undergrad. Admissions, 1987-92, coord. Coun. of Undergrad. Deans, 1987-92, acting Exec. Asst. to Provost, spring 1990, coord. Coun. of Grad. Deans, 1987-90, coord. Planning Com. on Undergrad. Edn., 1987-89, coord. Planning Com. on Doctoral Edn., 1987-89, faculty advisor Coll. Arts and Scis., 1990—, affiliated faculty Solomon Asch Ctr. for Study of Ethno-polit. Conflict, 1999—; exec. dir. Penn Pub. Talk Project, 1999—. Contbr. articles to profl. jours. Mem. bd. dirs. Jewish Cmty. Rels. Coun., Phila., 1984—; mem. bd. dirs., trustee Hillel of Greater Phila., 1988-98. Mem. Am. Philos. Assn., Soc. for Phenomenology and Existential Philosophy, Assn. for Study of Ethnicity and Nationalism. Avocations: horseback riding, wilderness camping. E-mail: sps@pobox.upenn.edu. Home: 515 S 22nd St Philadelphia PA 19146-1247 Office: Univ Pa 502 Hollenback Ctr 3000 South St Philadelphia PA 19104-6325

STEINBERG, WARREN LINNINGTON, school principal; b. N.Y.C., Jan. 20, 1924; s. John M. and Gertrude (Vogel) S.; m. Beatrice Ruth Blass, June 29, 1947; children: Leigh William, James Robert, Donald Kenneth. Student, U. So. Calif., 1943-44; BA, UCLA, 1949, MEd, 1951, EdD, 1962. Tchr., counselor, coach Jordan H.S., Watts, L.A., 1951-57; tchr., athletic coord. Hamilton H.S., L.A., 1957-62; boys' vice prin. Univ. H.S., L.A., 1962-67, Crenshaw H.S., L.A., 1967-68; cons. Ctr. for Planned Change, L.A. City Sch., 1968-69; instr. edn. UCLA, 1965-71; boys' vice prin. LeConte Jr. J.S., L.A., 1969-71, sch. prin., 1971-77; adminstrv. cons. on integration L.A. Unified Sch. Dist., 1977-81, adminstr. student-to-student interaction program, 1981-82; prin. Gage Jr. H.S., 1982-83, Fairfax H.S., 1983-90; pres. Athletic Coords. Assn., L.A. Unified Sch. Dist., 1959-60; v.p. P-3 Enterprises, Inc., Port Washington, N.Y., 1967-77, Century City (Calif.) Enterprises, 1966-88. Contbr. articles on race rels., youth behavior to profl. jours. and newspapers. V.p. B'nai B'rith Anti-Defamation League, 1968-70; mem. adv. com. L.A. City Commn. on Human Rels., 1966-71, 72-76, commr., 1976—, pres., 1978-87, also chmn. edn. com.; mem. human rels. commn. L.A. Unified Sch. Dist., 1999—, mem. citizens adv. com. for student integration, 1976-79; mem. del. assembly Cmty. Rels. Conf. So. Calif., 1975-91; chmn. So. Calif. Drug Abuse Edn. Month com., 1970; bd. dirs. DAWN, The Seedling, 1993-95, Project ECHO—Entrepreneurial Concepts, Hands-On, 1996—; mem., chmn. case conf. human rels. West L.A. Coordinating Coun. With USMCR, 1943-46. Recipient Beverly Hills B'nai B'rith Presdl. award, 1965, Pres.'s award Cmty. Rels. Conf. So. Calif., 1990, Lifetime Achievement award L.A. City Human Rels. Commn., 1996, award L.A. Unified Sch. Dist. Bd. Edn., 1997, commendation L.A. City Coun., 1968, 88. Mem. Beverly-Fairfax C. of C. (bd. dirs. 1986-88), Lions (bd. dirs. 1960-62), Kiwanis. Home: 2737 Dunleer Pl Los Angeles CA 90064-4303

STEINBERGER, JACK, physicist, educator; b. Bad Kissingen, Germany, May 25, 1921; came to U.S., 1935; s. Ludwig Lazarus and Berta (May) S.; m. Joan Beauregard, 1943, (div. 1962); children: Joseph, Richard Ned; m. Cynthia Eva Alff; children: Julia Karen, John Paul. BS in Chemistry, U. Chgo., 1942, PhD in Physics, 1948; hon. degree, Ill. Inst. Tech., 1989, U. Glasgow, 1990, Dortmund U., 1990, Columbia U., 1990, U. Autonoma de Barcelona, Spain, 1992, U. Blaise Pascal, Clermont-Ferrand, France, 1995, U. Würzburg, 1997. Mem. Inst. for Advanced Study, Princeton, N.J., 1948-49; asst. U. Calif., Berkeley, 1949-50; prof. Columbia U., N.Y.C., 1950-68, Higgins prof., 1968-72; staff mem. European Orgn. for Nuclear Research, Geneva, 1968-86, dir., 1969-72; prof. physics Scuola Normale, Pisa, Italy, 1986—. Pfc. U.S. Army, 1943-46. Co-recipient Nobel prize in physics, 1988; recipient Nat. Medal of Sci., 1988, Mateuzzi medal Societa Italiane delle Scienze, 1991; fellow Guggenheim Found., Sloan Found. Mem. NAS, Am. Acad. Arts and Scis., Heidelberg Acad. Scis., Academia Europea, Academia Nationale dei Lincei. Home: 25 Chemin des Merles, CH 1213 Onex Switzerland Office: European Ctr for Nuclear Rsch, CH 1211 Geneva 23, Switzerland

STEINBOCK, JOHN THOMAS, bishop; b. L.A., July 16, 1937. Student, L.A. Diocesan sems. Ordained priest Roman Cath. Ch., 1963. Aux. bishop Diocese of Orange, Calif., 1984-87; bishop Diocese of Santa Rosa, Calif., 1987-91; titular bishop of Midila, 1984; bishop Diocese of Fresno, Calif., 1991—. Fax: 559-488-7464. Office: Diocese of Fresno 1550 N Fresno St Fresno CA 93703-3711

STEINBOCK, OLIVER, chemistry educator; b. Hameln, Germany, June 18, 1966; s. Günther K. D. and Ursula (Voges) S.; m. Bettina S. Neumann, Mar. 27, 1998. Diplom-physiker, U. Göttingen, 1991, Dr.rer.nat., 1993. Rsch. scientist Max-Planck Inst., Dortmund, Germany, 1989-93; postdoctoral assoc. W.Va. U., Morgantown, 1993-94, vis. asst. prof., 1994-95; vis. asst. prof. Fla. State U., Tallahassee, 1995-96, asst. prof., 1998—; rsch. scientist U. Magdeburg, Germany, 1996-98. Contbr. articles to profl. publs. Recipient Achievement award Conf. So. Grad. Schs., 2000; scholar German Nat. Merit Found., 1992-93; Liebig fellow Found. of the German Chem. Industry, 1994-96. Mem. Am. Chem. Soc., German Phys. Soc., German Biochem. Soc. Office: Fla State U Dept Chemistry Tallahassee FL 32306-4390

STEINBOCK, PAIGE CARNEY, executive recruiter; b. Tampa, Fla., July 11, 1971; d. James Patrick and Mineta Jean Scott; m. Christopher Paul Steven Steinbock, Sept. 7, 1997. BA in French Lit., Wheaton Coll., 1993. Legal aide Furth, Fahrner & Mason, San Francisco, 1993-94; sr. recruiter Source Finance, San Francisco, 1994-98; sr. assoc. Korn/Ferry Internat., San Francisco, 1999—. Mem. Am. Soc. Woman Accts. (bd. dirs. 1998—), Fin. Women's Assn., Exec. Women's Golf Assn., No. Calif. Human Resources Assn. Avocations: travel, reading, collecting wine, gourmet cooking.

STEINBORN, ERNST OTTO H., physicist, educator; b. Dresden, Germany, May 8, 1932; s. Heinrich and Gertrud (Thomas) S.; m. Gudrun Mnich, Sept. 14, 1968. Diploma, Tech. U. Dresden, 1959; D of Natural Scis., U. Frankfurt-Main, Fed. Republic of Germany, 1965; Habilitation, Tech. U. Berlin, 1970. Cert. in physics, theoretical and phys. chemistry. Rsch. asst. U. Frankfurt-Main, 1961-67; rsch. assoc. Iowa State U., Ames, 1967-69; from instr. phys. chemistry to prof. Tech. U. Berlin, 1969-71; prof. U. Regensburg, Fed. Republic of Germany, 1971-97, prof. emeritus, 1997—. Mem. adv. edit. bd. Internat. Jour. Quantum Chemistry, 1988-92; contbr. articles to sci. jours. Mem. Am. Phys. Soc. (life), Deutsche Physikalische Gesellschaft, Deutsche Bunsen-Gesellschaft für Physikalische Chemie. Lutheran. Office: U Regensburg, Universitätsstrasse 31, D-93040 Regensburg Germany

STEINBRENNER, GEORGE MICHAEL, III, professional baseball team executive, shipbuilding company executive; b. Rocky River, Ohio, July 4, 1930; s. Henry G. and Rita (Haley) S.; m. Elizabeth Joan Zieg, May 12, 1956; children: Henry G. III, Jennifer Lynn, Jessica Joan, Harold Zeig. BA, Williams Coll., 1952; postgrad., Ohio State U., 1954-55. Asst. football coach Northwestern U., 1955, Purdue U., 1956-67; treas. Kinsman Transit Co., Cleve., 1957-63; pres. Kinsman Marine Transit Co., Cleve., 1963-67, dir., 1965—; pres., chmn. bd. Am. Ship Bldg. Co., Cleve., 1967-78, chmn. bd., 1978—; prin. owner N.Y. Yankees, Bronx, 1973-90, 93—; limited ptnr. N.Y. Yankees, 1990-93; owner Bay Harbor Inn, Tampa, Fla., 1988—; bd. dirs. Gt. Lakes Internat. Corp., Gt. Lakes Assocs., Cin. Sheet Metal & Roofing Co., Nashville Bridge Co., Nederlander-Steinbrenner Prodns. Mem. Cleve. Little Hoover Com., group chmn., 1966; chmn. Cleve. Urban Coalition; vice chmn. Greater Cleve. Growth Corp., Greater Cleve. Jr. Olympic Found.; founder Silver Shield Found., N.Y.C.; chmn. Olympic Overview Commn.; v.p. U.S. Olympic Com., 1989—. Served to 1st lt. USAF, 1952-54. Named Outstanding Young Man of Yr. Ohio Jr. C. of C., 1960, Cleve. Jr. C. of C., 1960; Chief Town Crier, Cleve., 1968; Man of Yr., Cleve. Press Club, 1968. Mem. Greater Cleve. Growth Assn. (bd. dirs.). Office: NY Yankees Yankee Stadium E 161st St & River Ave Bronx NY 10451

STEINDL, MICHAEL PAUL ARMIN, linguist, author; b. Scheidegg, Bayern, Germany, Mar. 4, 1924; s. Michael and Maria (Enzensberger) S.; m. Elisabeth Stegmann, July 22, 1952; children: Elisabeth, Barbara, Katharina, Rüpert. PhD, U. Munich, 1952. Lectr. secondary sch. Schulen Schloss Salem, Bodensee, Germany, 1952-56; lectr. Lindau, Bodensee, 1956-67; lectr., vice dir. German Sch., Rome, 1967-75; course dir. U. Munich, 1975-83; prof. Katholische U., Eichstätt, Bayern, Germany, 1983—. Author: Einheit und Einigung Europas, 1968, Zweitsprache Deutsch für Ausländerkinder, 1983, Reihe Bildschirm Nr 5-28, Video und Begleitheft 1989-1996, Fahr mit. Reisen in Deutschland, 1996. Lt. German Army, 1945. Mem. Görres-Gesellschaft. Roman Catholic. Home: Am Lerchenhang 24, D-85111 Adelschlag Bayern, Germany

STEINDLER, WALTER G., retired lawyer; b. N.Y.C., Dec. 2, 1927; s. Mortimer B. and Ray (Feingold) S.; m. Carol A. Halpin, June 28, 1969; children: Michael, Morty, Melissa, Amy, Ellen. BA, Queens Coll., 1950; JD, NYU, 1953. Bar: N.Y. 1953, U.S. Supreme Ct. 1965, U.S. Dist. Ct. (ea. dist.) N.Y. 1972, U.S. Dist. Ct. (so. dist.) 1974, U.S. Ct. Appeals (2d cir.) 1974. Ptnr. Borden Skidell Fleck & Steindler, Jamaica, N.Y., 1955-62; pvt. practice law Babylon, N.Y., 1962-67; town atty. Town of Babylon, 1967-69; asst. county atty. Suffolk County, N.Y., 1970-71; ptnr. Sarisohn, Carner, Steindler, Lebow, Braun & Castrovinci, Commack, N.Y., 1976-93; ret., 1993; capt., judge adv. 2d area command N.Y. Guard, N.Y.C., 1965-70; guardian ad litem 20th Jud. Cir. Lee County, Fla., 1995-98. With U.S. Army, 1946-47. Mem. Free Sons Israel (pres. 1953), Masons. Office: 350 Veterans Memorial Hwy Commack NY 11725-4330

STEINDORF, GERHARD, education educator; b. Friedeberg, Germany, June 30, 1929; s. Johannes and Gertrud (Ninnemann) S.; m. Gisela Rischmüller, July 14, 1962; children: Arne, Karen. B., Gymnasium, Bad Kreuznach, Fed. Republic Germany, 1949; PhD in Langs., U. Mainz, Fed. Republic Germany, 1959. Tchr. Rheinland-Pfalz, Fed. Republic Germany, 1951-60; lectr. Pädagogische Hochschule, Worms, Fed. Republic Germany, 1960-62; prof. gen. didactics and scholar pedagogy Pädagogische Hochschule, Bonn, Fed. Republic Germany, 1962-70, full prof. gen. didactics and scholar pedagogy, 1970-80; full prof. gen. didactics and scholar pedagogy U. Bonn, 1980—, dean faculty of pedagogy, 1992-94; dir. Seminary of Scholar Pedagogy, Pädagogische Fakultät Bonn, U. Bonn, 1980-94. Author: Von den Anfängen der Volkshochschule in Deutschland, 1968, Einführung in die Schulpädagogik, 3d edit., 1976, Pädagogikstudium-Planung und Gestaltung, 1975, Lernen und Wissen, 1985, Grundbegriffe des Lehrens und Lernens, 5th edit., 2000. Mem. Deutsche Gesellschaft für Erziehungswissenschaft. Office: Pädagogische Fakultät, U Bonn Römerstr 164, D 53117 Bonn Germany

STEINER, ADOLF MARTIN, seed science educator; b. Stuttgart, Germany, June 2, 1937; m. Renate Knauer; children: Martin, Bernhard. Student, U. Tübingen, Germany, 1956-58, U. Munich, 1959; D Natural Scis., U. Freiburg i. Br., Germany, 1964; Habilitation in Plant Physiology, U. Hohenheim, Stuttgart, Germany, 1972. Postdoctoral fellow Smithsonian Instn., Washington, 1964-65; rsch. assoc. U. Freiburg i. Br., 1966-68; rsch. assoc. U. Hohenheim, 1968-74, prof. seed sci., 1976—, mem. univ. bd., 1979—, chmn. univ. gen. assembly, 1980—; mem. univ. planning com., 1988—; univ. del. for the Hohenheim Gardens, 1988—; mem. adv. bd. German Agrl. Mus., 1990—; guest prof. U. Agrl. Scis., Vienna, 1990—. Mem. editorial bd. Seed Sci. and Tech., Genetic Resources and Crop Evolution; also numerous articles on plant physiology and seed sci. Recipient Sprengel-Liebig medaille in gold, 1995. Mem. Assn. German Agrl. and Exptl. Rsch. Stas., Internat. Seed Testing Assn., also others. Avocations: athletics, philosophy, poetry. E-mail: saffluff@uni-hohenheim.de. Office: U Hohenheim, 350/4, D-70593 Stuttgart 70, Germany

STEINER, HANS HERBERT, physician; b. Traunstein, Bavaria, Germany, Feb. 7, 1957; s. Hans and Anneliese Susanne (Pleil) S.; m. Hedwig Gertrud Milz, Dec. 14, 1985; children: Julia Kriemhild, Eva-Marie Agnes, Laurenz. MD, U. Erlangen, Nurenberg, Germany, 1982. Internist Dept. Anaesthesiology, Nurenberg, 1982, Dept. Ophthalmology, Nurenberg, 1983; resident Dept. Neurosurgery/U. Heidelberg, Germany, 1985-90, chief resident, 1991-94, asst. prof., 1995—; sec. Verein zur Foerderung der Neurochirurgie, 1993—; spkr. in field. Author: (books) Lesions of the peripheral nerve system, 1992, Neurocritical Care, 1994, Neurological Surgery, 1997, Acta Neurochirurgica jour., 1996, Jour. Neurosurgery, 1999, Jour. of Pain, 2000. Comdr. Bundesmarine Navy, 1984-85, Germany. Recipient Neuro-oncol. award Soc. for Cancer Treatment, 1995, 99, 2000. Mem. German Soc. Neurol. Surgeons (bd. mem.). Roman Catholic. Avocations: violinist, swimming, skiing, tennis, gardening. Office: Dept Neurosurgery/U Heidelberg, Im Neuenheimer Feld 400, 69120 Heidelberg Germany

STEINER, HANS-GEORG, mathematician; b. Witten, Germany, Nov. 21, 1928; s. Alfred and Johanna (Viol) S.; m. Erika-Luise Paecher, May 10, 1952; children: Johannes, Pamela, Gregor. MSc, U. Muenster, Fed. Republic Germany, 1955; PhD, U. Darmstadt, Fed. Republic Germany, 1969. Asst. prof. U. Muenster, 1957-67; dir. Ctr. Didactics of Math. U. Karlsruhe, Fed. Republic Germany, 1967—; prof. math. edn. U. Erlangen-Bayreuth, Fed. Republic Germany, 1970-73; prof., dir. Inst. Didactics of Math. U. Bielefeld, Fed. Republic Germany, 1973—; European co-dir. Comprehensive Sch. Math. Project, Carbondale, Ill., 1967-72; chief cons. Sec. Sch. Math. Improvement Study, N.Y.C., 1966-70; v.p. Assn. for Furtherance of Didactics of Math., Karlsruhe, 1969—. Author of 15 books in field; contbr. articles to profl. jours. V.p. Internat. Youth Ctr. of Arts, Bayreuth, 1974-84; mem. Adv. Bd. Inst. Music-Theatre, Bayreuth, 1970-85, Inst. Sci. Edn., Kiel, 1988-94. Mem. Internat. Commn. on Math. Instrs. (v.p. 1974-78), Hamburg Math. Soc., Math. Assn. Am., German Math. Soc., Am. Ednl. Rsch. Assn., German Soc. Didactics Math., Czechoslovak Mathematicians and Physicists (hon.). Home: Mars Str 16, D-33739 Bielefeld Germany Office: Bielefeld U Inst Didactics, Universitaetsstrasse 25, D-33615 Bielefeld Germany

STEINER, HANSRUEDI, management consultant; b. Uznach, Switzerland, July 1, 1954; s. Walter and Anna (von Niederhausern) S.; married; children: Yves, Janine, Pascal-Robin. Tchr.'s Diploma, Kantonsschule Wattwil, Switzerland, 1974; BA, Wheaton Coll., Ill., 1981, MA, 1982; PhD, Mich. State U., 1985. Dir. BESJ, Fallanden, Switzerland, 1974-80, cons., 1985-87; instr. SFB, Zurich, Switzerland, 1987-89; asst. to the dir. SFB, Zurich and Dietikon, 1989-92; cons. Wollerau, Switzerland, 1992—; journalist Hofner Volksblatt, Wollerau, Switzerland, 1986-92; cons. Schindler Aufzuge, Ebikon, Switzerland, 1991—, Securitas, Zollikofen, Switzerland, 1989—, Civil Protection, Bern, 1991—; coach Fed. Sch. for Instrs., Schwarzenburg, Switzerland, 1995—; co-owner McPaperLand/Andreas Kumin AG, Wollerau, 1995—. Author several books on econs. and vocat. tng., including: Schritte in die Zukunft, 1994; co-author: Das Jahr der Schweiz, 1991. Dir. media 700th Ann. of Switzerland, Celebration of Confedn., 1989-91; discussion moderator for various orgns., 1989—; mem. Maturity Commn., Canton of Schwyz, 1988-96, Adult Edn. Comm., 1996-99. Mem. Zentralstelle fuer betriebliche Ausbildung. Avocations: sports, nature, creative writing, travel. Office: Jostenstr 21, CH-8854 Galgenen Switzerland

STEINER, JEFFREY JOSEF, industrial manufacturing company executive; b. Vienna, Austria, Apr. 3, 1937; came to U.S., 1958; s. Beno and Paula (Bornstein) S.; m. Claude Angel, Apr. 11, 1957 (div. 1972); children: Eric, Natalia, Thierry; m. Linda Schaller, Mar. 6, 1976 (div. June 1983); children: Benjamin, Alexandra. Student textile design, U. London, 1956; student textile mfg., Bradford Inst. Tech., London, 1957; HHD (hon.), Yeshiva U., 1996. Mgmt. trainee Metals and Controls div. Tex. Instruments, Attleborough, Mass., 1958-59, mgr. internat., 1959-60; pres. Tex. Instruments, Argentina, Brazil, Mex., Switzerland, France, 1960-66, Burlington Tapis, Paris, 1967-72; chmn., pres. Cedec S.A. Engrng. Co., Paris, 1973-84; chmn., CEO Fairchild Corp., N.Y.C., 1985—, Banner Aerospace, 1993—; bd. dirs. Copley Fund, Fall River, Mass., Comms. Intelligence Corp., Corp. Express, Inc. Trustee Montefiore Med. Ctr., N.Y.C.; bd. dirs. Israel Mus., Yeshiva U. Bus. Sch. Decorated Knight of Arts (France), knight Indsl. Merit of France, chevalier de L'Ordre des Arts et des Lettres, 1990, chevalier de L'order National du Merite (France), commandatore de la Republica (Italy); recipient mayor's medal City of Paris, 1990. Mem. City Athletic Club, Racing Club, Polo Club. Jewish. Avocations: tennis, sailing. Office: Fairchild Corp 110 E 59th St Ste 31 New York NY 10022-1304

STEINER, RICHARD C., semitic linguist, educator; b. N.Y.C., Nov. 7, 1945; s. Frederick Steiner and Pearl Weiss; m. Sara K. Rosenschein, June 1, 1969; children: Chana, Shana, Rachel. BA, Yeshiva U., 1966; student, Hebrew U., Jerusalem, 1963-64; B in Hebrew Lit., Yeshiva U., 1966; postgrad., Uppsala (Sweden) U., 1966-67; PhD, U. Pa., 1974. Asst. prof. Dropsie U., Phila., 1972-73, Touro Coll., N.Y.C., 1973-75; asst. to assoc. prof. semitic langs. and lit. Yeshiva U., Bernard Revel Grad. Sch., N.Y.C., 1975-84, prof. semitic langs. and lit., 1984—; vis. assoc. prof. U. Chgo., 1981; Gerard Weinstock vis. prof. Jewish studies, Harvard U., 1999. Author: The Case for Fricative-Laterals in Proto-Semitic, 1977, Affricated Sade in the Semitic Languages, 1982; co-author: A Quantitative Study of Sound Change in Progress, 1972; contbr. articles to profl. jours. (Bibl. Archeology Soc. award 1984); editl. bd. Hebrew Ann. Rev., 1981-87, Jour. Afroasiatic Langs., 1986-92. Fellow Inst. Advanced Studies, Jerusalem, 1983-84, 94-95, Am. Scandinavian Found., 1966-67, Humphrey Inst. Social Ecology, Beersheba, Israel, 1989; rsch. grantee NEH, 1978-81, 84-88. Fellow Am. Acad. Jewish Rsch., Am. Friends of Acad. Hebrew Lang. (pres. 1998—). E-mail: rsteiner@ymail.yu.edu. Office: Yeshiva U Revel Grad Sch 500 W 185th St New York NY 10033-3299

STEINER, STUART, college president; b. Balt., July 24, 1937; s. Louis and Lillian (Block) S.; m. Rosalie Weiner, Sept. 12, 1962; children—Lisa, Susan, David, Robyn. AA, Balt. Jr. Coll., 1957; B.S., U. Md., 1959; grad. cert., Fla. State U., 1962; M.S.W., U. Pa., 1963; J.D., U. Balt., 1967; M.A., Tchrs. Coll., Columbia U., 1972; EdD, Columbia U., 1987. Caseworker, then supr. and dir. juvenile ct. services Balt. Dept. Social Services, 1960-64; dir. referral center Health and Welfare Council Met. Balt., 1964; dir. admissions and placement Harford Jr. Coll., Bel Air, Md., 1965-67; dean of students Genesee Community Coll., Batavia, N.Y., 1967-68; dean of coll. Genesee Community Coll., 1968-75, pres., 1975—; pres. SUNY West, acting dep. to chancellor for community colls., 1985, pres. of assn. Pres. of Pub. Community Colls., 1987-89; acting pres. Fashion Inst. Tech., N.Y.C., 1997-98; CEO Ednl. Found. Fashion Industries, 1997-98; bd. dirs. Workforce Investment Bd.; commr. Commn. of Higher Edn., Mid. States Assn., 1999. Contbr. articles to profl. jours. Bd. dirs. St. Jerome Hosp., Genesee County Community Chest, campaign chmn.; bd. dirs. Health Sci. Agy., Western N.Y., Girl Scouts Genesee Valley, 1989-90, Genesee Mercy Healthcare; trustee Villa Maria Coll.; trustee, v.p. N.Y. Chiropractic Coll.; bd. dirs. United Meml. Med Ctr.; pres. Genesee County United Way, Community Coll. of Balt. Hall of Fame. Named Sigma Delta scholar, 1958-59, Heuisler scholar U. Balt. Law Sch., 1960-61, Kellogg fellow, 1971-72; recipient CEO award Assn. of C.C. Trustees (N.E. region) 1997. Mem. Pvt. Indsl. Coun. (bd. dirs. 1983-2000, workforce investment bd. 2000—). Home: 33 Woodcrest Dr Batavia NY 14020-2721 Office: Genesee Community Coll 1 College Rd Batavia NY 14020-9703

STEINER, TIMOTHY JOHN, medical researcher; b. Hawkhurst, Kent, Eng., Apr. 26, 1946; s. Raymond Eugene and Barbara Ruth (Ward) S.; m. Susan Elizabeth George, 1967. BSc with honors, Chelsea Coll., London, 1969, PhD, 1975; MB, BS, Charing Cross Hosp. Med. Sch., London, 1976; LLM, U. Wales, 1991; MA, 1997. Cert. gen. med. council, 1978. Demonstrator in physiology Chelsea Coll., London, 1969-73; house physician, surgeon Charing Cross Hosp., London, 1977, lectr. in exptl. neurology, 1980-86, hon. cons., 1986—; sr. lectr. in clin. physiology Charing Cross and Westminster Med. Sch., London, 1986-96, reader in clin. physiology, 1997—; dir. head The Princess Margaret Migraine Clin., 1987—. Contbr. articles to profl. jours. Trustee, corr. The Way Ahead, London, 1987—, chmn. bd. trustees, 1989—. Research scholar Med. Research Council Gt. Brit. Chelsea Coll., London, 1967-69, research grantee. Fellow Faculty Pharm. Medicine, Royal Coll. Physicians, Med. Soc. London (coun. 1985-88), Am. Heart Assn. (stroke coun.); mem. European Headache Fedn. (bd. dirs., 1st v.p. 1998-2000, pres. 2000—), Internat. Headache Soc. (gen. sec. 1993-99, chmn. ethics sub-com., mem. clin. trials sub-com., mem. classification sub-com.), Inst. Med. Ethics, Medicolegal Soc., Soc. Pharm. Medicine, Royal Soc. Medicine, Assn. Brit. Neurologists, Brit. Assn. Study Headache (chmn. exec. com. 1992-94, mem. coun. 1994—), Anglo-Dutch Migraine Assn. (chmn. exec. com. 1992-93, sec. 1993-98, assoc. rsch. ethics com. 1999—, mem. coun. 1999—). Avocations: legal aspects of med. practice, flying, boating. Home: 95 Kingston Hill, Kingston Upon Thames England KT2 7PZ Office: Imperial Coll Sch Medicine, St Dunstans Rd, London England W6 8RP

STEINER, ULRICH ALFRED, chemist; b. Bombay, India, Mar. 26, 1922; came to the U.S., 1957; s. Jakob Alfred and Mathilde (Gass) S.; m. Ingeborg Maria Lauber, June 2, 1949 (dec. 1959); children: Gabriele Gertsch, Beat Ulrich; m. Claire Beulah Koss, Jul. 15, 1961. Diploma in chemistry, Federal Inst. Tech., Zurich, Switzerland, 1946, Dr. SC, 1948. Rsch. chemist Emser Werke, Domat/Ems, Switzerland, 1948-53, asst. dept. head, 1953-57; rsch. chemist Union Carbide, Boundbrook, N.J., 1957-86; rsch. assoc. Amoco Performance Products, Inc., Boundbrook, N.J., 1986-91; ret. Patentee in field. Recipient Thomas Alva Edison Patent award R&D Coun. N.J., 1992. Home: 237 Jefferson Ave N Plainfield NJ 07060-3927

STEINERT, TILMAN, psychiatrist, psychotherapist; b. Stuttgart, Germany, Nov. 23, 1957; s. Gerhard Reinhold and Ilse (Breuning) S.; m. Sabine Katharina Roschinski, July 25, 1986; children: Janina, Christoph. MD, U. Ulm, Germany, 1985; psychiatrist, Cen. of Psychiatry, Weissenau, 1991, Neurologist, 1992, psychotherapist, 1992. Asst. med. doctor Cen. of Psychiatry, Zwiefalten, 1985-86, Weissenau, 1987-92; sr. psychiatrist U. Ulm, 1992-96; head dept. Cen. Psychiatry, Weissenau, 1997—, head rsch. dept., 1998—; quality mgr. Cen. Psychiatry, 1999. Author: (book) Agression in Mentally Ill, 1995; contbr. articles to profl. jours. Dir. Assn. for Prevention of Violence in Psychiatric Hosps., 1997. Avocations: mountaineering, rock climbing. Office: Cen Psychiatry, PO Box 2044, D-88190 Ravensburg Germany

STEINETZ, BERNARD GEORGE, JR., endocrinologist; b. Germantown, Pa., May 30, 1927; s. Bernard George Sr. and Hazel Scott (Jefferds) S.; m. Jane Rutledge Nash, June 17, 1949; children: Scott Jefferds, Ann Rutledge Steinetz Barton. AB, Princeton U., 1950; PhD, Rutgers U., 1954. Sr. scientist Warner-Chilcott Co., Morris Plains, N.J., 1954-58; sr. rsch. assoc. Warner-Lambert Rsch. Inst., Morris Plains, 1958-67; head reprod. endocrinology CIBA Pharm. Co., Summit, N.J., 1967-71; mgr. cartilage rsch. and endocrinology CIBA-Geigy Corp., Ardsley, N.Y., 1971-84; rsch. assoc. prof. Lab. Exptl. Medicine and Surgery in Primates NYU Med. Ctr., Tuxedo, 1984—, rsch. prof., 1991—; rsch. prof. environ. medicine Nelson Inst. Environ. Medicine NYU Sch. Medicine, Tuxedo, 1997—; mem. conf. orgn. com. N.Y. Acad. Scis., N.Y.C., 1968-70. Contbr. more than 150 articles to profl. jours. Mem. Drug Utilization Rev. Coun. of the State of N.J., Trenton, 1977-86. Fellow CIBA Rsch. CIBA Pharm. Co., 1968, fellow N.Y. Acad. Sci., 1971; grantee March of Dimes, 1987-89, 95-97, Morris Animal Found., 1987-93, NIH (NICHHD) 1994—, Cancer Rsch. Found. of Am., 1999—. Mem. Endocrine Soc., Am. Physiol. Soc., Soc. for Study Reproduction, N.Y. Acad. Scis., Orthopaedic Rsch. Soc., Brookside Racket & Swim Club, Franklin Lakes Racket Club. Achievements include patent for method of determining pregnancy in dogs; patent pending for olive oil based margarine. Home: 336 Long Bow Dr Franklin Lakes NJ 07417-2122 Office: NYU Sch Med Nelson Inst Eviron Medicine 57 Old Forge Rd Tuxedo Park NY 10987-5007

STEINHAGEN-THIESSEN, ELISABETH ROSALIE, physician, medical educator; b. Flensburg, Germany, Sept. 6, 1946; d. Thorwald and Lisa Steinhagen-Thiessen; m. Lothar Diabo; 1 child, Maria. Degree in physics and chemistry, U. Marburg, Fed. Republic Germany, 1966, MD, 1967. Pvt. practice physician Hamburg, Fed. Republic Germany, 1986-87; chief physician Max-Bürger-Krankenhaus, Berlin, 1987—; prof. Free U. Berlin, 1987—. Mem. editl. bd. mags. Geriatrie Praxis, Age. Recipient prize G.E. Konjetzny, 1979, Martint, 1982. Mem. Acad. Scis., Am. Aging Assn. Home: Wittenauer Str 211, 13469 Berlin Germany Office: Charita Vischow Klinik/EGZB, Reinickendorfer Str 61, 13347 Berlin Germany

STEINHAUER, SHERRI, professional golfer; b. Madison, Wis., Dec. 27, 1962. Student, U. Tex. Golfer LPGA, 1986—; winner du Maurier Classic, 1992, Sprint Championship, 1994, Weetabix Women's British Open Championship, 1998, 99; mem. U.S. Solheim Cup Team, 1994, 98, Japan Airlines Big Apple Classic, 1999. Achievements include 3 LPGA career hole-in-ones. Office: c/o LPGA 100 International Golf Dr Daytona Beach FL 32124-1082

STEINHAUFF, DAVID MARK, geologist; b. Bakersfield, Calif., May 20, 1958; s. Fredrick Paul and Sara Ann (Taylor) S. AA in Gen. Edn., Chabot Coll., 1978; BS in Anthropology, U. Calif., Davis, 1981; BS in Geology, Calif. State U., Sacramento, 1983; MS in Geology, Ohio State U., 1985; PhD in Geology, U. Tenn., 1993. Registered profl. geologist, Tenn. Paper mill 3d hand Inland Container Corp., Newark, Calif., 1982; field asst. Calif. Divsn. Mines and Geology, Sacramento, 1983; geologist, micropaleontologist Shell Oil, U.S.A., Houston, 1985; rsch. assoc. Byrd Polar Inst., Columbus, Ohio, 1983-85; geologist Exxon U.S.A., Houston, 1987, ABB Environ., Inc., Knoxville, 1992; grad. tchg. asst. U. Tenn., Knoxville, 1987-91, instr., risk assessment advisor, 1995-97; hydrogeologist SciTek, Inc., Oak Ridge, Tenn., 1991-92; risk assessment team leader, project mgr. Oak Ridge Nat. Lab., 1993-96; carbonate sedimentologist Kans. Geol. Survey, U. Kans., Lawrence, 1997-98; sr. geologist Exxon Exploration Co., Houston, 1998—; instr. evening sch. U. Tenn., Knoxville, 1996-97. Contbr. articles to profl. jours. Ctr. of Excellence fellow U. Tenn., 1986. Mem. AAAS, Am. Inst. Profl. Geolotists (cert.), Geol. Soc. Am. (instr. short course St. Louis 1989, session chmn. Jackson, Miss. 1996, grantee 1988), Am. Assn. Petroleum Geologists (grantee 1985), Soc. for Sedimentary Geology (leader field trip 1992), Soc. for Risk Analysis, Houston Geol. Soc., East Tenn. Geol. Soc. (spkr. 1993, 96), Sigma Xi. Avocations: swimming, skiing. Office: ExxonMobil Exploration Co 233 Benmar Dr Houston TX 77060-2598

STEINHAUSEN, MICHAEL WILHELM EMIL, physiologist, researcher; b. Greifswald, Germany, June 28, 1930; s. Wilhelm and Marie-Helene (Colsman) S.; m. Brigitte Holtz, Apr. 22, 1957; children: Mechthild, Friedhelm, Almut, Ute, Wiltrud. MD, U. Kiel, Germany, 1958; habilitation, U. Heidelberg, Germany, 1966; DSc (hon.), U. Louisville, 1990. With Physiology Inst. U. Heidelberg, Germany, 1960-63, with dept. ophthalmology, 1963-64, mem. I. Physiol. Inst., 1966—, prof. physiology, 1972—; with dept. physiology Cornell Med. Sch., N.Y., 1965-66; vis. prof. Calif. Inst. Tech., Pasadena, 1976, U. Ariz., Tucson, 1982. Author: (textbook) Medical Physiology, 4th edit., 1996; author 9 sci. films on renal physiology, 1963—; contbr. articles to profl. jours. Leader Heidelberger Arzteorchester. Recipient Gold award Brit. Med. Assn. Film Competition, London, 1968, Price of Soviet Union, Internat. Sci. Film Assn., Kiew, 1971, Malpigi prize European Microcirculation Soc., Antwerpen, 1976, Universitätsmedaille Heidelberg, 1994. Mem. Microcirculation Soc. Germany (chmn. 1979, 87, 92), Physiology Soc., Nephrology Soc. Home: Wielandtstr 34, D-69120 Heidelberg Germany Office: Anat Zellbiol U Heidelberg, Im Neuenheimer Feld 307, D-69120 Heidelberg Germany

STEINHAUSER, JANICE MAUREEN, arts administrator, educator, artist; b. Oklahoma City, Okla., Apr. 3, 1935; d. Max Charles and Charlotte (Gold) Glass; m. Stuart Z. Hirschman, Dec. 30, 1954 (div. 1965); children: Shayle, David, Susan; m. Sheldon Steinhauser, May 2, 1965; children: Karen, Lisa Steinhauser Hackel. BFA, U. Colo., Denver, 1972; student, U. Mich., 1953-55. Community affairs adminstr. United Bank Denver, 1973-76; dir. visual arts program Western States Arts Found., Denver, 1976-79; exec. dir. Artreach, Inc., Denver, 1980-82; v.p. mktg. Mammoth Gardens, Denver, 1982-83; dir. pub. rels. Denver Ctr. for Performing Arts, 1983-86; founder, pres. Resource Co., Denver, 1986-88; dir. liberal studies div. Univ. Coll. U. Denver, 1992-97; sculptor, 1997—. Bd. dirs. Met. Denver Arts Alliance, 1982-85, Denver Internat. Film Festival, 1983-86, Colo. Nat. Abortion Rights Action League, 1991-95. Mem. Women's Forum Colo., Internat. Women's Forum, Colo. New Music Assn. (bd. dirs. 1987-91), Asian Performing Arts Colo. (bd. dirs. Mizel Mus. of Judaica, 1995-2000), Phi Beta Kappa, Kappa Delta Phi. Democrat. Jewish. Avocations: travel, reading, films.

STEINHOFF, BERNHARD JOCHEN, neurologist; b. Offenburg, Baden, Germany, Sept. 18, 1961; s. Gerd H. and Evamaria G. (Dettmer) S.; m. Astrid M. Schwoerer, Aug. 18, 1989; children: Stephan Richard Duane, Philipp Christophe Eric. MD, U. Freiburg, Germany, 1986; PhD, U. Goettingen, Germany, 1997. Asst. doctor Epilepsy Ctr., Kork, Germany, 1987-89; asst. neurologist U. Hosp., Munich, 1990-92; fellow doctor Cleve. Clinic, 1992; staff mem. Dept. Clin. Neurophysiology, Goettingen, Germany, 1993—; dir. Epilepsy Surgery Program Dept. Clin. Neurophysiology, Goettingen, 1993-2000; vice dir. Epilepsy Ctr. Kork, Kehl-Kork, Germany, 2000—. Contbr. articles to profl. jours. Recipient Promotion's prize German Soc. Epilepsy Forsch., Berlin, 1990. Mem. Internat. League Against Epilepsy (German sect.), German EEG Soc., German Soc. Neurology, Am. Epilepsy Soc. (corr.), German Soc. Presurg. Epilepsy Diagnostics and Epilepsy Surgery. Avocations: epileptology, music, modern literature.

STEINHOFF, FRANK LENNART, pharmacist; b. Trelleborg, Sweden, Oct. 12, 1959; s. Berthold and Ortrud (Graebner) S. MSc, U. Bonn., 1985; MBA, INSEAD, France, 1989; PhD, Tech. U. Braunschweig, 1990. Pharmacist 3M, Germany, 1983-84; clin. pharmacist Germany, 1985-90; cons., sr. cons. Arthur D. Little, Germany, 1990-94; sr. cons. ABB-MAC, Sweden, 1995-97; v.p. ABB-PTO, Germany, 1998; mng. dir. Steinhoff & Rendahl, Germany, 1999—. Home: Philosophenweg 18-1, D-69120 Heidelberg Germany

STEINHORN, IRWIN HARRY, lawyer, educator, corporate executive; b. Dallas, Aug. 13, 1940; s. Raymond and Libby L. (Miller) S.; m. Linda Kay Shoshone, Nov. 30, 1968; 1 child, Leslie Robin. BBA, U. Tex., 1961, LLB, 1964. Bar: Tex. 1964, U.S. Dist. Ct. (no. dist.) Tex. 1965, Okla. 1970, U.S. Dist. Ct. (we. dist.) Okla. 1972. Assoc. Oster & Kaufman, Dallas, 1964-67; ptnr. Parness, McQuire & Lewis, Dallas, 1967-70; sr. v.p., gen. counsel LSB Industries, Inc., Oklahoma City, 1970-87; v.p., gen. counsel USPCI, Inc., Oklahoma City, 1987-88; ptnr. Hastie & Steinhorn, Oklahoma City, 1988-95; mem., officer, dir. Conner & Winters, Oklahoma City, 1995—; adj. prof. law Oklahoma City U. Sch. Law, 1979—; lectr. in field. Mem. adv. com. Okla. Securities Commn., 1986—. Served to capt. USAR, 1964-70. Mem. ABA, Tex. Bar Assn., Okla. Bar Assn. (bus. assn. sect., sec.ptreas. 1986-87, chmn. 1988-89), Com. to Revise Okla. Bus. Corp. Act, Oklahoma City Golf and Country Club, Rotary, Phi Alpha Delta. Republican. Jewish. Home: 6205 Avalon Ln Oklahoma City OK 73118-1001 Office: Conner & Winters One Leadership Sq 211 N Robinson Ave Ste 1700 Oklahoma City OK 73102-7136

STEININGER, HERBERT, judge. Pres. Austrian Supreme Ct., Vienna. Office: Oberster Gerichshof, Museumstr 12, 1016 Vienna Austria*

STEININGER, KARL W., economics educator; b. Vienna, Austria, Sept. 1, 1965; s. Karl F. and Luise Sophie (Toyfl) S.; m. Ulrike Maria F. Neier, May 9, 1997. MS in Social Econs., U. Vienna, 1988, D in Social Econs., 1994. Asst. Tech. U. Vienna, 1988-89; lectr. U. Agr. and Renewable Resources, Vienna, 1991—; prof. econs. U. Graz, Austria, 1990—; cons. World Bank, Washington, 1990, 95; vis. scholar U. Calif., Berkeley, 1992, 95; guest prof. U. Trieste, Italy, 1997. Author: Trade and Environment, 1995, International Trade and Transport, 2000; contbr. articles to profl. jours. Grantee Fulbright Found., 1989. Mem. Am. Econ. Assn., European Econ. Assn.,

European Assn. Environ. and Resource Economists. Office: U Graz, Universitaetsstr. 15, A-8010 Graz Austria

STEINKE, BERTHOLD, physician, educator; b. Karlsruhe, Germany, Sept. 26, 1950; s. Max and Hilde S.; m. Baerbel Oechsle, 1978; 3 children. MD, U. Tübingen, 1975, habil., 1985. Asst. doctor Med. U. Clinic, Tübingen, Germany, 1979-84, doctor, 1984-92; chief med. clinic Kreiskrankenhaus, Rottweil, Germany, 1992—; prof. medicine U. Tübingen, 1991—. Author books, numerous articles in field. Office: Med Klin, Krankenhausstr 30, 78628 Rottweil Germany

STEINLE, WOLFGANG JOSEF, social scientist; b. Karlsruhe, Fed. Republic Germany, Apr. 3, 1953; s. Josef and Maria (Müller) S. BA, U. Stuttgart, 1974; Diploma Soc., U. Bielefeld, 1977; PhD, Bielefeld U., Bonn, Fed. Republic Germany, 1983. Researcher Regional Adminstrn., Toulouse, France, 1977; head unit EC Commn., Brussels, 1977-79, adviser, 1980-85; mng. dir. Empirica, Munich and Bonn, 1984—; pres. Empirica, Cologne and Brussels, 1989—; v.p. Infratest KG, Munich, 1984-88; bd. dirs. Hypermedia AG, Basel; dep. chmn., bd. dirs. Wimmex AG, Munich, 2000—. Editor: Telework, 1987, various publs. European Single Market, Regional Devel., Locational Analysis for Companies. Mem. Central and E. Europe Regional Sci. Assn. (auditor 1990—), Bd. Small and Mediums Sized Cos. German. Avocations: painting, car racing. Office: Empirica, DeLasasse Subbelrather Str 140, 50823 Cologne NRW, Germany

STEINMAN, EDWARD A., physicist; b. Yaroslavl, USSR, June 20, 1941; s. Alexander E. and Tat'ana F. Steinman; m. Olga I. Bobrovskaja, May 20, 1980; children: Olga, Alexandre. Cert. in physics. Sr. sci. rschr. Inst. Solid State Physics, Chernogolovka, Russia, 1974—. Avocations: mountain skiing, tennis. Fax: 007 096 5764111. E-mail: 142432. Office: Inst Solid State Physics, Institutskii prospect, 142432 Chernogolovka Moscow, Russia

STEINMANN, GERHARD GUSTAV, immunopathologist; b. Osnabrueck, Germany, June 10, 1948; s. Gustav Heinrich and Else Luise (Meyer-Buenemann) S.; m. Claudia Gertrud Foelger, Dec. 22, 1975; children: Julia, Sonja. Aerztl. prüfg, U. Hamburg, Fed. Republic Germany, 1975, approbation, 1977, Dr. med., 1977, diplom Psychologie, 1977; habilitation, U. Kiel, 1985. Diplomate German Bd. Pathology. Intern U. Krankenhaus Eppendorf, Hamburg, 1976-77; resident dept. pathology Kiel, 1977-79; asst. dept. pathology, 1980-85; rsch. fellow Meml. Sloan-Kettering Cancer Ctr., N.Y.C., 1979-80; rsch. group leader Thomae GmbH, Biberach, Germany, 1985—; prof. med. faculty U. Kiel, Germany, 1994—. Contbr. articles to profl. jours., chpts. to books. Served with Bundeswehr, 1967-69. Recipient Louise-Eylmann-Stiftung award, 1985; Ev. Studienwerk Villigst scholar, 1972, Deutsche Forschungsgemeinschaft-Bonn scholar, 1979; DFG grantee; Erich-Krieg prize, 1981. Mem. Internat. Soc. Lymphology, Am. Soc. Clin. Oncology, Am. Assn. for Cancer Rsch., Internat. Soc. for Exptl. Hematology, German Soc. for Pathology, Eurage, Internat. Soc. for Interferon and Cytokine Rsch. Achievements include contributions to understanding of aging of human immune system and the use of cytokines in clinical therapy. Office: Boehringer Ingelheim, D-88397 Biberach Germany

STEINMANN, JOHN COLBURN, architect; b. Monroe, Wis., Oct. 24, 1941; s. John Wilbur and Irene Marie (Steil) S.; m. Susan Koslosky, Aug. 12, 1978 (div. July 1989). BArch, U. Ill., 1964; postgrad., Ill. Inst. Tech., 1970-71. Registered architect, Wash., Oreg., Calif., N.Mex., Ariz., Utah, Alaska, Wis., Ill. Project designer C.F. Murphy Assocs., Chgo., 1968-71, Steinmann Architects, Monticello, Wis., 1971-73; design chief, chief project architect State of Alaska, Juneau, 1973-78; project designer Mithun Assos., architects, Bellevue, Wash., 1978-80; owner, prin. John C. Steinmann Assos., Architect, Kirkland, Wash., 1980-94; supr. head facilities sect. divsn. fin. Dept. Edn. State of Alaska, Juneau, 1994-96; docs. mgr. Loschky Marquardt and Nesholm, Architects, Seattle, 1996-98; project mgr. Dept. Gen. Adminstrn. Divsn. Engring. and Archtl. Svsc., State of Wash., Olympia, 1998-99; project mgr. URS Architects, Seattle, 2000—; bd. dirs. Storytell Internat.; lectr. Ill. Inst. Tech., 1971-72. Prin. works include Grant Park Music Bowl, Chgo., 1971, Menomonee Falls (Wis.) Med. Clinic, 1972, Hidden Valley Office Bldg., Bellevue, 1978, Kezner Office Bldg., Bellevue, 1979, The Pines at Sunriver, Oreg., 1980, also Phase II, 1984, Phase III, 1986, The Pines at Sunriver Lodge Bldg., 1986, 2d and Lenora highrise, Seattle, 1981, Bob Hope Cardiovascular Rsch. Inst. lab animal facility, Seattle, 1982, Wash. Ct., Bellevue, 1982, Anchorage Bus. Park, 1982, Garden Townhouses, Anchorage, 1983, Vacation Internationale, Ltd. Corp. Hdqrs., Bellevue, 1983, Vallarta Torres III, Puerto Vallarta, Mex., 1987, Torres Mazatlan (Mex.) II, 1988, Canterwood Townhouses, Gig Harbor Wash., 1988, Inn at Ceres (Calif.), 1989, Woodard Creek Inn, Olympia, Wash., 1989, Northgate Corp. Ctr., Seattle, 1990, Icicle Creek Hotel and Restaurant, Leavenport, Wash., 1990, Bellingham (Wash.), Market Pl., 1990, Boeing Hot Gas Test Facility, Renton, Wash., 1991, Boeing Longacres Customer Svc. Tng. Ctr. Support Facilities, Renton, 1992, Boeing Comml. Airplane Group Hdqrs., Renton, 1996, U. Wash./Cascade C.C., Bothell, Wash. State U., Pullman, Wash., Sea-Tac Airport Comm. Control Ctr., Seattle; also pvt. residences. Served to 1st lt. C.E., USAR, 1964-66, Vietnam. Decorated Bronze Star. Mem. AIA, Am. Mgmt. Assn., Nat. Coun. Archtl. Registration Bds., U. Wash. Yacht Club, Columbia Athletic Club, Alpha Rho Chi. Republican. Roman Catholic. Address: 4316 106th Pl NE Kirkland WA 98033-7919

STEINPARZ, FRANZ XAVER, information scientist, consultant, educator; b. Steyr, Austria, June 16, 1947; s. Franz and Juliane (Omer) S.; m. Waltraud Elizabeth Wirth, Sept. 13, 1985. Diploma in Math. Engring., Johannes Kepler U., Linz, Austria, 1980, Dr. in Tech. Scis., 1983. Lectr. in computer sci. Johannes Kepler U., Linz, 1980-86; sr. lectr. computer sci. U. Zürich, Switzerland, 1986-87, Johannes Kepler U., 1987-94; prof. computer sci. Hohere Technische Bundeslehranstalt (polytechnic), Leonding, 1994—. Author: Computer & Kommunikation, 1988, Message Handling Systems, 1988; contbr. articles to profl. jours. Mem. IEEE, Assn. Computing Machinery, Arbeitsgemeinschaft fur Datenverarbeitung (province chmn. 1985-92). Home: Starhembergstr 27, A-4020 Linz Austria

STEINRÜCK, HANS-PETER, physicist; b. Salzburg, Austria, Jan. 27, 1959; s. Gerd and Maria (Kirchgasser) S.; m. Hadwig Elisabeth Brandstatter, June 15, 1985; children: Hans-Georg, Philipp Christoph. Diploma in physics, Tech. U. Graz, 1983, DSc, 1985. Postdoctoral researcher Stanford (Calif.) U., 1985-86; asst. prof. Tech. U. Munich, Germany, 1986-94; prof. U. Wurzburg, Germany, 1994-98, U. Erlangen (Germany)-Nürnberg, 1998—. Mem. AAAS, Am. Physical Soc., Germany Physical Soc. Roman Catholic. Office: U Erlangen-Nürnberg, Egerlandstr 3, D-91058 Erlangen Germany

STEINSCHNEIDER, ROBERT HENRI, pediatrician; b. Paris, Aug. 29, 1937; s. David and Bertae (Simplatt) S.; m. Solange Genevieve Schwartz, Dec. 11, 1964; 1 child, Gaelle. MD, U. Paris, 1968. Intern Paris Hosp., 1964-68, chief clin., 1968-73; asst. Meaux (France) Hosp., 1975—; pediatrician Ctr. Hosp. Meaux, 1973—; dir. Ctr. for Cystic Fibrosis, Meaux Hosp., 1993—. Author: Practical Dictionary for Pediatric Therapy, 1980, Practical Dictionary for Medical Therapy, 1972, 6th edit., 1990. Under lt. French Med. Staff, 1963. Mem. French Pediat. Soc., Lions Club. Jewish. Avocations: stamps, photography. Home: 10 Rue Pasteur, 77100 Nanteuil les Meaux France Office: Ctr Hosp Meaux, 6-8 Rue St Fiacre, 77108 Meaux France

STEINVORTH, RONALD, civil and structural engineer, consultant; b. San José, Costa Rica, June 4, 1950; s. Mario and Margarita (Sauter) S.; m. Lilia Berrocal, July 1971 (div. 1981); children: Katia, Ronald; m. Marialaura Bonilla, Feb. 16, 1984; 1 child, Christine. Civil engr., U. Costa Rica, San José, 1973; MS, Stanford U., 1979; postgrad., Free U. Brussels, Belgium, 1986. Cert. structural and seismic engr. Programmer Program S.A., San José, 1971-73; structural engr. Franz Sauter & Assocs., S.A., San José, 1973-74, 79—, v.p., 1982—; v.p. Franz Sauter & Assocs., Managua, Nicaragua, 1974-77; rsch. asst. John Blume Earthquake Engring. Ctr., Stanford, Calif., 1978-79; pres. Ingenieros Estructurales Consultores Asociados S.A., San José, 1979—, Grupo IECA S.A., 1995—; bd. dirs. Costa Rican Seismic Code Com., San José. Recipient scholarships John Blume Earthquake Engring. Ctr., Stanford, 1978-79, Free U. Brussels, Belgium, 1986. Mem. Costa Rican Engrs. and Architects Assn., Nicaraguan Engrs. and Architects Assn., Costa Rican Assn. Structural Engring. (dir. 1985-87), Am. Concrete Inst., Costa Rican Chamber of Cons. (dir. 1986-88, 91, pres. 1996-2000), Costa Rican Chamber of Constrn. (bd. dirs. 2000—). Roman Catholic. Avocation: martial arts. Office: IECA SA, PO Box 10917-1000, San José Costa Rica

STEINWALL, PONTUS PER ROBERT, power plant engineer, consultant; b. Tranås, Sweden, Dec. 17, 1969; s. Åke Bertil and Ester Rut (Jonsson) Hjellstrom; m. Johanna Eva Marie Steinwall, July 16, 1994. Engr., Erik Dahlberg U., Jönköping, Sweden, 1989; MSc, Lund (Sweden) Inst. Tech., 1995. Engr. Abbflakt, Jönköping, Sweden, 1989-95, ABB Kraftwerke, Baden, Switzerland, 1994; rsch. engr. Lund (Sweden) Inst. Tech., 1995; cons. Sycon Energikonsult AB, Malmö, Sweden, 1996—; pres. Miljöföreningen vid L.U. Lund, Sweden, 1993-94. Sgt. Swedish Mil. Police, 1990. Mem. Mopedofilerna Kalmar. Avocations: sailing, trekking, travel. Home: Sankt Goransgatan 6, 39246 Kalmar Sweden Office: Sycon Energikonsult AB, Carl Gustafväg 4, 20509 Malmö Sweden

STEINWANDTER, HARALD, chemist; b. Klagenfurt, Austria, Mar. 12, 1939; s. Joseph and Luise (Krischay) S.; m. Meherangis Ghassemian, Dec. 29, 1966 (div. Sept. 1995); children: Dunja, Nora, Eva, Florian; m. Ulrike Ruhl, Apr. 14, 1999. PhD, U. Vienna, Austria. Rschr. Tech. U., Darmstadt, Germany, 1969-71; tchr. Tech. U., Darmstadt, 1971-73, dir. dept. organic residues in dairy products, 1973-75, dir. dept. organic residues in animal products, 1975-78, dir. dept. organic residues and environ. chems., 1978—; cons. Fgn. Min., Amman, Jordan, 1984, Manila, 1987, Addis Ababa, Ethiopia, 1988, Nicosia, Cyrus, 1989. Contbr. over 75 articles to profl. jours. Rep. Hessian Govt., Wiesbaden, 1985, 93, German Govt., 1989. Mem. Soc. German Chemists, N.Y. Acad. Scis. Avocations: human rights, ethics, ecology, music, sports. Home: Lichtenbergstr 39, D 64289 Darmstadt D 36287, Germany also: Ottersbacherstr 2, D 36287 Breiteubach Herzberg Germany

STEJSKAL, VLADIMIR, mechanical engineering educator; b. Jindrichuv Hradec, Czech Republic, July 5, 1936; s. Jan and Marie (Cimbůrková) S.; m. Marie Kaslová, Apr. 24, 1961 (div. 1981); children: Vladimir, Pavel; m. Libuše Krejčiková, June 15, 1984. Engring. Degree, Czech Tech. U., Prague, 1959, CSc, 1972, degree. Asst. prof. Czech Tech. U., Prague, Czech Republic, 1963-86, assoc. prof., 1986-93, prof., 1993—, head dept., 1993. Co-author: (book) Dynamics of Machines, 1996, Kinematics and Dynamic of Machinery, 1996. Home: Sudánská 597, 16000 Prague Czech Republic

STELLA, ANA MARIA, chemistry educator, researcher; b. Capital Federal, Argentina, July 11, 1944; d. Vencio Astro and Maria Rosario (Decono) S.; m. Guillermo Edgardo Rosellini, Feb. 2, 1940; children: Maria Claudia, Karina Valeria, Enzo. Licenciada, U. Buenos Aires, 1970, Dr, 1977. Asst. educator U. Buenos Aires, 1970-82; asst. dir. CONICET, Argentina, 1980-84, asst. rschr., 1984-94; adj. prof. Nat. U. Buenos Aires, 1982—; ind. rschr. CONICET, 1994—; mem. found. CIPYP, Argentina, 1970—; mem. edn. subcom. dept. biochemistry Faculty of Sci., U. Buenos Aires, 1989—. Author: Melanin: Its role in human photoprotection, 1995; contbr. articles to profl. jours. Fellow Argentine Assn. Dermatology, Tetrapyrole Discussion Group. Roman Catholic. Home: Antonino M Ferrari 1074, 1424 Buenos Aires Argentina Office: CIPYP, PAB II 20 p, Buenos Aires Argentina

STELLA, CLARA, agricultural educator, researcher; b. Firenze, Italy, June 8, 1920; d. Anchise and Nella (Salvi) S. Cert., Secondary Sch., Firenze, Italy, 1940; degree in chem., Univ. Firenze, 1945; degree in biological sci., Univ. Bologna, Bologna, Italy, 1950. Prof. asst. Univ. Firenze, 1960-70, assoc. prof., 1970-73, prof., 1973—; tchr. Univ. Firenze, 1970-90, researcher, 1955—; inst. dir. Agricultural Industry, Firenze, 1970-89; tech. com. presidentship Chianti Wine Consortium, Firenze, 1983—. Contbr. numerous articles to profl. jours. Mem. Acad. Italian della Vite e del Vino, Acad. dei Georgofili, Acad. Italian dell Olivo. Roman Catholic. Avocations: classical music listening, philosophy, detective story reading, cross words solving. Home: Via T Tozzetti 27, 50144 Firenze Italy

STELLAR, ARTHUR WAYNE, educational administrator; b. Columbus, Ohio, Apr. 12, 1947; s. Fredrick and Bonnie Jean (Clark) S. BS, Ohio U., 1969, MA, 1970, PhD, 1973. Tchr. Athens (Ohio) City Schs., 1969-71; curriculum coord., tchr. Belpre (Ohio) City Schs., 1971-72; prin. elem. schs., head tchr. learning disabilities South-Western City Schs., Grove City, Ohio, 1972-76; dir. elem. edn. Beverly (Mass.) Pub. Schs., 1976-78; coord. spl. projects and systemwide planning Montgomery County Pub. Schs., Rockville, Md., 1978-80; asst. supt. Shaker Heights (Ohio), 1980-83; supt. schs. Mercer County Pub. Schs., Princeton, W.Va., 1983-85, Oklahoma City Pub. Schs., 1985-92, Cobb County, Ga., 1992-93; dep. supt. Boston Pub. Schs., 1993-95, acting supt., 1995-96; supt. Kingston (N.Y.) Sch. Dist., 1996—; adj. prof. Lesley Coll., Cambridge, Mass., 1976-78; adj. faculty Harvard U., 1992-93. Author: Educational Planning for Educational Success, Effective Schools Research: Practice and Promise; editor: Effective Instructional Management; cons. editor, book rev. editor Jour. Ednl. Pub. Rels.; mem. editl. bd. Jour. Curriculum & Supervision, Reading Today's Youth; contbr. articles to profl. jours. Bd. govs. Kirkpatrick Ctr.; mem. Oklahoma City Com. Econ. Devel.; founding bd. dirs. Oklahoma Alliance Against Drugs, Oklahoma Zool. Soc. Inc.; selected for Leadership Oklahoma City, 1986; bd. dirs. Leadership Oklahoma City, ARC; bd. dirs. Okla. Centennial Sports Inc., Rip Van Winkle Coun. BSA; mem. Oklahoma Acad. for State Goals, State Supt.'s Adv. Coun.; mem. clin. experiences adv. com. U. Okla. Coll. Edn.; trustee Arts Coun. Oklahoma City, Omniplex Sci. and Arts Mus., Oklahoma City Area Vocat.-Tech. Dist. 22 Found.; mem. Urban Ctr. Ednl. Adv. Bd., U.S. Dept. Edn. Urban Supt. Network, Coun. Great City Schs. Bd., Urban Edn. Clearing House Adv. com., U. Okla. Adminstrn. cert. program com., Cmty. Literacy Coun. Bd.; chmn. bd. dirs. Langston U.; chairperson United Way Greater Okla., Sch. Mgmt. Study Group, Okla. Reading Coun. (Okla. literacy coun. reading award 1-89), Oklahoma City PTA; bd. dirs. Oklahoma County chpt. ARC, Jr. Achievement Greater Oklahoma City Bd., Oklahoma State Fair Bd., Horace Mann League Bd., Last Frontier Coun. Bd.; v.p. N.Y. State PTA, 1996—, Kingston Chpt. Rip Van Winkle Coun., Boy Scouts Am., 1996—, membership chmn., 1996-97; exec. bd. Nat. Dropout Prevention Ctr. Network, 1998—; mem. curriculum com. N.Y. State Coun. Sch. Supts., 1996—; bd. dirs. Friends Historic Kingston, 1996—, Friends Senate House, Kingston, 1996—. Charles Kettering Found. IDEA fellow, 1976, 78, 80; Nat. Endowment Humanities fellow, Danforth Found., 1987-88; recipient Silver Beaver award Boy Scouts Am., 1990, Amb. award Horace Mann League, 1995, 96, 97, 98, 99, 2000. Mem. ASCD (exec. coun., pres.-elect 1993-94, pres. 1994-95, rev. coun. 1997—), Mass. ASCD, Ohio ASCD, Okla. ASCD (Publ. award 1989), N.Y. ASCD, Internat. Soc. Ednl. Planning, Nat. Soc. Study Edn., Nat. Planning Assn., Nat. Assn. Gifted Children (life), Nat. Coun. Tchrs. English (life), Music Educators Nat. Conf. (life), Nat. Orgn. Legal Problems Edn., Nat. Policy Bd. Ednl. Adminstrn., Am. Assn. Sch. Adminstrs. (life, Leadership for Learning award 1991), Coll. Bd. Advanced Placement Spl. Recognition award 1991, Nat. Assn. Elem. Sch. Prins. (life), Am. Edn. Fin. Assn., Nat. Assn. Edn. Young Children (life), Nat. Sch. Pub. Rels. Assn. (Honor award 1991), Am. Mus. Natural Hist. (assoc.), World Coun. Curriculum and Instrn. (life, bd. dirs. N.Am. chpt. 1996-2000, pres. 2000—), Coun. Basic Edn., Ohio Assn. Elem. Sch. Adminstrs., Buckeye Assn. Sch. Adminstrs., Ohio U. Coll. Edn. (disting. alumnus award 1991), Okla. Assn. Sch. Adminstrs., Mass. Assn. Sch. Adminstrs., Okla. Coalaition Pub. Edn., Okla. Commn. Ednl. Leadership, Urban Area Supts. (Okla. br.), Ohio U. Alumni Assn. (nat. dir. 1975-78, pres. Ctrl. Ohio chpt. 1975-76, pres. Mass. chpt. 1976-78, life mem. trustee's acad.), World Future Soc. (life) Greater Oklahoma City C. of C. (bd. dirs.), Oklahoma Heritage Assn., H eritage Hills Assn. (bd. dirs.), Victorian Soc. (New England chpt.), Nat. Eagle Scout Assn., Aerospace Found. (hon. bd. dirs.), PLATO, Learning, Inc. (bd. dirs.), Am. Bus. Card Club, Coca Cola Collectors Club, Internat. Club, Mgmt. Consortium (bd. advisors), Rotary (Boston), Tau Kappa Epsilon Alumni Assn. (regional officer Mass. 1976-78, named Alumni Nat. Hall of Fame 1986, Nat. Alumnus of Yr. 1993, Excellence in Edn. award 1993), Kappa Delta Pi (life, advisor Cen. Okla. chpt., nat. publs. com.), Phi Delta Kappa (life). Methodist. Home: 225 N Manor Ave Kingston NY 12401-2503

STELLATO, GIOVANNI, physician; b. San Martino d'Agri, Potenza, Italy, Aug. 26, 1955; s. Agostino and Maria (Messina) S.; m. Liisa Tikkala, Aug. 23, 1992 (div. Oct. 1996); children: Stefan, Erika. MD, U. Naples, 1980, Specialization in Ob-Gyn, 1985; PhD, U. Helsinki, Finland, 1997. Med. Diplomate. Cons. Inst. Ob-Gyn. U. Naples, 1984-97; med. mgr. divsn. gynecology Nat. Tumor Inst., Naples, 1987—; vis. scientist Inst. Ob-Gyn. U. Helsinki, 1989-91. Author: Diagnosis and Treatment of Human Papilloma Virus (HPV) Infection in the Lower Female Genital Tract, 1987; contbr. articles to profl. jours. Mem. Italian Soc. Colposcopy and Cervical-Vaginal Pathology, Italian Soc. Ob-Gyn. Roman Catholic. Home: Via San Giacomo de Capri 4, I-80128 Napoli Italy

STELTER, REINHARD ERICH, sports scientist, educator, psychotherapist; b. Kiel, S.-Holts., Germany, Mar. 28, 1954; arrived in Denmark, 1984; s. Gottfried Erich and Brigitte Elisabeth (Nernst) S.; m. Annette Frandsen; 1 child, Nathali Christin; m. Sherene Anja Horami. BA in Sociology, U. Kiel, Germany, 1980, MA in Sport Sci. and History, 1980; PhD in Psychology, U. Copenhagen, 1994; cert. psychotherapist, Gestalt Sch. North Zealand, Denmark, 1987. Tchr. primary and secondary schs. Kiel, 1978-81; tchr. secondary sch. Hamburg, 1983-84; tchr. primary sch. Copenhagen, 1985-87, coll. tchr., 1986-87; tchr., rschr. U. Copenhagen, 1987-97, prof. Inst. Exercise and Sport Scis., 1997—; mem. mng. coun. Sch. Body Dynamics, Copenhagen, 1989-97; pres. Danish Forum Sport Psychology, 1994—; mem. mng. coun. European Assn. of Sport Psychology, 1999—; pres. European Congress Sport Psychology, Copenhagen, 2003. Author: (in Danish) Experiencing and Staging in Sport, 1995, (in German) You are Like Your Sport, 1996 (Karl-Hofmann award 1996), (in Danish) Focusing on the Body-Sport Psychology in Theory and Practice, 1999; co-author: (in Danish) Sport-Human and Social Science Related, 1991. Mem. Greenpeace, World Wildlife Found., Danish Refugee Help; sponsor Save the Children. Mem. Am. Psychol. Assn. (affil.), Danish Forum Sport Psychology (pres. 1994—), German Assn. Sport Sci., German Assn. Sport Psychology, European Coll. Sport Sci. Avocations: theater, films, music, exercise and sports, nature. E-mail: rstelter@ifi.ku.dk. Office: U Copenhagen Inst Exercise, Norre Alle 51, 2200 Copenhagen N, Denmark

STELZENMULLER, CYRIL VAUGHN, lawyer; b. Fairfield, Ala., Jan. 25, 1928; s. James Grey and Helen (Brennan) S.; m. Jeannette Faye Wood, Mar. 19, 1965; 1 child, James Wood. BA, Cornell U., 1950, LLB with distinction, 1952. Bar: Ala. 1952, U.S. Dist. Ct. (no. dist.) Ala. 1955, U.S. Ct. Appeals (5th cir.) 1955, U.S. Ct. Appeals (D.C. cir.) 1973, U.S. Ct. Appeals (6th cir.) 1975, U.S. Supreme Ct. 1980, U.S. Ct. Appeals (11th cir.) 1982. Law clk. to judge U.S. Ct. Appeals (5th cir.), New Orleans, 1954-55; assoc. Burr & Forman, Birmingham, Ala., 1955-64, ptnr., 1964—. Contbr. articles to law rev. Col. ANG. Mem. Order of Coif, Phi Beta Kappa. Avocation: stained glass. Home: 3537 Victoria Rd Birmingham AL 35223-1403 Office: Burr & Forman LLP Ste 3000 Southtrust Tower Birmingham AL 35203-3204

STELZER, FRANZ, chemist, educator; b. Fürstenfeld, Austria, Jan. 24, 1948; s. Franz and Hedwig S.; m. Christine Elisabeth Codan, Sept. 6, 1973 (dec. 1984); m. Susanna Maria Pucker, Aug. 1, 1986; children: Korbinian, Anna, Magdalena, Theresa. Diploma, Tech. Sch. Graz (Austria), 1972; Dr in Tech., Tech. U. Graz, 1975, Dozent, 1987. Vis. assoc. prof. Ca. Inst. Tech., Pasadena, 1988-89; assoc. prof. Tech. U. Graz, 1989—; dir. Christian Doppler Lab. for Catalytic Polymerisation, Graz, 1991-94. Contbr. articles to profl. jours. Mem. nat. bd. Boy Scouts and Girl Guides of Austria. Mem. Austrian Chem. Soc., Am. Chem. Soc. Roman Catholic. Avocations: music, sports. E-mail: stelzer@ictos.tu-qraz.ac.at. Home: Feuerbachg 15, A-8020 Graz Austria Office: Tech U Graz, Stremayrg 16, A-8010 Graz Austria

STELZER, IRWIN MARK, economist; b. N.Y.C., N.Y., May 22, 1932; s. Abraham and Fanny (Dolgins) S.; m. Marian Faris Stuntz, 1981. BA cum laude, NYU, 1951, MA, 1952; PhD, Cornell U., 1954. Fin. analyst Econometric Inst., 1952; tchg. fellow Cornell U., 1953-54; instr. U. Conn., 1954-55; rschr. Twentieth Century Fund, 1953-55; economist W.J. Levy, Inc., 1955-56; sr. cons., v.p. Boni, Watkins, Jason & Co., Inc., 1956-61; rschr. Brookings Instn., 1956-57; pres. Nat. Econ. Rsch. Assocs., Inc., 1961-85, I.M. Stelzer Assocs. Inc., 1986—; dir. Energy and Environmental Ctr., Harvard U., 1987-90; dir. regulatory policy studies Am. Enterprise Inst., 1990-98; dir. regulatory studies Hudson Inst., 1998—; adv. coun. Electric Power Rsch. Inst.; adv. com. revision of rules of practice and procedure FERC; chmn. com. on adequate power supply FPC; bd. dirs. The Energy Adv. Group of the Keystone Ctr; mng. dir. Rothschild, Inc.; assoc. mem. Nuffield Coll., Oxford U.; mem. publs. com. The Pub. Interest; lectr. in field. Author: Selected Antitrust Cases: Landmark Decisions, 1955, The Antitrust Laws: A Primer, 1993; econ. columnist The Sunday Times, London, 1986—; contbg. editor The Weekly Standard; columnist Courier Mail, Australia; contbr. articles to econs. field; mem. publ. com. The Pub. Interest. Mem. Mayor's Energy Policy Adv. Group for N.Y.C.; adv. panel Pres.'s Nat. Commn. for Rev. of Antitrust Laws and Procedures; mem. Gov.'s Adv. Panel on Telecom., bd. governing trustees Am. Ballet Theatre; bd. dirs. U.S. Nat. Com., World Energy Conf., Regulatory Policy Inst., Oxford U.; mem. Fed. Energy Regulatory Com. Task Force on Pipeline Competition. Mem. Am. Econ. Assn., Reform Club, Cosmos Club, Phi Beta Kappa. Home: PO Box 1008 Aspen CO 81612-1008 Office: 1101 17th St NW Ste 202 Washington DC 20036-4722

STELZER, JOHN FRIEDRICH, nuclear engineer, researcher; b. Leipzig, Saxony, Germany, Feb. 26, 1928; s. Karl and Johanna (Richter) S.; m. Marianne Rost, May 12, 1951; children: Mechthild, Roderich, Hermann. Dipl.-ing., Technische Hochschule, Aachen, Fed. Republic of Germany, 1964, Dr.-ing., 1971. Registered profl. engr. Farmer Altmittweida, Saxony, 1951-60; project engr. Nuclear Rsch. Ctr., Juelich, Fed. Republic of Germany, 1964-66; head of group thermodynamics Nuclear Rsch. Ctr. Inst. for Reactor Experiments, Juelich, 1967-72; head of tech. analysis subdivision Rsch. Ctr. KFA, Juelich, 1973-92; cons. in structural mechanics, 1992—; lectr. Fachnochschule Juelich, 1964-80, House of Techniques, Essen, Germany, 1977—; mem. organizing com. Conf. on Numerical Methods in Thermal problems, Stanford, Calif., 1991; cons. in the field of statics, dynamics, rigidity and temperature field analysis. Author: Heat Transfer and Fluid Flow, 1971, Physical Property Algorithms, 1984; contbg. author to numerous books; co-editor: Engineering Computations, Communications in Applied Numerical Methods, Numerical Methods for Heat and Fluid Flow; contbr. numerous papers to profl. jours.; patentee in field. Co-founder PROFEM GmbH, Aachen, 1984. Achievements include developments in the finite element method and computer graphics, reconstruction of historical farmhouses in Saxony.

STELZLE, JAMES JOSEPH, library administrator; b. Buffalo, Sept. 29, 1953; s. Roy J. and Eileen (Flynn) S.; m. Debra A. Kriegler, July 26, 1981 (div.). BA in Polit. Sci., SUNY, Buffalo, 1975, BA in Sociology, 1976, MLS summa cum laude in Info., Libr. Sci., 1985. Cert. profl. pub. libr. N.Y. Ins. agt. Prudential, Buffalo, 1979-83; mktg. rsch. analyst Barrister Info. Systems, Buffalo, 1984; automation cons., coord. project analysis & systems linkage Rochester (N.Y.) Inst. Tech. Wallace Meml. Libr.; bookmobile libr. Buffalo & Erie County Pub. Libr. Sys., Buffalo, 1986-87; asst. libr. mgr. Buffalo & Erie County Pub. Libr. Sys., 1987-88, libr. mgr., 1988—. Chair, co-chair various coms. Ellicott Dist. Coalition of Agys., Buffalo, 1988-95; mem. various coms. East Lovejoy Bus. & Taxpayers Assn., 1989-93; bd. dirs. Hennepin Pk. Cmty. Ctr. Redevel. Com., 1992-93, Broadway Area Bus. Assn., 1993—. Recipient $20,000 grant N.Y. State Libr. Resources Coun., 1986. Mem. ALA. Avocations: hunting, fishing, skiing, scuba diving. Home: 201 Lehavre Dr Cheektowaga NY 14227-3163 Office: Buffalo & Erie County Libr Dudley Libr 2010 S Park Ave Buffalo NY 14220-1837

STEMANS, WERNER, German language educator, artist; b. Duesseldorf, Germany, Apr. 3, 1929; s. Wilhelm Reuen and Johanna Stemans. PhD, U. Munich, 1958; postgrad., Max Müller/Bhavan, Calcutta, 1959-63. Dozent in German lang. Goethe Inst., Paris, 1964-95; vis. faculty Beida U., Peking, China, 1980, Pedagogic Inst., Samara, Russia, 1993. Drawings included in: N.Y. Rev. of Books, Minuit Rev. Paris, others; exhibited in Paris, N.Y., Moscow, Montreal, Samara, Munich, Peking, Basel, 1995-2000. Home: 16 rue du Parc Royal #105, 75003 Paris France

STEMMERMANN, GRANT NICHOLAS, pathologist, educator; b. N.Y.C., Oct. 28, 1918; s. Charles and Agnes Stuart (Grant) S.; m. Jean Elizabeth Gammon, Sept. 7, 1944 (dec. June 25, 1976); children: Ruth (dec.), Maile Anne; m. Nell Jane Nelson, Dec. 23, 1977; children: Mele, Rachel. Student, Trinity Coll., 1935-37, Cornell U., 1937-39; MD, McGill Coll., Montreal, Can., 1943. Intern Montreal Gen. Hosp., 1943-44; resident Halloran VA Hosp., Staten Island, N.Y., 1946-50; lab dir. Hilo (Haiwai)

Meml. Hosp., 1951-58, Kuakini Med. Ctr., Honolulu, 1952-83; pathologist Japan Hawaii Cancer Study, Honolulu, 1983-93; prof. U. Cin., 1993—; cons. Japan Hawaii Cancer Study, 1998—. Contbr. artilces to profl. jours. Capt. Med. Corps., 1944-46. E-mail: stemm gn@email.uc.edu. Office: U Cin Dept Pathology 231 Bethesda Ave Cincinnati OH 45267-0001

STEMMET, PIETER ANDREAS, lawyer; b. Montagu, South Africa, Jan. 7, 1959; s. Daniel Christoffel and Rosina Elizabeth (Kleynhans) S.; m. Monique Viljoen, Apr. 28, 1989; children: Gerda Rosalie, Ineke Monique. BA in Law, Stellenbosch (South Africa) U., 1982, LLB, 1984; BA in Internat. Rels. with honors, Pretoria (South Africa) U., 1987, LLM in Internat. Law, 1993. 3rd sec. South African Embassy, Tel Aviv, 1987-90; 1st sec. South African Embassy, Ankara, 1993-97; law adviser Dept. Fgn. Affairs, Pretoria, 1997—; organizer Jessup Moot Ct. Competition, Pretoria, 1999. Contbr. articles to profl. jours. Advocate High Ct. South Africa, 1997—. Lt. South African Air Force, 1978-79. Mem. Internat. Law Assn. Mem. Dutch Reformed Ch. Avocations: reading, writing, gardening. Office: Dept Fgn Affairs, PO Box X152, 0001 Pretoria South Africa

STEMPEL, ERNEST EDWARD, insurance executive; b. N.Y.C., May 10, 1916; s. Frederick Christian and Leah Lillian S.; m. Phyllis Brooks (dec. Mar. 1993); children: Diana Brooks Bergquist, Calvin Pinkcomb, Neil Frederick, Robert Russell. A.B., Manhattan Coll., 1938; LL.B., Fordham U., 1946; LL.M., NYU, 1949, D.J.S., 1951; LL.D. (hon.), Manhattan Coll., 1986. Bar: N.Y. 1946. With Am. Internat. Underwriters Corp., N.Y.C., 1938-53; v.p., dir. Am. Internat. Co. Ltd., Hamilton, Bermuda, 1953-63, chmn. bd., from 1963; ret.; chmn., dir. Am. Internat. Assurance Co. (Bermuda) Ltd., Am. Internat. Reins. Co. Ltd., Bermuda, Philippine Am. Life Ins. Co., Manila, Australian Am. Assurance Co., Ltd., Am. Internat. Assurance Co., Ltd., Hong Kong, AIG Life Ins. Co., Del. Am. Life Ins. Co., Wilmington, Del., Am. Internat. Life Assurance Co. of N.Y.; pres., dir. Starr Internat. Co. Inc.; sr. advisor Am. Internat. Group Inc.; dir. C.V. Starr & Co. Inc., N.Y.C., Am. Life Ins. Co., Wilmington, Seguros Interamericana (S.A.), Mexico, Mt. Mansfield Co., Inc., Stowe, Vt., Seguros Venezuela (C.A.), Caracas, dir. Am. Internat. Underwriters (Latin Am.), Inc., Bermuda, Am. Internat. Underwriters Mediterranean, Inc., Bermuda, Pacific Union Assurance Co., Calif., Underwriters Adjustment Co., Panama. Served to lt. (s.g.) USNR, 1942-46. Mem. Am. Bar Assn., N.Y. State Bar. Clubs: Marco Polo (N.Y.C.), Royal Bermuda Yacht (Bermuda), Mid-Ocean (Bermuda), Coral Beach & Tennis Club (Bermuda), Riddell's Bay Golf and Country (Bermuda). Office: Am Internat Co Ltd, Am Internt Bldg Richmond Rd, Pembroke HM 08, Bermuda*

STEMPEL, JOHN DALLAS, international studies educator; b. Easton, Pa., July 26, 1938; s. John Emmert and Mary Roberts (Farmer) S.; m. Nancy A. Dean, Feb. 11, 1961 (div. Jan. 1990); m. Susan Hodgetts, May 18, 1991; children: Amy, Alix, Jill. AB cum laude, Princeton U., 1960; MA with distinction, U. Calif., Berkeley, 1963, PhD, 1965. Jr. officer U.S. Embassy U.S. Fgn. Svc., Conakry, Guinea, 1966; acting dep. chief mission U.S. Embassy U.S. Fgn. Svc., Bujumbura, Burundi, 1966-68; watch officer State Dept. Ops. Ctr. U.S. Fgn. Svc., Washington, 1968-70, staff asst. to dep. sec. state, 1968-69; Ghana desk officer U.S. Fgn. Svc., 1970-72; polit.-econ. officer U.S. Embassy U.S. Fgn. Svc., Lusaka, Zambia, 1972-74; from sr. internal polit. reporter to dep. chief sect. to acting polit. counselor U.S. Embassy U.S. Fgn. Svc., Tehran, Iran, 1975-79; diplomat-in-residence, mem. faculty U.S. Naval Acad., Annapolis, Md., 1979-81; dir. ops. ctr. Dept. State U.S. Fgn. Svc., Washington, 1981-83, dir. Office Near East and South Asian Affairs Bur. Internat. Security Affairs Dept. Def., 1983-84, spl. asst. Persian Gulf affairs, 1984-85; consul gen. U.S. Fgn. Svc., Madras, India, 1985-88; prof. internat. studies, assoc. dir. Patterson Sch. Diplomacy and Internat. Commerce U. Ky., Lexington, 1988-93, prof. internat. studies, dir. Patterson Sch. Diplomacy, 1993—; adj. prof. George Washington U., Washington, 1968-72, 80-85, Am. U., Washington, 1975; prof. Regional Coop. and Devel. Coll., Tehran, 1975-78; rsch. assoc. Mershon Ctr. Ohio State U., 1972. Author: Inside the Iranian Revolution, 1981; (monograph) Theory and Practice in Foreign Affairs: Why Two Worlds Seldom Meet, 1972; contbr. articles to profl. jours. With USN, 1960-62, lt. USNR, 1962-70. Mem. Internat. Studies Assn., N.Y. Coun. on Fgn. Rels. (mem. U.S. Dept. Commerce Export Coun. Ky.). Avocations: tennis, reading, railroads. Office: U Ky Patterson Sch Diplomacy Patterson Tower Rm 455 Lexington KY 40508-2826

STEMPEL, WOLF-DIETER, Romance philology educator; b. Landau, Pfalz, Germany, July 7, 1929; s. Hans and Hilde (Panzer) S.; m. Elvina Simonianz. PhD, U. Heidelberg, 1954; habil. Romance Philology, U. Bonn, 1962. Prof. Romance Philology U. Bonn, 1963-67, U. Konstanz, 1967-73, U. Hamburg, 1973-85; prof. Romance Philology U. Munich, 1985-94, prof. emeritus, 1994—; sen. German Rsch. Coun., Bonn, 1982-88; mem. selection com. Alexander von Humboldt Found., 1986-2000; dean faculty, U. Munich, 1987-89. Author: Studies on Old French Sentence Connection, 1964, Texts of Russian Formalists II, 1972, Gestalt, Totality, Structure, 1978, Dictionary of Medieval Occitan, 1996—. Mem. Joachim Jungius Soc. of Scis. (mem. 1974-85, corr. 1985—, Hamburg), Bavarian Acad Scis. (ordinary 1988—), European Acad. London (ordinary 1990—). Office: U Munich Inst Romance Philology, Ludwigstr 25, 80539 Munich Germany

STENAGER, ELSEBETH NYLEV, physician; b. Herning, Denmark, Aug. 27, 1956; d. Bendt Nylev and Ruth Helga (Nielsen) Thuesen; m. Egon Stenager, Apr. 5, 1980; children: Kirstina, Maria, Søren, Jacob. MD, Odense (Denmark) U., 1987, PhD, 1996. Med. tng. Odense (Denmark) U. Hosp., Odense, 1987-90, rsch. fellow, 1990-93, physician, 1993-94; physician Dept. Social Medicine, Odense, 1994—. Author: Suicidal Behaviour, 1996, Disease, Pain and Sucidal Behavior, 1998; contbr. articles to profl. jours. Grantee Rockwool Found., Denmark, 1990-93. Mem. Danish Assn. Social Medicine, Danish Assn. Psychiatry. Home: Blåklokkevej 51, 5250 Odense Denmark Office: Dept Social Medicine, Tolder Lundsvej 2,5, DK 5000 Odense Denmark

STENBACK, GUY OLOF, import company executive; b. Borga, Finland, July 27, 1924; s. Axel A. and Mary M. (Nordberg) S.; married, June 2, 1949; children: Maria, Christel, Martin. BS in Econ., Swedish Comm. U., Helsingfors, 1950; Dr. Bus. Adminstrn. (hon), World U. Round Table, 1988. With Oy Alftan Ab, Helsinki, Finland, 1956—; gen. mgr. Oy Alftan Ab, 1966-91; bd. dirs. Robert Bosch Oy, Esbo, 1991-97. Recipient Councellor of Commerce award Pres. of Finland, 1975, White Rose of Finland, 1983, Grosses Verdienstzeichen, Pres. of Austria, 1983, Grosses Bundesverdienstkreuz, Pres. of Fed. Republic of Germany, 1986. Mem. German C. of C. (bd. dirs.) Swiss C. of C. (bd. dirs.), Finnish-German Assn. (vice-chmn. 1968-99), British-Finnish Trade Assn., Finnish-Austrian Assn. Home: Badetsvag 7, Grankulla 02700, Finland

STENBÄCK, PÄR (OLAV MIKAEL), international agency administrator; b. Borgå, Finland, Aug. 12, 1941; s. Mikael and Rakel (Granholm) S.; m. Sissel Lund, June 27, 1970; children: Anders, Matts. Student, Oxford (Eng.) U., 1965, Norwegian Inst. Fgn. Affairs, Oslo, 1969; MS in Polit. Sci., Helsinki (Finland) U., 1972. Editor Finnish Broadcasting Corp., Helsinki, 1963-68; mem. Finnish Parliament, Helsinki, 1970-85; mng. dir. Hanaholmen Cultural Inst., Esbo, Finland, 1974-85; min. edn. Govt. of Finland, 1979-82, min. fgn. affairs, 1982-83; sec. gen. Finnish Red Cross, Helsinki, 1985-88, Internat. Fedn. Red Cross and Red Crescent Socs. (formerly League Red Cross and Red Crescent Socs.), Geneva, 1988-92, Nordic Coun. Mins., Copenhagen, 1992-96; v.p. Internat. Youth Found., Helsinki, Finland, 1997—; free-lance journalist, 1961-68; freelance writer radio features and fgn. affairs commentaries Yleisradio, 1964-68, TV news commentator, 1966; mem. Commn. Law and Economy, 1970-74; substitute mem. Fgn. Rels. Commn., 1970-72; mem. Inter-Parliamentary Group, 1970-79; full mem., vice chmn. Fgn. Rels. Commn., 1972-79, 83-85; substitute mem. State Budget Commn., 1974-75, full mem., 1975-77; vice chmn. organizing com. Conf. on Security and Cooperation Interparliamentary Union, 1972-73; mem. Finland's delegation to Nordic Coun., 1976-79, 83-85; bd. trustees Tamro Oy, Vanda, Finland, 1986—, U. Åbo, Turku, Akademi Found., 1992—; dir. Internat. Youth Found., Balt., 1990-96; chmn. Swedish Norwegian Commn. on Reindeer Grazing. Editor Nya Argus, 1965-70, mem. editorial bd., 1965-86; editor in chief Svensk Framtid, 1967-70; dep. editor Ulkopolitiikka/Utrikespolitik, 1965-69; lead writer, Parliamentary corr. Västra Nyland, 1970-74. Chmn. Nyliberala Studentförbundet, Finland, 1965, Youth Orgns. Swedish Peoples' Party, 1965; bd. dirs. Nordic Liberal and Radical Youth, 1965-67; mem. Delegation for Cooperation between Centrist Parties, 1968-70; vice chmn. Fishermen's League, Nyland Province, 1970-71, chmn., 1971-85; mem. party bd. Swedish Peoples' Party, Finland, 1967-70, vice chmn., 1970-77, chmn., 1977-85; vice. chmn. Govt. Com. State Subsidies to Youth Orgns., 1970-71; chmn. youth and internat. scholarships sects. Finnish Nat. Commn. for UNESCO, 1970-77; mem. Ctrl. Bd. Pohjola-Norden, Finnish Assn. Nordic Cooperation, 1970-85; chmn. Nature and Environment Protection, 1971-74; bd. dirs. European North Atlantic Com. for Young Leaders, 1971-75; elected mem. Swedish Finland's Folkting, 1970-80; chmn. Cultural Coun. Swedish Nyland Province, 1975-77; mem. Finnish chpt. Bd. World Wildlife Found., 1972-78; chmn. Svartbäck Environment Protection Assn., 1971-76; chmn. Norwegian-Finnish Cooperation Fund, 1979-87; mem. fgn. rels. com. Lutheran Ch. Finland, 1987-88; chmn. Ctrl. Union for Adult Vol. Edn., 1986-88; dir. Swedish-Finnish Cultural Found., Helsinki, Stockholm, 1993—; pres. Finnish Red Cross, 1996-99, Found. for Swedish Culture in Finland, 1996—; bd. dirs. Nordic Baltic Film Fund, 1994—; bd. dirs. Internat. Crisis Group, Brussels, 1995—; del. European Cultural Found., 1996—; chmn. Swedish-Norwegian Commn. for Reindeer Grazing Conv., 1998—; vice chmn. EU com. European Found. Ctr., 1999—. Decorated Grand Cross Nordstjärneorden, Sweden, Grand Cross St. Olav's Orden, Norway, Grand Cross Dannebrogen, Denmark, Grand Cross Falkorden, Iceland, Grand Cross Santa Miranda, Venezuela, Comdr. Lion Orden, Finland, Comdr. White Rose Orden, Finland, Comdr. Ordre Santé, Ivory Coast; recipient Independence Commemorative medal, Zimbabwe, Holy St. Vladimir Orden class II, Russian Orthodox Ch., Axel Lille medal Swedish People's Party; Hon. tilte of Minister bestowed by Pres. of the Republic, 1999; Leadership grantee U.S. State Dept., 1969, 76. Evangelical Lutheran. Avocations: history, books, African stamps, fishing. Office: Found Swedish Culture Fin, PO Box 439, FIN00101 Helsinki Finland

STENBERG, ADAM W., financial advisor, investment company executive; b. Mpls., May 11, 9170; s. Michael Glenn and Donna Rae S.; m. Sharalyn V., June 20, 1992; children: Georgia, Everett. BS in Econs., U. Minn., 1992, BA in Polit. Sci., 1993. Registered investment adv., Minn. Sys. adminstr. U.S. Rep. Jim Ransted, Washington, 1994; sr. legis. asst. U.S. Rep. Gil. Gutknecht, Washington, 1996; fin. dir. Revier for Congress, Shakopee, Minn., 1996; fin. adv. Prudential Securities, Mpls., 1997-98, Paradigm Investments, Mpls., 1998—; cons. Am. Express Fin. Advs., Mpls., 1999—. Mem. First Bapt. Ch., 1988—, dir. men's ministry, 1998—, trustee, chmn., 1999—; candidate Minn. State Rep., Mpls., 1998, 00. Recipient Spl. Svc. award U.S. Treasury, 1991. Mem. U. Minn. Alumni Assn. Republican. Avocations: web development, politics, basketball, software. Office: Paradigm Investments 4920 Ewing Ave S Minneapolis MN 55410-1750

STENBY, ERLING HALFDAN, applied thermodynamics educator; b. Copenhagen, Denmark, Oct. 13, 1957; s. Arne Halfdan and Gertrud (Nilsson) S.; m. Annie Lone Oppermann, Aug. 22, 1981; children: Mette, Peter. MS, Tech. U. Denmark, Lyngby, 1982, PhD, 1985. Rsch. assoc. Tech. U. Denmark, Lyngby, 1985-87, asst. prof., 1987-91, assoc. prof., 1991-96; vis. prof. U. Pau, France, 1993-94; prof. Tech. U. Denmark, Lyngby, Denmark, 1996—; dir. IVC-SEP Dept. Chem. Engring. Tech. U. Denmark, Lyngby, 1994—; editor Mad Mag., Denmark, 1978-93. Assoc. editor: In Situ, J. Petroleum Science and Engineering. Recipient Rsch. award Jorck Found., 1995, Dong Hon. Rsch. award, 2000. Mem. Soc. Petroleum Engring., Danish Tech. Rsch. Coun. Office: IVC-SEP, Bldg 229-DTU, DK-2800 Lyngby Denmark

STENDIG-LINDBERG, GUSTAWA, physician, researcher, educator; b. Cracow, Poland, June 12, 1926; d. Jakub and Felicia (Infeld) S.; m. Per-Olov Lindberg, Nov. 2, 1953 (div. 1964); children: Miriam Felicia (dec.), Eva Ariela. Lic., Royal Coll. Physicians and Surgeons, Ireland, 1952; MD, Karolinska Inst., Sweden, 1961. Physician univ. and gen. hosps., London and Stockholm, 1952-58; psychiatrist Södersjukhuset & Beckomberga Hosp., Stockholm, 1962-65; psychiatry cons. Mental Health Sta., Jerusalem and Ashkelon, Israel, 1965-66; psychiatry cons., lectr. Ramat Chen Clinic, Tel-Aviv U., 1966-67; physician univ. and gen. hosps., Stockholm, 1967-69, State Work Assessment Clinic, Stockholm, 1969-70; dep. head dept. physical medicine and rehab. Karolinska Hosp., Stockholm, 1970-75; rsch. fellow dept. theoretical alcohol rsch. Karolinska Inst., Stockholm, 1975-79; 1st physician pain clinic Ichilov Hosp., Tel-Aviv, 1979-87; founder, dir. back rehab. clinic Ichilow Hosp., Tel-Aviv, 1987-96; vis. rsch. fellow Tel-Aviv U., 1966-67, vis. prof. dept. cell biology, 1977-82, vis. assoc. prof. dept. physiology and pharmacology, 1982—; mem. internat. sci. symposia on magnesium, 1981-. Author poetry, 1984; contbr. poetry to jours. Chmn. Miriam Lindberg Meml. Found., Ramat Aviv, Israel, 1976—; founder Miriam Lindberg Israel Poetry for Peace prize, 1993; chmn. com. against proliferation of nuc. technology, Stockholm, 1974-77. Rsch. grantee Sweden, Israel, U.S. Fellow Royal Soc. Great Britain, Swedish Soc. Medicine; mem. English Med. Assn., Swedish Med. Assn., Israel Med. Assn., N.Y. Acad. Scis., Am. Acad. Physical Medicine and Rehab. Jewish. Office: Tel Aviv U, Dept Physiology & Pharmacology, 69978 Ramat Aviv Israel

STENEROTH, ERIK ROBERT, naval architectural studies educator; b. Stockholm, July 21, 1923; s. Emil Robert and Ida Elisabeth (Peyron) S.; m. Margareta Gunvor Svea Brolin, Oct. 6, 1947; children: Marianne, Elisabeth. M of Engring., Royal Inst. Tech., Stockholm, 1949, D of Enring. Sci., 1953. 1st asst. dept. strength materials Royal Inst. of Tech., Stockholm, 1950-52; rschr. Swedish Bd. for Tech. Rsch., Stockholm, 1953-54; new bldg. supr. Johnson Line, Stockholm, 1955-56; prof. naval arch. Royal Inst. of Tech., Stockholm, 1957-91, prof. emeritus, 1991—; cons. in field Stockholm, 1957—; mem. Lloyd's Register Tech. Com., London, 1986—; mem. Swedish Bd. Maritime Accident Investigation, Stockholm, 1981-93; mem. Detnorske Veritas' Nordic Tech. com. Nordic Com. for Safety at Sea, 1969-91; mem. Internat. Ship Structures Congress, inaugural com., 1959-61, standing com., 1961-64, 73-79, tech. com., 1964-72, 79-82. Author: On the Transverse Strength of Tankers, 1955, Comparative Study of Different Icebreaking Bows, 1997, also textbooks; contbr. numerous articles, reports to profl. publs. Lt. Swedish Navy, 1949-50. Decorated Officer of Royal Order of Polar Star, Swedish Govt., 1967. Mem. Swedish Ship Rsch. Found. (mem. rsch. bd. 1960-80), Royal Swedish Acad. Engring. Scis., Swedish Acad. Engring. Scis. (Finland), Royal Instn. Naval Archs., Swedish Soc. Mech. Engrs., Swedish Welding Soc. Mem. Conservative Party. Avocations: woodland walks with dog, folk dancing, photography, boating, gymnastics. Home and Office: Stigbergsg 35, 11628 Stockholm Sweden

STENESTRAND, ULF, cardiologist; b. Karlskrona, Blekinge, Sweden, Jan. 31, 1961; s. Stig A. and Britt-Marie I. (Stenestrand) Håkansson; m. Carina E. Fröjdh, June 1998. BM, Uppsala (Sweden) U., 1982; MD, U. Linköping, Sweden, 1986. Fellow in clin. preventive cardiology Stanford (Calif.) U., 1986-87; intern Norrköping (Sweden) Hosp., 1987-89; resident in cardiology U. Hosp., Linköping, 1989-93, cardiologist, 1994—; cons. Nat. Bd. Medicine, Stockholm, 1995—. Capt. Royal Swedish Navy Res., 1990—. Scholar Rotary Internat., Stanford, 1986. Mem. Swedish Med. Assn., Swedish Cardiology Assn. Avocations: sports, music, traveling. E-mail: ulf.stenestrand e lio.se. Office: Dept Cardiology, U Hosp, S-581 85 Linköping Sweden

STENFLO, JAN OLOF, astronomy educator, science administrator; b. Nykyrka, Sweden, Nov. 10, 1942; s. Carl Daniel and Signe Emanuella (Rödén) S.; m. Joyce Elaine Tucker, Nov. 13, 1971; children: Erik Olof, Martin Roland. BS, U. Lund, Sweden, 1964, MS, 1966, PhD in Astronomy, 1968. Docent U. Lund, 1969-75; sr. rsch. sci. Swedish Nat. Rsch. Coun., Lund, 1975-80; prof. astronomy Eidg. Tech. Hochschule ETH, Zurich, Switzerland, 1980—; dir. Inst. Astronomy ETH Zurich, Zurich, Switzerland, 1980—; prof. astronomy U. Zurich, 1980—; pres. Large Earth-based Solar Telescope Found., Stockholm, 1983-97. Author: Solar Magnetic Fields, 1994; contbr. articles to profl. jours. Mem. Royal Swedish Acad. Scis., Royal Physiographic Soc., Norwegian Acad. Sci. and Letters. Avocations: classical music, mountain hiking. Office: Inst Astronomy, ETH Zentrum, CH-8092 Zurich Switzerland

STENFORS, LARS-ERIC, otolaryngology educator; b. Narpes, Finland, Oct. 3, 1941; s. Johan Lennart and Margareta Johanna (Lundquist) S.; m. Asta Ritva-Lisa Forsman, July 24, 1964; children: Nikolai, Alexis, Anton. MD, U. Aarhus, 1971; DPhil, U. Umea, 1980. Resident Ctrl. Hosp., Kokkola, Finland, 1971-75; resident U. Umea (Sweden), 1975-81, assoc. prof., 1982—; head dept. otolaryngology U. Kokkola (Finland), Kokkola, 1985-94; prof. U. Tromsoe (Norway), 1994—. Recipient Media prize Finnish Soc. Medicine, 1992. Mem. Norwegian Otolaryngologic Soc., Finnish Otolaryngologic Soc., Swedish Soc. Medicine, Russian Otolaryngologic Soc., Russian Acad. Otolaryngology, Head and Neck Surgery. Avocations: sports medicine, fishing, music. Office: Dept Otolaryngology, PO Box 34, N-9038 Tromsø Norway

STENGÅRD, JARI HANNU JOHANNES, family physician, genetic epidemiologist, educator; b. Pori, Finland, Feb. 18, 1953; s. Jorma Johannes and Jenny Sofia (Viitala) S.; m. Karin Lydia Elisabet Johansson, Feb. 18, 1993. BSc in Math., U. Turku, Finland, 1976; MD, U. Oulu, Finland, 1982, PhD in Medicine, 1987. Asst. in pharmacology U. Oulu, Finland, 1983-87; asst. physician dept. oncology U. Helsinki, 1988-89; sr. rschr. Nat. Pub. Health Inst., Helsinki, 1989—; asst. prof. U. Kuopio, Finland, 1994—; jr. fellow Acad. Finland, Helsinki, 1992-93; vis. rsch. investigator dept. human genetics U. Mich., Ann Arbor, 1991—. 2d lt. Finnish Air Force, 1982-83. Lutheran. Avocations: beekeeping, literature. Office: Nat Pub Health Inst, Mannerheimintie 166, 00300 Helsinki Finland

STENGER, VERNON ARTHUR, analytical chemist, consultant; b. Mpls., June 11, 1908; s. Laurence Arthur and Effie Harriet (Dahlberg) S.; m. Ruth Luella Day, Aug. 2, 1933 (dec. Oct. 1994); children: Robert, Emilie, Alan, Gordon, David; m. Eleanor Miller, Sept. 19, 1996. BS, U. Denver, 1929, MS, 1930; PhD, U. Minn., 1933; DSc (hon.), U. Denver, 1971. Chemist Eastman Kodak Co., Rochester, N.Y., 1929-30, N.W. Rsch. Inst., U. Minn., Mpls., 1933-35; chemist Dow Chem. Co., Midland, Mich., 1935-40, tech. expert, 1940-53, asst. lab. dir., 1954-61, rsch. scientist, 1961-73, cons., 1973—; chmn. subcom. on magnesium alloy analysis ASTM, Phila., 1941-54. Author: (with I.M. Kolthoff) Volumetric Analysis, Vol. I, 1942, Vol. II, 1947, (with Kolthoff and R. Belcher) Volumetric Analysis, Vol. III, 1957; contbr. 10 encyclopedia articles, 6 chpts. to books and articles to profl. jours. Bd. mem. Midland Symphony Orch., hon. mem. 1990—. Recipient Anachem award Soc. Analytical Chemists, Detroit, 1970. Fellow Am. Inst. Chemists, N.Y. Acad. Scis.; mem. Am. Chem. Soc. (chmn. com. on analytical reagts. 1967-73, mem. adv. bd. Analytical Chemistry 1953-56, Midland sect. award 1979), Geochem. Soc., Sigma Xi. Baptist. Achievements include patent for apparatus for instrumental determination of total organic carbon (TOC), widely used in water analysis, various analytical methods in industry. Home: 1108 E Park Dr Midland MI 48640-4275

STENGLER-LARREA, ERIK ARIS, educator, astronomer, science writer; b. Freigurg i.B., Germany, Sept. 30, 1969; s. Evaristo Larrea and Erika Stengler; m. Cristina Silvia Hansen-Ruiz, May 3, 1997. Degree in Physics, U. Cologne, Germany, 1990; MPhil in Astronomy, U. Cambridge, Eng., 1992, PhD in Astrophysics, 1995. Guest rschr. Royal Greenwich Obs., Cambridge, 1994-96; postdoctoral fellow Physics Inst., U. Cantabria, Santander, Spain, 1996-97; dir. Euroeducacion Profesional, Los Realejos-Tenerife, Spain, 1997; astronomy officer Blas Cabrera Sci. Ctr., Arrecife de Lanzarote, Spain, 1997; tchr. trainer Instituto de Astrofisica de Canarias, La Laguna-Tenerife, Spain, 1998; edn. and astronomy officer Miramon Sci. Ctr., San Sebastian, Spain, 1999—; const. and translator in astronomy Cambridge U. Press, Cambridge and Madrid, 1995, 98; sci. and tech. translator ADW Europe S.L., Durango, Spain, 1996-98. Translator: Our Evolving Universe, 1998; contbr. articles to profl. jours. Mem. N.Y. Acad. Scis., Astron. Soc. Pacific, Aranzadi Sci. Soc., Spanish Soc. Astronomy, Spanish Royal Soc. Physics, Assn. Astronomy Edn. Roman Catholic. Avocation: interpretation of quantum mechanics. E-mail: eriks@wauadoo.es. Office: Miramon Kutxaespacio, Ciencia P Mikeletegui 43, San Sebastian Spain 20009

STENIUS-AARNIALA, BRITA SIGNE MARIA, medical educator, consultant; b. Helsinki, Finland, Apr. 8, 1939; d. Sten Gunnar and Vesta Helena (Edgren) Stenius; m. Ilpo Sakari Aarniala, Aug. 28, 1976; children: Saara, Jaakko. MD, U. Helsinki, Finland, 1965, D in Med. Sci., 1973, docent in pulmonary medicine, 1976. House officer in internal medicine Aurora Hosp., 1965, 69, 70-72; house officer in anesthesia and internal medicine, 1965-68; rsch. asst. dept. clin. immunology Cardiothoracic Inst., Brompton Hosp., London U., 1966-67; house officer dept. pulmonary medicine Helsinki U., Finland, 1967, 68; house officer in pulmonary medicine Laakso Hosp./Helsinki U., 1967-70; rsch. asst. Cardiothoracic Inst., Brompton Hosp., London U., 1969-70; acting sr. lectr. pulmonary medicine Helsinki U., 1972-73, sr. lectr. pulmonary medicine, 1973-76, acting assoc. prof. pulmonary medicine, 1978-79, prof. pulmonary medicine, 1980—, acting prof. pulmonary medicine, 1980, acting chief dept. pulmonary medicine, 1991; mem. med. rsch. coun. Acad. Finland, 1990-95; spkr. in field. Contbr. articles to profl. jours., chpts. to books; mem. editl. bd. Allergy, 1983-92; consulting editor: European Jour. Respiratory Diseases, 1980-87. Recipient Duodecim's Writers award, 1969, 78, 90, The Medix award, 1984. Mem. Brit. Soc. Allergology, Internat. Coll. Chest Physicians and Surgeons, Swedish Assn. Chest Physicians, Finnish Soc. Allergy and Clin. Immunology (sec. for fgn. affairs 1974-75, sec. 1975-78), Finnish Assn. Chest Physicians (bd. dirs. 1984), Finnish Coll. Physicians, Finska Läkaresällskapet (libr. 1975-76, bd. dirs. 1978-79, vice chmn., 2000—, bd. mem. 2000—). Avocation: birdwatching.

STENKIN, YURI VASILIEVICH, physicist; b. Ulan-Ude, Russia, Dec. 10, 1948; s. Vasili and Olga S.; m. Natalia Mironova, Aug. 1, 1972; 1 child, Dmitri. BS, Moscow Phys. Engring. Inst., 1972; PhD, Russian Acad. Scis., Moscow, 1986. From engr. to sr. rschr. Inst. Nuclear Rsch. Russian Acad. Scis., 1973—; expert Russian Found. Basic Rsch., Moscow, 1999—. Office: Inst Nuclear Rsch, 60th Oct Anniv prospect 7a, 117312 Moscow Russia

STENLUND, BENGT GUSTAV VERNER, chemical engineering educator; b. Kristinestad, Finland, Aug. 17, 1939; s. Gustav Stenlund and Linda (Malmstrom) Hofman; m. Kerstin Ottosson, 1964; 1 child, Tomas. MS in Chem. Engring., Abo Akademi, 1965, D Tech. Chem. Engring., 1970; D in Tech. (hon.), U. Karlstad, Sweden, 2000. Rsch. assoc. Finnish Pulp and Paper Rsch. Inst., Helsingfors, Finland, 1965-77; acting prof. polymer tech. Abo Akademi U., 1977-79, prof., 1979—, dean dept. chem. engring., 1982-85, vice-rector, 1985-88, rector, vice-chancellor, 1988-97; mem. sci. del. Finnish Chem. Industry, 1984-89; chmn. LC Working Group EU Rsch. Policy, 1993-94; mem. European Sci. and Tech. Assembly, 1995-97. bd. dirs. AboaTech Ltd., chair, 1997-98; bd. mem. Finnish Inst. in Japan. Contbr. articles to profl. jours. Bd. mem. Assn. European Univs., 1994-98, Baltic Univ. Programme, 1995-98. Mem Finnish Acad. Engring., Royal Swedish Acad. Engring., Finnish Soc. Sci. and Letters, Coun. Tech. Finnish Acad. Scis. (chmn. 1986-88, main coun. 1986-88), Nordic Found. of Tech. (bd. dirs. 1987-90), Finnish Rector's Coun. (chmn. 1990-92). Avocations: art, univ. history, sailing. Office: Abo Akademi Univ, FIN-20500 Abo Finland

STENNER, ROBERT DAVID, environmental and health research engineer, toxicologist; b. Fennimore, Wis., Mar. 12, 1946; s. Arno F. and Edna M. (Mill) S.; m. Vicki S. Muller, June 12, 1965; children: James Brian, Heidi Diane. BS in Power Mechanics with honors, U. Wis., Menomonie, 1970; MS in Nuc. Engring., Idaho State U., 1981; PhD in Toxicology, Wash. State U., 1996. Environ. engr. Gaston County Air Pollution Control, Gastonia, N.C., 1973-77; environ. engring. specialist environ. divsn. State of Idaho, Pocatello, 1977-81; chem. and radiation protection engr. Pacific Gas and Electric Co., San Francisco, Eureka, Calif., 1981-84; rsch. engr. sci. III and IV Battelle N.W. Labs., Richland, Wash., 1984—; mem. audit team Assurance Program for Remedial Action, Dept. of Energy, Washington, 1984-86; risk assessment rep. Environ. Mgmt. Ops. Cons. Selection Team, Richland, Wash., 1988-89; mem. chem. protection initiative team Battelle N.W. Labs., 1989-90, point of contact-Life Sci. Ctr., 1993—; mem. tech. team Ctr. for Risk Excellence, Dept. of Energy, 1998—; pres., chmn. bd. SEA, Inc. Contbr. articles to profl. jours. Sec. Lions Club, Bessemer City, N.C., 1974-77; youth program counselor United Meth. Chs., numerous cities, 1973-95; vol. ARC, Kennewick, Wash., 1989; chmn. bd. dirs. Pacific N.W. Cross Connection Youth Mission; bd. mem. Ingalls Creek Enrichment Ctr. Recipient Merit award Menomonie Area C. of C., 1970. Mem. ASTM (chair E47.14 subcom.), Soc. Toxicology, Pacific N.W. Assn. Toxicologists, Soc. Risk Analysis. Democrat. Avocations: outdoor recreation, European sports car restoration, travel, music. Home: 1238 Glenwood Ct Richland WA 99352-9404 Office: Battelle NW Labs PO Box 999 Richland WA 99352-0999

STENROS, ANNE KAARINA, architect; b. Helsinki, Apr. 5, 1954; d. Helmer Erik and Pirkko (Vaara) S. MArch, U. Oulu, Finland, 1981, U. Calif., 1984; D in Tech., Helsinki U. Tech., 1992. Mng. dir. Design Forum Finland, Helsinki, 1995—. Editor-in-chief: Form Function Finland, 1995—; contbr. articles to profl. jours. Recipient awards Jenny and Antti Wihuri Found., 1990, Alfred Kordelin Found., 1990, Finnish Acad., 1993. Mem. Finnish Assn. Architects. Office: Design Forum Finland, Erottajankatu 15-17A, 00130 Helsinki Finland

STENSETHER, JOHN ELDON, minister; b. Mpls., Feb. 28, 1944; s. John H. and Gertie Marie (Stensaas) S.; m. Barbara L. Erickson, Sept. 3, 1966; children: Julie Lyn, Kevin John. BA, U. Minn., 1966; postgrad., Fuller Theol. Sem., Pasadena, 1966-69; PhD, Calif. Grad. Sch. Theology, Glendale, 1970; student, Dallas Theol. Sem., Trinity Evang. Div. Sch. Ordained to ministry Evang. Free Ch. Am., 1972. Sr. pastor Del Rey Hills Evang. Free Ch., Playa del Rey, Calif., 1968-72, Calvary Evang. Free Ch., Essex Fells, N.J., 1972-76, Trinity Evang. Free Ch., South Bend, Ind., 1976-80, Evang. Free Ch., Turlock, Calif., 1980—; vis. prof. Northeastern Bible Coll., Essex Fells, N.J., 1973-75; staley disting. Christian scholar; speaker various Colls., sems. and confs. Fellow Evang. Free Ch. of Am. Ministerial, Turlock Evang. Assn. of Ministers. Office: Evang Free Ch 1360 N Johnson Rd Turlock CA 95380-3507

STÊNSON, HENRY ORJAN, airline executive; b. Uppsala, Sweden, June 10, 1955; s. Stig and Helen (Tottie) S.; m. Carina Åkerwall, Sept. 21, 1986; children: Anna, Fredrik. Student, Linkoping U., 1976-77, 83-84. Commd. officer Swedish Army, 1979-84; asst. p.r. mgr. Saab Aircraft, 1984-86; pres. Expresshlipp, Stockholm, 1986-88; dir. pub. rels. Volvo Aero, Trollhattar, 1989-93; v.p. Volvo Group, Gothenburg, Germany, 1993-94; v.p. corp. comms. Saab Aircraft, Linkoping, 1994-95; sr. v.p. corp. comms. Volvo Cars, Gothenburg, 1995-98, SAS, Stockholm, 1998—. Mem. City Coun., Linkoping, 1975-84; vice chmn. Young Conservatives Sweden, 1984-86, bd. dirs. 1980-84; chmn. bd. European Ctr. Pub. Affairs, U. Surrey, U.K. Conservative. Avocations: skiing, golf, hunting. Home: Senapsgränd 6, 18245 Enebyberg Sweden Office: SAS, STODP, 195 87 Stockholm Sweden

STENSTROEM, THURE OSCAR, humanities educator; b. Roma, Sweden, Apr. 12, 1927; s. Oscar and Elisabeth Charlotta (Bjoerklund) S.; m. Marie-Louise Einarsdotter Hjorth, July 2, 1955; 1 child, Emma Elisabeth. MA, Uppsala U., 1951, fil.lic.-degree, 1957, PhD, 1961. Asst. prof., univ. lectr. Scandinavian lit. Uppsala (Sweden) U., 1961-68, prof. regius et ordinarius, 1971-93; vis. prof. Harvard U., Boston, 1968-69; rsch. worker Coun. of Humanities, Stockholm, 1969-71. Author: Existentialismen, 4th edit., 1991, Existentialismen i Sverige, 1984, Romantikern Eyvind Johnson, 1978, Gyllensten i hjärtats öken, 1996. Recipient Warburg prize Acad. Letters, History and Antiquities, 1969, Schuch prize Swedish Acad., 1985, Gold medal His Majesty King Charles Gustavus, 1994. Mem. Royal Soc. Humanities (pres. 1987-88), Royal Soc. Scis. (pres. 1992-93), Royal Danish Acad. Scis. and Letters, Royal Swedish Acad. Letters, History and Antiquities, Royal Norwegian Acad. Scis. Avocations: Baroque music, harpsichord, Gotlandic history. Office: Uppsala U Litteraturvet Inst, Slottet ing AO, S75237 Uppsala Sweden

STENSTROM, PER ORVAR, electrical engineering educator; b. Trelleborg, Sweden, Nov. 11, 1957; s. Nils Edvard and Anna Greta (Kernell) S.; m. Carina Ingrid Elmerstig; 1 child, Sofia. MSEE, Lund (Sweden) U., 1981, PhD in Computer Engring., 1990. Sys. engr. Kockumation, Malmo, Sweden, 1981-83, ABB, Lund, 1983-84; rsch. asst. Lund U., 1984-88, asst. prof., 1988-93, assoc. prof., 1993-95, docent, 1993; prof. in computer architecture Chalmers U., Gothenburg, Sweden, 1995—; vice-dean Sch. of Elec. and Computer Engring. Chalmers U., 1999—; sci. advisor Swedish Inst. Computer Sci., Stockholm, 1995-98. Author: 68000 Microcomputer Organization and Programming, 1992; editor Jour. of Parallel and Distributed Computing, 1993—, IEE Trans. on Computers; contbr. over 80 articles to sci. jours. and confs. Mem. IEEE (sr., guest editor IEEE Computer Jour. 1996). Avocations: music, sailing, photography. E-mail: pers@ce.chalmers.se. Fax: 46-31-772-3663. Home: Sjomarksvagen 2, SE423 61 Torslanda Sweden

STENUMGAARD, PETER FRANK, telecommunications researcher; b. Finspång, Sweden, Mar. 10, 1964; s. Frank Stenumgaard and Ulla-Britt Anna (Gustafsson) Mortensen; m. Helena Birgitta Aspeqvist, May 28, 1989; children: Sara, Jacob. MS in Applied Physics, Linköping Inst. Tech., Sweden, 1988; postgrad., Royal Inst. Tech., Stockholm, 1996—; licentiate degree, Royal Inst. Tech., 1999. Lab. engr. FFV Materials Tech., Linköping, 1988-89; sys. engr. Saab Mil. Aircraft, Linköping, 1989-95; scientist Swedish Def. Rsch. Establishment, Linköping, 1995—. Contbr. articles to profl. jours. Recipient Young Scientist award URSI Commn., 1998. Mem. IEEE. Office: Swedish Def Rsch Estab, PO Box 1165, S-58111 Linköping Sweden

STENVINKEL, PETER LARS, nephrologist, educator; b. Stockholm, Nov. 5, 1957; s. Bo and Siv (Jidell) S.; m. Katarina Tunell; children: Maria, Lisa, Fredrik. PhD, Karolinska Inst., 1994. Intern Huddinge Hosp., 1987-91; cons. in nephrology Sweden, 1992—; vis. assoc. prof. U. Calif. Davis, 2000—. Baxter Extramural grantee, 1995. Mem. Internat. Soc. Nephrology, Am. Soc. Nephrology. Home: Svardsvagen 4A, 19273 Sollentuna Sweden Office: Dept Renal Medicine, 14186 Huddinge Sweden

STENZL, JÜRG THOMAS, musicologist, music critic; b. Basel, Switzerland, Aug. 23, 1942; s. Hans and Heidi (Schoch) S.; divorced; 1 child, Tatjana Angelica; m. Nike Wagner, Oct. 1991. PhD, U. Bern, Switzerland, 1968; Habilitation, U. Fribourg, Switzerland, 1974; 2d Habilitation, U. Vienna, Austria, 1992. Asst. Inst. Musicology U. Fribourg, 1969-80, prof. Inst. Musicology, 1980-92; dir. Universal Edit., Vienna, 1992-93; prof. Music Acad., Graz, 1994-96, U. Salzburg, 1996—. Author: (books) music from Middle Ages to 20th Century, (monograph) Luigi Nono, 1998. Recipient Liszt medal Hungarian Acad. Sci., 1983. Mem. Swiss Musicol. Soc. (sec. 1972-80). Home: Lanserhofstr 69, A-5020 Salzburg Austria Office: U Salzburg Inst Musicology, Bergstr 10, A-5020 Salzburg Austria

STEPAK, ASA MARTIN, writer; b. Bklyn., Nov. 23, 1950; s. Louis and Anna (Leyter) S. BA cum laude, NYU, 1973. Author: Southern Rhapsody, 1995, Southern Heritage Potpourri, 1995.

STEPANEK, JOSEPH EDWARD, industrial development consultant; b. Ellinwood, Kans., Oct. 29, 1917; s. Joseph August and Leona Mae (Wilson) S.; m. Antoinette Farnham, June 10, 1942; children: Joseph F., James B., Antoinette L., Debra L. BSChemE, U. Colo., 1939; DEng in Chem. Engring., Yale U., 1942. Registered profl. engr., Colo. Engr. Stearns-Roger Mfg., Denver, 1939-45; from asst. to assoc. prof. U. Colo., Boulder, 1945-47; from cons. to dir. UN, various countries, 1947-73; cons. internat. indsl devel., U.S.-China bus. relations Boulder, 1973—; bd. dirs. 12 corps., 1973—. Author 3 books on indsl. devel.; contbr. 50 articles to profl. jours. Exec. dir. Boulder Tomorrow, 1965-67. Recipient Yale Engring. award Yale Engring. Assn., 1957, Norlin award U. Colo. 1978, Annual award India League of Am., 1982. Mem. AAAS. Democrat. Unitarian. Avocation: ranching. Home: 1622 High St Boulder CO 80304-4224

ŠTĚPÁNEK, PETR, computer science educator; b. Pardubice, Czech Republic, Jan. 24, 1943; s. Otakar and Ludmila (Brabcová) Š.; m. Olga Burešová, Dec. 19, 1970; children: Kateřina Barbora. Promovany matematik, Charles U., Prague, 1965, RNDr, 1968, postgrad., 1973, DSc in Logic, 1991. Asst. prof. computer sci. Charles U., Prague, 1965-87, assoc. prof., 1987-98, prof., 1998—; free-lance cons., Prague, 1992—. Author: Mathematical Logic, 1982. Mem. Fed. Assembly, Prague, 1992; chmn. Dist. Orgn. Civic Dem. Party, Prague, 1993-95. Rsch. grantee Ministry Edn., Prague, 1993, Czech Grant Agy., Prague, 1996—. Mem. Am. Math. Soc., Assn. Symbolic Logic, Assn. Logic Programming (hon.). Mem. Civic Democratic party.

STEPANENKO, VLADIMIR DANILOVICH, meteorologist, researcher; b. Runovschino, Ukraine, USSR, Oct. 5, 1922; s. Danilo Petrovich Stepanenko and Nataly Leontiovna Muravik; m. Vera Ivanovna Grishina, Oct. 18, 1944; 2 children. Grad., Hydrometerol. Inst., Moscow, 1944; postgrad., Hydrometerol. Inst., Leningrad, USSR, 1947-50; D Tech. Scis., Higher Cert. Commn., Moscow, 1965, prof. degree, 1967. Mil. engr. Soviet Black Sea Navy, USSR, 1944; sr. engr. Ctrl. Forecast Inst., Moscow, 1944-46; instr. Hydrometeorol. Inst., Leningrad, 1951-57; col., sr. instr. Mil. Engring. Acad., Leningrad, 1958-73; dep. dir. Main Geophys. Obs., Leningrad, 1974-86, chief dept., 1987-95; chief specialist Main Geophys. Obs., St. Petersburg, Russia, 1996—, co-chief Soviet-Am. working group on study air pollution, 1975-94, chief Methodical Ctr. Radar Meteorology of Socialist Country, 1977-92, pres. Nat. Commn. on Atmospheric Electricity, 1990—; chief State Commn., Hydrometeorol. Inst., Odessa, 1980—. Author: Radar in Meteorology, 1966, 2d edit., 1973, Intensity and Probabilities of Airplane Icing, 1994, Radio Means for Thunderstorm Investigation, 1983, Microwave Radiometrical Methods in Meteorology, 1988. Named Laureate of State Honors of USSR, 1986, Deserved Specialist on Sci. and Techniques of Russia, 1993, Honors Specialist of Russian Hydrometeorol. Svc., 1997. Mem. Petrovsky Acad. Scis. and Art Russia, N.Y. Acad. Scis., St. Petersburg Nature Protection Voluntary Soc. (pres.). Home: Krasnogo Kursanta 28 KV 29, 197110 Saint Petersburg Russia Office: A Voeikov Main Geophys Obs, Karbysheva 7, 194021 Saint Petersburg Russia

STEPANICHEV, MIKHAIL YUREVICH, biochemist; b. Souvorov, Russia, Feb. 13, 1968; s. Yuri and Roza (Koucherova) S.; m. Natalia Yershova, Mar. 5, 1994; 1 child, Anastasia. PhD, Inst. Higher Nervous Activity, Moscow, 1996. From jr. rschr. to sr. rschr. Inst. Higher Nervous Activity and Neurophysiology, Moscow, 1995-98. Office: Inst Higher Nerv Activity, Butlerov St 5a, 117865 Moscow Russia

STEPANIK, JOSEPH VINZENZ, retired physician, researcher; b. Vienna, Austria, Oct. 22, 1922; s. Vinzenz Josef and Anna (Chladek); m. Hanna Safar (dec. 1978); children: Ludwig, Constance, Martin; m. Louise Margarete Wolf, June 21, 1980. Grad., Real Gymnasium, Vienna, Austria, 1940; MD, U. Vienna, Vienna, Austria, 1947. Intern City Hosp., Vienna, Austria, 1947-48; resident 2nd Eye Clinic U. Vienna, 1949-52; resident eye dept. U. Cinn., Ohio, 1952-53; rsch. fellow Eye Inst. Columbia U., N.Y.C., 1953-54; asst. prof.2nd Eye Clinic U. Vienna, 1953-60, assoc. prof., 1961-87, prof. emeritus, 1972—; head eye dept. City Hosp., Vienna, 1960-87. Contbr. 125 articles to profl. jours. Recipient Austrian Cross of Hon. for Sci. and Arts Pres. of Austria, 1977, Disting. Svc. award-Golden Decoration Gov. of Vienna, 1986. Mem. European Glaucoma Soc. (hon.). Avocations: piano, classical music. Home: Schlösselgasse 22/11, A1080 Vienna Austria

STEPANOV, IGOR ALEKSANDROVICH, physicist, researcher; b. Riga, Latvia, Jan. 15, 1959; s. Alexandr Arhipovich and Galina Antonovna (Dobrovolsky) S. MS in Physics, Latvian U., Riga, 1982. Rschr. Riga Tech. U., 1982-85, 92-95, Solid State Physics Inst., Riga, 1985-87, Inst. of Physics, Riga, 1988-92, Microelectronics Ctr., Riga, 1995-98, Inst. of Chem. Physics, Riga, 1998—; cons. Microelectronics Ctr., 1998—. Contbr. articles to profl. jours. CIMO Nordic scholar, 1997, Swedish Inst. Nordic scholar, 1998; Danish Rectors Conf. grantee, 1997. Avocations: tourism, sports. Office: Inst of Chemical Physics, Rainis Bulv 19, LV-1586 Riga Latvia

STEPANOV, NIKITA VLADIMIROVICH, physicist; b. Moscow, USSR, Apr. 9, 1957; d. Vladimir Sergeevich and Raisa Vasilievna (Phunticova) S.; m. Marina Stepanov; children: Natalia, Victoria. MS, Moscow State U., 1981; PhD, Inst.for Theor. & Exper. Phys., Moscow, 1991. Permanent jr. rsch. staff Inst. for Theoretical and Experimental Physics, Moscow, 1981-83, permanent rsch. staff, 1983-90, permanent sr. rsch. staff, 1990—; unpaid assoc. European Lab. for Particle Physics, Geneva, Switzerland, 1992-96; project assoc. CERN, Geneva, Switzerland, 1996—; scientific cons. Novue Tech., Moscow, 1991—. Contbr. articles to profl. jours. Avocations: artificial intelligence in high energy physics, finance. E-mail address: Nikita.Stepanov@cern.ch. Fax: 41(22) 767-89-40. Office: CERN, EP Divsn, Ch-1211 Geneva Switzerland

STEPANOV, VICTOR GEORGIEVICH, chemical researcher, chemical engineer; b. Grozny, USSR, Nov. 20, 1955; s. Georgi Ivanovich and Nina Evgenievna (Kozlova) S.; m. Elena Sarkisovna Avetisyanz, Dec. 17, 1977 (div. 1987); children: Konstantin Victorovich, Marina Victorovna; m. Irina Victorovna Suhareva, Aug. 25, 1987. Chem. Engr., Oil Inst., Grozny, USSR, 1978; Candidate of Chemistry, Novosibirsk, USSR, 1985; D of Chemistry, Novosibirsk, Russia, 1997. Chem. engring. diplomate. Jr. scientific researcher Inst. Catalysis, Novosibirsk, USSR, 1978-86; scientific researcher Inst. Catalysis, Novosibirsk, 1986-88; sr. scientific researcher Inst. Catalysis, Novosibirsk, Russia, 1988-92; vice-dir. Scientific Engring. Ctr. Zeosit, Novosibirsk, 1992—. Co-author: Zeoforming Process: A new Motor Fuel Production Process; Contbr. articles to profl. jours. Avocations: philately. Home: Polevaya st 9 apart 8, Novosibirsk 630128, Russia Office: Scientific-Engring Ctr Zeosit, Lavrentieva Av 5, 630090 Novosibirsk Russia

STEPHAN, BODO, retired manufacturing company executive; b. Berlin, Mar. 9, 1939; s. Hans-Werner and Ilse Charlotte (Kretschmann) S.; m. Ingrid-Maria Seeger, Apr. 1, 1942; children: Viola-Dorothee, Katharina-Marguerite. Doctor's degree, U. Cologne, Fed. Republic Germany, 1966. Admitted to Bar, Berlin, 1970. Asst. prof. U. Berlin and Cologne, 1963-69; head sales mgr. F. Meyer Steelworks, Dinslaken, Fed. Republic Germany, 1970-73; div. mgr. lighting technique AEG-Telefunken, Springe/Hannover, Fed. Republic Germany, 1974-80; sr. mgr. internat. div. AEG Cables, Moenchengladbach, 1980-82; chief exec. internat. ops. telecom, electronics Krone AG, Berlin, 1983-85, chief exec. corp. controlling, 1986-87; pres., CEO, shareholder Kluessendorf AG, Berlin, 1988—, also bd. dirs.; ret. Author: Rechtsschutzbeduerfnis, 1966; contbr. articles to profl. jours. Consul ad honorem A.D. of Ecuador to Berlin. Fellow Assn. of C. of C., Berlin Industrialists Club, German Soc. Internat. Affairs, German Electronical Assn., Controllers Assn., Am. C. of C. Lutheran. Clubs: Club des Affaires, Econ. Politics Discussion Circle. Lodge: Kiwanis. Avocations: tennis, golf, skiing, internat. politics. Office: Kluessendorf AG, Aitadellenweg 20 D-F, D-13599 Berlin Germany

STEPHAN, ED, sociology educator; b. L.A., Dec. 27, 1939. Student, Calif. Poly. Inst., 1957, U. San Francisco, 1957-61, San Francisco State Coll., 1963-65; BA in Social Sci., U. Oreg., 1970, PhD in Sociology, 1970. Grad. asst., instr. social sci. San Francisco State Coll., 1964-65; NIMH fellow in methodology U. Oreg., 1965-69, rsch. asst. Ctr. for Advanced Study of Ednl. Adminstrn., 1966, instr. sociology dept., 1967-69, instr. Honors Coll., 1969-70; asst. prof. Western Wash. U. (formerly Western Wash. State Coll.), Bellingham, 1970-73, assoc. prof., 1973-76, prof., 1976—, assoc. dean Coll. Arts and Scis., 1972-73, chmn. sociology/anthropology, 1974-76, chmn. sociology, 1976-78. Author online book: The Division of Territory in Society, 1995; contbr. articles to profl. jours.; creator Demographic Rsch. Lab. Homepage, 1994-95, John Graunt Homepage, 1996, webpages for Western Wash. U., 1996. Fax: (360) 650-9295. Home: 523 13th St Bellingham WA 98225-6102 Office: Western Wash U Dept Demography/Sociology Bellingham WA 98225-9801

STEPHAN, EGON, SR., cinematographer, film equipment company executive; b. Leipzig, Germany, Nov. 25, 1933; came to U.S., 1952; 1 child, Egon Jr. Engr. Reeves Sound, Inc., N.Y.C., 1952-55, Camera Equipment Co., N.Y.C., 1955-57; instr. U.S. Army Signal Corps., 1957-59; camera rental mgr. F&B Ceco, Miami, Fla., 1959-66; freelance cinematographer, 1966—; owner, pres. Cine Video Tech., Inc., Miami, 1966—. Recipient Cine Golden Eagle award Coun. on Internat. Nontheatrical Events, 1973, Gold Camera award U.S. Indsl. Film Festival, 1974, Emmy award Nat. Acad. TV Arts and Scis., 1981, Fisher Meml. award South Fla. Film and Tape Prodrs. Assn., 1981. Mem. Soc. Motion Picture and TV Engrs., Fla. Motion Picture and TV Assn. (chmn. 1978), Internat. Assn. Theatrical Stage Employees. Office: Cine Video Tech Inc 7330 NE 4th Ct Miami FL 33138-5005

STEPHAN, MARK TYLER, radiologist; b. Lafayette, La., Dec. 14, 1955; s. John Edward and Beulah (Dupré) S.; m. Wanda Robertson, July 2, 1987; 1 child, Sophie Justinn. BS, U. Southwestern La., 1978; MD, La. State U., New Orleans, 1982. Diplomate Am. Bd. of Radiology with certification in diagnostic radiology, interventional radiology and neuroradiology. Fellow in radiology Ochsner Clinic, New Orleans, 1982-86, M.D. Anderson Hosp., Houston, 1986-87; angiographer Northwest Radiologists, Indpls., 1987-88; diagnostic radiologist Acadiana Radiology, Lafayette, 1988—. Contbr. articles to profl. jours. Recipient AMA Physician's Recognition award, 1985, 92, 95. Mem. Am. Coll. Radiology, Am. Roentgen Ray Soc., Am. Soc. Neuroradiology, Radiol. Soc. of La., Lourdes Physician Hosp. Orgn. (bd. dirs. 1995-98). Avocations: cooking, hi fi. Office: ARG Inc c/o Our Lady of Lourdes 611 Saint Landry St Lafayette LA 70506-4627

STEPHAN, PAULA ELIZABETH, economist, school administrator; b. Menomonie, Wis., Mar. 31, 1945; d. A. Stephen and Margaret (Shaffer) S.; m. William D. Amis, July 27, 1974; 1 child, David. BA, Grinnell Coll., 1967; MA, U. Mich., 1970, PhD, 1971. Asst. prof. econs. Ga. State U., Atlanta, 1971-76, assoc. prof. econs., 1976-81, prof. econs., 1981—, assoc. dean Andrew Young Sch., 1996—; vis. scholar Wissenschaftzentrum, Berlin, 1992, 93, 94. Author: Striking the Mother Lode in Science, 1992; contbr. over 30 articles to profl. jours. Mem. bd. dirs. Paideia Sch. Endowment, Atlanta, 1983—, chair, 1991-98. Recipient grants Alfred P. Sloan Found., 1993-95, 99, Andrew Mellon Found., 1995, 2000. Mem. NSF (com. on equal opportunities in sci. 1999—, grant 1990-91), NRC. Avocations: reading, traveling. E-mail: PSTEPHAN@GSU.edu. Home: 2101 Black Fox Dr NE Atlanta GA 30345-4124 Office: Ga State Univ Andrew Young Sch 33 Gilmer St SE Atlanta GA 30303-3083

STEPHANICK, CAROL ANN, dentist, consultant; b. South Amboy, N.J., Feb. 5, 1952; d. Edward Eugene and Gladys (Pionkowski) S. BS, Rutgers U., 1974; MS, Med. Coll. Pa., 1980; DMD, Temple U., 1984. Lic. dentist, Pa., N.J., Vt. Med. technologist Jersey Shore Med. Ctr., Neptune, N.J., 1975-76, South Amboy Meml. Hosp., 1976-78, Smith-Kline Clin. Labs., King of Prussia, Pa., 1981; instr. dept. biology St. Peter's Coll., Jersey City, 1976-78; instr., edn. coord. Coll. Allied Health, Hahnemann U., Phila., 1978-80; instr. dept. oral radiology Sch. Dentistry, Temple U., Phila., 1984-87; assoc. dentist Personal Choice Dental Assocs., South Amboy, 1985-86, Marcucci and Marcucci, P.C., Phila., 1986-90, Gwynedd Dental Assocs., Springhouse, Pa., 1990-92; spl. events coord. Liberty Dental Conf., Phila., 1990—. Neighbor patrol Sprague St. Neighbors Town Watch, Phila., 1986-93. Named to Legion of Honor, Chapel of Four Chaplains, 1987. Mem. ADA, Pa. Dental Assn., Philadelphia County Dental Soc. (publicity coord. 1990—, pub. info. coord. 1991, semi-finalist judge sr. smile contest 1990—, com. on concerns of women dentists, select com. 1988—), Delaware Valley Assn. Women Dentists, Am. Assn. for Functional Orthodontics, Am. Soc. Clin. Pathologists (med. technologist), Delta Sigma Delta. Roman Catholic. Avocations: reading, weight training, walking, sailing, dog training. Home: PO Box 386 Haddonfield NJ 08033-0310 Office: 777 White Horse Pike S Hammonton NJ 08037-2029

STEPHANOPOULOS, CONSTANDINOS, president of the Republic of Greece; b. Patras, Greece, 1926; s. Demetrius and Vrisiis Stephanopoulos; m. Eugenia El. Stounopoulou, 1959; 3 children. Pvt. practice; M.P. for Achaia Govt. of Greece, 1964-89, under sec. of commerce, 1974, min. of interior, 1974-76, min. of social svcs., 1976-77, min. to Prime Min., 1977-81, parliamentary rep. New Dem. Party, 1981-85, pres. Party of Dem. Renewal, 1985-94, pres., 1995—. Office: Presdl Palace, Herodou Atticou St, Athens Greece*

STEPHEN, JOHN ERLE, lawyer, consultant; b. Eagle Lake, Tex., Sept. 24, 1918; s. John Earnest and Vida Thrall (Klein) S.; m. Gloria Yzaguirre, May 16, 1942; children: Vida Leslie Stephen Renzi, John Lauro Kurt. JD, U. Tex., 1941; postdoctoral, Northwestern U., 1942, U.S. Naval Acad. Postgrad. Sch., Annapolis, 1944; cert. in internat. law, U.S. Naval War Coll., Newport, R.I., 1945; cert. in advanced internat. law, U.S. Naval War Coll., 1967. Bar: Tex. 1946, U.S. Ct. Appeals (D.C. cir.) 1949, U.S. Tax Ct. 1953, U.S. Supreme Ct. 1955, U.S. Dist. Ct. D.C. 1956, U.S. Ct. Appeals (2nd cir.) 1959, U.S. Ct. Appeals (7th cir.) 1964, U.S. Dist. Ct. (so. dist.) N.Y. 1964, U.S. Dist. Ct. (so. dist.) Fla. 1969, D.C. 1972, U.S. Dist. Ct. (no. dist.) Ill. 1974, U.S. Dist. Ct. (we. dist.) Wash. 1975, Mich. 1981, U.S. Dist. Ct. (we. dist.) Mich. 1981, U.S. Dist. Ct. (so. dist.) Tex. 1981. Gen. mgr., corp. counsel Sta. KOPY, Houston, 1946; gen. atty., exec. asst. to pres. Tex. Star Broadcasting Co. and affiliated cos., Houston, 1947-50; ptnr. Hofheinz & Stephen, Houston, 1950-57; sr. v.p., gen. counsel TV Broadcasting Co., Tex. Radio Corp., Gulf Coast Network, Houston, 1953-57; spl. counsel, exec. asst. Mayor, City of Houston, 1953-57; spl. counsel Houston C. of C., 1953-56; sr. v.p., gen. counsel Air Transp. Assn. Am., Washington, 1958-70; v.p., gen. counsel Amway Corp. and affiliated cos., Ada, Mich., 1971-82; counselor, cons. Austin, Tex., 1983—; chief protocol City of Houston, 1953-56; advisor Consulates Gen. of Mex., San Antonio, Houston, New Orleans, Washington, 1956-66; atty. Gen. Creighton W. Abrams, Comdr. U.S. Mil. Assistance Command, Vietnam, Saigon/Washington, 1970-71; mem. adv. bd. Jour. of Air Law and Commerce, 1966-72; vis. lectr. Harvard Bus. Sch., Pacific Agribus. Conf., The Southwestern Legal Found., Inter-Am. Law Conf.; apptd. by Pres. of U.S. legal advisor, del. U.S. Diplomatic Dels. to Internat. Treaty Confs., Paris, London, Rome, Tokyo, Madrid, Bermuda, Guadalajara, Dakar, 1961-71, Internat. Air-Rte. Dels. to U.K., France, Spain, Portugal, Belgium, The Netherlands, Japan, Rep. of Korea, Mex., Australia, Argentina, Soviet Union, and Brazil, 1960-70; legal advisor, del. U.S. dels. to UN Specialized Orgns., Montreal, Geneva, 1964-71; U.S. rep. Internat. Conf. on Aircraft Disturbance, London, 1966; hon. faculty mem., vis. lectr. sch. of law, sch. of bus., U. Miami, 1968—; accredited corr. UN, Rep. and Dem. Nat. Convs.; exec. officer USNR Pub. Affairs Co. 8-7, 1950-57. Author, editor, media prodr. Comm. and transp. group chief Harris County/Houston CD, 1952-56; chmn. legal com. Nat. Aircraft Noise Abatement Coun., Washington; mem. adv. bd. Houston Mus. Fine Arts, 1953-57; bd. dirs. Contemporary Arts Assn., 1952-57, Tex. Transp. Inst., 1964-72; conferee Global Strategy Conf., Naval War Coll., 1958. Comdr. USNR, 1941-46, PTO; mem. staff Supreme Allied Command, NATO. Recipient Jesse L. Lasky award RKO Pictures-CBS, Hollywood, Calif., 1939, H.J. Lutcher Stark prize U. Tex., 1939, 40, Walter Mack award PepsiCo, U. Tex., 1941, Best U.S. Pub. Svc. Broadcasts award CCNY, 1946, First-FM (West) award Frequency Modulation Assn., Houston, 1947, Tex. State Network award mobile coverage Nat. Presdl. Convs., Phila., 1948, Chgo., 1952, Trusonic Wireless Microphone award Acad. Motion Picture Arts & Scis., Beverly Hills, 1951, Frank White award, Mutual Broadcasting Sys., N.Y., 1953, C.R. Smith Aviation Devel. award, Am. Airlines, N.Y., 1955, KLM Royal Dutch Airlines award, Washington, 1956, Capt. Eddie Rickenbacker Air Transport Advancement award Eastern Air Lines, N.Y., 1956, Allied Rod & Gun Club Triple Crown trophy, Gander, Nfld., 1958, Iron Duke award No. Va. Lit. Soc., Arlington, 1962, President's Outstanding commendation, U.S. Naval War Coll., Newport, 1967, IBM Corp. Exec. Computer Concepts prize, San Jose, Calif., 1976, M.Y. ENTERPRISE award Peter Island, Brit. V.I., 1978, Glacier Bay award M.V. MALIBU, Sitka, Alaska, 1980. Mem. ABA (past chmn., mem. coun. sect. pub. utility, comms. and transp. law, standing com. on aero. law), The Am. Law Inst. (advisor Restatement (2d) of Torts), World Peace Through Law Ctr. Geneva (past chmn. internat. aviation law com.), The Fed. Bar Assn. (exec. com. transp. coun., comms. coun.), The D.C. Bar, State Bar Tex. (50 Yr. Meritorious Practice award 1996), State Bar Mich., Fed. Comms. Bar Assn., Assn. ICC Practitioners, A Judicature Soc., Washington Fgn. Law Soc. (vis. lectr. 1967-68), Japanese Air Law Soc. (hon. mem. 1966—), Venezuelan Air and Space Law Soc. (hon.), SOVEDAE (hon. Caracas), Naval Submarine League, Naval War Coll. Found., Internat. Club (Washington), Explorers Club (Washington), Houston Polo Club, Lakeshore Club (Chgo.), Nat. Aviation Club (Washington), Saddle and Cycle Club (Chgo.), Breakfast Club (Houston), Execs. Club (Houston), Order Ky. Cols., Ark. Travelers, Tex. Navy Adm., Flying Col., Phi Eta Sigma, Delta Sigma Rho (pres Tex. chpt. 1940). Home: 6904 Ligustrum Cv Austin TX 78750-8352

STEPHEN, MICHAEL, psychologist. BA in Psychology, U. Okla., 1973; MS, Okla. State U., 1977, PhD in Counseling Psychology, 1986. Lic. psychologist, Okla. Pvt. practice specializing in comm., relationships, children Oklahoma City, 1991—; mem. univ. faculty; active staff Mercy Hosp.; spkr. in field. Author: Cherry Lane: The Power of Abuse; Sex, Love, and God; and Healing, a woman's story; The Mental States Examination for Beginning and Advanced Professionals, Hypoglycemia: A Disease of the Mind, Biochemical/Systemic Treatment to Mental Health. Vol. child abuse prevention and related polit. issues. Mem. APA, Christian Athletes Assn., Okla. Thoroughbred Assn.. Okla. Psychol. Assn., Christian Assn. Psychol. Studies, numerous civic and arts orgns. Avocations: athletics, race horse training, ranching, film and acting. Home: 14025 Crossing Way W Unit G Edmond OK 73013-4756

STEPHEN, NINIAN MARTIN, judge; b. Oxford, Eng., June 15, 1923; s. Frederick and Barbara (Cruickshank) S.; m. Valery Mary Sinclair, June 4,

1949; children: Mary, Ann, Sarah, Jane, Elizabeth. LLB, U. Melbourne, 1949; LLD (hon.), U. Sydney, U. Melbourne, U. Griffith; DLitt (hon.), We. Australia U. Called to Victoria bar, 1952, created queen's counsel, 1966; judge Victorian Supreme Ct., 1970-72; justice High Ct. of Australia, 1972-82; U.K. privy councillor, 1979, gov.-gen. of Australia, 1982-89, amb. for the environ., 1989-92; chmn. Second Strand No. Ireland Talks, 1992; expert Group on Cambodia, 1998-99; mem. ethics commn. Internat. Olympic Com., 2000—. Served with Australian Army, 1941-146; judge internat. criminal tribunals former Yugoslavia & Rwanda, 1993-97. Decorated Knight of Garter, Knight, Order of Australia, Knight Grand Cross St. Michael & St. George, Knight Grand Cross Royal Victorian Order, Knight British Empire, Comdr. Légion d'Honneur, France, Knight St. John Jerusalem. Address: Flat 13/1 193 Domain Rd, South Yarra VIC 3141, Australia

STEPHENS, ANDREAS WILLIAM, mechanical engineer; b. Neuenkirchen, North-Rhine Westphalia, Germany, Apr. 24, 1967; arrived in Australia, 1983; s. William Raymond and Maria Katharina (Kentrup) S.; m. Sadhana, July 6, 1993; 1 child, Ravi Alex. B of Mech. Engring. with class 1 honors, U. New South Wales, Sydney, Australia, 1991, BSc in Physics, 1991, PhD in Elec. Engring., 1997. Rsch. asst. U. New South Wales, Sydney, Australia, 1994-95; mech. engr. Pacific Solar Pty. Ltd., Sydney, Australia, 1995-98; indsl. analyst Johnson Taylor Ltd. (formerly Paul Morgan Securities), Sydney, 1998; analyst M.J.H. Nightingale & Co., Ltd., Sydney, 1998-99; sr. investment analyst Flinders Asset Mgmt. Ltd., Sydney, 1999—; dir. Alpina Investments, Sydney, Australia, 1992—. Contbr. articles to profl. jours. Recipient Australian postgrad. rsch. award Australian govt., Sydney, 1991; supplementary engring. scholar U. New South Wales, Sydney, 1991. Avocations: fin. analysis, internat. cuisine, family. Office: Flinders Asset Mgmt Ltd, Level 6 4 O'Connell St, Sydney NSW 2000, Australia

STEPHENS, BRENDA WILSON, librarian; b. Durham, N.C., Oct. 22, 1952; d. Leroy Thomas and Lucy Mae (Umstead) Wilson; m. Gregory Frederick Stephens, Mar. 6, 1977; children: Seth, Sara. Student, Vincennes U., 1970-71; BA, Winston-Salem State U., 1974; MLS, N.C. Cen. U., 1981. Cert. pub. libr., N.C. From bookmobile coord. to county libr. Orange County Pub. Libr., Hillsborough, N.C., 1976-92; regional libr. dir. Orange County Pub. Libr., Hillsborough, 1992—. Sec. United Way of Greater Orange County, 1991-93; elected mem. Orange County Sch. Bd., 1998—. With U.S. Army, 1974-76. Mem. ALA, N.C. Libr. Assn. (chair adult sect. 1987-93, co-chair 1985-87, lit. com. 1983-85), N.C. Pub. Libr. Dirs. Assn. (officer), Kiwanis Club (pres. 1992-93), A.L. Stanback Mid. Sch. PTO (pres. 1991-92). Democrat. Baptist. Avocation: quilting. Home: 5807 Craig Rd Durham NC 27712-1008 Office: Orange County Pub Libr 300 W Tryon St Hillsborough NC 27278-2438

STEPHENS, CHRISTOPHER LUKE, writer, translator; b. Modesto, Calif., Nov. 8, 1964; s. David Eldee and Nancy Jane (Raymond) S.; m. Haruko Mizoguchi, Mar. 25, 1993. BA, Calif. State U. Fresno, 1985; postgrad., George Washington U., 1986; Cert. of Completion, YMCA Japanese Sch., Osaka, Japan, 1991. Tchr. Calif. State U. Fresno, 1983-85, George Washington U., Washington, 1986, ECC Lang. Sch., Osaka, Japan, 1986-87; tchr., mgr. Discovery English Sch., Osaka, Japan, 1988—; writer, translator (Japanese/English) freelance, Osaka, Japan, 1991—; lang. cons. various dance/music groups and individuals, Osaka, 1991—; radio DJ., 1998—. Editor-in-chief Kansai Forum, 1994-98; musical works include concerts Haco and CD (HACO, Happiness Proof), 1995; illustrator t-shirt design for music club; writer, mem. editl. staff Kansai Time Out mag, 1998—; various solo, duo, band performances. Mem. Amnesty Internat., Nishinomiya/Hyogo, 1995—. Recipient Full scholarship, internship George Washington U., 1986, scholarship YMCA Japanese Sch., 1990. Mem. Kansai Internat. Media Forum. Avocations: drawing, playing music, writing, riding bicycles, studying new langs. Home: 6-14 Kawahigashi-cho, Nishinomiya 662, Japan

STEPHENS, DEBORAH LYNN, health company executive; b. Newton, Iowa, May 30, 1952; d. Clarence Harry and Nancy Elizabeth (Gass) Wright; m. David K. Brender, Dec. 18, 1971 (div.); m. Michael E. Stephens, May 21, 1988 (div.). BS, U. Iowa, 1974; postgrad., U. Wis., Milw., 1978-80, U. Calif., Berkeley, 1987. Asst. to dean of fin. U. Iowa Coll. Medicine, Iowa City, 1975-77; contract audit acct. Miller Brewing Co., Milw., 1977-79; asst. contr. Unicare Health Facilities, Milw., 1979-81; v.p. fin. Sacred Heart Rehab. Hosp., Milw., 1981-84; COO, exec. v.p. Sacred Heart Rehab. Hosp., Med. Rehab. Inst., Milw., 1984-88; CEO, prin. founding mem. Behavioral Health Sys., Birmingham, Ala., 1989—, also bd. dirs.; cons. on rehab., fin., multi-corp. planning and zero-base budgeting 1988; founding mem. Am. Rehab. Network, Inc., Washington, 1986-87; mem. oral exam. bd. City of Milw., 1984-86, Jefferson County, Ala., 1995; mem. prospective payment adv. com. HHS, Washington, 1986; nat. presenter on zero-base budgeting, cor. reorgns., managed care, and planning. Contbr. articles to profl. jours. Mem. healthcare cost containment com. Bus. Coun. Ala., Rotary Club of Birmingham. Named one of Top 5 Thriving Bus. Women in Birmingham, Bus. to Bus., 1995, one of Top 78 nat. Entrepreneurs, Entrepreneur mag., 1996; featured in Healthwatch, Open Minds, Entrepreneur mag., Birmingham Post Herald, Birmingham News. Mem. Hosp. Fin. Mgmt. Assn. (governing bd. 1981-88), Nat. Forensic League (life), Nat. Assn. Accts., Nat. Assn. Rehab. Facilities (prospective payment adv. bd. 1986-88, com. on med. oriented facilities 1983-88), Ga. Managed Care Assn. (bd. dirs. 1995), Birmingham C. of C. (Small Bus. Person of Yr. award 1995), Venture Club, Kappa Kappa Gamma. Avocations: dancing, skiing, jogging, travel, reading. Office: Behavioral Health Systems 2 Metroplex Dr Ste 500 Birmingham AL 35209-6812

STEPHENS, ELTON BRYSON, bank executive, service and manufacturing company executive; b. Clio, Ala., Aug. 4, 1911; s. James Nelson and Clara (Stuckey) S.; m. Alys Varian Robinson, Nov. 28, 1935; children: James Thomas, Jane Stephens Comer, Elton Bryson Jr., Dell Stephens Brooke. B.A., Birmingham-So. Coll., 1932, LLD (hon.), 1977; LL.B., U. Ala., 1936, LHD (hon.), 1990; grad., Advanced Mgmt. Program, Harvard U., 1960; LHD (hon.), Faulkner U., 1992. Bar: Ala. 1936. Regional dir. Keystone Readers Service, Birmingham, 1937-43; partner, then founder and pres. Mil. Service Co., Inc. (predecessor of EBSCO Industries, Inc.), Birmingham, 1943-58; founder EBSCO Industries, Inc., and affiliates, 1958; since pres., chmn. bd. EBSCO Industries, Inc., and affiliates, Birmingham; now chmn. bd. EBSCO Industries, Inc. and affiliates, Birmingham; bd. dirs. R.A. Brown Ins. Agy. Ltd., 1966—; chmn. EBSCO Investment Svc., Inc., 1959—, Canebsco Subscription Svc., Toronto, Ont., Can., 1972—; founder, chmn. Ala. Bancorp divsn. Highland Bank; founder EBSCO Savs. and Profit Sharing Trust, Ala. Bancorp Savs. and Profit Sharing Trust. Mem. fin. and investment com., past chmn. bd. trustees, chmn. exec. com. Birmingham-So. Coll.; trustee So. Research Inst.; former pres., chmn. bd. trustee Birmingham Met. YMCA; mem. bd., chmn. econ. pension com. Tenn.-Tombigbee Waterway Authority; founder % Clubs of Ala., founder United Art Fund/Met. Arts Council; vice chmn., bd. dirs., hon. chmn.; vice chmn. Am. Coun. Arts, 1990-95; fundraiser Rebirth Symphony, Birmingham. Elton B. Stephens Expressway named in his honor, 1970, Elton B. Stephens Library, Clio, 1979. Mem. Birmingham C. of C. (bd. dirs.), The Club, Birmingham Press Club, Summit Club, Mountain Brook Country Club (Ala.), Rotary (pres. Homewood, Ala. 1979-80, Paul Harris fellow), Ala. Symphonic Assn. (chmn., CEI, prin. fund raiser), Ala. Acad. Honor, Alpha Tau Omega (past chmn. nat. found.), Omicron Delta Kappa, Phi Alpha Delta. Methodist.

STEPHENS, HEIDI MULTHOPP, physician, researcher; b. Balt., June 13, 1963; d. Heiko and Lorna Jean (Cook) Multhopp; m. Steven Scott Stephens, Aug. 1, 1987; children: Samantha Marie, Eric Robert. BA in Chemistry, Goucher Coll., Towson, Md., 1983; MD, U. Md., Balt., 1987; MBA, U. South Fla., 1998. Diplomate Am. Bd. Orthopedic Surgery. Intern U. South Fla., Tampa, 1987-88, resident, 1988-90; resident Union Meml. Hosp., Balt., 1990-92; fellow in orthopedic surgery Tampa Gen. Healthcare, 1992-93, mem. staff; mem. staff VA Med. Ctr., Tampa, Shriners Hosp., Tampa, H. Lee Moffitt Cancer Ctr., Tampa; asst. prof. U. South Fla., Tampa, 1993—. Co-author: Manual of Pediatric Orthopedics, 1996; contbr. articles to profl. jours. Mem. AMA, Fla. Med. Soc. Office: Harbourside Med Tower Ste 650 4 Columbia Dr Tampa FL 33606-3568

STEPHENS, HELEN JANSSENS, principal; b. Chgo., July 7, 1947; d. Albert Joseph and Lucille Catherine (Gietel) Janssens; m. James Richard Stephens, May 18, 1968; children: James Albert, Andrea Renée. Student, No. Ill. U., 1965-67; BA in Math., Northeastern Ill. U., Chgo., 1981; MEd, Loyola U., Chgo., 1991. Sec. ALD, Inc., Chgo., 1967-68; spl. typist Bankers Life & Casualty, Chgo., 1971-73; tchr. St. Edward Sch., Chgo., 1982-99; prin. St. Tarcissus Sch., Chgo., 1999—. Moderator St. Edward Student Coun., Chgo., 1989-99, handbook com., 1987; mem. Math. Curriculum Improvement Project, Chgo. 1986-89. Found. for Excellence in Teaching grant, 1988. Mem. Ill. Coun. Tchrs. Math., Nat. Coun. Tchrs. Math., Nat. Cath. Edn. Assn., Assn. for Curriculum Devel., Am. Legion Aux., Phi Delta Kappa. Roman Catholic. Avocations: reading, collecting bells. Home: 3100 N Kilbourn Ave Chicago IL 60641-5364 Office: St Tarcissus Sch 6040 W Ardmore Ave Chicago IL 60646-5320

STEPHENS, JAMES LINTON, mechanical engineer; b. Stamford, Conn., Nov. 1, 1956; s. James Regis and Beatrice Helen (Johnson) S.; m. Laura Lynn Holmes, Sept. 6, 1980; children: Mark Linton, Jaimee Lee, Matthew James. BS in Mech. Engring., BS in Biomed. Engring., Northwestern U., 1980. Registered profl. engr., Wis. Mfg. engr. Parker Hannifin Corp., Des Plaines, Ill., 1980-81, St. Mary's, Ohio, 1981-84; mfg. engr. Ohmeda divsn. BOC Group, Madison, Wis., 1984-91, sr. mfg. engr. Ohmeda divsn., 1991-95; sr. engr. Case Corp., Racine, Wis., 1995—. Mem. steering com. for engring. profl. devel. program U. Wis., Madison, 1994. Ill. State scholar, 1975. Mem. Soc. Mfg. Engrs. (treas. Madison chpt. 1984-85, 2d vice chmn. 1985-86, 1st vice chmn. 1986-87, chmn. 1987-88, certification chmn. 1988—, fundraiser 1987—, seminar and workshop leader 1987—, Chmn. plaque 1988, elected to machining tech. assn. bd. advisors 1996—). Avocations: swimming, tennis, reading science fiction. Office: Case Corp 7000 Durand Ave Racine WI 53406

STEPHENS, JEFFREY GARETT, architectural and construction management executive; b. Bellflower, Calif., Aug. 8, 1970; s. Gary Woodrow and Penny Ann Stephens. A in Arch., Phoenix Inst. Tech., 1992. Wood carpenter Pacific Western Builders, Cypress, Calif., 1984-88, Beckwith Constrn., Laughlin, Nev., 1988-89; drafting and field technician Ind. Roofing Consultants, Santa Ana, Calif., 1992-93; arch. project coord. Todd and Assocs., Phoenix, 1993-95; project mgr. CCA Archs., Newport Beach, Calif., 1995-97, MST Constructors, Inc., Lake Forest, Calif., 1997-99; owner The Progressive Way, Huntington Beach, Calif., 1999—. E-mail: jeff08@pacbell.net. Home and Office: The Progressive Way 8791 Baywood Dr Huntington Beach CA 92646-2611

STEPHENS, KENNETH GILBERT, electrical engineering educator, university dean; b. Coventry, Eng., May 3, 1931; s. George Harry and Christiana (Jackson) S.; m. Miriam Anne Sim, Dec. 7, 1957 (div. 1980); children: Jane, Ian; m. Elizabeth Carolynn Jones, Sept. 8, 1980. BS with honours, U. Birmingham, Eng., 1952, PhD, 1956. Chartered engr., U.K. Reactor rsch. physicist Assoc. Elec. Industries (AEI) Ltd., Aldermaston, Berkshire, Eng., 1955-62; sr. rsch. engr. Pye Ltd., Cambridge, Eng., 1963-66; lectr. elec. engring. U. Surrey, Guildford, Eng., 1966, reader, 1967-78, prof., 1978—, head dept. electronic and elec. engring., 1983-91, dean Faculty Engring., 1992-96, prof. emeritus, 1996—. Joint editor: (conf. procs.) Low Energy Ion Beams, 1978, 80, (book) Ion Implantation Technology, 1991. Bd. govs. Royal Grammar Sch., Guildford, 1979—, chmn., 1996—. Fellow Instn. Elec. Engrs., Inst. Physics; mem. Marylebone Cricket Club. Avocations: swimming, sports, gardening, reading, music. Home: 10 Brockway Close, Guildford GU1 2LW, England Office: U Surrey, Dept Elec Engring, Guildford GU2 5XH, England

STEPHENS, LARRY DEAN, engineer; b. Sterling, Colo., Sept. 1, 1937; s. John Robert and Shirley Berniece (Rudel) S.; m. Carol Ann Wertz, Sept. 1, 1957 (div. May 1975); children: Deborah Lynn, Janell Diane, Dana Larry, Hilary Elizabeth Melton. BS in Engring., 1959; Colo. State U., 1960; MBA, U. Colo., 1967. Registered profl. engr., Colo. Engr. Bur. Reclamation, Denver, 1960-90, cons., 1991—; exec. v.p. U.S. Com. on Irrigation and Drainage, Denver, 1971—; exec. dir. U.S. Com. on Large Dams, Denver, 1986—. V.p. Internat. Commn. on Irrigation and Drainage, 1989-92. With USNG, 1961-62. Mem. Am. Soc. Agrl. Engrs., Assn. State Dam Safety Ofcls., Colorado River Water Users Assn., Coun. on Engring. and Sci. Soc. Execs., Univ. Club Denver. Republican. Methodist. E-mail: stephens@uscid.org. Home: 1625 Larimer St Apt 1505 Denver CO 80202-1532 Office: USCID 1616 17th St Ste 483 Denver CO 80202-1277

STEPHENS, ROBERT DAVID, environmental engineering executive; b. La Follette, Tenn., Nov. 8, 1949; s. Robert Oscar and Billie Jean (Maples) S.; m. Donna Jean Reece, July 11, 1970 (div. Apr. 1984). BA in Biology, Berea (Ky.) Coll., 1971; postgrad., U. Cin., 1973-74. Cert. environ. assessor, Fla., environ. trainer; registered environ. property assessor. Environ. specialist Ky. Dept. Health, Ludlow, 1971-74; project mgr. Pedco Environ. Specialists, Cin., 1974-77; environ. control mgr. Mobil Chem. Corp., Richmond, Va., 1978-84; v.p. Environ. Analysis Corp., Richmond, 1984-85; mgr. Environ. Rsch. and Tech. Group GSX Corp., Greensboro, N.C., 1985-86; mgr. regulatory affairs and cmty. rels. Internat. Tech. Corp., Knoxville, Tenn., 1986-88; mgr. environ. studies Internat. Tech. Corp., Tampa, Fla., 1988-90; gen. mgr. First Environment, Inc., Tampa, 1990-91; co-owner Bruder Stephens, Inc., Tampa, 1991—; faculty Fla. C. of C. Environ. Seminars, 1988—; adj. faculty U. Fla. Treeo Ctr.; adj. faculty U. South Fla. Coll. Pub. Health; expert witness in environ. mgmt., sampling and analysis, environ. risk mgmt. Contbr. articles to profl. jours. Co-founder Berea Community Theater, 1970; bd. dirs. So. Waste Info. Exch., Inc.; mem. adv. bd. Ctr. for Environ./Occup. Risk Analysis and Mtmg., U. South Fla. Coll. Pub. Health. Mem. Fla. Bar Assn. (assoc., environ. and land use sect.), Fla. Environ. Assessors Assn. (pres. 1996-97, bd. dirs. 1993—), Water Polution Control Fedn., Va. Orchid Soc. (pres. 1980-85, del. World Orchid Congress, Miami 1984), Ridge Orchid Soc., Tampa Club (bd. dirs. 1999—). Republican. Avocations: orchid horticulture, guitar. Home: PO Box 145 Mango FL 33550-0145 Office: 14409 N Nebraska Ave Ste A Tampa FL 33613-2226

STEPHENS, STEVE ARNOLD, real estate broker; b. Irby, Cheshire, Eng., May 25, 1945; came to U.S., 1983; s. Harold Dennis George and Hilda Leonora (Howell) S.; m. Lynn Williams, Apr. 14, 1983. Student, Manchester U., Eng., 1967-69. Lic. pvt. detective, Ill.; cert. comml. investment mem. From cadet to detective Cheshire (Eng.) Police, 1961-69; acting detective sgt. Merseyside (Eng.) Police, 1969-75; acting sgt. Hampshire (Eng.) Police, 1975-77; retail store owner Horsham, West Sussex, Eng., 1977-79; pvt. detective Carratu Internat., London, 1979-83, D.A.C. Stephens, Aurora, Ill., 1983-86; broker Coldwell Banker Comml.-Primus Realty, Oswego, Ill., 1986-98; broker, owner Stephens Comml. Real Estate, Aurora, Ill., 1998—. Bd. dirs. Aurora Crimestoppers, pres., 1995-96. Recipient Rep. Legion of Merit award, Rep. Order of Merit award. Mem. Nat. Assn. Realtors (CCIM), Comml. Investment Real Estate Inst. (cert., bd. dirs. Ill. CCIM chpt. 1992-97, sec.-treas. 1994, v.p. 1995, pres. 1996, v.p. region 7 1999—), No. Ill. Comml. Assn. Realtors (dir. 1995-97), Internat. Assn. Chiefs of Police, Ill. Assn. Realtors, Greater Aurora C. of C., Aurora Country Club. Avocations: travel, literature, golf. Home: 7 Saddlewood Ct Aurora IL 60506-9175 Office: 518 N Lake St Aurora IL 60506-3105

STEPHENSON, ANTHONY EDGAR (TONY STEPHENSON), geoscientist, researcher; b. Melbourne, Australia, Oct. 3, 1954; s. Arthur Exley and Barbara Nancy (Green) S.; m. Monica Yeung, 1985. BS, U. Queensland, Brisbane, Australia, 1976, BS with honors, 1977. Geologist Noranda Australia Ltd., Perth, 1978-79; clk. Australian Govt., Perth, 1980-81; geoscientist Bur. Mineral Resources, Canberra, Australia, 1981-90, rsch. scientist, 1990-91; sr. rsch. scientist Bur. Resource Scis., Canberra, Australia, 1991-94, prin. rsch. scientist, 1994-98; prin. rsch. scientist Australian Geol. Survey Orgn., Canberra, 1998—; bd. dirs. Gondwana Dreaming Pty Ltd., Canberra, CPSU Advantage Ltd., Sydney. Nat. v.p. Profl. Officers Assn., Melbourne, 1990-91, nat. dep. pres. profl. divsn. pub. sector union, 1991-93, nat. pres. profl. divsn. cmty. and pub. sector union, 1993-99. Mem. AAAS, Am. Assn. Petroleum Geologists, Soc. Exploration Paleontologists Mineralologists, Geol. Soc. Australia, Petroleum Exploration Soc. Australia. Office: Australian Geol Survey Orgn, GPO Box 378, Canberra ACT 2601, Australia

STEPHENSON, FRANCIS RICHARD, astronomer; b. Newcastle-upon-Tyne, Eng., Apr. 26, 1941; s. Francis Joseph Stephenson and Evelyn Wanless Chipchase; m. Ellen Samson Stirling McNally, Oct. 19, 1974; children: Gillian, Susan, John. BSc with honors, U. Durham, 1963; MSc, Newcastle U., Newcastle-upon-Tyne, 1964, PhD, 1972, DSc, 1982. Asst. lectr. Marine & Tech. Coll., S. Shields, U.K., 1965-66; rsch. fellow U. Newcastle, 1973-79, U. Liverpool, 1979-82; sr. rsch. assoc. Jet Propulsion Lab., Pasadena, Calif., 1989-91; sr. rsch. fellow Durham (U.K.) U., 1982-96, professorial fellow, 1996—. Co-author: Historical Supernovae, 1977; author: Historical Eclipses and Earth's Rotation, 1997. Freeman, City of London, 1993; local preacher on trial Meth. Ch., Newcastle, 1997. Fellow Royal Astron. Soc. (Jackson-Gwilt medal 1992); mem. Internat. Astron. Union (pres. hist. astronomy 2000—, mem. earth rotation com. 1972—), Newcastle Astron. Soc. (pres.), Durham Astron. Soc. (hon. pres.), worshipful Co. of Clockmakers (freeman 1992—, Tompion Gold Medal 1992, liveryman 1998—). Methodist. Avocations: violin playing, travel. Home: 36 Grange Rd, Newcastle-upon-Tyne NE4 9LD, England Office: Univ of Durham, South Rd, Durham CH1 3LE, England

STEPHENSON, IRENE HAMLEN, biorhythm analyst, consultant, editor, educator; b. Chgo., Oct. 7, 1923; d. Charles Martin and Carolyn Hilda (Hilgers) Hamlin; m. Edgar B. Stephenson, Sr., Aug. 16, 1941 (div. 1946); 1 child, Edgar B. Author biorhythm compatibilities column Nat. Singles Register, Norwalk, Calif., 1979-81; instr. biorhythm Learning Tree Open U., Canoga Park, Calif., 1982-83, instr. biorhythm personality analysis, 1980—, instr. biorhythm compatibility, 1982—; owner, pres. matchmaking svc. Pen Pals Using Biorhythm, Chatsworth, Calif., 1979—; editor newsletter The Truth, 1979-85, Mini Examiner, Chatsworth, 1985—; rschr. biorhythm personality and compatibility, 1974—, biorhythm columnist Psyhic Astrology Horoscope, 1989-94, True Astrology Forecast, 1989-94, Psychic Astrology Predictions, 1990-94, Con Artist Types, 1995, Pedophile (child molester) Types, 1995-2000, Personality Types, 1996, Trouble-Addict (Suicide) Types, 1997, Domineering/Nag Types, 1998, Con Artists, Sweetheart Swindlers, Super Con Artist Types, 1998, Bully types, 2000, Deadly Compatibility Combination, 2000, Fatal Attraction Types, 2000, Sadism, Sadistic, Sadistic Predators, 2000, Salesperson, Practical Joker Types, 2000, Doormat Types, 2000, Famous/Queen Bee/Rescuer Types, 2000, Prostitution, 2000. Author: Learn Biorhythm Personality Analysis, 1980, Do-It-Yourself Biorhythm Compatibilities, 1982; contbr. numerous articles to mags. Office: PO Box 3893 Chatsworth CA 91313-3893

STEPHENSON, TONI EDWARDS, publisher, investment management executive, communications executive; b. Bastrop, La., July 23, 1945; d. Sidney Crawford (dec.) and Grace Erleene Little; m. Arthur Emmet Stephenson, Jr., June 17, 1967; 1 child, Tessa Lyn. Grad. owner/pres. mgmt. program, Harvard Bus. Sch. Pres., dir. Gen. Comm., Inc., Denver; sr. v.p., founder Stephenson & Co., Denver, 1971—; gen. ptnr. Viking Fund; ptnr. Stephenson Properties, Stephenson Ventures, Stephenson Mgmt. Co.; v.p. Stertek, Inc.; bd. dirs. Startek Europe Ltd., Startek Pacific, Ltd.; v.p. Startek, Inc. Past dir. The Children's Hosp., St. Joseph's Hosp., Cherry Creek H.S. Parent Tchr. Conf. Orgn.; past pres. Children's Hosp. Assn. Vols.; past troop leader Girl Scouts Am. Mem. Harvard Bus. Sch. Club Colo., DAR, Delta Gamma, Jonathan Club, Annabel's (London), Thunderbird Country Club, Glenmoor Country Club, Denver Petroleum Club.

STEPHERSON, BRIAN EDWARD, psychological social worker, artist, writer; b. N.Y.C.; s. Lemuel Arthur and Margaret Sue (Badgett) S. BA, Columbia U., 1965; postgrad., Hunter Coll., 1981-83. In psychol. social work N.Y.C. Writer prose, essays and non-fiction. Recipient Pres.'s achievement award Pres. Ronald Reagan, 1984. Mem. Columbia Coll. Club. Republican. Episcopal. Avocation: writing. Home: 454 W 35th St New York NY 10001-1505

STEPNIEWSKI, ALFRED DANIEL, mechanics educator; b. Pajaków, Radom, Poland, Jan. 19, 1939; s. Bolesław and Stanisława (Łyjak) S.; m. Wanda Kalewicz, Sept. 21, 1963 (div. Nov. 1983). M in Mechanics, Tech. U. Szczecin, Poland, 1962; M in Math., U. Poznań, Poland, 1971, D in Engring., 1974. Mechanist educator Tech. U. Szczecin, 1962—. Author: Treaty on Fundamentals of Mechanics, D'Alembert's Supplemented and Generalized Principle as Fundamental Law of Classical Mechanics, 1984, Primary Fundamentals of Classical Mechanics, 1992, Lectures on Mechanics, vol. 1, 1993, vol. 2, 1995. Mem. Polish Soc. Theoretical and Applied Mechanics, Polish Soc. Math. Avocations: music, bicycle trips. Home: Ruska 33 c/9, 70-132 Szczecin Poland Office: Tech U Szczecin, Al Piastów 19, 70-310 Szczecin Poland

STEPNOWSKI, ANDRZEJ, science educator; b. Baila Podlaska, Poland, Jan. 4, 1940; s. Jacenty and Maria (Daniluk) S.; m. Krystyna Krezcko, Sept. 17, 1966 (dec. May 1999); children: Rafal, Piotr. MSc, Tech. U. GdaŁsk, Poland, 1964, PhD, 1974, DSc, 1992. Asst., asst. prof. Tech. U. GdaŁsk, 1965-85, assoc. prof., 1988-90, prof., 1993—, dean sci., 1996-99; acoustic expert Seastar Instrument Inc., Dartmouth, Can., 1986-88; vis. prof. Middle East Tech. U., Turkey, 1990-91; acad. cons. Inst. Pertanian Bogor, Indonesia, 1991-92; acoustic expert Food and Agr. Orgn., Rome, 1976; dir., CEO C-Map Inc., GdaŁsk, 1993—. Assoc. editor: Acta Acoustica, 1999—; contbr. over 100 articles to profl. jours.; 7 patents in field. Recipient award Ministry of Sci., 1974, 76, 84, 86; named Fellow of Cross of Polonia Restituta, Pres. of Poland, 1999, Master of Polish Tech., Ministry of Rsch. Tech., Warsaw, 1974, 84, 86. Fellow Polish Acad. Scis. (Hydroacoustic Subcom.); mem. IEEE, Polish Acoustical Soc. (sec. gen. 1991-93). Roman Catholic. Avocations: music, archeology, sports, tennis. Home: De Gaulle'a 14/11, 80-261 GdaŁsk Poland Office: Tech U GdaŁsk, G Narutowicza 11/12, 80-952 GdaŁsk Poland

STEPNOWSKI, PIOTR, environmentalist, consultant; b. Gdansk, Poland, June 30, 1970; s. Andrzej and Krystyna (Kreczko) S. MSc, U. Gdansk, 1995, PhD, 1999. Rschr. U. Gdansk, 1994—. Editl. project leader: Ecological Engineering, 1997. Bd. dirs. Coalition Clean Baltic, Stockholm, 1997. Mem. Polish Acad. Sci. (mem. com. for marine rsch.), Polish Ecol. Club (cons. 1996—, bd. dirs. 1996-99). Avocations: jazz, art. Home: De Gaulle'A 14, 80-261 Gdansk Poland Office: U Gdahsk Faculty Chemistry, Ul Sobieskiego 18-19, 80952 Gdansk Poland

STEPTO, ROBERT FREDERICK THOMAS, chemistry educator, consultant; b. Morden, Eng., Nov. 13, 1937; s. Frederick James and Elsie Una (Coleman) S.; m. Joan Helena Morgan, June 21, 1958; children: Jon Morgan, Paul Morgan. BSc with spl honours in Phys. Chemistry, U. Bristol, Eng., 1958, PhD in Chemistry, 1962; DSc in Polymer Sci., U. Manchester, Eng., 1988. Chartered chemist, Eng. Rsch. fellow U. Manchester (Eng.) Inst. Sci. and Tech., 1961-63, asst. lectr., lectr., sr. lectr. polymer sci. and tech., 1963-79, reader, 1979-92, prof., 1992—; vis. lectr. Tech. U. Munich, 1972; vice dir. R&D Capsugel AG, Basle, Switzerland, 1985-88; vis. prof. U. Copenhagen, 1987-89; affiliate prof. U. Wash., Seattle, 1987-92; assoc., titular mem., chmn. Commn. IV.1, Internat. Union Pure and Applied Chemistry, 1987-99, titular and assoc. mem. Commn. IV.2, 1987-91, chmn. working party on polymer networks, 1987-91, v.p. macromolecular divsn., 1997—. Contbr. over 240 articles to sci. jours., chpts. to books, editor books; patentee in fields of thermoplastics processing of starch and synthesis of polyols; editor books in field. Recipient Interphex award for innovation in prodn. in pharm. industry, 1986; Francis-Francis scholar U. Bristol, 1958-61. Fellow Royal Soc. Chemistry, Statis. Mechanics and Thermodynamics Group, Polymer Networks Group (chmn. 1986-90, treas. 1990-92, sec. 1992-98), Macro Group U.K. (coms. 1988-92). Office: UMIST Polymer Sci-Tech Group, Manchester Materials Sci Ct, Manchester M1 7HS, England

STEPTOE, ANDREW PATRICK ARTHUR, psychologist, educator; b. London, Apr. 24, 1951; s. Patrick Christopher and Sheena Macleod Steptoe; m. Jane Furneux Horncastle, 1980 (div. 1984); 1 child, William; m. Jane Wardle, 1991; 1 child, Matthew. BA, Cambridge (Eng.) U., 1972, MA, 1976; DPhil, Oxford (Eng.) U., 1976, DSc, 1995. Rsch. lectr. Christ Ch., Oxford U., 1975-77; lectr. St. George's Hosp. Med. Sch., U. London, 1977-81, sr. lectr., 1981-87, reader, 1987-88, prof. psychology, 1988-2000, chair acad. bd., 1997-99; prof. psychology Univ. Coll., London, 1998—. Author: Psychological Factors in Cardiovascular Disorders, 1981, Essential Psychology for Medical Practice, 1988, The Mozart - Da Ponte Operas, 1988, Mozart-Everyman/EMI Music Companion, 1997; editor: Psychosocial Processes and Health, 1994, Genius and the Mind, 1998, Brit. Jour. of Health Psychology, 1995—; assoc. editor Annals of Behavioral Medicine, 1991-96, Psychophysiology, 1982-86. Fellow Brit. Psychol. Soc.; mem. Internat. Soc. Behavioral Medicine (pres. 1994-96), Soc. for Psychosomatic

Rsch. (pres. 1983-85), Swedish Soc. Behavioral Medicine (hon.). Avocations: music, theater, reading, family. Office: U Coll London Dept Epidemiology & Pub Health, 1-19 Torrington Pl, London WC1E 6BT, England

STERBA, OLDRICH JOSEF, veterinary surgeon, researcher; b. Bystřice Olši, Czechoslovakia, Mar. 23, 1930; s. Oldrich and Anna (Petrankova) S.; widowed, 1985; children: Jiří, Radovan, Katerina; m. Hedvika Sebelova, June 11, 1993. D of Vet. Medicine, U. Vet. Medicine, Brno, Czechoslovakia, 1954, PhD, 1963; D of Biol. Sci., Czech Acad. Sci., Prague, 1985. Lectr. U. Vet. Medicine, Brno, 1951-54, sr. lectr., 1954-65; sci. worker Czech Acad. Sci., Brno, 1965-80, sr. sci. worker, 1981-93; prof. U. Vet. Pharm. Sci., Brno, 1993—; head of dept. Inst. Vertebrate Zoology, Czech Acad. Sci., Brno, 1969-90, dir. Inst. Sys. and Ecol. Biology, 1990-93. Co-author: (textbook) Veterinary Anatomy, 1971, (book) Biology of Game, 1990, Kolda's Atlas of Veterinary Anatomy, 1999, Anatomy and Embryology of Game, Embryology of Dolphins, 2000. Recipient Golden medal Palacky U., 1990, Silver medal Masaryk U., 1995. Mem. Czech Anatomical Soc. (v.p. 1991-93), Czech Zool. soc. (J.E. Purkyne medal 1990), Internat. Com. Vet. Anat. Nomenclature. Roman Catholic. Avocations: history, prehistory, classic literature, philology. Office: U Vet and Pharm Scis, Palackeho 1-3, 61242 Brno Czech Republic

STERCHI, THOMAS NEAL, lawyer; b. Olney, Ill., Aug. 6, 1945; s. Alfred Rhodell and Gladys Marie (Chaplin) S.; m. Mary-Michael Kelly, Dec. 31, 1990; children: Laura, Neal, Sarah, Megan. BS, Ea. Ill. U., 1967; JD, U. Mo., 1972. Bar: Mo., U.S. Dist. Ct. Mo. (we. and ea. dists.), Kans., Nebr., U.S. Ct. Appeals (8th and 10th cirs.). Assoc. Watson, Ess, Marshall & Enggas, Kansas City, Mo., 1972-79; ptnr. Watson, Ess, Marshall & Enggas, Kansas City, 1979-82; founding ptnr. Baker Sterchi Cowden & Rice, L.L.C., Kansas City, 1982—; past chmn. pharm. med. device , litigation section Fedn. Insurance Corp. Counsel, 1997-99, mem. products liability section, mem. devel. com., new mems. com. and admissions com; mem. Defense Rsch. Inst.; nat. coordinating trial counsel E.R. Squibb & Sons, Inc., Bracco Diagnostics Inc.; adv. coun. product liability Defense Rsch. Inst. Author: Case notes and Comments Mo. Law Review, 1972, Mo. Product Liability Case Survey, 1991; contbr. author: TIPS Jour. 1999 Annual Survey. Mem. pub. relations com. Jackson Cmty. Med. Soc., Kansas City, Mo., 1979-80; Commr. Great Am. Basketball League, Johnson City, Kans., 1992-97. With U.S. Army, 1969-71. Mem. Am. Bar Assn. (litigation and tort and ins. practice sections), Internat. Assn. Insurance Law, Fedn. of Ins. and Corp. Counsel, Trial Attys. Am. (Mo. bar), Western Mo. Defense Lawyers Orgn. (pres. 1985-87), Mo. Orgn. of Defense Lawyers (bd. dirs. 1989-95), Kansas City Metropolitan Bar Assn., Kansas City Claims Assn. Avocations: golf, tennis. Fax: 816-472-0288. E-mail: sterchi@bscr-law.com. Office: 2100 Commerce Tower 2400 Pershing Rd Ste 500 Kansas City MO 64108-2504

STERCKX, LUC MARIE JAN, oil company executive; b. Leuven, Belgium, Mar. 8, 1952; s. Joseph and Josette (Vandecauter) S.; m. Christine Karel Maria Stymans; children: Katrien, Els, Marlies, Peter. Chem Engr, U. Leuven, 1975, PhD in Chem. Engring., 1979; postgrad., U. Brussels, 1982. Various positions Exxon, Belgium, 1979-85; gen. mgr. Indaver, Belgium, 1985-91; sr. v.p. Petrofina, Belgium, 1991-95; gen. mgr. Fina Deutschland, 1995-99; v.p. Oleo Chems., Totalfina, Belgium, 1999—; bd. dirs. Indaver, Belgium. Capt. Health Svcs., Belgian Mil., 1975-76. Home: Ericalaan 8, B-2930 Brasschaat Belgium Office: Totalfina, Nijverheidsstraat 52, B-1040 Brussels Belgium

STERLING, ARTHUR JAMES, legal assistant; b. Pineville, La., July 27, 1944; s. Leon Henry and Dorothy Mae S; m. Gwendolyn Sterling, June 28, 1964 (div. July 7, 1982); children: Eric, Hope, Monique, Heather. AA in Bus. Adminstrn., Compton C.C., 1986; student, U. Southern Calif., 1988-89; AA in Bus. Paralegal, Cerritos C.C., 1994. With U.S. Naval Weapons, Seal Beach, Calif., 1979-83, Norwalk Superior Ct., 1991; law clk. Recipient Dave Holt Meml scholarship, K.T. Skula meml. scholarship, Johnson Controls, Inc. Fund scholarship, Amy Welch Meml. scholarship. Mem. Soc. for Advancement of Mgmt., Phi Beta Lambda. Democrat. Avocations: computers, cooking, reading. Home: 4216 Carlin Ave Lynwood CA 90262-5208

STERLING, DAVID AKIBA, environmental and occupational health science educator; b. Tuscaloosa, Ala., Jan. 12, 1955; s. Theodor D. and Nora M. S.; m. Linda S. Leason, Mar. 31, 1979; children: Callen S., Ryan A. BS in Biol. Scis., U. Oreg., 1978; MS in Environ. Health/Sci., U. Cin., 1982; PhD in Environ. Occupl. Health Sci., U. Tex. Sch. Pub. Health, Houston, 1986. Environ. and occupl. health/indsl. hygiene cons. TDS Ltd., Vancouver, B.C., Can., 1975-81; sr. rsch. asst., field studies dir. Tex. Indoor Air Quality U. Tex., Houston, 1982-83, grad. instr. Indsl. Hygiene Lab., 1981-84; rsch. chemist IIT Rsch. Inst., Chgo., 1984-87, coord. Chgo. divsn. environ. health and safety program, 1986-87; asst. prof., asst. dir. for programs Environ. Health Old Dominion U., Norfolk, Va., 1987-93; asst. prof. environ., occupl. health Saint Louis U., 1993-99, assoc. prof. environ., occupl. health, 1999—. Contbr. articles to profl. jours./publs. Grantee in field, including Old Dominion U. Rsch. Found., 1993-94, IIT Rsch. Inst., St. Louis U. Mem. Am. Indsl. Hygiene Assn., Am. Conf. Govtl. Indsl. Hygienists, Am. Bd. Indsl. Hygienists, Am. Acad. Indsl. Hygiene, Internat. Soc. Exposure Analysis and Environ. Epidemiology. Avocations: snow skiing, back packing, akido, pottery. Office: Saint Louis Univ Sch of Pub Health 3663 Lindell Blvd Saint Louis MO 63108-3342

STERLING, RICHARD LEROY, English and foreign language educator; b. Atlantic City, Feb. 18, 1941; s. Richard Leroy and Anne (Bass) S. BA, Am. U., 1968; MA, Cath. U., 1971; PhD, Howard U., 1990. Head Start tchr. D.C. pub. schs., summer 1968; tchr. French and English, adult and continuing edn. D.C. Pub. Schs., Washington, 1969-71, 76-83; instr. French Howard U., Washington, 1973-76, grad. teaching asst., 1983-85, instr., lectr. in French, 1985-89; tchr. English Community-Based Orgns., D.C. Pub. Schs., Washington, 1989-91; asst. prof. French and English Bowie (Md.) State U., 1991-97, assoc. prof. French, 1997—; tchr. summer enrichment program for gifted children Sch. Edn., Howard U., summers 1985, 86; tchr. ESL, D.C. Pub. Schs., summer, 1989, 94; asst. coord. Humanities Immersion Program, Project Access for H.S. Students, Bowie State U., summer 1997-98; vice-chmn. World Centennial Conf.; French, Am. and Planetary Dimensions of Saint-John Perse, U. D.C., 1987; mem. adv. coun. Northeast Conf. Teaching Fgn. Langs; NAACP-ACT-SO competition humanities judge 1997—; adj. assoc. prof. English, Southeastern U. Washington, summer 1998—; presenter, book reviewer in field. Author: The Prose Works of Saint-John Perse: Towards an Understanding of His Poetry, 1994; contbr. articles to profl. jours. Active Assn. Democratique des Francais a L.Etranger, 1988—, Senegal friendship com. Office Cmty. and Ethnic Affairs, Prince George's County Govt., Md., 1993-94, Inst. for Haitian Cultural and Sci. Affairs, 1992-94, local arrangements com. Conf. Coll. Composition and Communication, Washington, 1995, Friends of the Corcoran, 1999—; membership com. and outreach com. St. John's Ch., Washington, 1993, ch. growth com., 1995. With U.S . Army, 1964-66. Mem. MLA, Coll. Lang. Assn., Middle Atlantic Writers Assn. (chmn. essay contest com. 1995—), Samuel Beckett Soc., Societe des Professeurs Francais et Francophones d'Amerique, Zora Neale Hurston Soc., Am. Assn. Tchrs. French (sec.-treas. Washington chpt. 1986-90), Nat. Cathedral Assn., Md. Fgn. Lang. Assn. (bd. dirs.), Friends Superior Ct. Washington D.C. (bd. dirs.), Univ. Club (Washington), Pi Delta Phi, Sigma Tau Delta. Democrat. *Episcopalian. Avocations: classical music, history, travel. Home: 4235 Alton Pl NW Washington DC 20016-2017 Office: Bowie State U Dept English & Modern Langs Bowie MD 20715

STERLING OF PLAISTOW, BARON JEFFREY MAURICE, transportation company executive; b. Dec. 27, 1934; s. Harry and Alice Sterling; m. Dorothy Ann Smith, 1985; 1 child. Ed., Guildhall Sch. Music, London; D (hon.) in Bus. Adminstrn., Nottingham Trent U., 1995; D (hon.) in Civil Law, Durham U., 1996. With Paul Schweder and Co., stock exch., 1955-57, G. Eberstadt & Co., 1957-62; fin. dir. Gen. Guarantee Corp., 1962-64; mng. dir. Gula Investments Ltd., 1964-69; chmn. Sterling Guarantee Trust plc (now merged with Peninsular and Oriental Steam Nav. Co.), from 1969; exec. Peninsular and Oriental Steam Nav. Co., London, 1980—, chmn., 1983—; spl. adviser to sec. state for industry, 1982-83, for trade and industry, 1983-90; pres. Gen. Coun. Brit. Shipping, 1990-91, European Cmty. Shipowners' Assns., 1992-94. Freeman City of London; elder bro. Trinity House, 1991; chmn. bd. govs. Royal Ballet Sch., 1983-99; bd. govs. Royal Ballet, 1986-99; chmn. Young Vic Co., 1975-83; vice chmn. Motability, 1977-95, chmn., 1995—; chmn. organizing com. World ORT Union, 1969-73, mem. exec. com., 1966—, mem. tech. svcs. com., 1974—; v.p. Brit. ORT, 1978; dep. chmn., hon. reas. London celebrations com. Queen's Silver Jubilee, 1975-83. Decorated knight and comdr. Order of Brit. Empire, knight in the Order of St. John, 1998; created baron life peer of Pall Mall in City of Westminster, 1991. Fellow Inst. Marine Engrs. (hon.), Inst. Chartered Shipbrokers (hon.), Inst. of Surveyors Valuers and Auctioneers; mem. Royal Inst. Chartered Surveyors (hon.), Royal Naval Reserve (hon.), Garrick Club, Carlton Club, Hurlingham Club. Avocations: music, swimming, tennis. Office: The Peninsular And Oriental Steam Nav Co, 79 Pall Mall, London SW1Y 5EJ, England

STERMER, DUGALD ROBERT, designer, illustrator, writer, consultant; b. Los Angeles, Dec. 17, 1936; s. Robert Newton and Mary (Blue) S.; m. Jeanie Kortum; children: Dugald, Megan, Chris, Colin, Crystal. B.A., UCLA, 1960. Art dir., v.p. Ramparts mag., 1965-70; freelance designer, illustrator, writer, cons. San Francisco, 1970—; founder Pub. Interest Communications, San Francisco, 1974; chmn. illustration dept. Calif. Coll. Arts and Crafts, 1994—; bd. dirs. Am. Inst. Graphic Arts, Illustration Partnership Am.; mem. San Francisco Art Commn., 1997—. Cons. editor: Communication Arts mag., 1974-90; designer: Oceans mag., 1976-82; editor: The Environment, 1972, Vanishing Creatures, 1980; author: The Art of Revolution, 1970, Vanishing Creatures, 1980, Vanishing Flora, 1994, Birds and Bees, 1994; designer 1984 Olympic medals; illustration exhbn. Calif. Acad. Scis., 1986; one-man show Jernigan Wicker Gallery, San Francisco, 1996. Mem. Grand Jury City and County San Francisco, 1989; bd. dirs. Delancey St. Found., 1990—. Recipient various medals, awards for design and illustration nat. and internat. competitions. Office: 600 The Embarcadero # 204 San Francisco CA 94107-2121

STERN, DAVID HOWARD, physician, journalist; b. Oakland, Calif., Nov. 8, 1959; s. Richard Ian and Judith Kay (Putzier) S.; m. Lan Thi Nguyen, June 29, 1996; 1 child, My Linh Saré. BS in Life Sci., U. Nebr., 1982; MD, U. Nebr., Omaha, 1986. Diplomate Am. Bd. Family Practice. Internship, resident U. Calif., L.A., 1986-89; ind. contractor So. Calif., 1988-93; assoc. Western Medical Group, Torrance, Calif., 1993-96; pvt. practice Torrance, Calif., 1996—; cons. Western Medical Group, Torrance, 1994-96; asst. dir. Centrala Hosp. Airport Medical, El Segundo, Calif., 1995-96. Contbr. articles to profl. jours.; editor Aspartame Advisory, 1997, Deep Times News Service, 1994-98. Founder Deep Politics Virtual Network, Internet, 1998; active Citizens for Truth in Kennedy Assasination, L.A., 1993—. Mem. Am. Assn. Family Practice (Calif. chpt.), Am. Assn. Physicians Surgeons, Am. Booksellers Assn., Am. Soc. Profl. Journalists, Union Am. Physicians Dentists. Mem. Zen Judaism Ch. Avocations: writing, photography, poetry, biking, computer system building. Home: PO Box 4270 Torrance CA 90510-4270

STERN, ERNEST, trust company executive. BA in Internat. Rels., Queens Coll., 1955; MA in Internat. Econs., Fletcher Sch. of Law and Diplomacy, 1956, PhD, 1964. Economist U.S. Dept. Commerce, 1957-59; program economist USAID, Turkey, 1959-68; asst. adminstr. policy and program adminstrn. USAID, 1968-72; sr. adv. office of the econ. adv. to the pres. World Bank Group, 1972, also dep. chmn. econs. com., dir.-devel. policy, 1974, v.p. South Asia region, 1975, v.p. ops., 1978, sr. v.p. ops., 1980, sr. v.p. fin., 1987, mng. dir., 1991-95, acting pres., 1995; mng. dir., corp. office sr. client relationship mgr. Morgan Guaranty Trust Co. N.Y. (subs. J.P. Morgan & Co. Inc), N.Y.C., 1995—; instr. dept. econs. and stats. Middle East Tech. U., Ankara, Turkey, 1960-61; lectr. Woodrow Wilson Sch. of Pub. and Internat. Affairs, Princeton U., 1971; trustee CommonFund Capital, Inc. Mem. internat. adv. bd. U. Pa. Ctr. for Advanced Study of India; mem. adv. com. Econ. Growth Ctr., Yale U.; trustee Endowment Advisors; mem. Group of Thirty. Mem. Coun. Fgn. Rels. Office: JP Morgan & Co Inc Morgan Guaranty Trust Co of NY 60 Wall St New York NY 10260-0001

STERN, GARY HILTON, bank executive, economist; b. San Luis Obispo, Calif., Nov. 3, 1944; s. Robert Earl and Joy Merdis (Shimon) S.; m. Mary Katherine Nelson, Aug. 17, 1969; children: Matthew Stuart, Meredith Faulkner. A.B., Washington U., St. Louis, 1967; M.A., Rice U., 1970, Ph.D., 1972. Economist Fed. Res. Bank of N.Y., N.Y.C., 1970-73, mgr. domestic research, 1973-77; mgr. fixed income research Loeb Rhoades, Hornblower, N.Y.C., 1977-78; sr. economist A.G. Shilling & Co., N.Y.C., 1978-81; sr. v.p. Fed. Res. Bank of Mpls., 1982-85, pres., 1985—; adj. assoc. prof. NYU, 1980-82; adj. asst. prof. Columbia U., 1976-79. Author: In the Name of Money, 1980. Trustee West Side Montessori Sch., N.Y.C., 1978-79. NDEA scholar, 1969-70; Bache & Co. scholar, 1963-67; univ. scholar Washington U.-St. Louis, 1964-67, Rice U.-Houston, 1967-70. Office: Fed Res Bank of Mpls PO Box 291 90 Hennepin Ave Minneapolis MN 55480-0291*

STERN, GEOFFREY HOWARD, educator; b. Liverpool, England, Feb. 5, 1935; s. Malcolm and Rose (Coleman) S.; m. Elisabeth Tucker, Sept. 4, 1967 (div. 1987); children: Tiffany, Jonathon. BS, London Sch. Econs., 1957. Lectr. Kilburn Polytech, 1958-59; asst. lectr. London Sch. Econs., 1960-62, lectr., 1962-95, sr. lectr., 1995—; coord. World Politics Dipl., 1980—; radio presenter and commentator. Author: The Rise and Decline of International Communism, 1990, Communism: An Illustrated History from 1848 to the Present Day, 1991, Leaders and Leadership, 1993, The Structure of International Soc., 2000. Avocations: musical composition, jazz piano, concerts, cabaret, cooking. Home: 8 Cyprus Rd, London N3 3RY, England Office: London Sch Econs, Houghton St, London WC2A 2AE, England

STERN, HAROLD PETER, business executive; b. Frankfurt, Germany, Oct. 16, 1923; s. Hugo H. and Lily C. (Strauss) S.; m. Annette B. Kaplan, Nov. 28, 1958; children: Steven B., Eric K., Robert (dec.). Student, NYU, Columbia U., 1940-43. V.p., pres. Rector Internat. Corp., Mt. Vernon, N.Y., 1948—, Rector Internat. Equipment Corp., Mt. Vernon, N.Y., 1984—, Rector Mineral Trading Corp., Mt. Vernon, N.Y., 1948—; exec. sec. Cork Inst. Am., N.Y.C. Elected to Rep. State Com., Albany, N.Y.; vice chmn. Rep. Town Com., Harrison, N.Y.; mem. Nat. Coun./Small Bus. Adminstrn., Washington; commr./chmn. Westchester County Police Bd. Lt. Col. N.Y. Guard. Recipient John Egar Hoover Gold medal Am. Police Hall of Fame, Excellent Police Duty medal Nat. Assn. Chiefs of Police, Police Disting. Svc. medal Westchester County Dept. Pub. Safety, Westchester County Disting. Svc. medal Westchester County Exec. Fellow Nat. Law Enforcement Acad. (hon.). Avocations: boating, skiing, hunting, fishing. Office: Rector Internat Corp 9030 Lakes Blvd West Palm Beach FL 33412-1560

STERN, ISAAC, violinist, performing arts executive; b. Kreminiecz, Russia, July 21, 1920; came to U.S., 1921; s. Solomon and Clara S.; m. Nora Kaye, Nov. 10, 1948; m. Vera Lindenblit, Aug. 17, 1951; children: Shira, Michael, David; m. Linda Reynolds, Nov. 3, 1996. Student, San Francisco Conservatory, 1930-37; numerous hon. degrees including, Dalhousie U., 1971, U. Hartford, 1971, Bucknell U., 1974, Hebrew U., Jerusalem, 1975, Yale U., 1975, Columbia U., 1977, Johns Hopkins U., 1979, U. Md., 1983, Tel Aviv U., 1983, NYU, 1989, U. Ill., 1992, Harvard U., 1992. Pres. Carnegie Hall, N.Y.C. Recital debut San Francisco, 1934; orchestral debut San Francisco Symphony Orch. (Pierre Monteux condr.), 1936; N.Y. debut, 1937; Carnegie Hall recital debut, 1943; N.Y. Philharm. debut (Arthur Rodzinski condr.), 1944; participated Prades Festival with Pablo Casals, 1950-52; soloist for first orchestral and recital performances at Kennedy Ctr., Washington; first Am. to perform in USSR after World War II, 1956; mem. Istomin-Rose-Stern trio, 1962-83 (Beethoven cycle w/Istomin & Rose 1970-71); performed in China at invitation of Chinese govt., 1979; performed world premieres of violin works by Bernstein, Dutilleux, Hindemith, Maxwell Davies, Penderecki, Rochberg and Schuman; has played with major orchestras, given countless recitals and performed at important festivals in the U.S., Europe, Israel, Far East, Australia and S. Am. Over 150 records, cassettes and CD's for CBS Masterworks, named Artist Laureate 1984 CBS Masterworks; made soundtrack for motion pictures Humoresque (Warner Bros.) and Fiddler on the Roof (United Artists); starred in soundtrack Tonight We Sing (20th Century Fox) and Journey to Jerusalem with Leonard Bernstein; documentary film From Mao to Mozart-Isaac Stern in China (Academy award 1981, Cannes Film Festival Special Mention), Carnegie Hall: The Grand Reopening, 1987 (Emmy award), Isaac Stern-A Life, 1991; author: My First 79 Years, 1999. Chmn. emeritus Am.-Israel Cultural Found.; founder Jerusalem Music Ctr.; originating mem. Nat. Endowment for the Arts; pres. Carnegie Hall, N.Y.C., 1960—. Decorated comdr. Order de la Couronne, comdr. Legion d'Honneur; comdr.'s cross (Order of Dannebrog (Denmark); recipient numerous Grammy awards, Grammy Lifetime Achievement award, 1987, Hall of Fame Induction medal Am. Classical Music, Nat. medal of Honor, 1991, Presdl. medal of Freedom, 1992, numerous local city awards, Gold Rays with Neck Ribbon Japan's Order of the Rising Sun, 1998; named Musician of Yr., ABC/Musical Am., 1986; Fellow of Jerusalem, 1986. Office: ICM Artists Ltd 40 W 57th St Fl 16 New York NY 10019-4098

STERN, JACQUES, information systems specialist; b. Paris, France, Mar. 21, 1932; s. Leon and Dora (Braejman) S.; m. Janine Riemer, Dec. 12, 1956; children: Marc-Henri, Paul-Eric, Laurent. Degree in engring., Ecole Poly., Sur'aero; MS, Harvard U. Mem. air def. computer sys. French Air, 1958-64; pres., founder Soc. d'Etudes des Systems d'Automation, 1964; chair, CEO BULL, 1980, hon. pres., 1989; chmn. Honeywell Bull Inc., 1987; founder Stern Computer Sys., 1989—; founder, pres. SYCOMORE, 1991—, Stern Sys. Info., 1997, SYNESYS, 1998—. Author numerous tech. books. Decorated Officer Ordre Nat. du Merite, Chevalier, Legion d'Honneur. Mem. Acad. Scis. Applications, Found. Fyssen (v.p.). Office: SYNESYS, 12 Boulevard des Iles, 92441 Issy les Moulineaux France

STERN, JAMES COPER, sales executive; b. N.Y.C., Dec. 12, 1925; s. George Charles and Ruth (Coper) S.; m. Judith Vinson, Oct. 31, 1963 (div. Mar. 1974); children: Hillary Anne, Renee Jean; m. Ruth Nussbacker Szold, Aug. 22, 1982. BA, NYU, 1949. Trainee, exec. asst. Gardner Advt. Co., N.Y.C., 1949-50; advt. mgr. NOPCO Chem. Co., Harrison, N.J., 1950-53; account exec. Ziv TV Programs, N.Y.C., 1954-56; sales rep. United Artists Associated, N.Y.C., 1957-61; v.p., sales mgr. Allied Artists TV, N.Y.C., 1961-70; exec. v.p., gen. sales mgr. ITC Entertainment, Inc., Studio City, Calif., 1970-89; pres. JCS Syndication Svcs., L.A., 1990—. Cpl. U.S. Army, 1944-46, ETO. Mem. Internat. Radio and TV Soc., Nat. Assn. TV Program Execs., Ind. TV Program Execs. Republican. Jewish. Avocations: watercolor painting, skiing, golf, art. Home: 8455 Fountain Ave Apt 515 Los Angeles CA 90069-2543 Office: JCS Syndication Svcs 8455 Fountain Ave Apt 515 Los Angeles CA 90069-2543

STERN, JOANNE THRASHER, elementary school educator; b. Norfolk, Va., Oct. 18, 1932; d. Thomas Williams and Mary Ellen Thrasher; m. Milford Josiah Stern, Apr. 29, 1956; children: Milford J. III, Thomas Thrasher, William Byrd. BS, James Madison U., 1952; MEd, U. Va., 1963. Cert. elem. tchr. Tchr. 5th grade City of Chesapeake, 1952-54; tchr. Va. Beach Pub. Schs., 1957-60, Norfolk (Va.) City Pub. Schs., 1966-68; life insurance agent Spain, 1977-78; tchr. Def. Dependent Schs., Fed. Republic Germany, 1985; tchr. English Madison Middle Sch., 1987-89; tchr. ESOL 1st grade, 1988-91; 1st grade tchr., reading tchr. Toussaint Louverture Elem. Sch., 1989-2000; tchr. grade 2 Campbell Dr. Elem. Sch., Homestead, Fla., 2000—; real estate agent Gregory Realty Corp., 1964-83; tchr. English Nan Ping Tchrs. Coll., summer 1993; tchr. piano Hess Conservatory Music, 1997—. Organist 1st Bapt. Ch. of North Miami Beach (Fla.); tchr. Holiday Bible Club, Pembrokeshire, Wales, 1996. Mem. AAUW, Women Leaders Round Table (life), Chesapeake Bay Bus. and Profl. Women, Kappa Delta Pi. Home: 225 Saint Croix Pl Key Largo FL 33037-4316

STERN, JOHN PETER, association executive; b. N.Y.C., Nov. 8, 1954; s. Walter and Marion (Tyson) S.; m. Sakumi Murakami, Mar. 17, 1982; children: George, Ken. AB summa cum laude, Princeton U., 1976; JD, Harvard U., 1979. Bar: Calif. 1980, N.Y. 1984, D.C. 1985; lic. real estate broker, Calif. With Graham & James, L.A., 1981-84; exec. dir. U.S. Electronics Industry Office, Tokyo, 1984-88; v.p. Asian ops. Am. Electronics Assn., Tokyo, 1988-95; sr. v.p. Asian Tech. Info. Prog., Tokyo, 1996—; speaker Deming Quality Control Awards Ceremonies, 1988; bd. dirs. Telecommunication Tech. Com., 1985—; mem. Japan Indsl. Standards Optoelectronic Tech. Com., Tokyo, 1987—, Telecommunications Tech. Study Coun. Standards Policy Working Group, 1990-96; mem. Japanese Ministry of Posts and Telecommunications Future Broadcast Satellite Procurement Study Group, 1990-91; testified before U.S. Senate, 1989; mem. Japan Indsl. Standards Info. Tech. Div. Coun., Tokyo, 1991—; advisor Walter F. Mondale, U.S. Amb. to Japan, 1993-96. Author: The Japanese Interpretation of the "Law of Nations", 1854-1874, 1979; editor: Yearbook of Japanese Data Transmission and Telecommunications, 1994; contbr. monthly column to newspaper, 1988; contbg. author: Interfirm Production Supply Systems, 1989, The Business Guide to Japan, 1996, The Bureaucrats' SuperPower, 1996, Japan's Technical Standards: Implications for Global Trade and Competitiveness, 1997, Unlocking the Bureaucrat's Kingdom: Deregulation and the Japanese Economy, 1998. Lectr., U.S. Info. Svc., Japan, 1985—; mem. Bilateral Working Group on Symmetrical Access, Washington, 1988; trustee, Princeton in Asia, 1980-85. Telecom Day award Japanese Ministry Posts and Telecomm., 1992. Mem. State Bar Calif., State Bar N.Y., Bar of D.C., Am. Arbitration Assn. (internat. arbitration panel 1983—), Tokyo Am. Club, Fgn. Corr. Club Japan. Fax: 81-3-3484-8366. E-mail: jme@consultant.com. Office: Soshigaya 3-11-1-404, Setagaya-ku Tokyo 157-0072, Japan

STERN, KURT, pathologist, educator; b. Vienna, Apr. 3, 1909; arrived in Israel, 1969; s. Leopold and Elsa (Heller) S.; m. Florence Shirley Sherman, May 28, 1939 (dec. May 1989); children: Elsa Libby, Josef Judah, David Michael. MD, U. Vienna, 1933. Cert. Am. Bd. Pathology. Resident physician State Inst. Study Malignant Disease, Buffalo, N.Y., 1943-45; asst. pathologist Mt. Sinai Hosp., Chgo., 1945-60; assoc. prof. pathology Chgo. Med. Sch., 1949-60; prof. pathology U. Ill. Sch. Medicine, Chgo., 1960-69; prof. life scis. Bar-Ilan U., Ramat-Gan, Israel, 1969-80; rsch. prof. Hebrew U., Hadassah Med. Sch., Jerusalem, 1980—; assoc. dir. rsch. Mt. Sinai Med. Rsch. Found., Chgo., 1946-60; dir. Blood Ctr., Mt. Sinai Hosp., Chgo., 1950-60. Co-author: Die Wege and Ergebnisse Chemisher Krebs Forschung, 1936, Biochemistry of Malignant Tumors, 1943; contbr. articles to profl. jours. and chpts. to books. Recipient Disting. Svc. award Am. Soc. Clin. Pathologists, 1968, Disting. Svc. award Am. Assn. Blood Banks, 1968, John Elliott Meml. award, 1972, award Internat. Soc. Blood Transfusions, 1999. Fellow AAAS, Am. Soc. Clin. Pathologists, N.Y. Acad. Sci. Home: 22 Pinsker St Apt 3, 92228 Jerusalem Israel Office: Hebrew U Hadassah Med Sch, PO Box 12272, 91120 Jerusalem Israel

STERN, PAUL CLINTON, social scientist; b. N.Y.C., Dec. 23, 1944; s. Sydney Clinton and Anne Lillian (Schechtman) S.; m. Susan Parkison, July 13, 1968; 1 child, Sarah R. (dec.). BA, Amherst Coll., 1964; MA, Clark U., 1969, PhD, 1975. From instr. to asst. prof. psychology Elmira (N.Y.) Coll., 1971-78; postdoctoral fellow, rsch. assoc. Yale U., New Haven, Conn., 1978-80; study dir., prin. staff officer U.S. Nat. Rsch. Coun., Washington, 1980—; rsch. prof. sociology George Mason U., Fairfax, Va., 1993—; pres. Social and Environ. Rsch. Inst., Leverett, Mass., 1996—; peer ptnr. Danish Environ. Rsch. Program, Denmark, 1997. Author: (book) Evaluating Social Science Research, 1979, (with others) Home Energy Conservation: Issues and Programs for the 1980s, 1981, Environmental Problems and Human Behavior, 1996, Evaluating Social Science Research, 2d edit., 1996; editor: (with others) Energy Use: The Human Dimension, 1984, Improving Energy Demand Analysis, 1984, Energy Efficiency in Buildings: Behavioral Issues, 1985, Perspectives on Deterrence, 1989, Behavior, Society, and Nuclear War, vol. 1, 1989, vol. 2, 1991, vol. 3, 1993, Global Environmental Change: Understanding the Human Dimensions, 1992, Perspectives on Nationalism and War, 1995, Understanding Risk: Informing Decisions in a Democratic Society, 1996, Environmentally Significant Consumption: Research Directions, 1997, People and Pixels: Linking Remote Sensing and Social Science, 1998, Making Climate Forecasts Matter, 1999, The Aging Mind: Opportunities in Cognitive Research, 2000, International Conflict Resolution After the Cold War, 2000; co-editor: Jour. Socio-Econs., 1991-98; assoc. editor: (jours.) Evaluation Rev., 1986-89, Environment and Behavior, 1997—; contbr. articles to profl. jours., chpts. to books. Fellow AAAS, APA; mem. Soc. for Psychol. Study of Social Issues, Soc. for Personality and Social Psychology, Soc. for Human Ecology. E-mail: pstern@nas.edu. Office: Nat Rsch Coun 2101 Constitution Ave NW Washington DC 20418-0007

STERN, ROBERT C., physician, educator; b. N.Y.C., Dec. 13, 1938; s. Samuel and Lily S. BA, Drew U., 1959; MD, Albert Einstein Coll. Medicine, 1963. Diplomate Nat. Bd. Med. Examiners, Am. Bd. Pediat., Am. Bd. Pediatric Pulmonology. Intern pediat. U. Hosps. Cleve., Babies and

Childrens Hosp. Divsn., 1963-64, jr. asst. resident pediat., 1964-65; sr. asst. resident pediat. Bronx Mcpl. Hosp. Ctr., N.Y.C., 1965-66; fellow cystic fibrosis/pediat. pulmonary diseases Case Western Res. U. Sch. Medicine, Cleve., 1968-70; sr. instr. pediat. Case Western Res. U., Cleve., 1970-71, asst. prof., 1971-77, assoc. prof., 1977-83, prof., 1983—; cons. Cystic Fibrosis Founds. various countries, 1990—, various pharm. and med. tech. cos., 1990—. Author: Treatment of Hospitalized Cystic Fibrosis Patients, 1998, Treatment of Cystic Fibrosis, 2000; contbr. numerous chpts. to Nelson's Textbook of Pediatrics, 1979—, also over 100 articles to med. jours. Pres. Children's Lung Found., Cleve., 1983—. Capt. USAF, 1966-68. Recipient David Stuckert award Cystic Fibrosis Rsch. Inst., San Francisco, 1997. Mem. Am. Thoracic Soc., Soc. Pediat. Rsch., Am. Pediat. Soc. Achievements include introduction of heparin lock for intermittent administration of intravenous drugs; research in cystic fibrosis. Avocations: reading, running, chess, writing humor, mathematics. Home: 2300 Overlook Rd Apt 406 Cleveland Hts OH 44106-2391 Office: Univ Hosp Cleve 11100 Euclid Ave Cleveland OH 44106-1736

STERN, S(EESA) BEATRICE, executive secretary, registered nurse; b. Atlantic City, Feb. 13, 1919; d. Max and Gussie (Thierman) Rosen; m. Francis H. Stern, June 29, 1958 (dec. Feb. 1973); m. Bernard N. Abelson, Dec. 5, 1973 (div. Feb. 1992). AA, Miami-Dade C.C., Fla., 1982, AS in Nursing, 1982. RN, Fla., N.J., Nev. Sec. N.J. State Highway Dept., Trenton, 1938-41; columnist N.J. Herald, Trenton, 1939-41; sec. U.S. Army, various locations, 1941-46; legal sec. Gus Feuer, Atty. at Law, Miami, 1946-47; exec. sec. to pres. Pharms., Inc., N.Y.C., 1947-58; med. sec. Phila., 1958-72; nurse Mt. Sinai Med. Ctr., Miami Beach, Fla., 1982-83, Atlantic City Med. Ctr., 1983-84. Vol. Hollywood Med. Ctr., 1992-96, Aventura Med. Ctr., 1992—; mem. bd. govs. Brith Sholom, 1970—. Mem. Brith Sholom Women (nat. pres. 1970-72), Phi Theta Kappa. Avocations: swimming, handcrafts, reading, crossword puzzles.

STERN, THOMAS LEE, physician, educator, medical association administrator; b. San Francisco, Jan. 14, 1920; s. Bernard Michael and Alice Sarah (Halberstadt) S.; m. Gladys Crawford, June 26, 1944; children: Donnel Bernard, Lee Crawford, Pamela Ann. BS, Willamette U., 1947; MD, U. Oreg., 1950; DSc (hon.), Med. Coll. Ohio, 1982. Rotating intern St. Vincents Hosp., 1950-51, resident in general surgery, 1951-52; tech. advisor Marcus Welby M.D.-TV, Universal City, Calif., 1970-75; residency dir. Santa Monica (Calif.) Hosp., 1969-74; lectr. preventive and social medicine UCLA, L.A., 1970-73; v.p. Am. Acad. Family Physicians, Kansas City, Mo., 1974-83; assoc. prof. family medicine Kans. U. Med. Ctr., Kansas City, 1975-83; pres. Internat. Ctr. for Family Medicine, Buenos Aires, 1982-83; prof. family medicine U. Fla. Med. Ctr., Gainesville, 1983-86; v.p. Am. Acad. Family Physicians Found., Kansas City, 1983-91, audio tape editor, 1991-97; cons. U.S. Naval Med. Corps, U.S. Army Med. Corps, Washington, 1975-82. Author: House Calls, Recollections of a Family Physician, 2000. With USN, 1941-45, PTO. Recipient F. Marian Bishop award Soc. Tchrs. Family Medicine, 1991. Fellow Am. Acad. Family Physicians (Thomas Johnson award 1985, Award of Merit 1983, John Walsh award 1991); mem. AMA. Avocations: wine, computer. Home: 24415 S Starcrest Dr Sun Lakes AZ 85248-0884

STERN, WALTER WOLF, III, lawyer; b. Cin., Mar. 25, 1946; s. Walter W. Jr. and Harriet Louise Stern; m. Judith M. Looker, Jan. 4, 1974; 1 child, Rachael Louise. BA, Carthage Coll., 1969; JD, Marquette U., 1974. Bar: Wis. 1974, U.S. Dist. Ct. (ea. and we. dists.) Wis. 1974, U.S. Ct. Appeals (7th cir.) 1981, U.S. Supreme Ct. 1983. Pvt. practice Kenosha, Wis., 1974-82, 85-91; sr. ptnr. Joling Rizzo Willems Stern & Burroughs, Kenosha, 1982-85; pvt. practice Union Grove, Wis., 1991—; lectr. criminal law Carthage Coll., Kenosha, Wis., 1976—. Educator, Domestic Violence Project, Kenosha, 1983-94; hearing examiner Gen. Relief, Kenosha, 1990-95. Fellow Am. Acad. Forensic Scis. Avocations: fishing, hunting, jogging, reading, creative writing. Office: Atty at Law PO Box 64 Union Grove WI 53182-0064

STERNBERG, AHUD, surgeon, surgical oncologist, educator; b. Haifa, Israel, May 27, 1945; s. Aharon and Shifra (Tamshes) S.; m. Meira Behrman, Sept. 22, 1971; children: Itay Aharon, Assaf. MD, Hebrew U., Jerusalem, 1969; MSurg, Tel Aviv U., 1981. Cert. in gen. surgery, Israel. Intern Beilinson Med. Ctr., Petah-Tikva, Israel, 1970, resident dept. surgery B, 1974-80, sr. surgeon, 1980-88; clin. fellow Roswell Park Cancer Inst., Buffalo, 1982-84; chief dept. surgery Hillel Jaffe Med. Ctr., Hadera, Israel, 1988—; sr. lectr. Tel Aviv U. Sackler Faculty Medicine, 1990—; sr. surg. cons. Meuchedet Sick Fund, Israel, 1991—; presenter in field at nat. and internat. confs.; mem. Bd. for Accreditation of Gen. Surgery Residency, Israel, 1991—. Contbr. over 150 articles to med. jours. Maj. Israel Def. Forces, 1971-74; mem. Res. 1963-70, 74-96. Recipient best clin. rsch. award Roswell Park Cancer Inst., 1983; scholar Hebrew U.-Hadassah Med. Sch., 1964-69. Mem. Israel Med. Assn. (bd. examiners for cert. in surgery 1990—), Israeli Surg. Soc. (coun. 1994-97, exec. com. 1997—, Milwiczki award 1982), Israeli Soc. Surg. Oncology (treas. 1998—), Israel Soc. Colorectal Surgery, Israel Soc. Preventive Oncology, Israel Trauma Soc., Israel Soc. Endoscopic Surgery, Am. Soc. Clin. Oncology, European Soc. Surg. Oncology, Roswell Park Surg. Soc., European Sch. Oncology Alumni Club. Jewish. Achievements include creation of new staging system for curatively resected colorectal cancer. Avocations: classical music, painting. Fax: 972-6-6331775. ote, hospital committees are not listed, per style. Home: 3 Moshe Sharet St, 38512 Hadera Israel Office: Hillel Jaffe Med Ctr, Dept Surgery A, 38100 Hadera Israel

STERNBERG, ESTHER MAY, neuroendocrinologist, immunologist, rheumatologist; b. Montreal, May 9, 1951; came to U.S., 1980, naturalized, 1991; d. Joseph and Ghitta (Wexler) Sternberg; 1 child, Penny Rebecca Herscovitch. BSc with great distinction, McGill U., 1972, MD, 1974. Diplomate Nat. Bd. Med. Examiners; lic. physician, Can., Mo. Intern Royal Victoria Hosp./McGill U., Montreal, 1974-75, resident II in medicine, 1977-78, clin. fellow rheumatology, 1978-79, clin. and rsch. fellow rheumatology, 1979-80; gen. practice medicine Mount Royal, Que., 1975-77; rsch. assoc. divsn. allergy/clin. immunology Washington U., St. Louis, 1981-83, rsch. assoc. Howard Hughes Med. Inst., 1983-84, assoc. Howard Hughes Med. Inst., 1984-86, instr. divs. rheumatology, 1984-86; attending physician Barnes Hosp., St. Louis, 1984-86; vis. scientist Nat. Inst. Arthritis, Musculoskeletal and Skin Disease/NIH, Bethesda, Md., 1987-90; tenured sr. scientist NIMH/NIH, Bethesda, 1991—, med. officer, chief unit on neuroendocrine immunology, 1991-95, assoc. br. chief clin. neuroendocrinology br., 1994-2000, med. officer, chief sect. neuroendocrine immunology, 1995—; dir. integrative neural-immune program NIMH/NIH, 1999—; vis. scientist NIAMS, NIH and head Inter-Inst. Unit on Neuroendocrine Immunology and Behavior, NIMH and Nat. Inst. Arthritis, Musculoskeletal and Skin Diseases, Bethesda, 1989-90; rsch. full prof. Am. U., Washington, 1995—; temporary advisor WHO, 1991; ad hoc mem. NIH/NIMH/Libr. Congress Human Genome Project liaison com., 1990-91; invited expert CDC, Atlanta, 1989-93; spl. cons. Inst. Health (Hygienic) Scis., Min. of Health, Japan, 1992-94; med. adv. bd. Scleroderma Fedn., 1993-95; cons. John D. and Catherine T. MacArthur Found. Network on Mind-Body Interactions, 1994—; participant WHO/Pan Am. Health Orgn. Collaborating Ctr. for Health of the Elderly Work Group meeting, 1995; mem. com. on military nutrition rsch. Inst. of Medicine of NAS, 1998—; advisor Nat. Libr. of Medicine Planning Com., Breath of Life: An Exhbn. on Asthma, 1997-98, NIMH/NIH Ctr. for Sci. Rev., 1998; reviewer FDA's Office of Women's Health, 1998; co-dir. Exhibition on Emotions and Disease Nat. Libr. Medicine, 1996-97, others; co-chair/chair/organizer numerous confs. Author: The Balance Within. The Science Connecting Health and Emotions; editl. bd. Brain, Behavior and Immunity, Jour. Neuroimmunology, Neuroimmunomodulation, Molecular Psychiatry, Immunologic Rsch.; invited guest series editor Jour. Clin. Investigation, 1997; reviewer Jour. Clin. Investigation, New Eng. Jour. Medicine, Jour. Immunology, Endocrinology, Jour. Clin. Endocrinology and Metabolism, Arthritis and Rheumatism, Am. Jour. Physiology, Jour. Neuroimmunology, Brain, Behavior and Immunity; editor: Stress: Mechanisms and Clinical Implications, 1995, Neuroimmune Interactions: Molecular, Integrative Systems and Clinical Implications, 1998; assoc. editor Brain, Behavior and Immunity, Neuroimmunomodulation; contbr. chpts. to books and articles to profl. jours.; patentee in field. Recipient Arthritis Found. Met. Washington William R. Felts award for excellence in rheumatology rsch. pubs., 1991, FDA Commr.'s Spl. Citation, 1991, USPHS Superior Svc. award, 1994; McGill U. scholar, 1967-68, 68-71; Am. Acad. Allergy/Schering Travel grantee, 1982, United Scleroderma Found. grantee, 1985-86, 86-87, Scleroderma Found. Greater Washington, 1987, 88; NIH New Investigator awardee, 1985-88, others. Fellow Am. Coll. Rheumatology; mem. AAAS, Soc. Neurosci., Am. Soc. Clin. Investigation, Am. Assn. Immunologists, N.Y. Acad. Scis., Can. Med. Assn., Internat. Soc. Neuroimmunology (mem. internat. adv. com. 1995), PsychoNeuroImmunology Rsch. Soc. (councillor 1997—), Soc. for Neuroimmunomodulation (sec. 1997-99, pres. 2000—). Fax: 301-402-1561. E-mail: ems@codon.nih.gov. Office: NIMH/NIH 10 Center Dr Msc 1284 Bldg 10 Bethesda MD 20892-0001

STERNBERG, HILGARD O'REILLY, geographer, educator; b. Rio de Janeiro, Brazil, July 5, 1917; s. Bruno Ludwig and Johanna Mary O'Reilly (Begg) S.; m. Carolina de Silveira Lobo, July 28, 1942; children: Hilgard, Maria Inês (Mrs. Francis Anthony Mangiola), Ricardo, Leonel, Cristina (Mrs. David L. Rausch). Bacharel, U. de Brasil, 1940, Licenciado, 1941, Doutor, 1958; Ph.D., La. State U., 1956; Docteur h.c., U. Toulouse, France, 1965. Faculty U. Brazil, 1942-64, prof. geography, 1944-64; dir. Center Research in Geography of Brazil, 1951-64; prof. geography U. Calif. at Berkeley, 1964-88, prof. emeritus, 1988—; First v.p. Internat. Geog. Union, 1956-60; mem. com. research priorities in tropical biology NRC, 1977-80. Author articles, books in field. Decorated comdr. Nat. Order Merit, Order Rio Branco Nat. Order Sci. Merit, Brazil; recipient Best Publ. award Nat. Council Geog. Edn., 1966. Fellow AAAS, Calif. Acad. Scis.; mem. Brazilian Acad. Scis., Deutsche Akademie der Naturforscher Leopoldina, Assn. de Géographes Français, Assn. Am. Geographers, Assn. de Geógrafos Brasileiros, Calif. Acad. Scis.; hon. mem. Soc. de Géographie (Paris), Gesellschaft für Erdkunde zu Berlin, Soc. Serbe de Géographie; hon. corr. mem. Royal Geog. Soc., Brazilian Hist. and Geog. Inst. (com. mem.), Rio Grande do Sul Hist. and Geog. Inst. Achievements include special research on geomorphology, settlement patterns, land-use in Amazonia, climatic variability in Amazonia, N.E. Brazil, West Central Brazil; environmental impact of development especially in tropics, geography of food, historical geography. E-mail: hilgards@socrates.berkeley.edu. Home: 466 Michigan Ave Berkeley CA 94707-1738

STERNBERG, SIR SIGMUND, foundation trustee; b. Budapest, Hungary, June 2, 1921; s. Abraham and Elizabeth Sternberg; m. Hazel Everett Jones, 1970; 4 children (2 from previous marriage). Chmn. Lloyd's Underwriters, 1969—, Martin Slowe Estates Ltd., 1971—, ISYS Ltd., 1986—; former mem. London Metal Exch.; co-chmn. arbitration com. Bur. Internat. Récupération, 1966; judge Templeton Found., 1988. Rsch. gp. Labor Shadow Cabinet, 1973-74; dep. chmn. Labor Fin. and Industry Gp.; chmn. St. Charles Gp., Her Majesty's Customs, 1974, Inst. for Archaeo-Metall. Studies, Internat. Coun. Christians and Jews, Friends of Oxford Ctr. of Postgrad. Hebrew Studies; mem. N.W. Met. Regional Hosp. Bds.; v.p. Coll. Speech Therapists; pres. Voluntary Orgn. Communications and Lang.; active CRUSE Nat. Orgn. for Widowed and Their Children; hon. treas. Coun. Christians and Jews; bd. dirs. Deps. of Brit. Jews; trustee Manor House Trust, 1984—; chmn. function com. Inst. Jewish Affairs; gov. Hebrew U. Jerusalem; co-chmn. Friends of Keston Coll.; bd. mgmt. Spiro Inst.; convenor Religious Press Gp. With Brit. armed forces, 1939-45. Decorated knight comdr. Order of St. Gregory; recipient Brotherhood award NCCJ, 1980, 1st class medal with star and badge of religion Order of Orthodox Hospitallers, 1986, Silver Pontifical medal, 1986, Benemerenti medal, 1988, Gold Star of Internat. Friendship Govt. of German Dem. Republic, 1988, Order of Merit Govt. of Polandm 1989. Fellow Soc. of Co. and Comml. Accts., Royal Soc. Arts, Royal Soc. Medicine, Coll. Speech Therapists (hon.); mem. Reform Club, City Livery Club, Rotary (chmn. London chpt. 1980-83, Paul Harris fellow 1989). Avocations: golf, swimming. Office: Sternberg Ctr for Judaism, 80 East End Rd, London N3 2SY, England

STERNIK, ALEXANDER VADIMOVICH, diplomat, historian, linguist; b. Moscow, Russia, Jan. 20, 1966; came to U.S., 1998; s. Vadim Isaakovich and Iolana Vassilievna S.; m. Anna Igorevna, Dec. 5, 1992; children: Milana, Maxim. Degree in World's History, Moscow State, 1989. Interpreter Embassy of USSR to Ethiopia, Addis Abeba, 1989-91, attaché, 1991-94; third sec. Ministry of Foreign Affairs, Moscow, 1994-95, second sec., 1995-97, first sec., 1997-98; first sec. Permanent Mission of the Russian Fedn. to UN, N.Y.C., 1998—. Avocations: horseback riding, swimming, bodybuilding. Office: Permanent Mission of the Russian Fedn to UN 136 E 67th St New York NY 10021-6137

STERRETT, JAMES MELVILLE, accountant, business consultant; b. Chicago, Dec. 25, 1949; s. James McAnlis and Antoinette (Galligan) S.; m. Joyce Mieko Motoda, Sept. 1, 1989; 1 child, Victoria Hanako. BS in Acctg., Chaminade U., Honolulu, 1988; MBA, Chaminade U., 1991. CPA, Hawaii. Cons. Profitability Cons., Honolulu, 1985-87; pres. Sterrett Cons. Group, Honolulu, 1987-88; auditor Deloitte & Touche, Honolulu, 1988-90; acct., cons. pvt. practice, Honolulu, 1990—. Mem. Nat. Soc. Pub. Accts., Nat. Assn. Tax Practitioners, Hawaii Soc. CPA's, Delta Epsilon, Sigma. Office: 1314 S King St Ste 855 Honolulu HI 96814-1979

STERRETT, SAMUEL BLACK, lawyer, former judge; b. Washington, Dec. 17, 1922; s. Henry Hatch Dent and Helen (Black) S.; m. Jeane McBride, Aug. 27, 1949; children: Samuel Black, Robin Dent, Douglas McBride. Student, St. Albans Sch., 1933-41; grad., U.S. Mcht. Marine Acad., 1945; BA, Amherst Coll., 1947; LLB, U. Va., 1950; LLM in Taxation, NYU, 1959. Bar: D.C. 1951, Va. 1950. Atty. Alvord & Alvord, Washington, 1950-56; trial atty. Office Regional Counsel, Internal Revenue Service, N.Y.C., 1956-60; ptnr. Sullivan, Shea & Kenney, Washington, 1960-68; municipal cons. to office vice pres. U.S., 1965-68; judge U.S. Tax Ct., 1968-88, chief judge, 1985-88; ptnr. Myerson, Kuhn & Sterrett, Washington, 1988-89; of counsel Vinson & Elkins, Washington, 1990—. Bd. mgrs. Chevy Chase Village, 1970-74, chmn., 1972-74; 1st v.p. bd. trustees, mem. exec. com. Washington Hosp. Center, 1969-79, chmn. bd. trustees, 1979-84, mem. bd. trustees, 1999—; chmn. bd. trustees Washington Healthcare Corp., 1982-87; chmn. bd. trustees Medlantic Healthcare Group, 1987-89; mem. audit com. Medstar Health, 1990—; mem. Washington Cathedral, 1973-81, 99—, mem. fin. com., 1998—, chmn., 1999—; mem. governing bd. St. Albans Sch., 1977-81; trustee Louise Home, 1979-89. Served with AUS, 1943; Served with U.S. Mcht. Marine, 1943-46. Fellow Am. Bar Found.; mem. ABA, D.C. Bar Assn., Am. Coll. Tax Counsel, Soc. of the Cincinnati, Coun. for Future, Am. Inns. of Ct., Chevy Chase Club (bd. govs. 1979-84, pres. 1984), Met. Club, Lawyers Club, Alibi Club, Alfalfa Club, Ch. of N.Y. Club, Beta Theta Pi. Episcopalian. Office: Vinson & Elkins 1455 Pennsylvania Ave NW Fl 7 Washington DC 20004-1013

STERZINSKY, GEORG MAXIMILIAN CARDINAL, archbishop; b. Feb. 9, 1936. Created cardinal Roman Catholic Ch., 1991. Ordained bishop of Berlin, 1989; former pres. Bishops' Conf., Roman Cath. Ch., Bonn, Fed. Republic Germany; now archbishop of Berlin, 1994—. Office: Wundstrasse 48-50, D14057 Berlin Germany*

STESMANS, ANDRE LEOPOLD, physicist, educator; b. Zonhoven, Limburg, Belgium, July 30, 1950; s. Eduard and Elisa (Welkenhuysen) S.; m. Jacqueline Philtjens; children: Wim, Ilse. BSc in Physics, U. Leuven, Belgium, 1972, D in Physics, 1977. Rsch. asst. Belgian Nat. Sci. Found., Leuven, 1972-77, sr. rsch. asst., 1977-79, rsch. assoc., 1979-90, professor physics, 1990—; Contbr. articles on solid state physics to internat. jours.; adv. bd. Jour. of Physics: Conds. Matter, 1996—. Mgr. Theatrical Co. Die Ghesellen, Zonhoven, 1987. Fellow Inst. Physics (U.K.); mem. IEEE, Am. Phys. Soc. Avocations: theatre, painting, sci. edn. Office: Katholieke U Leuven Physics Dept, Celestijnenlaan 200D, 3001 Leuven Belgium

STETINA, PAMELA ELEANOR, nursing educator; b. Cambridge, Mass., Nov. 11, 1964; d. Charles and Eleanor Mary (Jennison) Toth; m. Francis Lee Stetina Jr., Aug. 15, 1987. BSN, Salisbury (Md.) State U., 1987; cert. in gerontology, U. Denver, 1990; M in Nursing, U. Phoenix, Englewood, Colo., 1996. RN; cert. oncology nurse Oncology Nursing Certification Corp. Grad. nurse, RN Dorchester Gen. Hosp., Cambridge, Md., 1987-89; staff nurse Salisbury Med. Ctr., 1988-89; staff/charge nurse Porter Care Hosp., Denver, 1989-91; floating nurse Summit Health Profls., Denver, 1991-96; clin. nurse NMC Home Care, Englewood, 1992-95; mem. faculty, asst. dir. nursing Concorde Career Inst., Denver, 1994-96; coord. nursing Pueblo C.C.-S.W., Durango, Colo., 1996—; mem. curriculum com., all faculty com., nursing adv. com., Pueblo (Colo.) C.C., 1996—. Contbr. Jour. Nursing Jocularity. Instr. CPR Am. Heart Assn., Colo., 1994—. Named Educator of Yr., Colo. Pvt. Sch. Assn., Denver, 1995. Mem. Nat. Orgn. Assoc. Degree Nurses, Nat. League for Nursing, Oncology Nursing Soc. Avocations: reading, hiking. E-mail: pstetina@juno.com. Office: Pueblo C C SW Campus 701 Camino Del Rio Ste 118 Durango CO 81301-5466

STETSON, LAVERNE ELLIS, agricultural engineer; b. Crawford, Nebr., Aug. 26, 1933; s. Orville Earl and Anna Helena (Soester) St.; m. Shirley Ruth Wasserburger, Mar. 3, 1956; children: Patricia Ann, Erwin Duane, Ronald Dean, Helen Irene. BSc, U. Nebr., 1962, MSc, 1968. Registered profl. engr., Nebr. Agrl. engr. USDA, Agrl. Rsch. Svc., Lincoln, Nebr., 1962—. Recipient Disting. Svc. award Nat. Food & Energy Coun., 1979. Fellow IEEE (chmn. rural electric power com. 1982), Am. Soc. Agrl. Engrs. (dir. 1980-82, Kable award 1987, Packer Engring. Safety award 1990); mem. Irrigation Assn. (Man of Yr. 1980), Gamma Sigma Delta (award of merit 1990). Roman Catholic. Achievements include research on an analog model for neutral-to-earth voltages. Office: USDA Agrl Rsch Svc U Nebr 252 Chase Hall Lincoln NE 68583

STETTER, JOSEPH ROBERT, electric power industry executive; b. Buffalo, Dec. 15, 1946; s. John and Norma Susannah (Hartman) S.; m. Pamela A. Belke, July 2, 1999; children: Thomas J., Edward F., Suzanne M.; stepchildren: Danielle A., Kaehlene A. AAS in Chem. Tech., Erie County Tech. Inst., 1966; BA in Chemistry, SUNY, Buffalo, 1969, PhD in Phys. Chemistry, 1975. Rsch. asst. Linde div. Union Carbide corp., Tonawanda, N.Y., 1966-68, rsch. chemist, 1968-70; sr. rsch. chemist Energetics Sci. Inc., Elmsford, N.Y., 1974-77; dir. chem. rsch. E.S. div. Becton Dickinson & Co., Hawthorne, N.Y., 1977-80; sect. head, group leader Argonne (Ill.) Nat. Lab., 1980-85; pres., chief exec. officer Transducer Rsch., Inc., Naperville, Ill., 1983-96, also bd. dirs.; assoc. adj. prof. chemistry Ill. Inst. Tech., Chgo., 1985-97, assoc. prof., 1998—; sci. adv. bd. U.S. EPA, Washington, 1985-87. Contbr. articles to profl. jours.; patentee in field. Trustee Lakeland Cen. Sch. Dist., Peeksvill, N.Y., 1977-80; mem. St. Raphael Sch. Athletic Bd., Naperville, Ill., 1990-93. Recipient New Tech. award NASA, Washington, 1979, 93, Excellence in Tech. Transfer award Fed. Lab. Consortium, Washington, 1987, IR-100 award IR Mag., Chgo., 1979, 84, 93, Cert. of Appreciation, NAS, Washington, 1990. Mem. AAAS, ISEA, AWMA, Am. Chem. Soc., Am. Conf. Govt. Ind. Hygienists (energy com. 1984-86), Fed. Anlaytical Chemistry and Specialty Soc. (bd. dirs. 1980-99), Nat. Acad. Sci. (mem. com. 1987-90), Electrochem. Soc. (chmn. sensor divsn. 2000—), Sigma Xi. Avocations: keyboard, music, astromomy, psychology. Email: stetter@iit.edn. Home: 2243 Comstock Ln Naperville IL 60564-4337 Office: Ill Inst Tech IIT Ctr BCPS Dept Chicago IL 60616

STETTER, K. O., microbiologist, educator; b. Munich, July 16, 1941; s. Josef and Elisabeth (Huebner) S.; m. Heidi Zahradnik, Dec. 20, 1969; children: Sabine, Florian, Claudia. Abitur, Staatl. Luitpold-Oberrealschule, Munich, 1960; diploma in Biology, Tech. U., Munich, 1969, D (hon.), 1973; D (hon.), Ludwig-Maximilians U., Munich, 1977. Asst. Ludwig-Maximilians U., 1969-73; post doctoral fellow Max-Planck Inst. Biochemistry, Martinsried, Germany, 1974-75; asst. lectr. Ludwig-Maximilians U., 1975-77, lectr., 1977-80; prof. microbiology U. Regensburg, Germany, 1980—; vis. prof., faculty mem. UCLA, 1989—; co-founder Diversa Corp., San Diego, 1994; dir. Inst. Microbiology U. Regensburg, Germany, 1980. Mem. editl. bd. Systematic and Applied Microbiology, Extremophiles. Recipient Deutsche Ges. Hygiene award U. Microbiology, 1985, Gottfried-Wilhelm-Leibniz-Preis Deutsche Forschungsgemeinschaft, Germany, 1988, medal Lectr. The Internat. Inst. Biotech., London, 1994. Mem. Am. Soc. Microbiology, Deutsche Akademie der Naturforscher Leopoldina, Royal Netherlands Acad. Arts and Scis., Vereinigung f. Allg. U. Angew. Mikrobiologie, Deutsche Gesellschaft f. Hygiene und Mikrobiologie, Gesellschaft Deutscher Naturforscher und Ärzte, Gesellschaft Deutscher Chemiker, Gesellschaft f. Biologische Chemie, The Internat. Inst. Biotech. Avocations: origin of life, life scis., orchid cultivation. Office: U Regensburg Abt Mikrobiologie, Universitätsstrasse 31, D-93053 Regensburg Germany

STETTNER, LOUIS, photographer; b. Bklyn., Nov. 7, 1922; m. Janet Iffland, 1981; children: Patrick, Anton, Arion. Student engring., Princeton U., 1940-41; BA in Photography and Cinema, U. Paris, 1956. Freelance photographer for Life, Time, Fortune, Du, Paris-Match, Realites, 1965-70; lectr. Bklyn. Coll., Queensborough Coll., Cooper Union, 1972-73; prof. art C.W. Post Ctr., L.I. U., 1973-79; lectr. I.C.P., N.Y., Bennington (Vt.) Coll., 1976. Exhibited in group shows, 1949, including Milw. Ctr. for Photography, 1980, Photograph Gallery, N.Y.C., 1981, Photographers Gallery, London, 1982, Berner Photo-Gallerie, Switzerland, 1983, Midtown Y Gallery, N.Y.C., 1983, Union Square Gallery, N.Y.C., 1983, Retrospective Ctr. of Photography, Geneva, 1986, Photofind Gallery, N.Y.C., 1988, Comptoir de la Photographie, Paris, 1989, Kate Heller Gallery, London, 1990, Berinson Gallery, Berlin, 1990, Vision Gallery, San Francisco, 1990, Agatha Gaillard Gallery, Paris, 1990, Kunsthalle, Koblenz, Germany, 1999, Bonni Benrubi Gallery, N.Y., 1999, Marion Meyer Gallery, Paris, 2000, Musée Art Naif, Paris, 2000; represented in permanent collections Mus. Modern Art, I.C.P., Victoria and Albert Mus., London, Met. Mus. Art, Art Inst. Chgo., San Francisco Mus. Fine Art, Musee d'Elysee, Lausanne, Switzerland, Smithsonian Mus., Musée Carnavalet, Paris, also others; (books) Early Joys 1947-72, 1987, 1988, Wisdom Cries Out in the Street, 1999, Sous le Ciel de Paris, 1993, Comptoir de la Photografie. With inf. AUS, 1941-45. Decorated Chevalier d'Order des Arts et Lettres, France; recipient prize young photographers contest Life mag., 1951, 1st prize Pravada World Contest, 1975; Yaddo fellow, 1956-57; grantee Creative Artists Pub. Svc., 1973, Nat. Endowment for Arts, 1974. Home and Studio: 172 W 79th St New York NY 10024

STEUDEL, HEINZ, physicist; b. Langenwetzendorf, Germany, Aug. 31, 1935; s. Kurt and Helene (Strauss) S.; m. Brigitte Sacklowski, July 2, 1966; two children. DSc, Acad. Sci. Berlin, 1983. Scientist Acad. Sci., Berlin, 1960-91; sr. scientist Max Planck Soc., Berlin, 1992-96, Humboldt U., Berlin, 1997-99; guest prof. U. Jena, 2000—. Co-author: Solitonen—Nichtlineare Strukturen, 1991. Home: Neltestr 35, 12489 Berlin Germany

STEUER, RICHARD MARC, lawyer; b. Bklyn., June 19, 1948; s. Harold and Gertrude (Vengar) S.; m. Audrey P. Forchheimer, Sept. 9, 1973; children: Hilary, Jeremy. BA, Hofstra U., 1970; JD, Columbia U., 1973. Bar: N.Y. 1974, U.S. Dist. Ct. (ea. and so. dists.) N.Y. 1974, U.S. Ct. Appeals (2d cir.) 1974, U.S. Supreme Ct. 1979, U.S. Dist. Ct. (no. dist.) N.Y. 1984, U.S. Dist. Ct. (we. dist.) N.Y. 1997, U.S. Ct. Appeals (3d cir.) 1987, U.S. Ct. Appeals (5th cir.) 1995. Ptnr. Kaye, Scholer, Fierman, Hays & Handler LLP, N.Y.C., 1973—, co-chair antitrust practice group, 1996—; adj. assoc. prof. law NYU, 1985; lectr. in field; neutral evaluator U.S. Dist. Ct. Ea. Dist., N.Y, 1994-96. Author: A Guide to Marketing Law: Law and Business Inc., 1986; contbr. articles to profl. jours. Fellow Am. Bar Found.; mem. ABA (lectr. 1978, 85, 89, 96, 97, 98, 99, editl. bd. antitrust devel. vol. 1984-86, chmn. monograph com. refusals to deal and exclusive distributorships 1983, others, vice-chmn. program com. 1988-91, chmn. spring meeting program com. 1991-92, Sherman Act sect. 1 com. 1991-93, coun. sect. antitrust law 1993-96, chmn. publs. com. 1996-98, editl. chmn. Antitrust mag. 1998—), Assn. Bar City N.Y. (antitrust and trade regulation, internat. trade, lectures and CLE coms., lectr. 1983-99, chmn. antitrust and trade regulation 1995-98). Office: Kaye Scholer Fierman Hays & Handler LLP 425 Park Ave New York NY 10022-3506

STEUR, PETER P. M., physicist; b. Amsterdam, The Netherlands, Dec. 24, 1951; s. Henk W. J. Steur and Hillegonda T. M. Steur-Bleker; m. Bernardetta Gallus, July 6, 1991. BS, Vrije U., Amsterdam, 1974, MS, 1979; PhD, Rijks U., Leiden, The Netherlands, 1983. Rschr. Consiglio Nazionale delle Ricerche, Turin, Italy, 1986-96, 1st rschr., 1996—; mem. Nat. Orgn. Com. TempMeko, Turin, 1996. Contbr. articles to profl. jours. Mem. AAAS, European Phys. Soc., Working Group 4 of Consultative Com. for Thermometry. Avocations: early music, reading, jogging, bicycling. Office: Consiglio Nat Ric, Strada delle Cacce 73, I-10135 Turin Italy

STEURER, WOLFGANG, physician, surgeon, researcher; b. Innsbruck, Austria, Dec. 23, 1962; s. Ronald and Irmgard (Glavic) S.; m. Maria A. Wiedner, Aug. 30., 1986; children: Theresa, Magdalena. B, BRG Innsbruck, 1981; MD, U. Innsbruck, 1987. Resident U. Innsbruck, 1989-92, fellow,

1994-96, staff dept. transplant surgery, 1996-98, dir. pancreas transplant program, 1998—; rsch. fellow Harvard U., Boston, 1992-94. Mem. IPITA. Roman Catholic. Avocations: chamber music, mountain biking, skiing, travelling. Office: Dept Transplant Surgery, Anichstr 35, A-6020 Innsbruck Austria

STEVENS, DAVID RICHARD, corporate psychologist; b. Wokingham, Berkshire, Eng., Apr. 2, 1947; arrived in Australia, 1949; s. Peter Oliver and Evelyn (Rees) Tutte; m. Linley Anne Scott, Apr. 27, 1976; children: Veronica, Briony, Jillian. BA, U. Adelaide, Australia, 1975; MSc, U. Surrey, Guildford, Eng., 1981; MA, Sydney U, 1998; PhD, Calif. Coast U., 1991. Registered psychologist, Australia. Nat. mktg. exec. New Zealand Breweries, Wellington, Australia, 1976-78; ednl. psychologist Dept. of Edn., Adelaide, 1978-80; sr. cons. W.S. Atkins, Epsom, Eng., 1980-81, Coopers & Lybrand, Sydney, Australia, 1981-83; dir. Horwath & Horwath, Sydney, 1983-86; mng. dir. Strategic Thinking Pty. Ltd., Sydney, 1986—; adj. prof. U. Western Sydney Sch. Civic Engring. and Environ., 1998—; vis. prof. U. Nev., Las Vegas, 1987; chmn. Internat. Ctr. for Strategic Thinking, 1998—. Author: Participatory Business Planning, 1990, Strategic Thinking, 1997; contbr. numerous articles to profl. jours. Bd. dirs. Upper Mountain Area Health Authority, NSW,, 1985; chmn. Blue Mountains Tourism Authority, 1987, Standards Australia Com., 1994. Mem. Australian Psychol. Soc., Am. Psychol. Soc., World Futures Soc. Avocation: writing fiction (pen name De'ttut). Office: 50 Railway Parade, Wentworth Falls NSW 2782, Australia

STEVENS, DERRICK JOHN, research chemist; b. Warminster, Wiltshire, Eng., Dec. 29, 1925; s. Reginald John and Edwina Kathleen (Mounter) S.; m. Carol Anne Rayson, July 5, 1969; children: Nicholas Jeremy, Melanie Jayne. BS, Southampton U., Eng., 1945; PhD, London U., 1971. Chartered chemist. Rsch. chemist Brit. Rubber Prodrs. Rsch. Assn., Welwyn, Garden City, Eng., 1948-53, Rsch. Assn. Brit. Flour Millers, St. Albans, Eng., 1953-70; prin. sci. officer Flour Milling Baking Rsch. Assn., Chorleywood, Eng., 1970-72, sr. prin. sci. officer, 1972-76, head of group, 1976-88. Contbr. 50 publs. to sci. jours. Fellow Royal Soc. Chemistry (life, coun. mem. 1989-92, 95-98), Inst. Food Sci. and Tech. (life), London & S.E. Milling Soc. (hon. life, pres. 1985-86). Avocations: classical music, electronics, computing, wine. Home: 75 Stanley Hill Ave, Amersham HP7 9BA, England

STEVENS, GEOFF(REY), chemist, writer; b. West Bromwich, U.K., June 4, 1942; s. William James Stevens and Gladys Cochrane; m. Barbara Christine Smith (div. 1980); 1 child, Catharine Ann; m. Geraldine May Wall Goodwin, 1996. Devel. chemist Robinson Bros. Ltd., West Bromwich, 1958-63; asst. chief chemist W.H. Keys Ltd., West Bromwich, 1964-66; works chemist, supr. Raleigh Industries Ltd., Handsworth, U.K., 1966-79; devel. chemist Metal Closures Ltd., West Bromwich, 1979-95. Author: History of the Saltwells Spa, 1975, Field Manual for Poetry Lovers, 1992, A Comparison of Myself with Ivan Blatny, 1992, The Complacency of the English, 1995, For Reference Only, 1999, Been There, 1999, Central To Me, 1999; editor: Purple Patch, 1976—; U.K. editor SlugFest Ltd. (USA), 1995—. Avocations: artist, reading, art, watching cricket. Home: 25 Grittiths Rd, West Bromwich B71 2EH, England

STEVENS, GEOFFREY WAYNE, chemical engineer, educator; b. Melbourne, Australia, Australia, Sept. 3, 1954; s. Ashley Robert and Lillian Olive (Cosgrove) S.; m. Jennifer Lynne Carland, Feb. 5, 1994. B in Chem. Engring., Royal Melbourne Inst. Tech., Melbourne, 1976; PhD, Melbourne U., 1981. Registered profl. engr. Part-time lectr. Swinburne Inst., Melbourne, 1977-79; instrument designer Imperial Chem. Industries, Melbourne, 1981-83; lectr. U. Melbourne, 1983-87, sr. lectr., 1987-91, reader, 1992-98, prof., 1999—, head dept. chem. engring., 2000—; vis. rsch. fellow McMaster U., Can., 1986, Tech. U., Munich, Germany, 1990; sr. Fulbright fellow U. Minn., 1993. Author: (with others) Science and Practice of Liquid-Liquid Extraction, 1992; contbr. articles to profl. jours.; apptd. to editorial bd. of internat. jour. Hydrometallurgy, 1994, Solv Extn. and Ion Exchange, 1996, Chem. Engring. R&D, 1998. Sec. General of Internat. Solvent Extension Com., 1996. Fellow Australia Inst. Mining and Metallurgy, Inst. Chem. Engrs. Avocations: sailing, bushwalking, squash. Home: 84 Pickles St, Port Melbourne 3207, Australia Office: Univ Melbourne, Univ Melbourne, Dept Chem Engring, Parkville 3010, Australia

STEVENS, GEORGE ALEXANDER, realtor; b. Loma, Mont., Nov. 10, 1923; s. Otto Oliver and Josephine (Dale) S.; m. Martha Evie Fultz, Sept. 16, 1944 (div. 1978); children: Gary, Kathleen, Arlene, Tina; m. Arleen Dorothea Largent, Nov. 14, 1978. A in Bus Adminstrn., SUNY, 1992. Prin. George Stevens Farm, Loma, Mont., 1946-93, George Stevens, Realtor, Loma, Mont., 1957-93; pres. George A. Stevens COrp., Loma, 1976-93, Gold and Silver Realty, Inc., Great Falls, Mont., 1993—. Trustee Sch. Dist. # 32, Loma, 1947-50; election judge Precinct # 7, Loma, 1953-88. With USN, 1944-46, PTO. Mem. Nat. Assn. Realtors, VFW (life), Am. Legion (life), Elks (life), Eagles Lodge. Democrat. Lutheran. Home: 810 8th Ave N Great Falls MT 59401-1036

STEVENS, JANE, curator; b. Chgo., Oct. 1, 1947; d. John. J. and Mattie S. BA in Anthropology, U. Ill., 1972; MA in Media Study, SUNY, Buffalo, 1981; cert. arts mgmt., U. Mass., 1994. Asst. curator Chgo. Hist. Soc., 1978-85; instr. photography Morton Coll., Cicero, Ill., 1987—; curator, asst. adminstr. Ill. Art Gallery, Chgo., 1985—; coord. fine arts seminar Chgo. Met. Ctr., 1999-00; affiliate mem. Ceres Gallery, N.Y.C., 1993—; dir. ARC Ednl. Found., Chgo., 1992-93, mem. adv. bd., 1999—, grantwriter, 1996-99. Guest artist House of Good Shepherd, Chgo., 1997—; panelist Ill. Assn. Mus., 1996; city arts visual arts panelist City of Chgo., Cultural Affairs, 1994-97; moderator, panelist Art Culture Nature Assn., U. Wash., 1999; editor, writer (exhbn. catalogue) Artists Residents Chgo. Gallery, 20th Anniversary, 1995; curator, writer (exhbn. brochure) Ill. State Mus., 1996; guest writer (newsletter) YLEM/Internat. Soc. Electronic Arts Conf., 1996; editor, curator (exhbn. catalogue) Electronic Immersions, 1997. Recipient Purchase award Fla. State U., 1985, Spl. Projects award Ill. Arts Coun., 1998; Project Completion grantee Ill. Arts Coun., 1983. Mem. Am. Assn. Mus. (mem. curator com. 1996—), Assn. Humanistic Psychology, Coll. Art Assn., Chgo. Artists Coalition. Avocations: travel, reading, photography, film, modern dance. E-mail: jstevens@museum.state.il.us. Home: 1631 N Nagle Ave Chicago IL 60707-4016 Office: Ill Art Gallery Ill State Mus 100 W Randolph St Ste 2-100 Chicago IL 60601-3219

STEVENS, JEROME HEBERT, management consultant; b. Paris, Apr. 24, 1959; came to U.S., 1991; s. Francois Hébert-Stevens and Claude Arthaud; m. Valerie Travert, Dec. 28, 1996; 1 child, Arthur. MD, U. Paris VII, 1987; diploma in health economics, U. Paris V, 1989; MBA, U. Pa., 1994. Attending physician Hosp. de Paris, 1987-90; med. dir. Lyonnaise Santé, Paris, 1989-92; cons. CSC Healthcare, N.Y.C., 1994-99; founder Direct Medica, Paris, 2000—. Co-author: Reengineering the Operating Room, 1996; participant med. TV series Entretiens de Bichat, 1990. Bd. dirs. GERO 92 Geriat. Assn., Paris, 1989-92. With French Army, 1985-86. Mem. Am. Coll. Physician Execs. Avocations: sailing, golf, modern art. Home: 666 5th Ave # 239 New York NY 10103-0001

STEVENS, LEOTA MAE, retired elementary education educator; b. Waverly, Kans., Mar. 27, 1921; d. Clinton Ralph and Velma Mae (Kukuk) Chapman; m. James Oliver Stevens, Nov. 7, 1944 (dec.); children: James Harold, Mary Ann Hooker Tibbits. BA, McPherson Coll., 1954; MS, Emporia U., 1964, postgrad., 1969-77; postgrad., Wichita U., 1977. Educator Pleasant Mound Sch., Waverly, 1940-41; prin. educator Halls Summit Sch., Waverly, 1941-42; educator Waverly Grade Sch., 1942-43, Ellinwood (Kans.) Jr. H.S., 1943-45, Hutchinson (Kans.) Grade Sch., 1945-48, Lincoln Sch., Darlow, Kans., 1948-49; educator prin. Mitchell-Yaggy Consol. Sch., Hutchinson, 1949-57; educator elem. Hutchinson Sch. Dist. 308, 1957-85, ret., 1985; v.p. Reno County Tchrs. Assn. Hutchinson, 1956-57, pres. Assn. Childhood Edn. Internat., 1978-79. Author of numerous poems; compiler The Alexander-Kukuk Descendants: 1754 to 1998. Mem. Worker ARC Blood Mobile, 1986—, Hutchinson Cmty. Concerts 1970—; ch. sch. tchr. Trinity United Meth. Ch., 1959-71. (attendance chair, 1994); historian Women's Civic Ctr., 1988-92, art com. chmn., 1992-96; den mother Cub Scouts, 1963-66, leader Girl Scouts Ellinwood, 1944-45. Mem. AAUW (news reporter 1984-87, legis. chmn. program com. 1991-94, 2d v.p., 1994—), Ret. Nation State and Local Edn. Assn., Reno County Tchrs. Assn. (v.p. 1956-57), Assn. Childhood Edn. Internat. (pres. 1978-79), Reno County Extension Homemaker Coun. (rep. 1987—), Rainbow Extension Club (pres. 1986-92), Hutchinson Area Ret. Tchrs. Assn. (historian 1996-99), Am. Legion Aux., Friends of Preservation, Delta Kappa Gamma (sec., v.p. 1972-80, grant chmn. 1980-88, publicity com. 1990-93, legis. chmn. 1994—). Republican. Avocations: art, music, traveling, gardening, camping, genealogy. Home: 805 W 23rd Ave Hutchinson KS 67502-3765

STEVENS, LINDA LOUISE HALBUR, addiction counselor; b. Huron, S.D., Oct. 28, 1960; d. Alvin LeRoy and Esther Louise (Schroeder) Halbur; m. Lowell Eugene Stevens, July 26, 1980 (div. 1995); children: Lowell John, Tracie Lynn. BSW, U. N.D., 1991; MEd, N.D. State U., 1993. Lic. social worker, addiction counselor, N.D.; lic. addiction counselor; cert. counselor reciprocal, Minn. Tracker Luth. Soc. Svcs., Hillsboro, N.D., 1990-94; addiction counselor Heartland Med. Ctr., Fargo, N.D., 1993-94, S.E. Human Svc. Ctr., Fargo, 1994—; dual diagnosis Off Main Program, Fargo, 1995; addiction counselor, SMI day treatment provider Koochiching Counseling Ctr., International Falls, Minn., 1997; OTR driver Gainey Transp. Svcs., 1998; inpatient substance abuse case mgr. New Ulm Med. Ctr., 1998—. Local/state officer N.D. Women of Today, Hillsboro, 1982-87. Recipient Presdl. Excellence award N.D. women of Today, 1986-87. Mem. NASW, Am. Counseling Assn. Avocations: golf, sewing, pets, cross country skiing. Home: 1217 N Spring St New Ulm MN 56073-1131 Office: 1324 5th North St New Ulm MN 56073-1514

STEVENS, NORMAN DENNISON, retired library director; b. Nashua, N.H., Mar. 4, 1932; s. David P. and Ruth (Ackley) S.; m. Nora Bennett, Jan. 16, 1959; children: David P., Sara, Elizabeth. BA, U. N.H., 1954; MLS, Rutgers U., 1957, PhD, 1961. Acting dir. univ. librs. Howard U., Washington, 1961-63; assoc. libr. Rutgers U., New Brunswick, N.J., 1963-68; assoc. univ. libr. U. Conn., Storrs, 1968-75, univ. libr., 1975-87, dir. univ. librs., 1987-94, dir. emeritus univ. librs., 1994—, acting dir. Thomas J. Dodd Rsch. Ctr., 1995-96; exec. dir. The Molesworth Inst., Storrs, 1959—; condr. librs. N. Am. Sch. for the Artsy, White Bear Lake, Minn., 1988—; pres. The Bibliosmiles, 1993—, Am. Book Collectors of Children's Books, 1998—. Author: A Guide to Collecting Librariana Communications Throughout Libraries, 1983; editor: Library Humor, 1971, The Librarian, 1976, Postcards in the Library, 1995. Named Libr. of the 20th Century, Assn. of Disjunctive Librarianship, 2000. Mem. ALA, Libr. Cat Soc. (historian 1997—), Phi Beta Kappa, Phi Kappa Phi, Pi Sigma Alpha. Avocations: collecting library memorabilia, library humor, profl. writing. Home: 143 Hanks Hill Rd Storrs Mansfield CT 06268-2315

STEVENS, RICHARD JOHN, psychology educator; b. London, May 6, 1939; s. John Ernest and Ethel Maud (Lerwill) S.; m. Margaret Patricia Baker (div. 1984); children: Rhett, Aron, Dominic. MA with 1st class hons.(summa cum laude), U. Edinburgh, 1962; MA (hon.), Trinity Coll., Dublin, Ireland, 1979; PhD, Open U. TV dir. BBC-TV, London, 1962-65; lectr. psychology Trinity Coll., Dublin, 1965-72; from lectr. to sr. lectr. in psychology Open U., Milton Keynes, U.K., 1972—, head dept. psychology, 1992—. Author: Freud and Psychoanalysis, 1983, Erik Erikson: An Introduction to the Man and His Work, 1983, Personal Worlds, 1986, Understanding the Self, 1996. Mem. Assn. for Humanistic Psychology (chair). Humanist. Office: Open Univ, Walton Hall, Milton Keynes England

STEVENS, ROBERT BOCKING, lawyer, educator; b. U.K., June 8, 1933; naturalized, 1971; s. John Skevington and Enid Dorthy (Bocking) S.; m. Katherine Booth, Dec. 23, 1985; 1 child, Robin; children by previous marriage: Carey, Richard. BA, Oxford U., 1955, BCL, 1956, MA, 1959, DCL, 1984; LLM, Yale U., 1958; LLD (hon.), N.Y. Law Sch., 1984, Villanova U., 1985, U. Pa., 1987; D.Litt. (hon.), Haverford Coll., 1991. Grays Inn bencher, 1999. Barrister-at-law London, 1956; tutor in law Keble Coll. Oxford U., 1958-59; asst. prof. law Yale U., 1959-61, assoc. prof., 1961-65, prof., 1965-76; provost, prof. law and history Tulane U., 1976-78; pres. Haverford Coll., 1978-87; chancellor, prof. history U. Calif., Santa Cruz, 1987-91; of counsel Covington and Burling, Washington and London, 1991—; master Pembroke Coll., Oxford, 1993—; Essex Court Chambers, 1966—; vis. prof. U. Tex., 1961, U. East Africa, 1962, London Sch. Econs., 1963, Stanford U., 1966, Brookings Instn., 1967-68, U. Coll. London, 1991-94; cons. UN, HEW, U.S. Dept. State. Author: The Restrictive Practices Court, 1965, Lawyers and the Courts, 1967, In Search of Justice, 1968, Income Security, 1970, Welfare Medicine in America, 1974, Law and Politics, 1978, The Law School, 1983, The Independence of the Judiciary, 1993. Grantee Rockefeller Found., 1962-64, Ford Found., 1962-64, 73-74, Russell Sage Found., 1967-68, NEH, 1973-74, Nuffield Found., 1975; named Hon. fellow Keble Coll. Oxford U., 1985, Socio-Legal Ctr., 1992. Mem. Marshall Aid Meml. Commn. (chair), Rsch. com., Am. Bar Found. Home: Masters Lodgings, Pembroke Coll, Oxford OX1 1DW, England Office: Covington and Burling, Leconfield House Curzon St, London W1Y 8AS, England

STEVENS, ROBERT EDWARD, engineering company executive; b. Kansas City, Mo., Oct. 30, 1957; s. Kenneth E. and Nina (France) S. BS in Chem. Engring., U. Mo.-Rolla, 1980, MS in Engring. Mgmt., 1985. Process design engr. The Pritchard Corp., Kansas City, Mo., 1981-83; process engr. Procter & Gamble, Cape Girardeau, Mo., 1986-87; tech. mgr. Procter & Gamble, 1987-90; project engring. mgr. Bechtel, 1990, mgr. engring., 1990-93, project mgr., 1993-99, site mgr., 1998-99, engring. mgr. Mex., 1999-2000, project mgr., 2000—. Contbr. to Physical Properties of Gases and Liquids, 1987. Chairperson bd. dirs. Wesley Found., St. Louis, 1993-98; mem. corp. devel. coun., chair benchmarking com. U. Mo.-Rolla, 1996—. Recipient Stan Adams Reliability award P & G Paper Div., 1990, Pres.'s award for team excellence Shell Oil Co., 1994, Performance Plus award Bechtel, 1994; Nat. Merit scholar, 1976. Mem. AIChE, Nat. Fire Protection Assn., Project Mgmt. Inst., Am. Soc. Engring. Mgmt., U. Mo. Rolla-Wesley Found. Alumni Assn. (pres. 1988-97), Alpha Chi Sigma (Cert. Appreciation 1991), Tau Beta Pi. Methodist. Home and Office: 11220 W Florissant # 369 Florissant MO 63033-6741

STEVENS, SHEILA MAUREEN, teachers union administrator; b. Glendale, Calif., Nov. 1, 1942; d. Richard Chase and Sheila Mary (Beatty) Flynn; m. Jan Whitney Stevens, Sept. 12, 1964; children: Ian Whitney, Bevin Michelle. AA in Liberal Arts, Monterey Peninsula Coll., Calif., 1963; BA in Anthropology, Calif. State U., Long Beach, 1969; postgrad. studies in Edn., U. Guam, 1976-77. Tchr. U.S. Trust Territory of the Pacific, Koror, Palau Island, 1968-72, Kolonia, Ponape Island, 1972-76; tchr. Dept. Edn., Agana, Guam, 1976-79; newspaper editor Pacific Daily News (Gannett), Agana, 1979-83; comm. dir. Guam Fedn. of Tchrs., Agana, 1983-84, exec. dir., 1984-85; exec. dir. Alaska Fedn. Tchrs., Anchorage, 1985-87; labor rels. specialist N.Y. State United Tchrs., Watertown, 1987-93; regional staff dir. N.Y. State United Tchrs., Potsdam, 1993—; mem. Gov.'s Blue Ribbon Panel on Edn., Agana, Guam, 1983-85; leadership devel. coord. Am. Fedn. Tchrs., Washington, 1983—; trainer positive negotiations program Situation Mgmt. Sys., Hanover, Mass., 1988—. Author, editor: Pacific Daily News, 1981-83 (Guam Press Club awards 1981, 82, 83); contbr. articles to mag. and jours. Mem. task force on labor policy, com. on self determination, Govt. of Guam, Agana, 1984-85, Adult Basic Edn. Planning Com., 1985; mem. labor studies adv. bd., Anchorage, Alaska, 1989, regional compact coalition N.Y. State Edn. Dept., Albany, 1994. Named Friend of Edn., Carthage (N.Y.) Tchrs. Assn., 1990. Mem. NOW, ACLU, ASCD, AAUW, Am. Fedn. Tchrs. Comm. Assn. (Best Editorial award 1984), Indsl. Rels. Rsch. Assn. Democrat. Methodist. Avocations: travel, reading, free-lance writing, cross-country skiing. Office: NY State United Tchrs 11 Elm St Potsdam NY 13676-1812

STEVENS, STEPHEN EDWARD, psychiatrist; b. Phila.; s. Edward and Antonia S.; m. Isabelle Helen Gallacher, Dec. 27, 1953. BA cum laude, LaSalle Coll., 1950; MD, Temple U., Phila., 1954; LLB, Blackstone Sch. Law, 1973. Diplomate Am. Bd. Psychiatry and Neurology. Intern Frankford Hosp., Phila., 1954-55; resident in psychiatry Phila. State Hosp., 1955-58; practice medicine specializing in psychiatry Woodland Hills, Calif., 1958-63, Santa Barbara, Calif., 1970-77; asst. supt. Camarillo (Calif.) State Hosp., 1963-70; cons. ct. psychiatrist Santa Barbara County, 1974-77; clin. dir. Kailua Mental Health Ctr., Oahu, Hawaii, 1977—. Author: Treating Mental Illness, 1961, Survival and the Fifth Dimension, 1997, Psychiatry, Survival and God, 1998. Served with M.C., USAAF. Decorated Purple Heart. Fellow Am. Geriatrics Soc. (founding); mem. Am. Acad. Psychiatry and Law, AMA, Am. Psychiat. Assn., Am. Legion, DAV (Oahu chpt. 1), Caledonia Soc, Am. Hypnosis Soc., Am. Soc. Adolescent Psychiatry, Hawaiian Canoe Club, Honolulu Club, Elks (BPOE 616), Aloha String Band (founder, pres.). Home: PO Box 26413 Honolulu HI 96825-6413

STEVENS, WILBUR HUNT, accountant; b. Spencer, Ind., June 20, 1918; s. John Vosburgh and Isabelle Jane (Strawser) S.; m. Maxine Dodge Stevens, Sept. 28, 1941; children: Linda Maxine Piffero, Deborah Anne Augello. BS, U. Calif., Berkeley, 1949, MBA, 1949. CPA, Calif.; cert. fraud examiner, fin. svcs. auditor; diplomate Am. Bd. Forensic Acctg. Staff acct. McLaren, Goode, West & Co., San Francisco, 1949-52; mng. ptnr. Wilbur H. Stevens & Co., Salinas, Calif., 1952-70; regional ptnr. Fox & Co., CPAs, Salinas, 1970-73; nat. dir. banking practice Fox & Co., CPAs, Denver, 1973-80; pres., chmn. Wilbur H. Stevens, CPA, PC, Salinas, 1980-94; chmn. Stevens, Sloan & Shah, CPAs, 1994—; adj. prof. acctg. U. Denver, 1975-78; faculty mem. Assemblies for Bank Dirs., So. Meth. U., Dallas, 1976-81, Nat. Banking Sch., U. Va., Charlottesville, 1979-87; chmn., dir. Valley Nat. Bank, 1963-71, Pacific Ag Credit, Inc., 1997—; bd. dirs. La Presente, Inc., World Travel, Inc. Editor Issues in CPA Practice, 1975; contbr. articles to profl. jours. Capt. AUS, 1942-53. Decorated Bronze Star; Frank G. Drum fellow U. Calif., Berkeley, 1949. Mem. AICPA (v.p. 1971), Am. Acctg. Assn., Am. Assembly Collegiate Schs. Bus. (accreditation coun. 1975-78, 81-84), Nat. Assn. State Bds. Accountancy (pres. 1976-77, strategic initiatives com.), Calif. Soc. CPAs (pres. 1968-69, Disting. Svc. award 1988), Acctg. Rsch. Assn. (pres. 1973-75), Acad. Acctg. Historians, Assn. Cert. Fraud Examiners, Am. Coll. Forensic Examiners, Nat. Assn. Fin. Svcs. Auditors, Burma Star Assn., CBI Vets. Assn., 14 AF Assn., Hump Pilots Assn., Salinas C. of C. (pres. 1960), Commonwealth Club Calif., Masons (master 1992, 97, Hiram award 1998, grand lodge com. taxation), Knight Tamplar (comdr. 2000), Royal Arch (high priest 1998, grand chpt. inspector 1999—), Cryptic Masons (illus. master 2000), Knight Masons Am., Royal Order Scotland, 32 degree Scottish Rite, Nat. Sojourners (pres. Monterey Bay chpt. 1996), Heroes of '76 (comdr. John C. Fremont chpt. 1996-97), Fed. for Collingwood Libr. and Mus., Red Cross of Constantine, Salinas High Twelve Club (pres. 1995), QCCC, London, Rotary (dist. gov. 1983, chmn. internat. fellowship accounts 1994-96, Paul Harris fellow 1973), Phi Beta Kappa, Beta Gamma Sigma (v.p. 1949), Beta Alpha Psi. Republican. Methodist. Home: 38 Santa Ana Dr Salinas CA 93901-4136 Office: 975 W Alisal St Ste D Salinas CA 93901-1148

STEVENSON, DAVID JOHN DOUGLAS, physician, educator; b. Glasgow, Scotland, Jan. 6, 1933; s. Douglas Stuart and Mary Edith (Lang) S.; m. Anna Marie Skadegaard, July 29, 1967; children: Bjørn Douglas, Ellen Gilla, Alan Dorje. MB, B of Surgery, U. Glasgow, 1957; MA, U. Cambridge, Eng., 1958; MD, U. Glasgow, 1965. Diplomate Bd. Tropical Medicine and Hygiene, Eng., Pub. Health, Scotland. House surgeon, physician Glasgow Hosps., 1957-58; Diocesan med. officer Diocese of Nyasaland, Malawi, 1958-63; govt. med. officer Ministry of Health, Malawi, 1965-66; lectr. tropical diseases U. Edinburgh, Scotland, 1966-72; sr. lect. internat. cmty. health Liverpool Sch. Tropical Medicine, Eng., 1972-90; hon. fellow pub. health scis. U. Edinburgh, 1991—; vis. prof. Inst. Medicine, Kathmandu, Nepal, 1974-75; cons. Ministry of Health, Sierra, Leone, 1980, U. Yaoundé, Cameroon, 1985, Med. Emergency Relief Internat., Afghanistan, 1996. Author (wordlist) En Liten Skotsk-Norsk Ordliste, 1963; editor: (textbook) The Control of Disease in the Tropics, 5th edit., 1987. Parliamentary candidate Scottish Nat. Party, Glasgow, 1964, Edinburgh, 1970, European parliament candidate, Lothians, 1979, 84. Recipient Bronze medal Order of St. Lazarus, Scotland, 1962; named Chevalier, Order of St. Lazarus, Scotland, 1984. Fellow Faculty of Pub. Health Medicine, Royal Soc. Tropical Medicine and Hygiene (Scottish br. com. 1996); mem. Freshwater Biol. Assn. (life). Lutheran. Avocations: playing Scottish bagpipes for dancing, international music and dance, parapsychology, hypnotism, appropriate technology. E-mail: david.stevenson@ed.ac.uk. Home: 22 Blacket Pl, Edinburgh EH9 1RL, Scotland Office: Univ Edinburgh Pub Health, Teviot Pl, Edinburgh EH8 9AG, Scotland

STEVENSON, EDWARD WARD, retired physician, surgeon, otolaryngologist; b. Chester, S.C., Jan. 9, 1926; s. Thomas M. and Annie Lou (Ward) S.; m. Dorothy Giles, Sept. 2, 1947; children: Sally Anne Stevenson Yeilding, Laura Stevenson Healy, Nancy Stevenson Schonbeger (dec.), Molly Stevenson Walker. B in Medicine, Duke U., 1945; MD, U. Md., Balt., 1949. Intern Bapt. Meml. Hosp., Memphis, 1949-50; resident Med. Coll. Va. Hosp., Richmond, 1953-55; fellow Ochsner Found. Hosp., New Orleans, 1955-56; staff otolaryngologist Ochsner Clinic, New Orleans, 1956-57; pvt. practice Birmingham, 1957-60, 65-94; instr., clin. asst. prof. surgery U. Ala., Birmingham, 1957-94; pvt. practice Decatur, Ala., 1960-65; ret., 1994; faculty Tulane U. Sch. Medicine, 1956-57; mem. staff Bapt. Med. Ctr.-Montclair, Birmingham. Contbr. articles to profl. jours. Bd. dirs. So. Mus. Flight, Birmingham, 1989—, Ala. Aviation Hall of Fame; pres. Birmingham Aero Club, 1996. Mem. AMA, ACS, Am. Laryngol., Rhinol. and Otol. Soc. (sec.- treas. so. sect. 1990-93, v.p. so. sect. 1993-94), Am. Soc. Head and Neck Surgery, Am. Acad. Otolaryn., Am. Soc. Ophthal. and Otolaryn. Allergy, So. Med. Assn., Jefferson County Med. Soc., Am. Sleep Disorders Assn., Ala. Otolaryn. Soc. (founder, pres. 1971), Med. Assn. State Ala., Morgan County Med. Soc. (pres. 1964-65), Tri-State Otolaryn. Assembly (co-founder), Birmngham Otolaryn. Soc. (pres. 1984), Birmingham Aero Club (pres. 1996), Birmingham Downtown Rotary Club. Methodist. Avocations: aerobatic flying, world travel. Home: 4249 Antietam Dr Birmingham AL 35213-3221

STEVENSON, FRANCES KELLOGG, museum program director, inventor; b. Boston; d. Charles Summers and Alice deGueldry (Stevens) S.; m. James Richard Wein, 1971 (div. 1989). BA, Wells Coll., Aurora, N.Y., 1967; MA, Oxford U., 1972; MBA, U. Pa., 1992. News editor Sierra Club, San Francisco, 1970-71; copy editor Oxford (Eng.) U. Press, 1972-73; from editor to publs. officer Smithsonian Instn., Washington, 1974—; pres. Stevenso Concepts Inc., Washington. Co-editor: Abroad in America: Visitors to the New Nation, 1976; compiler: (book) National Portrait Gallery Permanent Collection Illustrated Checklist, 1982; patent pending PaddlePro. Mem. St. John's Episcopal Ch., Lafayette Sq. James E. Webb fellow Smithsonian Instn., 1988-89. Mem. Sulgrave Club. Episcopalian. Home: 2724 Ordway St NW Apt 4 Washington DC 20008-5047 Office: Smithsonian Instn Portrait Gallery 8th And F Sts NW Washington DC 20560-0001

STEVENSON, JAMES LARAWAY, communications engineer, consulting; b. Detroit, Oct. 25, 1938; s. Joseph Morley and Kittie Harriet (Laraway) S.; m. Jeanie Lorraine Minkstein, Aug. 7, 1965; children: Amy Jean, Brian Morley. AAS, U.S. Armed Forces Inst., 1958; BSEE, MIT, 1960, MSEE, 1962. Cert. master radio and telecommunications engr. FCC. With USN Mercury Space Project, 1957-63; engr. Sta. WBCM-FM, Bay City, Mich., 1964-65; chief engr. Sta. WCRM, Clare, Mich., 1965-66, Sta. WSMA, Marine City, Mich., 1966; engr. Sta. WWJ-AM-FM-TV, Detroit, 1966-79; owner, mgr. Twin Oaks Comms. Engring. (name now Twin Oaks Comms. Engring. P.C.), North Branch, Mich., 1972—; charter pilot, flight & ground instr. G. B. DuPont Co., Almont Marlette Aviation Inc., 1977-82; cons. electronics engr. various cos., 1968—; expert legal witness, 1968—; mem. corp. edn. adv. coun. Colls. Bus. Adminstr., Sci., Engring. & Tech., Saginaw Valley State U., 1997—. Contbr. articles to profl. jours. Sr. div. judge Detroit Met. Sci. and Engring. Fair, 1975—, Mich. State Sci. & Engring. Fair, 2000—; spl. awards judge Intel Internat. Sci. & Engring. Fair, Detroit, 2000; search & rescue pilot, mission comdr., capt. Mich. wing CAP, 1961-81; cubmaster Pack 457 Boy Scouts Am., North Branch, 1983-85; mem. adv. bd. jacknabbit.com., Issaquah, Wash., 1999—. Recipient appreciation award CAP, 1980, North Branch Area Schs., 1985, Century award Boy Scouts Am., 1984. Mem. AIAA, IEEE (sr., chmn. N.E. Mich. sect. 1987-88, 95—, bd. dirs. 1984—), NSPE, Nat. Assn. Radio Telecomm. Engrs. (sr.), Mich. Soc. Profl. Engrs. (flint chpt.), Saginaw Valley Engring. Coun. (chmn. 1990-91, sec.-treas. 1992-95), Engring. Soc. Detroit (profl.), Profl. Activities Coun. Engrs. (chmn. U.S. activities bd. 1985—), Nat. Pilots Assn. (sr. pilot citation, safe pilot award 1978), Aircraft Owners and Pilots Assn., North Branch C. of C. (charter), Am. Legion, Lions (pres. North Br. club 1990-91), Radio Club Am. Avocations: computers, amateur radio, flying. Office: Twin Oaks Comms Engring PC 2465 Johnson Mill Rd PO Box 340 North Branch MI 48461-0340

STEVENSON, JAMES RICHARD, radiologist, lawyer; b. Ft. Dodge, Iowa, May 30, 1937; s. Lester Lawrence and Esther Irene (Johnson) S.; m. Sara Jean Hayman, Sept. 4, 1958; children: Bradford Allen, Tiffany Ann, Jill Renee, Trevor Ashley. BS, U. N.Mex., 1959, JD, 1987; MD, U. Colo., 1963. Diplomate Am. Bd. Radiology, Am. Bd. Nuc. Medicine, Am. Bd. Legal Medicine, 1989; Bar: N.Mex. 1987, U.S. Dist. Ct. N.Mex. 1988. Intern U.S. Gen. Hosp., Tripler, Honolulu, 1963-64; resident radiology U.S. Gen. Hosp., Brook, San Antonio, 1964-67; radiologist, ptnr. Van Atta Labs., Albuquerque, 1970-88; radiologist, ptnr. Radiology Assocs. of Albuquerque, 1988—, pres., 1994-96; radiologist, ptnr. Civerolo, Hansen & Wolf, Albuquerque, 1988-89; adj. asst. prof. radiology U. N.Mex., 1970-71; pres. med. staff AT & SF Meml. Hosp., 1979-80, chief of staff, 1980-81, trustee, 1981-83. Author: District Attorney manual, 1987. Participant breast screening Am. Cancer Soc., Albuquerque, 1987-88; dir. profl. divsn. United Way, Albuquerque, 1975. Maj. U.S. Army, 1963-70, Vietnam; col. M.C. USAR, 1988—. Decorated Bronze Star; Allergy fellow, 1960; Med.-Legal Tort scholar, 1987. Fellow Am. Coll. Radiology (councilor 1980-86, mem. med. legal com. 1990-96), Am. Coll. Legal Medicine, Am. Coll. Nuc. Medicine, Am. Coll. Nuc. Physicians, Radiology Assn. Albuquerque; mem. AMA (Physicians' Recognition award 1969—), Am. Soc. Law & Medicine, Am. Arbitration Assn., Albuquerque Bar Assn., Soc. Nuc. Medicine (v.p. Rocky Mountain chpt. 1975-76), Am. Inst. Ultrasound in Medicine, N.Am. Radiol. Soc. (chmn. med. legal com. 1992-95), N.Mex. Radiol. Soc. (pres. 1978-79), N.Mex. Med. Soc. (chmn. grievance com.), Albuquerque-Bernalillo County Med. Soc. (scholar 1959), Nat. Assn. Health Lawyers, ABA (antitrust sect. 1986—), N.Mex. State Bar, Albuquerque Bar Assn., Sigma Chi, Albuquerque Country Club, Elks, Masons, Shriners. Republican. Methodist. Home: 3333 Santa Clara Ave SE Albuquerque NM 87106-1530 Office: Medical Arts Imaging Ctr A6 Med Arts Sq 801 Encino Pl NE Albuquerque NM 87102-2612

STEVENSON, JOSIAH, IV, cultural arts administrator; b. Jamaica, N.Y., Oct. 4, 1935; s. Josiah and Ruth Lillian (Leech) S.; m. Jane Margaret Kupfer, Sept. 1, 1957; children: Josiah V., Todd Sander. AB, Dartmouth Coll., 1957; MBA, Amos Tuck Sch. Bus., 1958. Instr. U. Md.-Far East, 1959-61; account supr. Benton & Bowles, Inc., N.Y.C., 1961-66; group product mgr., gen. mgr. Japan Chesebrough-Pond's Inc., Greenwich, Conn., 1967-77; dir. devel. Dartmouth Coll., 1977-84, Boston Symphony Orch., 1984-95; v.p. Curtis Inst. Music, Phila., 1995—; mng. ptnr. Dover Stevenson & Assocs., 1987—. With USAF, 1958-61. Mem. U.S. C. of C., Nat. Soc. Fund Raising Execs. (Mass. chpt. bd. dirs., v.p. 1993-95, bd. dirs. Greater Phila. chpt. 1996—), Dartmouth Club, Tokyo Lawn Twnnis Club, Yale-Dartmouth Club (N.Y.C.), Badminton and Tennis Club (Boston). Republican. Presbyterian. Home: Spring Pond Rd PO Box 1810 Norwich VT 05055-1810 Office: Curtis Inst Music 1726 Locust St Philadelphia PA 19103-6187

STEVENSON, KEVIN MICHAEL, accountant; b. Melbourne, Victoria, Australia, May 6, 1950; s. Kenneth George and Ellen Mary (McLeod) S.; m. Anne-Marie Rocke, Jan. 29, 1972; children: David, Kirsten, Timothy, James, Erin, Simone, Kieran. B of Commerce, U. Melbourne, 1971, MBA, 1976. From auditor to tech. rschr. Fell & Starkey, Melbourne, 1971-76; from tech. rschr. to exec. dir. Australian Acctg. Rsch. Found., Melbourne, 1976-89; nat. tech. ptnr. Coopers & Lybrand, Melbourne, 1989-98; sr. tech. ptnr. PricewaterhouseCoopers, Melbourne, 1998-99; founding ptnr. Stevenson McGregor, 1999—; standing interpretations com. Internat. Acctg. Stds. Com., London, 1997—. Contbr. articles to profl. jours. Urgent issues group Australian Acctg. Rsch. Found., Melbourne, 1995—. Named Acct. of Yr., Bus. Rev. Weekly, Melbourne, 1988. Fellow Australian Soc. Cert. Practising Accts., Inst. Chartered Accts. Australia (state councillor 1996—). Roman Catholic. Avocation: golf. Office: Stevenson McGregor & McCahey, 935 Station St Ste 10, Box Hill 3128, Australia

STEVENSON, MIRANDA FAYE, zoologist; b. Glasgow, Scotland, Mar. 26, 1947; d. Douglas Ardoch and Elizabeth Lindsay (Houston) S.; m. Christopher William Morris. BA, Dublin U., Ireland, 1969; PhD, Aberystwyth U., 1980; MBA, Edinburgh U., Scotland, 1996. Zoo keeper Chester Zoo, 1969-71; scientific officer Welsh Plant Breeding Sta., 1972; rsch. asst. Aberystwyth U., 1972-79; curator animals Edinburgh Zoo, Scotland, 1979-96, deputy dir., 1996-98; dir. Marwell 200, Eng., 1998—; presenter in field. Mem. Promate Soc. Gt. Britain, Internat. Primatological Soc., Am. Zoo Assn. Avocations: theatre, cinema, walking. Office: Marwell Zool Park, Colden Common, Winchester SO21 1JH, England

STEVENSON, NANCY NELSON, museum executive; b. Annapolis, Md., Oct. 23, 1950; d. Perry Waldemar and Grace Anne Nelson; m. Roger Stevenson Jr., Nov. 18, 1972; children: Jennifer Loren, Matthew Austin. BA, Sarah Lawrence Coll., 1972. Tchr. Montgomery County (Md.) Pub. Schs., 1972-76; bd. dirs. Jr. League of Washington, 1988-89, 90-92; trustee Nat. Mus. Women in the Arts, Washington, 1996—, sec. bd. of trustees, 1997-98, treas. bd. of trustees, 1998—. Co-author French immersion curriculum, 1974. Pres. Country Pl. Citizens Assn., Potomac, Md., 1983-84. Office: Nat Mus Women in the Arts 1250 New York Ave NW Washington DC 20005-3970

STEVENSON, ROBERT MURRELL, music educator; b. Melrose, N.Mex., July 3, 1916; s. Robert Emory and Ada (Ross) S. AB, U. Tex., El Paso, 1936; grad., Juilliard Grad. Sch. Music, 1938; MusM, Yale, 1939; PhD, U. Rochester, 1942; STB cum laude, Harvard U., 1943; BLitt, Oxford (Eng.) U.; Th.M., Princeton Theol. Sem.; DMus honoris causa, Cath. U. Am., 1991; LHD honoris causa, Ill. Wesleyan U., 1992; LittD honoris causa, Universidade Nova de Lisboa, 1993. Instr. music U. Tex., 1941-43, 46; faculty Westminster Choir Coll., Princeton, N.J., 1946-49; faculty research lectr. UCLA, 1981, mem. faculty to prof. music, 1949—; vis. asst. prof. Columbia, 1955-56; vis. prof. Ind. U., Bloomington, 1959-60, U. Chile, 1965-66, Northwestern U., Chgo., 1976, U. Granada, 1992; cons. UNESCO, 1977; Louis Charles Elson lectr. Libr. of Congress, Washington, 1969; inaugural prf. musicology Nat. U. Mex., 1996; spkr. Dumbarton Oaks Pre-Columbian Music Workshop, 1998, Internat. Colonial Music Congress, Lima, Peru, 2000; lectr. Turect Bach Rsch. Found., Gyford U., 2000. Author: Music in Mexico, 1952, Patterns of Protestant Church Music, 1953, La musica en la catedral de Sevilla, 1954, 85, Music Before the Classic Era, 1955, Shakespeare's Religious Frontier, 1958, The Music of Peru, 1959, Juan Bermudo, 1960, Spanish Music in the Age of Columbus, 1960, Spanish Cathedral Music in the Golden Age, 1961, La musica colonial en Colombia, 1964, Protestant Church Music in America, 1966, Music in Aztec and Inca Territory, 1968, Renaissance and Baroque Musical Sources in the Americas, 1970, Music in El Paso, 1970, Philosophies of American Music History, 1970, Written Sources for Indian Music Until 1882, 1972, Christmas Music From Baroque Mexico, 1974, Foundations of New World Opera, 1973, Seventeenth Century Villancicos, 1974, Latin American Colonial Music Anthology, 1975, Vilancicos Portugueses, 1976, Josquin in the Music of Spain and Portugal, 1977, American Musical Scholarship, Parker to Thayer, 1978, Liszt at Madrid and Lisbon, 1980, Wagner's Latin American Outreach, 1983, Spanish Musical Impact Beyond the Pyrenees, 1250-1500, 1985, La Música en las catedrales españolas del Siglo de Oro, 1993; contbg. editor: Handbook Latin Am. Studies, 1976—; editor Inter-Am. Music Rev., 1978—; contbr. to New Grove Dictionary of Music and Musicians, 17 other internat. encys. Served to capt. U.S. Army, 1943-46, 49. Decorated Army Commendation ribbon; fellow Ford Found., 1953-54, Gulbenkian Found., 1966, 81, Guggenheim Found., 1962, NEH, 1974, Comité Conjunto Hispano-Norteamericano (Madrid), 1989; recipient Fulbright rsch. awards, 1958-59, 64, 70-71, 88-89, Carnegie Found. tchg. award, 1955-56, Gabriela Mistral award OAS, 1985, Heitor Villa Lobos Jury award OAS, 1988, OAS medal, 1986, Cert. Merit Mexican Consulate San Bernardino, Calif., 1987, Silver medal Spanish Ministry Culture, 1989, Gold medal Real Conservatorio Superior, 1994, 97, 1st Lifetime Achievement award Sonneck Soc., 1999. Mem. Am. Musicol. Soc. (hon. life, Pacific SW chpt.), Real Academia de Bellas Artes, Hispanic Soc. Am., Am. Liszt Soc. (cons. editor), Heterofonia (cons. editor), Brazilian Musicol. Soc. (hon.), Portuguese Musicol. Soc. (hon.), Argentinian Musicol. Soc. (hon.), Orden Andrés Bello, Primera Clase, Venezuela, 1992, Sonneck Soc. Am. Music (lifetime achievement award 1999). Avocation: playing piano. Office: UCLA Dept Music 405 Hilgard Ave Los Angeles CA 90095-9000

STEVENSON, WILLIAM EDWARD, III, language educator; b. Balt., Aug. 4, 1948; s. William Edward and Gladys Margaret (Kaufman) S. BA, Johns Hopkins U., 1970, MA, 1972, MEd, 1974; PhD, U. Pa., 1975. Cert. tchr., Md. Grad. instr. Johns Hopkins U., Balt., 1970-72; cons. Stevenson & Kelly, Balt., 1975-78; tchr. lang. City of Balt. pub. schs., 1978—; cons. S.A.T. Prep, Balt., 1986-87, Morgan State U., Balt., 1989-90. Author: Pathological Grotesque in Greek and Roman Art, 1975. Head adult sch. Greek Meth. Ch., 1994—. Danver Coit Gilman fellow Johns Hopkins U., 1970-72, David and Lucille Packard fellow Am. Sch., athens, 1972, NEH fellow, 1998, Rockefeller fellow, 1998. Democrat. Methodist. Avocations: photography, painting, drawing, sculpture, coin collecting. Office: Roland Paul Sch (233) 5704 Roland Ave Baltimore MD 21210-1334

STEVENSON, WILLIAM ROBERT, retired military historian, genealogist; b. Vero Beach, Fla., Aug. 27, 1920; s. Albert "Bert" Noble and Laura Belle (Atkin) S.; m. Beatrice Ruth Levy, Dec. 13, 1947; children: Fredrick Philip (dec.), Robert John, William Rudolph, Earl Marion, Edith May Doland. AB, Ind. U., 1948. Enlisted USN, 1939, storekeeper 1st class, 1939-45; ednl. advisor USAF, Germany, 1950-51, mil. historian, 1951-56; mil. historian Mobile (Ala.) Air Material Area, 1956-58; tech. writer Missile Command, Huntsville, Ala., 1958-60; mil. historian White Sands (N.Mex.) Missile Range, 1960-63, Electronics Command, Eatontown, N.J., 1963-77. Merit badge councilor Boy Scouts Am., Vero Beach, Fla., 1984—, troop committeeman Troop 551, 1987—. SAR (registrar, genealogist Fla. chpt. 1985—), War of 1812 (registrar FLSSAR, registrar, genealogist Treasure Coast chpt., genealogist Fla. chpt. 1997—), Sons of the Revolution (registrar, genealogist Fla. chpt. 1989—), Descendants of Washington's Army at Valley Forge (registrar Fla. brigade). Republican. Methodist. Avocation: genealogy.

STEVENS-SOLLMAN, JEANNE LEE, artist; d. Ernest Gustave and Virginia Hawes; m. Philippus Steven Sollman, Oct. 16, 1971. BS, R.I. Coll., 1968, BFA, 1970; MFA in Ceramics, Pa. State U., 1972, postgrad., 1986-87. Artist in residence, instr. ceramics Juniata Coll., Huntington, Pa., 1975-76; artist in residence State Coll. (Pa.) Area H.S., 1995; instr. ceramics Haystack Mountain Sch. Crafts, Deer Isle, Maine, 1977, Pa. State U., University Park, 1978; coord., dir. Trout Run Medallic Symposium, St. Marys, Pa., 1997, 99—; juror Am. delegation Fedn. Internat. de la Medaille, The Hague, The Netherlands, 1998; cons. in field. One-person shows include Handcrafters Gallery, Portland, Maine, 1984, Soc. Arts and Crafts, Boston, 1984, Susan McLeod Gallery, Sarasota, Fla., 1984, Palisander Gallery, Taos, N.Mex., 1986, 15 Steps, Ithaca, N.Y., 1987, Am. Numismatic Soc., N.Y.C., 1999; recent group exhbns. include The Pen and Brush Club, N.Y., 1997, 98 (Medallic Art Co. award), 99 (Margaret Sussman Meml. award), Rack and Hamper Gallery, N.Y., 1997, 99, 2000, Gallery Heian, Kyoto, Japan, 1997, Art Alliance Gallery, Lemont, Pa., 1997, U. Park Campus Mall Pa. State U., University Park, 1998, Sculptures at Sea Mus., The Hague, 1998, Benson Park, Loveland, Colo., 1998, 99, 2000, Bedford (Pa.) Art Arts Coun., 1999, So. Alleghenies Mus. Art, Loretto, Pa., 1999, University Park Campus Pa. State U., 1999, 2000, Mus. of the Dog, St. Louis, 1999, Altoona (Pa.) Campus Pa. State U., 1999, Queensboro (N.Y.) C.C., 2000, Goethe Nat. Mus., Weimar, Germany, 2000, numerous others. Co-partitioner Patton Concerned Citizens, Centre County, Pa., 1990. Recipient Dutch Art Metal award Dutch Art Metal Soc., The Hague, 1998, Distinction in Sculpture award So. Alleghenies Mus. Art, Loretto, Pa., 1997, 1st prize sculpture Rural Am. 2000, Harrisburg, Pa., 2000. Fellow Am. Numismatic Soc. (J. Sanford Saltus award 1999); mem. Pen and Brush (Margaret Sussman Meml. award 1999), Fedn. Internat. de la Medaille (co. del.), Am. Medallic Sculpture Assn. (2d v.p. 1987—), Art in Common. Avocations: gardening, dog-trials & showing, shepherding. E-mail: stevsollmn@aol.com. Studio: Stevens Sollman Studios 318 N Fillmore Rd Bellefonte PA 16823-9047

STEVER, HORTON GUYFORD, aerospace scientist and engineer, educator, consultant; b. Corning, N.Y., Oct. 24, 1916; s. Ralph Raymond and Alma (Matt) S.; m. Louise Risley Floyd, June 29, 1946; children: Horton Guyford, Sarah, Margarette, Roy. A.B., Colgate U., 1938, Sc.D. (hon.), 1958; Ph.D., Calif. Inst. Tech., 1941; LL.D., Lafayette Coll., U. Pitts., 1966, Lehigh U., 1967, Allegheny Coll., 1968, Ill. Inst. Tech., 1975; D.Sc., Northwestern U., 1966; DSc, Waynesburg Coll., 1967, U. Mo., 1975; D.Sc., Clark U., 1976; DSc, Bates Coll., 1977; DH, Seton Hill Coll., 1968; D.Engring., Washington and Jefferson Coll., 1969, Widener Coll., Poly. Inst. N.Y., 1972, Villanova U., 1973, U. Notre Dame, 1974; DPS, George Washington U., 1981. Staff radiation lab. MIT, Cambridge, 1941-42; asst. prof. MIT, 1946-51, assoc. prof. aero. engring., 1951-56, prof. aero. and astro., 1956-65, head depts. mech. engring., naval architecture, marine engring., 1961-65, assoc. dean engring., 1956-59, exec. officer guided missiles program, 1946-48; chief scientist USAF, 1955-56; pres. Carnegie-Mellon U., Pitts., 1965-72; dir. NSF, Washington, 1972-76; sci. adviser, chmn. Fed. Council Sci. and Tech., 1973-76; dir. Office Sci. and Tech. Policy, sci. and tech. adviser to Pres., 1976-77, sci. cons., corp. trustee, 1977—; secretariat guided missiles com. Joint Chiefs of Staff, 1945; sci. liaison officer London Mission, OSRD, 1942-45; guided missiles tech. evaluation group Research and Devel. Bd., 1946-48; sci. adv. bd. to chief of staff USAF, 1947-69, chmn., 1962-69; steering com. tech. adv panel on aeros. Dept. Def., 1956-62; chmn. spl. com. space tech. NASA, chmn. rsch. adv. com. missile and spacecraft aerodynamics, 1959-65; mem. Nat. Sci. Bd., 1970-72, ex-officio, chmn. exec. com., 1972-75; mem. Def. Sci. Bd., 1962-68; adv. panel U.S. Ho. Reps. Com. Sci. and Astronautics, 1959-72; mem. Pres.'s Commn. on Patent System, 1965-67; chmn. U.S.-USSR Joint Commn. Sci. and Tech. Cooperation, 1973-77, Fed. Council Arts and Humanities, 1972-76; Pres. com. Nat. Sci. medal, 1973-77. Author: Flight, 1965; Contbr. articles to profl. jours. Past trustee Colgate U., Shady Side Acad., Sarah Mellon Scaife Found., Buckingham Sch.; truste Univ. Rsch Assn., 1977—, pres., 1982-85; trustee Woods Hole Oceanographic Inst., 1980—, Sci. Svc., 1982—, Univ. Corp. for Atmospheric Rsch., 1980-83; bd. dirs. Saudi Arabia Nat. Ctr. for Sci. and Tech., 1978-81; bd. govs. U.S. Israel Binat. Sci. Found., 1972-76, chmn., 1972-73; mem. Carnegie Commn. on Sci., Tech. and Govt., 1988-93. Recipient Pres.'s Cert. of Merit, 1948, Exceptional Civilian Svc. award USAF, 1956, Scott Gold medal Am. Ordinance Assn., 1960, Disting. Pub. Svc. medal Dept. Def., 1969, NASA, 1988, Nat. Medal of Sci., 1991, Vannevar Bush award NSF, 1997, Arthur M. Bueche award, 1999; comdr. Order of Merit Poland. Fellow AIAA (hon., pres. 1960-62), AAAS, Royal Aero. Soc., Am. Acad. Arts and Scis., Royal Soc. Arts, Am. Phys. Soc.; mem. NAS (chmn. assembly engring. 1979-83, chmn. policy divsn. 1995-97), NAE (chmn. aero. and space engring. bd. 1967-69, fgn. sec. 1984-88), Acad. Engring. of Japan (fgn. mem.), Royal Acad. of Engring. of Great Britain (fgn. mem.), Cosmos Club, Bohemian, Phi Beta Kappa, Sigma Xi, Sigma Gamma Tau, Tau Beta Pi. Episcopalian. Office: 588 Russell Ave Gaithersburg MD 20877-2868

STEWARD, JAMES BRIAN, lawyer, pharmacist; b. Cleve., Mar. 25, 1946; s. Louis Fred and Helen Elaine (Goodwin) S.; m. Betty Kay Krans, Dec. 14, 1968; children: Christina Lynn, Brian Michael. BS in Pharmacy, Ferris State Coll., 1969; JD, U. Mich., 1973. Bar: Mich. 1973, U.S. Dist. Ct. (we. dist.) Mich. 1979, U.S. Cir. Ct. (6th Cir.) 1980, U.S. Supreme Ct. 1986. Pharmacist Revco Pharmacies, Grand Rapids, Mich., 1969-70, Coll. Pharmacy, Ypsilanti, Mich., 1970-73; assoc. Bridges & Collins, Negaunee, Mich., 1973-80; ptnr. Steward, Peterson, Sheridan & Nancarrow, Ishpeming, Mich., 1980-94, Steward & Sheridan, Ishpeming, 1995—. Mem., chmn. Negaunee Commn. on Aging, 1974-86; mem., chmn., sec. Marquette County Commn. on Aging, 1976-82; trustee, v.p., pres. Negaunee Bd. Edn., 1984-88, 91-95; mem., chmn., adv. bd. trustee Ishpeming Area Cmty. Fund, 1995—; mem. combined ad hoc com. Marquette County Commn. on Aging, 1996. Mem. Mich. Bar Assn. (mem. awards com. 1996—), Marquette County Bar Assn. (sec.- treas., v.p., pres.), Am. Soc. for Pharmacy Law, Ishpeming Cross County Ski Club, Superiorland Cross Country Ski Club, Wawonowin Country Club, Phi Delta Chi, Rho Chi. Avocations: cross country ski racing, downhill and water skiing, running, biking, classic cars. Office: 205 S Main St Ishpeming MI 49849-2018

STEWARD, LESTER HOWARD, psychiatrist, academic administrator, educator; b. Burt, Iowa, Nov. 6, 1930; s. Walter and Helen Steward; m. Patricia Byrness Roach, June 17, 1953; children: Donald Howard, Thomas Eugene, Susan Elaine, Joan Marsha. BS, Ariz. State U., 1958, MA in Sci. Edn., 1969; postgrad., Escuela Nat. U., Mex., 1971-80; PhD in Psychology, Calif. Coast U., 1974; MD, Western U. Hahnemann Coll., 1980. Rschr. drug abuse and alcoholism Western Australia U., Perth, Australia, 1970-71; intern in psychiatry Helix Hosp., San Diego, Calif., 1971-72; rschr. drug addiction North Mountain Behavioral Inst., Phoenix, 1975-77; exec. v.p., CEO James Tyler Kent Coll., 1977-80; pres., CEO Western U. Sch. Medicine, 1980-86; instr. psychology USN Westpac, Subic Bay, Philippines, 1988-91; pvt. practice preventive medicine Tecate, Baja California, Mexico, 1971-88; instr. Modern Hypnosis Instrn. Ctr., 1974—, Maricopa Tech. Community Coll., Phoenix, 1975-77; mem. Nt. Ctr. Homeopathy, Washington, Menninger Found., Wichita, Kans. Contbr. numerous papers to profl. confs. Leader Creighton Sch. dist. Boy Scouts Am., Phoenix, 1954-58. Fellow Am. Acad. Med. Adminstrs., Am. Assn. Clinic Physicians and Surgeons, Internat. Coll. Physicians and Surgeons, Am. Coll. Homeopathic Physicians, Am. Counc. Sex Therapy; mem. numerous orgns. including Nat. Psychol. Assn., Am. Psychotherapy Assn., Royal Soc. Physicians, World Med. Assn., Am. Acad. Preventive Medicine, Am. Bd. Examiners in Psychotherapy, Am. Bd. Examiners in Homeopathy, Western Homeopathic Med. Soc. (exec. dir.), Ariz. Profl. Soc. Hypnosis (founder 1974). Home: 515 W Townley Ave Phoenix AZ 85021-4566

STEWART, ALAN VINCENT, plant breeder, executive; b. Reefton, Westland, New Zealand, May 12, 1955; s. Arthur Francis and Rita Emily May (Ellery) S.; m. Kerry Anne McEntee, Oct. 2, 1981 (div. Sept. 21, 1988); m. Linda Evelyn Flanagan Gray, Dec. 10, 1988 (div. Apr. 1999); children: Jessica, Wendy, Mark. B in Agrl. Sci., Lincoln (New Zealand) U., 1977, M in Agrl. Sci. with honors, 1979, PhD, 1987. Plant breeder, rsch. leader Pyne Gould Guinness Ltd., Christchurch, New Zealand, 1979—. Tchg. fellow biometrics Lincoln U., 1978. Mem. New Zealand Grassland Assn. (pres. 1997-98), New Zealand Genetical. Soc., New Zealand Agronomy Soc. (mem. com. 1990—), Grassland Soc. South Africa, Internat. Turfgrass Soc. Address: 16 Landy St, Christchurch 8006, New Zealand

STEWART, ALEXANDER CONSTANTINE, medical technologist; b. N.Y.C., Nov. 3, 1957; s. Dudley Constantine and Lillian Eunice (Mills) S.; m. Shirlene Denise Keys, June 22, 1985; children: Shechianh Faith, Akilah Danielle, Omari Joseph Constantine. Student, Herbert H. Lehman Coll., 1975-77; BS in Med. Tech., U. Kans., 1979; BTh, Northgate Bible Coll., 1989. Cert. med. technologist Am. Soc. Clin. Pathologists.$Dert. clin. lab. supr. Nat. Cert. Agy. Med. Lab. Pers. Chemistry technologist White Plains (N.Y.) Med. Ctr., 1979-89, Mt. Vernon (N.Y.) Hosp., 1987-89; chemistry supr. St. Agnes Hosp., White Plains, 1989-92, Westchester Sq. Med. Ctr., Bronx, N.Y., 1992-93; med. technologist Richland Meml. Hosp., Columbia, S.C., 1993—; instr. W. L. Bonner Bible Coll., 1995-97. Co-author: (with Sherry Sherrod DuPree) The Silent Spokesman, 1994, (with Shirlene Stewart) Write the Vision, 1996. Asst. historian Ch. of Our Lord Jesus Christ, 1989—; deacon Refuge Temple, Ch. of Our Lord Jesus Christ, 1993—, chmn. bd. trustees, 1993—; bd. dirs. New and Living Way Ministries, 1999-2000. Mem. NAACP, Soc. Pentecostal Studies (editl. com. 1992-99), Pentecostal Hist. Soc., African Am. Genealogical Soc., S.C. African Am. Hist. e Geneal. Soc. (sec. 1999—). Democrat. Pentecostal. Avocations: research and storage of African American Pentecostal materials. E-mail: stewart alexander@hotmail.com. Home: 801 Riverwalk Way Irmo SC 29063-9375 also: Refuge Temple 4450 Argent Ct Columbia SC 29203-5901 also: 4159 Grace Ave Bronx NY 10466-2015

STEWART, ALICE MARY, epidemiologist, researcher; b. Sheffield, Yorkshire, Eng., Oct. 4, 1906; d. Albert Ernest and Lucy (Wellburn) Nash; m. Ludovick Drumin Stewart, June 17, 1933 (div. 1952); children—Anne Katarine, Hugh Drumin. M.A., Cambridge U., 1930, M.D., 1933. Intern Royal Free Hosp., London, 1933, non-resident med. registrar, 1935-39; intern Childrens Hosp., Manchester, Eng., 1934; physician EGA Hosp., London, 1939-42, Radcliffe Infirmary, Oxford, Eng., 1942-45; reader in social medicine Oxford U., 1945-74; sr. research fellow Birmingham U., Eng., 1974—; cons. Nat. Council Occupational Health, 1968-74; epidemiologist Bur. Radiol. Health, Rockville, Md., 1970, Pitts. Sch. Pub. Health, 1975-76, Portland State U., 1984-85. Contbr. articles to various jours. Fellow Royal Coll. Physicians (London). Home: Evenlode Cottage, Fawler Charlbury Oxford OX7 3AZ, England Office: Dept Social Medicine, Univ Birmingham, Edgbaston Birmingham B15 2TH, England

STEWART, ARLENE JEAN GOLDEN, designer, stylist; b. Chgo., Nov. 26, 1943; d. Alexander Emerald and Nettie (Rosen) Golden; m. Randall Edward Stewart, Nov. 6, 1970; 1 child, Alexis Anne. BFA, Sch. of Art Inst. Chgo., 1966; postgrad., Ox Bow Summer Sch. Painting, Saugatuck, Mich., 1966. Designer, stylist Formica Corp., Cin., 1966-68; with Armstrong World Industries, Inc., Lancaster, Pa., 1968-96, interior furnishings analyst, 1974-76, internat. staff project stylist, 1976-78, sr. stylist Corlon flooring, 1979-80, sr. exptl. project stylist, 1980-89, sr. project stylist residential DIY flooring floor divsn., 1989-96, master stylist DIY residential tile, 1992-96; creative dir. Stewart Graphics, Lancaster, Pa., 1996—. Exhibited textiles Art Inst. Chgo., 1966, Ox-Bow Gallery, Saugatuck, Mich., 1966. Home and Office: 114 E Vine St Lancaster PA 17602-3550

STEWART, B(OBBY) A(LTON), soil scientist, educator; b. Erick, Okla., Sept. 26, 1932; s. William David and Anna Maude (Howard) S.; m. Jane Ann Nelson; children: Steven Mark, Gregory Neal, Judith Ann Stewart Meadow. BS in Soils, Okla. State U., 1953, MS in Soils, 1957; PhD in Soil Sci., Colo. State U., 1961. Cert. soil scientist. Rsch. soil scientist Agrl. Rsch. Svc., USDA, Stillwater, Okla., 1953-57, Ft. Collins, Colo., 1957-68; dir. Conservation and Prodn. Rsch. Lab. USDA, Bushland, Tex., 1968-93; dir. Dryland Agr. Inst., disting. prof. West Tex. A&M U., Canyon, 1993—, interim head divsn. agr., 1998. Contbr. over 175 articles to profl. jours. Fellow Am. Soc. Agronomy (bd. dirs. 1979-82), Soil Sci. Soc. Am. (assoc. editor jour. 1967-72, chmn. soil and water divsn. 1971-72, bd. dirs. 1971-72, 75-82, editor-in-chief jour. 1975-79, pres. 1981-82), Soil and Water Conservation Soc. (chmn. nat. meeting program com. 1972, chmn. waste mgmt. divsn. 1973, Pres.'s citation, 1972, Golden Spread Chpt. Achievement award 1975, Hugh Hammond Bennett award 1994); mem. Internat. Soil Sci. Soc. (vice chmn. divsn. soil conservation). Methodist. E-mail: bstewart@mail.wtamu.edu. Office: West Tex A&M Univ 2402 N 3 Rd Ave Canyon TX 79016-0001

STEWART, CHRIS, economist, researcher, educator; b. London, Dec. 24, 1967; s. Gordon Edward and Angela Stewart. BA in Polit. Economy with 1st class honors, Thames Poly., London, 1989; MSc in Econs., U. London, 1990; PhD in Econs., London Guildhall Univ., 1999. Rsch. asst. Kingston U., London, 1991-95, lectr. econs., 1991-99, rsch. fellow, 1996-99; econs. lectr. London Guildhall U., 1999—; freelance cons. Ecotech Ltd., Birmingham, Eng., 1992. Contbr. articles to refereed profl. jours. mem. Royal Econ. Soc., Brit. Mensa. Avocations: drumming, playing soccer, reading. Office: London Guildhall Univ, 84 Moorgate, London EC2M 6SQ, England

STEWART, CHRISTINE SUSAN, Canadian government official; b. Jan. 3, 1941; d. Morris Alexander Leishman and Laura Anne Doherty; m. David Ian Stewart, Aug. 24, 1963; children: Douglas Alexander, John David, Catherine Anne. Ed., Neuchatel Jr. Coll., Switzerland, U. Toronto, Ont., Can. Nurse; mem. Ho. of Commons, 1988—, mem. standing com. for external affairs and internat. trade, assoc. critic for human rights; official opposition critic Can. Internat. Devel. Agy.; sec. state L.Am. and Africa Cabinet of Prime Min. Jean Chrétien, Ottawa, 1993-97, min. environ., 1997—. Founding exec. dir. Horizons of Friendship. Liberal. Roman Catholic. Office: House of Commons, Confederation Bldg Rm 232, Ottawa, ON Canada K1A 0A6

STEWART, DAVID WITHERINGTON, aerospace engineer; b. Marion, Ind., Feb. 9, 1939; s. Edgar Allen Jr. and Faye Maxine (Cummings); m. Ruth Ada Valk, Aug. 26, 1961, (div.); m. Annette Louise Witherington, Dec. 17, 1962 (dec. Aug. 1999); children: Edna (dec.), Geoffrey. BS in Physics, U. Fla., Gainesville, 1959. Sr. engr. Atlas Gen. Dynamics/Convair, Cape Canaveral, Fla., 1959-63; lead engr. Gemini-Titan Martin Canaveral, Cape Canaveral, 1963-66; lead engr. Sprint Martin-Orlando, Orlando, Fla., 1966-67; lead engr. Apollo Rockwell Internat., Kennedy Space Center, Fla., 1967-74, lead engr. avionics, 1975-78, prime system integ. engr. shuttle, 1978-79, supr. orbiter software, 1979-81, project mgr. software, 1982-84, project mgr. design, 1984-85, project mgr. adv. programs, 1985-89, mgr. adv. program, 1989-91, project mgr. adv. program and bus. devel., 1991-92, program devel. mgr. Fla. ops. space sys. divsn., 1992-96; pres. Bus. Devel. Cons., Titusville, Fla., 1996—; pres. Rockwell Fla. Chpt. NMA, 1985-87. Author: Edie and

the Gobie, 1966. Pres. North Brevard Environ. Action Com., Titusville, 1970-73; chmn. Marine Resources Coun. East Fla., 1996-97; pres.-elect Space Coast Devel. Commn., 1995-96; sec. Space Coast Grant Profls. Network, 1997-99; pres. Brevard Adult Literacy Vols., Inc., 2000—. Mem. Inst. Cert. Prof. Mgrs. (cert. mgr.), Am. Cons. League (accredited profl. cons.). Republican. Unitarian. Fax: 321-264-1885. E-mail: bizwiz@mciworld.com. Home: PO Box 5869 Titusville FL 32783-5869 Office: Bus Devel Cons Rm 211 3880 S Washington Ave Titusville FL 32780-5864

STEWART, GEORGE, university dean. Exec. dean Faculty of Sci. U. Western Australia, Perth. Office: U Western Australia, Faculty Sci, Perth W 6907, Australia*

STEWART, GEORGE RAY, association executive, educator; b. Birmingham, Ala., Aug. 19, 1944; s. DeWitt and Ann (McCain) S.; m. Nancy Ann Norton, June 5, 1964; children: Steven Ray, Jeffery Alan. BA, Samford U., Birmingham, 1966, MA, 1967; MA, Emory U., 1971. Mem. staff Birmingham Pub. Libr., 1960-97, assoc. dir., 1970-76, dir., 1976-93, sys. dir., 1993-97; part-time instr. Grad. Sch. Libr. Svc. U. Ala., 1997—; exec. dir. Gift Mgmt. Assn., Pelham, Ala., 1997—; bd. vis. Coll. Comm. Info. Scis. U. Ala., 1997—. bd. dirs. Red Mountain Mus., 1972-79, Literacy Coun. Ctrl. Ala., 1990-94; bd. dirs. Indsl. Health Coun., Birmingham, 1972-85, sec., 1979-81, pres. bd. dirs. 1982, 83. Mem. ALA, Southeastern Libr. Assn. (treas. 1985-86, v.p. 1986-88, pres. 1989-90), Ala. Libr. Assn. (scholarship 1968, pres. 1976), Ala. Hist. Assn. Office: Gift Mgmt Assn PO Box 699 Pelham AL 35124-0699

STEWART, GORDON THALLON, public health educator; b. Paisley, Scotland, Feb. 5, 1919; s. John and Mary Lang (Thallon) S.; m. Joan Kego, Mar. 27, 1946 (div. Mar. 1975); children: Linda, Ian, Jane, Jonathan; m. Georgina Houston Walker, Mar. 21, 1975. BSc, U. Glasgow, Scotland, 1939, MB, ChB, 1942, MD, 1949; Diploma in Hygiene and Tropical Medicine, U. Liverpool, Eng., 1947. Med. diplomate in internal medicine, pathology and pub. health. Sr. resident City Hosp. Aberdeen, Scotland, 1946; rsch. fellow U. Liverpool, 1946-48; sr. registrar, tutor St. Mary's Hosp., London, 1949-52; vis. prof. WHO, Geneva, 1953-54; cons. microbiology SW Met. Hosp. Bd., London, 1954-63; prof. epidemiology U. N.C., Chapel Hill, 1963-68, Tulane U., New Orleans, 1968-71; prof. pub. health U. Glasgow, 1972-83, prof. emeritus, 1983—; vis. prof. Dow Med. Coll., Karachi, Pakistan, 1953, Cornell U., N.Y.C., 1971-72; cons. WHO, 1952-86, Research Triangle, N.C., 1964-70, N.Y.C. Health Dept., 1970-71. Author: Penicillin Group of Drugs, 1965; editor: Penicillin Allergy, 1971, Trends in Epidemiology, 1972; patentee in field. Dir. Drug Abuse Rsch. Team, New Orleans, 1968-72, inter-univ. Health Rsch. Tng., N.Y.C., 1971; sr. adviser Med. TV 4 Programmes, London, 1980—; commentator radio and TV, Europe and U.S.A., 1964—. Lt. Royal Navy, 1943-46. NSF fellow, 1964, Royal Coll. Physicians fellow, 1972, Royal Coll. Pathology fellow, 1964; NIH grantee, 1964-71. Fellow Med. Soc. London, Royal Soc. Medicine, Infectious Disease Soc. Am. Home: 3 Lexden Terr, Tenby SA70 7BJ, England

STEWART, HAROLD SANFORD, real estate investment and supply executive; b. Cookeville, Tenn., Nov. 22, 1949; s. Willie Sanford and Margaret Eula (Wassom) S.; m. Diana Gail Law, May 3, 1968; children: Rhonda Gail, Scott Harold. Diploma, Nashville Vocat.-Tech. Sch., 1969. Cert. ACCA-EPIC instr., Air Conditioning Contractors of Am. Sales and part mgr. Scotsman Supply Co., Nashville, 1967-73; salesman Brock-McVey Supply Co., Bowling Green, Ky., 1973-76; pres., gen. mgr. Eds Supply Co., Bowling Green, 1976-79, Nelsco Supply Co., Bowling Green, 1979-80; pres. Air Supply Co., Inc., Bowling Green, 1980-88; sales mgr. One Stop Supply, Inc., Bowling Green, 1988-89; pres. Bilt-Rite Constrn., Inc., Bowling Green, 1989-92; sec., treas. K&H Enterprises, Inc., Bowling Green, 1989-93; pres., gen. mgr. H.S. Properties, Bowling Green, Ky., 1989—; pres., gen. mgr., stockholder Stewart Supply, Inc., Bowling Green, 1993—; chmn. Ky. State Vocat. HVAC Craft Com., Frankfort, 1987, Bowling Green Vocat. HVAC Craft Com., 1980-88; nat. adv. coun. Thermaflex Mfg. Co., Kansas City, Mo., 1986-87. City clk. and trustee City of Plum Springs, Ky., 1975-79; treas. Bowling Green Civitan Club, 1973-78; trustee Jackson Grove Bapt. Ch., Bowling Green, 1975-86. Named Civitan of Yr., Bowling Green Club, 1973-75, Col., Hon. Order of Ky. Cols. Mem. Masons, Optimist. Avocations: reading, computers, tennis, jogging. Home: 536 Detour Rd Bowling Green KY 42101-6501 Office: 300 W 6th St Bowling Green KY 42101-1878

STEWART, IAN NICHOLAS, mathematics educator; b. Folkestone, Kent, Eng., Sept. 24, 1945; s. Arthur Reginald and Marjorie Kathleen (Diwell) S.; m. Avril Bernice Montgomery, July 4, 1970; James Andrew, Christopher Michael. BA, Cambridge U., Eng., 1966, MA, 1969; PhD, Warwick U., Coventry, Eng., 1970. Lectr. Warwick U., 1969-84, reader, 1984-90; prof., 1990—; Humboldt fellow U. Tübingen, Fed. Republic Germany, 1974-75; vis. fellow U. Auckland, New Zealand, 1976; assoc. prof. U. Conn., Storrs, 1977-78; prof. So. Ill. U., Carbondale, 1978, U. Houston, 1983-84. Author: Galois Theory, 1973, Concepts of Modern Mathematics, 1975, Catastrophe Theory and its Applications, 1978, The Problems of Mathematics, 1987, Does God Play Dice, 1989, Fearful Symmetry: Is God A Geometer?, 1992, The Collapse of Chaos, 1994, Nature's Numbers, 1995, From Here to Infinity, 1996, The Magical Maze, 1997, Figments of Reality, 1997, Life's Other Secret, 1998, The Science of Discworld, 1999; editor Dynamics and Stability of Systems, Oxford, Eng., 1986—. Recipient Faraday medal Royal Soc., 1995, comm. award Joint Policy Bd. for Math., 1999, Gold medal Inst. for Math. and Its Applications, 2000. Mem. AAAS, Math. Assn. Am., Internat. Soc. for Interdisciplinary Study of Symmetry, Am. Math. Soc., London Math. Soc., Cambridge Philos. Soc., Sci. Fiction Writers Am., Greenpeace. Avocations: writing science fiction, guitar. Office: U Warwick Math Inst, Gibbet Hill Rd, Coventry CV4 7AL, England

STEWART, J. DANIEL, air force official; b. Savannah, Ga., June 20, 1941; s. Benjamin F. and Bessie L. (Edenfield) S.; m. Rebecca M. Smith; children: Daniel, Laura. BS in Aero. Engring., Ga. Inst. Tech., 1963, MS in Aero. Engring., 1965, PhD in Aero. Engring., 1967; M. in Mgmt. Sci., Stanford U., 1979. Mem. tech. staff applied mechanics divsn. Aerospace Corp., El Segundo, Calif., 1967-74; br. chief tech. divsn. Air Force Rocket Propulsion Lab., Edwards AFB, Calif., 1974-78, asst. for R&D mgmt., 1979-81; divsn. chief Air Force Armament Divsn., Eglin AFB, Fla., 1981-83; dir. drone control program office 3246 Test Wing, Eglin AFB, Fla., 1983-85, joint dir. US/Allied munitions program office, 1985-86; tech. dir. rsch./devel./acquisitions Air Force Armament Divsn., Eglin AFB, Fla., 1986-88; asst. to comdr. Air Force Munitions Divsn., Eglin AFB, Fla., 1988-90; tech. dir. Air Force Devel. and Test Ctr., Eglin AFB, 1990-93, exec. dir., 1993-98; exec. dir. Air Armament Ctr., Eglin AFB, Fla., 1998-99, Air Force Materiel Command, Wright-Paterson AFB, Ohio, 1999—; mem. policy coun. Scientist and Engr. Career Program, Randolph AFB, Tex., 1994—, chmn. career devel. panel, 1994-96. Bd. dirs. Internat. Found. for Telemetering, Woodland Hills, Calif., 1991-95; mem. engring. adv. bd. U. Fla., Gainesville, 1988—; mem. citizens adv. com. U. West Fla., Pensacola, 1991—; mem. civilian exec. adv. bd. Air Force Materiel Command, 1990—, also former chmn.; mem. curricular adv. com. Def. Test and Evaluation Profl. Inst., 1991—. Recipient Presdl. Meritorious Rank award Pres. of U.S., 1993. Mem. Air Force Assn. (Lewis H. Brereton award 1994), Sr. Exec. Assn., Am. Def. Preparedness Assn., Internat. Test and Evaluation Assn. (Cross medal 1994), Assn. of Old Crows, Fed. Exec. Inst. Alumni, Gulf Coast Alliance for Tech. Transfer. Avocations: tennis, golf, fishing. Office: Air Force Materiel Command 4375 Chidlaw Rd Wright Pat OH 45433-5066

STEWART, JAMES HAMILTON, lawyer; b. Bradford, Yorkshire, Eng., May 2, 1943; s. Henry Hamilton and Edna Mary (Pulman) S.; m. Helen Margaret Whiteley, Apr. 19, 1972 (dec.); children: Alexandra, Georgina. LLB with honors, Leeds U., 1965. Bar: N.E. Cir. 1970, Queens Coun. 1982, Bencher of Inner Temple 1992. Dep. high ct. judge, 1993, master inner temple, 1993, joint head of chambers, 1996. Office: Park Court Chambers, 16 Park Pl, Leeds LS1 2SJ, England

STEWART, JANE, psychology educator; b. Ottawa, Ont., Can., Apr. 19, 1934; d. Daniel Wallace and Jessie Stewart; m. Dalbir Bindra, Aug. 5, 1959 (dec. 1981). BA with honours, Queen's U., Kingston, Ont., 1956; PhD, U. London, 1959; DSc (hon.), Queen's U., 1992. Sr. rsch. biologist Ayerst Labs., Montreal, Que., 1959-63; part-time instr. psychology Sir George, Montreal, 1962-63; assoc. prof. psychology Williams U., Montreal, 1963-69; prof., chmn. psychology SGW Univ. (now Concordia U.), Montreal, 1969-75; prof. psychology Concordia U., Montreal, 1975—; dir. Ctr. for Studies in Behavioral Neurobiology, Concordia U., Montreal, 1990—. Fellow AAAS, APA, Royal Soc. Can., Can. Psychol. Assn.; mem. Soc. for Neurosci., N.Y. Acad. Sci. Office: Concordia University, 1455 de Maisonneuve Blvd W, Montreal, PQ Canada H3G 1M8

STEWART, JOHN MURRAY, banker; b. Summit, N.J., Apr. 2, 1943; s. Robert John Stewart and Mary Catherine (Grabhorn) Stewart Yoder; m. Sandra Meyers Frazier, Feb. 26, 1966 (div. 1997); children: Jennifer Bricar, Catherine Dorothy; m. Rebecca Marie Mellen, July 10, 1998. BA, U. Va., 1965; MBA, NYU, 1983. Trust officer, v.p. Bankers Trust Co., N.Y.C., 1965-82, Morgan Guaranty Trust Co., N.Y.C., 1982-83; mgr., pres., dir. Morgan Trust Co. Fla., Palm Beach, 1983-89; pres., dir. Bankers Trust Co. Fla., 1989-93; pres. pvt. capital group SunTrust Bank, Orlando, Fla., 1993-96; chmn., dir. Harris Trust/Bank of Montreal, West Palm Beach, 1996—. Campaign chmn. Palm Beach Cmty. Chest, 1985, 86; vestryman Bethesda By the Sea Ch., Palm Beach, 1986-89, 92-94, treas., 1986-87; trustee Cathedral Ch. of St. Luke, Orlando, 1996; bd. dirs. Orlando Opera Co., 1994-96, Palm Beach Opera Co., 1996—; mem. exec. com. Palm Beach County Local Initiatives Support Corp. Mem. Fla. Bankers Assn. (chmn. trust bus. devel. com. 1989, planning commn., chmn. trust legis. com. 1990), N.Y. State Bankers Assn. (mem. trust bus. devel. com. 1978-82), N.Y. Yacht Club (N.Y.C.), Everglades Club (Palm Beach), Monmouth Boat Club (Red Bank, N.J.), Sailfish Club of Fla. (Palm Beach) (bd. govs. 1992-96), SAR (pres. Palm Beach chpt. 1997, 98).

STEWART, JOHN TODD, economist. AB, Stanford U., 1961; MA, Tufts U., 1962, MALD, 1970. With Am. Fgn. Svc., 1962-98; U.S. amb. to Republic of Moldova, 1995-98; dep. head U.S. diplomatic missions to Can., Costa Rica and Jamaica; dir. office maritime and land transport Dept. of State, Washington; dir. GATT affairs Pres.'s Spl. Rep. for Trade Negotiations; dep. dir. Inst. Internat. Econs., Washington, 1998—. Office: Inst Internat Econs 11 Dupont Cir NW Washington DC 20036-1207

STEWART, JON BARTLEY, philosophy educator; b. Dallas, Nov. 20, 1961; s. Joseph Edward and Lexie Dean (Clark) S. BA in Philosophy, U. Calif., Santa Cruz, 1984; MA in Philosophy, U. Calif., San Diego, 1986; student, Westfälische Wilhelms U., Münster, Germany, 1989-91; PhD in Philosophy, U. Calif., San Diego, 1992. Rsch. asst. Westfälische Wilhelms U., Münster, 1990-91; guest lectr. dept. philosophy U. Calif., San Diego, 1991, Westfälische Wilhelms U., 1992-93; assoc. rsch. prof. Søren Kierkegaard Rsch. Ctr. U. Copenhagen, 1996—. Editor: The Hegel Myths and Legends, 1996, The Phenomenology of Spirit Reader: Critical and Interpretive Essays, 1998, The Debate Between Sartre and Merleau-Ponty, 1998; author: The Unity of Hegel's Phenomenology of Spirit, 2000; co-editor Kierkegaard Studies Yearbook, 2000—. Heinrich Hertz-Stiftung grantee German govt., 1992-93, Belgian-Am. Ednl. Found. grantee, 1993-94, Alexander von Humboldt grantee Humboldt U., 1994-95, Nat. Acad. Edn. Spencer post-doctoral fellow, 1995-96. Mem. The Am. Philos. Assn., The Hegel Soc. Am., The John Dewey Soc. for Study of Edn. and Culture, The N.Am. Nietzsche Soc., The Northwest Soc. for Phenomenology, Existentialism, and Hermeneutics, The Soc. for Phenomenology and Existential Philosophy, The Jorge Luis Borges Ctr. for Studies and Documentation.

STEWART, LUCILLE MARIE, special education coordinator; b. Pittsburgh, Feb. 24; d. William H. and Edna (Hoffman) S. BEd Duquesne U.; MEd, U. Pittsburgh; postgrad. courses Columbia U., U. Calif., Calif. State U. Cert. elem. and secondary tchr., spl. edn. tchr., supr., adminstr. Tchr. Lincoln (Ill). State Sch., 1953; group leader Retarded Education Alliance, N.Y.C., 1954-58; tchr. mentally retarded Ramapo Cen. Sch. Dist., Spring Valley, N.Y., 1958-60, seriously emotionally disturbed, 1960-64; program dir. Pomona (N.Y.) Camp for Retarded, summers 1960-63; tchr. Stockton Sch., San Diego, 1964-65, supr. presch. program for educationally disadvantaged Ramapo Ctrl. Sch. Dist., Spring Valley, N.Y., 1965-67; tchr. Cathdral City (Calif.) Sch., 1967-78; prog. specialist edn. Palm Springs Unified Sch. Dist., Calif., 1978-95; prin. elem. summer schs. Palm Springs (Calif.) Unified Sch. Dist., 1971-72; prin.-tchr. Summer Extended Sch. for Spl. Students, 1979—; mem. exec. com. U. Calif. Extension area adv. com. Mem. NEA, AAUW, Calif. Tchrs. Assn., Palm Springs Tchrs. Assn., Palm Springs Ednl. Leadership Assn., Calif. Assn. Program Specialists, Assn. for Supervision and Curriculum Devel., Am. Assn., Calif. Adminstrs. of Spl. Edn. (Desert community mental health childrens com.), Coun. Exceptional Children (admin., early childhood-learning handicap divsns.), Childhood Edn. Alpha Kappa Alpha, Phi Delta Kappa, Delta Kappa Gamma. Club: Toastmistress. Office: Palm Springs Unified Sch Dist 980 E Tahquitz Canyon Way Palm Springs CA 92262-6786

STEWART, MAC A., educator; b. Forsyth, Ga., July 7, 1942; s. Alonzo and Zillia (Watson) S.; m. Tena Clemons, June 4, 1967; children: Bruce Kifle, Justin Che. BA, Morehouse Coll., 1963; MA, Atlanta U., 1965; PhD, Ohio State U., 1973. Lic. psychologist, Ohio. Tchr., counselor Jasper County Tng. Sch., Montivello, Ga., 1963-64; tchr. Crispus Attucks High Sch., Indpls., 1965-66; dir. student fin. aid Morehouse Coll., Atlanta, 1966-70, dir. upward bound, 1967-70; dir. residence hall Ohio State U., Columbus, 1970-71, grad. adminstrv. assoc. student fin. aid, 1971-73, asst. dean Univ. Coll., 1973-75, assoc. dean Univ. Coll., 1975-90, assoc. prof., dean Univ. Coll., 1991-98, assoc. provost for undergrad. studies, 1998—; Contbr. articles to profl. jours.; mem. editl. bd. The Negro Ednl. Rev., 1983—, editor-in-chief, 1999—. Bd. trustees The Columbus Acad., Gahanna, Ohio, 1990-96, Buckeye Boys Ranch, Grove City, Ohio, 1978-84, Mt. Carmel Coll. Nursing, 1998—, Internat. Found. Edn. & Self-Help, 1998—, Mt. Carmel Coll. Nursing, 1998—; mem. adv. coun. Internat. Found. Edn. and Self-Help, Phoenix, 1992—, bd. dirs., 1998—; bd. dirs. Urban Edn., Rsch. and Human Devel. Inst., Columbus, 1977-80. Mem. ASCD, Ohio Acad. Sci., Nat. Assn. Equal Opportunity in Health Edn., United Negro Coll. Fund, Phi Kappa Phi, Phi Beta Sigma, Sigma Pi Phi. Avocations: reading, collecting insulators, travel, jogging, weight lifting. Home: 930 Notchbrook Dr Delaware OH 43015-8996 Office: Ohio State U 154 E 12th Ave Columbus OH 43201-1806

STEWART, MALCOLM WILLIAM, psychologist, researcher; b. Lower Hutt, Wellington, N.Z., Dec. 19, 1959; s. Alan William and Christine Norma (Innes) S.; m. Janet Lynn Fanslow, May 25, 1991; children: Briony Fanslow, Geneva Fanslow. BS, Victoria U., Wellington, N.Z., 1980; Diploma of Mgmt., N.Z. Inst. Mgt., Wellington, 1983; Diploma Clin. Psychology, Otago U., Dunedin, N.Z., 1990, PhD, 1991. Registered psychologist, N.Z. Biomed. engr. Wellington Hosp., 1981-84; tutor/lectr. Otago U., Dunedin, 1985-90; asst. clin. psychologist Cherry Farm, Dunedin, 1990-91; clin. psychologist Cardiology dept. Dunedin Hosp., 1991; clin. psychologist, psychiat. liaison team Pain Clinic, Middlemore Hosp., Auckland, N.Z., 1991-94; prof. leader psychology Health Waikato, Hamilton, N.Z., 1994-97; adj. faculty Oglethorpe U., Atlanta, 1997-98; adj. clin. faculty Ga. Sch. Profl. Psychology, Atlanta, 1998; sr. lectr. sch. medicine U. Auckland, New Zealand, 1999—; vis. scientist Ctrs. for Disease Control and Prevention, Atlanta, 1998; clin. psychologist Early Intervention for Psychosis Team, Taylor Ctr., Auckland, 1999—. Editor Jour. N.Z. Pain Soc., 1994-97; contbr. articles to profl. jours. Mem. coun. Workers Ednl. Assn., Dunedin, 1989-91; group regional action network coord. Amnesty Internat., Dunedin, 1990-92; mem. Forest and Bird Soc., Auckland. Recipient Young Investigators Travel award N.Z. Health Rsch. Coun., 1989. Mem. N.Z. Coll. Clin. Psychologists, N.Z. Psychol. Soc. (com. mem., Best Student Paper award 1990), N.Z. Pain Soc. (mem. coun.), N.Z. Health Psychology Soc. Avocations: home renovation, freelance writing, hiking. Office: Taylor Ctr, PO Box 47-679, Ponsonby Auckland New Zealand

STEWART, MELINDA JANE, judge; b. Merced, Calif., Apr. 10, 1949; d. Donald Joel and Betty Yvonne (Santi) S.; m. Bruce G. Wilbur, Aug. 1998; children from previous marriage: Alexa Marie, Julienne Rose, Robert Patrick; stepchildren: Michelle, Keith, Kelly, Kevin. BA, Stanford U., 1972; JD, Golden Gate Law Sch., 1975. Bar: Calif. 1975, U.S. Dist. Ct. (no. dist.) Calif. 1975. Dep. dist. atty. Santa Clara County Dist. Atty., San Jose, Calif., 1976-80; atty. Miller & Hinkle Law Offices, San Jose, 1980; pvt. practice Tondreau & Goodman, San Jose, 1980-83; referee Santa Clara County Superior Ct., San Jose, 1983-89, judge, 1989—; faculty Calif. Ctr. for Jud. Edn. and Rsch., 1983—. Bd. dirs. Eastfield Ming Quong Childrens Ctr., 1993-98, pro bono project of Santa Clara County, 1992-95, YWCA Kids Connection, 1993-95, Hillbrook Sch., 1993-98. Named Calif. State Bar Assn. Family Law Judge of Yr., 1995; recipient Henry B. Collada Meml. award, 1995. Mem. Calif. Judges Assn., Assn. Family and Counciliation Cts. (Calif. chpt. bd. dirs.). Avocations: swimming, tennis, skiing. Office: Superior Ct Santa Clara County 191 N 1st St San Jose CA 95113-1001

STEWART, MICHAEL ALEXANDER, philosophy educator; b. Norwich, Eng., Oct. 21, 1937; s. Duncan Percy and Mary Phyllis (Skelton) S. MA, U. St. Andrews, Scotland, 1960; PhD, U. Pa., Phila., 1965. Tchg. fellow U. Pa., 1961-63; lectr. Bklyn. Coll., 1963-64, U. Western Ont., London, Can., 1964-65; lectr. Lancaster (U.K.) U., 1965-77, sr. lectr., 1977-93, prof. history of philosophy, 1993-97, rsch. prof., 1997—; hon. prof. U. Aberdeen, Scotland, 1999—; sr. fellow Harris Manchester Coll. U. Oxford, 2000—; gen. editor Oxford Studies in History of Philosophy, 1990—, Clarendon edition of The Works of John Locke, 1992—; joint gen. editor The Philos., Polit. and Lit. Works of David Hume, Oxford, U.K., 1992—; vis. fellow Inst. for Advanced Studies in the Humanities, Edinburgh, 1981-83, 86, 95, Rsch. Sch. Social Scis., Australian Nat. U., Canberra, 1991-92, 96. Author: The Kirk and the Infidel, 1995; editor: Selected Philosophical Papers of Robert Boyle, 1979, Law, Morality and Rights, 1983, Studies in the Philosophy of the Scottish Enlightenment, 1990, Studies in 17th Century European Philosophy, 1997, English Philosophy in the Age of Locke, 2000; co-editor, contbr.: Hume and Hume's Connexions, 1994; contbr. articles to profl. jours.; editl. cons. Br. Jour. History of Philosophy, 1993—; mem. editl. bd. Jour. History of Philosophy, 1994—. Gifford lectr. U. Aberdeen, Scotland, 1995, Robert Allen Meml. lectr. Presbyn. Hist. Soc. Ireland, 1994. Mem. Brit. Soc. for History of Philosophy (chmn. 1984-91), Mind Assn. (publs. officer 1988—), Royal Inst. Philosophy (mem. coun. 1986—). Avocations: music, opera, travel. Home: 17 Magdala Crescent, Edinburgh EH12 5BD, Scotland

STEWART, MICHAEL B., lawyer, mechanial and aerospace engineer; b. Royal Oak, Mich., Nov. 5, 1963; s. Colin M. and Jacqueline P. Stewart; m. Katherine Hewitt, May 1987; children: Elizabeth and Caitlin. BSME, U. Mich, 1987, BA in English, 1987, MS in Aerospace Engring., 1988, JD, 1991. Assoc. Dykema Gossett PLLC, Bloomfield Hills, Mich., 1991-96; founding ptnr. Rader, Fishman & Grauer PLLC, Bloomfield Hills, 1996—. Contbr. articles to profl. jours. Named 40 Under 40 Honoree Crain's Detroit Bus., 1998. Mem. ABA, Intellectual Property Law Assn., Mich. Patent Law Assn., Mich. Bar Assn., Oakland County Bar Assn. (chmn. continuing legal edn. subcom. for IP com. 1998), Optimists (bd. dirs. 1993-97), Delta Theta Phi (treas., bd. govs., Detroit alumni senate). Avocations: cycling, woodworking. E-mail: mbs@raderfishman.com. Office: Rader Fishman & Grauer PLLC 39533 Woodward Ave Ste 140 Bloomfield Hills MI 48304-5098

STEWART, MICHAEL MCFADDEN, professional speaker; b. Eupora, Miss., Aug. 24, 1938; s. Judge Ernest and Billie Rivers (McFadden) S.; m. Barbara Ann Dickerson, June 2, 1962; children: Michael Jr., Mark Robert (dec. Dec. 1997). BS, La. State U., 1961. Cert. speaking profl. Nat. Spkrs. Assn., 1996. Cons. E.K. Williams & Co., Birmingham, Ala., 1964-66, br. mgr., 1966-68; br. mgr. E.K. Williams & Co., Miami, Fla., 1968-69, Marcoin, Inc., Balt., 1969-73; dist. mgr. Marcoin, Inc., Falls Church, Va., 1973-74; v.p. Marcoin Western Ops., Inc., Houston, 1974-77; dir., v.p. Marcoin, Inc., Atlanta, 1977-85; ptnr. Cherokee/G & S Assocs., Atlanta, 1985-88; pres. Stewart & Stewart, Inc., Dunwoody, Ga., 1988—, The Sales Power Resource Group, Inc., Atlanta, 1991-95; cons., speaker AMA, N.Y.C., 1989—, Duffy-Vinet Inst., Langhorne, Pa., 1987-92, The Sullivan Group, Guilford, Conn., 1990-92; guest speaker SBA, Bell South Success Symposium Series, 1990-91. Author: How to Get Started with a Small Business Computer, 1984, Quality Customer Service, 1990, Using Your Financial Statements to Boost Your Bottom Line Profits, 1990, Computerizing Your Business, 1991, The Magic of Customer Service, 1991, Bring Home the Bacon, 1992, Customer Service Excellence: How to Implement a Corporate-wide Program, 1992, Strategic Relationship Selling, 1992, Transition into Sales Management, 1992, Sales Managememt Call Reluctance Workshop, 1992, Negotiating with Style, 1992, Meeting Today's Competitive Challenges, 1992, Creative Management in Tough Economic Times, 1993, Relationship Empowered Technical Selling, 1993, Consultative Relationship Selling, 1993, Customer-Centered Sales Management Leadership, 1993, Customer Centered Selling, 1993, Being Different in a Niche Market, 1993, Moving, Shaking and Prospecting, 1993, 50/250 The Smart Way, 1993, Customer-Centered Relationship Selling, 1994, Working Sucessfully with Others, 1994, Fundamentals of Quality Customer Service, 1994, Sales Are The Life-Blood Service is the Heart Beat, 1994, Customer-Centered Value Selling, 1994, Customer-Centered Sales Management, 1994, Make the Number by Selling Value, 1995, Hiring Smart, 1995, Customer-Centered Sales Management, 1995, Live the Spirit, 1996, Sell Value, Not Price, 1996; contbg. author: Chicken Soup for the Soul at Work, 1996, Relationship Centered Value Selling, 1997, Professional Sales Skills, 1997, Sales Negotiation for Higher Profits, 1998; contbg. author: Reach for the Stars, 1998, Close More Sales!, 1999, Close More Sales With Premise, 2000; contbr. numerous articles to profl. jours. Fin. officer Atlanta Colts Youth Assn., 1979; vol. speaker Am. Cancer Soc., 1994—. Capt. U.S. Army, 1961-64. Recipient Silver award Carlson Learning Co., Mpls., 1990. Mem. ASTD, Ga. Speakers Assn. (past pres., past dir., Mem. of Yr. 1996), Nat. Spkrs. Assn. (cert. speaking profl.), Dunwoody Country Club, Dunwoody Gridiron Club (pres. 1981), Lambda Chi Alpha. Episcopalian. Avocation: golf. Home: 490 Tavern Cir Atlanta GA 30350-4455

STEWART, PATRICIA RHODES, retired clinical psychologist, researcher; b. Vallejo, Calif., Feb. 11, 1910; d. Butler Young Rhodes and Sarah Virginia (Ryan) Rhodes; m. John Kenneth Stewart (div.); children: John K., Nancy Rush. AB summa cum laude, Stanford U., 1930; MA, San Jose State U., 1959; PhD, U. London, 1963. Tchg. asst. San Jose State U., 1959-60; staff psychologist Napa State Hosp., 1964-77; pvt. practice in psychotherapy Berkeley, Calif., 1978-94; pvt. rsch. in adolescent deviance Berkeley, 1979-85; staff psychologist Westwood Mental Health Facility, Fremont, Calif., 1985-88. Author: Children in Distress: American and English Perspectives, 1976. Chair criminal justice com. No. Calif. region Am. Friends Svc. com., San Francisco, 1977-80, chair exec. com. 1970-74, 80-83, bd. dirs., 1980-83; bd. dirs. Friends Com. on Legis., Sacramento, 1985-88, No. Calif. Ecumenical Coun., Oakland, Calif., 1989-95. Mem. APA, AAAS, Phi Beta Kappa. Mem. Soc. of Friends. Home: 1225 Monterey Ave Berkeley CA 94707-2718

STEWART, RALPH DAVID HUSTON, medical educator; b. Gillingham, Kent, Eng., May 7, 1933; arrived in New Zealand, 1939; s. Ralph William Truman Huston and Mary Barr (Stevenson) S.; m. Dorothea Elspeth Gibbs, Dec. 14, 1957; children: Ralph, Sara, Hamish, Timothy. MB, ChB, U. Otago, Dunedin, New Zealand, 1956, MD, 1968. Various appointments in hosps. and rsch. units New Zealand, Eng., Scotland and Australia, 1957-70; assoc. prof. medicine U. Otago, 1971-74, prof. medicine, 1974-83, dep. dean med. sch., 1983-85, dean med. sch., 1986-90, asst. vice chancellor health scis., 1991-98; vice chmn. senate U. Otago, 1985-87, mem. coun., 1991-94; mem. Otago Hosp. Bd., Dunedin, 1984-89; dir. Healthlink South, Christchurch, New Zealand, 1996-2000, HealthCare Otago, Dunedin, New Zealand, 1998—. Co-author: Fact Finding Group on Nuclear Power, 1977, The Present State and Future Needs of Cancer Research in New Zealand, 1983, Research for Health, 1989. Mem. Nat. Interim Provider Bd., New Zealand, 1992; chair Ministerial Adv. Group on Clin. Tng., 1992, steering com. Crown Health Enterprises Establishment Unit, 1993, clin. adv. group Crown Health Enterprises Monitoring Unit, 1994. Fellow Royal Coll. Physicians (London), Royal Australasian Coll. Physicians; mem. New Zealand Endocrine Soc. (pres. 1985-88). Avocations: bridge, reading, skiing, sailing.

STEWART, REBEKAH BROOKE, retired small business owner; b. Sycamore, Ga., Oct. 29, 1923; d. Robert Elijah and Ester (Cannon) Brooke; m. Robert E. Stewart (dec. July 1984); children: Richard Lamar, Elizabeth Anne. Student, Armstrong State Coll., Savannah, Ga., 1955-59. Co-owner, asst. mgr. Stewart's Inc., material handling equipment company, Savannah, 1955-95; ret., 1995. Mem. Nat. Assn. Women in Constrn. (past pres. Savannah). Baptist. Home: 1700 Fox Holw SW Lilburn GA 30047-3310

STEWART, ROBERT ARTHUR CHURCHILL (BOB STEWART), journal publisher, municipal official; b. Wellington, New Zealand, Nov. 1,

1939; s. Robert Arnold Stewart and Ethel Gwendolyn (Hansell) Cousins; m. Mary Jones, Jan. 2, 1971; children: Robert W.A., Peter G.A. Student, Christ's Coll., Christchurch, New Zealand, 1953-57; BA, U. New Zealand, Wellington, 1962; EdM, Harvard U., Cambridge, Mass., 1965; PhD, Massey U., Palmerston North, New Zealand, 1972. Lectr. in psychology Carleton U., Ottawa, Ontario, Can., 1965-66; lectr., sr. lectr. in edn. Massey U., Palmerston North, New Zealand, 1968-78; assoc. prof. of psychology Laurentian U., Sudbury, Ont., Can., 1975-78; reader, prof. of human devel. U. South Pacific, Suva, Fiji, 1978-89; head Sch. of Edn. U. of the South Pacific, Suva, Fiji, 1981-83, pro vice-chancellor (acad.), 1983-85, acting vice-chancellor, 1985, head Sch. Humanities, 1986-88; founder, governing dir. Scientific Jour. Publishers, Palmerston North, New Zealand, 1989—. Author: (book) Cultural Dimensions: Factor Analysis of Textor's A Cross-Cultural Summary, 1972; editor: (books) Adolescence in New Zealand: A Book of Readings 2 vols., 1976, From the South Pacific: Profiles in Human Experience, 1980, Pacific Profiles: Personal Experiences of 100 South Pacific Islanders, 1982; co-editor: (with J.P. Maas) Towards a World of Peace: People Create Alternatives, 1986; editor (jours.) Personality: An Internat. Jour., 1970-71, Social Behavior and Personality, An Internat. Jour., 1973—; contbr. 61 chpts. to books, articles to profl. jours. Am. Field Svc. scholar to Delavan, Wis., 1957-58; mem. Rotary Peace Forum Internat. Com., Evanston, Ill., 1988-89; elected councillor Palmerston North (New Zealand) City Coun., 1992—, chmn. City's Econ. Com., 1993-98, apptd. mem. Manawatu Bus. Devel. Bd., Palmerston North, 1994-98, deputy chmn., 1996-98; apptd. mem. Heritage Regent Theatre Trust Bd., 1999—; electorate chmn. New Zealand Nat. party, Palmerston North, 1992-95, divsn councillor, Wellington province, 1994-95. Recipient Ken Scheller Rotary award for writing excellence, Sydney, Australia, 1990. Mem. New Zealand Property Investors Fedn. (coun. mem., v.p. North Island, 1991-92), Palmerston North Rotary Club (comty. svc. dir. 1991-92), Manawatu Rose Soc., Lodge Rangitane #369. Avocations: rose growing, gardening, philately, telephone card collecting, music. Home: 30 Summerhill Dr, Palmerston North 5301, New Zealand Office: Sci Jour Publishers, PO Box 1539, Palmerston North 5331, New Zealand

STEWART, RODERICK DAVID, singer; b. North London, Eng., Jan. 10, 1945; m. Alana Collins, Apr. 6, 1979 (div. 1984); children: Alana, Sean; child with Kelly Emberg: Ruby Rachel; m. Rachel Hunter, Dec. 15, 1990, child, Renée. Singer with Jeff Beck Group, 1968-69, Faces, 1969-75; albums include (with Jeff Beck Group) Truth, 1968, Beck-Ola, 1969; (with Faces) The First Step, 1970, Long Player, 1971, A Nod Is As Good as a Wink...To a Blind Horse, 1971, Ooh La La, 1973, Coast to Coast/Overture & Beginners, 1973, Snakes and Ladders/The Best of Faces, 1976; (solo) An Old Raincoat Won't Ever Let You Down, 1969, Gasoline Alley, 1970, Every Picture Tells a Story, 1971, Never a Dull Moment, 1972, Sing it Again Rod, 1973, Smiler, 1974, Atlantic Crossing, 1975, The Best of Rod Stewart, 1976, The Best of Rod Stewart Vol. II, 1976, A Night on the Town, 1976, Foot Loose & Fancy Free, 1976, Blondes Have More Fun, 1978, Greatest Hits Vol. I, 1979, Tonight I'm Yours, 1981, Absolutely Live, 1981, Camouflage, 1984, (with Jeff Beck) Get Workin', 1985, Out of Order, 1988, Storyteller: The Complete Anthology 1964-1990, 1990, Downtown Train, 1990, Vagabond Heart, 1991, You Wear It Well, 1992, The Mercury Anthology, 1992, Once In A Blue Moon Vintage, 1993, Ridin High, The Rod Stewart Album, Unplugged...And Seated, 1993 (Grammy nomination, Best Pop Male Vocal for "Have I Told You Lately"), Spanner in the Works, 1995, Handbags and Gladrags, 1996, When We Were the New Boys, 1998; films include Rod Stewart - The Best of Rod Stewart, Rod Stewart and The Faces - The Final Concert, 1974, Rod Stewart and Faces, 1975, Rod Stewart Live at Los Angeles Forum, 1980, Rod Stewart-Tonight He's Yours, short and long versions, 1981, The Rod Stewart Concert Video, 1984, Rod Stewart - Storyteller 1984-91, 1991, Rod Stewart - Vagabond Heart. Named Rock Star of Year Rolling Stone mag., 1971; recipient British Rock and Pop Lifetime Achievement award, 1992; inducted into the Rock & Roll Hall of Fame, 1994. Office: Warner Bros Records 3300 Warner Blvd Burbank CA 91505-4694

STEWART, ROGER CHARLES, consumer products consumer executive; b. Indpls., Sept. 23, 1949; s. Charles Thomas and Mary Pearl Stewart. BS in Sci., Purdue, 1971, MS in Indsl. Admin., 1974. Staff disposable fin. analysis Procter Gamble, Cin., 1978-80, staff spl. assign analysis, 1980, assoc. dir. tissue, 1981-83; dir. soft drinks Procter Gamble, Lexington, Ky., 1983-85; dir. sys. RVI Procter Gamble, Wilton, Conn., 1986; dir. internat. treasury Procter Gamble, Cin., 1987-98, v.p. global treasury, 1998—; lectr. Krannert Sch., Purdue U., West Lafayette, Ind., 1992—. Past pres. Cancer Family Care, 1978—; fundraiser local charities. Avocations: playing marimba, travel, biking. E-mail: stewart.rc.@pg.com. Home: 9829 Villageview Ct Cincinnati OH 45241-3802

STEWART, T. BONNER, parasitology educator; b. São Paulo, Brazil, Nov. 24, 1924; came to U.S., 1933; s. Charles T. and Leonor (de Magalhães) S.; m. Jane Evans Simril, June 19, 1956; children: D. Alan, Janice R., Julia L., J. Todd. BS in Zoology, U. Md., 1949; MS in Zoo-Parasitology, Auburn U., 1953; PhD in Vet. Med. Sci., U. Ill., 1963. Vet. parasitologist USDA, Agrl. Rsch. Svc. Regional Lab., Auburn, Ala., 1950-53; dir. USDA, Agrl. Rsch. Svc., Swine Parasite Lab., Tifton, Ga., 1953-79; prof. Sch. Vet. Medicine La. State U., Baton Rouge, 1979—; cons. pharm.-swine anthelmintics, 1980—; vis. prof. Fed. Rural U. of Rio de Janeiro, 1986, Danish Ctr. for Exptl. Parasitology, 1997, collaborator, 1997—; collaborator USDA Agrl. Rsch. Svc., Watkinsville, Ga., 1992—. Contbr. more than 100 articles to profl. jours. Mem. exec. bd. Boy Scouts Am., Baton Rouge, 1985—, scouter, Tifton, Baton Rouge, 1957—; mem. Rotary Club, Tifton, 1964-79, pres., 1972; elder Presbyn. Ch., Tifton, 1972—. With U.S. Army, 1943-46, ETO. Recipient Silver Beaver, Boy Scouts of Am., 1969; named Wood Badge Dir., Boy Scouts Am., 1989. Mem. Am. Assn. Vet. Parasitologists (Disting. Vet. Parasitologist award 1996), World Assn. for Advancement of Vet. Parasitology, Am. Soc. Parasitology, Animal Disease Rsch. Workers in the So. States (pres. 1978), Wildlife Disease Assn. Achievements include research in prevalence, pathogenesis and control of swine parasites; in economics of parasitisms; in parasite effects on host nutrition; in taxonomy of Helminth parasites. Office: Sch Vet Medicine La State U Baton Rouge LA 70803-0001

STEWART, THOMAS CLIFFORD, trading and investment company executive; b. Portland, Oreg., Oct. 25, 1950; s. Jack Fry Stewart and Naomi June Gedney Cuyler; m. Susan Elizabeth Sample; children: Cortny, MacKenzie, Tommy, Andrew. Student, U. Gothenburg, Sweden, 1971; BS, U. Oreg., 1974; MBA, UCLA, 1982. Prin. Morgan Stanley & Co., N.Y.C., 1982-90; pres. Cort MacKenzie & Co., Virginia Beach, Va., 1990-92, Portland, Oreg., 1992-95, Lake Oswego, Oreg., 19955; chmn. Beijing Kang Mei Biol. Products Co., Ltd., 19955; dir. Acrymed, Lake Oswego, Oreg., 1995-96, Morley Fin. Svcs., Lake Oswego, Oreg., 1995-97; dir. bikerbill.com., Va., 2000—. Contbr. articles to profl. jours. Trustee U. Oreg. Found., 19945; chmn. U. Oreg. Pres.'s Assn., 1997-99; exec. com., Lundquist Coll. of Bus., Univ. Oregon, 1998—, bd. advisors Coll. Bus., U. Oreg., 1990—, Athletic Dept., Bd. Advisors, Univ. Oregon, 1998—; Oreg. State Commn. on Higher Bus. Edn., 1992-94; mem. leadership coun. U. Oreg., 1995-99, mem. adminstrn. com., mem. acad. affairs com., 1996-00; bd. dirs. Lake Oswego Sch. Found., 1996-2000; treas. adv. cabinet Oreg. State, 1993-94; adv. bd. sec. of Navy Nat. Naval Res. Policy Bd., Washington, 1987-89. Comdr. USN, 1974-80, USNR, 1980-91. Decorated Air medal, Navy Commendation for Valor; Baker scholar, 1981. Mem. Presdl. Roundtable, Naval Res. Assn. (Jr. Officer of Yr. 1988), U.S. Navy League, ROA, Am. Legion, VFW, Beta Gamma Sigma, Beta Alpha Psi, Alpha Mu Alpha, Skull & Dagger. Office: Cort MacKenzie 884 Park St Lebanon OR 97355-3204

STEWART, WARREN EARL, chemical engineer, educator; b. Whitewater, Wis., July 3, 1924; s. Earl Austin and Avis (Walker) S.; m. Jean Durham Potter, May 24, 1947; children—Marilyn, David, Douglas, Carol, Margaret, Mary Jean. B.S. in Chem. Engring, U. Wis., 1945, M.S. in Chem. Engring, 1947; Sc.D. in Chem. Engring, Mass. Inst. Tech., 1951. Project chem. engr. Sinclair Research Labs., Harvey, Ill., 1950-56; cons. Sinclair Research Labs., 1956-83; asst. prof. chem. engring. dept. U. Wis., Madison, 1956-58; assoc. prof. U. Wis., 1958-61, prof., 1961—, chmn. dept., 1973-78, McFarland-Bascom prof., 1983-96, prof. emeritus, 1997—; cons. Engelhard Industries, Inc., Newark, 1956-58; instr. spl. courses transport phenomena Chemstrand Corp., Pensacola, Fla., 1962, Nat. U. La Plata, Argentina, 1962, Esso Rsch. & Engring. Co., 1963, 66, Phillips Petroleum Co., 1963, Am. Inst. Chem. Engrs., 1965, 68, 69, Inst. Tec. Celaya (Mex.), 1983, Univ. Autonoma de Mex., 1985; Reilly lectr. Notre Dame U., 1993. Author: (with R.B. Bird and E.N. Lightfoot) Transport Phenomena, 1960, Special Topics in Transport Phenomena, 1965, (with R.B. Bird, E.N. Lightfoot and T.W. Chapman) Lectures in Transport Phenomena, 1969; editorial advisor: Latin Am. Applied Rsch.; editorial advisor: Computers and Chem. Engring. Served to ensign USNR, 1944-46. Recipient Benjamin Smith Reynolds teaching award, 1981, Byron Bird rsch. award, 1991. Fellow Am. Inst. Chem. Engrs. (Computing in Chem. Engring. award 1985); mem. NAE, Am. Chem. Soc. (Murphree award in indsl. and engring. chemistry 1989), Am. Soc. for Engring. Edn., (Chem. Engring. Lectureship award 1983), Phi Beta Kappa, Sigma Xi, Alpha Chi Sigma (research award 1981), Phi Eta Sigma, Tau Beta Pi, Phi Lambda Upsilon, Phi Kappa Phi. Conglist. (deacon, moderator). Home: 734 Huron Hl Madison WI 53711-2955

STEWART-BELL, LESLIE ANN, sculptor, moldmaker; b. Billings, Mont., Dec. 29, 1960; d. Robert Burns and Farrell Jane (Coffman) S.; m. Bruce E. Bell, Dec. 18, 1996. BA, Mont. State U., 1987; MFA, Ea. Ill. U., 1988. Owner, pres. LASH Quality Molds & Sculpture Supply, Portland, Oreg., 1991—; tchr. moldmaking: sculpting for bronze; moldmaker Remington Art Mus., 1997. Prodr. instructional video prodns. from moldmaking of sculpture to finished bronze fine art; contbr. article to profl. jour. Active Portland (Oreg.) Art Mus. Mem. NAIC Investment Club (v.p. 1996—). Avocations: windsurfing, kite flying, motorcycling, canoeing, rafting. Home: 28607 NE 49th Cir Camas WA 98607

STEWARTBY, IAN, bank executive; b. Aug. 10, 1935; s. H.C. Stewart; m. Deborah Charlotte Buchan, 1966; 3 children. Student, Haileybury, Jesus Coll.; MA, LittD, Cambridge U., 1978. Joined Brown, Shipley & Co. Ltd., 1960-63, asst. mgr., 1963-66, mgr., 1966; dep. chmn. Standard Chartered plc, 1993—, also bd. dirs.; bd. dirs. Diploma plc, Portman Bldg. Soc., others; chmn. Throgmorton Trust PLC, 1990—. Author: The Scottish Coinage, 1955, 2d edit., 1967, Scottish Mints, 1971; co-author: Coinage in Tenth Century England, 1989, New History of the Royal Mint, 1992; contbr. numerous articles to profl. jours. M.P. Conservative for North Hertfordshire, 1974-92, called Hitchin, 1974-83; parliamentary pvt. sec. to Chancellor of the Exchequer, Sir Geoffrey Howe, 1979-83; parliamentary undersec. of State for Def. Procurement, 1983; Econ. Sec. to the Treas., 1983-87; Min. of State for the Armed Forces, 1987-88, Min. of State, No. Ireland, 1988-89; hon. treas. Westminster Com. for the Protection of Children, 1960-70; trustee Sir Halley Stewart Trust, 1978—; county v.p. St. John Ambulance, Hertfordshire, 1978—; mem. Coun., Haileybury, 1980-95. Lt. commdr. Royal Naval Res. Named Baron of Portmoak, 1992. Mem. Beefsteak, MCC, Royal Automobile Club, Hawks Club, Pitt Club, The New Club. Office: Standard Chartered plc, 1 Aldermanbury, London EC2V 7SB, England

STEWART-COUSINS, ANDREA ALICE, legislator; b. N.Y.C., Sept. 2, 1950; d. Robert Lucius and Beryl Agatha (Phipps); m. May 5, 1979; children: Kevin, Steven, Candice. BSc, Pace U., 1986. Cert. bus. edn. tchr., N.Y. Customer svc. rep. N.Y. Tel., 1970-78; market adminstr. AT&T, N.Y.C., 1979-83; journalist Gannett Westchester Newspapers, Yonkers, N.Y., 1986-88; tchr. Yonkers (N.Y.) Pub. Schs., 1988-89; pers. mgr. Career Blazers, White Plains, N.Y., 1989-92; dir. cmty. affairs Mayor's Office, Yonkers, 1992-95; legislator Westchester County Bd. Legislators, White Plains, 1996—; sponsor Westchester County Human Rights Commn., N.Y., 1999—. Bd. dirs. Yonkers Gen. Hosp., 1999—; presenter, govt. liaison Westchester Black Women's Pol. Caucus, 1992— (Legislator of Yr. 2000). Racial justice award YWCA, White Plains, 2000, Civil Libertarian 2000 award Am. Civil Liberties Union, Weschester County, Trailblazer award N.Y. State Assn. of Human Rights Commn., 2000. Mem. NAACP (Legis. Excellence 2000), Westchester County Bd. Legislators (county legislator 1996—), Westchester County Dem. Com., N.Y., 1998—. Avocations: meditation, reading. Fax: 914-963-5831. Home e-mail: acyogi@aol.com. Office e-mail: ac9@Westchester.gov. Home: 293 N Broadway Yonkers NY 10701-2453 Office: Westchester County Bd Legislators 148 Martine Ave White Plains NY 10601-3311

STEWART NELSON, PAMELA, home health administrator, consultant; b. Chgo., June 27, 1948; d. Donald and Lena (Brevard) Paquet; m. William Frank Nelson, Mar. 25, 2000. Diploma, St. Elizabeth Hosp. Sch. Nursing, Chgo., 1969; B. Nursing, Governor State U., 1978. Staff nurse emergency rm. St. Elizabeth's Hosp., Chgo., 1969-72, charge nurse emergency rm., 1973-76; staff nurse trauma Christ Hosp., Oaklawn, Ill., 1972-73; staff nurse SO Suburban Home Health, North Riverside, Ill., 1976-79, supr., 1979, dir., 1979-81; cons. home health HQR, North Riverside, 1981-82; exec. dir. Superior Care, Great Neck, N.Y., 1982—; pres. Health Care Design, Plainfield, Ill., 1984—; cons. Steuben County Pub. Health, BAth, N.Y., 1986-88, Evang. Hosp. Systems, Oakbrook, Ill., 1989-90, Midwest Home Care, Chgo., 1991-92; adv. bd. chmn. Primary Care Svcs., Chgo., 1989—. Author: Nurse, Therapists Notes and Summaries, 1981, Modual Approach, 1984, 87, Computers in Health Care and Home Care Economics, Documentation for Home Care, 1992. Mem. APHA, Ill. Home Care Coun. (reimbursement com. 1986-88, bd. dirs. and edn. chmn. 1989-91). Avocations: reading, writing, decorating, debating issues. Office: Health Care Design 1400 N Penny Ln Plainfield IL 60544-9468

STEYAERT, JAN KAREL MARIE-ANTOON, corporate executive; b. Tielt, Belgium, Jan. 29, 1945; s. Valerius Desiderius Josephus and Gabrielle Josephine Alphonse Marie Antoine Van Daele; Anna Julia Godelieve Ghekiere; children: Tom, Carolien, Floris. Student, Sint Amandus Gent, Belgium, HITH Gent, Belgium. With Telindus Group NV, Heverlee, Belgium, 1970—, gen. dir., mng. dir., also bd. dirs.; bd. dirs. Telindus NV, Telindus GSM, Telindus Lux., Telindus France, Telindus U.K., Telindus Italy, Telindus Germany, Telindus Suisse, Datax NV, Mobistar NV, Mercator & Noordstar, Anima Eterna. Avocations: art, sailing. Office: Telindus Group NV, Geldenaaksebaan 335, 3001 Heverlee Belgium

STEYER, ROLF, psychologist, educator; b. Fulda, Hessen, Germany, Dec. 1, 1950; s. Karl-Heinz and Ursula (Neumann) S.; m. Anna-Maria Majcen, Jan. 17, 1992;; children: Anna Carolina, Christian Alexander. Diploma in Psychology, U. Goettingen, 1978; PhD in Psychology, U. Frankfurt, 1982; Dr.habil., U. Trier, Germany, 1988. Univ. asst. U. Frankfurt, 1978-82, U. Trier, 1982-94; rsch. dir. ZUMA, Mannheim, Germany, 1994-95; prof. U. Magdeburg, 1995-96; prof. psychology U. Jena, 1996—. Author: Theorie Kausaler Regressionsmodelle, 1992, Messen und Testen, 1993; editor European Jour. Psychol. Assessment. Mem. European Assn. Psychol. Assessment (gen. sec. 1996-99). Office: Inst for Psychology, Am Steiger 3 Haus 1, 07743 Jena Germany

STIBBE, AUSTIN JULE, accountant; b. St. Paul, Mar. 29, 1930; s. Austin Julius and Agnes Dorothea (Delaney) S.; m. Mary Elizabeth King, May 29, 1952; children: Anne Marie, Craig Jule, David King, Karen Lee. BSB in Acctg., U. Minn., 1952. CPA, Minn., Wis. Tax acct. Ernst & Ernst, Mpls., 1955-60; corp. tax mgr. EcoLab, Inc., St. Paul, 1960-65; audit mgr. Coopers & Lybrand, Mpls., 1965-74; v.p. Wilkerson, Guthmann & Johnson, Ltd., St. Paul, 1974-93, of counsel, 1993—. Exec. officer Twin Cities Squadron, U.S. Naval Sea Cadet Corps, Mpls., 1974-80; bd. dirs., treas., mem. Twin Cities coun. Navy League, 1970—, pres., 1979-81, treas., 1975-79, 81-91; mem. adv. coun. to dept. acctg. U. Minn., Mpls., 1983-86; bd. dirs., chmn. audit com. St. Paul Area Coun. Chs., 1985-87; mem. adv. bd. Headwaters Soc., 1987-88; mem. fin. reporting com. United Way St. Paul Area, 1981-93, mem. audit com., 1991-93; dist. commr. Indianhead coun. Boy Scouts Am., 1962-65. Lt. USN, 1952-55. Mem. Minn. Soc. CPAs (life), U.S. Naval Inst. (life), Belle Taine Lake Assn. (dir. 1995—, treas. 1996—), Hubbard County COLA Print Com., 1995-98, Friends of Heritage, 1996—. Presbyterian. Avocations: music, boating, history. Home: PO Box 41 Nevis MN 56467-0041

STIBLER, HELENA ELISABETH CHRISTINA, neurologist; b. Stockholm, July 24, 1943; d. Sture G.A. and Karin E. (Blanche) S. MSc, Karolinska Inst., Sweden, 1966, MD, 1971, Specialist Degree in Neurology, 1977, PhD in Neurology, 1978. Cert. Ednl. Coun. for Fgn. Med. Grads. Resident Karolinska Hosp., Stockholm, 1971-76, specialist ward physician, 1977-85, dir. Neurochemistry Rsch. Lab., 1982—, asst. chief physician, 1986-91, chief physician, 1991—, dir. neurooncology sect., 1993—; assoc. prof. Karolinska Inst., univ. lectr., 1986—; vis. prof., invited lectr. various univs., Scandinavia, France, Italy, Germany, Belgium, Can., U.S., 1977—. Author, editor: Acta Paediatrica Scandinavica, 1991; contbr. or co-contbr. numerous articles in clin. neurology and neurosci. to profl. publs. U. Toronto Rsch. fellow, 1980-81, INSERM Rsch. fellow, 1987; grantee Karolinska Inst., 1975—, Swedish Coun. for Planning Coord. of Rsch., 1980-82, 94, Swedish Med. Rsch. Coun., 1983—, Vivian Smith Found., 1984-87, INSERM, 1987, Cornell Found., 1990-94, others. Mem. Swedish Soc. Medicine (Lennmalms award 1979), Swedish Med. Assn., Swedish Soc. Neurology (auditor), Internat. Soc. Biomed. Rsch. Alcoholism, Internat. Soc. Developmental Neurosci., Internat. Fedn. Neurology. Avocations: gardening, antiquities, music, animals. Office: Karolinska Hosp, Dept Neurology, 17176 Stockholm Sweden

STICKELER, STEPHAN, educator; b. Altenhundem, Fed. Republic Germany, Sept. 2, 1960. MA, San Diego State U., Calif., 1985; State exam., U. Siegen, Siegen, Fed. Republic Germany, 1986. Intern Seminar, Paderborn, 1989-91; tchr. English and history Westfalen Kolleg Paderborn, 1991—. Youth worker Cath. Kolping Soc., Altenhundem, 1976—, pres., 1987—. Scholar German Acad. Exchange Svc., 1982-83. Mem. MLA. Roman Catholic. Home: Fichtenstr 5, 57368 Lennestadt 1, Germany Office: Westfalen Kolleg Fuerstenweg 17B, 33102 Paderborn Germany

STICKLE, DAVID WALTER, microbiologist; b. Boston, Apr. 18, 1933; s. Harold Edwards and Lucille Margaret (Magee) S.; m. Mary Elizabeth DeLong, July 29, 1972. BS in Chemistry, Biology, Tufts U., 1955; MS in Pharmacy and Health, Northeastern U., Boston, 1968; MPH, U. N.C., 1969, DrPH, 1971. Bacteriologist Mass. Dept. Pub. Health, Boston, 1959-63, supr. immunology unit, 1963-68; UNC/CDC lab. dir.'s program Ctrs. for Disease Control, Atlanta, 1968-71; chief, clin. lab. improvement program Divsn. Med. Labs./Minn. Dept. Health, Mpls., 1971-82, acting dir., 1977-78, asst. dir., 1978-88; ex-officio mem. Minn. Soc. Clin. Pathologists Exec. Com., Mpls., 1977-78; mem. Proficiency Testing Com., Minn. Acad. Family Physicians, Mpls., 1977-83; adj. asst. prof. U. Minn., Mpls., 1977-88; assoc. prof. emeritus, U. Minn., 1988—. Editor: Med. Lab. Forum periodical, 1973-88. Proctor Nat. Registry of Microbiology, Mpls. Examinations for Minn., 1987-92; instr. Edina Community Edn. Programs, Minn., 1992. With U.S. Army, 1955-57. Lab. tng. grantee Ctr. for Disease Control, HEW, Atlanta, 1977-78, 1978-80, 1979-81. Mem. Am. Soc. Microbiology, Phi Sigma, Sigma Xi. Achievements include serologic tests for systemic candidiasis which were in use for many years by the Ctrs. for Disease Control, U.S. Dept. of Health and Human Svcs.

STIEF, CHRISTIAN GEORG, urologist, consultant; b. Ensheim, Saar, Germany, Dec. 25, 1958; s. Franz and Ursula Stief; m. Judith Maria Carlen, June 30, 1987; children: Philipp Franziskus, Christopher Thomas. Grad., U. Freiburg, 1983, U. Montpellier, 1984; MD, U. Saarlandes, 1984. Staff urology Bundeswehrkrankenhaus Ulm, 1984-86, U. Freiburg, 1987, U. Calif., San Francisco, 1987-88; staff surgery U. Freiburg, 1988-89; prof. urology Med. Sch. Hanover, 1989—; cons., referee Jour. Urology, Urologic Rsch., World Jour. Urology, European Urology, Internat. Jour. Impotence Rsch., Andrologie, Aktuelle Urologie, Der Urologe, Clin. Nephrology, Urologia Internat. Mem. editl. bd. Urologic Rsch., World Jour. Urology, Internat. Jour. Impotence Rsch., Andrologie, Aktuelle Urologie; contbr. articles to profl. jours. Recipient Lower Saxony Cancer award 1992, prize Forum Urodynamicum, 1994, Innovation award U. Grosshadern/Munich, 1995, C.E. Alken prize, 1996, Poster prize VI Internat. Congress Andrology, 1997, J. Lapides prize, 1999. Mem. German Urol. Rsch. Soc. (1st prize 1990), Internat. Soc. for Impotence Rsch. (Herbert Newman prize 1990), German Urol. Assn. (Maximilian Nitze prize 1990, film prize 1995, Jack Capides prize 1998). Fax: 49 511 532 4941. E-mail: stief.christian@mh-hannover.de. Office: Med Sch Hannover, Dept of Urology, D-30623 Hannover Germany

STIEFEL, LINDA SHIELDS, lawyer; b. Syracuse, N.Y., Nov. 14, 1948; d. Harold F. and Ellen (Brown) Shields; m. John L. Stiefel, Sept. 20, 1969; 1 child, John L. BS, Tusculum Coll., 1988; JD, Akron Sch. Law, 1991. Bar: Ohio 1992, D.C. 1993, N.Y. 1998, U.S. Dist. Ct. (no. dist.) Ohio 1993, U.S. Supreme Ct. 1997. Judicial law clk. Stark County Common Pleas, Canton, Ohio, 1991-94; pvt. practice Louisville, Ohio, 1992-97, Cape Vincent, N.Y., 1998—. Active Ohio Dem. Nat. Com., Columbus, Stark County Dem. Party, Canton, Ohio, 1991-97; trustee, mem. exec. com. Am. Handweaving Mus.; trustee Cape Vincent Village Green, Cape Vincent Planning Bd. Mem. ABA, NOW, Ohio Bar Assn., Stark County Bar Assn., N.Y. State Bar Assn., Jefferson County Bar Assn. Methodist. Home and Office: 596 West Broadway Cape Vincent NY 13618

STIEGLITZ, THOMAS, biomedical engineering, researcher; b. Goslar, Germany, Nov. 9, 1965; s. Heinz and Luzia (Hartwig) S. MSEE, U. Karlsruhe, Germany, 1993; PhD, U. Saarland, Saarbruecken, Germany, 1998. Paramedic Landkreis Goslar, Germany, 1985-87, Promedic, Karlsruhe, 1990-93; rsch. asst. Fraunhofer Inst. Biomedical Engring., Sankt Ingbert, 1993-96, head resource neural prosthetics, 1996—; organizer internat. workshop, 1998. Contbr. articles to profl. jours.; patentee flexible artifical nerve plate, flexible interdigital cuff electrode. Mem. IEEE, Internat. Functional Elec. Stimulation Soc. (founding mem.), Verein Deutscher Ingenieure. Avocations: mountain biking, reading, singing, trekking. Fax: 49-6894-980-400. E-mail: thomas.stieglitz@ibmt.fhg.de. Office: Fraunhofer Inst Bio Engring, Ensheimer Strasse 48, D 66386 Sankt Ingbert Germany

STIEL, GEORG MARIAN, physician, engineer; b. Loslau, Silesia, Poland, Dec. 14, 1946; arrived in Germany, 1973; s. Boleslaus and Eugenia (Kroll) S.; m. Ludmilla S.G. Kostowa, Sept. 12, 1975. PhD, U. Warsaw, 1970; MD, U. Hamburg, Germany, 1989. Rsch. fellow U. Warsaw, 1970-73; rsch. engr. Siemens, Germany, 1974-79, Texaco, Germany, 1980-82; resident in medicine RWTH Aachen, Germany, 1989-90; resident in internal medicine, fellow cardiology U. Hosp. Eppendorf, Hamburg, 1991—; dir. QCA Lab. U. Hosp., Eppendorf, Hamburg, 1991—. Contbr. articles to profl. jours. Fellow ESC; mem. VDI, German Soc. Cardiology. Home: Saselbergweg 52, Hamburg 22395, Germany

STIENEKER, FRANK, pharmacist, pharmaceutical technology educator; b. Ibbenbueren, Westfalen, Germany, Feb. 11, 1960; s. Fritz and Christel (Wilhelm) S.; m. Birgit Fladerer, July 1, 1961. 1 State Examination, U. Frankfurt, 1984, 2 State Examination, 1986, 3 State Examination, 1987, Dr. Phil. Nat., 1992. Pharmacist. Rsch. assoc. U. Frankfurt, 1987-92, rsch. mgr., 1992-96; prodn. mgr., mgr. R&D GMNmbH, Walldorf, Germany, 1996-97; head pharmacy dept. APV, Mainz, Germany, 1997-99, mng. dir., 1999—; lectr. U. Frankfurt, 1996—. Author: Adjuvants for HIV-Vaccines, 1992, Controlled Delivery of Proteins and Peptides, 1994; contbr. articles to profl. jours. Home: Im Lorsbachtal 35, D-65719 Hofheim Germany Office: Internat Assn Pharm Tech, Kurfürstenstr 59, D-55118 Mainz Germany

STIENSTRA, STEPHANI ANN, editor; b. Baytown, Tex., Aug. 6, 1955; d. Herbert Howard and Janice Faye (Stowe) Cruickshank; m. George Keyston III, Oct. 8, 1983 (div. Mar. 1997); children: Jeremy George, Kristopher Samuel; m. Thomas Frank Stienstra, Dec. 4, 1998. AA with honors, Merced (Calif.) Coll., 1975; BA in Journalism with distinction, San Jose State U., 1976. Reporter Fresno (Calif.) Bee, 1974-75; reporter, photographer Merced (Calif.) Sun-Star, 1974-77; pub. info. officer Fresno City Coll., 1977-80; dir. comms. Aerojet Tactical Sys. Co., Sacramento, Calif., 1980-83; co-owner, v.p. Keyco Landscape Contractor Inc., Loomis, Calif., 1984-96; co-owner Tom Stienstra.com, 1999—. Co-coord. Aerojet United Way Campaign, 1981; Aerojet Tactical Sys. Co. coord. West Coast Nat. Derby Rallies, 1981-83; co-founder, pres. Calif. Lion Awareness. Mem. Internat. Assn. Bus. Communicators (dir. Sacramento chpt. 1983), Citrus Heights C. of C. (v.p. 1983), Outdoor Writers Assn. Calif. Republican. Office: Tom Stienstra.com PO Box 151 Mount Shasta CA 96067-0151

STIER, SERENA DEBORAH, law educator, psychologist, author; b. Chgo., Oct. 8, 1939; d. Morris Carren and Claire (Hadden) Auster; m. Herbert Allen Stier, June 4, 1961 (dec. Oct. 1969); m. Steven Jay Burton, Aug. 7, 1977; children: Daryn, Max, Sam. BA, Stanford U., 1960; MA, Boston U., 1961; PhD, UCLA, 1967; JD, U. Iowa, 1981. USPHS postdoctoral fellow Mt. Sinai Hosp., Los Angeles, 1968-70; asst. prof. med. psychology UCLA, 1970-73; policy studies officer Am. Psychol. Assn., Washington, 1974-77; assoc. prof. law Albany (N.Y.) Law Sch., 1988-93; cons. Kauffman Found. Ctr. for Entrepreneurial Leadership, 1994-2000;

founding faculty Calif. Sch. Profl. Psychology, Los Angeles, 1970-72; adj. prof. law U. Iowa, Iowa City, 1982-87. Bd. dirs. Iowa Civil Liberties Union, 1981-83, Iowa Children's Mus., 1995—; mem. nat. task force on committment guidelines Ctr. for State Cts., Williamsburg, Va., 1984-86; pres. Friends Devel. Coun., UIMA, 2000—. Mem. APA. Democrat. Jewish. Avocations: viewing and studying art. Home: 3691 Forest Gate Dr NE Iowa City IA 52240-7906

STIERLIN, HELM, psychiatry educator; b. Mannheim, Germany, Mar. 12, 1926; s. Paul and Elsbeth (Schöningh) S.; m. Satuila Zanolli; children: Larissa, Saskia. PhD in Philosophy, U. Heidelberg, Fed. Republic Germany, 1951, MD, 1953. Interpreter Brit. Mil. Govt., 1945-46; intern Univ. Poly., Munich, 1953-54; resident in neurology and psychiatry Munich U. Hosp. for Nervous and Mental Diseases, 1954-55; resident in psychiatry Sheppard and Enoch Pratt Hosp., Towson, Md., 1955-57; mem. staff Chestnut Lodge, Rockville, Md., 1957-62; sr. supervising analyst Sanatorium Bellevue, Kreuzlingen, Switzerland, 1963-64; head psychotherapy unit adult psychiatry br. NIMH, Bethesda, Md., 1966-71, acting chief family studies sect. adult psychiat. br., 1970-74; assoc. clin. prof. psychiatry U. Md., Balt., 1973-75; prof., chief dept. basic psychoanalytic rsch.-family therapy U. Heidelberg, 1974-91, prof. emeritus of psychiatry; vis. scientist adult psychiatry br. NIMH, 1965, acting chief, 1971-72; vis. lectr. univs. in N.Z. and Australia, 1965; writer, lectr., Europe, 1965-66; asst. prof. psychiatry Johns Hopkins U., Balt., 1969-74; mem. faculty Washington Sch. Psychiatry, 1971-74, Washington Psychoanalytic Inst., 1972-74. Author of 13 books in 12 langs.; editor, founder Familiendynamik, 1979-95; editor: Texte zur Familiendynamik; assoc. editor or mem. editorial bd. Psyche, Family Process, Jour. Family Therapy, Terapia Familiare, Psicoterapia y Familia, Thérapie Familial. Recipient ann. prize Md. Psychiat. Assn., 1961, ann. essay prize Psychoanalytic Rev., 1964, ann. rsch. essay prize Washington Psychoanalytic Soc., 1973. Fellow Am. Assn. for Marriage and Family Therapy (disting. profl. contbn. award 1985); mem. Am. Psychiat. Assn. (corr.), Internat. Assn. for Sys. Therapy, Nat. Coun. on Family Rels., Finnish Psychiat. Assn. (corr.), German Psychoanalytic Assn., German Med. Assn., German Workgroup for Family Therapy, Am. Family Therapy Assn., Inst. Family Therapy Assn. Avocations: hiking, theater, travel. Home and Office: Kapellenweg 19, D-69121 Heidelberg Germany

STIFF, P. ENOCH, corporate executive, lawyer; b. Cambridge, Mass., Sept. 7, 1947; s. Bernard and Eugenia (Neal) S.; m. Ruth L. Andersen, June 22, 1974; children: Tyler, Andrew, Christian. BA, U. Minn., 1969; JD, Suffolk U., 1977; MBA, Dartmouth Coll., 1983. Bar: Mass., 1977. Corp. counsel Xomox Corp., Cin., 1974-81; div. counsel Amca Internat., Hanover, N.H., 1983-86; v.p., gen. counsel U.S. ops. Atwood & Morrill Co., Inc., Salem, Mass., 1986-87; exec. v.p., chief operating officer Trak Internat., Inc., Port Washington, Wis., 1987-89, pres., chief exec. officer, 1989-95; pres., CEO Omni Quip Internat., Inc., 1995-99, Omni Quip Textron, Inc., 1999—. Lt. USN, 1969-74, Vietnam. Office: Trak Internat Inc 369 W Western Ave Port Washington WI 53074-2233

STIFTER, SABINE ANNA MARIA, software developer; b. Linz, Austria, Oct. 29, 1962; d. Adalbert and Erika (Bruckner) S. MSc in Engring., U. Linz, 1985, D of Tech., 1988, habilitation, 1994. Rsch. asst. Inst. Math. U. Linz, 1984-88, asst. prof. Rsch. Inst. for Symbolic Computation, 1988-94, mem. faculty Rsch. Inst. for Symbolic Computation, 1988—; mgmt. asst. U. Linz and Softwarepark Hagenberg, 1994-96; mng. dir., shareholder TuSZ GmbH, Hagenberg, Austria, 1996—. Editor: Advances in Robot Kinematics, 1990. Recipient Best Paper award Assn. Computing Machinery, Italy, 1988, German U. Software award U. Karlsruhe, 1991. Office: TuSZ GmbH, Hauptstr 99, A-4232 Hagenberg Austria

STIGALL, PHYLLIS GRAHAM, retired librarian; b. Ft. Wayne, Ind., Oct. 3, 1917; d. Edwin James and Mary Josephine (Palmer) Graham; m. Richard Patten Pooley, Apr. 4, 1943 (dec. Dec. 1950); 1 child, Samuel Graham Pooley; m. William Jasper Stigall Jr., Aug. 11, 1956. AA, Stephens Coll., 1937; AB, Northwestern U., 1939; MALS, U. Mich., 1952. Asst. counselor Stephens Coll., Columbia, Mo., 1939-42; asst. to dir. USO-YWCA Clubs, various locations, 1942-46; co-dir. U. Mich. Cmty. Ctr., Ann Arbor and Willow Run, 1946-47; libr., dean, instr. Lincoln (Ill.) Coll., 1952-66; mgr. publs. and librs. IBM Rsch. Ctr., Yorktown Heights, N.Y., 1966-88; ret. Author: Notes on 46 Women Writers, 1991, Journeys of the Brave, 1992, Ireland: Reader's Guide. Women, 1995; photographs exhibited, 1996. Mem. AAUW, LWV (chpt. bd. dirs., pres. 1947-66). Democrat. Episcopalian. Avocations: photography, research, biography, history, genealogy. Home: PO Box 211 Scarborough NY 10510-0711

STIGEBRANDT, ANDERS GÖSTA, oceanography educator; b. Uddevalla, Sweden, Nov. 10, 1942; s. Gösta Harald and Brita Elisabeth (Sandquist) S.; m. Siv Lilian Emanuelsson, Dec. 28, 1965; children: Fredrik, Henrik, Martin. PhD, Göteborg (Sweden) U., 1978. Ednl. and rsch. asst. Göteborg U., 1968-73; scholar Nordic U. Group for Phys. Oceanography, 1973-74; rschr. Sintef, Trondheim, Norway, 1974-76; asst. prof. Göteborg U., 1977-83, prof. oceanography, 1986—; sr. rschr. Swedish Natural Sci. Rsch. Coun., 1983-86; chmn. nomination com. Stockholm Water Prize, 1998—; cons. Inst. Marine Rsch., Bergen Norwegian Inst. of Water Rsch., 1980—. Author computer programs for computation of environ. effects of fish farming, sewage, etc.; contbr. articles to profl. jours., chpts. to books. Recipient Fridtjof Nansen medal European Geophys. Soc., 1996. Fellow Royal Swedish Acad. Scis. Avocations: family life, violin playing, gardening, tennis. E-mail: ANST@OCE.GU.SE. Office: Göteborg U/ Earth Scis, Guldhedsg 5A Box 460, SE-40530 Göteborg Sweden

STIGLIANO, JOSE MARIA, administrator, computer scientist; b. Buenos Aires, Argentina, Dec. 9, 1953; s. Jose and Yvonne Suzanne (Engel) S.; m. Daniela Saida Farinelli, Dec. 14, 1988; children: Veronica Maria, Carolina Maria, Jose Nicolas. Cert. in electronics, L.A. Huergo Tech. Coll., 1973; cert. systems analysis, U. Del Salvador, 1975; BSBA, Am. U., 1990; MS in Mgmt., Boston U., 1992; PhD in Mgmt., Clayton U., 1993; BS in Mgmt. Info. Systems, U. of State of N.Y., 1996; MSc in Computer Sci., Boston U., 1997. Programmer Ministry of Justice, Buenos Aires, 1973-76; analyst, programmer CTC Svc. Bur., Buenos Aires, 1976-77; systems analyst Aurora S.A., Buenos Aires, 1977-78; computer systems officer Internat. Fund Agrl. Devel. UN, Rome, 1981-88; info. tech.coord. Internat. Fund Agrl. Devel. of U.N., Rome, 1988—; lectr. U. Del Salvador, Buenos Aires, 1975-77; cons. in field. Inventor in field. Recipient UN Merit award, 1988, UN Svc. award, 1990. Mem. IEEE, IEEE Computer Soc., IEEE Comms. Soc., Engring. Mgmt. Soc., Software Engring. Tech. Coun., Soc. Internat. Devel. (life), Assn. Computing Machinery, Boston U. Gen. Alumni Assn. Avocations: music, bass guitar. Office: Internat Fund Agrl Devel, 107 Via Del Serafico, 00142 Rome Italy

STILES, MARY ANN, lawyer, author, lobbyist; b. Tampa, Fla., Nov. 16, 1944; d. Ralph A. and Bonnie (Smith) S.; m. Barry Smith. AA, Hills Community Coll., 1973; BS, Fla. State U., 1975; JD, Antioch Sch. Law, 1978. Bar: Fla. 1978. Legis. analyst Fla. Ho. of Reps., Tallahassee, 1973-74, 74-75; intern U.S. Senate, Washington, 1977; v.p., gen. counsel Associated Industries Fla., Tallahassee, 1978-81, gen. counsel, 1981-84, spl. counsel, 1986—; assoc. Deschler, Reed & Crichfield, Boca Raton, Fla., 1980-81; founding ptnr. Stiles, Taylor, & Grace, P.A., Boca Raton, Fla., 1982—; shareholder, dir. Stiles, Taylor, & Grace, P.A., Tampa; gen. dounsel Associated Industries Ins. Co., Inc., 1996—, Associated Industries Fla., Inc., 1997—, Associated Industries Ins. Svcs., Inc., 1997—; shareholder, dir. Six Stars Devel. Co. of Fla., Inc. Platnum Bank; br. chair Employers 1st Trust, Inc.; shareholder, pres. 42nd St., The Bistro. Author: Workers' Copmensation Law Handbook, 1980-94 edit. Bd. dirs., sec. Hillsborough C.C. Found., Tampa, 1985-87, 94-96; bd. dirs. Hillsborough Area Regional Transit Authority, Tampa, 1986-89, Boys and Girls Club of Tampa, 1986—; The Spring, 1992-93, What's My Chance, 1992-94; mem. Gov.'s Oversite Bd. on Workers' Compensation, 1989-90, Workers Comp. Rules Com., Fla. Bar, 1990-95, Workers Comp. Exec. Counsel Fla. Bar, 1990-95Jud. Nominating Commn. for Workers' Compensation Cts., 1990-93, trustee Hillsborough Cmty. Coll., 1994-99, vice-chair, 1995-96, chair, 1996-97; bd. dirs. Seminole Boosters, Inc., Fla. State U., 1996—. Mem. ABA, Fla. Bar Assn., Hillsborough County Bar Assn., Hillsborough Assn. Women Lawyers, Fla. Assn. Women Lawyers, Fla. Women's Alliance, Hillsborough County Seminole Boosters (past pres.). Democrat. Baptist. Club: Tiger Bay (Tampa, past pres., sec.). Avocations: boating, reading. Office: 315 S Plant Ave Tampa FL 33606-2325 also: 111 N Orange Ave Ste 850 Orlando FL 32801-2338 also: 317 N Calhoun St Tallahassee FL 32301-7605 also: PO Box 310397 Miami FL 33231-0397

STILGENBAUER, STEPHAN, physician, researcher; b. Kaiserslautern, Germany, Nov. 27, 1966; s. Hans and Anneliese (Köhler) S.; m. Franziska Beker, Aug. 10, 1996. Student, Baylor Coll. of Medicine, 1993; MD, U. Heidelberg, Germany, 1994. With M.D. Anderson Cancer Ctr., Houston, 1993; rsch. fellow Med. Clinic Poly. V, U. Heidelberg, 1994-99; postdoctoral rschr. German Cancer Rsch. Ctr., Heidelberg, 1996-98; fellow U. Ulm, Germany, 1999—. Contbr. articles to profl. jours. With German Air Force, 1986-87. Ednl. grantee German Acad. Exch. Svc., 1993, rsch. grantee Krebshilfe, Bonn, 1995, Wilhelm Sander Stiftung, 1997, European Cmty., 2000. Roman Catholic. Avocations: art, sports. Office: U Ulm Dept of Internal Med III, Robert Koch Str 8, 89081 Ulm Germany

STILL, ARTHUR WILLIAM, counseling psychologist; b. London, Aug. 22, 1935; s. Frank Ernest and Gladys Jane (Baker) S.; m. Shirley Christine Goodman, Nov. 5, 1955 (div. 1975); children: Charlotte, Melany, Lucy; m. Maureen McDermott; children: Maisie, Enid. BA, Cambridge (Eng.) U., 1960, MA, 1962, PhD, 1965. Asst. rschr. Cambridge (Eng.) U., 1963-65; psychology lectr. Durham (Eng.) U., 1965-79, sr. psychology lectr., 1979-88; vis. assoc. prof. Williams Coll., Williamstown, Mass., 1973-74; staff therapist Wellspring, Edinburgh, Scotland, 1993-97; counselling psychologist, Borders NHS Trust, 1998—. Editor: Against Cognitivism, 1991, Rewriting the History of Madness, 1992; editor History of the Human Scis., 1987-98; contbr. articles to profl. jours. including Nature, Jour. for the Theory of Social Behavior, others. Chmn., organizer Cruse Bereavement Care, Ctrl. Borders Br., Scotland, 1993-97. Fellow Brit. Psychol. Soc. Home and Office: 6-7 Hadden Farm Cottages, Kelso Roxburghshire TO5 84U, Scotland

STILL, JAMES, adult education educator, writer; b. LaFayette, Ala., 1906; s. James Alexander and Lonie (Lindsey) S. AB, Lincoln Meml. U., 1929; MA, Vanderbilt U., 1930; BS in Libr. Sci., U. Ill., 1930; LittD (hon.), Berea Coll., 1973, Morehead State U., 1978, U. Ky., 1979; HLD (hon.), Lincoln Meml. U., 1974, Ky. Wesleyan U.; degree (hon.), Transylvania U., 1983, Cumberland Coll., 1996. Mem. staff Hindman (Ky.) Settlement Sch., 1932-39, 51-61; assoc. prof. Morehead (Ky.) State U., 1962-70; commentator Nat. Pub. Radio, Washington, 1980-83; vis. prof. Appalachian Coll., 1987—. Author: (books) River of Earth, 1940, 2d edit., 1978, Sporty Creek, 1977, 2d edit., 1998, The Wolfpen Notebooks, 1991, (poetry) Hounds of the Mountain, 1937, 2d edit., 1968, (short stories) Pattern of a Man, On Troublesome Creek, 1977, The Run for the Elbertas, 1980, (children's books), Way Down Yonder on Troublesome Creek, 1974, The Wolfpen Rusties, 1974, Jack and the Wonder Beans, 1977, 2d edit., 1996, An Appalachian Mother Goose, 1998. Sgt. U.S. Army, 1942-45. Recipient O. Henry Meml. prize for short story, 1939, So. Authors award, 1940, award Am. Acad. Arts and Letters and Nat. Inst. Arts and Letter, 1947, 79, Algernon Sydney Sullivan award Lincoln Meml. U., 1971, medal of hon. DAR, 1973, medallion for intellectual excellence U. Ky., 1994, Ednl. Svc. award to Appalachia Carson-Newman Coll., 1991, award Fellowship of So. Writers, 1997, award Appalachian Coll. Assn., 1998; Guggenheim fellow, 1941, 46; named Poet Laureate of Ky., 1995-96; James Still fellowship estab. U. Ky., 1989; James Still room dedicated Johnson-Camden Libr., Morehead State U., 1961. Mem. South Atlantic MLA, Phi Beta Kappa. Avocations: Mayan civilization, gardening, travel. Home: PO Box 865 Hindman KY 41822-0865

STILLER, BEN, actor, director; b. N.Y.C., 1966; s. Jerry Stiller and Anne Meara. Student, UCLA. Acting debut Broadway revival The House of Blue Leaves, 1985; actor, writer Saturday Night Live; actor, writer, creator The Ben Stiller Show (Emmy award for writing); appeared in spl. House of Blue Leaves; dir., writer Colin Quinn Back in Bklyn., Working Trash; appeared in films Hot Pursuit, Empire of the Sun, Fresh Horses, Next of Kin, That's Adequate, Stella, 1990, Highway to Hell, 1992, Reality Bites, 1994, Heavyweights, 1995, Get Shorty, Flirting With Disaster, 1996, The Cable Guy, 1996, McClintock's Peach, Zero Effect, 1998, There's Something About Mary, 1998, Permanent Midnight, 1998, Your Friends and Neighbors, 1998, The Suburbans, 1999, McClintock's Peach, 1999, Black and White, 1999, Mystery Men, 1999, The Independent, 2000, Keeping the Faith, 2000, Meet the Parents, 2000; appeared on tv AFI's 100 Years, 100 Laughs: America's Funniest Movies, 2000. *

STILLER, CHRISTOPH, electrical engineer, researcher; b. Köln, Germany, Dec. 27, 1964; s. Arno Rudi and Renate (Bollhagen) S.; m. Susanne Werth, Oct. 22, 1988; children: Tobias, Anika, Maria. MSEE, Aachen (Germany) U. Tech., 1988, PhD in Engring., 1994; student, Norwegian Inst. Tech., 1987-88. Rsch. asst. Aachen U., 1988-94, Nat. Inst. Sci. Rsch.-Telecom, Can., 1994-95; rsch. project mgr. Bosch, Germany, 1995—. Grantee Deminex, Germany, 1987, Natural Scis. and Engring. Rsch. Coun. Can., 1994. Mem. IEEE (sr., assoc. editor IEEE Trans. Image Proc.), German Elec. Engring. Assn. Achievements include 8 patents in the area of image processing inventions for object-based image processing and image analysis. Office: Robert Bosch GMBH FV/SLH, PO Box 777777, 31132 Hildesheim Germany

STILLER, SHALE DAVID, lawyer, educator; b. Rochester, N.Y., Feb. 23, 1935; s. Maurice Aaron and Dorothy (Salitan) S.; m. Ellen M. Heller; children: Lewis B., Michael J., Kenneth R.; stepchildren: William Heller, Lawrence Heller. B.A., Hamilton Coll., 1954; LL.B., Yale U., 1957; M.L.A., Johns Hopkins U., 1972. Bar: Md. 1957. Ptnr. Piper & Marbury, Balt., 1992—; lectr. U. Md. Law Sch., 1963—. Contbr. articles to profl. jours. Trustee Johns Hopkins U., Assn. Jewish Charities, Peabody Inst., Weinberg Found.; trustee, vice chmn. Johns Hopkins Medicine; mem. adv. bd. Tax Mgmt., 1972-93; chmn. Jud. Nominating Commn., Balt., 1979-83; officer, bd. dirs. Park Sch., 1973-79, pres., 1982-86; pres. Jewish Family Agy., 1972-74. Mem. ABA, Am. Law Inst., Am. Coll. Tax Counsel, Am. Coll. Trust and Estate Counsel, Order of Coif. Democrat. Jewish. Club: 14 W Hamilton St (Balt.). Home: 807 St Georges Rd Baltimore MD 21210-1408 Office: Piper Marbury Rudnick & Wolfe 6225 Smith Ave Baltimore MD 21209-3600

STILLMAN, MICHAEL ALLEN, dermatologist; b. N.Y.C., Apr. 12, 1943; s. Aaron and Anne (Turansky) S.; m. Susan Fuchs, July 8, 1973; children: Julie, Jeremy. BA, Clark U., 1963; MD, SUNY, 1967. Diplomate Am. Acad. Dermatology. Med. intern Maimonides Hosp., Bklyn., 1967-68; dermatology resident NYU Med. Ctr. and Bellevue Hosp., N.Y.C., 1970-73; pvt. practice Mt. Kisco, N.Y., 1973—; cons. in dermatology U.S. Mil. Acad., West Point, N.Y., 1973-75. Contbr. essays and articles to profl. jours. and newspapers. Bd. trustees South Salem (N.Y.) Libr., 1990-98; boys varsity tennis coach John Jay H.S., Katonah, N.Y., 1996. Capt. USAF, 1968-70, Vietnam. Decorated Combat Inf. badge. Fellow Am. Soc. Dermatol. Surgeons, Am. Acad. Dermatology; mem. N.Y. State Med. Soc., Noah Worcester Dermatology Soc. Avocations: tennis, jogging, writing. Home: 33 Mead St Waccabuc NY 10597-1107 Office: PO Box 268 Mount Kisco NY 10549-0268

STILLMAN, RICHARD JOSEPH, retired army officer, consultant, publisher writer; b. Lansing, Mich., Feb. 20, 1917; m. Darlene Slater, Nov. 15, 1941 (dec. Oct. 1992); children: Richard, Thomas, Ellen. BS, U. So. Calif., 1938; postgrad., Harvard U., 1938-39; MS, Syracuse U., 1950, PhD, 1955; postgrad., Army War Coll., 1959-60, NATO Def. Coll., 1960-61. Commd. 2d lt. U.S. Army, 1938, advanced through grades to col., 1955, ret., 1965; dir. Ctr. for Econ. Oppty. and Mgmt. Devel., Ohio U., Athens, 1965-67; prof. bus. adminstrn. Ohio U., 1965-67; prof. mgmt. U. New Orleans, 1967-82; pres. R.J. Stillman Co., New Orleans, 1982—. Author: General Patton's Timeless Leadership Principles, 1997-98, video, 1999, Guide to Personal Finance, 5th edit., 1988, Willie: General Patton's Best Friend: The Story of General G.S. Patton, Jr. and His Beloved Dog, 2000; contbr. articles to profl. jours. Mem. Mayor's Mill Adv. Com., New Orleans. Decorated Legion of Merit, Bronze star, Luxembourg Order of the Crown. Named to Hon. Order Ky. Cols.; Maxwell scholar, 1949-50; recipient Scouters award Boy Scouts Am., 1955; Stillman prize and professorship named in his honor U. New Orleans. Mem. Army Navy C.C., Plimsoll Club of World Trade Ctr. Avocations: swimming, jogging, public speaking.

STILP, ALOIS JOSEF, retired physicist; b. Marienbad, Germany, Oct. 1, 1933; s. Josef Michael and Juliane (Richter) S.; m. Anni Weygand, May 17, 1961; children: Tanja, Thilo, Vera, Jarko. Degree in physics, U. Freiburg, Germany, 1960, PhD, 1965. Divsn. chief impact physics divsn. Ernst-Mach-Inst., Freiburg, 1966-97, dep. dir., 1975-97. Co-author: High Velocity Impact Dynamics, 1990. Fellow Aeroballistic Range Assn. (Ballistics award 1991), Hypervelocity Impact Soc. (Disting. Scientist award 1992). Home: Bussardweg 7, 79110 Freiburg Germany

STILWELL, DAVID WILLIAM, engineering company executive; b. Fleet, Hampshire, Eng., June 8, 1949; arrived in Portugal, 1951; s. Michael William and Maria Inez (Horgan) S.; m. Deolinda Monteiro, Dec. 13, 1974; children: Catherine Anne, Ana Maria, Inez Maria. Trainee Soc. Agricola Tabacos, Mozambique, 1969-72, sales exec., 1972-74, factory mgr., 1974-76; adminstrn. mgr. REXABEX, Brazil, 1977-78, tobacco buyer, 1978-80; mng. dir. Engring. Co. Portugal, Lda, Lisboa, 1980—. Mem. Royal Brit. Club (hon. sec. 1988-90), Club Golf Estoril, Sport Lisboa Benfica. Roman Catholic. Avocation: golf. Fax: (351.1) 355 3399. Office: Engring Co Portugal Lda, Rua S Sebastiao Pedreira 122 3, 1050 Lisbon Portugal

STIMPERT, ALISON KENDRA, marine biologist, researcher, ecologist; b. Cleve., Sept. 4, 1975; d. Donald William and Jacqueline S. BA magna cum laude, Carleton Coll., 1997. Intern Aquarium of Niagara, Niagara Falls, N.Y., 1995, Wolf Hollow Wildlife Rehab. Ctr., Friday Harbor, Wash., 1997; from intern to field agent Kewalo Basin Marine Mammal Lab., Honolulu, 1998, whale project field agent, 1998—. Vol. dolphin intelligence Earthwatch, Honolulu, 1992, Oceanic Soc. Expedition, Bahamas, 1993. Nat. Merit scholar Carleton Coll., 1992. Mem. Soc. Marine Mammalogy (Hawaii chpt.), Sigma Xi. Mem. Unitarian Ch. Avocations: synchronized swimming, dance, TV/movies. E-mail: stimpera@hotmail.com. Office: Kewalo Basin Marine Mammal Lab 1129 Ala Moana Blvd Honolulu HI 96814

STIMPSON, CATHARINE ROSLYN, English language educator, writer; b. Bellingham, Wash., June 4, 1936; d. Edward Keown and Catharine (Watts) S. AB, Bryn Mawr Coll., 1958; BA, Cambridge U., Eng., 1960, MA, 1960; PhD, Columbia U., 1967. Mem. faculty Barnard Coll., N.Y.C., 1963-80; prof. English, dean of grad. sch., vice provost grad. edn. Rutgers U., New Brunswick, N.J., 1980-92, Univ. prof., 1991—; chmn. bd. scholars Ms. Mag., N.Y.C., 1981-92; dir. fellows program MacArthur Found., 1994-97; Univ. prof., dean Grad. Sch. Arts and Sci. NYU, N.Y.C., 1998—. Author: Class Notes, 1979, Where the Meanings Are, 1988; founding editor: Signs: Jour. Women in Culture and Society, 1974-81; book series Women in Culture and Society, 1981; columnist Change Mag., 1992-93. Chmn. N.Y. Council Humanities, 1984-87, Nat. Council Research on Women, 1984-89 ; bd. dirs. Stephens Coll., Columbia, Mo., 1982-85; trustee Bates Coll., 1990—. Hon. fellow Woodrow Wilson Found., 1958; Fulbright fellow, 1958-60; Nat. Humanities Inst. fellow New Haven, 1975-76; Rockefeller Humanities fellow, 1983-84. Mem. MLA (exec. coun., chmn. acad. freedom com., 1st v.p., pres. 1990), PEN, AAUP, NOW, PBS (bd. dirs. 1994—), Legal Def. and Edn. Fund (bd. dirs. 1991-96). Democrat. Home: 29 Washington Sq W Apt 15C New York NY 10011-9199 Office: NYU 6 Washington Sq N New York NY 10003-6668

STINCHCOMB, ALBERT MONROE, producer, designer/realtor; b. Battle Creek, Mich., Apr. 6, 1944; s. Loid Monroe and Barbara Hough (Parks) S. Student, U. Mich., CUNY. Chmn. Stinchcomb and Monroe, Inc., N.Y.C., N.J., 1979—, Majestic Entertainment, Ltd., Jersey City, 1984—; pres. 275 Corp., Jersey City, N.J., 1983-95, Majestic Devel. Corp., Jersey City, 1989-95; exec. v.p. The Gyncyn Corp., 1994—, CJS Mgmt., 1996—; owner Majestic Theatre, 1980-95. Appeared in numerous prodns. including Life With Father, 1954, Wizard of Oz, 1955, She Stoops to Conquer, 1985; produced numerous prodns. including Macbeth, 1986, Royal Shakespear Co., 1987, The Golden Handshake, 1987, Why Father Won't Come Home, 1987, Scarpa the Magician, Liberty, The Ballet, 1988, The Adams Letters, 1988. Pres. Liberty Ctr. for Performing Arts, Jersey City, 1984-94; bd. dirs. Fraunces Tavern Mus., 1977-94, Acad. of Art, 1987—, Ednl. Art Team, 1988-95; active Preservation N.J. Mem. Nat. Film Inst., Am. Soc. Interior Designers, Sons of Revolution, Soc. Colonial Wars, Saint Nicholas Soc., N.J. Assn. Realtors (Burgdorff Realtors Million Dollar Club). Home: Grove Cottage PO Box 487 Jersey City NJ 07303

STINE, SUSAN MARIE, psychiatrist, health science facility administrator; b. Miami, Fla., Sept. 25, 1949; d. Carl William and Mary Elizabeth (Biggers) S. BS, Tulane U., 1971; PhD in Neurosci., U. Rochester, N.Y., 1979; MD, U. Miami, Fla., 1983. Diplomate Am. Bd. Psychiatry and Neurology with added certification in addictions. Rsch. asst. Ctr. for Brain Rsch., Rochester, 1977-78; staff fellow NIMH Lab. Preclin. Pharmacology St. Elizabeth's Hosp., Washington, 1978-81; intern St. Raphael's Hosp., New Haven, 1983-84; psychiatric resident Psychiat. Dept. Yale U., 1984-87, asst. prof. psychiatry, 1987-98; in-patient attending physician Conn. Mental Health Ctr., New Haven, 1987-89; clin. dir. out-patient substance abuse program VA Med. Ctr., West Haven, Conn., 1989-96, dir. opiate treatment program, 1996-98, dir. addiction psychiat. residency trng. program, 1998—; dir. substance abuse program Harper Hosp., 1998-99; assoc. prof. Wayne State U., 1998—; dir. psychiat. svcs. Jefferson Ave. Rsch. Clinic/Wayne State U., 1999—. Author articles in profl. jours.; author: (book) New Treatment for Opiate Depression, 1997. NIMH tng. grantee U. Rochester, 1972-76. Mem. AMA, AAAS, Soc. for Neurosci., N.Y. Acad. Scis., Am. Psychiat. Assn., Am. Acad. of Addiction Psychiatry, Am. Bd. Psychiatry and Neurology, Coll. Problems of Drug Dependence, Can. Coll. Neuropsychopharamacy, Sigma Xi. Avocations: sculpture, gold and silver smithing, graphic arts. Office: 2761 E Jefferson Ave Detroit MI 48207-4105

STING (GORDON MATTHEW SUMNER), musician, songwriter, actor; b. Newcastle Upon Tyne, Eng., Oct. 2, 1951; s. Ernest Matthew and Audrey (Cowell) Sumner; m. Frances Eleanor Tomelty, May 1, 1976 (div. Mar. 1984); children: Joseph, Fuschia Katherine; m. Trudie Styler, Aug. 22, 1992; children: Brigette, Michael, Jake, Eliot, Paulina, Giacomo Luke. Grad., Warwick U., Coventry, Eng.; hon. doctorate, Northumbria U., 1992; hon. degree, Berklee Coll. Music, Boston, 1994. Schoolmaster Newcastle Upon Tyne, Eng., 1975-77; songwriter, singer, bass player with rock group The Police, 1977-86; mng. dir. Kaliedescope Cameras, London, from 1982. Albums recorded with The Police include Outlandos D'Amour, 1978, Reggatta De Blanc, 1979, Zenyatta Mondatta, 1980, Ghost in the Machine, 1981, Synchronicity, 1983, The Singles; Every Breath You Take, 1986; stage appearance: (Broadway) Three Penny Opera, 1989; solo albums include The Dream of the Blue Turtles, 1985, Bring On The Night, 1986, Nothing Like the Sun, 1987, The Soul Cages, 1991, Ten Summoner's Tales, 1993 (Grammy award, Best Long Form Music Video, 1994), Demolition Man (soundtrack), 1993, Mercury Falling, 1996; appeared in films Quadrophenia, 1979, The Secret Policeman's Other Ball, 1981, Brimstone and Treacle, 1982, Dune, 1985, The Bride, 1985, Plenty, 1985, Julia and Julia, 1987, Stormy Monday, 1988, Resident Alien, 1990, The Grotesque, 1995, Lock, Stock and Two Smoking Barrels, 1998; voice artist tv series Captain Planet and the Planeteers, 1990-92; rec. soundtracks for films including Brimstone and Treacle, 1982, Party, Party, 1982, The Secret Policeman's Other Ball, 1982, The Emperor's New Groove, 2000. Recipient 13 Grammy awards with The Police and as solo artist; Downbeat mag. Readers' Poll Pop/Rock Musician of Yr. award, 1989, Downbeat mag. Readers' Poll Pop/Rock group award, 1989, Internat. Rock award for Video Legend, 1991, Star of the Walk of Fame, 2000. Mem. Performing Rights Soc., Amnesty Internat., Rainforest Found. (co-founder). Office: Kathryn Schenker Assocs 12th Fl 1776 Broadway New York NY 10019 also: Firstars 3520 Hayden Ave Culver City CA 90232-2413 also: A & M Records Inc 70 Universal City Plz Universal Cty CA 91608-1011*

STINGEL, ANA MARIA, psychology educator, psychotherapy researcher; b. São Paulo, Brazil, Apr. 2, 1955; d. Antonio and Leonor (Chimenez) S.; m. John Wallace-Collett, Sept. 18, 1980 (div. June 1983); m. Eduardo Gordilho Fraga, July 22, 1986; children: Leonardo Stingel-Fraga, Joana Stingel-Fraga. BSc in Psychology with honors, N.E. London U., 1984; MA in Clin. Psychology, Cath. U., Rio de Janeiro, 1991; D in Psychotherapy Rsch., Fed. U. Rio de Janeiro, 1998. Cert. in cognitive, social, and clin. psychology. Lang. instr. SENAC, São Paulo, 1974-79; contbr. BBC Overseas, London, 1980-84; radio prodr. fgn. office Cen. Office of Info., London, 1981-84; psychology prof. dept. psychology Cath. U., Rio de Janeiro, 1988—;

psychotherapy supr. psychiatry divsn. Santa Casa Gen. Hosp., Rio de Janeiro, 1989—; vice-dir WHO health divsn. Collaborating Ctr. for Rsch. in Psychotherapy, Rio de Janeiro, 1996—; supr. in psychotherapy Brazilian Navy, 1995-97; cons. on devel. of Brazilian tech. for biofeedback equipment, 1997-98. Editor: (book) Cognitive Processes, 1996; contbr. articles to profl. jours. Awarded Key of the City, Lincoln Park City Hall, 1974; grantee Aid for Rsch. Found. of Rio de Janeiro, 1991. Mem. Brazilian Asssn. of Psychiatry (head of rsch. in psychotherapy dept. 1996-98). Avocations: horseback riding, science fiction, cinema, traveling, music. Office: R Visconde de Piraja, 529/301 Ipanema, 22410003 Rio de Janeiro Brazil

STINGL, GEORG, dermatologist, scientist; b. Vienna, Austria, Oct. 28, 1948; s. Kurt and Elfriede (Wafek) S.; m. Laura A. Gazze, Dec. 13, 1980. MD, U. Vienna, 1973. Resident dept. dermatology I Univ. Vienna (Austria) Med. Sch., 1973-76; guest rschr. dermatol. br. Nat. Cancer Inst., NIH, Bethesda, Md., 1977-78; mem. staff dept. dermatology Med. Sch., U. Innsbruck, Austria, 1978-81, assoc. prof. dermatology, 1980; mem. staff dept. dermatology Med. Sch., U. Vienna, 1981-85, full prof., head div. cutaneous immunobiology, dept. dermatology I, 1985-91, prof., chmn. div. immunology, allergy and infectious diseases, dept. dermatology, 1991—; vis. scientist lab. immunology Nat. Inst. Allergy and Infectious Diseases, NIH, Bethesda, 1985-86. Section editor: Immunology of Jour. Invest Dermatology, 1987—; European deputy editor Jour. Invest. Dermatology, 1992—; contbr. chpts. to books and articles to profl. jours. Mem. Internat. Com. Dermatology, European Soc. Dermatol. Rsch., Soc. Investigative Dermatology, Am. Assn. Immunologists, Austrian Acad. Scis., German Acad. Scis. Roman Catholic. Avocations: classical music, swimming, sauna. Home: St Ulrichs Platz 2-7, A 1070 Vienna Austria Office: Univ Vienna Med Sch, Dept Dermatology, A 1090 Vienna Austria

STINNER, BENNO, surgeon; b. Kirchen, Germany, Feb. 11, 1958; s. Alban and Margarete S.; m. Gabi Horn, Aug. 8, 1987; children: Maria Rita, Heiner. Dr.med., Johannes-Gutenberg U., Mainz, Germany, 1985. Rschr. Inst. Physiology, Gottingen U., Germany, 1985-87; resident Marburg U., Germany, 1987-93, staff mem. dept. theoretical surgery, 1988—, cons. surgeon, 1993-98, substitute head dept., 1998—; cons. in field. Co-author: Lancet, 1994, Langenbecks Archiv Surgery, 1998. Fin. grantee Deutsche Forschungsgemeinschaft, Bonn, Germany, 1997, 99. Mem. Deutsche Gesellschaft Chirurgie, Internat. Soc. Colon and Rectal Surgeon, Working Group Surg. Oncology. Home: Gabelsberger Str 37 b, D-35037 Marburg Germany Office: Dept Gen Surgery, Baldingerstrasse, D-35033 Marburg Germany

STINNETT, MARK ALLAN, lawyer; b. Jackson, Miss., Sept. 15, 1955; s. Allan J. and Joan (Mouser) S.; m. Carol Fowler, Sept. 5, 1992; children: Michelle, Michael. BA in Polit. Sci. with honors, Tex. Tech U., 1977; JD with honors, U. Tex., 1980. Bar: Tex. 1980, U.S. Dist. Ct. (no. and ea. dists.) Tex. 1981, U.S. Ct. Appeals (5th cir.) 1993. Shareholder Cowles & Thompson, Dallas, 1980-2000; founding ptnr., mng. ptnr. Stinnett Thiebaud & Remington L.L.P., Dallas, 2000—. Mem. Philmont Ranch com. Boy Scouts Am. Mem. ABA, Am. Inns of Ct., Am. Coll. Legal Medicine, Am. Health Lawyers Assn., State Bar of Tex., Dallas Bar Assn., Tex. Assn. Def. Counsel, Dallas Assn. Def. Counsel, Def. Rsch. Inst., Inns Ct. (barrister Dallas chpt. 1988-91), Tex. Ctr. Legal Ethics and Professionalism, Nat. Eagle Scout Assn., Philmont Staff Assn. (pres. 1994-98). Avocations: backpacking, softball, military history. Home: 5541 Mallard Trce Frisco TX 75034-5058 Office: Stinnett Thiebaud & Remington LLP 1445 Ross Ave Ste 4800 Dallas TX 75202-2702

STINNETT, TERRANCE LLOYD, lawyer; b. Oakland, Calif., July 22, 1940; s. Lloyd Monroe and Gertrude (Hyman) S. BS, Stanford U., 1962; JD magna cum laude, U. Santa Clara, 1969. Bar: Calif. 1970, U.S. Dist. Ct. (no. dist.) Calif. 1970, U.S. Dist. Ct. (ea. ctrl. and so. dists) Calif. 1975, U.S. Ct. Appeals (9th cir.) 1970, U.S. Supreme Ct. 1975. Law clk. to judge Calif. Ct. Appeals, San Francisco, 1969-70; assoc. Hyman, Rhodes & Aylward, Fremont, Calif., 1970-71, Glicksberg, Kushner & Goldberg, San Francisco, 1972-77; mem. Goldberg, Stinnett Meyers & Davis, San Francisco, 1977—; bd. dirs. Fremont Bancorp, Fremont Bank, vice-chmn. bd., 1998-2000. Mem. ABA, Bar Assn. San Francisco (chmn. bench bar liaison com. for U.S. Bankruptcy Ct., No. Dist. of Calif. 1997). Republican. Roman Catholic. Home: 131 Alamo Hills Ct Alamo CA 94507-2243 Office: Goldberg Stinnett Meyers & Davis 44 Montgomery St Ste 2900 San Francisco CA 94104-4803

STIPIC MARKOVIC, ASJA, physician, researcher; b. Makarska, Dalmatia, Croatia, July 31, 1952; d. Ivan and Anka (Juras) Stipic; m. Marijo Markovic; 1 child, Marul. MD, Zagreb (Croatia) Sch. Medicine, 1976, MSc in Biomedicine, 1987, PhD, 1998. Mc. diplomate; cert. in allergy and clin. immunology. Intern Hosp. Sv. Duh, Zagreb, 1976-77, resident, 1978-82; specialist Dept. Clin. Immunology, Zagreb, 1982—; head lab. for functional pulmonary diagnosis Hosp. Sv. Duh, Zagreb, 1986—, subspecialist, 1999—. Contbr. articles to profl. jours. Mem. Croatian Soc. for Allergy and Clin. Immunology (sec. 1996-97, treas. 1982-90), Croatian Soc. for Internal Diseases (treas. 1997-99), European Acad. for Allergy and Clin. Immunology. Roman Catholic. Avocations: solo singing, fiction. Home: Trg N Subica Zrinjskog 6, 10 000 Zagreb Croatia

STIRITZ, WILLIAM P., food company executive; b. Jasper, Ark., July 1, 1934; s. Paul and Dorothy (Bradley) S.; m. Susan Ekberg, Dec. 4, 1972; children—Bradley, Charlotte, Rebecca, Nicholas. B.S., Northwestern U., 1959; M.A., St. Louis U., 1968. Mem. mktg. mgmt. staff Pillsbury Co., Mpls., 1959-62; staff Gardner Advt. Co., St. Louis, 1963; with Ralston Purina Co., St. Louis, 1963-97, pres., CEO, chmn., 1981-97; chmn., pres., CEO, Agribrands Internat., St. Louis, 1997—; bd. dirs. Am. Freightways, Angelica Corp., Ball Corp., Boatmen's Bancshares, Inc., Gen. Am. Life Ins. Co., May Dept. Stores, S.C. Johnson & Son, Reins. Group Am., Vail Resorts; bd. dirs., chmn. Ralston Purina, Ralcorp; chmn. Westgate Equity Group, LLC. With USN, 1954-57. Office: AgriBrands Internat 9811 S 40 Dr Saint Louis MO 63124-1103

STIRLING, CHARLES JAMES MATTHEW, organic chemistry educator; b. Croydon, Surrey, Eng., Aug. 12, 1930; s. Alexander Dickson and Isobel Millicent Stirling; m. Eileen Gibson Powell, 1956; 3 children. Grad. in chemistry with 1st class honors, St. Andrews U., Scotland, 1952; PhD, King's Coll., London, 1955, DSc, 1967; DSC (hon.), St. Andrews, 1994, Aix-Marseille, 1999. Rsch. fellow Civil Svc., Porton Down, Wiltshire, Eng., 1955-56, sr. rsch. fellow, 1956-57; Imperial Chem. Industries fellow U. Edinburgh, 1957-59; lectr. organic chemistry Queen's U., Belfast, No. Ireland, 1959-65; reader King's Coll., 1965-69; prof. U. Wales, Bangor, 1969-90, U. Sheffield, Eng., 1990—. Contbr. over 200 articles to sci. jours. Fellow Royal Soc., Royal Soc. Chemistry (award for organic reaction mechanisms 1988, Millenium award and fellow 1999). Avocations: choral music, travel, furniture restoration. Office: U Sheffield Dept Chemistry, Sheffield S3 7HF, England

STIRRAT, WILLIAM ALBERT, electronics engineer; b. Syracuse, N.Y., Nov. 5, 1919; s. Robert William and Doris (White) S.; m. Bernice Amelia Wilson, July 13, 1958; children: Valerie Lynne, Dorothy Grace, William Ellsworth. Student, Triuna (Yaddo) Arts of the Theater Sch., 1936, Saratoga Eastman Sch Bus., 1936-37; BS in Physics, Rensselaer Poly. Inst., 1942, postgrad., 1949-50; postgrad., Rutgers U., 1951-58, Fairleigh Dickinson U., 1971. Elecs. engr. GE, Schenectady, N.Y., 1941-44; instr. physics Clarkson Coll. Tech., 1947-49; electronic engr. rsch. and devel. U.S. Army, Fort Monmouth, N.J., 1950-87; prin. engr. Eagle Tech. Logicon, Inc., Northrop Grumman Corp., Eatontown, N.J., 1987-92; pres. Stirrat Arts & Scis., Freehold, N.J., 1992—. Author: (with Alex North) Unchained Melody, 1936 (Top song of Yr., A Top Song of the Century, Acad. award nomination 1955, Top ASCAP love song of the 50s decade), Why 3? (Army award 1985); assoc. editor IEEE Transactions on Electromagnetic Compatability, 1970-76; contbr. articles to profl. jours.; patentee in field. Chmn. pub. rels. Battleground dist. Monmouth coun. Boy Scouts Am., 1970-77; mem. Rep. Congl. Leadership Coun., 1989-91; mem. Rep. Campaign Coun., 1992-93, Rep. Nat. Com., 1992-99. Mem. SAR, IEEE (editor N.J. Coast sect. Scanner 1974-75), Internat. Songwriters Assn., Palgrave Soc., Internat. Platform Assn., Am. Soc. of Composers, Authors and Publishers. Episcopalian. Achievements include development of binomial pulse. Home and Office: 218 Overbrook Dr Freehold NJ 07728-1525

STITH, MARY BETH (RAE), marketing professional for graphic design; b. St. Louis, Jan. 19, 1945; d. William King and Ella Roe Barnett; 1 child, Elliot King. BA in Am. Studies, Grinnell Coll., 1966. Dir. spl. events March of Dimes, Chgo., 1982-86; dir. mktg. Gerhardt & Clemons, Chgo., 1986-95, v.p., 1995—. E-mail: rae@gerhardtelemons.com. Home: 2650 W Belden Ave Chicago IL 60647-3039

STITH, W(ILLIAM) MARK, real estate executive; b. Tucson, July 25, 1956; s. Sarah Josephine Lewis; m. Candace L. Starr, Mar. 18, 1991; children: Melissa Starr, Dawn Starr. BS in Pub. Adminstrn., U. Ariz., 1979, MEd in Counseling, 1981; student, Pima C.C., Tucson, 1990. Lic. profl. clin. counselor and marriage/family therapist, N.Mex.; lic. pvt. investigator, Ariz.; cert. emergency med. technician. Comml. realtor Breckenridge and eureka Realty, Tucson, 1982-88; dir. Childrens Protection Ctr. and Shelter, 7th Jud. Dist., Socorro, N.Mex., 1988-90; child protective svc. investigator State of Ariz., Pinal/Gila Counties, 1990; realty specialist, realtor Lauer & Assocs., Tucson, 1990-95; asst mgmt. realty specialist J.V. James & Assocs. Brokerage and Appraisals, Tucson, 1995—; lead investigator, chief rsch. Sierra Rsch., Tucson, 1991—; ind. contractor in asset mgmt. Dept. of Treasury/FDIC Resolution Trust Corp., Ariz. and N.Mex., 1991—. Author, developer: (book/manual) Operation Spiritfire, 1995. Bd. dirs. C.P.C. and S. Inc. Childrens Family Project, Tucson, 1994—. Mem. Nat. Assn. Realtors, Ariz. Assn. Realtors, Phi Alpha Alpha, Phi Theta Kappa. Address: 6657 E Victoria St Tucson AZ 85730-3226

STITT, DOROTHY JEWETT, journalist; b. Houston, Sept. 4, 1914; d. Harry Berkey and Gladys (Norfleet) Jewett; m. James Wilson Stitt, Feb. 14, 1939; children: James Harry, Thomas Paul. AB, Rice U., 1937; MS, Columbia U., 1938. Reporter Houston Post, 1936-38, asst. city editor, 1938; editor of publs. Jewett Family of Am., 1971-94, editor emeritus, 1994—; spl. asst. to pub. Jewett Genealogy Vols. III and IV, 1995-97; Jewett family Dir.-for-Life, 1995—; gen. chair Jewett Family Reunion, 1996; exec. com. Jewett 2000 Millennium Reunion. Author, editor: The 100th Anniversary Yearbook and History of the George Taylor Chapter, DAR, 1895-1995, 1994, Easton Red Cross Fiftieth Anniversary Booklet and History—Fifty Years of Service, 1967. Adv. bd. Easton Salvation Army, pub. chmn., 1956—, chmn. bd. dirs., 1964, bd. treas., 1981; bd. dirs., pub. chmn. Easton chpt. ARC, 1952-67, vol. Lehigh Valley chpt., 1995-96, 98; founding chmn., pres. Easton JC Wives, 1950-53; mem. fin. com. Little Stone House Mus. Assn., 1974-76, 80, organizing bd. dirs. sec. and pub. chmn., 1974-91; bd. dirs. Easton United Comty. Chest/United Way, 1957-60, publicity chmn. for 1st campaign, 1960; active Easton Civil Def. Comms., 1956-60; mem. bd. Montgomery County Pa. Girl Scouts USA, 1946-48, publicity chmn., initiator and editor county newsletter; den mother cub scouts Easton Boy Scouts Am., 1948-55; capt. renovation campaign area YWCA, 1956; mem. March Sch., Easton PTA, 1948-57, sec., 1952-54, v.p., 1954-56, bylaws chmn., 1953, Easton H.S., 1954-61, membership chmn., 1955-57, 59-60; bd. dirs. Easton Young Woman's Christian Assn., 1965-68, publicity chmn. Y-Teen com., 1953-68; class agent 60th reunion Grad. Sch. Journalism Class of 1938 Columbia U., 1998; mem. exec. com. Jewett 2000 Millennium Reunion. Recipient plaques Salvation Army, 1982, 91, Jewett Family of Am., 1993, cited for Outstanding Svcs., Easton chpt. ARC, 1967, cert. for Outstanding Svc. and Support, 1997, citation Hist. and Geneal. Soc. Northampton County for outstanding svc. in restoration and pub. of Little Stone House Mus., 1993, citation United Way of Easton, 1960, Molly Pitcher gold medal of appreciation SAR, 1980. Mem. AAUW (treas. Easton br. 1950-52, newsletter initiator and editor 1951-60, rep. of br. to UN N.Y.C. conf. 1961-68, internat. rels. chair 1960-68; Pa. achievement award 2000), UDC (Jefferson Davis chpt./Houston), DAR (George Taylor chpt. regent 1974-80, 89-95, vice regent 1980-83, historian 1971-74, 95—, pub. chair 1969—, Pa. state chair vol. svcs. 1995-98, DAR chmn. Kressler Meml. Garden, Easton, 1999—), PEO (chpt. AF Houston), Easton Tavern House Soc., World Affairs Coun. Phila., Woman's Club of Easton (pres. 1961-64, bd. dirs. 1957—, pub. chair 1952-68, 70-82, 92-96, parliamentarian 1984-92, 2000—, spl. fin. chair 1969-78, legis. chair 1982-84, internat. affairs chair 1996-2000, history update chair 1997—, Outstanding Woman of Yr. 1992, Gold Medal of Honor 1992), Pa. Northeastern Dist. Regents Club (pres. 1980-83, treas. 1997—), Northampton Country Club (Niners' Golf chair 1957-91), Women's Golf Assn. (constn. and bylaws chair, publicity chmn. 1957-92, parliamentarian 1960-92), Libr. of Congress Assn. (founding nat. mem., charter assoc.). Republican. Episcopalian. Avocations: antiques, historical research, golf, swimming, grandmothering. Home: 110 Upper Shawnee Ave Easton PA 18042-1377

STITT, THOMAS PAUL, SR., lawyer; b. Sellersville, Pa., Oct. 2, 1943; s. James Wilson and Dorothy (Jewett) S.; m. Suzanne Ruth Reifsnyder, June 19, 1970 (div. Sept. 1982); children: Alicia Ann, Rebecca Jean; m. Melinda May Millheim, Aug. 20, 1983 (div. June 2000); children: Thomas Paul, Victoria Elizabeth, Andrew James. AB, Duke U., 1965; JD, So. Meth. U., 1968. Bar: Tex. 1968, Pa. 1969, U.S. Dist. Ct. (ea. dist.) Pa. 1971, U.S. Supreme Ct. 1986. Assoc. Coffin and DeRaymond, Easton, Pa., 1971-73; jr. ptnr. Coffin, DeRaymond, Shipman & Stitt, Easton, 1973-75; sr. ptnr. Coffin, DeRaymond, Shipman, Stitt, Lewis & Walters, Easton, 1975-87, Stitt and Cordts, Easton, 1987-94; pvt. practice Easton, 1994—; sr. ptnr. Star Enterprises Partnerships, Lehigh Valley, Pa., 1986—; solicitor Borough of Stockertown, Pa., 1974-84, Easton Suburban Water Authority, 1987—; bd. dirs. Keystone Food Products, Inc., Easton, Premier Bank, Easton; bd. dirs., v.p. Jewett Family of Am., 1985-94, 96—. Solicitor Lehigh Valley chpt. ARC, 1988-90, bd. dirs., 1990-96, chmn. 1994-96; trustee, elder First Presbyn. Ch., Easton, 1973-79, 80-86; pres. State Theater, Inc., Easton, 1988-91; bd. dirs. Easton Pub. Libr., 1973-78, pres., 1978. 1st lt. U.S. Army, 1969-71. Mem. ABA (Silver Key award 1968), Northampton Country Club (bd. dirs. 1987-96), AAA Northampton County (v.p., bd. dirs. 1973—), Masons, Shriners, Rotary. Republican. Avocations: reading, golf, tennis, swimming, travel. Office: Thomas P Stitt Sr Law Office 101 S 3rd St Easton PA 18042-4524

STIVER, JAMES FREDERICK, pharmacist, health physicist, administrator, scientist; b. Elkhart, Ind., Jan. 27, 1943; s. Melvin Hugh and Pauline Anna (Schrock) S.; m. Joan Louise Trindle, Aug. 14, 1965; children: Gregory James, Richard Frederick, Kristin Louise, Elizabeth Ann. BS in Pharmacy and Pharm. Scis., Purdue U., 1966, MS, 1968, PhD, 1970. Lic. pharmacist, Ind., N.D. Asst. prof. N.D. State U., Fargo, 1969-73, radiol. safety officer, 1969-76, assoc. prof., 1973-76; radiation safety officer KMS Fusion Inc., Ann Arbor, Mich., 1976-80; mgr., pharmacist Kroger Sav-On Pharmacy Co., Elkhart, Ind., 1980-81; pharmacist Elkhrt Gen. Hosp., 1981; environ. regulatory affairs adminstr. Upjohn Co., Kalamazoo, Mich., 1981-88, patent liaison scientist, 1988-92, sr. patent liaison scientist, 1992-94; pharmacist, asst. mgr. Judd Drugs, Elkhart, 1994-95; pharmacist Meijer Pharmacy, Goshen, Ind., 1995-99; pharmacist, asst. mgr. Wal-Mart Pharmacy, Elkhart, 1999-2000, mgr., 2000—; cons., lectr. Contbr. articles, abstracts to publs. Named to Hon. Order Ky. Cols. Fellow Am. Inst. Chemists; mem. AAAS, Am. Pharm. Assn., Am. Chem. Soc., Health Physics Soc., Internat. Radiation Protection Assn., Am. Biol. Safety Assn., Ind. Pharmacists Assn., N.D. Pharm. Assn., Order Ky. Cols., Kappa Psi, Rho Chi, Phi Lambda Upsilon, Sigma Xi. Home: 505 S Skyview Dr Middlebury IN 46540-9427 Office: Wal Mart Elkhart IN 46514

STIVER, WILLIAM EARL, retired government administrator; b. Madison, Ind., Mar. 30, 1921; s. John Virgil and Anna Lynne (Ryker) S.; m. Norma A. Cull, June 11, 1944; children: Vicki, Raymond, Gena, John. Student, Hanover Coll., 1947-49; BS, U. Calif., Berkeley, 1951, MBA, 1952. With Fed. Ser. Bur. Census, Commerce Dept., Suitland, Md., 1952-79, chief budget and finance div., 1963-73, dep. assoc. adminstr. Social and Econ. Stats. Adminstrn., 1973-75; spl. asst., assoc. dir. adminstrn. and field ops. Bur. of Census, 1975-77, electronic data processing staff coordinator, 1977-78, ret., 1979. Served with USA, 1942-45, 45-46. Recipient Silver medal Commerce Dept., 1969. Mem. Phi Beta Kappa, Beta Gamma Sigma. Home: 8104 Kerby Pky Ct Fort Washington MD 20744-4756

STIX, GERULF, government official; b. Vienna, Austria, Jan. 28, 1935; s. Franz and Senta (Vogel) S; m. Helga Sprenger. D. in Econs., U. Innsbruck/Tirol, Austria, 1957. Mem. Austrian Parliament, Vienna, 1971-90; leader Tirol/Innsbruck region Liberal Party Austria, 1973-85; 3rd pres. Austrian Parliament, Vienna, 1983-90; mgmt. cons. for pvt. businesses Innsbruck/Tirol, 1972-99. Author: Die Arbeitslose Gesellschaft, 1978, Die Stunde des Euroliberalismus, 1991; editor Genius-Lesestücke. Avocation: sailing. E0mail: g.stix@tirol.com. Home: Winkelweg 17, A6060 Ampass Austria

STOBERSKI, MICHAEL EDWARD, lawyer; b. Troy, N.Y., Oct. 18, 1966; s. John S. and Winifred A. (Boland) S.; m. Holly S. Sedarat, Oct. 21, 1994. BA, U. San Diego, 1988, JD, 1991. Bar: Calif. 1991, Nev. 1992, U.S. Dist. Ct. (so. dist.) Calif. 1991, Nev. 1992, U.S. Ct. Appeals (9th cir.) 1992. Shareholder Rawlings, Olson, Cannon, Gormley & Desruisseaux, Las Vegas, Nev., 1991—; counsel Clark County Pro Bono Project, Las Vegas, 1992-96, named Rookie of Yr. 1992-93. Mem. ABA, Def. Rsch. Inst., Clark County Bar Assn. Avocations: golf, skiing, scuba diving. Office: Rawlings Olson Cannon Et Al 301 Clark Ave Ste 1000 Las Vegas NV 89101-6597

STOCK, IAN, marketing research company executive; b. Rugby, Eng., June 4, 1950; s. Alec and May (Allen) S.; m. Vivienne Frances Williams, May 11, 1984; 1 child, Clym Francis Stock-Williams. BSc in Econs. with honours, U. Wales, 1971. Diplomate in internat. mktg. mgmt. Mktg. exec. Deeko Plc, London, 1973-76, Whitbread & Co., London, 1976-78; sr. rsch. exec. Makrotest Ltd., London, 1978-82, Bus. and Market Rsch., Cheshire, Eng., 1982-83; prin. Ian Stock Mktg. Consultancy, Cheshire, 1983-87; ptnr. S.A.M.M., Cheshire, 1987-98; head mkt. rsch. Vichydrographic Office, Somerset, 1998—; cons. D.T.I. Enterprise Initiative for Mktg., U.K., 1989-94, C.I.M. Consultancy Svc., U.K., 1992-98, South and East Cheshire Tng. and Enterprise Coun., 1991-98, Shropshire Tng. and Enterprise Coun., 1991-98. Author rsch. reports. Advisor Young Enterprise, 1999—. Mem. Chartered Inst. Mktg., Jacob Sheep Soc., Crewe Bus. Chamber (pres. 1996-98), Crewe & Nantwich Chamber of Commerce (dir. 1996-98). Avocations: walking, chess, classical music.

STOCK, JEFFREY KEVIN, academic administrator; b. York, Pa., Aug. 27, 1971; s. Christine Berkheimer. BA, Gettysburg Coll., 1994; MBA, Frostburg State U., 1998. Dir. admissions Wilson Coll., Chambersburg, Pa. Office: Wilson Coll 1015 Philadelphia Ave Chambersburg PA 17201-1279

STOCK, KIM H., dance studio owner, choreographer; b. Miami, Feb. 27, 1943; m. Edward S. Stock, Nov. 22, 1984; stepdau.: Salena M. Stock. Dance student, McKinley Acad. Dance, Miami, 1947-60, Luigi, Miami, 1961, Roland Duprée, Hollywood, Calif., 1962. Profl. dancer various cities, 1959-84; dance tchr. Kennewick, Wash., 1993-96; owner Stock Ctr. Performing Arts, Nipomo, Calif., 1997—; choreographer Richland (Wash.) Light Opera, 1994-95, Pacific Light Opera, Richland, 1995-96. Mem. Nipomo C. of C. (entertainment dir., Octoberfest com. 1998, 99, Kids Day Celebration, 1998, 99), Rotary Club of Nipomo. Avocations: sewing, gourmet cooking, gardening, puzzles. E-mail: kstockcenter@cs.com. Office: Stock Ctr Performing Arts 330 W Tefft St Ste A Nipomo CA 93444-8876

STOCK, RODNEY CLIFFORD, musicologist, editor; b. Westcliff-On-Sea, Essex, Eng., Sept. 8, 1929; arrived in Switzerland, 1958; s. Clifford William Charles and Barbara Beatrice (McKeone) S.; m. Renée Jeanne Bathilde Hue, Aug. 26, 1954; children: Rodolphe, Marie-Astrid. Licence ès Lettres, Sorbonne U., Paris, 1952; postgrad., Ont. Inst. Studies in Edn., Toronto, 1974, U. Geneva, 1979-84. Tchr. various schs. and colls., Paris, 1950-51, Lons-le-Saunier, Jura, 1951-52, Le Mans, Sarthe, 1952-54; tchr. London, 1954-58, Geneva, 1958-66; chief English sect. UNESCO-Internat. Bur. Edn., Geneva, 1966-70; editor Internat. Bur. Edn., UNESCO, Geneva, 1970-77, sr. editor, 1977-89; editor Cahiers Suisses Pédagogie Musicale, Geneva, 1989-97; tchr. People's Univ. Geneva, 1995—; mem. council Faculty of Psychology and Edn. Geneva U., 1980-84; council mem. Archive Institut Jean-Jacques Rousseau, Geneva, 1982—; journalist Internat. Music Coun., 1999—. Author: (with others) Le Bureau International d'Education au Service du Mouvement Educatif, 1979; contbr. articles on comparative edn., literary and mus. criticism to profl. jours. Mem. Geneva Symphony Orch. Mem. Comparative Edn. Soc. Europe, Swiss Soc. for Rsch. in Edn., Music Edn. Rsch. Group, Inst. Romande Rsch. et Documentation Pédagogiques, Internat. Soc. Music Edn., European String Tchrs. Assn., Internat. Orgn. Journalists, Swiss Assn. Specialized Journalists. Home: 79 rue des Eaux-Vives, 1207 Geneva Switzerland

STOCKARD, JOE LEE, public health service officer, consultant; b. Lees Summit, Mo., May 5, 1924; s. Joseph Frederick and Madge Lorraine (Jones) S.; m. Elsie Anne Chamberlain, Dec. 27, 1957. BS, Yale U., 1945; MD, U. Kans., 1948; MPH, Johns Hopkins U., 1961. Med. officer U.S. Army Med. Corps, Korea and Malaya, 1952-55; asst. prof. preventive medicine Sch. Medicine U. Md., Balt., 1955-58; dep. dir. Cholera Rsch. Lab., Dhaka, Bangladesh, 1960-63; advanced through grades to capt., epidemiologist USPHS, Washington, 1960-76, 64-67; chief preventive medicine sect. USAID, Saigon, Vietnam, 1965-68; assoc. dir. Office Internat. Health, Office of Surgeon Gen. USPHS, Washington, 1967-69; epidemiologist, med. officer Agy. for Internat. Devel., Washington, 1969-87; mem. expert adv. com. WHO, Ouagadougou, Burkina, Faso, 1987-92; mem. joint programme com. AID project officer Onchocerciasis Control Program, West Africa, 1975-87; med. officer AID Africa Bur., Washington, 1976-87; guest spkr., prof. seminar on leptospirosis, 1956; organizer plague sect. meeting 8th Internat. Congress Tropical Medicine, 1969. Author: (with others) Communicable and Infectious Diseases, 1964; contbr. articles to U.S. Armed Forces Med. Jour., N.Y. Acad. Sci. Jour. Citizens rep. on regional water quality adv. com. Low Country Coun. of Govts., 1996-98. Recognized for support of onchocerciasis control in West Africa by Pres. Jerry Rawlings, Rep. of Ghana, 1986. Fellow Royal Soc. Tropical Medicine and Hygiene; mem. APHA, Am. Soc. Tropical Medicine and Hygiene, Retired Officers Assn. Achievements include discovery that massive doses of benadryl will not prevent shock in Korean epidemic hemorragic fever, gangrene is not a previously recognized manifestation of bubonic plaque in S.E. Asia; co-discovery that leptospirosis can be a significant problem in troops in Malayasia. Office: 1 Savage Ct Bluffton SC 29910-4430

STOCKBURGER, DAVID WEBB, psychologist, educator; b. Canton, Ohio, Sept. 2, 1947; s. Webb and Clara Stockburger; m. LeAnna Marie DeAngelo, May 23, 1999; 1 child, Stephanie. BA, Ohio U., 1969, MA, 1971, PhD in Math. Psychology, 1974. Prof. psychology S.W. Mo. State U., Springfield, 1974—. Author (Internet books) Indtoductory Statistics: Concepts, Models and Applications, 1996 (Math.com award 1999), Multivariate Statistics, 1996. Avocation: Web development. Office: SW Mo State U 901 S National Ave Springfield MO 65804-0088

STOCKDALE, SALLY BOYD, artist, realtor; b. Coral Gables, Fla., Apr. 20, 1941; d. Grant Stockdale and Alice Boyd (Magruder) Proudfoot; m. David Michael deWilde, Dec. 21, 1968 (div. 1978); children: Holland Stockdale, Christian duCroix; m. Mariano Eduardo Munoz-Lopez, Mar. 26, 1981. A.A., Bennett Coll., Millbrook, N.Y., 1961; postgrad., Trinity Coll., Dublin, Ireland, 1962; B.F.A., Am. U., 1979; postgrad., Corcoran Sch. Art, Washington, 1980-93; grad., Realtor Inst., 1994. Lic. realtor, Washington, Md., Va. Realtor Pardoe Real Estate ERA, Washington, 1987—. One-woman shows include: Tahiti Gallery, Marbella, Spain, 1978, Dumbarton Series, Washington, 1982; commd. murals include Children's Hosp., Washington; represented Folger Library, Washington; portraits state and fed. legislators, others; illustrator Holiday Mag., 1963-68, Spanien Jour., 1979, The Dreadful Day, 1981, Patrick, 16 Centuries, 1983. Mem. Nat. Trust for Historic Preservation. Work featured in Washington Evening Star, Washington Post, New York Times; recipient Top Prodr. award Washington Assn. Realtors, 1987-99. Mem. Nat. Mus. Women in Arts, Capital Spkrs., Club Nautico de Altea. Home: 4719 Chesapeake St NW Washington DC 20016-4465

STOCKENBERG, BO PETER, architect; b. Svdertdlje, Stockholm, Sweden, June 12, 1965; s. Hans Oscar and Gunvor Maria (Houmann) S. UC in Bus. Adminstrn., U. Uppsala, Sweden, 1988; BSc in Arch., Royal Sch. Tech., Stockholm, 1998. Internet media cons. Carat/Inter-Media AB, Stockholm, 1988-90; media dir. Indsl. News Svc. AB, Stockholm, 1991-92, Stockenberg Media, Stockholm, 1992—; arch./design cons. Vasahuset AB, Stockholm, 1992-93, Bergaliden AB, Stockholm, 1994-95, Catella Fvrvaltning AB, Stockholm, 1996-97, Ecuro Fvrvaltning AB, Stockholm, 1998-99, Form & Funktion Archs., Stockholm, 1999—. Tech. adviser Royal Swedish Army, 1984-85. Recipient 1st prize in design for CFL-dedicated lighting fixtures NUTEK/Ljuskultur, Stockholm, 1997. E-mail: peter.stock-

enberg@delta.telenordia.se. Office: Form & Funktion Archs, Brevallagatan 8, S-113 36 Stockholm Sweden

STOCKER, ARTHUR FREDERICK, classics educator; b. Bethlehem, Pa., Jan. 24, 1914; s. Harry Emilius and Alice (Stratton) S.; m. Marian West, July 16, 1968. A.B. summa cum laude, Williams Coll., 1934; A.M., Harvard U., 1935, Ph.D., 1939. Instr. Greek Bates Coll., 1941-42; asst. prof. classics U. Va., 1946-52, assoc. prof., 1952-60, prof., 1960-84, prof. emeritus, 1984—, chmn. dept., 1955-63, 68-78, assoc. dean Grad. Sch. Arts and Scis., 1962-66; vis. asst. prof. classics U. Chgo., summer 1951. Editor: (with others) Servianorum in Vergilii Carmina Commentariorum Editio Harvardiana, Vol. II, 1946, Vol. III, 1965; assoc. editor: Classical Outlook. Served with USAAF, 1942-46; col. (ret.). Sheldon traveling fellow from Harvard, 1940-41. Mem. Va. Classical Assn. (pres. 1949-52), Mid. West and South Classical Assn. (pres. So. sect. 1960-62, pres. 1970-71), Nat. Huguenot Soc. (pres. gen. 1989-91), Am. Philol. Assn., Mediaeval Acad. Am., Poetry Soc. Va. (pres. 1966-69), S.A.R. (chpt. pres. 1972, 91), Huguenot Soc. Va. (pres. 1981-83), Raven Soc. (Raven award 1977), Phi Beta Kappa, Omicron Delta Kappa. Republican. Presbyterian (elder). Clubs: Masons, Red-Land (Charlottesville, Va.), Colonnade (Charlottesville, Va.), Farmington Country (Charlottesville, Va.), Commonwealth (Richmond, Va.), Williams (N.Y.C.), Army and Navy (Washington). Home: 250 Pantops Mountain Rd Charlottesville VA 22911-8694

STOCKER, GEOFFREY LUFF, psychotherapist, researcher, educator; b. London, July 2, 1923; s. George Newton and Gertrude Else (Wright) S.; m. Irene Elsie Turner, Feb. 2, 1947 (div. May 5, 1956); 1 child, Christine; m. Pamela Elizabeth Ashcroft, Feb. 2, 1984; children: Pauline, Gary. BTh, Internat. Free Protestant U., London, 1961, MTh, 1962, PhD, 1964; lic., London Coll. Music, 1957. Ordained deacon Free Protestant Episcopal Ch., 1962. Apprentice Analytical Chem., London, 1945-47; propr. Belsize Chem. Products and Stocker & Walker Food Products, London, 1947-56; prin. Hampstead Sch. Speech & Drama, London, 1957-84; pvt. practice psychotherapy, London, 1958—; assoc. in psychology Brit. Tutorial Inst., London, 1957; cons. psychotherapist The Sleep Clinic Ealing, London, 1995—; cons. chemist Lafi Fine Foods, Ltd., London, 1949-52; mng. dir. The Sch. Psychol. Salesmanship, Ltd., London, 1961-69, Dynamic Motivation Ltd., London, 1964-70, Speed-Learn Ltd., London, 1970-74; dir. Subliminal Learning Methods Ltd., London, 1967-72; pres. The Sleep-Learning Assn., London, 1962—; presbyter Free Protestant Episcopal Ch., Tottenham, 1962-64; tchr. speech and drama. Author: Geoffrey Stocker Tapes, Sleep-Learning Assn., 1964-66; editor: Learning During Natural Sleep, English translation, 1965; editor Quarterly Jour. Sleep-Learning Assn., 1965-68. Hon. rsch. fellow St. Andrew's Ecumenical Rsch. Fellowship Intercollegiate, Tottenham, London, 1963. Fellow Hypnotherapy Soc. (London), Hypnotherapy Rsch. Soc. U.K. (founding), Royal Soc. Arts (London); mem. Sci. and Med. Network, Nat. Coun. for Hypnotherapy and Hypnotherapy Register, Brit. Soc. Hypnotherapists, Brit. Hypnotherapy Assn. (founding), New Era Acad. Music and Drama (assoc.), London Coll. Music (assoc.), London Acad. Music and Dramatic Art (assoc.), English Spkg. Bd. (founding). Avocations: classical piano music, reincarnation, esoteric philosophy, conjuring, sketching. Fax: 0181-998-0220.

STOCKER, JOYCE ARLENE, retired secondary school educator; b. West Wyoming, Pa., May 13, 1931; d. Donald Arthur and Elizabeth Mae (Gardner) Saunders; m. Robert Earl Stocker, Nov. 26, 1953; children: Desiree Lee Stocker Stackhouse, Rebecca Lois Stocker Genelow, Joyce Elizabeth Stocker Scrobola. Grad. cum laude, Coll. Misericordia, Dallas, 1953; Master's equivalency diploma, Pa. Dept. Edn., 1991. Cert. tchr., Pa. Tchr. music and lang. arts West Pittston (Pa.) Sch. Dist., 1953-60; tchr. music and choral Wyoming Area Sch. Dist., Exeter, Pa., 1970-78, tchr. English composition, 1978-93, chmn. lang. arts dept., 1982-90, dir. nat. history day activities, 1982-93; state cons. Nat. History Day, 1996—. Organist, choir dir. United Meth. Ch., Wyo., 1958—; dir. W. Wyo. Centennial Choir, 1998; mem. adminstrv. bd. West Wyo., 2000—; mem. worship com. United Meth. Ch. and Interch. Coun., Wyo. and West Wyo. Recipient DAR Tchr. of Yr. award, 1992-93, Wilkes U., 1990; named Outstanding Educator, Times Leader, 1993; honoree Wyo. United Meth. Ch. Choir, 1999. Mem. NEA, Pa. Edn. Assn., Wyo. Edn. Assn., N.E. Pa. Writing Coun., Nat. Coun. Tchrs. English, Women Educators Internat., Orgn. Am. History, Pa. Music Educators Assn., Music Educators Nat. Coun., Nat. Coun. Social Studies, Pa. Assn. Sch. Retirees (Vol. of Yr. 1998), Pa. Sch. Employees Retirement Sys. (social svcs. com.), Pa. Retired Pub. Sch. Employees Assn. (Luzerne-Wyoming counties chpt.), Pa. Coun. Social Studies, Delta Kappa Gamma (recording sec. 1991—, accompanist Pa. state chorus, 1999—, 2000—), Phi Mu Gamma. Methodist. Avocations: reading, writing, sewing, hunting, fishing. Office: Wyoming Area Sch Dist 20 Memorial St Exeter PA 18643-2659

STÖCKER, MICHAEL WILHELM, science educator, editor; b. Kassel, Hessen, Germany, Jan. 25, 1948; s. Michael and Sophia Anna (Tentrop) S.; m. Wencke Ophaug, Sept. 16, 1994; 1 child, Mikkel. Diploma, U. Münster, Germany, 1972, diploma in chemistry, 1975, D in Nat. Scis., 1979. Chemielaborant Hoechst AG, Frankfurt, 1964-67; sci. asst. U. Münster, 1974-79; sci. asst. U. Bergen, Norway, 1980-82, prof., 1999—; rsch. scientist Ctr. Indsl. Rsch., Oslo, 1982-89, sr. rsch. scientist, 1989-92; prin. rsch. scientist Found. Scientific & Indsl. Rsch. Norwegian Inst. Tech., Oslo, 1992—; dir. 10th Internat. Zeolite Summer Sch., Wildbad Kreuth, Germany, 1994; cons. European Space Agy., Paris, 1996; vis. scientist UBC, Vancouver, 1988-89. Editor: Advanced Zeolite Science and Applications, 1994; spl. issue and newsbrief editor Microporous and Mesoporous Materials jour., 1998—. Mem. Internat. Zeolite Assn. (synthesis commn. 1992—, catalysis commn. 1994—, chair 1998—, bd. mem. 1998—), Am. Chem. Soc., Norwegian Chem. Soc., German Zeolite Assn. Roman Catholic. Office: SINTEF Applied Chemistry, Forskningsveien 1 POB 124, Blindern Oslo N-0314, Norway

STOCKHAUSEN, KARLHEINZ, composer; b. Mödrath, Germany, Aug. 22, 1928; m. Doris Andreae, 1951; children: Suja, Christel, Markus, Majella; m. Mary Bauermeister, 1967; children: Julika, Simon. Student, Musikhochschule, Cologne, Germany, 1947-51; student acoustical scis., U. Bonn, 1954-56; studied with Werner Meyer-Eppler, Olivier Messiaen. composer, condr. first pub. score for electronic music; dir. Electronic Studio, Cologne; condr., tchr., editor rev. of serial music; performance own works, U.S., Can., 1958; with Westdeutscher Rundfunk Electronic Music Studio, Cologne, 1953—, artistic dir., 1963-77; guest prof. U. Pa., 1964, U. Calif., Davis, 1966-67; prof. Musikhochschule, Cologne, 1971-77. Composer: Kreuzspiel for six players, 1951; Spiel for orch., 1952; Eleven Piano Pieces, 1952-56; Punkte for orch., 1952; Kontrapunkte for ten instruments, 1952-53; Gruppen for 3 orchs., 1955-57; Zeitmasze, 1955-56; Gesang der Jünglinge, 1956; Zyklus, Refrain, Carré for 4 choirs and 4 orchs., 1959; Kontakte for electronic sounds, piano and percussion, 1959-60; Momente for 4 choirs, 13 instruments, solo-soprano, 1962—; also numerous works for solo instruments; Originale, mus. theatre, 1961; Plus-Minus, 1963; Mixture for orch. and electronic modulators, 1964; Mikrophonie I, 1964, Telemusik, 1966, Hymnen, 1967, Stimmung, 1968, Mantra, 1970, Trans, 1971, Inori, 1974, Cadenzas, 1978, Invisible Choirs, 1979, Donnerstag aus Licht, 1981, Samstag aus Licht, 1984, Montag aus Licht, 1988, Dienstag aus Licht, 1993, Freitag aus Licht, 1996, Mittwoch aus Licht, 1998; composer over 280 compositions; over 100 recs. of works; author: Towards a Cosmic Music, 1989, Texte zur Musik (10 vols.); subject of numerous books and articles. Foremost exponent of electronic music. Recipient German Critics award, 1964, Italian award for Orchestral Works, 1968, Grand Prix du Disque, 1968, 69, 71, Edison prize, 1974, German Record prize, 1983, Picasso medal UNESCO, 1992, Order of Merit Nordrhein-Westfalen, 1992. Fellow Royal Irish Acad. Music; mem. Royal Swedish Acad., Acad. Arts Berlin, Philharmonic Acad. Rome, Am. Acad. and Inst. Arts and Letters, European Acad. Sci., Arts and Letters, Royal Acad. Music (hon.), Am. Acad. Arts and Scis. (hon.), Nat. Acad. St. Cecelia (hon.). Office: Stockhausen-Verlag, 51515 Kurten Germany

STOCKMEYER, ROLF-PETER, accountant; b. Goettingen, Germany, Mar. 2, 1956; s. Rolf and Marilene (Behrens) S.; m. Renate Batsch, Sept. 1, 1981; 1 child, David. Diplom-Volkswirt, U. Cologne, Germany, 1981. Asst. Treuarbeit AG, Düsseldorf, Germany, 1981-87, prokurist, 1987-90; prokurist C & L Westdeutschland Wirtschaftsprüfungsgesellschaft AG, Essen, Germany, 1990—; ptnr. C&L Deutsche Revision AG, Essen, Germany, 1996-97, PricewaterhouseCoopers Deutsche Revision AG, Essen, Germany, 1998—; mcpl. councillor Linnich, 1975-81; tax advisor, apptd. by Finanzminister des Landes Nordrhein-Westfalen, Düsseldorf, 1986; chartered acct., apptd. by Minister fuer Wirtschaft, Mittelstand und Tech. des Landes Nordrhein-Westfalen, Düsseldorf, 1988. Avocations: music, literature. Home: Bienenhof 3, D 51519 Odenthal-Höffe Germany Office: Westdeutschland WPG AG, Weserstr 101, D 45043 Essen Germany

STOCKTON, JOHN HOUSTON, professional basketball player; b. Spokane, Wash., Mar. 26, 1962; m. Nada Stepovich, Aug. 16, 1986; 1 child, John Houston. Grad., Gonzaga U., 1984. With Utah Jazz, Salt Lake City, 1984—; mem. U.S. Olympic Basketball Team, 1992. Named to NBA All-Star team, 1989-94; holder NBA single season rec. most assists, 1991; NBA Assists leader, 1987-1992; NBA Steals leader, 1989, 92; named NBA All-Star Co-MVP, 1993, All-NBA First Team, 1994. Led NBA in most assists per game, 1988-93; led NBA with highest steals per game avg., 1989,1992; shares single-game playoff record for most assists, 24, 1988. Office: Utah Jazz 301 W South Temple Salt Lake City UT 84101-1216

STOCKWIN, JAMES ARTHUR AINSCOW, Japanese politics and modern studies specialist; b. Sutton Coldfield, U.K., Nov. 28, 1935; s. Wilfred Arthur and Edith Mary (Ainscow) S.; m. Audrey Lucretia Hobson Wood, Jan. 30, 1960; children: Katrina Mary, Jane Clare, Rupert Arthur, Timothy James (dec.). BA, Oxford (Eng.) U., 1959; PhD, Australian Nat. U., Canberra, 1965. Lectr. Australian Nat. U., Canberra, 1964-66, sr. lectr., 1966-72, reader, 1972-81; Nissan prof. modern Japanese studies Oxford U., 1982—; dir. Nissan Inst. Japanese Studies, 1982—, fellow St. Antony's Coll., 1982—; sub-warden St. Antony's Coll., 1999-2001. Author: The Japanese Socialist Party and Neutralism, 1968, Japan: Divided Politics in a Growth Economy, 1975, 2d edit., 1982, The Story of Tim, 1993, Governing Japan, 1999; author: (with others) Dynamic and Immobilist Politics in Japan, 1988; translator: (Junji Banno) The Establishment of the Japanese Constitutional System, 1992; contbr. articles to profl. jours. Mem. Brit. Assn. Japanese Studies (past pres. 1994-95), Japan Studies Assn. Australia, Australian Inst. Internat. Affairs, Australasian Polit. Studies Assn. Office: Nissan Inst Japanese Studies, 27 Winchester Rd, Oxford OX2 6NA, United Kingdom

STODDARD, SANDOL, writer; b. Birmingham, Ala., Dec. 16, 1927; d. Carlos French and Caroline (Harris) S.; m. Felix M. Warburg (div. 1966); children: Anthony, Peter, Gerald, Jason; m. Peter R. Goethals, May 1, 1984. BA magna cum laude, Bryn Mawr Coll., 1959. Author 26 books including: Growing Time, 1971, The Doubleday Children's Bible, 1983 (Lewis citation 1983), The Hospice Movement: Updated and Expanded Edition, 1992, Prayers, Praises and Thanksgivings, 1992. Bd. dirs., co-founder Hospice of Kona, Kailua-Kona, Hawaii, 1985; co-founder Kona Theol. Inst., 1990; bd. dirs. Choice in Dying, N.Y.C. Recipient Humanitarian Svc. award Forbes Health System, 1979, Notable Book award Am. Libr. Assn., 1964. Mem. AAUW, Nat. Writer's Guild, Cosmopolitan Club. Democrat. Episcopalian. Home and Office: 78-6646 Mamalahoa Hwy Holualoa HI 96725-9734

STODDARD, WILLIAM BERT, JR., economist; b. Carbondale, Pa., Oct. 6, 1926; s. William Bert and Emily (Trautwein) S.; student Lafayette Coll., 1944-45; BS, NYU, 1950, AM, 1952; m. Carol Marie Swartz, Feb. 28, 1970; 1 child, Emily Coleman. Asst. chief acct., budget dir. Hendrick Mfg. Co., Carbondale, Pa., 1952-54, asst. dir. prodn., 1956-68, also dir.; credit corr. U.S. Gypsum Co., N.Y.C., 1954-56; investment counselor, Carbondale, 1968-73, Ridgefield, Conn., 1973—; dir. First Nat. Bank Carbondale, 1968-73; bd. dirs. Lackawanna County Mfrs. Assn., Scranton, Pa., 1960-73. Treas., trustee Aldrich Mus. Contemporary Art, Ridgefield, 1976-90; bd. dirs. Ridgefield Library and Hist. Assn., 1977-85, 87-93; trustee Ridgefield Libr. Endowment Fund Trust, 1985—. Served with U.S. Army 1946-47. Mem. Inst. Mgmt. Accts., Nat. Def. Indsl. Assn., Phi Alpha Kappa, Phi Delta Theta. Republican. Methodist. Clubs: NYU (N.Y.C.), Waccabuc (N.Y.) Country, Princeton Club (N.Y.C.). Home: 59 Bridle Trl Ridgefield CT 06877-1401 Office: 23 Catoonah St Ridgefield CT 06877-4431

STODDART, LEYLAND KLING, stamp dealer, correspondence club director; b. L.A.; arrived in The Philippines, 1985; s. Leland Kling and Helen Isabel (Hancock) S.; m. Lillian May Pearson, 1967 (div. 1985); m. Nelly Deuna, Apr. 8, 1993. Grad., Hollywood H.S., L.A. Owner, dir. South Seas Corr. Club, The Philippines, 1965—. Recipient WWII Svc. medal U.S. Army. Mem. Am. Philatelic Soc., Am. Topical Assn., Royal Can. Philatelic Soc., China Stamp Soc. Office: Box 38, Alaminos Pangasinan The Philippines

STODDART, SIMON KENNETH, archaeology educator; b. London, Nov. 8, 1958; s. Kenneth Bowring and Daphne Elizabeth (Hughes) S.; m. Caroline Ann Malone, June 25, 1983; children: Charlotte, Lucy. BA, Cambridge (Eng.) U., 1980, MA, 1984, PhD, 1987; MA, Mich. U., 1983. Rsch. fellow Magdalene Coll., Cambridge, 1986-90; lectr. U. York, Eng., 1988-90, U. Bristol, Eng., 1990-94; sr. lectr. U. Bristol, 1994-96; lectr. U. Cambridge, 1996—. Joint author: (with N. Spivey) Etruscan Italy, 1990; editor: (with C. Mathers) Development of Decline in Mediterranean Bronze Age, 1994, (with C. Malone) Territory, Time of State, 1994; dep. editor: Jour. Antiquity, 1998—. Fellow Soc. Antiquaries. Office: Magdalene Coll, Cambridge CB3 OAG, England

STOEBNER, JOHN MARTIN, physician; b. Burlington, Tex., 1933; s. Alfred Walter Richard and Mary Evaleen (Martin) S.; m. Julia Bryan Fisher, Aug. 7, 1971; children: J. Eric, Richard, William Scott, Julia M., Kristin. BS, Loyola U., New Orleans, 1956; MD, U. Tex. Med. Br., Galveston, 1959. Intern Fitzsimons Gen. Hosp., Denver, 1959-60; resident Walter Reed Gen. Hosp., Washington, 1965-68; prof. Tex. A&M Coll. Medicine; vice-chmn. radiology Scott & White Clin., Temple, Tex., 1986-92, chmn. 1992-96. Comdr. 94th Gen. Hosp. USAR, Dallas, 1972-82. Mem. Am. Coll. Radiology, Texas Radiol. Soc. Office: Scott & White Clin Radiology Temple TX 76508-0001

STOETZEL, BERTHOLD, psychologist, educator; b. Siegen, NRW, Fed. Republic Germany, Nov. 13, 1938; m. Stoetzel Magdalene Knoche, Apr. 2, 1990; children: Martin, Katrin. Tchr., Univ., Colone, Fed. Republic Germany, 1968, diploma in Psychology, 1971, D in Natural Scis., 1980. Tchr. Tradeschool, Bruehl, Fed. Republic Germany, 1968-71; indsl. psychologist Philips, AM, Siegen, Fed. Republic Germany, 1971-72; prof. Univ., Siegen, Fed. Republic Germany, 1973—. Author several books; contbr. articles to profl. jours. Office: Univ Siegen, Hoeldeslinstr 3, Siegen North Rhine-Westphalia 59, Germany

STOEV, STOYTCHO MITREV, mineralurgist, educator; b. Haskovo, Bulgaria, Nov. 29, 1931; s. Mitru Stoev and Zlatka Ivanova (Tchilingirova) Sapunarov; m. Viliana Yankova Maneva, Dec. 18, 1960; children: Dimitar, Teodora Stoytcheva. Degree in engring., Mining Inst., Dnepropetrovsk, Ukraine, 1954; PhD, Mining Inst., Sofia, Bulgaria, 1963; DSc, Higher Inst. Mining & Geology, Sofia, 1979. Asst. prof. mineralurgy Mining Inst., Sofia, 1954-59; assoc. prof. mineralurgy Higher Inst. Mining and Geology, Sofia, 1960-67, prof. mineralurgy, 1968—; head mineral/coal processing dept. Inst. Mining, Sofia, 1961-76, head vibroacoustical lab., 1963—; head Sci.-Tech. Union, Sofia, 1971-90; cons. to various instns. Author: Vibroacoustical Technologies, 1980, Gravity methods for Mineral Processing, 1986; co-author: Technologies for Industrial Minerals, 1988; contbr. chpts. to numerous books. Capt. Bulgarian Army, 1955. Mem. Sci.-Tech. Union. Avocations: gardening, collecting mushrooms, dancing. Home: jk Drujba bl 420 ent B, Sofia Bulgaria Office: U Mining & Geology, 1100 Sofia Bulgaria

STOEVER, WILLIAM ALFRED, international business educator, lawyer, consultant; b. Ames, Iowa, May 30, 1939; s. Herman J. and M. Martha (Brown) S.; m. Sherron L. Smets, June 12, 1976; children: Susan Jane, Mary Roberta. BA, Amherst Coll., 1962; MEd, Makerere U., Kampala, Uganda, 1963; JD, Harvard U., 1969; MBA, NYU, 1972, PhD, 1978. Bar: N.Y. 1970. Edn. officer Govt. Tanzania, Dar-es-Salaam, 1963-64; atty. Fed. Res. Bank N.Y., N.Y.C., 1970-71; rsch. dir. Inst. Jud. Adminstrn., NYU Law School, N.Y.C., 1971-74; asst. prof. Bklyn. Coll., N.Y., 1974-77; assoc. prof. internat. bus. and law Rutgers U., Newark, 1977-84, rsch. fellow, 1986-87; rsch. fellow Woodrow Wilson Sch., Princeton (N.J.) U., 1984-86; sr. tchg. fellow Nat. U. Singapore, 1987-89; Keating-Crawford prof. bus., W. Paul Stillman Sch. Bus. Seton Hall U., South Orange, N.J., 1989—; cons. UN Ctr. Transnat. Corps, Dacca, Bangladesh, 1985, UN INdsl. Devel. Orgn., Jakarta, Indonesia, 1987; lectr. USIS, 1985, U. Internat. Bus. and Econs., Beijing, 1990, Warsaw (Poland) Sch. Econs., 1991, Plekhanov Econ. Acad., Moscow, 1994, 95; invited nat. and internat. lectr.; cons. on ct. adminstrn. Author Renegotiations in Internat. Bus., 1981, contbr. numerous articles to profl. jours. Mem. Citizens Budget Adv. Com., Maplewood, N.J., 1989—. Recipient numerous rsch. and teaching awards. Mem. Acad. Internat. Bus., Acad. Mgmt., Soc. Internat. Devel., North Am. Case Rsch. Assn., Beta Gamma Sigma. Presbyterian. Avocations: internat. travel, swimming, windsurfing, board and card games. Home: 46 Claremont Ave Maplewood NJ 07040-2118 Office: W Paul Stillman Sch Bus Seton Hall # U South Orange NJ 07079

STOFFLE, CARLA JOY, university library dean; b. Pueblo, Colo., June 19, 1943; d. Samuel Bernard and Virginia Irene (Berry) Hayden; m. Richard William Stoffle, June 12, 1964; children: Brent William, Kami Ann. AA, So. Colo. State Coll., Pueblo, 1963; BA, U. Colo., 1965; MLS, U. Ky., 1969; postgrad., U. Wis., 1980. Head govt. publ. dept. John G. Crabbe Library, Eastern Ky. U., Richmond, 1969-72; head. pub. services U. Wis.-Parkside Library, Kenosha, 1972-76, exec. asst. to chancellor, 1978, asst. chancellor edn. services, 1979-85; assoc. dir. U. Mich. Library, Ann Arbor, 1985-91, dep. dir., 1986-91; mem. adv. commn. Sch. Libr. Sci. U. Mich., Ann Arbor, 1986-92; dean librs. U. Ariz., Tucson, 1991—, acting dir. Sch. Info. Resources and Libr. Sci., 1999—; vol. Peace Corps, Barbados, W.I., 1965-67; mem. adv. bd. Bowker Libr., N.Y., 1985-90; mem. bd. advisors U. Ariz. Press, 1995-2000; mem. adv. coun. OCLC Rsch. Librs., 1995-2000; bd. dirs. Assn. for Rsch. Librs., chair com. on stats. and measurement, 1999—, mem. steering com. scholarly pub. and acad. resource program, 1998; mem. editl. bd. Internet and Higher Edn., 1998-99; bd. dirs. Ctr. for Rsch. Librs., treas., 1999—, budget and fin. com., 1994; presenter in field. Co-author: Administration Government Documents Collection, 1974, Materials and Method for History Research, 1979, Materials and Methods for Political Science Research, 1979; assoc. editor Collection Building, 1986-91, editorial bd., 1986-95; mem. editl. bd. The Bottom Line, 1989-95; contbr. numerous articles to profl. jours. Recipient Most Outstanding Reference Quar. Article award Reference Svc. Press, 1986, Woman on the Move award Tucson Young Women's Christian Assn., 1992, Pres.'s award Ariz. Ednl. Media Assn., 1993, Student Honor Soc. Mortar Bd. award for Faculty Excellence, 1995; named Outstanding Alumnus, Coll. Libr. and Info. Sci., U. Ky., 1989. Mem. ALA (treas. 1988-92, exec. bd. dirs. 1985-92, councilor 1983-92), Assn. Coll. Rsch. Librs. (pres. 1982-83, Bibliographic Instrn. Libr. of Yr. 1991, Acad. Rsch. Libr. of Yr. 1992). Office: U Arizona Main Libr 1510 E University Blvd Tucson AZ 85721-0001

STOIAN, IONELA MARINELA, internist, researcher; b. Pitesti, Arges, Romania, Mar. 1, 1964; d. Mihail and Maria (Serban) Dunitrescu; m. Bogdan Stoian, Dec. 7, 1991. MD, Med. U. Bucharest, Romania, 1989. Intern County Hosp., Pitesti, Romania, 1989-92; resident in internal medicine Univ. Hosp., Bucharest, 1989-92; asst. rschr. internal medicine Acad. Med. Scis., Bucharest, 1995—; asst. internal medicine Med. U. Bucharest, 1995—, asst. nephrology, 1995—. Lt. med. svc. Romanian Res. Mem. N.Y. Acad. Scis. Office: Med U Carol Davila Buch, str Dionisie Lupu nr 37 s 1, Bucharest Romania

STOICA, PETRE, engineering educator; b. Rm Valcea, Romania, July 23, 1949; arrived in Sweden, 1992; s. Petre and Marina (Tanase) S.; m. Anca Iuliana Marinescu, July 14, 1972. MSc, Poly. U., Bucharest, Romania, 1972, DSc, 1979; Doctor Honoris Causa (hon.), Uppsala (Sweden) U., 1993. Asst. prof. Poly. U., 1972-79, assoc. prof., 1980-89, prof. engring., 1990-95, assoc. dean, 1990-91; docent Uppsala U., 1995-97, prof., 1998—; guest prof. Uppsala U., 1992-93; Jubilee vis. prof. Chalmers U. Tech., Gothenburg, Sweden, 1994; vis. prof. U. Fla., 1995, Stanford U., 1997, 99. Author: System Identification, 1989, Optimization and Modelling, 1989 (Acad. prize), Introduction to Spectral Analysis, 1997; assoc. editor 5 jours. in field; contbr. articles to profl. publs. Bd. dirs. Time Series Analysis and Forecasting Soc., London, 1981-86. Recipient Best Paper award Conf. on Cybernetics, Bucharest, 1985. Fellow IEEE (Sr. award 1989, Technical Achievement award 1996, Sign. Processing Soc., Paper award 1999, Baker Paper prize award, 2000, The Third Millennium medal 2000), Royal Statis. Soc.; mem. Internat. Fedn. Automatic Control-Modelling, Identification and Signal Processing Com., Romanian Acad. (hon.). Avocations: travel, walking in the woods, biking, bird watching, reading science fiction. Office: Uppsala U Sys & Control Grp, Uppsala U Sys/Control Dept, PO box 27, SE 75103 Uppsala Sweden

STOICHITA, VICTOR IEEROMIM, art historian, writer; b. Bucharest, Romania, June 13, 1949; s. Sandu Stoichita and Michaela Papilian; m. Anna-Maria Coderch, Jan. 16, 1982; children: Pedro, Maria. Dottore in lettere, U. Rome, 1973; docteur de l'état ès lettres, Sorbonne, Paris, 1989. Asst. prof. Fine Arts Acad., Bucharest, 1973-82, U. Munich, 1984-91; U. prof. Fribourg, Switzerland, 1991—. Author: The Self-Aware Image, 1997, Visionary Experience in the Golden Age of Spanish Art, 1995, A Short History of the Shadow, 1997, Goya: The Last Carnival, 1999. Fellowship Alexander-von-Humboldt, 1982-84, Inst. for Advanced Study, 1989, Ctr. for Advanced History in Visual Arts, 1993; vis. scholar Getty Rsch. Inst., 1998. Mem. Carl-Justi-Vereinigung, Association Swisse des Historiens de e'Art. Home: Le Grand Clos, CH-1730 Ecuvillens Switzerland Office: Seminaire d'Histoire Art, U Misericorde, CH-1700 Fribourg Switzerland

STOICHKOV, HRISTO, professional soccer player; b. Plovdiv, Bulgaria, Feb. 8, 1966. Forward Maritsa Plovdiv Football Club, Bulgaria, Hebros Harmanli Football Club, Bulgaria, Barcelona Football Club, Spain, Parma Football Club, Italy; now forward CSKA Sofia Football Club, Bulgaria; forward, ctr. Bulgaria Nat. Team; winner Champion's Cup, European Cup Winner's Cup, 1997, Spanish Cup; forward MLS Chgo. Fire, 2000—. Recipient Golden Boot, Europe, 1994, League Championship medal, 1991-94; named European Footballer of Yr., 1994. Office: 3 Dragan Tsankov Blvd, Sofia Bulgaria Office: Chgo Fire Ste 444 311 W Superior Chicago IL 60610*

STOILOV, DIMITAR ILIEV, publishing executive; b. Plovdiv, Bulgaria, June 11, 1948; s. Ilia Dimitrov and Maria Dimitrova (Filipova) S.; m. Nedialka Peneva, Mar. 9, 1975; 1 child, Ilko Dimitrov. BS, Inst. Chem. Tech., Sofia, 1972; postgrad., U. Sofia, 1977. Pres. Rodopi newspaper, Plovdiv, Bulgaria, 1974-89; dep. editor-in-chief Svoboda newspaper, Plovdiv, 1989-90, Provintzia newspaper, Plovdiv, 1990-91; v.p. H.G. Danov Pubs., Plovdiv, 1991-93; dept. chief Hermes Pubs., Plovdiv, 1993—. Author: Missed Trains Timetable, 1986, Adultery Versions, 1990, Shockingly Charming, Voraciously Pretty, 1998. Recipient Innovations and Improvements Inst. awards, 1980-88. Mem. Bulgarian Journalists Union (Journalistic awards 1980-88). Eastern Orthodox. Avocations: football, mountaineering, collecting books. Home: 32 Preslav St, 4000 Plovdiv Bulgaria Office: Hermes Publishers, 16 Dobri Voynikov St, 4000 Plovdiv Bulgaria

STOILOVA, KRASIMIRA PETROVA, science educator; b. Sofia, Bulgaria, June 1, 1952; d. Peter Pavlov and Vasilka Stoilova (Velkova) Mitrova; m. Todor Atanasov Stoilov, May 6, 1975; children: Zlatka Todorova, Vasilka Todorova. Elec. engr., Tech. U. Sofia, 1975; PhD, Bulgarian Acad. Scis., Sofia, 1981. Cert. engr. Rschr. Inst. Tech. Cybernetics and Robotics Bulgarian Acad. Scis., Sofia, 1977-81, asst. prof. cen. lab. control sys., 1982-90, asst. prof. cen. lab. automation, 1990-94, assoc. prof. Inst. Computer and Comm. Sys., 1994—. Author: Theory and Application of Hierarchical Systems, 1989; contbr. articles to profl. jours. Mem. Union Automatics and Informatics (control com.). Avocations: touring, cooking, philately, singing. Home: Ljulin 220 str bl 210, 1336 Sofia Bulgaria Office: Bulgarian Acad Scis Inst Computer & Comm Sys, Acad G Bonchev str bl 2, 1113 Sofia Bulgaria

STOJKO, ELVIS, ice skater; b. New Market, Ont., Can., Mar. 22, 1972; s. Steve and Irene S. Winner Siver medal men's figure skating 1998 Winter Olympic Games. Recipient 3d Pl. award men's figure skating World Figure Skating Championships, 1992, 2d Pl. award, 1993, 1st Pl. award, 1994, 1st Pl. award, 1995, Gold medal men's figure skating Candian Championships,

1994, Silver medal men's figure skating Olympic Games, 1994, Silver medal World Championships, 2000. *

STOKER, DENNIS JAMES, consultant radiologist; b. London, Mar. 22, 1928; s. George Morris and Elsie Margaret (Macqueen) S.; m. Anne Sylvia Nelson Forster, Sept. 22, 1951 (dec. June 1997); children: Claire, Philip, Neil, Catherine; m. Sheila Mary Mercer, Oct. 30, 1999. MB, BS, U. London, 1951. Cons. physician Royal Air Force, 1964-68, St. George's Hosp., London, 1972-87, Royal Nat. Orthopaedic Hosp., London, 1972-93, 97—; dean Inst. of Orthopaedics U. London, 1987-90; dean, v.p. Royal Coll. Radiologists, 1989-91; editor Skeletal Radiology, 1984-96. Author: Knee Arthrography, 1980; co-author: Self Assessment-Orthopaedics, 1988, Radiology of Skeletal Disorders, 3rd edit., 1989. Chmn. spl. trustees Royal Nat. Orthopaedic Hosp., 1998. Wing comdr. RAF (med. br.), 1952-68. Recipient Knox medal Royal Coll. Radiologists, 1992, medal Internat. Skeletal Soc., 1993. Fellow Royal Coll. Radiologists, Royal Coll. Physicians, Royal Coll. Surgeons, Royal Soc. Medicine (v.p. radiology sect. 1978-80); mem. Internat. Skeletal Soc., European Soc. Musculoskeletal Radiology (hon.), RAF Club. Avocations: family history, med. history, philology, gardening. Address: 3, Pearces Orchard, Henley on Thames RG9 2LF, England

STOKES, ADRIAN VICTOR, computing executive; b. London, June 25, 1945; s. Alfred Samuel and Edna (Kerrison) S. BSC with 1st class honours, Univ. Coll. London, 1966, PhD, 1970; DSc (hon.), U. Hertfordshire, 1994. Chartered chmist, 1969, engr., 1990. Rsch. programmer GEC Computers Ltd., Borehamwood, Herts., 1970-71; sr. rsch. fellow Inst. Computer Sci. U. Coll. London, 1971-77; sr. lectr. The Hatfield Poly., Herts., 1977-81; dir. computing St. Thomas' Hosp., London, 1981-88; prin. cons. nat. Health Svc. Info. Mgmt. Centre, 1988-99; joint dir. Nat. Health Svc. Info. Authority, 1999-2000; vis. prof. Nene Coll., 1994—; mng. dir. C.A.t. Ltd., London, 1981—; chmn. European Workshop for Open systems Expert Group Healthcare, 1991-97; mem. tech. com. 251 Comité Européen de Normalisation, 1992—. Author: Concise Encyclopaedia of Information Technology, 1985, others; contbr. articles to profl. jours. Mem. Social Security Adv. Com., London, 1980—; mem. Minister of State for Transport's panel of advisers on disability, 1983-85; mem. Dept. Health and Social Security com. on restrictions against disabled people, 1979-81, Disabled Persons' Transport Adv. com., 1986-89; chmn. exec. com. Royal Assn. Disability and Rehab., 1986-92, v.p., 1999—; chmn. Disabled Drivers Motor Club, 1972-82, 91-94, 97-2000; trustee Independent Living Funds, 1993—; gov. Motability, 1978—. Order of Brit. Empire; officer of the Most Excellent Order, 1983, Freeman Worshipful Co. Info. Tech., 1988, Freeman City London, 1988. Fellow Brit. Computer Soc., Inst. Dirs., Royal Soc. Arts; mem. Computer Soc., Inst. Elec. and Electronic Engrs., Assn. Computing Machinery, Royal Soc. Chemistry, Inst. Mgmt. Avocations: philately, computing, Elvis Presley records. Home: 97 Millway, Mill Hill, London NW7 3JL, England

STOKES, ARCH YOW, lawyer, writer; b. Atlanta, Sept. 2, 1946; s. Mack B. and Rose Stokes; m. Maggie Mead; children: Jennifer Jean, Austin Christopher, Susannah Rose, Travis, Emmarose. BA, Emory U., 1967, JD, 1970. Bar: Ga. 1970, U.S. Dist. Ct. (no. dist.) Ga. 1970, U.S. Ct. Appeals (5th cir.) Ga. 1970, U.S. Ct. Mil. Appeals 1971, U.S. Ct. Appeals (9th cir.) Ga. 1980, (2d cir.) Ga. 1990, U.S. Supreme Ct. 1981, U.S. Dist. Ct. (no. dist.) Calif. 1981, U.S. Ct. Appeals (11th cir.) Calif. 1982, U.S. Ct. Appeals (7th cir.) Calif. 1986, U.S. Ct. Appeals (1st cir.) Calif. 1992, U.S. Ct. Appeals (8th cir.) Calif. 1991, U.S. Dist. Ct. (no. dist.) N.Y. 1991, U.S. Dist. Ct. (ea. dist.) Mich. 1986. Ptnr. Stokes Lazarus & Carmichael, Atlanta, 1972-92; ptnr. Stokes & Murphy, Atlanta, 1992—, San Diego, Pitts., Dallas, 1992—, Las Vegas. Author: The Wage & Hour Handbook, 1978, The Equal Employment Opportunity Handbook, 1979, The Collective Bargaining Handbook, 1981. Founding mem. adv. bd. William F. Harrah Hotel Coll., U. Nev., Las Vegas, also vis. spkr.; vis. spkr. Cornell U., Johnson and Wales U., U. Houston, Ga. State U. Mem. ABA, ATLA, Union Internat. des Avocats, Internat. Soc. Hospitality Cons., Confrérie de la Chaîne des Rôtisseurs, Am. Hotel and Motel Assn. Office: Stokes & Murphy PO Box 87468 College Park GA 30337-0468

STOKES, DONALD WILLIAM, shipping industry company executive; b. Wellington, N.Z., Nov. 7, 1936; s. Sidney William and Ada Louise Stokes; m. Leila Frances Edwards, Aug. 12, 1961; children: Michael William, Philippa Mary, Joanna Margaret. Cert. in customs law N.Z., 1961. Shipping clk. John Chambers & Son Ltd., Wellington, 1955-58; shipping mgr. Philips Elec. Industry N.Z., Wellington, 1958-60; shipping customs broker A.R. Guthrey Ltd., Christchurch, 1960; owner Stokes Shipping Co., Invercargill, N.Z., 1961; mng. dir. D.W. Stokes Shipping & Travel Ltd., Invercargill, N.Z., 1961—; chmn. bd. dirs. Southland 2000, Invercargill, 1988—; trustee, dir. Southland Millenium, Invercargill, 1997—. Mem. Invercargill C. of C. (chmn. 1972-78), Masons, Rotary (sec. 1972). Anglican. Avocations: tramping, walking, swimming. Office: DW Stokes Shipping & Travel, cnr Don & Deveron Sts, Invercargill 9500, New Zealand

STOKES, JOHN GÉRARD, forest products company executive; b. Perth, Australia, Oct. 16, 1923; s. John Placid and Mary Christina (White) S.; m. Audrey Joan Tilly (div. Oct. 1962); children: John Paul, Jane Winifred, Mary Anne; m. Inge Christine Elizabeth Straberger, May 21, 1963; children: Peter, Stephanie, Rebecca, James. BS in Engring., U. Western Australia, Perth, 1944. Chief engr., asst. mills. supt. State Saw Mills West Australia, 1946-56; gen. mgr. Kalangadoo Timber Ltd., South Australia, S.A., 1956-59; devel. mgr. Kauri Timber Ltd., Melbourne, Australia, 1959-63; mng. dir. Gang Nail Australia Ltd., 1963-76; v.p. internat. Gang Nail Sys. Inc., Brussels and Miami, Fla., 1976-82, Perth and Brussels, 1982-86; dir. Bunnings Ltd., Perth, 1992-96, Bunnings Forest Products Pty. Ltd., West Australia, 1985-99; also other related coms. in Australia; leader UN Food and Agr. Industry Coop. Program Mission to Sri Lanka, 1970, UN Devel. Program Industry Coun. for Devel. Mission to Amazonia, Brazil, 1984. Inventor in field; contbr. articles to profl. jours. Pres. Underwater Explorers Club West Australia, 1954-56; pres. Assn. for Blind West Australia, 1988-89, now life mem.; world pres. World Coun. Young Men's Svc. Clubs, 1963-64; nat. pres. Royal Guide Dogs for Blind, 1975-76, nat. vice patron, 1976—; inaugural chmn. Founds. for Mus. Contemporary Sci. and Tech., 1988-89; chmn. Info. Radio, 1990-92; mem. adv. bd. Found. for Internat. Tng. Decorated Order of Australia medal for svcs. to the blind, 1993. Mem. Instn. Engrs. Australia, Wood Turners Assn. Western Australia, Weld Club (Perth), Waratah Ski Club (Perishr Valley, Australia), Apex Club Claremont (life, pres. 1952), Assn. Apex Clubs Australia (life gov.). Roman Catholic. Avocations: skiing, scuba diving, bicycling. Home: 16 Grant St, Cottesloe 6011, Australia

STOKES, JOHN LEMACKS, II, clergyman, retired university official; b. Songdo, Korea, Aug. 23, 1908; s. Marion Boyd and Florence Pauline (Davis) S.; m. Alda Grey Beaman, June 20, 1933; children: John Lemacks III, Mary Anne (foster dau.). A.B., Asbury Coll., 1930; postgrad., Asbury Theol. Sem., 1930-31; M.Div., Duke U., 1932; Ph.D., Yale U., 1936; LL.D., Pfeiffer Coll., 1975. Ordained to ministry Meth. Ch., 1931. Pastor Meth. chs., Randleman, Franklin and Elkin, N.C., 1936-45, Rock Hill, St. John's, S.C., 1945-50; sec. religion higher edn., div. ednl. instns. Bd. Edn. Meth. Ch., Nashville, 1950-53; del. jurisdictional conf. Meth. Ch., 1952, 60, 68; pres. Pfeiffer Coll., Misenheimer, N.C., 1953-68; exec. sec. Quadrennial Emphasis, United Meth. Ch., 1968-69; asso. dir. N.C. Bd. Higher Edn., Raleigh, 1969-71; acting dir. N.C. Bd. Higher Edn., 1972; asso. v.p. U. N.C., Chapel Hill, 1972-75; spl. asst. in acad. affairs U. N.C., 1976-93; dir. numerous out-of-state programs in health professions, 1972-94; mem. Govs. Commn. Citizens for Better Schs. N.C., 1956-60, N.C. Com. on Nursing and Patient Care, 1956-64, N.C. Higher Edn. Facilities Edn., 1964-68, N.C. Com. on Drug Abuse, 1970-76, N.C. Com. on Aero. Edn., 1971-86; chmn. N.C. adv. com. Farmers Home Adminstrn., 1967-69, Marine Sci. Coun., 1969-72; dir. N.C. Inst. Undergrad. Curricular Reform, 1972-78; coordinator Fort Bragg-Pope Grad. Program, 1973-77; adv. com. Nat. Four-year Servicemens Opportunity Coll., 1973-78. Contbr. articles to religious pubs. Bd. dirs. ARC, 1940-48, YMCA, 1946-50; vice chmn. Western N.C. Conf. Bd. Missions, 1960-64; trustee Asbury Coll., 1945-51. Recipient Outstanding Svc. award N.C. Optometric Assn., 1988, Merit award So. Coun. Optometrists, 1990. Mem. Aircraft Owners and Pilots Assn., U.S. Lawn Tennis Assn., Am. Assn. Higher Edn., So. Srs. Golf Assn., NEA, Nat. Christian Edn. Assn., So. Philos. Soc., Woman's Soc. Christian Service, Echo Farms Country Club, Masons, Shriners, Rotary, Civitan, Lions. Address: 1402 Hospital Plaza Dr Apt 325 Wilmington NC 28401-6655

STOKES, JONATHAN HUGH, organizational psychologist, psychotherapist; b. London, Feb. 13, 1952; s. Harry Michael and Prudence Mary (Watling) S.; m. Fay Caroline Ballard; 2 children, Isabella, Matthew. MA, Oxford U., 1973. Cert. clin. psychologist. Chmn. adult dept. Tavistock Clinic, London, 1989-94; dir. Tavistock Consultancy Svc., London, 1994-99. Contbg. author: Unconscious at Work, 1994, Routledge, International Encyclopedia of Business and Management Routledge, 1996, Talking Cure, 1999. Mem. Brit. Psychol. Soc., Brit. Confedn. Psychotherapists, Internat. Soc. Psychoanalytic Study of Orgns. (pres.). Office: Tavistock Consultancy Svc Tavistock Ctr, 120 Belsize Ln, London NW3 5BA, England

STOKES, KERRY MATTHEW, company executive; b. Melbourne, Victoria, Australia, Sept. 13, 1940; s. Mathew Phillip and Irene Florence (Dudley) S.; children: Ryan Kerry, Bryant Mathew. Student, St. George Christian Bros., Melbourne, West Australian Tech. Coll., Melbourne. Chmn. Australian Capital Equity Pty. Ltd., 1980—; chmn. Seven Network Ltd., Australia, 1995—, exec. chmn., 1999—; lectr. in field. Chmn. Nat. Gallery of Australia, Canberra, 1996—, Gallery of Western Australia Found., 1989-91; bd. dirs. Canberra Theatre Trust, 1981-86; pres. appeal campaign Inst. Child Health Rsch., Western Australia, 1992. Fellow Australian Inst. Mgmt. Office: Australian Capital Equity, 30 Kings Park Rd Level 3, West Perth 6005 WA, Australia

STOKES, PETER HEDLEY, space debris analyst, researcher; b. Middlesbrough, Eng., Mar. 31, 1965; s. Peter Nelson and Sylvia (Burley) S. BS with honors, U. St. Andrews, Scotland, 1987; MS, Cranfield (Eng.) Inst. Tech., 1989; MPhil, U. Surrey, Guildford, Eng., 1994. Chartered physicist; chartered engr. Sci. officer Royal Aerospace Establishment, Farnborough, Eng., 1988-92; higher sci. officer Def. Rsch. Agy., Farnborough, 1992-95; sr. scientist Def. Evaluation and Rsch. Agy., Farnborough, 1995—%; chmn. U.K. Space Debris Coord. Group, 1996—; mem. interagy. space debris coord. com., 1997—. Contbr. rsch. articles to profl. jours. Fellow British Interplanetary Soc.; mem. AIAA, Royal Aero. Soc., Inst. Physics. Avocations: hill walking, travel, art collecting, sports. Office: Space Dept A8, Def Eval Rsch Agy, Farnborough GU14 0LX, England

STOKKE, TROND, geneticist; b. Karlstad, Sweden, Nov. 24, 1956; s. Hans and Berit (Stoemner) S.; m. Paula Mary DeAngelis, May 3, 1991; 1 child, Caroline. MS, U. Oslo, 1981, PhD, 1989. Fellow, postdoctoral rschr. The Norwegian Radium Hosp., Oslo, 1982-92; postdoctoral rschr. U. Calif., San Francisco, 1993; scientist The Norwegian Radium Hosp., 1994—. Mem. Internat. Soc. Analytical Cytometry. Office: Norwegian Radium Hosp, Montebello, Oslo Norway 0310

STOKROOS, ROBERT JAN, otorhinolaryngologist; b. Veendam, Groningen, The Netherlands, Mar. 13, 1967; s. Wiebrand Henderikus and Henderka Johanna (Beltman) S.; m. Rosina Petronella Maria Van der Holst, Aug. 30, 1996; children: Jasper Constantyn, Laurens Maryn. MD cum laude, Groningen (The Netherlands) U., 1992, PhD, 1997. Diplomate ear-nose-throat surgery. Resident in otolaryngology Univ. Hosp., Groningen, 1992-97, otolaryngologist, 1997; otolaryngologist Univ. Hosp., Maastricht, The Netherlands, 1997—, chmn. divsn. skull base surgery, 1998-99. Author: Idiopathic Sudden Sensorineural Hearing Loss, 1997; contbr. articles to profl. publs. Bd. dirs. Med. Sch., Groningen U., 1994-96. Mem. Dutch Ear Nose Throat Soc. (prize 1998, otological travel grantee 1997), Dutch Skull Base Soc., Dutch/Flemish Pediat. Ear Nose Throat Soc., European Soc. Otology and Neurology. Home: Bieslander weg 118, NL 6213 Maastricht Limburg, The Netherlands Office: Univ Hosp Maastricht, P Debeyelaan 25, 6202 AZ Maastricht Limburg, The Netherlands

STOKSTAD, MARILYN JANE, art history educator, curator; b. Lansing, Mich., Feb. 16, 1929; d. Olaf Lawrence and Edythe Marian (Gardiner) S. BA, Carleton Coll., 1950; MA, Mich. State U., 1953; PhD, U. Mich., 1957; postgrad., U. Oslo, 1951-52; LHD (hon.), Carleton Coll., 1997. Instr. U. Mich., Ann Arbor, 1956-58; mem. faculty U. Kans., Lawrence, 1958—; assoc. prof. U. Kans., 1961-66, prof., 1966-80, Univ. Disting. prof. art history, 1980-94, Judith Harris Murphy disting. prof. art, 1994—, dir. mus. art, 1961-67, research assoc., summers 1965-66, 67, 71, 72; assoc. dean Coll. Liberal Arts and Scis., U. Kans., 1972-76; research curator Nelson-Atkins Mus. Art, Kansas City, Mo., 1969-80, consultative curator medieval art, 1980—; bd. dirs. Internat. Ctr. Medieval Art, 1972-75, 81-84, 88-96, v.p., 1990-93, pres., 1993-96, sr. advisor, 1996-97; cons., evaluator North Ctrl. Assn. Colls. and Univs., 1972—, commr.-at-large, 1984-89. Author: Santiago de Compostela, 1978, The Scottish World, 1981, Medieval Art, 1986, Art History, 1995, rev. edit., 1999, Art: A Brief History, 2000. Recipient Disting. Service award Alumni Assn. Carleton Coll., 1983, Kans. Gov.'s Arts award, 1997; Fulbright fellow, 1951-52; NEH grantee, 1967-68. Fellow AAUW; mem. AAUP (nat. coun. 1972-75), Archeol. Inst. Am. (pres. Kans. chpt. 1960-61), Midwest Coll. Art Conf. (pres. 1964-65), Coll. Art Assn. (bd. dirs. 1970-80, pres. 1978-80), Soc. Archtl. Historians (chpt. bd. dirs. 1971-73).

STOL, MIROSLAV BOHUSLAV, biomaterials researcher; b. Heralec, East Bohemia, Czechoslovakia, Oct. 19, 1938; s. Josef and Josefa (Stejdirova) S.; m. Blanda Prochazkova, Apr. 28, 1964; children: Kristina, Jan. MSc, Inst. Chem. Tech., Prague, Czechoslovakia, 1966. Engineering diplomate. Technician FATRA, Napajedla, Czechoslovakia, 1953-64; technician IMC CSAV, Prague, 1964-66, researcher, 1966-81; researcher Rheumatol. Inst., Prague, 1981-95; cons. Prague, 1995—; rschr. Inst. Thermodynamics Czech Acad. Scis., 1999—; cons. Ministry of Health, Prague, 1985-96. Author and co-author 64 inventions (Golden medal Czech Ministry of Health 1989); contbr. articles to profl. jours. Grantee IGA Ministry Health, Prague, 1992. Mem. Rheumatology Soc., Clin. Biochemistry Soc., Czech Med. Soc., N.Y. Acad. Scis. Roman Catholic. Avocations: pets, nature's turistic, historical literature. Home: Nad Palatou 50, Prague 5 CZ-15000, Czech Republic

STOLIAR, LEONID MICHAEL, family physician; b. Kalinkovichi, Belorussion, Feb. 12, 1959; arrived in Israel, 1989; s. Michael Abraham and Eudokia Mark (Bondarin) S.; m. Alla Alex Gendler, Jan. 16, 1982; children: Maxim, Ori, Karin. MD, The First Leningrad Med. U., 1982; Family Physician, Ben Gurion U., Beer-Sheva, Israel, 1996. Intern City Hosp. # 25, Leningrad, 1982-83; resident Soroka Med. Ctr., Beer-Sheba, Israel, 1991-96; gen. practitioner First Aid Sta., Leningrad, 1983-85; ICU physician Nahimsong Hosp., Leningrad, 1986-89; family physician Soroka Med. Ctr., Beer-Sheva, 1990—. Mem. Israel Assn. Family Physicians, Nat. Geog. Soc. Avocations: biology, stamp collecting. Home: Shloma Zvi Rav 5, 84700 Beer-Sheva Israel Office: Ben Gurion Univ, Dept Family Medicine, 84105 Beer-Sheva Israel

STOLINSKY, DAVID C., physician; b. Fargo, N.D., Nov. 19, 1934; s. Aaron and Rose Meblin S.; m. Stefanie Auerbach, May 17, 1966. AB (hons.), Univ. Calif., 1955, MD, 1958. Diplomate Am. Bd. Internal Medicine. Asst. rsch. physician Univ. Calif., San Francisco, 1965-66; asst. prof. medicine Univ. So. Calif., L.A., 1966-98; attending physician Univ. So. Calif. Medical Ctr., L.A., 1966-92. Contbr. articles to profl. jours. Assoc. investigator Nat. Cancer Inst., 1966-76. Fellow Am. Coll. Physicians; mem. Internat. Wound Ballistics Assn., Am. Assn. for Cancer Rsch., Am. Soc. Clinical Oncology, Phi Beta Kappa. Republican. Jewish. Avocation: history. E-mail: stolinsky@prodigy.net. Office: 420 S Beverly Dr Ste 100 Beverly Hills CA 90212-4410

STOLL, HANS HEINRICH, retired law educator; b. Freiburg, Germany, Aug. 4, 1926; s. Heinrich and Doris (Eberle) S.; m. Elisabeth Walburga Schneider, Aug. 31, 1957; children: Andreas, Georg Heinrich, Veit, Eva Katharina, Angela Johanna. Staatsexamen in Law, U. Tübingen, Fed. Republic Germany, 1948, 52, JD, 1954. Bar: Stuttgart, Fed. Republic Germany 1954. Rsch. fellow Max Planck Inst. Pvt. and Internat. Law, Tubingen and Hamburg, 1955-60; prof. law U. Bonn, Fed. Republic Germany, 1960-65, U. Freiburg, Fed. Republic Germany, 1965-94; ret. U. Freiburg, 1994; mng. dir. Bibliothek Rechtswissenschaft U. Freiburg, 1985-93. Author: Handeln auf Eigene Gefahr, 1967, Haftungsfolgen im Bürgerlichen Recht, 1993. Mem. German Assn. Comparative Law (gen. sec. and v.p. 1965-81), German Coun. Pvt. Internat. Law (pres. 1987-97), Internat. Acad. Comparative Law (assoc.). Lutheran. Avocations: entomology. Home: Alemannensteige 9, 79117 Freiburg Germany

STOLL, HEATHER MARIE, geochemist, researcher, educator; b. Schenectady, N.Y., Feb. 21, 1973; d. Harry Gene and Patricia Donath Stoll; m. Alberto Tapia, Dec. 20, 1997. BA in Geology, Williams Coll., 1994; MA in Geochemistry, Princeton U., 1996, PhD in Geochemistry, 1998. Grad. fellow Princeton (N.J.) U., 1994-97; tchg. fellow Harvard U., Cambridge, Mass., 1997-98; postdoctoral rsch. fellow U. Oviedo, Asturias, Spain, 1998-2000; vis. prof. U. Oviedo, Spain, 2000—. Contbr. articles to profl. jours. Recipient Gretchen Bletschmidt award Geol. Soc. Am., 1996; winner Acad. Am. Poets Contest, 1994; grad. fellow Office Naval Rsch. and NSF, 1994, postdoctoral fellow NATO, 1998. Mem. Am. Geophys. Union, European Union Geoscis., Nat. Assn. Geology Tchrs. Avocations: hiking, piano, jewelry making. E-mail: heather.stoll@asturias.geol.uniovi.es. Fax: 34 985103103. Office: U Oviedo Dept Geology, Arias de Velasco, 33005 Oviedo Asturias, Spain

STOLL, JUTTA ANNE, lawyer; b. Nuernberg, Germany, May 5, 1956; d. Karl and Elisabeth (Riecker) S.; 1 child, Liisa. Dr jur (summa cum laude), U. Heidelberg, Germany, 1981; LLM, Georgetown U., 1984. Bar: Wash. 1985, Frankfurt 1986. Assoc. Puender Volhard & Weber, Frankfurt, Germany, 1986-89; atty. pvt. practice, Frankfurt, Germany, 1990—. Author: Agreements Between States and Foreign Investors, 1982; contbr. articles to profl. jours. Repicient Studienstiftung des Deutschen Volkes. Volles scholar, Bonn, Germany, 1975-81. Avocations: skiing, golf, art, music. Office: Hainer Weg 50, 60599 Frankfurt Germany

STOLL, NEAL RICHARD, lawyer; b. Phila., Nov. 7, 1948; s. Mervin Stoll and Goldie Louise (Serody) Stoll Wilf; m. Linda G. Seligman, May 25, 1972; children: Meredith Anne, Alexis Blythe. BA in History with distinction, Pa. State U., 1970; JD, Fordham U., 1973. Bar: N.Y. 1974, U.S. Dist. Ct. (ea. dist.) N.Y. 1974, U.S. Ct. Appeals (2d cir.) 19 4, U.S. Ct. Appeals (11th cir.) 1982, U.S. Dist. Ct. (ea. dist.) Mich. 1983, U.S. Dist. Ct. (so. dist.) N.Y. 1974, U.S. Supreme Ct. 1986. Assoc. Skadden, Arps, Slate, Meagher & Flom, LLP, N.Y.C., 1973-81, mem., 1981—; lectr. Practicing Law-Inst., N.Y.C. Author: (with others) Aquisitions Under the Hart Scott Rodino Antitrust Improvements Act, 1980; contbr. articles to profl. pubs. Mem. Assn. Bar City of N.Y. (mem. trade regulation com. 1983-85), ABA, N.Y. State Bar Assn. Democrat. Office: Skadden Arps Slate Four Times Sq New York NY 10036-6522

STOLL, PETER, ecologist; b. Stein am Rhein, Switzerland, Feb. 18, 1963; s. Kurt and Amalie S. MS, U. Basel, 1991; PhD, U. Zurich, 1995. Postdoctoral rsch. Swarthmore (Pa.) Coll., 1995-96, Royal Veterinary & Agrl. U., Copenhagen, 1996-97; rsch., tchg. asst. U. Bern Geobotanical Inst., Switzerland, 1997—. Mem. Ecol. Soc. Am., Br. Ecol. Soc. Office: U Bern Geobotanical Inst, Altenbergrain 21, CH-3013 Bern Switzerland

STOLL, WOLFGANG, plastic surgeon, educator; b. Gettenau, Hessen, Germany, Sept. 23, 1947; s. Walter and Gertrud (Möbs) S.; children: Sebastian, Andrea, Vera. Degree, U. Heidelberg, 1972, approbation, 1974; habilitation, U. Münster, Germany, 1981. Specialist plastic surgery, 1976—; univ. prof., clin. dir. U. Essen, 1989, U. Münster, 1991—; internat. tchr. European Rhinologic Soc. Author: Schwindel und Gleichgewichtsstörungen symptome, 1998. Recipient Anton-von-Tröltsch prize ENT Soc., 1983, special mention Festival du film medical de Liege, 1994. Mem. Am. Acad. Facial Surgery and Reconstructive Surgery of the Head and Neck, European Acad. Facial Surgery, Barany Soc. Avocations: tennis, painting. Home: Josef Pieper Str 12, 48149 Münster Germany Office: ENT Univ Clinic, Kardinal von Galen Ring 10, 48129 Münster Germany

STOLLEY, RICHARD BROCKWAY, journalist; b. Peoria, Ill., Oct. 3, 1928; s. George Brockway and Stella (Sherman) S.; m. Anne Elizabeth Shawber, Oct. 2, 1954 (div. 1981); children: Lisa Anne, Susan Hope, Melinda Ruth, Martha Brockway ; m. Lise Jane Hilboldt, 1997. BS in Journalism, Northwestern U., 1952, MS, 1953; LLD, Villa Maria Coll., 1976. Sports editor Pekin (Ill.) Daily Times, 1944-46; reporter Chgo. Sun-Times, 1953; mem. staff weekly Life mag., 1953-73; bur. chief weekly Life mag., Los Angeles, 1961-64, Washington, 1964-68; sr. editor weekly Life mag., Europe, 1968-70; asst. mng. editor weekly Life mag., N.Y.C., 1971-73; mng. editor monthly Life mag., N.Y.C., 1982-86; founding mng. editor People mag., N.Y.C., 1974-82, Picture Week mag., N.Y.C., 1985-86; dir. spl. projects Time Inc., N.Y.C., 1987-89; editl. dir. Time Inc. Time Warner Inc., N.Y.C., 1989-93, sr. editl. adviser, 1993—. Introd. to Leigh A. Wiener, Marilyn: A Hollywood Farewell: The Death and Funeral of Marilyn Monroe, 1990; editor People Celebrates People: The Best of 20 Unforgettable Years, 1994, rev. edit., 1996, Life: Our Century in Pictures, 1999, Life: Century of Change, America in Pictures, 1900-2000, 2000; exec. prodr. (TV show) Extra, 1995-96; editl. cons. Our American Century series Time-Life Books, 1998-99. Chmn. Twins Found., Providence; bd. govs. Nat. Parkinson Found., Miami, Fla.; chmn. Child Care Action Campaign, N.Y.C.; trustee N.Y.C. Citizens Crime Commn. With USN, 1946-48. Recipient Alumni merit award Northwestern U., 1977, Alumni medal Northwestern U., 1994, Henry Johnson Fisher award for lifetime achievement in mag. pub., 1997; inducted into Am. Soc. Magazine Editors' Hall of Fame, 1996, Hall of Achievement Medill Sch. Journalism Northwestern U., 1997. Mem. Am. Soc. Mag. Editors (pres. 1982-84), Nat. Press Club, Overseas Press Club, Century Assn., Kappa Tau Alpha, Sigma Delta Chi.

STOLL-KELLER, FRANÇOISE, biologist, educator; b. Strasbourg, Bas-Rhin, France, Oct. 15, 1951; d. Georges and Monique (Hollender) Stoll; m. Daniel Keller (div. oct. 1992); children: Nathalie, Pierre, Laetitia. MD, Sch. Medicine, Strasbourg, 1978. Asst. Sch. Medicine, Strasbourg, 1980-87; maitre de conf., assoc. prof. Praticien Hosp., Strasbourg, 1987-97, prof. Inst. Virologie, 1997—. Mem. Rotary. Office: Inst of Virologie, 3 rue Koeberle, 67000 Strasbourg France

STOLNITZ, GEORGE JOSEPH, economist, educator, demographer; b. N.Y.C., Apr. 4, 1920; s. Isidore and Julia (Jurman) S.; m. Monique Jeanne Delley, Aug. 26, 1976; children: Cindy, Wendy, Dia. BA, CCNY, 1939; MA, Princeton U., 1942, PhD, 1952. Statistician U.S. Bur. Census, 1940-41; rsch. assoc. Princeton U. Office of Population Rsch., 1948-56; asst. prof. Princeton U., 1953-56; prof. econs. Ind. U., Bloomington, 1956-90, prof. emeritus, 1990—; dir. Ind. U. Internat. Devel. Rsch. Ctr., Bloomington, 1967-72, Ind. U. Population Inst. for Rsch. and Tng., Bloomington, 1986-91; prin. officer Population and Econ. Devel. UN, N.Y.C., 1976-78; cons. Ford Found., U.S. Congress, Rockefeller Found., UN, U.S. Dept. Commerce, U.S. Dept. Energy, U.S. Dept. HHS, U.S. Dept. State; vis. rsch. scholar Resources for the Future, 1965-67; vis. scholar Population Reference Bur., 1987-88. Author books; contbr. numerous articles in population and devel. fields, testimonies on pub. utility costs of capital. Capt. USAF, 1942-46. Nat. Sci. Found. fellow, 1959-60. Mem. Population Assn. Am. (pres. 1983), Am. Econ. Assn., Am. Statis. Assn., Econometric Soc., Internat. Union Sci. Study of Population, Cosmos Club. Home: 2636 E Covenanter Ct Bloomington IN 47401-5408 Office: Ind U Population Inst CIPEC Bldg 408 N Indiana Ave Bloomington IN 47408-3742

STOLPIN, WILLIAM ROGER, artist, printmaker, retired engineer; b. Flint, Mich., June 25, 1942; s. William and Dorothy Florence (Mitchell) S.; m. Kathleen Diane Poyner, Aug. 14, 1970; children: Krishna Ann, James Mitchell. B of Mech. Engring., GMI Engring. and Mgmt. Inst., Flint, 1965; AA, Charles Stewart Mott C.C., Flint, 1978; postgrad., Ea. Mich. U., 1992. Jr. reliability engr. GM Corp., Flint, 1968-76, sr. reliability engr., 1976-80, quality control supr., 1980-83, product assurance mgr., 1983-89; asst. staff engr. GM Corp., Warren, Mich., 1990-93; printmaker, print pub. Flint, 1969-80; printmaker, print pub., co-founder Das Print Co., Holly, Mich., 1980—; resident artist Robert T. Longway Planetarium, Flint, 1975—. Printmaker: (lithograph) ...And the Santa Maria, 1969 (Smithsonian permanent collection 1973), (serigraph) One Giant Leap For Mankind, 1970 (Smithsonian permanent collection 1973), numerous published serigraphs, lithographs, intaglio prints and woodcuts, 1969—. Grant reviewer Greater Flint Arts Coun., 1989-90, v.p., 1973-74, programming and planning, 1988, mktg. & pub. rels., 1999—, bd. dirs., 1999—; pres. Buckham Fine Arts Project, Flint, 1993-94, bd. dirs., 1993—; bd. dirs. Whaley Hist. House, Flint, 1997-2000; adv. com. U. Mich. Flint Art Gallery, 1997—, Shiawassee Arts Coun., 1999—, Alma Coll., 1999—. Recipient 1st in Graphics award Internat. Platform Assn., 1969, Koegler Meml. award Left Bank Gallery, 1991, 1st in Overall Attitude, Mich. Renaissance Festival, 1993, 98, 1st prize

all media award Left Bank Gallery, 1998, purchase prize Saginaw Art Mus., 1994, 98. Mem. AAAS, AIAA, Internat. Assn. for Astron. Arts, Am. Soc. for Quality, Nat. Stereoscopic Assn., Soc. Automotive Engrs., Soc. Am. Graphic Artists, Flint Artist's Market, Left Bank Gallery, Detroit Artist's Market, Assn. Sci. Fiction and Fantasy Artists, Mich. Assn. Printmakers, Mich. Guild Artists and Artisans. Avocations: directing community theater, participant in Michigan Renaissance Festival, stereoscope imaging. Studio: Das Print Co 12201 Gage Rd Holly MI 48442-8339

STOLT, BIRGIT, foreign language educator; b. Lubeck, Germany, June 10, 1927; d. Bengt and Hildegard (Koenig) Paul; m. Bengt Stolt, Jan. 7, 1956; children: Veronica, Pelle. PhD, Stockholm U., 1964; ThD (hon.), Uppsala U., Sweden, 1996. Asst. prof. German Stockholm U., 1964-72, assoc. prof. German, 1973-79; prof. German philology Aarhus U., Denmark, 1976-77; prof. German Stockholm U., 1980-92. Author: Die Sprachmischung in Luthers Tischreden, 1964, Studien zu Luthers Freiheitstraktat, 1969, Wortkampf, 1974, Hier bin ich - wo bist Du? Heiratsanzeigen und ihr Echo, 1976, Die Seligenstadter Lateinpadagogik, 1989, Textgestaltung - Textverstandnis, 1990, Martin Luther, manniskohjartat och bibeln, 1994, Martin Luthers Rhetorik des Herzens, 2000; contbr. articles to profl. jours. Fellow Inst. Advanced Studies Berlin; mem. Royal Soc. Humanities, Royal Acad. Letters, History & Antiquities. Home: Tallbacksvagen 8, S-756 45 Uppsala Sweden

STOLTE, LARRY GENE, marketing executive, former computer and publishing company executive; b. Cedar Rapids, Iowa, Sept. 17, 1945; s. Ed August and Emma Wilhelmina (Tank) S.; m. Rebecca Jane Tappmeyer, June 13, 1970; children: Scott Edward, Ryan Gene. BBA with highest distinction, U. Iowa, 1971; MBA, Trinity U., 2000. CPA, Ill., Mo., Minn., Mich., Wis.; CMA, CME, CSE, CMC, CPCM. Tax & auditing acct. McGladrey Pullen & Co., Cedar Rapids, 1971-73; v.p., gen. mgr. TLS Co. (subs. CCH Computax Inc.), Cedar Rapids, 1973-92, also bd. dirs.; re-engring. cons. CCH, Inc., Riverwoods, Ill., 1992-94; nat. dir. mktg. McGladrey & Pullen, Cedar Rapids, 1994-97; sr. v.p., mng. dir. Web Site Dynamics, Cedar Rapids, 1997—. Sgt. USMC, 1964-67. Mem. AICPA (cert.), Nat. Assn. Computerized Tax Processors (pres.), Am. Mgmt. Assn., Am. Mktg. Assn., Inst. Mgmt. Accts. (cert.), Nat. Bur. Profl. Mgmt. Cons. (cert.), Sales and Mktg. Execs. Internat. (cert. CME & CSE), Inst. of Cert. Mgmt. Cons. (cert.). Republican. Methodist. Fax: 319-395-6575. E-mail: larrystolte@yahoo.com. Address: 3000-A Towne House Dr NE PO Box 2026 Cedar Rapids IA 52406-2026 Office: Web Site Dynamics PO Box 2879 Cedar Rapids IA 52406-2879

STOLTZFUS, NATHAN A., history educator, documentary and film consultant; b. Harrington, Del., July 24, 1954; s. Llewellyn Roy and Anna Elizabeth Stoltzfus. BA, Goshen (Ind.) Coll., 1978; MDiv, Harvard U., 1984, AM, 1988, PhD, 1993. Prof. history Fla. State U., Tallahassee, 1994—; cons. for documentary adaptations BBC, London, German TV, Berlin, 1992-93. Author: Resistance of the Heart, 1996. H.F. Guggenheim scholar, 1993-94; Fulbright Commn. exch. scholar, Germany, 1984-86; Albert Einstein Inst. fellow, scholar in residence, 1985-87; IREX Exch. scholar, East Germany, 1987-88. Avocation: gardening. Home: 1551 Live Oak Dr Tallahassee FL 32301-4907 also: 1615 Kenyon St NW Apt 59 Washington DC 20010-2776

STOLTZFUS, VICTOR EZRA, retired university president, academic consultant; b. Martinsburg, Pa., Mar. 24, 1934; s. Ira Mark and Elsie Rebecca (Shenk) S.; m. Marie Histand Althouse, June 19, 1955; children: Kristina, Rebecca, Malinda. BA in Social Sci., Goshen Coll., 1956; BD, Goshen Bibl. Sem., 1959; MA in Sociology, Kent State U., 1964; PhD in Sociology, Pa. State U., 1970. Pastor North Lima (Ohio) Mennonite Ch., 1959-66; instr. Youngstown (Ohio) U., 1964-66, Pa. State U., University Park, 1966-70; prof. Eastern Ill. U., Charleston, 1970-81; dean Goshen (Ind.) Coll., 1981-84, pres., 1984-96. Contbr. articles to profl. jours. Mem. Am. Assn. Higher Edn. Lodge: Rotary. Avocation: raquetball. Home: 607 College Ave Goshen IN 46526-4911

STOLYAROVA, VALENTINA LEONIDOVNA, physical chemist; b. Leningrad, Russia, Jan. 20, 1952; d. Leonid Semenovich Korotkov and Valentina Vasilievna (Rumyantzeva) Korotkova; m. Georgii Konstantinovich Stolyarov, Oct. 14, 1972 (dec. Jan. 1985); 1 child, Alexander; m. Bengt Ivan Thor, Nov. 4, 1994. MS, Leningrad State U., 1974; PhD, USSR Acad. Scis., Leningrad, 1979; ChD, Commn. Coun. Ministers USSR, Moscow, 1992. Jr. researcher Inst. Silicate Chemistry, USSR Acad. Scis., Leningrad, 1979-86, scientific researcher, chief of group, 1986-91, sr. researcher, 1991-93; chief rsch. scientist Inst. Silicate Chemistry, USSR Acad. Scis., St. Petersburg, 1993—; scientific sec. of coun. "glass materials" State Dept. of Sci., Highest Sch. and Scientific Policy of USSR, Moscow, 1989-93; assoc. mem. Russian Acad. Scis., 1997; vis. prof. Swedish Inst., Stockholm, 1995-98. Author: Mass Spectrometric Study of Vaporization of Oxide Systems, (Russian edit.) 1990 (prize Internat. Sci. Found. 1993), (English edit.), 1994; contbr. articles to profl. jours. Recipient scholarship Swedish Inst., Stockholm, 1993, Royal Acad. Scis., 1994, 95-96, 96-97. Mem. AAAS, Minerals, Metals and Materials Soc., Internat. Union of Pure and Applied Chemistry, Electrochem. Soc., N.Y. Acad. Scis., Russian Acad. Scis. Avocations: collecting post stamps and cactusti. Home: Moskovsky pr dome 197 Kv9, Metallurgy Dept, 196066 Saint Petersburg Russia Office: Inst Silicate Chem Acad Scis, ul Odoevskogo 24 korp 2, 199155 Saint Petersburg Russia

STOLZ, ALAN JAY, youth camp executive; b. N.Y.C., May 7, 1931; s. Irving H. and Pearl (Maltz) S.; m. Sandra Stolz (div.); m. Gail C. Stolz; children: Maryann Stolz Ross, Gary M. AB, Wabash Coll., 1953; LHD (hon.), London Inst., 1973. Cert., lifetime camp dir. Colo. Outdoor Inst., state instr. emergency med. svc. Pres. Camp Cody, Inc., Freedom, N.H.; ptnr., prin. 72d St Assocs. Real Estate Corp., N.Y.C.; cons., profl. witness U.S. Senate and Ho. Reps., White House, Washington; cons. youth camp health various govtl. agys., Washington; guest speaker Am. Free Enterprise program, Moscow and St. Petersburg, Russia, 1993; speaker Internat. Youth Conf., Toronto, Ont., Can., 1994, Orlando, 1995; pres. Alanor, Inc., Fla., 1994—; apptd. consumer affairs specialist N.H. Atty. Gen. Office, Dept. of Justice, Fraud and Anti-Trust Bur. Author: National Camp Directors Guide, 1990; contbr. articles to profl. jours. Founding mem. USAF Mus. in Brit.; primary instr. Emergency Med. Svcs., Westport, Conn., v.p., 1996—, bd. dirs.; instr. trainer ARC, 1999, Conn. and N.H.; advisor explorer adv. coun. Boy Scouts Am.; justice of peace State of N.H., quorum mem.; bd. govs. Judaica Mus., Riverdale, N.Y., 1994—; vol. dist. coord. N.H. marine patrol Aux. State Dept. Safety, 1991—; mem. Am. Friends British Museum, 1998—. Sgt. U.S. Army, 1955-57. Recipient honor award Emergency Med. Svcs., 1989, 97, 99, Environ. Youth Honors award White House-EPA, 1994, Citation for 55 yrs. svc. to Boy Scouts Am., Conn. State Legislature, 1994, Gov.'s Exec. Coun., N.H., 1995, Cold War Recognition cert. U.S. Dept. Def., 1999, numerous awards Boy Scouts Am., honored for safety patrol svc., 1996, White House Med. Corps Secret Svc. citation for svcs. on presdl. visit, 1999, Congressional Record Congratulations citation for 2 decades EMS vol. leadership, 1999, Congratulations citation from Conn. Gov., State Legislature and Town Mayor, 1999, Am. Red Cross Unsung Heroes award, 2000, EMS Vol. of Yr. award, 2000; named Conn. Vol. of Yr., Carosel Mag., 1990, Conn. Man of Yr., Spotlight Mag., 1991, EMS Vol. Yr., 2000. Republican. Jewish. Avocations: archeology, photography, aviation, history, medical research. Home: 5 Lockwood Cir Westport CT 06880-1640 Office: 46 Gailan Rd Freedom NH 03836

STOLZBERG, MARK ELLIOTT, psychologist; b. N.Y.C., Apr. 30, 1944; s. Seymour and Ruth (Petesky) S.; m. Marilyn Goldberg, Mar. 18, 1972; children: Susan Beth, David Jonathan, Daniel Jason. BA, Hofstra U., 1966, PhD, 1986; MA in Exptl. Psychology, C.W. Post Coll., 1970; postgrad. in clin. psychology, SUNY, Albany, 1973. Intern in clin. psychology Maimonides Hosp., Bklyn., 1972-73; pres. Stolzberg Rsch. Inc., Stony Brook, N.Y., 1976—; adj. lectr. Bklyn. Coll., 1973; mem. faculty Coll. Optometry, SUNY, 1985-86; cons. clin. psychologist to numerous nursing homes, 1994—. Contbr. articles to profl. jours. Chair com. on spl. edn. Port Jefferson Pub. Schs.; co-pres. North Shore SEPTA, 1999—. Grad. fellow C.W. Post Coll., 1968-70, SUNY, Albany, 1970-72, N.Y. State War Svc. scholar; recipient Disting. Achievement award for Rsch., N.Y. State Optometric Assn., 1983. Mem. Ind. Practitioners of Geropsychology (co-founder, pres. 1999—). Home and Office: 3 Seabrook Ct Stony Brook NY 11790-3305

STOLZY, SANDRA LEE, anesthesiologist; b. Washington, Nov. 30, 1952; d. Albert Donald Stolzy and LaVerne Ann Ludwig; m. James Alden Shook, Jr.; children: Bryan Alden, Brigitte Lee, brett Wesley; m. James Furman Cumpston, Dec. 21, 1996 (div. May 1999). BS, Widener Coll., 1981; MD, Med. Coll. Pa., 1981. Asst. prof. U. Louisville, 1984-86; chief anesthesia divsn. VA Med. Ctr., Louisville, 1984-86; staff anesthesiologist St. Mary's Hosp., Rogers, Ark., 1986-92; dir. anesthesiology Bates Med. Ctr., Bentonville, Ark., 1992-99; staff anesthesiologist Washington Regional Med. Ctr., Fayetteville, Ark., 1999—; paramedic instr. Northwest Ark. C.C., Rogers-Bentonville, 1986-99. Cub scout leader Boy Scouts Am., Rogers; asst. girl scout leader Girl Scouts Am., Rogers. Mem. Am. Soc. Anesthesiologists. Republican. Roman Catholic. Home: 3707 W Wood St Rogers AR 72756-1715 Office: Ozark Regional Anesthesia 133 Sunbridge Fayetteville AR 72701

STONE, ALEXANDER PAUL, mathematics educator; b. West New York, N.J., June 28, 1928; s. Samuel Bradford and Violet Elizabeth (Schuessler) S.; m. Mary Ann Majeski, July 23, 1960; 1 child, Christopher Bradford. BSEE, Columbia U., 1952; MSEE, Newark Coll. Engring., 1956; PhD, U. Ill., 1965. Field engr. Western Elec./Bell Telephone Labs., Whippany, N.J., 1952-56; instr. in elec. engring. Manhattan Coll., Riverdale, N.Y., 1956-58; asst. prof. physics Dickinson Coll., Carlisle, Pa., 1958-60; asst. prof. math. U. Ill., Chgo., 1965-69; assoc. prof. math. U. Ill., 1969-70, U. N.Mex., Albuquerque, 1970-76; prof. math. U. N.Mex., 1976—, chmn. dept. math. and stats., 1991-97; cons. Air Force Rsch. Lab., 1984—. Editor: Improperly Posed Boundary Value Problems, 1976; author: Transient Lens Synthesis, 1990; contbr. articles to profl. jours. With USN, 1946-48, 2d lt. U.S. Army, 1951-52. NSF grantee, 1966-70, AFOSR grantee, 1984-85, 95-96; IPA appt. AFRL, 1991-94, 97-99. Mem. Am. Math. Soc., Internat. Union of Radio Sci. (commn. E on electro-magnetic noise and interference). Avocations: tennis, golf, mountaineering. Office: Univ NMex Dept Math And Stats Albuquerque NM 87131-0001

STONE, DUANE SNYDER, school psychologist, clergyman; b. Turon, Kans., Nov. 10, 1935; s. Herman and Neva F. (Snyder) S.; m. Nancy R. Castillo, July 12, 1958; children: Patricia L. Stone Davis, Christopher D. AA, Graceland Coll., 1953; BA, San Jose State U., 1959, MA, 1961; EdS, Wichita State U., 1985. Ordained to ministry Reorganized LDS Ch., 1951. Tchr., adminstr., supt. Santa Clara County Schs., San Jose, Calif., 1959-63; commd. 2d lt. USAF, 1963, advanced through grades to maj., 1974; security police officer USAF, Altus AFB, Okla., 1963-66; instr. Officer Tng. Sch. USAF, Lackland AFB, Tex., 1966-69; base def. officer 35 TRW USAF, Phan Rang Air Base, Vietnam, 1969-70; asst. prof. aerospace sci. Memphis State U. AFROTC, 1970-73; comdr. security police squadron USAF, Minot AFB, N.D., 1973-76; clin. psychologist 91st Regional Hosp. USAF, Minot AFB, 1976-83; ret., 1983; sch. psychologist Wichita (Kans.) Pub. Schs., 1985-86, Butler County Sch. Bd., El Dorado, Kans., 1986—; pres. Reality Theapy Assocs., Wichita, 1983—. Author: The Ministry of Health and Healing, 1986, Ministry to Persons with Debilitating Lifestyles, 1988. Treas. Springhaven, Andover, Kans., 1955—. Recipient award Reorganized LDS Ch., 1995. Mem. NASP (cert.), DAV, NRA, Ret. Officers Assn. Avocations: flying, photography. Home: 1112 S Kansas St Wichita KS 67211-2724 Office: Butler County Sch Bd 1518 W 6th Ave El Dorado KS 67042-1425

STONE, EDWARD CARROLL, physicist, educator; b. Knoxville, Iowa, Jan. 23, 1936; s. Edward Carroll and Ferne Elizabeth (Baber) S.; m. Alice Trabue Wickliffe, Aug. 4, 1962; children: Susan, Janet. AA, Burlington Jr. Coll., 1956; MS, U. Chgo., 1959, PhD, 1964; DSc (hon.), Washington U., Saint Louis, 1992, Harvard U., 1992, U. Chgo., 1992; BA (hon.), UCLA, 1998. Rsch. fellow in physics Calif. Inst. Tech., Pasadena, 1964-66, sr. rsch. fellow, 1967, mem. faculty, 1967—, prof. physics, 1976-94, David Morrisroe prof. physics, 1994—, v.p. for astron. facilities, 1988-90, v.p., dir. Jet Propulsion Lab., 1991—; Voyager project scientist, 1972—; cons. Office of Space Scis., NASA, 1969-85, mem. adv. com. outer planets, 1972-73; mem. NASA Solar System Exploration Com., 1983; mem. com. on space astronomy and astrophysics Space Sci. Bd., 1979-82; mem. NASA high energy astrophysics mgmt. operating working group, 1976-84, NASA Cosmic Ray Program Working Group, 1980-82, Outer Planets Working Group, NASA Solar System Exploration Com., 1981-82, Space Sci. Bd., NRC, 1982-85, NASA Univ. Relations Study Group, 1983, steering group Space Sci. Bd. Study on Major Directions for Space Sci., 1995-2015, 1984-85; mem. exec. com. Com. on Space Research Interdisciplinary Sci. Commn., 1982-86; mem. commn. on phys. scis., math. and resources NRC, 1986-89; mem. adv. com. NASA/Jet Propulsion Labs. vis. sr. scientist program, 1986-90; mem. com. on space policy NRC, 1988-89; chmn. adv. panel for The Astronomers, KCET, 1989—. Mem. editl. bd. Space Sci. Instrumentation, 1975-81, Space Sci. Rev., 1982-85, Astrophysics and Space Sci., 1982—, Sci. mag. Bd. dirs. W.M. Keck Found. Recipient medal for exceptional sci. achievement NASA, 1980, Disting. Svc. medal, 1981, 98, Disting. Pub. Svc. medal, 1985, Outstanding Leadership medal, 1986, 95, Am. Edn. award, 1981, Dryden award, 1983, Aviation Week and Space Tech. Aerospace Laureate, 1989, Sci. Man of Yr. award ARCS Found., 1991, Pres.'s Nat. medal of Sci., 1991, Am. Acad. Achievement Golden Plate award, 1992, COSPAR award for outstanding contbn. to space sci., 1992, LeRoy Randle Grumman medal, 1992, Disting Pub. Svc. award Aviation/Space Writers Assn., 1993, Internat. von Karman Wings award, 1996, Alumni award S.E. C.C., Burlington, Iowa, 1998, CEO of Yr. award ARC, 1998, Carl Sagan award Am. Astronautical Soc. and Planetary Soc., Allan D. Emil Meml. award Internat. Astronautical Fedn.; Asteroid named for Edward C. Stone, 1996; Sloan Found. fellow, 1971-73; inducted to Hall of Fame Aviation Week and Space Tech., 1997; awarded Von Karman Lectureship in Astronautics, 1999. Fellow AIAA (assoc., Space Sci. award 1984, Von Karman lectureship in astronautics 1999), AAAS (award 1993), Am. Phys. Soc. (chmn. cosmic physics divsn. 1979-80, exec. com. 1974-76), Am. Geophys. Union, Internat. Astron. Union; mem. NAS, Internat. Acad. Astronautics, Am. Astron. Soc. (divsn. planetary scis. com. 1981-84, Space Flight award 1997), Am. Assn. Physics Tchrs., Am. Philos. Soc. (Magellanic award 1992), Calif. Assn. Rsch. in Astronomy (bd. dirs., vice chmn. 1987-88, 91-94, 97—, chmn. 1988-91, 94-97), Astron. Soc. Pacific (hon.), Nat. Space Club (bd. govs., Sci. award 1990), Calif. Coun. Sci. and Tech. Office: Jet Propulsion Lab 4800 Oak Grove Dr 180-904 Pasadena CA 91109-8001

STONE, EDWARD LUKE, private equity investor, realtor; b. Englewood, N.J., Jan. 18, 1937; s. James and Anna (Druskin) S.; m. Cassandra Reeve, Mar. 15, 1969. BA, Yale U., 1958; postgrad., Cambridge U., Eng., 1959; MBA, Harvard U., 1966. Dir. fin. planning Yale U., New Haven, 1966-69; pres. HDC, Inc., Boston, 1969-77; ptnr. Dane, Falb, Stone, Boston, 1977-81; exec. dir. White House Preservation Fund, Washington, 1981-90; trustee Newport Art Mus., 1991-94; chmn. Stone and Cranwell, Newport, R.I., 1995-99; pres. Hogan and Stone, Newport, 1996-99; broker, investor Benchmark Assocs., Middletown, R.I., 1999—; cons. Booz Allen Hamilton, Bethesda, Md., 1987-88. Trustee Nat. Mus. of Women in the Arts, Washington, 1988-90, Tudor Pl. Found., Washington, 1988-95, The Washington Home, 1988-95, Touro Synagogue Friends, 1996—; gov. Newport Health Care Corp., 1997—; co-chmn. The Isaac Bell House, 1995—. Mem. Newport Reading Rm., Spouting Rock Beach Assn., Somerset Club, Elizabethan Club, Phi Beta Kappa. Avocations: early 19th Century American decorative arts. Home: The Poplars 12 Leroy Ave Newport RI 02840-4106

STONE, FRANZ THEODORE, retired fabricated metal products manufacturing executive; b. Columbus, Ohio, May 11, 1907; s. Julius Frederick and Edna (Andress) S.; m. Katherine Devereux Jones, Feb. 23, 1935; children: Franz Theodore, Thomas Devereux Mackay, Raymond Courtney (dec.), Catherine Devereux Diebold. AB magna cum laude, Harvard U., 1929; hon. degrees, Canisius Coll., 1975, Ohio State U., 1976, Keuka Coll., 1999. Chmn. bd. Columbus McKinnon Corp., Amherst, N.Y., 1935-86. Chmn. emeritus Arts Council in Buffalo and Erie County, 1973-86; pres. Buffalo Philharmonic Orch. Soc., 1959-61, also life dir.; chmn. emeritus Studio Arena Theatre, Buffalo, 1968-86; Nat. Conf. of Christian and Jews Brother Sisterhood citation, 1986; First Arts award Arts Council and Greater Buffalo C. of C. Recipient Gold Key award Buffalo YMCA, 1966, Red Jacket award Buffalo & Erie County Hist. Soc., 1976, Disting. Citizen award SUNY, Buffalo, 1985, Conductor's award Buffalo Philharm. Orch., 1993. Mem. Gulfstream Bath & Tennis Club, Ocean Club of Fla., Boca Raton Country Club, Pundits Club, Buffalo Country Club, Buffalo Club, Buffalo Yacht Club, Saturn Club (Buffalo), The Little Club (Gulfstream). Home: 33 Gates Cir Apt 9G Buffalo NY 14209-1197

STONE, GERALD CHARLES, Slavonic studies researcher and educator; b. Surbiton, Surrey, Eng., Aug. 22, 1932; s. Albert Leslie and Grace Madeline (Varndell) S.; m. 1953 (div. 1974); children: Peter B., Christine A., David A.; m. Vera Fedorovna Konnova, Apr. 10, 1974; 1 child, Lydia Grace. BA, U. London, 1964, PhD, 1968. Asst. lectr. U. Nottingham, Eng., 1966-68; lectr. U. Nottingham, 1968-71; asst. dir. rsch. U. Cambridge, Eng., 1971-72; univ. lectr. Slavonic langs. Oxford (Eng.) U., 1972-99; fellow Hertford Coll., 1972-99, emeritus fellow, 1999—; ret. Author: The Smallest Slavonic Nation, 1972, A Dictionarie of the Vulgar Russe Tongue, Attributed to Mark Ridley, 1996; joint author: The Russian Language Since the Revolution, 1978; editor Oxford Slavonic Papers, 1982-99. Served with Brit. Army, 1951-53. Fellow Brit. Acad.; mem. Philol. Soc. (coun. 1981-86, 96-2000). Mem. Ch. of England. Home: 6 Lathbury Rd, Oxford OX2 7AU, England Office: Hertford College, Oxford OX1 3BW, England

STONE, HERMAN HULL, internist; b. Noble, Ill., Dec. 12, 1915; s. Roy Edson and Carrie (Michels) S.; m. Marie Carlson Christensen; children, Patricia Marie Soln, Richard Allen. BS, U. Ill., 1937, MD, 1941. Resident in internal medicine U.S. VA Hosp., Hines, Ill., 1946-49; chief of medicine VA Hosp., Oklahoma City, 1949-50; with Riverside (Calif.) Med. Clinic, 1950-91; dir. Med. Libr., 1991—; clin. prof. medicine Loma Linda (Calif.) U., 1963—; founder, dir. Patients' Info. Libr., Riverside, 1991—; pres. citizens univ. com. U. Calif. Riverside, 1979-81; trustee Calif. Blue Shield. Served to maj. M.C., AUS, 1942-46. Recipient Outstanding award Nat. Soc. Fund Raising Execs., 1996. Fellow ACP (life); mem. L.A. Acad. Medicine (trustee), Rotary Club. Avocations: golf, books, travel. Office: Patients Info Libr 3660 Arlington Ave Riverside CA 92506-3912

STONE, INGEBORG EDA, recording industry executive; b. Hamburg, Germany, June 15, 1923; d. Kurt Rudolf-Wilhelm and Gertrude Anna (Breihan) Lubahn; m. Gregory Stone, May 24, 1948 (dec. 1991); children: Cristina Karmas, Toranna Wermes. Grad., U. Calif., Berkeley, 1944, postgrad., 1944-45. Profl. ice skater Shipstad & Johnson's Ice Follies, 1945-47; choreographer Hielo & Estrellas, South America, 1947-48; educator City of L.A. Sch. System, 1957-68, Washoe County (Nev.) Schs., Reno, 1968-83; cofounder Reno Philharm. Symphony Orch., 1969—; pres. Credo Music Co., Impromptu Records, Mijas, Spain, 1991—. Author: Music Has No Frontiers, 1999, Operetta: My Liebestraum, 1969; CD: My Grisha's Gypsy Soul, 1999, The Virtuosi Septet (5 Violoncellos and 2 pianos), 2000. Bd. dirs. Reno Philharm. Symphony Orch., 1969-83; dir. Gregory Stone Music Libr., Mijas, 1991—. Mem. Knights Templar, Assn. Amigos Orquesta Ciudad De Malaga (hon.), Delta Kappa Gamma. Avocations: art, music, writing, swimming, sculpture. Home: Urbanizacion El Coto, Calle Los Zorzales 49, 29649 Mijas Spain

STONE, JAMES ROBERT, surgeon; b. Greeley, Colo., Jan. 8, 1948; s. Anthony Joseph and Dolores Concetta (Pietrafeso) S.; m. Kaye Janet Friedman, May 16, 1970; children: Jeffrey, Marisa. BA, U. Colo., 1970; MD, U. Guadalajara, Mex., 1976. Diplomate Am. Bd. Surgery, Am. Bd. Surg. Critical Care. Intern Md. Gen. Hosp., Balt., 1978-79; resident in surgery St. Joseph Hosp., Denver, 1979-83; pvt. practice Grand Junction, Colo., 1983-87; staff surgeon, dir. critical care Va. Med. Ctr., Grand Junction, 1987-88; dir. trauma surgery and critical care, chief surgery St. Francis Hosp., Colorado Springs, Colo., 1988-91; pvt. practice Kodiak, Alaska, 1991-92; with Summit Surg. Assocs., 1992-96; asst. dir. trauma Tristate Trauma System, Erie, Pa., 1996-99; med. dir. LifeStar Aeromed, Erie, Pa., 1997-99; dir. trauma, sr. assoc. physician, med. dir. emergency svcs. ISJ Mayo Health, 1999—; clin. prof. surgery U. Minn. Med. Sch., Minneapolis, 1999—, dir. trauma/EMS med. dir., sr. assoc.; asst. clin. prof. surgery U. Colo. Health Sci. Ctr., Denver, 1984-96; pres. Stone Aire Cons., Grand Junction, 1988—; owner, operator Jjnka Ranch, Flourissant, Colo.; spl. advisor CAP, wing med. officer, 1992-96; advisor med. com. unit, 1990-92; advisor Colo. Ground Team Search and Rescue, 1994-96. Contbr. articles to profl. jours.; inventor in field. Bd. dirs. Mesa County Cancer Soc., 1988-89, Colo. Trauma Inst., 1988-91. Colo. Speaks out on Health grantee, 1988; recipient Bronze medal of Valor Civil Air Patrol. Fellow Denver Acad. Surgery, Southwestern Surg. Congress, Am. Coll. Chest Physicians, Am. Coll. Surgeons (trauma com. Colo. chpt.), Am. Coll. Critical Care; mem. Am. Coll. Physician Execs., Soc. Critical Care (task force 1988—), Assn. Air Med. Physicians. Roman Catholic. Avocations: horse breeding, hunting, fishing.

STONE, JOHN OWEN, freelance journalist; b. Perth, Australia, Jan. 31, 1929; s. Horace Joseph and Eva Sydney (Hunt) S.; m. Nancy Enid Hardwick, July 14, 1954; children: Philippa Jane, John Owen Hardwick, Roland Hugh, Andrew Guy, Richard Ian. BS with honors class 1, U. Western Australia, 1950; BA with honors class 1, Oxford U., 1954. Various positions Australian Treasury, 1954-66; exec. dir. IMF and World Bank, Washington, 1967-70; dep. sec. to the Treasury Canberra, Australia, 1971-79; sec. to the Treasury Australian Treasury, 1979-84; senator for Queensland Parliament of Australia, 1987-90; weekly columnist various Australian major newspapers, 1985-98; vis. prof. Ctr. for Policy Studies, Monash U., Melbourne, 1984; econ. cons. Melbourne, 1985-87, 1990—; sr. fellow Inst. Pub. Affairs, Melbourne, 1985-87, 90-95; chmn. J.T. Campbell & Co., Melbourne, 1994-96; mem. Def. Efficiency Rev. Com., 1996-97; mem. No. Rep. Campaign Com., Victoria, 1999. Editor, pub.: Proceedings of The Samuel Griffith Soc., Upholding the Australian Constitution, Vols. 1-11, 1992-99; monthly columnist The Adelaide Rev., 1998—; contbr. numerous articles to profl. jours. Leader Nat. Party in Senate, 1987-90, Shadow Minister for Fin., 1987-90; mem. legal and constnl. affairs com., regulations and ordinances com. in Senate, 1987-90. Rhodes scholar for Western Australia, 1951, James Webb Medley scholar, Oxford U., 1953. Mem. Coun. for the Nat. Interest (Councillor 1985-94), H.R. Nicholls Soc. (pres. 1986-89, bd. dirs. 1990-95), The Samuel Griffith Soc. (bd. dirs. 1992—). Anglican. Avocations: reading, wine, travel.

STONE, JOHN TIMOTHY, JR., writer; b. Denver, July 13, 1933; s. John Timothy and Marie Elizabeth (Briggs) S.; m. Judith Bosworth Stone, June 22, 1955; children: John Timothy III, George Williams. Student, Amherst Coll., 1951-52, U. Mex., 1952; BA, U. Miami, 1955, postgrad., 1955; postgrad., U. Colo., 1959-60. Sales mgr. Atlas Tag, Chgo., 1955-57; br. mgr. Household Fin. Corp., Chgo., 1958-62; pres. Janeff Credit Corp., Madison, Wis., 1962-72, Recreation Internat., Mpls., 1972-74, Continental Royal Svcs., N.Y.C., 1973-74; dir. devel. The Heartlands Group/Tryon Mint, Toronto, Ont., Can., 1987-89; spl. cons. Creative Resources Internat., Madison, 1988-90, Pubs. Adv. Group, 1990—; spl. cons. art and antiques Treasure Hunt Assocs., 1994—; bd. dirs. Madison Credit Bur., Wis. Lenders' Exch. Author: Mark, 1973, Going for Broke, 1976, The Minnesota Connection, 1978, Debby Boone So Far, 1980, (with John Dallas McPherson) He Calls Himself "An Ordinary Man", 1981, Satiacum, The Chief Who's Winning Back the West, 1981, Runaways, 1983, (with Robert E. Gard) Where the Green Bird Flies, 1984, The Insiders Guide to Buying Art, 1993, Anyone's Treasure Hunt, 1995; syndicated columnist The Great American Treasure Hunt, 1983-87. Served with CIC, U.S. Army, 1957-59. Mem. Minarani Club, African First Shooters Club, Sigma Alpha Epsilon. Presbyterian. Office: Pubs Adv Group 1009 Starlight Dr Madison WI 53711-2724

STONE, LINDA CHAPMAN, physician, consultant, medical educator; b. Detroit, Apr. 20, 1943; d. Harry Walter and Kathryn Ann (Forshee) Chapman; m. Laurence B. Stone, July 10, 1965; 1 child, Robert Laurence. BA, Mich. State U., 1961-65; MA, Ohio U., 1971; MD, Ohio State U., 1979. Diplomate Am. Bd. Family Practice. Tchr. local high schs., Mich., 1965-69; instr. comms. Ohio U., 1970-71; resident physician Riverside Meth. Hosp., Columbus, Ohio, 1979-82, chief resident, 1981-82; family physician Beechwold Med. Ctr., Columbus, Ohio, 1983-93; family physician, instr. U. Mich., 1993; v.p. physician ednl. comms. U.S. Health Corp., Columbus, 1994, v.p. primary care devel., 1995-96; exec. v.p. Med. Group Ohio, 1996-99; clin. asst. prof. medicine Ohio State U., 1983—; bd. dirs. Elizabeth Blackwell. Healthcare adv. various women's orgns., 1983—. Fellow Am. Acad. Family Physicians (alt. del. 1999—); mem. AAUW, Am. Med. Women's Assn., AMA, Am. Coll. Physicians Execs., Ohio Acad. Family Physicians (bd. dirs. 1992—, v.p. 1997-99, pres.-elect 1999-2000,

pres. 2000—), Ohio Acad. Family Physicians, Ohio Acad. Family Physicians Found. (vice-chair 1998—), Ohio State Med. Assn., Soc. Tchrs. Family Medicine, Delta Gamma. Democrat. Methodist. Avocations: creative writing. Office: Ohio State Univ 456 W 10th Ave Columbus OH 43210-1240

STONE, MICHAEL WILLIAM, retired tax official; b. Sheffield, Yorks, Eng., Jan. 10, 1948; s. Ernest William and Lucy Jean (Matchett) S. BA, Open U., 1991. Ordained Aaronic priest LDS Ch., 1995, elder Melchizedek priesthood, 1995. Trainee clk. Thain Wildbur Accts., Kings Lynn, Norfolk, Eng., 1966-67; clk. Lincolnshire Canners, Kings Lynn, 1967-70; inland revenue officer HM Inspector of Taxes, Kingston, Surrey, 1970-84, London, 1984-85, Twickenham, Middlesex, Eng., 1985-92, Peterborough, Cambs., Eng., 1992-94. Fellow Brit. Interplanetary Soc.; mem. Brit. Sci. Fiction Assn., Mensa. Mem. LDS Ch. Avocations: astronomy, history, science fiction, genealogy. Home: 4 Cobbet Pl Cavendish St, Peterborough Cambs PE1 5EW, England

STONE, PHILIP JAMES, financial director; b. Southwick, Sussex, England, Sept. 8, 1955; s. James Edward and Patricia (Ann) S.; m. Karen Elaine Funnell, Aug. 2, 1980; children: Kevin James, Christopher Ian, Phillip Benjamin. Grad., Chartered Inst. Cost & Mgmt., Worthing, England, 1984. Fin. acct. Beecham Pharm., Worthing, 1974-81; mgmt. acct. GEC Marconi Process Control & Devel., Burgess Hill, W. Sussex, England, 1982-86; fin. dir. Lunnons, Ltd., Lewes, E. Sussex, England, 1987-96, L&S Printing Co., Ltd., Worthing, England, 1996—. Fellow Chartered Inst. Mgmt. Accts. Avocations: squash, tennis, cricket, swimming, walking. Home: 22 Croft Ave, Southwick BN42 4AB, England

STONE, RALPH KENNY, lawyer; b. Bainbridge, Ga., Aug. 7, 1952; s. Ralph Patrick and Joyce (Mitchell) S.; m. Julie Ann Waldren, Aug. 24, 1974; children: Laura Lee, Rebecca, Michael. BBA magna cum laude, U. Ga., 1974, JD cum laude, 1977. Bar: Ga. 1977, U.S. Dist. Ct. (so. dist.) Ga. 1977, U.S. Supreme Ct. 1980, U.S. Ct. Appeals (11th cir.) 1981. Staff acct. Price Waterhouse & Co., Columbia, S.C., 1974; assoc. Calhoun & Donaldson, Savannah, Ga., 1977; ptnr. Franklin & Stone, Statesboro, Ga., 1977-88, Edenfield, Stone & Cox, Statesboro, Ga., 1988-94; pres. R. Kenny Stone, P.C., 1994—; instr. taxation Ga. So. Coll., Stateboro, 1979-80. Sect. chmn. United Way S.E. Ga., campaign chmn., 1989, pres. 1991; charter pres. Leadership Bulloch, Inc., 1984; chmn. Bulloch County Dem. Com., 1984-90, Bulloch 2000 Com., 1986-88; alt. del. Dem. Nat. Conv., 1988; sec. Ga. Assn. Dem. County Chairs, 1985-89, pres. 1989-91; dist. chmn. Boy Scouts Am., 1985; pres. Forward Bulloch Inc., 1986; participant Leadership Ga., 1986; mem. Ga. Bd. Industry Trade & Tourism, 1991-96. Mem. ABA, State Bar Ga., Bulloch County Bar Assn. (pres. 1982-83), Statesboro-Bulloch C. of C. (pres. 1986, chmn. bd. dirs. 1987, chmn. devel. authority Bulloch County 1991—), Rotary (Statesboro), Optimist Club (pres. 1980-81, dist. lt. gov. 1981-82), Phi Kappa Phi, Beta Alpha Psi. Baptist. Home: 319 Dogwood Trl Statesboro GA 30461-4253 Office: R Kenny Stone PC PO Box 681 Statesboro GA 30459-0681

STONE, ROSS GLUCK, orthopedic surgeon; b. Pottsville, Pa., May 14, 1951; s. Jerome M. and Alma (Gluck) S.; m. Wendy E. Reiner, March 21, 1987; children: Melissa, Logan. BA in Philosophy, Yale U., 1973; MD, Columbia U., 1977. Diplomate Am. Bd. Orthopaedic Surgery. Intern, resident Harvard U., 1977-79; resident, vis. clin. fellow Columbia U., 1979-83; pvt. practice Atlantis, Fla., 1983—; clin. fellow in surgery Harvard Med. Sch., 1978-79; expert med. advisor Fla. Dept. Labor & Employment, 1995-97, 97—; editl. adv. bd. Am. Jour. Pain Mgmt., 1992—; chmn. surg. rev. com. Palm Beach Regional Hosp., 1995, institnl. rev. com. John F. Kennedy Med. Ctr., 1995-96, 97, 98, 99; divsn. ortho. surgery Columbia Hosp., 1994—; chmn. dept. surgery Palms West Hosp., 1998—. Contbr. chpt. to book and articles to profl. jours.; invented tension headache reliever device. Trustee Palms West Hosp., Loxahatchee, Fla., 1985-88. Recipient Physician's Choice award So. Med. Assn. 88th Assembly, 1994, Scientific Poster recognition So. Med. Assn. 88th Assembly, 1994, 89th Assembly, 1995, Sr. Resident award Eastern Ortho. Assn. 14th ann. meeting, 1983, Rsch. Manuscript award Assn. for the Advancement of Med. Instrumentation, 1996. Mem. Palm Beach County (Fla.) Med. Soc. (bd. dirs. 1995—, sec. 1998, 2nd v.p. 1999, 1st v.p. 2000, del. Fla. Med. Assn. 1995-2000, legis. com. 1995-96, 97, 98, 99, emergency med. svc. and disaster relief plan coms. 1994-95, health and human svcs. com. 1994-95, pub. rels. com. 1995-98, chmn. pub. rels. com., 1996, 97, 98, chmn. other coms., chmn. bd. censors and mediation 1999, chmn. membership 2000, sec. MEDPAC bd. dirs 1999, treas. MEDPAC bd. dirs. 2000). Republican. Jewish. Avocations: weight lifting, aerobic conditioning, reading, tennis. Office: 120 John F Kennedy Dr Ste 124 Lake Worth FL 33462-6623

STONE, SAMUEL BECKNER, lawyer; b. Martinsville, Va., Feb. 4, 1934; s. Paul Raymond and Mildred (Beckner) S.; m. Shirley Ann Gregory, June 18, 1955; children: Paul Gregory, Daniel Taylor. BSEE, Va. Polytech. Inst. & State U., 1955; JD, George Wash. U., 1960. Bar: Md. 1960, Calif. 1963, Patent and Trademark Office. Patent examiner, 1955-58; patent adv. Naval Ordinance Lab., Silver Spring, Md., 1958-59; assoc. Thomas & Crickenberger, Washington, 1959-61, Beckman Instruments Inc., Fullerton, Calif., 1961-65; assoc. Lyon & Lyon, L.A., 1965-72, ptnr., 1972; mng. ptnr. Lyon & Lyon, Irvine, Calif., 1982—; judge Disneyland Com. Svc. Awards, Anaheim, Calif., 1987. Mem. Orange County Bar Assn. (bd. dirs. 1988-91, travel seminar chair 1986-92), Orange County Patent Law Assn. (pres. 1987, bd. exec. com. 1987-90), Calif. Bar Assn. (intellectual property sect. bd. 1987-90), Am. Arbitration Assn. (intellectual property panel neutral arbitrators 1997-2000), Am. Electronics Assn. (lawyers com. 1988-99, co-chair 1996-97), Orange County Venture Group (dir. 1985-99, pres. 1996-97), Rams Booster Club (dir. 1984-90), Pacific Club (mem. legal adv. com., chair 1989-92, bd. dirs. 1999—). Republican. Avocations: tennis, waterskiing, music. Home: 1612 Antigua Way Newport Beach CA 92660-4344 Office: Lyon & Lyon 1900 Main St Fl 6 Irvine CA 92614-7317

STONE, THOMAS RICHARDSON, cultural center president; b. Milw., Feb. 1, 1939; s. Thomas S. and Ann Louise (Taplin) S.; m. Cynthia White Hutchinson, July 20 1963; children: Sarah, Thomas. BS, U.S. Mil. Acad., 1961; MA, Rice U., 1971, PhD, 1974. Commd. 2d lt. field artillery U.S. Army, 1961, advanced through grades to col., 1988; v.p. medicare support svcs. Pa. Blue Shield, Camp Hill, 1988-90; dir. devel. and fin. Metro Arts of the Capital Region, Harrisburg, Pa., 1990-93; pres., CEO Whitaker Ctr. for Sci. & the Arts, 1993—. Author: The Second World War: Europe and the Mediterranean, Vol. II, 1980; contbr. articles to profl. publs. Deacon St. Paul's United Ch. Christ, Mechanicsburg, Pa., 1987-90, pres. of consistory, 1989-92, elder, 1990-92; Pa. Heritage Soc.; mem. Cumberland-Perry Assn. for Retarded Citizens, 1980—, bd. dirs., 1980-82, 86-97, pres., 1984-86; mem. preservation com. Pa. Monuments at Gettysburg Battlefield; bd. dirs. Modern Transit and Partnership, 2000. Decorated Bronze Star, Legion of Merit; grantee Rice U., 1971-72; recipient Cmty. Svc. award, Am. Legion, Carlisle, Pa., 1987. Mem. Nat. Soc. Fund Raising Execs. (cert., bd. dirs. ctrl. Pa. chpt. 1994—, Outstanding Fund Raising Exec. Ctrl. Pa. chpt. award 1997), Technol. Coun. Central Pa. (edn. com.), Assn. U.S. Army, Capital Fedn. Cosmopolitan Internat. Club (Cosmo of Yr. award 1981-82, pres. 1980-82, lt. gov. 1983-86, gov. elect 1986-87, gov. 1987-88, internat. 2d v.p. 1991-92, internat. 1st v.p. 1992-93, internat. pres.-elect 1993-94, internat. pres. 1994-95, Patrick J. Hodgins award 1999), Cosmopolitan Diabetes Found. (dir. 1988-91, 97-99, chmn. 1999—). E-mail: tcstone@ix.netcom.com. Home: 6319 Stephens Xing Mechanicsburg PA 17050-2347 Office: Whitaker Ctr for Sci & the Arts 301 Market St Harrisburg PA 17101-2205

STONE, TREVOR WILLIAM, medical educator, researcher; b. Mexborough, Yorkshire, Eng., Oct. 7, 1947; s. Thomas William and Alice (Reynolds) S.; m. Anne Corina, Apr. 3, 1971. B in Pharmacy, U. London, 1969, DSc, 1983; PhD, U. Aberdeen, Scotland, 1972. Lectr. U. Aberdeen, 1970-77; sr. lectr. U. London, 1977-82, reader, 1982-86, prof. neuroscience, 1986-88; prof. pharmacology U. Glasgow, Scotland, 1989—; cons. Beechams, Eng., 1987. Author: Microiontophoresis, 1985; editor: Purines: Pharmacology, 1985, Purines: Basic and Clinical, 1991, Adenosine in the Nervous System, 1991, Neuropharmacology, 1995; editor: Quinolinic Acid, 1989, CNS Neurotransmitters, 1994-96, Pills, Potions, Poisons, 2000. Fellow Royal Soc. Medicine; mem. British Pharmacological Soc., Physiol. Soc., Soc. Neuroscience, N.Y. Acad. Scis. Avocation: photography, pool, snooker, classical music. Office: U of Glasgow, West Medical Building, G12 8QQ Glasgow UK

STONEBRIDGE, JERRY BERT, construction company executive, consultant; b. Issaquah, Wash., June 2, 1941; s. Harold William and Phoebe Kay (Hoye) S.; m. M. Suzanne Carlson, July 28, 1976; children: Jerry Edward, Jeffrey Scott. BS in Zoology and Chemistry, Wash. State U., 1963; cert. in operating engring., N.W. Heavy Equipment Sch., 1964; postgrad., U. Wash., 1970-75. Rsch. asst. rehab. medicine dept. U. Wash., Seattle, 1964-72, rsch. assoc., 1972-78; ophthalmic med. asst. Am. Assn. Ophthalmology, 1971-72; pres. Stonebridge Constrn. Co., Inc., Whidbey Island, Wash., 1978—; cons. on-site sewage disposal systems and their mgmt., 1978—. Contbr. articles to profl. jours. Pres. Freeland Cmty. Assn., 1980-82; trustee Saratoga Beach Cmty. Assn., 1982-91; mem. tech. rev. bd. Island County Health Dept., 1980-82; mem. Freeland C. of C., 1974—, also past pres. Wash State Environ. Health Assn., 1986—, Nat. Environ. Health Assn., 1993—, Island County/Stanwood Cmty. Network, 1996-99, Nat. On-Site Wastewater Recycling Assn., 1991—, bd. dirs., 1997—; founding mem., bd. dirs. Wash. State On-Site Sewage Assn., 1988—, v.p., 1988-95, pres., 1995-97; bd. dirs. Nat. Decentralized Water Resources Capacity Devel. Steering Com., 1998—, Island County Health adv. bd., 1990-94. Bausch & Lomb grantee, 1959-60, Nellie Martin grantee, 1960; recipient 1st place prize for rsch. exhibit Am. Phys. Therapy Assn., 1973, Silver medal Am. Congress Rehab. Medicine, 1974. Mem. Internat. Platform Assn., Am. Bibliography Inst., Pi Ti Iota. Republican. Fax: 360-331-5158. Home: 3333 SE Harbor Rd Langley WA 98260-9659 Office: PO Box 594 Freeland WA 98249-0594

STONECIPHER, HARRY CURTIS, manufacturing company executive; b. Scott County, Tenn., May 1936. BS, Tenn. Poly. Inst., 1960. With GE, 1960-61, 62-86, Martin Aircraft Co., 1961-62; exec. v.p. Sundstrand Corp., 1987, pres., COO, 1987-88, pres., CEO, 1988-94, chmn., 1991-94, also past bd. dirs.; pres., CEO McDonnell-Douglas Corp., St. Louis, 1994-97, Boeing Co., Seattle, 1997—, Boeing Corp., 1997—; bd. dirs. Milacron, Inc. Recipient John R. Allison award, 1996, Rear Adm. John J. Bergen Leadership medal Nay League, 1996. Fellow Royal Aero. Soc. Office: Boeing Co Mail Stop 10-26 Seattle WA 98124-2207

STONEHILL, LLOYD HERSCHEL, gas company executive, mechanical engineer; b. South Bend, Ind., May 20, 1927; s. Charles Myers and Louise Mary (Reed) S.; m. Jean Carole Herzer, Dec. 30, 1961; children: Mark, Bill, John, Rob. BSME, Purdue U., 1949. Registered profl. engr., La. Chief engr. Rothschild Boiler & Tank Works, Shreveport, La., 1949-54; chmn. bd. dirs. Frankfort (Ind.) Bottle Gas, Inc., 1956—. Patentee in field. Founding prs. Clinton County Hosp. Authority, Frankfort, 1974; membership chmn. Clinton County Hosp. Found., Frankfort, 1982-83, 89. With U.S. Army, 1954-56. Recipient Heroism award Elks Lodge, Frankfort, 1959. Mem. Nat. Propane Gas Assn. (mktg. awards 1986, 87), Am. Legion, Purdue Alumni Assn. (Clinton County Chpt. mem. pres.' coun.), Hudson Inst., Rotary (sec. 1963-65, Paul Harris fellow), Lambda Chi Alpha (sec. 1946-47). Republican. Mem. Christian Ch. Avocations: collecting old violins, sailing, reading. Home: 1258 Forest Dr Frankfort IN 46041-3230 Office: Frankfort Bottle Gas Inc 1555 McKinley Ave Frankfort IN 46041-1805

STONELEY, ROBERT, petroleum geologist, consultant; b. Horsforth, Yorkshire, Eng., July 22, 1929; s. Robert and Dorothy (Minn) S.; m. Hilda Mary Margaret Cox, Oct. 22, 1953; children: Elizabeth Mary Margaret, Robert Leslie Gayford. BA, U. Cambridge, Eng., 1951, MA, 1956, PhD, 1973. Geologist Falkland Islands Dependencies Survey, Antarctica, 1951-53, Brit. Petroleum Co., London and overseas, 1953-78; prof. petroleum geology Imperial Coll., U. London, 1978-94, prof. emeritus, 1994—; cons. petroleum geologist London, 1994—; non-exec. dir. Berkeley Exploration, London, 1980-85; chmn. Joint Assn. for Petroleum Exploration Courses U.K., 1980-89; dir. Petroleum Geology '86, London, 1986-99. Author: Introduction to Petroleum Exploration for Non-Geologists, 1995; contbr. articles to profl. jours. Liveryman The Worshipful Co. of Carpenters, London, 1994—. Recipient The Polar medal, 1953, Lyell Fund Coke Medal Geol. Soc. London, 1965, 88, The Mackay Hammer, Geol. Soc. N.Z., 1968, Petroleum Group medal The Geol. Soc., 1997. Fellow Geol. Soc. London (coun. 1980-83); mem. Geologists Assn. (gen. sec. 1993-99), Am. Assn. Petroleum Geologists, Petroleum Exploration Soc. G.B. (hon.). Mem. Ch. of Eng. Avocations: walking, gardening, music. Home: Red Cross Ln, Cambridge CB2 2QU, England Office: 1A Pelham Ct, 145 Fulham Rd, London SW3 6SH, England

STONEMAN, COLIN FRANK, economics educator, consultant, researcher; b. Nottingham, Eng., Aug. 3, 1939; s. Frank William and Patricia Kathleen (Lymbery) S.; m. Patricia Mary Wass, July 21, 1962; children: Catherine, Marianne. BSc in Chemistry, Univ. Coll. London, 1961, PhD in Chemistry, 1964; grad. with honours, Inst. Statisticians, London, 1968. Lectr. chemistry U. Hull (Eng.), 1964-80, 82; sr. rsch. fellow U. Zimbabwe, Harare, 1981; sr. rsch. fellow U. York (Eng.), 1983-86, lectr. econs., 1986—; hon. rsch. fellow Ctr. for Developing Area Studies U. Hull (Eng.), 1986-96; vis. rsch. fellow Ctr. for Devel. Studies U. Leeds, 1998—. Co-author: Zimbabwe: Politics, Economics and Society, 1989; co-editor: Education for Democracy, 1970, 72; editor: Zimbabwe's Inheritance, 1981, Zimbabwe's Prospects, 1988; mem. editorial bd. Jour. So. African Studies, 1985—, editor, 1988—; mem. editorial bd. Rev. Africa Polit. Economy, 1989—; contbr. numerous articles to profl. jours. Leverhulme Trust sr. rsch. fellow, 1983-86. Mem. African Studies Assn. U.K., Devel. Studies Assn. Avocations: opera, music, gardening, Spanish language and culture. Home: Old School Swine, Hull HU11 4JE, England Office: U York Ctr So African, U Leeds Ctr Devel Studies, Leeds LS2 9JT, England

STONER, JOYCE HILL, art conservator, art history educator, songwriter; b. Washington, Oct. 9, 1946; d. I. William and Catherine (Dawson) Hill; m. W. Patrick Stoner, July 4, 1970; children: Catherine Rebecca, Elizabeth Virginia. BA in Fine Arts summa cum laude, Coll. of William and Mary, 1968; MA in Art History, NYU, 1970, diploma in art conservation, 1973; PhD in Art History, U. Del., 1995. Conservation asst. Nat. Portrait Gallery Smithsonian Inst., Washington, 1968; grad. asst. library NYU Conservation Ctr., N.Y.C., 1968-69; conservation asst. Colonial Williamsburg, Va., 1969; computer cataloger registrar's dept. Mus. Modern Art, N.Y.C., 1969-70; mng. editor Art and Archaeology Tech. Abstracts, N.Y.C., 1969-85; pvt. practice art conservator Charlottesville, Va., 1970-73; intern in paintings conservation Washington, 1972-73; pvt. practice conservator Balt. and Phila., 1976—; painting conservator Winterthur Mus., 1976-80, sr. conservator, 1980-81; dir. art conservation program U. Del./Winterthur, 1982-97, prof., 1996—. Writer, dir. (off broadway show) I'll Die If I Can't Live Forever; contbr. chpts. to books. Trustee Williamstown Regional Art Conservation Lab., 1989-95; active Nat. Inst. for Conservation, 1991-93; vis. com. Getty Conservation Inst., 1991-97. Fellow Am. Inst. for Conservation (Gettens award for svc. to the field of art conservation 1991), Internat. Inst. for Conservation (mem. coun. 1997—); mem. Am. Assn. Mus., Internat. Coun. Mus., FAIC Oral History File (project dir. 1975—), Phi Beta Kappa, Theta Alpha Phi, Kappa Kappa Gamma. Presbyterian. Home: 1223 Arundel Dr Wilmington DE 19808-2145 Office: Old Coll U Newark DE 19716

STONNINGTON, HENRY HERBERT, physician, medical executive, educator; b. Vienna, Austria, Feb. 12, 1927; came to U.S., 1969; m. Constance Mary Leigh Hamersley, Sept. 19, 1953. MB, BS, Melbourne U., Victoria, Australia, 1950; MS, U. Minn., 1972. Diplomate Am. Bd. Phys. Medicine and Rehab., 1973. Pvt. practice Sydney, N.S.W., Australia, 1955-65; clin. tchr. U. N.S.W., Sydney, 1965-69; resident in Phys. Medicine and Rehab. Mayo Clinic, Rochester, Minn., 1969-72, mem. staff, 1972-83; assoc. prof. Mayo Med. Sch., Rochester, 1975-83; chmn. dept rehab. medicine Med. Coll. Va., Va. Commonwealth U., Richmond, 1983-88, prof. rehab. medicine, 1983-89, dir. rsch. tng. ctr., 1988-89; v.p. med. svcs. Sheltering Arms Hosp., Richmond, 1985-92; prof. and chmn. dept. phys. medicine and rehab. U. Mo., Columbia, 1992-94; med. dir. Meml. Rehab. Ctr., Savannah, Ga., 1994-97; clin. prof. rehab. medicine Emory U., Atlanta, 1997—; med. dir. rehab. svcs. Meml. Hosp., Gulfport, Miss., 1998—. Editor Brain Injury, 1987—, Pediatric Rehabilitation, 1997—; contbr. articles to profl. jours. Recipient award Rsch. Tng. Ctr. Model Sys., Nat. Inst. Disability and Rehab. Rsch., Washington, 1987, 88. Fellow Australian Coll. Rehab. Medicine, Australasian Faculty Rehab. Medicine, Royal Coll. Physicians Edinburgh (Scotland), Am. Acad. Phys. Medicine and Rehab., Am. Coun. Rehab. Medicine, Am. Assn. Acad. Physicians; mem. Internat. Brain Injury Assn. (v.p. for sci. affairs 1998—, bd. dirs.).

STOOPLER, MARK BENJAMIN, physician; b. N.Y.C., Sept. 29, 1950; s. Alex and Blanche Sylvia (Kappel) S.; m. Lynn Sara Fruchter, Jan. 10, 1982; children: David Andrew, Emily Rachel, Jesse Bryan. BS, Tulane U., 1971; MD, Cornell U., 1975. Diplomate Am. Bd. Internal Medicine, Am. Bd. Oncology. Intern and resident in internal medicine North Shore U. Hosp., Manhasset, N.Y., 1975-78; intern and resident in internal medicine Meml. Sloan-Kettering Cancer Ctr., N.Y.C., 1975-78, asst. chief resident in medicine, 1978, fellow in med. oncology, 1978-80; asst. attending physician Presbyn. Hosp., N.Y.C., 1980-93, assoc. attending physician, 1993—; asst. clin. prof. medicine Columbia U. Coll. of Physicians and Surgeons, N.Y.C., 1980-93; assoc. clin. prof. medicine, 1993—. Contbr. articles to profl. jours. Recipient U. scholar Tulane U., 1970-71. Fellow ACP; mem. Am. Soc. of Clin. Oncology, Am. Fedn. for Clin. Research, Internat. Assn. for the Study of Lung Cancer, Phi Beta Kappa. Office: Columbia-Presbyn Med Ctr 161 Fort Washington Ave New York NY 10032-3713

STOPFORD, MICHAEL JOHN, university administrator; b. June 22, 1953. MA in English Lang. and Lit., Oxford (Eng.) U., 1975. With U.K. Diplomatic Svc. London, N.Y.C. and Vienna, 1975-79; sec. UN, N.Y.C. and Geneva, 1980-95; dir. Info. Ctr. UN, Washington, 1992-95; chief media and pub. rels. Internat. Fin. Corp., Washington, 1996-97; sr. asst. to pres. Am. U., Washington, 1997—. E-mail: mjs@american.edu. Office: Am U 4400 Massachusetts Ave NW Washington DC 20016

STOPLER, TRAIAN IOSEF, microbiologist, researcher; b. Bacau, Moldavia, Romania, Mar. 30, 1924; s. Iosef and Jenny (Moscovici) S.; m. Sonia Kant, 1953 (div. 1957); 1 child, Mihaela; m. Ana Negreanu, 1962 (dec. May, 1985). MD, U. Bucharest, 1953. Sci. rschr. Inst. Hygiene, Bucharest, 1953-62; lab. chief infectious diseases Hosp. Colentina, Bucharest, 1962-72; lab. chief mycoplasma-pertussis Govt. Ctrl. Labs., Jerusalem, 1972-94. Contbr. articles to profl. jours. Recipient, Dipl. of Recognition, Internat. Congress of the Internat. Orgn. for Mycoplasmology, 1998. Home: Etzel 2/12, 32427 Jerusalem 91323, Israel Office: Govt Ctrl Labs, PO Box 6115, Jerusalem Israel

STOPPANI, ANDRES OSCAR MANUEL, research center director, educator; b. Buenos Aires, Aug. 19, 1915; s. Oscar Carlos and Julia Severa (Bahia) S.; m. Antonia Emmy Delius, July 1, 1967. MD, U. Buenos Aires, 1941, PhD in Chemistry, 1945; postgrad., U. Liege, Belgium, 1947, Nat. Inst. Med. Rsch., London, 1953, U. Calif., Berkeley, 1954; PhD, U. Cambridge, Eng., 1953. Prof. biochemistry U. La Plata, Argentina, 1947-48; prof. biochemistry Sch. Medicine U. Buenos Aires, 1949-55, prof., dir. Inst. Biochemistry, Sch. Medicine, 1955-80, prof. emeritus, dir. dept. physiol. scis., 1970-80; bd. dirs. NRC, Argentina, 1963-66, 80-83; pres. Nat. Acad. Exact, Phys. and Natural Scis., Buenos Aires; emeritus investigator NRC Argentina. Contbr. numerous articles to profl. jours. Recipient Weissman prize NRC, 1962, Campomar prize, 1970, Silver award Rotary, 1975, Bunge-Born prize, 1979, Am. States Orgn. Interam. Sci. prize, Bernardo A. Houssay, 1989, Platinum prize Konex Found., 1993, Nat. Sci. prize Argentina, 1993, award Hadassah Internat. Orgn., 1997; grantee Rockefeller Found., 1957-60, The Jane Coffin Childs Found. for Med. Rsch., 1961-63, USAF Office Sci. Rsch., 1969-71, WHO, 1977-82, Swedish Agy. for Rsch. Cooperation with Developing Countries, 1988-95. Fellow Royal Soc. Medicine, Third World Acad. Scis. Trieste, Chilean Acad. Scis., Latin Am. Acad. Scis., Am. Acad. Clin. Biochemistry; mem. Royal Nat. Acad. Medicine (Spain), Royal Nat. Acad. Pharmacy (Spain), Argentine Assn. for Advancement of Sci., Argentine Soc. for Biochem. Rsch. (pres. 1970-71), Argentine Soc. Biology (pres. 1980-83), Argentine Soc. Protozoologists (pres. 1980-81), Am. Chem. Soc., Biochem. Soc. U.K., Soc. Gen. Microbiology U.K., N.Y. Acad. Scis., Am. Soc. Biochemistry and Molecular Biology, Oxygen Soc., Soc. for Free Radical Rsch., Internat. Soc. for Study of Xenobiotics, Nat. Acad. Exact, Phys. and Natural Scis., Nat. Acad. Medicine (pres. 1996), Buenos Aires Nat. Acad. Scis., Chilean Acad. Medicine (hon.), Chilean Acad. Scis. (hon.), Brazilian Acad. Scis. (corr.), Nat. Rsch. Coun. Argentina (hon. pres. 1996), Paraguay Acad. Medicine (hon.), Uruguay Nat. Acad. Medicine (corr.), Nitric Oxide Soc., Am. Soc. Cell Biology, Societé de Chimie Biologique, Co. Biologists Unltd. U.K., Am. Soc. Microbiology, Protein Soc., Soc. Biol. Inorganic Chemistry. Home: Viamonte 2295, 1056 Buenos Aires Argentina Office: Facultad de Medicina, Paraguay 2155, 1121 Buenos Aires Argentina

STOPPARD, TOM (TOMAS STRAUSSLER), playwright; b. Zlin, Czechoslovakia, July 3, 1937; s. Eugene and Martha (Stoppard) Straussler; m. Jose Ingle, 1965 (div.); m. Miriam Moore-Robinson, 1972 (div.); 4 children. MLitt (hon.), U. Bristol, Eng., 1979, Brunel U., Eng., 1979, U. Sussex, Eng., 1980. Journalist Western Daily Press, Bristol, Eng., 1954-58, Evening World, Bristol, 1958-60; free-lance reporter, 1960-63; bd. dirs. Royal Nat. Theatre, London, 1989—. Author: (plays) The Gamblers, 1965, Rosencrantz and Guildenstern Are Dead, 1966 (Plays and Players Best Play award 1967, Best Play Tony award 1968), Enter a Free Man, 1968, The Real Inspector Hound, 1968, Albert's Bridge, 1969 (Prix Italia 1968), If You're Glad I'll Be Frank, 1969, After Magritte, 1970, Dogg's Our Pet, 1971, Jumpers, 1972 (Evening Standard Best Play award 1972, Plays and Players Best Play award 1972), Travesties, 1974 (Evening Standard Best Play award 1974, Best Play Tony award 1976), Dirty Linen and New-Found-Land, 1976, Every Good Boy Deserves Favor, 1974, Night and Day, 1978 (Evening Standard Best Play award 1978), Dogg's Hamlet, Cahoot's Macbeth, 1979, The Real Thing, 1982 (Evening Standard Best Play award 1982, Best Play Tony award 1984, Best Fgn. Play Tony award 1984), Hapgood, 1988, Artist Descending a Staircase, 1988, Arcadia, 1993 (Evening Standard Best Play award 1993, Oliver award 1994), Indian Ink, 1995, Invention of Love, 1997 (Evening Standard Best Play award 1997); (play adaptations) Tango by Slawomir Mrozek, 1966, The House of Bernarda Alba by Federico Garcia Lorca, 1973, Undiscovered Country (based on Das Weite Land by Arthur Schnitzler), 1979, On the Razzle (based on Einen Jux will er sich machen by Johann Nestroy), 1981, Rough Crossing (based on The Play's the Thing by Ferenc Molnar), 1984, Dalliance (based on Liebelei by Arthur Schnitzler), 1986; (radio plays) The Dissolution of Dominic Boot, 1964, M is for Moon Among Other Things, 1964, If You're Glad I'll Be Frank, 1966, Albert's Bridge, 1967, Where Are They Now?, 1970, Artist Descending A Staircase, 1972, The Dog It Was That Died, 1982, In the Native State, 1991, also episodes of radio serials The Dales, 1964, A Student's Diary, 1965; (screenplays) The Romantic Englishwoman, 1975, Despair, 1978, The Human Factor, 1980, (with Terry Gilliam and Charles McKeown) Brazil, 1985 (Best Screenplay Acad. award nominee 1985, Best Screenplay L.A. Critics Circle award 1985), Empire of the Sun, 1987, The Russia House, 1990; (author, dir.) Rosencrantz and Guildenstern Are Dead, 1990 (Grand prize Venice Film Festival 1990), Billy Bathgate, 1991, (with Marc Norman) Shakespeare in Love, 1998 (Golden Globe award and Oscar for best screenplay); (teleplays) A Walk on the Water, 1963, A Separate Peace, 1966, Teeth, 1967, Another Moon Called Earth, 1967, Neutral Ground, 1968, The Engagement (based on his radio play The Dissolution of Dominic Boot), 1970, One Pair of Eyes, 1972, (with Clive Exton) Boundaries, 1975, Three Men in a Boat, 1975, Professional Foul, 1977, Squaring the Circle: Poland 1980-81, 1985; (translator) Largo Desolato by Vaclav Havel, 1987; (novel) Lord Malquist and Mr. Moon, 1966; contbr. short stories to Introduction 2, 1964. Decorated knight comdr. Order Brit. Empire; Ford Found. grantee, 1964; recipient John Whiting award Arts Coun. Great Britain, 1967, Evening Standard Most Promising Playwright Drama award, 1972, Shakespeare prize Hamburg, Germany, 1979. Fellow Royal Soc. Literature. Office: Peters Fraser Dunlop, Drury Ho 34-43 Russell St, London WC2B 5HA, England

STORB, JOHN WILLIAM, civil engineer, consultant; b. New Holland, Pa., Apr. 26, 1924; s. Lewis Mentzer and Elizabeth (Baumler) S.; m. Louise Catherine Williams, June 17, 1950; children: Audrey Louise, Diane Elaine, John William Jr., Nancy Suzanne. BS in Mil. Art and Engring., U.S. Mil. Acad., West Point, N.Y., 1945; MSCE, Ga. Inst. Tech., 1951. Registered profl. engr., D.C., 12 states. Commd. 2d lt. USAF, 1945, advanced through grades to capt., 1952; fighter pilot USAF, Okinawa, Japan, 1946-48; ops. officer USAF, Mitchel Field, N.Y., 1948-49; mem. radar outfit Pope AFB, N.C., 1951-52; civil engr. USAF Hqrs. Europe, 1952-54; engr. USAF Corps of Engrs Office, Boston, 1954-55; chief engr. mktg. Gulf Oil Corp., Phila., 1955-64; owner Storb Inc., Willow Grove, Pa., 1964—; profl. engr. storage tank adv. com. Commonwealth of Pa., Harrisburg, 1992-96, mem. gov. com.

to rev. fire marshal regulations, 1964-65. Mem. fundraising com. Holy Redeemer Hosp., Huntingdon Valley, Pa., 1998. Mem. NSPE, Nat. Fire Protection Assn. Avocations: golfing, fishing. Home: 2725 Brendan Cir Huntingdon Valley PA 19006-5524 Office: Storb Inc 410 Easton Rd Willow Grove PA 19090-2511

STORBECK, MATTHEW LEE, finance director; b. Norway, Mich., May 1, 1961; s. Clayton Elmer Storbeck and Geraldine Marie Goodman-Storbeck; m. Sherri Lynn French, May 19, 1984; 1 child, Justin D. AAS in Mortuary Sci., Cin. Coll. Mortuary Sci., 1983; BBA magna cum laude, Western Mich. U., 1988. Funeral dir. Allore-Sprow Funeral Homes, Monroe, Mich., 1983-86; fin. dir., treas. City of Otsego, Mich., 1988—. Mem. Otsego/Plainwell (Mich.) Airport Bd., 1992-94; task force mem. to rsch. county wide tax adminstrn. sys. Allegan County Bd. Commrs., 1993. Mem. Mcpl. Treas. Assn. U.S. and Can. (cert. mcpl. fin. adminstr., cert. excellance award for mcpl. investment policy 1996), Mich. Mcpl. Fin. Dirs. Assn., Mich. Mcpl. Treas. Assn., Allegan County Treas. Assn. (sec. 1993, pres. 1994, 96),. Avocations: home remodeling, hunting, fishing, camping. E-mail: mattstorbeck@hotmail.com and storbeck@accn.org.

STORER, ROY, former dean of dentistry, educator; b. Wallasey, Cheshire, Eng., Feb. 21, 1928; s. Harry and Jessie (Topham) S.; m. Kathleen Mary Frances Pitman, May 16, 1953; children: Sheila Anne, Carolyn Mary, Michael Roy David. Lic. in dental surgery, U. Liverpool, Eng., 1950, MS, 1960. FDSRCS, Eng., DRDRCS, Edinburgh. House surgeon United Liverpool Hosps., 1950, house surgeon, registrar, 1952-54; lectr. in dental prosthetics U. Liverpool, 1954-61, sr. lectr., 1962-67; vis. assoc. prof. Northwestern U., Chgo., 1961-62; prof. prosthodontics U. Newcastle, Newcastle upon Tyne, Eng., 1968-92, prof. emeritus, 1992—, clin. sub-dean, 1970-77, dean dentistry, 1977-92; hon. cons. dental surgeon, United Liverpool Hosps., 1962-67; cons. restorative dentistry United Newcastle Hosps. (named changed to Newcastle Health Authority), 1968-91; mem. Gen. Dental Coun., London, 1977-92; chmn. Gen. Dental Coun. Edn. Com., London, 1986-91; mem. faculty bd. Royal Coll. Surgeons Eng., London, 1982-90; dental com. Univ. Grants Com., London, 1982-89; external examiner dental subjects Univs. of Belfast (Northern Ireland), Birmingham (Eng.), Bristol (Eng.), Dublin (Ireland), London, Dundee, Leeds, Newcastle upon Tyne, Royal Coll. Surgeons Eng.; chmn. div. dentistry Newcastle U. Hosps., 1972-75; mem. adv. com. tng. dental practioners Dental Com. European Community, Brussels, 1986-92; mem. med. com. Univs. Funding Coun., London, 1989-92; pres. Med. Rugby Football Club, Newcastle, 1968-82; mem. No. Sports Coun., 1973-88. Co-author: (with Smith) A Laboratory Course in Dental Materials for Dental Hygienists, 1963, (with Anderson) Immediate and Replacement Dentures, 3d edit., 1981; contbr. articles to med. jours. Capt. Army, 1950-52. Mem. East India, Devonshire Sports and Pub. sch. Clubs, Marylebone Cricket Club. Avocations: rugby football, cricket, gardening. Home: 164 Eastern Way, Darras Hall, Ponteland, Newcastle upon Tyne NE20 9RH, England

STORESLETTEN, KJETIL, economist, educator; b. Bergen, Norway, Feb. 1, 1967; arrived in Sweden, 1995; s. Leiv Gunnar and Anny (Nesheim) S.; m. Elie Kathrine Seierstad, Jan. 2, 1993; 1 child, Leiv. BS in Econs., Norges Handelshoyskole, Bergen, 1991; PhD, Carnegie Mellon U., 1995. Asst. prof. Stockholm U., 1995—; cons. Swedish govt., Stockholm, 1995—. Referee jours. in field; contbr. articles to profl. jours. Mellon Found. fellow, 1991-94, Mannerfeldt Fund, Stockholm, 1996-99. Avocations: skiing, church activities, hiking. Office: IIES, Stockholm U, 10691 Stockholm Sweden

STOREY, BOBBY EUGENE, JR., electrical engineer, engineering consultant; b. Bainbridge, Md., Jan. 26, 1958; s. Bobby E. Sr. and Rebecca J. (Seagraves) S.; m. Lynn M. Miller, May 24, 1976 (div. June 1988); 1 child, Christopher David; m. Mary H. Freeman, Feb. 14, 1992. AA in Math., Gordon Jr. Coll., 1986; BS in Applied Physics, Ga. Inst. Tech., 1988, M in Applied Physics, 1989; grad., N.Y. Inst. Photography, 1998. Engr. instrumentation and controls Va. Power Co., Mineral, 1982-85; engr. electro optics GEC Avionics, Norcross, Ga., 1988; v.p. EnerSci Inc., Norcross, 1989-94; project engr. LXE, Inc., Norcross, 1988-94; pres. E & H Enterprises, Inc., Duluth, Ga., 1994-96; mgr. engring. project office Sci. Atlanta, Inc., Norcross, Ga., 1995-96; dir. engring. project office Sci.-Atlanta Inc., 1996-98; dir. engring. Sci.-Atlanta Inc., Lawrenceville, Ga., 1998—. With USN, 1976-82. Mem. Internat. Orgn. Electrical and Electronic Engrs. Republican. Avocations: coins, woodworking, target shooting, photography. Home: 5311 Channel Dr Gillsville GA 30543-2800 Office: Sci Atlanta Inc 4386 Park Dr Norcross GA 30093-2906

STOREY, FRANCIS HAROLD, business consultant, retired bank executive; b. Calgary, Alberta, Can., June 20, 1933; s. Bertwyn Morrell and Hilda Josephine (Masters) S.; m. Willomae Saiter, Apr. 25, 1954; children: Daryl, Elizabeth, Brian, Shelley. Student, Gonzaga U., 1953, Pacific Coast Bankers Sch., 1974-76. Designated Certified Profl. Cons. Bank trainee Wash. Trust Bank, Spokane, 1950-56; owner Storey & Storey, Spokane, 1956-64; agt. Bankers Life Nebr., Spokane, 1964-67; sr. v.p. Old Nat. Bank, Spokane, 1967-87, U.S. Bank of Wash., Spokane, 1987-90; pvt. practice cons. Spokane, 1990—; bd. dirs. Output Tech. Corp. bd. dirs. Coalition for Women on Streets (treas., finance chmn.). Bd. dirs. Spokane Bus. Incubator, 1985-96, United Way of Spokane, 1987-95; bd.dirs., treas., fin. chair, gen. conv. dep. Episc. Diocese Spokane Dep., 1969—; trustee Spokane Symphony Soc., 1986-93, Spokane Area Econ. Devel. Coun., 1982-89; mem. adv. bd. Intercollegiate Ctr. Nursing Edn., 1990-96, chair, 1996. Mem. Acad. Profl. Cons. and Advisors, Inland N.W. Soc. Cons. Profls., Spokane Rotary, Spokane Country Club, Spokane Club. Episcopalian. Avocations: golf, reading, travel. Home: 214 E 13th Ave Spokane WA 99202-1115

STOREY, KEITH, forest products company executive; b. Auburn, Wash., Sept. 24, 1936; s. Harry George and Mildred G. Storey; m. Nancy C. Storey, Nov. 28, 1969; 1 child, Mark C. Student, Wash. State Coll., 1954-56; BA, Wash. State U., 1960. V.p. M. Ross Downs Assn., Seattle, 1960-63, First Met. Properties, Seattle, 1963-65; real estate specialist Weyerhaeuser Co., Tacoma, 1966-70, mgr. real estate, 1970-85, dir. real estate, 1986—. Bd. dirs. Highline Cmty. Hosp., Burien, Wash., 1980-87. With USN, 1956-58. Mem. Internat. Devel. Rsch. Coun. (bd. dirs. 1979-82, master profl. 1985), Nat. Assn. Corp. Real Estate (bd. dirs. 1974-76, Master corp. real estate 1980). Avocations: fishing, golfing, hiking, boating, skiing. E-mail: fishstorey@aol.com. Home: 17144 6th Pl SW Seattle WA 98166-3534

STOREY, ROBERT CLIFTON, financial consultant; b. Detroit, Nov. 9, 1930; s. Clifton L. and Jane Storey; children: Michael, Robert Jr., Diane, Frank; m. Stephanie Trombley, Oct. 18, 1975. Student, Dearborn (Mich.) Jr. Coll., 1949-50, Wayne State U., 1950-51. Mgr. br. U.S. Leasing, Detroit, 1960-61; regional v.p. Equilease Corp., Detroit, 1962-69; founder, pres. Master Lease Corp., Detroit, 1969-83, Capital Resource Mgmt., Columbia, S.C., 1986-90, Network Leasing Sys. Am., Columbia, 1990—; dir., v.p., founder Long Creek Equestrian Ctr., Blythewood, S.C., 1983—. Contbr. articles to profl. jours. Mem. Equipment Leasing Assn. (dir., v.p. 1982-83), Columbia Country Club. Methodist. Avocations: cross country motorcycling, tennis, golf, swimming. Office: Network Leasing Sys Am Inc 3031 Scotsman Rd Columbia SC 29223-1832

STÖRI, HERBERT, physics educator, consultant; b. Bad Ischl, Austria, May 23, 1951; s. Günther and Gertrude (Mühlbacher) S.; m. Larissa Schwed, Aug. 19, 1991. PhD, U. Innsbruck, Austria, 1977. Postdoctoral fellow U. Innsbruck, 1977-79, European Orgn. for Nuclear Rsch., Geneva, 1979-81; asst. prof. physics Tech. U. Vienna, 1981-89, assoc. prof., 1989—; dep. head Institut für Allgemeine Physik Technische Universität Wien, 1987-94, 2000—; cons. to number of cos. in Austria and abroad. Contbr. more than 80 articles to profl. jours. and conf. vols.; patentee in field. Mem. Austrian Phys. Soc., Am. Vacuum Soc., Yacht Club Austria. Roman Catholic. Avocation: offshore sailing. Office: Tech U Vienna, Wiedner Hauptstrasse 8-10, A-1040 Vienna Austria

STORK, GILBERT, chemistry educator, investigator; b. Brussels, Belgium, Dec. 31, 1921; s. Jacques and Simone (Weil) S.; m. Winifred Stewart, June 9, 1944 (dec. May 1992); children: Diana, Linda, Janet, Philip. B.S., U. Fla., 1942; Ph.D., U. Wis., 1945; D.Sc. (hon.), Lawrence Coll., 1961, U. Paris, 1979, U. Rochester, 1982, Emory U., 1988, Columbia U., 1993, U. Wis., 1997. Sr. research chemist Lakeside Labs., 1945-46; instr. chemistry Harvard U., 1946-48, asst. prof., 1948-53; assoc. prof. Columbia U., N.Y.C., 1953-55, prof., 1955-67, Eugene Higgins prof., 1967-92, prof. emeritus, 1992—, chmn. dept., 1973-76; plenary lectr. numerous internat. symposia, named Lectureships in U.S. and abroad; cons. several cos.; chmn. Gordon Steroid Conf., 1958-59. Recipient Baekeland medal, 1961, Harrison Howe award, 1962, Edward Curtis Franklin Meml. award Stanford, 1966, Gold medal Synthetic Chems. Mfrs. Assn., 1971, Nebr. award, 1973, Roussel prize in steroid chemistry, 1978, Edgar Fahs Smith award, 1982, Willard Gibbs medal Chgo. sect. Am. Chem. Soc., 1982, Nat. Medal of Sci., 1982, Linus Pauling award, 1983, Tetrahedron prize, 1985, Remsen award, 1986, Cliff S. Hamilton award, 1986, Mony Ferst award Sigma Xi, 1987, George Kenner award, 1992, Chem. Pioneer award Am. Inst. Chemists, 1992, Welch Found. Award in Chemistry, 1993, Allan R. Day award, 1994, Wolf prize, 1996, Phila. Chemists Club award, 1998; Guggenheim fellow, 1959. Fellow NAS (award in chem. sci. 1982), French Acad. Scis., Royal Soc. (U.K., fgn. mem.), Am. Acad. Arts and Scis., Am. Philos. Soc.; mem. Am. Chem. Soc. (chmn. organic chemistry divsn. 1967, award in pure chemistry 1957, award for creative work in synthetic organic chemistry 1967, Nichols medal 1980, Arthur C. Cope award 1980, Roger Adams award in organic chemistry 1991), Royal Soc. Chemistry (hon., London), Pharm. Soc. Japan (hon.), Chemists Club (hon. N.Y.). Home: 18 Chestnut St Englewd Clfs NJ 07632-1908 Office: Columbia U Dept Chemistry Chandler Hall New York NY 10027

STORK, JOHN JOSEPH, management consultant; b. Godalming, Eng., Dec. 25, 1935; s. Joseph W. and Kathleen (Waddington) S.; m. Delphine M. Bowie, Feb. 1, 1963; children: Adam, Matthew. B Commerce with honors, U. leeds, 1958. Buyer S. Simpson Ltd., London, 1958-60; client service exec. Attwood Stats. Ltd., London, 1960-62; research dir. Masius, Wynne-Williams Ltd., London, 1962-68; dir. D'Arcy MacManus & Masius Internat., London, 1968-74; chmn. John Stork Internat. Group, London, Amsterdam, Brussels, Frankfurt, Geneva, Oslo, Paris, Stockholm, 1974-88; mng. ptnr. Korn/Ferry Internat. Ltd., London, 1989-92; dir. Kitchen Range Foods Ltd., Huntingdon, 1993-98; chmn. Stork & May Ltd., London, 1995—; chmn. El. Pie Marine Ltd., London, 1983-93. Served with Royal Navy, 1953-55. Reform. Mem. Royal Thames Yacht Club (London). Office: Stork & May Ltd, 32 Old Burlington St, London W1M 3AT, England

STORM, RUTH ELLEN, venture capitalist; b. Reno, June 5, 1959. BA, Wartburg Coll., 1981; MBA, City U., London, 1988. Legal asst. Hon. Neal Smith U.S. Ho. of Reps., Washington, 1981-83; mgr. Citicorp Venture Capital, London, 1984-88; ptnr. Phildrew Ventures, London, 1988—. Office: Phildres Ventures, 100 Liverpool St, London EC2M 1RH, England

STÖRMER, HORST LUDWIG, physicist; b. Frankfurt-Main, Fed. Republic Germany, Apr. 6, 1949; came to U.S., 1977; s. Karl-Ludwig and Marie (Ihrig) S.; m. Dominique A. Parchet, 1982. PhD, U. Stuttgart, 1977. From tech. staff to dir. phys. rsch. lab. AT&T Bell Labs., Murray Hill, N.J., 1977-97; prof. physics and applied physics Columbia U., N.Y.C., 1998—; adj. physics dir. Lucent Tech., 1997—. Recipient Otto Klung prize Germany, 1985, Benjamin Franklin medal in physics, 1998, Nobel prize in physics, 1998; Bell Labs. fellow, 1983; Decorated Officier de la Legion d'Honneur (France), 1999, Germany, 1999. Fellow NAS, Am. Phys. Soc. (Buckley prize 1984), Am. Acad. Arts and Scis. Office: Columbia U Dept Physics 538 W 120th St New York NY 10027-6601 also: Lucent Technologies 700 Mountain Ave New Providence NJ 07974-1208*

STORMES, JOHN MAX, instructional systems developer; b. Manila, Oct. 7, 1927; s. Max Clifford and Janet (Heldring) S.; m. Takako Sanae, July 29, 1955; children: Janet Kazuko Stormes-Pepper, Alan Osamu. BS, San Diego State U., 1950; BA, U. So. Calif., 1957, MA, 1967. Cert. secondary and community coll. tchr., sr. profl. human resources. Editing supr. Lockheed Propulsion Co., Redlands, Calif., 1957-61; proposals supr. Rockwell Internat., Downey, Calif., 1961-62; publs. dir. Arthur D. Little, Inc., Santa Monica, Calif., 1962-63; publs. coord. Rockwell Internat., Downey, 1963-68; project dir. Gen. Behavioral Systems, Inc., Torrance, Calif., 1969-73; tng. and comm. cons. Media Rsch. Assocs., Santa Cruz, Calif., 1973—; instrl. design supr. So. Calif. Gas Co., L.A., 1985—; lectr. Calif. State U., Northridge, 1991—; tng. cons. Nat. Ednl. Media, Chatsworth, Calif., 1966-81, communications cons. Opinion Rsch. Calif., Long Beach, 1974—. Co-author: TV Communications Systems For Business and Industry, 1970; contbg. author: ASTD's In Action series of casebooks, 1996-99. Curriculum adv. bd. communications dept. Calif. State U., Fullerton, 1964-78. Sgt. U.S. Army, 1953-55, Japan. Mem. Soc. Tech. Communication (sr. mem., 2nd v.p. Orange County chpt. 1962-63), Internat. Soc. Performance and Instruction (v.p. L.A. chpt. 1989, pres. 1990). Democrat. Episcopal. Avocations: photography, sailing. Home: 9201 Florence Ave Apt 102 Downey CA 90240-3578 Office: So Calif Gas Co SC 720G PO Box 513249 Los Angeles CA 90051-1249

STORM-MATHISEN, JON, neuroscientist, educator; b. Oslo, Jan. 16, 1941; s. Haakon and Ardis Ingrid (Søvig) Storm-M.; m. Ingebjørg Selberg, Mar. 21, 1964; children: Ardis, Håkon, Per. MD, U. Oslo, 1965, PhD, 1976. Rschr. Norwegian Def. Rsch. Establishment, Kjeller, Norway, 1967-77; assoc. prof. U. Tromsø, Norway, 1975; assoc. prof. U. Oslo, 1978-85, prof., 1985—. Co-editor: Glutamate: Transmitter in the CNS, 1981, Excitatory Amino Acids, 1986, Understanding the Brain through the Hippocampus, 1990, Glycine Neurotransmission, 1990, Handbook of Chemical Neuroanatomy: Glutamate, 2000; contbr. 200 articles to profl. jours. Lt. Norwegian Army, 1967. Recipient Monrad Krohn's prize Norwegian Neurol. Soc., 1989. Fellow Norwegian Acad. Sci. and Lettes; mem. Soc. Neurosci., Internat. Soc. Neurochemistry. E-mail: jonsm@pons.uio.no. Office: Univ Oslo Anatomical Inst, PO Box 1105 Blindern, N-0317 Oslo Norway

STORMONT, CLYDE JUNIOR, laboratory company executive; b. Viola, Wis., June 25, 1916; s. Clyde James and Lulu Elizabeth (Mathews) S.; m. Marguerite Butzen, Aug. 31, 1940; children: Bonnie Lu, Michael Clyde, Robert Thomas, Charles James, Janet Jean. BA in Zoology, U. Wis., 1938, PhD in Genetics, 1947; DVM (hon.) U. Veterinaria & Pharmaceutica, Brno, Czech Republic, 1994. Instr., lectr. then asst. prof. U. Wis.-Madison, 1946-50; asst. prof. dept. vet. microbiology U. Calif.-Davis, 1950-54, assoc. prof., 1954-59, prof., 1959-73, prof. dept. reprodn., 1973-82, prof. emeritus, 1982—; chmn. Stormont Labs., Inc., Woodland, Calif., 1981—. Contbr. articles to profl. jours. Lt. (j.g.) USNR, 1944-46, PTO. Fulbright fellow, 1949-50, Ellen B. Scripps fellow, 1957-58, 64-65. Mem. Am. Genetic Assn., Genetics Soc. Am., Nat. Bison Assn., N.Y. Acad. Sci., Am. Soc. Human Genetics, Soc. Exptl. Biology and Medicine, Internat. Soc. for Animal Genetics, Sigma Xi. Office: Stormont Labs Inc 1237 E Beamer St Ste D Woodland CA 95776-6000

STORMS, LESTER C. (C STORMS), retired veterinarian; b. Camas, Wash., Oct. 13, 1920; s. Roy Lester and Helen Violet (Belshe) S.; m. Marjorie Louise Hudson, Apr. 10, 1943 (div.); children: Marjorie Maureen, Terry Jo, Sandra Diane. BS in Animal Husbandry, Wash. State U., 1951, DVM, 1952. Intern Portland, 1952; gen. practice vet. medicine Camas, 1952-54; dr.'s asst. pvt. practice vet. office, Hollywood, Calif., 1954, L.A., 1954, Whittier, Calif., 1954; vet. in charge pvt. practice vet. office, Artesia, Calif., 1955-56; owner, pvt. practice vet. medicine Buena Park, Calif., 1956-86; ret., 1986; mem. adv. bd. Guide Dogs for Blind, San Rafael, Calif., 1957-58; mem. steering com. Children's Hosp., Fullerton, Calif., 1960-61. With USN, 1940-51, PTO. Decorated Air medal with 3 gold stars, DFC.; recipient Pappy Pedigoe Meml. Trophy Calif. Sports Car Racing Assn., 1965. Mem. NRA, So. Calif. Vet. Medicine Assn. (life), Am. Vet. Medicine Assn., Orange County Vet. Medicine Assn. (pres. 1958), Olde '78 Fraser's Highlanders (chief-of-staff), Explorer's Club, Adventurer's Club L.A. (sec. 1984, bd. dirs. 1980-82, 95-97), Long Beach Yacht Club, Rotary (Paul Harris fellow, pres. Buena Park chpt. 1963), Masons, Shriners (capt., pres. 1999—, Legion of Honor, capt. Legion of Honor Shrine). Avocations: race car driving, sailing, fishing, shooting. Home: 78th Frasers Highlanders 4316 Latona Ave Los Angeles CA 90031-1426

STOROZHEV, VLADIMIR, physicist, researcher; b. Novosibirsk, Russia, Feb. 6, 1947; s. Boris Storozhev and Ludmila Dagestanskaya; m. Natalia Arsenyeva, Dec. 10, 1983; children: Vladimir, Sofia. Grad., Inst. Physics and Tech., Moscow, 1970; PhD, Inst. Energy Problems, Moscow, 1993. Engr. Inst. Chem. Physics, Moscow, 1970-87; scientist Inst. Energy Problems of Chem. Physics, Moscow, 1987—. Contbr. articles to profl. jours., including Russian Jour. Phys. Chemistry, Jour. Aerosol Sci., Surface Sci., others. Avocations: tennis, mountain skiing, football, volleyball. Office: Inst Energy Probs Chem Phys, Leninsky prospect 38 Bldg 2, 117829 Moscow Russia

STORR, ANTHONY, psychiatry consultant; b. Bentley, Surrey, Eng., May 18, 1920; s. Vernon Faithfull and Katherine Cecilia S.; m. Catherine Cole, Feb. 6, 1942 (div. Sept. 1970); children: Sophia Jane, Polly Cecilia, Emma Faithfull; m. Catherine Lisette Peters, Oct. 9, 1970. Student, Winchester Coll., 1933-38; MB, B. Chir., Christ's Coll., Cambridge, 1944, MA, 1946. Psychotherapist cons. Oxford (England) Health Authority, 1974-84, psychiatrist hon. cons., 1984—. Author: The Integrity of the Personality, 1960, The Dynamics of Creation, 1972, Jung, 1973, Solitude, 1989, Freud, 1989, Churchill's Black Dog, Kafka's Mice and Other Phenomena of the Human Mind, 1989, The Art of Psychotherapy, 1990, Human Destructiveness, 1991, Music and the Mind, 1992, Feet of Clay, 1996; editor: The Essential Jung, 1983. Fellow Royal Coll. Physicians, Royal Coll. Psychiatrists (hon.), Royal Soc. Lit.; mem. Savile Club. Avocation: music. Home and office: 45 Chalfont Rd, Oxford OX2 6TJ, England

STORR, MARTIN ALEXANDER, physician, gastroenterology; b. Munich, June 11, 1970; s. Peter Paul and Annette (Bader) S.; 1 child, Leopold. PhD, Tech. U., Munich, 1997. Intern, resident Tech. U., Munich, 1996, 97-99, physician, rschr., instr., 1996—. Author: Inhibitorische Mechanismen am Ileum der Ratte, 1998, Neurogastroenterology, 2000. Deutcher Akademischer Austausch Dienst grant, Bonn, Germany, 1993. Mem. Bund Deutscher Internisten, Deutscher Gesellschaft für Innere Medizin, Deutsche Gesellschaft für Verdauungskrankheiten. Home: Franz-Senn-Str 9, 81377 Munich Germany Office: Klinikum Rechts der ISAR, Ismaningerstr 22, 81675 Munich Germany

STORR-PAULSEN, ALLAN, ophthalmologist, educator, researcher; b. Copenhagen, Mar. 20, 1947; s. Erik and Evy (Storr) Paulsen; m. Annette Steglich-Petersen, mar. 30, 1974; children: Marie, Signe, Bertram. MD, U Copenhagen, 1976. Cert. gen. practitioner, ophthalmologist, Denmark. Resident in ophthalmology U. Lund, Sweden, 1981-82, U. Copenhagen, 1982-90; ophthalmic surgeon Holbaek, Denmark, 1990-93; chief surgeon in ophthalmology Hvidovre (Denmark) U. Hosp., 1993-96, Frederiksberg U. Hosp., 1997—; asst. prof. ophthalmology U. Copenhagen. Mem. Am. Soc. Cataract and Refractive Surgery, European Soc. Cataract and Refractive Surgery, Scandinavian Soc. Cataract and Refractive Surgery. E-mail: allanstorr@dadlnet.dk. Home: Ellinorsvej 30, DK-2920 Charlottenlund Denmark Office: Frederiksberg U Hosp, Dept Ophthalmology, DK-2000 Frederiksberg Denmark

STORTZ, CARLOS ARTURO, chemistry researcher, educator; b. Buenos Aires, Sept. 20, 1956; s. Zygmunt and Ada (Remz) S.; m. Miriam Liliana Fainberg, Sept. 1, 1983; children: Martin, Laura. Lic. in Chemistry, U. Buenos Aires, 1979, PhD in Chemistry, 1984. Lab asst. to assoc. prof. U. Buenos Aires, 1980—; rsch. assoc. Georgia State U., Atlanta, 1986-88; ind. rschr. NAt. Rsch. Coun. Argentina, 1998—; vice chmn. Dept. Organic Chem., U. Buenos Aires, 1995-99; assoc. editor Anales de la Asoc. Quim. Argentina, Buenos Aires, 1994—. Author: (with others) Techniques in Glycobiology, 1996; contbr. articles to profl. jours. Mem. Argentine Rsch. Soc. Organic Chem. (bd. dirs. 1993-96), Assn. Quimica Argentina. Avocation: Argentine soccer stats. Office: U Buenos Aires Quim Orgn, Fac Ciencias Exactas Pab 2, 1428 Buenos Aires Argentina

STORY, E(UGENE) JACK, physicist; b. St. Louis, Dec. 12, 1928; s. William Bryan and Edith (Wood) S.; m. Sally Elaine Dixson, Aug. 30, 1981; children: Michael, Michelle, Sandra. BS in Physics magna cum laude, S.E. Mo. State U., 1953; MS, Vanderbilt U., 1960. Staff Univ. Chgo., Ill., 1954-57; assoc. prof., dir. phys. scis. rsch., nuclear reactor labs. N.C. State Univ., Raleigh, 1957-63; physicist E G & G, Inc., Santa Barbara, Calif., 1963-66; dep. gen. mgr. E G & G Measurements Inc., Las Vegas, Nev., 1966-82; dir. advanced tech. E G & G, Inc., Boston, 1982-88; pres. EG&G Sci. Support Corp., 1989-94; assoc. dir. Superconducting Super Collider Lab., Dallas, 1989-94; cons. EG&G/U.S. Customs, EG&G/Rocky Flats, EG&G/Antarctica, PBF Inc., Lester Knight/ORNL Nat. Neutron Spallation Lab., 1994-98; mem. N.C. Atomic Energy Adv., State of N.C., Raleigh, 1960-63; cons. N.C. Rsch. Triangle, Carolinas Va. Nuclear Power Assn., NASA, Duke U., 1961-63. Contbr. articles to Health Physics, Nuclear Engring., Physics Rsch. Nuclear edn. adv. com. Univ. Nev., Reno, 1975-79; chmn. Nev. Safety Coun., 1977-80, Clark County (Nev.) C.C. Edn., 1979-81. Mem. AAAS, Rotary. Republican. Church of Latter Day Saints. Home: 2744 Crown Ridge Dr Las Vegas NV 89134-8318

STORZ, JOHANNES, veterinary microbiologist, educator; b. Hardt, Germany, Apr. 29, 1931; came to U.S., 1958; s. Johannes and Theresia (Klausmann) S.; m. Hannelore Roeber, Aug. 8, 1959; children: Gisela Therese, J. Peter K., Heidi Ella. DVM, Vet. Coll., Hannover, Germany, 1958; Dr.Med.Vet., U. Munich, Germany, 1959; PhD, U. Calif., Davis, 1961; Dr.honoris causae, U. Zurich, Switzerland, 1994. Diplomate Am. Coll. Vet. Microbiologists. Rsch. asst. Fed. Rsch. Ctr. Virology, Tubingen, Germany, 1957-58; lectr. U. Calif., Davis, 1958-61; asst. prof. vet. sci. Utah State U., Logan, 1961-63, assoc. prof., 1963-65; assoc. prof. vet. microbiology Colo. State U., Ft. Collins, 1965-67, prof., 1967-82; prof. and dept. head La. State U., Baton Rouge, 1982—; vis. prof. virology Justus Liebig U., Giessen, Germany, 1978-79, 90; cons. WHO, Geneva, Switzerland, 1970; pres. Workshop Human and Animal Chlamydial Infections, Buenos Aires, 1994; rsch. master Coun. on Rsch., La. State U., 1997. Author: Chlamydia and Chlamydia Ind. Disease, 1971; co-author: A Half Century of Progress in Microbiology: South Central ASM Branch,, 1997. Mem. Internat. Rels. Commn., Baton Rouge, 1989-94; chmn. European Exhibits, Internat. Heritage Celebration, Baton Rouge, 1994. Recipient Norden Tchg. award Colo. State U., 1975, A.C. Clark Rsch. award, 1978, Rsch. award AVMA, 1983, Svc. award Gamma Sigma Delta, 1992, Alexander Von Humboldt prize, 1978; SVM disting. scholar, 1989. Mem. Am. Soc. Microbiology (pres. south cen. br. 1994-96), Faculty Club. Republican. Roman Catholic. Avocations: biking, swimming, mountain hiking, travel. Home: 2942 Rene Beauregard Ave Baton Rouge LA 70820-5711 Office: La State Univ Sch Vet Medicine S Stadium Rd Baton Rouge LA 70803-0001

STOTHARD, JOHN, orthopaedic surgeon; b. Ripley, Derbyshire, Eng., Apr. 23, 1948; s. John Douglas and Doris Stothard; m. Elizabeth Ross, May 13, 1972; children: Debra, Pamela. MB, BChir, U. Edinburgh, Scotland, 1971, MD, 1980. Rotating registrar Yorkshire Region, Leeds, 1974-76; registrar traumatic and orthopaedic surgery Newcastle-Upon-Tyne, 1976; sr. rsch. assoc. Med. Rsch. Coun., 1976-78; sr. registrar traumatic and orthopaedic surgery No. Region, 1978-81; cons. traumatic and orthopaedic surgeon Stockton-on-Tees, 1981-93, Middlesbrough, 1993—; dir. MSc in Clin. Orthopaedics, U. Teesside, 1995—, vis. prof. Sch. of Health, 1996—; chmn. specialty tng. com. orthopaedic surgery U. Newcastle-Upon-Tyne, 1992-96; head tng. orthopaedic surgery No. Region, 1994-99; mem. spl. adv. com. on orthopaedic surgery, 2000—. Contbr. articles to profl. jours. Fellow Royal Coll. Surgeons Edinburgh, Brit. Orthopaedic Assn. (edn. com. 1994-96); mem. Brit. Orthopaedic Rsch. Soc., Brit. Soc. for Surgery of Hand (edn. com. 1999—). Home: Maple Lodge 622A Yarm Rd, Eaglescliffe, Stockton On Tees TS16 0DQ, England

STOTT, DAVID JAMES, physician; b. Rugby, Eng., Apr. 6, 1959; s. James Wilson and Agnes Catherine (Scott) S.; m. Shiona Margaret MacPhail, May 16, 1987; children: Kathryn, Alastair. MB, B in Surgery, U. Glasgow, 1981, MD, 1988. Intern Western Infirmary, Glasgow, 1982-84, resgistrar in internal medicine MRC Blood Pressure Unit, 1984-86; registrar in geriatric medicine Gartnaval Gen. Hosp., Glasgow, 1986-87; sr. registrar in geriatric and gen. internal medicine Western Infirmary/Garnavel Gen. Hosp., 1987-90; sr. lectr. in geriatric medicine, hon. cons. U. Dept. of Geriatric Medicine, So. Gen. Hosp., Glasgow, 1991-93, Glasgow Royal Infirmary, 1993-94; David Cargill prof. geriatric medicine, hon. cons. Acad. Sect. Geriatric Medicine, Royal Infirmary, Glasgow, 1994—. Editl. bd., Systematic Revs. editor Jour. Age and Ageing, 1998—. Fellow Royal Coll. Physicians (Glasgow, Edinburgh, Best Presentation prize 1992); mem. British Geriatrics Soc.(pharmacology and therapeutics sect., Taylor Brown prize Scottish br.

1995, 97, 99), Med. Rsch. Soc., Scottish Soc. of Explt. Medicine, Scottish Soc. of Physicians (Fitzgerald Peel Rsch. fellowship 1991, 95), British Stroke Rsch. Group, British Assn. of Stroke Physicians, British Med. Assn. Home: 5 Heather Ave, Bearsden, Glasgow G61 3AN, England

STOTT, ROBERT HENRY, journalist; b. Lower Hutt, Wellington, New Zealand, Dec. 4, 1940; s. Harry Ernest and Joan (Powles) S.; m. Janet Joy McGregor, Dec. 8, 1962; children: Karen Barbara, Joanne Audrey. Reporter The Dominion, Wellington, New Zealand, 1958-59, HB Herald Tribune, Napier, New Zealand, 1959-62, Rotorua Post, Whakatane, New Zealand, 1962-63; chief reporter Beacon, Whakatane, 1963-65, Evening Standard, Palmerston North, New Zealand, 1965-69; dep. chief reporter The Dominion, New Zealand, 1969-72; mng. dir. Southern Press Ltd., Porirua, Wellington, New Zealand, 1972—. Contbr. articles to profl. publs.; author books on tranport; radio commentator; editor Rails mag., 1971—. Recipient Queen's Svc. medal, 1986; Commonwealth Press Union fellow, 1966, Permanent Way Instn., U.K., 1985. Fellow Chartered Inst. Transport in New Zealand (hon. editor 1973-97); mem. Queen Elizabeth Nat. Trust New Zealand (life). Avocations: small boat sailing, classical music, rail hobbies. Home: High Ridge RDI, Porirua New Zealand Office: Southern Press Ltd, R D I, Porirua Wellington New Zealand

STOTTER, LAWRENCE HENRY, lawyer; b. Cleve., Sept. 24, 1929; s. Oscar and Bertha (Lieb) S.; m. Ruth Rapoport, June 30, 1957; children: Daniel, Jennifer, Steven. BBA, Ohio State U., 1956, LLB, 1958, JD, 1967. Bar: Calif. 1960, U.S. Supreme Ct. 1973, U.S. Tax Ct. 1976. Pvt. practice San Francisco, 1963—; ptnr. Stotter and Coats, San Francisco, 1981-97; sole practitioner, 1997—; mem. faculty Nat. Judicial Coll.; mem. Calif. Family Law Adv. Commn., 1979-80. Editor in chief: Am. Bar Family Advocate mag, 1977-82; TV appearances on Phil Donahue Show, Good Morning America. Pres. Tamalpais Conservation Club, Marin County, Calif.; U.S. State Dept. del. Hague Conf. Pvt. Internat. Law, 1979-80; legal adv. White House Conf. on Families, 1980—. Served with AUS, 1950-53. Mem. ABA (past chmn. family law sect.), Am. Acad. Matrimonial Lawyers (past nat. v.p.), Calif. State Bar (past chmn. family law sect.), San Francisco Bar Assn. (past chmn. family law sect.), Calif. Trial Lawyers Assn. (past chmn. family law sect.). Home: 2244 Vistazo St E Tiburon CA 94920-1970 Office: 1255 Columbus Ave # 200 San Francisco CA 94133-1326

STOUP, ARTHUR HARRY, lawyer; b. Kansas City, Mo., Aug. 30, 1925; s. Isadore and Dorothy (Rankle) S.; m. Kathryn Jolliff, July 30, 1948; children: David C., Daniel P., Rebecca Ann, Deborah E. Student, Kansas City Jr. Coll., Mo. 1942-43; BA, U. Kansas City, 1950; JD, U. Mo., Kansas City, 1950. Bar: Mo. 1950, D.C. 1979, U.S. Dist. Ct. (we. dist.) Mo., U.S. Dist. Ct. Kans., U.S. Dist. Ct. Ariz. Pvt. practice law, Kansas City, 1950—; chmn. U.S. Merit Selection Com. for Western Dist. Mo., 1981. Chmn. com. to rev. continuing edn. U. Mo., 1978-79; mem. dean search com. U. Mo. Law Sch., Kansas City, 1994-95; trustee U. Mo.-Kansas City Law Found., 1972—, pres., 1979-82; trustee U. Kansas City, 1979—. With USNR, 1942-45. Recipient Alumni Achievement award U. Mo., Kansas City, 1975, Law Found. Svc. award U. Mo.-Kansas City Law Found., 1987. Fellow Internat. Soc. Barristers (state mem. chmn.), Am. Bar Found. (life mem.); mem. ABA (ho. dels. 1976-80), Kansas City Met. Bar Assn. (pres. 1966-67, Dean of Trial Bar award 1991), Mo. Bar (bd. govs. 1967-76, v.p. 1972-73, pres. elect 1973-74, pres. 1974-75), Lawyers Assn. Kansas City Mo., Mo. Assn. Trial Attys. (sustaining), Assn. Trial Lawyers Am. (sustaining), So. Conf. Bar Pres.'s (life), Mobar Research Inc. (pres. 1978-86), Phi Alpha Delta Alumni (justice Kansas City area alumni 1955-56). Lodges: Optimists (pres. Ward Pkwy. 1961-62, lt. gov. Mo. dist. internat. 1963-64), Sertoma, B'nai B'rith. Home: 9002 Western Hills Dr Kansas City MO 64114-3566 Office: Palace Bldg Ste 250 1150 Grand Blvd Kansas City MO 64106-2317

STOUPEL, ELIJAH, medical educator; b. Kaunas, Lithuania, June 20, 1929; arrived in Israel, 1974; s. Gregory and Ester (Lan) S.; m. Sophia Danguole Nugaraite; children: Jannet, Ylana. MD, Vilnius (Lithuania) U., 1952, PhD in Medicine, 1960, D of Med. Sci., 1967. Dir. Dist. Dept. Health and Dept. Internal Medicine, Nementzine, Lithuania, 1952-55; faculty appointment, family physician Vilnius U. Hosp., 1955-58, cardiologist dept. thoracic surgery, 1958-62, asst. prof. faculty for postgrad. med. studies, 1962-66, assoc. prof., 1966-70, full prof. medicine, 1970-74; chief cons. in cardiology Heart Inst. Beilinson Med. Ctr. (now Rabin Med. Ctr.), Petah-Tiqva, Israel, 1975—; prof. cardiology Tel Aviv U., 1994—. Author: Prognosis in Cardiology, 1971, Mitral Valve Disease After Comissurotomy, 1973, Forecasting in Cardiology, 1976, Studies in Clinical Cosmobiology, 1968—. Pres. Israeli br. Internat. Physicians for Prevention of Nuclear War, 1984-91. Fellow Internat. Soc. Internal Medicine, European Soc. Cardiology, Israel Heart Soc. E-mail: stoupel@inter.net.ie. Home: 27 Habanim, Hod Hasharon 45268, Israel Office: Rabin Med Ctr Beilinson Campus, Petah Tiqwa 49100, Israel

STOUT, DAVID KER, economics educator; b. Bangor, Wales, Jan. 27, 1932; s. Alan Ker and Evelyn (Roberts) S.; m. Margaret Sugden, July 30, 1956; children: Nigel, Rowland, Lucy, Eleanor. BA in English and Econs. with honors, U. Sydney, Australia, 1953; MA in Philosophy, Politics & Econs., U. Oxford, Eng., 1956. Prize fellow Magdalen Coll., Oxford, 1958-59; ofcl. tutorial fellow in econs. U. Coll., Oxford, 1959-76; econ. dir. Nat. Econ. Devel. Office, London, 1970-72, 76-80; prof. econs. U. Leicester, Eng., 1980-82; head econs. and corp. devel. Unilever Plc, London, 1982-92; dir. Ctr. Bus. Strategy, London (Eng.) Bus. Sch., 1992-97; rsch. assoc. Nat. Econ. Rsch. Assocs., 1997—; assoc. Nat. Bur. Econ. Rsch., N.Y.C., 1970; advisor Commonwealth Govt., Canberra, Australia, 1973, 75-76; mem. exec. com. Nat. Inst. Econs. and Social Rsch., London, 1974—; chmn. industry and econ. com. Econ. and Social Rsch. Coun., London, 1989-92; chmn. Program on Info. and Comm. Tech., London, 1990-94; mem. mfg. and bus. process tech. Foresight Panel, 1994—; mem. tech. Interaction Bd. Biol. Scis. Rsch. Coun., 1994-96; spl. advisor Innovative Mfg. Initiative, 1996—. Mng. editor Bus. Strategy Rev., 1994-98; contbr. chpts. to books and articles to profl. jours. Rhodes scholar NSW Rhodes Trustees, 1954, Jr. and Sr. George Webb Medley scholar Oxford (Eng.) U., 1955, 56. Avocations: chess, music, bivalves. Fax: (44) 1732-780904.

STOUT, DONALD EVERETT, real estate developer, environmental preservationist; b. Dayton, Ohio; s. Thorne Franklin and Lovella Marie (Sweeney) S.; m. Gloria B. McCormick; children: Holly Sue, Scott Kenneth. BS, Miami U.; grad. courses in real estate. Lic. real estate broker, Ohio, U.S. V.I.; cert. gen. appraiser, Ohio. Pres. various real estate groups; developer 1st transp. ctr. for trucking in Ohio; pres. The Falls Estates, Wright Gate Tech. Ctr., Edglo Land Recycle, pres. Donald E. Stout, Inc.; developer, instr. real estate courses. Contbr. articles to profl. jours. With U.S. Army and U.S. Navy. Named Outstanding Real Estate Salesmen in the state, Ohio Bd. Realtors. Mem. Nat. Assn. Real Estate Bds., Appraisal Inst. (sr. real estate analyst, sr. residential appraiser), Soc. Indsl. Office Realtors, Dayton Area Bd. Realtors (co-founder, 1st pres. salesman divsn.), U.S. Naval Res. Officers Assn., Raymond M. Hughes Soc., Exhausted Roosters, Masons (32 degree), Shriner, Phi Delta Theta. Office: 1344 Woodman Dr Dayton OH 45432-3442

STOUT, ELIZABETH WEST, foundation administrator; b. San Francisco, Mar. 4, 1917; d. Claudius Wilson and Sarah (Henderson) West; m. Bruce Churchill McDonald, Mar. 19 1944 (dec. 1952); children: Douglas, Anne; m. Charles Holt Stout, Oct. 27, 1958 (dec. 1992); stepchildren: Richard, George (dec.), Martha Stout Gilweit. Student, U. Nev., 1934-37; grad., Imperial Valley Coll., 1990. Cashier, acct. N.Y. Underwriters, San Francisco, 1937-42; sec. supply and accounts USN, San Francisco, 1942-44. Contbr. articles to profl. jours. Mem. adv. bd. Anza-Borrego Desert, Natural History Assn., 1974-84; founder Stout Paleontology Lab., Borrego Springs, Calif., 1982; found. trustee Desert Rsch. Inst., Reno, 1989—; active Black Rock Desert Project, 1989, Washoe Med. Ctr. League, 1953—, St. Mary's Hosp. Guild, 1953—. Named Disting. Nevadan U. Nev., 1993. Mem. Anza-Borrego Desert Natural History Assn. (dir. emeritus 1984), Soc. Vertebrate Paleontology, De Anza Desert Country Club, Kappa Alpha Theta. Republican. Episcopalian. Avocations: travel, writing, reading, golf.

STOUT, LOWELL, lawyer; b. Tamaha, Okla., July 23, 1928; s. Charles W. and Rosetta (Easley) S.; m. Liliane Josue, Nov. 29, 1952; children: Georgianna, Mark Lowell. Student, Northeastern State Coll., Tahlequah, Okla., 1946-49, U. Okla., 1949-51; LLB, U. N.Mex., 1952. Bar: N.Mex. 1952. Ptnr. Easley, Quinn & Stout, Hobbs, N.Mex., 1954-58, Girand & Stout, Hobbs, 1958-60; pvt. practice Hobbs, 1960-80; ptnr. Stout & Stout, Hobbs, 1980—. Cpl. U.S. Army, 1952-54. Perenially listed in Best Lawyers in America. Fellow Am. Coll. Trial Lawyers; mem. Assn. Trial Lawyers Am., State Bar N.Mex., N.Mex. Trial Lawyers Assn., Lea County Bar Assn. Home: 218 W Lea St Hobbs NM 88240-5110 Office: Stout & Stout PO Box 716 Hobbs NM 88241-0716

STOVALL, RICHARD L., academic administrator; b. Springfield, Mo., Mar. 28, 1944; s. Wilbern Lee and Ernestine Patricia (Putman) S.; m. Susannah K. Young; children: Richard Christopher, Stacy Suzanne. BA, SW Mo. State U., 1966; MA, C.W. Post Coll. L.I. U., 1969; PhD, Ohio State U., 1975. Instr. SW Mo. State U., Springfield, 1969-72; asst. prof. U. S.C., Columbia, S.C., 1975-77; prof., asst. dept. head SW Mo. State U., Springfield, 1977—; cons. Cedar Hills High Sch., Dallas, 1986, Andrews Ins. Agy., 1984, Mo. Cosmetology Assn., 1983-84, Springfield Pers. Assn., 1982, Syntex Corp. 1981-82; pub. rels. Halcyon of Dallas, 1988-96, Hawthorne Group of Washington, 1995-96, The Harrell Group, Dallas, 1999. Contbr. articles to profl. jours. Tabulation room coord. for MSHSAA Dist. Speech Festival; lectr. Springfield Pub. Schs., City Utilities Citizens Adv. Bd.; pres. Boy Scouts Am. With ES USNR-TAR, 1962-69. Mem. Pub. Rels. Soc. Am., Am. Forensics Assn., Speech Communication Assn. Am., So. Speech Communication Assn., Pub. Rels. of the Ozarks, Pub. Rels. Soc. Mid-Mo., Cen. States Speech Assn., Speech and Theatre Assn. Mo., Cherokee Homeowners Assn. (pres.). Episcopal. Home: 1131 E Meadowlark St Springfield MO 65810-2961 Office: SW Mo State U 901 S National Ave Springfield MO 65804-0088

STOWASSER, BARBARA R.F., foreign language and culture educator. MA, UCLA, 1959; PhD, U. Munster, Germany, 1961; hon. degree, Georgetown U., 1991. Asst. prof. dept. Arabic studies Georgetown U., Washington, 1976-83, assoc. prof., 1983-94, prof., 1994—, dir. Ctr. for Contemporary Arab Studies, 1993—. Author: Women in the Qur'an, 1994; editor: The Islamic Impulse, 1987. Mem. Mid. East Studies Assn. (pres. 1998-99), Am. Assn. Tchrs. Arabic (pres. 1986-87), Am. Coun. for Study of Islamic Studies (bd. dirs. 1983—). Office: Georgetown U Ctr Contemp Arab Studies Washington DC 20057-0001

STOWE, CHARLES ROBINSON BEECHER, management consultant, educator, lawyer; b. Seattle, July 18, 1949; s. David Beecher and Edith Beecher (Andrade) S.; m. Laura Everett, Mar. 9, 1985. BA, Vanderbilt U., 1971; MBA, U. Dallas, 1975; JD, U. Houston, 1982; PhD, U. Warsaw, Poland, 1998. Bar: Tex. 1982, U.S. Dist. Ct. (so. dist.) Tex. 1984, U.S. Tax Ct. 1984. Acct. exec. Engleman Co., Dallas, 1974-75; instr. Richland Coll., Dallas, 1976; acct. Adthur Andersen & Co., Dallas, 1976-78; part-time pub. rels. cons.; dir. Productive Capital Assocs., 1975-81; pres. Stowe & Co., Dallas, 1978—; from asst. to prof. dept. gen. bus. and fin. Coll. Bus. Adminstrn., Sam Houston State U., 1982—; dir. Office Free Enterprise and Entrepreneurship, 1982-86, Office Internat. programs, 1998—; adminstrv. intern asst. to pres., spring, 1985. Author: Bankruptcy I Micro-Mash Inc., 1989, rev. edit., 1995, The Implications of Foreign Financial Instutions on Poland's Emerging Entrepreneurial Economy, 1999; co-author: CPA rev.; editor Houston Jour. Internat. Law, 1981-82; contbr. articles to profl. jours. Trustee Stowe-Day Found., 1979-80; mem. nat. adv. bd. Young Am.'s Found., 1979—; vol. faculty State Bar Tex. Profl. Devel. Program, 1988—; vol., mediator Dispute Resolution Ctr. Montgomery County; mediator so. dist. U.S. Dist. Ct. Tex. 1993; teach chief U.S. Mil. liaison Rep. Poland, 1994; pub. affairs officer George C. Marshall European Ctr. Security Studies, 1997. With USNR, 1971-74; capt. Res. Recipient Freedoms Found. award, Navy Achievement medal, Gold Star, Def. Meritorious Svc. medal with oak leaf cluster, Navy Meritorious Svc. award; Summer fellow Tex. Coordinating Bd., 1988, Prince-Babson fellow Entrepreneurship Symposium, 1991. Mem. ABA, Am. Arbitration Assn., State Bar Tex. (vol. faculty profl. devel. program 1988-90, vice chair profl. efficiency and econ. rsch. com. 1993, chair law office mgmt. com. 1993-94), Walker County Bar Assn. (pres. 1987-88), Pub. Rels. Soc. Am., Tex. Assn. Realtors, U.S. Navy League, Naval Res. Assn., Res. Officers Assn., Dallas Vanderbilt Club (pres. 1977-78). Office: PO Box 2144 Huntsville TX 77341-2144

STOWE, ROBERT LEE, III, textile company executive; b. Charlotte, N.C., July 3, 1954; s. Robert Lee Jr. and Ruth Link (Harding) S.; m. Christine Ruth Edwards, Jan. 15, 1983; children: Christine Ruth, Lillian Rhyne. BA, Davidson (N.C.) Coll., 1976. Dir., mgmt. trainee R.L. Stowe Mills, Inc., Belmont, N.C., 1976-77, v.p., 1977-79, exec. v.p., 1979-84, chmn. bd., 1984—; sec., treas. Lakeview Farms, Inc.; pres. Robrt Lee Stowe Jr. Found., Belmont, 1978—; bd. mgrs. Wachovia Bank of N.C., Gaston County; mem.-mgr. McAdams & Stowe, LLC. Trustee Belmont Abbey Coll., 1987-90, Mint Mus. Art, Charlotte, 1989-92, Crossnore (N.C.) Sch., 1987-98, Sci. Museums, Charlotte, 1989-91, Gaston Day Sch., 1994-97, Gaston County C of C., 1992-95, Mis. of New South; trustee Daniel Jonathan Stowe Conservancy, 1990, pres., 1996-2000, vice-chmn., 2000; deacon, elder local Presbyn. Ch.; bd. dirs. Downtown Belmont, Inc., Gaston County Edn. Found., Gaston County YMCA; bd. trustees Presbyn. Hosp. Found., Charlotte, N.C. Named one of Outstanding Young Men Am., 1979. Mem. Am. Textile Mfrs. Inst. (bd. dirs. 1989-92), Newcomen Soc. U.S., N.C. Textile Found. (bd. dirs. 1986—), Met. Club N.Y., Charlotte Country Club, Gaston Country Club. Republican. Avocations: golf, boating, church activities. Home: 135 N Main St PO Box 232 Belmont NC 28012-0232 Office: RL Stowe Mills Inc 100 N Main St Belmont NC 28012-3104

STOYAN, DIETRICH KURT, statistics educator; b. Berlin, Nov. 26, 1940; s. Kurt Karl and Margarete (Jakubski) S.; m. Helga Katharina Ringel, Sept. 5, 1964; children: Irene, Helmut. Dipl.-Math., Tech. U. Dresden (Germany), 1964; Dr.-Eng., Bergakademie Freiberg, Freiberg, Germany, 1967; Dr. rer. nat. habil., Bergakademie, Freiberg, Germany, 1975. Scientist Deutsches Brennstoff Inst., Freiberg, 1964-75; lectr. Bergakademie Freiberg, 1975-90; prof. Bergakademie Freiberg, Freiberg, 1990—; vice chancellor Bergakademie, 1991-97. Author: Methods of Queueing Theory, 1976, Comparison Methods for Queues and Other Stochastic Models, 1983, Stochastic Geometry and Its Applications, 1987, 95, Fractals, Random Shapes and Point Fields, 1994. Fellow Royal Stats. Soc.; mem. Deutscher Hochschul-Verband, Academia Europaea, Inst. Math. Stats., Internat. Stats. Inst. Avocations: reading, bicycling, gardening. Home: Stauffenbergstr 14, 09599 Freiberg Germany Office: Bergakademie Freiberg, 09596 Freiberg Germany

STOYANOV, EUGENIE STEPANOVICH, chemistry researcher, educator; b. Varna, Bulgaria, Dec. 26, 1948; arrived in Russia, 1955; s. Stefan Vasil'evich and Vasilka Nikolova (Kirilova) S.; m. Irina Vasil'evna Sheliakina, Nov. 13, 1971; children: Lillie, Alexander, Andrey. BS, Moscow State U., 1971; PhD, Vernadsky Inst. Geochemistry, Moscow, 1975; D in Chem. Tech., Mendeleyev U., Moscow, 1991. Cert. sr. rsch. assoc. Moscow; cert. prof. chemistry Moscow. Rsch. assoc. Inst. Inorganic Chemistry, Kemerovo, Russia, 1975-83; head lab. Inst. Hydrometallury Nonferrous Metals, Novosibirsk, Russia, 1983-88; sr. rsch. assoc. prof. Inst. Catalysis, Novosibirsk, 1991—; sr. lectr. Kemerovo (Russia) State U., 1978-83; prof. Novosibirsk State Pedagogical U., 1991-96, head chair chemistry, 1996—. Author: Employment of Electronic and Vibration Spectroscopy in Organic and Inorganic Chemistry, 1996; contbr. articles to profl. jours. Grantee Internat. Sci. Found., N.Y., 1994, Internat. Sci. Found. and Russian Govt., N.Y. and Moscow, 1995, German Acad. Exch. Svc., Bonn, 1995, Copernicus, Commn. of the European Commn., Brussels, 1998. Avocations: traveling, mountain walking. Home: App 19, Morskoi prospekt 32, 630090 Novosibirsk Russia Office: Inst Catalysis, Prospekt Lavrentieva 5, 630090 Novosibirsk Russia

STOYANOV, IVAN ILIEV, rector; b. Brashlianitsa, Bulgaria, Feb. 12, 1949; s. Ilia Stoyanov and Elena (Ivanova) Georgieva; m. Todorka Dimitrova, Sept. 6, 1970; children: Ilia Ivanov, Elena Ivanova. BA, U. Veliko Turnovo, Bulgaria, 1971; PhD, Bulgarian Acad. Scis., 1983. Tchr. Secondary Sch., Paissievo, Bulgaria, 1971-72; curator Mus. History, Pleven, Bulgaria, 1974-75; lectr. St. Cyril & St. Methodius U., Bulgaria, 1975—; vice dean faculty history U. Veliko, Turnovo, Bulgaria, 1989-91, vice rector, 1991-93; rector St. Cyril & St. Methodius U., Turnovo, Bulgaria, 1995-99; mem. Accreditation Coun., Bulgaria, 1995—, Rectors Coun., Bulgaria, 1995—, Soc. Historians, Bulgaria, 1995—. Author: The Liberal Party in the Principality of Bulgaria, 1879-1886, 1989, The Slav Committees and the Bulgarian Liberation Movement after the April Uprising, 1992, A Short History of Veliko Turnova in Modern Times, 1878-1940, 1993, Bulgaria: The Frontiers of National Grandeur, 1994, Policies and Programs of the National Liberation Movement, 1994, History of Bulgaria 681-1960, vol. 1, 1995, Bulgaria from Antiquity to the Present Day, vol. 1, 1997, History of the Bulgarian Revival, 1999. Avocations: basketball, literature, music. Home: 27-B Teodossi Turnovsku, 5003 Veliko Turnovo Bulgaria Office: U Veliko Turnovo, 2 Teodossi Turnovski, 5003 Veliko Turnovo Bulgaria

STOYANOV, PETAR, government official; b. Plovdiv, May 25, 1952. Grad., U. Sofia, Bulgaria, 1976. Lawyer Plovdiv, 1978; dep. min. justice Govt. Bulgaria, Sofia, 1992, mem. parliement, 1994-96, pres., 1997—. Mem. Union Dem. Forces. Office: 2 Dondoukov Blvd, 1000 Sofia Bulgaria*

STOYLE, PETER BLIN, academic administrator; b. Weston-super-mare, Somerset, Eng., Mar. 1, 1935; arrived in Argentina, 1979.; s. Clayton Cobb Stoyle and Grace Alethea Alway Jones; m. Els van der Stoel, July 7, 1958 (div. 1968); children: Philip, Daniel, Tamara; m. Susana Abergo, Dec. 26, 1969; children: Rupert, David, Giselle, Veronica. BA, Oxford (Eng.) U., 1958, Diploma in Edn., 1959, MA, 1962. Asst. tchr. Peterhouse, Marondela, Zimbabwe, 1959-63; adminstr. Coll. Careers, Cape Town, South Africa, 1963-64; headmaster Brit. Sch., Montevideo, Uruguay, 1964-78; dir. studies St. George's Coll., Buenos Aires, Argentina, 1979-91; coord. internat. edn. St. George's Coll., Buenos Aires, 1991-94; coord. internat. baccalaureate St. Andrew's Scots Sch., Buenos Aires, 1995—; regional rep. United World Colls., Buenos Aires, 1979—; examiner internat. baccalaureate, Buenos Aires, 1980—, workshop leader, regional dir., 1982—. Mem. Internat. Baccalaureate Coun. Found., Geneva, 1977-79. Mem. English-Speaking Scholastic Assn. River Plate (hon., pres. 1974-76, 80-84, founder and chair ctr. 1985-87). Avocations: piano and organ music, walking, reading. Home: Rivadavia 28/36, TI P7 San Isidro, 1642 Buenos Aires Argentina Office: St Andrew's Scots Sch, RS Peña 601, 1636 Olivos, Buenos Aires Argentina

STOYLOV, STOYL PESHEV, biophysics educator, researcher; b. Sofia, Bulgaria, Apr. 19, 1935; s. Kryakov Pesho and Radka Nedeva (Khadzhi Pencheva) S.; m. Elena Dyankova Ilieva, Dec. 18, 1935; children: Svetla, Peter. Physicist Degree, U. Sofia, 1959; PhD, Acad. of Scis., Sofia, 1965, DSc, 1973. Assoc. rsch. prof. Inst. Phys. Chemistry, Acad. of Sci., Sofia, 1968-75, rsch. prof., 1975-80; prof. biophysics, head dept. Med. Faculty, Sofia, 1980-86; prof., dir. Inst. Phys. Chemistry Acad. Sci., Sofia, 1989-93, prof., 1993—; prof. physics Nat Pedagogic Inst., Butare, Rwanda, 1971-72; prof. phys. chemistry U. Bejaia, Algeria, 1986-88; lectr. in physiochem. methods in biology Biology Faculty, Sofia, 1968-86; vis. prof. lab. biophysics Fac. Pharmacy, U. Louis Pasteur, Strasbourg, 1994-2000; hon. vis. prof. Sch. of Process, Environmental and Mat. Engring., U. Leeds, 2000—. Author: Physico-Chemical Methods in Biology, 1981, Colloid Electro-optics, 1991; co-author: Biophysics, 1985; co-editor: Colloid and Molecular Electro-optics, 1992. Mem. Bulgarian Phys. Soc. (v.p. 1983), Nat. Soc. for Biomed. Physics and Engring. (pres. 1981-84), nat. Biochem. and Biophys. Soc. (v.p. 1982-86), Internat. Com. for Molecular Electro-optics (v.p. 1991-94), N.Y. Acad. Sci. Avocations: travel, sports, music. Home: 48 Bul Simeonovsko Chaussee, 1434 Sofia Bulgaria Office: Bulgarian Acad Scis, Inst Phys Chemistry, 1113 Sofia Bulgaria

STOYTCHEV, LUBEN IVANOV, geologist; b. Sofia, Bulgaria, Mar. 6, 1932; arrived in Belgium, 1972; s. Ivan Kristev Stoytchev and Ludmila Petrova Berova; m. Louchka Radeva Findjikova, July 27, 1968; 1 child, Kristina. MSc in Mining Engring., High Poly. Sch., Sofia, 1955, MSc in Exploration Geology, 1967; PhD in Mining and Geol. Engring., Pacific Western U., 1990. Underground mining engr. States Collieries, Sofia, 1955-56; designing engr. MINPROEKT Coal Mining Inst., Sofia, 1957-61, sr. design engr., 1965-68, head operational rsch. team, 1968-72; sr. geologist States Mines, Botevgrad, Bulgaria, 1961-62; sr. engr. NIPROROODA Metal Mining Inst., Sofia, 1962-65; retrainee INIEX, Liege, Belgium, 1972-73; mgmt. cons. CEDEC, S.A., Brussels, 1973-78; chief engr. Gen. Carrieres et Mines (GECAMINES), Lubumbashi, 1978-79; assemblyman operation of studies Miniere de Bak Wanga (MIBA), Mbujimayi, 1980-91; control Mondial Engring. Constrn., Liege, 1991-92; project initator SAMI Engring., Herstal, Belgium, 1998—; cons. geologist J.J. Internat. Engring. Cons., Liege, 1999—. Contbr. articles to profl. jours. Avocation: reading about economy, history and politics. Home: Esplanade de la Pain 4194, 4040 Herstal Liege, Belgium

STOZICKY, FRANTISEK VACLAV, pediatrician; b. Budyne, Czech Republic, Aug. 8, 1941; s. Frantisek and Paulina (Mackova) S.; m. Olga Vera Vahalova, June 21, 1975; children: Frantisek, Jan, Jana. MD, Charles U., Prague, Czech Republic, 1966, D of Med. Scis., 1990. Pediatrician Regional Hosp., Ústí, Czech Republic, 1966-75; asst. prof. pediatrics Charles U., Prague, Czech Republic, 1975-82; assoc. prof. Charles U., Pilsen, Czech Republic, 1982—; cons. in field. Author: Apolipoproteins-Biochemistry and Clinical Significance, 1990; inventor in field. Mem. Czech Med. Soc., Czech Pediatric Soc., Czech Atherosclerosis Group (pres. 1992-96). Avocations: lawn tennis, football. Home: Kaznejovska 3, 323 20 Plzeň Czech Republic Office: Charles U Dept Pediatrics, Husova 13, 306 05 Plzeň Czech Republic

STRACHAN, WILLIAM JOHN, optical engineer; b. West Orange, N.J., Feb. 21, 1970. BS, Seton Hall U., 1992; MS, U. Mass., 1995. Tchg. asst. U. Mass., 1992-95; laser engr. Light Age, Inc., Somerset, N.J., 1995-98, sr. laser engr., 1998-99; applications engr. RD Automation, Piscataway, N.J., 1999-2000; rsch. and devel. engr. JDS Uniphase, W. Trenton, N.J., 2000—. Mem. assessment com., exec. bd. Lit. Vols. Am., chief fin. officer, Literacy Vols. Am., 1999—. Mem. Am. Phys. Soc., Optical Soc. Am. Office: JDS Uniphase Epitaxx Divsn 7 Graphics Dr West Trenton NJ 08628-1547

STRACHER, DOROTHY ALTMAN, education educator, consultant; b. N.Y.C., May 11, 1934; d. Joseph and Gussie (Newman) Altman; m. Alfred Stracher, July 4, 1954; children: Cameron Altman, Adam Reed, Erica Terri. BA, Bklyn. Coll., 1955; MA, Columbia U., 1957; postgrad., U. Copenhagen, 1958-59; acad. vis., Oxford (Eng.) U., 1973-74; PhD, Hofstra U., 1979. Cert. English and social sci. tchr., N.Y. Coordinator secondary reading Cen. Moriches (N.Y.) Sch. Dist., 1974-78; coordinator reading Ea. Williston (N.Y.) Sch. Dist., 1978-79; specialist reading and writing SUNY, Old Westbury, 1979-81; adj. prof. dept. reading Hofstra U., Hempstead, N.Y., 1979-82; asst. prof. edn. L.I. U., Bklyn., 1982-83, Coll. New Rochelle, N.Y., 1983-85; sr. learning diagnostic specialist child devel. div. L.I. Jewish Hosp., Bklyn., 1985-86; prof. Dowling Coll., Oakdale, N.Y., 1986—, acad. chair Sch. Edn., 1991-93; coord. elem. edn. dept. Dowling coll., Oakdale, N.Y., 1997-99; vis. prof. U. East London, London, 1994; cons. Johnson & Johnson, Inc., Princeton, N.J., 1982—, Sanford (Fla.) Sch. Dist., 1983, Lawrence (N.Y.) Sch. Dist., 1984, Sch. Dist. 7, N.Y.C., 1984—. Author: (with others) First the Fundamentals, 1980, What Do You Call a Well-Behaved Martian?, A Manual For Thinkers' Parents, 1981, Integrating Assessment, 1982; editor: Differentiated Curricula, 1986, A Literature Based Integrated Curriculum: Grades Pre-K-, 1989, Successful Strategies for Learning Disabled College Students: Reading, Writing and Reasoning, 1991; contbr. articles to profl. jours. Bd. dirs. Roslyn (N.Y.) Sch. Dist., 1975-84, v.p., 1980-82, pres., 1982-84; mem. adv. bd. Children's Sch. Sci., Woods Hole, Mass., 1976-82. Mem. Coun. for Exceptional Children, Orton Soc., Internat. Reading Assn., Nat. Assn. for Gifted Edn., LWV (bd. dirs. 1961-70), NOW, Kappa Delta Pi. Avocations: reading, writing, traveling. Home: 47 The Oaks Roslyn NY 11576-1704

STRACK, HAROLD ARTHUR, retired electronics company executive, retired air force officer, planner, analyst, author, musician; b. San Francisco, Mar. 29, 1923; s. Harold Arthur and Catheryn Jenny (Johnsen) S.; m. Margaret Madeline Decker, July 31, 1945; children: Carolyn, Curtis, Tamara. Student, San Francisco Coll., 1941, Sacramento Coll., 1947, Sacramento State Coll., 1948, U. Md., 1962, Indsl. Coll. Armed Forces, 1963. Commd. 2d lt. USAAF, 1943; advanced through grades to brig. gen. USAF, 1970; comdr. 1st Radar Bomb Scoring Group Carswell AFB, Ft. Worth, 1956-59; vice comdr. 90th Strategic Missile Wing SAC Warren AFB, Cheyenne, Wyo., 1964; chief, strategic nuclear br., spl. studies group Joint Chiefs of Staff, 1965-67, dep. asst. to chmn. JCS for strategic arms negotiations, 1968; comdr. 90th Strategic Missile Wing SAC Warren AFB, Cheyenne, 1969-71; chief Studies, Analysis and Gaming Agy. Joint Chiefs

Staff, Washington, 1972-74, ret., 1974; v.p., mgr. MX Peacekeeper Program v.p. strategic planning Northrop Electronics Divsn., Hawthorne, Calif., 1974-88; ret., 1988. 1st clarinetist, Cheyenne Symphony Orch., 1969-71. Mem. Cheyenne Frontier Days Com., 1970-71. Decorated D.S.M., Legion of Merit, D.F.C., Air medal, Purple Heart. Mem. Order Pour le Merite, Inst. Nav., Am. Def. Preparedness Assn., Air Force Assn., Aerospace Edn. Found., Am. Fedn. Musicians, Order Pour le Merite, Cheyenne Frontier Days "Heels". Home: 707 James Ln Incline Village NV 89451-9612

STRADA, MAURO, engineering educator; b. Padua, Italy, May 19, 1951; s. Ostelio and Ezia (Gallato) S.; m. Emma Riccio, May 27, 1993; children: Gianluca, Andrea, Angela. Degree in engring., U. Padua, 1974. Asst. prof. dept. mech. engring. U. Padua, Italy, 1974-83, prof., 1983-90; prof. Istituto Univ. di Architettura di Venezia, Venice, Italy, 1990—; dir. Steam s.r.l., Padua; owner, Studio Strada, Padua, 1980-92. Contbr. articles to profl. jours.; author: Technical Acoustic, 1983. Mem. Associazione Italiana Condizionamento Areazione Riscaldamento Refrigerazione. Roman Catholic. Avocation: bridge. Office: STEAM srl, Via Dante 58, 35139 Padua Italy

STRADLEY, WILLIAM JACKSON, lawyer; b. Houston, Oct. 27, 1939; s. Samuel H. and Mary Stradley; m. Emmalee H. Stradley, Apr. 16, 1960; children—Lisa D., William M. B.S., U. Houston, 1964; J.D., 1967. Bar: Tex. 1967, U.S. Dist. Ct. (so. dist.) Tex. 1967, U.S. Ct. Appeals (5th cir.)1967, U.S. Supreme Ct. 1970. Cert. Civil Trial Law, Personal Injury Trial Law Tex. Bd. of Legal Specialization. of coun. Mithoff & Jacks, L.L.P. mem. faculty trial advocacy course Law Sch. U. Houston, 1982. Pres., Police Adv. Com. 1981-84, sec., 1980-81; bd. dirs. Houston Council Human Relations, 1982-84; mem. adminstrv. bd. St. Luke's United Meth. Ch.; co-chair fed. judiciary appointments com. State Bar Tex., 1991, mem. continuing legal edn. com., 1991, adminstrn. justice com., spl. com. professionalsm. Recipient Pub. Service award Houston Police Dept., 1984. Mem. Houston Bar Found. (charter), Am. Bd. Trial Advocates (pres., treas. 1980-82, v.p. 1983-84 Houston), State Bar of Tex. (chmn. grievance com.), Supreme Ct. Tex. (mem. profl. ethics com. 1984-94), Houston Trial Lawyers Assn. (bd. dirs. 1980-82, v.p. 1983-84, pres. 1985-86), Houston Bar Assn. (chmn. tort and compensation sect. 1980-81, chmn. continuing legal edn. com., com. on professionalism), Tex. Trial Lawyers Assn. (dir. emeritus, chmn. ethics com., by-laws com.), Assn. Trial Lawyers Am., Houston Club, Met. Racquet Club. Home: 64 E Broad Oaks Dr Houston TX 77056-1226 Office: 3450 One Allen Ctr Houston TX 77002

STRAEDE, CHRISTEN ANDERSEN, research center administrator; b. Kloster, Denmark, Dec. 19, 1952; s. Anders Andersen and Christine (Christensen) S.; m. Lili Bay Kristensen, Apr. 29, 1989 (div.); m. Doris L. Larsen, Aug. 19, 2000. MSc in Physics and Math., U. Aarhus, Denmark, 1981; PhD in Physics, Cen. Bur. Nuclear Measurement, Geel, Belgium, 1985. Fellow CBNM European Atomic Energy Community, Geel, 1982-85; project mgr. Danish Technol. Inst., Aarhus, 1985-92; mgr. Ctr. for Surface Tech., Aarhus, 1989-94; sect. mgr. tribolog ctr. Danish Tech. Inst., Aarhus, 1992-93, mgr. tribolog centre, 1993—, frame program mgr. low temperature surface tech., 1994-97, mgr. Ctr. for Indsl. Material Physics and Tribology, 1996-99, mgr. Ctr. for Materials Tech., 1999—; EC expert, surface engr. Commn. European Communities-Basic Rsch. in Indsl. Techs. in Europe/European Rsch. on Advanced Materials, Brussels, 1989-95; Danish nat. rep. Versailles Project on Advanced Materials and Standards Tech. Working Area-Wear Test Methods, 1991—; conf. presenter in field.; mem. internat. com. Internat. Conf. Surface Modification of Metals by I on Beams; mem. adv. bd. surface techs. for Danish Rsch. Counsels, 1997—. Contbr. articles to sci. jours. and conf. proc. Fellow CEC, 1982-85. Home: Grundbirgsveg 22, DK-8600 Silkeborg Denmark Office: Danish Technol Inst, Teknologiparken, DK-8000 Århus Denmark

STRAHILEVITZ, MEIR, inventor, researcher, psychiatry educator; b. Beirut, July 13, 1935; s. Jacob and Chana Strahilevitz; m. Aharona Nattiv, 1958; children: Michal, Lior. MD, Hadassah Hebrew U. Med. Sch., 1963. Diplomate Am. Bd. Psychiatry and Neurology, Royal Coll. Physicians and Surgeons Can. Asst. prof. Washington U. Med. Sch., St. Louis, 1971-74; assoc. prof. So. Ill. U., Springfield, 1974-77, U. Chgo., 1977, U. Tex. Med. Br., Galveston, 1978-81; chmn. dept. psychiatry Kaplan Hosp., Rehovot, Israel, 1987-88; clin. assoc. prof. U. Wash., Seattle, 1981-88; prof. U. Tex. Med. Sch., Houston, 1988-92. Contbr. articles to profl. jours. Fellow Am. Psychiat. Assn., Royal Coll. Physicians and Surgeons Can. Achievements include patents for immunological methods for removing species from the blood circulatory system, for treatment methods for psychoactive drug dependence, for immunological methods for treating mammals; methods of improved targeting of drugs and visualization ligands, particularly in the treatment and diagnosis of cancer; invention of use of antibodies to receptors and their fragments as drugs, of immunoadsorption treatment of hyperlipidemia, cancer, autoimmune disease and coronary artery disease, immunoassay methods for psychoactive drugs; discovery of the protective effects of Nitric Oxide (NO) on psychiatric patients. Office: PO Box 25008 Seattle WA 98125-1908

STRAHLER, ALAN H., geography educator, author, researcher; b. N.Y.C., Apr. 27, 1943; s. Arthur Newell and Margaret Elizabeth S.; m. Kristi Margaret Schrader, Feb. 4, 1967; 1 child, Amy Leona. BA, The Johns Hopkins U., 1964, PhD, 1969. Asst. prof. U. Va., Charlottesville, 1969-74; asst. then assoc. prof. U. Calif., Santa Barbara, 1974-82; prof. Hunter Coll., N.Y.C., 1982-88, Boston U., 1988—; mem. (selected) Moderate-Resolution Imaging Spectometer Sci. Team, NASA, 1989. Author, co-author phys. geography textbooks including 9 major titles in 13 edits.; contbr. numerous articles to profl. publs. Recipient numerous grants NSF and NASA, 1978—, Outstanding Contbrs. to Remote Sensing medal Assn. Am. Geographers, 1993. Achievements include development of body of research on remote sensing of forests and vegetation emphasizing mathematical models of forest structure and viewing of forests by imaging instruments on space-borne platforms. Home: 225 Brattle St Cambridge MA 02138-4623 Office: Boston U Dept of Geography 675 Commonwealth Ave Boston MA 02215-1406

STRAIT, VIOLA EDWINA WASHINGTON, librarian; b. El Paso, Tex., Aug. 29, 1925; d. Leroy Wentworth and Viola Edwina (Wright) Washington; m. Freeman Adams, Mar. 6, 1943; 1 child, Norma Jean (Mrs. Louis Lee James); m. Clifford Moody, Jan. 8, 1950; 1 child, Viola Edwina III (Mrs. Paul M. Cunningham); m. Amos O. Strait, Dec. 9, 1972. Bus. cert., Tillotson Coll., 1946, BA, 1948; MS in Libr. Sci., U. So. Calif., 1954. Substitute tchr. El Paso Pub. Schs., 1948; sec., bookkeeper U.S.O.-YWCA, El Paso, 1948-50; libr. asst. Spl. Svcs. Libr., Ft. Bliss, Tex., 1950-53, libr., 1954-71; equal employment opportunity officer Ft. Bliss, 1971-72; dep. equal employment opportunity officer Long Beach (Calif.) Naval Shipyard, 1972-85; with Temp. Job Mart, Torrance, Calif., 1986-87; substitute tchr. Ysleta Ind. Sch. Dist., 1988-89; profl. libr. Eastwood Hts. Elem. Sch., 1989-90; sec. Shiloh Bapt. Ch., El Paso, 1991-92; br. mgr. El Paso Pub. Libr., 1992-96, retired, 1996. Sec. Sunday sch. Bapt. Ch., 1956-66, 92-96, min. music, 1958-72, supr. young adult choir, 1966-72, pres. sr. choir, 1969-71; disc jockey Sta. KELP, El Paso, 1970-72; host radio show Sta. KTEP, U. Tex., El Paso, 1994—. Mem. ALA, Border Region Libr. Assn. (chmn. scholarship com. 1970), NAACP (sec. 1996), Alpha Kappa Alpha. Democrat. Baptist. Avocations: playing the piano and organ, public speaking, reading, ocean view dining. Home: 1667 Nancy Lopez Ln El Paso TX 79936-5410

STRAJA, SORIN RADU, chemical engineer, mathematician, computer programmer; b. Bucharest, Romania; s. Radu and Sonica Straja; m. Mihaela Cirstea, Mar. 26, 1982. MS, Poly. Inst., Bucharest, 1979, PhD, 1987. Chem. engr. Plastics Processing, Bucharest, 1979-81; rsch. and devel. cons. Chem. and Biochem. Energetics Inst., Bucharest, 1982-89; cons., vol. USDA, Washington, 1991-92; chemist U. Md., Balt., 1992-93; dir. occupational health and safety dept. Temple U., Phila., 1993-95, asst. prof. stats., 1994—; v.p. Inst. Regulatory Sci., Columbia, Md., 1996—; cons. Montgomery Investment Tech., Radnor, 1995—. Editor: Environmental International, 1993-99; contbg. editor: Technology, 1996—; contbr. numerous articles to profl. jours. Recipient Nicolae Teclu award Romanian Acad. Scis., 1983. Mem. AIChE, ACS, N.Y. Acad. Sci., Soc. Risk Analysis. Avocations: history, geography. Office: Inst Regulatory Sci 5457 Twin Knolls Rd Ste 408 Columbia MD 21045-3297

STRAKA, HERBERT KARL, botany educator; b. Brünn, Moravia, July 14, 1920; s. Rudolf and Gisela (Petsch) S.; m. Gertrud Ketzler, Dec. 19, 1951. PhD, U. Bonn., Germany, 1951; PhD (hon.), U. Rennes, France, 1973. Asst. U. Kiel, Fed. Republic Germany, 1951-54, docent, 1954-60, prof. botany, 1960—. Author: Vulkaneifel, 1951, Mesembryanthemes, 1954, Madagascar/Mascarenes, 1964, Palynology, 1970. Named Chevalier Order Nat. Malgache, Antanavarivo, 1987. Mem. Swedish Soc. Plant Geography (corr. mem.), Madagascan Acad. (corr. mem.), Sudeto-Germany Acad., N.Y. Acad. Scis., Acad. Sci. Outre-Mer (Paris), Czech Bot. Soc. (hon.). Avocations: photography, folklore. Home: Forstweg 47, Schleswig-Holstein, D24105 Kiel Germany Office: U Botan Inst, Olshausenstrasse 40, D24098 Kiel Germany

STRAKA, JOHN ANTHONY, otolaryngologist; b. Pitts., 1942. MD, Creighton U., 1966. Diplomate Am. Bd. Otolaryngology. Intern Mercy Hosp., Pitts., 1966-67, resident, 1967-71; resident Allegheny Gen. Hosp., Pitts., 1967-71; pvt. practice; mem. staff Eye and Ear Hosp., Pitts.; mem. sr. active staff Children's Hosp. Pitts., St. Francis Hosp., Pitts., Suburban Gen. Hosp., Sewickley Valley Hosp., Allegheny Gen. Hosp., Western Pa. Hosp.; clin. asst. prof. U. Pitts. Mem. AMA, ACS, ARS, Am. Acad. Facial and Plastic Reconstructive Surgery, Am. Acad. Otolaryngology-Head and Neck Surgery, Soc. Univ. Otolaryngologists. Address: 1099 Ohio River Blvd Sewickley PA 15143-2056 also: 3471 5th Ave Pittsburgh PA 15213-3215

STRAKA, LASZLO RICHARD, publishing consultant; b. Budapest, Hungary, June 22, 1934; came to U.S., 1950, naturalized, 1956; s. Richard J. and Elisabeth (Roeck) S.; m. Eva K. von Viczian, Jan. 20, 1962 (div. May 1981); children: Eva M., Monika E., Viktoria K. B.A. cum laude, NYU, 1959. Acct. Greatrex Ltd., N.Y.C., 1952-53; pres. Maxwell Macmillan Internat. Pub. Group, N.Y.C., 1991-92; with Pergamon Press, Inc., Elmsford, N.Y., 1954-90, v.p., 1964-68, exec. v.p., treas., 1968-74, pres., 1974-75, 80-88, chmn. bd., 1975-77, 88-90, vice chmn. bd., 1977-80, 88-89, also dir.; vice chmn. bd. Pergamon Books Ltd., Oxford, Eng., 1986-88; group v.p. Macmillan Inc., N.Y.C., 1989-91; pub. cons., 1992—; treas. Brit. Book Centre, Inc., N.Y.C., 1956-67; pres. Pergamon Holding Corp., 1981-86; chmn. bd. Microforms Internat., Inc., 1971-87. d. dirs., sec. Szechenyi Istvan Soc., N.Y.C., 1967-80, 89-93. Mem. Phi Beta Kappa. Home and Office: 80 Radnor Ave Croton On Hudson NY 10520-2610

STRAKA, RONALD MORRIS, physicist; b. Reading, Pa., Apr. 22, 1935; s. Morris Richard and Irene (Gurtowski) S.; children: Erika Jane, Sonya Ellen. B of Engring. Sci., Johns Hopkins U., 1957, postgrad., 1957-58. Rsch. asst. Carnegie Instn., Washington, summer 1955, Astrophysics Lab., Johns Hopkins U., Balt., 1957-58; rsch. physicist Air Force Cambridge Rsch. Labs., Bedford, Mass., 1958-77; phys. scientist Air Force Sys. Command Hdqrs., Andrews AFB, Md., 1977-79; physicist Air Force Geophysics Lab., Bedford, 1979-91, ret., 1991; NATO fgn. sci. cons. U. Athens (Greece), 1964; sr. sci. cons. SENCOM Corp, Bedford, 1994-99. Photography exhbns. include Carl Siembab Gallery, Boston, DeCordova Mus., Lincoln, Mass., Boston Mus. Fine Arts, Mpls. Art Inst.; contbr. articles to profl. jours. Dir. photography Boston Ctr. Adult Edn., 1969-77; bd. dirs. Rockport Chamber Music Festival. Recipient Sci. Achievement award USAF, 1971, 84; NSF grantee, 1964. Mem. N.Y. Acad. Scis., Internat. Sci. Radio Union, Rockport Art Assn. (bd. trustees), North Shore Arts Assn. (pres. 1995-96), Acad. Arts Assn., Internat. Soc. Marine Painters, U.S. Senatorial Club, Air War Coll. Alumni Assn., U.S. Figure Skating Assn., Sigma Xi. Home: 40 Granite St Rockport MA 01966-1310 Office: AF Rsch Lab Hanscom AFB MA 01731

STRAKA, THOMAS JAMES, forester, educator; b. Chippewa Falls, Wis., Dec. 17, 1949; s. James Otto and Elieen Helen S.; m. Patricia Casciere, Feb. 14, 1976. BS, U. Wis., 1972, MS, 1973; MBA, U. S.C., 1978; PhD, Va. Tech. U., 1981. Registered forester, S.C., Miss. Porject forester Internat. Paper Co., Georgetown, S.C., 1974-78; grad. rsch. asst. Va. Tech. U., Blacksburg, 1978-81; assoc. prof. Miss. State U., Mississippi State, 1982-89; prof. Clemson U., S.C., 1989—. Mem. Appalachian Soc. Am. Foresters (chair 2000), Miss. Soc. Am. Foresters (chair 1987), Miss. Forestry Assn. (bd. dirs. 1984-89), Forest Products Soc., Lions, Kiwanis, Xi Sigma Pi, Sigma Xi. Republican. Episcopalian. Home: 130 Timber Trl Westminster SC 29693-5366 Office: Clemson U Dept Forest Resources PO Box 340331 Clemson SC 29634-0001

STRANADKO, EUGENY PHILIPPOVICH, oncologist, educator; b. Wiksa, Russia, July 14, 1937; m. Dina Michailovna Gorskaya, June 27, 1962 (div. Oct. 1980); children: Svetlana, Sergey; s. Lioudmila Michailovna Zelentsova, June 12, 1982. MD, State Med. Inst., Gorky, USSR, 1961; PhD, State Ctrl. Inst. Med. Edn., Moscow, 1969; prof. degree in oncology, Laser Acad. Scis. Russia, 1996. Head surg. dept. Vladimir (USSR) Dist. Hosp., 1961-65; aspirant oncology chair Ctrl. Inst. Postgrad. Med. Edn., Moscow, 1965-68; rschr. dept. esophageal and gastric surgery State Sci. Inst. Clin. and Exptl. Surgery, Moscow, 1968-75, sr. rschr., 1975-78; sr. rschr. P.A. Hertzen Moscow Cancer Rsch. Inst., 1978-83, head anticancer dept., 1983-88; gen. oncologist Med. Dir. Moscow, 1988-92; head dept. laser oncology and photodynamic therapy State Rsch. Ctr. Laser Medicine, 1992—. Co-author: Cancer of the Lung, 1971, Atlas of Oncological Operations, 1982; author: Photodynamic Therapy of Skin Cancer, 1996, Photodynamic Therapy of Malignant Tumors, 1999. Mem. SPIE, Cancer Soc. Russia, Oncologist's Club. Avocations: skiing, hunting, wind surfing. Fax: 007-095-249 3905. E-mail: geinic@cityline.ru. Home: Krivorozhskaya St 13-58, 113638 Moscow Russia Office: State Rsch Ctr Laser Med, Studentcheskaya St 40, 121165 Moscow Russia

STRAND, ERLING PETTER, computer and electronic engineering educator; b. Sarpsborg, Østfold, Norway, May 31, 1955; s. Reidar R. and Hjørdis A. (Olseng) S.; m. Bente Kristin Slommerud, July 14, 1979; children: Lars Kristoffer, Kristin Elise. Grad. in engring., Østfold Coll., 1977; MSc, U. Trondheim, Norway, 1981. Rschr. Alcatel Stk, Oslo, 1981-85; rsch. dir. Edas Målesystemer, Eidsvoll, Norway, 1985-88; instr. computer and electronic engring. Østfold Coll., Sarpsborg, 1988—; rsch. mgr. Project Hessdalen, Sarpsborg, 1983—; organizer 1st internat. workshop on unidentified atmospheric light phenomena in Hessdalen, 1994; participant numerous TV and radio programs throughout world. Co-author: UFO-Fenomenet-Kan det Umuligevaere Mulig, 1987; author: (tech. report) Project Hessdalen. Avocation: science on unknown phenomena. Home: Bukkholmveien, N-1747 Skjeberg Norway Office: Høgskolen i Østfold Coll, Tuneveien 20, N-1705 Sarpsborg Norway

STRANG, PETER MIKAEL, oncologist, researcher; b. Karleby, Finland, Aug. 1, 1957; s. Robert and Ulla (Wedenberg) S. MD, Uppsala (Sweden) U., 1983, PhD, 1987. Asst. physician Uppsala U. Hosp., 1981-84, resident in oncology and radiotherapy, 1985-88, oncologist, radiotherapist, 1989-93, assoc. prof., 1990-97, chief oncologist, 1993-97; prof. palliative medicine Linköping U., Norrköping, Sweden, 1997—; sci. counselor Swedish Nat. Bd. Health and Welfare, 1994—; prof. palliative medicine Linköping U., 1997—. Author 6 textbooks (Swedish); contbr. numerous articles to profl. jours. Mem. Internat. Gynecol. Cancer Soc., European Soc. Radiotherapy and Oncology, European Soc. Psychosocial Oncology, European Assn. Palliative Care. Avocations: music, sailing, jogging. Office: Linköping Univ, Palliative Rsch Unit, 60182 Norrkoping Sweden

STRANO, MARCO, criminologist, researcher; b. Rome, Aug. 12, 1959; s. Francesco and Maria Teresa (Visani) S. Degree in sociology, U. Rome, 1989; degree in clin. psychology, Italian Ctr. Clin. Psychology, Rome, 1992. Cert. psychologist. Rschr. U. Rome, 1990-98; rsch. mgr. Cath. U. Rome, 1998—, rschr., 1998—; pres. Inst. Criminology Rsch., Rome, 1998; cons. Italian Police Force, 1990. Author: Mafia Development and Criminal Technology, 1994, New Frontier of Crime, 1997, Research in Criminology, 1999, Criminology Handbook, 2000, Computer Crime, 2000; webmaster: www.criminologia.org. Mem. Am. Psychol. Assn., Acad. Tiberina, N.Y. Acad. Scis. E-mail: strano@skynet.it.

STRANSKY, MAREK, public relations company executive; b. Prague, Dec. 11, 1971; s. Karel Stransky and Jindra (Bicanova) Stranska; m. Gabriela Stejskalova, July 1998. BA, Carleton U., Ottawa, Can., 1991; MA, Charles U., Prague, 1995, PhD, 2000. Mgr. Honda Czech Republic (Fintraco), Prague, 1991-93; sr. assoc. Burson-Marsteller, Prague, 1993-97; exec. dir. AMI Comms. Edelman Public Rels. Worldwide, Prague, 1997—, mng. ptnr., 1998—; cons. Boeing, 1996-98, Bass Plc, U.K., 1998—, Orange Plc, U.K., 1998—, GE Capital, 1998. Contbr. articles to profl. jours. Active Freedom Union Party Polit. Affiliation, Prague, 1998—. Mem. Czech Pub. Rels. Club, Navy League U.S. Avocations: sports, political science, aviation, history, public relations. Home: Spanielova 1247, 16300 Prague 6, Czech Republic Office: AMI Comms Edelman Pub Rels, Michalska 3, 11000 Prague Czech Republic Address: M Stranskmy, Krolmusova 40, 163 00 Prague Czech Republic

STRASBURG, DUDLEY, investment counselor; b. Cleve., July 6, 1925; s. Roy Strasburg and Billye (Goldman) Donigian; m. Jacqueline Kretz (div. 1968); children: Tor, Robin. BA, UCLA, 1948; MA, Columbia U., 1949; postgrad., The Sorbonne, Paris, 1949-50. Editor Exposition Press, N.Y.C., 1950-51, World Pub. Co., N.Y.C., 1951-53, Harlem Book Co., N.Y.C., 1954-56; investment counselor Investors Overseas Svcs., Wiesbaden, Germany, 1957-59, reg. mgr., 1959-63, gen. mgr. for Europe, 1963-69; gen. mgr. for Europe Piedmont Mgmt. Co., Wiesbaden, 1969-72; founder, pres. Strasburg & Co., Wiesbaden, 1972—; pres. Assn. for Humanistic Psychology, Wiesbaden, 1972-93; lectr. in field. Author/editor: Assn. for Humanistic Psychology newsletter. With U.S. Army, 1944-46, ETO. Avocations: tennis, travel, music, lecturing and workshops for American, German and European groups on psychology, world history, music, and art. Home and Office: Kaiser Friedrichstr 11, 65193 Wiesbaden Hessen, Germany

STRASSBURG, HANS-MICHAEL, pediatrician; b. Buechenbeuren, Germany, June 2, 1948; s. Hans-Wolfgang and Ursel (Schueler) S.; m. Gabriele Wiedemann, May 24, 1974; children: Verena, Hans-Peter. MD, U. Tuebingen, 1972; habilitation in Pediatrics, U. Freiburg, 1987. Intern in pediatrics Children's U. Hosp., Freiburg, 1981, neuropediatrician, 1984, social medicine pediatrician, 1988; physician in social medicine Children's Ctr. Hosp., Munich, Bavaria, Germany, 1988; prof. in neuropediatrics Children's Univ. Hosp., Wuerzburg, Bavaria, Germany, 1991—; bd. dirs. Fruehdiagnosezentrum. Author: Cerebral Ultrasonography, 1985, The Crying Infant, 1989, Children With Developmental Disorders, 1997, 2000. Mem. Neuropediatric Soc., Pediat. and Social Pediat. Soc., Soc. Neurophysiology, Soc. Ultrasound in Medicine, Gegen Vergessen-für Demokratie, Aerzte für die Dritte Welt, Ethical Commn. Faculty Medicine Würzburg. Avocations: classical music, history, walking. Office: Childrens Univ Hosp, Josef Schneiderstr 2, 97080 Wuerzburg Bavaria, Germany

STRASSEN, VOLKER, retired mathematics educator; b. Dusseldorf-Gerresheim, Germany, Apr. 29, 1936; s. Otto Albert and Caroline Katharina (Lafrentz) S.; m. Edith Schienmann; children: Tyko, Till, Olaf, Otto, Katrin, Anna. Masters, U. Gottingen, Fed. Republic of Germany, 1961; PhD, U. Gottingen, 1962; Habil., U. Erlangen, Fed. Republic of Germany, 1966. Instr. dept. math. U. Calif., Berkeley, 1962-63, asst. prof. stats. dept., 1963-64, 1966-67, assoc. prof. stats. dept., 1967-68, vis. Miller prof., 1972-73; fellow Deutsche Forschungsgemeinschaft, 1964-66; prof. Inst. Applied Maths. U. Zurich, Switzerland, 1968-88; gastforscher Gesellsch. Mathematik Datenver., Bonn, Fed. Republic of Germany, 1976-77; prof. U. Konstanz, Fed. Republic of Germany, 1988-99. Recipient Cantor medal Deutsche Mathematiker Vereinigung, 1999. Mem. Deutsche Akademie der Naturforscher Leopoldina, Akademie der Wissenschaften zu Göttingen (corr.), Heidelberger Akademie der Wissenschafen. Home: Schubertstr 3, 78464 Konstanz Germany

STRASSER, HELMUT, ergonomics, educator, researcher; b. Dillingen, Germany, June 10, 1942; m. Ursula Strasser, Aug. 8, 1969; children: Angelika, Christian. Dipl.-ing., Tech. Univ., Munich, 1968, Dr.-ing., 1972. Group mgr. U. Munich, 1972-86, priv.-doz., 1981-86; prof. U. Siegen, 1986—; mem. sci. adv. bd. Zeitschrift fuer Arbeitswissenschaft, 1988, Zentralblatt fuer Arbeitsmedizin, 1990; adv. bd. Fed. Min. of Rsch. and Tech., Germany, 1977. Author: (in German) Ergonomic Methods for the Assessment of Strain, 1982, Favorable Movements for an Ergonomic Work Design - Electromyographic Investigations into the Hand-Arm System, 1992, Ergonomic Rating of Environmental Stress, 1995, Strain-Oriented Planning and Design of Manual Work, 1996. Mem. Gesellschaft für Arbeitswissenschaft, Soc. of Indsl. Ergonomics and Safety, Internat. Found. of Indsl. Ergonomics and Safety Rsch., Deutsche Physiologische Gesellschaft. Office: Univ Siegen, U Siegen, Paul Bonatz Str 9-11, D-57068 Siegen Germany

STRASSER, HERMANN, sociology educator; b. Altenmarkt/Pg., Salzburg, Austria, Nov. 28, 1941; arrived in Fed. Republic Germany, 1978; s. Franz and Elisabeth (Pichler) S.; m. Gudrun Brunhilde Hinz, Aug. 16, 1968; children: Sandra E., Mark H. Diploma in Econs., U. Innsbruck, Austria, 1964; Dr. rer. oec., U. Innsbruck, 1967; postgrad., Free U. Berlin, 1967-68; PhD in Sociology, Fordham U., 1974. Rsch. assoc. U. Innsbruck (Austria), 1968; teaching asst. Fordham U., Bronx, N.Y., 1968-69; teaching fellow Fordham U., 1969-71, rsch. asst., 1970-71; vis. prof. U. Okla., Norman, 1971-72; asst. prof. Inst. for Advanced Studies, Vienna, Austria, 1972-77; full prof. U. Duisburg, Fed. Republic Germany, 1978—, rsch. project dir., 1978—; dir. U. Placement Ctr. Akzent, 1997—; rsch. project dir. European Commn., Brussels, 1988-89; dir. verbal inst. prof. texts, Ratingen, 1992—. Author several books; contbr. articles to profl. jours. Fulbright grantee, Vienna, 1968-72, grantee German Sci. Found., 1985-89. Mem. Am. Sociol. Assn., Internat. Sociol. Assn., German Sociol. Assn., Austrian Sociol. Assn., German Am. Friendship Club, Rotary. Home: Forsthaus 9, D-40883 Ratingen 6, Germany Office: U Duisburg, Lotharstr 65, U Duisburg, D-47057 Duisburg 1, Germany

STRASSER, PATRICK, physicist; b. Bienne, Berne, Switzerland, June 4, 1963; s. Tony and Béatrice (Farine) S.; m. Ikuko Tanaka, Oct. 22, 1995; 1 child, Marina. Diploma in physics engring., Swiss Fed. Inst. Tech., Lausanne, 1988; DEng, U. Tokyo, 1994. Rsch. asst. Swiss Fed. Inst. Tech., Lausanne, 1988-89; COE postdoctoral rschr. Inst. Nuc. Study, U. Tokyo, 1995-97; postdoctoral fellow RIKEN, Muon Sci. Lab., Wako-shi, Japan, 1994-95, spl. postdoctoral rschr., 1997-2000; contract researcher RIKEN, Muon Sci. Lab., Wako-shi, 2000—; lectr. U. Tokyo, 1996-99. Mem. Japan Phys. Soc. Roman Catholic. Avocation: woodwork. Office: Inst Phys Chem Rsch, RIKEN, 2-1 Hirosawa, Muon Sci Lab, Wako-shi Saitama 351-0198, Japan

STRASSER, RUDOLF, law educator; b. Steyr, Austria, Feb. 9, 1923; s. Josef and Rosa Strasser; m. Margarethe Strasser; children: Helmuth, Klaus; m. 2d. Ilse Prischl, Dec. 23, 1969; 1 child, Thomas. LLD, U. Graz; LLD (hon.), U. Salzburg, 1988. Ofcl., dir. Bd. of Workers and Staff, Linz, Austria, 1949-67; mgr. Legal Dept. and Child Care Dept., Linz, 1949-67; adj. prof. law faculty U. Vienna, 1964; prof. law Acad. Soc. and Econ. Scis., Linz, 1965-75, Johannes-Kepler U., Linz, 1975-93; bd. dirs. Vöst-Alpine Stahl AG, Linz, Bauhütte Leitl GesmbH, Linz, Neuson AG, Linz, Inst. for Labor Law and Social Law, Linz; cons. Wissenschaft, Forschung und Kunst, Vienna, 1975-88; mgr. Rsch. Inst. for Univ. Law, Linz, 1980—, Inst. for Bus. Partnerships, Linz, 1973—; dir. steering adv. com. Inst. for Savs. Banks, Linz, 1975-96; dir. Inst. for Communal Scis., Linz, 1970-87. Author: Die Betriebsratswahl, 1953, 5th edit., 2000, Die Betriebsvereinbarung n. österr.udt. Recht, 1957, Der immaterielle Schaden im österr. Recht, 1964, Kollektivvertrag und Verfass, 1968, Die Beendigung d. Ges.n. bürgerl. Recht, 1969, Arbeitsrecht II, 1976, 3d edit., 1990, Betriebspension und Gleichbehandlung, 1991; co-author: Komm.z.Betr.rätegesetz, 1961, 2d edit., 1973, Die Universität als auton. Lehr-u., Forsch.unternehmen, 1968, Der Arbeitskampf, 1972, Kurzkomm.z.Arb.verfass.gesetz, 1974, 3d edit., 1999, Hdkomm.z. Arbverfass.gesetz m. dems. 75. Österr.Hochschulr., 1986, Labor-Law and Industrial Relations in Austria, 1992, Kommentar z. AktienG., 1993; contbr. articles to jours. and newspapers. Recipient Gold Svc. medal, 1967, Ring of Honor, City of Linz, 1968, Gold Svc. medal, 1971, Gold medal City of Vienna, 1979, Austria Cross for Sci. and Art 1st class, 1981, Gold Svc. medal, 1983, Culture prize of Upper Austria, 1991, Festschrifts in honor of Goth and Toth Birthdays. Mem. Social Dem. Party. Roman Catholic. Avocations: skiing, golf. Home: Hebenstreitrasse 11, A 4020 Linz Austria Office: Johannes-Kepler U, Altenbergerstrasse 69, 4040 Linz Austria

STRASSLER, JURG, linguist, researcher; b. Zurich, Switzerland, Feb. 17, 1951; s. Hanksjakob and Lilianne (Ruff) S. Diploma in philosophy, U. Zurich, 1977, DPhil, 1982; MPhil, U. Cambridge, Eng., 1980. Sr. tchr. Alte Kantonsschule, Aarau, Switzerland, 1981—; lectr. U. Zurich, 1994—; sr. asst. U. Berne, Switzerland, 1995—. Author: Idioms in English, 1982;

editor: Tendenzen Europaischer Linguistik, 1998; editl. asst. Multilingua, 1995—. Mem. Swiss Assn. Univ. Tchrs. English, Linguistics Assn. Gt. Britain, N.Y. Acad. Scis. Avocations: curling, athletics, folk music. Home: Stritengassli 44a, CH5000 Aarau Switzerland Office: U Berne, Langgassstrasse 49, CH3000 Bern Switzerland

STRATARIDAKIS, CONSTANTINE JOHN, aeronautical and mechanical engineer, consultant; b. Heraklion, Crete, Greece, Jan. 20, 1958; s. John Constantine and Aekaterina John (Chochlidakis) S.; m. Maria Emmanuel Segredakis, July 31, 1994; 1 child, Aekaterina. BS, U. Calif., Davis, 1980, MS, 1984, PhD, 1989. Rsch. asst./tchg. asst. U. Calif., 1980-86, assoc. instr., 1987-89; elected lectr. Tech. U. Crete, Chania, 1992—; cons. B.R. White Assocs.-Environ. Sci. Assocs., Inc., Davis, 1980-89; European interegional-projects coord. Regional Authority of Crete, 1991-93, 98—; project mgr. Ea. Crete Devel. Orgn., 1993-98; dir./founder Wind Farm Corp., Crete, 1993—; advisor Theseus S.A. Solar-Thermal Power Plant Devel., 1998—. Contbr. articles to profl. jours. Advisor to gov. Regional Authority Crete, 1991-93. Flight sgt. Greek Air Force, 1990-91. Recipient Edward Frank Graft scholarship U. Calif., 1977. Mem. AIAA (sr.), Tech. Chamber Greece. Home: Akadimias 95A, GR-71305 Heraklion Greece Office: SAM SA, 1770 str no 12, GR-71202 Heraklion Greece

STRATIL, ANTONÍN, animal geneticist, researcher; b. Nětčice, Czech Republic, June 11, 1941; s. Josef and Ludmila (Menšíková) S.; m. Anežka Ševčíková, Feb. 9, 1963; children: Přemysl, Jaromír. Ing. Agr., U. Agr., Brno, Czech Republic, 1963; PhD, Inst. Animal Physiol. Genetics, Liběchov, Czech Republic, 1968; DSc, U. Agr., Praha, Czech Republic, 1985. Rsch. scientist Inst. Animal Physiol. Genetics, Acad. Sci. Czech Republic, Liběchov, 1968-74, sr. scientist, 1974-82, chief scientist, 1982—, head rsch. group, 1973—, dep. dir., 1987-90. Co-author: Animal Genetics, 1978; contbr. articles to sci. jours. Recipient nat. prize Czech Nat. Assembly, Praha, 1977, prize Czechoslovak Acad. Sci., Praha, 1986, Hon. medal U. Agr., Brno, Czech Republic, 1989. Mem. Internat. Soc. Animal Genetics (com. mem. 1990-98), Gregor Mendel Genetics Soc., Czech Acad. Agrl. Sci. Roman Catholic. Home: Vinohradská 2229, 276 01 Mělník Czech Republic Office: Acad Sci Czech Republic, Inst Animal Physiology & Genetics, 277 21 Liběchov Czech Republic

STRATTON, JOHN ALFRED, mechanical engineer, educator; b. Rochester, N.Y., Sept. 12, 1941; s. Burton Elbridge Stratton and Alice Adele Howe; children: Thomas C., Linda S. Palmer, Ann-Marie O. AAS, Rochester Inst. Technology, 1962, BS, 1964; MSEE, Rensselaer Poly. Inst., Troy, N.Y., 1966. Profl. engr. Sys. planning engr. N.Y. State Elec. & Gas, Binghamton, 1966-69; asst. prof. Alfred (N.Y.) State Coll., 1969-71; from prof. elec. engring. technology to chair dept., dean Rochester Inst. Technology, 1971-99, chair mfg. & mech. engring. technology, pckg. sci., 1999—; cons. in field. Mem. IEEE, Inst. Power Engring. Soc., Am. Soc. Engring. Edn. Avocation: riding trains. e-mail: rit.edu. Home: 43 Queensway Rd Rochester NY 14623-4627 Office: Rochester Inst Technology 78 Lomb Memorial Dr Rochester NY 14623-5604

STRAUB, GERHARD HERBERT, manufacturing company executive; b. Munich, Aug. 11, 1936; s. Hugo and Maria (Jehle) S.; m. Gisela Ganzlin, Oct. 31, 1963; children: Stefan, Oliver, Florian. Diplom-kaufmann, Ludwig-Maximilian U., Munich, 1964. Comml. referee Mamnesmann AG, Huttenwerk Huckingen, Germany, 1964-66; substitute mgr. Suddeutsche Etna-Werk GmbH, Munich, 1966-73, gen. mgr., 1973—; mem. plenary meeting Industrie und Handelskammer, Munich, 1982—; pres. Walter Lehmann-Stiftung, Bonn, 1984—; chmn. EuropaausschuB im Landesverband der Bayerischen Industrie, Mittelstandsausschuss im Landesverband der Bayerischen Industrie, Munich, 1985—; vice chmn. foreign trade coun. IHK Munich, 1992—, dep. chmn., 1990—; comml. judge Landgericht Munich I, 1979—; bd. dirs., chmn. Vereinigung der Bayerischen, Munich 1998. Recipient order of merit award Fed. Rep. Germany 1st class. Mem. Bundesverband Heizung Klima Sanitar (exec. bd. 1980-84, pres. 1984—), Landesverband Heizungs-, Klima- u nd Sanitartechnik Bayern, Munich (exec. bd. 1975-78, 2d chmn. 1979-84, 1st chmn. 1985—). Avocations: painting, hockey. Office: Suddeutsche Etna-Werk GmbH, Einsteinstrasse 104 Pf 801623, 81616 Munich Germany

STRAUB, JOHANNES, mechanical engineer, educator; b. Ingolstadt, Bavaria, Germany; s. Otto Jakob and Katharin (Gutmann) S.; m. Barbara Dinter, Feb. 18, 1966; children: Florian Johannes, Markus Christoh, Bernhart Erich. M in Engring., Tech. U. Munich, 1957, DEng, 1965, Habilitation, 1976. Sci. asst. Tech. U. Munich, 1957-63, head engr., 1963-70, acad. dir., 1970-77, prof., 1977-98, prof. emeritus, 1998—; vis. prof., Ankara, Turkey, 1971, 76, Tokyo, 1975, Beijing, Wuhan, Nanjing, China, 1984, Tskuba, Japan, 1989, Fukuoka, Japan, 1995; head Inst. Thermodynamic, 1972-81; cons. in field. Editor: Water and Steam, 1979, Steam Tables, 1981, 3d edit. 1990, Heat Transfer, 1982; contbr. over 250 articles to profl. publs. Head European Youth Group, 1950-58. Mem. Alpine Club, Assn. German Engrs., Assn. for Space Rsch. Achievements include research in microgravity critical phenomena, heat transfer. Office: Tech U Munich, Thermodynamic, D85748 Garching Germany

STRAUB, LASZLO, engineering executive; b. Budapest, Hungary, Oct. 30, 1946; arrived in Germany, 1980; s. Elek Straub and Maria Szemerjay; m. Orsolya Rostas, Dec. 16, 1993; children: Gabriel Akos, Christoph Laszlo. MSc in Engring., Tech. U., Budapest, 1970, PhD in Engring., 1989. Sci. asst. Tech. U., Budapest, 1970-72; sci. mgr. Sci. Rsch. Inst. for Vehicle Safety, Budapest, 1972-74, sr. sci. mgr., 1974-80; sr. mgr. R & D Knorr-Bremse, Munich, 1980-94, v.p., 1994—; cons. Hwy. Traffic Safety Bd., Budapest, 1992—, Hwy. Vehicle Safety Adminstrn., Dept. of Transport, Bonn and Berlin, 1995—, Nat. Hwy. Traffic Safety Adminstrn., Washington, 1995—; chair German sect. UNO/ECE Expert Group Electronically Controlled Braking Systems, Geneva, Switzerland, 1995-96. Author: Vehicle Braking and Safety, 1972, Theory of Friction Processes, 1974 (sci. award), Theory of Vehicle Stability, 1976 (safety award Dept. of Transport), Vehicle Safety and Human Environment, 1979 (Environ. award Hungarian Acad. Scis.); inventor, patentee in field. Chair Vehicle Safety Bd., Hungary, 1978-80; senator Tech. U., Budapest, 1998—. Fellow German Assn. Vehicle Industry; mem. Inst. Mech. Engrs., Internat. Standardization Orgn. Avocations: tracking, sailing, literature, music.

STRAUB, LINDA CATHERINE, poet; b. Tampa, Fla., Sept. 12, 1948; d. Martin James and Alvena Mae (Carwile) Estep; m. Robert E. Straub, May 23, 1970 (div. Mar. 1991); children: Robert Jeffrey, Amy Catherine, Kyle Martin. Cert. exec. sec., Lansdale (Pa.) Sch. Bus., 1968. Mgr. adminstrv. br. Navy Resale and Support Svcs., Mechanicsburg, Pa., 1987-90; exec. sec. A.Z. Ritzman Assocs., Harrisburg, Pa., 1990-95; adminstrv. asst. HealthAm. of Pa., Harrisburg, 1996—. Contbr. poetry to profl. jours. Mem. Acad. Am. Poets. Avocations: guitar, reading, photography.

STRAUB, OTTO CHRISTIAN, veterinarian; b. Blaubeuren-Gerhausen, Germany, Dec. 11, 1930; s. Otto Friedrich and Babette (Mann) S.; m. Ursula Wannagat, May 8, 1965; children: Kristina Lotte, Ellen Babette, Christian Otto. D in Vet. Medicine, Vet. Coll., 1956; D in Vet. Medicine (hon.), U. Bucharest, 1994. Lectr., rsch. asst. specialist U. Calif., Davis, 1956-60; rsch. officer CSIRO, Parkville, Australia, 1960; scientific dir. Fed. Rsch. Ctr. Virus Diseases of Animals, Tubingen, Germany, 1961-95; pres. Vet. Coun., Baden-Württemberg, 1991; 1st v.p. Bundestierärztekammer, Germany, 1991-95. Author: Bovine Herpesvirusinfektioen, 1978; editor: Internat. Symposium on Bovine Leukosis, 1976, 80, 82, Tierärztl Umschau, 1978—. Decorated Order of Merit of the Fed. Republic of Germany, 1996; recipient Golden State medal of Baden-Württemberg, 1995. Mem. Acad. Tiergesundheit (v.p. 1991-97). Achievements include development of first proof of cell-mediated immunity caused by a virus; development of the first locally applicable vaccines against BHVI infections; introduction of the nowadays world-wide accepted procedure to combat bovine leukosis; first detection and description of Maedi/Visna and scrapie in sheep. Home: Im Schoenblick 71, 72076 Tübingen Germany Office: Paul Ehrlich-Str 28, D72076 Tübingen Germany

STRAUB, RAINER HANS, internist, rheumatologist, researcher; b. Freiburg, Germany, Mar. 29, 1960; s. Hans Paul and Ruth Maria (Ginter) S.; m. Verena Ursula Huber, Jul. 11, 1986; children: Isabella, Alexander, Volker. Staats examen, Univ., Freiburg, 1988, MD, 1988, habilitation, 1995. Jr. doctor Univ. Hosp., Freiburg, 1988-91, Regensburg, 1991-94; postdoctoral fellow Univ. Pharmacology, Vienna, Austria, 1994; sr. doctor Univ. Hosp., Regensburg, 1995—; rschr. in neuroendocrinoimmunology. Mem. German Soc. Immunology, German Soc. Internal Medicine, German Soc. Rheumatology. Roman Catholic. Office: Univ Hosp, Franz Josef Strauss Allee11, 93042 Regensburg Germany

STRAUBE, RICHARD HERMANN-PAUL, physician, clinical supervisor, researcher, inventor; b. Simmern, Germany, Feb. 27, 1957; s. Werner and Anna-Maria (Pfister) S.; m. Birgit Gudrun-Traudel Bialas, May 28, 1983; children: Alexander, Thomas, Jasmin, Yvonne. Diploma in Medicine, Johann-Wolfgang-Goethe U., Frankfurt, Germany, 1982, MD, 1983. Med. asst. Dist. Hosp. Lüdenscheid, Germany, 1983-90, chief diabetes edn. program, 1984-90, chief hyperbaric dept., 1988—, chief HIV/AIDS outpatient dept., 1989-90, chief asst. supr. dept. nephrology, 1990—, head apheresis care unit, 1991—; med. chief paramedic care unit Red Cross Germany, Lüedenscheid, 1983—, med. chief disaster rescue unit, 1985—, med. di8r., 1990; head med. edn. rescue medicine Dist. Hosp. Lüedenscheid, 1996—, dir. dept. rescue medicine, 1996-99. Inventor in field; contbr. articles to profl. jours. Co-pres. Assn. Med. Rehab., Lüedenscheid, 1992. Recipient Merit award Red Cross Germany, 1989, 92, 99. Fellow Internat. Soc. Apheresis, Clin. Nephrology Assn., Assn. Nephrology Germany, N.Y. Acad. Scis. Roman Catholic. Avocations: scuba diving, aquaristics, astronomy. E-mail: 0235149749@t-online.de. Home: Westerfelder Weg 65, 58515 Lüedenscheid Germany Office: Dist Hosp Lüedenscheid, Paulmannshoeherstrasse 14, 58515 Lüedenscheid Germany

STRAUCH, BERISH, plastic surgeon, hand and cosmetic surgeon; b. N.Y.C., Sept. 19, 1933; m. Rena Feuerstein, June 12, 1955; children: Robert, Laurie. BS, Columbia U., 1955, MD, 1959. Diplomate Am. Bd. Surgery, Am. Bd. Plastic Surgery, added qualification in hand surgery. Intern Bellevue Hosp., N.Y.C., 1959-60; resident gen. surgery Montefiore Med. Ctr., Bronx, 1960-63; hand surgery fellow Roosvelt Hosp., N.Y.C., 1961; resident plastic surgery Stanford U., Palo Alto, Calif., 1966-67, chief resident, 1967-68; asst. prof. plastic surgery Albert Einstein Coll. Medicine, Bronx, 1970-76, assoc. prof., 1976-81; chief plastic surgery svcs. Montefiore Med. Ctr. and Albert Einstein Coll. Medicine, Bronx, 1978-87; prof. plastic surgery Albert Einstein Coll. Medicine and Montefiore Med. Ctr., Bronx, N.Y., 1981—; acting chmn. dept. Montefiore Med. Ctr. and Albert Einstein Coll. Medicine, Bronx, 1987-89, chmn., 1989—; instr. Stanford U., 1967-68; vis. plastic surgeon Sing Sing (N.Y.) Prison, 1968-75. Co-author: (with others) Atlas of Microvascular Surgery: Anatomy and Operative Approaches, 1993 (Best Healt Sci. Book, Doody's Rating Svc. 1993); co-editor: (with A. Daniller) Textbook on Microsurgery, 1976, (with others) Grabb's Encyclopedia of Flaps, 3 vols., 1990, (Outstanding Publ. in Clin. Medicine, Assn. Am. Pubs. 1990), 2d edit. 1997; contbr. about 70 articles to profl. jours., and 20 chpts. to sci. books; assoc. editor Plastic and Reconstructive Surgery, 1982-88; founder, editor-in-chief Jour. Reconstructive Microsurgery, 1984—. Capt. Med. Corps. U.S. Army, 1964-66,. Mem. AAAS, ACS, Am. Soc. for Reconstructive Microsurgery (founder, past sec., treas. pres., chmn. Founder's Lectr. 1988), Am. Assn. Plastic Surgeons, Internat. Soc. Reconstructive Microsurgery (chmn. founding coun. 1983-84, pres. 1984-85). Med. Soc. State of N.Y., Am. Trauma Soc. (founding mem.), N.Y. Acad. Sci., Am. Soc. for Peripheral Nerve Surgery (pres. 1993-94), and others. Office: Montefiore Med Park 1625 Poplar St Ste 200 Bronx NY 10461-2653

STRAUCH, FRIEDRICH, paleontologist; b. Hamburg, Germany, Nov. 23, 1935; s. Friedrich and Auguste (Gruemmer) S.; m. Monika Luecke, Aug. 21, 1964; children: Konrad, Severin, Gereon. Diploma in Geology, U. Cologne, Germany, 1961, PhD, 1961. Asst. sci. U. Cologne, 1962-71; guest prof. U. Aarhus (Denmark), 1971-73; prof. U. Cologne, 1973-80; prof. and head of dept. geology and paleontology U. Münster, 1980—. Contbr. articles to profl. jours. Roman Catholic. Home: Suedostring 26, D-48329 Havixbeck Germany Office: U Muenster/Inst Geology, Corrensstr 24, D-48149 Münster Germany

STRAUER, BODO ECKEHARD, internal medicine educator; b. Babelsberg, Potsdam, Berlin, Jan. 16, 1943; s. Walter Karl and Ingeborg Johanna (Kludas) S.; m. Elisabeth Thea Alves, May 20, 1975; children: Wulf-Alexander, Mark-Benjamin. MD, U. Goettingen, Germany, 1966. Physician U. Goettingen, 1966-73, asst. prof. medicine, 1973-74; assoc. prof. medicine U. Munich, Germany, 1974-80, full prof. medicine, 1980-84; chmn. dept. internal medicine U. Marburg, Germany, 1984-87, U. Duesseldorf, Germany, 1987—; cons. German Soc. Cardiology, 1984—; chmn. European Working Group Heart and Hypertension, 1984-88; dir. dept. internal medicine U. Duesseldorf, 1987—, pres. rsch. in cardiology, 1989—; chmn. Working Group Angiology, 1989—; rsch. counselor Sci. Senate, Bonn, Germany, 1990—; senator German Rsch. Assn., Bonn, 1992. Author: (monographs) Dynamics of the Heart, 1975 (Paul Martini award 1976), Hypertensive Heart Disease, 1978 (Theodor Frerichs award 1980), Das Hochdruckherz, 1983 (Franz Gross award 1987). chmn. Convent, U. Duesseldorf, 1992-94. Fellow Internat. Coll. Angiology, Internat. Coun. Clin. Cardiology, Am. Coll. Cardiology, European Soc. Cardiology, Rotary. Home: Elmenweide 9, 40589 Düsseldorf Germany Office: Univ Duesseldorf, Mooren St 5, 40225 Düsseldorf Germany

STRAUGHAN, WILLIAM THOMAS, engineering educator; b. Shreveport, La., Aug. 2, 1936; s. William Eugene and Sara Chloetilde (Harrell) S.; m. Rubie Ann Barnes, Aug. 20, 1957; children: Donna Ann, Sara Arlene, Eugene Thomas. BS, MIT, 1959; MS, U. Tex., 1986; PhD, Tex. Tech. U., 1990. Registered profl. engr., Fla., Ill., Iowa., La., Tex., Wash. Project engr. Gen. Dynamics Corp., Chgo., 1959-60; chief project, design engr. Gen. Foods Corp., Kankakee, Ill., 1960-64; mgr. plant engring. Standard Brands Inc., Clinton, Iowa, 1964-66; regional mgr. Air Products & Chems., Inc., Creighton, Pa., 1966-68; gen. mgr. Skyline Corp., Harrisburg, N.C., 1968-70; cons. Charlotte, N.C., 1970-72; dir. engring. and Fla. ops. Zimmer Homes Corp., Pompano Beach, 1972-73; v.p. engring. and mfg. Nobility Homes, Inc., Ocala, Fla., 1973-78, Moduline Internat., Inc., Lacey, Wash., 1978-85; rsch. engr. U. Tex., Austin, 1985-86; lectr., rschr. Tex. Tech. U., Lubbock, 1987-90; assoc. prof. U. New Orleans, 1990-92; asst. prof. dept. civil engring. La. Tech. U., Ruston, 1992-98; tchr. 24 different courses, 1987—; cons. in field, Dubach, La., 1992—; condr. workshops in field; apptd. spokesman Mfrd. Housing Industry before U.S. Congress. Contbr. articles to profl. jours. Vol. engring. svcs. Lubbock Fire Safety House, 1990; judge sci. fair Ben Franklin H.S., New Orleans, 1990. Recipient T.L. James Svc. award La. Tech. U., 1994; grantee Urban Waste Mgmt. and Rsch. Ctr., New Orleans, 1991, Shell Devel. Co., 1993, La. Edn. Quality Support Fund, Insituform Techs., Inc., Trenchless Tech. Ctr., PABCO, Inc., InLiner USA, Inc., 1995, others; numerous grants in field. Mem. ASME (life), ASCE (Student chpt. Tchr. of Yr. award 1995, 98), NSPE, Am. Soc. Engring. Edn., Phi Kappa Phi, Sigma Xi, Chi Epsilon. Achievements include: designed, constructed and managed first plant for the prodn. of intermediate moisture pet food (Gainesburgers) in the world. Organized and directed all activities to allow Clinton, Iowa plant with a 1 mile shoreline to continue ops. during the greatest flood of the upper Miss. River in 1965. Avocations: flying, skiing, backpacking, golf, photography. Home: 199 Sellers Rd Dubach LA 71235-3218

STRAUSER, DAVID ROSS, healthcare educator; b. Sept. 4, 1968; m. Mary Ellen Chryst, Apr. 7, 1990; children: Matthew, David, John. MS, U. Wis., 1990, PhD, 1995. Asst. prof. U. Memphis, 1995—, dir. rehab. studies, 1998—; dir. cmty. based job readiness program U. Memphis, 1997—. Roman Catholic. E-mail: strauser.david@coe.memphis.edu. Office: University of Memphis 100B Ball Hall Memphis TN 38152-3570

STRAUSER, ROBERT WAYNE, lawyer; b. Little Rock, Aug. 28, 1943; s. Christopher Columbus and Opal (Orr) S.; m. Atha Maxine Tubbs, June 26, 1971 (div. 1991); children: Robert Benjamin, Ann Kathleen; m. Terri D. Seales, Oct. 17, 1998. BA, Davidson (N.C.) Coll., 1965; postgrad., Vanderbilt U., Nashville, 1965-66; LLB, U. Tex., 1968. Bar: Tex. 1968, U.S. Ct. Mil. Appeals 1971. Staff atty. Tex. Legis. Coun., Austin, 1969-71; counsel Jud. Com., Tex. Ho. of Reps., Austin, 1971-73; chief counsel Jud. Com., Tex. Constl. Conv., Austin, 1974; exec. v.p. and legis. counsel Tex. Assn. Taxpayers, Austin, 1974-85; assoc. Baker & Botts, Austin, 1985-87; ptnr. Baker & Botts, 1988—. Assoc. editor Tex. Internat. Law Jour., 1968. Mem. Tex. Ho. Speakers Econ. Devel. Com., Austin, 1986-87; assoc. dir. McDonald Obs. Bd. Visitors, 1988—; mem. adv. bd. Sch. of Social Work, U. Tex. Lyceum Assn., 1980-81, 84-88; mem. bd. dirs. Tex. Assn. Bus. and C. of C.; mem. Dean's Roundtable, U. Tex. Law Sch.; bd. dirs. Austin Symphony Orch. Soc., 1985—, v.p., 1993-94, nominating com., 1998. Capt. USNR, ret. Named Rising Star of Tex., Tex. Bus. Mag., 1983. Mem. State Bar of Tex. (coun. mem. tax sect.), Tex. Assn. Bus. and C. of C.s (bd. dirs. 1999), Travis County Bar Assn., Headliners Club (Austin). Home: 3312 Gilbert St Austin TX 78703-2102 Office: Baker & Botts 1600 San Jacinto Blvd Austin TX 78701

STRAUSS, ELLEN LOUISE FELDMAN, lawyer; b. Worcester, Mass.; d. William and Miriam (Jagodnik) Feldman; m. Douglas A. Strauss (div. May 1977). BA, Western Conn. State Coll., 1978; JD, Franklin Pierce Law Ctr., 1981. Bar: Conn. 1983, U.S. Dist. Ct., Conn., 1983, U.S. Dist. Ct., so. dist., N.Y., 1991, ea. dist., 1991. Self-employed Ellen L.F. Strauss, Esq., Weston, Conn., 1983—; bd. dirs. Human Lactation Ctr., Fairfield, Conn., 1987—, Efficacy, Hartford, Conn., 1997—. Contbr. columns to local newspapers. Founder, mem. Keep Weston Rural, Conn., 1984—. Mem. Am. Trial Lawyers Assn., Conn. Trial Lawyers Assn. Avocation: travel. E-mail: ELFS88LAW@aol.com. Office: Ellen LF Strauss Esq 88 Ladder Hill Rd N Weston CT 06883-1107

STRAUSS, RAYMOND BERNARD, otolaryngologist; b. N.Y.C., Mar. 25, 1930; s. Victor M. and Fannie (Price) S.; m. Lois Kelly, June 12, 1958; children: Steven Douglas, Keith Andrew. AB, Washington U., St. Louis, 1950; PhD, U. Fla., 1956; MD, Case We. Res. U., 1958. Diplomate Am. Bd. Otolaryngology, Am. Bd. Cosmetic Plastic Surgery. Intern dept. medicine, asst. resident surgery U. Hosps., Cleve., 1958-60; resident otolaryngology Columbia-Presbyn. Med. Ctr., N.Y.C., 1960-63; pvt. practice otolaryngology and facial plastic surgery Englewood, N.J., 1963—; attending otolaryngologist, past chief otolaryngology Englewood Hosp. and Med. Ctr.; assoc. attending otolaryngologist Vanderbilt Clinic and N.Y. Presbyn. Hosp.; past dir. facial plastic surgery clinic; assoc. prof. clin. otolaryngology Coll. Physicians and Surgeons, Columbia U. Dir., vice-chmn. bd. dirs. NVE Savs. Bank; past trustee Dwight-Englewood Sch.; past bd. dirs. No. Valley chpt. ARC; elder Presbyn. Ch., past clk. of session, past pres. bd. trustees. Recipient Coakley Meml. prize in otolaryngology Columbia U., 1958; Marie and Henry Heiner fellow in otolaryngology, 1961-62; decorated Army Commendation medal. Fellow ACS, Internat. Coll. Surgeons, Am. Acad. Facial Plastic and Reconstructive Surgery, Am. Acad. Cosmetic Surgery, Am. Acad. Otolaryngology and Head and Neck Surgery; mem. AMA, Royal Soc. Medicine, Am. Speech Lang. and Hearing Assn. (cert. clin. competence in speech pathology and audiology), N.Y. Laryngol. Soc. (past pres.), N.Y. Bronchoscopic Soc. (past pres.), N.Y. Otol. Soc. (past pres.), N.J. Soc. Cosmetic Surgery (trustee), N.J. Acad. Ophthalmology and Otolaryngology-Head and Neck Surgery (past pres.), N.J. Med. Soc., N.Y. County Med. Soc., Bergen County Med. Soc., Bergen County Soc. Otolaryngologists, Head and Neck Surgeons (past pres.), Englewood Surg.Soc. (past pres.), First Presbyn. Ch. Men's Assn. (past pres.), N.Y. Athletic Club, Englewood Club (past pres., Disting. Svc. award 1980), Knickerbocker Country Club, Rotary (past pres., dist. 7490 gov.), Phi Beta Kappa, Alpha Omega Alpha, Nu Sigma Nu. Home: 436 Lewellyn Cir Englewood NJ 07631-2021 Office: 1211 Hamburg Tpke Ste 205 Wayne NJ 07470-5000

STRAUSS, ROBERT PHILIP, economics educator; b. Cleve., May 11, 1944; s. Harry and Carrie S.; m. Celeste G. Meade, Jan. 11, 1980; children—Sarah Elizabeth, David Anthony, Elena Nicole. A.B. in Econs., U. Mich., 1966; M.A., U. Wis., 1968, Ph.D. in Econs., 1970. Fellow Inst. Research on Poverty, 1968-69; asst. prof. econs. U. N.C., Chapel Hill, 1969-73, assoc. prof., 1973-79; econ. policy fellow Brookings Instn., Washington, 1971-72; economist U.S. Congress Joint Com. Taxation, 1975-78; prof. econs. and pub. policy Carnegie-Mellon U., Pitts., 1979—, assoc. dean Sch. Urban and Pub. Affairs, 1981-83, dir. Ctr. for Pub. Fin. Mgmt., 1984-91; dir. research Pa. Tax Commn., 1979-81; vis. prof. econs. and pub. policy U. Rochester, 1992-94. Mem. Pa. Local Tax Reform Commn., 1987; sec. faculty Carnegie-Mellon U., 1991-92. Recipient Exceptional Service award U.S. Treasury, 1972, Disting. Service award Pitts. Tax Execs. Inst., 1987, Georgescun Roegen award, 1998; grantee NSF, U.S. Dept. Labor, U.S. Treasury, HUD, Social Security Adminstrn. Mem. Am. Econ. Assn., Econometric Soc., Nat. Tax Assn., Pub. Choice Soc., Assn. for Pub. Policy and Mgmt., Am. Soc. for Pub. Adminstrn., Nat. Tax Assn. (bd. dirs. 1995-98). Club: Cosmos. Home: 2307 Country Pl Export PA 15632-9059 Office: 5000 Forbes Ave Pittsburgh PA 15213-3815

STRAUSS-KAHN, DOMINIQUE GASTON ANDRÉ, government official; b. Neuilly-sur-Seine, France, Apr. 25, 1949; s. Gilbert Strauss-Kahn and Jacqueline Fellus; m. Anne Sinclair, 1991; 4 children. Asst. prof. econs. U. Paris X, 1975-78, prof. econs., 1978-81, 86-91; head Fin. Dept. Econ. Planning Agy., Paris, 1981-84, dep. commr., 1984-86; min. industry and trade Govt. France, 1991-93; mayor City of Sarcelles, 1995-97; min. econ. fin. and industry Govt. France, 1997-99. Mem. Socialist Party Bur. Avocations: piano, cinema, skiing, rugby. Office: Mairie de Sorcelles, 95200 Sorcelles France

STRAUSSLER, TOMAS See STOPPARD, TOM

STRAUTINS, VILNIS, flute educator, past symphony orchestra executive; b. Lubana, Madona, Latvia, Dec. 28, 1939; s. Fricis Strautins and Emma (Bundzis) Strautina; m. Dzidra Markevica, Dec. 31, 1964; children: Ineta, Peteris. Master's, Latvian Music, Riga, 1965. Prin. flutist Latvian Nat. Symphony Orch., Riga, 1961-89, mng. dir., 1989-97; prof. flute Latvian Music Acad., Riga, 1971—. Lutheran. Avocation: correspondence chess. Office: Latvian Music Acad, Kr Barona 1, LV-1050 Riga Latvia

STRAVORAVDI, PELAGIA, biologist, researcher; b. Serres, Greece, Aug. 31, 1954; d. Andreas and Vasiliki (Paschou) S.; m. Konstantinos Tzoanas, Apr. 12, 1980. Degree in biology, U. Patras, 1976; degree in pharmacology, U. Thessaloniki, 1982, PhD, 1986. Tng. for rsch. in electron microscopy and in lab. animals Theagenion Cancer Hosp., Thessaloniki, 1979-86, head of dept. electron microscopy, 1986—; rschr., cons. Symeonidis Rsch. Ctr., Thessaloniki, 1979—. Co-author: Cancer Treatment-An Update, 1994, Urology, 1992; contbr. articles to profl. jours. Mem. SOS Child Care Program, Thessaloniki, 1991; vol. Cancer Related Orgn., Greece, 1985, Ecological Activity in Recycling, Thessaloniki, 1990. Grantee Ministry of Health, 1986; recipient award 5th Hellenic Oncology Congress, 1989, award 6th Internat. Congress on Anti-Cancer Treatment, 1995. Mem. European Assn. for Cancer Rsch., Internat. Soc. for Interferon and Cytokine Rsch., Greek Soc. for Cancer Rsch., N.Y. Acad. Sci. Avocations: stamps collecting, swimming, travelling, book reading. Office: Theagenio Cancer Hosp, 2 Al Symeonidis, 54007 Thessaloniki Greece

STRAWA, ANTHONY WALTER, research scientist; b. Chgo., Apr. 22, 1950. BS, USAF Acad., Colorado Springs, Colo., 1973; PhD, MS, Stanford (Calif.) U., 1986. Rsch. asst. Stanford U., 1982-86; lead researcher ballistic range NASA-Ames Rsch. Ctr., Moffett Field, Calif., 1986-89, prin. investigator Aerosissit flight expt., 1990-91, rsch. scientist atmospheric scis., 1991—, acting br. chief atmospheric rsch. br., 1995-96; mem. NASA Aerodynamic Sensors Working Group, 1989-93, leader Cloud and Microphysics Group, 1999—. Mem. AIAA (sec. aerodynamic measurement tech. com. 1989-93), AAAS, Am. Assn. Aerosol Rsch., AMS, AGU. Office: NASA-Ames Rsch Ctr Mail Stop 245-4 Moffett Field CA 94035

STRAWN, DEBORAH, audiologist; b. Cedartown, Ga., Sept. 23, 1952; d. Kenchen Davis and Imogene Watson S.; m. William Boyd Burford, Aug. 20, 1988; 1 child, Tess Taylor Burford. BA, Auburn U., 1972; MA, U. Ala., 1976, Auburn U., 1981. Tchr. of deaf/blind Auburn (Ala.) U., dir. hearing impaired program; hearing specialist Auburn City Schs.; cons. State Dept. of Edn., Montgomery, Ala. Sec., v.p. Raritans, Loachapoka, Ala., 1992-95. Mem. Alexander Graham Bell Assn. for the Deaf. Avocation: stained glass artist. Office: Auburn City Schs 807 Wrights Mill Rd Auburn AL 36830-6801

STRAWSON, SIR PETER FREDERICK, philosophy educator; b. London, Nov. 23, 1919; s. Cyril Walter and Nellie Dora (Jewell) S.; m. Grace Hall Martin, Oct. 27, 1945; children: Julia Katharine, Galen John, Robert Neville,

Virginia Ann. MA, Oxford U., 1940; Dr. (hon.), Munich U., 1998. Lectr. Univ. Coll. N. Wales, Bangor, 1946-47; lectr. Univ. Coll., Oxford, 1947-48, fellow, 1948-68; prof. metaphysics Magdalen Coll., Oxford U., 1968-87, prof. emeritus, 1987—; lectr., vis. prof. in many countries, including U.S.A., Can., Argentina, Mex., India, Israel, Yugoslavia, France, Fed. Republic Germany, Belgium, Spain, China, Czech Republic. Author: Introduction to Logical Theory, 1952, Individuals, 1959, The Bounds of Sense, 1966, Logico-Linguistic Papers, 1971, Freedom and Resentment, 1974, Subject and Predicate in Logic and Grammar, 1974, Scepticism and Naturalism: Some Varieties, 1985, Analyse et Mètaphysique, 1985, Analysis and Metaphysics, 1992, Entity and Indentity, 1997, Autobiography and Replies to Critics in the Philosophy of P.F. Strawson, 1998. Served as capt. Brit. Army, 1940-46, U.K., Italy, Austria. Created knight bachelor, 1977. Fellow Brit. Acad.; mem. Am. Acad. Arts and Scis. (fgn. hon.), Acad. Europaea, Mind Assn., Aristotelian Soc. (pres. 1969-70), Athenaeum Club (London). Avocations: walking, reading English and French literature, travelling. Home: 25 Farndon Rd, Oxford OX2 6RT, England Office: University Coll, High St, Oxford England also: British Acad, 10 Cartlton House Terr, London NW1 4QP, England

STRAZDINS, INDULIS, mathematician, researcher, educator; b. Riga, Latvia, Mar. 31, 1934; s. Ernests Brastins and Liza S.; widowed; 1 child, Ivars. PhD in Physics and Math., Byelorussian Acad. Sci., Minsk, 1965; D of Physics and Math., Comput. Ctr. Acad. Sci., Moscow, 1989; D Habilitation in Math., Sci. Coun., Latvia, 1992. Mem. faculty Riga Poly. Inst. (now Riga Tech. U.), 1959—, assoc. prof. math., 1965-90, prof. math., 1990—. Author: (textbook) Elements of Discrete Mathematics, 1980; contbr. articles and revs. to profl. and popular jours. MP Parliament (Supreme Coun.) of Republic of Latvia, 1991-93. Mem. Latvian Math. Soc. (bd. dirs. 1992-97), Am. Math. Soc., Fibonacci Assn. Avocations: languages, literature, music, history. Office: Riga Tech U, Riga LV-1658, Latvia

STRAZEWSKI, PETER MARCIN, chemistry educator, researcher; b. London, Oct. 4, 1958; arrived in Switzerland, 1961; s. Jerzy Adam Strazewski (originally Rappaport) and Wanda Halina (Kurek) S.; m. Marianne Firouzeh Marcelle Farahmand, Dec. 29, 1988. Diploma in chemistry, U. Basel, 1981, PhD, 1986, Privatdozent, 1995. Rsch. assoc. U. Basel, 1986-88, asst. prof., 1991-95, assoc. prof., lectr. chemistry, 1995—; rsch. assoc. U. Cambridge, Eng., 1988-90; asst. prof. U. Basel, 1991-95, assoc. prof., lectr. chemistry, 1995—. Author: The Biological Equilibrium of Base Pairs, 1990, Recent Studies on the Synthesis, Structure and Function of Nucleic Acids, 1994, A Pleading For Chemistry, European Chemistry Chronicle, vol. 4-1, 1999; contbr. articles to profl. jours. Mem. New Swiss Chem. Soc., N.Y. Acad. Sci., German Chem. Soc., Eurosci., European Chem. Soc. E-mail: peter.strazewski@unibas.ch. Office: Inst Organic Chemistry, St Johanns-Ring 19, CH-4056 Basel Switzerland

STRAZHAV, VASSILY I., minister of education and science of Belarus; b. Rostov on Don, July 26, 1944; married. Student, Belarus Acad. Sci., 1963-66; diploma, Belarus State U., 1966, PhD. Sr. constrn. engr., jr. scientific rschr. Inst. Physics, Acad. Sci., 1970-72; sec. sci. dept. physics, math. Acad. Sci., 1972-75; instr. dept. edn. Minsk Dist. Communist Party Com., 1975-78; head dept. sci. Minsk City Communist Party Com., 1978-80; dept. head Belarus Inst. Agr. Mechanization, 1980-88; dep. min. Edn. and Sci., 1988-94, min., 1994—. Communist. Office: Min Edn & Sci, ul Sovetskaya St 9, 220010 Minsk Belarus*

STRAZZELLA, JAMES ANTHONY, law educator, lawyer; b. Hanover, Pa., May 18, 1939; s. Anthony F. and Teresa Ann (D'Alonzo) S.; m. Judith A. Coppola, Oct. 9, 1965; children: Jill M., Steven A., Tracy Ann, Michael P. AB, Villanova U., 1961; JD, U. Pa., 1964. Bar: Pa. 1964, D.C., 1965, U.S. Dist. Ct. (ea. and mid. dist.) Pa. 1969, U.S. Ct. Appeals (3rd cir.) 1964, U.S. Ct. Appeals (D.C. cir.) 1965, U.S. Ct. Appeals (4th cir.) 1983, U.S. Supreme Ct. 1969. Law clk. to Hon. Samuel Roberts Pa. Supreme Ct., 1964-65; asst. U.S. atty., 1965-69; vice dean, asst. prof. law U. Pa., Phila., 1969-73; faculty Temple U., Phila., 1973—; James G. Schmidt chair in law, 1989—, acting dean, 1987-89; chief counsel Kent State investigation Pres.'s Commn. Campus Unrest, 1970; chmn. Atty. Gen.'s Task Force on Family Violence, Pa., 1985-89; mem., chmn. justice ops. Mayor's Criminal Justice Coordinating Commn., Phila., 1983-85; Pa. Joint Coun. Criminal Justice, 1979-82; mem. Com. to Study Pa.'s Unified Jud. Sys., 1980-82; Jud. Coun. Pa., 1972-82; chmn. criminal procedural rules com. Pa. Supreme Ct., 1972-85; mem. task force on prison overcrowding, 1983-85, rsch. adv. com., 1988, Pa. Commn. on Crime and Delinquency; chmn. U.S. Magistrate Judge Merit Selection Com., 1991, mem., 1989, 90, 91; co-chair Mayor's Transition Task Force on Pub. Safety, Phila., 1992; designate D.C. Com. on Adminstrn. of Justice Under Emergency Conditions, 1968; del. D.C. Jud. Conf., 1985, 95. Contbr. articles to profl. jours. and books. Mem. adv. bd. dirs., past pres. A Better in Lower Merion; dir. Hist. Fire Mus., Phila., 1978—; bd. dirs. Lower Merion Hist. Soc., 1998-2000, dir. Neighborhood Civic Assn., Bala-Cynwyd, Pa., 1984-87; bd. dirs. Smith Meml. Playground in Fairmount Pk., 1997—, Coun. Legal Edn. Opportunity Bd., 1997—; bd. trustees Bala Cynwyd Pub. Libr., 1999—. Recipient award for disting. tchg. Linback Found., 1983, Advancement of Justice award Pa. Atty. Gen., 1989, Disting. Pub. Svc. award Assn. State and County Detectives, 1989, Spl. Merit award Pa. Assn. Police Chiefs, 1989, significant contbn. to legal scholarship and edn. Beccaria award Phila. Bar Assn. and Nat. IAB Assn., 1995. Fellow Am. Bar Found.; mem. Am. Law Inst., ABA (faculty appellate judges' seminars 1975, various coms., acad. advisor appellate judges edn. com. 1993—; reporter task force on Federalization Criminal Law 1998-99), FBA (Phila. crim. law com. adv. bd. 1988-93, chmn. nat. criminal law com. 1991-92), Pa. Bar Assn. (commn. profl. stds. 1981-84, chmn. criminal law sect. 1986-88, Spl. Merit award 1987), Phila. Bar Assn. (criminal justice sect., appellate cts. com.), Order of the Coif (exec. bd. U. Pa.), St. Thomas More Soc. (pres. 1985-86, past dir. Phila. area, St. Thomas More award 1996). Roman Catholic. Home and Office: 100 Maple Ave Bala Cynwyd PA 19004-3017 Office: Temple U Law Sch 1719 N Broad St Philadelphia PA 19122-6002

STREAN, BERNARD M., retired naval officer; b. Big Cabin, Okla., Dec. 16, 1910; s. Ralph Lester and Maude (Hopkins) S.; m. Janet Lockey, June 12, 1935 (dec. 1978); children: Bernard M., Richard Lockey, Judy (Mrs. William S. Graves); m. Susan Noble Webb, 1978. BS, U.S. Naval Acad., 1933; grad., Armed Forces Staff Coll., 1949, Nat. War Coll., 1958. Commd. ensign USN, 1933, advanced through grades to vice adm., 1965, designated naval aviator, 1935, assigned USS Pennsylvania, 1933-35; assigned Naval Air Sta. USN, Pensacola, Fla., 1935-36; assigned USS Saratoga USN, 1936-38, assigned San Diego Naval Sta., 1938-39; assigned Pearl Harbor Naval Air Sta. USN, Hawaii, 1939-40; assigned Naval Air Sta. USN, Jacksonville, Fla., 1940-42; comdr. Fighter Squadron 1, USS Yorktown USN, 1943-44, comdr. Air Group 98, 1944-45, comdr. Air Group 75, 1945-46, head tech. tng. program sect. Office Chief Naval Ops., 1950-51, comdg. officer Air Transp. Squdaron 8, 1951-54, comdg. officer Pre-Flight Sch., 1954-56, comdg. officer USS Kenneth Whiting, 1956-57, comdg. officer USS Randolph, 1958-59, chief staff, aide to comdr. Naval Air Force, U.S. Atlantic Fleet, 1959-60, comdr. Fleet Air Whidbey, 1960-61, comdr. Patrol Force 7th Fleet, also U.S. Taiwan Patrol Force, 1961-62, asst. chief naval ops. for fleet ops. Operation Navy, High Command of Navy, Comdr. Naval ops., 1962-64, comdr. Carrier Div. 2, Atlantic Fleet, 1964-65, comdr. World's 1st All-Nuclear Naval Task Force, 1964, comdr. round the world cruise; dep. asst. chief for pers., Bur. Naval Pers. Dept. Navy, Washington, 1965-68; chief naval air tng. Naval Air Sta. Dept. Navy, Pensacola, Fla., 1968-71; ret., 1971; v.p. O.S.C. Franchise Devel. Corp., 1971-75; chmn. bd. Solaray Corp., 1975-80; v.p. Huet-Browning Corp., Washington. Bd. dirs. U.S. Olympic Com., 1965-68; trustee No. Va. Community Colls., 1978-82. Decorated Navy Cross, (2) D.F.C. with 2 gold stars, Air medal with 7 gold stars, Legion of Merit, D.S.M., numerous area and campaign ribbons; Disting. Svc. medal (Greece); medal of Pao-Ting (Republic of China). Mem. Mil. Order World Wars, Loyal Order Carabao, Early and Pioneer Naval Aviators Assn. (pres. 1977-79), Arlington County Tax Assn. (vice chmn. 1978-80), Md. Aviation Hist. Soc. (founder, bd. dirs. 1978-82), U.S. Naval Acad. Alumni Assn. (pres. Class 1933, 1973-88), Army Navy Club (Washington), N.Y. Yacht Club, Washington Golf and Country Club (Arlington), L.A. Country Club. Home: 6251 Old Dominion Dr Mc Lean VA 22101-4818

STREAN, HERBERT SAMUEL, psychoanalyst, social work consultant; b. Montreal, Que., Can., Mar. 2, 1931; came to U.S., 1944; s. Lyon Peter and Lillian Ruth Strean; m. Marcia Ruth Strean, Mar. 21, 1954; children: Richard, William. BA, NYU, 1951; MSW, Boston U., 1953; D of Social Welfare, Columbia U., 1968. Cert. psychoanalyst, Nat. Psychol. Assn. for Psychoanalysis. 1st lt. U.S. Army, Ft. Dix, N.J.; psychotherapist Jewish Bd. of Guardians, N.Y.C.; instr. SUNY, Stony Brook; prof. Rutgers U., New Brunswick, N.J.; pvt. pratice psychotherapy N.Y.C. Author 35 books in field; contbr. over 100 articles to profl. jours. Bd. dirs. N.Y. Ctr. for Psychoanalytic Tng., 1986-93; pres. Soc. for Psychoanalytic Tng., 19890-82. Named Social Worker of Yr., N.J.-Nat. Assn. Social Workers, 1972, Alumnus of Yr., Boston U., 1998. Democrat. Jewish. Avocations: golf, theater, reading. Home: 1011 Sheffield Rd Teaneck NJ 07666-5627 Office: 7 W 96th St New York NY 10025-6540

STREBEL, HEINZ, business administration educator; b. Munich, Sept. 23, 1939; s. Heinrich and Sofie (Geymeier) S.; m. Sigrun Briesen, July 31, 1965; children: Eva, Michael, Anne-Katrin. Diploma, U. Karlsruhe, Fed. Republic Germany, 1963; Habilitation, Free U. Berlin, 1977. Asst. U. Karlsruhe, 1963-71; asst. prof. Acad. Pub. Adminstrn., Kehl, Fed. Republic Germany, 1971-76; assoc. prof. Free U. Berlin, 1976-84; prof. bus. adminstrn. U. Oldenburg, Fed. Republic Germany, 1984-90, U. Graz, Austria, 1990—. Author: Forschungsplanung mit Scoring-Modellen, 1975, Umwelt und Betriebswirtschaft, 1980, Industriebetriebslehre, 1984, Umwelt und Ökonomie, 1991, Betriebliche Umweltökonomie, 1993, Integriertes Deponiemanagement, 1995, Externes Recycling in Produktionsbetrieb, 1996, Kreislauforientierte Unternehmenskooperation, 1998, Okonomische Energienutzung, 1999. Home: Waltendorfer Hauptstr 147, A-8042 Graz Austria Office: Graz, A-8010 Graz 8010, Austria

STRECK, FREDERICK LOUIS, III, lawyer; b. St. Louis, Nov. 6, 1960; s. Frederick Louis Jr. and Joan Kathrine (Faerber) S.; m. Michelle Renee Harding; children: Frederick IV, Robert Harding, Joseph Walter, Samuel Franklin. BBA, Tex. Christian U., 1983; JD, St. Mary's U., 1986. Bar: Tex. 1986, U.S. Dist. Ct. (no. dist.) Tex. 1987, U.S. Ct. Appeals (5th cir.) 1987; bd. cert. in personal injury trial law, civil trial advocacy; diplomate Am. Bd. of Trial Advocacy. Atty. Kugle, Stewart, Dent & Frederick, Ft. Worth, 1986-89, The Dent Law Firm, 1990—. State del. Dem. Party, Tex., 1988. Fellow Tex. State Bar Coll.; mem. ABA, ATLA,, Tex. Trial Lawyers Assn., Million Dollar Adv. Forum. Democrat. Roman Catholic. Avocations: wine collecting, golf, fishing, scuba diving. Fax: 817-332-5809. E-mail: fstreck3@yahoo.com. Office: The Dent Law Firm 1120 Penn St Fort Worth TX 76102-3417

STRECKERT, HANS JUERGEN, virologist; b. Witten, Germany, Aug. 29, 1950; s. Hugo Hildegard (Schmuecker) S.; m. Gabriele Steinforth, July 17, 1981; children: Ilka, Svea, Uta. MS in Chemistry, Univ. Bochum, 1979; Dr. rer. nat., Ruhr Univ., 1982. Rschr. Ruhr Univ., Bochum, 1978-83; sr. rschr. Med. Sch., Bochum, 1983-94, lectr. virology, 1994—; with Found. of Dr. Streckert-Diagnostica, 1998; Contbr. articles to profl. jours. Grantee Deutsche Forschungsgemeinschaft, 1989, 95, Deutsche Vereinigung zur Bekaempfung der Viruserkrankungen, 1996. Mem. Gesellschaft fuer Virologie, Gesellschaft fuer Biologische Chemie. Home: Alte Strasse 41b, 58452 Witten Germany Office: Dr Streckert Diagnostica, Im Lottental 36, 44801 Bochum Germany

STREEB, GORDON LEE, diplomat, economist; b. Windsor, Colo., Dec. 24, 1935; s. Gerhard O. and Amelia (Martin) S.; m. Alice Junette Thomas, Aug. 11, 1962; children: Kurt, Kent, Kerry-Lynn. BSBA, U. Colo., 1959, BSChemE, 1959; PhD in Econs., U. Minn., 1978. Fgn. service officer U.S. Dept. State, Berlin, 1963-65; vice consul Am. Consulate, Guadalajara, Mex., 1965-67; instr. econs. U. Minn., 1968; examiner Bd. Examiners, 1972-73; internat. economist for trade policy Bur. Econ. and Bus. Affairs, Washington, 1973-77; econ. counselor U.S. mission European Office of the UN and other internat. orgns., Geneva, 1977-80; exec. asst. to undersec. of state on econ. affairs Washington, 1980-81; dep. asst. sec. state for econ. and social affairs Bur. Internat. Orgn. Affairs, Washington, 1981-84; dep. chief mission Am. Embassy, New Delhi, India, 1984-88; sr. inspector Dept. State, Washington, 1988-90; amb. to Zambia Am. Embassy, Lusaka, 1990-93; diplomat-in-residence The Carter Ctr., Atlanta, 1994-95; assoc. exec. dir. peace program, The Carter Ctr., 1995—. Home: 2680 Churchwell Ln Tucker GA 30084-2402 Office: The Carter Ctr One Copenhill Atlanta GA 30307

STREEP, MERYL (MARY LOUISE STREEP), actress; b. Summit, N.J., June 22, 1949; d. Harry Jr. and Mary W. Streep; m. Donald J. Gummer, 1978. BA, Vassar Coll., 1971; MFA, Yale U., 1975, DFA (hon.), 1983; DFA (hon.), Dartmouth Coll., 1981. Appeared with Green Mountain Guild, Woodstock, Vt.; Broadway debut in Trelawny of the Wells, Lincoln Center Beaumont Theater, 1975; N.Y.C. theatrical appearances include 27 Wagons Full of Cotton (Theatre World award), A Memory of Two Mondays, Henry V, Secret Service, The Taming of the Shrew, Measure for Measure, The Cherry Orchard, Happy End, Wonderland, Taken in Marriage, Alice in Concert (Obie award 1981); movie appearances include Julia, 1977, The Deer Hunter, 1978 (Best Supporting Actress award Nat. Soc. Film Critics, Acad. award nomination), Manhattan, 1979, The Seduction of Joe Tynan, 1979, Kramer vs. Kramer, 1979 (N.Y. Film Critics' award, Los Angeles Film Critics' award, both for best actress, Golden Globe award, Acad. award for best supporting actress), The French Lieutenant's Woman, 1981 (Los Angeles Film Critics award for best actress, Brit. Acad. award, Golden Globe award 1981, Acad. award nominiation), Sophie's Choice, 1982 (Acad. award for best actress, Los Angeles Film Critics award for best actress, Golden Globe award 1982), Still of the Night, 1982, Silkwood, 1983 (Acad. award nomination), Falling in Love, 1984, Plenty, 1985, Out of Africa, 1985 (Los Angeles Film Critics award for best actress 1985, Acad. award nomination), Heartburn, 1986, Ironweed, 1987 (Acad. award nomination), A Cry in the Dark, 1988 (named Best Actress N.Y. Film Critics' Circle, 1988, Best Actress Cannes Film Festival, 1989, Acad. award nomination), She-Devil, 1989, Postcards From the Edge, 1990, Defending Your Life, 1991, Death Becomes Her, 1992, The House of the Spirits,1994, The River Wild, 1994, The Bridges of Madison County, 1995 (Acad. award nominee for best actress 1996), Before and After, 1996, Marvin's Room, 1997, Dancing at Lugnasa, 1998, One True Thing, 1998; TV film The Deadliest Season, 1977; TV mini-series Holocaust, 1978 (Emmy award); TV dramatic spls. Secret Service, 1977, Uncommon Women and Others, 1978, First Do No Harm, 1997; TV (narrator) The Velveteen Rabbit, 1985 (Emmy award Best Children's Rec.), A Vanishing Wilderness, 1990, Music of the Heart, 1999 (Acad. award nominee for best actress). Recipient Mademoiselle award, 1976, Woman of Yr. award B'nai Brith, 1979, Woman of Yr. award Hasty Pudding Soc., Harvard U., 1980, Best Supporting Actress award Nat. Bd. of Rev., 1979, Best Actress award Nat. Bd. of Rev., 1982, Star of Yr. award Nat. Assn. Theater Owners, 1983, People's Choice award, 1983, 85, 86, 87. Office: Creative Artists Agy 9830 Wilshire Blvd Beverly Hills CA 90212-1825

STREET, BRIAN VINCENT, education educator, consultant; b. Manchester, Lancashire, Eng., Oct. 24, 1943; s. Harry and Margaret Nellie (Brown) S.; children: Chloe, Alice, Nicholas. BA in Eng. Lit. with hons., London U., 1966; diploma in Social Anthropology, U. Oxford, Eng., 1967; PhD, U. Oxford, 1970. Lectr. in Eng. lang. and lit. U. Mashad, Iran, 1970-71; lectr. in social anthropology U. Sussex, Eng., 1974; sr. lectr. in social anthropology U. Sussex, 1989-96; vis. assoc. prof. grad. sch. edn. U. Pa., Phila., 1988; prof. lang. in edn. Sch. Edn. King's Coll., London, 1996—; fellowship study tour Brit. Coun./Dept. for Internat. Devel., South Africa, Australia, 1992—; adj. prof. edn., Grad. Sch. of Edn., U. Pa., 1993—; cons. to Dept. for Internat. Devel., UK, Nepal, South Africa, 1998. Author: (books) The Savage in Literature, 1975, Literacy in Theory and Practice, 1984, Social Literacies: Critical Approaches to Literacy in Education, Development and Ethnography, 1995 (cited Nat. Coun. Tchrs. English, U.S., 1996); editor (book) Cross-Cultural Approaches to Literacy, 1993 (commended by judges for BAAL Ann Book prize 1993); co-author: Ordinary People Writing: Literacy Practices and Identity in the Mass-Observation Project, 1999, Language Learners as Ethnographers, 1999; joint series editor Mass-Observation Occasional Papers series, Sussex U., Written Lang. and Literacy, 1994—, J. Benjamins book series; co-editor International Handbook of Literacy, 1999, Student Writing in the University; Cultural and Epistemological Issues, 1999, Cultural Encounters representing otherness, 1999; editor: Literacy and Development Ethnographic Perspectives, 2000. Fellow Brit. Inst. of Persian Studies, Iran, 1969-70; vice chair, Bd. Chief Examiners Internat. Baccalaureate, UK, 1984-90; mem. bd. visitors Coll. Health, Edn. and Human Resources, U. Scranton, Pa., 1993-7; trustee Mass-Observation Archive U. Sussex, 1998—. Co-recipient Runner-up award Representations and Images of Primitive Peoples, Anthropology and Photography, Yale U. Press, 1993; recipient David S. Russell award for disting. rsch., 1996; co-recipient Brit. Assn. for Applied Linguistics, Ann. Book prize, 1994. Fellow Royal Anthrop, Inst.; mem. Brit. Assn. for Literacy in Devel. (vice chair 1995-98), Nat. Langs. and Literacy Inst., Melbourne, Australia (critical friend 1995—). Avocations: conversation, wine, travel, film, walking. Home: Flat 4 111 Marine Parade, Brighton BN2 1AT, England Office: King's Coll Sch of Edn, 120 Stamford St, Franklin-Wilkins Bldg London SE1 8WA, England

STREET, DANA MORRIS, orthopedic surgeon; b. N.Y.C., May 7, 1910; s. William Dana and Elizabeth (Clark) S.; m. Elna Alice Clare, June 18, 1940; children: Rosalyn Clare (Mrs. David R. Sprague), Dana Clark, Steven Morris, William Milo. B.S., Haverford Coll., 1932; M.D., Cornell U., 1936. Diplomate: Am. Bd. Orthopaedic Surgery. Intern pathology Duke Hosp., 1936-37, Duke Hosp. (orthopedics), 1937-38; asst. resident phys. medicine Albany (N.Y.) Hosp., 1938-39; fellow Nemour Found., 1939-40; intern orthopedics Boston City Hosp., 1940; asst. resident surgery Albany Hosp., 1940-41; intern, asst. resident orthopedics Johns Hopkins Hosp., 1941-42; fellow N.Y. Orthopaedic Hosp., 1942; chief orthopedic sect. Kennedy VA Hosp., Memphis, 1946-59; prof. surgery, chief orthopedic div. U. Ark., 1959-62; prof. surgery in residence UCLA, 1962-75; head orthopedic div. Harbor Gen. Hosp., Torrance, Calif., 1962-75, Riverside (Calif.) Gen. Hosp., 1975-77; chief orthopedic sect. Jerry L. Pettis Meml. VA Hosp., Loma Linda, Calif., 1977-80; prof. orthopedics Loma Linda U., 1975-80, emeritus, 1980—. Author: (with others) Science and Practice of Intramedullary Nailing, 1995; contbr. aricles on medullary nailing and joint replacement to med. jours.; also book chpts. Served to maj. M.C. USAAF, 1942-46. Mem. AMA, Am. Acad. Orthopaedic Surgeons, Am. Orthopaedic Assn., Calif. Med. Assn., Calif. Orthopaedic Assn., Western Orthopedic Assn., Assn. Bone and Joint Surgeons (treas. 1953-56, v.p. 1956-58, pres. 1959), Am. Fracture Assn. Presbyn. (elder, deacon, clk. sessions). Home: 5440 Ralston St # 249 Ventura CA 93003-6002

STREET, DAVID HARGETT, investment company executive; b. Oklahoma City, Dec. 4, 1943; s. Bob Allen and Elizabeth Anne (Hargett) S.; m. Betty Ann Nichols, Oct. 1, 1966; children: Elizabeth Ann, Randall Hargett, Jeffrey David. BA in English, U. Okla., 1965; MBA in Fin., U. Pa., 1970. Vice pres. SEI Corp., 1970; v.p., prin. Street & Street, Inc., N.Y.C., 1970-74; v.p., mgr. San Francisco regional office First Nat. Bank Chicago, 1974-78; sr. v.p., CFO, treas. Bangor Punta Corp., Greenwich, Conn., 1978-84; v.p., treas. Penn Cen. Corp., Greenwich, 1984-86, v.p. fin., 1986-87; sr. v.p. fin. Penn Cen. Corp., Cin., 1987-92; exec. v.p. Gen. Cable Corp., Highland Heights, Ky., 1992-94, also bd. dirs.; pres., CEO Street Capital Group, Duluth, Ga., 1994—; mem. adv. bd. Mfrs. Hanover Trust Co., 1982-88. Vice chmn. bd. dirs., treas. Greenwich Acad. for Girls, 1984-87, chmn. bd. trustees, 1987-88; trustee Cin. County Day Sch., 1990-91; mem. cmty. bd. Sta. WGUC-FM, 1988-94; trustee Bethesda Hosp., Inc., 1993-97; trustee Cin. Classical Pub. Radio, Inc., 1994-97, Cmty. Chest Cin. Area, Inc., 1993-97, treas., 1994-95; trustee John Austin Cheley Found., 1995—, treas., 1996—; trustee Fountain Valley Sch., 1995—, treas., 2000—. 1st lt. M.I. U.S. Army, 1966-67. Mem. St. Ives Country Club. Republican. Presbyterian. Home and Office: 103 Villamoura Way Duluth GA 30097-2068

STREET, MARYAN, industrial relations educator; b. New Plymouth, Taranaki, New Zealand, Apr. 5, 1955; d. Robert Sterry and Catherine Betty (Aylward) S.; 1 child. BA with honors, Victoria U. of Wellington, New Zealand, 1977; MPhil with honors, U. Auckland, New Zealand, 1994. Secondary tchr. pub. schs. Auckland, 1978-85; field officer NZ PPTA, Auckland, 1985-87; mgr. TUEA, Auckland, 1989; coord. NZCTU, Auckland, 1989-90; dir. Ctr. Labor Studies U. Auckland, 1990—, 1990-2000; employee rels. mgr. Waitemata Health Ltd., Auckland, 2000—. Author: The Scarlet Runners, 1993; contbr.: Business and NZ Society, 1995, Politics in NZ, 1997. Pres. New Zealand Labour Party, Auckland, 1993-95; v.p. Auckland CTU, 1987-88; convenor Combined State Unions, Auckland, 1984-87; regional chmn. NZPPTA, Auckland, 1983-85. Recipient Commemorative medal New Zealand Govt., 1990, Suffrage Yr. medal, 1993. Mem. Assn. Univ. Staff (br. exec. mem. 1990-96). Avocations: music, cooking, gardening. Office: University of Auckland, Waitemata Health Ltd, Private Bag 93-503 Takapuna, Auckland 1309, New Zealand

STREET, PATRICIA LYNN, secondary education educator; b. Lillington, N.C., May 3, 1940; d. William Banks and Vandalia (McLean) S.; m. Col. Robert Gest, June 2, 1962 (div. 1985); children: Robert, Roblyn Renee. BS, Livingstone Coll., 1962; MEd, Salisbury State U., 1974; postgrad., various, 1968—. Tchr. Govt. of Guam Marianas Island, Agana, Guam, 1962-64; sec., typist USAF, Glasgow AFB, Mont., 1964-65, Syracuse (N.Y.) U. AeroSpace Engring., 1966-67; tchr. Syracuse (N.Y.) City Sch. System, 1967-69; lectr. U. of Md., Eastern Shore, Princess Anne, Md., 1970-72; tchr. Prince George's County Pub. Schs., Upper Marlboro, Md., 1973—; instr. U. Guam, Anderson AFB, 1963, U.S. Armed Forces Inst., Anderson AFB, 1963, Yorktowne Bus. Inst., Landover, Md., 1987-90, Cheseapeake Bus. Inst., Clinton, Md., 1983-89; asst. advisor student tchrs. U. Md. Ea. Shore, Princess Anne, 1972; adj. instr. Bowie State U., 1990—; conv. speaker. Mem. AAUW, NEA, ASCD, Am. Vocat. Assn., Md. Bus. Edn. Assn. (pres.-elect 1987-88, pres. 1988-89, Educator of Yr. 1989), Md. Vocat. Assn. (regional rep. 1986-89, audit chmn. 1987-89, Vocat.-Tech. Educator of Yr. 1989), Ea. Bus. Edn. Assn. (co-editor newsletter 1990-91, secondary exec. dir. 1991-94, pres.-elect 1997-98, pres. 1998-99), Md. State Tchrs. Assn., D.C. Bus. Edn. Assn., Nat. Bus. Edn. Assn., Nat. Bus. Edn. Assn. (exec. bd. dirs. 1998-99), Internat. Soc. for Bus. Edn., Md. Bus. Edn. Com., Prince George's County Edn. Assn., Delta Pi Epsilon. Democrat. Baptist. Avocations: sewing, singing, modern creative dancing. Home: 10107 Welshire Dr Upper Marlboro MD 20772-6204 Office: Prince George's Pub Sch Upper Marlboro MD 20772

STREET, PICABO, Olympic athlete; b. Triumph, Idaho, Apr. 3, 1971. Silver medalist, women's downhill alpine skiing Olympic Games, Lillehammer, Norway, 1994; downhill skier U.S. Ski Team, 1994—. Named World Cup Downhill Women's Champion, 1995, 96; recipient Bronze and Gold medal World Championships, 1996, Gold Medals (3), Women's Super Giant Slalom Alpine Skiing, Nagano, Japan, 1998, Gold medal Super 6 Slalom, 1998 Winter Olympics, Nagano. Office: c/o US Ski and Snowboard Assn PO Box 100 Park City UT 84060-0100

STREET, ROBERT, retired academic administrator, physicist; b. Wakefield, Eng., Dec. 16, 1920; s. Joe and Edith Elizabeth (Jones) S.; m. Joan Marjorie Bere, June 26, 1943; children: Alison Mary, Nicholas Robert. M.Sc., U. London, 1944, Ph.D., 1948, DSc, 1966, D.Sc.(hon.) U. Western Australia, 1986, U. Sheffield, Eng., 1987. With Ministry Supply, London, 1941-45; lectr. in physics U. Nottingham (Eng.), 1945-54; sr. lectr. U. Sheffield (Eng.), 1954-60; Found. prof. Monash U. (Australia), 1960-74; dir. Research Sch. Phys. scis., Australian Nat. U., Canberra Act, 1974-78; vice-chancellor U. Western Australia, Perth, 1978-86; hon. sr. rsch. fellow U. Western Australia, 1987—. Research, publs. in field. Decorated officer Order of Australia. Fellow Australian Acad. Sci., Inst. Physics, Australian Inst. Physics; mem. Inst. Elec. Engrs. Club: Weld (Perth). Home: 60 Temby Ave, Kalamunda Western Australia 6076, Australia Office: U Western Australia, Nedlands, Perth 6907, Australia

STREETEN, BARBARA WIARD, ophthalmologist, medical educator; b. Candia, N.H., Mar. 3, 1925; d. Robert Campbell Wiard and Gertrude Sarah Matheson; m. David Henry Palmer Streeten, Aug. 2, 1952; children: Robert Duncan, Elizabeth Anne, John Palmer. AB magna cum laude, Tufts U., 1945, MD cum laude, 1950. Diplomate Am. Bd. Ophthalmology. Jr. resident in gen. pathology Mallory Inst., Boston City Hosp., 1951-52; fellow in ophthalmic pathology Mass. Eye and Ear Infirmary, Boston, 1952-53; resident in ophthalmology Wayne County Gen. Hosp., Eloise, Mich., 1953-56; from jr. to sr. clin. instr. ophthalmology U. Mich. Med. Sch., Ann Arbor, 1956-60; from asst. prof. to prof. ophthalmology SUNY Health Sci. Ctr., Syracuse, 1964—, dir. eye pathology lab., 1966—, from asst. prof. to prof. pathology, 1968—. Contbr. over 110 articles to profl. jours., chpts. to textbooks. mem. vision study sect. Nat. Eye Inst., NIH, Bethesda, Md., 1977-80, mem. bd. sci. counselors, 1982-86; mem. editl. bd., mem. editl. adv.

com. Ophthalmology jour., 1982-94; gen. editor Investigative Ophthalmology and Visual Sci., 1979-82, mem. editl. bd., 1987-92. Grantee Nat. Eye Inst., NIH, 1975-2000. Mem. Am. Assn. Ophthalmic Pathologists (charter, past pres., bd. dirs., Zimmerman medal 1997), Am. Acad. Ophthalmology (honor award 1990), Verhoeff Ophthalmic Pathology Soc. (past pres.), Assn. for Rsch. in Vision and Ophthalmology (past sect. chmn.), Internat. Soc. Ophthalmic Pathology (co-v.p. N.Am. 1990-92), Phi Beta Kappa, Alpha Omega Alpha. Episcopalian. Achievements include establishment of elastic system nature of the suspensory ligament of the ocular lens; ultrastructural and immunopathologic contributions to diseases of the ocular connective tissue matrix, particularly those related to cataract and glaucoma. Avocations: archeology, sailing, snorkeling, travel, art. Home: 334 Berkley Dr Syracuse NY 13210-3000 Office: SUNY Upstate Med Univ WH Rm 2107 766 Irving Ave Syracuse NY 13210-1602

STREETEN, DAVID HENRY PALMER, internist, educator; b. Bloemfontein, South Africa, 1921; came to U.S., 1951; s. Reginald Craufurd and Olive Gladys (Palmer) S.; m. Barbara Anne Wiard, Aug. 2, 1952; children: Robert Duncan, Elizabeth Anne, John Palmer. BSc, U. Orange Free State, South Africa, 1941; MB BCh, U. Witwatersrand, South Africa, 1946; DPhil, Oxford U., 1951. Diplomate in internal medicine and endocrinology Am. Bd. Internal Medicine. Asst. prof. internal medicine U. Mich., Ann Arbor, 1955-60; assoc. prof. SUNY Upstate Med. Ctr., Syracuse, 1960-64, prof. Health Sci. Ctr., 1964—, prof. emeritus, 1994—. Author: Orthostatic Disorders of the Circulation, 1987; mem. editl. bds. 5 clin. and rsch. jours.; contbr. numerous articles to profl. jours., chpts. to books. Recipient Irvine Page Lifetime Achievement award in hypertension rsch. Am. Heart Assn. Coun. for High Blood Pressure Rsch., 1998, Best Tchr. award Dept. Medicine, SUNY, Syracuse, 1994, Life-time Achievement awad Nat. Dysautonomia Rsch. Found., 2000; Nuffield Found. fellow, 1948-51; Rockefeller fellow, 1951-52; Howard Hughes fellow, 1959-60; NIH and NSF awardee; NIH grantee. Fellow AAAS, ACP (Laureate award 1993), Royal Coll. Physicians; mem. Am. Diabetes Assn. (pres. Syracuse chpt. 1981-83), Ctrl. Soc. Clin. Rsch., Endocrine Soc., Internat. Soc. Hypertension, Am. Autonomic Soc. (nat. pres. 1995-96). Episcopalian. Achievements include original descriptions of 4 clinical disorders: hyperbradykininism, orthostatic edema, delayed orthostatic hypotension, hypermedullipinemia. Home: 334 Berkeley Dr Syracuse NY 13210-3000 Office: 750 E Adams St Syracuse NY 13210-2306

STREETER, JOHN WILLIS, information systems manager; b. Topeka, Sept. 3, 1947; s. Jack and Edith Bernice (Vowels) S.; m. Nancy Ann Buck, June 15, 1968 (div. 1985); children: Sarah Beth, Timothy Paine; m. Linda Lea Wenrich Weisbender, Sept. 13, 1986; stepchildren: Michael Leon Weisbender II, Debra Ann Weisbender Johnson, Dawn Marie Weisbender. BS in Computer Sci., Kans. State U., 1973, MBA in Mgmt., 1974; postgrad., Harvard U., 1992. Computer programmer U.S.M.C., 1965-70, Kans. State U., Manhattan, 1970-74; cons., mgr., prin. Am. Mgmt. Systems, Inc., Arlington, Va., 1974-83; systems planning analyst Fed. Nat. Mortgage Assn., Washington, 1983-85; assoc. dir. computing and telecomm. Kans. State U., Manhattan, 1985-91, dir. info. systems, 1991—; mem. State of Kans. Info. Tech. Adv. Bd., 1997-98. Author: Streeter Genealogy, 1985. Staff sgt. USMC, 1965-70. Recipient Navy Achievement medal in data processing Sec. Navy, 1971. Mem. IEEE, SR, KC, IEEE Computer Soc., Assn. for Computing Machinery, Am. Inst. Cert. Computer Profls., Educause, Inc. (Kans. State U. voting mem. rep. 1987—), Streeter Family Assn. (bd. dirs. 1988—, v.p. 1990-95), Am. Legion. Republican. Roman Catholic. Avocations: genealogy, history, book collecting. Home: 6765 Salzer Rd Wamego KS 66547-9636 Office: Kans State U Info Sys 2323 Anderson Ave Ste 215 Manhattan KS 66502-2912

STREETMAN, LEE GEORGE, sociology educator, criminology educator; b. Port Neches, Tex., Sept. 29, 1953; s. George Bernard and Roberta Valmeta (Fry) S. BA, U. Del., 1983, MA, 1985, PhD, 1995. Lectr. Ursinus Coll., Collegeville, Pa., 1990-92; asst. prof. Del. State U., Dover, Del., 1991-93; assoc. prof. Del. State U., Dover, 1996—; instr. Temple U., Phila., 1994; asst. prof. Cheyney (Pa.) U., 1994-96; assoc. prof. Del. State U., Dover, 1996—; sr. rsch. analyst Admark, Inc., Horsham, Pa., 1986-88; rsch. specialist Del. Coun. Crime and Justice, Wilmington, Del., 1988-89. Author: Drugs, Delinquency, and Pregnancy, A Panel Study of Adolescent Problem Behavior, 1996, Crime Perception in Postmodern Society, 1997, Streetman Soldiers in the War of the Rebellion (1861-65), 2d edit., 2000; contbr. articles to profl. jours. Tutor Thresholds Inmate Pre-release Program, Smyrna, Del., 1995. Mem. Am. Sociol. Assn., Am. Soc. Criminology, Popular Am. Culture Soc., Pa. Sociol. Soc., Soc. Study Social Problems, Alliance Prevention Adolescent Pregnancy, Sons of Confederate Vets., Cherokee Nat. Hist. Soc., Living History Soc. of Del., Ctrl. Del. Civil War Round Table. Office: Dept Sociology and Criminal Justice Del State U Dover DE 19901

STREETO, JOSEPH MICHAEL, catering company official; b. New Haven, Dec. 12, 1942; s. Pasquale Joseph and Marie Veronica (Matazzaro) S. BS, Quinnipiac Coll., Mt. Caramel, Conn., 1964. Mng. dir. spl. events divsn. Culinary Enterprises, Inc., Chgo., 1986-97; project dir. Blue Plate at Symphony Ctr., Chgo., 1997—; mem. com. DePaul U. Awards for Excellence in the Arts Gala, 1998. Co-chmn. telethon Muscular Dystrophy Assn., Chgo., 1989; Horizon Hospice, Chgo., 1988, vol., 1990, 96, chmn. annual benefit, 1999, Horizon Hospice Annual Benefit, 1999; co-chmn. gourmet dinner Blackstone benefit DePaul U.; bd. dirs. Horizon Hospice, 1995—; active Cooks by the Books/The Chgo. Fund on Aging, 1994-96. Home: 253 E Delaware Pl Apt 10E Chicago IL 60611-1733

STREHBLOW, HANS-HENNING STEFFEN, chemistry educator; b. Berlin, Germany, Sept. 21, 1939; s. Otto Alfred Wilhelm and Johanna Annemarie (Herold) S.; m. Claudia Strehblow; children: Kaja Ines, Alexander Dirk, Corinna Christine. Diplom in Chemistry, Freie U. Berlin, 1967, PhD, 1971, Habilitation in Phys. Che, 1977. Asst. Freie U. Berlin, 1969-73, asst. prof., 1973-79; cons. scientist Bell Labs., Murray Hill, N.J., 1976-77; akademischer rat Heinrich-Heine Univ., Düsseldorf, 1979-82; prof. phys. chemistry Heinrich-Heine Univ., 1982—; vis. prof. Johns Hopkins U., Balt., 1987-88, U. Pierre et Marie Curie Paris, 1993, 95, 96, 97, 99; guest scientist NIST, Gaithersburg, Md., 1987-88. Contbr. articles to profl. jours. Mem. Electrochem. Soc., Bunsen Gesellschaft, Gesellschaft Deutscher Chemiker, Fachgruppe Angewandte Elektrochemie, Internat. Soc. Electrochemistry. Avocation: gardening. Office: Heinrich Heine U Inst Phys/Elec Chem, Düsseldorf Geb 2642, 40225 Düsseldorf Germany

STREHLITZ, BEATE, research scientist; b. Leipzig, Saxony, Germany, Jan. 29, 1960; d. Alfred and Annelies (Pfestorf) Körner; m. Holger Strehlitz, Aug. 9, 1980; children: Nora, Wiebke. Deg., Inst. Tech. Ilmenau, 1985, engr., 1985; D. U. Witten, 1995. Project engr. VEB Galvanotechnik, Leipzig, Germany, 1985-88; sci. coworker Inst. Biotech., Leipzig, 1988-93; sci. coworker Ctr. Environ. Rsch., Leipzig, 1993-95, head project, 1995—. Patentee in field; contbr. articles to profl. jours. Avocation: sports. Office: Umweltforschungszentrum, Permoser Str 15, D-04318 Leipzig Germany

STREHLOW, HANS, chemistry educator; b. Oberhausen, Fed. Republic Germany, July 29, 1919; s. Friedrich and Christine (Jaeger) S.; m. Inge Platz Strehlow; children: Ulrich, Renate, Joachim. Diploma, U. Bonn, Germany, 1948; PhD, 1949. Asst. Max-Planck Inst. Phys. Chemistry, Gottingen, Germany, 1950-53; dept. leader, 1953-84, scientific mem., 1958-95. Author: Magnetische Kernresonanz und Chemische Struktur, 1962, 68, (with W. Knoche) Fundamentals of Chemical Relaxation, 1977, Rapid Reactions in Solution, 1992. Office: Max-Planck Inst Biophys Chem, AM Fassberg, D37077 Gottingen Germany

STREIBIG, JENS CARL, agricultural studies educator; b. Copenhagen, Denmark, Mar. 16, 1945; s. Carl Johan Streibig and Magdalene Jørgensen; m. Lone Vibeke Ottosen, Dec. 20, 1969; children: Trine, Sarah. MS, Veterinaer og Landbohoejskole, Copenhagen, 1972, PhD, 1977, DSc, 1992. Rsch. fellow Veterinaerog Landbohoejskole, 1975-76; sr. rsch. fellow Veterinaerog Land Bohoejskole, 1977-81, sr. lectr., 1982-92, assoc. prof., 1992-96, prof., 1996—; vis. scientist KTRI, Melbourne, Australia, 1988, NPURU-USDA, Oxford, Miss., 1997-98. Editor: Herbicide Bioassay, 1993. Recipient Hon. Sci. merits Brink Found., Denmark, 1987. Mem. Weed Scis. Soc. of Am. (hon.), European Weed Rsch. Soc., (sci. sec. 1994—). Home: Kloeverprisvej 11, DK-2650 Hvidovre Denmark Office: KVL Dept Agrl Sci, Thorvaldsensvej 40, DK-1871 Frederiksberg C, Denmark

STREIBLOVA, EVA, microbiologist, educator; b. Praha, Czech Republic, Apr. 1, 1931; d. Frantisek and Ruzena Safrankova (Pankova) Panek. D Natural Resources, Charles U., Praha, 1961; PhD, Czech Acad. Scis., Praha, 1966, DSc, 1982. Rsch. scientist Inst. Microbiology, Praha, 1951-66, staff scientist, 1967-70, sr. staff scientist, 1970-82, head rsch. group, 1982-95, emeritus leading scientist, 1996—; lectr. faculty natural scis. Charles U., Praha, 1990—; vis. prof. faculty natural scis. U. Salzburg, Austria, 1992-98, faculty pharmacy U. Nancy, 1991-95, Japan Soc. Promotion Scis., 1990. Editor: The Microbial Cell Cycle, 1984, The Cytoskeleton, 1991; contbr. chpts. to books. Mem. Czechoslovak Biol. Soc. (hon., exec. com.). Home: Dr E Streiblova, Na Pernikarce 14, Praha 6, Czech Republic Office: Inst. Microbiology, 142 20 Praha 4, 1083 Videnska Czech Repubic

STREIFINGER, WOLFGANG, surgeon; b. Jan. 26, 1947; s. Hanns and Apollonia S.; m. Margitta Hehr, June 16, 1976. MD, Ludwig-Maximilian U., Munich, Germany, 1973. Physician Hosp. Schrobenhausen, Germany, 1973-74; home physician, med. specialist Surgical Clin., Augsburg, Germany, 1974-81; house physician urological dept. City Hosp. Thalkirchnerstrasse, Munich, Germany, 1981-82; asst. med. dir. Clin. St. Elisabeth, Neuburg/Donau, Germany, 1982-85; asst. physician Heart Surgical Clin., Augsburg, Germany, 1985-87; asst. med. dir. Chirurgical Dept. City Hosp., Friedberg, 1987-95; asst. med. dir. Co. Hosp., Wertingen, 1995-96, head physician, 1996—; Contbr. articles to profl. jours. Mem. Christian Soc. Union, Friedberg, Germany, 1987—. Office: County Hosp, Ebersberg 36, Schwaben D-86637, Germany

STREIKER, SUSAN L., law librarian; b. Phila., Dec. 11, 1959; d. Lowell Dean and Lois Suzanne Streiker. BA, Brigham Young U., 1981, MLS, 1983. Reference and media asst. Law Sch. Libr. Brigham Young U., Provo, Utah, 1981-83; instr. in legal rsch., reference and media libr. Sch. of Law Southwestern U., L.A., 1984-89; reference libr. Paul, Hastings, Janofsky & Walker, LLP, L.A., 1989-91; head law libr. Paul, Hastings, Janofsky & Walker, L.A., 1991—. Fellow ABA; mem. Am. Assn. Law Librs., Southern Calif. Assn. Law Librs., Phi Alpha Theta. Avocations: music, traveling, painting, gardening, ballooning. Office: Paul Hastings Janofsky & Walker LLP 555 S Flower St Fl 23D Los Angeles CA 90071-2300

STREISAND, BARBRA JOAN, singer, actress, director; b. Bklyn., Apr. 24, 1942; d. Emanuel and Diana (Rosen) S.; m. Elliott Gould, Mar. 1963 (div.); 1 son, Jason Emanuel; m. James Brolin, July 1, 1998. Grad. high sch., Bklyn.; student, Yeshiva of Bklyn. N.Y. theatre debut Another Evening with Harry Stoones, 1961; appeared in Broadway musicals I Can Get It for You Wholesale, 1962, Funny Girl, 1964-65; motion pictures include Funny Girl, 1968, Hello Dolly, 1969, On a Clear Day You Can See Forever, 1970, The Owl and the Pussy Cat, 1970, What's Up Doc?, 1972, Up the Sandbox, 1972, The Way We Were, 1973, For Pete's Sake, 1974, Funny Lady, 1975, The Main Event, 1979, All Night Long, 1981, Nuts, 1987; star, prodr. film A Star is Born, 1976; prodr., dir., star Yentl, 1983, The Prince of Tides, 1991, The Mirror Has Two Faces, 1996; exec. prodr.: (TV movie) Serving in Silence: The Margarethe Cammermeyer Story, 1995; TV spls. include My Name is Barbra, 1965 (5 Emmy awards), Color Me Barbra, 1966; actress, prodr., dir. The Mirror Has Two Faces, 1996; rec. artist on Columbia Records; Gold record albums include People, 1965, My Name is Barbra, 1965, Color Me Barbra, 1966, Barbra Streisand: A Happening in Central Park, 1968, Barbra Streisand: One Voice, Stoney End, 1971, Barbra Joan Streisand, 1972, The Way We Were, 1974, A Star is Born, 1976, Superman, 1977, The Stars Salute Israel at 30, 1978, Wet, 1979, (with Barry Gibb) Guilty, 1980, Emotion, 1984, The Broadway Album, 1986, Til I Loved You, 1989; other albums include: A Collection: Greatest Hits, 1989, Just for the Record, 1991, Back to Broadway, 1993, Concert at the Forum, 1993, The Concert Recorded Live at Madison Square Garden, 1994, The Concert Highlights, 1995, Higher Ground, 1997. Recipient Emmy award, CBS-TV spl. (My Name Is Barbra), 1964, Acad. award as best actress (Funny Girl), 1968, Golden Globe award (Funny Girl), 1969, co-recipient Acad. award for best song (Evergreen), 1976, Georgie award AGVA 1977, Grammy awards for best female pop vocalist, 1963, 64, 65, 77, 86, for best song writer (with Paul Williams), 1977, 2 Grammy nominations for Back to Broadway, 1994; Nat. Acad. of Recording Arts & Sciences Lifetime Achievement Award, 1994. Office: ICM c/o Jeff Berg 8942 Wilshire Blvd Beverly Hills CA 90211-1934

STREIT, BRUNO, biologist, ecotoxicologist, ecologist; b. Basel, Switzerland, Mar. 4, 1948; s. Kurt Walter and Maria Theresia (Lill) S.; m. Sigrid Hertha Wilhelmine Ohlsen, Sept. 21, 1978. Diploma, U. Basel, 1971, PhD, 1975, Habilitation, 1979. Scientist Limnologisches Inst., Konstanz, Germany, 1975-78; asst. Zoology Inst. U. Basel, 1978-79, asst. prof., 1979-82; rsch. assoc. dept. biology Stanford (Calif.) U., 1982-84; prof. U. Frankfurt, Germany, 1985—; cons. Büro Or. H. Schmassmann, Liestal, Switzerland, 1971-72, Motor Columbus, Baden, Switzerland, 1979-80. Author: Ökologie ein Kurzlehrbuch, 1980, Lexikon Ökotoxikologie, 1991, 2d edit., 1994; co-editor: Molecular Ecology and Evolution, 1994, Fish Ecotoxicology, 1998; editor: Evolutionary Ecology of Freshwater Animals, 1997, others. Mem. German Soc. Limnology (chmn. ann. meeting 1997), others. Office: Johann-Wolfgang-Goethe U, Dept Ecology & Evolution, D-60054 Frankfurt Germany

STREIT, LUDWIG P., physics educator; b. Leipzig, Germany, June 26, 1938; s. August G. and Marie-Therese (Adolph) S.; m. Margarida de Faria, June 6, 1988; children: Clara-C., Jan-D. PhD, U. Graz, Austria, 1962. Postdoctoral fellow univs. Graz, Hamburg, Zurich, 1962-68, asst. prof., 1968-69; assoc. prof. Suracuse (N.Y.) U., 1970-72; mem. tech. staff Bell Labs., N.J., 1969-70; prof. Bielefeld (Fed. Republic Germany) U., 1972—, dir. Ctr. for Interdisciplinary Rsch., 1981-85; hon. prof. U. Graz, 1973; chair prof. U. Minho, Portugal, 1989-91, U. Madeira, 1991—. Editor 16 books; author monograph; contbr. over 80 articles to sci. jours. Acad. fellow Volkswagen Found., 1980-82. Mem. Assn. Math. Physics (exec. com. 1979-85, sec. 1982-85). Office: U Bielefeld, Universitätsstrasse 25, 33501 Bielefeld Germany

STREITMAN, CHARLES MICHAEL, pediatrician; b. Mako, Csongrad, Hungary, July 24, 1937; . Charles and Cathrine (Nacsa) S.; m. Helen Tisza, Feb. 13, 1962; children: Agnes, Christina. MD, Szote Med. U., Budapest, Hungary, 1962; PhD, Hungarian Acad. Sci., 1983. Fellow Albert Szent-Györgyi Med. U., Szeged, 1962-66, asst. prof., 1966-77, assoc. prof., 1992—; chief pediat. Hodmezovasarhely, 1977-84; assoc. prof. Postgrad. Med. U., Budapest, 1984-92. Author: Nephrology, 1979. Recipient Heinrich Herz award U. Düsseldorf, 1964-65, Habilitation award Pediatric/Nephrology, 1998. Mem. World Fedn. Hungarians (v.p. 1996), European Soc. Pediat. Nephrology (award 1977), Internat. Pediat. Nephrology Assn. (award 1980), German Pediat. Assn. Roman Catholic. Avocations: swimming. Home: Vedres Str 22 B, 6726 Szeged Hungary Office: A Szent Gyorgyi Med U, Koranyi rkpt 14-15, 6725 Szeged Hungary

STREITWOLF, HANS WALDEMAR, retired physicist; b. Hirschfeld, Germany, Apr. 4, 1933; s. Karl and Gertrud (Bischoff) S.; m. Sonnhild Ulrich, June 10, 1966; children: Peter, Holger. Dr. rer. nat., U. Berlin, 1959, dr. habil., 1969. Rsch. scientist Acad. Sci. Berlin, 1957-91, Max Planck Gesellschaft, Berlin, 1992-96, Inst. für Physik, Humboldt Univ., Berlin, 1997-99. Author: Group Theory in Solid State Physics, 1967, 71; co-author: Theoretische Grundlagen der Halbleiterphysik, 1977. Mem. Deutsche Physikalische Gesellschaft.

STREJAN, GILL HENRIC, immunologist, educator; b. Galati, Romania, Sept. 24, 1930; s. Henric S. and Rita (Kleiner) S.; m. Odette Isabella Fischer, May 30, 1963. MS, U. Bucharest, Romania, 1953; PhD, Hebrew U., Jerusalem, 1965. Postdoctoral fellow Calif. Inst. Tech., Pasadena, 1965-68; asst. prof. U. Western Ont., London, Can., 1968-73, assoc. prof., 1973-80, prof., 1980-96, prof. emeritus, 1996—; scientist J.P. Robarts Rsch. Inst., London, Can., 1994—. Author: (chpt.) Modern Concepts and Developments in Immediate Hypersensitivity, 1978; contbr. articles to profl. jours. Grantee Med. Rsch. Coun., Can., 1968-96, Multiple Sclerosis Soc. Can., 1981—. Mem. Am. Assn. Immunologists, Can. Soc. Immunology, Sigma Xi. Office: U Western Ont Dept Micro & Immun, Health Sci Ctr, London, ON Canada N6A 5C1

STREJCEK, ELIZABETH GEIERMAN, reading specialist, educator; b. Chgo., Dec. 7, 1948; d. Aloysius Herman and Lillian Elizabeth (Cowan) Geierman; m. George Joseph Strejcek, Jan. 27, 1971; children: James Edwin, Theodore Eliot. BA in History, U. Ill., Chgo., 1971, MA in Ednl. Leadership, 1981. Cert. reading specialist, Ill. Subs. tchr. pub. schs., Berwyn, Ill., 1972-74; tchr. reading grades 5-8 South Berwyn Pub. Sch., Berwyn, 1974-77; tchr. reading lab. grades 9-12 Bolinbrook (Ill.) High Sch., 1979-83; tchr. reading grades 7-8 Westview Mid. Sch., Romeoville, Ill., 1983-84, tchr. grades 6-8, 1984-85; chpt. I reading tchr. grades K-5 Northview Elem. Sch., Bolingbrook, 1985-91; tchr. grades 9-10 Morton East H.S., Cicero, 1991—, tchr. spl. program on attendance, chpt. I-title I tchr., 1991, 94, tchr. truancy and attendance program, 1993—, mem. various coms., 1991—; presenter lectures, demonstrations on reading and writing and using technology in classroom, 1989—, Title I Summer Sch. Curriculum (reading and writing), 1997. Mem. AAUW, Internat. Reading Assn., Ill. Reading Coun. (bd. dirs. 1994-95), Ill. Computing Educators, Nat. Coun. Tchrs. English, Czech Cache, ICREARY, Secondary Reading League (pres. 1993-95, 99-00). Avocations: pottery/ceramics, computer applications, reading, drawing. Office: 2423 S Austin Blvd Cicero IL 60804-2616

STREK, PAWEL, surgeon, educator; b. Cracow, Poland, June 9, 1959; s. Jozef and Jrena (Stelmaszek) S.; m. Weneta Hejnar, Sept. 26, 1983. MD, Jagiellonian U., Cracow, Poland, 1984, PhD, 1991. Med. diplomate Otolaryngology. Asst. dept. otolaryngology Jagiellonian U., Cracow, 1984-93, lectr., 1993-99, assoc. prof., 1999—. Contbr. articles to profl. jours. Mem. Polish Soc. Otorhinolaryngologists (sec. 1998—), European Rhinologic Soc. Roman Catholic. Avocations: tennis, windsurfing, skiing, travel, music. Phone: 4812-421-00-38. Office: Dept Otolaryngology CM UJ, Sniadeckich 2, 31-501 Cracow Poland

STRELAU, RENATE, historical researcher, artist; b. Berlin, Feb. 1, 1951; came to U.S., 1960; d. Werner Ernst and Gerda Gertrud (Bargel) S. BA, U. Calif., Berkeley, 1974; cert. Arabic lang. proficiency, Johns Hopkins U., 1976; MA, Am. U., 1985, MFA, 1991. Rsch. asst. Iranian Embassy, Washington, 1976-80. One-woman shows include Cafe Espresso, Berkeley, Calif., 1973, Riggs Bank, Arlington, Va., 1994-95; exhibited in group shows at Watkins Gallery, Washington, 1999; represented in permanent collections at C. Law Watkins Meml. Collection, Am. U. Mem. Am. Hist. Assn., Orgn. Am. Historians, Soc. for Historians Am. Fgn. Rels. (life). Home: 1021 Arlington Blvd Apt 1041 Arlington VA 22209-2255

STRELETS, VALERIA BORISOVNA, neurophysiologist, researcher; b. Charkhov, USSR, June 26, 1939; d. Boris Samojlovich Beilin and Julija Ivanovna Guy; m. Vitaliy Alekseevich Strelets; 1 child, Natalia Vitalievna. Diploma in Medicine, Moscow Med. Inst., 1962; Diploma in Psychology, Moscow U., 1980; Candidate of Med. Scis., 2d Moscow Med. Inst., 1970; D of Med. Scis., Inst. Higher Nervous Activity and Neurophysiology, Russian Acad. Scis., 1985. Postgrad. fellow Ctr. Mental Health, 1965-68; with Serbsky Inst. Gen. and Forensic Psychiatry, 1970-77; from jr. sci. rschr. to head of lab. clin. electrophysiology Inst. Higher Nervous Activity and Neurophysiology, 1977-97, leading rschr., 1997—; lectr. psychol. dept. Moscow U., Moscow Youth Inst. Contbr. articles to profl. jours. Russian del. Internat. Fedn. Clin. Neurophysiologists. Grantee Intas Found., Russian Found. for Humanitarian Rsch. Avocation: foreign languages. Home: Prospect Vernadskogo 38A 7, 117454 Moscow Russia Office: Inst Higher Nervous Activ, Russia Acad Scis, 117865 Moscow Russia

STRELKOV, LEONID ALEKSEEVICH, biologist, researcher; b. Moscow, Feb. 12, 1945; s. Aleksei Ivanovich and Zinaida Grigorievna (Tronova) S.; m. Ludmila Borisovna Milova, Mar. 9, 1966 (div. 1970); 1 child, Dmitriy; m. Nana Borisovna Chiaureli; 1 child, Rusudan. Diploma, Second Med. Inst., Moscow, 1969; DSc, Inst. Molecular Biology, Kiev, Ukraine, 1976. Asst. Inst. Molecular Biology, Moscow, 1971-82; sr. scientist Inst. Phys. Chem. Medicine, Moscow, 1983-86, Inst. Immunology, Moscow, 1986-89, Inst. Bioorganic Chemistry, Moscow, 1989—. Contbr. articles to profl. jours. Home: 117574, Odoevskiy Str 7-2-238, Moscow Russia Office: Shemyakin and Ocvhinnikov, Inst Biorg Chem 16-10, 117871 Moscow Russia

STRELKOV, ROSTISLAV BORISOVICH, physician, radiologist; b. Alapaevsk, Sverdlovsk, Russia, Jan. 9, 1929; s. Boris Michailovich and Ludmila Wasilievna (Strachova) S.; m. Grigozievna Traida Partin-Oslonovskaja, Feb. 19, 1947; 1 child, Natalia Rostislavovna. Student, Moscow Med. Inst., 1948-52, Samara Med. Inst., 1954; MD, Ural State U., Swerdlowk, Russia, 1963. Asst. prof. Swerdlowsk Med. Inst., Russia, 1959-62; rschr. worker Inst. of Pathology and Therapeutics Acad. Med. Sci., Sukhumy, USSR, 1962-68; chief of lab. Inst. Brain Rsch. Acad. Med. Sci., Moscow, 1969-78, Inst. Med. Radiology, Obninsk, Russia, 1978-84; prof. Russian State Med. U., Moscow, 1984-89; dir. Med. Ctr. of Hyposittherapy, Moscow, 1989-93; pres. Acad. Hypoxic Problems Russian Fedn., Moscow, 1993—. Author: (with others) Normobaric Hypoxia, 1988, Radioprotection Method for Animals and Humans, 1994; inventor, patentee in field; contbr. numerous articles to profl. publs. Pres. pub. charity fund Care, Support Initiative, Moscow, 1999—. Mem. Internat. Sci. for Pathophysiology (Russian nat. adv. bd. 1992), Russian Med. Tech. Acad., N.Y. Acad. Scis. Home and Office: Malaja Filyevskaja, Ulitza 22-7, 121433 Moscow Russia

STRELNIKER, YAKOV MIKHAILOVICH, physicist, researcher; b. Gnivan, Vinnitsa, USSR, May 23, 1956; arrived in Israel, 1990; s. Mikhail Isaakovich and Sophia L'vovna (Livshits) S. MSc, Perm U., 1978, PhD, 1989. Sr. rsch. scientist Vinnitsa Med. U., 1987-90; postdoctoral rsch. assoc. Tel Aviv (Israel) U., 1991-94, rsch. scientist, 1994-2000; sr. rsch. scientist Bar-Ilan U., 2000—. Gileadi fellow Ministry of Absorption of the State of Israel, 1996—. Office: Bar-Ilan U, Minerva Ctr & Dept Physics, 52900 Ramat-Gan Israel

STREL'NITSKIJ, VLADIMIR EVGEN'EVICH, physicist; b. Kharkov, Ukraine, Sept. 19, 1946; s. Evgenij Venedictovich and Olga Romanovna Strel'nitskij; m. Irina Semenovna Shilina, July 19, 1972; 1 child, Natasha. Master's degree, Kharkov State U., 1970, PhD, 1980. Engr., jr. scientist, sr. scientist, head of lab. Kharkov Inst. Physics and Tech., 1972—. Sr. lt. Russian Army, 1970-72. Recipient State Premium of Soviet Union, Govt. of Soviet Union, 1987. Mem. Ukrainian Phys. Soc. Fax: 057 2350755. E-mail: strelnitskij@kipt.kharkov.ua. Home: Elizarova 4 Fl 281, 61098 Kharkov Ukraine Office: Kharkov Inst Physics/Tech, Akademicheskaya 1, 61108 Kharkov Ukraine

STREMPEL, ULRICH, political scientist; b. Kiel, Germany, Dec. 8, 1953; s. Juergen and Erika Margarete Marie (Sander) S.; m. Lise AnnePerreault, Aug. 9, 1975 (div. Nov. 1979). BA (hons.), U. Alta, Edmonton, Can., 1975, PhD, 1982; MA, Carleton U., Ottawa, Ont., Can., 1977. Lectr. polit. sci. U. Alta, 1979-80, 81-82; adminstrv. intern Commn. of European Communities, Brussels, 1977-78; rsch. fellow German Soc. for Fgn. Affairs, Bonn, 1982-84; editor Press and Info. Office of German Govt., Bonn, 1984-86, sr. officer, govt. spokesman's group, 1986-90; 1st sec. press and info. German Embassy, Paris, 1990-94; dep. head France, EU, OECD German Embassy, Bonn, Berlin, 1994—. Contbr. articles to jours. and books; translator articles and monographs on internat. politics. Mem. Christian Dem. Union, 1982—; v.p. Can. Wolf Defenders, Edmonton, 1980-81. Carleton U. grad. scholar, 1975-76; dissertation fellow U. Alta, 1980-81. Mem. German Soc. for Can. Studies, German-Can. Soc., Europa Union. Lutheran. Avocations: chess, tennis, fine automobiles. Home: Danglerstr 66, D-53173 Bonn Germany Office: Informationsamt Bundesregierung, Neustädtische Kirchstr 5, D-10117 Berlin Germany

STRENA, ROBERT VICTOR, university research laboratory manager; b. Seattle, June 28, 1929; s. Robert Lafayette Peel and Mary Oliva (Holmes) S.; m. Rita Mae Brodovsky, Aug. 1957; children: Robert Victor, Adrienne Amelia. AB, Stanford U., 1952. Survey mathematician Hazen Engring., San Jose, Calif., 1952-53; field engr. Menlo Sanitary Dist., Menlo Park, Calif., 1954-55; ind. fin. reporter Los Altos, Calif., 1953-59; asst. dir. Hansen Labs. Stanford U., 1959-93, asst. dir. emeritus Ginzton Lab., 1993—; ind. fin. cons., Los Altos, 1965—; mem. restoration adv. bd., Moffett Fed. Airfield,

1994—. Active Edn. System Politics, Los Altos, 1965-80, local Boy Scouts Am., 1968-80, Maj. USAR, 1948-70. Mem. AAAS, Mus. Soc., Big X (Los Altos), Cherry Chase Golf Club. Republican. Avocations: golf, sailing. Home: 735 Raymundo Ave Los Altos CA 94024-3139 Office: Stanford U Ginzton Lab Stanford CA 94305

STRENGER, HERMANN JOSEF, chemicals executive; b. Cologne, Germany, Sept. 26, 1928; married; 4 children. With Bayer AG, 1949, Brazil, 1954-57; bd. mem. Bayer AG, 1972-84, chmn. mgmt. bd., 1984-92; chmn. supervisory bd. Bayer AG, Leverkusen, Germany, 1992—; with Bayer subs. AB Anilin Kemi, Gothenburg, Sweden, 1958-61, sales mgr., coatings, 1961-65, head dept. polyurethanes, 1965-72; mem. supervisory bd. Commerzbank AG, Degussa AG, Linde AG; chmn. Veba AG; founder Hermann Strenger Found. for the Promotion of Internat. Profl. Experience. Pres. supporting body U. Cologne, Germany. Recipient Centenary medal Soc. Chem. Industry, Great Britain, 1991. Mem. Assn. German Chem. Industry (pres. 1990-91). Office: Veba AG Postfach 30 10 51, Bennigsenplatz 1, D-40474 Düsseldorf Germany also: Bayer AG, D-51368 Leverkusen Bayerwerk, Germany*

STRENGTH, ROBERT SAMUEL, manufacturing company executive; b. Tullos, La., May 14, 1929; s. Houston Orion and Gurcie Dean (Cousins) S.; m. Janice Lynette Grace,Sept. 12, 1954; children: Robert David (dec.), James Steven (dec.), Stewart Alan, James Houston (dec.). BS in Indsl. Mgmt., Auburn U., 1956. Registered profl. engr., Calif.; cert. safety profl. Engr., supr. plant safety Monsanto Co., 1956-74; engring. stds. mgr. Corp. Fire Safety Ctr., St. Louis, 1974-78; mgr. product safety and acceptability Monsanto Polymer Products Co. (formerly Monsanto Plastics and Resins Co.), St. Louis, 1978-82; mgr. product safety Monsanto Chem. Co., St. Louis, 1982-87; founder, pres. Product Safety Mgmt. Inc., 1987—; mem. com. on toxicity of materials used in rapid rail transit, NRC, 1984-87. Editor testile sect. newsletter Nat. Safety Coun., 1961-62. Pres. Greenwood (S.C.) Citizens Safety Coun., 1966-68; U.S. del., tech. expert on fire safety of elec. products, Internat. Electrotech. Commn. With USAF, 1948-52. Recipient S.C. Outstanding Svc. to Safety award Nat. Safety Coun., 1968. Mem ASHRAE, Am. Soc. Safety Engrs., Nat. Safety Coun. (pres. textile sect. 1966), So. Bldg. Code Congress, Internat. Conf. of Bldg. Ofcls., Bldg. Ofcls. and Code Adminstrs. Internat., Nat. Fire Protection Assn., (mem. code making panel 7 nat. elec. codes), ASTM Fire Test Com. (chmn. fire hazard and risk assessment subc0m., mem. exec. com. fire test), Nat. Inst. Bldg. Scis., Plastic Pipe and Fittings Assn., Soc. Plastics Industries (past chmn. coord. com. on fire safety 1985-87), Nat. Acad. Scis., Cherry Hills C.C., Raintree Plantation Golf and C.C., Tiger Point C.C. Republican. Methodist. Home and Office: 3510 Hillside Ave Gulf Breeze FL 32561-3322

STRETTON, JOHN EDWARD HALLYBURTON, surgeon, consultant, writer; b. London, Jan. 17, 1916; s. Hallyburton Tom and Mary Lucy (Barber) S. BA, Cambridge (Eng.) U., 1939, MBBS, MA, 1947. Registered med. practitioner, Gen. Med. Coun. Eng. Asst. gen. practitioner surgeon; gen. house surgeon Staines Hosp., 1944-45, traumatic house surgeon, 1945-46; surg. registrar Aylesbury Hosp., 1946; surg. registrar, veneriologist Dreadnought Seamen's Hosp., Greenwich, 1947; surg. registrar The Princess Beatrice Hosp., London, 1947-49; surgeon Isle of Jersey, Channel Islands, 1949; surg. registrar Kings Coll. Hops. Group, London, 1950-58; cons. trauma surgeon Princess Alice Hosp., Eastbourne, Eng., 1958, Royal East Sussex Hosp., Hastings, Eng., 1958; physician 7520th USAF Hosp., London, 1958-62; chmn. Chalk Blue Estates Ltd., Heathfield, Eng., 1962, Jomay Bldg. Co. Ltd., Heathfield, Eng., 1962, Cala San Esteban, Soc. Anomina, Menorca, Spain, 1970; lectr. history of art Nat. Gallery, London. Author: (as Hallyburton Stretton) Columbus: Rival to King Ferdinand, 1994; contbr. articles to catologues and jours. With Brit. Home Guard, 1939-45. Recipient diving medal Club Mediteranee. Fellow Inst. Dirs. London; mem. Royal Coll. Surgeons Longon, Royal Coll. Physicians London (lic.), Inst. Profls., Mgrs. and Specialists Eng., Guild of Sommeliers, Brit. Med. Assn., Med. Protection Soc., Royal Automobile Club (Sr. 100 mem.). Home: Apt 10 Es Castell Menorca, Baleares 07720, Spain

STRETTON, ROSS, ballet dancer; b. Canberra, Australia; came to U.S., 1979.; Student, Australian Ballet Sch. Mem. corps de ballet Australian Ballet, 1972-74, soloist, 1974-78, prin. dancer, 1978-79; with Joffrey Ballet, 1979-81; joined No. Ballet Theatre, Manchester, Eng.; guest artist Am. Ballet Theatre, 1980-81, soloist, 1981-83, prin. dancer, 1983-90, asst to the dirs., 1990-91, regisseur, 1991-93, asst. dir., 1993—; art. dir. Australian Ballet, Melbourne, Victoria, Australia, 1997—. Created role in Martine van Hamel's Amnon V'Tamar; other repertoire includes: Bach Partita, La Bayadere, Bouree Fantastique, Giselle, Duets, Pillar of Fire, La Sylphide, The Wild Boy, Cinderella, Don Quixote, The Nutcracker, Swan Lake, The Sleeping Beauty, others. Office: care Am Ballet Theatre 890 Broadway New York NY 10003-1211

STREVETT, KEITH ANTHONY, bioenvironmental engineer, educator; b. Chgo., June 14, 1967; s. Alan Dalton and Janet Marie Strevett; m. Stacy Frances Huck, Dec. 15, 1990; children: Anthony Joseph, Theresa Marie. BS in Microbiology and Pub. Health, Mich. State U., 1992, BS in Civil and Environ. Engring., 1992; PhD in Environ. Engring., U. Conn., 1995. Cert. Engr. in tng., Mich. Rsch. asst. Mich. Biotech. Inst., East Lansing, 1986-90; rsch. asst. dept. biochemistry Mich. State U., East Lansing, 1989-92; rsch. asst. Sch. Civil and Environ. Engring., U. Conn., Storrs, 1992-95; engr. Hoag and Grasso, Inc., Storrs, 1993-95; asst. prof. Sch. Civil Engring. and Environ. Sci., U. Okla., Norman, 1995—; rsch. engr. Bioenviron. Engring. and Sci. Lab., U. Okla., 1996—. Developer theory on environ. sci. and tech.; inventor, contbr. articles in field. Recipient NSF Career award, 1998. Mem. ASCE, Assn. Environ. Engring., Assn. Sci. Profs., Am. Soc. Engring. Educators, Am. Soc. Microbiology, Sigma Xi, Chi Epsilon. Fax: 405-325-4217. E-mail: strevett@ou.edu. Office: Univ Okla Sch Civil Eng Environ Sci 202 W Boyd St Rm 334 Norman OK 73019-1027

STREZH, PETR EVGENYEVICH, physicist, educator; b. Moscow, Apr. 8, 1937; s. Evgeniy Grigoryevich Strezh and Elena Petrovna Artemkina. Diploma in physics, Moscow State U., 1961, degree in phys. and math. scis., 1968. Engr. Ctrl. Sci. Rsch. Inst. Mech. Engring., Kaliningrad, Russia, 1961-64; rsch. asst. Russian Peoples' Friendship U., Moscow, 1968, sr. lectr., 1969, asst. prof., 1970—; sr. rschr. Contractual Works, Moscow, 1979-83; supr. studies for postgrad. students, Moscow, 1975-82. Author: Electrical Oscillations and Waves, 1997; contbr. articles to profl. publs. Dep. Dist. Soviet, Moscow, 1973-79. Recipient Honor of Higher Sch., Ministry of Higher and Secondary Spl. Edn., 1987, Vet. of Labor award, 1990. Avocations: piano, oil painting, collecting books. Home: 15 Ostrovityanova Str, Bldg 1 Apt 42, 117 437 Moscow Russia Office: Russian Peoples Friendship, 6 Miklukho-Maklai Str GSP, 177 198 Moscow Russia

STRIBLIN, LORI ANN, critical care nurse, Medicare coordinator, nursing educator; b. Valley, Ala., Sept. 23, 1962; d. James Author and Dorothy Jane (Cole) Burt; m. Thomas Edward Striblin, Oct. 26, 1984; children: Natalie Nicole, Crystal Danielle. AAS in Nursing, So. Union State Jr. Coll., Valley, Ala., 1992. RN, Ala.; cert. ACLS, BLS, in fitness nutrition ICS. Surg. staff nurse East Ala. Med. Ctr., Opelika, 1992-93, surg. charge nurse, 1993-95, critical care ICU staff nurse, 1993-95; RN case mgr. East Ala. Home Care, Opelika, 1995-96; staff devel. coord., medicare coord. Lanett (Ala.) Geriatric Ctr., 1996-97; case mgr. Lanier Home Health Svcs., Valley, Ala., 1996-97; med. advisor Nu Image Weight Loss Ctr., Opelika, Ala., 1996-97, nurse case mgr. weight loss ctr., counselor, diet educator, 1996-98; RN case mgr. Chattahoochie Hospice, Valley, Ala., 1998; case mgr. Chattahoochee Hospice, 1998; critical care nurse cardiovasc. ICU and telementry unit East Ala. Med. Ctr., Opelika, 1999—; clin. instr. educator So. Union C.C., Valley, 1994-97. Mem. AACN, Ala. State Nurses Assn. Baptist. Avocations: crafts, horseback riding, hiking, swimming, reading, arts. Home: 1608 31st St Valley AL 36854-2925

STRICKER, ANDREAS, banking executive; b. Grabs, Switzerland, Mar. 31, 1959; s. Andreas and Gertrud Pauline (Irgang) S.; m. Marie-Carmen Carmona, Jan. 31, 1981; children: Valerie, Bruno. Diploma, Swiss Comml. Sch., Buchs, Switzerland, 1978, Swiss Higher Banking, Berne, Switzerland, 1985. Head of securities ops. Union Bank Switzerland, London, 1986-90; head of worldwide securities dept. Citibank N.A., Zurich, Switzerland, 1991-94; mem. exec. bd. Bordier & Cie, Geneva, Switzerland, 1994—; Bd. dirs. Swiss Fin. Svcs. Group AG, Zurich, SIS Sega Intersettle AG, Zurich. Mem. Société Litteraire (bd. dirs.). Avocations: tennis, cross-country skiing. Home: Chemin de la Californie 12, 1222 Vesenaz Geneva, Switzerland Office: Bordier & Cie Pvt Bankers, 16 Rue de Hollande, 1204 Geneva Switzerland

STRICKER, JACK MAURICE, architect, designer; b. Zurich, Aug. 2, 1943; s. Jakob and Emma Catherina (Largo) S.; m. Barbara Dwyer Miller, Aug. 25, 1968 (div. 1974); m. Hedy D. Dubacher, Sept. 25, 1985. BS, U. Pa. Designer Grob AS, Zollikon, Switzerland, 1960-61; design dir. Dr. Farner, Zurich, 1961-62; asst. creative dir. Sauter, Zurich, 1962-63; designer Pitts. Studios, 1963-64; art dir. Gateway Studios, Pitts., 1964-66; prin. Jack M. Stricker Assoc., Pitts., 1966-73, Zurich, 1974—; tchr. Ivy Sch. Profl. Art, P itts., 1965-67, prof., 1967-70. Mem. Optimists. Home: Melchrutistrasse 55, CH-8304 Wallisellen Switzerland Office: Jack M Stricker Assocs, Melchrütistrasse 55, 8304 Wallisellen Switzerland

STRICKLAND, MELANIE ANN, pharmacist; b. Longview, Tex., Sept. 13, 1966; d. Josh S. and Carolyn F. (Wimber) S.; m. Jerry Ray McClain, Feb. 14, 1998. AS, Kilgore Coll., 1987; BS in Pharmacy, U. Houston, 1991. Registered pharmacist, Tex. Staff pharmacist Hermann Hosp., Houston, 1991-92; clin. pharmacist Baylor Med. Ctr., Garland, Tex., 1992—; chmn. profl. studies adv. coun. U. Houston Coll. Pharmacy, 1994-97. Vol. Red Cross Disaster Svcs., Denton, Tex., 1995—. Mem. Am. Soc. Health Sys. Pharmacists, Metroplex Soc. Hosp. Pharmacists.

STRICKLAND, ROBERT LOUIS, former investment company executive; b. Florence, S.C., Mar. 3, 1931; s. Franz M. and Hazel (Eaddy) S.; m. Elizabeth Ann Miller, Feb. 2, 1952; children: Cynthia Anne, Robert Edson. AB, U. N.C., 1952; MBA with distinction, Harvard U., 1957. Bd. dirs. Lowe's Cos., Inc., North Wilkesboro, N.C., 1961-2000, sr. v.p., 1970-76, with, 1957-98, exec. v.p., 1976-78, chmn. bd., 1978-98, chmn. exec. com., 1988-98, mem. office of pres., 1970-78, chmn. emeritus, 1999; founder Sterling Advt., Ltd., 1966; v.p., mem. adminstrv. com. Lowe's Profit-Sharing Trust, 1961-87, chmn. ops. com., 1972-78; mgmt. com. Lowe's ESOP Plan, 1978-97; bd. dirs. T. Rowe Price Assocs., Balt., Hannaford Bros., Portland, Krispy Kreme Corp., Winston-Salem; panelist investor rels. field, 1972—; spkr., panelist employee stock ownership, 1978—; spkr. on investor rels., London, Edinburgh, Glasgow, Paris, Zurich, Frankfurt, Milan, Vienna, Singapore, Tokyo. Author: Lowe's Cybernetwork, 1969, Lowe's Living Legend, 1970, Ten Years of Growth, 1971, The Growth Continues, 1972, 73, 74, Lowe's Scoreboard, 1978, also articles. Mem. N.C. Ho. of Reps., 1962-64, Rep. Senatorial Inner Circle, 1980-95; exec. com. N.C. Rep. Com., 1963-73; trustee U. N.C., Chapel Hill, 1987-95, chmn. bd., 1991-93; dir., dep. chmn. Fed. Res. Bank of Richmond, 1996-98; com. on bus. laws and the economy N.C., 1994-97; dir. U.S. Coun. Better Bus. Burs., 1981-85; bd. dirs., v.p. Nat. Home Improvement Coun., 1972-76; bd. dirs. N.C. Sch. Arts Found., 1975-79, N.C. Bd. Natural and Econ. Resources, 1975-76; bd. dirs., govt. affairs com. Home Ctr. Inst.; trustee, sec. bd. Wilkes C.C., 1964-73; chmn., pres. bd. dirs. Do-It-Yourself Rsch. Inst., 1981-89; pres. Hardware Home Improvement Coun. City of Hope Nat. Med. Ctr., L.A., 1987-89. With USN, 1952-55, lt. Res. 1955-62. Named Wilkes County N.C. Young Man of Yr., Wilkes Jr. C. of C., 1962; recipient Bronze Oscar of Industry award Fin. World, 1969-74, 76-79, Silver Oscar of Industry award, 1970, 72-74, 76-79, Gold Oscar of Industry award as best of all industry, 1972, 87, Excellence award in corp. reporting Fin. Analysts Fedn., 1970, 72, 74, 81-82, cert. of Distinction Brand Names Found., 1970, Retailer of Yr. award, 1971, 73, Disting. Mcht. award, 1972, Spirit of Life award City of Hope, 1983, Free Enterprise Legend award Students Free Enterprise, 1994; named to Home Ctr. Hall of Fame, 1985. Mem. Nat. Assn. Over-Counter Cos. (bd. advisers 1973-77), Newcomen Soc., Employee Stock Ownership Assn. (pres. 1983-85, chmn. 1985-87), James Madison Club, Federalist Soc., Forsyth Country Club, Piedmont City Club, Hound Ears Club (Blowing Rock, N.C.), Elk River Club (Banner Elk, N.C.), Roaring Gap Club (N.C.), Ponte Vedra Inn and Club (Fla.), Scabbard and Blade, Phi Beta Kappa, Pi Kappa Alpha. Home: 226 N Stratford Rd Winston Salem NC 27104-3132 Office: 2000 W 1st St Winston Salem NC 27104-4225

STRICKLAND, WILTON L., lawyer; b. Ft. Myers, July 1, 1942; s. Lorenzo Strickland and Mary Voncille Singletary; m. Barbara Hathaway Lahna (div. July 1984); children: Amy Beth Strickland-Quattlebaum, Wilton Hathaway Strickland. BA, U. Fla., 1964; JD, Stetson U., 1969. Bar: Fla. 1969, U.S. Dist. Ct. (so. dist.) Fla. 1969, Trial Bar (so. dist.) Fla. 1983, U.S. Dist. Ct. (mid. dist.) Fla. 1988, U.S. Ct. Appeals (5th cir.) 1978, U.S. Ct. Appeals (11th cir.) 1981, U.S. Supreme Ct. 1977. Ptnr. Howell, Kirby, Montgomery et al, Ft. Lauderdale, Fla., 1969-73, Ferrero, Middlebrooks & Houston, Ft. Lauderdale, 1974-77, Ferrero, Middlebrooks & Strickland, Ft. Lauderdale, 1977-91, Strickland & Seidule, Ft. Lauderdale, 1991-98; pvt. practice Wilton L. Strickland, P.A., Ft. Lauderdale, 1998—. Chmn. bd. Hospice Care Broward County, Inc.; bd. dirs. Salvation Army Broward County; mem. Helping Abandoned and Dependent Youth. Mem. ABA, ATLA, Fla. Bar (mem. ethics com.), Acad. Fla. Trial Lawyers (dir. 1980-84), Broward County Trial Lawyers Assn. (past pres. 1981), Broward County Bar Assn., Am. Bd. Trial Advs. (founder Broward County chpt.), Million Dollar Advocates Forum, The Bar Register of Preeminent Lawyers, Phi Alpha Delta (former pres. Brewer chpt.). Democrat. Presbyterian. Avocations: winter skiing, reading, hiking, boating, white water rafting. Home: 2897 NE 25th St Fort Lauderdale FL 33305-1722 Office: # 303 1401 E Broward Blvd Ste 303 Fort Lauderdale FL 33301-2100

STRICKON, HARVEY ALAN, lawyer; b. Bklyn., Nov. 9, 1947; s. Milton and Norma (Goodhartz) S.; m. Linda Carol Meltzer, July 2, 1972; children: Joshua Andrew, Meredith Cindy, Erica Stacey. BBA, CCNY, 1968; JD, NYU, 1971. Bar: N.Y. 1972, U.S. Dist. Ct. (so. and ea. dists.) N.Y. 1973, U.S. Ct. Appeals (2d cir.) 1973, U.S. Supreme Ct. 1975, U.S. Dist. Ct. (no. dist.) N.Y. 1980, U.S. Dist. Ct. (we. dist.) N.Y. 1981, U.S. Dist. Ct. Ariz. 1991, U.S. Dist. Ct. Conn., 1996. Law clk. U.S. Dist. Ct. (ea. dist.) N.Y., Bklyn., 1971-73; assoc. Moses & Singer, N.Y.C., 1973-80; from assoc. to ptnr. Kaye, Scholer, Fierman, Hays & Handler, N.Y.C., 1980-91; from ptnr. to counsel Paul, Hastings, Janofsky & Walker LLP, N.Y.C., 1991—; mem. complaint mediation panel, departmental disciplinary com. appellate div., 1st dept. Supreme Ct. State N.Y.; mem. mediation panel U.S. Dist. Ct. (ea. dist.) N.Y.; mem. mediation register U.S. Bankruptcy Ct. (so. dist.) N.Y. Co-author: Enforcing Judgments and Collecting Debts in New York, 1996. Mem. Nassau County Rep. Com., Great Neck, N.Y., 1982—; chmn. bd. dirs. Flushing Community Vol. Ambulance Corps. Inc., N.Y., 1981-86, vice chmn., 1987-92. Mem. ABA, N.Y. State Bar Assn., Assn. Bar City N.Y. (chmn. complaint mediation panel com. on profl. discipline), Am. Judicature Soc., Assn. Comml. Fin. Attys., N.Y. Law Inst., Bankruptcy Lawyers Bar Assn., (bd. govs. 1987-89, corr. sec. 1989—), Am. Bankruptcy Inst. Republican. Jewish. Home: 11 West Brook Rd Great Neck NY 11024-1219 Office: Paul Hastings Janofsky & Walker LLP 399 Park Ave New York NY 10022-4697

STRIEBEL, HANS-MARTIN, biochemist; b. Esslingen, Baden-Wurttemberg, Germany, Apr. 24, 1961; s. Martin and Dorothea (Ziegler) S. Diploma in Chemistry, U. Munich, 1989, PhD, 1993. Chem. diplomate. Postdoct. fellow Yale U., New Haven, Conn., 1993-96; rsch. scientist Inst. Molecular Biotech., Jena, Germany, 1997—. Contbr. articles to profl. jours. Pvt. 1st class German Army, 1980-81. Mem. Gesellschaft Deutscher Chemiker. Office: Inst Molekulare Biotech, Beutenbergstr 11, D-07745 Jena Germany

STRIEFLER, FRANK, consumer products company executive; b. Kleinwallstadt, Bavaria, Germany, Oct. 27, 1966; s. Rainer and Karla (Meiss) S.; m. Nikolina Del Eisinger, July 13, 1999. Bachelor, Fachhochschule, Frankfurt, Germany, 1991; cert. in mktg., U. Calif., Berkeley, 1997. Jr. account mgr. Lowe & Ptnr., Frankfurt, 1991; account mgr. Young & Rubicam, Frankfurt, 1992; group head account GPP, Leonberg, 1993-94; brand mgr. Hugo Boss, Metzingen, Germany, 1994; advt. mgr. Wrangler, Mörfelden, Germany, 1995-97; brand comm. mgr. Nike Internat., Mörfelden, 1998—. Recipient German Media prize Innovative Strategy, 1999, Silver Trailers Art Dirs. Club, 1996. Avocations: snowboarding, running, football. Office: Nike Internat, Hessenring 13A, 64546 Mörfelden Hessen, Germany

STRIJDOM, PETER, import-export company executive; b. Pretoria, Transvaal, South Africa, May 26, 1969; s. Peter and Martha Maria (Raath) S. BA, U. Pretoria, 1989. Pers. mgr. Dept. Fgn. Affairs, South Africa, 1990-92; sales/tour mgr. Amiel Tours, Israel, 1993-98; mng. dir. Ostritrade, Belgium, 1998—. Recipient Acting award for drama Republic of South Africa Bd. Performing Arts, 1986, Acting award for comedy, 1986. Avocations: photography, interior design, cooking, flower arranging, private pilot. Home and Office: Residentie Charlotte, Koninklijke Baan 40, 8420 De Haan Belgium

STRILER, RAY, distance education consultant; b. Crystal City, Mo., Dec. 21, 1938. BS in Edn., S.W. Mo. U., 1961; MS, Peabody Coll., Vanderbilt U., 1978; MA, Rider U., 1984; EdD, U.S. Internat. U., 1989. Prof., dept. chmn. Rider U., N.J.; tchr. coll. prep., Carlsbad, Calif.; dir. acad. programs and v.p. mil. programs Inst. for Profl. Devel., Phoenix; tech. cons. Voltek Inc., Belleville, Ill.; ptnr. Global Learning Techs., Oceanside, Calif.; pres. Edn. 2020 Inc. Alumni bd. dirs. U.S. Internat. U. Lt. col. U.S. Army, 1962-86.

STRIMBU, VICTOR, JR., lawyer; b. New Philadelphia, Ohio, Nov. 25, 1932; s. Victor and Veda (Stancu) S.; m. Kathryn May Scrote, Apr. 9, 1955 (dec. 1995); children: Victor Paul, Michael, Julie, Sue; m. Marjorie Bichsel, Oct. 23, 1999. BA, Heidelberg Coll., 1954; postgrad., Western Res. U., 1956-57; JD, COlumbia U., 1960. Bar: Ohio 1960, U.S. Supreme Ct. 1972. With Baker & Hostetler LLP, Cleve., 1960—, ptnr., 1970—. Bd. dirs. North Coast Health Ministry; mem. Bay Village (Ohio) Bd. Edn., 1976-84, pres., 1978-82; mem. indsl. rels. adv. com. Cleve. State U., 1979—, chmn., 1982, 98; mem. Bay Village Planning Commn., 1967-69; life mem. Ohio PTA; mem. Greater Cleve. Growth Assn.; trustee New Cleve. Campaign, 1987—, North Coast Health Ministry, 1989—, Heidelberg Coll., 1996—; mem. indsl. rels. adv. com. Cleve. State U., 1979—, chmn., 1982, vice chmn., 1998. With AUS, 1955-56. Mem. ABA, Ohio Bar Assn., Greater Cleve. Bar Assn., Ohio Newspaper Assn. (minority affairs com. 1987—), Ct. of Nisi Prius Club, Cleve. Athletic Club, The Club at Soc. Ctr. Republican. Presbyterian. Office: Baker & Hostetler LLP 3200 National City Ctr 1900 E 9th St Ste 3200 Cleveland OH 44114-3475

STRINATI, GIANCARLO, physics educator, scientist; b. Viareggio, Lucca, Italy, July 13, 1951; s. Aristide and Diana (Conti) S.; m. Miriam Rosini, Oct. 4, 1973 (div. May 1990); 1 child, Emilio; m. Claudia Romero, June 25, 1991; children: Adriano, Marcello. Laurea in Physics, U. Rome, 1973; MS, U. Chgo., 1975, PhD, 1977. Rsch. assoc. U. Chgo., 1977-78, Max-Planck Inst., Stuttgart, Germany, 1978-79; asst. prof. U. Rome, 1980-82, assoc. prof., 1983-86, 91-94; assoc. prof. Scuola Normale Superiore, Pisa, Italy, 1987-91; prof. U. Camerino, Italy, 1994—; cons. E.N.I. Corp., Venice, Italy, 1988-89. Contbr. articles to profl. jours. Fulbright fellow, 1974-77, Von Humboldt fellow, 1978-79. Mem. Sigma Xi (assoc.). Roman Catholic. Home: Localita Colleromano 71, 00060 Riano Rome, Italy Office: U Camerino, Dept Physics, 62032 Camerino Macerata, Italy

STRINGER, CHRISTOPHER BRIAN, paleontologist, educator; b. London, Dec. 31, 1947; s. George Albert and Evelyn Beatrice (Brien) S.; m. Rosemary Susan Lee, Apr. 2, 1977; children: Katherine, Paul, Thomas. BSc in Anthropology with honours, Univ. Coll., London, 1969; PhD in Anatomy, U. Bristol, Eng., 1974, DSc in Anatomy, 1990, LLD (hon.), 2000. Sci. officer Natural History Mus., London, 1969-70, sr. rsch. fellow, 1973-76, sr. sci. officer, 1976-90, head human origins program, 1990—; vis. lectr. Harvard, Cambridge, Mass., 1979; vis. prof. Royal Holloway Coll., London, 1995—; Lyell lectr. Brit. Assn., 1988; Radcliff lectr. Green Coll., Oxford (Eng.) U., 1996. Author: (with Clive Gamble) In Search of the Neanderthals, 1993 (Archaeology Book of Yr. award 1994), (with Robin McKie) African Exodus, 1996; assoc. editor Jour. Human Evolution, 1986—, Quaternary Sci. Revs., 1993—. Trustee L.S.B. Leakey Trust, 1993—. Hon. rsch. fellow Univ. Coll., 1980—; grantee for Pleistocene cave studies Nat. Geog. Soc., 1995, 96, for prehistory of Egypt, Leakey Found., 1996, Gibraltar cave excavations Brit. Acad., 1996, 97, 98, 99; recipient Stopes medal Geologists Assn., 2000. Mem. Primate Soc. (coun. 1995-98, Napier medal 1998), Quaternary Rsch. Assn. (coun. 1980-85), Internat. Assn. for Human Palaeontology (nat. rep. 1986—). Avocations: astronomy, soccer, music, current affairs, writing. Office: Natural History Museum, Dept Palaeontology, London SW7 5BD, England

STRINGER, GRETCHEN ENGSTROM, consulting volunteer administrator; b. Pitts., Feb. 25, 1925; d. Birger and Gertrude Anne (Schuchman) Engstrom; m. Loren F. Stringer, Oct. 3, 1953 (dec. Sept. 1992); children: Lizbeth, Pamela, William E., Frederick E. BA, Oberlin Coll., 1946; Cert. in Teaching, U. Pitts., 1951, SUNY, Buffalo, 1964; M, SUNY, Buffalo, 1996. Cert. vol. adminstr. Owner, founder, pres. Vol. Cons., Clarence, N.Y., 1979—; owner, founder, officer Non Profit Mgmt. Ctr., Buffalo, 1995—; Founding pres., bd. dirs. Ctrl. Referral Svc. Author: The Board Manual Workbook, 1980, rev., 1993, The Instructors Guide, 1982, A Magical Formula, 1980; co-author: Non Profit Management Education, 1998; contbr. articles to profl. jours. Exec. dir. Vol. Action Ctr., United Way Buffalo and Erie County, 1978-81; founding vice chair Erie County Commn. on Status of Women, 1989-93; pres. Girl Scout Coun. of Buffalo and Erie County, chair, gen. mgr. cadette encampment; bd. dirs. Clarence Ctrl. Sch. Dist., 1976-86; chair, gen. mgr. Buffalo and Erie County Bicentennial Parade, 1976, Erie County Ski Swap; active Longview Protestant Home for Children Bd., Millard Fillmore Jr. Bd., Prevention is Primary, N.Y. Bd. State Foster Care Youth Ind. Project, others; Cmty. Hero Torch Bearer Summer Olympics, 1996; del. White House Conf. on Small Bus., 1995. Recipient Pinny Wilson Vol. award Buffalo and Erie County, 1981, Continuing Svc. award Mass. Mutual, 1987, Girl Scouts Thanks Badge, 1983, Susan Reid Greene Russell award Jr. League of Buffalo, 1994. Mem. Nat. Assn. Women Bus. Owners (bd. pres. Buffalo chpt. 1998-2000), N.Y. Assn. Vol. Ctrs. (founding exec. bd.), Vol. Admisntrs. Western N.Y. (founding pres. 1980), Buffalo Ambassadors of C. of C. (bd. dirs.), Women's Pavilion PanAm. 2001 (chair bd. dirs. 1999-2000), Jr. League Buffalo, Inc. (sustainer v.p. 1998-2000), Assn. Vol. Adminstrn. (chair, gen. mgr. nat. conf. 1986, nat. trainer, re-cert. chair, subcom. vol. adminstrn. higher edn.). Office: Non Profit Mgmt Ctr 9015 Cliffside Dr Clarence NY 14031-1460

STRINGER, HOWARD, media executive; b. Cardiff, Wales, U.K., Feb. 19, 1942; came to U.S., 1965, naturalized, 1985; s. Harry and Marjorie Mary (Pook) S.; m. Jennifer Kinmond Patterson, July 29, 1978; children: David, Ridley, Harriet, Kinmond. BA, MA, Oxford (Eng.) U., 1964. Prodr., dir. CBS News, N.Y.C., 1973-76; exec. prodr. CBS Reports, 1976-81, Evening News, 1981-84; exec. v.p., 1984-86; pres. CBS News, 1986-88, CBS Broadcast Group, 1988-95; chmn., CEO Tele-TV, 1995-97, Sony Corp. Am., 1998; chmn. Sony Can.; bd. dirs. Applied Graphics Technologies. Chmn. Am. Film Inst.; bd. dirs. Am. Theatre Wing; trustee Presbyn. Hosp., Mus. Radio and TV; bd. govs. Nature Conservancy, United Cerebral Palsy. Served to sgt. U.S. Army, 1965-67, Vietnam. Recipient Emmy awards Nat. Assn. TV Arts and Scis., 1973, 79 (2), 81 (2), 83 (4), Columbia Dupont award Columbia Journalism Sch., 1979, 81, Overseas Press Club awards, 1974, 79, 82, IRTS Found. award, 1994, Pres.'s award Stage Dirs. and Choreographers Found., 1994, First Amendment Leadership award Radio & TV News Dirs. Found., 1996; inductee to Broadcasting and Cable Hall of Fame, 1996, Royal TV Soc. Wales, 1999; hon. fellow Merton Coll., Oxford, 2000. Presbyterian. Office: Sony Corp of Am 550 Madison Ave New York NY 10022-3211

STRINGER, PAMELA MARY, retired headmistress; b. Birmingham, Eng., Aug. 30, 1928; d. Edwin Allen and Margherita Mary (Holland) S. MA, Oxford U., 1950. Asst. classics mistress Sherborne Sch. for Girls, 1950-59; head of classics Pate's Grammar Sch. for Girls, Cheltenham, 1959-64, dep. headmistress, 1963-64; headmistress Clifton H.S. for Girls, 1965-85. Mem. Secondary HEADS Assn., Girls Schs. Assn. Roman Catholic. Avocations: travel in Tuscany and Umbria, reading, cooking, Italian art and culture. Home: 36 Henleaze Gardens, Bristol BS9 4HJ, England

STRIPLING, BETTY KEITH, artist, nurse; b. Stephenville, Tex., Aug. 22, 1930; d. Fred Lancaster and Myrtle Ethel (Patton) Keith; m. Warren Lee Stripling, Mar. 22, 1952 (div. 1961); children: Keith, Kelley, David (dec.). Student, John Tarleton Agrl. Coll., 1948-50, Tarleton State U., 1980-85. LVN, Tex. Clk.-typist Kimbell-Food Products Co., Ft. Worth, 1950-52; LVN Stephenville Hosp. and Clinic, 1963, LVN floor duty, 1963-64, LVN surgery, 1964-66; LVN surgery Ft. Worth Osteo. Hosp., 1966-68; LVN,

charge nurse Sunset Nursing Home, Stephenville, 1968-80, LVN, DON, 1973-78; LVN, charge nurse Cmty. Nursing Home, Stephenville, 1980-86, 89-94, pvt. duty nurse, 1986-89; cmty. nursing home LVN Cmty. Nursing Home, 1998-99; freelance painter, 1999-2000. Democrat. Avocations: painting, television, reading, studying computers and medicine, shopping.

STRIZHALO, VOLODYMYR OLEXANDROVYCH, science administrator; b. Lutsk, Volynska, USSR, Oct. 9, 1940; s. Alexander Zakharovych and Tatiana Ivanivna (Kyslyan) S.; m. Valentyna Anatoliivna Yermolieva, Sept. 20, 1966; children: Olexiy, Maxym. Diploma in Mech. Engring., Kyiv Poly. Inst., Ukraine, 1962; postgrad., Inst. Problems Material Sci., Kyiv, 1963-66, Cand. Sci. Engr., 1967; Dr. Sci. Engr., Inst. Problems of Strength, Kyiv, 1979. Mech. engr. Asst. Kyiv Poly. Inst., Ukraine, USSR, 1962-63; prof. Kyiv Poly. Inst., Ukraine, 1979—; jr. rsch. assoc. Inst. Problems of Strength, Kyiv, Ukraine, USSR, 1967-69, sr. rsch. assoc., 1969-77, head dept., 1977—; dep. dir. Inst. Problems of Strength, Kyiv, Ukraine, 1988—. Author 7 books; contbr. articles to profl. jours. George Soros grant Soros Fund, 1994, Soros Fund and Govt. of Ukraine, 1995; recipient Order of the Badge of Honour Govt. of the USSR, 1986, State prizes of Ukraine in Sci., 1990, 97. Mem. N.Y. Acad. Scis. Avocations: gardening, vine growing. Home: 15 Bastionnaya str Apt 58, 01014 Kyiv Ukraine Office: Inst Problems of Strength, 2 Timiryazevska str, 01014 Kyiv Ukraine

STRNAD, ERNST, translator, writer; b. Mikulasovice, Czechoslovakia, July 5, 1928; came to Germany, 1946; s. Josef and Pauline (Schamal) S.; m. Galina Logvinovna Shkurenko, Jan. 28, 1967; 1 child, Jelena. Maturity, Vorstudienanstalt, 1947; diploma in econs., Humboldt *U., 1951, habilitation, 1980; PhD in Philosophy, Pieck U., 1968. Translator various works in fields of economics (on J.M. Keynes, U.S. mgmt.), philosophy (M.B. Mitin, N. Merker, Alfarabi), memoirs (St. Poplawski, K. Philby, men-of-war (B. Ireland); author: Essays on Etruscan Economy and Language, 1979, 86, Ausgewählte etruskologische Arbeiten, 1996, (with brother) Der Befehl "Ans Tor!", 1994; co-editor: Grosses Okonom Worterbuch Russisch-Deutsch, 1983; co-author: Einleitung in die Klassischen Altertumswissenschaften, 1986. Mem. Hermann Duncker Club (Bernau). Avocations: horticulture, protection of animals. Home: Berlinerstrasse 6, 16321 Bernau Germany

STROBEL, STEFAN MICHAEL, technical development director; b. Kuenzelsau, Germany, Mar. 1, 1970; s. Günter Strobel and Renate Giese. Diploma in med. info., U. Heidelberg, Germany, 1996; ingenieur de conaissance DESS, U. de Savoie, Chambery, France, 1994. Programmer Orgaplus Unternehmensberatung, Heilbronn, 1990-94; Internet cons. Steinbeis Transferzentrum/Xlink Heilbronn, 1994-95; sr. cons., tech. mgr., founding mem. Centaur Comm. GmbH, Heilbronn, 1995-99; tech. devel. dir. IntegralisCentaur GmbH, Heilbronn, 1999—. Author: (books) Linux—Unleashing the Workstation in Your PC, 1993, Firewalls fuer das Netz der Netze, 1997, (book and CD) Linux Universe, 1994. Avocations: volleyball, diving. E-mail: strobel@integraliscentaur.de. Office: Integralis-Centaur GmbH, Urbanstrasse 68, 74074 Heilbronn Germany

STROBEL, STEPHAN, pediatric immunologist, researcher, medical educator; b. Hamburg, Germany, Oct. 9, 1947; arrived in Eng., 1980; s. Theodor Martin Maria and Margund Johanna (Schroeder) S.; m. Margarita Magdalena Neumann, 1971; children: Patrick, Christian. MD, U. Frankfurt, 1972; PhD, U. Edinburgh, 1984. Cons. pediatrician U. Frankfurt, 1979—, privatdozent, 1987—, prof., 1991; reader U. London, 1992—, consulting pediatric immunologist, 1992—, dir. pediat. edn. and tng., 1995, prof., 1999; vice dean Inst. Child Health, London, 1992—, vice head Grad. Sch. U. Coll. London, 1999; prof. U. London, 1996; advisor Dept. Health, U.K., 1998. Contbr. articles to profl. jours. Recipient Adalbert V. Czerny prize and medal German Paediatric Assn., 1984; named Hon. Amigo of Venezuela, Venezuela Positive Found., 1995. Fellow Royal Coll. Physicians (hon. mem.), Royal Coll. Pediatrics and Child Health. Avocations: early 20th century and contemporary studio pottery, sailing, cinema. Office: Inst Child Health, 30 Guilford St, London WC1N NEH, England

STROBL, GERHARD FRANZ XAVER, engineer; b. Stuttgart, Germany, Feb. 8, 1956; s. Xaver Franz and Gertrud Elisabeth (Raible) S.; m. Ingrid Helga Elisabeth Holzer, July 2, 1982; children: Frederik, Felix, Philipp-Marcel. MS, U. Ariz., 1982; diploma in engring., U. Stuttgart, 1983; diploma d'etudes approfondies, U. Nice, France, 1989, Doctorate, 1993. Cert. physics and engring. R&D engr. Telefunken Electronic, Heilbronn, Germany, 1983-88; rsch. scientist Ctr. Nat. Recherce Sci. Physique Solide et Energie Solaire, Sophia Antipolis, France, 1988-90; R&D engr., project leader Deutsche Aerospace AG, Heilbronn, 1991-94; R&D engr., project leader Angewandte Solarenergie ASE, Heilbronn, 1994-96, mgr. R&D, 1996-98, dir. R&D, 1998—. Contbr. articles to profl. jours.; patentee in field. Avocations: jazz music, classical music, tennis, skiing. Office: Angewandte Solarenergie, Theresienstr 2, D-74072 Heilbronn Germany

STROBLE-THOMPSON, COLETTE MARY HOULE, plastering and stucco company executive; b. Manchester, N.H., Aug. 10, 1947; d. George Albert and Mary Agnes (Sala) Houle; children: B.J., Danielle, Alden; m. Dennis W. Thompson. Student, CAP Regional Staff Coll. Tex., 1985, 86. Lic. real estate agt., stucco/plasterer. Switchboard operator Leavitt's Dept. Store, Manchester, N.H., 1965-66, with credit office, 1966-67, merchandizer, advertiser, 1966-69; advt. marketer Ariz. wide K-Mart, Mesa; owner, mgr. Colette's Boutique, Mesa, 1980-82; co-founder, CEO, pres. Stroble Plastering, Gilbert, Ariz., 1977—; cons. area wide constrn. firms, Phoenix, 1979—; contractor plastering and stucco, Phoenix, 1987-90; realtor personal real estate property, Phoenix, 1988-90. Author, editor Wing Tips, 1985-86; co-inventor, electronic locator transmitter. Maj., squadron leader, fin. officer, personnel officer CAP, Mesa, 1990; active Dept. Disabled/Disadvantaged, Phoenix, 2000. Recipient Humanitarian award Dept. Econ. Security, Mesa, 1989, Letters of Appreciation, Leper Colony, Mexico, 1989. Mem. Nat. Assn. Search and Rescue (life), World Wing Kung Fu Assn., Rosicrucian Order Amorc (dep. master, master). Avocations: collector of masks & fetishes of all cultures, fishing, traveling, real estate, boating. Office: Stroble Plastering & Stucco 721 N Monterey St Ste 103 Gilbert AZ 85233-3835

STROCKA, VOLKER MICHAEL, archaeologist; b. Frankfurt, Hassia, Germany, Feb. 26, 1940; s. Gerhard and Mathilde (Dafeldecker) S.; m. Brigitte Auchter, Feb. 2, 1941; children: Cordula, Wolfgang, Gregor. Dr.phil., U. Freiburg, Germany, 1965; Dr.habil., U. Bochum, Germany, 1973. Asst. Inst. Classical Archaeology U. Bochum, 1965-74; dozent Inst. Classical Archaeology, U. Göttingen, 1974-75; 1st dir., prof. Ctrl. German Archaeology Inst., Berlin, 1975-81; ord. prof. Inst. Classical Archaeology, U. Freiburg, 1981—; sci. mem. Austrian excavations of Ephesos, Turkey, 1967-78, 93; dir. archaeol. project "Houses of Pompeii," 1975-95; co-dir. archaeol. excavations in Thugga/Tunisia, 1996-2000; mem. scholarship com. Alexander von Humboldt-Stiftung, Bonn, 1976-82, 95—; senator German Rsch. Coun., 1987-93. Author: Piräusreliefs und Parthenosschild, 1967, Die Wandmalerei der Hanghäuser in Ephesos, 1977, Häuser in Pompeji: Casa del Principe di Napoli, Vol. I, 1984, Häuser in Pompeji: Casa del Labirinto, vol. 4, 1991. Fellow German Archaeol. Inst., Österreichisches Archäologisches Inst. Roman Catholic. Home: Hochrüttestrasse 3, D-79117 Freiburg Germany Office: U Freibury Inst Archaeology, Br Fahnenbergplatz, D-79085 Freiburg Germany

STROE, ION, mechanical engineering educator; b. Moraresti, Arges, Romania, June 9, 1952; s. Vasile and Elena (Giubega) S.; m. Elvira Sendroiu, Oct. 15, 1977. Degree in engring., Poly. U., Bucharest, Romania, 1976, PhD, 1986; postgrad., Internat. Space U., Stockholm, 1995. Engr. Flight Test Ctr., Craiova, Romania, 1976-78; rschr. Nat. Inst. Fluid Mechanics, Bucharest, 1978-82; asst. Poly. U., Bucharest, 1982-86, asst. prof., 1986-92, assoc. prof., 1992-98, prof., 1998—. Co-author: (with R. Voinea and M.V. Predoi) Technical Mechanics, 1996; contbr. articles to profl. jours. Mem. Romanian Soc. Acoustics (founder), Acad. Scientists Romania, Planetary Soc. Home: Apt 70, Dristor 96 Bl 12B Sc B, 74322 Bucharest Romania Office: Politehnica U Bucharest, Splaiul Independentei 313, RO-77206 Bucharest Romania

STROETMANN, KARL ANTONIUS, company executive; b. Burgsteinfurt, Fed. Republic Germany, Feb. 4, 1944; s. Paul; and Isabella (Bachem) S. Diploma in Bus., Free U., Berlin, 1968; PhD, U. B.C., Vancouver, Can., 1974. Rsch. fellow Inst. for Systems Tech. and Innovation Rsch., Karlsruhe, 1974-77; v.p., ptnr. Abt. Assocs. Economic and Social Rsch. GmbH, Heidelberg and Bonn, 1978-80; mng. dir. Social Scis. Info. Ctr., Bonn, 1980-89; sr. rsch. fellow German Nat. Rsch. Ctr. for Computer Sci., St. Augustin, 1990-95; dir. German Social Scis. Infrastructure Svcs., Mannheim, 1986-88. Editorial bd. Internat. Jour. Info. and Libr. Rsch., London, 1989, editor: Innovation, Economic Change and Technology Policy, 1977, Informationslogistik, 1992, Information Management for Information Services, 1992; author: New Media and Information Technology, 1980; contbr. articles to profl. jours. Can. Coun. scholar, 1969-73; recipient several fellowships and grants. Mem. Soc. for Informatics, German Soc. for Documentation, Royal Soc. Medicine-Telemedicine Forum, Am. Telemedicine Assn. Free Democratic Party. Roman Catholic. Office: Empirica GmbH, Oxfordstr 2, D-53111 Bonn Germany

STROH, RAYMOND EUGENE, personnel executive; b. Bloomington, Ill., Aug. 13, 1942; s. Harry William and Felcie Cleo (Weaver) S.; m. Peggy Jane Whitacre, June 12, 1966; children: Rebecca Jane, David Ray. BA, So. Ill. U., 1966, U. Ill., 1977. Pers. technician Ill. Dept. Mental Health, Springfield, Ill., 1966-67; pers. officer Andrew McFarland Mental Health Ctr., Springfield, 1967-68, Manteno (Ill.) State Hosp., 1968-69; chief pers. officer Ill. Dept. Law Enforcement, Springfield, 1969-75, Ill. Dept. Revenue, Springfield, 1975-81, Ill. Dept. Mental Health, Springfield, 1981-82; pers. exec. Ill. Dept. Cen. Mgmt. Svcs., Springfield, 1982—; state govt. chmn. U.S. Savs. Bond Campaign, Springfield, 1978-82. Bd. dirs. Consumer Credit Counseling Svc., Springfield, 1988-94, sec., 1994; coun. exec. bd. Boy Scouts Am., Springfield, 1987—, v.p., 1987-99, dist. commr., 1979-86, unit commr., 1970-79; bd. dirs. Ill. State Employees Credit Union, 1984-85. Recipient Patriotic Svc. awards U.S. Treasury Dept., 1979-82, Silver Beaver award Boy Scouts Am., 1987, Dist. award of merit, 1981, Area Pres. awards, 1985, 86, Scouters Key award, 1976, Order of the Arrow Vigil Honor, 1998, James E. West Fellowship award, 1998. Mem. NRA, U. Ill. Alumni Assn., So. Ill. U. Alumni Assn., Exptl. Aircraft Assn., Aircraft Owners and Pilots Assn., Ponce De Leon Inlet Lighthouse Assn., Nat. Geog. Soc., Cornell U. Lab. of Ornithology, Abraham Lincoln Gun Club, Appalachian Trail Conf., Union County (Tenn.) Hist. Soc., Bass Anglers Sportsman Soc., Lionel Railroader Club, Wabash R.R. Hist. Soc., Theta Delta Chi. Republican. Lutheran. Avocations: aviation, hunting, fishing, bird watching, model railroading. Home: 2111 Warwick Dr Springfield IL 62704-4147 Office: Ill Dept Cen Mgmt Svcs 501 Stratton Ofc Bldg Springfield IL 62706-0001

STROH, RÜDIGER JOACHIM, physicist; b. Leverkusen, Germany, Oct. 16, 1962; m. Kirsten Engelbrecht, Oct. 7, 1995; 1 child, Karen. PhD, Cambridge (Eng.) U., 1991. Rsch. assoc. Cambridge U., 1990-91; rsch. engr. Thomson CSF, France, 1991-93; tech. engr. ITT Intermetall, Freiburg, Germany, 1993-94, sect. head defect engring., 1994-96, mgr. process engring., 1996-98, mgr. waferfab, 1999—. Contbr. articles to profl. jours.; patentee in field. Office: Micronas GmbH, Hans-Bunte-Str 19, D-79108 Freiburg Germany

STROHAL, PETAR, Energy company executive; b. Zagreb, Croatia, June 17, 1932; arrived in Austria, 1979; s. Petar and Mira (Werner) S.; m. Jelisaveta Svoboda, Nov. 17, 1962; children: Marko, Marija. Diploma, Faculty Chem. Engring., Zagreb, 1956; PhD, U. Zagreb, 1960. Rschr. Inst. R. Boskovic, Zagreb, 1960-62, head nuclear chem. lab., 1962-66, asst. dir. gen., 1977-78; prof. U. Zagreb, Croatia, 1966-74; dir. Ctr. for Marine Rsch., Rovinj, Croatia, 1975-77; rep. to internat. orgn. Min. of Fgn. Affairs, Vienna, Austria, 1979-83; sect. head Internat. Atomic Energy Agy., Vienna, 1984—; sr. advisor to hazardous waste mgmt. agy. Ministry of Economy of the Republic of Croatia, Zagreb, 1996—, R. Boskovic Inst., Zagreb, 1996—. Contbr. articles to profl. jours. Tech. editor Croatian Chem. Soc., Zagreb, 1966-68; chmn. Nat. Commn. for Coop. in Nuclear Energy, Belgrade, 1967-78; mem. City Coun., Zagreb, 1969-71; coord. Mediterranean Radiol. Program, Geneva, 1972-74. Mme. Croatian Chem. Soc., Yugoslav Radiol. Soc., Croatian Med. Acad., Geographic Soc., European Nuclear Soc. Roman Catholic. Avocations: human rights, fine arts, culture of small nations, gardening. Home: Dalmatinska 11, 10000 Zagreb Croatia

STROHECKER, LEON HARRY, JR., orthodontist; b. Schuylkill Haven, Pa., Aug. 14, 1932; s. Leon Harry and Anna (Fabian) S.; m. Juanita Mary Puyoou, Apr. 13, 1957; children: Sandra Lee Strohecker Beckett, Leon Harry III. Student, U. Pa., 1950-53, DDS, 1957, orthodontic cert., 1960. Bd. cert. Am. Bd. Orthodontics. Pres., pvt. practice Lansdale, Pa., 1961—; dir. Face Head & Neck Pain and Trauma Ctr., Lansdale, 1987-99; bd. dirs. Artman Home Retirement Ctr., Ambler; treas., bd. dirs. Valley Ctr. Mental Health Clinic, Lansdale, 1984—; guest lectr. in field. Pres. Lansdale Rotary Club, 1967-68; coun. mem. Trinity Luth. Ch., Lansdale, 1977-85, chmn. fin. com., 1980-85. Lt. (j.g.) USN, 1957-59. Recipient Wisdom award of honor. Mem. ADA, Internat. Acad. Head, Neck and Facial Pain, Internat. Coll. Cranio-Mandibular Orthopedics, Am. Acad. Pain Mgmt. (diplomate), Am. Assn. for Functional Orthodontics, Am. Profl. Practice Assn., Am. Soc. Dentistry for Children, Am. Acad. Oral Medicine, Am. Assn. Orthodontists, Am. Assn. Stomatologists, Am. Acad. Oral Medicine, Middle Atlantic Orthodontic Soc., Pa. Orthod ontic Soc., Phila. Orthodontic Soc., Pa. Dental Assn., Second Dist. Dental Assn., Montgomery-Bucks Dental Soc., Alpha Omega, Omicron Kappa Epsilon. Avocations: tennis, travel, bridge, water sports. Home: 1512 Cedar Hill Rd Ambler PA 19002-1406 Office: 456 E Hancock St Lansdale PA 19446-3803

STROHM, WOLF DIETER, medical administrator; b. Danzig, Germany, Sept. 28, 1941; s. Eberhard Walter and Annemarie Ursula (Reimer) S.; m. Inge Wahl, Nov. 2, 1966 (dec. 1983); children: Oliver, Timmo; m. Jutta Magdalena Nawrath, Sept. 28, 1984; children: Corinna Andrea, Philipp Sebastian. MD, U. Heidelberg, Germany, 1967, U. Montpellier, France, 1964; PhD, U. Frankfurt, Germany, 1983. Asst. med. dir. Dept. Gastroenterology Med. Clin. U. Frankfurt, 1983-85; med. dir. Med. Clinic II Clinicum, Heilbronn, Germany, 1985—; lectr. in field. Contbr. articles to profl. jours., chpts. in books. Recipient Nitrolingual prize Pohl-Boskamp Hamburg, 1981. Mem. Lions. Evangelical. Home: Kraemerstr 15, D-74076 Heilbronn Germany Office: Med Clinic II, Am Gesundbrunnen 20-24, D-74078 Heilbronn Germany

STROHMAIER, WALTER LUDWIG, urologist, educator; b. Stuttgart, Germany, May 27, 1957; s. Otto Georg and Katharina Luise (Eckes) S.; m. Barbara Elisabeth Schaal, May 4, 1984; children: Georg, Carolina, Jakob. Med. Staatsexamen, Eberhard-Karls-U., Tuebingen, Germany, 1983; MD, Eberhard-Karls-U., 1983. Diplomate Bd. Urology. Resident in urology Eberhard-Karls-U., Tuebingen, 1983-86, 87-88, resident in surgery, 1986-87, registrar, 1988-96, asst. prof., 1992-98, assoc. prof., 1998—; head dept. urology Klinikum Coburg, 1996—. Editor: Nephrocalcinosis and Kidney Calcium Antagonists, 1988, Therapie des Harnblasenkarzinoms, 1988, Hyperthermia of the Prostate, 1992, Urolithiasis, 1996, Diagnostik und Therapie des Harnblasenkarzinoms, 1998. Mem. Ortschaftsrat Rottenburg-Wendelsheim, 1994-96. Recipient Peter Bischoff prize Norddeutsche Gesellschaft for Urology, 1988, Poster prize Deutsche Gesellschaft of Urology. Mem. Am. Urology Assn. (corr.), Deutsche Gesellsch. of Urology, European Assn. Urology, European Soc. Urolithiasis Rsch. (adv. bd.), Internat. Urol. Soc. Avocations: horseback riding, piano playing, studying south-west Germany history. Home: Eschenweg 12, D-96450 Coburg Germany Office: Urol Dept Klinikum Coburg, Ketschendorfer Str 33, D-96450 Coburg Germany

STROHMEYER, GEORG W.W.F., physician; b. Freden, Germany, Nov. 6, 1928; s. Güstav and Lea (Wallenstein) S.; m. Sibylle Colpe; children: Torsten, Silke, Henning. MD, U. Hamburg, Germany, 1954. Rsch. fellow dept. biochemistry U. Hamburg, 1955-57, resident dept. internal medicine, 1957-60; rsch. assoc. Harvard U., Boston, 1960-61; sr. resident dept. internal medicine U. Marburg, Germany, 1962-66; assoc. prof. dept. internal medicine U. Marburg, 1966-72; prof. medicine, chair U. Düsseldorf, Germany, 1972-94, prof. emeritus, 1994—; med. dir. U. Hosps. Düsseldorf, 1980-88; prorector Heinrich Heine U., Düsseldorf, 1989-93. Contbr. chpts. to books. Col. Med. Svc. German Army, 1969-73. Recipient Hon. award Internat. Soc. Hemochromatosis, Boston, 1995; grantee German Rsch. Soc. Mem. German Med. Soc. (pres. 1980-81), Internat. Assn. for the Study of the Liver (pres. 1981), Internat. Soc. Iron Rsch. (pres. 1992-93). Avocations: sports, music. Office: Univ Hosp, Moorenstreet 5, D-40225 Düsseldorf Germany

STRÖKER, ELISABETH, philosophy educator, administrator; b. Dortmund, Germany, Aug. 17, 1928; d. Wilhelm and Luise (Hüttemann) S. MA in Math., Chemistry & Philosophy, U. Bonn, Germany, 1953, PhD in Philosophy, 1954, PhD (hon.), 1992. Rschr., tchr. math., chemistry & philosophy U. Bonn, Germany, 1955-60; asst. prof. U. Hamburg, Germany, 1961-63, pvt. dozent, 1963-64; prof. philosophy U. Braunschweig, Germany, 1965-71, dean faculty, 1968-70; prof. philosophy, dir. Hussere Archives U. Cologne, Germany, 1972—, dean faculty, 1976-77; guest prof. in most of European countries, U.S.A. and Can., 1968—. Author 14 books; contbr. 100 articles to philos. jours. Mem. Gen. Soc. Philosophy Germany, German Soc. Phenomenology, Am. Soc. Phenomenology (hon.), German Soc. History Scis. Lutheran. Office: Sem Philosophie U Koln, Albertus-Magnis-Platz, D-50923 Cologne Germany

STRØM, EVALD JON, lawyer; b. Oslo, Feb. 15, 1942; s. Harald and Petra Jenny (Ødegaard) S.; m. Siri Kristiansen, June 19, 1966; children: Kjersti, Guro. JD, U. Oslo, 1970. Bar: Norway 1973. Asst. rschr. U. Oslo, 1967-68; asst. judge Byfogden, Stavanger, Norway, 1971-72; pvt. practice Oslo, 1972—; chmn. bd. Skovly-Gruppen As, Oslo, Cerealia Uni Bake As, Ski, Norway, As Avisdrift (Fjell-Ljom), Roros; mem. bd. Bia Kors Ciculom, Hotel Røros (Norway) As, Roros Kultur-og Yonferansesenter Stiftelsen Det Brinner En Eld, Roros, Stiftelsen Vinterfestspilli Bergstaden, Roros, Blue Cross Norway, Oslo. Author: Odelsloven, 1975, Husnøkkelen, 1985, Røros-loven Av 1901, 1995. Mem., sec. Mcpl. Com. of Lumber to Peasantry, Røros, Norway, 1994-95. Mem. Norwegian Lawyer Assn., Norwegian Assn. Agrl. Law, Lions Internat. Avocations: genealogy, local history, law history, cultural history, farming. Office: Advokatfirmaet, Linda Stabel H Haakon VII's GT.2, 0114 Oslo Norway

STROM, MILTON GARY, lawyer; b. Rochester, N.Y., Dec. 5, 1942; s. Harold and Dolly (Isaacson) S.; m. Barbara A. Simon, Jan. 18, 1975; children: Carolyn, Michael, Jonathan. BS in Econ., U. Pa., 1964; JD, Cornell U., 1967. Bar: N.Y. 1968, U.S. Dist. Ct. (W. dist.) N.Y. 1968, U.S. Ct. Claims 1969, U.S. Ct. Mil. Appeals 1969, U.S. Ct. Appeals (D.C. cir.) 1970, U.S. Supreme Ct. 1972, U.S. Dist. Ct. (so. dist.) N.Y. 1975. Atty. SEC, Washington, 1968-71; assoc. Skadden, Arps, Slate, Meagher & Flom, N.Y.C., 1971-76, ptnr., 1977—. Served with USCGR, 1967-73. Mem. ABA, N.Y. State Bar Assn. (corp. law sect.), Assn. of Bar of City of N.Y., Internat. Bar Assn. Republican. Jewish. Club: Beach Point. Avocations: tennis, skiing, golf. Office: Skadden Arps Slate Meagher & Flom 4 Times Sq Fl 24 New York NY 10036-6595

STROMHOLM, STIG FREDRIK, university administrator, lawyer, educator; b. Boden, Sweden, Sept. 16, 1931; s. Fredrik and Gerda (Janson) S.; m. Gunilla Margareta Forslund, Aug. 9, 1958; children: Christina, Fredrik, Katarina. BA, Uppsala (Sweden) U., 1952, LLB, 1957, LLD, 1966; diploma in comparative law, Cambridge (Eng.) U., 1958; LLD, U. Munich, 1964; LLD (hon.), Lyons (France) U., 1980; PhD (hon.), U. Helsinki, Finland, 1990, U. Uppsala, 1992; LLD (hon.), U. Copenhagen, 1996. Jr. judge Stockholm Ct. Appeals, 1961-66; lectr. Uppsala U., 1966-69, prof. law, 1969—, dean faculty law, 1973-79, vice rector, 1978-89, rector, pres., 1989-97. Author various legal works, also fiction and criticisms. Served to capt. Swedish Army, 1968. Decorated Grand Cross, Grand Officer, comdr., officer and knight various orders. Mem. Royal Swedish Acad. Sci., Royal Swedish Acad. Letters, History and Antiquities (pres. 1985-93), Royal Uppsala Acad. Arts and Scis. (pres. 1979—), Academia Europaea, London (pres. 1997—). Lutheran. Home: Norra Rudbecksg 5, 75236 Uppsala Sweden

STROMNES, AASMUND LONNING, education educator; b. Trondenes, Norway, Oct. 14, 1927; s. Martin and Petra (Lonning) S.; m. Margot Holmen, July 21, 1951; three children. MA, U. Oslo, 1961, PhD, 1968. Tchr. primary schs., Volda, Trondheim, Oslo, Norway, 1951-61; rsch. fellow, then lectr., asst. prof. U. Oslo, Norway, 1961-73; prof. U. Tromso, 1973-85, U. Trondheim, Norway, 1985-97. Author: The Development of School Children's Color Concepts and Their Referents, 1968, Governing of Schools and Democracy, 1983, Epistemologies and Education, 1993, Beginning Teachers, 1980; editor: Teacher's Thinking, 1987, Theory and Practice in Pedagogy, 1991, Scandinavian Jour. of Ednl. Rsch., 1985—. Mem. Norwegian Soc. Scis. & Letters, Am. Ednl. Rsch. Assn., European Assn. Rsch. & Learning & Instrn. Home: Helge Neumanns veg 8, N-2080 Eidsvoll Norway

STRØMNES, FRODE JENS, psychologist; b. Jan. 4, 1937; s. Martin Olav Konrad and Petra Johane (Lønning) S.; m. Bjørg Imsland, 1 child, Gro; m. 2d Liisa Helena Sulkakoski, 1968; children: Sunniva Johanna, Hogne Martinus, Ingunn Loviisa. Mag. art., Oslo U., 1963; fil. tri., Turun Yliopisto, 1971. Lectr. Aarhus U., 1970; docent Åbo Akademi, 1972-75, 87—, acting prof. psychology, 1974; prof. psychology U. Tromsø, 1975-89, U. Bergen, 1990—; rsch. prof. Royal Norwegian Dept. Edn., 1990—; dosentti Turun Yliopisto, 1976—. Author: Prolegomena to a Theory of Semiotics, 1969, Associations or Addresses: A Study in Serial Verbal Learning, 1971, A New Physics of Inner Worlds, 1976; contbr. to profl. jours.; rsch. on verbal learning. Active preservation old neighborhoods Turku, also ecology. Grantee Suomen Kulttuurirahasto, 1974; rsch. fellow Norwegian Rsch. Coun., 1963-68, 71-74. Mem. Norsk Statsstipendiatfor. Home: Karstadvg 11, N-6100 Volda Norway

STRONACH, FRANK, automobile parts manufacturing executive. Chmn., dir., founder Magna Internat. Inc., Aurora, Ont., Can., 1971—. Founder The Fair Enterprise Inst. Office: Magna Internat Inc, 337 Magna Dr, Aurora, ON Canada L4G 7K1

STRONG, GEORGE HOTHAM, private investor, consultant; b. Johnstown, Pa., July 15, 1926; s. George Hite and Mary Elizabeth (Hotham) S.; m. Mary Louise Lyon, Sept. 19, 1953; children: Cynthia Strong Hibbard, Dexter, Sarah Strong Bornstein. AB magna cum laude, Allegheny Coll, 1949; MBA, Harvard U., 1951. V.p. Smith Barney & Co., N.Y.C. & Boston, 1951-67, Norlin Corp., N.Y.C., 1967-73, Am. Medicorp, Bala-Cynwyd, Pa., 1974-78; cons. A.D. Little, Cambridge, Mass., 1973-74; sr. v.p., dir. Universal Health Services, King of Prussia, Pa., 1978-84; pvt. practice investor N.Y.C., 1985—; bd. dirs. AmerSource, Malvern, Pa., Health South Rehab., Birmingham, Ala., Balanced Care Corp., Camp Hill, Pa., Pocantico Devel. Assn., N.Y.C., Managed Care USA, Charlotte, N.C. Served to sgt. U.S. Army, 1944-46, Italy. Mem. Phi Beta Kappa. Republican. Episcopalian. Clubs: Harvard (N.Y.C.); Union League (Phila.); Seabright (N.J.) Lawn Tennis, Seabright Beach, Rumson Country (N.J.). Home: 946 Navesink River Rd Rumson NJ 07760-2330

STRONG, KARIN HJORT, artist, educator; b. N.Y.C., Jan. 30, 1956; d. Corrin Peter and Mette Hjort (Matthiesen) S. BA, Boston U., 1981; AA, Pratt U., 1985. Art tutor Hampshire Coll., Amherst, Mass., 1977; co-founder, mgr., tchr. Poland Springs (Maine) Cmty. Program, 1977-79; tchr. Southampton Cultural Ctr., 1989-96; tchg. asst. master workshop on art L.I. Univ., Southampton, N.Y., 1990; bd. mem. Catharine Lorillard Wolfe Art Club, Inc., N.Y.C., 1989-96; painting judge Pen and Brush Club, Inc., N.Y.C., 1995; art show judge J.L.C. Art Ctr., Inc., Stony Brook, N.Y., 1995. Artist represented by Gallery East, Images Gallery, Lizan Tops Gallery, others. Vol. coord. Appalachian Mountain Club, Boston, 1981; monkey trainer to aid quadreplegics Boston U., 1981; spkr., event M.C. CLWAC, Nat. Arts Club, N.Y.C., 1992-95; spkr., lectr. Jimmy Ernst Artist Alliance, East Hampton, N.Y., 1993, Southampton Artists, 1994. Mem. Soc. Animal Artists, Southampton Artists (bd. mem., exhbn. chair, publicity com. 1988-90), Catharine Lorillard Wolfe Art Club, Inc. (pres. 1992-95). Avocations: music, playing guitar, flute and dulcimer, sports, writing.

STRONG, LIAM, telecommunications executive; b. Jan. 6, 1945; s. Gerald and Geraldine (Crozier) S.; m. Jacqueline Gray, 1970; 2 children. Degree, Trinity Coll., Dublin. With Proctor and Gamble, 1967-71, Reckitt and Coleman, 1971-86, Sunset Designs, U.S., 1980-82, R&C Pharmaceuticals, 1982-86; pres. Durkee French Foods, U.S., 1986-88; dir. mktg. and ops. Brit. Airways, 1988-91; CEO Sears plc, 1991-97, World Comm. Internat., 1997; bd. dirs. Skystream Inc.; chmn. London Health Partnership, 1994-97. Fax:

44 (0)207 675 3393. E-mail: liam.strong@wcom.co.uk. Office: Worldcom Fox Ct, 14 Grays Inn Rd, London WC1X 8HN, England

STRONG, SIR ROY COLIN, historian, garden writer, diarist, former museum director; b. London, Aug. 23, 1935; m. Julia Trevelyan Oman, 1971. Grad., Queen Mary Coll., U. London; PhD, Warburg Inst., London. Asst. keeper, then, dir., keeper, sec. Nat. portrait Gallery, London, 1959-74; dir. Victoria and Albert Mus., London, 1974-87; lectr. Eng., U.S., also contbr. to radio and TV; Ferens prof. fine art, U. Hull, Eng., 1972; Walls lectr. Pierpont Morgan Libr., 1974; arranger numerous mus. exhbns. Author books on garden design and on life and art of Tudor, Stuart and Victorian Eng., including, Art and Power, Renaissance Festivals, 1450-1650, 1984, Cecil Beaton: The Royal Portraits, 1988, Creating Small Formal Gardens, 1989, Lost Treasures of Britain, 1990, A Celebration of Gardens, 1991, Royal Gardens, 1992, Small Period Gardens, 1992, Successful Small Gardens, 1994, The Story of Britain, 1996, The English Arcadia, 1996, The Roy Strong Diaries, 1967-87, 1998, The Spirit of Britain, 1999, The Artist and the Garden, 2000; contbr. articles to profl. jours.; reviewer for newspapers, radio and TV. Recipient Shakespeare prize, 1980; knighted, 1982. Fellow Soc. Antiquaries, Royal Soc. Lit.; mem. Royal Archaeol. Inst., Garrick Club London. Office: The Laskett, Much Birch, Hertfordshire HR2 8HZ, England

STRONG, SELDEN RICE, advocate; b. Hartford, Conn., Jan. 24, 1927; s. Edward Winslow and Maude Emily (Foster) S.; m. Dorothy May Lewis, July 4, 1947 (div. July 1981); children: Thor M., Nathan B., Jill P., Amanda C. BA, U. N.H., 1954; postgrad., U. Va. Child welfare worker State of N.H., Dover, 1954-56; buyer II Concord, 1963-64; dep. purchasing agts. aide L.A. County, 1956-61; purchasing agent Imperial Co., El Centro, Calif., 1961-62; contract splst. D.C. Gov., Washington, 1964-71; owner, mgr.r Bikers' and Hikers' Retail, Woodbridge, Va., 1972-77; social worker Elder Svc. of Merval, Lawrence, Mass., 1959-91, ret. 1991. Founder Relevance, Reality, Reason & Peace, 1999. Avocations: writing, walking, bicycling, camping. Home: 464 Suncook Valley Hwy Unit D5 Epsom NH 03234-4351

STRONG, SUSAN CLANCEY, writer, communication consultant, editor; b. Cin., Nov. 10, 1939; d. William Power and Elizabeth (Browne) Clancey; m. Oliver Swigert, 1957 (div. 1972); children: Silvia, David Mack; m. Richard Devon Strong, 1977. BA, Northwestern U., 1965; MA, U. Calif., Berkeley, 1972, PhD, 1979. Tchr. Helen Bush Parkside Sch., Seattle, 1965-66, Taipei (Taiwan) Lang. Inst., 1967-68; acting instr. U. Calif., Berkeley, 1972-78, teaching fellow, 1979, lectr., 1979-84; lectr. St. Mary's Coll., Moraga, Calif., 1982-85; pvt. practice Orinda, Calif., 1985-90, 97—; sr. rsch. assoc. Ctr. for Econ. Conversion, 1990-96; mem. Contra Costa County Conflict Resolution Panels, Calif., 1987-90; affiliate Support Ctr./CTD, San Francisco, 1987-90; del. UN Conf. on Econ. Conversion, Moscow, 1990; cofounder The Who's Counting?" Project, 1996; founder The Metaphor Project, 1997, Y2K in Orinda, 1998. Author: The GDP Myth: How It Harms Our Quality of Life, and What Communities are Doing About It, 1995; editor Deficit Delirium, 1993, Shaping A New Conversion Agenda, 1995; author poetry; columnist, book reviewer, film reviewer. Mem. Bay Area Global Tomorrow Com., 1986; co-founder Peace Economy Working Group, 1988; co-founder Peace Economy Campaign, 1988; mem. Peace Action Nat. Strategy Com., 1989-95, co-chair strategy com., 1992-93; conf. cochmn. Nat. Sane/Freeze Congress, 1989-90, rep. nat. bd. advisors Nat. Peace Action, Washington, 1989-95; mem. bd. advisors Peace and Environ. Project, San Francisco, 1986-88; chmn. No. Calif. Sane Freeze, San Francisco, 1985-89; convenor The Natural Step Open Space Com. Conf., San Francisco, 1997. Mem. Phi Beta Kappa. Mem. Green Party. Episcopalian. Avocation: music.

STRONG-CUEVAS, ELIZABETH, sculptor; b. St. Germain en Laye, France, Jan. 22, 1929; Am. citizen; d. George and Margaret (Strong) de Cuevas; 1 child, Deborah Carmichael. Student, Vassar Coll., 1946-48; AB, Sarah Lawrence Coll., 1952; postgrad., Art Students League, 1963-68. One-woman shows include Lee Ault Gallery, N.Y.C., 1977-78, Tower Gallery, Southampton, N.Y., 1980, Iolas-Jackson Gallery, N.Y.C., 1983, 85, Guild Hall Mus., East Hampton, N.Y., 1985, Kerr Gallery, N.Y.C., 1988—, Ruth Vered Gallery, East Hampton, 1988, Grounds for Sculpture, Hamilton, N.J., 1999—; group shows include Guild Hall, East Hampton, 1980, Art Students League of N.Y., 1982, Bruce Mus., Greenwich, Conn., 1984, 85, Tower Gallery, N.Y.C., 1985, Kouros Gallery, N.Y.C and Ridgefield, Conn., 1985, Susan Blanchard gallery, N.Y.C., 1985-86, Ruth Vered Gallery, East Hampton, 1986-87, Benton Gallery, Southampton, 1987—, Kerr Gallery, N.Y.C., 1988—, Elaine Benson Gallery, Bridgehampton, N.Y., 1989, Portico, Inc., Cologne Art Fair, 1990, Feingarten Galleries, N.Y. Art Show, 1990, Marisa del Re Biennale IV, 1993, Parrish Mus., Southampton, N.Y., 1994, Grounds for Sculpture, Hamilton, N.J., 1994-95, Shidoni, Tessuque, N.Mex., 1995-98, Bernard Biderman Fine Art, Southampton, N.Y., 1997, The Tolman Collection, Singapore, 1997-98; represented in pvt. collections at Bruce Mus., Greenwich, Conn., Grounds for Sculpture, Hamilton, N.J. Mem. Vassar Club (N.Y.).

STROTHER, SHERRIE KAYE CARTER, county official; b. Charleroy, Pa., July 2, 1948; d. Thomas Earl Jordan and Mary Anne (Fair) Lightner; m. Ronald O. Strother, Feb. 14, 1982; m. Phillip E. Carter, June 6, 1967 (dec. Sept. 1975); 1 child, Staci Dione. BA, La. State U., 1979; postgrad., Tex. A&M U., 1984, FBI Nat. Acad., 1984; M in Criminal Justice, FBI Nat. Acad., 1988. Lic. polygraph examiner; lic. pilot. Sec. Aetna Life & Casualty Co., Shreveport, La., 1967-68; investigator Fed. Civil Svc., Ariz., Okla., La., 1969-75; supr. pub. rels., crime prevention and internal affairs divs. Caddo Sheriff's Dept., Shreveport, 1979—; editor The Caddo Star, 1981—; capt. ops. and corrections investigations, patrol, narcotics, chief of security Caddo Detention Ctr., 1992-95, chief of support, 1998—; adj. instr. Northwestern State U., La. Cmty. Policing Inst.; Bossier Parish Cmty. Police Acad. Co-editor: Captain's Corner Newsletter, 1998—. Bd. dirs. dept. Bossier C.C., 1985-86; adviser Law Enforcement Explorers Group, 1980-85. Mem. La. Sheriff's Assn., La. Polygraphy Assn., La. Peace Officers Assn., Nat. Sheriff's Task Force, Am. Bus. Women's Assn., La. State U. Shreveport Alumni Assn. (alumni bd. dirs. 1981-83), Women in Law Enforcement Assn. (merit award 1983). Republican. Baptist. Avocations: flying, motor cycling, bowling, reading, karate. Home: 263 Pomeroy Dr Shreveport LA 71115-2621 Office: Caddo Sheriff's Dept 501 Texas St Shreveport LA 71101

STROUD, BRADLEY LYN, ballet company executive; b. Three Rivers, Mich., Oct. 3, 1958; s. Harley Allen Stroud and Sandra Lou (Hill) Hansen; m. Claudia Marie Doll, Aug. 2, 1980; children: Carolyn, Matthew, Michael. BS, Ctrl. Mich. U., 1980. Regional adminstrv. mgr. Harris/Lanier, Boston, 1982-86; exec. dir. Met. Ballet Theatre, Detroit, 1992-94; compt. Comcast Cablevision, Flint, Mich., 1986-87; asst. compt. M&B Distbg., Flint, 1987-91; compt. Midwest Wholesale Foods, Flint, 1991-92; dir. dance Detroit Opera House, 1996—. Co-dir. Cath. Youth Group St. Ives Cath. Ch., Southfield, Mich., 1986-92. Mem. Eisenhower Dance Ensemble, Cortez & Co. Contemporary, Music Movement Bd., Toney Powell (bd. dirs.), Plum Hollow Country Club. Avocations: skiing, golf. Home: 18120 Kinross Ave Beverly Hills MI 48025-3151 Office: Detroit Opera House 1526 Broadway St Detroit MI 48226-2115

STROUD, JOHN FRANKLIN, engineering educator, scientist; b. Dallas, June 29, 1922; s. Edward Frank and Ethel A. Stroud; m. Dorcas Elizabeth Stroud, Feb. 4, 1944; children: Kevin, Karen, Richard. BSME, Stanford (Calif.) U., 1949, postgrad., 1949-53; cert. in fin. mgmt. for sr. execs., U. Pa., 1984. Aero. rsch. scientist NASA Ames Rsch. Lab., Moffett Field, Calif., 1949-53; thermodynamics engr. Lockheed, Burbank, Calif., 1953-55, group engr. (mgr.) propulsion, 1955-63, dept. engr. (mgr.) propulsion, 1963-70, from dept. engr. to divsn. engr. (mgr.) propulsion, 1970-83, chief engr. (mgr.) flight scis., 1983-85, divsn. engr. (mgr.), 1985-90, ret., 1990; cons. spl. studies in econs. and engring. sci., 1990—; mem. ad hoc adv. congrl. subcom. on high tech wind tunnels, 1985. Contbr. articles to profl. jours.; author and speaker in field. Charity fund raiser United Way, 1970-80, others. Lt., naval aviator USN, 1942-45, ETO. Decorated Battle of Atlantic. Fellow AIAA (assoc., airbreathing propulsion com. 1966-68, 80-83, chmn. many sessions 1970—); mem. Soc. Automotive Engrs. (aviation div. air transport com., propulsion com., chmn. many sessions nat. confs. 1970—, co-chmn. AIAA/SAE nat. propulsion conf. 1978). Achievements include patent for low drag external compression supersonic inlet; design and development of integrated F-104A inlet and air inductions system, integrated inlet/air induction system into the total propulsion system and airframe; management of team that developed, designed, and integrated the aeropropulsion systems on the L1011 commercial transport; devised new theory for turbulent boundary layers in adverse pressure gradients; numerous other patents pending.

STRUBE, JUERGEN F., chemical company executive. Chmn. bd. BASF Group, Ludwigshafen, Germany; chmn. exec. bd. dirs. BASF Aktiengesellschaft, Ludwigshafen. Office: BASF Aktiengesellschaft, Carl-Bosch Strasse 38, 67056 Ludwigshafen Germany*

STRÜCKER, GERHARD, analytical chemist, educator; b. Dortmund, Fed. Republic Germany, Nov. 13, 1954; s. Hans-Walter and Martha (Schoof) S.; m. Sylvia Flachmann, Aug. 15, 1985; children: Juliane, Thomas. Diploma in chem. engring., Fachhochschule Münster, Burgsteinfurt, Germany, 1978; BS, Juniata Coll., 1979. Sci. tchr. Fachhochschule Münster, Burgsteinfurt, 1980-81; dept. chmn. Stadtwerke Hagen AG, Hagen, 1981—; mem., chmn. working com. on chemistry Arbeitsgemeinschaft der Wasserwerke an der Ruhr, Essen, Germany, 1981—, mem. commn. on water quality of the River Ruhr, 1993—, bd. dirs.; mem. working com. on gen. affairs Arbeitsgemeinschaft Trinkwassertalsperren, Siegburg, Germany, 1986—, bd. dirs. Contbr. articles to profl. jours. including VGB Kraftwerks Chemie, Ruhrwassergütebericht, and Gas-und Wasserfach. Mem. Am. Chem. Soc., N.Y. Acad. Scis. Lutheran. Avocations: photography, hiking, collecting stamps. Home: Derner Strasse 375, D-44329 Dortmund Germany Office: Stadtwerke Hagen AG, Hohenzollernstrasse 5-7, D-58095 Hagen Germany

STRUCKMEIER, JUERGEN, physicist, researcher; b. Frankfurt am Main, Germany, Sept. 11, 1952; s. Werner and Ilse (Krueger) S.; m. Maria Helena Schoenenberg, July 24, 1992. Diploma in physics, U. Frankfurt, 1978, PhD, 1985. Postdoctoral assoc. U. Frankfurt, 1985; vis. scientist U. Md., College Park, 1986; rsch. fellow Inst. Heavy Ion Rsch., Darmstadt, Germany, 1979-84; staff scientist Gesellschaft für Schwerionenforschung, Darmstadt, Germany, 1986—. Contbr. articles to sci. jours., including Particle Accelerators, Phys. Rev. E. Recipient award IEEE Particle Accelerator Conf., 1995. Mem. German Phys. Soc. Avocation: sailing. Home: Berger Strasse 174, 60385 Frankfurt am Main Germany Office: Ges fuer Schwerionenforsch, Planck Strasse 1, 64291 Darmstadt Hessen, Germany

STRUFF, RICHARD HEINRICH, science administrator; b. Bochum, North Rhine-Westphalia, Germany, Dec. 16, 1935; s. Richard Heinrich and Maria Agnes (Harpen) S. Degree in Agriculture Econs., Bonn. U., 1960, PhD in Agriculture Econs., 1973. Scientific employee Soc. Agriculture, Policy Rsch. and Rural Sociology, Bonn, 1960—, staff, 1964—, mgr., 1980—. Author: Regional Dimensions of Economic Development, 1973, Regional Differences of Per Capita Income: Convergence or Divergence?, 1973, Regional Incidence of Public Expenditures, 1980, Regional Living Conditions, vol. 1: To Dwell, Work and Get Welfare Assistance in Town and Rural Areas, 1992, vol. 2: Village and Community Studies in Germany, 1999, others; editor: pub. series FAA, 1980—, annual report, 1980—. Mem. European Soc. Rural Sociology, German Sociology Soc. (mem. agrl., rural sociology sect.), Fed. Rsch. Insts. (mem. working group socio-econ. rsch.). Roman Catholic. Office: Soc Agrl Policy Rsch, Meckenheimer Allee 125, D-53 115 Bonn Germany

STRUG, KERRI, former gymnast, Olympic athlete; b. Tucson, Ariz., Nov. 19. Student, Stanford U., 1996-97, UCLA, 1997—. Mem. Jr. Pacific Alliance Team, Indpl., 1989, Jr. Pan Am. Games Team, Tallahassee, Fla., 1990, World Gymnastics Championship Team, Indpls., 1991, U.S. Olympic Team, Barcelona, Spain, 1992, Hilton Challenge Team, L.A., Calif., 1993, Team World Championship Team, Dortmund, Germany, 1994, World Champion Team, Sabae, Japan, 1995, U.S. Olympic Team, Atlanta, 1996, John Hancock Gymnastics Tour, 1997—; spokesperson Nu Skin IVH Inc. Placed 1st all around Am. Classic, Calif., 1989, 2d all around Am. Classic, Tex., 1989, 2d uneven bars, balance beam Dutch Open, Holland, 1990, 1st vault U.S. Gymnastics Championships, Ohio, 1991, 1st vault U.S. vs. Romania, Tex., 1991, 1st vault, balance beam U.S. Gymnastics Championships, Ohio, 1992, 2d all around, floor exercise U.S. Gymnastics Championships, Ohio, 1992, 1st all around, uneven bars, balance beam, floor exercise Am. Classic/World Championships Trials, Utah, 1993, 1st uneven bars and 2d all around, balance beam, floor exercise U.S. Olympic Festival, Tex., 1993, 2d uneven bars Coca Cola Nat. Championships, Utah, 1993, 1st balance beam, 2d all around, McDonald's Am. Cup, Fla., 1993, 2d (with Waller) all around Reebok Internat. Mixed Pairs, 1993, 2d all around NationsBank World Team Trials, Va., 1994, 1st all around, uneven bars U.S. Olympic Festival, Colo., 1995, 1st all around, balance beam, floor exercise, 2d vault, uneven Bars McDonald's Am. Cup, Tex., 1996; recipient Silver medal World Championships, 1991, Olympic Bronze medal, 1992, Silver medal Team World Championships, 1994, Bronze medal World Championships, 1995, Olympic Gold medal, 1996. Mem. Karolyi's Gymnastics. Avocations: reading, shopping.

STRUIF, L. JAMES, lawyer; b. Alton, Ill., Sept. 18, 1931; s. Leo John and Clara Lillie (Bauer) S.; m. Shirley Ann Spatz, Mar. 24, 1965; children: Scott B., Jamie Lynn, Susan Marie, Jeffrey James. BS, Northwestern U., 1953; JD, U. Ill., Champaign, 1960. Bar: Ill. 1960, U.S. Dist. Ct. (so. Dist.) Ill. 1960. Gen. counsel So. Ill. U., 1960-64; pvt. practice Struif Law Offices, Alton, Ill., 1964—; lectr. So. Ill. U., Edwardsville, 1960-65. Author: Guide to Law for Laymen, 1987, Field Guide to 150 Prairie Plants of S.W. Ill., 1989. Scoutmaster Boy Scouts Am., Alton, 1966-69; active civil rights worker, Miss., 1964; trustee The James and Anne Nelson Found. With USN, submarines 1953-57, Pacific. Recipient Chmns. award Madison County Urban League, 1989, Blazing Star award The Nature Inst., 1990. Mem. Assn. Trial Lawyers Am., Ill. Trial Lawyers Assn., Ill. Bar Assn. Democrat. Mem. United Ch. of Christ. Avocations: nature, gardening, science, piano. Office: The Struif Law Offices 2900 Adams Pkwy Alton IL 62002-4857

STRUIK, PAUL CHRISTIAAN, agronomy educator; b. Haarlemmermeer, The Netherlands, Nov. 27, 1954; s. Jacobus and Philippijntje (Bokhorst) S.; m. Andrea Elisabeth Molengraaf, Aug. 31, 1978; children: Eelco Jeroen, Roeland Floris. Degree in Agronomy, Wageningen Agrl. U., Netherlands, 1978, Doctoral Degree, 1983. Rschr. Wageningen Agrl. U., 1978-81, asst. prof., 1982-86, prof. field crops sci., 1986-95, prof. crop and grassland sci., 1995-97, prof. crop physiology/agronomy, 1997—; main organizer Internat. Confs. on Agronomy and Crop Sci. Author: Seed Potato Technology, 1999; editor: Plant Production on the Threshold of a New Century, 1994; coordinating editor Potato Rsch., 1990—, Jour. Agronomy and Crop Sci., 1994—. Chairperson exec. bd. Protestant Secondary Sch., Zetten, The Netherlands, 1994—. ZWO fellow, 1984. Mem. ASA, CSSA, IIRB, European Assn. Potato Rsch. (sec., treas. 1990—), Gesellschaft Pflanzenbauwissenschaften Germany (chair working groups 1995—). Home: Schweitzerpark 9, 6671 BR Zetten The Netherlands Office: Wageningen Univ, Haarweg 333, 6709 RZ Wageningen The Netherlands

STRUNA, NANCY L., social historian and American studies educator; b. Painesville, Ohio, May 24, 1950; d. Edward A. and Betty J. (Hoffacker) S. BS, U. Wis., 1972; PhD, U. Md., 1979. Social studies tchr. The Andrews Sch., Willoughby, Ohio, 1972-74; grad. asst. U. Md., College Park, 1974-76; tchr. 1-8 grades St. Mark's Elem., Adelphi, Md., 1976-78; instr. U. Md., College Park, 1978-80; asst. prof. U. Minn., Mpls., 1980-82; prof. U. Md., College Park, 1982—; spl. asst. to pres. women's issues U. Md., 1998-2000, fellow Acad. Affairs, 1998-99, campus legis. liaison, 1999. Author: People of Prowess, Sport, Leisure and Labor in Early America, 1996; contbr. articles to profl. jours., chpts. to books. Chairperson Pres. Commn. on Women's Issues, U. Md., 1996-98; mem. Omohundro Inst. for Early Am. History and Culture, Soc. Early Americanists. Named Disting. scholar Nat. Assn. Phys. Edn. in Higher Edn., 1993. Fellow Am. Acad. Kinesiology; mem. N.Am. Soc. Sport History (pres. 1995-97), Orgn. Am. Historians, Am. Hist. Assn., Am. Studies Assn., U.S. Capitol Hist. Assn. Office: U Md 2133 Taliaferro Hall Coll College Park MD 20742-0001

STRUNK, HORST PAUL, physicist; b. The Hague, The Netherlands, June 13, 1940; arrived in Germany, 1944; s. Paul and Helene (Hess) S.; m. Helga Elisabeth Stumpf, May 18, 1968; children: Niko, Isa-Katrin. Diploma in physics, Univ., 1968, Dr.rer.nat., 1973. Rsch. scientist Max Planck Inst., Stuttgart, Germany, 1968-83; prof. materials sci. Tech. U., Hamburg-Harburg, Germany, 1983-89, U. Erlangen, Germany, 1989—; vis. assoc. prof. Cornell U., Ithaca, N.Y., 1979-80, vis. prof., 1983; vis. scientist Siemens Rsch. Lab., Munich, Germany, 1986-87. Achievements include relaxation mechanisms in heteroepitaxial misfitting semiconductor layer systems; micro mechanisms in crystal growth and quantum structure formation; laser crystallization. Office: U Erlangen Dept Mater Sci, Cauerstr 6, 91058 Erlangen Germany

STRUNK, KLAUS ALBERT, educator; b. Dusseldorf, Germany, Aug. 22, 1930; s. Albert Friedrich and Hedwig (Schaefer) S.; m. Marion Renate Kriegeskotte, Aug. 17, 1957; children: Stefan, Albert, Reinhard Curt, Almuth. DPhil, U. Cologne, Germany, 1957, DPhil habilitation, 1965. Asst. prof. U. Cologne, Germany, 1965-67; prof. U. Saarland, Saarbruecken, Germany, 1967-77, U. Munich, Germany, 1977—; sec. Indogermanische Gesellschaft, Wiesbaden, Fed. Republic of Germany, 1969-83. Author: Die sogennaten Aeolismen der homerischen Sprache, 1957, Nasalpraesentien and Aorista, 1967, Lachmanns Regel fuer das Lateinische, 1976, Typische Merkmakle von Fragesaetzen und die verische Pluti, 1983. Mem. Indogermanische Gesellschaft (pres. 1983-87), Soc. Linguistique Parus, Bayerische Akademie Wissenschaften. Home: Ringbergstr 11, D-83707 Bad Wiessee Germany Office: U Munich, Geschwister Sch Platz 1, D-80539 Munich Germany

STRUNK, MARTIN, atmospheric chemist, researcher; b. Osnabrueck, Germany, Aug. 21, 1969; s. Georg and Elisabeth Strunk; m. Bianca Maria Schimmel, June 10, 1998; 1 child, Simon Leonard. Diploma in chemistry, Phillipps U., Marburg, 1996. Rschr. Goethe U., Frankfurt. Mem. Am. Geophys. Soc., European Geophys. Union. E-mail: m.strunk@meteor.uni-frankfurt.de. Home: Schlosstrasse 121, 60486 Frankfurt Germany Office: U Frankfurt, Georg-Voigt Strasse 14, 60325 Frankfurt Germany

STRUNK, ORLO CHRISTOPHER, JR., psychology educator; b. Pen Argyl, Pa., Apr. 14, 1925; s. Orlo Christopher and Katherine Elizabeth (Glasser) S.; m. Mary Louise Reynolds, July 3, 1947; children: Laura Louise, John Christopher. Certificate, Churchman Bus. Coll., Easton, Pa., 1948; A.B., W. Va. Wesleyan Coll., Buckhannon, 1953; S.T.B., Boston U., 1955, Ph.D., 1957. Exec. sec. Inst. Pastoral Care, Mass. Gen. Hosp., 1955-57; grad. asst. Boston U., 1955-57, instr. psychology of religion, 1956; instr. Boston U. (Sch. Theology), 1957-58, 62; assoc. prof. psychology W. Va. Wesleyan Coll., 1957-60, dean, prof. psychology, 1959-69; prof. psychology of religion Boston U., 1969-86; also faculty counselor, supr. Albert V. Danielsen Inst.; part-time faculty Webster U., 1994—; pastoral psychotherapist The Coastal Samaritan Ctr., Myrtle Beach, S.C., 1986—; assoc. dir., staff psychologist Ecumenical Counseling Svc., Inc., Melrose, Mass.; rsch. cons. Religion in Edn. Found., Calif. Author: Readings in the Psychology of Religion, 1959, Religion: A Psychological Interpretaton, 1962, Mature Religion: A Psychological Study, 1965, The Choice Called Atheism, 1969, The Psychology of Religion, 1971, Dynamic Interpersonalism for Ministry, 1973, The Secret Self, 1976, Privacy: Experience, Understanding, Expression, 1983; mng. editor: Jour. Pastoral Care. Served with USAAF, 1943-46. Decorated Air medal with five oak leaf clusters. Fellow Am. Psychol. Assn.; mem. W.Va. Assn. Acad. Deans (pres.). Methodist (elder). Home: 1068 Harbor Dr SW Calabash NC 28467-2300

STRUPCZEWSKI, WITOLD GUSTAW, hydrologist, educator; b. Gdynia, Poland, June 8, 1937; s. Jan and Mieczyslawa (Gniazdowska) S.; m. Krystyna Sokolowska, Dec. 6, 1969; 1 child, Piotr. MS in Engring., Tech. U., Warsaw, Poland, 1960, D of Tech. Scis., 1966, Habil., 1970. Prof. geophys. scis., 1983. Asst. State Hydrology and Meteorology Inst., Warsaw, 1958-61; from sr. asst. to asst. prof. Sanitary and Water Engring., Tech. U., 1961-72; from assoc. prof. to prof. Inst. Geophysics, Polish Acad. Scis., Warsaw, 1972—; lectr. univs. in Iraq, 1975-76; chief hydrologist WAKUTI Consulting Office, Germany, 1981-82; project mgr. UN Dept. Tech. Coop. for Devel., Liberia, 1982-86; vis. prof. U. Calgary, Can., 1992; vice chmn. Internat. Hydrological Programme, UNESCO, 1998—. Assoc. editor Jour. Hydrological Scis., 1993—, Jour. Stochastic Hydrology and Hydraulics, 1990-95; author: Historical Extraordinary Hydro-Meteorological Phenomena of the Polish Territories, 1964; co-author: Geostatistical Methods: Recent Developments and Application in Surface and Subsurface Hydrology, 1992, New Uncertainty Concepts in Hydrology and Water Resources, 1995, Surface Water Hydrology, 1996, Integrated Approach to Environmental Data Management Systems, 1997; contbr. over 80 articles to profl. jours. Recipient Golden Cross of Merit, Bd. Polish Govt., Warsaw, 1984. Mem. Internat. Assn. Hydrological Scis. (v. chmn. internat. hydrology program, 1998-2002), European Geophysical Soc. Roman Catholic. Avocations: mountaineering. E-mail: wgs@igf.edu.pl. Home: Dzierzby 5 Apt 1A, 02 836 Warsaw Poland Office: Inst Geophysics Pol Acad Sc, Ksiecia Janusza 64, 01 452 Warsaw Poland

STRUTZ, FRANK MANFRED, nephrologist; b. Mainz, Germany, Oct. 17, 1961; s. Wolfgang and Irmgard A. (Frey) S.; m. Annette M. Kreidler, Sept. 17, 1993; children: Karen, Christin. MD, U. Tuebingen, 1990. Intern U. Tuebingen, Germany, 1991-92; fellow U. Pa., 1992-94; resident U. Goettingen, Germany, 1994-2000, chief resident, 2000—. Author: Immunologic Renal Diseases, 1997; contbr. articles to profl. jours. Grantee Carl-Duisberg, 1987, German Rsch. Found., 1992-94, 97. Mem. German Soc. of Nephrology, Am. Soc. Nephrology. Office: Georg August U Med Ctr, Robert-Koch Str 40, Goettingen Germany

STRUVE, GUY MILLER, lawyer; b. Wilmington, Del., Jan. 5, 1943; s. William Scott and Elizabeth Bliss (Miller) S.; m. Marcia Mayo Hill, Sept. 20, 1986; children: Andrew Hardenbrook, Catherine Tolstoy, Frank Leroy Hill, Guy Miller, Beverly Marcia Wise Hill (dec.), Elena Wise Struve-Hill. AB summa cum laude, Yale U., 1963; LLB magna cum laude, Harvard U., 1966. Bar: N.Y. 1967, D.C. 1986, U.S. Dist. Ct. (so. dist.) N.Y. 1970, U.S. Dist. Ct. (ea. dist.) N.Y. 1973, U.S. Dist. Ct. (no. dist.) Calif. 1979, U.S. Dist. Ct. D.C. 1987, U.S. Ct. Appeals (2d cir.) 1969, U.S. Ct. Appeals (D.C. cir.) 1973, U.S. Ct. Appeals (8th cir.) 1976, U.S. Ct. Appeals (9th cir.) 1979, U.S. Supreme Ct. 1971, U.S. Dist. Ct. (we. dist.) N.Y. 1991. Law clk. Hon. J. Edward Lumbard, Chief Judge United States Ct. Appeals for 2d Circuit, 1966-67; assoc. Davis Polk & Wardwell, N.Y.C., 1967-72, ptnr., 1973—; ptnr. Ind. Counsel's Office, 1987-94. Mem. ABA, N.Y. State Bar Assn., Assn. of Bar of City of N.Y. (chmn. com. antitrust and trade regulation, 1983-86, chmn. com. fed. cts. 1998—), Am. Law Inst. Home: 116 E 63rd St New York NY 10021-7325 Office: Davis Polk & Wardwell 450 Lexington Ave Fl 31 New York NY 10017-3982

STRUZAK, RYSZARD, radio scientist; b. Janow, Poland, Apr. 2, 1933; s. Robert and Maria (Miazga) S.; m. Irena Kolodziejczak, Sept. 21, 1956; children: Maria, Marcin. Engr., U. Tech., 1954, MSc, 1956, PhD, 1962, DSc, 1968. Rsch. asst. Nat. R&D Ctr., Wroclaw, Poland, 1953-54; instr., prof. U. Tech., Wroclaw, 1954-56, 69-85; head Inst. of Telecomm., Wroclaw, 1973-85, Tech. Dept. Int. Telecomm. Union, Geneva, Switzerland, 1985-93; cons. World Bank, Ankara, Turkey, 1993-94; elected mem. RRB-ITU, Geneva, 1995-98, 99—; co-founder Internat. Symposium on Electromagnetic Compatibility, 1972—; co-dir. Internat. Sch. on Data and Multimedia Comms., Internat. Ctr. for Theoretical Physics, Italy, 1999, 2000; cons., 193—; chmn. Tech. Cnsl. Union R&TV Broadcast, Poland, 1981-82, ITU-CCIR IWP, Geneva, 1975-85; vice chmn. URSI-E, Brussels, 1984-87; co-chmn. URSI-WGEI, Brussels, 1996—. Co-author: EMC Radio Engineering, 1982; editor: Global Communications Series, 1993—; contbr. articles to profl. jours. With Polish Army, 1961-63. Recipient Gold Cross of Merit Govt. of Poland, 1969, Cavallier's Cross, 1982, Gold M. Distinction Assn. Polish Electric Engrs., Medal of Internat. Telecom. Union, 1998. Fellow IEEE, Internat. Telecomm. Acad. Home: Route Du Boiron 45, CH 1260 Nyon Switzerland Office: Inter Telecom Union, Place des Nations, CH 1211 Geneva Switzerland

STRYKER, JAMES WILLIAM, automotive executive, former military officer; b. Grand Rapids, Mich., Apr. 20, 1940; s. John Alvin and Marian (Anderson) S.; m. Eleanor Marie Finger, Sept. 26, 1964; children: James William II, Marian Marie Jenkins, Kathryn Alison Greenbauer. BS, U.S. Mil. Acad., 1963; MA, U. Mich., 1972; postgrad., U.S. Army Command and Gen. Staff Coll., 1978. Commd. 2d lt. U.S. Army, 1963; battery exec. officer 6th/20th field arty. U.S. Army, Ft. Carson, Colo., 1964-65; advisor U.S.

Army, Vietnam, 1965-66; battery comdr. 4th/3d field arty. U.S. Army, Ft. Hood, Tex., 1967-68; advisor U.S. Army, Thailand, 1969-70; S-3 ops. officer 1st/7th F.A., Ft. Riley, Kans., 1972-73; assoc. prof. history U.S. Mil. Acad., West Point, N.Y., 1973-77; chief nuclear ops. Ctrl. Army Group NATO, Heidelberg, Germany, 1978-81; dir., project mgr. tank-automotive command U.S. Army, Warren, Mich., 1981-86; ret. U.S. Army, 1986; program mgr. military vehicles operation GMC Truck, Pontiac, Mich., 1987-95; cross brand portfolio mgr. Pontiac-GMC Divsn. GM Corp., Detroit, 1996-98, asst. brand mgr. product full size and mid size vans, 1999—. Author: (with others) Encyclopedia of Southern History, 1977; co-author: Early American Wars, 1978. Decorated Legion of Merit, Bronze Star medal, Def. Meritorious Svc. medal, Meritorious Svc. medal with oakleaf cluster, Army Commendation medal with oakleaf cluster, U.S. Army/Vietnamese Cross of Gallantry with palm and gold star. Mem. NRA (endowment), Nat. Def. Indsl. Assn. (dir. Detroit chpt. 1991-92, 94-97, 2d v.p. 1995, 1st v.p. 1995-96, pres. 1996-97, adv. 1997-2000), Assn. U.S. Army (dir. Detroit chpt. 1990-95), Gordon Setter Club Am., Nodrog Setter Club Mich., Ruffed Grouse Soc. (banquet com. Detroit 1998, 99, 2000), Trout Unltd. Avocations: hunting, skeet shooting, trout fishing, field training English and Gordon Setters. Home: 168 First St Romeo MI 48065-5000 Office: GM Fleet & Comml Orgn MC 482-A19-B66 PO Box 100 100 Renaissance Ctr Detroit MI 48243-1001

STRYKER, STEVEN CHARLES, lawyer; b. Omaha, Nebr., Oct. 26, 1944; s. James M. and Jean G. (Grannis) S.; m. Bryna Dee Litwin, Oct. 20, 1972; children: Ryan, Kevin, Gerrit, Courtney. BS, U. Iowa, 1967, JD with distinction, 1969; postgrad. studies, Northwestern U. Grad. Sch. Bus, 1969-70, DePaul U., 1971. Bar: Iowa 1969, Tex. 1986; CPA Ill., Iowa. Sr. tax acct. Arthur Young & Co., Chgo., 1969-72; fed. tax mgr. Massey Ferguson, Des Moines, 1972-74; fed., state tax mgr. FMC Corp., Chgo., 1974-78; gen. tax atty. Shell Oil Co., Houston, 1978-81, asst. gen. tax counsel, 1981-83, gen. mgr., 1983-86, v.p., gen. tax counsel, 1986—. Mem. ABA, AICPA, Tex. Bar Assn., Iowa Bar Assn., Ill. Soc. CPAs, Iowa Soc. CPAs, Tax Execs. Inst., Am. Petroleum Inst. Home: 2121 Kirby Dr Unit 124 Houston TX 77019-6068 Office: Shell Oil Co 1 Shell Plz Ste 4570 Houston TX 77001

STRYSICK, MICHAEL OTTO, terrestrial ecologist, researcher; b. Sheboygan, Wis., Jan. 13, 1931; s. Michael Sr. and Agnes (Czaja) S.; m. Carol Ann Greiner, June 25, 1955 (dec. July 1992); children: Peter Michael, Mary Susan. Terrestrial ecologist, rschr. Sheboygan, Wis., 1954—; cons. Master Gardner program U. Wis. Ext. Svcs., Sheboygan Falls, Wis., 1988—; rschr. Neem Oil Margosan-O, 1992. Cubmaster to commr. Boy Scouts Am.; pres. Cath. Com. Scouting, Sheboygan, 1970-97. With U.S. Army, 1952-54, Korea. Recipient St. George medal Boy Scouts Am., 1984. Mem. AAAS, Korean War Vets. Assn., VFW, Am. Legion. Achievements include Neem Oil development in the 1980s and field studies; Hanta Virus verification in Ams. as med. problem, 1990—; researcher in Myology 2000, a post-genome 30 protein complex of the nucleus of human cells; and use of woodchip mulch, adverse effects in anerobic conditions in 1970-80. Avocation: travel to gain information on interrelationships of life forms and symbiotic associations required for survival.

STRZALKOWSKI, IRENEUSZ, physicist, educator; b. Pabianice, Poland, June 3, 1939; s. Henryk and Eufemia Anna (Majkowska) S.; m. Malgorzata Halina Krzyzanowska, July 9, 1967. MSc, U. Warsaw, 1962; PhD, Warsaw Tech. U., 1969; DSc, D Habilitation, Warsaw U. of Tech., 1988. Asst. dept. chemistry Warsaw Tech. U., 1962-64, sr. asst., 1964-70, adj. prof. Inst. Physics, 1970-89, docent, 1989-93, prof., 1993—; head semiconductor structures group Inst. Physics, Warsaw Univ. Tech., 1975-93, head MOS structures lab., 1993, vice-dir. acad. affairs, 1981-92. Contbr. articles to profl. jours. Fellow Inst. of Physics (U.K.); mem. European Phys. Soc. (coun. mem. 1994, mem. editl. bd. European Jour. Phys. 1995), Polish Phys. Soc. (sec.-gen. 1993-97, pres. 1997), Foundation Pro Physica (bd. dirs. 1997), Polish Acad. Scis. (mem. sci. coun. High Press. Rsch. Ctr. 1994, Comm. of Physics 1999, Counc. Scientific Socs., 1999), Soc. Europeenne Pour La Formation Des Ingenieurs Working Group on Physics, Am. Physics Soc., Inst. Exptl. Physics (scientific coun. 1999). Roman Catholic. Avocations: tourism, skiing, gardening. Home: Wawozowa 21 m 27, 02-796 Warsaw Poland Office: Warsaw U Tech Inst Physics, Koszykowa 75, 00-662 Warsaw Poland

STRZEMBOSZ, ADAM JUSTYN, chief justice; b. Warsaw, Poland, Sept. 11, 1930; s. Adam and Zofia (Gadomska) S.; m. Zofia Mont, June 1, 1957; children: Katarzyna, Anna, Piotr, Marcin. Student, Jagiellonian U., Cracow, Poland; MA in Law, Warsaw U., 1953, PhD in Law, 1969. Legal adviser Ministry Labour and Social Security, Warsaw, 1953-56; judge County Ct., Warsaw, 1956-81, Provincial Ct., Warsaw, 1968-81; sr. lectr., prof. Lublin (Poland) Cath. U., 1982-90; vice min. Ministry Justice, Warsaw, 1989-90; judge Supreme Ct., Warsaw, 1990-98; first pres. Supreme Ct. Poland, Warsaw, 1999—; rschr. Rsch. Inst. of Judicial Law, Warsaw, 1974-81. Author: Juvenile Thieves in Urban Environment, 1971, Prevention of Social Child and Juvenile Maladjustment, 1979, Statute on the Proceedings on the Minors Cases, 1983, Legal Proceedings in Juvenile Cases Under Polish Law, 1984, System of Judicial Means to Protect Children and Juveniles from Maladjustment, 1985; author, editor: Family Courts: An Empirical Research, 1983, For the Criminal Law Based on Justice, Human Rights and Caritas, 1988; contbr. 80 articles to profl. jours. Head Solidarity group commn. Ministry Justice, Warsaw, 1980-81; bd. dir. Solidarity Mazowsze Region, Warsaw, 1980; del. to 1st Solidarity conf., elected mem. and joint leader Commn. Appeal, Oliwa, Gdańsk, Poland, 1981. Mem. Polish Sociological Assn., Lublin Cath. U. Scientific Assn., Penal Law Assn. Roman Catholic. Avocations: cycling, literature. Home: Stanislawa Augusta #73, app.20, 03-846 Warsaw Poland Office: The Supreme Ct, Ogrodowa 6, 00-951 Warsaw Poland*

STUARDO P., JAIME, ophthalmologist; b. Temuco, Chile, Feb. 18, 1943; s. Marta A. Bahamondes, May 14, 1968; children: Susana Elizabeth, Jaime Alejandro. Medical Degree, U. Chile, Santiago, 1968, postgrad., 1974-75. Bd. cert. diplomate. Med. dir. Losvilo's Hosp., Losvilos, Chile, 1968-71; chief physician Rural Health/Nat. Health Svc., La Serena, Chile, 1972-73; cons. ophthalmology Nat. Health Svc., Santiago, 1975-76; ophthalmologist Codelco, El Salvador, 1977-80; chmn. dept. ophthalmology Vina Del Mar's Hosp., Chile, 1985-89; cons. San Martin's Hosp., Quillota, Chile, 1995-97; cons. ACHS, Vina Del Mar, 1990—, Mut. Security, Vina Del Mar, 1990—; cons., instr. Firemen Corp., Vina Del Mar, 1995-96; cons. Lions, Vina Del Mar, 1981-98. Mem. Lions Club (pres. Losvilos club 1969), Chilean Ophthalmology Soc., Valparaiso Ophthalmology Soc. Avocations: gardening, golf, bowling. Home: 556 Holmden St Miraflores, Viña del Mar Chile Office: SB Ltd, 160 Of 6 Arlegui St, Viña Del Mar Chile

STUART, ALAN EDWARD, retail executive; b. Boston, May 19, 1962; s. Donald Edward and Joan Edith (Teed) S. BS, U. N.H., 1984. Store asst. mgr. Toys R Us, Inc., Northboro, Mass., 1985; corporate auditor Toys R Us, Inc., Rochelle Park, N.J., 1986-87; office mgr. Toys R Us, Inc., Northboro, 1988-89, support svc. mgr., 1989; support svc. dir. Toys R Us, Inc., Atlanta, 1990—; frieght audit and claims mgr. Toys R Us, Inc., Paramus, N.J., 1993—; dir. internat. traffic Toys R Us, Inc., 1996—, dir. analytical svcs., 1998—; entrepreneur Stuart Assocs., Powder Springs, Ga., 1991. Republican. Unitarian Universalist. Avocations: currency and coin collector, sports memorabilia, white water rafting, golf, swimming. Home: 12 Silver Fox Ln Sussex NJ 07461-4800

STUART, CYNTHIA MORGAN, university administrator; b. Harrisburg, Pa., June 29, 1949; d. Paul William and Bernice Leona (Boyer) M.; m. David Edward Stuart, June 14, 1971. Student, Elizabethtown (Pa.) Coll., 1967-69; BA, U. N.Mex., 1971, MPA, 1982. Admissions counselor U. N.Mex., Albuquerque, 1974-77, asst. dir. admissions, 1977-80, assoc. dir. admissions, 1980-83, dir. admissions, 1983—, univ. articulation officer, 1989—, dir. student outreach svcs. (secondary appointment), 1991-95, enrollment mgmt. team mem., 1998—; mem. N.Mex. Coordinating Coun. Secondary Schs. and Colls., 1983-92; chair Coun. for Common Concerns, Albuquerque, 1987-95; mem. N.Mex. Articulation Com., Santa Fe, 1983-95; mem. adv. bd. Albuquerque Tech. Vocat. Inst., 1991—. Compiler, editor Statewide Statistical Profile Report, N.Mex. H.Ss., 1983-90; cover photographer Prehistoric New Mexico, 2d edit., 1994, Glimpses of the Ancient Southwest, 1995. Coord. United Way, Albuquerque, 1980-81; elected del. N.Mex. Dem. Conv., 1982; mem. issues and advocacy com. Albuquerque Bus. Edn. Compact, 1991-93; mem. Am. Indian Edn. Initiative, Albuquerque, 1992—; Coll. Bd. del., 1991—. Recipient sys. devel. grant Commn. on Higher Edn., Santa Fe, 1995. Mem. Am. Assn. Collegiate Registrars and Admissions Officers (reporting officer of transfer credit N.Mex. 1979—), Rocky Mountain Assn. Collegiate Registrars and Admissions Officers (v.p. 1979-81, pres. 1983-84), N.Mex. Assn. Collegiate Registrars and Admissions Officers (sec.-treas. 1978-82, pres. 1991-92, Outstanding Svc. award 1990), N.Mex. Am. Coll. Testing Coun. (chair 1996-97, state rep. 1997—, trustee Am. Coll. Testing 1999—, del. to Coll. Bd. 1991—). Democrat. Avocations: photography, travel, drawing, music. Home: 423 Tulane Dr SE Albuquerque NM 87106-1417 Office: Univ New Mex Office of Admissions Student Svcs Ctr Albuquerque NM 87131-0001

STUART, HAROLD CUTLIFF, lawyer, business executive; b. Oklahoma City, July 4, 1912; s. Royal Cutliff and Alice (Bramlitt) S.; m. Joan Skelly, June 6, 1938 (dec. 1994); children: Randi Stuart Wightman, Jon Rolf; m. Frances Langford, Nov. 18, 1994. J.D., U. Va., 1936. Bar: Okla. 1936, D.C. 1952. Ptnr. Stuart, Biolchini, Turner & Givray, Tulsa; judge Common Pleas Ct., 1941-42; asst. sec. air force, 1949-51; chmn. bd. 1st Stuart Corp., radio, oil, real estate and investments, Tulsa; dir. Lowrance Electronics, Inc., Tulsa; spl. cons. to sec. Air Force, 1961-63; mem. Okla. Hwy. Commn., 1959-63; bd. dirs. Great Empire Broadcasting Inc., Wichita, Kans. Trustee emeritus Lovelace Found., Albuquerque; trustee N.Am. Wildlife Fedn; mem. Nat. Eagle Scout Coun. Boy Scouts Am., Disting. Eagle Scout; past pres. Air Force Acad. Found., chmn. bd. Served from 1st lt. to col. USAAF, 1942-46, ETO. Decorated Bronze Star (U.S.) and 6 battle stars; comdr. Order of St. Olav; King Haakon 7th Victory medal; medal of Liberation (Norway); Croix de Guerre (Luxembourg); named to Okla. Aviation and Space Hall of Fame, Okla. Hall of Fame. Mem. Am., Okla., D.C. bar assns., Air Force Assn. (dir., nat. pres., chmn. bd. 1951-52), Tulsa C. of C., Tulsa Headliner, Falcon Found. (vice chmn.), Ducks Unltd. (trustee), Delta Kappa Epsilon. Democrat. Clubs: Southern Hills Country, The Boston (Tulsa); Burning Tree (Washington), Willoughby Golf, The Amb. (Stuart, Fla.). Home: PO Box 96 2460 Palmer St Jensen Beach FL 34958-0096 also: 4590 E 29th St Tulsa OK 74114-6208

STUART, JAMES FORTIER, musician, artistic director; b. Baton Rouge, Dec. 22, 1928; s. Evander Morgan and Jeanne (Fortier) S. Mus.B., La. State U., 1950, B.Music Edn., 1950, Mus.M., 1954; Mus.D., U. Rochester, 1968; DFA (hon.), Coll. of Wooster, 2000. Asst. prof. voice, dir. opera Boston U.; also Boston Conservatory, 1964-68; prof. music, dir. opera Kent (Ohio) State U., 1968—; founder, artistic dir. Kent Light Opera Co., 1969—, Nat. Light Opera Co., 1977—; artistic dir. Ohio Light Opera Co., Wooster, 1979—; pres. Stuart Prodns., Ltd., Cleve., 1974—; mus. cons. Internat. Hospitality Mgmt., Inc., Cleve., 1974. Tenor soloist maj. opera cos. and symphonies, N.Y.C., Boston, Phila., Atlanta and New Orleans, 1950-70; leader tenor Am. Savoyards, 1956-60, Martyn Green Gilbert and Sullivan Co., 1961-67; translator into English from original French texts: Auber's Fra Diavolo, 1988, Lecocq's Fille de Madame Angot, 1989, Ciboulette (Reynaldo Hahn), 1990, Offenbach's M. Choufleuri, 1996, Millöcker's Der Bettelstudent, 1996, Kálmán's Der Bajadere, 1998, Strauss's Eine Nacht in Venedig, 1999, Kálmán's Kaiserin Josephine, 2000. Recipient Significant Sig Outstanding Achievement in Lyric Theatre award Sigma Chi, 1995; inducted Coll. of Fellows of Am. Theatre, 1996. Office: Ohio Light Opera 1600 Via De Luna Pensacola Bch FL 32561-2350

STUART, JOAN MARTHA, fund raising executive; b. June 2, 1945; d. Ervin Wencil and Flora Janet (Applebaum) S. Student, Boston U., 1963-67. Cert. fund raiser. Prodn. asst. Random House, N.Y.C., 1968-69; book designer Simon & Schuster, N.Y.C., 1969-71; feature writer Palm Beach (Fla.) Post, 1971-72; co-founder, comm. dir. Stuart, Gleimer & Assocs., West Palm Beach, 1973-84, pres., 1982—; fin. devel. dir. YWCA Greater Atlanta, 1984-86, Ctr. for the Visually Impaired, Atlanta, 1986-90; ea. divsn. dir. City of Hope, 1990-94; devel. dir. Jewish Family Svcs., Atlanta, 1994-99, Ctr. for Visually Impaired, 1999—; adj. prof. Kennesaw Coll. Contbr. articles to profl. jours. Mem. crusade com. Am. Cancer Soc. Bd., 1981—; bd. dirs. Theatre Arts Co., 1980-81; cmty. svcs. chmn., bd. dirs. B'nai B'rith Women, 1980-82; chmn. publicity Leukemia Soc. Atlanta Polo Benefit, 1983; com. chmn. Atlanta Zool. Beastly Feast Benefit, 1984; mem. Atlanta Symphony Assocs.; chmn. Salute to Women of Achievement, 1987-90; founder, advisor Lauren's Run, 1992—. Recipient Nat. award B'nai B'rith Women, 1978, Regional award, 1979, Cert. of Merit, Big Bros./Big Sisters, 1976. Mem. Nat. Soc. Fund Raising Execs. (cert.), Ga. Exec. Women's Network, Diabetes Assn. (bd. dirs. 1990—), Jerusalem House (bd. dirs. 1991-94), Parent to Parent (bd. dirs. 1993-95). Democrat. Jewish. Office: 763 Peachtree St NE Atlanta GA 30308-1205

STUART, JOHN TREVOR, mathematics educator; b. Leicester, England, Jan. 28, 1929; s. Horace and Phyllis Emily (Potter) S.; m. Christine Mary Tracy, Aug. 31, 1957; children: Andrew Mark, David Michael Addis, Katherine Maria Teresa. BS, U. London, 1949, PhD, 1951; ScD (hon.), Brown U., 1986, U. East Anglia, Norwich, Eng., 1987. Scientific officer Nat. Physical Lab., Teddington, Eng., 1951-66; prof. Imperial Coll., London, 1966-94, emeritus, 1994—; vis. lectr. Mass. Inst. Tech., Cambridge, 1956-57, also vis. prof., 1965-66; vis. prof. Brown U., Providence, R.I., 1988-89; dean royal coll. sci. Imperial Coll., 1990-93. Fellow Imperial Coll., 1998. Fellow Royal Soc. London (coun. mem. 1982-84); mem. London Math. Soc. (pres. 2000-2002, Sr. Whitehead prize 1984), Am. Phys. Soc. (Otto Laporte award 1987), Soc. for Indsl. and Applied Math. Home: 3 Steeple Close Church Rd, SW195AD Wimbledon England Office: Imperial Coll, Dept Math, SW72BZ London England

STUART, MAXWELL CHARLES, film and television distribution company executive; b. Melbourne, Victoria, Australia, June 23, 1936; s. Archibald John and Flora (Morrison) Wilson; m. Jill Maree Leslie, Nov. 26, 1960 (div. Mar. 1991); children: Grant, Paul, Timothy, Anthony; m. Patricia Margaret Spicer, Apr. 13, 1991; children: Emily, Victoria. Grad., Austral. Adminstrv. Staff Coll., Mt. Eliza, 1964. Acct. Broken Hill Associated Smelters Pty. Ltd., Melbourne, 1954-58; co. sec. Gippsland Acceptance Ltd., Dandenong, Australia, 1958-60, GTV9, Melbourne, 1960-69; gen. mgr. ATVO-TV, Melbourne, 1969-79; mng. dir. M.C. Stuart Assocs. Pty. Ltd., Melbourne, 1979—; syndicate leader Ansett Mgmt. Program, Ansett Transport Industries Ltd., Melbourne, 1974-78; cons. Energy Source TV Ltd., Wellington, New Zealand, 1985-86, Sandown Park Motor Raceway, Melbourne, 1990-95; dir. Bojima Transworld Trading Pty Ltd., Melbourne, 1981-84, Bojar Pty Ltd., Melbourne, 1983-84. Mem. Monash Mt. Eliza Alumni Assn., Australia Soc. Accts. (assoc.), Melbourne Cricket Club. Liberal. Mem. Ch. of Eng. Avocations: golf, gardening. Office: MC Stuart Assocs Pty Ltd, 34 Power St Unit 2, Balwyn 3103 VIC, Australia

STUART, (CHARLES) MURRAY, manufacturing executive; b. Gourock, Scotland, July 28, 1933; s. Charles Maitland and Grace Forrester (Kerr) S.; children: David Charles Thomson, Caroline Alison. MA, Glasgow U., Scotland, 1957; LLB, Glasgow U., 1957; chartered acct., 1961. Internal auditor Ford Motor Co., Brentwood, Eng., 1962-65; fin. dir., sec. Sheffield (Eng.) Drill & Steel Co., 1965-69; fin. dir., asst. mng. dir. Unicorn Industries Ltd., Stafford, Eng., 1969-73; fin. dir. Hepworth Ltd., Leeds, Eng., 1973-74; fin. dir. and dep. mng. dir. ICL plc, London, 1974-81; fin. dir. MB Group plc and predecessor co., Reading, Eng., 1981-83; dir. fin. planning and adminstrn. MB Group plc and predecessor co., Reading, 1983-86, mng. dir., 1986-87, group chief exec., 1988-89; chmn. MB Group plc, Reading, 1989-90; vice chmn. CMB Packaging SA, Brussels, 1989-90; dir., chief fin. officer Berisford Internat., London, 1990-91. Mem. Audit Commn. for Local Authorities in Eng. Wales, 1986-95, dep. chmn., 1991-95; non-exec. dir. Scottish Power, 1990-2000; mem. West Surrey and N.E. Hampshire Health Authority, 1990-93. Fellow Royal Soc. of Arts, Assn. of Corp. Treas.; companion British Inst. of Mgmt.

STUART, NANCY RUBIN See RUBIN, NANCY ZIMMAN

STUART, PAMELA BRUCE, lawyer; b. N.Y.C., Feb. 13, 1949; d. J. Raymond and Marion Grace (Cotins) S. AB with distinction, Mt. Holyoke Coll., 1970; JD cum laude, U. Mich., 1973. Bar: N.Y. 1974, D.C. 1975, U.S. Dist. Ct. D.C. 1979, U.S. Ct. Appeals (D.C. cir.) 1980, U.S. Supreme Ct. 1980, U.S. Dist. Ct. Md. 1989, Md. 1992, Va. 1993, U.S. Ct. Appeals (4th cir.) 1993, Fla. 1994, U.S. Dist. Ct. (ea. dist.) Va. 1994, U.S. Dist. Ct. (no. dist.) N.Y. 1996, U.S. Dist. Ct. (so. dist.) Fla. 1998, U.S. Dist. Ct. (so. dist.) N.Y. 1999, U.S. Dist. Ct. (ea. dist.) N.Y. 1999. Trial atty., deputy asst. dir. Bur. of Consumer Protection, FTC, Washington, 1973-79; asst. U.S. atty. U.S. Atty's Office, Washington, 1979-85; sr. trial atty. Office of Internat. Affairs, U.S. Dept. Justice, Washington, 1985-87; atty. Ross, Dixon & Masback, Washington, 1987-89; mem. Lobel, Novins, Lamont & Flug, Washington, 1989-92; pvt. practice, Washington, 1992—; instr. Nat. Inst. for Trial Advocacy, Atty. Gen.'s Advocacy Inst., Legal Edn. Inst., Fed. Practice Inst.; mem. Jud. Conf. D.C., 1985-88, 91-98; mem. Jud. Conf., D.C. Cir., 1996, 98, 2000; assoc. mem. Consular Corps Washington; legal analyst CNN, MSNBC, Fox News, other TV networks. Author: The Federal Trade Commission, 1991; contbr. articles to profl. jours. Bd. dirs. Anacostia Econ. Devel. Corp., 1993—, Anacostia Holding Co., Inc., Anacostia Mgmt. Co., Inc., 1997—. Mem. ABA (mem. internat. criminal law com., chmn., 1993-96, chmn. fed. crim rules subcom. white collar crime com. sect. criminal justice 1997-99), Bar Assn. D.C. (bd. dirs. 1995—), Asst. U.S. Attys. Assn. D.C. (exec. coun. 1993-99, pres. 1998-99), Assn. Trial Lawyers Am., Women's Bar Assn. D.C., Fla. Bar (mem. exec. coun. real property probate and trust law sect. 1999—), Alumnae Assn. Mt. Holyoke Coll. (bd. dirs. 1986-89, 92-95, Alumnae medal of honor 1990), Edward Bennett Williams Inn of Ct. (master of bench), Fed. City Club (bd. govs. 1992—), Cosmos Club. Avocations: writing, interior design, investments, piano. Home: 5115 Yuma St NW Washington DC 20016-4336 Office: 888 16th St NW Washington DC 20006-4103 also: 111 Johns Island Dr Apt 7 Vero Beach FL 32963-3274

STUART, SANDRA JOYCE, computer information scientist; b. Wheatland, Mo., Aug. 15, 1950; d. Asa Maxville and Inez Irene (Wilson) Friedley; m. John Kendall Stuart, Apr. 17, 1971; 1 child, Whitney Renee. Student, Cen. Mo. State U., 1968-69; AA (hon.), Johnson County Community Coll., 1980; BS in Bus. Adminstrn. cum laude, Avila Coll., 1992. Statis. asst. Fed. Crop Ins. Corp., Kansas City, Mo., 1978-83; mgr. Fed. Women's Program, Kansas City, 1979-80; mgmt. asst. Marine Corps Fin. Ctr., Kansas City, 1983-85, analyst computer systems, 1985-88; computer programmer analyst Corps. of Engrs., Kansas City, 1988-91; regional program mgr. FAA, Kansas City, 1991—. Author: The Samuel Walker History, 1983. Asst. supt. Sunday sch. Overland Park (Kans.) Christian Ch., 1979-80, supt., 1980-82. Mem. Wheatland High Sch. Alumni Assn. (pres. 1990-91), Mo-Kan High Tech. Crime Investigation Assn. (charter, 2d v.p. 1998-99, 1st v.p. 1999—). Avocations: needlework, genealogy, reading, traveling.

STUBBE, MICHEL MARIE, economist, statistician; b. Gent, Belgium, May 1, 1959; s. Andre and Jeanine (Opsomer) S.; m. Maria Antonia Sastre Alonso, Nov. 3, 1989; children: Luis Edouard, Emma Béatrice. Lic.Sci.Econ., U. Gent, 1981; DEA, U. Grenoble, France, 1982, PhD, 1986. Rschr. U. Grenoble, 1982-85; cons. European Commn., Luxembourg, 1985-88; stats. officer Sec. Com. European Commn. Govs., Basle, Switzerland, 1988-90, prof. mem., 1990-93; dep. head divsn. European Monetary Inst., Frankfurt, Germany, 1994-98; head divsn. European Ctrl. Bank, Frankfurt, 1998—. Pres. Club Belge de Bale et du Jura, Switzerland, 1992-93. French Govt. scholar, 1981-84. Mem. European Econ. Assn., Am. Econ. Assn. Office: European Ctrl Bank, PO Box 16 03 19, D-60066 Frankfurt am Main Germany

STUBBE, RAY WILLIAM, minister, chaplain, author; b. Milw., Aug. 15, 1938; s. Clarence Arnold and Ruby Ottilie (Mueller) S. BA, St. Olaf Coll., 1962; MDiv, Northwestern Luth. Theol. Sem., 1965; postgrad., U. Chgo., 1967. Ordained to ministry Evang. Luth. Ch. Am., 1965. Mission devel. bd. Am. missions Luth Ch. in Am., Oak Creek, Wis., 1965-66; organizer, pastor All Saints Luth Ch., Oak Creek, 1966-67; enlisted USN, 1955; commd. ensign USNR, 1963, advanced through grades to lt., comdr. chaplain corps, 1971; augmented to USN, 1971, ret., 1985; chaplain, 1967-85; ret. USN, 1985; asst. pastor Evang. Luth. Ch. of Redeemer, Milw., 1985—. Author: Inside Force Recon, 1989, Khe Sanh Chaplain, 1970, Paddles, Parachutes, Patrols, 1979, Aarugha, 1989, Valley of Decision, 1991, The Final Formation, 1995, Psalms of the Revised Common Lectionary Pericope System, 1998; editor Khe Sanh Veteran/Red Clay, 1996-98; contbr. articles and poems to profl. jours. and books. Chaplain Wis. Vietnam Vets., Milw., 1984—, 3d Marine Div. Assn., 1988; founder, pres. emeritus Khe Sanh Vets., Inc., 1988—. Recipient Legion of Honor award Chapel of Four Chaplains; decorated Bronze Star medal with combat V. Mem. Am. Assn. Rel., VFW (life), DAV (life), Retired Officers Assn. (life), Wis. Vietnam Vets. (chpt. 1), Force Reconnaissance Assn. (life), Spl. Forces Assn. (life), Marine Corps Hist. Found. (life), 3d Marine Divsn. Assn. (life), Vietnam Vets. of Am. (life), Spl. Ops. Assn. (life), Soc. Bibl. Lit., Wis. Acad. Scis., Arts and Letters. Home: 8766 Parkview Ct Milwaukee WI 53226-2729 Office: Redeemer Luth Church 631 N 19th St Milwaukee WI 53233-2152

STUBBERUD, ALLEN ROGER, electrical engineering educator; b. Glendive, Mont., Aug. 14, 1934; s. Oscar Adolph and Alice Marie (LeBlanc) S.; m. May B. Tragus, Nov. 19, 1961; children: Peter A., Stephen C. B.S. in Elec. Engring, U. Idaho, 1956; M.S. in Engring, UCLA, 1958, Ph.D., 1962. From asst. prof. to assoc. prof. engring. UCLA, 1962-69; prof. elec. engring. U. Calif., Irvine, 1969—; assoc. dean engring. U. Calif., 1972-78, dean engring., 1978-83, chair elec. and computer engring., 1993-98, interim dean engring., 1994-96; chief scientist U.S. Air Force, 1983-85; dir. Elec. Communications and Systems Engring. divsn. NSF, 1987-88. Author: Analysis and Synthesis of Linear Time Variable Systems, 1964, (with others) Feedback and Control Systems, 2d edit., 1990, (with others) Digital Control System Design, 2d edit., 1994; contbr. articles to profl. jours. Recipient Exceptional Civilian Svc. medal USAF, 1985, 90, Meritorious Civilian Svc. medal, 1996. Fellow IEEE (Centennial medal 1984, Millennium medal 2000), AIAA, AAAS, NYAS; mem. INFORMS, Sigma Xi, Sigma Tau, Tau Beta Pi, Eta Kappa Nu. Office: U Calif Dept Ece Irvine CA 92697-0001

STUBBING, THOMAS JOHN, airless drying technology executive, inventor; b. Buntingford, Eng., June 19, 1932; s. Harold Rolfe and Violet Emily (Chapman) S.; m. Ann Peters, Feb. 4, 1956; children: Martin Rolfe, Penelope Claire, Juliet Emily. Student, Sir John Cass Coll., London, 1950-51. Area mgr. G.B. Ollivant Ltd., Nigeria, 1954-63, Initial plc, Bristol, Eng., 1963-69; mng. dir. Hokatex GmbH, Castrop-Rauxel, Germany, 1969-75; area mgr. Rethwisch K.G., Bochum, Germany, 1975-80; chmn., ptnr. Heat-Win Ltd., Bitterley, Ludlow, Eng., 1980—; presenter and cons. in field. Contbr. articles to profl. jours.; patentee for method and apparatus for energy efficient drying and continuous drying in superheated steam now in commercial use in the ceramic industry and being developed for use in other industries. Mem. Parish Coun., Bitterley, 1990-95. Sgt. Edn. Corps, Royal Army, 1952-54. Recipient Brit. Innovation award for mfg. tech. Sunday Times/Honeywell, 1989. Avocations: photography, gardening. Home and Office: Spout House, Bitterley Ludlow SY8 3HQ, England

STUBBS, MICHAEL WESLEY, English linguistics educator; b. Glasgow, Scotland, Dec. 23, 1947; s. Leonard Garforth and Isabella (McGavin) S. BA, King's Coll., Cambridge, U.K., 1970, MA, 1973; PhD, U. Edinburgh, U.K., 1975. Rschr. U. Birmingham, U.K., 1973-74; lectr. U. Nottingham, U.K., 1974-85; prof. Inst. of Edn. U. London, U.K., 1985-90; prof. U. Trier, Germany, 1990—. Author: (books) Language, Schools and Classrooms, 1976, Language and Literacy, 1980, Discourse Analysis, 1983, Educational Linguistics, 1986, Text and Corpus Analysis, 1996. Hon. rsch. fellow U. Birmingham, 1994—. Mem. Brit. Assn. for Applied Linguistics (chair 1988-91). Avocation: walking. Office: U Trier, FB2 Anglistik, D-54286 Trier Germany

STUBBS, SUSAN CONKLIN, statistician; b. Washington, July 26, 1935; d. Maxwell Robertson and Marcia (Nye) Conklin; m. LeRoy Carter Hostetter, May 20, 1975 (div. 1988); m. Joel Richard Stubbs, Sept. 20, 1992. BA, Pa. State U., 1957. Economist Bur. of Census, Suitland, Md., 1973-74; economist Bur. of Labor Statistics, Washington, 1974-78, supervisory economist, 1978-84; statistician IRS, Washington, 1984-95, chief rschr. stats. of income divsn., 1989-92, coord. for indsl. classification, 1994-95; ret., 1995; cons. joint com. on taxation U.S. Congress, 1992-94; OPM legis. fellow, 1988. Contbr. articles to profl. jours.; editor govtl. statis. publs. Leader, del., com. mem., v.p., bd. dirs., chmn. nominating com. Girl Scout Coun. Nation's Capital, Washington, 1968-99; sec., treas. Middlesex Beach Assn., Bethany, Del., 1991-94; jobs editor Caucus for Women in Stats., Wash-

ington, 1992-95; mentor Mentors Inc., Washington, 1992-94; bd. dirs. Rice's Hotel/Hughlett's Tavern Found., 1998-2000; treas. Smith Point Sea Rescue, 1998—; docent, chmn. Christmas on Cockrell's Creek, Reedville Fisherman's Mus., 2000; active Boy Scouts Am. Campaign for Family Values, Lee Coun., VA Capital Fund Dr., coord. Northumberland County; treas. Episc. Diocese of Va., Region II, 1999—. Mem. Am. Statis. Assn., Woman's Club Northumberland County (pres. 1996-98, treas. 1998), Rivers Bend Assn. (v.p., bd. dirs. 1996-98, chair bylaws com., chair long range planning com. 1998-2000), Va. Federated Woman's Clubs (pres. Eastern area Lee dist. 1998-2000), Bus. and Profl. Women Essex County and Northern Neck (sec. 1999—), People Helping People Tutor and Mentor Program (tutor and mentor). Avocations: sailing, swimming, gardening, reading. Home: 776 Riverview Ln Heathsville VA 22473-4011

STUBIČAR, NADA KRISTINA, physical chemistry, researcher, chemistry educator; b. Duga Resa, Karlovac, Croatia, Nov. 1, 1939; d. Čedomir and Kristina Istina Miku Puzigaća; m. Mirko Stubičar, Feb. 11, 1967; 1 child, Silvija Sunčana. BS in Chemistry, U. Zagreb, Croatia, 1966, MSc in Phys. Chemistry, 1973, DSc in Natural Scis., 1978. Rsch. and tchg. asst. Inst. Phys. Chemistry, Faculty Natural Scis. & Math., Zagreb, 1968-84; sr. scientist, asst. prof. Faculty Natural Scis. and Math., Zagreb, 1984—. Contbr. more than 30 articles to sci., profl. jours., and books. Fulbright-IREX scholar SUNY, Buffalo, Ga. Inst. Tech., Atlanta, 1982-83. Mem. European Colloid and Interface Soc., Croatian Soc. Surfactants, Croatian Chem. Soc., Croatian Soc. Engrs. and Technicians, Soc. Univ. Tchrs. Achievements include research in emulsion polymerisation, crystal growth of sparingly soluble salts from solution and aggregation of inorganic and organic colloids (amphilphiles), mainly by potentiometric and dynamic laser light scattering method. Avocations: painting, needlework. Home: ul Matije Jandrića 38, HR 10000 Zagreb Croatia Office: Univ Zagreb Fac Natural Sci, PO Box 163, HR 10001 Zagreb Croatia

STUBOS, ATHANASSIOS, chemical engineer, research consultant; b. Kalamata, Greece, Sept. 7, 1960; s. Constantinos and Vassiliki (Tsolkas) S.; m. Efimia Palli, June 4, 1994. Diploma in Chem. Engring., Nat. Tech. U. of Athens, Greece, 1984; postgrad. diploma in Fluid Mechanics, Von Karman Inst. for Fluid Dynamics, Brussels, 1985; PhD in Applied Scis., U. Libre de Bruxelles, 1990. Rsch. asst. Von Karman Inst., Brussels, 1985-89, postdoctoral rsch. fellow, 1990-91; advanced physics instr. St. John's International Sch., Brussels, 1986-87; sr. rschr. Nat. Rsch. Ctr. Demokritos, Athens, 1992—; vis. rsch. assoc. U. So. Calif., L.A., 1991; rsch. cons. Inst. Mechanics of Materials and Geostructures, S.A., Pendeli, Greece, 1992—. Author chpts. to books; contbr. articles to profl. jours.; patentee in field. Recipient Math. award Greek Math. Soc., 1978, Von Karman prize, 1985. Mem. Greek Assn. Chem. Engrs., Internat. Solar Energy Soc. (Greek sect.), Nat. Geog. Soc., Tech. Chamber of Greece. Greek Orthodox. Avocations: travelling around globe, cinema, basketball, soccer. Home: Xiroyianni 57, 15771 Zografos Greece Office: Nat Rsch Ctr Demokritos, 15310 AG Paraskevi Greece

STUCHEBRUKHOV, ALEXEY ALEXANDROVICH, chemistry educator; b. Moscow, Russia, Dec. 2, 1957; s. Alexander N. and Nina S. S.; m. Olga A., Nov. 16, 1960. MS, Moscow Phys. & Tech. Inst., Russia, 1981, PhD, 1985. Prof. chemistry U. Calif., Davis, 1994—. Contbr. articles to profl. jours. Named Beckman Young Investigator, Beckman Found., 1997; Arthur A. Sloan Found. fellow, 1997. Office: U Calif 1 Shields Ave Davis CA 95616-5200

STUCK, ROGER DEAN, electrical engineering educator; b. Ventura, Calif., Nov. 6, 1924; s. William Henry and Marian Grace (Ready) S.; m. Opal Christine Phillips, July 25, 1948; children: Dean, Phyllis, Sandra. BSEE, Calif. Inst. Tech., 1947; MSEE, N.C. State U., 1957. Elec. engr. Warren Wilson Coll., Swannanoa, N.C., 1947—, instr. elec. engring. physics, 1948-69, dean students, 1969-72, instr. physics, elec. engr., 1972-86. Author: (charts) The Periodic Table of Physical Concepts, 1977, The Periodic Table of Physical Concepts with Economic Concepts, 1980; (book) The Periodic Table of Physical Concepts Book of Definitions, 1980. Lt. (j.g.) USNR, 1942-46. Mem. Sigma Xi. Republican. Presbyterian. Achievements include identification of gravitational inductance, capacitance and splendor (MVVV) and energy-spread (hc) as the fundamental initial concept of physical creation. Home: 65 Green Forest Rd Swannanoa NC 28778-2246

STUCKY, JEAN SEIBERT, lawyer; b. Berkeley, Calif., Feb. 9, 1951; d. Edward Raymond and Frances Selma (Berg) S.; m. Scott Wallace Stucky, Aug. 18, 1973; children: Mary-Clare, Joseph. BA in Econs., Wellesley (Mass.) Coll., 1973; JD, Cornell U., 1978; MA in Econs., Trinity U., San Antonio, 1980; postgrad., George Washington U., Washington, 1991—. Bar: D.C. 1978. Atty.-advisor Adminstrv. Conf. U.S., Washington, 1978-79, Divsn. Advice, NLRB, Washington, 1979-94; contractor labor counsel U.S. Dept. Energy, Office Gen. Counsel, Washington, 1994—. Mem. Washington Cathedral Altar Guild, 1988—. Mem. D.C. Bar, Dames of Loyal Legion of U.S., Washington Wellesley Club (pres. 1992-94), Wellesley Coll. Alumnae Assn. (regional chmn. 1995-97). Republican. Episcopalian. Avocations: gardening, flower arranging. Home: 11004 Homeplace Ln Potomac MD 20854-1406 Office: US Dept Energy Office Gen Counsel 1000 Independence Ave SW Washington DC 20585-0001

STUCKY, SCOTT WALLACE, lawyer; b. Hutchinson, Kans., Jan. 11, 1948; s. Joe Edward and Emma Clara (Graber) S.; m. Jean Elsie Seibert, Aug. 18, 1973; children: Mary-Clare, Joseph. BA summa cum laude, Wichita State U., 1970; JD, Harvard U., 1973; MA, Trinity U., 1980; LLM with high honors, George Washington U., 1983; postgrad., Nat. War Coll., 1993. Bar: Kans. 1973, U.S. Dist. Ct. Kans. 1973, U.S. Ct. Appeals (10th cir.) 1973, U.S. Ct. Mil. Appeals 1974, U.S. Supreme Ct. 1976, D.C. 1979, U.S. Ct. Appeals (D.C. cir.) 1979. Assoc. Ginsburg, Feldman & Bress, Washington, 1978-82; chief docketing and svc. br. Nuclear Regulatory Commn., Washington, 1982-83, legis. counsel U.S. Air Force, 1983-96; gen. counsel sen. com. on armed svcs. Nuclear Regulatory Commn., 1996—; lectr. bus. law Maria Regina Coll., Syracuse, N.Y., 1977; congrl. fellow Office Senator John Warner, 1986; res. judge adv. USAF Res., Washington, 1982—; col. Appellate Mil. Judge, USAF Ct. Criminal Appeals, 1991-95, 97-98; sr. reservist USAF Judiciary, 1995-97, Air Res. Personnel Ctr., 1998-99, Air Force Legal Svcs. Agy., 1999—. Contbr. articles to profl. jours. Capt. USAF, 1973-78. Decorated Air Force Meritorious Svc. medal with two oak leaf cluster. Mem. Fed. Bar Assn., Judge Advs. Assn. (bd. dirs. 1984-88), Res. Officers Assn., Wichita State U. Alumni Assn. (pres. chpt. 1981-86, nat. bd. dirs. 1986-92), Adoption Svc. Info. Agy. (bd. dirs. 1998—), Army and Navy Club (Washington), Mil. Order of Loyal Legion U.S. (state comdr. and recorder 1984-92, nat. treas. 1987-89, nat. vice comdr. 1989-93, nat. comdr.-in-chief 1993-95), Sons of Union Vets Civil War (chpt. vice-comdr 1986-88), Phi Delta Phi, Phi Alpha Theta, Phi Kappa Phi, Omicron Delta Kappa, Sigma Phi Epsilon. Republican. Episcopalian. Home: 11004 Homeplace Ln Potomac MD 20854-1406 Office: Sen Armed Svcs Com 228 Senate Office Bldg Washington DC 20510-0001

STUCKY, WOLFFRIED, computer science educator; b. Bad Kreuznach, Germany, Nov. 5, 1939; s. Karl J. and Auguste (Schweitzer) S.; m. Ingrid C. Koch, Dec. 24, 1942; 1 child, Alexandra. Diploma in math., U. Saarbruecken, Germany, 1965, D Natural Sci., 1970. Asst. lectr. U. Saarbruecken, 1965-70; with Boehringer, Mannheim, Germany, 1970-71, E. Merck, Darmstadt, Germany, 1971-75; prof. applied informatics U. Karlsruhe, Germany, 1976—. Co-author: Database Systems: Concepts and Models, 2d edit., 1983, Programming With Modula-2, 2d edit., 1994, Automata-Languages-Computability, 1992, Problem-Algorithm-Program, 1993. Mem. IEEE, Assn. Computing Machinery, German Informatics Soc. (pres. 1996-97), Coun. European Profl. Informatics Socs. (v.p. 1998—). Home: Klarastr 11, D-67549 Worms Germany Office: U Karlsruhe, Inst Applied Informatics, D-76128 Karlsruhe Germany

STUCLEY, HUGH GEORGE, land owner; b. Bideford, Devon, England, Jan. 8, 1945; s. Dennis Bankes and Sheila Margaret (Bampfylde) S.; m. Angela Caroline Toller, Jan. 22, 1969; children: George, Peter, Charlotte, Lucinda. Cert. of merit, Royal Agrl. Coll., Cirencester, Eng., 1970. chmn. bd. dirs. Hartland Quay Hotel Co. Chmn. Devon br. Country Landowners Assn., 1995-97; pres. Devonshire Assn., 1997-98; chmn. Badcworth Land Co., 1999—; lt. Royal Horse Euands (The Blues), 1963-68. Episcopalian. Avocations: shooting, skiing, tennis, surfing. Home: Affeton Castle, Worlington, Crediton Devon, England

STUDER, JAMES EDWARD, geological engineer; b. Aurora, Colo., Sept. 1, 1961; s. Fredrick Ernest and Patricia Dora (McWilliams) S.; m. Anita Louise Palmer, Apr. 19, 1986; 1 child, Matthew Bernard. BS in Geol. Engring., U. Mo., Rolla, 1984, MS in Geol. Engring., 1985. Registered profl. engr., Kans., Fla., Tex., N.Mex., Okla., Ariz.; registered geologist, Ky. Engring. aide engring. divsn. pub. works City of Kansas City, Mo., 1981-83; civil engr. tech. U.S. Army Corps Engrs., Kansas City, 1984; staff engr. Woodward-Clyde Cons., St. Louis, 1985; staff to asst. project engr. Woodward-Clyde Cons., Overland Park, Kans., 1986-89, project engr., 1989-90; grad. teaching asst. U. Mo., Rolla, 1985; sr. project engr. Coastal Remediation Co., Norman, Okla., 1990-92; program dir. Hall Southwest Corp., Austin, Tex., 1992-93; S.W. region program mgr. Envirogen, Inc., Austin, 1993-94; sr. engr. Duke Engrg. and Svcs., Albuquerque, 1995-98, sect. mgr., 1998—; pres., founder Funding Resource LLC, 1997—; lectr. grad. sch. seminars, 1987-96, Nat. Seminar on RCRA Corrective Action, 1990, Internat. Symposium on Bioremediation, 1995, 97, 99, Superfund Conf., 1996, U.S. EPA Tech. Transfer Conf., 1996, 98, Internat. Symposium on Chlorinated and Recalcitrant Compounds, 1998, 2000; adv. bd. Albuquerque Tech.-Vocational Inst., 1995-99; youth soccer coach, 1997-2000. Contbr. articles on environ. sci. and engring. to profl. jours. and books. Environ. adv. bd. City of Round Rock, Tex., 1993. Eagle Scout Boy Scouts Am. Mem. ASCE, Am. Cash Flow Assn., Assn. Ground Water Scientists and Engrs., N.Mex. Optics Industry Assn., Albuquerque C. of C., Coronado Venture Forum, N.Mex. Entrepreneurs Assn., Sigma Gamma Epsilon (W.A. Tarr award 1984). Roman Catholic. Achievements include leading first full-scale vadose zone partitioning interwell tracer test for in-situ quantification of dense non-aqueous phase liquid (DNAPL); leading design of first US EPA-permitted arid-land final cap for hazardous waste landfill; on team that discovered and mapped previously unrecorded cave in Missouri; devel. of innovative technologies for characterization and restoration of hazardous waste sites and water resources. Office: Duke Engring and Svcs 1650 University Blvd NE Ste 300 Albuquerque NM 87102-5619

STUDER, WILLIAM JOSEPH, library educator; b. Whiting, Ind., Oct. 1, 1936; s. Victor E. and Sarah G. (Hammersley) S.; m. Rosemary Lippie, Aug. 31, 1957; children: Joshua E., Rachel Marie. BA, Ind. U., 1958, MA, 1960, PhD (Univ. fellow), 1968. Grad. asst. div. libr. sci. Ind. U., 1959-60, reference asst., 1960-61; spl. intern Libr. of Congress, 1961-62, reference libr., sr. bibliographer, 1962-65; dir. regional campus librs. Ind. U., Bloomington, 1968-73; assoc. dean univ. librs. Ind. U., 1973-77; dir. librs. Ohio State U., Columbus, 1977-2000, prof. libr. sci., 2000—; mem. Libr.Svcs. and Constrn. Act Adv. Com. of Ind., 1971-76, Adv. Coun. on Fed. Libr. Programs in Ohio, 1977-85, chmn., 1980-81; mem. adv. coun. Libr. Svcs. and Tech. Act, 1997-99; mem. ARL Office Mgmt. Studies Adv. Com., 1977-81, ARL Task Force on Nat. Libr. Network Devel., 1978-83, chmn., 1981-83, com. on preservation, 1985-88, vice-chmn., 1989-90, chmn., 1991-92, task force on scholarly comm., 1983-87, bd. dirs., 1981-84, com. stats. and measurement, 1993-99, chmn., 1997-98; mem. network adv. com. Libr. of Congress, 1981-88; mem. libr. study com. Ohio Bd. Regents, 1986-87; mem. steering com. Ohio Libr. and Info. Network (Ohio Link), 1987-90; bd. dirs. Ctr. Rsch. Librs., 1989-96, vice-chmn., 1993-94, chmn., 1994-95, sec., chmn. membership com., 1990-93; mem. adv. coun. Ohio Link Libr., 1990-2000, chmn., 1991-92, policy adv. coun., governing bd., 1991-92. Contbr. articles to profl. jours. Trustee On Line Computer Libr. Ctr. Inc., 1977-78; del. On Line Computer Libr. Ctr. Users Coun., 1983-91; mem. rsch. librs. adv. com. OnLine Computer Libr. Ctr., 1989-95, vice chair, chair-elect, 1993-94, chair, 1994-95; bd. dirs. Ohio Network of Librs. Ohionet, 1977-87, chmn., 1980-82, 86-87, treas., 1983-86; mem. Columbia U. Sch. Library Svc. Conservation Programs, vis. com., 1987-90; mem. nat. adv. coun. to commn. on preservation and access, 1989-92; treas. Monroe County (Ind.) Mental Health Assn., 1966-76; active Mental Health Social Club, 1971-73; budget rev. com. United Way, 1975-77; bd. dirs. Mental Health Assn. Recipient citation for participation MARC Insts., 1968-69; Louise Maxwell award Ind. U., 1978. Mem. ALA, Ohio Libr. Assn. (bd. dirs. 1980-83), Assn. Coll. and Rsch. Librs. (bd. dirs. 1977-81, com. on activities model for 1990, 1981-82, chmn. libr. sch. curriculum task force 1988-89), Acad. Libr. Assn. Ohio, Torch Club (pres. 1993-94), Phi Kappa Phi (pub. rels. officer 1982-83, sec. 1983-85), Phi Eta Sigma, Alpha Epsilon Delta., Beta Phi Mu. Home: 724 Olde Settler Pl Columbus OH 43214-2924 Office: Ohio State U William Oxley Thompson Meml Libr 1858 Neil Ave Columbus OH 43210-1225

STUEBNER, JAMES CLOYD, real estate developer, contractor; b. Phila., Dec. 15, 1931; s. Erwin A. and Frances (Quinn) S.; children: Kathleen, Stephen, James, Susan, Elizabeth; m. Susan Rae Peterson, June 16, 1990. BA, Dartmouth Coll., 1953. Sales engr. Rohm & Haas Co., Phila., 1956-69; pres. Structural Plastics Corp., Mpls., 1961-69; pres., gen. ptnr. Stuebner Properties, Mpls., 1969—; pres. Northland Inn and Exec. Conf. Ctr., 1988—; CEO Five Star Realty and Devel. Co., Mpls., 1992—, Boone 94 Properties (Sleep Inn Hotel), 1998. Mem. Minn. Conv. Ctr. Commn., St. Paul, 1988; commr. Minn. Econ. Devel. Commn., St. Paul, 1985; bd. dirs. Bach Soc. of Minn., Mpls., 1986—, Minn. Orchestral Assn., Mpls., 1988-91. Sgt. U.S. Army, 1953-55. Mem. Nat. Assn. Office and Indsl. Parks (bd. dirs. Minn. chpt. 1976-85, 81-90, pres. 1978-80, 92-93, nat. pres. 1983-84, v.p. 1981-81, Developer of Yr. award 1987, Minn. Bus. Person of Yr. award 1990, vice chmn. indsl. devel. forum 1996, chmn. 1997). Avocations: sailing, running, singing. Office: Five Star Realty and Devel Co 7000 Northland Dr N Minneapolis MN 55428-1502

STUERMER, HANS-DIETER, chemist; b. Eberbach, Baden, Germany, Oct. 30, 1950. Diploma in chemistry, U. Freiburg (Germany), 1975, B in Econs., 1977. Scientist U. Freiburg, 1975-79; lectr. Pedagog Coll., Esslingen, Germany, 1979-81; exec. Stuermer & Schuele OHG, Freiburg, 1981-90; dir. Freiburg Inst. of Environ. Chemistry, 1987—. Editor: Chemicals in Environment, 1984; patentee in field. Mem. state parliament Baden-Wurttemberg, 1984-88; mem. county coun. Breisgau-Hochschwarzwald, 1989-94; mem. regional coun. (Green Party) Sudlicher Oberrhein, 1995—. Office: Freiburg Inst Environ Chem, Wilhelmstrasse 24a, D-79098 Freiburg Germany

STUERMER, MICHAEL, historian; b. Kassel, Germany, Sept. 29, 1938; s. Bruno and Ursula (Schorbening) S. PhD, Marburg U., 1965; habilitation, TH Darmstadt, Germany, 1971. Lectr. European history Sussex U., Brighton, Eng., 1970-71; prof. U. Technische Hochschule, Darmstadt, 1971-73, Erlangen (Fed. Republic Germany) U., 1973-88; rsch. fellow Harvard U., Cambridge, Mass., 1976-77; mem. Inst. for Advanced Study, Princeton, N.J., 1977-78; assoc. prof. Sorbonne U., Paris, 1979-85; dir. SWP Ebevnhausen, Fed. Republic Germany, 1988-98; columnist FAZ Frankfurt, Fed. Republic of Germany, 1985-94, Neue Zürchet Zeitung, 1994-98, Die Welt, 1998—. Author: Scherben des Glueck, Klassizismus und Revolution, 1987, Waegen und Wagen Sal Oppenheim Jr. & Cie. Geschichte einer Bank und einer Familie, 1989, Das Ruhelose Reich-Deutschland 1866-1918, 1990, Die Grenzen der Macht. Begegnuno der Deutschen mit Geschichte, 1992, The German Century, 1999. Officer Legion of Honor, 1990. Office: SWP, Die Welt Axel-Springer, Strasse 65, D-10888 Berlin Germany

STUETZ, ANTON, chemist, researcher, educator; b. Schärding, Austria, June 11, 1947; s. Leopold and Hilda (Wallner) S.; m. Edelfriede Nisslmüller, July 4, 1970; children: Werner, Irmgard. PhD, U. Vienna, 1972, univ. dozent, 1987, univ. prof., 1994. Cert. medicinal chemist. Postdoctoral rsch. scientist Max Planck Inst. Biophys. Chemistry, Göttingen, Germany, 1972-74; head lab. Novartis formerly Sandoz Rsch. Inst., Vienna, 1974-86, dep. head dermatology, 1986-91, head dermatology rsch., 1992-94, head rsch., 1995-96, acting head Inst., 1995-97, head chemistry and pharmacology, 1997-99, head inflammatory skin diseases, 1999—. Contbr. articles to profl. jours.; patentee in field. Mem. German/Austrian Chemists, Soc. Investigative Dermatology, N.Y. Acad. Sci. Avocations: music, playing piano, mountaineering, jogging. Home: Haymogasse 140, A-1230 Vienna Austria Office: Novartis Rsch Inst, Brunnerstrasse 59, A-1235 Vienna Austria

STUFANO, THOMAS JOSEPH, criminologist, author, inventor; b. Newport, R.I., July 23, 1955; s. Thomas and Zoe Anne (Halsey) S.; 1 child, Christine Anne; m. Rene Ellen Goldfarb, Nov. 10, 1994. BSc in Criminal Justice, Pacific Western U., 1988, MBA, 1990; PhD in Criminal Justice, Clayton U., 1992; disting. grad., U.S. Air U., 1992; DSc in Mil. Scis., Eurotechnical Rsch. U., 1997. Legis. rschr. R.I. Ho. of Reps., Providence, R.I., 1978-79; sub com. investigator U.S. Ho. of Reps., Washington, 1979-81; law enforcement staff rschr. State of Fla., 1981-88; intelligence officer U.S. Govt., Washington, 1988-96; CEO, dir. Diversified Intelligence Group, Inc., Coral Springs, Fla., 1995—; exec. dir. Diversified Technologies and System Inc., Fort Lauderdale, Fla., 1995—; cons. crime commn. State of Fla., 1986-87, U.S. Govt., Washington, 1990-92, State of R.I., 1979-80; mem. Pres.' Commn. on Aviation Security and Terrorism. Author: Human Element in Business, 1992, Combating Terrorism, 1994, Investigators Pretext Investigation Manual, 1998, BEA Training Manual, 1998; Applied Impact Theory patentee, 1999; contbr. articles to profl. jours. Mem. Rep. Senatorial Inner Circle, Washington, 1992—; instr. ARC, Fla., 1994—; mem. adv. bd. Nat. Civil Def., Washington, 1988—; mem. Presdl. Round Table. Recipient Presdl. Commendation Pres. of U.S., 1988, 91, 94, Commendation U.S. Ho. of Reps. and Senate, 1982, 91, 94, commendation Prime Minister Lady Margaret Thatcher, 1991, Citation R.I. Ho. of Reps., 1980, Gov. of Mass., 1980, Tenn., Fla., Ky., 1990, Commendation U.S. Dept. of State, 1992, Min. Intelligence Security, Eng., 1996, Meritorious Achievement award for global antiterrorism, 1997, 20th Century Achievement award ABI, 1998, Millennium Hall of Fame award, 1998, 500 Leaders of Influence award IBI, 1998. Mem. Air Force Assn., Internat. Narcotic Enforcement Officers Assn., Res. Officers Assn., World Assn. of Investigators, Internat. Assn. Counter Terrorism and Security Profls., USAF/SARCAP (instr. search and recovery pilot), Aircraft Owners and Pilots Assn., Profl. Assn. of Diving Instrs. (instr., Platnuim Diving award 1989), Am. Shorin Kempo Karate Assn. (5th degree blackbelt), Order of Ky. Cols. Roman Catholic. Avocations: scuba diving, airplane pilot, parachuting, bicycling, karate.

STUHL, OSKAR PAUL, scientific and regulatory consultant; b. Dec. 23, 1949; s. Johannes Alexander and Johanna Wilhelmine (Hoelling) S. S. Dipl. Chem., U. Duesseldorf, 1976, Dr.rer.nat., 1978. Tutor Inst. Organische Chemie U. Duesseldorf, 1975-76, sci. assoc., 1976-79; mgr. product devel. Drugofa GmbH, Cologne, Fed. Republic of Germany, 1980; mgr. sci. rels. RJRN, Cologne, 1981-88, mgr. sci. svcs., 1989-94; co-founder, co-owner WRKM Internat., 1996—; cons. in field, 1995—. Mem. editl. bd. Beitraege zur Tabakforschung Internat., 1986-96; contbr. articles to profl. jours.; patentee in field. Mem. Duesseldorf Mus. Verein, Verein der Freunde des Hetjens-Museums, Verein der Freunde des Stadtmuseums Duesseldorf, Met. Mus. Art, N.Y.C., Friends Royal Acad. Arts, London, Friends of Tate Gallery, London, Art Soc. of Rheinlande and Westfalen, Gesellschaft der Freunde der Kunstammlung NRW, Gesellschaft der Freunde und Foerderer der Univ. Duesseldorf, Zuercher Kunstgesellschaft, Freundeskreis Theatermuseum, Duesseldorf, Foerderverein NRW-Stiftung, Forum fuer Film, Duesseldorf, Freunde und Foerder der Akademie fuer Kommunikations Design, Duesseldorf, Deutsch-Japanische-Gesellschaft. Mem. AAAS, Gesellschaft Deutscher Chemiker, Gesellschaft Deutscher Naturforscher und Aerzte, Max-Planck-Gesellschaft, Deutsche Gesellschaft fuer Arbeits hygiene, Am. Chem. Soc. (including various divsns.), Chem. Soc. Japan, N.Y. Acad. Scis., Royal Soc. Chemistry, Am. Pharm. Assn., Acad. Pharm. Rsch. and Sci., Internat. Union Pure and Applied Chemistry, Am. Soc. Pharmacognosy, Fedn. Internat. Pharmaceutic, Christlich Demokratische Union, Vereinigung AC Club Duesseldorf, PCL Club (London), KDStV Burgundia-Leipzig Club, Golf Club Velbert. CDU-Mittelstands und Wirtschaftsvereinigung. Roman Catholic. Office: PO Box 140544, D-40075 Düsseldorf Germany

STUHLMACHER, PETER OTTO JOHANNES, religion educator; b. Leipzig, Germany, Jan. 18, 1932; s. Johannes and Elise (Hoffmann) S.; m. Irmgard Kuehl, June 7, 1960; children: Walther, Mechthild, Reinhart, Konrad, Gertraud. ThD, U. Tübingen, Germany, 1962, Habilitation for N.T., 1967. Prof. N.T., U. Erlangen, Germany, 1968-72, U. Tübingen, 1972-2000. Lutheran. Home: Untere Schillerstrasse 4, D-72076 Tübingen Germany

STÜHMER, WALTER, medical institute scientist; b. Bogota, Colombia, Nov. 4, 1948; m. Synnöve Beckh; 1 child, Jaro. Diplomphysiker, Tech. U. Munich, 1975, PhD in Physics, 1980. Postdoctoral and vis. scientist U. Wash. Sch. Medicine, Seattle, 1980-83; group leader Max-Planck Inst. for Biophys. Chemistry, Göttingen, Germany, 1992—; dir. dept. molecular biology Max-Planck Inst. for Exptl. Medicine, Göttingen, 1992—. Humboldt grantee; Max-Kade fellow, N.Y., 1981. Avocations: flying, diving. Office: Max-Planck-Inst for exp Medizin, Hermann-Rein-Str 3, 37075 Gottingen Germany

STUKALOV, SERGE YEPHIMOVICH, ophthalmologist, researcher; b. Voronezh, Russia, Aug. 28, 1929; s. Yephim Egorovich and Varvara Paul-na (Svistunova) S.; m. Nathalie Sergeevna Moiseeva, Oct. 14, 1958; 1 child, Alexei. MD, Inst. Kuybyshev, Russia, 1952; Averbakh hon. diploma, USSR Acad. Med. Sci., 1978. Diplomate ophthalmology. Ophthalmologist Eye Clinic, Kuybyshev, 1954-56, aspirant, 1956-59, asst., 1959-66, docent, 1966-70; prof. Eye Clinic, Voronezh, 1970—. Author: Immunological Investigations in Ophthalmology, 1975, Pigmental Dystrophia of Retina, 1980, Primary Glaucoma, Immunity and Old Age, 1989, Uveapathies, 1990; contbr. 250 articles to profl. jours. Maj. Russian mil., 1952-53. Named Honor Scientist, Russia, 1992. Mem. Voronezh Assn. Ophthalmologists (chmn.). Home: Nikitinskaya St 35/29, 394018 Voronezh Russia Office: Eye Regional Hosp, Revolutii 1905 Year 22, 394036 Voronezh Russia

STUKENBROEKER, BERTHOLD KARL-HEINZ, management consultant; b. Berlin, Jan. 9, 1945; s. Herbert and Marianne (Felderhoff) S.; m. Helga Goerner, June 24, 1968. Diploma, U. Kiel, Federal Republic of Germany, 1970, PhD, 1973. Sci. U. Kiel, 1970-74; mgr., info. systems Goedecke AG (Warner Lambert), Freiburg, 1974-77; cons., lectr. Sci. Control Systems GmbH, Hamburg, 1977-78; exec. cons. Diebold Group, Frankfurt, 1978-82; mgr., new media pub. group Bertelsmann AG, Munich, 1982-85; v.p., corp. devel. Bertelsmann AG, Guetersloh, 1985-87, v.p., printing and svcs. div., 1987-93; exec. dir. eps Bertelsmann Electronic Printing Svc. GmbH, Guetersloh, 1991-93; ptnr. Consulting Trust GmbH, Düsseldorf, 1993—; mem. adv. bd. Infobase and Frankfurt Fair, 1985-93; expert Commn. of the European Communities, Brussels and Luxembourg, 1985—; v.p. bus. devel. Bundesdruckerei GmbH, Berlin, 1996-99; founder, exec. dir. D-Trust GmbH, Berlin, 1998-2000; mem. expert com. electronic pub. Open Soc. Inst. Soros Found., Budapest, 1997-2000. Editor-in-chief: (newsletter) Fuchsbriefe Neue Medien, 1983-85. Home: Weisses Venn 105, D-33442 Herzebrock Germany Office: Consulting Trust, Heltorfer Str 12, D-40472 Duesseldorf Germany

ŠTULÍK, KAREL, chemical researcher, educator; b. Kolín, Czechoslovakia, Feb. 13, 1941; s. Karel and Marta (Stolínová) S.; m. Madeleine Hyman, July 10, 1969; 1 child, Martin. MSc, Czech Tech. U., Prague, 1963; PhD, Heyrovsky Inst., Prague, 1967; DSc, Charles U., Prague, 1990. Lectr. Charles U., Prague, 1967, researcher, 1970-90, prof., dept. head, 1990-97, dean faculty natural scis., 1997—; asst. lectr. U. Strathclyde, Glasgow, 1968-69; vis. prof. U. Padova (Italy), 1988-89; chmn. Czech Grant Agy., Prague, 1992—. Co-author: Electrochemical Stripping, 1976, Ion-Selective Electrodes, 1982, Electroanalytical Measurements, 1987 (award Charles U. 1990), Czech-English Chemical Dictionary, 1988. Recipient Gordon Meml. award Talanta Pergamon Press, Oxford, Eng., 1972, award for instrument devel. Acad. of Sci., Prague, 1987. Mem. Czech Chem. Soc., Internat. Union Pure and Applied Chemistry, Fedn. European Chem. Socs. Avocations: traveling, visual arts, music, mountain hiking. Office: Charles U Dept Analyt Chem, Albertov 2030, 128 40 Prague 2, Czech Republic

STULL, FRANK WALTER, elementary school educator; b. Easton, Pa., June 4, 1935; s. George Washington and Minnie Elizabeth S.; m. Darlene Joy Hunsicker, Aug. 2, 1958; children: James, Ronald, Wendy. BS, East Stroudsburg State Coll., 1956; MEd, Lehigh U., 1966. Cert. tchr., N.J. Tchr. Korea Heung-Up Bank, Seoul, Korea, 1957-58, Howell Twp. Elem. Sch., Freehold, N.J., 1958-59, Holland Twp. Elem. Sch., Milford, N.J., 1959-91. Bd. dirs., sec., treas., mgr. Hunterdon County Sch. Employees Fed. Credit Union, Phillipsburg, N.J., 1969-87, mem. adv. com., 1995; merit badge counselor Boy Scouts Am., 1970-84, cubmaster, 1971-72; treas., mem. Hist. Preservation Commn. Holland Twp., 1993—; bd. govs. Riegel Ridge Cmty. Ctr., 1997—; trustee, scholarship coord. C&E Found., 1997—. Recipient Meritorious Svc. award N.J. Credit Union League, 1988, Tchr.

Recognition award State N.J. Gov., 1987, Disting. Achievement award for rsch. and preservation of history of Holland Twp. and surrounding areas; named Outstanding Elem. Tchr. Am., 1972; Experienced Tchr. in Geography fellow Pa. State U., 1967. Mem. NEA, Holland Twp. Edn. Assn., Hunterdon County Edn. Assn., N.J. Edn. Assn., Phi Delta Kappa (chartered mem. Zeta Gamma chpt.). Avocations: photography, travel. Home and Office: 806 Rugby Rd Phillipsburg NJ 08865-2033

STULTS, LAURENCE ALLEN, airline pilot; b. Evanston, Ill., Nov. 2, 1940; s. Allen Parker and Elizabeth Van Horne; m. Karen Frashure, Feb. 13, 1965 (div. 1986); m. Takako Yajima, Mar. 25, 1986; children: Sam Taku, Mark Edwin, Rex Allen. AB in Econs., Colgate U., 1962; MS in Adminstrn. of Sci. and Technology, George Washington U., 1978; postgrad., Cath. U., 1977; cert. in Japanese Lang., U. Guam, Maniglao, 1991. Real estate lic. U. Hawaii. Commd. 2d lt. U.S. Marine Corps, 1962, fighter pilot, 1962-83; flight instr., 1966-68; test pilot, mgr. fighter test br. Naval Air Test Ctr., 1971-75; advanced through grades to lt. col. commdg. officer USMC, 1980-82; capt. Continental Air Micronesia, 1984-91; chief pilot World Fish and Agriculture, 1991; capt. B-727 Continental Airlines, Denver and Guam, 1991-94; capt. B-757 Continental Airlines, Newark, 1994-95; capt. B-737 Continental Airlines, Cleve., 1996-97; capt. DC-10 Continental Airlines, Honolulu, 1997—; cons. real estate sales, Honolulu, 1983-86; gen. ptnr. Transpac Translations, 1987—; cons. aviation transportation matters, 1991—. Pres. Mariners Ridge Homeowners, Honolulu, 1980-86, Tumon View (Guam) Homeowners, 1987-91; active Boy Scouts Am. Decorated D.F.C. (3), Bronze star, Cross of Gallantry, Meritorious Svc. medal, Navy Achievement medal, Air medal (30), Eagle Scout. Mem. Soc. Exptl. Test Pilots, Ind. Assn. Continental Pilots, Continental Ops. Group, Marine Corps Assn., Order of Arrow, Hash-House Harriers, AARP, The Ret. Officers Assn., Gainey Ranch Golf Club, The Honolulu Club, The Spa, Sigma Nu. Republican. Congregationalist. Avocations: sailing, running, bicycling, tennis, golf. Home: #1202 Nuuanu Parkside 2047 Nuuanu Ave Honolulu HI 96817-2500 Office: Continental Airlines Honolulu Internat Airport PO Box 11 Honolulu HI 96810-0011

STUMBLES, JAMES RUBIDGE WASHINGTON, multinational service company executive; b. Harare, Zimbabwe, Aug. 13, 1939; came to U.S., 1980; s. Albert R.W. and Mary Dallas (Atherstone) S.; m. Vyvienne Clare Shaw, Dec. 19, 1964; children: Christopher, Timothy, Jonathan. BA, U. Cape Town, Republic of South Africa, 1960, LLB, 1962. Adv. Supreme Ct. of S. Africa. Mng. dir. Rennies Confirming & Fin. Pty. Ltd., Johannesburg, 1971-72; group mng. dir., chmn. subsidiaries Pritchard Svcs. Group South Africa, Pty., Ltd., Johannesburg, 1972-80; dir. security, pres. subs. Pritchard Svcs. Group Am., Columbus, Ohio, 1980-83; exec. v.p., pres. subs. Mayne Nickless/ Loomis Corp., Seattle, 1984-87; v.p. N.W. Protective Svc. Inc., Seattle, 1987-91, pres., CEO, 1991—; pres., CEO Western Security Svc. Inc., Spokane, 1991—, Northwest Protective Svc. Inc.-Oreg., Portland, 1992—; chmn. Clarington Inc., 1996—, Washington Law Enforcement Exec. Forum, 1999—. Sec. Boy Scouts, Johannesburg, 1978-80. Mem. Rand Club, Rainier Club, Rotary, Kiwanis, Round Table (officer 1969-80). Avocations: tennis, boating, fishing. Office: NW Protective Svc Inc 2700 Elliott Ave Seattle WA 98121-1189

STUMBLES, ROBERT ATHERSTONE, lawyer; b. Harare, Zimbabwe, Sept. 1, 1934; s. Albert Rubidge Washington and Mary Dallas (Atherstone) S.; m. Pamela-Anne Mason, Apr. 30, 1960; children: Dana Lynette Stumbles Barbour, Rodney John, Richard Kevin. BA in Law, Rhodes U., South Africa, 1954, Oxford U., 1958; MA, Oxford U., 1964. Admitted as legal practitioner Zimbabwe 1964, Malawi 1986, Botswana 1988; notary and conveyancer Zimbabwe, Malawi. Asst. and legal practitioner Stumbles and Rowe, Harare, 1960—, ptnr., 1965—, sr. ptnr., 1983—; sole proprietor Sacranie Gow & Co., Malawi, 1986—, Stumbles & Co., Botswana, 1988—; mem. Jud. Svc. Commn., Zimbabwe, 1985—; dir. various cos. in Malawi and Zimbabwe; chmn. Brit. Airways, Zimbabwe, 1980—, Goksel (Pvt.) Ltd., 1981—, I Conforzi (Tea and Tobacco) Ltd., 1995—, J.R. Gobey and Sons (pvt.) Ltd., 1999—; bd. dirs. Total (Malawi) Ltd., ude Holdings, Ltd., Gulliver Consol. Ltd., chmn., 1987—; bd. dirs. Stone Holdings (Pvt.) Ltd., chmn., 1995—; bd. dirs. James North (Pvt.) Ltd., chmn., 1989-99. Author: Central African Association of Round Tables Handbook, 1973, The Three Golden Keys (population degrowth, economic growth and environmental regrowth), 1998; editor African Rehab. Jour., 1984. Trustee numerous trusts including Zimbabwe Devel. and Trust, Zimbabwe Welfare & Charitable Orgns. Trust, Africa Environment, Population Svcs., Bernard Mziki, Women's Vol. Svcs., Childline; chmn. Round Table Race Rels. Endowment Trust; diocesan registrar Diocese of Harare, 1972-90, acting chancellor, 1987-90, chancellor, 1990—; dep. chancellor Province of Ctrl. Africa, 1989—; mem. Nat. Constnl. Com., Zimbabwe, 1978; commr. Zimbabwe Constitutional Commn., 1999, The Sandura Commn.; com. Investment Guidlines for Malawi, Unit Trusts in Malawi; past chmn. Avondale Sch. PTA, past mem. adv. coun.; past mem. parent-tchrs. liaison com. Arundel Sch.; mem. Prince Edward Sch. PTA; sec. Prince Edward Sch. Adv. Coun., 1982-83; mem. St. George's Coll. PTA; founder, chmn. Nat. Pledge Assn., 1976; past chmn. St. John's Amb. Assn. fundraising com.; mem. St. John's Ctr. and exec. com.; past mem. Outward Bound Nat. Coun.; adv. bd. Salvation Army, Mashonaland, 1973-85; chmn. Round Table of Salisbury (Harare) Round Table #1, 1967, chmn., 1969; others. Named Outstanding Young Man of the Yr., Jaycees, 1971; Paul Harris fellow Rotary, 1988; invested mem. Order of St. John of Jerusalem, 1999; Order of Epiphany for Distinguished Svc. to Anglican Ch. of Province of Ctrl. Africa. Mem. Oxford Soc., Fellows Club (life, founder pres.), Harare Club, Rotary, Blantyre Sports Club, Mulika Club, Assn. Round Tables of Ctrl. Africa (hon. life), Round Table Joint Venture Club (1st hon. life), World Coun. Young Men's Svc. Clubs (world pres. 1973-74). Avocations: tennis, fishing, music. E-mail: sturow!harare.iafrica.com. Fax: 263-4-738909. Office: Stumbles and Rowe, Union Ave PO Box 495, Harare Zimbabwe

STUMER, MARK BRADLEY, lawyer, restaurateur; b. N.Y.C., May 31, 1969; s. Nathan and Roberta Adele (Klau) S. LLB, SUNY, Albany, 1991; JD, N.Y. Law Sch., 1995. Bar: N.Y. 1995, U.S. Dist. Ct. (ea. and so. dists.) N.Y., 1995. Pres. Mark B. Stumer & Assoc., P.C., N.Y.C., 1995—; owner Tja! Restaurant, N.Y.C., 1999—; pres. Soho Consulting Group, Inc., N.Y.C., 1996—. Contbr. articles to profl. jours. including Nat. Restaurant Assn., Restaurant Law, and The Restaurateur; pub. "Restaurant Law", Entertainment Law & Fin., Bus. Lawyer. Mem. ABA, N.Y. State Bar Assn. (former chmn. copyright sect. student divsn. 1993-94), Nat. Assn. Trial Lawyers, Nat. Employment Lawyers Assn. (N.Y. chpt.), Young Entreprenuers Orgn., Nat. Restaurant Assn., N.Y. State Restaurant Assn., N.Y. County Lawyers Assn. Office: Mark B Stumer & Assocs PC 101 5th Ave New York NY 10003-1008

STUMP, M. PAMELA, sculptor; b. Detroit, July 8, 1928; d. Clarence Homer S. and Gladys Greening Bogue; m. David Everet Walsh, Aug. 1950 (div. 1975); children: Kimberly Klaerr, Sara Greening Walsh Munro, John Klaerr II; m. Richard Taylor White, March, 1989. B of Design, U. Mich., 1950, M of Design, 1951. Educator Ann Arbor (Mich.) Adult Edn., 1950-51, Saginaw (Mich.) Mus. Sch., 1963-68, Birmingham (Mich.) Bloomfield Art Assn., 1969, Washtenaw C.C., Ypsilanti, Mich., 1968-69, Cranbrook Ednl. Cmty., Bloomfield Hills, Mich., 1969-90. One-woman shows include Cranbrook Kingswood, Bloomfield Hills, 1969-90, Mich. Women's Hist. Ctr. & Hall of Fame, Lansing, 1994, Swann Gallery, Detroit, 1997; exhibited in group shows at Cranbrook Kingswood, 1950, 70, 87, City Art Mus., St. Louis, 1951, Terry Art Inst., Miami, Fla., 1951, Temple Israel, Detroit, 1951, 58, Ceceile Gallery, N.Y.C. (3rd prize), 1956, Pa. Acad. Fine Arts, Phila., 1958, Horace H. Rackham Sch. Grad. Studies, Detroit, 1960, Detroit Artists Market, 1961, R and R Robinson Gallery, Naples, Fla., 1962, Rubiner Gallery, West Bloomfield, Mich., 1963, Mich. Fine Arts Competition (Juror's award), 1983, 87, Slusser Gallery, U. Mich., 1989, Outdoor Sculpture II, III, Southfield, Mich., 1990, 91, N.Y. Acad. Scis., N.Y.C., 1991, Oakland U., 1991-92, Urban Park, Detroit, 1991, 92, Arc Gallery, Chgo., 1992, 1 Heritage Place, Southgate, Mich., 1993; prin. works include courtyard sculpture Kingswood Sch., steel sculpture Sister City, Tokushima, Japan, 10 bronze sculptures for Cranbrook Schs., Bloomfield Hills, Civic Ctr., Saginaw, bronze fountain at Presbyn. Ch., Grosse Ile, Mich, bronze sculpture of history of U. of Mich. Women, Ann Arbor, Mich. Bell Telephone Co., Saginaw, bronze sculpture at Providence Hosp., Southfield, meml. for poet T. Roethke Saginaw Valley State U., bronze sculpture at First Presbyn. Ch., Pompano Beach, Fla.; commissioned works for Rochester Hills Libr., Saginaw Mus., Western Mich. U., Kalamazoo, numerous others. Mem. Emily's List, Planned Parenthood. Mem. ACLU, NOW, LWV, Nat. Assn. Women Artists, Nat. Mus. Women in Arts (charter), Detroit Artist Market, Detroit Inst. Arts Founders Soc., Internat. Sculptors. Avocations: reading, writing. Home and Studio: 19629 Parke Ln Grosse Ile MI 48138-1024

STUMP, T(OMMY) DOUGLAS, lawyer, educator; b. Cushing, Okla., Jan. 7, 1957; s. Thomas Burl and Lindsey L. Stump; children: Kelli Jo and Matthew Douglas. BA in English, E. Ctrl. U., Ada, Okla., 1979; JD, Oklahoma City U., 1982. Bar: Okla. 1983, U.S. Dist. Ct. (we. dist.) Okla. 1983, U.S. Ct. Appeals (10th cir.) 1983, U.S. Dist. Ct. (ea. and no. dists.) Okla. 1986, U.S. Ct. Appeals (5th cir.) 1986, U.S. Supreme Ct. 1986. Founding atty. T. Douglas Stump & Assocs., Oklahoma City, 1990—; adj. prof. law Oklahoma City U.; lectr. various continuing legal edn. programs, immigration seminars, 1983-98. Author: Matrimonal Maladies and the Alien, 1983, General Information Concerning United States Immigration Laws, 1989, L-1 Intracompany Transfers, 1995, Employment Based Immigration Law, 1995. Bd. dirs. Lyric Theater, mem. exec. com., co-sponsor various prodns., 1992-95, Oklahoma City Econ. Roundtable, founder and provider Focus on Success Scholarship Fund, Drumright H.S., Oklahoma City, 1993—. Fellow Okla. Bar Found., mem. ABA (young lawyers divsn. del. 1988, 1989, exec. mem. young lawyers divsn. com. on immigration law), Am. Immigration Lawyers Assn. (Okla., Tex., N.M. chptrs., chmn. com. on nonimmigrant visas 1986-88, Oklahoma City sect. chmn. 1987-91, chmn. membership com. 1988-90, treas. 1991-92, vice chmn. 1992-93, chmn. legis. action com., Okla. City INS liaison 1995—, pres. Tex. chpt. 1998-99, bd. govs. 1998-99, AILA/INS Tex. Svc. Ctr. liaison, sr. editor publs. com., no. border task force), Okla. Bar Assn. (treas. 1988, sec. 1989, mem. com. on legal specialization 1987-91, mem. spl. com. on Unauthorized Practice of Law 1988-90, mem. house counsel sect. 1988—, mem. com. on legal ethics 1990-92, com. on civil procedure 1991-94, mem. solo and small firm task force 1993—, bd. dirs. young lawyers divsn. 1986-90, dir. com. on alien/refugee assistance 1986-89, chmn. com. on alien/refugee assistance 1986-90, Outstanding Dir. award 1987), Oklahoma County Bar Assn. (mem. fee grievance com. 1990-91), Okla. Soc. Human Resource Mgmt. (gen. counsel), Oklahoma City U. Law Sch. Alumni Assn. (bd. dirs. 1989-94, pres. 1992-94, Outstanding Law School Alumni award 1993). Republican. Office: 50 Penn Pl Ste 1320 Oklahoma City OK 73118

STUMPERS, FRANS LOUIS, retired electrical engineering educator; b. Stratum, the Netherlands, Aug. 30, 1911; s. Caspar and Antoinette (Etmans) S.; m. Maria A. H. Driessen, Aug. 26, 1954; children: Hans, Ingrid, Annette, Marc, Monique. MSc, U. Utrecht (the Netherlands), 1937; DSc, U. Delft (the Netherlands), 1946. Rsch. asst. Philips Rsch., Eindhoven, the Netherlands, 1928-34, rsch. scientist, 1938-53, group leader, 1954-60, chief scientist, 1960-68, sci. counsellor, 1968-72, cons., 1973-74; prof. Nymegen (the Netherlands) U., 1968-82, Utrecht U., 1976-81; guest prof. Ruhr U., Bochum, Fed. Republic Germany, 1974-75; rsch. assoc. MIT, Cambridge, Mass., 1952-53. Mem. Polish Soc. Engrs. (hon.), Dutch Soc. Radio Engrs.-Electronics (hon.), Royal Dutch Acad. Scis., Hungarian Acad. Scis., IEEE (bd. dirs. region 8 1975-76), Com. Internat. Spl. Perturbations Electriques (pres. 1967-73), URSI (hon. pres. 1990), N.Y. Acad. Scis. Home: Elzentlaan 11, 5611LG Eindhoven The Netherlands

STUMPF, HELMUT, mechanical engineering educator; b. Bad Kreuznach, Germany, Jan. 17, 1934; s. Friedrich and Wilhelmine (Stahlschmidt) S.; m. Renate Pohler, Jan. 27, 1961; 1 child, Christoph Alexander. Diploma in engring., Tech. U. Aachen, Fed. Republic Germany, 1959; diploma in econ. engring., Tech. U. Aachen, 1964, D Engring., 1965, cert. univ. prof., 1969. Univ. asst. Tech. U. Aachen, 1959-67, chief engr., 1967-70, lectr., 1970-71, prof. mech. engring., 1971-72; prof. mech. engring. U. Bochum, Germany, 1972-99, prof. emeritus, 1999—. Author 1 book, more than 100 sci. publs. Home: Brunsteinstrasse 25, 447890 Bochum Germany Office: Lehrstuhl Allgemeine Mech, Ruhr U Bochum, 447800 Bochum Germany

STUMPF, ISTVÁN, political scientist, academic administrator; b. Sárospatak, Hungary, Aug. 5, 1957; m. Andrea Horváth, 1983; children: Anna, András, Kata, Sara. Law degree, Eötvös U., Budapest, Hungary, 1982, sociology degree, 1985, PhD in Polit. Sci., 1995. Asst. prof. Eötvös U., 1982-87, founder, dir. Bibó Profl. Law Coll., 1982-88; sr. rschr. Inst. Polit. Sci., Hungarian Acad. Scis., Budapest, 1987—; assoc. prof. polit. sci. Eötvös U., 1997—; dir. Budapest Sch. Politics, 1991—; min. Prime Minister's OFfice, 1998—. Author: Reconceptualizing Politics, Socialization and Education, University of Oldenburg, 1993, Articulation of Political Interest in Hungary, 1996; editor: Youth and Politics, 1992, Between Two Elections, 1997. Mem. Internat. Polit. Sci. Assn. (bd. mem. 1997—), Hungarian Polit. Sci. Assn. (sec. 1995—), Hungarian Sociol. Assn., Hungarian UN Assn. (mem. bd. 1990—). Avocations: football, tennis. Office: Budapest Sch of Politics, Benczur Str 33, H-1068 Budapest Hungary

STUPP, ROGER, physician, clinical researcher; b. Basel, Switzerland, Sept. 17, 1959; s. Robert and Anita (Gablinger) S. MD, U. Zurich, 1987. Bd. cert. European Soc. Med. Oncology. Fellow U. Chgo., 1991-94; attending physician Cantonal Hosp., Aarau, Switzerland, 1994-96, Univ. Hosp., Lausanne, Switzerland, 1996—. Contbr. chpts. to books, articles to profl. jours. Mem. European Soc. Med. Oncology, Am. Soc. Clin. Oncology, Am. Soc. Hematology. Home: 9 Ave de Beaumont, 1012 Lausanne Switzerland Office: Univ Hosp CHUV, Ctr for Oncology, 1011 Lausanne Switzerland

STURDEE, DAVID WILLIAM, obstetrician-gynecologist; b. Walmer, Kent, England, May 13, 1945; s. Peter Doveton and Daphne S.; m. Elizabeth Morton Muir, Sept. 4, 1971; children: Simon, Claire. MB, BChir, St. Thomas' Hosp. Med. Sch., London, 1969; MD, U. Birmingham, Eng., 1979. Rsch. fellow U. Birmingham, 1975-77, clin. lectr., 1981—; sr. registrar Coventry and Birmingham Hosps., West Midlands, Eng., 1978-81; cons. obstetrician-gynecologist Solihull Hosp., West Midlands, 1981—, clin. dir., 1991-95; bd. mem. European Menopause and Andropause Soc., 2000—. Editor: Managing The Menopause, 1993, HRT and Thromboembolism, 1997; contbr. articles to profl. jours. Fellow Royal Coll. Ob-gyn (higher tng. com., subsplty bd. 1988-90, jour. editor 1994-99, publs. officer, chmn. publs. mgmt. com. 1999—); mem. Internat. Menopause Soc. (founding mem., internat. editl. bd. Menopause Digest, editor-in-chief Climacteric Jour. 1997—), Brit. Menopause Soc. (founding mem., coun. mem. 1989—, hon. treas. 1991-95, chmn. 1996-97), Brit. Med. Assn. (chmn. Solihull divsn. 1991-93), Brit. Soc. Colposcopy and Cervical Pathology, Copt Heath Golf Club. Anglican. Avocations: singing: church choir and close harmony group, golf. Office: Solihull Hosp, Dept Ob-Gyn, Solihull B91 2JL, England

STURDEVANT, CHARLES OLIVER, retired physician, neuropsychiatrist; b. Atkinson, Nebr., Aug. 8, 1907; s. John Newton and Clara Katherine (Zimmerman) S.; m. Helen Henricks; children: William, Charles, John; m. Nancy Elizabeth Quick, May 8, 1945; 1 child, Richard Anthony. BSc, U. Nebr., 1929, MD, 1932. Diplomate Am. Bd. Psychiatry and Neurology. Student asst. in neuropsychiatry U. Nebr., 1930-32; rotating intern Emanuel Hosp., Portland, Oreg., 1932-33; fellow in psychiatry Columbia U., N.Y.C., 1933-35; assoc. in neurology and psychiatry U. Oreg. Med. Sch., 1935-42; assoc. clin. prof. UCLA, 1951-74; mem. hon. staff St. John's Hosp., Santa Monica, Calif., 1976-98, Santa Monica Hosp., 1946-98; mem. hon. staff Hoag Hosp. Presbyn., Newport Beach, Calif., 1994-98, ret.; chief of psychiatry St. John's Hosp., Santa Monica, 1954-76; med. dir. Capistrano by the Sea Hosp., Dana Point, Calif., 1976-90; clin. prof. psychiatry U. Irvine, Calif., 1981—. Author: (with others) Psychiatric Emergencies, 1964; contbr. articles to profl. jours. Mem. counter propaganda com. State of Oreg., 1941-42; bd. dirs. Travelers Aid Soc., Portland, 1939-42, Multiple Sclerosis Soc., L.A., 1949-50; mem. Social Svc. Com., L.A., 1949-50. Maj. U.S. Army, 1942-46. Fellow AMA, Am. Psychiat. Assn. (life), North Pacific Soc. Neurology and Psychiatry (life); mem. Orange County Psychiat. Soc. (Excellence award, 1998), Calif. Med. Soc., Med. Rsch. and Edn. Soc. (founder), Newport Harbor Yacht Club, Skunk Point Yacht Club, Sigma Xi. Avocations: sailing, NHYC, gardening. Home: 13 Taywood Ct Laguna Niguel CA 92677-4131

STURDEVANT, WAYNE ALAN, computer software executive; b. Portland, Oreg., Apr. 3, 1946; s. Hervey Sturdevant and Georgia (Rawls) Bright; m. Helen F. Radbury, Sept. 24, 1976; children: Wayne Jr., Stephen, John, Brian, Daniel. BS in Edn., So. Ill. U., 1980. Enlisted USAF, 1964, supt. on-job-tng. adv. svc., 1978-82, chief on-job-tng. ops., 1982-85; ret., 1985; lead engr. McDonnell Douglas Corp., 1985-88; br. mgr. Southeastern Computer Cons., Inc., 1988-2000; pres. Apollo Software Inc., Austin, 2000—; developed advanced concepts in occupational edn., interactive multimedia instrn. design, innovations in support of ISO 9000. Contbr. articles on mgmt., ops., and tng. innovations in the work place to profl. jours. Bishop LDS Ch., 1983-84, 98—, stake presidency, 1990-96; exec. bd. Boy Scouts Am., 1986—. Recognized for leadership in multi-nat. programs; recipient Citation of Honor Air Force Assn., 1980, Silver Beaver award Boy Scouts Am., 1998; named Internat. Man of Yr., Internat. Biog. Ctr., 1992. Republican. Avocations: reading, camping. E-mail: wsturdevant@apolloUSA.com. Home: 9214 Independence Loop Austin TX 78748-6312

STURESON, JOHAN BENGT ANDERS, lubricating grease company executive; b. Linköping, Sweden, Mar. 8, 1958; s. Nils Sture Torsten and Gunnel Ebba (Bengtsson) S.; m. Birgitta Kristina Larsson, June 10, 1984; children: Carl, Per, Karin. MS, Swedish U. Agr., 1983. Cons. Hushållningssällskapet, Sweden, 1983-86; area mgr. ICI Agro, Sweden, 1986-89; mktg. mgr. ICI Agro Nordic, Copenhagen, 1989-91; project mgr. ICI Nordic, Gothenburg, 1991-93; sales mgr. ICI Chems. & Polymers, Gothenburg, 1994-98; mng. dir. ICI Norden AB, Gothenburg, $, 1994-99; mng. ptnr., CEO, Axel Christiernsson Internat. AB, Nol, Sweden, 2000—; chmn. LHS, Uppsala, Sweden, 1982. 2d lt. Lappland Rangers, 1977-78. Avocations: boating, gardening, family. Home: Gladiolvägen 9, S-434 46 Kungsbacka Sweden Office: Axel Christiernssen Inter, PO BOX 2100, S-449 11 Nol Sweden

STURGES, JOHN SIEBRAND, management consultant; b. Greenwich, Conn., Feb. 12, 1939; s. Harry Wilton and Elizabeth Helen (Niewenhous) S.; m. Anastasia Daphne Bakalis, May 6, 1967; children: Christina Aurora, Elizabeth Athena. AB, Harvard U., 1960; MBA, U. So. Calif., 1965; postgrad., NYU, 1972, U. Mich., 1982; PhD, Columbia U., 1997; ThD, Am. Coll., 1997, PhD, 2000. Cert. profl. mgmt. cons., sr. profl. in human resources; cert. mgmt. cons.; cert. profl. cons. to mgmt. With Equitable Life Assurance Soc. U.S., N.Y.C., 1965-79, mgr. sys. devel., 1965-70, dir. compensation and benefits, 1971-75, v.p. pers. and adminstrv. svcs., 1975-79; sr. v.p. pers. Nat. Westminster Bank U.S.A., N.Y.C., 1979-82; corp. sr. v.p. adminstrn. and human resources Willis-Corroon Corp., N.Y.C., 1982-84; mng. dir. human resources Marine Midland Bank, N.Y.C., 1984-87; mng. dir. Siebrand-Wilton Assocs., N.Y.C., 1986-87, pres., 1987—. Lay reader, Stephen minister St. Peters Episcopal Ch., Freehold, N.J., 1972—. Lt. USNR, 1960-65. Mem. Internat. Found. Employee Benefit Plans, Commerce Assocs., Soc. for Human Resource Mgmt. (dir. 1979—), Am. Compensation Assn., Human Resources Planning Soc., Inst. Mgmt. Cons. (bd. dirs. 1992—), Cons. Bur., Harvard Club (N.Y.C., Boston, Princeton; dir. 1991-97), Nassau Club, Monmouth Boat Club, Beta Gamma Sigma (dir. N.Y. 1978—), Phi Kappa Phi. Republican. Office: Siebrand-Wilton Assocs Inc PO Box 2498 New York NY 10008-2498

STURGES, SHERRY LYNN, recording industry executive; b. Long Beach, Calif., Dec. 11, 1946; d. Howard George and Alice Myrtle Fairbairn; m. Jeffery Alan Sturges, Dec. 30, 1969; children: Allisun Malinda, Jay. Grad. high sch., Las Vegas, Nev. V.p. Soultime, Inc., Las Vegas, 1968-69, Universe, Inc., Las Vegas, 1971-76; co-developer, owner Fun Trax Music Video and Audio Recording Studios, Westwood, Calif., 1986—; creative cons. John Debella Show, 1990, M.T.V., L.A., 1990, KCET-TV, L.A., 1990, KTLA-TV, L.A., 1991. Co-writer song The Sharing of Love for TV series Murder, She Wrote, 1996, feature film The Ride, 1997; song writer (film) The Ride, 1997. Officer PTA, Woodland Hills, Calif., 1977-86, pres., 1984-86; vol. Connie Stevens Charity Orgn., Beverly Hills, Calif., 1980-84; vol. Crossroads Sch. for Arts and Sci., Westwood Meth. presch., West L.A. Bapt. Sch., Northridge United Meth. Ch., St. Vincent's Parents Coun., St. Joseph the Worker Sch., Chatsworth H.S., Sepulveda Nursery Sch., Nat. Neurofibromatosis Found., Life Steps Found., Westwood Village Assn., San Joaquin Valley Actors Repertory Co., 1997—. Recipient Outstanding Contribution award L.A. Unified Sch. Dist., Oxnard Unified Sch. Dist., 1998, 99. Mem. Am. Soc. Composers, Authors and Pubs. Republican. Avocations: collecting dolls, plates and figurines.

STURM, GERHARD, chemistry educator, chemist; b. Karlsbad, Germany, Oct. 31, 1937; s. Rudolf and Antonia (Loessl) S.; m. Annemarie Popp, May 10, 1964; children: Silke, Gunnar, Kerstin, Ingrun. Diploma in chemistry, U. Bonn, Germany, 1960, Dr.rer.nat., 1964. Lab. dir. U. Women's Hosp., Marburg, Germany, 1970—. Inventor in field. Mem. German Soc. Clin. Chemistry, German Soc. Endocrinology, Internat. Steroid Study Group. Avocation: cultivation and research of orchids. Home: Baumgarten 11, D-35043 Marburg Germany Office: U Womens Hosp, Pilgrimstein 3, D-35033 Marburg Germany

STURMA, MICHAEL THOMAS, historian, educator; b. Phila., July 9, 1950; arrived in Australia, 1976; s. Rudolph Albert and Joan Marie (Koslowsky) S.; m. Ying Chu Yue, July 5, 1990. BA, Centre Coll., Danville, Ky., 1972; MA, U. N.C., 1975; PhD, Australian Nat. U., Canberra, 1980. Tutor Australian Nat. U., 1980; lectr. U. New Eng., Armidale, Australia, 1981-91; sr. lectr. Murdoch U., Perth, Australia, 1991—. Author: Vice in a Vicious Society, 1983, Australian Rock 'n' Roll, 1991; contbr. articles to profl. jours. Convenor Amnesty Internat., Armidale, 1990-91. Mem. Australian Hist. Assn., Pacific Hist. Assn., Inst. Commonwealth Studies, Fremantle History Soc., Australian Conservation Found. Office: Murdoch U, South St, Perth 6150, Australia

STURMAN, ANDREW PHILIP, geography educator; b. South Pickenham, Norfolk, Eng., Sept. 5, 1950; arrived in New Zealand, 1977; s. Leslie George and Margaret Ivy (Atkins) S.; m. Anne Ruth Pashley, July 21, 1973; children: Joanna, James, Adam. BSc with honors, U. Birmingham, Eng., 1973, PhD in Geography, 1976. Vis. prof. Meml. U., Nfld., Can., 1976-77; lectr. U. Canterbury, Christchurch, New Zealand, 1977-83, sr. lectr., 1983-96, assoc. prof. geography, 1997—, dir. Ctr. Atmospheric Rsch., 1999—; dir. Sturman Holdings Ltd., Christchurch, 1996—; vis. rsch. fellow Coop. Inst. Rsch. in Environ. Sci., Boulder, Colo., 1983-84, dept. geography Postgrad. Sch. Climatology and Applied Meteorology U. Birmingham, 1984; mem. Ministry Rsch., Sci. and Tech. rev. team, 1990; referee Found. for Rsch., Sci. and Tech., Australian Rsch. Coun., 1991-92, 92-93, 93-94, 94-95, 95-96. Rev. editor New Zealand Geographer, 1980-81; author: Weather and Climate of Australia and New Zealand, 1996; referee local and internat. jours.; contbr. articles in field to profl. jours. Recipient Marsden Fund award Royal Soc. New Zealand, 1996, Erskine fellowship, 1989. Fellow Royal Meterol. Soc.; mem. New Zealand Geog. Soc., Meteorol. Soc. New Zealand (v.p., Canterbury local br. organizer 1986-89). Avocations: music, photography. Office: U Canterbury, Dept Geography Pvt Bag 4800, Christchurch New Zealand

STURRUP, CHANDRA, Olympic athlete. Winner Gold medal 4x100 meter relays Sydney, 2000. Office: Bahamas Amateur Athletic Assn, PO Box 55, Nassau 5517, Bahamas*

STUSEK, ANTON, mechanical engineer, researcher; b. Trbovlje, Slovenia, Slovenian, Jan. 14, 1932; s. Friderik and Antonia Stusek; m. Cecilia Abram; children: Andrew, Natasha. Student, Engring. Coll., 1949; BSME, U. Ljubljana, Slovenia, 1959; postgrad., U. Mo., 1963; MS in Mech. Engring., U. Zagreb, Croatia, 1971. Designer Mil. Tech. Inst., Belgrad, Yugoslavia, 1949-52; researcher, project engr. Shipbuilding Inst., Zagreb, 1959-73; sr. lectr. dept. mech. engring. U. Ljubljana, 1973-96, ret., 1996. Author: Hydraulics and Pneumatics, 1969. Lt. col. Yugoslavian Navy, 1949-73. Decorated Medal with Silver Swords, Medal with Golden Swords, Silver medal Shipbuilding Inst. Zagreb. Mem. ASME, Slovenian Soc. Engrs. and Techs., Slovenian Fluid Power Soc. (hon. mem., ex-pres.), Soc. for Devel. and Promoting of Hydraulics and Pneumatics Aachen. Roman Catholic. Achievements include innovations of an axial piston pump, EH servovalve, EH steering systems for ships, hydraulic alternating current generator; research project on fluid power in Slovenia. Home: Ellerjeva 45, 1000 Ljubljana Slovenia

STÜSSI-LAUTERBURG, JÜRG FRED, librarian, historian; b. Zürich, Switzerland, Mar. 4, 1954; s. Alfred and Klara (Von Kanel) Stüssi; m. Barbara Lauterburg, Mar. 26, 1983; children: Bernhard, Adrian. Lic. phil.,

Zurich U., 1979, PhD, 1982. Asst. Zurich U., 1979-83; librarian Fed. Mil. Libr., Berne, 1984—. Author: Das Schweizer Militarwesen, 1982, Helvetias Töchter, 1989, Füderalismus Und Freiheit, 1994, Weltgeschichte im Hochgebirge, 1999. Mem. local govt., Windisch, 1986-97. Lt. col. Swiss Army, 1973—. Fellow Swiss Mil. History Assn., Friends of Swiss Fed. Archives. Mem. Union of Centrist Dems. Avocations: trekking, mountain studies. Home: Scheuerrain 1, Postfach, CH-5210 Windisch Aargau, Switzerland Office: Fed Mil Libr, Bundeshaus Ust, CH-5210 Windisch Aargau, Switzerland

STUTZ, ROLF HARRY, trading company executive; b. Zürich, Switzerland, Oct. 25, 1945; s. Theo and Jenny (Trachsler) S.; m. Liselotte Meier, Oct. 23, 1984; children: Danielle, Caroline. Diploma, Swiss Comml. Sch., Zürich, 1964, Swiss Mercantile Sch., London, 1966, Swiss Mgr. Sch., Zürich, 1985. Buying mgr. IBM, Zürich, 1969-72; sales mgr. Firmenich SA, Quito, Ecuador, 1972-76; mktg. mgr. Moos Textile Co., Weisslingen, Switzerland, 1976-82; owner ELEC Handels AG, Zürich, 1982—. Avocation: golf.

STUTZMAN, L. LEE, pastor; b. Clinton, Okla., June 13, 1953; s. Clamens L. Stutzman and Viola Darlene (Waters) Bonn; m. Connie R. Stutzman, June 3, 1972; children: Elizabeth, Jonathan, Rebecca. BA in Theology, Vision Christian U., MS in Theol. Studies, D in Ministry. With traveling ministry, 1972-78; founder Liberty Temple, Lima, Ohio, 1978-88, Liberty Christian Cathedral, 1988—; with nat. traveling ministry; apostle Liberty Network of Chs., Dayton, Ohio, 1986—. Author: From the Ground Up, 1987, Order Out of Chaos, 1995, Spiritual Gifts, 1992; prodr. (TV show) Life Without Limit, 1985—. Republican. Office: Christ Cathedral 295 E Salem St Clayton OH 45315-9719

STUTZMAN, THOMAS CHASE, SR., lawyer; b. Portland, Oreg., Aug. 1, 1950; s. Leon H. and Mary L. (Chase) S.; m. Wendy Jeanne Craig, June 6, 1976; children: Sarah Ann, Thomas Chase Jr. BA with high honors, U. Calif., Santa Barbara, 1972; JD cum laude, Santa Clara U., 1975. Bar: Calif. 1976; cert. family law specialist. Pvt. practice San Jose, Calif., 1976-79; pres., sec., CFO Thomas Chase Stutzman, PC, San Jose, Calif., 1979—; legal counsel Cypress Human Resources, Inc., DMJ Pro Care, Inc., Sparacino's Foods, Tax Firm, Inc., United Charities, Marina Assocs. Inc., Midnight Fraction Mine Inc., D.A.M. Good Engring./Mfg., Inc., E.M.I. Oil Filtration Systems, Inc., China Villa, Inc., Creative Pacifica, Inc., Am. West Furniture Mfg., Inc., Advanfab Corp., Am. First Tech., Analop Engring., Inc., Excel-Law Video, Inc., First Am. Real Estate Financing Co., Hoffman Industries, Inc., Info. Scan Tech., Inc., PRD Construction Mgmt. Svcs., Unifed Homes, Inc., Marine Biogenic Pharm. USA, Inc., Miller Networks, Mi Pueblo Mt. View, Inc., others; instr. San Jose State U., 1977-78. Bd. dirs. Santa Cruz Campfire, 1978-80, Happy Hollow Park, 1978-80, 83-86, Pacific Neighbors, pres., 1991-92. Mem. Calif. Bar Assn., Santa Clara County Bar Assn. (chmn. environ. law com. 1976-78, exec. com. family law, exec. com. fee arbitration com.), Assn. Cert. Law Specialist, San Jose Jaycees (Dir. of Yr. 1976-77), Rotary, Lions (dir. 1979-81, 2d v.p. 1982-83, 1st v.p. 1983-84, pres. 1984-85), Scottish Rite, Masons, Phi Beta Kappa. Congregationalist. Office: 1625 The Alameda Ste 626 San Jose CA 95126-2207

STUTZMAN, WARREN LEE, electrical engineer, educator; b. Elgin, Ill., Oct. 22, 1941; s. James Earl and Christina Louise (Steidinger) S.; m. Claudia Janeanne Morris, Dec. 20, 1964; children: Darren Morris, Dana Lynn. BEE, U.Ill., 1964, AB in Math., 1964; MEE, Ohio State U., 1965, PhD in Elec. Engring., 1969. Asst. prof. Va. Poly. Inst. and State U., Blacksburg, 1969-74, assoc. prof., 1974-79, prof., 1979—, Thomas Phillips prof. engring., 1992—. Author: (with G. Thiele) Antenna Theory and Design, 1981, 2d edit., 1998, Polarization in Electromagnetic Systems, 1993. Fellow IEEE. Office: Va Poly Inst & State U Elec Engring Dept Blacksburg VA 24061-0111

STUVINSKI, B. C. See FELKER, WILLIAM H.

STÜWE, HEIN PETER, physicist, educator; b. Königsberg, Ostpreussen, Germany, Sept. 14, 1930; s. Kurt and Gertraude (Werner) S.; m. Ursula Biermann, Jan. 10, 1957; children: Kurt, Gertraud, Klaus. Dr.rer.nat., U. Göttingen (Germany), 1955; dozent habil., RWTH Aachen, 1961; Dr.h.c., U. Miskolc (Hungary), 1985. Rsch. assoc. U. Ill., Urbana, 1956-58; rsch. asst. RWTH Aachen, 1958-62, asst. prof., 1962-66; prof. Tech. U. Braunschw (Germany), 1967-71, Montanuniv Leoben, Austria, 1971—; rsch. vis. Kinsei Ken, Tokyo, 1966-67; vis. prof. Indian Inst. of Tech., Madras, 1970; guest prof. Univ. Politecnica, Madrid, 1986; dir. Inst. for Solid State Physics Österreichische Akademie der Wissenschaften, Leoben, Austria, 1971—, dir. Inst. Metal Physics; rector, vice rector Montanuniversität, Leoben, 1978-84. Fellow ASM Internat.; mem. Austrian Acad. Scis. (corres.). Avocation: go-game. Home: Schillerstr 7a, Leoben Styria A-8700, Austria Office: Erich-Schmid-Inst, Jahnstr 12, Leoben Styria A-8700, Austria

STYLIANOPOULOS, LEONIDAS CONSTANTINOS, civil engineer, educator, consultant; b. Athens, Greece, June 5, 1929; s. Constantinos Leonidas and Chryssanthi (Katsalidou) S.; m. Sophia Leonidas Douros Stylianopoulos, Dec. 25, 1965; children: Constantinos, Areti, Demetrios, Chryssanthi, Georgios. Sci. diploma, Athens Coll., Greece, 1948; BSCE, Cornell U., 1952; MSCE, Purdue U., 1955. Project mgr. Ammann and Whitney, Athens, Greece, 1957-58; hwy. engr. Doxiadis Assoc.s, Athens, Greece, 1958-67; traffic engr. Buchart-Horn, Inc., York, Pa., 1967-68; deputy dir. Dot of Pa., Harrisburg, 1968-69; resident mgr. Airways Engring. Corp., Washington, 1969-74; chief civil engr., project mgr. Frank E. Basil, Inc., Washington, 1974-86; value engr., cons. SH&G, V.E. Divsn., Washington, 1986-88; resident project mgr. URS Internat. Inc., San Francisco, 1988-99; prof. Greek Air Cadet U., Dekelia, Greece, 1994-98; rsch. engr. dept. civil engring., lab. transp. work U. Patras, Greece, 1998—; bd. dirs. Geomechaniki of Greece, Athens, 1960-65; cons. UN Spl. Fund, N.Y.C., 1963-64; adv. bd. Min. of Coord., Athens, 1970-72; prof. urban engring. Athens Ctr. of Ekistics, 1960-65. Editor: Bibliography 18, 1958; guest editor Ekistics, 1989—; contbr. articles to profl. jours. Exec. bd. Christian U. Scientists, Athens, 1960-2000; adv. bd. Student Christian Union, Athens, Greece, 1969-86. 2nd lt. Greek Corps. of Engrs., 1957-58, Europe. Recipient Delta Price award Athens Coll., Psychicon, Greece, 1948, All-American Soccer award Am. Soccer Assn., Washington, 1951. Mem. ASCE, ASPE, Greek Soc. Civil Engrs., Transp. Rsch. Bd., Technical Chamber of Greece. Republican. Avocations: soccer, basketball, tennis, track, fishing. Office: 29 Kalisperi St, GR 152 34 Chalandri Greece

STYLIANOPOULOU, FOTINI, biology educator; b. Athens, Greece, Mar. 15, 1948; d. Leonidas and Niki (Stambouli) S.; m. Theodoros Papapolychroniou, June 8, 1980. AB in Biochemistry, Vassar Coll., 1970; MS in Chemistry, Rensselaer Poly. Inst., 1972; PhD in Neuro and Biobehavioral Scis., Stanford U., 1976. Lectr. histology Med. Sch., U. Athens, 1977-85, prof. biology faculty nursing Sch. Health Scis., 1985—; vis. prof. dept. human genetics and devel. Columbia U., N.Y.C., 1987; project officer in charge biomed. rsch. projects Sci. Rsch. and Tech. Agy., Greek Ministry Coordination, Athens, 1979-80. Contbg. author: Greek Educational Ency., Vol. 9, 1989; contbr. over 75 articles to sci. jours. Recipient Sotiris Papastamatis 3d prize for biomed. rsch. Hellenic Med. Assn., 1981, 82, 1st prize, 1984. Mem. AAAS, Greek Soc. for Neurosci. (exec. coun.), Greek Biochem. and Biophys. Soc. (exec. coun. 1981-83), Greek Soc. Endocrinology, Greek Soc. Biol. Scis., N.Y. Acad. Scis., Internat. Soc. for Devel. Neurosci., Phi Beta Kappa. Greek Orthodox. Avocations: philosophy of science, music, swimming. Home: Korytsas 41- Papagou, 15669 Athens Greece Office: U Athens, PO Box 14224, 11510 Athens Greece

STYNEN, DIRK EDMOND, biologist; b. Geel, Belgium, July 5, 1957; s. Robert and Lydia (Derboven) S.; m. Lieve Hens, Aug. 3, 1979; children: Katrien, Bram, Hanne. Lic. in Biology, Katholieke U., Leuven, Belgium, 1979; PhD, 1984. Postdoctoral fellow U. Pa., 1984-86; rsch. mgr. Sanofi Diagnostics Pasteur, Genk, Belgium, 1987-93; mgr. quality assurance and regulatory affairs Innogenetics, Zwijnaarde, Belgium, 1994-2000; pres. Qarad G.N.G.a., Mol, Belgium, 2000—. Contbr. articles to sci. publs. and profl. jours. Pres. Rugby Football Club, Laakdal, 1986-92, sec., 1982-84. Jean and Rose Hoguet Found. rsch. fellow, 1984, Instituut voor Aanmoediging van Wetenschappelijk in Nijverheid en Landbouw scholar, 1979-82. Mem. Am. Soc. Microbiology, Regulatory Affairs Professionals Soc. Avocations: rugby, travel, reading, tennis. Home: 13 Volmolenheide, B2400 Mol Belgium Office: Qarad, Volmolenheide 13, B2400 Mol Belgium

STYRON, ROSE, human rights activist, poet, journalist; b. Balt., Apr. 4, 1928; d. Benjamin Bernei and Selma (Kann) Burgunder; m. William Styron, May 4, 1953; children: Susanna, Polly, Thomas, Alexandra. BA, Wellesley Coll., 1950; MA, Johns Hopkins U., 1952; LHD (hon.), Briarcliff Coll., 1976, SUNY, Purchase, 1991, Trinity Coll., 2000. Bd. dirs. Amnesty Internat., USA, N.Y.C., 1973-83, chair nat. adv. coun., 1984-94. Author: (poems) From Summer to Summer, 1965, Thieves' Afternoon, 1973, By Vineyard Light, 1995; co-author, translator: Modern Russian Poetry, 1972; contbr. editorials, profiles, articles, book revs. and poetry to maj. newspapers and mags. Chair, judge Robert F. Kennedy Meml. Human Rights Award, 1983—; mem. adv. bd. Reebok Found. for Human Rights, 1987—; mem. exec. bd. Human Rights Watch, N.Y.C., 1975-94; bd. dirs. Acad. of Am. Poets, 1995—, Equality Now, 1993—; chmn. adv. coun. Roxbury (Conn.) Libr., 1990-92; bd. dirs. N.Y. Found. for Arts, N.Y.C., 1986-94, Lawyers Com. for Human Rights, N.Y.C., 1981—, Rainforest Found., 1989-95, Assn. to Benefit Children, 1993—, Folger Shakespeare Libr., 1994-00; bd. overseers NYU Faculty of Arts and Scis., 1994—. Mem. P.E.N. (chair freedom-to-write com. 1983-89, bd. dirs. 1983-93), Coun. Fgn. Rels., Vineyard Haven Yacht Club. Democrat. Home: 12 Rucum Rd Roxbury CT 06783-1906

STYRON, WILLIAM, writer; b. Newport News, Va., June 11, 1925; s. William Clark and Pauline Margaret (Abraham) S.; m. Rose Burgunder, May 4, 1953; children: Susanna Margaret, Paola Clark, Thomas, Claire Alexandra. Student, Christchurch Sch., Davidson Coll.; Litt.D., Davidson Coll., 1986; A.B., Duke U., 1947, Litt.D., 1968. Fellow Am. Acad. Arts and Letters at Am. Acad. in Rome, 1953; fellow Silliman Coll., Yale, 1964-99; jury pres. Cannes Film Festival, 1983. Author: novels Lie Down in Darkness, 1951, The Long March, 1953, Set This House on Fire, 1960, The Confessions of Nat Turner, 1967 (Pulitzer prize 1968, Howells medal Am. Acad. Arts and Letters 1970), Sophie's Choice, 1979 (Am. Book award 1980), In the Clap Shack (play), 1972, This Quiet Dust, 1982, Darkness Visible, 1990, A Tidewater Morning, 1993; also articles, essays, revs.; editor: Best Stories from the Paris Rev., 1959; adv. editor: Paris Rev., 1953—; mem. editorial bd. The Am. Scholar, 1970-76. Decorated Commandeur de l'Ordre des Arts et des Lettres, Commandeur Legion d'Honneur (France); recipient Duke U. Disting. Alumni award, 1984, Conn. Arts award, 1984, Prix Mondial del Duca, 1985, Elmer Holmes Bobst award for fiction, 1989, Edward MacDowell medal for excellence in the arts, 1988, Nat. Mag. award, 1990, Nat. medal of Arts, 1993, Medal of Honor, Nat. Arts Club, 1995, Common Wealth award, 1995, F. Scott Fitzgerald award, 1996. Mem. Am. Acad. Arts and Scis., Am. Acad. Arts and Letters, Soc. Am. Historians, Signet Soc., Harvard, Académie Goncourt, Phi Beta Kappa. Democrat. *

STYRYLSKA, TERESA BRONISLAWA, mechanical engineer; b. Turaszowka-Krosno, Poland, July 30, 1934; d. Aleksander and Helena S.; m. Jerzy Kazimierz, June 7, 1958. MSc, Cracow Univ. Tech., Cracow, Poland, 1958, PhD, 1965, DSc, 1974. Asst. Cracow Univ., Cracow, 1958-59, sr. asst., 1959-65, first asst., 1965-80, asst. prof., 1980-91, prof., 1991—. Contbr. articles to profl. jours. Recipient Edn. Ministry award Min. of Edn., 1975, 1982, Gold Cross of Merit award People's State Coun., 1980. Mem. Polish Soc. Theoretical and Applied Mechanics, Polish Acad. Sci. (applied mech. com.), Gesselschaft fur Angewandte Mathematik und Mechanik. Avocations: novels, theatre, cinema, skiing, hiking. Office: Cracow Univ Tech, Warszawska 24, 31-155 Cracow Poland

SU, CHING-HUA, materials scientist; b. Taipei, Taiwan, Oct. 10, 1954; s. Draw-Ming Su and Kuo-In Ho; m. Yuk Yin Ma Su, May 19, 1995; children: Jeanne, Wynne. BS in Materials Science, National Tsing-Hua U., Taiwan, 1976; PhD in Materials Science, Marquette U., Milw., 1985. Rsch. asst. Marquette U., 1979-84; sr. scientist U. Space Rsch. Assn., Huintsville, Ala., 1985-93, dir., 1993-94; rsch. scientist NASA/Marshall Space Flight Ctr., Huintsville, Ala., 1994—; cons. in field. Author: (books) Semiconductor & Semimetals, 1983, Current Research Topics in C. Growth, 1995. Avocations: travel, bridge, basketball. Office: SD47 NASA Marshall Space Flight Ctr Huntsville AL 35812

SU, CHING-TZONG, engineering educator, researcher, consultant; b. Koou Hwu, Yung-Lin, Taiwan, Sept. 10, 1949; s. Chen Su and Feen Lee; m. Chin-Mei Lee, Mar. 30, 1973; children: Cheng-Ming, Cheng-Lun, Cheng-Xin. BS, Cheng Kung U., Tainan, Taiwan, 1972, MS, 1977, PhD, 1986. Prof. engring.; patent atty. Sr. engr. Indsl. Devel. Bur., Taipei, 1980-81; sect. chief Bur. Commodity Inspection and Quarantine, Tainan, Taiwan, 1982-87; assoc. prof. Yung-Lin (Taiwan) Inst. Tech., 1987-89; prof. elec. engring. Chung Cheng U., Chia-Yi, 1989—; prin. cons. Bao-Dao Cons. Ltd., Taichung, Taiwan, 1984—; patent rev. Bur. Nat. Stds., Taipei, 1997-99; tech. cons. preparatory office Chung Cheng U., Chia-Yi, Taiwan, 1988-89. Contbr. articles to profl. jours. Recipient Rsch. award Ministry of Econ. Affairs, 1983, Nat. Sci. Coun., 1997, 98, 99, 2000, Medal and Citation Ministry of Edn., 1995. Mem. IEEE (sr.), Electro-Mech. Security Protection Assn. (vice chmn. bulk power network). Avocations: golf, bowling, table tennis. Home: 21 Lane 220, An-Ho St, 60021 Chia-Yi Taiwan, Taiwan Office: Chung Cheng U Dept Elec Engring, 160 San-Hsing, 621 Ming-Hsiung Chia-Yi, Taiwan

SU, CHIUNG-CHIEH JACK, mechanical engineer, researcher; b. Hsin-chu, Taiwan, Nov. 11, 1950; s. York and Hwa-In (Liu) S.; m. Su-Rong Hsieh, Nov. 12, 1977; 1 child, Yen-Chu. BSME, Nat. Cheng-Kung U., Tainan, Taiwan, 1972, MSME, 1975; PhD, Ariz. State U., 1984. Tchg. asst. Nat. Cheng-Kung U., 1972-75; rsch. asst. Ariz. State U., Tempe, 1979-83, rsch. assoc., 1983-84; assoc. engr. Chung-Shan Inst. Sci. and Tech., Lungtan, Taiwan, 1977-79, rsch. assoc., 1984-88, tech. supt., 1988—; invited spkr. on thermal design and analysis electronic equipment Nat. Ctrl. U., Chung-Li, Taiwan, 1989-92, Unicorn Internat. Pvt. Ltd., Singapore, 1995, Electronics Rsch. and Service Org., ITRI, Taiwan, 1998, mem. organizing com. 3rd Internat. Symposium on Transport Phenomena in Thermal Control, Taipei, 1988. Author (with others): Heat Transfer and Fluid Flow in Rotating Machinery, 1987, Transport Phenomena in Thermal Control, 1989, Design Guide of Electronic Equipment, 1994. 2nd lt. mil. batteries factory Chinese Mil., 1975-77, Taiwan. Fellow AIAA (assoc.); mem. ASME, Chinese Inst. Engrs. Avocations: music, hiking, swimming, travel, photography. Home: Apt 1, 41 Pai-Nien Rd 15th Fl, Lungtan 325, Taiwan Office: 2 Chung-Shan Rd, Chia-An Village, Lungtan 325, Taiwan

SU, DAIZHONG, mechanical engineering educator, researcher; b. Shenyang, Liaoning, China, July 26, 1948; arrived in Eng., 1987; s. Yiqun and Xiulan (Guan) S.; m. Jian An Zhang, Apr. 21, 1981; 1 child, Zhan. B in Engring., Harbin (China) Inst. Tech., 1976, MPhil, 1980; PhD, U. Strathclyde, Glasgow, Scotland, 1991. Engr. Harbin Boiler Works, 1969-78; lectr. Harbin Inst. Tech., 1981-86; rsch. fellow U. Surrey, Guildford, Eng., 1990-92; sr. lectr., reader in design The Nottingham Trent U., 1992—; vis. scholar U. Strathclyde, Glasgow, 1987-90; guest prof. U. Miskolc, Hungary, 1995—; vice chmn. Internat. Conf. Theory and Practice of Gearing, Izhevsk, Russia, 1996, 98; chmn. Internat. Conf. on Gearing Transmission and Mechanical Systems, Nottingham, 2000. Author: (with P.J. Garden and G. Druce) Contact Stress in a Disk Cam with Roller Follower, 1993, Analysis of Cam Roller Follower, 1991; mem. edit. bd. Jour. Gearing and Transmissions, 1996—; contbr. articles to profl. jours. including Jour. Mech. Engring., Internat. Jour. Computer Meths., Jour. Materials Processing Tech., Concurrent Engring., others. Recipient Oversea Rsch. Scholar award Com. of Vice Chancellors and Prins. of the U. of U.K., 1987, Henry Lester award, The Henry Lester Trust Ltd., 1988; Tchg. Co. Schem grantee Sec. State for Trade and Industry, 1995. Mem. Share Experience Engring. Design, Chinese Mech. Engring. Soc., Internat. Infomatization Acad. Home: 1 Heddington Gardens, Arnold, Nottingham NG5 8NW, England Office: The Nottingham Trent U, Dept Mech and Mfg Engring Burton St, Nottingham NG1 4BU, England

SU, DONGWEI, economist, educator; b. Xiamen, Fujian, People's Republic China, Dec. 12, 1970; s. Jinyu Su and Yuande Lin. BA, Xiamen U., 1992; MA, Ohio State U., 1993, PhD, 1997. Asst. prof. U. Akron, 1997—; expert Inst. of Fin. Rsch. and Edn., McGill U., Montreal, Can., 1997—. Contbr. articles to profl. jours. Dir. Chinese Fin. Assn. in Am., Columbia U., 1996. Rsch. fellow Sandra-Ann Morsillis Pacific-Basin Capital Markets Rsch. Ctr., 1997—. Avocations: biking, cooking, reading, movies, classical music. E-mail: su@uakron.edu. Home: 2751 Parkplace Dr Uniontown OH 44685-8758 Office: Univ of Akron Dept Econs Akron OH 44325-0001

SU, FONG-CHIN, bioengineer, educator; b. Tainan County, Taiwan, Sept. 1, 1958; s. Won-chun and Kuei-Hwa (Wu) Su; m. Rey-Chuan Chang, May 3, 1959; children: Vicky, Elmer. BS, Nat. Cheng Kung U., Tainan, 1980; MS, Nat. Taiwan U., Taipei, 1982, U. Rochester, 1987; PhD, U. Rochester, 1989. Assoc. prof. biomech. engring. Nat. Cheng Kun_ U., Tainan, 1989-97, prof. biomech. engring., 1997—; vis. scientist Mayo Clinic, Rochester, Minn., 1993-94; dir. Motion Analysis Lab., Nat. Cheng Kung U., 1989—; chmn. Inst. Biomech. Engring., 2000—. Author: Clinical Biomechanics, 1998; contbr. articles to profl. jours., including Jour. Hand Surgery; dep. editor in chief Chinese Jour. Med. Bio Engring., 1997—. Jr. lt., Chinese Combined Svc. Force, 1982-84. Li Found. scholar, N.Y., 1993, Nat. Sci. Coun. (Taiwan) fellow, 1994, 99; recipient rsch. award Nat. Sci. Coun., 1990-97, 99. Mem. Internat. Soc. Biomechs., Formosan Soc. Biomechs. (sec. gen. 1995-97, exec. bd. 1993—). Fax: 886 6 2760659. E-mail: fcsu@mail.ncku.edu.tw. Office: Nat Cheng Kung U, Inst Biomed Eng 1 Univ Rd, Tainan 701, Taiwan

SU, NINGHU, hydrologist, research scientist; b. Longde, Ningxia, China, Nov. 24, 1959; arrived in Australia, 1988; s. Dehai Su and Xiuying Zhao; m. Qi Ma; 1 child, Teng. BSc in Agriculture, Ningxia Coll. Agrl. Scis., China, 1982; MSc in Agriculture, Chinese Acad. Scis., Yangling, China, 1985; PhD, Australian Nat. U., Canberra, 1994. Probational rsch. fellow Chinese Acad. Scis., 1985-88, asst. rsch. prof., 1988-91; rsch. asst. Australian Nat. U., 1991-92; scientist Landcare Rsch. New Zealand Ltd., Lincoln, 1993-2000; sr. rsch. assoc. Sch. Math. Scis. Queensland U. Tech. Gardens Point Campus, Brisbane, Australia, 2000—. Rschr. in field. Recipient achievement award Ningxia Govt., China, 1987; PhD scholar Australian Nat. U., Canberra, 1989-93; grantee Australian Rsch. Coun., 1997. Mem. Internat. Assn. Hydrological Scis.

SU, SHENG-HUI (GEORGE S. SU), medicinal chemist, researcher; b. Shanghai, China, Mar. 9, 1941; came to U.S., 1992; s. Cheng-Ye and Zao-Fu (Hwang) S.; m. Qi-Qi Zhang, Mar. 8, 1967; 1 child, Jun-Jie. BS in Pharmacy, Shanghai Med. U., 1962, PhD in Med. Chemistry, 1966. Vis. rsch. fellow Inst. Microbial Chemistry, Tokyo, 1981-83; v.p., R&D dir. Shanghai Inst. Pharm. Industry, 1983-89, rsch. prof., 1989-92; rsch. scientist BioGenex Labs., San Ramon, Calif., 1992-95, sr. rsch. scientist, mgr. R & D, 1995—; guest prof. Shanghai Inst. Pharm. Industry, 1993—. Contbr. articles to sci. jours. Mem. Am. Chem. Soc., AAAS, Chinese Am. Chem. Soc. Achievements include patents in field; development of novel synthetic process for antibiotics, e.g. Amikacin, Tobramycin, cephalosporins and penicillins; invention and development of novel technology for DNA synthesis applied in oligonucleotide labeling and signal amplification. Home: 2 Craydon Ct San Ramon CA 94583-3906 Office: BioGenex Labs 4600 Norris Canyon Rd San Ramon CA 94583-1320

SU, SOPHIA SEH-YI, consultant; b. Taipei, Taiwan, Mar. 27, 1964; d. Yann-Huei and Ching-Yun (Wang) S. BS, UCLA, 1987; PhD, Columbia U., 1993. Cons. Arthur Andersen, Taipei, Taiwan, 1999—. Postdoctoral fellow Kyoto U., Japan, 1993-96, vis. rsch. fellow Nat. Taiwan U. Hosp., 1996-99. Office: TNS Corp Fin Co, 13F 156 Min Sheng E Rd, Taipei 105, Taiwan

SUAREZ, CARLOS, otolaryngologist, educator, hospital administrator; b. Langreo, Asturias, Spain, Mar. 17, 1944; s. Carlos Suarez and Carmen Nieto; m. Carmen Maria Alvarez-Escudero, July 4, 1970. MD, U. Valladolid, Spain, 1967; degree in otolaryngology, Autonomous U., Madrid, 1972; Phd, U. Oviedo, Spain, 1978. Resident Hosp. La Paz, Madrid, 1968-71, staff physician, 1971-75; chmn. Hosp. Ctrl. de Asturias, Oviedo, 1975—; prof. U. Oviedo, 1979—; med. dir. Hosp. Cen. de Asturias, Oviedo, 1983-84, dir. skull base surgery unit, 1993—; vis. prof. UCLA, 1984-85, U. Pitts., 1994; mem. Nat. Bd. Otolaryngology, Spain, 1987—; rschr. head and neck cancer. Contbr. articles to profl. jours. Recipient Corr. Acad. award Royal Acad. Medicine Cataluña, Barcelona, 1974, Corr. Acad. award Royal Acad. Medicine Galicia, La Coruña, Spain, 1975. Mem. Am. Soc. Head Neck Surgery, Am. Acad. Otolaryngology (honor award 1996), European Base Skull Soc., Spanish Soc. Otolaryngology (v.p. 1993—, César Beltrán award 1985, 90, Garsi award 1990, Tecnobio award 1995, Bristol-Myers Squib award 1996), European Soc. Otolaryngology. Avocations: classic music, literature, history, politics, sports. Home: Cardenal Cienfuegos 3, 9oB, 33007 Oviedo Spain Office: Hosp Ctrl de Asturias, Celestino Villaamil s/n, 33006 Oviedo Spain

SUAREZ, GERMAN, banker. Pres. Ctrl. Bank Peru. Office: Banco Central Reserva del Peru, Avenida Miro Quesada 441, Lima 1, Peru*

SUÁREZ, HORACIO GUILLERMO, biologist, researcher; b. Buenos Aires, Sept. 26, 1936; arrived in France, 1969; s. Manuel Suárez de Deza and Amelia Mercedes Mella Villar; m. Françoise Monsaingeon, July 7, 1967; children: Sebastian, Manuel. MD, Faculty Medicine, Buenos Aires, 1961; PhD in Biochemistry, Faculty Biochemistry, Buenos Aires, 1968; DSc, Faculty Sci., Paris, 1974. Rschr. Academia de Medicina, Buenos Aires, 1958-69, Inst. Cancer, Villejuif, France, 1969—; head lymphomas lab. Acad. Medicine, Buenos Aires, 1962-69; head cell transformation lab. Inst. Cancer, Villejuif, 1983-2000; cons. prof. Inst. Microbiology, Buenos Aires, 1981-89. Contbr. rsch. articles to profl. jours. Mem. Buenos Aires Cricket Rugby Club (mem. directory 1960-69). Roman Catholic. Avocations: athletics, polo, rugby, football, boxing. Home: 9 Ave Mirebeau, 92340 Bourg la Reine France Office: Inst Rsch Cancer, Inst Rsch Cancer, 7 Rue Guy Mocquet, 94801 Villejuif France

SUAREZ, LOUIS A., cardiothoracic surgeon; b. Havana, Cuba, Dec. 30, 1947; came to U.S., 1962; s. Louis A. and Irma C. (Abate-Daga) S.; m. Denise Marie Boland, June 2, 1973; children: Louis A. III, Megan, Michael. BS, Loyola U., Chgo., 1970; MD, U. Ill., Chgo., 1974. Diplomate Am. Bd. Surgery, Am. Bd. Thoracic Surgery, Am. Bd. Surg. Critical Care. Intern U. Wis. Hosp., Madison, 1974-75, resident in surgery, 1977-81, resident in cardiothoracic surgery, 1981-83; staff surgeon Appleton (Wis.) Med. Ctr., 1983—; chief cardiac surgery Appleton Heart Inst., 1993—; staff surgeon Theda Clark Med. Ctr., 1992—; chief of staff Theda Care Hosps.; chief surgery Unified Med. Staff, Appleton, 1994-96. Lt. comdr. USNR, 1975-77. Fellow ACS, Am. Coll. Cardiology, Am. Coll. Chest Physicians, Soc. for Thoracic Surgery, Wis. Surg. Soc. (coun. 1990-96), Wis. Surg. Travelling Club. Roman Catholic. Home: 2011 N Nicholas St Appleton WI 54914-2211 Office: Appleton Heart Surgeons 820 E Grant St Appleton WI 54911-3483

SUAREZ-ARRIAGA, MARIO-CESAR, geothermal reservoir engineer, educator; b. Mexico City, Mex., Oct. 22, 1950; s. Maria Loreto Arriaga; m. Elke Amanda Bosche Jung, Dec. 12, 1980; children: Nadia, Karina, Karsten. BS, Paul Sabatier U., 1977, MS, 1979; PhD, Nat. Aut. U. of Mex., 2000. Prof. H.S., Mexico City, 1970-73; technician Farbar Labs., Mexico City, 1973-74; scientist asst. Inst. of Applied and Theoretical Mechanics, Paris, 1980-81; modeling and engr. Brigade of the Mexican Volcanic Belt, Los Azufres, Michoacan, 1981-82; prof., rschr. Faculty of Scis., Morelia, Michoacan, 1982—; cons. engr. Petroleos Mexicanos, Mexico City, 1999—; reservoir engr. Comision Fed de Electricidad, Morelia, 1981—; scholar Lawrence Berkely Lab. Author: (with others) Stories From a Heated Earth, 1999; contbr. articles to profl. publs. Co-founder Geotermia-Rev. Mex. de Geoenergia, 1985. Mem. AAAS, Internat. Geothermal Assn., Soc. Matematica Mexicana, Am. Math. Soc., Mex. Geothermal Assn. (founder). Democrat. Buddhist. Avocations: mathematics, computing, swimming, movies. Fax: 43-227060. E-mail: msuarez@zeus.ccu.umich.mx. Home: Patzimba 438 Vista Bella, Morelia, 58090 Michoacan Mexico Office: Comision Fed Electricad, Alejandro Volta 655, 58290 Morelia Mexico

SUÁREZ BATISTA, LILIA ESTHER, chemist, researcher; b. Havana, Cuba, Apr. 26, 1963; d. Gabriel Aurelio Suárez O. and Delfina Batista Pérez; m. Pedro Ulises Ostoa Saloma, Dec. 23, 1991 (Sept. 1993). BS in Chemistry, U. Havana, 1988, M in Molecular Immunology, 1998; postgrad., U. Salamanca, Spain, 1998—. Rschr. Inst. Hematology and Immunology, Havana, 1988-, Ctr. Molecular Immunology, Havana, 1994-98. Contbr.

articles to profl. jours.; patentee in field. Recipient award Ministry Pub. Health, 1992, 96, Annual award of health, Cuba, 1999. Mem. Cuban Soc. Hematology, Canarian Assn. Cuba. Avocations: reading, classical and digital music, travel, going to theater, cinema. Home: F 26 between 1ra y 3ra, Havana 10400, Cuba Office: Inst Hematology & Immunol, E y Aldabó PO Box 8070, Havana 10800, Cuba

SUAREZ-CAVELIER, LUIS, lawyer; b. Hamburg, Germany, May 29, 1951; s. Cayetano Suarez-Pinzon and Beatriz Cavelier-Gaviria; m. Patricia Jimenez-Garbrecht; children: Isabel Suarez-Jimenez, Ignacio Suarez-Jimenez, Cristina Suarez-Jimenez, Luis Suarez-Jimenez. D Sci. Law, U. Javeriana, Bogota, Colombia, 1976; grad. in Criminology, U. Complutense, Madrid, 1978; grad., Internat. and Comparative Law Ctr., 1980. Gen. sec. Correa-Ayay Uribe Holquin, Bogota, 1973-74, Bogota Stock Exch., 1976; lawyer Cavelier, Perdomo, Cavelier, Bogota, 1978-82; sr. ptnr. Suarez Y Metke, Bogota, 1982-88; sec. Govt. of Bogota, 1988; sr. ptnr. Suarez Y Metke, 1989—. Mem. Colegio De Abogados Javerianos, Internat. Bar Assn., Jockey Club Bogota. Roman Catholic. Home: Calle 70 #00-80, Bogota 2, Colombia Office: Suarez Y Metke, Carrera 13 # 38-29, Bogota Colombia

SUAREZ RIVERA, ADOLFO ANTONIO, archbishop; b. San Cristobal de las Casas, Mexico, Jan. 9, 1927. Ordained priest Roman Cath. Ch., 1952; bishop of Tepic, 1971-80, Tlalnepantla, 1980-83; archbishop of Monterrey, Mex., 1980—; cardinal of Coll. of Cardinals, Monterrey, Mex., 1994—. Office: Porfirio Barba Jacob No 906, Col Anahuac, CP 66450 San Nicolas de Graza Nuevo Leon, Mexico also: Aptdo Postal 7 Loma Larga, 2429 con Sierra Madre, 6400 Monterrey Nuero Leon, Mexico

SUBASIC, DAMIR, environmental program and project manager, consultant, environmentalist; b. Bugojno, former Yugoslavia, Feb. 15, 1946; s. Stjepan and Mira (Cop) S.; m. Natasa Kirinic, Dec. 27, 1976; children: Marko, Hrvoje. BS in Physics, Faculty Natural Sci., Zagreb, Croatia, 1970; MS, U. Zagreb, 1974. Rschr. Inst. of Physics, Zagreb, 1971-77; safety and licensing coord. Croatian Electricity, Zagreb, 1977-86; head Ministry Energy and Industry, Zagreb, 1986-91; dir. APO-Hazardous Waste Mgmt. Agy., Zagreb, 1991-97; unit head IAEA, Vienna, Austria, 1997-98; dir. APO-Hazardous Waste Mgmt. Agy., Zagreb, 1998—; cons. NPP Krsko, Slovenia, 1980-82; extern expert for radwaste IAEA, 1993—, lectr., 1993—, project supr., 1996—, v.p. diplomatic conf., 1997; mem. steering com. Risk Abatement Ctr. Ctrl. and Ea. Europe, 1997—; part-time sr. lectr. Higher Sch. for Safety at Work, U. Zagreb, 1998—; pres. steering com. Croatian Toxicology Inst., Zagreb, 1997—; mem. steering com. KRKA Nat. Park, Zagreb, 1999—. Contbr. articles to profl. jours. and chpts. to books. V.p. Friend of Nature Movement Lijepa naša, 1997—. Recipient State Environ. award on waste mgmt. State Directorate for Environment, 1996, Cert. of Acknowledgement Croatian Radiation Protection Assn., 1992, Friend of Nature Movement Lijepa Nasa, 1996. Mem. Internat. Solid Waste Assn., Am. Nuc. Soc., Croatian Nuclear Soc., European Nuclear Assn., Nuclear Soc. Slovenia, Croation Assn. Risk Assessment, N.Y. Acad. Scis. Avocations: skiing, sailing, football. Home: Zeleni trg 7, 10 000 Zagreb Croatia Office: APO-Hazardous Waste Mgmt, Savska cesta 41/IV, 10 000 Zagreb Croatia

SUBBARAJ, RAMANUJAM, biology educator; b. Tirunelveli, Tamil Nadu, India, Apr. 1, 1951; s. Subbiah Ramanujam and Chinnappan Ramalakshmi; m. Natarajan Vijayalakshmi, Mar. 22, 1978; children: Renuka, Sriram, Venkatesh. BSc, St. John's Coll., Tirunelveli, India, 1971; MSc, Sch. of Biology, Madurai, 1974, PhD, 1979. Lectr. Madurai Kamaraj U., Madurai, 1980-87, reader, 1987-95, prof., 1995—. Mem. Indian Soc. for Chronobiology (pres. 1993—), Soc. for Biol. Rhythms, Soc. for Light Treatment and Biol. Rhythms, Nat. Geographical Soc. Avocations: photography, television, reading, volleyball. Home: North St 4 Palkalainagar, 625 021 Madurai/Tamil Nadu India Office: Madurai Kamaraj U, Palkalanagar, 625 021 Madurai/Tamil Nadu India

SUBBIAH, VEERANAN, engineering educator, researcher; b. May 12, 1942; s. Muthiah Veeranan and Muthammal Subbiah. BE, Govt. Coll. Tech., Coimbatore, India, 1965; ME, Bengal Engring. Coll., Howrah, India, 1968; PhD, PSG Coll. Tech., Coimbatore, India, 1981. Assoc. lectr. Govt. Coll. Tech., Coimbatore, 1965-66; tech. tchr. trainee Bengal Engring. Coll., Howrah, 1966-69; lectr. PSG Coll. Tech., Coimbatore, 1969-81, asst. prof., 1981-84, prof., 1984-95, head dept., 1995—, placement officer, 1990-92, dean student affairs, 1995-98. Grantee All India Coun. Tech. Edn., 1996, Univ. Grants Commn., 1996. Fellow Instn. Engrs. (Best Paper award 1988); mem. IEEE, Indian Soc. for Tech. Edn. Avocations: reading magazine, watching TV, Internet activities. E-mail: subbiah@flashmail.com. Office: PSG Coll Tech, Peelamedu, Coimbatore, Tamil Nadu 641 004, India

SUBBOTSKY, EUGENE VASILEVITCH, psychologist; b. Suhe-Bator, Mongolian Republic, Jan. 15, 1948; arrived in the U.K., 1991; s. Vasili and Maria (Turutina) S.; children: Alexei, Natasha. MSc in Psychology, Moscow (USSR) U., 1972, candidate psychology, 1975, D in Psychology, 1985. Cert. lectr. in psychology. Rsch. asst. Moscow (USSR) U., 1975-78, sr. lectr., 1975-82, docent psychology, 1982-90; vis. rsch. fellow U. Konstanz, Germany, 1990-91; lectr. psychology U. Lancaster, Eng., 1991-94, reader in devel. psychology, 1994—. Author: Psychology of Partnership in Preschoolers, 1976, Child Discovers the World, 1991, Foundation of the Mind, 1992, The Birth of Personality, 1993, The Child as a Cartesian Thinker, 1996. Recipient Alexander von Humboldt award Alexander von Humboldt Found., Germany, 1989-91. Mem. Internat. Soc. for the Study Behavioral Devel., Brit. Psychol. Soc. Avocations: skiing, swimming, fishing, cycling. Home: 11 Haydock Rd, Lancaster LA1 4ND, England Office: Psychology Dept, Lancaster Univ, Lancaster LA1 4YF, England

SUBERT, EDOARDO CARLO, banking executive; b. Milan, Italy, Nov. 2, 1960; s. Alberto and Evelina (Vismara) S.; m. Mariangela Acquadro, Apr. 10, 1989; 1 child, Alberto. B in Econs. and Bus., Bocconi, Italy, 1985. Jr. cons. CAST, Milan, 1986-87; dir. Citibank, Milan, 1987-90; responsible Italian desk N.M. Rothschild and Sons, Ltd., London, 1990-93; mng. dir. Rothschild Italia, Milan, 1993—. Office: Rothschild Italia Spa, Cso Magenta 12, 20123 Milan Italy

SUBHIRUN, PREECHA, military officer; b. Mounglopburi, Lopburi, Thailand, Jan. 6, 1957; s. Preecha and Prunnee Subhirun; m. Chidchanok Somproa, May 1, 1993; 6 children. BSEE, 1969. Commd. officer Thailand Arty., 1981, advanced through grades to col., 1997—; detachment comdr. 1st Spl. Force Regiment Thailand Arty., Lopburi, 1981-87; antiaircraft arty. battery comdr. 4th Antiaircraft Arty. Bn. Thailand Arty., 1987-88, 89-96; dep. dir. civil air Army Def. Command Unit Thailand Arty., Bangkok, 1997—. Home: 51/61 Tahan Rd, Dusit Bangkok 10300, Thailand Office: Army Air Def Command, Dechatugka Rd, Donmueng Bangkok 10210, Thailand

SUBRAHMANYA, SUSHEELA, journalist, editor, publisher; b. Hassan, Karnataka, India, Sept. 6, 1934; d. Shri. K.V. Venkataramanaiah and Smt. Venkataramanaiah Parvathamma; m. Kandikere Narasimhiah Subrahmanya, May 20, 1960 (dec. Feb. 1985). BA in Econs. with honors, Maharaja's Coll., Mysore, Karnataka, India, 1956, MA in Econs., 1959. Editor, publisher Southern Economist, Bangalore, India, 1962—, journalist, 1962—. Mem. Indian Fedn. Small and Medium Newspapers (pres. 1990-96, south zone pres. Karnataka Unit 1996—).

SUBRAHMANYAM, AVANIDHAR, management educator; b. Chennai, Tamilnadu, India, Sept. 16, 1962; came to U.S., 1984; s. Manohar and Vasanti Subrahmanyam; m. KaveriKrishnamurthy, July 16, 1987; children: Divya, Jayant. BTech., Indian Inst. Tech., Kanpur, 1984; MBA, Tulane U., 1986; PhD, UCLA, 1990. Asst. prof. Columbia U. Grad. Sch. Bus., N.Y.C., 1990-92, assoc. prof., 1992-93; assoc. prof. Anderson Sch. Mgmt., UCLA, 1993-96, prof., 1997—. Editor Jour. FIn. Markets, 1996; contbr. articles to profl. jours. Recipient Best Paper award Western Fin. Assn., 1997, 2d Pl. Best paper award Jour. Fin. Econs., 1998, Best Paper award Jour. Fin., 1999. Democrat. Hindu. E-mail: subra@anderson.ucla.edu. Home: 682 Via Santa Ynez Pacific Palisades CA 90272-2840 Office: U Calif Anderson Sch Mgmt 110 Westwood Plz Los Angeles CA 90095-0001

SUBRAMANI, MUNIRATHINAM, neuroscience researcher; b. Vadakkupattu, India, Mar. 9, 1966; s. Subramani Muniswamy and Sharada Ellan; m. Suma Bhaskar, Nov. 29, 1998; 1 child, Varsha. BSc in Zoology, Islamiah Coll., Vaniyambadi, 1987; MSc in Biochemistry, U. Madras, India, 1989; MPhil in Neurophysiology, Nat. Inst. Mental Health & Neuroscis. Deemed U., Bangalore, India, 1992; PhD in Neurophysiology, Nat. Inst. Mental Health & Neuroscis. Deemed U., 1998. Sr. rsch. fellow Nat. Inst. Mental Health & Neuroscis., Bangalore, 1997-98; postdoctoral fellow U. Conn., Storrs, 1999—; cons. scientist RARE Clinic, Bangalore, 1993—; postdoctoral mem. Scholars Club PROMEGA. Contbr. articles to profl. jours. Fellow Royal Soc. of Netherlands, Amsterdam, 1997; studentship Asia Specfic Soc. Regeneration, Hong Kong U., 1998; travel grantee Kalyani Exporters, Bombay, 1997. Mem. AAAS, ASCB, Am. Soc. Neurochemistry, Assn. Chemoreception Scis., Internat. Brain Rsch. Orgn., N.Y. Acad. Sci. Home: 1 S Eagleville Rd Storrs Mansfield CT 06268-2502 Office: Dept Pharmacol & Neurosci R #215 Storrs Mansfield CT 06269

SUBRAMANIAM, B., metallurgical engineer; b. Kallidaikurichi, Tamil Nadu, India, Nov. 16, 1951; s. R. Balachandran and Sakuntala Balachandran S.; m. Lakshmi, June 1, 1977; children: Karthik, Archana. BE in Metallurgy Engring., Regional Engring. Coll., Trichy, India, 1973. Engr. Cominco Ltd., Trail, B.C., Can., 1974-75; process engr. Carborundum Universal Ltd., Palghat, India, 1976-84; plant mgr. Carborundum Universal Ltd., Palghat, 1984-89; dep. gen. mgr. Carborundum Universal Ltd., Cochin, 1990-94, gen. mgr., 1994-2000, v.p., 2000—. Patentee in field. Nat. bridge master conferred gy Am. Contract Bridge League. Mem. Kerala High Tension Extra High Tension Electricity Assn. (pres. 1997-98), Confedn. Indian Industry, Kerala Mgmt Assn., Rotary (past pres., Rotary Internat. presdl. citation 1989-90), The Indian Inst. of Metals (assoc.). Avocations: cricket, bridge, cricket commentator. E-mail: subbub@tvk.cvmi.co.in. Home: The Kasl Yamuna Nagar, 682033 Cochin India Office: Carborundum Universal Ltd, PO Box 2272 Thiruvottiyur, 600 019 Chennai India

SUBRAMANIAN, GANAPATHY, chemist, consultant, editor; b. Madras, India, July 15, 1935; arrived in Eng., 1962; s. Manuvadhyar Pallikundum and Tarakad Ramaswamy (Krishnambal) S.; m. Anny Mauricette Thomasson, July 15, 1968; 1 child, Olivier Ananda. BSc, U. Madras, 1956; MSc in Organic Chemistry, Sardar Vallabhbhai Vidyapeeth, Gujerat, India, 1960; PhD, U. Glasgow, 1966. Postdoctoral rschr. U. Glasgow and U. Kent, 1966-68; rsch. chemist Proprietary Perfumes, Ltd., Ashford, Kent, 1968-70; asst. flavor rsch. mgr. Bush Boake Allen, London, 1970-74; analytical mgr. Life Sci. Rsch., Essex, 1974-76; rsch. mgr. Barnett and Foster, Northants, 1976-79; rschr., adminstr. Chelsea Coll. U. London, 1979-82; assoc. prof. Higher Inst. Tech., Libya, 1982-86; chem. engring. rschr. Loughborough (Eng.) U., 1988-91; chem. and biotech. cons., Kent, 1991—. Editor: Preparative and Process Scale Liquid Chromatography, 1991, A Practical Approach to Chiral Separations by Liquid Chromatography, 1994, Process Scale Liquid Chromatography, 1995, Quality Assurance in Environmental Monitoring, 1995, Bioseparation and Bioprocessing, vols. I and II, 1998; contbr. numerous articles to profl. jours. including Phytochemistry, Brit. Jour. Pharmacology, Jour. Internal Medicine Rsch., among others. Mem. Indian Red Cross Soc. Mem. Royal Inst. Chemistry.

SUBRAMANIAN, RAMACHANDRAN, applied mathematician, researcher, educator; b. Tiruchirapalli, India, Sept. 15, 1937; s. Subramanian and Akilandam (Rangaswamy) Ramachandran; m. Kalpakam Krishnamurthy, Sept. 6, 1962; children: Ramakrishnan, Latha. BA with honors, MA, Madras U., Chennai, India, 1959, MSc, 1960; PhD in Math., Indian Inst. Tech. Madras, Chennai, India, 1965. Jr. tech. asst. Indian Inst. Tech. Madras, 1960-61, sr. tech. asst., 1961-65, lectr., 1965-71, asst. prof., 1971-80, prof., 1980-98, prof. emeritus, 1998—; bd. acad. courses, bd. acad. rsch., libr. adv. com., head dept., mem. fin. com., bd. govs., Indian Inst. Tech. Madras; vis. prof. U. Port Harcourt, Nigeria, 1983-84; vis. scientist U. Kerala, India, 1980, U. Bielefeld, Germany, 1988, Hindustan Coll. Engring., Padur, 1999, Valliammai Coll. Engring., Kattanghlathur, 2000; spkr. in field. Mem. editl. bd. Jour. Indian Soc. Probability and Stats.; reviewer Math. Reviews, Zentralblatt für Mathematik; referee (jours.) IEEE Transactions on Reliability, Reliability Engring. and Sys. Safety, Opsearch, Pramana, Microelectronics and Reliability, Jour. Math. and Phys. Scis.; contbr. over 90 articles to profl. jours. Alexander von Humboldt Found. fellow, Germany, 1971-72, 76, 88. Mem. Indian Math. Soc. (life), Operational Rsch. Soc. India (life), Assn. Maths. Tchrs. India (life), Indian Soc. Probability and Stats. (life), Am. Math. Soc. Hindu. Avocations: reciting/teaching vedas, reading books, walking, music. Office: Indian Inst Tech Madras, Dept Maths, Chennai 600 036, India

SUBRAMANIAN, RAMASWAMY, physicist, educator, researcher; b. Coimbatore, Tamil Nadu, India, Oct. 31, 1964; arrived in Sweden, 1992; s. Naduvilmadam Ramaswamy and Saradha (Harihara) S.; m. Preethi Vaidyanathan, Oct. 25, 1994; 1 child, Aditya. BSc in Physics, Bharathi Dasan U., India, 1985, MSc in Physics, 1987; PhD, Indian Inst. Sci., 1992. Postdoctoral fellow in molecular biology Swedish U. Agrl. Scis., Uppsala, 1992-94, asst. prof., 1994-97, assoc. prof., 1997—. Author: Of Carbonyl Metabolism Enzymology and Molecular Biology, 1999; contbr. articles to profl. jours. Achievements include patent in Synthesis of New Antibiotics. Office: Swedish U Agrl Scis, Dept Molec Biology, Box 590, 75124 Uppsala Sweden

SUBRAMANIAN, RAVI, electrical engineer; b. Geneva, Switzerland, Oct. 22, 1965; came to U.S., 1983; s. Muthu and Dakshayini (Srikantiah) S. BSEE with honors, Calif. Inst. Tech., 1987; PhDEE and Computer Sci., U. Calif., Berkeley, 1991. From assoc. engr. to co. scientist Teknekron Comm. Sys., Inc., Berkeley, Calif., 1988-91; mem. tech. staff AT&T Bell Labs., Holmdel, N.J., 1991-95; tech. mgr. Synopsys, Inc., Mountain View, Calif., 1995-96, dir., 1997—; invited spkr. in field. Assoc. editor IEEE Transactions on Circuits & Sys., 1995-97; contbr. articles to profl. jours.; patentee in digital comms. U. Calif. fellow, 1988-89. Mem. AAAS, IEEE (chmn. 1996 workshop on VLSI Comms.), N.Y. Acad. Scis. Avocations: soccer, mountain biking, traveling. Office: Synopsys 700 E Middlefield Rd Mountain View CA 94043-4033

SUBRAMANIAN, SERMADEVI RAMALINGAM, university researcher, educator; b. Villupuram, Tamil Nadu, India, Oct. 6, 1938; s. S. Ramalingam and G.R.S. Kannammal; m. A.S. Gomathi, Dec. 11, 1962; 1 child, S. Ramalingam. BSc in Agr., Agrl. Coll., Coimbatore, 1960, MSc in Agr., 1964; PhD, Tamil Nadu Agrl. U., Coimbatore, 1975. Extension officer Dept. Agr., Madras, India, 1960-64; rsch. asst. Agrl. Coll., Coimbatore, 1964-69, asst. prof., 19670-75, assoc. prof., 1975-82, prof. dept. agrl. econs., 1982-93, dir. rural devel. studies, 1994-97, dir. planning and monitoring, 1997-98; program coord., 1998—. Editor: Readings in Integrated Rural Development, 1987, Participatory Rural Appraisal for Agricultural Research, 1992; co-author: Basic Economics, 1989. Recipient T. Konda Reddy Shield, Madras Agrl. Students Union, 1966; Ford Found. Postdoctoral fellow, 1981. Mem. Soc. of Social Scientists, Indian Soc. Agrl. Econs. Home: 14 Periyar Nagar First St, Vadavalli Coimbatore 641 041, India Office: Tamil Nadu Agrl Univ, Dept Agrl Econs, Coimbatore 641 003, India

SUBRAMANIAN, VAIDYANATHAN, environmental science educator; b. Tiruchy, India, May 11, 1942; s. K.S.V. and S. (Ponnammal) Iyer; m. Mera Iyengar, Jan. 26, 1976; children: Kalpana, Sridhar. BSc with honors, Jadavpur U., Calcutta, India, 1964, MSc, 1966; PhD, Northwestern U., Evanston, Ill., 1973. Postdoctoral fellow Northwestern U., Evanston, 1972-73; asst. prof. McGill U., Montreal, Que., Can., 1973-75; asst. prof., assoc. prof., prof. Jawaharlal Nehru U., New Delhi, 1975—, dean Sch. Environ. Scis., 1992-94, coord. ENVIS Ctr., 1994—, coord. UGC Spl. Assistance Programme, 1994—. Contbr. articles to profl. jours.; patentee in field. Fulbright scholar, 198-73; recipient numerous rsch. grants from Indian and internat. agys. Avocations: music, jogging, debate, religion, philosophy. Home and Office: Jawaharlal Nehru U, 47 Dakshinapuram JNU Campus, New Delhi 110067, Inda

SUBRAMANIYAN, S., biotechnologist; b. Trivandrum, India, Mar. 1, 1969; s. G. Sivaramakrishnan and S. Meenakshi; m. G.S. Sandhia, Sept. 8, 1998; 1 child. BSc, U. Kerala, 1989, MSc, 1992; PhD, Cochin U. Sci. & Technology, 2000. Jr. rsch. fellow Regional Rsch. Lab., Trivandrum, 1994-96, sr. rsch. fellow, 1996-99, project fellow, 1999—. Min. Human Resources fellow, India, 1993, 94, UGC/CSIR, 1993. Mem. Am. Soc. Microbiology, N.Y. Acad. Sci., Assn. Microbiologists India. Hindu. Avocations: reading, creating Web pages, websurfing. E-mail: subr44@yahoo.com, subr44@rediffmail.com. Home: TC 15-124 (1) Althara, Nagar Vellayambalam, Trivandrum 695010, India

SUBRAMANYA, SRIKANTIA, educator; b. Karnataka, India, Oct. 1, 1956; s. Srikantiah and Saroja Ramachandran; m. Revathi Rao, Dec. 8, 1993; children: Suneet, Suhas. BE, Bangalore (India) U., 1979; ME, Indian Inst. of Sci., 1981; MS, Ind. U., 1991; PhD, George Washington U., 1999. Asst. exec. engr. Indian Telephone Industries, Bangalore, 1981-84; software engr. ASEA AB, Vasteras, Sweden, 1984-87, Nokia OY, Helsinki, Finland, 1987-88; computer systems engr. Kuwait U., 1992-93; asst. prof. U. Mo., Rolla, 1998—. Grad. scholarship Indian Inst. of Sci., 1979-81, Nat. Merit scholarship Govt. of India, 1972-79; recipient Grant-in-Aid of Rsch. award Sigma Xi, 1997, Richar Merwin Meml. award George Washington U., 1996. E-mail: subra@umr.edu. Fax: 573-341-4501. Home: 1319 Truman Ave Rolla MO 65401-2517 Office: U Mo 1870 Miner Cir Rolla MO 65409-0001

SUCCI, SAURO FAUSTO, research executive; b. Forli, Romagna, Italy, Jan. 15, 1954; s. Luciano and Maria Luisa (Gavelli) S.; m. Claudia Gentile, Sept. 25, 1982; 1 child, Caterine. D Nuclear Engring., U. Bologna, Italy, 1979, specialist, 1981; PhD in Physics, Poly. Sch., Lausanne, Switzerland, 1987. Cert. engr. Scholar Ente Nat. Energie Alternative, Bologna, 1980-81, European Atomic Agy., München, Germany, 1981-82; postdoctoral Ecole Poly. Fed. Lausanne, 1982-86; rschr. IBM, Rome, 1986-90, sr. rschr., 1990-93, sci. coord., 1993-95; rsch. dir. Inst. Applied Computing, Nat. Rsch. Coun., Rome, 1995—; chmn. European Mech. Coun., Cagliari, Italy, 1992; chmn. fluid conf. IBM, Oberlech, Austria, 1992; mem. adv. group Centro Ricerche Sviluppo Studi Superiori Sardegna, Cagliari, 1992; asst. dept. physics Poly. Fed. de Lausanne, 1984-85; vis. prof. U. Paris, 1994, U. Chgo., 1995, MIT, 1996, 97. Author: Automi Cellulari, 1991, Parallel Fluid Dynamics, 1996; mem. editl. bd. Internat. Jour. Modern Physics, 1996, Jour. Scientific Computing, 1997, Applied Rheology, 1999; contbr. articles to profl. jours. Pres. Cath. Mission, Lausanne, 1986. Specialist Italian Air Force, 1979-80. Recipient Gold medal for disting. non-resident citizens Forli, 1997; scholar Harvard U., 2000. Fellow Am. Phys. Soc.; mem. AAAS, Am. Phys. Soc., European Phys. Soc., Am. Soc. Indsl. and Applied Math., Italian Soc. Indsl. and Applied Math, N.Y. Acad. Scis. Avocations: theatre, music, basketball. Home: Via Pianeta Terra Z7OB, 00144 Rome Italy Office: Inst Computing Applications Nat Rsch Coun, Viale Policlinico 137, 00161 Rome Italy

SUCESKA, MUHAMED, chemist, researcher; b. Han-Pijesak, Bosnia and Herzegovina, Dec. 10, 1954; s. Enes and Emina (Hafizovic) S.; m. Ljiljana Halavanja, May 26, 1979; children: Ines, Dino. BSc, Mil. Tech. Acad., Zagreb, Croatia, 1977, PhD, 1991; MSc, U. Zagreb, 1986. Lectr. Mil. Tech. Acad., Zagreb, 1982-91; technologist Pires, Zagreb, 1991-93; leading rschr. Brodarski Inst., Zagreb, 1993—; cons. SUIS-Spl. Equipment and Sys., Kumrovec, Croatia, 1998—. Author: Test Methods For Explosives, 1995, Propellants, 1996, Pyrotechnics Devices, 1998; editor-in-chief Secondary Publ. Brodarski Inst., 1994, 95, 96, 98, 2000. Maj. Former Yugoslav Army, 1977-91. Recipient Croatian Annual award for sci. Ministry Sci. and Tech., Zagreb, 1998. Mem. Internat. Pyrotechnics Soc., Croatian Soc. for Explosives. Avocations: sports, music. E-mail: suceska@brod.hrbi.hr. Fax: 385 1 650 43 60. Home: Ljerke Sram 4, 10000 Zagreb Croatia Office: Brodarski Inst, Av V Holjevca 20, 10000 Zagreb Croatia

SUCH, JOSE, physician, researcher; b. Alicante, Spain, Feb. 23, 1958; s. Jose Such and vincenta Ronda; m. Maria Del Carmen Sanchez, Aug. 27, 1983; children: Carmina, Paula, Pepe, Luis. MD, U. Cadiz, Spain, 1990. Mil. physician Spanish Navy, 1982-93; gastroenterologist SVS, Spain, 1993-96; hepatologist Univ. Hosp., Alicante, 1996—; rsch. scholar LLUMC, Loma Linda, Calif., 1997-98. Co-author: Spontaneous Bacterial Peritonitis, 1999; contbr. articles to profl. jours. Mem. AEEH, EASL. Avocations: reading, fishing, hunting. Home: Urb. La Pinada 1., c/Las Brisas 7, 03016 Alicante Spain Office: Hosp Gen Univ, Liver Unit, c/Pintor Baeza s/n, 03010 Alicante Spain

SU CHEE CHEN (CHAN DUKI), obstetrician, gynecologist; b. Fianarantsoa, Madagascar, Jan. 23, 1949; arrived in Taiwan, 1962; s. Kwok Pon Chan and Lucile Chu; m. Yin Kao, July 19, 1975; children: John Chen Shao Chieh, Joe Chen Shao Chiu. BM, Taipei Med. Coll., Taiwan, 1975. Med. diplomate ob-gyn. Intern Tri-service Gen. Hosp., Taipei, Taiwan, 1974-75; resident Vet. Gen. Hosp., Taipei, 1977-81; attending Vets. Gen. Hosp., Taipei, 1982-91; fellow Hosp. Bichat, Paris, 1981, Hosp. Antoine Beclere, Paris, 1981; dir. assisted reproductive unit Cathay Gen. Hosp., Taipei, 1991—; clin. assoc. prof. Nat. Yang Ming U., Taipei, 1989—. Mem. Fertility Soc. Taiwan (pres. 1997—), Assn. ObGyn (Taiwan), Am. Soc. for Reproductive Medicine. Achievements include being member of in vitro fertilization team that produced first test tube baby in Taiwan or in all Chinese people. Avocations: soccer, golf, swimming. Home: 5F No 2 Lane 246, Yenchi St, 106 Taipei Taiwan Office: Cathay Gen Hosp, 280 Jen-Ai Rd Sec 4, 106 Taipei Taiwan

SUCHODOLSKI, HENRYK SZIGNIEW, primary school educator; b. Głubczyce, Opole, Poland, Jan. 21, 1959; s. Piotr and Bronisława (Łanowa) S.; m. Krystyna Jaśków, Feb. 4, 1989; children: Justyna, Joanna. MA, U. Rostov-on-don, Russia, 1983. Tchr. Pilszcz, Poland, 1983-87, Branice, Poland, 1987—. Mem. Polish Tchrs. Assn. Avocations: geography, history, foreign languages, travel.

SUCHOJAD, HENRYK, modern history educator, librarian; b. Szumsko, Poland, May 1, 1947; s. Antoni and Jozefa (Zal) S.; m. Czeslawa Maria Wypior, Apr. 28, 1973; children: Kamil, Damian. MA in History, Wroclaw (Poland) U., 1972, PhD, 1989. Tchr. history H.S. No. III, Kielce, Poland, 1972-84; acad. tchr. Pedagogical U., Kielce, 1984—, dir. main libr., 1995—. Author: History in School, 1985; editor: Kosciuszko's Insurrection, 1995, Library and Information in Educational System, 1999, Research and Didactic Functions of Academic Libraries, 1996. Mem. Polish Soc. History (dept. mgr. 1996—). Home: Toporowskiego 81/59, 25-547 Kielce Poland Office: Biblioteka Glowna WSP, Lesna 16, 25-509 Kielce Poland

SUCHOZEBRSKI, MAREK JAN, economist; b. Warsaw, Poland, Aug. 20, 1940; s. Czeslaw and Maria (Walicka) S.; ; m. Ewa Bialkowska, May 29, 1969 (div. 1972); m. Elzbieta Krasucka, June 26, 1994. Diploma, SGPiS, Warsaw, 1968, DS, 1976. Asst. to prof. SGPiS, Warsaw, 1968-76, prof.'s asst., 1976—. Contbg. author: Political Economy of Socialism, 1972, 76, 78 (Minister of Edn. award 1971); contbr. articles to profl. jours. Avocations: tourism, fine arts, classical music. Home: Etiudy Rewolucyjnej, Belska 14 m 3, 02 638 Warsaw Poland Office: Coll Sch of Econ and Arts, Mazowiecka 1 B, 96-100 Skierniewice Poland

SUCIU, EMIL, military officer; b. Targu-Mures, Romania, Nov. 26, 1950; s. Emil and Eva (Toarniczky) S.; m. Angela Dragnea, Sept. 10, 1971; 1 child, Emil. BA, U. Bucharest, 1973, MA, 1982; postgrad., Min. Def., Bucharest, 1994. Philological diplomate. Commd. lt. Romanian Armed Forces, 1973, advanced through grades to col., 1999; jr. officer Romanian Navy, Constanta, 1973-81; sr. officer Gen. Staff, Bucharest, 1981-94, Min. Def., Bucharest, 1994-95; dep. def. attaché Embassy of Romania, Budapest, 1995-99; def. attaché Embassy of Romania, Ankara, 2000—; external co-worker, rschr. Inst. Linguistics, Bucharest, 1981—. Author: Drama iugoslava, 1992; contbr. chpts. to books and articles to profl. jours. Decorated Mil. Merit 1st class medal Gen. Staff, Bucharest, 1998. Avocations: music, fishing. Home: bl N 14 sc 1 ap 7, St Estacadei 12, 77598 Bucharest Romania Office: Embassy of Romania, Ankara Turkey

SUCKALE, ROBERT, art historian; b. Königsberg, Prussia, Germany, Oct. 30, 1943. D of Philosophy, U. Munich, Germany, 1970, Dr. phil. habil., 1976. Asst. prof. U. Munich, Germany, 1971-80; prof. U. Bamberg, Germany, 1980-90, Tech. U., Berlin, Germany, 1990—; dir. d'études associé Ecole des Hautes Etudes en Sciences Sociales, Paris; vis. prof. Harvard U., Cambridge, Mass., 1992; Richard- Krantheimer prof., Rome, 1997-98. Co-author: Gotische Architektur in Frankreich 1140-1270, 1985; author: Die Hofkunst Kaiser Ludwigs des Bayern, 1993, Kunst in Deutschland. Vor

Karl dem Grossen bis Heute, 1998. Office: Tech U Berlin Sekr A56, Strasse des 17 Juni 152, 10623 Berlin Germany

SUCUPIRA, MARIA SILVA, endocrinologist, nuclear physician; b. Maranguape, Brazil, Nov. 22, 1941; d. Julio Lima and Cione (Silva) S. PhD in Medicine, U. São Paulo, 1973. Resident in internal medicine Ribeirãi Preto U. Sao Paulo (Brazil) Faculty Medicine, Brazil, 1966-69, trainee Hormone Lab., 1968; asst. prof. endocrinology U. Sao Paulo, Brazil, 1972-73; asst. prof. internal medicine U. Brasilia, 1969-72; fellow in nuclear medicine U. Sao Paulo, 1973; physician in nuclear medicine and endocrinology Inst. Nat. Assistencia Medica, Previdência Social Hosp., Brasilia, 1973-93; founder nuclear medicine clinic Inst. Nacional Assistencia Medica Providencia Social Hosp., Brasilia, 1974, chief nuclear medicine clinic, 1977-79, 82-85, chief imagenology svc., 1990-93; nuclear physician U. Hosp., U. Brasilia, 1995—; pres. med. ethic commn. Brazilian Congress, 1986-87, 1990-95, mem. med. ethic com., 1985-87, 1995-98, physician in internal medicine and endocrinology, 1984-98; med. cons. Nat. Sci. and Tech. Devel. Commn., Brasilia, 1984-97; computer rschr. in nuclear medicine Pan Am. Health Orgn., 1981; fellow in nuclear medicine Johns Hopkins Med. Instns., Balt., 1979-82; dir. sec. of med. and social assistance Brazilian Congress (Fed. Senate), 1995-97, chief health and work sect., 1997—, spl. sec. of edit. and pub., 1997-98; mem. Ethic Regional Coun. Medicine, Brasilia, 1978-83. Mem. Brazilian Soc. Endocrinology and Metabolism, Brazilian Coll. Radiology, Brazilian Soc. Biology and Nuclear Medicine, Brazilian Soc. Diabetes, Med. Assn. Brasilia, Med. Assn. Brazil, Soc. Latino Am. de Tiroides, Soc. Nuclear Medicine, Johns Hopkins Radiol. Alumni Assn., Assn. Diplomats Superior Sch. War, N.Y. Acad. Scis. Roman Catholic. Avocations: painting, photography, music, graphology, chiromancy. Fax: 55-61-4434544. E-mail: mssucupira@ambr.com.br. Home: SQS 207 Bloco D Apt 508, 70253040 Brasilia DF, Brazil Office: U Hosp Nuclear Medicine Svc, Av L 2 Norte Quadra 605, Cep-70840-050 Brasilia DF, Brazil

SUDA, HIROSHI, rail transportation executive; b. Kyoto, Japan, Jan. 28, 1931. LLB, Kyoto U., 1954. With Japanese Nat. Railways, 1954-87; dir. adminstrn. Nagoya Railway Operting Divsn., 1966-68; investment contr. Ctrl. Japan Region, Nagoya, Japan, 1968-69; dep. dir. passenger dept., 1969, dep. dir. facilities passenger dept., 1969-71, dep. dir. comml. ops., 1971-74, dep. dir. adminstrn. passenger dept., 1974-79; supt. Nagoya Railway Operating Divn., 1979-81; dir. passenger dept., 1981-83; pres., rep. dir. Ctrl. Japan Railway Co., 1987-95, chmn., rep. dir., 1995—, chmn. bd. dirs. Office: Ctrl Japan Railway Co, 2-14-19 Meieki-Minami, Nakamura-ku Nagoya 450, Japan*

SUDA, MINORU, liberal studies educator; b. Mukoh, Japan, Nov. 5, 1931; s. Kyuitiroh and Aya (Okugawa) S.; m. Kayo Kuwayama, Jan. 6, 1961; children: Makoto, Asaki. BA, Kyoto U., 1955. Tchr. Kyoto Prefectural Sr. H.S., 1956-64; lectr. Ritsumeikan U., 1964-66, asst. prof., 1966-72, from prof. to prof. emeritus, 1972-97; part-time lectr. Kyoto City U. of Arts and Music, 1988-96. Co-author: The Liberation and Literature of African Americans, 1979, The Resonating Rise of Civic Cultural Movements, 1994, The Thought and Literature of African Americans, 1994. Chmn. Kyoto Cultural Orgns. Coordinating Coun. Mem. Am. Lit. Soc. of Japan, Cultural Econs. Soc. of Japan, Black Studies Assn. of Japan. Avocations: seeing movies, plays and going to concerts. Home: 82-7 Miyatani, Hirono, Uji-si Kyoto 611, Japan Office: Ritsumeikan U, 56-1 Tohji-in Kitamati, Kitaku Kyoto 603, Japan

SUDAKOV, MICHAEL YURIEVICH, physicist, researcher; b. Ryazan, Russia, Nov. 2, 1960; s. Yurij Ivanovich and Valentina Danilovna (Yprunina) S.; m. Tatyana Vladimirovna Glazunova, Jan. 16, 1980; children: Tamara, Michael. Student, Radio Engring. Inst., Ryazan, 1980; M of PHysics, Moscow Physics Engring. Inst., 1984; PhD in Physics, USSR Acad. Sci./Physics Inst., Moscow, 1989. Asst. Radio Engring. Inst., Ryazan, 1989-93; docent Inst. of Mgmt., Ryazan, 1994-99; mem. faculty Pedagogical U., Ryazan, 1999—. Contbr. articles to profl. jours. Avocation: carpentry. Home: Bratislava 21/1 5, 390035 Ryazan Russia Office: Physics Dept/Pedagogical U, Svoboda St 46, 390000 Ryazan Russia

SUDAKOV, SERGEY KONSTANTINOVICH, neurobiologist, researcher; b. Moscow, Sept. 17, 1955; s. Konstantin Victorovich and Polina Atonasevna (Mamaeva) S.; m. Ekaterina Leonidovna Ryndina, Nov. 21, 1978; 1 child, Darya. Md, 1st Moscow Med. Inst., 1978; Candidate Med. Scis., Inst. Normal Physiology, Moscow, 1981; D in Med. Scis., Inst. Nervous Activity Neuro., Moscow, 1989. Med. diplomate. Jr. scientist Med. Inst., Moscow, 1978-81; jr. scientist Inst. Normal Physiology, Moscow, 1981-84, sr. scientist, 1984-89; head lab. State Rsch. Ctr. Addictions, Moscow, 1989—; prof. pharmacology. Author: Neurodynamic of Mental Processes and Correction of Psychical Functions, 1986; contbr. articles to profl. jours. Mem. Nat. Narcotic Control Bd., Moscow, 1989—. Grantee Russian Fedn. Basic Rsch., Moscow, 1994, 97, European Commn., 1994. Mem. Internat. Acad. Scis., Med. Comm. Internat. Olympic Comm., 1998—. Home: Kutuzovsky prospect 30/32940, 121165 Moscow Russia Office: Rsch Inst on Addictions, Malij Mogiltzevskij per 3, 121002 Moscow Russia

SUDANOWICZ, ELAINE MARIE, government executive; b. Dorchester, Mass., Aug. 3, 1956; d. John Anthony and Helen Mary (Budzinski) S. Student, Fontbonne Acad., Milton, Mass., 1974; BA, Boston State Coll., 1978; MPA, Suffolk U., Boston, 1986; grad. Exec. Leadership Devel. Program, Dept. of Def., 1993. Cert. level 2 contractor, level 3 in program mgmt., Mass. Pub. rels. office mgr. MacDonald & Evans Inc. Litho., Dorchester, 1974-78; rsch. asst. Nat. Commn. Neighborhoods, Washington, 1978; polit. cons. various nat., state and local polit. campaigns, 1974-86; telephonist supr., cons. ARC, Boston, 1980-81; adminstrv. asst. Suffolk County Courthouse Commn., Boston, 1981-82; exec. asst. sheriff Suffolk County Sheriff's Office, 1982-86; presdl. mgmt. intern ESD/PK Air Force Systems Command, Hanscom AFB, Mass., 1986-89; advanced copper CAP Air Force Systems Command, Andrews AFB, Md., 1989-90; contract negotiatior Hdqrs., Electronic Systems divsn. Joint STARS Program, Hanscom AFB, Mass., 1990-92; program mgr. Hdqrs., Electronic Sys. Ctr., EN-1, Hanscom AFB, 1992-95; asst. program dir. bus. acquisition re-engring. Elec. Sys. Ctr., Hanscom AFB, 1994-95; dep. commr. for transp. City of Boston, 1995—; Mayor's interagency liaison Boston Emergency Mgmt. Agy., 1995—. Author: Constitutional Vignette, Separation of Powers and Contracting in the Bureaucrat, 1987; contbr. PMInformer, 1989—; also articles; agt., cons Theatre Arts-Play 1988—. Vol., cons. City & State Pub. Agys.-Pub. Sector, Boston; literacy vol., 1988-89; task force Transp. Rsch. Bd. on Critical Transp. Infrastructure Security, 1999—. Recipient Spl. Achievement award U.S. Dept. Transp., 1989, Outstanding Alumnus award Suffolk U., 1990. Mem. Am. Soc. Pub. Adminstrn. (coun. mem. 1996—, mem. exec. bd. emergency and crisis mgmt. sect. 1999—), Nat. Contract Mgmt. Assn. (bd. dirs. 1996—, photographer No. Va. chpt. 1989-90, cert. profl. contracts mgr., nat. chair program mgmt. spl. topics com.), Presdl. Mgmt. Alumni Group (nat. bd. dirs. 1989-90, N.E. field bd. dirs. 1990—, Outstanding Alumnus award 1990), Trustees of Reservations Mass., Dept. Def. Sr. Profl. Women's Assn., Boston Network for Women in Govt. and Politics, Pi Alpha Alpha (pres. Suffolk U. chpt.). Democrat. Roman Catholic. Avocations: art, cross country and downhill skiing, hiking, outdoors, gardening. Home: 108 Alban St Dorchester MA 02124-3711 Office: Boston Emergency Mgmt Agy Boston Fire Alarm 59 The Fenway Boston MA 02115-3700

SUDAR, SUBBIAH, mathematician educator, researcher; b. Madurai, India, May 31, 1962; s. Palamadai Ramasany and Subbiah (Gomathi) S.; m. Vaidyanathan Nagarajan Sreemathi Sudar, Sept. 7, 1994; 1 child, Subashini. BA in Math., U. Madras, India, 1982; MS in Applied math., MIT, Madras, India, 1984; PhD in Math., IIT, Madras, India, 1989. Fellow AG Technomathematik U. Kaiserslautom, Germany, 1989-91; rsch. assoc. Indian Inst. Sci., Bangalore, India, 1991-94; lectr. Indian Inst. Sci., Kharagpur, India, 1994-95, asst. prof., 1995—. Contbr. over 20 articles to profl. jours. Fellow German Acad. Exchange Svc., 1989, 94, 99. Mem. Indian Soc. for Indsl. and Applied Math., Indian Soc. for Theoretical and Applied Mechanics (life). Avocation: singing. Home: BF-2/4 IIT Campus, Kharagpur 721302, India Office : Dept Math, Indian Inst Technology, Kharagpur 721302, India

SUDARSKY, JERRY M., industrialist; b. Russia, June 12, 1918; s. Selig and Sara (Ars) S.; m. Mildred Axelrod, Aug. 31, 1947; children: Deborah, Donna (dec.). Student, U. Iowa, 1936-39; BS in Chem. Engrging., Poly. U. Bklyn., 1942; DSc (hon.), Poly. U. N.Y., 1976. Founder, CEO Bioferm Corp., Wasco, Calif., 1946-66; cons. to Govt. of Israel, 1966-67; founder, chmn. Israel Chems., Ltd., Tel Aviv, 1967-72; chmn. I.C. Internat. Cons., Tel Aviv, 1971-73; vice chmn., bd. dirs. Daylin, Inc., L.A., 1972-76; pres., chmn. J.M.S. Assocs., L.A., 1976—f; vice chmn. bd. dirs. Jacobs Engring. Group Inc., Pasadena, Calif., 1982-94; chmn., CEO Health Sci. Prop. Holding Corp., 1994-97; chmn. Alexandria Real Estate Equities Inc., Pasadena, 1997—. Patentee in field of indsl. microbiology. Bd. govs. Hebrew U., Jerusalem; trustee Polytechnic U. N.Y., 1976—; bd. dirs. Mgmt. Edn. Assn., UCLA, 1990-99. Served with USNR, 1943-46. Mem. AAAS, Am. Chem. Soc., Brentwood Country Club (L.A.), Sigma Xi. Office: JMS Assoc 2220 Ave Of Stars Ste 111 Los Angeles CA 90067-5656

SUDARSONO, JUWONO, government administrator; b. 1942. Deputy gov. Nat. Resilience Inst.; min. Dept. Environ. Affairs., Dept. Edn. & Culture, 1998—, Dept. of Def. Office: Dept Pertahanan, Medan Merdeka Barat 13-14, Jakarta 10110, Indonesia Office: PO box 4104, Jakarta Pusat, Indonesia*

SUDHARSONO, JUWONO, federal official. Min. of def. and security Indonesia, 1999. Office: Ministry of Def & Security, Jl Medarka Barat 13-14, Jakarta 10110, Pusat*

SÜDI, JANOS, biologist, researcher; b. Budapest, Hungary, Feb. 20, 1931; s. Janos Sr. and Ottilia (Foerk) S.; m. Aranka Merschitz, June 29, 1956 (div. Sept. 1973); children: Peter, Eszter; m. Ingrid Otte, Sept. 9, 1982. PhD, Eötvös U., Budapest, 1963; D in Habilitation, U. Kiel, 1978. Rschr. Inst. Plant Protection, Budapest, 1955-63, Inst. Biochemistry of Hungarian Acad. Scis., Budapest, 1964-70, Ges. Biotech. Forsch., Braunschweig, Germany, 1971-73, U. Kiel (Germany) Med. Sch. Inst. Biochemistry, 1974-78, U. Kiel (Germany) Med. Sch. Inst. Toxicology, 1989—, Dairy Rsch. Ctr. Inst. Hygiene, Kiel, 1979-88. Contbr. articles to profl. jours. Fellow Internat. Atomic Energy Agy., Oxford (Eng.) U., 1962-63; European Molecular Biology Orgn. scholar, Bristol, Eng., 1970-71; grantee German govt., Kiel, 1974-76. Mem. AAAS. Roman Catholic. Avocations: hiking, botany. Home: Preusserstr 17, D-24105 Kiel Germany Office: U Kiel Inst Toxicology, Brunswiker Str 10, D-24105 Kiel Germany

SUDIBYO, BAMBANG, Indonesian minister of finance; b. Temanggung, Indonesia, Oct. 8, 1952. Degree in acctg., Gajah Mada U., Indonesia, 19977; MBA, U. N.C., 1980; D Econs., U. Ky., 1985. Econs. prof. Gadjah Mada U.; dir. gen. for budget Indonesia, inspectorate gen.; sec.-gen. Indonesian Ministry of Fin.; min. fin. Indonesia Jakarta, 1999—. Office: Ministry of Fin Timur 2-4, Jl Lapangan Banteng, Jakarta Pusat Indonesia*

SUDO, SHINJI, languages educator, historian; b. Takasaki, Japan, Aug. 6, 1939; s. Takeshi and Kaoru (Kato) S.; m. Kazuko Tomura, May 30, 1970; 1 child, Hideya. BA, Keio U., 1963, MA, 1965, PhD, 1987. Lectr. Chubu Women's Jr. Coll., Gifu, Japan, 1968-69; from lectr. to prof. Kyoto Sangyo U., Japan, 1970—; vis. prof. Nangyang U., Singapore, 1973-74, Stanford (Calif.) U., 1977-78; chief dept. internat. studies Kyoto Sangyo U., 1982-92. Autholr: The Studies of U.S.-Japanese War in Diplomatic Relations, 1986; editor: The History of After World War II, 1992. Japan Found. fellow, 1973-74; Fulbright Found. grantee, 1977-78. Mem. Japan Def. Soc., Japan Politics and Laws Assn., Japan United Nations Assn. in Kyoto. Avocations: golf, tennis, igo. Home: 103-8 Kitazono-cho, Shimogama Sakyo ku, Kyoto 606-0831, Japan Office: Kyoto Sangyo U, Motoyama Kamigamo Kita-ku, Kyoto 603-8555, Japan

SUDRE, MARGUERITE JOSETTE GERMAINE, anesthetist; b. Vinh, Vietnam, Oct. 17, 1943; arrived in France, 1951; d. Robert Charles Henri and Thi-Khue (N'Guyen) Demaiche. PhD in Medicine, U. Marseilles, France, 1976. Pres. Region Reunion, Reunion Island, France, 1993—; sec. state for French lang. Govt. of France, 1995; mem. European Parliament, Brussels, Belgium. Roman Catholic. Office: Parliament European, Rue Wiertz, ASP 13E217 Brussels B-1047, Belgium*

SUDYATMIKO, DJOKO (LIE GIOK HAUW), wholesale trading executive; b. Pati, Java, Indonesia, Apr. 6, 1944; s. Hie Thiong Lie and Trien Nio Tong; m. Vera Tjahja, Sept. 20, 1970; children: Rinaldy Sudyatmiko, Karina Sudyatmiko. BSEE, Bandung Inst. Technology, Indonesia, 1965. Mem. parliament Parliament of the Rep. of Indonesia, Jakarta, 1971-77, 77-82, 1982-87, 87-92; mem. People's Coun. of Rep. of Indonesia, Jakarta, 1992-98; mem. bd. mgmt. MAKRO, 1992—; co-chmn. devel. and indsl. com. Parliament of Rep. of Indonesia, 1984-89, chief del. of Indonesian Parliament in Inter-Parliamentary Union, 1988; mem. com. for internat. cooperation Indonesian Parliament, 1982-92; participant numerous internat. confs., 1977-92. Pres. Indonesian Student Action Coalition, Bandung, 1966-67, Indonesian Cath. Student Orgn., Bandung, 1967-68; chmn. dept. Internat. Rels. of Ruling Party, Golkar, Jakarta, 1988-93; dep. majority leader Parliament of Rep. of Indonesia, 1983-88. Recipient Satyalencana Penegak medal Minister of Def., Jakarta, 1967. Mem. Trisakti U. Found., Cath. U. Atmajaya in Jakarta (trustee 1990—), Panca Bhakti U. (supr. bd. 1982—). Roman Catholic. Avocations: tennis, guitar.

SUEN, SHING-YI, science educator; b. Matou, Tainan, Taiwan, Nov. 26, 1965; parents Wen-Bin Sun and Su-Hsiueh Wang; m. Wen-Hwa Wu, June 2, 1994; children: Sz-Wei, Ying-Wei. BS, Nat. Taiwan U., Taipei, 1987, MS, 1989; PhD, U. Wis., 1994. Assoc. prof. Nat. Chung Hsing U., Taichung, 1994-2000, prof., 2000—. Editor: Jour. Engring., Nat. Chung Hsing U., 1997. Mem. Internat. Adsorption Soc., Chinese Colloid & Interface Soc., Chinese Inst. Chem. Engrs., Phi Tau Phi. Avocations: reading, badminton, hiking. Fax: 886-4-2854734. E-mail: sysuen@nchu.edu.tw. Office: Nat Chung-Hsing, 250 KuoKuang Rd, 402 Taichung Taiwan

SUENAGA, SHIGEAKI, dentist, dental radiologist; b. Kagoshima, Japan, Dec. 8, 1953; s. Shigeshi and Masako Suenaga; m. Chieko Midori, May 3, 1982; children: Yoko, Nobuaki. PhD, Kagoshima U., 1991. Asst. Kagoshima U. Dental Sch., 1980-93, lectr., 1993—. Office: Kagoshima U Dental Sch, 8-35-1 Sakuragaoka, Kagoshima City 890, Japan

SUENOBU, MINEO, applied linguistics educator; b. Kobe, Hyogo, Japan, Mar. 10, 1941; s. Koji and Misao S.; m. Yoko Yamamoto, Sept. 25, 1971; children: Toshio, Tomoko, Misako, Takeshi. BA, Kwansei Gakuin U., Nishinomiya, Japan, 1964, MA, 1966. Tchr. Kobe Coll., Nishinomiya, Japan, 1965-66, Kwansei Gakuin High Sch., Nishinomiya, Japan, 1966-69; lectr. Kobe (Japan) U. of Commerce, 1969-79, assoc. prof., 1979-87, prof., 1987—; rsch. U. Hawaii, Honolulu, 1975-76; chmn. faculty meeting Kobe (Japan) U. of Commerce, 1990-91, head English dept., 1992-93, chmn. entrance examination instn. com., 1993-94, chmn. regional improvement promoting com., 1996—; vis. prof. Jinan U. China, 1997, 99, U. New Eng., Armidale, Australia, 1998. Author: (book) From Error to Intelligibility, 1989, Communicability within Errors, 1995, Japanese English, 1999; contbr. articles to profl. linguistics jours.; referee various jours. and confs. Named for Excellent Results in Edn., Hyogo Prefecture, 1989. Mem. Japan Assn. Coll. English Tchrs. (exec. com. rev. 1985-93), Japan Assn. for Study of Teaching English to Children (councilor, rev. 1980-91), English Lang. Edn. Soc. (com. mem. 1983-91), Internat. Soc. Applied Psycholinguistics (treas.), Internat. Assn. World Englishes, Japan Assn. for Asian English (councilor 1997—), Lang. Lab. Assn. Japan (exec. com.), Internat. Conf. on Fgn. Lang. Edn. and Tech. (chmn. exec. com.), Tenrikyo. Home: 3-24-10 Ohtani-cho, Nagata-ku Kobe 653-0838, Japan Office: Kobe U of Commerce, 8 Gakuen-nishi Nishi-ku, Kobe 651-2197, Japan

SUERO, JOSÉ AGUSTIN, company executive; b. Santo Domingo, Dominican Republic, May 3, 1947; s. Justiniano Vasquez and Amelia Suero; m. Josefina Cuello, Mar. 19, 1972; children: Juan Carlos, Arlene Suero Cuello. Student, Mahatmagandy, Santo Domingo, 1967-68, Corp. Argentina de Production, Buenos Aires, 1970, NYU, 1983, 84, Ctrl. Ednl. Caribe, N.Y.C., 1987. Mgr. prodn. Super Maquet Domincano, Santo Domingo, 1966-71; pres. adminstrn. Products Gaucho, Santo Domingo, 1971-76; mgr. meat Fedco Foods, Bronx, N.Y., 1976-82, Pioneer Super Marquet, 1982-84, Associated Super Marquet, 1984-87, Read Apple Super Marquet, N.Y.C., 1987—. Bd. mem. Esperanza Ctr., 1974-94, Dominican Parade, 1981-84, La Gran Parade of Bronx, 1990; v.p. Ceduca Centro Ednl. Caribe, 1976-90, 34 Police Precinct coun., 1989-92; active Presdl. Commn. Am. Agenda. Mem. U.S. Families of Am., Lions Club. Republican. Roman Catholic. Office: High Power Coalition 580 W 161st St Apt 26 New York NY 10032-6210

SUESS, JAMES FRANCIS, clinical psychologist; b. Evanston, Ill., Aug. 8, 1950; s. James Francis and Rae Love (Miller) S.; m. Linda Grace Powell, July 31, 1976; 1 child, Misty Lynne. BS, U. So. Miss., 1974, MS, 1978, PhD, 1982. Lic. psychologist, N.Y., Ala.; diplomate Am. Bd. Profl. Psychology, Am. Bd. Med. Psychotherapists, Profl. Assn. Custody Evaluators, Am. Coll. Forensic Examiners, Am. Bd. Forensic Medicine. Assoc. psychologist State of Miss., Ellisville, 1978-80; clin. psychologist SUNY Med. Sch./Erie County Med. Ctr., Buffalo, 1982-84, supervisiong clin. psychologist, 1984-87, assoc. dir., 1987—; dir. practica SUNY Med. Sch., 1982-90, faculty counsel, 1988—; cons. Buffalo Dept. Social Svcs., 1985—; mem. spkrs. bur. Erie Alliance for Mentally Ill, 1986—; vis. prof. U. Guadalajara Sch. Medicine, 1985—; clin. dir. Stickney Adolescent Ctr. Mobile Met. Hosp. Ctr., 1993-97; chmn., dir. Physicans' Psychiat. Clinic, 1997—; CEO Stillwood Clin. Group, 1998—. Author: Annotated Bibliography of Sex Roles, 1972, Personality Disorder and Self Psychology, 1991; contbr. articles to refereed jours. including Perceptual and Motor Skills, Jour. Clin. and Consulting Psychology, Am. Annals of Deaf. With USAR, 1969-76. Fellow Am. Orthopsychiat. Assn., Soc. Personality Assessment; mem. Am. Psychol. Assn., Ala. Lic. Psychol. (pres.), Mobile Assn. Psychol. (pres.). Fax: 334-479-8172. E-mail: drfrsuess@cs.com. Home: 507 Evergreen Rd Mobile AL 36608-3845 Office: The Stillwood Clin Grp 717 Executive Park Dr Ste B Mobile AL 36606-2843

SUESS, JOCHEN RICHARD, gynecologist, obstetrician; b. Nuremberg, Bavaria, Germany, July 3, 1959; s. Georg Johann and Ingeborg Maria Anna (Roscher) S. MD magna cum laude, U. Friedrich-Alexander, Erlangen-Nuremberg, 1986. Cert. in sports medicine, emergency medicine, human genetics, psychotherapy. Asst. dept. human genetics U. Friedrich-Alexander, Erlangen-Nuremberg, 1988-91; asst. dept. ob-gyn. Klinikum St. Marien, Amberg/Oberpfalz, Bavaria, 1987-88, 91-98, sr. physician, 1998—; mem., cons. European Found. Quality Mgmt. (EFQM). Contbr. articles to profl. jours. Capt. Med. Corps German Army, 1986-87. Mem. German Soc. Human Genetics, Fedn. Med. Genetics, German Soc. Ob-Gyn., Fedn. German Gynecologists, German Soc. Med. Ultrasound (DEGUM), Fedn. Bavarian Sport Physicians, German Soc. Mil. Medicine, Bavarian County Med. Chamber (del.). Roman Catholic. Avocations: history of female sex hormones, collecting semi-precious stones, U.S. manned space covers Apollo, modern literature and classic movies, pop music of 1960's and 1970's. Home: Laufamholzer Kirchensteig 28, 90482 Nuremberg Bavaria, Germany Office: Klinikum St Marien, Amberg Mariahilfbergweg 7, 92224 Amberg Oberpfalz Bavaria, Germany

SUEYOSHI, SHUZO, forester, researcher; b. Himeji, Hyogo, Japan, Apr. 23, 1952; s. Tadao and Sakae (Takeuchi) S.; m. Chieko Fujimoto, Feb. 9, 1954; children: Sakura, Sumire. BAS, Kyoto U., 1976, MAgr, 1978, PhD in Agr., 1995. Rschr. Forestry and Forest Products Rsch. Inst., Tsukuba, Japan, 1980-88, sr. rschr., 1988-92, head dwelling physics lab. wood tech. divsn., 1992—. Office: Forestry/Forest Prod Rsch, Inst PO Box16 Tsukuba Norin, 305-8687 Tsukuba, Ibaraki 305-8687, Japan

SUFALKO, DYNAH NAOMI JULIETTE, marketing communications manager; b. Harrogate, York, Eng., July 18, 1964; came to U.S., 1967; d. Robert Duncan-White and Lesley Marigold Elizabeth Nordyke; m. Arnold Felix Sufalko, Aug. 11, 1990 (div. Oct. 1998). AS, Elgin (Ill.) C.C., 1993, basic vocat. specialist in mgmt.-mktg., 1993; BS in Bus. Adminstrn., Roosevelt U., Chgo., 1999. Cert. trade show marketer San Francisco State U.; cert. mgr. of exhibits Trade Show Exhibitors Assn. Office mgr. Ko-Pack Corp. of Am., Bensenville, Ill., 1982-86; Midwest rep. LDC Am. divsn. Pioneer Electronics, Rosemont, Ill., 1986-87; project mgr. Star Displays, Elgin, 1994-95; exhibit mgr. Richardson Electronics, LaFox, Ill., 1995-97; account mgr. Exhibitgroup/Giltspur, Roselle, 1997-99; sr. corp. account exec. Contempo Design, Libertyville, Ill., 1999; fin. officer Windy City chpt. oper. coun. Tradeshow Exhibitors Assn.; mktg. comm. mgr. Gen. Exhibits and Design, Inc., Chgo., 2000; records coord., fin. officer Windy City chpt. Operating Coun. Tradeshow Exhibitors Assn., Chgo.; advisor, rev. com. mem. Cert. Trade Show Marketers Program, Boulder, Colo. Scholastic scholar Roosevelt U., 1993-99. Mem. Phi Theta Kappa, Mu Alpha Theta. Avocations: dance, theater, golf, pets. Office: General Exhibits and Design Inc 4925 W Lawrence Ave Chicago IL 60630-3824

SUFFCZYNSKI, MACIEJ JOZEF, physicist; b. Cracow, Poland, Oct. 25, 1926; s. Edmund Jerzy and Zofia Antonina (Uziemblo) S.; m. Danuta Kosmowska, 1965; children: Michel, Peter, Jan. MSc in Physics, Jagiellonian U., Cracow, 1950; PhD in Physics, Warsaw (Poland) U., 1954. Head chmn. theory solid state physics Warsaw U., 1959-70; prof. Inst. Physics, 1970-96; head theoretical physics Inst. Physics, 1970-73; vis. prof. physics U. Rochester, N.Y., summer, 1962, Mich. State U., 1964, U. Los Andes, Merida, Venezuela, 1972, U. Bilkent, Ankara, Turkey, 1990. Contbr. articles to profl. jours. Decorated Cavalier Cross Polonia Restituta. Mem. Polish Phys. Soc., Inst. Physics, Com. on Data Sci. and Tech. (nat. com. 1972—). Avocation: travel. Office: Inst Physics, Al Lotnikow 32/46, 02-668 Warsaw Poland

SUGA, HITOSHI, investment company executive; b. Tokyo, Chiyoda-ku, Japan, Sept. 6, 1952; s. Sohsuke and Kiyoko (Takayanagi) S.; m. Midori Nakajima, May 21, 1978; children: Yumiko, Eiichi-David. BA in Polit. Sci., Waseda U., Tokyo, 1976; MBA, Harvard U., 1985. Staff Mitsui & Co. Ltd., Tokyo/Osaka, 1976-83, Mitsui Co. (USA) Inc., N.Y.C., 1985-86; sub-mgr., asst. mgr., mgr., asst. gen. mgr. corp. planning divsn. Mitsui & Co. Ltd., Tokyo, 1986-96; pres., CEO MVC Corp., Tokyo, 1996—; mergers and acquisitions com. mem. Japan Ctr. for Internat. Fin., Tokyo, 1995; initial pub. offering com. mem. Ministry of Internat. Trade and Industry, Tokyo, 1998; dir. Cosmo PR Inc., Tokyo, 1998. Editor: (book) How to Do a Leveraged Buyout, 1988; co-author: (books) Entrepreneur Strategy Through Case Method, 1994, How to Do a Venture Capital Investment, 1997. Mem. Am. C. of C., Fgn. Corrs. Club Japan (assoc.), Harvard Club Japan. Avocations: jogging, skiing. Office: MVC Corp, 1-2-3-5F Kudan-Kita, 102-0073 Chiyoda-ku Tokyo, Japan

SUGA, SHIGEMASA, material physics educator; b. Okayama, Japan, Nov. 24, 1945; s. Seiichi and Tamiko (Yamamoto) S.; m. Sachiha Osada, Aug. 8, 1971; children: Koichiro, Miyuki, Masaki, Yasuhiko. Bachelor's degree, U. Tokyo, 1968, Master's degree, 1970, PhD, 1973. Asst. prof. Meisei U., Tokyo, 1971-73; rsch. scientist Max Planck Inst. für Festkörperforschung, Stuttgart, Germany, 1973-76; assoc. prof. U. Tokyo, 1976-89; prof. Osaka U., 1989—, Inst. for High Energy Physics, Tsukuba, Japan, 1990-96; chmn. SPring-8 Beam Line Com., 1994-96. Co-author: (books) Advances in Material Science, 1980, Synchrotron Radiation, 1986, Materials Technology, 1985, Experimental Physics, Spectroscopy, 1999; patentee in field. Recipient Japanese Jour. Applied Physics prize, 1992. Mem. Japan Soc. for Synchroton Radiation Rsch. (com. mem. 1987-98, sec. 1987-91). Avocations: tennis, swimming. E-mail: suga@mp.es.osaka-u.ac.jp. Home: 3-22-5 Shin Kofudai, 563-0105 Toyonogun Osaka, Japan Office: Osaka U Grad Sch Engrg Sci, 1-3-Machikaneyama, 560-8531 Toyonaka Osaka, Japan

SUGANTHAN, PONNUTHURAI NAGARATNAM, electrical engineering educator, researcher; b. Jaffna, Sri Lanka, Dec. 20, 1967; arrived in Singapore, 1999; s. Ponnuthurai and Vallinayagy (Kanagasundram) Nagaratnam; m. Sashikala Rajasingham, 1999. BA in Elec. Engring., Cambridge (Eng.) U., 1990, cert. postgrad. studies, 1992, MA, 1994; PhD in Elec. and Computer Engring., Nanyang Technol. U., Singapore, 1996. Rsch. asst. Nanyang Technol. U., 1992-93, tchg. asst., 1993-95; predoctoral rsch. asst. U. Sydney, Australia, 1995-96; lectr. elec. engring. U. Queensland, St. Lucia, Australia, 1996-99; asst. prof. elec. engring. Nanyang Technol. U., Singapore, 1999—; rschr. in neural networks and pattern analysis. Contbr. articles to sci. jours., including Image and Vision Computing Jour., Pattern Recognition Jour., others. Scholar Overseas Devel. Adminstrn. U.K., 1987, U.K. Rsch. Coun., 1990, Christ Coll. scholar Cambridge U., 1990. Fellow Cambridge Commonwealth Trust (life); mem. IEEE (sr., newsletter editor Queensland 1998), Instn. Elec. Engrs. (U.K.). Hindu. Avocations: playing squash, badminton, chess, cards, watching television.

SUGAR, ALAN MICHAEL, company executive; b. Mar. 24, 1947; s. Nathan and Fay Sugar; m. Ann Simons, 1968; 3 children. DSc (hon.), London City U., 1988. Chmn. bd. Amstrad Plc, Brentwood, Eng., 1968-97; exec. dir. Betacam, 1997—; chmn. Tottenham Hotspur plc, London; chmn. Tottenham Hotspur plc, 1991—. Avocation: tennis. Office: Tottenham Hotspur plc, 748 High Rd Tottenham, London N17 0AP, United Kingdom*

SUGÁR, JÁNOS, consulting pathologist, researcher; b. Polgár, Hajdu, Hungary, Jan. 27, 1922; s. Antal and Mária (Horovitz) S.; m. Márta Müller, June 6, 1961; 1 child, Katalin. MD, U. Debrecen, Hungary, 1950; spceialist in pathology, Postgrad. Med. Sch., Budapest, Hungary, 1956; PhD, Nat. Inst. Oncology, Budapest, 1957; DSc, Hungarian Acad. Scis., Budapest, 1969. Cert. specialist in pathology and diagnostic cytology, Hungary. Rsch. fellow Nat. Inst. Oncology, 1954-62, sci. dir., prof., dir. tumor pathology dept., 1974-92; Am. Cancer Soc. rsch. fellow Royal Cancer Inst., London, 1963-64; chief exptl. morphology dept. Rsch. Inst. Oncopathology, Budapest, 1973-74; ret., 1992; cons. pathologist City Hosp. Budapest, 1993—; prorector edn. Postgrad. Med. Sch., 1977-83; v.p. Nat. Bd. Med. Specialization, Budapest, 1984-88; mem. fellowship com. Union Internat. Contre le Cancer, Geneva, 1985-88. Author: Early Diagnosis and Pathohistology of Malignant Tumors of the Skin, 1965; contbr. over 250 articles to internat. jours., chpts. to books. Lt. Hungarian Army Res. Decorated Star Order (Hungary); recipient J. Baló award, 1981, O. Krompecher award, 1986, award Hungarian Acad. Scis., 1988. Mem. Internat. Acad. Cytology, Internat. Inst. Life Scis., Soc. Hungarian Oncologists (pres. 1984-91), European Cell Proliferation Study Group (bd. dirs. 1980—), European Soc. Pathology (bd. dirs. 1985-88), Collegium Ramazzini. Home: Utas St 7, 1025 Budapest Hungary

SUGAR, JOSEPH ROBERT, educator, musician, conductor; b. Worcester, Mass., Dec. 14, 1928; s. Elias George and Emily Angeline (David) S.; m. Clara Anne Steele, Dec. 26, 1955; children: Thomas Elias, Robert Albert. AA, Bergen Jr. Coll., Teaneck, N.J., 1948; BA, L.I. U., 1950; MA, Columbia U., 1955; profl. diploma, 1956. Brass instr. L.I. U., N.Y., 1949; asst. in bands. Ind. U., Bloomington, Ind., 1950; band dir. Upsala Coll., East Orange, N.J., 1956-57; band. dir., instr. music Bethpage (N.Y.) Elem. Sch., 1957-66; instr. baton twirling Bethpage High Sch., 1957-67; band. dir. Hewlett-Woodmere (N.Y.) Jr. High Sch., 1966-78; asst. band dir., instr. baton twirling Hewlett High Sch., 1967-69, band dir., 1983-84, dir. jazz ensemble, 1983-89; band dir. Dowling Coll., Oakdale, N.Y., 1977-79; dist. dir. music Hewlett-Woodmere Pub. Schs., 1978-89; advisor to music chmn. for courses music edn. C.W. Post Coll. L.I. U., Greenvale, N.Y., 1990—; prof., 1990—, dir. music edn., 1990—; summer band sch. co-dir Manasquan, N.J., 1955-64; creative music cultural workshop, Bethpage, 1959-62; youth choir dir. Levittown (N.Y.) Presbyn. Ch., 1966; dir. N.Y. Jazz Ensemble, Hempstead, 1976; dir. Kismet Shrine Temple Band, 1997—; clinician numerous music festivals, 1970—. Performer Indpls. Symphony Orch., 1950, Joe Sugar and the Big Band, 1980—; accompanist numerous entertainers including Vic Damone, Diahann Carroll, Al martino, Jerry Vale, Georgia Gibbs, Toni Arden, Johnny Ray, Eddie Fisher, Cab Calloway, Marilyn Michaels, Frankie Lane, Henny Youngman, Anna Maria Alberghetti, Patti Page, Bobby Rydel, Buddy Grecco, Billy Eckstine, Julius La Rose, The Four Aces, Don Cornell, Connie Francis; rec. artist with Audio-Fidelity, 20th Century Fox, Paramount, MGM, 1958-61; author: Presidents march, 1982, Twirling Tips in 3 Volumes, 1963, Where Are We Headed in Music Education?, 1960; composer, condr. (album) Ten Nights in a Harem, 1963. Mem. Boy Scouts Am. With USAF, 1950-52. Grantee Ford Found., 1962; recipient Merit award Music Belongs, 1972, 1st pl. award East Nat. Music Festival, 1977, Appreciation of Outstanding Leadership award Black Music Caucus, 1982, Cert. of Merit award N.Y. State Senate, 1982, citation Town of Hempstead, 1982; named Man of Yr. Wantagh C. of C., 1979. Mem. Music Educators Na.t Conf. (life, pres. Eastern divsn. 1985-87), N.Y. State Adminstrs. Music Edn. (pres. 1987—), N.Y. State Sch. Music Assn.(pres. 1980-82, Disting. Svc. award 1989), Nassau Music Educators (pres. 1970, Pres. award 1970, Svc. awards 1973, 87), Nat. Assn. Jazz Educators, Internat. Trumpet Guild, N.Y. State Coun. Music Adminstrs., DAV (life), Wantagh Friends of Libr., Am. Legion (past commander, award 1978), Jones Beach Power Squadron (sr.), Kiwanis (past pres. award 1979), Masons, Wantagh Dads and Booster (pst pres.), Wantagh Spiked Shoe (past pres. award 1979), Phi Delta Kappa, Phi Mu Alpha (life), Kappa Kappa Psi, Phi Mu Alpha, Tri M. Republican. Home: 1594 Milburn Ct Wantagh NY 11793-3330

SUGAR, SHERRY D., computer operator, administrative assistant; b. St. Joseph, Mo., May 6, 1962; d. Robert and Floy Hitzelberger. Student, Mo. Western State Coll., 1980, So. Ill. U., 1980-82; sec. II cert. completion, Profl. Bus. Sch., 1982; student, Lindenwood U., 1999—. Acct. Swift Ind., National City, Ill., 1982; computer operator, dirs. asst. Western Union, Bridgeton, Mo., 1982—; dispatcher, office mgr. Associated Maintenance Svcs., St. Peters, Mo., 1989-91. Mem. World Wildlife Fund, Nat. Wildlife Fedn., Nature Conservancy, Defenders Wildlife. Avocations: amateur photography, reading, flower gardening, computers.

SUGARMAN, ROBERT P., lawyer; b. Passaic, N.J., Aug. 29, 1949; s. Meyer and Sylvia (Schwartz) S.; m. Louise Aufiero, June 29, 1980; children: Lauren, Jason. BA, Rutgers Coll., 1971; JD, Columbia U., 1975. Bar: N.Y. and N.J. 1976, U.S. Dist. Ct. (so. dist.) N.Y. 1976, U.S. Dist. Ct. (ea. dist.) N.Y. 1977, U.S. Ct. Appeals (2d cir.) 1992. Assoc. Paul, Weiss, Rifkind, Wharton & Garrison, N.Y.C., 1975-79; assoc. Milberg Weiss Bershad Hynes & Lerach, N.Y.C., 1979-82, ptnr., 1983-99; ptnr. Office Robert Sugarman, Uniondale, N.Y., 2000—. Office: Ste 400 50 Charles Lindberg Blvd Uniondale NY 11553

SUGASAWA, TOSHINARI, pharmacologist, biochemist; b. Tokyo, Dec. 29, 1959. BS, Kyoto U., 1979; DSc, U. Paris VII, 1996. Rsch. mgr. Sumitomo Pharms. Rsch. Ctr., Osaka, Japan, 1983—. Office: Sumitomo Pharms Rsch Ctr, 3-1-98 Kasugadenaka Konohana-ku, Osaka 554-0022, Japan

SUGATHAN, SHEELA KANDDENKATTIL, microbiologist; b. Trichur, Pudukad, India, Oct. 1, 1960; d. Shankaran Krishnan and Kausalya Karappan (Koppatil) Kanddenkattil; m. Sugathan Thoppil, Dec. 12, 1982; children: Roshan, Shweta. MSc, Topieala Nat. Med. Coll., Bombay, 1985; postgrad., M.G. U., Kottayamn, India, 1999—. Microbiologist Doctors Diagnostic Ctr., Cochin, India, 1986-87, Green Crescent Hosp, Cochin, 1990-92, M.O.S.C.M.M. Hosp., Cochin, 1994—. Mem. Indian Assn. Med. Microbiologists, Indian Leptospirosis Soc. Avocations: reading, music, philately, coins. Office: MOSCMM Hosp, Kolenchery, Ernakulam 682311, India

SUGAWARA, MASUMI, psychologist; b. Tokyo, Japan, Apr. 17, 1958; d. Morio Kazue (Furusawa) Takeuchi; m. Kensuke Sugawara, Nov. 9, 1986; children: Ryousuke, Shyunsuke. BA, Tokyo Metro. U., 1981, MA, 1983, PhD, 1990. Registered Psychologist. Lectr. Meiji-Gkuin U., Tokyo, 1987-91, Tokyo Women's U., 1991-95, Tokyo Metro. U., 1996-97, Keio U., Tokyo, 1999—; chief sect. family study NIMH, Chiba, Japan, 1995—; Mem. editl. bd. Japanese Assn. Devel. Psychology, 1997—, Japenese Assn. Personality Psychology, 1997—, Archives of Psychiatric Diagnostics and Clinical Evaluation, 1997—. Contbr. articles to profl. jours. Cons. cmty. edn., Yokohama, 1990-92. Recipient Devel. Sci. Rsch. award, Cen. Devel. Sci., Tokyo, 1989, Clin. and Devel. Rsch. award, Yasuda Life Welfare Found., Tokyo, 1997, 98, Mental Health Rsch. award, Daiwa Health Found., Tokyo, 1999. Mem. Japanese Assn. Psychology, Japanese Assn. Devel. Psychology, Japanese Assn. Personality Psychology. Avocations: violin, travel. E-mail: sugawara@ncnp-k.go.jp. Office: Nat Inst Mental Health, Khonodail-7-3, 272-0827 Ichikawa Japan

SUGAWARA, MICHIO, architectural company executive; b. Tokyo, Nov. 22, 1937; m. Ryoko Nishikawa, Oct. 30, 1967; 1 child, Yuichiro. B of Engring., U. Waseda, Tokyo, 1961; BArch, U. Calif., 1965. Registered 1st class arch. Staff Shimuzu Corp., Tokyo, 1961-62; designer Office of Charles Eames, Calif., 1962-67; staff Ishimoto A&E, Tokyo, 1967—, gen. mgr., 1981—, mng. dir., 1987—, sr. exec. dir., pres., 1997—. Mem. Japanese Inst. Archs., U. Calif. Japan Alumni Assn. Avocations: painting, music, tennis, golf. Home: 3-7-10 kita Aoyama Minatoku, Tokyo Japan Office: Ishimoto Arch & Engring Firm Inc, 4-6-12 Kudan Mimami, Tokyo 102, Japan

SUGAWARA, SATOSHI, space systems engineer; b. Sapporo, Hokkidoo, Japan, Mar. 30, 1961; s. Tetsuzoo Sugawara; m. Fusae Kogure, May 5, 1987; 1 child, Masashi. BS, Sci. U. Tokyo, 1983, M of Tech., 1985; postgrad., Calif. Inst. Tech., 1994. Engr. Hitachi (Japan) Ltd., 1985-90, asst. sr. engr., 1990-96, sr. engr., 1996—. Mem. AIAA, Japan Soc. Mech. Engring., Soc. Automotive Engring. Avocations: golf, playing saxophone, tennis. Home: 1-7-11 Daihara-cho, Hitachi-shi 316-0021, Japan Office: 1-1 Saiwai-cho 3-chome, Hitachi-shi 317-8511, Japan

SUGAYA, EIICHI, physiology educator; b. Tokyo, Mar. 25, 1929; s. Tsuneshino and Huchi (Yamada) S.; m. Aiko Sugaya, May 3, 1967. MD, Keio U., Tokyo, 1953, PhD, 1958. Asst. dept. physiology Keio U., Tokyo, 1954-58; boursier (French govt.) dept. physiology Sorbonne, Paris, 1956-58, Neurophysiology Lab. Musee Oceanographique, Monaco, 1958; asst. dept. surgery Keio U., Tokyo, 1958-64; gen. surgeon Ichikawa (Japan) Hosp., Tokyo Dental Coll., 1959-60; surgeon neurosurgery 2d Tokyo Nat. Hosp., 1960-64; rsch. fellow div. neurol. surgery Washington U., St. Louis, 1962-63; prof. physiology dept. physiology Kanagawa Dental Coll., Yokosuka, Japan, 1964-96; prof. divsn. oriental medicine Sch. Medicine Tokai U., Tokyo, 1996—; cons. Tsumura (Pharm.) Co., Tokyo, 1983-2000; specialist doctor Rappongi Hosp. (Oriental medicine), Tokyo, 1964-96; vis. prof. Inst. for Oriental medicine Sch. of Medicine, Keio U., Tokyo, 1992-96; chief rschr. lab. molecular & devel. medicine Inst. Exptl. Animals, Kawasaki, 1996-99; dir. Aieido Clinic Oriental Medicine, Tokyo, 1999—. Mem. Japan Soc. Oriental Medicine (specialist), Japan Autonomic Nerve Soc. (councilor, editing exec.), Japan Physiol. Soc. (councilor 1964-99). Avocation: violin. Fax: 81-422-42-0532.

SUGDEN, ROBERT, economics educator; b. Leeds, Eng., Aug. 26, 1949; s. Frank Gerald and Kathleen (Buckley) S.; m. Christine Margaret Upton, Mar. 26, 1982; children: Joe Robert, Jane Sarah. BA, U. York, 1970, DLitt, 1978; MSc, Univ. Coll., Cardiff, Wales, 1971. Lectr. in econs. U. York, Eng., 1971-78; reader in econs. U. Newcastle upon Tyne, 1978-85; prof. econs. U. East Anglia, Norwich, Eng., 1985—. Author: (with others) The Principles of Practical Cost-Benefit Analysis, 1978, The Political Economy of Public Choice, 1981, The Economics of Rights, Co-operation and Welfare, 1986. Office: U East Anglia, Sch Econs and Social Studies, Norwich NR4 7TJ, England

SUGGS, MICHAEL EDWARD, lawyer; b. Conway, S.C., Nov. 9, 1962; s. Edward and Rebecca S. BSBA, U. S.C., 1985, JD, 1992. Bar: S.C. 1992, U.S. Dist. Ct., S.C., 1995. Asst. pub. defender Def. Corp. Horry County, Conway, S.C., 1993—. Troop 847 com. Boy Scouts Am., Loris, S.C., 1985—; coun. City of Loris, 1994—, mayor pro-tem, 1998-00. Recipient Eagle Scout award Boy Scouts Am., 1976. Mem. S.C. Assn. Criminal Def. Lawyers, Horry County Bar Assn., Loris C. of C. Methodist. Home: 4932 Circle Dr Loris SC 29569-3146 Office: Def Corp Horry County PO Box 1666 114 Laurel St Conway SC 29526-5134

SUGIANTO, mechanical engineer; b. Dumened, Indonesia, Feb. 19, 1966; s. Tan Hok Djien and Kwee Kim Nio; m. Oey Oy Kim, Oct. 8, 1995. Degree in engring., Inst. Tech. Surabaya, Indonesia, 1990. Fabrication supt. Pt. Capitama Equindo Indah, Batam Island, Indonesia, 1990-92; MDT inspector level II Pt. Cwamac Citra Prakarsa, Java, Indonesia, 1992-93; mech. supr. Pt. Satyamitra Surya Perkasa, Denpasar, Bali, Indonesia, 1993-94, Samsung Heavy Industries, Merak, Indonesia, 1994-96; mech. maintenance foreman Pt. Amoco Mitsui, Merak, 1996—. Mem. Am. Welding Soc., Nat. Assn. Corrosion Engrs., Am. Soc. Non-destructive Testing, Singapore Welding Soc. Home: J Karet Belakang Gang Anggr, VI No 20 Rt 013/02, Jakarta 12940, Indonesia Office: Pt Amoco Mitsui Pta, Jl Raya Merak Rm 116, Merak West Java Indonesia

SUGIHARTA, ASEP, national park administrator, educator; b. Sumedang, West Java, Indonesia, Feb. 29, 1964; s. Satja and Mamah Ukamah; m. Tati Saukah, July 8, 1989; children: Yaumi Fauziah, Dini Nurdiani, Muhammad Fihri. Grad. in forestry, Bogor (Indonesia) Agrl. U., 1987; MS in Wildlife Sci., N.Mex. State U., 1994. Mem. staff Ministry Forestry, Bogor, 1987-92, Las Cruces, N.Mex., 1992-94; head sect. Bromo T.S., Ministry Forestry, Malang, Indonesia, 1994-97; head nat. park Taka Bonerate, Ministry Forestry, Benteng, Indonesia, 1997—; lectr. Malang (Indonesia) Agrl. Inst., 1995-97. Office: Taka Bonerate Nat Park, JL S Parman 40, Selayar Benteng Sulawesi, Indonesia

SUGIKI, SHIGEMI, ophthalmologist, educator; b. Wailuku, Hawaii, May 12, 1936; s. Sentaro and Kameno (Matoba) S.; m. Bernice T. Murakami, Dec. 28, 1958; children: Kevin S., Boyd R. AB, Washington U., St. Louis, 1957; MD, Washington U., 1961. Intern St. Luke's Hosp., St. Louis, 1961-62; resident ophthalmology Washington U., St. Louis, 1962-65; chmn. dept. ophthalmology Straub Clinic, Honolulu, 1965-70, Queens Med. Ctr., Honolulu, 1970-73, 80-83, 88-90, 93—; clin. prof. ophthalmology Sch. Medicine U. Hawaii, 1997. Maj. M.C., AUS, 1968-70. Decorated Hawaiian NG Commendation medal, 1968. Fellow ACS; mem. Am., Hawaii med. assns., Honolulu County Med. Soc., Am. Acad. Ophthalmology, Contact Lens Assn. Opthalmologists, Pacific Coast Oto-Ophthal. Soc., Pan-Pacific Surg. Assn., Am. Soc. Cataract and Refractive Surgery, Am. Glaucoma Soc., Internat. Assn. Ocular Surgeons, Am. Soc. Contemporary Ophthalmology, Washington U. Eye Alumni Assn., Hawaii Ophthal. Soc., Rsch. To Prevent Blindness. Home: 2398 Aina Lani Pl Honolulu HI 96822-2024 Office: 1380 Lusitana St Ste 714 Honolulu HI 96813-2443

SUGIMOTO, SEIJI, biochemist; b. Chuoh-Ku, Tokyo, Japan, July 6, 1958; s. Mitsuyoshi and Toshiko (Iwasaki) S.; m. Hiroko Nodake, Sept. 15, 1987; children: Yuko, Saho, Tatsuhiro. BS, Waseda U., 1981, MS, 1983, PhD, 1992. Rschr. Tokyo Rsch. Labs., Kyowa Hakko Kogyo Co., Ltd., 1983-90, staff scientist, 1990-95; rsch. fellow Harvard Med. Sch., Boston, 1992-93; lectr. Tokyo Inst. Technology, 1996; sr. rschr. Tokyo Rsch. Labs., 1995—. Author: Recombinant Microbes for Industrial and Agricultural Applications, 1994; contbr. articles to profl. jours. Mem. Japanese Biochem. Soc., Japanese Cancer Assn. Avocations: skiing, driving. E-mail: ssugimoto@kyowa.co.jp. Office: Kyowa Hakko Kogyo Co Ltd, 3-6-6 Asahimachi, 194-8533 Machida Japan

SUGIMOTO, TADAO, chemistry educator; b. Chiba, Japan, Jan. 11, 1941; s. Yasutsugu and Yasu (Ishimoto) S.; m. Taeko Tarao, Jan. 18, 1969; children: Mikio, Shigeki, Hideki. BS in Engring., Tokyo U., 1964, MS in Engring., 1966, D of Engring., 1977. Researcher Fuji Photo Film Co., Minami-ashigara, Japan, 1966-80, sr. researcher, 1980-91; prof. Tohoku U., Sendai, Japan, 1991—. Co-author: Colloid Science, 1995, Fine Particles Science and Technology, 1996, Gel Technology, 1997, (handbook) Ceramic Data Book, 1991. Recipient Photographic Tech. prize Soc. Photographic Sci. and Tech. of Japan, 1983, Internat. Metallographic Contest award Internat. Metallographic Soc., 1993, vinci d'Excellence, Moët Hennessy-Louis Vuitton, France, 1997. Mem. Chem. Soc. Japan, Japan Inst. Metals, Am. Chem. Soc. Avocations: Japanese history, classical music, kendo. Office: Tohoku U Inst Adv Matl Proc, Katahira 2-1-1, Sendai 980-8577, Japan

SUGIMOTO, YUKIHIRO, chemist, educator; b. Ichinomiya, Aichi, Japan, Feb. 1, 1959; s. Haruo and Tomiko Sugimoto; m. Norie Koike, Oct. 12, 1985; children: Miyuki, Yuki. BS, U. Tokyo, 1982, MS, 1984; PhD, Kyoto U., 1991. Rschr. Kao Corp., Tokyo, 1984-92; lectr. Tottori (Japan) U., 1992-93, assoc. prof., 1993—. Co-author: Mannual for Plant Molecular and Cell Engineering (Japanese), 1992, Handbook of Roots (Japanese), 1994, Dictionary of Roots (Japanese), 1998, Biotechnology in Agriculture and Forestry Vol. 43 Medicinal Plants XI, 1999. Grantee Fujisawa Found., 1993, Agrl. Chem. Rsch. Found., 1993, Ministry of Edn., Sci., Sports and Culture, 1995, 98—, Kampou Sci. Found., 1997, Saneyoshi Scholarship Found., 1997-98, Sumitomo Found., 1998-99, Novartis Found., 1999. Mem. Japan Soc. Biosci., Biotech. and Agrochemistry, Japanese Soc. Plant Cell and Molecular Biology, Japanese Soc. Plant Physiologists. Achievements include patents for alkaloid production by plant tissue cultures. Office: Tottori U Arid Land Rsch, Ctr 1390 Hamasaka, Tottori 680-0001, Japan

SUGIMURA, KAZUHISA, bioengineering educator; b. Toyama, Japan, Apr. 14, 1948. Prof. engring. Kagoshima U., Japan. Fax: 81 99 258 4706. Home: Koutokujidai 5-20-5, Kagoshima 891-0103, Japan Office: Kagoshima U Faculty Engring, Dept Bioengring 1-21-40 Korimoto, Kagoshima 890 0065, Japan

SUGIOKA, YOICHI, academic administrator. Pres. Kyushu U, Fukuoka, Japan. Office: Kyushu U, Hakozaki Higashi-ku, Fukuoka 812-8591, Japan*

SUGISAKI, SHIGEMITSU, international bank official; b. 1941; married; three children. BA, U. Tokyo, 1963; M Internat. Affairs, Columbia U., 1967. Mem. Minister's Secretariate, to various banking positions Min. of Finance, Japan, 1964-76; various to dep. vice min. of finance for internat. affairs Min. of Fin., Japan, 1979-90, 90-91, dep. dir. gen. Internat. Fin. Bur., 1991-92; personal asst. to pres. Asian Devel. Bank, 1976-79; commr. Tokyo Regional Taxation Bur., 1992-93; sec. gen. Exec. Bur. Securities and Exch. Surveillance Commn., 1993-94; spl. advisor to mng. dir. IMF, Washington, 1994-97, dep. mng. dir., 1997—. Office: Internat Monetary Fund 700 19th St NW Washington DC 20431-0001*

SUGITA, KATSUYUKI, bank executive; b. Oct. 13, 1942. Grad. in Econs., Gokyo U., 1966. With The Nippon Kangyo Bank, Ltd., Tokyo, 1966-74, asst. mgr. Overseas Bus. Divsn., 1974-76, asst. mgr. of N.Y. Br., 1976-81, mgr. Internat. Adminstrn. Divsn., 1981-83, mgr. Internat. Planning Divsn., 1983-84, mgr. Overseas Bus. Divsn., 1984-87, asst. gen. mgr. Personnel Divsn. II/asst. to gen. mgr. I, 1987-90, gen. mgr. of Corporate Banking Divsn. V, 1990-92, gen. mgr. Associated Cos. Divsn., 1992-94, gen. mgr. Planning and Coord. Divsn., 1994, dir., gen. mgr. Planning and Coord. Divsn., 1994-95, mng. dir., gen. mgr. Planning and Coord. Divsn., 1995-96, mng. dir., gen. mgr. Nat. Banking Adminstrn. Divsn. V, 1996-97; pres., CEO Dai-Ichi Kangyo Bank, Ltd., Tokyo, 1997—. Office: The Dai-Ichi Kangyo Bank Lt, 1-5 Uchisaiwaicho 1-chome, Chifoda-ku, Tokyo 100-0011, Japan*

SUGITA, NOBUO, publisher; b. Osaka, Japan, Sept. 8, 1921; s. Tsukumo and Tama S.; m. Aiko Tsutsui, Jan. 23, 1948; children: Keizo, Takako. LLB, Doshisha U., Kyoto, Japan, 1943. Pres. Minerva Shobo Co. Ltd., Kyoto, 1948—. Mem. Japan Book Pubs. Assn. (councillor 1960-85, dir. 1969-80, advisor 1986—, dir. 1996-2000), Rotary. Office: Minerva Shobo Co Ltd, 1 Tsutsumidani-cho Hinooka, Yamashinaku Kyoto 607-8494, Japan

SUGITA, TAKAAKI, surgeon; b. Abeno, Osaka, Japan, May 17, 1959; s. Takazumi and Akiko (Kimura) S.; m. Sayuri Matsubara, June 13, 1996. MD, Shiga U. Med. Sci., 1985. Resident Shiga U. Med. Sci., Otsu, 1985-86; staff Shiga Seijinbyo Hosp., Moriyama, 1986-89, Amagasaki Hosp., 1989-91, Shiga U. Med. Sci., Otsu, 1991-96; staff surgeon Tenri Hosp., Tenri, 1996—. Home: Sashiyanagi 318-1 505, Tenri 632-0093, Japan Office: Tenri Hosp Dept Cardio Vasc Surg, 200 Mishima, Tenri 632-8552, Japan

SUGIURA, NOBUAKI, electronic and mechanical engineer; b. Toyota, Aichi, Japan, Feb. 1, 1956; s. Rokurou and Sakiyo (Suzuki) S.; m. Hisae Ueno, Oct. 6, 1984; children: Hidenobu, Akihiro, Munehisa. BS, Nagoya (Japan) Inst. Tech., 1979; MS, Nagoya U., 1981, PhD, 1996. Staff mem. Nippon Tel. & Telegraph Corp. Elec. Comm. Labs., Tokyo, 1981-88; sr. rsch. engr. Nippon Tel. & Telegraph Corp. Applied Electronics Labs., Tokyo, 1989-93; sr. rsch. engr. supr. Nippon Tel. & Telegraph Network Svc. Systems Labs., Tokyo, 1994—. Mem. IEEE, The Inst. of Electronics, Info. and Comm. Engrs., Internat. Microelectronics and Packaging Soc., Internat. Electrotech. Commn. (tech. com. 48, subcom. 48D). Avocations: jogging, soccer. Home: 1458-9 Kitairiso, Sayama 350-1315, Japan Office: Aich U of Tech 50-2 Manori, Nishihazama-cho Gamagorishi, Aichi 443-0047, Japan

SUGIYAMA, KAZUNORI, music producer; b. Tokyo, Aug. 18, 1950; came to U.S., 1976; s. Hiroshi and Michiko (Maeda) S.; m. Emi Fukui, Aug. 11, 1981. BS, Waseda U., 1974, postgrad., 1974-75; MA, Boston U., 1977. Jr. adminstrv. officer Japanese Mission to UN, N.Y.C., 1978-88; rep. N.Y. Toshiba EMI Records, Jazz Div., Tokyo, 1990-93; rep. U.S., exec. producer DIW/Avant Records, Tokyo, 1991—; exec. producer Tzadik Records, N.Y.C., 1995—; mem. adv. bd. The New Grove Dictionary of Jazz, 1997—; corr. Jazz Life, Tokyo, 1980-88; columnist OCS News, N.Y.C., 1982-90; columnist Asahi Newspaper, 1998-99. Rec. engr. (album) Bud and Bird/Gil Evans, 1988 (Grammy); prodr. V/Ralph Peterson, 1990 (Jazz Album of Yr.); co-prodr. The Nurturer/Geri Allen, 1991 (2d pl. Jazz Album of Yr.), Big Band & Quartet/David Murray, 1992 (Best Prodn. Jazz Album of Yr.), Picasso/David Murray, 1993 (3d pl. Jazz Album of Yr.); translator Autobiography of Miles Davis, 1989. Mem. NARAS, USTA. Avocations: tennis, travel. Office: 93 Mercer St Apt 3W New York NY 10012-4452

SUGIYAMA, SATORU, cardiologist, researcher; b. Nagoya, Aichi, Japan, Nov. 23, 1947; s. Sachio and Haruko (Chimura) S.; m. Masako Wakiya, June 4, 1978; children: Yuichiro, Mariko. MD, U. Nagoya, Japan, 1972, PhD, 1976. Diplomate Ednl. Coun. for Fgn. Med. Grads. Asst. prof. U. Nagoya, Japan, 1977-82; dir. dept. gerontology The Chunichi Hosp., Japan, 1982-83; chief instr. Inst. Applied Biochemistry, Gifu, 1984-93, dir. dept. biomed. chemistry, 1994-99; dir. Sugiyama (Japan) Med. Clin., 1999—. Co-author: The Cardiomyopathic Heart, 1994, Lipid Chromatographic Analysis, 1994; contbr. over 200 articles to profl. jours. including New England Jour. of Medicine, Am. Heart Jour., Jour. of Electrocardiology; contbr. chpts. to more than 2 dozen sci. books and presented 16 papers to internat. sci. symposia. Recipient Med. Excellence award, 1997. Fellow Am. Coll. Chest Physicians; mem. Am. Heart Assn. (mem. coun.), Am. Thoracic Soc., N.Y. Acad. Scis. Home: 205 Ohshima-cho 2-97-1, Chikusa Nagoya 464-0833, Japan Office: Ikeshita 1-11-10, Chikusa Nagoya 464-0677, Japan

SUGIYAMA, TAKASHI, electric company executive; b. Osaka, Kansai, Japan, Aug. 10, 1924; s. Koichi and Mitoko (Ohtsubo) S.; m. Shizuko Sakata, May 5, 1953; children: Tadashi, Noriko. Grad., U. of Tokyo, 1947, ED, 1970. Sr. v.p., advisor Yokogawa Elec. Co., Tokyo, 1978-83; chief exec. officer GE-Yokogawa Med. Sys., 1982-91; advisor Yokogawa Rsch. Inst., Tokyo. Chmn. Project Hope Japan. Recipient Award of Dir. of Sci. and Tech. Agy., 1971; honored with Purple Ribbon medal Japanese Govt., 1975. Fellow IEEE (life); mem. Soc. Instrument and Control Engrs. (hon.). Avocations: golf, swimming, gardening. Home: 3-19-4 Sakai, Musashinoshi 180, Japan Office: Yokogawa Electric Corp, 2-9-32 Nakacho, Musashinoshi 180-0022, Japan

SUGIYAMA, TOKU MARY, retired school administrator; b. Sacramento, Sept. 6, 1921; d. Sakae and Kuniko (Kosaka) Koda; m. Yone J. Sugiyama, Apr. 5, 1952; m. George Y. Morishita, Mar. 23, 1942; (dec. Mar. 1949); children: Maeona, Carolyn, George. Jr. cert. U. Calif.-Berkeley, 1941; BA, Towson State U., 1980, MA, 1984. Tchr., Poston Relocation Ctr., Ariz., 1941-44; purchasing agt. U.S. Dept. Def., Tokyo Ordnance Depot, 1952-56; instr. Ikebana Sogetsu Sch., Tokyo, 1956-67, exec. dir. Sogetsu USA, sch. Japanese flower arrangement, 1967-93, ret., 1993. Author: Sogetsu Ikebana Notes, 1997. Recipient Mohan Sho, Sogetsu Sch., 1960, Sofu Sho, 1967, Flower Arranger of Yr. award Nat. Council State Garden Clubs, 1979, 1st Sofu Teshigahara Meml. award, 1991. Mem. Md. Fedn. Garden Clubs, Ikebana Internat. (charter), Balt.-Kawasaki Sister City Cultural Com. Home: 959 Ellendale Dr Baltimore MD 21286-1511

SUGIYAMA, TORU TOM, automotive executive; b. Hiratsuka, Japan, Aug. 15, 1956; s. Tadatsugu and Hatsue S. MBA, Calif. State U., 1994, MS in Acctg., 1997; MS in Engring., Oakland U., 1997. Mgr. Denny's Japan Co., Ltd., Tokyo, 1979-80; indsl. engr. NHk Spring Co., Ltd., Yokohama, Japan, 1980-82, acct. mgr., 1983-89; mgr. NHK Internat. Corp., Southfield, Mich., 1992-96, corp. sec., treas., 1996—; lectr. Oakland U., Rochester, Mich., 1998—. Avocations: golf, tennis, swimming. Office: NHK Internat Corp 300 Galleria Office 314 Southfield MI 48034

SUGUMARAN, SAMUEL THOMSON, physician; b. Thanjavur, Tamil Nadu, India, July 4, 1950; s. Samuelraj Vadivel Thomas Davidson and Viola Thangabai Agnes; m. Prema Gethsi Dawson, Feb. 16, 1979; children: Dagny, Gracia. BSc in Zoology, Madurai U., Palayamkottai, India, 1970; MB, BChir, Madras U., Thanjavur, India, 1978, diploma in psychol. medicine, 1983. Sr. ho. surgeon Thanjavur Med. Coll., 1978-80; med. officer Damien Found., Thiruchirapalli, India, 1980, Ch. of South India Mission Hosp., Erode, 1981, Emmaus-Suise Ales, Kumbakonam, India, 1983-88, 89-97, German Leprosy Relief Assn., Madras, India, 1988-89; specialist Schieffelin

Leprosy Rsch. and Tng. Ctr., Karigiri, India, 1997—. Mem. N.Y. Acad. Scis. Avocations: reading science and literature, listening to pop music. Home and Office: Schieffelin Leprosy Rsch, Karigiri, Vellore 632 106, India

SUH, CHANG-JIN, health economist, researcher; b. Seoul, Korea, Aug. 8, 1958; s. Jeong-Hoon and Sung-Ran (Kim) S.; Yeesook Kim Suh, June 9, 1984; children: Suah, Sueon. BA, Hanyang U., Seoul, Korea, 1982, MA, 1984; PhD, Vanderbilt U., Nashville, 1994. Sr. rschr. Korea Inst. Health Svcs. Mgmt., Seoul, Korea, 1994-96, rsch. fellow, 1997—; temporary adv. WHO, Beijing, China, 1994; lectr. Hanyang Grad. Sch., Seoul, Korea, 1994-95, Chung-Ang Grad. Sch., Seoul, Korea, 1997; cons. prof. Cath. Grad. Sch. Health Mgmt. and Policy, Seoul, Korea, 1998—. Author: Impacts of WTO on Health Care Market in Korea, 1996, Designing a Demonstration Program to Implement DRG-based Payment System in Korea, 1997, Health Insurance and Resource Constraints in Developing Countries, 1997, Impacts of OECD Membership on Korean Health and Health Care Industry, 1998, Evaluation of 1997 Demonstration Program of DRG-based Payment System in Korea, 1998. Mem. Korean Health Econ. Assn. (exec. com. 1998—, edtl. bd. 1998—, editor 2000—), Internat. Health Econ. Assn. Fax: 82-02-824-1765. E-mail: cjsuh@Khidi.or.kr. Office: Korea Health Industry Devel Inst, 57-1 Nolyanjin-Dong, Dongjae-Gu Seoul 156-050, Korea

SUH, DONG JIN, chemical engineer, researcher; b. Taegu, Korea, June 12, 1958; s. Dal-Soo Suh and Choon-sun Paek; m. Sun-Ae Kim, May 4, 1986; children: Ka-Eun, Ye-Rin. BS, Seoul Nat. U., 1982; MS, Korea Advanced Inst. Sci. & Tech., Seoul, 1984; PhD, Korea Advanced Inst. Sci. & Tech., Taejon, 1991. Rsch. engr. Korea Inst. Sci. and Tech., Seoul, 1984-91, sr. rsch. engr., 1991-98, prin. rsch. engr., 1998—; vis. rsch. scholar Caregie Mellon U., Pitts., 1992-93; rsch. fellow U. Tokyo, 1995-96. Contbr. articles to profl. jours.; spkr. in field. Mem. AIChE, Korean Inst. Chem. Engrs. Avocations: listening to classic music, climbing. Office: Korea Inst Sci & Tech, PO Box 131 Cheongryang, 136-791 Seoul Korea

SUH, HAK SOO, agronomist; b. Changyoung, Kyongnam, Republic of Korea, Sept. 8, 1941; s. Im Sul Suh and Sun Ak Gam; m. Ha Ja Shin; children: Eun Jung, Eun Young, Eun Sil, Dong Hyuk. BS in Agronomy, Seoul Nat. U., 1970, MS in Plant Breeding, 1973, PhD, 1977. From asst. prof. to prof. Yeungnam U., Kyongsan, Korea, 1977-85; prof. Yeungnam U., Kyongsan, 1985—, asst. dean coll. agr. animal sci., 1989-91; dean Coll. Agr. Animal Sci., Kyongsan, 1991-93; rsch. advisory Yongnam Crop Experimental Sta., Milyang, Korea, 1983-93, Crop Aexperimental Sta. RDA, Suwon, Korea, 1998—; vis. prof. Nat. Inst. Genetics, Mishima, Japan, 1994-95. Author: Biological Statistics, 1987, Agricultural Genetics, 1994; inventor in field. Postdoc. fellow Internat. Rice Rsch. Inst., 1981-83; recipeint Korean Soc. Crop Sci. award, 1988, Best Rsch. award Korean Fedn. Sci. Tech., 1992, Korean Breeding Soc. award, 1993. Home: 38-6 Sangdong Suseong-gu, Taegu Republic of Korea Office: Dept Bioresources, Yeungnam U Kyongsan, Kyongsan Republic of Korea

SUH, HWAL, medical materials educator; b. Seoul, May 29, 1953; s. Young-mo and Yoon-ok (Cheong) S.; m. Kyunghee Lee, May 6, 1978; children: Hyun, Lin. DDS, Yonsei U., Seoul, 1978, MSD, 1984; PhD, Osaka (Japan) U., 1992. Lic. dentist, Korea; diplomate Implant Dentistry, Korea. Attending rschr. Columbia Inst. Materials Sci. and Tech., N.Y.C., 1985-87; spl. rschr. Seoul Nat. U., 1992-95; assoc. prof. Yonsei U., Seoul, 1995—, chair rsch. ctr. for tissue regeneration, 2000—; vice chair Yonsei Med. Tech. and Quality Evaluation Ctr., Seoul, 1997-99, chair, 1999—; exec. dir. Korean Health and Med. Tech. Planning and Evaluation Bd., 1995-96; team leader Nat. Project Health & Medicine, Tissue Engring. Team, 1999—; mem. internat. com. Internat. Conf. on Cellular Engring., 1999—. Author: (books) Introduction of Biomaterials, 1992, Tissue Engineering for Artificial Organs, 1998; patentee in field. Capt. Korean Army, 1978-81. Recipient Sci. Presentation award Internat. Implant Symposium, 1990, Madison Bioengring. award Korean Soc. for Med. and Biol. Engring., 1997. Mem. Internat. Std. Orgn. (chair tech. com. 150 Korean sect. 1997—), Korean Inst. Sci. and Tech. (affiliated prin. rschr. 1998—), Korean Soc. for Biomaterials (exec. dir. 1996—, chair com. sci. affair 1999—). Office: Yonsei U Coll Medicine, 134 Shinchon-dong, Seoul Korea

SUH, JUNG HO, engineering educator; b. Pusan, South Korea, Apr. 17, 1965; s. Sam Joon Suh and Sun Yeo Tak; m. Bok Soon Shin, Jan. 27, 1991; children: Young Jin. BS, Pusan Nat. U., 1988, Ms, 1990, PhD, 1997. Rschr. Suhrytung Material R&D Ltd., Yang San, 1990-95; prof. Ulsan (Republic of Korea) Coll., 1998—. Avocation: collecting. E-mail: josuh@mail.ulsan-c.ac.kr. Office: Ulsan Coll Dept Indsl Chem, Mugeodong Namgu, Ulsan 680-749, Republic of Korea

SUH, SOONG-HYUCK, chemical engineer, educator, researcher; b. Kwangju, Korea, Jan. 11, 1956; s. Soo-Hyun and Kwi-Soon (Hong) S.; m. So-Eun Kim, Nov. 7, 1981; children: Jin-Hyang, Jin-Wook. BS, Chonnam Nat. U., Kwangju, Korea, 1980, MS, 1982; MA, U. Mo., Rolla, 1985, PhD, 1986. Rsch. assoc. U. Lethbridge, Can., 1987-88, U. Minn., Mpls., 1988-90; sr. rschr. Korea Atomic Energy Rsch. Inst., Taejon, 1990-91; prof. Keimyung U., Taegu, 1991—; vis. rsch. scholar Minn. Supercomputer Inst., Mpls., 1988-90, Imperial Coll., London, 1997, 98, U. Dublin, 1998, Tohoku U., Sendai, Japan, 1998, Cornell U., Ithaca, N.Y., 1995, IBM Almaden Rsch. Ctr., San Jose, Calif., 1993. Contbr. articles to profl. jours. including Jour. Chem. Physics, Molecular Physics, and Korean Jour. Chem. Engring.; mem. editl. bd. Molecular Simulation, 1999—. Recipient Bisa Rsch. award Keimyung U., 1994, Shimkang Rsch. award Korean Inst. Chem. Engring., 1995. Presbyterian. Home: Hyundai Apt 105-902, Sangin-dong Dalseo-ku, Taegu 704-370, Korea Office: Keimyung U Dept Chem Engr, Shindang-dong Dalseo-ku, Taegu 704-701, Korea

SUH, SUK-HWAN, manufacturing engineer, educator; b. Changsung, South Korea, May 24, 1952; s. Jung-Ok Suh and Bu-Gui Bai; m. Eunsook Choi; children: Jinny, Sunny. BS, Korea U., 1976; MS, KAIST, Seoul, Korea, 1978; PhD, Ohio State U., 1986. Dep. mgr. Hyundai Motor Co., Seoul, 1978-81; instr., rschr. Ohio State U., Columbus, 1982-86; rschr. U. Mich., Ann Arbor, 1986-87; from asst. prof. to prof. Postech, Pohang, Korea, 1987—. Mem. IEEE, ASME, Soc. Mech. Engring. Home: Gyosu Apt 4-1404 Jigok-dong, 790-390 Pohang Kyungbuk, Republic of Korea Office: Postech Dept Indsl Engring, San 31 Hyoja-dong, 790-784 Pohang Kyungbuk, Republic of Korea

SUH, YOO-HUN, molecular neurobiology educator, administrator; b. Kimchun, Kyungbook, South Korea, Feb. 8, 1948; s. Kyung-Duk and Yoon-Soo (Kim) S.; m. Sook-Hee Lee, Apr. 6, 1974; children: Won-Hyuk, Jee-Kyung. MD, Seoul Nat. U. Med. Coll., 1973, PhD, 1980. Intern Seoul Nat. U. Hosp., 1973-74, resident, 1974-76; rschr. Army Def. Devel. Inst., Seoul, 1976-79; instr. pharmacology Seoul Nat. U. Med. Coll., 1979-82, asst. prof., 1983-84; vis. prof. Cornell Med. Coll., N.Y.C., 1984-86; assoc. prof. Seoul Nat. U. Med. Coll., 1986-92; exch. prof. Ctr. for Molecular Biology U. Heidelberg, Germany, 1989-90; chmn. dept. molecular biology Neurosci. Rsch. Ctr., Seoul, 1990—; prof. Seoul Nat. U. Med. Coll., 1992—; dean Kangwon Nat. U. Coll. Medicine, 1997—; dir. Biomed. Brain Rsch. Ctr., NIH, 1998—; vis. prof. Imperial Coll., 1996—. Author: Neurotransmitter, 1990, Mystery of the Brain, 1994, Pharmacology, 1994, Amazing Brain, 1995, Know the Brain and Use the Brain, 1996, The Brain and Longevity, 1996, The Brain Scape, 1997, The Brain World, 1997; editor: Jour. Neurochemistry, 1994, Jour. Molecular Neurosci., Jour. Neurosci. Rsch., 1998. Maj. Korean Army, 1976. Recipient Excellent Achievement award Korean Engring. and Sci. Found., 1991, Med. Achievement award Yuhan Pharm. Co., 1992, Drug Devel. award Ministry Sci. and Tech., 1992, Kwang Hae prize, 1995, Sejony Cultural award, 1997, Korean Publ. award, 1997. Mem. Am. Soc. Neurosci., Internat. Soc. Neurchemistry, Internat. Brain Rsch. Orgn., Asian Pacific Soc. Neurochemistry (pres. 1996—), Korean Brain Soc. (pres. 1998—). Achievements include patents in field. Office: Seoul Nat U Coll Med Dept Pharm, 28 Yongondong Chongno-ku, Seoul 110-799, Republic of Korea

SUHADI, F.X. BUDHIANTO, pathologist; b. Surabaya, E. Java, Indonesia, June 26, 1939; s. Suhadi and Liana; m. Bernadette Widyastuti, Feb. 27, 1967; children: Stefanus Sofyan, Johannes Adrian. MD, Airlangga U., Indonesia, 1965. cons. pvt. labs. Surabaya, Indonesia, 1965—, Siloam Gleneagles Hosp., Jakarta, Indonesia, 1995—. Staff of dept. of clin. pathology Airlangga U. Sch. of Medicine, Surabaya, Indonesia, 1965-85; head of dept. clin. pathology Airlangga U. Sch. of Medicine, Surabaya, 1985-95; coord. Nat. Quality Assurance Program Dept. of Health, Jakarta, 1978-90; sec. Indonesian Assn. for Clin. Chemistry, Jakarta, 1980-86; chmn. Indonesian Assn. for Pathology, Surabaya, 1985-95, Indonesian Assn. for Clin. Chemistry, Surabaya, 1985-95, Quality Control Implementation & Data Processing Unit, Jakarta, 1985-87; mem. Cen. Health Lab./DOH, Jakarta, 1987-95; com. mem. Surabaya Assn. for Diabetes, 1986—; dep. chmn. Diabetes and Nutrition Ctr., Surabaya, 1987—; chmn. Subteam for Processing and Evaluation of DATA/DOH, Jakarta, 1987-95; cons. pvt. labs. Surabaya, 1965—, Siloam Gleneagles Hosp., Jakarta, 1995—. Recipient 30 yrs.-Gold medallion Pres. Rep. of Indonesia, Jakarta, 1997. Fellow Nat. Acad. Clin. Biochemistry, Am. Soc. Clin. Pathologists; mem. Internat. Soc. Hematology, Am. Assn. Clin. Chemistry, Clin. Lab. mgmt. Assn., Asian Pacific Fedn. of Clin. Biochemistry (v.p. 1991-94), Indonesian Med. Assn., Indonesian Assn. for Pathology, Indonesian Endocrin Soc., others. Avocations: jogging, swimming, fitness, tennis. Home: Tomang Raya, J1 Kosambi No 1, 11430 Jakarta Indonesia Office: Dept Clin Path, Siloam Gleneagles Hosp, 15811 Tangerang Indonesia

SUHARA, TOSHIAKI, electronics engineering educator; b. Yuasa, Wakayama, Japan, Nov. 13, 1950; s. Susumu Suhara and Yoshiko Suhara; m. Masako Nomura, Apr. 29, 1980; 2 children. B Engring., Osaka (Japan) U., 1973, M Engring., 1975, D Engring., 1978. Rsch. assoc. Osaka U., 1978-90, asst. prof., 1990-91, assoc. prof., 1991—; guest rsch. scientist Tech. Rsch. Ctr. Finland, Helsinki, 1980; guest rsch. fellow Glasgow (Scotland) U., 1986-87; guest prof. Chalmers (Sweden) U. Tech. Author: Optical Integrated Circuits, 1987, Quantum Electronics, 1994, Fundamentals of Semiconductor Lasers, 1998, Optical-Wave Engineering, 1998; contbr. articles to profl. publs. Recipient Paper award Laser Soc. Japan, 1990, Sci. prize IBM Japan, 1995. Mem. IEEE (sr.), Inst. Electronics, Info. and Commn. Engrs. (Young Engr. award 1980, Paper award 1978, 87, 96), Japan Soc. Applied Physics. Achievements include invention of integrated-optic disc pickup head. E-mail: suhara@ele.eng.osaka-u.ac.jp. Fax: 81-6-6879-7793. Home: M-905 29 Shin-Ashiya-Kami, Suita 565-0804, Japan Office: Osaka U Dept Electronics, 2-1 Yamada-Oka, Suita 565-0871, Japan

SUHARTA, HERLIYANI, physics engineer, materials engineer; b. Surabaya, East Java, Indonesia, Aug. 8, 1952; d. Wijaya Lie and Rr. Soetarti (R.M. Hardjopraseto) Herli; m. Nyoman Suharta, Mar. 24, 1979; children: N. Vita Anggreini, M. Yuda Mahatma, K. Yoga Mahatma. Physics engr., Inst. Tech., Surabaya, 1978; MPh in Phys. Metallurgy, Sheffield U., 1987; postgrad., Hertfordshire U. Project leader tech. transfer project Indonesia & Germany Coop., Jakarta, 1989-93; project liaison coop. devel. of solar dehydration Indonesia & Japan Coop., Jakarta, 1993-97; sr. rschr. BPP Teknologi (AhPMdy), Jakarta, 1979—; group leader thermal & mech. energy divsn. BBP Teknologi, Jakarta, 1987-96; rschr. in solar thermal energy tech. and its field testing; mem. team formulation Indsl. Dept., Jakarta, 1989-90; lectr. in field of solar thermal pump and solar oven; presenter confs.; prin. investigator Ctr. for Field Rsch. at EarthWatch, Mass., 1995-99, NRC RUT II, 1994-97, RUSNAS Fuel Cell, 1997. Contbr. articles to profl. pubs. Candidate UNESCO Sci. prize, Bangkok, 1995. Mem. Am. Solar Energy Soc., Internat. Solar Energy Soc. (survey contact 1991), Indonesia Soc. Engrs. and Technicians (bd. dirs. 1992—), World Sustainable Energy Coalition, Indonesia Physics Soc., Himpunan Ahli Perpindahan Kalor. Roman Catholic. Avocations: travel, swimming. E-mail: herli@mimo.bppt.go.id. Home: Perum Puspiptek Blok 4 H3, Serpong, W Java Tangerang 15314, Indonesia Office: UPT LSDE BPP Teknologi, PUSPIPTEK, Serpong Tangerang 15314, Indonesia

SUHR, PAUL AUGUSTINE, lawyer; b. Sonwunri, Chonbuk, Korea, Jan. 20, 1940; came to U.S. 1966; s. Chong-ju and Oksuk (Pang) So; m. Angeline M. Kang Suhr; 1 child, Christopher. BA, Campbell Coll., Buies Creek, N.C., 1968; MA, U. N.C., Greensboro, 1970; MS, U. N.C., Chapel Hill, 1975; JD, N.C. Cen. U., 1988. Bar: N.C. 1989, U.S. Dist. Ct. (ea. and mid. dist.) N.C. 1989, U.S. Ct. Appeals D.C. 1990, U.S. Ct. Appeals (4th cir.) 1992. Bibliographer N.C. Div. of State Libr., Raleigh, 1975-78; dir. Pender County Pub. Libr., Burgaw, N.C., 1978-80; libr. Tob. Lit. Svc., N.C. State U., Raleigh, 1980-85; pvt. practice law Law Offices of Paul A. Suhr, PLLC, Raleigh and Fayetteville, N.C., 1989—. Author short stories and novelettes various lit. mags., jours. and revs. Mem. Human Resources and Human Rels. Adv. Commn., City of Raleigh, 1990-95, chmn., 1994-95. N.C. Humanities Com. grantee, 1979-80; recipient Presdl. award President of Korea, 1992. Mem. ABA, ATLA, AILA, N.C. Bar Assn., N.C. Trial Lawyers Assn., Wake County Bar Assn. (bd. dirs. 1996-97), D.C. Bar Assn. Democrat. Roman Catholic. Avocations: gardening, fishing, writing. Office: 1110 Navaho Dr Ste 502 Raleigh NC 27609-7322

SUIFFET, NORMA JULIETA, language professional; b. Montevideo, Uruguay, Sept. 2, 1933; d. Raul Abelardo and Julia Juana (Bianchi) S.; m. Rubinstein Moreira, Dec. 21, 1970; 1 child, Igor Augusto. Diplomate U. Salamanca, 1954. dir. Casa del Poeta Latinoamericano Montevideo, Uruguay, Capitulo Montevideo Acad. Iberoamericana de Poesia; mem. Grupo de Los 9, Aude, Grupo Erato, Montevideo. Author: Tres Poetas Uruguayos, 1955, Garcilaso de la Vega, 1958, Rafael Barret, 1958, Analisis Estilistico de Tabaré, 1960, Las Voces Incandescentes, 1965, Los Cuentos de Alda, 1967, Tres Poetas de Cerro Largo, 1978, El poema de la Cruz, 1981, Horizontes Intactos, 1985, Los Juegos del Tiempo, 1991, Horizontes de Luz, 1993, Jose Enrique Rodo, 1995; editor: La Urpila. Recipient Lit. prize Ministry Edn. and Culture, 1958, 67, 70, 94, Lit. prize Inttendencia Mcpl. de Montevideo, 1960, 78, others. Avocations: gobelino tapestry, filatelia. Home: 1225 Rambla Republica Argentina, 11000 Montevideo Uruguay

SUIN DE BOUTEMARD, BERNHARD, religion educator, clergyman, publisher; b. Berlin-Dahlem, Feb. 10, 1930; s. Guenther and Louise (Loeffler) S. de B.; m. Annemargret Pfautsch (dec. 1986); children: Christoph-Amand, Cordula, Dorothee. Grad. in theology, 1958; diploma in pedagogy, U. Osnabrück, Germany, 1973; D Social Sci., U. Bielefeld, Germany, 1974. Ordained to ministry Luth. Ch., 1958. Min. Luth. Ch., Niedersachsen, Germany, 1958-75, Evang. Ch. Hessen-Nassau, Germany, 1975—; prof. social sci. Protestant Coll. Social Work, Darmstadt, Germany, 1975-95, rector, 1981-86, dean, 1993-95; prof. social work and religious edn. Theol. U. Friedensau, Sachsen-Anhalt, Germany, 1995—; mem. synod Luth. Ch. Niedersachsen, 1965-76, Protestant Chs. Germany, 1966-72, Evang. Ch. Hessen-Nassau, 1986-92; dir. children's village Terre des Hommes, Libreville, Gabon and Biafra, Africa, 1969; pub. Suin-Buchverlag, Lindenfels, Germany, 1975—; cons. marriage and family guidance, mediation, Darmstadt, 1993-98; pres. Soc. for Projektdidaktik of Bundesrepublik Deutschland, 1995—; cons. Agenda 21 town Lindenfels, 1997—. Author: Schule, Projektunterricht, 1975; editor: The Alternative Free Neighborhood Universities Catalogue, 1977-83. Fellow German Soc. for Sociology. Fax: 06255 2657. Home: Kappstrasse 29, D-64678 Lindenfels Germany Office: Theol U Friedensau, Dept Social Work, D-39291 Friedensau Germany

SUISSA, ELI, Israeli government official; b. Casablanca, Morocco, 1956; arrived in Israeli, 1956; married; 4 children. Mem. Shas Party; asst. to the min. Israeli Ministry of Interior, 1984-86, Jerusalem dist. commr., 1986-96, min. interior, 1996—; min. nat. infrastructure Tel Aviv. With Israeli Army Golani Brigade, officer in army chaplaincy. Office: Min Nat Infrastructure, Derekh Petah Tikva 48, Kiryat Ben-Gurion Tel Aviv 61171, Israel*

SUITNER, OTMAR, conductor; b. Innsbruck, Austria, May 16, 1922; s. Karl and Maria (Rizzi) S.; grad. Hochschule Musik, Mozarteum, Salzburg, 1943; m. Marita Wilckens, Feb. 14, 1948. Condr., Tiroler Landestheater, Innsbruck, 1943-44; condr., pianist, 1945-52; mus. dir., Remscheid, W.Ger., 1952-57; gen. mus. dir. Pfalzorch., Ludwigshafen, 1957-60, Staatsoper, Dresden, E.Ger., 1960-64, Staatsoper, Berlin, E.Ger., 1964-89; hon. condr. NHK Symphony Orch., Tokyo, 1973-88; prof. Hochschule Musik, Vienna, 1977-88; guest condr. in San Francisco, Japan, Europe, Teatro Colon, Buenos Aires, also festivals in Bayreuth, Prague and Vienna; rec. artist EMI, Teldee, Deutsche Grammophon, Eterna, Denon records. Decorated commendatore Gregorius Order. Roman Catholic.

SUJBERT, LASZLO, pharmacist, pharmaceutical and medical educator; b. Ujpest, Hungary, Sept. 19, 1933; s. Pal and Anna (Boza) S.; m. Rozalia Miczan, Apr. 20, 1963; 1 child, Laszlo. Grad. in Pharmacy, Budapest (Hungary) Sch. Medicine, 1957, PharmD, 1961; PhD, Hungarian Acad. Sci., 1987; DrMed habil, Semmelweis U. Medicine, Hungary, 1995. Asst. Budapest Sch. Medicine, 1957-70; 1st asst. Semmelweis U. Medicine, 1970-88, assoc. prof., 1988-97, prof., 1997—; vice dir. Inst. Hygiene, 1995-97; invited mem. subcom. on water supply and canalization Hungarian Acad. Sci., 1986, mem., 1995—. Mem. editorial bd. Népegészégügy. Mem. Magyar Hig. Tars, Magyar Gyogysz. Tars, N.Y. Acad. Scis. Office: Semmelweis U Inst Hygn, Nagyvaradter 4, 1089 Budapest Hungary

SUJUDI, Indonesian government official; b. Bogor, West Java, Indonesia, Sept. 9, 1930. Student, Stanford U., 1956-57, U. Indonesia, 1959, 72. Officer Bank Rakyat Indonesia; head microbiology dept. U. Indonesia, 1966-79, asst. dean III dept. medicine, 1974-77, asst. rector I, 1977-81, head rsch. bd., 1983-86, rector, 1986-93; min. health Govt. of Indonesia, Jakarta, 1993—. Office: U Indonesia Dept Health J1 HR Rasuna Sd, Blok X-5 Kav 4-9, Jakarta 12950, Indonesia*

SUKARNOPUTRI, MEGAWATI, government official; b. Jogjakarta, Indonesia, Jan. 23, 1947; married; three children. Grad., Padjajaran U., Indonesia. Leader Indonesian Democratic Party of Struggle. Avocation: flower-arranging. E-mail: pd@insprint.net.id. Office: Indonesian Dem Pty Struggle, Jalan Lenteng Agng Nomor 99, Jakarta Indonesia*

SUKERNIK, REM, geneticist, researcher; b. Kiev, Ukraine, Dec. 9, 1934; s. Israil and Khasya (Gordon) S.; m. Lydia Raicher, Nov. 4, 1958; 1 child, Mikhail. MD, Med. Inst., Barnaul, Russia, 1960; degree in internal medicine, Med. Inst., Novosibirsk, Russia, 1965; degree in genetics, D in Biol. Sci., Russian Acad. Sci., Novosibirsk, Russia, 1987. Gen. practice physician Dist. Hosp., Turochak Village, Russia, 1960-62; asst. prof., rschr. Med. Inst., Novosibirsk, 1962-65; head lab. human genetics Inst. Clin. and Exptl. Medicine, Novosibirsk, 1965-90; head lab. human molecular genetics Inst. Cytology & Genetics, Russian Acad. Scis., Novosibirsk, 1990—. Contbr. articles to profl. jours., chpts. to books. Lt. Soviet Army Res., 1960-90. Mem. Vavilov Soc. Geneticists. Avocations: hunting, fishing, social activities. Home: Zolotodolinskaya 33-4, 630090 Novosibirsk Russia Office: Rus Acad Sci Inst Cytol/Gen, 10 Prospect akadem Lavrenty, 630090 Novosibirsk Russia

SUKHANOV, VICTOR ALEXANDROVICH, biochemist, researcher; b. Krasnojarsk, Siberia, Russia, Oct. 24, 1947; s. Alexander Dmitrijevich and Natalija Ignatievna (Goncharova) S.; m. Tatijana Jurievna Fedorova, Dec. 4, 1973; 1 child, Ekaterina. First class honour degree, State Acad. Fine Chem. Tech., Moscow, 1973, PhD, 1976; D in Biol. Scis., Russian Acad. Scis., Moscow, 1997. Cert. engr.-chemist-technologist, sr. rschr. Rschr. Rsch. Inst. for Biol. Testing of Chem. Compounds, Moscow, 1977-80, head biochem. lab., 1980-85, head exptl. molecular pathology dept., 1982-85; head cell mediators lab. Rsch. Ctr. for Molecular Diagnostic and Treatment, Moscow, 1986-95; sr. rschr. Russian State Med. U., Moscow, 1995-97; leading rschr. Inst. Chem. Physics, Russian Acad. Scis., Moscow, 1997—; head metabolic portraitition & control lab. Ctr. Theoretical Problems Phys. Chem. Pharmacology, Moscow, 2000—; dir. for sci. Simka Internat., Moscow, 1993-97, gen. dir. Biotech-Sapris Ltd., Moscow, 1997—. Author: (with R. Zhdanov) Paramagnetic Models of Biologically Active Compounds, 1981, Spin Labels in Biology and Medicine, 1984, Bioactive Spin Labels, 1992; contbr. articles to profl. jours. Mem. Internat. Orgn. Folk Art, Internat. Soc. Oncodevelopmental Biology and Medicine, Russian Biochem. Soc., N.Y. Acad. Sci. Avocations: bicycling, walking, water skiing, chess. Home: Nakhimovsky prosp 7/1-98, 113149 Moscow Russia Office: Inst Chem Physics, Kosyhina 4, 117977 Moscow Russia

SUKHORUKOV, ANATOLY NIKOLAEVICH, mechanician, researcher; b. Moscow, Feb. 4, 1944; s. Nikolay Romanovich and Nataliya L'vovna (Yagudina) S.; m. Nina Borisovna Sotina, Mar. 27, 1965; 2 children. MS, Moscow State U., 1966, PhD in Mechanics, 1981. Asst. prof. Inst. for Machine-Tool Engring., Moscow, 1966-68, 71-74; rschr. Inst. of Mechanics, Moscow State U., 1974-85, sr. rschr., 1985—; lectr. Moscow State U., 1974—. Author articles and inventions. Chmn. trade union com. Inst. of Mechanics, Moscow U., 1993-95. Recipient P.L. Kapitsa medal for sci. discovery, Moscow, 1996; Russian Fund Fundamental Investigation grantee, 1997. Mem. Moscow U. Scientist Club, N.Y. Acad. Scis. Avocations: tennis, music, travel. Office: Moscow State U Inst Mechs, Mitchurinsky Pr 1, 119899 Moscow Russia

SUKHORUKOV, VICTOR LEV, physicist; b. Novosibirsk, Russia, May 30, 1951. D of Physics, Rostov State U., Rostov-na-Donu, Russia, 1973, PhD in Solid State Physics, 1977, Hab. Dr. in Solid State Physics, 1985, prof. physics, 1988. Cert. prof. physics. Lectr physics Rostov State U., Rostov-na-Donu, 1977-81, docent of physics chair, 1981-86, prof. of physics chair, 1986-88, chief math. chair, 1988—; habilitated dr. bd. advisor Rostov State U., Rostov-na-Donu, 1989—. Contbr. papers to sci. jours. Avocations: climbing, building. Office: Rostov State U TC, N Opolcheniya sq 2, Rostov-na-Donu 344038, Russia

SUKHOV, DMITRY LVOVICH, engineering executive, consultant; b. Moscow, Apr. 23, 1967; s. Lev Vasiljevich and Galina Alexeevna S.; m. Tatjana Andreevna Samozvon, July 28, 1989; 1 child, Ekaterina. Engr., Moscow Aviation Inst., 1990, MS, 1999; Bus. Adminstr., TACIS Levi-Lovanium, Brussels, 1999. Engr. Scientific CAD Ctr., Moscow, 1990-93; CAD engr. Aerosoft Ltd., Moscow, 1993-94; mgr. JV "SiV", Moscow and Pretoria, South Africa, 1994-96; mktg. mgr. "Vympel" Design Bur., Moscow, 1996-99; head comml. dept. JSC "Russian Sugar", Moscow, 1999—; weapons sys. cons. "Vympel" Design Bur., Moscow, 1998—. Contbr. articles to profl. jours. Youth leader Komsomol, Moscow, 1984-90. Mem. TACIS Assn. Avocation: basketball. Home: 5-1-162 Sratovskaya str, Moscow 109518, Russia

SUKMONO, SIGIT, geology and geophysics educator; b. Banyuwangi, East Java, Indonesia, July 15, 1964; s. Suryamin and Dal (Karsini) S.; m. Riauli Sukmono, June 14, 1989; children: Krisna Adhi, Widhia Kurnia. IR, Inst. Tech. Bandung, Indonesia, 1987, DSc, 1997; MSc, Asian Inst. Tech., Bangkok, 1992. Lectr. Inst. Tech Bandung, 1988—, acad. sec. geophysics program, 1992—; cons. Pt. CPI, Jakarta, Indonesia, 1988—, Pertamina, Jakarta, 1993—, Pt.PTK, Jakarta, 1997—. Contbr. articles to profl. jours. Recipient Internat. Publ. awards Ministry of Edn. and Culture, Indonesia, 1998; named Best Indonesia Rschr., Toray Sci. Found., 1998. Mem. AAAS, Seismol. Soc. Am., Am. Geophys. Union. Home: Jl Lamongan 7, Bandung West Java 40291, Indonesia Office: ITB Dept Geophys Engring, Jl Ganesha 10, Bandung West Java 40132, Indonesia

SUKPANICHNANT, SANYA, pathologist, consultant; b. Bangkok, Oct. 23, 1961; s. Chaiyong and Chaweewan S.; m. Bussara Jennapar, Aug. 5, 1986; 1 child, Puris. MD, Mahidol U., Bangkok, 1986, grad. diploma in clin. sci., 1987. Diplomate Thai Bd. Anatomic Pathology. Resident in anatomical pathology Siriraj Hosp. Mahidol U., Bangkok, 1986-89, instr. pathology, 1989-94, asst. prof. pathology, 1994-97, assoc. prof. pathology, 1997—, dir. hematopathology divsn., 1993—; rsch. fellow in hematopathology Vanderbilt U., Nashville, 1990-93. Contbr. articles to profl. jours. Recipient Stowell-Orbison award cert. of merit USCAP, 1993. Mem. Royal Coll. Pathologists Thailand, U.s. and Canadian Acad. Pathology (Stowell-Orbison award cert. of merit 1993), European Assn. Haematopathology. Avocations: reading, listening to and singing music, traveling. Office: Siriraj Hosp Dept Path, 2 Pranok Rd Bangkok No 1, Bangkok 10700, Thailand Address: Dept Path Mahidol U, Siriraj Hosp Fac Med, Bangkok 10700, Thailand

SUKUL, LOMASH, power generation equipment and design manufacturing executive; b. Kanpur, India, Aug. 15, 1953; s. Rama Kant and Kamala Shukla; m. Veena Shukla, May 4, 1978; children: Priyank, Manali. B of Engring., MACT, Bhopal, India, 1975, M of Tech., 1981; MBA, Bhopal U., 1986. Design engr. Bharat Heavy Elecs., Bhopal, 1976-81, sr. design engr., 1981-85, dep. mgr., 1985-88, mgr., 1988-92, sr. mgr., 1992-95, dep. gen. mgr., 1995-2000, sr. dep. gen. mgr., 2000—; designer, cons. Bharat Heavy Elecs. Author: Value Management, 1997, Business Process Reengineering, 1998; contbr. articles to profl. jours. Fellow Instn. Engrs. India; mem. All India Mgmt. Assn., Tribology Soc. India (life). Avocations: painting, vocal

music, writing stories, cooking, sports. Home: 26 Challet A-Sector, 462021 Bhopal India Office: Bharat Heavy Elecs, Hydrogenerator Engring, 462021 Bhopal India

SUKUMARAN, GOPU KUMAR, electrochemist; b. Coimbatore, Tamilnadu, India, June 30, 1959; s. K.l and Leela (Parameshwaran Pillai) S.; m. Jalaja Kumari Vijayan,ly 11, 1988; 1 child, Deepika. BSc in Chemistry, U. Calicut, India, 1978; MSC in Chemistry, U. Delhi, India, 1981; PhD in Chemistry, U. Dibrugart, Assam, India, 1986. Postgrad. tchr. chemistry Kendriya Vidyalage, Assam, 1981-82; jr. rsch. fellow Regional Rsch. Lab. Ctrl. Electrochem. Rsch. Inst., Jorhat, Assam, 1982-84, sr. rsch. fellow, 1984-87; rsch. asoc. Ctrl. Electrochem. Rsch. Inst., Karaikudi, Tamilnadu, India, 1987-88, scientist B, 1988-93, scientist C, 1993—; chmn. PhD adjuction com. S.V. U., Tirupati, India, 1994. Contbr. articles to profl. jours.; patentee in field. Recipient sr. DAAD fellowship, Germany, 1997, DAAD fellowship, Germany, 1999; grantee Coun. Sci. and Indsl. Rsch. India and Dept. Sci. and Tech., India, 1986, UNESCO and Com. on Sci. and Tech. in Developing Countries, 1987, Coun. Sci. and Indsl. Rsch., New Delhi and TamilNadu State Coun. Sci. and Tech., Madras, 1994, Coun. Sci. and Indsl. Rsch., New Delhi, 1997, Indo-French Ctr. for Promotion Advanced Sci. Rsch., New Delhi, 1998, DAAD, 1999. Fellow Soc. Advancement Electrochem. Sci. and Tech. (life); mem. Indian Chem. Soc., Swedeshi Sci. Movement (life). Hindu. Avocations: stamp collecting, aquariums, pets. Home: J-41 CECRI, Karaikudi, Tamilnadu 630006, India Office: Ctrl Electrochem Rsch Inst, Karaikudi, Tamilnadu 630 006, India

SUKUN, KAMIL MEHMET, publisher; b. Istanbul, Turkey, July 18, 1948; s. Ismail Nacil and Fatma Ayten (Akar) S.; m. Perran Oztunc, Feb. 13, 1981; 1 child, Mehmet. BA in Fgn. Trade, Ankara Acad. Econ., 1974. Free-lance photographer, 1971-74, Veb Ofset Ileri Matbaacilik A.S., Istanbul; photog. cons. Ilbas Pub. Co., Istanbul, 1974; art dir., editor-in-chief Adam mag., Istanbul, 1975; editor-in-chief EV (decorating) mag., 1976-83, Vizon (fashions) mag., 1977-83; founder pres. Profesyonel Ltd., Istanbul, 1983—; publisher Who's Who in Turkey-Gunumuz Turkiy esinde Kim Kimdir, 1984—. Photo exhbns. in Turkey, Yugoslavia, Belgium; producer Vizon Show Internat., Istanbul, 1979—, Sofia & Cairo, 1982; editor: The Fifty Residences of Turkey, 1981; author Adam mag. cover photograph selected and pub. in Photographis, 1978 (Zurich). Cons. Istanbul C. of C., 1986—. Lt. Turkish Navy, 1979-80. Recipient Diploma award 7th Internat. Biennial Exhbn. Photography, 1971, Turkish Found. Naval Forces Supporting Found. award, 1984, Turkish Found. Against Cancer cert., 1984, Ankara Coll. cert., 1988, Turkish Kidney Found. & Yesilkoy Lions Club cert., 1989, Lions Dist. 118T cert., 1990, Istanbul-Masiak Rotary Club cert., 1994, UNICEF Nat. Com. award, 1984, 85, UNICEF Presdl. award, 1985, Turkish Ministry Health award, 1985. Mem. Istanbul Journalists Assn., Royal Photog. Soc. Gt. Brit., IADP, Ciragan Group (gen. sec. 1991), Internat. Computer Users' Fellowship of Rotary Istanbul Hi-Fi Club (pres. 1995), Inernat. Advertisers Assn., Lions. Home: Nisantasi 5/7 Rumeli C, Istanbul 80220, Turkey

SULAIMAN, AFSAR MOHAMMED, environmentalist, consultant; b. Begusarai, Bihar, India, Dec. 12, 1956; s. Mohammed and Waliya (Sultana) S.; m. Farhana Afsar, Nov. 10, 1977; children: Saima, Ahmad, Athar, Omar. BSc with honors, AMU, Aligarh, India, 1977, MSc, 1979, MPhil, 1981, PhD, 1983. Qualified environ. profl. Inst. Profl. Environ. Practice USA, 1996; registerednenviron. mgr. NREP, USA, 1999. Jr./sr. rsch. fellow Aligarh Muslim U., 1980-83; rsch. scientist Indian Inst. Tech., Bombay, 1983-84; supr. Ctrl. Lab. Saudi Kuwaiti Cemer, Dammam, Saudi Arabia, 1984-88; lectr. Zakir Hussain Coll. Engring. and Tech., Aligarh, 1988-89; facility mgr., tech. advisor Nat. Environ. Preservation Co. (BeeA'h), Jubail, Saudi Arabia, 1989-96; dep. gen. mgr., tech. mgr. Saudi Co. for Environ. Work, Al-Khobar, Saudi Arabia, 1996-97; mgr. environ. affairs United Med. Group, Riyadh, 1998-99; mgr. environ. divsn. AHG, Jeddah, Saudi Arabia, 1999—. Named Internat. Man of the Yr. IBC, 1998-99; recipient 20th Century Achievement award Am. Biog. Inst., Washington, 1999; jr. rsch. fellow Dept. Environment New Delhi, 1980, sr. rsch. fellow, 1981. Mem. Air and Waste Mgmt. Assn., Internat. Solid Waste Assn. (Denmark). Avocations: reading, writing, traveling, photography. Office: United Medical Group, PO Box 93692, Riyadh 11683, Saudi Arabia Address: Abdullah Hashim Indus Gases & Equipment Co, PO Box 44, Jeddah 21411, Kingdom of Saudi Arabia

SULAIMAN, SALLEHUDIN BIN, medical entomology educator; b. Kuala Lumpur, Malaysia, July 21, 1947; s. Sulaiman Bin Osman and Zaitun Binti Gantam; m. Salma Binti Mohd Ali, Nov. 1979; children: Shazli, Khairunnisa, Hanisah. BSc, Bandung Inst. Tech., 1973, MSc in Entomology, 1974; MSc in Parasitology, Liverpool Sch. Tropical Med., 1975, PhD in Med. Entomology, 1982. Lectr. U. Kebangsaan Malaysia, Kuala Lumpur, 1975-83; assoc. prof. dept. parasitology and med. entomology U. Kebangsaan Malaysia Faculty Medicine, Kuala Lumpur, 1983-94, prof. med. entomology dept. parasitology and med. entomology, 1994; prof. med. entomology dept. biomed. sci. U. Kebangsaan Malaysia-Faculty Allied Health Scis., Kuala Lumpur, 1996, dep. dean. Author: Medical Entomology in Malay, 1990, Insecticide and Control of Vectors of Diseases' in Malay, 1995; contbr. articles to profl. jours. Commonwealth scholar Assn. Commonwealth Univ., 1978; grantee in field. Fellow Royal Entomological Soc. London; mem. Am. Mosquito Control Assn., Am. Soc. Tropical Medicine and Hygiene, Malaysian Soc. Parasitology and Tropical Medicine, Malaysian Soc. Health, Malaysian Soc. Applied Biology, Japanese Soc. Med. Entomology and Zoology, Soc. Vector Ecology. Islam. Avocations: reading, swimming. Home: Lot 11551 Taman Mesra, Batu 13 Jalan Ceras, Kajang 43000, Malaysia Office: Fac Allied Health Scis, Jln Raja Muda Abdul Aziz, Kuala Lumpur 50300, Malaysia

SÜLE, TAMÁS GYULA, physician, researcher; b. Budapest, Hungary, Mar. 6, 1937; s. Gábor and Katalin (Gömöri) S.; m. Magdolna J.C.D. Etter, Dec. 15, 1963; children: Agnes J.C.D., Katalin. MD, Med. U., Pécs, Hungary, 1962. Asst. II Clinic for Internal Medicine, Pécs, 1967-75, asst. prof., 1975-86; head physician Cardiology Rehab. Sta. County Hosp., Pécs, 1986—; mem. com. med. ethics Hungarian Chamber Physicians, Budapest, 1990—; pres. com. med. ethics Baranya County Chamber Physicians, Budapest, 1990—. Author: Medical History of Baranya County and Pécs As It Is Represented by Medals, 1989, Medical Medals of Pécs of the Past 150 Years, 1996; contbr. articles to profl. jours. Mem. Hungarian Numismatic Soc., Budapest, 1990—, Hungarian Assn. Collectors Medals, Budapest, 1980—; found. mem. St. Eligius Soc., Pécs, 1992. 1st lt. Hungarian Armed Forces Med. Regiment, 1962. Recipient award for excellent work Min. Edn., Budapest, 1979, Széchényi Ferenc award Hungarian Assn. Collectors of Medals, 1995. Fellow Transdanubian Soc. Internal Physicians (sec. gen. 1991—, Itinerary Congress award 1995), Hungarian Assn. Med. History (leading bd. dirs. 1985—), Hungarian Soc. Cardiology. Avocations: medical numismatology, medical history. Home: Maria U 25, 7621 Pécs Hungary Office: Cardiology Sta County Hosp, Angyan J U 2, 7635 Pécs Hungary

SULEIMAN, BASHIR MOHAMED, physicist, educator, researcher; b. Benghazi, Libya, Jan. 22, 1955; s. Mohamed Suleiman Hamad and Zainab Suleiman Saeed; m. Madiha Ali El Fagai; children: Abdel-Wahab, Abdel-Aziz. BSc, U. Calif., Santa Barbara, 1979; MSc, U. Garyounis, Benghazi, 1983; PhD in Material Physics, U. Gothenburg, Sweden, 1994. Asst. lectr. U. Garyounis, Benghazi, 1983-87, lectr., 1987-89; rschr. U. Gothenburg, 1989-94, sr. rschr., 1994-95, asst. prof., 1995-97, assoc. prof. physics, 1998—. Contbr. articles to profl. jours. Min. of Edn. scholar, 1975-79, U. Garyouris scholar, 1983. Mem. Union of Swedish Univ. Tchrs. Avocations: running, badminton, tennis, football. Home: PO Box 29128, Sharjah United Arab Emirates Office: Univ of Sharjah, PO Box 27272, Sharjah United Arab Emirates

SULEIMAN, MOHAMMED-SAADEH, physiologist; b. Damascus, Syria, Mar. 22, 1953; arrived in U.K., 1988; s. Ahmed and Mariam S.; m. Helen Mary Skatun; children: Amir, Tariq, Miriam. Diploma in sci., Bir Ziet U., 1973; BSc, Am. U., Beirut, 1975; PhD, Essex U., Colchester, U.K., 1980. From asst. prof. to assoc. prof. An-Najah U., Palestine, 1980-88; from rsch. assoc., fellow to sr. lectr. Bristol (Eng.) U., 1988-2000, reader, 2000—; pres. asst. An-Najah U., Nablus, 1985-86, dean rsch. and grad. studies, 1986-88. Contbr. articles to profl. jours. Exec. com. Bristol Heart Inst., 1995—. U.K. Med. Rsch. Founds. grantee, 1990-99; Fulbright fellow, 1988. Mem. The Biochem. Soc., The Physiol. Soc., British Soc. for Cardiovascular Rsch. (exec. com. 1998—). E-mail: m.s.suleiman@bris.ac.uk. Office: Bristol Heart Inst, Bristol Royal Infirmary, BS2 8HW Bristol England

SULEMAN, AMER, internist, cardiologist; b. Lahore, Punjab, Pakistan, Mar. 21, 1967; s. Sheikh Mohammad and Nusrat Suleman; m. Mahvash Amer, May 31, 1999. BA, Punjab U., Lahore, 1986, BS, 1986; MB, BChir, King Edward Med. Coll., Lahore, 1990. Diplomate Am. Bd. Internal Medicine. House officer internal medicine and cardiology Mayo Hosp., Lahore, 1991; clin. instr. dept. pathology SUNY, Buffalo, 1991-92, clin. instr. dept. medicine, 1992-95; fellow dept. cardiology Alton Ochsner Med. Ctr., New Orleans, 1995-97; staff cons. internal medicine and cardiology Denton (Tex.) Regional Med. Ctr., 1997—. CME editor: Internet Text Book of Medicine; mem. editl. adv. bd.: Internat. Jour. Family Practice; contbr. articles to profl. jours. Founding mem. Muscular Dystrophy Welfare Assn., Pakistan, 1986-87, Art and Cultural Orgn. Pakistan, 1985; incharge youth wing Internat. Red Cross, Punjab, 1986; vol. physician AlShifa Clinic, Bedford, Tex., 1999—. Recipient Sci. Poster Recognition awards So. Med. Assn., 1999; Merit scholar Govt. Pakistan, 1982; Rsch. grantee KOS Pharm., 2000. Fellow Royal Soc. Medicine, Am. Inst. Stress; mem. ACP, Am. Soc. Hypertension. Avocations: poetry, literature, community service, playing chess. Fax: (940) 381-2613. E-mail: asuleman@pol.net. Home: # 3324 1408 Teasley Ln Apt 3324 Denton TX 76205-5257 Office: Heart Ctr North Tex Ste 16 4405 I 35 N Denton TX 76207

SULEMAN, SYED MOHAMMAD, postmaster general; b. Karoli, Rajisthan, India, Oct. 3, 1942; arrived in Pakistan, 1948; s. Syed Masood and Maimoona Begum Ahmad; m. Begum Fehmida Azmat; children: Noah Syed, Maria Syed, Musfira Syed. BSc, D. J. Coll., Karachi, Pakistan, 1960; MA, U. Karachi, Pakistan, 1970. PMG/gen. mgr. Postal Life Ins., Karachi, 1986-89; dep. dir. gen. Pakistan Post Office, Islamabad, 1989-92; gen. mgr. Spl. Svcs., Islamabad, 1992-96; dir. Postal Staff Coll., Islamabad, 1996; postmaster gen. Pakistan Post Office, 1997—. Editor: Tarikhul Islam. Mem. D.J. Coll. Old Boys' Assn., Japan Internat. Cooperation Agy. Alumni Assn. (exec. mem.). Avocations: hockey, chess, music, sight seeing, reading informative books. Home: House #17 St 32 Sector F7/1, Islamabad Pakistan Office: Postmaster Gen, Islamabad 44000, Pakistan

SULESKI, RONALD, publishing executive; b. Erie, Pa., June 11, 1942; children: Kiyomi, Valerie. BA cum laude, U. Pitts., 1966; MA, U. Mich., 1968, PhD, 1974. Prof. history U. Tex., Arlington, 1974-79; mng. dir. Pergamon Press, Tokyo, 1983-88, Harpercollins, Tokyo, 1988-91; pres. Commerce Clearing House Japan, Tokyo, 1991-93; provost Huron U., Tokyo, 1994—. Author: Affective Expressions in Japanese, 1982, The Red Spears, 1985, The Modernization of Manchuria, 1994. Pres. Asiatic Soc. Japan, Tokyo, 1987-94. With U.S. Army, 1960-63. Avocation: reading. Home: 4-22-8 Inogashira, Mitaka Tokyo 181, Japan

SULIAMAN, FAWZI A., pediatrician, immunologist; b. Nablus, Jordan, May 18, 1949; came to U.S., 1976; s. Ahmad S. and Izziyeh (Dawood) S.; m. Sondus Dawood; children: Ehab, Sana, Mansa, Amal. MBChB, Baghdad (Iraq) Med. Sch., 1974. Diplomate Am. Bd. Pediat., Am. Bd. Allergy and Immunology. Pediat. resident Christ Hosp., Oaklawn, Ill., 1977-80; pediatrician Evergreen Park, Ill., 1980-83, Aramco, Dhahran, Saudi Arabia, 1983-85; allergy-immunology fellow Creighton U., Omaha, 1985-87; allergist-immunologist Aramco, Dhahran, 1987—. Contbr. articles to profl. jours., chpt. to book. Fellow Am. Acad. Pediat., Am. Coll. Allergy, Asthma and Imunology. Office: Dhahran Health Ctr, PO Box 76, Aramco Dhahran Saudi Arabia

SULIMANI, RIAD ABBAS, endocrinologist; b. Mecca, Saudi Arabia, Feb. 2, 1954; s. Abbas Abdullah and Salha Saleh (Abu Al-Naja) S.; m. Soha Abdulhameed Al-Khateeb; children: Ramy, Roba, Rawan, Mohammed, Shahd. BS, King Saud U., Saudi Arabia, 1977. Demonstrator King Saud Med. Coll., Riyadh, Saudi Arabia, 1978; resident Dalhousie U., Halifax, Can., 1979-83; asst. prof. medicine King Saud U., 1986-89, assoc. prof., 1989-99, prof. medicine, 1999—; chief dept. internal medicine King Saud U., 1989-93, Security Forces Hosp., 1993—. Contbr. articles to profl. jours. Endocrinology fellow McGill U., Montreal, Can., 1983-85. Mem. Saudi Diabetes Assn. Avocation: reading. Home: PO Box 2861, Riyadh 11461, Saudi Arabia Office: King Saud U, Dept Internal Medicine, Riyadh Saudi Arabia

SULKES, AARON, physician; b. Mexico, Jan. 26, 1948; arrived in Israel, 1977; s. Szepsel Sulkes and Tatiana Litvak Schein; m. Jaqueline Beatriz Eksztejn, June 22, 1978; 1 child, Shabtiel. MD, Nat. U. of Mex., Mexico City, 1971. Resident Nat. Inst. of Nutrition, Mexico City, 1972-74, staff physician, 1976-77; fellow MD Anderson Cancer Ctr., Houston, 1974-76; staff physician Hadassah Med. Orgn., Jerusalem, 1977-90, Rabin Med. Ctr., Petach Tikva, Israel, 1990—; acting head dept. of oncology Hadassah Med. Orgn., Jerusalem, 1989; head Inst. of Oncology Rabin Med. Ctr., 1990—. Editl. bd. Israel Jour. of Med. Scis., European Cancer News. Mem. Israel Soc. for Clin. Oncology and Radiotherapy, Am. Soc. of Clin. Oncology, European Soc. of Med. Oncology. Jewish. Avocation: photography. Office: Inst Oncology Rabin Med Ctr, Beilinson Campus, 49100 Petach Tikva Israel

SULKOWSKI, HUBERTUS VICTOR, lawyer; b. Csikszereda, Hungary, Apr. 1, 1943; arrived in U.S., 1957; s. Alfred Viktor and Ingeborg (Brumowski) S.; m. Christine Barbara Joosten, July 26, 1969 (div. Jan. 1994); children: Nikolas Alexander, Erica Elizabeth, Christopher Victor. BA, Trinity Coll., Hartford, Conn., 1966; JD, Boston Coll., 1969. Bar: N.Y., U.S. Supreme Ct.; avocat Paris Bar. Assoc. Jackson Nash, N.Y.C., 1969-71, Mendes & Mount, N.Y.C., 1971-72; ptnr. Donovan Leisure, N.Y.C., 1984-87; assoc. Shearman & Sterling, N.Y.C., 1972-84, ptnr., 1987—, founder, mng. ptnr. Budapest office, 1991-97, mng. ptnr. Paris office, 1992-97. Mem. The Univ. Club of N.Y.C., Cercle d l'Union Interaliée (Paris), Hungarian Knights of Malta. Roman Catholic. Office: Shearman & Sterling, 114 Avenue des Champs-Elysees, 75008 Paris France

SULLEBARGER, JOHN THOMPSON, physician, educator; b. Plainfield, N.J., May 2, 1957; s. Franklyn Jackson and Joanne Abbott (Aspinall) S.; m. Lorrie Jeanne Miller, June 14, 1980; children: Jeffrey Franklyn, Melissa Jeanne. Student, U. Mainz, 1977; AB, Dartmouth Coll., 1979; MD, Johns Hopkins U., 1983. Intern U. Rochester, N.Y., 1983-84; resident in medicine U. Rochester, 1984-86, fellow in cardiology, 1986-89, from sr. instr. to asst. prof., 1989-92; asst. prof. U. South Fla., Tampa, 1992-96, assoc. prof., 1997-99; dir. CCU Tampa Gen. Hosp., 1997—; dir. interventional cardiology Fla. Cardiovascular Inst., 1999—; dir. Cardiac Catheterization Lab., James Haley VA Hosp., Tampa, 1992-99; dir. interventional cardiology U. South Fla., 1994-99; attending physician Strong Meml. Hosp., Rochester, 1989-92. Author: (with others) book chapters; contbr. articles to profl. jours. Chmn. Bd. Christian Svc., 1st Bapt. Ch., Rochester, 1991-92. Fellow ACP, 1992, Am. Coll. of Cardiology, 1991, Counc. on Clin. Cardiology of Am. Heart Assn., 1991, N.Y. Cardiological Soc., 1992. Fellow Soc. Cardiac Angiography and Interventions. Avocations: music. Office: 508 S Habana Ave Ste 340 Tampa FL 33609-4191

SULLIVAN, BARRY, law educator; b. Newburyport, Mass., Jan. 11, 1949; s. George Arnold and Dorothy Bennett (Furbush) S.; m. Winnifred Mary Fallers, June 14, 1975; children: George Arnold, Lloyd Ashton. AB cum laude, Middlebury Coll., 1970; JD, U. Chgo., 1974. Bar: Mass. 1975, Ill. 1975, Va. 1995, U.S. Dist. Ct. (no. dist.) Ill. 1976, U.S. Ct. Appeals (7th cir.) 1976, U.S. Ct. Appeals (10th cir.) 1977, U.S. Supreme Ct. 1978, U.S. Ct. Appeals (11th cir.) 1986, U.S. Ct. Appeals (5th and 9th cirs.) 1987, U.S. Ct. Appeals (fed. cir.) 1993, U.S. Ct. Appeals (D.C. cir.) 1994, U.S. Ct. Appeals (4th cir.) 1997. Law clk. to judge John Minor Wisdom U.S. Ct. Appeals (5th cir.), New Orleans, 1974-75; assoc. Jenner & Block, Chgo., 1975-80; asst. to solicitor gen. of U.S. U.S. Dept. of Justice, Washington, 1980-81; ptnr. Jenner & Block, Chgo., 1981-94; prof. law Washington and Lee U., Lexington, Va., 1994—, dean, 1994-99, v.p., 1998-99; Fulbright prof. U. Warsaw, Poland, 2000—; spl. asst. atty. gen. State of Ill., 1989-90; lectr. in law Loyola U., Chgo., 1978-79; adj. prof. law Northwestern U., Chgo., 1990-92, 93-94, vis. prof., 1992-93; Jessica Swift Meml. lectr. in constnl. law Middlebury Coll., 1991. Assoc. editor U. Chgo. Law Rev., 1973-74; contbr. articles to profl. jours. Trustee Cath. Theol. Union at Chgo., 1993—; mem. vis. com. U. Chgo. Divinity Sch., 1987—. Yeats Soc. scholar, 1968; Woodrow Wilson fellow, Woodrow Wilson Found., 1970. Mem. ABA (chmn. coord. com. on AIDS 1988-94, mem. standing com. on amicus curiae briefs 1990-97, mem. coun. of sect. of individual rights and responsibilities 1993-98, mem. sect. of legal edn. com. on law sch. adminstrn. 1994-98, chair sect. legal edn. com. on professionalism 1999-2000), Va. Bar Assn., Va. State Bar (chair sect. on edn. of lawyers 1998-99), Bar Assn. 7th Fed. Cir. (vice chmn. adminstrv. justice com. 1985-86), Am. Law Inst., Lawyers Club Chgo., Phi Beta Kappa. Democrat. Roman Catholic. Home: PO Box 372 Fairfield VA 24435-0372 Office: Washington and Lee U Sch Law Sydney Lewis Hall Lexington VA 24450

SULLIVAN, CHARLES R., engineering educator; b. Princeton, N.J., Dec. 1, 1964; s. Roger D. and Margaret Peplow Sullivan. BS with highest honors, Princeton U., 1987; PhD, U. Calif., Berkeley, 1996. Design and devel. engr. Lutron Electronics, Coopersburg, Pa., 1987-90; asst. prof. engring. Dartmouth Coll., Hanover, N.H., 1996—; cons. Volterra, Fremont, Calif. Assoc. editor IEEE Transactions on Power Electronics; contbr. articles to profl. jours. Recipient Ross N. Tucker Electronic Materials award Am. Inst. Mining, Metallurgical & PEtroleum Engrs., 1995, Career award NSF, 1999. Mem. IEEE, Am. Soc. for Engring. Edn. Achievements include patent for circuit and method for improved dimming of gas discharge lamps. Avocations: bicycling, music. E-mail: charles.r.sullivan@dartmouth.edu. Fax: 603-646-3856. Home: 7 S Park St Hanover NH 03755-2119

SULLIVAN, DEBRA KAE, elementary education educator; b. Iowa City, Iowa, Jan. 27, 1962; d. Raymond Francis and Jo Adele (Meyers) S. Cert. specialization in mgmt. devel., Am. Hotel & Motel Assn., 1985; BA, U. Iowa, 1989. Nev. tchg. lic. grades K-8. Reservations mgr. Holiday Inn, Iowa City, 1981-83; reservations clk. Holiday Inn Mart Plaza, Chgo., 1983-85; substitute tchr. grades K-12 Iowa City Sch. Dist., 1989-90; tchr. K-8 Clark County Sch. Dist., Las Vegas, Nev., 1990—; tchr. cons. Geog. Alliance in Nev., Las Vegas, 1994—; mem. geography curriculum task force Clark County Sch. Dist., Las Vegas, 1995; mem. geography task force State of Nev., Reno, 1996, 99, mem. social studies task force, 1996; mem. Advanced Geography Inst., Geog. Alliance in Nev., Moscow, Russia, 1996, summer geography workshop Nat. Geographic Soc., Washington, 1998; chairperson 2d ann. GeoFest '96, Las Vegas. Host family Home Away From Home Program, U. Nev., Las Vegas, 1994-97. Mem. NEA, Nat. Coun. Social Studies, Nat. Coun. for Geog. Edn., People to People Internat., Social Studies Coun. Nev. (Elem. Sch. Social Studies Tchr. of the Yr. 1995-96), Am. Mensa. Avocations: reading, walking, collecting geography related objects, current events, cats. Home: 5709 Berwick Falls Ln Las Vegas NV 89149-5157 Office: Quannah McCall Elem Sch 800 E Carey Ave North Las Vegas NV 89030-5557

SULLIVAN, DOROTHY RONA, state official; b. Boston, Jan. 7, 1941; d. Lewis Robert and Dorothy (Hopkins) S.; B.A., Boston U., 1963; M.Ed., State Coll. Boston, 1966; C.A.G.S., Boston U., 1972; postgrad. Northeastern U., 1970-71, Boston Coll., 1974-78, U. Mass., 1980. Rsch. asst. Boston Lying-in Hosp., 1963-64; employment counselor Mass. Div. Employment Security, Boston, 1964-66, sr. employment counselor, 1966-67, prin. employment counselor, 1967-70, employment office mgr., 1970-75, supr., 1975-78, chief rsch. dept., 1978-88, dir. def. employment analysis, 1985-87; chief rsch. dept. Mass. Divsn. Employment and Tng., 1989-98, chief rsch. dept., 1998—. Supr. community counselor interns and rehab. adminstrn. interns Northeastern U. Grad. Sch. Edn., 1968-74; supr. public adminstrn. interns Suffolk U., 1976; supr. econ. interns Boston U., 1979, Regis Coll., 1984, U. Mass.-Boston, 1998; presenter in field. Recorder Gov.'s Conf. on Rehab., 1970, mem. Gov.'s Commn. Employment of Handicapped, 1972-78, Pres.'s Com. Employment of Handicapped, 1975-78; exec. bd. Greater Boston council Camp Fire Girls, 1971-73; R.S.V.P. adv. bd. Boston Commn. Affairs of the Elderly, 1977-78; mem. adv. com. equal employment opportunity practices Dept. Personnel Adminstrn., 1984-85; mem. adv. group Mass. Occupl. Info. Coordinating Com., 1991-98. Recipient Recognition award Nat. Occupl. Info. Coordinating Com., 1994. Mem. ACA (recorder), AACD, ASPA, APGA (nat. recorder conf. 1968), Nat. Career Devel. Assn., Nat. Rehab. Assn. (Mass. sec. 1971-72, exec. bd. 1972-74, v.p. 1974-75, pres. 1976-77), Am. Fedn. State, County and Mcpl. Employees (exec. bd. local 164 1972-73, 74-76), Am. Acad. Polit. and Social Sci., Rockport Art Assn. (patron), Am. Econ. Assn., Am. Bus. Women's Assn. (del. nat. conv. 1980, 83, pres. Boston chpt. 1982, Woman of Yr., Boston chpt. 1983), Am. Soc. Pub. Adminstrn. (life, region I-II liaison, sect. women in pub. adminstrn. 1988-90, Mass. chtp. coun. mem., officer, treas. 1997, sec. 1998, v.p. 1998—, pres. elect 1999, pres. 2000, nat coun. mem. campaign for internat. rels.), Boston Ctr. for Internat. Visitors, Charitable Irish Soc., Chatham Swim Club. Author: Boston Employment Service Guide, 1969, Careers and Training in the Allied Health Field, 1989, Higher Skills, Higher Wages and Higher Achievement, 1997, Career Families and Career Paths, 1997, Massachusetts Cities and Towns, 1978-82, Outplacement Program, 1993, Presentation and Performance Portfolio, 1998; editor Mass. Trends, 1978-82; contbr. articles to profl. jours. Home: 33 Morey Rd Roslindale MA 02131-1037 also: Eldredge Sq Chatham MA 02633 Office: 19 Staniford St Charles F Hurley Bldg Boston MA 02114

SULLIVAN, EDWARD LAWRENCE, lawyer; b. Boston, May 8, 1955; s. Edward L. and Dorothy L. (Gregory) S.; m. Susan M. Griffin, Dec. 2, 1983; children: Erica A., Brittany M. BA in Polit. Sci., St. Anselm Coll., 1977; JD, St. Louis U., 1980. Bar: Mo. 1980, U.S. Dist. Ct. (we. dist.) Mo. 1980, Mass. 1981, Ill. 1981, D.C. 1986. Atty., Ill. divsn. Peabody Coal Co., Fairview Heights, 1980-85; legis. counsel Peabody Holding Co., Washington, 1985-88; dir., legal and pub. affairs, western divsn. Peabody Coal Co., Flagstaff, Ariz., 1988-90; sr. counsel Peabody Holding Co., St. Louis, 1990-94; gen. counsel Powder River Coal Co., Gillette, Wyo., 1994; gen. counsel, western region Peabody Holding Co., St. Louis, 1995—. Industry rep. royalty policy com. U.S. Dept. Interior, Washington, 1995—. Mem. Bar Assn. Met. St. Louis. Office: Peabody Holding Co Inc 701 Market St Ste 700 Saint Louis MO 63101-1895

SULLIVAN, EDWIN PERCY ALBERT, retired chemistry and physics educator, researcher; b. Sydney, NSW, Australia, Feb. 16, 1924; s. Percy Albert and Annie (King) S.; m. Eva Weiszberger, Feb. 16, 1962; children: Gregory, Kim Anne. BSc with honors, U. Sydney, 1950, MSc, 1951, PhD, 1954. Cert. in phys. chemistry and physics. Lectr. chemistry U. Malaya, Singapore, 1954-56; tchg. fellow U. Sydney, 1956-57; lectr. chemistry U. NSW, 1958-61, U. Sydney, 1961-65; sr. lectr. spectroscopy Victoria U. Wellington, New Zealand, 1965-67, reader spectroscopy, 1967-69; lectr. physics NSW Inst. Tech., Sydney, 1969-70, sr. lectr. physics, 1971-84; vis. prof. McGill U., Can., 1974-75, 82, Mich. State U., 1978; asst. sec., editor Sci. Soc. Malaya, Singapore, 1954-56; coord. Australian and New Zealand Assn. for Advancement of Sci., 1962, Electronics for Scientists in New Zealand, Victoria U., Wellington, 1967; hon. assoc. physics U. Tech., Sydney, 1984—. Contbr. rsch. articles to profl. jours. Life mem. U. Sydney Union, U. Tech. Sydney Union. Pvt. Australian Army, Australian Imperial Forces, 1942-45. Rsch. grantee New Zealand Rsch. Grant Com., 1967, 68, Australian Rsch. Grant Com., 1981, 82, 83. Mem. Australian Inst. Physics, N.Y. Acad. Sci., Returned Servicemen's League of Australia. Avocations: scientific research, camping, sailing, boating. Home: 29 Howard St Randwick, 2031 Sydney NSW, Australia

SULLIVAN, GARY, psychiatrist; b. Manchester, England, Mar. 2, 1955; s. Arnold and Marion (Evans) S. BS, U. Wales, Cardiff, 1976, MB BCh, 1982, MS in Psychiatry, 1995, MBA, 1999. Med. practitioner Mid Glamorgan, Wales, 1983-90; psychiatrist Gwent (Wales) Health, 1990-93, South Wales Tng. Scheme, 1993-97. Contbr. rsch. papers to profl. pubs. Mem. Royal Coll. Psychiatrists (chmn. collegiate trainees com. 1996), Royal Coll. Gen. Practitioners. Office: Dept Psyc Med St Tydfil's Hosp, Merthyr Tydfil, Cardiff CF47 0SJ, Wales

SULLIVAN, IAN DOUGLAS, pediatric cardiologist; b. New Zealand, Feb. 8, 1952. BMedSc, Otago U., New Zealand, 1974, MBChB, 1976. Cons. Great Ormond Street Hosp. Children, London, 1989—. Contbr. articles to profl. jours. Fellow Royal Australasian Coll. Physicians. Office: Great Ormond Street Hosp Children, WCIN 3JH London England

SULLIVAN, JAMES F., physicist, educator; b. Cin., Mar. 7, 1943; s. James E. and Alma L. (Lienesch) S.; m. Sylvia J. Kasselmann, Aug. 16, 1969; 1

child, Robert L. BS, Xavier U., 1965, MS, 1969. Instr. physics Brebeuf Prep. Sch., Indpls., 1965-67; instr. physics OMI Coll. Applied Sci., U. Cin., 1968-71, asst. prof. physics, 1971-77, assoc. prof. physics, 1977-88, prof. physics, 1988—; summer faculty researcher Solar Energy Rsch. Inst., Golden, Colo., 1980; mem. high sch. evaluation team N. Ctrl. Assn., Cin., 1983, 84, 85. Author: Technical Physics, 1988; Co-author: Laboratory Manual for General Physics, 1973, 83, 90, 92, Physics for Technology Laboratory Manual, 1995, 97. Organizer of events St. Xavier H.S. Alumni, Cin., 1983—; vol. examiner Am. Radio Relay League for U.S. Fed. Comm. Commn., Newington, Conn., 1984—; judge physics category Ohio State Sci. Fair, Delaware, Ohio, 1986—; chief negotiator faculty and librs. U. Cin., 1995. Named Faculty Mem. of Yr., Gamma Alpha chpt. Tau Alpha Phi, 1983. Fellow Ohio Acad. Sci.; mem. AAUP (v.p. U. Cin. chpt. 1994-96), Am. Assn. Physics Tchrs. (founder, past pres., assoc. sec. So. Ohio sect. 1993—, com. on instrnl. media 1994-98, chief organizer and presenter Fundamentals of Radio workshop Toronto 1985, Columbus, Ohio 1986, Bozeman, Mont. 1987, Orono, Maine 1992, Boise, Idaho 1993, South Bend, Ind. 1994, College Park, Md. 1996, Denver, 1997), Ohio Valley Amateur Radio Assn. (pres. 1997—), Am. Soc. Engring. Edn. Achievements include supervising successful attempt of OMI Coll. Applied Sci. contact of shuttle Challenger during STS-51F mission, 1985. Office: Univ Cin 2220 Victory Pkwy Cincinnati OH 45206-2822

SULLIVAN, JAMES STEPHEN, bishop; b. Kalamazoo, July 23, 1929; s. Stephen James and Dorothy Marie (Bernier) S. Student, St. Joseph Sem.; BA, Sacred Heart Sem.; postgrad., St. John Provincial Sem. Ordained priest, Roman Cath. Ch., 1955, consecrated bishop, 1972. Assoc. pastor St. Luke Ch., Flint, Mich., 1955-58; assoc. pastor St. Mary Cathedral, Lansing, Mich., 1958-60, sec. to bishop, 1960-61; assoc. pastor St. Joseph (Mich.) Ch., 1961-65, sec. to bishop, 1965-69; assoc. pastor Lansing, 1965, vice chancellor, 1969-72; aux. bishop, vicar gen. Diocese of Lansing, 1972-85, diocesan consultor, 1971-85; bishop Fargo, N.D., 1985—. Pres. World Apostolate Fatima; episc. liaison Cath. Mktg. Network; nat. episcopal liaison to the Cath. Cursillo Movement. Mem. Nat. Conf. Cath. Bishops. Office: Chancery Office PO Box 1750 1310 Broadway Fargo ND 58102-2639

SULLIVAN, JERRY STEPHEN, electronics company executive; b. Havre, Mont., July 17, 1945; s. Patrick Joseph and Evangeline (O'Neil) S.; m. Sharon Lee Horton, June 17, 1967; children: Garrett, Mindy, Darren. BS, U. Colo., 1967, MS, 1969, PhD, 1970; advanced mgmt. program, Harvard U. Bus. Sch., 1986. Tech. mgr. N.V. Philips Co., Eindhoven, The Netherlands, 1971-75; group dir. N.Am. Philips Corp., Briarcliff Manor, N.Y., 1975-80; dir. Tektronix, Beaverton, Oreg., 1981-83, div. gen. mgr., 1983-85, corp. dir., 1985-88; v.p. Microelectronics & Computer Tech. Corp., Austin, Tex., 1988-92; pres., CEO, Design Techs. Inc., Austin, 1992—; chmn. bd. MBA Techs., Inc., Phoenix; bd. dirs. Sherpa Corp., San Jose, Calif., Ontos, Inc. Boston, MBA Tech. Inc., Phoenix; mem. adv. bd. Ctr. Integrated Sys., Stanford U., Palo Alto, Calif., 1982—. Mem. adv. com. Coll. Engring., U. Tex., Austin, 1989—, bd. dirs. Edn. Found., 1990—. Mem. IEEE, Am. Phys. Soc., Assn. Computing Machinery, Am. Mgmt. Assn., Nat. Assn. Corp. Dirs. Avocations: scuba diving, golf, chess, sailing. Office: Design Techs Inc 107 Ranch Rd 620 S Austin TX 78734-3942

SULLIVAN, JOHN FOX, publisher; b. Phila., Oct. 19, 1943; s. Neil Joseph S. and Mary (Fox) Cullumbine; m. Beverly Knight Lilley, June 10, 1978; stepchildren: Buchanan, Brooke, Whitman, Justin Lilley. BA, Yale U., 1966; MBA, Columbia U., 1968. Staff econ. analyst U.S. Dept. Def., Washington, 1968-69; asst. to pub. Newsweek Internat., N.Y.C., 1970-73, asst. mng. dir., 1974-75; pres., pub. Nat. Jour. Group, Inc., Washington, 1975—, The Atlantic Monthly, 1999—. Mem. editl. adv. bd. Who's Who. Bd. dirs. Arena Stage, Times Mirror Found., Nat. Gallery Cartoon Art; trustee Monterey Inst. Internat. Studies. Mem. Yale Club (N.Y.C.). Episcopalian. Home: 22 Old Vineyard Ln Flint Hill VA 22627-1735 Office: Nat Jour Group 1501 M St NW Ste 300 Washington DC 20005-1700

SULLIVAN, KEITH FREDERICK, education educator; b. Northampton, Eng., Oct. 11, 1948; s. George Garrett and Hilda Emily (Williams) S.; m. Ginette Louise Dunn, Feb. 24, 1978; children: Jacob, Hannah, Amy. BA, Sir George Williams U., Montreal, 1972; PhD, Inst. of Dialect and Folk Life, Studies/U. Leeds, Eng., 1978; MPhil, U. Cambridge, 1984; D Bus. Studies, Massey U., New Zealand, 1997. Rsch. fellow Ctr. for Maori Studies and Rsch./Waikato U., 1979-80; asst. lectr. Massey U., 1981; dir. U. of the South Pacific, Kiribati, 1982-83; rschr. Justice Dept., Wellington, New Zealand, 1985-87; chair edn. Victoria U., Wellington, 1994-95, dir. of postgrad. studies Sch. of Edn., 1996-98; cons. New Zealand Police, Wellington, 1998; vis. fellow U. South Australia, 1996; Charter fellow in human rights Wolfson Coll., U. Oxford, 1995-96. Editor/author: (book) Education and Change in the Pacific Rim, 1998; author: (book) What Should Count as Work in the 'Ivory Tower'?, 1997, The Anti-Bullying Handbook, 2000, others; contbr. articles to profl. jours., chpts. to books in field. Recipient Can. Govt. Faculty Enrichment award, Can., 1992, 99. Office: Victoria U of Wellington, Box 600, Wellington New Zealand

SULLIVAN, MARK HUBBARD FITZMAURICE, biochemist, researcher; b. London, Apr. 22, 1958; s. Vernon Fitzmaurice and Shirley Annette (Hubbard) S.; m. Susan Marianne Sealey, Apr. 23, 1983. BA, U. Oxford, Eng., 1980; PhD, U. London, 1984. Postdoctoral rsch. asst. Royal Free Hosp., London, 1984-87; lectr. Royal Postgrad. Med. Sch., London, 1987-98; sr. lectr. Imperial Coll. Sch. Medicine, 1998—. Contbr. articles to profl. jours. Mem. Biochem. Soc., Soc. for Endocrinology, Soc. for Immunology. Avocation: philately. Office: Hammersmith Hosp, Du Cane Rd, London W12 0HS, England

SULLIVAN, MICHAEL JOHN, ambassador, former governor; b. Omaha, Sept. 23, 1939; s. Joseph Byrne and Margaret (Hamilton) S.; m. Jane Metzler, Sept. 2, 1961; children: Michelle, Patrick, Theresa. BS in Petroleum Engring., U. Wyo., 1961, JD, 1964. Bar: Wyo. 1964; 10th Circiut Ct. Appeals, 1968; U.S. Supreme Ct., 1980. Assoc. Brown, Drew, Apostolos, Barton & Massey, Casper, Wyo., 1964-67; ptnr. Brown, Drew, Apostolos, Massey & Sullivan, Casper, 1967-86, 95-98; gov. State of Wyo., Casper, 1987-95; amb. to Ireland Dublin, 1998—. Trustee St. Joseph's Children's Home, Torrington, Wyo., 1986-87; bd. dirs. Natrona County Meml. Hosp., Casper, 1976-86. Mem. ABA, ATLA, Wyo. Bar Assn., Wyo. Trial Lawyers Assn., Rotary (pres. Casper club). Democrat. Roman Catholic. Avocations: fly fishing, golf, tennis, jogging. Office: Am Embassy Dublin Ireland Dept State Washington DC 20521-0001

SULLIVAN, PATRICIA ANN, administrative assistant; b. Oct. 1, 1941; d. Louis William and Ruby Lee Hounsel; divorced; children: Leslie Rene, Michael Shawn. Grad., Lererett's Chapel H.S., Overton, Tex., 1960. Subs. tchr. East Feliciana Parish Schs., Slaughter, La., 1968-72, Henderson (Tex.) Ind. Sch. Dist., 1976-77; sec. Pool Well Svc. - Rocky Mountain Region, Casper, Wyo., 1980-81; legis. aide State of Tex. - Rep. McWilliams, Henderson, 1982-90; adminstrv. asst. Rusk County Commrs., Henderson, 1990—; chmn. phys. environ. adv. com. Ea. Tex. Coun. of Govts., Kilgore, Tex., 1994-2000. Grant writer in field. Chmn. Rusk County Flag Design Contest, 1996; mem. Cmty. Residency Com., Henderson, 1999-2000. Mem. Nat. Trust Forum for Hist. Preservation. Democrat. Baptist. Avocations: decorating, reading, collecting blue and white china, travel. Office: Rusk County Commrs Office 115 N Main St Ste 500-a Henderson TX 75652-3147

SULLIVAN, PATRICIA W. (TERRY SULLIVAN), real estate trainer; b. Hempstead, N.Y., July 25, 1936; d. Gilbert Hudson and Vera (Morgan) Wehmann; m. Richard J. Sullivan, June 8, 1957 (div. Apr. 1982); children: Katherine Sullivan-Irwin, Gillian Stewart, Adam W. BS, Skidmore Coll., 1958; MS, Syracuse U., 1965. Mgr. Purtell & Wigdale, Inc., Cedarburg, Wis., Merrill Lynch Real Estate, Cedarburg; office mgr. Coldwell Banker Real Estate, Cedarburg; sales mgr. Coldwell Banker Residential Brokerage, Mequon, WI; owner, trainer, cons. Terry Sullivan Tng. and Seminars, Belgium, Wis., 1991—; sales mgr. Coldwell Banker, Mequon, Wis. Contbr. articles to profl. jours. Named Wis. Cert. Real Estate Brokerage Mgr. of Yr., 1990. Mem. Nat. Assn. Realtors (bd. dirs. 1989-90, Omega Tau Rho award 1983, Outstanding Educator of the Year award for medium states, 1989), Nat. Women's Coun. Realtors (pres. 1990), Women's Coun. Realtors (pres. Milw. chpt. 1982, bd. dirs. 1983-90, named WCR of Yr. 1983, LTG 1985), Ozaukee Bd. Realtors (pres. 1979, bd. dirs. 1977-79, Realtor of Yr. 1979), Realtors Nat. Mktg. Inst. (dir. RS coun. 1983-86, CRS 1978, CRB 1981), Wis. Realtors Assn. (v.p. 1982-83, bd. dirs. 1983-86, Instr. of Yr. 1988, Disting. Svc. award 1992, GRI 1975), Wis. Cert. Residential Specialists (cert.; pres. 1982, Cert. Residential Specialist of Yr. 1983), Wis. Cert. Residential Brokers (cert.; pres. 1988). Address: Terry Sullivan Tng & Seminars 5342 Sandy Beach Ln Belgium WI 53004-9731

SULLIVAN, ROBERT EMMET, JR., lawyer; b. Detroit, Oct. 2, 1955; s. Robert Emmet Sr. and Gloria Marie (Lamb) S. BA in Polit. Sci. and Sociology, Wayne State U., 1977; M Urban Planning, U. Mich., 1979; JD, U. Detroit, 1983; postgrad., Oxford (Eng.) U., 1981. Bar: Mich. 1984, U.S. Dist. Ct. (we. dist.) Mich. 1984, U.S. Dist. Ct. (ea. dist.) Mich. 1984, U.S. Ct. Appeals (6th cir.) 1984, U.S. Ct. Appeal (D.C. cir.) 1984, U.S. Tax Ct. 1984, D.C. 1985, U.S. Supreme Ct. 1987. Planning commr. City of Detroit, 1982-85; shareholder Sullivan, Ward, Bone, Tyler & Asher, P.C., Detroit, 1984—; bd. dirs. Internat. Inst. of Met. Detroit. Contbr. articles to profl. jours. Active St. Scholastica Parish Ch., North Rosedale Park Civic Assn., Detroit Hist. Soc. Moffitt scholar, 1982, 83. Mem. AIA, Detroit Bar Assn., Mich. Soc. Planning Ofcls., Am. Inst. Cert. Planners. Roman Catholic. Home: 7464 Wilshire West Bloomfield MI 48322-2875 Office: Sullivan Ward Bone Tyler & Asher 25800 Northwestern Hwy Southfield MI 48075-1000

SULLIVAN, SCOTT, journalist; b. Cleve., Sept. 5, 1937; s. Maurice and Beatrice (Adams) S.; m. Hélène Henry, Dec. 8, 1973; children: Judith, Rebecca, Stéphane. BA, Yale U., 1958, Cambridge U., 1960; MA, Cambridge U., 1965. Reporter, city editor, Paris bur. chief Balt. Sun, 1963-72; Paris bur. chief, chief diplomatic corr. Newsweek, N.Y.C., 1972-82, European regional editor, 1983-98; pub. affairs adviser Internat. Energy Agy., 1988—. Author: The Shortest Gladdest Years, 1973, The Lerner and Loewe Songbook, 1960. Recipient Cunningham award Overseas Press Club, 1985. Mem. Travellers Club, Phi Beta Kappa. Democrat. Episcopalian. Avocations: bridge, poker, tennis. Home: 2 Sq. de L'Opera-Louis-Jouvet, F-75009 Paris France Office: IEA, 9 rue de la Federation, F-75015 Paris France

SULLIVAN, SHIRLEY ROSS (SHIRLEY ROSS DAVIS), art collector; b. Berkeley, Calif.; d. Edwin M. Ross; m. George Freeborn (dec.); children: George, Tita, Nelly, Mary; m. Thomas Davis (dec.); m. Charles Sullivan, Sept. 6, 1997. Interior designer Woodside, Calif., 1963-90; tchr., lectr., Woodside, 1965-70; art collector, Woodside and San Francisco, 1968—. Trustee San Francisco Mus. Modern Art, 1986—; pres. Collectors' Art Forum, San Francisco, 1983-85; mem. collectors' com. Nat. Gallery Art, 1998—. Office: ICMS 790 Laurel St San Carlos CA 94070-3164

SULLIVAN, THOMAS JAMES, retired manufacturing company executive; b. Franklin, N.H., Mar. 26, 1923; s. James J. and Helen (Mullin) S.; m. Anne Clark, Aug. 31, 1963. A.B., Holy Cross Coll., 1947; J.D., Harvard U., 1949. With Gen. Dynamics Corp., 1949-61, asst. div. mgr., 1959-61; sr. assoc. Harbridge House, Cambridge, Mass., 1961-63; with Hydraulic Research & Mfg. Co., Valencia, Calif., 1963-71; v.p. Hydraulic Research & Mfg. Co., 1964-68, exec. v.p., 1968-69, pres., 1969-71; v.p. Textron, Inc., Providence, 1971-73; pres. Walker/Parkersburg (W. Va.) Co., 1973-81, Sprague Meter, Bridgeport, Conn., 1981-84, Dimetrics Inc., Diamond Springs, Calif., 1984-86. Served with USAAF, 1943-46. Fellow Nat. Contract Mgmt. Assn. Home: 2186 Augusta Ct San Luis Obispo CA 93401-4500

SULLOWAY, FRANK JONES, psychologist, historian; b. Concord, N.H., Feb. 2, 1947; s. Alvah Woodbury and Alison (Green) S.; 1 child, Ryan. AB summa cum laude, Harvard U., 1969, AM in History of Sci., 1971, PhD History of Sci., 1978. Jr. fellow Harvard U. Soc. Fellows, 1974-77; mem. Sch. Social Sci. Inst. for Advanced Study, Princeton, N.J., 1977-78; rsch. fellow Miller Inst. for Basic Rsch. in Sci., U. Calif., Berkeley, 1978-80; rsch. fellow MIT, Cambridge, 1980-81, vis. scholar, 1989-98; postdoctoral fellow Harvard U., Cambridge, 1981-82, vis. scholar, 1984-89; rsch. fellow Univ. Coll., London, 1982-84; Vernon prof. biography Dartmouth Coll., Hanover, N.H., 1986; vis. Miller rsch. prof. U. Calif., Berkeley, 1999—, vis. prof., 2000—. Author: Freud, Biologist of the Mind, 1979 (Pfizer award History Sci. Soc. 1980), Born to Rebel, 1996; contbr. numerous articles on Charles Darwin and Sigmund Freud to profl. jours. Fellow NEH, 1980-81, NSF, 1981-82, John Simon Guggenheim Meml. Found., 1982-83, MacArthur Found., 1984-89, Dibner Inst., MIT, 1993-94, Ctr. for Advanced Study in Behavioral Scis., Stanford, Calif., 1998-99; recipient Randi award Skeptics Soc., 1997, Golden Plate award Am. Acad. Achievement, 1997. Fellow AAAS (mem. electorate nominating com. sect. L 1988-91, 94-97); mem. Am. Psychol. Soc., Human Behavior and Evolution Soc., History of Sci. Soc. (fin. com. 1987-92, com. on devel. 1988-92). Home: 1709 Shattuck Ave Apt 205 Berkeley CA 94709-1753 Office: U Calif Dept Psychology IPSR 4125 Tolman Hall Berkeley CA 94720-1603

SULTAN, ABDUL HAMEED, obstetrician and gynecologist, consultant; b. Pinetown, Natal, South Africa, Aug. 29, 1954; arrived in England, 1984; s. Abdul Razack and Saleemah (Wahed) S.; m. Razia Rahamet, Dec. 18, 1976; children: Shaista, Kabeer. M.B.Ch.B., U. Natal, 1979, MD, 1995. Sr. house officer Greenwich Hosp., London, 1987; registrar North Middlesex Hosp., London, 1988-89; rsch. registrar St. Mark's and St. Bartholomew's Hosp., London, 1990-92; sr. registrar Whipps Cross Hosp., London, 1993, St. George's Hosp., London, 1994-95; cons. ob-gyn. Mayday Hosp., London, 1996—. Contbr. articles to profl. jours. Recipient The Victor Bonney shield Victor Bonney Soc., London, 1993; The Well Being Trust grantee, 1994. Mem. Royal Coll. Obstetrician and Gynecologists (Gladys Dodds prize 1993), Internat. Continence Soc., Brit. Med. Assn., St. Mark's Assn. Avocations: football, cycling, fishing, travel. Office: Mayday University Hosp, Mayday Rd, Croydon CR7 7YE, England

SULTAN, ABDURAZZAQ MOHAMMED NOUR, medical educator, biochemist, researcher; b. Makkah, Saudi Arabia, May 14, 1953; s. Mohammed Nour and Hanoufa Husien Ali (Al-Daly) S.; m. Nawal E. A. Mohammed Raheem, 1990; children: Noran, Camellia, Sultan, Qusai. PhD in Biochemistry, Edinburgh U. Med. Sch., 1981. Prof. clin. biochemistry, head med. scis. dept. Umm Al-Qura U., Makkah, Saudi Arabia, 1983-90, dean faculty of medicine and med. scis., 1990—, head dept. biochemistry, 1990—. Author: Cellular and Molecular Biochemistry, 1993. Mem. Biochem. Soc., Am. Assn. Clin. Chemistry, Am. Diabetes Assn. Muslim. Office: UMM Al-Qura U, PO Box No 6503-31, Makkah Saudi Arabia

SULTAN, GILBERT DAVID, physicist, researcher; b. La Goulette, Tunisia, June 21, 1938; arrived in France, 1962; permanent resident, 1967; s. Sauveur Ychova and Eugenie (Cohen) S.; m. Ursula Gerda Hartmann, July 2, 1966; children: Marc, Carole, Alain. B degree in Physics and Math., U. Paris, 1959, diploma in math., 1960, diploma in physics, 1963. Tchr. H.S. Carthage, Tunisia, 1959-62, H.S. St. Denis, 1962-63; asst. prof. Le Mans U., France, 1963-66; sci. rschr. U. Paris, Orsay, 1964-66, asst. prof., 1966-68; sci. rschr. Nat. Ctr. Sci. Rsch., Orsay, 1966-99; cons. French Telem. Nat. Ctr. Lannion, 1986-87, French Army Rsch. Ctr., Arcueil, 1987-90, Electricity of France and Oven Mfg., Lyon, 1990-92, Innovatique (HIT Group), Chassieu, 1992-97. Author: Spectral Line Shapes, 1987, Resonance Ionization Spectroscopy, 1990; contbr. more than 50 articles to profl. jours. including Phys. Rev., Jour. Applied Physics, Chem. Physics, Applied Physics Letters, Zeitschrift fur Physik, Surface and Coatings Tech., among others. Mem. Nouvelles Frontieres, Bridge Club, Tennis Club. Avocations: bridge, tennis, travel, walking, chess. Home: 18 rue de Valois, 91940 Les Ulis France Office: U Paris 11 Nat Ctr Sci Rsch, LPGP Bat 212, 91405 Orsay France

SULTAN, H.E. SHEIKH FAISAL BIN, banking executive; b. Ras Al Khaimah, United Arab Emirates, 1940; s. Sheikh Sultan bin Salim; m. Sheikha Mousa bint Al Hilal Nahyan. Mil. adviser Crown Prince of Abu Dhabi, 1970; under-sec. Ministry of Def., Abu Dhabi, 1971; chief of staff Def. Forces, Abu Dhabi, 1973; chmn. GIBCA Group of Cos./United Arab Bank, 1974—. Maj.-Gen. mil. United Arab Emirates. Decorated Jordanian Star 1st Class, King Hussein, medal of Merit 1st class, Al Sadat, Egypt, Superior Order Staff Gen. Officer Class, Al Nilein medal 1st class: Sudan, Emirates Mil. medal, Ruler United Arab Emirates. Avocations: camel breeding and racing. Office: GIBCA Grp/Sheikh Khalifa St, PO Box 2570, Abu Dhabi United Arab Emirates

SULTAN, RABIH FAYEZ, chemist, educator; b. Beirut, Jan. 1, 1958; s. Fayez and Sobhieh (Akram) S.; m. Amal Mohamad Abou-Hatab, Aug. 15, 1968; children: Fares, Kifah. BSc, Am. U. Beirut, 1979, MSc, 1981; PhD, Ind. U., 1986. Rsch. asst. Geochem Rsch. Assocs., Bloomington, Ind., 1984-86; asst. prof. United Arab Emirates U., Al-ain, 1988-92; instr. Am. U. Beirut, 1981-82, lectr., 1986-88, asst. prof., 1992-96, assoc. prof., 1996—, chmn. dept. chemistry, 1997—; mem. coun. Syndicate of Chemists in Lebanon, 1994-96. Co-author: General Chemistry Laboratory Manual, 1991; contbr. articles to profl. jours. Mem. Am. Chem. Soc., N.Y. Acad. Scis. Avocations: reading, classical music, nature, collecting model planes, swimming. Office: Am U Beirut, Dept Chemistry, Beirut Lebanon

SULTAN, RANA MUHAMMAD, mining engineer, consultant; b. Lahore, Pakistan, Sept. 1, 1934; s. Abdul Majid and Mumtaz Begum (Majid) Rana; m. Shahida Chughtai, Oct. 4, 1964; 4 children. BSc in Engring., Punjab U., Lahore, 1957; MSc in Engring., Stanford U., 1962. Cert. 1st class colliery mgr., Pakistan; cert. mines rescue and safety Nat. Coal Bd. U.K. Lectr. Govt. Engring. Coll., Lahore, 1957-58; mineral devel. officer Lahore, 1958; mine mgr. Govt. of West Pakistan, Warcha, 1958-60; asst. mine engr. Govt. of Pakistan, Khewra, 1960-62; mine mgr. Pakistan Indsl. Devel. Corp., Khewra, 1962-69; chief insp. of mines Labour Dept. of Punjab, Lahore, 1969-94; mining engr. IMEP Consultancy Svcs. (Pvt) Ltd., Lahore, 1994—; chmn. Mining Bd. of Examiners, Lahore, 1969-94; vice chmn. Miners Welfare Bd., Lahore, 1969-94; chmn. Cento Coal Symposium, Lahore, 1979. Mem. adv. Welfare Orgn. for Handicapped, Lahore, 1996-97; chmn. Friends Welfare Soc. for Handicapped Children, Lahore, 1990-96. Recipient Gold medal Inst. Mining Engrs. Pakistan, 1983. Mem. Rotary Club (dist. gov. 1995-97), Lahore Gymkhana. Islamic. Home: 9-B Bahawalpur House GOR-2, Lahore Pakistan Office: IMEP Consultancy Svcs Ltd, 10/3 Sharif Complex, Gulberg Lahore Pakistan

SULTANBAWA, M. U. S., science academy executive. Pres. Nat. Acad. Scis., Colombo, Sri Lanka. Office: Nat Academy of Sciences, 120/10 Wijerama Mawatha, Colombo 7 Sri Lanka*

SULTAN BIN MUHAMMAD AL-QASIMI, SHEIKH **See AL-QASIMI, SHEIKH SULTAN BIN MUHAMMAD**

SULTANIK, JEFFREY TED, lawyer; b. N.Y.C., July 26, 1954; s. Solomon and Anna (Tiger) S.; m. Judith Ann Clyman, Nov. 14, 1981; children: Evan A., Sara A. BA cum laude, U. Pa., Phila., 1976; JD, Hofstra U., 1979. Bar: Pa. 1979, Fla. 1980, U.S. Dist. Ct. (ea. dist.) Pa., U.S. Ct. Appeals (3d cir.). Ptnr. Fox, Rothschild, O'Brien & Frankel, L.L.P., Lansdale, Pa., 1979-81; solicitor Upper Merion Sch. Dist., 1995—; solicitor Boyertown (Pa.) Area Sch. Dist., 1981—, Perkiomen Valley Sch. Dist., Rahns, Pa., 1983—, North Montco Vocat.-Tech. Sch., Lansdale, 1981—, Souderton (Pa.) Area Sch. Dist., 1989—, Wallingford-Swarthmore Sch. Dist., 1999—; spl. counsel Penn Delco Sch. Dist., Aston, Pa., Coun. Rock Sch. Dist., Newtown, Pa., 1998, Kennett Consolidated Sch. Dist., 1999—, Colonial Sch. Dist., 1996—, Owen J. Roberts Sch. Dist., 1999—, Wissahickon Sch. Dist., 1999—, Norristown Sch. Dist., 1999—, Marple Newtown Sch. Dist., 2000—; spl. counsel Owen J. Roberts Sch. Dist., 1999—; chair pers. com., mktg./admissions com., sec. bd. trustees Germantown Acad., Ft. Washington, Pa., 1991—; presenter Coun. Sch. Attys., Anaheim, Calif., 1997, Milken Found., L.A. Regular columnist Your School and the Law, 1992. Mem. Nat. Orgn. Legal Problems of Edn., Nat. Assn. Sch. and Coll. Attys., Pa. Sch. Bds. Assn., Inc. (continuing edn. in sch. law award 1990, sch. mgmt. in-svc. edn. award 1985), Pa. Assn. Sch. Bus. Ofcls. (cert. of appreciation 1991), Pa. Bar Assn. (labor and edn. sects.), Montgomery County Bar Assn. (mcpl. law com. 1983—), Lehigh U. Law Forums, Assn. Del. Valley Ind. Schs. Republican. Jewish. Avocations: automobiles, travel. E-mail: jsultanik@frof.com. Home: 2056 Spring Valley Rd Lansdale PA 19446-5114 Office: Fox Rothschild O'Brien & Frankel LLP 1250 S Broad St Ste 1000 Lansdale PA 19446-5343

SULTEN, PHILIPPE FERNAND, engineering executive; b. Kinshasa, Zaire, May 7, 1953; arrived in France, 1982; s. Firmin Marie and Marcelle Anne (Mersch) S.; m. Mireille Bernadette Rimlinger Sulten, Aug. 14, 1987; children: Emeline, Anne, Pierre, Estelle. Diploma in Elec. Engring., U. Liege, Belgium, 1976; diploma in Nuclear Engring., 1977; training in bus. mgmt., Inst. Francais de Gestion, 1998-99. Asst. U. Liege, Belgium, 1976-77; jr. expert Internat. Labor Orgn., Geneve, Suisse, 1977-82; commn. engr. GEC Alsthom, Belfort, France, 1982-88; engr. and devel. mgr. Alsthom Intermagnetics, Belfort, France, 1988-96; deputy mng. dir., 1996-98; quality mgr. mfg. Abb Alstom Power, 1999—. Two patents, 1992, 96. Mem. Societe des Electriciens et Electroniciens (sr., France), Assn. des Ingenieurs de L'Inst. Montefiore (Belgium), Assn. des Ingenieurs de la Region Belfort-Montbeliard (France). Home: 26B rue D'Evette, 90350 Evette Salbert France Office: Abb Alstom Power, Avenue des 3 Chenes, 90018 Belfort France

SULTONOV, OTKIR, Uzbek government official; b. Tashkent, July 14, 1939; married; 1 child. Grad., Tomsk Polytechnical Inst., 1964. Electrician, mechanic, sr. engr., chief of lab., chief of design bur., chief of dept., dep. chief engr., dep. gen. dir. amalgamation Tashkent Aviation Indsl. Assn., 1962-85; dir. gen. Sci.- Indsl. Amalgamation "Vostok", 1985-91; chmn. Goskomvneshtorgsvyaz, 1991; dep. fgn. min. Govt. of Uzbekistan, Tashkent, 1990-95, prime min., 1995—, min. fgn. econ. rels., 1995-98. Office: Cabinet of Ministers, Government House, 700008 Tashkent Uzbekistan*

SULYK, STEPHEN, archbishop; b. Balnycia, Western Ukraine, Oct. 2, 1924; s. Michael and Mary (Denys) S. Student, Ukrainian Cath. Sem. of Holy Spirit, Fed. Republic Germany, 1945-48, St. Josaphat's Sem., 1948-52; Licentia in Sacred Theology, Cath. U. Am., 1952. Ordained priest Ukrainian Cath. Ch., 1952. Assoc. pastor Omaha, 1952; assoc. pastor Bklyn., 1953, Minersville, Pa., 1954, Youngstown, Ohio, 1955; pastor Ch. Sts. Peter and Paul, Phoenixville, Pa., 1955, St. Michael's Ch., Frackville, Pa., 1957-61, Assumption of Blessed Virgin Mary Ch., Perth Amboy, N.J., 1962-81; sec. Archeparchy Chancery, 1956-57; adminstr. St. Nicholas, Phila., 1961; archbishop Met. of Ukraine-Rite Catholics of Archeparchy, Phila., 1981—; vice chmn. Priests Senate, 1977-78; bd. dirs. Diocesan Adminstrn., 1972-79; pres. Ascension Manor, Inc.; archbishop Ukranian Rite Caths. Archeparchy Phila., Met. Ukranian-Rite Caths. U.S.A.; chmn. Priest's Senate; chmn. ad-hoc inter-rite com. Nat. Cath. Conf. Bishops/U.S. Cath. Conf., 1991. Mem. Providence Assn. Am. (Supreme Protector), Coll. Bishops of Roman Cath. Ch., Presidium of Synod of Ukranian Cath. Bishops (treas.). Office: Archdiocese of Philadelphia 827 N Franklin St Philadelphia PA 19123-2004

SUM, JOHN PUI-FAI, computer science educator; b. Hong Kong, Nov. 11, 1967. BEng, Hong Kong Poly. U., 1992; MPhil, Chinese U. Hong Kong, 1995, PhD, 1998. rschr. in field of neural networks. Avocation: badminton. Office: Hong Kong Bapt U, Dept Computer Sci, Kowloon Tong Hong Kong

SUMA, HISAYOSHI, health facility administrator; b. Nishiwaki, Hyogo, Japan, Mar. 1, 1950; s. Keizo Kiyose and Tazuko Mimura; m. Fumie Morii, Mar. 1, 1975. MD, Osaka Med. Coll., 1974, PhD, 1988. Resident surgery Toranomon Hosp., Tokyo, 1974-78; staff surgeon Juntendo U., Tokyo, 1978-83, Osaka (Japan) Med. Coll., 1983-89; chief cardiac surgery Mitsui Meml. Hosp., 1989-94; vis. prof. cardiac surgery Cath. U., Rome, 1994-96; chief cardiac surgery Shonan Kamakura (Japan) Gen. Hosp., 1996-97, dir., 1998-99; dir. Hayama Heart Ctr., 2000; cons. Cardiothoracic Ctr. Monaco, 1997—. Author: Coronary Artery Graft Disease, 1994, Alternative Bypass Conduit and Methods for Surgical Coronary Revascularization, 1994, Arterial Conduits in Myocardial Revascularization, 1996, Ischemic Heart Disease: Surgical Management, 1998. Active Kioicho Rotary Club, Tokyo, 1997, Japan Animal Welfare Soc., 1998; counselor Nippon Music Found., Tokyo, 1998. Recipient Mitsui Welfare Found. award Mitsui Welfare Found., Tokyo, 1993. Fellow Japanese Coll. Cardiology; mem. Am. Assn. for Thoracic Surgery, European Assn. for Cardio-thoracic Surgery. Avocations: skiing, golfing, music, traveling, cooking. Office: Shonan Kamakura Gen Hosp, 1202-1 Yamazaki, Kamakura 247-8533, Japan

SUMANTH, DAVID JONNAKOTY, industrial engineer, educator; b. Machilipatnam, India, Jan. 28, 1946; came to U.S., 1972; s. John Devraj and

Nancy (David) Jonnakoty; m. Chaya J. Victor, June 26, 1974; children: John J., Paul J. BME, Osmania U., India, 1967, MME, 1969; MS in Indsl. Engring., Ill. Inst. Tech., 1974, PhD in Indsl. Engring., 1979. Tchg./rsch. asst. Ill. Inst. Tech., Chgo., 1973-78, instr., 1979; asst. prof. indsl. engring. U. Miami, Coral Gables, Fla., 1979-83, founding dir. productivity research group, 1979—, dir. grad. studies, 1980-83, assoc. prof. indsl. engring., 1983-88, Coll. Engring. coordinator MBA/MSIE, 1984-93; prof. indsl. engring. U. Miami, Coral Gables, 1988—; chmn. 1st and 2d Internat. Conf. on Productivity Rsch., 3d, 4th, 5th Internat. Conf. on Productivity and Quality Rsch. Author: Productivity Engineering and Management, 1984, internat. student edit., 1985, Spanish edit., 1990, Indian edit., 1990, coll. custom series edit., 1994, also instrs. manual, (script) Total Productivity Management, 1985; editor: Productivity Management Frontiers-I, 1987, II, 1989, Productivity and Quality Management Frontiers III, 1991, IV, 1993, V, 1995, VI, 1997, VII, 1998, Total Productivity Management, 1998. Recipient over 60 honors, awards and recognitions including YMCA Edn. Gold medal, 1969, Freedoms Found., 1987; fellow U. Miami Eaton Honors Coll., 1986, fellow World Acad. Productivity Sci., 1989; gov.'s appointee as sr. judge Fla. Sterling award, 1992-93, judge, 1993-98. Mem. Am. Inst. Indsl. Engrs. (sr. mem., pres. Miami chpt. 1982-83, bd. dirs. 1983-84, nat. asst. dir. productivity mgmt. 1984—, chairperson rsch. com. 1987, Outstanding Indsl. Engr. of Yr. Miami chpt. 1983, 84); Productivity Ctr. (trustee 1985-89), Internat. Soc. for Productivity and Quality Rsch. (founder 1993, founding pres. 1993-95, chmn. 1995—). Republican. Baptist. Avocations: reading, writing, people. Office: U Miami Productivity Rsch Group Coral Gables FL 33124

SUMAYE, FREDERICK TLUWAY, prime minister of Tanzania; married;. Dep. min. agriculture Govt. of Tanzania, min. agriculture, livestock devel. and coops., 1994-95, prime min., 1996—. Office: Office of the Prime Min, Box 980, Dodoma Tanzania*

SUMBERG, ALFRED DONALD, professional association executive; b. Utica, N.Y., Nov. 22, 1928; s. Samuel M. and Rachel Frances (Silverstein) S.; m. Dolly Primakow, June 26, 1955; children: Susan Diane Beldon, Laurie Darlene Sumberg. Student, Utica Coll., 1946-48, Hebrew Union Coll., 1948-50; AB, U. Cin., 1950, MA, 1951; PhD, U. Wis., 1960; LHD (hon.), U. Cin., 1994. Exec. dir., founding dir. Am. Jewish Tercentenary Com. Wis. Wis. Jewish Archives, 1954-55; instr. history U. Wis., Parkside, 1955-56; prof. history and econs. East Stroudsburg (Pa.) U., 1956-67; vis. prof. history U. Cin., Cin., 1954, 58, 67; assoc. gen. sec., dir. govt. rels. AAUP, Washington, 1967-94; founding pres. N.E. Pa. Sch. Employees Fed. Credit Union, 1960-67; mem. exec. com. educator's ad hoc com. on copyright law, 1976-94, co-chair ad hoc com. for the creation of a cabinet-level dept. of edn., 1978-80, com. for edn. funding v.p.-treas., 1980-82, pres., 1982; bd. dirs. The Tuition Exch., 1988-96. Contbr. articles to profl. jours., chpts. to books. Bd. dirs., chair edn. com. The Hist. Found. of Pa., 1961-67; pres. The Hist. Assn. Northeastern Pa., 1963-67, Monroe County (Pa.) Hist. Soc., 1965-67; edn. coord. Mondale-Ferraro campaign, 1984; vol. Nat. Exec. Svc. Corps, 1994-96. Mem. AAUP, Am. Hist. Assn., Nat. Trust for Hist. Preservation, U.S. Capitol Hist. Soc., Am. Econs. Assn., Nat. Economists Club, Nat. Dem. Club, Libr. of Congress Assocs., U. Cin. Alumni Assn. (life, pres. Washington chpt. 1972-74), U. Wis. Alumni Assn. (life, pres. Washington chpt. 1978-80), Phi Alpha Theta, Kappa Delta Pi, Utica Coll. Alumni Assn. Democrat. Jewish. Home and Office: 1309 Fallsmead Way Rockville MD 20854-5523

SUMERS, ANNE RICKS, ophthalmologist, museum director; b. Beverly, Mass., May 8, 1957; d. David Frank and Anne Russell (Russell) Ricks; m. Elliott H. Sumers, May 31, 1983; children: Ben, Ted. BA in English Lit. with honors, U. Mich., 1979; MD, U. Cin., 1983. Diplomate Am. Bd. Ophthalmology. Intern in internal medicine Mt. Auburn Hosp., Cambridge, Mass., 1984; resident in ophthalmology NYU/Bellevue Hosp., 1984-87; ptnr. Ridgewood (N.J.) Ophthalmology, PC, 1990—; dir. N.J. Childrens Mus., Paramus, N.J., 1992—; co-owner Saddle River (N.J.) Market, 1995—; team ophthalmologist N.Y. Giants Football Team, 1994—, N.J. Nets, 1999—; state coord. N.J. Turn Off Your TV Week, 1994, 95, 96; spkr. in field. Author: The Offical M.D. Handbook, 1983, Be A Better Mother—Today!, 1999; writer, host Channel 11/WPIX Wonder Zone, 1993; interviewed on Good Morning Am., Am.'s Talking, CBS This Morning, NJN Discover N.J., Comcast Cablevision, Cablevision, Fox Channel 5 Good Day N.Y., 1992—, NBC Nightly News, numerous radio shows; writer (essays) Newsweek, USA Today. Named one of 10 N.J. Women of Yr., N.J. Woman Mag., 1993; profiled in AMA News, Med. Econs., The N.Y. Times, Star Ledger, Argus and other newspapers and mags. Fellow Am. Acad. Ophthalmology (media spokesperson, media info. com.); mem. AMA, Assn. Youth Museums, N.J. Acad. Ophtholmology (bd. govs. 1997), Alpha Omega Alpha. Office: Ridgewood Ophthalmology PC 1200 E Ridgewood Ave Ridgewood NJ 07450-3937

SUMERS, REBECCA ANN, interior designer; b. Marengo, Iowa, Sept. 9, 1947; d. Russell Dean and Arvena Maxine (Seaton) S. BFA, Drake U., 1969; postgrad., Venezia Isola di Studies, Venice, Italy, 1969-71. Lic. interior designer, Tex. Arts advisor Office of the Mayor, Washington, 1971-73; apparel mgr. Apogee Internat., Boston, 1973-75; dir. World Fine Arts Ctr., Atlanta, 1975-77; arts advisor Dept. Human Resources, San Antonio, 1977-79; interior designer/buyer Leonard's Furniture, 1979-95; interior designer Coles Drexel Heritage, Fairfax, Va., 1995-98, Colony House, Arlington, Va., 1998—; lectr. in field. Mem. San Antonio Artists Alliance. Mem. Am. Soc. Interior Designers, Alpha Xi Delta.

SUMI, CHIKAYOSHI, medical engineer, educator; b. Tokyo, Dec. 2, 1968; s. Yoshio and Miyoko (Hiraiwa) S. B in Engring., Sophia U., Tokyo, 1991, M in Engring., 1993, D in Engring., 1996. Assoc. rschr. Sophia U., Tokyo, 1996-97, lectr., 1998—; vis. scholar Keele U., Stoke, Eng., 1997, U. Ill., Urbana, 1997. Contbr. articles to profl. jours. including Jour. Applied Physics. Grantee Japan Soc. for Promotion of Sci., 1996-97. Mem. IEEE, Japan Soc. Ultrasonics in Medicine, Japan Med. Electronics and Biol. Engring. Office: Sophia U Elec & Electron En, 7-1 Kioi-cho Chiyoda-ku, Tokyo 102-8554, Japan

SUMI, SHIGEMASA, psychology educator; b. Gifu, Japan, Nov. 21, 1932; s. Seisho and Ito (Kaneyama) S.; m. Michiko Iwano, May 26, 1963; children: Makiko, Masato, Jyunko, Reiko. BA, Chiba U., Japan, 1959; MA, Keio U., Tokyo, 1961, PhD, 1976. Lic. psychologist, Japan. From asst. prof. to assoc. prof. psychology Keio U., Tokyo, 1964-77, prof. psychology, 1977-97, prof. emeritus, 1997—; prof. psychology Japan Women's U., Tokyo, 1997—; editor Japanese Psycholog. Assn., Tokyo, 1990-95, Japanese Psychonomic Soc., 1990-99. Editor: New Horizons in the Study of Gestalt Perception, 1996; contbr. articles to profl. jours. Mem. Japanese Psycholog. Assoc., Japanese Psychonomic Soc. Fax: 81-3-3981-4470. Home: 3-40-5 Minamiotsuka, Toshima-ku, Tokyo 170-0005, Japan Office: Japan Women's U Dept Psych, Nishiikuta Tama-ku, Kawasaki 214-8565, Japan

SUMIDA, GERALD AQUINAS, lawyer; b. Hilo, Hawaii, June 19, 1944; s. Sadamy and Kimiyo (Miyahara) S. AB summa cum laude, Princeton U., 1966; JD, Yale U., 1969. Bar: Hawaii 1970, U.S. Dist. Ct. Hawaii 1970, U.S. Ct. Appeals (9th cir.) 1970, U.S. Supreme Ct. 1981. Rsch. assoc. Ctr. Internat. Studies, Princeton U., 1969; assoc. Carlsmith, Ball, Honolulu, 1970-76, ptnr., 1976-99; gen. counsel Asian Devel. Bank, 1999—; mem. cameras in courtroom evaluation com. Hawaii Supreme Ct., 1984-86. Co-author: (with others) Legal, Instiutional and Financial Aspects of An Inter-Island Electrical Transmission Cable, 1984, Alternative Approaches to the Legal, Instiutional and Financial Aspects of Developing an Inter-Island, Electrical Transmission Cable System, 1986; editor Hawaii Bar News, 1972-73; contbr. chpts. to books. Mem. sci. and statis. com. Western Pacific Fishery Mgmt. Coun., 1979-99; mem. study group on law of armed conflict and the law of the sea Comdr. in Chief Pacific, USN, 1979-82; chmn. Pacific and Asian Affairs Coun. Hawaii, 1991, pres., 1982-91, bd. govs., 1976-96; bd. govs. ARC, 1994-2000, mem. exec. com., 1996-2000, chmn. human resources com., 1996-2000, chmn. Hawaii chpt., 1983-99, bd. dirs., 1983-99, vice chmn., 1990; chmn. Hawaii C. of C., 1997-98, bd. dirs., 1990-99; vice chmn. Honolulu Com. Fgn. Rels., 1983—; pres., dir., founding mem. Hawaii Ocean Law Assn., 1978—; mem. Hawaii Adv. Group for Law of Sea Inst., 1977-85; pres. Hawaii Inst. Continuing Legal Edn., 1979-83, dir., 1976-87; pres., founding mem. Hawaii Coun. Legal Edn. Youth, 1980-83, dir., 1983-88; chmn. Hawaii Commn. Yr. 2000, 1976-79; mem. Honolulu Cmty. Media Coun., 1976-99, exec. com., 1976-84, legal coun., 1979-83; bd. dirs. Hawaii Imin Centennial Corp., 1983-90, Hawaii Pub. Radio, 1983-88, Legal Aid Soc. Hawaii, 1984; founding gov., exec. v.p., chmn. rules and procedures Ctr. Internat. Comml. Dispute Resolution, 1987—; exec. com. Pacific Aerospace Mus., 1991—; exec. com. Pacific Islands Assn., 1988—; exec. com. Asia-Pacific Ctr. Res. Internat. Bus. Disputes, 1991-95; mem. Coun. Asia-Pacific Dispute Rsch. Ctrs., 1991-95; bd. dirs. U.S. C. of C., 1998—; mem. Pacific Basin Econ. Coun., 1993—; mem. mgmt. com. PBEC-U.S. Nat. Com., 1994-99. Recipient cert. of appreciation Gov. of Hawaii, 1979, resolutions of appreciation Hawaii Senate and Ho. of Reps., 1979; grantee Japan Found., 1979. Mem. ABA, Hawaii Bar Assn. (pres. young lawyers sect. 1974, v.p. 1984), Japan-Hawaii Lawyers Assn., Am. Soc. Internat. Law, Internat. Bar Assn., Am. Judicature Soc., Inter-Pacific Bar Assn., Internat. Law Assn., Plaza Club (Honolulu), Colonial Club (Princeton). Democrat. E-mail: gsumida@adb.org. Office: Office Gen Coun Asian Devel Bank, 6 ADB Ave, 0401 Metro Manila Mandaluyong, Philippines also: Gen Coun Asian Devel Bank, PO Box 789, 0980 Manila Philippines

SUMIDA, GREGORY ZIO, artist, photographer, musician; b. L.A.. Grad., Alhambra H.S. One-man shows include Palm Springs Desert Mus., 1973, Desert S.W. Art Gallery, 1974, Pioneer Mus. and Haggin Art Gallery, 1975, Potlatch Art Gallery, 1976, Maxwell Galleries, San Francisco, 1977, Smith Gallery, N.Y.C., Troy's Gallery, Ariz., 1984, 86, 88, Zantman Galleries, Palm Desert, Calif., 1990, Legacy Gallery, 1991; group shows include Americana Gallery, Carmel, Calif., 1978, Fireside Gallery, Carmel, Calif., 1979, De Colores Gallery, Denver, 1979, Stremmel Galleries, Reno, 1980, Period Gallery West, Scottsdale, Ariz., 1981, Artist Union Gallery, 1982, 84, 85, Smith Gallery, N.Y.C., 1983, Artist Union Gallery, 1982, 84, 85, Hunter Art Gallery, San Francisco, 1984, For Art Lovers Only, Denver, 1984, Classic-Am. Show, 1988, 89, Legacy Gallery, Scottsdale, 1990, 2000, Zantman Galleries, Carmel, Calif., 1996, Urubamba Gallery, Paris, 1996, Artist FocusShow Legacy Gallery, Scottsdale, 2000; represented in numerous pub. and pvt. collections; included in numerous publications including S.W. Art, 1977, Contemporary We. Artists, 1982, We. Art Digest, 1986, Palm Springs Desert Life, 1987, Calif. Rev., 1989, Palm Springs Life, 1991, Am. Reference, 1991, Le Peintre Sumida, 1991, International Fine Art Collector, 1992, Art West, 1999. Office: PO Box 9210 Stockton CA 95208-1210

SUMIHARA, KIYOHIDE, mechanical engineering researcher, consultant; b. Kiya-Kyushu City, Japan, Jan. 29, 1955; s. Hideomi and Kazuko (Naka) S. PhD, MIT, 1983; DSc in Engring., Tokyo U., 1985. Engr. Nissan Motor Co., Tokyo, 1987-89; asst. prof. mech. engring. Nihon U., Tokyo, 1989-90; sr. rschr. Nomura Rsch. Inst., Tokyo, 1991-92; asst. mgr. Daimler-Benz AG, Tokyo, 1993-95; rep. Hybrid Rsch. Lab., Fukuoka, Japan, 1996—. Contbr. articles to profl. jours. Civic ombudsman, Fukuoka, 1997—. Mem. Japan Soc. Mech. Engrs., Japanese Econ. Assn., Japan Soc. Indsl. and Applied Math., Japan Critics Assn., N.Y. Acad. Scis. Avocations: Japanese fencing, noh, bowling, golf, guitar. Office: Hybrid Rsch Lab, 4-47-4 Najima Higashi-ku, Fukuoka 813-0043, Japan

SUMINO, KOJI, steel company executive, educator; b. Kanazawa, Ishikawa, Japan, May 8, 1931; s. Saburo and Sono (Sentani) S.; m. Masae Paula Tanioka, Apr. 1, 1958; children: Akira, Kaoru. BA in Sci., Kanazawa (Japan) U., 1953; MA in Sci., Tohoku U., Sendai, Japan, 1955, DSc, 1962. Rsch. assoc. Tohoku U., 1956-64, assoc. prof., 1965-73, prof., 1974-95, prof. emeritus, 1995—; exec. advisor Nippon Steel Corp., Tokyo, 1995-2000; chmn. Internat. Con. Defect Control in Semiconductors, Yokohama, Japan, 1988-90, 7th Internat. Symposium Silicon Materials Sci. & Tech., San Francisco, 1993-94, 18th Internat. Conf. Defects in Semiconductors, Sendai, 1993-95; dir. Japan Inst. Metals, Sendai, 1991-92. Author: Crystal Plasticity, 1977; editor: Dislocations in Solids, 1985, Defect Control in Semiconductors, I & II, 1990, The Science and Technology of Defect Control in Semiconductors, 1993. Recipient Meritorious prize Japan Inst. Metals, 1972; hon. fellow N.Y. State U., Albany, 1991; invited prof. Nanjing (China) U., 1994, Zhejiang (China) U., 1994. Mem. Japan Inst. Metals, Japanese Soc. Applied Physics, Phys. Soc. Japan. Avocation: playing cello. Home: Aoba-ku, 4-6-4 Kunimigaoka, Miyaqi Sendai 989 3201, Japan

SUMIYOSHI, TOMIKI, psychiatrist, researcher; b. Tokyo, Dec. 18, 1964; s. Hiroshi and Fusako (Naganuma) S.; m. Sawako Suemasa, Apr. 4, 1993. MB, Kanazawa U., Japan, 1989, MD, 1989, PhD, 1993. Med. diplomate. Resident Fukui Prefectural Psychiat. Hosp., Japan, 1990; ward adminstr., dir. neurochemistry rsch. Kanazawa U. Hosp., Japan, 1991-93; rsch. assoc. dept. psychiatry Case Western Res. U., Cleve., 1993-95; asst. prof. dept. psychiatry, dir. psychopharmacology rsch. Saitama Med. Sch., Japan, 1995-96; asst. prof. dept. neuropsychiatry, dir. neurochemistry rsch. Toyama Med. and Pharmaceutical U., Japan, 1996—; apptd. psychiatrist Health and Welfare Ministry Japan, 1996—; cons. Janssen, Inc., Tokyo, 1993—, Fujisawa, Inc., Toyko, 1999—. Author: Neurobiological Aspects of Schizophrenia, 1996; contbr. articles to profl. jours. Rep. athlete The Nat. Athletic Meeting, Hachinohe, Japan, 1993. Recipient psychiat. rsch. award Saburo Matsubara Meml. Fund, Kanazawa, Japan, 1993, young investigator award Nat. Alliance for Rsch. on Schizophrenia and Depression, Chgo., 1995, rsch. prize Japanese Soc. Biological Psychiatry, Tokyo, 1996; scholar Rotary, 1994-95. Mem. Soc. Neuroscience, N.Y. Acad. Scis., World Fedn. Socs. Biol. Psychiatry, Japanese Soc. Psychiatry and Neurology, Nat. Geog. Soc., Japanese Soc. Biological Psychiatry, Japanese Soc. Neuropsychopharmacology, Japanese Soc. Clin. Neuropsychopharmacology. Avocations: foreign languages, classical music, figure skating, foreign travel. Home: 3-7-5-307 Shin-nezuka-machi, Toyama 939-8205, Japan Office: Psychiat Hosp at Vanderbilt 1601 23d Ave South Ste 306 Nashville TN 37212-8645

SUMMALA, HEIKKI, traffic psychology educator; b. Joengsuu, Finland, Dec. 2, 1948; m. Sirkka Summala; children: Anna, Antti, Elli. PhD, U. Helsinki, Finland, 1981. Rschr. U. Helsinki, 1971-75, jr. lectr., 1981-85, acting prof. gen. psychology, 1986-89, prof. traffic psychology, 1989—; jr. rschr. The Finnish Acad., Helsinki, 1975-81; Recipient Traffic Safety medal of honor Ministry of Transport and Comm., Finland, 1995, Golden medal of honour for sci. rsch. City of Kerava, 1999. Co-author: (with R. Näätänen) Road-User Behavior and Traffic Accidents, 1976; mem. editl. bd. Accident Analysis and Prevention, Transportation Human Factors, Transportation Rsch. F.: Traffic Psychology and Behavior; contbr. articles to profl. jours. Mem. Human Factors and Ergonomics Soc. (A.R. Lauer award 1988), Ergonomics Soc. Home: Aleksis Kiven tie 59, 04200 Kerava Finland Office: U Helsinki Dept Psychology, PO Box 13, 00014 Helsinki Finland

SUMMERFIELD, JOHN ARTHUR, gastroenterologist, educator; b. Nov. 14, 1946; s. John Crampton and Patrica Sandra (Musgrave) S.; m. Lesley Regan, Mar. 10, 1990; children: Nuala, Oliver, Jessica, James, Clare, Jenny. MB, BS, London U., 1970, MD, 1976. Intern London Hosp., 1970-71; resident gastroenterology Royal Free Hosp., London, 1973-75, lectr. Sch. Medicine, 1976-80, sr. lectr., cons. physician, 1981-87; practice medicine specializing in gastroenterology London, 1981—; vis. scientist NIH, Bethesda, Md., 1980-81; sr. fellow in clin. sci. Wellcome Trust, London, 1981-87; reader in medicine, St. Mary's Hosp. Med. Sch., London, 1988-92, prof. medicine, 1993—. Author: Colour Atlas of Liver Disease, 1979; editor: Jour. Hepatology, 1984—, Clin. Sci., 1984; contbr. sect. to books, numerous articles to profl. jours. Fellow Royal Coll. Physicians (London); mem. Med. Rsch. Soc., Brit. Soc. Gastroenterology, Internat. Assn. Study of Liver, European Assn. Study of Liver (sec. 1985-87), Brit. Assn. Study of Liver, Am. Assn. Study of Liver Diseases, Athenaeum Club. Office: Imperial Coll Sch Medicine, Praed St, London W2 1NY, England

SUMMERFIELD, PETER WILLIAM, solicitor; b. Berlin, Germany, June 3, 1933; arrived in Eng., 1939; s. Frank and Margot Summerfield; m. Susan Evelyn Wharton, July 15, 1963; children: Mark, Amanda, David; m. Marianne Dorothee Granby, July 5, 1973; children: Janette, Suzanne. BA with honours, U. Oxford, Eng., 1957, MA with honours, 1960. Articled clk. Oppenheimers, London, 1957-60, asst. solicitor, 1960-65, ptnr., 1965-88; ptnr. Nabarro Nathanson, London, 1988-96; cons., 1988—; hon. solicitor in U.K. to Swiss and Austrian Govts.; lectr. in field. Contbr. numerous articles to profl. jours. Past chmn. internat. bd. advisers McGeorge Sch. Law, U. Pacific, Sacramento. Mem. ABA, Internat. Bar Assn., Inst. of Dirs., Law Soc. Eng. and Wales, Japan Assn., Brit-German Jurists Assn., Soc. English and Am. Lawyers, Am. C. of C. (U.K.), Brit. C. of C. in Germany, Brit.-Swiss C. of C. (past chmn. London chpt.), Brit.-Swiss C. of C., German-Brit. Chamber of Industry and Commerce in U.K., Brit C. of C. in Spain, Finnish-Brit. Trade Guild, Norwegian C. of C., others. Jewish. Office: Summerfields, 86 Kingsley Way, London N2 0EN, England

SUMMERS, ANDREW, marketing professional; b. London, June 19, 1946; s. Basil and Margaret (Hunt) S.; m. Frances Halestrap, Aug. 14, 1971; children: Sarah, Kate, Bennet. MA, Cambridge U., 1968. Dir. mktg., dir. mng. J.A. Sharwood Ltd., U.K., 1975-85; dir. comml., dir. mng. RHM Foods Ltd., U.K., 1986-90; chief exec. Mgmt. Charter Initiative, U.K., 1991-94, Design Coun., U.K., 1995—; dir. S. Daniels PLC, U.K., 1991—; bd. dirs. Brit. Trade Internat. Bd. dirs. Brit. Overseas Trade Bd., 1997-99, Food From Britain, 1982-86; chmn. DTI European Trade Com., 1998—; tutor Leadership Trust, 1986-94. Fellow Royal Soc. Arts; mem. Inst. Mgmt. (companion), Design Mgmt. Inst.USA (advisory coun. 1998—). Avocations: tennis, theatre. Office: 34 Bow St, London WC2E 7DL, England

SUMMERS, GABRIEL JEFFREY, chemistry educator, consultant; b. Kimberley, No. Cape, South Africa, Oct. 29, 1957; s. George James and Iris Josephine (Campher) S.; m. Carol Ann Larey; children: Jeremy, Darryl, Graeme, Claudia. BSc, U. Western Cape, Bellville, South Africa, 1979; BSc with honours, U. Stellenbosch, South Africa, 1982; higher edn. diploma, U. South Africa, Pretoria, 1984; MSc, U. Akron, 1987, PhD, 1990. Sr. lab. technician U. Western Cape, 1980, mem. coun., 1996—; lectr. Peninsula Technikon, Bellville, 1980-87; rsch. scientist U. Akron, Ohio, 1986-91, Edison Polymer Innovation Corp., Akron, 1991-92; assoc. prof. Vista U., Port Elizabeth, South Africa, 1993-96; prof. chemistry U. South Africa, 1997—; rschr. Found. for Rsch. Devel., 1994-96, Water Rsch. Commn., 1995-99. Contbr. articles to sci. jours., incuding Polymer Internat.; patentee in field (U.S. and Republic of South Africa). Com. mem. Ednl. Opportunities Coun., South Africa. Recipient Africare Intership award, 1990, Disting. Corp. Inventor award Am. Assn. Patent Holders, 1995; grantee UN Edn. and Tng. Program for So. Africa, 1988. Mem. South African Chem. Inst. (exec. com. 1993-97, coun. 1995-97), Macromolecule Soc. South Africa. Mem. African Nat. Congress. Avocations: rugby, golf, cricket. Office: U South Africa, Dept Chemistry, PO Box 392, Pretoria 0003, South Africa

SUMMERS, SANDRA LEE, nursing educator; b. Lamar, Colo., Oct. 20, 1958; d. John William and Velma Bernadine Jackson; m. Ronald Lee Summers, July 2, 1977; children: Jeremy Keith, Jerrod Ray, Sarah Jean. MSc in Nursing, U. Colo., 1997, MSN, 1997. RN, Colo. Dir. Sonshine Presch., Wiley, Colo., 1988-90; staff nurse Ft. Lyon (Colo.) VA Med. Ctr., 1990-93; dir. nursing program Lamar (Colo.) Cmty. Coll., 1993—; chair Wellness Conf. com., 1997—; bd. dirs. High Plains Cmty. Health Ctr., Lamar. Recipient Masonic Excellence in Edn. award Masonic Temple, Lamar, 1997. Republican. Mem. Ch. of Christ. Avocations: camping, reading. E-mail: sandy.summers@lcc.cccoes.edu. Office: Lamar Community Coll 2401 S Main St Lamar CO 81052-3912

SUMMERS, THOMAS CAREY, lawyer; b. Frederick, Md., Feb. 9, 1956; s. Harold Thomas and Doris Jean (Culler) S.; m. Robin Ann Stalnaker, May 12, 1990; children: Kristin, Heather, Lindsay. BA, Dickinson Coll., 1978; JD, U. Balt., 1981. Bar: Md. 1981, U.S. Dist. Ct. Md. 1981, D.C. 1986. Assoc. Ellin & Baker, Balt., 1979-89, Peter G. Angelos, Balt., Md., 1989—; adj. prof. law U. Balt. Sch. of Law. Mem. ABA, Md. State Bar Assn., Md. Trial Lawyers Assn. Democrat. Lutheran. Avocation: golf. Office: Law Offices of P G Angelos One Charles Ctr Baltimore MD 21201

SUMMERSCALES, JOHN, engineer, educator; b. Wakefield, Eng., Apr. 9, 1952; s. Stanley and Mavis (Kershaw) S. BSc, U. Wales Inst. Sci. Tech., Cardiff, Wales, 1974; MSc, Thames Polytech., London, 1976; PhD, Plymouth (Eng.) Polytech., 1984; postgrad. diploma in edn., U. Plymouth, 1998. Registered profl. incorporated engr., Eng. Editorial coder Derwent Publs., London, 1976-77; rsch. asst. Plymouth Polytech., 1977-81; cons. Diving Diseases Rsch. Ctr. Ltd., Plymouth, 1982; materials technologist Western Approach Cons., Torquay, Eng., 1982-84; higher sci. officer Ministry of Def., Plymouth, 1984-87; sr. lectr. U. Plymouth, 1987-2000, reader in composites engring., 2000—; external examiner U. Manchester (Eng.) Inst. Sci. and Tech., 1990-99, U. Loughborough, Eng., 1991, U. Limerick, Ireland, 1993-95, Warwick U., 1996-99, U. Leeds, Eng., 1997, Strathclyde U., Scotland, 1998, U. Bournemouth, Eng., 2000. Editor (textbook) Non-Destructive Testing of Fibre-Reinforced Plastics, 1987-90; editor Composites Manufacturing, 1991-95, Microstructural Characterisation of Fibre-Reinforced Composites, 1998; sword-sequence arranger (Morris tradition cutlass dance) Shoelaces, 1992—. Fellow Inst. of Materials, Inst. of Non-Destructive Testing, Internat. Assn. Quality Practitioners; mem. Soc. for the Advancement of Materials and Process Engring. Avocations: cotswold Morris dancing, music, theater, photography, travel. Office: U Plymouth, U Plymouth, DMME Smeaton 101, Plymouth PL4 8AA, England

SUMMERS-POWELL, ALAN, lawyer. BA, Yale Coll., 1985; JD, U. Pa., 1988. Bar: N.Y. 1989, N.J. 1989, U.S. Dist. Ct. (fed. dist.) N.J. 1989, D.C. 1990, Fla. 1993, U.S. Dist. Ct. (mid. dist.) Fla. 1996, U.S. Ct. Appeals (11th cir.) 1996, U.S. Tax Ct. 1997. Pvt. practice Palm Harbor, Fla.; chmn. David Leasing and Devel., Inc. Office: PO Box 6043 Palm Harbor FL 34684-0643

SUMNER, GORDON MATTHEW See STING

SUMSION, JOHN WALBRIDGE, information scientist; b. Gloucester, Eng., Aug. 16, 1928; s. Herbert Whitton and Alice Hartley (Garlichs) S.; m. Annette Dorothea Wilson (div. 1979); children: Bridget, Christopher, Michael, Kate; m. Hazel Mary Jones, 1979. BA in Modern History, Cambridge (Eng.) U., 1952, MA, 1981; MA in Econs., Yale U., 1953. Prodn. mgr. K Shoemakers, Kendal, Eng., 1954-62, dir., 1962-81; registrar Pub. Lending Right, Eng., 1981-91; dir. libr. and info. stats. unit Loughborough (Eng.) U., 1991-96, sr. fellow dept. info. scis., 1996—; mem. Copyright Tribunal, Eng., 1990-93; non-exec. dir. TeleOrdering Ltd., Alton, Eng., 1992-94;mem. Libr. & Info. Svcs. Coun., Eng., 1992-95. Author: PLR in Practice, 1st edit., 1988, 2d edit., 1991; joint author: Perspectives of Public Library Use, 1995, Library Performance Indicators and Library Management tools, 1995; contbr. articles to profl. jours. Decorated Order Brit. Empire. Fellow Libr. Assn.; mem. Internat. Fedn. Libr. Assns. (hon. chmn. stats. sect. 1995-99). Liberal Democrat. Anglican. Avocations: singing, flute, walking. E-mail: j.w.sumsion@lboro.ac.uk. Home: The Granary, 29 Main St, Rotherby, Melton Mowbray, Leicestershire LE14 2LP, England Office: Loughborough U, Dept Info Sci, Loughborough LE11 3TU, England

SUN, ANDY, dentist; b. Ping-Dong, Taiwan, Nov. 23, 1953; s. Shi-Kia Sun and Su-Ju Chen; m. Shu-Yun Hsiung, Mar. 11, 1978; children: Han-Wei, Wan-Lin. DDS, Nat. Taiwan U., 1978, PhD, 1992. Attending physician Nat. Taiwan U., 1989—; assoc. prof. Fu-jen Cath. U., Taipei, 1993-94, World U. Journalism, Taipei, 1996—; vis. prof. Tianjin (China) Med. U., 1999—, Hu-Bei (China) Traditional Chinese Med. Coll., 1999—; vis. assoc. prof. Shanghai (China) Traditional Chinese Med. U., 1999—. Contbr. articles to profl. jours. Mem. cen. com. KMT, Taipei, 1995-98. Lt. Taiwan armed forces, 1978-80. Recipient Outstanding in Immunology Rsch. award Found. Immunology Rsch., 1987. Mem. Univ. and Coll. Lectrs. Assn. (pres. 1998—), Straits Acad. and Cultural Exch. Assn. (v.p. 1997—), Chinese Soc. Immunology, N.Y. Sci. Coun., Formosan Med. Assn. Roman Catholic. Avocations: speech, singing, mediation, qigong. Office: Nat Taiwan U Hosp, No 1 Chang-te St, Taipei 100, Taiwan

SUN, CHAO, artist, consultant; b. Hsuchou, China, Apr. 20, 1929; s. Weifang and Jy (Hwu) S.; m. Cheng Kuan, Apr. 8, 1978; 1 child, Yilin. Diploma, Nat. Taiwan (China) Acad. Arts, 1968. Soldier Ministry Nat. Def. China, 1946-62; artist sculpture, ceramics Nat. Palace Mus., Taipei, 1969-78; artist Taipei, 1978—, Tienshin Art and Pottery Corp., Taipei, 1982—; mem. exhbn. com., collection com., jury com. Taipei Fine Arts Mus., 1984—, Nat. Mus. History, Taipei, 1984—, Taiwan Mus. Art, Taichung City, 1984—, Kaohsiung Mus. Fine Arts, Kaohsiung City, 1984—; cons. Taiwan Internat. Artists' Village Planning Office, Taipei, 1999—. One-man exhibitions include Nat. Mus. History, Taipei, 1987, 94, Galerie Jacques Barrere, Paris, 1989, Sochaux Art Ctr., France, 1990, Übersee Mus., Germany, 1993, Staatliche Museen Kassel, Germany, 1993; long term

exhbns. include Nat. Palace Mus., Taipei, 1974—; represented in permanent collections at Victoria and Albert Mus., London, 1988, Brit. Mus., London, 1994. Everson Mus. Art, N.Y., 1992. Recipient Nat. Cultural award China Govt., 1987. Avocations: shooting, photography, travelling. Home and Office: 32-1 Tienshintz Sanchih, 252 Taipei Hsien Taiwan, China

SUN, CHING-CHERNG, optics science edcuator; b. Tainan, Taiwan, Jan. 6, 1965. BS, Nat. Chiao Tung U., Taiwan, 1988; PhD, Nat. Ctrl. U., Taiwan, 1993. Postdoct. Nat. Ctrl. U., 1993; assoc. prof. Nat. Ctrl. U., Taiwan, 1996—, Chine Hsin Coll. Tech. and Commerce, Taiwan, 1995-96. Contbr. articles to profl. jours. 2nd lt. Chinese Air Force, 1993-95. Mem. Optical Soc. Am., SPIE. Avocations: playing ball, reading, travel. Office: Nat Ctrl U, Inst Optical Sci, 320 Chung-Li Taiwan

SUN, DA-WEN, engineering educator, researcher; b. Chaozhou, Guangdong, China, Dec. 18, 1960; s. Guangbin Sun and Younong Zheng; 1 child, Angelina Meiling. BSME, South China U. Tech., 1982, MSME, 1985, PhD in Chem. Engring., 1988. Lectr. South China U. Tech., Guangzhou, 1988-89; rsch. fellow U. Stuttgart, Germany, 1989-90; rsch. assoc. Queen's U., Belfast, No. Ireland, 1990-91, U. Newcastle, Newcastle-upon-Tyne, Eng., 1991-94; sr. rsch. assoc. U. Sheffield, Eng., 1994-95; lectr. Univ. Coll., Dublin, Ireland, 1995-99; sr. lectr. U. Coll., Dublin, 1999—; dir. FRCFT Rsch. Group Univ. Coll., Dublin, 1995—, chmn. CIGR Internet svc. working group, sec. CIGR WG1 and EurAgEng SIG 12. Mem. editl. bd. CIGR Jour. Agrl. Engring. Internat.; contbr. articles to profl. jours. Recipient 1st Natural Sci. prize Higher Edn. Commn., Guangdong, 1994, 3d Natural Sci. prize Sci. and Tech. Commn., Guangdong, 1994. Mem. Instn. Mech. Engrs. (Eng., corp.), Inst. Materials (Eng., corp., E. Gaspar award 1991, PMDA award 1991), Am. Soc. Agrl. Engring. (corp.), Internat. Inst. of Refrigeration (corp.). Avocations: sports, gardening, travel, reading, internet. Office: Nat U Ireland, Earlsfort Terr, Dublin 2, Ireland

SUN, DONGCHU, statistics educator; b. Shanghai, People's Republic of China, May 8, 1956; s. Zenze Sun and Yun Chen; m. Zhuoqiong He, May 5, 1987; children: Abby P., Tony K. BS in Math., East China Normal U., 1982; MS in Statistics, Ohio State U., 1988; Phd in Statistics, Purdue U., 1991. Lectr. East China Normal U., Shanghai, 1985-87; fellow Ohio State U., Columbus, 1987-88; tchg. asst., fellow Purdue U., West Lafeyette, Ind., 1988-91; vis. asst. prof. U. Mich., Ann Arbor, 1991-92; asst. prof. U. Mo., Columbia, 1992-99, assoc. prof., 1999—; rsch. fellow Nat. Inst. of Statis. Scis., Research Triangle Park, N.C., 1998-99. Contbr. articles to profl. jours. Grantee NSF, 1999—, Nat. Inst. of Statis. Sci., 1996-99; fellow U. Calif., Berkeley, 1987; recipient I.W. Burr award Purdue U., 1991. Mem. Am. Statis. Assn., Inst. of Statis. Scis., Intrnat. Chinese Statis. Assn., Internat. Statis. Inst. Avocations: stamp collecting, exercise. Office: U Mo Dept Stats 316 Math Scis Bldg Columbia MO 65211-0001

SUN, HAIYIN, optical engineer, educator; b. Kunming, Yunnan, China, July 27, 1958; came to the U.S., 1990; s. Qiyuan Sun and Shouzheng Wang; m. Nan Yang, Oct. 3, 1987; children: Tobias Y., Christina N. BS in Physics, Shanghai (China) Tchrs. U., 1982; MS in Photonics, Shanghai (China) Inst. Optics, and Fine Mechanics, 1985; PhD in Photonics, U. Ark., 1994. Instr. Shanghai Tchr.'s U., 1982; asst. prof. Shanghai Inst. Optics and Fine Mechanics, 1986-88; vis. scientist Telecom. Network Rsch. Ctr. of Germany's Post, Darmstadt, 1988-90; optical engr. Power Tech., Inc., Little Rock, 1994-96; sr. optical engr. Coherent Inc., Auburn, Calif., 1996—; adj. prof. U. Ark., Little Rock, 1996—; prin. investigator various projects; editor Jour. Optical Comm. Contbr. chpt. to book and numerous articles to profl. jours.; inventor several optical devices. Named Outstanding Rschr., The Justice Dept. USA Govt., 1995; rsch. grantee Ark. Sci. & Engring. Authority, 1993. Avocations: classical music, watching TV movies and sports, cooking. Home: 8328 Northvale Way Citrus Heights CA 95610-0803

SUN, HUAFEI, mathematics educator; b. Dalian, Liaoning, China, Oct. 2, 1958; s. Changshan Sun and Shan Zhou; m. Mingze Chen; 1 child, Xiao Sun. BS, Northeastern U., Shenyang, China, 1987, MS, 1990; PhD, Tokyo Met. U., 1999. Asst. lectr. Northeastern U., 1990-93, lectr., 1993-94; postdoctoral Kumamoto U., 1999-01. Contbr. articles to profl. jours. Recipient Outstanding Thesis awards Liaoning Sci. Com., 1991, 92. Avocations: sports, music. Home: Hakozaki 5 chiome 4-12-504, Fukuoka 812-0053, Japan Office: Faculty Math, Kyushu Univ, Fukuoka 812-8581, Japan

SUN, JEFFREY C., legal educator; b. San Francisco, 1971; s. Gary and Ruth Sun. BBA, Loyola Marymount U., L.A., 1993, MBA, 1994; JD, Ohio State U., 1998; postgrad., Columbia U., 1998—. Bar: Ohio 1998. Dir. student activities Santa Monica (Calif.) Cath., 1993-95, dir. mktg. and admissions, 1993-95; assoc. Thompson, Hine & Flory, Columbus, Ohio, 1995; rsch. asst. Ohio State U., Columbus, 1997, rsch. assoc., 1998; rsch. asst. to pres. Tchrs. Coll. Columbia U., N.Y.C., 1998, instr., 1999—; mem. adv. bd. St. Monica Cath., Ohio Ctr. for Law Related Edn.; adj. asst. prof. NYU, N.Y.C., 1998—. Mem. Ohio State Bar Assn., Coun. on Law and Higher Edn., Edn. Law Assn. E-mail: jcs81@columbia.edu. Home: 1230 Amsterdam Ave # 918 New York NY 10027-6602

SUN, JENNIFER KATHERINE, physician; b. Princeton, N.J., Mar. 19, 1972; d. Pershing Bit-Sing Sun and Betty Chang; m. David Samuel Friedman, June 15, 1996. BA, Harvard Coll., 1993, MD, 1999. Rsch. fellow Cornell U. Med. Coll., N.Y.C., 1993-94, Nat. Eye Inst., Bethesda, Md., 1997-98; med. intern Lahey Clinic Med. Ctr., Burlington, Mass., 1999-2000; opthalmology resident Mass. Eye and Ear Infirmary, Boston, 2000—. Contbr. articles to profl. jours. Educator Prevention Health Awareness & Choice through Edn., Boston, 1994-95. NEH grantee, 1989; John Harvard scholar Harvard U., 1991-93, Elizabeth Cary Agassiz scholar Harvard U., 1991-93. Mem. AMA, Mass. Med. Soc. Avocations: theater, literature, cooking, travel. Home: 1135 Beacon St Apt 5 Brookline MA 02446-5505

SUN, JI WU, energy economist, educator; b. Shanghai, Mar. 6, 1948; Arrived in Finland, 1990; parents XinFu Sun and Xue AnMao; m. Du XiaoLing, Jan. 1, 1984; children: Jian, Jin, Maria. MSc, Elec. Power Rsch. Inst. China, Beijing, 1984; Licentiate, Turku (Finland) Sch. Econs., 1993, Dr., 1996. From lectr. to asst. prof. XinJiang Industry U., 1971-78; sr. fellow State Statis. Bur. China, Beijing, 1984-86, Youth Polit. Inst., Beijing, 1986-89, Turku Sch. Econs., 1990—. Contbr. articles to profl. jours. Avocation: reading. E-mail: jsun@abo.fi. Home: Kamnerinpolku 3 A 12, 20750 Turku Finland Office: Turku Sch Econs, Box 110, 20521 Turku Finland

SUN, JIAZHENG, Chinese government official; b. 1944. Grad. Chinese Lang. Dept., Nanjing (China) U., 1968. Employee Liuhe County, Jiangsu province, China, 1968-78; sec. Nanjing City Communist Party of China Youth League Com., Jiangsu Provincial Communist Party of China Youth League Com; sec. gen., standing com. Jiangsu Provincial Communist Party of China Com.; sec. Xuzhou City Communist Party of China Com.; dep. sec. Jiangsu Provincial Communist Party of China Com.; alternate mem. 14th Communist Party of China Ctrl. Com.; min. radio, cinema, and television Beijing People's Govt., 1994—, min. culture. Mem. Communist Party of China, 1966—. Office: Min of Culture, JIA 83/Dong An Men Bei Jie, Beijing 100722, China*

SUN, JIE, mathematics educator, researcher; b. Qingdao, China; s. Zhenxian and Xuewen Sun. Diploma in Engring., Tsinhua U., China, 1970; MS, Chinese Acad. Sci., China, 1981, U. Washington, 1983; PhD, 1986. Tchr. Tsinghua U., China, 1972-78; asst. prof. Northwestern U., 1986-92; sr. lectr. Nat. U. Singapore, 1993-97, assoc. prof., 1998—; cons. Chinese Industries, China, 1972-78; prin. investigator NSF, 1988-90; dir. MBAM Program Nat. U. Singapore, 1994-95; assoc. editor Asia-Pacific Jour. Oper. Rsch., Singapore, 1994—. Editor: Advances in Optimization and Appoximation, 1994; contbr. rsch. papers in field. Recipient Outstanding Univ. Rschr. award, 1999. Mem. Math. Programming Soc.

SUN, JI-YAO, immunologist, researcher; b. Tunchen, China, Nov. 25, 1960; came to u.S., 1996; s. Qizhen and Yimung Sun; m. Jing Han, Aug. 2, 1988; 1 child, Qishan. MB, Med. U. Anhui, Hefei, China, 1986; MD, The Acad. Amms, Beijing, 1991. Asst. rschr. The Acad. Amms, 1991-93, assoc. rschr., 1993-94; postdoctoral fellow U. Madrid, Spain, 1995-96; rsch. fellow City of Hope Nat. Med. Ctr., Duarte, Calif., 1996—. Author: Primary Immunodeficiency Disease, 1998; contbr. articles to profl. jours. Ministry of Edn. and Scis. scholar, Spain, 1995. Mem. AAAS, Am. Soc. Gene Therapy, N.Y. Acad. Scis. Home: 5305 Rosemead Blvd Apt 9 San Gabriel CA 91776-2243 Office: City of Hope Nat Med Ctr Familian & BMT 1500 Duarte Rd Duarte CA 91010-3012

SUN, JUNHONG, surgeon, educator; b. Fenghua, Zhejiang, China, July 24, 1951; d. Changxing Sun and Youjun Yu; 1 child, Ren. Diploma of medicine, Second Mil. Med. U., Shanghai, China, 1974, M in Medicine, 1984, PhD, 1989. Med. diplomate. Surgeon Changzheng Hosp., Shanghai, 1974-86; assoc. prof. surgery Second Mil. Med. U., Shanghai, 1989-91; dep. dir. surgeon Hepatobiliary Surgery Inst., Shanghai, 1989-91; fellow Australian Nat. Liver Transplantation Unit, Sydney, 1991-93; prin. hosp. scientist Royal Prince Alfred Hosp., Sydney, 1993—, dir. transplantation rsch., 1997—; clin. assoc. prof. U. Sydney, 1999—; vis. prof. surgery 2d Mil. Med. U., Shanghai, 1996—; vis. prof. surgery Sun Yat-Sen U. Med. Scis., Guangzhou, 1998—, Chinese PLA Gen. Hosp. and Mil. Postgrad. Med. Sch., Beijing, 1999—. Editor: Liver Tumors and Diseases, 1991, Science and Technology—Advancing into the New Millennium, 1999, Transplantation Surgery, 2000. V.p. Australia-China Scholars Assn., Sydney, 1995-97, pres., 1997-99. WHO fellow, N.Y., Pitts., 1987-88. Fellow Australasian Coll. Biomed. Scientists; mem. Chinese Med. Assn., Internat. Transplantation Soc., Internat. Soc. for Exptl. Microsurgery (councillor), Ausinan Sci. and Tech. Soc. (pres. Sydney 1999—, Coun. Australian Chinese Orgns. (dep. sec. gen. 1999—). Office: Dept Surgery, Univ Sydney, Sydney 2006 NSW, Australia

SUN, LUORUI, physics educator, researcher; b. Yanshi, Henan, China, Nov. 7, 1942; s. Naixin Sun and Yin Chen; m. Shuanglian Sun, Feb. 11, 1969; children: Shaocong, Shaofeng. BSc, U. Sci. and Tech. China, Beijing, 1968; MSc, U. Sydney, Australia, 1983. Technician Geol. Bur. Shanxi Province, China, 1968-77, Coal Geol. Bur. Henan Province, China, 1977-80; rschr. U. Sydney, 1980-83; tchr. Zhengzhou (China) U., 1983-86, assoc. prof., 1986-92, prof. physics, 1992—; vis. scholar U. Leeds, Eng., 1991, 97, U. Utah, Salt Lake City, 1994-95; cons. Sun Wah Pub. Co., Hong Kong, 1996—; dir. sci. project Zhengzhou Cosmic Ray Detecting Array, 1991—. Contbr. articles to profl. jours. Nat. scholar Edn. Dept. China, 1978, 93, China Nat. Scholarship Coun., 1996; recipient Sci. prize Henan Province, 1993, Outstanding prof. prize and May Day medal of Henan, 1994. Mem. Chinese Physics Soc. Avocations: table tennis, electronics, computers. Achievements include design of Zhengzhou cosmic ray air shower array. Office: Zhengzhou Univ, Dept Physics, Zhengzhou, Henan 450052, China

SUN, ROBERT ZU JEI, inventor, manufacturing company executive; b. Shanghai, July 5, 1948; s. David C.H. and Evelyn (Lee) S.; m. Nan Jennifer Ronis, Sept. 20, 1986; children: Matthew Nyland, Michael Elias. B.S. in Elec. Engring., U. Pa., 1970. Sr. project engr. Drexelbrook Engring. Co., Horsham, Pa., 1970-78; pres., chmn. bd. Suntex Internat., Inc., Easton, 1981—. Inventor 24 Math Game, Mhing Card Game; 5 patents in field. Pres. Coalition of Religious and Civic Orgns., Easton, 1979-81; mem. transition team Pa. Gov.-elect Tom Ridge, 1994; apptd. by Gov. Ridge to Pa. State Bd. Edn., 1995, Team Pa. Amb. Coun., 1999. Recipient 2 Excellence awards for Mhing pkg. Nat. Paperbox and Pkg. Assn., 1984-85. Office: 118 N 3rd St Easton PA 18042-1804

SUN, RON, computer scientist, cognitive scientist; b. Shanghai, Oct. 8, 1960. BS, Fudan U., Shanghai, 1983; MS, Clarkson U., Potsdam, N.Y., 1986; PhD, Brandeis U., Waltham, Mass., 1991. Rsch. engr. SRIEA, 1983-85; lectr. computer sci. Iona Coll., 1986-88; asst. prof. computer sci., psychology U. Ala., Tuscaloosa, 1992-98, assoc. prof. computer sci., psychology, 1998-99, assoc. prof. computer engring. and sci., 1999—; spkr. in field. Author: Integrating Rules and Connectionism for Robust Commonsense Reasoning, 1994, (chpts.) Neual and Intelligent Systems Integration, 1991, Neural Networks for High Level Knowledge Representation and Inference, Artificial Intellignece and Neural Networks: Steps Towards Principled Integration, Vol. 1, 1994, Progress in Neural Networks, Vol. 5, 1995; co-author: (chpts.) Neural and Intelligent Systems Integration, 1991, Neural Network Perspectives on Cognition and Adaptive Robotics, 1997, A Companion to Cognitive Science, 1999, Deep Fusion of Computational and Symbolic Processing, 1999, others; co-editor: Computational Architectures Integrating Neural and Symbolic Processes, 1994, Connectionist Symbolic Integration, 1997, Hybrid Neural Systems, 2000, Sequence Learning, 2000; editor-in-chief Cognitive Sys. Rsch.; editor Neural Computing Surveys, 1997—, Applied Intelligence, 1997—, Connection Sci., 1995—; guest editor Connection Sci., 1993, IEEE Transaction Neural Networks, 1998; reviewer MIT Press, John Wiley and Sons, Kluwer Acad. Pubs., Blackwell Pubs., World Sci. Lawrence Erlbaum Assocs., Acad. Press, Oxford U. Press; contbr. articles to Artificial Intelligence, Connection Sci., IEEE Transaction on Neural Networks, IEEE Transaction on Knowledge and Data Engineering, IEEE Transaction on Systems, Man, and Cybernetics, Neural Networks, Fuzzy Sets Sys., Applied Intelligence, Internat. Jour. Intelligent Sys., Info. Scis., Jour. Intelligent Sys., Philosoph. Psychology, Knowledge Acquisition, AISB Quar., AI Mag., Neural Network Revs., Jour. Math. Psychology, Consciousness and Cognition, Cognitive Sci., Adaptive Behavior, Cognitive Sys. Rsch. Grantee Office Naval Rsch., U. Ala., 1993, Army Rsch. Inst., 2000. Mem. IEEE (sr. mem.), Cognitive Sci. Soc. (David Marr award 1991), Am. Assn. Artificial Intelligence, Internat. Neural Network Soc., Assn. Computing Machinery, Soc. Psychology Philosophy, Upsilon Pi Epsilon. Address: CECS Dept Univ of Missouri 201 Engineering Building W Columbia MO 65211-2060

SUN, RONGQI, organic chemistry educator, researcher; b. Zhen Jiang City, Jiangsu, China, Jan. 23, 1960; s. Sun Shoukang and Li Lansheng; m. Yangsheng Wang, Aug. 14, 1987; 1 child, Jie. BSc, Lanzhou (China) U., 1982, MSc, 1985, PhD, 1988. Asst. prof. Shanghai Inst. Pharm. Industry, 1988-90; assoc. prof. organic chemistry East China U. Sci. and Tech., Shanghai, 1991-96, prof., 1996-99, dean dept. fine chem. tech., 1992—, v.p. Coll. Pharm. Tech., 1996—; vis. scholar Rutgers U., N.J., 1999—. Contbr. articles to sci. jours., including Phytochemistry, Planta Medica, Chinese Sci. Bull., Chinese Jour. Organic Chemistry. Recipient Shanghai edn. prize City of Shanghai, 1997. Mem. Chinese Pharm. Assn. Avocations: sports, travel. Office: East China U Sci and Tech, 130 Meilong Rd, Shanghai 200237, China

SUN, SIAO FANG, chemistry educator; b. Shaoshing, China, Feb. 19, 1922; came to U.S., 1949; s. Yuan and Yu C. Sun; m. M. Emily Chao, June 23, 1951; children: Patricia Viane, Caroline Marie, Diana Kate. MA, U. Utah, 1950; MS, Loyola U., 1956; PhD, U. Chgo., 1958, U. Ill., 1962. Prof. math. Northland Coll., Ashland, Wis., 1960-64; asst. prof. chemistry St. John's U., Jamaica, N.Y., 1964-70, assoc. prof. chemistry, 1970-75, prof. chemistry, 1975-92, adj. prof., 1992—; vis. scientist Nat. Ctr. Sci. Rsch., Strasbourg and Meudon-Bellevue, France, 1975-78, Carlsberg Lab., Copenhagen, 1981; staff scientist Max Planck Inst. Biophysical Chemistry, Gottingen, Germany, 1976. Contbr. articles to profl. jours. Office: St John's Univ Dept Chemistry Jamaica NY 11439-0001

SUN, SIYING, mechanical engineer, educator; b. Tainjin, China, Aug. 5, 1941; d. Jaifang Sun and Shuwen Ya; m. Yaowu Shi, Dec. 30, 1967; 1 child, Xuan Shi. BSc, Xi'an (China) Jiaotong U., 1964. Cert. engr., China. Engr. Shenyang (China) Gas Compressor Inst., 1964-70, Xi'an Cable Works, 1970-74; assoc. prof., then prof. Xi'an Jiaotong U., 1974-95; prof. Beijing Poly. U., 1995—; vice dir. Jiaoda-Wanbao Compressor Engring. Rsch. Ctr., Xi'an, 1988-90; sec., mem. compressors and cryogenics engring. discipline subcom. Nat. Tchg. Supervision Com. for High Edn., Xi'an, 1986—. Author: Theory of Reciprocating Compressors, 1987, Handbook of Chemical Machinery Wires, 1989, Gas Pulsation and Piping Vibration of Reciprocating Compressor, 1988 (2d Class award Nat. Excellent Books); contbr. articles to profl. jours. Recipient 1st class award Tech. Progress of Tainjin, 1982, 2d class Nat. Sci. Tech. Progress award, 1986, 3d class Sci. Tech. Progress award Nat. Edn. Com., 1994. Mem. China Compressor Assn. (cons. tech. com. 1990—). Avocation: dancing. Home: Mo-Fang-Na-Li 28-1-101, 100021 Beijing China Office: Beijing Poly U Environ Engr, 100 Ping Le Yuan, 100022 Beijing China

SUN, TUNG-TIEN, medical science educator; b. Chung King, Szechuan, People's Republic of China, Feb. 20, 1947; s. Chung-Yu and Wen (Lin) S.; m. Brenda Shih-Ying Bao, Aug. 14, 1971; children: I-Hsing, I-Fong. BS in Agrl. Chemistry, Nat. Taiwan U., Taipei, 1967; PhD in Biochemistry, U. Calif., Davis, 1974. Rsch. assoc. dept. biology MIT, Cambridge, 1974-78; asst. prof. depts. dermatology, cell biology and anatomy Johns Hopkins Med. Sch., Balt., 1978-81, assoc. prof. depts. cell biology and anatomy, dermatology, ophthalmology, 1981-82; assoc. prof. depts. dermatology and pharmacology NYU Med. Sch., N.Y.C., 1982-86, prof., 1986-90, Rudolf L. Baer prof., 1990—, prof. dept. urology, 1996—, assoc. dir. Skin Disease Rsch. Ctr., 1989-93, dean's lectr., 2000; mem. cell biology study sect. NIH, 1984-88; adj. prof. dept. dermatology U. Pa. Med. Sch., Phila., 1992—; chair Gordon Conf. Keratinization & Epithelial Differentiation, 1995; Angus lectr. U. Toronto, 1986, Pinkus lectr. Am. Acad. Dermatopathologists, 1986, Liu lectr. Stanford Med. Sch., 1987, Susan Swerling lectr. Harvard Med. Sch., 1991, Kihei Tanioku Meml. lectr. Japanese Soc. Investigative Dermatology, 1998; adj. prof. Coll. Life Sci. Peking U., 1998—; hon. prof. Third Mil. Med. U., Chung King, China, 1998—. Mem. editl. bd. Differentiation, 1984—, Epithelial Cell Biology, 1990-93; assoc. editor Jour. Investigative Dermatology, 1990—, Jour. Dermatol. Sci., 1992—; U.S. mng. editor Molecular Biology Report, 1994-96. Recipient Career Devel. award Nat. Eye Inst., 1978-82, Monique Neill-Caulier Career Scientist award, 1984-89, Alcon award in vision rsch., 1993, Wu Jieping Urololgy Found. award Chinese Med. Assn., 1998. Fellow AAAS; mem. Am. Soc. Biol. Chemists, Am. Soc. for Cell Biology, Internat. Soc. Differentiation (bd. dirs. 1985-88), Nat. Inst. Arthiritis and Musculoskeletal and Skin Diseases (bd. sci. counselors), Soc. Investigative Dermatology (Montagna lectr. 1989, bd. dirs. 1993-98), Assn. Rsch. in Vision Sci. and Ophthalmology. Office: NYU Med Sch Dept Dermatology 560 1st Ave New York NY 10016-6402

SUN, VINCENT CHINGWEN, medical educator, scientist; b. Chia-Yi, Taiwan, China, Sept. 27, 1966; s. Ta-ke Sun and Yi-Fen Chang. BS, Chengchi U., Taipei, Taiwan, 1988; MS, Taiwan U., 1990; PhD, U. Chgo., 1998. Rsch. asst. Nat. Sci. Coun. Taiwan Univ., 1992-93; rsch. assoc. Visual Scis. Ctr. Univ. Chgo., 1994-97; asst. prof. Chung Shan Med. Sch., Taichung, Taiwan, 2000—. Contbr. chpts. to books. Lt. Taiwanese Army, 1990-92. Mem. Am. Psychol. Assn., Optical Soc. Am., 523 Mountaineering Club (trustee 1999). Avocations: photography, mountaineering, shooting. Home: 129 Wan-Ning St #2, Taipei 116, China Office: Chang Gung Meml Hosp, 5 Fu Hsian St, Kwei-Shan 333, China

SUN, XIAN-HE, computer science educator; b. Beijing, Apr. 26, 1955; s. Chang-Xiang Sun and Yu Lin; m. Hang Zhang-Sun, Sept. 18, 1983; children: Alan Y., Linda Z. MS in Maths., Mich. State U., 1985, MS in Computer Sci., 1987, PhD in Computer Sci., 1990. Computer scientist Ames (Iowa) Nat. Lab., 1990-91; vis. asst. Clemson (S.C.) U., 1991-92; staff scientist ICASE NASA Langley, Hampton, Va., 1992-94; asst. prof. La. State U., Baton Rouge, 1994-99, assoc. prof., 1999; assoc. prof. Ill. Inst. Tech., Chgo., 1999—; guest scientist Argonne Nat. Lab., Darien, Ill., 1999—; vis. sr. scientist Navy Rsch. Lab, Stennes Space Ctr., 1999; vis. scientist NASA Langley, Hampton, 1994, 95, 96. Editor: spl. issue Jour. Parallel and Automated Computing, 1994, spl. issue Jour. Supercomputing, 1998; assoc. editor: (book) Proceedings of PDPTA Conf., 1998; contbr. chpt. to book. Recipient Cert. of Recognition Office of Naval Rsch., 1999, rsch. award NSF, 1999, TGEF award La. Bd. Regents, 1999. Mem. IEEE (sr.), Assn. Computing Machinery, Phi Kappa Phi. Office: Ill Inst Tech Dept Computer Sci Chicago IL 60616

SUN, XIE, hospital administrator, medical educator; b. Wuxi, Jiangsu, People's Republic of China, Jan. 19, 1933; d. Chunpu Sun and Minyi Ding; m. Deming Huang, Dec. 1, 1955; children: Huang Jihong, Huang Weiguo, Huang Weimin. BS, Nanjing U., Jiang Su, People's Republic of China, 1950, MD, 1956. Physician Med. Coll. Jiang Su, Zhenjian, 1956-60; physician Nanjing Gu Lou Hosp., 1960-65, physician-in-charge, 1965-83, chief gastroenterology, 1983-86, pres., 1986-90, dir. dept. gastroenterology and dept. internal medicine; prof. Med. Coll. Nanjing U., 1987—; adviser Nanjing Govt. Hosp., 1990—; cons. JingLin Expert Consultative Svc. Ctr., 1987—; well-known veteron experts com. mem. Nanjing Gu Lou Hosp., 2000; mem. coun. Jiang Su Province Vet. Experts Assn. in Sci. and Tech., 1999. Author: Clinical Pancreatology, 1989; contbr. articles to profl. jours. Mem. 8th Nanjing Com. of Communist Party of China, Nanjing, 1984-89. Rsch. assoc., recipient diploma of honor Internat. Biographical Ctr., Cambridge, Eng., 1994. Mem. Jiang Su Province Veteron Experts Assn. in Sci. and Tech. (coun. mem. 1999). Office: Nanjing Gu Lou Hosp, 321 Zhong Shan Rd, Nanjing Jiangsu 210008, China

SUN, XUECHUAN, physiologist, educator, researcher; b. Chengdu, China, Nov. 19, 1958; s. Liayu and Yuanfang (Lin) S.; m. Ronghui Zhou, Feb. 1, 1993; 1 child. BS, Chengdu Inst. Phys. Edn., 1982; MSc, Shanghai Inst. Phys. Edn., China, 1987; DSc, West China U. Med. Scis., Chengdu, 1997. Cert tchr., China. Clin. physician, asst. rschr. Nat. Inst. Sports Injuries, Chengdu, 1982-84; asst. prof. dept. sports medicine Chengdu Inst. Phys. Edn., 1984-87, lectr. dept. sports medicine, 1987-91, chmn., asst. prof. dept. sports medicine, 1991-95, dir., prof. dept. postgrad. studies, 1995-97; dir. Phys. Tng. and Rsch. Ctr. JUN Phys. Edn. Inst., Guangzhou, China, 1997—; mem. experts group for key disciplines of sports scis. State Bd. Phys. Culture and Sports, China, 1994-98, mem. tchg. materials com., 1996—. Chief editor, author: Exercise Chronobiology, 1994, Applied Chronobiology, 1995; author: Chronopharmacology and Chronomedicine, 1995; editor Jour. Chengdu Inst. Phys. Edn., 1989-96. Recipient awards. Mem. N.Y. Acad. Scis., Internat. Soc. for Chronobiology, China Sports Sci. Soc. (standing mem.). Avocations: soccer, tennis. Office: JUN Phys Edn Inst, No 38 Yudong Western Rd, Guangzhou Guangdong 510502, China

SUN, XUE-ZHI, physician, researcher; b. Liaoyuan, China, Sept. 3, 1963; s. Gui-Sheng and Yao-Xian (Pei) S.; m. Rui Zhang, Feb. 3, 2000. B Medicine, Norman Bethune U. Med. Scis., Changchun, China, 1985; PhD, Nagoya (Japan) U., 1996. Med diplomate. Intern Changchun Hosp., China, 1984-85; rschr., physician Lab. Industry Hygiene, Ministry Pub. Health China, Beijing, 1985-91; asst. Sch. Medicine, Tokushima (Japan) U., 1996-97; rschr. Nat. Inst. Radiol. Scis., Chiba, Japan, 1998—; vis. prof. Nagoya U., Japan, 2000—. Author: The World of Human Being, 1996; contbr. articles to profl. jours. Recipient award for best essay Chounichi Newspaper Agy., Japan, 1995, Tokushima Newspaper Agy., 1996, Internat. Edn. Ctr., Japan, 1997, China Central Television Quiz for Overseas Viewers, 1999, best cover design of "Radiological Scis." Jitsugyokoho Press, Japan, 2000. Fellow Japanese Teratology Soc. (Acad. award 1998), Japanese Assn. Anatomists, Japan Radiation Rsch. Soc., Med. Soc. China (Acad. award 1990); mem. AAAS, Japan Internat. Assn. (editor 1994). Buddhist. Avocations: reading books, writing essay and novel, sports, listening to music, watching movies. Home: 2-2-15-306 Chigusadai, Chiba 263-0013, Japan Office: Nat Inst Radiol Scis, 4-9-1 Anagawa, Chiba 263-8555, Japan

SUN, YAN, electrical engineer; b. Chengdu, Sichuan, China, Oct. 5, 1964; came to U.S., 1989; s. Shaokang and Yuan (Ye) S.; m. Rong Pan, Sept. 7, 1991. BS, Shandong Normal U., Jinan, China, 1984; MS, U. Elec. Sci. and Tech. China, Chengdu, 1987; PhD, Stanford U., 1995. Rsch. asst. Shandong Normal U., 1984, U. Elec. Sci. and Tech. China, Chengdu, 1984-87; mem. faculty U. Sci. and Tech. China, Hefei, 1987-89; rsch. asst. Stanford (Calif.) U., 1989-95; mem. tech. staff Bell Labs. Lucent Tech., Holmdel, N.J., 1995-98, sr. mgr., 1998—; guest prof. S.W. Jiaotong U., Chengdu, 1997—, Tsinghua U., Beijing, 1999. Contbr. articles to profl. jours. Named Innovator of Yr., Jour. of Telephone, Paris, 1998; Dr. Boi-Wei Chen Meml. scholar, 1995. Mem. IEEE (sr.), Optical Soc. Am., Photonic Soc. Chinese-Ams. (sec.). Achievements include research in long distance transmissions,. Office: 3B-528 101 Crawfords Corner Rd Holmdel NJ 07733-1900

SUN, ZHEN-DONG, laser and physics researcher; b. Laizhou, Shandong, China, June 22, 1963; s. Fu-Ling Sun and Yu-Xiang Zhang; m. Fa-Hua Qu, Dec. 6, 1987; 1 child, Wan-Peng. BSc in Physics, Shandong Normal U., 1984; M in Tech., Tsinghua U., Beijing, 1995; MSc, Toyama (Japan) U., 1997, PhD, 2000. Lectr. physics Yantai (Shandong, China) U., 1984-92; lectr. electronics engring. Tsinghua U., Beijing, 1992-95. Contbr. articles to profl. jours. Mem. Optical Soc. China, Phys. Soc. Japan, N.Y. Acad. Scis. Avocations: basketball, badminton, playing the Erhu. E-mail: d982264@ems.toyama-u.ac.jp. Fax: 81-764-938195. Office: Toyama U Dept Physics, Gofuku, Toyama 930-8555, Japan

SUN, ZHENG, research scientist; b. Mudanjang, China, Jan. 9, 1962; s. Yishao Sun and Shuqin Guo; m. Haishan Xing, Nov. 23, 1987; children: Hansen, William. B of Engring., Tsinghua U., Beijing, 1984; M of Engring., Harbin (China) Inst. Tech., 1987; Lic. Tech., Lappeenranta U. Tech., Finland, 1991; D of Tech., Lappeenranta U. Tech., 1992; MBA, Golden Gate U., 1997. Chartered engr. U.K. Engring. Coun. Engr. Cen. Iron and Steel Rsch. Inst., Beijing, 1987-89; rsch. engr. Lappeenranta U. Tech., 1989-92; sr. engr. Metalock (Singapore) Ltd., 1994-95; rsch. fellow Gintic Inst. Mfg. Tech., Singapore, 1995—; vis. scientist Tech. Rsch. Ctr. Finland, Espoo, 1992-94. Editor, guest editor: Internat. Jour. Materials and Product Tech., 1996; contbr. numerous papers to profl. jours. Recipient Nat. Tech. awards Nat. Sci. and Tech. Bd., 1995. Mem. Inst. Materials London (profl. mem.), Am. Welding Soc., Singapore Welding Soc. (coun. mem.). Avocations: music, sports, travel.

SUN, ZHENG MING, mechanical engineer; b. Jiangsu, China, Dec. 16, 1964; s. Yadong Sun and Chenglan Jiang; m. Hong Shan, Dec. 28, 1990; 1 child, Ye. Bsc, Southeast U., Nanjing, China, 1985; MSc, Chinese Acad. Scis., 1988, PhD, 1992. Asst. prof. Chinese Acad. Scis., Shenyang, 1992-93; rsch. fellow U. Vienna, Austria, 1993-94, Toyohashi U. Technology, Japan, 1994-97; rsch. scientist Tohoku Nat. Indsl. Rsch. Inst., Sendai, Japan, 1997-99, sr. rsch. officer, 1999—. Mem. Japan Inst. Metals. Avocations: tennis, reading. Home: Nishimiyagino 8-7-32, Sendai 983, Japan Office: Tohoku Nat Indsl Rsch Inst, 4-2-1 Nigatake Miyagino-ku, Sendai Japan

SUNAMURA, TSUGUO, coastal geomorphologist, coastal engineer; b. Tokyo, Apr. 1, 1941; s. Teiji and Jun (Hidaka) S.; m. Reiko Ogiwara, Jan. 17, 1971. B.Sc. in Phys. Geology, Tokyo Kyoiku U., 1964; M.Sc. in Civil Engring., U. Tokyo, 1969; Ph.D. in Coastal Engring., 1972. Coastal engr. rsch. sect. Nippon Tetrapod Co., Ltd., 1964-67; rsch. engr., then rsch. assoc. Coast Engring. Lab. U. Tokyo, 1969-78; assoc. prof. Inst. Geosci. U. Tsukuba, 1978-87; prof., 1987-96; prof. dept. earth and space sci. Osaka (Japan) U., 1996—; vis. prof. civil engring. U. Del., 1978-79; instr. Chuo U., 1970-78, Chiba U., 1975-76. Author: Geomorphology of Rocky Coasts; mem. editl. bds. profl. publns; contbr. articles to profl. jours. Mem. Geol. Soc. Am., Soc. Sedimentary Geology, Japanese Goemorphol. Union, Japanese Soc. Civil Engrs., Assn. Japanese Geographers, Brit. Geomorphol. Rsch. Group. Home: 4-37-7-302 Senriyama-nishi, Suita Osaka 565-0851, Japan Office: Osaka U, Dept Earth and Space Sci, Osaka 560-0043, Japan

SUNANDANA, CHANNAPPAYYA SHAMANNA, physics educator, researcher; b. Kunigal Town, Karnataka, India, June 17, 1949; s. Amrutur Channappayya Shamanna and Shamanna Indiramma; m. Sunandana Prabha, Oct. 13, 1975; 1 child, Sumohan. BSc, U. Mysore, India, 1968; MSc in Physics, Indian Inst. Tech., Madras, 1970, PhD, 1976; diploma in creative writing in English, Indira Gandhi Nat. Open U., New Delhi, 1992. Postdoctoral fellow Indian Inst. Tech., 1976-81; fellow in physics U. Hyderabad, India, 1981-84, lectr., 1984-86, reader, 1986-98; prof. U. Hyderabad, 1998—. Author: (poetry) Anukampana, 1983. Mem. Materials Rsch. Soc. India (life), Indian Physics Assn. (life). Avocations: music, literature, popularizing science, poetry recitals. Office: U Hyderabad, Sch Physics, Hyderabad 500 046, India

SUND, BENGT CHRISTIAN, chemistry researcher, educator; b. Vaasa, Finland, Oct. 22, 1958; arrived in Sweden, 1988; s. Bengt Vilhelm and Berit Ann-Marie (Norrgård) S. MS, Turku (Finland) Acad., 1985; PhD, Uppsala (Sweden) U., 1992. Chemist Wallac Oy, Turku, 1984-88; rschr. Uppsala U., 1992-97; researcher Medivir AB, Huddinge, Sweden, 1997—. Contbr. articles to profl. jours. With Finnish Army, 1977-78. Recipient award Swedish Tech. Rsch. Coun., Uppsala, 1993-95, Swedish Rsch. Coun. Natural Scis., Uppsala, 1996. Mem. Finnish Chem. Soc., Swedish Chem. Soc. (cartoonist comic strip). Mem. Eckankar Religion of Light and Sound. Achievements include rsch. publications for new syntheses of novel DNA and RNA analogs as biomimickal tools for biological processes and patent applications for syntheses of new medical diagnostical tools and new medical drugs. Avocations: spiritual matters, cartooning. Office: Medivir AB, Lunastigen 7, S-14144 Huddinge Sweden

SUNDARAM, RAMAKRISHNAN, research consultant; b. New Delhi, Delhi, India, Oct. 12, 1959; came to US, 1982; s. Ramakrishnan and Rajeswari S. B. Tech., Indian Inst. Tech., New Delhi, 1982; degree in elec. engring., MIT, 1985, MS, 1987; PhD, Purdue U., 1994. Scientist Tektronix Inc., Beaverton, Oreg., 1985, Beaverton, 1987; tech. staff AT&T Bell Labs., Holmdel, N.J., 1987-88; rsch. cons. Info. Sys. Inc., W. Lafayette, Ind., 1994-95; designer fast computing architectures Info. Sys. Inc., W. Lafayette, 1995—. Contbr. articles to profl. jours. Mem. IEEE, Optical Soc. Am., SPIE. Avocations: classical music, tennis, reading.

SUNDARESHAN, TAMBARAHALLI SUBRAMANIAM, cytogeneticist, educator; b. Mysore, Karnataka, India, June 30, 1955; s. Tambarahalli Subramaniam and Krishna Iyer Rajammal; m. Suma Dhavale, Aug. 29, 1982; children: Shilpa, Sneha. BS, Mysore U., 1974, MS, 1976; PhD, Bangalore (India) U., 1995. Rsch. asst. Indian Inst. of Sci., Bangalore, 1977-81; cons. cytogeneticist Med. Genetics Ctr., Kuwait, 1981-88; asst. prof. cytogenetics Kidwai Meml. Inst. of Oncology, Bangalore, 1990—. Contbr. over 40 articles to profl. jours. Avocations: tennis, cricket. Home: 599 SWATI 10th B Cross, 4th Main WCR II Stage, Bangalore 560 086, India Office: Dept Pathology, Kidwai Meml Inst Oncology, Bangalore 560029, India

SUNDAR RAJAN, ASOKAN, physicist, educator; b. Madras, Tamil Nadu, India, Oct. 2, 1960; s. Chakravarthy and Shanbagam Sundar Rajan; m. Kadambi Venkatachar Rajshri, Sept. 15, 1988; 1 child, Siddarth Asokan. BS in Physics, Madras U., 1981; MS in Materials Sci., Anna U., Madras, 1983; PhD in Physics, Indian Inst. Sci., Bangalore, 1987. Rsch. assoc. Indian Inst. Sci., Bangalore, 1986-87, sci. officer, 1987-90, sr. lectr., 1990-93, asst. prof., 1993-99, assoc. prof., 1999—. Editor: (book) Advances in Instrumentation, 1996; contbr. articles to internat. jours. Recipient Young Scientist award Indian Nat. Sci. Acad., 1990, Young Scientist Rsch. award Dept. Atomic Energy, 1995. Mem. Materials Rsch. Soc. India, Semi-Condr. Soc. India (life), Instrument Soc. India (gen. sec.). Avocations: listening to music, reading books. Home: Indian Inst Sci, DV-127 Vignanapura Campus, Bangalore 560 094, India Office: Indian Inst Sci, C V Raman Ave, Bangalore 560 012, India

SUNDBERG, CARL-ERIK WILHELM, telecommunications executive, researcher; b. Karlskrona, Sweden, July 7, 1943; came to U.S., 1984; s. Erik Wilhelm and Martha Maria (Snaar) S. MEE, U. Lund, Sweden, 1966, PhD, 1975. Tchr., rsch. asst., lectr. U. Lund, 1966-75, rsch. prof. (docent), 1977-84; rsch. fellow European Space Agy., Nordwijk, The Netherlands, 1975-76; disting. mem. tech. staff AT&T Bell Labs., Murray Hill, N.J., 1984-96, Lucent Technologies, Bell Labs., 1997—; cons. L.M. Ericsson, Gothenburg, Sweden, 1976-77, Bell Labs., Crawford Hill, N.J., 1981-82; instr. Carl Cranz Gesellschaft, Oberpfaffenhofen, Fed. Republic Germany, 1990-93. Co-author: Digital Phase Modulation, 1986, Source-Matched Mobile Communications, 1995; contbr. articles to profl. jours.; patentee in field. Served in Swedish Navy, 1968. Fellow IEEE (Best Paper award 1986, guest editor Jour. on Selected Areas in Comm. 1988-89), IEE Marconi Premium (Best Paper award 1989); mem. Swedish Union Radio-Scientifique Internationale, Svenska Electric Engrs., Riksförening (Sweden), CF Civil Engrs. förbundet (Sweden). Lutheran. Avocations: travel, history, photography. Home: 25 Hickory Pl Apt A11 Chatham NJ 07928-1465 Office: Lucent Technologies Bell Labs RM 2D-547 600 Mountain Ave New Providence NJ 07974-2008

SUNDBERG, EDWARD AUGUST, consulting executive; b. Chgo., May 14, 1947; s. Edward B. and Ruth (Wildebush) S.; m. Leslie Dahn, June 17, 1972; children: Edward, Liisa, Lindsey, Lori. BS, U.S. Naval Acad., 1968; MBA, Boston U., 1974. Commd. ensign USN, 1968, served to lt., resigned, 1973; ret. capt. USNR, 1991; dir. sales Norlin Mus. Instruments, Lincolnwood, Ill., 1975-79; v.p. Burns Internat. Security Svc., Chgo., 1979-80; pres. Odgen Security, Inc., Boston, 1981-85, Blydenstein Willink, U.S.A., Inc., Boston, 1985-88; v.p. Blydenstein Willink, N.V., Enschede, The Netherlands, 1985-88; prin., ptnr. CRD, 1999—; bd. dirs. ConsultAmerica, Inc., Atlanta, pres., 1987-99; vis. prof. Boston U. Sch. Mgmt., 1983-84; pres. ISS Oxford Svcs., Atlanta, 1989-92; exec. v.p. ISS Internat. Svc. System, Inc., 1990-92; chmn. Sundberg Communications Co., Inc., 1992-95. Cubmaster Boy Scouts Am., Concord, Mass., 1984; chmn. bd. dirs. Thermomizer Environmental Corp., 1996-99, Big Bros. and Big Sisters of Metro Atlanta, 1991-94. Capt. USN R, 1973-92. Mem. Young Pres's. Orgn., Naval Res. Assn. (life), Res. Officers Assn., U.S. Naval Alumni Assn. (life), Boston U. Alumni Assn. (bd. dirs. MBA Alumni Bd. 1984-85). Avocations: racquetball, tennis, coins, golf.

SUNDBERG, JOHAN EMIL FREDRIK, music educator, researcher; b. Stockholm, Mar. 25, 1936; s. Halvar G.F. and Margit F.K. (Hammarberg) S.; m. Agneta Sundberg, 1968 (div.); 1 child, Susanna; m. Ulla E.M. Ahlesten, Dec. 3, 1983; children: Martin, Erik. Degree filosofie kandidat, Uppsala U., 1961, degree filosofie licentiat in musicology, 1963, degree filosofie doktor, docent in musicology, 1966; D (honoris causa), U. York (Great Britain), 1996. Guest researcher Royal Inst. Tech., Stockholm, 1962-66, rsch. scientist, 1967-79, prof. music acoustics, 1979—. Author: The Science of the Singing Voice, 1987, The Science of Musical Sounds, 1991; editor Harmony and Tonality, 1987, Gluing Tones, 1992; contbr. more than 150 articles to scientific jours. Mem. Stockholm Bach Choir, 1964-79, pres. 1973-79. Fellow Acoustical Soc. Am.; mem. Swedish Royal Acad. Music, Swedish Acoustical Soc. (pres. 1976-81). Avocation: singing. Office: KTH Royal Inst Tech, SE 10044 Stockholm Sweden

SUNDERARAJ, FRANCIS, religious organization administrator; b. Madras, Tamil Nadu, India, Apr. 7, 1937; s. Abraham Devaraj James and Sophip David; m. Sheila Bhanumathy Devasahayam, Dec. 29, 1965; children: Mallika Ruth, Vinodh Samuel. BS, Madras Christian Coll., 1957; B in Divinity, Union Biblical Sem., Pune, India, 1965; M in Theology, Princeton (N.J.) Theol. Sem., 1971; MA, Wheaton Coll., 1993; D (hon.), Biola U., La Mirada, Calif., 1995. Chemist Corp. Madras, 1958-59, Tube Products India, Madras, 1960-61; assoc. pastor Emmanuel Meth. Ch., Madras, 1965-67; pastor, dist. supt. Meth. Ch., Malaysia, 1967-70, 72-76; sec. christian edn. Evang. Fellowship India, 1976-90, gen. sec., 1984—; gen. sec. Evang. Fellowship Asia, 1994—. Editor Aim, 1984—, Asian Ch. Today, 1994—. Mem. World Evang. Fellowship (mem. internat. coun.). Avocations: reading, television, meeting people. Home & Office: c/o Victoria Chambers, 4 1 826 JN Rd, Hyderbad 500001, India

SUNDERLAND, ERIC, university president; b. Ammanford, Carmarthensmire, U.K., Mar. 18, 1930; s. Leonard and Mary Agnes (Davies) S.; m. Jean Patricia Watson, Oct. 19, 1957; children: Helen Rowena, Frances Anne. BA, U. Wales, U.K., 1950, MA, 1951, LLD (hon.), 1997; PhD, U. London, 1954. Rsch. asst. U. London, 1953-54; rsch. scientist Nat. Coal Bd., U.K., 1957-58; lectr. in anthropology U. Durham, Eng., 1958-66, sr. lectr. in anthropology, 1966-71, prof. of anthropology, 1971-84, pro-vice chancellor, 1979-84; prin., vice chancellor U. Wales, Bangor, 1984-95, vice chancellor, 1989-91, prof. emeritus, 1995—; pres. U. Wales, Lampeter, 1998-2001; sec.-gen. Internat. Union Anthropol. and Ethnol. Scis., 1978-98, pres. 1998—; chmn. bd. dirs. Gregynog Press, 1991—; mem. Broadcasting Coun. for Wales (BBC), 1996-2000. Editor: Genetic Variation in Britain, 1973, The Exercise of Intelligence, 1980, Genetic and Population Studies in Wales, 1986. Chmn. local govt. boundary commn. for Wales, 1994—; chmn. Environ. Agy's adv. com. for Wales, 1996—; mem. bd. Brit. Coun., 1996—; chmn. Welsh com. Brit. Coun., 1996—; high sheriff of Gwynedd, 1998-99, also dep. lt., 1998-99, lord lt. of Gwynedd, 1999—. Commd. officer Royal Arty., 1954-56. Decorated Order Brit. Empire, 1999; recipient M. Gandhi Freedom award Coll. William and Mary, Williamsburg, 1989; Lampeter fellow U. Wales (hon.), 1995, Bangor fellow U. Wales (hon.), 1996. Fellow Royal Anthopol. Inst. (various positions including pres. 1989-91), Inst. Biology London, Croatian Anthropol. Soc. (hon.); mem. Gorsedd of Bards (hon.), Internat. Union Anthropology and Ethnolog. Scis. (pres. 1998—). Congregationalist. Avocations: traveling, book collecting, gardening, water colors. Home: Y Bryn, Ffriddoedd Rd, Bangor Gwynedd LL57 2EH, United Kingdom

SUNDERLAND, NORMAN RAY (NORM SUNDERLAND), health physicist, nuclear engineer educator; b. Lone Wolf, Okla., Aug. 1, 1933; s. Alva Franklin and Octava Pearl (Purcell) S.; m. Marilyn NMN Stanworth, Aug. 27, 1970; children: Melody, Larry, Derreck, Toni, James, Jo Lynn, Stacie, Thomas. BS, Okla. State U., 1960; MEd, U. Nev., Las Vegas, 1973; PhD, Columbia-Pacific U., 1985. Registered radiation protection technologist. Asst. dir. environ. sci. REECO (Nev. Test Site), Mercury, Nev., 1966-77; univ. sys. radiation safety officer U. Mo., Columbus, 1977-80; prof. N.E. Mo. State, Kirksville, 1978-84; dir. environ. health, safety U. Mo., Columbia, 1980-82; nuc. power cons. AWC, Inc., Cedar Rapids, Iowa, 1982-85; asst. dir. nuc. assessment divsn. EPA, Las Vegas, 1985-91; dir. environ. health, safety Utah State U., Logan, 1991-98; dir. Envirocare of Tex., Andrews, 1998—; chair radiation control, Utah, 1987-1992; EPA rep. to Ea. Europe (Poland, Russia), 1989-96; cons. French AEC. Author: Bio-Physics of Radiation, 1997; co-author: Rad Emergency Response Operations, 1968, (Jour.) Transfer of Radiocesium to Grass, 1993, Transfer of Radiocesium to Soil, 1994; patentee in field. Pres. Mo. Higher Ednl. Assoc., Columbia, 1980-81; bishop LDS Ch., Cedar Rapids, Iowa, 1982-85. With combat engring. U.S. Army, 1953-56, Alaska. Fellow Nat. Health Physics Soc. (pres. MidAm. chpt. 1981-82, Lake Mead chpt. 1988-89, Great Salt Lake chpt. 1994-95, chmn. bd., mem. membership com. 1998—), Nat. Registry Radiation Protection Technicians (sec., mem. nat. bd. 1975-98, emeritus 1992, Arthur Humm Jr. Meml. award 1998); mem. Jaycees. Republican, Democrat. Mem. LDS Ch. Achievements include TRUclean process patent which removes radioactive material from soil (now owned by Lockeed Internat.). Home: 1851 N 1600 E North Logan UT 84341-2114

SUNDERMAN, ROBERT ALLEN, artist, set designer; b. Clarinda, Iowa, Nov. 11, 1956; s. Lavern Charles and Jenny Lee Sunderman; m. Michele Ann Dunne, Jan. 15, 1983. BFA, U. Iowa, 1979, MA, 1981, MFA, 1982. Artist, scenic designer Sunderman Enterprises, Des Moines, 1982—; scenic designer Iowa Pub. TV, Johnston, 1984-2000; art instr. Des Moines Art Ctr., 1986—; asst. prof. tech. and design theatre Iowa State U., Ames, Iowa, 2000—; asst. sculptor to Chungi Choo, 1982-96; scenic designer, painter World Food Prize, Theatre Coll., Des Moines, 1999; scenic designer in residency Grinnell, Iowa, 1999. Prin. works include Meml. Wall, Des Moines, Little Boxes, Johnston, Iowa, Ceremonial Mate, Des Moines. Recipient Jury award Sedona Art Assn., 1992, Best in Metal award Two Rivers Art Assn., 1997, Windsor Newton award 6th Nat. Art Exhbn. Northern Colo. Art Assn., 1997, Excellence award Iowa Film Assn., 1998, Merit award Iowa Film Assn., 1998. Mem. U.S. Inst. Theatre Tech., Soc. Am. Silversmiths, Des Moines Art Ctr., Iowa Craft Assn., Kansas City Artists Coalition, Arts Iowa City. Avocations: hiking, biking, traveling, skiing, volleyball. E-mail: rsunder@iastate.edu. Office: Iowa State U 210 Pearson Hall Ames IA 50311 Also: Sunderman Enterprises 1134 46th St Des Moines IA 50311-3310

SUNDIN, MATS JOHAN, professional hockey player; b. Sollentuna, Sweden, Feb. 13, 1971. Selected 1st round NHL entry draft Que. Nordiques, 1989; traded Toronto Maple Leafs, 1994, right wing, 1994—; played in Europe during 1994-95 NHL lockout; named to Swedish League All-Star Team 1990-91, 91-92; selected NHL All-Star Game, 1996. Office: c/o Toronto Maple Leafs, 60 Carlton St, Toronto, ON Canada M5B 1L1

SUNDIUS, TOM ROBERT, physicist, educator, researcher; b. Helsinki, Dec. 21, 1942; s. Robert Waldemar and Mary Alma (Askolin) S.; m. Carola Elisabeth Karlsson, June 21, 1974; children: Annemarie Elisabeth, Erik Robert Christian. MSc, U. Helsinki, 1965, LicPhil, 1971, PhD, 1981. Rsch. scientist Rsch. Inst. for Theoretical Physics, Helsinki, 1972-74; rsch. asst. Finnish Acad., 1975-77; teaching asst. dept. physics U. Helsinki, 1978-84, amanuensis dept. physics, 1985—, docent in physics, 1977—; vis. scientist, Fulbright scholar U. Mich., Ann Arbor, 1981-82. Mem. Phys. Soc. in Finland (chmn. 1993-96), Finnish Phys. Soc. Lutheran. Avocations: astronomy, genealogy. Office: U Helsinki Dept Physics, PO Box 9, FIN00014 Helsinki Finland

SUNDNES, KNUT OLE, physician, consultant; b. Oslo, Norway, Oct. 18, 1946; s. Jon Sigurd and Marte (Westre) S.; m. Sissel Koller, Apr. 19, 1969; children: Ane Kristin, Jon Erlend. Student, U. Basel, Switzerland, 1972, Ednl. Coun. Fgn. Med. Grads., 1972, Nat. Def. Coll., Norway, 1986, Staff Officers Course, UN, Sweden, 1994. Lic. physician, Norway, 1974, specialist in anesthesiology and intensive care, 1981. Med. registrar Akershus Cen. Hosp., Norway, 1972-73; surg. registrar Oslo City Hosp., Norway, 1974-76; anesthesiology registrar Baerum County Hosp., Norway, 1976-78; anesthesiology registrar Akershus Cen. Hosp., Norway, 1978-79, sr. registrar anesthesiology, 1979-82; sr. registrar anesthesiology Nat. Hosp., Oslo, Norway, 1982-87; cons. Dept. Anesthesiology Baerum County Hosp., Norway, 1987-96; head Anaesthetic Svcs. Norway Def. Forces, 1996—, dir. Ctr. for War Surgery and Emergency Medicine, 1999—; med. officer UNIFIL, South Lebanon, 1979; med. del. Internat. Com. Red Cross, Thailand, 1983-84, Kabul, Afghanistan, 1990, 92, med. coord., Mekele, Ethiopia, 1991; force med. ops. and planning officer UNPF, Zagreb, 1994-95; guest lectr. U. Bergen, Norway, 1991—, U. Oslo, 1992—, European Ctr. Disaster Medicine; chmn. Task Force on Quality Control of Disaster Mgmt., 1994—. Contbr. numerous articles to profl. jours. Union rep. Akershus Cen. Hosp., Norway Med. Assn., 1981-82, National Hosp., 1985-86; chmn. Physicians Adv. Bd., Baerum County Hosp., 1993-96. Lt. col. UNPF, Zagreb, 1994-95. Recipient UNIFIL medal UN, 1979, UNPF medal UN, 1995. Mem. Norwegian Assn. for Disaster Medicine (pres. 1993-94), Nordic Soc. for Disaster Medicine (mem. bd. dirs. 1993—, pres. 1998—), Rotary Internat., Norwegian Med. Assn., World Assn. Disaster and Emergency Medicine (bd. dirs. 1995—, pres.-elect World Assn. Disaster and Emergency Medicine 1999—). Avocations: hunting, sailing. Office: Norwegian Defense Forces-Med Regiment, Lahaugmoen, 2026 Skjetten Norway

SUNDQUIST, HELGE ERIK, communications executive; b. Vaasa, Finland, Aug. 2, 1930; s. Hugo Erik and Dagny Sigrid (Krook) S.; m. Ruth Linnea Blomqvist, Dec. 30, 1956; children: Nils Eirik, Hans Kristian, Britt-Marie Ingeborg. Diploma in Econ. Scis., Abo Akademi, Turku, Finland, 1954. Acct. Vasabladet, Vaasa, 1955, office mgr., 1956-62, editor-in-chief, 1962-64, fin. mgr., 1964-67, mng. dir., 1968-89; mng. dir. Ab Suncas Investment Ltd., Vaasa, 1990—. Mem. Regional Planning Com., Vaasa, 1965-70. Grantee Amerikan Suomen Lainan Apuraha, 1961; recipient Ekonomierad Titel Pres. of Finland, 1989. Mem. Internat. Newspapers Promotion Assn. in Europe (nat. sec. Finland chpt. 1979-84), Swedish Press Assn. Finland (chmn. 1975-89, named Chmn. of Honor 1990), Graphic Club (chmn. Vaasa chpt. 1968-2000), Swedish Club (sec. Vaasa chpt. 1970-80), Masons (sec. Österbotten chpt. 1976-80). Avocations: golf, slalom, music. Home: Strandgatan 15 B, SF-65120 Vaasa Finland Office: Ab Suncas Investment Ltd, Radhusgatan 21, 65100 Vaasa Finland

SUNDSTØL, FRIK, agronomy and agricultural sciences educator; b. Birkenes, Norway, Feb. 26, 1940; s. Georg Berner and Randi Sofie Sundstøl; m. Turi Elin Fredriksen, Aug. 1, 1964; children: Arnt, Bent Asbjørn. BSc, Agr. U. of Norway, 1965, PhD, 1969, D of Agr., 1975. Scientist Agr. U. of Norway, Ås, 1970-74, assoc. prof., 1975-87, prof., 1987-99; tech. advisor So. African Ctr. Cooperation Agrl. Rsch. Tng.-So. African Devel. Cmty., Gaborone, Botswana, 1999—; advisor Internat. Found. for Sci., Stockholm; cons. FAO,Rome, China, Greece. Co-editor proceedings Utilization of Low Quality Roughages in Africa, 1981, Energy Metabolism of Farm Animals, 1982; editor Handbook - Straw and other Fibrous By-Products as Feed, 1984; contbr. articles to sci. and profl. jours. Lt. Norwegian Army. Grantee Fullbright Found., Cornell U., 1995. Mem. Scandinavian Assn. of Agrl. Scientists, European Assn. of Animal Scientists (chmn. nutrition sect. 1994-98). Lutheran. Avocations: skiing, athletics, fishing. E-mail: fsundstol@gov.bw.

SUNDSTROM, BERNT OLOF, fiber optics researcher, consultant, educator; b. Hammerdal, Jamtland, Sweden, Apr. 18, 1946; s. Jons and Augusta Annie (Jonsson) S.; m. Viviann Birgit Bergman, Aug. 13, 1988; children: Anna Helena, Ulla Magdalena, Johan Olof. MS, Royal Inst. Technology, Stockholm, 1973, PhD in Physics, 1981. Rsch. engr. Ericsson Cables, Sundbyberg, Sweden, 1982-95; rschr. Ericsson Microelectronics, Kista, Sweden, 1995—; ITU Expert Internat. Telecomms. Union, Bangalore, India, 1988, 94. Author: (book) Luminescence and Absorption Studies of Zinc Phosphide and Indium-Doped Silicon, 1981. Mem. Swedish Nat. Com. Internat. Electrotechnical Commn., 1993—, Swedish Standards Assn., 1994—. Mem. Swedish Optical Soc. Avocations: Mozart music, etymology, astronomy, physics, chess. Office: Ericsson Microelectronics, Isafjordsgatan 16, S-16481 Kista Sweden

SUNDSTRÖM, GEORG OLIVER ZACHARIAS, lawyer; b. Helsinki, Mar. 16, 1936; m. Lena Sundström; children: Pamela, Filip, Alexander. LLM, U. Helsinki, 1961, LLD, 1965; MCL, U. Chgo., 1963; MLitt, Cambridge U., 1966. Lawyer Finnish Steamship Corp., Helsinki, 1958, 59, 70; asst. Espoo (Finland) Dist. Ct., 1960; judge Helsinki Mcpl. Ct., 1962; assoc. Haight, Gardner, Poor & Havens, N.Y.C., 1963; legal advisor European Commn., Brussels, 1971-72; ptnr. Nordic Law, Helsinki, Brussels, 1972—. Office: Nordic Law, Unioninkatu 39 A 9, FI-00170 Helsinki Finland

SUNDVALL, LARS, materials science engineer; b. Stockholm, Feb. 16, 1962; m. Sussanne Bergman, May 29, 1993. MSc, Royal Inst. Tech. Stockholm, 1986. From mgr. sys. to mgr. planning and control Ericsson Components AB, Stockholm, 1987-95, mgr. project, 1996-97; operational devel. and quality mgr. Ericsson Radio Sys., AB., Stockholm, 1998—; mem. gen. assembly Swedish Assn. Grad. Engrs., Stockholm, 1994—. Grantee Royal Inst. Tech. Sweden, 1985. Avocations: running, cross-country skiing, downhill skiing. Home: Runsavägen 26, 16854 Stockholm Bromma, Sweden Office: Ericsson Radio Sys AB, S-16480 Stockholm Sweden

SUNDY, GEORGE JOSEPH, JR., engineering executive; b. Nanticoke, Pa., Apr. 22, 1936; s. George Joseph Sr. and Stella Mary (Bodurka) S.; m. Stella Pauline Miechur, May 21, 1966; children: Sharon Ann, George Joseph III. BS, Pa. State U., 1958. Rsch. engr. Bethlehem (Pa.) Steel Corp., 1959-85; reliability engr. Flo-Con Systems, Inc. (name now Vesuvius USA), Champaign, Ill., 1985-90; reliability mgr., 1990-96, slide gate product line specialist, 1996—. Patentee in field. Mem. Am. Soc. Materials, Am. Ceramics Soc., Iron and Steel Soc. AIME, Keramos, Sigma Tau. Democrat. Roman Catholic. Home: 604 E South Mahomet Rd Mahomet IL 61853-3602 Office: Vesuvius USA 1404 Newton Dr Champaign IL 61822-1069

SUNG, DAE DONG, chemistry educator; b. Sichunmyon, Kyung Nam, Republic of Korea, June 17, 1945; s. Cha Sung and Soon Agh (Ha) S.; m. Buyng Hee Yoon, Apr. 13, 1975; children: Myo Ya, Yun Duck. BS, Dong-A U., Pusan, Republic of Korea, 1969, MS, 1977, DSc, 1981. Lectr. Pusan Nat. U., 1977-78, Kyung Nam Tech. Coll., Pusan, 1978-79; lectr. Dong-A U., 1979-81, from asst. prof. to assoc. prof., 1981-90, prof. chemistry, 1990—, head lab. basic scis., 1982-83, head Basic Sci. Inst., 1989-91, dean Coll. Natural Scis., 1997—; rschr. Princeton U., N.J., 1983; rsch. fellow Liverpool U., 1997; dean Coll. Natural Scis. Dong-A U., 1997—; lectr., spkr. Internat. Conf. Boron Chem. and Internat. Conf. Physical Organic Chem., 1984, 86, 90-99; spkr., invited lectr. Conf. on the Internat. Correlation Analysis in Chemistry, Kyushu, Japan, 1996, Madras, India, 1999. Contbr. articles to profl. jours. Grantee Republic of Korea Sci. and Engring. Found., 1984, 87, 88, 90, 93, 94-98, 2000, Ministry of Edn., Republic of Korea, 1987, 91-98, 99-2000. Fellow Eng. Royal Soc. (rschr.); mem. Korean Chem. Soc. (author bull. 1985, 87, 90, 91-2000), Am. Chem. Soc. Avocation: swimming. Office: Dong-A U, Dept Chemistry, Saha-Gu Pusan 604-714, Republic of Korea

SUNG, FUNG YEE CAROL, solicitor; b. Hong Kong, Hong Kong, July 14, 1970; d. Shui Lun and Ying Ming (Chan) S. Diploma in legal studies, U. Hong Kong, 1992, postgrad. cert. in law, 1994; LLB 2d Class Hons., Manchester Met. U., Eng., 1998. Bar: solicitor, Hong Kong, Eng., Wales. Trainee solicitor Haldanes Solicitors, Hong Kong, 1994-96, solicitor, 1996—. Roman Catholic. Avocations: swimming, cyling, playing badminton and squash, reading, listening to music.

SUNG, MI SOOK, radiologist, educator; b. Kwang-Ju, Korea, Feb. 14, 1962; d. Byung Ho Sung and Jung Yim Kim. BA, Chunnam U., Kwang-Ju, 1987; Master, Cath. U. Korea, Seoul, 1993, PhD, 1997. Med. diplomate; diplomate radiology. Intern Korea Vets. Hosp., Seoul, 1987; resident St. Mary's Hosp., Cath. U. Korea, Seoul, 1988-90; fellow Cath. U. Korea, Seoul, 1991-92; instr. Holy Family Hosp./Cath. U., Puncheon, Korea, 1992-97, asst. prof., 1998-99; rsch. scholar U. Calf./Dept. VA Med. Ctr., San Diego, 1999—; sec. Korean Soc. Musculoskeletal Imaging, Seoul, 1995-97; com. mem. resident tng. com. Radiol. Soc., Seoul, 1997—. Author: Skeletal Radiology, 1998, Diagnostic Imaging Asia Pacific, 1998; reviewer Korean

Jour. Radiology, 1996—; contbr. articles to profl. jours. Mem. Radiologic Soc. N.Am. (cum laude 1997), Radiologic Soc. Korea (Bronz award 1989, 93, 98), Radiologic Soc. Magnetic Resonance Imaging. Avocations: writing, art appreciation, traveling, ping pong. Home: Apt B-1001, GongJak Apt Yoido-Dong, Seoul 510-010, Korea Office: Holy Family Hosp Cath Univ, Sosa-dong, Pucheon 420-717, Korea also: Dept VA Med Ctr/UCSD Osteoradiology Sect 3350 La Jolla Village Dr San Diego CA 92161-0002

SUNGUR, MEHMET ZIHNI, psychiatrist, educator, consultant; b. Adana, Cukurova, Turkey, Jan. 1, 1957; s. Refik and Azize (Ögütcü) S.; divorced; children: Kale Refikcan, Lara Hannah. Diploma with honors, Tarsus Am. Coll., Turkey, 1974, Hacettepe U., Ankara, Turkey, 1982. Registered pvt. therapist, U.K. Gen. practitioner Ministry of Health, Erzincan, Turkey, 1982-84; registrar dept. psychiatry Med. Sch. of Ankara U., 1984-88, sr. registrar, 1988-90, assoc. prof. dept. psychiatry, 1992—; sr. registrar Med. Mil. Hosp., Ankara, 1990-92; dir. Cognitive and Behavior Therapy Ctr., Ankara, 1995—, Smoking Cessation Ctr., Ankara, 1994—, Sexual Dysfunction Assessment and Treatment Ctr., Ankara, 1993—; cons. Ctr. for Improvement of Mental Health in Turkey, Ankara. Contbr. articles to profl. jours. Fellow Queen's Med. Ctr., Coun. of Europe, 1985, Inst. Psychiatry, Brit. Coun., London, 1986-88; recipient Eli Lilly Meditteranean Schizophrenia Reintegration award, 1998, Prof. Nusert Fisek Pub. Health award, 1999, Best Rsch. Project award, 1999. Mem. Turkish Assn. for Behaviour and Cognitive Psychotherapy (pres.), Turkish Assn. for Postgrad. Trainees and Specialists (establisher, hon. mem.), Turkish Asn. Sexual Edn. Training Rsch. (establisher), Brit. Assn. for Behaviour and Cognitive Psychotherapy, Turco-Brit. Fellowship Club, World Assn. for Psychosocial Rehab., Lions, Assn. of European Psychiatrists, Assn. of Turkish Psychiatrists (establisher), European Assn. Behavior Cognitive Therapies (pres.), Am. Psychiat. Assn. Avocations: cross-cultural exchange, travel, diving, singing, sports. Fax: (90) (312) 4666209. Home: Mehmet 2 Sungur, Yuksel Sitesi A Blok # 17, Balgat-Ankara Turkey Office: Ankara U, Tlp Fakultesi, Psikiyatri, Anabilim Dali Cebeci Ankara, Turkey

SUNIL, MUKALUVILAYIL SAMUEL, zoology educator; b. Enathu, Kerala, India, Mar. 11, 1960; d. Mukaluvilayil Mathew Samuel and Madathil John Sosamma; m. Pappy Thomas; 1 child, Prince Sunil Thomas. BEd, M.T. Tng. Coll., Pathanapuram, India, 1983; MSc, N.S.S.H. Coll., Changanacherry, India, 1986; MPhil, Aquatic Biol./Fisheries U., Trivandrum, India, 1988, PhD, 1994. Tchr. Novadaya Vidyalaya, Vechoochira, 1989; part-time lectr. G.V. Raja V.H.S., Trivandrum, 1989-92; lectr. V.H.S.S., Parassala, India, 1993, Catholicate Coll., Pathanamthitta, India, 1995—. Patentee in field. Sec. Rsch. Scholars Union, Trivandrum, 1990. Recipient Rsch. award U.G.C., 1998-99. Avocations: travel, writing, collecting stamps. Home: Mukaluvilayil Elangamangala, Enathu Kerala 691526, India Office: Catholicate Coll, Makkamkunnu PO, Pathanamthitta Kerala, India

SUNWARD, JUSTIN HUGO, artist, writer; b. Chgo., Feb. 20, 1939; s. Arthur Peter and Dorothy Irene Johnsen. Student, Sch. of Art Inst. of Chgo., 1951-52; diploma with honors, Frances Harrington Profl. Sch. Interior Decoration, Chgo., 1958. Represented in permanent collections Mus. Modern Art, N.Y.C., Met. Mus. Art, N.Y.C., Whitney Mus. Am. Art, N.Y.C., Mus. Contemporary Modern Art, Uuskila, Finland, others; contbr. art revs. to publs. Recipient numerous nat. art competition awards. Mem. Chgo. Art Critics Assn. (founding mem.). Avocations: cooking, gardening, history, architecture, traveling.

SUNWOO, MYUNG HOON, science and technology educator; b. Seoul, Korea, Mar. 25, 1958; s. Young Joon and Sunbong (Ahn) S.; m. Chun Hee Kim, July 7, 1985; children: Joon, Kyung. BS, Sogang U., Seoul, 1980; MS, Korea Adv. Inst. Sci. & Tech., Taejun, Korea, 1982; PhD, U. Tex., 1990. Cert. 1st class electronic engr., Korea. Mem. tech. staff ETRI, Taejun, 1982-85, Motorola, Austin, Tex., 1990-92; asst. prof. Ajou U., Suwon, Korea, 1992-96, assoc. prof., 1996—; mem. adv. com. Samsung Elecronics and Korea Mobile Telecomm.;active program coms. of various internat. confs. Author: (book chpt.) Parallel Architectures and Algorithms for Image Understanding, 1991; contbr. articles to profl. jours. Recipient Outstanding Paper award Inst. Electronics Info. and Comm. Engr. Asian Conf. on Computer Vision, 1994, Outstanding Contbn. award IEEE Asian Pacific Con. on Circuits and Systems, 1996, Outstanding Paper award Samsung, 1996. Mem. IEEE (mem. tech. com. VLSI systems and applications tech. com.), Korea Inst. Telematics and Electronics, Korean Inst. Comm. Scis. Avocations: traveling, swimming, listening to music. Fax: 82-31-212-9531. E-mail: sunwoo@madang.ajou.ac.kr. Office: Ajou U, San 5 Wonchun-Dong PaldalKu, Suwon 442-749, Korea

SUOMALAINEN, TAUNO OLAVI, orthopaedic surgeon; b. Iisalmi, Finland, May 20, 1939; s. Tauno Johannes and Helena (Kettunen) S.; m. Seija Sinikka Korpi, May 16, 1964; children: Merja, Mette, Merita, Martina, Etta, Merike. Licenciate of Medicine, U. Helsinki, Finland, 1966; Grad. Gen. Surgery, U. Kuopio, Finland, 1971; spl. orthopaedics and traumatology, Helsinki (Finland) U., 1973; PhD, Kuopio U., 1986. Resident orthopaedics and traumatology Helsinki U., 1971-73, Invalid Found. Hosp., Helsinki, 1973-74; specialist in orthopaedics and traumatology Kuopio U. Ctr. Hosp., 1974-85, surgeon-in-chief dept. orthopaedics and traumatology, 1985—; pvt. practice Hosp. Lasaretti, Kuopio, 1989—. Contbr. articles to profl. jours. Mem. Soc. Internat. de Chirurgie Orthopedique et de Traumatologie, Finnish Orthopaedic Assn., Scandinavian Orthopaedic Assn., European Hip Soc. Avocations: jogging, skiing, fishing, literature, family. E-mail: olavi.suomalainen@kuh.fi. Office: Kuopio Univ Hosp, FIN70211 Kuopio Finland

SUONINEN, EERO JUHANI, retired materials science educator; b. Vipuri, Finland, May 14, 1929; s. Herman and Helvi Irene (Rosendal) S.; m. Pirkko Kaarina Kovanen, June 28, 1958 (dec. Aug. 1986); children: Liisa Maria, Mikko Juhani, Marja Kaarina; m. Vuokko Valvikki Koskela, Sept. 22, 1990. Diploma in engring., Finnish Inst. Tech., Helsinki, 1952; MS, MIT, 1954, PhD, 1957. Rsch. asst. MIT, Cambridge, 1954-57; rsch. worker Norelco, Mt. Vernon, N.Y., 1957; chief physicist Outokumpu Co., Helsinki, 1958-61; rsch. assoc. U. Ariz., Tucson, 1961-62; prof. tech. physics U. Oulu, Finland, 1962-69; prof. materials sci. U. Turku, Finland, 1969-94; vis. prof. U. Conn., Storrs, 1972-73, Oreg. State U., Corvallis, 1983-84. Contbr. over 150 articles to tech. jours. U.S. Loan to Finland Found.-Fulbright grantee, 1953-54. Mem. Finnish Acad. Tech. Scis., Acad. Finland (natural sci. rsch. coun. 1986-91), Sigma Xi. Lutheran. Home: Rykmentintie 45 Apt 22, FIN20880 Turku Finland Office: U Turku Lab Materials Sci, Vesilinnatie 5, FIN-2052 Turku Finland

SUPACHAI, PANITCHAPHAK, federal official; b. May 30, 1946. BA in Econs., The Netherlands, MA in Econs., PhD in Devel. Planning. Mem. Ho. of Reps., 1986, 95, 96; dep. min. Ministry of Fin., 1986; dep. prime min. Office of Prime Min., 1992, 97—; mem. Senate, 1992-95; min. Ministry of Commerce, 1997—. Democrat. Office: Govt House, Thanon Sanam Chai, Bangkok 10200, Thailand*

SUPHIOGLU, CENK, medical researcher; b. Nicosia, Cyprus, Feb. 28, 1966; arrived in Australia, 1977; s. Celal and Zehra (Mustafa) S.; m. Dianna Margaret Hocking, May 1, 1994. BSc with honors, LaTrobe U., Bundora, Australia, 1989; PhD, U. Melbourne, Parkville, Australia, 1994. Rsch. scientist ICI Rsch., Ascotvale, Australia, 1988-89; rsch. officer U. Melbourne, 1994-96, sr. officer, 1997; sr. med. rsch. fellow dept. allergy and clin. immunology Monash U. Med. Sch., 1998—. Contbr. articles to profl. jours.; inventor rye-grass pollen allergen. Recipient Melbourne U. postgrad. scholar, 1990-93, Lillian Roxon Meml. Asthma Rsch. Trust award Asthma Found. of Victoria, 1992, Channel 10 Young Achiever award in Sci. & Tech., 1991. Mem. AAAS, Australian Soc. Clin. Immunology & Allergy, Australian Soc. Immunology, Am. Acad. of Allergy, Asthma and Immunology. Avocations: swimming, gardening, films, travel, classical music. Office: Monash Med Sch/Clin Immunol, Commercial Rd, 3181 Prahran Victoria, Australia

SUR, SERGEI VLADIMIROVICH, pharmacist, researcher, consultant; b. Zaporozhie, Ukraine, July 24, 1961; s. Vladimir Vladimirovich and Larissa Avramovna (Moskalenko) S.; m. Larissa Ivanovna Guba, Apr. 16, 1983; 1 child, Olena Sergeevna. Degree in pharmacy with honors, Med. U., Zaporozhie, 1983; candidate of sci., Ukrainian Acad. Scis., Kiev, 1989. Dep. dir. pharmacy, Odessa, Ukraine, 1983-85; rsch. scientist Inst. Colloid Chemistry and Chemistry of Water Ukrainian Acad. Scis., Kiev, 1985-92; rsch. scientist Ukrainian Hygienic Ctr., Kiev, 1992; head of lab. Inst. Pharmacology and Toxicology, Kiev, 1993-98; dir. of lab. Ctr. Lab. for Quality Control of Medicines, Kiev, 1998—; cons. Ukrainian Pharmacopeia, Kharkiv, 1990—; advisor WHO, Geneva, Switzerland, 1998—. Contbr. articles to profl. jours. Mem. Internat. Pharm. Fedn., Pharm. Assn. of Ukraine. Office: Ctrl Lab for Quality Control of Meds, ul Kudravska 10G, 04053 Kiev Ukraine

SUR, WILLIAM KENNETH, executive search consultant; b. Toledo, Ohio, Apr. 6, 1932; m. Margaret C. Sur, Oct. 6, 1956; 4 children. BS in Econs., Villanova (Pa.) U., 1954. Sales rep. Olin Ma Thieson Chem. Corp., N.Y.C., 1958-61; sr. fin. analyst Merck & Co., Inc., Rahway, N.J., 1961-66; sr. v.p., dir. SpencerStuart, N.Y.C., 1966-82; pres. Sollis, Sur & Assocs., N.Y.C., 1982-89, Stricker, Sur & Assocs., N.Y.C., 1989-91; sr. v.p., dir. Canny, Bowen Inc., N.Y.C., 1991-98; mng. dir. Conboy, Sur & Assocs., N.Y.C., 1998—. Lt. j.g. USN, 1954-58. Office: Conboy Sur & Assocs 545 5th Ave Rm 630 New York NY 10017-3620

SURACI, PATRICK JOSEPH, clinical psychologist; b. Rochester, N.Y., May 31, 1936; s. Frank and Josephine Rosalie (Marino) S. PhD in Psychology, New. Sch. for Social Rsch., N.Y.C., 1981. Cert. clin. psychologist, N.Y. Intern in clin. psychology Morrisania Neighborhood Family Care Ctr., Montefiore Hosp., N.Y.C., 1979-80; staff psychologist N.Y. Police Dept., 1981-83; pvt. practice N.Y.C., 1982—; adj. lectr. N.Y. Inst. Tech., N.Y.C., 1975-78, John Jay Coll. Criminal Justice, CUNY, 1973-81; adj. asst. prof. Baruch Coll. Psychology Dept., CUNY, 1983-92; vol. Manhattan Ctr. for Living, 1994-96. Author: Male Sexual Armor. Erotic Fantasies and Sexual Realities of the Cop on the Beat and the Man in the Street, 1992. Mem. The Nat. Arts Club. With U.S. Army, 1959-62. Mem. APA, N.Y. State Psychol. Assn. (task force on AIDS), Actors Equity. Office: 8 Gramercy Park S New York NY 10003-1718

SURAMO, ILKKA, radiologist, educator; b. Teuva, Finland, Oct. 22, 1942; s. Otto and Aili (Muttilainen) S.; m. Marja-Liisa Järkkälä, Dec. 30, 1968; 1 child, Riikka Maria. MD, U. Turku, Finland, 1968; PhD, U. Oulu, 1973. Assoc. prof. roentgenology U. Oulu, Finland, 1980-84, prof. diagnostic radiology, 1990—; assoc. prof. radiology U. Helsinki, 1984-90, acting prof. radiology, 1985-89; prof. diagnostic radiology U. Oulu, Finland, 1990—. Assoc. editor Acta Radiologica, Stockholm. Mem. Radiol. Soc. Finland (v.p. 1981-84, pres. 1988-89). Office: U Oulu Dept Diagnostic Rado, Kajaanintie 50, 90220 Oulu Finland

SURANA, CHANDRA SINGH, civil engineering educator, consultant, researcher; b. Udaipur, Rajasthan, India, Jan. 17, 1937; s. Khyali Lal and Mohan Bai (Kothari) S.; m. Kusum Matta, Nov. 22, 1960; children: Rina, Vidhi, Vipul. BSc in Engring., Banaras (India) Hindu U., 1959; ME in Structures, U. Roorkee, India, 1962; PhD in Civil Engring., U. Edinburgh, Scotland, 1968. Lectr. Delhi Coll. Engring., New Delhi, 1962-65; lectr. civil engring. Indian Inst. Tech., New Delhi, 1969-70, asst. prof., 1970-74, 76-79, prof., 1979-97, emeritus fellow, 1997—, chmn. dept., 1988-90; mem. vis. faculty U. Edinburgh, 1975; vis. prof. Carleton U., Ottawa, Ont., Can., 1981-82, Tribhuvan U., Kathmandu, Nepal, 1998; cons. on bridges to govt. and nongovtl. orgns., India, 1980—; organizing sec. World Conf. on Bridges, New Delhi, 1983; core mem. tech. coms. Indian Ministry Transport, New Delhi, 1986—; rep. All India Coun. Tech. Edn., 1992—. Author: Grillage Analogy in Bridge Deck Analysis; contbr. articles on bridge engring. to nat. and internat. jours.; developer comprehensive computer package analysis of bridges. Active Jain Cmty., New Delhi, 1970—; founder Juvenile Diabetic Assn., Mother's Internat. Sch., New Delhi, 1985—. Fellow Coun. for Sci. Indsl. Rsch., U. Roorkee, 1959-62, Brit. Coun. Commonwealth scholar U. Edinburgh, 1965-68; rsch. grantee Coun. for Sci. and Indsl. Rsch., Indian Inst. Tech., New Delhi, 1968-71. Fellow Indian Roads Congress (referee, expert various bridge code coms. 1985—). Jain-Hindu. Avocations: playing squash, swimming, reading. Office: Indian Inst Tech CE Dept, Hauz Khas, New Delhi 110 016, India

SURANA, PRAKASH CHAND, accountant, consultant; b. Taranagar, Rajasthan, India, Nov. 1, 1955; s. Khem Chand and Munni Devi (Dugar Munni) S.; m. Kiran Daga, Jan. 25, 1977; children: Rashmi, Kuldeep, Alka, Alok. B of Commerce with honors, Calcutta (India) U., 1974, LLB, 1978. Cert. in auditing, co. law adv., tax consultancy, mgmt. svcs. Proprietor Prakash Surana & Assocs., Calcutta, 1978—; sec. Uttar Howrah Sabha, Howrah, India, 1990-95, Mitra Parishad, Calcutta, 1995-97, Shri Jain Swetamber Terapanthi Sabha, Calcutta, 1998—; v.p. Uttar Howrah Shri Jain Swetamber Sabha, Howrah, 1995—; organizer Purbanchal Samiti, Salt Lake, India, 1999; bd. dirs. Khem Chand Fin. Pvt. Ltd., Calcutta; sr. cons. Richhold Group, Calcutta, 1988—. Author: (book) The Chartered Accountant, 1998, Lions Mirror, 1999 (Outstanding Devel. 1999); editor: (book) Vigyapti, 1993-99. Village svc. Lions Club Calcutta, Lake Gardens, India, 1990-93; social worker West Bengal Welfare Soc., Calcutta, 1991-95; convenor Terapanthi Sabha, Taranagar, India, 1997; educator Karyavahini, Calcutta, 1997-99; trustee Jain Swetamber Terapanthi Mahasabha, 2000—. Fellow Inst. Chartered Accts. of India, Assn. Secs. and Mgrs.; mem. Inst. Co. Secs. of India, Brit. Inst. Mgmt., Inst. Internal Auditors, Direct Tax Profls. Assn. (exec. 1993-98), Ea. India Coun. (adv., exec. 1991-93), Hindusthan Club Ltd. (exec. 1995—). Jain. Avocations: child welfare, public speaking, educating, social service, working for moral upliftment. Fax: 91 33 238 9559. E-mail: pcsurana@cal3.vsnl.net.in. Home: CJ-72 Salt Lake, Calcutta 700 091, India Office: Prakash Surana & Assocs, 157 Netaji Subhas Rd, Calcutta 700 001, India

SURANA, VINOD S., lawyer, consultant; b. Coonoor, Nilgiris, India, July 7, 1974; s. Shikermal S. and Leela (Jhabakh) S. BA, Madras (India) U., 1994, B in Law, 1996; LLM, Cornell U., 1997; Program of Instrns. for Lawyers, Harvard U., 1999. Ptnr. Surana & Surana Internat. Attys., Madras, 1996—; vis. prof. Madras U., 1998—; pres. Internat. Law Students Assn., Washington, 1999—; dir. ILSA, Washington, 1996-99, Surana & Surana Corp. Cons. Ltd., Madras, 1999—. Proofreader: Cases & Materials on Banking Laws, 1996. Sec. Gandhi Forum, Madras, 1998—. Nominated to Outstanding Young Person India Jr. Chamber Internat., 1996. Office: Surana & Surana, 224 NSC Bose Rd, Madras 600001, India

SURANYI, GYORGY, bank executive. Pres. Magyar Nemzeti Bank, Budapest. Office: Magyar Nemzeti Bank, Szabadság tér 8-9, 1850 Budapest Hungary*

SURASSAVADEE, SURAT, communications executive, consultant; b. Bangkok, Oct. 21, 1954; s. Suraphat and Somying (Srisuriwonase) S.; m. Patlin Suknonthalat, May 10, 1980; children: Sommai, Somwang, Semkid,, Somchai. BSc, Assumption Coll., 1977, MSc, 1979, PhD, 1980; PhD, U. Mich., 1981. Mng. dir. Siam Architectures & Co., Bangkok, 1982—; exec. dir. Siam Comm., Bangkok, 1982—; bd. dirs. Ruaysarptawee, Bangkok, Grand Inncome, Bangkok, Inncome Ste., Bangkok, City Residence, Bangkok. Author: Siam Today, 1982 (Excellent Book award 1985), The Role of Politics from Past to Present,, 1984 (Excellent Book award 1987). Lt. Bangkok Mil., 1973. Fellow Siam Club, Lions Club, French Club. Democrat. Buddhist. Avocations: reading and writing, collecting stamps, playing tennis, swimming, teaching. Home and Office: 286/67 Surwonove Rd, Bangkok 10500, Thailand

SURAUD, ERIC, physicist, educator; b. Lyon, France, Feb. 28, 1959; s. Joachim and Raymonde (Boiron) S.; m. Marie Gabrielle Pedotti, Feb. 22, 1986; children: Pierre, Céline, Jean-Philippe. Ecole, Polytech., France, 1981; DEA, Univ. Paris, 1982, PhD, 1984; habilitation, Univ. Grenoble, France, 1989. Asst. prof. Grenoble Univ., 1985-88; vis. scientist Groningen Univ., The Netherlands, 1988; physicist C.E.A., France, 1988-92; assoc. prof. Toulouse Univ., France, 1992-98; vis. prof. Kyoto Univ., Japan, 1992-93; prof. Toulouse Univ., 1998—; bd. mem. IUF, France, 1997-99; coord. Exchange program, France, Germany, 1992-94, 95-97, 99—. Author: La Matière Nucléaire, 1998, Physique des Collisions Nucléaires, 1998, (with D. Durand and B. Tamain) Nuclear Dynamics in the Nucleonic Regime, 2000; contbr. articles to profl. jours.; co-editor Jour. Phys. G., 1992-95, Annales de Physique, 1996—, Le Temps des Savoirs, 2000—, Internat. Jour. Molecular Sci., 2000—. With French Army, 1981. Mem. Soc. Francaise de Physique, Am. Physical Soc., Anciens Eleves de l'x. Avocations: reading, classical music, movies, skiing. Home: 2 rue des Coteaux, 31520 Ramonville France Office: Lab Phys Quantique U Paul Sabatier, 118 Rte de Narbonne, 31062 Toulouse cedex France

SURBER, CHRISTIAN, pharmacologist, researcher; b. Basel, Switzerland, Jan. 27, 1955; s. Hansjórg and Vivian (Jórgensen) S.; m. Gabriela Maria Cueni, Oct. 27, 1958; children: Jakob, Jonathan. PharmD, U. Basel, Switzerland, 1979, PhD, 1982. Cert. pharmacist. Rsch. asst. Hoffmann La Roche Inc., Basel, 1982-86, U. Calif., San Francisco, 1986-89; rsch. asst. dept. dermatology U. Hosp., Basel, 1989-94; chmn. dept. pharmacy St. Claire Hosp., Basel, 1989-94, U. Hosp., Basel, 1995—; cons. Bundesgesundheitsamt, Berlin, 1991—; mem. med. faculty U. Basel, 1997—, Fed. Pharmacy and Therapeutics com. Editor: Topical Corticosteroids, 1992, Exogenous Dermatology, 1995, Skin Pharmacology, 1999; patentee in field. Maj. Switzerland Army. Recipient grant Swiss Nat. Sci. Found., 1988. Mem. Am. Assn. Pharm. Sci., Am. Soc. Hosp. Pharm., Skin Pharmacology Soc. Avocation: photography. Office: U Basel Inst Hosp Pharmacy, Spitalstrasse 26, CH-4031 Basel Switzerland

SURBER, DAN CLIFFORD, system engineer; b. Spokane, May 29, 1951; s. James Clifford and Virginia Louise (Wey) S.; m. Sara Marion Gustafson, June 3, 1978; children: David Andrew, Katherine Elizabeth, Amy Lois, Anne Kristen. BS in History, USAF Acad., 1974; MS in Aero. Sci., Embry-Riddle Aero. U., 1983; PhD in Eng. Mgmt., Kennedy-Western U., 2000. Enlisted USAF, 1969, commd. major, 1974; ret., 1998; instr. pilot, T-37B 43d Tng. Squadron, Craig AFB, Ala., 1975-77; flight examiner, T-37B 71st FTW, Det OL-F 43d Tng. Squadron, Grissom AFB, Ind., 1977-79; flight comdr., F-111F aircraft comdr. 492d Tactical Fighter Squadron, RAF Lakenheath, U.K., 1979-83; wing safety officer, F-11D aircraft comdr. 522d Tactical Fighter Squadron, Cannon AFB, N.Mex., 1983-86; sgt. USAR Mil. Intelligence, Ft. Dix, N.J., Ft. Worth, Tex., 1986-91; sr. engr., advanced human factors tech. YF2ZA, X30 NASP, AFTIF-16 Gen. Dynamics, Ft. Worth, 1991-93; engr., sr. tech. specialist RAH66 Comanche Program Boeing Helicopter Divsn., Phila., 1991-93; mission equipment and flight control sys. mgr. RAH66 Comanche Joint Program Office, Shelton, Conn., 1993-95; software sys. safety staff engr. Beoing Def. & Space Group, Helicopters, Phila., 1995-97; sys. engring. mgr. Functional Engring. Case—New Holland NV, Burr Ridge, Ill., 1997—. Inventor in field. Asst. scoutmaster, Boy Scouts Am., Wallingford, Pa., 1994-97, Naperville, Ill., 1997-98, cubmaster, Benbrook, Tex., 1990-91. Mem. SAE, Interrrnat. Coun. Sys. Engrs., Assn. Grads. USAF Acad. (life), DAV (life), Tex. Army Nat. Gaurd Assn. (life). Evangelical Protestant. Republican. Avocations: golf, strategy war gaming, camping, bicycling, model airplanes. E-mail: dcsurber@earthlink.net. Office: CNH Global (NV) 7 S 600 County Line Rd Burr Ridge IL 60521

SURBER, DAVID FRANCIS, public affairs consultant, syndicated television producer and journalist; b. Covington, Ky., 1940; s. Elbert and Dorothy Kathryn (Mills) S. BA in Physics, Thomas More Coll., 1960; LLD (hon.), London Inst. Applied Rsch., 1973. Owner The P.R. Co., pub. affairs counseling, Covington, 1960—. Spl. corr. Am. newspapers to Vatican II, Rome, 1965; prodr. (syndicated weekly TV series) Make Peace with Nature, WKRC-TV, Cin., 1973—, Strip Mining: Two Views, 1972, Energy: Where Will It Come From, How Much Will It Cost, 1975, Atomic Power for Ohio, 1976, A Conversation With The Vice President, 1976, The Bad Water, 1977, The Trans-Alaska Pipeline: A Closeup Report, 1977, Acid Rain: A World View, 1986-89, Energy Independence in the U.K., 1992, Unhappy Prospects: Acid Rain & Global Climate Change, 1995, The Kyoto Summit: Was it Global, and Will it Work, 1997-98. Mem. Bd. Zoning Appeals, Covington, 1964-84, chmn., 1971-84; chmn. Covington Environ. Commn., 1971-72, Commn. Strip Mining, 1967-68; pub. interest adv. com. Ohio River Valley Water Sanitation Commn., 1976-82; water quality adv. com. Ohio-Ky.-Ind. Regional Coun. Govts., 1975-82; environ. adv. coun. City of Cin., 1981-84; apptd. by Sec. of Energy to Nat. Coal Coun., 1992, 94, 96, 98—, chmn. comm. com., 1999—; rehab. com. Cmty. Chest Greater Cin., 1972-78, mem. agy. admissions com., 1972-78, priorities com., 1972-78; pres. bd. dirs. Cathedral Found., 1968-70; trustee Montessori Learning Ctr., 1973-75, Bklyn. Spanish Youth Choir; founding mem. Mayor's Task Force on the Environment, Cin., 1972-73; Dem. candidate for U.S. Ho. Reps., 1972; mem. Ky. Nature Preserves Commn., 1976-79. Recipient Cmty. Svc. award Thomas More Coll., 1975. Mem. AFTRA, ACLU, Tri-State Air Com. (chmn. 1973-74), Izaak Walton League (pres. Ky. 1973, dir. Ky.; nat. dir.), Mousquetaires d'Armagnac, Nat. Inst. Urban Wildlife (bd. dirs. 1987-96). Office: PO Box 15555 Covington KY 41015-0555

SURBER, JOE ROBERT, assistant superintendent of schools; b. Pawhuska, Okla., Apr. 11, 1942; s. Hugh Richard and Odema (Harris) S.; m. Jo Del Novak; children: Robert Brian, Karrie Jo. BA in Edn., Northeastern State U., 1964; MS in Edn., Okla. State U., 1969, EdD, 1974. Cert. supt., sch. psychologist, sch. counselor. High sch. prin. Unity Bd. Govs., Ponca City, Okla., 1970-71; sch. psychologist Bi-State Mental Health Found., Ponca City, 1971-74; adj. prof. Okla. State U., Ponca City, 1976-84; asst. supt. Ponca City Pub. Schs., 1984—. Pub. The Blue Book of Counseling: Concrete Tools and Techniques, 1976. Past dir. ARC, Ponca City Crime Stoppers, Kay County Youth Shelter, Okla. Assn. Schs. with Impacted Svcs. Staff sgt. USAR, 1966-72. Named One of 3 Outstanding Oklahomans, 1976; recipient Disting. Svc. award, 1973, Outstanding Educator award, 1972. Pres. Okla. Dirs. Spl. Svcs. (past pres.), Okla. Sch. Psychol. Assn. (v.p.). Home: 1308 Desoto Ponca City OK 74604

SUREAU, CLAUDE GUY, obstetrician, gynecologist, educator; b. Paris, Sept. 27, 1927; s. Maurice and Rita (Jullian) S.; m. Janine Murset, Oct. 6, 1956; children: François, Véronique, Agnès. MD, U. Paris, 1955. Resident Paris Hosp., 1951-55; vis. fellow Columbia Presbyn. Med. Ctr., N.Y.C., 1955; chief resident Paris U., 1956-59; asst. attending physician, asst. prof. St. V. de Paul Hosp., 1959-61, prof., chmn. ob-gyn. dept., 1974-76; assoc. attending physician, assoc. prof. U. Clinic Baudelocque, 1967-74, prof., chmn., 1976-89; chmn. ob-gyn. unit Am. Hosp. of Paris, 1990-93, dir. med. affairs, 1994-95; pres. Theramex Inst. Bioethics, Women's Health and Society, Paris, 1996—; dir. Unit 262 Pathophysiology of Reprodn. INSERM, 1983-90. Author: Le Danger de Naitre, 1978, Clinical Perinatology, 1980, Immunologie de la Reproduction, 1983, La Maitrise de la Contraction Utérine, 1987, Aux débuts de la vie, 1990, Ethical Aspects of Human Reproduction, 1995, Ethical Dilemmas in Assisted Reproduction, 1997, Alice au pays des clones, 1999, Ethical Problems in Obstetrics and Gynaecology, 2000. Decorated chevalier et officier de la Légion d'Honneur (France). Fellow Royal Coll. Obstetricians and Gynecologists, Am. Coll. Obstetricians and Gynecologists (hon.); mem. Intern. Fedn. Gynecologists and Obstetricians (pres. 1982-85, ethical com. pres. 1985-94), French-Speaking Fedn. Gynecologists and Obstetricians (pres. 1986-88), European Asn. Gynecologists and Obstetricians (pres.1988-91), French Acad. Medicine (pres. 2000). Roman Catholic. Office: Inst Theramex, 38-40 Avenue de New York, BP 398-16 Paris Cedex 16, France

SURESH KUMAR, SIVANPILLAI, science educator; b. Pathanapuram, Kerala, India, May 14, 1970; s. Sivanpillai and P. Kallyanikutty. BSc in Zoology, Kerala (India) U., 1990; MSc in Marine Biology, Cochin U. Sci. and Tech., India, 1993, PhD, 1998. Sr. rsch. fellow Cochin U. Sci. and Tech., Kerala, India, 1993-97; lectr. MES Ponnani Coll., Kerala, India, 1997—. Contbr. articles to profl. jours. Active Marine Biol. Assn. India, Soc. Fisheries Technologists India. Avocations: aquarium keeping, swimming. Home: Vrindavanam Kannankara, Pathanapuram, Kollam 689695, India Office: MES Ponnani Coll, Ponnani, Malappuram Kerala 679 586, India

SURGY, ALBERT DE, anthropologist; b. Nantes, Bretagne, France, Jan. 11, 1934; s. Paul and Anne (Pelliet) S.; m. Nancy Van Der Horst, Dec. 02, 1967 (div. May 1996); children: Gilles, Viviane. Lic. in psychology, U. Rennes, France, 1956; D of Ethnology, U. Paris-V, Paris, 1970, D of Letters, 1974; DEUG in Japanese, U. Paris VII, Paris, 1987. Chargé de mission Commissariat Au Plan, Paris, 1960-63; rschr. Nat. Ctr. Sci. Rsch., Paris, 1965—. Author: La Géomancie et le Culte D'Afa Chez les Evhé du Littoral, 1981, La Divination par les Huit Cordelettes Chez les Mwaba-Gurma, Vol. I, 1983, Vol. II, 1987, La Voie des Fétiches, 1995, De L'Universalité d'Une

Forme Africaine de Sacrifice, 1988. Mem. Soc. Africanistes. Office: CNRS URA 221, 27 Rue Paul Bert, 94204 Ivry-sur-Seine France

SURI, DEEPIKA, nephrologist, internist; b. Chandigarh, UT, India, June 1, 1964; d. Lalit Mohan and Usha Suri. MBBS, Panjab U., Punjab, India, 1988. Diplomate Am. Bd. Internal Medicine, Am. Bd. Nephrology. Intern, resident Good Samaritan Hosp./Johns Hopkins, 1991-94; fellow Stanford U. Med. Ctr., 1994-97; assoc. H.A. Rodiles, Inc., El Centro, Calif., 1997-99; house physician Alpena (Mich.) Gen. Hosp., 1999-2000; med. dir. Alpena Dialysis Unit, 2000—. Mem. AMA, ACP, ASN. Office: Alpena Gen Hosp 1501 W Chisholm St Alpena MI 49707-1498

SURI, JASJIT S., research scientist. BS in Computer Engring., Regional Engring. Coll., Bhopal, India, 1988; MS, U. Ill., Chgo., 1991; PhD in Elec. Engring., U. Wash., 1997. Lectr. dept. electronic and computer engring. Regional Engring. Coll., Bhopal, 1988-89; rsch. asst. biomed. visualization dept. U. Ill., Chgo., 1989-90; rsch. programmer image sci. group IBM Palo Alto (Calif.) Sci. Ctr., summer 1990-91; rsch. assoc. U. Wash., Seattle, 1992-97; rsch. software engr. radiation treatment planning group Siemens Med. Sys., Calif., 1991-92; rsch. scientist Gammex Inc., Middleton, Wis., 1997, Sch. Medicine, U. Wis., Madison, 1997; rsch. scientist software devel. TSI, N.Y., 1997; rsch. staff scientist image guided surgery dept. Image Processing and Computer Graphics Picker Internat., Cleve., 1999—; with Bharat Heavy Elec. Ltd., Bhopal, summer 1986, Larson & Tubro Ltd., Bombay, India, summer 1987, Nat. Info. Tech. Ltd., Bhopal, summer 1987; presenter in field; mem. Mayo Clinic Procs., Rochester, Minn.; mem. rev. com. Internat. Conf. in Pattern Analysis and Applications, Plymouth, Eng., 1998. Author: (with others) Model Based Segmentation, 2d. rev. edit., 2000; mem. rev. bd. bd. Radiology, Jour. Computer Assisted Tomography, Internat. Jour. Pattern Analysis and Applications, Internat. Conf. Pattern Analysis and Applications; contbr. articles. to profl. jours. Scholar Regional Engring. Coll., 1985-88. Mem. IEEE, Assn. Computing Machinery, Artificial Intelligence, Optical Engring. Soc. Am., Engring. in Medicine and Biology Soc. (mem. editl. bd.), Am. Assn. Artificial Int., USENIX-Tcl/Tk. E-mail: jsuri@mr.marcoimed.com. Office: Marconi Med Sys Cleveland OH 44143

SURI, RAMA SUBBARAYA SASTRI, engineer, researcher; b. Nuzvid, India, Nov. 16, 1942; s. Krishna Murti and Rukmini (Kolachala) S.; m. Sumathi Veluri, Mar. 19, 1971; children: Naga Anilkumar, Naga Kirtana. B Tech. Chem. Engring., Andhra U., Waltair, India, 1962. Sr. sci. asst. Nat. Chem. Lab., Coun. Sci. and Indsl. Rsch., Pune, India, 1963-68; scientist Regional Rsch. Lab., Coun. Sci. and Indsl. Rsch., Bhubaneswar, India, 1968-81, scientist, asst. dir., 1981-93, dep. dir., 1993—, head mineral beneficiation divsn., 1999—; guest scientist Niproruda, Sofia, Bulgaria, 1975-76; cons. instnl. Tata Iron & Steel Co. Ltd., Jameshedpur, India, 1988-93, Nat. Mineral Devel. Corp. Ltd., Hyderabad, India, 1991-92, Birla Periclase Ltd., Visakhapatnam, India, 1995-96, Mecon (India) Ltd., Ranchi, 1995-96, Uranium Corp. India Ltd., Jadhuguda, 1995-96, Hindustan Zinc Ltd., Udaipur, India, 1995-99, Rajasthan State Mines & Minerals Ltd., Udaipar, 1999. Assoc. editor: International Series on Chemical Engineering: Utilisation of Natural Resources: Chemical Engineering Approach, 1994; co-editor: Indian Mineral Industry: Energy Environment and Resource Development, 1995, Benefication, Agglomeration and Environment, 1999, Mineral Processing, Waste and Environment Management, 2000, Mineral Resources and Beneficiation Plant Practices in India, 2000; co-patentee in field; contbr. numerous articles to profl. publs. Fellow Indian Inst. Chem. Engrs. (life, hon. vice chmn. Bhuabneswar region 1991-92, hon. chmn. 1992-93); mem. Indian Inst. Metals (life, hon. sec. Bhuabneswar chpt. 1985-86), Indian Inst. Mineral Engrs. (life). Avocations: reading, travel. E-mail: srs sastri@yahoo.com. Home: 503 RRL Colony, Bhubaneswar Orissa 751013, India Office: Regional Rsch Lab, Bhubaneswar Orissa 751013, India

SURIKOV, IGOR MICHAELOVITCH, biologist, politician; b. Saint Petersburgh, Russia, June 1, 1930; s. Michael Joannovitch and Nadegda Vasilievna (Sretenskaya) S.; m. Kira Kirillovna Kusnetzova, Oct. 27, 1951; children: Olga, Dmitry. Cand., Inst. Biology, Minsk, 1957; D, Inst. Plant Breeding, Saint Petersburg, 1973. Sci. worker Inst. Cytology, St. Petersburg, 1959-65, sr. sci. worker, 1966-83; chief lab. Inst. Plant Breeding, St. Petersburg, 1983-87, Inst. Agric. Biotechnology, Moscow, 1987-90; prof. Inst. Gen. Genetics, Moscow, 1992—; part. Constitutional Conf., Moscow, 1993; asst. deputy Fed. Assembly, 1994-96; v.p. N.I. Vavilov Fund, 1996—. Author: Incompatibility and Embryo Sterility in Plants, 1991; editor: Problems of Distant Hybridization in Gramineae and Solanaceae, 1992; contbr. articles to profl. jours. Co-pres. Party of Constitutional Dem., Moscow, 1990-91; mem. cen. coun. Movement Dem. Russia, Moscow, 1990-91, Constitutional Dem. Party, 1991-92, Movement Forward Russia, 1995—. Recipient Saros Fund grant, 1993. Mem. Russian Acad. Natural Scis., N.Y. Acad. Scis. Avocations: history, poetry, music, horticulture, bicycle. Home: Menzinskogo 23-1-181, 129327 Moscow Russia Office: Inst Gen Genetics, Gubkina 3, 117809 Moscow Russia

SURIN, PHITSUWAN, federal official; b. Nakron, Si, Thammarat Province, Oct. 29, 1949; married, 3 children. Grad. in polit. sci. cum laude, Claremont Men's Coll., 1972; PhD, Harvard U., 1982. Univ. tchr., journalist; elected Ho. of Reps., 1986, sec. of the Spkr. of the Ho. of Reps., 1986; asst. sec. Min. of Interior, 1988, dep. fgn. min., 1992-95; min. of fgn. affairs Ministry of Fgn. Affairs, Bangkok, 1997—. Democrat. Office: Min Fgn Affairs Wang, Saranrom Thanon Sanamcahi, 10200 Bangkok Thailand*

SURIN, VITALY IVANOVICH, physicist, researcher, educator; b. Feodosia, Crimea, Russia, Sept. 30, 1956; s. Ivan Fedorovich and Raisa Petrovna (Ivanova) S.; m. Galina Borisovna Dubkova, June 21, 1957; children: Andrew, Margaret. Degree, Engring. Physics Inst., Moscow, 1979; postgrad., Engring. Physics Inst., 1985-88. Sr. engr. Engring. Physics Inst., Moscow, 1980-85, rsch. asst., 1988—; cons. Inst. Info., Moscow, 1989-91. Contbr. articles to profl. jours. Chmn. Trade Union of the Chair, Engring. Physics Inst., 1989—. Recipient 2d prize of br. Physics of Radiation Damage, 1986, cand. of Engrg., 1999. Home: Caucastan Blvd, 115516 Moscow Russia Office: Moscow Engring Physics Inst, 115409 Moscow Russia

SURIS, JOSEP M., science educator, administrator; b. Barcelona, Catalunya, Spain, Aug. 13, 1945; s. Josep I. Suris and Montserrat Jorda; m. Marta Suñer; children: Anna, Pau, Daniel. Degree in econs., Autonomous U. Barcelona, 1975; PhD in Econs., Faculty of Sci. and Econs., Barcelona, 1984. Cert. economist. Prof. ESADE, Barcelona, 1975-87; dir. PYCASA, Barcelona, 1987-91; prof. U. Autonoma De Barcelona, 1991—; dir. Fundació Empresa i Ciència, Barcelona, 1992—; cons. in field; vis. prof. Harvard U., Cambridge, Mass., 1985. Editor and author books in field; contbr. articles to profl. jours. Bd. dirs. Intermon, Barcelona, 1984—. Avocations: mountain biking, tennis. Home: P Manuel Girona 46, 08034 Barcelona Spain Office: Fundació Empresa Ciencia, Campus UAB Edificio, 08193 Barcelona Spain

SURJÁN, PÉTER, physicist, educator; b. Budapest, Hungary, Aug. 30, 1955; s. László and Margit (Göttinger) S.; m. Zsuzsa Károly; children: Eszter, Zsuzsa, Katalin, Márta, Péter. MSc, Eötvös U., Budapest, 1978, PhD, 1980. Rschr. Chinoin Pharm. Works, Budapest, 1978-88; sr. rschr. Tech. U., Budapest, 1989; assoc. prof. Eötvös U., Budapest, 1990-98, prof. theoretical chemistry, 1998—. Author: Second Quantized Approach to Quantum Chemistry, 1989; co-author: Applied Quantum Chemistry, 1986; contbr. articles to profl. jours. Fellow World Assn. Theoretically Oriented Chemists; mem. Internat. Soc. Chem. Physics (bd. mem.), Internat. Soc. Math. Chemistry. Roman Catholic. Office: Eötvös Univ Dept Theor Chemistry, PO Box 32, 1518 Budapest Hungary

SURMA, STANISŁAW ANTONI, physicist; b. Majdan Stary, Tarnopol, Poland, May 8, 1940; s. Karol and Bronisława (Razik) S.; m. Małgorzata Maria Wiszniewska, Sept. 8, 1974 (dec. Mar. 1985); 1 child, Jakub; m. Krystyna Czajkowska, Oct. 25, 1986; 1 child, Antoni. MS, Wrocław (Poland) U., 1966, PhD, 1991. Trainee asst. IEP (Inst. Exptl. Phy.) Wrocław U., 1966-67, asst., 1967-74, sci.-tech. specialist, 1975—. Contbr. articles to profl. jours. Mem. Polish Phys. Soc., Soc. Wrocław City Amateurs. Solidarity Union. Roman Catholic. Avocations: reading, radio and electronics, parapsychology. Office: Wrocław U Inst Exptl Phy, pl M Borna 9, PL 50204 Wrocław Poland

SURMAN, OWEN STANLEY, psychiatrist; b. Boston, Apr. 21, 1943; s. Aaron Harry and Edith Anne (Silver) S.; m. Lezlie Anne Humber, July 19, 1969 (dec. Nov. 5, 1994); children: Craig Bruce Hackett, Kathleen Bridget Lezlie. BSc with honors, McGill U., 1964, MD, CM, 1968. Diplomate Am. Bd. Psychiatry and Neurology. Intern Balt. City Hosp., 1968-69; clin. fellow in medicine Johns Hopkins U., Balt., 1968-69; resident in psychiatry Mass. Gen. Hosp., Boston, 1969-72; clin. fellow in psychiatry Harvard Med. Sch., Boston, 1969-72; clin. asst. in psychiatry Mass. Gen. Hosp., Boston, 1975-76, asst. in psychiatry, 1977-80, asst. psychiatrist, 1980-86, assoc. psychiatrist, 1986-89, psychiatrist, 1990—; instr. psychiatry Harvard U. Med. Sch., Boston, 1975-80, asst. prof., 1980-90, assoc. prof., 1990—; psychiat. cons. Boston Ctr. Heart Transplant, 1988-94; mem. ethics com. Mass. Ctr. Organ Transplantation, 1988—; mem. subcom. Human Studies, Mass. Gen. Hosp., 1982—, acting chmn., 1996-97, co-vice-chmn., 1999—, cons. transplant unit, 1975—, vice-chmn. xenotransplant adv. com., 1997-98, living related partial liver donor oversight com., 2000—; mem. Inst. for Study of Smoking Behavior and Policy, John F. Kennedy Sch. Govt., 1982-89. Mem. editorial bd. Jour. Geriatric Psychiatry and Neurology, 1988—; contbr. articles to profl. jours., chpts. to books. Bd. dirs. Unitarian-Universalist Area Ch., Sherborn, Mass., 1983-86, 93-96; advancement officer troop 1 Boy Scouts Am., Sherborn, 1983-91. Lt. comdr. M.C., USNR, 1972-75. Grantee Milton Fund, 1969-70, Upjohn Corp., 1982-84, Burroughs Wellcome Co., 1984-85, Eli Lily Corp., 1989, 90-92. Fellow Am. Psychiat. Assn., Am. Acad. Psychosomatic Medicine (ethics com., awards com. 1994-97); mem. AAAS, Mass. Med. Soc., Boston Bar Assn., N.Y. Acad. Scis., Hastings Ctr. (assoc.), Johns Hopkins Med. and Surg. Soc., Mass. ACLU, Libr. of Boston Athenaeum, Ford Hall Forum, New Eng. Poetry Club. Republican. Avocation: creative writing. Office: Mass Gen Hosp Wang ACC 815 15 Parkman St Boston MA 02114

SURMANN, HARTMUT, electrical engineer; b. Duelmen, Germany, Sept. 18, 1963; s. Johannes and Helga (Willezelek) S.; married, Feb. 19, 1999; 1 child, Hendrik Leonard. MSc, U. Dortmund, 1989, PhD, 1995. Postdoctoral rschr. German Nat. Rsch. Ctr. Info. Technology, St. Augustin, 1994-00, sr. rschr., 1996—. Mem. Assn. German Elec. Engrs. Avocations: swimming, bicycling, skiing, diving. Home: Lessingstr 2, 53757 Saint Augustin Germany Office: Nat Rsch Ctr Info Tech, Schloss Birlinghoven, 53754 Saint Augustin Germany

SURMANN, JOHANNES PETER, pharmaceutical analysis educator; b. Vechta, Germany, May 26, 1947; s. Franz Hermann and Elisabeth (von Heesen) S.; m. Ursula Schroeder, Oct. 22, 1971; children: Jan Clemens, Kai Alexander, Frauke Elisabeth. BS in Pharmacy, U. Marburg, Germany, 1971, diploma in Chemistry, 1974, PhD in Chemistry, 1976, habilitation chemistry, 1982. Mem. sci. staff U. Marburg, 1971-78, asst. prof., 1978-86; prof. U. Würzburg, Germany, 1986-93, Humboldt U., Berlin, 1993—. Author: Quantitative Analyse von Arzmeistoffen, 1987; co-author: Praktische Mathematik in der Pharmazie, 1981, Ionempaarchromatographie, 1989; editor: Hagers Handbook, Vol. 2, 1991. Avocations: literature, music (plays clarinet). Office: Humboldt U Inst Pharmacy, Goethestr 54, 13086 Berlin Germany

SUROWIEC, ANDREW JULIUS, biophysicist, researcher; b. Lwów, Poland, Apr. 13, 1940; came to U.S., 1986; s. Jan Jakub and Maria (Knobloch) S.; m. Irene Regina Baranowski, Apr. 27, 1977; 1 child, Caroline Maria. Engr., Tech. U., Gliwice, Poland, 1962, MS, 1964; PhD, Silesian U., Katowice, Poland, 1972. Cert. elec. engring. Asst. prof. Silesien Sch. Medicine, Katowice, 1964-82; postdoctoral fellow Ctr. d'Etude L'Energie Nucleaire, Mol, Belgium, 1973-74; disting. vis. scientist U. Ottawa, Ont., Can., 1983-87; asst. prof. Bowman U. Sch. Medicine, Winston-Salem, N.C., 1987-88, U. So. Calif., L.A., 1988-93; sr. physicist Centennial Med. Ctr., Nashville, 1993—. Peer reviewer: Cancer, Internat. Jour. Am. Cancer Soc., 1993; contbr. articles to Physics in Medicine and Biology, Bioelectromagnetics, IEEE Transactions Biomed., Internat. Jour. Hyperthermia, Biopolymers, Jour. Chem. Soc. Faraday Transactions. Grantee Nat. Sci. and Engring. Rsch. Coun., 1985. Fellow Radiation Rsch. Soc.; mem. Internat. Clin. Hyperthermia Soc., N.Y. Acad. Scis. Achievements include patent for recording system for rotating viscometer; finding of simulated materials for electromagnetic studies and cancer treatment; findings of dielectric spectroscopy of normal and cancer tissues; finding of dielectric and hydrodynamic properties of DNA. Avocations: music, modern history, swimming. Home: 8209 Londonberry Rd Nashville TN 37221-4640 Office: Centennial Med Ctr Radiation Therapy 2300 Patterson St Nashville TN 37203-1528

SURPATEANU, GHEORGHE, chemist, educator; b. Ciineni, Vilcea, Romania, Oct. 10, 1944; arrived in France, 1995; s. Nicolae and Joita (Sofilca) S.; m. Mioara Georgescu, Dec. 17, 1970; 1 child, Georgiana. Grad., Chemistry Faculty, Jasi, Romania, 1967; PhD in Chemistry, Jasi U., 1972. Asst. prof. U. Al. J. Cuza, Jasi, 1968-74; asst. assoc. U. Lille, France, 1974-76; asst. prof. Politech. Inst., Jasi, 1976-88; prof. U. Jasi, 1988-95; prof. U. Littoral, Dunkerque, France, 1995—, dir. Laboratoire de Synthese Organique et Environement. Editor: Fundamentals of Chemical Reactivity, 1982; author reports, articles and patents. Recipient prize Romanian Acad. Mem. AAAS. Office: U Littoral MREID, 145 Ave Maurice Schumann, Dunkerque 59140, France

SURTANI, JACKIE BHAGWANDAS, banker; b. Bombay, Maharastra, India, Mar. 31, 1967; arrived in Hong Kong, 1979; s. Bhagwan Parmanand and Lata Bhagwan S.; m. Seema Balani, Dec. 18, 1993. BSc, U. East Anglia, Eng., 1988; MPhil, Balliol Coll., U. Oxford, Eng., 1990. Dir. Chase Manhattan Bank, Hong Kong, 1990-95, Credit Suisse First Boston, Hong Kong, 1995-97; head of proj. fin. KBC Bank, Hong Kong, 1997—. Dervorguilla scholar Oxford U., 1988. Home: Upper Baguio Villa Block 27, 17/F C 550 Victoria Rd, Pokfulam Hong Kong

SURUCU, HUSEYIN SELCUK, physician, researcher; b. Ankara, Turkey, Jan. 12, 1966; s. Ahmet Cengiz and Fatma (Mualla) S. MD, U. Ankara, 1989, PhD in Anatomy, 1994. Physician Suruc Hosp. Min. Health, Urfa, 1990-91; rsch. asst. anatomy Hacettepe Med. Faculty U. Ankara, 1990-94, asst. prof. anatomy, 1996—. Mem. adv. bd. Jour. Med. Rsch., 1998; contbr. articles to profl. jours. including Cancer Letters, Surg. and Radiologic Anatomy, Jour. Andrology, and Okajimas Folia Anatomica. 1st lt. GATA Mil. Med. Fac., Turkish mil., 1995-96. Recipient Assoc. Prof. award Higher Coun. Edn., 1999. Avocations: basketball, diving, windsurfing, guitar playing. Office: Hacettepe Med Fac, Dept Anatomy, 06100 Sihhiye Ankara, Turkey

SURVEYOR, RATAN DINSHAW, civil engineer; b. Bombay, India, June 15, 1923; s. Dinshaw Maneckji and Ratanbai (Nazir) S.; m. Nerges Sorab Kapadia, Feb. 22, 1965; children: Darius, Rashna. BSc, St Xavier's Coll., 1943; BE, NED Engring. Coll., 1946. Engr. Gannon Dunkerly & Co., Bombay, 1946-50; prin. Ratan Surveyor & Co., Bombay, 1950-2000; arbitrator Indian Coun. of Arbitration, New Delhi, 1991-2000. Spl. exec. magistrate Maharashtra, 1988-96, spl. exec. officer, Maharashtra, 1997-2000; mem. Parsi Panchayat Anjuman Com., 1982-2000. Recipient Bus. Excellence award Global Bus. Forum, 1994, Rattna Shiromany award India Internat. Soc. for Unity, 1993, Vikas Rattan award Internat. Friendship Soc. of India, 1995, Glory of India Internat. award 1995, Internat. Gold Star award Internat. Forum for NRI's, London, 1999, Indira Ghandi Excellence award NRI, London, 1999. Fellow Royal Soc. of Health (life, London)), Instn. of Engrs. India (life); mem. Ripon Club, Bombay Presidency Radio Club Ltd., Breach Candy Swimming Bath Trust. Avocations: astronomy, physics, poetry, history, general reading. Home: 91B Paradise Apts, 44 Nepean Sea Rd, Bombay 400036, India Office: Ratan Surveyor & Co, Peninsula House Dr DN Rd, Bombay 400001, India

SURYANARAYANAN, ANANTHANARAYANAN, finance company executive; b. Bombay, Apr. 25, 1957; s. Ananthanarayanan and Ananthanarayanan Renganayaki; m. Lakshmi Sundaram, Nov. 11, 1984; 1 child, Anand S. Bharadwaj. B of Comm., Bombay U., 1977. Gen. acct. Union Carbide Ltd., India, 1981-84; logistics mgr. Nicholas Labs. India Ltd., 1984-88; dir. fin. Recon Ltd., Bangalore, India, 1988-2000; CEO Medybiz.com Pvt. Ltd., Bangalore, 2000—. Fellow Inst. Chartered Accts. India. Avocations: reading, music appreciation, golf. Home: 971 14th Cross 16th Main, Banashankari II Stage, Bangalore Karnataka 560 070, India Office: Medybizcom Ltd, 971 14th Cross 16th Main, Basavanagudi Bangalore 560070, India

SURYAPRANATA, HARYANTO, cardiologist; b. Pangkalpinang, Bangka, Indonesia, June 24, 1951; arrived in Belgium, 1973; s. Joesoef and Surti (Widjaja) S.; m. Godelieve Maria De Spiegelaere, Sept. 3, 1983; children: Franciska, Alexandra, Frederieke. MD, Cath. U., Leuven, Belgium, 1977; PhD, Erasmus U., 1988. Physician St. Lucas Gen. Hosp., Brugge, Belgium, 1977-82; cardiology fellow Thorax Ctr., Erasmus U., Rotterdam, The Netherlands, 1982-85; clin. head catheter lab. Thorax Ctr., Erasmus U., Rotterdam, 1986-91; interventional cardiologist Hosp. Weezen Landen, Zwolle, The Netherlands, 1992—; dir. clin. rsch. Hosp. Weezen Landen, Zwolle, 1996—. co-author: Acute Coronary Hemodynamic Effects of Diltiazem in Patients with Coronary Artery Disease, 1984, (chpt.) Prognosis of Coronary Heart Disease. Progression of Coronary Atherosclerosis, 1984, Facts and Hopes in Thrombolysis in Acute Myocardial Infarction, 1986, The First 24 Hours of Acute Myocardial Infarction, 1986, Reforzo G., 1987, Invasive Cardiovascular Therapy, 1987, New Developments in Quantitative Coronary Arteriography, 1988, Reperfusion and Revascularization in Acute Myocardial Infarction, 1988, Interventional CArdiology and Angiology, 1989, Nitrate, Kalziumantagonisten, Beta-Blocker, 1989, PTCA an Investigational Tool and a Non-Operative Treatment of Acute Ischemia, 1990, Nitrates in Heart Failure, 1991, Medically Refractory Rest Angina, 1992, Quantitative Coronary Angiography in Clinical Practice, 1994, Progress in Quantitative Coronary Arteriography, 1994; mem. editl. bd. Rev. Contemporary Pharmacotherapy, 1995—; contbr. over 150 articles to profl. jours. Fellow European Soc. Cardiology (working group coronary circulation 1990—, scientific com. 1995—); mem. Czech Soc. Cardiology (editl. bd. 1993—), Am. Coll. Cardiology, Dutch Interventional Cardiology Soc. Avocations: tennis, reading. Home: Kloosterbrink 4, 8034 PV Zwolle The Netherlands Office: Hosp Weezenlanden, Groot Wezenland 20, 8011 JW Zwolle The Netherlands

SURYAVANSHI, ARVIND KRISHNAJIRAO, research and development engineer; b. Sirsi, India, Oct. 13, 1957; came to Singapore, 1997; s. Krishnaji Rao Srinivas Rao and Leelavati Krishnaji Rao; m. Vani Arvind Marati Krishnaveni Bai, Dec. 12, 1988; children: Manisha, Pranay. B of Engring., BVB Coll. Engring. Tech., Hubli, India, 1979; M of Tech., Indian Inst. Tech., Mumbai, 1988; PhD, U. Manchester Inst. Sci./Tech., Eng., 1994. Planning engr. Suri & Nayar Ltd., Bangalore, India, 1981-82; scientist C Nat. Inst. Oceanography, Goa, India, 1982-91; rsch. assoc. U. Sheffield, Eng., 1995-97; mgr. concrete consultancy A.C.C., Mumbai, 1997; rsch. fellow Nat. U., Singapore, 1997-99; sr. R&D engr. Poh Cheong Concrete, Singapore, 1999—. Contbr. tech. articles to profl. jours. Commonwealth fellow Commonwealth Commn., Eng., 1991-94. Avocations: reading, music, traveling, cricket, watching TV. E-mail: arvks@hotmail.com. Home: Blk 116 #02-633 Yishun, 760116 Singapore Singapore

SUŠA, OLEG, social science educator; b. Prague, Czech Republic, Nov. 26, 1947; s. Milan and Jarmila (Kratochvílová) S.; m. Eva Truncová, Apr. 17, 1971; children: Veronika, Jan. BA, Charles U., Prague, Czech Republic, 1971, MA, 1972, PhD, 1983. Rsch. fellow Czech Acad. Scis., Prague, Czech Republic, 1974-86, sr. rsch. fellow, 1986; asst. prof. Charles U., Prague, Czech Republic, 1990; vis. rsch. fellow J.F.K. Inst. Free U., Berlin, 1992; vis. fellow Inst. Advanced Studies in Humanities U. Edinburgh (Scotland), 1993; cons. Dept. Environ. Protection, Prague, Czech Republic, 1991-94, expert Com. Environ., Prague, Czech Republic, 1995; vis. fellow Ctr. for Environ. Change, U. Lancaster, U.K., 1996. Author: Human Potential Development as a Global Problem, 1989, Social Context of Environmental Responsibility, 1998, Modern Society, Ecological Problem and Human Dignity, 1999; (journals) Studia Humanistica, 1992, ACTA Universitatis Carolinae, 1994, 98, 99, Jour. of Philosophy, 1993, 95, 97, 99, Czech Sociological Review, 1989, 92, Greek Sociological Review, 1996, 97, Czech Sociological Review, 1996. Grantee Czech Grant Agy., Prague, 1991-92, 94-96. Mem. Masaryk's Czech Sociol. Assn., League of Czech Philosophers, Czech Future Studies Assn. (bd. dirs. 1990—). Avocations: wood carving, sculpture, painting, graphics. Home: Staropramenná 16/973, 150 00 Prague 5, Czech Republic Office: Inst Philosophy, Czech Acad Sci Jilská 1, 110 00 Prague 1, Czech Republic

SUSEENDIRARAJAH, SWAMINATHAN, language educator, researcher; b. Jaffna, Sri Lanka, Oct. 9, 1933; s. Sithamparanathan Swaminathan and Poothapillai Poothathaipillai; m. Ponnampalam Kamala Devi, Aug. 31, 1965; children: Thiruvarulchelvi, Aravindan, Giridaran. MA, U. Madras, India, 1958, Annamalai U., India, 1962; Postgrad. Diploma in Sanskrit, Annamalai U., India, 1965, PhD, 1967. Journalist Assoc. Newspapers of Ceylon Ltd., Sri Lanka, 1958-60; lectr. Annamalai U., 1963-67, Jaffna Coll., Sri Lanka, 1968-70; sr. lectr. U. Sri Lanka, 1971-83; prof. U. Jaffna, Sri Lanka, 1984—, head dept. linguistics and English, 1983—; cons. govt. textbook com., Sri Lanka, 1972-80; convenor Internat. Conf. on Tamil Linguistics, Sri Lanka, 1992; rep. Internat. Jour. Dravidian Linguistics, 1974-80. Author: Jaffna Tamil, 1993; contbr. articles to profl. jours. Commonwealth Acad. staff fellow U. Edinburgh, 1987-88. Mem. Linguistics Soc. India (life), Internat. Assn. Dravidian Linguistics (life). Hindu. Avocations: gardening, stamp collecting. Office: U Jaffna PO Box 57, Sir Pon Ramanathan Rd, Jaffna Sri Lanka

SUSENO, GIRI HADIHARJONO, Indonesian government official. Minister of comms. Govt. of Indonesia, Jakarta, 1998—. Office: Dept Comms, Jl Medan Merdeka Barat 8, Jakarta 10110, Indonesia*

SUSIC, MICHAEL, marine chemist, researcher, consultant; b. Hamburg, Germany, Jan. 19, 1947; arrived in Australia, 1950; s. Ljubisa and Irmgard Herta (Pehmoller) S.; m. Pamela Joyce Florance, 1970 (div. 1998); children: Christine Bianca, Kathryn Naomi; m. Maria-Isabel Sanchez, 1999. BSc, U. Melbourne, Victoria, Australia, 1969. Cert. in ednl. psychology Victoria Dept. Edn. Tutor Victorian Coll. Pharmacy, Melbourne, 1969; chemist Oxy Chems., Melbourne, 1970-72; sr. chemist E. R. Squibb and Sons., Melbourne, 1973-80; scientist Australian Inst. Marine Sci., Townsville, Queensland, 1980-98; cons. referee Jour. Chromatography, Amsterdam, The Netherlands, 1990—. Contbr. articles to profl. pubs. Sch. advisor Kirwan State H.S., Townsville, 1991-93. Australian Govt. Commonwealth scholar, 1965. Mem. N.Y. Acad. Scis., Royal Australian Chem. Inst., Planetary Soc., Cmty. and Pub. Sector Union, North Star Athletic Club, Queensland Masters Athletic Club. Avocations: competitive athletics, computers, travel. E-mail: michaels@ecn.net.au. Home: 12/15 Brian St, Kingston Qld 4114, Australia Office: Quality Home Tuition, PO Box 282, Sunnybank Qld 4109, Australia

SUSKI, JAN, physicist, researcher; b. Lodz, Poland, Jan. 19, 1946; arrived in France, 1981; s. Stanislaw and Barbara (Wielowieyska) S.; m. Anna Maria Szweycer, Sept. 14, 1969; children: Maria, Katarzyna, Barbara. MSc, U. Torun, Poland, 1968; PhD in Physics, Inst. Nuclear Rsch., Poland, 1978. Rschr. Inst. Nuclear Rsch., Poland, 1968-81; postdoctoral fellow U. Paris VI, 1981-83; sci. advisor Schlumberger Industries, France, 1984—; asst. rsch. dir. CNRS, Lille, France, 1989-95; mem. European Network Nexus, 1993-97; expert European Commns., Brussels, 1992—. Author, referee papers and articles; patentee in mech. and chem. sensors. Avocations: reading, bridge. Home: 8 Place de l'Hotel de Ville, 92160 Antony France Office: Schlumberger Industries, 50 Av J Jaures, 92542 Montrouge France

SUSKIND, SIGMUND RICHARD, microbiology educator; b. N.Y.C., June 19, 1926; s. Seymour and Nina Phillips S.; m. Ann Parker, July 1, 1951; children: Richard, Mark, Steven. A.B., NYU, 1948; Ph.D., Yale U., 1954. Research asst. biology div. Oak Ridge Nat. Lab., 1948-50; USPHS fellow NYU Med. Sch., N.Y.C., 1954-56; mem. faculty Johns Hopkins U., Balt., 1956—, prof. biology, 1965-96, univ. prof., 1983-96, prof. emeritus, 1996—, Univ. ombudsman, 1988-91, dean grad. and undergrad. studies, 1971-78, dean Sch. Arts and Scis., 1978-83; head molecular biology sect. NSF, 1970-71; cons. NIH, 1966-70, Coun. Grad. Schs., Mid States Assn. Colls. and Secondary Schs., 1973—, NSF, 1986; vis. scientist Weizmann Inst. of Sci., Israel, 1985; trustee Balt. Hebrew U., 1985-93; mem. adv. bd. La. Gheriatric Ctr., 1990—. Author: (with P.E. Hartman) Gene Action, 1964, 69, (with P.E. Hartman and T. Wright) Principles of Genetics Laboratory Manual, 1965; editor: (with P.E. Hartman) Foundations of Modern Genetics series, 1964, 69; mem. sci. editorial bd. Johns Hopkins U. Press, 1973-76, 88-91.

With USNR, 1944-46. NIH grantee, 1957-76. Fellow AAAS; mem. Am. Soc. Microbiology, Genetics Soc. Am., Am. Assn. Immunology, Am. Soc. Biol. Chemistry and Molecular Biology, Coun. Grad Schs., Assn. Grad. Schs., Northeastern Assn. Grad. Schs. (exec. com. 1975-76, pres. 1977-78). Avocations: research in microbial biochemical genetics and immunogenetics. Office: Johns Hopkins U Dept Biology and McCollum-Pratt Inst 34th and Charles Sts Baltimore MD 21218

SUSKO, CAROL LYNNE, lawyer, accountant; b. Washington, Dec. 5, 1955; d. Frank and Helen Louise (Davis) S. BS in Econs. and Acctg., George Mason U., 1979; JD, Cath. U., 1982; LLM in Taxation, Georgetown U., 1992. Bar: Pa. 1989, D.C. 1990; CPA, Va., Md. Tax acct. Reznick Fedder & Silverman, P.C., Bethesda, Md., 1984-85; sr. tax acct. Pannell Kerr Forster, Alexandria, Va., 1985; tax specialist Coopers & Lybrand, Washington, 1985-87; supervisory tax sr. Frank & Co., McLean, Va., 1987-88; mem. editl. staff Tax Notes Mag., Arlington, Va., 1989-90; adj. faculty Am. U., Washington, 1989—; tax atty. Marriott Corp., Washington, 1993-94; sr. tax mgr. Host Marriott Inc., Washington, 1994-99, KPMG LLP, McLean, Va., 1999—. Mem. ABA, AICPAs, Va. Soc. CPAs, D.C. Soc. CPAs, D.C. Bar Assn. Office: KPMG LLP Rm 6184 1676 International Dr Ste 6184 Mc Lean VA 22102-4832

SUSLA, JEFFREY JONATHAN, English language educator; b. Bridgeport, Conn., Oct. 30, 1958; s. Nicholas Jonathan and Betty Irene (Stavnitzky) S.; m. Patricia Anne Plumb, June 25, 1995. BA in English and History, Wesleyan U., 1982; MALS, Dartmouth Coll., 1991. English tchr. U.S Peace Corps, Illassit, Kenya, 1988-89, Woodstock (Conn.) Acad., 1993—. co-advisor Woodstock Acad. Student Coun., 1995—; dir. Woodstock Acad. Theatre, 1994, 96; mem. supt. search com. Town of Woodstock, 1995. Fellowship Conn. Writing Project U. Conn., 1994, Nat. Endowment for the Humanities, 1996, Fulbright Meml. Fund., Japan, 1997, Tchg. Excellence award, Kazakhstan, 1998; named Educator of Yr. 21st Century Newspaper, 1996. Avocations: reading, travel. Home: PO Box 27 Woodstock CT 06281-0027 Office: Woodstock Acad Woodstock CT 06281

SUSLOV, ALEXANDER VICTOROVICH, bank executive; b. Saratov, Russia, Sept. 1, 1949; s. Victor Stepanovich and Maria Petrovna (Arefieva) Suslov; m. Tatiana Alexandrovna Mizinova, Feb. 8, 1975; children: Helen, Matthew. Economist, Econ. Inst., Saratov, 1972. Sr. inspector credits Saratov regional bd. Stroybank of USSR, 1970-72, 73-74, mng. dir. Leninsky br. Saratov regional bd., 1974-81; sr. economist of authorized rep. office Stroybank of USSR, Ulan-Bator, Mongolia, 1981-86; dep. chief tech. dept. Saratov regional bd. Stroybank of USSR, 1986, head dept. financing Saratov regional bd., 1986, mng. dir. Saratov regional bd., 1986-87; head Saratov regional bd. Promstroybank of USSR, 1987-90; chmn. bd. comml. bank for reconstrn. and devel. Econombank, Saratov, 1991-92, chmn. bd. Joint Stock Comml. Bank for Reconstrn. and Devel., 1993-97, chmn. bd. Joint Stock Close Co., 1997—; mem. bank Coun. at Gov. of Saratov Region, 1998—. Capt. res., 1972-73. Recipient medal of the laureate of All-Russian Businessmen Contest Career, 1995, 98, Golden Eagle prize-diploma, 1998; named Honored Economist of Russian Fedn. Mem. Interbank Assn. (chmn. bd. dirs. 1994-96), Regional Bank Club. Home: Lermontov St 12a Fl 4, 410002 Saratov Russia

SUSSE, SANDRA SLONE, lawyer; b. Medford, Ma., June 1, 1943; d. James Robert and Georgie Coffin (Bradshaw) Slone; m. Peter Susse, May 10, 1969 (div. May 1993); 1 child, Toby. BA, U. Mass., 1981; JD, Vt. Law Sch., 1986. Bar: Mass. 1986, U.S. Dist. Ct. Mass. 1988, U.S. Ct. Appeals (1st cir.) 1995. Staff atty. Western Mass. Legal Svcs., Springfield, 1986—. Mem. ABA, Mass. Bar Assn., Women's Bar Assn. Mass. Avocations: hiking, German literature, films, skating. Address: Western Mass Legal Serv 127 State St Fl 4 Springfield MA 01103-1905

SÜSSMUTH, RITA, government official, education and French educator; b. Wuppertal, Germany, Feb. 17, 1937; m. Hans Süssmuth; 1 child, Claudia. PhD, Münster, 1964. Asst. U. Stuttgart, Osnabruck, Germany, 1963-66; lectr. Coll. of Edn., Bochum, 1966; prof. Ruhr U., Bochum, 1971; prof. (on leave) U. Dortmund; dir. Rsch. Inst. Women and the Society, Hannover, 1982-85; min. youth, family affairs, women and health, 1985-88; mem. German Bundestag, Bonn, 1987—, pres., 1988-98; mem. Sci. Adv. Com. on Family Affairs, 1971-85; v.p. Family Assn. German Catholics, 1980-85; chairwoman Commn. Elaboration 7th Report on Youth, 1984; chmn. Ind. Commn. on Immigration, 2000—. Author: Studies on the Subject of Child Anthropology, 1968, Women-Do not Give Resignation a Chance, 1985, Aids-Ways of Overcoming Fear, 1987, Fighting and Setting in Motion, 1989, When Time Changes its Rhythm, 1991. Chairwoman Women's Assn. within CDU, 1986—, German AIDS Found., 1988—. Mem. German Soc. for Fgn. Policy (bd. dirs. 1990), Inst. for East-West Security Studies, German Assn. Adult Edn. (pres. 1989). Democrat. Roman Catholic. Avocations: tennis. Office: Platz Der Republik 1, 11011 Berlin Germany

SUSSO, ALHAJI PAPA, musician; b. Sotuma Sere, The Gambia, Sept. 29, 1947; came to U.S., 1985; s. Alhaji Bunka and Alhaja Mariama (Sakiliba) S.; children: Sankung, Fatoumata, Karano, Alhassan, Mariama, Binta, Muhammad, Musa, Kinda, Sarjo. BA in Bus. Adminstrn., Cuttington U., Suakoko, Liberia. Agrl. asst. Ministry of Agr., The Gambia; sr. acct. Ministry of Works, The Gambia; liaison officer Gambia Embassy, Sierra Leone, Liberia; mgr. The Bayo Co., Monrovia, Liberia; chief musician Gambia Natl. Troupe, Banjul, The Gambia; dir. Koriya Musa Ctr., Sotuma Sere, U.R.D. Address: # 3G 333 E 181st St Apt 3G Bronx NY 10457-2325

ŠUŠTAR, ALOJZIJ, retired bishop; b. Trebnje, Ljubljana, Slovenia, Nov. 14, 1920. Studied philosophy, Ljubljana; studied theology, Gregoriana U., Rome, 1941; attended, Theological Sem. Germanicum, Rome. Ordained priest, 1946. Chaplian St. Moritz, Switzerland, 1947-51; prof. philosophy of religion Schwyz Coll., 1951-63; prof. moral theology Theological Sem., Chur, 1963-68; rector Theological Higher Sch., Chur, 1968; vicar gen. Chur; sec. European Bishops Conf., 1971; returned to Slovenia, 1977; archbishop and metropolitan Ljubljana Archdiocese, 1980-97; v.p. Roman Cath. Bishop Conf. and Primate of Slovenia. Office: St Stanislavs Instn, Stula 23, SI 1210 Ljubljana Sentvid, Slovenia*

SUSTER, ZELJAN, business educator, dean; b. Split, Yugoslavia, Nov. 18, 1958; came to the U.S., 1989; s. Emil and Olga (Jelenkovic) S.; m. Sanja Grubacic, Dec. 3, 1988. BA in Econs. and Fin., U. Belgrade, Yugoslavia, 1981, MA in Econs., 1984, PhD in Econs., 1988. Rsch. assoc. Inst. Econ. Scis., Belgrade, 1983-89; assoc. prof. U. New Haven, West Haven, Conn., 1990—; chair dept. econs. and fin. U. New Haven, West Haven, 1996-97, assoc. dean Sch. Bus., 1997—; vis. fellow Mellon Found., Yale U., 1990-91; rsch. assoc. U. Ill., Champaign-Urbana, 1995-96; sr. analyst Analytic Resources, Woodbridge, Conn., 1995—; mem. adv. bd. Charter Oak State Coll., Newington, Conn., 1996—. Author: Historical Dictionary of FR of Yugoslavia, 1999; mem. editl. bd. Serbian Studies, 1993—, Dialogue, 1998—, New Serbian Political Thought, 1998—; contbr. articles to profl. jours. Mem. N.Am. Soc. for Serbian Studies (mem. governing bd. 1993—, v.p. 1998—, pres. 1999—), Ea. Econ. Assn., Atlantic Econ. Soc., Multinational Fin. Soc., Internat. Soc. for Intercomm. of New Ideas, Am. Assn. for the Advancement of Slavic Studies, Kiwanis Internat. Avocation: chess. Office: U New Haven Sch Bus 300 Orange Ave West Haven CT 06516-1916

SUTCLIFFE, ERIC, lawyer; b. Calif., Jan. 10, 1909; s. Thomas and Annie (Beare) S.; m. Joan Basché, Aug. 7, 1937; children: Victoria, Marcia, Thomas; m. Marie C. Paige, Nov. 1, 1975. AB, U. Calif., Berkeley, 1929, LLB, 1932. Bar: Calif. 1932. Mem. firm Orrick, Herrington & Sutcliffe, San Francisco, 1943-85, mng. ptnr., 1947-78. Trustee, treas., v.p. San Francisco Law Libr., 1974-88; founding fellow The Oakland Mus. of Calif.; bd. dirs. Merritt Peralta Found., 1988; past bd. dirs. Hong Kong Bank of Calif., Friends of U. Calif. Bot. Garden, sec. Fellow Am. Bar Found (life); mem. ABA (chmn state regulation securities com. 1960-65), San Francisco Bar Assn. (chmn. corp. law com., 1964-65), San Francisco C. of C. (past treas., dir.), State Bar Calif., Pacific Union Club, Bohemian Club, Phi Gamma Delta, Phi Delta Phi, Order of Coif. Home: 260 King Ave Oakland CA 94610-1231 Office: Old Fed Reserve Bank Bldg 400 Sansome St San Francisco CA 94111-3304

SUTCLIFFE, HAYDN, chemistry educator, European education consultant; b. Lincoln, Eng., Nov. 25, 1930; s. Wilfred Hewitt and Dora (Price) S.; m. Florence Begg, Apr. 9, 1955; children: Martin, Niel. BSc, London U., 1953; PhD, Manchester (Eng.) U., 1962. Sr. chemist Imperial Smelting Co., Bristol, Eng., 1956-58; lectr. in chemistry U. Salford, Eng., 1961-96; cons. in European edn. Dept. Environ. Resourses, Salford, 1996—; postdoctoral fellow U. Manchester Inst. Sci. & Tech., 1959-60. Author: Practical Inorganic Chemistry, 1960; author numerous articles on aspects of fluorine and zirconium chemistry and articles on edn.; use of novel zirconium compounds for the conservation fo archaeological wood artifacts. Avocation: wood. Office: U Salford, The Crescent, Salford M5 4WT, England

SUTER, LUDWIG HERMANN, dermatologist, educator; b. Berlin, May 24, 1938; s. Emil Otto Hermann and Margarete Johanne Luise (Paul) S.; m. Jacoba-Johanna Braaksma, Nov. 12, 1971; children: Margrit, Elke. Student, Free U., Berlin, 1957-63; med. state exam., U. Würzburg, Germany, 1964. Approbation for physicians; diploma for dermatology. Intern Evangelisches Krankenhaus, Holzminden, Germany, 1965-66; rsch. fellow Max-Planck-Inst., Göttingen, Germany, 1966-70; rsch. assoc. Albert Einstein Coll. Medicine, N.Y.C., 1970-72; asst. dept. dermatology U. Münster, Germany, 1972-78; asst. med. dir. dept. dermatology U. Münster, 1978-80; med. dir. Fachklinik Hornheide, Münster, 1980—. Contbr. articles to biochem., immunol., and dermatol. jours. Rsch. grantee Deutsche Forschungsgemeinschaft, 1971-72, 72-80, Deutsche Krebshilfe, 1987-90. Mem. European Soc. for Dermatol. Rsch., Deutsche Dermatologische Gesellschaft, Gesellschaft für Immunologie. Avocations: hiking, cross-country skiing, jogging, swimming. Home: In der Stroth 37, D-48157 Münster Germany Office: Fachklinik Hornheide, Dorbaumstr 300, D 48157 Münster Germany

SUTER, ROBERT MERLE, physicist, educator; b. Washington, Oct. 8, 1947; s. Merle and Marion Thayer S.; m. Cynthia M. Nelson, May 24, 1986; children: Daniel, Christopher, Samuel. BSEE, N.C. State U., 1970; PhD, Clark U., 1978. Rsch. scientist IBM Watson Rsch., Yorktown Heights, Pa., 1979-80; from asst. prof. Carnegie Mellon U., Pitts., 1981-96, prof., 1996—. mem. AAAS, Am. Physical Soc., Material Rsch. Soc. E-mail: suter@andrew.cmu.edu. Office: Dept Physics Carnegie Mellon U 5000 Forbes Ave Pittsburgh PA 15213-3815

SUTHAHARAN, SHANMUGATHASAN, computer science educator; b. Batticaloa, Sri Lanka, Oct. 26, 1958; s. Subramaniam and Jeiyaluckshmi (Sivasubramaniam) Shanmugathasan; m. Manimehala Suthaharan, Sept. 15, 1985; children: Lovepriya, Praveen. BSc, U. Jaffina, Sri Lanka, 1980, BSc with honors, 1981; MSc, Dundee (Scotland) U., 1988; PhD, Monash U., Melbourne, Australia, 1995. Cert. in computers. Asst. lectr. U. Jaffna, 1981-85; lectr. Middlesex U., London, 1988-90; computer courseware developer CompuTeach Coll., Melbourne, 1990; sr. instr., UNIX adminstr. Computer Power Tng. Inst., Melbourne, 1991-96; postdoctoral rsch. fellow Monash U., 1995-96, lectr., 1996-98; dept. head, prof. computer sci. Tenn. State U., Nashville, 1999—; adj. prof. Ctr. Excellence in Info. Sys. Engring. and Mgmt., Tenn. State U., Nashville, 1997-98; chief investigator Monash U., 1997-98; vis. prof. U. Tex., Arlington, 1997-98; rschr., presenter in field. Editor jour. Real-Time Imaging, 1998-99; editor conf. procs. in field; contbr. articles to profl. jours., chpts. to books. Grantee FIT, 1995-96, Australian Rsch. Coun., 1998, Monash U., 1997-98. Mem. IEEE (sr. mem., mem. tech. com. 1997, 98). Office: Tenn State U 3500 John A Merritt Blvd PO Box 9604 Nashville TN 37209-1561

SUTHAT, NGOENMUN, federal official; b. May 18, 1945; married. LLB, Thammasat U. Elected Ho. of Reps., 1975, 83, 88, 92, 95, 96, dep. min. of pub. health, 1988-90; dep. min. of agrl. and coops., 1990-91, dep. min. of interior, 1992-95, chmn. ho. of standing com. on justice and human rights, 1996-97, dep. leader of Democrat Party; min. of justice Ministry of Justice, Bangkok, 1997—. Democrat. Office: Ministry of Justice, 6 Thanon Rachini, 10200 Bangkok Thailand*

SUTHEP, THAUGSUBAN, federal official; b. Suratthani, July 7, 1949. BA in Polit. Sci., Chiang-Mai U.; M in Polit. Sci., Middle Tenn. State U. Sec. to min. Ministry of Commerce, 1980; sec. to min. Ministry of Agr. and Coops., 1981, dep. min., 1986; sec. Prime Min. Office, 1983; min. Transport and Comm., 1997—. Democrat. Office: Ministry Transport Comm, Khet Pom Prab, Bangkok 10100, Thailand

SUTHERLAND, DAVID WILLIAM, educator; b. Breckenridge, Minn., Dec. 14, 1967; s. William George and Cynthia Marie S. Laborer Progress Enterpris, Jamestown, N.D., 1993-94; peer adv. Mental Health Consumers of N.D., Jamestown, 1994-95; one-on-one instr. Alpha Opportunities, Jamestown, 1995—. Mem. Assembly of God. Avocations: computers, writing, electronics, ministry. Home: 1023 Western Park Vlg Jamestown ND 58401-6013

SUTHERLAND, DONALD, actor; b. St. John, N.B., Can., July 17, 1935; m. Lois Hardwick; m. 2d, Shirley Douglas; children: Kiefer, Rachel; m. 3d, Francine Racette; children: Roeg, Rossif, Angus. Grad., U. Toronto, 1958. Actor: London Acad. Music and Dramatic Art, Perth Repertory Theatre, Scotland, also Nottingham, Chesterfield, Bronley, Sheffield, (plays) The Spoon River Anthology, The Male Animal, The Tempest, August for People (London debut), On a Clear Day You Can See Canterbury, The Shewing Up a Blanco Posnet, (films) The World Ten Times Over, 1963, The Castle of the Living Dead, 1964, Dr. Terror's House of Horrors, 1965, Fanatic, 1965, The Bedford Incident, 1965, Promise Her Anything, 1966, The Dirty Dozen, 1967, Sebastian, 1968, Oedipus the King, 1968, Interlude, 1968, Joanna, 1968, The Split, 1968, Start the Revolution Without Me, 1969, The Act of the Heart, 1970, M*A*S*H, 1970, Kelly's Heroes, 1970, Little Murders, 1970, Alex in Wonderland, 1971, Klute, 1971, Johnny Got His Gun, 1971, Steelyard Blues, 1972, Lady Ice, 1972, Alien Thunder, 1973, Don't Look Now, 1973, S*P*Y*S, 1974, The Day of the Locust, 1975, End of the Game, 1976, Casanova, 1976, 1900, 1976, The Eagle Has Landed, 1977, Animal House, 1978, Invasion of the Body Snatchers, 1978, The Great Train Robbery, 1979, The Kentucky Fried Movie, 1978, Murder by Decree, 1979, Bear Island, 1979, A Man, A Woman and a Bank, 1980, Nothing Personal, 1980, Ordinary People, 1980, Eye of the Needle, 1981, Gas, 1981, The Disappearance, Blood Relative, Threshold, 1983, Max Dugan Returns, 1983, Crackers, 1984, Heaven Help Us, 1985, Revolution, 1985, The Trouble with Spies, 1987, The Wolf at the Door, 1987, Apprentice to Murder, 1988, The Rosary Murders, 1988, Lock Up, 1989, Lost Angels, 1989, A Dry White Season, 1989, Backdraft, 1991, JFK, 1991, Eminent Domain, 1991, Buffy the Vampire Slayer, 1992, Younger and Younger, 1993, Shadow of the Wolf, 1993, Six Degrees of Separation, 1993, The Puppet Masters, 1994, Quicksand, Disclosure, 1994, Outbreak, 1995, Bethune: The Making of a Hero, FTA, The Shadow Conspiracy, 1997, The Assignment, 1997, Fallen, 1997, Without Limits, 1998, Free Money, 1998, Toscano, 1999, CSS Hunley, 1999, Virus, 1999, Instinct, 1999; TV shows and movies include Marching to the Sea, The Death of Bessie Smith, Hamlet at Elsinore, The Saint, The Avengers, Gideon's Way, The Champions, The Winter of Our Discontent, 1984, Ordeal By Innocence, 1985, Buster's Bedroom, Citizen X, 1995 (Emmy award). Decorated officier dans l'Ordre des Artes et des Lettres (France); officer Order of Can. Office: c/o CAA care Katherine Olin 9830 Wilshire Blvd Beverly Hills CA 90212-1804

SUTHERLAND, JOHN BENNETT, chemical engineer; b. Burlingame, Kans., Feb. 21, 1918; s. Earl Wilbur and Edith May (Hartshorn) S.; m. Maxine Louise Turvey, Oct. 13, 1935; children: John Walter, Max Earl, Lynn Ann Sutherland Bradshaw. BS in Chem. Engring., Kans. State U., 1939, MS in Chem. Engring., 1940; PhD in Chem. Engring., U. Pitts., 1946. Rsch. engr. Texaco, Port Arthur, Tex., 1940-41; rsch. asst. Mellon Inst. Pitts., 1941-43; asst. prof. Northwestern U., Evanston, Ill., 1943-46; pres. Sutherland-Becker Lab., Burlingame, Kans., 1946-62; exec. dir. Kans Sate Indsl. Devel. Commn. State of Kans., Topeka, 1953-56; dir. planning and rsch. Butler Mfg. Co., Kansas City, Mo., 1956-65; dir. indsl. rsch. and ext. U. Mo. System, Columbia, 1966-80; exec. dir., v.p. Master Practitioners, Inc., Sedalia, Mo., 1983-84; prof. emeritus U. Mo., Columbia, 1980—; cons. Kans. Indsl. Devel. Commn., 1946-53; dept. dir. econ. devel. Office Indsl. Devel. Studies Report Series, 1966; mem. Sci. Adv. Commn., Kansas City, Mo., 1962. Mem. Gov.'s Energy Adv. Com., State of Mo., 1970; treas. Pub. Sch. Dist., Burlingame, Kans., 1948. Mem. AIChE, Am. Chem. Soc., Rotary Club (pres. 1949-50). Achievements include development of new state-wide technology transfer system coordinating field specialists serving manufacturers backed by a referral system, campus experts and a technical library; avocations: gardening, fishing, reading. Home: 3021 SW Burlingame Rd Topeka KS 66611-2003

SUTHERLAND, MELANIE JAN, theatre director and producer; b. Johnson City, N.Y., Jan. 17, 1957; d. Rudolph Blake and Diane Thomas Sutherland. AB in Theatre, Kirkland-Hamilton Coll., 1979. Lic. massage therapist, N.Y. Resident and artistic dir. AAI Prodns., N.Y.C., 1986—; resident dir. Circle Rep Theatre, N.Y.C., 1992-95, Rattlestick Prodns., N.Y.C., 1995—, Circle East, N.Y.C., 1995—; freelance dir., 1979—; judge Joseph A. Callaway Award, N.Y.C., 1992—, Susan Smith Blackburn Award, N.Y.C., 1993—; dir. John Golden Award for directing, 1990; program dir. Directors Nite Out, 1991—; resident dir. Women's Project and Prodns., N.Y.C.; prodr. Blatant Selt-Interest Networking Event, N.Y.C. Dir. Easterinan Alley, The Love of the Nightingale, The Misanthrope, A Pirate's Lullaby, Doves on a Lark, H'r Story. Bd. dirs. Coalition, sec., 1994—; mem. FIDO in Prospect Park. Avocations: running, hiking, raising my border collie, travel. Fax: 775-522-00617. E-mail: msuther766@aol.com.

SUTHERLAND, PETER DENIS, banker, lawyer; b. Dublin, Ireland, Apr. 25, 1946; s. William George and Barbara (Nealon) S.; m. Maruja Cabria Valcarcel, Sept. 18, 1971; children: Shane, Ian, Natalia. B of Civil Law (hons.), U. Coll. Dublin, 1967; LLD, St. Louis U., doctorate (hon.); doctorate (hon.), Nat. U. Ireland, Dublin City U., Holy Cross U., U. Bath, Suffolk U., Mass., Open U. of Trinity Coll. Barrister at law King's Inn, Dublin, Mid. Temple, Dublin; bar: N.Y., U.S. Supreme Ct. Tutor law U. Coll. Dublin, 1968-81; atty. gen. to Ireland, 1981-84, commr. of the European Communities, 1985-89; chmn. Allied Irish Banks, PLC, Ireland, 1989-93; dir.- gen. General Agreement on Tariffs and Trade (GATT), Geneva, Switzerland, 1993-94, World Trade Orgn., Geneva, 1995—; chmn., mng. dir. Goldman Sachs Internat., London, 1995—; non exec. dir. British Petroleum plc, London, 1995-97, non exec. chmn., 1997-98; non exec. co-chmn. BP Amoco plc, London, 1998—; dir. Investor AB, 1995—, ABB Ltd., 1996—, Telefonaktiebolager LM Ericsson, 1 996—; vis. fellow Kennedy Sch., Harvard U., 1990, U. Coll. Dublin, 1990—. Author: 1st Janvier 1993-6 le qri va changer, 1988. Mem. strategy com. Fine Gael Party, 1979-81. Recipient First European Law prize Found. de la Liberté, Paris, 1988, Grand Cross of Civil Merit, King of Spain, 1989, Grand Cross of King Leopold II, King of Belgium, 1989, Gold medal European Parliament, 1988; named European Person of the Yr., Coun. of the European Movement, Ireland, 1988; Chevalier Legion d'Honneur (France), 1993, Commdr. du Wissau (Morocco), 1994, New Zealand Commemorative medal 1990, The Order of Rio Branco, Brazil, 1996, The Grand Cross of the Order of Infante Dom Henrique, Portugal, 1998. Mem. N.Y. Bar, Irish Bar Assn. (sr. counsel), United Svcs. Club, Royal Irish Yacht Club. Roman Catholic. Avocations: sports, reading. Office: Goldman Sachs Internat, Peterborough Ct 133 Fleet St, London EC4A 2BB, England

SUTHERLAND, SIR STEWART, university vice chancellor; b. Scotland, Feb. 25, 1941; s. George A.C. and Ethel (Masson) S.; m. Sheena Robertson, 1964; children: Fiona, Kirsten, Duncan. MA, U. Aberdeen, Scotland, LLD (hon.), 1991; MA, Corpus Christi Coll., Cambridge, Eng.; LHD (hon.), Coll. Wooster, Ohio, 1986; LLD (hon.), Va. Commonwealth U., 1992, Nat. U. of Ireland, 1992; DUniv., U. Stirling, U.K., 1993; Dr.h.c., U. of Uppsala, 1995—; DLitt (hon.), Richmond Coll., 1995, U. Wales, 1996, U. Glasgow, 1999. Lectr. philosophy U. Coll. North Wales, 1965; lectr. philosophy U. Stirling, 1968, sr. lectr., 1972, reader, 1976; prof. history and philosophy of religion King's Coll., London, 1977-85, vice prin., 1981-85, prin., 1985-90; vice chancellor U. London, 1990-94; vice chancellor, prin. U. Edinburgh, Scotland, 1994—; vice chmn. Com. Vice Chancellors and Prin., 1989-92, chmn. acad. std. group, 1988-92, London Conf. on Overseas Students, 1989-94; fellow King's Coll., London, 1983—; freeman Goldsmith's Co., 1987—, Liveryman, 1992; hon. fellow Corpus Christi Coll., 1989—, U. Coll., Bangor, 1991—; Her Majesty's Chief Inspector for schs. in Eng., 1992-94, chmn. com. on appeals cts. procedure; active Hong Kong Coun. Acad. Accreditation, 1992-95; mem. Univ. Grant Com., Hong Kong, 1995—, Coun. Sci. and Tech., 1993—, Higher Edn. Funding Coun. Eng., 1996—; chmn. Royal Commn. on Long Term Care of the Elderly, 1997-99. Author: Faith and Ambiguity, 1984, God, Jesus and Belief, 1984, Atheism and The Rejection of God, 1977, 80; editor Religious Studies, 1984-90; joint editor: The Philosophical Frontiers of Christian Theology, 1982, The World's Religions, 1988, Religion, Reason and the Self, 1989; contbr. articles to profl. jours. Fellow Brit. Acad. (chmn. Postgrad. Studentships Com., 1987-84), Royal Soc. Edinburgh, Coll. Preceptors (hon.); mem. Royal Inst. Philosophy (chmn. of coun. 1988—). Avocations: tassie medallions, theater, jazz. Office: U Edinburgh, Old Coll South Bridge, Edinburgh EH8 9YL, Scotland

SUTHERLAND, WILLIAM JAMES, ecologist; b. Accra, Ghana, Apr. 27, 1956; arrived in Eng., 1957; s. Alasdair Cameron and Gwyneth Audrey (Campbell-James) S.; m. Nicola Jane Crockford, May 25, 1996. BS, U. East Anglia, Norwich, Eng., 1977; PhD, Liverpool (Eng.), 1980. Postdoctoral fellow Oxford (Eng.) U., 1980-82; lectr. Liverpool U., 1982-83; demonstrator U. East Anglia, Norwich, 1983-85, lectr., 1985-93, reader, 1993-96, prof., 1996—. Author: From Individual Behavior to Population Ecology, 1996, The Conservation Handbook 2000; editor: Managing Habitats for Conservation, 1995, Ecological Census Techniques, 1996, Conservation Science and Action, 1998, Behaviour and Conservation 2000, The Conservation Handbook, 2000; contbr. to sci. publs. Recipient Sci. medal Zool. Soc. London, 1997; Nuffield fellow, 1993. Office: U East Anglia, Sch Biol Scis Norwich NR4 7TJ, England

SUTHERS, HANNAH LOUISE BONSEY, biologist; b. Lorain, Ohio, Oct. 4, 1931; d. William Edwin and Hannah Elisabeth Bonell B.; m. Derwent Albert Suthers, June 20, 1953 (div. Oct. 1968); children: Daniel Derwent, Hannah Marie Suthers McCabe, Edwin Bonsey. BA, Oberlin Coll., 1953, MS equivalent in biology, 1998, MA equivalent in thology, 1998. Master permitee Bird Banding, USGS, Migratory Bird Mgmt.; cert. avian rehabilitator USDI Fish and Wildlife Svc. Sec./clk. Union Theol. Seminary, N.Y.C., 1953-54; nursery sch. tchr. Berkeley (Calif.) Unified Sch. Dist., 1954-55; sec./clk. Ch. Divinity Sch. of the Pacific, Berkeley, 1955; nursery sch. tchr. Edgewood People's Ch., East Lansing, Mich., 1964-65; overseas missionary Protestant Episcopal Ch., Brazil, 1965-68; lab. tech. Princeton (N.J.) Labs., Inc., 1968; profl. rsch. staff Princeton U., 1968-89, profl. tech. staff, 1989-96; reviewer Am. Jour. of Botany, 1971-73, 83, N.Am. Bird Bander, 1977—; chair Profl. Rsch. and Tech. Staff Grievance Com., Princeton U., 1978-80, area rep., 1982-89, coord. com. Princeton U. Women's Orgn., 1982-89; cons. Bracco Rsch. USA, Inc., Princeton, 1996—, Williams Transcontinental Gas Pipeline Corp., Lawrenceville, N.J., 1996—, FMC Corp., Princeton, 1997—, Allelix Neurosci., Inc., Cranbury, N.J., 1997-99, Johnson & Johnson Consumer Products, Inc., Skillman, N.J., 1998—, Purdue Bio Pharma LP, Princeton, N.J., 1999—. Contbr. articles to profl. jours. Bird bander U.S. Geol. Survey, 1953—; leader Bits and Boots 4-H Horse Club, Mercer County, N.J., 1969-75; county coach Mercer County 4-H Competitive Trail Ride and Mercer County 4-H Horse Judging Team, 1973-75; rep. Mercer County Horse Coun., 1970-75; participant N.J. Audubon Breeding Bird Atlas, 1980-85, 91-95; mem. Migratory Bird Rehab. Policy and Permit Rev. Com., N.J., 1988-90, others; trainer N.Am. Banding Coun., 1998—; vol. cons. Woodrow Wilson Nat. Fellowship Found., Princeton, 1997. Recipient Outstanding Layperson award Diocese of Mich. Bishop's award 1955, Frank M. Chapman Meml. award Am. Mus. of Natural History, 1986, Paul A. Stewart award Wilson Ornithol. Soc., 1986, 87, Small Grants, Audubon/Washington Crossing Chpt., 1986-88, 94—, others. Mem. Sigma Xi. Democrat. Episcopalian. Achievements include the discovery of day-length sensitivity of Xanthium seedlings, allowing aseptic culture of sprouts for plant hormone bioassays; developed aseptic culture techniques of Xanthium hypocotyl tissue for bioassays; teammate in discovery of the chemoattractant in the cellular slime mold Polysphondylium violaceum and in the discovery of the role of ammonia in chemotaxis; discovered the trans-continental tranport of cellular slime molds (Dictyostelids) by migratory songbirds.

SUTO, KEIICHI, pharmaceutical company research executive; b. Isesaki, Japan, Mar. 13, 1956; s. Kozaburo and Hatsuko (Kaneko) S.; m. Yoshiko Yaginuma Suto, Apr. 7, 1985; children: Eiichi, Sayaka. Pharm. doctor, Tokyo U. Pharmacy and Life Sci, 1998. Rsch. assoc., gen. mgr. Taisho

Pharm. Co. Ltd., Ohmiya, Japan, 1980—. Avocations: swimming, playing guitar. Office: Taisho Pharm Co Ltd, 403 Yoshino-cho 1 chome, Ohmiya 330-8530, Japan

SUTOO, DEN'ETSU, neuroscientist, researcher; b. Tendo, Yamagata, Japan, May 29, 1952; s. Den'ichiro and Kikue (Shinohara) S.; m. Sumi Inoue, Mar. 20, 1976; children: Lemi, Ken'etsu. B of Hygienic Sci., Kitasato U., Tokyo, 1975, PhD, 1989. Rschr. U. Tsukuba, Japan, 1975—, expert officer, 1990-92, head officer, 1992—; cons. Tosoh Corp., Tokyo, 1977-90, Jeol Ltd., Tokyo, 1978-97, Nikon Corp., Tokyo, 1983—, Taisho Pharm. Co. Ltd., Tokyo, 1996—, Yamato Scientific Co., Ltd., Tokyo, 1999—. Author: The Vulnerable Brain and Environmental Risks, 1994; contbr. articles to profl. jours. Fellow Japanese Sci. Jamboree, Tokyo, 1970—, Tsukuba Sci. Fair, Tokyo, 1984-97; exec. mem. Tsukuba Children's Art Contest, Tokyo, 1984—; headman of town, 1997-99; adviser preservation of stickleback, Yamagata, Japan, 1998—. Recipient Spl. award U.S. Patent Office, 1969, Prime Min. award Japanese Govt., 1969, Grant award Toyota Found., Tokyo, 1987. Fellow Japanese Pharmacological Soc., Japanese Finalist Club; mem. N.Y. Acad. Scis. Buddhist. Avocations: classical music, cycling, photography, gardening, fishing. Fax: (81) 298-54-9817. E-mail: dsutoo@md.tsukuba.ac.jp. Home: 3-22-13 Namiki, Tsukuba 305-0044, Japan Office: Univ Tsukuba Inst Med Sci, 1-1-1 Tennoudai, Tsukuba 305-8575, Japan

SUTOWSKI, THOR BRIAN, choreographer; b. Trenton, N.J., Jan. 27, 1945; s. Walter X. and Kathryn (Tang) S.; m. Sonia Arova, Mar. 11, 1965; 1 dau., Ariane. Student San Diego Ballet, 1958-63, San Francisco Ballet, 1963-64, Nat. Ballet, 1964. Cert. solotanzer (solo dancer), Genossenschaft Deutscher Buhnen-Angehorigen, West Germany. Soloist, Norwegian State Opera, Oslo, 1965-70; 1st soloist Hamburgische Staatsoper, Hamburg, Ger., 1970-71; dir. San Diego Ballet, 1971-76, Ballet Ala., Birmingham, 1978-81; dir. State of Ala. Ballet, Birmingham, 1982-83; chmn. Ala. Sch. Fine Arts, Birmingham, 1976-96; assoc. dir. Calif. Ballet Co., San Diego, 1996-98; artistic prodr. San Diego Ballet Co., 1998—; artistic advisor, choreographer Asami Maki Ballet, Toyko, 1976-79; choreographer Atlanta Ballet, 1980-87, resident choreographer Atlanta Ballet Co., 1987-93; dance advisor Ala. State Arts Council, Montgomery, 1977-78; advisor Tenn. Ballet Co.; dance advisor Miss. Arts Council; choreographer Ballet South and State of Ala. Ballet; mem. City of Atlanta Mayor's Review Fellowship panel, 1987; adj. prof. choreography U. Ala., Tuscaloosa, 1988—; lectr. U. Calif., San Diego, 1998—; commd. choreograher Bavarian State Ballet-State Opera, Munich, 1994. Recipient Pub. TV Emmy award, 1976; Obelisk award for Choreography, 1977, 78, 79, 80; grantee Ford Found., 1964, Nat. Endowment Arts, 1973-74. Mem. Am. Guild Mus. Artists. Republican. Lutheran.

SUTTER, JANE ELIZABETH, educator, writer; b. St. Louis, Nov. 27, 1939; d. Richard A. and Elizabeth Henby Sutter. AB in Sociology and English, Vassar Coll., 1961; MA in Health Facilities Mgmt., Webster Coll., St. Louis, 1979. Healthcare analyst Chgo. and St. Louis, 1966-83; asst. dir. radio, TV and motion picture dept. AMA, Chgo., 1966-67; staff coord., rsch. assoc. Chgo. water quality study and environ. health study Inst. of Medicine of Chgo., 1967-69; dir. environ. health planning Comprehensive Health Planning, Inc., Chgo., 1969-73; planning assoc., spl. asst. to med. dir. Sutter Clinic, Inc., St. Louis, 1975-84; vol. activist, educator; founder, dir. Wild Birds for the 21st Century Inc., 1996—; dir., corr. www.wildbirds.org; corr., dir. wildbirds.org. Chmn. Opera Theatre of St. Louis Newsletter, Vol. 1, No. 1, 1980, Vol. 1, No. 2, 1980; co-founder, com. mem. 1st Internat. Alewife Festival of Chgo., Chgo. Yacht Club, summer 1968; appointee Gov.'s Com. for Pure Air and Water, Chgo., 1968; spl. advocate N.Am. Migratory Birds particularly hummingbirds; mem. Ladue Chapel. Mem. Nat. Coun. State Garden Clubs, Inc., Federated Garden Clubs of Mo., Inc., Clayton Garden Assn., Mo. Bot. Garden, St. Louis Artists' Guild (mem. artists' sect. 1992-95, portraitist), Inst. Religion in an Age of Sci., Univ. Club, Neotropical Bird Club (U.K.). Avocations: artist, music, landscaping for birds. E-mail: jesutter@wildbirds.org. Home: 7376 Pershing Blvd Saint Louis MO 63130-4206

SUTTER, JOHN RICHARD, manufacturer, investor; b. St. Louis, Jan. 18, 1937; s. Richard Anthony and Elizabeth Ann (Henby) S. BA, Princeton U., 1958; MBA, Columbia U., 1964. CPA, N.Y., Mo. Mgr. Price Waterhouse, N.Y.C., 1964-71; pres. John Sutter and Co., Inc., St. Louis, 1972-86, Handlan-Buck Co., St. Louis, 1975-88; investor, 1988—; pres. Pamlico Jack Group, Oriental, N.C., 1989—; pres. Sutter Mgmt. Corp., St. Louis, 1972-79. Mem. Chpt. Christ Ch. Cathedral, 1987-88. Lt. (j.g.) USNR, 1959-63. Mem. AICPAs, Mo. Soc. CPAs, Neuse Sailing Assn., Sailing Club of Oriental. Episcopalian. Clubs: Princeton, Oriental Dinghy. Avocations: painting, sailboat racing, ocean cruising, ceramic arts. Home and Office: 410 Whittaker Point Rd PO Box 481 Oriental NC 28571-0481

SUTTER, MADELINE ANN, landscape architect; b. Chgo., Oct. 13, 1941; d. William Charles Matthew Traugott and Antonette Florence Geller; m. Gray Carroll Stribling Jr., June 3, 1967 (div. Aug. 1982); 1 child, William Charles Matthew Stribling. BA, U. Wis., 1965; A of Horticulture, Meramec Coll., 1982; M of Landscape Arch. with honors, N.C. State U., 1999. Sys. analyst McDonnell-Douglas Corp., St. Louis, 1965-67; mem. faculty Washington U., St. Louis, 1967-70; pres. Inside/Outside, Inc., St. Louis, 1971-89; v.p. Handlan-Buck Co., St. Louis, 1983-88; pres. Madeline Sutter, ASLA, Oriental, N.C., 1989—; lectr. Pamlico C.C., Grantsboro, N.C., 1990-94; cons. Hist. Beaufort (N.C.) Preservation, 1992-95, Coalition for Cmty. Conservation, Raleigh, N.C., 1995—. Author: Trees for Small Towns, 1999, Ma: An Investigation Into the Making of Exterior Meditative Physical and Sequential Space, 1999; creator: (urban forest program) Trees for Oriental, 1992-96 (Tree City U.S.A. award 1996). Chmn. Tree Bd. of Oriental, 1992-96; mem. phys. environment com., campus planning and design N.C. State U. Named Disting. Woman of N.C., N.C. Coun. for Women, 1996; grantee Trees for Oriental Phase I, II and II Am. the Beautiful, 1992, 94, 95, Phase III Small Bus. Adminstrn., 1995, Trees for Small Towns Urban and Comty. Forestry Grant Program, 1996. Mem. Am. Soc. Landscape Archs., Herb Soc. Am. (mem.-at-large 1971—), N.C. Soc. Landscape Archs., N.C. League Landscape Archs., St. Louis Herb Soc. (pres., all offices 1967—), N.C. Urban Forest Coun. (mem. exec. bd., treas. 1992—), Tau Sigma Delta Natl. Honor Soc. for Architecture and the Allied Arts, Neuse Sailing Assn., Sailing Club Oriental. Avocations: sailboat racing, offshore and coastal cruising, harpsichord. Home and Office: PO Box 481 Oriental NC 28571-0481

SUTTLE, HELEN JAYSON, retired education educator; b. Plattsburgh, N.Y., Dec. 13, 1925; d. Harold Lincoln Jayson and Blanche Rabideau Jayson Woods; widowed, 1993; 1 child, Adolpha Helen Suttle Blanton. BA in Edn., Limestone Coll., 1961; MA in Edn., Winthrop U., 1973. Cert. tchr., S.C. Tchr. Madden Elem. Sch., Spartanburg, S.C., 1961-71, West Jr. High Sch., Gaffney, S.C., 1971-81, L.L. Vaughn Elem. Sch., Gaffney, S.C., 1981-88; substitute tchr. Gaffney Dis. 1, 1988—. vol. S.C. Budget Control bd., Upstate Carolina Med. Ctr., Meals on Wheels, local soup kitchen, Literacy Assn.; v.p. Ch. Women's Guild, pres., 1998—; pres. Sacred Heart Sr. Citizen's Club, treas. Ch. comm. Greenville Deanery; Eucharistic min., lector; chmn. Cherokee County Rep. Com.; mem. exec. bd. S.C. Coun. Cath. Women, 1998—, chair family commn., 1998—; trustee Limestone Coll., 1998—. Named woman of Yr., S.C. Coun. Cath. Women Greenville Deanery, 1996. Fellow Internat. Biog. Assn. (life, dep. gov. Am. chpt.), Limestone Coll. Alumni Assn. (pres., chpt. pres.), Fountain Club (charter mem.), Kalosophia Honor Soc. Roman Catholic. Avocations: writing, art, gardening, crafts. Home: 201 Trenton Rd Gaffney SC 29340-3626

SUTTNER, ERNST CHRISTOPH, religious studies educator; b. Regensburg, Bayern, Germany, Oct. 4, 1933; arrived in Austria, 1975; s. Johann and Johanna (Weiss) S. Lic. philosophy, Gregorian U., Rome, 1956, lic. theology, 1960; D in Theology, U. Würzburg, Germany, 1967, Venia Legendi, 1974. Ordained priest Roman Cath. Ch., 1960. Parish priest, 1960-62; asst. U. Würzburg, Germany, 1962-75; prof. Cath. theology Vienna, Austria, 1975—. Author: (books) Offenbarung, Gnade und Kirche bei A.S. Chomjakov, 1967, Beiträge zur Kirchengeschichte der Rumänen, 1978, Das Evengelium in Farbe-Glaubensverkündigung durch Ikonen, 1982, Church Unity: Union or Uniatism? Catholic-Orthodox Ecumenical Perspectives, 1991, Die katholische Kirche in der Sowjetunion, 1992, Das wechselvolle Verhältnis zwischen den Kirchen des Westens im Lauf der Kirchgeschichte, 1996, Kirche und Nationen, 1997, Die Christenheit aus Ost und West auf der Suche nach dem sichtbaren Ausdruck fur ihre Einheit, 1999; contbr. numerous articles to profl. jours. Office: Inst Theologie und Geschichte des christilichen, Schottenring 21, A-1010 Vienna Austria

SUTTNER, JON RICHARD, elementary education educator; b. Brentwood, Pa., Apr. 17, 1952; s. Ulrich Walter Suttner and Ruth Madeline Morrow. BS in Edn., Lock Haven (Pa.) State Coll., 1974. Cert. elem. edn., Pa. Elem. tchr. Hempfield Area Sch. Dist., Greensburg, Pa., 1975—. Ct. supr. Hempfield Recreation, Greensburg, 1979-92. Mem. NEA, Pa. State Edn. Assn., Hempfield Educators Assn., Elks. Lutheran. Avocations: sports, reading, electronics. Home: 181 Bonita St Greensburg PA 15601-4949 Office: Hempfield Area Sch Dist W Newton Rd Greensburg PA 15601

SUTTON, ANNE FRANCES, archivist; b. Kent, Eng., Nov. 3, 1942; d. Philip Henry and Catherine Elizabeth (Howard) S. BA, Oxford U., 1962-65; dipl. archive studies, London U., 1973, PhD, 1995. Asst. archivist Corp. London, London, 1973-80; archivist Mercers Co., London, 1981-99, historian, 1999—; mng. trustee Richard III and Yorkist History Trust, 1985—. Co-author: The Hours of Richard III, 1990; co-author, editor: The Coronation of Richard III, 1983, Medieval London Widows, 1300-1500, 1994; editor: The Ricardian, 1972—; contbr. hist. articles to profl. jours. Fellow Soc. Antiquaries London, Royal Hist. Soc. Home: 44 Guildhall St, Bury Saint Edmunds, Suffolk IP33 1QF, England Office: Mercers Co, Mercers Hall Ironmonger Ln, London EC2 8HE, England

SUTTON, BETTY SHERIFF, elementary education educator; b. Orangeburg, S.C., Jan. 16, 1933; d. Luther Doyle and Mattie (White) Sheriff; m. William Bryan Nunn, June 19, 1954; 1 child, Lisbeth Sheriff Nunn (Mrs. William Reid Clark); m. James Carlton Sutton, Dec. 28, 1979 (dec., 1998). Student, Columbia Coll., 1949-52; BS, U. S.C., 1953. Tchr. grade 4 State of S.C. Pub. Sch., Blackville, 1953-54; tchr. grade 2 Dream Lake Elem. Sch., Apopka, Fla., 1954-64; tchr. spl. edn. Leon County Sch., Tallahassee, Fla., 1965-66; page mother Fla. Ho. Reps., Tallahassee, 1966-67; tchr. grade 3 Timberlane Elem. Sch./Leon County Schs., Tallahassee, 1967-71; tchr. grades 3 and 4 Golfview Elem. Sch./Brevard County Schs., Rockledge, Fla., 1972-86; tchr. grade 1 Cambridge Elem. Sch./Brevard County Schs., Cocoa, Fla., 1987-98; ret., 1998; pres. Bits of Brevard, Inc., Rockledge. Chmn. Democrats for Conner, 1988, Keep Brevard Beautiful, 1990; active Brevard Symphony Orch. Guild, Brevard Mus. Guild, 1973—, Brevard Heritage Coun., Inc., Episcopal, St. Marks Guild. Recipient S.C. Forestry award State of S.C. Forestry Commn., 1977; ART grantee J. Paul Getty Ctr. for Edn. in the Arts, 1990. Mem. AAUW (pres. 1968-70), Apopka Woman's Club (pres. 1960-62), Apopka Garden Club, Brevard Reading Coun. (v.p. 1980-82), Am. Mothers, Inc., Columbia Coll. Column Club, Columbia Coll. Alumni Club. Ctrl. Fla., U. S.C. Alumni Club (life), Country Club of Rockledge, Delta Kappa Gamma (pres. 1992-94). Avocations: volunteering, reading, swimming, travel, farming. Home: 2201 Royal Oaks Dr Rockledge FL 32955-5440

SUTTON, DAVID AINSLEY, real estate company executive; b. Christchurch, New Zealand; s. Frederick Ira and Marjorie (Webb) S.; m. Dianne Fleming, Oct. 14, 1967. Degree, Christs Coll., Christchurch, 1960. Dir. Simes Ltd., Christchurch, 1972—; bd. dirs. Christchurch Multiple Listing Bur., Real Estate Network Ltd. Mem. Rotary (pres. Christchurch club 1996-97, dir., v.p., 1993-96). Avocations: water sports, boating, snow skiing. Office: Simes Ltd, Box 13341, Christchurch New Zealand

SUTTON, DOUGLAS HOYT, nurse; b. McHenry, Ill., Oct. 27, 1962; s. Hoyt Douglas Sutton and Barbara (Sutton) Hensley. Cert. in emergency med. tech., Polk Community Coll., Winter Haven, Fla., 1985; ADN, SUNY, Albany, 1990, BS in Nursing, 1991, BS in Psychology, 1993; MSN, U. Fla., 1995; MPA, Troy State U., 1997; EdD, Fla. Internat. U., 2000, master's cert., 2000. Cert. adv. nursing adminstrn., Post Master's Cert. Adult Health Nurse Practitioner, Fla. Internat. U., 2000. Paramedic Polk County Emergency Med. Svcs., Bartow, Fla., 1984-88; edn. cons. Moore Pubs., 1990-94; mgr. orthopedics and skilled care programs Columbia Healthcare, Inc., Gainesville, 1995-97; dir. med. surg. nursing U. Cmty. Hosp., Tampa, 1997-98; dir. patient svcs. Bethesda (Fla.) Meml. Hosp., 1998-2000; nursing instr. Broward C.C., Davie, Fla., 2000—. Mem. Fla. Orgn. Nurse Execs., Am. Coll. Healthcare Execs., Sigma Theta Tau. Home: 1623 NE 16th Ter Fort Lauderdale FL 33305-3409

SUTTON, ERNEST SHAW, chemical engineer; b. Burlington, N.J., May 22, 1922; s. Ernest Shaw Sr. and Elizabeth Bauer (Sholl) S.; m. Janet Gilbertson, July 1, 1950 (dec. Mar. 1974); children: Jane M., Douglas S., Andrea L.; m. Lois Williams, June 12, 1975. BSChemE, U. Pa., 1943. Analytical chemist Nat. Synthetic Rubber Corp., Louisville, 1943-44; polymer chemist Hewitt Robins, Inc., Buffalo, 1946-48, United Aircraft, Inc., Hartford, Conn., 1948-50, Thermoid Rubber Co., Trenton, N.J., 1950-53; propellant chemist Thiokol Corp., Elkton, Md., 1953-54, head R&D labs., 1954-84; head preliminary design Morton-Thiokol, Inc., Elkton, 1984-86, dir. mktg., 1986-87, v.p., gen. mgr., 1987-88; pvt. practice aerospace cons. West Grove, Pa., 1988—; bd. dirs. Cecon, Inc., Wilmington, Del., So. Chester County Med. Ctr., West Grove. Author: History of Thiokol and Rockets, 1996. Pres. residents coun. Jenners Pond Retirement Cmty., West Grove, 1996—. With U.S. Army, 1944-46. Mem. AAAS, AIAA, Am. Chem. Soc., Planetary Soc. Achievements include 8 patents in solid rocket propellants and rocket motor componants. Avocations: skiing, community theater, gardening, computers, investing. Home: 252 Azalea Ln West Grove PA 19390-9479 Office: Cecon Inc 242 N James St Wilmington DE 19804-3168

SUTTON, GERARD, university administrator. Vice-chancellor, prin. U. Wollongong, N.S.W., Australia. Office: Uni Wollongong, Northfields Ave, Wollongong NSW 2522, Australia*

SUTTON, HAL EVAN, professional golfer; b. Shreveport, La., Apr. 28, 1958; s. Howard Everett and Mary Alice (Rogers) S.; m. Ashley; children: Samantha, Sara, Sadie. B.S. in Sci., Centenary Coll. Professional golfer, 1981-. Named Player of Yr., Profl. Golf Assn., 1983; winner Disney Classic, 1982, Profl. Golf Assn. Championship, 1983, Tournament Player's Championship, 1983, 2000, Memphis Classic, 1985, Phoenix Open, 1986, Meml. Tournament, 1986, Ryder Cup Team, 1987; B.C. Open, 1995; Westin Texas Open, 1998; The Tour Championship, 1998, Bell Canadian Open, 1999, Greater Greensboro Chrysler Classic, 2000. Home: 30 Provident Oaks Bossier City LA 71111-5456 Office: Sutton Enterprises 212 Texas St Ste 117 Shreveport LA 71101-3287

SUTTON, JOHN ANDREW, physician, business executive; b. London, Feb. 7, 1943; s. Philip Reginald John and Mabel Constance (Buist) S.; m. Jeanette Filshie, Mar. 30, 1970; 1 child, Theodora. MBBS, U. London, MD, 1990. Med. adviser Glaxo Labs., Greenford, London, 1970-74; dir. clin. pharmacology unit Abbott Labs., Inc., U.K., 1978-80; dir. clin. pharmacology SmithKline Beecham, Harlow, Eng., 1980-85, Roussel Labs. U.K., 1985-89; med. dir. Knoll AG, Maidenhead, Eng., 1989-90; founder, dir. Guildford (Eng.) Clin. Pharmacology Ltd., 1994—; hon. cons. Royal Surrey County Hosp., Guildford, 1997—. Patentee board game, novel method of measuring stomach emptying. Biol. Rsch. Coun. U.K. grantee, 1996-99. Fellow Coll. Anaesthetists Ireland, Brit. Pharmacol. Soc., Assn. Clin. Pharmacologists in the Pharma Industry (founder); mem. Soc. for Medicines Rsch. Avocations: chess, bridge, desktop publishing. Home: Cedars, Vanzell Rd, Midhurst West Sussex, England Office: Guildford Clin Pharm Ltd, Royal Surrey County Hosp, Guildford Surrey GU2 5XX, England

SUTTON, JOHN E.G., archeologist; b. Reading, Berkshire, Eng., May 22, 1937; s. Edward C. and Nora Ruby (Giles) S.; m. Inez B. Jarrick, 1970; children: Tamar, Ruth. MA, Oxford (Eng.) U., 1961; PhD, U. East Africa, Makerere (Uganda), 1965. Lectr., sr. lectr. U. Dar es Salaam, Tanzania, 1965-73; head dept. archeology Ahmadu Bello U., Zaria, Nigeria, 1974-77; prof. archeology U. Ghana, Legon, 1977-82; vis. fellow Wolfson Coll. Oxford U., 1982-83; dir. British Inst. Ea. Africa, Nairobi, 1983-98; Leverhulme emeritus fellow British Inst. Ea. Africa, East Africa, 1998-2000. Author: The Archaeology of the Western Highlands of Kenya, 1973, A Thousand Years of East Africa, 1990, Archaeological Sites of East Africa, 1999; editor: Jour. of Ea. African Hist. and Archeol. Rsch. Azania, 1983—, Tanzania Notes and Records, 1967-71; contbr. articles to profl. jours. Mem. gov. bd. Ghana Nat. Mus., Accra, 1979-81; mem. coun. Pan African Congress of Prehistory, 1983-95. Fellow Soc. of Antiquaries. Avocations: hill-walking, ornithology, boating, classical music. Office: British Inst in E Africa, Box 30710, Nairobi Kenya

SUTTON, JOHN EWING, lawyer; b. San Angelo, Oct. 7, 1950; s. John F. Jr. and Nancy (Ewing) S.; 1 son, Joshua Ewing; 1 stepson, Michael Brandon Ducote. BBA, U. Tex., 1973, JD, 1976. Bar: Tex. 1976, U.S. Tax Ct. 1977, U.S. Ct. Claims 1977, U.S. Ct. Appeals (5th cir.) 1978, U.S. Dist. Ct. (we. dist.) Tex. 1979, U.S. Supreme Ct. 1980; CPA, Tex. Tax specialist Peat, Marwick, Mitchell & Co., CPAs, Dallas, 1976-77; ptnr. Shannon, Porter, Johnson, Sutton and Greendyke Attys. at Law, San Angelo, Tex., 1977-87; judge 119th Dist. Ct. of Tex., 1987-99; pvt. practice Law Offices of John E. Sutton, 1999—. Treas. Good Shepherd Episcopal Ch., San Angelo, 1979-81; co-chmn. profl. divsn. United Way, San Angelo, 1980-82; trustee Angelo State U. Found., 1987-99, pres., 1988-91, 95-97, v.p., 1992-94, 98-99, sec.-treas., 1991-92. Mem. ABA, Tex. Bar Assn., Tom Green County Bar Assn. (sec.-treas. young lawyers 1977-78), AICPAs, Tex. Soc. CPAs (bd. dirs. 1980-87, pres. San Angelo chpt. 1980-81, mem. state exec. com. 1981-82, 86-87, state sec. 1986-87, chmn. profl. ethics com. 1985-86, Young CPA of Yr. 1984-85), Concho Valley Estate Planning Coun. (v.p. 1979-80, also dir.). Office: Law Office of John E Sutton 117 S Irving St San Angelo TX 76903-6419

SUTTON, KERRY PETER, exhibition and graphic designer; b. Matamata, Waikato, New Zealand, Sept. 22, 1944; s. Alfred and Beatrice Frances Sutton. Diploma in indsl. design, Wellington (New Zealand) Poly., 1964; ed., Art Ctr. Coll. Design, L.A., 1966-68. Freelance designer, photographer Auckland, 1990—. Designer, inventor I-ching lucky chime, I-ching incense burner. Mem. Royal Overseas League. Avocation: traveling. Home and Office: 18/10 Hutton St, Otahuhu Auckland New Zealand

SUTTON, L. PAUL, criminal justice educator; b. Munich, Aug. 16, 1948; s. William L. Sutton and Paulette Mikkelson. BS in Polit. Sci. and History, U. Kans., 1970; MA in Criminal Justice, SUNY, Albany, 1971, PhD in Criminal Justice, 1975. Asst. prof. sociology U. N.Mex., Albuquerque, 1976-78; rsch. assoc. Hindelang Criminal Justice Rsch. Ctr., Albany, N.Y., 1974-76; prof. criminal justice San Diego State U., 1981—; sr. rsch. assoc. Nat. Ctr. for State Cts., Williamsburg, Va., 1978-81; ind. filmmaker, N.Mex., Calif., 1982-92; cons. State of Calif. Dept. of Corrections, 1997-98; commr. cmty.-based punishment planning com., San Diego, 1996-97; bd. dirs. Nat. Forum on Criminal Justice, Springfield, Ill., 1980-81; expert witness on sentencing reform Nat. Acad. Scis., Washington, 1981. Producer documentary film Doing Time: Ten Years Later, 1991, Doing Time, 1979; co-author: The Search Warrant Process, 1984, Sentencing by Mathematics, 1982. Grantee Calif. State Dept. Corrections, 1997, NEH, 1979. Mem. AAUP, Am. Soc. Criminology,Acad. Criminal Justice Scis., Western Soc. Criminology, Phi Beta Kappa. Avocations: filmmaking, sailing, jogging. Office: San Diego State U Dept Criminal Justice San Diego CA 92182-4505

SUTTON, LOUISE NIXON, retired mathematics educator; b. Hertford, N.C., Nov. 4, 1925; d. John Calhoun and Annie Mariah (McNair) Nixon. BS, N.C. A&T State U., 1946; MA, NYU, 1951, PhD, 1962. Cert. tchr. sci. and math., N.C. Tchr. math./sci. Willis Hare H.S., Pendleton, N.C., summer 1946; tchr. math. Dudley High Sch., Greensboro, N.C., 1946-47; instr. math. N.C. A&T State U., Greensboro, 1947-57; asst. prof. math. Del. State U., Dover, 1957-62; assoc. prof. to prof. and dept. head math. Elizabeth City (N.C.) State U., 1962-87, prof. emeritus, 1987—; adv. com. math. cert. Del. State Bd. Edn., Dover, 1961-62, adv. com. cert. in math. and sci., 1959-61. Bd. dirs. Perquimans County Indsl. devel. Corp., Hertford, 1967-72; NAACP rep. adv. com. N.C. Bd. Social Svcs., Raleigh, 1969-71; mem. fin. bd. Pearson St. YWCA, Greensboro, 1954-56; AME Zion rep. Com. on Christian Edn. of Exceptional Persons, Nat. Coun. Chs., N.Y.C., 1963-65, rep. 150th Anniversary Advance, Am. Bible Soc., 1964-66; bd. dirs. Divsn. Higher Edn., N.C. Assn. Educators, 1969-72; mem. St. Paul AME Zion Ch., 1972-97, trustee, 1972-73, ch. treas., 1997-98. Recipient Disting. Tchr. award Elizabeth City (N.C.) State U. Gen. Alumni Assn., 1974, Tchr. of Yr., 1980, Woman of Yr. award NAUW, 1976, Plaque St. Paul AME Zion Ch., 1999; honoree Daughter of Isis, Arabia Ct. # 23, 1998, Elizabeth City State U. Gen. Alumni Assn., 1997. Mem. NAUW (pres. 1974-80, regional dir. 1976-80), NAACP (life), Nat. Coun. Tchrs. Math. (life), N.C. Coun. Tchrs. Math. (v.p. colls. 1979-80), Order Ea. Star (grand assoc. dean 1993-95, worthy matron 1994-97), George Washington Carver Floral Club (pres. 1991-99), Daus. of Isis, Delta Sigma Theta (life, pres. Dover, Del. and Elizabeth City Alumnae chpts.). Republican. Avocations: mini-golf, bowling, quilting, crochet, fishing. Home: 4 Driftwood Rd Hertford NC 27944-9684

SUTTON, NIGEL JAMES, aeronautical engineer, test flight officer; b. Kingston, Jamaica, June 19, 1963; came to U.S., 1982; s. Harold James and Sheila Claire (Murray) S.; m. Gail Ann Burris, Sept. 5, 1998. BS in Computer Sci., Park Coll., 1987; MS in Indsl. Engring., U. Tenn., 1995; MS in Aero. Engring., Naval Postgrad. Sch., 1998; MBA, Fla. Inst. of Tech., 2000. Enlisted USAF, 1983-87; commd. ensign USN, 1987; advanced through grades to lt. comdr.; student flight officer VT-10/VAW-110, San Diego, 1988-89; mission comdr. VAW-114, San Diego, 1989-92; flight instr. VAW-110, San Diego, 1992; test naval flight officer Navy Test Pilot Sch., Patuxent River, Md., 1993-94; test naval flight officer Force Aircraft Test Squadron, Patuxent River, Md., 1994-96, chief test project leader, 1998—; acquisition profl., aerospace engr. duty officer Force Aircraft Test Squadron, Patuxent River, 1998—; asst. program mgr. test and evaluation, 1998—. Contbr. articles to profl. jours. Named Navy Test Flight Officer of Yr., 1994; recipient Officer of Yr. award for leadership, USN, 1994. Mem. AIAA (tech. com. on aircraft survivability), Soc. Flight Test Engrs., Toastmasters Internat. (v.p. membership 1996-98, Best Spkr. award 1997), Nat. Naval Officer Assn. Republican. Roman Catholic. Achievements include research in radar discrimination between moving objects and free floating objects in UHF band; in critical component identification and combat kill modes of the JSF.

SUTTON, PAUL ROBERT, graphic designer, computer programmer; b. Columbia, Md.; s. Frederick James and Catherine W. Sutton. Student, Boston Coll., 1999—. Acct. Just Gardens, Columbia, 1996-98; web designer, graphics designer Cotter Integrated, Ellicott City, Md., 1998—. E-mail: suttonp@bc.edu.

SUTTON, PETER ALFRED, former archbishop; b. Chandler, Que., Can., Oct. 18, 1934. BA, U. Ottawa, 1960; MA in Religious Edn, Loyola U., Chgo., 1969. Ordained priest Roman Catholic Ch., 1960, bishop, 1974; oblate of Mary Immaculate; high sch. tchr. St. Patricks, Ottawa, Ont., 1961-63, London (Ont.) Cath. Cen. Sch., 1963-74; bishop of Labrador-Schefferville, Que., Can., 1974-86; archbishop Missionary Diocese of Keewatin-Le Pas, Man., 1986, apptd. coadjustor archbishop, 1986-98, archbishop, 1986-98; mem. Can. Conf. Cath. Bishops, mem. social affairs commn.; mem. Western Cath. Conf. of No. Bishops, Man. Bishops; Canadian accompanying Bishop L'Arche Internat. (homes for mentally handicapped), 1983—. Contbr. religious articles to newspapers. Address: PO Box 270, 108 1st St W, The Pas, MB Canada

SUTTON, RICHARD, cardiologist; b. Newport, Eng., Sept. 1, 1940; s. Dick Brasnett and Greta Mary (Leadbeter) S.; m. Anna Gunilla Cassö, Nov. 28, 1964 (div. 1998); 1 child, Edmund. MBBS, U. London, 1964, DSc (Med), 1988. Registrar in cardiology St. George's Hosp., London, 1967-68; fellow in cardiology U. N.C., Chapel Hill, 1968-69; registrar, then sr. registrar Nat. Heart Hosp., London, 1970-76; cons. cardiologist Westminster Hosp., London, 1976-93, Royal Brompton and Chelsea and Westminster hosps., 1993—; hon cons. cardiologist Italian Hosp., 1977-89. Author: Foundations of Cardiac Pacing, part 1, part 2, 1991, 98; editor: European Jour. Cardiac Pacing and Electrophysiology, 1991-96, editor Europace, 1997—; contbr. chpts. to book, articles to med. jours. Fellow Royal Coll. Physicians, Am. Coll. Cardiology (Gov.'s award 1979, 82); mem. Brit. Med. Assn., Brit. Pacing and Electrophysiology group (co-founder, pres. 1990-95, past sec., past coun. mem.), Med. Rsch. Soc., Royal Soc. Medicine, European Working Group on Cardiac Pacing (chmn. 1998-2000). Anglican. Avocations: opera,

tennis, cross-country skiing. Office: 149 Harley St, London W1N 1HG, England

SUTTON, ROBERT EDWARD, investment company executive; b. Burlington, Vt., July 3, 1943; s. Rollin Robert and Blanche Margaret (Deforge) S.; m. Julie Robin Levine, Feb. 1, 1975; children: Katherine Vanessa, David Robert. BA in Econs., St. Michaels Coll., 1962-66. V.p. Compretic, Inc., Beverly Hills, Calif., 1967-70; brokerage cons. Conn. Gen. Life Ins. Co., Denver, 1970-74; pres. The Core Corp., Denver, 1975-80; mng. dir. Willshire Investments & Holding Co., Denver, 1981-91; pres., chmn. Gen. Capital, Inc., Denver, 1991-93; pres, CEO WK Capital Advisors, Inc., Denver, 1994—; dir. NAt. Assn. Indep. Contr., Denver. 1991—, Nat. Endowment Trust, Denver, 1990—, Tri Corp, Denver, 1980-89, Nat. Acceptance Corp., L.A., 1991—, Nat. Investment Holdings, L.A., 1990—; chmn. Centrix Findmiol, LLC, 1998—, EIF, Inc., 1998—. Mem. Nat. Rep. Eagles, Washington, 1986-90, Inner Circle, Washington, 1985-90, Denver Ctr. Performing Arts, 1976-86. Mem. Am. Cancer League, Glenmoor Country Club. Home: 57 Glenmoor Cir Cherry Hl Vlg CO 80110-7121 Office: WK Capital Advisors Inc 7900 E Union Ave Ste 1100 Denver CO 80237-2746

SUTTON, WILLIAM DWIGHT, lawyer; b. Butler, Pa., Oct. 22, 1916; s. James S. Sutton and Ada Elizabeth Emrick; m. Mary Ella Newsome, Dec. 4, 1943; children: Ann, Melissa. BA, Washington & Jefferson, 1938; JD, U. Mich., 1941. Bar: Pa. 1946, U.S. Ct. Appeals (3d cir.) 1946, U.S. Supreme Ct. 1946. Assoc. atty. Donovan, Leisure, Newton & Irvine, N.Y.C., 1941-42; ptnr. Thorp Reed & Armstrong, Pitts., 1952-90, sr. ptnr., 1991—. Major U.S. Army, 1942-46, PTO. Decorated Bronze Star, 1944. Mem. ABA, Pa. Bar Assn., Allegheny County Bar Assn. Home: 605 Scenic View Dr Pittsburgh PA 15241-3999 Office: Thorp Reed & Armstrong 20 Stanwix St Fl 9 Pittsburgh PA 15222-4802

SUVIRANTA, ANTTI JOHANNES, retired judge; b. Helsinki, Finland, Nov. 30, 1923; s. Bruno Kaarle and Aino (Tarjanne) S.; m. Alma Annikki Elosuo, Jul. 5, 1953 (dec. Oct. 1999); children: Leena Marjatta, Raili Annikki, Outi Kyllikki. Cand. of law, Univ. Helsinki, 1948; M in law, Harvard Univ., 1952; D in law, Univ. Helsinki, 1963; D in law (hon.), Univ. Stockholm, 1984. Dist. judge's clerk and deputy Dist. Ct. of Janakkala, Hämeenlinna, Finland, 1951; civil servant Finnish Ministry of Finance, Helsinki, 1956-59; acting prof. of labour law Univ. Helsinki, 1962-67, prof. labour law, 1967-82; pres. Finnish Labour Ct., Helsinki, 1970-82; chief justice Supreme Adminstrv. Ct. of Finland, Helsinki, 1982-93; ret., 1993; docent of fiscal law Univ. Turku, Turku, Finland, 1963-70; vice chmn. Finnish Labour Ct., 1968-70; chmn. Finnish Labour Coun., 1973-79; chmn. several govt. commn. on Tax, Labour & Adminstrv. Law, Helsinki, 1962-85. Author: The Notion of Employment in Tax Law, 1961, Joint Taxation of Spouses, 1962, The Role of the Member States in the Unification Work of the Internat. Labour Orgnaisation, 1966, Finland International Encyclopaedia for Labour Law and Industrial Relations, 1980, rev. edit., 1999. Mem. exec. com. Internat. Soc. Labour Law and Social Security, Geneva, 1970-85; mem. com. application of conventions and recommendations of the Internat. Labour Orgn., Geneva, 1984-93; pres. Internat. Assn. Supreme Adminstrv. Jurisdictions, Paris, 1986-89; mem. European Commn. for Democracy Through Law, Venice, Italy, 1990-98. 1st lt. Finnish Artillery, 1941-44. Recipient Grand Cross of the Order of Judiciary Merit of Labour Pres. Supreme Labour Ct. of Brazil, 1980, Grand Cross of the Order of Finnish White Rose Pres. of Republic of Finland, Helsinki, 1987, Grand Cross of Royal Swedish Order of North Star King of Sweden, 1988. Mem. Finnish Acad. Arts & Scis. (chmn. of section for legal sci. 1985-90), Soc. Finnish Lit., Internat. Acad. Comparative Law. Avocations: gardening, international meetings. Home: Vuorimiehenkatu 19 A8, FIN00140 Helsinki Finland

SUVOROV, NICKOLAI FEDOROVITCH, physiologist, researcher; b. Urei, Pensa, Russia, Feb. 3, 1919; s. Fedor Ivanovich and Akulina Pavlovna (Logunova) S.; m. Natalia Michailovna Usievitch, Oct. 22, 1945; children: Olga Nickolaevna, Alexander Nickolaevitch. MD, I Med. Inst., St. Petersburg, Russia, 1946; PhD in Sci. in Medicine, Inst. Exptl. Medicine, St. Petersburg, 1949; DMS, Inst. Physiology, RAN, St. Petersburg, 1966, prof. (hon.), 1971. Jr. rschr. Inst. Brain, St. Petersburg, 1949-50; sr. rschr. Inst. Physiology, St. Petersburg, 1950-64, head of lab., 1964-78; head of dept. Inst. Physiology, 1978-90, prin. rschr., 1990—; vis. prof. Beijing U., 1953-56; vice-dir. rsch. Inst. Physiology, St. Petersburg, 1974-89. Author: (books) Central Mechanisms of Vascular Pathology, 1974, Striatal System and Behavior, 1984, Psychophysiol. Mechanisms of Selective Attention, 1985, Neurophysiol. Structure of Human Emotional State, 1981; editor: Jour. Physiology, Jour. Physiology of Higher Nervous Activity. Lt. Med. Force, 1941-43. Decorated Order of Honor, USSR Govt., 1971, 81, Order 2d World War, USSR Govt., 1985, Order of Russia, Russian Govt., 1999. Mem. Russian Physiol. Soc. (v.p. 1980-90), Am. Physiol. Soc. (hon.), Phys. Soc. (head 1975-99), Inst. Physiology (sci. coun. 1964—). Social Democrat. Orthodox. Avocations: Eastern poetry, gardening, volleyball, skiing. Home: Petrovskaya 2-2-25, 197046 Saint Petersburg Russia Office: Inst Physiology, Makarova 6, 199034 Saint Petersburg Russia

SUVOROVA, ANNA ISAAKOVNA, chemistry educator, researcher; b. Serdlovsk, Russia, Aug. 24, 1934; d. Isaak Jakovlevitch and Amalia Albertovna (Denner) Postovsky; m. Alexey Leonidovitch Suvorov, Aug. 10, 1956; children: Elena, Anthon. Degree in chemistry, Ural State U., Sverdlovsk, 1957; D in chemistry, Ural State U., 1968; DSc, U. Moscow, 1996. Asst. Ural State U., 1958-75, docent, 1975-93, prof., 1993—; chair macromoleucles chemistry, 1991—. Contbr. over 70 articles to profl. jours. Mem. Mendeleev's Soc. Avocations: classical music, painting. E-mail: anna.suvorova@usu.ru. Office: Lenin St 51, 620083 Ekaterinburg Russia

SUWALSKY, MARIO, chemistry educator; b. Santiago, Chile, June 19, 1936; s. Gregorio and Lea (Weinsymer); m. Susana Dueñas, Jan. 6, 1961; children: Jana Debora, Yahel Rebeca. Pharm. Chemist, U. Concepcion, Chile, 1959; PhD, Weizmann Inst. Sci., Rehovoth, Israel, 1969. Instr. U. Concepcion, Chile, 1959-60, chief-instr., 1960-69, prof., 1969—; dir. dept. analytical and inorganic chemistry, Faculty Chemistry Scis., U. Concepcion, Chile, 1970-76, dir. dept. polymers, 1982-86, dir. grad. studies, 1984-93, dir. rsch. and grad. studies, 1993—. Pres. Jewish Comty. Concepcion, Chile, 1984-88, 1997—. Recipient Guggenheim fellowship, Guggenheim Found., U.S., 1975, Mcpl. prize in Sci., Mcplty. Concepcion, 1996; named hon. corresponding mem Acad. Arts and Scis. Puerto Rico, 1991. Mem. Latin. Am. Fedn. Chem. Socs. (pres. 1972-76), Chem. Soc. Chile (pres. 1969-73), N.Y. Acad. Scis., Rotary Club Concepcion (v.p. 1997). Avocations: tennis, music, paintings, travel. Home: Caupolican 67 Dep 401, Concepción Chile Office: U Concepción Faculty Chem, Casilla 160-C, Concepción Chile

SUWANJUTHA, SUBHAREE, pediatrician, educator; b. Nakornratchasima, Thailand, Dec. 25, 1941; d. Chalieu and Subha (Mulapalalaksna) Tongudai; m. Tasana Suwanjutha; 2 children. MD, Faculty Medicine Siriraj Hosp., Bangkok, 1965; Cert. in Pediat. Respiratory Disease, Temple U., Phila., 1971. Diplomate Am. Bd. Pediatrics. Chief divsn. pediat. respiratory diseases Ramathibodi Hosp., Bangkok, 1973-99, chief pediat. intenstive care, 1973-99, prof. pediats. faculty of medicine, 1985—, assoc. dean postgrad. edn., 1992-95; chmn. respiratory care com. Ramathibodi Med. Sch., Bangkok, 1982—, chmn. dept. pediat. Faculty Medicine, 1998—; chmn. dept. pediatrics Ramathibodi Hosp., 1998—; selected expert in respiratory diseases for children by Med. Coun. Thailand as cons. Labour Ct., Ministry of Justice; rep. of S.E. Asia region 1st World Congress in Pediat. Intensive Care as WHO advisor, organizer, 1991; exec. com., regional amb. World Fedn. for Pediat. Intensive Care and Critical Care Soc., 1997—. Editor/author: Text Book of Pediatrics, 1979, Textbook on Respiratory Care in Pediatrics, 1991. Mem. com. Inst. for Devel. of Children and Family of Thailand, 1994—. Recipient Outstanding Prof. award Mabidol U., 1996, Outstanding Alumni award St. Christopher's Hosp. for Children, 1991. Fellow Am. Coll. Chest Physicians, Am. Assn. for Respiratory Care; mem. Royal Coll. Pediatricians of Thailand (chmn. exec. subcom. on pediat. pulmonology 1987—), Med. Coun. Thailand (chmn. sub-bd. com. on tng. of pediat. pulmonology 1989—), Thai Soc. Critical Care Medicine (pres. 1991-97), Asia-Pacific Assn. for Respiratory Care (chmn. med. adv. bd. 1993—), Asthma Assn. Thailand (com. mem. 1992—), Assn. for Healthy Lungs in Children (chmn. 1996—), Thai Thoracic Soc. (subcom. of cmty. pediats. for environ. control and anti-smoking activities 1991—), Thai Assn. Pediatric Pulmonology and Critical Care (pres. 1998—). Buddhist. Avocations: reading, jogging, aerobic exercise. Fax: (662) 201-1850. Home: 8 Soi Samsen 24 Samsen Rd, Dusit Bangkok 10300, Thailand Office: Ramathibodi Hosp Dept Pediatrics, Rama VI Rd, Bangkok 10400, Thailand

SUWANTO, ANTONIUS, microbiologist, researcher; b. Jember, Indonesia, Nov. 30, 1959; s. Adi Widjaja and Tan Kin Nio; m. Annita Florence Chandrah, Dec. 28, 1986; 1 child, Harry C. BSc, Bogor (Indonesia) Agrl. U., 1983; MS in Microbiology, U. Ill., 1989, PhD in Microbiology, 1992. Tchr. sr. h.s. Regina Pacis, Bogor, 1982-84; gen. mgr. North Aspac Ind. Co., Lampung, Indonesia, 1984-85; faculty staff Bogor Agrl. U., 1985—; profl. staff Inter Univ. Ctr. Biotech., Bogor, 1992—; cons. shrimp hatchery/farm, Besuki, Indonesia, 1992—; cons. on cocoa butter substitute, Jakarta, Indonesia, 1997—; sci. counterpart Can.-Indonesian Devel. Project, Manado, Ambon, 1994; biotech. adv. bd. Nat. Rsch. Strategy, Jakarta, 1996; molecular biology program coord. Biol. Tropics S.E. Asian, Bogor, 1997. Rschr.: (invention) Biocontrol of Soybean Disease, 1995 (Best Young Rschr. award 1995). Recipient Internat. Tng. Program in Biotech., German Rsch. Ctr. for Biotechnology, 1997, Carl Zeiss award Marine Biol. Lab., 1994; Biotech. Career fellow Rockefeller Found., 1995-97, short-term biotech. fellow UNESCO, 1994. Mem. Indonesian Soc. for Microbiology (pub. svc. coord. 1997), Am. Soc. for Microbiology, Am. Soc. for Photobiology. Avocations: swimming, hiking, traveling, teaching. Office: Bogor Agrl U, Dept Biology FMIPA, 16144 Bogor Indonesia

SUWAT, LIPTAPANLOP, politician; b. Ratchaburi Province, Feb. 9, 1955; married. BS in Civil Engring., Kasetsart U.; MS in Transport Engring., Purdue U. Dep. min. Ministry of Transport and Comm., 1990-92, min., 1996; min. Ministry of Sci., Tech. and Environ., 1995, Ministry of Industry, Bangkok, 1998—. Sec. gen. Chart Pattana Party. Office: Ministry of Industry, Rama VI Rd Ratchathewi, Bangkok 10400, Thailand

SUYU, CARLOS TAGUIBAO, sales professional; b. Tuguegarao, Cagayan, The Philippines, Aug. 24, 1950; s. Victoriano Cusipag S.; m. Filomena Hipolito Callueng, Oct. 15, 1975; children: Angelo, Maria Concepcion, Michelle Issah. BS in Elem. Edn., St. Paul U., Tuguegarao, 1970, M in Guidance and Counseling, 1972. Head tchr. Dept. Edn. and Culture, Tuguegarao, 1973-76; sr. adminstr. Nat. Manpower and Youth Coun. Region 2, Tuguegarao, 1976-86, provicial dir., 1986-89, chief adminstr., 1989-90; unit mgr. Insular Life Ins. Co., Ltd., Tuguegarao, 1982-90, dist. sales mgr., 1990—. Bd. dirs. YMCA, Tuguegarao, 1989—, Rotary Club, Tuguegarao, 1996—, Boy Scouts Am., Tuguegarao, 1998—. Mem. Life Underwriters Assn. (cert.). Roman Catholic. Avocations: reading, table tennis, darts, fishing, mountaineering. Office: Insular Life Sychangco Bldg, Bonifacio 57, Cagayan Tuguegarao 3500, The Philippines

SUZDALEV, IGOR PETROVITCH, physicist; b. Moscow, Sept. 4, 1938; s. Peter Kirillovitch and Tatiana Ivanovna (Emelianova) S.; m. Irina Semenovna Charina, Apr. 15, 1972; children: Feodor, Peter. Engring. - Physics Diploma, Engr. Physics Inst., Moscow, 1962; PhD, Inst. Chem. Physics, Moscow, 1965, DSc, 1974. Jr. rschr. Inst. Chem. Physics, Moscow, 1965-68, sr. rschr., 1968-81, head of lab., 1981—, prof. chem. physics, 1983—; mem. scientific bds. Inst. Chem. Physics, 1990—, Internat. Adv. Bd. on Mossbauer Effect (IBAME), Mainz U., Germany, 1995—. Author: Dynamic Effects in Mossbauer Spectroscopy, 1979, Mossbauer Spectroscopy of Proteins and Model Compounds, 1988, Physical Review B 45, 1992, Nuclear Instrumen and Methods, Phys. Res. B76, 1993, Z. Phys. D36, 1996, Z. Phys. D37, 1996; contbr. articles to profl. jours. Mem. scientific bd. Russian Basic Rsch. Found., Moscow, 1995—. Grantee Internat. Sci. Found., Washington, 1993-95, Deutscher Forschung Gemeinschaft, Bonn, Germany, 1994-96, Russian Basic Rsch. Found., Moscow, 1993—. Mem. Russian Phys. Soc. (bd. dirs. 1992—). Avocations: piano, guitar, singing, writing poetry, cross-country skiing. Office: Inst Chem Physics, Kosygina 4, 117977 Moscow Russia

SUZUKI, AKIRA, language educator; b. Hirosaki, Aomori, Japan, Oct. 6, 1957; s. Takashi and Kinu (Sudo) S.; m. Akiko Kimura, Mar. 7, 1994. BA, Hirosaki U., 1980; MA, U. Tokyo, 1982. Asst. lectr. U. Tokyo, 1982-85; asst. prof. Meiji U., Tokyo, 1985-87; assoc. prof. Gakushuin U., Tokyo, 1987-91, Tokyo U. Fgn. Studies, 1991—. Author: The Vision of an Ending: W.B. Yeats and Modern Europe, 1996. Mem. English Soc. Japan (trustee 1998—), Shakespeare Soc. Japan, Yeats Soc. Japan, The Nabokov Soc. Japan.

SUZUKI, AKIRA, physics educator; b. Tokyo, Apr. 14, 1949; s. Masatsugu and Takako (Tanbo) S.; m. Keiko Sawamura, Sept. 13, 1992. BSc, Sci. U. Tokyo, 1973; PhD, U. Reading, Eng., 1982. Rsch. assoc. Purdue U., West Lafayette, Ind., 1982-85; chief scientist Canon Inc. Rsch. Ctr., Atsugi, Japan, 1986-93; assoc. prof. Sci. U. Tokyo, 1993-98, prof. sci., 1999—. Contbr. articles to profl. jours. Mem. IEEE, Am. Phys. Soc., N.Y. Acad. Scis. Avocations: tennis, golfing, music. Office: Sci U Tokyo Ctr Solid State, Physics 1-3 Kagurazaka, Tokyo 162, Japan

SUZUKI, BARNABAS TATSUYA, import/export manufacturing company executive; b. Hokkaido, Japan, Jan. 29, 1938; s. Mamoru and Hideko (Miura) S.; m. Tamiko Niwa, May 28, 1967; children: Lena, Mina. BL, Sophia (Jochi) U., Tokyo, 1963. Mgr. internat. div. Sanken Electric Co. Ltd., Tokyo, 1963-75; pres. Transtekne Internat. Inc., Tokyo, 1975—; corp. rep. Japan Airpax Corp., Frederick, Md., 1975—; bd. dirs. Sanken-Airpax Co., Ltd., Tokyo. Author: The First English Pipe-smoker in Japan, 1997, A Historical Study of Smoking Introduction into Japan, 1999; co-author: All about Pipes, 1978. Mem. The Pipe Club of Japan (chmn.), Com. Internat. des Pipe Club (v.p.), Paris, Academie Internationale de la Pipe, Confrerie des Maitres-Pipiers de Saint Claude. Home: 9-17-11 Chiyoga-oka, Asawo-ku, Kawasaki 215-0005, Japan Office: Transtekne Internat Inc, 6F AI Bldg 1-2-4 Honmachi, Shibuya-ku Tokyo 151-0071, Japan

SUZUKI, DAVID TAKAYOSHI, geneticist, science broadcaster; b. Vancouver, B.C., Can., Mar. 24, 1936; s. Kaoru Carr and Setsu (Nakamura) S.; m. Joane Setsuko Sunahara, Aug. 20, 1958 (div. 1965); children—Tamiko Lynda, Troy Takashi, Laura Miya; m. Tara Elizabeth Cullis, Dec. 10, 1972; children—Severn Setsu, Sarika Freda. BA cum laude, Amherst Coll., Mass., 1958; PhD, U. Chgo., 1961; LLD (hon.), U. P.E.I., 1974, Queen's U., Ont., 1987; DSc (hon.), Acadia U., N.S., 1979, McMaster U., Ont., 1987, U. Windsor, Ont., 1979, Trent U., Ont., 1981, Lakehead U., Ont., 1986; DHL (hon.), Gov.'s State U., Ill., 1986. Research assoc. Oak Ridge Nat. Lab., 1961-62; asst. prof. U. Alta., Edmonton, Can., 1961-63; asst. prof. dept. zoology U. B.C., Vancouver, 1963-65, assoc. prof., 1965-69, prof., 1969—; vis. prof. UCLA, 1966, U. Calif.-Berkeley, 1969, 1976-77, U. Utah, Salt Lake City, 1971-72, U. P.R., 1972, U. Toronto, 1978. Host TV programs Suzuki on Sci., CBC, Vancouver, 1971-72, Sci. Mag., Toronto, 1974-79, Quirks & Quarks, Vancouver, 1974-79, Nature of Things, Toronto, 1979—; host series on sci. TV programs Interface, 1974-75, Just Ask, Inc., 1980, Night Video, 1984, Futurescan, 1984; radio program Discovery, 1983—; author: (textbook) Introduction to Genetic Analysis, 1976, David Suzuki Looks at Plants, 1985, David Susuki Looks at Insects, 1986, David Suzuki Looks at Senses, 1986, Egg-Carton Zoo, 1986, Sciencescape: The Nature of Canada, 1986, British Columbia: Frontier for Ideas, 1986, From Pebbles to Computers, 1986; contbr. articles to profl. and popular publs. and mags. Bd. dirs. B.C. Civil Liberties Assn., 1973, Can. Civil Liberties Assn., 1982—. Decorated officer Order of Can.; recipient W.R. Steacie Meml. award Nat. Research Council Can., 1969-72; Sci. and Engring. medal Sci. Council B.C., 1981; UN Environ. Programme medal, 1985; grantee Can. Nat. Research Council, AEC, Nat. Cancer Inst. Can., NIH also others; recipient UNESCO Kalinga prize, 1986, Royal Bank award, 1986. Mem. Alliance of Can. TV and Radio Artists (award 1986), Genetic Soc. Am., Sci. Council Can. Mem. New Democratic Party. Avocations: scuba diving, fishing, skiing. Address: 2211 W 4th Ave # 210, Vancouver, BC Canada V6K 4S2

SUZUKI, HIDEKAZU, medical educator; b. Konosu, Japan, Dec. 1, 1963; s. Kazuo and Kazuko (Mimaru) S.; m. Kimiko Kino, Apr. 29, 1998; 1 child, Kieko. MD, Keio U., Tokyo, 1989, PhD, 1994. Instr. Keio U. Sch. Medicine, Tokyo, 1995—. Recipient Young Investigator award Asian Microcirculatory Soc., 1997; rsch. fellow Am. Heart Assn., 1993, U. Calif., San Diego, 1993-95. Mem. Am. Assn. Study of Liver Disease, Japanese Soc. Helicobacter Rsch. (exec.), Japanese Soc. Autonomic Nervous Systems (exec.), Japanese Soc. Exptl. Ulcer (exec.). Avocations: swimming, reading. Home: 5-14-6-802 Sendagaya, Shibuya-ku Tokyo 151-0051, Japan Office: Keio U Sch Medicine Dept Internal Med, 35 Shinanomachi, Shinjuku-ku Tokyo 160-8582, Japan

SUZUKI, HIROKAZU, electrical engineer, researcher; b. Yokohama, Kanagawa, Japan, Feb. 27, 1958; s. Tomie and Saburou (Hosaka) S.; m. Hiromi Sano, Feb. 22, 1986; children: Takahiro, Chihiro. BS, Tokyo Denki U., 1980, MS, 1982, PhD, 1995. Engr. Numadu (Japan) br. office Tokyo Electric Power Co., 1982-85, sr. engr. tech. rsch. divsn., 1985-91, asst. mgr., 1991-93, rschr. power electronics dept., 1993-97, sr. rschr., 1997—; vis. rschr. U. Tokyo, 1986-87; vis. lectr. Tokyo Denki U., 1998—. Mem. editl. bd. Jour. Magnetics Soc. Japan, 1991-2000, Trans. Inst. Elec. Engr. Japan, 1991-93; co-author: Fundamentals of Applied Magnetics, 1997; inventor new control method of large power ac/dc converter, 1996. Recipient OHM tech. award Elec. Tech. Found. Japan, Tokyo, 1996. Mem. IEEE, Inst. Elec. Engr. Japan (excellent presentation prize 1992, excellent transactions paper award 1998, outstanding devel. award 2000), Magnetics Soc. Japan. Home: 5-214, Moto-Machi, Naka-Ku, Yokohama 231-0861, Japan Office: Tokyo Elec Power Co, 4-1 Egasaki-Cho, Tsurumi-ku, Yokohama 230-8510, Japan

SUZUKI, HIROSHI, manufacturing company executive; b. Tokyo, Dec. 25, 1946; s. Yoshikazu and Kimie (Yamada) S.; m. Chigusa Segawa, Oct. 5, 1974 (dec. June 1993); children: Satoko, Takahisa, Masayuki; m. Nobuko Ikuta, Sept. 7, 1997. BS, Tokyo U., 1969, MS, 1971, PhD, 1974. Mgr. Mitsubishi Elec. Corp., Tokyo, 1990-94, gen. mgr., 1994—. Co-author: NEw Energy Era, 1988, Electricity in Global Age, 1993. Vis. fellow Nat. Inst. Sci. & Tech. Policy, Tokyo, 1995-97, Tokyo U., 1997—. Fellow IEEE; mem. Engring. Acad. Japan (dir.). Avocations: scuba diving, golf, Go. Office: PSTEC Mitsubishi Elec Corp, 2-2-3 Marunouchi, Chiyoda, Tokyo 100-8310, Japan

SUZUKI, HITOMI, organic chemistry educator, researcher; b. Kyoto, Japan, May 19, 1935; s. Seiji and Harue (Hojo) S.; m. Misao Sakane, Apr. 8, 1963; children: Hiroatsu, Eiki. BS, Kyoto (Japan) U., 1958, MS, 1960, DSc in Chemistry, 1963; PhD in Chemistry, London (Eng.) U., 1967. Asst. prof. Kyoto (Japan) U., 1963-71; assoc. prof. Hiroshima (Japan) U., 1971-78; prof. Ehime U., Matsuyama, Japan, 1978-89; emeritus prof. Kyoto U., 1989—; prof. organic chemistry Kwansei Gahuin U., Nishinomiya, Japan, 2000—. Author and patentee in field; contbr. over 450 rsch. articles. Recipient Japan Chem. Soc. award, 1997; Ramsay Meml. fellow Ramsay Meml. Fellowships Trust, 1965-67. Home: 930-71 5-chome Higashino, Matsuyama 790-0903, Japan Office: Kwansei Gakuin U, Sch Sci, Dept Chemistry, Nishinomiya 662-8501, Japan

SUZUKI, ISAO, physical chemist; b. Akiruno, Tokyo, Jan. 6, 1945; s. Risuke and Ai (Hirano) S.; m. Chikako Handa, May 21, 1972; 3 children. BS, U. Tokyo, 1967, MS, 1970, DS, 1977. Rschr. Electrotech. Lab., Tokyo, 1970-77, sr. rschr., 1977-90, sect. chief, 1990—. Author: (in Japanese) Synchrotron Radiation Technique, 1990; chief editor jour. Progress in Atomic Collision Rsch. in Japan, 1992-94; contbr. articles to profl. jours. Mem. Chem. Soc. Japan, Phys. Soc. Japan, Japanese Soc. Applied Physics. Achievements include development of x-ray monochromatizing and focusing device, mass spectrometer system, digital scanning system. Office: Electrotech Lab, 1-1-4 Umezono, Tsukuba Ibaraki 305-8568, Japan

SUZUKI, JIRO, psychiatry; b. Osaka, Japan, Feb. 11, 1936; s. Keikichi and Toshiko S.; m. Hiroko Kaihara, Nov. 17, 1964. MD, Tokyo U., 1961, PhD, 1966. Chmn. rsch. staff Psychiat. Inst. Tokyo, 1973-87; prof. psychiatry Toho U., Japan, 1987—. Author: Art and Science of Epilepsy, 1967. Mem. Japanese Soc. Neurology & Psychiatry (dir. bd. trustees 1993—, pres. 1997—), Japanese Soc. Epilepsy (dir. bd. trustees 1993—), Japanese Soc. Biol. Psychiatry (dir. bd. trustees 1997—, rep. WPA zone 17). Avocations: tennis, golf. Office: 6-11-1 Ohmori-Nishi Ohtaku, Tokyo 143, Japan

SUZUKI, JUN-ICHI, cardiologist; b. Tokyo, Aug. 19, 1954; s. Hitoshi and Fumiko (Ando) S.; m. Yoko Shimazaki, Dec. 7, 1985; three children. instr. health ctr. U. Tokyo, 1994—. Editor: Textbook of Cardiac Magnetic Resonance Imaging, 1998; contbr. articles to profl. jours. Grantee for MRI rsch. Banyu Pharm. Co., 1995—, grantee for sci. rsch. Ministry Edn., 1997—. Mem. Japanese Circulation Soc., Japanese Coll. Cardiology. Office: U Tokyo Faculty Medicine, Hongo 7-3-1, Bunkyo-ku Tokyo 113-8655, Japan

SUZUKI, KAZUSHIGE, cosmetics company executive; b. Osaka, Japan, Apr. 8; m. Yuriko Kzauko Adachi; children: Yasuko, Tomuko. B Engring, Nihon U., Tokyo, 1953; D Agr, Osaka (Japan) Prefecture U., 1968. Dir. Noevir Co., Ltd., Kobe, Japan, 1978-82, mng. dir., 1982-83, exec. dir., 1983-87, exec. pres., 1989-96, supreme advisor, 1997—. Mem. Soc. Cosmetic Chemists of Japan (v.p., dir. Osaka chpt.). Home: 5-53 Rokubuncho, Nishinomiya Hyogo 662-0086, Japan Office: Noevir Co Ltd, 6-13-1 Minatoshima nakamach, Kobe Hyogo 650-8521, Japan

SUZUKI, KUNIHIRO, microelectronics company executive, researcher; b. Hachinohe, Japan, Jan. 8, 1959; s. Fukushi and Yae (Hayashi) S.; m. Kyoko Abe, Mar. 25, 1984; 4 children. BS, Tokyo Inst Tech., 1979, MS, 1981, PhD, 1996. Cert. engr. Sr. rschr. Fujitsu Labs. Ltd., Atsugi, Japan, 1983—. Contbr. articles to profl. jours. Mem. IEEE. Avocation: running. Home: Kamikasuya 2533-35, Isehara Kanagawa, Japan Office: Fujitsu Labs Ltd, 10-1 Morinosato-Wakamiya, Atsugi Kanagawa, Japan

SUZUKI, OSAMU, automotive industry executive; b. Gero, Gifu, Japan, Jan. 30, 1930; s. Shunzo and Toshiko S.; m. Shoko Suzuki, 1958; 3 children. Student, Chuo U., Japan, 1953. Joined Suzuki Motor Co. Ltd., 1958, various mgmt. positions, 1958-63, dir., 1963-66, jr. mng. dir., 1967-72, sr. mng. dir., 1973-77, pres., 1978-2000, chmn., 2000—. Recipient Sitara-i-Pakistan award Govt. of Pakistan, 1985, Honor with Blue Ribbon medal, 1987, Mid. Cross of Order of Rep. Hungary, 1993, Second Class Order of the Rising Sun, Gold and Silver Star, 2000. Avocation: golf. Office: Suzuki Motor Corp, 300 Takatsuka-cho, Hamamatsu 432-8611, Japan

SUZUKI, SHIGERU, mineralogist; b. Shinjuku, Tokyo, May 23, 1948; s. Shinichi and Masako (Sakai) S.; m. Sakiko Kumagai, Oct. 26, 1980; children: Shoko, Ryo. BS, Waseda U., 1972, M in Engring., 1974, D in Engring., 1977. Lic. tchr., sr. x-ray tech.; instr. first aid. Postdoctoral fellow Waseda U., Tokyo, 1978-79; scientist Power Reactor and Nuclear Fuel Devel. Corp., Tokyo, 1979-81, rschr., dep. gen. mgr., 1981-90; from vis. lectr. mineral chemistry to rsch. fellow U. Hull, England, 1994-98—; spl. advisor, chmn. edn. and rsch. affairs Scientists and Technologists Forum, Tokyo, 1999-2000, dir., 2000—; lectr. global environment study Dokkyo U., Saitama, Japan, 2000—; spl. monitor Sci. and Tech. Agy., Tokyo, 1985-86; vis. scholar U. Leicester, England, 1992-94. Mem. Friends of East Riding Youth Orch., East Yorkshire, England, 1993-98. Fellow The Minerol. Soc.; mem. AAAS, The Clay Minerals Soc. Avocations: traveling, male chorus. Home: 3-30-15-305 Namiki, 332-0034 Kawaguchi-shi Saitama, Japan Office: Faculty Econs Dokkyo U, 1-1 Gakuen-cho Soka-shi, Saitama 340-0042, Japan

SUZUKI, SHIN'ICHI, comparative education educator; b. Changchun, China, Jan. 1, 1933; arrived in Japan, 1946; s. Yoshio and Haruno (Katho) S.; m. Noriko Koike, Feb. 15, 1962 (div. Apr. 1975); children: Satoko Suzuki Nagai, Akitaka, Hidetaka; m. Akiko Ishihara, Mar. 21, 1996. BA, Waseda U., Tokyo, 1958, MA, 1960; PhD in Edn., Ashiya (Japan) U., 1984. Cert. secondary tchr., Tokyo. Sr. lectr. Waseda U., 1964-69, assoc. prof., 1969-77, prof., 1977—, vice dean sch. edn., 1984-86, chairperson, dep. edn., 1992-95, 98—, dir. dep. tchr. edn., 2000—; vis. prof. De La Salle U., Manila, The Philippines, 1987-89, Tonpei U., Shengyang, China, 1990—, Kent (Ohio) State U., 1994, Beijing Normal U., 1997—. Author and editor: Modernization and Educational Reforms: Prospects for 21st Century, 1994 (Tokyo Club's prize 1994), Europe: Illumination or Illusion: Lessons from Comparative x International Education, Education in Europe: A Comparative Approach, 1996, Shifts in Education Space, 2000; contbr. articles to profl. jours. Mem. Ministry of Edn. Adv. Coun. on Tchr. Edn., Japan, 1978-88. Mem. Japan Assn. Tchr. Edn. (dir., mgr., internat. dep.), Japan Soc. Studies in Ednl Policies (academic mgr.), Japan Soc. Edn. Law (academic mgr.), Japan Assn. Pvt. Univs. Tchr. Edn. (sec. gen. 1974-94), China-Japan Forum

Studies in Edn. (sec. gen. 1990—), U.K.-Japan Forum Ednl. Rsch. (pres. 1990—), Comparative Edn. Soc. of Asia (co-pres. 1995-98), Japan Soc. Internat. Edn. Avocation: gardening. Home: Plz 90-10, Ohmiya Saitama 331-0063, Japan Office: Waseda U Sch Edn, Nishiwaseda 1 6 1, Tokyo 169 8050, Japan

SUZUKI, SHINZO, researcher; b. Nagoya, Japan, Sept. 1, 1960. DS, Kyoto U., Japan, 1990. Tech. assoc. Inst. Molecular Sci., Okazaki, Japan, 1985-90; rsch. assoc. Tokyo Met. U., 1990—. Office: Tokyo Met U Dept Chemistry, Hachioji, Tokyo 192-0397, Japan

SUZUKI, TADAO, executive; b. Japan, Jan. 16, 1930; m. Takako Suzuki. Grad., Keio U., 1951; postgrad., Northwestern U., 1952. Chmn. Ajinomoto Co, Inc., 1951; pres. Mercian Corp., Tokyo. Office: Mercian Corp, 5-8 Kyobas Hi 1-Chrome, Chuo-ku Tokyo 104, Japan*

SUZUKI, TOSHIFUMI, food service and retail executive; b. Dec. 1, 1932. Chmn. Seven-Eleven Japan Co. Ltd., Tokyo; with Ito Yokado Co., Tokyo, 1963, various mgmt. positions, 1963-85, v.p., from 1985, now pres., CEO. Office: Ito Yokado Co Ltd, 1-4 Shiba-Koen 4-chome, Minato-ku Tokyo 105-8571, Japan*

SUZUKI, TOSHIO, publishing executive; b. Tokyo, May 26, 1923; 1 child, Ichiro. Student Hosei U., Tokyo, 1942-46. Prodn. mgr. Time-Life Internat., Tokyo, 1946-59; prodn. mgr. and Tokyo office mgr. Asia Mags. Ltd., Hong Kong, 1960-71; pres. Japan Communications Ltd., Tokyo, 1971—, INCOM Co., Ltd., Tokyo, 1972—; pres. INCOM Mktg. Inc., 1989; apptd. dir. ABC-Japan, Japan Audit Bur. Circulation, 1995. Buddhist. Home: 1-6-23 301 Sengoku, Bunkyo-ku, Tokyo 112, Japan Office: INCOM Co Ltd, 1-23-6 Sekiguchi Bunkyo-ku, Tokyo 112, Japan

SUZUKI, TOSHIO, electrical engineer; b. Utsunomiya, Japan, Sept. 15, 1938; s. Kinnichiro and Ei (Sakairi) S.; m. Kanae Hirota, Dec. 7, 1971; children: Rieko, Kentaro. B in Engring., U. Tokyo, 1962, PhD in Engring., 1972. Rschr. engr. Ctrl. Rsch. Inst. Electric Power Industry, Tokyo, 1962-79, mgr., 1979-93, assoc. v.p., 1993-95, v.p., 1995-99; sr. v.p. Ctrl. Rsch. Inst. Electric Power Industry, 1999—; rsch. assoc. U. Calif., Berkeley, 1969-70; chmn. Japan com. IECTC36, Tokyo, 1990-95. Co-author: Electrical Engineering Handbook, 1988. Fellow IEEE; mem. SIGRE SC 33, Inst. Elec. Engrs. Japan (v.p. 1995-96, Tech. Devel. award 1991, Outstanding Achievement award 1993), Phys. Soc. Japan. Avocations: golfing, music, football. Home: 2065-85 Ohzenji Asao, Kawasaki 215 0013, Japan Office: Ctrl Rsch Inst Elec Power, 1-6-1 Ohtemachi Chiyoda-ku, Tokyo 100 8126, Japan

SUZUKI, TSUTOMU, pharmacology and toxicology educator; b. Nagai, Yamagata, Japan, Nov. 19, 1949; s. Shinichi and Matsuno (Tezuka) S.; m. Michiko Matumura, Apr. 8, 1976; children: Tatsunori, Haruka. BS, Hoshi U., Tokyo, 1972, M Pharm. Scis., 1974, D Pharm. Scis., 1979. Rsch. and teaching assoc. Hoshi U., Tokyo, 1979-89, asst. prof., 1989-93, assoc. prof. pharmacology, 1994-98, chair, prof. toxicology, 1999—; rsch. assoc. U. Minn., Mpls., 1984-85; vis. scientist NIH, NIDA, ARC, Balt., 1985-86. Mem. editorial adv. bd. Life Sci., 1996—, Analytical Pharmacology, 1997—; asst. editor Addiction Biology, 1996—; mem. editorial acad. Internat. Jour. Molecular Medicine, 1997—. Mem. Internat. Soc. Biomed. Rsch. on Alcoholism, Behavior Genetic Assn., Japanese Pharmacol. Soc. (councilor 1980—, award for encouragement of young investigators 1990), Japanese Soc. Toxicological Scis. (editor 1996-98), Japanese Soc. Neuropsychopharmacology (trustee 1991-94, 99—, Sci. award 1993). Avocations: skiing, tennis. Home: 5-4-23-401 Yokodai Isogo-ku, Yokohama Kanagawa 235-0045, Japan 235 Office: Hoshi U Dept Toxicology, 2-4-41 Ebara, Shinagawa-ku, Tokyo 142-8501, Japan

SUZUKI, YOSHIHIKO, industrial gas company executive; b. Tokyo, July 12, 1951; s. Tomeji and Hiro (Baba) S.; m. Chiyomi Murota, Apr. 3, 1982; children: Mana, Tatsuhiko. B Econs., Keio U., Tokyo, 1976. Dir. Suzuki Shokan Co., Ltd., Tokyo, 1985—, pres., 1992—. Avocation: music. Office: Suzuki Shokan Co Ltd, 1-12-11 Funado Itabashi ku, Tokyo 174-8567, Japan

SVANBORG, CATHARINA, clinical immunology educator; b. Stockholm, Nov. 23, 1949; d. Alvar and Marianne (Lindh) Svanborg; children: Arvid, Gustav. MD, Göteborg U., Sweden, 1974, PhD, 1978; postgrad., U. Mich., 1979-80. Asst. prof. med. microbiology Göteborg U., 1979-89; prof. clin. immunology Lund (Sweden) U., 1989—; vis. prof. dept. microbiology and immunology U. Ala., Birmingham, 1981-85; mem. study sect. microbiological Med. Rsch. Coun., 1988-95, chmn. bd. cell biology study sect., 1999—; mem. Fernström Award Com., 1990-96; appointed Swedish EC-R&D Coun., 1994; mem. faculty appointments com., med. faculty, Lund U., 1996—; govt. advisor on sci. issues, 1999—; spkr. in field. Mem. editl. bd. Infection and Immunity, European Jour. Clin. Microbiology, Jour. Infectious Diseases, Microbial Pathogenesis, Internat. Jour. Molecular Medicine, Microbial Drug Resistance; reviewer numerous jours.; contbr. over 35 articles to profl. jours. Recipient Thord Gray fellowship, 1979, Fogarty fellowship, 1979-80, Swedish-Am. Found. fellowship, 1979-80, Fernström award, 1983, Ann. award Am. Acad. Pediat., 1985, Domagk award Bayer Internat., 1992, Windemere award Brit. Pediat. Soc., 1996, Disting. Achievement award Bristol-Myers Squibb, 1999. Fellow Vitterhetsakademin (Sweden), Royal Swedish Acad. Scis.; mem. Internat. Soc. Mucosal Immunity, Infectious Disease Soc. Am. (Spl. lectureship 1987), Swedish Med. Assn. (chmn. sect. clin. immunology 1990-96, Ann. Jubilee award 1997), Am. Soc. Microbiology, Scandinavian Soc. Immunology, Am. Soc. Nephrology, European Soc. Clin. Microbiology, Academia Europaea, Royal Physiographic Soc. Office: Lund U Dept Med Microbiol, Solvegatan 23, 223 62 Lund Sweden

ŠVANCARA, JOSEF STANISLAV, psychology educator; b. Bohuňoy, Svitavy, Czechoslovakia, Apr. 2, 1924; s. Josef and Františka (Bušinová) Š; m. Lea Müllerová, Sept. 28, 1948; children: Pavel, Jan, Vít, Jiří, Marie. PhD, Masaryk U., Brno, Czech Republic, 1950; Candidate of Sci., Slovac Acad. Sci., Bratislava, 1964. Prof. gen. psychology and developmental psychology Min. of Edn., Prague, Czech Republic, 1991. Clin. psychologist Faculty Childrens Hosp., Brno, 1950-64; rsch. psychologist Pediat. Inst., Brno, 1964-68; prof. psychology Masaryk U., Brno, 1968-86, 90—; rsch. psychologist, chief dept. Czech Acad. Scis., Brno, 1967-77; cons. postgrad. program psychology Masaryk U., Brno, 1990—. Author: Biological Determinants of Behavior, 1975; author, editor: Diagnostic of Psychological Development, 1971, 3rd edito., 1980, Russian edit., 1978, Bulgarian edit., 1986; contbr. articles to profl. jours. Mem. Czech-Moravian Psychol. Soc. (hon., v.p. 1994—), Soc. for High Abilities (v.p. 1990—). Roman Catholic. Avocations: chamber music, violoncello. Home: Kounicova 51, 602 00 Brno Czech Republic

SVANHOLM, POUL JOHAN, former brewing company executive; b. Aalborg, Jutland, Denmark, June 7, 1933; s. Poul and Gerda (Stougaard) S.; m. Lise Andersen, July 5, 1957; children: Michael, Louise. LLB, U. Copenhagen, 1958. Pres. Vingaarden, Odense, Denmark, 1962-72; pres. Carlsberg A/S, Copenhagen, 1972-96, chief exec. officer, 1974-82, group chief exec. officer, 1982-96; mem. European adv. com. N.Y. Stock Exch.; chmn. bd. Den Danske Bank, Copenhagen, Thomas B. Thriges Found., Copenhagen; bd. dirs. D/S Svendborg, Copenhagen; owner Raunborg Estate. Address: Helleruplund Allé 15, DK 2900 Hellerup Denmark

SVARC, ALFRED, physicist, researcher, consultant; b. Zagreb, Croatia, Nov. 15, 1952; s. Ljubomir and Nada (Valic) S.; m. Jadranka Popovic, May 28, 1980; 1 child, Denis. BSc, U. Zagreb, 1976; MSc, Rudjer Boskovic Inst., Zagreb, 1979, PhD in Theoretical Nuclear-Med. Physics, 1981. Asst. Rudjer Boskovic Inst., 1976-80, sr. asst., 1980-85, rsch. assoc., 1985-89, sr. rsch. asst., 1989-98, sci. advisor, 1998—; cons. on med. physics. Contbg. author: Advances in Nuclear Physics, 1986. Recipient Fed. Young Scientist award Govt. of Croatia, 1982. Fellow Croatian Phys. Soc., Am. Phys. Soc. Avocations: tennis, chess. Home: Gunduliceva 53, 10000 Zagreb Croatia Office: Rudjer Boskovic Inst, Bijenicka 54, 10000 Zagreb Croatia

SVARDSUDD, KURT FOLKE, internist, educator; b. Pitea, Sweden, Sept. 7, 1942; s. Ernst Folke and Karin Cecilia (Lundmark) S.; m. Gudrun Katharina Elisabeth Sundberg, Oct. 16, 1965; children: Charlotte, Ulf, Mats. MB, Göteborg U., Gothenburg, Sweden, 1964, PhD, 1978; MD, Umea (Sweden) U., 1968. Intern, resident Boden & Gothenburg, 1968-80; rsch. assoc. U. Minn., 1980-81; lectr. internal medicine Göteborg U., 1982-87; lectr. family medicine Uppsala (Sweden) U., 1987-90, prof. epidemiology, 1990-95, prof., chmn. dept. family medicine, 1995-97, chmn. dept. pub. health and caring scis., 1998—. Contbr. numerous sci. papers to internat. jours. Med. capt. Swedish Army, 1970-89. Rsch. grantee various orgns., 1980—. Fellow Swedish Med. Soc. (bd. dirs. 1995-97), Swedish Med. Assn.; mem. Swedish Epidemiology Assn. (chmn. 1993-95), Internat. Soc. and Fedn. Cardiology. Avocation: skiing. Home: Kronparksv 5, S 75752 Uppsala Sweden

SVARICEK, FERDINAND, control engineer; b. Krefeld, Germany, Sept. 23, 1955. Diploma in Engring., U. Duisburg, Germany, 1982, D Engring., 1987, Venia Legendi, 1994, Private Dozent, 1995. Lic. mech. engr. Rsch. asst. U. Duisburg, 1982-86, chief engr., 1987-94; R&D engr. ITT Automotive, Germany, 1995-98; project mgr. ContiTech, Germany, 1998-2000, Continental AG, 2000—. Author: Zuverlässige numerische Analyse linearer Regelungssysteme, 1995; contbr. articles to profl. jours. Mem. IEEE, Planetary Soc., Verein Deutscher Ingenieure. Achievements include contributions to computer-aided analysis and design of linear and nonlinear control systems. Office: Continental AG, Jaedekamp 30, 30419 Hamburg Germany

SVASTI, JISNUSON, biochemistry educator; b. Bangkok, Sept. 25, 1947; s. Prince Arjuna and Princess Chandra (Paribatra) S.; m. Phromchatra Vudhijai, Aug. 8, 1968; children: Sasibha, Chandrabha. BA with hons., U. Cambridge, 1968, MA, 1972, PhD, 1972. Lectr. Mahidol U., Bangkok, 1972-75, asst. prof., 1975-77; sr. rsch. assoc. U. Tex., Galveston, 1976-77; assoc. prof. Mahidol U., Bangkok, 1978-82, prof. biochemistry, 1982—, v.p. internat. rels., 1997-99; head lab. biochemistry Chulabhorn Rsch. Inst., Bangkok, 1991—; pres. Fedn. Asian and Oceanian Biochemists, 1990-92. Author/editor: Laboratory Experiments and Basic Principles in Biochemistry, 1978; editor-in-chief: Jour. of the Sci. Soc. of Thailand, 1985-87; author: (book) Biochemistry, 1987, revised edit., 1999. Named Knight Grand Cordon of the Most Exalted Order of the White Elephant, Thailand, 1998, Knight Grand Cordon of the Most Noble Order of the Crown of Thailand, 1993. Fellow Third World Acad. Sci.; mem. Biochem. Soc./U.K., Sci. Soc. Thailand (chmn. biochem. sect. 1986-87), Fedn. Asian Biochemists and Molecular Biologists (hon.). Buddhist. Avocations: photography, computers, reading.

SVEBAK, SVEN EGIL, psychology medicine educator; b. Verdal, Middle Norway, Norway, Dec. 17, 1941; s. Hans Georg and Dagny (Strand) S.; m. Randi Myrseth, Apr. 2, 1971; children: Annette, Teresa. Grad. in Psychology, U. Oslo (Norway), 1970; D in Philosophy, U. Bergen, Norway, 1982. Lic. Psychologist. Instr. of psychology U. Oslo, 1967-68; rsch. asst. U. Bergen, 1968-70, asst. prof., 1970-76, assoc. prof. to prof., 1976-95; vis. prof. Queens U. of Belfast, No. Ireland, 1987; adj. prof. U. Utah, 1990; prof. of medicine, U. of Trondheim, Norway, 1993—; lectr. of Behavioral Medicine Physiotherapy Coll. of Bergen, 1977-92; cons. in Archtl. Design CUBUS A-S, 1970—, Inst. Psychol. Counseling, Bergen, 1988-92; co-organizer 3d Internat. Conf. Reversal Theory, Amsterdam, 1987; organizer 6th Internat. Conf. Reversal Theory, Bergen, 1993; pres. Internat. Soc. Humor Studies, 1998, organizer 10th internat. ISHS conf., Bergen, 1998. Editor: Psychological Service Armed Forces, 1986, Stress and Health: A Reversal Theory Perspective, 1997; assoc. editor Internat. Jour. of Psychophysiology, 1983-95; contbr. articles to profl. jours. Recipient numerous research grants, 1972—. Mem. Psychophysiology Soc., Internat. Orgn. of Psychophysiology, Reversal Theory Soc., Internat. Soc. for the Study of Individual Differences, Am. Psychosomatic Soc. Avocations: boating, fishing, wildlife, jogging, skiing. Office: Faculty Medicine, ISMUT MTFS NTNU, N-7489 Trondheim Norway

SVEDBERG, BJORN MAGNUS IVAR, bank executive; b. Stockholm, July 4, 1937; s. Inge and Anna-Lisa (Lundstrom) S.; m. Gunnel Richardsdotter Nilsson, June 21, 1960; children: Camilla, Nina, Oscar, Rickard. M.S., Royal Inst. Tech., Stockholm, 1962; postgrad. U. Lausanne (Switzerland), 1972; D in Tech. (hon.) U. Lund, Sweden. With Telefonaktiebolaget L.M. Ericsson, Stockholm, 1962—, dept. mgr., 1970-72, chief engr., 1972-76, sr. v.p. R & D, 1976-77, pres., 1977—, chmn. bd. dirs., 1990—; pres., CEO Skandinaviska Enskilda Banken, 1992-97; dir. AB Volvo, 1994—; bd. dirs. ASEA Brown Boveri, Incentive, STORE, Volvo. Chmn. ABB AB, Chalmers U. Tech. Home: Telefonaktiebolager, LM Ericsson, S126 25 Stockholm Sweden*

SVENDSEN, ALF, artist, art educator; b. Bklyn., Mar. 24, 1930; s. Alf and Anna Thordina (Fjeldberg) S. BFA cum laude, Syracuse U., 1955; MFA summa cum laude, U. Notre Dame, 1965. Asst. sculptor Ivan Mestrovic, Notre Dame, Ind., 1955-56; sculptor Hall of African Man Am. Mus. Natural History, N.Y.C., 1966-68; tchr. art Mt. Anthony H.S., Bennington, Vt., 1969-71; prof. Delaware County C.C., Media, Pa., 1971-89. Exhibited work at New Sch. Social Rsch., N.Y.C., 1958, N.Y. Six Gallery, 1962, Berkshire (Mass.) Mus., 1970, Gallery 14 Sculptors, N.Y.C., 1974, Darmouth (N.H.) Coll., 1978, Deshong Mus., Chester, Pa., 1981, Art Sutton, Que., 1998, Mary Bryan Gallery, Jeffersonville, Vt., 1999. With USN, 1948-52. Home: 465 Daigle Rd Enosburg Falls VT 05450-5088

SVENDSEN, OLE LANDER, physician; b. Denmark, May 31, 1962; s. Otto Lander and Grethe (Pedersen) S.; m. Lone Kjaersgård Sørensen, May 30, 1992; children: Sune, Nina. MD, U. Copenhagen, 1989, D Med. Sci., 1996. Houseofficer Copenhagen U. Hosps., 1989, registrar in internal medicine, 1994-97; rsch. fellow dept. clin. chemistry Glostrup (Denmark) Hosp., 1990-92; registrar Steno Diabetes Ctr., Gentofte, Denmark, 1993; sr. registrar internal medicine and endocrinology Copenhagen U. Hosps., 1997—; lectr. internal medicine U. Copenhagen, 1998—; cons. Danish Nutrition Coun., Copenhagen, 1993-97, Ctr. Clin. Basic Rsch., Ballerup, Denmark, 1996—; delegate Coun. European-Internat. Assn. Obesity, 1999—; external examiner human nutrition, Royal Veterinary and Agrl. U., Copenhagen, 1997—. Contbr. articles to profl. jours. Mem. Danish Assn. Study Obesity (sec./bd. dirs. 1992-96, 98—). E-mail: ols@ccbr.dk. Home: Bakkevaenget 23, DK 3460 Birkerøed Denmark Office: Ctr Clin Basic Rsch, Ballerup Byvej 222, DK 2750 Ballerup Denmark

SVENSON, CHARLES OSCAR, investment banker; b. Worcester, Mass., June 28, 1939; s. Sven Oscar and Edahjane (Castner) S.; m. Sara Ellen Simpson, Nov. 15, 1968; children: Alicia Lindall, Tait Oscar. A.B., Hamilton Coll., 1961; LL.B., Harvard U., 1964; LL.M., Bklyn. Law Sch., 1965. Bar: N.Y. 1965, U.S. Dist. Ct. (so. dist.) N.Y. 1965, U.S. Ct. Appeals (2d. cir.) 1965. Atty. Dewey, Ballantine, Bushby, Palmer & Wood, N.Y.C., 1964-68; v.p. Goldman Sachs & Co., N.Y.C., 1968-75; sr. v.p. Donaldson, Lufkin & Jenrette, N.Y.C, 1975-89; mng. dir., 1989—. Trustee Kirkland Coll., Clinton, N.Y., 1976-78; trustee Hamilton Coll., Clinton, 1979-83, 90—. Mem. ABA, N.Y. State Bar Assn., Assn. of Bar of City of N.Y. Clubs: Tuxedo (Tuxedo Park, N.Y.); Harvard (N.Y.C.). Home: 1185 Park Ave New York NY 10128-1308 Office: Donaldson Lufkin & Jenrette Securities Corp 277 Park Ave Fl 7 New York NY 10172-3400

SVENSSON, ARNE, communications systems educator, consultant; b. Västerstad, Sweden, Oct. 22, 1955; s. Bertil and Nannie (Olsson) S.; m. Gunbritt Arvidsson, Sept. 5, 1992; 1 child, Arvid. PhD, U. Lund, Sweden, 1979, Lic., 1982, DSc, 1984. Rsch. engr. U. Lund, 1980, rsch. asst., 1980-85, docent, 1984-88; rschr. Ericsson Radio Sys., Mölndal, Sweden, 1987; specialist Ericsson Radar Electronics, Mölndal, Sweden, 1988-94; prof. dept. signals and sys. Chalmers U. Tech., Gothenburg, Sweden, 1993—; cons. Ericsson Radio Systems, Stockholm, 1982-84, 98, Mölndal, 1987, Ericsson Microwave Systems, Mölndal, 1994—, Ericsson Radio Access, Stockholm, 1995, Ericsson GE Mobile Com., Raleigh, N.C., 1993-94; mem. coun. Svenska Elektro och Dataingenjörers Riksförening, 1998—, Stiftelsen Nordiska Radiosamfundet, 2000—. Contbr. articles to profl. jours. Pres. European IFYE Assn., 1991-95; bd. dirs. Swedish 4-H, Katrineholm, 1984-85. Recipient Young Scientists award Union of Radio Sci., 1984, Best Paper award Vehicular Tech. Soc., 1986. Mem. IEEE (sr.), Svenska Elektro Och Dataingenjörers Riksförening, Swedish Union Radio Sci. Avocations: gardening, outdoor activities. Home: Göksäter 6290, SE-47396 Henån Sweden Office: Chalmers U Tech, Dept Signals and Systems, SE-41296 Göteborg Sweden

SVENSSON, LARS GEORG, cardiovascular and thoracic surgeon; b. Barbeton, Republic South Africa, Aug. 11, 1955; came to U.S., 1986; s. Karl-Georg and Marianne S.; m. Marion Frances Robinson, June 14, 1986. MB, BCh, U. Witwatersrand, Johannesburg, South Africa, 1978, MSc (Med.), 1983, PhD, 1986. Diplomate Gen., Vascular and Cardiothoracic Surgery. Resident in surgery Johannesburg Hosp., 1981-86; fellow cardiovascular surgery Cleve. Clinic Found., 1986-87; fellow cardiovascular surgery Baylor Coll. of Medicine, Houston, 1987-89, resident cardiothoracic surgery, 1989-91; attending surgeon Meth. Hosp., VA Med. Ctr., Houston, 1991-92; attending surgeon Lahey Clinic, Burlington, Mass., 1993—, dir. Aortic Surgery Ctr. and Marfan Syndrome Clinic, 1993—; spkr. in field. Contbr. numerous articles to profl. jours. including Jour. Vascular Surgery, Chest, Ann. Thoracic Surgery, Jour. Thoracic, Cardiovascular Surgery and Anesthesia.; mem. editorial bd. Annals of Thoracic Surgery, Annals of Cardiovasc. and Thoracic Surgery. Recipient Good Fellowship award Treverton Coll., 1970, Cert. of Merit South African Sugar Assn., 1972, Robert Niven award 1974-76, DeBakey Heart Fund Rsch. award 1988, 89, 90, 91, V.A. Rag Rsch. Fund award 1992; Dana Fund Rsch. fellowship, 1994, David Lurie Rsch. fellowship 1985; Davis and Geck Surg. Rsch. scholarship, 1985. Fellow Am. Coll. Surgeons, Royal Coll. Surgeons, Coll. Surgeons and Physicians of South Africa, Royal Coll. Surgeons in Can. in Vascular and Cardiothoracic Surgery, Am. Coll. Cardiology; mem. AMA, Soc. Thoracic Surgeons. Achievements include animal research to find methods of intraoperatively locating the spinal cord blood supply and methods to prevent paraplegia after aortic surgery; investigation of methods to protect the brain, spinal cord and kidneys; study of hydrogen injection to localize spinal cord supply in humans, study of intrathecal papaveine in patients undergoing aortic surgery, minimizing use of homologous blood for major aortic surgery, particularly of the ascending and aortic arch; novel operations for ascending and aortic arch surgery; first reported replacement of the entire aorta from the heart to the aortic bifurcation during a single operation; pioneered a technique for doing minimal access "keyhole" heart surgery; (with E. Stanley Crawford) wrote the first definitive textbook on the aorta entitled Cardiovascular and Vascular Disease of the Aorta; devel. an approach for minimal access to the heart for heart operations.

SVENSSON, PALLE, political scientist; b. Herning, Denmark, Feb. 4, 1944; s. Peter and Karla Astrid Ingeborg (Petersen) S.; m. Alissa Lomholt, Oct. 8, 1973; children: Kasper, Nikolaj. Cand. polit. sci., Aarhus Univ., Denmark, 1972, D of Polit. Sci., 1996. Asst. prof. Aarhus U., 1972-76, assoc. prof., 1976—; dir. dept. polit. sci. Aarhus U., 1988-89; exec. com. The Open U., Aarhus, 1989—, chmn. 1992—; cons. in field. Editor Politica, 1989-91, mem. editl. bd., 1983-97. With Royal Danish Navy, 1964-66. Jean Monnet fellow European U. Inst., Florence, Italy, 1985-86. Home: Tulshojvej 23, 8270 Hojbjerg Denmark Office: Aarhus Univ, Dept Polit Sci, 8000 Århus Denmark

SVENSSON, PETER JOHNNY, physician; b. Nässjo, Sweden, May 25, 1958; s. Bertil Harry and Inga-Karin Tyra (Johansson) S.; m. Ingrid Margareta Rogius, June 10, 1989; children: Ulf, Claes. MD, Lund (Sweden) U., 1991. Specialist in internal medicine U. Hosp. Malmö, Sweden, 1995—, specialist in coagulation and bleeding disorders, 1996—, specialist in hematology, dept. medicine, 1997—. Office: U Hosp Malmö, Dept Coagulation Disorders, S205 02 Malmö Sweden

SVENUNGSSON, BO DAVID, physician, researcher; b. Stockholm, Mar. 29, 1945; s. David and Margit (Larsson) S.; m. Elisabet Karin Hillebrant, Dec. 22, 1985; children: Arvid, Frida, Gustaf. MD, Karolinska Inst., Stockholm, 1971, PhD in Infectious Diseases, 1979, Diploma in Tropical Medicine, 1981. Resident Roslagstull Hosp., Stockholm, 1974-80, sr. cons., 1980-92; sr. cons. Huddinge U. Hosp., Sweden, 1992—; assoc. prof. Huddinge U. Hosp., 1984—; mem. human ethics com. Karolinska Inst., 1984-93; fellowship Infectious Diseases and Clin. Bacteriology, 1980. Editor: (anniversary book) Swedish Society of Infectious Diseases, 1998, (textbook) Intestinal Infections, 1998; contbr. articles to profl. jours. Mem. Swedish Soc. of Infectious Diseases (v.p. 1998—), Swedish Soc. Tropical Medicine, Scandinavian Soc. for Antimicrobial Chemotherapy. Avocations: ornithology, magic, playing accordion. Office: Karolinska Inst/Dept Inf Di, Huddinge Univ Hosp, 14186 Huddinge Sweden

SVESHNIKOV, PETER GEORGIEVICH, science administrator, researcher; b. Moscow, Nov. 20, 1953; s. Georgiy Petrovich and Erlena Alexandrovna (Evteeva) S.; m. Elena Vasilievna Churdaljova, Jan. 9, 1983 (div. July 1994); m. Marika Stavrovna Frolova, Feb. 3, 1995; children: George, Tatiana, Maria. Master's degree, Moscow State U., 1977, PhD, 1982; D of Biology, Rsch. Ctr. Molec. Diagnostics, Moscow, 1993, prof., 1997. Cert. in biophysics. Jr. rschr. Inst. Molecular Biology, Russian Acad. Scis., Moscow, 1977-79; rschr. IMB, Moscow, 1979-82; sr. rschr. Moscow State U., 1985-86; sr. rschr. Inst. Applied Molecular Biology, Moscow, 1986-90, head immunochem. dept., 1990-92; dep. dir. Rsch. Ctr. for Molecular Diagnostics, Moscow, 1992—; co-dir. Joint Biotechnol. Co. Biomed. Rsch., Berlin, 1995—. Patentee in field; reader, reviewer Jour. Biotech., 1986-97. Recipient Medal for Outstanding Rsch., Russian Ministry of Health, 1991, Medal for 850 Anniversary Moscow, Pres. Russian Fedn., 1999. Mem. Internat. Acad. for Info. Techs. (corr. mem.), Russian Biochem. Soc. (cen. coun. mem. 1988-94), Moscow Antibody Club/Inst. Bioorganic Chemistry, Russian Acad. Scis. Russian Orthodox. Avocations: music, theater, skiing, traveling. Office: Rsch Ctr Molec Diagnostics, Sympheropolsky Blvd 8, 113149 Moscow Russia

SVESTKA, ZDENEK F., solar physicist; b. Prague, Czechoslovakia, Sept. 30, 1925; s. Frantisek and Jarmila (Treybalova) S.; m. Tatjana Krizkova, 1951 (div. 1960); 1 child, Jiri; m. Ludmila M. Fritzova, May 26, 1962; children: Marta-Helen, Petr (dec.). Grad., Charles U., 1949; PhD, Acad. Scis. Prague, 1956, DSc, 1966. Head solar dept. Astronomical Inst. Acad., Ondrejov, Czechoslovakia, 1956-70; vis. scientist European Space Tech. Ctr., The Netherlands, 1970-74; prin. scientist AS&E, Cambridge, Mass., 1974-77, SRON, Utrecht, The Netherlands, 1977-90; rsch. physicist U. Calif. San Diego, La Jolla, 1990—. Author: Solar Flares, 1976; editor jour. Solar Physics, 1967—; contbr. articles to profl. jours. Pres. com. on solar activity Internat. Astron. Union, 1964-70. Recipient Guggenheim award astronautics, 1968, gold medal Czechoslovak Acad. Scis., 1995. Mem. Internat. Acad. Astronautics., Sci. Com. Solar-Terrestrial Physics (hon.). Office: U Calif San Diego 9500 Gilman Dr La Jolla CA 92093-5004

SVETINA, ANTE STIPE, pathophysiologist, researcher; b. Čitluk, Dalmatia, Croatia, Feb. 2, 1947; s. Stipan and Manda (Džaja) S.; m. Maja Antončic, Aug. 5, 1989; children: Lana, Iva, Stjepko. DVM, Faculty Vet. Medicine, Zagreb, Croatia, 1974; MS, Ctr. Postgrad. Studies, Zagreb, Croatia, 1978; PhD, Faculty Vet. Medicine, Zagreb, Croatia, 1982. Asst. Inst. R. Boškovic, Zagreb, 1975-78; asst. dept. pathophysiology Vet. Faculty, Zagreb, 1978-85; asst. dept. pathophysiology Vet. Medicine Faculty, Zagreb, 1985-95, prof. pathophysiology, 1995—. Author: Blood Pathophysiology, 1988. Mem. Croatian Soc. Physiology, Croatian Soc. Biophysics, Croatian Soc. Pharmacology, N.Y. Acad. Sci. Roman Catholic. Avocations: mountaineering, cooking. Office: Faculty Vet Medicine, Heinzelova 55, 10000 Zagreb Croatia

SVETITSKY, BENJAMIN, physicist, educator; b. Jerusalem, Sept. 11, 1955; s. Shmuel and Sara (Rapoport) S.; m. Sara Beck, Dec. 19, 1976; children: Shulamit, Elisha, Batsheva. SB, MIT, 1974; MA, Princeton U., 1976, PhD, 1980. Rsch. assoc. U. Calif., Santa Barbara, 1980-81, Cornell U., Ithaca, N.Y., 1981-84; rsch. scientist MIT, Cambridge, 1984-88; sr. lectr. Tel Aviv U., 1988-92, assoc. prof., 1992—, chmn. dept. nuclear physics, 1998-2000; vis. scientist Weizmann Inst. Sci., Rehovot, Israel, 1987-88; collaborator Los Alamos (N.Mex.) Nat. Lab., 1989—; fgn. collaborator Ctr. for Study of Saclay, Gif-sur-Yvette, France, 1992; vis. assoc. prof. U. Colo., Boulder, 1993-94. NSF grad. fellow, 1974, Allon fellow Israel Coun. for Higher Edn., 1990; recipient Wolfson Rsch. award Israel Acad. Scis., 1990. Mem. Am. Phys. Soc., Israel Phys. Soc. Office: Tel Aviv Univ, Sch Physics and Astronomy, 69978 Tel Aviv Israel

SVETTSOV, VLADIMIR VLADIMIROVICH, physicist, researcher; b. Moscow, Russia, July 18, 1948; s. Vladimir Nikitich and Tamara Nikolayevna (Guseva) S.; m. Tatyana Semyonovna Karelova, Sept. 3, 1971; 1 child, Nickolay Vladimirovich. Engr. physicist, Moscow Inst. Physics and Tech., 1972; PhD in Physics and Math., Schmidt Inst. for Physics, Moscow, 1983. Jr. rschr. Schmidt Inst., Moscow, 1972-86, sr. rschr., 1986-91; sr. rschr. Inst. Dynamics of Geospheres, Moscow, 1991—. Recipient certificate of Good Work, Russian Acad. Scis., Moscow, 1999. Avocation: karate. Office: Inst Dynamics of Geospheres, Leninskiy prospekt 38-6, 117979 Moscow Russia

SVINKELSTIN, ABRAHAM JOSHUA, information technology executive; b. Stuttgart, Germany, Nov. 14, 1948; came to U.S., 1950; s. Emanuel and Sabina (Lederman) S.; m. Janet Mostel, Nov. 7, 1976; children: Jeremy David, Rachel Sabina, Ilana Michelle. BS in Aerospace Engring., Poly. U. N.Y., 1970; MS in Ops. Rsch. and Engring. Math., Columbia U., N.Y.C., 1971; MS in Computer Sci., SUNY, Stony Brook, 1972. Programmer/analyst Bank Leumi, Tel Aviv, Israel, 1973-74; assoc., cons. Monchik Weber Assocs., N.Y.C., 1974-79; ptnr., cons. Computer Programming Assocs., N.Y.C., 1979-84; project leader Shearson Lehman Bros., N.Y.C., 1984-87; asst. v.p. Warner Ins. Svcs., Fair Lawn, N.J., 1988-92; v.p. software devel. Everlink Corp., N.Y.C., 1992-94; project mgr. Am. Internat. Group, N.Y.C., 1994-97; prin. cons. CAP GEMINI, N.Y.C., 1997—. Pres. Seminole Condominiums, Forest Hills, N.Y., 1979-86; Cub Scout den leader Boy Scouts Am. Mem. Data Processing Mgmt. Assn., MIS Network Assocs. (v.p. adminstrn./fin. 1992-94), Sigma Gamma Tau. Libertarian. Jewish. Home: 13-61 Finn Ter Fair Lawn NJ 07410-5135 Office: CAP GEMINI 1114 Ave of Americas New York NY 10036

SVIRIDOV, ANDREI VALENTINOVITSH, entomologist, researcher; b. Moscow, Dec. 22, 1946; s. Valentin Petrovitsh and Mariamna Borisovna (Grakova) S.; m. Irina Konstntinovna Matysko, Oct. 27, 1972 (div. Feb. 1977); 1 child, Darya. Diploma, Lomonosov State U., Moscow, 1970; PhD in Biol. Scis., Lomonosov State U., 1985. Sr. lab. asst. Faculty of Biology and Soils Lomonosov State U., Moscow, 1970-71, jr. researcher dept. entomology, 1971-86, researcher lab. taxonomic zoology Zool. Mus., 1987-92; sr. researcher Zool. Mus. Lomonosov State U., 1992—, curator lepidoptera collections Zool. Mus., 1977—; cons. univs., nature reserves, mus., insts., 1994—. Author: Types of the Biodiagnostic Keys and their Applications, 1994, Biodiagnostical Keys: theory and practice, 1994; editor: Russian Jour. Scientific Lepidopterology, 1994-96; sec. invertebrate animal sect. (terrestrial) Commn. of Red Book of Russia, 1992—, Commn. of Red Book of the Concord of the Ind. Staats, 1998—; contbr. over 90 articles to profl. jours. Grantee Internat. Sci. Found. (G. Soros), 1994, grantee ecol. security of Russia Min. Nature and Preservation, 1995; decorated 850 Yrs. of Moscow medal Pres. of Russia, 1998. Mem. Russian Entomol. Soc., Moscow Soc. Naturalists, Soc. Europaea Lepidopterolo., Systematic Zoology/Biology, Descendants Coun. of the Great War of 1812-1814 Vets., Hist.-Geneal. Soc. Moscow. Avocations: genealogy, philosophy of science, sociology. Home: Bolshaya Tsherkizovskaya St, 1-2-52, 107061 Moscow Russia Office: Zool Mus Moscow Lomonosov U, Bolshaya Nikitskaya 6, 103009 Moscow Russia

SVIRIDOV, KONSTANTIN NIKOLAEVICH, physicist; b. Moscow, Feb. 12, 1947; s. Nikolai Fedorovich Sviridov and Nadejda Antonovna Kuyshinnikova; m. Galina Yureyna Homich, Oct. 28, 1969; 1 child, Georgievskaya Maria. Grad. with honors, Moscow Aviation Inst., 1971; Cand. Tech. Sci., Astrophysica, Moscow, 1978, D Tech. Sci., 1997. Engr. Cen. Design Office/Astrophysica, Moscow, 1971-78, sr. scientific worker, 1978-81; lab. head SPA Astrophysica, Moscow, 1981-88, head of rsch. dept., 1988-91, chief scientific worker, 1991-97, dep. dir., 1997—; dir. gen. Assn. with Limited Liability Intellect, Moscow, 1992-99, Co. with Limited Liability Intellect, Moscow, 1999—; cons. in field; lectr. in field. Inventor in field; contbr. articles to profl. jours. Tchr. Chair of Quantum Optical Systems in the MPTI, Moscow, 1998-99; expert Scientific Coun. in SSC SPA Astrophysica, Moscow, 1998-99; mem. Trade Union of the Workers of Min. of Def. Industry, 1971-99. Laureate of the Lenin Komsomol prize in the field of sci. and technology, Cen. Com. of ALYCL, Moscow, 1977; named Best Inventor of City of Moscow, 1987; honored Inventor of the Russian Fedn., Pres. of Russian Fedn., Moscow, 1998. Mem. Optical Soc. of Russia, Astronomic Scientific Coun./Russian Acad. of Sci., EOS, SPIE, IEEE. Avocations: travels, hunting, nature recreation. Home: Stroginsky Bulvar b 15 a 90, 123592 Moscow Russia Office: State Sci Ctr/Astrophysica, Volokolamskoye Shosse b 95, 123424 Moscow Russia

SVIRNOVSKI, ARCADI IOSIFOVICH, hematologist, researcher; b. Minsk, Belarus, Feb. 14, 1938; s. Iosif Abramovich and Dora Arcadyevna (Eidelman) S.; m. Esfir Lasaryevna Geller, May 23, 1961; 1 child, Vadim Arcadyevich. Physician, State Med. Inst., Minsk, 1955-61; educator, Pedagogical Inst. Fgn. Langs., Minsk, 1955-60; cert. specialist, State Inst. Med. Tng., Moscow, 1963; PhD Med. Scis., Nat. Ctr. Hematology, Moscow, 1968, MD, 1979. Rsch. fellow Hematology and Blood Transfusion Rsch. Inst., Minsk, 1961-66, head lab. for leukemia pathophysiology, 1967—; prof. hematology and blood transfusion Higher Qualification Com. for Acad. Degrees and Titles, Moscow, 1990; part-time tchr. High Med. Sch., Minsk, 1964-79, State Med. Inst., Minsk, 1988-89; cons. Hosp. N 9 Hematol. Dept., Minsk, 1977—, Bone Marrow Transplantation Ctr., Minsk, 1994—, Children's Oncohematol. Ctr., Minsk, 1996—; sec. of expert coun. Nat. Higher Qualification Com. for Acad. Degrees and Sci. Titles, Minsk, 1994-2000; chmn. spl. for acad. degrees in hematology and blood transfusion for Belarus, 2000—. Dep. editor-in-chief: Theoretical and Practical Problems of Hematology and Blood Transfusion, 1982, The Ways of Correction of Hematopoietic Disorders in Experimental and Clinical Conditions, 1984, Means and Methods of Biospecific Correction in Hematology and Transfusiology, 1988, Clinical and Theoretical Aspects of Transfusiology, 1990; mem. editl. bd. Hematology, 1996—; inventor in field. Mem. Internat. Soc. for Hemotherapy and Graft Engring. (complimentary mem.), European Hematology Assn. The Netherlands, Nat. Soc. Hematologists and Transfusiologists (v.p. 1978—), Belarussian Acad. Ecological Anthropology. Avocations: theater, music, garden plants. Office: Hematology and Blood Transfusion Inst, 160 Dolginovski Tract, 223059 Minsk Belarus

SVIRSKII, ALEXEY VICTOROVICH, neurologist, educator; b. St. Petersburg, Russia, Oct. 22, 1954; s. Victor Grigoryevich and Ida Alexeyevna (Krushinskaya) S.; m. Galina Zosimovna Lapina, July 10, 1982; 1 child, Dmitriy. MD, Pediat. Med. Acad., St. Petersburg, 1978; PhD, Moscow State U., 1997. Head dr. dept. pediat. Dist. Hosp., Arkhangelsk, Russia, 1978-88; asst. prof. neurology Univ. Med. Acad., Arkhangelsk, 1991—; chief city pediat. neurologist City Dept. Health, Arkhangelsk, 1996—. Avocations: sports, music. Office: Arkhangelsk Med Acad, Troitzkii Pr 51, 163045 Arkhangelsk Russia

SVOBODA, JOANNE DZITKO, artist, educator; b. Dec. 24, 1948; d. John Richard and Joanna Frances (Rygiel) Dzitko; m. Peter W. Svoboda, Sept. 3, 1972; children: Kimberly Anne, Lauren Anne. Student, Parsons Sch. Design, 1966, Kean Coll., 1970; BA, Jersey City State Coll., 1970, MA, 1975; postgrad., Tchrs. Coll., Columbia U., 1972, Chubb Inst., 1983-84. Art tchr. Jersey City, 1966-70, Henry Snyder H.S., Jersey City, 1970-80; tng. specialist Johnson & Johnson Baby Products, Skillman, N.J., 1984-89; cons., 1989—; pres. Mgmt. Strategies Internat., 1991—; adj. instr. Raritan Valley C.C., 1999—. Exhibited Courtney Gallery, Jersey City State Coll., 1970, 74, Long Valley, 1979-80; contbr. articles in field to various publs. Trustee Jersey City Mus. Assn., 1973-79, chmn. fine arts dept., 1972-79; mem. curriculum revision com. Jersey City Bd. Edn., 1976; mem. Washington Twp. Shade Tree Commn., 1979-81, chmn., 1981; mem. Washington Twp. Hist. Heritage Commn., 1981-85; active encouraging establishment of hist. zone Long Valley, landmarks, Jersey City and Washington Twp. Grantee N.J. State Dept. Edn., 1973; recipient awards N.J. Fedn. Jr. Woman's Clubs: black and white photography, 1979, crafts, 1979, 1st pl. color photography, 1980, free form, 1981. Mem. Am. H.S. Assn. (asst. exec. dir. 1997-99). Office: PO Box 336 Oldwick NJ 08858-0336

SVOBODA, LADISLAV, chemistry educator; b. Pardubice, Czech Republic, Mar. 15, 1954; s. Ladislav and Zdenka (Miklasova) S.; m. Hana Kubesova, July 1, 1978; children: Ladislav, Hana. Grad., Inst. Chem. Tech., Pardubice, 1978, PhD, 1982; Habilitation, U. Pardubice, 1996. Asst. Inst. Chem. Tech., Pardubice, 1982-96; assoc. prof. U. Pardubice, 1996—, head of dept., 1996—; cons. PPD Chems., Pardubice, 1994—. Contbr. articles to profl. jours. including Jour. Chromatography and Collection of Czechoslovak Chem. Comms. Mem. Soc. Indsl. Chemistry, Czech Chem. Soc. Avocations: sports, literature, music. Home: L Matury 813, 53012 Pardubice Czech Republic Office: U Pardubice, nam Cs legli 565, 53210 Pardubice Czech Republic

SVOBODA, MIROSLAV, veterinary medicine educator; b. Trebic, Czech Republic, Sept. 18, 1952; s. Martin and Emilie (Linhartova) S.; m. Vlasta Zatloukalova, Sept. 27, 1975; children: Linda, Martin. DVM, U. Vet. and Pharm. Scis., Brno, Czech Republic, 1977, PhD, 1985. Asst. prof. Faculty Vet. Medicine, Brno, 1980-89, assoc. prof., 1989-98, head small animal clinic, 1993—, prof. small animals medicine, 1998—. Contbr. articles to profl. jours.; author: Dermatology of the Dog and Cat, 1994, Infectious Diseases of the Dog and Cat, 1996, Endocrinology of the Dog and Cat, 1998; co-author: Parasitology of Small Animals, 1995. Mem. Czech and Slovak Small Animal Vet. Assn. (v.p. 1991-93), Czech Small Animal Vet. Assn. (pres. 1993-97), Fedn. European Companion Animal Vet. Assn. (rep. Czech Small Animal Vet. Assn. 1994-97), World Small Animal Vet. Assn. (rep. Czech Small Animal Vet. Assn. 1995—). Avocations: tennis, windsurfing, bicycling. Home: Rozhledova 1a, 62100 Brno Czech Republic Office: U Vet and Pharm Scis, Palackeho 1/3, 612 42 Brno Czech Republic

SVOBODA, OLGA, linguist, information professional, educator; b. Pelhrimov, Czechoslovakia, Mar. 27, 1947; arrived in South Africa, 1983; d. Frantisek and Marie (Syrovatkova) Studnicka; m. Jan Svoboda, July 4, 1969; children: Vojtech, Simona. BA with honors, U. Witwatersrand, 1989; MA, Charles U., 1969, PhD, 1981. Specialist libr. Slavonic Libr., Prague, Czech Republic, 1971-82; from info. scientist to info. mgr. Mintek, Randburg, South Africa, 1983-97; dir. Minerals and Energy Edn. and Tng. Inst., U. Witwatersrand, Johannesburg, 1997—; translator Advanced Techs. Worldwide, Johannesburg, South Africa, 1990—; lectr. U. Witwatersrand, Johannesburg, 1990. Mem. South African Inst. Info. Sci., South African Online User Group, South African Inst. Energy. Avocations: collecting African masks and wood carvings, hiking. Home: PO Box 73508, 2030 Fairland South Africa Office: MEETI, PO Box 395, Wits 2050, South Africa

SVOBODA, PETR, hockey player; b. Most, Czech Republic, Feb. 14, 1966; married. Hockey player LITV/CZECH, 1982-84, 94-95, MONT/NHL, 1984-91, 91-92, BUFF/NHL, 1991-92, 92-95, PHIL/NHL, 1994-97, 97-99, CZEC/OLYM, 1997-98, TAMP/NHL, 1998-99, 2000—. Recipient ice hockey Gold medal, Olympic Games, Nagano, Japan, 1998. Avocations: golf, tennis, Bermuda vacations. Office: Tampa Bay Lightening Ice Palace 401 Channelside Dr Tampa FL 33602-5400*

SVOBODA, PETR, biochemist, educator; b. Prague, Czechoslovakia; s. Bedrich and Jarmila (Petrachøva) S.; m. Jaroslava Solcova; 2 children: Petr, Zuzana. D of Natural Scis., Charles U., Prague, 1972, PhD, 1977, DSc, 1998. Rschr. Inst. Physiology, Prague, 1976-82, prin. investigator, 1982-87, head of dept., 1988-91; rsch. scientist Stockholm and Glasgow U., 1992-93, Glasgow U., 1993-94; prin. investigator Inst. Physiology, Prague, 1994-96; head of dept. Faculty of Sci., Prague, 1997—, Inst. Physiology, Prague, 1998—. Contbr. numerous articles to sci. jours. Grantee Wellcome Trust Fellowship, 1993-94, Collaborative Rsch. Initiative, 1996—, Agy. of Czech Ministry of Edn. for Support of Sci. at Univs. in Czech Republic, 1997—. Mem. Czech Biochem. Soc., Czech Physiol. Soc., Czech Macrochem. Soc. Home: U Smaltovny 22/B, 170 00 Prague Czech Republic Office: Inst Physiology, Ul Denska 1083, 142 20 Prague Czech Republic

SVOBODA, PETR, gastroenterologist; b. Brno, Czechoslovakia, Jan. 19, 1950; s. Jan and Vera (Simankova) S.; m. Ivana Krtickova, Aug. 11, 1973; children: Ivana, Jana. MD, Purkynje U., 1974, PhD, 1985. Registrar Dist. Hosp., Bruntal, Czechoslovakia, 1974-77, specialist in medicine, 1977-79, head cardiology and ICU, 1979-85; head dept. medicine U. Hosp., Brno, 1986-89; head dept. medicine Rsch. Inst., Brno, 1990—, assoc. prof. medicine, 1999—; chmn. sci. bd. Ministry Health, Brno, 1993—. Contbr. articles to profl. jours.; co-editor: Traumatology, 1996, guest-editor: Hepato-Gastroenterol., 1996. Specialist Highest Ct. Czech Republic, Praha, 1983—. Grantee Czech Republic, 1991—, European Econ. Com., 1994-96. Mem. European Assn. Endoscopic Surgery, Czech and Moravian Club Invasive Endoscopy (pres. 1993—), N.Y. Acad. Scis., Soc. Am. Gastrointestinal Endoscopic Surgeons, Internat. Gastrosurgical Club (chmn. chpt. Czech Rep.). Avocations: swimming, alpine skiing, bridge. Home: Barvicova 11, 602 00 Brno Czech Republic

SVOBODA, PETR, polymer engineer, researcher; b. Zlin, Czech Republic, Jan. 15, 1967; s. Jiri and Miroslava (Jenackova) S.; m. Dagmar Opatova, Dec. 15, 1990; children: Hana, Alena. Degree in engring., Tech. U. Brno, Czech Republic, 1989; D in Engring., Tokyo Inst. Tech., 1995. Tchr. Tech. U. Brno, 1989-91; chief rschr. Beltyr Ltd., Czech Republic, 1995—; prof. dept. organic and polymeric materials Tokyo Inst. Tech., 1998—. Contbr. articles to profl. jours. Avocations: dancing, skiing, swimming. Fax: 03-5734-2876. Office: Dept Organic and Polymeric Materials, Tokyo Inst Tech, Ookayama Meguro-ku Tokyo 152, Japan

SVOBODA-BEUSAN, IVNA, immunologist, researcher; b. Slavonski Brod, Slavonia, Croatia, June 16, 1948; d. Dalibor and Branka (Pilar) Svoboda; m. Mario Beusan, Aug. 28, 1976; children: Filip, Damjan. MSc, U. Zagreb, Croatia, 1975, PhD, 1986. Fellow in tumor immunology Paris, 1998; rsch. assoc. Inst. Immunology, Zagreb, 1988-99, sr. rsch. assoc., 1999—; lectr., mentor, participant sci. and profl meetings, 1975-99. Author/co-author over 100 sci. and profl. texts. Mem. Croatian Immunol. Soc., Croatian Soc. Allergology and Clin. Immunology, Croatian Microbiol. Soc., Croatian Med. Assn. Immunology. Avocations: classical music, literature, dogs, yoga. Home: Pod Zidom 3, 10000 Zagreb Croatia Office: Inst Immunology, Rockefellerova 10, 10000 Zagreb Croatia

SVYAZHIN, ANATOLY GRIGORIEVICH, metallurgy educator, researcher; b. Verkhnaya Tura, Russia, Oct. 11, 1934; s. Grigory Antonovich and Pavla Andrianovna S.; m. Galina Yakovlevna Kozlova, Apr. 30, 1964; 1 child, Alexey Anatolievich. Diploma in engring., Moscow Steel & Alloys Inst., 1962, PhD, 1966, DSc, 1987, prof., 1989. Sr. rsch. scientist steel metallurgy Moscow Steel & Alloys Inst., 1967-71, head steelmaking divsn. rsch. lab., 1972-76, head Rsch. Lab. of Metals and Alloys, 1977—; rsch. scientist Inst. Ferrous Metallurgy-Aachen (Germany) U. Tech., 1970; vis. prof. Tech. U. Czestochowa, Poland, 1994-99; mem. sci. com. for resources and ecology Ministry of Sci. and Tech. of Russian Fedn., Moscow, 1996—, mem. sci. com. high nitrogen steels, 1990—. Contbr. over 200 articles to sci. jours. and conf. procs.; patentee in field. Recipient prize Bd. Ministers of the USSR, Moscow, 1987, award Min. of Edn./Min. of Ferrous Metallurgy of the USSR, Moscow, 1980-95. Fellow Internat. Biog. Assn. (life); mem. Assn. Steelmakers Commonwealth Ind. States, Internat. Commonwealth Ind. States Metallurgist Union. Fax: 70952372127. Office: Steel & Alloys Inst Tech U, Leninsky Prospect 4, 117936 Moscow Russia

SWAFFIELD, DAVID RICHARD, lawyer; b. Norwich, Norfolk, Eng., Nov. 11, 1951; s. James and Elizabeth Margaret (Maunder) S.; m. Barbara Dianne Pilkington, Oct. 20, 1979 (div. 1998); children: James William, Robin Alexander. Attended, Dulwich Coll., London, 1962-69; BA, MA, Downing Coll., Cambridge, Eng., 1975; Chester (Eng.) Coll. Law, 1976; Law Degree, London Coll. Law, 1978. Admitted: solicitor Supreme Ct. Eng., Wales, 1979. Investment analyst Rowe & Pitman, London, 1973-75; articled clerk Hill Dickinson & Co, Liverpool, Eng., 1976-79, solicitor, 1979-82, ptnr., 1982-89; dir. Grayhill Ltd., Liverpool, Eng., 1984-85; ptnr. Hill Dickinson, various cities, Eng., 1989—; joint mgr. War Risks Assn. Ltd., Liverpool, London, 1991—, mgr., sec., 1994-99. Contbr. articles to profl. jours. Gov. Birkenhead Sch., 1994—; amb. Merseyside, 1997—. Mem. Liverpool Law Soc. (pres. 2000). Office: Hill Dickinson Davis Campbell, Pearl Assurance Hse Derby S, Liverpool L2 9XL, England also: 45 Ludgate Hill, London EC4, England

SWAFFORD, LESLIE EUGENE, physician assistant, consultant; b. Long Beach, Calif., Aug. 31, 1950; s. Leslie Eugene Swafford, Sr. and Kathryn Shirley (Gros) Jarvis; children: Jayson Patrick, Jonathan Allyn, Jude Christopher, Joshua Douglas; m. Cheryl Kaleen Killman, Apr. 10, 1993; 1 child, Lesli Tayte. BS in Allied Health, physician asst. degree of completion, George Washington U., 1978; postgrad. in Occupl. Medicine, U. Cin., 1994-95. Cert. physician's asst. NCCPA, ACLS, PALS, CDC AIDS Counselor, EBT (Alco-Sensor IV), EBT (EC/IR) QAP, TTT. Chief EEG technologist Group Health Assn., Washington, 1974-76; physician asst. Pediat. Assocs., Frederick, Md., 1978-81, Heart Inst. for Care, Amarillo, Tex., 1981-84, Maricopa County Medicine Assocs., Avondale-Goodyear, Ariz., 1984-89; mgr. Samaritan Occupl. Health Svcs. Samaritan Health System, Phoenix, 1989-98; dir. employee health/occupl. medicine, worker's comp program Maryvale Hosp. Med. Ctr., Phoenix, 1998, MRO asst., dir. adminstr. respiratory protection program, 1998—; adminstr. drug test program Samaritan Health Svcs., Phoenix, 1991-95; mem. com. Ariz. Rural Health Conf., 1992-96; adj. asst. prof. physician asst. tng. program Kirksville Coll. of Osteo. Medicine, Phoenix, 1995—; instr. Calif. Tech. Contbr. articles to profl. jours. Chmn. sex edn. com. North Ctrl. Accreditation-Aqua Fria H.S., Avondale, Ariz., 1991; physician asst. Camp Geronimo (Boy Scouts of Am.), Phoenix, 1989-94; team mem. Young People's Beginning Experience Grief Recovery Program for Children, Phoenix, 1989-93; mem. com. Ariz. Dept. Health Svcs.-Robert Wood Johnson Application, Phoenix, 1992-93. With USN, 1969-74. Recipient scholarship NIH, 1976, Squibb Pharm. Rural Physician Asst. of Yr. award honorable mention Am. Acad. Physician Assts., 1987, Dr. Paul L. Singer award for disting. cmty. svc. Samaritan Found., 1991. Fellow Ariz. State Assn. Physician Assts. (pres.-elect 1990-91, pres. 1991-92, chmn. Ariz. physician asst. tng. program task force 1990-94); mem. Am. Coll. Forensic Examiners. Republican. Roman Catholic. Avocations: fishing, hiking, softball, basketball, golfing. Home: 17723 Cactus Flower Dr Goodyear AZ 85338-5232 Office: Maryvale Hosp Med Ctr 5102 W Campbell Ave # 503 Phoenix AZ 85031-1703

SWAIM, JOHN FRANKLIN, physician, health care executive; b. Bloomingdale, Ind., Dec. 24, 1935; s. Max DeBaun and Edna Marie (Whitely) S.; m. Joan Dooley, Sept. 19, 1957 (div. Apr. 1979); children: John Franklin, Parke Allen, Pamela Ann; m. Peggy Lou Sankey, May 30, 1979; one child, Anne-Marie. BS cum laude, Ind. State U., 1959; MD, Ind. U., Indpls., 1963. Diplomate Am. Bd. Family Practice with added cert. in geriatrics. Med. dir. Newport (Ind.) Chem. Depot, 1968—, Parke Clinic, Rockville, Ind., 1969—, Rockville Correctional Facility, 1970—; pres. Parke Investments Inc., Rockville, 1972—, Vermillion Health Care Corp., Clinton, Ind., 1977—, Parke County Coroner, 1980, Swaim Farm Corp., 1998—, Parke County Health Officer, 1999—. Author: One Year and Eternity, 1978; contbr. articles to profl. jours. Coroner, Parke County, Ind., 1972-82. Capt. USAF, 1963-67, Vietnam. Decorated Bronze Star. Mem. Am. Acad. Family Physicians, AMA, Ind. Med. Assn. (dist. pres. 1986—), Hoosiers Assocs. Club, Elks, Masons, Shriners. Republican. Avocations: reading and investing. Home and Office: Parke Clinic PO Box 185 Rockville IN 47872-0185

SWAIM, MARK WENDELL, hepatologist, molecular biologist, gastroenterologist, educator, photographer; b. Winston-Salem, N.C., Dec. 4, 1960; s. Donnie Lee and Bernice Earline (Brown) S. BA summa cum laude, U. N.C., 1983; MD, Duke U., 1990, PhD with honors, 1990. Diplomate Am. Bd of Internal Medicine, Am. Bd. Gastroenterology and Hepatology. Resident Dept. of Med. Duke U. Med. Ctr., Durham, N.C., 1990-93, fellow gastroenterology, 1993-97, clin. med. instr., 1994-2000, fellow in advanced hepatology and endoscopy, 1997-98, attending physician, 1998-2000; attending physician Durham VA Med. Ctr., 1998-2000; asst. prof. medicine Gastrointestinal Ctr., U. Tex.-M.D. Anderson Cancer Ctr., Houston, 2000—; assoc. Dept. of Medicine Duke U., 1998-2000; instr. clin. medicine Duke U. Sch. Medicine, 1994-2000, mem. admissions com.; asst. prof. medicine Gastrointestinal Ctr., U. Tex. M.D. Anderson Cancer Ctr., Houston; vis. med. resident Nat. Taiwan U., Taipei, 1991, 92; vis. physician Saratov (Russia) Med. U., 1995; book rev. panelist The Pharos of Alpha Omega Alpha; consulting physician Al-Jazeira Hosp., Abu Dhabi, United Arab Emirates. Contbr. articles to profl. jours., Ency. Brit. Great Ideas Today, 1996; photography pub. in Am. Photo. Recipient Brody award for history of medicine, 1998, Davison award for tchg. excellence, 2000; NIH Med. Sci. Tng. Program fellow, 1983-90, numerous acad. scholarships. Mem. ACP (winner assocs. competition 1994), Am. Coll. Gastroenterology, Am. Soc. for Gastrointestinal Endoscopy, Am. Assn. for Study Liver Diseases, Reticuloendothelial Soc., Am. Coll. Forensic Examiners, Engel Soc., Am. Liver Found. (bd. dirs. Tex. chpt.), Houston Acad. Medicine, Alpha Omega Alpha (pres. Duke chpt. 1989), Phi Beta Kappa, Sigma Xi, Phi Lambda Upsilon, Sigma Pi Sigma. Avocations: photography, traveling, chamber music. Home: 6301 Almeda Rd Apt 116 Houston TX 77021-1056 Office: Dept GI Oncology & Digestive Diseases U Tex M D Anderson Cancer Ctr Holcombe Blvd Houston TX 770[illegible]

SWAIMAN, KENNETH FRED, pediatric neurologist, educator; b. St. Paul, Nov. 19, 1931; s. Lester J. and Shirley (Ryan) S.; m. Phyllis Kammerman Sher, Oct. 1985; children: Lisa, Jerrold, Barbara, Dana. BA magna cum laude, U. Minn., 1952, BS, 1953, MD, 1955; postgrad., 1956-58. Diplomate Am. Bd. Psychiatry and Neurology, Am. Bd. Pediatrics, Am. Bd. Psychiatry and Neurology with Spl. Competence in Child Neurology. Intern Mpls. Gen. Hosp., 1955-56; resident in pediatrics, fellow in pediatrics to chief resident U. Minn. Hosp., 1956-58, spl. fellow in pediatric neurology, 1960-63, dir. pediatric neurology tng. program, 1968-94, various to interim head dept. neurology, 1994-96; chief pediatrics U.S. Army Hosp., Ft. McPherson, Ga., 1958-60; asst. prof. pediatrics, neurology U. Minn. Med. Sch., Mpls., 1963-66; prof., dir. pediatric neurology U. Minn. Med. Sch., 1969-96, mem. internship adv. coun. exec. faculty, 1966-70, interim head dept. neurology, 1994-96; postgrad. fellow pediatric neurology Nat. Inst. Neurologic Diseases and Blindness, 1960-63, assoc. prof., 1966-69; cons. pediatric neurology Hennepin County Gen. Hosp., 1963—, Mpls., St. Paul-Ramsey Hosp., St. Paul Children's Hosp., Mpls. Children's Hosp.; vis. prof. numerous univs. including Loyola U., 1982, U. N.Mex., 1982, U. Ind. Med. Sch., 1983, U. Kyushu, Shiga, Nagoya, Tokyo, 1985, Driscoll Children's Hosp., Corpus Christi, Tex., 1986, Inst. Nacional de Pediatria, Mexico City, 1986, U. de Concepion, Chile, 1989, Beijing U. Med. Sch., 1989, Xian Med. U., China, 1989, Children's Hosp. of Mich., Detroit, 1990, Hong Kong Child Neurology Soc., 1995, Tartu, Estonia, 1997, Krem, Austria, 1997, Santiago, Chile, 1997, Kaunas, Lithuania, 1998, ICNA Ednl. Seminar, Tartu, 1998, Montevideo, Uruguay, 1999, others; lectr. in field; guest worker NIH, NICHD, Bethesda, Md., 1978-79, 79-81. Author: (with Francis S. Wright) Neuromuscular Diseases in Infancy and Childhood, 1969, Pediatric Neuromuscular Diseases, 1979, (with Stephen Ashwal) Pediatric Neurology Case Studies, 1978, 2d edit., 1984, Pediatric Neurology: Practice and Principles, 1989, 3d edit., 1999; editor: (with John A. Anderson) Phenylketonuria and Allied Metabolic Diseases, 1966, (with Francis S. Wright) Practice Pediatric Neurology, 1975, 2d edit., 1982; mem. editorial bd.: Annals of Neurology, 1977-83, Neurology Update, 1977-82, Pediatric Update, 1977-85, Brain and Devel. (Jour. Japanese Soc. Child Neurology), 1980—, Neuropediatrics (Stuttgart), 1982-92; editor-in-chief: Pediatric Neurology, 1984—; contbr. articles to sci. jours. Chmn. Minn. Gov.'s Bd. for Handicapped, Exceptional and Gifted Children, 1972-76; mem. human devel. study sect. NIH, 1976-79, guest worker, 1978-81. Served to capt. M.C. U.S. Army, 1958-60. Fellow Am. Acad. Pediatrics, Am. Acad. Neurology (rep. to nat. coun. Nat. Soc. Med. Rsch.); mem. Soc. Pediatric Rsch., Ctrl. Soc. Clin. Rsch., Ctrl. Soc. Neurol. Rsch., Internat. Soc. Neurochemistry, Am. Neurol. Assn., Minn. Neurol. Soc., AAAS, Midwest Pediatric Soc., Am. Soc. Neurochemistry, Child Neurology Soc. (1st pres. 1972-73, Hower award 1981, Founder's award 1996, chmn. internat. affairs com., 1991-96, mem. long range planning com. 1991-97, chmn. fin. com. 1995—), Internat. Assn. Child Neurologists (exec. com. 1975-79, chmn. global edn. com. 1996-99), Profs. of Child Neurology (1st pres. 1978-80, mem. nominating com. 1986-92), Japanese Child Neurology Soc. (Segawa award 1986, mem. nominating com. 1986-92, chair internat. affairs com. 1991—, mem. long range planning com. 1991-98), Soc. de Psiquiatria y Neurologia de la Infancia y Adolescencia, Internat. Child Neurology Assn. (chair internat. edn. com. 1996-99), Lithuanian Child Neurology Soc. (hon.), Phi Beta Kappa, Sigma Xi. Office: U Minn Med Sch Dept Pediatric Neurology 1821 University Ave W Saint Paul MN 55104-2801 also: UMHC Box 486 420 Delaware St SE Minneapolis MN 55455-0374

SWALES, JOHN DOUGLAS, medical educator, scientist; b. Leicester, Eng., Oct. 19, 1935; s. Frank and Doris Agnes (Flude) S.; m. Kathleen Patricia Townsend; children: Philip, Charlotte. BA with honors, first class, Clare Coll., Cambridge, Eng., 1957; MB, BChir, Westminster Med. Sch.,

U.K., 1960; MA, Clare Coll., Cambridge, Eng., 1961; MD, Cambridge U., 1971. House officer Westminster Hosp., 1961-62; sr. house officer Queen Mary's Hosp., Ruehampton, Eng., 1962-63; med. registrar Westminster Hosp., 1964-68; rsch. fellow Royal Postgrad. Med. Sch., 1968-70; sr. lectr. Manchester (Eng.) U. Med. Sch., 1970-74; prof. medicine Leicester (Eng.) U. Med. Sch., 1974—; dir. R&D Dept. Health, London, 1996-98; Lloyd-Roberts lectr. Royal Soc. Medicine, 1997. Author: Manual of Hypertension, 1995, Sodium Metabolism in Disease, 1974, Clinical Hypertension, 1979, Platt versus Pickering, 1985; editor: Textbook of Hypertension, 1994, Manual of Hypertension, 1995. Recipient Passingham prize Cambridge U., 1957, BUPA/RSM price for best testbook, 1995. Fellow Am. High Blood Pressure Coun., Australian High Blood Pressure Rsch. Coun. (hon.), Royal Coll. Physicians (Bradshaw lectr. 1987, Croonian Lectr. 1991, Harveian orator 1995), Acad. Med. Scis.; mem. Assn. Physicians, Athenaeum Club. Avocation: bibliophile. Home: 21 Morland Ave, Leicester LE2 2PF, England Office: Clin Sci Bldg Royal Inf, PO Box 65, Leicester LE2 7LX, England

SWALES, MARTIN WILLIAM, German language educator; b. Victoria, B.C., Can., Nov. 3, 1940; arrived in Eng., 1946; s. Percy Johns and Doris (Davies) S.; m. Erika Marta Meier, Sept. 23, 1996. BA, Cambridge (Eng.) U., 1961; PhD, U. Birmingham, Eng., 1963. Lectr. in German U. Birmingham, 1964-70; assoc. prof. German U. Toronto, Can., 1970-72; prof. U. Toronto, 1975-76; reader in German King's Coll., U. London, 1972-75; prof. German U. Coll., London, 1976—, dean faculty arts, 1982-85; hon. dir. Inst. German Studies, London, 1989-93. Author: Arthur Schnitzler, 1971, The German Novelle, 1977, The German Bildungsroman, 1978, Epochenbuch Realismus, 1997. Recipient Officer's Cross of Order of Merit, Fed. Republic Germany, 1994. Fellow Brit. Acad. Avocations: music, theater, conversation. Home: 11 De Freville Ave, Cambridge CB4 1HW, England Office: Dept German U Coll London, Gower St, London WC1E 6BT, England

SWALLOW, PETER GEORGE, engineering educator; b. Nottingham, Eng., Sept. 24, 1947; s. Geoffrey and Winifred Mary (Ellwood) S.; m. Lynne Louise Farhall, June 12, 1971; children: John Richard, Robert Geoffrey. Diploma in surveying, Leicester (Eng.) Poly., 1971, post grad. diploma in archtl. bldg. conservation, 1978. Chartered bldg. surveyor. Archtl. asst. Brit. Shoe Corp., Leicester, 1968-69; bldg. surveyor Bruton Knowles & Co., Gloucester, Eng., 1971-73, Eric Cole Design Co., Eng., 1973-74; lectr. Leicester Poly., 1974-89; prof. bldg. surveying De Montfort U., Leicester, 1989—, head of dept., 1990-99; prin. Swallow Enterprises, Leicester, 1990—. Author: Measurement and Recording of Historic Buildings, 1993, Building Maintenance Management, 1996, Surveying Historic Buildings, 1996; contbr. articles to profl. jours. Hon. sec. Fleckney Village Trust, Leicester, 1990-98; specialist, advisor in conservation Leicester City Coun., 1994—. Fellow Royal Inst. Chartered Surveyors, Assn. Bldg. Engrs., Royal Soc. Arts, Inst. Hist. Bldg. Conservation. Avocations: historic bldgs. and landscapes, industrial archaeology, walking. Home: 41 Highfield St Fleckney, Leicester LE8 8BD, England Office: De Montfort U Sch Arch, The Gateway, Leicester LE1 9BH, England

SWAMINATHAN, KUMAR, electrical engineer, researcher; b. Madras, India, Apr. 11, 1959; s. Mannargudi Venkatraman and Saroja Swaminathan; m. Giayatri Iyer, June 26, 1994. B in Tech., Indian Inst. Tech., Madras, 1981; MS, Calif. Inst. Tech., 1982, PhD, 1986. Mem. tech. staff AT&T Bell Labs, Whippany, N.J., 1986-91; prin. engr. Hughes Network Sys., Germantown, Md., 1991-93, sr. prin. engr., 1993-99, adv. engr., 1999—. Mem. IEEE (sr.), Sigma Xi. Achievements include 15 patents in speech communication technology. Avocations: jogging, swimming, reading, cycling, movies. Office: Hughes Network Sys 11717 Exploration Ln Germantown MD 20876-2799

SWAMINATHAN, MONKOMBU SAMBASIVAN, agricultural researcher; b. Tamil Nadu, India, Aug. 7, 1925; d. M.K. and S. (Thangam) Sambasivan; m. Mina Bhoothalingam Swaminathan, 1955; children: Soumya, Madhura, Nitya. BSc, Travancore U., India, 1945; BSc in Agr. Coimbatore Agrl. Coll., Madras U., 1947; Assoc., Indian Agrl. Rsch. Inst., New Delhi, 1949; PhD, U. Cambridge, Eng., 1952; DSc (hon.), The Sardar Pater U., Vllabh Vidyanagar, 1970; The Andhra U., 1972, Andhra Pradesh Agrl. U., Hyderabad, 1973, Haryana Agrl. U., Hissar, 1973, G.B. Pant U., Pantnagar, 1974, Jodhpur U., 1975. Tchr., researcher, rsch. adminstr. Ctrl. Rice Rsch. Inst. Cuttack, Indian Agrl. Rsch. Inst., New Delhi, 1954-72; dir. gen. Indian Coun. Agrl. Rsch., 1972-79; sec. Govt. India, 1972-79, sec. to India Ministry Agr. and Irrigation, 1979-80, acting dep. chmn. Planning Commn., 1980, mem. Agr., Rural Devel., Sci. and Edn. Planning Commn., 1980-82; dir. gen. Internat. Rice Rsch. Inst., Los Banos, Philippines, 1982—; vice chmn. tech. adv. com. Consultative Group on Internat. Agrl. Rsch., 1971-77, Protein-Calorie Adv. Group UN, 1972-77; chmn. first quinquennial rev. Internat. Rice Rsch. Inst., 1976; chmn. UN Adv. Com. on Sci. and Tech., for Devel., 1980-83, chair in ecotechnology UNESCO; pres. Internat. Fedn. Agrl. Sys. for Devel., 1976-83; chmn., bd. trustees Internat. Coun. Rsch. in Agroforestry, U.K., 1977-82; ind. chmn. FAO Coun., Rome, 1981-85; mem. sci. and tech.a dv. com. tropical diseases rsch. WHO, 1983-85; hon. v.p. World Wildlife Fund, Geneva, 1985—; pres. Internat. Union for Conservation of Nature and Natural Resources, Geneva, 1986-90; gen. pres. Indian Sci. Congress, Waltair, 1976; pres. SV Internat. Congress Genetics, New Delhi, 1983, World Wide Fund Nature; mem. Nat. Commn. on Agr., 1971-77. Recipient Shanti Swarup Bhatnagar award, 1961, Mendel Meml. award Czechoslovak Acad. Scis., 1965, Birbal Shani medal Indian Bot. Soc., 1966, Padma Shri, Prs. India, 1967, Ramon Magsaysay award, 1971, Padma Bhushan Pres. India, 1972, Barclay medal Asiatic Soc., 1978, K.L. Moudgill prize, 1978, Borlaug award, 1979, Mghnad Saha medal Indian Nat. Sci. Acad., 1981, Rathindranath Tagore prize Visva Bharati U., 1981, R.D. Misra medal Indian Environ. Soc., 1982, R.B. Bennett Commonwealth prize, 1984, Dr. B.P. Pal medal, 1996, award Assn. for Women in Devel., Washington, 1985, Bicentenary medal U. Ga., 1985, Gen. Foods World Food prize, 1987, albert Einstein Sci. award, 1986, Golden Hearth Presdl. award, 1987, Padman Bibhushan, India, 1989, Tyler prize Environ. Achievement, 1991, Honda prie Eco-tech, 1991, UNEP-Sasakawa Environ. prize, 1994, Asian Productivity Orgn. Regional award, 1994, Blue Planet prize Asashi Glass Found., 1996, Shatabdi Puraskar award Indian Sci. Congress Assn., 1999, Legend in his Lifetime awad World Wilderness Trust, 1999, Asutosh Mookerjee Meml. award Indian Sci. Congress Assn., 2000, Indira Gandhi prize for Peace, Disarmament and Devel., 1999, UNESCO Gandhi Gold medal, 1999, Franklin D. Roosevelt Four Freedoms award Franklin and Eleanor Roosevelt Inst., Planet and Humanity medal Internat. Geog. Union. Fellow AAAS, Indian Nat. Sci. Acad.(Silver Jubilee Commemoration medal 1973), Royal Soc. London, Third World Acad. Scis., Nat. Acad. Scis. India (hon.), Swedish Seed Assn.(hon.), Nat. Acad. Sci. Italy (hon., fgn.), Nat. Acad. Agrl. Scis. (pres.), Royal Soc. Arts, Lodnon Linnean Soc.; mem. Nat. Acad. Scis. U.S. (fgn. assoc. 1977), All-Union Acad. Agrl. Scis. USSR (fgn.) Royal Swedish Acad. Agr. and Forestry (fgn.), Nat. Acad. Arts and Scis. (hon., fgn.). Home: 11 Rathna Nagar, Madras 600018, India Address: 3d Cross St, Taramani Instl Area Chennai 600113, India

SWAMINATHAN, NATARAJAN (SAM SWAMINATHAN), storyteller; b. Coimbatore, Tamil Nadu, India, Sept. 4; s. Natarajan Krishnaswamyand Meenakshi Balasundaram Natarajan; m. Vanitha Swaminathan Rajan, 1973; children: Anand, Aditya. Degree in elec. engring., Banaras (India) Hindu U., 1971; MBA, Jamnalal Bajaj Inst., Mumbai, 1978. Head IT Shell, Muscat, Oman, 1981-88; cons. mgr. KPMG, Dubai, United Arab Emirates, 1989-90; lectr. Higher Colls. Tech., Dubai, 1990-94; storyteller Ctr. for Creative Thinking, Dubai, 1995—, mng. dir.; tchr. Higher Colls. Tech., Dubai. Contbr. weekly bus. column to Mgmt. Notebook, 1994-97, management.com, 1998—; spkr. video Becoming A World Class Company, 1999. Lt. Indian armed forces, 1970-80. Mem. ASTD, Dubai Quality Group. Avocations: writing, squash, tennis. Fax: 971-4-268-5496. E-mail: sam@cthinking.com. Office: Ctr for Creative Thinking, Po Box 14133, Dubai United Arab Emirates

SWAMY, M. R. KUMARA, financial management researcher; b. Mysore, Karnataka, India, Jan. 23, 1938; s. Rama and Subbamma Rao; m. Shaila Rao Swamy, Aug. 25, 1966; 2 children. BA with honors, India, 1958, MA, 1960; PhD, U.S.A., 1965. Social worker Bharat Sevak Samaj, Delhi, 1956-57; rsch. fellow Delhi Sch. of Econs., 1960-61; econ. investigator Nat. Coun. Applied Econ. Rsch., Delhi, 1961-62; cons. Cassa Per Il Mezzogiorno, Rome, 1965-66; adv. oil economist Govt. of Qatar, Doha, 1967-69; sr. rsch. officer Commerce Rsch. Bur., Bombay, 1969-77; prof. econs. and fin., head dept. Inst. Mgmt. and Tech., Anambra State U. Tech., Enugu, Nigeria, 1977-87; dir., mng. editor Jour. Fin. Mgmt. and Analysis Om Sai Ram Ctr. for Fin. Mgmt. Rsch., Mumbai, India, 1987—; chmn. pub. lectures com. Inst. Mgmt. and Tech., Enugu, 1979-87; mem. com. of experts on low-cost housing Govt. of Nigeria, 1980-81, expert mem. appts. and promotion com. professorial appts. U. Ibadan, Nigeria, 1998—; disting. economist guest spkr. U. Rome, 1965-66. Founder, editor Nigerian Jour. Fin. Mgmt., 1982-87, Jour. Fin. Mgmt. and Analysis, 1987—; contbr. over 180 articles to profl. jours.; lectr. and rschr. in field. Lisle fellow, 1963—. Mem. Fin. Mgmt. Assn. Internat., Indian Econ. Assn. Avocations: collecting words of wisdom, stamps, coins, traveling. Office: 15 Prakash Coop Housing Soc, Relief Rd Santacruz West, Mumbai 400054, India

SWAN, GEORGE STEVEN, law educator; b. St. Louis. BA, Ohio State U., 1970; JD, U. Notre Dame, 1974; LLM, U. Toronto, 1976, SJD, 1983. Bar: Ohio 1974, U.S. Dist. Ct. (so. dist.) Ohio 1975, U.S. Supreme Ct. 1987, U.S. Ct. Appeals (6th and 11th cirs.) 1993, U.S. Ct. Appeals (10th cir.) 1994, D.C. 1997, Ga. 1997, U.S. Dist. Ct. (no. dist.) Ga. 1997, Fla. 1997, Minn. 1998, Nebr. 1998, N.D. 1998, U.S. Ct. Appeals (7th cir.) 1998, La. 1999, Mass. 1999; ChFC, CLU, CFP; registered investment advisor. Sec. of state N.C., 1990; asst. atty. gen. State of Ohio, Columbus, 1974-75; jud. clk. Supreme Ct. Ohio, Columbus, 1976-78; asst. prof. Del. Law Sch., Wilmington, 1980-83, assoc. prof., 1983-84; prof. law St. Thomas U. Law Sch., Miami, Fla., 1984-88; jud. clk. U.S. Ct. Appeals (7th cir.), Chgo., 1988-89; assoc. prof. N.C. Agrl. & Tech. State U., Greensboro, 1989-96, 97-99; vis. prof. John Marshall Law Sch., Atlanta, 1996-97, 2000—. Contbr. articles to law jours. Mem. Ohio State Bar Assn., D.C. Bar, State Bar Ga., Fla. Bar, Mass. Bar Assn., Nebr. State Bar Assn., La. State Bar Assn., N.D. State Bar Assn., Soc. of Fin. Svc. Profls., Fin. Planning Assn., Am. Polit. Sci. Assn. Office: John Marshall Law Sch 1422 Peachtree St NE Atlanta GA 30309-3002

SWAN, SIR JOHN (WILLIAM DAVID), former premier of Bermuda; b. July 3, 1935; s. John N. and Margaret E. Swan; m. Jacqueline A. D. Roberts, 1965; 3 children. B.A., W.Va. Wesleyan Coll.; LLD (hon.), U. Tampa, 1986, W.Va. Wesleyan Coll., 1987. Salesman real estate Rego Ltd., 1960-62; founder, chmn., CEO John W. Swan Ltd., 1962—; mem. Parliament of Bermuda, 1972—, min. for marine and air svcs., 1976-77, min. for labor and immigration, 1977-78, min. for home affairs, 1978-82, premier of Bermuda, 1982-95; formerly parliamentary sec. for fin.; chmn. Dept. Civil Aviation; mem. Lloyd's of London; chmn. Swan Groups of Cos., 1996—. Chmn. bd. dirs. Bermuda Hosps. Recipient St. Paul's A.M.E. Anniversary Citation, 1969, Internat. Medal of Excellence, Poor Richard Club of Phila., 1987, Outstanding Learning Disabled Achiever award Lab Sch. of Washington, 1992; named Outstanding Young Man of the Yr., 1969, Hon. Citizen of City of London, 1985. Fellow Jr. Chamber Internat. (senator 1992); mem. Chief Execs. Orgn., World Bus. Coun., The Bohemian Club of San Francisco, Royal Bermuda Yacht Club, Rotary (hon.). Mem. United Bermuda Party. Avocations: tennis, sailing. Address: Swan Bldg, 26 Victoria St, Hamilton HM 12, Bermuda

SWAN, SUSAN LINDA, history educator; b. Everett, Wash., May 31, 1943; d. Joseph William Franckevitch and Doris Aline (Doolittle) Berry; m. Victor LaMarr Swan, June 19, 1965 (div. Apr. 1994); 1 child, Kerrigan Aline. BA in History, U. Wash., 1965, BA in English, 1965; MA in History, Western Wash. U., 1969; PhD in History, Wash. State U., 1976. Employment interviewer Wash. State Employment Security, Tacoma, 1971-72; asst. prof. history Wash. State U., Pullman, 1977-82, student affairs officer III, 1984-94, assoc. prof. gen. edn. program, 1994—; rsch. assoc. Nat. Coord. Spl. Hist. Projects, Mex., 1991-92. Co-author: Breve Historia de las Sequias en Mexico, 1995; contbg. editor: Reading About the World, I, II and III, 1999; contbr. articles to profl. publs. Mem. student affairs com., advisor, chair acad. advising and reinstatement subcom., mus. adv. subcom. Wash. State U., chpt. advisor Alpha Phi Omega, 1995-99; vol. Pullman Meml. Hosp. Aux., 1983-92; group leader Sacajawea coun. Camp Fire, Pullman, 1984-90. Mem. AAUP, AAAS, World History Assn., Am. Mus. Women in the Arts, Seattle Art Mus., Assn. Faculty Women (treas. 1998-99), Phi Alpha Theta (pres. 1974-75), Phi Kappa Phi. Avocations: watercolors, gardening. Home: PO Box 3195 Pullman WA 99165-3195 Office: Wash State U Dept History Pullman WA 99164-0001

SWANK, HILARY ANN, actress; b. Bellingham, WA, July 30, 1974; m. Chad Lowe, Sept. 28, 1997. Appeared in feature films: Buffy the Vampire Slayer, 1992, The Next Karate Kid, 1994, Sometimes They Come Back...Again, 1996, Kounterfeit, 1996, The Way We Are, 1997, Heartwood, 1998, Boys Don't Cry, 1999 (Golden Globe award for Best Actress, 2000, Oscar award for Best Actress, 2000), Affair of the Necklace, 2000, The Gift, 2000; (tv movies) Cries Unheard: The Donna Yaklich Story, 1994, Terror in the Family, 1996, Dying to Belong, 1997, The Sleepwalker Killing, 1997; (tv series) Camp Wilder, 1992, Beverly Hills, 90210, 1997-98, Leaving L.A., 1997; (tv appearances): Growing Pains, 1985, Evening Shade, Harry and the Hendersons, 1991. Avocations: sky diving, river rafting, skiing, swimming. *

SWANKE, THOMAS AQUINAS, economist, educator; b. Chgo., Mar. 25, 1961; s. John Walter and Kathleen (Battle) S.; m. Susan Palmer, Aug. 4, 1984: children: Peter Alden, Heidi Nicole. BA in Econs., U. San Diego, 1983; MA in Econs., U. Colo., Boulder, 1988; PhD in Econs., U. Colo., 1993. Assoc. prof. W. Va. State Coll., Institute, 1993—. Contbr. articles to profl. jours. Bd. dirs. Catholic Cmty. Svcs., Hamblin, W. Va., 1998—. Mem. Union of Radical Political Economists, Assn. for Evolutionary Economists, Am. Economics Assn. E-mail: tswanke@mail.wvsc.edu. Office: W Va State Coll PO Box 1000 Institute WV 25112-1000

SWANN, BARBARA, lawyer; b. N.Y., Sept. 15, 1950; d. George Arthur. BA summa cum laude, Montclair State U., 1988; JD, Rutgers Law, 1992. Bar: N.J. 1992, D.C. 1994, N.Y. 1995, U.S. Dist. Ct. N.J. 1992, U.S. Ct. Appeals (3rd cir.) 1994, U.S. Dist. Ct. N.Y. 1996. Correspondent The Associate Press, Newark, N.J., 1974-80; reporter, bureau chief The Hudson Dispatch, Union City, N.J., 1973-80; editorial page editor The Paterson (N.J.) News, 1980-81; v.p., acct. supr. Gerald Freeman, Inc., Clifton, N.J., 1981-86; pres. LePore Assoc., Inc., West Caldwell, N.J., 1986-89; law clk. to Hon. Robert N. Wilentz N.J. Supreme Ct., 1992-93; law clk. to Hon. Leonard I. Garth U.S. Ct. Appeals (3rd cir.), 1993-94; assoc. Cahill, Gordon & Reindel, N.Y., 1994-97; liaison Republic of Ga. ABA Cen. and East European Law Initiative, 1997-98, media law specialist, 1998—. Editor-in-chief: Rutgers Computer & Technology Law Jour., 1991-92. Founding trustee Ctr. for Children's Advocacy, Riverdale, N.J. 1994—. Mem. ABA, Assn. of the Bar of the City of New York, N.J. State Bar Assn., N.Y. County Lawyers' Assn. Am. Inn of Ct., D.C. Bar Assn.

SWANN, HUMPHREY VENABLES, occupational psychologist, educator; b. London, Aug. 6, 1943; s. Bernard Burrows and Mary Hamilton (Cooke) S.; m. Joan Margaret Swainston; children: Philippa Jane, Juliet Tessa, Richard Alexander. BA, Cambridge U., 1965; MPhil, Birkbeck Coll., 1974. Author programmed instrn. materials Internat. Tutor Machines, 1965-66; tng. officer English Elec. Computers, 1966-67; rsch. officer Coll. of Estate Mgmt., 1967-69; media rsch. mgr. Austin Knight, 1969-71; sr. lectr. London Guildhall U., 1972—; specialist tng., selection, and motivation. Mem. Br. Psychol. Soc. Avocations: sports, cricket, hockey, skiing, sketching. Home: 120 Dukes Ave Muswell Hill, N10 2QB London England Office: London Guildhall U, E1 7NT London England

SWANNELL, RICHARD PAUL, research and development administrator; b. Chelmsford, Essex, Eng., Apr. 7, 1963; s. Brian Edward and Kathleen Anne (Harland) S.; m. Afsaneh Sabokbar, July 20, 1991; children: Sasha, Omid, Edward. BSc, U. Liverpool, Eng., 1984; MPhil, U. Newcastle, Newcastle Upon Tyne, Eng., 1989. Sr. rsch. officer U. Essex, Colchester, 1987-89; higher sci. officer Warren Spring Lab., Stevenage, Eng., 1990-94; sr. scientist AEA Tech., Harwell, Oxford, Eng., 1994—. Contbr. articles to Nature, Microbiology Ecology, Microbiology Revs., Spill Sci. Technol. Bulletin. Mem. Am. Soc. Microbiology, Soc. Gen. Microbiology. Mem. Liberal Dem. Party. Roman Catholic. Avocations: hiking, horseback riding, badminton, squash. Office: AEA Tech plc, Nat Envtl Tech Ctr, Culham Oxford OX143DB, England

SWANSBURG, RUSSELL CHESTER, medical administrator educator; b. Cambridge, Mass., Aug. 6, 1928; s. William W. and Mary A. (Pierce) S.; m. Laurel Clark, Sept. 1951; children: Philip Wayne, Michael Gary, Richard Jeffrey. Diploma, N.S. Hosp. Sch. Nursing, 1950; BSN, Western Res. U., 1952; MA in Nursing Edn., Columbia U., 1961; PhD, U. Miss., 1984. CNAA. Asst. adminstr. U. of S. Ala. Med. Ctr., Mobile; v.p. U. South Ala., Mobile; prof. Auburn U., Montgomery, Ala., Med. Coll. of Ga., Augusta; mil. cons. USAF Surgeon Gen., 1972; sr. med. svc. cons., 1973-76; nurse cons. VA Med. Ctr., Tuskegee, Ala., 1987-88; mem. editl. adv. bd. Nursing Adminstrn. Manual. Author: Team Nursing: A Programmed Learning Experience, 1968, Inservice Education, 1968, The Measurement of Vital Signs, 1970, The Team Plan, 1971, Management of Patient Care Services, 1976, Strategic Career Planning and Development, 1984, The Nurse Manager's Guide to Financial Management, 1988, Management and Leadership for Nurse Managers, 1990 (Book of Yr. Selection, Am. Jour. Nursing 1990), 2d edit. 1996, Introductory Management and Leadership for Clinical Nurses, 1993, 2d edit., 1999 (Book of the Yr. Selection, Am. Jour. Nursing 1999), Staff Development: A Component of Human Resource Development, 1994, Budgeting and Financial Management for Nurse Managers, 1997, (audiovisual course) Nurses & Patients: An Introduction to Nursing Management, 1980; contbr. articles to profl. publs. Bd. dirs. Air Force Village Found., Alzheimer's Care and Research Found. Col. USAF, 1956-76. Decorated Air medal with oak leaf clusters, Legion of Merit; recipient award for outstanding work in hosp. adminstrn. Ala. State Nurses' Assn., 1985, Outstanding Nursing Svc. Adminstrn. award, 1981, Outstanding Nurse Rschr. 1984, Disting. Svc. award Air Force Village Found., 1999. Fellow AONE, Ala. Orgn. Nurse Exec's (past state pres.); mem. Council Grad. Edn. Adminstrn. in Nursing (sec.), Ala. Acad. Sci., Sigma Xi, Phi Kappa Phi, Sigma Theta Tau. Home and Office: 4917 Ravenswood Dr Apt 1711 San Antonio TX 78227-4356

SWANSON, BARRY ERNEST, securities company executive; b. Buffalo, June 23, 1940. BS, St. Lawrence U., 1962; lang. cert., U. Heidelberg, 1969. Registered investor-advisor; CFP. V.p. Intervest Internat. Corp., Heidelberg, Germany, 1980-86; pres., chief exec. officer Integrated FIn. Planning Corp., Heidelberg, 1986—. Contbr. articles to newspapers and mags. Lt. col. U.S. Army. Mem. NAACP Europe, Internat. Assn. Fin. Planning Europe (pres. 1991-92), Internat. Bd. Cert. Fin. Planners (cons. 1988—, cert.), Heidelberg Internat. Ski Club (pres. 1974-76), Heidelberg Internat. Toastmasters Club (pres. 1990-91), Am./German Bus. Club (pres. 1997—). Home: Cmr 420 Box 21 APO AE 09063-0021 Office: Integrated Fin Planning Cor, Integrated Fin Planning Svc, Karl Strasse 20, 69117 Heidelberg 6900, Germany

SWANSON, CAROL ANN, lawyer; b. West Point, Nebr., Aug. 8, 1944; d. Ora Elmer Jr. and Florence Marguerite (Witt) Underwood; m. Leonard Jelkren, Oct. 5, 1962 (div. 1983); children: Le Ann Jelkren Mandici, Bradley Grant Jelkren; m. Dan Whalen Swanson, Dec. 29, 1989. BS, U. Ctrl. Fla., 1987; JD, U. Fla., 1990. Bar: Fla. 1990. Assoc. Law Offices of Thomas Pilacek, Maitland, Fla.; owner Law Offices of Carol Swanson, Orlando, Fla., 1994—. Mem. Fla. Bar, Seminole County Bar, Orange County Bar. E-mail: swanson.carol@worldnet.att.net. Office: Law Offices of Carol Swanson 801 N Magnolia Ave Ste 301 Orlando FL 32803-3843

SWANSON, DAVID HEATH, agricultural company executive; b. Aurora, Ill., Nov. 3, 1942; s. Neil H. and Helen J. (McKendry) S.; m. Carolyn Breitinger; children: Benjamin Heath, Matthew Banford. B.A., Harvard U., 1964; M.A., U. Chgo., 1969. Account exec. 1st Nat. Bank Chgo., 1967-69; dep. mgr. Brown Bros. Harriman & Co., N.Y.C., 1969-72; treas. Borden, Inc. Internat., N.Y.C., 1972-75; v.p., treas. Continental Grain Co., N.Y.C., 1975-77, v.p., CFO, 1977-79, gen. mgr. European div., 1979-81, exec. v.p. and gen. mgr. World Grain div., 1981-83, corp. sr. v.p., chief fin. and adminstrv. officer, 1983-86, group pres., 1985-86; pres., CEO Cen. Soya, Ft. Wayne, Ind., 1986-93; chmn., CEO Explorer Nutrition Group, N.Y.C., 1994-96; pres., CEO, Countrymark, Inc., Indpls., 1996-98; mem. adv. bd. U.S. Export-Import Bank, 1985-86; bd. dirs. Fiduciary Trust Internat., Conrail. Founding bd. dirs. Internat. Policy Coun. on Agr. and Trade; mem. adv. bd. Purdue U. Agr. Sch.; mem. Gov.'s Econ. Devel. Ind. Bd.; bd. govs. Exec. Coun. on Fgn. Diplomats and U.S. Agr. Libr.; gov. Found. for U.S. Constn. Mem. Coun. Fgn. Rels., Nat. Assn. Mfrs. (bd. dirs.), Ind. C. of C. (bd. dirs.), Am. Alpine Club (bd. dirs.), Links Club, Racquet and Tennis Club, Explorers Club (bd. dirs., sec., pres.), Millbrook Golf and Tennis. Republican. Congregationalist. Office: Explorer Nutrition and Fiber Group 46 E 70th St New York NY 10021-4928

SWANSON, DENNIS MICHAEL, religious institution librarian, pastor; b. Inglewood, Calif., May 6, 1956; s. Robert Clayton and Virginia Lee (Johnson) S.; m. Jeanette Marie Farr, Sept. 10, 1977; children: Andrew Michael, Amy Michelle. BS in Biblical Studies, The Master's Coll., 1990; MDiv, The Master's Sem., Sun Valley, Calif., 1994; MLS, San Jose State U., 1996. Officer L.A. Police Dept., 1977-90; sr. pastor Calif. Heights Bapt. Ch., Long Beach, 1990-93; dir. acad. advancement The Master's Coll., Newhall, Calif., 1993; sem. libr., asst. prof. The Master's Sem., 1994—; interim pastor Bethel Bapt. Ch., Lancaster, Calif., 1997-98, Pine Mtn. (Calif.) Cmty. Ch., 1996. Asst. editor: Introduction to Biblical Counseling, 1994, The MacArthur Study Bible, 1997 (gold medallion 1998); contbr. articles to profl. publs. Mem. Evang. Theol. Soc., Soc. Biblical Lit., Am. Theol. Libr. Assn., Am. Schs. Oriental Rsch. Republican. Baptist. Avocations: golf, hiking, camping, reading. Home: 30038 Abelia Rd Santa Clarita CA 91351-1509 Office: The Master's Sem 13248 Roscoe Blvd Sun Valley CA 91352-3739

SWANSON, JACK ELMER, economist, investment consultant; b. Santa Monica, Calif., Nov. 24, 1931; came to Eng., 1959; s. Jack Elmer and Lillian Mae (King) S.; m. Heidi Helga Eartly, Aug. 13, 1958; children: Noel, Mitzi. BA in Bus. Adminstrn., U. Wash., 1956. Cert. secondary tchr., Can., Eng. Contract adminstr. Keiser Internat. Engrs., London, 1965-67; progress officer John Mowlem, London, 1967-72; br. mgr. Hambro Life Ins., London, 1972-74; lectr. econs. and bus. studies Birmingham (Eng.) Edn., 1974-79; lectr. econs. Alberdink Thijm Coll., Hilversum, The Netherlands, 1984-90; investment cons., 1980—; chmn. bd. govs. Hammersmith Coll., London, 1967-69; dir. Gandeamus Ltd., Douglas, Isle of Man, 1986—. Author: Time to Invest, 1982, The European Options Markets: A New Approach to Investment, 1984. Mem. Greater London Coun., 1967-69, Inner London Edn. Authority, 1967-69. Avocations: sailing, marquetry.

SWANSON, JENNIE ELIZABETH WILLIAMS, healthcare administrator, mentor, volunteer; b. Atlanta, Aug. 5, 1932; d. Chester Arthur and Cleo Annie Williams; m. Richard Scott Edward Swanson, Apr. 24, 1954; children: Laurel Dee, Jeffrey Richard, Scott Edward. BS, Northwestern U., 1954; MS, No. Ill. U., 1972, EdD, 1976. Pub. sch. tchr., 1954-69, psycho-ednl. diagnostician, 1969-72; faculty Loyola U., Chgo., 1976-82, asst. prof. ob-gyn and pediat., 1979-82; dir. pre-start project depts. ob-gyn and pediat. Stritch Sch. Medicine, 1978-82; dir. spl. svcs. Cmty. Unit Sch. Dist. 220, 1982-92; hospice bereavement vol., 1997—; coun. mem., mentor Cong. Unitarian Ch.; antique dealer; mem. Gov. Ill. Com. Preventive Svcs., 1979-80; chair B-3 subcom. First Chance Consortium, 1978-80; chair INTER-ACT, 1979-80; cons. in field. Author: (with others) Partners in Child Development, 1978. Grantee HEW, 1973-76, 78-82. Mem. Coun. Exceptional Children, Assn. Maternal and Child Health, Nat. Perinatal Assn., Nat. Acad. Neuropsychology, Nat. Assn. Edn. Young Child, Northwestern U. Alumni Assn., Delta Delta Delta, Delta Kappa Gamma (scholar 1974). Unitarian.

SWANSON, JERRY WILLIAM, neurologist; b. Peoria, Ill., Dec. 15, 1950; s. Clarence William and Joanne Krull S.; m. Kristine Kay Haugen, Dec. 28, 1974; children: Elizabeth, Rachel. BA, Wartburg Coll., 1973; MD, Northwestern U. Med. Sch., Chgo., 1977. Diplomate Am. Bd. Psychiatry and Neurology. Cons. in neurology Mayo Clinic, Rochester, Minn., 1982—; assoc. prof. neurology Mayo Med. Sch., Rochester, 1992—; vice-chmn. edn., dept. neurology Mayo Clinic, 1996-98, program dir. dept. neurology, 1996-98, chmn. headache divsn., dept. neurology, 1996—, head clin. sect., dept. neurology, 1998—. Co-editor: (book) Mayo Clinic Examinations in Neurology, 7th edit., 1998; contbr. more than 40 articles to profl. jours. and publs. Fellow Am. Acad. Neurology; mem. Am. Neurol. Assn., Minn. Soc. Neurol. Scis., Am. Headache Soc. (ann. scientific mtg. co-chair 1999—).

Lutheran. Avocations: canoeing, Nordic skiing, hiking. Office: Dept Neurology/Mayo Clin 200 1st St SW Rochester MN 55905-0001

SWANSON, KARIN, hospital administrator, consultant; b. New Britain, Conn., Dec. 8, 1942; d. Oake F. and Ingrid Lauren Swanson; m. B. William Dorsey, June 26, 1965 (div. 1974); children: Matthew W., Julie I., Alison K.; m. Sanford H. Low, Oct. 14, 1989. BA in Biology, Middlebury Coll., 1964; MPH, Yale U., 1981. Biology tchr. Kents Hill (Maine) Sch., 1964-66; laboratory instr. Bates Coll., Lewiston, Maine, 1974-78; asst. to gen. dir. Mass. Eye and Ear Infirmary, Boston, 1979-80; v.p. profl. services Portsmouth (N.H.) Hosp., 1981-83; v.p. Health Strategy Assn. Ltd., Chestnut Hill, Mass., 1983-85; v.p. med. affairs Cen. Maine Med. Ctr., Lewiston, 1986-89; health care mgmt. cons. Cambridge, Mass., 1989-91; CEO Hahnemann Hosp., Brighton, Mass., 1991-94; adminstr. Vencor Hosp., Boston, 1994-95; pres., CEO The Laser Inst. New Eng., Newton, Mass., 1996-97; health care mgmt./real estate devel. cons. Damariscotta, Maine, 1997—. Mem. Phi Beta Kappa. Avocations: reading, gardening, walking. Home and Office: PO Box 1281 Damariscotta ME 04543-1281

SWANSON, LAUREN A., consultant, entrepreneur, educator, researcher; b. Apr. 17, 1951. BS, U. Wyo., 1973; MS, 1974; postgrad., Wheaton Coll., 1977; PhD, U. Ga., 1983. Instr. mktg. U. Wyo., Laramie, 1974-76; grad. instr. mktg., mgmt. sci. U. Ga., Athens, 1978-79; vis. prof. mktg. Grad. Sch. Bus. Adminstrn. Atlanta U., 1980-81; asst. prof. mktg. U. Mass., Boston, 1981-86; rsch. cons. Hill-Holliday-Connors-Cosmopulos Inc., Boston, 1983-86; assoc. in rsch. Fairbank Ctr. for East Asian Rsch. Harvard U., Cambridge, Mass., 1986—; fgn. expert, prof. mktg. and econs. U. Internat. Bus. and Econs., Beijing, 1986-87; assoc. prof. mktg. Chinese U. Hong Kong, 1987-98, assoc. dir. MBA programs, 1991-96; v.p. Dalton (Nebr.) Telecom, 1998-99; cons. in mktg. and telecomms. Dalton, 1999—; cons. to industry; examiner Hong Kong Quality Award, 1991-95. Guest editor: Internat. Jour. Advtsg.; contbr. numerous articles to profl. jours.

SWANSON, LESLIE KEATING, financial services executive; b. Wilmington, Del., Sept. 27, 1952. BS, U. Del., 1974, postgrad., 1980-83. Registered securities broker and ins. broker. Registered securities broker Merrill Lynch Pierce Fenner & Smith, Wilmington, 1984-89; fin. advisor, rule 144 specialist Morgan Stanley Dean Witter, Phila., 1989—. Avocations: golf, photography, skiing, tennis. Fax: 215 963-3925. Home: PO Box 4046 Wilmington DE 19807-0046 Office: Morgan Stanley Dean Witter Two Logan Sq 18th And Arch Sts Philadelphia PA 19103-1199

SWANSON, ROY ARTHUR, classicist, educator; b. St. Paul, Apr. 7, 1925; s. Roy Benjamin and Gertrude (Larson) S.; m. Vivian May Vitous, Mar. 30, 1946; children: Lynn Marie (Mrs. Gerald A. Snider), Robin Lillian, Robert Roy (dec.), Dyack Tyler, Dana Miriam (Mrs. Jon Butts). BA, U. Minn., 1948, BS, 1949, MA, 1951; PhD, U. Ill., 1954. Prin. Maplewood Elementary Sch., St. Paul, 1949-51; instr. U. Ill., 1952-53, Ind. U., 1954-57; asst. prof. U. Minn., Mpls., 1957-61, assoc. prof., 1961-64, acting chmn. classics, 1963-64, prof. classics, chmn. comparative lit., 1964-65; prof. English Macalester Coll., St. Paul, 1965-67, coord. humanities program, 1966-67; prof. comparative lit. and classics U. Wis.-Milw., 1967—, prof. English, 1990-96, chmn. classics dept., 1967-70, 86-89, chmn. comparative lit., 1970-73, 76-83, coord. Scandinavian studies program, 1982-96; cons. St. Paul Tchrs. Sr. High Sch. English, 1964. Author: Odi et Amo: The Complete Poetry of Catullus, 1959, Heart of Reason: Introductory Essays in Modern-World Humanities, 1963, Pindar's Odes, 1974, Greek and Latin Word Elements, 1981, The Love Songs of the Carmina Burana, 1987, Pär Lagerkvist: Five Early Works, 1989; editor Minn. Rev., 1963-67; Classical Jour., 1966-72; contbr. articles to profl. jours. With AUS, 1944-46. Decorated Bronze Star; recipient Disting. Teaching award U. Minn., 1962, Disting. Teaching award U. Wis.-Milw., 1974, 91, 99. Mem. Am. Philol. Assn., Am. Comparative Lit. Assn., Modern Lang. Assn., Soc. for Advancement Scandinavian Study, Phi Beta Kappa (pres. chpt. 1975-76). Home: 11618 N Bobolink Ln Mequon WI 53092-2804 Office: U Wis Dept Fgn Langs/Linguistics PO Box 413 Milwaukee WI 53201-0413

SWANSON, SHIRLEY JUNE, registered nurse, adult education educator; b. Dade City, Fla., Feb. 26, 1942; d. Alan John and Ollie Mae (Jackson) S.; m. James A. Whatley, 1960 (div. 1962); 1 child, Marsha L. Glunt; m. Jerald Ward Steen, Sr., June 7, 1963; children: Linda A. Stanley, Jerald Ward, Jr., Jerald Wagner. AA, Hillsborough C.C., 1974; BA, U. South Fla., 1975; AS, Gupton-Jones Coll., 1992, No. Maine Tech. Coll., 1996; postgrad., St. Joseph's Coll., Windham, Maine, 2000—. RN; cert. in elem. and adult edn. scis., Maine; mortician. Personal life underwriter Home Ins. Co., N.Y.C., 1979-82; with L.L. Bean, Freeport, Maine, 1988-90; tchr. biology Caribou (Maine) Adult Edn., 1994-96; owner Alan's Dau.'s Place, 1988—, Angel Quilts, 1996—; spkr. in field. Author, editor Coffee Break, 1963-64. Ofcl. spinner Fla. State Fair, Tampa, 1984-85; spinner East Animal Farm/Westshore Mall, Tampa, 1984-85; guest spinner Town of Westfield (Maine) Jubilee Days, 1995; hospice vol. Vis. Nurses of Aroostook County, Caribou, 1995—. Billerica, Mass. O.E.S. scholar, 1975, Am. Bd. Funeral Svc. Edn. scholar, 1992, Caribou Adult Edn. Sys. scholar, 1995. Mem. Phi Theta Kappa, Pi Sigma Eta. Roman Catholic. Avocations: wool spinning, commission quilting, tutoring, weaving, amateur radio W4EFM. Home: PO Box 3314 Portland ME 04104-3314 Office: Caribou Adult Edn Ctr Sweden St Caribou ME 04736

SWANSON, THOMAS RICHARD, manufacturing, supply chain and systems executive; b. St. Paul, June 4, 1954; s. John Richard and Lorraine Ann (Meline) S.; m. Carol Ann Kraemer, June 26, 1976; children: Brian, Christopher. BS in Mech. Engring., U. Minn., 1976. Engring. positions 3M Co., St. Paul, 1976-79, supr. positions, 1979-81, office supr., 1981-84, materials control mgr., 1984-92, mfg. systems mgr., 1992-99; ptnr. T.R.S. Enterprises, Shoreview, Minn., 1981-84; pres. T.R.S. Enterprises, Forest Lake, Minn., 1984—, CEO, 1990-91; CFO MTR Holdings Ltd., St. Paul, 1990—; speaker-cons. Council of Logistics Mgmt., Oak Brook, Ill., 1985, Minn. Soc. Packaging and Handling, Mpls., 1985, Material Handling Inst., Pitts., 1984—, Am. Prod. and Inventory Control Soc., Oaks Church, Va., 1987—; pres. MTR Holdings, Ltd., 1989—; corp. cons., 1992—. Contbr. articles to profl. jours. Mem. Coun. Logistics Mgmt., Minn. Snowmobilers Assn., Am. Power Boat Assn. (chair region 8), Twin City Power Boat Assn. (bd. dirs.), Deep South Racing Assn. Republican. Methodist. Avocations: boating, fishing, snowmobiling. Home and Office: 4800 Centerville Rd North Oaks MN 55127-2202

SWANSON, WALLACE MARTIN, lawyer; b. Fergus Falls, Minn., Aug. 22, 1941; s. Marvin Walter and Mary Louise (Lindsey) S.; m. Susan Windsor Swanson; children: Kristen Lindsey, Eric Munger. B.A. with honors, U. Minn., 1962; LL.B. with honors, So. Methodist U., 1965. Bar: Tex. 1965. Since practiced in Dallas; assoc. Coke & Coke, Dallas, 1965-70; ptnr. firm Johnson & Swanson, Dallas, 1970-88; prin. Wallace M. Swanson, P.C., Dallas, 1988—; chmn., CEO Ace Cash Express Inc., Irving, Tex., 1987-88, State St. Capital Corp., 1990—. Served with USNR, 1960-65. Mem. Tex. Bar Found., State Bar Tex. (securities com. 1972-86, chmn. 1978-80, coun. bus. law sect. 1980-86), Crescent Club. Methodist. Address: 6234 Fm 879 Enuis TX 75119

SWART, LYNDSEY, occupational therapist; b. Boksburg, Transvaal, South Africa, July 23, 1963; d. Raymond Peter and Gwendolen Ruth (Harvey) Banks; m. Nicolaas Jacob Swart, Oct. 8, 1988; 1 child, Stephen James. BSc in Occupl. Therapy, U. Witwatersrand, Johannesburg, South Africa, 1985; MSc in Occupl. Therapy, U. Orange Free State, Bloemfontein, South Africa, 1995; postgrad. diploma in vocat. rehab., U. Pretoria, South Africa, 1998; cert. in advanced labor law, U. South Africa, Pretoria, 1999. Occupl. therapist State Hosp. Svcs., Vereeninging, South Africa, 1986-88, Bloemfontein, 1988-93; pvt. practice occupl. therapist Johannesburg, 1993—; cons. in field; external examiner U. Pretoria, 1997-98, 2000. Contbr. articles to profl. jours.; author, team leader Codes of Good Practice — Disability, 1999—, Technical Assistance Manual on Codes of Good Practice Disabilty, 1999—; contbg. author: Good Practice-Disability-Employment Equity Act, 1999—. Mem. Johannesburg Diocesan Guild of Servers Ch. of the Province of South Africa, 1998—; ch. counselor St. Peter's Anglican Ch., Gauteng, South Africa, 1999—. Grantee U.S. AID, 1999—. Mem. South African Soc. Vocat. Rehab. (vice chair 1997—). Anglican. Avocations: clay target shooting, golf, wildlife. Address: PO 2765, Krugersdorp 1740, South Africa Office: Mayo No 9 1st Fl, William Nicol St, Roodepoort South Africa

SWARTZ, CHRISTOPHER JOHN, musician, instrument designer and builder; b. El Paso, Tex., Dec. 25, 1951; s. Grant Leroy and Mildred Charlotte (Zass) S. AA, Trident Tech., 1980. Co-owner Perimeter Records, Atlanta, 1986-96, Outer Loop Prodns., Atlanta, 1996—; recorded numerous audio cassettes, 1983—; played numerous live concerts, 1970—; lectr. in field. Albums include ISO, 1986, Music for Home Built Instruments, 1987, 11 X 2, 1988; video cassettes include Solo/Live at Klang, 1991, The Music of Stockhausen, 1993; author: Percussion, String and Wind Instruments, 1990. Office: Outer Loop Prodns PO Box 451376 Atlanta GA 31145-9376

SWARTZ, JAMES D., education educator; b. Akron, Ohio, Aug. 13, 1944; s. oscar Tower and Laura Ann S.; m. Dorothy, Sept. 8, 1978. BA, Kent State U., 1967; MA, Ohio State U., 1982, PhD, 1989. Dir. media edn. svcs. Marion (Ohio) Tech. Coll., 1982-84, sociology instrn., 1982-84; prof. U. Ark., Fayetteville, 1991—; adj. asst. prof. Ohio State U., Columbus, 1984-89. Lt. USN, 1967-84. Mem. Am. Edn. Rsch. Assn. (chair spl. interest group for media curriculum culture 1999), Am. Film Inst., Assn. for Edn. Comms. and Technology, Soc. for Philosophy Higher Edn. (sec./treas. 1997-98), Phi Kappa Phi.

SWARTZLANDER, EARL EUGENE, JR., engineering educator, former electronics company executive; b. San Antonio, Feb. 1, 1945; s. Earl Eugene and Jane (Nicholas) S.; m. Joan Vickery, June 9, 1968. BSEE, Purdue U., 1967; MSEE, U. Colo., 1969; PhD, U. So. Calif., 1972. Registered profl. engr., Ala., Calif., Colo., Tex. Devel. engr. Ball Bros. Rsch. Corp., Boulder, Colo., 1967-69; Hughes fellow, mem. tech. staff Hughes Aircraft Co., Culver City, Calif., 1969-73; mem. rsch. staff Tech. Svc. Co., Santa Monica, Calif., 1973-74; chief engr. Geophys. Systems Corp., Pasadena, Calif., 1974-75, staff engr. to sr. staff engr., 1975-79, project mgr., 1979-84, lab. mgr., 1985-87; dir. ind. R&D TRW Inc., Redondo Beach, Calif., 1987-90; Schlumberger Centennial prof. engring. dept. elec. and computer engring. U. Tex., Austin, 1990—; gen. chmn. Internat. Conf. Wafer Scale Integration, 1989, Internat. Conf. Application Specific Array Processors, 1990, 94, 11th Internat. Symposium on Computer Arithmetic, 1992, 31st Ann. Asilomar Conf. on Signals, Sys., and Computers, 1997, others; chmn. 3d Internat. Conf. Parallel and Distributed Sys., Taiwan, 1993. Author: VLSI Signal Processing Systems, 1986; editor: Computer Design Development, 1976, Systolic Signal Processing Systems, 1987, Wafer Scale Integration, 1989, Computer Arithmetic Vol. 1 and 2, 1990, Application Specific Processors, 1996; editor-in-chief Jour. of VLSI Signal Processing, 1989-95, IEEE Transactions on Computers, 1991-94, IEEE Transactions on Signal Processing, 1995; editor: IEEE Transactions on Computers, 1982-86, IEEE Transactions on Parallel and Distributed Systems, 1989-90; hardware area editor ACM Computing Revs., 1985—; assoc. editor: IEEE Jour. Solid-State Circuits, 1984-88; contbr. more than 200 articles to profl. jours. and tech. conf. procs. Bd. dirs. Casiano Estates Homeowners Assn., Bel Air, Calif., 1976-78, pres., 1978-80; bd. dirs. Benedict Hills Estates Homeowners Assn., Beverly Hills, Calif., 1984—, pres., 1990-95. Recipient Disting. Engring. Alumnus award Purdue U., 1989, U. Colo., 1997, Outstanding Elec. Engr. award Purdue U., 1992, knight Imperial Russian Order St. John of Jerusalem (Knights of Malta), 1993. Fellow IEEE; mem. IEEE Computer Soc. (bd. govs. 1987-91, Golden Core mem. 1996), IEEE Signal Proc. Soc. (bd. govs. 1992-94), IEEE Solid-State Cirs. Coun. (sec. 1992-93, treas. 1994-97), Eta Kappa Nu, Sigma Tau, Omicron Delta Kappa. Office: U Tex Austin Dept Elec Computer Engring Austin TX 78712

SWASH, MICHAEL, neurologist, educator; b. Woodford, Essex, U.K., Jan. 29, 1939; s. Edwin Frank and Kathleen (Burton) S.; m. Caroline Mary Payne, Jan. 12, 1966; children: Jesse Edward, Thomas Henry, Edmond Joseph. MB BS, London U., 1962, MD, 1973. Neurology resident U. Hosp., Cleve., Case Western Res. U., Cleve., 1965-67; fellow neurophysiology Washington U. Sch. Medicine, St. Louis, 1967-68; registrar, MRC rsch. fellow, sr. registrar London Hosp., 1968-72; cons. neurologist Royal London Hosp., 1972—; med. dir. Royal London Nat. Health Svc. Trust, 1990-94; sr. lectr. in neuropathology London Hosp. Med. Coll., 1976-95; prof. neurology St. Bartholomew's and Royal London Sch. Medicine & Dentistry; CMO Swiss Re Life and Health, 1984—; adj. neurologist Cleve. Clinic Found., 1985-99. Author: Clinical Neurology, 1991, Muscle Biopsy Pathology, 2d edit., 1992, Neuromuscular Disorders, 3d edit., 1997, Hutchison's Clinical Methods, 21st edit., 2000, others. Fellow Royal Coll. Physicians, Royal Coll. Pathologists; mem. Am. Neurolog. Assn., Athenaeum Club, London Rowing Club, other. Avocations: rowing, music, opera, country life, art. Fax: 44 181 299 6395. E-mail: mswash@btinternet.com. Office: Royal London Hosp, London E1 1BB, England also: London Ind Hosp, London E1 4NL, England

SWEDBERG, KARL BIRGER, cardiologist, scientist; b. Solna, Sweden, Sept. 28, 1944; s. Birger and Eivor (Carlsson) S.; m. Ingela Thylén, June 27, 1966; children: Benjamin, Lisa. MD, Umeå (Sweden) U., 1970; PhD, Gothenburg (Sweden) U., 1978, assoc. prof., 1980. Intern County Hosp., Halmstad, 1971-74; fellow in cardiology Sahlgren's Hosp., Gothenburg, 1974-79; head cardiology dept. Ostra U. Hosp., Gothenburg, 1985-93, chief medicine, 1994-99, area mgr., 1995-96, staff physician, 1979—, assoc. prof., 1980-99, prof. medicine, 1999—; vis. assoc. prof. U. Calif., San Francisco, 1981-82. Contbr. chpts to med. textbooks; contbr. articles to various profl. jours. Fellow European Soc. Cardiology (chmn. working group on heart failure); mem. Am. Heart Assn., Am. Coll. Cardiology, Swedish Soc. Cardiology (pres. 1991-93), Chilean Soc. Cardiology (hon.). Avocations: golf, downhill skiing. Office: Sahlgrenska U Hosp/Ostr, Dept Medicine, S-41685 Göteborg Sweden

SWEDENBURG, ERIC, lawyer; b. Apr. 15, 1971. BS, U. Va., 1993; JD, Cornell U., 1999. CPA, Va.; Bar: N.Y. Sr. acct. PriceWaterhouse, Washington, 1993-96; assoc. Simpson, Thacher & Bartlett, N.Y.C., 1999—. Mem. Atty./CPA Found. (scholarship recipient 1998-99), Order of Coif. Office: Simpson Thacher & Bartlett 425 Lexington Ave New York NY 10017-3903

SWEENEY, BONNY E., lawyer; b. Wenatchee, Wash., May 17, 1959; d. James K. and Violet G. Sweeney; m. David O. Brink; children: Benjamin Brink Sweeney, Samuel Sweeney Brink. BA, Whittier Coll., 1981; MA, Cornell U., 1985; JD summa cum laude, Case Western Res. U., 1988. Bar: Mass. 1988, Calif. 1995, U.S. Dist. Ct. (no. dist., so. dist., ea. dist., ctrl. dist.), U.S. Ct. Appeals (10th cir.). Assoc. Foley, Hoag & Elliot, Boston, 1988-94; assoc. Milberg Weis Bershad et al., San Diego, 1996-99, ptnr., 1999—. Mem. ABA. Office: Milberg Weiss Bershad et al 600 W Broadway Fl 18 San Diego CA 92101-3311

SWEENEY, GEORGE BERNARD, petrochemical industry executive, investor, broadcast executive, travel agency executive; b. Cleve., May 9, 1933; s. George Bernard and Ethel E. (Wise) S.; m. Molly Jane O'Neill, July 13, 1963; children: Brian, Kelly, Mark, Kevin, Kim. BSBA, John Carroll U., 1955; MBA, U. Pa., 1957; DHL (hon.), John Carroll U., 2000. With Exxon Corp., 1956-78; chmn., pres. Esso Pakistan Fertilizer Co., Karachi, 1969-74; v.p. Exxon Corp. and Exxon Chem. U.S.A., Houston, 1974-78; dir., prin., exec. v.p. Chagrin Valley Co. Ltd., Cleve., 1977-83; dir. Nevamar Corp., Odenton, Md.; pres., prin. Questers, Inc., Houston, 1979-86; pres., prin. Stas. KMUV/KPHD/KSSO, Conroe, Tex., 1984-89, Sweeney Broadcasting Co., 1984-89, Travel Network, Sweeney Travel Quest, Inc., 1987-93. Bd. dirs., v.p., bd. advs. Houston Symphony, 1976—; trustee John Carroll U., Cleve., 1977—, Strake Jesuit Coll. Prep., Houston, 1979-85; trustee, chmn. bd. Trinity Coll., Washington, 1974-80; exec. bd. Wharton Grad. Sch., U. Pa., 1980-85; trustee, bd. dirs., exec. com. U. St. Thomas, Houston, 1982-88; mem. parents com. U. Va., Charlottesville, 1984-91; bd. dirs. Tex. Hunter-Jumper Assn., 1981-87, U. Miami (Fla.) Ctr. for Family Studies, 1999—; dir., v.p. Houston Hunter Jumper Charity Horse Show, 1983-88; founding trustee, bd. dirs. Franciscan Mission Svc., Silver Springs, Md., 1987-91, mem. audit com.; mem. nat. bd. dirs. U.S. Equestrian Team, Gladstone, N.J., 1989-94; bd. dirs. Ctr. for Family Studies of U. Miami, 1999—. Served to 1st lt. Transp. Corps., U.S. Army, 1958. Recipient in Pakistan U.S. State Dept. citation of appreciation, 1974, John Carroll U. Centennial medal, 1986, Sullivan award John Carroll U., 1980, 85, 90, 95, 2000, Alumni Svc. award, 1995, Bus. Sch. 50 Finest award, 1995, Silver Quill award, 1999. Mem. Houston Club, Palm Beach Polo and Country Club, Houston Oaks Golf Club, Ancient Order of Hibernians. Home: 24112 Macedonia Rd Hockley TX 77447-6010 also: 12563 Mallet Cir Wellington FL 33414-8408

SWEENEY, JOHN FRANCIS, lawyer; b. Washington, Nov. 26, 1946; s. Albert Eugene and Mildred (Mattimore) S.; m. Noreen Marie Castelli, Aug. 9, 1969; children—Matthew John, Laura Marie. B.S. in Math., Carnegie-Mellon U., 1968; J.D., Georgetown U., 1973. Bar: N.Y. 1974, U.S. Supreme Ct. 1980, U.C. Ct. Appeals (Fed. cir.) 1982, U.S. Ct. Appeals (2d cir.) 1975, U.S. Ct. Appeals (3d cir.) 1981, U.S. Dist. Ct. (so. dist.) N.Y. 1975, U.S. Dist. Ct. (ea. dist.) N.Y. 1984. Mathematician, U.S. Army Strategy and Tactics Analysis Group, Bethesda, Md., 1968-70; computer analyst U.S. Army Computer Systems Support and Evaln Command, Arlington, Va., 1970-73; assoc. Morgan & Finnegan and predecessor firm Morgan Finnegan Pine Foley & Lee, N.Y.C., 1973-81, ptnr., 1981—, mem. exec. com. 1983—. Author: (poems) Rhymes, 1984. Mem. ABA Assn. of Bar of City of N.Y. (mem. patent com. 1983—), N.Y. Patent, Trademark and Copyright Law Assn.,. Democrat. Roman Catholic. Club: Head of the Bay (Huntington Bay, N.Y.). Home: Tulipwood Lloyd Ln Lloyd Neck NY 11743 Office: Morgan & Finnegan 345 Park Ave Fl 22 New York NY 10154-0053*

SWEENEY, LUCY GRAHAM, psychologist; b. Davenport, Iowa, Nov. 14, 1946; d. B. Graham and Dorothy (Lawson) S.; m. Richard N. Tiedemann, Dec. 2, 1978 (div. 1989); 1 child, Susan Lee; m. Rogers Stolen, June 28, 1997. AA, William Woods Coll., 1966; BA with honors, U. Denver, 1968; MA in Devel. Psychology, Columbia U., 1977; PsyD, Rutgers U., 1990. Cert. family therapist. Profl. actress, 1968-73; dir. therapeutic play and recreation program St. Luke's Med. Ctr., N.Y.C., 1973-78; child life coord. St. Francis Hosp., Hartford, Conn., 1978-80; clinician Resolve Community Counseling Ctr., Scotch Plains, N.J., 1981-84; staff psychologist women's inpatient unit Lyons (N.J.) VA Med. Ctr., 1990; psychologist women's treatment program Fair Oaks Hosp., Summit, N.J., 1990-92; cons. Kessler Inst. for Rehab., East Orange, N.J., 1992-94, Resolve Community Counseling Ctr., Scotch Plains, N.J., 1992—; pvt. practice Westfield, N.J., 1993-99, Blacksburg, Va., 1999—. Contbr. articles to profl. jours. Recipient John Weyandt award for Outstanding Student in Theatre U. Denver, 1968. Mem. APA, Va. Psychol. Assn. Home: 704 Cedarview Dr Blacksburg VA 24060-5906

SWEENEY, PATRICE ELLEN, health administration executive; b. Denver, Sept. 19, 1953; d. Floyd L. and Martha Lou (Ray) S.; m. Steven Michael Wilk, June 25, 1977; children: Adam, Kristen, Ryan. AB, Princeton U., 1975; MHA, Duke U., 1977. Adminstrn. resident U. Hosp. Jacksonville, Fla., 1977-78; fellow Am. Hosp. Assn., Blue Cross Blue Shield, Chgo., 1978-79; from dir. corp. svcs. to sr. corp. planner Md. Health Care System, Balt., 1979-82; spl. asst. to pres. Am. Hosp. Assn., Chgo., 1982-85; from dir. hosp. rels. to asst. v.p. hosp. rels. Premier Hosps. Alliance, Westchester, Ill., 1985-89, v.p. hosp. rels., 1989-95; v.p., owner, affiliate svcs. Premier, Inc., Westchester, 1996-99, sr. v.p. relationship mgmt., 1999—. Contbr. articles to profl. jours. NCAA wrestling announcer Princeton (N.J.) U., 1975, 81; nursing home visitor Manor Care, Balt., 1980-81; head room mother Lane Sch., Hinsdale, Ill., 1990-98; Sunday Sch. tchr. Union Ch., Hinsdale, 1992-96; bd. dirs. Rape Crisis Ctr., Balt., 1980-82. Population Inst. fellow, 1976-77; King Edward's Hosp. Fund fellow, 1977. Avocations: gardening, piano, cooking, needlework. Office: Premier Inc 700 Commerce Dr Oak Brook Mall IL 60521

SWEENEY, RICHARD JAMES, economics educator; b. San Diego, Jan. 13, 1944; s. John Joseph and Catherine Scott (Spahr) S.; m. Joan Long, June 19, 1965; children: Robin Scott, Erin Michaela. BA, UCLA, 1965; PhD, Princeton U., 1972. Acting asst. prof. econs. UCLA, 1968-71; asst. prof. Tex. A&M U., College Station, 1971-73; dep. dir. office of internat. monetary research U.S. Dept. Treasury, Washington, 1973-77; Charles M. Stone prof. econs. and fin. Claremont (Calif.) McKenna Coll., 1977-89, chmn. dept. econs., 1987-89; Bolton Sullivan & Thomas A. Dean chair internat. fin. Georgetown U., Washington, 1989—; vis. assoc. prof. econs. U. Va., Charlottesville, 1975; vis. prof. bus. adminstrn. Dartmouth Coll., Hanover, N.H., 1979; vis. prof. fin. Gothenburg (Sweden) Sch. Econs., 1991—. Author: A Macro Theory with Micro Foundations, 1974, Principles of Microeconomics, Macroeconomics, 1980, Wealth Effects and Monetary Theory, 1988, Profit-Making Speculation in Foreign Exchange Markets, 1992; author, editor: Capital Control in Emerging Market Economies, 1997, Exchange-Rate Policies for Emerging Market Economies, 1999; contbr. articles to profl. jours. Fellow NSF 1966-68, Woodrow Wilson Found. 1965; grantee Gen. Electric Found., 1980, Mid.-Am. Found., 1987, Earhart Found., 1988. Mem. Western Econ. Assn. (editor Econ. Inquiry jour. 1984-96), Am. Econ. Assn., Am. Fin. Assn., Western Fin. Assn., Phi Beta Kappa. Democrat. Avocations: writing, weightlifting, walking, aerobics. Office: McDonough Sch Bus Georgetown U Washington DC 20057-0001

SWEENEY, RONALD TERENCE, marketing and media professional; b. Hull, Yorkshire, Eng., Sept. 1, 1932; s. Harold Sweeney and Doris Taylor; m. Amy Holmes, May 23, 1959; 1 child, Alison Jane. Diplomate in archtl. studies, Hull Coll. (now U. Humberside); Postgrad. diploma in Race Rels., U. Bradford, Eng., 1987, postgrad. in Arts, 1996—. Mktg. and pub. rels. exec. Nevin D. Hirst Ltd., Leeds and London, Eng., 1955-61; sr. exec. Farmer-Herbert Mktg., Eng., 1961-68; dir. Rowlinson-Broughton, Manchester and London, Eng. and Europe, 1968-72; feature writer Thomson Newspapers, Manchester and London, Eng., 1972-80; editor, head mktg. Bradford and Ilkley Coll., Eng. and overseas, 1980-97; mng. dir. Internat. Travel Conf., Newsline, Burley-in-Wharfedale, Ilkley, U.K., 1993; sr. lectr. Park Lane Coll., Leeds, Leeds Poly., 1962-71; sr. mgr. Bradford & Ilkley Coll., U. Bradford, 1981—; cons. Ministry Nat. Edn., Warsaw, 1994-95, computer divsn. U. Warsaw, 1994-95; mem. various ednl. orgns. Ctrl. and Eastern Europe; spkr., lectr. various univs., Eng.; cons. ednl. confs., 1992—, internat. travel confs., 1993—; Cambridge rep. found. studies tng. for learning and serving United Reformed Ch./Scottish Chs. Open Coll., 1998—. Founding editor: (newspaper) Education and Training News, 1985— (Higher Edn. Info. Svcs. Trust award 1990, 91, 92, Award of Merit Communicators in Bus. 1994, 95); editor: Adult Education Programme, 1980—. elder Uniformed Ch., Yorkshire, 1983—; founder, chmn. Good Neighbor Sch., 1968-80; chmn. Windmill Mental Health Trust, Eng., 1981—; vice-chmn. Lord Mayor of Bradford's Appeal com., chmn. Christian outreach Scheme. With Brit. Air Force, 1951-54. Ednl. grantee Brit. Govt., European Union. Mem. Brit. Communicators in Bus., Nat. Union Journalists, Internat. Fedn. Journalists, European Fedn. Journalists. Avocations: cycling, swimming, drama, travel, reading. Home: Tirconnell, 11 Endor Crescent, Burley-in-Wharfedale Ilkley LS29 7QH, England

SWEENEY, ROSEMARIE, medical association administrator; b. Fall River, Mass., Sept. 2, 1950; d. John Francis and Phyllis (Field) S.; m. Edmund Burke Rice, Feb. 24, 1978; 1 child, Jonathan Field Rice. Student, Hillsdale Coll., 1968-69; BA, Am. U., 1972, MPA, 1978. Profl. staff mem. Office of Rep. Margaret Heckler, Washington, 1972-74; staff assoc. fed. agy. affairs Am. Osteo. Assn., Washington, 1974-78, govt. affairs rep., 1978-79; dir. Washington office Am. Acad. Family Physicians, Washington, 1979-82; v.p. socioeconomic affairs and policy analysis, 1992—; mem. family practice adv. com. George Washington U., Washington, 1990-96. Vol. Montgomery County Sexual Assault Svc., Rockville, Md., 1984-93; mem. Glen Echo Fire Dept., Bethesda, Md., 1986-92, Victim Svcs. Adv. Bd., Md., 1987-93; chmn. victim svc. adv. bd. Montgomery County, Md., 1991-93; bd. dirs. Westmoreland Children's Ctr., Bethesda; treas. Washington Episcopal Sch. Parent Assn., 1999—; mem. adv. bd. Capital Area Rural Roundtable; bd. trustees Washington Episcopal Sch., 2000-03. Recipient Outstanding Svc. award Montgomery County Crisis Ctr., Md., 1986, Outstanding Performance award Montgomery County Sexual Assault Svc., Md., 1987, Recognition award Soc. Tchrs. Family Medicine, Kansas City, Mo., 1990, Govs.' Sixth Annual Victim Assistance award, Balt., 1991. Mem. Women in Govt. Rels., Am. Soc. Assoc. Execs. Avocations: running, volunteer work, reading. Office: Am Acad Family Physicians 2021 Massachusetts Ave NW Washington DC 20036-1011

SWEENY, CHARLES DAVID, chemist; b. May 22, 1936; s. Charles A. and Ruth (Beale) S.; m. Barbara K. Scheid, Feb. 12, 1977. BS, Pa. State U., 1960; PhD, Calif. Coast U., 1990. Technician Alcoa Rsch. Labs., New Kensington, Pa., 1954-58; spectroscopist Am. Color & Chem. Corp., Lock Haven, Pa., 1963-66, supr. analyt. labs., 1966-78; mgr. quality control Am.

Color and Chem., 1978-81; pres. CDS Labs., Inc., 1982—. Contbr. articles to profl. jours.; patentee effluent treatment. Scoutmaster W. Branch coun. Boy Scouts Am., 1966-76, counselor, 1976—, chmn. adminstrv. bd., 1975—; mem. emergency planning com., econ. devel. Clinton County Planning Commn. With AUS, 1960-63. Fellow Am. Inst. Chemists; mem. Am. Chem. Soc., Inter Soc. Color Coun. (chmn. strength of colorants-dyes com. 1975-78), Am. Assn. Textile Chemists and Colorists (chmn. weathering com. 1978-81, chmn. color measurement com. 1984-87), Pa. State U. Sci. Alumni Assn. (pres. bd. dirs. 1985-95). United Methodist. Office: Mt Vernon St Lock Haven PA 17745

SWEENY, DONNA BOZZELLA, writer, editor; b. Bklyn., Apr. 11, 1945; d. Joseph and Kaarin (Pajula) Bozzella; m. H.W. Allen Sweeny, Jan. 2, 1981; stepchildren: Peter, Christine, Catherine, David. BA, St. John's U., 1966; MBA, Fordham U., 1982; postgrad., CUNY, 1982-84. Employment interviewer, divsn. employment N.Y. State Dept. Labor, Bklyn., 1967-72; travel coord. Am. Jewish Com., 1974-75; adminstrv. asst. to pres. Bell & Howell Edn. Group, Evanston, Ill., 1976-78; legal coord. Internat. Std. Brands (later Nabisco Brands), N.Y.C., 1978-80; dir. tng. and adminstrn. Arthur Andersen, Tokyo, 1984-86; freelance writer and editor 1986—. Cooking columnist Tokyo Weekender, 1986-90; staff writer Coconut Grove Times, 1997—, Brickell Post, 1997—, South Miami Times, 1999—; publicity writer Streets of Mayfair Mall, 1997-99; editor Voice of the Grove, 1994-97; assoc. editor: Coconut Grove Mag., 1998—. Pres. Coconut Grove (Fla.) Federated Rep. Women's Club, 1992-93; mem. exec. com. Ambs. of Mercy Hosp., Miami, Fla., 1993—; trustee Miami Mus. Sci., 1994, mem. adv. bd., 1995; mem. adv. coun. La Salle H.S., Miami, 1996-98; committeewoman dist. 20 Dade County Rep. Exec. Com., 1997-98; mem. spl. events com. Coconut Grove Playhouse, 1998-99; bd. dirs. Coconut Arts Festival, 1999—. Mem. Coconut Grove C. of C. (bd. dirs. 1997-2000, Coconut Club award 1997). Roman Catholic. Avocations: photography, ikebana, collecting political memorabilia, cooking. Home: 2000 S Bayshore Dr Coconut Grove FL 33133-3256

SWEET, CYNTHIA KAY, business administrator; b. Highland, Kans., Feb. 21, 1949; d. Jack Wendull and Ruthanna (Dittemore) Hedrick; m. Roger Keith Alexander, 1968; children: Karen Joyce, Melinda Ruth Anne; m. Erich Christian Sweet, Oct. 31, 1990. Student, U. Kans., 1968, North Peralta Coll., 1973-74, U. Colo., 1976-79; BS in Bus. Tech., Empire State Coll., 1984. Computer operator Computer Ctr. U. Colo., Boulder, 1977-79; subscription coord. Inst. Arctic & Alpine Rsch., Boulder, 1979; computer operator Computer Ctr. Rensselaer Poly. Inst., Troy, N.Y., 1979-80, dir. devel. info. svcs., 1982-85; rsch. analyst N.Y. State Mus., Albany, 1979-80, project mgr., 1980-82; product mgr. Info. Assocs., Rochester, N.Y., 1985-89, sr. program mgr., 1990-92; applications mgr. Claris Corp., Santa Clara, Calif., 1989-90; custom programming mgr. Datatel, Fairfax, Va., 1992-94; exec. dir. advancement solutions TRG, Phoenix, 1994-96; dir. profl. svcs. USA Group Info. Solutions, Phoenix, 1996-97; v.p. InfoSolutions.edu, Phoenix, 1997-99; higher edn./pub. sector practice mgr. The Hunter Group, San Francisco, 1999—; freelance fundraising cons., Albany and Rochester, 1984-89. Contbr. articles to profl. jours. Activity coord. Info. Assocs./United Way, Rochester, 1985-89, 91-92; mem. festival staff meml. Art Gallery, Rochester, 1987-89; bd. dirs. Draper Dance Theatre, Rochester, 1988-92. Mem. NSFE, Coun. for Advancement and Support of Edn., Project Mgmt. Inst., Am. Mgmt. Assn. Avocations: camping, hiking, gardening, gourmet cooking, reading. Office: The Hunter Group 300 Montgomery St Ste 200 San Francisco CA 94104-1904

SWEET, HARVEY, theatrical set designer, lighting designer; b. Detroit, Oct. 27, 1943; s. Sam and Rose Sweet; m. Susan Perrett, Mar. 16, 1964 (div. Mar. 1975); children: Deborah Anne, Rebecca Lynn, Jason Aaron; m. Patricia Ravn, Sept. 9, 1978 (div. July 1987). BS, Ea. Mich. U., 1965; MS, U. Wis., 1967, PhD, 1974. Instr. U. N.D., Grand Forks, 1967-69; asst. prof. Boise (Idaho) State Coll., 1972-73; instr. U. Wis., Madison, 1973-74; prof. of theater arts U. No. Iowa, Cedar Falls, 1974-89; dir. lighting Landmark Entertainment Group, L.A. and Tokyo, 1989-91; cons. Advanced Tech., Tokyo, 1991; tech. writer Walt Disney Imagineering, Glendale, Calif., 1992; project mgr., sr. designer, sr. estimator, tech. writer Tru Roll, Inc., Glendale, Calif., 1993-99; project mgr. estimator tech. sales LVH Entertainment Sys., Oxnard, Calif., 1999—; owner, operator Sweet Studios Theatrical Equipment, Cedar Falls, 1981-89; dir. theater tech. and design U. No. Iowa, 1974-87. Author: Graphics for the Performing Arts, 1982, Handbook of Scenery, Properties and Lighting I and II, 1988, 2nd edit., 1995, The Complete Book of Drawing for the Theatre, 1995; scenic designer Summer Repretory Theatre, 1988, Timberlake Playhouse, 1988-89; lighting designer, scenic designer, tech. dir. various coll. theatrical prodns., 1964-89; themed lighting designer Sanrio Puroland, Tokyo, 1989, exec. dir. lighting, 1990. Mem. U.S. Inst. for Theatre Tech. (vice commr. 1979-81, commr. 1981-87, mem. graphic stds. bd. 1979-86, evaluation commn. 1983-88, mem. publs. com. 1986-89, bd. dirs. 1989). Avocations: tennis, cooking. Office: LVH Electric 1653 Pacific Ave Ste 311 Oxnard CA 93033-1875

SWEET, WILLIAM, education educator; b. Edmonton, Alberta, Can., Apr. 22, 1955; s. William Donald and Joyce Leila (Taylor) S. DEA, U. Sorbonne, Paris, 1987; PhD, U. Ottawa, Can., 1994; DPh, St. Paul U., Can., 1996. Lectr. U. Kaskatchewan, Saskatoon, Can., 1980-83, Coll. de l'Outaouais, Hull, Que., Can., 1983-85, U. Ottawa, 1983-85, 87-88, Carleton U., Ottawa, 1989-90; asst. prof. to prof. St. Francis Xavier U., Antigonish, Nova Scotia, 1990—; sec.-gen. World Union of Cath. Philos. Socs., Washington, 1998—. Author: (book) Idealism and Rights, 1997; editor: Collected Works of Bernard Bosanquet, 1999, The Bases of Ethics, 2000, God and Argument, 1999. Chair of senate. St. Francis Xavier U., Antigonish, 1995-96, chair of faculty of arts, 1998-2000; mem. St. Martha's Regional Hosp. Mission Assurance Adv. Coun., 1999—; mem. ethics com. Ea. Regional Health Bd., Nova Scotia, 1999—. Rsch. grantee Social Scis. and Humanities Rsch. Coun. of Can., 2000; Nimishakkavi K. Subbaiah Naidu Endowment lectr. U. Madras, India, 1999, Royal Inst. of Philosophy lectr. U. Wales, Cardiff, 1999. Mem. Can. Jacques Maritain Assn. (pres. 1999—), Can. Soc. for Study of Religion (mem. exec. and mem. sec. 1999), Can. Philos. Assn. (bd. dirs. 1997-99), Can. Soc. Christian Philosophers (v.p. 1996—), Am. Soc. Christian Philosophers (chair com. on outreach to Christian philosophers 1996—). Avocations: travel, mountain climbing, literature. Office: St Francis Xavier Univ, PO Box 5000, Nova Scotia, Canada B2G 2W5

SWEETING, LINDA MARIE, chemist; b. Toronto, Ont., Can., Dec. 11, 1941; came to U.S., 1965, naturalized, 1979; d. Stanley H. and Mary (Robertson) S. BSc, U. Toronto, 1964, MA, 1965; PhD, UCLA, 1969. Asst. prof. chemistry Occidental Coll., L.A., 1969-70; asst. prof. chemistry Towson (Md.) State U., 1970-75, assoc. prof., 1975-85, prof., 1985—; guest worker NIH, 1976-77; program dir. chem. instrumentation NSF, 1981-82; vis. scholar Harvard U., 1984-85; contractor U.S. Army MRICD, 1991-93; vis. lectr. Johns Hopkins U., 1999—. Bd. dirs. Chamber Music Soc. Balt., 1985-91. Exec. com. Exptl. NMR. Conf. 1985-87, local arr. chair 1986. Mem. Md. Acad. Scis. (mem. sci. council 1975-83, 89-94), Assn. for Women in Sci. (treas. 1977-78, Woman of Yr. 1989), Am. Chem. Soc. (mem. women chemists Com. 1983-89), AAAS, Nature Conservancy, Sierra Club, Phi Lambda Upsilon, Sigma Xi (sec. TSU Club 1979-81, Towson chpt. pres. 1987-88, 91-92, 98-99, sec. 1995-98, mid-Atlantic nominating com. 1987-90, regional dir. 1988-89, nat. nominating com. 1991-94), Assn. for Practical and Profl. Ethics. Office: Towson U Dept Chemistry Baltimore MD 21252-0001

SWEETING, MARTIN NICHOLAS, electrical engineer; b. London, Mar. 12, 1951; s. Frank Morris and Dorothy May (Skelton) S.; m. Christine Ruth Taplin, Sept. 27, 1974. BSc with honors, U. Surrey, Eng., 1973, PhD, 1980. Chartered engr., Eng. With Marconi Space & Def. Systems, London, 1971-72, U. Surrey/MEL Ltd., 1974-79; rsch. fellow U. Surrey, 1979-84, lectr., 1984-90, sr. lectr. to prof., 1990—; tech. dir. Surrey Satellite Tech., Ltd., Guildford, 1985-90, CEO, 1990—; mem. Brit. Nat. Space Ctr., Space Tech. Adv. Bd., London, 1989-99. Contbr. numerous articles to profl. jours. Marconi Premium, IERE, 1987; recipient G. Pardoe Space award, RAES, 1990, Royal Acad. Engring. Silver medal, 1995, U.K. Engring. Coun. Gold medal. 1998; named Officer of the Order of the Brit. Empire, 1995. Fellow Royal Acad. Engring., Inst. Elec. Engrs. (U.K.), IEEE, AIAA, Brit. Interplanetary Soc. (U.K.), Royal Soc.; mem. Internat. Acad. Astronautics, Internat. Acad. Astronauts. Achievements include pioneering development of low cost microsatellites. Fax: 44 0 1483 259503. E-mail: m.sweeting@ee.surrey.ac.uk. Office: Surrey Space Ctr, Univ Surrey, Guildford Surrey England GU2 5XH

SWEIS MUSSA, RAFIQ, consular general, activist; b. Amman, Jordan, Aug. 8, 1946; came to U.S., 1971; s. Mussa Abdullah Sweis and Rida Ta'amneh; m. Rehab Bajes Shaktah, Jan. 1, 1974; children: Jeannette, Mirdad, Jackie, Violet. MS in Philosophy, U. Lateran, Vatican, Rome, 1967. Dir. fgn. affairs King Hussein, Amman, Jordon, 1967-71; mem. staff Gulf Oil Co., L.A., 1971-73, oil exec., 1973-74; pvt. practice Albuquerque, 1976-79, Chgo., 1979-84; pres. Fuheis Assn., Chgo., 1990-94; honorary consul Jordan, Amman, 1994-99; pres., editor-in-chief Fuheis Mag., Chgo., 1990-95. Editor-in-chief Fuheis Assn. Fuheis Mag., 1992-94. Democrat. Roman Catholic. Avocations: speak, read and write 5 languages. Office: Super-Fair Foods Inc 6319 S Vernon Ave Chicago IL 60637-3320

SWE-KHINE, MYINT, educational technology educator, consultant, resea; b. Rangoon, Burma, Mar. 27, 1945; s. Aung Khine and Khin Nu; m. Elizabeth Khin-San-Thwe; 1 child, Emily El Thinzar. MS in Edn., U. So. Calif., 1975; MS, U. Surrey, U.K., 1983; PhD, U. Sci., Malaysia, 1995; MBA, U. Leicester, U.K., 1997. Lectr. U. Sci., Malaysia, 1979-86; head Ednl. Tech. Ctr. U. Brunei Darussalam, 1986—. Office: Univ Brunei Darussalam, Ednl Tech Ctr, Bandar Seri Begawan 2028, Brunei

SWELLER, JOHN, educational psychology educator; b. Poland, Jan. 26, 1946; arrived in Australia, 1948; s. Bernard and Maria (Han) S.; m. Susan Sandor, Feb. 1, 1977; children: Naomi, Tamara. BA with honors, U. Adelaide, Australia, 1969, PhD, 1972. Lectr. Tasmanian Coll. Advanced Edn., Launceston, Australia, 1973; lectr. U. NSW, Sydney, 1974-78, sr. lectr., 1979-89, assoc. prof., 1990-91, prof., 1992—. Author: Instructional Design in Technical Areas, 1999; contbr. articles to profl. jours. Fellow Acad. of Social Scis. in Australia. Office: U NSW, Sch of Edn, 2052 Sydney Australia

SWENSON, KATHLEEN SUSAN, music and art educator; b. Reno, Nev., Oct. 23, 1938; d. Harold Ruthaford McNeil and Hollyce Margaret (Scruggs) McNeil Biggs; m. James Michael Phalan, 1956 (div. 1974); children: David Michael, Jeanine Louise Phalan Lawrence, Gregory Sean; m. Gerald Allen Swensen, Nov. 1976 (div. 1987); stepchildren: Craig Allen, Sarah Ann, Eric Sander. Student, U. Nev., Reno, 1956-58, Foothill Coll., 1966-68; AA, West Valley Coll.; BA, U. Calif., Santa Cruz, 1983. Concert pianist Nev.,Calif, 1950-64; pvt. piano instr. various locations, 1963—, pvt. art instr., 1970—, pvt. astrology instr., 1973—; founder, pres. AAM Triple Arts, Aptos, Calif., 1974—; founder, owner Aptos (Calif.) Acad. Music, 1991—. Producer, instr. art instrn. videos, music instrn. films, books. Mem. Soc Western Artists, Calif. Piano Tchrs. Assn., Los Gatos Art Assn. (pres. 1985-86), Saratoga Contemporary Artists (v.p. 1984-85), Nat. League Am. Pen Women (honorarian 1985), Soroptomists, Phi Beta Kappa. Republican. Episcopalian. Home and Office: Aptos Acad Music 3000 Wisteria Way Aptos CA 95003-3318

SWENSON, L. ANNE, publisher; b. Blue Island, Ill., Mar. 27, 1936; d. Eugene Martin and Golda Merle (Standard) S.; m. Douglas Hieber, Feb. 15, 1957 (div. May 1959); m. Warren Tunis Wognum, Nov. 25, 1965 (div. May 1997); children: Nicholas Evan Wognum, Sandra Anne Wognum. Student, Cornell Coll., Mt. Vernon, Iowa, 1954-56, U. Minn., 1964, Roosevelt U., 1964-65. Book buyer Maeyama's, Park Forest, Ill., 1960-63; pub./owner Milestones, Inc., Ely, Minn., 1977—; chmn. Donald G. Gardner Humanities Trust, Ely, 1995-00, design rev. com., City of Ely, 1993-94, Ely Greenstone Pub. Arts, 1998—. Editor: (book) Ely, Since 1888, 1988; pub. (weekly newspaper) The Ely Echo, 1977—; columnist/writer, 1976—. Com. chmn. Ely C. of C., 1994-96; bd. dirs. No. Lakes Arts Assn., Ely, 1995-2000, Voyageur Winter Festival, Ely/Winton Bicentennial Com., Ely, 1975-76; troop leader Girl Scouts, Rome, 1956-57. Mem. St. Louis Co. Hist. Soc., Ely/Winton Hist. Soc. Home: 2647 Van Vac Rd Ely MN 55731-8426 Office: Milestones Inc/Ely Echo 2 E Sheridan St Ely MN 55731-1257

SWENSON, RICHARD ALLEN, business owner, animal trainer; b. Willmar, Minn., Dec. 1, 1950; s. LeRoy Oswald Boe and Delores G. (Malghist) S.; children: Kristen, Richard Andrew, Kevin. Author: Secrets of Long Distance Sled Dog Racing. Treas. Pride, Alaska, 1993—. Recipient 1st pl. Iditarod, 1977, 79, 80, 81, 91 among others. Office: Denali Sled Dog Tours PO Box 86 Denali Park AK 99755-0086*

SWENSON, ULF, botany educator, researcher; b. Ljungby, Sweden, June 11, 1959; s. Göte and Ingrid (Karlsson) S. BSc, Uppsala (Sweden) U., 1991, Fil Lic, 1994, PhD in Systematic Botany, 1995; Docent, U. Lund, 1999. Rsch. assoc. Natural History Mus. Los Angeles County, L.A., 1996-99; rsch. assoc. dept. systematic botany Uppsala U., 1996-97, lectr. Biology Edn. Ctr., 1997-98; rsch. fellow Lund U., 1998-99; assoc. prof. Stockholm U., 1999—. Mem. Soc. Systematic Biologists, Swedish Bot. Soc. (bd. dirs. 1996—), Uppsala Bot. Assn. (bd. dirs. 1993—), Am. Soc. Plant Taxonomists, Willi Hennig Soc. Avocations: travel, botany, wine, hiking, snorkling. Home: Norrlandsgatan 36C, 75229 Uppsala Sweden Office: Stockholm U, Dept Botany, 10691 Stockholm Sweden

SWERDLOFF, MARK HARRIS, lawyer; b. Buffalo, Sept. 7, 1945; s. John and Joan (Harris) S.; m. Ileen Pollock, Dec. 24, 1967; 1 child, Jonathan Edward. BA, SUNY, Buffalo, 1967; JD, U. Conn., 1975. Bar: Conn. 1975, U.S. Dist. Ct. Conn. 1975, U.S. Ct. Appeals (2d cir.) 1983, U.S. Supreme Ct. 1985, Fla. 1977. Assoc. Wilson, Asbel & Channin, Hartford, Conn., 1975-78; ptnr. Swerdloff & Swerdloff, West Hartford, Conn., 1978—; pres. Arpus Enterprises, Old Saybrook Conn., 1993—; trial fact finder Superior Ct., Hartford, 1990—; arbitrator Dispute Resolution Inst., Hartford, 1990—. Mem. ABA, Conn. Bar Assn., Conn. Trial Lawyers Assn. Democrat. Jewish. Avocations: photography, travel, cooking. Home: 9 Beacon Heath Farmington CT 06032-1524 Office: Swerdloff & Swerdloff 61 S Main St West Hartford CT 06107-2486

SWETEL, LESTER F., mobile home park executive, wastewater consultant; b. Mt. Vernon, Ohio, Dec. 4, 1951; s. Frank and Helen Swetel; m. Lillian M. Varner, Sept. 14, 1974 (div. 1981). AA, Youngstown State U., 1992. Cert. Wastewater Class I. Svc. mgr. Don Casule, Inc., McDonald, Ohio, 1980-96; CEO Fowler (Ohio) Mobile Home Park, 1995—; wastewater ops. mgr. Dis Stull Inc., Newton Falls, Ohio, 1996-99; wastewater treatment operator Superior Mobile Homes, Dover, Ohio, 1999. Mem. Am. Water Works Assn., Nat. Soc. Profl. Engrs., Ohio Rural Water Assn., Ohio Housing Assn. Office: Fowler Mobile Home Park 2819 Sodom Hutchings Rd Fowler OH 44418-9745

SWETMAN, GLENN ROBERT, English language educator, poet; b. May 20, 1936; s. Glenn Lyle and June (Read) S.; m. Margarita Ortiz, Feb. 8, 1964 (div. 1979); children: Margarita June, Glenn Lyle Maximilian, Glenda Louise. BS, U. So. Miss., 1957, MA, 1959; PhD, Tulane U., 1966. Instr. U. So. Miss., 1957-58, asst. prof., 1964-66; instr. Ark. State U., 1958-59, McNeese U., 1959-61; instr. English Univ. Coll. Tulane U., 1961-64, spl. asst. dept. elec. engring., 1961-64; assoc. prof. La. Inst. Tech., 1966-67; prof., head dept. langs. Nicholls State Coll., Thibodaux, La., 1967-69, head dept. English, 1969-71, prof., 1971-91; prof. emeritus William Carey Coll., Gulfport, Miss., 1991—; writer in residence, prof. English William Carey Coll., Gulfport, 1991—; ptnr. Breeland Pl., Biloxi, 1960—; stringer, corr. Shreveport (La.) Times, 1966—; ptnr. Ormuba, Inc., 1975—; cons. tech. writing Union Carbide Corp., Am. Fedn. Tchrs. State v.p. Nat. Com. to Resist Attacks on Tenure, 1974—. Book reviewer Jackson (Miss.) State Times, 1961; contbr. poetry to various publs. including Poet, Prairie Schooner, Trace, Ball State U. Forum, Film Quar., Poetry Australia, numerous others worldwide; author: (books of poems) Tunel de Amor, 1973, Deka #1, 1973, Deka #2, 1979, Shards, 1979, Concerning Carpenters, 1980, Son of Igor, 1982, Poems of the Fantastic, 1990; contbr. numerous articles to encys.; cons. editor (poetry) Paon Press, 1974—, Scott-Foresman, 1975; mem. editl. bd. Scholar and Educator, 1980—. Subdivsn. coord. Rep. Party, Hattiesburg, Miss., 1964. With AUS, 1957. Recipient Poetry awards KQUE Haiku contest, 1964, Coll. Arts contest, L.A., 1966, Black Ship Festival, Yoqosuka, Japan, 1967, Green World Brief Forms award Green World Poetry Editors, 1965. Mem. MLA, S. Cen. MLA, So. Literary Festival Assn. (v.p. 1975-76, 82-83, pres. 1984-85), Coll. Writers Soc. La. (pres. 1971-72, exec. dir. 1983—), IEEE, Am. Assn. Engring. Edn., La. Poetry Soc. (pres. 1971-74, 86—), Internat. Boswellian Inst., Nat. Fedn. State Poetry Socs. (2d v.p., nat. membership chmn. 1972-74, pres. 1976-77), Nat. Soc. Scholars and Educators (bd. dirs. 1982—, sec. exec. bd. 1986—, sec. bd. dirs. 1968—, sec. soc. 1989—), Am. Fedn. Tchrs. (chpt. pres. 1973-78), Nat. Fedn. State Poetry Socs. (1st v.p. 1975-76, exec. bd. 1972—), Phi Eta Sigma, Omicron Delta Kappa. Home: PO Box 146 Biloxi MS 39533-0146 Office: William Carey Coll 1856 Beach Dr Gulfport MS 39507-1508

SWETNAM, DANIEL RICHARD, lawyer; b. Columbus, Ohio, Dec. 22, 1957; s. Joseph Neri and Audrey Marguerite (Mason) S.; m. Jeannette Deanna Dean, June 7, 1980; children: Jeremiah Daniel, Laura Janelle, Andrew Michael. BA, Ohio State U., 1979; JD, U. Cin., 1982. Bar: Ohio 1982, U.S. Dist. Ct. (so. dist.) Ohio 1982, U.S. Ct. Appeals (6th cir.) 1986, U.S. Supreme Ct. 1986. Assoc. Schwartz, Warren & Ramirez, Columbus, 1982-88, ptnr., 1989-96; prin. Schottenstein, Zox & Dunn, Columbus, 1997—. Deacon Grace Brethren Ch., Worthington, Ohio, 1989—; mem. Grace Brethren Christian Schs. Commn., 1993-98. Mem. ABA, Ohio State Bar Assn., Columbus Bar Assn., Comml. Law League Am., Order of Coif. Republican. Avocations: golf, tennis. Home: 2178 Stowmont Ct Dublin OH 43016-9563 Office: Schottenstein Zox & Dunn 41 S High St Columbus OH 43215-6101

SWIATEK, KAZIMIERZ CARDINAL, archbishop; b. Walga, Oct. 21, 1914. Archbishop archbishop of Minsk- Mohilew, Belarus; elevated to cardinal Roman Cath. Ch., 1994. Office: ul Szewczenki 12/1, 225710 Pinsk Belarus also: Pl Swobody 9, 220030 Minsk Belarus*

SWIBEL, STEVEN WARREN, lawyer; b. Chgo., July 18, 1946; s. Morris Howard and Gloria S.; m. Leslie S.; children: Deborah, Laura. BS, MIT, 1968; JD, Harvard U., 1971. Bar: Ill. 1971, U.S. Dist. Ct. (no. dist.) Ill. 1971, U.S. Tax Ct. 1973, U.S. Ct. Appeals (7th cir.) 1981. Assoc. Sonnenschein Carlin Nath & Rosenthal, Chgo., 1971-78, ptnr., 1978-84; ptnr. Rudnick & Wolfe, 1984-93, Schwartz, Cooper, Greenberger, Krauss Chartered, 1993—; adj. prof. taxation Ill. Inst. Tech. Kent Coll. Law, Chgo., 1989—; lectr. in field; contbr. articles to profl. jours. Ednl. counselor MIT, 1979—; bd. dirs. MIT Alumni Fund, 1992-95, Ragdale Found., 1987-00, treas, 1987-92; bd. dirs. Kids In Danger, 1998—. Recipient Lobdell Disting. Svc. award MIT Alumni Assn., 1989. Mem. ABA (com. partnerships sect. taxation), Ill. Bar Assn., Chgo. Bar Assn. (fed. taxation com., exec. subcom. 1984—, chmn. subcom. on real estate and partnerships 1986-87, vice chmn. 1988-89, chmn. 1990), Met. Club, MIT Club (dir. Chgo. chpt. 1980-91, 96—, sec. 1980-87, pres. 1987-89), Sigma Xi, Tau Beta Pi, Eta Kappa Nu. Office: Schwartz Cooper Greenberger & Krauss Chartered 180 N La Salle St Ste 2700 Chicago IL 60601-2757

SWIEGOT, ELMAR JOSEF, company executive; b. Wertheim, B.-W., Germany, Apr. 25, 1949; s. Josef Michael and Rosa Maria (Grein) S.; m. Gerlinde Maria Weis, Oct. 19, 1970; children: Mario, Marina. Diploma in econs., high sch., Heidelberg, Germany, 1975. Export mgr. Witeg Laborterchnik GmbH, Wertheim, 1975-82, head clk., sales mgr., 1982-95, gen. mgr., mng. dir., 1995—. Mem. Dechema. Mem. Christian-Dem. Union. Roman Catholic. Achievements include patents for liquid handling products. Avocations: painting, reading books, theater, tennis. Office: Witeg Labortechnik GmbH, 1m Bildacker 16, 97877 Wertheim Germany

SWIERŻ, JERZY WIKTOR, urologist, oncologist, consultant; b. Poznan, Poland, Nov. 5, 1954; s. Wiktor and Hermina Swierż; m. Halina Kasiak, May 19, 1982; 1 child, Angelika. MD, Med. Acad., Warsaw, 1981, Postgrad. Med. Acad., Warsaw, 1986; cert. in oncourology, European Sch. Oncology, Davos, Switzerland, 1994. Physician dept. radiotherapy Ctrl. Mil. Hosp., Warsaw, 1981, asst. dept. oncology, 1981-88, asst., cons. dept. urology, 1989—. Contbr. over 60 articles to med. jours., including Polish Urology. Mem. Polish Urol. Assn., Polish Oncological Assn., European Assn. Urology. Avocations: tennis, travel, swimming, volleyball. E-mail: jerzy.932572@pharmanet.com.pl. Office: Ctrl Mil Hosp Dept Urology, Szaserów 128, 00 909 Warsaw Poland

SWIFT, STEPHEN CHRISTOPHER, lawyer; b. N.Y.C., Jan. 7, 1954; s. James Stephen and Rhoda Emma Jean (Howd) S. AA, Lansing C.C., 1980; BA, Mich. State U., 1983; JD, Wayne State U., 1988. Bar: Mich. 1988, Hawaii 1989, D.C. 1991, Va. 1995, Md. 1998, U.S. Dist. Ct. D.C., , U.S. Dist. Ct. Md., U.S. Dist. Ct. (ea. and we. dists.) Va., U.S. Dist. Ct. Hawaii, U.S. Ct. Fed. Claims, U.S. Ct. Internat. Trade, U.S. Bankruptcy Ct. (ea. and we. dists.) Va., U.S. Tax Ct., U.S. Ct. Appeals (fed., D.C., 4th, 9th cirs.), U.S. Supreme Ct.; registered patent atty. Pvt. practice Honolulu, 1989-94, Arlington, Va., 1995—. Mem. ABA, Fed. Bar Assn., Fed. Cir. Bar Assn., Am. Intellectual Property Law Assn. Fax: 703-486-5757. E-mail: steve@swift-law.com. Office: Swift Law Office 2231 Crystal Dr Ste 500 Arlington VA 22202-3722

SWIG, ROSELYNE CHROMAN, community consultant; b. Chgo., June 8, 1930; m. Richard Swig, Feb. 5, 1950 (dec.); children—Richard, Jr., Susan, Marjorie, Carol. Student, U. Calif.-Berkeley, UCLA; MFA (hon.), San Francisco Art Inst., 1988, DHL (hon.), 1988. Founder, pres. Roselyne C. Swig Artsource, San Francisco, 1977-94; apptd. by Pres. Clinton as dir. Art in Embassies Program U.S. Dept. of State, 1994-97; founder, pres. Comcon Internat., 1998—; founder Ptnrs. Ending Domestic Abuse, San Francisco. Trustee San Francisco Mus. Modern Art, U. Art Mus., Berkeley, Calif.; ex officio bd. mem. Jewish Mus. San Francisco; bd. dirs., former treas. Am. Jewish Joint Distbn. Com.; vice chair fine art adv. panel Fed. Res., Washington; past trustee Mills Coll., Oakland, Calif.; past past pres., bd. dirs. Jewish Cmty. Fedn. San Francisco, the Peninsula, Marin and Sonoma Counties; past commr. San Francisco Pub. Libr.; past bd. dirs. San Francisco Opera, Am. Coun. for Arts, KQED Broadcasting Sys.; past. pres. Calif. State Summer Sch. Arts, past chair bd. trustees San Francisco Art Inst.; past pres. San Francisco Arts Commn.; past nat. v.p. Am./Israel Pub. Affairs Com.; past trustee United Jewish Appeal; past chair bd. trustees Univ. Art Mus. Mem. Women's Forum West (bd. dirs.), Internat. Women's Forum. Avocations: skiing, boating, tennis, fishing. *

SWIGER, MARK, social studies educator; b. Elkins, W.Va., Aug. 3, 1960; s. Arden Leo and Ethel Marie (Welch) S.; m. Dawn Schwertfeger, July 2, 1983; children: Amanda, Shane. BA in History, Bethany Coll., 1982; MA in Curriculum and Instrn., W.Va. U., 1993. Cert. tchr., W.Va. Social studies tchr. Cameron (W.Va.) H.S., 1982-97, cross country coach, 1983-90; social studies tchr. Moundsville (W.Va.) Jr. H.S., 1997—; track coach John Marshall H.S., Glen Dale, W.Va., 1985-92; cross country coach Wheeling (W.Va.) Jesuit U., 1990—, track & field coach, 1992—; mem. tech. com. Marshall County Schs., Moundsville, 1995-97. Mem. local sch. improvement coun. Cameron H.S., 1995-97; mem. accreditation team North Ctrl. Assn., Wheeling, 1991, 96; mem. rating com. Nat. Assn. Intercollegiate Athletics, 1993-95. Named Cross-Country Coach of Yr. men W.Va. Intercollegiate Athletic Conf., 1992, 93, women, 1993, 94, 94, Nat. Assn. Cross-Country Intercollegiate Athletic Conf., 1993, 94; Fulbright-Hayes study abroad fellow U.S. Dept. Edn., 1995; grantee IBM, 1998, 99, Local Unified Sch. Improvement Efforts, 1996-97, Lewis and Clark Rediscovery, 1999—. Mem. NEA, W.Va. Edn. Assn., Marshall County Edn. Assn., Nat. Geog. Soc., Nat. Coun. Social Studies, W.Va. Geog. Alliance, NCAA Coaches Assn., U.S. Track & Field Coaches Assn.

SWIHART, JAMES W., JR., diplomat; b. Washington, DC, July 25, 1946; s. James Wilbur and Ruth (Inge) S.; m. Ellen Jane Cendo Mar. 30, 1968; children: Jennifer Anne, Christopher John. BA, Columbia Coll., 1968. Vice consul Am. Embassy, Belize, Brit. Honduras, 1970-72; 2nd sec., polit. officer Am. Embassy, Belgrade, Yugoslavia, 1972-74; ops. officer ops. ctr. Dept. State, Washington, 1974-75, country officer for Italy and the Vatican, 1975-78; polit./mil. officer for U.S. Mission Berlin Dept. State, 1978-82; officer C.S.C.E. Bur. European Affairs Dept. State, Washington, 1982-83, officer for Fed. Republic of Germany, 1983-84; consul gen., prin. officer U.S. Consulate Gen., Zagreb, Yugoslavia, 1984-1988; mem. sr. seminar Dept. State, Washington, 1988-89, dir. Bur. for Ea. European and Yugoslavia Affairs, 1989-1991; min. counselor, deputy chief of mission Am. Embassy, Vienna, Austria, 1991-94, Chargé d'Affaires ad interim, 1993; amb. to Lithuania Am. Embassy, Vilnius, 1994-97; sr. fellow Inst. for Strategic Studies/Nat. Def. U., Washington, 1997-99; polit. advisor U.S. Space Command, Colorado Springs, Colo., 1999—. Avocations: piano, harpsichord, jogging, classical

music appreciation. Home: 40 Church St Tarrytown NY 10591-4806 Office: US Space Command Peterson AFB 250 S Peterson Blvd Ste 116 Colorado Springs CO 80914-3285

SWINBURNE, RICHARD GRANVILLE, philosopher, educator; b. Smethwick, Eng., Dec. 26, 1934; s. William H. and Gladys E. (Parker) S. BA with first class honors, Oxford (Eng.) U., 1957, BPhil, 1959, diploma in theology with distinction, 1960. Lectr., then sr. lectr. philosophy U. Hull, Eng., 1963-72; prof. philosophy U. Keele, Eng., 1972-84; Nolloth prof. philosophy Christian religion Oxford U., 1985—, Wilde lectr. natural and comparative religion, 1975-78; vis. assoc. prof. philosophy U. Md., College Park, 1969-70; Forwood lectr. history and philosophy religion U. Liverpool, Eng., 1977; Marrett Meml. lectr. Exeter Coll., Oxford U., 1980; Gifford lectr. Aberdeen, Eng., 1982-84; Edward Cadbury lectr. U. Birmingham, Eng., 1987; vis. prof. philosophy Syracuse (N.Y.) U., spring 1987; Wade Meml. lectr. St. Louis U., 1990; Indian Coun. for Philosophica Rsch. lectr., 1992; Dotterer lectr. Pa. State U., 1992, Aquinas lectr. Marquette U., 1997. Author: Space and Time, 1968, rev. edit., 1981, The Concept of Miracle, 1971, An Introduction to Confirmation Theory, 1973, The Coherence of Theism, 1977, rev. edit., 1993, The Existence of God, 1979, rev. edit., 1991, Faith and Reason, 1981, The Evolution of the Soul, 1986, rev. edit., 1990, (with Sydney Shoemaker) Personal Identity, 1984, Responsibility and Atonement, 1989, Revelation, 1992, The Christian God, 1994, Is There a God?, 1996, Providence and the Problem of Evil, 1998; editor: The Justification of Induction, 1974, Space, Time and Casuality, 1983, Miracles, 1988; contbr. articles to profl. jours. Fereday fellow St. John's Coll., Oxford U., 1958-61, Leverhulme research fellow in history and philosophy sci. U. Leeds, Eng., 1961-63; disting. vis. scholar U. Adelaide, Australia, 1982. Fellow The Brit. Acad. Home and Office: Oxford U Oriel Coll, Oxford 0X1 4EW, England

SWINERD, GRAHAM GEORGE, astronautical engineer, educator; b. Dover, Kent, Eng., Aug. 10, 1950; s. Frederick George and Amy (Wright) S.; m. Marion Prescott, Sept. 13, 1975; children: Victoria May, James Alasdair. BSc with honors, U. Kent, Canterbury, Eng., 1972, PhD, 1976. Chartered engr. Rsch. fellow Dundee (U.K.) U., 1976-79, Earth Satellite Rsch. Unit, Birmingham, U.K., 1979-83; spacecraft engr. Brit. Aerospace Space Systems, Stevenage, U.K., 1983-87; sr. lectr./rschr. dept. aeronautics and astronautics U. Southampton, U.K., 1987—; tech. cons. to various cos. and govt., 1990—. Co-author: Spacecraft Systems Engineering, 2d edit., 1995; contbr. numerous articles to profl. jours. Recipient numerous rsch. grants Engring. and Phys. Scis. Rsch. Coun., Natural Environment Rsch. Coun., Ministry of Def., others, 1990—. Fellow Royal Astron. Soc.; mem. Royal Aero. Soc. Avocations: mountain walking, photography, cycling. Office: U Southampton Astronautics Rsch Group, Sch Engring Scis Aero/Astronautics, Southampton S017 1BJ, England

SWINSON, ANGELA ANTHONY, physician; b. Washington, Nov. 5, 1960; d. Edgar and Phosia Lee (Hanna) Anthony; m. Kevin Lamont Swinson, June 28, 1986; 1 child, Erik Alan. BA, Johns Hopkins U., 1983, MPH, 1991; MD, Georgetown U., 1987. Diplomate Am. Bd. Forensic Examiners, Am. Bd. Forensic Medicine. Phlebotomist Georgetown U. Hosp., Washington, 1984; med. resident Homewood Hosp. Ctr., Balt., 1987-88; clinic physician Ea. Chest Clinic, Balt., 1990-91; resident in preventive medicine Johns Hopkins Sch. Hygiene and Pub. Health, Balt., 1990-92; asst. med. dir. Occupl. Med. Svc., NIH, Bethesda, Md., 1992-97; physician Med-Therapy PA, Balt., 1998—; mem. workgroup Prince George's County, Cheverly, Md., 1991-92. Contbr. articles to profl. jours. Sr. leader Girl Scouts Cen. Md., Balt., 1981-83; mem. inspirational choir Faith African Meth. Episcopal Ch., Laurel, Md., 1993—, mem. mass choir, 1993—, mem. inspirational choir, 1993-99, mem. scholarship com., 1995—, instr. vacation Bible sch., 1995, mem. health ministry, co-chair health and fitness ministry, 1999—; bd. dirs. Nat. Consortium for African Am. Children, Inc., 1995—. Grantee Nat. Med. Fellowships, 1983-85. Mem. Am. Coll. Occupl. and Environ. Medicine, Am. Coll. Forensic Examiners, Md. State Med. Soc., Delta Sigma Theta (Golden Life, co-chair phys. and mental health com. 1996-99, Columbia, Md. alumnae chpt. treas., Mu Psi chpt. 1980-82, pres. Mu Psi chpt. 1982-83, Minerva award 1981, chpt. award 1983). Avocations: music, art, aerobic exercise, religious activities. Office: Med-Therapy PA 3306 Eastern Ave Baltimore MD 21224-4108

SWINSON, BETTY WHITE, composer; b. New Castle, Ind., Aug. 20, 1934; d. Odie Paul and Ella Mildred (Dragon) White; m. Owen Isaac Swinson, Sept. 21, 1963; children: Jo Ann Swinson King, Lea Etta Swinson Walker. Grad. high sch., Mt. Summit, Ind. Author: (song book) A Song to Sing-A Story to Tell, vol. 1, 1983, vol. 2, 1988, vol. 3, 1996. Mem. Broadcast Music Inc., Traditional Country Gospel Music Assn. Avocations: traveling, crocheting, bird watching.

SWINSON, JEREMY MARK, psychology educator; b. St. Albans, Hertfordshire, Eng., Feb. 6, 1950; s. Cyril William and Brenda (Scul) S. BSc, London U., 1972; MEd, Univ. Wales Swansea, 1977. Lic. Psychologist. Tchr. Inner London Edn. Authority, 1973-76; ednl. psychologist Sefton Metropolitan Borough, Eng., 1977-84; sr. ednl. psychologist Sefton Mil. Base, Eng., 1984—. Co-author: Parental Involvement in Children's Reading, 1985; co-editor: (collection of papers) Improving Behaviour in Schools, 1994; author papers, contbr. articles to profl. jours. Chmn. Sefton Social Democrats, 1982, Woodlands Sch. Govs., 1982—. Fellow Brit. Psychol. Soc. (assoc.); mem. Waterloo Southport Rugby Football Club, Waterloo Football Club. Roman Catholic. Home: 54 Duke Street, L37 4AT Formby Liverpool, England

SWINTON, JEFFREY CHEEVER, lawyer; b. Salt Lake City, June 22, 1947; s. Kenneth Perry and Venice (Cheever) S.; m. Heidi Sorensen, Apr. 14, 1972; children: Cameron, Daniel, Jonathan, Ian. BA, U. Utah, 1971, JD, 1974. Bar: Utah 1974, U.S. Ct. Appeals (10th cir.) 1985, U.S. Supreme Ct. 1985. Ptnr. Stringham, Larsen, Mazuran & Sabin, Salt Lake City, 1974-79; sr. v.p. Ruti-Sweetwater, Inc., Salt Lake City, 1979-84; ptnr. Larsen, Mazuran & Verhaaren, Salt Lake City, 1984-85, Jensen & Swinton, Salt Lake City, 1986-87; ptnr., v.p., bd. dirs. Woodbury, Jensen, Kesler & Swinton, Salt Lake City, 1988-91; ptnr. Stoker & Swinton, Salt Lake City, 1991—. Assoc. editor Utah Bar Jour., 1973-74; editor Summation: Jour. Utah Law, 1973. Chmn., v.p., del. Salt Lake City Rep. Com., 1975-88; trustee Bus. Industry Cmty. Edn. Partnership, Salt Lake City, 1979-80; mem. panel judges Utah Pub. Employees Assn., 1980-83, 85-87; bd. dirs., pres. Work Activities Ctr. for Handicapped Adults, Salt Lake City, 1987-93; chair Utah state bd. svcs. People with Disabilities, 1993-99, govs. coun., 1996; dist. chmn. Boy Scouts Am., Salt Lake City, 1987-94; bd. dirs. Homeless Youth Resource Ctr., 1998-2000; exec. dir. Salt Lake Inner City Project, 1996—; chmn. Pioneer Region Welfare Com., 1998—; bishop Mormon Ch., 1977-85, stake pres., 1994—. Mem. ABA, ATLA, Utah State Bar Assn. (chair franchise law sect.), Nat. Futures Assn. (arbitrator 1991), U. Utah Law Sch. Alumni Assn. (treas., trustee 1979-83), Young Alumni Assn. U. Utah (pres. 1981-83), Soc. Bar and Gavel (pres. 1976-78), Beehive, Owl and Key, Skull and Bones, Rotary (pres. 1993). Mormon. Avocations: tennis, golf, singing. Home: 12ll East 100 South Salt Lake City UT 84102 Office: 311 S State St Ste 400 Salt Lake City UT 84111-2382

SWISHER, STACEY ELAINE, mechanical engineer; b. Columbus, Ohio, Nov. 12, 1966; d. George Monroe and Lnida Sue Swisher. BSME, Tenn. Tech. U., 1989; MSME, Va. Poly. Inst. and State U., 1991. Engr. in tng., Tenn. Process engring. mech. engr. Eastman Chem. Co., Kinsport, Tenn., 1991-94, devel. mech. engr., 1994-97; plant mech. engr. Eastman Chem. Co., Kinsport, 1997-98, maintenance gen. supr., 1998—. Contbr. articles to sci. jours.; patentee in field. Supporter United Way, Kingsport, 1991—, Safehouse, Kingsport, 1991—; free engring. svcs. Kingsport Ctr. for Opportunity, 1993. Mem. ASME (Young Engr. of Yr. 1997, plant engring. and maintenance technical divsn. 1999-2000, panel mem. Young Engrs. Forum with PBS 1998-99), NSPE.

SWITHINBANK, CHARLES WINTHROP, glaciologist, consultant; b. Pegu, Burma, Nov. 17, 1926; arrived in Eng., 1933; s. Bernard Winthrop and Dorothea (Molesworth) S.; m. Mary Stewart, Aug. 17, 1960; children: Carol, Kelvin. BA, Oxford U., 1949, DPhil, 1955; DEng (hon.), Milw. Sch. Engring., 1989. Glaciologist Norwegian-Brit.-Swedish Antarctic Expdn., 1949-55; rsch. assoc. U. Mich., Ann Arbor, 1959-63; chief glaciologist Brit. Antarctic Survey, Cambridge, Eng., 1971-74, head earth scis., 1974-86; cons. glaciologist Cambridge, 1986—; rsch. fellow Scott Polar Rsch. Inst., Cambridge, 1955-59, rsch. appointment, 1963-71, sr. rschr., assoc., 1987—; field work in Gambia, Iceland, Ross Ice Shelf, Transantarctic Mountains, Soviet Antarctic, North Pole, Greenland, Antarctic Peninsula, Ellsworth Mountains, others, 1947—; v.p. Internat. Commn. on Snow and Ice, 1979-83. Contbr. articles to profl. jours. Sub-lt. Royal Naval Vol. Res., 1944-47. Recipient medal of merit King Haakon VII, 1952, Watkins award Scott Polar Rsch. Inst., 1953, Polar medal Queen Elizabeth II, 1956, 2d prize Pictures of Yr. Competition, 1964, Retzius medal King Gustav VI, 1966, U.S. Antarctic Svc. medal, 1974, Mungo Pk. medal Royal Scottish Geog. Soc., 1990. Fellow Royal Geog. Soc. (life; Mrs. Patrick Ness award 1954, Patron's medal 1971), Am. Geog. Soc. (hon. life), Arctic Inst. N.Am. (life); mem. Swedish Soc. Anthropology and Geography (life), AAAS (life), Nat. Geog. Soc., Antarctican Soc., Internat. Glaciological Soc. (pres. 1981-84), Antarctic Club, Arctic Club, Sigma Xi (life). Home: 7 Home End Fulbourn, Cambridge CB1 5B5, England Office: Scott Polar Rsch Inst, Lensfield Rd, Cambridge CB2 1ER, England

SWITLO, JANICE GEORGINA ALICE E., barrister, solicitor, mediator, negotiator, legal and business consultant; b. Vancouver, B.C., Can., Jan. 10, 1959; d. Alexander Donald and Mary (Shutka) Switlo; married; 1 child. LLB, Osgoode Hall, Toronto, 1986; B.Commerce, U. B.C., 1981. Mgmt. cons. Control Data Can. Ltd., Vancouver, 1981-83; barrister, solicitor Aydin & Co., Vancouver, 1987-88; legal counsel Dept. Justice of Can., Vancouver, 1989-93; gen. counsel Westbank Indian Band, Westbank, B.C., 1993-94; barrister, solicitor, cons. Switlo & Co., Peachland, B.C., 1993-97; candidate fed. election Okanagan-Coquihalla, 1997; legal advisor Ministry Aboriginal Affairs, Govt. N.W.T., 1999-2000; mem. adv. coun. on multiculturalism, adv. coun. to Minister of Multiculturalism, B.C., 1996-98. Author: (book/screenplay) Sookinchute, 2000, (treatise) Trick or Treaty?, 1995, (book) Gustafsen Lake: Under Seige, 1997, (treatise) Apple Cede: First Nations Land Management Regional, 1999. Dir. B.C. Parents in Crisis Soc., Vancouver, 1991-93, Orpheum Kids Club Soc., Vancouver, 1991. Recipient various univ. scholarships. Mem. Internat. Bar Assn., Internat. Commn. Jurists (Can. sect.), Can. Counsel on Internat. Law, Can. Bar Assn., York U. Alumni Assn., U.B.C. Commerce Alumni Assn., Phi Delta Phi. Office: Switlo & Co, PO Box 1565, Yellowknife, NT Canada XIA 2P2

SWITZER, BRIAN CARL, strategic systems designer; b. Cleve., Sept. 13, 1938; s. Robert Charles and Patricia Davison S.; m. Nicole S., Dec. 31, 1964; children: Michelle, Stephanie. BA, Ohio Wesleyan U., 1960; MBA, Ohio State U., 1964. Founder, pres. M.C.O. Solutions, Inc., Shaker Heights, Ohio, 1962—; bd. dirs. Cons. Assocs. Internat., Inc., Pepper Pike, Ohio, 1998—. Author: How to Sell Overseas, 1966. Mem. Rotary. Republican. Episcopal. Avocation: photography. Home: 11615 Pleasant Ridge Pl Cleveland OH 44136-4523 Office: MCO Solutions 23400 Stanford Rd Shaker Heights OH 44122

SWITZER, MAURICE HAROLD, journalist; b. Toronto, Ont., Can., Mar. 28, 1945; s. Harold Switzer and Ruby (Marsden) Hicks; m. Mary Helene Pavlik; children: Andrea Zimperi, Adin, Lisa Doracka. Student, Trent U., Peterborough, Ont., 1964-65. Journalist Belleville (Ont.) Intelligencer, 1965-67, sports editor, 1967-72, mng. editor, 1972-79; mng. editor Oshawa (Ont.) Times, 1979-81; pub. Timmins (Ont.) Daily Press, 1981-86, Sudbury (Ont.) Star, 1986-92, Winnipeg (Man.) Free Press, 1992-94; ret.; owner Media Help Svcs., 1994—; facilitator Aboriginal Media First Nations Tech. Inst., 1996-97; dir. comms. Assembly of First Nations, Ottawa, 1997—. Author: Bruno Cavallo a Conversation, 1991. Mem. elders coun. Mississaugas of Rice Lake First Nation.

SWOGER, JAMES WESLEY, magician; b. Wilkinsburg, Pa., Jan. 26, 1918; s. George Edmond and Iva Edna (Heacox) S.; m. Willie Williams, Jan. 8, 1944 (div. 1967); children: Melinda, James Michael, Andrina; m. Violet Elizabeth Pettit, Oct. 29, 1968. Owner House of Enchantment, Oceanside, Calif., 1937—; owner, magician Magicum of Magic, 1937, Magic Follies of Tomorrow, 1938-41; active numerous war bond drive shows, camp shows, ship entertainment and concert tours in Australia, New Guinea and the Philippines, 1943-46; starred in Magic on Showboat Rhododenron Season, 1965—, Mr. Roger's Neighborhood; lectr. Magic Castle, 1995; magician Pitts. Children's Theatre, 1941-43, Bascom Prodns., 1941-43, Austin Prodns., 1941-43; bd. dirs. Awesome Balloons, Inc. Magician for more than 77 yrs. Named Magician of Yr. 1960, 50 Yrs Svc. Magic, Internat. Magicians Ring 13 IBM, 1973, Faithful Yr. Svc. Magic, 42d Annual Magicfest, 1973, 60 Yr. Svc. Magic, 1983; named to Order of Arrow Boy Scouts Am. Mem. Soc. Am. Magicians (pres.), Internat. Brotherhood Magicians (pres., Order of Merlin Excalibur 1995), Craftsmen Printers Guild, Mystic 52 (pres.), Acad. Magical Arts Scis., Fellowship Christian Magicians, San Diego Ring 76 IBM, Awesome Balloons (bd. mem. 2000). Republican. Avocations: inventing stage effects, model illusions. Home: 3542 Mira Pacific Dr Oceanside CA 92056-3932

SWOOPES, SHERYL DENISE, professional basketball player; b. Brownfield, Tex., Mar. 25, 1971; d. Louis Swoopes; m. Eric Jackson; 1 child, Jordan. Student, South Plains Jr. Coll., Tex.; BA, Tex. Tech. U., 1993. Basketball player USA Women's Nat. Team, 1995-96, Houston Comets, 1997—; mem. 1995 Pan Am. Games Womens Basketball Team. Recipient bronze medal as mem. 1994 World Championship Team, gold medal as mem. 1994 Women's Goodwill Games Team; named 1993 Nat. Player of the Yr., MVP 1993 NCAA Final Four, 1992 and 1992 SWC Player of Yr., 1992 SWC Newcomer of the Yr.; mem. WNBA champion Houston Comets, 1997, 98, 99. Achievements include having a Nike basketball shoe named in her honor. Office: Houston Comets Two Greenway Plz Ste 400 Houston TX 77046 Address: 908 E Felt St Apt 111 Brownfield TX 79316-3703

SWOPE, ALAN JOSEPH, psychologist, educator; b. Cleve., Apr. 24, 1942; s. Floyd Keene and Leone Louise Swope; m. Bonnie Lee Swope, June 1976 (div. Oct. 1997); children: Alison, Laura. BA, Hiram Coll., 1964; PhD, Columbia U., 1969. Lic. psychologist, Calif. Psychologist City of Berkeley, Calif., 1970-81; pvt. practice as psychotherapist Berkeley, 1971—; prof. Wright Inst., Berkeley, 1978—, Calif. Sch. Profl. Psychology, Alameda, 1982—; hon. life bd. mem. Calif. Psychology Internship Coun., Berkeley, 1992—. Contbr. articles to profl. jours. Fellow Am. Bd. Profl. Psychology (diplomate); mem. APA. Avocations: writing, reading, tennis, piano. Office: 3155 College Ave Berkeley CA 94705-2755

SWORT, ARLOWAYNE, retired nursing educator and administrator; b. Bartlesville, Okla., Dec. 9, 1922; d. Arlington L. and Clara E. (Church) S. Diploma, St. Luke's Hosp. Sch. Nursing, Kansas City, Mo., 1944; BSN, U. Colo., 1958; MS in Nursing, Cath. U. Am., 1961; EdD, Columbia U., 1973. Assoc. prof., assoc. dean Sch. Nursing U. Pitts., 1974-77; dean, prof. Sch. Nursing U. Tex. Health Scis. Ctr., Houston, 1977-83, prof. nursing, 1983-85; prof., assoc. in adminstrn. Johns Hopkins U. Sch. Nursing, Balt., 1985-87; prof., assoc. dean for adminstrn. and grad. acad. affairs Johns Hopkins U. Sch. Nursing, Balt., 1987-89, sr. assoc. dean, 1990-91; mem. profl. adv. com. Home Health Care, 1998-2000. Mem. aux. Medina County Cmty. Hosp., Hondo, Tex., 1997-99, charity ball chmn., 1998-99. Recipient numerous rsrch. grants. Mem. Am. Assn. for History of Nursing Inc., Nat. League for Nursing, Sigma Theta Tau, Kappa Delta Pi. Home: 1317 Kollman Dr Hondo TX 78861-1014

SWYERS, DONALD G., information scientist; b. Syracuse, N.Y., Mar. 30, 1958; s. William A. Swyers and Corinne Prall Neville; m. Nancy C. Bargesser, Jan. 2, 1993; 1 child. BS in Mgmt. Sci., SUNY, Geneseo, 1980; MBA in Corp. Investment, U. Hartford, 1991. Cert. computer profl. Inst. Cert. Computing. Database analyst Xerox, Webster, N.Y., 1980-87; computer automated sys. engring. tool cons. Aetna, Hartford, Conn., 1987-94; cons. Hartford, 1994-99; information engr. Citigroup-Travelers Life & Annuity, Hartford, 1999—. Home: 575 Bridge Rd Unit 10-6 Florence MA 01062-1089 Office: Citigroup Travelers Life and Annuity 1 Tower Sq # 9ms Hartford CT 06183-0001

SXRENSEN, THORKILD INGVOR ARRILD, epidemiology educator, administrator; b. Copenhagen, Dec. 7, 1945; s. Poul Hjalmer and Helene Cathrine Sxrensen; m. Karen Bodil Valling Andersen, July 1, 1972; children: Nikolaj, Signe, Kristoffer. MD, U. Copenhagen, 1971, DMS, 1983. Cert. specialist in internal medicine and hepatology Danish Nat. Health Bd. Resident surg. dept. Copenhagen County U. Hosp., 1971-74, asst. prof., 1974-78; resident med. dept. Copenhagen Municipality U. Hosp., 1978-80; sr. resident Copenhagen U. Hosps., 1980-85; chief physician Copenhagen Municipality U. Hosp., 1985-89; rsch. prof. Danish Rsch. Coun., 1989-94; chief physician clin. epidemiology Copenhagen U. Hosp., 1994—; prof. clin. epidemiology med. faculty U. Copenhagen, 1994—; dir. Inst. Preventive Medicine, Copenhagen, 1993—; dean med. faculty U. Copenhagen, 1995-96. Contbr. numerous rsch. articles to profl. jours. Lt. Danish Armed Forces, 1973. Recipient Hagedorn award Danish Soc. for Internal Medicine, Codan award Med. Assn. Codan Ins. Co. and Med. Soc. Copenhagen, 1999. Mem. Danish Epidemiol. Soc., Danish Assn. for Study of Obesity, Danish Soc. for Med. Philosophy (ethics and methodology pres. 1996—), Danish Soc. for Med. Priority Setting (v.p. 1999—). Lutheran. Avocations: classical and modern music, classical and modern art, plays, movies, philosophy. Fax: 4533324240. E-mail: tias@ipm.hosp.dk. Home: 13 Fuglebakkevej, DK 2000 Copenhagen Denmark Office: Inst Preventive Medicine, 3-5 Xster Farimagsgade, DK 1399 Copenhagen Denmark

SY, DALISAY CHIONGLO, biochemistry educator; b. Perez, Philippines, June 9, 1941; d. Jose Lee and Dominga (Tan) Chionglo; m. Benito Gan Sy, Apr. 30, 1966; children: Jonathan B., Benjamin M., Albert B., Belinda M. BS in Pharmacy, U. Santo Tomas, 1962, PhD iin Biol. Scis., 1988; MS in Biochemistry, U. Ill., 1967. Rsch. asst. U. Ill., Chgo., 1964-66, rsch. assoc., 1966-68; chmn. U. Santo Tomas Coll. of Pharmacy, 1983-92, U. Santo Tomas Coll. of Medicine, 1992—; prof. biochemistry U. Santo Tomas, 1992-96. Contbg. editor Santo Tomas Jour. of Medicine, 1992-96. Mem. Phila. Soc. of Biochemistry and Molecular Biology (dir. 1988—), Am. Assn. for Clin. Chemistry, U. Ill. Alumni Assn. (life), Nat. Rsch. Coun. of the Philippines. Roman Catholic. Avocations: gardening, reading. Home: 35 Speaker Perez St, Quezon City 1114, The Philippines Office: De La Salle U Coll Med, Dept Biochemistry, Dasmariñas Cavite, The Philippines

SYBESMA, JACOB PHILIP, bloodbank executive, hematologist; b. Larantuka, Indonesia, Jan. 7, 1937; came to The Netherlands, 1946; s. Jan Francois and Rosette (van Staveren) S.; m. Iris Johanna Koopmans, Apr. 10, 1965; children: Tiddo, Marc. MD, U. Utrecht, The Netherlands, 1963; PhD, U. Utrecht, 1974. Intern U. Hosp. Utrecht, 1961-63; staff mem. in internal medicine U. Utrecht, 1969-75; resident U. Hosp. Utrecht, The Netherlands, 1967-69, Mil. Hosp. Utrecht, The Netherlands, 1964-65, St. Elisabeth's Hosp. Curaçao, 1965-67. Contbr. articles to profl. jours. Pres. Med. Dispute Soc., Dordrecht, The Netherlands. Mem. Am. Assn. Bloodbanks, Internat. Soc. Blood Transfusion (Paris), Am. Soc. for Apheresis, Dutch Soc. Hematology, N.Y. Acad. Scis., European Soc. Hemapheresis, Dutch Soc. Internal Medicine. Avocations: sailing, gardening. Home: Kloevelaan 33, 3381 LG Giessenburg The Netherlands Office: Bloodbank ZWN Rotterdam, PO Box 9010, 3301 AA Dordrecht The Netherlands

SYCHOV, ALYAKSANDR, diplomat; b. Homel, Belarus, Sept. 19, 1951; married; 2 children. Ministry Fgn. Affairs, Belarus, 1979-84; With Belarus permanent mission to UN office, Geneva, 1984-90; head internat. econ. rels. dept. Ministry Fgn. Affairs, Belarus, 1991-92, dep. fgn. min., 1992-94; permanent rep. of Belarus UN, N.Y., 1994—; mem. bur., chmn. of session com. Econ. Commn. for Europe, 1988-90; chmn. com. on internat. security and disarmament matters 51st Session UN Gen. Assembly, 1996-97, chmn. 1st com. 19th spl. session UN Gen. Assembly, 1997, vice-chmn. ECOSOC, 1998-99. Office: Permanent Mission of Belarus to UN 136 E 67th St New York NY 10021-6137

SYCIP, WASHINGTON, accountant; b. Manila, Philippines, June 30, 1921; s. Albino and Helen (Bau) S. m. Anna Yu, Nov. 27, 1948; children: Victoria, George, Robert. BS in Commerce, U. Sto. Tomas, Manila, 1940, MS in Commerce, 1942; MS in Commerce, Columbia U., 1943. Chmn. Euro-Asia Ctr. INSEAD, Fontainebleau, France, 1981-88; mem. internat. adv. bd. Caterpillar Tractor Co., Peoria, Ill., 1985-90, AT&T Internat., N.J., 1987-88; chmn. Asian Inst. Mgmt., Manila, 1968—; mem. adv. coun. Columbia U., N.Y.C., 1982—; mem. internat. adv. bd. Am. Internat. Group, N.Y.C., 1983—; bd. dirs. Joseph H. Lauder Inst. Mgmt. and Internat. Studies, Phila., 1983—; mem. internat. adv. bd. United Technologies Corp., Hartford, Conn., 1984—; cons. Henkel KG, Duesseldorf, Fed. Republic Germany, 1984—; mem. internat. adv. bd. Chem. Bank, N.Y.C., 1985—. Fellow Internat. Acad. Mgmt.; mem. Philippine Inst. CPA's (pres., Hall of Fame award 1980), Mgmt. Assn. of the Philippines (Man of Yr. 1967), Internat. Fedn. Accts. (pres. 1982-85), Makati Bus. Club. Home: 60 Cambridge Cir Forbes, Park Makati, Manila The Philippines Office: SGV Group, 6760 Ayala Ave Makati, Manila The Philippines*

SYCIP-WALE, FE LEE, physician; b. Cebu City, Philippines, July 19, 1935; d. Daniel Zarate Sycip and Tim Wa Lee; m. Sebellon M. Wale; children: Levi Japheth D. Wale, Mercedes Leah S. Wale. BS, U. Philippines, 1955; MD, Far Ea. U., Manila, 1961; diploma, London Sch. Hygiene and Tropical Medicine, 1973. Rotating resident Sillimal U. Med. Ctr., Dumaguete City, Philippines, 1961-63; cons. pediatrics Silliman U. Med. Ctr., Dumaguete City, Philippines, 1967-72, head extension service program rural communities, 1972—; intern Pittsfield (Mass.) Affiliated Hosps., 1963-64; resident pediatrics Children's Mercy Hosp., Kansas City, Mo., 1964-66; gen. practice resident Sweddish Covenant Hosp., Chgo., 1966. Recipient Bayaning Pilipino Regional award, region VII ABS-CBN, 1995, Albert Schweitzer award, 1996, Women Centennial award Province of Negros Oriental, 1998. Mem. Philippine Pediatric Soc., Maternal and Child Health Assn. Philippines, Philippine Med. Assn., Rotary, Gideon's Aux. Home: Oracion subdiv Banilad, Dumaguete, Negros Oriental, The Philippines Office: Silliman U Med Ctr, Extension Program, Dumaguete, Negros Oriental, The Philippines

SYDDALL, THOMAS HAROLD, patent lawyer; b. Auckland, New Zealand, Dec. 23, 1938; s. Clifford Walter and Lucy Ellen (Rolls) S.; m. Miriam Ann Antrobus, Dec. 24, 1983. BSc, U. New Zealand, 1960; LLB, Victoria U., Wellington, New Zealand, 1966. Barrister and solicitor High Ct. New Zealand, 1966; registered patent atty.; notary pub. With A.J. Park (formerly A.J. Park & Son), Wellington, 1960-65, ptnr., 1966—. Contbr. articles to profl. jours. Fellow New Zealand Inst. Patent Attys. (pres. 1980-82, exam. bd. 1991—); mem. Chartered Inst. Patent Agts. (Brit. oversea mem.), New Zealand Inst. Chemistry, New Zealand Assn. Scientists (mem. coun. 1992—), Wellington Dist. Law Soc., New Zealand Group Asian Patent Attys. Assn. (mem. of exec. 1985—), New Zealand Group Internat. Assn. for Protection of Indsl. Property, New Zealand Sect. Internat. Fedn. Indsl. Property Attys., Royal Soc. New Zealand. Avocations: the performing arts, reading, walking. Office: AJ Park, Post Office Sq, Wellington New Zealand

SYDOROVA, LUDMILLA VICTOROVNA, chemist, research scientist; b. Gayseen, Ukraine, Nov. 25, 1953; d. Victor Ivanovich and Vera Michaylovna (Peresada) S.; m. Rostislov Arsenievich Yatsyuk, Sept. 6, 1980 (div. Jan. 1985); 1 child, Dmitry. Grad., State U. Odessa, Ukraine, 1976; postgrad., State U. Svivska Polytech., Lviv, Ukraine, 1995-2000. Teaching lab. asst. State U., Odessa, Ukraine, 1976-77; engr. Inst. Phys. Mechs., Lviv, Ukraine, 1977-88; jr. rsch. scientist State U. Lvivska Polytech., Lviv, Ukraine, 1988-90, rsch. scientist, 1990—; head Analytical Ctr., Lviv, 1991-96; dir. SPPE, San-Dez. Inventor in field. Grantee USAID, 1996, U.S. Info. Agy., 1996, 97, 99. Mem. ACS. Avocations: badminton, travel, driving, cooking, music. Home: 11 Dovzenko St ap 55, 79070 Lviv 70, Ukraine Office: State U Lvivska Polytech, 12 Bandera St, 290646 Lviv Ukraine

SYDOW, MICHAEL DAVID, lawyer; b. Dec. 12, 1950; m. Kelli McDonald; children: Kristen, David, Wyatt. BA, Southwestern U., 1973; JD with honors, U. Tex., 1976. Bar: Tex. 1976, U.S. Ct. Claims 1977, U.S. Ct. Appeals (5th cir.) 1977, U.S. Dist. Ct. (so. dist.) Tex. 1977, U.S. Dist. Ct. (ea. dist.) Tex. 1979, U.S. Supreme Ct. 1980, U.S. Dist. Ct. (no. dist.) Tex. 1985, U.S. Dist. Ct. (we. dist.) Tex. 1986; cert. in civil trial law Tex. Bd. Legal Specialization. Trial atty. Office Gen. Counsel USN, Arlington, Va., 1976-77; mem. firm Eastham, Watson, Dale & Forney, Houston, 1977-84, Hagans & Sydow, LLP, Houston, 1985-90, Reynolds & Sydow, LLP, Houston, 1993-94; pvt. practice, 1990-93; with Sydow & McDonald, LLP, 1995-97; shareholder Verner, Liipfert, Bernhard, McPherson & Hand, Houston, 1997—. Fellow Tex. Bar Found., Houston Bar Found.; mem. Houston Bar Assn. (chmn. jud. liaison com. 1988-90, Pres.'s award 1990), Maritime Law Assn. U.S. (mem. com. on gen. average 1977-88, practice and

procedures com. 1988—), State Bar Tex., Phi Delta Phi. Address: Verner Liipfert Bernhard McPherson & Hand Chartered 1111 Bagby St Ste 4700 Houston TX 77002-2543

SYE, WEN FA, chemistry educator; b. Keelung, Taiwan, Apr. 26, 1946; s. Li Fu and Chang Kuei (Chang) S.; m. Kuei Yin Lu, Nov. 13, 1986; children: Hui-Yin, Shih-Hui. BS, Tam Kang U., Tamsui, Taiwan, 1972; MS, U. Tex., El Paso, 1978; PhD, U. Houston, 1981. Rsch. assoc. U. Tex. Med. Br., Galveston, 1981-83; assoc. prof. chemistry Tam Kang U., 1983-87, prof. chemistry, 1987—, chmn. dept. chemistry, 1988-93; vis. prof. Brigham Young U., Provo, Utah, 1990; dean, Coll. Sci. Tam Kang U., 1993-99; cons. Environ. Protection Agy., Taipei, 1991-92. Inventor, rschr. in field. Corporal, Taiwan Army, 1972-74. Mem. Chinese Chem. Soc., Tamsui Parents' Assn. (hon.), Tamsui Bd. Edn. (hon.), Phi Tau Phi. Buddhist. Avocations: painting, travel, music, sports. Home: 4th fl No. 10 Lane 73, Hsueh-Hu St, Tamsui 25137, Taiwan Office: Tam Kang U Dept Chemistry, 151 Ying-Chuan Rd, Tamsui 25137, Taiwan

SYED, AMIN TABISH, medical scientist; b. India, Mar. 30, 1957; m. Farhat Mubin; 2 children. MBBS, AIIMS; MD, AIIMS, New Delhi, India, 1981; MAMS, Nat. Acad. Med. Scis., New Delhi, 1989; student, U. Bristol, England; DLitt (hon.), City U., L.A., 1985. Diplomate Nat. Bd. Examinations. House surgeon Govt. Hosp. for Bone & Joint Surgery, Srinagar, India, 1981-82; med. officer J&K Health Svcs., Srinagar, 1982-84; house officer dept. surgery and allied specialities Inst. Med. Scis., Srinagar, 1984-86; hosp. adminstr. Inst. Med. Svcs., Srinagar, 1987-89, All India Inst. Med. Scis., New Delhi, 1989-91; cons. hosp. and health svcs. mgmt., med. adminstr. Inst. Med. Svcs., Srinagar, 1991-94; postdoctoral fellow faculty of medicine U. Bristol, 1995-96; assoc. prof. pub health medicine, med. adminstr. S.K. Inst. Med. Scis., Srinagar, 1997—; Indian rep. World Health Forum, Dallas, 1998. Author: Khush-hal Riyasat, 1975, Hussaini Karvanuk Saffer, 1980, Sher-i-Kashmir Aur Kashmiriyat, 1984, Health Care Management: Principles & Practice, 1998, State-of-the-Art Planning of Health Care Institutions, 1999, Essential Skills in Clinical Medicine, 1999, Management of Intensive Care, 1999, Health Care Financing in Developing Countries, 1998; chief editor: Koshur Akhbar (literary newspaper), 1982-86; editor: Kashmed, 1978-79; editor Jour. Med. Scis., 1997—; contbr. articles to profl. jours. Fellow Royal Inst. Pub. Health and Hygiene (England), N.Y. Acad. Scis., Internat. Med. Scis. Acad.; mem. Nat. Acad. Med. Scis. (life), Inst. Health Svcs. Mgmt. (England), Acad. Hosp. Adminstrn. (life, hon. faculty mem., exec. editor jour.), Indian Soc. Health Adminstrs. (life), India Hosp. Assn. (life, convenor), Internat. Hosp. Fedn. (London), Am. Hosp. Assn., rep. India at World Health Forum on Emergence of Infectious Diseases, Dallas, Tex., 1998. Home: Takhlique 64/III Hamzah, Colony Bemina PO Box 826 GPO, Srinagar 190001, India Office: Inst Med Scis, PO Box 826 GPO, Srinagar 190011, India

SYED, IBRAHIM BIJLI, medical educator and physicist, writer, philosopher, theologist, public speaker; b. Bellary, India, Mar. 16, 1939; came to U.S., 1969, naturalized, 1975; s. Ahmed Bijli and Mumtaz Begum (Maniyar) S.; m. Sajida Shariff, Nov. 29, 1964; children: Mubin, Zafrin. BS with honors, Veerasaiva Coll., Bellary U., Mysore, 1960; MS with honors and distinction, Bangalore U., Mysore, 1962; diploma, U. Bombay, 1964; DSc, Johns Hopkins U., 1972; PhD (hon.), Malta, 1985. Cert. hazard control officer, 1980, internat. health care safety profl., 1980; diplomate Am. Bd. Radiology, Am. Bd. Health Physics. Lectr. physics Veerasaiva Coll., Bellary U., Mysore, 1962-63; med. physicist, radiation safety officer Victoria Hosp., India, 1964-67, Bowring and Lady Curz on Hosp. & Postgrad. Med. Rsch. Inst., Bangalore, India, 1964-67; cons. med. physicist, radiation safety officer Ministry of Health, Govt. of Karnataka, India, 1964-67, Bangalore Nursing Home, India, 1964-67; med. physicist, radiation safety officer Baystate Med. Ctr., Springfield, Mass., 1973-79; assoc. prof. Springfield Tech. C.C.; also adj. prof. radiology Holyoke (Mass.) C.C., 1973-79; asst. clin. prof. nuclear medicine U. Conn. Sch. Medicine, Farmington, 1975-79; cons. med. physicist Mercy Hosp., Springfield, 1973-79, Wing Meml. Hosp., Palmer, Mass., 1973-79; med. physicist, radiation safety officer VAMC, Louisville, 1979—, exec. officer radiation safety com., 1979—; prof. medicine U. Louisville Sch. Medicine, 1979—, dir. nuclear med. scis., 1980—; guest lectr. religious studies program U. Louisville, 1979—; vis. prof. Bangalore U., 1987-88, Gulbarga U., India, 1987-88; vis. scientist Bhabha Atomic Rsch. Ctr., Bombay, India; invite spkr. Veerasaiva Coll., Bellary, India, 1996, Vijayanagar Coll., Hospet, 1996, Vijayanagar Inst. Med. Scis., Bellary, 1996, Deccan Coll. Med. Scis., Hyderabad, India, 1996, Bhabha Atomic Rsch. Ctr., Bombay, 1997; invited spkr. 15th Ann. Islamic Conf. New Eng., Islamic Coun. New Eng., 1999, Coun. for a Parliament of the World's Religions, Cape Town, South Africa, 1999; PhD thesis examiner Allahabad U., 1996—; course dir. licensing for nuclear cardiologists U. Louisville, 1980—, mem. admissions com. nuclear medicine program, 1980—; guest relief examiner Am. Bd. Radiology, 1991; examiner in radiol. physics, 1995, 97, 98, 2000; mem. panel of examiners Am. Bd. Health Physics; PhD thesis examiner U. Delhi, Internat. Inst. for Advanced Study, Clayton, Mo., 1985—, Allahabad (India) U., 1996—; faculty mem. Med. Physicists of India Ann. Meeting, 1987; IAEA tchr. expert in nuclear medicine on mission to People's Republic of Bangladesh, 1986, to Guatemala, 1994; founder, pres. Islamic Rsch. Found. for Advancement of Knowledge, Louisville, 1988—; convener Internat. Conf. on Islamic Renaissance: Action Plan for the 21st Century, Chgo., 1995; cons. Coun. Sci. and Indsl. Rsch., Govt. India, 1980—, Am. Coun. Sci. and Health, 1980—; cons. gastroenterology and urology divsn. FDA, HHS, 1988—, cons. radiopharm. divsn., 1989—; cons. Govt. India in nuclear medicine, diagnostic radiol. physics, therapeutic radiol. physics and radiation safety, 1992; cons. radiol. and med. nuc. physics, Govt. India, Un Devel. Program, 1992; convenor Internat. Conf. on Islamic Renaissance, Chgo., 1995; guest spkr. Muslim Cmty. Ctr., Chgo., 1988—; invited spkr. objective studies and Islamic voice, Bangalore, 1996, Parliament of World Religions, Chgo., 1993, Cape Town, South Africa, 1999. Author: Radiation Safety for Allied Health Professionals, Radiation Safety Manual, 1979; contbg. editor Jour. of Islamic Food and Nutrition Coun. of Am., 1986—, health and sci. column Muslim Jour., 1989—; freelance writer Minaret Biweekly, N.Y.C., 1975—, AL'FURQAN Internat., Norcross, Ga., 1990, Message Internat., Jamaica, N.Y., 1990, Minerate Monthly Mag., L.A., 1995—; editor: Science and Technology for the Developing World, 1988; mem. editl. bd. Jour. Islamic Med. Assn., 1981—; regular contbr. Pres.'s Page; manuscript reviewer for sci. and med. jours., 1973; assoc. editor AAlim, 1998—; contbr. more than 100 articles to sci. jours.; pub. internat. more than 90 articles on various topics of Islam in jours. and mags. Pres. Springfield Islamic Ctr., 1973-79, India Assn., Louisville, 1980-81; v.p. Islamic Cultural Assn., Louisville, 1979-80, trustee, 1980—, vice chmn. bd. trustees, 1980-84, chmn. bd. trustees, 1984-86; vice chmn. bd. trustees Islamic Cultural Assn. of Louisville, Inc., 1987-89; ordained minister for Islamic marriages, 1983—; vol. Muslim Chaplain to Ky. State Reformatory, LaGrange, Ky., 1989—, to VAMC, Louisville, 1990—, Luther Luckett Correctional Instn., LaGrange, Roederer Correctional Complex, West Liberty, 1995—, Ky. Correctional Instn. for Women, Pee Wee Valley, 1995—, Green River Correctional Complex, Central City, Ky., 1998—, Imam and Khatib Friday Khutbah, Islamic Ctr., Louisville, St. Mary's Correctional Instn., Lebanon, Ky., 1990—; Imam and Khatib Muslim Friday Prayers; legal advisor Islamic Cultural Assn. Louisville, 1986-87; notary pub. Commonwealth of Ky., 1983—; mem. spkrs. bur. Louisville C. of C., 1980—, U. Louisville, 1980—; invited spkr. Muslim Cmty. Ctr., Chgo., 1986—, Islamic Ctr. Kansas City, Mo., 1989—, Islamic Ctr. Dayton, Ohio, 1989, Muslim Soc. Memphis, 1989, Islamic Ctr. Lawrence, Kans., 1989, Kalamazoo (Mich.) Islamic Ctr., 1989, Muslim Students Assn. U. Mo., Kansas City, 1989, Islamic Ctr. Worcester, Mass., 1989, Miami Valley Islamic Ctr., Springfield, Ohio, 1990, The Islamic Ctr. Greater Toledo, Ohio, 1990, Islamic Soc. Iowa City, 1990, Islamic Ctr. Cedar Rapids, Iowa, 1990, 92, Islamic Ctr. Waterloo, Iowa, 1990, Islamic Ctr. Columbus, 1990, Islamic Ctr. Tallahassee, 1993, Islamic Ctr. Madison, Wis., 1994, Majid Baitijr Rahman, Silver Spring, Md., 1995, Islamic Soc. Balt. Islamic Ctr., 1995, Islamic Found., Villa Park, Ill., 1995, Islamic Ctr. Greater Indpls., 1995, Islamic Ctr. Greater Little Rock, 1996, Islamic Soc. N.Am. and Muslim Students Assn., St. Louis, 1998, Islamic Ctr. Nashville, 1999, Islamic Ctr. Tucson, Ariz., 2000; chmn. Ky. State Nat. Alumni Schs. com. John Hopkins U.; judge Ky. State Sci. Fair, 1985—; dir. Ctr. for Qur'an and Sci. Studies, 1988—; trustee India Cmty. Found. Louisville, 1980—, chmn. bd. 1984—; trustee Karnataka Cmty. Found. Louisville, 1980—, chmn. bd. 1988—; bd. dirs. Child Guidance Clin., Springfield, 1973-79, Heritage Corp., Louisville, 1981—, others; active ACS, Heart Fund; vol. Muslim chaplain Ky. State Reformatory, La Grange, Dept. Vets. Affairs Med. Ctr., Louisville, 1990—. Recipient Disting. Cmty. Svc. award India Cmty. Found., 1982, Hind Rattan Jewel of India Title award Govt. India, 1994; WHO fellow, Govt. India scholar Bhabha Atomic Rsch. Ctr., Bombay, 1963-64; USPHS fellow Johns Hopkins U., 1969-72. Fellow Inst. Physics (U.K.), Am. Inst. Chemists, Royal Soc. Health, Am. Coll. Radiology, Internat. Acad. Med. Physics; mem. Am. Assn. Physicists in Medicine, Am. Coll. Nuclear Medicine, Health Physics Soc., Am. Acad. Health Physics, Soc. Nuclear Medicine (faculty mem. ann. meeting 1987, convenor internat. conf. 1995), Nat. Assn. Ams. of Asian Indian Descent (chmn. state pub. rels. com. 1982—), Islamic Med. Assn. N.Am. (life, faculty 1994, 96, 98), Internat. Inst. Islamic Medicine (faculty Orlando, Fla. 1996, 97, Birmingham, U.K. 1998), Islamic Soc. N.Am. (faculty Chgo. 1998), Islamic Soc. Balt. (founding mem.), Islamic Cultural Ctr., Louisville, Islamic Assn. Maritime Provinces Can., Halifax, N.S. (asst. sec. 1967-69), Health Physics Soc. (chmn. med. health physics com. 1989—, affirmative action com. 1984—), Am. Assn. Physicists in Medicine (biol. effects com.), Assn. Muslim Scientists and Engrs. N.Am. (program chmn. ann. conf. 1987, treas. 1987-88, sec. 1988—), AAUP, Soc. Nuclear Medicine India (life, faculty mem. ann. meeting 1987, invited spkr. and faculty ann. meeting 1996), Assn. Med. Physicists India (life, invited spkr. and faculty ann. meeting Maas 1996), Med. and Biol. Physics (divsn. Can.) Assn. Physicists, Hosp. Physicists Assn., N.Y. Acad. Scis., Islamic Assn. Maritime Provinces of Can., Ky. Med. Assn., Jefferson County Med. Soc. (assoc.), Sigma Xi. Islamic. E-mail: irfi@iname.com. Home: 7102 W Shefford Ln Louisville KY 40242-6462 Office: 800 Zorn Ave Louisville KY 40206-1433

SYED, MUBIN AKHTAR, psychiatrist, consultant; b. Lahore, Pakistan, Jan. 2, 1933; s. Mamud Ali Syed and Qudsia Khatoon; m. Sultana Ashraf; children: Mehjabeen, Mahrukh, M. Salahudin, Mehwish; m. Kausar Parveen; children: Haider Ali, Abdur Rehamn. MBBS, King Edward Med. Coll., Lahore, 1956. Diplomate Am. Bd. Psychiatry and Neurology. House phys. Mayo Hosp., Lahore, 1957; pvt. practice Lahore, 1957-62; intern Deaconess Hosp., St. Louis, 1962-63; resident in psychiatry Ypsilanti (Mich.) Gen. Hosp., 1963-64, Mo. State Hosp., St. Louis, 1964-66; staff psychiatrist Mo. State Hosp., St. Joseph, 1966-69; dir. Karachi (Pakistan) Psychiat. Hosp., 1970—. Author: The Diagnosis and Treatment of Psychosexual Disorders in Pakistan, 1991, Sexual Problems of Youngsters, 1992. Pres. Coun. of Psychol. and Edn. Rsch., 1977. Mem. Islamic Med. Assn. (founder, pres. 1967). Islam. Office: Karachi Psych Hosp, Nazimabad No 3, Karachi Sindh, Pakistan

SYED, SHAHABUDDIN HUSAINY, electrical engineer, researcher; b. Kolar, Karnataka, India, July 22, 1967; s. Nizamuddin Syed and Khamarunnisa S. Diploma in Elec. Engring., Govt. Poly., Chintamani, India, 1986; BEE, Siddaganga Inst. Tech., Tumkur, India, 1991; diploma in Bus. Mgmt., Hindustan Inst. Mgmt., New Delhi, 1987. Lectr. Bharath Poly., Bangarapet, India, 1991-93; maintenance engr. USHA Telehoist Ltd., Kolar, India, 1993-94; dep. engr. NGEF Ltd., Bangalore, India, 1994-96, sr. engr., 1996—. Contbr. articles to profl. jours. Recipient scholarship S.J. Jindal Trust, Bangalore, 1986-91. Mem. Indian Soc. Tech. Edn. (life). Avocations: essay writing, articles of public interest, cricket, technical trainer. Home: #4448 Opp Camping Grounds, Vijayanagar Bangarapet, Kolar Bangalore 563 114, India Office: NGEF Ltd Sr Engr EHV Test, PB #3876, Bangalore 560 038, India

SYGNECKI, CHRISTINA, sales executive; b. Forest Hills, N.Y., Aug. 30, 1954; d. Rene Julien and Marie Helene (Popovic) S.; m. Mark Spencer Conroy, May 22, 1977 (div. Dec. 1988). BA, U. Miami, 1974. Outside sales mgr. Cream of the Valley, Sacramento, Calif., 1983-84; dept. mgr. Oakville Grocery, San Francisco, 1984-85; store mgr. La Ferme Beaujolaise, San Francisco, 1985-86; chef, owner Nina Rent-A-Chef, San Francisco, 1986-88; mdse. coord. Carnival Cruise Lines, Miami, 1988-93; sales mgr. duty free Greyhound Leisure Svcs., Miami, 1993-95; sales mgr. cruise ships Weitnauer Am. Trading, Miami, 1995-96; mgr. Pertex Textile Products, Bloomfield Hills, Mich., 1996-97; metro mgr. Artisans and Estates of Kendall Jackson Winery, Santa Rosa, Calif., 1997—; mem. Seigneurs de Corbieres, France. Mem. Chaine des Rotisseurs (vice echanson, Merit award 1996), Sommelier Guild (v.p. 1993—), Ordre des Canardiers. Republican. Roman Catholic. Avocations: yoga, travel, wine collecting, literature, music. Home and Office: 914 SE 10th St Deerfield Beach FL 33441-5718

SYKA, JOSEF NICHOLAS, neuroscientist, educator; b. Prague, Czech Republic, Sept. 18, 1940; s. Josef and Vera (Postranecka) S.; m. Eva Sykorova, Feb. 14, 1969; children: Josef, Michael. MD, Charles U., Prague, 1965, DSc, 1991; PhD, Acad. Scis., Prague, 1971. Scientist Inst. Physiology Acad. Sci., Prague, 1971-74, head of lab. Inst. Exptl. Medicine, 1975—, dir. Inst. Exptl. Medicine, 1994—; assoc. prof. medicine Charles U., Prague, 1991-96, prof. medicine, 1996—; vis. scientist dept. physiology U. Western Australia, Perth, 1985-86; chmn. Commn. Auditory Physiology, Internat. Union Physiol. Scis., 1993-97. Editor: Acoustical Signal Processing in the Central Auditory System, 1997; co-editor: Neuronal Mechanisms of Hearing, 1981, Auditory Pathway—Structure and Function, 1988; co-author: Physiology and Pathophysiology of Vision and Hearing, 1981. Vice-chmn. rsch. and devel. coun. of Govt. of Czech Republic, 1992—. Mem. Czech Neurosci. Soc. (chmn. 1992—), Czech Physiol. Soc. (coun. mem. 1982-95), Internat. Brain Rsch. Orgn. (Czech. rep. 1993—), European Sci. Found. (coun. mem. 1998—), Italian Audiol. Soc. (hon.), Czech Med. Soc. (hon.). Avocations: classical music, gardening, skiing, tennis. Office: Inst Exptl Medicine, Acad Sci Videnska 1083, 142 20 Prague 4 Czech Republic

SYKAS, EFSTATHIOS D., electrical and computer engineering educator; b. Athens, Greece, Feb. 28, 1956; s. Dimitrios E. and Eleni V. (Tsavalia) S.; m. Xenia G. Anagnostou, Apr. 23, 1993. Diploma, Nat. Tech. U. Athens, 1979, Doctorate, 1984. Diplomate in engring. Teaching asst. dept. elec. engring., div. computer sci. Nat. Tech. U. Athens, 1979-84, lectr., 1986-88, asst. prof., 1988-92, assoc. prof., 1992-96; prof. Nat. Tech. U., Athens, 1996—, dir. computer sci. divsn., 1997-2000; bd. govs. Inst. Comm. and Computer Sys., 1999—; work package leader several projects. Contbr. articles to profl. jours. I.K.Y. fellow, Greek State, 1974-79. Mem. IEEE, Assn. for Computing Machinery, Tech. Chamber of Greece (T.E.E. award 1976-79). Office: Nat Tech U Athens Dept Elec Engring, Heroon Polytechneiou 9, Athens 15 773, Greece

SYKES, ALFRED GEOFFREY, chemist, educator; b. Huddersfield, Jan. 12, 1934; s. Alfred H. and Edith Wortley S.; m. Elizabeth Blakey; 3 children. PhD, Huddersfield Coll., 1958; DSc, U. Manchester, 1973. Lectr. U. Leeds, Eng., 1961-70, reader, 1970-80; prof. inorganic chemistry U. Newcastle-upon-Tyne, 1980-99, prof. emeritus, 1999; panel mem. SERC Inorganic Chem., 1980-83, EPSRC/BBSRC com., writing panels; vis. prof. Argonne Nat. Labs., 1968, Heidelberg U., 1975, Northwestern U., 1978, U. Berne, 1981, U. Sydney, 1984, U. Kuwait, 1989, U. Adelaide, 1992, U. Melbourne, 1992, Meml. U. Nfld., 1995, U. of the West Indies, 1997, U. Lausanne, 1998, South Africa, 1999, U. La Laguna, Spain, 2000. Author: Kinetics of Inorganic Reactions, 1964; editor: Advanced Inorganic Chemistry, Vols. 32-51; contbr. 450 articles to chemistry jours. Recipient Tilden medal Royal Soc. Chem., 1984; JSPS fellow, 1984. Fellow Royal Soc. Avocations: travel, classical music, sports. Home: 73 Beech Ct, Newcastle-upon-Tyne NE20 9NE, England Office: Univ Newcastle-upon-Tyne, Dept Chemistry, Newcastle-upon-Tyne NE1 7RU, England

SYKES, DAVID MICHAEL, office supplies executive; b. Nottingham, England, June 10, 1954; s. Michael Le Gallais and Joan (Groome) S.; m. Margaret Lynne McGreavy, Apr. 1, 1950; children: Stephen David, Joanna Lauren. Sales dir. Frank Groome (Nottingham) Ltd., Ilkeston, England, 1974-85; mng. dir. Sykes Office Supplies, Nottingham, 1985—, Libra Office Equipment Ltd.

SYKES, NIGEL PHILIP, palliative medicine physician, consultant; b. London, Oct. 10, 1954; s. Basil and Margaret (Knee) S.; m. Anne Charlotte Lloyd, Aug. 11, 1984; children: Catherine, Rachel, Peter. BA, Oxford (Eng.) U., 1977, BM, BCh, 1980, MA, 1981. Registrar in gen. practice Airedale (Eng.) Health Authority, 1981-84; Macmillan lectr. palliative medicine U. Leeds, Eng., 1987-91, mem. faculty bd. medicine, 1988-91; registrar, sr. registrar in palliative medicine St. Christopher's Hospice, London, 1985-87, cons. in palliative medicine, 1991—; chmn. palliative care working group Yorkshire (Eng.) Cancer Orgn., 1988-91; hon. cons. St. Thomas' Hosp., London, 1991—, Guy's Hosp., London, 1991—; sr. lectr. King's Coll., U. London; mem. regional specialist subcom. for palliative medicine South Thames Regional Health Authority, 1993-97; invited spkr. numerous internat. meetings, including U. Chgo., 1995, Hospice Assn. So. Africa, 1995, Portuguese Palliative Care Assn., 1996, Brit. Coun., Zimbabwe, 1998, Krakow Hospice Conf., Poland, 1999, Pain in Europe, Nice, 2000. Contbg. author: Oxford Textbook of Palliative Medicine, 1993, 2d edit., 1997; co-editor: The Management of Terminal Malignant Disease, 1993; mem. editl. adv. com. Hospice Jour., 1995-99, Jour. Palliative Medicine, 1998—; contbr. numerous articles to med. jours., including Lancet, Palliative Medicine, Jour. Pain and Symptom Mgmt., Geriatric Medicine, also chpts. to books. Spkr. all-party hospice com. Houses of Parliament, London, 1995. Fellow Royal Coll. Gen. Practitioners; mem. Assn. for Palliative Medicine Gt. Britain and Ireland (treas., exec. com. 1988-92, mem. ethics com. 1995—, Evans prize for rsch. 1991), European Assn. for Palliative Medicine, Brit. Med. Assn., Oxford Med. Grads. Soc. Anglican. Office: St Christopher's Hospice, Lawrie Park Rd, London SE26 6DZ, England

SYKOVA, EVA, neuroscientist, researcher; b. Rozmital, Czechoslovakia, July 24, 1944; d. Karel and Anna (Rokytova) S.; m. Josef Syka, Feb. 16, 1969; children: Josef, Michael. MD, Charles U., Prague, Czechoslovakia, 1970; PhD, Czechoslovak Acad. Scis., Prague, Czechoslovakia, 1976; DSc, Masaryk U., Brno, Czechoslovakia, 1990. Postdoctoral rschr. Inst. Physiology Czechoslovak Acad. Scis., Prague, 1976-83, head lab. neurohumoral regulation, 1983-90; head lab. cellular neurophysiology Inst. Exptl. Medicine Acad. Scis. Czech Republic, Prague, 1991—; assoc. prof. Charles U., Prague, 1994—; chmn. dept. neuroscis. Second Med. Sch., Charles U., Prague, 1996—; chairperson sect. for med. scis. Grant Agy. of the Czech Rep., Prague, 1995—; mem. sci. adv. com. Inst. of Developmental Neurosci. and Aging, Denver, 1996—; presenter, spkr. numerous lectrs. and seminars. Author: Ionic and Volume Changes in the Microenvironment of Nerve and Receptor Cells, 1992; editor: Neuronal-Astrocytic Interactions: Implications for Normal and Pathological CNS Function, 1992, Ion-Selective Microelectrodes and their Use in Excitable Tissues, 1981; author more than 23 chpts. to books; mem. editl. bd. The Neuroscientist, 1994—, Glia, 1997—; contbr. more than 65 articles to profl. jours. including Jour. Physiology, Jour. Neurophysiology, Neurosci., Brain Rsch., Glia, Jour. Cerebral Blood Flow and Metabolism, The Neuroscientist, among others. Recipient awards Czech Med. Soc. J.E. Purkyne, 1992, 94, Czech Acad. Scis., 1997, Czech Neurosci. Soc., 1993. Mem. Czech Physiol. Socy. (sci. sec. 1990—, prize 1984), European Biomed. Rsch. Assn. (internat. exec. com. 1994—), Am. Soc. for Neurosci., N.Y. Acad. Scis., Internat. Union Physiol. Scis., Internat. Brain Rsch. Orgn. Office: Inst Exptl Medicine ASCR, Videnska 1083, 142 40 Prague 4, Czech Republic

SYLVESTER, LYNDA JOANN, product designer; b. Chgo., Apr. 30, 1950; d. Kenna (Gunderson) S. Student, U. Wis., Boston Mus. Fine Arts, Parsons Sch. of Design. Owner Kegonsa Gen. Store, Madison, 1969-75, Windward Specialties, Captiva Island, Fla., 1975-80, Lynda Sylvester Designs, N.Y.C., Sag Harbor, N.Y., 1980—; pres. Sylvester & Co. Inc., Sag Harbor, 1987—; owner Harbor Mercantile, Sag Harbor, 1993-97, Sylvester Co. Wholesale. patentee in field. Mem. Village Planning Bd., Sag Harbor, 1993-98. Democrat. Avocations: drawing, painting, photography. Home: PO Box 1192 Sag Harbor NY 11963-0039

SYLVESTER, NANCY KATHERINE, speech educator, management consultant; b. Evansville, Ind., July 17, 1947; d. Leonard Nicholas and Marjore (Moore) Jochim; m. James Andrew Sylvester, Aug 21, 1971; children: Marcy Dee, Holly Nicole. BS, Ind. State U., 1969; MA, U. Mich., 1970. Registered profl. parliamentarian; cert. prof. parliamentarian; leadership/team/meeting mgmt. specialist; cert. tchr. of parliamentary procedure. Assoc. prof. speech Rock Valley Coll., Rockford, Ill., 1970—; co-owner Jimmy's Frozen Custard, 1996—; bd. dirs., chmn. bd. First Fed. Savs. Bank, Belvidere, Ill., 1996-98. Author: Basics of Parliamentary Procedure, 1997, Handbook for Effective Meetings, 1993; contbr. articles to profl. jours. Bd. dirs. Jr. League Rockford, 1974-78, Rock River Homeowners Assn., 1990-91; pres. Children's Devel. Ctr. Aux. Bd., Rockford, 1984-85; parliamentarian Winnebago County Dem. Caucus, 1991; vice-chmn. Commn. on Am. Parliamentary Practice, 1989-90, chmn., 1990-91; nat. parliamentarian Girl Scouts U.S., 1996-97, bd. dirs. Rock River coun., 1979-81. Recipient Jardene medal Ind. State U., 1969, RVC Faculty of Yr. award, 1994, Athena award Rockford Area C. of C., 1999; Rockham scholar U. Mich., 1969-70. Mem. Am. Inst. Parliamentarians, Am. Soc. Women Accts. (parliamentarian 1980—), Am. Women Soc. CPAs (parliamentarian 1991-96), Nat. Coun. State Bds. Nursing (parliamentarian 1992-99), Am. Vet. Med. Assn. (parliamentarian 1998—), Ill. Assn. Parliamentarians, Am. Assn. Nurse Anesthetists (parliamentarian 2000—), Nat. Assn. Ins. Women (parliamentarian 1983-91), Nat. Assn. Parliamentarians (bd. dirs. 1997—, chmn. nat. nominating com. 1997-99, chmn. bylaws com. 1999-01), Assn. Quali ty and Participation, Speech Commn. Assn., Coun. Better Bus. Burs. (parliamentarian 1993), Nat. League Nursing (parliamentarian), Rockford C. of C. (ex-officio bd. dirs., Athena award 1999), Phi Rho Pi (region 4 v.p. 1972-73, nat. v.p. 1973-74), Am. Soc. Pain Mgmt. Nurses (nat. parliamentarian 1994-97), Ind. Accts. Assn. Ill. (parliamentrian 1990—), Info. Sys. Audit and Control Assn. (parliamentarian 1994-98), Am. Speech-Lang.-Hearing Assn. (parlia mentarian 1999—). Fax: 815-877-5290. E-mail: nancysylvester@home.com. Home and Office: 4826 River Bluff Ct Loves Park IL 61111-5836

SYMONDS, EDWARD, energy economist, consultant; b. Rugby, Eng., 1919; s. Henry Herbert and Gwendolen (Wortley) S.; m. Margaret Elizabeth Holness, Nov. 12, 1949; children: Matthew, Katharine, Hugh, John. Student, Mil. Coll. Sci., Woolwich, Eng., 1944; MA, Oriel U., Oxford, Eng., 1947. Editor Economist Jours., London, 1947-53, World Bank, Washington, 1953-59; v.p. Citibank, N.Y.C., 1959-74; dep. asst. sec. U.S. Dept. Treas., Washington, 1974-75; cons. Energy Econs. and Fin., Dorchester, Eng., 1976—; chmn. Environ. Commn., New Vernon, N.J., 1982-85. Author: Petroleum Economist, 1949—. Capt. Brit. Army, 1939-46. Mem. Protection Rural Eng. (coun. mem. 1987). Democrat. Avocations: hill climbing, cycling. Home and Office: Energy Econs & Fin, Rly Cottage Toller Porcorum, Dorchester DT2 ODJ, England

SYMONS, HUGH WILLIAMS, food technologist; b. Kosgama, Sri Lanka, Jan. 4, 1927; came to U.S., 1978; s. William Shawe and Olive Margaret (Mansell) S.; m. Judith Mary Tatlock, Feb. 27, 1965; children: Lucy, Victoria. MA, Queens' Coll., Cambridge, Eng., 1951. Chartered biologist; mastership in food control. Chemist Hector Whaling, London, 1953-58; co. quality contr. Birds Eye Foods Ltd., Surrey, Eng., 1958-78; sr. v.p. Am. Frozen Food Inst., McLean, Va., 1978-92. Editor: Processing and Handling of Quick Frozen Foods, 1985. Sub-lt. Royal Naval Vol. Res., 1946-48. Fellow Inst. Food Sci. and Tech. (v.p. 1972-74), Inst. of Biology, Inst. of Refrigeration, Internat. Acad. Food Sci. & Tech.; mem. Cherry Mktg. Inst. (Okemos, Mich., bd. dirs. 1988-92). Home and Office: 35 Knights Park, Kingston upon Thames KT1 2QH, England

SYMONS, MARTYN CHRISTIAN, chemistry educator; b. Suffolk, Eng., Nov. 12, 1925; s. Stephen White and Marjorie (Lebraseur) S.; m. Janice Olive O'Connor, Jan. 12, 1970 (dec. 1995); children: Rebecca, Richard; ptnr. Irene White, 1998. BS, Battersea Poly., London, 1946, PhD, 1953, DSc, 1960. Lectr. Battersea Poly., 1948-53, Southampton (Eng.) U., 1953-60; prof. phys. chemistry Leicester (Eng.) U., 1960-88, rsch. prof. chemistry, 1988-93; vis. rsch. prof. chemistry DeMontfort U., 1993—, Nottingham Trent U., 1997—; vis. prof. biol. chemistry U. Greenwich, 1997—; Cancer Rsch. Campaign sr. fellow, Leicester, 1988-93; vis. prof. biol. chemistry U. Essex, 1997—, chemistry St. Bartholomew Med. Sch., London, 1997—. Author: Structure of Inorganic Radicals, 1967, Chemical Aspects of Electron Spin Resonance Spectroscopy, 1978, Techniques in Free Radical Research, 1991, Iron and Free Radicals: Chemistry, Biology and Medicine. Fellow Royal Soc., Royal Soc. of Chemistry (Brucker lectr. 1986, R.A. Robinson lectr. 1987), Am. Chem. Soc., Royal Soc. Arts. Avocations: watercolor painting, piano. Home: 33 Castle Rd, Hadleigh, Southend S57 2AU, England Office: De Montfort Universtiy, LE 19 BH Leicester England

SYMS, HELEN MAKSYM, educational administrator; b. Wilkes Barre, Pa., Nov. 12, 1918; d. Walter and Anna (Kowalewski) Maksym; m. Louis

Harold Syms, Aug. 16, 1947; children: Harold Edward, Robert Louis. BA, Hunter Coll., 1941; MS, Columbia U., 1947; teaching credentials, Calif. State U., Northridge, 1964. Statis. clk. McGraw Hill Pub. Co., N.Y.C., 1941-42; acct. Flexpansion Corp., N.Y.C., 1943-47, Oliver Wellington & Co., N.Y.C., 1947-48, Broadcast Measurement Bur., N.Y.C., 1948-51; tchr. Calif. State U., Northridge, 1964, Burbank (Calif.) Unified Sch. Dist., 1964-79; chmn. bus. edn. dept. Burbank H.S., 1974-79; docent, acct. arts coun. Calif. State U., Northridge, 1979—; tchr. MEND-Meet Each Need with Dignity Learning Ctr., Pacoima, Calif., 1987-89; assoc. dir. M.E.N.D. (Meet Each Need with Dignity) Learning Ctr., Pacoima, Calif., 1989-96. Mem. Phi Beta Kappa, Delta Kappa Gamma (pres. 1972-74, treas. Xi chpt. 1982-90, 92—, treas. area IX 1975-78). Home: 9219 Whitaker Ave Northridge CA 91343-3538

SYNEK, MIROSLAV, physicist, chemist, world affairs independent consultant, researcher; b. Prague, Czechoslovakia, Sept. 18, 1930; came to U.S., 1958, naturalized, 1963; s. Frantisek and Anna (Kokrment) S.; children: Mary Rose, Thomas Robert. Student, Indsl. Chemistry Tech. Sch., Prague, 1946-50; cert. in liberal arts, Prague, 1951; MS in Physics with distinction, Charles U., Prague, 1956; PhD in Physics, U. Chgo., 1963. Analytical chemist Indsl. Medicine Inst., Prague, 1950-51; rsch. physicist Acad. Scis., Prague, 1956-58; from asst. to assoc. prof. De Paul U., Chgo., 1962-67; prof. Tex. Christian U., Ft. Worth, 1967-71; lectr., rschr. U. Tex., Austin, 1971-75; tenured faculty U. Tex., San Antonio, 1975-95; sci. advisor Tex. Edn. Agy., Austin, 1971-73, U. Tex., 1971-73; advisor Student Physics Soc., active numerous univ. coms. Contbr. numerous articles to sci. jours., abstracts to presentations. Campaigner United Way, San Antonio, 1975-95; judge Alamo Sci. Fair and Tex. Acad. of Sci. Fairs; grand award judge Internat. Sci. and Engring. Fair, 1998, 99. Rsch. grantee Robert A. Welch Found., 1968-71, 76-83, 93-95. Fellow AAAS, Am. Phys. Soc. (life), Tex. Acad. Sci., Am. Inst. Chemists; mem. NEA, Tex. State Tchrs. Assn., AAUP, DAV Comdrs. Club, Am. Assn. Physics Tchrs., Am. Mus. Natural History, Libr. Congress, Smithsonian Instn., Internat. Platform Assn., N.Y. Acad. Scis., Am. Chem. Soc., Czechoslovak Nat. Coun. (dist. sec. Chgo. 1961-63, chmn. 1967), Czechoslovak Soc. Arts and Scis. Am., Internat. Soc. Poets (disting. mem.), Sheriffs' Assn. Tex. (assoc.), San Antonio Astronomical Assn., World Affairs Coun. (diplomat mem.), Bexar County Czech Heritage Soc., Sigma Xi (life), Sigma Pi Sigma. Roman Catholic. Achievements include research in atomic structure calculations of laser-active lanthanides, analytical relativistic self-consistent field theory, approximate estimate of the extra-terrestrial intelligence probability, nuclear age requiring free elections. E-mail: m.synek@juno.com. Home and Office: PO Box 4911 San Antonio TX 78280-4911

SYNOVITZ, LINDA BAILY, health studies educator; b. Omaha, Apr. 11, 1943; d. Michael John and Gladys E. Harris; m. John Hayes Baily, Oct. 18, 1964 (div. May 1981); children: Blake Harris, Jared Hayes; m. Robert Joseph Synovitz, Aug. 11, 1985. RN, Meth. Hosp. Sch. Nursing, Peoria, Ill., 1964; BA in Health Scis., Western Ill. U., 1981, MS in Cmty. Health, 1985; PhD in Curriculum and Instrn., Kent State U., 1993. RN, Ill., La.; cert. health edn. specialist; cert. health edn. secondary tchr., Ill. Nurse, psychiat. nurse Abbot Ctr. Ward for Children Peoria State Hosp., Bartonville, Ill., 1964-65; nurse, psychiat. nurse, asst. head nurse med. ward Meth. Hosp., Peoria, 1965-67; nurse post-surg. ward McDonough Dist. Hosp., Macomb, Ill., 1967-68, 69-72; nurse post-surg. ward and emergency rm. McDonough Dist. Hosp., Macomb, 1976-78; nurse BEU Health Ctr. Western ill. U., Macomb, 1978-79; instr., placement counselor, faculty specialist Robert Morris Coll., Carthage, Ill., 1981-86; dir. audiovisual dept. Robert Morris Coll., Carthage, 1981-86; instr. dept. health scis. Western Ill. U., Macomb, 1986-87; DON Macomb Manor Nursing Home, 1987; instr. CNA program Spoon River Coll., 1988; instr. dept. health scis. Western Ill. U., 1988-89; instr., tchg. fellow dept. adult, counseling, health Kent State U., 1989-92; asst. prof. health edn. dept. phys. edn./health edn. divsn. No. Ill. U., DeKalb, 1992-96; asst. prof. health edn. dept. kinesiology and health studies Southeastern La. U., 1996—, co-grad. program coord., dept. curriculum chair, 1996—; substitute tchr. Macomb Pub. Sch. Sys., 1987-89; cons. health edn. curriculum revision Main Twp. H.S., Chgo., summer 1996; presenter in field. Contbr. articles to profl. jours. Recipient Cert. Appreciation, Nat. Injury and Violence Prevention Task Force, 1999; W.I. Taylor Health Sci. scholar Western Ill. U. Coll. Health, Phys. Edn., Recreation Found., 1980, Dorothy R. Hansen scholar, 1981, Eta Sigma Gamma scholar, 1981; grantee Ill. HIV/AIDS Prevention PRoject, 1993, 94, 95, U.S. Dept. Health and Human Svcs., Maternal and Child Health, 1997, Office of Adolescent Pregnancy Program, 1997, Southeastern La. U., 1998, 98, 99, Kellogg, Ford, Asian, Luce, Rockefeller, GE and Spencer Founds., 1998. Fellow Am. Sch. Health Assn. (mem. continuing edn. and program evaluation 1991-94, mem. conv. program planning com. 1991, 93-96, mem. awards com. 1995-97, nat. injury and violence prevention task force 1997, 98, tchg. techniques com. reviewer 1997, co-chair awards com. 1997, vice-chair sexuality coun. 1997-98, chair sexuality coun. 1998-99, bd. reps. 1998-2000, tchg. techniques com. reviewer 1998, violence prevention coun. rep. to health edn. sect. 1998, bd. dirs. 1998, rep. to nat. adv. panel to evaluation Am. Social Health Assn. teen sexual health web site 1999, mem. nominating com. 1999, Disting. Svc. award 1998); mem. Am. Alliance for Health, Phys. Edn., Recreation and Dance, La. Alliance for Health, Phys. Edn., Recreation and Dance, So. Dist. Alliance for Health, Phys. Edn., Recreation and Dance, Am. Assn. for Health Edn. (sch. health edn. adv. 1995, rsch. coordinating bd. proposal reviewer 1997), Am. Coll. Health Assn., Am. Sch. Health Assn., Sex Info. and Edn. Coun. of the U.S., Ill. Sch. Health Assn. (treas. 1996), La. Coun. on Comprehensive Sch. Health Edn. Program, PEO Sisterhood (sec., treas., v.p.), Phi Kappa Phi, Eta Sigma Gamma (mem. Gamman of the yr. com. 1992-95, chmn. Gamman of the yr. com. 1993-95). E-mail: lsynovitz@selu.edu. Office: Southeastern La Univ Slu 10845 Hammond LA 70402-0001

SYPHERS, MARY FRANCES, music educator; b. Floresville, Tex., Sept. 26, 1912; d. Little Fleming and Lillian Frances (Herrington) Spruce; m. Ansel James Syphers, July 23, 1959 (dec. 1972). BA in English, U. Tex., 1938; MEd, So. Meth. U., Dallas, 1950; studied voice with Dr. Wilcox, 1947, studied composition with Roy Harris, 1947, studied Music Edn. with Augustus Zansig. Cert. high sch. music tchr., cert. elem. tchr., Tex. Tchr. music Ehlers Country Sch., Poth, Tex., 1931-35, Poth Ind. Sch. Dist., 1936-40, Sinton (Tex.) Ind. Sch. Dist., 1941, Stephen J. Hay Sch., Dallas, 1942-50, Alamo Sch., Dallas, 1951—, Edwin J. Kiest Sch., Dallas, 1955—, Lakewood Elem., Dallas, 1976-81; voice, drama tchr. Poth Ind. Sch. dist., 1936-40. Contbg. author: New England To Texas, 1986. Choir dir. 1st Meth. Ch., Sinton, Tex., 1941-42; soloist, jr. choir dir. Oaklawn Meth. Ch., Dallas, 1942-43; soloist 1st Presbyn. Ch., Dallas, 1943-46, Highland Park Presbyn. Ch., Dallas, 1946-47; symphony chorus Dallas Music Staff, 1944-60; mem. choir St. Michael and All Angels Episocpal Ch., Dallas, 1949-91; organizer jr. female vols. USO, Dallas, 1960-70, coordinator jr. female vols. anniversary celebration, Dallas, 1966; mem. publicity com. So. Meml. Assn., Dallas, 1981; life mem. PTA; mem. Shakespeare Study Club. Recipient Citation as member of concert choir Am. Culture and Lang. Ctr., Salzburg, Austria, 1987. Mem. New Eng. Women (pres. Tex. chpt. 1985-87), Dallas Coun. World Affairs, Dallas Inst. Humanities (sponser), Buckland Hist. Soc. (life), Nat. Soc. Colonial Dames (chmn. 1981-90), DAR (Jane Douglas chpt.), Standard Club Dallas (recreation sec. 1981-91), Delta Kappa Gamma (pres. Epsilon chpt. 1960-62). Democrat. Episcopalian. Avocations: genealogy, book binding, picture taking, reading, family history. Home: 2729 Laurel Oaks Dr Garland TX 75044-6939

SYRISTOVA, EVA, psychologist, philosopher; b. Prague, Nov. 7, 1928; d. Josef and Miroslava (Vitvarova) Voparil; m. Jaroslav Syriste, Dec. 5, 1925; 1 child. DPhil, Charles U., Prague, 1951. Editor SPN Pubs., Prague, 1951-53; clin. psychologist Inst. Psychiatry, Prague, 1953-57; lectr. psychopathology, psychotherapy U. Charles, Prague, 1957-67, prof., 1967-94, prof. emeritus, 1994. Author: The Possibilities and Limitations of the Psychotherapy of Schizophrenic Diseases, 1965, The Imaginary World, 1973, Normality of the Personality, 1973, The Cracked Time, 1989, The Group Psychotherapy of Psychoses, 1989, Man in Crisis, 1994, The Poem as a Home in the Homeless of Paul Celan, 1994. Recipient Hon. prize Cultural Ctr. Prague, 1983. Mem. Internat. Assn. of Applied Psychology, Internat. Brain Rsch. Orgn., Czech Med., Psychiat., Psychol. and Artistic Assn., N.Y. Acad. Scis., Internat. Soc. Phenomenology and Scis. of Life, Assn. White Raven for Nonprofl. Art in Prague (bd. dirs.). Avocations: poetry, painting, sculpture, music. Home: Sluknovska 316, 190 00 Prague 9, Czech Republic

SYROMYATNIKOV, VLADISLAV GENRIKHOVICH, physicist; b. Kolchugino, Vladimir, Russia, Apr. 17, 1954; s. Genrikh Anatol'evich and Tamara Aleksandrovna S.; m. Ol'ga Vasil'evna Razvodovskaya, May 7, 1977; children: Arsenii, Dar'ya. Grad., Petersburg State U., St. Petersburg, Russia, 1977. Field worker-rschr. Petersburg Nuclear Physics Inst. Russian Acad. of Scis., Gatchina, Russia, 1977-79, major lab. asst., 1979-80, jr. rsch. worker, 1980-89, rsch. worker, 1989—; dep. chmn. Coun. Young Scientists, Petersburg Nuclear Physics Inst., 1983-87. Contbr. articles to profl. jours.

SYRON, MARTIN BERNARD, business executive; b. Man., Can., Sept. 27, 1936; married; children—Karra, Julie, Kristie. Grad., U. Windsor, Ont., Can., U. Ottawa, Ont., Can. Legal counsel Harvey's Foods Ltd., Toronto, Ont., Can., 1968-69; v.p., dir. Foodcorp Ltd., Toronto, Ont., Can., 1969-72, pres., dir., 1972-84; dir., pres., chief operating officer Cara Ops., Toronto, Ont., Can., 1977-90, chmn. bd., CEO, 1990—; chmn. Cara Ops., Mississauga, Ont.; dir. Swiss Chalet Bar-B-Q, Inc., Toronto, Devco, Toronto, Marbe, Toronto. Club: Granite (dir.) (Toronto). Home: 49 Highland Ave, Toronto, ON Canada M4W 2A2 Office: Cara Ops Ltd, 6303 Airport Rd, Mississauga, ON Canada L4V 1R8*

SYRON, RICHARD FRANCIS, financial executive, economist; b. Boston, Oct. 25, 1943; s. Dominick Richard and Elizabeth (McQuire) S.; m. Margaret Mary Garatoni, Oct. 21, 1972; children: Erin Elizabeth, Brendan Paul. BS in Econs.-Acctg. with high honors, Boston Coll., 1966; MA in Econs., Tufts U., 1969, PhD in Econs., 1971. Dep. dir. budget Commonwealth of Mass., 1973-74; v.p., economist Fed. Res. Bank of Boston, 1974-82, sr. v.p., econ. advisor, 1982-85; exec. asst. to sec. U.S. Treasury, Washington, 1979-80; dep. sec. for econ. policy U.S. Treasury, 1980-81; asst. to Chmn. Volcker Fed. Res. Bd., Washington, 1981-82; pres., CEO Fed. Home Loan Bank of Boston, 1986-88; pres., chief exec. officer Fed. Res. Bank of Boston, 1989-94; chmn. Am. Stock Exch., N.Y.C., 1994-99; chmn., pres., CEO Thermo Electron, Waltham, Mass., 1999—; past chmn. Boston Coll.; past chmn. Boston Pvt. Industry Coun.; bd. dirs. John Hancock Mut. Life Ins. Co., Boston, Dreyfus Corp. Author: Urban Fire Insurance, 1972; contbr. articles to profl. jours. Teaching fellow Tufts U., 1966-69. Mem. Boston Econ. Club (past pres.), Comml. Club Boston, Clover Club (Boston), Wianno Yacht Club, N.Y. Athletic Club, N.Y. Athletic Club Yacht Club, Siwanoy Country Club. Office: Thermo Electrons 81 Wyman St Waltham MA 02454

SYROPOULOS, APOSTOLOS, computer scientist, educator; b. Bad Wimpfen, Germany, Dec. 4, 1965; s. Georgios and Vassiliki (Rentzos) S.; m. Styliani Charisis, May 14, 1994 (div.); 1 child, Demetrios-Georgios. BSc in Physics, U. Ioannina, 1989; MSc in Computer Sci., U. Göteborg, 1993. Computer programmer U. Ioannina, 1988-89, Democritus U. Thrace, 1990-91, Tech. Editions, Athens, 1996; computer educator Secondary Edn., Greece, 1996—; pres. Greek Tex Group. Author: LaTex, 1998; co-author: Tex and Digital Typography: 110 questions and answers, 1998; editor: (Greek Tex Users Group newsletter) Eutupon. With Greek Army, 1993-94. Mem. Assn. for Computer Machinery (spl. interest group on programming langs.), Greek Tex's Group, Sigplan. Avocations: digital typography, astronomy, philosophy, coin and stamp collection. Home: 366 28th October St, GR 67100 Xanthi Greece

SYROS, CONSTANTIN ELIAS, physics educator; s. Elias and Panajota (Korasidis) S.; m. Gerda Maria Marbach, Dec. 18, 1963. Diploma, U. Athens, 1955; PhD in Physics and Math., U. Cologne, 1961; diploma, Nuclear Rsch. Ctr., Karlsruhe, Germany, 1962. Asst. Inst. Theoretical Physics U. Cologne, 1959-61; rschr. Euratom Reactor Physics, Ispra, Italy, 1961-67; sci. sec. Euratom CBNM, Geel, Belgium, 1967-68, European Am. Nuclear Data Com., Brussels, 1967-68, European Working Group for Reactor Dosimetry, Brussels, 1967-68; advisor Commn. of the European Commn., Brussels, 1968-75; prof. physics and nuclear tech. U. Patras, 1969—, rector, 1976-77, dir. physics sect., 1983-92, chmn. engring. sci. dept., 1991-93; Inventor device for reduction of neutron flux in reactors and new propeller type; contbr. articles to profl. jours. Sec. Inf., 1952-54. Grantee German Rsch. Cmty., 1959-61, European Commn., 1991-94. Mem. Am. Math. Soc., European Phys. Soc., German Phys. Soc., Hellenic Nuc. Phys. Soc., Union Greeek Physicists, Rotary. Avocations: jogging, accordion. Office: U Patras Lab Nuclear Tech, PO Box 1418, 26110 Patras Greece

SYTKO, VLADIMIR, physicist, educator, researcher; b. Grodno, Belarus, Oct. 11, 1951; s. Vladimir Alexander and Alexandra Ivan (Rudenya) S.; m. Olga Yakov Yunakova, June 16, 1990; m. Natalia Vladimir Chashchina, July 6, 1974 (div. Jan. 1988); 1 child, Andrew. DS in physics, Gomel (Belarus) State U., 1974. Rschr. Belarus State U., Minsk, 1974-77; rschr. Gomel State U., 1977-87, prof., 1987—, chief metrologist, 1997—, mem. sci. degree coun., 1995-97; mem. Belarus Metrological Acad., Minsk, 1994-97. Author: Theoretical Metrology, 1997; contbr. articles to profl. jours; patentee in field. Recipient Testimonial award World Exhbn. of Achievements of Young Inventors, 1985. Russian Orthodox. Avocations: fishing, travel. Home: Sovetskaya St 106-72, 246028 Gomel Belarus Office: Gomel State U, Sovetskaya St 104, 246028 Gomel Belarus

SYVÄLAHTI, ERKKA KARL, pharmacology educator; b. Turku, Finland, Aug. 17, 1946; s. Erkki Karl and Sisko (Valtonen) S.; m. Riitta Kristina Väisänen, June 10, 1972; children: Pekka, Hanne. MD, U. Turku, 1972; specialist psychiatry, Sweden, 1984; PhD, 1976; Docent Psychiatry, Helsinki U., 1986. Rsch. assoc. U. Turku, 1972-75, lectr., 1976-77, prof. pharmacology, 1989—; clin. pharmacologist Astra Co., Stockholm, 1977-80; sr. researcher Acad. Finland, Helsinki, 1981-87; permanent advisor Ministry of Health Affairs, Finland, 1989—. Contbr. articles to profl. jours. Med. lt. Finnish mil. Recipient Hon. Rsch. award Ciba-Geigy Found., 1987. Mem. Scandinavian Soc. Psychopharmacology (bd. mem. 1987—), Finnish Pharmacol. Soc. (bd. mem. 1989—), Brain Rsch. Soc. (bd. mem. 1984-88), Ethical Com. (chmn. 1989—). Home: Nahkurinpiha 1 A 9, FIN20110 Turku Finland Office: U Turku Dept Pharmacology, Kiinamyllynk 10, FIN20520 Turku Finland

SYVÄNNE, MIKKO SAKARI, cardiologist, consultant; b. Helsinki, Finland, Sept. 5, 1951; s. Niilo Viktor and Sirkka Helena Syvänne; m. Mirja Anneli Suomalainen, Feb. 28, 1975. Lic. medicine, U. Helsinki, 1977, MD, PhD, 1995. Gen. practitioner Vantaa (Finland) Mcpl. Health Svc., 1977-84; resident in internal medicine Jorvi Dist. Hosp., Espoo, Finland, 1984-86; resident in internal medicine Helsinki U. Ctrl. Hosp., 1986-88, specialist clin. investigator, 1988-95, fellow in cardiology, 1995-98, consulting cardiologist, 1998—. Contbr. articles to profl. jours. Fellow Finnish Cardiac Soc.; mem. Finnish Soc. Internal Medicine. Fax: 358-9-471-74047. Office: Helsinki U Ctrl Hosp, PO Box 340, 00029 Helsinki Finland

SZABADI, JUDITH, art historian, educator; b. Pápa, Hungary, Nov. 24, 1940; d. Bela and Vilma (Bartha) S. MA, U. Budapest, 1964, PhD in Art History, 1981. Editor Corvina Press, Budapest, 1964—; sr. lectr. Acad. of Art, Budapest, 1984—; sr. curator Hungarian Nat. Gallery, Budapest, 1990-95; dept. head Acad. Fine Arts, Budapest, 1993—. Author: Endre Bálint, 1969, L. Gulacsy, 1969, J. Rippl-Ronay, 1978, Art Nouveau in Hungary, 1979, A magyar szecesszió művészete, 1979, Jugendstil in Ungarn, 1982, The Life and Art of Lajos Gulácsy, 1983, Tradition and Modernity, 1987, Art Nouveau in Hungary, 1989, Igy elt Rippl-Rohai, 1990, Manet A Modern elet heroizmusa, 1995, The Kieselbach Collection, Hungarian Painting 1900-1945, 1996; contbr. articles to profl. jours. Research grantee Hungarian Acad. Scis.-Soros Found., 1986, 88. Mem. Hungarian Art Soc., Hungarian Art Found. Office: Acad Fine Arts, Andrassy ut 69-71, 1062 Budapest Hungary

SZABADOS, TAMAS, mathematician, educator; b. Budapest, Hungary, May 14, 1948; s. Istvan and Ibolya (Kardos) S.; m. Eva Kosa, Aug. 14, 1974; children: Gabor, Kinga. Diploma in Elec. Engring., Tech. U., Budapest, 1972; Diploma in Math., Lorand Eotvos U., Budapest, 1978, PhD in Math., 1982. Rsch. fellow Tech. U., Budapest, 1972-74, asst. prof., 1974-96, assoc. prof. math., 1996—; vis. rschr. Carleton U., Ottawa, Can., 1979-80; vis. instr. Spokane Falls Coll., Wash., 1991-92; adj. prof. Budapest Semester in Math., 1996—, Western Md. Coll. Budapest br., 1998-99; external fellow math. immunology group Math. Rsch. Inst. of Hungarian Acad. Scis., 1997—; cons. Videoton Electronics Co., Budapest, 1981-88. Author: (book) Vektoranalizis, 1983; contbr. articles to profl. jours. and publs. Mem. Janos Bolyai Math. Soc., Am. Math. Soc., Bernoulli Soc. Avocations: reading, tennis. Office: Tech U Dept Math, EGRY U 20-22, 1521 Budapest Hungary

SZABO, CSABA ATTILA, telecommunications educator; b. Judenburg, Austria, July 18, 1945; s. Sandor Szabo and Rozalia Fesus; m. Zsuzsanna Okordi, July 31, 1974 (div. 1990); children: Levente, Gyongyver; m. Eva Agnes Mramurácz, Sept. 8, 1990. MSEE, State U. Telecomms., St. Petersburg, Russia, 1968; DS, Tech. U. Budapest, 1975; PhD, Hungarian Acad. Scis., Budapest, 1986, DS, 1986. R&D engr. Videoton, Szekesfehervar, Hungary, 1968-70; faculty mem. Tech. U. Budapest, 1970—, prof., 1996—; founder, pres. BCN, Ltd., Budapest, 1990—; dir. rsch. dept. telecomms. TUB, Budapest, 1990-91, head lab. of comms. networks, 1991—. Co-author: (book) Statistical Communication Theory and its Applications, 1982, Integrating Voice and Data in Telecommunication Networks, 1998; contbr. articles to profl. jours.; patentee in field. Mem. IEEE. Avocations: mountaineering, running. Home: 10 Verecke Lepcso, H-1025 Budapest Hungary Office: Tech U Budapest, Sztoczek u 2, H-1111 Budapest Hungary

SZABÓ, DEZSÖ, retired physician, medical research administrator; b. Szeged, Hungary, July 12, 1925; s. Ernö and Ilona (Robicsek) S.; m. Éva Vass, Dec. 23, 1968. MD, Sch. Med. Budapest (Hungary) U., 1953; PhD, Hungarian Acad. Scis., Budapest, 1969; prof. pathology, Semmelweis U., Budapest, 1989; DSc, Hungarian Acad. Scis., Budapest, 1992. Asst. prof. dept. pathol. anatomy Sch. Medicine Budapest U., 1953-63; head lab. electron microscopy Inst. Exptl. Medicine, Hungarian Acad. Scis., 1963-90, dep. dir., 1990-93, ret., 1993; guest investigator Wenner-Gren Inst., Stockholm, 1968; vis. prof. McGill U., Montreal, Que., Can., 1971-72. Author: Medical Colour Photomicrography, 1967; co-author: The Microscope Handbook, 1979; contbr. over 100 articles to sci. jours. Mem. Hungarian Microscopical Soc., Sci. Soc. for Optics and Acoustics, Internat. Acad. Pathology. Home: Madách tér 7, 1075 Budapest Hungary Office: Hungarian Acad Scis POBx 67, Inst Exptl Med Szigony u 43, 1450 Budapest Hungary

SZABO, FRANZ GEORG, computer artist, science journalist, computer mathematician, pipe sculptor; b. Vienna, Austria, June 26, 1948; s. Stephan and Rose Marie (Redtenbacher) S.; m. Susanne, July 31, 1974; 1 child, Lorenz. Student, U. Vienna, 1967-69, Tech. U. Vienna, 1967-73. Exhibited computer art in Austria, in Concordia Press Club, Vienna, 1994, 97, in Wolfsberg, Carinthia, 1999, 00; permanent collection pipe sculptures Austrian Tobacco Mus., Vienna. Mem. N.Y. Acad. Scis. Avocations: cooking, photography.

SZABO, GABRIELA, Olympic athlete; b. Bistrita, Romania, Nov. 14, 1975; m. Gyongyossy Zsolt, 1999. Winner Silver medal 1500 meter race Atlanta, 1996; winner world title 5000 meter race, 1997; winner 3000 meter Golden League meets Berlin, 1999; winner 5000 meter title World Championships, 1999; winner Gold medal 5000 meter race Sydney, 2000. Named Women's Athlete of Yr. Track and Field News/AIPS, 1999. finished 5000 meter in Sydney in record time; first athlete to win more than 1 million in one yr. Office: Federacio Romana Atletism, 16 Vasile Conta St, Bucharest 70139, Romania*

SZABÓ, GYULA, physician, educator; b. Makó, Csongra'd, Hungary, Mar. 23, 1955; s. János Szabó and Anna Kiss; m. Anna Bujdosó, May 20, 1984; 1 child, Aaron. MD, Szeged (Hungary) Med. Sch., 1979; PhD, Hungarian Acad. Sci., Budapest, 1993, DSc, 1999. Cert. specialist clin. chemistry, neuroendocrinology, pathophysiology. Intern Szegedi Orvostudo-Ma'nyi Egyetem, Szeged, Hungary, 1979-84; asst. prof. Albert Szent-Györgyi Med. Univ., Szeged, 1979-96, assoc. prof., 1996-2000; prof. U. Szeged, Albert Szent-Györgyi Med. & Pharm. Ctr., 2000—; vis. asst. prof. U. Colo. Health Scis. Ctr., Denver, 1994-95. Office: Albert Szent Györgyi Med & Pharm Ctr U Szeged, Semmelweis u 1 PF 427, 6701 Szeged Hungary

SZABO, ISTVAN, film director; b. Budapest, Hungary, Feb. 18, 1938; s. Istvan and Maria (Vita) S.; m. Vera Gyurey, Dec. 29, 1961. Dir., Budapest Acad. Theatre and Film Arts, 1961. Began career as mem. Balazs B. Studio, Budapest; leading mem. Hungarian Film Studios, Budapest, 1961—, dep. head Objektiv studio, 1980-92; prof. Hungarian Film Sch., Budapest, 1970—; prof., docent Deutsche Film Fernsehakademie, Berlin, 1982-84. Dir. short films: Concert, 1961, Variations Upon a Theme, 1961, Te (You), 1963, (Grand prix de Tours) Budapest, amiert szeretem (Budapest, Why I Love It), (series segment) Alom a hazrol (Dream About the House), 1971, (documentary) Kegyelet (Piety), 1967, Varosterkep (City Map) (Grand prix of Oberhausen 1977); TV plays: Osbemutato (Premier), 1974, Katzenspiel (Cat Play), 1982; full-length films: Almodozasok kora (The Age of Day-Dreaming), 1964, Apa (Father) (Grand prix of Moscow 1966), 1966, Szerelmes film (love film), 1970, Tuzolto utca 25 (25 Fireman's Street) (Grand prix of Locarno 1974), 1973, Budapesti mesék (Budapest Tales), 1976, Bizalom (Confidence) (Silver Bear of Berlin 1980, Acad. award nomination 1981), 1979, Der Grüne Vogel (The Green Bird), 1979, Mephisto (Acad. award for best fgn. lang. film 1982, David di Donatello prize 1982, prize of Italian Critics, prize of Critics U.K. 1982), 1981, Redl ezredes (Col. Redl), (Brit. Acad. award 1986, Acad. award nomination 1986, Cannes Internat. Film Festival Jury Prize), 1985, Hanussen, 1989 (Acad. award nomination 1989), Meeting Venus, 1991, Sweet Emma Dear Böbe 1992 (Silver Bear of Berlin 1992, prize Itlaian Critics 1992), (TV play) Offenbach, 1995, Steadying the Boat (BBC-TV), 1996, Sunshine, 1998-99. Recipient Euro. Film Acad. award, 1999, Gemie award (Canada), 1999, Bela Balázs prize, 1967, Kossuth prize, 1975; named Hon. Citizen City of New Orleans. Mem. Acad. Motion Picture Arts and Scis., Assn. Hungarian Film Dirs. and Artists.

SZABÓ, ISTVÁN, obstetrician-gynecologist, educator; b. Máramarossziget, Hungary, June 6, 1942; s. István Szabó and Katalin Ladányi; m. Mariann Modensieder, July 20, 1968; 1 child, István. MD, Med. U. Pécs, Hungary, 1966, cert. ob-gyn., 1970, PhD, 1984; DSc, 1999. Instr., fellow dept. ob-gyn. Med. U. Pécs, 1968-78, asst. prof. dept. ob-gyn., 1978-89, assoc. prof. dept. ob-gyn., 1989-93, prof., chmn. dept. ob-gyn., 1993—; mem. European Assn. Gynecologists and Obstetrics, 1988. Author: Labor and Delivery, 1997; editor: Jour. Hungarian Gynecologists, 1993, Early Pregnancy, Biology and Medicine, 1994; contbr. articles to profl. jours. Recipient Gold Medal Pres. Hungary, 2000. Mem. World Assn. Perinatal Medicine, Sci. Com., Internat. Assn. for the Lung Surfactant Sys., European Assn. Perinatal Medicine, Endoscopic Soc. Hungarian Gynecologists (pres. 1996), Hungarian Soc. Perinatal (pres.) 1996—, Hungarian Soc. Ob-Gyn. (pres. 1998—). Avocations: photography, collecting paintings and artwork. Home: 4/1 Erreth Lajos St, H-7623 Pécs Hungary Office: Med U Pécs Dept Ob-gyn, 17 Édesanyák St, H-7623 Pécs Hungary

SZABÓ, IVÁN, Hungarian government official; b. Budapest, Hungary, Jan. 8, 1934; s. Ferenc Szabó and Maria Sallai; m. Ildikó Zemenszky; 2 children. PhD, Budapest Tech. U. & Ec. U. Structural engr. Rd. and Railway Bldg. Co., 1957-59; tech. dir. Bldg. Mechanization Co., 1959-69; chief engr. Civil Engring. Co., 1969-78; export mgr. Water Constrn. Trust, 1978-85; pres. Engring. and Constructing Co-operative, 1985-90; M.P. Országgyűlés, Budapest, 1990-98; min. trade and industry Govt. of Hungary, 1991-93, min. of fin., 1993-94; leader parliamentary group, dep. party sec. Hungarian Dem. Forum, Budapest, 1994-96, adminstrv. pres., 1994-96. Founder Hungarian Dem. People's Party, 1996, leader parliamentary group, bd. dirs., 1996-98, hon. pres., 1998—. Mem. Hungarian Consumer Protection Assn. (pres.). Avocation: gardening. Office: Hungarian Dem Peoples Party, Iskola u 16, 1011 Budapest Hungary

SZABO, JENÖ IMRE, endocrinologist, immunologist, educator; b. Eger, Hungary, July 21, 1942; s. Jenö and Erzsebet (Sziraki) S.; m. Adrienne Boros, June 27, 1970; children: Adrienne, Krisztina. MD, U. Debrecen (Hungary), 1967, PhD, 1988. Pathologist U. Debrecen, 1967-77, ednl. advisor, 1988—, endocrinologist, assoc. prof., 1989—, immunologist, 1990—. Author (chpt. in book) Clinical Immunology, 1992; contbr. articles to profl. jours. mem. European Thyroid Assn. Avocations: 20th Century history, dogs, computers. Home: Tessedik S 53, H 4032 Debrecen Hungary Office: 1st Dept Medicine, Debrecen U Med Sch, H 4012 Debrecen Hungary

SZABÓ, LÁSZLÓ, financial executive, economist, chemical engineer; b. Budapest, Hungary, May 21, 1952; s. Imre and Erzsébet (Forschner) S.; m.

Eszter Sebestyén, Jan. 21, 1978; 1 child, Imre. BS in Chem. Engring., Budapest (Hungary) Tech. U., 1976; Economist, Budapest U. Economic Sci., 1986; MBA, Strathclyde Grad. Bus. Sch., Glasgow, Scotland. Project engr. petroleum design Olajterv, Budapest, Hungary, 1976-83; project mgr. sect. head State Devel. Bank, Budapest, 1983-86; dep. dir., chief internal auditor Inter-Europa Bank Ltd., Budapest, 1987-91; CFO Graphisoft Group, Budapest, 1991-93; mng. dir. OTP Deutsche Leasing Kft., Budapest, 1993-95; CFO Raiffeisen Lizing Ltd., Budapest, 1996—; instr. high sch. for fin. and acctg., Budapest, 1990-92; lectr. Internat. Chem. Industry Sys. Conf., Tech. Chem. Systems, 1979-81, Banking Tng. Ctr., Budapest, 1991—. Author: (books) Banking Operations, 1992, Special Bank Operations, 1994. Mem. Assn. of Orgn. and Mgmt. (bd. dirs. fin. sect. 1984-92, Orgn. award 1989), Hungarian Leasing Assn. (bd. dirs. 1992—). Office: Raiffeisen Lizing Rt. 19-21 Váci u, H-1052 Budapest Hungary

SZABO, MAGDA (MRS. TIBOR SZOBOTKA), author; b. Debrecen, Hungary, Oct. 5, 1917; d. Alexis and Lenke (Jablonczay) Szabo; m. Tibor Szobotka, June 5, 1948. D. Phil. in Latin Philology, Debrecen U. Author numerous novels, short stories, dramas, others, trans. into 33 langs.; novels include: Fresko, 1958, The Fawn, 1959, Island-Blue, 1959, Night of the Pig-Killing, 1960, Pilate, 1963, The Danaid, 1964, Genesis I, 22, 1967, Kathlin-Street, 1969, Lala the Fairy, 1965, Old Well, 1970, Old-Fashioned Story, 1977, The Battle, 1982, The Onlookers, 1974, The Door, 1987, Noises, 1957, Outside of the Circle, 1985, Meranian Boy, 1981, The Battle, 1981, King Bella, 1983, On the Heights of Age, 1987, The Wednesday of the Cats, 1989, The Moment, 1990, (essays) The Apathy of the Semigods, 1992, The Logic of the Butterflies, 1996. Recipient József Attila prize, 1959, 72, Kossuth prize, 1978, Getzs Corp. prize, 1992. Mem. Acad. Europienne (Beaux arts sect.), Acad. Scéchenyi of Lit. and Arts in Hungary, Internat. Pen Club. Home: Julia utca 3, H-1026 Budapest II, Hungary*

SZABÓ, MÁTÉ, political scientist, educator; b. Budapest, Hungary, June 13, 1956; s. György Szabó and Mária Horváth; m. Mária Bábosik; children: Daniel, Viola. MA in Law, Eötvös Loránd U., Budapest, 1980; PhD in Polit. Sci., Hungarian Acad. Scis., 1987. Jour. editor Világosság, Budapest, 1980-84; rschr., tchr. U. ELTE, Budapest, 1985—. Editor Hungarian Polit. Sci. Rev., 1992-99; contbr. articles to profl. jours. Recipient Ference Erdei prize Hungarian Sociol. Assn., Budapest, 1988. Mem. Hungarian Polit. Sci. Assn. (sec. gen. 1992-97). Office: Univ ELTE Faculty State, Egyetem tér 1-3, 1364 Budapest Hungary

SZABO, PETER JOHN, investment company executive, financial planner, mining engineer, lawyer; b. Bklyn., Nov. 22, 1946; s. Paul Simon and Marita Ellen (Coughlin) S.; m. Dorothy Anne Steward, Nov. 14, 1970; children: Peter, David, John Paul Steward. BS in Mining Engring., Columbia U., 1968; LLB, LaSalle Law Sch., 1975; MS in Fin. Planning, Coll. Fin. PLanning, 1994. registered profl. engr., CFP. Mining engr. Halecrest Co., Mt. Hope, N.J., 1973-74; mgr. solid fuels & minerals Ford, Bacon & Davis, N.Y.C., 1974-75; asst. v.p. Mfrs. Hanover Trust Co., N.Y.C., 1975-77, Irving Trust Co., N.Y.C., 1977; v.p. Republic Nat. Bank of Dallas, 1977-80; mgr. bus. devel. AMOCO Minerals, Denver, 1980-84; investment broker B.J. Leonard, Denver, 1984-85; investment exec. Wedbush Nobel Cook, Denver, 1985; regional sr. v.p. Alliance Fund Distbrs., N.Y.C., 1985-92, sr. v.p., 1992—; mining engr. U.S. Bur. Mines, Dallas, 1971-72, IRS, Washington, 1972-73. Treas. Columbia Sch. Engring., 1968—. Lt. USMC, 1969-71, Vietnam, capt. Res. Mem. VFW (post sr. vice comdr. 1993-94, post comdr. 1994-95, all state team post comdrs. 1995, 16th dist. jr. vice comdr. 1995—, 16th dist. sr. vice comdr. 1996—, nat. aide-de-camp 1995-96), Mil. Order of the Cootie (sr. vice comdr. 1994-95). Republican. Roman Catholic. Avocations: sailing, golf, tennis, jogging, scripophily. Home and Office: Alliance Fund Distbrs 810 Oxford Way Benicia CA 94510-3646

SZABÓ, SÁNDOR, mathematician, researcher; b. Karcag, Hungary, Apr. 16, 1954; arrived in Bahrain, 1992; PhD, Eötvös U., Budapest, Hungary, 1980; DSc, Hungarian Acad. Sci., 1995. Faculty Tech. U., Budapest, 1978-92, U. Bahrain, 1992—; vis. prof. U. Dundee, U.K., 1987-88, U. Calif., Davis, 1989-90, U. of the Pacific, Stockton, Calif., 1990-91. Author: Algebra and Tiling, 1994. Recipient Beckenbach Book prize Math. Assn. Am., 1998. Mem. Hungarian Math. Soc., Am. Math. Soc. Avocation: sailing. Home: Flat 24 Bldg 1118 Rd 2925, Manama Bahrain Office: Dept Math U Bahrain, PO Box 32038, Isa Town Bahrain

SZABO, TIBOR, philosophy educator; b. Szeged, Hungary, Mar. 30, 1945; s. Ferenc and Erzsebet (Terhes) S.; m. Katalin Kürtösi; children: Timea, Szilard. MA in French, Attila Jozsef U., Szeged, 1970, MA in Italian, 1970; PhD in Philosophy, Hungarian Acad. Scis., Budapest, 1983. Asst. prof. dept. philosophy Attila Jozsef U., 1970-84, assoc. prof., 1984—, assoc. chmn. dept. philosophy, 1990-92; chmn. dept. social scis. Gyula Juhasz Tchrs. Tng. Coll., Szeged, 1992-98, assoc.dir., 1995-98; dir. Langs. Tchrs. Inst., 1999—; Bd. dirs. Lukacs Circle, Szeged, 1979—. Author: Political Philosophy of Gramsci, 1991, The End of Silence, 1991, Gramsci and Lukács - Today, 1993, Quite Free, 1994; editor: Lukács and Modernity, 1996, The Crossroads of the Philosophy, 1998, Naive Country, 1999. Recipient Lukacs medal George Lukacs Found., 1985, Foscolo medal U. Pavia, Italy, 1990, Dante award Accademia Casentinese, 1997. Mem. Hungarian Philos. Assn. (bd. dirs. 1986-89), Hungarian Polit. Sci. Assn. (bd. dirs. 1985-95), Internat. Gramsci Soc., Group d'Etudes Sartreiennes, N.Y. Acad. Scis., Hungarian Applied Philosophy Assn. (bd. dirs. 1998—). Home: Rigo u 24/b, 6724 Szeged Hungary Office: Juhasz Guyula Tanarkepzo Foiskola Szedegi Tudomanyegyetem, Boldogasszony sgt 6, 6701 Szeged Hungary

SZABO, YURIKA LIN, marketing executive, advertising executive; b. Long Beach, Calif., Mar. 1, 1967; d. Sandor Alex and Taeko (Tsujimura) S. Student, Calif. State U., Long Beach, 1985-90. Dir. mktg. Adolphs Food Svc., Lakewood, Calif., 1991—; publicist, cons. L.A. Access Video, 1996—; graphic designer Peepod Prodns., Los Alamitos, Calif., 1996—; reporter Studio 12, Lakewood, 1997, camera operator, 1997; cons. L.A. Access Video, 1996—. Author of poems. Recipient Editor's Choice award Nat. Libr. Poetry, 1996; Calif. Scholar Fedn. Svc. scholar, 1981-85. Mem. Internat. Soc. Poets (disting.). Avocations: writing, computer graphics, body sculpting, acting, skating.

SZABOLCSI, MIKLOS, Hungarian literary historian, educator; b. Budapest, Hungary, Mar. 3, 1921; s. Lajos and Elizabet (Meszaros) S.; m. Hedvig Margulesz, 1948; 1 child, Janos. PhD, Budapest U. Scis., 1943. Tchr. secondary sch. Budapest, 1945-49, 50-53; head dept. Ministry Religious and Ednl. Affairs, Budapest, 1949-50; dep. editor Literary Mag. Csillag, Budapest, 1953-56; rschr., head Literary Inst., Budapest, 1956-81; prof. Kossuth Lajos U., Debrecen, Hungary, 1964-70; prof. Eotvos Lorand U., Budapest, 1979-94, prof. emeritus, 1999—; dir. gen. Hungarian Nat. Inst. Edn., Budapest, 1981-88; vis. prof. Sorbonne, Paris, 1965-66. Author: Life and Work of Attila jozsef, 1963, 77, 93, 98, Methods of Poetry Analysis, 1968, 69, Sign and Cry, Problems of Avantgard and Neo-Advantgard, 1967, 82, The Clown as Self-Portrait of the Artist, 1971, Main Currents of XXth Century World Literature, 1987; co-editor: A Short Story of Hungarian literature, 1955-75, history of Hungarian Literature, Modern Period, 1975-76. Recipient state prizes for excellence in lit. Mem. Internat. Fedn. Modern Lang. and Lit. (pres. 1981-84), Soc. European de Culture. Office: U of Budapest Fac of Phil, Piarista Koz 1-3, 1051 Budapest 5, Hungary

SZAFRAŃSKI, ANDRZEJ, surgeon, researcher; b. Warsaw, Nov. 21, 1966; s. Jerzy and Helena (Żeleźniakowicz) S.; m. Kamila Anna Sokołowska, July 29, 1989; 1 child, Mikołaj. Grad. vet. dept., Agrl. Acad., Warsaw, 1986; grad., Med. U., Białystok, Poland, 1988; MD, Med. U., Warsaw, 1992, Masters in Medicine, 1992, specialization in pediat. surgery, 1996, specialization in oncological surgery, 2000. Intern Praski Hosp., Warsaw, 1992-93; resident dept. oncological surgery Inst. Mother and Child, Warsaw, 1994-96, asst. dept. oncological surgery, 1996-2000; asst. dept. human anatomy Med. U., Warsaw, 1993—, cons. dept. oncological surgery, 2000—. Mem. Polish Pediat. Surgeons Assn., Polish Assn. Clin. Oncology, Polish Anatomical Assn. Achievements include treatment of metastases in osteosarcoma patients. Avocations: informatics, photography, mountain climbing, diving. E-mail: szafran@supermedia.pl. Home: 64 Korfantego St, 01-496 Warsaw MZW, Poland Office: Inst Mother & Child, 17a Kasprzaka St, 01 211 Warsaw MZW, Poland

SZAJDAK, LECH WOJCIECH, soil scientist, researcher; b. Sroda Wlkp, Poznań, Poland, Feb. 10, 1953; s. Stefan and Zofia (Bednarek) S.; m. Hanna Maria Grzemska, July 1, 1978; children: Wojciech, Maciej, Marianna. MS, Med. Acad., Poznań, Poland, 1977, PhD, 1986; graduate in First Grade Specialization, Ministry Health Social Welfare, Poland, 1986. Asst. Med. Acad., Poznań, 1977-80, sr. asst., 1980-86, sr. asst. prof., 1986-88; sr. asst. prof. Polish Acad., Poznań, 1988—. Avocations: jogging, antique china.

SZAJNA, JOZEF, painter, stage designer, theater director; b. Rzeszow, Poland, Mar. 13, 1922; s. Julian and Karolina S.; m. Bozena Sieroslawska, July 19, 1953; 1 child, Lukasz. Diploma graphics, Acad. Fine Arts, Cracow, Poland, 1952, diploma stage designing, 1953. Mem. faculty Acad. Fine Arts, Cracow, 1954-65; prof. scene-designing Acad. Fine Arts, Warsaw, Poland, 1972—; mgr., supr., dir., stage designer Nowa Huta (Poland) Theatre, 1955-66; stage dir. Teatr Stary, Cracow, 1966-70; mgr., theatre dir., designer Studio Teatr Galeria, Warsaw. Scenographer: Princess of Turandot, 1956, Akropolis, 1962, Macbeth, 1970; dir. plays: The Empty Field, 1965, The Bath House, 1968; author's performances: Faust, 1971, Replika I, 1971, Witkacy, 1972, Replika II, 1972, Replika III, 1973, Gulgutiera, 1973, Dante, 1974, Cervantes, 1976, Majakowski, 1978, The Death on the Pear-Tree, 1978, Dante Alive, 1981, Dante Contemporary, 1985, Replika VII, 1986, Dante, 1992, Earth, 1993, Trace, 1993, Trace II, 1993, vida Y Muerte Del Poeta Cervantes, 1993, The Rest's, 1995, Deballage, 1997; numerous one-man and group exhbns. include Venice XXXV Biennial, 1970, Prague Quadrennial (gold medal), 1971, Warsaw (1st prize and gold medal), 1972, Munich (Silver medal), 1974, São Paulo Bienniale, 1979, 89, Berlin, 1980, 88, Moscow, 1987, Paris, 1987, Venice Biennale, 1990, Warsaw, Poznan, 1992, Gdansnk, 1992, Internat. Triennale, Majdanek, 1994, Auschwitz, Frankfurt A/M, Düsseldorf, Bochum, Warsaw, Weimar-Buchenwald, 1995, Opole, Weimar-Buchenwald, Kalisz, 1996, Rzeszow, Warszawa, Graz, Oronsko, 1997, Szajina Galéria, Rieszow, 1997, Szczecin-Zamek, 1998, Wroclaw Nat. Mus., 1998, Osaka Nat. Mus., 1998, Polish Kultur Inst., Budapest, 1999, Polish Kultur Inst., Rome, 2000, Milan Mus. Permanente, 2000; prin. works include European Art Banner Italian Accademia d'Europa, Statue of Victory, Centro Studi E Richerche Delle Nazioni in Salsmaggiore, 1984, numerous others. Held prisoner concentration camps, Oswiecim and Buchenwald. Decorated knight and comdr. Cross of Order of Polonia Restituta, also comdr. Cross with star of Polonia Restituta, Big Cross of Polonia Restituta; recipient Polish Reviewers award, 1957; Nowa Huta Artistic award, 1959; Minister of Culture and Arts (Poland) award, 1962, 71, 79; City of Cracow award, 1971; Gold medal Accademia Italia delle Arti e del Lavoro, 1981, Order Banner of Labour 1st Class, 1985, Medal Meritorious for Nat. Culture, 1986; Gold Centaur award Accademia Italia delle Arti del Lavoro, 1981, Oscar d'Italia '85 Accademia Italia, Artistic award Warsaw, 1986, Gold Mask award Bielsko Biala, 1994, Alfred Jurzykowski Found. award, 1995, Replika VI award Internat. Que. Theatre Festival, 1986. Mem. Internat. Assn. Soc. Européene de Culture, Art-AIAP (UNESCO) (hon. counsellor 1979 for Leonardo da Vinci world award - Mex.), Internat. Coun. Auschwitz-Birkenau. Home: 14m8 Smulikowskiego, 00-389 Warsaw Poland

SZALAI, CSABA, molecular biologist; b. Budapest, Hungary, June 17, 1961; d. Bela and Roza (Toronyai) S.; m. Ildiko, Oct. 4, 1997; 2 children. BA, Tech. U., Budapest, Hungary, 1983, MA, 1985, PhD, 1990; PhD, Med. U., Budapest, Hungary, 1999. Rschr. Toxicological Rsch. Co., Budapest, Hungary, 1985-90; chemist Heim Pal Pediatric Hosp. Ctrl. Lab., Budapest, Hungary, 1990-92, rschr., 1992-94, leader molecular biology lab., 1994—; cons. in field. Author: 1000 Questions in Pediatrics, 1996; contbr. articles to profl. jours. Mem. Hungarian Soc. Clin. Lan., Hungarian Soc. Biologists, Soc. Human Genetics. Avocations: sports, reading, television. Home: Szel 14 IV/13, 1035 Budapest Hungary Office: Heim Pal Pediatric Hosp, Ulloi ut 86, 1089 Budapest Hungary

SZALAPSKI, ROBERT FRANCIS, theoretical physicist; b. St. Paul, Minn., Dec. 21, 1964; s. Edward William and Judith Mary (Raines) S.; m. Jeanne Therese Larson, Sept. 17, 1985; children: Jacob Daniel, Maxwell Martin. BS in Physics, U. Minn., 1988; PhD in Physics, U. Wis., 1994. Rsch. assoc. Nat. Lab. for High Energy Physics, Tsukuba, Japan, 1994-96, rsch. fellow, 1996—. Contbr. articles to profl. jours. Fellowship NSF, 1996-97, postdoctoral fellowship Japan Soc. for the Promotion of Sci., 1996-97, grad. fellowship Dept. of Edn., 1989-93. Avocations: tennis, running. E-mail: robs@avanticorp.com. Home: 43 Smallwood Dr Pittsford NY 14534-3433 Office: Avant! Sys Divsn 117 Victor Heights Pkwy Victor NY 14564-8938

SZALEK, BENON ZBIGNIEW, logistics and heuristics educator; b. Szczecin, Poland, Nov. 3, 1948; s. Henryk and Aleksandra (Rozanowicz) S. From head chair logistics to head heuristics & praxiology U. Szczecin, Poland, 1990—, asst. prof., 1987-91, assoc. prof., 1991-96; prof. U. Szczecin, 1996—. Author: Interpretation of Phaistos Disk, 1977, Decipherment and Interpretation of Ancient Inscriptions, 1984, Outline of Logistic Heuristics, 1994, Roots of Easter Island, 1995, Easter Island and Indus Valley Scripts, 1997, Proto-Dravidian Origin of the Easter Island and Indus Valley Script, 1998, Inscription of the Phaistos Disk, 1999, The Narmini Report, 2 vols., 1999, The Axis 27N-27S (Mohenjo Daro-Easter Island), 2000; contbr. articles to profl. jours. Mem. Polish Soc. Polit. Scis., Narmini Found. Home: Mazurska 20 m7, PL 70444 Szczecin Poland

SZALEWICZ, KRZYSZTOF, physics educator; b. Gdansk, Poland, Jan. 19, 1950; came to U.S., 1985; s. Zygmunt and Helena (Nowogrodzka) S.; m. Halina Gajda; 1 child, Magdalena; m. Lidia Jankowska; children: E. Agnieszka, Monika H. MS, U. Warsaw, Poland, 1973, PhD, 1977, DSc, 1984. Asst. prof. dept. chemistry U. Warsaw, 1977-85; assoc. rsch. scientist dept. physics U. Fla., Gainesville, 1985-88; asst. prof. dept. physics U. Del., Newark, 1988-90, assoc. prof. dept. physics, 1990-94, prof. dept. physics, 1994—; adj. rsch. asst. prof. U. Fla., 1980-82; vis. prof. U. Cologne, Fed. Republic of Germany, 1982, 83, 84, U. Uppsala, Sweden, 1990; referee NSF, U.S. Dept. of Energy. Author: Numerical and Statistical Methods for Chemists, 1987; contbr. over 110 articles to profl. jours. Mem. Am. Phys. Soc. Achievements include solution of several problems in theory of intermolecular interaction; creation of a novel perturbational method for computing interaction of many-electron systems; development of explicitly correlated coupled cluster expansion; calculation of various properties of muonic molecular ions relevant for muon catalyzed fusion. Home: 412 Jaymar Blvd Newark DE 19702-2837 Office: U Del Dept of Physics Newark DE 19716

SZALLER, JAMES FRANCIS, lawyer; b. Cleve., Jan. 22, 1945; s. Frank Paul and Ellen Grace (O'Malley) S.; m. Roberta Mae Curtin, Oct. 23, 1967 (div. Aug. 1975); m. Charlene Nancy Smith, Apr. 28, 1984. AA, Cuyahoga Community Coll., 1967; BA, Cleve. State U., 1970, JD cum laude, 1975. Bar: Ohio 1975, U.S. Dist. Ct. (no. dist.) Ohio 1975, U.S. Supreme Ct. 1982, U.S. Ct. Appeals (6th cir.) 1983, U.S. Ct. Appeals (4th cir.) 1986. Assoc. Metzenbaum, Gaines & Stern, Cleve., 1975-79; sr. ptnr. Brown & Szaller Co., L.P.A., Cleve., 1979—; lectr. law Cleve. State U., 1977-81. Mem. editorial bd. Cleve. State U. Law Rev., 1973-75.; contbr. articles to profl. jours. Mem. Ohio State Bar Assn., Greater Cleve. Bar Assn., Cleve. Acad. Trial Lawyers, Ohio Acad. Trial Lawyers (Disting. Svc. award 1996), Assn. Trial Lawyers Am., Nat. Coll. Advocacy (advocate). Democrat. Roman Catholic. Avocations: gourmet cooking, automobile racing. Office: Brown & Szaller Co LPA 14222 Madison Ave Cleveland OH 44107-4510

SZALLER, ZSUZSANNA, chemical engineer and researcher; b. Budapest, Hungary, Aug. 23, 1960; d. János and Erzsébet (Grámer) S. MSc, Tech. U. Budapest, 1985. Chem. engr. Rsch. Lab. for Crystal Physics, Hungarian Acad. Scis., Budapest, 1982—. E-mail: szaller@szfki.hu. Office: Rsch Inst Sol St Phys Opt, Konkoly Thege 29-33, H-1121 Budapest Hungary

SZAMOSI, TAMAS, pediatrician, educator; b. Budapest, Hungary, Sept. 30, 1936; s. Jozsef and Jozsefne (Lusztig) S.; m. Tamasne Anna Doncsecz, Jan. 7, 1962; children: Anna, Tamas. MD, U. Budapest, 1961. Cert. specialist in clin. pathology and pediatrics. Rsch. worker dept. biochemistry Med. U. Budapest, 1961-72; physician, pediatrician Semmelweis U. Medicine, Budapest, 1972-82, from asst. to assoc. prof. dept. pediatrics, 1982—; cons. Gen. Hosp. Tajoura, Lybia, 1976-79; dir. Hungarian Group of Tajoura Cardiac Ctr. Lybia, 1988-90; chmn. Internat. Group for Prevention of Atherosclerosis in Childhood, 1996—. Editor: The Prevention of Chronic Adulthood Illnesses in Children, 1993, Current Trends of the Prevention of Atherosclerosis in Childhood 1, 1994, 2, 1996, 3, 1999. Recipient award for excellent work Hungarian Ministry Edn., 1989. Fellow Am. Coll. Nutrition, Assn. Pediatric Edn. in Europe (exec. com. 1997—); mem. Hungarian Atherosclerosis Soc. (chmn. pediatric sect. 1983—), Internat. Atherosclerosis Soc., European Soc. Social Pediatrics. Avocation: playing piano. Office: Semmelweis U Med Dept Ped 2, Tuzolto u 7, H-1094 Budapest Hungary

SZANTAY, CSABA, chemist; b. Budapest, Hungary, Nov. 29, 1958; s. Csaba Szantay and Judit Imre; m. Erika Salamon, Dec. 7, 1987; 1 child, Gina. MSc, Tech. U. Budapest, 1982, PhD, 1987. Rsch. asst. Tech. U. Budapest, 1982-87; postdoctoral fellow U. Leeds, England, 1988-89; from scientific advisor to head spectroscopic divsn. Gedeon Richter Ltd., Budapest, 1990—. Editor: Methods for Structure Elucidation by High-Resolution, 1997; contbr. articles to profl. jours. Avocation: body building. Office: Gedeon Richter Ltd, Budapest 10 PO Box 27, H-1475 Budapest Hungary

SZÁNTÓ, BORISZ, nuclear engineer, educator, researcher; b. Moscow, Russia, July 1, 1936; arrived in Hungary, 1945; m. Györgyi Dénes, Dec. 26, 1958; children: Viktor, Vera. MSc in Mech. Engring., Tech. U., Budapest, 1958, MSc in Nuclear Engring., 1963; PhD in Econs., Hungarian Acad. Scis., Budapest, 1984, D Habilitation in Tech. Sci., 1996. Rsch. fellow Ctrl. Rsch. Inst. Physics, Budapest, 1958-65; head divsn. Metrimpex, Budapest, 1965-69; head dept. Nat. AEC, Budapest, 1969-73; 1st comml. sec. Hungarian Embassy, Tokyo, 1973-77; sr. counsellor Coun. Ministers Sci. and Tech. Policy Secretariat, Budapest, 1977-90; sr. rsch. fellow Tech. U. Budapest, 1989—. Author: Innovation as a Means of Economic Development, in Hungarian, 1985, in Russian, 1990, Creative Technology. The Theory of Socio-Technical Evolution, 1990; contbr. articles to profl. jours. Mem. Internat. Coun. Sci. Policy Studies, Hungarian Sci. Soc. on Econs. of Progress in Sci. (pres. 1995—). Home: Dobos u 67, H-1202 Budapest Hungary Office: Tech U Budapest, Muegyetem rkp 9, st ep 15, H-1111 Budapest Hungary

SZAPIRO, TOMASZ JERZY, economist, researcher; b. Warsaw, Poland, Dec. 23, 1950; s. Jerzy and Maria Danuta (Ksiazkiewicz) S.; m. Ewa Maria Podedworna, Jan. 17, 1981; children: Katarzyna, Hanna, Michal. MSc in Physics, U. Warsaw, 1973; PhD in Math., Polish Acad. Scis., 1981; habilitation in economy, Warsaw Sch. Econs., 1992. Rsch. asst. Warsaw Sch. Econs., 1973-78, sr. rsch. asst., 1978-81, asst. prof., 1981-93, assoc. prof., 1992—, dean grad. sch., 1992-96; vice dir. Sch. Reflective Practitioners, Warsaw, 1994-97. Author: Pondering Decisions, 1993; co-author: Calculus, 1996; contbr. articles to profl. jours. Mem. Internat. Soc. for MCDM, Polish Math. Soc., INFORMS (exec. bd. Polish chpt. 1995-97). Avocations: music, reading, walking. Office: Warsaw Sch Econs, Al Niepodleglosci 162, 02-554 Warsaw Poland

SZAREWSKI, ANNE, gynecologist; b. London, Sept. 1, 1959. MBBS, U. London, Middlesex Hosp., 1982. Sr. clin. med. officer family planning Margaret Pyke Ctr. Rsch. & Tng. in Family Planning, London, 1986—; sr. clin. rsch. fellow gynecol. oncology Imperial Cancer Rsch. Fund, London, 1991—; instr. family planning Faculty Family Planning, London, 1986—, regional assessor instructing doctors in family planning, 1993—, mem. coun. faculty family planning and reproductive healthcare, 2000—. Co-author: (with Albert Singer): Cervical Smears; What Every Woman Should Know, 1988, (with John Cochrane) The Breast Book, 1989, (with John Guillebaud) Contraception: A User's Handbook, 1994, 3d edit., 2000; author: Hormonal Contraception: A Woman's Guide, 1991, The Cervical Smear Test: A Woman's Guide, 1994. Office: Imperial Cancer Rsch Fund, Lincolns Inn Fields, PO Box 123, London WC2A 3PX, England

SZAROTA, TOMASZ MARCELI, history educator, researcher; b. Warsaw, Poland, Jan. 2, 1940; s. Rafał Marceli Blüth and Elida Maria Szarota; m. Anna Manteuffel, Dec. 1, 1962; 1 child, Piotr. MA, U. Warsaw, 1962; PhD in History, Polish Acad. Scis., Warsaw, 1966. Asst. then adj. Inst. History, Polish Acad. Scis., 1962-77, asst. prof., 1978-84, extraordinary prof., 1985-90, ord. prof., dept. chief, 1991—. Author: Daily Life in Occupied Warsaw, 1973, 3d. edit., 1988, Stefan Rowecki "Grot" A Biography, 1983, 2d edit., 1985, Warschau unter dem Hakenkreuz. Leben und Alltag im besetzten Warschau, 1985, V as Victory. Symbols, Signs and Patriotic Demonstrations in Fighting Europe, 1994, Daily Life in Capitals of Occupied Europe, 1995, Germans and Poles. Reciprocal Apperception and Stereotypes, 1996, Der deutsche Michel.Die Geschichte eines nationalen Symbols und Autostereotyps, 1998, Antijewish Incidents and Pogroms in Occupied Europe, 2000. Grantee German Acad. Exch. Svc., 1974-75, A. v. Humboldt-Stiftung, 1983-84, 88, 97, Ministry Higher Tchg. and Rsch., France, 1996; disting. fellow Inst. Wissenschaften Menschen, Vienna, 1998; recipient award Polityka, 1970, 72, 75, 78. Mem. Authors Soc. Roman Catholic. Avocation: travel. Home: Madalińskiego 69/4, 02-549 Warsaw Poland Office: Polish Acad Scis Inst Hist, Rynek St Miasta 29/31, 00-272 Warsaw Poland

SZASZ, ANDRAS, physicist, educator, researcher; b. Budapest, Hungary, Nov. 4, 1947; s. István Szasz and Maria Rozsa; m. Susan Szasz-Csih, Aug. 8, 1971; children: Oliver, Nora. MS, Eötvös U., Budapest, 1972, PhD, 1974; CSc, St. Petersburg U., Russia, 1983; Habilitation, Hungary, 1996. Assoc. prof. Eötvös U., Budapest, 1974-84, 1984-94; head metal lab. Eötvös U., Budapest, 1983-87, head surface physics lab., 1987-96; vis. prof. Strathclyde U., Glasgow, Scotland, 1987—; vis. prof. Szent Istvan, Hungary, 1996—. Author 3 books; contbr. more than 250 sci. papers to profl. jours.; patentee in field. Mem. IEEE, European Hyperthermia Soc., European Physics Soc., Am. Elec. Chem. Soc., Am. Phys. Soc., Eötvös Physics Soc., N.Y. Acad. Sci. Avocation: travel. Home: Ibolya Utca 2, H-2071 PA'TY Hungary Office: OncoTherm Ltd, 20 Szent Istvan Krt, H-1137 Budapest Hungary

SZASZ, GYÖRGY, pharmaceutical chemist; b. Budapest, Hungary, Oct. 31, 1927; m. Maria Zacsko, July 19, 1958; 3 children. PhD, Semmelweis U. Medicine, Budapest, 1968, DSc, 1980. Pharm. diplomate. Prof. pharm. chemistry U. Medicine, Budapest, 1974—, dean pharm. faculty, 1972-84; dir. Inst. Pharm. Chemistry, Budapest, 1974-94; Author: Pharmaceutical Chemistry, 1972, Pharmaceutical Chemistry of Hypotentives, 1989. Mem. Hungarian Pharm. Soc. (pres. 1991-95), German Pharm. Soc. (hon.). Home: Szamos u 5, 1122 Budapest Hungary Office: Inst Pharm Chemistry, Högyes E u 9, 1092 Budapest Hungary

SZATHMÁRY, EÖRS, biologist, educator; b. Budapest, Hungary, Dec. 18, 1959; s. Géza and Katalin (Nagy) S.; m. Edina Földessy; 1 child, Eörs Jr. MSc in Biology, Eötvös U., Budapest, 1984, PhD, 1987, DSc, 1995. Rsch. fellow dept. plant taxonomy and ecology Eötvös U., 1987-95, prof. biology, 1997—; Soros scholar Sch. Biol. Sci., Brighton, U.K., 1987-88; rsch. fellow Nat. Inst. Med. Rsch., London, 1991-92; fellow inst. Advanced Study, Berlin, 1992-93; guest prof. U. Zurich, 1993-94; fellow Collegium Budapest, 1994-95, permanent fellow, 1995—. Author: (with J. Maynard Smith) The Major Transitions in Evolution, 1995, The Origins of Life, 1999, Prize of the Academy, 1999. Recipient New Europe prize Stanford U., 1996. Mem. European Soc. for Evolutionary Biology, Internat. Orgn. Systematic and Evolutionary Biology (pres. 1996—). Roman Catholic. Achievements include development of stochastic corrector model, coexistence of parabolically growing replicators, explanation for the size of the genetic alphabet, coding coenzyme handle hypothesis for the origin of the genetic code, common principles in the major evolutionary transitions. Avocation: horseback riding. Home: Mátyaskiraly Út 38A, H-1125 Budapest Hungary Office: Collegium Budapest, Szentháromságu 2, H-1014 Budapest Hungary

SZATMÁRI, MARIANNE, physician, consultant; b. Budapest, Apr. 27, 1931; d. Tibor and Magda (Altai) S.; m. Bela Takacs, Mar. 3, 1956 (dec. 1977). MD, Semmelweis U., Budapest, 1955. Internist Tetenyi U Korhaz, Budapest, 1955-58; gen. practice medicine Budapest, 1958-79, gen. practice chief cons., 1979-85; head dept. primary health care and rehab. Min. of Pub. Welfare, 1985-91, dep. head dept. med. care, 1989-91; vis. prof. sociology faculty Budapest Elte U.; liaison officer Hungary, head dept. internat. rels. MOW, 1991-98; nat. profl. officer WHO, 1998—. Author: Special Problems of General Practice, 1978; author numerous articles in field. Recipient award for extraordinary work Min. of Health, Hungary, 1979; Heim medal German Sci. Soc., 1985, Purkinje medal Tschechoslov. Purkinje. Soc., 1987, Outstanding Physician award 1988, Order of Merit of the Hungarian Officer's

Cross, 1995, Batthyany Strattman medal 1997, Internat. Generaliste d'honneur medal, 1991, others. Mem. Societas Internationalis Medicinsae Generalis (v.p. 1973—, Internat. Hippokrates medal 1985, Extraordinary Physician medal 1988, v.p.), Hungarian Sci. Soc. Gen. Practitioners (vice sec. gen. 1967—, Medicus Anonymus award 1977), Brit. Royal Coll. Gen. Practitioners, European Workshop on Rsch. in Gen. Practice, World Assn. of Med. Law (coun. of pres. 1994—), MOIF (Cambridge). Home: Balzac utca 48/b, 1136 Budapest Hungary Office: Arany János u 6-8, Ministry of Health, H-1051 Budapest Hungary

SZÁVA-KOVÁTS, ENDRE, library and information scientist, researcher; b. Budapest, Hungary, July 12, 1928; s. József and Katalin (Resch) S.; m. Klára Bán, Sept. 10, 1960. DSc, U. Budapest, Hungary, 1965, PhD, 1971. Various posts, rschr. Budapest, Hungary, 1950-88; dir.-gen. Libr. Hungarian Parliament, Budapest, 1991-96; ret., rschr. Budapest, 1988-90, 96—. Author: Literature Half-Life, 1979, Citation Analysis "Refutation" of the "Ortega Hypothesis", 1994; editor: History of the Library of Parliament, 1995; contbr. numerous articles to profl., sci. jours. in Germany, India, Switzerland, U.K., U.S., USSR and Hungary. Home: Magyari István u 0, H-1114 Budapest Hungary

SZAZ, ZOLTAN MICHAEL, association executive; b. Budapest, Hungary, Jan. 3, 1930; came to U.S., 1950; s. Geza and Magda (Nagy) S.; m. Jayne Anne Davis, Sept. 7, 1957 (div. Nov. 1995); children: Claire Anne, Anna Maria, Mary Carol, Christopher Michael; m. Elizabeth Susan Almassy, Nov. 11, 1995. BA cum laude, St. John's U., Collegeville, Minn., 1951; MA in History, Cath. U. Am., 1953, PhD in Polit. Sci., 1956. Instr, asst. prof. history St. John's U., Jamaica, N.Y., 1960-64; assoc. prof. polit. sci. Seton Hall U., South Orange, N.J., 1965-68, Troy (Ala.) State U., 1971-72; exec. v.p. Am. Fgn. Policy Inst., Washington, 1968-98, pres., 1998—, immigration cons., 1987-97, pres., 1998—; exec. v.p. Nat. Confedn. Am. Ethnic Groups, Washington, 1979-90, nat. sec., 1990—, pres., 1998—. Author: Germany's Eastern Frontiers, 1960, Die deutsche Ostgrenze, 1961, Southeast Asia, 1984, Erdely Vedelmeben (In Defense of Transylvania), 1996. Speechwriter on ethnic issues 1960 Nixon Campaign; founding mem. Rep. Nat. Heritage Group Coun., Washington, 1970; sec. Internat. Rels. Am. Hungarian Fedn., 1965-90; founding pres. U. Profs. for Acad. Order, 1970-71. Recipient Ellis Island Medal of Honor, N.Y. State Bicentennial Commn., 1986, Medal of Honor, Transylvanian World Fedn., São Paulo, Brazil, 1983, Little Cross of the Order of Merit, Republic of Hungary, 1998, Hungarian Am. Order Hon., 1999. Mem. World Affairs Coun., Internat. Studies Assn. Roman Catholic. Home: 9419 Leesburg Pike Vienna VA 22182-1460

SZCZEPANIAK, CZESLAW, electrical engineer, educator; b. Warsaw, Poland, July 16, 1928; s. Jan and Marianna (Bogucka) S.; m. Janina Kowalska, Apr. 21, 1956; children: Robert, Konrad. MSEE, Tech. U., Warsaw, 1956; PhD, In. Electrotech., Warsaw, 1966. Registered profl. engr., Warsaw. Engr. Electrotech. Inst., 1956-69, section and dept. leader, 1969—, tchr., 1991, prof. electrical, 1991—. Author: Direct Current Potentiometers, 1972, Alternating Current Potentiometers, 1976, Electrical Measuring Comparators, 1979; inventor in field. Mem. Warsaw Sci. Soc., Polish Acad. Scis. (chmn. electrometrology sect. electrotech. com. 1993-95). Roman Catholic. Avocations: walking, bicycling, car. Home: Zeganska 24d/13, 04-713 Warsaw Poland Office: Inst Elektrotechniki, M Pozarskiego 28, 04-703 Warsaw Poland

SZCZEPANIAK, PIOTR STANISLAW, computer scientist, educator; b. Pabianice, Poland, Apr. 29, 1953; s. Zygmunt and Janina (Denuszek) S.; m. Ewa Maria Hartman, Apr. 21, 1977; children: Katarzyna, Bartek. MSc, Tech. U., Lodz, Poland, 1977; PhD, Tech. U., Dresden, Germany, 1982, DSc, 1990. Asst. Tech. U., Lodz, 1977-78, 81-82, asst. prof., 1982-94, assoc. prof., 1994—; editor Springer books. Contbr. articles to profl. jours. TEMPUS program grantee European cmty., 1991, 92, 95, 96, 97. Mem. IEEE (sr.), Polish Cybernetical Soc., Polish Neural Networks Soc. Roman Catholic. Avocations: swimming, sailing.

SZCZEPANIK, EDWARD FRANCISZEK, economist, educator, government official; b. Suwalki, Poland, Aug. 22, 1915; s. Franciszek and Wladyslawa (Stepien) S.; m. Hanna Maria Janikowska, June 29, 1946; children: Barbara, Tadeusz, Zofia, Tomasz. MS in Econs. and Commerce, Prin. Sch. Commerce, Warsaw, Poland, 1936; MS in Econs., London Sch. Econs., 1953; PhD in Econs., U. London, 1956. Asst. lectr. Prin. Sch. Commerce, Warsaw, 1938-39; asst. prof. Polish U. Coll., London, 1947-53; sr. lectr. U. Hong Kong, 1953-61; advisor Harvard U. Adv. Team, Karachi, Pakistan, 1961-63; sr. economist Food & Agr. Orgn. UN, Rome, 1963-77; sr. rsch. fellow U. Sussex, Sussex, England, 1978-81; prof. econs. Polish U. in London, 1981—; cons. UN High Commr. for Refugees, Hong Kong, 1954, Food & Agr. Orgn. UN, Hong Kong, 1954-55, Econ. Commn. for Asia & Far East UN, Bangkok, Thailand, 1956, Internat. Coffee Orgn., London, 1975. Author: The Economic Growth of Hong Kong, 1958, Agricultural Policies, 1975; co-author: The National Income of Hong Kong, 1955, New Limits of European Agriculture, 1985. Chmn. Rsch. Inst. for Polish Affairs, London, 1951-53, 83-86; pres. Polish Soc. Arts and Scis. Abroad, London, 1981—; minister Polish Govt. in Exile, London, 1981-86, prime minister, 1986-90; chmn. Liquidation Commn., Polish Govt. in Exile, 1991; chmn. Coun. for Rsch. on Poles Abroad, 1996—. Capt. Polish Army, 1939-46, maj., 1990. Decorated Silver Cross of Merit with sword and Cross Mil. Valour, Polish Army; decorated knight Polonia Restituta (Polish Govt. in Exile), comdr. Polonia Restituta with grand sash. Fellow Royal Econ. Soc., Polish Hearth. Conservative. Roman Catholic. Home: By the Way Bradford Rd, Lewes BN7 1RD, England Office: Chmn/Polonia Aid Found Trst, Polish Soc Arts/Sci Abroad, 240 King St, London W6 0RF, England

SZCZESNY, RONALD WILLIAM, lawyer; b. Detroit, Nov. 26, 1940; s. Raymond Joseph and Sophie (Welc) S.; children: Timothy, Laurie, Kristen; m. Susan Joy Feragne, May 25, 1985. BA in Chemistry, Wayne State U., 1963, JD, 1972. Bar: Mich. 1975, U.S. Dist. Ct. (ea. dist.) Mich. 1975, U.S. Tax Ct. 1975, U.S. Supreme Ct. 1983, U.S. Ct. Appeals 1985. Rsch. chemist Wyandotte Chems., Mich., 1961-64; exptl. chemist Cadillac Motor Car Co., Detroit, 1964-66, gen. supr. material lab., 1966-69, materials engr., 1969-72; staff analysis engr. GM Co., Warren, Mich., 1972-77; assoc. Zeff and Zeff & Materna, Detroit, 1977-89, Stern Cohan and Stern, Southfield, Mich., 1989-97; pvt. practice Madison Heights, Mich., 1997—. Mem. ATLA, Mich. Trial Lawyers Assn., Detroit Bar Assn., Oakland County Bar Assn., Macomb County Bar Assn., Soc. Automotive Engrs., Advocates Bar Assn., Am. Acad. Forensic Scis., Internat. Assn. Arson Investigators, Mich. Assn. Arson Investigators, U. Mich. Pres.'s Club, Am. Soc. Safety Engrs., Nat. Assn. Fire Investigators, Nat. Fire Protection Assn., Million Dollar Advs. Forum. Democrat. Roman Catholic. Home: 27333 Spring Arbor Dr Southfield MI 48076-3543 Office: 28051 Dequindre Rd Madison Heights MI 48071-3001

SZCZURASZEK, TOMASZ WIESLAW, engineering educator; b. Inowroclaw, Bydgoskie, Poland, Mar. 9, 1949; s. Stefan and Anna (Glowacka) S.; m. Martyna Bogumila Czuchra, Sept.1 8, 1975; children: Agnieszka, Pawel. MS, Tech. U. Gdansk, Poland, 1976, PhD, 1980, prof., 1991. Asst. to older asst. Engr. H.S., Bydgoszcz, Poland, 1972-80; prof. asst. U. Tech., Bydgoszcz, Poland, 1980-90, readership, 1990-92, prof., 1992—, vics dean rsch. and edn., 1981-84, head dept. traffic engring., 1984—; rd. bldg. older inspector Regional Rd.'s Hdqs., Bydgoszcz, 1989-90. Co-author: Traffic Flow Simulation, 1980 (Rector's award 1981), Model of Traffic Flow on Double Lane Road, 1990 (Rector's award 1991); patentee in field (Rector's award 1989); contbr. articles to profl. jours. Head Consulative Coun. Woivodship Rd. Safety Bd., Bydgoszcz, 1995—. Mem. Polish Acad. Scis. (traffic engring. soc. 1996—, traffic control soc. 1996—), Transp. Engrs. and Technicians Assns. (appraiser's coun. 1987—, Golden medal 1994). Roman Catholic. Avocations: painting. Home: Tunczykowa 1, 85 436 Bydgoszcz Poland Office: Dept Traffic Engring, Kaliskiego 7, 85 791 Bydgoszcz Poland

SZE, DANIEL YUNG-HO, medical educator; b. Pitts., June 5, 1961; s. Tsung Wei and Frances Tung Sze; m. Cynthia Ruth Harris, Aug. 14, 1993; children: Katherine Lily, Michael Jason. BA, Harvard U., 1983; PhD, MD, Stanford U., 1991. Asst. prof. Stanford U., 1997—. Office: Divsn Cardiovascular and Interventional Radiology Stanford U Stanford CA 94305

SZE, FRANK KAI-HOI, physician, researcher; b. Chung Ching, China, Jan. 2, 1944; s. James Sze and King-Yi Ng; m. Amay Pun, Sept. 18, 1978 (dec. Sept. 1997). MD, Shanghai Second Med. U., China, 1969; diploma in palliative medicine, U. Wales, United Kingdom, 1996. Resident Lu-Wan Dist. Hosp., Shanghai, 1970-80; licentiate Queen Mary Hosp., Hong Kong, 1981-83; med. officer Princess Margaret Hosp., Hong Kong, 1983-89, Chinese U. Hong Kong/Prince of Wales Hosp., 1989-91; sr. med. officer Shatin Hosp., Hong Kong, 1991-95, sr. med. officer in-charge palliative care unit, 1996—, sr. med. officer in-charge stroke unit, 1996—; clin. fellow Oxford (Eng.) U., 1995-96; hon. assoc. prof. faculty medicine Chinese U. Hong Kong, 1996—. Contbr. articles to med. jours. Fellow Hong Kong Coll. Physicians, Hong Kong Acad. Medicine, Royal Coll. Physicians, Edinburgh; mem. Hong Kong Soc. Palliative Medicine (hon. sec. 1997-99). Avocation: long distance running. Office: Shatin Hosp Dept Med/Geriat, 33 A Kung Kok St, Hong Kong China

SZEBERÉNYI, JÓZSEF, physician, cell biologist, educator; b. Kaposvár, Hungary, Feb. 20, 1950; s. György and Erzsébet (Fikár) S.; m. Gyöngyi Burus. MD, Pécs Med. Sch., 1974; PhD, Pecs Med. Sch. Hungary, 1986, DSc, 1997. Cert. clin. chemistry. Postdoctoral fellow Washington U., St. Louis, 1982-84; postdoctoral fellow, vis. prof. Harvard Med. Sch., Boston, 1987-92; prof. Pécs Med. Sch., 1992—; lectr. Pecs Med. Sch., 1975-92. Author: Molecular Genetics for Students, 1982; contbr. articles to profl. jours. Grantee U.S.-Hungarian Joint Fund, 1994-96. Mem. Hungarian Biol. Soc. (sect. pres. 1995), Hungarian Biochem. Soc., Hungarian Soc. Med. Edn. Office: Pécs Univ Fac Med, Szigeti út 12, H-7643 Pécs Hungary

SZECSY, RICHARD SAMUEL, civil engineer; b. Champaign, Ill., Mar. 18, 1969; s. Richard Elmer and Ellen Kay (Collier) S.; m. Amanda Caryl Lindley, Apr. 6, 1994. BSCE, Tex. A&M U., 1992, MSCE, 1993; PhD in Civil Engring., U. Ill., 1997. Strategic planning and analysis Pioneer Concrete Tex., Irving, 1997, tech. dir., 1997-98; tech., dir. new bus. devel. Pioneer USA, Houston, 1998—. Mem. ASCE, ACI Internat. (tech. dir. N.E. Tex. chpt. 1997-98), Tex. Soc. Profl. Engrs. Office: Pioneer USA 800 Gessner Rd Ste 1100 Houston TX 77024-4257

SZEFNER, ZBIGNIEW PIOTR, welding engineering educator, researcher; b. Szczecin, Poland, Mar. 5, 1951; s. Alfons Pawel and Danuta Regina (Bruska) S.; m. Bozena Barbara Skalmierska, Apr. 9, 1977; children: Mariusz, Anna. MS, Tech. U. Szczecin, 1974, DS, 1984; diploma in edn., Wyzsza Pedagogic Acad., Poland, 1986. Cert. mech. engr. Demonstrator welding Tech. U. Szczecin, 1973-74, asst., 1974-83, lectr., 1983-84, tutor, 1984—; supr. welding FMB Hydroma State Enterprise, Szczecin, 1985-86, Promus, Szczecin, 1994-95; cons. Eko-Wark, 1992-93; vice-chmn. Mgmt. Bldg. Coop., Szczecin, 1989-95. Patentee in field; contbr. articles to profl. jours. Chmn. Sch. Bd., Szczecin, 1995-97; mem. Trade U. Solidarnosc, 1979—. Recipient Prize of Rector for jour. articles and patents, Outstanding Achievement award The Lincoln Electric Co., 1994. Mem. Polish Soc. Mech. Engring. (sec. 1983-87, hon. 1989, province directorship). Roman Catholic. Avocations: science, tinkering, touring, fishing. Home: Dubois 34/69, 71-610 Szczecin Pomorze Zachodnie West Pomeranian, Poland Office: Tech U Szczecin, Al Piastów 19, 70-310 Szczecin Pomorze Zachodnie, Poland

SZEGEDY-MASZÁK, MIHÁLY, educator, editor, literary historian; b. Budapest, Hungary, June 23, 1943; s. György and Valéria (Holló) S-M; m. Márta Ákom, Dec. 27, 1966 (div. Jan. 1971); children Zoltán; m. Agnes Szemerkényi, Aug. 1, 1975; children: Anna, Zsuzsanna. MA, Eötvös U., Budapest, 1966, PhD, 1967. Assoc. prof. Eötvös U., Budapest, 1981-90, prof., 1990—; editor Hungarian Studies, Budapest, 1987—; vis. prof. Ind. U., Bloomington, 1984, 87, 91—. Author: Világkép és Stilus, 1980, A Regény, amint Irja önmagát, 1980, 87, Kubla Kán és Pickwick ur, 1982, Kemény Zsigmond, 1989, Márai Sándar, 1991, Ottlik Géza, 1994, Minta a Szönyegen, 1995, Irodalmi Káhonok, 1998; editor: A Mindentudás Igézete, 1985, Tanulmányok Kosztolànyi Deasöröl, 1998, Epoche-Text-Modalität, 1999. Mem. Internat. Comparative Lit. Assn. (coordinating com.), Hungarian Acad. Scis., Acad. Europaea, Internat. Comparative Lit. Assn. (v.p.). Home: Völgy u 25, 1021 Budapest Hungary Office: Eötvös U, Pesti B u 1, 1052 Budapest Hungary

SZÈKELY, LA'SZLO', philosophy educator; b. Baja, Hungary, July 3, 1954; s. Zsuzsanna Papp, Dec. 29, 1987; 1 child, La'szlo'. M Math., József Attila U., Szeged, Hungary, 1978; PhM, Eötvös Lorand U., Budapest, Hungary, 1982; PhD, Hungarian Acad. Sci., Budapest, 1990. Lectr. Juha'sz Gyula Tchr. Tng. Coll., Szeged, 1979-85; rsch. fellow Tech. U., Budapest, 1985-88; prof. Inst. Philosophy Hungarian Acad. Sci., Budapest, 1989—. Author: (in Hungarian) From Einstein's Cosmos to Inflationary Universe, 1990, Cosmos with a Human Face: the Anthropic Principle, 1997, (in English) Why Not Lukacs? Studies in East European Thought, 1999. Avocations: music, literature, sports, humanities. Office: Inst Philosophy, Hungarian Acad Sci POB 594, 1398 Budapest 62, Hungary

SZEKERES, MARIA, medical physiologist; b. Budapest, Hungary, May 8, 1970; d. Bela and Maria (Nagy) S.; m. Gyorgy Laszlo Nadasy, May 24, 1997; 1 child, Veronika. MD, Semmelweis U., 1994. Postdoctoral fellow, then rsch. fellow, then asst. prof. Semmelweis U., Budapest, 1994—; postdoctoral fellow N.Y. Med. Coll., N.Y.C., 1997-98. Recipient award Internat. Union Angiology Congress, Budapest, 1996. Mem. Hungarian Physiol. Soc. Avocations: reading, travel. Office: Semmelweis U Clin Rsch Dept, 78/A Ulloi U, 1082 Budapest Hungary

SZEKERES-VARSA, VERA, linguistics educator, translator; b. Budapest, Hungary, Apr. 27, 1933; d. József and Ilona (Garai) Varsa; m. György Konra'd Aug. 8, 1955; György Szekeres, March 30, 1960 (dec. 1973); m. Andra's Roma'n, Aug. 7, 1975. Cert. tchr., Hungarian U. Sci., 1955, 60, 75, 80, cert. psychology, 1965, cert. in art history, 1975, cert., 1980. Tchr. Budapest Pub. Schs., 1955-60; sr. tchr. Hungarian U. Sci. Philological Dept., 1960-79; head linguistic dept. Hungarian Acad. Drama and Film, 1979—; head, tchr.'s group Hungarian U. Sci., 1975-79; sect. Pedagogical Soc., 1970-75. Author: Salamandre in the Fire, 1985; contbr. articles to pedagogical pubs. Chairperson Amnesty Internat., Hungary, 1996—, Hungary Univ. Women, 1997-99; councilor, pres. cultural com., Budapest local govt., 1990-94. Named Outstanding Tchr. Minstry of Edn., Hungary, 1985. Mem. Internat. Coun. Monuments and Sites. Avocations: swimming, rowing, tourism. Home: Aulich 3, 1054 Budapest Hungary

SZELECZKY, ZOLTÁN, biologist; b. Budapest, Feb. 29, 1940; s. Zoltán and Klára (László) S.; m. Judit Szabó, Oct. 21, 1974; children: Balázs, Zsófia. PhD, Eötvös L. U., Budapest, 1963. Rsch. fellow Agrl. Rsch. Inst. of Hungarian Acad. Sci., Martonvásár, Hungary, 1963-70; sr. mem. Inst. for Drug Rsch., Budapest, 1970—. Mem. Hungarian Parliament, 1990-94. Mem. Hungarian Democrats' Forum. Roman Catholic. Avocations: touring, gardening. Home: Bánffyhunyad u 24B, 1182 Budapest Hungary Office: Inst for Drug Rsch, PO Box 82, H-1325 Budapest Hungary

SZELÈNYI, JÁNOS, petroleum engineer, oil industry executive; b. Eger, Heves, Hungary, Aug. 8, 1958; s. János and Jánosnè (Pèntek) S.; m. Zsuzsanna Miegend, Dec. 20, 1980; children: Barbara, Krisztina. MS in Petroleum Engring., U. Miskolc (Hungary), 1982, MS in Gas Engring., 1990; Part 1-Open DMS, The Buckinghamshire Coll., Budapest, Hungary, 1991-92. Drilling engr. Mecsek Ore Mining Co., Pècs, Hungary, 1982-84; prodn. mgr., prodn. engr. Nagyalfold Oil & Gas Prodn. Co., Eger, Hungary, 1984-92; head R&D DEP (exploitation) Mol Hungarian Oil & Gas Co., Szolnok, 1992-95; concession mgr. Mol Hungarian Oil & Gas Co., Budapest, 1995—. Contbr. articles to profl. jours.; patentee in field. Mem. Soc. Hungarian Miners and Metallurgists, Soc. Petroleum Engrs. Avocations: tennis, recording videos, music. Office: Mol Hungarian Oil & Gas Co, Oktober Huszonharmadika u18, 1117 Budapest Hungary

SZÉLL, KÁLMÁN ELEMER, anesthesiologist, educator; b. Herény, Vas, Hungary, May 29, 1926; s. Elemér Ödön and Márta (Nemeth) S.; m. Mária Erzsebet Röthy, Dec. 31, 1957; children: Annamária, Kálmán. MD, Med. Sch. Budapest, Hungary, 1952; specialist in surgery, Budapest, 1956, specialist in traumatolgy, 1960, specialist in anesthesia, 1962; PhD, 1981. Surgeon, trauma surgeon, anesthetist in training Markusovszky Tchg. Hosp., Med. Sch. U. Pécs, Szombathely, Hungary, 1952-62; asst. lectr. Markusovszky Tchg. Hosp., Med. Sch. U. Pécs, Szombathely, 1963-67, head dept. anesthesia and ICU, 1968-92; prof. univ. coll. Sect. Med. Sch., U. Pécs, Szombathely, 1993—; chmn. Health Workers Trade Union, Szombathely, 1971-89; asst. dir. Nat. Inst. Anesthesia and Intensive Care, Budapest, 1979—; vice chmn. Hungarian Soc. Anesthesia and Intensive Care, Budapest, 1981-89; vice-rector Coll. Szombathely Sect. of the Med. Sch., U. Pécs, 1993-97; chmn. Coll. Anesthesia and Intensive Care, Adv. Bd. Ministry Health, 1997-2000. Author: The History of the Markusovszky Hospital, 1979; author, co-editor: Anesthesia and Intensive Care, 1971; contbr. articles to profl. jours. Chmn. Soc. for Popularization of Sci. Knowledge, Vas County, Hungary, 1972-89; councillor Local Coun., Szombathely, 1990-94; chmn. Secular Coun. of the Diocese, Szombathely, 1990—. Capt. Hungarian Artillery, 1944-46. Recipient Golden award for highest std. of work Hungarian State, Budapest, 1983, Medal of Merit Officer's Cross, Pres. Rep. of Hungary, Budapest, 1992. Mem. Dr. Batthyany László Soc. (pres. 1990—), Soc. for Mil. Traditions, Assn. Recsk. Avocations: watercolor painting, Hungarian literature, philosophy, classical music, swimming. Home: Szent Imre Herceg Utca 100A, H-9700 Szombathely Vas, Hungary

SZEMEREY, JOHN, European Commission official; b. Budapest, Hungary, Aug. 15, 1940; arrived in Gt. Britain, 1949; s. Zoltán Szemerey and Irma G.E. (Fleischmann) Hardy; m. Josepha V.E. Newsome, Jan. 28, 1984; stepdaughter, Sandra; children: Samantha, Mark. Student, Uppingham Sch., Eng., 1954-58, Hotchkiss Sch., 1958-59; cert. in fin. and adminstrv. mgmt., Cath. U. Louvain, Belgium, 1979. Features writer London Internat. Press., 1959-61; jr. pub. rels. exec. Lamb, Ruck Keene Ptnrs., London, 1961-62; pub. rels. exec. Campbell-Johnson Ltd., London, 1962-64; sec. group pub. rels. com., house mag. editor P&O Group, London, 1964-69; sr. pub. rels. exec. Howard Panton Ltd., London, 1969-71; journalist, pub. rels. cons. London, 1971-73; ofcl. European Commn., Brussels, 1974—; chmn. Europe Today confs., Cath. U. Louvain, Belgium, 1989-91. Author: Reforming the Institutions of the European Union, 2000; co-author: (with Sir Angus Maude) Why Electoral Change? (booklet), 1982; prin. editor (report) Europe-A Conservative Way Ahead, 1976; Westminster columnist Jour. of Commerce, 1971-73; London polit. columnist Sunday Chronicle, Durban, South Africa, 1961-62; contbr. articles to profl. jours., newspapers. Councillor London Borough of Islington, 1968-71; parliamentary conservative candidate, Islington South-West, 1970, Islington South and Finsbury, 1974; founder, chmn. European Conservative Forum, Brussels, 1974-78; candidate European Parliament for the Pro Euro Conservative Party, 1999. Mem. Chartered Inst. Journalists, Inst. Pub. Rels., English-Speaking Union (Belgium chmn. 1976-77, 85-91), Carlton Club. Office: European Commn, 200 Rue de la Loi, B-1049 Brussels Belgium

SZENCI, OTTO FERENC, veterinarian; b. Ujpest, Hungary, Aug. 20, 1949; s. Gyozo and Zsuzsanna (Kovats) S.; m. Piroska Ozsvari, May 25, 1974; children: Ildiko, Krisztina, Anna. DVM, U. Vet. Sci., Budapest, Hungary, 1972; PhD, Hungarian Acad. Scis., Budapest, 1985, DSc, 1999. Asst. prof. U. Vet. Sci., Budapest, Hungary, 1978-80, 1st asst., 1980-90, assoc. prof., 1990-93, prof., 1993—. Author: Practical Advices for Calving Assistance, 1977 (2d prize 1976), Practical Advices for Foaling Assistance, 1979, Practical Advices for Artificial Insemination and Breeding of Domestic Animals, 1984. Rsch. scholar U. Vet. Sci., Budapest, 1972-78. Mem. Hungarian Assn. Buiatrics (pres. 1989—), Hungarian Vet. Clin. Assn. (com. mem. 1993—, Hungarian Assn. Reprodn. (com. mem. 1994—), World Assn. Buiatrics (exec.com. 1992—), European Assn. Animal Products, Mgmt. and Health Comm. (sec. 1998—). Presbyterian. Home: Uzsoki 32/A, H-1145 Budapest Hungary Office: U Vet Sci, Szent Istvan U Fac Vet Sci, Istvan 2, H-1078 Budapest Hungary

SZENDE, BÉLA, pathologist; b. Budapest, Hungary, July 29, 1936; s. Béla and Júlia (Mesterházy) S.; m. Beláné Gabriella Kiss; children: Katalin, Gabriella. BA, Vörösmarty Grammar, Budapest, 1954; MA, Budapest U., 1960. Resident Budapest U., 1960-63, asst., 1963-71, sr. lectr., 1971-75, reader, 1975-82, prof., 1982—. Contbr. articles to profl. jours. Recipient J. Balo award Hungarian Soc. Pathologists, Budapest, 1995. Mem. Coll. Hungarian Pathologists (pres. 1995—), Pathol. Soc. Gt. Britain, Internat. Acad. Pathologists. Home: Üllöi ut 55, 1091 Budapest Hungary Office: Semmelweis U, Üllöi ut 26, Budapest Hungary

SZENTES, TAMAS, economics educator, researcher; b. Dunakeszi, Hungary, Mar. 8, 1933; s. Vilmos and Vilma (Varga) S.; m. Ilona Papy, Feb. 4, 1955. MA, Univ. Econ. Sci., Budapest, 1955, D, 1959; PhD, Hungarian Acad. Sci., Budapest, 1964, D of acad., 1974. Editor Pub. of Econ. & Law, Budapest, 1955-62; sr. lectr. Budapest Univ. Econs., Budapest, 1962-67; prof., head econ. dept. Univ. of Dar Es Salaam, Dares Salaam, Tanzania, 1967-71; prof. Budapest Univ. of Econ. Sci., 1971-85; rsch. dir. Inst. of Social Sci., Budapest, 1985-89; prof. Budapest Univ. of Econ. Sci., 1989—; part time rsch. fellow Afro-Asian Rsch. Ctr. of Acad., Budapest, 1963-74, part time head dept. Inst. of World Econ., 1973-74, prof. rsch. fellow, 1974-85, head of PhD program internat. rels. Budapest Univ. of Econ. Sci., 1993—. Author: The Political Economy of Underdevelopment, 1971, 73, 76, 83, 88, Theories of World Capitalist Economy, 1985, The Transformation of World Economy, 1985, Fundaments of World Economics, 1995. Bd. dirs. Hungarian UN Assn., 1976—. Recipient Silver Order of Labour award Pres. of Rep., 1971, Golden Order of Labor award, 1981, State Prize, 1985. Mem. Hungarian Acad. Sci. (mem. presdl. coun. 1999). Office: Budapest Univ of Econ Scis, Fovam Ter 8, 1093 Budapest Hungary

SZENTGYORGYI, PAUL, nuclear chemist, researcher; b. Burgisch, Rumania, June 25, 1932; arrived in Hungary, 1990; s. Paul and Piroska (Lorinczi) S.; m. Judith Turak, Dec. 27, 1960; children: Judith-Ann, Peter, Paul, Stephen. B of Phys. Chemistry, U. Cluj, Romania, 1955, D of Phys. Chemistry, 1966. Rsch. scientist Inst. Isotope Tech., Cluj, 1956-89, Nat. Inst. Pharmacy, Budapest, Hungary, 1990—. Co-author: Deuterium and Heavy Water, 1975; contbr. articles to profl. jours. Mem. Hungarian Assn. Nuclear Medicine. Home: Vasarhelyi 33, 2330 Dunaharaszti Hungary Office: Nat Inst Pharmacy, Zrinyi 3, 1051 Budapest Hungary

SZENTMIKLOSI, ANDRAS JOZSEF, pharmacologist; b. Szikszo, Hungary, July 6, 1948; s. Jozsef Szentmiklosi and Maria Csurko; m. Agnes Aniko Cseppento; children: Agnes Adrienn, Kornel Zsolt. MD, U. Med. Sch. Debrecen, Hungary, 1972; PhD, Hungarian Acad. Scis., Budapest, 1993. Instr. U. Med. Sch. Debrecen, 1972-73, asst. prof., 1973-82, asst. lectr., 1982-91, assoc. prof., 1991—; sec. regional ethics com. sci. bd. U. Med. Sch. Debrecen, 1995—; advisor Curatorium Internat. Found. Pulmonology, Allergology and Immunological Related Disorders, Debrecen, 1999—. Editor (with Szabo): Novel Results in Cardiovascular Pharmacology, 1990. Recipient medal Hungarian Ministry Edn., 1984; Szechenyi Profl. grantee Curatorium Szechenyi, 1997. Fax: 36-52-427-899. Home: Bem ter 11, H-4026 Debrecen Hungary Office: U Med Sch Debrecen, Nagyerdei krt 98, H-4012 Debrecen Hungary

SZENTPÁLI, BÉLA, physicist, researcher; b. Budapest, Hungary, Jan. 30, 1943; s. Béla and Mária (Bernátsky) S.; m. Ágnes Cziráki, Aug. 15, 1967 (div. 1975); children: Áron, Péter; m. Ilona Parais, Mar. 8, 1980; childr en: Zsófia, Márton. Physicist, Eötvös Loránd U., Budapest, 1967; PhD in Electronics, Hungarian Acad. Scis., Budapest, 1980; DTech in Electronic and Elec. Engring., Tech. U. Budapest, 1981. Registered expert in Hungary. Rschr. Rsch. Inst. for Tech. Physics and Math. Sci., Budapest, 1967—, sr. rsch. fellow, 1980—, head of dept., 1985—; mem. com. electronic devices and techs., Hungarian Acad. Scis., 1989—; mem. state examining bd. electronic and elec. engring., Tech. U. Budapest; regular referee Nat. Scientific Found. and similar bds., 1985—. Co-author: Microelectronics and Electronics Technology, (in Hungarian) 1994; patentee in field. Recipient Scientific award Presidium Hungarian Acad. Scis., 1980. Mem. IEEE (sr.), Scientific Soc. Telecomm., Eötvös Loránd Phys. Soc. Roman Catholic. Avocations: sailing, angling, gardening, history. E-mail: szentpa@mfa.kfhi.hu. Office: Konkoly-Thege u 29-33, H-1121 Budapest Hungary

SZÉP, JENÖ, mathematician, educator; b. Budapest, Jan. 13, 1920; s. Pal Szép and Arabella Liebert; m. Gabriella Tésy, Jan. 14, 1948; children: Gabriella, Katalin, Zsófia, Jenö. Diploma in Math. and Physics, U. P. Pázmány, Budapest, 1943. Asst. prof. U. Pedagogy, Budapest, 1941-46, prof., 1947-49; prof. U. Pedagogy, Szeged, 1950-60, U. Economy, Budapest,

1961-90; vis. prof. U. Florence (Italy), Siena (Italy), Lecce (Italy). Co-author: Theory of Games, 1985, 2d edit., 1999, Semigroups, 1991, Vector Products and Applications, 1998; co-editor: Pure Math. and Appl. Jour., 1989—; author/co-author several math. books; contbr. articles to profl. jours. Recipient Academician prize Acad. Scis. Hungary, 1957, V.J. Eötvös prize, 1999; A. Szentgyörgyi prize Ministry Pub. Edn., 1993. Mem. Math. Program Soc., Gesellschaft fur Angewandte Mathematik und Mechanik. Roman Catholic. Office: U Econs/IX Fővámtér 8, PO Box 489, Budapest Hungary

SZEPESY, KENNETH STEPHEN, charity organization administrator; b. Trenton, N.J., Aug. 31, 1956; s. Stephen and Joan (Stevens) S.; m. Mariann Lydia Moore, June 3, 1995; 1 child, Alexis Noel. BA, LaSalle U., Phila., 1979; student, St. Mary Sem. and U., Balt., 1980-83, 87-88. Counselor Youth and Family Svcs., Trenton, 1984-86; tchr. Holy Cross H.S., Delran, N.J., 1986-87; priest Cath. Ch., Trenton, 1989-93; parish outreach coord. Cath. Charities, Perth Amboy, N.J., 1994—; dir. HIV Lunch Program, New Brunswick, N.J., 1994-97; coord. vols., Cath. Charities, 1997—. Contbr. articles to profl. jours. Adv. bd. United Way, Milltown, N.J., 1997—. Democrat. Roman Catholic. Avocations: reading, baseball, walking. Office: Catholic Charities 271 Smith St Perth Amboy NJ 08861-4005

SZEPESY, LÁSZLÓ ELEK, chemist, researcher; b. Györ, Hungary, Apr. 15, 1928; s. Elek and Ilona (Boda) S.; m. Márta Csury, June 2, 1951; children: László, Gábor, Márta. Diploma in Chem. Engring., Tech. U. Budapest, 1950, Dr.Tech., 1961; CSc, Hungarian Acad. Sci., Budapest, 1960, DSc, 1980. Cert. chem. engr. Sci. co-worker Hungarian Oil and Gas Rsch. Inst., Veszprém, 1950-55, dep. head of dept., 1955-61, head dept., 1961-77; sci. advisor Tech. U. Budapest, 1977-93, part-time rschr., 1993-2000; cons. UNESCO, Basrah, Iraq, 1973-74. Author: Gas Chromatography, 1963, Gas Chromatography, 1970 (Highest Standard award 1971), (in English), 1971; regional editor Chromatographia, Germany, 1968-71; contbr. more than 170 articles to profl. jours.; holder 29 patents in field. Recipient Zwet Meml. awards Russian Acad. Sci., 1979, 93; rsch. fellow E.S.P.C.I., Paris, 1980-81, Yale U., 1987-88. Mem. Hungarian Chem. Soc. (chmn. chrom group 1963-94, K. Than Meml. award 1983, v.p. analytical divsn. 1975, MTESZ award 1988), Hungarian Acad. Sci. (chmn. chrom com. 1970-99). Avocations: bridge, swimming. Office: Tech U Budapest Dept Chem Tech, Budafoki ut 8, 1521 Budapest Hungary

SZEPIELOW, WŁODZIMIERZ JERZY, neurologist, researcher; b. Łodż, Poland, Dec. 27, 1946; s. Mikołaj and Zenobia Janina (Makowska) S.; m. Jadwiga Maria Malec, Dec. 18, 1976 (div. Nov. 1995); children: Agnieszka Anna, Małgorzata Maria. MD, Mil. Med. Acad. Medicine, 1970; Neurologist Cert. Specialist, Mil. Med. Acad. Medicine, Warsaw, 1976; Electroencephalographer, Inst. Psychiatry & Neurology, Warsaw, 1978; cert. med. informatics specialization, European Edn. in Med. Informatics Statistics and Epidemiology, Prague, 1995; Aviation Medicine Cert. Specialist, Polish Air Force Inst., Warsaw, 1997. Cert. med. informatics European Edn. in Med. Informatics, Stats. and Epidemiology. Asst. Ctr. Postgrad. Med. Edn. of Mil. Med. Acad., Warsaw, 1970-72, sr. asst., 1976-87; med. officer, gen. practitioner The 1st Kosciuszko Warsaw Army Divsn., 1972-76; adj. prof. Polish Air Force Inst. Aviation Medicine, Warsaw, 1987-97; exec. dir. Telemedicine and Elec. Health Records Inst., Warsaw, 1999—; sec. country coun. Polish Medicine Econ. Chamber, Warsaw, 1995—, Microsoft Healthcare Users Group Europe, 1999—; med. officer UN Disengagement Observer Force, Syria, 1980-81; head local br. Polish Tourist Hiking Soc., Warsaw, 1984-94. Lt. col. Polish Air Force Inst. Aviation Medicine, 1964-97. Recipient UN Medal, 1981, Gold Cross of Merit, Pres. Republic Poland, 1992. Mem. Polish/European Sleep Rsch. Soc., European Bioelectromagnetics Assn., Polish Soc. Clin. Neurophysiology (treas. exec. bd. Warsaw br. 1979-97), Polish Neurol. Soc., World Fedn. Neurology (space and underwater neurology rsch. group, rsch. group on neuroimaging), Microsoft Healthcare Users Group Europe, Polish C. of C. (com. privatization 1997—). Avocations: sailing, mountain trekking, computing/internet surfing, tourist organization and guiding, scuba diving. E-mail: vovoszep@plearn.edu.pl. Office: PO Box 64, 03-606 Warsaw 24, Poland

SZERGENYI, ISTVAN, diplomat; b. Miskolc, Hungary, Oct. 11, 1933; s. Istvan Szergenyi and Margit Zsembovits; m. Magdolna Lelbach; 1 child, Istvan. Grad., U. Veszprem, 1958; PhH, 1995. Engr. Raffineire Petrol, Budapest, 1958-60, Plant GAMMA, Budapest, 1960-65; counselor Office of Planning, Budapest, 1965-90; dir. gen. Min. Industry, Budapest, 1990—; prof. Tech. U., Budapest, Hungary, 1986—; chmn. com. ECE, 1993-95. Author 4 books; contbr. orver 100 articles to profl. jours.

SZERLETICS TURI, MARIA, chemical engineer; b. Budapest, Apr. 30, 1955; d. lazos Turi and Maria Bors; m. Antal Szerletics, Aug. 21, 1976; children: Akos, Antal. MSc in Chem. Engring., Tech. U. Budapest, 1978, PhD in Biochemistry, 1992; PhD, St. Stephen U., 2000. Chemist Temaforg, Kunszentmiklos, Hungary, 1978-83; tchr. J. Damjanich Secondary Sch., Kunszentmiklos, 1978-80; analyst Nat. Inst. of Food Hygiene and Nutrition, Budapest, 1983—; cons., speaker in field; mem. Hungarian group FAO/WHO Pesticide Residues Com. Contbr. articles to sci. and profl. jours. Mem. Hungarian Chem. Soc. Avocations: travel abroad, flower gardening, teaching. Home: Reguly u 43, H-1089 Budapest Hungary Office: Nat Inst Food Hygiene Nutri, Gyali u 3/A, H-1097 Budapest Hungary

SZIGETI, JÁNOS, physicist; b. Budapest, Hungary, Oct. 11, 1936; s. György and Zsuzsanna (Ziffer) S.; m. Boglárka Gulyás, Aug. 7, 1967; children: Andrea, Zsófia. Diploma, Roland Eötvös U., 1960; PhD, U. Leningrad, 1972; acad. dr., 1996. With Ctrl. Rsch. Inst. for Physics, 1960-91; sr. scientist Rsch. Inst. for Particle and Nuclear Physics, 1991-96, sci. advisor, 1996—, head dept. laser spectroscopy, 1991—; asst. scientific co-worker, 1960-66; scientific co-worker Acad. of Sci., 1966-72, sr. scientist, 1972-96, head dept. laser spectroscopy, 1993—, sci. advisor, 1996—; head of dept. Rsch. Inst. of Particles and Nuclear Physics, 1991—. Contbr. numerous articles to profl. jours. Mem. Roland Eötvös Phys. Soc., European Phys. Soc. Avocation: rowing on the Danube. Home: Erzsebet u 27 app 40, 1045 Budapest Hungary Office: Rsch Inst Particle & Nuc Physics, PO Box 49, H-1525 Budapest Hungary

SZIKLAI, ISTVAN, surgeon; b. Kalocsa, Hungary, Feb. 28, 1954; s. Istvan and Veronika (Zsigmondi) S.; m. Marianna Hejja, Feb. 23, 1956; children: Gerda, Nora, Emese. MD, U. Szeged, Hungary, 1978; PhD, Semmelweis Med. U., Budapest, 1986; DS, Hungarian Acad. Sci., Budapest, 1995. Medical diplomate. Sr. asst. Semmelweis Med. U., Budapest, 1986-87; assoc. prof. Semmelweis Med. U., 1993—; rsch. fellow Paris 7 Univ., 1987-88; adj. prof. Semmelweis Med. U., 1988-91; Hugh Knowles vis. prof. Northwestern U., Evanston, Ill., 1991-92. Author: (book) Oto-Rhino-Laryngology, 1994. Recipient Politzer prize Internat. Soc. Ear Surgeons, 1995. Mem. Coll. ORL Amic. Sacrum, Assn. Rsch. Otolaryngology, N.Y. Acad. Sci. Avocations: swimming, classical music. Office: U Debrecen, ORL Clinic Nagyerdei Krt 98, H 4012 Debrecen Hungary

SZILASSY, SANDOR, retired lawyer, library director, educator; b. Magyarbarnag, Hungary, Apr. 9, 1921; came to U.S., 1957; s. Sandor Sr. and Jolan (Fenyves) S.; m. Clara Ida Varkonyi, July 21, 1951; children: Peter S., Thomas S., Paul A.D. LLD, U. Budapest, Hungary, 1944, Lawyer-Judge Dipl., 1949; MA, Ind. U., 1959. Practicing atty., pres. law firm Veszprém, Hungary, 1944-56; asst. libr. Anderson (Ind.) Coll. Libr., 1959-61; head div. sci. and tech. Auburn (Ala.) U. Libr., 1961-68; head libr., assoc. prof. Ind. State U., Evansville, 1968-69; dir. libr., prof. U. Tampa, Fla., 1969-72; dir. librs. Rowan U. of N.J., 1972-94; v.p. Ala. Acad. Sci., 1963-68; pres. Coun. N.J. Coll. and Univ. Librs., 1978-79, 89-90, Librs. Unltd., N.J., 1981-82, 88-89; cons. numerous orgns; radio commentator, Sta. WTEL, Phila., 1987-91. Author: Revolutionary Hungary, 1971 (Arpad Acad. Gold medal 1972), Ein Amerikanischer Diplomat uber Ungarn, 1974, Hungary's Road to Trianon, 1988, numerous others; author book chpts.; mem. editorial bd. Ency. Hungarica, 1989—; contbr. essays, studies, articles to profl. jours., newspapers, mags.; editor Egyesült Amerikai Magyarság. Bd. elders Presbyn. Ch., Lakeland, Fla., 1970-72; 1st Hungarian United Ch. of Christ, Miami, 1996—. Recipient Legion of Honor award Chapel of Three Chaplains, 1981. Mem. N.J. Acad. Libr. Network (exec. bd. 1988—), Tri-State Coll. Libr. Coop. (pres. 1975-76, 88-89, Johanniter Order Knights (Germany), Arpad Acad. (sect. pres. 1979—), Miami Kossuth Club (pres.), Phi Alpha Theta. Mem. Reformed Ch. Avocations: research, writing, reading, swimming, hiking. Home: 133 N Pompano Beach Blvd Pompano Beach FL 33062-5720

SZIRÁNYI, TAMÁS, computer science researcher, educator; b. Budapest, Hungary, Aug. 31, 1957; s. Zoltán and Marianne (Kiss) S.; m. Krisztina Keresztes, June 21, 1986; children: Barbara, Levente, Marcell. MSc in Elec. Engring., Tech. U. Budapest, 1980, specialist engr., 1982, univ. doctorate, 1983; PhD in Computer Sci., Hungarian Sci. Qualification, 1992. Rsch. emgr. Videoton, Budapest, 1981-91, group leader R&D, 1983-87, head R&D dept., 1988-91; assoc. prof. Veszpém U., Hungary, 1992—; sr. rsch. fellow Hungarian Acad. Sci., Budapest, 1991—. Contbr. 60 sci. papers and articles to profl. jours. 1st Class scholar Minister Culture, Budapest, 1978. 79. Mem. IEEE, Internat. Soc. Optical Engring., J. Neumann Computer Soc., Hungarian Image Processing and Pattern Recognition Soc. (pres. 1997—). Roman Catholic. Avocations: music, mountaineering, skiing, boating, playing the flute. Home: Jávorka A u 20, 1147 Budapest Hungary Office: MTA Sztaki, Lágymányosi 11, 1111 Budapest Hungary

SZIRTES, LÁSZLÓ, nuclear scientist; b. Budapest, Hungary, Feb. 25, 1930; s. László and Lászlóné Regina (Fischoff) S.; m. Lászlóné Eva Varga, Dec. 14, 1960; 1 child, Katalin. Diploma in engring., Lomonosov State U., Moscow, 1955, PhD, 1968, DSc, 1986. Head of labor Lardoline Oil Refinery, Budapest, 1955-59; head sci. team Inst. Isotopes, Budapest, 1955-63, head dept., 1963-85, mem. sci. bd., 1985—. Contbr. chpt. to: Inorganic Ion Exchangers in Chemical Analysis, 1991; contbr. or co-contbr. over 100 articles to sci. jours. Mem. Internat. Assn. Radiopharmaceutics, Hungarian Nuclear Med. Soc., Hungarian Chem. Soc., N.Y. Acad. Scis., Inst. Isotope and Surface Chemistry, Chem. Rsch. Ctr. fo Hungarian Acad. Sci. Avocations: gardening, woodworking, swimming. Office: Hungarian Acad Sci, PO Box 77, Inst Isotopes, H-1525 Budapest Hungary

SZLACHETKO, DARIUSZ LUCJAN, botanist; b. Gdańsk, Poland, July 27, 1961; s. Henryk and Danuta (Karol) S.; m. Alina Jusis, Apr. 30, 1983; children: Jakub, Aleksandra. MSc, Gdańsk U., 1985, PhD, 1990; Dr. Habilitation, Poznań (Poland) U., 1996. Asst. Gdańsk U., 1985-90, lectr., 1990-97, prof., 1998—, head lab. plant taxonomy, 1998—, head dept. plant taxonomy and nature conservation, 1999—; vis. prof. Mus. Nat. Natural History, Paris, 1992, 95, 96, 98. Author: Systema Orchidalium, 1995 (Prime Min. award 1997, Gdańsk U. Chancellor award 1997, W. Szafer Meml. award 1998); co-author: Orchids of Poland, 1996, Flore du Cameroun, Orchidaceae, 3 vols., 1998, Flore du Gabon, Orchidaceae, 1998. Com. for Sci. Rsch. grantee, 1992-94, 95-97, 98—. Mem. Polish Bot. Soc., Internat. Soc. for Plant Taxonomy, Polish Acad. Sci. (bot. com.). Roman Catholic. Avocations: cultivating orchids, gardening, travel, books. Home: Kochanowskiego 98/1, PL 80405 Gdańrsk Poland Office: Gdańsk U, Al Legionów 9, PL 80441 Gdanńsk Poland

SZMAJA, WITOLD, physicist, researcher; b. Sieradz, Poland, Nov. 4, 1963. M in Physics, U. Lodz, Poland, 1987, PhD in Physics, 1996. Asst. dept. solid state physics U. Lodz, Poland, 1988-96; adj. dept. solid state physics U. Lodz, 1996—. Contbr. articles to Jour. Magnetism and Magnetic Materials, Physica B. Recipient Grotowski's award for master thesis Lodz divsn. Polish Soc. Physics, 1988. Avocations: football, mountain climbing, digital image processing. Office: U Łódź Dept Solid State Physics, Pomorska 149/153, 90 236 Lodz Poland

SZMITKOWSKI, MACIEJ, medical researcher; b. Czeremcha, Bialystok, Poland, May 8, 1946; s. Jerzy and Czeslawa (Frydrych) S.; m. Krystyna Siwicka, Dec. 21, 1945; children: Dorota, Agata. MD, Med. U., Bialystok, Poland, 1973, PhD, 1979. Asst. dept. clin. biochemistry Med. U., Bialystok, 1970-74, sr. rschr., 1974-78, asst. prof., 1979-88, prof., 1988—, vice dean faculty med. analytics, 1984-87, head dept. biochem. diagnostics, 1983—, dean Faculty of Pharmacy, 1998—; regional cons. Med. Lab. Diagnostics, Bialystok, Poland, 1984—; mem. com. analytical chemistry Polish Acad. Sci., Warsaw, 1996-99. Mem. editl. bd. Lab. Diagnostics, 1992—; author: Medical Laboratory Diagnostics Tests, 1994; contbr. articles to profl. jours. Recipient sci. awards Ministry of Health, 1978, 79, 86, 87, 92. mem. Polish Soc. Lab. Diagnostics (dep. pres. 1987-90, nat. rep. exec. bd. 1986—), Polish Coll. Lab. Medicine (exec. bd. 1994). Avocations: handiwork. Office: Med U Dept Biochem Diagnos, M Sklodowska Curie 24A, 15-276 Bialystok Poland

SZMYT, PRZEMYSLAW ALEKSANDER, media executive; b. Poznan, Poland, Dec. 16, 1962; s. Aleksander and Regina (Wojciechowski) S.; m. Ewa Malgorzata Marcinkowski, Aug. 30, 1986; children: Klaudyna, Kamil, Kornel. M of Law, A. Mickiewicz U., Poznan, 1987; postgrad., Leyden (The Netherlands) U., 1990, Asser Coll. of Law, The Hague, The Netherlands, 1991, U. Calif.-Hastings, San Francisco, 1991-92. Admitted to practice law, Poland. Lectr. A. Mickiewicz U. Law Sch., Poznan, 1987-91; atty. Soltysinski Kawecki Szlezak, Warsaw, Poland, 1991-95; country dir. Mees Pierson, Warsaw, 1995-97; sr. v.p., gen. counsel At Entertainment, Inc., Hartford, Conn., 1997-2000; pres. Ctrl. Capital Ptnrs. (Poland) S.A., 2000—; Canal Plus Polska dir., Warsaw, 1994-96; Eurocash dir., Poznan, 1994-95; Huta Kunice dir. St. Gobain, Kunice, Poland, 1994-95; bd. dirs. Vistula S.A.; pres. Wizja TV, 1998-99. Author: (book) Product Liability, 1988; contbr. articles to profl. jours. Dir. Litewska Children's Hosp., Warsaw, 1997—, United Way Poland, Warsaw, 1998—. Recipient Prof. Jakubowski's award Polish C. of C., 1987; Fulbright fellow U. Calif.-Hastings, 1991-92. Mem. Warsaw Bar Assn., Young Pres. Orgn., Fulbright Alumni Assn. Roman Catholic. Home: Saneczkowa 27, 05-510 Konstancin Warsaw, Poland Office: PTK, Pawinskiego 5A Blok D, Warsaw Poland

SZNERCH, ANTONI, advanced materials company executive; b. Wrexham, Rossett, U.K., Oct. 15, 1956; s. Emil and Janina (Czerwinska) S.; m. Janice Colley, Sept. 26, 1981 (div.). BSc with honors, U. Wales, Cardiff, 1978; MBA, Open U., Milton Keynes, U.K., 1991; diploma, Inst. Indsl Mgrs. Diploma in indsl. mgmt. Asst. works mgr. Burmah Oil, Wrexham, 1980-82; plant supr. Cytec Aerospace, Wrexham, 1982-85, adminstrn. mgr., 1985-87, mfg. mgr., 1987-92, sales analyst global sales devel., 1992-93, product mgr., 1993—. Found. gov. St. Marys Roman Cath. Primary Sch., Wrexham, 1990—. Mem. Assn. of MBA's. Avocations: golf, exercise, motorsports. Home: 27 Valley Way Hermitage Pk, Wrexham LL13 7GW, Wales Office: Cytec Aerospace Ltd, Abenbury Way Wrexham Indsl, Wrexham LL13 942, Wales

SZODFRIDT, ISTVÁN, forestry engineering educator; b. Gyúr, Hungary, Nov. 7, 1930; s. István and Istvánné (Dukavits) S.; m. Julia Dölles, Mar. 21, 1960; children: Gábor, Tamás. Forest engr. degree, U. for Forestry, Sopron, Hungary, 1953; Hon. D, U. for Forestry, 1999. Referent State Forestry Enterprise, Keszthely, Hungary, 1954-58; rschr. Forest Rsch. Inst., Budapest, Hungary, 1958-65; rsch. sta. chief Forest Rsch. Inst., Kecskemét, Hungary, 1965-83; prof. forestry engring. U. for Forestry, 1983-96, prof. emeritus, 1996—. Author: Forest Site Diagnosis, (in Hungarian) 1994, Forest Site Survey, (in Hungarian) 1966. recipient Bedö-Dij award Soc. Hungarian Foresters, Visegrád, 1994. Mem. Forestry Com. Hungarian Acad. Scis. Avocations: travel, classical music, literature. Home: Határör u. 17, H-9400 Sopron Hungary Office: Univ for Forestry, Bajcsy-Zs. u. 4, H-9401 Sopron Hungary

SZOKA, EDMUND CASIMIR CARDINAL, archbishop; b. Grand Rapids, Mich., Sept. 14, 1927; s. Casimir and Mary (Wolgat) S. B.A., Sacred Heart Sem., 1950; J.C.B., Pontifical Lateran U., 1958, J.C.L., 1959. Ordained priest Roman Catholic Ch., 1954; asst. pastor St. Francis Parish, Manistique, Mich., 1954-55; sec. to bishop Marquette, Mich., 1955-57, 59-62; chaplain St. Mary's Hosp., Marquette, 1955-57; tribunal, notary, defender of bond Marquette, 1960-71; asst. chancellor Diocese of Marquette, 1962-69, chancellor, 1970-71; pastor St. Pius X Ch., Ishpeming, Mich., 1962-63, St. Christopher Ch., Marquette, 1963-71; bishop Diocese of Gaylord, Mich., 1971-81; archbishop of Detroit, 1981-90; elevated to cardinal, 1988; pres. Pontifical Commn for Vatican City State, Vatican; sec.-treas. Mich. Cath. Conf., Lansing, 1972-77; chmn. region VI Nat. Conf. Cath. Bishops, 1972-77; treas., mem. adminstrv. bd. and adminstrv. com., budget and fin. com. Nat. Conf. Cath. Bishops/U.S. Cath. Conf., 1981-84; trustee, mem. exec. com., chmn. com. for univ. relations Cath. U. Am., 1981-90; trustee Nat. Shrine of the Immaculate Conception, Washington, 1981-90; chmn. bd. trustees Cath. Telecommunications Network Am., 1984-90; pres. Prefecture for Econ. Affairs of the Holy See, 1990; mem. Secretariat of State, 2d sect. Coun. for Rels. with States. Mem. Congregation for Insts. Consecrated Life and Socs. Apostolic Life, Congregation for Causes of Saints, Congregation for Bishops, Congregation for Evangelization of Peoples, Congregation for Clergy. Address: Prefecture Econ Affairs, 00120 Vatican City Vatican City

SZOKOLOCZY-SYLLABA, PHILIPPE BELA, tax and estate planning specialist; b. Aigle, Vaud, Switzerland, July 31, 1964; s. Janos Lajos and Adrienne Francoise (Grobet) S.; m. Gina Palffy de Erdoed, May 18, 1996. BSBA, Presbyn. Coll., 1984; degree in law, U. Geneva, 1987. Bar: Geneva 1990, Paris 1993; cert. European fin. analyst. Assoc. Borel & Barbey, Geneva, 1987-90, Shaw, Pittman, Potts & Trowbridge, Washington, 1990-91, Freshfields, Paris, 1991-92, Archibald/Andersen, Paris, 1993-94; mem. mgmt. Banque Paribas (Suisse) SA, Geneva, 1995-99, Heritage Fin. and Trust Co., Geneva, 1999—. Mem. All Am. Academic Tennis Team, 1983-84. Office: Heritage Fin & Trust Co, 12 Cours des Bastiens, 1205 Geneva Switzerland

SZOLNOKI, JOHN FRANK, special education educator, administrator; b. N.Y.C., Apr. 16, 1956; s. Jacob and Anna (Reinwald) S.; m. Judy Lynn Gitterman, June 7, 1981; children: Melissa Beth, David Jacob. BS, Manhattan Coll., 1978; MS, Coll New Rochelle, 1981; MEd, Columbia U., 1983, EdD, 1988. Cert. tchr. spl. edn., sch. adminstr., supr., dist. adminstr., N.Y. Therapy aide Office Mental Health, N.Y. State Bronx Psychiat. Ctr., 1978; tchr. sci. 6th-8th grades St. Philip and James Sch., Archdiocese of N.Y., 1978-79; program supr. occpl. edn. classes St. Mary's Habibilitation Inst. Inst. Applied Human Dynamics, Bronx, N.Y., 1979-83; sch. supr. Assn. for Help of Retarded Children Bronx Habilitation Ctr., N.Y.C., 1983-87; spl. educator Mt. Pleasant-Blythedale Union Free Sch. Dist., Valhalla, N.Y., 1987-88; spl. edn. educator Bd. Coop. Ednl. Svcs. So. Westchester, White Plains, N.Y., 1988-98, Dobbs Ferry (N.Y.) H.S., 1995-96, Harrison (N.Y.) H.S., 1996-97; adj. prof. Western Conn. State U., Danbury, 1988-89, St. Thomas Aquinas Coll., Sparkill, N.Y., 1990, 91, Coll. New Rochelle, N.Y., 1994, CUNY Hunter, 1994—; team leader Bd. Coop. Ednl. Svcs., So. Westchester, 1989-93, site coord. extended sch. yr. program Rye Lake campus, 1991-95; presenter in field; Ctr. Spl. Edn. and Tng. Resource Ctr., workshop presenter supts. day, 1995. Vol. firefighter, sec. hook & ladder Harrison (N.Y.) Fire Dept., 1993-95, lt., 1996, 97, capt., 1998 (Firefighter of Yr. 1990); mem. com. Very Spl. Arts,White Plains, N.Y., 1990; parent rep. exec. bd. Harrison Children's Ctr., 1991-93, 95—; lector, tchr. catechism St. Gregory the Gt. Roman Cath. Ch., 1994-95; EMT vol. Harrison Ambulance Corps, 1993-94; aux. police officer N.Y.C. Police Dept., 1975-77; mem. Ctrl. Westchester Vicariate Coun., Archdiocese of N.Y., 1998—; mem. parish coun. St. Gregory the Great, 1998—; panel mem. surrogate decision making com. N.Y. State Commn. on Quality Care for the Mentally Disabled, 1999—. Grantee: Readers Digest Found., Westchester Edn. Coalition, 1990, Innovation Network, Westchester, Rockland Impact II, Adaptor award, 1991, 92, 93, 94, 95, 97, 98. Mem. Am. Assn. on Mental Retardation (rsch. project norming examiner adaptive behavior scale 1991), Coun. for Exceptional Children (pres. Hunter Coll. chpt. 1997—, regional rep. to bd. dirs. N.Y. State Fedn. 1990-93, treas. 1993-96, exec. bd. dirs. 1993-96, del. Nat. conv. 1998, co-chair N.Y. state conv. 1997), Kappa Delta Pi, Phi Delta Kappa. Avocation: marathon runner (finisher N.Y.C. 1989, 92, 93). Home: 127 Webster Ave Harrison NY 10528-2913 Office: Bd Coop Ednl Svcs So Westchester 1606 Old Orchard St White Plains NY 10604-1049

SZONDY, ZSUZSANNA JULIANNA, biochemist, researcher; b. Ózd, Hungary, July 23, 1959; d. György Szondy and Teréz Marsi. MD, Univ. Debrecen, Hungary, 1983; MSc, Oxford (Eng.) U., 1987; PhD, Hungarian Acad. Sci., 1990. Rsch. asst. dept. biochemistry Univ. Debrecen Sch. Medicine, 1983-90, asst. prof., 1990-95, assoc. prof., 1995—, head oral biochemistry dept., 1999—; vis. scientist Ind. U. Lab. Exptl. Oncology, 1985, Oxford U. Dept. Biochemistry, 1988-89, Karolinska Inst., Dept. Toxicology, Stockholm, 1992, Pasteur Inst. Dept. Viral Oncology, 1998. Co-author: Biochemistry for Medical Students, 1994; patentee in field; contbr. articles to profl. jours. Recipient High Ednl. Study medal Ministry of Edn., Hungary, 1983; Széchenyi professorial fellow Ministry of Edn., 1997. Mem. Hungarian Biochem.Soc. (Gerendás prize 1982), Hungarian Immunology Soc., Hungarian Biology Soc., European Cell Death Orgn., N.Y. Acad. Scis. Avocations: choir singing, travel, languages, jogging. Office: Debrecen U Sch Medicine Dep, Biochemist Nagyerdei krt 98, H-4012 Debrecen Hungary

SZÖVÉNYI, ESZTER, ministerial counselor, international specialist; b. Sopron, Hungary; d. Sándor and Sarolta (Boross) S.; m. Laszlo Husvar (div. 1985). MA in Latin and Russian Lit./Linguistics, ELTE U., Budapest, Hungary, 1970, postgrad., 1975. Comml. specialist Electroimpex Fgn. Trade Co., Budapest, 1969-72; interpreter FMV Telecomms. Co., Budapest, 1972-81; sr. officer Fedn. Tech. and Sci. Socs., Budapest, 1981-85, Nat. Authority for Environment and Nature Conservation, Budapest, 1985-88, Ministry for Environment and Water Mgmt., Budapest, 1988-93; chief counselor Ministry for Environment and Regional Policy, Budapest, 1993—; bd. dirs. Environ. Mgmt. Tng. Ctr., Budapest, 1994—. Co-translator: Literary Essays, 1976, The Physiology of Success, 1978, Dostoyewski--Myth and Reality, 1978, Russian and Soviet Philology, 1983. Recipient Cert. of Merit, Fedn. Tech. and Sci. Socs., 1983, Ministry for Environ. and Water Mgmt., 1988. Mem. Assn. Classical Studies. Roman Catholic. Avocations: reading, learning, travel, theater. Office: Ministry for Environment, Fo u 44-5o, H-1011 Budapest Hungary

SZTANDERA, LES MARK, computer science educator; b. Zabrze, Poland, Dec. 19, 1961; came to U.S., 1989; s. Felix and Regina (Sowa) S.; m. Wanda Monica Wietrzycka, Apr. 5, 1986; 1 child, Claudia Sabrina. Diploma, Cambridge (Eng.) U., 1989; MS, U. Mo., 1990; PhD, U. Toledo, Ohio, 1993. Rsch., tchg. asst. U. Mo., Columbia, 1989-90, U. Toledo, 1991-93; asst. prof. Phila. U., 1993-98, assoc. prof., 1998—, head computer sci. dept., 1997—; reviewer coll. textbooks Prentice Hall Co., Englewood Cliffs, N.J., 1993—, McGraw-Hill Co., N.Y.C., 1993—, profl. jours. in field; organizer, mem. coms., chmn. various internat. confs. Contbr. numerous articles to profl. jours. Rsch. grantee Am. Heart Assn., Washington, 1991, Cray-Pitts. Supercomputing Ctr., 1992, 94, 96, NSF, Washington, 1996, Nat. Textile Ctr., Wilmington, 1998—, Dept. Commerce, Washington, 1998—. Mem. Assn. for Computing Machinery, N. Am. Fuzzy Info. Processing Soc., Can. Soc. for Fuzzy Info. and Neural Systems. Achievements include development of fuzzy neural trees, contributions to fuzzy set theory. Avocations: travel, literature. Office: Phila Univ Dept Computer Sci Philadelphia PA 19144

SZTANISZLAV, ANNA DANIELNE, chemical science company administrator, researcher; b. Nagybarát, Hungary, Nov. 20, 1944; c. Sztefan Sztefanov Ivanov and Cena Simeonova Ganeva; m. Daniel Pál Sztaniszlav, Nov. 21, 1969; children: Daniel, Szabolcs, Gabor. MS, Eötvös LoranD U., Budapest, Hungary, 1968, PhD in Chem. Scis., 1978. Scientist Rsch. Inst. for Telecom., Budapest, 1968-78, sr. scientist, 1979-84, head divsn., 1984-91, head dept., 1991-94; head dept. Innovation Co. for Telecom., Budapest, 1994—. Inventor in field; contbr. articles to profl. jours. Fellow Sci. Soc. Telecom. Budapest; mem. Internat. Conf. on Microwave Ferrites (internat. orgn. com. 1988—). Avocation: travelling. Home: Tas vezer ut 3, H-1029 Budapest Hungary Office: Innovation Co for Telecom, Ungvar u 64-66, H-1142 Budapest Hungary

SZUBKA, TADEUSZ, philosophy educator; b. Radkow, Poland, Sept. 19, 1958; s. Jan and Maria (Salachna) S.; m. Krystyna Handzel, Oct., 1985. MA in Philosophy, Cath. U. Lublin, 1982, PhD, 1992. Teaching asst. Cath. U. Lublin, Poland, 1986-93, lectr., asst. prof., 1993—. Author: Metafizyka analityczna P.F. Strawsona, 1995; co-editor: The Mind-Body Problem, 1994; editor, translator: Metafizyka w filozofii analitycznej, 1996, Filozofia brytyjska u schylku XX wieku, 1998. Rsch. fellow Brit. Coun., 1993, U. Notre Dame, 1994-95, U. Queensland, 1996-97, U. Edinburgh, 2000, U. Pitts., 2000—. Mem. Am. Philos. Assn. (internat. assoc.), Aristotelian Soc., Soc. Christian Philosophers. Roman Catholic. Avocations: walking, music. Office: Cath U Lublin Faculty Philo, Al Raclawickie 14, 20-950 Lublin Poland

SZUCS, ANDREW ERIC, training manager; b. Cleve., Apr. 25, 1946; s. Andrew Elmer and Katherine (Krizsak) S.; m. Laura Jean Nyhan, June 4, 1971; children: Andrew Edward, Eric Stephen. BA, U. Dayton, 1968;

Diploma, Cleve. Inst. Electronics, 1972; MBA, Wright State U., 1984. Pub. affairs specialist USAF, Laughlin AFB, Tex., 1968-70; exhibit rschr., writer USAF Orientation Group, Wright-Patterson AFB, Ohio, 1970-73; cmty. rels. dir. Wright-Patterson AFB, 1973-77; publ. mgr. Air Force Logistics Command, Wright-Patterson AFB, 1977-85, chief pub. officer, 1985-90; civilian command tng. mgr./adminstrn. Air Force Materiel Command, Wright-Patterson AFB, 1990—. Contbr. articles to profl. jours. (AWA Jour. award 1986). Staff sgt. USAF, 1968-73. Named Disting. Alumnus, St. Ignatius High Sch., Cleve., 1994. Mem. Soc. Aerospace Communicators, Nat. Press Club, Am. Radio Relay League, Amateur Satellite Corp., U.S. Soccer Fedn. (referee), Ohio High Sch. Athletic Assn. (referee), Wright State U. Bus. Alumni Assn. (rec. sec. 1985-89), Nat. Assn. Sports Ofcls. Roman Catholic. Avocations: ham radio operator, creative writing, trainer for pvt. soccer team. Home: 1135 Mint Springs Dr Fairborn OH 45324-5728 Office: Edn and Tng Divsn HQ AFMC/DPEO Wright Patterson AFB OH 45433

SZUCS, MIHALY, soil science educator; b. Csolyospalos, Hungary, Feb. 4, 1947; s. Mihaly and Maria (Csaki) S.; m. Ljudmila Satravko, Nov. 14, 1970; children: Natalia, Viktoria. BSc, Agrl. U., 1971, D, 1975, PhD, 1987, Habilitation, 1996. Engr. Inst. of Quality, Mosonmagyaróvár, 1971-75; asst. Agrl. U., Mosonmagyaróvár, 1975-87, assoc. prof. soil sci., 1987-99, prof., 1999—, head dept., 1995—; mem. European Netwok on Trace Elements, Hungary, 1980-87. Contbr. articles to profl. jours. Cochran fellow U.S. Govt., 1992; Cooperation in Sci. and Tech. fellow European Union, 1993, sci. fellow, 1994, Tempus fellow, 1995; sci. fellow NATO, 1998. Avocations: swimming, reading. Office: U West Hungary, Var u 2, H-9200 Mosonmagyarovar Hungary

SZUECS, ERVIN, mechanical engineer, educator; b. Budapest, Hungary, Jan. 23, 1930; s. Ödön Stemmer and Regina Braun; m. Ludmilla Szuecs, Oct. 14, 1965; children: Andras, Katalin, Imre. MS in Mech. Engring., Tech. U., Budapest, 1960; PhD, Hungarian Acad. Sci., 1965, DSc, 1973. Head dept. Rsch. Inst. for Heat Tech., Budapest, 1959-69; head computer ctr. Rsch. Isnt. for Bldg. Sci., Budapest, 1969-78; sci. advisor Rsch. inst. for Traffic Studies, Budapest, 1978-79; head dept. gen. tech. Eotvos Lorand U., Budapest, 1979-95, prof., 1980-95; head dept. Janus Pannonius U., Pecs, Hungary, 1982-86; sci. advisor Pedagogical Inst., Budapest, 1986-89, Inst. for Edn., Budapest, 1989-95. Author: Dialoge Über Technische Prozesse, 1976, Beszélgessünk a Technikáról, 1979, Similitude and Modeling, 1980, A Számítógép Tegnaptól, 1987, Technikatörténet, 1992, Komputervilág, 1994, Informatics, 1999, Word '97 Manual, 2000, others; chief editor, contbr. ency. Képes Diáklexikon, Technika, 1989. Sgt. Hungarian mil., 1950-53. Avocation: dogs. Home: Romai Ut 11, H 2440 Szazhalombatta Hungary Office: Eotvos Lorand U, Rakoczi Ut 5, H 1088 Budapest Hungary

SZUFLADOWICZ, MAREK, cardiac surgeon, educator; b. Warsaw, Poland, Mar. 8, 1955; s. Roman and Zofia Szufladowicz; m. Ewa Maria Marcisz, Apr. 29, 1979; children: Karol, Monika. MD, Med. Acad., Warsaw, 1980; PhD, 1989. Trainee in cardiac surgery Nat. Inst. Cardiology, Warsaw, 1981-85, 87-89; fellow tng. in pediat. cardiothoracic surgery U. Utrecht, The Netherlands, 1985-86; registrar unit cardiothoracic surgery Hosp. for Sick Children, London, 1990-91; cons., asst. prof. unit cardiac surgery Nat. Inst. Cardiology, Warsaw, 1991—. Contbr. articles to profl. jours. Recipient Profl. Achievements award Ministry of Health, Poland, 1996. Mem. European Soc. Cardiology, Polish Cardiol. Soc. Office: Nat Inst Cardiology, Alpejska 42, 04-628 Warsaw Poland

SZUMIEC, MARIA ANNA, geophysicist, researcher; b. Bielsko-Biala, Poland, Jan. 10, 1930; d. Jan and Wanda Florentyna (Fritz) G.; m. Jan Stanislaw, May 31, 1952 (div. Mar. 1995); 1 child, Andrzej. Diploma, Jagiellonian U., Cracow, Poland, 1952; MA in Geophysics, Warsaw (Poland) U., 1961; D., Jagiellonian U., 1967; D Habilitation, Warsaw U., 1979. Asst. of sci. Inst. Ichthyobiology and Aquaculture Polish Acad., Golysz, Poland, 1954-60, sr. asst., 1960-67, adj. prof., 1967-76, dozent, 1976-85, prof., 1985—; dep. pres. sci. bd. Inst. Water Biology, Polish Acad. Sci., Cracow, 1994-98; cons. thermal stratification of lakes Freshwater Assn. Windermere Labs., Eng., 1975, teaching methodology of monitoring of physical properties of fish ponds Fisheries Rsch. Inst., Vodnany, 1976, teaching physical environment of inland water bodies Symposium on Mgmt. of Inlandwaters for S.Am. Sao Carlos U.. Sao Paulo, 1987; cons. thermal properties of carp ponds Catholic Univ., Lyon, France, 1987. Contbr. numerous articles to profl. jours. Recipient Scientific Rsch. Achievement award Pres. Province Bielsko, 1985. Mem. Polish Soc. Hydrobiology, World Wetlands Partnership. Avocations: skiing, swimming, gardening. E-mail: maszumic@polbox.com. Home: Kalinowa 12, 43-520 Chybie Poland Office: Polish Acad Sci Inst, Ichthyobiology& Aquaculture, 43 520 Chybie Poland

SZUMIEL, IRENA, radiation biologist, researcher; b. Warsaw, Poland, Feb. 10, 1936; d. Wacław and Janina (Porzezinska) S. MSc, U. Warsaw, 1960, PhD, 1965, DSc, 1978. Rsch. asst. U. Warsaw, 1960-68; rsch. asst. Inst. Nuc. Rsch., Warsaw, 1968-78, assoc. prof. radiation biology, 1979-90; prof. radiation biology, head dept. Inst. Nuc. Chemistry and Tech., Warsaw, 1990—; Contbr. over 100 articles to internat. scientific jours. Mem. N.Y. Acad. Scis., Polish Biochem. Soc., European Soc. Radiation Biology. Avocations: flower composition, mushrooms, cats. Office: Inst Nuc Chem & Technology, Dorodna 16, PL-03195 Warsaw Poland

SZUMSKI, HENRYK, NATO official, military officer; b. Apr. 6, 1941; married; 4 children. Grad., Armoured Forces Officer Sch., Poznan, 1964. Commd. 2d lt. Armed Forces of Republic of Poland, 1964, advanced through grades to lt. gen., 1997, early assignments include platoon leader, co. comdr., 1964-68, chief of staff, then comdr. 24th Tank Regiment, 1971-80, divsn. comdr. 12th mechanized divsn., 1983-84, comdr. Pomeranian mil. dist. staff, 1984-86, dep. chief of Gen. Staff, Polish Armed Forces for Ops., 1986-87, Silesian mil. dist. comdr., 1987-89, with Polish Armed Forces Gen. Staff and Nat. Security Office, 1989-93, chief of Gen. Staff of Polish Armed Forces, 1997—. Avocations: history, literature, sports. Office: Gen Staff, Ul Rakowiecka 4a, 00-904 Warsaw Poland also: NATO Hdqrs, Blvd Leopold III, 1110 Brussels Belgium*

SZURKOWSKI, JANUSZ WIKTOR, physicist, educator; b. Leszno, Poland, June 20, 1955; s. Wiktor and Marianna (Klukowska) S.; m. Ewa Chmiel, Jan. 14, 1989. MSc, A. Mickiewicz U. Poznań, Poland, 1980; PhD in Physics, U. Gdańsk, Poland, 1990. Asst. Inst. Physics Tech. U. Poznań, 1980-88; rschr. Inst. Exptl. Physics U. Gdańsk, 1988-94, asst. prof., 1994—, leader photoacoustic group, 1990—. Co-author: Biospectroscopy vol. 5, 1990; contbr. articles to profl. jours. Recipient 1st order Ministry of Sci. and H.S. Tchg., Poland, 1985, 2nd order Ministry of Nat. Edn., Poland, 1988. Mem. Am. Soc. for Photobiology, Polish Acoustic Soc., N.Y. Acad. Scis. Avocations: sailing, horsemanship. Office: U Gdańsk Inst Expt Phys, Wita Stwosza 57, 80-952 Gdańsk Poland

SZUSZKIEWICZ, EWA, astronomer, educator; b. W—dro469e Wielkie, Legnica, Poland, Nov. 20, 1958; d. Stefan and Helena (Kowalska) S.; m. Franco Ferrari, Aug. 8, 1992. M in Astronomy, U. Wrocław, Poland, 1982; M in Astrophysics, Inter. Sch. Advanced Studies, Trieste, Italy, 1986, PhD in Astrophysics, 1988; postgrad. Ctr. for Astronomy, Nicolaus Copernicus Univ., Torun, Poland, 2000. Rsch. asst. U. Wrocław, 1982-88, lectr., 1989-92; rsch. fellow Max Planck Inst. for Astrophysics, Garching, Germany, 1989-90; rsch. assoc. U. London, 1990-93; rsch. fellow Internat. Sch. for Advanced Studies, Trieste, 1993-95; rsch. assoc. U. Leicester, Eng., 1996-98; lectr. Ctr. for Astronomy Nicolaus Copernicus U., Torun, 1998—; tchr. Internat. Sch. for Advanced Studies, Trieste, 1994-98; chmn. Workshop on Accretion Disks, Lund, Sweden, 1993, Workshop on Basic Physics of Accretion Disks, Kyoto, Japan, 1995; invited spkr. U. Kyoto, 1995; vis. fellow Internat. Ctr. for Theoretical Physics, Trieste, 1989, 96, Max Planck Inst. for Astrophysics, Garching, 1993. Contbr. articles to profl. jours. including Astrophys. Jour., Geophys. and Astrophys. Fluid Dynamics, Royal Astron. Soc. Fellow Royal Astron. Soc.; mem. Polish Astron. Soc., Italian Astron. Soc., N.Y. Acad. Scis. Avocations: singing, playing guitar, musical compositions, dancing, choreography.

SZUTA, MARCIN, physicist; b. Gdynia, Poland, Sept. 19, 1937; s. Walery and Cecylia (Yoskowska) S.; m. Teresa Dioniza Dobrowolska, Aug. 4, 1943; children: Marcin, Jaroslaw, Erwin. MS, Tech. U. Gdansk, 1961; PhD, Inst. Nuclear Rsch., 1976; DS, Tech. U. Warsaw, 1997. Head operators, adj. Inst. Nuclear Rsch., Warsaw, Poland, 1962-84; head lab., adj. Inst. Atomic Energy, Warsaw, 1984-93; vis. scientist Berkeley Tech. Ctr., Bristol, Eng., 1993-94; group head Inst. Atomic Energy, Warsaw, 1994—, assoc. prof., 1999—. Patentee in field; contbr. articles to profl. jours. Mem. European Nuclear Soc., Polish Nuclear Soc. Roman Catholic. Avocations: historical literature, sports, coaching judo. Home: Pazinskiego 1C/10, 04-643 Warsaw Poland Office: Inst Atomic Energy, 05-400 Otwock Swierk, Poland

SZUTS, GABOR GYÖRGY, agricultural science educator; b. Veszprem, Hungary, May 27, 1950; s. György Szuts and Sandorné (Végbeli) Novák; m. Gaborné Zsuzsanna Mohácsi, Apr. 13, 1974; children: Krisztina, Gabor Jr. MSc, Veszprémi U. Georgikon, Keszthely, Hungary, 1975; PhD, Hungarian Acad. Scis., Budapest, 1990. Cert. engr. Grad. asst. U. Keszthely, 1975-79, asst. lectr., 1979-80; assoc. prof. animal nutrition Pannon U. Agr., Keszthely, 1980—. Contbr. numerous articles to profl. jours. Irex grantee, 1985. Avocations: photography, swimming, sailing. Home: Szèchenyi St 1-3, H 8360 Keszthely Hungary Office: Veszprémi U Georgikon, Deák F St 16, H 8361 Keszthely Hungary

SZWAJCZAK, ELZBIETA TERESA, physicist educator; b. Potok Stany, Poland, Nov. 12, 1947; d. Czeslaw Franciszek and Anna Helena Mech; m. Zdzislaw Szwajczak, Nov. 22, 1969; children: Wojciech, Ewa. MS, Marie Curie-Sklodowska U., Lublin, 1970. Mathematician Inst. Aviation Branch of Warsaw Inst., Rzeszow, Poland, 1971-72; constructor Rsch. and Devel. Ctr., PZL, Rzeszow, Poland, 1972-73; rsch. asst. Rzeszow U. Tech., Dept. Physics, 1973-75, asst., 1975-84, adjunct, 1984—. Mem. Solidarity, Rzeszow, Poland, 1980—. Grantee State Com. for Scientific Rsch., 1979, 1987; recipient Rsch. and Scientific Work-Rector award, Rzeszow, 1978, 79, Scientific Work-Rector award, Rzeszow, 1985, Rsch. Work-Rector award, Rzeszow, 1992. Mem. Polish Phys. Soc., Biomechanics Soc. Avocations: walking, mountaineering, reading. E-mail address: etsz@ewa.prz.rzes zow.pl.

SZYBICKI, EDMUND, executive; b. Bulkowo, Poland, June 7, 1927; s. Jan and Ewa (Turbacz) S.; m. Margareta Anna Persson, Nov. 7, 1957. B Engring., Stockholm Tekniska Inst., 1948; BS in Maths., U. Stockholm, 1954. Head group Ericsson L.M., Stockholm, 1958-70, ITT-Teleco. Labs., Madrid, Spain, 1970-74; coord. ITT-Teleco. Labs., Paris, 1974-77; mgr. Bell No. Rsch., Montreal, Can., 1977-80, Soc. Gen. Industry, Geneva, 1980-82; cons. Internat., Geneva, 1982-86; tech. dir. IST Systems, Geneva, 1986—; cons. in field. Inventor in field. Mem. N.Y. Acad. Scis. Avocation: tennis.

SZYMAŃSKI, ZBIGNIEW, endocrinologist, medical educator; b. Lublin, Poland, Sept. 1, 1938; s. Marian and Nina (Romańczuk) S.; m. Krystyna Sawińska, Dec. 25, 1964; children: Halina, Przemysław, Anna, Justyna. Physician, Pomeranian Med. Acad., Szczecin, Poland, 1961, MD, 1970, asst. prof., 1991; specialist of internal diseases, 1969; endocrinologist, Postgrad. Med. Ctr., Warsaw, Poland, 1974. Physician Hosp. Depts., Szczecin, 1961-62; asst. The 3rd Dept. Internal Disease, Szczecin, 1963-66, asst. lectr., 1966-70, tutor, 1970-72; tutor The Inst. Ob-Gyn., Szczecin, 1972—, asst. prof., 1992-97; physician endocrinologist Clinic of Endocrinology, Szczecin, 1971-97; fellow The Coun. for Natural Family Planning Promotion, Warsaw, 1992—; prof. The Inst. of Family Studies, Łomianki near Warsaw, 1993—; mem. Seym Lower House of Polish Parliament, 1997—, vice-chmn. health commn., mem. commn. for contacts with Poles abroad, mem. Assembly for Seym members of Republic of Poland and Seymas members Republic of Lithuania, chmn. Polish-Belorussian bilateral group. Author: Influence of Gonadotropins on Synthesis of Adrenal Steroids, 1991; contbr. articles to profl. jours. Bd. fellow Solidarity-The Pomeranian Med. Acad., Szczecin, 1980— ; pres. The Responsible Parenthood Soc., Poland, 1981-91; advisor Humane Life Internat.-Europe, Gdansk, Poland, 1993—. Participant auditor The World Synod of Bishops/Family in the Contemporary World, Rome, 1980, Hon. fellow The Responsible Parenthood Soc., Poland, 1996; recipient Golden Merit Cross for the pedagogic activity, 1987. Mem. Polish Internists' Soc., Polish Endocrinol. Soc., Polish Physicians. Roman Catholic. Avocations: travel, history and political geography of Middle Europe.

SZYMBORSKA, WISLAWA, poet; b. July 2, 1923; m. Adam Wlodek (div.); m. Kornel Flipowicz (dec.). Student, Jagiellonian U., Cracow. Mem. editl. staff Zycie Literackie, 1953-81. Author: (poetry) Questions Put to Myself, 1954, Calling Out to Yeti, 1957, Salt, 1962, No End of Fun, 1967, A Large Number, 1976, The People in the Bridge, 1986, The End and the Beginning, 1993. Decorated Knight's Cross, Order of Polonia Restituta, 1974; recipient Gold Cross of Merit, 1955, Goethe award, 1991, Polish PEN Poetry award, 1996, Nobel Lit. prize, 1996. Office: Zwigzel Literalow Polskich, ul Krolewska 82m 18, 30-079 Cracow Poland*

SZYMCZAK, EDWARD JOSEPH, mechanical engineer; b. Anderson, Tex., Sept. 28, 1938; s. Harold and Verna (Walkoviak) S.; m. Lorena Jane Sharp, Sept. 26, 1964; children: Denise, Lisa, Brian. Student, U. St. Thomas, 1958; BSME, Tex. A&M, 1961; MBA, U. Houston, 1970. Registered profl. engr., Tex. Engr. trainee to engring. mgr. Cameron Iron Works, Houston, 1961-90; dir. engring. ea. hemisphere Cooper Oil Tool Div./Cooper Industries, London, 1990-91; dir. engring. Cooper Oil Tool Div./Cooper Industries, Houston, 1991-95, Cameron div. Cooper Cameron Corp., Houston, 1995-97; mgr. design process tech. ABB Vetco Gray, Houston, 1998—; past chmn. indsl. adv. bd. U. Southwestern La., Lafayette; councilor Tex. A&M U. Rsch. Found., College Station, 1994—; mem. mech. engring. adv. bd. U. Tenn., Knoxville, 1996-2000. Patentee (8) on oil tool equipment. Mem. ASME, Tex. A&M Former Students Assn., Tex. A&M 12th Man Found., Tex. A&M Mech. Engring. Acad. Disting. Grads., Soc. Petroleum Engrs., Nat. Assn. Corrosion Engrs., Tau Beta Pi. Republican. Roman Catholic. Avocations: ranching, farming, mechanic, investing, technical and personnel recruiting. Home: 4002 Cypress Hill Dr Spring TX 77388-5717

SZYSZKA, ROSWITA EVELYN, artist; b. Chgo., Apr. 5, 1955; d. John and Regina (Rizinger) Schilli; m. Michael C. Szyszka, Jan. 29, 1977; children: David M., Eric S. AA, Am. Acad. Art, 1976. Graphic artist Sargent & Lundy Engring. Cons., Chgo., 1976-77, Arthur Young & Co., Chgo., 1977-79; painter, artist Kleinert/The Woodstock (N.Y.) Guild, 1989—, Woodstock Artist Assn., 1989—. Mem. Woodstock Artist Assn., The Woodstock Guild. Office: PO Box 637 Bearsville NY 12409-0637

SZYSZKOWITZ, RUDOLF HANS GEORG, physician, educator; b. Graz, Austria, May 23, 1941; s. Franz and Theresia (Tagger) S.; m. Gertraud Kutschera, Aug. 4, 1967; children: Aglaia, Cornelia, Roswitha, Gwendolin. MD, U. Graz, Austria, 1966, postgrad., 1980; postgrad., Med. Sch., Hannover, Germany, 1972, 75. Asst. Chirurgische U.-Klinik, Graz, 1966-70; oberarzt Unfallchir. Klinik Hochschule, Hannover, 1970-75; head dept trauma surgery Univ. Klinic f. Chirurgie, Graz, 1976-93; head, chair Univ.-Klinik f. Unfallchirurgie, U. Graz, 1993—. Contbr. articles to profl. jours. Bd. dirs. AO/ASIF Found., Chur/Davos, Switzerland, 1997—. Mem. Styrian Assn. for Traumatology (pres. 1987-93), Austrian Assn. for Traumatology (pres. 1992-93), Arbeitsgemeinschaft für Osteosynthesefragen Austria (pres. 1995—), Girdlestone Orthopaedic Soc. (chair 1997-98), Orthopedic Trauma Assn. N.Am. (corr.), German Assn. Plastic and Reconstructive Surgery (corr.), Brit. Orthopaedic Assn., German Assn. Traumatology (corr.), Swiss Assn. Traumatology (corr.), Am. Assn. Surgery of Trauma (hon.). Avocations: skiing, mountaineering, history and drama. E-mail: rudolf.szyszkowitz@funigraz.ac.at. Office: U Klinik Unfallchirurgie, Auenbruggerplatz 7a, A-8036 Graz Austria

SZYSZKOWSKI, ANTONI WALENTY, architect; b. Poznan, Poland, Jan. 4, 1925; s. Bronislaw and Aniela (Nowak) S. BArch, U. Ill., 1960. Registered arch., Ill. Arch. various firms Chgo., 1960-72, pvt. practice, 1972-90, ret., 1990. Staff sgt. U.S. Army, 1950-52. Recipient 2d prize Nat. Inst. for Archl. Edn., Marble Inst. Am., 1957, prize Midwest TV, Inc., 1957; decorated U.S. Infantry Combat badge. Mem. Alpha Rho Chi. Avocations: collecting art, swimming, gardening. Home: Dyminska 9/m29, 01-519 Warsaw Poland

TA, TAI VAN, lawyer, researcher; b. Ninh Binh, Vietnam, Apr. 16, 1938; came to U.S., 1975; s. Duong Van and Loan thi (Pham) T.; m. Lien-Nhu Tran, Oct. 26, 1967; children: Becky, John, Khuong Virginia, Dora. LLB, U. Saigon, Vietnam, 1960; MA, U. Va., 1964, PhD, 1965; LLM, Harvard U., 1985. Bar: Mass. 1986, U.S. Dist. Ct. Mass. 1987. Prof. U. Saigon Law Sch., 1965-75, Nat. Sch. Adminstrn., 1965-75; ptnr. Tang thi Thanh Trai & Ta Van Tai, 1968-75; legal rschr. Reed Smith Shaw & McClay, Pitts., 1975; rsch. assoc. Harvard U. Law Sch., Cambridge, Mass., 1975—, adj. lectr., 1998—; pvt. practice, Brookline, Mass., 1986—; rsch. scholar NYU Law Sch., N.Y.C., 1990-94; cons. Milbank Tweed Hadley & McCloy, N.Y.C., 1979, Shearman & Sterling, N.Y.C., 1979, Paul Weiss Rifkind Wharton and Garrison, N.Y.C., 1989, 90. Co-author: The Laws of Southeast Asia, 1986, The Le Code: Law in Traditional Vietnam, 1987, Investment Law in Vietnam, 1990; author: Vietnamese Tradition of Human Rights, 1988; contbr. articles to profl. jours. V.p. Vietnamese Refugees Assn., Mass., 1976-79; advisor to Vietnamese community, Mass., 1989—. Fulbright scholar 1960-62; grantee Asia Found., 1972, Ford Found., 1975-76, Aspen Inst. 1993. Avocations: piano, swimming, foreign languages. Home: 145 Naples Rd Brookline MA 02446-5748 Office: Harvard U Law Sch Pound 423 1563 Massachusetts Ave Cambridge MA 02138-2903

TAALAS, JUKKA PETTERI, atmospheric scientist; b. Helsinki, Finland, July 3, 1961; s. Jaakko Adolf and Marja-Leena (Kauhanen) T.; m. Anni Helena Minkkinen, Oct. 27, 1986; children: Ara, Anna, Hilla, Okko, Aada. M of Philosophy, U. Helsinki, 1988, PhD, 1993. Weather technician Finnish Meteorol. Inst., 1983-85, rsch. scientist, 1986-90, sr. scientist, 1990-92, project mgr., 1992-97, head of rsch., 1997—; lectr. U. Helsinki, 1989-92, U. Kuopio, Finland, 1996—; cons. Ekono oy, Finland, 1990-92; mem. scientific adv. group on UV radiation UN/WMO , 1995—; mem. EU sci. panel on stratospheric ozone, 1997—; chmn. Nordic Ozone and UV group, 1991-96. Contbr. articles to profl. jours. Chmn. meteorol. students union U. Helsinki, 1984-86, mem. environtl. sect., 1987-89. 2d lt. Naval Acad., 1980-81. Recipient numerous grants. Lutheran. Avocations: nature, Lake Saimaa, hunting, cross-country skiing. Home: Karhuniitynkuja 6, 02810 Espoo Finland Office: Finnish Meteorol Inst, POB 503, 00101 Helsinki Finland

TABACHUK, EMELIA, banker; b. Passaic, N.J., Aug. 3, 1926; d. Michael and Fannie (Stefanyk) T. Student, Drake Bus. Coll., 1956, N.Y. Inst. Credit, 1978-80. With Marine Midland Bank, N.Y.C., 1946—; adminstrv. asst. Marine Midland Bank, 1975-76, ops. asst., 1976-78, comml. banking officer, 1978—, asst. v.p., 1982-85, retired, 1985. Mem. Nat. Assn. Bank Women, Nat. Assn. Female Execs., Am. Soc. Profl. and Exec. Women. Home: 78 Stadtmauer Dr Clifton NJ 07013-2513 Office: 140 Broadway New York NY 10005-1101

TABAGARI. SERGI ILYICH, biochemist, educator; b. Khashuri, Georgia, May 9, 1946; s. Illyia Sergeevich and Nina Semenovna (Latsabidze) T.; m. Nia Sergeevna Bregvadze, Oct. 30, 1978; children: Gvantsa, Ilyia. MD, Med. Inst., Tbilisi, Georgia, 1976. Postdoctoral fellow Med. Inst., Tbilisi, 1971-73, asst. prof. dept. biochemistry, 1973-83, assoc. prof. dept. biochemistry, 1983-96; head dept. biochemistry "AIETI" Highest Med. Sch., 1992—, dean, 1995—; postdoctoral fellow N.I. Pirogov Med. Inst., Moscow, 1977; sr. scientist Inst. of Pharmacochemistry, Tbilisi, 1981-86; sci. collaborator Inst. of Nutrition, Moscow, 1989-91; head neurochemistry lab. Inst. Neurology, Tbilisi, 1991-95; dep. dir. Inst. Hygiene, Tbilisi, 1994, dean, 1995—; cons. Rep. Ctr. of Sci. Med. Info., Ministry of Health, Tbilisi, 1991-95, Joint Swiss-Georgian Med. Ctr. CITO, 1997—; founder, v.p. Biphar Tech. Ltd., Tbilisi, 1992. Editorial bd. Health Jour., 1991-94; founder, coeditor Jour. of Georgia Medicine, 1991; author: Biochemistry, 1993. Mem. Am. Assn. Clin. Chemistry, Georgia Biochem. Soc., Sci. Soc. of Clin. Pharmacology, N.Y. Acad. Scis., 1995. Christian Orthodox. Office: Med Inst, Vazha-Pshavela Ave 33, Tbilisi 380077, Georgia

TABAGARI, SERGO ILYA, dean; b. Khashuri, Caucasus, Georgia, May 5, 1946; s. Ilya Sergo and Nina Semion (Latsabidze) T.; m. Nia Sergo Bregvadze, Oct. 30, 1978; children: Gvantsa, Ilya. PhD, Med. Inst., Tbilisi, Georgia, 1976. From asst. prof. to assoc. prof. dept. biochem. Med. Inst., Tbilisi, 1973-96; dean AIETI Highest Med. Sch., Tbilisi, 1995—; v.p., founder Biphar Tech. Ltd., Tbilisi, 1992-96, Biphar Co. Ltd., Tbilisi, 1996—; head neurochem. lab. Inst. Neurology, Tbilisi, 1991-96; dep. dir. Inst. Hygiene, Tbilisi, 1994-97; head dept. biochem. AIETI Highest Med. Sch., Tbilisi, 1992—; head clin. chem. dept. Swiss-Georgian Joint Med. Ctr. CITO, 1998—; cons. in field. Co-editor Jour. Georgian Medicine. Coun. dirs. Sci. and Edn. for Life, Tbilisi, 1997; gen. dir. New Tech. Analytical Ctr., Tbilisi, 1997. Mem. Am. Assn. Clin. Chemistry, Georgian Biochem. Soc., Georgian Assn. Family Drs. (bd. dirs.), N.Y. Acad. Scis. Christian Orthodox. Avocations: music, football, swimming. Office: Biphar Co Ltd, PO Box 172, 380079 Tbilisi Georgia

TABAKIN, RALPH, actor, communications executive, industrial engineer; b. San Antonio, Sept. 22, 1921. instr. corp. comms., legal and social svc. activities. Appeared in films Rain Man, Good Morning Vietnam, Tin Men, Young Sherlock Holmes, The Natural, Diner, Toys, Bugsy, Wag the Dog, Sleepers, Sphere, Liberty Heights, others; appeared on numerous TV programs and in TV commls., also in indsl. films. Served with U.S. Army, World War II. Recipient mil. decorations, also citations and awards for career accomplishments. Mem. AFTRA, SAG, Actors Equity Assn., Internat. Platform Assn., Am. Theatre Assn., Nat. Soc. Lit. and the Arts. Home: 12600 Parkland Dr Rockville MD 20853-3431 Office: Md Acad Dramatic Arts 11141 Georgia Ave Ste 505 Wheaton MD 20902-4660

TABAKOV, EMIL, orchestra conductor; b. Rousse, Bulgaria, Aug. 21, 1947; s. Russi Dimitrov and Biserka Mincheva (Vandeva) T.; m. Burjana Nikolaeva; children: Julian, Martian. Student, Bulgarian State Conservatoire, Sofia, 1974. Conductor Rousse Philharm. Orch., 1976-79; conductor-chief Sofia Soloists Chamber Orch., 1979; chief conductor Sofia Philharm. Orch., 1985, music dir., chief condr., 1988—. Composer Symphonies 1981, 84, 88, 98, Concert for 15 Strings, 1979, Concert for Double Bass, Concerto for Percusions, Concerto-piece for Symphonica Orch., others. Award Nikolai Malko Competition award for conductors, Kopenhagen, 1977. Office: Sofia Philharm, Benkovski Str 1, 1000 Sofia Bulgaria*

TABAKOV, TODOR DIMITROV, barrister; b. Sofia, Bulgaria, Oct. 18, 1955; s. Dimitar Todorov and Mina Petkova (Popova) T.; m. Milena Lubenova Georgieva, Mar. 24, 1979; children: Lubomir Todorov, Yvonne Todorov. Grad., French Sch., Sofia, 1974; LLB, Sofia Law Sch., Sofia, 1980. Lic. trade marks and patent rep. Patent Inst. Rep. Bulgaria, 1998. Judge City Ct., Sofia, 1981-83, Mcpl. Ct., Sofia, 1985-86; legal adviser Ministry of Fin., Sofia, 1986-88, head div., 1989-90, head dept., 1990-91; expert Ministry of Economy, Sofia, 1988-89; pres. Interlex, Sofia, 1991-93; barrister Bulgarian Bar Assn., Sofia, 1993—; cons. Orgn. Econ. Cooperation and Devel.; mem. Coun. on New Tax Legis., Ministry of Fin., 1997—. Author: Bulgaria Tax Treaties, 1991, Part II, 1994, Commentary of the Law on Individual Income Taxation, 1998; co-author: VAT in Bulgaria, 1994. Mem. supervisory bd. Open Soc. Fund, Sofia, 1990, chmn., 1997—; bd. dirs. Internat. Found. Ciril and Metodius, Sofia, 1991. Lt. Bulgarian Air Forces, 1974-76; corr. Internat. Bur. Fiscal Documentation, 1992, Tax Notes Internat., 1991. Mem. Internat. Fiscal Assn., European Fedn. Accts. and Tax Cons., Bulgarian C. of C. and Industry (chmn. bd. contrs. 1991-93), bd. dirs.), Bulgarian Assn. Tax Experts and Cons. (dep. chmn. 1997—). Christian Orthodox. Home: 118 James Boucher Ave, Sofia 1407, Bulgaria Office: 6th fl, 116 James Boucher Ave, Sofia 1407, Bulgaria

TABAKSBLAT, LAZAR SIGIZMUNDOVICH, geochemistry educator; b. Berdichev, Ukraine, May 23, 1935; s. Sigizmund Abramovich and Sima Moiseevna (Polonskaya) T. Bachelor's degree, State Poly. U., Novocerhkassk, 1960; Master's degree, Inst. Geology and Geochemistry, Sverdlovsk, USSR, 1968; D of Geology, Tumensk State Oil U., Tumen, Russia, 1999. Cert. mining engr., hydrogeologist, geochemist. Postgrad. fellow Geol. Inst., Kazan, Russia, 1963-66; prof. Poly. U. North Kazahstan, Pav Lodar, 1970-74; sr. rschr. Ros Niivtt, Sverdlovsk, 1974-76; prof. Urals Mining U., Yekaterinburg, 1976—. Author: (book) The Basics of Soil Science and Geochemistry, 1998; contbr. reports to profl. jours. Avocation: traveling. Home: PO Box 42, 620026 Yekaterinburg Russia Office: ul Kuibysheva 30, 620219 Yekaterinburg Russia

TABAQCHALI, SOAD, medical microbiology educator, consultant; b. Baghdad, Iraq, Dec. 15, 1934; naturalized Brit. citizen, 1962; d. Mahmoud Nadim and Munira (Kadri) T.; m. Peter Shiakallis, 1959 (div. 1968); m. Christopher Charles Booth, (div. 1999); 1 child, Nadya Christina. MB, BChir, St. Andrew's U., Scotland, 1958. House physician Maryfield Hosp., Dundee, Scotland, 1959; rsch. fellow med. unit Royal Free Hosp., London, 1959-62; asst. lectr. Royal Postgrad. Med. Sch., London, 1965-70; from lectr. to reader St. Bartholomew's Hosp., London, 1973-86, prof. med. microbiology, head dept., 1986-98; prof. med. microbiology, head dept. St. Bartholomew's & Royal London Sch. Medicine and Dentistry, 1995-98; prof. emeritus Queen Mary Westfield Coll., London U., 1998—; hon. cons. N.E. Thames Regional Health Authority, London, 1974-94, Royal Hosp. Nat. Health Svc. Trust, London, 1994-98, former mem. com. for pathogenic organisms; adv. bd. Priz Galien Awards, 1994-99; expert panelist Inco-Copernicus Programme, 1997—; adv. bd. Med. Rsch. Coun., 1997—. Contbr. over 250 articles to sci. jours., chpts. to books; patentee in field. Fellow Royal Coll. Pathologists (London), Royal Coll. Physicians (London). Avocations: opera, music, travel, charity work. E-mail: s.tabaqchali@mds.qmw.ac.uk. Home: 9 Kent Ter, London NW1 4RP, England Office: St Bartholomew's Hosp Dept, Med. Micro, West Smithfield, London EC1A 7BE, England also: Wolfson Inst Preventive Med, Charterhouse Sq, London EC1M 6BQ, England

TABARES-MESA, JAIME, infosystems and education technology consultant, engineering educator; b. Medellín, Antioquia, Colombia, Feb. 4, 1943; s. Juan Tabares and Graciela Mesa; m. Mary Toledo, Dec. 26, 1970; children: Ivan Felipe, Santiago, Daniel. BSc, U. Calif., Berkeley, 1969; MSc, Stanford U., Palo Alto, Calif., 1971; Magister, U. Antioquia, Medellín, 1993. Registered profl. engr. Prof. U. Nacional Colombia, Medellín, 1972—, dean, 1981-84, v.p., 1991; disting. prof. U Nacional Colombia, Bogotá, 1992; v.p. Ingeominas, Bogotá, 1977-79, Colciencias, Bogotá, 1991-94; CEO InterRed, Bogotá, 1995; leader internet developers for Colombia; internet cons. Contbr. articles to profl. jours. Avocations: listening to music, computers. Home: A A 56156, Medellín Colombia

TABATA, TATSUO, physicist, researcher; b. Kanazawa, Ishikawa, Japan, Apr. 17, 1935; s. Kunika and Chiyoko (Kawamura) T.; m. Teiko Murata, Nov. 6, 1960; children: Yuko, Yasuko. BS, Kyoto (Japan) U., 1958, MS, 1960, DSc, 1967. Researcher Radiation Ctr. of Osaka Prefecture, Sakai, 1960-69, sr. researcher, 1969-85, chief researcher, 1985-90; prof. Osaka Prefecture U., Sakai, 1990-99, emeritus prof., 1999—; part-time researcher Japan Atomic Energy Rsch. Inst., Naka-gun, Ibaraki Prefecture, 1984-99. Co-author: Brush Up English for Science, 1989, Radiation Dosimetry of Electron Beams for Radiation Processing, 1990; contbr. more than 85 articles to more than 20 profl. jours. in fields of computers, physics, med. physics, nuclear engrng., biology, psychology. Mem. Citizens' Assn. for Fostering the Culture of Sakai; mem. Friends of Tuva Japan. Grantee for Defect Detection by Electron Beams, Sci. and Tech. Agy. of Japanese Govt., 1982-85. Mem. Am. Phys. Soc., Phys. Soc. Japan, Japan Soc. Applied Physics, Japanese Scientists Assn. Home: 198-51 Kami, Sakai Osaka 593-8311, Japan

TABATA, YASUHIKO, biomedical engineering educator; b. Osaka, Japan, Feb. 18, 1959; s. Takashi and Sachiko (Kohiro) T.; m. Yoko Tomibe, May 28, 1989; 2 children. BS, Kyoto (Japan) U., 1981, MS, 1983, PhD, 1988. Rsch. fellow Kyoto (Japan) U., 1986-88, rsch. assoc. biomed. engrng., 1996-00, prof. biomed. engrng., 2000—; assoc. prof. AIST/MITI, Tsukuba, Japan, 1988-89; vis. scientist MIT, Boston, 1991-92. Office: Inst Frontier Med Kyoto U, 53 Kawahara-cho Shogoin, Sakyo-ku Kyoto 606-8507, Japan

TABATONI, PIERRE, economics educator, consultant; b. Cannes, France, Feb. 9, 1923; s. Joseph and Rose (Altavelle) T. Educated, Lycé de Cannes, Faculties of Letters and Law, Aix-en-Provence, London Sch. Econs., Harvard U.; Dr. Honoris Causa, U. Brussels, U. Liege, U. Waseda, U. Sussex, U. Koblenz. Assoc. prof. econs. U. Algiers and Aix-en-Provence, 1950-54; dir. Inst. Bus. Adminstrn., prof. Aix-Marseilles U., 1950-60; prof. U. Paris, 1961-75; adminstr. u. Paris-Dauphine, 1968; counsellor for higher edn. Ministry of Edn., 1969-73; dir. cultural affairs French Embassy, Washington, 1973-75; dir. internat. univ. rels. Ministry Univs., 1975-79; rector of acad. chancellor Univs. of Paris, 1978-81; rector intern U. Senghor, Alexandria, 1989-90; pres. Europe Inst. Edn., Paris, 1989-96; expert European Union, 1991-94, Assn. European Univs., Geneva, 1994-98. Author: On Shifting and Incidence of Taxation, 1950; (with others) Economics of Financial Institutions, 1963, Policy and Structures in Management Systems, 1975, Business and Financial Innovation, 1987, Strategic Management in University, 1998, History of European Moneys, 1999, Privacy Issues, 2000. Decorated Officer Legion d'honneur; comdr. Palmes academiques, Ordre Mérite (Fed. Republic of Germany), Order de Léopold (Belgium). Mem. Acad. Moral and Polit. Scis. (Paris), Acad. Mediterranée, Acad. Polit. Sci. (Madrid) (corr.).

TABATZNIK, BERNARD, retired physician, educator; b. Mir, Poland, Jan. 8, 1927; came to U.S., 1959, naturalized, 1966; s. Max and Fay (Ginsberg) T.; m. Marjorie Turner, Jan. 8, 1956; children: Darron Mark, Keith Donald, Ilana Wendy; m. Charline Edwards Harmon, Aug. 7, 1992. BSc, U. Witwatersrand, South Africa, 1945, MB, BChir, 1949. Intern Baragwanath Hosp., Johannesburg, South Africa, 1950-51, Hillingdon Hosp., Ashford Hosp., also research unit Canadian Red Cross Meml. Hosp., Taplow, Eng., 1951-54; med. registrar Ashford Hosp., 1954-56, Johannesburg Gen. Hosp., 1956-58; physician Baragwanath Hosp., 1958-59; fellow in medicine Sch. Medicine Johns Hopkins U., Balt., 1959-60, fellow in cardiology, 1960-61, asst. prof. medicine, 1966-97, ret., 1997; head cardiopulmonary divsn. Sinai Hosp., Balt., 1961-72; assoc. chief medicine Sinai Hosp., 1964-72; chief cardiology dept. North Charles Gen. Hosp., Balt., 1972; also dir. med. edn., dir. Postgrad. Inst., coord. ambulatory svcs.; med. dir. Nurse Practitioner-Physician Asst. Program, Ch. Hosp., Balt., 1987-90. Contbr. articles to profl. jours. Recipient Save-A-Heart Humanitarian award, 1977, Maimonides award, 1983, Shaarei Zion Humanitarian award, 1987. Fellow Royal Coll. Physicians (London); mem. South African Cardiac Soc., Am. Heart Assn., Md. Heart Assn. (chmn. health careers 1964-66), Laennec Cardiovasc. Sound Group. Home: HC 3 Box 180 Monterey VA 24465-9313

TABAU, ROBERT LOUIS, rheumatologist, researcher; b. Marseille, France, May 10, 1928; s. Victor and Valentine Tabau; m. Mireille Thonney de Blonay, Sept. 18, 1962; children: Laurence, Valerie, Herve. Grad., Faculty Pharmacy Marseille, 1950, D of Pharmacology, 1952; MS, U. Aix-Marseille, France, 1950; MD, Faculty Medicine Marseille, 1959, M of Human Biology, 1960, diploma in human biology rsch. Cert. specialist in rheumatology, med. biology, thermal, climatic and nuclear medicine, homeopathy and acupuncture. Chief doctor U. Med. Clin. Ctr. Hosp. U. Vaudois, Lausanne, Switzerland, 1961-62; pvt. practice in rheumatology, thermal and climatic medicine Aix Les Bains, France, 1962—; rsch. worker, then rsch. supr. Nat. Inst. for Health and Med. Rsch., France, 1965; dir. rsch. ctr. in osteoarticulary pathology Nat. Inst. for Health and Med. Rsch., Marseille, 1965-79; asst. ctrl. lab. Hosp. de Conception, Marseille, 1952-56, head lab. of functional explorations, 1958-65; asst. radiobiology lab. Ctr. de Lutte contre Cancer, Marseille, 1953-57; med. cons. Hosps. in Marseille Ctr. Rheumatology, 1970-75; master rschr. and med. counselor Auvergne Thermale, Rhone Alpes Thermal. Co-author: Applied Radiations and Isotopes, 1957, Cesium 137 in Téléthé rapie, 1963, Goutte and Lithiase Urique, 1964, L'osteoporose, 1964, La Polyarthrite Rhumatoide, 1965; reporter various med. confs. and symposia. Named Chevalier for work in insecticides and pesticides Nat. Inst. Agronomic Rsch., 1966, Chevalier for svcs. to Edn. Govt. of France, 1980, Officer, Palmes Academiques, 1990, Chevalier Nat. Order of Merit, 1980, Officier, 1986, Chevalier Nat. Order legion of honor. Mem. French Chem. Soc., Marseille Soc. Pharmacie, Soc. Biology, Soc. Functional Medicine (hon.), Lyonnais Group Med. Studies, Internat. Ctr. Auricular Medicine and Acupuncture, European Coun. Drs. for Plurality in Medicine Brussels, Cir. of Rhematologists, French Soc. Clin and Biol. Rsch. (chmn. 1980—), Portuguese Inst. Rheumatology (hon.), Rotary (chmn. 1994—). Avocations: skiing, tennis, golf. Address: 23 Chem BELLEVUE, 73100 Aix les Bains France Office: Le Chambord 3 Roche du Roi, 73100 Aix les Bains France

TABB, PHILLIP JAMES, architect, educator, director, consultant; b. Richland, Wash., July 6, 1945; s. Frank George and Tryphosa Ruth Tabb; m. Myfanwy Lloyd, Sept. 31, 1977; children: Michael Lloyd, David Phillip. BSc in Architeture, U. Cin., 1969; MArch, U. Colo., 1976; PhD in Architecture, Archtl. Assn., London, 1990. Lic. arch., Colo. Archtl. desinger Office Econ. Opportunity, Calverton, N.Y., 1969, Earl R. Flansburgh and Assoc., Cambridge, Mass., 1970-71, RNL Archs., Denver, 1971-72, ABR Partnership, Denver, 1972-73; prin. arch. Joint Venture Arch., Boulder, Colo., 1974-79, Phillip Tabb Arch., Boulder, 1979-84, 89-98; asst. prof. U. Colo., Boulder, 1983-84; prof., dir. Sch. Architecture Wash. State U., Pullman, 1998—; prin. planner Phillip Tabb Cons., Pullman, 1999—. Author: Solar Energy Planning, 1984, First Principles, 1999; co-author: Community Energy Decision Support, 1996. Pres. Boulder Ctr. Arts and Humanity, 1982-83. Fellow Colo. Energy Rsch. Inst., 1975-76. Mem. AIA. Home: 1015 NE B St Pullman WA 99163-3946 Office: Wash State U Sch Architecture Pullman WA 99164-0001

TABBAH, HACHEM NADIM, obstetrician-gynecologist; b. Beirut, Jan. 23, 1952; arrived in Saudi Arabia, 1988; s. Nadim Hachem Tabbah and Esmet Hassan Kabbani; m. Therese Elisabeth Laffourcade, Aug. 1, 1987; 1 child, Nadim-Julien. MD, U. Pierre Marie Curie Paris VI, Paris, 1980; Laureat, Faculty Medicine, Paris, 1981; diploma ultrasound medicine/ob-gyn., Fac. Medicine Cochin Pt. Royal, Paris, 1982; qualification in ob-gyn., U. Rene Descartes Paris V, 1985. Cert. cons. obstetrician-gynecologist Ordre Medicine Paris. Cons. ultrasound attache d'echographie generale Ctr. Hosp. de Meaux, France, 1981-84; cons. obstetrician-gynecologist Ctr. Hosp. Dourdan, France, 1984, King Fahd Armed Forces Hosp., Jeddah, Saudi Arabia, 1985, Ctr. Hosp. de Neuilly, Neuilly sur Seine, France, 1986; sr. cons. obstetrician gynecologist Dr. Nagib N. Pharaon Hosp., Jeddah, Saudi Arabia, 1987-96, head ob-gyn. dept., 1996-98; cons. obstetrician-gynecologist infertility, fetal med. Dr. Esam Hashem Specialist Clinic, Jeddah, 1999—; cons. advisor Air France, Jeddah, French Consulate, Jeddah. Contbr. articles to med. jours. V.p. Cercles d'Affaires Francais de Jeddah, 1997—; pres. Club des Medecins Francophones, Jeddah, 1996. Mem. Saudi Ob-Gyn. Soc., Mid. East Fertility Soc. Avocations: judo, computer/Internet, theater. Fax: 9662 6060629. E-mail: hachemtabbah@yahoo.com. Office: Dr EAH Specialist Clinic, Prince Abdullah St PO 14606, 21434 Jeddah Saudi Arabia

TABBAH, KHALDOUN, immunologist, educator; b. Aleppo, Syria, Dec. 15, 1961; s. Abdl-Razak Tabbah and Chokri Kodimati. MD, U. Aleppo, 1986, postgrad. med. studies, 1991; MD, U. Southampton, Eng., 1999. Cert. physician, U.K., Syria. House officer Aleppo Univ. Hosps., 1986-87, sr. house officer in gen. and respiratory medicine, 1987-89, registrar in gen. and respiratory medicine, 1989-91; sr. lectr. chest medicine, hon. cons. Alleppo U. Hosp., 2000—; army physician Aleppo Mil. Hosp., 1991-93; lectr. respiratory medicine Aleppo U., 1993-94; registrar in respiratory and gen. medicine Southampton Gen. Hosps., 1995-96; specialist registrar in respiratory med., clin. rsch. fellow U. Southampton, 1997-2000; expert reviewer Clin. and Exptl. Allergy Jour., 1998—. Contbr. rsch. articles to profl. jours. Lt. Syrian Army, 1991-93. Mem. Brit. Soc. for Allergy and Clin. Immunology, Arab Thoracic Assn., Syrian Soc. Chest Physicians, Syrian Med. Assn. Avocations: reading, walking, stamp collecting, slide photography. Fax: 00963 21 2223764. E-mail: ktabbah@Doctors.net.uk. Home: PO Box 8348, Alleppo Syria Office: Dept Internal Medicine, Aleppo U Hosp, Aleppo Syria

TABIDZE, VAZHA, biochemist; b. Telavi, Georgia, Oct. 13, 1948; s. Dimitry and Sophie (Makharadze) T. BS in Chemistry, Tbilisi (Georgia) State U., 1971; PhD in Biochemistry, Inst. Plant Biochemistry, Tbilisi, 1981. Jr. rschr. Inst. Plant Biochemistry, 1971-81, sr. rschr., 1981—; postdoctoral scientist Inst. de Biologie Moleculaire Des Plantes, Strasbourg, France, 1992, Johns Hopkins U., Balt., 1995, 96-97; lectr. in biochemistry Tbilisi State U., 1990-91. Contbr. articles to profl. jours. Mem. N.Y. Acad. Scis. Achievements include demonstration of significant intramolecular heterogeneity in chloroplast DNA in higher plants; research in chloroplast DNA fine structure, gene organization, and nucleotide sequence analysis. Home: 166 Barnov St, Tbilisi 380062, Georgia Office: Inst Plant Biochemistry, Georgian Mil Rd 10th KM, Tbilisi 380059, Georgia

TABIEI, ALA, aerospace and mechanical engineer, educator; b. Tehran, Iran, Sept. 9, 1961; came to U.S., 1985; m. Entessar Tabiei, Mar. 19, 1986; children: Omeed, Sherein, Ameen. BSME, Damascus (Syria) U., 1985; MS in Aeronautical Engrng., Wichita State U., 1988; MS in Math., U. Cin., 1992, PhD in Aerospace Engrng., 1994. Sr. structural engr. Altair Engrng. Inc., Troy, Mich., 1994-95; asst. prof. U. Cin., 1995—; dir. Ctr. of Excellence in DYNA3D Analysis, Cin., 1997—. D. Eisenhower fellow Dept. Transp., 1993-94. Home: 4221 N Haven Dr Mason OH 45040-8623

TABLER, SHIRLEY MAY, retired librarian, artist; b. Washington, Mar. 18, 1936; d. Howard Leon and Ella May (Miles) Bosley; m. Edward Charles Sepelak, July 30, 1954 (div. 1965); children: David Edward, Linda May, William Bryan; m. Carlton Byard Tabler, June 27, 1968 (dec. May 1993); stepchildren: Roger Byard, Charlotte Virginia. BS in Art Edn., U. Md., 1977, BA in Libr. Sci., 1978, MA in Art Edn., 1981, MLS, 1990. Sec. Nat. Capital Housing Authority, Washington, 1954-55; clk. Vitro Corp., Silver Spring, Md., 1956-57; hostess, cashier Hot Shoppes, Wheaton, Md., 1960-63; new accounts sec. State Nat. Bank, Bethesda, Md., 1966-68; media aide, art tchr. Montgomery County Pub. Schs., Rockville, Md., 1968-86, libr., cataloguer, computer tech., 1986-93. Exhibited in group shows at Arts Club, Washington, 1990, 91, 92, 93, 94, 95, 96, 97, Rockville Mcpl. Gallery, 1992, 93, 94, 95, 97, 98, 99, Sugar & Fricht Gallery 1994, 95, Ten Oaks Gallery-Clarksville, 1994, 95, 97, 98, 99, 2000, Town Ctr. Gallery, 1994, Kensington Gallery, 1994, 95, 96, 97, 98, 99, 2000, Strathmore Hall, 1998, 99, 2000, World-Wide Internat. Miniature Art Show, Eng., 1995, Hobart, Tasmania, 2000; one-person shows include Rockville Mcpl. Gallery 1989, Landon Gallery, Bethesda. Md., 1990, Washington Printmakers Gallery, 1994, 97, 2000Galleries at Savage Mill, 1996, 97, Cafe Monet Gallery, 1997, 98, 99, 2000; juried into Washington Area Printmaker's calendar, 1994, 95, 96, 98, 99, 2000. Leader, advisor Girl Scouts U.S., Rockville, 1964-82. Mem. ALA, Soc. Librs. Internat., Am. Art League, Nat. League Am. Pen Women (past pres. Chevy Chase), Md. Printmakers, Washington Printmakers Gallery, Miniature Painters, Sculptors and Gravers Soc., D.C., Cider Painters Am., Art Gallery of Fells Point, Miniature Art Soc. Fla., Olney Art Assn. (newsletter editor 1984-91, show chmn. 1993, 98, libr. show chmn. 1992-94, program chmn. 1995, 96, 97, 98, joint show chair 1998), Rockville Art League, Phi Kappa Phi. Democrat. Methodist. Avocations: camping, leather tooling, painting, quilting, ceramics. Home and Studio: 123 Charles St Rockville MD 20850-1510 Office: Genevieve Roberts Studio 17521 Shenandoah Ct Ashton MD 20861-9774

TABONE, CENSU, former president of Malta, ophthalmic consultant, former diplomat, educator; b. Gozo, Malta, Mar. 30, 1913; s. Nicolo and Elisa Calleja; m. Maria Wirth, Nov. 1941; children: Marilise, Colin, Helen, Monica, Vincent, Patricia, Francis, Joseph (dec.), Anna. MD, U. Malta, 1937; Diploma in Ophthalmology, Oxford U., 1946; Diploma in Ophthalmic Medicine and Surgery, London U., 1947; Diploma in Med. Jurisprudence, S.A. London U., 1962; MD (hon.), Beijing Med. Coll.; LLD (hon.), U. Malta. Army med. officer, 1939-46; clin. officer Royal Eye Hosp., London, 1946; cons. St. Luke's Hosp., Victoria Hosp., King George V Hosp., Malta; med. cons. WHO, 1952-59; mem. Parliament, Malta, 1966-89; min. of labour Malta, 1966-71, min. fgn. affairs, 1987-89; Pres. of Malta, 1989-94; mem. panel Trachoma experts WHO; vis. prof. internat. affairs, U. Malta. Sec. gen. Nationalist Party, Malta, 1962-74, dep. leader, 1974-77, pres. exec. com. Decorated Grand Cross Order of Merit (Germany), Kavalier ta l-Unur Ordni tal Meritu (Malta), Grand Cross Order of Makarios III (Cyprus), Cavaliere di Gran Croce al Merito con Gran Collare (Italy), Knight Grand Cross Order of the Bath (Great Britain), Knight Grand Cross Order of Merit, Sovereign Mil. Order of St. John Jerusalem and Malta, Pro Merito medal Coun. of Europe of Found. Merite Europeen. Fellow Royal Coll. Surgeons (Edinburgh). *

TABOR, ANNA MARIE, writer; b. Feb. 28, 1972. BA, St. Mary's Coll., Notre Dame, Ind., 1994; postgrad., U. Notre Dame, 1995-97. English tchr. Orden Bunka Ctr., Tsu City, Japan, 1994-95; ESL tchr. Nishikawa, Bremen, Ind., 1996; Japan program adminstr., asst. and tour guide coord. St. Mary's Coll., Notre Dame, 1996; writer 1st Books, Indpls., 1997—. Author: The Wager, 1997.

TABOR, CURTIS HAROLD, JR., librarian, minister; b. Atlanta, July 3, 1936; s. Curtis Harold and Gertrude Olive (Casey) T.; m. Dorothy May Corbin, June 30, 1957 (dec. June 1996); m. Paulene C. Pennington, July 12, 1997; children: Timothy M., John M. AA, Fla. Coll., Temple Terrace, 1957; BA, Harding Coll., 1960; MA, Butler U., 1967; MDiv, Bapt. Missionary Assn. Theol. Sem., Jacksonville, Tex., 1974; MLS, Tex. Woman's U., 1977. Min. Ch. of Christ, Bowling Green, Ky., 1960-61, Hamilton, Ont., Can., 1961-64, Indpls., 1964-67, Nacogdoches, Tex., 1967-75, Dallas, 1976-77, Columbus, Miss., 1977-79, Tampa, Fla., 1993-97, Maryville, Tenn., 1997—; reference libr. Blount County Pub. Libr., 1998—; tchr. Great Lakes Christian Coll., Beamville, Ont., Can., 1961-64; Bible chair dir. Stephen F. Austin State U., Nacogdoches, 1967-75; participated archaeol. excavations, Tell Gezer, Israel, 1969, Tell Lachish, Israel, 1980; prof. libr. sci., Fla. Coll., Temple Terrace, 1979-85, libr. dir., 1985-97. Author: (with others) Resurrection, 1973, Biblical Authority, 1974, The Lord of Glory, 1980, Making a Difference: Florida College, the First Fifty Years, 1996. Cub master Cub Scouts Am., Nacogdoches, 1970-75; pres. Nacogdoches Baseball Assn., 1974-75; vol. driving instr. 55 Alive AARP, 1998—. Recipient scouters key Cub Scouts Am., 1975. Mem. Nat. Geneal. Soc., Tampa Bay Libr. Consortium (treas. 1986-89), Sons of Am. Revolution, Eta Beta Rho, Beta Phi Mu. Republican. Mem. Ch. of Christ. Avocation: Am. radio operator-KC4XS-Locksmith. Home: 1906 Raulston View Dr Maryville TN 37803-2868

TABUTIN, JACQUES, orthopaedic surgeon; b. Moulins, France, Aug. 22, 1948; s. Jean and Denise (Jacon) T.; m. Chantal Gounot, June 12, 1976; children: Sophie, Berengere, Mayeul, Clemence. BA, Lycee Banville, Moulins, France, 1966; MD, U. Lyon, France, 1977, CES in Biomechanics and Kinesiology, 1979, CES in Gen. Anatomy and Organogenesis, 1980, MA in Human Biology, 1980. Cert. Orthopaedic Surgeon, 1983. Intern, resident Lyon, 1972-77, attache anatomie, 1974-77, chef de clinique, fellow, 1977-81; head orthopaedic surgery Hosp., Cannes, France, 1981—; expert pres. les Tribunaux, Aix En Provence, 1990; cons. Etablissement Francais Des Greffes, 1995; pres. Gradual Elongation Nail Com., 1996. Recipient Antonin Poncet prize U. Lyon, France, 1979. Mem. SOFCOT, SICOT, ESSKA, ESSES, European Hip Soc., Gerhard Kuntscher KREIS, Internat. Soc. Technology in Arthoplasty. Roman Catholic. Avocations: golf, skiing, riding. Home: 8 Rue de Madrid, 06110 Le Cannet France Office: Centre Hospitalier, 13 Ave des Broussailles, 06401 Cannes Cedex, France

TACAL, JOSE VEGA, JR., retired public health official, veterinarian; b. Ilocos Sur, Philippines, Sept. 5, 1933; came to U.S., 1969; s. Jose Sr. and Cristina (Vega) T.; m. Lilia Caccam, 1959; children: Joyce, Jasmin, Jose III. DVM, U. Philippines, Quezon City, 1956; diploma, U. Toronto, 1964. Diplomate Am. Coll. Vet. Preventive Medicine; lic. vet., Calif. Provincial veterinarian Philippine Bur. Animal Industry, Manila, 1956-57; instr. vet. medicine U. Philippines, Quezon City, 1957-64, asst. prof., chmn. dept. vet. microbiology, pathology and pub. health, 1965-69; pub. health veterinarian San Berandino (Calif.) County Dept. Pub. Health, 1970-83, sr. pub. health veterinarian, program mgr., sect. chief, 1984-2000; zoonotic diseases lectr. Calif. State U., San Bernardino, spring 1984; lectr. U. Calif. Extension, Riverside, spring, 1985; vis. prof. vet. pub. health U. Philippines at Los Banos, Laguna, 1988; participant 1st Internat. Conf. on Emerging Zoonoses, Jerusalem, 1996; program presenter 4th Internat. Symposium on Ectoparasites of Pets, U. Calif., Riverside, 1997; poster presenter 8th Ann. Rabies in the Ams. Conf., Kingston, Ont., Can., 1997; mem. rabies and ferret adv. group Calif. Dept. Health Svcs., 1998; program presenter 48th Western Poultry Disease Conf., Vancouver, B.C., Can., 1999, 10th Ann. Rabies in Ams. Meeting, San Diego, 1999. Columnist L.A. Free Press, 1991, Pilipinas Times, 1993, Mabuhay Times, 1994-95; contbr. more than 50 articles to profl. jours. Pres. Filipino Assn. of San Bernardino County, Highland, Calif., 1979; charter mem. Greater Inland Empire Filipino Assn., Highland, 1986-99; del. First Filipino Media Conf. N.Am., L.A., 1993; mem. San Bernardino County Africanized Honey Bee Task Force, 1993-2000; participant 1st Internat. Conf. on Emerging Zoonoses, Jerusalem, 1996. Recipient Donald T. Fraser Meml. medal U. Toronto, 1964, Cert. of Merit, Philippine Vet. Med. Assn., 1965, Cert. of Appreciation Calif. State Bd. Examiners in Vet. Medicine, 1979, 84, Cert. of Recognition, Congressman George E. Brown Jr., 42d Congl. Dist. Calif., 1994, Assemblyman Joe Baca, 62d Assembly Dist., Calif. State Legis., 1994, Vet. Medicine/Journalism award Greater Inland Empire Filipino Assn., 1999; Colombo Plan Study fellow Can./Philippine Govts., 1963-64. Mem. AAAS, AVMA, Orange Belt Vet. Med. Assn., Western Poultry Disease Conf., Soc. for Advancement of Rsch., Calif. Rare Fruit Growers (Inland Empire chpt.), San Bernardino City Libr. Found., Phi Kappa Phi, Phi Sigma. Office: PO Box 1023 Highland CA 92346-1023

TACCHELLA, JEAN-CHARLES, film director, screen writer; b. Cherbourg, France, Sept. 23, 1925. Pres. French Cinematheque; pres. French Cinematheque, 2000. Dir. films (short) The Last Winters, 1971, A Nice Day, 1972; (features) Voyage to Grand Tartarie, 1973, Cousin Cousine, 1975, The Blue Country, 1977, Soupcon (It's a Long Time That I've Loved You), 1979, Croque la vie, 1981, Staircase C, 1985, Travelling Avant, 1987, Dames Galantes, 1990, The Man of My Life, 1992, Seven Sundays, 1994, People Who Love Each Other, 1999; dir. TV film Criminal Court, 1986. Home: 8 bis Boulevard de Lesseps, Versailles 78000, France Office: VMA, 20 Ave Rapp, 75007 Paris 75008, France

TACHAKRA, SPITMAN SAVAK, physician, consultant; b. Surat, Gujerat, India, Aug. 30, 1939; s. Savak Byramji and Mehra Savak (Kapadia) T.; m. Almitra Spitman Dotiwalla, May 3, 1976; 1 child, Farzahn. MB BS, U. Bombay, 1963, MS, 1967. Intern, sr. house officer, registrar J.J. Group of Hosps., Mumbai, 1963-69; registrar orthopaedics and trauma Ashford, Eng., 1970-72; registrar, acting cons. Birmingham Accident Hosp., 1972-76; fellow RJ and AH Orthopaedic Hosp., Oswestry, 1976-78; cons. Ctrl. Middlesex Hosp., London, 1978—; hon. cons. St. Mary's Hosp., London, 1988—; undergrad. subdean St. Mary's, Ctrl. Middlesex Hosp., 1988-92; hon. sr. lectr. Middlesex Hosp. Med. Sch., London, 1978-83, Imperial Coll. S.M., London, 1983—; clin. div. Ctrl. Middlesex Hosp., London, 1990—. guest editor Archives Emergency Medicine, 1988; contbr. articles to profl. jours. including Jour. Royal Soc. Health, Jour. Telemedicine and Telecare. Founder, chmn. Cmtys. Cope in Med. Disaster, 1987-91, 98—. Fellow Royal Coll. Surgeons (Edinburgh) (Eng.), Royal Soc. Medicine (telemedicine forum 1996—); mem. Assn. Emergency Svc. Mgrs. Developing World (founder, pres. 1987—), Brit. Assn. Emergency Medicine. Avocations: motor racing, opera. Home: 83 Barn Hill, Wembley, Middlesex HA9 9LN, England Office: Ctrl Middlesex Hosp, Acton Ln, London NW10 7NS, England

TACHAU, HERMAN, structural engineer; b. Braunschweig, Germany, Nov. 12, 1920; came to U.S., 1936; s. Paul and Ilse Lea (Sternthal) T.; m. Heidi Elisabeth Mazur, Jan. 18, 1948; children: Judith Ilse, Robert David, Paul Alfred. BSCE, Ill. Inst. Tech., 1942; MSCE, Harvard U., 1946. Registered prof. engr. N.Mex., Ariz. Asst. prof. civil engring. U. Iowa, Iowa City, 1949-53; bridge designer N.Mex. State Hwy. Dept., Santa Fe, 1953-63; bridge design engr. N.Mex. State Hwy. Dept., 1963-68, asst. bridge engr., 1968-73, bridge engr., 1973-82; structural engr. H.W. Lochner Inc., Santa Fe, 1983-87; bridge engr. Scanlon & Assocs., Santa Fe, 1987-93; mem. subcom. bridges and structures Am. Assn. State Hwy. Ofcls., Washington, 1973-82; chmn. tech. com. concrete masonry design, 1978-82, mem. nat. coop. hwy. rsch. project, 1975-82. Contbr. tech. papers. Recipient 1st award Welding Contest, J.F. Lincoln Arc Welding Found., 1956. Mem. ASCE (v.p. N.Mex. sect. 1975-76), NSPE, Am. Concrete Inst. (bridge com. 1981-94).

TACHAUER, ALLAN DINU, internist; b. Timisoara, Romania, Mar. 26, 1960; came to U.S., 1987; s. Ernest and Ecaterina T.; m. Alessandra, June 9, 1986; 1 child, Allana. MD, Carol Davila Inst. Medicine, Bucharest, 1985. Diplomate Am. Bd. Internal Medicine. Resident Ravenswood Hosp., Chgo., 1989-92; fellow in med. ethics U. Chgo., 1992-93; assoc. program dir. Ravenswood Hosp., 1997-99; pvt. practice Chgo., 1993—; clin. asst. prof. U. Ill., Chgo., 1997—. Fellow ACP; mem. Am. Soc. Bioethics & Humanities, AAAS. Avocations: violin, foreign languages, computers. E-mail: atachauer@rhmc.com. Office: RMPG 4211 N Cicero Ave Chicago IL 60641-1604

TACHI, DOUGLAS PAUL, architect, interior designer; b. Chgo., Mar. 1, 1945; s. Sadayoshi and Ruth Nobuko (Shikami) T.; m. Fleta Ross Collins, Dec. 27, 1987; children: Erin Paige, Brett Spencer. BS in Arch., Wash. U.,

St. Louis, 1968, MArch, 1974. Apprentice in arch. Mies van der Rohe, Chgo., 1961-63; designer Anselevicius & Rupe, St. Louis, 1974-76; project designer Harry Weese & Assocs., Washington, 1976-77; chief designer, v.p. in charge of design Harry Weese & Assocs., Miami, Fla., 1977-83; ptnr., v.p. Tilden, Tachi and Pales, Miami, 1983-87; ptnr., pres. Loggia Arch., Orlando, Fla., 1987—; master plan cons. Rollins Coll., Winter Park, Fla., 1996-97; chief designer Miami Metrorail, 1977-83; project mgr. stas. L.A. Rapid Transit Dist., 1981. Exec. prodr. documentary: Manzanar, Only What They Could Carry, 2000. Mem. master plan com./architect Miami Downtown Govt. Ctr., 1979-84; architect Art in Transit Screening Com., Miami, 1979-82. With U.S. Army, 1969-71. Recipient Master Plan award U. Miami, 1985, Architecture award Downtown Devel. Assn., Orlando, 1989. Mem. AIA (assoc., Henry Adams Cert. for Excellence in Arch. 1972). Avocations: Biblical archaeology, fly fishing, yacht design.

TACHIIRI, MASAYUKI, art historian, assistant curator; b. Utsunomiya, Tochigi, Japan, Sept. 7, 1968; s. Yoshikuni and Setsuko Tachiiri; m. Naoko Umenai, July 3, 1994. B of Art History, Keio U., Tokyo, 1991, M of Art History, 1994. Rschr. Keio U., 1993-94; rschr. Yamanashi Prefectural Mus. Art, Kofu, Japan, 1994, asst. curator, 1995—; lectr. Tokyo U., 1996, Yamanashi U., Kofu, 1995-96. Author: Reconsidering J.F. Millet, 1996 (Sankei prize 1996), J.F. Millet, His Life and Works, 1997, Return to Nature--Millet and the Barbizon Artists, and the Renewal of Rural Tradition, 1998; translator (with Y. Ide et al) J.F. Millet, His Life and Works, 1998; contbr. articles to profl. jours. including Bull. of Yamanashi Mus. Ministry Culture and Edn. grantee, 1995, 96, Ministry Home Affairs grantee, 1996, POLA Art Found., 1998. Fellow Japan Art History Soc.; mem. Met. Mus. Art, Mus. Modern Art N.Y. Avocations: skiing, mountain climbing, driving. Office: Yamanashi Prefect Mus Art, 1-4-27 Kugawa, 400-0065 Yamanashi Kofu, Japan

TACHIKI, DENNIS SHIGEO, sociologist, researcher; b. Santa Monica, Calif., Mar. 10, 1952; arrived in Japan, 1988; s. Joseph H. and Miyoko Tachiki; m. Satoko Fujita, Feb. 11, 1977; children: Rumi, Miya. BA, UCLA, 1974; MA, U. Mich., 1985. Program dir. U. Minn., Mpls., 1974-79; rsch. assoc. U. Mich., Ann Arbor, 1979-87; sr. rsch. fellow Sakura Inst. Rsch., Tokyo, 1988-98; program officer Asian Productivity Orgn., 1998-99; sr. rsch. fellow Fujitsu Rsch. Inst., 1999—; instr. Sophia U., Tokyo, 1988-92; cons. in field. Author: Total Quality Management, 1995, Developing Human Resources for Sustainable Economic Growth, 1994; contbr. articles to profl. jours. Chair Japan Am. Student Conf., 1974-75. Grantee Ford Found., 1980-82. Mem. Am. Sociol. Assn. (fellow 1980-85), Indsl. Rels. Rsch. Assn., Assn. for Asian Studies. E-mail: tachiki@dd.catv.ne.jp. Office: Fujitsu Rsch Inst, 1-16-1 Kaigan Minato-ku, Tokyo 105-0022, Japan

TACHIWAKI, TOKUMATSU, chemistry educator; b. Kyoto, Japan, Oct. 27, 1938; s. Sensuke and Yasu (Kishimoto) T.; m. Teruko Otsubo, May 25, 1965; children: Kenji, Yasushi, Yuuko. B. Tech., Doshisha U., Kyoto, 1961, M. Tech., 1963; D Tech., Osaka (Japan) U., 1992. Asst. prof. dept. chem. engring. Doshisha U., Kyoto, 1963-83, lectr. prof. dept. chem. engring., 1983-88, assoc. prof. dept. chem. engring., 1988-94, prof., 1994—. Contbr. articles to profl. jours. Mem. Am. Inst. Chem. Engrs. Avocations: golf, gardening, fishing. Home: 11-41 Tenjinyama Miyamaki, Kyotanabe City, Kyoto 610-0313, Japan Office: Doshisha U Dept Chem Engring & Material Sci, 1-3 Miyakotani Tatara, Kyotanabe City Kyoto 610-0321, Japan

TACIK, HENRYK M., NATO official; b. Ostrów Wielkopolski, Poland, Dec. 5, 1947; m. Alicja Tacik; children: Joanna, Bartosz. BA in Engring., Engr Officer Sch., 1968; MA in Mil. Ops., Mil. Acad. of Gen. Staff, Poland, 1976; MBA in Mil. Strategy, Mil. Acad. Gen. Staff, Russia, 1988; MA in Nat. Security, Nat. Def. U., Nat. War Coll., U.S., 1997. Commd. 2d lt. Polish Armed Forces, 1968; advanced through grades to brig. gen. Western European Union; platoon leader, then co. comdr. Polish Armed Forces, 1968-73, comdr. 17th engr. bn., 12th mechanized divsn., 1976-79; comdr. 7th pontoon regiment Polish Armed Forces, Deblin, 1979-83; comdr. 2d engring. brigade Polish Armed Forces, Kazun, Poland, 1983-86; dep. chief of engrs., Silesian Mil. Dist. Polish Armed Forces, 1988-89, chief of engrs., 1989-91; dep. chief of engrs., Gen. Staff Polish Armed Forces, Warsaw, 1991-92; chief of engrs., Gen. Staff Polish Armed Forces, 1992-96; chief of command dept. Gen. Staff Polish Armed Forces, Warsaw, 1997-98; mil. rep. to NATO Mil. Com. Polish Armed Forces, Brussels, 1998—; also Polish mil. rep. Western European Union, 1998—. Avocations: military history, hunting. Office: NATO Hdqrs, Blvd Leopold III, 1110 Brussels Belgium*

TACK, THERESA ROSE, women's health nurse; b. Lunenburg, Vt., Nov. 10, 1940; d. Gustave L. and Blanche Rose Fournier; m. Dennis M. Tack, Sept. 2, 1961; children: Lynelle Scullard, Karyn Terry, LeAnn Gomez. Diploma, Cen. Maine Gen. Hosp., 1961. Cert. ACLS, neonatal resuscitation Am. Heart Assn. Staff nurse neurosurgery unit Hillcrest Med. Ctr., Tulsa, 1961-62; staff nurse cardiovascular unit Meth. Hosp., Houston, 1962-65; staff nurse St. John's Hosp., Red Wing, Minn., 1979-85, Wasatch County Hosp., Heber City, Utah, 1985-97. columnist, Nurses Notes in Wasatch Wave, Heber City, Utah, 1990-97. Open heart vol. liaison Naples Cmty. Hosp., Naples, Fla., 1998—.

TACKOWIAK, BRUCE JOSEPH, lawyer; b. Milw., July 10, 1956; s. Eugene Charles and Bernadine Tackowiak. BA in History and Polit. Sci., U. Wis., 1979; cert. emergency med. technician, Madison Area Tech. Coll., 1981; Diploma in Internat. and Comparative Law, Magdalen Coll., U. Oxford, Eng., 1986; JD, U. San Diego, 1988. Bar: Calif. 1990, Ill. 1991, U.S. Dist. Ct. (ctrl. and so. dists.) Calif. 1990, U.S. Ct. Appeals (4th cir.) 1990. Atty. LaFollette, Johnson, De Haas, Fesler & Ames, L.A., 1990-92, Hillsinger & Costanzo, L.A., 1992-93, Roxborough, Pomerance & Gallegos, LLP, L.A., 1993-97; prin. Law Offices of Bruce J. Tackowiak, L.A., 1997—; assoc. Am. Inns of Ct., 1992—. Sr./mng. editor U. San Diego Jour. Contemporary Legal Issues, 1987-88. Mem. ABA, ATLA, Calif. Bar Assn., Los Angeles County Bar Assn., Ill. Bar Assn., Chgo. Bar Assn., World Futurist Soc. (profl.). Avocations: team sports, running, tennis. Office: 6500 Wilshire Blvd Fl 16 Los Angeles CA 90048-4920

TAÇON, PAUL STEPHEN CHARLES, anthropologist, archaeologist; b. Windlesham, Surrey, Eng., July 4, 1958; arrived in Australia, 1991; s. Paul Henry Dwight and Sheila Fraser (Young) T.; m. Susan Margaret Davies, Jan. 11, 1997; 1 child, Astrid Nicole. BA with honors, U. Waterloo, Ont., Can., 1980; MA, Trent U., Peterborough, Can., 1984; PhD, Australian Nat. U., Canberra, 1990. Assoc. prof. Trent U., Peterborough, 1989-90; sci. officer Australian Mus., Sydney, 1991-93, rsch. scientist, 1994-96, sr. rsch scientist, 1996-99, prin. rsch. scientist, 1999—; rock art and mus. cons. Australian Mus., 1991—; profl. sci. photographer, Sydney, 1989—; head People and Pl. Rsch. Ctr., 1996—. Contbr. articles to profl. jours. Rsch. grantee Australian Inst. Aboriginal Studies, 1986, Australian Mus., 1991-97, MacDonald Found., 1991-95. Mem. Australian Rock Art Rsch. Assn. (life), Australian Archaeol. Assn., Soc. for Am. Archaeology. Avocation: photography. E-mail: pault@austmus.gov.au. Office: Australian Museum, 6 College St, Sydney 2010 NSW, Australia

TADA, TOMIO, immunologist, researcher; b. Yuki, Ibaraki, Japan, Mar. 31, 1934; s. Susumu and Umé (Kubo) T.; m. Norie Isaka, July 4, 1968; children: Chris, Oko, Aya. MD, Chiba (Japan) U. Sch. Medicine, 1959, PhD, 1964; D Honoris Causa, Copernicus Med. Sch., Crakow, Poland, 1988. Prof. immunology Chiba U., 1974-77, Tokyo U., 1977-94; dir. Life Sci. Inst. Sci. U. Tokyo, 1995-99. Author: Semantics of Immunity, 1993 (Jiro Osaragi award 1993); editor-in-chief (internat. jour.) International Immunology, 1989—. Recipient Emil von Behring prize Marburg (Germany) U., 1980, Asahi award Asahi Newspaper Co., 1982. Mem. Internat. Union of Immunol. Socs. (pres. 1995-98). Avocation: drums. Home: 6-24-5 Hongo Bunkyo-ku, Tokyo 113-0033, Japan Office: Takasakiya Bldg 5F, 1-1-17 Mukogaoka Bunkyo-ku, Tokyo 113-0023, Japan

TADA, TOSHIO, literature classicist; b. Toyama, Japan, Nov. 20, 1924. BA, Kansai U., Osaka, Japan, 1951; MA, Kansai U., 1954, LittD, 1980. Asst. Kansai U., Osaka, 1953-57; lectr. Kansai U., 1957-60, asst. prof., 1960-66, prof., 1966-95; prof. (hon.) Kansai U., Osaka, 1995—, Kansai Gaidai U., Hirakata, 1996—. Author: (books) Between Irony & Sympathy-Studies on Henry James and Others, 1981.

TADASA, KOJI, biochemistry educator; b. Mihara, Hiroshima, Japan, Mar. 16, 1940; s. Yutaka and Shizue (Muraoka) T.; m. Chiseko Kitahara, Apr. 3, 1975. PhD in Engring., U. Osaka Prefecture, Sakai, Japan, 1979. Asst. prof. biochemistry U. Shinshu, Ina, Japan, 1972-85, assoc. prof., 1986-97, prof., 1998—. Contbr. articles to sci. jours. on microbial Ttansformation, enzyme chemistry, bioorganic chemistry. Mem. Chem. Soc. Japan, Japan Soc. Biosci., Biotech. and Agrochemistry, Japan Biochem. Soc. Buddhist. Avocations: tennis, skiing. Home: 11470 Nakazawa, Komagane 399-4231, Japan Office: Shinshu U Dept Biosci, 8304 Mimaniminowa, Nagano 399-4598, Japan

TADDEY, GERHARD, archivist, historian; b. Gelsenkirchen, Germany, Nov. 16, 1937; s. Gerhard and Antonie (Bühler) T.; m. Ute Thiele, Jan. 1, 1966; children: Robert, Regine. DrPhil, U. Göttingen, Germany, 1964; Privatdozent, U. Tübingen, Germany, 1999. Archivist Main State Archives, Stuttgart, Germany, 1965-71; chief Hohenlohe-Zentralarchiv, Neuenstein, Germany, 1971-86; head dept. Landesarchivdirektion, Stuttgart, 1986-93; chief State Archives, Ludwigsburg, Germany, 1993—; chmn. Kommission für geschichtliche Landeskunde, Stuttgart, 1995—. Author: Kein Kleines Jerusalem, 1992; editor: Lexikon der deutschen Geschichte, 1977, 3d edit., 1998, Handbuch der hist. Stätten: Baden-Württemberg, 1980; editor Lebensbilder aus Baden-Württemberg. Roman Catholic. Office: Staatsarchiv, Arsenalplatz 3, 71638 Ludwigsburg Germany

TADIĆ, DUBRAVKO, physics educator, research scientist; b. Zagreb, Croatia, Oct. 31, 1934; s. Radoslav and Gizela (Majnarić) T.; m. Gordana Indjic, 1976. PhD, U. Zagreb, 1961. Asst. prof. U. Zagreb, 1964-67, assoc. prof., 1967-73, prof., 1973—, dept. head theoretical physics, 1988—. Contbr. over 100 articles to sci. jours. Mem. Croatian Acad. of Scis. Home: Barciceva 9, 10 000 Zagreb Croatia Office: Faculty Nat Scis, Bijenicka 32 Physics Dept, 10 000 Zagreb Croatia

TADI-UPPALA, PADMA PAULINE, toxicologist; b. Nuzvid, Andhra, India; came to U.S. 1985; d. Paul Raj and Mary Paul T.; m. Gurunatha Rao Uppala, Dec. 23, 1991; children: Danny S. Uppala, Michael R. Uppala. MS, Kakatiya U., Warangal, India, 1978; B. Ed., Osmania U., Hyderabad, India, 1985; PhD, Loma Linda U., 1991. Rsch. asst. Loma Linda (Calif.) U., 1991-92; adj. instr. Riverside (Calif.) Coll., 1992-93; instr. U. Calif., Riverside, 1993-94; asst. prof. Atlantic Union Coll., Lancaster, Mass., 1993-95; assoc. prof. Oakwood Coll. and U. Ala., Huntsville, 1995—; advisor Triana Med. Bd., Hunstville, Ala., 1997—. Contbr. articles to profl. jour., L.A. Times. Recipient Zappara Excellence in Tchg. award Gen. Conf. Seventh Day Adventists, 1998. Mem. Am. Assn. Cancer Rsch., Am. Soc. Microbiology, Sigma Xi, Phi Eta Sigma. Mem. Seventh Day Adventist Ch. Avocations: camping, gardening, hiking, travel. Office: Oakwood Coll 7000 Adventist Blvd NW Huntsville AL 35896-0001

TADMOURI, GHAZI OMAR, molecular biologist, geneticist, agriculture engineer; b. Cairo, Egypt, Nov. 8, 1969; s. Omar Abdusalam and Fawkiye Abdulghani (Manakhli) T.; m. Nisrine Mohamad Ali Bissar, Aug. 2, 1995. B, Nat. Orthodoxe Coll., Mina, Lebanon, 1986; BS, Am. Univ. Beirut, Beirut, Lebanon, 1992; MS, Bosphorus U., Istanbul, Turkey, 1994, PhD, 1999. Rsch. asst. Bogazici Univ., 1993-97; writer Al-Adib Newspaper, Tripoli, Lebanon, 1992—; researcher Bogazici Univ., 1992-2000. Author: Life & Genetics, 1997; editor: Tripoli City Web pages, 1997—; contbr. articles to profl. jours. Recipient Masters and PhD Student scholarships Scientific and Tech. Rsch. Coun. Turkey, 1994-99, Best Phd Dissertation award Bohaziçi U., Turkey, 1999. Fellow Transfer of Know-how Through Expatriate Nationals for Lebanon Project, 1994—, Middle East Genetics Assn., 1997—. Avocations: translation of scientific works, reading, stamp collecting, radio listening. Fax: 90 212 265 97 78. E-mail: tadmouri@boun.edu.tr or OTADMORI@cyberia.net.lb. Office: Bogazici Univ, Dept Molecular Biology, Istanbul 80815, Turkey

TADOKORO, TERUO, interior design firm executive, architect; b. Tokyo, Oct. 7, 1947; s. Kamajiro and Chiyoko (Muramatsu) T.; m. Saori Yuasa, May 8, 1977; children: Chika, Hiroshi. B Engring., Sci. U. of Tokyo, 1971, M Engring., 1974. Cert. architect, Japan. Architect design divsn. Kajima Corp., Tokyo, 1974-79, engr. constrn. divsn., 1979-83; chief. engr. Kajima Sdn. Bhd., Kuala Lumpur, Malaysia, 1983-85; procurement mgr. Hong Kong office Kajima Corp., 1985-88; sr. mgr. Kajima U.K. Engring., London, 1988-91; gen. mgr. Taiko Trading Co., Ltd., Tokyo, 1991-98, Ilya Corp., Tokyo, 1998—. Contbr. articles to profl. jours. Office: Ilya Corp 5-13, Akasaka 6-chome Minato-ku, Tokyo 107-0052, Japan

TADROS, AIDA BOTROS, chemist, educator; b. Alexandria, Egypt, Apr. 13, 1952; d. Abd-El Said Botros and Gad Alla Aziza (Marcos) T.; m. Mounir Fouad Missak, Jan. 20, 1989; 2 children. BS in Chemistry, Nat. Inst. Oceang. & Fisheries, Alexandria, 1974, MSc, 1979, PhD, 1984. Specialist Nat. Inst. Oceanography & Fisheries, 1976-81, rsch. asst., 1981-85, dr. rschr., 1985-90, assoc. prof., 1990-95, prof., 1995—. Contbr. numerous articles to profl. jours. Postdoctoral fellow, Holland, 1985-86, Peace fellow, U.S.A., 1989-90. Avocations: reading, listening to music, research. Home: 16 Mourtada Basha, Alexandria Shots, Egypt Office: Nat Inst Oceanography &Fisheries, Kayet Bay, Alexandria Egypt

TADROS, MARLYN RAMZI, human rights activist, feminist; b. Cairo, May 21, 1959; came to U.S., 1998; d. Ramzy I. Tadros; m. S. Samuel, Feb. 16, 1982 (div. 1998); 1 child: Nabil Samuel. MA, Cairo U., 1986, PhD in Comparative Lit., 1996. Dep. dir. Legal Rsch. and Resource Ctr. for Human Rights, Cairo, 1991-99; exec. dir. nat. NGO steering com. Internat. Conf. on Population and Devel., Cairo, 1994; sr. dir. programs Unitarian Universalist Svc. Com., Cambridge, Mass., 1999—; exec. dir. Assn. for Devel. and Enhancement of Women, Cairo, 1991. Author: Rightless Women/Heartless Men, 1997, Copts Between Modernism and Fundamentalism, 1992, Sodom, Sodom, 1997. Human rights activist Legal Rsch. Ctr., Cairo, 1991—; feminist activist Arab Women Solidarity Assn., Cairo, 1987-91. Ford Found. grantee, Harvard U. Law Sch., 1998-99. Mem. Egyptian Enlightenment Assn. Avocations: politics, reading, foreign movies. E-mail: mannina@hotmail.com. Home: 61 Sacramento St Cambridge MA 02138-1925

TAEGI, YU, publisher; b. Namhae-gun, Kyungnam, Republic of Korea, Nov. 15, 1957; s. Yu Chaemun and Park Okyup; m. Lee Shinae, July 30, 1980; children: Sujung, Dongseok. BA, Seoul Nat. U., 1983. Mktg./tng. staff profl. Ssang-yong Cement Industry Ltd., Seoul, 1984-85; editor-in-chief Keorum Pub. Co., Seoul, 1985-92; mng. dir. Hongik Media Ltd., Seoul, 1992-95, pres., 1995—. Exec. mgr. Coun. for the Free Press, Seoul, 1986. Recipient award Minister of Culture and Sports award Korean Govt., Seoul, 1997. Mem. Korean Pubs. Assn. (bd. dirs. 1995-98), Paju Pub. City Cooperatives (auditor 1995-99). Avocations: korean chess, table tennis, golf. Office: Hongik Media Ltd 4th Flr, Chunwoo bld/Dangsan-dong5ga, 150-045 Yongdungpo-gu Seoul 150-045, Republic of Korea

TAEYUKI, OSHIMA, pharmaceutical educator; b. Nagoya, Aichi, Japan, Aug. 4, 1959. BS, Kyoto (Japan) Pharm. U., 1982, MS, 1985; ABD, PhD, Nagoya U., 1989. Lic. pharmacist, hygienic technologist, counselor Japan Soc. Health Counseling. Assoc. prof. Hokuriku U., Kanazawa, Japan, 1989—. Author: (books) On Taking Your Medication Correctly, 1995, Notebook of Your Medication, 1995; editor: (video) Pharmaceutical Instruction for Deaf-Mute Patients, 1997; inventor in field. Vol. Osaka Lighthouse, Inc., 1995. Recipient grant-in-aid for sci. rsch. Japanese Ministry of Edn., Sci. and Culture, 1994, 95. Mem. Japan Pharm. Assn., Pharm. Soc. Japan, Am. Soc. Health-Sys. Pharmacists. Avocations: judo (4th-degree black belt), fishing. Office: Hokuriku U, Ho-3 Kanagawa-machi, 920-1181 Kanazawa Ishikawa, Japan

TAFANI, JEAN-PIERRE J., physiologist; b. Creteil, France, Feb. 20, 1957; s. Jean M.J. and Lucette M. (Sollier) T.; 1 child, Marion A.L. Vet. medicine cert., Maisons-Alfort, France, 1979; MS in Physiology, U. Paris VI, 1981; DVM, U. Creteil, France, 1982. Product mgr. Pioneer-France-Mais, Paris, 1982-83; project leader Pioneer Overseas Corp., Paris, 1983-85; dir. R&D nutrition Brit. Petroleum, Paris, 1985-89; pres., CEO S.A. APCIS, Marne La Vallee, France, 1990—; expert pharmaco-toxicologist New Drug Applications, France, 1990—; expert pharmacologist Ct. Appeal, Reims, France, 1995—; vis. lectr. Inst. Nat Agronomique, Paris, 1995. Inventor pulsatile liquid drug dispenser, pulsatile delivery sys. electrochemically driven, new feed additive using membrane stabilization properties of silybinine, new betacarbolines. Founder Marta's Coop. for Contemporary Art, 1996—. Mem. Controlled Release Soc., Wildlife Photographers Assn. Office: SA APCIS, 17 Rue Victor Hugo, 94700 Maisons-Alfort France

TAFDRUP, PIA, poet; b. Copenhagen, Denmark, May 29, 1952; d. Finn and Elin (Hannover) T.; m. Bo Hakon Joergensen, June 30, 1978; children: Philip Tafdrup Joergensen, Daniel Tafdrup Joergensen. BA, Copenhagen U., 1977. Author: (poems) When an Angel's Been Grazed, 1981, Nohold, 1982, The Innermost Zone, 1983, Spring Tide, 1985, White Fever, 1986, The Bridge of Moments, 1988, The Crystal Forest, 1992, Territorial Song-A Jerusalem Cycle, 1994, The Queen's Gate, 1998, Thousand Born, 1999, (poetics) Walking Over the Water, Outline of a Poetics, 1991, (plays) The Death in the Mountains, 1988, The Earth is Blue, 1991, (libretto) The Town of Viso, 1999; editor: Constellations--an Anthology of Danish Poems, 1982, Transformations, Poetry 1980-85, 1985; contbr. to numerous books and publs. in several countries. Chmn. lit. com. Danish State Art Found., 1993-95. Recipient lit. prize Weekend Avisen, 1995, Emil Aarestrup medal, 1996, Danish lit. prize for women Ragna Sidin's Found., 1997; Holger Drachmann grantee, 1986, Henri Nathansen grantee, 1987, Otto Rung grantee, 1987, Tagea Brandt grantee, 1989, Edith Rode grantee, 1991, Einar Hansens grantee, 1991, N. Bang grantee, 1992, Anckerske grantee, 1994, Morten Nielsen grantee, 1995, Lifelong Artists' grantee, 1998; scholar Danish State Art Found., 1984-86. Mem. Danish Lang. Coun., Danish Acad. Rungstedlund, Danish Pen Copenhagen. E-mail: tafdrup@post6.tele.dk. Home: Rosenvaengets, Sidealle 3 2th, 2100 Copenhagen Denmark

TAFELSKI, MICHAEL DENNIS, psychologist; b. Wyandotte, Mich., Apr. 12, 1949; s. Chester John and Veronica (Machcinski) T. BA in Sociology and Psychology, Wayne State U., 1973, MSW, 1975, MEd, 1976. Lic. med. social worker, Mich. Caseworker home attendent divsn. N.Y.C. Dept. Human Resouces, 1976-78; intake case mgr. Phoenix House Found., Inc., N.Y.C., 1978-81; ptnr. GR Social Svcs., Grand Rapids, Mich., 1982-84; founding ptnr. Tafelski, Tafelski & Gatz and predecessor firm Tafelski, Tafelski, Gatz & Robaskewicz, P.C., Grand Rapids, 1984—. Contbr. to Profl. Jour. of Social Work, 1984-86, DNC, 1992—, Democrats 2000. Contbg. mem. Gen. Election Legal and Acctg. Compliance Fund and the Clinton Legal Expense Trust, GORE 2000, Inc., state dist. mem.; state dist. mem. Mich. Victory Fund 2000; mem. Dem. Senatorial Campaign Com.; Dem. Congressional campaign com. U.S. Ho. Reps. State of Mich. Higher Edn. grantee, Lansing, 1969. Mem. Polish Falcons Soc., KC (Grand Knight). Democrat. Roman Catholic. Avocations: photography, psychopathology, lit. Office: Tafelski Tafelski Gatz 4254 Lamdale Ct SE Ste 9 Grand Rapids MI 49546-2403

TAFT, FREDERICK IRVING, lawyer; b. New Haven, June 26, 1945; s. Seth Chase and Frances (Prindle) T.; m. Susan Hoefflinger, July 28, 1973; children: Amanda, Joshua. BA, Yale U., 1967, JD, 1971. Bar: Ohio 1972. Probation officer Ohio Dept. Corrections, Norwalk, 1971-72; asst. atty. gen. State of Ohio, Columbus, 1972-73; sole practice Cleve., 1973-77; assoc. Spieth, Bell, McCurdy & Newell Co. L.P.A., Cleve., 1977-82, ptnr., 1982—; pres. Ideaspace, Inc. Author: Stan Mahoney, 1978, Welcome to the Friday Forum, 1992, Strategic Atlas--U.S. Health Care Reform, 1993. Pres. Your Schs., Cleveland Heights and University Heights, Ohio, 1986-89; trustee Children's Aid Soc., Cleve., 1982-91, Ohio Venture Assn., 1984-86, Family Health Assn., Cleve., 1985-90; mem. vis. com. Colls. of Case Western Res. U., 1986-89; mem. Council, Pepper Pike, 1998—. Grantee AHS Found., 1976. Mem. ABA, Cleve. Bar Assn. (chmn. corp., banking and bus. law sect. 1987-88), Cleve. City Club (program chmn., trustee 1988, v.p. 1989-90, pres. 1990-91, v.p. Forum Found. 1997-99, pres. 1999—). Democrat. Unitarian. Avocations: snorkeling, travel, photography. Home: 4 Pepper Ridge Rd Pepper Pike OH 44124-4904 Office: Spieth Bell McCurdy & Newell Co LPA 925 Euclid Ave Ste 2000 Cleveland OH 44115-1407

TAFT, JOHN THOMAS, television producer, writer; b. Dublin, Ireland, July 7, 1950; came to U.S., 1957; s. William Howard and Barbara (Bradfield) T.; m. Christine Rinehart Jordan, June 28, 1990; children: Stephen Alexander Rinehart. BA, Yale U., 1972, U. Oxford, Eng., 1974; MA, U. Oxford, Eng., 1979, Johns Hopkins U., 1981. Stringer New Republic mag., Washington, 1977-79; pres. Taft Assocs./TV Prodn., Washington, 1984—; Washington editor Harper's mag., N.Y.C., 1987-89; cons. Panoptic Prodns., London, 1984-89. Contbr. articles to profl. jours.; author: Mayday at Yale, 1976, American Power, 1989; producer TV documentary: After the War, 1987, America's Century, 1989; mem. adv. bd. Jour. Popular Film and TV, 1991—. Mem. Author's League of Am., Manuscript Soc. (trustee 1979-85, 92—), Elizabethan Club (bd. govs. 1970-72), 1925 F St. Club. Avocations: skiing, skating, golf. Home: 3013 44th Pl NW Washington DC 20016-3556 Office: Taft Assocs TV Prodn 1015 33rd St NW Apt 501 Washington DC 20007-3531

TAFT, NATHANIEL BELMONT, lawyer; b. Tarrytown, N.Y., Aug. 12, 1919; s. Louis Eugene and Etta Minnie (Spivak) Topp; m. Norma Rosalind Pike, May 22, 1943 (dec. Dec. 1997); children: Charles Eliot, Stephen Pike. BS in Econs., Fordham U., 1940; JD, Harvard U., 1948. Bar: N.Y. 1949. Asst. to gen. counsel N.Y. State Ins. Dept., Albany, 1948-50; law dept. N.Y. Life Ins. Co., N.Y.C., 1951-65, group dept., 1965-84, ret. as group v.p., 1984; sole practice law White Plains, N.Y., 1985—; lectr., author on healthcare reform, 1992—. Contbr. articles to profl. jours.; author monographs on group ins. regulation. Bd. dirs. Westchester Philharmonic, 1991—, v.p., gen. counsel, 1999—. Mem. ABA, N.Y. State Bar Assn., Nat. Assn. Physicians (sec.-treas. 1991—). Republican. Jewish. Avocations: golf, writing. Home and Office: 16 Sparrow Cir White Plains NY 10605-4624

TAFT, NELLIE LEAMAN, artist; b. Cin., May 22, 1937; d. Hulbert and Elizabeth (Brady) Sutphin; m. A.M. Gammell, Dec. 1, 1973 (div. Apr. 1981). AB, Briarcliff Jr. Coll., 1957; BA, Columbia U., 1968; MA, Tchrs. Coll., 1970. Counselor Oreg. State Sch. for Deaf, Salem, 1960; asst. tchr. art Brearley Sch., N.Y.C., 1961; tchr. pottery Greenwich House Pottery, N.Y.C., 1965-66; tchr. Lexington Children's Ctr., N.Y.C., 1965-66; intern New World Sch., Hackensack, N.J., 1969-70; tchr. The Caedmon Sch., N.Y.C., 1970-73; founder, prin. The Learning Ctr., East Greenwich, R.I., 1978-81; cons. in field. One-woman shows include Carnegie Art Ctr., Ky., 1984, Closson's Gallery, Cin., 1986, 89, 95, Wooden Tent Gallery, Mass., 1990, Gallery 68, Belfast, Maine, 1992, Between the Muse Gallery, Rockland, Maine, 1996; group shows include John S. Ames Gallery, Belfast, Ireland, 1994, Contemporary Art Ctr., Cin., 1994, Nielsen Gallery, Boston, 1998, 99, Muse Gallery, 1998, 99, Maine Coast Artist Gallery, 1999; represented in permanent collections at Cin. Art Mus., Cin. Bell Telephone. Bd. dirs. Cambridge Art Assn.; nat. com. mem. Whitney Mus. Clarissa Bartlett Traveling scholar, 1991, Albert H. Whitin Traveling scholar, 1991. Mem. St. Botolph Club (art com.), Camargo Club. Avocations: tennis, golf, kayaking, flying, dancing.

TAGÁNYI, ZOLTÁN, sociologist; b. Budapest, Hungary, July 16, 1940; d. László Taeubel and Judit (Tholt) T.; m. Judith Kolosváry, Sept. 2, 1995. MA in Ethnography, U. Poznan, 1968; PhD in Sociology, Hungarian Acad. Sci., 1986. Lectr. U. Budapest, 1970-71; with Dept. History/Agr., Budapest, 1971-91, Inst. of Sociology/Hungarian Acad. Scis., Budapest, 1991—. Contbr. articles to profl. jours. Mem. Internat. Soc. for Human Ethology, European Soc. for Sociobiol. Home: Bogár u 5, 1022 Budapest Hungary Office: Hungarian Acad Sci Inc, Inst Sociology Uri u 49, 1014 Budapest Hungary

TAGAYA, NOBUMI, surgery educator; b. Ashikaga, Tochigi, Japan, Sept. 20, 1956; s. Tomikichi and Kaoru (Endo) T.; m. Akemi Sugita, Mar. 9, 1991; children: Yuka, Mayuko. MD, Dokkyo U., Mibu, Tochigi, Japan, 1983, PhD, 1990. Resident Dokkyo Univ. Hosp., 1983-85; clin. instr. Dokkyo U., Mibu, 1985-86; chief surgeon Takagi Pvt. Hosp., Gunma, Japan, 1990-92; instr. Dokkyo Univ. Hosp., Mibu, 1992-94; transplant fellow Queensland Liver Transplant Svc., Brisbane, Australia, 1994-96; asst. prof. Dokkyo U., Mibu, 1998—; chief surgeon Kyowa Cen. Hosp., Ibaraki, Japan, 1985-86, Utsunomiya Cen. Hosp., Tochigi, 1987-88. Contbr. articles to med. jours. Fellow Collegium Internat. Chirurgiae Digestivae, Transplantation Soc., Asian Surg. Assn. Home: 3-2-6 Sugito, 345-0036 Sugito Saitama, Japan

Office: Dokkyo U Sch Medicine, 880 Kitakobayashi, 321-0293 Mibu Tochigi, Japan

TAGER, ROMIE, barrister, queen's counsel; b. London, July 19, 1947; s. Osias and Minnie M. (Mett) T.; m. Esther Marianne Sichel, Aug. 29, 1971; children: (twins) Joseph Peter and Simon Jonathan. LLB, U. Coll. London, 1969. Barrister-at-law Inns of Ct. Sch. of Law, London, 1970. Barrister London, 1971-95, Queen's Counsel, London, 1995—; chmn. Greenquest Group, London, 1997—. Hon. sec. Jewish Book Coun., London, 1989—. Mem. Hon. Soc. of the Middle Temple. Conservative. Jewish. Avocations: opera, theatre, travel, walking. Office: Hardwicke Bldg, New Sq Lincolns Inn, London WC2A 3SB, England

TAGGART, HELEN M., adult education educator, nurse; b. Savannah, Ga., Dec. 6, 1946; d. Thomas Anthony and Ruth Elizabeth (Sisson) McKenzie; m. Thomas Robert Taggart, Mar. 9, 1968; children: Kathleen Taggart Swanner, Thomas Robert Jr. BSN, Armstrong State Coll., 1978; MSN, Ga. So. U., 1992; postgrad., U. Ala., Birmingham, 1995—. Staff nurse St. Joseph's Hosp., Savannah, 1967-68, 77-89; head nurse St. Joseph's Hosp., Ga., 1971-74, St. Mary's Hosp., Athens, Ga., 1968-71; instr. Armstrong State Coll., Savannah, 1989-92; asst. prof. Armstrong Atlantic State U., Savannah, 1992—; profl. adv. com. Nat. Multiple Sclerosis Soc., Atlanta, 1992-96; bd. mem. Ga. Bd. Nursing, Atlanta, 1994—; mem. Clin. Simulation Task Force Nat. Coun. State Bds. Nursing, Chgo., 1996-99. Editor, contbr.: Adult Nursing in Acute Community, 1998; contbr. articles to profl. jours. and chpts. to books. Counselor Multiple Sclerosis Support Group, Savannah, 1989-97. Nat. Assn. Orthop. Nurses rsch. grantee, 1996, U. Ala. (Birmingham) traineeship grantee, 1997, Armstrong Atlantic State U. rsch. grantee, 1997-98. Mem. Nat. League Nurses (exec. bd. 1996-98), Assn. Bus. Women Am. (exec. bd. 1994-96), Nat. Assn. Orthop. Nurses (rsch. com. 1995-99), Ga. Nurses Assn. (exec. bd. 1992-96). Avocations: gardening, swimming, snow skiing. Home: 6 Mulberry Bluff Dr Savannah GA 31406-3226 Office: Armstrong Atlantic State University 11935 Abercorn St Savannah GA 31419-1989

TAGGART, HUGH MCALLISTER, geriatrician; b. Sheffield, England, Nov. 29, 1949; s. James McAllister and Helen Margaret (Thompson) T.; m. Grace Ann Campbell, July 5, 1974; children: Christopher, Kathryn. MB, Queen's U. Belfast, 1973, MD, 1979. Rsch. fellow Queen's U. Belfast, 1977-78, sr. lectr., 1980-92, hon. lectr., 1993—; sr. registrar in geriatric medicine Belfast City Hosp., 1978-79, cons. physician, 1980—; sr. postdoctoral rsch. fellow U. Wash., 1979-80; mem. adv. bd. Nat. Osteoporosis Soc., England, 1988—; mem. adv. panel Dairy Coun., No. Ireland, 1989—; examiner MRCP Royal Coll. Physicians and Surgeons Glasgow, 1999—. Contbr. articles to profl. jours. Fellow Royal Coll. Physicians London, Royal Coll. Surgeons Glasgow; mem. Am. Soc. Bone and Mineral Rsch. Avocations: golf, badminton, bridge, travel, walking. E-mail: hugh.taggart@bch.n-i.nhs.uk. Home: 1 Crawfordsburn Wood, Crawfordsburn BT19 1XB, Northern Ireland Office: Belfast City Hosp, Lisburn Rd, Belfast BT9 7AB, Northern Ireland

TAGGART, KEITH ANTHONY, physicist, systems analyst; b. Cleve., July 10, 1944; s. Earl W. and Eva A. T.; m. Rita M. Kopczewski, Aug. 3, 1968; children: Mark T., Christopher A., Karen A. BS in Physics, Case Inst. Tech., 1966; MS in Physics, Case Western Reserve U., 1968, PhD in Physics, 1970. Officer, scientist Air Force Weapons lab. USAF, Kirkland AFB, N.Mex., 1970-73; post doctoral fellow plasma physics lab. Princeton (N.J.) U., 1973-74; group leader Los Alamos (N.Mex.) Nat. Lab., 1974-85; dir. countermeasures office Strategic Def. Initiative Orgn., Washington, 1985-88; prin. scientist Sci. Applications Internat. Corp., McLean, Va., 1988—. Contbr. articles to profl. jours. Coach Los Alamos Youth Soccer, 1979-83; pack master Boys Scouts Am., Los Alamos, 1978-81, scoutmaster, 1982-85; troop com. chmn. Boy Scouts Am., Springfield, Va., 1985-86. Capt. USAF, 1970-73. Fellow NSF, 1969-70. Fellow AIAA (assoc.); mem. Armed Forces Comm. and Electronics Assn., Tau Beta Pi. Republican. Roman Catholic. Avocations: art collecting, science fiction, computer technology, chess. Office: Sci Applications Internat Corp 1410 Spring Hill Rd Ste 400 Mc Lean VA 22102-3055

TAGGART, THOMAS MICHAEL, lawyer; b. Sioux City, Iowa, Feb. 22, 1937; s. Palmer Robert and Lois Allette (Sedgwick) T.; m. Dolores Cecilia Baroway Renfro, Jan. 4, 1963; children: Thomas Michael Jr., Theodore Christopher; m. Mary Ann Gribben, Feb. 7, 1976. BA, Dartmouth Coll., 1959; JD, Harvard U., 1965. Bar: Ohio 1965, U.S. Dist. Ct. (so. dist.) Ohio 1967, U.S. Dist. Ct. (no. dist.) Ohio 1981, U.S. Supreme Ct. 1997. Ptnr. Vorys, Sater, Seymour & Pease, Columbus, Ohio, 1965—; lectr. Ohio Legal Ctr. Inst., Ohio Mfrs. Assn., Capital U. Ctr. for Spl. and Continuing Legal Edn. Capt. USMC, 1959-63. Mem. ABA, Ohio Bar Assn. (bd. govs. 1991-99, liability ins. com. 1996-97, 99-00, pres. 1997-98, trustee Found. 1996-98, 2000—, chair commn. on jud. evaluations 2000, Ohio Bar medal 1999), Columbus Bar Assn. (bd. govs., pres. 1989-90), Ohio Assn. Civil Trial Attys., Am. Arbitration Assn., Columbus Area C. of C. Methodist. Home: 145 Stanbery Ave Columbus OH 43209-1465 Office: Vorys Sater Seymour & Pease 52 E Gay St Columbus OH 43215-3161

TAGLIAFERRI, GUIDO ALFONSO, physics educator; b. Rome, Jan. 27, 1920; s. Romeo and Beatrice (Corsi) T.; m. Carla Silvia Pinto, Nov. 11, 1953; children: Federico, Beatrice. D of Physics, U. Pisa, Italy, 1941; diploma in physics, Scuola Normale Superiore, Pisa, 1942. Asst. prof. U. Milan, 1945-53, 56-59; rsch. assoc. U. Princeton, N.J., 1954-55; prof. U. Bari, Italy, 1960, U. Milan, 1960-96; dir. sect. Nat. Inst. Nuclear Physics, Milan, 1964-67. Author: Storia della fisica quantistica, 1985; co-author: Un viaggio in Europa nel 1786, 1994; contbr. articles to profl. jours. Mem. Italian Phys. Soc. (Gold medal 1994), Istituto Lombardo-Accademia di Scienze e Lettere, N.Y. Acad. Scis. Roman Catholic. Home: Corso Garibaldi 22, 20121 Milan Italy Office: Inst Gen Physics, via Brera 28, 20121 Milan Italy

TAGLIAFERRI, ROBERTO, computer science educator and cybernetics researcher; b. Naples, Italy, Aug. 30, 1960; s. Federico and Lidia (Guerrini) T.; m. Anna Rose Castaldo, Sept. 16, 1993. Degree in computer sci. cum laude, U. Salerno, Italy, 1984. Young rschr. Internat. Inst. for Advanced Sci. Studies, Naples, 1984-86; rsch. asst. U. Salerno, 1986-89, assoc. rschr., 1989-2000, prof., 1991—; dir. Internat. Inst. for Advanced Sci. Studies, Vietri s/m, Italy, 1990—. Contbr. articles to profl. jours. Pres. Cinecircoli Giovanili Sociocultural Novità, Naples, 1986-93; v.p. Cinecircoli Giovanili Sociocultural Campania, C/mare, Italy, 1990-93. Mem. IEEE (NNC regional interest group com. 1996—), Internat. Neural Network Soc. (v.p. Italian regional SIG), Societa Italiana Reti Neuroniche (sec. 1994—). Roman Catholic. Avocations: cinema, theatre, voluntary service. Office: U Salerno Dept Math & Info, Via S Allende, I-84081 Baronissi Italy

TAGLIENTE, JOSEPHINE MARLENE, artist; b. Chisholm, Minn., Nov. 23, 1939; d. Joseph and Carmela (DeLuca) T.; m. Wayne W. Brown, May 28, 1960 (div. 1972); children: Michael Anthony, Troy Tagliente, Roben Tagliente, Angela Monique, Ninon Terese, Anina Maria (dec.). Student, Mpls. Coll. Art and Design, 1957-59, Mankato State Coll., 1966, Kansas City Art Inst., 1972; MFA, U. Guanajuato, Mex., 1974. artist-in-residence Jewish Cmty. Ctr., Wilmington, 1969; illustration chairperson, mem. faculty Ray Coll. of Design, Chgo., 1980-87; adj. faculty Paradise Valley C.C., Phoenix; spkr. in field. One-woman exhbn. Natalini Gallery, Chgo., 1986; group exhbns. include Windbell Gallery, Wilmington, Del., Newark (Del.) Gallery, Galeria San Miguel, Mex., Galeria Osman, Mex., Galeria Condor, Mex., Torres Gallery, Albuquerque, Dartmouth Gallery, Albuquerque, Edith Lampert Gallery, Santa Fe, La Luna Nueva, Santa Fe, Herberger Theatre, Phoenix Little Theatre, Artesimo Gallery, Scottsdale, Ariz., Del. Art Mus., Wilmington, others; represented in corp. collections Collins, Miller & Hutchins, Chgo., Mt. Sinai Hosp., N.Y.C.; also pvt. and pub. permanent collections; represented by Artisimo Gallery, Scottsdale; illustrations published in books; poetry published in anthologies; inventor garden products, office implements. Vol. art educator St. Anne's Intercity, Wilmington, 1967-68, Recreation Intercity, Chgo., 1978-79; cultural advocate for homeless Cultural Labor Party, Chgo., 1980-87, cultural advocate for minority concerns, 1985-88. Recipient Fine Art award Artist's Guild of Chgo., 1977, Print Drawing award, 1978, Educator/Svcs. award Sauk Area Career Ctr., 1984. Mem. Nat. Mus. Women in Arts, The Drawing Soc. Avocations: writing, digital painting, raising turtles and studying their habitat.

TAGUCHI, KIICHIRO, otolaryngologist; b. Matsumoto, Japan, Aug. 23, 1933; s. Masao Imae (Ito) T.; m. Teruyo Kanzawa, Sept. 20, 1967; 3 children. MD, Shinshu U., Matsumoto, Japan, 1958, PhD, 1970. Assoc. prof. Shinshu U., Matsumoto, 1969-79, prof. sch. medicine, 1979-99, prof. emeritus, 1999—; dir. Nagano Occupl. Health Promotion Ctr., 1999—. Editor: Vestibular and Neural Front, 1994, (monograph) Early Diagnosis for Head & Neck Cancers, 1987, Ten Years Research and Clinical Reports, 1990. Clin. fellow U. Toronto, 1967-69. Mem. Internat. Soc. Postural Gait Rsch. (pres. 1994-97), Japan Soc. Equilibrium Rsch. (chmn. 1995-97). Avocations: video-taping, jogging, mountain climbing. Home: 1102 Satoyamabe, Matsumoto 390-0221, Japan Office: Nagano Occupl Health Promotion Ctr, 215-1 Okadamachi 3F, Nagano 380-0936, Japan

TAGUCHI, SHINICHI, cardiovascular surgeon; b. Okayama, Okayama, Japan, Dec. 20, 1958; s. Kazumi and Aiko (Kurihara) T.; m. Takako Sunaga, Dec. 10, 1989; children: Kenichi, Ayumi. MD, Keio U., 1984, PhD, 1989. Clin. clk. Mayo Clinic, Rochester, Minn., 1983; resident Keio U. Hosp., Tokyo, 1984-90; chief resident Keio U. Hosp., 1990-91, clin. instr., 1992-93; clin. fellowship Pitié-Salpétrière Hosp., Paris, 1991-92; vice dir. 2d Tokyo Nat. Hosp., 1993-97, Nat. Saitama Hosp., Wako, Japan, 1997-2000; dir. Ashikaga Red Cross Hosp., Ashikaga-City, Tochigi, Japan, 2000—. Contbr. articles to profl. jours. Recipient ann. award Japanese chpt. Am. Coll. Chest Physicians, 1990. Fellow Japanese Soc. for Artificial Organs; mem. Soc. Thoracic Surgeons, Japanese Assn. for Thoracic Surgery, Am. Soc. for Artificial Internal Organs. Avocations: walking, swimming, skiing, tennis. Office: Ashikaga Red Cross Hosp, 3-2100 Honjo, Ashikaga-City 326-0808, Japan

TAHA, ALI ABDALLA MOHAMED, veterinary science educator; b. Al-Gureir, Sudan, Jan. 1, 1949; arrived in Saudi Arabia, 1988; s. Abdalla Mohamed Taha and Amma Al-Hassan Siddeeq; m. Shadia Abdel-Aati Omer, Sept. 21, 1977; children: Azza, Mohamed, Mamoun, Mostafa. B in Vet. Sci., U. Khartoum, Sudan, 1973, M in Vet. Sci., 1978; PhD, U. Liverpool, Eng., 1982. Vet. officer Ministry Animal Resources, Khartoum, 1973-74; tchg. asst. Faculty Vet. Sci., Khartoum, 1974-78; asst. prof. U. Khartoum, 1982-87, assoc. prof., 1987-88; assoc. prof. King Saud U., Buraidah, Saudi Arabia, 1988—; mem. Khartoum U. Senate, 1986-88; sec. Faculty Rsch. Bd., Khartoum, 1986-88; acting head Dept. Anatomy, Khartoum, 1988; sec. dept. vet. medicine Faculty Agr. and Vet. Medicine, King Saud U., 1988-92, mem. sr. scholar com., 1994-98, mem. com. Jenadriah exhbn., 1998, others; chmn. libr. com. Coll. Agr. and Vet. Medicine, Buraidah, 1991-93. Editor: (translation) Outlines of Avian Anatomy, 1998, Guide to the Dissection of Domestic Animals, 2000; contbr. articles to profl. jours. Mem. Khartoum U. Trade Union, 1982-86, Staff Affairs Com., Shambat, 1982-86, Staff Coop. Shop, Shambat, 1983-85; supr. Vet. Student Soc. Faculty Vet. Sci., 1987-88. Scholar Brit. Coun., Eng., 1978. Mem. Sudan Vet. Assn., Saudi Biol. Soc., World Assn. Vet. Anatomists. Islamic. Avocations: soccer, athletics, table tennis. Home: PO Box 10158, Buraidah Qassim, Saudi Arabia Office: Coll Agr & Vet Medicine, PO Box 1482, Buraidah Qassim, Saudi Arabia

TAHA, ALI OSMAN MOHAMMED, federal official. Min. soc. planning, min. fgn. affairs Govt. of Sudan, 1995—, 1st v.p. Office: Ministry Fgn Affairs, PO Box 873, Khartoum Sudan*

TAHA, FARAG ABDIL KADIR, psychology educator, researcher; b. Minofia, Egypt, May 1, 1937; s. Abdil Kadir Ahmed and Magda Yasseen (Abdel Hady) T.; m. Azza Ihab Samah, July 19, 1962. BA, Ain Shams U., Cairo, 1959, MD, 1965, PhD, 1968. Prof. psychology Mohamed V U., Rabat, Morocco, 1973-77; lectr. psychology Ain Shams U., Cairo, 1969-73, prof., 1981—, head dept. psychology, 1985-89. Author: Psychology and Current Issues, 1979, Industrial and Organizational Psychology, 1980; editor, co-author: Encyclopedia of Psychology and Psychoanalysis, 1993 (Zeewar prize 1998); editor-in-chief Periodical Jour. of Psychology, 1996, Jour. Psychol. Rsch. Egyptian Psychologists Assn., 1996-99. Exec. mem. Intenrat. Assn. Applied Psychology, 1984-94. Mem. Egyptian Assn. for Psychol. Studies (pres.), Institut d'Egypte (life). Avocations: reading, travel, writing and editing. E-mail: amrhegazi@yahoo.com. Office: Ain Shams U Faculty of Arts, Abbassia, Cairo Egypt

TAHA, HIND SAYED, psychology educator; b. Cairo, Egypt, Nov. 16, 1951; s. Sayed Taha Abdelbar and Bossayna Amin Mohei Eldin; m. Amr Abdelmoneim AbouSamra, Jan. 28, 1971; children: Soliman, Hossam. BA, Cairo U., 1973, MA, 1985, PhD in Psychology, 1988. Asst. prof. Nat. Ctr. for Social and Criminological Rsch., Cairo, 1979—; advisor Adv. Sci. Com., Nat. Coun. for Addressing Drug Abuse and Addiction, Cairo, 1990-96; mem. psychology com. High Coun. for Culture, 1999. Author: Disengagement: A Theoretical and Psychometric Study of a Concept, 1994, Public Opinion Measurement: In Methods and Ethics, 1994, Drug Abuse Among Secondary School Students in Egypt, Vol. 8, 1999. Mem. APA, World Assn. for Public Opinion Rsch., Egyptian Psychologists Assn. E-mail: samra@access.com.eg. Office: Nat Ctr Social/Criminol Rsh, Ibn Khaldoun Sq-Imbaba, Giza Egypt

TAHA, ZAHARI, engineering educator, consultant; b. Kuala Lumpur, Malaysia, Sept. 21, 1960; s. Mohd Isa and Sutan Rejab (Salbiah) T.; m. Syed Abd Rashid Sharifah Norazizan; children: Zayd, Sarah, Ammar, Muhammad. BS in Engring., U. Bath, Eng., 1983; PhD, U. Wales, 1987; diploma in Islamic Studies, Internat. Islamic U., Kuala Lumpur, 1993. Chartered engr., Eng. Assoc. prof. U. Malaya, Kuala Lumpur, 1992-2000, prof., 2000—; rsch. fellow U. Wales Inst., Cardiff, 1995—. Contbr. articles to profl. jours. Recipient Hitachi fellowship Hitachi Scholarship Found., 1992, Malaysian Young Scientist award, 1997. Mem. Instn. Engring. Designers U.K., Mensa, N.Y. Acad. Scis. Muslim. E-mail: zahari@fk.um.edu.my. Office: CAD/CAM/Faculty of Engring, U. Malaya, 50603 Kuala Lumpur Malaysia

TAHARA, EIICHI, pathologist, educator; b. Yokohama, Japan, July 19, 1936; s. Yoshinori and Sadako T.; m. Yoshie Shimamoto, Mar. 28, 1963; children: Hidetoshi, Makoto, Eiji. MD, Hiroshima U., 1963, PhD, 1968; dipolma nat. exam. dor med. practitioners. Asst. dept. pathology Hiroshima U. Sch. Medicine, 1968-72, asst. prof., 1972-77, assoc. prof., 1977-78, prof., chmn., 1978—; chief rsch. facilities for lab. animal sci. Hiroshima U., 1994-96; councilor Hiroshima U., 1985-87; chief divsn. anatomical pathology Hiroshima U. Hosp., 1986-92, dir. faculty of medicine, 1996-98; rep. Cancer Rsch. Project of Cancer Stromal Interaction, 1993-98, Project of Gastric Intestinal Metaplasia, 1994-97; chief rsch, fac, for lab. Animal Sci. of Hiroshima U., 1994—; mem. cancer Rsch. Project of Genetic Instability in Human Cancer, 1994—. Author, editor: Gastric Cancer, 1993, Gann Monograph on Cancer Research, 1994, Molecular Pathology of Gastroenterological Cancer-Application to Clinical Practice, 1997; editor Differentiation, Jour. Cancer Rsch. and Clin. Oncology, Jour. Exptl. Therapeutics and Oncology, Jour. Pathology, Exptl. and Toxicologic Pathology, others; contbr. articles to profl. jours. Grantee Found. for Promotion Cancer Rsch., 1991, 94, 97, Princess Takamatsu Cancer Rsch. Fund, 1990, Ministry Health and Welfare, 1989-91, Ministry of Edn. Sci. and Cult., Japan, 1990-93, 94—; recipient award Hiroshima Med. Assn., 1972, R.E. "Bob" Smith award, 1997; hon. fellow Royal Coll. Pathologists, 1999. Mem. Internat. Soc. Differentiation (pres. 1996-98, organizer 8th internat. conf. 1994), Internat. Soc. Gastroenterological Carcinogenesis(sec. gen. 1996—, organizer 1st internat. conf. 1996), Japanese Soc. Pathology (bd. dirs. 1991-93, 95—, pres. 1998), Japanese Cancer Assn. (pres. 1999, assoc. editor 1995—), Hiroshima Soc. for Cancer Therapy (pres.), U.K. Soc. Pathology (hon.), Japanisch-Deutsche Gesellschaft Hiroshima (v.p. 1990—), Hiroshima Cancer Seminar Found. (chmn. 1999—), Hiroshima Humboldt Club (chmn.). Buddhist. Office: Hiroshima U Sch Medicine, 1-2-3 Kasumi Minami-ku, Hiroshima 734-8551, Japan

TAHER, FOUAD, consulting company executive; b. Cairo, Oct. 26, 1923; m. Enaya Ahmad Hassan, 1949. BS, Cairo U., 1945; PhD, Stanford U., 1951. Lectr. Cairo U., 1951-59, assoc. prof., 1959-61; dir. gen. Ministry of Pub. Works, Cairo, 1961-64; inspector gen. Electricity Authority, Cairo, 1964-71; v.p. Rural Electrification, Cairo, 1971-77; counsellor Electricity Corp., Saudi Arabia, 1977-82; chmn. Elec. Power Systems Engring. Co., Cairo, 1982—; cons. Indsl. Devel. Ctr., League of Arab States, Cairo, 1974-76; bd. mem. Egypt Electricity Authority, 1998—. Contbr. articles to profl. jours. Recipient Decoration of the Republic, Govt. Egypt, 1971. Fellow IEEE. Lodge: Rotary (pres. 1987-88). Home: 22 Ibn Zanki St Zamalek, Zamalek, Cairo Arab Republic of Egypt Office: Electric Power Systems Co, PO Box 90, 11799 Cairo Arab Republic of Egypt

TAHER, ZAINAB ABDULHUSAIN, educational administrator; b. Surat, Gujarat, India, June 6, 1936; d. Yahya and Asma Yahyabhoy (Rasoolbhoy) Mohyuddin; m. Abdulhusain Taher Bhoy; children: Tasneem, Nisreen, Arwa. BA, Sophia Coll., Bombay, 1958; BEd, St. Xaviour U., Bombay, 1966. Tchr. English, Young Ladies Sch., Bombay, 1963-74; prin. Arab Unity Sch., Dubai, United Arab Emirates, 1974—. Office: Arab Unity Sch, Rashidiya, PO Box 10563, Dubai United Arab Emirates

TAHERE, ANAS, medical administrator; b. Aleppo, Syria, July 20, 1954; arrived in France, 1982; s. Salah Tahere and Daed Msouti; m. Yveline Isabelle Tahere, May 9, 1985; 1 child, Diana-Eve. MD, Faculty of Medicine, Aleppo, 1978; CES Radiodiagnostics, U. Nantes, France, 1985. Physician Aleppo, 1978-82; attache CHU de Nantes Svc. de Radiologie Centrale, Nantes, 1983-88; practice hosp. CH de St. Quentin, France, 1988-89, CH de Laval, France, 1989; chief svc. med. imaging, practice hosp. Ctr. Hospitalier de nord Mayenne, France, 1989—. Contbr. articles to profl. jours. Mem. JCE, French Soc. Radiology and Med. Imaging, Radiol. Soc. N.Am. (corr. mem.), Rotary Club. Fax: 33 243087641. E-mail: anas.tahere@worldonline.fr. Office: Ctr Hosp Nord Mayenne, 5 Rue Roullois, 53100 Mayenne France

TAHERZADEH, MOHAMMAD J., biochemical engineer; b. Esfahan, Iran, Mar. 22, 1965; s. Mohammad and Beigom (Madhkhan) T.; m. Arezoo Keivandarian, May 19, 1971. BSc, Isfahan U. Tech., Esfahan, 1989; MSc, Sharif U. Tech., Tehran, Iran, 1991; PhD, Chalmers U. Tech., Göteborg, Sweden, 1999. Rschr. Jahad Daneshgahy, Esfahan, 1986-91; lectr. Isfahan U. Tech., 1992-94; with dept. chem. reaction engring. Chalmers U. Tech., Göteborg; asst. prof. Lund U. of Tech., Sweden, 1999—. Contbr. articles to sci. publs. Recipient diploma award Pres. of Iran, 1992. Office: Chem Reaction Engr, Chalmers U Tech, Kemivägen 10, 412 96 Göteborg Sweden

TAHIR, MUHAMMAD AEJAZ ALI, editor; b. Punjab, Pakistan, June 14, 1952; s. Mian Muhammad and Hajira (Bibi) Ali; m. Naheed Zaidi (div. Apr. 1994); m. Razia Sultana, Nov. 18, 1972; children: Sibtain Muhammad, Aejaz Sadia, Aejaz Andleeb, Ahmed Umair. BA, U. Karachi, Pakistan, 1981. Asst. project dir. UNICEF, Karachi, Pakistan, 1972-74; sr. acct. clk. Pakistan Indsl. Devel. Corp., Karachi, 1977-84; editor, publisher Pakistan Chess Mag., Karachi, 1986—. Exec. editor ILM.E. Computer, 1991—, Weekly Urdu Spl. Report, 1999—; mem. editl. bd. Weekly Urdu Crimes Time, 1998—. Coord. Arain Rabita Markaz, Karachi, 1989; chmn. Arain Welfare Trust, Karachi, 1996; incharge Arain-Hajjl Umrah Group, 1997—. With Pakistan Army, 1971-72. Mem. Karachi Union Journalists. Muslim. Avocations: photography, chess, social work. Home: R-1008 Block 14, Gulistan-E-Mustafa, 75950 Karachi Pakistan Office: Pakistan Chess Mag, PO Box 179, 74200 Karachi Pakistan

TAHIROV, TAHIR HAJI OGLU, crystallographer; b. Nakhichevan, Azerbaijan, June 5, 1961; s. Haji Tahir oglu and Farida Ibrahim gyzy (Mehdiyeva) T.; m. Nigyar Davud gyzy Babayeva, Nov. 18, 1988; children: Narmin, Emin. BS, MS, Kiev Polytech. Inst., 1984; PhD, Rostov State U., 1989. Lab. asst. Inst. of Physics, Baku, Azerbaijan, 1984; postgrad. rschr. Inst. of Chem. Physics, Chernogolovka, Russia, 1985-87; rschr. Inst. of Inorganic and Phys. Chemistry, Baku, 1988-91; postdoctoral fellow Nat. Tsing Hua U., Hsinchu, Taiwan, 1991-94; sr. scientist Inst. for Protein Rsch., Osaka U., Japan, 1996-97; sr. scientist Kanagawa Acad. Sci. and Tech. and Yokohama (Japan) City U. Sch. of Medicine, 1997—; vis. scientist Himeji Inst. of Tech., Harima Sci. Garden City, Japan, 1994-96. Contbr. articles to profl. jours.; patentee in field. Avocations: travel, music, science, sport, family.

TAHMINDJIS, PHILLIP VICTOR, law educator; b. Sydney. BA, Sydney U., 1972, LLB, 1975; LLM, U. London, 1977; SJD, Dalhousie U., Can., 1996. Barrister. Lectr. Inst. of Edn., Melbourne, 1977-78; lectr. Queensland U. of Tech., Brisbane, 1978-80, sr. lectr., 1980-93, assoc. prof., 1993-97, assoc. dean of law, 1997—; cons. Human Rights Commn., Brisbane, 1987-96, Anti-Discrimination Commn., Brisbane, 1992—, Electoral and Adminstrv. Rev. Commn., Brisbane, Queensland Rail, 1996-97. Editor: (books) Australian and New Zealand Equal Opportunity Law, 1990—, The Law and Sexual Harassment in the Workplace: Comparative Perspectives, 2000; contbr. articles to profl. jours. Pres. Amnesty Internat., Queensland, 1981-83, Free Bus. Assn., Queensland, 1986-88; trustee Queensland AIDS Coun., 1984-87. Mem. Internat. Bar Assn. (chmn. com. II discrimination law 1995-98, chmn. com. 19 human rights law 1999—), Australasian Law Tchrs. Assn. (convenor discrimination law group 1993—). Avocation: figure skating. Office: Queensland U Tech Fac Law, 2 George St, 4000 Brisbane Australia

TAHVANAINEN, ESA PETRI, physician, researcher; b. Lappeenranta, Finland, Mar. 22, 1965; s. Martti Ilmari and Soile Hellevi (Lipiainen) T.; m. Pia Johanna Salo, Aug. 1, 1998. MD, U. Helsinki, 1995. Biochemistry rschr. U. Kuopio, 1987-91; med. genetics rschr. U. Helsinki, 1992-95; resident dept. biochemistry Nat Pub. Health Inst., Helsinki, 1996-99; project leader Merck, Sharp and Dohme, Helsinki, 1999; pvt. practice Helsinki, 2000—; vis. rschr. Coriell Inst. for Med. Rsch., Camden, 1989; vis. rschr. dept. med. coll. physicians and surgeons Columbia U., N.Y.C. Contbr. articles on med. genetics to profl. jours. Avocations: soaring, diving. Home: Raisiontie 11 A3, 00280 Helsinki Finland Office: Sturenkatu 8, 00510 Helsinki Finland

TAHVANAINEN, PIA JOHANNA, medical researcher, physician; b. Pori, Finland, Dec. 31, 1969; d. Kalervo and Anja-Riitta (Rantala) S.; m. Esa Tahvanainen, Aug. 1, 1998. MD, PhD, U. Helsinki, 1995. Rschr. dept. med. genetics U. Helsinki, Finland, 1993-95; resident in internal medicine Maria Hosp., Helsinki, 1996—; vis. rschr. Columbia U., N.Y.C., 1997. Home: Raisiontie 11 A 3, 00280 Helsinki Finland

TAI, ELIZABETH SHI-JUE LEE, library director; b. Si-Ann, China, Aug. 12, 1942; came to the U.S., 1965; d. Jun-Yee Lee and Fang-Yee Liu; m. Hsiang Tai, Dec. 29, 1969; children: Alan C., Victoria C., Brian C. BA in English Lang. and Lit., Nat. Cheng Kung U., Taiwan, 1965; M in Libr. and Info. Sci., Tex. Woman's U., 1967. Sr. libr. Queens (N.Y.) Borough Pub. Libr., 1967-73; asst. regional libr. Cin. Pub. Libr., Libr. for Blind and Physically Handicapped, 1973-75; libr. Ga. State Liby., Atlanta, 1975-78; dir. Poquoson (Va.) Pub. Libr., 1979—. Vol. ARC-York County, Va. Chpt., 1980—; vice-chair Peninsula Ret. Sr. Vol. Program Coun., Newport News, Va., 1994-99, chair, 2000; mem. York County (Va.) Sch. Sys. Extend Program Coun., 1997. Named City Employee of Yr., City of Poquoson, 1989. Mem. ALA, Va. Libr. Assn., Va. Pub. Libr. Dirs. Assn. (Outstanding Pub. Rels. award 1998, Outstanding Facility award 1998, Outstanding Young Adult Program award 1999, Outstanding Children's Program award 1999), Tidewater Area Libr. Dirs. Coun. Avocations: reading, gardening, swimming, tennis. E-mail: etai@ci.poquoson.va.us. Home: 129 Loblolly Dr Yorktown VA 23692-4254 Office: 500 City Hall Ave Poquoson VA 23662-1996

TAI, JOHN JEN, biostatistician; b. Taipei, Taiwan, Oct. 15, 1953; s. Hong-Wen and Ya-Fang (Yao) Tai; m. Szu-Hua Kuo; children: Albert Hua, Ting-Yu. PhD, Med. U. S.C., 1984. Assoc. rsch. fellow Academia Sinica, Taipei, Taiwan, 1984-90; assoc. prof. Nat. Taiwan U., Taipei, 1989-90; prof. Fu-Jen Catholic U., Taipei, 1990-98, Nat. Yang-Ming U., Taipei, 1990-98; rsch. fellow Academia Sinica, Taipei, 1990-98; prof. Nat. Taiwan U., 1998—; protocol statistician Nat. Health Rsch. Insts., Taipei, 1986—; dir. secretariat Academia Sinica, Taipei, 1992-94; cons. Taipei Vet. Gen. Hosp., Taipei, 1996—. Author (with others): Biomedical Statistics, 1998; contbr. articles to profl. jours.; edit. bd. Science, 1996. Mem. Internat. Statistical Soc. Home: F 3 no 6 alley 441 ln 150, Hsin Yi Rd Sec 5, Taipei 110, Taiwan Office: Inst Epid Nat Taiwan U, 1 Jen-Ai Rd Sec 1, Taipei 100, Taiwan

TAI, LI-MING, school principal, consultant; b. Taipei, Taiwan, Oct. 30, 1951; d. Shih-Chang Tai and I-Tseng Chen; m. Tai-Sheng Wei, Apr. 23, 1978; 1 child, Ting-Han Wei. BA in Edn., Nat. Cheng-chi U., Taipei, 1974,

MA in Edn., 1976; MEd, UCLA, 1989, PhD, 1998. Sch. supr. County Govt. Bur. Edn., Taipei County, 1977-80; dir. ext. & pub. rels. Pub. Libr., Kaohsiung, Taiwan, 1980-82; sch. supr. Kaohsiung, Taiwan, 1982-84; prin. Mcpl. Shih-Chia Jr. H.S., Kaohsiung, Taiwan, 1984-95, Nat. Exptl. H.S., Hsinchu, Taiwan, 1995—; exec. dir. ext. br. Nat. Sun-Yat Sen U. Alumni Assn., Kaohsiung, 1987-88; mem. com. Task Force on Amendment of Tchr. Tng. Act, Ministry of Edn., Taipei, 1998-99; cons. China Youth Corps counseling divsn., So. Taiwan and Gtr. Hsinchu area, 1989—. Contbr. articles to profl. jours., chpt. to book. Mem. Comparative and Internat. Edn. Soc. Avocations: travel, music, art, reading, cooking. Office: Nat Exptl High Sch, 300 Chieh-Shou Rd Sc Ind Pk, Hsinchu 300, Taiwan

TAIFOUR, MAJED GHALEB, editor, journalist; b. Damascus, Syria, Apr. 5, 1962; s. Ghaleb Farid and Nermine Fakhri (Zambarakji) T.; m. Enass Mahmoud Soussan, Oct. 3, 1996; 1 child, Tala. BA, Am. U. Beirut, 1984, MA in Middle Eastern Studies, 1989. Reporter The Daily Star, Lebanon, 1983-85; rschr. Ctr. for Arab Unity Studies, 1985-89; freelance journalist Lebanon, 1983-91; sr. bus. reporter Gulf News, Dubai, 1991-95; sr. editor ADNOC, Abu Dhabi, 1996—. Recipient Pan Asia Journalism award Citibank, N.Y.C., 1994. Avocations: internet, reading, tennis. Office: ADNOC, PO Box 898, Abu Dhabi United Arab Emirates

TAILLEFER DE HAYA, LIDIA, English educator, translator; b. Málaga, Spain, Oct. 20, 1963; d. Eugenio Taillefer Pérez and María de Haya Gálvez; m. José Luis Manjón-Cabeza Marín, June 15, 1996. BS, U. Málaga, 1988; MS, CUNY, 1989; Doctorate, U. Complutense, Madrid, 1995. Dir. Translation Bureau, Málaga, 1989-92; prof. English U. Málaga, 1991—, coord. doctorate program, 1998—; freelance translator, 1990-94; mem. editl. bd. Analecta Malacitana, Málaga, 1996—. Editor: Nueva Lectura de la Mujer: Crítica Histórica, 1995, El Sexismo en el Lenguaje, 1999; translator: (poetry) Poesia Reunida de Marianne Moore, 1996;. Dep. mem. Women's Coun., Málaga, 1996. Recipient Cambridge Seminar grantee Brit. Coun., 1995; rsch. grantee U. Málaga, Andalusian Coun., U.K., 1997. Mem. MLA, Assn. Colegial de Escritores de Espana, Traductores, Assn. Espanola De Linguistica Apuicada. Avocations: reading, writing, old movies, music, dancing. Office: Univ Málaga Fac Letras, Campus de Teatinos s/n, 29071 Málaga Spain

TAIMUTY, SAMUEL ISAAC, physicist; b. West Newton, Pa., Dec. 20, 1917; s. Elias and Samia (Hawatt) T.; BS, Carnegie Inst. Tech., 1940; PhD, U. So. Calif., 1951; m. Betty Jo Travis, Sept. 12, 1953 (dec.); children: Matthew, Martha; m. Rosalie Richards, Apr. 3, 1976; stepchildren: Charles Scott Holman, Martha Ruth Holman, Elizaeth Ann Holman. Physicist, U.S. Naval Shipyard, Phila. and Long Beach, Calif., 1942-46; rsch. asst. U. So. Calif., 1947-51; sr. physicist U.S. Naval Radiol. Def. Lab., 1950-52, SRI Internat., Menlo Park, Calif., 1952-72; sr. staff engr. Lockheed Missiles & Space Co., Sunnyvale, Calif., 1972-89; cons. physicist, 1971—. Mem. Am. Phys. Soc., Sigma Xi. Episcopalian. Contbr. articles to sci. publs. Patentee in field. Home: 3346 Kenneth Dr Palo Alto CA 94303-4217

TAINTER, JOSEPH ANTHONY, archaeologist; b. San Francisco, Dec. 8, 1949; s. George Washington and Elizabeth Anne (O'Reilly) T.; m. Bonnie Catherine Bagley, Nov. 4, 1977; 1 child, Emmet Bagley. BA, U. Calif., 1972; MA, Northwestern U., 1973, PhD, 1975. Asst. prof. U. N.Mex., Albuquerque, 1975-78; rsch. asst. prof. Eastern N.Mex. U., Portales, 1978-80; archaeologist USDA Forest Svc., Albuquerque, 1980-94; project leader Rocky Mountain Rsch. Sta., Albuquerque, 1994—; pres. N.Mex. Archaeol. Coun., Albuquerque, 1979-80; cons. U.S. Nat. Com. of Scientific Com. on Problems of the Environ., UN, 1995, Monts Mandingues Classified Forest, Bamako, Mali, 1992-93, Nat. Directorate of Arts and Culture, Mali, 1998, 99; dirs. lectr. Getty Rsch. Ctr., 1994; plenary address Internat. Soc. Ecological Econs., 1994. Author: The Collapse of Complex Societies 1988, 10th printing, 1999, Korean edit., 1999; co-editor: Evolving Complexity and Environmental Risk in the Prehistoric Southwest, 1996; co-editor: The Way the Wind Blows: Climate, History and Human Action, 2000. Grantee NSF, 1974-75. Mem. AAAS, Am. Anthropol. Assn., Soc. for Am. Archaeology. Achievements include developed and tested new theory explaining why societies and civilizations collapse; developed and tested new theory that relates economic sustainability to sociopolitical complexity; developed first archaeological research program in USDA Forest Service Research. Home: PO Box 145 Corrales NM 87048-0145 Office: Rocky Mountain Rsch Sta 2205 Columbia Dr SE Albuquerque NM 87106-3222

TAIPALE, KAARIN HANNA IRENE, architect; b. Helsinki, July 22; d. Pentti and Saara Elisabeth (Pesonen) T. MArch, Eidgenössische Technische Hochschule, Zurich, Switzerland, 1972; MS in Hist. Preservation, Columbia U., 1983. Project architect Kalle Vartola Architects, Helsinki, 1974-81, Robert A. M. Stern Architects, N.Y.C., 1983-84; owner, prin. Kaarin Taipale Architects, Helsinki, 1985—; dep. city architect City of Helsinki, 1992-93, dir. bldg. dept., 1993—; mem. exec. com. Internat. Coun. for Local Environ. Initiatives, 1998—. Editor-in-chief Arkkitehti, Finnish Archtl. Rev., 1988-91; contbr. articles to profl. jours., newspapers. Fulbright scholar, N.Y.C., 1981. Mem. Finnish Assn. Architects, Internat. Council on Monuments and Sites. Lutheran. Avocations: architecture, traveling.

TAIRA, KAZUNARI, chemistry educator; b. Kazusa, Nagasaki, Japan, Apr. 15, 1952; s. Makoto and Tomiyo T.; m. Matsuo Masako, Apr. 2, 1983; children: Gene, Kay, Ai. Assoc., Nat. Sasebo Coll. Tech., Japan, 1973; BS, So. Ill. U., 1977; MS, U. Ill., Chgo., 1980, PhD, 1984. Rsch. asst. Nagasaki (Japan) U., 1973-76; postdoctoral fellow U. Ill., Chgo., 1984, Pa. State U., University Pk., 1984-87; sr. rsch. fellow Nat. Inst. Biosci. & Human Tech., Tsukuba, Ibaraki, Japan, 1987-94; prof. inst. applied biochemistry U. Tsukuba, 1994-99; prof. dept. chem. biotech. Grad. Sch. Engring. U. Tokyo, 1999—; cons. Japan Rsch. Industry Assn., Tokyo, 1991—; adj. rschr., rsch. group leader Nat. Inst. Biosci./Human Tech., 1994-99; adj. rschr., project leader Nat. Inst. Adv. Interdisciplinary Rsch., 1997—. Patentee in field; mem. editl. bd. Internat. Jour. Nucleic Acids Rsch., 1995—, Jour. Biochem., 1995—, Gene Therapy Mol. Biol., 1998—. Recipient Tsukuba prize The Sci. & Tech. Promotion Found. of Ibaraki, 1992, Unique Invention prize Sci. & Tech. Agy. of Japan, 1993, Minister Ministry of Internat. Trade & Industry award, 1993. Mem. Molecular Biology Soc. Japan, Chem. Soc. Japan, Antisense DNA/RNA Soc. Japan (com. mem. 1991—), Phi Lambda Upsilon. Avocations: bird watching, tennis. Home: 2-4-3 Higashi, Tsukuba 305-0046, Japan Office: U Tokyo Grad Sch Engring, Dept Chem Biotech Hongo, Tokyo 113-8656, Japan

TAIRAKO, TOMONAGA, philosophy educator; b. Funabashi, Chiba, Japan, Feb. 20, 1951; s. Daihachiro and Fumiko (Takahashi) T.; m. Reiko Hirose, Apr. 25, 1976; 1 child, Yukino. B.sociology, Hitotsubashi U., Tokyo, 1974, M.Sociology, 1976. Assoc. prof. faculty econs. Hokkaido U., Sapporo, Japan, 1981-87; assoc. prof. faculty social sci. Hitotsubashi U., Tokyo, 1987-94, prof., 1994—. Author: Socialism and Contemporary World (in Japanese), 1991; co-author: Time and Temporality in Intercultural Perspective, 1996, Elemente zur Kritik der Werttheorie, 1997. Home: RA204 Naka 2-1, Kunitachi 186-0004, Japan Office: Hitotsubashi U, Fac of Social Sci, Kunitachi 186-8601, Japan

TAIRBEKOV, MURAD GARUN, cell biologist; b. Baku, Azerbaijan, USSR, Oct. 9, 1937; s. Garun Dadash and Saltanat Kazim Tairbekov; m. Nora Manvel Mkrtumiyan, 1961; children: Michael, Renata. Grad., State U., Baku, 1960; PhD, Inst. Biophysics, Moscow, 1968; DSc in Biology, Inst. Biomed. Problems, Moscow, 1988. Jr. rschr. Inst. Biophysics, Moscow, 1964-66, sr. rschr., 1966-71; sr. rschr. Inst. Biomed. Problems, Moscow, 1972-87, leading rschr., 1988—; prof., rsch. fellow, prin. scientist Inst. Biomed. Problems, 1997—. Author: Gravitational Cell Biology, 1997. Grantee Russian Found. Basic Rsch., 1996—, Wolkswagen-Schtiftung Coop. with Natural Sci., 1996-98. Home: Artsimovich St 16-346, 117437 Moscow Russia Office: Inst Biomed Problems, Khoroshevskoye sh 76A, 123007 Moscow Russia

TAISHOFF, LAWRENCE BRUCE, publishing company executive; b. Washington, Aug. 30, 1933; s. Sol Joseph and Betty (Task) T.; m. Nancy Lee Stuckey, Sept. 17, 1962 (div. 1979); children: Robert Paul, Randall Lawrence, Jonathan Bradford. AB, Duke U., 1955. Asst. dir. Sta. WTOP-TV, Washington, 1955-56; with Broadcasting Publs., Inc., Washington, 1958—, pres., pub., 1971-91, chmn., 1991—, also dir.; adviser Cahners Consumer/Entertainment Pub. divsn. Cahners Pub. Co., Washington, 1991—; v.p. Jolar Corp., Washington, 1952-72, dir., 1958-72; gen. ptnr. Jolar Assocs., Washington, 1972—; chmn. bd., pres. Graphictype, Inc., 1976-86, also dir.; chmn., pres. Solar Corp., 1982-86; chmn. Broadcasting-Taishoff Found., 1982—; chmn., CEO Chuckie Broadcasting, Ardmore, Okla., 1993—, Trustco, Washington, 1988—. Co-author radio and TV segment Britannica Book of the Yr., 1983—. Trustee Washington Journalism Ctr., 1982-93, Nat. Press Found., 1993—, mem. adv. bd., 1993—; bd. dirs. Ardissone, Naples, Fla., 1994—, Nat. Press Found., 1982—, mem. exec. com., 1990-94; mem. journalism and comms. exec. com. Capital Campaign for Arts and Scis., Duke U., 1984—, mem. athletic adv. bd., 1999—; bd. advisors Am. Journalism Ctr., Budapest, 1991-95; mem. White House Press Corps, 1983—; mem. Met. Washington Bd. Trade, 1970—; team capt. pubs. divsn. United Givers Fund drive, 1965; mem. admissiosn adv. com. Duke Alumni Assn., 1968-70; mem. U.S. Senate and Ho. of Reps. Periodical Press Gallery, 1958—; trustee Broadcast Pioneers Ednl. Fund Inc., 1985; judge VFW Voice of Democracy contest, 1978—; mem. bd. judges Peabody awards, 1985-91; mem. Am. U. Sch. Comms. Disting. Adv. Commn., 1985—; mem. Founders Soc. Duke U., 1985—, Duke Athletic Adv. Bd., The Mus. of TV and Radio Roundtable, 1988-89; bd. dirs. Ardissone, Naples, Fla., 1994-99; chmn., trustee Taishoff Family Found.; chmn., CEO Solar L.C., Naples, Fla. With AUS, 1956-58. Mem. IEEE (sr.), Internat. Radio & TV Soc., Broadcast Pioneers (life, bd. dirs., exec. com. Broadcast Pioneers Libr.), Am. Sportscasters Assn. (exec. com. 1990—), White House Corrs. Assn., Nat. Press Club, Woodmont Country Club (Rockville, Md.), Bryce Resort Club (Basye, Va.), Cosmos Club (Washington), Sigma Delta Chi, Zeta Beta Tau. Jewish. Office: 4420 Mercantile Ave Naples FL 34104-3348

TAIT, JAMES FRANCIS, retired biophysicist, endocrinologist; b. Stockton-on-Tees, Eng., Dec. 1, 1925; s. Herbert and Constance Levinia (Brotherton) T.; m. Sylvia Agnes Wardroppes, Sept. 1, 1956. BSc in Physics with 1st Class Honors, Leeds U., Yorkshire, Eng., 1942, PhD, 1947; DSc (hon.), Hull U., 1979. Lectr. in med. physics Middlesex Hosp. Med. Sch., U. London, 1948-55, external staff, 1955-58; sr. sci. Worcester Found. for Exptl. Biology and Medicine, Shrewsbury, Mass., 1958-70; Joel prof., head dept. med. physics Middlesex Hosp. Med. Sch., U. London, 1970-82, joint head biophys. endrocrinology unit dept. med. physics, 1970-85; emeritus prof. med. physics U. London, 1989—; mem.-at-large Howard Florey Inst. for Exptl. Physiology and Medicine, Melbourne , Australia, 1973—; mem. Laurentian Hormone Conf. Com., 1960-70. Recipient Tadeus Reichstein award Internat. Soc. for Endocrinology, 1976, Ciba award Am. Heart Assn. for Hypertension USA, 1977, Douglas Wright medallion U. Melbourne, 1989; MRC Rehirement fellow, 1982-86. Fellow Royal Soc. London, Royal Soc. Medicine London; mem. Am. Diabetic Assn., Endocrine Soc. (hon.), Soc. for Endocrinology (hon., medal 1969, Sr. Henry Dale medal 1979), Biochem. Soc. (hon.). Liberal Democrat. Avocations: walking, chess, photography, art appreciation, gardening. Home and Office: Moorlands Main Rd E Boldre, Brockenhurst Hants SO42 7WT, England

TAIT, JOHN REID, lawyer; b. Toledo, Apr. 7, 1946; s. Paul Reid and Lucy Richardson (Ruddew) T.; m. Christina Ruth Bjornstad, Mar. 12, 1972; children: Gretchen, Mary. BA, Columbia U., 1968; JD, Vanderbilt U., 1974. Bar: Idaho 1974, U.S. Dist. Ct. Idaho 1974, U.S. Ct. Appeals (9th cir.) U.S. Supreme Ct., Nez Perce Tribal Ct. Assoc. Keeton & Tait, Lewiston, Idaho, 1974-76, ptnr., 1976-86, 89—; ptnr. Keeton, Tait & Petrie, Lewiston, 1986-88. Chmn. bd. No. Rockies Action Group, Helena, Mont., 1985-86, bd. dirs., 1981-88; mem. Lewiston Hist. Preservation Commn., 1975-94, chmn., 1988-94; bd. dirs. Idaho Legal Aid Svcs., Boise, 1975-99, Idaho Housing Agy., Boise, 1984-91, St. Joseph Regional Med. Ctr. Found., Inc., 1989-94, Lewiston Ind. Found. for Edn., Inc.; Dem. precinct committeeman, 1976-86, state committeeman, 1977-94; del. Sem. Nat. Conv., 1980, 84; regional coord. Idaho State Dem. Party, 1996-99; treas. Larry LaRocco for Congress, 1990, 92. With U.S. Army, 1968-71. Recipient Pro Bono Svc. award Idaho State Bar, 1988, Cmty. Recognition award Lewiston Intergovtl. Coun., 1992, Spl. Recognition award Idaho Legal Aid Svcs., 1993. Mem. ABA, ATLA, Idaho Trial Lawyers Assn. (regional dir. 1976-77, 86-88, 97—), Clearwater Bar Assn. (sec. 1974-76, pres. 1984-86), Consumer Attys. Calif., Workplace Injury Litigation Group. Office: Keeton & Tait Box E 312 Miller St Lewiston ID 83501-1944

TAIT, MADELE, marketing professional, educator; b. Stellenbosch, Republic of South Africa, Mar. 30, 1967; d. Thys and Ria Jacobs; m. Mark Tait. June 23, 1990; 2 children. B. Econ., U. Free State, Rep. South Africa, 1987; M.Comm., Vista U., Rep. South Africa, 1991; D.Comm., U. Port Elizabeth, Rep. South Africa, 1996. Lectr. Vista U., Port Elizabeth, Rep. South Africa, 1989-91; sr. lectr. U. Port Elizabeth, 1991—. Co-author: (book) Applied Business Economics, 1993, Contemporary Management Issues, 1996; contbr. articles to profl. jours. Mem. So. African Inst. Mgmt. Scientists, Afrikaans Cultural Orgn. Mem. Dutch Reformed Church. Avocations: travel, gardening, squash, correspondence. Home: 10 Titian Rd Walmer Heights, 6070 Port Elizabeth Republic South Africa Office: U Port Elizabeth, PO Box 1600, Port Elizabeth Republic South Africa

TAIT, RICHARD, editor-in-chief. BA, Bradfield Coll., New Coll., Oxford, MA, DPhil, 1978. Jr. rsch. fellow St. Edmund Hall Oxford, 1972-74; rschr. Money Programme BBC TV, 1974-75; prodr. Nationwide, 1976-82; editor People and Power, 1982, Money Programme, 1983-85, Newsnight, 1985-87, BBC Gen. Election, 1987, Channel Four News/Ind. TV News, 1987-95; editor-in-chief Ind. TV News, 1995—. Fellow Royal TV Soc.; mem. Internat. Press Inst. (vice chmn.). Office: ITN, 200 Grays Inn Rd, London WC1X 8XZ, England

TAIT, SIMON JOHN ANDERSON, journalist; b. Herford, Germany, Jan. 30, 1948; s. William Anderson and Alice Mary (Crowther) T.; m. Ann Sandra Williams, Nov. 24, 1979; 1 child, Adam. With Telegraph mag., London, 1984-88; arts corr. The Times, London, 1988-92; freelance journalist, broadcaster London, 1992—; editl. dir. Arcadia Internat., London, 1997—; chmn. Arts Corrs.' Group, London, 1994—; editor Arts News, 1998—. Author: Palaces of Discovery, 1989, Times Guide to Museums, 1989-90. Mem. Savile Club, Nat. Union Journalists.

TAIT, SYLVIA AGNES SOPHIA, retired endocrinologist; b. Tumen, Siberia, Russia, Jan. 8, 1917; arrived in Eng., 1920, U.S., 1958; d. James William and Ludmila (Zaharof) Wardropper; m. Anthony James Simpson, Apr. 6, 1940 (dec. Oct. 1941); m. James Francis Tait, Sept. 1, 1956. BSc in Zoology with honors, Univ. Coll., London, 1939; DSc (hon.), Hull U., 1979. Rsch. asst. anatomy dept. Oxford (Eng.) U., 1941-44; biol. rsch. asst. Courtauld Inst. Biochemistry Middlesex Hosp. Med. Sch., London U., 1944-55, mem. MRC external sci. staff biochemistry dept., 1955-58, joint head dept. med. physics MRC biophys.-endocrinology, 1970-82; sr. scientist Worcester Found. for Exptl. Biology, Shrewsbury, Mass., 1958-70; ret.; mem.-at-large Howard Florey Inst. Exptl. Physiology and Medicine, Melbourne, Victoria, Australia, 1973—. Contbr. over 200 sci. papers to profl. jours. Recipient Tadeus Reichstein award Internat. Soc. for Endocrinology, 1976, Ciba award Am. Heart Assn. for Hypertention, 1977, Sir Henry Dale medal Soc. for Endocrinology, 1979, Douglas Wright medallion U. Melbourne, 1989. Avocations: bird watching in New Forest, gardening, cooking. Home: Moorlands Main Rd, Brockenhurst SO42 7WT, England

TAITTINGER-WARREN, BRIGITTE TAITTINGER, business executive; b. Reims, Marne, France, July 8, 1959; d. Claude Taittinger and Catherine De Suarez d'Aulan; m. Sept. 4, 1989; children: Cyril, Bérénice, François, Judith, Grégolte. Bachelor, U. Reims, 1977, MS in History, 1981; grad., Polit. Sci. Sch., Paris, 1984. With budget dept. Publicis, 1984-88; dir. mktg. Groupe du Louvre, 1988-90; dir. mktg. Annick Goutal, Paris, 1990—, pres. bd. dirs. Office: Annick Goutal, Exelmans Blvd, Paris France

TAJIMA, HAJIME, education educator; b. Saitama-ken, Japan, July 6, 1947; s. Kakuo and Masae Tajima; m. Emiko Imai, Aug. 31, 1972. BEd, Tokyo U., 1971, MEd, 1973, postgrad., 1979. Lector Kokugakuin U., Tokyo, 1980-83, asst. prof., 1984-90, prof. faculty gen. edn., 1991—; dir. Assn. for Ednl. Evaluation in Japan, 1990—. Author: (with others) The Total Research on the Group Educational Century, 1984, On the Educational Movements in the Jiyū-Minken Movement, 1984, The Modernization of Japanese Education, vol. 1 Thought and System, vol. 2 Contents and Method, 1986, Historical Study on the Science of Education in Japan, 1997, Principles of Education, 1997. Mem. Japanese Soc. for Study Edn., Japanese Soc. for Study Ednl. History. Home: 508-32 Ichigao-cho, Aoba-ku Yokohama 225-0024, Japan Office: Kokugakuin U, 4-10-28 Higashi, Shibuya Shibuya-ku Tokyo 150, Japan

TAJIMA, OSAMU, psychiatrist, researcher; b. Sakai-Machi, Japan, Feb. 17, 1950; s. Mitsuji and Sumiko (Kinugasa) A.; m. Yasuko Kasuga, Jan. 10, 1979; children: Ai, Ken, Hayato, Maria. MD, Kyorin U., Tokyo, 1976, PhD, 1982. Asst. dept. neuropsychiat. Kyorin U., Tokyo, 1982-84, lectr., 1984-91, 1991-96, assoc. prof., 1996-2000; prof. psychiatry, dept. health sci. Kyorin U. Sch of Medicine, Tokyo, 2000—; vis. lectr. Sch. Socio-Medical Sci. Occupational & Physical Therapist, Tokyo, 1987-93; medical cons. Joy Pack Leisure Corp., Tokyo, 1988—; cons. psychiatrist Tokyo Met. Mitaka Health Ctr., Tokyo, 1990—; cons. psychiatrist Workshop for Chronic Mentally Ill., 1992—. Co-author: Antidepressants, Past, Present and Future, 1992, Drug Treatment in Psychiatry, 1988; mem. editl. bd. Jour. Japanese Soc. Neuropsychopharmacology, 1997—. V.p. The Com. Group Home Svc. for Chronic Mentally Ill in Fuchu-City, Tokyo, 1992—. Recipient Anzu Soc. Pres. award, 1976. Fellow Japanese Soc. Biological Psychiatry, Japanese Soc. General Hosp. Psychiatry; mem. N.Y. Acad. Scis., Am. Assn. Advancement of Sci. Avocations: reading, cycling, walking, traveling, music. Home: 2-3-10 Shin-Machi, Fuchu Tokyo 183-0052, Japan Office: Kyorin U Dept Health, 476 Miyashit-cho, Hachioji Tokyo 192-8508, Japan

TAJIRI, MASAYOSHI, physicist; b. Himeji, Hyogo, Japan, Nov. 30, 1937; s. Tatsuji and Mitsue (Watanabe) T.; m. Yoshiko Ohashi, Mar. 21, 1971; children: Michiko, Hiroko, Masao. BS, Kobe U., 1960; DSc, Nagoya (Japan) U., 1967. Rsch. assoc. Osaka Prefecture U., Sakai, Japan, 1961-66, asst. prof., 1966-74, assoc. prof., 1974-94, prof. dept. math. scis., 1994—; sr. vis. fellow U. of Newcastle upon Tyne, 1972-73. Editl. bd. Jour. of Nonlinear Math. Phys., 1996—; co-author: Nonlinear Wave Motion, 1989; contbr. articles to profl. jours. Mem. Japanese Phys. Soc., Japan Soc. of Fluid Mechanics, Japan Soc. of Plasma and Nuclear Fusion Rsch. Home: 7-17-7 Ohno-dai, Osaka-Sayama 5890023, Japan Office: Osaka Prefecture Univ, 1-1 Gakuencho, Sakai 5998531, Japan

TAJON, ENCARNACION FONTECHA (CONNIE TAJON), retired educator, association executive; b. San Narciso, Zambales, Philippines, Mar. 25, 1920; came to U.S., 1948; d. Espiridion Maggay and Gregoria (Labrador) Fontecha; m. Felix B. Tajon, Nov. 17, 1948; children: Ruth F., Edward F. Teacher's cert., Philippine Normal Coll., 1941; BEd, Far Eastern U., Manila, 1947; MEd, Seattle Pacific U., 1976. Cert. tchr., Philippines. Tchr. pub. schs. San Narciso and Manila, 1941-47; coll. educator Union Coll. Manila, 1947-48; tchr. Auburn (Wash.) Sch. Dist., 1956-58, Renton (Wash.) Sch. Dist., 1958-78; owner, operator Manila-Zambales Internat. Grill, Seattle, 1980-81, Connie's Lumpia House Internat. Restaurant, Seattle, 1981-84; founder, pres. Tajon-Fontecha, Inc., Renton, 1980—, United Friends of Filipinos in Am. Found., Renton, 1985—; founder Labrador Fontecha and Baldovi-Tajon Permanent Scholarship Fund of The Philippine Normal U., 1990; co-founder The United Filipino-Am. Coll. Fund for the USA and the Philippines, 1995; bd. mem. World Div. of the Gen. Bd. of Global Ministries of the United Meth. Ch., 1982-84, Ch. Women United Seattle Chapt.; mem. advisory bd Univ. Wash. Burke Mus., 1991—; mem. King TV Asian Am. Adv. Forum, 1993. Editor bull. Renton 1st United Meth. Ch., 1994. Bd. dirs. women's divsn. Gen. Bd. Global Ministries United Meth. Ch., 1982-84, Renton Area Youth Svcs., 1980-85, Girl's Club Puget Sound, Ethnic Heritage Coun. Pacific N.W., 1989—; mem. Mcpl. Arts Commn., Renton, 1980—; chairperson fundraising steering com. Washington State Women's Polit. Caucus, 1985-89; governing mem. nat. steering com. state coun. Nat. Women's Polit. Caucus, 1990—; mem. vol. action, 1990 Goodwiil Games, Seattle; vol. worker Native Am. Urban Ministries, 1990—; mem. adv. bd. Renton Cmty. Housing Devel.; mem. cmty. adv. bd. U. Wash. Thomas Burke Meml. Mus., 1990—; mem. program com. UN, 1992—; mem. Asian Pacific task force Ch. Coun. Greater Seattle, 1993—; mem. Renton-Rainier area planning com. World Day of Prayer, 1997; coord. establishment and devel. Seattle-Renton area United Filipino-Am. Coll. Fund, 1995, coord. internat. buffet dinner United Filipino-Am. Coll. Fund for U. Wash., Filipino Youth Empowerment Project and Mentor's Child Sponsoring Program; emeritus bd. mem. Ethnic Heritage Coun. Pacific N.W., 1993—; co-chmn. Ann. Filipino and Filipino Am. youth Activities Pres.'s Day Spelling Bee Greater Seattle and Vicinity, 1990-96; coord. Ecumenical World Cmty. Day celebration luncheon Greater Seattle unit Ch. Women United, 1994. Recipient spl. cert. of award Project Hope, 1976, U.S. Bicentennial Commn., 1976, UNICEF, 1977, Spirit of Liberty award Ethnic Heritage Coun. Pacific Northwest, 1991; named Parent of Yr. Filipino Community of Seattle, Inc., 1984, One of 500 Seattle Pacific U. Centennial "Alumni of a Growing Vision", 1991. Mem. NEA, Wash. State Edn. Assn. (bd. dirs. 1990-92), Am. Assn. Ret. Persons, Nat. Ret. Tchrs. Assn., Renton Ret. Tchrs. Assn., U. Wash. Alumni Assn. (life), U. Wash. Filipino Alumni Assn. (pres. Wash. state chpt. 1985-87), Renton Hist. Mus. (life), Internat. Platform Assn., United Meth. Women, Pres.'s Forum, Alpha Sigma, Delta Kappa Gamma. Democrat. Avocations: reading, bowling, crocheting, cooking, walking. Home and Office: 2033 Harrington Pl NE Renton WA 98056-2303

TAJTI, JÁNOS, neurologist; b. Gyula, Hungary, Sept. 17, 1958; s. János and Piroska (Fehér) T.; m. Ilona Tarkanyi, Sept. 3, 1983; children: János, Máté. MD, U. Med. Sch., Szeged, Hungary, 1983, PhD, 1994. Resident Albert Szent-Györgyi U. Med. Sch., Szeged, Hungary, 1985-89, asst. prof., 1989-94, assoc. prof., 1994—. Author: Textbook on Neurology, Chapters on Neurology. Grantee Ministry Welfare, Hungary, 1993-96; rsch. fellow dept. anatomy Albert Szent-Györgyi U. Sch. Medicine, 1983-85, postdoctoral fellow dept. neurology, 1989-92; postdoctoral fellow dept. neurology Baylor Coll. Medicine, 1989-91. Mem. Hungarian Headache Assn. (bd. dirs.), Hungarian Pain Assn. (sec.). Avocations: chess, hiking. Office: Albert Szent-Györgyi U Med Sch, Semmelweis U 6, 6721 Szeged Hungary

TAK, TAHIR, cardiologist, researcher; b. Lahore, Punjab, Pakistan, July 18, 1951; came to U.S., 1985; s. E. Tak and E. Nathaniel. BS, Govt. Coll., Lahore, 1971; MD, U. Nijmegen, Holland, 1980; PhD, U. Maastricht, Holland, 1989. Asst. prof. medicine U. So. Calif., L.A., 1989-96; assoc. prof. medicine U. Nev., Las Vegas, 1996-98; cardiologist Scott and White Clinic, Temple, Tex., 1998—. Fellow ACP, European Soc. Cardiology, Am. Coll. Chest Physicians; mem. Am. Coll. Cardiology. Home: 216 Cypress Springs Dr Belton TX 76513-5360 Office: Scott and White Clinic 2401 S 31st St Temple TX 76508-0001

TAKACS, ANDRAS, veterinarian; b. Kassa, Slovakia, Sept. 21, 1941; s. Andras and Ilona Takacs; m. Katalin Nagy, Nov. 7, 1966; children: Andras, Denes, Peter. DVM, U. Budapest, 1964. Food hygiene controller Baz County Animal Health and Food Control Sta., Miskolc, Hungary, 1964-66, regional veterinarian, 1966-73; leading veterinarian State Farm, Sarospatak, Hungary, 1973-86; food hygiene specialist Baz County Animal Health & Food Control Sta., 1986&. Avocations: hunting, movies, football, internet.

TAKACS, GABOR, engineering educator; b. Gyongyosmellek, Somogy, Hungary, Jan. 16, 1947; s. Gyula and Jolan (Nemenyi) T.; m. Beata Gobbi, July 7, 1973; children: Zsolt, Reka. MS, U. Miskolc, Hungary, 1970; PhD, Hungarian Acad. Scis., Budapest, 1985. Asst. U. Miskolc, 1970-78, assoc. prof. engring., 1978-88, 89-97, prof., 1997—; vis. prof. Tex. Tech U., Lubbock, 1988-89. Author: Modern Sucker-Rod Pumping, 1993. Mem. Soc. Petroleum Engrs. (sect. chmn. 1992-94, Disting. lectr. 1995-96). Roman Catholic. Avocations: windsurfing, sailing, computers. Home: Toldi 3, H-3525 Miskolc Hungary Office: Univ Miskolc, Egyetemvaros, H-3515 Miskolc Hungary

TAKÁCS, JENÖ, research engineer, consultant; b. Kispest, Hungary, July 15, 1929; s. Janos and Roza (Kosztolanyi) T.; m. Judith Sara Hidegh, Feb. 7, 1959; children: Reka Judith, Ester Csilla. BSc, Univ. Tech. Sci., Budapest, 1951, MSc, 1956; PhD, U. Surrey, Eng., 1971. Cert. in engring./physics. Lectr. Univ. Tech. Scis., Budapest, 1951-56; sr. engr. Epsylon Rsch. Co., London, 1957-61; prin. engr. Brandenburg Ltd., Croydon, Eng., 1961-62, R.B. Pullin and Co., London, 1962-63; sr. rsch. engr., nuclear physics U. Oxford, Eng., 1963-85, rsch. assoc., engring. sci., 1985-93, assoc. engring. sci., 1993—; vis. prof. LNETI, Lisbon, 1993, Chiang Mai U., Thailand, 1995, 98. Author 1 book; contbr. 1 book; contbr. to over 50 profl. jours. Capt.

Signal Co., 1951-56. Fellow IEE; mem. Internat. Soc. Optical Engring. Avocations: music, sport, theatre, games. Office: U Oxford Dept Engring Sci, Parks Rd, Oxford OX1 3PJ, England

TAKACS, MIKLOS, librarian; b. Kamon, Hungary, Dec. 3, 1933; s. Janos and Janosne (Maria Hende) T.; m. Valeria Rainer, Oct. 15, 1966; children: Thyra, Dora, Veronika. Grad. in libr. scis., U. Budapest, 1954. From reference libr. to dir. County Libr., Szombathely, Hungary, 1954-94. Mem. Assn. Hungarian Librs. (v.p. 1968-73). Avocations: family, reading, music, driving. Home: Szell Kalman u 15, 9700 Szombathely Hungary Office: County Libr Berzsenyi Daniel, Petofi Sandor u 43, 9700 Szombathely Hungary

TAKÁCS, SÁNDOR, public health physician; b. Karcag, Hungary, Feb. 3, 1931; s. Sándor and Sándorné (Nádházi) T.; m. Sándorné Tóth, Sept. 17, 1955; 1 child, Ágnes. Diploma, Med. U., Debrecen, Hungary, 1955, Postgrad. U., Budapest, 1961; PhD, Hungarian Acad. Sci., Budapest, 1970, DSc, 1986. Gen. practice medicine Dist. Coun., Edelény, Hungary, 1955-57, pub. health supr., 1957-61; chief environ. health dept. County Coun., Miskolc, Hungary, 1961-76, dir., 1976-91; chief rsch. dept. Nat. Pub. Health Ctr., Budapest, 1991-98; prof. Tech. U. Miskolc, 1978—; lectr. U. Veszprém, Hungary, 1978—. Author: Environment, Human, Microelements, 1993, The Human Environment, 1994; contbr. articles to profl. publs. (Fodor József medal 1992); editor in chief Hungarian Jour. of Pub. Health, 1995-98. Recipient Pro Environ. Protection award Min. Environ. Protection, Budapest, 1989. Fellow Assn. Hungarian Hygienics (bd. dirs. 1960—), Assn. Hungar Labour Hygienics, Soc. Hungarian Hydrologists (Pro Aqua award 1993); mem. Soc. Polish Hygienics (hon.), Assn. Hungarian Doctors for Healthy Environment (pres. 1994). Avocations: philately, working in orchard, numismatics, music. Home: Almos u 10, 3526 Miskolc Hungary Office: U Miskolc, Egyetemváros Mész u 2, 3515 Miskolc Hungary

TAKADA, GORO, pediatrician, educator; b. Pyong Yang, Korea, Sept. 27, 1941; s. Tetsutaro and Kino (Endo) T.; m. Hiroko Ogawa, Nov. 3, 1967; children: Hiroyuki, Akiko. MD, Tohoku U., Sendai-shi, Japan, 1967; PhD, Osaka (Japan) City U., 1975. Asst. prof. Tohoku U. Sch. Medicine, Sendai-shi, 1978-82; assoc. prof. Akita (Japan) U. Sch. Medicine, 1982-88, prof., chmn., 1988—; pres. 42nd annual meeting Pediat. Soc. North Japan, Akita-shi, 1990, 38th annual meeting Japanese Soc. Inborn Errors of Metabolism, Akita-shi, 1995. Contbr. articles to profl. jours. Chmn. Com. for Child Health in Akita Prefecture, 1993—. Recipient Osaka Mayor's award Osaka City, 1975, award of Osaka Med. Soc., Osaka City U. Sch. Medicine, 1975, Arakawa award Tsuneo Arakawa, Sendai-shi, Japan, 1981. Avocations: travel, camera, swimming. Home: 3-12-20 Sakuraga-oka, 010-0043 Akita shi, Japan Office: Akita Univ Sch Medicine, 1-1-1 Hondo, Akita-shi 010-8543, Japan

TAKAGAKI, TASUKU, bank executive; b. Tokyo, 1928; married; 2 children. BA in Econs., U. Tokyo, 1953. With The Bank of Tokyo Ltd., 1953—, gen. mgr. internat. investment divsn., planning divsn., 1975-79, dir., gen. mgr. personnel divsn., 1979-82, resident mng. dir. for Europe, 1982-84, mng. dir. head office, 1984-86, sr. mng. dir., 1986-89, dep. pres., 1989-90, pres., 1990-96; dep. treas. Asian Devel. Bank, 1966-71; pres. Bank Tokyo-Mitsubishi Ltd., 1996—; chmn. Bank of Tokyo-Mitsubishi Ltd., 1998—, sr. adviser, 2000—; mem. Coun. Fgn. Econ. Cooperation (advisory body to prime min.), Customs Tariff Coun., Ministry Fin., Internat. Trade Ins. Coun., Ministry Internat. Trade and Industry; chmn. Latin Am. com. Keidanren; chmn. Export and Import Transaction Coun., Ministry Internat. Trade and Industry; chmn. com. internat. rels. Keizai Doyukai. Dep. chmn. Internat. Econ. Affairs Com., Tokyo Chamber of Commerce and Industry. Decorated Gran Cruz Orden Nacional al Merito, Govt. Republic of Colombia, 1991, Medal of Honour with Blue Ribbon, Govt. of Japan, 1994, Gra-Cruz Ordem do Merito Agricola, Comml. Indsl., Govt. Portugal, 1995, Orden del Libertador en el grado de Comendador, Govt. Republic Venezuela, 1996. Office: Bank Tokyo-Mitsubishi Ltd, 7-1 Marunouchi 2-chome, Chiyoda-ku Tokyo 100-8388, Japan

TAKAGI, HIDEAKI, computer scientist, mathematician; b. Mihara-cho, Hyogo-ken, Japan, Mar. 23, 1950; s. Yoshio and Kiyo (Kashu) T.; m. Yoko Aida, Dec. 6, 1974; children: Mayu, Takuma, Hayato. Diploma, U. Tokyo, 1972, MS, 1974; PhD, UCLA, 1983. Systems engr. IBM Japan, Ltd., Tokyo, 1974-79; researcher IBM Japan Sci. Inst., Tokyo, 1983-84, mgr. communication networks, 1984-85; mgr. distributed systems IBM Tokyo Rsch. Lab., 1985-87, mgr. founds. systems, 1987-90, mgr. project planning, 1990-93; cons. researcher, 1993; prof. U. Tsukuba, 1993—. Author: Analysis of Polling Systems, 1986, Queueing Analysis, Vol. I, 1991, Vols. II and III, 1993; editor: Stochastic Analysis of Computer and Communication Systems, 1990; jour. editor IEEE/ACM Transactions on Networking Communications Soc., N.Y., 1986-94, Performance Evaluation, 1984—, Queueing Systems, 1988—. Fellow IEEE; mem. Ops. Rsch. Soc. Am. Avocation: world trotting. Home: 747-3 Serizawa, Chigasaki-shi, Kanagawa 2530008, Japan Office: U Tsukuba-Inst Policy and Planning Scis, 1-1-1 Tennoudai, Tsukuba 305 8573, Japan

TAKAGI, TAKAKO FRANCES, theology educator; b. Kumamoto, Japan, Aug. 7, 1948; d. Keiichi Dominic and Aiko Mary (Kataoka) T. BA, Sacred Heart U., Tokyo, 1972, MA, 1974; PhD in Theology, Cath. U., Washington, 1985. Lectr. in theology Notre Dame Seishin U., Okayama, Japan, 1976-81; assoc. prof. theology Notre Dame Seishin U., Okayama, 1985-92, prof. theology, 1993—. Author: (books) A History of Christian Education of Women in Japan, 1991 (Acad. Rsch. prize 1992), Christianity and the Religious View of the Japanese, 1991; (with others), A Way of Human Relations, 1993, Women and Men Through Christianity, 1993. Mem. Cultural Coun. of Okayama Prefecture, 1986—, Profl. Coun. Okayama Prefecture, 1997—, Coun. of Okayama City, 1996—; pres. Assn. of Death and Dying, Okayama, 1992—. Recipient scholarship Philantrophic Ednl. Orgn., Washington, 1981-85. Mem. Am. Cath. Hist. Assn., Soc. Hist. Studies of Christianity, Japan Soc. Christian Studies. Avocations: reading, music. Office: Notre Dame Seiskin U, 2-16-9 Ifukucho, Okayama Okayama 700, Japan

TAKAHARA, RYOJI, public health officer, health economist; b. Okayama, Japan, May 16, 1947; s. Michiharu and Michiko (Ukida) T.; m. Yuko Takahara, Aug. 1, 1972; children: Nogusa, Sion. AA, Okayama U., 1968, MD, 1972; MPH, U. Tex., Houston, 1980. Resident Toshima Met. Hosp., Tokyo, 1972-74; chief health statistician Ministry of Health, Tokyo, 1976-77, dep. dir. Health Econs., 1976-82; 1st sec. embassy of Japan Ministry of Fgn. Affairs, Manila, 1982-85; dir. divsn. Ministry of Health and Welfare, 1989-91; dir., dir. gen. Ministry of Health and Environment, Okayama, 1991-93, dir. food sanitation, 1993-95, dir. nat. hosp. adminstrn., 1995-97, dir. cmty. health, health promotion disease prevention and nutrition, 1997-98, dir. divsn. health sci. policy, 1998-99; dir. gne. health med. affairs Japan Def. Agy., Tokyo, 1999—; cons. Japan Internat. Coop. Agy., 1974, WHO, Geneva, 1989; adj. asst. prof. dept. Hygiene Med. Sch. Okayama U., 1995—, Sch. Medicine Tokushima U., 1995—, Kyoshu U., 1997—. Contbr. more than 50 articles to profl. jours. Fellow Royal Soc. Health (London); mem. APHA, Am. Coll. Preventive Medicine, Am. Econs. Assn., Japan Clin. Epidemiology Network (founder 1986—), Japan Pub. Health Assn. (mem. bd. dirs. 1997—). United Ch. of Christ. Avocations: art, travel, music. Home: 1-4-33-606 Takanawa Minato, Tokyo 108-0074, Japan Office: Japan Def Agy, 5-1 Honmuracho Ichigaya, Shinjyuku-ku, Tokyo 162-8801, Japan

TAKAHASHI, AKIRA, hospital executive; b. Nagoya, Japan, Feb. 22, 1930; s. Kenzo and Tetsuko (Katsumata) T.; m. Yoshiko Ishikawa, Dec. 17, 1961; children: Masaru, Osamu, Satoshi. MD, Nagoya (Japan) U., 1955, PhD, 1960. Assoc. prof. dept. internal medicine Nagoya (Japan) U. Sch. Medicine, 1968-78; prof. dept. internal medicine Aichi Med. U., Nagakute, Aichi, Japan, 1978-85; prof. dept. neurology Nagoya U. Sch. Medicine, 1985-93; emeritus prof. U. Nagoya, 1993—; dir. Nagoya U. Hosp., 1989-91, Tokai Ctrl. Hosp., Kakamigahara, Gifu, Japan, 1993-2000; hon. dir. Tokai Ctrl. Hosp., 2000—. Author: (book) Internal Medicine, 1991, 100 Cases of Neurological Diseases, 1994, Merck Manual, 17th edit., 1999; editor Clin. Neurology, 1983-94, Autonomic Nervous System, 1989—, Clinical Autonomic Rsch., 1996—. Mem. N.Y. Acad. Scis., Am. Neurol. Assn., Am. Autonomic Soc., Internat. Soc. History of Neuroscis. Avocations: classic music, mountaineering, butterfly-watching, history of medicine. Home: 126 4-chome Momoyama-cho, Obu Aichi 474-0026, Japan Office: Tokai Ctrl Hosp, 4 Sohora Higashijima-machi, Kakamigahara Gifu 504-8601, Japan

TAKAHASHI, KATSUHISA, school administrator; b. Kannonji-shi, Kagawa-ken, Japan, May 7, 1941; s. Takehisa and Kimie (Imai) T.; m. Miyako Mori, Apr. 29, 1970; children: Akihisa, Yuri. BS, Ehime U., Matsuyama, Japan, 1964; MA in Edn., Internat. Christian U., Tokyo, 1966. Cert. h.s., sci., 1st grade tchr. Sci. tchr. Takamatsu Minami Sr. H.S., 1966-71; rschr. Kagawa-Ken Edn. Ctr., Takamatsu, 1972-73; sci. tchr. Sanbonmatsu Sr. H.S., Ouchi, Kagawa, 1974-76, Kannonji-Daiichi Sr. H.S., Kannonji, 1977-93; head of instrn. dept. Kannonji-Chuo Sr. H.S., Kannonji, 1994-97; vice-prin. Marugame Sr. H.S., 1998—. Mem. Am. Assn. Physics Tchrs., Physics Edn. Soc. Japan. Avocations: chorus, yoga. Home: 957 Shusaku-cho Kannonji, Kagawa 768-0011, Japan Office: Marugame Sr High Sch, 1-6 Bancho, Marugame, Kagawa 763-8512, Japan

TAKAHASHI, KENJI, imaging company research associate; b. Takasaki, Gunma, Japan, May 31, 1951; s. Tooru and Fumie Takahashi; m. Sanae Taniguchi, Mar. 19, 1978; 1 child, Gaku. B in Engring., U. Tokyo, 1974. Rschr. Fuji Photo Film Co., Ltd., Minamiashigara, Kanagawa, Japan, 1974-87; rsch. assoc. Fuji Photo Film Co., Ltd., Kaisei, Kanagawa, Japan, 1987—; part-time lectr. Nagoya (Aichi, Japan) U., 1997. Contbr. chpt. to book. Recipient Umetani prize Soc. Japan Radiologic Tech., 1989, Spl. prize Japan Crystallographic Soc., 1992, Grand Tech. prize Nikkei BP Co., 1997. Mem. Electrochem. Soc., Japan Soc. Applied Physics, Japan Chem. Soc., Japan Phosphor Soc. Achievements include patents in field. Avocations: hiking, skiing, reading novels. E-mail: gsk-t@aurora.dti.ne.jp and takahasi@miya.fujifilm.co.jp. Fax: 81-465-85-2078. Home: 331-10 Horinouchi, Odawara Kanagawa 250-0853, Japan Office: Miyanodai Tech Devel Ctr, 798 Miyanodai, Kaisei Kanagawa 258-8538, Japan

TAKAHASHI, KIYOSHI, research educator; b. Warabishi, Saitamaken, Japan, Sept. 26, 1937; s. Shichiro and Tsune (Fukuda) T.; m. Emiko Nakano, Nov. 30, 1963; 3 children. B of Engring., U. Tokyo, 1961, D of Engring., 1975. Cert. in engring. Rsch. engr. NKK Corp., Kawasaki, Japan, 1961-64; rsch. assoc. U. Tokyo, 1964-67, lectr., 1967-77; assoc. prof. Kyushu U., Fukuoka, Japan, 1977-80; prof. Kyushu U., Kasuga, Japan, 1980—; dir. Rsch. Inst. for Applied Mech. Kyushu U., Kasuga, Japan, 1999—; vis. rschr. Fraunhofer Inst. for Solid Mechanics, Freiburg, Germany, 1976-77; vis. prof. Fed. Inst. Tech., Lausanne, Switzerland, 1990, U. Mich., Ann Arbor, 1991; mem. internat. sci. com. Internat. Conf. on Deformation, Yield and Fracture, U.K., 1989—. Editor: (books) Progress in Acoustic Emissin Vol. VI, 1992, Impact Fracture of Polymers, 1992; contbr. articles to profl. jours.; mem. editl. adv. bd. NDT & E Internat., 1995—, Jour. Macromolecular Sci., 1987—. Recipient Achievement award Material Sci. Soc. Japan, 1989; MIDAF grantee Mech. Industry Devel. and Assistance Found., 1990, Iketani grantee, 1992, Paper Awd., Jour. of Japan Soc. of Composite Materials, 1998. Avocations: golf, skiing, gardening. Home: 2-3-11 Nagaoka, 815-0075 Fukuoka Japan Office: Kyushu U, 6-1 Kasugakoen, 816-8580 Fukuokaken Japan

TAKAHASHI, KOJI, physician, radiologist; b. Sapporo, Hokkaido, Japan, Oct. 19, 1957; s. Kikuo and Tomie Takahashi; m. Noriko Hayashi, Mar. 27, 1983; children: Mayu, Ryo, Shyo. BM, Asahikawa Med. Coll., Hokkaido, 1982. Mem. jr. staff Asahikawa Med. Coll., 1982-86; resident Jichi Med. Sch., Tochigi, 1986-87, mem. jr. staff, 1987-91, instr., 1991-98; assoc. prof. Asahikawa Med. Coll., 1998—. Contbr. articles to profl. jours. Mem. Japan Radiol. Soc., Japanese Coll. Radiology, Japanese Soc. Angiography and Interventional Radiology, Japanese Soc. Magnetic Resonance in Medicine, Radiol. Soc. N.Am. Avocation: football. Home: 6-5-5-5 Kaguraoka, Asahikawa 078-8316, Japan Office: Asahikawa Med Coll Dept Radiology, 2-1 Midorigaoka Higashi, Asahikawa 078-8510, Japan

TAKAHASHI, MASAO, cardiac surgeon; b. Fukui, Japan, Aug. 5, 1963; s. Yoshinori and Kinue (Makino) T.; m. Kyoko Ukegawa, Sept. 15, 1989; children: Saeko, Ryo. MD, Kanazawa (Japan) U., 1988, PhD, 1995. Resident Kanazawa U. Sch. Medicine, 1988-89; med. staff, 1990-93; resident Yokohama (Japan) Sakae Kyosai Hosp., 1989-90, med. staff, 1993-95; instr. dept. cardiovascular surgery Fukui (Japan) Prefectural Hosp.; chief dept. thoracic & cardiovascular surgery Chigasaki Tokushukai Hosp., Kanagawa, Japan, 1997—. Contbr. articles to profl. jours., patentee in field. Fax: 81-467-86-7127. Office: Chigasaki Tokushukai Hosp, 14-1 Saiwai-Cho, 253-0052 Chigasaki Kanagawa, Japan

TAKAHASHI, NAOKO, Olympic athlete; b. Gifu, Japan, May 6, 1972. Winner marathon Asian Games, 1998; winner Gold medal women's marathon Sydney, 2000. Reported to be fastess marathon run by a woman without assistance of pacesetters, 1998. Office: Japan Amateur Athletic Fedn, 1-1-1 Jinnan Shibuya-ku, Tokyo 150-50, Japan*

TAKAHASHI, RYUICHI, computer science educator; b. Chiba City, Japan, Jan. 31, 1954. BS in Physics, Waseda U., Tokyo, 1978; ME in Info. Processing, Tokyo Inst. Tech., 1981. Rschr. VLSI computer engr. NEC Corp., Tokyo, 1981-91; asst. prof. computer sci. Tokyo Inst. Tech., 1991-94; assoc. prof. info. scis. Hiroshima City U., Japan, 1994—. Mem. IEEE, Inst. Electronics, Info. and Comm. Engrs., Info. Processing Soc. Japan, Assn. for Computing Machinery. E-mail: ryuichi@ce.hiroshima-cu.ac.jp. Office: Hiroshima City U Info Scis, 3-4-1 Ozukahigashi Asaminami-ku, Hiroshima City 731-3194, Japan

TAKAHASHI, SHIN, CEO, representative director; b. Chigasaki, Kanagawa, Japan, Mar. 19, 1963; s. Minoru and Hisayo (Yamaguchi) T. BA in Polit. Sci., Keio Univ., 1986, Brown U., 1986; MBA, INSEAD, 1989. Salesman Mitsubishi Corp., Tokyo, 1986-88; asst. to the chmn. Club Med. Mgmt. Asia, Tokyo, 1989-96; brand mgr. Coco Cola (Japan) Co. Ltd., Tokyo, 1996-97; pres., CEO, rep. dir. Piaget, Baume & Mercier Japan, Ltd., Tokyo, 1997—. Corr. (newsletter) US Express, 1986. Mem. Brown Univ. Alumni Club (exec. v.p.). Avocations: arts, horseback riding, swimming. Office: Toranomon 45 Mori Bldg 8F, 5-1-5 Toranomon Minato-ku, Minato-ku Tokyo 195-0001, Japan

TAKAHASHI, SHOTARO, retired communications executive, former ambassador; b. Oita, Japan, Dec. 25, 1920; s. Shichinosuke and Shin (Odakara) T.; m. Nobu Nagasaku, June 8, 1947. Grad., Tokyo U. of Commerce (now named Hitotsubashi U.), 1943. With Ministry Fgn. Affairs, Japan, 1943-87; councillor Embassy, Washington, 1966-67; external dir. EXPO '70 Assn., Osaka, Japan, 1967-70; min. Embassy, London, 1971-74; amb. Embassy, Kuwait, 1974-77; consul gen. Consulate-Gen., N.Y., 1977-81; ambassador Embassy, Tehran, Iran, 1981-83, Helsinki, Finland, 1984-87; pres. Radiopress, Inc., Tokyo, 1987-97, retired, 1997. 2nd lt. Japanese Army (in Japan and China), 1944-45. Decorated Grand Cross of Order of Lion of Finland, Finnish govt., 1986, Order of Rising Sun, Gold and Silver Star, Japanese govt., 1991; named hon. comdr. Victorian Order, Brit. govt., 1971. Avocation: golf. Home: 4-11-5-701 Sendagaya, Shibuya-ku Tokyo 151-0051, Japan

TAKAHASHI, SUSUMU, mechanical engineer, educator; b. Fukushima City, Japan, Mar. 10, 1929; s. Jinchirow and Ima (Tatugoyama) T.; m. Hisako Chiba, Feb. 2, 1957; children: Atsuko, Shouko, Yuko. BA in Engring., Tohoku U., 1953, D of Engring., 1978. Prof. Kanto-Gakuin U., Yokohama, Japan, 1970—, dean, 1976, pres., 1979; cons. Yokohama, 1990-94. Author: Stress-Strain Analysis, 1986, Strength of Materials, 1989; author, editor: Handbook of Non-Destructive Inspection, 1992, The Basic Applied Mathematics, 1995, Photomechanics, 1997. Recipient Meritorious Deed award Japan Soc. Non Destructive Inspection, 1992, Best Paper award, 1994. Fellow Japan Soc. Photoelasticity (Best Paper award 1997); mem. Asian Pacific Congress for Strength Evaluation (pres. 1992—), Japan Soc. Mech. Engrs. Buddhism. Home: 207 Shimoyagiri, Matudo 271, Japan Office: Kanto-Gakuin Univ, 4834 Matuura-cho Kanazawaku, Yokohama 236, Japan

TAKAHASHI, SUSUMU, internist, educator; b. Namerikawa, Toyama, Japan, June 23, 1937. MD, Nihon U. Sch. Medicine, 1964, PhD, 1969. Assoc. prof. Nihon U. Sch. Medicine, 1983-92; dir. Nishi-Kot-U Nat. Hosp., 1992-98, Yokosuka Nat. Hosp., 1998-99; prof. Nihon U. Grad. Sch. Bus., 1999—. Recipient Oshima award Kidney Found. Japan, 1990. Office: Nihon U Grad Sch Bus, 8-24 Kudan-Minami 4-Chome, Chiyoda-Ku, Tokyo 102-8275, Japan

TAKAHASHI, TADASHI, agricultural studies educator; b. Tenmabayashi, Aomori, Japan, Sept. 12, 1955; s. Katsuo and Tsuki (Nozuki) T.; m. Makiko Karatsuya; children: Mariko, Yu, Jun. BAS, Tohoku U., Sendai, 1979, DAgr, 1989. Rsch. assoc. Akita Prefectural Coll. Agr., Ohgata, Japan, 1979-87; lectr. Akita Prefectural Coll. Agr., 1987-91, assoc. prof., 1991-99; assoc. prof. Akita Prefectural U., 1999—; tech. advisor Akita Prefectural Govt., 1994—. Contbr. sci. papers to profl. jours. Mem. Japanese Soc. Soil Sci. and Plant Nutrition (Progress award 1992), Soil Sci. Soc. Am., Clay Sci. Soc. Japan. Home: 52-6 Uenodai, Tennou 010-0201, Japan Office: Akita Prefectural Univ, Shimo-Shinjo, Akita 010-0195, Japan

TAKAHASHI, TAKEO, anesthesiology educator emeritus; b. Otaru-city, Japan, Mar. 4, 1922; s. Chokichi and Sumi (Nemoto) T.; m. Tamiko Hiraki, Oct. 17, 1951; children: Masako, Hiroo, Muneo, Arihiro, Makio. MD, Hokkaido U. Sch. Medicine, 1945, PhD, 1950. Assoc. prof. surgery Sapporo (Japan) Med. Coll. and Hosp., 1955-57, prof. dept. anesthesiology, 1957-87; prof. emeritus Sch. Medicine Sapporo Med. U., 1987—; pres. Noboribetsu (Japan) Gen. Hosp., 1987-89; chair bd. dirs. Sapporo Med. U. Found. Promotion of Med. Sci., 1997—. Mem. Japan Soc. Anesthesiology (hon.), Japan Soc. Pain Clinicians, Japan Soc. Circulation Control. Avocations: music, ceramic art, drawing. Home: 3-7 1-jyo 7-chome Nishi-ku, 063-0001 Sapporo Hokkaido, Japan Office: Sapporo Med U Found, Promotion Med Sci, 060-0001 Sapporo Hokkaido, Japan

TAKAHASHI, YASUNARI, English literature educator; b. Tokyo, Feb. 9, 1932; s. Yasunobu and Toyo (Ishigami) T.; m. Michi Hashii, Nov. 18, 1958; Nobuya, Mihoko. BA, U. Tokyo, 1953, MA, 1955. Lectr. English Chuo U., Tokyo, 1958-62; lectr. U. Tokyo, 1962-65, assoc. prof., 1965-76, prof., 1976-92, prof. emeritus, 1992—; prof. Showa Women's U., Tokyo, 1992—; vis. prof. U. Toronto, Can., 1981; vis. fellow commoner Trinity Coll., Cambridge, Eng., 1986-87; vis. scholar Pembroke Coll., Cambridge, 1994; short-term fellow Princeton (N.J.) U., 1997. Author: Summa Nonsensica, 1977, (play) The Braggart Samurai, 1991; translator: Collected Plays Samuel Beckett, 3 vols., 1967-86; editor: A Shakespeare Handbook, 1994. Named Comdr. Brit. Empire, Govt. Eng., 1993. Mem. English Literary Soc. Japan (pres. 1989-92), Shakespeare Soc. Japan (pres. 1989-97), Internat. Shakespeare Assn. (v.p. 1996—). Avocations: table tennis, skiing. Home: 1-2-4 Aobadai Meguro-ku, Tokyo 153-0042, Japan

TAKAHASHI, YOSHINDO, retired transport company executive; b. Tokyo, Apr. 21, 1931; s. Yoshio and Antonina Nikolaiuna (Razmowa) T.; m. Noriko Masago, Oct. 7, 1955; children: Hiroshi, Kaoru, Yukie. BS, Aoyama Gakuin U., Tokyo, 1955. Mgr. Hino Motors Ltd., Tokyo, 1961-77; mgr. overseas ops. Hino Motors Ltd.; mng. dir. Hino Motors Hellas S.A., Athens, 1963-68; comptroller Thai Hino Motor Sales Ltd., Bangkok, 1970-71; mng. dir. Okamoto Freighters Ltd., Tokyo, 1977-94, ret., 1994. Home: No 3-15-4-816, Higashi-nogawa Komae-Shi, Tokyo 201-0002, Japan

TAKAISHI, NOBORU, psychiatrist, educator; b. Kobe, Hyogo, Japan, Jan. 2, 1928. MD, Nippon Med. Sch., Japan, 1954; D Med. Sci., Osaka (Japan) U., 1959. Diplomate Japanese Nat. Bd. Med. Examiners, 1955. Intern Osaka U. Hosp., 1954-55; sr. vis. fellow psychiatry U. Oreg. Med. Sch., 1964-65; rsch. fellow psychiatry Albert Einstein Coll. Medicine, 1983; asst. prof. psychiatry Osaka U. Med. Sch., 1966-69, lectr. psychiatry, 1969—; chief dept. psychiatry Osaka U. Br. Hosp., 1966-69; pvt. practice psychiatry Takaishi Clinic, Osaka, 1969—; clin. prof. psychiatry Nippon Med. Sch., 1999—. Contbr. articles to profl. jours., chpts. to books; translator various articles. Fellow Internat. Soc. Hypnosis (rep.), Am. Soc. Clin. Hypnosis (approved cons.), Assn. for Advancement Behavior Therapy; mem. Japanese Psychiatry Assn. (mem. bd. 1979-81), Japanese Soc. Psychosomatic Medicine (mem. bd. 1996—, approved cons. 1966—), Japanese Soc. Clin. Hypnosis (founding pres. 1999—), Japanese Soc. Behavior Therapy (mem. bd. 1976—), Japanese Union Assn. for Psychomed. Therapy, Am. Acad. Psychoanalysis (sci. assoc.), Soc. Exploration Psychotherapy Integration, Swedish Soc. Clin. and Exptl. Hypnosis. Avocations: tennis, Japanese classical song, brush writing. Office: Takaishi Clinic, 1-2-2-200 Umeda Kita-ku, Osaka 530-0001, Japan

TAKAKUWA, YASUO, education educator; b. Nagoya, Aichi, Japan, Aug. 21, 1929; s. Kenshichiro and Taka (Baba) T.; m. Moeko Shinoda, May 28, 1961; children: Yoshiro, Yuji, Yasuhiko. BA, U. Tokyo, 1952. Tchg. asst. Tokyo Inst. Tech., 1952-57; asst. prof. Kokugakuin U., Tokyo, 1957-60, assoc. prof., 1960-63; assoc. prof. Nagoya U., 1963-73, prof., 1973-84, prof. emeritus, 1996—; prof. Sophia U., Tokyo, 1984-96, Edogawa U., Chiba, Japan, 1996-2000; policy adviser Japan Audiovisual Info. Ctr.; chmn. of bd. dirs. Audiovisual Sci. and Tech. Ctr., 1991—; vis. prof. U. of the Air in Japan, 1995—. Author: Audiovisual Education in an Age of Innovation, 1976, Media and Education, 1995; editor: Invitation to Media Education, 5 vols., 1987; Media and Education Revised, 1999. Bd. dirs. SONY Found. for Sci. Edn., 1972—. Mem. Japanese Audiovisual Edn. Assn. (bd. dirs. 1978—, Leadership Honor award 1989), Japanese Soc. Study Audiovisual Broadcast Edn. (pres. 1988-94), Internat. Visual Literacy Assn. (bd. dirs. 1993-95), Internat. Coun. Ednl. Media (dep. rep. Japan 1995—), Japan Assn. for Ednl. Media Study (pres. 1994-97). Avocations: travel, collecting stamps, Mozart. Home: 2-19-16 Shimomeguro, Meguro-ku, Tokyo 153-0064, Japan

TAKAMI, MICHIO, physicist, chemist, researcher; b. Kumamoto, Japan, Apr. 17, 1938; m. Yuko Murata, Dec. 21, 1943; children: Michihiro, Michiaki. BSc, Tokyo U., 1962, MSc, 1964, DSc, 1967. Rsch. scientist RIKEN, Saitama, Japan, 1966-80, sr. scientist Inst. Phys. and Chem. Rsch., 1981-85, chief scientist Inorganic Chem. Phys. Lab., 1986-99; fellow Inst. Laser Sci. U. Electro-Comm., Tokyo, Japan, 1999—. Contbr. articles in physics and chemistry rsch. to profl. jours. Office: Inst Laser Sci, U Electro-Comm, Chofu Tokyo 182-8585, Japan

TAKAMIYA, TOSHIYUKI, language educator; b. Tokyo, Feb. 23, 1944; s. Yukio and Kiyoko (Masuda) T.; m. Mieko Edamatsu, Mar. 29, 1971. BA in Econs., Keio U., 1966, BA in English, 1968, MA in English, 1970; DLitt (hon.), U. Sheffield, 1998. Asst. lectr. Keio U., Tokyo, 1971-78, assoc. prof., 1978-85, prof., 1985—; vis. assoc. Darwin Coll., Cambridge, 1993; vis. scholar St. John's Coll., Cambridge, 1993-94. Author, co-editor: Aspects of Malory, 1981; co-editor: Medieval English Studies Past and Present, 1990; co-author: New Science Out of Old Books: Studies in Manuscripts and Early Printed Books, 1995, Chaucer in Perspective, 1999; editor-in-chief Poetica, 1993—. Trustee The New Chaucer Soc., 2000—; councillor of bd. English Lit. Soc. Japan, Tokyo, 1995—; trustee Japan Soc. Medieval English Studies, Tokyo, 1995—; dir. The Humanities Media Interface Project, Keio U., Tokyo, 1999—. Fellow Soc. Antiquaries London. Office: Keio Univ Dept English, Mita Minatoku, Tokyo 108, Japan

TAKANAKA, KIMIO, economist; b. Tokyo, Aug. 14, 1961; s. Tokujiro and Rinko (Kobayashi) T.; m. Miki Takada, Feb. 12, 1994; children: Haruka Clara, Kazuki. BA in Econs., St. Paul's (Rikkyo) U., 1986, D of Internat Econs, 1992; D of Engring., Tokyo Inst. Tech., 2000. Economist Japan External Trade Orgn., Tokyo, 1986-89; rsch. assoc. World Econ. Info. Svcs., Tokyo, 1989-91; rsch. assoc., project coord. Stanford (Calif.) U., 1991-93; dir., chief economist Jetro, Toronto, Ont., Can., 1993-96; dep. dir. Japan External Trade Orgn., Tokyo, 1996-97; dir., assoc. prof. Takushoku U., Tokyo, 1997-2000, prof., 2000—, assoc. dean faculty internat. devel., 2000—; prof. disting. fellow World Econ. Info. Svcs., Tokyo, 1997—; com. mem. Govtl. Indsl. Structure Com. of Japan, Tokyo, 1991, chmn. sub-com. for internat. rels. Govtl. Com. for Econ. Structure of Japan, Tokyo, 1991. Author: (books) Asia Sogo-izon no Jidai, 1990, Nichi-bei Sogo-izon no Keizaigaku, 1993 (Mitsui award, Suntory award 1993), Foreign Direct Investment in the United States, 1993. Chmn. Hiroshima-area Indsl. and Internationalization Com., Horoshima, 1989; rep. Rikkyo U. Alumni Assn., Tokyo, 1991—. Recipient Nitobe Inazo award Nitobe Inazo Meml. Orgn., Tokyo, 1984, Mitsui Meml. award for Internat. Trade, Mitsui Trade and Econ. Inst., Tokyo, 1993. Avocations: scuba diving, golf. Office: Takushoku U, 4-14 Kohinata 3-chome, Bunkyo-ku 112-8585, Japan

TAKANISHI, LILLIAN K., elementary school educator; b. Koloa, Hawaii, May 19, 1935; d. Saburo and Ayano (Ishida) Kunioka; m. Kenso Takanishi, July 11, 1959; children: Kendra Shizuyo, Kendace Tami. BS in Edn., N.E. Mo. State Tchrs. Coll., 1956; postgrad., U. Hawaii. Cert. profl. edn. Tchr. grade 4 Eleele (Hawaii) Sch., ret., 1990, site coord. After Sch. Plus Program, 1990-97, facilitator parent cmty. network ctr., 1990-97; facilitator parent community network ctr., Eleele Sch., 199-97; asst. dir. Eleele/Kamehameha Summer Sch., 1991, 92, 93; tchr. Waimea/Kamehameha Summer Sch., 1994. Adv. jr. Girl Scouts of the U.S., sr. 4H Club, jr. Y-Teens, Civil Air Patrol. Recipient Kauai Dist.'s Dept. of Edn. Sustained Superior Performance and Employee of Yr. award, 1992-93. Mem. Hawaii State Tchrs. Assn. (v.p., sec., treas. Kauai chpt.), Parent Teacher Student Assn. (treas., grade level chmn.), Kau Ele Pepe Safety Action Team, Nana's House (bd. dirs. 1997—), Ho'o Lokahi, Delta Kappa Gamma (2d v.p. Eta chpt., sec.). Home: PO Box 396 Eleele HI 96705-0396

TAKANO, SUSUMU, gastroenterologist; b. Mitaka, Japan, May 4, 1957; parents Atsuto and Mieko Takano; children: Satoru, Yutaka. MD, Chiba U., 1982. Physician Chiba (Japan) U. Hosp., 1982-92; dir. palliative care unit, med. record mgr. Kawasaki (Japan) Social Ins. Hosp., 1992—. Author: Viral Hepatitis and Liver Diseases, 1994; contbr. articles to profl. jours. Avocations: playing violin, travel. Office: Kawasaki Social Ins Hosp, Tamachi 2-9-1, Kawasaki 210-0822, Japan

TAKAO, KUNORI, surgeon; b. Sendai, Japan, Jan. 5, 1945; s. Masao and Mine (Okuyama) K.; m. Keiko Nishi, Mar. 14, 1971; children: Takayoshi, Emiko, Takahiro. B, Tohoku Univ., Sendai, 1969. Researcher Tohoku Univ., Sendai, 1971-79, asst. prof., 1979; rsch. fellow Karolinska Inst., Stockholm, Sweden, 1977-78; surgeon Iwaki-kyoritsu Hosp., Iwaki-shi, Japan, 1979—. Contbr. articles to profl. jours. Leader Kuze Field String Orchestra, Iwaki-Shi, 1990—; com. mem. Nat. Health Ins. Assn., Fukushima-ken, Japan, 1996—. Mem. Japanese Soc. for Surgery, Japanese Soc. Transplantation, Japanese Cancer Assn. Avocation: playing violin. Office: Iwaki-kyoritsu Hosp, Uchigo Mimaya, Iwaki shi 973-8402, Japan

TAKASAKI, AKITO, engineering educator, researcher; b. Kyoto, Japan, June 5, 1959; s. Hideo and Emiko (Egawa) T.; m. Kiyoko Minami, Aug. 30, 1989; 1 child, Kento. B Engring., Shibaura Inst. Tech., Tokyo, 1982; M Engring., Tokyo Inst. Tech., 1984, D Engring., 1988; DSc, Hiroshima (Japan) U., 1996. Rschr. Japan Atomic Energy Rsch. Inst., Ibaraki, Japan, 1987-88, 90-91, OECD Halden (Norway) Reactor Project, 1988-90; rsch. assoc. Nat. Def. Acad., Yokosuka, Japan, 1991-96; asst. prof. Shibaura Inst. Tech., 1996-98, assoc. prof., 1998—; reviewer Israel Sci. Found., 1995. Contbr. articles to profl. jours. Rsch. grantee Kato Sci. Found., Tokyo, 1995; rsch. grantee Hosakawa Powder Tech. Found., Osaka, 1999. Mem. AIME, ASM Internat., Materials Rsch. Soc. Achievements include research on mechanical engineering and materials science. Home: 83-1-107 Minami-Nakano, Omiya, Saitama 330-0826, Japan Office: Shibaura Inst Tech, Omiya, Saitama 330-8570, Japan

TAKASE, KENJI, biochemist, researcher; b. Kounosu, Saitama, Japan, Jan. 9, 1950; s. Noboru and Sumi (Nishio) T.; m. Akiko Iino, Dec. 5, 1993. B degree, Hokkaido U., Sapporo, Japan, 1972, M degree, 1974, PhD, 1978. Rsch. assoc. U. Kans. Med. Ctr., Kansas City, 1978-82, Brandeis U., Waltham, Mass., 1982-83, N.Y. Dept. Health, Albany, 1984; sr. rsch. scientist Nat. Inst. Agrobiol. Resources, Tsukuba, Japan, 1984—. Mem. Japanese Vegetarian Soc. (bd. dirs.). Avocations: playing the piano, listening to classical music, skiing, tennis. Office: Nat Inst Agrobiol Resources, 2-1-2 Kannondai, Tsukuba Ibaraki 305-8602, Japan

TAKASE, KENSAKU, neurosurgeon, neurosonologist; b. Tokushima, Japan, Nov. 12, 1955; s. Hiroshi and Hiroko (Murao) T.; m. Katsuko Ikezoe, Sept. 15, 1986; children: Ayako, Yukako. Grad., U. Tokushima (Japan), 1980, MD (hon.), 1992. Diplomate Japanese Bd. Neurological Surgery. Resident dept. anesthesiology U. Tokushima, 1986-87, resident dept. neurological surgery, 1987-88, asst. tchr. dept. neurological surgery Sch. Medicine, 1988-89; dir. neurological surgery Taoka Hosp., Tokushima, 1989-91; chief neurological surgery Tokushima Prefectural Ctrl. Hosp., 1991—. Author: TCD Manual, 1996; mem. editl. bd. Neulosonology, 1995—. Mem. Japan Neurosurgical Soc., Japan Acad. Neurosonology (exec. com. 1999—). Home: 2-28 Shinnkura-cho, 770-0855 Tokushima Japan Office: Tokushima Prefectural Ctrl Hosp, 1-10-3 Kuramoto-cho, 770-8539 Tokushima Japan

TAKASE, SHIGEHIRO, chemist; b. Nagoya, Aichi, Japan, Aug. 5, 1953; s. Asaichi and Fumiko (Sugiura) T.; m. Toshiko Wada, Oct. 17, 1983; children: Chihiro, Yuki. BS, Nagoya U., Japan, 1976, MS, 1978, PhD, 1987. Rschr. Fujisawa Pharm. Co., Ltd., Osaka, Japan, 1979-85; rsch. chemist Fujisawa Pharm. Co., Ltd., Tsukuba, 1985-92, sr. rsch. chemist, 1993—; vis. Kobe Gakuin U., Japan, 1985; vis. rsch. scientist U. Ill., Urbana, 1992-93. Inventor in field. Avocations: travel, movies, dogs. Office: Fujisawa Pharm Co Ltd, Tokodai 5-2-3, 300 2698 Tsukuba/Ibaraki Japan

TAKASHIMA, SHIRO, biophysics educator; b. Tokyo, May 12, 1923; s. Atsuharu and Yoshie (Miyoshi) T.; m. Yuki Morita, June 26, 1953; children: Nozomi L., Makoto D. BS, U. Tokyo, 1947, PhD, 1955. Assoc. prof. Osaka U., Japan, 1959-63; rsch. scientist Walter Reed Med. Ctr., Washington, 1963-64; asst. prof. U. Pa., Phila., 1964-70, assoc. prof., 1970-76, prof. bioengring., 1976-92; prof. emeritus, 1993—; mem. editorial bd. J. Biol. Physics., The Netherlands, 1977-97. Author: Electrical Properties of Biopolymers and Membrane, 1989; (book chpt.) Principles and Technics of Protein Chemistry, 1968; contbr. articles to profl. jours.; organizer internat. confs. Bd. dirs. Japanese Assn. of Greater Phila., 1983-90. Recipient Vis. Prof. grants Ministry of Edn., Italy, 1984, Japan Soc. of Sci., 1977, Yamada Found., 1990, Disting. Svc. award overseas Japanese Edn., Kensho-Kai, Japan, 1997; decorated for disting. achievements in sci. and edn., Japanese Govt., 1997. Mem. IEEE, Biophysical Soc., N.Y. Acad. Scis. Democrat. Methodist. Achievements include rsch. into dielectric relaxation of biopolymers, electrical properties of excitable mempranes from nerves and muscles. Home: 659 Niblick Ln Wallingford PA 19086-6675 Office: U Pa Dept Bioengring Philadelphia PA 19104-6392

TAKASHIMA, SHOJI, sociology educator; b. Osaka, Japan, Dec. 13, 1931; m. Keiko Ibuki, Mar. 20, 1964; 1 child, Masato. BA, Kobe (Japan) U., 1955; MA, Kyoto (Japan) U., 1957, LittD, 1964. Asst. prof. Kyoto U., 1960-64; assoc. prof. Aichi U. Edn., Kariya, Aichi, Japan, 1964-73; prof. Aichi U. Edn., Kariya, 1973-79; prof. Kyoto Prefectual U., 1979-83, dean faculty of arts and scis., 1981-83; prof. Ryukoku U., Kyoto, 1983-98, dean faculty sociology, 1993-95; prof. Kogakkan U., Nabari, Japan, 1998—, dean faculty of social welfare, 1998—; counselor and mediator Nagoya Family Ct., Nagoya, 1969-81, Kyoto Family Ct./ 1981—. Author: Foundations of Contemporary Sociology, 1981, The Family, Social Welfare and State in Sweden, 1997; co-author: Readings on Japanese Political Society, 1987; editor: Sociology: Theories, History and Problems, 1979, Comtemporary Sociology at the Cross Roads, 1980. Avocations: travel, stamp collecting. Home: 304 Karamaguchi-cho, Teramachi-higashiiru, Karamaguchi-dori, Kita-ku Kyoto 603 8137, Japan Office: Kogakkan U Faculty Social W, 7 Kasugaoka, Nabari Mie 518 0498, Japan

TAKASUNA, MIKI, psychology educator; b. Hitachi, Japan, Feb. 9, 1962; s. Tsuneyoshi and Kiyoshi (Yosoi) T.; m. Toshiaki Hara, Nov. 1990. BA, U. Tsukuba, Japan, 1984, MA, 1986, PhD, 1991. Asst. U. Tsukuba, Japan, 1992-95; lectr. Yamano Coll. Aesthetics, Hachiouji, Japan, 1995-2000; assoc. prof. Yamano Coll. Aesthetics, Hachiouji, 2000—. Co-author: General History of Japanese Psychology, 1997. Recipient Kamitake award Shin-Yuh-Kai, Inst. Psychology, U. Tsukuba, Japan, 1996; postdoctoral fellow U. Mich., Ann Arbor, 1991-92. Mem. Japanese Psychol. Assn., Soc. Neurosci., N.Y. Acad. Scis. Avocation: history of European rock music. Home: Hashimoto 6-36-1-1802, Sagamihara 229-1103, Japan Office: Yamano Coll Aesthetics, 530 Yarimizu, Tokyo 192-0396, Japan

TAKATA, HITOSHI, engineering educator, researcher; b. Kurate, Fukuoka, Japan, Apr. 16, 1944; s. Kumaki and Harue (Kurihara) T.; m. Nahoko Nakashima, July 27, 1971; children: Hiroto, Masae. BS, Kyushu Inst. Tech., Japan, 1968; MS, Kyushu U., 1970, PhD, 1974. Asst. Kyushu U., 1973-74; asst. prof. Kyushu Inst. Tech., 1974-75, assoc. prof., 1975-94; prof. Kagoshima (Japan) U., 1994—. Contbr. articles to profl. jours. Mem. IEEE, Inst. Elec. Engring. Japan, Soc. Instrument and Control Engring. Home: 3-37-26 Seiryo, Kagoshima 890-0032, Japan Office: Kagoshima U, Korimoto, Kagoshima 890-0065, Japan

TAKAYAMA, MACHIKO, humanities educator; b. Tokyo, Apr. 16, 1940; d. Teruhiko and Toshiko (Tabayashi) Onabe; m. Akira Takayama, Jan. 30, 1970 (dec. Jan. 1996). BA, Tokyo U., 1966, MA, 1968; PhD, So. Ill. U., 1990. Lectr. Tsudo Coll., Tokyo, 1968-70; assoc. prof. Edogawa U., Chiba, 1991-94, prof., 1994—; vis. lectr. Tokyo Christian Women's Coll., 1992-94, Surugadai U. saitama, 1996-97, Ibaragi U., Mito, 1998-99, Tokyo U., 1999. Contbr. articles to profl. jours. Mem. Am. semiotic Soc., Japanese Soc. Religious Studies, Japanese Sociol. Soc. Avocations: modern dance, rowing, travel. Office: Edogawa Univ, 474 Komaki, Nagareyama-shi 270-01, Japan

TAKEBAYASHI, SHIGEO, radiologist, educator; b. Tokyo, Nov. 18, 1953; s. Yuhsaku and Keiko (Sugihara) T.; m. Kumiko Watanabe, Mar. 3, 1979; children: Tomoko, Akiko. MD, Yokohama (Japan) City U., 1978, Dr. of Med. Scis., 1986. Resident Yokohama City U. Hosp., 1978-80, staff, 1981-85, instr., 1986-88, asst. prof., 1989-92; chief of radiology Yokohama Kowau Hosp., 1993-96; asst. prof. Yokohama City U. Hosp., 1997-99, assoc. prof., 1999—; vis. fellow Washington U. Med. Ctr., St. Louis, 1988; dir. diagnostic radiology Yokohama City U., Urafune Hosp., 1996-99, assoc. prof., 1999—. Contbr. articles to profl. jours. Mem. Am. Roentogen Ray Soc., Radiol. Soc. of N.Am. (Cum Laude 1997), N.Y. Acad. Scis. Avocation: playing flute. Home: 214 Yamashita-cho Naku-ku, Yokohama 231, Japan Office: Yokohama City Univ Hosp, 3-46 Urafune-cho Minami-ku, Yokohama 232, Japan

TAKEDA, MASAKO, English educator; b. Matsumoto, Nagano, Japan, Sept. 1, 1945; d. Masazo and Ikuko (Nakata) T. BA in Japanese Lit., Kyoto (Japan) U., 1968, BA in Am. Lit., 1970, MA in Am. Lit., 1972. Asst. lectr. Mie U., Tsu, Japan, 1972-73; lectr. Mie U., Tsu, 1973-76, assoc. prof., 1976-88, prof., 1988-91; prof. Osaka (Japan) Shain Women's Coll., 1991—; bd. dirs. Kota Lit. Pochette, Osaka, 1989—. Author: From Japan to Amherst: My Days with Emily Dickinson, 1996; contbr. articles to profl. jours. Mem. Higashi-Osaka Internationalization Com., 1992, 95—, Higashi-Osaka Social Edn. Com., 1993-94. Grantee Japanese Ministry Edn., U. Mass. and Harvard U., 1986-87, Am. Coun. Learned Socs., Amherst Coll., 1993-94, The Fulbright, Mount Holyoke Coll., 1999. Mem. Am. Lit. Soc. Japan, Emily Dickinson Soc. Japan (exec. dir. 1986—), Emily dickinson Internat. Soc. Avocations: music, calligraphy, flower arranging, movies. Office: Osaka Shoin Womens Coll, 4-2-26 Hishiya-nishi, Higashi-Osaka 577-8550, Japan

TAKEDA, RYOYU, hospital administrator; b. Shiga, Japan, Dec. 2, 1928; Ryokan and Tamao (Minamoto) T.; m. Chikuda Masako; 1 child, Yuko. MD, Kanazawa U., Japan, 1952, PhD, 1987. Prof. Kanazawa U., Japan, 1972-94; chmn. rsch. group disorders adrenal hormones Japanes Min. Health & Welfare, 1983-88; pres. Kanazawa U. Hosp., 1984-86, dean, 1993-94; pres. KKR-Hokuriku Hosp., Kanazawa, 1994-99. Recipient Kanazawa Culture award, 1998. Avocation: reading. Home: Kasamai 1-5-20, Kanazawa 920-0965, Japan Office: KKR Hokuriku Hosp, Izumigaoka 2-13-43, Kanazawa 921-8035, Japan

TAKEDA, TAKESHI, chemistry educator; b. Tokyo, July 9, 1949; s. Yoshio and Chiyo (Ohoki) T.; m. Yukiko Aikawa, Mar. 12, 1978; 1 child, Mariko. BSc, Tokyo Inst. Tech., 1972, MSc, 1974, PhD, 1977. Asst. prof. chemistry U. Tokyo, 1977-80; assoc. prof. chemistry Tokyo U. Agr. and Tech., 1981-94, prof. chemisry, 1994—. Patentee in field; contbr. articles to profl. jours., including Chem. Comm., Jour. Am. Chem. Soc., Jour. Organometallic Chemistry, Synlett. Recipient Progress award in synthetic organic chemistry Soc. Synthetic Organic Chemistry, Japan, 1986. Mem. Am. Chem. Soc., Chem. Soc. Japan. Avocations: fishing, gardening. Home: 1-28-9 Kamisoshigaya, Setagaya, Tokyo 157-0065, Japan Office: Tokyo U A&T Dept Appl Chem, 2-24-16 Nakacho, Koganei, Tokyo 184-8588, Japan

TAKEDA, TSUNEHIRO, brain science educator; b. Toyohashi City, Aichi, Japan, July 31, 1948; s. Motokichi and Shizue (Suzuki) T.; m. Harumi Uchiyama, Jan. 1, 1978; children: Tsuneharu, Mika. B, Tokyo U., 1972, M, 1974, PhD, 1977. Rschr. Nat. Inst. Biosci. and Human Tech., Japan, 1977-84; sr. rschr. Nat. Inst. Biosci. and Human Tech., 1984-92, head lab., 1992-97; prof. Tokyo U., 1997—. Inventor in field. Recipient Minister's prize Agy. Sci. and Tech., Tokyo, 1991, Ministry Internat. Trade and Industry, 1992, Tsukuba (Japan) prize Ibaraki Prefecture, 1993. Office: Tokyo U Dept Complexity of Sci and Engrg, Hongo 7-3-1, Tokyo 113, Japan

TAKEDA, YASUTSUGA, manufacturing executive; b. Tokyo, Jan. 8, 1935; s. Rokuro and Shizu (Inaba) T.; m. Tomoko Matsumoto, Oct. 3, 1966; children: Yukiko, Yohko, Hiroko. BS, Tokyo U., 1958, D Engring., 1973; DS (hon.), Trinity Coll., Dublin, Ireland, 1990. Sr. rschr. electro-optics group Ctrl. Rsch. Lab. Hitachi Ltd., Tokyo, 1970-75; dep. gen. mgr. Hitachi rsch. lab. Hitachi Ltd., Omika, Japan, 1978-80; gen. mgr. Ctrl. Rsch. Lab. Hitachi Ltd., Tokyo, 1982-89, exec. dir. bd., 1989-93, sr. exec. dir. bd., 1993-99; pres. Hitachi Koki Co., Ltd., Tokyo, 1999—; guest prof. Osaka (Japan) U., 1997—; presenter in field; pres. Japan Applied Math. Soc., Tokyo, 1991-92, Japan TV Soc., Tokyo, 1994-95. Author: Holography, 1974; contbr. articles to profl. jours. Mem. sci. coun. Ministry of Edn. Japan, Tokyo, 1998—; profl. mem. Sci. Coun., Japan, 1998-99; v.p. World Acad. Biomed. Tech., UNESCO, Paris, 1997-99; chmn. subcom. policy affairs Keidanren Indsl. Tech., Tokyo, 1994-99. Recipient Contbn. award Japan Laser Soc., 1993, Japan TV Soc., 1996. Fellow IEEE (chmn. LEOS Tokyo chpt. 1989-90); mem. Japan Acad. Engring., World Acad. Biomed. Tech. Avocations: golf, go, contract bridge, piano, classical music. Office: Hitachi Knko Co Ltd 20th Fl, Shinagawa Innercity Tower A, Konan 2 Minato-ku Tokyo 108-6020, Japan

TAKEI, NORIYOSHI, psychiatrist, epidemiologist, educator; b. Oyama, Tochigi, Japan, Aug. 3, 1955; s. Yoshio and Sayoko Takei; m. Atsuko Takei, Sept. 15, 1985; children: Tomohide, Hyu. MD, Iwate Med. Coll., Morioka, Japan, 1982; MSc, London Sch. Hygiene/Trop. Med., 1994; PhD, U. Tokyo, 1997. Intern, then resident Tokyo Women's Med. Coll. Hosp., 1982-83, asst. psychiatrist, 1984-89; vis. rsch. psychiatrist Inst. Psychiatry, London, 1989-92, rsch. psychiatrist, 1992-93, hon. lectr., 1993-95, sr. lectr., 1995-98, hon. sr. lectr., 1998—; asst. prof. psychiatry Hamamatsu (Japan) U. Sch. Medicine, 1998-2000, assoc. prof., 2000—; vis. rsch. fellow U. Tokyo, 1994—, Nat. Inst. Mental Health, Japan, 1996—. mem. editl. bd. European Psychiatry, 1997—, Schizophrenia Rsch., 1998—, Internat. Rev. of Psychiatry, 1998—, Acta Psychiatrica Scandinavica, 2000—; contbr. articles to profl. jours. Wellcome Trust travel grantee, 1992, tng. fellow, 1993; rsch. fellow Stanley Found. Rsch. Ctr. Japan, 1999. Mem. AAAS, Brit. Assn. Advancement Sci., Japanese Soc. Psychiatry and Neurology. Fax: 03081 (0)53 435 3621. E-mail: ntakei@hama-med.ac.jp. Office: Hamamatsu U Sch Medicine, Dept Psy, 3600 Handa-cho, Hamamatsu 431-3192, Japan

TAKEKAWA, SHOICHI DANIEL, radiologist, researcher; b. Nagoya, Aichi, Japan, Jan. 18, 1931; s. Satoshi and Fumiko (Kawabe) T.; m. Richi Saito, Jan. 11, 1958; children: Elika, Shunji, Tomoko. MD, Hirosaki (Japan) U., 1957, PhD, 1968; MS in Radiology, Mayo Grad. Sch. Medicine, Rochester, Minn., 1965. Diplomate Japanese Bd. Radiology (examiner 1975-94). Asst. prof. dept. radiology Hirosaki U. Sch. Medicine, 1970, prof., chair dept. radiology, 1987-96; chief dept. radiology Aomori Prefecture Ctrl. Hosp., Japan, 1970-75; chief dept. diagnostic radiology Tokyo Met. Komagome Hosp., 1975-84; prof., chair dept. radiology Dokkyo U. Koshigaya Hosp., Saitama, Japan, 1984-87; dir. ctr. diagnostic imaging Oyokyo Found., Hirosaki, 1996-97; chmn. 70th ann. meeting Japanese Assn. Radiol. Physicists, 1995; pres. 25th ann. meeting Japanese Soc. Angiography and Interventional Radiology, 1996, 6th internat. symposium Interventional Radiology and New Vascular Imaging, Aomori and Hirosaki, 1996; Reese-Hartman vis. prof. diagnostic radiology Mayo Med. Sch., Mayo Grad. Sch. Medicine, Mayo Found., Rochester, 1995; vis. lectr. Hirosaki U. Sch. Medicine, 1997; radiology cons. Akita (Japan) Social Ins. Hosp., 1997; vis. rsch. assoc. in radiology U. Tex. Health Sci. Cctr. at San Antonio, 1997; dir. chmn. rsch. inst. Diagnostic and Therapy Viscular Disease, So. Tohoku Rsch. Inst. Neurosci., Koriyama, Japan, 1998—. Contbr. chpts. to books. Mem. Com. for Assessment of Health Injury from Air Pollution, Kita-ku, Tokyo, 1979-84; mem., chair exam. com. licensing radiology technicians Ministry of Health and Welfare, 1980-83, 86-88; mem. com. for surveillance of radiation from nuc. fuel cycle factory in Rokkasho Village, Aomori Prefecture, 1989-99; judge physician assessment of patients with pneumoconiosis Ministry of Labor, Japan, 1991-97. Carman fellow Mayo Found., Rochester, 1965; recipient Disting. Achievement in Medicine award Aomori Prefecture, 1995, Hirosaki City, 1995. Mem. Japanese Radiol. Soc., Japanese Soc. Magnetic Resonance Medicine, Japanese Soc. Angiography and Interventional Radiology, Radiol. Soc. N.Am., Cardiovascular Interventional Radiology Soc. Europe, others. Avocations: music, golf, playing Go, audio and electronics.

TAKEKUMA, SHINICHI, economist, educator; b. Otaru, Hokkaido, Japan, May 27, 1950; s. Ryoichi and Kiyo Takekuma (Nakata) T.; m. Masayo Kiyohara, Dec. 12, 1981; children: Midori, Yuichi. BA in Econs., Hitotsubashi U., Kunitachi, Tokyo, 1972; MA in Econs., U. Rochester, 1978, PhD in Econs., 1979. Asst. prof. Hitotsubashi U., Kunitachi/Tokyo, 1981-83, assoc. prof., 1983-90, prof. econs., 1990—. Author: Microeconomics, 1989, The Fundamental Theory of Macroeconomics, 1998; contbr. articles to profl. jours. Mem. The Econometric Soc., Soc. for Promotion of Econ. Theory, Nihon-Keizai-Gakkai. Home: 3-21-3 Inogata, Komae 201-0015, Japan Office: Hitotsubashi Univ/Econs, 2-1 Naka, Kunitachi 186-8601, Japan

TAKEMOTO, KIICHI, chemistry educator; b. Osaka, Japan, Feb. 14, 1930; s. Kenzo and Hatsue (Asakura) T.; m. Etsuko Tamaki, Apr. 26, 1959; children: Tatsuo, Mariko. B of Engring., Osaka U., Japan, 1953, DEng, 1962. Asst. fellow Osaka City U., 1953-59, lectr., 1959-64, assoc. prof., 1964-69; prof. Osaka U., 1969-93, Ryukoku U., 1993-2000. Author: Functional Polymers, 1987. Recipient Award for Chem. Soc., 1989, Award for Polymer Sci. Achievements, 1991. Mem. Am. Chem. Soc., Chem. Soc. Japan, Soc. Polymer Sci. Japan. Avocations: travel, railways, stamp collections. Home: Sakae 4-10-26, Takatsuki Osaka 569, Japan Office: Ryukoku U Ext Ctr (REC), Sci Technol Faculty, Seta Otsu Shiga 520-21, Japan

TAKEMURA, KATSUMI, nephrologist; b. Tsuchiura, Japan, Nov. 30, 1959; s. Takeshi and Kazuko (Adachi) T.; m. Miki Kataoka, Dec. 18, 1988; 1 child, Tsubasa. MD, Tsukuba U., Japan, 1984, PhD, 1990. Chief resident Tsukuba U., Japan, 1989-91; dir. nephrology Mito Ctrl. Hosp., Japan, 1991-92, Kamitsuga Gen. Hosp., Kanuma, Japan, 1992—. Author: Guanidino Compounds in Biology and Medicine, 1992; contbr. articles to profl. jours. Congress grantee European Renal Assn., 1998. Fellow Bank Renal Transplantation. Avocations: golf, basketball. Home: 446-4 Kaijima-machi, Kanuma 322, Japan Office: Kamitsuga Gen Hosp, 1-1033 Shimoda-machi, Januma Japan

TAKENAKA, HIROYUKI, pharmacist, radiologist, corporation executive; b. Godo, Anpachi, Japan, Dec. 7, 1957; s. Toshio and Terumi (Kondo) T.; m. Yoko Esaki, June 16, 1985; children: Yuya, Narie. Bachelor Degree, U. Shizuoka, Japan, 1980, Master Degree, 1982, PharmD, 1985; DMedSci, Pacific Western U., 1997. Rschr. Toyobo Co., Ltd., Osaka, Japan, 1985-87; sr. rschr. Nikken Sohonsha Corp., Gifu, Japan, 1987-90, chief rschr., 1991-92; pres. MicroAlgae Corp., Tokyo, 1993—; head MAC Gifu Rsch. Inst., Gifu, Japan, 1994—; vice-chmn. Japan Sound Transmission Analysis of Bone Assn., 1995—. Author: What's MicroAlgae?, 1996. Recipient Honor award China Nat. Coun. Industry, 1996, 2000. Mem. Vitamin Soc. Japan (councilor 1996—), Japan Soc. for Marine Biotech. (ofcl. 1996-98, councilor 1999—). E-mail: takenaka@mac-bio.co.jp. Office: MAC Gifu Rsch Inst, 4-15 Akebono, Gifu 500-8148, Japan

TAKENAKA, TOSHIFUMI, physiologist; b. Tokyo, Jan. 1, 1933; s. Shigeo and Yoshiko (Aso) T.; m. Yoshiko Kitagawa, Nov. 29, 1965; children: Noriko Sakai, Kazuko Mera, Yuko, Naoko. MD, Tokyo Med. and Dental U., 1958, PhD, 1963. Med. diplomate. Vis. fellow NIH, NIMH, Washington, 1963-64; rsch. fellow Dept. Anatomy UCLA, 1967-73; assoc. prof. Tokyo Med. and Dental U., 1973-98; prof. Yokohama City Univ., Japan, 1991-93, dean med. sch., 1991-98; rsch. cons. Riken, Wako, Japan, 1991-99; dir. Kanagawa (Japan) Rehab. Ctr., 1998—; prof. Kokushikan U., 1998—. Editor Jour. of Theoretical Biology. Recipient Nissan Sci. award Nissan Sci. Found., 1981. Avocations: golf, karate, Taichiken. Home: 2-1-5 Kichijojikitamachi, Musashinoshi, Tokyo Japan Office: Kokushikan U Dept Phys, 7-3-1 Nagayama, Tama Tokyo Japan

TAKEOKA, YUKIKAZU, chemist, researcher; b. Hirakata, Osaka, Japan, Jan. 6, 1968; s. Yukiharu and Kazuko Takeoka. PhD, Sophia U., Tokyo, 1996. Postdoctoral fellow MIT, 1996-98; rsch. asst. prof. Yokohama (Japan) Nat. U., 1998—. Recipient Uehara Meml. Found. award, 1996. Mem. Am. Chem. Soc., Am. Phys. Soc. E-mail: ytakeoka@ynu.ac.jp. Office: Yokohama Nat U, 79-5 Hodogaya-ku, Yokohama, Kanagawa 240-8501, Japan

TAKESHIGE, CHIFUYU, university president, retired physiology educator; b. Japan, Oct. 16, 1926; s. Kaoru and Masako (Tsuchiya) T.; m. Kazuko Miyazaki, 1956; children: Fumitaka, Maya, Yoji. MD, Showa Med. Coll., Tokyo, 1952; DMS, Chiba (Japan) U., 1955. Prof. physiology Sch. Medicine, Showa U., Tokyo, 1970-91, prof. emeritus, 1991—, pres., 1994—. Editor book, 1981. Nihon Ryodoraku Assn. (pres. 1994). Home: 4-5-32 Meguroku, Tokyo 153, Japan Office: Showa U, 1-5-8 Hatanodai Shinagawaku, Tokyo 142, Japan

TAKESHITA, OSCAR YASSUO, engineering educator; b. Sao Paulo, Oct. 28, 1966. PhD in Elec. Engring., U. Tokyo, 1997. Postdoctoral rsch. assoc. U. Notre Dame, Ind., 1997-99; asst. prof. Ohio State U., Columbus, 1999—. Mombusho scholar Ministry of Edn. of Japan, 1991-97; grantee Ind. Space Grant Consorium, 1998, Ohio State U., 1999. Mem. IEEE Info. Theory Soc., IEEE Comms. Soc. Fax: (614) 292-7596. Office: Ohio State U 2015 Neil Ave Columbus OH 43210-1210

TAKEUCHI, AKIRA, neurophysiologist, educator; b. Tokyo, May 5, 1927; parents Naohiko and Toshi (Sawabe) T.; m. Noriko Tanaka, Apr. 25, 1954; 1 child, Keiko. MD, U. Tokyo, 1951, PhD, 1958. From assoc. prof. to prof. Juntendo U., Tokyo, 1956-93; prof. emeritus Juntendo U., 1993—; dep. dir. City of Hope Med. Ctr., Duarte, 1966-68; dean Juntendo U., 1988-91. Recipient purple ribbon medal Govt. Japan, 1990. Mem. AAAS, Japan Physiol. Soc., N.Y. Acad. Scis. Home: 1-11-10 Wakamiya Nakanoku, Tokyo 165-0033, Japan

TAKEUCHI, HIROSHI, marketing professional; b. Edogawa-ku Tokyo, June 26, 1946; s. Sotoyuki and Nobuko (Tsujiguchi) T.; m. Noriko Yamazaki, Apr. 29, 1973; 1 child, Riho. BS, Waseda U., 1969, MS, 1971, PhD, 1976. Sr. researcher ctrl. rsch. lab. Hitachi Ltd., Tokyo, 1984-90, sr. engr. med. systems divsn., 1990-91, dept. mgr., 1991—. Contbr. articles to profl. jours. Recipient Richard M. Fulrath Pacific award Am. Ceramic Soc., 1991. Mem. IEEE (sr., adminstrv. com. ultrasonics, ferroelectrics and frequency control soc. 1991-93), N.Y. Acad. Scis., Internat. Soc. for Optical Engring. Avocations: piano, guitar, hiking, swimming, gardening. Home: Minoridai 700-15, Matsudo 270-2231, Japan Office: Hitachi Ltd Med Sys Divsn, Marunouch 1-5-1 Chiyoda-ku, Shinagawa-ku Tokyo 100-8220, Japan

TAKEUCHI, KATSUHIKO, chemical engineer; b. Tokyo, Apr. 10, 1941; s. Ken Hisamoto and Fusako Takeuchi; m. Hiroko Tsuji; children: Masahiro, Toshiki, Makoto. B in Engring., Kyoto U. With Toyo Engring. Corp., Japan, 1966—, tech. advisor, 1976—. Contbr. articles to profl. jours. Mem. AIChE, Am. Chem. Soc., DECHEMA. Avocations: sports, Japanese chess. Office: Toyo Engring Corp, 8-1- Akanehama 2-chome, Narashino-shi Chiba 275, Japan

TAKEUCHI, KEIICHI, geography educator; b. Chigasaki, Japan, Dec. 7, 1932; s. Kyoichino and Yasuko (Chikami) T.; m. Matelda Lamperti, Aug. 1, 1963; children: Noemi, Sarinah. BS, U. Tokyo, 1956, MS, 1956. Lectr. Hitotsubashi U., Tokyo, 1966-68, assoc. prof., 1968-74, prof., 1974-92, prof. emeritus, 1992—; prof. Komazawa U., Tokyo, 1992—; chmn. Commn. on the History of Geog. Thought, Internat. Geog. Union, 1988-94; dir. Japan Cultural Inst. Rome, 1989-92. Recipient Premio Guido Donso, Assn. Mezzogiorno-Europa, Naples, 1993. Mem. Società Geografica Italiana (corr.),

Human Geog. Soc., Assn. Am. Geographers, Japan Assn. Econ. Geography (pres. 1993-2000), Assn. Japanese Geographers (pres. 1993-95). Home: 4-14-23 Higashi, Kunitachi Tokyo 186-0002, Japan

TAKEUCHI, SEIICHI, dean, engineering educator; b. Kanazawa, Japan, Jan. 17, 1936; s. Kinzo and Mitsue (Nakata) T.; m. Gleda Gaye Hall, June 12, 1971; children: Seiichi Jr., Toshiharu, Yasuyo. BS, Tokyo Denki U., 1960; MS, Poly. Inst. Bklyn., 1969; PhD, NYU, 1974. Rsch. scientist Microwave Rsch. Inst. Poly. Inst. Bklyn., 1972-74; dep. gen. mgr. fiber optic divsn. Sumitomo Elec. Industries, Yokohama, Japan, 1984-85, gen. mgr. opto electronics labs., 1986-88, sr. gen. mgr. rsch. and devel. group, 1989-91, corp. sr. gen. mgr., 1991-97; dean, prof. Tokyo Denki U., 1997—. Fellow IEEE. Avocations: golf, tennis. Home: 460 Izumicho Izumiku, Yokohama City Japan Office: Tokyo Denki U 2-2 Kanda, Nishiki-cho Chiyoda-ku, Tokyo Japan

TAKHAR, HARMINDAR SINGH, scientist, engineering educator; b. Dist. Jalandhar, Panjab, India, Sept. 10, 1933; arrived in U.K., 1961; s. Narajan Singh and Hukam Kaur Takhar; m. Vidya Devi, Dec. 23, 1962; children: Sonyan, Indra, Rajinder Singh. BSc, Delhi U., 1953; MSc, Birmingham (Eng.) U., 1964; PhD, Manchester (Eng.) U., 1967, DSc, 1991. Scientist India Meteorol. Dept., Delhi, 1957-60, Trent River Bd., Nottingham, U.K., 1961-63; lectr., reader dept. engring. U. Manchester, 1966-99. Contbr. over 250 articles to profl. jours. Recipient Merited Students award Govt. of India, 1950-53, Rsch. Studentship award D.S.I.R. U.K., London, 1963-66. Fellow Royal Meteorol. Soc. (pres. Manchester br. 1975-79), Royal Aero. Soc. London. Sikh. Avocations: reading Indian poetry, classical music, history. Home: 75 The Avenue, Sale, Manchester M33 4GA, England

TAKIGAWA, TADAHIRO, physicist; b. Saitama, Japan, May 13, 1945; s. Koichi and Yuko (Ariyama) T.; m. Masako Katou, Nov. 14, 1975; 2 children. Bachelors degree, U. Tokyo, 1969, masters degree, 1971, doctoral degree, 1974. Sr. mgr. Toshiba Corp., Kawasaki, Japan, 1990-96, sr. fellow, 1996—; chairperson PhotoMark Japan, 1998—. Editor: ULSI Lithography Innovation, 1994; adv. editor Microelectronic Engring., 1990—. Recipient prize Japanese Soc. for Promotion of Machine Industry, 1995. Mem. Soc. Photo-Optical Instrumentation Engrs., Assn. Super-Advanced Electronics Techs. (mgr. 1996), Japan Soc. Applied Physics (bd. dirs. 1997-98), Vacuum Soc. Japan (bd. dirs. 1988-97). Home: 3-6-2-1012 Hisamoto, Takatsu-ku, Kawasaki 213-0011, Japan Office: Toshiba Semicon Co Microele, 8 Shinsugita-cho, Isogo-ku, Yokohama 235-8522, Japan

TAKIN, MANOUCHEHR, think tank member; b. Tehran, Mar. 15, 1942; s. Ali-Mohammad Takin and Batoul Khormachi; m. Maryam Shakibnia, Aug. 10, 1973; children: Sharmin, Ramin. BSc in Geology with honours, Manchester U., 1963; PhD in Geophysics, Cambridge U., 1967; MBA, Indsl. Mgmt. Inst., Tehran, 1977. Geologist, geophysicist The Oil Consortium, Tehran, 1967-70, Geolog. Survey of Iran, Tehran, 1970-74; sr. geologist AMOCO Internat., Iran-PanAm., Chgo. and Tehran, 1974-75; exploration mgr. Ultramar Iran Oil Co., Tehran, 1975-78; acting head exploration/prodn. rsch. Nat. Iranian Oil Co., Tehran, 1978-81; sr. officer OPEC, Vienna, 1981-90; sr. petroleum upstream analyst Ctr. for Global Energy Studies, London, 1990—; part-time instr. various univs., Iran; participant various radio and TV programs including BBC, CNN, CNBC, Canada BC, others. Contbr. articles to profl. jours. Mem. Am. Assn. Petroleum Geologists, Am. Geophys. Union, Inst. Petroleum Iran, Petroleum Exploration Soc. of Gt. Britain, Soc. for Contemporary Iranian Studies (mem. coun. 1995—), Inst. Petroleum London, Iran Islamic Soc. Engrs., Soc. Petroleum Engrs. Moslem. Avocations: swimming, tennis, hiking, Persian calligraphy, social studies. E-mail: takin@cges.co.uk. Home: 38 Viceroy Ct, Prince Albert Rd, London NW8 7PR, England Office: Ctr Global Energy Studies, 17 Knightsbridge, London SW1X 7LY, England

TAKIZAWA, HIDEAKI, gastroenterologist; b. Saitama, Japan, July 17, 1960; s. Eiichi and Youko Takizawa; m. Kyoko Kimura, Nov. 10, 1991; children: Hiroki, Naoki. MD, Niigata U., Japan, 1985, DPhil, 1992. Resident Niigata U. Hosp., 1985, physician, 1988-90; rsch. fellow gastroenterology Niigata U., 1986-87; physician Kouseiren Murakami Hosp., Murakami, Japan, 1991; asst. chief gastroenterology Nagaoka Red Cross Hosp., Japan, 1992-96; chief gastroenterology Kido Hosp., Niigata, 1997—. Author: Digestion, 1995; contbr. articles to profl. jours. Mem. Japanese Soc. Gastroenterology, Japanese Soc. Internal Medicine, Japan Gastroenterol. Endoscopy Soc. Office: Kido Hosp, 5-2-1 Kamikido, Niigata 950-0891, Japan

TAKIZAWA, KUNIHARU, optoelectronics researcher, educator; b. Fukaya, Saitama, Japan, Aug. 11, 1945; s. Shohei and Take (Maruyama) T.; m. Teruko Hirashima, Oct. 25, 1976; children: Ayako, Taeko, Naoko. B in Engring., Tohoku U., Sendai, Japan, 1968, D in Engring., 1987. Sr. rschr. Sci. and Tech. Rsch. Labs. NHK (Japan Broadcasting Corp.), Tokyo, 1986-93, dir. advanced material rsch. divsn., 1994-97, dir. advanced imaging devices rsch. divsn., exec. rschr., 1997-00; prof. optoelectronics Seikei U., 2000—; mem. dept. Japan Nat. Com. for Radio Sci., Tokyo, 1991—; mem. optoelectronics 130 com. Japan Soc. for the Promotion of Sci., Tokyo, 1992—, chmn. optoelectronics 130 com., 1997—; mem. organizing com. Conf. on Lasers and Electro-Optics/Pacific Rim, Tokyo, 1995-97; part-time lectr.Tokyo U. Agr. and Tech., 1998—, Chiba U., 1999—; vis. prof. Sci. U. Tokyo, 1999-00. Co-author: Optical Computing in Japan, 1990, Data Book of Applied Optics, 1994, Glossary of Optoelectronics, 1996. Recipient award Motion Picture and TV Engring. Soc. Japan, 1992, Tech. award Lighting Designers and Engrs. Assn. Japan, 1992. Mem. Inst. Electronics, Info. and Comm. Engrs. Japan, Japan Soc. Applied Physics, Optical Soc. Japan (Optical prize for excellent papers 1981). Avocations: cycling, walking, gardening, fishing. E-mail: takizawa@apm.seikei.ac.jp. Office: Seikei U Dept Applied Phys Anal Math Lab, 3-3-1 Kichijyouji Kita-machi, Musashino City Tokyo 180-8633, Japan

TAKIZAWA, MAKOTO, computer science educator; b. Tokyo, Dec. 6, 1950; s. Kinjiro and Utako Okamoto T.; m. Etsuko Hoshizawa, Mar. 21, 1982. B in Applied Physics, Tohoku U., Sendai, Japan, 1973, M in Applied Physics, 1975, D in Computer Sci., 1983. Mgr. JIPDEC, Tokyo, 1975-86; asst. prof. Tokyo Denki U., Hatoyama, Japan, 1986-87, assoc. prof., 1987-94, prof., 1994—; vis. prof. GMD, Darmstadt, Germany, 1989-90, Keele U., 1990—; co-chair Internat. Symposium on Object-oriented Reliable Computing Systems, 2000. Author: (books) Distributed Processing, 1996, Database Systems, 1989. Recipient Best Paper awards IEEE/Internat. Conf. on Info. Networking, 1995, IEEE/Internat. Conf. on Parallel and Distributed Systems, 1996. Fellow Info. Processing Soc. Japan (exec. bd. 1999—); mem. IEEE (co-chair 18th internat. conf. distributed computing sys. 1998). Avocation: swimming. Home: 6-20-21-106 Kita-karasuyama, Setagaya-ku/Tokyo 157-0061, Japan Office: Tokyo Denki U/Dept Computer, Ishizaka Hatoyama, Saitama 350-0394, Japan

TAKUMIDA, MASAYA, medical educator; b. Hiroshima, Japan, Jan. 26, 1958; s. Takaaki and Tsuyako (Yamamoto) T.; m. Yoshiko Dewa, Oct. 10, 1984; 3 children. MD, Hiroshima U., 1982, PhD, 1985; PhD, Karolinska Inst., Stockholm, 1988. Clin. asst. Hiroshima U. Hosp., 1985-86, 89-90; guest rschr. Karolinska Inst., Stockholm, 1986-88; asst. prof. Hiroshima U., 1991—; guest asst. prof. Hiroshima Bunka Women's Coll., 1990—; spl. rschr. for intractable disease Ministry for Health and Welfare, Japan, 1996—. Author: (books) Dynamic Properties of the Endolymphatic Sac, 1988, Second International Symposium on Meniere's Disease, 1989, The Vestibula and Oculomotor System, 1990. Recipient Years award Kojinkai, 1994. Mem. Japan Soc. for Equilibrium Rsch. (mem. program com. 1994—, Years award 1997), Prosper Meniere Soc., Barany Soc. Office: Hiroshima U Sch Med, 1-2-3 Kasumi Minamiku, Hiroshima 434-8551, Japan

TAL, JACOB, electronics executive; b. Tiberias, Israel, Nov. 29, 1940; s. Refael and Seniora Tboul; 1 child, Tomer; m. Rivka Barlev. BS, Technion, Haifa, Israel, 1966; MS, U. Minn., 1968, PhD, 1970. Research fellow U. Minn., Mpls., 1970-71; elec. engring. prof. U. Utah, Salt Lake City, 1971-78; research engr. Hewlett Packard, Palo Alto, Calif., 1978-81; founder, owner Motion Control Seminar, Mountain View, Calif., 1981—; founder, pres. Galil Motion Control, Mountain View, 1983—; cons. Control Data, Mpls., 1970-75, Electro Craft, Mpls., 1970-78, Ford Motor Corp., Detroit, 1976-78, Burroughs Corp., Westlake, Calif., 1981-82. Author: Motion Control by Microprocessors, 1984, (with others) Incremental Motion Control, 1978, Motion Control Applications, 1989; contbr. articles to profl. jours. Mem. IEEE, Electronic Motion Control Assn. Avocations: folk dancing, hiking, windsurfing. Home: PO Box 1885 Los Altos CA 94023-1885 Office: Galil Motion Control 3750 Atherton Rd Rocklin CA 95765-3717

TAL, JOSEF, composer; b. Pinne, Germany, Sept. 18, 1910; arrived in Israel, 1934.; s. Julius and Ottilie (Bloch) Gruenthal; m. Rosie Loewenthal, 1933 (div. 1938); 1 child, Reuwen; m. Pola Pfeffer, Jan. 1940; 1 child, Etan. Student, Staate Acad. Music, Berlin; Dr. (hon.), Tel Aviv U., Acad. Music, Hamburg, 1996, Hebrew U., 1998. Dir. Israel Acad. Music, Jerusalem, 1948-52, Israel Centre Electronic Music, Jerusalem, 1961-81; head dept. musicology Hebrew U., Jerusalem, 1965-71; prof. musicology Hebrew U., 1970-84. Composer numerous operas and symphonies. Recipient Israel State prize, 1971, Arts prize City Berlin, 1975, Wolf prize Wolf Found., Jerusalem, 1983; fellow for Rsch. in Electronic Music UNESCO, Paris and U.S., 1955-56, Inst. for Advanced Studies, Berlin, 1984. Mem. Acad. Arts Berlin, Am. Acad. Inst. Arts and Letters (hon.), Verdienstkreuz (1 Klasse), l'Ordre Artes et Lettres (comdr. 1985), Israel Sect. Internat. Music Coun. (pres. 1974-82). Avocations: theatre, film. Home: Hod Jerusalem, 3 Guatemala St Apt 1203, Jerusalem 96704, Israel

TALA, EERO OTTO, internist, chest diseases educator; b. Kiikka, Finland, Sept. 26, 1931; s. Otto Jalmari and Olga Maria (Järvinen) T.; m. Maija-Leena Teinilä, Dec. 4, 1955; children: Juhani, Leena, Marianna, Eeva. MD, U. Turku, Finland, 1957, DMS, 1967, Prof., 1970. Rsch. fellow in pharmacology U. Turku, 1958-61, resident in chest diseases and medicine, 1962-67; assoc. chief physician, chief physician Paimio Hosp., Preitilä, Finland, 1968-94; prof. diseases of chest U. of Turku, 1970-94, dean med. faculty, 1983-85; ret., 1994—; temporary expert WHO, Geneva, 1989—; pres. for Europe, Internat. Union Against Tb, 1982-90, assessor Uppsala Univs./U. Coll. London Med. Sch. Editor: Eurpoean Respiratory Jour., 1976-90; contbr. over 200 articles on pharmacology, medicine and chest diseases to med. jours. Decorated Order of White Rose (Finland). Mem. Finnish Lung Assn. (pres. Turku 1973-76), Hungarian Chest Assn. (hon.), Latin Am. Lung Assn. (hon.), Royal Sci. Soc. Uppsala. Avocation: art. Home: Myllyhaantie 4, FIN-21530 Paimio Finland Office: Paimio Hosp, FIN-21540 Preitilä Finland

TALABATTULA, SRINIVAS, engineering educator, consultant; b. Khammam, India, Sept. 26, 1962; s. Ramabrahmacharyulu and Challapalli (Kamakshi) T.; m. Lakshmi Kaligotla Uma, Apr. 20, 1942; 1 child. BSc with honors, Osmania U., Hyderabad, India, 1983; M Engring., Indian Inst. Sci., 1987, PhD, 1993. Rsch. assoc. Indian Inst. Sci., Bangalore, 1996-98, asst. prof., 1998—. Co-author: Optical Communications, 2000. Recipient nat. merit scholarship Indian Govt., 1978, Mombusho fellowship Japanese Govt., 1992. Mem. IEEE. Avocations: classical Indian music on violin. Office: Indian Inst Sci, Elec Comm Engring Dept, Bangalore 560012, India

TALAMANTES, ROBERTO, developmental pediatrician; b. Juarez, Chihuahua, Mex., June 19, 1952; came to U.S., 1955; s. Cruz and Viviana (Monarez) T.; m. Blanca Yolanda Chavez, Aug. 19, 1972; children: Christian, Steven. BS in Biology, U. Colo., 1972; MD, U. Autonoma Ciudad Juarez, 1979. Rotating intern Baylor Coll. Medicine, Houston, 1980-81, pediat. resident, 1981-84, devel. pediat. fellow, 1984-86; pvt. practice Gen. Devel. Pediatrics, Las Cruces, N.Mex., 1986—; pres. IPA N.Mex., 1993-98; chmn. bd. dirs. Cimarron HMO, 1997—; pres. elect med. staff Meml. Med. Ctr., Las Cruces, 1993-94, pres., 1994-95, sec., 1992-94. With U.S. Army, 1972-74. Fellow Am. Acad. of Pediatrics, Soc. of Devel. Pediatrics; mem. N.Mex. Podiatric Soc., N.Mex. Med. Soc. Republican. Avocations: chess, guitar. Office: Hillside Circle Las Cruces NM 88011

TALANDIER, JACQUES MARCEL, geophysicist, consultant; b. Paris, June 11, 1933; s. Pierre Jean-Marie and Adrienne (Barbe) T.; m. Lucie Moux, Nov. 23, 1972; children: Claude, Cyril. D. U. Paris, 1972. Seismologist Lab. Geophysique CEA, Tahiti, 1959-67, chief, 1968-76, dir., 1976-93; cons. Dept. Analyse et Surveillance de l'Environment, Paris, 1993—, Lab. de Detection et Géophysique, Paris, 1993—, Commissariat à l'Energie Atomique, Paris, 1993—. Contbr. articles to profl. jours. Home: Chateau de Saussiqnac, 24240 Saussignac France

TALÁŠEK, VLADIMÍR KAREL, engineering executive; b. Hranice, Moravia, Czech Republic, Jan. 1, 1938; s. Vladimír and Marie (Pařízková) T.; m. Marie Věra Podivínová, Oct. 28, 1966; children: Ellen, Nelly. Dipl.Ing., Inst. Chem. Tech., Prague, Czech Republic, 1961, Dr., 1967. Asst. prof. Inst. Chem. Tech., Prague, 1961-71, vice-rector, 1991-92; sr. rschr. Ustav Technického Rozvoje A Informaci, Prague, 1971-84, dep. dir., 1984-87; head TUEV Rheinland CR, Prague, 1993-2000, TUEV Umwelt Cent CR, Prague, 2000—; vice gen. chmn. Conf. on Nuclear Waste Mgmt., Prague, 1993. Contbr. articles to profl. jours.; author: EC-Research and Development, 1991; patentee in field. Deutscher Akademischer Austauschdienst fellow U. Munich, 1968-69. Mem. Czech Mech. Engring. Soc. (steering com. 1990—), PANGEA-Nadation Prague, Ambassador Club (Frankfurt). Mem. Citizen Dem. Party. Roman Catholic. Avocations: tennis, skiing, history paintings. Home: Kurkova 1209, CZ 18200 Prague Czech Republic

TALATI, KHUSHROO JAMSHED, software applications architect; b. Bombay, India, Oct. 25, 1955; s. Jamshed Dadabhai and Daulet Jamshed (Tarapore) T.; m. Roshni Phiroze Engineer, Feb. 11, 1985; children: Rutty, Anaita. B of Tech., Kakatiya U., 1977; M of Tech., Indian Inst. of Tech., 1979. Sys. analyst Tata Consultancy Svcs., India, 1979-83, project mgr., 1983-86; project leader Natwest Australia Bank, 1986-88; cons. Westpac Bank, Australia, 1988-90, sys. mgr., 1990-92; chief designer IBM Australia, Sydney, 1992-94; application devel. mgr. IBM, Thailand, 1994-97; practice mgr. Oracle Fin. Svcs. Industry, South Asia, Bangkok, 1997—; cons. IBM, Thailand, 1994-97, Sydney, 1992-94, Australia; tech. dir. Oracle, South Asia. Architect Application architecture of Oracle based distributed (Performance award 1995); chief designer DB2 based client server application, 1992-94. Avocations: reading, travelling, tennis, squash, swimming. Home: Apt 5A Regent Garden Ct, 23/2 Soi 13 Sukhumvit Rd, Bangkok 10110, Thailand Office: Oracle Sys (Thailand) Co, 952 Rama IV Rd Ramaland Bld, Bangkok 10500, Thailand

TALAY, MUSTAFA ISTEMIHAN, federal official; b. 1945; married; 2 children. Grad. in polit. sci., U. Ankara, Turkey. Min. Ministry of Culture, Ankara, 1997—. Democratic Left Party. Office: Min Culture Kultur Bakanligi Opera, Ataturk Bulvari no 29 06050, Ankara Turkey

TALBĂ, LIVIU-IOAN N., electronics company executive; b. Bucharest, Romania, Sept. 10, 1960; s. Neculai V. and Georgeta V. (Irimia) T.; m. Cornelia V. Calin, Oct. 11, 1982; 1 child, Liviu-Nicolae; m. Roxana V. Sturzu, Oct. 2, 1993; 1 child, Cosmin-Mihai. MSc, Poly. Inst. Bucharest, 1985, PhD in Electronics, 1997; Msc in Adminstrn. & Polit. Studies, U. Bucharest, 1992. Engr. Electronica SA, Romania, 1985-91, MIS dir., 1991-92; gen. dir. Pro-Cons. Ltd., Romania, 1992-93; network dir. World Trade Ctr., Bucharest, 1994; CEO Jaclyn SA, Romania, 1994-99, Microelectronica SA, Bucharest, 1999—; expert Romanian Nat. Agy. for Valuation, 1996. Author: Vocal Signal Algorithm for GSM Communication, 1999; editor: Discret and Analogue Signals, 1997; inventor delaying circuit for very high voltage on CRT, 1988, audio-video digital letter with smart card, 1999. V.p. Limba Noastra cea Romania, Chisinau, 1996, Republic of Moldova, Georgeta Jalba Humanitarian Activities, Bucharest, 1999. Recipient awards Sony Mfg. Co. U.K., 1992, AOTS, Japan, 1992, Total Quality Mgmt. Tng. Svcs., Wales, 1992, Harvard U. Sch. Govt., 1999. Mem. Nat. Assn. Microtechs. Romania (pres. 1999), Romanian Industry Assn. Mem. Orthodox Ch. Avocations: piano playing, tennis, philosophy. Home: Str Dumbrava Rosie No 26, Bucharest Sector 2, Romania Office: Microelectronica SA, Str Erou Iancv Nicolae 126, 72996 Bucharest Romania

TALBOT, DAVID KEITH, environmental geochemist; b. Chesterfield, U.K., Feb. 12, 1965; s. Keith D. and June (Goodwin) T.; m. Sarah J. Sidebotham, Mar. 20, 1995; children: Sophie Frances Meradith, Emily Grace Victoria. BA with honors, Open U., 1991; MSc, Loughborough U. of Tech., 1994. Chartered chemist. Mineral surveyor Sharrock Oakes, Derby, U.K., 1985-87; exploration geologist B & H Fuel, Worksop, U.K., 1987; land reclamation specialist DCC, Matlock, U.K., 1988; environtl. engr. CH&P, London, 1988-91; rsch. scientist British Geol. Survey, Nottingham, U.K., 1991—. Contbr. articles to profl. jours. Fellow Assn. of Exploration Geochemists, British Interplanetary Soc. Avocations: astronomy, hill walking, music, caving. Office: British Geol Survey, Keyworth, Nott NG12 5GG, United Kingdom

TALBOT, PETER JENNINGS, financial services executive; b. Norwalk, Conn., June 11, 1961; s. Edward Richmond Talbot and Ellen Jennings Grevatt; m. Kathryn Lynn Nichols, Aug. 18, 1984; children: Kaitlyn Elizabeth, Peter Jennings II. BBA, U. North Fla., 1987. Republican. Episcopalian. Dealer svcs. rep. Chrysler First Comml. Corp., Atlanta, 1987-88; acct. mgr. Chrysler First Comml. Corp., Bloomington, Minn., 1988-89; sr. acct. mgr. Chrysler First Comml. Corp., St. Louis, 1989-91; dist. sales mgr. Chrysler First Comml. Corp., Irving, Tex., 1991-92; credit and collections mgr. PHH-NTS, Ft. Worth, 1992-93; region mgr. Transamerica Comml. Fin. Corp., Schaumburg, Ill., 1993-97; ops. mgr. GE Capital Vendor Fin. Svcs., Danbury, Conn., 1997-98; internat. ops. mgr. GE Capital Telecom Fin. Svcs., Danbury, 1998—. Corp. sec. Cmty. Christmas, Inc., Cary, Ill., 1993-97. Mem. Water's Edge Country Club, Sigma Nu. Avocations: sailing, genealogy, golf, gardening. E-mail: peter.talbot@gecapital.com. Home: 12 Gardan Rd New Milford CT 06776-5200 Office: GE Capital Telecom Fin Svcs 10 Riverview Dr Danbury CT 06810-6268

TALBOT, STEPHEN H., television producer, writer; b. Hollywood, Calif., Feb. 28, 1949; s. Lyle and Margaret (Epple) T.; m. Pippa Gordon; children: Dashiell, Caitlin. BA, Wesleyan U., 1970. Asst. to pres., lectr. Am. studies SUNY, Old Westbury, 1970-73; reporter Internews, Berkeley, Calif., 1973-79; producer, reporter KQED-TV, San Francisco, 1980-89; producer, writer Frontline (PBS), San Francisco, 1992—. Appeared in Leave It To Beaver as Gilbert, 1958-63, also Twilight Zone, Perry Mason, Lassie, others; prodr., co-writer for Frontline: The Best Campaign Money Can Buy (Columbia U. Dupont award), 1992, Rush Limbaugh's America, 1995, The Long March of Newt Gingrich, 1996, Justice for Sale, 1999; prodr.: (PBS-TV) Beryl Markham, 1986, Ken Kesey, 1987, Carlos Fuentes, 1989, Maxine Hong Kingston, 1990, John Dos Passos, 1994, Frontline: Spying on Saddam, 1999; producer, writer: (documentary) The Case of Dashiell Hammett, 1982 (Peabody award, Edgar Allan Poe award), 1968: The Year That Shaped a Generation, 1998; co-producer, reporter: (documentary) Broken Arrow, 1980 (George Peabody & George Polk award), others; prodr., writer: (Frontline spl.) The Battle Over School Choice, 2000. Recipient Thomas Storke Internat. Journalism award World Affairs Coun. No. Calif., San Francisco, 1983, 86, Golden Gate award San Francisco Film Festival, 1986, 89, Emmy award, NATAS, 1980-81, 82-83, 87-88, 90-91. Mem. Writer's Guild Am. West, Am. Fedn. TV and Radio Artists. Office: Ctr Investigative Reporting 500 Howard St Ste 206 San Francisco CA 94105-3027

TALBOTT, BEN JOHNSON, JR., lawyer; b. Louisville, May 2, 1940; s. Ben Johnson and Elizabeth (Farnsley) T.; m. Sandra Riehl, Oct. 19, 1963; children: Elizabeth, Betty, John, Ben, Sandra. AB magna cum laude, Xavier U., Cin., 1961; LLB, Harvard U., 1964. Bar: Ky. 1965, U.S. Ct. Appeals (6th cir.) 1967. Law clk. to presiding justice U.S. Dist. Ct. Ky., Louisville, 1964-65; assoc. Middleton, Reutlinger & Baird, Louisville, 1965-68, ptnr., 1968-80; ptnr. Westfall, Talbott & Woods, Louisville, 1980-2000, Talbott & Talbott, PLLC, Louisville, 2000—; atty. Stitzel-Weller Distillery, 1970-72, Louisville Gen. Hosp., 1974-83, Louisville and Jefferson County Bd. Health, 1974-80, U. Louisville, Louisville, 1980—. Mem. adv. bd. Louisville 15, Sta. WKPC-TV, Bd. dirs., 1972-74, pres. 1974; past bd. dirs. U. Louisville Found., U. Louisville Med. Sch. Fund Orgn.; bd. dirs. Louisville Theatrical Assn., 1971—, pres., 1975-76, chmn., 1977-78; bd. dirs. Def. Enterprise Fund, 1994—; bd. dirs. Macauley Theatre, 1975, TARC Adv. Com., 1971, Jefferson County Capital Constrn. Com., 1971, Louisville Orch., 1976-86, pres., 1979-81; bd. trustees, trustee U. Louisville, 1970-79, sec., 1974, vice chmn., 1975, chmn. fin. com., 1976; bd. dirs. Ky. Ctr. for the Arts, 1983—, Louisville Lung Assn., 1974-75, treas., 1975; bd. dirs. Historic Homes Found., 1972-78, 95-97, 2000—, v.p. 1978, advisor, atty. 1978-98; bd. regents Whitehall, 1993—. Named Outstanding Young Man of Louisville, Louisville Jaycees, 1976. Mem. ABA, SAR, Ky. Bar Assn. (chmn. 1989, Gen. Practice Session of the CLE), Louisville Bar Assn. (past mem. exec. com.), The Def. Rsch. and Trial Lawyers Assn., Harvard Law Sch. Assn. of Ky. (sec. 1965, pres. 1989—), Mayflower Soc., Soc. Colonial Wars, Filson Club, Pendennis Club, Louisville Country Club, Louisville Boat Club, Big Sand Lake Club, Phi Kappa Phi. Avocations: golf, tennis, skiing. Home: 566 Blankenbaker Ln Louisville KY 40207-1167 Office: Talbott & Talbott 501 S 2nd St Louisville KY 40202-1864

TALBOTT, GEORGE ROBERT, physicist, mathematician, educator; b. San Diego, Oct. 1, 1925; s. George Fletcher and Mary (Lanz) T.; BA with honors, UCLA, 1960; DSc, Ind. No. U., 1973. Physicist, mem. tech. staff Rockwell Internat. Co., Anaheim, Calif., 1960-85; mem. faculty thermodynamics Pacific States U., 1971-77, prof., 1972-80, chmn. dept. math. studies, 1973-80; lectr. computer sci. Calif. State U., Fullerton, 1979—; cons. physics, computer sci.; disting. guest lectr. Brunel U., London, 1974, 76; spl. guest Forschungsbibliothek, Hannover, W. Ger., 1979; assoc. editor KRONOS jour., Glassboro (N.J.) U., 1978—; chief computer scientist and edml. videotape dir. Specialized Software, Wilmot, Wis., 1982—; phys. scientist and rsch. assoc. San Diego Mus. Man, 1993—. With M.C., U.S. Army, 1956. Recipient Vis. Scholar's award Western Mich. U., 1979; elected to Herbert Hoover H.S. Hall Fame, San Diego, 1998. Mem. Am. Soc. Med. Technologists, Am. Math. Soc., Math. Assn. Am., Am. Soc. Clin. Pathologists (lic. med. lab. technologist), Sigma Xi. Buddhist. Author: Electronic Thermodynamics, 1973; Philosophy and Unified Science, 1977, Computer Applications, 1989, Sir Arthur and Gravity, 1990, Fermat's Last Theorem, 1991, The Signal Processing Library, 1995; co-inventor burner. Home: 4031 E Charter Oak Dr Orange CA 92869-2611

TALEB, AHSENE MEBAREK, school administrator, criminologist, educator; b. Taher, Jijel, Algeria, Sept. 16, 1948; arrived in Saudi Arabia, 1993; s. Mebarek Salah and Yamna (Grine) T.; m. Nadira Yamina Boulassel, May 28, 1983; children: Mouna, Yasmine, Samia, Samir, Anis, Karim. BA, Coll. Arts, Baghdad, Iraq, 1970; grad. studies diploma, Internat. Sch. Grad. Studies, Stockholm, 1974; MA in Sociology, Stockholm U., 1976; PhD in Comparative Studies, U. Essex, Colchester, Eng., 1987. Lectr. U. Constantine, Algeria, 1980-84, sr. lectr., 1984-87, assoc. prof., 1987-93, chmn. sociology dept., 1987-93, sci. coun. dir., 1991-93; chmn. social sci. dept. Naif Arab Acad., Riyadh, Saudi Arabia, 1994—; sci. cons. Naif Arab Acad., Riyadh, 1993-99, mem. sci. coun. Naif Arab Acad., 1997-98, cons. Coun. Arab Mins. of Interior, Tunis, 1996-99. Author: (books) The City and the Crime, 1987, Criminology, 1987, Crime and Punishment, 1988, Prisoners-Work, 1999; co-author: (books) Media, Youth and Crime, 1998, Police-Selection, 1999; contbr. sci. articles to profl. jours. With Algerian mil., 1982-84. Recipient Honor Cert., U. Benghazi, 1988, Abu Dhabi Police, 1995. Mem. Arab Youth Rehab. Coun., Algeria Emigrants Assn. (dir. 1998—). Avocations: philately, sports, reading, equitation.

TALEBI, JALAL, professional soccer coach, former player. Player Iran Nat. Team; coach United Arab Emirates, Singapore, Indonesian Olympic Team, 1996; tech. adviser Iran Nat. Team, coach. Office: c/o IR Iran Football Fedn, Mirdamad Ave Razan Jonoobi St, PO Box 15875-6967 Tehran 15875, Iran*

TALEN, WILLIAM CLAIRE, bank executive, financial consultant; b. Ogilvie, Minn., Dec. 28, 1924; s. Clare and Anna (Minnema) T.; m. June Sieswerda (dec.); children: Deborah Ann, William Claire Jr., Julie, Ruth Elizabeth, Mary June; m. Caroline Sarah Hall, July 31, 1982; children: Caroline Rich, Robert Lassiter. BA, Calvin Coll., 1948; student in Banking, U. Wis., 1950; student in Fin. Pub. Rels., Northwestern U., 1955; cert., Am. Inst. Banking, 1961. Pres., bd. dirs. Farmers & Merchants Bank, Watertown, S.D., 1960-62, Univ. State Bank, Green Bay, Wis., 1962-70, New Franken (Wis.) Bank, 1963-71, Algoma (Wis.) Bank, 1964-71; exec. v.p., bd. dirs. Bankers Trust Co., Des Moines, 1970-73; bd. dirs., chair exec. com. First Bank & Trust, Menomonie, Wis., 1973-81; chmn., pres. First State Bank, Edgerton, Wis., 1973-88; pres., bd. dirs. Farmers Savings Bank & Trust, Traer, Iowa, 1974—; pres., chair Talen, Inc.-Bank Holding Co., Traer,

Iowa, 1976—, Farmers Savings Bank & Trust, Vinton, Iowa, 1988—; bank cons., Northfield, Minn., 1973—; v.p. Iowa, Am. Bankers Assn., Washington, 1974-76; pres., owner Farmers & Merchant Bank, Greenwood, Wis., 1992-94. Pres. Menomonie (Wis.) C. of C., 1954-55, Green Bay Symphony, 1968-70, Des Moines Symphony, 1972-73; dir. Green Bay YMCA, Jr. Achievement. 1st lt. U.S. Army, 1943-46. Mem. Am. Mgmt. Assn., Am. Consulting League, Nat. Cert. Profl. Mgmt. Cons., Iowa Ind. Bankers, Iowa Bankers Assn., Bank Mktg. Assn., Am. Bankers Assn., Am. Legion, VFW, Toastmasters (pres. 1953-54), Internat. Fellowship Flying Rotarians, Des Moines C. of C. (dir.), Rotary (Paul Harris fellow 1978, 94), 50 Year Club, Wis. Bankers Assn., 50th Yr. Club, Iowa Bankers Assn. Republican. Presbyterian. Avocations: flying (commercial pilot), Ham radio. Office: PO Box 535 Northfield MN 55057-0535

TALESNICK, STANLEY, lawyer; b. Indpls., June 4, 1927; s. Louis and Rose (Galerman) T.; m. Joan Goldstone, Mar. 16, 1952 (div. Feb. 1967); children: Jill Wilkins, Jane Talesnick, Kay Gilmore; m. Claudia Jean Ferrell, Nov. 28, 1969 (dec.). AB, Ind. U., 1948, LLB, 1950, JD, 1967. Bar: Ind. 1950, U.S. Dist. Ct. (no. and so. dists.) Ind. 1950, U.S. Dist. Ct. (ea. dist.) Wis. 1991, U.S. Ct. Appeals (7th cir.) 1961, U.S. Supreme Ct. 1980; cert. bus. bankruptcy law Am. Bd. Cert. Ptnr. Dulberger, Talesnick, Claycombe & Bagal, Indpls., 1952-57, Bagal & Talesnick, Indpls., 1957-67, Talesnick & Kleiman, Indpls., 1967-74, Dann Pecar Newman Talesnick & Kleiman, Indpls., 1974-94; bankruptcy and creditor's rights counsel Leagre, Chandler & Millard, Indpls., 1995-1999; of counsel Ancel & Dunlap, LLP, —, 2000—; asst. city atty. City of Indpls., 1959-67; instr. bus. law Butler U., Indpls., 1981-82. Chmn. Ind. bd. NCCJ, 1974-76; v.p. Jewish Fedn. Greater Indpls., 1985-89, pres. 1989-91; bd. dirs. Coun. Jewish Fedns., 1986-90; treas. Indpls. Hebrew Congregation, 1967-70; v.p. Indpls. Hebrew congregation Found., 1992-96. With USN, 1945-46, USNR. Disting. fellow Ind. Bar Assn.; recipient Liebert I. Mossler Cmty. Svc. award outstanding & enduring vol. svcs. Jewish Fedn. Greater Indpls. Inc., 1997. Fellow Comml. Law Found.; mem. Ind. State Bar Assn. (ho. of dels. 1985—), Indpls. Bar Assn. (v.p. 1989-90, chmn. comml. and bankruptcy sect. 1985, bd. mgrs. 1994-96), Lawyers Assn. Indpls., Comml. Law League Am., Am. Bankruptcy Inst., B'nai Brith (local pres. 1957-58). Democrat. Jewish. Fax: 317-263-3871. E-mail: st@ancel.net. Home: 8342 Eagle Crest Ln Indianapolis IN 46234-9528

TALGAM, YOAV, electronics manufacturing company executive; b. Tel-Aviv, Israel, Dec. 23, 1954; s. Moshe and Ruth (Yavin) T.; m. Daphna Gornitzky, Sept. 14, 1976; children: Inbal, Erez, Tomer. BSc in Elec. Engring. hons., Technion, Haifa, Israel, 1979; MSc in Elec. Engring. hons., U. Tex., 1987; MBA, Tel-Aviv (Israel) U., 1992. Computer architect, designer Intel, Haifa, Israel, 1979-84; sr. mem. tech. staff Motorola Semiconductors, Tel-Aviv, Austin, Tex., 1984-92; mng. dir. Radway Internat. Ltd, Tel Aviv, 1992-95; pres. Fujitsh Microelec. Israel Ltd., Herzelia, Israel, 1995—. Major, Israel Defense Force, 1973-76. Mem. IEEE. Office: Fuitsh Microelec Israel Ltd, PO Box 12398, 46733 Herzliyya Israel

TALGO, HARRISON, chief administrator tribal government; b. Bylas, Ariz., Feb. 7, 1950; s. Oliver B. Sr. and Eunice Talgo; m. Elouise Talgo, Oct. 13, 1972; children: Geron Randall, Elina Louise, Harrison Jr., Randall Lee. AA, Ea. Ariz. Coll., 1976; student, U. Ariz., 1992. Livestock mgr. Slaughter Mt. Livestock, San Carlos, Ariz., 1980-2000; with early childhood/head start Human Health Svc., San Carlos, 1980-2000; tribal councilman San Carlos Tribal Govt., 1986-2000, tribal govt. chief adminstr., 1993-96; tribal coun. chmn. San Carlos Apache Tribe; cons. U. Ariz., Tucson, U.S. Dept. Agrl., Billings, Mont., 1996-98; housing bd. commr. San Carlos Housing Authority, 1998-2000; bd. commr. Bur. of Land Mgmt., Satford, Ariz., 1998-2000. Active Bylas Luth. Ch. Coun., 1976-86, Ft. Thomas Sch. Bd., 1984-98; bd. dirs. Migrant Head Start, Phoenix, 1986-90; chmn. strategic planning San Carlos Apache, 1994-99; mem. Rep. Party Tax Reform, 1998-99. With USMC. Recipient recognition Inter Tribal Coun. Ariz., 2000. Mem. Nat. Congress Am. Indian, Nat. Indian Gaming Assn., VFW, Am. Legion (post #36), Marine Corps League. Home: PO Box 47 Bylas AZ 85530-0047 Office: Tribal Govt Box O Tonto Ave San Carlos AZ 85550

TALI, TOM, clergyman; b. Port Vila, Efate, Vanuatu, Aug. 1, 1948; s. Tom and Leah Iatehe (Namuli) Kapen; m. Loloma Tukai Tali, Nov. 29, 1978; children: Grace, Alitia, Tom Kapan, Esther. Student, Tangoa Tng. Inst., 1966-68; diploma in theology, Rarongo Theol. Coll., Rabaul, Papua New Guinea, 1974. Ordained min. Presbyn. Ch., 1975. Pastor Presbyn. Uripive Session, Lakatoro and Malekula, 1975-78, Middle Bush Tanna, Tafea, Vanuatu, 1979-82, Pankumu Session, East Malekula, Vanuatu, 1983-84, Paton Meml. Ch., Port Vila, 1985-98; student welfare officer Onescia Presbyn. Coll., 2000—; clk. No. Island Presbytery, Vanuatu, 1976-78, So. Island Presbytery, 1979-82; moderator Presbyn. Ch. Vanuatu, 1993-95. Active in preparing villages to prepare for polit. independence, Malekula and Middle Bush Tanna, 1975-80. Recipient Vanuatu 10th Anniversary medal of honor from Pres. Republic of Vanuatu. Mem. Vila Mins. Fraternal Orgn. (sec. 1988-96). Avocations: diving, hunting, gardening, soccer, singing. Address: Presbyn Ch of Vanuatu, PO Box 150, Port Vila Vanuatu

TALIAFERRO, ROBERT See BROOKE, TAL

TALIB, MOHAMMAD, computer science educator; b. Lucknow, India, June 15, 1965; s. Wasi and Akhtar (Jehan) Husain. BSc, Lucknow U., 1984, PhD in Computer Sci. and Engring., 1998; MSc, Kanpur U., 1986; MS, Birla Inst. Tech. and Sci., 1994; postgrad., Aligarh Muslim U., 1988. Coord. Inst. of Computer Edn., Shahjahanpur, India, 1987; asst. dir. Shia P.G. Coll., Lucknow U., India, 1988-91, head dept. computer sci., 1991-98; reader dept. computer sci. and engring. Shri Ram Murti Smarak Coll. Engring. and Tech., Bareilly, 1998-99; lectr. Multimedia U., Malaysia, 1999—; software engr. Technics, Inc., Pleasanton, Calif., USA, 1996; asst. coord. Indira Gandhi Nat. Open U., Lucknow, 1990-92; dir. Isabella Thouburn P.G. Coll., Lucknow, 1993-94; dir. Nat. P.G. Coll. Lucknow, 1996-97; cons. Trade Tax Tng. Ctr., Lucknow, 1997—; cons. bd. Tech. Edn., Lucknow, 1996—; acad. advisor Bd. of Tech. Edn., Lucknow, 1996—. Contbr. articles to profl. publs.; tech. editor Recent Advances in Scis. and Tech., 1997—, Indian Jour. of Bio Rsch., 1997—. Organizing sec. Mehfil, Lucknow, India, 1984—. Nat. Merit scholarship Govt. of Uttar Pradesh, 1979-81, 81-83. Mem. IEEE, Computer Soc. of India (Lucknow chpt.). Avocations: creative writing, reading, excursion, watching television. E-mail: mohammad.talib@mmu.edu.my or drtalib@hotmail.com. Fax: 603-8312 5264 or 91-522 299810 or 91-522 224563. Office: Fac of Info Tech Multimedia U FoE Bldg, Jalan Multimedia CR 4093 3rd Level, 63100 Cyberjaya Selangor, Malaysia

TALISMAN, RAN, plastic surgeon; b. Haifa, Israel, May 7, 1961; s. Heinrich Fima and Shira Talisman; m. Shlomit Zyskind, Sept. 18, 1989; children: Shiran Roth, Sarah Sonia, Or Haim. MD, Tel Aviv U., 1991. Resident in plastic and reconstructive surgery Hebrew U., Jerusalem, 1991-94; fellow in burn and reconstructive surgery SUNY, Stony Brook, 1994-96; fellow in craniofacial surgery Med. Coll. Wis., Milw., 1996-97; attending staff plastic, reconstructive-craniofacial surgery Haim Sheba Med. Ctr.-Sackler Sch. Medicine, Tel Hashomer, Israel, 1997—. Author: From Infancy to Adulthood, 1998. Lt. Israel Air Force, 1979-82. Mem. AMA, Israel Med. Assn., Am. Burn Assn., Am. Cleft Palate Craniofacial Assn., Am. Soc. Maxillo-Facial Surgery. Jewish. Avocations: painting, football. Fax: 972-3-531-3142. E-mail: rtalisma@netvision.net.il. Home: Hazohar 20, 62339 Tel Aviv Israel Office: Haim Sheba Med Ctr, Dept Plastic Surgery, 52621 Tel Hashomer Israel

TALLÁR, FERENC, philosopher, educator; b. Budapest, Hungary, Nov. 6, 1950; s. ferenc and Gabriella (Vértessi) Teichmann; m. Sára Fedor; children: Márton, Ágnes. MA, Eötvös U., Budapest, 1975, PhD, 1984; Dr.habil., Kossuth U., Debrecen, Hungary, 1996. Assoc. prof. Eötvös U., 1980-85; sr. rsch. fellow Hungarian Acad., Budapest, 1985—; Humboldt fellow U. Konstanz, Germany, 1989-91; vis. prof. U. Hamburg, 1993; dir. Inst. Social Scis. Berzsenyi Coll., Szombathely, Hungary, 1996—; vis. prof. U. Sussex, Brighton, Eng., 1997. Author: Fascination of Utopia, 1984, In Two Items, 1988, Limited Scepticism, 1994, Freedom and the European Tradition, 1999. Fellow Soros Found., 1985-87, Humboldt Found., 1989-91. Mem. Hungarian Soc. Philosophy, German Assn. Analytical Philosophy, German Assn. for Aesthetics. Avocations: cinema, theatre, hiking. Office: BDTF Dept Sociology, Károlyi Gáspár 4, H-9704 Szombathely Hungary

TALLBOYS, RICHARD GILBERT, trade consultant, lecturer; b. Chadwell St. Mary, Essex, Eng., Apr. 25, 1931; s. Harry and Doris (Gilbert) T.; m. Margaret Evelyn Strutt, Mar. 27, 1954; children: Roger, Prudence, Sarah, Peter. B of Commerce, U. Tasmania, Australia, 1960; LLB, U. London, 1968. Pvt. practice acctg. Australia, 1955-62; trade commr. Australian Govt., 1962-68; with Brit. Diplomat Svc., 1968-88, amb. to Vietnam, 1985-87; chief exec. World Coal Inst., London, 1988-93. Co-author: Fifty Years of Business in Indonesia, 1995; editor: Developing Vietnam, 1995. Mem. coun. Royal Inst. of Internat. Affairs, London, 1995—councillor City of Westminster, 1998—. Lt. comdr. Royal Australian Naval Res.; mcht. marine nav. officer, 1947-55, U.K. and Australia. Decorated officer Order Brit. Empire, companion Order St. Michael and St. George. Fellow Inst. Chartered Accts. in Eng. and Wales, Inst. Chartered Accts. in Australia, Chartered Inst. of Co. Secretaries and Adminstrs., Australian Soc. of Cert. Practising Accts.; mem. Traveller's Club (London). Avocations: skiing, cautious adventure. Office: 7 Chapel Side, London W24LG, England

TALLENT, ROBERT GLENN, chemical and environmental engineer, entrepreneur; b. Nashville, July 4, 1954; s. Glenn Oliver and Virginia Jo (Bell) T.; m. Sandra Marie McKenzie, Aug. 2, 1986; 1 child, Emily Suzanne (dec.). BE, Vanderbilt U., 1976; MS, George Washington U., 1996. Cert. Scuba diving instr. trainer, emergency med. technician. Dir. tng. Am. Watersports Co., Oxon Hill, Md., 1980-83; chem. engr. Naval Sea Systems Command, Washington, 1980-87; pres. Caribbean Ventures, Alexandria, Va., 1984-88; dist. course dir. Profl. Assn. Diving Instrs., Va., Md., Del., Washington, 1984—; staff Am. Systems Corp., Chantilly, Va., 1988-89; account exec. Data Link Info. Solutions, Inc., Falls Church, Va., 1989-90; pres. Internat. Diving Inst., 1988-91, Nut'N But Nuts, Stafford, Va., 1990-91, Earthworks Internat., Stafford, 1991-96; engr. Info. Spectrum, Inc., 1994-96, SEMCOR, 1996-97; pres. The Triton Found., 1997—; project mgr. MACI, 1998-2000; exec. v.p. The Curran Group, Inc., 2000—. Author: Caribbean Ventures Dive Travel Notebook, 1986. Commr. Boy Scouts Am., Stafford, Va., 1988-97. Lt. (j.g.) USN, 1976-80. Recipient Wood Badge Boy Scouts Am., 1994, Internat. Cmty. Svc. award PADI, 1994, 98, Silver Beaver award Boy Scouts Am., 2000. Mem. Nat. Eagle Scout Assn. (life mem.), Luv-N-Laffs Clowns, Undersea Med. Soc., Clowns of Am. Internat. Republican. Methodist. Avocations: squash, Chinese culture, music, clowning, scuba diving. Home: 30 Larkwood Ct Stafford VA 22554-1585

TALLENT, WILLIAM HUGH, chemist, research administrator; b. Akron, Ohio, May 28, 1928; s. Charles Othar and Agnes Annette (Johnson) T.; m. Joy Anne Redfield, Aug.23, 1952; children: Elizabeth Ann, Cinda Marie, Raymond Charles. BS, U. Tenn., 1949, MS, 1950; PhD, U. Ill., 1953. Chemist Nat. Heart Inst., Bethesda, Md., 1953-57, G.D. Searle & Co., Skokie, Ill., 1957-64; head new crops evaluation investigations Agr. Rsch. Svc., USDA, Peoria, Ill., 1964-69, chief indsl. crops lab., 1969-74, asst. dir., 1974-75, ctr. dir. No. Regional Rsch. Ctr., 1975-83, regional adminstr. N.E. region, 1983-84; asst. adminstr. Agr. Rsch. Svc., USDA, Washington, 1984-94; tech. transfer advisor Agr. Rsch. Svc., USDA, Beltsville, Md., 1994—. Editor Jour. Am. Oil Chemists Soc., 1998—. Recipient Merit award Gamma Sigma Delta, 1979, Presdl. Rank award for Sr. Execs., 1988, NASA Tech. 2002 award for lifetime achievement in tech. transfer, 1992. Mem. AAAS, Am. Oil Chemists' Soc., Am. Chem. Soc., Soc. Econ. Botany. Fax: 319-354-4059. Home and Office: 831 West Side Dr Iowa City IA 52246-4309

TALLEY, HAYWARD LEROY, communications executive; b. Nov. 3, 1923; s. Roy and Reta (Hayward) T.; m. Emma Mae Chandler, Sept. 2, 1950; children: Brian, Kevin. BS, U. Ill., 1948. Chief engr. Sta. WOKZ-AM-FM, Alton, Ill., 1948-50; pres., gen. mgr. Talley Broadcasting Corp. (sta. WSMI AM and FM), Litchfield, Ill., 1950—; pres. Talley Broadcasting Co. (sta. KBKB AM and FM), Ft. Madison, Iowa, 1960-99, North Cen. Iowa Broadcasting Co. (stas. KLSS, KSMN), Mason City, 1963-83, WAOX, Staunton, Ill., 1999—. Chmn. ofcl. bd. Meth. Ch., 1961-63, 65-66; adv. bd. Lewis & Clark Coll., 1978—. With Signal Corps, U.S. Army. Mem. Nat. Assn. Broadcasters, Ill. Broadcasters Assn., Rotary (pres. Litchfield Club 1989-90), Masons, Am. Legion. Home: 1414 N Harrison St Litchfield IL 62056-1209 Office: Sta WSMI PO Box 10 Litchfield IL 62056-0010

TALLEY, RICHARD WOODROW, accountant; b. Birmingham, Ala., Sept. 10, 1941; s. Alton Woodrow and Alta O. (Tittle) T.; m. Anita Marcell Moses, Jan. 14, 1966; children: Richard Woodrow Jr., Leah Michelle. BS in Commerce and Bus. Adminstrn., U. Ala., 1984. CPA, Ala. Pres. Smither, Talley & Mauldin, P.C., Decatur, Ala., 1964—. Officer Boy Scouts Am., Decatur, Austin Band Boosters, Decatur, PTA, Decatur; mgr., coach Dixie Youth Baseball, Decatur; deacon Ch. of Christ. Served as sgt. USAR, 1964-70. Named Boss of Yr. Decatur Jaycees, 1980. Mem. AICPA, Tenn. Soc. CPAs, Ala. Soc. CPAs, Commerce Execs. Soc. U. Ala., Lions (sec. 1982-83, treas. 1985-86, sec.-treas. 1994-95). Avocations: genealogy, photography. Home: 1266 Brandywine Ln SE Decatur AL 35601-4582 Office: Smither Talley & Mauldin PC PO Box 2067 Decatur AL 35602-2067

TALLEY, TRUMAN MACDONALD, publisher; b. N.Y.C., Feb. 3, 1925; s. Truman Hughes and Helen Nicholson (Macdonald) T.; m. Madelon DeVoe, Oct. 17, 1953 (dec. 1997); children: Melanie, Macdonald, Marina. Student, Buckley Sch., Deerfield Acad., Sorbonne, 1945-46; grad. cum laude, Princeton U., 1949. Assoc. editor New Am. Libr. of World Lit., N.Y.C., 1949-59; editorial v.p. New Am. Libr. of World Lit., 1959-64; pres., editl. dir. Weybright & Talley, N.Y.C., 1966-78; pub. Truman Talley Books with Times Books, 1978-82; with E.P. Dutton, 1983-98, St. Martin's Press, N.Y.C., 1998—; mem. grad. bd. Princeton Tiger, 1950—. Trustee Clinton Hall Assn. Merc. Libr., N.Y.C. With AUS, 1943-46, ETO. Decorated Purple Heart. Mem. P.E.N. Clubs: Anglers, Brook, Maidstone, Southampton Beach. Office: Truman Talley Books St Martin's Press 175 5th Ave New York NY 10010-7703

TALLMAN, ROBERT HALL, investment company executive; b. Creston, Iowa, Aug. 10, 1915; s. Ralph H. and Hazel Verne (Hall) T.; m. Elizabeth Childs, Sept. 19, 1938; children: Susan, Mary, Timothy. BS, U. Nebr., 1937. Trainee to dist. mgr. Firestone Tire & Rubber Co., Akron, Ohio, 1937-50; pres. Tallman Oil Co., Fargo, N.D., 1950-80; chmn. bd. State Bank of Hawley, Minn., 1966-70, 1st Nat. Bank of Barnesville, Minn., 1965-88; pres. Tallman Investment Ent., Fargo, 1980—; pres., dir. Dak Tech. Inc.; dir. Bell Farms. Past pres. Fargo Bd. Edn., N.D. Petroleum Coun.; past pres. St. Lukes Hosp. Assn.; past chmn. trustees 1st Congl. Ch. of Fargo; trustee U. Nebr. Found., 1987—. Mem. Fargo C. of C. (past pres.), Am. Assn. Ret. Persons, Nat. Rifle Assn., N.D. State U. Teammakers Club (past pres.), Fargo Country Club, Kiwanis (past pres.), Masons, Shriners, Elks. Republican. Congregationalist. Avocations: golf, hunting, fishing, travel, photography. Home: 3201 16th Ave S Fargo ND 58103-4517 Office: Box 9723 2108 S University Dr Fargo ND 58103-5342

TALLURI, SRINIVAS, education educator; b. Rajahmundry, India, Nov. 15, 1966; s. Prasada Rao and Prabhavathi Chaganti T.; m. Manogna Anantabhotla, July 31, 1992; 1 child, Dinakar. BS, Nagarjuna U., India, 1989; MS, U. Tex., 1992, PhD, 1996. Engr. trainee VST Industries, Hyderabad, Andhra, India, 1989-90; instr. U. Tex., Arlington, 1992-96, prof., 1996-97; prof. Fairleigh Dickinson U., Teaneck, N.J., 1997-99; cons. Gateway 2000, Iowa. Contbr. articles to profl. jours. Faculty advisor Indian Student Assn., 1999; student mentor, Teaneck, 1997-98. Mem. Inst. for Opers. Rsch. and Mgmt. Scis., Decision Scis. Inst. Hindu. Avocations: bridge, tennis, music. E-mail: talluri@alpha.fdu.edu. Office: Fairleigh Dickinson U 1000 River Rd Teaneck NJ 07666-1914

TALMACI, LEONID, banker. Gov. Nat. Bank Moldova, pres. Address: Nat Bank Moldova, 7 Renasterii Ave, 2006 Chisinau Moldova*

TALMI, YOAV, conductor, composer; b. Kibbutz Merhavia, Israel, Apr. 28, 1943; m. Erella Cottesmann; 2 children. Diploma, Rubin Acad. Music, Tel Aviv; postgrad., Julliard Sch. Music. Artistic dir., condr. Gelders Symphony Orch., Arnhem, 1974-80; prin. guest condr. Munich Philham. Orch., 1979-80; artistic dir. Israel Chamber Orch., 1984-88; music dir. New Israeli Opera, 1985-89, San Diego Symphony Orch., 1990-96, Waterloo Festival, N.J., 1994-95, Que. Symphony, Can., 1999—, Hamburg (Germany) Symphony, 2000—; guest condr. Berlin Philharm., Munich Philharm., London Philharm., Philharmonia, Royal Philharm., Concertgebouw, Paris Orch. Nat., Israel Philharm., Tokyo Symphony, New Japan Philharm., Vienna Symphony, St. Petersburg Philharm., Pitts. Symphony, Detroit Symphony, St. Louis Symphony, Houston Symphony, Dallas Symphony, Montreal Symphony, N.Y. Chamber Symphony, L.A. Chamber Orch., Oslo Philharm., Tonhalle Orch., Zurich, others. Composer: Dreams for choir a capella, Music for Flute and Strings; Overture on Mexican Themes (recorded), 3 Monologues for Flute Solo (pub.), Inauguration Fanfare, Elegy for Strings, Timpani, and Accordion, 1997; recs. include: Bruckner 9th Symphony (Oslo Philharm.), Gliere 3d Symphony, Brahms Sextet/4 Serious Songs, Rachmaninov's Isle of the Dead, Berlioz Overtures, Harold in Italy, Romeo and Juliette, (San Diego Symphony), Tchaikowsky/Schoenberg, Bloch/Barber/Grieg/Puccini (Israel Chamber Orch.); (with Erella Talmi) works for flute and piano. Recipient Boskovitch prize for composition, Israel, 1965, Koussevitzky Meml. Conducting prize, Tanglewood, 1969, Ruppert Found. Condr. competition award, London, 1973, Ahad Ha'am award L.A. Ctr. Jewish Culture and the Am.-Israel Cultural Found., 1997. Fax: 972-9-765-6553. E-mail: talmi@netvision.net.il. Home: PO Box 1384, Kfar Sava 44113, Israel Office: ICM Artists 40 W 57th St Fl 16 New York NY 10019-4098

TALMOR, SASCHA, editor; b. Balti, Romania, Nov. 1, 1925; d. Gershon Starosta and Lily (Lewinson) Ronen; m. Ezra Talmor; children: Edna, Avital. BA with honors, London U., PhD in Aesthetics, 1959. Sr. lectr. in English lit. Haifa U.; editor History European Ideas, 1980-95, The European Legacy, 1996—; mem. Kibbutz Nachshonim, 1945—. Author: Glanvill: The Uses and Abuses of Scepticism, 1981, The Rhetoric of Criticism: From Hobbes to Coleridge, 1984; contbr. articles to profl. publs. Avocation: reading and reviewing novels.

TALONOV, ALEXANDER V., management educator; b. Moscow, Apr. 28, 1958; s. Vladimir M. and Sophia Talonov; m. Maria L. Lvova, 1999. MA, Moscow Inst. Mgmt., 1980, PhD in Econs., 1984; D Econs., State U. Mgmt., Moscow, 1998. Asst. prof. Moscow Inst. Mgmt., 1984-94, assoc. prof., 1994-95, dep. head of chair state and mcpl. mgmt., 1995-98, dep. head of chair facility mgmt., 1998—; mem. Expert Bd. on Innovations in Govt. of Moscow, 1999—; mem. Com. on Support Market Reforms in Mcpl. Sphere, Moscow, 1998—; mem. sci. coun. Ministry of Bldg. and Arch. Policy of Russian Fedn., 1998—. Author: (monographs: Market Economy in Municipal Sphere, Reforming Municipal Economy, 1997. Grantee Internat. Cooperation, USIA, 1999; rsch. grantee State Acad. Mgmt., Groningen, The Netherlands, 1995, Rsch. Triangle Inst., U.S. Agy. Internat. Devel., 1996. Mem. N.Y. Acad. Scis., Geog. Soc. Russian Acad. Scis. Avocations: jogging, travel. Fax: 7 (095) 954-5109. E-mail: tav@edu.ru. Home: Chernitsinsky Pr 6-1-65, 107241 Moscow Russia Office: State U Mgmt, 99 Ryazansky Prospekt, 109542 Moscow Russia

TALT, ALAN R., lawyer; b. Stockton, Calif., June 17, 1929; s. Daniel Henry and Josephine (LeSaffre) T.; m. Marjorie Schutte, Sept. 12, 1953; children: Bradley Alan, Stephen Scott, Mark Kevin, Karen Talt Beardsley. BA, U. Calif., Berkeley, 1951, JD, 1954. Bar: Calif. 1955, U.S. Dist. Ct. (no. and so. dists.) Calif. 1955, U.S. Ct. Appeal (9th cir.) 1955. Law clk. to the chief judge U.S. Ct. Appeal (9th cir.), San Francisco, 1954-55; pvt. practice, L.A. and Pasadena, Calif., 1955—; gen. counsel Kirkhill Rubber Co., Brea, Calif., 1988—; gen. counsel, bd. dirs. KAPCO, Brea, 1985—; gen. counsel Caine, Farber & Gordon, Pasadena, 1986—. Asst. editor: Williston Casebook Contract Law, 1953. Pres. San Gabriel Valley Learning Soc., Pasadena, 1976-77; nat. v.p. Newman Clubs Am., 1949-50. Samuel Bell-McKee fellow, 1948; U. Calif. Berkeley Alumni scholar, 1947. Mem. Calif. State Bar, Jonathan Club, Valley Club (pres.), Ironwood Country Club. Avocations: fly fishing, philately. Home: 1375 St Albans Rd San Marino CA 91108-1860 Office: 790 E Colorado Blvd Ste 710 Pasadena CA 91101-2190

TALUKDAR, BANDANA, biochemistry educator, researcher; b. Calcutta, India, Mar. 21, 1941; d. Sailendra Nath and Sati (Bhaduri) T.; m. Dulal Chandra Majumdar, July 29, 1964; children: Barnali, Debashis, Mahalaxmi. MB, BS, U. Calcutta, 1962, diploma obstetrics-gyn., 1966, PhD, 1980. Biochemistry rsch. officer Ctrl. Rsch. Inst. for Yoga, Delhi, India, 1976; blood bank officer Indian Ministry Health, Delhi, 1977-80; lectr. biochemistry G.B. Pant Hosp., New Delhi, 1980-82, asst. prof., 1983-86, assoc. prof., 1986-89; assoc. prof. Maulana Azad Med. Coll., New Delhi, 1989-91, prof., 1991—, head biochemistry, 1997—; vis. assoc. prof. dept. internal medicine U. Va. Coll. Medicine, Charlottesville; tech. expert Bd. Tech. Edn., Delhi; mem. expert com. for setting up nat. ctr. for yoga Indian Ministry Health and Family Welfare, 1994—. Contbr. numerous articles and abstracts to sci. jours. WHO fellow, U.S., U.K., 1987. Fellow Indian Coll. Geriatrics; mem. Am. Assn. Clin. Chemistry, Internat. Fedn. Clin. Chemistry (life), Assn. Clin. Biochemists India (life), N.Y. Acad. Scis., Assn. Med. Biochemists India (life). Avocations: reading, music. Home: BT-31 Shalimar Bagh, Delhi 110 052, India Office: Maulana Azad Med Coll, Bahadurshah Zafar Marg, Delhi 110 002, India

TALVIK, TIINA, pediatric neurologist; b. Tartu, Estonia, Apr. 21, 1938; d. Alfred Johannes and Liidia (Kôrts) Tanimäe; m. Raul Talvik, Sept. 21, 1961; children: Katrin Gross-Paju, Inga Talvik. MD, U. Tartu, 1962, PhD, 1974, D Med. Scis., 1992. Pediatric neurologist Children's Hosp. Tartu, 1962-68; head Medico-genetics Ctr. Hosp. of Tartu, 1968-75; asst. prof. dept. neurology and neurosurgery U. Tartu, 1975-82, assoc. prof., 1982-91, head dept. pediatrics, 1991-92, prof., 1992; head, prof. Children's Hosp. of U. Tartu, 1991—, head hosp. and dept. pediatrics, 1992—; mem. Med. Commn. on Rehab. Internat., Denmark, 1989; chief pediat. neurologist of Republic of Estonia, Ministry of Health, Tallinn, 1975-93; mem. all union bd. of pediat. neurology Ministry of Health of USSR, Moscow, 1978-89. Contbr. articles to profl. publs. Mem. Baltic Child Neurology Assn. (pres. 1989-94, v.p. 1995—), Am. Acad. Cerebral Palsy and Developmental Medicine (corr.). Lutheran. Avocations: jewelry, art. Home: J Hurda St 10-2, EE2400 Tartu Estonia Office: Children's Hosp U Tartu, 6 N Lunini St, EE2400 Tartu Estonia

TALVITIE, JYRKI KALEVI, lexicographer; b. Hameenlinna, Finland, Dec. 2, 1941; s. Yrjö K.K. and Liili (Lahdentaus) T.; m. Riitta Helena Parpola, July 30, 1966 (div. May 1983); children: Sari, Eeva; m. Maria Cristina Mujica Chiuminatto, July 1, 1983. Mng. dir. Tietoteos Pub., Espoo, 1970—; v.p. Ibero-Am. Found., Helsinki, 1990—; hon. consul Guatemala in Finland, 1987—. Author 17 technical dictionaries in Finnish, Sweden, German, English, and French, 1972-2000; co-author two Spanish-Finnish Dictionaries, 1974-97; author: Mexico and Central America, 1995; contbr. articles to profl. jours. Pres. Suomen DX-Kuuntelijat, Helsinki, 1963-70, Finnish-Mex. Soc., 1975-84; sec. gen. European DX Coun., Helsinki, 1969-70. Avocations: Mayan culture, Latin America culture, car racing, history. Office: Tietoteos Pub, PO Box 22, FIN02881 Veikkola Finland

TAM, ALFRED YAT-CHEUNG, pediatrician, consultant; b. Hong Kong, Aug. 28, 1953; s. Fun and Yun-Ha (Ko) T.; m. Rosana Chan; children: Joyce Joy-Yee, Jonathan Joy-Man, Sebastian Zai-De. MB, BS, U. Hong Kong, 1977; MRCP (U.K.), Royal Coll. Physicians, 1982. Med. officer Queen Mary Hosp., Hong Kong, 1978-79, med. officer pediatric dept., 1979-84; lectr. pediatrics dept. U. Hong Kong, 1984-89; cons. paediatrician Grantham Hosp., Hong Kong, 1989-92; cons. pediatrician Canossa Hosp., Hong Kong, 1992—, Matilda Hosp., Hong Kong, 1992—; hon. clin. assoc. prof. pediatrics dept. U. Hong Kong, 1992—; fellow U. Hong Kong Centre of Asian Studies, 1989—. Sch. mgr. Sunnyside Sch., Hong Kong, 1984-90; bd. dirs. Haven of Hope Christian Svcs., Hong Kong, 1986-92; chmn. Haven of Hope Hosp., Hong Kong, 1990-92; mem. admissions, budget and allocations com. Cmty. Chest, 1992-93. Brit. Commonwealth scholar, 1982-83. rellow Hong Kong Acad. Med., Royal Coll. Physicians of Edinburgh, Hong Kong Coll. Pediatricians (mem. coun. 1990—, found. chmn. 1998—), Am. Coll. Chest Physicians, Hong Kong Asthma Soc. (mem. exec. com. 1989-97), Hong Kong Soc. Pediatric Respirology (v.p. 1997-98, pres. 1998—), Asian Pacific Soc. on Respirology (coun. mem. 1998—); mem. European Soc. Respirology, Am. Thoracic Soc., Am. Acad. Pediat., Asian Pacific Assn. Pediat. Allergy, Respirology and Immunology (v.p. 1998—). Avocations: badminton, golf. Office: 1106 Melbourne Plz, 33 Queens Rd Ctrl, Hong Kong China

TAM, FREDERICK WAI KEUNG, medical researcher, physician; b. Hong Kong, Jan. 3, 1960; arrived in Eng., 1977; s. Mon Kaw and Shing Yuke (Lin) T.; m. Kathy Yuen Ping Cheung. BA, U. Cambridge, Eng., 1982, MB,

B of Surgery, 1984, MA, 1986; PhD, U. London, 1996. Sr. house officer Leicester, Eng., 1986-87, St. James's Hosp., Leeds, Eng., 1987-88; med. registrar Hillingdon Hosp., Eng., 1988-89, Hammersmith Hosp., London, 1989-90; tng. fellow Med. Rsch. Coun., Eng., 1990-93; sr. rsch. fellow Nat. Kidney Rsch. Fund, Eng., 1993-99. Contbr. articles to profl. jours. Mem. Royal Coll. Physicians Eng., Brit. Renal Assn., Brit. Soc. Immunology. Office: Hammersmith Hosp, Ducane Rd Renal Unit, London W12 0NN, England

TAM, KIN YIP, chemist; b. Hong Kong, May 29, 1966; s. Chuen and Chung Kui (Fung) T. BS, Hong Kong Bapt. Coll., 1990; MPhil, Hong Kong Poly., 1992; PhD, Oxford U., 1996. Chemistry tchr. Maryknoll Tech. Coll., Hong Kong, 1989-90; rsch. asst. Hong Kong Poly., 1992-93, vis. lectr., 1992-93; rsch. chemist Sirius Analytical Instruments, Forest Row, England, 1996—. Scholar Elkhon Enterprises, 1989. Office: Sirius Analytical Instrumen, Riverside Forest Row Bus Pk, Forest Row RH18 5DW, England

TAM, NORA FUNG-YEE, science educator; b. Hong Kong, Guangdong, China, Jan. 5, 1954; d. Kam Tam and Lai-ha Wong. BSc with honors, Chinese U. of Hong Kong, 1976, MPhil, 1979; MSc, U. Sheffield, U.K., 1979; DPhil, U. York, U.K., 1982. Tchg. asst. Chinese U. of Hong Kong, 1976-79; demonstrator U. York, U.K., 1979-82; lectr. to sr. lectr. Hong Kong Polytech., 1982-90; sr. lectr. City U. of Hong Kong, 1990-96, assoc. dean, 1996-99, prof., 1997—; gov. Friends of the Earth, Hong Kong, 1990—; hon. prof. U. Xiamen, People's Republic of China, 1997, Nanjing U., People's Republic of China, 1999. Author six books; contbr. articles to profl. publs.; patentee in field. Mem. wetland adv. com. Agrl. and Fisheries Dept., Hong Kong, 1998—; mem. election com. for legis. coun., Hong Kong, 1998; mem. Environtl. Conservation Fund, Hong Kong, 1996; external examiners various univs. and colls. Mem. Soc. of Hong Kong Scholars (chmn. coun. 1999—), Hong Kong Instn. of Sci. (founder, coun. 1992—), Internat. Soc. for Mangrove Ecosystems (life), others. Avocations: traveling, sports, reading. Office: Dept Biol/Chem City U of HK, Tat Chee Ave, Kowloon Hong Kong

TAM, PAUL WING MING, engineering consultant; b. Hong Kong, Hong Kong, July 27, 1956; arrived in Can., 1987; s. Park Shing Tam and Li Kun Koo. BS, U. Edinburgh, Scotland, 1980; PhD, U. Waterloo, Can., 1992. Engr. Vallentine, Laurie & Davies Ltd., Hong Kong, 1985-87, Hong Kong Govt., 1987, 1993-95; rsch. asst. U. Waterloo, 1988-92; exec. engr. Meinhardt Ltd., Hong Kong, 1992-93; lectr. U. Hong Kong, 1995-98; asst. v.p. Parsons Brinckerhoff Ltd., Asia, 1999—. Co-author: The Organization and Management of Construction, vol. 2, 1996, vol. 3, 1996; contbr. articles to profl. jours. Mem. Inst. Civil Engr., Hong Kong Inst. Engrs. (chartered engr.). Roman Catholic. Avocations: tennis, swimming, singing, flute. Home: Flat 2708 Hing On House, Sui Wo Ct, Shatin Hong Kong China Office: 23 Fl AIA Tower, 183 Electric Rd N Point, Hong Kong China

TAM, ROSALINE, payment industry management executive; b. Hong Kong, Feb. 9, 1952; d. Yan Hing and Sin Kwan (Wong) Tam. BA in Math., U. Hawaii, Honolulu, 1971, MS in Info. Sci., 1972. Mktg. mgr. Philips, Hong Kong, 1984; v.p. systems and data processing East Asia/North Pacific, Am. Express, Hong Kong, 1984-88; v.p. strategic bus. sys. Am. Express, N.Y.C., 1988-89; v.p. project mgmt. and coordination Am. Express, Sydney, Australia, 1989-90; gen. mgr. product mgmt. Citibank, Sydney, 1991-95; mng. dir. Continuous Techs. Internat., Sydney, 1995-97; with MasterCard Internat., Hong Kong, 1997—. Custodian prin. State Libr. of New South Wales, Sydney, 1995—. Mem. IEEE, Assn. for Computing Machinery, Australian Computer Soc. Baptist. Avocations: travel, reading, movies. Office: MasterCard Internat, 1401-1404 Dah Sing Fin Ctr, Wanchai Hong Kong

TAM, SHEUNG WAI, educational administrator; b. Hong Kong, July 29, 1934; s. Nai Fat and Sau Mui (Lam) T.; m. Arleta Yau-Ling Chang, Mar. 30, 1963; 2 children. BSc, Hong Kong U., 1958, MSc, 1961; PhD, U. Nottingham, Eng., 1964. Chartered chemist. Lectr. Chinese U. of Hong Kong, 1965-70, sr. lectr., 1970-78, reader, 1978-81, prof. chemistry, 1981-95; pres. Chung Chi Coll. Chinese U. of Hong Kong, Hong Kong, 1976-81, 88-90; dean of grad. sch. CUHK, 1981-92, pro vice-chancellor, 1990-94; pres. Open Univ. of Hong Kong, Hong Kong, 1995—. Chmn. Alice Homiuling Nethersole Hosp., Hong Kong, 1984-87, 91-95, United Christian Hosp., Hong Kong, 1987-90, Pamela Youde Nethersole Ea. Hosp., Hong Kong, 1992-97, Supplementary Med. Professions Coun., Hong Kong, 1990-94; Justice of the Peace Hong Kong Govt., 1978. Named Officer of the British Empire, 1992. Fellow Royal Soc. Chemistry; mem. Internat. Coun. for Open and Distance Edn. (v.p. 1998—), Asian Assn. Open Univs. (pres. 1999—). Avocations: swimming, hiking, classical music, golf. Home: 3A Bauhinia Ct, World Wide Gardens, Shatin Hong Kong Office: Open Univ Hong Kong, 30 Good Shepherd st, Homantin Hong Kong

TAM, WING KEUNG, engineering company executive; b. Hong Kong, May 2, 1962; s. Fai Kuen and Ken (Tsui) Tam; m. Pui Ling Wong; children: Victor Tam, Nicholas Tam. B in Engring. with honors, Salford (Eng.) U., 1989; PhD, Royal Melbourne Inst. Tech., Australia, 1997. Chartered engr. Tech. officer Hong Kong Govt., 1985-87; sr. elecronics engr. Elite Bus. Machines Mfg. Co., Ltd., Hong Kong, 1989-90; application engr. Hewlett Packard Hong Kong Ltd., 1990-92, 92-93; sys. engr. Hong Kong Telecom CSL, 1992; project mgr. Group Sense Ltd., Hong Kong, 1996—; part-time lectr. Vocat. Tng. Coun., Hong Kong, 1989-92, Hong Kong Coll. Tech., 1992-93; vis. lectr. Hong Kong Poly. U., 1990-91; tutor, Royal Melbournen Inst. Tech., 1995. Mem. IEEE, Instn. Elec. Engrs., Hong Kong Instn. Engrs. Avocations: badminton, reading. Home: Fl B, Bl 6, 18/F, City One, Shatin, Shatin Hong Kong NT, China Office: Group Sense Ltd 27/F Wu Chu, 213 Queen's Rd East, Wanchai Hong Kong China

TAMAI, TERUHIRO, urban planner, architect, consultant; b. Kitakyushu, Fukuoka, Japan, Dec. 1, 1951; s. Etsuhiro and Yuino (Miyamoto) T.; m. Masako Ohtsubo, Oct. 8, 1980; 1 child, Ippei. BE in Architecture, Kyoto U., 1975, ME in Architecture, 1977; MPA-URP, Princeton (N.J.) U., 1988. Sect. chief Fukuoka City Govt., Japan, 1977-89; gen. mgr., v.p. S&E Internat., Inc., 1989-91; mgr. Fukuoka Jisho Co., Ltd., 1991-92; lectr. JKUCAT, Kenya, 1992-93; pres. abc Rsch. and Design, Japan, 1994-99; lectr. Towa U., 1995-96, Kyushu U., Japan, 1994-95; vis. prof. Saga U., 2000—. Contbr. articles to profl. jours. Chief officer The League of Global Enterprises, Fukuoka (mem. RKB Broadcasting Cos. bd. advs.), the Movement for Preserving Hist. Bldgs., Fukuoka. Recipient Highest award Fukuoka City Govt., 1983. Mem. Architectural Inst. of Japan, Japan Urban Design Inst., City Planning Inst. of Japan, Urban Land Inst. Avocations: travel, art, reading. Office: abc Rsch and Design Inc, 3F 4-6-12 Nakasu Hakata-ku, Fukuoka 810-0801, Japan

TAMAMA, TETSUO, electronics engineer; b. Tokyo, May 6, 1933; s. Hideo and Toshi (Hattori) T.; m. Emiko Sanekata, Oct. 6, 1962; children: Shigeo, Michio, Nobuo, Yoshio. BS, Tokyo U., 1956, MS, 1958. Engr. Mitsubishi Electric Corp., Amagasaki, Japan, 1958-76; mgr. radar dept. Mitsubishi Electric. Corp., Amagasaki, Japan, 1976-87; mgr. def. systems devel. Mitsubishi Electric. Corp., Tokyo, 1987-91, chief engr., 1991-94; sr. rschr. Def. Rsch. Ctr., Tokyo, 1994—; spl. rschr. Nat. Inst. Sci. and Tech. Policy, Tokyo, 1988-90; rsch. com. Def. Rsch. Ctr., Tokyo, 1991-94. Co-author: Electronic Communications Handbook, 1979, Electronic Communications and Informations Handbook, 1988, Electromagnetic Engineering Handbook, 1988; patentee in field. Mem. Japanese Soc. Aero. and Space Scis. (chmn. electronics com. 1989-91), Inst. Electronics Info. and Comm. Engrs. (chmn. space and nav. electronics com. 1991-93). Mem. United Ch. of Christ. Achievements include invention of interferometric 3-dimensional radars, leading developer of air defense radars for Japanese self-defense forces. Home: 3-41-4 Tsukaguchi-cho, Amagasaki, Hyogo-Ken 661-0002, Japan Office: Def Rsch Ctr Hirayama Bldg, 2 Ichiban-Cho Chiyoda-Ku, Tokyo 102 0082, Japan

TAMAOKI, BUN-ICHI, retired endocrinology biochemistry educator; b. Tokyo, Japan, July 24, 1925; s. Bunjiro and Michi (Takeuchi) T.; children: Hidehiko, Shigeto. BS, U. Tokyo, 1947, PhD, 1958. Rsch. assoc. U. Tokyo, 1947-61; sect. chief Nat. Inst. Radiol. Science, Chiba, Japan, 1961-74; dir. div. pharm. sci. Nat. Inst. Radiol. Science, Chiba, 1974-86; prof. faculty of pharm. sci. Nagasaki (Japan) U., 1986-92. Recipient prize Ministry of Sci. & Tech., Japanese Govt., Tokyo, 1981, Decoration and diploma Emperor Japan, 1995, rsch. grantee, NIH, Washington, 1962-72. Avocations: collector, antique cameras, porcelain, wrist watches. Home: 238-21 Sonno-cho, Inage-ku Chiba-shi 263-0051, Japan

TAMAYO, EDUARDO EMILIANO (EDDY TAMAYO), college educator; b. Miami Beach, Fla., Aug. 21, 1964; s. Pedro Luis and Josefina Maria T. AA in Chemistry, Oxford (Ga.) Coll., 1984; BS in History, Ga. Coll., 1986, MPA, 1991. Student activities adv., instr. Hillsborough Cmty. Coll., Tampa, Fla., 1992—; d. Creator cover photo Ctr. for Marine Conservation Annual Report, 1999. Bishops adv. bd. San Jose Mission, Dover, Fla., 1996—; task force Hillsborough County Recycling, Tampa, 1995—; academic adv. Phi Theta Kappa, Tampa, 1997—; v.p. Keep Hillsborough County Beautiful, Tampa, 1996—. Recipient Beautification Svc. award Mayor, 1994, Svc. award Dale Mabry Campus Disabled Student Assn., 1996, Nat. Marrow Donor Program award 1995. Mem. Am. Legion, Tampa Bay Young Reps., Knights of Columbus, Pi Kappa Phi, Pi Sigma Alpha. Republican. Roman Cath. Avocations: photography, scuba, sci-fi modeler, harmonica. E-mail: etamayo@hcc.cc.fl.us. Home: 125 Danube Ave Tampa FL 33606-3521 Office: Hillsborough Cmty Coll 2001 N 14th St Tampa FL 33605-3662

TAMBOLI, AKBAR RASUL, consulting engineer; b. Babhulgon, India, July 20, 1942; s. Rasul M. and Chandbi T.; m. Rounkbi A. Tamboli, May 21, 1969; children: Tahira, Ajim, Alamgir. BS, U. Poona, India, 1965; MS, Stanford U., 1967. Sr. engr. Miller Assocs., Pottsville, Pa., 1967-69; assoc. Edwards & Hjorth, N.Y.C., 1970-76; sr. project engr. Engrs. Inc., East Orange, N.J., 1977-80; v.p. Office of Irwin G. Cantor PC, N.Y.C., 1981-91; cons. engr. CUH2A Inc., Princeton, N.J., 1992-98; v.p. Thornton-Tomasetti Group, N.Y.C., 1999—. Editor: Steel Design LFRD Method Handbook, 1996. Vol. Cancer Fund Drive, N.J., 1986. Fellow ASCE; mem. Am. Steel Constrn., Am. Soc. Welding. Avocations: golf, boating. Home: 10 Davenport Dr Princeton Junction NJ 08550-3001 Office: Thornton-Tomasetti Group 641 Ave of the Americas New York NY 10011-2014

TAMBOURATZIS, GEORGE DEMETRIUS, electrical engineer, researcher; b. Sheffield, Eng., Aug. 31, 1966; arrived in Greece, 1969; s. Demetrius and Helen T. Diploma in elec. engring., Nat. Tech. U. Athens, Greece, 1989; MS in Digital Systems, Brunel U., London, 1990, PhD in Pattern Recognition and Neural Networks, 1993. Lectr. Hellenic Naval Acad., Piraeus, Greece, 1995-96; lectr. Sch. Petty Officers, Hellenic Air Force, Athens, 1995-96; rschr. Inst. Lang. and Speech Processing, Athens, 1996; engr. O.T.E. Telecomm. Co., Athens, 1996-99; rschr. Inst. Lang. and Speech Processing, Athens, 1999—. Contbr. chpt. to book Neural Networks: Techniques and Applications, 1993; articles to profl. jours. including Pattern Recognition Letters, Network: Computation in Neural Systems, others. Scholar, Evgenidion Found., 1989-90, Sci. and Engring. Rsch. Coun., 1989-93, Bodosakion Found., 1990-91, Greek Scholarship Found., 1991-93, Faculty Tech. Brunel U., 1990-93. Mem. IEEE, Tech. Chamber of Greece. Home: 10-14 Laskaridou Str, 176 76 Kallithea Athens Greece

TAMBOURIN, PIERRE EDMOND, science administrator, researcher; b. Vouziers, Ardennes, France, Sept. 23, 1943; s. Edmond and Blanche (Paulin) T.; m. Brigitte Gruest, Jan. 5, 1980; children: Marie, Julien. Engr. grad., French Ecole Poly., Paris, 1966; rsch. assoc., Nat. Inst. Health & Med. Rsch., Paris, 1967; degree in molecular biology, U. Paris-Sorbonne, 1970, PhD in Molecular Biology, 1974. Rsch. assoc., dir. unit 22 Nat. Inst. Health/Med. Rsch. Inst. Curie, Orsay-Paris, 1967-82; vis. scientist, guest worker lab. cellular oncology NIH-NCI, 1982-85; head of oncology lab. unit 152 Nat. Inst. Health/Med. Rsch. Hosp. Cochin, Paris, 1985-89; dir. biology sect. Inst. Curie, Paris, 1989-93; head of life scis. dept. Nat. Ctr. Sci. Rsch., Paris, 1993-97; ofcl. rep. Genopole, Evry, 1998—; pres. dept. structural molecular biology Ctr. Nuclear Studies Grenoble, 1982; pres. Ecole Normale Supérieure Lyon, 1991; v.p. INSERM Sci. Bd., 1991, Nat. Commn. on Animal Experimentation, 1989; mem. sci. bd. several univs. and insts.; lectr. in field; organizer meetings and workshops. Mem. editl. bd. internat. and French jours. Decorated Chevalier de l'Ordre Nat. du Mérite, 1989, Chevalier de la Légion d'Honneur, 1997; recipient Rosen Award of Cancer, French Found. Med. Rsch., 1993, Gallet-Breton award French Nat. Acad. Medicine, 1989, Cochin Award of Cancer and Hematology, 1987, French Nat. League Against Cancer award, 1982, ESSEC Award of Cancer, 1974. Office: Genopole, 2 rue Gaston Crémieux, CP5723 91057 Evry cedex France

TAMBS, LEWIS ARTHUR, diplomat, historian, educator; b. San Diego, July 7, 1927; s. Fred B. and Marguerite Johanna (Tambs) Jones; m. Phyllis Ann Greer, 1982; children: Kari, Kristin, Jennifer, Heidi, Greer, Michael, Alexa. B.S., U. Calif.-Berkeley, Berkeley, 1953; M.A., U. Calif.-Santa Barbara, 1962, Ph.D., 1967. Plant engr. Standard Brands, San Francisco, 1953-54; pipeline engr. Creole Petroleum Co., Caracas, Maracaibo, Venezuela, 1954-57; gen. mgr. Cacyp, Maracaibo, 1957-59; instr. Creighton U., 1965-67, asst. prof., 1967-69; prof. history Ariz. State U., Tempe, 1969-82, 87—, dir. Center Latin Am. Studies, 1972-76; cons. Nat. Security Council, 1982-83; U.S. ambassador to Colombia, 1983-85, U.S. ambassador to Costa Rica, 1985-87. Author: East European and Soviet Economic Affairs, 1975, Historiography, Method and History Teaching, 1975, (with others) Hitler's Spanish Legion, 1979; editor: United States Policy Toward Latin America, 1976, Inter-American Policy for the 80's; co-author periodical guides; contbr. articles to profl. jours. Bd. dirs. Ariz.-Mex. Commn., 1974-82, Coun. Inter-Am. Security, 1979-90. With U.S. Army, 1945-47, 50-51. Faculty grantee Ariz. State U., 1970, 71, 74, 78, 79. Roman Catholic. Office: Ariz State U Dept History Tempe AZ 85287-2501

TAMBURRINI, MAURIZIO, biochemist, researcher; b. Casagiove, Caserta, Italy, Oct. 7, 1958; s. Edmondo Tamburrini and Elide Moro; m. Maria Antonietta Ciardiello, Apr. 27, 1996; 1 child, Francesca. Grad., U. Naples, Italy, 1982; PhD, Rsch. Doctorate, U. Naples, 1988. Fellow Nat. Rsch. Coun., Naples, 1983; postdoctoral fellow Hoffman-LaRoche, Nutley, N.J., 1988—; rschr. Nat. Rsch. Coun., 1989—; scientist 6th Italian Antarctic Expedition, 1990-91, 9th Italian Antarctic Expedition, 1993-94; guest scientist Alfred Wegener Inst. ANT-X3 Expedition, 1992; project coord. Nat. Program for Antarctic Rsch., 1999—. Editor: (book) Newsletter of the Italian Biological Research in Antarctica, 1997-99; contbr. sci. articles to profl. jours. Mem. Italian Soc. Biochemistry, Nat. Order Biologists. Roman Catholic. Avocations: basketball, guitar. E-mail: tamburr@dafne.ibpe.na.cnr.it. Office: Inst Protein Biochem/Enzymo, Via Marconi 10, 80125 Naples Italy

TAMBWEKAR, UNMESH AJAY, management consultant; b. Bombay, Nov. 4, 1971; s. Ajay B. and Ujwala Tambwekar. BS, St. Peter's Coll., Jersey City, 1992; M in Engring. Mgmt., Stevens Inst. Tech., 1996; Exec. M in Tech. Mgmt., U. Pa., 1999. Fin. analyst PaineWebber Group, Weehawken, N.J., 1990-92; sys. analyst Toys R Us, Somerset, N.J., 1992-94; mgr. Baker & Taylor, Bridgewater, N.J., 1994-96, Noblestar Sys., Parsippany, N.J., 1996-97; founding ptnr., chief info. officer Brownstone Techs., Hoboken, N.J., 1995-97; sr. mgr. Ernst & Young, Lyndhurst, N.J., 1998-2000; mgr. Answerthink Cons. Group, N.Y.C., 2000—. Contbr. articles to profl. jours. Mem. Internat. Soc. Strategic Mgmt., N.Y. New Media Assn. Avocations: reading, triathalons, skiing, travel. Fax: 212-629-4818. E-mail: utam@home.com. Home: 1109 Green Hollow Dr Iselin NJ 08830-2942 Office: Answerthink Cons Group 1 Penn Plz Ste 1628 New York NY 10119-1628

TAMIN, AZAIBI, molecular virologist, researcher; b. Muar, Johor, Malaysia, Mar. 9, 1959; came to U.S., 1984; s. Hj Tamin Sahandan and Kamisah Hassan; m. Zabedah Ismail, Sept. 1, 1984; children: Adam Zulfaqar Azaibi, Afiq Zulfaiz Azaibi. BS in Microbiology with honors, U. Leeds, Eng., 1983; PhD in Microbiology, Oregon State U., 1989. Tutor in microbiology Nat. U. Malaysia, 1983-84; teaching asst. Oreg. State U., Corvallis, 1985-86; rsch. asst. Oregon State U., Corvallis, 1986-88; rsch. fellow U.S. NRC & Ctrs. for Disease Control & Prevention, Atlanta, 1989-91; rsch. scientist Ctrs for Disease Control & Prevention measles sect., Atlanta, 1991—; cons. Min. of Sci., Tech. and Environment, Malaysia. Contbr. articles to profl. jours. Capt. Outward Bound Sch., Malaysia (Merit award), 1978; boy-sgt. Royal Military Coll., Malaysia, 1978; pres. Malaysian Student Union, U. Leeds, Eng., 1983. Recipient scholarship Ministry of Edn., Malaysia, 1978-83, scholarship Dept. Pub. Svc., 1984-89, N.L. Tartar fellowship, 1989, postdoctoral fellowship U.S. NRC, CDC, 1989-91. Islamic. Achievements include first to report a mutation in the cis-acting element in a gene responsible for both temperature sensitivity and drug resistant phenotypes in poxvirus; first to report a enhanced in vitro neutralizati activity against certain strains of wildtype measles virus in the presence of both anti-fusion and anti-hemagglutinin antibodies to measles glycoproteins; a mem. of the first group to identify and determine the nucleotide sequence of Nipal virus research in molecular pathobiology and evolution studies of continental U.S. orthopoxviruses; research in poxvirus expression systems, molecular biology immune response and antigenic studies of measles virus, Hendra virus and Nipah virus. Office: Ctrs Disease Control & Prevention Measles Sect MS C22 Atlanta GA 30333

TAMKIN, CURTIS SLOANE, real estate development company executive; b. Boston, Sept. 21, 1936; s. Hayward and Etta (Goldfarb) T.; m. Priscilla Martin, Oct. 18, 1975; 1 child, Curtis Sloane. BA in Econs., Stanford U., 1958. V.p., treas., dir. Hayward Tamkin & Co., Inc., mortgage bankers, L.A., 1963-70; mng. ptnr. Property Devel. Co., L.A., 1970-82; pres. The Tamkin Co., 1982—. Mem. bd. govs. Music Ctr. L.A., 1974-98; pres. L.A. Master Chorale Assn., 1974-78; mem. vis. com. Stanford U. Librs., 1982-86; bd. dirs. L.A. Philharm. Assn., 1985—. Lt. (j.g.) USNR, 1960-63. Mem. Mem. Founders League L.A. Music Ctr. (pres. 1988-98, chmn. emeritus 1998), L.a. Jr. C. of c.. (dir. 1968-69), Pacific Coun. Internat. Policy, Burlingame Country. Home: 1230 Stone Canyon Rd Los Angeles CA 90077-2920 Office: 9460 Wilshire Blvd Beverly Hills CA 90212-2732

TAMM, CARL OLOF SEBASTIAN, ecology educator; b. Stockholm, Oct. 11, 1919; s. Olof Filip Sebastian and Ingegard (Bergman) T.; m. Gullevi Ehrlin, Apr. 2, 1947; children: Staffan O.H., Martin C.A. MA, U. Stockholm, 1944, PhD, 1953; Dr.agr.forest, U. Helsinki, 1977, Norwegian U. Agrl., 1984; Dr.forest, Swedish U. Agrl. Scis., Uppsala, 1988. Rsch. asst. U. Lund, Sweden, 1946-47, asst. lectr., 1948; rschr. Swedish Forest Rsch. Inst., Stockholm, 1949-56, prof., 1957-62; prof. forest ecology Royal Coll. Forestry, Stockholm, 1963-77, Swedish U. Agrl. Scis., Uppsala, 1978-84; guest prof. Sch. Forestry, Christchurch, New Zealand, 1981; chmn. Swedish IBP Com., Stockholm, 1971-74, Swedish SCOPE Com., Stockholm, 1982-88. Author: Studies in Forest Nutrition I-IV, 1955-56, Nitrogen in Terrestrial Ecosystems, 1991. With Swedish Army, 1940-43. Mem. Royal Swedish Acad. Forestry and Agr., Royal Swedish Acad. Scis., Norwegian Acad. Sci. and Letters, Finnish Acad. Scis., Deutsch Acad. Leopoldina. Avocation: nature conservation. Home: Stavgardsgatan 11, S-16756 Bromma Sweden Office: Swedish U Agrl Scis, PO Box 7042, S-75007 Uppsala Sweden

TAMM, DITLEV, law and history educator; b. Copenhagen, Denmark, Mar. 7, 1946; s. Henrik and Lizzie Tamm. LLM, U. Copenhagen, 1970, DrJur, 1977, DrPhil, 1984; D Hon., U. Helsinki, 2000. Prin. Ministry of Justice, Copenhagen, 1970-72; asst. U. Copenhagen, 1972-78, prof., 1978—. Author: Retsopgøret efter besaettelsen, 1984, Roman Law and European Legal History, 1997. Chmn. Danish Audit Commn. Mem. Royal Danish Soc. Scis., Royal Danish Soc. Danish History, Beirat Max-Planck-Institut für europäische Rechtsgeschichte. Lutheran. Avocations: foreign languages, literature. Home: Svanemoellevej 13, DK-2100 Copenhagen OE, Denmark Office: Det retsvidenskabelige Inst, Studiestraede 6, DK-1455 Copenhagen K, Denmark

TAMMET, HANNES, physics educator, researcher; b. Tallinn, Estonia, Aug. 5, 1937; s. Feliks Tammann and Linda (Mägi) T.; m. Eve-Reet Sepper, Aug. 30, 1958; children: Tanel, Joel. PhD, U. Tartu (Estonia), 1964; DSc, Main Geophys. Observatory, St. Petersburg, Russia, 1979. Mem. faculty U. Tartu (Estonia), 1964-67, dir. air electricity lab., 1983-92, prof. environ. physics, 1992—, head inst. environ. physics, 1993—; mem. faculty Pedag. U. Tallinn (Estonia), 1967-83. Author: The Aspiration Method for the Determination of Atmospheric Ion Spectra, 1970; mem. editl. bd., contbr. Jour. Aerosol Sci, 1995—. Fulbright scholar U.S. Govt., 1995-96; grantee Internat. Sci. Found. Mem. Am. Inst. Biomed. Climatology (hon.), Internat. Com. Atmospheric Electricity, Estonian Nat. Com. Internat. Geosphere-Biosphere Programme, Inst. Physics (U.K.), Estonian Phys. Soc. Avocations: hiking, skiing. Home: Ravila 56-6, 50408 Tartu Estonia Office: U Tartu, 18 Ülikooli Str, 50090 Tartu Estonia

TAMMI, OLLI EINO, educator emeritus; b. Helsinki, Finland, Dec. 24, 1924; s. Eino Vilhelm and Aili Dagmar (Julku) T.; m. Annikki Tolsa, July 28, 1951; children: Pekka, Eeva, Heikki. MSc, U. Helsinki, 1949, PhD, 1952. Asst. prof. U. Helsinki, 1950-60; assoc. prof. Tech. U. Helsinki, 1961-64; assoc. prof. U. Helsinki, 1964-70, prof., 1971-91; vis. prof. Stanford (Calif.) U., 1963-64, 68. Author: Extremum Problems for Bounded Univalent Functions I, 1976, II, 1982. With Finnish Army, 1943-45. Home: Ohjaajantie 20A9, 00400 Helsinki Finland

TAMMINEN, KALEVI REINO, retired religion educator, researcher; b. Maaria, Finland, Apr. 5, 1928; s. Artturi Reino and Sylvi Dagmar (Honkaniemi) T.;m. Lea Annikki Viljakainen, Mar. 25, 1961; 1 child, Kaisa. PhD, ThD, U. Helsinki, Finland, 1967. Lectr. Tchr. Tng. Coll., Savonlinna, 1952-54, Tchrs. Coll., Helsinki, 1961-62; gen. sec. edn. Evang.-Luth. Ch. of Finland, 1955-63; asst. in practical theology U. Helsinki, 1958-68, docent in pedagogy, 1967-70, prof. religious edn., 1970-91; ret., 1992; dean faculty theology U. Helsinki, 1984-87. Editor: Kristillinen Kasvatus Jour., 1955-67, Religious Development in Childhood and Youth, 1991, and several other studies and publs. mainly in field of religious devel. and religious edn. Pres. Finnish Theol. Lit. Soc., 1978-83, Christian Soc. Tchrs., 1966-84; pres. commn. on edn. Evang.-Luth. Ch. of Finland, 1986-89. Recipient William James award APA, 1995. Mem. Assn. Profs. and Researchers in Religious Edn. Home: Gunillankuja 5 A 3, SF-00870 Helsinki Finland Office: U Helsinki Faculty Theology, Neitsytpolku 1 B, 00140 Helsinki Finland

TAMMISTO, KALLE ANTERO, academic administrator; b. Eura, Finland, Sept. 5, 1949; s. Vaino and Eva (Inkeri) T.; m. Marja-Liisa, Oct. 16, 1976; children: Tommi, Kalle, Kristian. MBA, Turun Kauppakorkeakoulu, Finland, 1975, BBA, 1973. Tchr. Kauppaoppilaitos, Forssa, Finland, 1973-74; dir. Wurth Suomiloy, Helsinki, Finland, 1975-79; controller Turun Muna Oy, Kiukainen, Finland, 1977-75; tchr. Helsinki Sch. Bus., Finland, 1979-86; prin. Forssa Vocat. Inst. Bus. Coll., Forssa, 1986—. Home: Lamminolankat 19, FIN30420 Forssa Finland Office: Fai-Kauppaoppilaitos, Saksank 46, FIN30100 Forssa Finland

TAMMIVUORI, JUHANI TAPIO, wholesale company executive; b. Helsinki, Finland, June 6, 1941; s. Jouko and Inkeri (Ahola) T.; children: Mirka, Tiia, Tuomo, Tuuli. BSc in Econs., Helsinki Sch. Econs., 1965. Group mgr. Finnish Coop. Wholesale Soc., Helsinki, 1965-82; asst. mgr. Fazer Music, Inc., Helsinki, 1982-90; mng. dir. Levypiste Oy Ltd., Espoo, Finland, 1990-92; export mgr. Suomen Vientiverkko Oy Ltd., Helsinki, Finland, 1993; mktg. dir. Mobinter Oy Ltd., Helsinki, Finland, 1994-2000; gen. mgr. Lietmobinter, Lithuania, 1994-2000; mng. dir. Mobinter Baltic, S/A, Latviaž, 1994—. Office: Kutomotie 9C, FIN-00380 Helsinki Finland

TAMULIS, ARVYDAS, physicist, researcher; b. Taurage, Lithuania, Mar. 18, 1948; s. Vincas and Zofija (Dapkute) T.; m. Regina Gaidamaviciute, Nov. 11, 1972 (div. Sept. 1982); children: Vykintas, Aiste; m. Jelena Giceviciute, Apr. 21, 1995; 1 child, Gintare. M. Theoretical Physics, Vilnius (Lithuania) U., 1971, PhD of Theoretical and Math. Physics, 1985. Jr. rsch. fellow Inst. Physics and Math., Lithuania, 1971-75; jr. rsch. fellow Inst. Physics, Lithuania, 1975-85, rsch. fellow, 1985-90; rsch. fellow Inst. Theoretical Physics and Astronomy, Vilnius, 1991-96, sr. rsch. fellow, 1996—; lectr. in field; vis. scientist Chalmers U. of Tech., Gothenburg, Sweden, 1992, Inst. Study Stereochem. and Energetica Composti Coordinazione, Florence, Italy, 1996, Groupe Composants Organiques, Commr. Atomic Energy, Service de Physique Electronique, 1998, 99, Max-Planck-Inst. of Colloids and Interfaces, Berlin, 1997, U. Calif.-Davis., 2000. Contbr. 129 articles to profl. publs.; exhibited photography, 1974-83. Fellow Swedish Inst., 1992, NATO Sci. Com., 1996; grantee G. Soros Found., Vilnius, 1994-95, Inco-Copernicus grantee European Commn., 1997—. Mem. Internat. Soc. for Molecular Electronics and BioComputing (founding mem. 1989—), Internat. Soc. Optical Engring., European Optical Soc., Internat. Soc. for Study of the Origin of Life. Roman Catholic. Avocations: tennis, travel, swimming, philately,

photography. Home: Didlaukio 27-40, 2057 Vilnius Lithuania Office: Inst Theoretical Phys/Astrn, A Goštauto 12, 2600 Vilnius Lithuania

TAMURA, SABURO, mathematics educator; b. Higashi-osaka, Osaka, Japan, July 13, 1927; s. Mori-ichi and Teruko (Saeki) T.; m. Youko Tsujimoto, Mar. 21, 1955; children: Naoyuki, Shinji. BS, Osaka U., 1955; DSc, Kobe U., 1995. Asst. prof. Osaka Tech. Coll., 1962-66; prof. Ube (Yamaguchi, Japan) Coll., 1966-70; asst. prof. Yamaguchi U., 1970-73, prof., 1973-79; prof. Kobe (Hyogo, Japan) U., 1979-91, Osaka Sangyo U., 1991-00. Author: Introduction to Symbolic Logic, 1975, The Paradoxical World, 1981, Logical Design, 1982, Mathematicians in French Revolution, 1989, Puzzle Land in Mathematics, 1992, Why Do You Learn Mathematics, 1994, Logic and Thought, 1996. Fellow Soc. Kinki Math. Educators, Assn. Hyogo Math. Educators; mem. Math. Soc. Japan, Japan Soc. Math. Edn., Japan Soc. Edn. Tech. Avocations: puzzle maker, tanka (Japanese short poem). Home: 207 6-20 Nishimiyahara 2, Yodogawa-ku, Osaka 532 0004, Japan

TAMUZS, VITAUTS, mechanics educator, researcher; b. Riga, Latvia, Dec. 2, 1935; s. Peters and Emma (Helmane) T.; m. Daina Tamuzs (div. 1995); 3 children. Diploma higher edn., Moscow U., 1959, PhD, 1963; DSc, Acad. Sci., Latvia, 1973; Dr. Habilitation Engring., Riga Tech. U., 1992. Head of lab. Inst. Polymer Mechanics, Riga, 1964—; prof. mechanics Latvian U., 1975—; pres. Latvian Nat. Com. for Mechanics, 1992—. Co-author: (with A. Malmeisters & G. Teters) Mechanik der Polymerwerkstoffe, 1977 (Latvian State prize 1983), (with K.S. Kuksenko) Fracture Micromechanics of Polymer Materials, 1981, (with A. Lagzdins, G. Teters & A. Kregers) Orientational Averaging in Mechanics of Solids, 1992; editor: (procs. of U.S.-USSR symposia) Fracture of Composite Materials, 1979, 82; editor-in-chief: Mechanics of Composite Materials, 1988—. Recipient USSR State Sci. prize, 1985. Fellow Academia Europaea, Acad. Sci. Latvia. Avocations: traveling, climbing. Home: Ozolciema iela 24/1-48, LV-1058 Riga Latvia Office: Inst Polymer Mechanics, Aizkraukles 23, LV 1006 Riga Latvia

TAN, ALEXANDER JUNIOR UY, internist, nephrologist, educator; b. Manila, Mar. 11, 1960; s. Lin Sim and Soledad (Uy) T.; m. Jean Un, Sept. 10, 1995. BS in Biology summa cum laude, Cebu Drs. Coll. Arts and Scis., The Philippines, 1981; MD magna cum laude, Cebu Doctors Coll. Medicine, 1985. Diplomate Am. Bd. Internal Medicine, Am. Bd. Nephrology, Philippine Splty. Bd. Internal Medicine and Nephrology. Clin. instr. Cebu Doctors Coll. Arts and Scis., 1981-82; postgrad. intern CEBU Doctors Hosp., The Philippines, 1985-86; resident in internal medicine Nat. Kidney Inst., The Philippines, 1987-90, Lincoln Med. and Mental Health Ctr., N.Y.C., 1990-92; fellow in nephrology VA Med. Ctr. UCLA, 1992-94; rsch. scientist UCLA-West Los Angeles VA Med. Ctr., 1994-96, acting dir. Hypertension Clinic,, 1995-96; asst. prof. medicine UCLA Sch. Medicine, 1995-96; assoc. prof. medicine Cebu Doctors Coll. Medicine, 1997-98, prof., 1998—, chief med. clinics, 1997—; pvt. practice, 1997—; chief sect. nephrology Cebu Cardiovasc. Ctr., Cebu Doctors Hosp., 1997—; chmn. dept. medicine Cebu City Med. Ctr., 1998—. Contbg. author: Current Nephrology, 19th edit., 1996, 20th edit., 1997; editor-in-chief Stethoscope,, Cebu, 1979-81; contbr. articles to med. jours., including Jour. Am. Soc. Nephrology, Nephrology Dialysis and Transplantation, Kidney Internat. Vis. cons. Samantabhadra Charitable Med. Missions, Cebu, 1997—. Fellow ACP, Philippine Coll. Physicians, Philippine Soc. Nephrology; mem. Cebu Doctors Alumni Assn. (bd. editors 1985), You We Tong Frat. Assn. Roman Catholic. Avocations: swimming, chess. Office: Cebu Doctors Hosp, Osmena Bldg Ste A201, Cebu 6000, The Philippines

TAN, ANDY H.M., physicist, educator; b. Singapore, Jan. 8, 1972; m. Lynn L.E. Poh, May 18, 1999. BS with honors, Nat. U. Singapore, 1996; postgrad. diploma in edn., Nanyang Tech. U. Nat. Inst., 1998. Gen. edn. officer Nat. Jr. Coll., Singapore, 1997—. Tchg. scholar Pub. Svc. Commn., Singapore, 1991. Mem. Inst. Physics, N.Y. Acad. Scis. Avocations: tennis, music, reading. E-mail: andylynn@pacific.net.sg and andy@moe.edu.sg. Fax: 65-4684535. Home: #08-313, Blk276 Choa Chu Kang Ave 2, Singapore 680276, Singapore Office: Nat Jr Coll, 37 Hillcrest Rd, Singapore 288913, Singapore

TAN, BENJAMIN YEN-JING, physics educator, researcher; b. Kwang Tung, Republic of China, Feb. 4, 1942; s. Franklin Chau-Ched Tan and Li Set Huang; m. Lily K.C. Wu; m. Bertrand, Michael. Bachelor, Nat. Taiwan Normal U., Taipei, China, 1966; master, Western Mich. U., 1972; postgrad., Ohio U., 1989-90. Tchr. high sch., Taipei, 1965-66; instr. Nat. Chiayi (China) Tchrs. Coll., 1974—. Co-author: Physics for Teachers, 1985; contbr. articles to profl. publs. Mem. Am. Phys. Soc., Chinese Physics Assn. Avocations: jogging, music. Office: Chiayi Tchrs Coll, Dept Math & Sci Edn, Chiayi 62100, Republic of China

TAN, CHEE-BENG, anthropology educator; b. Batu Pahat, Johor, Malaysia, Apr. 29, 1950; p. Song-Hoo Tan and Chew-Chang Tey; m. Swee-Hiang Guan; 1 child, Vincent Youci. BA, U. Sains Malaysia, 1974; MA, Cornell U., 1976, PhD, 1979. Lectr. U. Singapore, Republic of Singapore, 1979-80; lectr. U. Malaya, Kuala Lumpur, Malaysia, 1980-85, assoc. prof. dept. Chinese studies, 1985-89, assoc. prof. dept. anthropology and sociology, 1989-96; prof. dept. anthropology Chinese U. Hong Kong, 1996—; mem. adv. panel Prime Minister's Dept. of Nat. Unity, Malaysia, 1985-89; history advisor Leisure and Cultural Svcs. Dept., Hong Kong, 2000. Author: The Baba of Melaka, 1988, Bibliography on Ethnic Relations, 1992, Communal Associations of the Indigenous Communities of Sarawak, 1994; editor spl. jour. issue The Preservation and Adaption of Tradition: Studies of Chinese Religious Expression in Southeast Asia, 1990; co-editor: The Chinese in Malaysia, 2000. Mwm. civil rights orgn. Allran, Kuala Lumpur, 1983—. Mem. Am. Anthropol. Assn., Assn. for Asian Studies, Malaysian Social Sci. Assn., Internat. Sociol. Assn., N.Y. Acad. Scis. Office: Chinese U Hong Kong, Dept Anthropology, Shatin NT Hong Kong Hong Kong

TAN, CHIN KIAN, freight forwarding merchant; b. Chaozhou, Guandong, China, Oct. 3, 1947; arrived in Singapore, 1954; s. Peng Bak Tan and Ah Thong Yeow; m. Geok Hua Chng; children: Terence, Daphne, Vivien. Mng. ptnr. Chap Ann Co., Singapore, 1973-80; mng. dir. Lotango Forwarders, Singapore, 1980—. Avocation: golf.

TAN, DANIEL YUNAN, minister; b. Palembang, Indonesia, Mar. 17, 1967; s. Tung Heng Tan and Lenny Kusuma. BS, Toyohashi (Japan) U. Tech., 1992. Lic. to ministry Indonesian Full Gospel Fellowship, 1999. Engr. Toshiba Comm. Tech. Corp., Tokyo, 1992-97; assoc. pastor IFGF Agape Tokyo, 1998-99; pastor IFGF Kansai, Osaka, 1999—; country rep. World Harvest, Japan, 1997—. Avocations: music, reading, travel, history. Home: Midori Mansion # 402, 4-12 Tenno-Cho, Takatsuki-shi Osaka 569-0088, Japan

TAN, HUNG MING JOHNNY, management professional; b. Petaling Jaya, Malaysia, June 6, 1961; parents Heng Chai Tan and Lee Hun Lim; m. Chin Chng Soong, Nov. 30, 1985; children: Joel Tan Kah Wai, James Tan Jia Jun, Joy Tan Jia Yi. B in Math. (hon.), U. Waterloo, Can., 1982; M in Applied Fin., U. Western Sydney, 1998. Cert. mgmt. cons. Head credit & mktg. DBS Fin. Ltd., Singapore, 1982-88; asst. v.p. Overseas Union Bank Ltd., Singapore, 1988-90; mgr., v.p. ABN Amro Bank, Singapore, 1990-92; mng. dir. Impact Cons. & Tng., Singapore, 1992—, Impact Mgmt. Cons. (KL) Ctr., Sdn Bhd, Malaysia, 1994—. Mem. Inst. Mgmt. Cons., Singapore Inst. Mgmt. Home: 73 Jalan Tua Kong 06-07, 457266 Singapore Singapore Office: Impact Cons & Tng, Robinson Rd PO Box 370, 900720 Singapore Singapore

TAN, KEVIN YEW-LEE, investment consultant; b. Singapore, Aug. 29, 1961; s. Richard Leng-Poh and Gayle Poo-Neo (Chia) T.; m. Meng Lang, Dec. 9, 1989; children: Krystal, Kimberley. LLB, U. Singapore, 1986; LLM, Yale U., 1988, JSD, 1995. Sr. tutor Nat. U. Singapore, 1986-87, lectr., 1987-94, sr. lectr., 1994-98, assoc. prof., 1998-2000. Author: The Legal Framework, 1995, 5th edit., 2000; author, editor: Constitutional Law in Malaysia and Singapore, 1991, 2d edit., 1997, Managing Political Change in Singapore: The Elected President, 1997, Lee's Lieutenants: Singapore's Old Guard, 1999, The Singapore Legal System, 1999, Change and Continuity: Forty Years of the Law Faculty, 1999. Nat. program commr. Singapore Scout Assn., 1992-95, aux. mem., 1996— Meritorious award 1992); coun. mem. Preservation of Monuments Bd., Nat. Youth Achievement Award Coun., Singapore Red Cross Soc. Sgt. Singapore Armed Forces, 1979-82. Mem. Yale Club (exec. com. 1992—), The Roundtable (pres. 1999—, excopres. 1996-98). Avocations: classical music, camping, hiking, reading, scouting. Office: Tecity Mgmt Pte Ltd, 83 Clemenceau Ave, Singapore SE239920, Singapore

TAN, KIM LEONG, pediatrician, neonatologist, medical educator; b. Malaysia, Oct. 30, 1936; s. Chim Ean Tan and Siew Bo Yeoh, m. Kwok Yee Leng, June 15, 1963; children: Min-Li, Min-Ching, Wei-Liang. MBBS, U. Singapore, 1962; DCH, U. London, 1967. Fellow Royal Coll. Physicians, 1977, Fellow Royal Australasian Coll. Physicians, 1978. Med. officer Ministry of Health, Singapore, 1963-68; head neonatal unit Kandang Kerbau Hosp., 1968-89; lectr. U. Singapore, 1968-71, sr. lectr., 1971-75, assoc. prof., 1976-79; prof. Nat. U. Singapore, 1980-98; head neonatal unit Nat. U. Hosp., 1985-89; chief dept. neonatology Nat. U. Hosp. Singapore, 1990-98; ret., 1999; pvt. practice Specialist Infant-Child Ctr. Mt. Elizabeth Med. Ctr.; cons. Mt. Elizabeth Hosp.; mem. WHO Expert Adv. Panel on Maternal and Child Health, 1993-97, World Assn. Perinatal Medicine, 1994—, Nat. Sci. Com. on Hepatitis and Related Disorders, Singapore, 1985—; chmn. Expert Com. on Immunization Program, Singapore, 1988-98, chmn. Chpts. of Pediatricians, Acad. of Medicine, Singapore, 1989-90. Co-editor Procs. of 1st Asia Oceana Congress of Perinatology, 1979; mem. editl. bd. Jour. AMA (SEA), 1984—; referee Pediats., Health Devices, Jour. AMA, Acta Pediat., European Jour. Pediats, Early Human Devel., Asia-Pacific Jour. Pub. Health, Anns. Acad. Med. Sing, Sing Med. Jour. Mem. panel of doctors Kim Seng Community Ctr. Night Clinic, Singapore, 1981—; mem. exec. com. Children's Aid Soc., Singapore, 1981-91. Mem. Singapore Pediat. Soc. (life, chmn. rsch. fund 1975—, Haridas Meml. lectr. 1972, 77), Ob-gyn. Soc. Singapore (Benjamin Henry Sheares lectr. 1976), Brit. Med. Assn., Singapore Med. Assn., Acad. of Medicine. Home: 259 6th Ave, Dynasty Garden Ct 1, Singapore 276557, Singapore Office: Mt Elizabeth Med Ctr, 3 Mt Elizabeth #17-16, Singapore 228510, Singapore

TAN, KONG-MENG, radiologist; b. Malacca, Malaysia, Nov. 9, 1943; came to U.S., 1965; s. Hin Jin and May (Woon) T.; m. May Chen; 1 child, Jennifer Mei-Sim. BS, U. Ill., Chgo., 1967; MD, U. Ill., 1971. Intern Ill. Masonic Med. Ctr., Chgo., 1971-72, resident in radiology, 1972-75; instr. radiology U. Ill. Coll. Medicine, Chgo., 1974-75; chief dept. radiology Kaiser Permanente Med. Ctr., Richmond, Calif., 1976—, dir. med. edn., 1976-83, dir. quality assurance, 1983-89; dir. Permanente Med. Group, Inc., 1982-88; asst. physician-in-chief Kaiser Richmond, 1989—; mem. gov. bd. Alameda Contra Costs Health Sys. Agy., 1979-83, vice chmn., 1982. Contbr. articles to profl. jours. Mem. adv. coun. Bay Area Air Quality Mgmt. Dist., 1978-86, chmn., 1982; bd. dirs. Oakland Chinese Cmty. Coun., 1981-90, 96—, pres., 1983; chmn. Bay Area Asian Health Alliance, 1980; trustee Audio Digest Found., 1986—. Fgn. scholar U. Ill., 1966-67, fgn. travel scholar, 1970. Mem. AMA (chmn. com. house staff affairs 1974-75, adv. com. continuing medm. edn. 1979-83, com. on continuing med. edn. 1985—, chmn. 1986-92, com. quality care 1986—), Alameda Contra Costa Med. Assn., Phi Delta Epsilon, Omega Beta Pi. Home: 952 Sunnyhills Rd Oakland CA 94610-2415 Office: Kaiser Med Center 901 Nevin Ave Richmond CA 94801-3143

TAN, LI-SU LIN, accountant, insurance executive, investment consultant; b. Keelung, Taiwan, Republic of China, Mar. 7, 1956; came to U.S. 1985; d. I-Chang and Sung-Mei (Chen) Lin; m. Bert T. Tan, Aug. 19, 1985; children: Patricia Tan, Peter Puwen Tan, Lotus Tan. BBA, Nat. Taiwan U., 1978; MBA, Ill. Inst. Tech., 1991. CPA, Ill., Taiwan; lic. ins. agt., Ill.; registered investment advisor. Asst. mgr. T.N. Soong & Co. (mem. firm of Arthur Anderson & Co., SC), Taipei, 1978-85; practitioner Li-Su Lin, CPA, Taipei, 1981-85, Li-Su Lin Tan, CPA, Naperville, Ill., 1988-90; pres. Lisu L. Tan & Co., Ltd., CPAs, Naperville, Ill., 1990—; agt. Mut. of Omaha Co., Lombard, Ill., 1991-94, Met. Life and Affiliated Cos., Bloomingdale, Ill., 1993-98, GE Fin. Assurance, Oak Brook, Ill., 1999—. Chair family Naperville Chinese Assn., 1990. Mem. AICPA (tax divsn., quality control program), Ill. Soc. CPAs, Taipei First Girls High Alumni Assn. (treas. 1990-94), Greater Chgo. Area Taiwanese Am. C. of C. (bd. dirs. 1995—), Taiwanese C. of C. N.Am. (treas. 1998-99), World Taiwanese C. of C. (dep. treas. 1998-99), Nat. Taiwan U. Alumni Assn. Greater Chgo. (bd. dir. 1999—). Buddhist. Avocations: travel, art collecting, photography. Office: Lisu L Tan & Co Ltd CPAs 6S235 Steeple Run Dr #200 Naperville IL 60540-3754

TAN, LUCIO C., airline, tobacco and beer company executive; b. Amoy, China, July 17, 1934; married. Chmn., CEO Philippine Airlines, Manila; chmn. Allied Banking Corp., Asia Brewery Inc. Fax: 63-2-813-3474. Office: 8th Fl Allied Bank Bldg, 6754 Ayala Ave, Makati The Philippines also: 1059, Metro Manila The Philippines*

TAN, MASAKI, surgeon; b. Akita, Japan, Feb. 13, 1946; s. Chiyoshi and Masae (Akahira) T.; m. Keiko Takahashi, Jan. 28, 1975; children: Hiroki, Chihiro. MB, Tohoku U., Sendai, Japan, 1971, MD, 1978; LLB, Kinki U., Osaka, Japan, 1985. Asst. prof. dept. surgery Tohoku U., Sendai, 1973-85; head dept. surgery Ohfunato (Japan) Prefectural Hosp., 1985-88, Kitakami (Japan) Prefectural Hosp., 1988-94, Isawa Prefectural Hosp., Mizusawa, Japan, 1994-98; vice dir. Wakayanagi NHI Hosp., Kurihara, 1998—. Author: Recent Advances in Chemotherapy, 1985, New Applications of OK-432, 1986. Mem. AAAS, ISPO, N.Y. Acad. Sci. Avocations: reading, movies, music, traveling. Office: Wakayanagi NHI Hosp, 130-5 Kawakitafurukawa Wakayanagi, Kurihara Miyagi 989-5501, Japan

TAN, NELLIE ANN LIM, salesperson, consultant; b. Manila, Sept. 18, 1952; d. Teodoro Lim and Sonia (Yii) Lim; m. Emerson Beyaoju Tan, Dec. 10, 1983; 2 children. Grad. in Bus. Adminstrn., St. Joseph Coll., The Philippines, 1974; grad. in Hotel and Restaurant Mgmt., The Philippines, 1980, grad. in Ins. Mgmt., 1986. Unit mgr. Insular Life, The Philippines, 1988—; br. mgr. Coll. Assurance Plan, The Philippines, 1989—; dist. mgr. Manila Meml. Pk., The Philippines, 1990—; unit mgr. Pacific Meml. Plans, The Philippines, 1995—; dir. Youthful Looks and Skin Care, The Philippines, 1988—, Gioelli, The Philippines, 1988-95. Mem. Quota Club Internat., The Philippines, 1990-98, Nat. Prestige Club, The Philippines, 1994-98. Recipient Young Achiever award Young Achiever's Found., The Philippines, 1985, Golden Scroll award Young Achiever's Found., 1991, 95, Parangal Ng Bayan award, The Philippines, 1995, Celebrity Mother of Yr. award Golden Mother/Father Found., The Philippines, 1995. Avocation: hobby-selling. Office: Insular Life, SKK Bldg 3d Fl, Pasay City Manila The Philippines

TAN, RICHIE REYNAN CHUA, finance officer; b. Cebu City, The Philippines, Jan. 4; s. Teotimo and Yolanda (Chua) T. BA in Psychology, De La Salle U., Manila, 1996. Auditor Fortune Tobacco Corp., Manila, 1997-98; jr. cons. Asia Brewery Inc., Manila, 1998, project mgr. reengring. distbn. sys., 1999; fin. officer fin. audit/sys. study Basic Holdings Corp., Manila, 1999—. Art editor Sound-Off, 1994, SC Jour., 1996. Recipient Best Editl. Cartoon award Green & White, 1996. Home: 24 Magnas St, Quezon City 1100, The Philippines

TAN, RODELENE PENEQUITO, psychologist; b. Bacolod City, The Philippines, Apr. 7, 1970; d. Rudy Alarcon Penequito and Crispina Villon Castro; m. Juancho Castillo, Oct. 10, 1989; children: John Rothmann Jeffrey Ralph, Jacqueline Rose. BS in Psychology, Far Eastern U., The Philippines, 1991, MA in Indsl. Psychology, 1995, EdD, 1999. Propr. Rothmann Trading, The Philippines, 1991—; nat. security specialist II Nat. Security Coun., The Philippines, 1993—; psychologist Philippine Nat. Police, 1996—; employee-rep. Nat. Security Coun., The Philippines, 1999—, Nat. Adv. Coun. WINGS, The Philippines, 1995—; neuro-psychiat. evaluator Philippine Nat. Police, 1996—. Mem. APA, Psychol. Assn. of the Philippines (bd. dirs. 1999—), Philippine Mental Health Assn., Pers. Officers Assn. of the Philippines, Inc., Internat. Coun. Psychologists,Assn. Govt. Psychologists of the Philippines. Avocations: psychological evaluation, training, swimming, tennis, volleyball. Home: 19 road 5 Pag-asa, 1100 Quezon City The Philippines Office: Nat Security Coun, V Luna Rd, Quezon City The Philippines

TAN, ROLAND KIM CHAY, research scientist; b. Singapore, Sept. 5, 1964; s. Eddie Hock Hoe and Linda Siew Eng (Foo) T.; m. Leena Hong Ling Goh. B in Engring., U. Essex, 1990, PhD, 1994. Cert. Inst. Patent Attys. Australia, 1998. Rsch. engr. Def. Sci. Orgn., Singapore, 1994-96; rsch. fellow Ctr. for Signal Processing, Singapore, 1996-99; head audio group Kent Ridge Digital Labs., Singapore, 1999—; audio cons. Singapore, 1994—; mem. Singapore Digital Audio Broadcasting and the Singapore Digital TV Working Group Com. Contbr. articles to profl. jours. and audio mags. Lt. Singapore Armed Forces, 1985-86. Recipient Project prize Philips Electronics, 1990, Overseas Rsch. Studentships award, AMIC award for excellence in Asian radio writing, 1998; grantee Meridian Audio, 1991-93. Mem. IEEE (Signal Processing), Audio Engring. Soc. (Singapore sect chmn. 1996-98, founding mem. Singapore sect. 1994, advisor Singapore sect. 1998-2000, student counselor Singapore sect. 1998—, Web master Singapore sect. 1999—). Avocations: music, arts, reading, swimming. Fax: (65) 774-4498. E-mail: roland@krdl.org.sg. Home: Apt Block 181, Stirling Rd 08-212, S140181 Singapore Singapore Office: Kent Ridge Digital Labs, 21 Heng Mui Keng Terr, S119613 Singapore Singapore

TAN, SIAUW KOAN, radiologist; b. Bandung, West Java, Indonesia, Mar. 5, 1951; s. Tjin Hong Tan and Kim Hong Liem; m. Bernadette Yvonne Sutandi, Aug. 8, 1979. MD, Maranatha Christian U., Bandung, 1979; cert. radiologist, Padjadjaran U., Bandung, 1989; cert. ultrasonologist, U. Zagreb, Yugoslavia, 1991. Head Pub. Health Ctr., Binong, Indonesia, 1980-84; head radiology dept. Dr. Abdul Azis Hosp., Singkawang, Indonesia, 1990-92, St. Borromeus Hosp., Bandung, 1992—. Mem. AAAS, Am. Coll. Radiology, Radiol. Soc. N.Am., Indonesian Radiol. Soc., N.Y. Acad. Scis., Am. Inst. Ultrasound in Medicine. Avocations: classical music, sports. Home: Galunggung 30, 40263 Bandung Indonesia Office: St Borromeus Hosp, IR H Juanda 100, 40132 Bandung Indonesia

TAN, TJIAUW-LING, psychiatrist, educator; b. Pemalang, Java, Indonesia, June 2, 1935; came to U.S., 1967; naturalized, 1972; s. Ping-Hoey and Liep-Nio (Liem) T.; m. Esther Joyce Kho, June 2, 1961; children: Paul Budiman, Robert Yuling, Alice Ayling. BS, U. Indonesia Faculty Medicine, 1957, MD, 1961; postgrad., U. Indonesia, Jakarta, 1961-65, UCLA, 1967-71, Pa. State U., 1971-72. Diplomate Am. Bd. Psychiatry and Neurology, Am. Bd. Gen. Psychiatry, Am. Bd. Geriat. Psychiatry. Lectr. psychiatry U. Indonesia, Jakarta, 1965-67; psychiat. cons. Ctrl. Gen. Hosp., Jakarta, 1965-67; postdoctoral fellow UCLA Brain Rsch. Inst., 1967-69; asst. rsch. psychiatrist, dept. psychiatry Neuropsychiat. Inst., UCLA, 1969-70; asst. prof. psychiatry Pa. State U., 1972-87, assoc. prof. psychiatry, 1987-99, prof. psychiatry, 1999—; chief inpatient psychiatry Univ. Hosp. Milton S. Hershey Med. Ctr., 1972—, dir. Behavioral Medicine Clinic, co-dir. Biofeedback Lab., 1975—; cons. psychiatry Family and Children's Svc. Lebanon County, Lebanon, Pa., 1971-79. Contbr. articles to profl. jours. Bd. dirs. Retarded Children's Assn. Dauphin County, Inc., 1971-73. Fellow Am. Psychiat. Assn. (life); mem. Pa. Psychiat. Soc., Ctrl. Pa. Psychiat. Soc., Assn. Advancement Behavior Therapy, Assn. Applied Psychophysiology and Biofeedback, Soc. Behavioral Medicine, Assn. Psychophysiol. Study of Sleep, Am. Acad. Sleep Disorder Medicine, Am. Assn. for Geriat. Psychiatry, Am. Geriat. Soc. Home: 1478 Bradley Ave Hummelstown PA 17036-9143 Office: Pa State U Coll Medicine Dept Psychiatry 500 University Dr Hershey PA 17033-2360

TAN, XUELIN, geneticist; b. Kaiyuan, China, July 7, 1957; child Wanning Tan and Qiongxing Jiang; m. Yaqing Tan, Jan. 31, 1988. BS, Yunnan Agrl. U., Kunming, China, 1982, MS, 1987; PhD in Plant Breeding and Genetic, Kasetsart U., Bangkok, 1998. Mem. staff Yunnan Agrl. U., Kunming, 1982-84, rice breeder Rice Rsch. Inst., 1987-92, assoc. prof., rschr., dir. Rice Rsch. Inst., 1998—; vis. scientist Kasesart U., Bangkok, 1992-93; acad. cons. Yunnan Agrl. U., Kunming, 1998—. Mem. Yunnan Soc. Crop Sci. (sec. 1988-92, vice chmn. 1989-92). Avocations: swimming, computer, reading, chess. Fax: 86-871-5150303. Home: Luoshuopo, Kunming 650201, China Office: Yunnan Agrl U, Rice Rsch Inst, Yunnan 650201, China

TAN, Y., research scientist; b. Badong, Hubei, China, Nov. 27, 1962; arrived in Australia, 1985; p. Wenbang Tan and Kemei Wang; m. Zoya Xu, Oct. 8, 1994; children: Anton, Anney . BSc, Ctrl. China U. Agr., Wuhan, 1983; PhD, Australian Nat. U., Canberra, 1989. English cert. Shanghai U. Fgn. Langs. Fellow Cornell U., Ithaca, N.Y., 1989-90; rsch. scientist Australian Nuc. Sci. and Tech. Orgn., Sydney, 1990-93, Ctr. Environ. Mechanics, Commonwealth Sci. and Indsl. Rsch., Canberra, 1993-94; sr. rsch. scientist Commonwealth Sci. and Indsl. Rsch. Orgn., Canberra, 1994-98, prin. rsch. scientist, 1999—. Contbr. chpt. to book and articles to profl. jours. Sec. Canberra br. Soil Sci. Soc. Am., 1996; pres. Assn. for Internat. Cooperation Australia, Canberra, 1998-2000; advisor Marco Polo Award Found., Hong Kong, 1999; founding mem. Australian Tech. Experts Network, 1999-2000. Mem. Soil Sci. Australia, Australian Soc. Limnology. Avocation: tennis. Office: Commonwealth Sci & Indsl, GPO Box 1666, Canberra ACT 2601, Australia

TANABE, MAKOTO, computational mechanics educator; b. Kamiichi, Toyama, Japan, Nov. 30, 1946; s. Tomomasa and Midori (Mori) T.; m. Yasuko Kondo, Apr. 8, 1972; children: Hiraku, Satoshi. BS in Math., Tokyo U. Edn., 1969; PhD in Engring., U. Tokyo, 1981. Registered cons. engr. Sr. specialist CRC Rsch. Inst. Inc., Tokyo, 1970-83; pres. Tanabe Cons. Office Ltd., Zama, Kanagawa, Japan, 1984—; assoc. prof. Kanagawa Inst. Tech., Atugi, Japan, 1985-92, prof., 1992—; advisor Nonlinear Analysis Program Rsch. Assn., Tokyo, 1984—; cons. NEC Info. System Co., Ltd., Tokyo, 1984—; head CAE Ctr., Kanagawa Inst. Tech., 1996—. Contbr. articles to profl. jours. Mem. ASME, Japan Soc. Mech. Engrs., Japan Cons. Engrs. Assn. Avocations: tennis, skiing, jogging. Office: Kanagawa Inst of Tech, 1030 Shimo-Ogino, Atsugi 243-02, Japan

TANABE, SETSUHISA, material scientist, glass researcher; b. Nagoya, Aichi, Japan, June 29, 1963; s. Zen-ichi and Midori Tanabe; m. Reiko Tanabe. BS in Engring., Kyoto (Japan) U., 1986, M of Engring., 1988, D of Engring., 1993. Asst. prof. materials sci. Kyoto U., 1990—. Author: Science of Rare Earths, 1997; mem. editl. bd. New Glass Forum, Tokyo; contbr. articles to profl. jours.; presenter in field. Recipient Young Scientists and Engrs. award Material Rsch. Soc., 1988, Inoue Sci. award for young scientists, 1994, Young Scientist award Ceramic Soc. Japan, 1996, Rsch. award Optical Sci. & Engring., 1995, Young Scientist award Chem. Soc. Japan, 1998. Avocations: tennis, baseball. Office: Kyoto U, Sakyo-ku, 606-01 Kyoto Japan

TANABE, TADASHI, biochemist, educator, researcher; b. Konan, Aichi, Japan, Sept. 23, 1941; s. Shizuo and Tsuyako (Sato) T.; m. Sumiko Yukawa, Jan. 15, 1974; 2 children. BS, Osaka U., Japan, 1965, MSc, 1967, PhD, 1971. Post doctral fellow Kyoto U., Japan, 1971-72, asst. prof., 1972-79; assoc. prof. Nat. Cardiovascular Ctr. Rsch. Inst., Osaka, 1979-89, prof., 1989—; prof. Osaka U., 1995—. Recipient The Soc. prize The Vitamin Soc. Japan, 1988. Mem. N.Y. Acad. Scis., Am. Soc. Biochemistry and Molecular Biology. Home: 3-18-3 Higashitoyonaka-cho, Toyonaka Osaka 560-0003, Japan Office: Nat Cardiovas Ctr Rsch Inst, 5-7-1 Fujishiro-dai, Suita 565-8565, Japan

TANAHASHI, JUNJI, historian science and technology, educator; b. Kyoto, Japan, May 7, 1929; s. Hatsutaro and Masago (Ikegami) T.; m. Eiko Tamao, Aug. 29, 1957; 1 child, Shuichi. BSc, Ritsumeikan U., Kyoto, Japan, 1952; MSc, Kyoto (Japan) U., 1956, DSc, 1961. Asst. prof. Shoin Women's U. (now Kobe Shoin Women's U.), Kobe City, Japan, 1966-73, prof., 1973—; founder, curator Biidoroshiryoko, Kobe City, 1970—; exhbn. supr. Edo period Japanese glass, Navio Mus. of Art, Osaka, 1981, Kobe City Mus., 1983, 90, 2000; exhbn. supr. Meiji period Japanese glass, Kobe City Mus., 1987. Co-author: (with others) A History of Glass in the Orient, 1977, A History of Social Problems of Technology in Japan (vol. 4 Ceramics), 1984, The Survey of Glass in the World (vol. 5 Japan), 1992; contbr. numerous articles on history of glass making to profl. jours. Merit award The Glass Mfrs. Assn. of Japan, 1983, Hyogo Prefecture, 1998. Fellow Assn. for Glass Art Studies, Japan (pres. 1997—); mem. The History of Sci. Soc. Japan, Japan Soc. for History of Indsl. Tech. Home: 5-8-10 Kitagoyo Kitaku, Kobe 651-1131, Japan Office: Kobe Shoin Women's U, 1-2-1, Shinohara-Obanoyamacho, Nadaku Kobe 657-0015, Japan

TANAKA, ATSUSHI, psychologist, researcher; b. Tokyo, Apr. 18, 1971; s. Tadashi and Miki (Yarita) T. M, Tohoku U., Sendai, 1996. Rsch. fellow Japan Soc. Promotion of Sci. for Young Scientists, Tokyo, 1996-97; staff

rschr. Vocat. Devel. Divsn. Nat. Inst. Vocat. Rehab., Chiba, Japan, 1997—; lectr. U. Electro-Comms., Tokyo, 1998-99; tchg. asst. Tohoku U., 1995-97. Author: Recent Advances in Physiological Anthropology, 1999; contbr. articles to profl. jours. Avocations: swimming, tennis, travel. Fax: 81-43-297-9057. E-mail: atanaka@nivr.jaed.or.jp. Office: Nat Inst Vocat Rehab, 3-1-3 Wakaba, Mihamaku Chiba 261-0014, Japan

TANAKA, HIDEYUKI, physicist, researcher; b. Kawaguchi, Japan, June 17, 1961. BS, Tohoku U., Sendai, Japan, 1985, MS, 1987; Dr.Engring., Waseda U., Tokyo, 2000. Rschr. Matsushita Rsch. Inst. Tokyo, Inc., Kawasaki, Japan, 1987-2000; rschr. Advanced Tech. Rsch. Labs. Matsushita Elec. Indsl. Co., Ltd., Kawasaki, Japan, 2000—; rsch. scientist Joint Rsch. Ctr. Atomic Tech., Tsukuba, Japan, 1994-97; vis. rschr. U. Tokyo, 1989. Mem. Phys. Soc. Japan, Japan Soc. Applied Physics. Office: Matsushita Elec Indsl Co Lt, 3-10-1 Higashimita Tama-ku, Kanagawa Kawasaki 214-8501, Japan

TANAKA, HIROSHI L., atmospheric scientist; b. Sibata, Niigata, Japan, Dec. 22, 1957; came to U.S. 1981; s. Wazoh and Chieko T.; m. Masayo Takagi, Oct. 18, 1981; children: Daiki, Lisa. BSc in Geosci., U. Tsukuba, Japan, 1980; PhD in Atmospheric Sci., U. Mo., 1988. Sr. rsch. specialist U. Mo., Columbia, 1981-88; asst. prof. Geophys. Inst. U. Alaska, Fairbanks, 1988-91; asst. prof. U. Tsukuba, Japan, 1991—. Mem. Am. Meteor Soc. (Fathest North pres. 1990-91), Japan Meteor Soc. (Yamamoto Shono award 1992), Sigma Xi (Grad. Student award 1988). Home: 2511-1 Saiki, Tsukuba 305-0028, Japan Office: U Tsukuba, Inst Geosci, Tsukuba 305-8571, Japan

TANAKA, HISAO, economist, educator; b. Tokyo, Feb. 11, 1924; s. Hanjiro and Hana (Tsuchiya) T.; B.C., Tokyo U. of Commerce, 1948; m. Reiko Ishiko, Feb. 18, 1953; children: Juichi, Mikihisa, Satoko. With Bank of Japan, Tokyo, 1948-80, assoc. advisor econ. rsch. dept., 1966, sr. rsch. officer Inst. Developing Econs., 1974-80; prof. econs. Kyoto Sangyo U., Kyoto, Japan, 1980-94; prof. faculty internat. studies Suzuka Internat. U, Mie, Japan, 1994-98; rschr. Japanese Ministry Fgn. Affairs, 1961-62; vis. prof. Nagoya U. of Commerce, 1977-78. Vis. scholar Chinese U. of Hong Kong, 1986-87; vis. prof. Chinese U. of Hong Kong, 1992. Mem. Am. Econ. Assn., Japan and Yugoslavia Assn. (dir. 1980—), Acad. for Hong Kong and Taiwan in Japan (v.p. 1988—). Buddhist. Author: Finance and Banking in Eastern Europe, 1978, Oil Money and Asian Dollar in International Money Market, 1978, World Economy and Monetary Problems, 1980, Interest Rates in the World, 1983, Reorganization of World Economy, 1988, Financial Perestroica in Soviet Economy, 1990, Rapid Economic Growth and Political Unrest in Asia, 1992, History of Hong Kong's Banking System, 1997. Home: 4-18-6 Minaminagasaki, Toshima-ku, Tokyo 171-0052, Japan

TANAKA, JUNJI, educational administrator; b. Osaka, Japan, Nov. 22, 1929; s. Waichiro and Hide T.; m. Chieko, Mar. 5, 1957; children: Keiji, Eiko. BA in Econs., Kinki U., Japan, 1956; cert. in librarianship, Doshisha U. Local employee USIA, 1957; sr. advisor Am. Ctr., Osaka, Japan, 1970; exec. dir. Japan Inst. for Internat. Study, Osaka, Japan, 1973—; pres. JIIS Corp. Ltd., 1988—; ednl. counseling svcs. internat. student and personnel exchange programs; pres. Japan Youth Devel. Assn., 1996; bd. dirs. Brain Dynamics Co., Ltd. Recipient Meritorious Honor award USIA, 1968. Mem. Nat. Assn. Fgn. Student Advisors, Osaka C. of C. and Industry, Japan-Am. Soc., Rotary. Home: 17-20, 4 chome, Kumano-cho, Toyonaka City, Osaka 560 0014, Japan Office: Kyoiku Ctr Bldg 5-1-1, Honmachi Toyonaka-shi, Osaka 560-0021, Japan

TANAKA, KAZUHIRO, orthopaedic surgeon, educator; b. Fukuoka, Japan, Sept. 6, 1964; s. Chitoshi Yamanaka and Kimiko Tanaka; m. Masako Nagata, Mar. 30, 1996. MD, Kyushu U., Fukuoka, Japan, 1989, PhD, 1995. Resident Kyushu U. Hosp., Fukuoka, 1989-90; med. staff Fukuoka Teishin Hosp., 1990-91; asst. prof. Kyushu U., Fukuoka, 1995—. Contbr. articles to profl. jours. Recipient Encouraging award Japanese Orthopedic Assn., Tokyo, 1997, award Japanese Soc. Cartilage Metabolism; named Overseas Rschr., Ministry Edn., Sci., Sports and Culture Japan, Tokyo, 1996. Mem. AAAS, Am. Assn. for Orthopaedic Surgeons, Orthopedic Rsch. Soc. (New Investigator Recognition award 1999), N.Y. Acad. Scis. Office: Kyushu U Dept Ortho Surgery, 3-1-1 Maidashi, Higashi-ku Fukuoka 812-8582, Japan

TANAKA, KAZUNORI, science educator; b. Hakodate, Hokkaido, Japan, May 24, 1929; s. Koichi and Yae (Yasuoka) T.; m. Chiyoko Yamato, Mar. 15, 1958; children: Hikaru, Makoto, Kiyoshi. BS, Hokkaido U., Sapporo, Japan, 1953, DSc, 1964. Asst. Hokkaido U., Sapporo, 1953-64, assoc. prof., 1964-68; prin. scientist Inst. Phys. and Chem. Rsch., Wako, Japan, 1968-90; prof. Shizuoka U., Hamamatsu, Japan, 1990-95; lectr. Nihon U., Tokyo, 1996—; assoc. rsch. scientist NYU, 1966; cons. M. W. Kellogg, 1967; vis. fellow Mellon Inst., Pitts., 1967-68. Home: 1199-41 Shimohiroya, Kawagoe Saitama 350-0804, Japan

TANAKA, KAZUO, optical engineer; b. Tokyo, Dec. 11, 1948; m. Kumiko Tanaka, Apr. 17, 1982; children: Naoki, Sachi. BSc in Precision Engring., Chuo U., Tokyo, 1971, MS, 1973; DrEng in Applied Physics, Tokyo Inst. Tech., 1984. Optical sys. designer Optics divsn. Canon Inc., Tokyo, 1973-78, sr. scientist Rsch. Ctr., 1979-83, sr. lens designer video divsn., 1984—, mgr. R & D hdqrs., 1986—; vis. lectr. Chuo U., 1995—, Chulalongkorn U., Bangkok, 1997—. Author: Progress in Optics, vol. XXIII, others; contbr. over 60 articles to profl. jours.; holder over 40 Japanese patents, 35 U.S. patents. Recipient Hatakeyama award Japan Soc. Mech. Engrs., 1971; JMA award Japan Mgmt. Assn., 1991. Mem. N.Y. Acad. Scis., Japan Soc. Applied Physics (Optics Best Paper award 1983), Optical Soc. Japan, Optical Soc. Am., Internat. Soc. Optical Engrs., Kanagawa Sci. Acad. E-mail: User494704@aol.com. Home: 1-38-2 Yayoi-cho, Nakano-ku, Tokyo 164-0013, Japan Office: Canon Inc R&D Hdqrs, 3-30-2 Shimomaruku Ohta-ku, Tokyo 146-8501, Japan

TANAKA, NOBORU, pathologist, educator, laboratory administrator; b. Tokyo, Mar. 19, 1921; s. Keitaro and Michie Tanaka; m. Hiroko Tanaka (dec. Apr. 1979); children: Mie Morita, Chie; m. Masue Tanaka, Nov. 15, 1981. DDS, Tokyo Med. and Dental U., 1941, MD, 1950, PhD, 1957. Lectr. Tokyo Med. and Dental U., 1951-54; dir. med. lab., chief pathologist Japan Red Cross Med. Ctr., Tokyo, 1954-72; resident in pathology Mt. Sinai Hosp., Chgo., 1958-59; guest faculty prof. pathology U. Chgo., 1962; prof. pathology Nihon U. Sch. Medicine, Tokyo, 1970—; dir. Chiba (Japan) Cancer Ctr. Rsch. Inst., 1972-86; cons. Saitama (Japan) Cancer Ctr., 1975-91; lectr. Yamanashi (Japan) Med. Coll., 1981-90; vis. prof. Chiba U., 1972-86; mem. editl. adv. bd. Am. Cancer Assn. Mem. editl. adv. bd. Cancer-Cytopathology. Recipient award Tokyo Mcpl. Assn. Social Welfare, 1990, award Japanese Soc. Social Welfare, 1992. Fellow Internat. Acad. Cytology (Maurice Goldblatt Cytology award 1985), Am. Coll. Angiology, Internat. Coll. Angiology; mem. Internat. Acad. Pathology (hon. mem. Bolivian div.), Bolivian Soc. Cancerology (hon.), Japanese Soc. Clin. Cytology (hon.; Cytopathologist award 1973), Japanese Cancer Assn. (Merit mem.). Lutheran. Avocations: photography, video, audio. Home: 2-7-26 Komagome, Toshima-ku, Tokyo 170, Japan Office: Biomed Labs, 1-34-5 Koenji Minami, Suginami-ku Tokyo 144, Japan

TANAKA, NORIHITO, manufacturing executive; b. Tokyo, Jan. 9, 1937; s. Minoru and Chiyo (Yoshizawa) T.; m. Eiko Osone, Jan. 17, 1967; children: Emi, Atsumi, Satoru. Grad. from econ. faculty, Keio U., Tokyo, 1959. With Nihon Bed Mfg. Co. Ltd., Tokyo, 1959-70, mng. dir., 1970—; mng. dir. Nihon Tekko Co. Ltd., Tokyo, 1970—, pres., 1988—; mng. dir. Nihon Bed Sales Co. Ltd., Tokyo, 1970-87, v.p., 1987—. Home: 1-22-22 Minami Kugahara, Ota-Ku Tokyo 146-0084, Japan Office: Nihon Bed Mfg Co Ltd, 5-6-3 Ikegami, Ota-ku Tokyo 146-0082, Japan

TANAKA, SACHIKO SAKO, educator; b. Hayama, Japan, Mar. 19, 1936; d. Hiroshi and Koh (Shibaoka) Sakomizu; m. Kazumi Tanaka, Nov. 8, 1964; 1 child, Kazusa. BA, Tsuda Coll., Tokyo, 1958; MS, UCLA, 1961, postgrad., 1987—. Lectr. YWCA, Social Welfare Coll., Tokyo, 1969-86; tchr. English Myojo Gakuen High Sch., Tokyo, 1967-63; internat. rels. Nat. Recreation Assn. Japan, Tokyo, 1963-65; prof. Tsuda Coll., Tokyo, 1969—; specialist Torrence (Calif.) Recreation Dept., 1961-62. Co-author: Games of the World, 1969, Arts & Crafts, 1971, Recreation Handbook, 1990, Liesure Counseling, 1994. Advisor Min. Labor, Tokyo, 1988-98; bd. dirs. Nat. Camping Assn., 1976-92, Mhojo Gakuen High Sch., 1990—, Japan Youth Hostel, Tokyo, 1997&. Recipient Mikasa award Nat. Recreation Assn. Japan, Tokyo, 1996, Camping award Nat Camping Assn. Russia, St. Petersburg, 1997. Mem. Internat. Psychol. Coun., World Leisure & Recreation Assn. Avocations: Japanese flower arrangement, tea ceremony, swimming, piano. Home: 2-10-19 Wakabacho Chofu-shi, Tokyo 182-0003, Japan Office: Tsuda Coll, 2-1-1 Tsuda-machi, Tokyo 186-8755, Japan

TANAKA, SATOSHI, sociologist; b. Hikari, Yamaguchi, Japan, Nov. 4, 1958; s. Toshiichi and Reiko (Torieda) T.; m. Keiko Shimada, June 14, 1986; 1 child, Yutarow. MEd, Waseda U., Tokyo, 1985, PhD, 1988. Asst. prof. Sch. Humanity Komazawa U., Tokyo, 1995-97; assoc. prof. Sch. Edn. Tokyo Gakugei U., Tokyo, 1997—; dir. History of Ednl. Thought Soc., Tokyo, 1995—. Editor: (book) Decodage of Education, 1997; contbr. articles to profl. jours. Democrat. Buddhist. Avocation: playing keyboards. Home: Kabemachi 3-1111, 198-0036 Oume Tokyo, Japan Office: Tokyo Gakugei U, Nukuikitamachi 4-1-1, 184 Koganei Tokyo, Japan

TANAKA, SHIGEKI, neurologist; b. Asahikawa, Hokkaido, Japan, Aug. 23, 1953; s. Tsuneo and Mutsu (Nogawa) T.; m. Kumiko Sakai, Nov. 2, 1980; children: Hiroki, Yoshiki, Genki. MD, Juntendo U., Tokyo, 1979. Cons. Shonan Hosp., Kanagawa, Japan, 1976—; resident Juntendo Hosp., Tokyo, 1979, sr. resident, 1980, asst. prof., 1982; neurologist Nat. Kohnodai Hosp., Chiba, Japan, 1981, Nat. Fuji Hosp., Shizuoka, Japan, 1982; assoc. prof. Juntendo Urayasu Hosp., Chiba, 1983-99; dir. neurology Juntendo Urayusa Hosp., Chiba, 1999—. Contbr. articles to profl. jours. Rsch. grantee Ministry of Edn., Japanese Govt., 1988. Fellow Royal Soc. Medicine (London) (overseas); mem. Japanese Soc. Neurology, Am. Acad. Neurology (corr. assoc.). Avocations: reading, jazz, tennis, movies. E-mail: urayn@air.linkclub.or.jp. Home: 1-19-12 Himonya Meguroku, Tokyo 152-0003, Japan Office: Juntendo Urayusa Hosp Dept Neur, 2-1-1 Tomioka, Urayasu 279-0021, Japan

TANAKA, TAKAJI, English educator; b. Tokyo, Japan, June 3, 1934; s. Kametaro Tanaka and Tsuru (Ishii) T.; m. Kyoko Makino, Mar. 1961; children: Toshiaki, Emiko, Eriko. BA in Eng., Rikkyo Univ., Tokyo, 1958, MA in Eng., 1960. Tchr. Rikkyo Elem. Sch., Tokyo, 1960-67; lectr. Tokai Univ., Kanagawa, Japan, 1967-70, assoc. prof., 1970-76, prof., 1976-80; chair Eng. dept. FLC Tokai Univ., 1980-95, asst. dir. FLC, 1995-98; program dir. Tokai H.S. English tchrs. tng., 1981-97. Author: Basic English Pronunciation, 1970, English Pronunciation and Its Speech Clinic, 1973; editor: LL Reports of Tokai Univ., 1976-80. Adv. City Bd. Edn. Kanagawa, 1983-90. Mem. Language Lab. Assn., The Phonetic Soc. Japan, Liberal and Gen. Edn. Soc. Japan. Avocations: travel, gardening. Home: 2559-1 Hon-Machida, Machida Tokyo 194-0032, Japan Office: Tokai Univ, 1117 Kita-kaname Hiratsuka, Kanagawa 259-1207, Japan

TANAKA, TAKESHI, electrical engineering educator; b. Hiroshima, Japan, Jan. 31, 1960; s. Osamu and Yoshie (Kihara) T.; m. Chisako Miyasaki, Dec. 21, 1991; children: Mare, Sou. BEngring., Hiroshima U., 1982, MEngring., 1984, DEngring., 1990. Asst. Hiroshima Inst. Tech., 1987-90, lectr., 1990-94, assoc. prof. engring., 1994—. Contbr. articles to Vacuum, Japan Jour. Applied Physics, Thin Solid Films, Jour. Vacuum Sci. Tech., others. Mem. IEEE, Am. Vacuum Soc., Japan Soc. Applied Physics, Inst. Electronics, Info. and Comm. Engrs. Avocations: driving, reading, walking, running. Home: 5-7-302 Minamisaiwaimachi, Kaita-cho Aki-gun, Hiroshima 736-0032, Japan Office: Hiroshima Inst Tech, 2-1-1 Miyake Saiki-ku, Hiroshima 731-5193, Japan

TANAKA, TOSHIJIRO, physicist; b. Ooda, Shimane, Japan, July 12, 1944; s. Takeshiro and Masayo (Tanaka) T.; m. Hiroko Kodashiro, Apr. 27, 1983; children: Haruna, Hideki, Yoshiki. BS, Ibaragi U., Mito, Japan, 1967; MS, Kobe (Japan) U., 1969; PhD, Osaka (Japan) U., 1976. Lectr. Kagoshima (Japan) Prefectural Coll., 1977-78, assoc. prof., 1978-84, prof., 1984—; vis. scholar U. Calif., Santa Barbara, 1979-80. Mem. com. Kagoshima Indsl. Tech. Assn., 1990—. Recipient MBC prize Minami Nihon Broadcasting Co. Ltd., Kagoshima, 1990. Mem. Inst. Elec., Info., Com. Engring., Phys. Soc. Japan, Am. Phys. Soc., Physics Edn. Soc. Japan. Avocations: tennis, igo, Japanese folk music, dance. Home: 7-13-10 Takaya Takamigaoka, Higashihiroshima Higashi-Hiroshima 739-2115, Japan Office: Hiroshima Prefecture U, 562 Nanatsuka Shobara, Hiroshima 727-0023, Japan

TANAKA, YASUO, otorhinolaryngology educator; b. Kyoto, Kansai, Japan, Mar. 14, 1931; s. Shuichiro and Take (Kamio-Tanaka) T.; m. Reiko Nakagawa, Oct. 3, 1960; 1 child, Akio. MD, Kyoto Prefecture U. Medicine, 1956, PhD, 1964. Instr. otolaryngology Kyoto Prefecture U. Medicine, 1959-63, vis. assoc. prof., 1967-75; instr. physiology Tokyo Med. and Dental U., 1963-65; asst. rsch. scientist NYU, N.Y.C., 1965-67; vis. assoc. prof. Tsurumi U. Sch. Dentistry, Yokohama, Japan, 1975-79; assoc. prof. Dokkyo U. Sch. Medicine, Tochigi, Japan, 1979-83, prof., 1983-96, prof. emeritus, 1996—; head dept. otolaryngology Kaibara Red Cross Hosp., Hyogo Prefecture, Japan, 1961, Yodogawa Christian Hosp., Osaka, Japan, 1961-63, Dokkyo U. Koshigaya Hosp., 1983-96; dir. Nagokakyo City Med. Clinic, 1967-79. Contbr. articles to profl. jours. Grantee Ministry of Edn., Japan, 1985, 88, 89, 90, 91, 94, 95. Mem. Japan Audiol. Soc. (councilor 1993—, del. Otoacoustic Emission sect. 1993-96, chmn. com. terminology 1998—), Japan Otological Soc. (councilor 1993—), Soc. of Practical Otolaryngology (com. mem. 1993—). Avocation: collecting wooden Dharma images. Office: Tanaka ENT Clinic, Nagaokakyoshi 4-5 Takenodai, Kyoto fu 6170827, Japan

TANAKA, YOSHIHIRO, engineering educator, researcher; b. Kobe, Hyogo, Japan, Feb. 21, 1960; s. Yoshiharu and Satsuki (Fukuhara) T. B of Engring., Kyoto U., Japan, 1982, M of Engring., 1984, DEng, 1988. Sr. rschr. CRIEPI, Tokyo, 1989-91; assoc. prof. Hokkaido U., Sapporo, Japan, 1991—; Mem. br. com. of OR Soc. of Japan, Sapporo, 1992-94. Contbr. articles to profl. jours. Rsch. fellow U. Calif. Berkeley, Japan Ministry of Edn., 1994-95. Mem. AAAS, Math. Program Soc. (Amsterdam), Soc. Insl. Appl. Math., N.Y. Acad. Scis. Avocations: reading, shogi (l-dan). Office: Hokkaido U Econs, Kita 9 Nishi 7 Kita-ku, Sapporo 060-0809, Japan

TANAKAWA, NOBUO, pediatrician, hospital administrator; b. Kitami City, Hokkaido, Japan, Nov. 25, 1946; s. Moriyoshi and Ayako (Mitobe) T.; m. Ritsuko Ichikawa, Mar. 30, 1972. MD, Hokkaido U., Sapporo, 1971. Intern Michael Reese Hosp., Chgo., 1973-74, resident, 1974-75; fellow Nat. Asthma Ctr., Denver, 1975-76, Baylor Coll. Medicine, Houston, 1976-77; staff pediatrician Chuo Hosp., Sapporo, 1977-84, City Hosp., Asahikawa, Japan, 1984-86, Tenshi Hosp., Sapporo, 1986-90; chief pediatrician Fukazawa Hosp., Sapporo, 1990—, dir., 1999—. Mem. Japan Med. Assn., Hokkaido Med. Assn., Sapporo Med. Assn. Avocations: tennis, baseball, table tennis, movies. Home: 2-4-24 Fushimi, Hokkaido Sapporo 064-0942, Japan Office: Fukazawa Hosp, 2-4-6-8 Nijuyonken, Hokkaido Sapporo 063-0802, Japan

TANAKOL, REFIK, endocrinologist, educator; b. Bolu, Turkey, May 29, 1952; s. Fuat Rahmi and Emine Necla (Kuleli) T.; m. Meral Ünsal, July 6, 1984; children: Ali, Ahmet. MD, Istanbul Faculty Medicine, Turkey, 1977, degree in internal medicine, 1982, degree endocrin., nutrition, metabolism, 1993, assoc. prof., 1993, prof., 1999. Obligatory svc. Social Security Hosp., Sanliurfa, Turkey, 1983-89; resident Istanbul Faculty Medicine, 1978-82, resident in endocrinology, 1989-93, lectr., 1993—. Contbr. manuscripts to profl. jours. With Turkish Main Hdqs., 1982-83. Mem. Interant. Osteoporosis Found. (rep. Soc. Turkish Endocrinology and Metabolism 1998-2000), European Calcified Tissues, Osteoporosis Coun. Turkey. Avocations: literature, chess, skiing, basketball.

TANCREDI, LAURENCE RICHARD, law and psychiatry educator, physician; b. Hershey, Pa., Oct. 15, 1940; s. Samuel N. and Alvesta (Pera) T. AB in English, Franklin and Marshall Coll., 1962; MD, U. Pa., 1996; JD, Yale U., 1972. Diplomate Am. Bd. Neurology and Psychiatry; Bar: N.Y. 1982. Sr. profl. assoc. Inst. Medicine, NAS, Washington, 1972-74; fellow in psychiatry Columbia U. Coll. Physicians and Surgeons, N.Y.C., 1974-75; postdoctoral fellow in psychiatry Yale U. Med. Sch., New Haven, 1975-77, assoc. prof. psychiatry, 1977-84; Kraft Eidman prof. medicine and law U. Tex. Health Sci. Ctr., Houston, 1984-92, dir. health law program, 1983-92; clin. prof. psychiatry NYU, 1992—; clin. prof. health care scis. U. Calif., San Diego, 1993—; mem. staff Brookhaven nat. Labs. Clin. Ctr., 1994-96; pvt. practice N.Y.C., 1994—; v.p. Internat. Acad. Law and Mental Health, 1987-95; mem. tech. bd. dirs. Milbank Meml. Fund, N.Y.C., 1981-84; mem. adv. com. on transplantations Health Care Fin. Adminstrn., Dept. Health and Human Svcs., 1981-84; nat. adv. bd. NIMH Ctr. for the Study of Pub. Mental Health N.Y. State Office Mental Health, 1994—; mem. cmty. svcs. bd. Dept. Mental Health, Mental Retardation and Alcohol Svcs., City of N.Y., 1995—; mem. sci. adv. com. Am. Suicide Found., 1995—; cons. Commn. on Med. Profl. Liability, co-prin. investigator study ABA, 1978-80; cons. in field. Office: 129B E 71st St New York NY 10021-4201

TANDE, JOHN OLAV GIAEVER, research scientist; b. Trondheim, Norway, Mar. 22, 1962; arrived in Denmark, 1990; s. Severin and Birgit (Giaever) T. BSEE, Trondheim Ingeniere Hoyskole, 1985; MS in Elec. Power Engring., Norwegian Inst. Tech., 1988. Scientist Risø Nat. Lab., Roskilde, Denmark, 1990—; convenor W610 Internat. Electrotech. Commn. TC88, 1996—; scientist Norwegian Elec. Power Rsch. Inst., Trondheim, 1997—. Editor: (book) IEA Expert Group Study on Estimation of Cost of Energy from Wind Energy Conversion Systems, 1994; contbr. articles to profl. jours. Avocations: Shotokan karate, hiking, skiing. Office: EFI, Sintef Energy Rsch, 7465, Trondheim Norway

TANDON, OM PRAKASH, neurophysiologist, educator, researcher; b. Lahore, India, July 3, 1944; s. Rallia Ram and Raj Rani (Sumitra Chopra) T.; m. Indu Vadehra, May 27, 1973; children: Shruti, Tripti. Student, S.D.B. Coll., Simla, India, 1961-62; MB, BChir, Med. Coll., Amritsar, India, 1967; MD in Physiology, All India Inst. Med. Scis., New Delhi, 1971. From tutor physiology to lectr. All India Inst. Med. Scis., 1969-75; postdoctoral fellow UCLA, 1975, Sch. Medicine Yokohama (Japan) City U., 1980; head dept. physiology U. Delhi, India, 1992-96, dean faculty med. scis., 1993-96; reader physiology Univ. Coll. Med. Scis., Delhi, 1975-82, prof., 1983—, officiating prin., 1999-2000; rsch. fellow WHO, Geneva, 1975; exch. scientist Indian Nat. Sci. Acad. and Japan Soc. for Promotion of Sci., 1980; vis. prof. Indo-U.S. cultural program U. Tex. Med. Sch., Houston, 1985; univ. grants com. exchange scientist Postgrad. Inst. Medicine, Budapest, 1989; expert, examiner Univ. Sains, Malaysia, 1991; cons. Commonwealth Higher Edn. Mgmt. Svc., London, 1995—; expert scientific adv. group Indian Coun. of Med. Coun., 1999. Author: Multiple Choice Questions in Human Physiology, 3d edit., 1996, Synopsis of Human Physiology Part I, Part II, 2nd edit., 1998; co-author: Med. Physiology, 1995; editor: (physiology) Indian Jour. Physiology and Pharmacology; contbr. articles to profl. jours.; spkr. Talks on Health program All India Radio, 1984-88. Warden Civil Home Def., Amritsar, India, 1965. Fulbright scholar UCLA, 1992; recipient A.V. Tilak Parvati Devi award in neuroendocrinology, 1984, B.K. Anand award in neurophysiology, 1989, Hari Om Ashram Alembic award for rsch. in basic med. scis., 1994, Maj. Gen. SL Bhatia Oration award for outstanding rsch. publs. in physiology, 1998, Prof. A.K. Mukherjee Meml. oration Physiol. Soc. India, 1999. Fellow Indian Assn. Biomed. Scientists, Nat. Acad. Med. Scis.; mem. Assn. Physiologists and Pharmacologists India (pres. Delhi br. 1982-84, 96—), Indian Med. Assn., Neurosci. Soc. India, Assn. Gerontology India (v.p.), Internat. Brain Rsch. Orgn. (elected), Internat. Assn. Gerontology (mem. regional coun. 1995-96), Fedn. of Indian Physiol. Soc. (gen. assembly). Avocations: singing, stamp collecting, gardening, badminton. Office: U Coll Med Scis, GTB Hosp, Dept Physiology, 110095 Delhi India

TANDON, RAJIV, training company executive; b. Allahabad, India, May 9, 1944; came to U.S., 1969; s. Jagdish Bihari and Vimla Devi (Mehrotra) T.; m. Priti Khanna, Sept. 1969; children: Ribhu Dev, Veeti. BTech with honors, Indian Inst. of Tech., 1966, MS in Ops. Rsch., 1972; MBA, U. Minn., 1972, PhD, 1987. Trainee Kumardhubi (India) Engring. Works, 1966-67, prodn. control officer, 1967-69; ops. rsch. analyst Nat. Car Rental, Mpls., 1971-72, mgr. ops. rsch., 1972-75, dir. fin. analysis, 1975-77, corp. v.p., MIS, 1977-81, corp. v.p., gen. mgr. car rental, 1981-86; dir. venture mgmt. U. St. Thomas, Mpls., 1988-93, dir. corp. venturing, 1993-95; pres., CEO Learning Byte Internat. (formerly Inst. for Advanced Tech.), Mpls., 1995—; mgmt. cons., 1986-95;. Exec. editor New Venture Rev., 1985-90; contbr. articles to profl. jours. Pres. Planners League, 1978. Mem. Am. Mgmt. Assn., Inst. of Noetic Sci., Inst. of Mgmt. Scis. (sec. upper Midwest chpt. 1975-76, v.p. 1976-77, pres. 1977-78). Avocations: reading, news. Home: 8109 Rhode Island Ave S Bloomington MN 55438-1146 Office: Learning Byte Internat 300 Highway 169 S Ste 350 Minneapolis MN 55426-1107

TANDON, VEENA, parasitology educator, researcher; b. Kashipur, Uttar Pradesh, India, Sept. 7, 1949; d. Pratap Narain and Pushpalata (Tandon) Mehrotra; m. Pramod Tandon, June 15, 1978; 1 child, Prateek. BS with honors, Panjab U., Chandigarh, India, 1967, MS with honors, 1968, PhD, 1973. Asst. prof. Zoology Himachal Pradesh U., Shimla, India, 1974-80; lectr. N.-Ea. Hill U., Shillong, India, 1980-84, reader, 1984-91, prof. parasitology, 1991—; postdoct. jr. spls. U. Calif., Irvine, 1978-79. Nat. Merit Scholar Govt. of India, 1967. Fellow Zool. Soc. India, Helminthol. Soc. India, NAS; mem. Indian Soc. Parasitology (life), Indian Sci. Congress Assn. (life), Zoo Outreach Organ. (life). Avocations: gardening, travel. Home: 12 NEHU-Quarters, 793022 Shillong Meghalaya, India Office: N-Ea Hill U, Mawkynroh, 793022 Shillong Meghalaya, India

TANDON, VINOD KUMAR, engineering educator; b. Sargodha, Punjab, India, Mar. 11, 1942; s. Madan Mohan and Janak (Kapoor) T.; m. Shubhra Kumar Aurora, Nov. 22, 1971; children: Vishesh, Vaibhav. BE, Coll. of Mil. Engring., 1967; MSc, Def. Coll., 1973. Cons. J.C. Mgmt. Cons., Ahmedabad, 1986-89; mng. trustee J.M. Charitable Edn. Trust, Ahmedabad, 1987—; mng. dir. Vishesh Security Svcs., Ahmedabad, 1987-98, Vishesh Laminators Ltd., Ahmedabad, 1996—. Mem. Cantonment Bd., Ahmedabad, 1983-86. Col. Elec. and Mech. Br., 1983-86. Avocations: golf, music, travel, reading, yoga. E-mail: kabir@adivasnl.net.in. Fax: 0091-79-402261. Home: Janak Kutir NR Army, Firing Range Hansol Gujart, Ahmedabad 382475, India Office: 60 Kamdhenu Complex OPP, Sahjanand Coll Ambawadi, Ahmedabad 380018, India

TANDY, JEAN CONKEY, art educator; b. Reese, Mich., May 17, 1931; d. Samuel Hall and Christine Margaret (Walker) Conkey; m. Norman Edward Tandy, Jan. 25, 1952; children: Michelle Tandy Ryan, Kristen, Peter Spence. BA, Mich. State U., 1962, MA in Fine Arts, 1965. Instr. French French Bath (Mich.) Cmty. Schs., 1961-62, designer program art curriculum, instr., 1962-67; instr. art Mahar Regional Schs., Orange, Mass., 1966-67, Athol (Mass.)-Royalston Regional Schs., 1967-68; invited designer, developer art curriculum Mt. Wachusett C.C., Gardner, Mass., 1968, chair art dept., 1968—, prof. art, 1968—. Watercolors and clay exhibited on regular basis, 1950—. Mt. Wachusett C.C. grantee, 1970-96, Fed. Govt. grantee, 1968; chosen for subject of Mount Wachusett C.C. Most Valuable Faculty Series film. Mem. Women's Caucus for Art, Mass. C.C. Coun., Women in Arts, Teaching Faculty Assn. (v.p. 1979-80, pres. 1980-81, grievance officer 1981-82). Independent. Avocations: gardening, writing poetry and children's stories, reading, travel. Home: 539 Whipple Hill Rd PO Box 2 Winchester NH 03470-0002

TANEJA, DALIP SINGH, soil and water engineer, researcher; b. Punjab, India, Feb. 29, 1944; s. Sadhu Ram Taneja and Lal Devi Huria; m. Sheela Devi Arora, Sept. 21, 1974; children: Menka, Rajinder, Vimi. BS, D.A.V. Coll., Abohar, India, 1965; BS in Agrl. Engring., Coll. Agrl. Engring., Ludhiana, India, 1969, MS in Agrl. Engring., 1973, PhD in Soil and Water Engring., 1993. Program assoc. Ford Found., Ludhiana, 1969-71; lectr. agrl. engring. Punjab Agrl. U., Ludhiana, 1974-75, asst. rsch. engr., 1975-87, assoc. prof., 1987-88, rsch. engr., 1988-95, sr. rsch. engr., 1995—; state engr. Ministry of Hydraulics, Algeria, 1979-83. Author: A Manual on Centrifugal Pumps for Irrigation, 1986, Handbook of Indian Pumps for Irrigation, 1988; editor: Optimization of Groundwater Utilization, 1993; contbr. articles to profl. publs. Councillor Punjab Agrl. Univ. Tchrs. Assn., 1988, 97-98. Recipient Commendation medal Punjab Pump Mfrs. Assn., 1992. Mem. Bur. Indian Stds. (mem. pump sectional com. 1996—), Indian Soc. Tech. Edn. (life), Indian Soc. Agrl. Engrs. (life, bd. dirs. 1996-97, vice-chmn. Punjab chpt. 1997-98, various awards 1987-89, 92, 91-92, 96, 98). Fax: 0161-400945. Home: 51-E Bhai, Randhir Singh Nagar, Ludhiana 141004 Punjab, India Office: Punjab Agrl U, Dept Soil & Water Engring, Ludhiana 141004, India

TANEYA, SHIN'ICHI, food science and technology consultant, rheologist; b. Sapporo, Hokkaido, Japan, Dec. 4, 1931; s. Ichiro Watanabe and Midori Tokuno Taneya; m. Chieko Matu'ura, Mar. 17, 1957; children: Yasuo, Nobuo, Yasuyo. BS, Sci. U. Tokyo, 1955; DSc, Tokyo Met. U., 1970. Sr. rschr. Tech. Inst., Snow Brand Milk Products Co., Ltd., Kawagoe, Japan, 1955-85, pres. Tech. Inst., 1985-92; prof. Faculty of Agr. Nat. Iwate U., Morioka, Japan, 1992-97, prof. Union Grad. Sch., 1992-97; gen. mgr. engring. divsn. Dalton Corp., Fujieda, Japan, 1997—; pres. Nat. Membrane Rsch. Com., Tokyo, 1989-90; food tech. advisor Iwate (Japan) Province, Morioka, 1994—, Akita (Japan) Province, 1996—. Author book; contbr. articles to profl. jours. Recipient Letter of Appreciation, Japan Soc. Powder Tech., 1996, Jilin U. Tech., 1996. Mem. Japan Soc. Sci. and Tech. (councilor 1996-98). Avocations: fishing, swimming. Home: 625-18 Hirashima, Fujieda, Shizuoka 426-0011, Japan Office: Dalton Corp, 407-3 Yawata, Fujieda, Shizuoka 426-0009, Japan

TANG, BEN ZHONG, science educator, researcher; b. Qianjiang, Hubei, China; arrived in Canada, 1989; s. Jia Fu Tang and Hua Zhen Yin; m. Xiao Jun Tuo; children: Michael, Natalie, Felicity. BS, South China U. Tech., Guangzhou, China, 1982; MS, Kyoto U., Japan, 1985, PhD, 1988. Vis. scientist Sumitomo Chem. Co., Ltd., Osaka, Japan, 1988-89; rsch. assoc. U. Toronto, 1989-94; sr. scientist Neos Co., Ltd., Shiga, Japan, 1989-94; asst. prof. Hong Kong U. Sci. & Tech., China, 1994-2000; assoc. prof. Hong Kong U. Sci. & Tech., 2000—; exec. com. Joint Lab. Nanostructured Materials and Tech., 1997—. Mem. editl. bd. Acta Polymerica Sinica, 1997—; contbr. articles to profl. jours.; inventor in field; reviewer: Nat. Natural Sci. Found., Beijing, 1997—, Rsch. Grants Coun., Hong Kong, 1996—. Mem. ACS (reviewer book series 1999), Hong Kong Instn. Sci., Hong Kong Chem. Soc., Soc. Plastics Engrs. (Hong Kong chpt., exec. com. 1995—). Avocations: reading, singing. Home: Apt 15 HKUST, 1 University Rd, Kowloon Hong Kong China Office: Hong Kong U Sci & Tech, Dept Chemistry, Kowloon Hong Kong China

TANG, DAWSON, private banker; b. Hong Kong, Nov. 26, 1956; s. T.C. and Sheila (Wang) T.; m. Polly Chang; children: Stephanie, Kevin. BA, U. Calif., Berkeley, 1974; MBA, UCLA, 1977. Lic. real estate broker, Calif. Officer Chase Manhattan Bank, N.Y.C., 1977-80; v.p. Bank of Am., San Francisco, 1980-83; pres. Crane Group Inc. Ltd., San Francisco, 1983-88; sr. mgr., head Paribas Capital Mkts., Taiwan, 1988-92; mng. dir. Royal Trust Asia Group Ltd., Taipei, Taiwan, 1992—; bd. dirs. Enstrust Securities Investment Trust, Taipei; mng. dir. Royal Trust Bank Asia Ltd., Singapore, 1993. Mem. Rotary (treas. Ctrl. Taipei club 1992, 97). Avocations: photography, reading, hiking, travel, music. Fax: 886 22875-8188. E-mail: tangda@tpts5.seed.net.tw. Office: Royal Trust Asia Gp 16F, 196 Chung Cheng Rd Sec 2, Taipei Taiwan

TANG, DECHAO, manager of computer software company; b. Shanghai, China, Sept. 4, 1950; arrived in Scotland, 1981; s. Shaoming Tang and Lijuan Wang; m. Yuan Zhang, June 1, 1985 (div. 1998). BSc, Harbin (China) U., 1978; MEngring., Tong Ji U., Shanghai, China, 1981; PhD, U. Strathclyde, Glasgow, Scotland, 1985. Assoc. prof. Tong Ji U., Shanghai, China, 1985-88; post-doctoral rsch. engr. U. Liege, Belgium, 1988-89; post-doctoral rsch. fellow U. Strathclyde, Glasgow, Scotland, 1989-92; lectr. U. Abertay, Dundee, Scotland, 1992-95; application devel. mgr. Integrated Environ. Solutions, Ltd., Glasgow, Scotland, 1995—. Contbr. articles to profl. jours., chpt. to book. Recipient Overseas Rsch. award Com. Vice-Chancellors and Prins. Univs., UK, 1983-84. Fellow Chartered Inst. Bldg. Svcs. Engrs., Inst. Energy; mem. Royal Acad Engring (chartered engr.), European Fedn. Nat. Engring. Assns. (European engr.). Mem. Free Ch. of Scotland. Avocations: hill walking, classical music, fishing, history. Fax: 0141 226 3747. E-mail: dechao@ies4d.com. Home: 73 Allander Rd, Bearsden Glasgow G61 1LX, Scotland Office: Orgn Int Environ Solutions, 1 Atlantic Quay, Broomielaw, Broomielan Glasgow G2 8JE, Scotland

TANG, FANG-FU, civil and structural engineer, consultant; b. Nanchong, Sichuan, China, Nov. 20, 1962; came to U.S., 1988; p. Nen-Zhi and Sui-Fang (Zhang) T.; m. Guangrong (Grace) Liu, May 29, 1991; children: Azalea, Becky. BSc, Chongqing U. Arch./Engring., China, 1984; MSc, Wuhan U. Hydro-Elec. Engring., China, 1987; PhD, U. Ariz., 1992. Registered profl. engr., Fla., Pa., W.Va. Vis. scholar U. Ariz., Tucson, 1988-89, rsch. asst., 1989-92; staff engr. Woodward-Clyde Cons., Overland Park, Mo., 1992; engr., sr. engr. Parsons Brinckerhoff, Tampa, Fla., 1992-95; sr. engr. Michael Baker Corp., Pitts., 1995-99, Burgess & Niple, Ltd., Columbus, Ohio, 1999—. Author: Mechanics of Jointed Rock, 1992; contbr. articles to profl. jours. Recipient award for sci. progress China Ministry of Energy, 1991. Mem. ASCE, Am. Concrete Inst., Am. Segmental Bridge Inst. Achievements include design method for composite cable-stayed bridge; bonded overlay construction on concrete segmental box-girder bridges; surface effects and energy characterization for brittle material response through ultrasonic scanning; energy dissipation, heterogeneity and stability of brittle materials, engineering fracture mechanics; stress-seepage coupled analysis for geomaterials and water induced seismicity; borehole scale effects and related instabilities. Avocations: football, swimming, bicycle riding, chess. Office: Burgess & Niple Ltd 5085 Reed Rd Columbus OH 43220-2513

TANG, GORDON YU NAM, business management educator; b. Hong Kong, China, July 6, 1960; s. Ho Hang and Kwan Tip (Wong) T.; m. Lai Wah Ng, Dec. 21, 1986; children: Enoch K.H., Shana I.Y., Seth K.W. BSc in Econs., Univ. Coll., London, 1983; MSc, Imperial Coll. Sci. and Tech., London, 1984; PhD, U. Strathclyde, Glasgow, Scotland, 1995. Stats. officer Hong Kong Polytech. U., 1985-86; asst. lectr. City U. of Hong Kong, 1986-88, lectr., 1988; lectr. Hong Kong Bapt. U., 1988-95, sr. lectr., 1995, assoc. prof., 1995-99, prof., 1999—. Contbr. articles to profl. jours. Mem. Am. Fin. Assn., Asia Pacific Fin. Assn. (founding), Vocat. Tng. Coun. (banking tng. bd.), Hong Kong Securities Inst. (examiner). Baptist. Avocations: reading, swimming. Office: Hong Kong Bapt U, Dept Fin and Decision Scis, Kowloon Hong Kong China

TANG, GRACE W.K., dean. MBBS, 1971. Prof. dept. ob-gyn. U. Hong Kong, dean faculty medicine, 1998—. Office: U Hong Kong 1/F Patrick, Manson Bldg 7 Sassoon Rd, Pok Fu Lan Hong Kong

TANG, HANSONG, computational fluid dynamics researcher; b. Hunan, China, Aug. 13, 1961; came to U.S., 1998; s. Zemin Tang and Degui Zeng; m. Yan Qin, Sept. 30, 1989; 1 child, Da. BS, Wuhan U. Electric-Hydraulic Engring., Wuhan, China, 1983, MEng, 1986; DSc, Peking U., Beijing, 1993. Lectr. Changhsa Comm. Inst., China, 1986-90; rsch. fellow Beijing U. Aeronautics and Astronautics, 1993-95, assoc. prof., 1995-98; rsch. fellow Ga. Inst. Tech., Atlanta, 1998—; cons. Dictionary Chinese Educationalists, Hong Kong, 1998; mem. Sci. Com. on China Aerospace Corp., Beijing, 1997. Editor: Jour. Hydrodynamics, Shanghai, 1999—, Comm. on Nonlinear Scis. and Numerical Simulations, Beijing, 1999—; contbr. articles to sci. jours., including Jour. Computational Physics, Math. Numerical Sinica, SIAM Jour. on Numerical Analysis. Grantee Natural Sci. Found. China, 1996, Aeronautics Sci. Found. China, 1996. Avocations: table tennis, swimming. Office: Ga Inst Tech Sch Civil And Environ Eng Atlanta GA 30332-0001

TANG, JIANMING, electrical engineer, researcher; b. Leting, Hebei, China, Jan. 28, 1968; s. Baishan Tang and Rongyan Liu; m. Ping Li, Dec. 8, 1993; 1 child, No. BSc, Northwest Polytech. U., Xian, China, 1990; MSc, Acad. Sinica, Xian, China, 1993; PhD, U. Wales, Bangor, 1999. Rsch. staff Inst. Optics and Precision Mechanics, Xian, 1993-95; vis. scholar U. Wales, Bangor, 1995-96, rsch. staff, 1999—. Contbr. articles to profl. jours. Mem. Inst. Physics. Avocations: reading, gardening. Office: Sch Elec Engring Computer, Univ Wales Dean St, Bangor LL57 1UT, Wales

TANG, JIAXUAN, Chinese government official; b. Zhenjiang City, China, Jan. 1938. Grad., Peking U. Joined Chinese Communist Party, 1973; first sec. then min. Embassy Chinese Communist Party, Japan; vice min. fgn. affairs Chinese Communist Party, 1993—, mem. 15th ctrl. com., 1997—; min. fgn. affairs Ministry Fgn. Affairs, Beijing. Office: Ministry Fgn Affairs, 225 Chaoyangmennei Daile, Dongsi Beijing 100701, China*

TANG, KALUO, chemistry educator; b. Shanghai, China, Aug. 7, 1939; d. Yuqing Tang and Yongqing Sun; m. Xianglin Jin, May 1, 1967; 1 child, Jing Jin. BS, Peking U., China, 1963, PhD, 1966. Lectr. Peking U., China, 1979-84, assoc. prof., 1987-94, prof., 1994—; vis. prof. SUNY, Albany, 1984-86, 89. Contbr. more than 70 articles to profl. jours. Vice chmn. Tchr. Union Peking U., Beijing, 1995-99; bd. dirs. Internat. Coun. on Main Group Chemistry, 1993-96. Recipient Nat. Natural Sci. Prize (second class), China, 1987, Sci. and Tech. Progress Prize, Nat. Edn. Com. China, 1987; rsch. fellow Chongqing Pharm. Inst., China, 1969-78. Achievements include synthesis and structure investigation of several series of transition metal organometallic and cluster compounds and metallo-fullerence compounds. Avocations: music, piano. Office: Peking U, Chemistry Dept, Beijing 100871, China

TANG, LOON CHING, engineering educator, consultant; b. Singapore, Oct. 25, 1962. BEng with 1st class honors, Nat. U. Singapore, 1987, MEng, 1988; MSc, Cornell U., 1991, PhD, 1992. Assoc. prof. dept. indsl. and sys. engring. Nat. U. Singapore, 1992—, dep. head dept., 1998—, sub-dean engring., 1999—; cons. various govt. agys. & pvt. orgns. Co-editor: OR Applications in Sinagpore, 1995; contbr. numerous articles to sci. jours. Mem. IEEE, Operational Rsch. Soc. Singapore (treas. 1994-97). Fax: 03065-777-1434. E-mail: isetlc@nus.edu.sg. Office: NUS Dept Ind & Sys Engring, 10 Kent Ridge Crescent, Singapore 119260, Singapore

TANG, MAN-CHUNG, engineer, administrator; b. Xiao Qing, China, Feb. 22, 1938; came to U.S., 1968; s. Yu-Fung and Jing Tse Tang; m. Yee-Yun Fung, Aug. 26, 1966; children: Chin-Chung, Chin-Ning. BSc, Chu-Hai Coll., Hong Kong, 1959; MS, Tech. U. Darmstadt, Germany, 1964, PhD, 1965; DLitt (hon.), Chu-Hai U., Hong Kong, 1997. Registered profl. engr., N.Y., Mass., Fla., Ill., Wash., others. Bridge engr. GHH, Germany, 1965-68; sr. engr. Severud & Assocs., N.Y.C., 1968-70; v.p., chief engr. Dyckerhoff & Widmann, N.Y.C., 1970-78; pres. DRC Cons. Inc., N.Y.C., 1978—; chmn. bd. T.Y. Lin Internat., San Francisco, 1995—. Contbr. more than 100 articles to profl. jours. Recipient Leadership award Am. Segmental Bridge Inst., 1991, Roebling Life Achievement award Internat. Bridge Conf., 1998. Mem. ASCE (hon.; named N.Y. Civil Engr. of Yr. 1989), Nat. Acad. Engring. (life). Achievements include pioneer work in design and construction of cable-stayed and segmental bridges. Office: TY Lin Internat 825 Battery St San Francisco CA 94111-1528

TANG, PAUL CHI LUNG, philosophy educator; b. Vancouver, B.C., Can., Jan. 23, 1944; came to U.S., 1971; s. Pei-Sung and Violet (Wong) T. BSc with high distinction, U. B.C., 1966; MA in Edn., Simon Fraser U., Vancouver, 1971; MA, Washington U., St. Louis, 1975, PhD, 1982; cert. in ethics, Kennedy Inst. Ethics, 1983; diploma in piano, Royal Conservatory Music, Toronto, 1962. Teaching asst. philosophy of edn. Simon Fraser U., 1969-71; instr. philosophy St. Louis C.C. at Meramec, Kirkwood, Mo., 1975-82; instr., lectr. philosophy Washington U., 1972-76; adj. asst. prof. Harris-Stowe State Coll., St. Louis, 1980-82; asst. prof. philosophy Grinnell (Iowa) Coll., 1982-85; asst. prof. to assoc. prof. to prof. dept. philosophy Calif. State U. Long Beach, 1985—, chmn. dept. philosophy, 1988-94, acting chmn., 1998; vis. lectr. philosophy So. Ill. U., Edwardsville, 1978-79. Contbr. numerous articles and revs. to profl. publs.; editor Philosophy of Sci. Assn. Newsletter, 1985-90; asst. editor Philosophy of Sci. acad. jour., 1972-75. Senator Internat. Parliament for Safety and Peace, Palermo, Italy. Decorated knight Templar Order of Jerusalem, knight Order Holy Cross of Jerusalem, knight comdr. Lofsenic Ursinius Order, chevalier Grand Crois de Milice du St. Sepulcre; recipient cert. of merit Student Philosophy Assn., 1988-90, 93-94, spl. award, 1992, Calif. State Senate Recognition award for commitment to edn., 1997; named faculty advisor of yr. Assoc. Students, 1987, 90, 91, 95, Highland Lord of Camster, Scotland, 1995; Paul Tang prize in philosophy named in his honor, 1996-99; fellow Washington U., 1971, summer rsch. fellow Calif. State U., 1988, 96, NEH fellow Harvard U., 1988, NEH Summer Seminar fellow, 1988; internat. scholar Phi Beta Delta, interdisciplinary scholar Phi Kappa Phi, 1993, Phi Beta Kappa, 2000; grantee vis. philosophers program Coun. for Philos. Studies, 1987, 91, 92; Disting. Vis. Scholars and Artists Fund, Calif. State U., 1988, 89, rsch. grantee, 1995, 97, 99. Fellow World Lit. Acad.; mem. Am. Philos. Assn. (Excellence in Tchg. award 1995, 97), Philosophy of Sci. Assn., History of Sci. Soc., Kennedy Inst. Ethics, Hastings Ctr., Iowa Philos. Soc. (pres. 1985-86), Brit. Soc. Philosophy of Sci., Soc. Philosophy and Psychology, Maison Internat. des Intellectuels de l'Acad. Francaise, Internat. Order Merit (Eng.), Golden Key Hon. Soc. (Internat. Man of Yr. 1995-96), Order Internat. Fellowship (Eng.), numerous others. Avocations: hiking, tennis, chess, music, travel. Home: 5050 E Garford St Apt 228 Long Beach CA 90815-2859 Office: Calif State U Dept Philosophy 1250 N Bellflower Blvd Long Beach CA 90840-0006

TANG, SHENGMING, sociology educator; b. Shanghai, China, Sept. 5, 1951; s. Wenching Tang and Yunyu Wu; m. Qilin Gu, Aug. 30, 1981; 1 child, Shawn Tang. BA, East China Normal U., Shanghai, 1982, MA, 1985; PhD, U. Nebr., 1992. Lectr. East China Normal U., Shanghai, 1985-88; asst. prof. Kenyon Coll., Gambier, Ohio, 1992-93; asst. prof. Western Ill. U., Macomb, 1993-97, assoc. prof., 1997—, dir. sociology grad. program, 1998—. Authro: Practical Approaches to Social Research, 1998; contbr. articles to profl. jours. Advisor Chinese Student Orgn., Western Ill. U., 1997—. Summer Rsch. grantee Western Ill. U., Macomb, 1999. Mem. Am. Sociol. Assn., Ea. Sociol. Soc., Western Sociol. Soc. Avocations: reading, classical music, playing piano, table tennis. E-mail: mfst@wiu.edu. Home: 310 Jamestown Rd Macomb IL 61455-9328 Office: Western Ill Univ 1 University Cir Macomb IL 61455-1390

TANG, SHUANG, computer programmer, researcher; b. Beijing, Dec. 24, 1957; s. Yijie and Diayun (Yue) T.; m. Joy Z. Zhang, June 12, 1983; 1 child, Brady. BS, U. Sci. and Tech. China, Hefei, 1982; PhD, SUNY, Stony Brook, 1988. Rsch. assoc. U. Md., College Park, 1988-92, Oreg. State U., Corrallis, 1992-95; sr. program developer Veson Computer Inc., N.Y.C., 1995—. Contbr. articles to profl. jours. Avocations: bridge. E-mail: shuangtang@yahoo.com. Home: 171 E 84th St Apt 23A New York NY 10028-2082 Office: Veson Computer Inc 29 Broadway Rm 1002 New York NY 10006-3101

TANG, TUCKHON ALEX, pediatrician; b. Malaysia, Feb. 12, 1955; s. Sikhung Tang and Wongfoo Leong; m. Agnes Tan, June 3, 1981; children: Kayin, Poyin. MD, Nat. U. Malaysia, 1981; Diploma in Child Health, Royal Coll. Physicians, Glasgow, Scotland, 1987. Med. officer Ministry of Health, Johor, 1982-85, registrar, 1985-87, clin. specialist, 1988; postgrad. fellow U. Edinburgh, 1987; cons. paediatrician Med. Ctr. Johor, 1988-89, Johor Specialist Hosp., 1989—; dir. T.H. Tang Baby & Child Clinic, Inc., Johor, 1990—. Com. mem. Hilltop Pvt. Sch. Bd., Johor, 1989—, Johor Spastic Assn., 1988—. Fellow Royal Coll. Physicians, Coll. Chest Physicians, Royal Coll. Physicians (Edinburgh), Acad. Medicine Malaysia; mem. Royal Coll. Physicians London, Royal Coll. Physicians Edinburgh, Malaysian Med. Assn., Internat. Child Health Group, Malaysian Pediat. Assn., Rotary Club of Tebrau (chair heart fund 1994—, cmty. svc. chair 1995). Christian Ch. Avocations: reading, book collecting, internet cybersurfing. Office: Johor Specialist Hosp, 39B Jalan Abdul Samad, 80100 JB Johor Bahru Malaysia

TANG, WALTER ZHONGHONG, environmental engineer; b. Hubei, China, Nov. 12, 1962; came to U.S., 1986; s. Yuxiang Tang and Yongcui Hu; m. Yinghua Zhang, July 19, 1993; 1 child, William Warren. BS in Sanitary Engring., Chongking (China) U., 1983; MS in Environ. Engring., Tsinghua U., Beijing, 1986, U. Mo., Rolla, 1988; PhD in Environ. Engring., U. Del., 1993. Registered profl. engr., Fla. Rsch. asst. U. Mo., Rolla, 1986-89, U. Del., Newark, 1989-91; asst. prof. environ. engring. Fla. Internat. U., Miami, 1991-97, assoc. prof., 1997—; mem. Asian studies program com. Fla. Internat. U., 1996, mem. com. Internat. Hurricane Rsch. Ctr., 1996—; referee Jour. Environ. Engring., Water Rsch., Chemosphere, Jour. Hazardous and Toxic Materials, Jour. Hazardous Wastes, Jour. Waste Mgmt., Environ. Tech., Rsch. on Chem. Intermediates; ozone sci. and engring. cons., environ. sci. and tech. cons. Fla. Internat. U., 1991—, U. Del., 1989-91, U. Mo.-Rolla, 1986-89; vis. prof. Chongqing U., 1998—, Chongqing Civil and Archl. U., 1998—. Co-author book; contbr. more than 30 articles to profl. publs. Recipient Faculty Excellence in Rsch. award Fla. Internat. U., 1997, Tchr. of Yr. award Fla. Internat. U. Engring. Honor Soc., 1997, Faculty Teaching award Fla. Internat. U., 1997; grantee U.S. EPA, 1993-95, 96—, NSF, 1993-95, Fla. Internat. U. Rsch. Found., 1993; China-Cornell Rsch. fellow Rockefeller Found., 1994-97, NIH, 1997—, Nat. Natural Sci. Found., China, 1998, China Ministry Edn., 1998. Mem. Am. Environ. Engring. Profs., Internat. Assn. on Water Quality, Am. Water Works Assn. Avocations: violin, fitness, running. Office: Fla Internat U Dept Civil Environ Engring Miami FL 33199-0001

TANG, YI, radiologist, researcher; b. Yichang, Hubei, China, Dec. 20, 1963; s. Zhongni and deying (Liu) T.; m. Xuling Huang, Oct. 2, 1988; 1 child, Zhicao. MD, Sun Yat-Sen U. of Med. Scis., Guangzhou, China, 1987; PhDd., Kumamoto (Japan) U., 2000. Resident Guangdong Provincial People's Hosp., Guangzhou, 1987-93, attending physician, 1993-95; guest rschr. Kumamoto U., 1995-96. Reviewer Jour. of Magnetic resonance Imaging, 1999; contbr. articles to profl. jours. Higo Yiyoku Seshikai scholar, 1998, Konan Asia Internat. Found. scholar, 1999. Mem. Radiol. Soc. N.Am., Japanese Soc. of Magnetic Resonance Imaging. Avocations: table tennis, swimming, driving. Office: univ Tex MD Andersen Cancer Str Dept Diag Radiology 1515 Holcombe Blvd Houston TX 77030-4009

TANG, YUAN YAN, computer science educator; b. Chengdu, Sichuan, China, Dec. 28, 1943; s. Yong Xi Tang and Shu Yu Wei; m. Liang Yun Wang, Apr. 25, 1972; 1 child, Zhaoping. B, Chongqing (China) U., 1966; M, Beijing U. Posts and Telecom., 1981; D, Concordia U., Montreal, Que., Can., 1990. Elec. engr. Beijing Inst. Data Processing, 1966-78; assoc. prof. Beijing Inst. Info. and Control, 1981-82; sr. rschr. Concordia U., Montreal, 1990-95; prof. Hong Kong Bapt. U., 1995—; dir. database divsn. Beijing Inst. Info. and Control, 1981-82; chair 17th Internat. Conf. on Computer Processing of Oriental Langs., 1997; chair, 2nd Internatl. Conf. on Multimodel Interface (ICMI99), 1999. Author: Electronic Designer's Graphics, 1981, Electronic Power Amplifier, 1987, Computer Transformation of Digital Images and Patterns, 1989; Wavelet Theory and its Application to Pattern Recognition, 1999; contbr. over 160 articles to profl. jours.; assoc. editor, guest editor to 14 books, Internat. Jour. Pattern Recognition and Artificial Intelligence, 1997—. Chmn. Chinese Student Soc., Montreal, 1983-89. Mem. IEEE (sr.), Chinese Lang. Computer (life), Pattern Recognition Soc. Office: Hong Kong Bapt U, Dept Computer Sci, Kowloon Hong Kong China

TANG, YUAN-LIANG, technology educator; b. Yuan-Lin, Taiwan, May 2, 1964; s. Bio-chao and Huei-Ping (Lee) T. BSc, Chung-Yuan Christian U., Taiwan, 1986; MS, Pa. State U., 1991, PhD, 1994. Software deisgner TAISEL, Taipei, 1988-89; tchg. asst. Pa. State U., 1990-91, rsch. asst., 1991-94; assoc. prof. Nat. Ping-Tung (Taiwan) Inst. Comemrce, 1994-97, Chaoyang U. Tech., Taichung, Taiwan, 1997—; mem. Nat. Assembly, Taiwan, 1996—. Mem. New Party. Office: Info Mgmt/Chaoyang U Tech, 168 Gifeng E Rd, Wufeng, Taichung Taiwan

TANG, ZHENG YU, lawyer; b. Wuxi, Jiangsu, China, Sept. 6, 1962; s. Qu Fei Tang and Feng Xing Hu; m. Ying Guo, Dec. 31, 1998. BA in Econs., Shanghai Maritime U., 1983; LLM, Chinese Acad. Social Scis., Beijing, 1986; JD, U. Maine, 1992. Bar: Pa. Arbitration clk. China Legal Affairs Ctr., Beijing, 1986-88, lawyer, 1988-89; assoc. Hancock Rothert & Bunshoft, L.A., 1992-94; ptnr. Commerce & Fin., Beijing, 1994; assoc., legal cons. Denton Hall, Beijing, 1994-98, ptnr., 1998—. Avocations: classical music, ballet, swimming, reading, travel. Office: Denton Hall, China World Tower Rm 3325, Beijing 100004, Chin

TANG, ZHI-LIAN, polymer engineering educator, researcher; b. Shanghai, China, Oct. 14, 1929; s. Chi-Xian Tang and Xiu-Yin Chen; m. Xue-Hong Wang; 1 child, Wei Tang. Grad., China Textile U., Shanghai, 1952; student, Dairen (China) U. Sci. Tech., 1954-55. Asst. lectr. China Textile U., 1952-80; assoc. prof. polymer engring. China Textile U., 1980-83; vis. scholar Rutgers U., New Brunswick, N.J., 1983-86; prof. polymer engring. China Textile U., 1986—, advisor PhD program, 1988—; joint projects rschr. Noyvallesina Eng. SpA, Parre, Italy, 1993-97, Karl Fischer GmbH, Berlin, 1993—, Hosokawa Bepex Corp., Mpls., 1997—, DuPont Nylon, Wilmington, Del., 1998—, BASF, Ludwigshaven, Germany, 1997—; cons. Chem. Fibre Rsch. Inst., China Textile U., 1988—. Contbr. articles to profl. jours. Recipient award of progress in sci. and tech., Shanghai Municipality, 1993, award for dir. outstanding young scholars, 1995. Office: China Textile U, 1882 West Yan An Rd, Shanghai 200051, China

TANG, ZHI-PING, mechanical engineer, educator; b. Changzhou, China, Sept. 22, 1945; s. Xiao-sheng Tang and Xing-yu Qin; m. Xiang-li Liao; children: Yan, Yang. BS, U. Sci. and Tech. China, Beijing, 1968; MS, U. Sci. and Tech. China, Hefei, China, 1981. Technician, Ministry of Railway, Sichuan, China, 1968-74; lectr. Neijiang Railway Engring. Sch., Sichuan, 1974-78; lectr. U. Sci. and Tech. China, Hefei, 1981-85, assoc. prof., 1988-94, prof. mech. engring., 1996—; vis. scientist Wash. State U., Pullman, 1985-88; vis. prof. N.C. State U., Raleigh, 1994-96; mem. acad. com. Nat. Key Lab. Shock Wave and Detonation Physics Rsch., Sichuan, 1991—; cons. S.W. Rsch. Inst., San Antonio, 1996; dep. dir. Rsch. Lab. Mech. Behavior and Design, Hefei, 1997—; vice-chmn. dept. modern mechanics U. Sci. and Tech. China, Hefei, 1997—. Author: Introduction to Shock-Induced Phase Transitions, 1992, (chpt. in book) High Pressure Shock Compression of Solids IV: Response of Highly Porous Solids to Shock Loading, 1997; patentee in field; mem. editl. bd. Explosion and Shock Waves, 2000—. Mem. The Chinese Assn. Theoretical and Applied Mechanics. Avocations: travel, fishing. Home: 7-601 North Campus, 96 Jinzhai Rd, Hefei 230026, China Office: Dept Modern Mechanics, U Sci & Tech 96 Jinzhai Rd, Hefei 230026, China

TANGA, RAVINDRA J., gynecologist-obstetrician, consultant; b. Belgaum, Karnataka, India, Nov. 23, 1948; s. Jaikumar R. and Shantabai J. Tanga; m. Kamal R. Tanga, Mar. 26, 1976; children: Rohit, Kaveri. MB BChir, KMC Mangalore, Karnataka, India, 1971. DABOG Am. Bd. Ob-Gyn.; ECFMG, FMG Bd. Asst. lectr. SUNY, Buffalo, 1975-78; lectr. Georgetown U., Washington, 1979-80; fellow in gynecology Georgetown U., 1978-79; lectr. M. R. Med. Coll., Gulbarga, Karnataka, 1981-84, asst. prof., 1984-93, prof., 1993—; cons. Arlington Hosp., Fairfax, Va., 1979-80, Health Plan, Indpls., 1980-81. Author: (book chpt.) The Adolescent Girl, 1991; contbr. articles to med. jours. Fellow ACOG; mem. Gulbarga Ob-Gyn. Soc. (sec. 1983-94, v.p. 1995-99), Rotary Internat. (charter mem., Best GGR dist. 3160 1995-96), Rotary Club Gulbarga North (pres. 1993-94). E-mail: ravindratanga@yahoo.com. Office: Dr Ravindra Tanga Hosp, Garden Rd, Gulbarga 585102, India

TANGE, HIROYUKI, economics educator; b. Tainan, Taiwan, Apr. 14, 1932; s. Tokuichiro and Shizuka (Fujii) T.; m. Yuko Suzuki, May 3, 1959; 1 child, Shizuko. B of Social Sci., Saitama U., Urawa, Japan, 1958; M of Lit., Ednl. U. Tokyo, 1961. Lectr. Saitama U., 1966-67, assoc. prof., 1967-74, prof. econs., 1974-98; prof. emeritus, 1998—; councilor Saitama U., 1979-81, 93—, dean student affairs, 1988-90; Co-author: The World Economy, 1965, The Postwar World Economy, 1968, The Japanese Economy, 1978, The Current Trends in World Economy, 1987. Mem. Consumer Protection Bd., Saitama Prefecture, Urawa, 1987—; mem. Housing Commn., Saitama Prefecture, Urawa, 1993. Avocations: photography, Haiku and Renku poetry, golf. Home: 4-6-3 Oto, Yono 338, Japan

TANG SEE KIONG, ADRIAN, electronic company executive, marketing consultant; b. Singapore, Aug. 13, 1958; s. Hon Siang Tang and Lin Heh Huay; m. Meng Hee Foo, Mar. 3, 1958; children: Li Meng, Benny, Wei Siong, Alan. Diploma in mktg. with distinction, London C. of C., 1981; diploma in telecomm. engring., City & Guilds London Inst., 1985; diploma in mktg., Chartered Inst. Mktg., U.K., 1990; Bachelor of Bus., Curtin U. Tech., Australia, 1996. Regional sales mgr. AMP Singapore Pte. Ltd., 1981-84; Asia Pacific sales mgr. Methode Electronics, Singapore, 1985-87; country mgr. Asean region Framatome Connector, Singapore, 1987-92; regional sales mgr. Asean region Thomas & Betts, Singapore, 1993—; mng. dir. Champ Electronics & Systems, Singapore, 1995—, also bd. dirs., vice chmn. & publicity sub-com. chmn. Publicity chmn. Pro-Tem Com., Singapore, 1997. With Singapore Armed Forces, 1986. Mem. IEEE (assoc.), Chartered Inst. Mktg., Singapore Inst. Mgmt., Mktg. Inst. Singapore & British Inst. of Mgmt. Avocations: golf, karate-do, jogging, reading. Fax: 65-2716988. E-mail: atang@cyberway.com.sg. Home: Apt Blk 727, Bedok Reservoir Rd 08-5036, Singapore 470727, Singapore Office: Champ Electronics & Sys Ltd, Blk 201 Ntuc Income 04-06A, Singapore 159545, Singapore

TANGUY, YANN, university president. Pres. U. de Nantes, Nantes Cedex, France. Office: U de Nantes, 1 Quai Tourville BP 13522, 44035 Nantes Cedex 1, France*

TANIEWSKI, MARIAN, chemist, educator; b. Radom, Poland, Feb. 5, 1930; s. Michal and Krystyna (Morawska) T.; m. Barbara Teresa Milowka, July 17, 1954. BS, Silesian Tech. U., Gliwice, Poland, 1952, MS, 1954, DS, 1959, Dr.Habil., 1962. Asst. lectr. Silesian Tech. U., Gliwice, 1955-62, docent, 1962-69, prof., 1969-75, 1975—, head of lab. of organic technology and petrochemistry, 1964—; postdoctoral Brit. Coun. scholar Oxford U., 1960-61; dep. vice-chancellor Silesian Tech. U., Gliwice, 1964-72, dean Faculty of Chemistry, 1981-84; mng. dir. Rsch. Inst. of Heavy Organic Synthesis, Kedzierzyn, Poland, 1985-89; mem. of head office, chief scientific adviser Polish Chamber of the Chem. Industry, Warsaw, 1990—. Author: (book) Industrial Organic Synthesis Development Trends, 1991; 1999 (2nd edit.) author/editor: (book) Chemical Technology - Raw Materials, 1997; contbr. articles to profl. jours.; editl. bd.: Chem. Industry jour., 1994—, Polish Jour. of Applied Chemistry, 1970—; patentee in field. Mem. State Com. of Scientific Rsch., 1994—, State Com. of Scientific Title and Degrees, Warsaw, 1997. Decorated Cavalier's Cross of the Order "Polonia Restituta", 1977, Officer's Cross of the Order "Polonia Restituta", 1987, Commander's Cross of the Order "Polonia Restituta", 1995, numerous medals and awards. Mem. Acad. of Engrs. in Poland, Polish Chem. Soc. (v.p. 1954—), Royal Soc. of Chem., Permanent Com. Chem. Tech. Congresses (pres. 1997—). Office: Silesian Tech Univ/Inst Chm, B Krzywoustego 4, 44-101 Gliwice Poland

TANIGAMI, AKIRA, researcher; b. Kobe, Hyogo, Japan. MD, Osaka (Japan) U., 1983. Cert. rschr. Rsch. fellow Cancer Inst., Tokyo, 1990-93; vis. fellow Baylor Coll. Medicine, Houston, 1993; vis. assoc. Nat. Ctr. for Human Genome Rsch., Bethesda, Md., 1993-95; sect. leader Nat. Cancer Ctr. Rsch. Inst., Tokyo, 1995-98; dir. Otsuka GEN Rsch. Inst., Tokushima, 1998—. Mem. Am. Soc. Human Genetics, Am. Diabetes Assn. Office: Otsuka GEN Rsch Inst, 463-10 Kagasuno Kawauchicho, Tokushima 771-0192, Japan

TANIGAWA, ATSUSHI, art educator; b. Tokyo, Jan. 7, 1948. BA, Tokyo U., 1971, MA, 1974. Asst. of faculty of letters Tokyo U., 1978-80; assoc. prof. Kokugakuin U., Tokyo, 1989-93, prof. art, 1994—. Author: Figures and Time, 1986, Labyrinth of Representations, 1992, Paradoxes of Aesthetics, 1993, Mirror and Skin, 1994, Skin of Literature, 1997. Mem. Japanese Soc. Aesthetics (com. mem. 1993—). Home: 2-32-5 Matsunoki, Suginami-ku, Tokyo 166-0014, Japan Office: Kokugakuin U 4-10-28, Higashi Shibuya-ku, Tokyo 150-8440, Japan

TANIGAWA, NOBUHIKO, medical educator; b. Tairen, Manshu, Japan, Aug. 26, 1943; s. Masaji and Teruko (Yoneda) T.; m. Yoko Shimazaki, Oct. 17, 1972; children: Nobuyuki, Junko. MD, Kyoto (Japan) U., 1970, PhD, 1979. Intern Kyoto U. Hosp., 1970-71; staff surgeon Tenri Hosp., Nara, Japan, 1971-74; asst. prof. second dept. surgery Kyoto U. Sch. Medicine, 1977-80; vis. rschr. dept. surg. oncology U. Calif., L.A., 1980-82; assoc. prof. second dept. surgery Fukui (Japan) Med. Sch., 1982-97; prof., chmn. dept. gen. and gastroenterol. surgery Osaka (Japan) Med. Coll., 1997—. Recipient award 8th Japanese Found. Multi-disciplinary Treatment Cancer, 1989. Fellow ACS, Internat. Coll. Surgeons; mem. Soc. Surg. Oncology. Avocations: golf, movies. Home: 310-10 Iwakuramiyake-Cho, Sakyo-Ku, Kyoto 606, Japan Office: 2-7 DaigakuMachi, Takatsuki City Osaka 569, Japan

TANIGUCHI, HIROSHI, mechanical engineering and architecture educator; b. Tokyo, Dec. 5, 1930; s. Sotoe Hongo and Chiyoko Taniguchi; m. Yoko Kuroiwa, Nov. 3, 1956; children: Masayuki, Nobuyuki. B of Engring., Hokkaido U., Sapporo, Japan, 1953, D of Engring., 1973. Engr. Mitsubishi Heavy Ind., Yokohama, Japan, 1953-62; assoc. prof. Hokkaido U., Sapporo, 1963-79, prof., 1979-94, hon. prof., 1994—; prof. Hokkai-Gakuen U., Sapporo, 1994—; hon. prof. Zhejiang U., Hangzhou, China, 1985—. Author: Computer Application, 1979, Steam Primover, 1986, Radiation Heat Transfer, 1994, Advances in Heat Transfer, 1995, Combustion Handbook, 1995, Quality Control, 1997, Thermal Energy Technique, 1999. Chmn. new tech. com. Hokkaido Govt., 1989—; chmn. environ. com. Tomakomai City, 1991—. Recipient Japanese Thermo-Tech. award Tanigawa Found., 1995, Hokkaido Sci. and Tech. award, 1998. Mem. Japanese Soc. Mech. Engrs., Japanese Soc. Architecture, Soc. for Heating, Air Conditioning and San. Engrs. (rsch. paper award 1986), Soc. Thermal Nuc. Power, Soc. Thermal Properties (rsch. paper award 1995), Japan Soc. Combustion (Rsch. award 1996), Rotary. Home: N22 E18-6-27 Higashi-ku, Sapporo Hokkaido 065-0022, Japan Office: Hokkai-Gakuen U Fac Engring, S26 W11-1-1 Chuo-ku, Sapporo 064-0926, Japan

TANIGUCHI, ICHIRO, electrical and electronics industry executive; b. Hyogo, 1936; married; 2 children. BS, Kyoto U., D in Engring., 1972. Rschr. Ctrl. Rsch. Lab. Mitsubishi Electric Corp., 1959; numerous mgmt. positions Mitsubishi Electric Corp., Kamakura, Japan, pres. and CEO, 1998—; also bd. dirs. Mitsubishi Electric Corp., gen. mgr. Electronic Products and Sys. Group, 1995, sr. mng. dir., 1997, pres., 1998—. Avocations: cooking, mystery novels, golf. Office: Mitsubishi Electric Corp, 2-2-3 Marunouchi, Chiyoda-ku Tokyo 100-8310, Japan*

TANIGUCHI, KEIJI, engineering educator; b. Tuyama, Okayama, Japan, Nov. 20, 1934; s. Teijyu and Kazue (Ebara) T.; m. Jyunko Ariki, Mar. 25, 1962; children: Yosikazu, Teruaki, Haruko. B in Engring., Kinki (Japan) U., 1964; DEng, Osaka (Japan) U., 1972. Designer Osaka Gear Works Japan, 1952-55; enlisted Japanese Air Force, 1955, advanced through grades to 1st lt., 1962, resigned, 1964; rsch. assoc. Osaka U., 1964-73; assoc. prof. engring. Fukui (Japan) U., 1973-75, prof., 1975-2000; hon. prof. Xi'an U. Tech., China, 1996, Fukui U., 2000. Avocations: coaching swimming, skiing instructor. Office: Bunkyo 3-9-1, Fukui-ken, Fukui 910-8507, Japan

TANIGUCHI, TADAAKI, oncologist; b. Mizokuchi-town, Tottori, Japan, Jan. 28, 1967; s. Takashi Tsukamoto and Yoshimi T.; m. Katsuno Onozawa Apr. 23, 1995. MD, Tottori U., Yonago, Japan, 1991; postgrad., U. London, 1997—; PhD, Univ. London, 1999. Med. diplomate in Japan. Jr. resident in gen. medicine Met. Komagome Hosp., Tokyo, 1991-93; sr. resident surgery and surg. oncology Met. Komagome Hosp., 1993-95, chief resident dept. surgery, 1995-97; rsch. fellow Imperial Cancer Rsch. Fund oncology unit Imperial Coll Sch. of Medicine, Hammersmith Hosp., London, 1997-2000; rsch. dir. Megro Inst. for Clin. Devel., Banyu Pharm. Co., Ltd., Tokyo, 2000—. Contbr. articles to profl. jours. Mem. AAAS (internat.), Am. Assn. for Cancer Rsch., Japan Surg. Soc., Japanese Cancer Soc. Avocations: tennis, skiing, volleyball. Office: Megro Inst Clin Devel/Banyu, 9-3-Shimo-Meguro 2 chome, Meguro-ku 153-8680, Japan

TANIGUCHI, YOSHIHIRO, chemist, educator; b. Kyoto, Japan, Dec. 12, 1941; s. Shinpachi and Hatsuno Taniguchi; m. Michiko Kadono; children: Mami, Gakuto. BS, Ritsumeikan U., Kyoto, Japan, 1962, MEng, 1964, DEng, 1970. Rsch. assoc. Ritsumeikan U., 1969-78, assoc. prof., 1978-85, prof., 1985—; dir. Rsch. Inst. Sci. and Engring., Ritsumeikan U., 1992-94, vice dean faculty sci. and engring., 1994-96, dean faculty sci. and engring., dean grad. sch. sci. and engring., 1998—; lectr. Hokkaido U., Sapporo, Japan, 1990, Fukuoka U., Hakata, Japan, 1990-92, Kobe (Japan) U., 1994-95. Co-author: Basic and Applied High Pressure Biology, 1994; co-editor: High Pressure Liquids and Solutions, 1994, Biological Systems Under Extreme Conditions, 2000. Recipient Young Scientist award Matsunaga Sci. Found., 1974. Office: Ritsumeikan U App Chemistry, 1-1-1 Nojihigashi, Shiga 525-8577, Japan

TANIISHI, NAOTOSHI, food company executive; b. Osaka, Japan, June 13, 1941; s. Kisaji and Masako Taniishi; m. Akiko Harada, Apr. 2, 1970; children: Hiroko, Yukihiro, Tomoko, Shouhei. Student, Kyoto (Japan) U., 1965. With sales divsn. Asahi Chem. Co., Tokyo, 1965-72; sales mgr. Asahi Chem. Co., Osaka, Japan, 1984-88, P.T. Indaci, Jakarta, Indonesia, 1972-80; dir. Asahi Europe, Brussels, 1980-84; sr. dir. Asahi Foods Co., Tokyo, 1988—. Avocations: travel, painting, golf, skiing, swimming. Home: 1-9-7 Kukotoricho, Izuma Osaka 594-0022, Japan

TANIMURA, TAKASHI, anatomist, teratologist; b. Kizu-cho, Kyoto, Japan, Jan. 10, 1931; s. Kazuharu and Chiyoko (Takahashi) T.; m. Haruyo Takaya, Oct. 22, 1961 (dec. Sept. 1992); children: Mutsumi, Makoto. MD, Kyoto U., 1956, D Med. Sci., 1967. Med. diplomate. Staff ob-gyn. Kyoto Nat. Hosp., 1957-60; asst. anatomy Kyoto U., 1960-65, lectr. anatomy, 1965-72, assoc. prof., 1972-78; prof. anatomy Kinki U., Osakasayama, Japan, 1978-98; prof. Life Sci. Rsch. Inst. Kinki U., Osakasayama, 1998-2000, emeritus prof., 2000—; mem. pharm. affairs coun. Ministry Health and Welfare, Tokyo, 1972-97, mem. expert com. on new chems., 1987—. Author: Clinical Aspects of Teratogenicity of Drugs, 1976; author, editor: Biological Reference Data Book on Experimental Animals, 1989, Developmental Toxicity, 1992; editl. bd. Congenital Anomalies, 1977—, Biology of Neonates, 1988—; editl. adv. bd. Neurotoxicology and Teratology, 1990-99. Mem. Japanese Teratology Soc. (dir. 1970-98, emeritus mem. 1999—, pres. 1984-85), Teratology Soc., Japanese Assn. Anatomists (councilor 1978-97, hon. mem. 1997—). Avocations: collection of folk dolls, history, travel. Home: 1-14-10 Shiroyamadai, Sakai Osaka 590-0137, Japan

TANIUCHI, KIYOSHI, retired mechanical engineering educator; b. Kahoku-choo, Kami-gun, Kōchi-ken, Japan, Aug. 8, 1926; s. Takeshi and Toshi (Yoshimoto) T.; m. Teiko Wakamatsu, Jan. 7, 1960; 1 child, Satoshi. Student, Kanto Gakuin Tech. Coll., Yokohama, Japan, 1946; BEng, Meiji U., Tokyo, 1952, DEng (hon.), 1980. Asst. Meiji U. Sch. Sci. and Tech., Kawasaki-shi, Japan, 1957-81, lectr. mech. engring., 1981-91, assoc. prof., 1991-95; ret. Meiji U. Sch. Sci. and Tech., 1995; instr. engring. Shibaura Inst. Tech., Ohmiya-shi, Saitama-ken, Japan, 1974-90. Co-author: Mechanical Design and Drawing, 1973, Descriptive Geometry, 1974, An Introduction to Mechanical Engineering, 1975; contb. sci. papers and presentations to nat. and internat. sci. meetings. Mem. ASTM, Internat. Soc. Optical Engring., Soc. Exptl. Mechanics, Japanese Soc. Mech. Engrs. Avocations: photography, art appreciation. Home: 5-10-12 Wakamatsu, Sagamihara 229-0014, Japan

TANK, ANDREW GEORGE, association administrator, writer; b. Sutton, Surrey, Eng., Mar. 23, 1958; s. Meyric Johnson and Audrey Victoria (Axon) T. BA, Cambridge (Eng.) U., 1979, MA, 1983. Mktg. mgr. Rank Strand, Brentford, U.K., 1979-80; vol. Internat. Vol. Svc. Bangladesh, 1980-81; journalist Haymarket Pub., London, 1982-85; Asia corr. Automotive News, Detroit, 1985-87; mgmt. editor Economist Intelligence Unit, London, 1987-88; rsch. assoc. Conf. Bd. Europe, Brussels, 1989-93, dir. Europe Rsch. & Couns., 1993—, exec. dir. Europe, 1997—. Author: Making Alliances Work, 1990, Building Flexible Companies, 1991; editor: The BI50: Case Studies in Management Success, 1988, also numerous reports in field. Mem. choir Holy Trinity Pro-Cathedral, 1990—. Mem. Royal Soc. Arts London. Avocations: singing, cycling, cooking. Home: Chaussee de la Hulpe 439, B-1170 Brussels Belgium Office: Conf Bd Europe, Chausee de la Hulpe 130, B1000 Brussels Belgium

TANKARD, JAMES WILLIAM, JR., journalism educator, writer; b. Newport News, Va., June 20, 1941; s. James William and Eileen (Looney) T.; m. Sara Elaine Fuller, July 21, 1973; children: Amy Elizabeth, Jessica Hope, Margaret Elaine. BS, Va. Poly. Inst., 1963; MA, U. N.C., 1965; PhD, Stanford U., 1970. Newswriter AP, Charlotte, N.C., 1965; reporter The Raleigh (N.C.) Times, 1965-66; vis. asst. prof. U. Tex., Austin, 1970, U. Wis., Madison, 1970-71; asst. prof. Temple U., Phila., 1971-72; asst. prof. U. Tex., Austin, 1972-76, assoc. prof., 1976-82, prof., 1982—, Jesse Jones prof. in journalism, 1989—. Author: The Statistical Pioneers, 1984; co-author: Basic News Reporting, 1977, Communication Theories, 1979, 4th edit., 1997, Mass Media in the Information Age, 1990; editor Journalism Monographs, 1988-94. Mem. AAUP, Assn. for Edn. in Journalism and Mass Communication (chair rsch. com. 1987-88), Internat. Communication Assn., Soc. Profl. Journalists. Avocations: hiking, jogging, bicycling. Home: 3300 Jamesborough St Austin TX 78703-1132 Office: U Tex Dept Journalism Austin TX 78712

TANKO, ADAMU IDRIS, geography educator; b. Kano, Nigeria, Aug. 27, 1966; s. Abdullahi Tanko Idris and Hawwa'u Abdullahi; m. Binta Adamu Aminu Kwalli, Sept. 9, 1993; children: Abdullahi, Aminu, Hauwa'u-Shukuriyya. BSc in Geography, Bayero U., Kano, 1989, MSc in Land Resources, 1993, PhD in Geography, 1999. Tchr. Govt. Secondary Sch., Tsaure, Kano, 1984-85, Sardauna Meml. Coll., Kaduna, Nigeria, 1989-90, Govt. Girls Sch., Sumaila, Kano, 1990-94; asst. lectr. Bayero U., Kano, 1994-97, lectr. II, 1997-99, lectr. I, 1999—; cons. WK & Assocs., Kano, 1996—, Natural Resource Inst., London, 1996-97, Reslarc, Kaduna, 1996-97, Inter-Tropical Cons., Kano, 1998—. Author: An Emotional Suicide, 1997; contbr. articles to profl. jours. Facilitator Nat. Population Commn., Nigeria, 1991; supr., key supr. West African Examination Coun., Nigeria, 1993-94. State and fed. govt. scholar Kano State and Fed. Govt., Nigeria, 1984-92; vis. rsch. fellow Sch. African and Asian Studies-U. Sussex, Brighton, U.K., 1998, travel fellow Am. Geophys. Union, San Francisco, 1999. Mem. Am. Geophys. Union, Nigerian Geog. Assn., Assn. Nigerian Authors (editor and asst. sect. 1993-95). Islam. Avocations: reading, writing, football, basketball, table tennis. Office: Bayero Univ, Gwarzo Rd PMB 3011, Kano NIgeria

TANN, JENNIFER, innovation studies educator; b. Bedford, Eng., Feb. 25, 1939; d. Alfred John and Frances (Ruddle) Booth; m. Roger William Tann, Oct. 12, 1963; children: Edmund John, Oliver Richard. BA, U. Manchester, Eng., 1960; PhD, U. Leicester, Eng., 1964. Rsch. asst. Historic Towns Project, Oxford, Eng., 1964-65; lectr. Aston U., Birmingham, Eng., 1969-72, reader, 1973-86; head dept. U. Newcastle-upon-Tyne, Eng., 1986-89; prof. innovation studies U. Birmingham, 1989—, head of sch., 1989-94, dean, 1993-96, dir. rsch. Bus. Sch., 1999—; cons. Dept. Health, U.K., Anglican Ch., U.K., English Heritage, various blue chip mfg. cos. Author: The Development of the Factory, 1971, Selected Papers of Boulton and Watt, 1993, A History of the Assay Office, Birmingham, 1993; contbr. numerous papers on innovation management. Home: Thanet House, High St Chalford, Stroud GL6 8DH, England Office: U Birmingham, Bus Sch, Birmingham B15 2TT, England

TANNA, SHASHI JAMNADAS, investment banking executive; b. Lindi, Tanzania, Mar. 13, 1950; s. Jamnadas J. and Kanta J. (Rabheru) T.; m. Jay S. Barai, Dec. 3, 1978; children: Anita, Sheena, Neil. BSc in Aeronautical Engring. with hons., Univ. Manchester, Eng., 1972. Fin. assoc. Touche Ross & Co., London, 1972-78; mgr. Arthur Andersen & Co., London, 1978-83; fin. exec. Unilever PLC, London, 1983-84; exec. dir. CIBC World Markets PLC, London, Eng., 1984—. Fellow Inst. Chartered Accts., Inst. Dirs.; mem. Inst. of Taxation (assoc.). Avocations: cricket, compulsory gardening, current affairs, business reading. Home: 16 Southfield Way, St Albans, Herts AL4 9JJ, England Office: CIBC Wood Gundy PLC, CIBC World Markets PLC, Cottons Ctr, Cottons Ln, London SE1 2QL, England

TANNER, BRIAN KEITH, physics educator; b. Raunds, Eng., Apr. 3, 1947; s. Edward Sydney and Gladys May Tanner; m. Ruth Hilda Simmonds, Aug. 16, 1969; children: Robert Edward, Thomas Matthew. BA, Oxford (Eng.) U., 1968, MA, DPhil, 1972. Chartered physicist. Jr. rsch. fellow Linacre Coll., Oxford, 1971-73; from lectr. to sr. lectr. U. Durham, 1973-86, reader in physics, 1986-90, prof. physics, 1990—, chmn. physics dept., 1996-99; sci. dir. Bede Sci. Instruments, Ltd., Durham, 1978—. Author: X-Ray Diffraction Topography, 1976, Introduction to the Physics of Electrons in Solids, 1995; co-author: High Resolution X-ray Diffractometry and Topography, 1998; co-editor: Characterization of Crystal Growth Defects by X-Ray Methods, 1980, X-Ray and Neutron Dynamical Diffraction: Theory and Applications, 1996. Radiation safety advisor Durham County Fire and Rescue Svc., 1984-00; organist Elvet Meth. Ch., Durham, 1981—. Fellow Inst. Physics, Royal Soc. Arts. Avocations: music, walking. Office: U Durham Dept Physics, South Rd, Durham DH1 3LE, England

TANNER, DANIEL, curriculum theory educator; b. N.Y.C., Sept. 22, 1926; s. Jack and Lillian (Jupiter) T.; m. Laurel Nan Jacobson, July 11, 1948 (div. 1988). BS with honors, Mich. State U., 1949, MS, 1952; PhD, Ohio State U., 1955. Asst. prof. edn. San Francisco State Coll., 1955-60; assoc. prof. edn., coord. Midwest program on airborne TV instrn. Purdue U., 1960-62; assoc. prof. edn., assoc. dir. internat. program for edn. leaders Northwestern U., 1962-64; assoc. prof. rsch. divsn. tchr. edn. CUNY, 1964-66; prof. edn., dir. Ctr. for Urban Edn., U. Wis.-Milw. Sch. Edn., 1966-67; prof. edn., dir. grad. programs in curriculum theory and devel. Grad. Sch. Edn., Rutgers U., New Brunswick, N.J., 1967—; chmn. dept. curriculum and instrn. Grad. Sch. Edn., Rutgers U., 1969-72, faculty rsch. fellow, 1974-75, 88-89; vis. lectr. U. Kansas City, summer 1956, Tchrs. Coll. Columbia, summer 1966; vis. prof. Emory U., summer 1968, SUNY, Binghamton, winter 1968, U. London, 1975, King Abdulaziz U., Saudi Arabia, winter 1992, U. Iowa, summer 1996; disting. lectr. ASCD, 1985, 86, Dewey Meml. lectr., 1984, Raths Meml. lectr., SUNY, 1984; Leadership Inst. lectr. U. Del., summer 1990; disting. lectr. Rider U., 1996; vis. scholar U. London Inst. Edn., 1974-75; mem. rev. bd. coll. work-study program U.S. Office Edn., 1965; mem. symposium on comparative curriculum history Inst. Sci. Edn. Kiel U., Fed. Republic Germany, 1989; del. leader Citizen Amb. Program, People-to-People Internat., Republic of South Africa, 1996, China, 1997, Dem. Citizenship Project Czech Republic, USIA, 1996-98; cons. U. Tex. Med. Ctr., 1961-62, Chgo. Sch. Survey, 1964-65, ctr. Urban Edn., N.Y.C., 1964-65, West Chgo. Sch. Survey, 1963-64, Nat. Ednl. TV Ctr., N.Y.C., 1963, Campbell County (Va.) Sch. Survey, 1970, Memphis Schs., 1977-78, ASCD Commn. on Gen. Edn., 1980-81, West Orange, N.J., Curriculum Study, 1984, ASCD Commn. on Secondary Sch. Practices, 1985, ASCD Ednl. Policy Task Force, 1985, NASSP Curric Coun., 1985-95; SUNY Buffalo External Evaluation, 1988; dir. Nat. Curriculum Inst., 1987, Perth Amboy (N.J.) Schs., 1996-97; delivered Founder's Day address Delaware Valley Coll., 1985, Keynote address Nat. Conf. Citizen Edn., Czech Rep., 1998. Author: Schools for Youth: Change and Challenge in Secondary Education, 1965, Secondary Curriculum: Theory and Development, 1971, Secondary Education: Perspectives and Prospects, 1972, Using Behavioral Objectives in the Classroom, 1972, Curriculum Development: Theory into Practice, 3rd edit., 1995, Supervision in Education, 1987, History of the School Curriculum, 1990, Crusade for Democracy: Progressive Education at the Crossroads, 1991; cons. editor, contbg. author: Ann. Rsch. Rev. for Sch. Leaders, 1996, 98, 00, Philosophy of Edn. Ency., 1996, Curriculum Issues, 87th Yearbook NSSE, 1988, 98th Yearbook, 1999, Ency. of Ednl. Rsch., 5th edit., 1982, Readings in Education Psychology, 1965, Yearbook of the Association for Student Teaching, 1962, The Great Debate, Our Schools in Crisis, 1959, Educational Issues in a Changing Society, 1964, Programs, Teachers and Machines, 1964, Views on American Schooling, 1964, The Training of America's Teachers, 1975, Curriculum and Instruction, 1981; co-author: Teen Talk: Curriculum Materials in Communications, 1971; co-editor: Improving the School Curriculum, 1988, Restructuring for an Interdisciplinary Curriculum, 1992, Curriculum Issues and the New Century, 1995; contbg. editor: Ednl. Leadership, 1969-74; mem. editl. bd.: Tex. Tech. Jour. Edn., 1984-89, Tchg. Edn., 1986-90, Jour. Curriculum Supervision; editorial cons.: Ency. of Ednl. Rsch., 5th edit., Jour. Ednl. Psychology; founding editor: Ann. Rev. of Rsch. Rev. for Sch. Leaders; contbr. Atlantic Monthly, Bull. of Atomic Scientists and other nat. mags., ednl. jours. Trustee Delaware Valley Coll., Doylestown, Pa., 1981-95; bd. dirs. Ohio State Alumni Assn. N.J., 1990-96. Recipient Excellence award Edn. Press Am., 1989, Distinguished Educator award Rider U., 1996; Univ. scholar Ohio State U., 1955. Fellow AAAS, John Dewey Soc. (bd. dirs. 1985-88, archivist 1989—, chmn. lectrs. commn. 1999—, pres. elect 2000); mem. AAUP, Am. Ednl. Rsch. Assn., N.Y. Acad. Scis., Am. Polit. Sci. Assn., Am. Ednl. Studies Assn., Nat. Soc. Study Edn., Phi Kappa Phi, Phi Delta Kappa (Svc. award 1957). Home: Highwood Rd Somerset NJ 08873 Office: Grad Sch Edn Rutgers U New Brunswick NJ 08903

TANNER, DEE BOSHARD, retired lawyer; b. Provo, Utah, Jan. 16, 1913; s. Myron Clark and Marie (Boshard) T.; m. Jane Barwick, Dec. 26, 1936 (div. Aug. 1962); children: Barry, Diane McDowell; m. Reeta Walker, Dec. 6, 1981. BA, U. Utah, 1935; LLB, Pacific Coast U., 1940; postgrad., Harvard U., 1936, Loyola U., L.A., 1937. Bar: Calif. 1943, U.S. Dist. Ct. (so. dist.) Calif. 1944, U.S. Ct. Appeals (9th cir.) 1947, ICC 1964, U.S. Dist. Ct. (ea. dist.) Calif. 1969, U.S. Supreme Ct. 1971. Assoc. Spray, Davis & Gould, L.A., 1943-44; pvt. practice L.A., 1944; assoc. Tanner and Sievers, L.A., 1944-47, Tanner and Thornton, L.A., 1947-54, Tanner, Hanson, Meyers, L.A., 1954-64; ptnr. Tanner and Van Dyke, L.A., 1964-65, Gallagher and Tanner, L.A., 1965-70; pvt. practice Pasadena, Calif., 1970-95; retired, 1995. Mem. L.A. Bar Assn., World Affairs Assn., Harvard Law Sch. Assn., Lawyers' Club L.A. Home and Office: 1720 Lombardy Rd Pasadena CA 91106-4127

TANNER, ERIC BENSON, lawyer; b. St. Louis, Aug. 27, 1949; s. Robert H. and Delores (Benson) T.; m. Rosalind Grace Tanner, June 23, 1978; children: Jacob, Adam. BA, U. Mo., Columbia, 1971; JD, U. Mo., Kansas City, 1975; cert., Coll. Fin. Planning, Denver, 1988. Bar: Mo. 1975. Instr. paralegal program Avila Coll., Kansas City, 1982-84; staff atty. Legal Aid Western Mo., Kansas City, 1975-83; pvt. practice, Kansas City, 1983-86; asst. v.p. trust dept. United Mo. Bank, NA, Kansas City, 1986-90; staff atty. Shook, Hardy & Bacon, Kansas City, 1990-93; v.p. trust dept., sr. trust atty. Commerce Bank, N.A., Kansas City, 1993—; CLE lectr. on estate planning topics to various bar assns. and univs., 1975—. Contbr. articles to law jours. Mem. planned giving com. Nat. Kidney Found., Kans. and Kansas City met. area, 1995-97; vol. Habitat for Humanity, 1997, 99; bd. dirs. Prime Health, 1980-86. Mem. ABA, Mo. Bar Assn., Kansas City Met. Bar Assn., Lawyers Assn. Kansas City, Kansas City Corp. Fiduciaries Assn. (pres. 1997), Estate Planning Soc. Kansas City. Office: Commerce Bank NA 1000 Walnut St Ste 800 Kansas City MO 64106-2160

TANNER, JORDAN, state legislator; b. Provo, Utah, July 26, 1931; s. Vasco Myron and Annie (Atkin) T.; m. Patricia Nowell, Sept. 16, 1960; children: Eric, Jeffrey, Timothy. BS, U. Utah, 1954; MBA, U. Calif., Berkeley, 1961. Fgn. svc. officer USIA, Washington, 1960-87; state rep. Utah Ho. of Reps., Salt Lake City, 1990—. Commr. Utah Centennial Commn., Salt Lake City, 1993—. Lt. USN, 1954-56. Republican. Mem. LDS Ch. Home and Office: 677 Lakeview Dr Alpine UT 84004-1322

TANNER, MAURI UUNO ENSIO, aerodynamicist; b. Närpiö, Finland, June 9, 1930; s. Uuno Oskar and Kerttu (Wahlroos) T.; m. Virpi Elina Pukonen, Nov. 30, 1952; children: Pekka, Leena. Diploma in engring., Tech. U., Helsinki, Finland, 1958; D in Engring., Tech. U., Brunswick, Fed. Rep. Germany, 1967. Chief research rock drill dept. Tampella Engring. Works, Tampere, Finland, 1958-61; aerodynamicist Deutsche Forschungsanstalt für Luft und Raumfahrt, Göttingen, Fed. Republic Germany, 1961-93; pvt. practice Göttingen, 1993—. Contbr. articles to profl. jours. Avocations: classical music. Home: Richard-Courant-Weg 13, 37077 Göttingen Germany

TANNER, MICHAEL CARL, mental health services professional; b. Bklyn., June 7, 1962; s. Carl F. and Mary J. Tanner; m. Pattie M. Albanese, Dec. 31, 1989 (div. 1998); 1 child, Gabrielle Kirsten. Mental health therapy aide Pilgrim Psychiat. Ctr., Brentwood, N.Y., 1988-96; devel. aide L.I. Devel. Ctr., Ridge, N.Y., 1996—; cashier Suffolk County Regional Off-Track Betting Corp., Hauppauge, N.Y., 1997—; grievance rep. Civil Svc. Employees Assn., Inc., N.Y. State, 1988—; congl. liaison Assn. State, County and Mcpl. Employees, Washington, 1988—. Coord. Neighborhood Watch, 1995; v.p. Bay Area Civic Assn., Shirley, N.Y., 1999; mem. Legis. Adv. Com., Shirley, 1997—. With N.Y. Army Nat. Guard, 1990-93. Recipient Proclamation, Suffolk County Legis., Shirley, 1996. Mem. Nat. Assn. Chiefs Police, Am. Police Hall of Fame (guardian angel), Hispanic Nat. Law Enforcement Assn. N.Y. (hon.), Internat. Brotherhood Teamster, Hauppauge, 1997—, Teamsters for a Dem. Union, Am. Legion (adjutant 1998), K.C. (2nd degree 1998—). Roman Catholic. Home: PO Box 389 Rocky Point NY 11778-0389 Office: LI Devel Ctr 64 Ridge Rd Ridge NY 11961-1008

TANNER, NORMAN PHILIP, clergyman, educator; b. Woking, Surrey, Eng., Feb. 26, 1943; s. John Basil and Agnes Emily (Tolhurst) T. Student, Sacred Heart Convent, 1948-51, Avisford Sch., 1951-56, Ampleforth Coll., 1956-61; LPh in Philosophy (hon.), Heythrop Coll., Oxfordshife, 1966; BA in History and Medieval Ch. History, Oxford (Eng.) U., 1969, MA, 1974, DPhil, 1974; BTh (hon.), Gregorian U., Rome, 1976. Joined Soc. of Jesus, 1961; ordained priest Roman Catholic Ch., 1976. Curate Farm Street Ch., London, 1977-78; tutor medieval history Campion Hall, Oxford U., 1978—, sr. tutor, 1981-97; lectr. ch. history Heythrop Coll., London U., 1981—; u. rsch. lectr. Oxford U., 1997—; expert ecumenical/gen. couns.of Western Ch.; lectr. Medieval Ch. History, 1982; vis. prof. Ecumenical Couns. Hekima Coll., Nairobi, Kenya, 1991, 96, 99, Chishawasha Sem., Harare, Zimbabwe, 1991, 96, 2000, Cedara Coll., Pietmaritzburg, 1991, St. Augustine Coll., Johannesburg, 1999, St. John Vianney Sem., Pretoria, South Africa, 1999,

Vidyajyoti Theol. Coll., Delhi, 1996, 99, Jnana Deepa Vidyapeeth, Pune, India, 1999, Centre Sèvres, Paris, 2000, Gregorian U., Rome, 2000; respected scholar Medieval Ch. Author: Heresy Trials in the Diocese of Norwich 1428-31, 1977, The Church in Late Medieval Norwich, 1370-1532, 1984, Decrees of the Ecumenical Councils, 1990, Kent Heresy Proceedings 1511-12, 1997; contbr. articles in field. dedicating time for work in parishes, giving retreats, other pastoral work. Fellow Royal Historical Soc.; mem. Soc. Jesus, Modern History Faculty, Theology Faculty, Oxford U. Eccles. History Soc., Cath. Theol. Assn. Great Britain. Address: Campion Hall,, Oxford OX1 1QS, England

TANNO, DAI, social sciences educator; b. Onagawa, Miyagi-ken, Japan, Dec. 16, 1952; s. Yugo and Kazuko (Abe) T. BA, Waseda U., Tokyo, 1976, MA, 1978; BA, Ga. So. Coll., 1986; PhD, U. Ga., 1993. Grad. asst. Ga. So. Coll., Statesboro, 1986-87, U. Ga., Athens, 1987-90; asst. prof. Salem-Teikyo U., Salem, 1993-95; dept. chairperson Salem-Toikyo U., Salem, 1996-98; assoc. prof. Aomori (Japan) Pub. Coll., 1998—. Contbr. articles to profl. jours. including Internat. Jour. Group Tensions, Coll. Student Jour., Cultural Dynamics. Grantee Aomori Found. Sci., Rsch. and Culture, 1999; recipient Best Article award Kagami Meml. Found. Tokyo Marine, 1992. Mem. Sci. Rsch. Soc. (assoc.). Office: Aomori Pub Coll, 153-4 Yamazaki, Goshizawa, Aomori 030-0196, Japan

TANNOCK, CHARLES, psychiatrist, consultant, legislator; b. Aldershot, Hampshire, Eng.; s. Robert and Anne (England) T.; m. Rosa Maria Vega Pizarro 1983 (div. Nov. 1988); 1 child, Thomas. BA with honors, Oxford (Eng.) U., 1980, MA, 1992; MB BS, London U., 1983. Rsch. fellow Charing Cross & Westminster Med. Sch., London, 1989-90; sr. registrar in psychiatry London U., 1991-93; sr. registrar in old age psychiatry Princess Alexandra Hosp., 1994; hon. sr. lectr. in psychiatry London U., 1995; cons. psychiatrist U. Coll. Hosp., London, 1995-99; local councillor Royal Borough of Kensington and Chelsea, London, 1998—; mem. London region European Parliament, 1999—. Contbr. articles to profl. jours. including Brit. Jour. Psychiatry and Quar. Jour. Medicine. Sec. Bow Group Health Com., London, 1988; vice chmn. South Stanley Ward, Kensington and Chelsea Conservative Assn., 1985—; mem. mcpl. elections Local Borough Coun., Conservative Party Candidate, London, 1994. Mem. Royal Coll. Psychiatrists. Roman Catholic. Avocations: foreign languages, travel, skiing, politics, finance. Home: 3 Kensington Mansions, Trebovir Rd, London SW5 9TF, England Office: Conservative Ctrl Office, 32 Smith Sq, London SW1P 3HH, England

TÄNNSJÖ, TORBJÖRN, philosopher, educator; b. Västerås, Sweden, Dec. 13, 1946; s. Harald and Carin (Mohlund) T.; m. Unni Beltzikoff, Apr. 30, 1968; children: Josef, Olga, Marja; m. Anita Dalgren, Mar. 18, 1995. BA, Stockholm U., 1967, PhD, 1974. Assoc. prof. Stockholm U., 1976-92; rsch. fellow Swedish Rsch. Coun. Humanities, 1992-95; prof. practical philosophy Gothenburg U., Sweden, 1995—. Author: Moral Realism, 1990, Conservatism for Our Time, 1990, Populist Democracy, 1992, Hedonistic Utilitarianism, 1998, Coercive Care, 1999, others; contbr. articles to profl. jours. Avocations: clarinet. Home: Swedenborgsgaten 27, 118 27 Stockholm Sweden Office: Gothenburg U, Dept Philosophy, 412 98 Gothenburg Sweden

TANOUE, KOJI, engineering educator, researcher; b. Kumamoto, Japan, Jan. 26, 1942; m. Junko Mukai, May 18, 1971; children: Masayo, Chie. B Engring., Kumamoto U., 1967; DEng, Kyushu U., Fukuoka City, Japan, 1980. Asst. Kyushu Inst. Tech., Kitakyushu, 1970-82, lectr. engring., 1982-84, assoc. prof., 1984—. Avocations: fishing, yachting, diving, travel, reading. Home: 9-3 Chiyo 5-chome, Yahata-nishi-ku, Fukuoka Kitakyushu 807-1112, Japan Office: Kyushu Inst Tech, 1-1 Sensui-cho, Tobata-ku, Fukuoka Kitakyushu 804-8550, Japan

TANOUS, HELENE MARY, radiologist, educator; b. Zanesville, Ohio, Oct. 22, 1939; d. Joseph and Rose Marie (Mokarzel) T.; m. John Camp, 1986 (dec. 1990). BA, Marymount Coll., 1961; MD, U. Tex., 1967. Diplomate Am. Bd. Radiology. Intern County Hosp., L.A., 1967-68; resident in radiology Cedars-Sinai Med. Ctr., L.A., 1968-69, U. So. Calif. Hosp., L.A., 1969-71; pvt. practice medicine specializing in radiology L.A., 1972-73; instr. radiology U. So. Calif. Med. Sch., L.A., 1971-72; asst. prof. diagnostic radiology Baylor Med. Sch., Houston, 1973-75; dir. med. student elective in diagnostic radiology Ben Taub Hosp., Houston, 1973-75; pvt. practice diagnostic radiology Largo, Fla., 1975—; chief Radiology Diagnostic Clinic, Largo, Fla.; asst. prof. diagnostic radiology U. South Fla. Med. Sch., 1980—; asst. prof., dir. med. student edn. in diagnostic radiology U. Tex., Galveston, 1988-91. Pres., founder Children's Advs., Inc., 1977-85; bd. dirs. Fla. Endowment for Humanities, 1979-83. Decorated Chevalier des Palmes Academiques Govt. of France, 1988. Mem. AMA, So. Med. Assn., L'Alliance Francaise of Tampa (bd. dirs. 1984—, pres. 1985-87), Fedn. Alliances Francaises U.S.A. (bd. dirs. 1987-89), Houston Com. Fgn. Rels. Home: 661 Bering Dr Unit 108 Houston TX 77057-2137

TANOUS, PETER JOSEPH, banker; b. N.Y.C., May 21, 1938; s. Joseph Carrington and Rose Marie (Mokarzel) T.; m. Barbara Ann MacConnell, Aug. 18, 1962; children: Christopher, Helene, William. BA in Econs., Georgetown U., 1960. With Smith Barney & Co., Inc. (now Salomon Smith Barney, Inc.), N.Y.C., 1963-78, 2d v.p., mgr. Paris office, 1967, v.p., 1968-78; resident European sales mgr. in Paris Smith Barney & Co., Inc. (now Salom0n Smith Barney, Inc.), N.Y.C., 1969-71; internat. sales mgr. Smith Barney & Co., Inc. (now Salomon Smith Barney, Inc.), N.Y.C., 1971-78, 1st v.p., 1975-78; chmn. bd. Petra Capital Corp., N.Y.C., 1978-81; pres. Lynx Investment Advisory Inc., Washington, 1992—; exec. v.p. Bank Audi (USA), N.Y.C., 1984-92; del. U.S.-Saudi Arabian Joint Econ. Commn. Bus. Dialogue; trustee Browning Sch., N.Y.C., 1987-93; bd. dirs. Cedars Bank, L.A., Interstate Resources, Inc., Rosslyn, Va., Modis Profl. Svcs., Inc., Jacksonville, Fla., Kistler Aerospace Corp., Seattle. Author: Investment Gurus, 1997, The Wealth Equation, 1999. Office: 1100 Connecticut Ave NW Washington DC 20036-4101

TANPARSERT, SRIVILAI, physician; b. Bangkok, Thailand, Jan. 7, 1939; d. Varapoj and Sumniang Chaivarat; m. Cherdchai Tanprasert, May 9, 1965; children: Thitiping, Songpoj, Tosapol. Diploma, Mater Dei Coll., Bangkok, Saipunya Sch., Bangkok, 1958; MD, Chulalongkorn U., Bangkok, 1964. Physician Nat. Blood Ctr., Bangkok, 1969-76, head routine lab. sect., 1976-82, asst. dir., acting head lab. sect., 1982-89, dep. dir., acting head routine lab. sect., 1989-98, dir., 1998—; expert physician Thai Red Cross Soc., Bangkok, 1994. Author: (texts) Blook Bank Technic, Hematology, Blood Bank, Urinalysis and Body Fluid, 1994, (manual) Standard Operating Prodecure Manual of Blood Testing. chmn. project on safe blood donation Nat. Blood Ctr. mem. adv. com., 1993—; mem. subcom. prevention and control of AIDS Ministry of Pub. Health; initiator 12 regional blood ctrs.; spkr. in field. Recipient Royal Thai Orders and Decorations, Royal Household and Prime Min. Office, Bankgok, 1976, 79, 81, 86, Commendation medal Thai Red Cross Soc., 1985, Outstanding Adminstr. in social svcs. Thai Soc. Found. and Econ. Newspaper, 1998. Mem. Thai Soc. Hematology (subcom. 1991-97), Med. Assn. Thailand, Assn. Virology, Bangkok Golf Club. Avocations: reading, travel, tennis, music. Home: 633/7 Sol Uthane 22, Sukhaphaban 1, Bangkapi Bangkok 10240, Thailand Office: Thai Red Cross Nat Blood Ct, Henri Dunant Rd, Bangkok 10330, Thailand

TANPHAICHITR, KONGSAK, rheumatologist, allergist, immunologist, internist; b. Bangkok, Feb. 22, 1946; came to U.S., 1971; s. Boonchoo and Hong (Nayakovit) T.; m. Sirirat Tareesung, June 17, 1973; children: Saksiri Marc, Marisa. Student, Mahidol U., Bangkok, Thailand, 1964-66, MD cum laude, 1970. Diplomate Am. Bd. Internal Medicine, Am. Bd. Rheumatology, Am. Bd. Allergy and Immunology; cert. Rheumatologist Royal Coll. Physicians Can. Straight med. intern Detroit Gen. Hosp.-Wayne State U., 1971-72; resident Barnes Hosp.-Washington U., St. Louis, 1972-74, fellow in rheumatology and immunology, 1974-76; instr. in medicine Washington U., St. Louis, 1976-77, asst. prof. medicine, 1977-97, assoc. prof. medicine, 1997—; attending physician Barnes Hosp., St. Louis, 1976—, Jewish Hosp. of St. Louis, 1981—; dir. Allergy, Rheumatology & Immunology Specialists, St. Louis; cons. rheumatology Washington U., St. Louis, 1976—. Author: Amyloid Fibrils in Joint Fluid, 1976, Studies of Tolerance in NZB/NZW Mice, 1977, Vasculitis and Multiple Sclerosis, 1980, Buddhism and Science, 1987, Buddhism: Answers to Common Questions, 1990, Buddhism Answers Life, 1995, Mindfulness: The Key to Perfect One's Life, 1997, Mind and Universe, 1998, Mindfulness and Stress Management, 1998, Awakened Life for the New Millennium, 2000, Ethics and Morality, 2000. Dharma tchr., bd. dirs., sec. Wat Phrasriratanaram Buddhist Temple, St. Louis, 1983—; co-dir. Buddhist Coun., St. Louis, 1985-90; chmn. Buddhist Coun. Greater St. Louis, 1999—. Fellow ACP, Am. Acad. Allergy, Asthma, and Immunology, Am. Coll. Rheumatology, Royal Coll. Physicians Can.; mem. Thai Physicians Assn. Am. (nat. treas. 1998, 00, treas. Midwest chpt. 1994, sec. 1997. bd. dirs. 1999—), Thai Assn. Greater St. Louis (pres.), Thai Temple Karate Shorinryu Club (Black Belt). Avocations: karate, karaoke, insight meditation, swimming. Home: 12413 Ladue Rd Saint Louis MO 63141-8100 Office: Allergy Rheum & Immun Specs 11115 New Halls Ferry Rd Florissant MO 63033-7613

TANPHAICHITRA, DEJA, internist, educator, consultant, clinician, researcher; b. Bangkok, Dec. 7, 1943; s. Boonchu and Hongs (Nayakovit) T.; m. Orasa Sukathat, Nov. 22, 1968; 1 child, Daniel. MD, Mahidol U., Bangkok, 1967. Diplomate Am. Bd. Internal Medicine, Am. Bd. Infectious Diseases. Fellow in medicine Tufts U., Medford, Mass., 1970-71; resident Boston City Hosp. and Boston VA Hosp., 1970-72, East Orange (N.J.) VA Hosp., 1970-72; instr. infectious diseases Med. Coll. Pa., Phila., 1972-74; resident Phila. VA Hosp.-U. Pa., 1973-74; fellow in immuno-endoscopy Boston City Hosp., Lahey Clinic Found., Brooks and Deaconess Hosps., Harvard U. Med. Sch., 1974-75, Harvard U., Boston, 1974-75; prof. medicine Mahidol U., 1983—; vis. physician in host def. Radcliff Infirmary, Oxford, Eng., and Nat. Heart and Lung Inst., London, 1991; vis. lectr. Chulalongkorn U., Bangkok, 1979—; participant sympsia in field. Contbr. articles to med. jours., chpts. to books. Fellow ACP; mem. Internat. Soc. for Infectious Diseases (hon.), Brit. Soc. for Study Infection (overseas mem.), Brit. Soc. for Antimicrobial Chemotherapy (overseas mem., vis. lectr. 1991). Office: Dan Clin, PO Box 4-217, Bangkok 10400, Thailand

TANQUARY, OLIVER LEO, minister; b. Springfield, Ill., Nov. 18, 1918; s. Lawrence Henry and Minnie (Potter) T.; m. Winifred Lillian Keen, June 24, 1939; children: Sylvia June, Lowell Emerson. BA, U. Pacific, 1933; MA, Boston U., 1940, STB, 1941; EdD, Fla. State Christian Coll., 1972; postgrad., Walden U., 1977-79. Ordained to ministry United Meth. Ch., 1941; cert. tchr., pub. sch. adminstr., Calif. Min. Hughes Meml. Meth. Ch., Edmonds, Wash., 1941-44; dir. guidance and rsch. County of Humboldt, Calif., 1948-52; min. Union Congl. Ch., Braintree, Mass., 1952-58, Paradise Hills Congl. Ch., San Diego, 1958-62; dir. guidance and counseling Paso Robles (Calif.) City Schs., 1962-68; dir. guidance and vocat. counseling County of Inyo, Calif., 1968-72; min. 1st Congl. Ch., Big Timber, Mont., 1972-77, 1st Meth. Ch., Big Pine, Calif., 1979-84, United Ch. of Christ, Quartz Hill, Calif., 1984-91; chaplain Mayflower Gardens Retirement Cmty., Quartz Hill, 1986-91; dir. vocat. counseling YMCA, San Diego, 1958-61; del. So. Calif. Conf., United Ch. of Christ, Pasadena, Calif., 1984-91, moderator Kern Assn., Calif., 1990; pres. Big Timber Ministerial Assn., 1967. Author: Choosing My Vocation, 1968, Foundations to Fulfillment, 1991, Our Rewarding Responses, 1997, (booklets) At Home in the Universe, 1944, Providential Guidance, 1954; contbr. articles to denominational publs. Mem. Inter-County Libr. Bd. So. Calif., 1982, Inyo County Schs. Adv. Bd., 1982-83, Inyo County Grand Jury, 1983-84. 1st lt., chaplain USAAF, 1944-48. Recipient svc. award Kiwanis Club, Paso Robles, Calif., 1965. Mem. Masons.

TANSEY, LISA REBECCA, database administrator, dancer, masseuse, musician; b. Palo Alto, Calif., Sept. 25, 1959; d. David Arthur and Beverly Joy Tansey. BS, U. Victoria, B.C., Can., 1983. Rsch. assoc. Syntro Corp., San Diego, 1983-87; programmer analyst Electronic Online Systems, Inc., Carlsbad, Calif., 1988-98; database adminstr. Litton PRC, La Mesa, Calif., 1998—; prin. Virtually There, San Marcos, Calif., 1992—. Pres. Moreton Bay Fig Morris, San Diego, 1986, 2000; leader San Dieguito Drum Cir., Solana Beach, Calif., 1997—. Avocations: dancer, musician. E-mail: Tansey-Lisa@prc.com and lisaware@aol.com. Home: 6135 Mohler St San Diego CA 92120-3515

TANTAOUI-ELARAKI, ABDELRHAFOUR, agronomy engineer, microbiology educator; b. Settat, Settat, Morocco, Apr. 27, 1948; s. Mohamed and Malika (Benjelloun) T.; m. Fatima Essalama, July 23, 1973; children: Fatin, Omar, Kawthar, Zaynab. Degree in Agronomy Engring., Ecole Nat. Superieure Agr., Montpellier, France, 1970; MS, Faculté des Scis., Caen, France, 1972, PhD, 1977. Prof. engring. Hassan II Inst., Rabat, Morocco, 1977-82, rsch. dean, 1982-84, head dept. engring., 1987-95, prof. engring., 1997—; sec. gen. Cen. Nat. de Coord. de Planitication de la Recherche (CNR), Rabat, Morocco, 1984-87; dir. Inst. Superieur de Formation en Tech. Alimentaire (ISFORT), Casa Blanca, Morocco, 1995-97. Author: Culture Industrielle des Microorganisms, 1996; editor Oleagenous Plants & Derivatives, 1995; contbr. articles to profl. jours.; patentee in field. Recipient Chimistes Ingenieurs en Industries Alimentaire medal, France, 1984. Mem. Soc. Marocaine de Microbiologie, Assn. Marocaine de Ingenieurs en Industries Alimentaires. Avocations: poetry and novel writing, painting. Home: Cite Al-Khadra-Guich Oudaya, 10100 Rabat Morocco

TANTAWI, MOHAMMED HUSSEIN, government official; married; 2 children. Grad., Mil. Acad., Egypt, 1956. With Egyptian Army, 1956—; advanced through grades to gen. Egyptian Mil., 1991; mil. attache Pakistan, Afghanistan; comdr. Egyptian Army, Rep. Guard; head Armed Forces Ops.; Min. of Def. and Mil. Prodn., 1991—. Office: Ministry of Defense Ministry of Justice, Sharia 3 July, Kobry al-Kobba Cairo Egypt*

TANTHAPANICHAKOON, WIWUT, chemical engineering educator; b. Bangkok, Dec. 1, 1949; s. Khiak Tong Tang and Boon Hua Kuay; m. Rachanee Chayasirisophon, Dec. 2, 1978; children: Winyu, Wiroon. B of Engring., Kyoto (Japan) U., 1973; M of Engring., U. Tex., 1975, PhD, 1978. Cert. prof. indsl. engr. Rsch. asst. U. Tex., Austin, 1973-78; from instr. to asst. to assoc. prof. Chulalongkorn U., Bangkok, 1978-93, dep. dean engring., 1991-95, prof., 1993—, chair chem. engring. dept., 1996-98; mem. internat. adv. com. Internat. Drying Symposium, Asia, Am. and Europe, 1984—; dir. Engring. Inst. for R&D, Bangkok, 1991-95; dep. dir. Thai Powder Tech. Ctr., Bangkok, 1993—; regional coord. World Filtration Congress, Nagoya, Japan, 1993; head chem. engring. com. Engring. Inst. Thailand, Bangkok, 1996-99; mem. organizing com. Internat. Symposium on Combustion and Energy Utilization, Bangkok, 1997; sec. Thai Assn. of Particle Tech., Bangkok, 1998—; mem. internat. adv. com. World Congress on Particle Tech., Brighton, Eng., 1998; mem. exec. com. Tech. Promotion Inst., Bangkok, 1998—. Author: (book) Industrial Heat Exchangers, 1993; coauthor: (book) Air Pollution, 1988; contbr. rsch. papers to profl. jours. Sec. gen. Fed. S.E. Asian AOTS Alumni Scis., Bangkok, 1990-92; pres. Asia Bunka Kaikan-Assn. Overseas Tech. Scholarships Alumni Assn., Bangkok, 1994-98. Recipient Sci. and Tech. award Thailand Toray Sci. Found., 1998. Fellow Engring. Inst. Thailand; mem. AIChE, Japan Assn. Heat Pipes, Soc. Powder Tech. Japan, Japan Assn. Aerosol Sci. and Tech., Sci. Soc. Thailand (life), Thai Acad. Sci. and Tech., Technol. Promotion Assn. (life mem., exec. com. 1985-94), Soc. Chem. Engrs., Union of Kyoto Club (pres. 1992-96). Avocations: reading books, classical music. Office: Chulalongkorn U Fac Engring, Payathai Rd Patumwan, Bangkok 10330, Thailand

TANTI, CHARMAINE CARUANA, education educator; b. Attard, July 17, 1971; d. Tanti Fortunato and Mary Grech T.; m. Mark Caruana, Jan. 17, 1999. BA in English and Theatre, U. Malta, 1993, MA in English Lit., 1998. Journalist U. Observer, Malta, 1993-94; tchr. St. Dorothy's Sch., Malta, 1993—. Contbr. articles to profl. jours.; author poems. Mem. Missionary Movement (youth leader 1987—), Assn. Freelance Writers, The Folio Soc., Internat. Socl Poets, Sharpe Appreciation Soc., Keats-Shelley Meml. Assn. Roman Catholic. Avocations: photography, ballroom dancing, drawing, reading, Spanish dancing. Home: St Mary 70, P Muscat St RBT08, Rabat Malta Office: St Dorothys Sch, Mdina Rd, ZBG08 Zebbug Malta

TAO, KAIYUAN, judge; b. Xiang Tan, Hunan, China, Mar. 12, 1964; d. Jinghua Tao and Jingdi He; m. Yapu Zhang; 1 child, Zitao. LLB, Wuhan U., China, 1985, LLM, 1988; LLD, Wuhan U., 2000. Lectr. of law Jinan U., Guangzhou, China; assoc. prof. law Jinan U., dep. dean of law dept., hon. prof. law; lawyer Guangzhou 2nd Fgn. Econ. Law Office, KingPound Law Firm, Guangzhou; internat. law cons. Leeda Law Firm, Guangzhou; v.p., sr. judge High Court of Guangdong Province; commr. examination com. on law degrees of Jinan U., 1996—, acad. com., 1996—. Author: (books) China's Law Dictionary (International Law) 1996, Basis Legal Systems, 1997, Comments on Cases on Partnership Law, 1996, Hong Kong Dictionary, 1994, China's Legal Regulation on Real Estate Business, 1994, Economic Law Aspects on Investment in China, 1991, Comments on Commercial and Banking Laws, 1992 (Best Seller/Hong Kong 1994), Research in China's Conflict of Laws, 1993, China's Legal Regulation on Foreign Economic Relations and Trade, 1991, China's Economic Laws, 1990; author/editor: (books) English-Chinese Dictionary of Commercial Law, 1996, International Commercial Law, 1999, Comments on Commercial Cases, 1994; contbr. articles to profl. jours. Mem. Guangdong Province Judges Assn. (vice-chmn. 1999—), Guangdong Province People's Government Econ. Law Rsch. Inst. (bd. dirs. 1996—), China Internat. Econ. Law Assn., Guangdong Province Internat. Law Rsch. Assn. (vice gen. dir. 1993—), Woman Judges Fedn. (standing com.). Avocations: tennis, touring, classical arts, literature.

TAO, MARIANO, biochemistry educator; b. Davao, Philippines, Mar. 3, 1938; came to U.S., 1963; s. Bong-Hua and Siu-Hua (Co) T.; m. Pearl Koh, June 3, 1967; children: Stephen, Kevin. BSChemE, Cheng Kung U., Tainan, Taiwan, 1962; PhD in Biochemistry, U. Wash., 1967. Sr. fellow U. Wash., Seattle, 1967-68; guest investigator Rockefeller U., N.Y.C., 1968-70; asst. prof. U. Ill., Chgo., 1970-74, assoc. prof., 1974-78, prof. dept. biochemistry and molecular biology, 1978-98, prof. emeritus, 1998—, acting head, 1979-80; biochemistry study sect. NIH, 1985-89; established investigator Am. Heart Assn., 1973-78. Mem. Am. Soc. Biochemistry and Molecular Biology, Am. Chem. Soc. Achievements include membrane abnormality and diseases I and II. Home: 1305 Darien Club Dr Darien IL 60561-3671 Office: U Ill Chicago 1853 W Polk St Chicago IL 60612-4316

TAO, WANG, ophthalmologist; b. Huai Ren, China, July 25, 1968; s. Wang Zilu and Zhao Yulan; m. Zhang Yun, Aug. 28, 1996. MBBS, Capital U. Med. Scis., 1991, MD, 1997. Resident in ophthalmology Beijing Tong Ren Hosp., 1991-96, chief resident in ophthalmology, 1996—. Mem. Chinese Med. Assn. Ophthalmology. Avocations: traveling, table tennis, websurfing, spectator sports. Office: Tong Ren Hosp Dept Opth, 2 Chong Nei St, 100730 Beijing China

TAO, XU TANG, research scientist; b. Xin Jian, Jiang Xi, China, Sept. 6, 1962; s. Qu Zao Tao and Xiu Zhen Hu; m. Qi Feng Gai, Dec. 15, 1987; 1 child, Fei Yang. BS, Shan Pong U., Jinan, China, 1983, MS, 1986; D.Eng., Tokyo U. Agr. and Tech., 1995. Asst. prof. Shan Dong U., Jinan, 1986-88, lectr., 1989-91; researcher RIKEN, Wako, Sataima, Japan, 1996—. Author: Functional Monomers and Polymers, 1997; contbr. articles to profl. jours. Recipient 1st Class Invention prize Ministry Edn. China, 1996, Good Presentation award Material Rsch. Soc. Japan, 1994. Mem. Internat. Soc. Optical Engring., Materials Rsch. Soc.

TAO, XUE-HENG, engineering educator; b. Dalian, Liaoning, China, Jan. 5, 1963; s. Long-Xiang Tao and Duo-Xiu Zou. BS, Dalian Inst. Light Industry, 1985; MS, Dalian U. Tech., 1988, PhD, 1997. Cert. univ. tchr., rschr.; cert. engr. in mech. engring. Tchg. asst. Dalian U. Tech., 1986-87, assoc. prof., 1995-97; asst. prof. Dalian Inst. Light Industry, 1988-89, lectr., engr., 1989-95, assoc. prof., 1995-98, prof., 1999—. Author: (book) Industrial Robots, 1999; patentee in field (Excellent Patent award 1998); contbr. rsch. articles to profl. publs. Recipient New Product award Chinese Ministry of Light Industry, 1992. Mem. Chinese Mech. Engring. Soc., Chinese Assn. Light Industry Machines. Home: #37-1-2 Xian St Xigang Dist, 116011 Dalian Liaoning, China Office: Dalian Inst Light Industry, Qinggong Yuan Ganjinzi Dist, 116034 Dalian Liaoning, China

TAOFINU'U, PIO CARDINAL, archbishop; b. Falealupo, Samoa, Dec. 8, 1923. Ordained priest Roman Catholic Ch., 1954, joined Soc. of Mary, 1962, consecrated bishop, 1968. Bishop of Apia Samoa and Tokelau, 1968-73; elected to Coll. Cardinals, 1973, archbishop of Samoa-Apia and Tokelau, 1982—. Mem. Congregation Causes of Saints. Address: Archdiocese of Samoa-Apia, PO Box 532, Apia West Samoa

TAORMINA, CHARLES ANTHONY, writer, editor, artist; b. Johnstown, Pa., Apr. 2, 1948; s. Anthony James and Shirley Ruth (Wagner) T.; m. Brenda Gail Gilbert, Aug. 8, 1970 (div. 1981); 1 child, Angela Loraine. BA in Liberal Arts, Indiana U. of Pa., 1970. Contbg. editor/reporter Times of Charlottesville, Va., 1976-78; editor Blue Ridge Rev., Charlottesville, 1978-79, VIRTÙ, Uniontown, Pa., 1993—; writer, editor, mgr. The Renaissance Workshop, Uniontown, 1990—; spkr. World Future Soc., Bethesda, Md., 1989, 93; mem., actor Actors & Artists of Fayette County, Scottdale, Pa., 1993; contbg. author/mem. writing workshop project-Projects, Inc. Author: (novels) Abbas & Merdan, Endgames, Karma Bums, Gratuity, Legacy, (novella) Of Rifles & Butterflies, (drama) Freedom One, Tauromenium, Rally!, Catalyst, (nonfiction) Along the Journalistic Path, Infinity, Vision, Ardour, Keystone, Quintessence, (story collections) Early Tales, Moments, Shared Lives, (poetry) Rain Folio, also monographs,(audio cassette) Renaissance: An Introduction; editor: Commercial Book and Story Editing; contbr. fiction to Blue Ridge Rev., Samisdat, Gargoyle, Fool's Jour., William and Mary Rev.; contbr. nonfiction to Daily Progress, The Sun, Harper's Weekly, others; contbr. photography to Washington Post, Gargoyle, others; contbr. on-line arts newsletter PRIVY; dramas staged Gemini Theater, Pitts., 1998. Freedom writer Amnesty Internat., N.Y.C., 1989—; mem. regeneration project Rodale Press, Emmaus, Pa., 1989; workshop leader VISTA Literacy Project, Ravenna, Ohio, 1988; pub. rels. worker Nat. Road Heritage Park Project, Uniontown, 1993. Recipient Honorable Mention award Soc. for Am. Cuisine, 1987. Mem. Dramatists Guild (assoc.), Am. Christian Writers Assn., Renaissance Soc. Am., Internat. Freelance Photographers Assn., Union of Concerned Scientists. Roman Catholic. Avocations: sketching, cosmology, travel, music listening, hiking. Office: The Renaissance Workshop 860 Chalker St Fl 1 Akron OH 44310-2116 also: 103 Camden Ave Johnstown PA 15904-2302

TAPAN, SEMA SAKARYA, marketing educator; b. Caycuma, Turkey, July 12, 1951; s. Sevket and Mualla (Gonenc) S.; m. Okan Rifat, Sept. 24, 1978; 1 child. BSc, Mid. East Tech. U., 1973; MBA, Bogazici U., 1975; PhD, Istanbul U., 1981. Assoc. prof. Bogazici U., Istanbul, Turkey, 1976—; founder, dir. Bogazici U. Sch. Applied Disciplines, Istanbul Technical U. Inst. Social Scis.; founder Turkish Mktg. Assn. and Ymir Found. Home: Kormac 1, Yenikoy 80870, Turkey

TAPANES, EDWARD EDUARDOVICH, fiber optic sensing company executive, physicist, research engineer; b. Odessa, Ukraine, Feb. 4, 1966; s. Eduardo R. and Paulina V. (Zelitskaya) T.; m. Cheryl Lee Beazley, Dec. 14, 1991; 1 child, Alexander Edward. BS, Royal Mil. Coll. Can., 1988; M of Applied Sci., U. Toronto, Can., 1990. Aerospace engr. Dept. Nat. Def., Can., 1984-91; computer sales rep. Social Engring. Assocs. Inc., Toronto, 1987-90; rsch. engr. Coop. Rsch. Ctr.-Aerospace Structures, Melbourne, Australia, 1991-92, Ctr. Advanced Materials Tech., Melbourne, Australia, 1992-94; dir. Future Fibre Techs. Pty. Ltd., Melbourne, Australia, 1994—, Smart Monitoring Technolgies Pty. Ltd., Melbourne, Australia, 1997—; hon. rsch. assoc. Monash U., Melbourne, 1994-97; cons. Mission Rsch. Corp., USA, 1994; cons. Aeronautical and Maritime Rsch. Labs., Melbourne, Australia, 1995—; mem. Australian Photonics Steering Com., 1997-99. Patentee in field; contbr. articles to profl. jours. Organizer Emancipate Sri Lankan Children From Prostitution and Exploitation, Melbourne, 1994; co-founder So. Spirit Inc., 2000. Recipient Postgrad. Rsch. fellowship U. Toronto, 1988, grant Australian Rsch. Coun., 1993, 94, 95, grants (2) Fed. Govt. Industry Innovation Program, 1995, Fed. Govt. R&D Start Program, 1998, 2000, Pursuit of Excellence award Australian Small Bus. Awards; nominated Australian Young Bus. Achiever award Fed. Govt., 1995. Mem. Australian Composite Structures Soc., Internat. Soc. Optical Engring., Internat. Soc. Optical Engring. (internat. tech. working group on smart structures 1991—). Avocations: music, fishing, snorkelling, sports, reading. Office: Future Fibre Techs Pty Ltd, 20 Viewtech Pl, Rowville VIC 3178, Australia

TAPER, HENRYK STANISLAW, pathologist; b. Wejherowo, Gdansk, Poland, Mar. 17, 1924; arrived in Belgium, 1964; s. Stanislaw and Anna (Pokora) T.; m. Danuta Barbara Sobkiewicz, July 10, 1948; children: Gilis Elzbieta, Jan. MD, Jagiellonian U., Cracow, Poland, 1949; D Med. Scis., Med. Acad., Cracow, 1951; PhD, Cath. U. Louvain, Belgium, 1975. Diplomate in pathology Acad. Medicine Gdańsk, Poland. Asst. Jagiellonian

U., 1949-50; lectr. Acad. Medicine, Gdansk, Poland, 1956-62; postdoctoral rsch. fellow Sloan-Kettering Inst. for Cancer Rsch., N.Y.C., 1962-63; lectr. Cath. U. Louvain, 1964-89; hon. lectr., cons. Cath. U. Louvain, Brussels, 1989—; vis. prof. Inst. Pathology U. Montreal, Que., Can., 1972; rsch. fellow German Cancer Inst., Heidelberg, Germany, 1974. Contbr. articles to profl. jours. Named Officer of Ordre de Léopold II, Kingdom of Belgium, 1988. Mem. European Assn. for Cancer Rsch., N.Y. Acad. Scis. Avocations: sports, touring. Home: Roeselbergweg 8, B-3012 Wilsele Belgium Office: Cath U Louvain Biochim Toxicologique Cancerol, Ave E Mounier 73, B-1200 Brussels Belgium

TAPLIN, MARK ALLARD, foreign service officer; b. Washington, Feb. 15, 1957; s. Winn Lowell and Ellajean Allard Taplin; m. Kathleen Ann Kavalec, Dec. 15, 1984; children: Benjamin C., Samuel C. BS in Fgn. Svc., Georgetown U., 1978; MSc in Econs. Strategic Studies, Univ. Coll. Wales, Aberystwyth, 1982. Cert. career counselor U.S. Fgn. Svc. Dir. policy and evaluation Bur. Ednl. and Cultural Affairs USIA, Washington, 1996-97, team leader econ. security team, 1997-98; counselor for pub. affairs U.S. Embassy, Kiev, Ukraine, 1999—. Author: (book) Open Lands Travels Through Russia's Once Forbidden Places, 1997. E-mail: mtaplin@exchange.usia.gov. Office: US Embassy, Kiev Ukraine

TAPLIN, RUTH, writer, editor, journalist, export company executive, researcher; b. San Francisco, Jan. 1, 1953; arrived in Eng., 1976; PhD, London Sch. Econs., 1985. Rsch. fellow U. Durham, 2000—; dir. ctr. for japanese and east asian studies Birkbeck Coll. Univ. London, 1989—; former East Asian editor CBI News, 1991-97; writer The Times; cons. Fedn. of Electronics Industry, 1997—; trainer Inst. of Exports, Telecoms, 1990—; rep. Asian Economic Bus. Forum, 1999—. Author Japanese Decision Making, 2 others; editor Jour. of Interdisciplinary Econs.; contbr. over 50 articles to profl. jours.; spkr. in field. Address: Ctr for Japanese & E Asian, Studies PO Box 427, Pinner HA5 3FX, England

TAPPER, COLIN FREDERICK, lawyer, educator; b. West Draytion, Middlesex, Eng., Oct. 13, 1934; s. Herbert Frederick and Florence Gertrude (Lambard) T.; m. Margaret White, Apr. 1, 1961; 1 child, Lucy. BA in Law, Oxford (Eng.) U., 1958, B of Civil Law, 1959. Lectr. London (Eng.) Sch. Econs., 1959-65; fellow Magdalon Coll., Oxford, 1965—; prof. law U. Oxford, Eng., 1980—; vis. prof. NYU Law Sch., 1971, Stanford U. Law Sch., 1975-76, U. Sydney, Australia, 1989; cons. Masons, Eng., 1989—. Author: Computers and the Law, 1973, Computer Law, 1978, 4th edit., 1990, Cross on Evidence, 1985, 6th edit., 1995, Handbook of European Software Law, 1999, Cross and Tapper on Evidence, 9th edit., 1995. Avocations: reading, writing, computing. Home: Corner Cottage, Woodstock Rd, Stonesfield Witney OX8 8QA, England Office: Magdalen Coll, Oxford OX1 4AU, England

TAPPER, UNA REID, administrative law judge; b. Jamaica, June 26, 1932; came to U.S., 1979; d. Uriah and Beatrice (King) Reid; m. Lloyd G. Tapper, Sr., Aug. 9, 1964; children: Patricia, Lloyd Jr. BA in Psychology, Temple U., 1957; MSW, U. Pa., 1959; JD, St. Louis U., 1982. Bar: Mo. 1982, N.Y. 1985. Chief med. social worker Univ. Hosp., Mona, Jamaica, 1964-79; sr. atty. Mo. Dept. Revenue, Jefferson City, 1982-85; protest atty. Housing Preservation & Devel., N.Y.C., 1985-88; adminstrv. law judge N.Y. State Social Svcs., N.Y.C., 1988-90; adminstrv. law judge N.Y. State Parole, N.Y.C., 1990-95, supervising adminstrv. law judge, 1995—. Avocation: gardening. Office: NY State Divsn of Parole 314 W 40th St New York NY 10018-1404

TAPROGGE, RAINER HERBERT, plastics engineer, consultant; b. Schwerte/Ruhr, Germany, Oct. 14, 1937; s. Paul and Sophia (Betten) T.; m. Ingrid Maria Gelueck Taprogge, Mar. 30, 1968; children: Carsten, Birga. Diploma in engring., Tech. U., Aachen, Germany, 1962, diploma in indsl. econs., 1966, PhD in Engring., 1966, Prof. degree, 1974. Mgr. Tech. U. RWTH, Aachen, 1962-66; vice head Inst. Plastics Tech., Aachen, 1966-70; mng. dir. Inst. for Future tech., Hamburg, Germany, 1970-73; consulting engr. Plastics Tech., Hamburg, 1973—; pres. Arbeitskreis Selbständiger Kunststoffingenieure und-berater, Frankfurt, 1978-88. Author: Engineering Design with Plastics, 1971, 74, High Performance Composites, 1974. Recipient Borchers award, Tech. U., Aachen, Germany, 1966. Mem. Verein Deutscher Ingenieure, Soc. Plastics Engrs., Arbeitsgemeinschaft Verstärkte Kunststoffe, Arbeitskreis Selbständiger Kunststoff-Ingenieure und Berater, Gesamt Verband Kunststoff Verarbeitende Industrie. Avocations: skiing, offshore sailing. Office: Taprogge Cons Engr, Stockkamp 10, D-22607 Hamburg Germany

TAPSCOTT, CHRISTOPHER PETER, sociologist; b. Edgeware, Middlesex, U.K., Sept. 5, 1952; s. Peter Gordon and Elizabeth Catherine (Smyth) T.; m. Gretta Eve Melck, July 29, 1985; children: Kimberley, Claire. BS with honors, U. Cape Town, S. Africa, 1974, M Pub Adminstrn, 1977; MSc, U. Birmingham, 1978; PhD, London Sch. Econs., 1992. Urban studies officer Cape Town City Coun., S. Africa, 1975-77, prin. urban studies officer, 1979-81; dir. Inst. for Mgmt. and Devel. Studies/U. Transkei, Umtata, S. Africa, 1981-86, Namibian Inst. for Social/Econ. Rsch., Windhoek/Nambia, 1990-93; head Social Scis. Divsn. U. Nambia, Windhoek/Nambia, 1993-94; dir. Sch. Govt. U. Western Cape, Cape Town, S. Africa, 1994—; task team mem. Presdl. Rev. comm. on Pub. Sector Reform, S. Africa, 1997-98; coord. tech. drafting team white paper on Transformation of Pub. Svc., S. Africa, 1995; mem. core adv. group on Inter-Govtl. Rels., Pretoria, S. Africa, 1998—; mem. Inter-Agy. World Congress on Agrl. Reform and Rural Devel., Rev. Mission to Nambia, 1994; trustee Joint Univs. Pub. Mgmt. Edn. Trust, chmn. 1997-99. Contbr.: (books) Power of Development, 1995, The Two-Edged Sword, 1996, When Refugees Go Home: African Experiences, 1996, The Worldwide Diffusion of The European Model of the State, 1999; contbr. articles to profl. jours. Mem. exec. com. Cmty. Peace Found., Cape Town, 1995-98; mem. So. Democracy Ctr. Coun., Cape Town, 1997-98; trustee Local Govt. Learning Network Trust, 1997—, We. Cape Pub. Adminstrn. and Mgmt. Forum, 1995—. Grantee Soc. for Protection of Sci. and Learning, London, 1987, Canon Collins Trust, London, 1988, Africa Edn. Trust, London, 1988. Mem. Internat. Inst. Adminstrv. Scis. Avocations: scuba diving, tennis. Office: Sch Govt/Univ Western Cape, Pvt Bag X17, Bellville 7535, South Africa

TAQIEDDIN, SALAH ABDULHAMID, mining and civil engineer, educator; b. Zarqa, Jordan, Feb. 19, 1944; s. Abdulhamid Ibrahim and Aysha Rashid (Domani) T.; m. Hanan Omar Jadid, May 29, 1973; children: Ranya, Ehab, Eyad, Lara. BSc in Mining Engring., Mid. East Tech. U., Ankara, Turkey, 1970, MSc in Mining Engring., 1972; BSc in Civil Engring., U. Mo., Rolla, 1983, PhD in Mining Engring., 1982. Process engr. Jordan Phosphates Mines Co., Ruseifa, 1970-71, shift engr., 1972-73; mine supt. Jordan Phosphates Mines Co., El Hassa, 1973-76; prof. mech. engring. Yarmouk U., Irbid, 1983-85; prof. civil engring. Jordan U. of Sci. and Tech., Irbid, 1986—; vis. prof. U. Mo., Rolla, 1985. Mem. AIME, ASCE, Internat. Soc. Explosives Engrs. (U.S.). Avocation: sports. Home: PO Box 606/Main Office, Irbid Jordan Office: PO Box 606 Main Office, Irbid Jordan

TARA, research chemist, publishing executive, writer; b. Kotdata, Punjab, India, June 11, 1921; came to U.S., 1966; naturalized, 1972; s. Nand and Isar (Kaur) Singh; m. Rani Surinder, Dec. 29, 1954; children: Nina, Roopinder, Sylvia, Sonya. BS with honors, Punjab U., 1944, MS with 1st class honors, 1946; AM, Harvard U., 1949, PhD, 1950. Post doctorate fellow with Prof. R.B. Woodward Harvard U., 1950-51; Post doctorate fellow NRC, Can., 1953-54; prof. chemistry govt. colls., Punjab, India, 1954-58; prin. govt. colls., India, 1958-64; rsch. and devel. chemist PEBOC Ltd., Northolt, Eng., 1964-65, Unilever Rsch. Lab., Isleworth, Eng., 1965-66; prin. investigator rsch. projects Aldrich Chem.Co., Milw., 1966-76; rsch. and devel. chemist Polyscis., Inc., Warrington, Pa., 1976-88, Calbiochem, La Jolla, Calif., 1989-94; pres. One World Publ. Co., San Diego, 1996—; prin. investigator rsch. projects. Author: The Educational Problem of India, 1955, An Outline of the Philosophy of Creative Education, 1959, Evolution of the Soul, 1970, Universal Creative Religion for Peace, Love and Light, 1978, 2d edit., 1994, Human Sacrifice and Cannibalism in the Holy Bible, 1996, Sex Stories of the Holy Bible, 1996; contbr. numerous articles to profl. jours. Mem. Am. Chem. Soc. Avocations: studies in comparative religions, meditation. Home: 4202 Appleton St San Diego CA 92117-1901 Office: One World Publ Co PO Box 178206 San Diego CA 92177-8206

TARACENA, ANTONIO, cement company executive; b. Mexico City, Sept. 5, 1951; s. Antonia T. and Hilda Sosa; m. Margarita Oliveras, Sept. 9, 1977; children: Antonio, Erick. Chem. Engr., U. Nat. Autonoma Mex., Mexico City, 1975; MBA, IPADE, Mexico City, 1993. Dist. mgr. Gates Rubber, Mexico City, 1975-78; divsional mgr. Hoechst, Mexico City, 1979-90; v.p. Eureka, Mexico City, 1990-93; pres. Corp. Moctezuma, Mexico City, 1993—; math tchr. U. Nat. Autonoma Mex., Mexico City, 1978-84. Avocations: running, reading, computing. Home: Ave del Rey 35, 55116 Naucalpan Mexico, Mexico Office: Corp Moctezuma, Monte Elbruz 134 PH, 11000 Mexico City Mexico

TARAFDAR, MUSTAFIZUR RAHMAN, civil engineer, consultant; b. Bogra, Bangladesh, Feb. 1, 1933; s. Mofiz Uddin and Genduli Bibi (Khan) T.; m. Naseem Akhtar Haque, July 6, 1958; children: Reni Kaiser, Reema Sharmeen, Luna Nasreen. BSc in Civil Engring. 1st class honors, U. Engring & Tech., Dhaka, Bangladesh, 1956; DIC PG Diploma in Hydrology, London (Eng.) U., 1962; MS in Civil Engring., Stanford U., 1967. Chartered engr., Eng.; registered engr. Nigeria. Asst. engr. Bangladesh Irrigation Dept., Dhaka, Comilla, Jessore, 1956-59; dep. dir. Bangladesh Water Devel. Bd., Dhaka, 1963-72, dir., 1972; chief water sect. Nat. Planning Commn., Dhaka, 1972-78; irrigation and drainage engr. World Bank, Washington, 1978-81; chief lectr. (assoc. prof.) Polytech. U., Ibadan, Nigeria, 1981-87; sr. lectr. and dir. agrl. rsch. U. Agr., Abeokuta, Nigeria, 1987-90; sr. lectr. and head hydraulic rsch. unit U. Lagos, Nigeria, 1990-96; chief engr. PMWR, AIM cons. Ltd., Lagos, Nigeria, 1997—; civil, irrigation engr. Confedn. Brit. Industries, London, 1959-62; irrigation engr. cons. World Bank Roster, Washington, 1983—; irrigation, dam engr. Water & Dam Svcs. Co., Lagos, 1992. Co-editor: (with others, books) UNESCO Paris Teaching Hydrology, 1973, Vol. II, 1973, textbooks in Hydrology; contbr. over 125 articles and papers to profl. jours. and to seminars and sci. proceedings worldwide. Mem. exec. coun. Inst. of Engrs., Dhaka, 1973-78; sec. Nat. Com. Internat. Hydrological Decade UNESCO, Dhaka, 1966-72, Earth Resources Satellite Technology (ERTS), Landsat Nat. Com., Dhaka, 1975-78. Recommended for Civil award Govt. E. Pakistan, 1971; (unfulfilled due to Bangladesh Independence). Fellow Dhaka Inst. Engrs.; mem. ASCE, Instn. Civil Engrs. (UK), Coun. of Registered Engrs., Alumi Fedn. U. Engring, Dhaka (v.p. 1976-78), CBI Scholars Assn. (Eng.). Islamic. Avocations: photography, reading, gardening. Home: 72 Segun Bagicha 1st Fl, Dhaka 1202, Bangladesh Office: AIM Cons Ltd, PO Box 267A Etim Inyang Crescent, Victoria Isalnd Lagos, Nigeria

TARAKANOV, BORIS VASILJEVICH, microbiologist; b. Wichuga, Russia, Apr. 19, 1933; s. Vasily and Zinaida (Jamchikova) T.; m. Ludmila Isaeva, May 23, 1959; two children. DVM, Agrl. Inst. Ivanovo, 1956; D in Biol. Sci., All-Russian Rsch. Inst., 1985. Veterinarian Sovkhoz, Chitinsky, Russia, 1956-62; from aspirant to chief dept. biotechnology All-Russian Rsch. Inst. Animal Physiology, Biochem. and Nutrition, Borovsk, Russia, 1962—, prof., 1996; chmn. Coun. Agrl. Sci. Scientific Ctr., Kaluga, Russia, 1993-97; assessor Australian Rsch. Coun., Canberra, 1996—. Author: Study the Microflora in Forestomaches of Ruminant, 1977, Microbiology of the Digestion of Ruminants, 1982, Methods of Study of the Digestive Tract Microflora in Farm Animals and Poultry, 1998. Recipient Gold medal All Russian Exhbn. Ctr., 1997. Mem. Russian Soc. Microbiology, Meritorious Sci. Worker Russia. Office: All Russian Rsch Inst Animal Physiology, Biochem & Nutrition, 249010 Borovsk Russia

TARAN, EVGENY YURIEVICH, mathematician; b. Malaya Pereshchepina, Poltava, Ukraine, Oct. 1, 1945; s. Yury Ivanovich and Lukeria Filippovna (Zimovets) T.; Liudmila Nikolaievna Krestinina, Feb. 13, 1966; children: Oleg, Dmitry. MS in Applied Math., Taras Shevchenko Kyiv Nat. U., Ukraine, 1967, PhD in Physics and Math., 1970, DS in Physics and Math., 1994. Lectr. to prof. Taras Shevchenko Kyiv Nat. U., 1969-95, prof., 1995—, dean fgn. students, 1984-85, prof., cons. math. Havana U., Cuba, 1971-73, 77-79, Camaguey U., Cuba, 1979-80. Co-author: Higher Mathematics: Book of Mathematical Problems, Book 2, 1994, Higher Mathematics: Special Sections, University Manual, Book 2, 1996; contbr. articles to profl. jours. Mem. Inst. Petrochemical Synthesis, Rheological Soc. Avocations: fishing, swimming. Office: Taras Shevchenko Kyiv Nat U, Vladimirskaya St 64, 01033 Kyiv Ukraine

TARANCZEWSKI, PAWEL MARIA, painter; b. Kraków, Poland, Jan. 21, 1940; s. Waclaw and Wanda (Hryniewiecka) T.; m. Marta Helena Umińska, Mar. 29, 1964; children: Dominika, Mateusz, Julia. MA, Acad. Fine Arts, Kraków, 1963; PhD, Jagiellonain U., 1988. Asst. prof. Dept. Architecture Tech. U. Kraków, 1982-97, prof., 1997-98; chair history of art Acad. Fine Arts, Cracow, 1998—. Group exhbns. include: Festival of Contemporary Polish Painting, Nat. Mus., Szczecin, 1996, Misiak, Michalski, Wiktor, Taranczewski, Regio Gallery, Freiburg, 1994, Painting in Kraków, Palac Sztuki Gallery, 1992, 1976, Ozas Gallery, 2000, others; solo shows include: Format Gallery, Kraków, 1994, 1994, Desa Gallery, Kraków, 1989, others. Office: Acad Fine Arts Cracow, pl Jana Matejki 13, 31-157 Krakow Poland

TARANTINO, LOUIS GERALD, business executive, consultant, lawyer; b. Bridgeport, Conn., Sept. 7, 1934; s. Louis Gerald and Mary Louise (Boyle) T. BA, U. Pa., 1955, LLB, 1958. Bar: Conn. 1958, N.Y. 1960. Assoc. Beekman & Bogue, 1959-67, ptnr., 1968-76; pres., bd. dirs. Berkeley Mgmt. Assocs., Inc., Boston, 1984—; mem. enterprise adv. bd. Photonics Ctr., Boston U.; ptnr. Berkeley Investment Ptnrs., N.Y.C., Wintzen Pharms, L.P., The Netherlands, Startup Ptnrs., Boston; bd. dirs. SiteLab Corp., Portsmouth, N.H., EachNet.com.Ltd.,Cayman Islands, Shanghai and Hong Kong, Anyparty.com.inc., Boston, Comml. Exch. Co. Inc., Boston; bd. dirs. The Inst. for New Medicine, Washington. Mem. Bar Assn. City N.Y., N.Y. Bar Assn., Conn. Bar Assn., SAR, Huguenot Soc. Pa., St. Anthony Hall, Knickerbocker Club, India House (N.Y.C.), St. Anthony Club (Phila.). Home: One Devonshire Pl Apt 3409 Boston MA 02109

TARAPOOM, VORAVAN, mutual fund executive; b. Ayudthya, Thailand, June 7, 1955; d. Decha and Prapas (Sawetakanit) Komolpis; m. Nirut Tarapoom. BArch, Silpakorn U., Thailand, 1977; MBA, North Tex. State U., 1981. Accounts exec. Datamat Ltd., Thailand, 1984-86; v.p. Bank of Asia, Thailand, 1986-93; sr. v.p. Thana One Fin. & Securities, Thailand, 1993-95; mng. dir. Thai Asia Mut. Fund, Thailand, 1995—; compliance dir. Assn. of Investment Mgmt., Thailand, 1995—. Mem. UNICEF, Wildlife Protection Found. (hon.), Elephant Found. (hon.). Home: 529/806 Merlin Tower 1, Thanurat Kwang Thung-Wat-Don Sathorn, Bangkok 10120, Thailand Office: Thai Asia Mut Fund Co Ltd, 183 Rajanakarn Blvd 11th Fl, Bangkok 10120, Thailand

TARAR, MUHAMMAD RAFIQ, president of Pakistan; b. Pir Kot, Pakistan, Nov. 2, 1929; married; four children. FSc, Guru Nanak Khalsa Coll., 1947; grad., Islamia Coll., Gujranwala, Pakistan, 1949; degree in law, U. Law Coll., Lahore, 1951. Law practice Gujranwala, 1951-66; sessions judge Bahawalnagar and Sargodha, 1966-74; judge Lahore High Ct., 1974-80, chief justice, 1989-91; judge Supreme Ct., Pakistan, 1991-94; sen. Pakistan Muslim League/Islamic Republic of Pakistan, 1997-98; pres. Islamic Republic of Pakistan, 1998—; mem. Election Commn. of Pakistan, 1980—. Avocation: classical Persian lit. Office: Office of the Pres, Aiwan-e-Sadr, Islamad Pakistan

TARASI, LOUIS MICHAEL, JR., lawyer; b. Cheswick, Pa., Sept. 9, 1931; s. Louis Michael and Ruth Elizabeth (Records) T.; m. Patricia Ruth Finley, June 19, 1954; children: Susan, Louis Michael III, Elizabeth, Brian, Patricia, Matthew. BA, Miami U., Ohio, 1954; JD, U. Pa., 1959. Bar: Pa. 1960, U.S. Dist. Ct. (we. dist.) Pa. 1960, U.S. Ct. Appeals (3d cir.) 1964, U.S. Supreme Ct. 1969, U.S. Dist. Ct. (we. dist.) Tex. 1988, U.S. Ct. Appeals (5th cir.) 1989, U.S. Ct. Appeals (4th cir.) 1994, U.S. Ct. Fed. Claims 1987, U.S. Dist. Ct. Colo. 1998; cert. civil trial adv. Nat. Bd. Trial Advocacy. Assoc., owner Burgwin, Ruffin, Perry & Pohl, Pitts., 1960-68; ptnr. Conte, Courtney & Tarasi, Beaver County, Pa., 1968-78, Tarasi & Tighe, Pitts., 1978-82, Tarasi & Johnson, P.C., Pitts., 1982-95, Tarasi & Assocs. P.C., Pitts., 1995—. Mem. parish coun. St. James Ch., Sewickley, Pa.; mem. Sewickley Borough Allegheny Coun., 1978-1982. With U.S. Army, 1954-56. Fellow Internat. Soc. Barristers; mem. Assn. Trial Lawyers Am. (gov., rep.), Pa. Trial Lawyers Assn. (pres. 1979-80), Acad. Trial Lawyers Allegheny County, Allegheny County Bar Assn., Pa. Bar Assn., West Pa. Trial Lawyers Assn. (pres. 1975), St. Thomas More Soc. (award 1991), Melvin Belli Soc. Democrat. Roman Catholic. Avocations: reading, golf, lecturing. Home: 1 Way Hollow Rd Sewickley PA 15143-1192 Office: The Tarasi Law Firm PC 510 3rd Ave Pittsburgh PA 15219-2107

TARASIEWICZ, HELENA PUZANOWSKA, chemist, researcher; b. Zgierszczanskie, Poland, Feb. 15, 1940; d. Franciszek and Apolonia (Szkiladz) Puzanowski; m. Mikolaj Tarasiewicz, Dec. 31, 1964; children: Arthur, Miroslaw. MS, Torun, Poland, 1963, PhD, 1970, DSc, 1976. Lectr. Tech. U., Bialystok, Poland, 1963-70, sr. lectr., 1970-76; assoc. prof. Warsaw U. Br., Bialystok, 1976-89; prof. Bialystok U., Bialystok, 1989—, head dept. inorganic and analytical chemistry, 1978—. Co-author: Chemistry of Complexes Compounds, 1988, Guide for Inorganic Proseminar, 1994; contbr. articles to profl. jours., chpt. to book. Recipient medal for edn. achievement Commn. Nat. Edn., Warsaw, 1978, award for sci. achievement Polish Ministry Edn., 1970, 82. Mem. Polish Chemistry Soc. (Rsch. Paper award 1974), Polish Toxicology Soc. Roman Catholic. Avocations: travel, gardening. Home: Rowna 15, 15-336 Bialystok Poland Office: U Bialystok, Pilsudskiego 11/4, 15-443 Bialystok Poland

TARASIEWICZ, MIKOLAJ, chemist, researcher; b. Bialowieza, Poland, Feb. 25, 1931; s. Stefan and Nadzieja (Gryko) T.; m. Helena Puzanowska, Dec. 31, 1964; children: Arthur, Miroslaw. MS, U. Minsk, USSR, 1956; PhD, U. Torun, Poland, 1970, DSc, 1974. Prof. Bialystok U. Lectr. Tech. U., Bialystok, 1964-70, sr. lectr., 1970-75; assoc. prof. Warsaw U. Branch, Bialystok, 1975-91; prof. Bialystok U., Bialystok, 1991—, head, prin. chemistry lab., 1978—. Co-author: Chemistry of Complexes Compounds, 1988, Guide for Inorganic Proseminar, 1994; contbr. articles to profl. jours. Lt. Polish Army, 1956-74, Bialystok. Recipient Polish State medal in sport and social achievement, Warsaw, 1960, Polish Ministry Edn. award for sci. achievement, 1982. Mem. Polish Chemistry Soc. (Rsch. Paper award 1974), Polish Edn. Soc. Avocation: sport. Home: Rowna 15, 15-336 Bialystok Poland Office: U Bialystok, Pilsudskiego 11/4, 15-443 Bialystok Poland

TARASOV, ALEKSANDR, physicist, researcher; b. Leningrad, USSR, Jan. 3, 1949; s. Anatoly Tarasov and Shafika Baichurina; m. Ludmila Babok, Aug. 13, 1988; 1 child, Eugene. MSc in Engring., Electrotech. Inst., Leningrad, USSR, 1972; PhD, State Optical Rsch. Inst., Leningrad, 1984. Cert. in laser engring. Jr. scientist State Optical Rsch. Inst., Leningrad, 1972-86, sr. scientist, 1986-89; leading scientist Nuclear Problems Rsch. Inst., Minsk, Belarus, 1989—. Contbr. numerous articles to sci. publs. Recipient USSR Leninsky Komsomol prize, 1982. Mem. Byelorussian Engring. and Tech. Acad. (grand engr.), Byelorussian Phys. Soc. Avocations: cars, dogs, sports. Office: Nuclear Problems Rsch Inst, 4 Bobruyscaya Str, 220050 Minsk Belarus

TARASSOLI, ABBAS, chemist, researcher; b. Kashan, Isfahan, Iran, Dec. 20, 1944; s. Ali Tarassoli and Fatemeh Secongi; m. Nahid Pourreza, Aug. 28, 1982. BS in Chemistry, Tehran (Iran) U., 1966, MS in Organic Chemistry, 1969; PhD in Organometallic Chemistry, U. London, 1975; diploma, Brit. Coun., London, 1975. Lectr. Jundi Shapur U., Ahwaz, Iran, 1969-72, asst. prof., 1975-83; assoc. prof. Shahid Chamran U., Ahwaz, 1983-88, prof., 1988—, acting dean, 1979-81, chmn. chemistry dept., 1986-90; acad. registrar Faculty Scis., Ahwaz, 1976-78; rsch. assoc. U. London, 1977; vis. prof. U. Colo., Boulder, 1978-79, vis. fellow, 1985-88, 99; mem. higher edn. coun. Shahid Chamran U., Ahwaz, 1989-99. Editor Univ. Scis. Jour., 1975-98; mem. adv. bd. Iranian Jour. Chemistry and Chem. Engring., 1987—; mem. reader's panel Inorganic Chemistry Communication, 1988; contbr. articles to profl. jours. Postdoctoral fellow U. B.C., Vancouver, Can., 1975. Fellow Chem. Soc. London; mem. Iranian Chem. Soc. (mem. high coun. 1989-00, pres. 1994-98), Am. Chem. Soc., N.Y. Acad. Scis. Avocations: jogging, swimming, reading, traveling. Office: Shahid Chamran U, Dept Chemistry, Ahwaz Iran

TARASZKIEWICZ, MARGARET, psychologist; b. Warsaw, Poland, Dec. 15, 1957; d. Wlodzimierz and Krystyna Budnicka; 2 children: Susan, Sophie. MA, U. Warsaw, 1982. Tchr., rschr. U. Warsaw, 1982-90; cons., trainer, 1990-93; mgr., educator Nat.-in-Svc. Tchr. Tng. Ctr., Warsaw, 1993—. Author: How to Teach Better. A Reflective Practitioner in Action, 1996 (Best Seller of Yr. 1996), Project of A Book Which is Not on an Educational Market, 1995 (First prize). Mem. Edn. for the Future Assn. (bd. dirs.), Devel. for the Future Assn. (bd. dirs 1996), Open Club for Innovations (co-head 1996). Avocations: gardening, travel. Home: Anielewicza 15/14, 00-167 Warsaw Poland Office: Nat In Svc Tchr Tng Ctr, Al Uyazdowskie 28, 00-478 Warsaw Poland

TARAVELLA, ROSIE, actress, writer; b. Mt. Morris, N.Y., July 8, 1962; d. Charles James and Carrie (Sardinia) T.; m. Michael Anthony Valerio, May 27, 1994. BA in Dramatic Arts, San Diego State U., 1985. Entertainment dir., staff trainer Johnny Rockets, Inc., L.A., 1986-98; staff writer, voice talent The Rick Dees Weekly Top 40, L.A., 1990-93; freelance writer, voice talent The Premiere Comedy Radio Network, L.A., 1992-98; actress L.A., 1992—; writer L.A. Times Calendar Live! Website, 1999—; theatrical prodr., cons. The Tamarind Theater, L.A., 1993-94. Author (plays) Rose's Bowl-O-Rama, 1992, The Wives, 1994, Pa's Funeral, 1995; (with Diane Kelber) Blue Grass, 1999; screenwriter: Carlo's Wake, 1997; actress (commls.) AT&T, Dial, Radio Shack and others, 1992—, (TV) Who's the Boss, Ellen, Full House, Married with Children, The Client, Almost Perfect, Brooklyn South, Sinatra, Norma Jean and Marilyn, George and Leo, Roswell; actress, co-writer (film) Carlo's Wake, 1999; writer Los Angeles Times Calendar Live! Web site, 1999—. Pres. Boards and Boards Prodns., North Hollywood, Calif., 1994-98. Recipient Am.'s Best Sitcom Writing Competition award, 1999. Mem. Mus. TV and Radio, KCRW-Nat. Pub. Radio, Am. Soc. Prevention Cruelty Animals, Nat. Geog. Soc. Democrat. Roman Catholic. Avocations: cooking, genealogy, Internet, film and TV history. Office: Broads and Boards 12828 Victory Blvd Ste 334 North Hollywood CA 91606-3013

TARAZOV, PAVEL GADELGARAEVICH, radiologist, researcher; b. Kizel, Perm, Russia, July 20, 1958; s. Gadelgarai Gabdrachmanovich and Galina Konstantinovna (Smirnova) T.; m. Lidiyua Ilyinichna Slavutskaya, Apr. 26, 1979 (div. Nov., 1983); children: Grigory, Tatiana; m. Irina Vasilievna Grischenkova, June 16, 1989; 1 child, Ekaterina. MD, 1st St. Petersburg Med. Inst., Russia, 1981; PhD, Rsch. Inst. Roentgenology, St. Petersburg, 1988, DSc in Medicine, 1996. Med. diplomate. Surgeon St. Petersburg Hosp. No. 26, 1981-84; jr. rschr. Rsch. Inst. Roentgenology, St. Petersburg, Russia, 1984-89; rschr. Rsch. Inst. Roentgenology, St. Petersburg, 1989-93, sr. rschr., 1993-96; head dept. angio/intervent. radiology —, 1996—; cons. The Sailor Hosp., St. Petersburg, 1988-94, The Acad. Postgrad. Edn. Radiographers, St. Petersburg, 1991—; presenter 25th Seminar of Radiology, Obninsk, Russia, 1995; cons., prof. Cathedra Surg. Hepatology, St. Petersburg Med. U., 1997—. Reviewer (jour.) Probl. Oncol (Russia), 1993—; contbr. articles to profl. jours. including Am. Jour. Roentgenology, Jour. Cardiovascular Surgery, Am. Jour. Gastroenterology, Cardiovascular Intervention Radiology, Acta Radiologica, Jour. Interventional Radiology, Jour. Vascular Intervent. Radiol., Surgery. Active mem. Wealth and Health for Children of Former Soviet Union, Chgo., 1994—;. Mem. European Congress of Radiology, European Congress of Internat. Hepatic, Pancreatic and Biliary Surgery Assn., Internat. Conf. Minimally Invasive Therapy, World Congress Endourology, N.Y. Acad. Sci., Radiology Soc. of St. Petersburg, Asia Pacific Cancer Conf., European Soc. Digestive Surgery. Home: POB 371, 195297 Saint Petersburg Russia Office: Rsch Inst Roetgenology, ul Leningr 70/4 Pesochny 2, 189646 Saint Petersburg Russia

TARBA, CORNELIU, science educator; b. Bucharest, Romania, Aug. 17, 1942; s. Nicolae S. and Veronia I. (Suciu) T.; m. Veronica V. Cosma, Dec. 27, 1971; children: Nicolae Adrian, Ioana Olivia. Diploma in biology, Babes-Bolyai U., Cluj-Napoca, Romania, 1965, diploma in physics, 1972; PhD, Cornell U., 1978. Biologist Zool. Sta., Sinaia, Romania, 1966-68; from tchg. asst. to assoc. prof. biophysics and cell biology Babes-Bolyai U., 1968-96, prof., 1996—, chmn. dept. animal physiology, 1990—, dir. dept. biology, 1997—. Author: Biomembranes, Transport and Cell Energetics, 1996. Mem. Romanian Soc. Pure and Applied Biophysics, Nat. Soc. Cell Biology (counsellor), European Cell Biology Orgn., N.Y. Acad. Scis. Home: Peana Str No 5, 3400 Cluj-Napoca Cluj, Romania Office: Dept Biology, Babes-Bolyai U, 3400 Cluj-Napoca Romania

TARCĂ, MIHAI, economist, educator; b. Pascani, Romania, Aug. 4, 1941; s. Vasile and Ecaterina (Popoaia) T.; m. Ana Lazăr, June 19, 1970; children: Viorel, Mihaela. Degree, Acad. Econ. Studies, Bucharest, 1965; Phd in Econs., Acad. of Econ. Studies, 1972. Asst. Al I Cuza U., Iasi, Romania, 1965-69, lectr., 1969-74, assoc. prof., 1974-90, prof., 1990—, chief dept. econs., 1974-91, dean faculty of econs., 1991-95; vis. prof. U. N.C., Chapel

Hill, 1975-76, Univ. Paris XI, 1994; fellow U. Nebr. Omaha, 1994; dir. Inst. of Enterprise Adminstrn., Iasi, 1994—, pres., 1998. Author, editor: Statistics, 1970, Privatization and the Market Economy, 1993; author: An Introduction to Demographic Prognosis, 1974, Statistics, 1979, Statistics, 1980, The Romanian Population: Past, Present and Future Trends, 1993, Regression and Correlation, 1994, Demography, 1997, Treatise of Applied Statistics, 1998; editor-in-chief University Annales, 1976-94; contbr. articles to profl. jours. Mem. Assn. of Romanian Statisticians, Gen. Assn. of Economists, World Population Soc., Internat. Union for the Sci. Study of Population, European Assn. for Population Studies, Acad. of Sci. (v.p. 1987). Home: Aleea Rozelor #9, 6600 Iasi Romania Office: Univ Al I Cuza IEAI, Bd Copou nr 11, 6600 Iasi Romania

TARGHETTA, RÉMI DOMINIQUE, internist; b. Sousse, Tunisia, Dec. 12, 1952; s. Charles and Marie Josèphe (Battistini) T.; m. Catherine Moynier, 1981 (div. 1984); 1 child, Karelle; m. Roseline Chavagneux, Aug. 11, 1990; children: Hugo, Renan. MD, U. Montpellier, France, 1982; PhD, U. Montpellier, Tours, France, 1993; M.Mgmt. Med., Ecole Super. de Commerce Paris, Paris, 1993. Intern Univ. Hosp., Nimes, France, 1978-82, head of clinic, 1982-84, staff internist, 1984—. Contbr. articles to profl. jours. Recipient Hosp. prize Faculty of Medicine, Montpellier, 1982, 83. Mem. Assn. of Departmental Lung Diseases (pres. 1992—), Am. Thoracic Soc., French Nat. Internal Medicine Soc., French Nat. Pneumology Soc. Home: 8 Rue de Garons, 30230 Bouillargues France Office: Gaston Doumergue Hosp, 5 Rue Hoche, 30006 Nimes France

TARI, GIULIANO, ceramics engineer; b. Bologna, Italy, May 17, 1970. DChemEng, U. Bologna, 1995; PhD, U. Aveiro, Portugal, 1999. Cert. materials engr. Postgrad. rschr. Italian Ceramic Ctr., Bologna, 1995; postdoctoral rschr. U. Aveiro, 1999; sr. rschr. CERAM, Stoke on Trent, U.K., 2000. Mem. European Ceramic Soc., Portuguese Soc. Rheology, Italian Soc. Rheology. E-mail: gtari@cv.ua.pt. Office: CERAM Rsch Ltd, Queens Rd Penkhull, Stoke-on-Trent ST4 7LQ, England

TARIFA, ENRIQUE EDUARDO, chemical engineer, educator, researcher; b. San Salvador de Jujuy, Argentina, Apr. 22, 1964; s. Fenelon Meliton and Maria Celia (Mamani) T. Grad. in Chem. Engring., Nat. U. Jujuy, 1990; D in Chem. Engring., Nat. U. Litoral, Argentina, 1995. Prof. Nat. U. Jujuy, 1995-99; rschr. CONICET, San Salvador de Jujuy, 1999—. Author: Simulacion Dinamica en Tiempo Real. Pasteurizador HTST, 1998; contbr. aritcles to profl. jours. Avocation: music. E-mail: eetarifa@cootepal.com.ar. Home: Gaspar Rosso No84, 4600 San Salvador de Jujuy Argentina Office: Nat Univ de Jujuy, Gorriti 237, 4600 San Salvador de Jujuy Argentina

TARIN, PERE, chemist; b. Barcelona, Spain, Sept. 30, 1955; s. Pere Tarin and Magdalena Manubens; m. Chantal Tarin (div. Oct. 1998); children: Cristina, Aniol. Degree in chemistry, U. Autonoma Barcelona, 1979, PhD in Chemistry, 1985. Asst. prof. Engr. Sch., Barcelona, 1979-80; collaborating prof. U. Autonoma Barcelona, 1981-87; responsible analytical methods devel. Esteve Quimica S.A., Barcelona, 1987-90; head dept. analytical chemistry R & D ctr. Pierre Fabre Iberica S.A., Barcelona, 1991—. Avocations: photography, dancing. Office: Pierre Fabre Iberica, Aptdo 91, Cerdanyola Spain

TARINO, GARY EDWARD, lawyer; b. Jersey City, Oct. 3, 1951; s. Edward G. and Veronica Tarino; m. Maureen Fitzpatrick, May 9, 1987. BA summa cum laude, Rutgers U., 1973, JD, 1976. Bar: N.J. 1976, U.S. Dist. Ct. N.J. 1976, D.C. Ct. Appeals 1978, U.S. Supreme Ct. 1980, N.Y. 1982, U.S. Dist. Ct. (so. dist.) N.Y. 1988, U.S. Dist. Ct. (ea. dist.) N.Y. 1990. Assoc. Winne, Banta, Rizzi & Harrington, Hackensack, N.J., 1976-79; asst. pros. Bergen County Pros. Office, Hackensack, 1979-83, chief organized crime squad, 1981-83; atty. Automatic Data Processing, Inc., Roseland, N.J., 1983—; assoc. gen. counsel, staff v.p. Automatic Data Processing, Inc., Roseland, 1994—; pub. defender Borough of Maywood, N.J., 1978; bd. dirs. N.J. Coun. Econ. Edn., 1990—; master Sidney Reitman Employment Law Am. Inn Ct., 1995—. Bd. dirs. Am. Heart Assn., N.J., 1976-81, Middlesex County (N.J.) chpt., 1973-81; trustee Integrity, Inc., 1991-97; grad. Leadership N.J., 1989; cubmaster pack III Boy Scouts Am., 2000—. Recipient cert. of appreciation U.S. Treasury Dept., 1983, letter of commondation PBA, 1983, Alumni Vol. Leadership award 1st Ann. Leadership N.J., 1991. Office: Automatic Data Processing 1 A D P Blvd Roseland NJ 07068-1786

TARIS, TOON, psychologist, researcher, consultant; b. Bussum, The Netherlands, Aug. 9, 1962; s. John Herman Taris and Helen Elisabeth Kuit; m. Inge Alida Bok, June 12, 1991; children: Marit Jasmin, Kiki Hester, Crispin Prosper. MA in Adminstrv. Sci., Free U. Amsterdam, The Netherlands, 1988, PhD in Work and Orgnl. Psychology, 1994. Lectr. stats. Free U. Amsterdam, 1988-92, rsch. fellow, 1989-93, sr. rsch. fellow, 1993-98; sr. rsch. fellow Utrecht (The Netherlands) U., 1999—; dir. B & T Consultancy, Hilversum, The Netherlands, 1996—; sr. cons. Inst. Work and Stress, Bilthoven, The Netherlands, 1997—. Author: A Primer in Longitudinal Data Analysis, 2000; editor Jour. Social Psychology, 1998—; contbr. articles to profl. jours., including Jour. Vocat. Psychology, Work and Stress, Jour. Applied Social Psychology. Office: Utrecht U, PO Box 80.140, 3508 TC Utrecht The Netherlands

TARLOW, MICHAEL JACOB, retired pediatrician, researcher; b. London, Dec. 27, 1939; s. Samuel and Fanny (Young) T.; m. Olwynne Frank, Sept. 11, 1965; children: Sarah, Joanna, Benjamin. MB, BS, Guy's Hosp. Med. Sch., London, 1962; MSc in Biochemistry, Univ. Coll., London, 1965; LLM, U. Wales, 2000. Cert. MRCP, FRCP. Rsch. fellow Univ. Coll. Hosp. Med. Sch., London, 1965-67; med. registrar Barnet Gen. Hosp., London, 1967-68; house physician registrar Hosp. for Sick Children, London, 1968-70; pediatric fellow Mayo Clinic, Rochester, Minn., 1971; sr. registrar Royal Aberdeen (Scotland) Hosp. for Sick Children, 1972-73; sr. lectr. in pediatrics U. Birmingham, Eng., 1974-99. Mem. editorial bd. Brit. Jour. Hosp. Medicine, Eng., 1985-95; co-author: Revision Pediatrics, 1989; contbr. articles to profl. jours. and chpts. in books. Mem. European Soc. Pediatric Infectious Disease Coun. (vice chmn. 1993-94, pres. 1994-95). Avocations: chess, squash, hill walking. Home: 43 Silhill Hall Rd, Solihull West Midlands B91 1JX, England

TARNEY, KAREN, organization executive; b. Milw., Apr. 18, 1940; d. Nathan and Myn (Apter) Paschen; children: Charles Green, Roberta Green Young; m. Richard Tarney, Oct. 6, 1985. BS with honors, U. Wis., Milw., 1978, MS in Nursing with honors, 1982. Tchg. asst. U. Wis., Milw., 1982, lectr., 1984; instr. Med. Coll. Wis., 1984-87; guest spkr., workshop creater-presentor in grief and loss, wellness, prevention and community. Book reviewer; contbr. articles to profl. jours. Mem. exec. com. Nat. Safety Coun., Milw.; co-founder Citizens Against Drug-Impaired Drivers. Address: PO Box 170970 Milwaukee WI 53217-8086

TARNOPOLSKII, YURI, mechanical engineer, researcher; b. Sevastopol, The Crimea, USSR, Dec. 16, 1929; s. Matvej and Anna Tarnopolskii; m. Rita Kalnberzina; children: Alla, Yelena. Grad., Latvian State U., Riga, 1952, CadnTechScis, 1957; HabilDrTechScis, Moscow Inst Problems of Mechs., 1968. Sci. worker Latvian Acad. Scis., 1954—; head of lab. Inst. Polymer Mechanics, Riga, 1963—; prof. mechanics Riga Tech. U., 1969—. Co-author: Static Test Methods for Composites, 1985, Spatially Reinforced Composites, 1993; co-editor: Handbook of Composites, Vol. 2. Structures and Design, 1989, Composite Engineering Handbook, 1997, Lubin's Handbook of Composites II, 1998. Recipient Latvian State prize, 1965, USSR State prize, 1985, Canders prize Latvian Acad. of Sci., 1998; named Honoured Sci. Worker of Latvia, 1990. Mem. Latvian Acad. Scis., Internat. Com. for Composite Materials, Nat. Com. on Theoretical and Applied Mechanics. Home: 79/81 Flat 41, Kr Valdemara St, LV 1013 Riga Latvia Office: Inst Polymer Mechanics, Aizkraukles St 23, LV 1006 Riga Latvia

TARNOPOLSKY, OLEG BORISOVICH, English educator; b. Dnepropetrovsk, Ukraine, Dec. 21, 1950; s. Boris and Sophia (Norkina) T.; m. Natalia Tolstikh, Sept. 20, 1969; 1 child. Diploma, Dnepropetrovsk State U., 1972; DSc, Moscow State U., 1992. From sr. libr. to instr. English Dnepropetrovsk Med. Inst., 1972-75; from instr. English to prof. English Dnepropetrovsk State Tech. U. Railway Transport, 1975—. Author: Methods of Teaching English to First Year Technical Students, 1989, Methods of Teaching English to Second Year Technical Students, 1993; contbr. articles to profl. jours. Home: ul Chkalova 4 apt 8, 49029 Dnepropetrovsk Ukraine

TARNOW, JÖRG, anesthesiologist educator; b. Wilhelmshaven, Germany, May 22, 1940; s. Otto Siegfried and Brigitte (Wichmann) T.; m. Katrin Bredekamp, July 19, 1968; children: Ulrike, Lisa. Med. degree, Kiel U., 1966. Resident anesthesiology, asst. prof., assoc. prof. Free Univ., Berlin, 1970-87; prof., chmn. Anesthesiology Dept. Heinrich Heine U., Dusseldorf, Germany, 1987—. Author: Cardiac Anesthesia, 1983; editor: Textbook of Anesthesia, 1992, (jour.) Der Anaesthesist. Recipient Dr. Heinrich Draeger award Critical Care Soc., 1987. Fellow Royal Coll. Anaesthetists. Office: Heinrich Heine U, Dept Anesthesiology, Moorenstr 5, 40225 Dusseldorf Germany

TARONE, ELAINE ELIZABETH, linguistics educator; b. Modesto, Calif., Feb. 13, 1945; d. Ernest Albert Tarone and Ellen Elizabeth Sutherland; m. Grant Hinkle Abbott, July 28, 1973; children: Rachel Abbott, David Abbott. BA, U. Calif., 1966; diploma, Edinburgh (Scotland) U., 1969; MA, U. Wash., 1970, PhD, 1972. Secondary tchg. credential, Calif. Tchr. Encinal H.S., Alameda, Calif., 1967-68; grad. asst. U. Wash., Seattle, 1969-72; dir. devel. skills Roxbury C.C., Boston, 1973-74; coord. ESL program U. Wash., Seattle, 1976-79; prof. linguistics U. Minn., Mpls., 1979—; part-time instr. Seattle Cen. C.C., 1972-73, 74-75; dir. ESL program U. Minn., Mpls., 1979-82, 83-86, 87-97; dir. Ctr. for Advanced Rsch. on Lang. Acquisition, U. Minn., Mpls., 1993-94, 96—. Author: (book) Variation in Interlanguage, 1988; co-author: (books) Connected!, 1999 (ETS award 1999), Focus on the Language Learner, 1989; co-editor: (book) Issues in Second Language Research, 1994. Episcopalian. E-mail: etarone@tc.umn.edu. Office: U Minn 320 16th Ave SE Minneapolis MN 55455-0135

TARPEH-DOE, LINDA DIANE, controller; b. Laramie, Wyo., Mar. 19, 1957; d. Leland Dean and Marilyn Lee (McClurg) Wheeler; m. Nyenpan Tarpeh-Doe, Jan. 16, 1982 (div. Nov. 1985); 1 child, Nyenpan Tarpeh-Doe II. BS in Acctg., U. Colo., 1979. CPA, Cert. Govt. Fin. Mgr. Asst. auditor First Bank Holding Co., Lakewood, Colo., 1979-80; internat. devel. intern USAID, Monrovia, Liberia, 1981-82; systems acct. USAID, Washington, 1982-84; fin. analyst USAID, Kingston, Jamaica, 1984-88; macs coord. USAID, Washington, 1988-93; controller USAID, Colombo, Sri Lanka, 1993-97, Nairobi, Kenya, 1997-2000; controller USAID/Ethiopia, Addas Ababa, 2000—. Mem. AICPA, Assn. Govt. Accts. Democrat. Methodist. Avocations: music, reading. Home: 3851 Paseo Del Prado St Boulder CO 80301-1527 Office: USAID Addis Ababa Dept State Washington DC 20521-0001

TARPGAARD, PETER THORVALD, naval architect; b. Knoxville, Tenn., Sept. 25, 1937; s. Peter Thorvald and Edith Margurite (Mees) T.; m. Judith Ann Burgess; 1 child, Andrew Christian. BS, U.S. Naval Acad.; SM mech. engr., MIT, 1968, naval engr., 1968, PhD, 1970. Spl. project asst. Office of the Chief of Naval Devel., Washington, 1970-73; profl. staff U.S. Arms Control & Disarmament Agy., Washington, 1973-76; design supr. Portsmouth Naval Shipyard, Portsmouth, N.H., 1976-79; prin. analyst Congressional Budget Office, Washington, 1979-85; mgr. submarine programs Draper Lab., Cambridge, Mass., 1985-92; prof. U.S. Naval War Coll., Newport, R.I., 1992-97; mgr. Noesis Inc., Newport, 1997—; cons. Congressional Office of Tech. Assessment, Washington, 1991-92. Contbr. articles to profl. jours. With U.S. Navy, 1959-79. Mem. Soc. Naval Architects & Marine Engrs., Assn. for Public Policy Analysis & Mgmts., U.S. Naval Inst. Episcopalian. Home: 5 Longmeadow Ave Middletown RI 02842-5225 Office: Noesis Inc 83 Dr Marcus F Wheatland Bd Newport RI 02840

TARPOHZY, DIMITRI NICOLAS, insurance broker; b. Alexandria, Egypt, Nov. 21, 1919; s. Nicolas Dimitri and Victoria (Klidjian) T.; m. Dorothy Farrell (dec. 1943); m. Janine Dahan, June 17, 1967. Chartered Inst. Inst., London. Mgr. Soc. Egyptienne de Bois et Matériaux, Alexandria, Egypt, 1950-61; pres., mng. dir. D. Tarpohzy & Co. S.A., Athens, 1975—; mgr. Mercury Ins. Agys., Athens, 1985—. Mem. Athens Club, Glyfada Golf Club, Lions Club (zone chmn. Greece-Cyprus). Home: 29 Ypsilantou St Kolonaki, 10675 Athens Greece Office: 44 Vasileos Constantinou Av, 11635 Athens Greece

TARPY, ELEANOR KATHLEEN, social worker; b. Pawtucket, R.I.; d. Stephen and Mary F. (Nolan) T. AB, Brown U., 1937; MS in Social Work, Boston U., 1947. Lic. social worker, Mass. Social worker R.I. Child Welfare, Providence, 1937-47, supr., 1947-49; supr. VA Regional Office, Providence, 1949-54, VA Med. Ctr., Brockton, Mass., 1954-90; ret., 1990. Contbg. author: Current Psychiatric Therapies, vol. 4, 1964. Mem. Nat. Assn. Social Work, (past com. chair). Home: 929 Armistice Blvd Pawtucket RI 02861-3321

TARR, IAN JAMES, publisher; b. Ammanford, Dyfed, Wales, Aug. 15, 1960; s. Vivian John and Olive (Francis) T. BSc in Biochemistry, Bath (Eng.) U., 1982. Sr. info. scientist Glaxo plc, London, 1983-87; editor Resources PJB Publs., London, 1988, mng. editor Pharmaprojects, 1989-90; editl. dir. Current Drugs Ltd., London, 1991-93, mng. dir., 1994—; mng. dir. Electronic Press Ltd., London, 1994—; dir. Current Sci. Group, London; pres. Electronic Press Inc., Boston. Author: Cancer Chemotherapy, 1989; contbg. author: Comprehensive Medicinal Chemistry, 6 vol., 1990; mng. editor (electronic database) The Investigational Drugs Database, 1993, 94, 95, (reference work) Pharmaprojects, 1990. Trustee CSA Trust, London, 1992—. Mem. Inst. Info. Scientists, Chem. Structure Assn. (treas. 1984-88), Am. Chem. Soc. Avocations: skiing, Internet, Welsh culture. Office: Current Drugs Ltd, 34-42 Cleveland St, London W1P 5FB, England

TARRANT, DEIRDRE ELIZABETH ANNE, dancer, educator, dance company director; b. Wellington, New Zealand, Jan. 25, 1946; d. Alfred Edward and Brigitte Esme (Rendle) T.; m. Peter Leo McKenzie, Apr. 13, 1971; children: Justin Daniel Edward McKenzie, Bret Peter Tarrant McKenzie, Jonathon Matthew REndle McKenzie. BA with honors, Victoria U., Wellington, 1967; advanced tchrs. cert., Royal Acad. Dancing, London. Licentiate Imperial Soc. Tchrs. of Dancing. Prin. Tarrant Dance Studios, New Zealand, 1968—; tchr. Royal Acad. Dancing, U.K., 1968-71; tchr. master class Can., 1972-84; dancer New Zealand Ballet Co., 1963-65; trustee Nat. Dance Archive, New Zealand, 1974-2000; dir. Footnote Dance Co., New Zealand, 1985—; dep. chair New Zealand Sch. Dance, 1990-95; maj. examiner Royal Acad. Dancing, U.K., 1984—; mem. dance adv. New Zealand Qualifications Authority, 1996—. Choreographer: (classical ballets) Sleeping Beauty, Alice in Wonderland, Graduation Ball, Wizard of Oz, others, (contemporary dance) Pieces of 8, Masques, Wheel of Fortune, The Stranger, others; choreographer dir.: (operas) La Boheme, Carmen, Marriage of Figaro, Hansel and Gretel, Madama Butterfly. Mem. sch. coms., New Zealand, scout assn. coms., New Zealand. Recipient Queen Elizabeth II award, 1967; grantee New Zealand Govt., 1994-99, Wellington Coun. grantee for youth work, 1997. Fellow Trinity Coll. (London). Avocations: walking, needlepoint, traveling, cooking, drama. Office: PO Box 3387, Wellington New Zealand

TARRANT, DESMOND, English and American literature educator; b. Southampton, Hampshire, U.K., Sept. 17, 1924; s. Richard George and Alice Maud (Pepper) T.; m. Dorrie Kathleen Mason, Dec. 24, 1947 (dec. June 1995); children: Paul, Leigh, Mandy. BA with honors, U. London, 1951, MA, 1956; tchr. diploma, U. Southampton, 1953. Tchr. Scottish Coll. of Commerce, Glasgow, 1955-57; vis. prof. U. Pa., 1957-58; lectr. dept. adult edn. U. London, 1958; lectr. Poole Tech. Coll., Dorset, 1969-71. Author: James Branch Cabell: The Dream and the Realty, 1967, Priceless Souls, 1998, The Firebrand, 2000; contbr. articles to profl. publs. With Royal Air Force, 1941-47. Recipient awards for poets and fiction. Mem. Soc. of Authors, N.Y. Acad. of Scis., Internat. P.E.N., Amnesty Internat. Socialist. Mem. Ch. of Eng. Avocations: poetry, novels, literary criticism, science and religion. Fax: 01202757278. Home: Forest Glade, 13 Cassel Ave, Poole Dorset BH13 6JD, England

TARRANT, JOHN See EGLETON, CLIVE (FREDERICK)

TARRIN, NIMMANHEMIN, federal official; b. Chiangmai, Oct. 29, 1945; married. BA in Govt. with honors, Harvard U., 1968; MBA, Stanford U. Banker, pres., CEO Siam Comml. Bank, Ltd., 1984-85; mem. Ho. of Reps., 1996; min. Ministry of Fin., Bangkok, 1997—. Democrat. Office: Ministry of Fin, Rama VI Rd, Bangkok 10400, Thailand*

TARRO, GIULIO, virologist; b. Messina, Italy, July 9, 1938; s. Emanuele and Emanuela (Iannello) T. MD, U. Naples, 1962, postgrad. in Nervous Diseases, 1968, PhD in Virology, 1971; postgrad. in Med. and Biol. Scis., Roman Acad., 1979; hon. degree in Medicine, U. Pro Deo, Albany, N.Y., 1989; hon. degree in immunology, St. Theodora Acad., N.Y., 1991; hon. degree in bioethics, Constantinian U., Cranston, R.I., 1996. Asst. in med. pathology Naples U., Italy, 1964-66; rsch. assoc. divsn. virology and cancer rsch. Children's Hosp., Cin., 1965-68; asst. prof. rsch. pediat. U. Cin. Coll. Medicine, 1968-69; rsch. fellow Nat. Rsch. Coun., Naples, 1966-74, rsch. chief, 1974; prof. oncologic virology Coll. Medicine U. Naples, 1971-85, prof. microbiology and immunology Sch. Specialization, 1972—; chief divsn. virology D. Cotugno Hosp. for Infectious Diseases, Naples, 1973—; dean faculty natural and phys. scis. Nobile Accademia di Santa Teodora Imperatrice, Capua, Italy, 1993—; sr. scientist Nat. Cancer Inst. Frederick (Md.) Ctr., 1973; project dir. Nat. cancer Inst., Bethesda, Md., 1971-75; edn. min. rep. Zool. Sta., Naples, 1975-79; cons. Italian Pharmacotherpic Inst., Rome, 1980-98; pres. De Beaumont Bonelli Found. for Cancer Rsch., Naples, 1978—, nat. com. on bioethics, 1995-98. Author: Virologia Oncologica, 1979 (award 1985), Patologia dell'AIDS, 1991, Con il Cancro si Può Vivere, 1992, AIDS Cosa Possiamo Fare Cosa Dobbiamo Sapere, 1994, Pocket File Research Collection, 1997, 3d edit., 1999, To Prevent Is To Win, 1998; editor in chief Internat. Jour. Clin. Investigation, 2000—; contbr. over 300 articles to profl. jours.; patentee in field. Pres. Sci. Cultural Com., Torre Annunziata, Italy, 1984, Tumor Prevention Assn., Rome, 1984; mem. acad. senate Constantinian U., Providence, 1990, U. Pro Deo, N.Y., 1994; mem. UNESCO-Hebrew U. Jerusalem Internat. Sch. of Molecular Biology and Microbiology; great officer Italian Republic, 1999. Maj. Italian Navy, 1982-84, lt. col., 1993-95. Decorated comdr. Nat. Order of Merit, Star of Europe, knight grand cross Sovereign Constantinian Order St. George; recipient Internat. Lenghi award Lincei Acad., 1969, Gold Microscope award Italian Health Min., 1973, Knights of Humanity award Internat. Register of Chivalry, Malta, 1978, gold medal of Culture, Pres. of Italian Republic, 1975, Culture award, 1985, 1st prize in Biomed. Rsch., Italian Acad. Arts and Scis., 1987, Castello di Pietrarossa award, Italy, 1991, gold Cesare award Padova, 1991, 20th Century award in Medicine, 1994, Gold Little Horse, Transnat. European Fedn., Rome 1996, Man of Yr. award Am. Biog. Inst., 1998, King Manfredi award Manfredonia, 1999, Equestris Ordinis S. Sepulcri of Jerusalem, Rome, 1999, Gold medal of Health Pres. of Italian Republic, 1999. Fellow AAAS; mem. Am. Soc. Microbiology, Am. Assn. for Cancer Rsch., Internat. Assn. for Leukemias, Internat. League Drs. for Abolition of Vivisection (pres. 1992—), Italian Soc. Immuno-Oncology (v.p. 1975—, pres. 1990—), Italian Assn. for Viral Study and Rsch. (pres. 1995—), Assn. Res. Prevention of Cancer (sci. com. 1995), AIDS Soc. Asia and the Pacific, Nat. Order Journalists, N.Y. Acad. Scis., UNESCO, Internat. Sch. for Molecular Biology and Microbiology, Lions (pres. Pompei chpt. 1987-89, vice gov. dist. 108y 1991-92, pres. com. to fight cancer 1992-94, pres. com. sci. and life 1994-95, pres. com. to fight drug addiction and AIDS 1995-97, pres. com. transplant and donations 1998-99, pres. com. oncology 2000—, Melvin Jones fellow 1993), European Soc. Clin. Virology. Roman Catholic. Achievements include discovery of RSV virus in infant deaths in Naples and of tumor liberated protein as a tumor associated antigen, 100 kilodalton protein overexpressed in lung tumors and other epithelial adenocarcinomas. Home: 286 Posillipo, 80123 Naples Italy Office: A O D Cotugno Hosp, 54 Quagliariello, 80131 Naples Italy

TARSCHYS, DANIEL, political science educator; b. Lidingö, Sweden, July 21, 1943; m. Bernhard T. and Karin (Alexanderson) T.; m. Regina Rehbinder, Oct. 16, 1970; children: Amelie, Charlotte. LLB, Stockholm U., 1965; PhD, Princeton U., 1972, Stockholm U., 1972. Prof. Soviet and East European Studies Uppsala U, Sweden, 1983-85; prof. polit. sci. Stockholm U., Sweden, 1985—; sec. gen. Coun. of Europe, 1994-99. M.P., 1976-82, 85-91, chmn. social affairs com., 1985-94, chmn. fgn. affairs com., 1991-94. Home: Däldvägen 9, S-181 62 Lidingö Sweden

TARSH, DEREK NICHOLAS, retired international tour operator; b. Liverpool, Eng., May 22, 1934; s. Jack and Edith Vera (Cohen) T.; m. Cynthia Helen Lucas, Aug. 27, 1959; children: David Jack, Benjamin Henry, Jeremy Gershon, Anna Miranda. BA in Econs. and Law, Cambridge U., 1956. Bar: Lincoln's Inn 1956. Mgr. Courts Bros. (Furnishers) Ltd., London, 1957-58; dir. Overseas Visitors Club Ltd., London, 1958-64, mng. dir., 1964-68; mng. dir. Trafalgar Travel Ltd., London, 1964-77, Insight Internat. Tours Ltd., London, 1978-94; mng. dir., chmn. Evan Evans Tours Ltd., London, 1983-94; dir. Insight Group PLC (formerly Black & Edgington Holdings PLC), Blacks Travel Agy. Ltd., Black & Edgington Travel Ltd., Interworld Tour Planners, Can.; chmn. Insight Internat. Tours (Pty.) Ltd., Australia, 1983—, Insight Internat. Tours (N.Z.) Ltd., 1983—, Insight Internat. Tours, West Coast Div. Inc. U.S.A., 1983-94. Mem. exec. coun. Kensing and Chelsea C. of C., 1965-68; chmn. Richmond Shelter Group, 1969-77; chmn. travel trade com. Joint Israel Appeal, 1976; mem. appeal com. Richmond Day Care Ctr. for the Elderly, Eng., 1978-81; dir. Foster Parents Plan (U.K.) Ltd., 1982—; treas. Richmond and Hounslow Marriage Guidance Coun., 1984-2000; trustee Richmond Parish Lands Charity, 1994—, chmn., 1997—; chmn. Potack's House Edn. Trust, 1993—; mem. coun. Clifton Coll., Bristol, 1995—. Company recipient awrad for export achievement Queen of Eng., 1983; Clare Coll., Cambridge U. scholar, 1956. Mem. European Tour Operators Assn. (chmn. 1990-93, treas. 1994-96), Rotary, Roehampton Club, Coombe Hills Golf Club, Hawks Club. Jewish. Avocations: golf, civic work.

TARSNANE, TERENCE JAMES, artist, educator; b. Hong Kong, Apr. 16, 1939; s. Laurence James and Maud Alicia (Pope) T. Diploma in fine arts, U. London, 1960, diploma in tchg., 1960. Art educator, cons. cultural activties Am. Sch., The Hague, The Netherlands, 1964—; lectr. in field. Exhibited in one-man and groups shows including Brit. Coun. Gallery, Amsterdam, Gallery V.D. Vlist, Leiden, The Netherlands, 1969, Gallery De Fiets, Delft, , The Netherlands, 1972, Gallery Liernur, The Hague, The Netherlands, 1972, 75, Gallery Flambard, The Hague, 1978, Gallery Munsterman, The Hague, 1988, Andres Art Gallery, The Hague, 1990, Gallery Jan Van Munster, The Hague, 1991, 93, 96, Liberty Gallery, London, 1980, Isis Gallery, Wiltshire, Eng., 1982, Chimney Mill Gallery, Suffolk, Eng., 1983, Gallery São Mamede, Lisbon, Portugal, 1974, 83, Gallery Gilde, Guimaraes, Portugal, 1984, 87, Gallery Adjectivo, Santarem, Portugal, 1988, Gallery Zen, Porto, Portugal, 1988, Harlee Gallery, N.C., 1994, Art Miami 1992, Fla., Smelik and Stokking Galleries, The Hague, 1998, 2000, Hague Salon, 1998, Groeneveld Gallery, Almelo, The Netherlands, 1999; one-man shows include Smelik and Stokking Galleries, The Hague, 2000; exhibited in group shows at Groeneveld Gallery, Almelo, The Netherlands, 2000, others; represented in permanent collections; prodr. of comml. artwork in U.S. and Europe. Avocations: reading, bicycling, natural history, gardening.

TART, CHARLES THEODORE, psychologist, educator; b. Morrisville, Pa., Apr. 29, 1937; s. Charles Samuel Tart and Alma Mathilda Pfleger; m. Judith Ann Bamberger, Feb. 11, 1958; children: Catherine Lucinda Tart Walker, David Theodore. Student, MIT, 1955-57; BA in Psychology, U. N.C., 1960, MA in Psychology, 1962, PhD in Psychology, 1963. Diplomate in exptl. hypnosis Am. Bd. Examiners Psychol. Hypnosis. Radio engr. various comml. broadcasting stas., 1955-59; rsch. asst. Round Table Found., Glen Cove, Maine, 1957; rsch. asst. psychophysiology lab. Duke U., 1958-60; tchg. asst. U. N.C., 1960-61, rsch. asst., 1961; lectr. in psychology Stanford U., 1964-65; instr. in psychiatry Sch. Medicine U. Va., 1965-66; prof. psychology U. Calif., Davis, 1966-94, prof. emeritus, 1994—; sr. rsch. fellow Inst. Noetic Scis., Sausalito, Calif., 1987—; prof. psychology Inst. Transpersonal Psychology, Palo Alto, Calif., 1994—; cons. SRI Internat., 1977-78; vis. prof. East-West psychology Calif. Inst. Integral Studies, San Francisco, 1994-95; disting. vis. prof., Bigelow chair consciousness studies U. Nev., Las Vegas, 1997-98. Author: Altered States of Consciousness, 1969, On Being Stoned: A Psychological Study of Marijuana Intoxication, 1971, Transpersonal Psychologies, 1975, States of Consciousness, 1975, (with P. Lee, R. Ornstein, D. Galin and A. Deikman) Symposium on Conciousness, 1975, Learning to Use Extrasensory Perception, 1976, Psi: Scientific Studies of the Psychic Realm, 1977, (with H. Puthoff and R. Targ) Mind at Large: Institute of Electrical and Electronic Engineers Symposia on the Nature of Extrasensory Perception, 1979, Waking Up: Overcoming the Obstacles to Human

Potential, 1986, Open Mind, Discriminating Mind: Reflections on Human Possibilities, 1989, Living the Mindful Life, 1994, Body Mind Spirit: Exploring the parapsychology of Spirituality, 1997; editor: Archives of Scientists' Transcendent Experiences. Bd. advisors Albert Hoffman Found., Ctr. for Study of Personality and Spirituality; mem. adv. bd. Forge Inst. for Spirituality and Social Change, Internat. Transpersonal Ctr. USPHS rsch. fellow U. N.C., 1961-63, Stanford U., 1963-65; recipient Elmer and Alyce Green award Internat. Soc. for Study of Subtle Energies and Energy Medicine, 1994, Disting. Sci. Contbns. award APA, 2000. Mem. Acad. Religion and Psychical Rsch. (adv. coun.), Am. Soc. Psychical Rsch., Internat. Assn. for Near-Death Studies, Multidisciplinary Assn. for Psychedelic Studies, Parapsychol. Assn. (Outstanding Career award 1999), Soc. for Sci. Exploration. Avocations: hiking, cmaping, mediation. E-mail: cttart@ucdavis.edu. Office: Inst Transpersonal Psychology 744 San Antonio Rd Palo Alto CA 94303-4632

TARTER, FRED BARRY, advertising executive; b. Bklyn., Aug. 16, 1943; s. Irving and Edna (Kupferberg) T.; m. Lois; children: Scott Andrew, Heather Michelle, Megan Elizabeth. BS, CCNY, 1966. Pres. Jamie Publs. Hootenanny Enterprises, Inc., 1962-65; mdse. dir. Longines Symphonette Soc., 1965-67; with Universal Communications, Inc., N.Y.C., 1967—, pres., CEO, 1969-74; exec. v.p. Deerfield Communications, Inc., N.Y.C., 1974-87, pres., CEO, 1977-88; pres. Deerfield Books, Inc., N.Y.C., 1988-89; pub. S.E.W. mag., N.Y.C., 1977-88; pres. The Rainbow Group Ltd., N.Y.C., 1988—; chmn. Stagebill Mag., 1997—; pres., CEO The Lakeside Group of Cos.; bd. dirs. Caribbean Internat. News Corp., Lakeside Group, Inc., Boardwalk Entertainment, Ltd.; chmn. Stagebill Enterprises, LLC; vice chmn. Affinity Comm., Inc.; exec. prodr. Joanne Carson's VIP's Miss Am. Teenager Pageant, 1972-73; pres. The Programme Exch., U.K. Ltd.; prodr. Spenser Judas Goat, 1995, Ceremony, 1996, Wounded Heart, 1996, Lover's Leap, 1996, Hearts Adrift, 1995, Marriage Counselor, 1994, Spenser: Pale Kings & Princes, 1995, Spenser: A Savage Place, 1995, Reasons of the Heart, 1996. Mem. Friars Club, The Reform Club (London), Met. Club (N.Y.). Home: 578 Westport Tpke Fairfield CT 06430-1670 Office: The Lakeside Group Ltd 210 E 39th St New York NY 10016-2754

TARTES, URMAS, science institute director; b. Tartu, Estonia, Sept. 19, 1963; s. Lembit and Kanni (Koiva) T.; m. Inga Maasik, Dec. 7, 1985; children: Annika, Saale. MS, Tartu U., Estonia, 1993, DPhil, 1995. Sr. lab. asst. Inst. Zoology & Botany, Tartu, Estonia, 1991-92, mng. dir., 1992-96, dir., 1996—. Councillor Village Cmty. Coun., Tahtiere, Estonia, 1993-96, v.p., 1996—. Sgt. Soviet Army, 1983-85. Mem. Estonian Naturalists Soc., Estonian Scientists Union. Avocation: nature photography. Office: Inst Zoology & Botany, Ria 181, EE 51014 Tartu Estonia

TARTTER, PAUL IAN, breast surgeon, educator; b. Edinburgh, Scotland, Aug. 21, 1951; came to U.S., 1956; s. Jean Royal and Jean (Walker) T.; m. Vivien Carol Rothman, Oct. 13, 1972; children: Eric Walter, Alexander Charles. BS in Biology, Brown U., 1973, MD, 1977. Resident in surgery Mt. Sinai Med. Ctr., N.Y.C., 1977-82, instr. in surgery, 1982-84, asst. prof. surgery, 1984-87, assoc. prof. surgery, 1987—; chief breast svc. Mt. Sinai Med. Ctr., 1989-98. Author: Immunologic Aspects of Blood Transfusion, 1992; co-author: Non-Palpable Breast Cancer, 1992; contbr. articles to profl. jours. Mem. AAAS, Assn. Acad. Surgery, Collegium Internat. Chirugiae Digestive, Internat. Soc. Preventive Concology, N.Y. Cancer Soc., N.Y. Met. Breast Group, N.Y. Surg. Soc., Soc. Italiana di Chirurgia et Immunobiologia, Soc. for Surg. of Alimentary Tract, Soc. Surg. Oncology, Surg. Infection Soc. Avocations: sailing, skiing. Office: 425 W 59th St # 7A New York NY 10019-1104

TARZIA, DOMINGO ALBERTO, mathematics researcher, educator; b. Rosario, Santa Fe, Argentina, Dec. 20, 1950; s. Giuseppe and Catuzza (Brogna) T.; m. Norma Dominga Gurruchaga, Apr. 18, 1975; children: Maria Silvina, Pablo Alberto. Lic. in Math., U. Nac. Rosario, Argentina, 1972, Lic. in Physics, 1977; DEA in Numerical Analysis, U. Paris VI, 1977; PhD, U. Paris, 1979, habilitation, 1991. Asst. U. Nac. Rosario, 1970-76, prof., 1979-90; researcher CONICET, Rosario, 1983—; prof., head dept. math. U. Austral, Rosario, 1991—; dir. rsch. project "Free Boundary Problems" CONICET-UNR-UA, 1979—. Author: (book) A Bibliography on Moving Free Boundary Problems, 1988, Curso de Nivelación de Matemática, 2000. Grantee for rsch. in math. CONICET, Buenos Aires, 1985—; recipient Best Lic. en Math. Assoc. Prof. U. Nac. Rosario, Argentina, 1972, Alberto Gonzalez Dominguez award in math., Ex. Sci. Nat. Acad., Argentina, 1996. Mem. Am. Math. Soc., Unión Matemática Argentina, Unione Matematica Italiana, Soc. for Industrial and Applied Math. Avocations: chess, athletics, football. Home: Pasaje Espora 61, Santa Fe, S2000DAA Rosario Argentina Office: FCE U Austral, Paraguay 1950 Santa Fe, S2000FZF Rosario Argentina

TASMAN-JONES, CLIFFORD, physician, gastroenterologist, hepatologist; b. Darfield, Canterbury, New Zealand, Dec. 21, 1928; s. Ernest Tasman and Mabel Olive (Ford) Jones; m. Beverley Anne North, Dec. 8, 1956; children: Timothy Charles, Christopher Andrew, Michael Hugh, David Jonathan. BSc, U. New Zealand, 1950; MB BS, Otago (New Zealand) U., 1956. House physician Royal Postgrad. Med. Sch., London, 1960; rsch. fellow U. Birmingham, Eng., 1961-62; med. specialist, tutor Green Lane Hosp., Auckland, New Zealand, 1962-66; specialist physician, gastroenterologist Auckland Hosp., 1965-71; sr. lectr. in medicine U. Auckland, 1971-73, assoc. prof. medicine, 1973-85, assoc. prof. gastroenterology and human nutrition, 1985-93; chmn. nutrition task force, chair hepatitis work parties Ministry of Health, New Zealand; chair nutrition adv. com. Pub. Health Commn., New Zealand; sec. Asian Pacific Orgn. Contbr. chpt. to books, articles to profl. jours. Mem. bd. govs. Kings Coll., Auckland, 1979-96; patron Tibetan Children's Relief Soc., Auckland, 1971-75. Capt. New Zealand Mil., 1956-60. Recipient Silver medal U. Bologna, Italy, 1991; Tasman/Glans fellow Gastroenterology Soc. Australia, 1995; Paul Harris fellow Rotary Internat.; high chief title Seiuli conferred by His Highness Malietoa Tanumafili II, Head of States of Samoa. Fellow Royal Coll. Physicians (London), Royal Australasian Coll. Physicians; mem. New Zealand Soc. Gastroenterology (sec. 1964-66, pres. 1966-68, 96—), New Zealand Nutrition Found. (dep. chair and chair), Orgn. Gastroenterologie Mondiale (exec. coun., chmn. nominations), Nutrition Soc. New Zealnd (pres.), New Zealand Soc. Gastroenterology (pres. 1996-98), others. Anglican. Avocations: swimming, croquet, cultivation of native plants, classical music, New Zealand history. Home: 34 Fern Glen Rd, 1005 Auckland New Zealand Office: Mercy Specialist Centre, 100 Mountain Rd, 3 Auckland New Zealand

TASNÁDI, ATTILA, economist, software developer; b. Budapest, Mar. 8, 1969; s. József and Judit Ilona (Karácsony) T. MBA, Budapest U. Econs. Sci., 1993; BSc, Eötvös U., 1994, MSc, 1997; PhD, Budapest U. Econ. Sci. Pub. Adminstrn., 2000. Dep. mgr. 3T+C, Budapest, 1993—; tchg. asst. Budapest U. Econ. Sci., 1999—. Contbr. articles to profl. jours.; developer software for econs. and statistics. Office: Budapest U Econ Sci D Math, Fövám tér 8, 1093 Budapest Hungary

TASSET, FRANCIS JOSEPH EMMANUEL, physicist; b. Mercury, France, Aug. 15, 1944; s. Emmanuel Emile and Cécile Raymonde (Duchaille) T.; m. Marie-Eglé Colette Marthe Chastagnier, Aug. 4, 1967; children: Cécile, Anne, Rémy. MSc, Faculty of Scis., 1968; PhD, U. Joseph Fourier, 1975. Physicist Inst. Laue-Langevin, Grenoble, France, 1972-75, staff scientist, 1976-99; vis. scientist Oak Ridge Nat. Lab., Oak Ridge, 1975-76; sr. fellow Inst. Laue-Langevin, Grenoble, 1999—; expert Conseil de la Neutronique, France, 1992-96; expert/lectr. IAEA, 1998—; conf. chmn. Polarized Neutron for Condensed Matter Investigation, Grenoble, 1998; E.C. coord. European Neutron Polarisation Initiative (ENPI). Guest editor: New Tools for Neutron Instrumentation, 1996; contbr. articles to profl. jours. Mem. European Phys. Soc., Soc. Francaise Physique, Soc. Francaise Neutronique (mem.), European Neutron Scat. Assn. (substitute French del. 1995-97). Avocations: cross-country skiing, hiking. Home: 16 rue Anatole France, F-38100 Grenoble France Office: Inst Laue-Langevin, BP 156, 6 Rue J Horowitz, F-38042 Grenoble Cedex 9, France

TASSI, GÉZA, civil engineer, educator; b. Budapest, Hungary; s. Imre Tassi and Emma Károly; m. Márta Rostás, Aug. 28, 1953 (dec. Oct. 1991); children: Gábor, Judit. D in Tech., Tech. U. Bldg. Civil & Transp. Enging., Budapest, 1960; D in Tech. Sci., Hungarian Acad. Sci., Budapest, 1976. Cert. engr. Rsch. fellow Hungarian Acad. Sci., Budapest, 1951-54; dep. chief technologist State Bldg. Contractors No. 31, Budapest, 1961-62; assoc. prof. Tech. U. Budapest, 1962-76, prof., 1976-93; semi-retired prof., 1993—; asst. to prof. Tech. U. Budapest, 1949-50; sr. asst. to prof. Tech. U. Bldg., Civil Transport Engrng., Budapest, 1954-61; cons. structural engrng. Enterprize Surveying Soil Mech., Budapest, 1957-60; head lab. Lab. Reinforced Concrete Structures, Tech. U., Budapest, 1974-91. Co-author: Prestressed Concrete Girders, 1970 (Niveau prize 1972). With Hungarian Air Force, 1950-51. Recipient Order of Labour, Presdl. Coun. Hungary, 1971. Mem. Internat. Orgn. Devel. Sturctural Concrete (FIP medal 1992), European-Interrnat. Com. Concrete, Sci. Soc. Transport, Sci. Soc. Bldg., Internat. Fedn. Béton (hon. pres. Hungarian group 1998). Avocations: family activities, international relations. Home: Veres Péter ut 181, H1165 Budapest Hungary Office: Budapest Univ Tech & Econs, Bertalan Lajos Utca 2, H1521 Budapest Hungary

TASSIOS, THEODOSSIOS PANAYOTIS, engineering educator; b. Kastoria, Greece, Jan. 22, 1930; s. Panayotis Theodossios and Chrise Christos (Economou) T.; m. Rea Polyvios Ioannidou, Nov. 10, 1966; 1 child, Panayotis. Cert., Etudes Superieures, Paris, 1954; Civil Engring. Degree, Nat. Tech. U., Athens, 1953, DrEngring, 1958; Dr honoris causa, U. Liege, Belgium, 1986. Cons. Bridge Design Office, Athens, 1957-64; dir. gen. Hellenic Found. Co., Athens, 1960-65; expert UNESCO/UNIDO, Paris and Vienna, 1966-86; prof. Nat. Tech. U., Athens, 1965-97; dir. Lab. Reinforced Concrete, Athens, 1969-97; cons. in civil engring. Athens, 1997—; dean Faculty of Civil Engring., Athens, 1975-76; vice chair Nat. Rsch. Coun., Athens, 1979-81; prof. honoris causa Nanjing S.E. U. China; expert rsch. in dam construction and tunneling European Union, 1990-99. Author 25 books; contbr. some 250 articles to profl.jours.; mem. editl. com. 5 internat. jours. Lt. mil. engring. Greek Army, 1954-56. Recipient medal City of Paris, 1986. Fellow Am. Concrete Inst.; mem. Hellenic Humanistic Soc. (v.p. 1990), Greek Assn. Philosophy (v.p. 1998), European Concrete Assn. (pres. 1983-87), Assn. Ancient Greek Tech. (pres. 1993—). Greek Orthodox. Avocations: mouth harmonica, gardening. Home: 4 Agias Lauras, 15236 P Pendeli Athens, Greece Office: Nat Tech U, Heroon Poly 5 Zografou, 15773 Athens Greece

TASSO, HENRI, theoretical research physicist; b. Beirut, Lebanon, June 21, 1937; arrived in Germany, 1964; s. Nagib and Augustine (Chakhtoura) T.; m. Heide Weinert, Sept. 7, 1963; 1 child, Nadia. Diploma, St. Joseph's U., 1958, INSTN, Saclay, France, 1959; PhD, Paris U., 1963. Rsch. scientist CEN Fontenay-aux-Roses, France, 1959-64; from Euratom officer to prin. Euratom officer Max-Planck-Inst., Garching, Germany, 1966—. Mem. N.Y. Acad. Scis.

TAST, HANS-JÜRGEN, book editor; b. Neugersdorf, Germany, Aug. 31, 1948; s. Hans and Margarethe (Schmidt) T.; m. Brigitte Tast, June 6, 1969; 1 child, Isadora. Grad. in Design, Fachhochschule Hildesheim HBK, Braunschweig, Germany. Book editor Verlag Kulleraugen, Schellerten, Germany. Author: Falsche 50er, 1983, Normalprogramm, 1983, Film/100-Uelzen, 1988, TV, TV, TV, 1994, Medienkompetenz, 1996, Jugend-Medien-Treff, 1998, Cross Over, 2000; co-author: Frances Farmer—Eine Fotogeschichte, 1979, Porträt-Foto-Mappe, 1992, Marion Michael-Eine Fotogeschichte, 1982. Mem. NLM, Hannover, Germany, 1994—. Mem. Nieders. Landesmedienanstalt Verband der dt. Filmkritik, LAG Jugend und Film Nds. Home and Office: Kulleraugen, Laaseweg 4, D-31174 Schellerten Germany

TASTET-LAMBERT, CATHERINE, marketing executive; b. Pau, France, Sept. 30, 1959; d. Jean Tastet and Christiane Camy; children: Marie Lambert, Benjamin Lambert. BS, U. Bordeaux, 1982. Application devel. coord. to global procurement team leader IBM, France, 1983-98, global procurement mktg. comms. mgr., 1998—. Office: IBM France, 5 ave des quarante journaux, Bordeaux Cedex 33041, France

TATA, JAMSHED RUSTOM, researcher, consultant; b. Bombay, India, Apr. 13, 1930; s. Rustom Jamshed and Gool (Contractor) T.; m. Renee Suzanne Zanetto, Nov. 4, 1954; children: Sylvie, Philip, Frederick. BSc, Bombay Univ., 1949; MSc, Indian Inst. of Sci., 1951; PhD, Univ. Paris, 1954. Postdoc. fellow Sloan-Kettering Inst., N.Y., 1954-56, Medical Rsch. Coun., London, 1956-60; vis. scientist Univ. Stockholm, Stockholm, Sweden, 1960-62; staff scientist Nat. Inst. Medical Rsch., London, 1962-73, head of dept., 1973-96, sr. scientist, 1996—; adv. dept. of Biotech., India, 1987—, Merind Ltd., India, 1993-98; chmn. Wellcome Trust Panel, U.K., 1990-92, 1997—; trustee Oxford Internat. Biomed. Ctr., U.K., 1992—. Author: The Thyroid Hormones, 1959, The Chemistry of Thyroid Diseases, 1960, Hormonal Signaling and Postembryonic Development, 1998; editor: Metamorphosis, 1996. Fellow The Royal Soc., India Nat. Sci. Acad., Third World Acad. Of Sci.; mem. European Mol. Biol. Orgn., Sigma Xi Soc., Biochem. Soc. E-mail: jtata@nimr.mrc.ac.uk. Home: 15 Bittacy Park Ave, NW7 2HA London United Kingdom Office: Nat Inst Medical Rsch, Mill Hill, NW7 1AA London United Kingdom

TATAI, MÁRIA, architectural firm executive; b. Budapest, Hungary, Sept. 7, 1952; d. Miklós Tatai and Mária Kozák. MArch, Tech. U. Budapest, 1978. Arch. Mcpl. Zoning and Planning Office, Budapest, 1978-83, Ráépterv Assn., Budapest, 1985-86; arch., mgr. Marton KFT, Budapest, 1995-98, arch., dir., 1998—; lectr. Eötvös Loránd U., Budapest, 1989-96; specialist Office of Hungarian Bldg. Industry, Budapest, 1997-98. Translator: Rudolf Wittkower: Architectural Principles, 1986; author: Environmental Culture in Education, 1990; editor Hungarian Bldg. Industry, 1997-98. Mem. Hungarian Sci. Soc. for Bldg., Assn. Hungarian Archs., Chamber Hungarian Archs. Avocations: dance, choreography, traveling. Home: Bártfai U 8/A, 1119 Budapest Hungary

TATÁR, BÉLA, English and Russian educator; b. Mezőkaszony, Bereg, Hungary, July 5, 1933; s. Imre Tatár and Piroska Majoros; m. Csilla Judit Fichtner, July 15, 1971; 1 child, Miklós Béla. Diploma in philology, U. Odessa, Ukraine, 1959; D of Philology, Eötvös Loránd U., Budapest, Hungary, 1966; habilitation, Eötvös Loránd U., 1995; candidate of linguistics, Hungarian Acad. Sci., Budapest, 1976. Asst. L. Eötvös U., Budapest, 1962-67, lectr., 1968-77, assoc. prof., 1978-97, prof., 1998—. Author: The Russian Lexicography, 1985 (High prize Ministry of Edn. 1987), The Modern Russian Phraseology, 1992, Russian-Hungarian, Hungarian-Russian Business Dictionary, 1994; editor Studia Russica, 1978—. Mem. Societas Linguistica Europaea, European Assn. Lexicography, Hungarian Soc. Linguistics. Avocations: cacti, viticulture. Home: Erkel utca 1, H-2094 Budapest-Nagykovácsi Hungary Office: Múzeum krt 4 D ft 7, H-1088 Budapest Hungary

TATARANNI, PIETRO ANTONIO, research endocrinologist, educator; b. Matera, Italy, Oct. 4, 1964; came to U.S., 1993; s. Angelo Michele and Maria Rosaria (Di Caro) T.. MD, Cath. U., Rome, 1990, splty. diploma in endocrinology, 1995. Rschr. Cath. U., 1991-93, lectr., 1999—; assoc. dir. clin. rschr. Merck & Co., Rahway, N.J., 1997-99; vis. assoc. NIH Nat. Inst. Diabetes, Digestive and Kidney Diseases, Phoenix, 1993-97, sr. scientist, 1999—; sci. reviewer for sci. jours., including Am. Jour. Physiology, Obesity Rsch., Jour. Clin. Endocrinology and Metabolism, 1997—. Contbr. chpt. to books. Mem. Am. Diabetes Assn., N.Am. Assn. for Study Obesity (young investigator award 1997). Roman Catholic. Avocations: tennis, hiking, horseback riding. E-mail: antoniot@mail.nih.gov.

TATARELLI, ROBERTO, psychiatrist, researcher; b. Fara Sabina, Italy, Sept. 14, 1940; s. Giacinto and Maria (Cersini) T.; m. Uta Godai, Jan. 25, 1969; children: Andreas, Caterina, Francesca Maria, Alessandro, Giulia, Susanne. MD, U. Rome, 1965; neurologist and psychiatrist degree, U. Pisa, 1970. Asst. prof. U. Rome, 1973-80, assoc. prof., 1980-94, full prof., 1994—; dir. Residency Sch. Psychiatry, Rome, 1994—; dir. Dept. Psychiatric Sci. and Psychol. Med., Rome, 1998—; cons. expert Civil and Criminal Ct., Rome, 1972—. Author: Suicide: Psychopathology and Prevention, 1992, The Elderly Patient, 1996; co-author: Treating With the Patient, 1989, Handbook of Elderly Psychopharmacotherapy. Lt. Italian Mil. Marine, 1966-67. Mem. Italian Soc. Psychiatry (regional sec. 1999—), Assn. European Psychiatrists (corr.), Lancisian Acad. (Italy). Roman Catholic. Avocations: jogging, tennis, swimming, gardening. Home: via monte di casa 65, I-00138 Rome Italy Office: U Rome Dept Psychiatric Sci, Piazzale A Moro 5, I-00185 Rome Italy

TATARENKO, VALENTIN ANDRIYOVYCH, physicist, researcher; b. Kyyiv, Ukraine, Sept. 19, 1958; s. Andrij Ivanovych and Lyudmila Dmytrivna Tatarenko; m. Helena Mikhajlivna Shargorodska Zapolsky, Apr. 16, 1985 (div.); 1 child, Lavrenty. MSc in Theoretical Physics with honors, Taras Shevchenko Kyyiv Nat. U., Ukraine, 1980; PhD in Solid State Physics, Inst. Metal Physics Nat. Acad. Scis. Ukraine, Kyyiv, Ukraine, 1986. Rsch. scientist Inst. Metal Physics Nat. Acad. Scis. Ukraine, Kyyiv, 1980-89; sr. staff rsch. scientist G.V. Kurdyumov Inst. Metal Physics Nat. Acad. Scis. Ukraine, Kyyiv, 1989—; exec. mng. editor internat. rsch. jour. Metallofizika i Noveishie Tekhnologii, Kyyiv, 1994—; exec. sec. editl. bd. rsch. jour. Metal Physics and Advanced Technologies, 1995—. Co-author: Interaction and Arrangement of Atoms in Interstitial Alloys, 1989; contbr. articles to profl. jours. Recipient All-Union Youth award, 1986. Avocations: history of science, philately. Fax: (380) 44 4442561. Home e-mail: 42297828@pagermirabilis.com; office e-mail: tatar@imp.kiev.ua. Home: Prospekt Pravdy 92/86, UA04208 Kyyiv 208, Ukraine Office: GV Kurdyumov Inst Metal Phy NASU, 36 Acad Vernadsky Blvd, UA03142 Kyyiv 142, Ukraine

TATARINTSEVA, RAISA YAKOVLEVNA, physician, manual therapy healer; d. Agaphia. MD, PhD. Head dept. clin. physiology and nonmedicamental methods Russian U. of People's Friendship. Mem. Acad. Med.-Tech. Sics. of Russian Fedn. Fax: (095) 4340-66-46. Office: Russian U People Friendship, Mikluho-Maklaya St 21/3, Moscow Russia 103055

TATARSKII, VALERIAN IL'ICH, physics researcher; b. Kharkov, USSR, Oct. 13, 1929; s. Il'ya A. and Elizabeth A. (Lapis) T.; m. Maia S. Granovskaia, Dec. 22, 1955; 1 child, Viatcheslav V. MS, Moscow State U., 1952; PhD, Acoustical Inst. Acad. Scis., 1957; DSc, Gorky State U., 1962. Scientific rschr. Geophys. Inst. Acad. Sci. USSR, Moscow, 1953-56; scientific rschr. Inst. Atmospheric Physics, Acad. Sci. USSR, Moscow, 1956-59, sr. scientific rschr., 1959-78, head lab., 1978-90; head dept. Lebedev. Phys. Inst. Acad. Sci., Moscow, 1990-91; sr. rsch. assoc. U. Colo. Coop. Inst. for Rsch. in Environ. Sci., Boulder, 1991—, NOAA/ERL. Environ. Tech. Lab., Boulder. Author: Wave Propagation in a Turbulent Medium, 1961, 67, The Effect of the Turbulent Atmosphere on Wave Propagation, 1971, Principles of Statistical Radiophysics, 1989; contbr. articles to profl. jours. Recipient of Max Born award, 1994, Optical Soc. of Am., USSR State prize, 1990. Fellow Optical Soc. Am. (Max Born award 1994), Inst. of Physics; mem. Russian Acad. Sci., U.S.A. Nat. Acad. Engring., N.Y. Acad. Sci. Avocations: classical music, kayaking. Office: NOAA ERL ETL 325 Broadway St Boulder CO 80305-3337

TATE, JOHN ELTON, lawyer; b. Rochester, Pa., July 26, 1955; s. William John and Elinor Effie Tate; m. Jeri Lee Decker, Oct. 19, 1996. BA in Econs. and Bus., Washington & Jefferson Coll., 1977; JD, Georgetown U., 1980. Bar: Ohio. Assoc. Smith & Schnacke, LPA, Dayton, Ohio, 1980-86; shareholder Smith & Schnacke, Cin., 1986-89; ptnr. Thompson Hine & Flory, Cin., 1989-90; assoc. gen. counsel Crown Equipment Corp., New Bremen, Ohio, 1990—. Mem. Phi Beta Kappa. Avocations: golf, reading. E-mail: john.tate@crown.com. Office: Crown Equipment 102 S Washington St New Bremen OH 45869-1249

TATE, ROBERT BRIAN, retired Renaissance studies educator; b. Belfast, No. Ireland, Dec. 27, 1921; s. Robert and Jane Grantie (Boyce) T.; m. Beth Ida Lewis, Dec. 21, 1951; children: Caroline Jane, Marcus Lewis. BA, Queens U., No. Ireland, 1948; MA, Queens U., 1953, PhD, 1957. Asst. lectr. Manchester (Eng.) U., 1949-52; lectr. Queens U., Belfast, 1952-56; reader in Hispanic studies Nottingham (Eng.) U., 1956-58, prof., 1958-83, prof. emeritus, 1983—. Author: Ensayos Sobre la Historiografia Peninsular del Siglo XV, 1970, El Cardenal Joan Margarit, 1976, The Pilgrim Route to Santiago de Compostela, 1987, Two Medieval Itineraries to Compostela, 1998; editor: Don Juan Manuel, 1974, Anon Directorio de Principes, 1977, Alfonso de Palencia, 1982, Fernando del Pulgar, 1985, others; translator: Pierre Vilar A Brief History of Spain, 1967, Alfonso de Palencia Gesfa Hispaniensi, 1998; contbr. articles to profl. jours. Capt. Indian Army, 1942-46. Fellow Inst. d'Estudis Catalans Barcelona (corr.), Real Acad. de Historia, 1974, Real Acad. de Buenas Letras, Brit. Acad. Avocations: art, architectural history. Home: 42 Main St, Sutton Bonington, Near Loughborough LE12 5PF England also: 11 Hope St Beeston, Nottingham NG9 1DJ England Office: U Nottingham Hispanic Studies, University Park, Nottingham NG7 2RD England

TATEIBA, MITSUO, communication engineering educator; b. Beppu, Oita, Japan, May 24, 1944; m. Junko Satoh, Apr. 4, 1974; children: Yoshiyuki, Haruko, Hideo. B Engring., Kyushu U., Fukuoka, Japan, 1967, M Engring., 1969, D Engring. (hon.), 1977. Assoc. prof. Nagasaki U., 1977-83; rsch. assoc. Kyushu U., 1969-77, assoc. prof., 1983-90, prof., 1990—, head dept. computer sci. and comm. engring., 1993, 97—. Co-editor: PIER 13 Electromagnetic Theory and Network Methods, 1996, PIER 14 Electromagnetic Scattering by Rough Surfaces and Random Media, 1996; contbr. articles to profl. jours. Recipient Yonezawa Meml. prize IECE, 1975, 7th Internat. Comm. Rsch. prize KDD Engring. and Cons., 1986, Rsch. for the Future Japan Soc. for Promotion of Sci., 1996—. Fellow Inst Physics; mem. Inst. Electronics, Info. and Comm. Engrs., Inst. Elec. Engrs. Japan. Home: 3-14-3 Miwadai Higashi-ku, Fukuoka 811-0212, Japan Office: Kyushu U, 6-10-1 Hakozaki Higashi-ku, Fukuoka 812-8581, Japan

TATEISHI, RYUTARO, engineering educator; b. Osaka, Japan, Nov. 25, 1950; s. Masahiko and Yukiko (Numai) T.; m. Kiyomi Ninomiya, June 28, 1986; 3 children. B of Agrl. Sci., U. Tokyo, 1974, DEng, 1982. Rsch. assoc. U. Tokyo, 1976--79; lectr. Chiba (Japan) U., 1979-88, assoc. prof., 1988—; vis. rschr. Clark U., Worcester, Mass., 1992. Mem. Japan Soc. Photogrammetry and Remote Sensing (sec. gen. 1992-2000), Asian Assn. on Remote Sensing (chmn. working group 1993-99), Internat. Soc. Photogrammetry and Remote Sensing (chmn. working group 1992—). Avocations: swimming, Japanese chess, skiing. Office: Ctr for Environ Remote Sens, 1-33 Yayoi-cho, Inage-ku Chiba 263, Japan

TATENO, YUKIO, physician, researcher; b. Moka-shi Tochigi-ken, Japan, Mar. 30, 1934; s. Chujiro and Yomi (Ueno) T.; m. Midori Nakamura, Apr. 24, 1960; children: Madoka, Mutsumi, Atsushi, Amane. MD, Chiba (Japan) U., 1959, PhD, 1964. Asst. Chiba U. Sch. of Medicine, 1964-71, lectr., 1971-74, assoc. prof., 1974-75; dir. dept. of radiology Chiba U. Hosp., 1974-75; chief divsn. clin. rsch. Nat. Inst. of Radiol. Scis., Chiba, 1975-83, dir. divsn. clin. rsch., 1983-93, dir. divsn. of radiation, health and clin. rsch., 1993-94, guest scientist, 1994-96, sr. rsch. counselor, 1996—. Author: History of Radiology (Japanese), 1973; editor: Positron Emission CT (Japanese), 1983, Computed Radiography, 1987, Brain Imaging for Neurotransmission (Japanese), 1994, Automated Diagnosis of X-ray Imaging (Japanese), 1994. Mem. Japan Radiol. Soc., Japanese Soc. of Nuclear Medicine, Japan Soc. of Magnetic Resonance in Medicine (pres. 1994-96), Japan Soc. of Computer Aided Diagnosis of Med. Images (pres. 1991-92), Soc. of Chest Screening by CT (pres. 1993—). Avocation: Haiku. Office: Nat Inst Radiol Scis, 4-9-1 Anagawa, Chiba-shi 263-8555, Japan

TATERA, JAMES FRANK, chemist, process analysis specialist; b. Milw., June 27, 1946; s. Frank and Agnes Rose (Szymanowski) T.; m. Kaaren Marie Piekarski, Sept. 9, 1972; children: Patrick, Monica, David. BS in Chemistry, Math., U. Wis., Oshkosh, 1968; postgrad., U. Minn., 1968, 71-73; MBA, Cen. Mich. U., 1982. Cert. specialist in analytical tech. Tchg. rsch. assoc. chemistry dept. U. Minn., Mpls., 1968, 71-73; analytical chemist Dow Corning Corp., Midland, Mich., 1973-76, scale up engr. new products commercialization, 1976-78, prodn. bldg. supt. prodn. dept., 1978-80; analytical systems specialist project and plant engring. Dow Corning Ltd., Barry, Wales, 1981-84; analytical systems supr. plant engring. & maintenance Dow Corning Corp., Carrollton, Ky., 1984-85, analytical systems specialist plant engring. and maintenance, 1985-87, sr. analytical and control specialist project engring., 1988-90, sr. analytical systems specialist strategic change program, 1991-98, sr. analytical sys. specialist Process Analysis Expertise Ctr., 1998—; session developer, panelist, presenter in field; U.S. nat. com. Internat. Electrotech. Commn., Paris, 1993, Milan, 1994, Montreal, 1996, Houston, 1998, U.S. nat. com. tech. advisor subcom. 65D, 1993—. Editl.

adv. bd. InTech mag., 1998—; contbr. articles to profl. jours., chpts. to books. 1st lt. U.S. Army, 1969-71. Decorated Bronze Star, Bronze Star with oak leaf cluster. Fellow Instrument Soc. Am. (dir.-elect, sec.-treas. analysis divsn. 1994-96, dir. 1996-98, chmn. SP 76 stds. com. 1991-96, pres. N.E. Mich. sect. 1979-80, various sect. offices 1976-79, Louisville sect. del. 1995—, com. mem. 1998—); mem. Am. Chem. Soc. (Louisville sect. chair 1999—, rep. vol. in pub. outreach program Louisville sect. chmn.-elect 1998-99, sect. careers program and nat. chemistry week com. 1992-99), Air and Waste Mgmt. Assn. (optical sensing divsn. indsl. issues and applications com. on enhanced monitoring 1993-99), Elks, Am. Legion, VFW, KC, Delta Sigma Phi, Phi Lambda Upsilon, Sigma Iota Epsilon. Roman Catholic. Home: 2038 Ridgewood Dr Madison IN 47250-2729 Office: Dow Corning Corp 4770 Hwy 42 E Mail Stop 32 Carrollton KY 41008

TATEYAMA, ICHIRO, gynecologist; b. Fukuoka, Japan, Aug. 21, 1952; s. Chikayoshi and Katsuyo Tateyama; m. Hiroko Uchino, Nov. 2, 1980; children: Ryoko, Ayako, Yuko. MD, Kyoto U., 1979, MD, PhD, 1989. Diplomate Bd. Obs.-Gyn. Resident Faculty of Medicine Kyoto U., 1978-79, Niigata (Japan) Prefectural Hosp., 1979-82; asst. Fukui (Japan) Med. Sch., 1982-84; chief dr. Tomita Hosp., Kyoto, 1984-86; co-chief dr. Kurashiki (Japan) Cen. Hosp., 1986-88, Tenri (Japan) Hosp., 1988-89; chief dr. Kishiwada (Japan) City Hosp., 1989—. Contbr. articles to profl. jours. Mem. Japan Soc. Cancer Therapy, Japan Soc. Cancer Rsch., Japan Soc. Fertility and Sterility, Japan Soc. Obs.-Gyn., Japan soc. Clin. Electron Microscopy. Avocations: piano, fishing. Home: 2-303 Shimomatsu-cho, Kishiwada 596 0823, Japan Office: Kishiwada City Hosp, 2 Gakuhara-cho, Kishiwada 596 0822, Japan

TATEYAMA, YOSHIYUKI, vegetables grower and exporter; b. Nishigoshi, Japan, May 25, 1940; arrived in Dominican Republic, 1956; s. Yoshinosuke and Fusako Tateyaam; m. Setsuko Hamada, Oct. 2, 1965; 1 child, Kazuyo. Student, Matsushiro Nagano, Nagano-Ken, Japan, 1981. Founder fruit exportation co. Exporte of Vegetables of Comayagua (Exveco), Comayagua, Honduras, 1990—. Mem., capt. Patronato Cuerpo Bomberos (Firemen), Jarabacoa, Dominican Republic, 1990; v.p. Assn. Dominico-Japones, Inc., Santo Domingo, Dominican Republic, 1980-92. Avocation: golf. Office: Exportadora Tateyama SA, Prol 7 N 1 Colonia Agricola, Jarabacoa LV, Dominican Republic

TATHAM, DAVID EVERARD, diplomatic consultant, retired government official; b. June 28, 1939; s. Francis Everard Tatham and Eileen Mary Wilson; m. Valerie Ann Mylechreest, 1963; 3 children. Grad., St Lawrence Coll.; BA in History, Wadham Coll., Oxford U. With HM Diplomatic Svc., 1960; 3d sec. United Kingdom Mission to the UN, N.Y.C., 1962-63; vice-counsul comml. HM Con. Gen., Milan, 1963-67; with ME Ctr. for Arabic Studies, Jeddah, 1967-70, Fgn. and Commonwealth Office, Muscat, 1971-77; asst. head ME dept. Fgn. and Commonwealth Office, Dublin, 1977-80, counsellor, 1981-84; amb. Yemen Arab Republic, 1984-87, Republic of Djibouti, 1984-87; head dept. Fgn. and Commonwealth Office, 1987-90; amb. Lebanese Republic, 1990-92; gov. Falkland Islands, 1992-95; commr. South Georgia and Sandwich Islands, 1992-95; Brit. High Commr. to Sri Lanka Colombo, 1996-99; accredited to Republic of Maldives; ret., 1999; adv. diplomatic tng. Palestinian Ministry Planning, 2000. Chmn. U.K. com. Sheckleton Scholarship Fund. Avocations: walking, historical research. Office: South Parade, Ledbury HR8 2HA, England

TATIKOLOV, ALEXANDER SERGEEVICH, chemist, researcher; b. Moscow, Russia, Oct. 27, 1946; s. Sergei Fedorovich and Praskovia Nikolaevna (Komrakova) T.; m. Ina Georgievna Panova, Aug. 12, 1977; 1 child, Dmitry Alexandrovich. Grad., Moscow State U., 1970; degree in chem. sci., Inst. Chem. Physics, Moscow, 1978, D of Chem. Sci., 1996. Engr. Inst. Chem. Physics, Moscow, 1970-72, jr. rsch. fellow, 1972-84, sr. rsch. fellow, 1984-97; leading rsch. fellow Inst. Biochem. Physics, Moscow, 1997—; editor Russian Chemistry Abstracts, 1996—. Contbr. articles to profl. jours. Grantee Russian Found. Basic Rsch., 1999. Avocations: photobiology research, teaching. Home: Otkrytoe shosse, 107370 Moscow Russia Office: Inst Biochem Physics, Kosygin St 4 Russ Acad Sci, 117977 Moscow Russia

TATIPAMULA, MALLIKARJUN, telecommunications and networking engineer; b. Warangal, India, Dec. 20, 1968. BTech, Regional Engring. Coll., Warangal, 1988; MTech in Electrical Engring., Indian Inst. Tech., Madras, India, 1990. Rsch. scholar, tchg. asst. Indian Inst. Tech., Madras, 1989, sr. project officer, sys. designer electrical engring. dept., 1990-92; asst. exec. engr. R&D transmission labs. Indian Telephone Industries, Bangalore, 1990; rsch. asst. electrical engring. dept. Queen's U., Kingston, Canada, 1993; sr. mem. sci. staff, team leader Northern Telecom Broadband Networks & Wireless Network Divsn, Ottawa, Canada, 1993-97; prin. staff engr. ground sys. divsn. Motorola Cellular Infrastructure Group, Chandler, Ariz., 1997-98; sr. sys. architect Cisco Sys., Inc., San Jose, Calif., 1998—; Spkr. in field; tech. cons. GTE, MCI, Pacific Bell, Bell Canada. Lead editor: Multimedia Communication Networks: Technologies and Services, 1998. Mem. IEEE (sr. mem., mem. tech. com. on computers and comms., others), Software Project Mgrs. Network (register mem.). Achievements include development of bringing together the telecommunications and networking communities, integration of legacy networks and new networks, existing and emerging technologies, and new architectures and revamped/extended architectures, and others. Fax: 408-527-1221. Office: Cisco Sys Inc MS SJ-9/2 170 W Tasman Dr San Jose CA 95134-1706

TATLONGHARI, CARMELITO ARELLANO, health physicist; b. Batangas City, The Philippines, Aug. 14, 1950; s. Modesto Azucena and Elena (Arellano) T.; m. Milagrosa Aquisap, Jan. 26, 1985; children: Mildred Rose, Carson Bryan, Catherine Rose. BSc in Physics, Mapua Inst. Tech., Manila, 1971. Nuclear rschr. Philippine Nuclear Rsch. Inst., Quezon City, 1971-72; instr. Mapual T U. Santo Tomas, Manila, 1974-79; lectr. U. Philippines, Quezon City, 1980-81; health physicist Philippine Nuclear Power Plant, Baqac Moronq, Bataan, The Philippines, 1979-85, radiation control supt., 1985-94; social environ. planning mgr. Nat. Power Corp., Quezon City, 1994-97; energy program mgr. USAID, Manila, 1997—; mem. exec. com. Scientists, Technologists and Engrs. for the People, 1986-96; bd. dirs. Binhi Agrl. Found., Quezon City, Scientists Action Ctr., Quezon City, Vol. in Sci. and Tech., Quezon City. Mapua Inst. Tech. acad. scholar, 1967-70, Asean-USAID environ. scholar, 1992. Fellow Philippine Bus. for Environ.; mem. Nat. Rsch. Coun. Philippines (assoc.), Radioisotopes Soc. Philippines, Nat. Radiol. Protection Assn., Philippine Orgn. Med. Physicists, Air and Waste Mgmt. Assn. Roman Catholic. E-mail: ctatlonghari@usaid.gov. Home: 19 London St Capitol Homes, Quezon City MM 1119, The Philippines Office: USAID, 1680 Roxas Blvd 17/F RMC, Manila The Philippines

TATO, ANTONIO CARLOS, bank executive; b. Aug. 5, 1944. Diploma in Economics, Universidade do Porto, 1969. Staff Banco de Angold, 1972-74; mgr. Banco Pinto & Sotto Mayor, 1974-80; mng. dir. Credito Predial Portugues, 1980-87; chmn. bd. dirs./CEO Banco Borges & IRMAO, 1987-95; dep. CEO Banco Mello, 1995—. Office: Banco Mello, Luxembourg Belgium

TATÒ, FRANCESCO, company executive; b. Lodi, Aug. 12, 1932; married; 2 children. Degree in letters and philosophy, U. Pavia. Pers. mgr. Olivetti, 1956, Deutsche Olivetti, 1978-81; mng. dir. Austro Olivetti, 1974, Internat. Rizzoli, 1974, Brit. Olivetti, 1975-78, Deutsche Olivetti, Frankfurt, Germany, 1976-81; mng. dir. fgn. sales Olivetti Group, 1982-84; mng. dir. Kienzle (Mannesmann Group), 1982-84; CEO Mondadori Editore S.p.A., 1984-86; pres. TA Triumph-Adler AG, Nürnberg, Germany, 1986-89; CEO Olivetti Office, 1984-86, Arnoldo Mondadori Editori-S.p.A., 1993-94, S.B.E.-Silvio Berlusconi Editore (Fininvest Group), 1993-96; mng. dir. Arnoldo Mondadori Editore S.p.A., 1984-86, ENEL Società per Azioni; chmn., CEO Sottrici Distbiruzione S.p.A., 1993-94; dep. chmn. Cartiere Sottrici Binda S.p.A., Olgiate Olona/Verese, 1994-96. Contbr. articles to profl. publs. Office: ENEL, Viale Regina Margherita 137, 00198 Rome Italy*

TATROV, ALEXANDER SERGEEVICH, information analyst, educator, researcher; b. Orjonikidze, Russia, Dec. 8, 1961; s. Serjei Serjeevich and Tamara Mussaevna (Kokoeva) T.; m. Zalina Tlatovna Dztieva, Dec. 5, 1992; 1 child, Tatrov Akhshar Alexandrovich. Diploma in medicine with honors, N. Ossetian State Med. Inst., Vladikavkaz, 1985, diploma in psychiatry, 1985, PhD, 1991; diploma in philology, N. Ossetian State U., 1997-99. Physician Regional Hosp., Kaliningrad, Russia, 1984-85; psychiatrist Hosp. Mental Diseases, Vladikavkaz, 1985-87; asst. prof. Dept. Normal Human Physiology North Ossetian State Med. Inst., 1990-95; asst. prof., chair gen. psychology North Ossetian State U., 1992-97, asst. prof. Faculty Tng. & Adapting, 1993-96, dir. analysis dept., 1995—; faculty internat. rels. NOSU, 1999—, sr. lectr., chair psychology NOSU; cons. North Ossetian Inst. Practical Psychology, 1995; referee Sci. Info. Analysis, 1990-95; mem. rsch. N. Ossetian U., 1995-97. Contbr. articles to profl. jours. Lt. Med. Svc. Res. Internat. Sci. Found. internat. grantee, 1993, Ctrl. European Univ. curriculum resource devel. grantee, 1996. Mem. Russian Sci. Soc. Physiologists, Russian Sci. Soc. Psychologists, N.Y. Acad. Scis. Freedom democrat. Avocations: music, literature, tennis, fishing, films. Home: Kuibisheva St 17 Apt 52A, 362040 Vladikavkaz Russia Office: North Ossetian State U, Vatutina 46, 362025 Vladikavkaz Russia

TATSUMI, KOUICHI, radiation biologist, internist; b. Haerhpin, Manchuria, Aug. 6, 1943; s. Shoushi and Miyoko (Sonoda) T.; m. Michiko Majima, May 13, 1973; children: Miho, Takashi, Miki. MD, Kyoto (Japan) U., 1968, PhD, 1975. Resident Koga Hosp., Shiga, Japan, 1969-71; rsch. assoc. dept. microbiology U. Chgo., 1976-79; lectr. dept. medicine Kanazawa Med. U., Ishikawa, Japan, 1979-81; assoc. prof. Radiation Biol. Ctr. Kyoto U., 1981-85; assoc. prof. dept. molecular oncology Kyoto U. Sch. Medicine, 1985-93; dir. divsn. biology and oncology Nat. Inst. Radiol. Sci., Chiba, Japan, 1993—; cons. Nuclear Safety Rsch. Assn., Tokyo, 1988—. Author: Low Dose Irradiation and Biological Defense Mechanisms, 1992; contbr. 80 articles to profl. jours.; mem. editl. bd. Japanese Jour. Cancer Rsch., 1988—, Jour. Radiation Rsch., 1990—, Internat. Jour. Radiation Biology, 1999—. Fellow Japan Soc. for Promotion of Sci., 1975-76, Leukemia Soc. Am., 1977-79. Mem. Japanese Radiol. Rsch. Soc. (sec. 1996-97), Japanese Cancer Rsch. Soc. (councilor 1997—), Environ. Mutagen Soc. Japan (Incentive award 1990). Buddhist. Avocations: skiing, sailing dinghy. E-mail: tatsumi@nirs.go.jp. Home: I-407 Todoroki 3-1, Inage-ku Chiba 263-0021, Japan Office: Nat Inst Radiol Scis, 4-9-1 Anagawa, Inage-ku Chiba 263-8555, Japan

TATSUMURA, TOSHIKI, thoracic and abdominal surgeon; b. Palembang, Sumatra, Indonesia, Aug. 21, 1943; s. Soo Guan and Kiok Neo (Ong) Lauw; m. Sawako Higashi, Jan. 10, 1970; children: Mie, Minako. MD, Kanazawa (Japan) U., 1971, PhD, 1976. Asst. prof. dept. thoracic surgery Sch. Medicine Toyama (Japan) Med. and Pharm. U., 1979-88, assoc. prof. dept. emergency, 1988—; vis. rsch. scientist dept. pharmacology Yale U., New Haven, 1984-85; vis. prof. Dalian Med. U., China. Editor Practical Emergency Medicine, 1993, 2nd edit., 1996, Color Atlas of Practical Emergency Medicine, 2000; contbr. articles to profl. jours. Fellow Internat. Coll. Angiology, Am. Coll. Chest Physicians; mem. Japanese Soc. Bronchology (councilor 1991-96, 2000—, mem. future planning com. 1991-96), Japanese Soc. for Chest Surgery (councillor 1989-99, mem. editorial bd. 1993-99, election com. mem. of chest surgery specialist and insts. 1988-93), Japan Lung Cancer (award for developing nebulization chemotherapy for lung cancer 1982), Japanese Assn. for Thoracic Surgery (councilor 1988-90), Am. Assn. for Broncology, Am. Inst. Ultrasound in Medicine, Am. Coll. Chest Physicians, Am. Soc. Clin. Oncology, Am. Assn. for Cancer Rsch. (corr.), Am. Coll. Chest Physicians, Japanese Cancer Assn., Japanese Soc. for Clin. Surgery (councilor 1983—), Japan Soc. coloproctology (councilor 1983—), PanAm. Trauma Soc., Internat. Trauma Anasthesia and Critical Care Soc. Avocations: golf, skiing, fishing, reading, music. Office: Toyama Med Pharm U Dpt Emer, 2630 Sugitani, Toyama 930-01, Japan

TATSUTA, MISAO, law educator; b. Kobe, Hyogo, Japan, Sept. 6, 1933; s. Saburo and Fukiko (Shiura) T.; m. Fumiko Takaku, Mar. 20, 1960; children: Yuriko Wada, Ken Tatsuta, Sho Tatsuta. LLB, Kyoto (Japan) U., 1956; LLM, U. Calif., Berkeley, 1966. Asst. faculty of law Kyoto U., 1956-58, lectr. faculty of law, 1958-59, assoc. prof. law, 1959-70, prof. law, 1970-97, dean faculty of law, 1985-87; prof. law Kobe (Japan) Gakuin U., 1997—; dir. Sumitomo Life Ins. Mutual Corp., 1999—; chmn. Japanese br. Commn. on Internat. Securities Regulations, Tokyo, 1989-96. Author: Securities Regulation in Japan, 1970, Corporation Law, 1st edition, 1989, Introduction to Business Law, 1997; editor: Commentaries on Commodity Exchange Law, 1995. Mem. Japan Econ. Law Assn. (bd. dirs. 1977—), Fin. Law Assn. (bd. dirs. 1984—). Avocation: fishing. Home: 3-3-8 Minami Tamondai, Tarumi-ku Kobe shi 655-0043, Japan Office: Faculty Law Kobe Gakuin U, 518 Arise Igawadani-cho, Nishi-ku Kobe 651-2180, Japan also: Oh-ebashi Law Office, 1-5 Dojima 1 chome 8th Fl, Kita-ku Osaka 530-0003, Japan

TATTERSFIELD, JOHN JULIAN FREDERICK, company executive, engineer; b. Milngavie, Scotland, Jan. 17, 1963; came to U.S., 1999; s. James Frederick and Gillian Mortimer Tattersfield; m. Nicola Anne Tattersfield, Aug. 3, 1985; children: Regan, Calum, Henry, Helena. BSc with honors, Royal Naval Engring., Plymouth, U.K., 1985; MSc, Cranfield (U.K.) Inst. Tech., 1988. Mgr. prodn. and machine shop Instron Ltd., High Wycombe, U.K., 1986-93; mng. dir. Instron Wolpert GmbH, Ludwigshafen, Germany, 1993-96; v.p., mng. dir. Instron Schenck Testing GmbH, Darmstadt, Germany, 1996-99; v.p., ops. dir. Instron Schenck Testing Corp., Canton, Mass., 1999—. Sch. gov. Aston Clinton (U.K.) Combined Sch., 1994. Sub lt. Royal Navy, 1980-86. Fellow in mfg. mgmt. Engring. Industry Tng. Bd., 1990. Fellow Engring. Industry Tng. Bd. (U.K.); mem. NSPE, SME, SAE, Brit. Inst. Mgmt. Avocations: yachting, sailing, renovating old cars, computer programming, speaking German. E-mail: rick tattersfield@instron.com. Office: Instron Corp 100 Royall St Canton MA 02021-1089

TATTEVIN, PIERRE, physician, researcher; b. Vannes, Bretagne, France, Oct. 6, 1968; s. Pierre and Annick Tattevin; m. Mariam Tinor, Mar. 13, 1999; 1 child, Lina. MD, Bichat-Claude Bernard, Paris, 1999. Intern Htpitaux de Paris, 1993-99; chef de clinique Ctr. Hospitalo-Univ., Rennes, France, 1999—. Author: Infections Respiratoires de l'adulte, 1997, Infection VIH, 1997, Du Symptome au Diagnostic; co-author: Clinical Infectious Diseases: A Practical Approach. Physician French Cooperation, 1995-96. Recipient Diplomes d'Etudes Approfondies, Mithodes d'Experimentation des Agents Anti-Infectieux, Paris, 1995, Prix Fred Siguier, SNFMI, France, 1998, Thhse de Midecine, Faculti Bichat, Paris, 1998. Avocations: travel, windsurfing, music, running. E-mail: tattevin@club-internet.fr. Fax: 0033142417388. Home: 114 rue Petit, 75019 Paris France Office: Clinique Rianimation, 46 rue Henri Huchard, 75018 Paris France

TATUM, ARTHUR, III, educator, lexicographer, pianist; b. Sumpter, S.C., July 7, 1935; s. Art Tatum and Lillie Bell. Cert. tchr. Prin. Youth in Action, N.Y.C., 1964-67; prin., tutor Cmty. Action, N.Y.C., 1968-72; performer Jazz Hall of Fame, L.A., 1975-79; music tutor Morgan Coll., Balt., 1980-83; music tutor Coppin State Coll., Balt., 1985-90, lang. tutor, 1995-96. Author: (Ebonese dictionary) Afro American Language, 1994, (gospel in ebonese) Gospel According to St. Matthew, 1996, Solar-Harmonic Systems (original method for reading and writing music). Lang. tutor Neighborhood Youth Corp., Charles Villa Balt., 1995-97. Avocations: sandlot baseball, golf, table-tennis. Office: Tatum Publs 2330 Guilford Ave Baltimore MD 21218-5206

TAUB, STANLEY, plastic surgeon, sculptor; b. N.Y.C., Aug. 15, 1931; m. Patricia Taub, Aug. 15, 1960; 1 child, Ari. BS, NYU; MD, N.Y. Med. Coll. Diplomate Am. Bd. Plastic Surgery. Intern Beth Israel Hosp., N.Y.C., 1957-58, resident in surgery, 1958-59; resident in surgery Martland Med. Ctr., Newark, 1959-61; resident in plastic surgery Kings County Hosp., 1961-63; pvt. practice N.Y.C.; attending plastic surgeon Cabrini Med. Ctr., 1965—, Westchester Sq. Hosp. Med. Ctr., 1963—. Sculptor works include portrait commns. for Richard Grossman Burn Ctr., 1996, Vladimir Horowitz and Arthur Rubinstein; inventor Taub oral panendoscope, 1963, artificial larynx "voicebak", 1968-78. Recipient Ignacio Barrequer award Smith Kline French, 1963. Mem. Am. Soc. Plastic and Reconstructive Surgeons. Avocations: concert piano, acting, ventroloquism. Office: 737 Park Ave New York NY 10021-4256

TAUB, STEPHEN RICHARD, lawyer; b. N.Y.C., Oct. 5, 1944; s. Irving Robert and Sylvia T.; m. Alyson Zoe Winter, Dec. 23, 1968. BA, Queens Coll., 1965; JD, NYU, 1968. Bar: N.Y. 1969, U.S. Dist. Ct. (ea. and so. dists.) N.Y. 1970, U.S. Ct. Appeals (2nd cir.) 1971, U.S. Supreme Ct. 1972. Asst. dist. atty., bur. chief Kings County Dist. Attys. Office, Bklyn., 1970-77; pvt. practice Garden City, N.Y., 1977-96; ptnr. Ostrow and Taub, LLP, Garden City, from 1996; counselor Schlissel, Ostrow, Karabatos, Poepplein & Taub, PLLC, Mineola, N.Y.; matrimonial case neutral evaluator Nassau County Supreme Ct., Mineola, 1997—. Village Justice Village Kensington, Great Neck, N.Y., 1986-98; Acting Village Justice Village Old Brookville, N.Y., 1998—. Fellow Am. Acad. Matrimonial Lawyers; mem. ABA, N.Y. Family Law Am. Inn of Ct. (master), N.Y. State Bar Assn., N.Y. State Magistrates Assn., Nassau County Bar Assn., Nassau County Magistrates Assn. (pres. 1993-94). Avocation: tennis. Office: Schissel Ostrow Et Al 190 Willis Ave Mineola NY 11501

TAUB, THEODORE CALVIN, lawyer; b. Springfield, Mass., Jan. 1, 1935; s. Samuel and Sara Lee (Daum) T.; m. Roberta Mae Ginsburg, Aug. 23, 1959; children: Tracy, Andrew, Adam. AB, Duke U., 1956; JD, U. Fla., 1960. Bar: Fla., 1960, U.S. Supreme Ct. Atty. Broad and Cassel, Tampa; asst. city atty. City of Tampa, 1963-67; city atty. City of Temple Terrace, Fla., 1974—; panelist in field. Contbr. articles to profl. jours. Chmn. Tampa-Hillsborough (Fla.) County Expy. Authority, 1974-84; mem. Hillsborough County Charter Commn., 1966-69, Local Govt. Mgmt. Efficiency Com., 1979, State of Fla. Environ. Efficiency Study Commn., 1986-88; founder Tampa Bay Performing Arts Ctr. Fellow: Am. Bar Found; mem. ABA (chmn. real property litigation com. 1981-86, chmn. com. on housing and urban environ. 1989-91), Am. Coll. Real Estate Lawyers (bd. govs.), Am. Land Title Assn. (lenders' counsel group), Fla. Bar Assn. (bd. cert. real estate lawyer), Fla. Jaycees (pres.), Tau Epsilon Phi. Democrat. Jewish. Home: 4937 Lyford Cay Rd Tampa FL 33629-4828 Office: 100 N Tampa St Ste 3500 Tampa FL 33602-5869

TAUBE, HENRY, chemistry educator; b. Sask., Can., Nov. 30, 1915; came to U.S., 1937, naturalized, 1942; s. Samuel and Albertina (Tiledetski) T.; m. Mary Alice Wesche, Nov. 27, 1952; children: Linda, Marianna, Heinrich, Karl. BS, U. Sask., 1935, MS, 1937, LLD, 1973; PhD, U. Calif., 1940; PhD (hon.), Hebrew U. of Jerusalem, 1979; DSc (hon.), U. Chgo., 1983, Poly. Inst., N.Y., 1984, SUNY, 1985, U. Guelph, 1987; DSc honoris causa, Seton Hall U., 1988; Lajos Kossuth U. of Debrecen, Hungary, 1988; DSc, Northwestern U., 1990; hon. degree, U. Athens, 1993. Instr. U. Calif., 1940-41; instr., asst. prof. Cornell U., 1941-46; faculty U. Chgo., 1946-62, prof., 1952-62, chmn. dept. chemistry, 1955-59; prof. chemistry Stanford U., 1962-90; prof. emeritus chemistry Stanford U., 1990—; Marguerite Blake Wilbur prof. Stanford U., 1976, chmn. dept., 1971-74; Baker lectr. Cornell U., 1965. Hon. mem. Hungarian Acad., Scis., 1988. Guggenheim fellow, 1949, 55; recipient Harrison Howe award, 1961, Chandler medal Columbia U., 1964, F. P. Dwyer medal U. NSW, Australia, 1973, Nat. medal of Sci., 1976, 77, Allied Chem. award for Excellence in Grad. Tchg. and Innovative Sci., 1979, Nobel prize in Chemistry, 1983, Bailar medal U. Ill., 1983, Robert A. Welch Found. award in Chemistry, 1983, Disting. Achievement award Internat. Precious Metals Inst., 1986, Brazilian Order of Sci. Merit award, 1994, Hon. fellowship Royal Soc. Can., 1997. Fellow Royal Soc. Chemistry (hon.), Indian Chem. Soc. (hon.); mem. NAS (award in chem. scis. 1983), Am. Acad. Arts and Scis., Am. Chem. Soc. (Kirkwood award New Haven sect. 1965, award for nuclear applications in chemistry 1955, Nichols medal N.Y. sect. 1971, Willard Gibbs medal Chgo. sect. 1971, Disting. Svc. in Advancement Inorganic Chemistry award 1967, T.W. Richards medal NE sect. 1980, Monsanto Co. award in inorganic chemistry 1981, Linus Pauling award Puget Sound sect. 1981, Priestley medal 1985, Oesper award Cin. sect. 1986, G.M. Kosolapoff award Auburn sect. 1990), Royal Physiographical Soc. of Lund (fgn. mem.), Am. Philos. Soc., Finnish Acad. Sci. and Letters, Royal Danish Acad. Scis. and Letters, Coll. Chemists of Catalonia and Beleares (hon.), Can. Soc. Chemistry (hon.), Hungarian Acad. Scis. (hon. mem.), Royal Soc. (fgn. mem.), Brazilian Acad. Scis. (corr.), Engring. Acad. Japan (fgn. assoc.), Australian Acad. Scis. (corr.), Chem. Soc. Japan (hon. mem. 1993), Phi Beta Kappa, Sigma Xi, Phi Lambda Upsilon (hon.). Office: Stanford U Dept Chemistry Stanford CA 94305-5080

TÄUBER, UWE CLAUS, physicist; b. Rehau, Germany, Sept. 12, 1963; s. Adolf and Gertraud (Dietrich) T.; m. Karin Ziegler, July 19, 1990; children: Lilian Alexandra, Judith Melanie. Physics Diploma, Tech. U. Munich, Germany, 1988, DrRerNat, 1992; DrRerNatHabil, Tech. U. Munich, 1999. Rsch. staff Tech. U. Munich, 1988-93; postdoctoral fellow Harvard U., Cambridge, Mass., 1993-95; rsch. assoc. Oxford (Eng.) U., 1995-97; habilitation fellow Tech. U. Munich, 1997-98; asst. prof. physics Va. Tech., 1998—. Contbr. articles to Phys. Rev. B/E, Phys. Rev. Letters, Ency. of Applied Physics, others. Recipient various scholarships; DFG postdoctoral rsch. fellow, 1993, Marie Curie fellow, 1996, DFG habilitation fellow, 1997. Mem. Deutsche Physikalische Gesellschaft, Am. Phys. Soc., Babenbergia (chmn. 1990-92), European Phys. Soc. Lutheran. Avocations: golf, piano. Home: 6104 Albemarle Ln Blacksburg VA 24060-8116 Office: Va Polytechnic Inst and U Physics Dept Blacksburg VA 24061-0435

TAUBØLL, ERIK, neurologist; b. Oslo, July 3, 1957; s. Gunnar and Oddrun (Solberg) T.; m. Tone-Marcelle Rudene, Aug. 14, 1983; children: Henrik, Elisabeth. MD, U. Oslo, 1983, PhD, 1994. Sr. registrar dept. neurology Rikshospitalet, The Nat. Hosp., Oslo, 1986-88; scientist Norwegian Rsch. Coun. for Sci. and Humanities, Oslo, 1988-91; sr. registrar dept. neurology Rikshospitalet, The Nat. Hosp. and U. Oslo, 1991—. Contbr. over 50 articles to profl. jours. 1st lt. Royal Norwegian Air Force, 1987-88. Recipient Forsberg Legacy grant, 1988. Mem. N.Y. Acad. Scis. Office: Rikshospitalet, Dept Neurology, 0027 Oslo Norway

TAUDIEN, EDWARD PAUL, retired construction executive; b. N.Y.C., Jan. 25, 1932; s. Edward Peter Paul and Lucia Sylvia (Linder) T.; m. Patricia A. Dean, June 14, 1958; children: Mark, Glenn, Evan. BS in Engring., Cooper Union Sch. Engring., N.Y.C., 1959. Registered profl. engr., N.Y., N.J., Fla. V.p. Skinner & Cook, Inc., Roselle Pk., N.J., 1954-81; mgr. ops. So. Bldg. Divsn. Perini Corp., West Palm Beach, Fla., 1981-86; v.p., gen. mgr. Proctor Constrn. Co., Vero Beach, Fla., 1987; area ops. mgr. Dawson Constrn. Co., Fla., N.C., 1988-93. Mayor Branchburg (N.J.) Twp., 1980; committeeman, 1975, 77-81; mem. Branchburg Planning Bd., 1977-81, Zoning Bd. Appeals, Palm Beach Gardens, Fla., 1984-87. Trustee Plainfield (N.J.) Masons Welfare & Pension Funds, 1974-77. Cpl. U.S. Army, 1952-54. Decorated Occupation Medal Germany, 1952, Nat. Def. Svc. Medal, 1953. Republican. Presbyterian. Avocations: world travel, history. Home: 4992 SE Mariner Village Ln Stuart FL 34997-2151

TAUFER, VENO, poet, playwright, essayist; b. Ljubljana, Slovenia, Feb. 19, 1933; s. Veno and Marija (Bizjak) T.; m. Jasna Skrinjar, Aug. 30, 1958; children: Vito, Matej, Lara Simona. MA Comparative Lit., U. Ljubljana, 1960. Editor Revija 57 mag., Yugoslavia, 1957-59; freelance writer, translator Yugoslavia, 1960-66; mem. external svcs. staff BBC, London, 1966-69; mem. editorial bd. for cultural and lit. affairs Ljubljana Broadcasting House, 1969-90; counselor to the Slovenian govt. Ministry Fgn. Affairs, 1991-95; chmn. Vilenica, 1996—; group mem., editorial counsel, Perspektive mag., 1960-64; mng. dir. exptl. theater, Oder 57, 1961-63; burse for theater studies, Govt. of France, Paris, 1972; vis. Fulbright prof., writer-in-residence, U. Md., Balt., 1982; mem. coun., Nova Revija mag., 1981—; jurist, jury sec., Slovene Writers' Assn. Vilenica award, 1985—; founder-dir. Internat. Poetry Festival, Vilenica, 1996. Author poetry collections; playwright: Prometheus or the Dark in the Pupil of the Sun, 1968, The Wood of Birngham, 1975, Ulysses & Son or the World and Home, 1989; books of essays, including On the Stage, 1977; translator modern poetry; author children's verse books. Chmn. Com. for Freedom of Speech and Writing, Ljubljana, 1985-89; mem. exec. collegium Human Rights Com., Ljubljana, 1987—; mem. exec. com. Slovene Democratic Alliance, Ljubljana, 1989-93. Recipient Nat. Presern award for lit., 1973, 96, Macedonian Writers Assn. award, 1975, Anton Sovre award Slovene Lit. Translators, 1975, Branko Miljkovic award, 1986, Simon Jenko award for poetry, 1987, Gábor Bethlen Internat. Literary award, 1989, Internat. Mitteleuropa prize, 1995. Mem. Slovene Writers' Assn. (sec. 1985-89, exec. bd. 1985—), PEN (exec. bd. 1994—, v.p. 1996-2000, pres. 2000—), Internat. PEN Writers for Peace Com. (chmn. 2000—), Assn. Internat. Critics of Theater. Avocations: diving, skiing, old music. Fax: 386 1 25 4847. Home: Ilirska 4, 1000 Ljubljana Slovenia Office: Slovene Writers Assn, Tomsiceva 12, 1000 Ljubljana Slovenia

TAULAVUORI, KARI MIKKO JUHANI, plant physiologist, researcher; b. Posio, Finland, Aug. 5, 1964; s. Kyösti Mikael and Liisa (Häkkinen) T.; m. Erja Birgitta Salonen, Mar. 4, 1995; 1 child, Mira-Sofia. BSc, U. Oulu, Finland, 1990, MSc, 1993, Lic. in Philosophy, 1996, PhD, 1998; postgrad., U. Oulu, 2000. Timberjack Haukipudas, Finland, 1985; garden worker Bot.

Gardens, U. Oulu, 1988-92; trainee Agrl. Rsch. Ctr., Tyrnävä, Finland, 1990, Jokioinen, Finland, 1991; rsch. asst. dept. botany U. Oulu, 1993, tchr. plant physiology dept. biology, 1995—; referee Physiologia Platarum, Lund, Sweden, 1996—; reviewer Grant Agy. Czech Republic, 1996—. Contbr. articles to profl. jours. Recipient Rsch. grants Maj & Tor Nessling Found., Finland, 1994-96, Emil Aaltonen Found., Finland, 1997-99; fellow Forest Rsch. Inst. Warsaw, Poland, 2000. Mem. Scandinavian Soc. Plant Physiologists. Office: Univ Oulu Dept Biology, PO Box 333, FIN90571 Oulu Finland

TAULBEE, THOMAS LESTER, psychotherapist, educator; b. Normal, Ill., June 12, 1947; s. Marion L. and Marjorie S. T. BS, Ill. State U., 1970; MS, Tex. A&M U., 1971, EdD, 1973. Cert. marriage and family therapist; cert. sports counselor. Psycotherapist Human Resource Devel. Ctr., Dallas, 1974-76; prof. psychology Richland Coll., Dallas, 1976—; prof. history Richland Coll., 1994—; bd. advisors Revival Fires Ministries, Branson West, Mo., 1997-99. Co-author: Psychology from a Personal Perspective, 1992, rev. edit., 1997; editor, co -author: Personal Applications of Psychology, 1997. Dir. Superior Student Roundtable, Parker, Tex., 1993, 1996—. Scholar Ctr. Behavioral Studies U. North Tex., Denton, 1973-74. Mem. Tex. Jr. Coll. Teachers Assn., Nat. Assn. Scholars, Assn. Behavior Analysis. Avocations: world travel, scuba diving, cooking. E-mail: taulbee@flash.net. Office: Richland Coll 12800 Abrams Rd Dallas TX 75243-2173

TAUR, YUAN, physicist, researcher; b. Nanchang, Jiangxi, China, Sept. 27, 1946; came to U.S., 1968; s. Tang and Ping-Chung Seh Taur; m. Betty Chu, Apr. 20, 1974; children: Ying, Hsuan. BS in Physics, Nat. Taiwan U., 1967; PhD in Physics, U. Calif., Berkeley, 1974. Postdoctor U. Calif., Berkeley, 1974-75; rsch. assoc. Goddard Inst. Space Studies NASA, N.Y.C., 1975-79; mem. tech. staff Rockwell Internat. Sci. Ctr., Thousand Oaks, Calif., 1979-81; rsch. staff mem., mgr. T. J. Watson Rsch. Ctr. IBM, Yorktown Heights, N.Y., 1981—; adj. prof. Rutgers U., Piscataway, N.J., 1977-79. Co-author: Fundamentals of Modern VLSI Devices, 1998; contbr. articles to profl. jours. Fellow IEEE (subject editor Electron Device Letters 1996-99, editor-in-chief 1999—). Achievements include 10 patents. Avocations: tennis, skiing, bridge, mahjong. Office: IBM T J Watson Rsch Ctr PO Box 218 Yorktown Heights NY 10598-0218

TAUZIAT, NATHALIE, tennis player; b. Bangui, Central African Republic, Oct. 17, 1967; d. Bernard and Regine Tauziat. Profl. tennis player. Established tennis acad., Cabreton, France, 1994. Winner Wimbledon, 1989, Birmingham, 1997, Eastbourne 1995, Quebec City 1993, Futures/Val d Oise-FRA, 1990, 92, Bayonne 1990, Futures/Limoges-FRA, 1987, Wimbledon, 1989; placed 2nd Australian Open; 3 time champion U.S. Open; winner 4 singles titles, 14 doubles titles. Mem. WTA Tour Players Assn. (bd. dirs. 1997-98). Avocations: music, playing golf, watching soccer. Office: care USTA 70 W Red Oak Ln White Plains NY 10604-3602*

TAVARE, NARAYAN SANABA, chemical engineering educator, researcher; b. Wayphale, Maharashra, India, July 1, 1950; arrived in Eng., 1978; s. Sonaba Krishna and Narmada Sonaba (Sapate) T.; m. Vasanti Narayan Tavare, Jan. 22, 1980; children: Aniket, Abhijeet. B in Chem. Engring., UDCT, Mumbai, India, 1972, M in Chem. Engring., 1974, PhD in Chem. Engring., 1978; DSc, UMIST, Manchester, Eng., 1995. Assoc. lectr. UDCT, Mumbai, India, 1974-78; rsch. asst. U. Coll., London, 1978-81; rsch. fellow UMIST, Manchester, Eng., 1981-95; lectr. Bradford (Eng.) U., 1995-99, reader in indsl. crystallization, 1999—. Author: (book) Industrial Crystallization, 1995. Mem. Inst. Chem. Engring. Avocations: swimming, walking. Office: U Bradford, Dept Chem Engring, W Ykshir Bradford BD7 1DP, England

TAVARTKILADZE, GEORGE ABEL, otorhinolaryngologist; b. Tbilisi, Republic of Georgia, Aug. 23, 1948; s. Abel T. and Nelli G. (Georgadze) T.; m. Natalia V. Baltijskaya, Dec. 24, 1977. B, Russian State Med. U., Moscow, 1972, M, 1973; MD, Moscow ENT Rsch. Inst., 1975, PhD, 1977. Med. diplomate. Sr. rschr. Moscow ENT Rsch. Inst., 1978-83, head lab., 1983-88; dir. Rsch. Ctr. Audiology and Hearing Rehab., Moscow, 1988—; academician Internat. Acad. Scis., 1994; audiologist in charge Russian Ministry Health Care, Moscow, 1989—, head Commn. on New Med. Equipment, 1989—; mem. expert adv. panel WHO, Geneva, 1994—. Contbr. articles to profl. jours., chpts. to books. Program dir. Internat. Found. Child Health Care, Moscow, 1990—, Lions Club Internat., Moscow, 1995-96. Named to Russian Order of Friendship, Pres. Russian Fedn., Moscow, 1996; grantee Commn. European Cmtys. Directorate, 1995-96, Open Soc. Inst., N.Y.C., 1997. Fellow Am. Acad. Audiology; mem. N.Y. Acad. Scis., Russian ENT Soc. (v.p.), Assn. Rsch. Otorhinolaryngology, Internat. Evoked Response Audiometry Study Group. Avocations: tennis, music. Home: 3 Romanov Per Apt 69, Moscow 103009, Russia Office: Rsch Ctr Aud/Hearing Rehab, 18 Bakulev St, 117513 Moscow Russia

TAVECCHIO, LOUIS W(ILLEM) C(ORNELIS), psychology educator; b. The Hague, The Netherlands, Mar. 10, 1946; s. Willem Cornelis Tavecchio and Maria Elisabeth Voorbraak; m. Marjan Wilma Brandina Meyer, Dec. 11, 1969; children: Wouter, Lotte, Gusta. BSc in Psychology, U. Amsterdam, The Netherlands, 1968, MSc in Psychology, 1971, PhD in Social Scis., 1977. Rsch. asst. U. Amsterdam, 1969-71, asst. prof., 1972-75; asst. prof. pedagogy Leiden (The Netherlands) U., 1976-78, assoc. prof., 1979—; chmn. rsch. com. on family rsch. Netherlands Orgn. for Sci. Rsch., 1989-94, chmn. rsch. com. on family and youth rsch., 1995, mem. com. on family and youth rsch., 1996—. Editor (with M.H. Van Ijzendoorn), author: Attachment in Social Networks, 1987; contbr. articles to profl. jours., including Jour. Marriage and Family, Jour. Moral Edn. Advisor on child care and center day care to various orgns., 1997—. Mem. Dutch Assn. Pedagogy. Avocations: listening and playing music (jazz), camping in a caravan, surfing on the net. Home: Doornenburg 10, 1121 GP Landsmeer The Netherlands Office: U Leiden Ctr Child-Fam Stds, Wassenaarseweg 52, 2333 AK Leiden The Netherlands

TAVERAS, JUAN MANUEL, physician, educator; b. Dominican Republic, Sept. 27, 1919; came to U.S., 1944, naturalized, 1950; s. Marcos M. and Ana L. (Rodriguez) T.; m. Bernice Helen McGonigle, June 12, 1947 (dec. 1990); children: Angela Forbes Summers, Louisa Helen Taveras Koranda, Jeffrey Lawrence; m. Mariana Margarita Bucher, Mar. 18, 1991. BS, Normal Sch. Santiago, Dominican Republic, 1937; MD, U. Santo Domingo, Dominican Republic, 1943, U. Pa., 1949; MS honoris causa, Harvard Med. Sch., 1971; Dr. honoris causa, Univ. Nacional Pedro Henriquez Ureña, Dominican Republic, 1987; Doctor Honoris Causa, U. Catolica Madre Y Maestra, Santiago, Dominican Republic, 1992. Diplomate: Am. Bd. Radiology. Instr. anatomy U. Santo Domingo, 1943-44; fellow radiology Grad. Hosp. U. Pa., 1945-48; rotating intern Misericordia Hosp., Phila., 1949-50; asst. radiologist Presbyn. Hosp., N.Y.C., 1950-52; asst. attending radiologist Presbyn. Hosp., 1953-56, assoc. attending radiologist, 1956-60, attending radiologist, 1960-65; dir. radiology Neurol. Inst., N.Y.C., 1952-65; cons. USPHS Hosp., S.I., N.Y., 1952-65, Morristown (N.J.) Meml. Hosp., 1957-65, St. Barnabas Hosp., N.Y.C., 1959-65, VA Hosp., Bronx, N.Y., 1960-65; asst. instr. radiology U. Pa. Sch. Medicine, 1947-48; faculty Columbia Coll. Phys. and Surg., 1950-65, prof. radiology, 1959-65; prof. radiology, chmn. dept., dir. Mallinckrodt Inst. Radiology, Washington U. Sch. Medicine, St. Louis, 1965-71; radiologist-in-chief Barnes and Allied Hosps., St. Louis, 1965-71; cons. neuroradiology service Unit 1 St. Louis City Hosp., 1966-71; cons. radiology Jewish Hosp., St. Louis, 1966-71; prof. radiology Harvard Med. Sch., 1971-89, prof. radiology emeritus, 1989—; radiologist-in-chief Mass. Gen. Hosp., Boston, 1971-88; pres. VII Symposium Neuroradiologieum, 1964; hon. prof. U. Chile, 1978, Peruvian U. Cayetano Heredia, 1994; founder, cons. Diagnosis and Advanced Medicine Ctr. in Juan M. Taveras Health Plaza, Santo Domingo, Dominican Republic, 1997—. Author: Neuroradiology, 1996, (with Ross Golden) Roentgenology of the Abdomen, 1961, (with Ernest H. Wood) Diagnostic Neuroradiology, 1964, 2d edit., 1976, (with Norman Leeds) Dynamic Factors in Diagnosis of Supratentorial Brain Tumors by Cerebral Angiography, 1969, (with F. Morello) Normal Neuroradiology, 1979, (with James Provenzale) Clinical Cases in Neuroradiology, 1994, (with Laszlo Szlavy) Noncoronary Angioplasty, 1994; editor: (with others) Recent Advances in the Study of Cerebral Circulation, 1970, Cysticercosis of the Central Nervous System, 1983, Radiology: Diagnosis, Imaging, Intervention, 1986, Radiologia e Imagen, Diagnostica y Terapeutica, 1998, 99; chief editor: Am. Jour. Neuroradiology, 1980-89; contbr. numerous articles to profl. jours. Bd. dirs. Edward Mallinckrodt, Jr. Found., 1980-96. Decorated knight Order of Duarte Sanchez y Mella (Dominican Republic) 1972; Juan M. Taveras professorship established in his honor Harvard Med. Sch., 1988. Fellow Am. Coll. Radiology (gold medal 1985); mem. AMA, Am. Neurol. Assn., Am. Roentgen Ray Soc. (gold medal 1988), Radiol. Soc. N.Am. (gold medal 1981), Mass. Med. Soc., Inter-Am. Coll. Radiology, World Fedn. Neurology, Am. Soc. Neuroradiology (pres. 1962-64, gold medal, 1995), N.Y. Acad. Scis., Nat. Acads. of Practice, Am. Assn. Neurol. Surgeons (assoc.), Assn. U. Radiologists (gold medal 1985), Mass. Radiol. Soc., Costa Rica Soc. Radiology, Colombia Neurol. Soc., Brazilian Radiol. Soc., New Eng. Roentgen Ray Soc.; pres. Iberrian Latin Am. Soc. of Neuroradiology 1988-91, pres. IV Congress of Iberian Latin Am. Soc. of Neuroradiology 1992, hon. mem. Phila. Roentgen Ray Soc., Radiol. Soc. Venezuela, Rocky Mountain Radiol. Soc., Tex. Radiol. Soc., Radiol. Assn. Ctrl. Am. and Panama, Hungarian Radiologic Soc., European Soc. Neuroradiology (hon.), Alpha Omega Alpha, Mexican Neuroradiology Soc. (hon., price of merit award). Republican. Home: 85 E India Row Apt 40F Boston MA 02110-3394 Office: Mass Gen Hosp 55 Fruit St Boston MA 02114-2696

TAVMAN, ISMAIL HAKKI, education educator; b. Karabuk, Turkey, Sept. 13, 1949; s. Mahmut Cemalettin and Armagan (Hosgor) T.; m. Sebnem Demir, July 17, 1992; children: Timur, Tayfun. BS, Robert Collage, 1975; MS, ENSAM Paris, 1983, PhD, 1987. Rsch. asst. Robert Coll., Istanbul, 1971-72, Va. Polytechnic and State U., Blacksburg, 1973; project mgr. Taris, Izmir, Turkey, 1979-81; rsch. asst. ENSAM, Paris, 1982-88; assoc. prof. Dokuz Eylul U., Izmir, 1989—. Contbr. articles to profl. jours. Mem. Turkish Chamber of Mech. Engrs., Club of Turkish-French Engrs. (adminstrv. bd.), Izmir Tennis Club. Avocations: tennis, jogging, swimming. Office: Dokuz Eylul Univ, Bornova 35100, Turkey

TAVORMINA, VINCENZO ANTONIO, surgeon; b. Castelvetrano, Trapani, Italy, Oct. 19, 1942; s. Antonio Tavormina and Caterina Viviani; m. Marisa Scuderi; children: Antonio, Licia. MD, U. Torino, Italy, 1967, Prof., 1969. Medical diplomate. Asst. prof. human anatomy U. Torino, 1969—, asst. prof. surg. anatomy; registrar sr. dept. emergency surgery U. Palermo, 1984-92, cons. surgeon, 1992—; specialist in surgery gen., U. Torino, 1972, thoracic surgery, 1975, cardiovascular surgery, 1979. Med. officer Army and Red Cross, 1968, 74. Fellow Tennis Club Palermo; mem. Rotary (past pres. 1995), Cath. Med. Assn. Democrat. Roman Catholic. Avocations: agriculture, films, classical music, books, sports.

TAWA, SHUNSUKE, retired law educator; b. Kobe, Japan, Dec. 6, 1929; s. Tasuku and Sadayo (Fujii) T.; m. Atsuko Oka, Mar. 18, 1954; children: Shigekazu, Isaki Mitsue, Michika. LLB, Kyushu U., 1954; LLM, Kobe U., 1965; LLD, Kokugakuin U., 1992. Tchr. Kannabe (Japan) Sr. High Sch., 1956-69; lectr. Tottori (Japan) U., 1969-70, asst. prof., 1970-76, prof. law, 1976-95; prof. criminal proceeding law Osaka Economy and Law U., 1995-2000; lectr. Tottori Women;s Short Coll., 1973-83, Tajima Tech. Sch., Toyooka, Japan, 1985-94. Author: Doitsu Kenjiseido no Hikakuhotekikenkyu, 1992, Hogakutsuron, 1983, About the Influence of European Community's Politically Unifying for the Criminal Proceeding Laws of United Kingdom and Germany, 1996, About Crown Porsecution Service in England and Wales, 1998, The Transition and the Change of the Conception about the Investigation and the Public Prosecution, 1999. Chief com. Tottori Ken Clean Election Promoting Assn., 1970-95; mem. standing com. Fukuyama City Clean Election Promoting Assn., 1995—; com. mem. Tottori Labor Stds. Office, 1970-80. Named hon. prof. Tottori Univ., 1995; recipient reward Min. Self-Govt., 1995. Mem. The Criminal Law Soc. Japan, The Comparative Law Soc. Japan, Japanese Legal and Polit. Sci. Assn., Japanese-German Assn. Rechtswissenschaft. Buddhist. Avocations: model ships, swords, travel, classical music. Home: 423 Hojyoji Ekiyachyo, Hiroshima Prefecture Fukuyama City 720-2413, Japan

TAWATA, SHINKICHI, agricultural engineering educator; b. Ginowan, Okinawa, Japan, Aug. 28, 1949; s. Shinki and Yoshiko Tawata. M of Agrl., Kyushu U., 1974, PhD, 1978. Postdoctoral assoc. SUNY, Stony Brook, 1979, U. Calif., Berkeley, 1979-82; asst. prof. U. Ryukyus, Japan, 1982-95, assoc. prof., 1995-98, prof., 1998—; cons. Japan Internat. Corp. Agy., Japan, 1986, Agrl. and Fishery Ministry, Japan, 1986-91, Okinawa Prefecture, Japan, 1989—. Author: Pesticides and Alternatives, 1990; contbr. articles to profl. jours. including Bioscience, Biotech., Biochemistry, Jour. Pesticide Science, others. Grantee Bank of Okinawa, 1991, Okinawa Prefecture, 1992. Achievements include patent in growth regulation method using mimosine, patent in simple reduction method of mimosine and its decomposed product from leucaena. Home: 45 Aichi, Ginowan 901-2206, Japan Office: Faculty Agrl U Ryukyus, 1 Senbaru, Nishihara 903-0129, Japan

TAWFIK, RUHIYAH MOHAMAD TAWFIK, artist; b. 1927; married; 1 child. Student, Faculty of Fine Arts, Cairo, 1953; PhD in Fine Arts, Prague Acad. Fine Arts. Sculptor, head dept. ceramics Agrl. Mus., 1955-65; dir. Mohammad Mahmoud Khalil Mus. Min. of Culture, 1967-69, cons. tech. office, 1981—. Mem. Sculptor's Assn., Fine Arts Fedn., Gezira Sporting Club. Avocation: classical music. Address: Manzil 17, Shareh al-Brazil Zamalek, Cairo Egypt

TAWIL, GEORGE, psychiatrist; b. Syria, Apr. 14, 1947; s. Santik and Aimilia (Roufkaki) T.; m. Eleftheria Tsakalou, Apr. 24, 1986. MD, U. Athens, Greece, 1981; PhD in Psychosomatics, U. Athens, 1986; postgrad., U. Wis., 1991, Baylor U., Houston, 1991; Fulbright doctorate program, Athens, 1991. Staff U. Athens Dromokaition Hosp., 1982-86; rschr. U. Athens, 1982-86; asst. prof. Psychiat. Clinic, Athens, 1983-93; Psychiat. Adminstrv. Coun., Athens, 1981; acad. advisor LaSalle U., Athens, 1996—. Contbr. articles to profl. jours. Fulbright scholar, 1991. Mem. Greek Soc. Neurology and Psychiatry, Greek Soc. for Mental Health of Child, Hellenic Psychiat. Assn., Am. Psychiat. Assn., Ill. Psychol. Assn., Am. Psychosomatic Soc., Nat. Geog. Soc., Advance Scientist Placement. Orthodox. Avocations: writing, reading, listening to music. Home and Office: Michalakopoulou 54, 115-28 Athens Greece

TAY, JOHN SIN HOCK, pediatrics educator; b. Tangkak, Johor, West Malaysia, Oct. 8, 1942; s. Seng Hoon Tay and Hoon Hock Loh; m. Ivy Kim Kee Goh, Aug. 10, 1968; children: Faith, Say Luan, Tay, David, Say Kong, Tay. MBBS with hons., U. Sydney, Australia, 1967; BD with hons., U. London, 1971; M of Medicine in Paediatrics, U. Singapore, 1973; MD, PhD, Nat. U. Singapore, 1977, 85. House officer Gen. Hosp. Malacca, Malaysia, 1967-68; med. officer Ministry of Health, Johor, West Malaysia, 1968-72; univ. trainee dept. pediatrics U. Singapore, 1972-73, lectr., 1973-76, sr. lectr., 1976-80; assoc. prof. dept. pediatrics Nat. U. Singapore, 1980-84, prof., 1985-95, prof., head dept., 1988-95. Editor: (book) A Practical Manual On Acute Paediatrics, 1989. Hon. priest Diocese of Singapore (Anglican), Singapore, 1980-95, dean St. Andrew's Cathedral (Anglican), Singapore, 1996—. Recipient Colombo Plan scholarship, Australia, Sydney, 1961-66, Med. Univ. Sydney, 1967. Fellow Royal Australasian Coll. Physicians, Am. Coll. Cardiology, Am. Coll. Med. Genetics, Royal Coll. Physicians, Acad. of Medicine (Young Investigator's award Singapore 1977), Singapore Paediatric Soc. (officer, 9th Haridas Meml. Lectr. 1982), Assn. S.E. Asian Nations Paediatric Fedn. (v.p. countries 1983-86, pres. 1986-88). Avocations: music, reading, chess. Fax: 262 1214. Home: 21 Corporation Rise, Singapore 618335, Singapore

TAY, TONG-EARN, mechanical engineering educator, researcher; b. Malacca, Malaysia, Nov. 25, 1961; s. Cheng-Seng Tay and Kim-Puay Poh; m. Lydia Hin-Pheng Loy; children: Clara Ying-Sui, William Ying-Wen. B Engring., U. Melbourne, Australia, 1984, PhD, 1988. Registered profl. engr., Singapore. Lectr. mech. engring. Nat. U. Singapore, 1989-93, sr. lectr., 1994-97, assoc. prof., 1998—; vis. prof. Ctr. for Composite Materials, U. Del., Newark, 1997-98. Contbr. articles to sci. jours., including Jour. Composite Materials, Composite Structures, Engring. Fracture Mechanics. Postgrad. scholar U. Melbourne, 1985. Mem. ASME, Bioengring. Soc. Singapore. Achievements include patent for energy storing composite prosthetic foot. Office: Nat U Singapore Dept M&PE, 10 Kent Ridge Crescent, Singapore 119260, Singapore

TAYA, MAAOUYA OULD SID AHMED, president of Islamic Republic of Mauritania; b. 1943. Min. def. Mauritania, 1978-79, 81-92; pres. Mauritania; minister in charge of Permanent Sec., mil. com. for nat. recovery, 1979-81, army chief of staff, 1980-81, prime minister, 1981-84, pres., 1984—; chmn. mil. com. for Nat. Salvation, 1984—. Office: Presidence de la République, BP 184, Nouakchott Mauritania*

TAYAMA, YOSHIO, insurance company executive; b. Tokyo, July 16, 1926; married; 2 children. Jurisprudence, Tokyo U., 1952. With Kyoei Life Ins. Co., Ltd., Tokyo, 1952-68, bd. dirs., 1968-74, mng. dir., 1974-80, sr. mng. dir., 1980-83, dep. pres., 1983-86, pres., 1986-94, chmn., bd. dirs., 1994-98, sr. advisor, 1998—; auditor Japan Inst. Life Ins., 1994—; mem. internat. bd. Bank Austria Aktiengesellschaft, 1993-98. Dir. Rsch. Inst. of Software Engring., 1988-98, Inc. Found., Oriental Life Ins. Cultural Development Ctr., 1991-98, hon. dir., 1998—; dir., Japan Brazil Ctrl. Assn. Recipient Blue Ribbon medal Japanese Govt., 1991. Mem. ALMANIJ (internat. coun. 1992—), Japan Inst. Life Ins. (auditor 1994-99), The Life Ins. Assn. of Japan (vice chmn. 1991-94). Office: Kyoei Life Ins Co Ltd, 4-4-1 Hongokucho Nihonbashi, Chuo-ku Tokyo 103-0021, Japan

TAYANC, METE, engineering educator; b. Nicosia, Cyprus, Dec. 31, 1966; s. Ali and Cihan (Hasan) T. MS, Bogazici U., Istanbul, Turkey, 1991, PhD, 1995; Assoc. Prof., Marmara U. Fac. Engring., Istanbul, Turkey, 1997. Meterol. sta. operator Meterol. Office, Nicosia, 1984-88; project coord. Inst. Environ. Scis. Bogazici U., Istanbul, 1990-95; with dept. info. systems and software translation Digital Equipment Corp., Istanbul, 1990-92; environ. cons. AS Ic Ve Dis Ticaret AS, Istanbul, 1993-95; engring. educator Marmara U., Istanbul, 1995-97, assoc. prof. engring., 1997—; cons., project coord. Istanbul Greater Municipality, Istanbul, 1995—; dir. Environmental Impact Assessment Report for a Pvt. Hosp., Pvt. Ozkan Hosp., Istanbul, 1997. Editor: MS WORD Student's Manual, 1996, 99; contbr. articles to profl. jours. Ranked first amongst 2754 grads. Istanbul Tech. U., Maslak, 1988; recipient 3rd prize chemistry Turkish Sci. and Tech. Rsch. Found., Kavaklidere, 1984; fellow Turkish Sci. and Tech. Rsch. Found., 1993-95, NATO/CCMS pilot project fellowship, 1997—. Mem. Am. Geophys. Union. Avocation: vis. hist. and scenic sites. Office: Marmara U/Fac Engring, Kuyubasi/Kadikoy, Istanbul 81040, Turkey

TAYAR, RENE BENEDICT, radiologist, consultant; b. Sliema, Malta, Oct. 3, 1945; arrived in England, 1971.; s. Oscar and Violetta (Riccardi) T.; m. Margaret Rose Tortell, Jan. 25, 1971; 1 child, Benjamin. MD, Royal U. Malta. Registrar Bristol (England) Royal Infirmary, 1974-77, sr. registrar, 1977-81; cons. radiologist St. Helier Hosp., Carshalton, Surrey, England, 1981—, Parkside Hosp., Wimbledon, London, 1985—, St. Anthony's Hosp., Cheam, Surrey, 1995—; hon. sr. lectr. St. George's Hosp. Med. Sch., U. London, 1985—. Co-founder, organizer Sir Harry Secombe Ct. Scanner Pub. Appeal, 1985, Sir Harry Secombe M.R. Scanner Pub. Appeal, 1992. Fellow Coll. Radiologists (London); mem. and hon. sec., Magnetic Resonance Radiologists Assn. (hon. sec., Royal Automobile Club (Pall Mall). Avocations: tennis, motor vehicles, jazz.

TAYLOR, ALAN BROUGHTON, judge; b. Oldbury, Eng., Jan. 23, 1939; s. Valentine James Broughton and Gladys Maud (Williams) T.; m. Diana Hindmarsh, Aug. 15, 1964; children: Stephen James, Robert David. Student, Malvern Coll., Worcester, U.K., 1952-57, Geneva U., 1957; LLB, Birmingham (U.K.) U., 1960; MLitt, Oxford (U.K.) U., 1962. Barrister at law, 1961. Practice bar Birmingham, U.K., 1963-91; cir. judge Crown and County Cts., Birmingham, 1991—; FCIArb, 1994. Contbr.: A Practical Guide to the Care of the Injured, 1964. Baptist. Avocations: philately, fell walking. Office: Cir Adminstrs Office, Priory Cts 33 Bull St, Birmingham B4 6DW, England

TAYLOR, ALLAN RICHARD, retired banker; b. Prince Albert, Sask., Can., Sept. 14, 1932; s. Norman and Anna Lydia (Norbeck) T.; m. Shirley Irene Ruston, Oct. 5, 1957; children: Rodney Allan, Leslie Ann. LLD (hon), U. Regina, Sask., 1987, Concordia U., Montreal, Can., 1988; DBA (hon.), Laval U., Quebec City, Can., 1990; LLD (hon.), Queen's U., Kingston, Ont., 1991; Doctorate of Univ. (hon.), U. Ottawa, 1992. With Royal Bank of Can., Toronto, Ont., Can., 1949-95; pres., COO, dir. Royal Bank of Can., Toronto, 1983-86, chmn., CEO, dir., 1986-94, chmn., 1994-95, ret., 1995; bd. dirs. Royal Bank of Can., Can.-Pacific Ltd., Calgary, Alta., GM Can. Ltd., Oshawa, Ont., Max Bell Found., Calgary, The Can. Ditchley Found., Toronto, Can. Inst. for Advanced Rsch., Toronto, NeuroScience Can. Found., Montreal; mem. adv. coun. Can. Exec. Svc. Overseas; former chmn. Can. Bankers Assn.; past pres. Internat. Monetary Conf. Former chmn. corp. program IMAGINE; mem. adv. bd. Can. Found. AIDS Rsch.; chmn. hon. adv. bd. Can. Assn. for Cmty. Living. Decorated officer Order of Can. Address: 200 Bay St 18th Fl North Tower, Toronto, ON Canada M5J 2J5

TAYLOR, ANGELO, Olympic athlete; b. Albany, Ga., Dec. 28, 1978. Student, Ga. Tech. Champion 400 meter hurdles NCAA Championship, 1998; 2nd place U.S. Championships, 1998; winner 1st nat. title; co-winner Gold Medal 4X400 relay World Championships, 1999; winner Gold Medal 400 meter hurdles Sydney, 2000. ranked no. 3 400 meter hurdles. Office: USA Track and Field Team One RCA Dome Ste 140 Indianapolis IN 46225*

TAYLOR, ANN (WINIFRED), British government minister; b. Motherwell, Scotland, July 2, 1947; m. David Taylor, 1966; 2 children. Past student, U. Bradford, U. Sheffield. Past tchr. Open U.; M.P. Bolton West, 1974-83, Dewsbury, 1987—; parliament pvt. sec. to sec. state edn. and sci., 1975-76, parliament pvt. sec. to sec. state def., 1976-77, asst. govt. whip, 1977-79, opposition spokesman edn., 1979-81, opposition spokesman housing, 1981-83, opposition spokesman home affairs, 1987-92, opposition spokesman environ., 1992-94, opposition spokesman edn., 1992-97; shadow leader House of Commons, 1997—; pres. coun., leader Ho. of Commons, London, 1997-98; spokesperson citizen's charter, 1994-95, parliamentary sec. to the Treasury, govt. chief whip, 1998—; past part-time tutor Open U.; spokesperson citizen's charter, 1994-95; mem. select com. stds. and privileges, 1995-97; chair select com. on modernisation Ho. of Commons, 1997-98. Hon. Fellow Birkbeck Coll., London. Office: Govt Chief Whip, 12 Downing St, London SW1A 2AA, England

TAYLOR, ANTHONY BALDWIN, civil engineer; b. Nassau, Bahamas, Nov. 25, 1971; came to U.S., 1990; s. Anthony Baldwin Sr. and Ruth Inez (McKenzie) T.; m. Kaaryn Wilaine Rogers, July 2, 1994; children: Anthony Baldwin III, Andrew Benjamin. BSCE, N.C. State U., 1994; PhD, Columbia State U., 1997. Owner/engr. TNT Constn., Nassau, 1992-94; constrn. engr. Greenman Pedersen Inc., Durham, N.C., 1994-96; resident engr. Parsons, Butner, N.C., 1996—. Mem. Am. Soc. Civil Engr., Assn. for the advancement of Cost Engring. Avocations: reading, writing, basketball, sport shooting, fishing. Home: 4885 E Wolf Tree Ave Terre Haute IN 47805-9414

TAYLOR, AUBREY ELMO, physiologist, educator; b. El Paso, Tex., June 4, 1933; s. Virgil T. and Mildred (Maher) T.; m. Mary Jane Davis, Apr. 4, 1953; children: Audrey Jane Hildebrand, Lenda Sue Taylor Brown, Mary Ann. BA in Math. and Psychology, Tex. Christian U., 1960; PhD in Physiology, U. Miss., 1964. Fellow biophysics lab. Harvard U. Med. Sch., Boston, 1965-67; from asst. prof. to prof. dept. physiology U. Miss. Coll. Medicine, Jackson, 1967-77; prof., chmn. dept. physiology U. South Ala. Coll. Medicine, Mobile, 1977—; pulmonary score com. Nat. Heart, Lung and Blood Inst., 1976; with Surgery and anesthesiology, 1979-82, and Manpower Com., 1985-95; chmn. RAP, 1983. Author 9 books; contbr. chpts. to books, over 725 articles to profl. jours.; mem. editl. bd. Jour. Applied Physiology, 1984—, Critical Care Medicine, 1991-97; N.Am. editor Clin. Scis., 1998—; mem. editl. bd. Circulation Rsch., Am. Jour. Physiology, Microvascular Rsch., Internat. Pathophysiology, Microcirculatory and Lymphatic Rsch., Microcirculation, Chinese Jour. Physiology, Jour. Biomed. Sci., Am. Rev. Resp. and Critical Care Jour., Internat. Soc. Pathology. With U.S. Army, 1953-55. Grantee NIH, 1967-98; recipient Lederle Faculty award, 1967-70, Philip Dow award U. Ga., 1984, NIH Merit award, 1987-97, Lucian award McGill U., 1988, John Whitney award U. Ark., 1990, Gelen award Intestinal Shock Soc., 1991, Arthur C. Guyton award U. Miss. Coll. Medicine, 1993, Disting. Alumnus award Tex. Christian U., 1998, Disting. Svc. award USA Med. Alumni Assn., 2000; named Disting. Physiologist Am. Coll. Chest Physicians, 1994, Myerson-De Luzio Lectr., Tulane

Sch. Medicine, 1997, Disting. Lectr., La. State U., Shreveport, 1997, Abreu Meml. Keynote Spkr., Med. Student Rsch. Conf., U. Tex. Sch. Medicine, Galveston, 1998, Wu-Ho-Su Meml. Symposium Spl. Lectr.; Louise Lenoir Locke eminent scholar. Fellow AAAS, Am. Heart Assn. (circulation coun., cardiopulmonary and critical care coun. 1977—, chmn. elect, chmn. 1993-98, basic sci. cons. 1998—, So. regional rev. com. 1977-81, chmn. 1979-81, EIA Rev. Com. 1986-95, pulmonary and devel. rev. com. 1987-95, chmn. grant/rev. com. 1994-95, chmn. med. student rsch. award com. 1992-94, nat. rsch. com. 1990-95, coun. affairs com. 1994-98, nominating com. 1998-99, del. assembly 1990-99, Dickinson W. Richards award 1988, Bronze award Miss. AHA 1976, Outstanding Ala. AHA program 1993, Sci. Coun. Achievement award 1995, Rsch. Achievement award 1997, Assn. Dept. Chairs Physiology Svc. award 1995, mem. basic sci. com. 1998, So. Ala. Dist. Achivement award 2000, Gala honoree 2000), Royal Soc. Medicine; mem. NAS (com. for Internat. Union Physiol. Sci.), Am. Physiol. Soc. (hon. com., chmn. 1993-96, coun. 1984-87, chmn. membership com. 1985-87, pres. 1987-90, Wiggers award 1987, chmn. Perkins fellow com. 1996-98), Assn. Dept. Chairs of Physiology (exec. com. 1996—, sec.-treas. 1998—, Cannon lectr. 1999), Microcirculatory Soc (coun. 1977-81, pres. 1981-83, Eugene Landis Rsch. award 1985), Ala. Acad. Scis. (State Rsch. award 1988), Internat. Lymphology Soc., N.Am. Soc. Lymphology (pres. 1988-90, Cecil Drinker Rsch. award 1988), Internat. Pathophysiology Soc. (v.p. 1991-99), N.Y. Acad. Scis., Biophys. Soc., Fedn. Am. Socs. for Exptl. Biology (bd. dirs. 1988-90, reorganizing com.), Am. Thoracic Soc., European Respiratory Soc. (sec. lung injury group), Alpha Omega Alpha, Sigma Xi. Democrat. Presbyterian. Achievements include rsch. in cardio-pulmonary physiology, fluid balance, edema, microcirculation and capillary exchange of solute and water. E-mail: ataylor@jaguard1.unsouthal.edu. Home: 11 Audubon Pl Mobile AL 36606-1907

TAYLOR, BARBARA ANN OLIN, writer, educational consultant; b. St. Louis, Feb. 8, 1933; d. Spencer Truman and Ann Amelia (Whitney) Olin; m. F. Morgan Taylor Jr., Apr. 5, 1954; children: Frederick M. III, Spencer O., James W., John F. AB, Smith Coll., 1954; M of Mgmt., Northwestern U., 1978, PhD, 1984; LHD, U. New Haven, 1995. Mem. faculty Hamden (Conn.) Hall Country Day Sch., 1972-74; cons. Booz, Allen & Hamilton, Inc., Chgo., 1979; program assoc. Northwestern U., Evanston, Ill., 1982; co-founder, exec. dir. Nat. Ctr. Effective Schs. Rsch. & Devel., Okemos, Mich., 1986-89, rsch. assoc., 1987; cons. on effective schs. rsch. and reform Nat. Ctr. Effective Schs. R&D, U. Wis., Madison, 1990-96; pres. Excelsior! Found., Chgo., 1994—; mem. exec. com. Hudson Inst., New Am. Schs. Devel. Corp. Design Team, 1990-94; Danforth Disting. lectr. U. Nebr., Omaha, 1993. Co-author: Making School Reform Happen, 1993, Keepers of the Dream, 1994, The Revolution Revisited: Effective Schools and Systemic Reform, 1995; editor: Case Studies in Effective Schools Research, 1990; contbr. articles to profl. jours. Pres. Jr. League of New Haven, 1967-69; pres. NCCJ, New Haven, 1971-73; co-chair Coalition Housing and Human Resources, Hartford-New Haven, 1970-73; co-chair steering com. Day Care Conn., Hartford, 1971-73; trustee U. New Haven, 1961-71, Smith Coll., Northampton, Mass., 1984-90, Choate Rosemary Hall Sch., 1973-78, Lake Forest Coll., 1996—, Hudson Inst., 1989-97, Northwestern U., 1998—. Recipient Humanitarian award Mt. Calvary Bapt. Ch., 1988, Outstanding Alumna award John Burroughs Sch., 1994, Pres.'s award U. New Haven. Mem. ASCD, Nat. Commn. Citizens Edn. (bd. dirs. 1980-86), Nat. Staff Devel. Coun., Phi Delta Kappa. Episcopalian. Office: Nat Ctr Effective Schs Rsch & Devel 222 E Wisconsin Ave Ste 301 Lake Forest IL 60045-1723

TAYLOR, BRUCE STEVENSON, architect, planner; b. N.Y.C., Sept. 3, 1946; s. James Stevenson and Linnea Sarrah (Hendrickson) T.; m. Sandra Dee Butzman, Oct. 9, 1970; 1 child, Eric Stevenson. BArch, Miami U., Oxford, Ohio, 1969. Registered architect, Mass., Conn., N.H., Vt., Maine, N.Y. Design craftsman Architects Collaborative, Cambridge, Mass., 1969-73; project architect W.M. Design Group, Nahant, Mass., 1973-76; pvt. practice architecture West Newbury, Mass., 1976-78; corp. dir. Claude Miquelle Assocs., Inc., Melrose, Mass., 1978-85; architect, planner Bruce S. Taylor, Architect, West Newbury, 1985—; vis. critic Boston Archtl. Ctr., 1976-77; student counselor Students from Boston Archtl. Ctr., 1980-85. Archtl. projects featured in mags. Bd. dirs. Bd. Health, West Newbury, 1981-83, chmn., 1984-85. Recipient Merit award Builder Mag., 1984, 1st Honor award Soc. Am. Registered Architects, 1984, Grand award Nat. Assn. Home Builders and Better Homes and Gardens, 1984. Mem. Nat. Council Archtl. Registration Bds., AIA, Boston Soc. Architects. Lutheran. Avocations: skiing, fishing, model railroading, historical architecture. Home and Office: 248 Main St West Newbury MA 01985-1414

TAYLOR, BRYAN WILSON, II, computer company executive, educator, consultant; b. Alexandria, La., Apr. 17, 1957; s. Bryan Wilson Taylor and Doris Llewellyn Loftus. BA, Rhodes Coll., 1979; MA, U. S.C., 1981; PhD, Claremont Grad. U., 1986. Asst. prof. Franklin Coll., Lugano, Switzerland, 1985-86, Pitzer Coll., Claremont, Calif., 1986-87, Calif. Poly. U., Pomona, 1987-88, Calif. State U., L.A., 1988-94; pres. Global Fin. Data, L.A., 1995—; cons. The Productivity Ctr., L.A., 1993—, Am. Pacific Bus. Inst., L.A., 1994—. Author: Guide to the Global Financial Database, 1999; contbr. articles to profl. jours. Mem. Internat. Banknote Soc., Am. Econ. Assn. Avocations: banknote collecting, financial history, tennis. E-mail: btaylor@pacifienet.net and btaylor@globalfindata.com. Fax: 323-258-9452. Office: Global Fin Data 784 Fremont Villas St Los Angeles CA 90042-5164

TAYLOR, CAROL ANN, educational administrator; b. Chgo., June 17, 1951; d. Clifford A. and Betty L. Taylor. BS, Evangel Coll., 1973; MA, Assemblies God Sch. Theology, Springfield, Mo., 1978; PhD, Fla. State U., 1987. Tchr. Koraes Greek Orthodox Sch., Chgo., 1973-76; instr. ESL U. Nebr., Omaha, 1978-80; dir. ESL program, tchr. Millard Pub. Schs., Omaha, 1980-83; instr. Fla. State U., Tallahassee, 1983-87; cons. S.E. Multifunctional Resource Ctr., Fla., 1984-87; program rsch. administr. Ednl. Testing Svc., Princeton, N.J., 1998-2000; vice provost for undergrad. edn. Biola U., LaMirada, Calif., 2000—; vis. prof. Ea. Mich. U., Ypsilanti, 1987-88. Contbr. articles to profl. jours. Mem. Com. Nebr. State Dept. Edn., Lincoln, 1981; mem. task force Mich. State Dept. Edn., 1987-88; chair sch. bd. Washington Crossing (Pa.) Christian Sch., 1996-98. Mem. Internat. Lang. Testing Assn., Am. Assn. Applied Linguists, Nat. Coun. Measurment Edn., Tchrs. English Speakers Other Langs., Phi Kappa Phi. Office: Biola U 13800 Biola Ave La Mirada CA 90639

TAYLOR, CHARLES GHANKAY, Liberia government president. Chief procurement officer Govt. of Liberia; with civil insurrection Liberia, 1991-96; pres. Govt. of Liberia, 1996—; mem. Transitional Exec. Coun. of State, Liberia, 1996-97. Mem. Nat. Patriotic Front of Liberia. Office: Coun of State Exec Mansion, PO Box 9001, Monrovia Liberia*

TAYLOR, CHRISTOPHER MALCOLM, mechanical engineer; b. Leeds, U.K., Jan. 15, 1943; s. William and Esther (Hopkinson) T.; m. Gillian Walton, Aug. 31, 1968 (div. Dec. 1985); 1 child, Sarah Jane; m. Diane Shorrocks, July 1, 1994. BSc, London U., 1964; MSc, U. Leeds, 1965, PhD, 1967, D of Engring., 1989. Chartered engr. Rsch. engr. English Electric Co. Ltd., Leicester, Eng., 1964-67; sr. engr. indsl. unit tribology U. Leeds, Eng., 1968-71, lectr., prof. mech. engring., 1971—, dean Faculty of Engring., 1996-97, pro-vice-chancellor, 1997—; cons. many cos.; rschr. in field. Contbr. numerous articles to profl. jours. Recipient Tribology Silver medal Tribology Trust, 1992. Fellow Royal Acad. Engring., Instn. Mech. Engrs. (v.p. 1997, Donald Julius Groen prize 1993), City Inst. London. Avocations: fell walking, cycling. Home: Sunnybank Crag Ln Huby, Leeds LS17 0BW, England Office: Univ Leeds Dept Mech Engrs, Woodhouse Ln, Leeds LS2 9JT, England

TAYLOR, CLIFFORD OTIS, retired principal; b. Ft. Pierce, Fla., Jan. 4, 1926; s. Thomas Archie and Margaret Emeline (Tyler) T.; m. Dorothy Ann Pearce, Dec. 27, 1952. BA, Fla. State U., 1950; MEd, U. Ill., Urbana, 1954; postgrad., U. Miami, Appalachian State U. Cert. tchr., prin. Tchr. Fairlawn Sch., St. Lucie County, Ft. Pierce, North Grade Sch., Palm Beach County Bd. Edn., West Palm Beach, Fla.; prin. South Grade Sch., Palm Beach County Bd. Edn., West Palm Beach, Fla.; prin. Kirklane Elem. Sch., Palm Beach County Bd. Edn., West Palm Beach, Fla., ret., 1991. Hon. mem. state and nat. PTA. With USN, 1944-46. Kirklane Elem. Sch. renamed Clifford O. Taylor/ Kirklane Elem. Sch. in his honor. Mem. ASCD, NAESP, Palm Beach County Prins. Assn., So. Assn. Schs. and Colls., Fla. Assn. Sch. Adminstrs., Retired Educators Assn., Lions, Phi Delta Kappa. Episcopalian. Home: 1811 N J Ter Lake Worth FL 33460-6523

TAYLOR, DAVID MARSHALL, radiotoxicology educator, consultant; b. London, Feb. 5, 1927; s. Frederic and Violet Florence (Beazley) T.; m. Mary Patricia Williamson, Dec. 13, 1952; children: Carolyn Lesley, Sarah Kirsten. BSc with honors, U. Liverpool, Eng., 1952; DSc, U. Liverpool, 1972; PhD, U. London, 1959. Lectr. Inst. of Cancer Rsch., London, 1953-64, sr. lectr., 1964-79; prof. U. Heidelberg, Germany, 1979-92; dir. Inst. Genetics and Toxicology Kernforschungszentrum, Karlsruhe, Germany, 1979-92; biochemist pharm. industry, 1992-93; assoc. sr. lectr. U. Surrey, Guildford, Eng., 1970-79; hon. prof. U. Wales, Cardiff, 1989—; part-time cons. Author: Basic Science of Nuclear Medicine, 1978, 84, Trace Element Medicine Chelation Therapy, 1995; contbr. over 300 articles to jours. in field; editor-in-chief Applied Radiation and Isotopes. Mem. Fed. Reactor Safety Commn., Germany, 1981-86; gov. schs., London, Cardiff, 1969—; mem. Llandaff Diocesan Coun. for Edn., 1993—. Recipient Roentgen prize Brit. Inst. Radiology, 1982, medal Faculty of Medicine, Pilsen, Czech Republic, 1990, Ganguly medal Indian Radiation Protection Assn., 1991. Fellow Royal Soc. Chemistry (chartered chemist), Royal Coll. Pathologists. Anglican. Avocations: travel, reading. Home: 5 Branwen Close, Cardiff CF5 4NE, Wales

TAYLOR, DAVID MATHIESON, microbiologist; b. Edinburgh, Scotland, Jan. 4, 1940; s. John Melville Mathieson and Eliza (Walkingshaw) T.; m. Isabella Hunter Gibson, Apr. 30, 1960; children: Lynne Agnes Marr, John Melville Mathieson, David William Gibson. PhD, Open U., Milton Keynes, Eng., 1983. Technician City Hosp., Edinburgh, 1936-65; sr. technician Royal Infirmary, Edinburgh, 1965-67; from higher rsch. scientist to sr. rsch. scientist Animal Breeding Rsch., Edinburgh, 1967-81; sr. rsch. scientist neuropathogenesis unit SEDECON, Edinburgh, 1981-99, prin. rsch. scientist, 1991—; pvt. cons., 1999—; cons. Ares Serono, Geneva, 1985-87, Microbiol. Assoc., Bethesda, Md., 1991-93. Decorated mem. Order Brit. Empire. Fellow Inst. Biomed. Scis., Inst. Sci. and Tech.; mem. Inst. Biology. Avocations: music, reading. Office: SEDECON 2000, 147 Oxgangs Rd North, Edinburgh EH13 9DX, Scotland

TAYLOR, DEREK EDMUND, business consultant; b. Farnworth, Lancashire, Eng., Nov. 30, 1925; s. John Evans and Mary Jane (Quigley) T.; m. Pamela Margaret Seymour, Sept. 28, 1965; children: Margaret Jane, Kathleen Anne. BSc, London U., 1951. Physicist Imperial Chem. Industries Ltd., Manchester, Eng., 1951-56; sr. scientist Nat. Coal Bd., London, 1956-59; sr. cons. H.B. Maynard Inc., Pitts., 1959-61; mng. dir. English Velvets Ltd., Salford, 1961-64; sr. supervising cons. Coopers & Lybrand Assocs., London, 1965-73; dir. mgmt. and bus. devel. unit Kingston Poly., 1975-90; mng. dir. Derek Taylor Assocs. Ltd., London, 1973—; non-exec. dir. Glaxo Ins., Bermuda, 1986-94, Market Garages Ltd., London, 1965-96; liveryman Bakers Livery Co., 1963—; gov. Benedict First Sch., Mitcham, 1999—. Joint author: New Organizations From Old, 1982, Management Development Through Applied Open Learning, 1989. Mem. Roehampton Club, Royal Wimbledon Golf Club, City Livery Club. Avocations: golf, reading, bridge, music, opera. Home and Office: 37 Edge Hill, London SW19 4NP, England

TAYLOR, DORIS DENICE, physician, entrepreneur; b. Indpls., Sept. 19, 1955; d. Eugene and Mary Catherine (Ryder) T. BA, U. Minn., 1976, cert. behavior analyst, 1977, MD, 1983; BS, Purdue U., 1979. Diplomate Nat. Bd. Med. Examiners. Pvt. practice Locumtenens, 1989—; mng. dir. Sebree-Watkins-Ovbokhan Meml. Cancer Fund, Indpls.; pres., CEO Taylors of Indy Corp., Indpls.; oncologic svcs. cons. and developer. Lange scholar, U. Minn., 1980, Joseph Collins Found. scholar, 1980-81, Nat. Med. Fellowship scholar, 1980-81. Mem. AMA, Am. Soc. for Therapeutic Radiology and Oncology, Am. Soc. Clin. Oncologists. Office: Taylors of Indy Corp 79 Prairiewood Dr Fargo ND 58103-4651

TAYLOR, DOUGLAS HOWARD, translator; b. Washington, Apr. 4, 1961; s. Richard Powell and Barbara Jo Anne (Harris) T. BA, Amherst Coll., 1984; MA, Am. U., 1990, cert. translator. Freelance Russian and French translator Germantown, Md., 1988—; v.p. Taylor Enterprises, Germantown, 1996—. Editor-in-chief Landon News, 1979-80; editor mag. Nat. Soc. for Children of Am. Revolution, 1979-80; contbr. articles to profl. jours. Mem. fin. com. Md. Reagan/Bush Campaign, Potomac, 1984; asst. to chmn. Md. Bush/Quayne Campaign, Bethesda, 1988. Mem. Phi Beta Kappa. Republican. Episcopalian. Avocations: numismatics, bowling, tennis, running, reading. Home and Office: 14914 Spring Meadows Dr Germantown MD 20874-3444

TAYLOR, EDNA JANE, retired employment program counselor; b. Flint, Mich., May 16, 1934; d. Leonard Lee and Wynona Ruth (Davis) Harvey; children: Wynona Jane MacDonald, Cynthia Lee Zellmer. BS, No. Ariz. U., 1963; MEd, U. Ariz., 1967. Tchr. high sch. Sunnyside Sch. Dist., Tucson, 1963-68; employment program counselor employment devel. State of Calif., Canoga Park, 1968-98, ret., 1998. Mem. adv. coun. Van Nuys Cmty. Adult Sch., Calif., 1983-96, steering com., 1989-91, leadership coun., 1991-92; mem. adv. coun. Pierce C.C., Woodland Hills, Calif., 1979-81; first aid instr., recreational leader ARC. Mem. NAFE, Internat. Assn. of Pers. in Employment Security, Calif. Employment Counselors Assn. (state treas. 1978-79, state sec. 1980), Delta Psi Kappa (life). Avocations: writing, tennis, health and fitness, gardening.

TAYLOR, EDWARD MICHAEL, insurance, enterprise risk management consultant; b. Cambridge, Mass., June 26, 1947; s. Edward D. and Rita P. (Collins) T.; children from previous marriage: Philip A., Donandrea M.; m. Leslie Foxen, 1996; children: Erica Arruda, Lindsay Ingraham. BSA, Bentley Coll., Waltham, Mass., 1970. V.p. J.H. Albert Internat. Ins. Advisors, Needham, Mass., 1974-80; prin., exec. v.p. Pine Ins. Agy., Melrose, Mass., 1980-83; pres., chief exec. officer, founder Taylor Risk Mgmt. Assocs., New Bedford, Mass., 1983-92; sr. v.p., prin. cons. Kevin F. Donoghue and Assocs., Boston, 1992-97; practice leader, risk mgmt. cons. PriceWaterhouseCoopers, LLP, Boston, 1997—. 2d lt. USNG, 1971-76. Decorated Internat. Order of Merit; recipient Leadership award for contbns. to risk mgmt. profession. Mem. Internat. Ins. Soc., Soc. Risk Mgmt. Cons., Risk and Ins. Soc. Am., Am. Biog. Inst. (Disting. Leadership award 1988, apptd. hon. mem. rsch. bd. advisors 1988), Am. Arbitration Assn. (appointed to nat. panel of arbitrators), Am. Soc. Safety Engrs., KC (dep. grand knight), Assn. of Contingency Planners, Global Assn. of Risk Profls. Office: PricewaterhouseCoopers LLP 160 Federal St Fl 9 Boston MA 02110-1707

TAYLOR, ELDON, psychological researcher; b. Anchorage, Utah, Jan. 27, 1945; s. Blaine Eldon and Helen Gertrude (George) T.; children: Roy, William, Angela, Eric, Cassandra, Hillarie, Preston. Student, Weber State Coll., Ogden, Utah, 1971-74; BS, MS, DD, U. Metaphysics, L.A., PhD in Pastoral Psychology, 1986; PhD in Clin. Psychology, St. John's U., Springfield, La., 1990; HHD (hon.), Sem. Coll., 1987; PhD in Pastoral Psychology (hon.), World U. Roundtable, Benson, Ariz., 1988. Diplomate Am. Psychotherapy Assn. Dir. Bulwark, Salt Lake City, 1977-84; pres., dir. Progressive Awareness Rsch., Spokane, Wash., 1984—; bd. dirs. World U. Roundtable, Benson, Ariz.; mem. adj. faculty St. John's U., 1989—. Author: Thinking Without Thinking, 1995, Subliminal Communication, 1986, Subliminal Learning, 1988, Simple Things and Simple Thoughts, 1989, Wellness: Just a State of Mind, 1993, Just Be: A Little Cowboy Philosophy, 1997, Subliminal Technology, 1998, Self Empowerment, 1999, others; contbr. numerous articles and poetry to various publs.; author numerous audiocassettes on self-improvement; patentee whole brain info. audio processor. Spiritual advisor Intermountain Hospice Ctr., Salt Lake City, 1987-88; counselor Utah State Prison, Draper, 1986-88; sports motivation trainer U.S. Judo Team, Colorado Springs, Colo., 1989—. Named Ky. Col., State of Ky., 1984; recipient Golden Poet award Am. Poetry Soc., 1985-87. Fellow Nat. Assn. Clergy Hypnotherapists; mem. Am. Psychol. Practitioners Assn., Am. Law Enforcement Officers Assn., Internat. Assn. for Forensic Hypnosis, Am. Counselors Soc., Internat. Soc. Stress Analysts, Am. Assn. Religious Counselors. Avocations: physics, horses. Home: PO Box 13249 Spokane WA 99213-3249 Office: Progressive Awareness Rsch 21203 W Beechwood Rd Medical Lake WA 99022-8630

TAYLOR, ELIZABETH ROSEMOND, actress; b. London, Feb. 27, 1932; d. Francis and Sara (Sothern) T. Student, Byron House, Hawthorne Sch., Metro-Goldwyn-Mayer Sch. Motion pictures include There's One Born Every Minute, 1942, Lassie Come Home, 1943, The White Cliffs of Dover, 1944, Jane Eyre, 1944, National Velvet, 1944, Courage of Lassie, 1946, Cynthia, 1947, Life with Father, 1947, A Date with Judy, 1948, Julia Misbehaves, 1948, Little Women, 1950, Conspirator, 1950, The Big Hangover, 1950 Father of the Bride, 1950, Father's Little Dividend, 1951, A Place in the Sun, 1951, Callaway Went Thataway, 1951, Lover is Better Than Ever, 1952, Ivanhoe, 1952, The Girl Who Had Everything, 1953, Elephant Walk, 1954, Rhapsody, 1954, Beau Brummel, 1954, The Last Time I Saw Paris, 1954, Giant, 1956, Raintree County, 1957, Cat on a Hot Tin Roof, 1958, Suddenly Last Summer, 1959, Scent of Mystery, 1960, Butterfield 8, 1960 (Acad. award best actress), Cleopatra, 1963, The V.I.P.'s, 1963, The Sandpiper, 1965, Who's Afraid of Virginia Woolf?, 1966 (Acad. award best actress), The Taming of the Shrew, 1967, The Comedians, 1967, Reflections in a Golden Eye, 1967, Dr. Faustus, 1967, Boom!, 1968, Secret Ceremony, 1968, The Only Game in Town, 1970, Under Milkwood, 1971, X, Y and Zee, 1972, Hammersmith is Out, 1972, Night Watch, 1973, Ash Wednesday, 1973, That's Entertainment, 1974 (guest star), The Driver's Seat, 1974, Blue Bird, 1975, Winter Kills, 1977, A Little Night Music, 1977, The Mirror Crack'd, 1980, Young Toscanini, 1988, The Flintstones, 1994, The Visit, 1999; TV appearances include Divorce His/Divorce Hers, 1973, Victory at Entebbe, 1977, Return Engagement, 1979, Between Friends, 1982, Hotel (series), 1984, Malice in Wonderland, 1986, North and South (miniseries), 1986, There Must Be a Pony, 1986, Poker Alice, 1987, Sweet Bird of Youth, 1989; theatre appearances in The Little Foxes, 1981 (Broadway debut), Private Lives, 1983; narrator film documentary Genocide, 1981; author: (with Richard Burton) World Enough and Time, poetry reading, 1964, Elizabet Taylor, 1965, Elizabeth Taylor Takes Off: On Weight Gain, Weight Loss, Self Esteem and Self Image, 1988; lics. (fragrances) Elizabeth Taylor's Passion, Passion for Men, White Diamonds/Elizabeth Taylor, Elizabeth Taylor's Diamonds & Emeralds, Diamonds and Rubies, Diamonds & Sapphires, Elizabeth Taylor Black Pearls. Active philanthropic, relief, charitable causes internationally, including Israeli War Victims Fund for the Chaim Sheba Hosp., 1976, UNICEF, Variety Children's Hosps., med. clinics in Botswana; initiated Ben Gurion U.-Elizabeth Taylor Fund for Children of the Negev, 1982; supporter AIDS Project L.A., 1985; founder, nat. chmn. Am. Found. for AIDS Rsch. (AmFAR), 1985—, internat. fund, 1985—; founder Elizabeth Taylor AIDS Found., 1991—. Named Comdr. Arts Letters (France), 1985; recipient Legion of Honor (France), 1987 (for work with AmFAR), Aristotle S. Onassis Found. award, 1988, Jean Hersholt Humanitarian Academy award, 1993 (for work as AIDS advocate), Life Achievement award Am. Film Inst., 1993; honored with dedication of Elizabeth Taylor Med. Ctr. Whitman-Walker Clinic, Washington, 1993.

TAYLOR, FRANK EDWARD, forensic computer and communication consultant; b. Risley, Lancashire, Eng., Jan. 22, 1936; s. John and Hilda (Hughes) T.; m. Ann Horsfield, Apr. 2, 1966; children: Jane M. Crook, Sarah Ann Toulmin. BSc, U. Manchester, Eng., 1956, MSc, 1958; PhD, U. Durham, Eng., 1961. Chartered engr., U.K. Rsch. engr. Ferranti Ltd., Manchester and Bracknell, Eng., 1961-63, computer design engr., 1963-64; applications cons. Internat. Sys. Control, Wembley, Eng., 1964-67; dep. prin. cons. Nat. Computing Ctr., Eng., 1967-78; prin. cons. Sys. Tech. Consultants, Knutsford, Eng., 1978—; sales dir. Microtech, Knutsford, 1979-96; hon. prof. computer sci. U. Hull, 1996—; chmn., pres. Nat. Computer Users' Forum, U.K., 1984-91; spkr. in field. Author: Teleprocessing Monitor Packages, 1978; co-author: Why Distributed Computing?, 1976; patentee in field. Fellow Brit. Computer Soc. (founder chmn. security com. 1977-92, coun. mem. 1971-74, 77-84); mem. Instn. Elec. Engrs. (assoc.), Brit. Stds. Instn. (founder chmn. com. on open sys. interconnection 1975-81), Confedn. European Computer Users (EC adv. com. 1986-88). Anglican. E-mail: 100334.72@compuserve.com. Office: Sys Tech Cons, PO Box 5, Knutsford WA16 9GA, England

TAYLOR, FRANK HENRY, accountant; b. Weymouth, Dorset, England, Oct. 10, 1907; s. George Henry and Emma Rebecca (Hodder) T.; m. Dora Margaret Mackay, 1936 (dec. 1944); 1 child; m. Mabel Hills, Nov. 15, 1948 (dec. 1974); 2 children; m. Glenys Mary Edwards, Jan. 28, 1978. Grad., Rutlish Sch., Merton, London, 1925. Prin. Frank H. Taylor Chartered Accts., London, 1930—; fin. dir. Ministry of Food, 1942-44, Ministry of War Transport, 1944-47. Author: (autobiography) Called to Account, 1993. Gov. Rutlish Sch., 1946-84; MP Moss Side, Manchester, 1961-74. Lt. col. Home Guard, 1943-45. Fellow Inst. Chartered Accts., Chartered Inst. Secs.; mem. Royal Automobile Club (golf capt. 1961), City Livery Club, Worshipful Co. of Bakers (master 1981), Ct. of Co. of World Traders, Dinosaurs Club Ho. of Lords. Anglican. Avocations: Surrey County rugby, sculling (Thames championship), punting (Thames championships). Home: 4 Barrie House, Lancaster Gate, London W2 3QJ, England

TAYLOR, FREDERICK WILLIAM, JR. (FRITZ TAYLOR), lawyer; b. Cleve., Oct. 21, 1933; s. Frederick William Sr. and Marguerite Elizabeth (Kistler) T.; m. Mary Phyllis Osborne, June 1, 1985. BA in History, U. Fla., 1957; MA in Near East Studies, U. Mich., 1959; JD cum laude, NYU, 1967. Bar: N.Y. 1968, Calif. 1969, U.S. Dist. Ct. (cen. dist.) Calif. 1969. Govt. rels. rep. Arabian Am. Oil Co., Dhahran, Saudi Arabia, 1959-63; oil supply coord. Arabian Am. Oil Co., N.Y.C., 1963-68; sr. counsel Arabian Am. Oil Co., Dhahran, 1969-71, gen. mgr. govt. rels. orgn., 1971-74, v.p. indsl. rels., 1974-78; assoc. O'Melveny & Myers, L.A., 1968-69; ptnr. Burt & Taylor, Marblehead, Mass., 1978-80; pres., chief exec. officer Nat. Med. Enterprises Internat. Group, L.A., 1980-82; counsel Chadbourne, Parke & Afridi, United Arab Emirates, 1982-84; ptnr. Sidley & Austin, Cairo, 1984-87, Singapore, 1987-93; spl. counsel Heller Ehrman White & McAuliffe, L.A. and Singapore, 1993-95; legal advisor, corp. counsel law divsn. Lucent Techs. Internat. Inc., Riyadh, Saudi Arabia, 1995—. Contbr. articles to profl. jours. Mem. ABA, Calif. Bar Assn., Order of Coif, Singapore Cricket Club, Tanglin Club, Changi Sailing Club, Singapore Am. Club, Dirab Golf Club. Home: 9875 E Shadowlake Ct Claremore OK 74017-1444 Office: Lucent Techs Int Inc, PO Box 4945 Khurais Rd, Riyadh 11412, Saudi Arabia

TAYLOR, FREDRIC WILLIAM, physicist; b. Amble, Eng., Sept. 24, 1944; s. William and Ena Lloyd (Burns) T.; m. Doris Jean Buer, June 28, 1969. BSc, Liverpool U., 1966; PhD, Oxford U., 1970. Staff scientist Jet Propulsion Lab. Calif. Tech. U., Pasadena, 1970-79; head Atmospheric, Oceanic and Planetary Physics Dept. Oxford (U.K.) U., 1979—; disting. vis. scientist Jet Propulsion Lab., 1996—. Author: Cambridge Atlas of Planets, 1986, Remote Sensing of Atmospheres, 1984; editor: Planetary and Space Sci. Jour., 1992—; patentee in field. Recipient Rank prize Rank Found., 1990, prize Sci. Instrument Makers Guild, 1991. Fellow Royal Meteorol. Soc., Royal Astron. Soc. Achievements include notable findings concerning atmospheres of earth and planets, using innovative experiments on satellite and space probes. Office: U Oxford Dept Physics, Clarendon Lab, Oxford OX1 3PU, England

TAYLOR, GAGE, artist, writer; b. Ft. Worth, Jan. 20, 1942. BFA, U. Tex., 1965; MFA, Mich. State U., 1967. Author, illustrator: Bears at Work, 1995; writer, composer CD ROM: Bears at Work, 1996; exhibited in group shows at Rosicrucian/Egyptian Mus., San Jose, Calif., 1993, U.S. State Dept. Caribbean Tour, 1987, Oakland Mus., 1985, Ortona, Italy, 1981, India Triennale, 1978, Huntsville Mus. of Fine Art, 1977, San Francisco Mus. Modern Art, 1976, Nat. Collection of Fine Art, Washington, 1976, Mus. Contemporary Art, Chgo., 1976, Paris Biennale, 1975, Whitney Mus., N.Y.C., 1973. Avocations: music composition and playing. Home: PO Box 2163 Sausalito CA 94966-2163

TAYLOR, GEORGE ALLEN, advertising agency executive; b. Lake City, Iowa, Oct. 26, 1906; s. Bertrand Franklin and Mabel (Minard) T.; m. Regina Helen Wickland, July 3, 1938 (div. 1956). PhB in Fine Arts, Northwestern U., 1947, MEd, 1951, postgrad., 1951-54; art edn. diploma, U. No. Iowa, 1926. Art supr. pub. schs. Indianola, Iowa, 1926-29; instr. art Simpson Coll., Indianola, 1926-29; designer Modern Art Studios, Chgo., 1929-30; display designer W.J. Rankin Corp., Chgo., 1930-35; creative dir. Arthur Meyerhoff Assocs., Inc., Milw., 1935-38; br. mgr. Arthur Meyerhoff Assocs., Inc., L.A., 1938-42; account exec. Arthur Meyerhoff Assocs., Inc., Chgo., 1942-59, account supr., 1959-61, v.p. adminstrn., 1961-65, vice chmn., 1965-80; pres. GATA Ltd.; lectr. semantics Ill. Inst. Tech., Chgo., 1947-50, Northwestern U. Sch. Commerce, 1948. Lyricist popular songs. Reader Recs. for Blind, Inc., 1956-94, CRIS Radio, 1981-85; mem. Chgo. Architec-

ture Found., Landmarks Preservation Coun. Ill. Recipient 1st place awards in copy and layout L.A. Advt. Club, 1940. Mem. AAAS, Friends of Downtown, Art Inst. Chgo. Home: Apt 29A-South 1212 N Lake Shore Dr Chicago IL 60610-2371 also: 4767 Ocean Blvd Apt 201 San Diego CA 92109-2475

TAYLOR, IRVING, surgeon, educator; b. Leeds, Eng., Jan. 7, 1945; s. Sam and Fay (Valkovich) T.; m. Berenice Penelope Brunner, July 31, 1969; children: Justine Samantha, Tamara Zoe, Gabrielle Rivka. MB ChB, U. Sheffield, Eng., 1968, MD, 1973, ChM, 1978; FMed Sci., 2000. Sr. registrar Sheffield Hosps., 1973-77; sr. lectr., cons. surgeon U. Liverpool, 1977-81; prof. surgery, head dept. surgery U. Southampton, 1981-93, U. Coll., London, 1993—. Author: Complications of Lower Gastrointestinal Surgery, 1985; editor: Progress in Surgery, Vol. 1, 1984, Vol. 2, 1986, Vol. 3, 1987, Recent Advances in Surgery, Vol. 14, 1989, Vol. 15, 1991, Vol. 16, 1993, Vol. 17, 1995, Vol. 18, 1996, Vol. 19, 1997, Vol. 20, 1997, Vol. 21, 1998, Vol. 22, 1999, Vol. 23, 2000, Surgical Principles, 1996, Essential General Surgical Oncology, 1996, editor European Jour. Surg. Oncology. Fellow Royal Coll. Surgeons (examiner); mem. Surg. Rsch. Soc. (sec. 1986-88), Assn. Surgeons (editl. sec. 1986-91), Assn. Profs. Surgery (sec. 1987-90, editor-in-chief European Jour. Surg. Oncology), Brit. Assn. Surg. Oncology (pres.). Avocations: swimming, tennis, golf, theatre. Office: U Coll London Dept Surgery, 67-73 Riding House St, London W1P 7LD, England

TAYLOR, JAMES FRANCIS NUTTALL, pediatric cardiologist; b. Singapore, Oct. 19, 1938; arrived in Eng., 1945; s. Evan Nuttall and Margaret Susie (Howes) T.; m. Ann Ensor, Sept. 18, 1965; children: Jonathan, Andrew, Richard, Michael. BA, Cambridge (Eng.) U., 1959, MBChir, 1962, MA, 1964, MD, 1976. House officer Burton-on-Trent Gen. Hosp., 1962-65; jr. med. staff St. Thomas' Hosp., London, 1965-66; research fellow Yale U. Sch. of Med., New Haven, Conn., U.S.A., 1971-72; jr. med. staff Hosp. for Sick Children, London, 1966-71, research fellow, 1972-75, paediatric cardiologist, 1975—; sr. lectr. Inst. Child Health, London, 1975. Mem. editorial bd. Brit. Heart Jour., 1972-78, Archives Disease in Childhood, 1978-91; joint editor Pediatric Cardiology, 1990-91, editor, 1991-99; contbr. articles on congenital heart disease to med. jours. Decorated knight Order of Falcon (Iceland). Fellow Royal Coll. Physicians (London), Royal Coll. Pediats. and Child Health (London), Am. Coll. Cardiology, European Soc. Cardiology, Brit. Cardiac Soc., Assn. European Paediatric Cardiologists, Royal Soc. Medicine. Anglican. Avocations: photography, walking, museums, music. Office: Hosp for Sick Children, Cardiac Wing / Great Ormond St, London WC1N 3JH, England

TAYLOR, JANE ELLEN, elementary educator; b. Port Clinton, Ohio, Feb. 2, 1955; d. Santo Thomas and Martha Zelma (Finefrock) Cipti; m. William Michael Taylor, Apr. 30, 1976; children: Aaron, Molly. BS in Edn., Ohio State U., 1979; MEd in Curriculum and Instrn., Ashland U., 1995. Paralegal cert. Am. Paralegal Assn. Mid. sch. team leader Discovery Sch., Mansfield, Ohio, 1979-82; tchr. 3rd/4th grade St. Edward's Sch., Ashland, Ohio, 1984-86; tchr. 4th grade St. Joseph's Sch., Libertyville, Ill., 1987-88; tchr. 2nd grade South Jordan (Utah) Elem. Sch., 1990-91; tchr. 1st grade Bataan Elem. Sch., Port Clinton, 1995-96, tchr. 2nd grade intervention class, 1996—, tchr. 3rd grade, 1997-98, tchr. 1st grade, 1998-99, tchr. 2nd grade, 1999—; com. mem. Blue Ribon Com., Port Clinton, 1996—. Author: Mrs. T. and the Can-Do Kids, 1997. Active Bataan Parent/Tchr. Orgn., Bataan Sch., 1997—. Recipient Wal-Mart Tchr. of the Yr. award, 1997. Mem. Future Educators Am. (co-advisor 1996—), Port Clinton Athletic Boosters, Port Clinton Music Boosters, Port Clinton Acad. Boosters. Republican. Roman Catholic. Avocations: reading, swimming, computers, home decorating, family activities. Office: Bataan Elem W 6th St Port Clinton OH 43452

TAYLOR, JOB, III, lawyer; b. N.Y.C., Feb. 18, 1942; s. Job II and Anne Harrison (Flinchbaugh) T.; m. Mary C. August, Oct. 24, 1964 (div. 1978); children: Whitney August, Job IV; m. Sally Lawson, May 31, 1980; 1 child, Alexandra Anne. BA, Washington & Jefferson Coll., 1964; JD, Coll. William and Mary, 1971. Bar: N.Y. 1972, U.S. Dist. Ct. (no., so. ea. and we. dists.) N.Y. 1973, U.S. Ct. Appeals (2d cir.) 1973, U.S. Ct. Claims 1974, U.S. Tax Ct. 1974, U.S. Supreme Ct. 1975, U.S. Ct. Appeals (9th cir.) 1976, U.S. Ct. Mil. Appeals 1977, U.S. Ct. Appeals (D.C. and 10th cirs.) 1977, D.C. 1981, U.S. Ct. Internat. Trade 1981, U.S. Ct. Appeals (fed. cir.) 1982, U.S. Dist. Ct. (no. dist.) Calif. 1983, U.S. Ct. Appeals (6th cir.) U.S. Dist. Ct., 1987, U.S. Ct. Appeals (3d cir.) 1990, U.S. Dist. Ct. Conn. 1996. Ptnr. Olwine, Connelly, Chase, O'Donnell & Weyher, N.Y.C., 1971-85, Latham & Watkins, N.Y.C., 1985—. Served to lt. USN, 1964-68. Mem. ABA, Assn. Bar City N.Y., La Confrerie des Chevaliers du Tastevin, Racquet and Tennis Club, Wee Burn Country Club (Darien, Conn.), New Canaan Country Club. Republican. Episcopalian. Avocations: squash, tennis, golf, reading. Office: Latham & Watkins 885 3rd Ave Fl 9 New York NY 10022-4834

TAYLOR, JOHN CALVIN, missionary, dentist; b. Cin., July 22, 1914; s. John Calvin Taylor V and Magdala Elizabeth Siehl; m. Adah Packard Boggs, Mar. 7, 1941; children: Sarah, Margaret, Virginia, John, Frederick, Alison, Carla. BSc, Muskingum Coll., 1937; BD, Xenia Theol. Sch., 1939; DDS, U. Pitts., 1949; cert. excellence in Hindi and Urdu, Lang. Sch., Landour, India, 1940, 41. Diploma Acad. Gen. Dentistry. Missionary Reformed Presbyn. Synod, Roorkee, India, 1939-46; moderator, pastor Reformed Presbyn., Pitts., Fairview, Pa., 1946-47; nat. missions missionary Presbyn. Bd. Home Missions, Pitts., Tyre, Pa., 1947-52; missionary dentist United Presbyn., Pitts., Seattle, 1953-59; dir. Dental Clinic Meth. Mission Hosp., Bariely, India, 1954-55; founder Dental Clinic Landour Cmty. Hosp., Mussoorie, India, 1955-59; pres. Rotary Club Internat., Mount Union, Pa., 1964-65; founder Dental Clinic Shanta Bhawan Hosp., Katmandu, Nepal, 1968; dental missionary Missionary Dentist, Inc.-E.L.W.A. Hosp., Liberia, 1977; dental missionary Missionary Dentist, Inc., Pakistan, 1980-81, Shell, Equador, 1983; dentist Dental Care, India, 1984—; founder Oral Clinic Ctr., Dera Dun, India, 1981—; tchr. emergency dentistry Vellore (India) Med. Coll., 1958; free dentist, India, 1984—; dentist Youth With a Mission, Mercy Ship, Hawaii, 1985. Author: Wildlife in India's Tiger Kingdom, 1980, Face the Devil's Roar, 1995. Co-founder, life mem. Wildlife Preservation Soc., Dehra-Dun, India, 1954—, organizer, founder Rajpur Wildlife Park, 1954—. Mem. ADA (hon., life), Herminie Lions Club (fgn. chmn. 1988—, Lions Hat award 1993), N.Am. Hunting Club, NRA. Republican. Presbyterian. Avocations: zoology, hunting, taxidermy, photography, music. E-mail: pcrooke@westol.com. Home: 110 Highland Ave Herminie PA 15637-1310

TAYLOR, JOHN MICHAEL, research director; b. Birmingham, Eng., Feb. 15, 1943; s. Eric John and Dorothy Irene T.; m. Judith Moyle, 1965; children: Michael James, Miranda Elizabeth, David Charles, Lydia Jane. MA, U. Cambridge, U.K., 1965, PhD, 1969. Rsch. engr. Gen. Electric Co., London, 1965-66; sr. sci. officer Signals R & D Establishment, Christchurch, U.K., 1969-77; head divsn. Royal Signals and Radar Establishment, Malvern, U.K., 1978-80; head divsn. Admiralty Surface Weapons Establishment, Portsmouth, U.K., 1980-81, head dept., 1982-84; lab. dir. Hewlett Packard Labs., Bristol, U.K., 1984-86, dir., 1986-98; exec. dir. Hewlett Packard Ltd., U.K., 1992-98; dir. gen. rsch. couns. Office of Sci. and Tech., U.K. DTI, 1999—; vis. prof. Bristol U., 1986—, Imperial Coll., London U., 1990—. Contbr. articles to profl. jours.; patentee in field. Fellow Royal Soc., U.K. Instn. Elec. Engrs. (pres. 1998-99), Brit. Computer Soc., Royal Soc. Arts, Royal Acad. Engring. Avocations: family, sailing, photography, theatre. Office: OST, Albany House, 94-98 Petty France, London SW1 9ST, England

TAYLOR, JOHN PATRICK, controller; b. Waterburgy, Conn., Mar. 17, 1964; s. Robert John and Natalie Ann T.; m. Diane Zoeller, Oct. 13, 1990; 1 child, Sydney May. BS in Acctg., Ctrl. Conn. Univ., New Britain, 1987. Sr. acct. John Garrity CPA, Prospect, Conn., 1986-91, Early Learning Ctr., Milford, Conn., 1991-92; mgr. acctg. TechnoSvc., Inc., Norwalk, Conn., 1992-96; contr. new bus. TechnoSvc., Inc., Norwalk, 1997—; contr. Milkron Corp. USA, Monroe, 1996-97.

TAYLOR, JOHN READ, JR., financial management company executive; b. N.Y.C., July 16, 1943; s. John Read and Patricia (Green) T.; m. Sandra Shackelford Brown, June 28, 1969 (div. 1988); 1 child, Louise Tiffany; m. Joyce Manis, Jan. 28, 1989; 1 child, John Read III. AB, Princeton U., 1966; postgrad. in polit. sci., U. N.C., 1966-69. Asst. mgr. Chem. Bank, N.Y.C., 1969-73; asst. v.p. First Nat. Bank Chgo., 1973-74; v.p. Citibank, N.Y.C., 1974-78, Gesellschaft fur Trendanalysen, N.Y.C., 1978-79; pres. EMCOR Mgmt., N.Y.C., 1979-81; chmn. FX Concepts, Inc., N.Y.C., 1981—; chmn. J3 Biologics, Inc., N.Y.C., 1992-98, U.S. Transgenics, Inc., 1999—. Bd. dirs. Franklin Coll. Switzerland, Lugano, 1975—, chmn., 1980-90, vice chmn. 1995—; bd. dirs. Hemophilia Assn. N.Y., 1990—; chmn. Coalition for Hemophilia B, N.Y., 1990—. Home: 45 E 89th St New York NY 10128-1251 Office: FX Concepts Inc 225 W 34th St Ste 710 New York NY 10122-0710

TAYLOR, JOSEPH HOOTON, JR., radio astronomer, physicist; b. Phila., Mar. 29, 1941; s. Joseph Hooton and Sylvia Hathaway (Evans) T.; m. Marietta Bisson, Jan. 3, 1976; children: Jeffrey, Rebecca, Anne-Marie. BA in Physics, Haverford Coll., 1963; PhD in Astronomy, Harvard U., 1968; DSc (hon., U. Chgo., 1985, U. Mass., 1994. Research fellow, lectr. Harvard U., 1968-69; asst. prof. astronomy U. Mass., Amherst, 1969-72; assoc. prof. U. Mass., 1973-77, prof., 1977-81; prof. physics Princeton U., 1980—, James McDonnell Disting. prof. physics, 1986—, dean of faculty, 1997—. Author: Pulsars, 1977. Recipient Dannie Heineman prize in astrophysics Am. Inst. Physics/Am. Astron. Soc., 1980, Tomalla Found. prize in gravitation and cosmology, 1985, Magellanic Premium award Am. Philos. Soc., 1990, Einstein prize laureate Albert Einstein Soc., 1991, Wolf Prize in Physics, Wolf Found., 1992, Nobel Prize in Physics, Nobel Foundation, 1993; MacArthur fellow, 1981. Fellow Am. Acad. Arts and Scis., Am. Phys. Soc.; mem. NAS (Henry Draper medal 1985, John J. Carty medal Advancement Sci. 1991), Am. Philos. Soc., Am. Astron. Soc., Internat. Sci. Radio Union, Internat. Astron. Union. Mem. Soc. of Friends. Home: 272 Hartley Ave Princeton NJ 08540-5656 Office: Princeton U Dept Physics 215 Jadwin Hall PO Box 708 Princeton NJ 08544-0001

TAYLOR, KENDRICK JAY, microbiologist; b. Manhattan, Mont., Mar. 17, 1914; s. William Henry and Rose (Carney) T.; m. Hazel Marguerite Griffith, July 28, 1945; children: Stanley, Paul (dec.), Richard. BS, Mont. State U., 1938; postgrad. (fellow), U. Wash., 1938-41, U. Calif., Berkeley, 1952, Drama Studio of London, 1985. Rsch. microbiologist Cutter Labs., Berkeley, Calif., 1945-74; microbiologist Berkeley Biologicals, 1975-86. Committeeman Mount Diablo coun. Boy Scouts Am., 1955, dist. vice-chmn., 1960-61, dist. chmn., 1962-65, cubmaster, 1957, scoutmaster, 1966; active Contact Ministries, 1977-80; bd. dirs. Santa Clara Cmty. Players, 1980-84; vol. instr. ESL, 1979-80; vol. ARC Blood Ctr., 1985-96, VA Hosp., 1986-96, San Jose; life mem. PTA; census taker, 1980; mem. Berkely Jr. C. of C., 1946-49. With AUS, 1941-46, lt. col. Res., ret. Recipient Scout's Wood badge Boy Scouts Am., 1962, Golden Diploma Mont. State U., 1988, Silver Diploma, 1998. Mem. Am. Soc. Microbiology (chmn. local com. 1953, v.p. No. Calif. br. 1963-65, pres. 1965-67), Sons and Daus. Mont. Pioneers, Mont. State U. Alumni Assn., Mont. Hist. Soc., Gallatin County Hist. Soc., Headwaters-Heritage Hist. Soc., Am. Legion (post 89), PTA Calif. (life). Presbyterian (trustee 1951-53, elder 1954—). Home: 550 S 13th St San Jose CA 95112-2361

TAYLOR, LAWRENCE DOW, geologist, educator; b. Boston, Oct. 6, 1932; s. Theodore and Dorothea Mae (Dow) T.; m. Jean Ann Ryland, Sept. 24, 1955; children: Charles, Keith. AB, Dartmouth Coll., 1954, MA, 1958; PhD, Ohio State U., 1962. Geologist geophysics br. U.S. Geol. Survey, Boston, and Greenland, 1954-55; geologist fuels br. U.S. Geol. Survey, Denver, 1958; rsch. assoc. Dartmouth Coll., Hanover, N.H., and Greenland, 1957-58; rsch. assoc. Ohio State U. Inst. Polar Studies, Columbus, Ohio, and Antarctica, 1962-63, Glacier Bay, Alaska, 1959-60; asst. prof. Coll. of Wooster, Ohio, 1963-64; asst. prof. Albion (Mich.) Coll., 1964-68, assoc. prof., 1968-77, prof., 1977-98, prof. emeritus, 1998—, chair dept. geol. scis., 1968-85; chief glaciologist Trans-Antarctic Traverse, NSF, U.S. Antarctic Rsch. Program, 1962-63. Contbr. articles to profl. jours. With U.S. Army, 1955-57. Grantee NSF, 1960, 62-63, 65, 69, Hewlett Melon Found., 1981, Pew Sci. Program, 1991, Albion Coll., 1992-97; recipient Exemplary Tchr. award United Meth. Ch., 1997, Antarctic Svc. Congl. medal; Taylor Hills, Antarctica, named in his honor. Fellow Geol. Soc. Am., Am. Quaternary Assn., Am. Geophys. Union, Nat. Assn. Geology Tchrs. (pres. East Ctrl. sect. 1984-85), Explorers Club, Rotary, Sigma Xi. Avocations: mountain climbing, backpacking, cross country skiing, tennis. Office: Albion Coll Dept Geol Scis Albion MI 49224

TAYLOR, LESLIE GEORGE, mining and financial company executive; b. London, Oct. 8, 1922; came to U.S., 1925; s. Charles Henry and Florence Louisa (Renouf) T.; m. Monique S. Schuster, May, 1964 (div. 1974); children: Leslie G. Anthony II, Sandra J. Mira, Linda S. Marshall; m. Wendy Ann Ward, July 4, 1979. BBA, U. Buffalo, 1952. Asst. to pres. Kelsey Co., 1952-60; pres. Aluminum Industries and Glen Alden Co., Cin. and N.Y.C., 1960-63; pres., chmn. bd. dirs. DC Internat. (and European subs.), Denver, 1963-68; prin. Taylor Energy Enterprises, Denver, 1968—, Taylor Mining Enterprises, Denver, 1968—, Leslie G. Taylor and Co., Denver, 1968—; del. Internat. Astronautical Soc., Stockholm, 1968, London, 1969, Speditur Conv., 1976; bd. dirs. AlFresh Foods, Ft. Lauderdale, Fla., Merendon Mining Internat., Calgary, Alta., MicroStockSearch.com, Vancouver, Can. Zinc Co., Vancouver; sr. advisor Voice Mobility, Inc., Richmond, B.C., Can. Mem. USCG Aux. Mem. Soc. Automotive Engrs., Shriners, Masons, Scottish Rites. Republican. Episcopalian. Fax: 541-956-9699. Office: Voice Mobility Inc, 13777 Commerce Pkwy, Richmond, BC Canada V6V 2X3

TAYLOR, LEWIS JEROME, JR., priest; b. Norfolk, Va., Feb. 22, 1923; s. Lewis Jerome and Roberta Page (Newton) T.; m. Pauline Rector Green, Nov. 24, 1945; children: Lewis J. III, Michael R., John B., Mary F., Joan E. BS in Engring., U.S. Naval Acad., 1944; MDiv, Seabury-Western Theol. Sem., Evanston, Ill., 1961; PhD in Religion, Duke U., 1972. Ordained priest Episcopal Ch., 1962. With George R. Green, Inc., White Post, Va., 1949-52, Travelers Ins. Co., Norfolk, 1956-58; chaplain Coll. William and Mary, Williamsburg, Va., 1961-63; rector St. Aidan's Episc. Ch., Virginia Beach, Va., 1963-68; prof. theology St. Andrews Sem., Manila, The Philippines, 1971-76; rector Ch. of the Messiah, Chester, N.J., 1978-86; interim rector of various parishes Diocese of Southern Va., 1986-93; instnl. chaplain Indian Creek Correctional Ctr., Chesapeake, Va., 1993-98; mem. Dept. Missions Diocese of Newark, 1965-68, Commn. on Ministry, Newark, 1979-82; dean Lay Sch. of Christian Studies, Newark, 1977-82; chmn. Commn. on Racism, Southern Va., 1992-95. Author: In Search of Self: Life, Death, and Walker Percy, 1985; contbr. articles to profl. jours. Bd. dirs. Samaritan House, Virginia Beach, 1995—. Comdr. USN, 1944-49, 52-56; PTO. Trinity Inst. grantee, 1986. Mem. Rotary (pres. 1980-86). Democrat. Avocations: tennis, camping, reading.

TAYLOR, MARGARET CAROL, social studies educator; b. Carshalton, Surrey, Eng., Nov. 3, 1936; d. Albert William and Ellen (Hughes-Jones) Maynard; m. John Bernard Taylor, Aug. 18, 1962; children: Matthew, Stephen, Eleanor. BA with honors, Bedford Coll., U. London, 1958; Post-grad. Cert. Secondary Edn., Hughes Hall, U. Cambridge, Eng., 1959. Asst. history tchr. Chislehurst (Eng.) Girls Grammar Sch., 1959-62; English and Latin tchr. H.S. of Montreal, 1962-64; sr. history tchr. Coll. du Leman, Geneva, Switzerland, 1976-78, head social studies dept., 1978—; mem. adv. bd. Model UN, The Hague, Netherlands, 1990—; mem. social studies com. European Coun. Internat. Schs., 1982-88, chmn., 1990-94. Mem. Hist. Assn. Great Britain. Anglican. Avocations: travel, mountain walking, cross-country skiing, opera, music. Home: L'Echappee, St Cergue, Vaud CH 1264, Switzerland Office: Coll du Leman, Rte de Sauverny, Versoix, Geneva 1290, Switzerland

TAYLOR, MARGARET TURNER, clothing designer, architectural designer, economist, writer, planner; b. Wilmington, N.C., May 7, 1944. A.B. in Econs., Smith Coll., 1966; M.A. in Econ. History, U. Pa., 1970, now Ph.D. candidate in City and Regional Planning. Tchr. Jefferson Jr. High Sch., New Orleans, 1966-69; instr. econs. U. Tex.-El Paso, 1974-75; adj. prof. econs., Salisbury State U., Md., 1976-78; prin. mgr., designer Margaret Norriss, women's clothing, Salisbury, Md., 1980-95; owner Functional Design Ideas, Inc., 1995—; planner at Wharton Ctr. Applied Research, Phila., 1985-86; planning cons., writer.

TAYLOR, MARGARET WISCHMEYER, retired English language and journalism educator; b. Terre Haute, Ind., Aug. 5, 1920; d. Carl and Grace (Riehle) Wischmeyer; m. John Edward Taylor, Sept. 5, 1942 (dec. 1988); children: Deborah Ann, Tobin Edward, Mary Leesa. BA magna cum laude, Duke U., Durham, 1941; MA, John Carroll U., Cleve., 1973. Feature writer Dayton Daily News, Dayton, 1945-53; freelance writer Cleve., 1953—; asst. to Dr. Joseph B. Rhine Duke U. Parapsychology Lab., Durham, 1941; asst. prof. English and journalism Ea. Campus, Cuyahoga C.C., Cleve., 1973-92, prof. emeritus, 1992—, advisor campus newspaper, 1973-84, dir. Writers Conf., 1975-90; writing cons., editor various cos. and pubs., Cleve., 1973—; founder, operator Grammar Hot Line, 1987-92. Author: Crystal Lake Reflections, 1985, English 101 Can Be Fun, 1991, The Basic English Handbook, 1995. Recipient top state honors Ohio Newspaper Women's Assn., 1947, award for best edn1., best overall stories Am. Heart Assn., 1970, Besse award for tchg. excellence, 1980, Profl. Excellence award, 1985, Provost's Pride award, 1987, Nat. Tchg. Excellence award Coun. for Advancement and Support of Edn., 1989; named Ohio Outstanding Citizen, Ohio Ho. Reps., 1987, 89, Innovator of Yr., League for Innovations in C.C.s, 1988, Pres.'s award Cuyahoga C.C., 1992. Mem. Mensa, Phi Beta Kappa, Pi Beta Phi. Presbyterian. Avocations: tennis, reading, writing. Home: 27900 Fairmount Blvd Cleveland OH 44124-4616

TAYLOR, MARTIN GIBBESON, accountant; b. Jan. 30, 1935; s. Roy G. and Vera Constance (Farmer) T.; m. Gunilla Chaterina Bryner, 1960; 2 children. MA, St. Catharine's Coll., Cambridge, 1962. Chartered acct. Co. sec. Dow Chem. U.K., 1963-69; with Hanson plc, 1969-95, vice chmn., 1988-95; non-exec. dir. UGI plc, 1979-82, Vickers plc, 1986-99, Securities Assoc., 1987-90, Nat. Westminster Bank plc, 1990-2000; chmn. Nat. Westminster Life Assoc., 1992-2000; dep. chmn. Charter plc, 1995—; bd. dirs. Millenium Chems., Inc. Gov. Mall Sch. Trust., 2000. Mem. Confederation Brit. Industry (mem. coun. 1981-96, mem. cos. com. 1981-94, mem. city/industry task force 1987, mem. pres.'s com. 1990-94, chmn. cos. com. 1990-94, mem. steering group on long termism and corp. governance 1990-92, rep. on take-over panel 1989-95). Avocations: art, books, sport, theatre. Office: 150 Brompton Rd, London SW3 1HX, England

TAYLOR, MARTIN JOHN, mathematics educator; b. Leicester, Eng., Feb. 18, 1952; married; 4 children. BA first class, Oxford U., 1973; PhD, King's Coll., London, 1976. Rsch. asst. King's Coll., London, 1976-77; jr. lectr. Oxford U., 1977-78; lectr. Queen Mary Coll., London, 1978-81; fellow Trinity Coll., Cambridge U., 1981-85; univ. asst. lectr. Cambridge U., 1984-85; chair pure math. U. Manchester (Eng.) IST, 1986—; chercheur assoc. CNRS, Besancon, 1979-80, NSF researcher U. Ill., Urbana, 1981; assoc. prof. Bordeaux, 1984, Besancon, 1988; invited prof., Geneva, 1989, Bordeaux, 1992; invited visitor Newton Inst., 1993; mem. editorial com. Sem. de Théorie des Nombres de Bordeaux, 1989, chmn. dept. math., 1989-91; external examiner U. Sheffield, 1990-92, U. E. Anglia, 1994-95; external assessor chair in pure math. Leicester U., 1993; organizer Erasmus exch. between UMIST, U. Manchester, Compultense U. Madrid, U. Iraklion, U. Bordeaux, 1990; editor press grad. texts series Oxford U.; EPSRC sr. rsch. fellow, 1999—. Recipient Jr. LMS Whitehead prize, 1982, Adams prize, 1983; Royal Soc. Leverhulme sr. rsch. fellow, 1991-92. Fellow Royal Soc.; mem. London Math. Soc. (coun. 1991-98—, prizes com. 1991—, progam com. 1992—, publs. com. 1992—, 98-2000, pres. 1998-2000). Home: 92 Ack Ln E, Bramhall, Cheshire SK7 2BH, England Office: U Manchester IST, PO Box 88, Manchester England

TAYLOR, MAURICE, bishop; b. Hamilton, Scotland, May 5, 1926; s. Maurice and Lucy (McLaughlin) T. Grad., Pontifical Scots Coll., Rome, 1951; STD, Pontifical Gregorian U., Rome, 1954. Ordained priest Roman Cath. Ch, 1950. Lectr. St. Peter's Coll., Cardross, Scotland, 1955-65; rector Royal Scots Coll., Valladolid, Spain, 1965-74; parish priest Our Lady of Lourdes Ch., East Kilbride, Scotland, 1974-81; bishop Diocese of Galloway, Ayr, Scotland, 1981—; episcopal sec. Bishops' Conf. Scotland, 1984—; v.p. Cath. Inst. for Internat. Rels., London, 1984—; chmn. Internat. Commn. on English in Liturgy, Washington, 1997—. Author: The Scots College in Spain, 1971, Guatemala: A Bishop's Journey, 1990, El Salvador: Portrait of a Parish, 1992; co-author: Opening Our Lives to the Saviour, 1995; co-author: Listening at the Foot of the Cross, 1996. E-mail: stninian@globalnet.co.uk. Home and Office: Bishops House, 8 Corsehill Rd, Ayr KA7 2ST, Scotland

TAYLOR, MICHAEL PAUL GORDON, solicitor; b. Hoylake, Cheshire, Eng., Mar. 2, 1949. LLB, St. John's Coll., Cambridge, Eng., 1974. Solicitor Norton rose, London, 1974-79, ptnr., 1979—. Author: Joint Operating Agreements, 1989, 2d edit., 1992; mem. editl. bd. Internat. Energy Law and Taxation Rev., 1989—; contbr. articles to profl. jours. Mem. Law Soc. Eng. and Wales, Internat. Bar Assn., U.K. Oil Lawyers Group (com. mem. 1987-89). Avocations: sports, reading, theatre. E-mail: taylormpg@norton-rose.com. Office: Norton Rose, Norton Rose, Kempson House Camomile St, London EC3A 7AN, England

TAYLOR, NICHOLAS C., state agency administrator, energy executive; b. Washington, Sept. 18, 1937; s. James Spear Taylor and Helen Livingston MacGregor Strauss; m. Catherine Blaffer, Jan. 1, 1999; children: Nicholas Van Kempen, Katherine C., Christie. AB, Harvard U., 1959; JD, Georgetown U., 1963. Assoc. Wilson, Woods & Villalon, Washington, 1964-65, Shearman & Sterling, N.Y.C., 1965-70, Locke, Liddell, Sapp, Dallas, 1970-74; shareholder Stubbeman, McRae, Sealy, Laughlin & Browder, Inc., Midland, Tex., 1974-93; atty. Midland, 1993—; pres. Mexco Energy Corp., Midland; chmn. State Securities Bd. of Tex. Mem. Tex. Jud. Coun., 1990. Recipient Am. Jurisprudence prizes for constnl. law, oil, and gas taxation So. Meth. U. Law Sch. Mem. Natural Gas Prodrs. Assn., Permian Basin Petroleum Assn., Midland Downtown Lions Club. Episcopalian. E-mail: mexco@msn.com. Office: Mexco Energy Corp PO Box 10502 Midland TX 79702-7502

TAYLOR, PATRICK JONATHAN, researcher; b. Newport News, Va., Aug. 28, 1967; s. Robert Theodore and Patricia Rae Taylor. BS, Hampden-Sydney Coll., 1989; MS, U. Va., 1993, PhD, 1997. Rsch. scientist NASA, Hampton, Va., 1989-91; postdoctoral rsch. scientist NAS, Ft. Belvoir, Va., 1997-98; rsch. staff mem. MIT Lincoln Lab., Lexington, Mass., 1998—; cons. for infrared detectors U.S. Army Rsch. Lab., Adelphi, Md., 1997-98. Contbr. articles to profl. jours. Edmund Madison Chitwood scholar, 1986. Mem. Materials Rsch. Soc., Chi Beta Phi. Avocations: snowboarding, surfing. Office: MIT Lincoln Lab 244 Wood St Group 83 Lexington MA 02420

TAYLOR, PETER WILLIAM EDWARD, counsel; b. Newbury, Berkshire, Eng., July 27, 1917; s. Peter and Julia (North) T.; m. Julia Mary Brown, Jan. 2, 1948; children: Malcolm Charles Vernon, Nigel William Gervase. BA in Maths., Cambridge (Eng.) U., 1937, BA in Law, 1939, MA, 1942. Bar: Eng. 1946. Pvt. practice London, 1947-81, pvt. practice Queen's counsel, 1981—; lectr. Inns Ct. Sch. of Law, London, 1952-70; conveyancing counsel of the Ct., Supreme Ct. of Judicature, London, 1974-81. Co-editor: (ency.) Halsbury's Laws of England, Title on Deeds, 1975; contbr. articles to profl. jours. Mem. Gen. Coun. of Bar, London, 1971-74, Senate of Inns of Ct. and the Bar, London, 1974-75, Land Registration Rule Com., London, 1976-81, Standing Com. on Conveyancing, London, 1985-87. With Royal Artillery, 1939-46, lt. col., 1945. Mem. Lincoln's Inn (bencher 1976—), Inner Temple. Anglican. Avocations: sailing, shooting, music. Office: Lincoln's Inn, Lincoln's Inn, London WC2A 3TL, England

TAYLOR, RALPH ORIEN, JR., real estate developer, investor; b. Kansas City, Mo., Jan. 6, 1919; s. Ralph Orien Sr. and Genevieve (Sturgeon) T.; m. Betty Boswell, Dec. 7, 1940 (dec. Oct. 1959); children: Ralph Bradley, Nancy Virginia Stevens; m. Deborah Rosemary Berger, Oct. 10, 1982. BS in Bus. and Pub. Adminstrn., U. Mo., 1940. Ptnr. Sturgeon & Taylor, Kansas City, Mo., 1940-42; chmn., pres. Sturgeon & Taylor, Inc., Kansas City, Prairie Village (Kans.), 1946, Sturgeon & Taylor Devel. Co., Inc., Prarie Village, Kans., 1949—, Sturgeon & Taylor, Co., Prarie Village, Kans., 1955-90, Roth & Taylor Devel. Co., Inc., Prarie Village, Kans., 1989—; ptnr., co-founder ScripTpro LLC, Pharmacy Robotics & Automation, Mission, Kans., 1994; mem. Johnson County (Kans.) Real Estate Bd., Kansas City Real Estate Bd. Lt. comdr. USNR, 1942-46, PTO, ETO. Decorated Bronze Star with combat V.; recipient Alumnus of Yr. award Phi Delta Theta Fraternity, 2000; Ralph & Debbie Taylor Baseball Stadium dedicated in his honor, U. Mo., 2000. Charter mem. Nat. Assn. Home Builders (life bd. dirs.), Home Builders Assn. Greater Kansas City (pres. 1951-52, life bd. dirs., Builder of Yr. award 1979); mem., Indian Hills Country Club (Mission Hills, Kans.), Ft. Lauderdale Country Clu b, Lauderdale Yacht Club, Phi Delta Theta (Raymond L. Gardner Alumnus of Yr. award 2000). Republican. Mem. Christian Ch. Avocations: golfing, boating. Home: 411 W 46th Ter Apt 903

Kansas City MO 64112-1437 also: Penthouse B 1050 Seminole Dr Ph B Fort Lauderdale FL 33304-3225 Office: Sturgeon & Taylor Devel Co Inc PO Box 8205 Prairie Vlg KS 66208-0205

TAYLOR, RICHARD BERTROM, accountant; b. Cuthbert, Ga., Nov. 1, 1951; s. Wilburn Bertrom and Marjorie (Hixon) T.; m. Sherrie L. Lieber; children: Kenneth, Douglas, Andrew. AS cum laude, Andrew Coll., 1971; BBA, U. Ga., 1973. CPA, Ga., Fla. Staff acct. Lester Witte & Co., Atlanta, 1973-79; mgr. HLB Gross Collins, PC, Atlanta, 1979-84, ptnr., 1984—; also v.p., bd. dirs. Gross, Collins & Cress, PC, Atlanta; adv. bd. acctg. dept. Kennesan State U., 1995—; exec. com. HLB-USA, Inc., 1997—. Bd. dirs. North Cobb Christian Sch., 1989-90. Mem. AICPAs, Ga. Soc. CPAs, Pinetree Country Club (bd. dirs. 1983-87, 91-93, treas. 1984-85, 91, v.p. 1986), Optimists (sec. 1982-84), French-Am. C. of C. (dir. Atlanta chpt. 2000—), Phi Kappa Phi, Beta Alpha Psi, Phi Theta Kappa. Methodist. Avocations: gardening, football, travel, golf, dance. Office: HLB Gross Collins PC 2625 Cumberland Pkwy SE Ste 400 Atlanta GA 30339-3911

TAYLOR, RICHARD EDWARD, physicist, educator; b. Medicine Hat, Alta., Can., Nov. 2, 1929; came to U.S., 1952; s. Clarence Richard and Delia Alena (Brunsdale) T.; m. Rita Jean Bonneau, Aug. 25, 1951; 1 child, Norman Edward. BS, U. Alta., 1950, MS, 1952; PhD, Stanford U., 1962; Docteur honoris causa, U. Paris-Sud, 1980; DSc, U. Alta., 1991; LLD (hon.), U. Calgary, Alta., 1993; DSc (hon.), U. Lethbridge, Alta., 1993, U. Victoria, B.C., Can., 1994; D honoris causa, U. Blaise Pascal, 1997; DSc honoris causa, Carleton U., Ottawa, Ont., 1999; DSc (hon.), U. Liverpool, U.K., 1999. Boursier Lab. de l'Accelerateur Lineaire, Orsay, France, 1958-61; physicist Lawrence Berkeley Lab., Berkeley, Calif., 1961-62; staff mem. Stanford (Calif.) Linear Accelerator Ctr., 1962-68, assoc. dir., 1982-86, prof., 1968—. Fellow Guggenheim Found., 1971-72, von Humboldt Found., 1982; recipient Nobel prize in physics, 1990. Fellow AAAS, Am. Acad. Arts and Scis., Am. Phys. Soc. (W.K.H. Panofsky prize div. particles and fields 1989), Royal Soc. Can., Royal Soc. London; mem. Can. Assn. Physicists, Nat. Acad. Scis. (fgn. assoc.). Office: Stanford Linear Accelerator Ctr M/S 96 2575 Sand Hill Rd Menlo Park CA 94025-7015

TAYLOR, RICHARD JAMES, lawyer; b. Merrill, Wis., Jan. 19, 1939; s. M.N. and Billie (Mead) T.; m. Nancy Hildebrand, Nov. 25, 1966. BA, U. Wis., 1962; DEF, U. Orleans, France, 1963; JD, U. Mich., 1966; postgrad., U. Paris II, 1971-72. Bar: N.Y. 1968. Assoc. Langner Parry Card & Langner, N.Y.C., 1966-68, Conboy Hewitt O'Brien & Boardman, N.Y.C., 1968-71; asst. prof. U. Paris I Law Sch., 1973-78; trademark and copyright counsel Colgate-Palmolive Co., N.Y.C., 1978—; seminar leader Am. Law and Lang., N.Y.C., 1987—; pro bono counsel Hearts and Voices, N.Y.C., 1992—; mem. com. of experts World Intellectual Property Orgn. Trademark Law Treaty, Geneva, 1993-94; lectr. intellectual property symposia. Co-author: Doing Business in France, 1973, Worldwide Trademark Transfers, 1992; contbr. chpt. to book, articles to Nat. Law Jour., Trademark Reporter, Jour. Japan Trademark Assn., Bus. Latin Am., others. Mem. ABA (chair com. on internat. trademark treaties and laws 1990-91, del. to World Trademark Symposium 1992), Internat. Trademark Assn. (chair internat. com. 1987-89, mem. internat. task force 1989-90, bd. dirs. 1992-95, mem. task force on trademark law treaty 1991-95, publ. bd. 1995—).

TAYLOR, RICHARD KENNETH STANLEY, education educator; b. Harrow, Middlesex, Eng., Nov. 18, 1945; s. Kenneth Charles and Jeanne Ann (Walton) T.; m. Jennifer Teresa Frost, Sept. 9, 1967; children: Joanna Teresa, Lucy Katherine, Matthew William Richard. BA, U. Oxford, 1967, MA, 1973; PhD, U. Leeds (Eng.), 1983. Adminstrv. asst. U. Lancaster (Eng.), 1967-70, U. Leeds, 1970-73; lectr. in politics, warden of U. Leeds Ctr., 1973-83, sr. lectr., 1983-86, dir. extramural courses, 1986-97, prof. cont. edn., 1990—. Author: Against the Bomb: The British Peace Movement 1958-65, 1988; co-author: University Adult Education in England and the USA: a reappraisal of the Liberal Tradition, 1985, Learning Independence: a political outline of Indian Adult Education, 1995, Lifelong Learning and the University: a post-Dearing Agenda, 1998. Chair West Yorkshire European Nuclear Disarmament Campaign; dir. Bangladesh Acid Survivors Trust, 1999. Mem. Univs. Assn. Cont. Edn. (sec. 1994-98), Nat. Inst. Adult Cont. Edn. (vice chair 1995-98, chair 1999—), Yorkshire County Cricket Club. Avocations: hill walking, climbing, running, cricket. Office: U Leeds, Sch Cont Edn, Leeds Yorkshire LS2 9JT, England

TAYLOR, RICHARD THOMAS, rheumatologist; b. Manchester, Eng., July 7, 1934; s. Thomas and Mabel (Hickley) T.; m. Elizabeth Ann Brett, Sept. 1, 1962; children: Sally, Caroline, Stephen; m. Christine Helen Miller, Sept. 12, 1990; 1 child, Georgina. BA, Cambridge U., 1956, MB, BChir, 1959. House physician Westminster Hosp., London, 1959, sr. med. registrar, 1968-72; med. registrar St. Stephen's Hosp., London, 1966-67; cons. physician Kidderminster Gen. Hosp., Worcestershire, Eng., 1972-95; ret., 1995; mem. Kidderminster and Dist. Health Authority, 1983-87. Chmn. Kidderminster Hosp. League Friends, 1996—, Save Kidderminster Hosp. Campaign, 1997—. Fellow Royal Coll. Physicians (London); mem. Brit. Soc. for Rheumatology, West Midlands Physicians Assn. Methodist. Avocation: gardening. Home: 11 Church Walk, Kidderminster Worcestershire DY11 6XY, England

TAYLOR, ROBERT EDWARD, foreign language educator; b. Portland, Oreg., Nov. 22, 1919; s. Dolph J. and Lula May (Nicholas) T.; m. Naomi Ellen Klatt, Feb. 13, 1943 (div. 1962); 1 child, Thomas Robert; m. Olga Zazuliak, May 19, 1962; 1 child, Anne-Marie. BA, Reed Coll., 1943; MA, Columbia U., 1947, PhD, 1951. Instr. french Columbia Univ., N.Y.C., 1947-50; instr. to prof. french NYU, N.Y.C., 1950-62, prof. french, 1962-63; prof. French U. Mass., Amherst, 1963-90, dept. head, 1963-70, prof. emeritus, 1990—; seminar assoc. Columbia Univ., 1959-80; chair Nat. Fulbright Com. for France, N.Y.C., 1963-65; dir. programs in France, Univ. Mass., 1971, 1990-91, 1997-98. Cons. editor Merriam-Webster's 3rd Internat. Dictionary, 1961; contbg. editor: Bibliographie Internat. de l'Humanisme et de la Renaissance; contbr. articles to Renaissance Soc. of Am., Modern Lang. Assn. 1st lt. USAAF, 1942-46. Decorated Chevalier dans l'Ordre des Palmes Académiques. Mem. Modern Lang. Assn. (asst. ed. 1950-55), Am. Assn. Tchrs. French, Assn. des Prof. de Lang. Modernes. Avocations: music, theatre. Home: 154 Lincoln Ave Amherst MA 01002-2011

TAYLOR, ROBERT MURRAY ROSS, retired surgeon; b. Calcutta, India, Dec. 10, 1932; s. George and Helen Bailey (Murray) T.; m. Margaret Rose Cutland; children—Linda, Jill, Anne, Bill. M.B., Ch.B., U. Glasgow, Scotland, 1956, Ch.M., 1968. Registrar surgery Royal Victoria Infirmary, Newcastle upon Tyne, Eng., 1962-64, sr. registrar surgery, 1966-70; research fellow U. Newcastle upon Tyne, 1964-66, hon. lectr. transplantation surgery, 1970-95; cons. surgeon Newcastle Health Authority, 1970—. Chmn. Transplant Sports Assn. Gt. Britain, 1984—. Served to capt. parachute regt., 1957-59. Fellow Royal Coll. Surgeons Edinburgh, Royal Coll. Surgeons London; mem. Internat. Transplantation Soc. (founding), Brit. Transplantation Soc. (founding, pres. elect 1985, pres. 1986-89), Surg. Research Soc. Gt. Britain, Assn. Surgeons Gt. Britain, North of Eng. Surg. Soc. Avocations: golf, running. Home: The Croft House, Hexham Slaley England NE47 OAA Office: Royal Victoria Infirmary, Queen Victoria Rd, Newcastle upon Tyne NE1 4LP, England

TAYLOR, RUSSELL BENTON, mining executive; b. Eskridge, Kans., May 16, 1925; s. Bayard Charles and Eva May (Russell) T.; m. Arlene Marie Krehbiel, Aug. 14, 1959; 1 child, Bruce Charles. BSBA, U. Kans., 1949; JD, U. Kans, 1951. Asst. cashier Eskridge (Kans.) State Bank, 1951-57, cashier, 1957, pres., 1958-69, chmn., 1969-78; v.p., dir South Standard Mining Co., Salt Lake City, 1978-96. Mayor City of Eskridge, Kans., 1959. Decorated Purple Heart. Mem. Kans. Bar Assn., Kiwanis, Masonic, Arab Shrine. Republican. Methodist. Avocations: traveling, ranching. Home and Office: 6th & Locust Eskridge KS 66423

TAYLOR, STUART ROSS, geochemist, author; b. Ashburton, New Zealand, Nov. 26, 1925; s. Thomas Stuart and Anne Grace (Lloyd) T.; m. Noel Elvie White, May 21, 1958; children: Susanna, Judith, Helen. BSc, U. New Zealand, 1948, MSc, 1951; PhD, Ind. U., 1954; DSc, Oxford U., 1978. Lectr. U. Oxford, Eng., 1954-58; sr. lectr. U. Cape Town, South Africa, 1958-60; professorial fellow Australian Nat. U., Canberra, 1961-90, vis. fellow, 1990-99, prof. emeritus, 1997; prof. U. Vienna, 1992, 96; vis. scientist Lunar and Planetary Inst., Houston, 1969-90. Author: Lunar Science: Post-Apollo View, 1975, Planetary Science, 1982, Solar System Evolution, 1992, (with others) Continental Crust, 1985, Destiny or Chance: Our Solar System and Its Place in the Cosmos, 1998; contbr. more than 220 articles to profl. jours. Recipient Goldschmidt medal Geochem. Soc., 1993, Gilbert award Geol. Soc. Am., 1994; Asteroid 5670 named Rosstaylor, 1997. Fellow Royal Soc. New Zealand (hon.), Australian Acad. Sci., Geol. Soc. London (hon.), Geol. Soc. India (hon.); mem. NAS (fgn. assoc.), Meteoritical Soc. (pres. 1989-90, Leonard medal 1998). Office: Australian Nat U, Dept Geology, Canberra 0200, Australia

TAYLOR, THOMAS FULLER, religious society administrator; b. Evanston, Ill., May 7, 1937; s. Lewis Archer and Margaret Fox (Nicholson) T.; m. Nancy Louise Emmons, June 16, 1963; children: Jennifer Louise, Clarke Bentley. BA in Physics, Earlham Coll., 1959; MusM, Northwestern U., 1962, PhD in Musicology, 1967. Instr. Oakwood Sch., Poughkeepsie, N.Y., 1959-61, Earlham Coll., Richmond, Ind., 1962-64; lectr. Northwestern U., Evanston, 1964-66, Ind. U., Bloomington, 1966-67; assoc. prof. musicology U. Mich., Ann Arbor, 1967-87; assoc. sec. Friends World Com. Consultation (Quakers), London, 1986-91, gen. sec., 1992-98. Author: The Catalog of Works of Jeremiah Clarke, 1973, Cheerfully over the World, a Handbook for Isolated Friends, 2000; editor Soc. of Friends publs. Clk., chmn. Ann Arbor Friends Meeting, 1974-78. Avocations: walking, music, travel.

TAYLOR, VICKY ANN, telephone company executive; b. Fairfield, Ala., July 31, 1958; d. Eddie Richardson and Ruth Hans Bogar. BS, Miles Coll., Fairfield, Ala., 1981. Info. case analyst FBI, Washington, 1981-89; adminstrv. sec. D.C. Pub. Schs., 1991-95; maint. adminstr. Bell Atlantic, Greenbelt, Md., 1995—; sub. tchr. Prince George's County Pub. Schs., Md., 1996—. poet/writer Nat. Libr. of Poetry, Owing Mills, Md., 1996—. Alto Mass Choir Glendale Bapt. Ch., Landover, Md., 1998, mem. newsletter ministry, 1998—, asst. ch. clk., 1999—. Avocations: bowling, baseball, volleyball, cooking, singing. Home and Office: 2002A Fort Davis St SE Washington DC 20020-1306 Office: PO Box 1056 Forestville MD 20753

TAYLOR, WILLIAM BROCKENBROUGH, engineer, consultant, management consultant; b. Norfolk, Va., Mar. 11, 1925; s. Lewis Jerome and Roberta Page (Newton) T.; m. Nancy Dare Aitcheson, June 12, 1945; children: William B. Jr., Anne P. Taylor Cregger, Paul K., Katharine C.Taylor Nace, David A. BS, U.S. Mil. Acad., West Point, N.Y., 1945; MS in Engring., Johns Hopkins U., 1951. Profl. engr., D.C., Va. Commd. 2d lt. U.S. Army Corps of Engrs., 1945, advanced through grades to maj., 1953, retired, 1954; gen. engr. Army AEC Nuclear Power Program, Washington, Ft. Belvoir, Va., 1955-60; engring. mgr. Army Mapping R&D, Ft. Belvoir, 1960-62; aerospace engr. NASA, Washington, 1962-67; R&D mgr. staff Army Hdqrs., Washington, 1967-69; tech. dir. Army R&D Lab., Ft. Belvoir, 1969-73; chief R & D U.S. Army Corps of Engrs., Washington, 1973-77; prin. engr. Planning Rsch. Corp., McLean, Va., 1978-80; consulting engr. and mgmt. cons. Alexandria, Va., 1980—; mem. study com. Nat. Rsch. Coun., Washington, 1983; mem. constrn. mgmt. task force Grace Commn. on Cost. Control, Washington, 1982. Contbr. articles to The Mil. Engr. jour., Wash. Acad. Scis. jour., others. Participant various civic activities. Fellow Soc. Am. Mil. Engrs. (pres. Fort Belvoir chpt. 1972); mem. AIAA, Wash. Acad. Scis., Sigma Xi. Republican. Episcopalian. Achievements include program definition of NASA's Apollo applications program; designs for geothermal energy power plant for Dominica; 5 military nuclear power plants; international technology transfer among U.S., U.K., Germany, Sweden, and Russia involving governmental and industrial clients. Home and Office: 4001 Belle Rive Ter Alexandria VA 22309-3004

TAYLOR, WILLIAM HALSTEAD, chemical pathologist, metabolic medicine physician; b. Wardle, Lancashire, Eng., Apr. 26, 1924; s. Thomas Halstead and Alice May (Hallett) T.; m. June Helen Thorniley, Sept. 7, 1950; children: Susan, John, Philippa, Rowena. BA, U. Oxford, Eng., 1946, BM, BCh, 1948, DM, 1957. House physician Postgrad. Med. Sch., London, 1948-49, Radcliffe Infirmary, Oxford, 1949; lectr., then sr. lectr. in clin. biochemistr U. Oxford, 1949-59, fellow, tutor St. Peter's Coll., 1957-59; head dept. chem. pathology Royal Liverpool (Eng.) Hosp., 1959-89; dir. studies chem. pathology U. Liverpool, 1962-74; dir. Mersey Regional Metabolic Unit, 1965-89; emeritus cons. Liverpool Health Authority, 1989—; emeritus cons. in metabolic medicine Halton Gen. Hosp., Runcorn, Eng., 1989—. Author: Fluid Therapy and Disorders of Electrolyte Balance, 1965; mem. editorialbd. Clin. Sci. Jour., 1962-67; contbr. articles to profl. jours. U. Oxford Christopher Welch scholar, 1946. Fellow Royal Coll. Physicians; mem. Med. Research Soc., Assn. Clin. Pathologists. Club: 41 (Liverpool), Rotary. Home: 16, Salisbury Rd, Cressington Pk, Liverpool L19 0PJ, England Office: Royal Liverpool U Hosp, Duncan Bldg Dept Med Microbiology, Liverpool L7 8XW, England

TAYLOR, WILLIAM JESSE, JR., international studies educator, research center executive; b. Florence, S.C., Dec. 28, 1933; s. William J. and Dorothy (Byrd) T.; m. Louise Inger Haegerstrom, Apr. 9, 1977; 1 child, Nicolaus; children by previous marriage: Juliana C., William J. III, L. Scott, Christopher B., Helen B. B.S., U. Md., 1962; M.A., Am. U., 1964, Ph.D., 1967. Enlisted U.S. Army, commd. 2d lt., 1955, advanced through grades to col., 1976; prof. U.S. Mil. Acad., West Point, N.Y., 1970-81; vis. prof. U.S. Nat. War Coll., 1975-76; ret. col. U.S. Army, 1981; dir. polit. mil. studies Ctr. for Strategic and Internat. Studies Georgetown U., Washington, 1980-83; exec. dir., chief operating officer Ctr. for Strategic and Internat. Studies, 1983-87, v.p. internat. security programs, 1987-92; sr. v.p. Internat. Security Affairs, 1992-99, sr. advisor, 1999—; pres. Taylor Assocs. Inc., 1984—; internat. lectr., debater, T.V. mil. analyst, 1970—. Author: Future of Conflict: U.S. Interests, 1982, Future of Conflict into the 21st Century, 1987; co-author: American National Security: Policy and Process, 1981, 83, 89, 93, 99; co-editor: Defense Manpower Planning, 1980, The Future of Conflict in the 1980's, 1982, Strategic Requirements for the Army to the Year 2000, 1983, Strategic Responses to Conflict in the 1980's, 1984, Nordic Defense: Comparative Decisionmaking, 1985, Strategic Dimensions of Military Manpower, 1987, The Future of U.S.-Republic of Korea Security Ties, 1989, The Korean Peninsula: Prospects for Arms Control, 1990, Korea 1991: The Road to Peace, 1991, Elvis in The Army, 1995, 97. Mem. Presiding Bishop's Nat. Episc. Roundtable, 1983-86. Decorated Bronze Star with oak leaf cluster, Legion of Merit (2), Air Medal (3), Air medal for valor, Vietnam Cross of Gallantry, Combat Infantry Badge; recipient Pitman Potter Medal Am. U., 1964; named to Infantry Officer Hall of Fame, 1976; named Disting. Alumnus, Episcopal Acad., 1995. Mem. St. Anthony Club. Republican. Episcopalian. Home: 6010 Maiden Ln Bethesda MD 20817-6261

TAYLOR, WILLIAM MICHAEL, author; b. Hickory, N.C., Sept. 4, 1949; s. William I. and Barbara S. Taylor. BA in English Lit., Ga. State U., 1976. Author poetry, essays; portrait artist. With U.S. Army, 1969-71. Home and Office: Gsp B 4 21 Ef122808 100 Hwy 147 Reidsville GA 30499-0001

TAYLOR, WILLIAM RAMSAY, computational molecular biophysicist; b. Larne, No. Ireland, Dec. 21, 1954; s. Ramsay and Kathleen Hawkins (Gilmore) T.; m. Sheelagh Maya Leith, Apr. 12, 1986; children: Laura Leith, Samuel Leith. BSc, Kings Coll., London, 1976; DPhil, Oxford (Eng.) U., 1980. Rsch. fellow IBM (U.K.), Winchester, 1980-81; rsch. fellow dept. crystallography Birkbeck Coll., London, 1981-87; staff scientist Nat. Inst. for Med. Rsch., London, 1987—, head divsn. math. biology, 1994—; vis. prof. dept. informatics Univ. Bergen, Norway; mem. Wellcome Trust Math. Biology Com. Assoc. editor Jour. Molecular Biology and Evolution; contbr. 150 articles to profl. jours. Achievements include research in algorithms for protein sequence and structure analysis and protein structure prediction. Avocation: doodling. Office: Nat Inst Med Rsch, The Ridgeway Mill Hill, London NW7 1AA, England

TAYLOR, WILSON H., diversified financial company executive. Grad., Trinity Coll. With Conn. Gen., 1954-82, sr. v.p., chief fin. officer, 1980-82; v.p. Aetna Ins. Co., 1975; exec. v.p. Cigna Corp., Phila., 1982-88, pres. property casualty group, 1983-88, corp. vice-chmn., chief operating officer, from 1988, chief operating officer, 1988, pres., chief exec. officer, 1988—, then chmn., pres., chief exec. officer, now chmn., chief exec. officer. Phi Beta Kappa. Office: Cigna Corp 1650 Market St 1 Liberty Pl Bldg St Philadelphia PA 19192-0001

TAYLOR-ROBINSON, ANDREW WILLIAM, immunoparasitologist; b. Salisbury, Wiltshire, Eng., Sept. 1, 1965; s. David and Valerie Elizabeth (Partridge) T.-R.; m. Lisa Rachel Brannan, Jan. 19, 1991; children: Ewan Carl, Seona Niamh, Ruaridh James. BS, U. Coll. London, 1987; PhD, U. Glasgow, Scotland, 1990. Rsch. scholar U. Glasgow, 1987-90, rsch. fellow, 1991-95; rsch. assoc. U. Edinburgh, Scotland, 1990-91; vis. rsch. fellow Max Planck Inst. for Immunology, Frieburg, Germany, 1992-93; Wellcome Trust rsch. fellow U. Leeds, 1995-2000, asst. prof., 2000—; grant referee Wellcome Trust, 1994, 98. Referee for jours. Nature, 1993, Transaction of Royal Soc. Tropical Medicine and Hygiene, 1993, Exptl. Parasitology, 1993, Parasite Immunology, 1993, The Lancet, 1995, Parasitology, 1995; contbr. articles to profl. publs. Recipient Best Contributed Poster award Scottish Parasitology Ann. Residential Meeting, 1993; rsch. grantee Wellcome Trust, Med. Rsch. Coun. U.K., 1991—, 94—. Fellow Royal Soc. Tropical Medicine and Hygiene; mem. Brit. Soc. Immunology (parasite immunology group 1998—, Best Contributed Paper award 1993), Brit. Soc. Parasitology (mem. coun., trustee 2000—), Brit. Soc. Cell Biology, Com. of Learned Socs. Episcopalian. Avocations: running, hill walking, soccer, church choral singing. Achievements include first direct demonstration that CD4 T cells are protective against bloodstage Plasmodium chabaudi malaria, first direct demonstration that Th2 cells are protective against any malaria, first direct demonstration that nitric oxide is produced during malaria infection and performs a protective function. Office: U Leeds, Sch Biology, Leeds LS2 9JT, England

TAYLOR-WILLIAMS, BONNIE JEAN, cosmetics executive; b. Chgo., Oct. 26, 1959; d. William Crawford and Juanita J. (Parker) Dunbar; m. Paxton G. Williams, Aug. 30, 1987. Grad., Pivot Point Beauty Sch. Lic. cosmetologist, Ill. Mgr., cosmetologist Selena's House of Beauty and Sch. HairWeev Tech., Chgo., 1978—; technician, instr. Sch. Hair Weev Tech., Chgo.; pres. Beautee, Inc., Chgo., 1989—, E-Z Beautee Extraordinary Maintenance Sys. & Hairgasm; instr. First Internat. Indep. Hair Weevers Assn., Chgo., 1974—. Choir mem. First Ch. Deliverance, 1978-88, Christ Universal Temple, 1996—. Avocations: professional writing, dancing, writing, travel. Office: Beautee Inc 444 E 83rd St Chicago IL 60619-5726

TAZAWA, MASASHI, biologist, educator, researcher; b. Yokohama, Japan, Jan. 12, 1930; s. Tomekichi and Hana (Takano) T.; m. Keiko Oana, Sept. 10, 1955; children: Akihiro, Mariko Yamada. PhD, Osaka U., 1960. Instr. biology Osaka (Japan) U., 1955-68, assoc. prof., 1968-77; prof. biology U. Tokyo, 1977-90, prof. emeritus, 1990—; prof. Fukui (Japan) U. Tech., 1990—. Editor: Cell Dynamics (Protoplasma), 1989, Plant Water Relations and Growth under Stress, 1989; editor in chief The Bot. Mag., Tokyo, 1981-82; editor Protoplasma, Vienna, 1982-90. Recipient prize of the Japan Acad., 1990. Mem. Am. Soc. Plant Physiologists (corr. mem.), German Bot. Soc. (hon.). Home: Chadomachi 6-15, Otsu, Shiga-ken 520-0066, Japan Office: Fukui U Tech, Gakuen 3-6-1, Fukui 910-8505, Japan

TCHA, DONG-WAN, educator; b. Seoul, Korea, Jan. 31, 1947; s. Kyung-Soon and Yong-Soon (Lee) T.; m. Young-Ja Sull; children: Jin-Young, Jong-Hyun. BS, Seoul Nat. U., 1969; MSc, Northwestern U., 1972, PhD, 1975. From asst. to assoc. prof. Korea Advanced Inst. Sci. and Tech., Seoul, Korea, 1975-85, prof., 1985—; bd. dirs. Ctr. for Telecomm. Mgmt. and Policy; chmn. telecomm. MBA program Korea Advanced Inst. Sci. and Tech. Grad. Sch. Mgmt., 1996-99; gen. co-chair INFORMS Internat. Congress, Seoul, 2000; dir. acad. activities, chmn. SIG on telecomm. mgmt. Korean Inst. Comm. Scis., 1993-94; guest scientist digital network group German Aerospace Rsch. Agy., 1986-87; vis. scientist IBM Japan Sci. Inst., Tokyo, 1983, IBM Thomas J. Watson Rsch. Ctr., Yorktown Hts., N.Y., 1981-82; rschr. Korea Inst. Sci. & Tech., 1979-80, Korea Atomic Energy Rsch. Inst., 1979; vis. scholar dept. engring.-econ. sys. Stanford U., 1977. Author: Telecommunications World (in Korean), 1996; mem. editl. bd. Jour. of Info. Tech. and Mgmt.; contbr. articles to profl. jours. Recipient The Goodeve medal The Operational Rsch. Soc., 1998; Humboldt Found. fellow U. Darmstadt, Germany, 1987. Mem. IEEE (sr.), Korea Ops. Rsch. and Mgmt. Sci. Soc. (v.p. 1990-92, pres. 1997-98, editor-in-chief 1983-85), Korea Comms. Soc. (dir. acad. activities 1993-94), Nat. Acad. Engring. Korea. E-mail: tchadw@sorak.kaist.ac.kr. Office: 207-43 Chongryangri-dong, Dongdaimum-gu, Seoul 130-012, Korea

TCHABAN, VASYL JOSEPH, mathematics, modelling & electrodynamics educator; b. Stary Zahoriv, Volhyn, Ukraine, Feb. 4, 1940; s. Joseph and Luba (Vasylchuk) T.; m. Roma Palanytsa, Feb. 21, 1965 (dec. Oct. 1969); children: Andrew, Ostap. 1st class diploma, Lviv (Ukraine) State Poly. U., Ukraine, 1965, Candidate Sci., 1970, DSc, 1987. Miner Coal Mine No. 1, Novovolhynsk, Ukraine, 1958-59; asst. prof., prof. Lviv State Poly. U., 1965—; prof. Rzeszow (Poland) Pedagogical U., 1993—, Lutsk (Ukraine) State Tech. U., 1997—. Author: The Fundamentals of Transient Processes of Electric Machine Systems (in Russian), 1980, The Methods of Analysis of Electromechanical Systems (in Russian), 1985, The Methods of Non-Linear Electrotechnics (in Ukrainian), 1990, Mathematical Modelling of Electromagnetic Processes, 1992, English-Ukrainian Electrotechnical Dictionary, 1995, Mathematical Modelling of Electromechanical Processes (in Ukrainian), 1997, Theoretical Electric Engineering (in Ukrainian), 1998, Physical Fundamentals of Electrotechnics (in Polish), 2000, Surrealistci Short Story, 1998, Electric Engineering. Electric Machines and Transformers (in Ukrainian), 1998, Electric Engineering. Electric Devices (in Polish), 1999; contbr. articles to profl. jours.; editor in chief Tech. News. Mem. Assn. Advancement Modelling & Simulation Techniques in Enterprises, Polish Neural Networks Assn., Ukrainian Acad. Engring. Sci., N.Y. Acad. Sci., Ukrainian Engring. Soc. (pres. 1991—). Avocations: surrealistic short-story writing, cycling, mountain skiing, photography. Home: 95/34 Lubinska Str, 79054 Lviv 54, Ukraine Office: Lviv State Poly U, 12/110 Bandera Str, 79013 Lviv Ukraine

TCHAICOVSKY, BENY, artist, composer, musician; b. Rio de Janeiro, Brazil, Nov. 3, 1954; came to U.S., 1976; s. Jacob and Fany T. Owner, pres. Zoe Prodns., Fairfax, Calif., 1993-98; cons. Artnetwork Comms., Sausalito, Calif., 1994—. Composer record album Explorer, 1983; executed poster at Cannes Film Festival (first place award), 1996, 3D animation home video program, 1997. Recipient Gold Medal award Internat. Exhibition ABD, Rio, Brazil, 1982, Best of Show award Natsoulas Novelozo Gallery, Davis, Calif., 1988, Comendator of the Brazilian Assn. Fine Arts title, Rio, 1990, Hon. Mention award Eurographic's, 1998. Avocations: travel. E-mail: zoe@3dzoe.com. Fax: (415) 454-4925. Home and Office: 92 Piper Ln Fairfax CA 94930-1022

TCHESNOVA, LARISSA VASSILIEVNA, zoologist, science historian, researcher; b. Moscow, Mar. 30, 1931; d. Vassiliy Ilyitch and Tina Veniaminovna (Zelmans) Svetlitchniy; m. Mikhail Parfyonovitch Tchesnov, Apr. 10, 1954; 1 child, Vassiliy. Diploma, Moscow Lomonosvov State U., 1954; DSc in Zoology, Russian Acad. Scis., 1957. Rsch. asst. Inst. History Natural Scis. and Tech. Russian Acad. Scis., Moscow, 1957-70, sr. rsch. asst. Inst. History Natural Scis. and Tech., 1970-80, sr. rschr. Inst. History Natural Scis. and Tech., 1980—; expert Russian Found. Humanitarian Rsch., Moscow, 1995—. Author: Essays from the History of Applied Entomology in Russia, 1968, Problems of General Entomology, 1974, Evolutionary conception in Parasitology, 1978, Main Stages of Development of Ecology of Insect in Russia, 1988, (with B.R. Striganova) Soil Zoology--Science of the 20th Century, 1999. Mem. russian Soc. Entomologists, Russian Soc. Protozoologists, Moscow Soc. Investigators of Nature. Home: 14-14/16 Zemlianoy val, 103064 Moscow Russia Office: Russian Acad Scis Inst Nat Hist and Tech, 1/5 Staropansky per, 103012 Moscow Russia

TCHURIKOV, NICKOLAI ANDREEVICH, molecular geneticist; b. aul Elburgan, Russia, Oct. 21, 1949; s. Andrew S. and Matrena V. (Serbina) T.; m. Tatiana Veniaminovna Tchurikova, July 12, 1972; children: Andrew N., Konstantin N. MD, Stavropol State Med. Inst., 1972; PhD, Moscow Inst., 1977, DSc, 1989. Physician Kirov's (Russia) Dist. Hosp., 1972-74; scientist Inst. Molecular Biology Russian Acad. Scis., Moscow, 1974-77, sr. scientist, 1983-89, leading scientist, 1989-90, dept. head, 1990—; prof. molecular biology Engelhardt Inst. Molecular Biology, 1997—. Contbr. articles to profl. jours. Recipient USSR State Prize, 1983. Mem. Three Balls Tennis Club. Avocations: classical music, tennis, underwater sports. Office: Engelhardt Inst Molec Biol, Russian Acad Scis Vavilov Str 32, 117984 Moscow Russia

TCHURUK, SERGE (SERGE TCHURUKDICHIAN), engineering executive; b. Marseilles, France, Nov. 13, 1937; s. Georges and Mathilde (Dondikian) Tchurukdichian; m. Héléna Kalfus; 1 child, Valérie. BS, École Nationale Supérieure de l'Armement; MS, École Polytech. Various positions in refining and rsch. Mobile Oil, France and U.S., 1964-68; dir. ctr. rsch. Mobile Oil, France, 1968-70, dir. info. sys., 1971-73; attaché to internat. planning Mobile Oil, N.Y.C., 1973-77, attaché to external rels., 1977-79; pres., CEO Mobil Oil/BV, Rotterdam, The Netherlands, 1979-80; dir. divsn. fertilizer Rhône Poulenc, 1980-81, head basic chemistry, 1981-83, head chem. specialties, 1983; chmn. Rhône Poulenc Inc., 1983; asst. gen. dir. Group Rhône Poulenc, 1982, pres., 1983; pres. directorate CdF Chimie S.A., 1986; chmn., CEO Orkem (formerly CdF Chimie S.A.), 1987-90; adminstr. Total Compagnie Française des Pétroles S.A., Paris, 1989, pres., CEO, chmn., 1990—; chmn., CEO Alcatel, 2000. Decorated chevalier Legion of Honor, officer Ordre National du Mérite (France). Avocations: music, skiing, tennis. Office: Alcatel Alsthom Group, 54 Rue la Boetiet, 75008 Paris France*

TEACI, DUMITRU M., soil scientist, researcher; b. Tarnova, Romania, Nov. 25, 1925; s. Mihai I. and Eufrosina G. (Zac) T.; m. Eleonora P. Popescu, Jan. 20, 1955 (dec. Mar. 1998); 1 child, Danulet Daniela. Engr., Agrl. Inst., Timisoara, Romania, 1952; Dr in Agr., Agrl. U., Bucharest, Romania, 1966, PhD, 1975. Head of sect. Ministry of Agr., Bucharest, 1952-62; head sect. rsch. Inst. Soil Sci., Bucharest, 1962-76; sec.-gen. Acad. of Agr., Bucharest, 1976-87; rschr. I, Inst. Soil Sci., Bucharest, 1987-92; soil scientist, rschr. Academia destinte Agrl. Sci., Bucharest, 1992—; cons. FAO, Rome, 1965-85, Romanian Project in Iran, 1967-72, in Buenos Aires, 1974, in Lagos, Nigeria, 1975. Author: Soils of Romania, 1965, Agricultural Land Evaluation, 1967, Economia Funciara, 1979, Roman Agriculture and Forestry, 1999. Pres. Dem. Agrarian Party, Bucharest, 1990; v.p. Romanian Nat. Party, 1999. Mem. Romanian Acad. Agr. (prize 1985), Romanian Acad. Scientists, Romanian Soil Sci. Soc. (sec.-ten. 1970). Christian Orthodox. Avocations: music, literature. Home: Sos M Bravu 3, Bl 3 Ap 114, 73259 Bucharest Romania Office: Acvademia Agrl Sci, Bd Marasti 59, Bucharest Romania

TEAGUE, CHARLES WOODROW, lawyer; b. Thomasville, N.C., May 27, 1913; s. Lonnie Edwards and Dora Mae (Lassiter) T.; m. Jessie Randle Perry (div. 1976); m. Julia Brent Byrum, July 25, 1980; children: Kathy Randle Teague Jennings, Penny Randle Teague Eubanks, Charles W. Teague Jr. LLB, Wake Forest U., 1934. Bar: N.C. 1934, U.S. dist. Ct. (ea. and mid. dists.) N.C., U.S. Ct. Appeals (4th cir.), U.S. Supreme Ct. Claims atty. Liberty Mut. Ins. Co., Boston, 1934-35, High Point, N.C., 1936-38; claims atty. Lumber Mut. Casualty Ins. Co., Raleigh, N.C., 1938-42; ptnr. Teague, Campbell, Dennis & Gorham, Raleigh, 1946—; sec. N.C. R.R., Raleigh, 1960-64. Chmn. bd. elections Wake County, Raleigh, 1960-64. Lt. comdr. USN, 1942-46, PTO. Mem. N.C. Bar Assn. (chmn., bd. govs. 1960-64, councilor 1968-76, pres. 1977-78)), ABA (del.), Carolina Club, Country Club of N.C., Elk River Country Club, Kiwanis. Democrat. Presbyterian. Avocation: golf. Office: Teague Campbell Dennis & Gorham 1621 Midtown Pl Raleigh NC 27609-7553

TEAGUE, CHERYL JEAN, research institute official; b. Manchester, Eng., Aug. 6, 1956; d. Tom and Jean Mary (Gates) Muskett; m. Jeremy Charles William Teague, Sept. 24, 1977 (div. Aug. 1996); m. Peter Cyril White, Aug. 30, 1997. Degree in genetics, U. Nottingham, 1978. Med. rep. Eli Lilly & Co., Basingstoke, 1978-80; advt. and sales promotion exec. Royal Soc. Chemistry, Nottingham, 1980-89, dep. sales promotion mgr., pub. rels. mgr., 1989-95; comml. liaison mgr. U. Glasgow, 1995-99; comm. devel. mgr. Hannah Rsch. Inst., Ayr, Scotland, 1999—; ptnr., mktg. dir. Teague-Sands Lit. Svcs., Nottingham, 1986-89; cons. Royal Pharm. Soc., London, 1994; lectr., pub. spkr. at various events; leader, sec. Ayrshire Biosci. Network. Author: International Online Meeting, 1986; contbr. articles to profl. publs. Mem. Scottish BioNetwork Assn., Scottish Dairy Assn., Licensing Execs. Soc. Avocations: creative writing, curling, travel, the arts, scuba diving. Office: Hannah Rsch Inst, Ayr KA6 5HL, Scotland

TEAGUE, LAVETTE COX, JR., systems educator, consultant; b. Birmingham, Ala., Oct. 8, 1934; s. Lavette Cox and Caroline Green (Stokes) T. Student, Auburn U., 1951-54; BArch, MIT, 1957, MSCE, 1965, PhD, 1968; MDiv with distinction, Ch. Div. Sch. Pacific, 1979. Cert. computer profl. Inst. Cert. Computer Profls. Archtl. designer Carroll C. Harmon, Birmingham, 1957, Fred Renneker, Jr., Birmingham, 1958-59; architect Rust Engring. Co., Birmingham, 1959-62, Synergetics, Inc., Raleigh, N.C., 1962-64, Rust Engring. Co., Birmingham, 1964-68; rsch. asst., instr., rsch. assoc. MIT, Cambridge, 1964-68; dir. computer svcs. Skidmore Owings & Merrill, San Francisco, Chgo., 1968-74; postdoctoral fellow UCLA, 1972; adj. assoc. prof. arch. and civil engring. Carnegie-Mellon U., Pitts., 1973-74; archtl. systems cons. Chgo., 1974-75, Berkeley, Calif., 1975-80, Pasadena, 1980-82, Altadena, Calif., 1982—; lectr. info. systems Calif. State Poly. U., Pomona, 1980-81, prof., 1981-98, prof. emeritus, 1998—, asst. chair, 1990-91, chair, 1991-93, 96-98; Fulbright lectr., Uruguay, 1985. Author: Event-Based Analysis and Design: An Introduction to Structured Methods, 2000; co-author: Structured Analysis Methods for Computer Information Systems, 1985. Recipient Tucker-Voss award MIT, 1967; Fulbright scholar, 1985. Mem. AIA (Arnold W. Brunner scholar 1966), Assn. Computing Machinery, Sigma Xi, Phi Eta Sigma, Scarab, Scabbard and Blade, Tau Beta Pi, Chi Epsilon, Beta Gamma Sigma. Episcopalian. Home: 1696 N Altadena Dr Altadena CA 91001-3623 Office: 3801 W Temple Ave Pomona CA 91768-2557

TEARE, RICHARD WALLACE, ambassador; b. Cleve., Feb. 21, 1937; m. Jeanie Walter; 3 children. BA, Harvard U., 1958; student, Naval War Coll., 1977-78. Joined Fgn. Svc., 1959; vice consul U.S. Consulate, Bridgetown, Barbados, 1960-62; consular officer U.S. Embassy, Manila, The Philippines, 1962-64; polit. officer U.S. Embassy, Saigon, Vietnam, 1965-67, Mexico City, 1971-74; counselor for polit. affairs U.S. Embassy, Vientiane, Laos, 1974-76; dep. chief mission U.S. Embassy, Wellington, New Zealand, 1983-86, Canberra, Australia, 1986-89; dep. and acting prin. officer U.S. Consulate Gen., Nha Trang, Vietnam, 1973; intelligence and rsch. specialist Vietnam Working Group Dept. State, 1967-69, desk officer, 1969-71, spl. asst. to asst. sec. for East Asian and Pacific Affairs, 1976-77, dep. dir. Office Philippine Affairs, 1978-80, dep. and acting U.S. rep. for Micronesian Status Negotiations, 1980-83, dir. Office of Indonesia, Malaysia, Brunei and Singapore Affairs, 1989-92, spl. projects officer Office of Dir. Gen., 1992-93, U.S. amb. to Papua New Guinea, Solomon Islands and Vanuatu, 1993-96; fgn. policy advisor to the Commander in Chief U.S. Pacific Command, Camp Smith, Hawaii, 1996-98; dir. Ctr. Australian & New Zealand Studies, Sch. Fgn. Svcs. Georgetown U., 1999—. Mem. Am. Fgn. Svc. Assn., Sr. Fgn. Svc. Assn., Asia Soc., Nat. Trust Hist. Preservation. Office: Georgetown U Bldg ICC Rm 305 M 27th and O St NW Washington DC 20057*

TEASLEY, ELLA LORAINE, educational association administrator; b. Memphis, Oct. 6, 1951; d. Pete Turner and Ruth Roberta Teasley. Student, Wayne State U., 1969, Madonna Coll., Livonia, Mich., 1993, Marygrove Coll., Detroit, 1970—; B of Mgmt., Detroit Inst. Tech., 1973. Tchr. Semi-Quois Cmty. Ctr., Detroit, 1983; pres., CEO Mich. Latchkey Assn., Inc., Detroit, 1984—; v.p. Detroit Sch. Age Inc., 1991—; bd. dirs. Wayne County Child Care Coordinating Coun., Detroit, 1998—. Co-author: How to Start a Latchkey Program, 1990; presenter workshops. Mem. Wayne County Sch. Age Coalition, 1985—; mem. Detroit Pub. Sch. Latchkey Task Force, 1988; mem. Mich. Dept. Edn. Office of Spl. Edn. Svcs., 1997. Mem. Ch. of Christ. Avocations: travel, reading, movies. Home: 3352 Kendall St Detroit MI 48238-3817 Office: Mich Latchkey Assn Inc PO Box 27132 Detroit MI 48227-0132

TEATHER, DEREK, medical statistician, educator; b. Nottingham, Eng., Aug. 29, 1948; s. Harold and Vera Teather; m. Briony Ann Morton, July 16, 1983. BSc in Stats. with honors, City Univ., London, 1970; MSc in Advanced Stats., Univ. Coll., London, 1971; PhD, Coun. Nat. Acad. Awards, London, 1981. Lectr. in stats. Poly. Ctrl. London, Eng., 1974-76; sr. lectr. Leicester (Eng.) Poly., 1977-81, prin. lectr., 1981-82, reader, 1982-87; prof. De Montfort U., Leicester, 1987—, head dept. med. stats., 1994—, dir. grad. studies Sch. Computing Scis., 1994-98; mem. health svcs. bd. Coun. for Nat. Acad. Awards, London, 1985-87; assessor civil svc. stats. Civil Svc., London, 1989—. Fellow Royal Statis. Soc., C Stat. Avocations: mountain walking, trail cycling. Office: De Montfort Univ, De Montfort Univ, The Gateway, Leicester LE1 9BH, England

TEATHER, ELIZABETH KENWORTHY, geography educator; b. Halifax, Yorkshire, Eng., Apr. 2, 1943; d. Edward and Joyce Mary (Oakes) Kenworthy; m. David Charles Teather; children: Ceri Jane, Ian Kenworthy. BA with Honors, U. Coll. London, 1964; Cert. in Edn., U. Birmingham, Eng., 1965; PhD, U. Coll. London, 1970; BA with Honors, U. New Eng., Armidale, Australia, 1986. Sr. lectr. U. New Eng., Armidale, Australia, 1988—. Editor: Embodied Geographies, 1999; co-editor: Country Women at the Crossroads, 1994; contbr. articles to profl. jours. Fellow Royal Geog. Soc.; mem. Inst. Australian Geographers, Am. Geog. Soc., Country Women's Assn. New South Wales, Zonta. Avocations: singing, bushwalkng, riding horse, embroidery. Office: U New Eng, Sch Human & Environ Studies, Armidale 2351, Australia

TEBBY, JOHN CAESAR, chemist, researcher; b. London, Apr. 4, 1933; s. Archibald Harold and Marjory Louise (Jervis) T.; m. Margaret Lillian Heron-Elliott, Apr. 1, 1961; children: Susan Jane, Michael John, Kathryn Sarah, William Frazer. Grad., Royal Inst. Chemistry, London, 1958; PhD in Organic Chemistry, Nottingham (Eng.) U., 1961, DSc in Organic Chemistry, 1987. Sr./prin. lectr. North Staffordshire Poly., Stoke-on-Trent, 1964-80; head of chemistry dept./divsn. Staffordshire U., Stoke-on-Trent, 1980-98, prof. emeritus, 1998—; advisor on chemistry courses, external examiner specialist various univs., U.K.; cons. to various cos., U.K. Editor: (handbook) Phosphorus 31 Nuclear Magnetic Resonance DaVa, 1990; sr. reporter SPR Organophosphoras Chemistry, 1999—. Fellow Royal Soc. Chemistry (chartered); mem. North Staffordshire Royal Soc. Chemistry (chmn. and vice-chmn. local sect. 1982-86). Achievements include research on phosophorylation and organophosphorus chemistry. Avocations: tennis, bridge.

TECKLENBURG, HELGA ANNA, mathematics educator; b. Soltau, Fed. Republic Germany, June 19, 1954; d. Helmut and Edith (Dittfach) T. Degree in secondary teaching, U. Hannover, Fed. Republic Germany, 1979, Doctor's Degree, 1980, habilitation, 1988. Asst. U. Hannover, 1979-83, asst. lectr., 1984-90; substitute prof. math. U. Hamburg, Fed. Republic of Germany, 1991-92; lectr. Tech. Coll., Lüneburg, Fed. Republic Germany, 1989-91, U. Giessen, Germany, 1992-93; prof. math. Acad. Tech., Economy and Culture, Leipzig, Germany, 1993—. Contbr. articles to internat. jours. Recipient Christian Kuhlemann prize Hannoveran U. Community, 1983, Thales prize Diercks-von Zweck Found., 1991. Mem. German U. Assn., German Math. Assn., Math. Soc. Hamburg. Lutheran. Office: Hochschule für Technik Wirtschaft, Karl-Liebknecht-Strasse 132, D-04277 Leipzig Germany

TEDER, PRIIT, physician; b. Tartu, Estonia, Apr. 14, 1964; s. Vello and Taimi (Mets) T.; m. Elo Kirsimäe, Apr. 25, 1987 (div. June 9, 1998); children: Ingrid and Karina (twins). MD, Tartu U., 1988, postgrad., 1990-91; PhD, Uppsala (Sweden) U., 1996. Physician/intern, pulmonary fellow Tartu U. Lung Hosp., 1988-90, head of ward, 1991-92; head endoscopy unit ICU Tartu Univ. Lung Hosp., 1991-92, 1997; vis. scientist Uppsala U. Lung Hosp., 1992-93; postgrad. student, 1993-96; postdoctoral fellow Uppsala U., 1996-97; jr. phys., 1997-98; asst. prof. Uppsala U., 2000—; postdoctoral assoc. Section of Pulmonary and Critical Care, Yale Univ., 1998-2000. Contbr. articles to profl. jours. Head med. students labour union Tartu U., 1985-88. Swedish Heart Lung Found. grantee, 1995-98. Mem. Estonian Med. Assn., Swedish Assn. for Lung Medicine, European Respiratory Soc., The Swedish Soc. of Med. Avocations: tennis, Japanese martial arts, sailing, tennis. blues and jazz music, German literature. Office: Uppsala Univ Dept Lung Med, Akademiska sjukhuset, S-75185 Uppsala Sweden

TEDESCHI, RICHARD GLENN, psychologist, educator; b. Stamford, Conn., Sept. 19, 1950; s. Richard and Grace Mary Ellen (Dobelstein) T.; m. Joan Elizabeth Tedeschi, Jan. 30, 1988; 1 child, Michael. BA, Syracuse U., 1972; PhD, Ohio U., 1976. Lic. psychologist, N.C.; cert. health svc. provider in psychology. From lectr. to prof. U. N.C., Charlotte, 1976—. Co-author: Trauma and Transformation, 1995, Facilitation Posttraumatic Growth, 1999; co-editor: Posttraumatic Growth, 1998. Mem. APA, Assn. for Dental Edn. and Counseling, N.C. Psychol. Assn. (bd. dirs. 1995—). Democrat. Lutheran. Avocations: saxophone playing, horses. E-mail: rtedesch@email.uncc.edu. Office: Univ NC Charlotte Dept Psychology 9201 University City Blvd Charlotte NC 28223-1000

TEDIN, DELIA MARIE, interior decorator; b. Buenos Aires, Nov. 17, 1942; d. Horacio V. and Delia (Iriarte Udaondo) T.; m. Horadio Mazza (div.); children: Horacio, Delia, Sofia; m. Mariano T. Noblia; 1 child, Tristan.. BA, U. Buenos Aires, 1975; postgrad., Cátedra de Diseño, Buenos Aires; studied with, Michael Ham, Jesus Maria, Sagrado Corazon. With decorating firms Una Casa Diferente, 1982-85, Casa en Barrio Norte, Buenos Aires, 1984, Diseno, 1983; prin. Delia Tedin Ideas, Buenos Aires, 1976, 85, Estudio Delia Tedin y Asociados, 1989—. Contbr. to numerous publs. Mem. Decorators Assn. Republic Argentina (bd. dirs.), Orgn. Ferias Multiples, Colaboration Grupos Danza y Teatro. Clubs: Tennis Argentina, Yate Argentina.

TEDROFF, JOAKIM MIHKEL, neuroscientist; b. Göteborg, Sweden, Oct. 30, 1961; s. Sven and Elna (Kann) T.; m. Kristina Birgitta Ekesbo, May 17, 1986; children: Antonia, Carl Johan, Hugo, Marika. MD, Uppsala (Sweden) U., 1989, PhD, 1990. Intern Löwenströms Hosp., Stockholm, 1990-92; resident Univ. Hosp., Uppsala, 1993-97, cons. neurology, 1998; cons. neurologist Huddinge U. Hosp., 1999—; assoc. prof. neurology Uppsala U., 1995—; cons. Pharmacia & Upjohn Inc., Stockholm, 1998—; dir. A. Carlsson Rsch. AB, Sweden, 1998—. Lt. Nordlands Cavalry Regiment, Sweden, 1980-82. Mem. N.Y. Acad. Scis., Movement Disorder Soc. Home: Skiljev 2, SE-18256 Danderyd Sweden Office: Huddinge U Hosp, Divsn Neurology, SE-14186 Huddinge Sweden

TEDROS, THEODORE ZAKI, real estate broker, appraiser, educator; b. Cairo, June 25, 1910; Naturalized, 1966; s. Zaki and Faika (Lotfi) T.; married 1962; 1 child, Samuel N. BA in Math., Tex. Christian U., 1957, MEd with honors, 1958; postgrad., Fla. State U., 1961. Tchr. pub. schs., Addis Ababa, Ethiopia, 1947-56, The American Inst., Addis Ababa, Ethiopia, 1952-56; instr. math. Fla. State U., Tallahassee, 1958-59; tchr. math. Fla. Mil. Sch. and Coll., Deland, Fla., 1961-64; tchr. Volusia County Bd. Instrn., Deland, 1964-75; real estate broker Daytona Beach, Fla., 1975-98, appraiser, 1978-92; prof. ednl. sociology U. Man., Winnipeg, Can., summers 1962-64. Sunday sch. tchr., Fla.; mem. Nat. Coun. Math. Tchrs., 1959-75, Phi Delta Kappa, 1960-80. Mem. Nat. Assn. Master Appraisers (v.p. 1985-86), Fla. Assn. Realtors, Daytona Beach Area Bd. Realtors, Nat. Assn. Realtors (cert. 1978-90). Democrat. Home: 227 Kensington Ave Deland FL 32724-2321

TEEKE, KATAOTIKA, Kiribati government official; b. Tarawa, Kiribati, Sept. 8, 1947. Student, St. Joseph's Coll., Kiribati, U.S.P. Suva Sch. Arts & Tech., U.K., INTAN, Malaysia, UNCRD, Nogoya, Japan. Rschr. indigenous politics in Kirabati and other islands Pacific; mem. Parliament, Govt. of Kiribati, Tarawa Atoll, 1994—, min. of health, fam. planning and social welfare, 1994—; min. environment and social devel., 1998—. Office: Ministry Health Fam Plan, PO Box 268 Bikenibeu, Tarawa Kiribati

TEEM, PAUL LLOYD, JR., bank executive; b. Gastonia, N.C., Mar. 10, 1948; s. Paul Lloyd Sr. and Ruth Elaine (Bennett) T. BA, U. N.C., 1970; Cert., Inst. Fin. Edn., Chgo., 1984, Diploma, 1985, Degree of Distinction, 1989. Cert. tchr. N.C., cert. consumer credit exec.; lic. real estate broker. Exec. v.p., sec. Gaston Fed. Bank, Gastonia, N.C., 1983—; exec. v.p., sec., bd. dirs. Gaston Fin. Svcs. Inc., Gastonia, N.C., 1988—; exec. v.p., sec. Gaston Fed. Holdings, Mut. Holding Co., Gastonia, 1998—, Gaston Fed. Bancorp, Inc., Gastonia, 1998—. Bd. dirs. Gastonia Mchts. Assn., Inc., 1981-83; lay reader Episcopal Ch. Decorated Order Purple Cross, Legion of Honor; named Ky. Col., 1995. Fellow Soc. Cert. Credit Execs.; mem. Nat. Soc. Sons and Daus. of Pilgrims, SAR, Sons of Confederate Vets., Mil. Order of Stars and Bars, Masons (32d degree, bd. dirs. 1981—, Disting. Svc. award 1987, Gold Honor award 1988, Active Legion of Honor 1989, Order of the Purple Cross of York 1990), Shriners, KT, Royal Order of Scotland, Hon. Order Ky. Cols., Phi Alpha Theta. Democrat. Avocation: genealogy. Home: 1208 Poston Cir Gastonia NC 28054-4634 Office: Gaston Fed Bank PO Box 2249 Gastonia NC 28053-2249

TEETS, WALTER RALPH, accounting educator; b. Boulder, Colo., Oct. 1, 1950; s. Otis E. and Elsie (Purchase) T.; m. Mary Anne Clougherty; stepchildren: Katherine Wierman, Elizabeth Wierman. B in Music Edn., U. Colo., 1973; MMus, U. Wis., Madison, 1976; MS in Edn., U. Wis., Whitewater, 1981, MS in Acctg., 1985; PhD, U. Chgo., 1989. CPA. Asst. prof. Wash. U., St. Louis, 1986-89, U. Ill., Urbana-Champaign, Ill., 1989-94, Gonzaga U., Spokane, Wash., 1994-99; assoc. prof. Gonzaga U., Spokane, 1999—; continuing profl. edn. spkr. Gonzaga U., 1996-2000, Wash. Soc. CPAs, numerous others; vis. assoc. prof. U. Notre Dame, 2000. Editor Fin. Reporting Jour., 1998—; contbr. articles to profl. jours. Recipient Outstanding Acctg. Educator award Wash. Soc. CPAs, 1998-99; Acad. acctg. fellow Office of Chief Acct., U.S. SEC, 1997-98. Mem. Am. Acctg. Assn. (editor Fin. Reporting Jour. newsletter Fin. Acctg. and Reporting sect. 1998—), K.C. (fin. sec. 1990-93, 99—). Avocations: music, cross-country skiing, four-wheeling. E-mail: teets@gem.gonzaga.edu. Fax: 509-323-5811. Office: Gonzaga Univ 502 E Boone Ave Spokane WA 99258-0001

TEGHEM, JACQUES, mathematics educator; b. Brussels, Feb. 3, 1948; s. Jean and Claire (Desirs) T.; m. Anne Marie Vanopdenbosch, Oct. 24, 1969; 1 child: Stephanie. MS, Free U. of Brussels, 1969, PhD, 1976. Asst. prof. Faculte Poly. de Mons, Belgium, 1976-90, prof. math. and ops. rsch., 1990—; prof. Free U. Brussels, 1982—. Author: Multiobjective Linear Programming Under Uncertainty, 1990; editor European Jour. Ops. Rsch., 1999—. Home: 27 Av Marechal Joffre, 1190 Brussels Belgium Office: Faculte Poly Mons, Rue de Houdain 9, 7000 Mons Belgium

TEGNER, IAN NICOL, financial executive; b. London, July 11, 1933; s. Sven Stuart and Peggy (Nicol) T.; m. Meriel Helen Lush, May 13, 1961; children: Kirstin Ruth Neill Edwards, Luke Nicol. Grad. advanced mgmt. program, Harvard U. Bus. Sch., 1974. Apprenticed chartered acct. Jenks Percival Pigeon & Co., 1952-57; acct. Clarkson Gordon & Co., Chartered Accts., Toronto, Ont., 1958-59; acct. Barton Mayhew & Co., Chartered Accts., London, 1959-65, ptnr., 1965-71; fin. dir. Bowater plc, 1971-86; dir. group fin. Midland Bank plc, London, 1987-89; chmn. Control Risks Group Ltd., London, 1990—; non-exec. chmn. Crest Packaging plc, 1993-99; non-exec. dir. Arjo Wiggins Appleton plc, Teesside Power plc, Coutts & Co., 1996-98, T.I.P. Europe plc, 1992-93; mem. acctg. stds. com. CCAB, 1984-86; external mem. M.O.D. Mgmt. Audit Bd., 1987-97; mem. editl. adv. coun. Corp. Governance, 1992—. Founder, trustee Latimer Housing Soc., 1964-80; trustee Lindley Ednl. Trust, 1977-93, English Touring Opera Ltd., 1990-99, Gower St. Sec. Mechanisms Trust, MacIntyre Care, 1993-95, Prince Consort Found., 1994—; v.p. The Country Trust, 1987—; steward The Argyllshire Gathering, 1992-97. Mem. Inst. Chartered Accts. of Scotland (pres. 1991-92), Hundred Group of Fin. Dirs. (chmn. 1988-90). Avocations: travel, book collecting, music, walking. Office: Control Risks Group Ltd, 83 Victoria St, London SW1H 0HW, England

TEGNER, YELVERTON S. R., medical consultant; b. Halmstad, Sweden, June 20, 1946; s. Sven O. and Myra J. (Fex) T.; m. Monica G. Ågren, Nov. 8, 1975; children: Andreas, Cecilia. BA, U. Lund, 1974, MD, 1974; PhD, U. Linkoping, 1985. Register Region Hosp., Lulea, Sweden, 1974-80, Ctrl. Hosp., Boden, Sweden, 1980-81; cons. U. Linkoping, Sweden, 1981-85, Ctrl. Hosp., Boden, 1985-91, The Ermine Clinic, Lulea, 1991—; assoc. prof. U. Umea, Sweden, 1991—. Author: Cruciate Ligament Injures in the Knee, 1985. Mem. Rotary. Avocations: golf, reading, riding. Office: The Ermine Clinic, PO Box 195, Luleå Sweden

TEGOS, STERGHIOS MICHALIS, neurosurgeon; b. Grevena, Macedonia, Greece, Mar. 25, 1950; s. Michalis Miltiadis and Soultana Sterghios (Michi) T.; m. Athina George Kleovoulou, Feb. 21, 1981; children: Georgia, Michalis. MD, U. Ferrara, 1976; neurosurgeon, U. Milan, 1982. House officer Neurosurg. Clinic, Ferrara, Italy, 1977-78; sr. registrar Neurosurg. Clinic, Milan, Italy, 1977-82, Neurosurg. Polyclinic, Athens, Greece, 1982-86; dept. chief neurosurgery Army VA Hosp., Athens, 1986—. Editor: Microneurosurgery with Video Tapes, 1998. Avocations: archery, shooting, diving. Home: 6 Bacopoulou St, 15451 Athens Greece

TEGZE, MIKLOS, physicist; b. Budapest, Hungary, Dec. 7, 1954; s. Miklos and Judit (Farkas) T.; m. Maria Putsay, Aug. 12, 1985; children: Anna, Borbala. Diploma, Eötvös U., Budapest, 1979, PhD, 1981; Candidate of Phys. Sci., Hungarian Acad. Sci., Budapest, 1991. Sci. co-worker Ctrl. Rsch. Inst. for Physics, Budapest, 1982-91; sr. sci. co-worker Rsch. Inst. for Solid State Physics, Budapest, 1991—; guest scientist U. Groningen (The Netherlands), 1982-84, Tech. U. Vienna (Austria), 1987-88. Contbr. over 70 articles to sci. jours. Recipient Széchenyi prize Republic of Hungary, 1999. Mem. Eötvös Phys. Soc. (Rezső Schmid award 1994). Achievements include work on the first experimental realization of atomic resolution X-ray holography. Office: Rsch Inst Solid State Physics, PO Box 49, H-1525 Budapest Hungary

TEICH, ALBERT HARRIS, professional society administrator; b. Chgo., Dec. 17, 1942; s. Maurice and Ina (Szuldiner) T.; m. Carolyn R. Richmond, June 3, 1965 (div. 1987); children: Mitchell Craig, Kenneth David; m. Jill H. Pace, Jan. 29, 1989; 1 child, Samantha Lynne. BS, MIT, 1964, PhD, 1969. Rsch. fellow Syracuse (N.Y.) U. Rsch. Corp., 1969-71, dir., sci. and tech. studies, 1971-73; coord. rsch. SUNY, Binghamton, 1973-74; dir. rsch. SUNY Inst. for Pub. Policy Alternatives, Albany, 1974-76; assoc. prof. pub. affairs and dep. dir., grad. program sci. tech. and pub. policy George Washington U., 1976-79; mgr., sci. policy studies AAAS, Washington, 1980-84, head, office of pub. sector programs, 1984-89, dir. sci. and policy programs, 1989—; cons. Nat. Acad. Scis., Office of Tech. Assessment, Washington, 1976-95, Orgn. for Econ. Cooperation and Devel., Paris, 1994—; chmn. SRS adv. com. NSF, Washington, 1988-90; pres. Technoscience Assocs., Inc., Silver Spring, Md., 1977-82. Editor: Science and Technology in the U.S.A., 1986, Technology and the Future, 8th edit., 2000; editor, author: Scientists and Public Affairs, 1974; mem. editl. bd. Science Communication, 1991—, Science, Technology and Human Values, 1994—, Prometheus, 1999—. Fellow AAAS (chmn. sect. X 1988); mem. Tech. Transfer Soc. (v.p. 1985-91), Am. Soc. for Pub. Adminstrn. (mem. editl. bd. 1985-89), Soc. for Social Studies of Scis., Sigma Xi. Avocations: swimming, photography, travel writing. Office: AAAS 1200 New York Ave NW Washington DC 20005-3941

TEICH, HOWARD BERNARD, lawyer, activist, public affairs specialist; b. Huntington, N.Y., Nov. 1, 1946; s. Samuel and Beatrice Ann (Kay) T. AB, U. Pa., 1967; JD, Boston U., 1970. Bar: N.Y., 1971, U.S. Dist. Ct. (so. dist.) N.Y. 1984. Counsel N.Y. State Senator Emanuel Gold, N.Y.C., 1971-72; law sec. N.Y. State Supreme Ct. Justin Martin Evans, N.Y.C., 1972-75; assoc. pub. Firehouse mag., N.Y.C., 1975-79; pub. Midtown South Bus., N.Y.C., 1985-87; prin. Law Offices Howard B. Teich, N.Y.C., 1980—; sr. cons. The Kamber Group, Washington, 1995—; sr. counsel McLaughlin & Stein, P.C., N.Y.C., 1997—. Founder, chair New Dem. Dimensions, N.Y.C., 1981-91, Nat. Task Force on Life Safety for Handicapped, Washington, 1979-81; bd. dirs. Boys Choir of Harlem, N.Y.C., 1983-85, Assn. on Am. Indian Affairs, 1990-97, adv. bd., 1997—; chmn. New Leadership of Israel Bonds, N.Y.C., 1977-79; pres. Am. Jewish Congress Met. Region N.Y.C., 1992—, past nat. v.p.; bd. dirs. Jewish Comty. Rels. Coun., N.Y., 1995—, past v.p., 1995-98; co-chair Jewish Heritage, N.Y.C., 1997—;dep. dir. N.Y. state citizens com. McGovern for Pres., 1972, Samuels for Gov., 1974, Carey for Gov., 1974; dep. dir. N.Y. state primary campaign Carter for Pres., 1980; co-chair N.Y. state citizens com. Glenn for Pres., 1984, Mondale/Ferraro '84, 1984; bd. dirs. Manhattan Playhouse. Recipient Robert Briscoe award Emerald Isle Immigration Soc., 1996, Israel Leadership award Israel Bonds, 1979, Martin Luther King Jr. Living-the-Dream award, Gov. George Pataki, N.Y., 1999. Mem. AJ Congress Met Region (pres. 1992—), U. Pa. Club, Assn. on Am. Indian Affairs (bd. dirs., nat. adv. bd.). Democrat. Jewish. Avocations: N.Y.C. marathon, softball, tennis, reading, theatre, dance. Home: 185 E 85th St New York NY 10028-2140 Office: 260 Madison Ave New York NY 10016-2401

TEICH, JEFFREY ERNEST, business educator, entrepreneur; b. Rush City, Minn., June 11, 1960; s. Ernest Albert and Evelyn Ann Teich; m. Gabriele Teich, Feb. 26, 1999; 1 child, Lara Margareta. BS, Ariz. State U., 1982, MS, 1984; PhD, SUNY, Buffalo, 1991. Faculty assoc. Ariz. State U.,

Tempe, 1984-86; grad. asst. SUNY, Buffalo, 1986-90; from asst. to assoc. prof. N.Mex. State U., Las Cruces, 1990—; vis. prof. Helsinki Sch. Econs., 1998, vis. scholar, 1989. Contbr. articles to profl. jours. including Electronic Markets, Decision Support Sys.; inventor (software) NegotiAuction, 2000. Mem. Internat. Soc. Multiple Criteria Decision Making, Decision Scis. Inst., INFORMS, Alpha Iota Delta, Sigma Iota Epsilon, Beta Gamma Sigma, Alpha Iota Delta. Avocations: computers, tennis, beach paddle ball, backgammon, travel. Office: NMex State U Dept Mgmt Las Cruces NM 88003

TEICHLER, STEPHEN LIN, lawyer; b. Charleston, W.Va., Jan. 30, 1952; s. Alfred H. and Marjorie R. (Dunbar) T.; m. Dana Ruth Hegerle, Aug. 6, 1977; children: Adam Reed, Ryan Stephen. BA, U. Va., 1974, JD, 1977. Bar: Va. 1977, D.C. 1977. Atty. Dept. Air Force Office of Gen. Counsel, Washington, 1977-80, Baker & Botts, Washington, 1980-95; Metzger & Hollis, 1995-97; atty. Duane Morris & Heckscher, Washington, 1997—. Capt. USAF, 1977-80. Lutheran. Home: 8315 Chapel Lake Ct Annandale VA 22003-4401 Office: Duane Morris & Heckscher 1667 K St NW Ste 700 Washington DC 20006-1608

TEICHLER, ULRICH CHRISTIAN, higher education educator, researcher; b. July 23, 1942; s. Johannes and Erika (Petersen) T.; m. Yoko Urata; children: Nils-Erik Shinichiro, Matthias Tim Yoshio. Diplom-Soziologe, Free U. Berlin, 1968; Dr.Phil, U. Bremen, 1975. Rsch. fellow Max-Planck Inst. Edni. Rsch., Berlin, 1968-78; guest rschr. Nat. Inst. Ednl. Rsch., Tokyo, 1970-72; prof. for rsch. on higher edn. and work Comprehensive U. Kassel, Hessen, Fed. Republic Germany, 1978—, v.p., 1980-82; dir. Ctr. for Rsch. on Higher Edn. and Work, Kassel, 1978—; fellow Netherlands Inst. for Advanced Study, Wassenaar, 1985-86; vis. prof. Sch. Edn. and Social Policy Northwestern U., Evanston, Ill., 1986-92; Japan SAP fellow Nagoya U., 1992; prof. Coll. Europe, Bruges, 1994-96. Author: Bibliography on Japanese Education, 1974, Theologie und gesellschaftliche Praxis, 1974, Der Arbeitsmarkt für Akademiker in Japan, 1975, Geschichte und Struktur des Japanischen Hochschulwesens, 1975, Das Dilemma der modernen Bildungsgesellschaft, 1976, Admission to Higher Education in the United States, 1978, Aspekte der Studienreform, 1979, Die neuen Beamtenhochschulen, 1980, Higher Education and the Needs of Society, 1981, Der Arbeitsmarkt für Hochschulabsolventen, 1981, Gesamthochschule-Erfahrungen, Hemnisse, Zielwandel, 1981, Bildung und Beschäftigung, 1981, Beispiele praxisorientierten Studiums, 1981, Implementation of Higher Education Reforms: The German Gesamthochschule, 1981, HIgher Education and the Labour Market in the Federal Republic of Germany, 1982, Hochschulzertifikate und betriebliche Einstellungspraxis, 1984, Higher Education in the European Community: Recognition of Study Abroad in the European Community, 1986, Hochschule-Studium-Berufsvorstellungen, 1987; Convergence of Growing Variety: The Changing Organisation of Studies, 1988, Auslandsstudium im Vergleich, 1988, Erträge des Auslandsstudiums für Studierende und Absolventen, 1988, Changing Patterns of the Higher Education System, 1988, Europäische Hochschulsysteme, 1990, The Impact of Study Abroad Programmes on Students and Graduates, 1990, Experiences and Careers of Science and Engineering Fellows Supported by the European Community, 1990, Bestand und Perspektiven der Weiterbildung, 1991, Learning in Europe, 1991, Handbook of Higher Education Diplomas in Europe, 1992, Transition to Work, 1994, Durchfürung von EG-Bildungsprogrammen in Deutschland, 1994, Berufsbild der Lehrenden und Forschenden an Hochschulen, 1995, Study Abroad and Early Career, 1996, Bestand und Entwicklungsrichtungen der Weiterbildung in Schleswig-Holstein, 1996, The ERASMUS Experience 1997, Integrating Europe through Co-operation Among Universities, 1997, European Research Fellowships 1987-1993, 1997, Tertiary Professional and Vocational Education in Central and Eastern Europe, 1998, Der Übergang von Bildungs zum Beschäftigungssystem in Japan, 2000; editor: Praxisorientierung des Studiums, 1979, Hochschule und Beruf, 1979, Praxisorientierung als institionelles Problem der Hochschule, 1980, Hochschule und Beruf-Forschungsperspektiven, 1981, Gesamthochschule Kassel 1971-81, 1981, Hochschuleund Beruf in Polen und in der Bundesrepublik Deutschland, 1983, Berufstätigkeit von Hochschulabsolventen, 1983, The Compleat University: Break from Tradition in Germany, Sweden and the U.S.A., 1983, Hochschule und gesellschaftliche Entwicklung in Polen und der Bundersrepublik Deutschland, 1984, Forschungsgestand Hochschule, 1984, Hochschulentwicklung in den 60er Jahren, 1986, Hochschule - Beruf - Gesellschaft, 1988, Der Berufsstart von Hochschulsbsolventen, 1990, Das Hochschulwesen in der Bundesrepublik Deutschland, 1990, Hochschulabsolventen im Beruf, 1992, Higher Education and Work, 1995, Academic Mobility in a Changing World, 1996, Berufliche Kompetenzentwicklung im Bildungs und Beschäftigungssystem in Japan und Deutschland, 1998, Brennpunkt Hochschule, 1998; Higher Edn. Rsch., 2000; contbr. articles to profl. jours. Mem. Higher Edn. Coun. State of Bremen, 1981-85. Recipient Coun. Internat. Ednl. Exch. prize, 1997, Comenicus prize UNESCO, 1998. Mem. Internat. Acad. Edn., Acad. Europe, Consortium Higher Edn. Rschrs. Home: Haroldstr 11, D-34128 Kassel Hessen, Germany Office: Wissenschaftliches Zentrum für Berufs und Hochschul forsc, Univ Gesamthochschule Henschelstr 4, D-34109 Kassel Hessen Germany

TEIG, MARLOWE GILMAN, investment banker; b. Fargo, N.D., Sept. 13, 1938; s. Julius Berner Teig and Anita (Hedlund) Teig-Erickson; m. Carole Lynne Werner, Nov. 25, 1961; children: Jennifer Lynne, Alan Gilman. B.A., U. Mich., 1961; postgrad., CCNY, 1962-64. With Harcourt Brace Jovanovich, 1964-80, Houghton Mifflin Co., 1980-87, Macmillan, Inc., 1987-88; mng. dir. Berkery, Noyes & Co., Newton, Mass., 1990—. Home: 40 Kirkstall Rd Newton MA 02460-2218

TEIGE, SCOTT WERNER, physicist; b. Chgo., Oct. 15, 1957; s. Roy and Elaine Lenore Teige; m. Kathryn Preston, Sept. 9, 1984; children: Jill, Amy. BA, U. Wis., 1979; MS, Ind. U., 1981, PhD, 1985. Fellow Rutgers U., Piscataway, N.J., 1985-90; Chester Davis fellow Ind. U., Bloomington, 1990, asst. scientist, 1990-92, assoc. scientist, 1992-99, sr. scientist, 1999—. E-mail: teige@kiva.net or teige@dustbunny.physics.indiana.edu. Office: Ind Univ Dept Physics 727 E 3rd St Bloomington IN 47405-7105

TEIKARI, VEIKKO OLAVI, industrial psychology educator; b. Jyväskylä, Finland, July 21, 1943; s. Onni Edward and Tyyne Hilja (Putkonen) T.; m. Eira Marjaana Eräntie, Nov. 1, 1969; children: Taru, Mika. D in Social Scis., U. Jyväskylä, 1977. Asst. Inst. Psychology U. Jyväskylä, 1967-68; sr. asst. Lab Indsl. Psychology U. Tech., Espoo, Finland, 1969-73, lab. mgr., 1973-84, prof., 1985—; leader dept. prodn. mgmt. Helsinki U. Tech., 1986-91. Author: Vigilanssi-ilmiön mittaamisesta ja sietysmahdollisuuksista, 1977, Vartiainen, M., Teikari, V. and Pulkkis, A. Psykologinen työnopetus, 1989, The Work Flow Game for Knowledge Work, A Handbook, 1998, others; contbr. articles to profl. jours. With Finnish mil., 1963-64. Mem. Psychol. Soc. Finland, Ergonomic Soc. Finland. Avocation: fishing. Home: Särkiniementie 10 C 16, 00210 Helsinki Finland Office: U Tech HUT, Box 9500, 02150 Espoo Finland

TEISSIER, HENRI, archbishop; b. Lyon, France, July 21, 1929; s. Henri and Marie-Claire (Richard) T. Licence de lettres, U. de Rabat, Morocco, 1948; Licence de philosophie, U. Paris, 1950; Licence de théologie, Cath. Inst., Paris, 1955. Ordained priest Roman Cath. Ch., 1955, bishop, 1973, archbishop, 1981. Dir. Study Centre of Ch. in Algiers, Algeria, 1966-73; bishop of Oran West Algeria, 1973-81; archbishop of Algiers, 1981—; pres. Bishop Conf. of North Africa, Algiers, 1981; mem. Vatican Sec. for Interreligious Dialogue, 1978-81, coun. Synod of Bishops, Vatican City, 1983-87, 89—, v.p. Caritas Internat., 1981-87; com. cons. Internat. Interligieux de l'UNESCO, 1998. Author: Eglise en Islam, 1984, La Mission de l'Eglise, 1985; coord.: Histoire des chrétiens d'Afrique du Nord, 1991, Lettres d'Algérie, 1998. Office phone: 213-2-74-41-22. Home phone: 213-2-92-56-67. Address: Archbishopric of Algiers, 13 rue Khélifa-Boukhalfa, DZ-16000 Algiers Algeria*

TEISSONNIERE, GERARDO, musician, educator; b. Ponce, PR. MMus, Cleve. Inst. Music. Mem. piano faculty Cleve. Inst. Music, 1989—. Recipient Arthur Loesser Meml. award Cleve. Inst. Music, 1985. Mem. Music Tchrs. Nat. Assn. Office: Cleve Inst Music 11021 East Blvd Cleveland OH 44106-1705

TEITELBAUM, JOAL, engineering executive, consultant; b. Uruguaiana, Brazil, June 9, 1937; s. Jose and Celina (Gus) T.; m. Raquel Foguel, Jan. 21, 1962; children: Silvio, Jader, Claudio, Flavio. Degree in civil engring., Fed. U. Rio Grande do Sul, Porto Alegre, Brazil, 1960. Founder, pres. Joal Teitelbaum Engring. Bur., Porto Alegre, 1961—; gen. dir. dept. airports Brazil, 1965-69, gen. sec. constrn. industry coun., 1976-89; v.p. Brazilian Chamber Constrn. Industry Brazil, 1981-95; gen. coord. Brazilian Program Quality and Productivity, 1991-94; mem. bd. dirs., pres. strategic planning com. Inter-Am. Fedn. of the Constrn. Industry, 1983-95; president Brazil/Chile C. of C. and Industry, 1995—; del. steering com. Confedn. Internat. Contractors Assn., 1987-95. Contbr. articles to profl. jours. Bd. dirs. ENCO, 1971-88; mem. Inter-Am. Planning Assn., 1965-85, steering com. Free Trade Area of Ams., 1997—. 2d lt. Brazilian Army, 1956-58. Recipient Merit and Medal Order of Pub. Svc., 1986, Honor Merit award Brazil Chamber of Constrn. Industry Quality Program, 1994, 97, 98, 99, Merit award RS Sys. Quality and Productivity, 1997, 98, 99, 2000, Merit trophy, 1999, 2000, Environ. Nat. First Prize award Brazil's Nat. Industry Confedn., 2000. Mem. Rio Grande do Sul Engring. Assn., Constrn. Industry Employers Assn., Brazil-USA Cultural Inst., So. Cone Integration Routes Com. (pres. 1998—), Rotary (bd. dirs. Porto Alegre club 1972-94). Avocations: tennis, soccer, travel, music, making video films. E-mail: eejt@zaz.com.br. Fax: 55 51 222 63 83. Office: Rua Tobias Silva 253, Porto Alegre 90570020, Brazil

TEITTINEN, PENTTI JOHANNES, retired agriculturist; b. Korpilahti, Finland, May 26, 1927; s. Toivo and Aili (Aaltonen) T.; m. Aino Penttila, 1950 (div. 1984); children: Leena, Riitta, Jukka, Matti; m. Pirkko Marttila (dec. 1998). MScAgr, U. Helsinki, Finland, 1951, DScAgr, 1975. Agronomic Diplomate. Rschr. Agrl. Rsch. Ctr., 1950-58, rsch. sta. dir., 1958-73, 75-80; chief inspector Ministry Agriculture and Forestry, 1973-74; dir. Seed Testing Sta., 1981-89, Nat. Bd. of Agriculture, 1990-92; ret., 1992; lectr. agroecology U. Helsinki, 1977-92, prof., 1981—; with Coun. for Agrl. and Forestry in Finland's Acad., 1980-85. Co-author, author several books and periodicals. Chmn., bd. dirs. several schs. and mcpl. bodies. Corp. Anti-Aircraft Artillery, 1944. Decorated World War II Commemorative medal; named Knight Order of the White Rose in Finland, Comdr. Order of the Lion in Finland. Mem. Union of Agrl. Socs. (bd. dirs. 1976-91), Finnish Beekeeper's Assn. (chmn. 1986-91), Kallio (Helsinki) Rotary Club (pres. 1994-95). Avocations: forestry, genealogy. Home: Halssilanperä 2B, 40400 Jyväskylä Finland

TEIXEIRA, FERNANDO LISBOA, electrical engineer, researcher; b. Rio de Janeiro, Nov. 24, 1969; came to U.S., 1996; s. Fernando Alberto de Castro and Maria Lucia Mello (Lisboa) T. BSEE, Cath. U., Rio de Janeiro, 1991, MSEE, 1995; PhD, U. Ill., 1999. Rschr. Ctr. for Telecommunication Studies, Rio de Janeiro, 1991; staff engr. Brazilian Army R&D Inst., Rio de Janeiro, 1992-94; engr. Satellite Transmission Dept. Embratel MCI Worldcom, Rio de Janeiro, Brazil, 1994-96; rsch. asst. U. Ill., Urbana, 1996-99; postdoctoral assoc. MIT, Cambridge, 1999—. Contbr. articles to profl. jours. 1st lt. Brazilian Army, 1992-94. Decorated Marshal Hermes medal. Mem. IEEE (fellowship 1998), Phi Kappa Phi. Roman Catholic. Avocations: reading Shakespearian drama, listening to Western classical music, tennis, jogging. E-mail: fernando@ewt.mit.edu. Office: MIT 77 Massachusetts Ave # 26-305 Cambridge MA 02139-4307

TEIXEIRA, GAIL, Guyanese government official; b. July 18, 1952; married; 2 children. BA in History, U. Toronto, 1974; MA in Polit. Sci., York (Eng.) U., 1976. Mem., exec. com. People's Progressive Party; sec. Women's Progressive Orgn.; personal sec. to Pres. Jagan Govt. of Guyana, 1977-92, MP, 1992—; sr. min. of health Govt. of Guyana, Brickdam, Georgetown, Guyana; min. of culture, youth and sports Govt. of Guyana, Brickdam, Guyana. Mem. People's Progressive Party. Office: Min Culture/Youth & Sports, 71 Main St/N Commonsburg, Georgetown Guyana*

TEIXEIRA, PAULA CRISTINA MAIA, microbiologist, researcher; b. Maia, Portugal, June 4, 1967; d. Carlos Santos Teixeira and Maria Emilia Campos Maia; m. Rui Alves Costa Maia, Sept. 21, 1991; children: Manuel Carlos, Francisca. BS, Escola Superior Biotech, Porto, Portugal, 1990; PhD, Escola Superior Biotec, Porto, Portugal, 1995. Tchr., researcher Escola Superior Biotecnologia, Porto, 1990—. Contbr. articles to profl. jours. and books. Tchr. Maia's Catholic Ch., 1991-95. Roman Catholic. Avocation: sports. Office: Escola Superior Biotec, R Dr António Bernardino, de Almeida 4200 Porto Portugal

TEIXEIRA-LEITE, MANUEL ADALBERTO LEONARDO, architect, consultant; b. Lisboa, Portugal, Nov. 29, 1951; s. Manuel Rodriguez Teixeira-Leite and Maria De Lurdes G. Fernandes Leonardo Teixeira-Leite; m. Teresa De Jesus Afonso Bravo, May 15, 1989. MS, Escola Superior Belas Artes Porto, Porto, Portugal, 1982. Tech. adv. Uniao De Bancos Portugueses, Porto, Lisboa, Portugal, 1984-87, sr. cons., 1987-90; dir. Icon-Image Consultancy, Porto, 1989—; lecturer Curso Superior de Arquitectura, Porto, 1987-88. Mem. Assn. Deficientes das Forças Armadas, Lisboa, Porto, 1975-93. Capt. Infantry, 1971-74. Recipient Premio Eng. Ant. Almeida Fundacao Eng. Ant. Almeida, Porto, 1983. Mem. Smithsonian Inst., Am. Assn. Advancement Scis., N.Y. Acad Sci., Morgan Sports Car Club. Avocations: painting, sailing, scuba diving. Office: Icon-Image Consultancy, R Estado da India 660-H66, 4430 Vila Nova de Gaia Portugal

TEJADA, SILVIA, chemistry educator, researcher in microbiology corrosion; b. Mexico City, June 20, 1945; d. Zoilo and Concepcion Tejada; children: Eduardo, Carlos. BS in Biol. Pharm. Chemistry, Nat. U. Mex., 1969. Coord. lab. Nat. U. Mex., 1993-95, head prodn. and quality control, 1968, prof. electrochemistry, 1995—; cons. Sci. Mus., Mex., 1995-97. Co-author: Electrochemistry Past and Present, 1989, Quimica en Mexico Ayer, Hoy Y Manana, 1991, Glosario de Terminos de Corrosion, 1995; patentee in field. Recipient spl. prize on rsch. project Nat. U. Mex., 1991, 3rd Pl. on Software Game, 1995, 1st Nat. prize Sciencefair, Nat. U. Mex., 1998. Mem. Chem. Soc. Mex., Soc. Mex., Mex. Soc. Electrochemicals. Avocations: movies, theater, reading, music, swimming. Home: 132 Asturias, 03400 Mexico City Mexico Office: FQ Ciudad U, Nat Univ Mexico, 04500 Mexico City Mexico

TE KANAWA, KIRI, opera and concert singer; b. Gisborne, N.Z., Mar. 6, 1944; d. Thomas and Eleanor Te Kanawa; m. Desmond Park, Aug. 30, 1967 (div. 1997); children—Antonia Aroha, Thomas Desmond. Student, St. Mary's Coll., Auckland, N.Z., 1957-60, London Opera Centre, 1966-69; DMus (hon.), Oxford U., 1983. Joined Royal Opera House, London, 1971; appeared in role of Countess in Le Nozze di Figaro, 1971; U.S. debut in Santa Fe Festival, 1971; Met. Opera debut as Desdemona in Otello, 1974; appearances with all major European and Am. opera houses, including Australian opera cos., Royal Opera House, Covent Garden, London, Paris Opera, Munich Opera, La Scala, others; opera appearences include Boris Gudonov, Carmen, Don Giovanni, the Magic Flute, Eugene Onegin, La Boheme, Manon Lescaut, many others; appeared in film Don Giovanni as Elvira, 1979; recs. include Blue Skies, 1986, Kiri Sings Gershwin, 1987, Kiri Te Kanawa: Italian Opera Arias, 1991, Kiri Her Greatest Hits, Ave Maria, Kiri on Broadway, The Kiri Selection, Kiri Side Tracks, My Fair Lady, Maori Songs; PBS appearance: Great Performances: West Side Story, 1985; author: Land of the Long White Cloud, 1989, Opera for Lovers, 1996. Decorated comdr. Order Brit. Empire, 1973, Dame Comdr. Brit. Empire, 1983, Order of Australia, 1990, Order of New Zealand, 1995. Address: care Nick Grace Mgmt Ltd, 2 Union Ct Sheen Rd, Richmond TW9 1AA, England

TEKIN, MUSTAFA, physician, geneticist; b. Ankara, Turkey, Jan. 29, 1970; came to U.S., 1998; MD, Ankara U., 1992. Clin. pediatric resident Ankara U. Sch. Medicine, 1992-97; clin. genetics fellow Med. Coll. Va. Va. Commonwealth U., Richmond, 1998—. Contbr. articles to profl. jours. Mem. AMA, Am. Soc. Human Genetics, Turkish Med. Assn. Office: Med Coll Va, Dept Human Genetics PO Box 980033 1101 E Marshall St Richmond VA 23298-5008

TELEGDY, GYULA, physiologist, educator; b. Nagyszeben, Romania, June 5, 1935; s. Bela and Margit (Sinkó) T.; m. Ibolya Haszon, Jan. 10, 1980; children: Enikö, Ildikó, Gergely. MD, Med. Sch., Pécs, Hungary, 1959, Phd, 1966; DSc, Med. Sch., Budapest, 1974. Docent physiology Med. U., Pécs, 1966-75; prof., chmn. dept. pathophysiology U. Med. Ctr., Szeged, 1975—, dean med. faculty, 1985-90. Contbr. over 600 articles to profl. jours. Mem. Hungarian Acad. Scis. (pres. regional com. 1990). Office: Inst Pathophysiology, Semmelweis 1, 6701 Szeged Hungary

TELEPAS, GEORGE PETER, lawyer; b. Kingston, N.Y., Nov. 20, 1935; s. Peter G. and Grace Telepas; m. Regina Tisiker, Sept. 6, 1969 (div.); m. Patricia Kilstofte, Apr. 30, 1995. BS, U. Fla., 1960; JD, U. Miami, 1965. Bar: Fla. 1965, Colo. 1986. Assoc. Preddy, Haddad, Kutner & Hardy, 1966-67, Williams & Jabara, 1967-68; pvt. practice Miami, Fla., 1968—. Mem. citizens bd. U. Miami. With USMC, 1954-56. Mem. ATLA, ABA, Fla. Bar Assn., Colo. Bar Assn., Dade County Bar Assn., Fla. Trial Lawyers Assn., Dade County Trial Lawyers Assn., Delta Theta Phi, Sigma Nu. Address: 1905 Sunburst Dr Vail CO 81657-5166

TELESETSKY, WALTER, government official; b. Boston, Jan. 22, 1938; s. Keril and Nellie (Krelka) T.; m. Sharron-Dawn Lamp, July 15, 1961; children: Stephanie Ann, Anastasia Marie. BS in Mech. Engring., Northeastern U., 1960; MBA, U. Chgo., 1961; postgrad., Harvard U., 1977. Engr. trainee Chrysler Corp., Detroit, 1956-59; rsch. asst. Microtech Rsch. Co., Cambridge, Mass., 1959-60; engr. Allis Chalmers Mfg. Co., Milw., 1960-61; mem. tech. staff The Mitre Corp., Bedford, Mass., 1962-68; sr. mem. tech. staff Data Dynamics, Inc., Washington, 1969; phys. scientist NOAA, Rockville, Md., 1970-71, U.S. Gate Project coord., 1972-74, dir. U.S. Global Weather Experiment Project Office, 1974, dir. Program Integration Office, 1975-77, dir. Programs and Tech. Devel. Office, 1977-79, dir. Programs and Internat. Activities Office, 1979-81; dep. assoc. dir. for tech. svcs., chief AFOS ops. div. Nat. Weather Svc., Silver Spring, Md., 1981-86, dir. Office of Systems Ops., 1986—; liaison to NAS coms. on atmospheric scis., geophysics studies and internat. environ. programs, 1975-81; U.S. coord. U.S./Japan Coop. Program in Natural Resources, 1980-88; chmn. U.S.-Japan Marine Resources and Engring. Coordination Com., 1980-88; U.S. del. governing coun. UN Environ. Program and World Meteorol. Orgn.; mem. commn. for Basic Systems World Meteorol. Orgn., 1988—; speaker in field. Contbr. articles to profl. publs. Recipient Silver medal Dept. Commerce, 1975, Gold medal Dept. Commerce, 1998. Mem. AAAS, Am. Geophys. Union, Am. Meteorol. Soc., Am. Soc. Mech. Engrs., Marine Tech. Soc. Home: 16 Eton Overlook Rockville MD 20850-3003 Office: 1325 E West Hwy Silver Spring MD 20910-3280

TÉLESSY, ISTVÁN GÁBOR, pharmacist, economist; b. Mözs, Hungary, Dec. 8, 1954; s. István and Gabriella (Svegedi) T.; m. Kornélia Fóris, Nov. 27, 1976; children: Szilveszter, Berta. Degree in pharmacy, Szeged (Hungary) U. Med. Sch., 1978, PharmD, 1983; PhD, Hungarian Acad. Sci., Budapest, 1995; degree in econ., U. Econ. Soc., Budapest, 1999. Asst. scientist Nat. Inst. Pharmacy, Budapest, 1981-85; head med. comm. Biogal Pharm. Works, Debrecen, Hungary, 1985-88; head med. divsn. Human Rsch. Inst., Gödöllo, Hungary, 1988-91; country exec. pharm. B. Braun Med., Budapest, 1991—; lectr. Postgrad. Med. Sch., Budapest, 1983-87; vis. prof. Szeged U. Med. Sch., 1989—; mem. editl. bd. Nutrition-Metabol-Diet, Budapest, 1985—. Author: Nutritional Therapy, 1996. Mem. Hungarian Soc. Pharmacists, European Soc. Ent-Parent. Nutrition, Am. Soc. Ent.Parent. Nutrition. Avocations: gardening, skiing, driving, classical jazz. Home: Fácán sor 25, H-2100 Gödöllo Hungary Office: B Braun Med Ltd, Felhévizi u5, H-1023 Bucharest Romania

TELFER, MAX LESLIE, engineering consultant; b. Preston, Australia, Mar. 6, 1940; s. William Robert Leslie and Elsie Elizabeth (McKenzie) T.; m. Josephine Margaret Carthew, Aug. 29, 1964; children: Ronald, Sharon. B Engring. Sci., Melbourne U., 1962, M of Engring. Sci., 1974. Engr. GAF, Melbourne, 1962-63; sr. lectr. Chisholm, Caulfield, 1964-90, Monash U., Caulfield, 1990-96; cons. BMJ Cons. Svc., Albert Park, 1996—; mgr. BMJ Cons. Svc., 1985—. Chmn. Com. for Persons with Disabilities, Monash U., 1994. Mem. IEEE, ACS, IE Australia. Avocation: organist.

TELFORD, TED GARY, computer company executive; b. Salt Lake City, Aug. 3, 1967; s. L. Gary and Jalene Faye Telford; m. Mindy P. Telford, Dec. 1, 1989; children: Taylor, Carson, Shae, Mady. AA, Weber State U., 1990; BA, U. Utah, 1992; MIM, Am. Grad. Sch. Internat. Mgmt., 1995. Comm. specialist AT&T, Salt Lake City, 1988-93; real estate analyst Intel, Chandler, Ariz., 1995-96; site selection mgr. Intel, Chandler, 1996—. Vol. tchr. LDS Ch., Fortaleza, Brazil, 1986-88. Mem. Am. Polit. Sci. Honor Soc., Internat. Devel. Rsch. Coun. Avocations: history, skiing, carpentry, music, family activities. E-mail: ted.g.telford@intel.com. Home: 3615 E Indigo Bay Ct Higley AZ 85236-3026 Office: Intel 4500 S Dobson Rd # Oc2-151 Chandler AZ 85248-4907

TELGENHOF, ALLEN RAY, lawyer; b. Flint, Mich., Jan. 31, 1964; s. Gerald H. and Bernice Kay Telgenhof; m. Judy Michele Campbell, Sept. 5, 1986; children: Tyler, Allyson, Will, Luke. BA, Mich. State U., 1987; JD cum laude, Thomas M. Cooley Law Sch., 1989. Bar: Mich. 1989, U.S. Dist. Ct. (ea. dist.) Mich. 1992, U.S. Ct. Appeals (6th cir.) 1992, U.S. Dist. Ct. (we. dist.) Mich. 1997. Legis. analyst Mich. Ho. of Reps., Lansing, 1989; assoc. Hicks & Schmidlin, P.C., Flint, 1990-93; pvt. practice law Clio, Mich., 1993-94; ptnr. Pointner, Joseph, Corcoran & Telgenhof, P.C., Charlevoix, Mich., 1994-98, Joseph, Corcoran & Telgenhof, P.C., Charlevoix, 1998-2000, Joseph, Corcoran, Telgenhof & Barnes, P.C., Charlevoix, 2000—; advisor Clio H.S. Law Club, 1992-94; founder, pres. Clio Area Edn. Found., 1992-94; presenter in field. Trustee Clio Bd. Edn., 1992-94, Charlevoix Bd. Edn., 1995—, pres., 1997—; commr. City of Charlevoix Planning Commn., 1995-96. Named Alumnus of Yr. Clio H.S., 1999. Mem. ABA, Charlevoix-Emmet Bar Assn. Avocations: sports, sailing, family activities. E-mail: atelgenhof@unnet.com. Fax: 231-547-3014. Office: Joseph Corcoran Et Al PO Box 490 203 Mason St Charlevoix MI 49720-1337

TELIŠMAN, SPOMENKA, biochemist, scientific consultant; b. Zagreb, Croatia, Mar. 1, 1945; d. Milivoj and Nada (Holetić-Pavičić) T.; m. July 3, 1971 (div. 1973). BSc in Chemistry, U. Zagreb, 1971, MSc, 1974, DSc in Biomedicine, 1983. Rsch. asst. Inst. for Med. Rsch. and Occupl. Health, Zagreb, 1971-83, sci. assoc., 1984-86, sr. sci. assoc., 1986-93, sci. cons., 1993—; vis. rschr. Regional Toxicology Lab., Dudley Road Hosp., Birmingham, Eng., 1979; vis. rschr. health and safety exec. Occupl. Medicine Labs., London, 1979; mem. sci. com., session chmn. 6-9th Internat. Confs. Heavy Metals in Environ., New Orleans, 1987, Geneva, 1989, Edinburgh, Scotland, 1991, Toronto, Ont., Can., 1993; invited lectr. Brookhaven Nat. Lab., Upton, N.Y., 1987, Internat. Symposium on Lead and Cadmium Toxicology, Beidaihe, China, 1990, 12th N.Am. Ann. Conf. on Lead and Health, Montreal, Que., Can., 1990; mem. permanent internat. sci. com. on metal toxicology Internat. Commn. on Occupl. Health, 1994—. Contbr. articles to sci. jurs. and ency., including Scandinavian Jour. Work Environ. Health, Internat. Archives Occupl. Environ. Health, Bull. Environ. Contamination Toxicology, Environ. Health Perspectives, ILO Ency. Occupl. Health and Safety. Rsch. grantee Commn. European Cmtys., 1982-84, EPA, 1986-89, Internat. Lead Zinc Rsch. Orgn., Inc., 1989-91. Mem. Croatian Toxicological Soc. Roman Catholic. Office: Inst Med Rsch-Occupl Health, POB 291, Ksaverska cesta 2, HR-10001 Zagreb Croatia

TELL, LEONID, pathophysiologist, writer, inventor, researcher; b. Kazakhstan, USSR, Aug. 11, 1942; s. Zisman Tell and Eda Gertner; m. Svetlana Auzhanova, Feb. 12, 1971; children: Damilya, Dana, Dinna. MD, Karaganda Med. Sch., Kazakhstan, 1965; PhD in Pathophysiology, Novosibirsk (Russia) Med. Sch., 1967; DSc in Pathophysiology, Internat. Friendship U., Moscow, 1984. Prof. pathophysiology Tselinograd (Kazakhstan) Med. Sch., USSR, 1965-96; chief clin. pathophysiology Akmola (Kazakhstan) Med. Sch., 1996—; rep. Med. Ministry of Kazakhstan to U.S. and Can., 1996—. Author: Central Nervous Mechanisms of Pulmonary Edema, 1989, General Physiology, 1992, Human Physiology and General Mechanisms of Diseases, 1994, Lectures on Pathophysiology, 1995, Intensive Therapy, 1996, The Code of Health, 1998, more than 300 textbooks. Holds 52 patents in field. Mem. Am. Physiol. Soc., N.Y. Acad. Scis., Kazakhstan Acad. Med. Scis., Kazakhstan Acad. Preventive Medicine. Avocations: running, rock climbing. Home: 2634 Brentwood Rd Beachwood OH 44122-1504

TELLEFSEN, GEORG, dentist; b. Ranea, Sweden, Oct. 26, 1951; s. Olaf and Margit (Bjalfve) T.; m. Monica Elisabeth Thell; children: Fredrik, Henrik, Gustav. DDS, Karolinska Inst., Stockholm, 1976, Periodontist, 1985. Asst. prof. Karolinska Inst., 1977-86, 1989-92, 94-95; assoc. head

dept. periodontology Stockholm Pub. Health Svc., 1986-89; assoc. prof. Loma Linda (Calif.) U., 1992-94; pvt. practice, Danderyd, Sweden, 1995—; cons. Guidor, Stockholm, 1996-97. Contbr. articles to profl. jours. Mem. Internat. AAP, Swedish Dental Assn., Internat. Acad. Dental Rsch. Lutheran. Avocations: skiing, long expedition-skating, travel, music. Home: Granhallsvagen 22A, 18275 Stocksund Sweden Office: Dana Clinic, Morby Centrum, 18231 Danderyd Sweden

TELLEGEN, JAN WILLEM, public affairs consultant, historian; b. Amsterdam, The Netherlands, Apr. 20, 1956; s. Gerrit Tellegen and Emma Bergman. Doctorandus, U. Amsterdam, 1984. Cons. Adviesbureau Bennis, The Hague, The Netherlands, 1985-88; mng. dir. Adviesbureau Bennis, The Hague, 1988-92; gen. mgr. JWT European Affairs, 1993—; chmn. Amsterdam Telematics Coun., 1994—, European Affairs Platform, Brussels, 1992-97. Author: Industriebeleid, 1998; author, editor: Logizticke Lobbies, 1998. Candidate European Parliament, Straatsburg, 1994, Provinciale State NH, Haarlem, The Netherlands, 1995. Avocations: reading history, culture, music. Office: JWT European Affairs, Linnaeusstraat 61, 1093 EH Amsterdam The Netherlands

TELLENNE, ERIC FRANÇOIS, writer, journalist; b. Paris, Nov. 22, 1953; s. Guy Albert and Annick (Lemoine) T. BA, Sorbonne U., Paris, 1975. Translator Practitioner's Psychologists Inst., Paris, 1978-79; literary reviewer Valeurs Actuelles mag., Paris, 1980-84; prodr., host Radio Nova, Paris, 1985-87; contbg. writer Canal Plus TV, Paris, 1988—; literary advisor Table Ronde Publs., Paris, 1989-92. Author: Collected Poems, 1998, (under pen name Raoul Rabut) Fried Eggs, 1985, short stories; translator: Neo-Natal Assessment Birth-Scale, 1978; columnist, contbr. Jalons mag., 1987-97. Recipient prizes in poetry French Writers Soc., 1998, French Acad., 1999. Roman Catholic. Avocations: astrology, classical music, American literature (1790-1977). Home and Office: 4 Square de Robiac, 75007 Paris France

TELLERIA, ANTHONY F., lawyer; b. Nicaragua, June 6, 1938; s. Carlos E. and Melida (Amador) T.; m. Dolores A. Rockey, Nov. 3, 1962; children: Matthew J., Andrea F. LLB, Southwestern U., 1964. Bar: Calif 1964. Sr. ptnr. Telleria, Townley & Doran, L.A., 1971-75; pvt. practice, L.A., 1964-71, 75—. Mem. Calif. Trial Lawyers Assn., L.A. County Bar Assn., Am. Arbitration Assn. (L.A. adv. coun., accident claims com.), Consumer Attys. Assn. of L.A. Home: 1615 Rose Ave San Marino CA 91108-3001 Office: 150 E Colorado Blvd Ste 206 Pasadena CA 91105-3722

TELLERIA, CARLOS MARCELO, reproductive endocrinologist; b. Los Toldos, Argentina, Sept. 24, 1964; s. Juan Carlos and Vilma Nelida (Giordano) T.; m. Alicia Alejandra Goyeneche, July 31, 1987; children: Nahuel, Micaela. MSc in Chemistry, U. San Luis, Argentina, 1986, MSc in Biochemistry, 1989, PhD in Reproductive Endocrinology, 1993. Postdoctoral fellow Fogarty Internat. Ctr., NIH, 1995-98; postdoctoral fellow Nat. Rsch. Coun. Argentina, 1994-95, asst. prof., 1998—. Recipient Perkins Meml. award Am. Physiol. Soc., 1996; PLACIRH rsch. grantee, 1998; Conicet fellow, 1990-95. Mem. Soc. for Study of Reprodn., Endocrine Soc. Office: Larlac-Conicet, CC 855, Mendoza 5500, Argentina

TELLEZ KUENZLER, LUIS, government official; b. Mexico City, Mex., 1958. Grad., Inst. Tech.; PhD in Econs., MIT. Gen. dir. fin. & planning Sec. Fin. & Pub. Credit, 1988; undersec. planning Sec. Agrl. & Hydraulic Resources, chief staff to pres., 1994; sec. Energy, Mines & Parastatal Industry, Mex., 1997—. Office: Sec Energy Mines Industry, Avenida Insuirgentes 552, Piso 06769, Mexico*

TELLEZ-MINOR, SAUL, physics educator and researcher; b. Mexico City, Oct. 16, 1949; s. Quirino Tellez-Aguilar and Celia Minor-Conde; m. Laura Perez Tejada-Granados, Aug. 29, 1979; children: Saul, Laura. BSc, ESFM-IPN, Mexico City, 1974, PhD, 1976; MSc, Hebrew U., Jerusalem, Israel, 1977. Diplomate in physics and math. Engrng. cons. Promasa Co., Mexico City, 1968-72; prof. physics ESIME-IPN, Mexico City, 1973—; prof. physics ESFM-IPN, Mexico City, 1974-77, titular prof., 1986—; exec. sec. Fundacion Hertel, Mexico City, 1995—; mem. jury Banamex award, 1981-82; mem. rsch. coun. jury CONACYT, Mexico City, 1981-82, IPN, Mexico City, 1982-87; creator, dir. Summer Inst. of Modern Physics, IPN-Fermilab, 1987-94; creator, jury pres. internat. rsch. awards Leon M. Lederman Award, 1992—, St. Louis U. Physics Award, 1992—, Ohio State U. Physics Award, 1996—, Los Alamos Nat. Lab. Summer Stay, 1997—. Dir., editor Profisica Rev., 1992-95. Recipient Ruta de la Independencia award SEP/MEX, 1962, others. Mem. Mexican Soc. Physics Tchrs. (pres. coun. 1992-95), Mexican Phys. Soc., Am. Assn. Physics Tchrs. Achievements include theory of dispersion pion deuteron; design, construction and test of solar energy concentrator, solar still, solar corn dryer; design of the International Science Education Center of the Superconducting Supercollider in Texas. Home: Calle 45 No 39, 15000 Mexico City Mexico Office: Fundacion Hertel, Managua 715 Colonia Linda Vista, 07300 Mexico City Mexico

TELLIER, PAUL M., railway transportation executive; b. Joliette, Que., Can., May 8, 1939; s. Maurice J. and Eva M. (Bouvier) T.; m. Andree Poirier, June 6, 1959; children: Claude, Marc. BA, U. Ottawa, 1959, LLL, 1962; BLitt, Oxford U., 1966; LLD (hon.), U. Alta., Can., 1996, U. Ottawa, Can., 2000. Bar: Que. bar 1963. Sr. gov. official Can., 1967-92; dep. minister Indian affairs and no. devel., 1979-82, dep. minister energy, mines and resources, 1982-85; chmn. governing bd. Internat. Energy Agy., 1985-92; clk. of Privy Council and sec. to Cabinet Govt. of Can., Ottawa, 1985-92; dir. Petro Can., 1985-92; pres., CEO Canadian Nat. Railway Co., 1992—; bd. dirs. Grand Trunk Corp., Detroit, Alcan Aluminum Ltd., Montreal, Can., BCE/Bell Can., Montreal, McCain Foods Ltd., Florenceville, Can., Bombardier, Montreal, Can.-Japan Bus. Coun., Conf. Bd. Can. Decorated companion Order of Can.; recipient Pub. Policy Forum Outstanding Achievement award, 1988, Gov. Gen.'s Outstanding Achievement award, 1990, Right Hand Man award Greenbrier, 1996, B'nai Brith award of merit, 2000; named to Queen's Privy Coun., Her Majesty Queen Elizabeth, 1992; Queen's counsel, 1981; named Transp. Person of Yr., 1997, Railroader of Yr., 1997, Grand Montréalais, 1998, CEO of Yr., 1998. Mem. Que. Bar, Railway Assn. Can. (dir.), Assn. Am. Railroads (dir.). Roman Catholic. Office: Can Nat Railway Co, 935 De La Gauchetiere St West, Montreal, PQ Canada H3B 2M9 also: PO Box 8100, Montreal, PQ Canada H3C 3N4

TELLO, RICHARD J., radiologist, researcher; b. Mexico City, Dec. 24, 1960; s. Mona Joan Lener; m. Jeanette M. Pratt, Dec. 27, 1983; 1 child, Rebecca. BS in Math., MIT, 1982, BSE in Mech. Engrng., 1982, MSME, 1983, postgrad. in mech. engring., 1984—; MD, Stanford U., 1989; MPH, Harvard U., 1998. Diplomate Am. Bd. Med. Examiners, Am. Coll. Radiology; certificate Diagnostic Radiology 1994, Special Competence Nuclear Medicine 1995. Rsch. asst. The Kidney Ctr., Boston, 1979, Beth Israel Hosp., Boston, 1980-81; rsch. engr. Extracorporeal Med. Specialties, King of Prussia, Pa., 1980; engr. IBM, Boulder, Colo., 1981-82; researcher, engr. IBM, Palo Alto, Calif., 1982-83; internal med. intern St. Mary's Hosp., San Francisco, 1989-90; radiology resident New England Deaconess Hosp., Boston, 1990-94; fellow nuclear medicine Harvard U., Boston, 1993-94; fellow MRI Brigham & Women's Hosp., Boston, 1994-95; dir. clin. MRI rsch. U. Melbourne, Australia, 1995-96; assoc. radiologist Alfred Hosp., Melbourne, Australia, 1996; assoc. prof. of radiology Boston U., 1996—, assoc. prof. of epidemiology and biostats., 1999—; dir. cardiac MRI, radiology rsch. —, 2000—; adv. bd. Magnetic Resonance Imaging & Single Photon Emission Computed Tomography St. Mary's Hosp., 1990, Digital Radiology New England Deacness Hosp., 1991, Internet Tech. and Care, Boston U.; admissions panel Stanford Med. Sch., 1983; tchr., lectr. and presenter in field. Author tech. reports and conf. proceedings; contbr. articles to profl. jours. Nat. Hispanic Scholarship Fund scholar, 1979-88, Leopold Schepp Found. scholar, 1979-84, 1987-89, Nat. Med. Found. scholar 1983-84, Paul W. Mayer scholar Alliance for Engrng. in Med. and Biology, 1986; Recipient Clapp and Poliak Eng. and Design award, 1980, Luis de Flores award MIT, 1982, special projects award and Rolex award for Innovation, 1993; MIT rsch. fellow 1983, MIT-Harvard HST/Whitaker Found. fellow 1984-87; grantee Sigma Xi, 1981, Hearst Found., 1985-87. Mem. ASME, Internat. Soc. Magnetic Resonance in Medicine, Radiological Soc. of No. Am. (rsch. resident award 1992), N.Y. Acad. Sci. (Otto P. Bergdorf honor 1978), Am. Roentgen Ray Soc. (New England chpt., pres. award 1994), Internat. Soc. of Magnetic Resonance in Medicine, Pi Tau Sigma, Sigma Xi. Achievements include patents in field of biomedical extracorporeal blood perfusion and filtration with additional work on continuous monitoring of blood pressure via development of new instrumentation; notable work in image analysis with emphasis on three dimensional anatomic reconstruction, on biomedical flow analysis with emphasis on cardiac and kidney function. Fax: 617-638-6616. E-mail: tello@alum.mit.edu. Home: 279 Weston Rd Wellesley MA 02482-4530

TELLO MACIAS, MANUEL, diplomat; s. Manuel Tello and Guadalupe Macias Viadero. Amb. to Gt. Britain Govt. of Mexico, London, 1977-79, under-sec. fgn. affairs, 1979-82; permanent rep. internat. orgns. Govt. of Mexico, Geneva, 1983-89; amb. to France Govt. of Mexico, 1989-92; sec. fgn. rels. Govt. of Mexico, Mexico City, 1994-95; now permanent rep. of Mexico to UN N.Y.C. Office: Permanent Mission of Mexico 2 United Nations Plz Fl 28 New York NY 10017-4403*

TELNOV, VALERY IVANOVICH, physicist, educator; b. Tomsk, USSR, Apr. 6, 1950; s. Ivan and Anna T.; m. Lilia Yakolevna, Dec. 1973; 1 child, Alexander. BS, MS, Novosibirsk State U., USSR, 1972; PhD, Inst. Nuclear Physics, Novosibirsk, USSR, 1982; D in Phys. Math. Scis., Inst. Nuclear Physics, 1993. Rsch. scientist Inst. Nuclear Physics, Novosibirsk, USSR, 1972-82, sr. rsch. scientist, 1982-88, leading rsch. scientist, 1988—; lectr. Novosibirsk Stae U., 1972-88, assoc. prof., 1988-93, prof., 1994—; vis. scientist Stanford Linear Accelerator Ctr., Stanford, 1978, 88, 91, 92, 96, European Lab. for Particle Physics, Geneva, 1986, 94, Linear Accelerator Lab., Orsay, France, 1994, DESY Particle Physics Lab., Hamburg, Germany, 1996, 99, KEK Particle Physics lab., Tsukuba, Japan, 1998. Contbr. articles to profl. jours. Outstanding Scientist scholar Govt. of Russia, 1993; named Soros Prof., 1999. Mem. Am. Phys. Soc. Avocations: mountain tourism, cross country skiing, diving. Office: Inst Nuclear Physics, Lavrentyeva 11, 630090 Novosibirsk Russia

TELNOV, VITALIY IVANOVITCH, radiobiologist, researcher; b. Novosibirsk, Russia, Jan. 8, 1950; s. Ivan Egorovitch and Ksenya Vasilyevna (Poltcherednikova) T.; m. Larisa Nikolaevna Dmitriy. MD, Med. Inst., Novosibirsk, Russia, 1973; PhD (hon.), Inst. Biophysics, Moscow, 1986. Physician Hosp. and Br. No. 1 Biophysics Inst., Ozyorsk, Russia, 1974-80; scientist Br. No. 1 Biophysics Inst., Ozyorsk, Russia, 1981-88, sr. scientist, 1989—; instr. Ozyorsk Tech. Inst., Moscow Engrng.-Phys. Inst., 1996—; chief lab. clin. biochemistry Br. No. 1 Biophysics Inst., 1989—; dean chem.-ecol. faculty Ozyorsk Tech. Inst. Moscow Engrng.-Phys. Inst., 1996-98, chief dept. common and radiation energy, 1999—. Contbr. articles to profl. jours. Mem. Trade Union Engrng. Industry Worker. Mem. Russian Biochem. Socs., Nuclear Soc. Moscow Internat., N.Y. Acad. Scis. Avocations: reading, tourism. Home: Parkoviy per 4-2, 456784 Ozyorsk Russia Office: Br No 1 Biophysics Inst, Ozyorsk Rd 19, 456780 Ozyorsk Russia

TELOW, SUSAN TAN, accountant, business executive; b. Cagayan de Oro, The Phillipines, Sept. 21, 1960; d. Vicente Yu and Adelia Ty (Yap) Tan; m. Tani Uy Telow, Dec. 27, 1987; children: Tani Stevenson Ten Telow, Tania Stephanie Tan Telow. BS in Commerce, Xavier U., Cagayan de Oro, 1981. CPA, The Philippines. Bank employee Cagayan de Oro, 1982-87. Treas. Venture Club, Cagayan de Oro, 1985. Office: GST Rice Trader, 128 Dona Nieves Ya Capin St, Misamis Cagayan de Oro City 9000, The Philippines

TEMAM, ROGER M., mathematician; b. Tunis, Tunisia, May 19, 1940; s. Ange M. and Elise (Ganem) T.; m. Claudette Cukorja, Aug. 21, 1962; children: David, Olivier, Emmanuel. M in Math., U. Paris, 1962, DSc, 1967. Asst. prof. math. U. Paris, 1960-67, prof., 1967—; prof. Ecole Polytechnique, Paris, 1968-85. Author: Numerical Analysis, 1969, Navier-Stokes Equations, 1977, 79, 84, Mathematical Problems in Plasticity, 1983, Infinite Dimensional Dynamical Systems in Mechanics and Physics, 1988, 2nd edit., 1997, (with I.Ekeland) Convex Analysis and Variational Problems, 1999, (with T. Dubois and F. Jauberteau) Dynamic Multilevel Methods and the Numerical Simulation of Turbulence, 1999; editor Physica D.; assoc. editor profl. jours.; contbr. articles to profl. jours. Recipient Grand Prize Joannidès, Acad. Sci. Paris, 1993. Mem. AAAS, Am. Math. Soc., Am. Phys. Soc., Soc. Indsl. and Applied Math., Soc. for Math. in Applications and Industry (founding pres. 1983-87), N.Y. Acad. Scis.

TEMANEL, BILLY ESTOQUE, agronomy director, educator, consultant; b. Buenavista, Agusan, The Philippines, Jan. 11, 1958; s. Aniceto Tolledo and Laureana Selga (Estoque) T.; m. Delores Oloan, Dec. 27, 1996; children from previous marriage: Billson, BilleChristian. BS in Agr., Mindanao State U., Marawi City, The Philippines, 1979; MS in Agr., Isabela (Phillipines) State U., 1984. Irrigation supr. Cocoa Investors Inc., Digos, Davao Sur, The Philippines, 1980-81; sci. rsch. asst. I Isabela State U., 1982-87; bd. sec. Quirino State Coll., Diffun, The Philippines, 1987-88, instr. I, 1989-92, asst. prof. IV, 1992—; cons. Farming Systems Devel. Econ. Rehab. Program CASCADES, Nueva Vizeaya, 1999; agr. advisor RP-German Cmty. Forest Mgmt. & Agroforest Project, Nagtipunan, Quirino, The Philippines, 1993; adv. Regional Advisory com. Found. Phil. Environment; provincial coord. Dept. Sci. and Tech., Diffun, Quirino, 1992—; coord. Linkages Spl. projects, Diffun, 1989—; program leader Banana R&D Project, Diffun, 1990—, peanut R&D project, Quirino, 1987—. Dir. CARD Found. Inc., Diffun, 1990—, v.p., 1991; mem. CVARRD Regional Tech. Working Group; v.p., bd. dirs. Diffun Water Dist, 1993—. Recipient Cert. Achievement, ICRISAT, 1989, Cert. Appreciation award Dept. Agr., 1990, United Meth. Ch., 1989, Dept. Sci. Tech., 1992, Dept. Agr., 1992, FFP-FAHP-FFPCC, 1992, Tech. Panel Agr. Edn., 1991, DOST-DECS, 1991, ICRISAT, 1992, Presdl. Cert. Recognition, 1991, Plaque of Recognition, Dept. Sci. Tech., 1992, 93, CUARRD, 1993, Plaque of Recognition Australian Agy. for Internat. Devel., 1999. Mem. Soc. for Advancement Vegetable Industry, Philippines Assn. Rsch. Mgrs., Philippines Assn. Vocat. Educators, Internat. Network Banana Plantains, Cereals Legumes Asia Network, Crop Sci. Soc. Philippines, Low-external Input Sustainable Agr. Network, Conservation Farming Movement Inc., Forests, Trees People Programme Network, Katipunam Multipurpose Coop. (ctrl. com.), Masons. Avocations: playing lawn tennis, walking, discoing, going to movies. Office: Quirino State Coll, Diffun 3401, The Philippines

TEMBO, CHRISTON S., federal official; b. May 28, 1944. Diploma, Mons Cadet Tng. Coll., Eng.; grad., Camberley Command and Staff Coll., Eng.; completed Form V, Zambia, 1965; achieved A level overseas. Chief army staff Govt. of Zambia, 1978-80, dep. comdr., chief of staff, 1987-84, comdr. army, 1985-87, ret. lt. gen. army, amb. to Fed. Republic Germany, 1987-88, minister tourism, 1991-95, minister fgn. affairs, 1995-96, minister mines and mineral devel., 1996-97, v.p., 1997—. Office: Office of VP, PO Box 30208, Lusaka Zambia*

TEMBO, SYDNEY DOUGLAS, science educator, researcher; b. Chipata, Zambia, Mar. 23, 1951; s. Symeon Bernard and Estele Nyendwa Tembo; m. Philomena Chiulemu Phiri, July 8, 1978; children: Emily, Benjamin, Peter. BS, U. Zambia, Lusaka, 1977; MPhil in Biochem./Immun./Bact. cum laude, U. Helsinki, Finland, 1987; PhD, Med. U. So. Africa, 1997. Chief hydrochemist Govt. Zambia, Lusaka, 1977-80, bacteriologist, 1980-81; rsch. scientist FAO/UNDP/Govt. Zambia, Lusaka, 1982-89; vaccine prodr. FAO/UNDP (Nat. Inst. Vet. Investigations), Maputo, Mozambique, 1981; bacterial vaccine prodr. FAO/UNDP, Lelystad, The Netherlands, 1984-85, Helsinki, Finland, 1983-87; lectr. biol. scis. Med. U. So. Africa, Pretoria, 1989-91, sr. lectr. in med. microbiology, 1986—; supr. postgrad. students Med. U. So. Africa, Pretoria. FAO/UNDP scholar U. Helsinki, 1982; Medunsa grantee, 1987; Medunsa fellow Med. U. So. Africa, 1989. Roman Catholic. Avocations: chess and indoor games, writing, reading, traveling. Fax: 27 12 521 5727. E-mail: tembos@yahoo.com. Home: Celliers, Pretoria Gauteng 0001, South Africa Office: Med U So Africa, Dept Microbiology Box 211, Pretoria Gauteng 0204, South Africa

TEMBROCK, GÜNTER ERWIN FRANZ, zoologist, ethologist, researcher; b. Berlin, June 7, 1918; s. Erich and Franziska (Schmidt) T.; m. Maria Luise Haller, Oct. 27, 1945 (dec. May 1991); m. Sylvia Wendland, Oct. 30, 1997. PhD, U. Berlin, 1941, habilitation, 1955; Dr.h.c., Martin-Luther-U., Halle, Germany, 1987, U. Rostock, Germany, 1992. Aux. asst. U. Berlin, 1941-44, rsch. asst., 1944-52, prin. asst., 1952-55, lectr., 1955-61, asst. prof., 1961-69, prof. zoology, 1969-83; dir. dept. Humboldt-U., Berlin, 1968-83, senator, 1992-94. Author: Grundzüge der Schimpansenpsychologie, 1949, Das Verhalten des Rotfuchses, 1957, Tierstimmen, Einführung in die Bioakustik, 1959, Verhaltensforschung, Einführung in die Tierethologie, 1961, 2d edit., 1964, Grundlagen der Tierpsychologie, 1963, 3d edit., 1971, Grundriss der Verhaltenswissenschaften, 1968, 3d edit., 1980, Biokommunikation, Teil I und II, 1971, Ethologie der Fortpflanzung bei Tieren, 1974, Tierstimmenforschung, 1977, Spezielle Verhaltensbiologie der Tiere, 1982-83, Verhalten bei Tieren, 1984,Verhaltensbiologie, 1987, 2d edit., 1992, Akustische Kommunikation bei Säugetieren, 1996, Angst, 2000; editor: Das Verhalten landwirtschaftlicher Nutztiere, 1969, Mechanismen der Bewegung und Orientierung der Tiere, 1973, Sexuologie, 1974, Biophonetik, 1975, Evolution and determination of animal and human behavior, 1982, Forschungen zu stammesgeschichtlichen Verhaltens-anpassungen beim Menschen und aktuelle Probleme der Soziobiology, 1982, Verhaltensbiologie, 1986, Verhaltensentwicklung, 1987, Natürliche Evolution von Lernstrategien, 1990, Humanethologie im Spektrum der Wissenschaften, 1990. Fellow German Acad. Naturalists Leopoldina; mem. German Ethological Soc. (hon.), Berlin Soc. Naturalists, German Soc. Mammalogy, Soc. for Sci. and Philosophy (pres.), Soc. Human Ontogenetics, German Soc. for Gen. and Applied Entomology. Avocations: classical singing, painting, drawing. Office: Humboldt U Inst Biology, Invalidenstrasse 43, 10115 Berlin Germany

TEMIZ, MUSTAFA, electrical engineering educator; b. Gümüshane, Turkey, June 15, 1948; s. Aziz and Ayse Temiz; m. Semra Kartal, Jan. 20, 1959; children: Ahmet Sakir, Rabia Nur. BS in Elect. Engrng., Istanbul Tech. U., Turkey, 1973, PhD in Elec. Engrng., 1984. Cert. electronic engrng. Control engr. Nitrogen Factory, Samsun, Turkey, 1974-76; rsch. asst. in engrng. Coll. Sakarya, Turkey, 1976-80; lectr. in engrng. Coll. Sakarya, 1976-85; asst. prof. Pamukkale U., Denizli, Turkey, 1985-93, chmn. elec.-electronic engrng. dept., 1993—. Author: The Society of Knowledge, 1989. Islam. Avocations: the history of knowledge, science fiction, writing in religious activities, writing in cosmology and cosmogony. E-mail: mustafatemiz@yahoo.com. Fax: 90 (258) 212 55 38. Home: Erle Yapi Kooperatifi2 Blok Kat 6, 17 PTT Arkasi Yenisehir, Denizli Turkey Office: Pamukkale Univ, Engring Faculty Elec-Elect Dept, Camlik Denizli Turkey

TEMNIKOV, ALEKSEI NIKOLAEVICH, physics educator; b. Village Platkovo, Jaroslavl, Russia, Mar. 30, 1952; s. Nikolai Grigor'evich and Anastasija Ivanovna (Smirnova) T.; m. Tatjana Vladimirovna Kureneva, June 30, 1973; 1 child, Dmitry. MA in Physics, Kazan State U., Russia, 1975, PhD in Physics/Math., 1987; docent, Kazan State Tech. U., 1993. Engr. Kazan State Tech. U., 1976-88, asst., 1988-93, docent of chair of physics, 1993—. Patentee in field; contbr. articles to profl. jours. Grantee Internat. George Soros Found., 1994, NATO Internat. Linkage grantee, 1998. Mem. N.Y. Acad. Scis. Avocations: drawing and painting, electronics, computers. Home: Karbyshev St 40-233, 420087 Kazan Russia Office: Kazan State Tech U, K Marx St 68, 420015 Kazan Russia

TEMPERLEY, HOWARD REED, historian, educator; b. Sunderland, Eng., Nov. 16, 1932; s. Fred and May (Holland) T.; m. Rachel Stephanie Hooper, Sept. 29, 1966 (wid. 1990); m. Kathryn Mary Lapp, Sept. 24, 1998; children by previous marriages: Alison, Rebecca, Nicholas. BA, Oxford U., 1956; MA, Yale U., 1957, PhD, 1961. Asst. lectr. U. Wales, 1960-61; lectr. U. Manchester, Eng., 1961-67; sr. lectr. history U. East Anglia, Eng., 1967-80, prof. Am. history, 1980—. Author: British Antislavery, 1972, White Dreams Black Africa: The Antislavery Expedition to the Niger, 1841-42, 1991; coauthor: Introduction to American Studies, 1981; editor: Gubbins's Journals, 1980, After Slavery: Emancipation and its Discontents, 2000; editor Jour. Am. Studies, 1977-86. Served to 2nd lt. British Army, 1951-53. Mem. Brit. Assn. of Am. Studies (chmn. 1986-89). E-mail: H.Temperley@uea.ac.uk. Home: Arlington House, Arlington Ln, Norwich NR2 2DB, England Office: U of East Anglia, Sch English & Am Studies, Norwich NR4 7TJ, England

TEMPERLEY, TOM GROOME, engineering executive, consultant; b. Lytham, England, Nov. 22, 1930; s. Thomas and Mabel Alberta (Gaskell) T.; m. Edith Kay, Jan. 11, 1961; children: Tom Gaskell, Elizabeth Katherine. DS cum laude, Etude U., Luxemburg, 1964. Chartered engr., England, 1965; chartered in fuel tech., England; accredited corrosion engr. U.S.A. Chemist Brit. Electricity Authority, 1948-53; cheif chemist Kuwait Min. Electricity & Awster, 1953-70; v.p., pres. Conam Svcs., Inc., U.S.A, Saudi Arabia, 1970-78; chmn., pres. Jahz Al0Amri Tradingand Contracting Co., Saudi Arabia, 1978-84; tech. dir. Global Chem. and Maintenance Systems, Inc., U.S.A., 1978—; dir. Environ. Engrng. Ltd.; chmn. Enviroserv Ltd.; underwriting mem. Lloyds of London, 1980—; worldwide cons. desalination field, 1954—. Author: Arabian Days, Desalination Operation; contbr. articles to profl. jours. Chmn. bd. govs. Continental Sch., Jeddah, Saudi Arabia, 1976—; founding mem. Brit. Businessman's Luncheon Club, Jeddah, 1980-82; v.p. English fed. Body-Builders, London, 1982—. Decorated officer Order Brit. Empire. Fellow Inst. Energy, Inst. Corrosion Sci. and tech., Inst. Nuclear Engrs., Inst. Petroleum, Royal Soc. Health; mem. Am. Inst. Chem. Engrs., Am. Chem. Soc. (sr. mem.), Nat. Assn. Corrosion Engrs. (v.p. 1995—), Internat. Desalination Assn. (bd. dirs. 1983—), Masons, Rowland Chadwick Club. Conservative. Mem. Ch. of England. Home: Lovely Hall, Salesbury, Blackburn Lancashire BB1 9EQ, England Office: PO Box 3240, 21471 Jeddah Saudi Arabia

TEMPLE, CHRISTOPHER LAWRENCE, financial editor, publisher, foundation executive; b. Binghamton, N.Y., Aug. 24, 1961; s. Christopher Lewis and Frieda Mae (Diana) T.; m. Susan Marie Luce, June 12, 1980; children: Christopher, Deborah, Jennifer, Daniel, Stephen, David, Andrew, Rachel. Cert. fin. planner, estate counselor. Fin. planner Lesko Fin. Assocs., Binghamton, 1979-85; gen. securities prin. New Decade Capital Corp., Binghamton, 1981-85; fin. planner Phoenix Fin. Svcs., Cortland, N.Y., Kalispell, Mont., 1986—, Spooner, Wis., 1986—; editor, pub. Your Money Today, Cortland and Kalispell, 1986-95, The Nat. Investor, Kalispell and Spooner, 1996—; mng. editor The Citizens Informer, Spooner and Washington, 1999—; founder, pres. Found. for Am. Renewal, 1999. Youth hockey coach, Kalispell, Spooner, 1994—. Mem. Am. Media Assn. (dir. 1997—), Nat. Assn. of Charitable Estate Counselors. Republican. Avocations: hockey, fishing, hunting, conservation, history. Office: Nat Investor Publishing 410 River St Spooner WI 54801

TEMPLE, ROBERT KYLE GRENVILLE, writer, historian, businessman; b. N.Y.C., Jan. 25, 1945; m. Olivia Moyra Nockolds, Dec. 30, 1972. BA, U. Pa., 1965. Sr. editor Second Look Mag., 1978-80; cons. Brit. Aerospace PLC, 1991, Cable & Wireless PLC, 1995; pres., CEO China InfoNet Ltd., 1995, China Vocat. Videos Corp. Ltd., 1995; dir. Vitacom Corp., Inc., 1997-98; cons. Carlton Comm. PLC, 1996, Xerox Corp., Inc., 1998; jt. dir. Project for Hist. Dating, 1999; pres., CEO Chinatech Enterprises Ltd., 1999; vis. prof. humanities, history and philosophy sci., U. Louisville, 1999; vis. rsch. fellow Archeol. Scis. Inst. Aegean, Alexandria, Egypt, U. Aegean, Greece, 2000; sr. vis. fellow Ctr. Sci., Tech. and Soc. Tsinghua U., Beijing, China, 2000; cons. Apple Computer Asia Pacific Ltd., 2000. Author: The Sirius Mystery, 1976, Goetter, Orakel, Und Visionen, 1982, Strange Things, 1983, Conversations with Eternity, 1984, China: Land of Discovery and Invention (The Genius of China in USA), 1986, reissued in Eng. as The Genius of China, 1991, 1998, Open to Suggestion: The Uses and Abuses of Hypnosis, 1989, He Who Saw Everything: A Verse Translation of the Epic of Gilgamesh, 1991, adaptor for stage version, 1992; TV producer: Blind to Science, 1989 (Spl. Merit award British Assoc. Advancement Sci. 1990), pilot films of The Thoughts of Charles, 1991; contbr. to Dictionary of Nat. Biography, 1990; editor: The Illustrated Golden Bough, 1997, The Sirius Mystery, expanded edit., 1998, (with Olivia Temple) Aesop: The Complete Fables, 1998, The Crystal Sun: Rediscovering a Lost Technology of the Ancient World, 2000, Conversations with Eternity, expanded edit., 2001; coprodr., co-dir. (2 episodes of 13 part series) Frontiers of the Unknown, 1990; video prodr. Red Carpet series, 1995; multiple contbr. Dictionary Nat. Biography Missing Persons vol., 1990. Sponsor Com. for the Def. of the Unjustly Prosecuted, 1980—. Recipient 5 nat. awards; New Horizons Rsch. Found. fellow, 1985. Fellow Royal Astron. Soc., London Coll. Optometrists (assoc.); mem. AAAS, PEN, Royal Hist. Soc., Fgn. Press Assn. in London, Royal United Svcs. Inst. for Def. Studies, Inst. Hist. Rsch., Internat. Assn. Egyptologists, Soc. for Ancient Greek Philosophy, Egypt Exploration Soc., Inst. Classical Studies, Hellenic Soc., Brit. Sch. Athens, Brit. Sch. Rome, Soc. Promotion Hellenic Studies. E-mail: robert.temple@china-infonet.demon.co.uk. Office: 16 Red Lion Sq, London WC1R 4QT, England

TEMPLETON, JOHN MARKS, JR., pediatric surgeon, foundation executive; b. N.Y.C., Feb. 19, 1940; s. John Marks and Judith Dudley (Folk) T.; m. Josephine J., Aug. 2, 1970; children: Heather Erin, Jennifer Ann. BA, Yale Coll., 1962; MD, Harvard U., 1968; hon. degree, Beaver Coll., Buena Vista U., Va. Commonwealth U. Intern Med. Coll. Va., Richmond, 1968-69, resident, 1969-73; prof. pediat. surgery U. Pa. and Children's Hosp. Phila., 1995, dir. trauma program, 1989-95; chmn. bd. Templeton Growth Fund, Ltd. Assoc. editor: Textbook of Pediatric Emergencies, 1993; pub. 6000 Name Geneology, 1997, A Searcher's Life, 1999. Chmn. health and safety, exec. bd. Cradle of Liberty Coun., Boy Scouts Am.; Ea. Coll., Fgn. Policy Rsch. Inst., Nat. Recreation Found., Melmark Charitable Found.; nat. bd. dirs., pres. Pa. divsn. Am. Trauma Soc.; bd. dirs. Nat. Bible Assn., Nat. Liberty Mus., Phila.; elder Proclamation Presbyn. Ch.; pres. John Templeton Found. With M.C., USNR, 1975-77. Barclay fellow Templeton Coll., Oxford U.; mem. Order of Charlemagne. Mem. ACS, AMA, Am. Pediat. Surg. Assn., Am. Acad. Pediats., Am. Assn. Surgery Trauma, Ea. Assn. Surgery Trauma, Phila. Coll. Physicians, Union League, Lyford Cay Club, Merion Cricket Club, Athenaeum Club London, Rotary Internat., White's London. Republican. Evangelical. Office: 5 Radnor Corp Ctr Ste 100 Radnor PA 19087-4534

TEMPLIN, JOHN LEON, JR., healthcare consulting executive; b. New Brunswick, N.Y., Aug. 5, 1940; s. John Leon and Theresa Veronica (Revolinski) T.; m. Barbara Maria Ribley, Sept. 12, 1970; children: John, Joseph, Kevin, Nan, Danielle, Christopher. BS in Mgmt. Engring., Rensselaer Poly. Inst., 1962, MS in Mgmt., 1969. Cert. healthcare cons. Am. Assn. Healthcare Cons. Mgr. customer svc. Norton Abrasives, Troy, N.Y., 1968-70; cons., sr. cons. Hosp. Assn. N.Y. State, Albany, 1970-79, dir. mgmt. svcs., 1979-80, sr. dir. mgmt. svc., 1981-83; dir. productivity improvement Applied Leadership Technologies, Inc., Greenfield Center, N.Y., 1983-84, v.p., productivity improvement div., 1984-85, pres., 1985-86; pres. Templin Mgmt. Assocs., Inc., Greenfield Center, 1987—, The Northeastern Cons. Alliance, Albany, N.Y., 1995-98. Editor quar. jour. Healthcare Supr., 1983—; mem. editorial com. ann. Manual for Workload Recording, 1978-91. Mem. budget com. Greater Saratoga Sch. Dist., Saratoga Springs, N.Y., 1978-79; mem. energy com. Blue Cross Assn., Chgo., 1978-81; mem. Gov.'s Task Force on Nursing, Albany, 1980; mem. parish coun. St. Joseph's Ch., Greenfield Center, 1981-87. Capt. U.S. Army, 1962-64. Fellow Am. Coll. Healthcare Execs., Healthcare Info. and Mgmt. Sys. Soc. (liaison Coll. Am. Pathologists 1978-91, chair edn. com. 1995-96, 97-98); mem. Am. Hosp. Assn. (seminar spkr. 1980-93), Clin. Lab. Mgmt. Assn. (bd. dirs. 1980-84), KC. Republican. Roman Catholic. Avocations: golf, computers, gardening, fishing. Home and Office: Templin Mgmt Assocs Inc 265 Locust Grove Rd Greenfield Center NY 12833-1501

TEN, JEFFREY RONALD, cosmetics executive; b. Phila., July 18, 1958; s. Henry Z. and Erika (Eisenstein) T. B in Mktg., Temple U., 1979. Export mgr. Elizabeth Arden, N.Y.C., 1980-86; worldwide export mgr. Monet Inc., N.Y.C., 1986-87; export mgr. Estee Lauder Cosmetics, N.Y.C., 1987-91; dir. Western hem export sales Estee Lauder Internat., 1989-91; v.p. internat. Avon Products-Giorgio Beverly Hills, Calif., 1991-94, Procter & Gamble, 1994-98; v.p. consumer products Hambrecht and Quist Asia Pacific, 1998-99; sr. v.p. internat. Del Labs., 1999—. Mem. Am. Mktg. Assn. E-mail: Jefften@worldnet.att.net. Home: 914 Avalon Court Dr Melville NY 11747-4285 Office: DEL Labs 178 EAB Plaza Unionville NY 89418

TEN BRINK, STEPHAN, communications engineer, researcher, consultant; b. Backnang, Germany, Dec. 5, 1970. Diploma in elec. engring., U. Stuttgart, 1997, postgrad. Cons. mobile comms. AT&T Bell Labs., Holmdel, N.J., 1995-96, Lucent, Bell Labs., Swindon, U.K., 1997—; rschr. U. Stuttgart, Germany, 1997—. Referee/reviewer IEE/IEEE, 1999—; patentee in field. RecipientPhysics award Bosch Telecom., 1990, Comm. Engring. award Richard-Hirschmann Found., 1995; scholarship German Nat. Scholarship Found., 1991. Mem. German ACM, IEEE. Office: Inst Telecomms U Stuttgart, Pfaffenwaldring 47 Dep 0408, 70569 Stuttgart Germany

TENDLER, MICHAEL, physics educator, scientific association executive; b. Leningrad, USSR, Aug. 28, 1947; arrived in Sweden, 1976; s. Boris and Deborah (Gerskowits) T.; m. Anna Taubes, May 7, 1980; children: Cecilia, Salomon. M, Leningrad U., 1971; PhD, Uppsala U., Sweden, 1978. Lectr. Mining Acad., Leningrad, 1973-75; rschr. Herzen Inst., Leningrad, 1973-75; scientist Siemens AG, Germany, 1978-79; bd. dirs. Internat. Ctr. for Dense Magnetized Plasma, 1998—; cons. Canada Coun., Ottawa, 1996; evaluator Weizmann Inst., Israel, 1996; pres. Internat. Congress Plasma Physics, 1996—; chmn. Inst. Plasma Physics, Prague, 1995—; lectr. in field. Co-author: Reviews of Plasma Physics, 1996; editor conf. proceedings; co-editor spl. issue Jour. Plasmaphysics. Mem. human rights com. Am. Phys. Soc., Anaheim, Calif., 1989; mem. Swedish com. Freedom of Sci., Stockholm, 1976-98; lectr. on human rights, Anaheim, 1989. Recipient E. Mach prize in physics Czech Acad. of Scis., 1999. Mem. Swedish Phys. Soc. (chmn. plasmaphysics divsn. 1996—), PPD European Phys. Soc. (bd. dirs. 1999—). Avocations: opera, ballet, arts, swimming, football. Home: Angsullsvagen 23, 16246 Stockholm Vallingb, Sweden Office: Royal Inst Technology, Alfvenlaboratory, 10044 Stockholm Sweden

TENENBAUM, GERSHON, psychologist; b. Cracow, Poland, Oct. 8, 1947; arrived in Australia, 1994; s. Bernard Dov and Tsipora (Kraus) T.; m. Hony Michal Bar-Tal, Sept. 26, 1954; children: Ravid, Noam, Sharon. BA, Tel-Aviv U., 1972, MA, 1976; PhD, U. Chgo., 1982. Lic. psychologist. From head dept. rsch. to head ctr. rsch. & sport medicine Wingate Inst., Israel, 1986-94; assoc. prof. psychology U. So. Queens, Australia, 1994-2000; prof. sport & exercise physiology Fla. State U. Coll. Edn., Tallahassee, 2000—. Editor Internat. Jour. Sport Psychology, 1995—. Officer Israeli Def. Forces, 1966-71. Mem. AAAS, Internat. Soc. Sport Psychology (sec. gen. 1987), Nat. Acad. Phys. Edn. and Sport, N.Y. Acad. Scis. E-mail: tenenbau@coe.fsu.edu. Office: Fla State U Coll Edn, 307 Stone Bldg, 4350 Tallahassee Australia

TENER, CAROL JOAN, retired secondary education educator; b. Cleve., Feb. 10, 1935; d. Peter Paul and Mamie Christine (Dombrowski) Manusack; m. Dale Keith Tener, Feb. 13, 1958 (div. Aug. 1991); children: Dean Robert, Susan Dawn Tener Belair. Student, Cleve. Mus. Art, 1948-53, Cleve. Art Inst., 1953-54; BS in Edn. cum laude, Kent State U., 1957; MS in Supervision, Akron U., 1974; postgrad., Kent State U., 1964, 81, 88-90, Akron U., 1975, 79, John Carroll U., 1982, 83, 85-86, Ohio U., 1987, Baldwin Wallace Coll., 1989. Cert. permanent K-12 tchr., Ohio. Stenographer Equitable Life Iowa, Cleve., 1953-54; tchr. elem. art Cuyahoga Falls (Ohio) Bd. Edn., 1957-58, 62-63, 1965-68, tchr. jr. h.s., 1968-69; tchr. h.s. Brecksville (Ohio)-Broadview Heights Sch. Dist., 1969-94; chmn. dept. art Brecksville-Broadview Heights (Ohio) H.S., 1979-94; ret.; chmn. curriculum devel. Brecksville-Broadview Heights (Ohio) H.S., 1982, 89; instr. for children Kent State U., 1956; advisor, prodr. cmty. svc. in art Brecksville Broadview Heights Bd. of Edn., 1969-94; former tchr. recreation and adult art edn. 1967-68, City of Cuyahoga Falls, 1967-68; com. mem. North Ctrl. Evaluation Com., Nordonia City, Ohio, 1978, Solon City, Ohio, 1989; chmn. north ctrl. evaluation com. Garfield Heights H.S., 1991; chair pilot program curriculum devel. com. in art/econs. Brecksville-Broadview Heights H.S., 1985-86, 86-87. Contbr. articles to newspapers, brochures, mags.; commd. artist for mural Brecksville City's Kids Quarters, 1994, Christopher Columbus/John Glen portraits in relief commemorating Columbus Day, 1961, Wooster (Ohio) Products Co.; editor Greater Cleve. chpt. Ohio Ret. Tchrs. Assn., 1998—. Chmn. Artmart Invitational Exhibit PTA, 1982-94; active Meals on Wheels program in Brecksville and Broadview Hts., 1995-98, Heart Disease collection, 1995, Stow-Glen Assisted Living Visitations, 1994-95, NCR Assisted Living transp. provision to hosps. and dr. in neighboring county; trustee, sec. Gettysburg Devel. Block Group Parma, 1995-96, Kids Quarters, 1994; Med Save fraud vol. Cuyahoga County Dept. Sr. and Adult Svcs., 2000—. Recipient Ohio Coun. on Econ. Edn. award, 1985-86, award for significant svc. to cmty. Ret. and Sr. Vol. Program of USA, 1996, GCC/ORTA Svc. award, 1998; Pres.'s scholar Kent State U., 1954-57. Mem. AAUW, ASCD, NAFE, Nat. Art Edn. Assn., Ohio Ret. Tchrs. Assn. (Cleve. chpt. pres.-elect 1998, registration chair 1997-98, co-chair 1996-98, program chair 1998, chpt. pres. 1999, interim editor 1998, editor 1999-2000, circulation mgr. 1998-2000, editor/circulation mgr. 2000—, by-law chair 2000—, nominating chair 2000—), Internat. Platform Assn., Brecksville Edn. Assn., Acad. Econ. Edn., Cleve. Mus. Art, Nat. Mus. Women in Arts, S.W. Area Ret. Educators (program chair 1996-98, program coord. 1999-2000), Phi Delta Kappa Pi. Roman Catholic. Avocations: European and American museum tours, photography, collecting books on architecture, painting. Home: 7301 Sagamore Rd Parma OH 44134-5732

TENER, GEORGE E., investor; b. Edgeworth, Pa., May 5, 1917; s. Alexander Campbell and Marion (Clement) T.; m. Patricia Ann Buehner Talcott, Apr. 13, 1945 (div. June 1964); children: Roberta T. Kerkam, Jenifer E.; m. Anne Powell Potts Faber, Oct. 11, 1966. BA, Yale U., 1940. Fgn. svc. officer Dept. State, Italy, Philippines, 1948-54; fin. analyst J&W Seligman & Co., N.Y.C., 1957-64; bd. dirs. Inst. Philos. Rsch., Chgo., 1967-93. Dir. Nat. Assn. for the So. Poor, 1965—. Lt. Am. Field Svc., 1942-44. Decorated Brit. Empire medal, 1945. Mem. Univ. Club (N.Y.), Met. Club, City Tavern Club. Democrat. Episcopalian. Avocations: writing, travel, photography. Home: 3202 Scott Pl NW Washington DC 20007-2946

TENET, GEORGE JOHN, government agency official; m. A. Stephanie Glakas; 1 child. BS in Fgn. Svc., Georgetown U., 1976; MIA, Columbia U., 1978. Legis. asst. to Sen. H. John Heinz III Senate Select Com. on Intelligence, Washington, 1985-86, designee to vice chair Sen. Patrick J. Leahy, 1986-89, dir. oversight of arms control negotiations Soviet Union/US, 1989-93, staff dir., 1993; mem. presdl. transition team Nat. Security Coun., Washington, 1993-95, spl. asst. to pres., sr. dir. intelligence programs, 1995-97; dep. dir. CIA, Washington, 1995-96, acting dir., 1996-97, dir., 1997—. Author: The Ability of U.S. Intelligence to Monitor the Intermediate Nuclear Force Treaty. Office: CIA Puf Affairs Office Washington DC 20505-0001

TENFELDE, KLAUS, historian; b. Erkelenz, Germany, Mar. 29, 1944; s. Paul and Toni (Deters) T.; m. Ellen Siepenkoetter, Mar. 6, 1973; children: Lars, Jan. PhD, U. Muenster, 1975; Dr.phil.habil., U. Muenchen, 1981. Apprentice Mining, Essen, Germany, 1958-62; policeman German Border Police, 1962-65; rschr. U. Munich (Germany), 1973, 75-81, dozent, 1981-86; prof. U. Innsbruck (Austria), 1986-90, U. Bielefeld (Germany), 1990-95, U. Bochum (Germany), 1995—; Author: Sozialgeschichte der Bergarbeiterschaft an der Ruhr, 1977, 2d edit., 1981, Proletarische Provinz, 1982, Arbeiter im Deutschen Kaiserreich, 1992; contbr. articles to profl. jours. Elected mem. Penzberg (Germany) City Coun., 1981-90. Mem. Verband Deutscher Historiker. Home: Bethanienstr 18, 44805 Bochum Germany Office: U Bochum, U Bochum, Inst Soziale Bewegungen, D-44789 Bochum Germany

TENG, JIANFU, electronics engineer, educator; b. Shandong Province, Shandong, China, Nov. 1, 1954; s. Teng Shufen and Zhang Guilan; m. Zhang Weina, Dec. 22, 1980; 1 child, Ying. MSc, Tianjin U., 1983; PhD, King's Coll., London, 1988. From lectr. to prof. Tianjin U., China, 1988—. Mem. China Inst. Electronics, N.Y. Acad. Scis. Office: Tianjin U, Dept Electronic Engring, 300072 Tianjin China

TENG, YONGHONG, chemist, researcher, translator; b. Dalian, Liaoning, China, Nov. 10, 1966; d. Weipan Teng and Yuncui Jiang; m. Masayuki Tatsumi. BS, Beijing Normal U., 1988, MS, 1991; PhD, Okayama (Japan) U., 1995. Guest rschr. Osaka U., Ibaraki, Japan, 1995; domestic sci. and tech. rschr. Osaka Nat. Rsch. Inst., Ikeda, Japan, 1995-98; new energy & indsl. tech. devel. orgn. fellow rschr. Rsch. Inst. Innovative Tech. for Earth, Kyoto, Japan, 1998—. Contbr. articles to sci. jours. Mem. Chem. Soc. Japan (presentation prize 72th nat. meeting 1997), Catalysis Soc. Japan. Achievements includg patent on catalyst for production of acrolein. Avocations: scuba diving, reading, travel. Office: Rsch Inst Innovative Tech, for Earth, 9-2 Kizugawadai, Kyoto Soraku-gun 619-0292, Japan

TENGBERG, JOHN T.U., investment company executive; b. Goteborg, Sweden, Apr. 6, 1949; s. John G.A. and Violet B. (Englund) T.; m. Magdalena K.C. Claesson, July, 1985; children: Anna, John, Carl, Lisa. BA, Stockholm U., 1974. Asst. to mng. dir. Gumperts, Goteborg, 1972-74, dir., 1974-79; rsch. asst., asst. lectr. Stockholm U., 1977-79; auditor Dahlgrens, Stockholm, 1979-81; dir., Provisor AB Certus, Stockholm, 1981—; ptnr. AV Havsfrun, Stockholm, 1989-98, main shareholder, 1995—. Mem. Stora Sällskapet. Home: Overasgatan 4, S-41266 Goteborg Sweden Office: AB Havsfrun, Strandvagen 1, 114 51 Stockholm Sweden

TENGBOM, ANDERS, architect; b. Stockholm, Nov. 10, 1911; s. Ivar J. and Hjordis (Nordin) T.; m. Margareta Brambeck, May 21, 1937; children—Jonas, Anna, Svante, Lisen. Architect, Royal Inst. Tech., Stockholm, 1934; postgrad. Cranbrook Acad., 1936, Royal Acad. Stockholm, 1941. Pvt. practice architecture, Stockholm, 1938—; asst. prof. architecture Royal Inst. Tech., 1947-48; mem. bd. Swedish Hosp. Fedn., 1962-70. Prin. archtl. works include Swedish Embassy Moscow, hosps. in Sweden, Venezuela, Saudi Arabia. Fellow AIA (hon.); mem. Nat. Assn. Swedish Architects (pres. 1963-65), Swedish Assn. Cons. Architects (pres. 1972-75), Royal Inst. Brit. Architects (hon. corr. mem. 1963), Royal Acad. Fine Arts (pres. 1980-86). Home: Canton 2, 17893 Drottningholm Sweden Office: Kornhamnstorg 6, 11127 Stockholm Sweden

TENGELYI, LÁSZLÓ, philosophy educator; b. Budapest, July 11, 1954. MA in Classical Philology (Latin), Eötvös Loránd U., Budapest, 1977, MA in History and Philosophy, 1979, MA in Classical Philology (Greek), 1985, PhD, 1984. Asst. prof. Eötvös Loránd U., Budapest, 1979-89, assoc. prof., 1989-99; prof. Eötvös Lánd U., Budapest, 1999—; head dept. Eotvos Loraud U., Budapest, 1997—. Author: Der Zwitterbegriff Lebensgeschichte, 1989, Kant, 1995, Guilt as an Event of Destiny, 1992, Autonomy and World Order, 1984; contbr. articles to profl. jours. Scholar Soros Found., 1988-89, A. von Humboldt-Stiflung, 1993-96, A. Mellon, Paris, 1998. Mem. Deutsche Gesellschaft für Phänomenologie, Hungarian Assn. of Philosophy; guest professorship U. de Poitiers (France), academic yr. of 1998-99, spring, 2000. Home: Halmi u 14, H1115 Budapest Hungary Office: Eötvös Lorbánd U, Pesti B u 1, H-1052 Budapest Hungary

TENGEN, THOMAS L., financial planner, finance educator; b. Lafayette, Ind., June 4, 1938; s. William E. and Marie C. (Faustich) T.; m. Rebecca R. Hawtin, Jan. 27, 1962 (div. Jan. 1978); 1 child, Scott A.; m. Judith Laurence, May 25, 1994; step children: Michael B. Laurence, Valerie Laurence. BS, Ind. State U., 1957. CFP; chartered fin. cons.; CLU. Gen. agent Lafayette Life, Ft. Wayne, Ind., 1960-63; supr. Mass Mutual Life, Ft. Wayne, 1963-66, gen. agent, 1966-80; gen. agent Penn Mutual Life, Cin., 1980-85; pres. Mercantile Fin. Group, Cin., 1985—. Chmn. Lucas County fund Rep. Party, Toledo, Ohio, 1974. Mem. Gean. Agents and Mgrs. Assn. (dir. Toledo, Ohio 1974-80, pres. Toledo, 1977-78, dir. Cin. 1981-83), Queen City Assn. (bd. dirs. 1988-94, pres. 1991), Cin. Estate Planning Coun., Hyde Park Golf and Country Club, Cincinnatus. Republican. Avocations: golf, hiking, horticulture. Office: Mercantile Fin Group 2444 Madison Rd Ste 105 Cincinnati OH 45208-1278

TEN HAVE, HENK AMJ, medical ethicist, educator; b. Voorschoten, The Netherlands, June 24, 1951; s. Henk and Agnes (Niersman) Ten H.; m. Nancy Lemmens, June 27, 1980; 1 child. MD, U. Leiden, 1978, PhD, 1983. Rschr. U. Leiden, The Netherlands, 1976-78; mcpl. physician Health Svcs. Rotterdam, The Netherlands, 1978-79; from lectr. to prof. philosophy U. Limburg, The Netherlands, 1982-91; prof. med. ethics Catholic U. Nijmegen, 1991—. Mem. European Soc. Philosophy Medicine & Health Care, Inst. Soc., Ethics & Life Sci., European Soc. Rsch. in Ethics, European Pub. Health Assn., Rotary. Office: Catholic U Nijmegen, Dept Ethics PO Box 9101, 6500 HB Nijmegen The Netherlands

TENKOTTE, PAUL ALLEN, history and international studies educator; b. Covington, Ky., June 30, 1960; s. Harry Vincent and Mary Margaret (Meier) T. BA in History, Thomas More Coll., 1982; MA in History, U. Cin., 1983, PhD in History, 1989. Charles P. Taft fellow U. Cin., 1982, 84, 85, grad. asst. Carl Blegen Libr., 1983, Lenore McGrane fellow, 1986-87; prof. history Thomas More Coll., Crestview Hills, Ky., 1987—; dir. internat. studies Thomas More Coll., 1991—; regional coord. 3 U.S. Congl. dists for Nat. Bicentennial Competition on the Constn. and Bill of Rights, Ctr. for Civic Edn., 1987-89. Author: A Heritage of Art and Faith; contbr. articles to profl. jours. and encyclopedias. Active Miami Purchase Assn. Historic Preservation, Cin., 1985-92; coord. historic restoration Mother of God Ch., Covington, 1986-94, v.p. governing bd., 1987-89; trustee Internat. Visitors Coun. Greater Cin., 2000—; mem. Ky. Underground Railroad Adv. Com., 1997—. Groesbeck scholar for historic preservation Nat. Soc. Colonial Dames Am. in Ohio, 1986; Cultural Exch. grantee Japan Travel Bur., 1991; recipient Thomas More Coll. Alumni Assn., 1999. Mem. Dinsmore Homestead Found. (adv. coun. 1989-92), Kenton County Hist. Soc. (v.p. 1981-82, pres. 1982), Phi Alpha Theta (Dr. A.F. Zimmerman scholar 1982, Dr. John Pine scholar 1985). Avocations: photography, architecture, bicycling, travel. Office: Thomas More Coll 333 Thomas More Pky Covington KY 41017-3428

TENNENBAUM, MICHAEL ERNEST, private investor; b. St. Petersburg, Fla., Sept. 17, 1935; s. Reubin and Frieda (Miller) T.; m. Suzanne Stockfisch; children by previous marriage—Mark Stephen, Andrew Richard. BS, Ga. Inst. Tech., 1958; MBA with honors, Harvard U., 1962. Assoc. Burnham & Co., N.Y.C., 1962-64; assoc. Bear, Stearns & Co., N.Y.C., 1964-69, sr. mng. dir., 1969-96, vice chmn. investment banking div., 1988-93; chmn. bd. dirs. Tech. Park, Atlanta, 1978-81; mng. mem. Tennenbaum & Co., LLC, L.A., 1996—; bd. dirs. ICF Kaiser Internat., Inc., 1998—; chmn. fin. com., mem. exec. com. ICF Kaiser Internat., Inc., 1998—; bd. dirs. TelePacific Corp. Bd. govs., nat. bd. trustees Boys and Girls Clubs Am.; mem. nat. adv. bd. Ga. Inst. Tech., 1971-77; mem. vis. com. Harvard U. Sch. Bus., Cambridge, Mass., 1986-92, bd. assocs., 1992—; bd. trustees Ga. Inst. Tech. Found., Inc., Atlanta, 1988-96; bd. dirs. Joffrey Ballet, 1990-92, chmn. exec. com., 1991-92; bd. dirs. Music Ctr. L.A. County Unified Fund Cabinet, 1990-91; chmn. L.A. Mayor's Spl. Adv. Com. on Fiscal Adminstrn., 1993-94; commr. Calif. Intercity HighSpeed Ground Transp. Commn.; chmn. Calif. High Speed Rail Authority, 1998—. Mem. Malibu Racquet Club. Home: 118 Malibu Colony Rd Malibu CA 90265-4642 Office: Tennenbaum & Co LLC 11100 Santa Monica Blvd Ste 210 Los Angeles CA 90025-3335

TENNEY, FRANK PUTNAM, marketing executive; b. Orono, Maine, Oct. 6, 1937; s. Carl Bither and Velma May (Williamson) T.; m. Margaret Anne Seymour, Apr. 23, 1960; children: Jane Dossiere, Carl B., Janet M., Alan F., Janice M. Lovell. Cert. notary public, Maine. Nat. sales mgr. Shaw & Tenney Oar & Paddle Co., Orono, 1958-68; sales mgr. George D. Wetherill, Phila., 1968-69; with R.M. Flagg, Veazie, Maine, 1968-69; salesman DuBois Chem., Cin., 1969-76; Maine sales mgr. Rochester (N.Y.) Midland Co., 1976-82; with H.A. Manning Co., BellowsFalls, Vt., 1982-86; dist. sales mgr. U.S. West Mktg. Resources, Loveland, Colo., 1986-90; mgr. dist. sales City Directory, Inc., Belmond, Iowa, 1990-92; with RAK Industries, 1993; v.p. Maine Mktg. Resources, Brewer, Maine, 1994—; assoc. Prepaid Legal. Adv. bd. Salvation Army. Tech. sgt. Maine ANG, 1955-87, ret. Mem. VFW (past comdr. Am. legion), Profl. Sales Club Bangor, Greater Bangor C. of C., Am. Legion (past vice comdr. II, Americanism officer 1997), 40/8, Golden Cir. (Averill plaque), KC (past grand knight Pine Cone coun., 4th degree, past faithful navigator Pine Cone assembly). Republican. Roman Catholic.

TENNO, ROBERT, electrical engineer, educator; b. Nuia, Viljandi, Estonia, Mar. 27, 1949; s. Alfred and Tamara (Perosti) T.; m. Reet Tromp, Oct. 19, 1973; 1 child, Ander. MSc, Tallinn U. Tech., 1973; PhD, Moscow U. Power Engring., 1979, DSc, 1989. Engr., rschr. USSR Rsch. Inst. Elec. Engring., Tallinn, Estonia, 1973-79; head group, sr. rschr. Estonian Acad. Scis., Tallinn, 1979-91; assoc. prof. Helsinki (Finland) U. Tech., 1991—. Contbr. articles to profl. jours. Office: Helsinki Univ Tech, Vuorimiehentie 1A, 02150 Espoo Finland

TENNYSON, EDSON LEIGH, transportation administrator, consultant; b. Orange, N.J., July 6, 1922; s. William Edwin and Jane Virginia (Leigh) T.; m. Shirley Louise Forward, July 15, 1944; children: Marilyn Elizabeth, Constance Virginia, Marjorie Leigh. BS in Mgmt. Engring., Carnegie Inst. Tech., 1947, BEngring. in Mgmt., 1947. Registered profl. indsl. engr., Ohio, Pa. Rsch. analyst Pitts. Railways Co., 1947-49; v.p. Kenosha Motor Coach Inc., Milw., 1949-51; traction commr. Youngstown (Ohio) City, 1951-56; dep. commr. Dept. Pub. Property, Phila., 1956-71; dep. sec. Dept. Transp., Harrisburg, Pa., 1972-79; planning coord. Pub. Works, Arlington County, Va., 1983-92; transp. cons. San Diego, Md., Del., N.J., 1980-82, 93-94; cons. to Nat. Capital Transit Agy., Washington, 1962-63. Mem. Citizens Adv. Com. No. Va., 1997—, transp. rsch. bd. Nat. Rsch. Coun., 1972—; mem. budget com. Nat. Capital Presbytery, Washington, 1993-96; chmn. tech. adv. com. Del. Valley Regional Planning Commn., 1970-76; asst. scoutmaster Boy Scouts Am., Mt. Lebanon, Pa., 1947-49; chmn. planning commn. Middletown, Pa., 1980-83; elder, Presbyn. Ch., Chestnut Hill, Phila., 1962-68; trustee Vienna Presbyn. Ch., Va., 1998—. 1st lt. U.S. Army, 1946. Westinghouse Meml. scholar, Pitts., 1940-45; recipient Disting. Svc. award U.S. Dept. Transp., Washington, 1978; named Arlington's Most Valuable Employee, 1987. Mem. Westwood Country Club, Tau Betea Pi, Omicron Deltea Kappa. Avocations: tennis, swimming, travel, transit research. Home and Office: 2233 Abbotsford Dr Vienna VA 22181-3220

TEN RAA, THIJS, economist; b. Bentveld, Holland, The Netherlands, Oct. 8, 1952; s. Cristiaan and Eva (Sachs) ten R.; m. Anna de Voogt, Oct. 2, 1992. Degree in math., U. Groningen, The Netherlands, 1977; PhD in Econs., NYU, 1981. Asst. prof. Erasmus U., 1981-85; assoc. prof. Tilburg U., 1986—. Author: Linear Analysis of Competitive Economies, 1995. Econ. adviser Labor Party, The Netherlands. Fulbright fellow, 1977-81, 84-88, Sloan fellow, 1978-80, Royal Netherlands Acad. of Arts and Scis. fellow, 1987-91. Mem. Assn. for Can. Studies in the Netherlands (v.p. 1986-90). Mem. Labor Party. Avocation: academic exchange. Home: Herengracht 31, 1015 BB Amsterdam Holland, The Netherlands Office: Tilburg U, Box 90153, 5000 LE Tilburg Brabant, The Netherlands

TENTER, ASTRID MARGARETA, parasitologist, researcher, educator; b. Oberhausen, Germany, Jan. 19, 1959; d. Friedhelm and Edith Elisabeth (Immig) Tenter; 1 child, Tim Friedhelm. Grad. in Vet. Medicine, Tierärztliche Hochschule, Hannover, Germany, 1982, DVM, 1984, Venia Legendi for Parasitology, 1995. Mem. faculty Tierärztliche Hochschule, Hannover, 1984—, privatdozentin, 1995—; vis. scholar U. Tech., Sydney, Australia, 1992-93; vis. rsch. fellow Flinders U. South Australia, Adelaide, 1989-91; courtesy asst. prof. Oreg. State U., Corvallis, 1988. Contbr. numerous articles to profl. jours. Deutsche Forschungsgemeinschaft rsch. fellow, 1988, 89-91. Mem. Am. Soc. Parasitology, Deutsche Gesellschaft für Parasitologie (mem. coun. 1992-96), World Assn. for Advancement of Vet. Parasitology, Australian Soc. for Parasitology, Brit. Soc. Parasitology. Avocations: literature, classical music, ballet. Office: Inst Parasitologie, Bünteweg 17, D-30559 Hannover Germany

TENTOA, TEWAREKA, I-Kiribati government official. V.p. Govt. of Kiribati, Tarawa Atoll. Office: Ministry of Home Affairs and Rural Devel, PO Box 75, Bairiki Tarawa Kiribati*

TENYI, JENO, physician, researcher; b. Gorcsony, Baranya, Hungary, Dec. 20, 1932; s. Geza and Gezane (Koos Olga) T.; m. Ilse Klein, Dec. 22, 1962; children: Aniko, Ildiko. MD, Med. U., Pecs, Hungary, 1957; PhD, Social Medicine, 1969. Resident Clinic of Internal Medicine Med. U., Pecs, 1957, asst. lectr., 1962, univ. lectr. Inst. for Pub. Health, 1962-69, prof. Inst. for Social Medicine, dir., 1970-91, prof. Inst. for Pub. Health, 1991—; dir. Nat. Inst. for Gen. Medicine, Pecs, 1979-91. Mem. Internat. Assn. Agrl. Medicine and Rural Health (pres. 1987-2000, past pres. 2000—). Avocation: gardening. Home: Szegfu u 19, 7624 Pecs Hungary Office: Inst of Pub Health, Szigeti ut 12, 7643 Pecs Hungary

TENZIN GYATSO See DALAI LAMA

TEO, FELETI PENITALA, Tuvaluan government official; b. Tarawa, Kiribati, Oct. 9, 1962; s. Fiatau Penitala and Uimai (Tofiga) T.; m. Tausaga Talake, Sept. 24, 1989; children: Kasipo, Losaline. LLB, U. Canterbury, Christchurch, New Zealand, 1987; LLM, Australian Nat. U., Canberra, 1996. Lic. barrister and solicitor, New Zealand and Tuvalu. Crown counsel Govt. Tuvalu, Funafuti, 1987-91, atty. gen., 1992—. Avocations: fishing, soccer, tennis, reading. Home: Nanumasa, Funafuti Island Tuvalu Office: Office Atty Gen, Pvt Mail Bag, Funafuti Tuvalu*

TEO, TAT-KAI, computer executive, consultant; b. Singapore, Singapore, Jan. 17, 1961; s. Choon-Hong Teo. BSc in Info. Sys. & Computer Sci., Nat. U. Singapore, 1986. Software engr. Inst. Sys. Sci., Singapore, 1986-88;

project leader Nortel Asia Ptd. Ltd., Singapore, 1989-91; sr. mgr. NorTel Asia South Pacific, 1993-96; regional dir.-Asia Stentofon ASA, Singapore, 1996—; sr. mgr. strategic software mktg. Asia Pacific Intel, 1999; CEO internet subsidiary Popular Holdings Ltd., 2000—; cons., inventor, rschr. in field, 1992-93. Designer ednl. games. Mem. Rediffusion Youth & Children Drama Group, 1971-79. Mem. IEEE (chairperson Singapore Computer Chpt. 1994-97), Singapore Computer Soc., Mensa. Avocations: Chinese chess, reading, traveling, cross-country.

TEODOR, DAN G.H., archaeologist, researcher; b. Bacău, Romania, Sept. 23, 1933; s. Gheorghe V. and Maria C. (Zarojanu) T.; m. Silvia G.H. Iacob, Oct. 25, 1958; children: Lucian, Andrei Ligia-Otilia. Student, U. Alex I. Cuza, Iasi, Romania, 1956. Rschr. Inst. History, Iasi, Romania, 1956-69, prin. rschr., 1969-89; dir., prin. rschr. Inst. Archaeology, Iasi, Romania, 1990—; prof. archaeology U. Alex. I. Cuza, Iasi, Romania, 1995—. Author: Teritoriul Est-Carpatic în Veacurile V-XI e.n., 1978 (Vasile Pârvan-Academia Română award 1978), Romanitatea Carpato-Dunăreană si Bizantul în Veacurile V-XI, 1981, The East-Carpathian Area of Romania V-XI Centuries A.D., 1980, Civilizatia Romanică la est de Carpati în Sec. V-VII e.n., 1984, Continuitatea Populatiei Autohtone la est de Carpati în Sec. VI-XI, 1984, Sisteme de Fortificatie Medievale Timpurii î Sec. VIII-XI, 1987, Crestinismul la est de Carpati de la Origini Până în Sec. XIV, 1991, Istoria Veche a României de la Origini Până în Sec. VIII, 1995, Mestesugurile la nordule Dunarii de Jos in secolele IV-XI, 1996, Descoperiri archeologice si numismatice la Est de Carpati in secolele V-XI, 1997; contbr. over 167 articles to profl. jours. Recipient U. Alex I. Cuza award, Iasi, 1984. Mem. Permanent Com. Internat. Union Slavonic Archaeology, Permanent Com. Internat. Union Pre and Proto-History, Historians Nat. Com., Romanian Assn. Byzantine Studies (v.p. 1985). Avocations: classical music, literature, philology, fine arts. Home: St Splai Bahlui 37 apt 3, 6600 Iasi Romania Office: Inst Archaeology Iasi, St Lascăr Catargi 18, 6600 Iasi Romania

TEODORESCU, GEORGE, industrial designer, educator, consultant; b. Bucharest, Rumania, Jan. 27, 1947; arrived in Fed. Republic of Germany, 1980; MArch, Inst. Architecture, Bucharest, 1972. Architect Trade Show Enterprise IPA, Bucharest, Rumania, 1972-76; indsl. designer Ministry for consumer art MIU, Bucharest, 1976-77; design mgr. Ministry for Edn., Bucharest, 1977-80; devel. engr. Leybold-Heraeus, Cologne, Fed. Republic of Germany, 1981-86; indsl. designer Leybold A.G., Cologne, 1986-90, design. mgr., 1990-93; prof. Art Acad. Stuttgart, 1993—; founder, leader Inst. for Capital Goods Design, Stuttgart, 1997—; gen. mgr. Steinbers Transfer Ctr. for Capital Goods, 1997—; mng. dir. Internat. Inst. for Integral Design, 2000—; prof. U. Wuppertal, 1991-93. Recipient Silver medal Eurodidac, 1986, Best Design award, Design Coun. NRW, Essen, Fed. Republic of Germany, 1988, 99, Industrie Form Hannover, Fed. Republic of Germany, 1990, State award, 1991, Design award Design Coun. Stuttgart, Fed. Republic of Germany, 1989, 90, Chgo. Atheneum award, 1995, 96, 98, 99. Mem. Indsl. Designer Soc. Am. (hon. mention 1989, Silver award 1990), Verein Deutscher Industrie Designer, Design Mgmt. Inst. Achievements include 6 patents for modular systems for physics (Germany), 1 patent for screen changing device for electron-welding (Germany), patents for wind tunnel experiment kit (Germany, France). Home: Alarich Str 19, D-70469 Stuttgart Germany Office: Tesign Design Consultancy, Bonnerstr 498, D-50968 Cologne 51, Germany also: Art Acad Stuttgart, Am Weissenhof 1, 70191 Stuttgart Germany

TEODORESCU, HONORIU DAN, engineer, researcher; b. Pitesti, Arges, Romania, Feb. 26, 1928; s. Cicerone Teodorescu and Zoe (Caridis) Kottaki; m. Stana Stella Guran, June 27, 1959; children: Roxana Iris, Dana Corina. BS, Poly. Inst., Timisoara, Romania, 1952, MS in Engring., 1967. Design engr. Inst. Studii Proiectari Energetice, Bucharest, Romania, 1952-54; rsch. engr. Inst. Cercetari Electrotehnice, Bucharest, 1954-55; rsch. engr. Electromotor Ltd., Timisoara, 1955-70, head Rsch. Ctr., 1970—; asst. prof. Poly. Inst., Timisoara, 1965-67, prof., 1967-70. Author: Nonlinear Systems Design, 1973, Automatic Control Systems, 1974, Biological Engineering, 1978, Optimized Stochastic Models, 1982, Deterministic Control Systems, 1984, An Introduction to Microelectronics, 1985, Microelectronic Control Systems, 1989; contbr. articles to profl. jours.; patentee in field. Recipient Gold medals Internat. Exhbn. for Inventions, Vienna, 1968, Oberhausen, 1970, Cologne, Germany, 1972. Mem. Romanian State Com. Electronics and Automation, Jury of Inventions Internemo. Avocations: pre-classic music, literature (short stories), walking. Home: Piata Victoriei 1A, 1900 Timisoara Romania

TEODORESCU, NICOLAE GHEORGHE, economics researcher, educator; b. Lipova, Arad, Romania, Nov. 14, 1947; s. Gheorghe Moise and Magdalena Nicolae (Munteanu) T.; m. Virginia Constantin Gherghe, Apr. 24, 1971. Grad. in Econs., Acad. Econ. Studies, Bucharest, Romania, 1970, D of Econs., 1980. Rschr. Market Rsch. Inst., Bucharest, 1970-92; mng. dir. Mia Mktg. Inst. Ltd., Bucharest, 1992-99, Mia Mktg. Internat., Bucharest, 1999—; assoc. prof. Acad. Econ. Studies, 1971-92, prof., 1992—. Author: Consumer Behaviour Investigation Patterns, 1984, Consumer Behaviour, 1997, Marketing-Grid Tests, 1999, Marketing Handbook, 2000. Lt. Romanian Mil., 1970. Mem. European Soc. for Opinion and Mktg. Rsch., Am. Mktg. Assn. Christian Orthodox. Avocations: reading, motoring, fishing. Home and Office: 10 Fibrei St, 72304 Bucharest Romania

TEODORU, GEORGE VASILE MARIUS, materials and structural engineer, consultant; b. Craiova, Romania, Sept. 8, 1932; s. Alexandru Stefan and Paula (Tuculescu) T.; m. Cornelia Popa, June 17, 1961. BS and MS magna cum laude, Tech. U., Bucharest, Romania, 1956; grad. in Radioactive Isotope Tech., Inst. for Atomic Physics, Bucharest, Romania, 1961; postgrad., Tech. U., 1971; PhD, Tech. RWTH, Aachen, Germany, 1983. Registered profl. engr., Germany. Supr. Intreprinderea Prefabricate Progres, Bucharest, 1956-57; supr., tech. mgr. Enterp. Bridges Constrn., Bucharest, 1957-61; chief rsch. engr. Inst. Rsch. in Constrn., Bucharest, 1961-71; tchr., rsch. asst. Tech. U., Bucharest, 1970-71; design and project mgr. P. Bauwens, Cologne, Germany, 1971-83; expert/cons. Verein Deutscher Ingenieure for Bldg., Cologne, Germany, 1983—; sr. lectr. Tropical Inst. Tech., Cologne, Germany, 1983—; vis. lectr. univs., Brazil, Thailand, 1990-94; advisor rsch. and PhD thesis Indian Inst. Sci., Bangalore, India, 1992; mem. organizing com. ACI Symposium NDT, San Antonio, 1987; mem. tech. orgn. com. 14th World Conf. Nondestructive Testing, New Delhi, 1996; presenter and chmn. session civil materials 9th Internat. Symposium on Nondestructive Characteristics of Materials, Sydney, Australia, 1999; execution of some first bridges in prestressed concrete in Romania; UNO, UNESCO roster of experts; presenter 12th, 13th, and 14th World Conf. on NDT, Amsterdam, 1989, São Paulo, 1992, New Delhi, 1996; presenter 7th, 8th, and 9th World Conf. Chemistry Cements, Paris, 1980, Rio de Janeiro, 1986, New Delhi, 1992, others; presenter 1st 2nd RILEM/CEB Symposium Quality Control of Concrete Structures, Stockholm, 1979, Gand, Belgium, 1991. Author: Hydrothermally Cured/Treated Concretes and Their Nondestructive Testing, 1983, Nondestructive Testing of Concrete (Beton-Verlag), 1989; mem. editl. bd. Internat. Advances in NDT Gordon and Breach Sci. Publ., 1994; reviewer numerous mags., 1989—; contbr. over 120 articles to profl. jours. Rsch. grantee German Soc. for Rsch., 1986-89. Fellow Am. Concrete Inst.; mem. ASTM, AAAS, Engring. Soc. Cologne (pres. 1993—), Réunion Internat. des Laboratoiree Essais Matériaux, N.Y. Acad. Sci. Achievements include pioneering work in NDT of concrete, multiple simultaneous use of several NDT methods, the first application rigor, statis. in evaluation of NDT results in quality control of concrete products, New criterion (logarith decrement) for frost resistance of concrete; being among the first to establish the qualitative and quantitative influence of curing conditions of concrete on the relations between non-destructively measured values (velocity or attenuation of ultrasound and rebound indices) and its compressive strength (for hydrothermally treated concrete, these relations are exponential); establishing the values of standard deviations (for ultrasonic pulse velocities and rebound indices) corresponding to a good quality of concrete production; presenting an original "pressure chamber" with video camera and monitor, which, for the 1st time, followed the process of crystallization in cement suspensions at high temperatures; discovery of the limited nature of applicability of some existing methods for structural analysis; pioneering work in the execution of pre-stressed concrete bridges and deep foundations on caissons with high compressed air. Avocations: tennis, chess composer (worldlevel) of endings (FIDE award 1966) of moremovers (FIDE award 1958) of problems with retro-analysis (FIDE Album 1962-64), pianist.

TEOREANU, ION, solid state chemistry educator, researcher; b. Topalu, Romania, Nov. 12, 1929; s. Ion Iorgu and Elena Alexandru (Gheorghiu) T.; m. Justina Alexandru Martin, Dec. 24, 1954; 1 child, Mihaela Teoreanu-Popescu. MS in Chemistry, Poly. U. Bucharest, Romania, 1953, PhD in Chem. Engring., 1961, DSc, 1970. Lectr. Poly. U. Bucharest, 1952-59, sr. lectr., 1959-61, reader, 1961-68, prof. solid state chemistry, 1968—; dep. dean Faculty Indsl. Chemistry, Poly. U. Bucharest, 1960-62, dean, 1978, head dept. Tech. of Silicate and Oxide Compounds, 1972-78. Author: Technology of Ceramic and Refractory Products, 2 vols., 1985, Introduction to the Science of Inorganic Materials, 2 vols., 1987, Fundamentals of the Inorganic Binders Technology, 1993; patentee in field; editor-in-chief Jour. Bldg. Materials, 1971—. Pres. Nat. Coun. Engrs. from Romania, Bucharest, 1980-82. Recipient Order Scientific Merit, State Coun. Romania, 1986. Mem. N.Y. Acad. Scis., Am. Ceramic Soc., European Ceramic Soc. (coun. mem. 1992—), Romanian Ceramic Soc. (pres. 1991—), Inst. Materials Gt. Britain. Eastern Orthodox. Avocations: music, travel, literature. Office: Poly U-Catedra SIMO, PO Box 12-134, Bucharest Romania

TEOULE, ROBERT AUGUSTE, biochemist; b. St. Germain, Ardeche, France, Dec. 5, 1933; s. Henri and Victoria (Tastevin) T.; m. Nicole Marguerite Armand, Aug. 13, 1959; children: Francoise, Christine. PhD, U. Lyon. Asst. U. Lyon (France), 1959-62; researcher CEA/Atomic Energy Commn., Grenoble, France, 1963-67; dir. lab. CEA, Grenoble, France, 1968-93; cons. ORIS, Grenoble, France, 1994—; dir. lab. ORIS, Grenoble, 1983-93; tchr. U. Grenoble, 1972-93. Author/editor: (with others) Effects of Ionizing Radiation on DNA, 1978; contbr. articles to profl. jours. Chmn. Nucleic Acids Probes Biotech. Program, 1986-88. Recipient prize Acad. Scis. France; decorated knight Order Nat. of Merit. Mem. Soc. Chemistry France (chmn. Alpes region 1981-82), Soc. French Biochemistry, European Soc. Radiation Biology (bd. dirs. 1988-92), Internat. Soc. Nucleic Acids Chemistry. Achievements include the identification of the major DNA lesions induced by ionizing radiation and by oxidative damage, the total chemical synthesis of natural tRNA, the discovery of alacali-labile protecting groups for rapid synthesis of oligonucleotides (DNA fragments) and an electrochemical method to manufacture DNA biochips. Home: 52 rue Thiers, 38000 Grenoble France

TEPENIER, DANIEL, sales and marketing professional; b. Boulogne Billancourt, France, Oct. 28, 1957; s. Fernand Tepenier and Sylvia Decottegnie; m. Sabine Bailly, May 2, 1964; 1 child, Lisa. DSc in Biology, U. Paris, Orsay, France, 1986. Sales rep. Organon Teknika, France, 1986-87, dist. mgr., 1987-88, product mgr., 1988, mktg. mgr., 1990-91, sales/mktg. mgr., 1991-95; bus. mgr. France Becton Dickinson, France, 1996-99, divsn. mgr. western Europe, 1996-99, divsn. mgr. France bioscis., 1999—. Office: BD, 11 rue Aristide Berges, 38800 Le Pont de Claix France

TEPFERS, RALEJS KRIŠJĀNIS, building technology educator; b. Rezekne, Latgale, Latvia, Dec. 28, 1933; arrived in Sweden, 1944; s. Ilmars and Irene (Zupans) T.; m. Ira Majors, June 22, 1961; children: Marlene, Janis, Beatrice. MSc in Civil Engring., Chalmers U. Tech., Göteborg, Sweden, 1958, Tekn. Lic., 1966, PhD, 1973; D in Engring. (hon.), Latvian Acad. Scis., Riga, 1996. Rsch. asst. Chalmers U. Tech., Göteborg, 1960-69, assoc. prof., 1969-94, prof., 1995—; Swedish nat. del. Com. Euro-Internat. du Beton, Lausanne, Switzerland, 1982-98. Author: A Theory of Bond Applied to Overlapped Tensile Reinforcement Splices for Deformed Bars, 1973, An Investigation of Fatigue of Concrete, 1978, Building Materials, 1985, revised 1995. Pres. Assn. Technique in Göteborg, 1987-88, Latvian Coun. in Sweden, Stockholm, 1992—. Cpl. Swedish Arty., 1959-60. Grantee Japan Soc. for the Promotion of Sci., Sendai, 1988. Mem. Swedish Concrete Assn., Concrete Assn. Latvia, Am. Concrete Inst. Avocations: open air life. E-mail: Tepfers@bm.chalmers.se. Home: Brödragatan 44, SE-41274 Göteborg Sweden Office: Chalmers U Tech, Sven Hultins Gata 8, SE-41296 Göteborg Sweden

TEPING, CHRISTIAN, ophthalmologist educator; b. Fulda, Hessen, Germany, Sept. 12, 1952; s. Heinrich and Margot (Runge) T.; m. Birgit Dagmar; children: Julia, Niklas; m. Claudia Katharina Backes; childran: Fritz, Paul. Med. exam., RWTH, Aachen, Germany, 1977; MD, RWTH, 1978. Med., sci. asst. Physiology and Clinic Forschung Max Planck Inst., Frankfurt, Bad Nauheim, Germany, 1978-80; med. asst. eye clinic RWTH, Aachen, 1980-84, habil., 1987; chief eye clinic Klinikum, Saarbrücken, Saarland, Germany, 1989—; prof. ophthalmology RWTH, Aachen, 1993. Contbr. articles to profl. jours. Recipient Sci. award for Ophthalmology Surgery, German Ophthalmology Assn., 1988. Office: Augenklinik, Augenklinik Klinikum, Saarbrucken Winterberg, 66119 Saarbrucken Germany

TEPLYKH, VISSARION, chemistry educator; b. Village Elovka, USSR, June 28, 1932; s. Fedor and Uljana (Solovjeva) T.; m. Larisa Virigradova, Mar. 7, 1953; children: Elena, Marija. Engr.'s degree, Inst. Tech., Leningrad, USSR, 1957, PhD, 1971. Mgr. of lab. Inst. Tech., Leningrad, USSR, 1957-59, postgrad. student, 1959-62, engr., 1962-70, asst., 1970-71, sr. rsch. worker, 1971-83, assoc. prof., 1983—; mgr. radioactive security,1962-70, vice dean of faculty, 1970-87, mem. faculty scientific coun., 1975-87, Inst. Tech., Leningrad, USSR; mem. coordinational coun. on phys. constants measuring Minatom, Moscow, 1982-90. Author: (with K.A. Petrzhak, E.V. Platygina) The Basis of Nuclear Energy Cycle, 1985, (with K.A. Petrzhak, E.V. Platygina) The Nuclear Properties and the Interaction of Radiation with Substance, 1989; inventor: (with E.C. Platygina) The Method of Measuring of Fission Products Yield, 1972, (with E.V. Platygina) Film Threshold Counter, 1988. Sr. lt. 1957-87, Leningrad. Recipient Bronze medal Exhbn. of Achievements of USSR Nat. Economy, Moscow, 1986, Diploma The Honorable Award of State Com. of Russian Fedn. on Highest Edn., 1993, Honorable award Atomic Energy Min. of Russian Fedn., 1999. Avocations: lake, river, forest, fishing. Home: Budapesskaja, 17-2-214 Saint Petersburg Russia Office: Technol Inst, Moskovskii pr 26, 198013 Saint Petersburg Russia

TEPPER, LYNN MARSHA, gerontology educator; b. N.Y.C., Mar. 16, 1946; d. Jack Mortimer and Ida (Golembe) Drukatz; m. William Chester Tepper, Aug. 27, 1967; children: Sharon Joy, Michelle Dawn. BS, SUNY, Buffalo, 1967; MA, Wayne State U., 1971; MS, Columbia U., 1977, EdM, 1978, EdD, 1980. Instr. John F. Kennedy Sch., Berlin, 1967-68, ednl. counselor, 1968-69; ednl. coordinator Army Edn. Ctr., Berlin, 1969-71; psychologist U.S. Dept. Def., Berlin, 1971-73; prof. Gerontology L.I. U., 1979-99, Columbia U., N.Y.C., 1982—; cons. NATO, Naples, Italy, 1969-71, SHAPE, Brussels, 1969-71, also numerous nursing homes, N.Y., 1978—, Found. for Long Term Care, 1992—; prof. gerontology Mercy Coll., Dobbs Ferry, 1979—; dir. Gerontology Resource Ctr., Ctr. for Geriatrics and Gerontology, Columbia U., N.Y.C., 1980-85, dir. Behavioral Sci. Program, 1982—; del. White House Conf. on Aging, 1980. Author: (textbooks) Long Term Care, 1993, Respite Care, 1993; contbr. articles to profl. jours., chpts. to books. Advisor Office on Aging, State of N.Y., Albany, 1980-90; dir. Mercy Coll., Inst. Gerontology, 1990—; trustee, St. Cabrini Nursing Home, 1988-98, Morningside Nursing Home, 1998—. Brookdale Inst. on Aging fellow, 1983; rsch. grantee NIH, Nat. Inst. on Aging, U.S. Dept. Edn., U.S. Bur. Health Professions, interdisciplinary geriat. tng. U.S. Dept. Health Resources Svcs. Adminstrn. Fellow Gerontol. Soc. Am.; mem. Northeastern Gerontol. Soc., N.Y. Assn. Gerontol. Edn., Am. Psychol. Assn. Avocations: physical fitness. Home: 50 Burnside Dr Hastings Hdsn NY 10706-3013 Office: Columbia U Med Campus Box 20 630 W 168th St New York NY 10032-3702

TERADA, MARCO ANTONIO, electrical engineer; b. Sao Paulo, Brazil, Nov. 27, 1966; s. Ramon and Maria (Prado) T.; m. Mires Freitas, Jan. 25, 1986; children: Marco, Monica. BSEE, U. Brasilia, 1989, MSEE, 1991; PhD, Va. Tech. U., 1995. Prof. U. Brasilia, 1995-98; sr. engr. satellite sys. Internat. Telecom. Satellite Orgn., Washington, 1998—; cons. Comtech Antenna Sys., Inc., St. Cloud, Fla., Prodelin Corp., Conover, N.C. Contbr., author: The Wiley Encyclopedia of Electrical and Electronics Engineering, 1999. Mem. IEEE, Brazilian Microwave & Optoelectronics Soc. Roman Catholic. Avocations: music, sports, computers, traveling. Office: INTELSAT Mailbox 33A 3400 International Dr NW Washington DC 20008-3006

TERAKAWA, AKIRA, solar cell engineer, materials scientist; b. Nara, Japan, July 13, 1967; s. Makoto and Katsuko (Yoshimura) T. DEng, Kyoto (Japan) U., 1990, postgrad., 1997-99. Rschr. Sanyo Electric Co. Ltd., Hirakata, Japan, 1990—. Contbr. articles to profl. jours. Mem. The Japan Soc. Applied Physics, Japan Solar Energy Soc. Home: Tomio-kita 2-2-1, Nara 631-0076, Japan Office: Sanyo New Mat Rsch Ctr, Dainichi Higashimuchi 1-1, Moriguchi Osaka 570-8502, Japan

TERAMOTO, TETSU SATOSHI, architect; b. Kumamoto, Japan, Jan. 19, 1954; s. Seiichi and Reiko (Kimura) T. MArch, Kumamoto U., 1980. Staff architect Azusa Sekkei Co. Ltd., Tokyo, 1980-82; sub-chief architect Osaka br. Azusa Sekkei Co. Ltd., Osaka, 1983-85; prin. Tetsu Teramoto Architect Office, Kumamoto, 1986—; lectr. Kumamoto YMCA Vocat. Coll. Arch., 1987-91. Pres. Kumamoto Daiichi Leo Club, 1978-79. Avocations: reading, aikido. Office: 1-12-1 Hirata, 860-0826 Kumamoto Japan

TERAMURA, SHOJI, linguist, educator; b. Osaka, Japan, Feb. 25, 1949; s. Iwao and Kimie (Nakamura) T. BA, Osaka U., Toyonaka, Japan, 1971, MA, 1973. Instr. linguistics Wakayama (Japan) U., 1973—; vis. scholar Lancaster (Eng.) U., 1988-89. Co-author: The Kenkyusha Dictionary of English Linguistics and Philology, 1982; co-editor: Shogakukan Random House English-Japanese Dictionary, 2d edit., 1994; contbr. articles to profl. jours. including Bull. of the Faculty of Edn. Wakayama U. Mem. English Lit. Soc. Japan, English Linguistic Soc. Japan, Japan Assn. Coll. English Tchrs. Home: Nagasone-cho 1180, Sakai Osaka 591-8025, Japan

TERANO, TOSHIRO, retired educator, mechanical engineering; b. Tokyo, Japan, Mar. 31, 1922; s. Takuji and Misao (Kasuya) T.; m.Kimiko Kamibayashi, Nov. 8, 1950; children: Takao, Masao. B in Engring., Tokyo U., 1945, D in Engring., 1960. Tech. official Ministry Transp., Tokyo, 1947-50; rschr. Transp. Rsch. Inst., Tokyo, 1950-62; prof. Tokyo Inst. Tech., 1962-82, Hosei U., Tokyo, 1982-92; head Lab, for Internat. Fuzzy Engring. Rsch., Yokohama, 1989-95; vis. prof. MIT, Boston, 1957-58. Author: (book) Systems Engineering-Challenge to Complex Problems; editor, author: Advances Applications of Fuzzy Engineering, 1993, Intelligent Information Processing by Fuzzy Methodology, 1995. Councilor Honda Found., Tokyo, 1978—, Tateishi Sci. Promotion Found., Kyoto, 1990—, Internat. AI Found., Tokyo, 1990—; dir. Fuzzy System Rsch. Inst., Iizuka, 1990—. Recipient Japan Soc. Mech. Engrs. prize, Tokyo, 1969, Japan Soc. for Ship Bldg. prize, Tokyo, 1972, Japan Soc. Instrument and Control prize, Tokyo, 1975, Moisil Internat. prize in Fuzzy System, Moisil Found (Rumania) Internat. Svcs., 1993, Kampe de Feriet award, Internat. Conf. on Info. Processing and Mgmt. of Uncertainty, France, 1996; decorated Third Order of Merit, 1968, The Order of the Sacred Treasure. Fellow IFSA (spl. mem.); mem. Japan Soc. Fuzzy Theory and Systems (bd. dirs., Svc. award 1994, Book awards 1994, 96), Internat. Fuzzy System Assn. (pres. 1985—), Japan Soc. Mech. Engrs. (com. chmn. Tokyo), Soc. System Control and Info. (v.p., com. chmn. Kyoto). Avocations: golf, travel, reading, studying fuzzy engring. E-mail: toshiro@mbc.infosphere.or.jp. Home: 4-24-12 Eifuku Suginami, Tokyo 168, Japan

TERAO, TOSHIO, physician, educator; b. Shimizu, Japan, Jan. 18, 1930; s. Eiji and Mitsuko (Katagiri) T.; m. Setsuko Nishigaki, Nov. 13, 1961; children: Toshiya, Yasuo, Yoshio. Diploma U. Tokyo, 1953, M.D., 1960. Intern, Tokyo U. Hosp., 1953-54; sr. scientist Nat. Inst. Radiol. Sci., Chiba, Japan, 1963-67; research assoc. Mayo Clinic, Rochester, Minn., 1970-72; asst. U. Tokyo, 1972-77, lectr. in medicine 1977-79; prof. medicine Teikyo U., 1980-91, prof. neurology, 1991—; pres. Teikyo U. Med. Hosp., 1987-93, dean, 1993-95, pres. North Tokyo Jueien, 1995—. Author, editor in field. Mem. Am. Acad. Neurology, Japanese Soc. Internal Medicine, Japanese Soc. Neurology, Japanese Soc. Neuropathology, Japanese Soc. EEG and Electromyography, Japanese Soc. Psychiatry and Neurology, Japanese Soc. Cerebrovascular Disease, Sigma Xi. Office: Teikyo U, 2-11-1 Kaga Itabashiku, Tokyo 173, Japan

TERAO, YASUO, physician, researcher; b. Shizuoka, Japan, Oct. 23, 1964; s. Toshio and Setsuko (Nishigaki) T. MD, U. Tokyo, 1989, PhD, 1998. Physician internal medicine U. Tokyo, 1989-90; physician dept. neurology divsn. neurosci. Grad. Sch. Medicine, 1993—; physician internal medicine Tokyo Met. Geriatric Hosp., 1990-91; physician dept. neurology Red Cross Med. Ctr., Tokyo, 1991-92, tokyo Met. Neurol. Hosp., 1992-93. Mem. Japanese Soc. Neurology, Japanese Soc. Internal Medicine, Japanese Soc. EEG and Electroencephalography. Office: U Tokyo Dept Neurology, 7-3-1 Hongo Bunkyo-ku, 113-8655 Tokyo Japan

TERÄSVIRTA, TIMO, economics educator; b. Helsinki, Finland, Jan. 24, 1941; s. Einari Allan and Sirkku Sylvia (Ilvessalo) T.; children from a previous marriage: Teemu, Eljas; m. R.K. Marikki Junnila, Nov. 6, 1987. MPolSc, U. Helsinki, Finland, 1964, LicPolSc, 1968, DPolSc, 1970. Rsch. fellow Acad. Finland, Helsinki, 1972-76; prof. U. Helsinki, 1976-80; rsch. fellow Rsch. Inst. Finnish Economy, Helsinki, 1980-89, Ctrl. Bank Norway, Oslo, 1993-94, 2000; prof. Stockholm Sch. Econs., 1994—; vis. prof. U. Calif., San Diego, 1984-85, 89-91, 98. Author: Stepwise regression and economic forecasting, 1970; co-author: Modelling nonlinear economic relationships, 1993. Mem. Soc. Scientiarum Fennica (E.J. Nyström's prize 1993), Internat. Statistical Inst. Office: Stockholm Sch Econs, Sveavägen 65, S-113 83 Stockholm Sweden

TERAUCHI, HAJIME, language educator; b. Maebashi-City, Gunma, Japan, Jan. 7, 1960; s. Haruo and Hisae (Enomoto) T.; m. Mayumi Koinuma, Mar. 30, 1997. BA, Keio U., Japan, 1983; MA, U. Warwick, Coventry, Eng., 1993, PhD, 1997. Cert. univ. lectr. Clk. Taiyo Kobe Bank, Tokyo, 1984-85; dep. headmaster Sano Dress Making Spl. Tng. Sch., 1985-98; assoc. prof. Takachiho U., Tokyo, 1998—; part-time lectr. Otsuma Women's U., Tokyo, 1995-98, Keio U., Tokyo, 1996—, Rikkyo U., Tokyo, 1997—. Author, editor: (book) English for Academic Purposes in Japan: An Investigation of Language Attitudes and Language Needs in a Department of Law, 1997; contbr. articles to profl. jours. Pres. Warwick Grad. Assn., Tokyo, 1997—. Fellow Japan Assn. Coll. English Tchrs.; mem. Brit. Assn. Applied Linguistics. Avocations: golf, rugby. Home: 2-5-40-529, Minami-Koshigaya Koshigaya, Koshigaya Saitama 343-0845, Japan Office: Takachiho U, Suginami-ku Tokyo, Japan

TERAZAWA, HIDEZUMI, physicist, educator; b. Amagasaki, Hyogo, Japan, July 25, 1942; s. Usami and Shigeko (Nakajima) T.; m. Atsuko Kuroda, Oct. 17, 1967 (dec. Oct. 1978); children: Tomozane, Waka; m. Keiko Hiraide, Feb. 1, 1980. BS, U. Tokyo, 1965, MS, 1967, DS, 1970. Instr., rsch. assoc. Cornell U., Ithaca, N.Y., 1969-71; asst. prof. Rockefeller U., N.Y.C., 1971-75; assoc. prof. Inst. for Nuclear Study U. Tokyo, 1975-97, acting head theoretical physics divsn. Inst. Nuc. Study, 1994-97, dir. Ctr. Asia and Oceania for Sci., 1989—; dep. rep. Theory Group, Inst. Particle & Nuclear Studies Tanashi br. High Energy Accelerator Rsch. Orgn. Min. Edn., Sci., Sports & Culture Japan, Tokyo, 1997-2000, acting dir., 2000; dep. rep. Hadron and Nuc. Theory Group, Inst. Partide and Nuc. Studies, High Energy Accelerator Rsch. Orgn., Min. Edn., Sci., Sports and Culture Japan, Tsukuba, Ibaraki, 2000—. Author: Prephysics and Pregeometry, 1982, Unification of Quarks and Leptons, 1982, Two-Photon Processes for Particle Productions at High Energies, 1973, Unified Model of the Nambu-Jona-Lasinio Type for All Elementary-Particle Forces, 1977, Gravity and Electromagnetism as Collective Phenomena of Fermion and Antifermion Pairs, 1978, Subquark Model of Leptons and Quarks, 1980, Pregeometric Origin of the Big Bang, 1983; editor: Particles and Nuclei, 1986, New Particles and the Structure of Hadrons, 1978, Quark and Lepton Physics, 1980, Composite Models of Quarks and Leptons, 1984; contbr. articles to profl. jours. Recipient award Gravity Rsch. Found., 1982, honorable mention awards, 1977, 79, 86. Mem. AAAS, Internat. Soc. Outer Space Law, Phys. Soc. Japan, Am. Phys. Soc., N.Y. Acad. Scis., Planetary Soc. Avocations: tennis, mountaineering, painting, composing music, traveling. Home: 3-11-26 Maesawa, Higashi-Kurume Tokyo 203-0032, Japan also: 4-201-312 Azuma, Tsukuba Ibaraki 305-0031, Japan Office: Inst Particle/Nuc Studies Engy Accel Rsch, Min Edn Sci Sports & Culture 1-1 Oho, Tsukuba Ibaraki 305-0801, Japan

TERBLANCHE, PETRO, environmental scientist, consultant; b. Brits, Northern, South Africa, Feb. 2, 1959; d. Jacobus Petrus and Maria Susanna (Meyer) T.; m. Francois Hermanus Roux; children: Su-Mari, Marlette. BS,

U. Pretoria, 1980, BS with honors, 1981, MS, 1984, DSc, 1987. Rsch. officer med. oncology dept. H.F. Verwoerd Hosp., Pretoria, 1982-88; sr./chief med. rschr. Med. Rsch. Coun., Pretoria, 1988-91; specialist scientist Med. Rsch. Coun., 1991-92; project mgr. atmospheric process and mgmt. advice Ematek Coun. for Scientific Indsl. Rsch., Pretoria, 1992-93; mgr. environ., health and safety svcs. Coun. for Scientific Indsl. Rsch., 1993-96, dir. divsn. food, biol. & chem. techs., 1996—; vis. scientist Harvard U. Sch. Pub. Health, 1989; enrolled advanced leadership program CSIR, 1994-95: South African rep. Internat. Stds. Orgn. work group for internat. stds. on environ. performance evaluation, 1994—; mem. UN Environ. Program steering com. for chem. risk assessment, 1994—; cons. in field. Contbr. over 200 scientific papers to profl. jours. Trustee Internat. Life Scis. Inst., 1997-98; mem. Gencor Health, Safety and Environ. Bd. Named Corp. Businesswoman of Yr. No. Transvaal Region, 1995; recipient Merit award Rotary Club of Vanderbijl Pk., 1994. Mem. Nat. Assn. for Clean Air (pres. 1996-98). Avocation: long distance running. Home: Waterkloof, 56 Dely Rd, Pretoria 0081, South Africa Office: Coun for Sci Indsl Rsch, PO Box 395, Pretoria 0001, South Africa

TERENCE, SIM CHET HONG, trade specialist; b. Singapore, Apr. 21, 1948; s. Sim and Tan (Alice) William; m. Chng Phaik Gan Grace, July 10, 1980; children: Sabrina (dec.), Sherene. B in Commerce, St. Olav's Acad., Paris, 1972. Chartered cons. Am. Cons. League. Rep. Vavasseur Levetus Export Ltd., England, 1968-72, Am. Minerals & Petroleum Corp., 1973, Dominion Shippers Ltd., England, 1974-78, Gordon & Gotch Export Svcs. Ltd., England, 1979-80, Dalgety Export Svcs. Divsn., England, 1981-83; co. dir. Global Exports Network Ltd, Singapore, 1986-92; pres. Beneficial Offshore Trading House, Singapore, 1984—. Avocations: securities markets, investments, finance. Home: Blk 108 Simei St #04-740, Singapore 520108, Singapore Office: Beneficial Offshore Trading House, Katong PO Box 3, Singapore 914301, Singapore

TERENTJEFF, JORMA KALEVI, engineering company executive; b. Oulainen, Finland, Mar. 4, 1949; s. Pauli and Bertta (RKistolainen) T.; m. Tarja Liisa Kangasniemi, Jan. 31, 1987 children: Timo, Heidi, Mikko. MSc, U. Oulu. Dir. radio prodn. Salora Oy, Oulu, Finland, 1973-79; plant mgr. Salcomp Oy, Oulu, 1979-82; mgmt. cons. Hansacon Oy, Oulu, 1983; pres. Oy Edacom, Oulu, 1983-87, Aspocomp Oy, Oulu, 1987-93, Teknoventure Oy, Oulu, 1993-95; pres., CEO Jot Automation Group PLC, Oulu, 1995—. Office: Jot Automation Group PLC, Automaatiotie 1, 90460 Oulunsal Finland

TERENTJEVA, ALEXANDRA K., astronomer, researcher; b. Solonikha, Russia, Apr. 28, 1933; d. Konstantin I. and Larissa I. (Volkova) T.; m. Igor S. Astapovich, Mar. 2, 1963 (dec. Jan. 1976); 1 chld, Vsevolod. Grad., U. Nizhnij Novgorod, Russia, 1956; postgrad., U. Kiev, Ukraine, 1962-65; PhD in Physics and Math., Pulkovo Obs., St. Petersburg, Russia, 1971. Rsch. scientist Astron. Obs. of U. Kiev, 1956-71, sr. rsch. scientist, 1972-77; sr. rsch. scientist Inst. of Astronomy/Acad. Sci., Moscow, 1978—; founding mem. Internat. Meteor Orgn., Belgium, 1988—, mem. coun., 1989-93. Contbr. articles to profl. jours. Mem. Internat. Astron. Union (commn. 1982—), European Astronomical Soc. Russian Orthodox. Avocations: travel, photography. Office: Acad Sci/Inst of Astronomy, 48 Pyatnitskaya, 109017 Moscow Russia

TERENZIO, MARION ANN, college program executive; b. Stamford, Conn., Aug. 8, 1954; d. Emanuele and Josephine Ann Terenzio. AB in Music, Vassar U., 1976; MA in Music Therapy, Tex. Woman's U., 1979; MA in Cmty. Psychology, Sage Grad. Sch., Troy, N.Y., 1989; PhD in Cmty. Psychology, Mich. State U., 1991. Prof. psychology and arts The Sage Colls., Troy, v.p. campus life; cons. music therapy various allied health agencies, 1985-98, Albany (N.Y.) Med. Ctr., 1993-96, colls. and univs., 1998—. Founding editor N.Am. Assn. Masters in Psychology newsletter, 1994-97. Bd. dirs. Troy Area United Ministries, 1994-98, Troy Savs. Bank Music Hall, 1996—, Rensselear County C. of C., Troy, 1999; mem. program com. Regional Art Ctr., Troy, 1994-98. Recipient Rubin Found. grant, 1998, Faculty Study award Pew Charitable Trust, 1998, grant Very Spl. Arts Washington, 1999, Disting. Svc. award Hudson McHawk Assn., 1999, Alumnae award Friend of Russell Sage Coll., 2000. Mem. Soc. Rsch. (chair com. on women 1995). Avocation: karate (black belt). E-mail: terenm@sage.edu. Office: The Sage Colls 45 Ferry St Troy NY 12180-4115

TERESHKO, IRENE VASILJEVNA, physicist, educator; b. Mariinsk, Russia, Aug. 7, 1941; d. Vasily and Klavdiya (Kucherinova) A.; m. Michael Tereshko, Apr. 24, 1963; two children. MSc, Tomsk State U., 1963, PhD, 1970. Jr. rschr. Inst. Geophysics, Novosibirsk, Russia, 1965-66; asst. prof. Inst. Comm., Novosibirsk, 1966-67; jr. rschr. Siberian Phys. Technol. Inst., Tomsk, 1971-72; from assoc. prof. to prof., sr. rschr. Mech. Engring. Inst., Mogilev, Belarus, 1973—. Author: Deformational Hardening of the Ordered Alloys, 1979; contbr. articles to profl. jours. Mem. N.Y. Acad. Scis. Fax: 375-222-225-518. E-mail: tereshko@phys.belpak.mogilev.by. Office: Mech Engring Inst, Lenin St 70, 212005 Mogilev Belarus

TEREZ, EDWARD IVAN, astrophysics and atmospheric physics educator; b. Leningrad, Russia, May 6, 1939; s. Ivan Ignatius Terez and Valentina Michail Mitrofanova; m. Galina Andrei Yatsenko, Oct. 3, 1964; children: Dmitry, Ivan. MSc in Aerospace Tech., Leningrad Inst. Tech., 1962; PhD, Crimean Astrophys. Obs., Crimea, Ukraine, 1973; D (hon.), Nat. Acad. Scis. Ukraine, Moscow, 1989. Rsch. engr. Leningrad Inst. Aerospace Tech., 1962-63; scientist Crimean Astrophys. Obs., 1963-75; assoc. prof. astrophysics and atmospheric physics Simferopol (Ukraine) State U., 1975-90, dept. head, prof., 1990—. Author: Photometric and Polarimetric Investigation of Celestial Bodies, 1985; contbr. articles to sci. jours., including Moon, Soviet Astron. Jour., Jour. Atmospheric and Terrestrial Physics. Recipient Pallas award Crimean Ministry Coun., 1995, State Crimean award, 1997. Mem. Am. Geophys. Union, Crimean Acad. Scis. (com. Simferopol), Petrov Acad. Scis. and Arts. Avocations: Russian, English, French, and German literature and poetry. Office: Simferopol State U, St Yaltinskaya 4, 333036 Simferopol Crimea, Ukraine

TERGAU, FRITHJOF, neurologist; b. Hildesheim, Germany, June 13, 1968; s. Hermann and Dorothea (Kittel) T.; m. Ulrike Weddig, Sept. 19, 1994. MD, U. Goettingen, Germany, 1995. Scientific asst. dept. anatomy U. Goettingen, Germany, 1995, jr. house officer dept. clin. neurophysiology, 1996-97, sr. house officer, 1997—; cons. in field. Author: Restless Legs Patient Information, 2000; contbr. articles to profl. jours. Capt. German Mil., 1987-88. European Cmty. fellow, London, 1997. Mem. Internat. Soc. Transcranial Magnetic Stimulation. Lutheran. Avocations: music, sports. Home: Schiffhornfeld 22D, D-30655 Hannover Germany Office: U Goettingen, Robert-Koch Str 40, D-37075 Göttingen Germany

TERHAL, PETRUS HENDRICUS, retired economist; b. Heerlen, The Netherlands, Sept. 10, 1935; s. Hendricus Jacobus and Johanna Gerardina (Verhagen) T.; m. Eleonora Maria Wellink, May 2, 1966. MSc in Math., U. Leyden, The Netherlands, 1966; PhD, Erasmus U., Rotterdam, The Netherlands, 1988. Sci. rschr. Ctrl. Computing Ctr., Leyden, 1967-69, Ctrl. Planning Bur., The Hague, The Netherlands, 1969-70, Netherlands Econ. Inst., Rotterdam, 1970-78; sci. rschr. Erasmus U., 1970-78, asst. prof. Ctr. Devel. Planning, 1978-96, dir., 1988-96; cons. Novib Dutch Govt. European Commn., India, 1980, 86, 92. Co-author: Towards Employment Guarantee in India, 1994, Economics of International Security, 1994; editor: Development, Transformation and State Policy, 1995; contbr. articles to profl. jours. Founding chmn., bd. dirs., 1st pres. Economists for Peace, The Netherlands, 1992; dep. chmn. sect. internat. affairs Dutch Coun. Chs., Amersfoort, 1985-96; chmn. Oecumenical Inst. Ch. & Devel. Cooperation, Utrecht, The Netherlands, 1996—. Green Left. Roman Catholic. Avocations: chess, choir singing, piano. Office: Erasmus U Cr Devel Planning, PO Box 1738, 3000DR Rotterdam The Netherlands

TER HOFSTEDE, ARTHUR HARRY MARIA, information systems specialist, educator; b. Nymegen, The Netherlands, Aug. 9, 1966; s. Joseph Maria and Johanna Margaretha (van der Maas) ter H. MSc cum laude, U. Nymegen, 1989, PhD, 1993. Rschr. Software Engring. Ctr., Utrecht, The Netherlands, 1989-93; asst. prof. U. Nymegen, 1993-95; lectr. U. Queensland, Brisbane, Australia, 1996; lectr. Queensland U. Tech., Brisbane, 1997-98, dep. dir. Coop. Inf. Sys. Rsch. Ctr., 1998, sr. lectr. info. sys., 1999-2000, assoc. prof., 2000—, dir. Coop. Internat. Sys. Rsch. Ctr., 1999—; cons. ID Rsch., Gouda, The Netherlands, 1994; project leader Ctr. for Info. Tech. and Comms., Brisbane, 1996-97. Contbr. articles to profl. jours. Roman Catholic. Avocations: classical music, history, reading, weight lifting, British comedy. Office: Queensland U Tech, GPO Box 2434, 4001 Brisbane Australia

TERJUNG, BIRGIT, internist, researcher; b. Bonn, Germany, Feb. 17, 1966; came to U.S., 1998; d. Sigurd and Brigitta (Goerbing) T.; m. Stephan Repges. Grad. in Arch., U. Bonn, 1985-88, 89-91, MD, 1996; student, U. Vienna, Austria, 1988-89; lic. physician, U. Munich, 1993. Resident dept. internal medicine U. Munich, 1991-93; fellow dept. internal medicine U. Bonn, 1993-97, 2000—; postdoctoral rsch. fellow dept. medicine Columbia U., N.Y., 1998-2000. Contbr. chpt. to Autoimmune Liver Disease, 1998, articles to profl. jours. Postdoctoral fellow Deutscher Akademischer Austauschdienst, Bonn, 1998—, Lise-Meitner award, 2000—. Mem. Am. Gastroenterol. Assn., German Assn. for Internal Medicine, German Assn. for the Study of the Liver. Home: Gut Capellen 4, 53913 Swisttal Germany

TER-KAZARIAN, SERGEI See ROSEN, SERGEI

TERNEYRE, GERARD M., metallurgical company executive; b. Lourdes, France, July 21, 1951; s. René A. and Huguette D. (Troc) T.; m. Sylvie M. Desoutter, Oct. 5, 1991; children: Clement, Eugenie, Benoit. MS, Ecole Centrale de Paris, 1974; MBA, Insead, Fontainebleau, France, 1978. Drill pipe mgr. Vallourec, Paris, 1979-81; plant mgr. Vallourec, Persan, France, 1982-84; human resources profl. Vallourec, Paris, 1985, v.p. fittings, 1986-89, v.p. devel., 1990-92, v.p. automotive br., 1993—; bd. dirs. Tubauto, Sens, France, No-Sag, Meaux, France, Sopretac (vallourec), Paris, Vallourec Automotive, Vitry, France, Perdriel, Buenos Aires, Vallourec do Brasil Autopecas, Jacot, Etupes, France. Home: 49 rue de la Tour, 75116 Paris France Office: Vallourec, 130 Rue De Silly, 92100 Boulogne France

TERNUS, MONA PEARL, critical care nurse, flight nurse, educator; b. Levittown, N.J., Nov. 3, 1961; d. William Joseph and Sarah (Tanne) Tillis; married, July 1998; 1 child, Kattey; stepchildren: Dale, Brian, Megan, Duncan. BA, NYU, 1982; MSN, Pace U., 1986. Cert. critical care nurse, trauma nurse, staff devel. nurse; instr. ACLS and critical care. Nursery nurse No. Westchester Hosp. Ctr., Mt. Kisco, N.Y., 1987-88; ICU nurse Meth. Hosp., Houston, 1988-89; dir. nursing Golden Age and Winslow Nursing Homes, Houston, 1989; hospice case mgr. Vis. Nurse Assn., Houston, 1989-91; critical care charge nurse Woodlands (Tex.) Meml. Hosp., 1990-92; commd. 1st lt. USAF, 1992, advanced through grades to capt., 1992; charge nurse surg. ICU 59th Med. Wing USAF, Lackland AFB, Tex., 1992-94, critical care educator, 1994-95; flight nurse 23d Aeromed. Evacuation Squadron, Pope AFB, N.C., 1996-97; 2nd in command Mobile Aeromed. Staging Facility NATO Implementation Force, Tuzla AB, Bosnia-Herzegovina, 1996-97; res. officer 433d Aeromed. Evacuation Squadron, Kelley AFB, Tex., 1997-98, 908th Aeromed. Evacuation Squadron, Maxwell AFB, Ala., 1998—; edn. specialist U. Tex., MD Anderson Cancer Ctr., Houston, 1997-98; prof. Auburn U., Montgomery, Ala., 1998—. Mem. AACN, ANA, Ala. Nurses State Assn., Air Force Assn., Officers Club, Assn. Mil. Surgeons U.S., Res. Officers Assn., Ret. Officers Assn., Aerospace Med. Assn., Pi Alpha Alpha, Pi Sigma Alpha, Sigma Theta Tau (v.p. Kappa Omega chpt.). Jewish. Avocations: travel, reading, holistic healing. Home: 7144 Heathermoore Loop Montgomery AL 36117-7461

TERNYIK, STEPHEN, economist, educator; b. Hamm, Ruhr, Germany, July 29, 1960; s. Istvan and Marianne (Hochgeladen) T.; m. Lisa Steven, Nov. 4, 1988; children: Simon, Daniel, Lea. MA, Tech. U., Berlin, 1986; postgrad., Henry George Sch., SUNY. Expert/advisor in human devel. and monetary learning, 1986—; vis. rsch. fellow dept. precision machinery engring. Yoshikawa lab. Tokyo U., 1993. Author: Social Learning Processes, 1989; contbr. poems to profl. publs., essays, reports, and abstracts. Decorated Internat. Order of Merit. Mem. Am. Cons. League (accredited profl. cons.). Mem. Hungarian Dem. Forum. Avocations: gymnastics, gourmet. Fax: 49 89 744 140 33. E-mail: e.ternyik@kjr-muenchen-land.de. Home: Foutca 13, H-6120 Kiskun Majsa Hungary Office: Ternyik R&D/Techno Logos, POB 201, D-82043 Pullach Germany

TERP, DANA GEORGE, architect; b. Chgo., Nov. 5, 1953; s. George and June (Hansen) T.; m. Lynn Meyers, May 17, 1975; children: Sophia, Rachel. BA in Architecture, Washington U., St. Louis, 1974; postgrad., Yale U., 1975-76; MArch, Washington U., 1977. Registered architect, Ill., Calif., Fla. Architect Skidmore Owings & Merrill, Chgo., 1976, 1978-84, Terp Meyers Architects, Chgo., 1984—; prin. Arquitectonica Chgo. Inc., 1986—. Exhibited in group shows at Moming Gallery, Chgo., 1980, Printers Row Exhibit, 1980, Frumkin Struve Gallery, Chgo., 1981, Chgo. Art Inst., 1983; pub. in profl jours. including Progressive Architecture, Los Angeles Architect; work featured in various archtl books; exhibited 150 Yrs. of Chgo. Architecture. Bd. dirs. Architecture Soc. Art Inst. Chgo. Recipient hon. mention Chgo. Townhouse Competition, 1978, award Progressive Architecture mag., 1980, Archtl. Record Houses, 1989, GLOBAL Architecture Ga. Houses/26, 1989, Casa Vogue, 1989, 2d place award Burnham Prize Competition, 1991. Office: Terp Meyers Architects Inc 919 N Michigan Ave Ste 2402 Chicago IL 60611-1664

TERPENING, VIRGINIA ANN, artist; b. Lewistown, Mo., July 17, 1917; d. Floyd Raymond and Bertha Edda (Rodifer) Shoup; m. Charles W. Terpening, July 5, 1951; 1 child by previous marriage, V'Ann Baltzelle Deatrick. Student, William Woods Coll., Fulton, Mo., 1936-37, Washington U. Sch. Fine Arts, St. Louis, 1937-40. lectr. on art; jurist for selection of art for exhibits Labelle (Mo.) Centennial, 1972; chmn. Centennial Art Show, Lewistown, 1971, Bicentennial, 1976; dir. exhibit high sch. student for N.E. Mo. State U., 1974; supt. ann. art show Lewis County (Mo.) Fair, 1975-90. One-woman shows include Culver-Stockton Coll., Canton, Mo., 1956, Creative Gallery, N.Y.C., 1968, The Breakers, Palm Beach, Fla., 1976, others; group shows include Mo. Ann. Show, City Art Mus., St. Louis, 1956, 65, Madison Gallery, N.Y.C., 1960, Ligoa Duncan Gallery, N.Y.C., 1964, 78, Two Flags Festival of Art, Douglas, Ariz., 1975, 78-79, Internat. Art Exhibit, El Centro, Calif., 1977, 78, Salon des Nations, Paris, 1985, UN World Conf. of Women, Narobi, Kenya, 1985, William Woods Coll., Fulton, Mo., 1992-95, La Junta Coll. Art League Internat., 1992, 94, Coffret Musée, Paris, 1995; represented in permanent collection Nat. Mus. of Women in Art, 1990; executed Mississippi RiverBoat oil painting presented to Pres. Carter by Lewis County Dem. Com., Canton, 1979. Mem. Lewistown Bicentennial Hist. Soc.; charter mem. Canton Area Arts Coun. of N.E. Mo. Recipient Cert. of Merit Latham Found., 1960-63, Mo. Women's Festival of Art, 1974, Bertrand Russell Peace Found., 1973, Gold Medallion award Two flags Exhibit, 1977, 1st Pl. award LaJunta (Colo.) Fine Arts League, 1981, diploma Univ. Delle Arti, Parma, Italy, 1981, Purchase award Two Flags Art Festival, 1981, award Assn. Conservation and Mo. Dept. Conservation Art Exhibit, 1982, Purchase award Canton Area Arts Coun., 1988, Colorado Springs Art Festival, 1989; paintings selected for Competition '84 Guide by Nat. Art Appreciation Soc., 1984, 1st Pl. award New Orleans Internat. Art Exhibit, 1984, Two Flags Festival of Art, 1986, Sunflower Judges award Harlin Mus., West Plains, Mo., 1994, Key to City, Lifetime award, 1998; named artist laureate, Nepenthe Mondi Soc., 1984. Mem. Artist Equity Assn., Internat. Soc. Artists, Internat. Platform Assn., Nat. Mus. Women in Art (charter), Animal Protection Inst. Mem. Disciples of Christ Ch. Address: 105 S Vine St PO Box 117 Lewistown MO 63452-0117

TERPUGOV, EUGENI L'VOVICH, biophysicist, researcher; b. Schuchin, USSR, Belorussia, June 19, 1948; s. Lev Nikolaevich and Antonina (Pavlovna) T.; m. Svetlana Dmitrievna Pislyakova, Mar. 10, 1969 (div. Sept. 1987); children: Boris, Artem; m. Olga Vasilevna Degtyareva, July 15, 1988; 1 child, Sophy. MS in Physics, St. Petersburg State U., Leningrad, 1972; PhD in Physics and Math., Russian Acad. Scis., Pushchino, USSR, 1984. Engr. Inst. Biol. Physics Russian Acad. Scis., Pushchino, 1972-74, sr. engr., 1974-84, jr. rsch. scientist, 1984-94, sr. rsch. scientist, 1994—. Contbr. articles to profl. jours. including Physics of Solid State, Biophysica, Biochim. Biophys. Acta, and Microchim. Acta. Mem. Biochem. Soc., Goblenz Soc. Avocations: tennis, music. E-mail: terpugov@ibfk.nifhi.ac.ru. Office: Inst Cell Biophys, Institutscaja 3, 142290 Pushchino Moscow, Russia

TERRA, JEAN-LOUIS, psychiatrist, educator; b. Lyon, France, Sept. 24, 1950; s. Pierre and Paule (Champagnon) T.; m. Marie-Paule Mesmin, June 26, 1975; children: Florence, Isabelle, Xavier, Jean-Baptiste. BA, Chartreux U., 1969; MD, Alexis Carrel U., 1981; degree in psychiatry, U. Lyon, 1983. Intern Hospices Civils de Lyon, 1976-81, asst., 1981-84; asst. Ctr. Vinatier, Bron, France, 1984-89, prof., 1989—, dept. head, 1995—; project mgr. Agence Nat. pour le Dével. de L'Evaluation Médicale, Paris, 1993—; temporary advisor WHO, Romania, 1992, Copenhagen, 1993; mem. Intercommn. INSERM, France, 1995. Author, editor: Qualité de vie Subjective et Santé-Mentale, 1994, Epidemiologie en Psychiatrie, 1995; author: L'Evaluation des Pratiques Professionnelles dans les Etablissements de Santé, 1994; contbr. articles to profl. jours. Mem. Internat. Fedn. Psychiat. Epidemiology (treas. 1993), French Group of Psychiat. Epidemiology (treas. 1985), Comité Lyonnais pour la Recherche Thérapeutique en Psychiatrie (pres. 1990—), Romanian Psychiat. Assn. (hon.). Office: Ctr Hospitalier Vinatier, 95 Blvd Pinel, 69677 Bron France

TERRADAS, JAUME, ecologist; b. Barcelona, Catalonia, Spain, Dec. 19, 1943; s. Antoni and Josefina (Serra) T.; m. Marina Mir, Oct. 26, 1966; children: Guillem, Berta. D. en Ciencias, U. Barcelona, 1973. Adj. prof. botany U. de Barcelona, 1968-69; adj. prof. botany U. Autonoma de Barcelona, Bellaterra, Spain, 1971-74, prof. agregado ecology, 1974-81, chmn. ecology, 1981—; mem. Com. MAB-Spain, Madrid, 1983-93; dir. Ctr. de Recerca Ecològica i Aplicacions Forestals, Bellaterra, 1988-98. Author: Ecologia Avui, 1971, 4th edit., 1981, Ecologia y Educacion Ambiental, 1979, Barcelona: Ecologia D'Una Ciutat, 1986; editor: Els Sistemes Naturals, 1989, Quercus ilex ecosystems: function, dynamics and management, 1992, Ecologia del Foc, 1996, Barcelona 1985-99, Ecologia d'una Ciutat, 1999. Mem. Consell de Benestar Social Municipality, Barcelona, 1989-94, Consell de Protecció de la natura de la Generalitat de Catalunya, 1995-97, Consell de Medi Ambient Municipality, Barcelona, 1998—. Recipient Environment award Generalitat de Catalunya, 1998, Medal Narcis Monturiol in Scientific and Tech. Rsch., 1992. Mem. Ecol. Soc. Am., Brit. Ecol. Soc., Assn. Española de Ecologia Terrestre (pres. 1989-91), Inst. Catalana D'Historia Natural (v.p. 1977-78), Soc. Espanola de Ciencias Forestales. Office: U Autonoma, CREAF, 08193 Bellaterra Spain

TERRELL, DEANE, university vice chancellor; married; 3 children. Degree in econs. with honors, U. Adelaide; PhD, Australian Nat. U. Past dep. vice-chancellor Australian Nat. U., Canberra, vice chancellor, 1994—, past chmn. bd. faculties, dean faculty of econs. & commerce; vis. prof. London Sch. Econs., Wharton Sch. Bus. at U. Pa.; chmn. AARNet Bd. Mgmt., 1997—; v.p. IDP Edn. Australia; bd. dirs. Australian Vice-Chancellor's Com., Australian Edn. Office, Tertiary Edn. Superannuation Scheme; dir. Open Learning Australia Pty. Ltd., 1997-98; mem. CanTrade bd., 1996—; dir. Internat. Devel. Program Edn., Australia, 1996—, v.p., 1995—; dir. TESS, 1994—. Mem. Bus./Higher Edn. Roundtable, Can Trade, Canberra Bus. Coun., Assn. of Pacific Rim Univs. (steering com.), High Performance Com. Com. Interim Bd., Australian Partnership Advanced Computing, Bus. Higher Edn. Roundtable, Rhodes Scholar Com. for Scholars at Large. E-mail: Vice-Chancellor@anu.edu.au. Office: Sir Roland Wilson Bldg 120, The Australian Nat U, Canberra ACT 0200, Australia*

TERRIER, JEAN-MICHEL, administrator; b. Chalon, France, Nov. 5, 1955; s. Roger Philippe and Josette (Gibaud) T.; children: Christel, Stephane. D, Soils & Structure, Paris, 1980. Rschr. Ecole Ctrl. Paris, 1979-80; project engr. Mecasol, Paris, 1982-84; sr. engr. Geodynamic, Paris, 1984-86; rschr. SNPE Rsch. Ctr., Paris, 1986-91; gen. mgr. Dynalis, Paris, 1991—. Contbr. articles to profl. jours. Mem. French Assn. Aeronautics, Soc. Ingenieurs l'automobile, Assn. Francaiswe Mecaninque, des sols, Am. Phys. Soc., N.Y. Acad. Scis. Avocations: movies, skiing, literature. Home: 14 rue Vincente d Indy, F-91590 Guigneville France Office: Dynalis BP 24, 9 rue Lausisin, F91710 Vert-Pe-Petit France

TERRIS, LILLIAN DICK, psychologist, association executive; b. Blooomfield, N.J., May 5, 1914; d. Alexander Blaikie and Herminia (Doscher) Dick; m. Louis Long, Apr. 22, 1935 (dec. Sept. 1968); 1 son, Alexander Blaikie Long; m. Milton Terris, Feb. 6, 1971. BA, Barnard Coll., 1935; PhD, Columbia U., 1941. Diplomate Am. Bd. Examiners in Profl. Psychology. Instr. psychology Sarah Lawrence Coll., Bronxville, N.Y., 1937-40; jr. pers. tech. SSA, Washington, 1941; sr. pers. clk. OWI, N.Y.C., 1941-43; dir. profl. examination svc. Am. Pub. Health assn., N.Y.C., 1943-70; pres., 1970-79, pres. emeritus, 1979—. Assoc. editor: Jour. Pub. Health Policy, 1979—; contbr. articles to profl. jours. Recipient Nat. Environ. Health assn. award, 1976, Cert. Svc. award Bd. Preventive Medicine, 1979. Fellow Am. Psychol. Assn., Am. Coll. Hosp. Adminstrs. (hon.); mem. Am. Pub. Health Assn., N.Y. State Psychol. Assn., Phi Beta Kappa, Sigma Xi. Home: 208 Meadowood Dr S Burlington VT 05403-7401 Office: 475 Riverside Dr New York NY 10115-0122

TERRIS, VIRGINIA R., writer; b. Bklyn., Aug. 26, 1917; d. Edward Sutherland and Edith (Staines) Rinaldy; m. Albert Terris, Feb. 1942; children: Susan, Abby, David, Enoch. BA, N.J. Coll. for Women, 1938; MA, Adelphi U., 1964; PhD, NYU, 1973. Libr., translator Morristown (N.J.) Nat. Hist. Park, 1940-41; instr. Morris Jr. Coll., Morristown, 1941-42; free-lance editor, 1944—; prof. Adelphi U., Garden City, N.Y., 1964-83; workshop tchr., N.Y., Minn., 1971; lectr., N.Y., Sweden, 1971. Author: (poetry) Tracking, 1976, Canal, 1981, Folding/Unfolding, 1992, The Metaphysical Raisin, 1996; co-editor: The Many Worlds of Poetry, 1969, Living Is What I Wanted, 1999; editor: Meaningful Differences: The Poetry and Prose of David Ignatow, 1994, At My Ease: Uncollected Poems of the Fifties and Sixties (David Ignatow), 1998. Mem. MLA, Poetry Soc. Am., Common Cause. Avocations: gardening, travel. Home: 84 N Bayview Ave Freeport NY 11520-1938

TERRY, ARTHUR HUBERT, literary critic, educator; b. York, Yorkshire, Eng., Feb. 17, 1927; s. Arthur and Beatrice (Hardisty) T.; m. Mary Gordon Sellar, June 25, 1955; children: Richard, Sally, Philip. BA in Modern Langs., Trinity Hall, Cambridge, Eng., 1947, MA in Modern Langs., 1950. Asst. lectr. Spanish Queen's U., Belfast, No. Ireland, 1950-54; lectr. in Spanish Queen's U., Belfast, 1954-60, sr. lectr. in Spanish, 1960-62, prof. Spanish, 1962-72; prof. lit. U. Essex, Colchester, Eng., 1973-93; prof. lit. emeritus U. Essex, Colchester, 1993—; pres. Internat. Catalan Studies, Barcelona, Spain, 1982-88. Author: La poesia de Joan Maragall, 1963, An Anthology of Spanish Poetry 1500-1700, Vol. 1, 1965, Vol. 2, 1968, Catalan Literature, 1972, Antonio Machado. "Campos de Castilla", 1973, Selected Poems of Ausiàs March, 1976, Joan Maragall, Antologia Poética, 1981, Sobre poesia catalana contemporània: Riba, Foix, Espriu, 1985, Quatre poetes catalans: Ferrater, Brossa, Gimferrer, Xirau, 1991, Seventeenth-Century Spanish Poetry: The Power of Artifice, 1993. Sgt.-instr. Royal Army Edn. Corps, 1947-49. Recipient Internat. Ramom Llull prize Catalan Govt. and Inst Catalan Studies, 1995; decorated Cross of St. George Catalan Govt., 1982. Fellow Inst. Romance Langs. (sr.); mem. Brit. Comparative Lit. Assn. (pres. 1986-92), Inst. Catalan Studies (corr.). Avocation: amateur music making. Home: 11 Braiswick, C04 5AU Colchester Essex C04 5AU, England Office: U Essex Dept Literature, Wivenhoe Park, C04 3SQ Colchester Essex C04 3SQ, England

TERRY, CRAIG ROBERT, lawyer; b. Lake Charles, La., Oct. 18, 1955; s. Robert J. and Elodie S. (Shattuck) T.; m. Linda N. Smith, Feb. 20, 1990; children: Ian W., Lindsay N. BA, U. Tex., 1980; MA, U. Ariz., 1985, JD, 1987. Bar: Tex. 1994. Law clk. Linden, Chapa & Fields, Tucson, 1985-86, Barassi & Burris, Tucson, 1986-87; tchg. asst. dept. psychology U. Ariz., Tucson, 1984-88; contractor litigation support Tucson, 1988-90; pvt. practice Austin, Tex., 1994—; mem. adv. com. Nat. Forest Mgmt. of Ariz., Tucson, 1984. Mem. Travis County Bar Assn. (mem. alt. dispute resolution sect., family law sect., entertainment/sports law sect.), Coll. of State Bar of Tex. Office: 1201 Rio Grande St Ste 200 Austin TX 78701-1709

TERRY, DAVID WILLIAM, lawyer; b. Temple, Tex., May 21, 1958; s. Victor Lewis and Jon Gayle (Kirschner) T.; m. Katherine Ellen Noll, Dec. 5, 1987; children: Nicholas William, John Benjamin. BA, Colo. Coll., 1981; JD, South Tex. Coll. Law, 1985. Bar: Tex. 1986, U.S. Dist. Ct. (no. and ea. dists.) Tex. Briefing atty. U.S. Ct. Appeals (4th cir.), San Antonio, 1986-87; pvt. practice Dallas, 1987—. Exec. editor South Tex. Law Rev., 1985. Pres. East Dallas Cppr. Parish, 1992. Mem. Tex. Trial Lawyers Assn. (bd. dirs.

1992—), Am. Assn. Portrait Artists, Dallas Trial Lawyers Assn. (bd. dirs. 1994—), ATLA, Coll. State Bar Tex. (pro bono coll.). Democrat. Methodist. Avocations: oil painting, portraits and landscapes. Office: 12221 Merit Dr Ste 1650 Dallas TX 75251-3102

TERRY, ELIZABETH HAYS, calligrapher, needlepoint designer; b. Bryn Mawr, Pa., July 29, 1935; d. James Franklin and Mary Ellen (Carmichael) Hays; m. Charles L. Terry, III, Feb. 8, 1958; children: Elizabeth Harllee Carmichael Terry Moran, Charles L. IV. AB, Smith Coll., 1957. Asst. to profs. Harvard U., Cambridge, Mass., 1957-58; art tchr. Exeter (N.H.) Day Sch., 1968-72; asst. editor Phillips Exeter Acad. Alumni Quarterly, 1972-75, dir. alumni records, 1975-85; owner Elizabeth Terry, Needlepoint Design, Exeter, N.H., 1980—; tchr. needlepoint Guild of Strawbery Banke, Portsmouth, N.H. Dir. for Town of Exeter-Save Our Shores, 1972. Mem. Smith Coll. Class of 1957 (class fund agt. 1972-77, alumnae fund com. 1977-80, class bequest chair 1982—, com. on deferred giving 1990—), N.H. Colonial Dames (pres. 1989-92, nat. historian 1992-94, nat. v.p. 1994—). Episcopalian. Avocations: tennis, needlepoint, historic preservation. Home and Office: 77 Brookside Dr Stratham NH 03885-2128

TERRY, ELIZABETH JOANNA, publisher, editor; b. Leeds, Yorkshire, Eng., Oct. 3, 1960; d. John and Margaret Terry; m. Michael Emmerson, June 29, 1991. BA with honors, U. Warwick, Eng., 1983. Editl. asst. Leisure Publs. Ltd., Hitchin, Eng., 1983-84, asst. editor, 1984-85, mng. editor, 1985-86; editor Dicestar Ltd., Hitchin, 1986-93, editor, pub., 1993-95; editor, pub. Leisure Media Co. Ltd., Hitchin, 1995—; mng. dir., 1996, also bd. dirs. Avocations: swimming, skiing, photography, reading, cooking. Office: Leisure Media Co Ltd, Portmill House Portmill Ln, Hitchin Herts SG5 1DJ, England

TERRY, GLENN A., retired nuclear chemist; b. St. Paul, Aug. 26, 1922; s. Claude Alexander and Loretta (Glenn) T.; m. Evelyn Jean Lehmann, Aug. 16, 1947; 1 child, Stephen Allan. BS, So. Ill. U., 1947; PhD, U. Wis., 1951. Rsch. chemist Mallinckrodt Chem. Works, St. Louis, 1951-56; process improvement head Mallinckrodt Chem. Works, St. Louis, 1956-59; sect. leader Spencer/Gulf, Kansas City, Mo., 1959-68; tech. dir. Nuclear Fuel Svcs., Erwin, Tenn., 1968-73; nuclear process engr. U.S. Nulcear Regulatory Com., Washington, 1973-81, sect. leader, 1981-88, ret., 1988. Contbr. articles to profl. jours.; patentee in field. Lt. (j.g.) USN, 1942-46, PTO. Mem. Am. Chem. Soc. (emeritus), Am. Nuclear Soc. (emeritus), Am. Legion, VFW, Elks, Sigma Xi, Phi Lambda Upsilon. Republican. Achievements include patents in field. Home: 122 Mcclain Ct Gray TN 37615-3904

TERRY, JOHN JOSEPH, transportation investor; b. Chgo., July 29, 1937; s. Michael Parnell and Honore (Ryan) T.; m. Terese Rose Mulkern, Dec. 31, 1960; children—Michael P., Gregory, Deirdre. B.S., Loyola U., Chgo., 1959; postgrad., U. So. Fla., 1967. C.P.A., Ill. With Touche, Ross & Co., 1959-65; v.p. Nat. City Lines, Denver, 1965-71; v.p. fin. Pepsico Transp., Inc., Tulsa, 1971-74; v.p. U.S. Rwy. Assn., Washington, 1974-76; chmn. P.I.E. Transport Europe, 1976-79; exec. v.p. IU Internat. Corp., Wilmington, Del., 1976-85; pres. Transp. Mgmt. Investment Group, Inc., Phila., 1985—; v.p.-at-large Am. Trucking Assn., Washington, 1984-85, chmn., internat. competitiveness task force, 1991, tax policy com., 1987—; bd. dirs. Caldwell Freight Lines, Lenoir, N.C., Basin Western, Inc., Roosevelt; cons. freight transp. World Bank and European Bank for Reconstrn. and Devel., 1986—. Served with U.S. Army, 1960-63. Recipient Best Motor Carrier Rsch. award Transp. Rsch. Forum, 1991. Office: Transp Mgmt Investment Group Inc 210 Locust St Apt 11B Philadelphia PA 19106-3923

TERRY, LEE R., congressman, lawyer; b. Omaha, Jan. 29, 1962; s. Leland R. Terry; m. Robyn L. Terry, Feb. 14, 1992; 1 child, Nolan E. BS, U. Nebr., 1984; JD, Creighton U., Omaha, 1987. Bar: Nebr. 1987, U.S. Dist. Ct. Nebr. 1987. Staff atty. Schrempp & Salerno, Omaha, 1987-92; ptnr. Schrempp, Salerno & Terry, Omaha, 1992-93, Terry & Kratville, Omaha, 1993-98; mem. 106th congress from 2d Nebr. dist., 1999—; mem. banking and fin. svcs. com., 1999—, mem. govt. reform and oversight com., mem. transport and infrastructure com., 1999—. Co-author: Trying the Soft Tissue Case in Nebraska, 1995. Mem. Omaha City Coun., 1991—, pres., 1995-97; chair elect Am. Diabetes Assn., Great Plains, 1996-97, chair Nebr. area, 1997-99. Named One of Ten Outstanding Young Omahans, Omaha Jaycees-C. of C., 1994. Mem. Nebr. Assn. Trial Attys. (dir. 1995—), Suburban Rotary. Republican. Methodist. Avocations: travel, playing, spending time with family. Home: 3210 N 97th St Apt 177 Omaha NE 68134-5320 Office: Ho Reps 1728 Longworth Hob Washington DC 20515-0001

TERSCHAN, FRANK ROBERT, lawyer; b. Dec. 25, 1949; s. Frank Joseph and Margaret Anna (Heidt) T.; m. Barbara Elizabeth Keily, Dec. 28, 1974; 1 child, Frank Martin. BA, Syracuse U., 1972; JD, U. Wis., 1975. Bar: Wis. 1976, U.S. Dist. Ct. (ea. and we. dists.) Wis. 1976, U.S. Ct. Appeals (7th cir.) 1979, U.S. Ct. Appeals (10th cir.) 1989, U.S. Supreme Ct. 1992. From assoc. to ptnr. Frisch, Dudek & Slattery Ltd., Milw., 1975-88; ptnr. Slattery and Hausman Ltd., Milw., 1988-94, Terschan & Steinle Ltd., Milw., 1994-96, Terschan, Steinle & Ness, Milw., 1996—. Treas., sec. Ville du Park Homeowners Assn., Mequon, Wis., 1985-86; cub scout packmaster pack 3844 Boy Scouts Am., 1989-90, asst. scoutmaster Troop 865, 1991-93. Mem. ABA, Am. Bd. Trial Advocates, Wis. Bar Assn., Milw. Bar Assn., Assn. Trial Lawyers Am., Wis. Acad. of Trial Lawyers (bd. dirs. 1996—), 7th Cir. Bar Assn., Order of Coif. Republican. Lutheran. Avocations: swimming, coin collecting, reading, outdoor activities. Home: 10143 N Lake Shore Dr Mequon WI 53092-6109 Office: 2600 N Mayfair Rd Ste 700 Milwaukee WI 53226-1314

TERSMAN, FOLKE BENGT RUNESSON, philosophy educator, researcher; b. Stockholm, Nov. 2, 1964; s. Rune Folke Baltzar and Brita Maria (Hultman) T.; m. Ninna Kristina Charlotta Torstensson, May 30, 1993; children: Hugo Eli, Maja Elsa Matilda. BA, Stockholm U., 1987, PhD, 1993. Rschr. Nat. Bd. Spent Nuc. Fuel, Stockholm, 1989-91; asst. prof. philosophy Stockholm U., 1993-95, rsch. fellow, 1995—. Author: Nuclear Waste and Social Science, 1991, Reflective Equilibrium, 1993, The Analysis of Argumentation, 1994; editor: Uncertainty and Decision, 1991. Mem. Swedish Philos. Assn. Office: Stockholm Univ, Dept Philosophy, S-106 91 Stockholm Sweden

TERTÁK, ADAM, tax consultant; b. Budapest, Jan. 22, 1953; s. Elemér and Mária Sartory T.; m. Elisabeth Terták; children: Nikolett, Linda. BBA, Coll. of Acctg., 1976; Diploma in Econs., Budapest U., 1988; postgrad., Harvard Bus. Sch., 1997. Economist diplomate. Computer software specialist SZKI, Budapest, 1971-75; head of computer ctr. EGSZI, Budapest, 1975-82; dir. SZAMREND, Budapest, 1982-87; advisor Gen. Venture and Trust Co., Budapest, 1987-88; dir. Bontas, Budapest, 1988-89; mng. ptnr. Ernst and Young, Budapest, 1990—. Treas. Am.-Hungarian C.of C., Budapest, 1994-96, 99; chmn. Transparency Internat., 1998—; bd. dirs. Joint Venture Assn. Hungarian Mgr. Assn., Budapest, 1991, United Way, Budapest, 1997. Mem. Rotary. Avocations: skiing, tennis, sailing, photography. Office: Ernst and Young Hungary Ltd, 20 Vaci ut, 1132 Budapest Hungary

TERUTUNG, HENDRA, mechanical engineer; b. Jakarta, Indonesia, July 28, 1960; s. Pubara and Helena (Luwia) T.; m. Gwenda Kandouw, Nov. 8, 1992; children: Crystalle, Beata Carmen. BSME, Tuskegee U., 1986, MS, 1989. Rsch. asst. materials sci. lab. Tuskegee (Ala.) U., 1983-87; rsc. assoc. Carver Rsch. Found., Ala., 1987-90; sales mgr. Atlas Asia Pacific, Jakarta, 1990-96; pres., dir. Bima Teresna Perkasa, Jakarta, 1994—; pres., dir. automotive mag. Mekanik, Jakarta, 1994-96. Contbr. articles to profl. jours. Mem. ASME, Ikatan Ahli Otomotif Indonesia, Sigma Xi, Pi Tau Sigma, Beta Kappa Chi. Roman Catholic. Avocations: swimming, tennis, golf, cars. Home: JL Tanjung Duren Timur 2A, Jakarta 11470, Indonesia

TERVAHARTIALA, PEKKA OLAVI, radiologist, researcher; b. Valkeala, Finland, Jan. 12, 1956; s. Olavi and Aira (Kuparinen) T.; m. Barbara Anna Rüfenacht, May 24, 1986; children: Tero, Anna, Eeva. MD, U. Helsinki, 1981, PhD, 1993. Lic. radiologist. Radiologist U. Hosp., Helsinki, 1988—; cons. radiologist TESLAMED, Helsinki, 1990. Mem. TEESI, UK-65 Soc., Finnish Radiol. Soc. Evangelic Lutheran. Avocations: fishing, woodworking. Office: U Hosp Dept Radiology HUCS, Haartmaninkatu 4, 00290 Helsinki Finland

TERVEER, JOYCE ANN, academic administrator, English language educator; b. Freeburg, Ill., Aug. 21, 1936; d. Oliver Andrew and Elsa Pearl (Davis) Klopmeyer; m. Russell Benjamin Terveer, Dec. 29, 1973; children: Robert Scott France, Tab France. BA, McKendree Coll., 1957; MA, So. Ill. U., 1974. English tchr., libr. Freeburg (Ill.) H.S., 1957-64; English tchr., adminstr. Althoff Cath. H.S., Belleville, Ill., 1965-98. Mem. Nat. Coun. Tchrs., Nat. Assn. Secondary Sch. Prins., Ill. Assn. Tchrs. English, Delta Kappa Gamma. Church of Christ. Home: 33 Fawnlily Dr Belleville IL 62221-4344 Office: Althoff Cath HS 5401 W Main St Belleville IL 62226-4734

TERWILIGER, GWEN H., education educator; b. Olney, Ill., Dec. 18, 1946; d. Carl G. Huber and Deloris J. Edwards; m. Richard K. Terwiliger, Aug. 31, 1968; 1 child, Eric. BS, Bowling Green State U., 1968, MEd, 1981; PhD, U. Toledo, 1995. Tchr. Oregon (Ohio) City Schs., 1968-72; part-time instr. U. Toledo, 1981-85, 86-87, assoc. prof., 1987—; vis. instr. Bowling Green (Ohio) State U., 1985-86; cons. Health Sys. Concepts, Longwood, Fla. Grantee U. Toledo Found., 1993. Mem. Am. Math. Assn. Two Yr. Colls., Nat. Coun. Tchrs. Math., Greater Toledo Coun. Tchrs. Math. (contest cood. 1988-95). Avocations: reading, cards. E-mail: drtwig@hotmail.com and gterwil@utoledo.edu. Fax: 419-730-3984. Office: Univ Toledo 2801 W Bancroft St Toledo OH 43606-3390

TERZEON, PAUL BERNARD, solicitor; b. Somerset, Eng., Sept. 3, 1951; s. Reginald and Anastasia (Traynor) T.; m. Hilary Janet Brooks, June 21, 1977; children: Rebecca, James. BSc with honours, London U., 1973. Solicitor Supreme Ct. Eng. and Wales. Solicitor Hempsons, London, 1975-78, Bird & Bird, London, 1978-81, Kingsley Napley, London, 1981—. Mem. Brit. Acad. Forensic Scis., Law Soc., City of Westminster Law Soc. (com. 1991), City of London Law Soc., London Criminal Cts. Solicitors Assn., Internat. Bar Assn. Avocations: country pursuits, walking. Office: Kingsley Napley, 14 St John's Ln, London EC1M 4AJ, England

TERZIAN, SHOHIG GARINE SHERRY, mental health facility administrator; d. Ebraxé Momjian and Ardashes Garabed T. AB in Eng. Literature cum laude, Radcliffe Coll., 1937; MS in Libr. and Info. Sci., Columbia Univ., 1942, student; student, UCLA, Univ. Wis., New Sch. for Social Rsch., 1940-65. First libr. neurol. inst. Columbia Presbyn. Med. Ctr., N.Y.C., 1940-41; reference asst. Vassar Coll. Libr., Poughkeepsie, N.Y., 1942-43; picture editor, rsch. asst. U.S. Office War Info., N.Y.C., 1943-46; rsch. libr. Time, Inc., N.Y.C., 1947-48; libr. Prudential Ins. Co. Western Home Office, L.A., 1948-61; mem. faculty dept. psychiatry & biobehavioral scis. UCLA Med. Sch., 1961-86; dir. mental health info. svc. UCLA Neuropsychiatric Inst., 1961-86; rsch. cons., 1987—; picture editor, rsch. asst. U.S. War Dept. Civil Defense, U.S. Dept. of State, Office Internat. Info. and Cultural Affairs, N.Y.C., 1943-46. Bibliographer; contbr. Bertrand Russell Soc. Quarterly, Santayana Soc. Bulletin, Ararat Quarterly, LA Times. Mem. Armenian Gen. Benevolent Union, UCLA Emeriti, UCLA Faculty Ctr., Spl. Libr. Assn. Washington, Saroyan Soc. Calif., Santayana Soc., Calif. Libr. Soc., Statue of Liberty Ellis Island Found. Armenian Orthodox. Avocations: reading, writing. Home: 11740 Wilshire Blvd # A1602 Los Angeles CA 90025-6536

TERZOLO, HORACIO RAUL, veterinarian, researcher; b. Buenos Aires, Aug. 23, 1948; s. Eduardo Raul and Carmen Rosa Joaquina (Pijoan) T.; m. Graciela Electra Boffi, May 14, 1977; 1 child, Mariano Sergio. B in Biol. Scis., San Jose Sch., Buenos Aires, 1965; Vet., U. Buenos Aires, 1971; PhD, U. Edinburgh, Scotland, 1984. Microbiology diagnostician Salisbury Lab.-Kahl Co., Cordoba, 1971-72; microbiologist Merck, Sharp & Dohme, Buenos Aires, 1972-74; bacteriologist Nat. Inst. Agrotech (INTA), Balcarce, 1974—; referee Argentine Soc. for Microbiology, Buenos Aires, 1990—; cons. Sci. Com. on Animal Diseases, Buenos Aires, 1988-94, Bovine Campylobacteriosis com.; rschr. infectious Coryza Pilar Labs (LAPSA), 1990-96; rschr. IgY tech. BIOTAY, 1997-98; bacteriologist FAO, Balcarce, 1974-75. Editor: Laboratory Methods, 1992; contbr. articles to profl. jours. Recipient scholarship Nat. Inst. Agrotech., 1981-84; grantee French Govt., 1987, Nat. Inst. Agrotech. Rsch., 1987, U. Queensland, Australia, 1993, Pilar Labs, 1993, Francisco C. Rosenbusch award, 1994, U. Berlin, Charité, Germany, 1998. Mem. Am. Soc. Microbiology, Sociedad de Medicina Veterinaria, Asociacion Argentina de Microbiologia, Asociacion Argentina de Veterinarios de Laboratorios de diagnostico, Soc. Gen. Microbiology, Nat. Acad. Agr. & Vet. Scis. (Rosenbusch award 1994), Prolf. Coun. of Vet. Surgeons, Argentinean Soc. of Infectology, Soc. Gen. Microbiology. Roman Catholic. Avocations: swimming, fishing. E-mail: hterzolo@balcarce.inta.gov.ar or terzolo@lacapitalnet.com.dr. Home: Rodriguez Pena 4081 Dept 2, 7600 Mar del Plata Argentina Office: INTA, Ruta 226 Km 73 and 1/2, 7620 Balcarce Argentina

TERZOPOULOS, JOHN E., electrical company executive; b. Athens, Apr. 3, 1928; m. Aikaterini Louka, June 26, 1960; children: Sarah, Emmanouella. Tech. eng., Tech. U., Athens, 1950. Constrn supr. Ministry of Pub. Works, Alexandroupolis, Greece, 1950-51; pub. contractor Ministry of Pub. Works, Greece, 1953-65; mng. dir. Electroimpex S.A., Athens, 1965—. Served to 2d lt. Greek Army, 1952-53. Mem. Greek C. of C. (Export award 1983). Mem. Christian Orthodox Ch. Lodge: Rotary. Avocations: bibliophile, electronic information. Home: 24 Vroutou St, 11141 Athens Greece Office: Electroimpex SA, PO Box 52019, 14410 Metamorfosi Greece

TESCHEMACHER, HANSJOERG, medical educator, pharmacologist; b. Augsburg, Germany, Dec. 18, 1938; s. Hans and Elisabeth (Gruber) T.; children: Anja Gabriele, Gudrun Jennifer. MD, U. Munich, 1966. Rsch. assoc. Max-Planck Inst. Psychiatry, Munich, Germany, 1968-78; prof. Justus-Liebig U., Giessen, Germany, 1978—; guest scientist Addiction Rsch. Found., Stanford, Calif., 1974-75. Rschr. in field. Recipient Wilhelm-Stepp award, German Soc. Biology of Nutrition, 1980. Office: Rudolf-Buchheim Inst Pharm, Frankfurter Str 107, D-35392 Giessen Germany

TESCHER DE CRANLEY, MICHEL (BARON DE FARNEY), gynecologist, obstetrician, surgeon; b. Paris, June 5, 1939; s. Alexandre Tescher de Cranley and Marcelle Chevalier; m. Christine Alice Masle; children: Jean Marc, Sandrine, Philippe; m. Dominque Jeanne Laurent; 1 child, Diane Alexandra. Degree in Medicine, U. Paris, 1969, Degree in Pathology, 1969, M in Human Ecology, 1970. Extern medicine Paris Hosp.-Pub. Assistance, 1961-64, internal medicine staff, 1964-69, assst. medicine, 1970-74; clin. chief U. Paris, 1970-74; chief ob-gyn. dept. Ctr. Hosp. Regional, Orleans, France, 1974—; chief plamfication ctr. Hosp. Regional Ctr., Orleans, 1974—; jud. expert Orleans Tribunal, 1976-96; joint gen. sec. Nat. Syndicate Gynecologic-Obstetrics, 1985-96. Contbr. articles to profl. jours. Mayor La Chapelle Saint Mesmin, 1995—. Recipient European Excellence cert., 1995. Mem. French Gynecologic Soc., French Gynecologic-Obstetric Soc., Gynecologic-Obstetricians Coll. French Democracy Union. Roman Catholic. Avocations: lecturing, tennis, swimming. Home: 36 Rte d Orleans PacPigeon, 45380 La Chapelle Mesmin Centre, France Office: Ctr Hosp Regional, 1 rue Porte Madeleine, 42032 Orleans Centre, France

TESFAI, GHEBRESELASSIE, minister of energy of Eritrea; b. Feb. 7, 1946. MSc in Petroleum Geology, Acad. Mining Metallurgy, Cracow, Poland, 1974. With Eritrean Liberation Front, Addis Ababa, 1965; fighter Eritrean Peoples Liberation, 1975-84, periodicals, radio program editor, 1976-84, adminstr. provisional high commn. econ. planning, 1984-87, mem. ctrl. com., head mfg. commn., 1987-91; sec. industry Provisional Govt. Eritrea, 1991-92; min. energy, mines, water resources, mem. nat. assembly Govt. Eritrea, 1993—. Office: Min Energy Mines, PO Box 5285, Asmara Eritrea

TESFAYE, SOLOMON, physician; b. Asmara, Hamasien, Eritrea, Dec. 21, 1958; arrived in the U.K., 1976; s. Ashebir Tesfaye and Mihret Tsegue. MB, BChir, Bristol (Eng.) U., 1984, MD, 1994. House officer Frenchay Hosp., Bristol, 1984-85; sr. house officer Bridgend (Eng.) Hosp., 1985-86, Walsgrave Hosp., Coventry, Eng., 1986-88; med. registrar Royal Hallamshire Hosp., Sheffield, Eng., 1988-90, med. rsch. registrar, 1990-93, cons. physician and diabetologist, 1997—; sr. registrar Royal Liverpool (Eng.) Hosp., 1993-96. Assoc. editor Diabetologia; contbr. chpts. to books and articles to profl. jours. Mem. Royal Coll. Physicians, European Assn. for Study of Diabetes, Brit. Diabetic Assn., Brit. Med. Assn. Avocations: music, sports, Impressionist painting, traveling. Office: Royal Hallamshire Hosp, Glossop Rd, Sheffield S10 2JF, England

TESNER, PAVEL ALEXANDR, chemist, researcher; b. Moscow, Aug. 31, 1910; s. Alexandr Andrew and Margarita Leopold (Herzberg) T.; m. Tamara Sergei Gerasimovich, Apr.. 29, 1939; 1 child, Elena. Degree in chem. engrng., Mendeleev Chem. Technol. Inst., Moscow, 1936, PhD, 1940; D of Chem. Sci. (hon.), Russian Acad. Sci., Moscow, 1950. Asst. Mendeleev Chem. Technol. Inst., Moscow, 1940-41; chief lab. Sci. Liquid Fuel and Gas Inst., Moscow, 1943-48; chief lab. All Russian Rsch. Inst. Natural Gases and Gas Techs., Moscow, 1948-88, chief sci. assoc., 1988—, dir., 1965-68. Author: Soot Formation, 1972, Chemistry and Physics of Carbon, 1984; co-author: Carbon black, 1952; contbr. articles to profl. jours.; patentee in field. Capt. Russian Army, 1941-43. Grantee Soros Internat. Sci. Found., 1994-95; recipient Russian State prize, 1952, Lenin prize, 1963, Lenin award, 1968. Avocations: skiing, tennis. Home: B Spasskay 33 Apt 96, 129090 Moscow Russia Office: VNIIGAS, p Razvilka, 142717 Moscow Russia

TESS, NIKOLAI LEONYD, marketing and sales professional; b. Riga, USSR, Oct. 19, 1956; s. Leonyd Vladimir and Nina Vassiliy (Cherkasova) T.; m. Olga Nikolay Kaftailova, Aug. 30, 1965; children: Anna, Anastasia, Olga. Degree in navigation and engring., Leningrad Maritime Acad., 1979; degree in linguistics, Latvian State U., 1987; MBA, INSEAD, 1993. Various positions Latvian Shipping Co., Riga, 1979-85, chief officer, 1985-88, capt., 1988-92; product mgr. S.C. Johnson (Johnson Wax), St. Ouen L'Aumone, 1994-96, analyst, 1996-2000; ind. cons., 2000—. Co-author: The Baltic Sea: New Developments in National Policies and International Cooperation, 1993. Russian Orthodox. Avocations: jogging, psychoanalysis, history of civilization, sports, arts. Home: 126 rue du Gen de Gaulle, 95620 Parmain France

TESSENSOHN, JOHN ALVIN, lawyer, author, playwright; b. Singapore, Oct. 28, 1967; s. Edward Anthony and Magdalene Theresa (Lioe) T. LLB with honors, Nat. U. Singapore, 1992; LLM with honors, Fordham U., 1998. Advocate and solicitor Supreme Ct. of Singapore, 1993. Assoc. in litig. Abraham Low & Ptnrs., Singapore, 1992-94; intellectual property counsel Shusaku Yamamoto Patent Law Offices, Osaka, Japan, 1994—; pvt. practice N.Y., 1999—. Mem. editl. bd. I.P. Asia, 1995—, Trademark World, 1999—, Patent World, 1999—; country corr. European Intellectual Property Rev., 1996—; author: (plays) The Breasts of Tiresias, Too Glam One, A Cup of Coffee, So Glam One, Mission of the Coming Day, 1988-94; columnist Singapore Internet Cmty., 1997; mem. adv. bd. World INtellectual Property Report, 1998, World Licensing Law Report, 1999; contbr. articles to profl. jours. Resident playwright Gung-Ho Theater Ensemble, Singapore, 1988-94. Recipient Outstanding Contbn. to the Arts award Victoria Jr. Coll., Singapore, 1986, Presdl. citation for Nat. Vol.'s Month, Pres. Republic of Singapore, 1991. Mem. Law Soc. of Singapore, Internat. Trademark Assn. (model law com. 1995-96), Osaka Internat. Lawyers Assn. Roman Catholic. Avocations: drama, travel, writing, swimming, film. Office: Shusaku Yamamoto Patent Law, 1-2-27 Shiromi Chuo-ku, Osaka 540, Japan

TESSLER, ALEXANDER, aerospace engineer; b. Kiev, Ukraine, Apr. 5, 1950; came to U.S., 1973; s. Leonid Tessler and Ida Ryabinskaya; m. Barbara Sue Feldsher, June 27, 1982; children: Lee, Veronica, Michael. BS in Structural Engring., Inst. Civil Engring., Kiev, 1972; MS in Structural Mechs., UCLA, 1976, degree in engring., 1978, PhD in Structural Mechs., 1979. Sr. engr. Northrop Corp., Hawthorne, Calif., 1980-83; mech. engr. U.S. Army Materials Tech. Lab., Watertown, Mass., 1983-91; aerospace engr. NASA Langley Rsch. Ctr., Hampton, Va., 1991—; adj. prof. mech. engring. Northeastern U., Boston, 1986-91, George Washington U., Washington, 1992—, Old Dominion U., Norfolk, Va., 1993—; cons. Internat. Space Sta., NASA, Huntsville, Ala., 1996; structures expert NASA/Russian Joint Working Group on Aeronautics, Hampton, 1995—; spkr. in field. Contbr. articles to profl. publs., chpt. to book. Recipient Spl. Act award U.S. Army, 1985, 89, Tech. Excellence Dual Career Ladder award NASA, 1992, Superior Accomplishment award NASA, 1993, 95. Mem. AIAA (structures tech. com.), U.S. Assn. Computational Mechs., Internat. Cmty. for Composites Engring. Achievements include pioneering of anisoparametric interpolation approach for penalty-type finite elements; development of innovative higher-order thick-composite beam, plate and shell theories applicable for computational mechanics. Avocations: running, photography. Home: 137 Chinquapin Orch Yorktown VA 23693-2322 Office: Langley Rsch Ctr Mail Stop 240 Hampton VA 23681-0001

TESSLER, NIR, physicist, electrical engineer, educator; b. Haifa, Israel, June 1, 1962; s. Moshe and Rebeca (Niego) T.; m. Shoshi Richter; children: Chen, Adi, Shahar. BSc summa cum laude, Technion Israel Inst. Tech., Haifa, 1989, MSc, 1992, DSc, 1995. Cert. elec. engr. Rsch. assoc. Cambridge (Eng.) U., 1995-97, sr. rsch. assoc., 1997—; sr. lectr. Technion, Haifa, Israel, 1999—. Fellow Gutvirt Found., 1991, Israel Min. Comm., 1993, Charles Clore Found., 1994, Rothschild Found., 1995, ESPRC, 1999, ALON, 1999. Mem. IEEE, Material Rsch. Soc. Office: EE Dept Technion, Haifa 32000, Israel

TESSUN, FRANZ, aerospace executive; b. Munich, Bavaria, Germany, Sept. 23, 1947; m. Renate Hauser, May 28, 1971; children: Silvia, Martin, Christina. Dipl. math., U. Hamburg, 1974. Developer databases Siemens, Germany, 1976-79; from head ops. rsch. to dir. study group Messerschmitt-Bolkow-Blohm, Germany, 1979-90; head strategy Intertraffic, Germany, 1990-92; v.p. mktg. rsch. DASA, Germany, 1992-97, v.p. knowledge mgmt. and scenarios, 1997—; chmn. supervisory bd. Scenario Mgmt. Internat., 1999—. Maj. German Reconnaisence, 1969-70. Recipient Esomar award 1997. Mem. Soc. Competitive Intelligence Profls. (spkr., com.), European Soc. Opinion and Mktg. Rsch. (cons.), Deutsche Gesellschaft für Luft-u. Rammfahrt (spkr.). Avocations: mountain walking, opera, classical music. Office: Daimler Chrysler Aerospace, PO Box 801109, 81663 Munich Bavaria, Germany

TEST, STACY MARIE, network engineer; b. Niskayuna, N.Y., Dec. 3, 1971; d. Ronald Allen and Lillian Mary Kane; m. Christopher Loren Test, Mar. 9, 1996. BSEE, Trenton State Coll., 1994. From cons. to sr. cons. Booz-Allen & Hamilton, Eatontown, N.J., 1994—. Mem. IEEE, Soc. Women Engrs. Roman Catholic. Avocations: softball, volleyball, music, sewing. Home: 353 Hilltop Rd Toms River NJ 08753-4221

TESTER, LEONARD WAYNE, psychology educator; b. Nampa, Idaho, Aug. 21, 1933; s. Walter Vernon and Dora Dorothy (Peters) T. BTh, Kansas City Coll., Overland, Kansas, 1957; MA, Abilene Christian Coll. (now Abilene Christian U.), 1961; STB, Harvard U., 1969; EdM, Columbia U., 1971, EdD, 1976, MPhil, 1979, PhD, 1981. Lic. psychologist, N.Y. Pers. mgr. Boston Safe Deposit & Trust Co., 1966-69; adj. instr. clin. counseling N.Y. Inst. Tech., Westbury, 1971-80, adj. asst. prof., 1980-84, sr. counselor, 1980-92, assoc. prof., 1984-92, dir., 1992-95, sr. counselor, 1980-92, prof., 1992—, prof., chmn., 1992-93, prof., dir., 1993-95; cons., grad. asst. Bus. Sch. and Tchrs. Coll. Columbia U., 1977-81. Contbr. articles to profl. jours.; presenter workshops in field. Exec. dir. Ho. of the Carpenter, Boston, 1967-68; bd. dirs. Pierre (S.D.) Coun. of Arts, Counseling Ctr. Episcopal Ch., Great Neck, N.Y., Tech. Sch. in N.Y.C. William Wayne Jackson honors scholar Harvard Div. Sch. Fellow Am. Orthopsychiat. Assn.; mem. APA, N.Y. Soc. Clin. Psychologists, N.Y. Soc. Hypnosis and Psychotherapy, others. Home: PO Box 20107 New York NY 10023-1477 Office: NY Inst of Tech 1855 Broadway New York NY 10023-7692

TESTORI, TIZIANO N., physician, oral surgery educator; b. Como, Italy, Sept. 2, 1956; s. Ferdinando N. and Matilde A. (Spinelli) T.; m. Giovanna Perrotti, July 5, 1987; 1 child, Veronica Bapu. MD, U. Milan, 1981, DDS, 1984, PhD, 1986. Pvt. practice Milan, 1986—; vis. prof. U. Milan, 1991—; head implantology section, dept. periodontology U. Milan, S. Paolo Hospital, Milan, Italy, 1998—, chmn. R.L. Weinstein prof., 1998—; scientific advisor Ctr. for Advanced Dental Studies in Milan, 1994—. Contbr. 70 scientific papers to profl. jours. Mem. Am. Acad. Osseointegration, Am. Acad. Implant Dentistry, N.Y. Acad. Sci., Knights of Malta, Rotary. Avocations: photography, travel, sports. Office: Via Maurizio Monti 1, 22100 Como Italy

TETERIN, YURY ALEXANDROVICH, physicist, researcher, educator; b. Krasnodar, Russia, Dec. 31, 1939; s. Alexandr Yakovlevich and Yevdokiya Vaselisovna (Ulanova) T.; m. Nataliya Alekseevna Petrusevich, May 10, 1966; children: Aleksey, Anna, Alexandr, Anton. Grad. in engring., Moscow Phys.-Tech. Inst., 1962-68, PhD, 1975; D Phys.-Math. Sci, Inst. Chem. Physics, Moscow, 1989. Jr. scientist Russian Rsch. Ctr. Kurchatov Inst., Moscow, 1968-79, sr. scientist, 1979-89, leading scientist, 1989-93, prin. scientist, 1993-98, chief lab., prof. physics, 1998—. Author: (in Russian) The Inner Valence Molecular Orbitals and Character of Chemical Bond, 1985, X-ray Photoelectron Spectroscopy of Actinoid Compounds, 1986, X-ray Photoelectron Spectroscopy of Lantnanoid Compounds, 1987, (in Serbian) Zbirka Zadataka iz Fizike, 1999. Mem. Russian Acad. Natural Scis., Acad. Engring. Sci. Russian Fedn., N.Y. Acad. Scis. Home: Narodnogo, Opolcheniya 22-2-172, 123 423 Moscow Russia Office: RRC Kurchatov Inst, IV Kurchatov Sq 1, 123 182 Moscow Russia

TETHER, ANTHONY JOHN, aerospace executive; b. Middletown, N.Y., Nov. 28, 1941; s. John Arthur and Antoinette Rose (Gesualdo) T.; m. Nancy Engle Pierson, Dec. 27, 1963 (div. July 1971); 1 child, Jennifer; m. Carol Suzanne Dunbar, Mar. 3, 1973; 1 child, Michael. AAS, Orange County C.C., N.Y., 1961; BS, Rensselaer Poly Inst., 1963; MSEE, Stanford (Calif.) U., 1965, PhD, 1969. V.p., gen. mgr. Sys. Control Inc., Palo Alto, Calif., 1968-78; dir. nat. intelligence Office Sec. of Def., Washington, 1978-82; dir. strategic tech. DARPA, Washington, 1982-86; corp. v.p. Ford Aerospace, Newport Beach, Calif., 1986-90, LORAL, Newport Beach, 1990-92; corp. v.p., gen. mgr. Sci. Application Internat., Inc., San Diego, 1992-94; CEO Dynamics Tech. Inc., Torrance, Calif., 1994-96; CEO, pres. Sequoia Group, Newport Beach, Calif., 1996-2000; chmn., bd. dirs. Condyne Tech., Inc., Orlando, Fla., 1990-92; dir. Orincon, La Jolla, Calif.; mem. def. sci. bd. Army Sci. Bd. Task Forces, 1998—; cons. Army Sci. Bd., Def. Sci. Board. Contbr. articles to profl. jours. Recipient Nat. Intelligence medal DCI, 1986, Civilian Meritorious medal U.S. Sec. Def., 1986. Mem. IEEE, Cosmos Club, Sigma Xi, Eta Kappa Nu, Tau Beta Pi. Avocations: ham radio, skiing. Home: 4518 Roxbury Rd Corona Del Mar CA 92625-3125

TETHER, MELANIE GEORGIA, barrister; b. London, June 30, 1956; d. Cyril Henry Gordon and Iris Evelyn (Lawson) T. MA, Oxford (Eng.) U., 1977. Cert. solicitor. Assoc. law Lawford & Co., London, 1981-83; with Brit. Coal Nationalised Industry, London, 1983-86; assoc. law Baker & McKenzie, London, 1986-89, Norton Rose, London, 1989-95; ptnr. Old Square Chambers, London, 1995—. Mem. Indsl. Law Soc. (v.p.). Office: Norton Rose, Old Square Chambers, 1 Verulan Bldgs Grays Inn, London WC1R 5LH, England

TETIK, CIHANGIR, orthopedic surgeon, educator; b. Ankara, Turkey, Sept. 28, 1960; s. Ahmet and Mukaddes (Sertel) T.; m. Sevgi Ersen, Sept. 11, 1984; 1 child, Hilal. MD, Ondokuz Mayis U. Som, Samsun, Turkey, 1984; surgeon, Ankara Hosp., 1990. Instr. Ankara Hosp., 1992-93, 94-95; rsch. fellow U. Utah, Salt Lake City, 1993-94; instr., rsch. fellow Cleve. Clinic Found., CCF, Cleve., 1995-96; instr. Marmara U., Istanbul, Turkey, 1996-97, asst. prof., 1997-99, assoc. prof., 1999—. Lt. Turkish Army, 1991-92. Mem. SICOT, Turkish Soc. for Surgery of the Hand, Turkish Orthopedic Soc., Turkish Reconst. Microsurg. (historian), Lions. Avocations: tennis, carpet collection. Home: B4/21, Barbaros Mah Bahar Sitesi, 81150 Istanbul Turkey Office: Marmara U Hosp, Tophanelioglu Cad 13/15, 81190 Istanbul Turkey

TETLIE, HAROLD, priest; b. Madison, Minn., Aug. 24, 1926; s. H. Ben and Anna (Mauland) T. BA cum laude, St. Olaf Coll., Northfield, Minn., 1951; MBA, U. Denver, 1956; postgrad., Cornell U., 1959-60; MDiv, Luther Sem., St. Paul, 1965. Ordained to ministry Am. Luth. Ch., 1965. Pastor Christ the King Chs. (Evang. Cath. Ch.), Alice, Tex., 1965—, congregation supr., 1969—; cir. parish priest, Nuevo Leon, Tamaulipas, Hidalgo, San Luis Potosi, Mex. Author numerous poems. Coord. Joint Action in Cmty. Svc., Inc., Alice, 1970—. Sgt. U.S. Army, 1945-46, PTO. Recipient Svc. to Mankind award Sertoma Club, Corpus Christi, Regional Vol. of Yr. award Joint Action in Cmty. Svc., 1991, Michael Madhusudan award for poem, Calcutta, 1996; Ky. Col., 1992. Mem. NEA (life), VFW (life), Am. Legion (life), 40 et 8 (life), Family Motor Coach Assn., Sons of Norway, Order of Ky. Col., Internat. Platform Assn., Thousand Trails, WWII Tank Destroyer Soc. (chaplain). Home and Office: Christ the King Chs PO Box 1607 Alice TX 78333-1607

TETLOW, ELISABETH MEIER, writer, researcher, scholar, lawyer; b. Cin., Mar. 26, 1942; d. Carl L. and Margaret (Hersey) Meier; m. L. Mulry Tetlow, July 5, 1970; children: Tania C., Maria A., Sonia M., Sarah A. BA, Columbia U., 1964; MA, Fordham U., 1967, Fordham U., 1970, Columbia U., 1973; STM, Woodstock Coll., 1974; MDiv, Jesuit Sch. Theology, Berkeley, 1979; JD, Loyola U., New Orleans, 1984. Bar: La. 1984. Instr. Coll. of Mt. St. Vincent, Riverdale, N.Y., 1968-69, Fordham U., 1970, Loyola U., New Orleans, 1979-82; law clk. La. Supreme Ct., New Orleans, 1984-85; staff atty. U.S. Ct. Appeals (5th cir.), New Orleans, 1985-87; rsch. atty. Kierr, Gainsburgh, Benjamin, New Orleans, 1988; law clk. La. Ct. Appeals (4th cir.), 1989-91. Author: Women and Ministry in the New Testament, 1980, 2d edit., 1984, Partners in Service, 1983, The Spiritual Exercises of St. Ignatius Loyola, 1987, 2d edit., 1996; contbr. articles to profl. jours. Active Amnesty Internat., Bread for the World, Pax Christi, Oxfam, Epilepsy Coun., Spl. Olympics, Sierra Club, Audubon Soc., Women's Ordination Conf.; bd. dirs. New Orleans region Dystonia Med. Rsch. Found.; v.p., bd. dirs. Greater New Orleans region Nat. Assn. Riding for the Handicappedm, 1995-97. Recipient Disting. Svc. award Alliance for Affordable Energy, 1992. Mem. ABA, Cath. Bibl. Assn. Am., Cath. Theology Soc. Am., Am. Acad. Religion, Soc. Bibl. Lit., Coll. Theology Soc., La. Bar Assn., La. Karate Assn., USA Karate Fedn. (U.S. Gold Medal Nat. Championships 1989), Internat. Shotokan Karate Fedn., New Orleans Tai Chi Assn., Symphony Chorus New Orleans (bd. dirs. 1996—), Met. Opera Regional Auditions. Democrat. Roman Catholic. Avocations: shotokan karate, swimming, piano, choral music, hiking. Home and Office: 16 Fontainebleau Dr New Orleans LA 70125-3452

TETLOW, WILLIAM LLOYD, infotech consultant; b. Phila., July 2, 1938; s. William Lloyd and Mary Eleanor (Ferris) T.; m. Amber Jane Riederer, June 13, 1964; children: Jennifer Kay, Rebecca Dawn, Derek William. Student, Cornell U., 1956-60; B in Gen. Edn., U. Omaha, 1961; MA, Cornell U., 1965, PhD, 1973. Dir. instl. research Cornell U., Ithaca, N.Y., 1965-70; dir. planning U. B.C., Vancouver, Can., 1970-82; dir. NCHEMS Mgmt. Products, Boulder, Colo., 1982-85; pres., dir. Vantage Info. Products, Inc., Boulder, 1985-87; pres., propr. Vantage Computer Svcs., Boulder, 1986-96; infotech cons. U. Colo., 1986-2000; cons. various univs. U.S., Can. and Australia, 1970—. Editor/author: Using Microcomputers for Planning and Decision Support, 1984; contbr. numerous articles to profl. jours. Mem. Mt. Calvary Luth. Ch. Coun., 1985-86, 89-92, pres., 1991-9. Served to 1st lt. AUS, 1961-63. Recipient U. Colo. medal, 1987; Kiwanis Hixon fellow, 1996, Kiwanis Lusche fellow, 1996. Mem. Assn. Inst. Rsch. (sec. 1973-75, v.p. 1980-81, pres. 1981-82), Concordia, Kiwanis (pres. 1996-97). Avocations: outdoor sports, woodworking. Home: 312 Diamond Cir Louisville CO 80027-3202

TETSU, NAKAMURA, education educator; b. Kobe, Japan, June 2, 1948; s. Teizo and Kusae Nakamura; m. Nakamura Toyota, Oct. 2, 1980; 1 child, Yukiharu. Bachelor, Hiroshima (Japan) U., 1971, master, 1973; doctor, Tokyo Inst. of Tech., 1993. Asst. prof. Akita (Japan) U., 1975-77, lectr., 1977-80, assoc. prof., 1980-85; assoc. prof. Hyogo U. of Tchr. of Edn., Yashiro, Japan, 1985-94, prof., 1995—. Author: Explication of the General Principles in Instructional Practice of Social Studies, 1991, 2d edit., 1996, Construction of a Systematic Framework for Social Studies Practice and Case Studies in the Framework, 1996; editl. bd. Nat. Coun. for the Social Studies, 1988-91. Mem. Japan Social Studies Rsch. Assn. (bd. dirs.). Avocations: kendo, Iaido. Home: 13-146-2006 Yamaguni, Yashiro, Hyogo 673-1421, Japan Office: Hyogo U of Tchr Edn, 942-1 Shimokume, Yashiro 673-14, Japan

TETZNER, KARL, editor; b. Duisburg, Germany, Oct. 26, 1914; s. Paul Gustav and Anna (Kriegel) T.; m. Annemarie Johanna Hossbach, Sept. 16, 1941; 1 child, Andrea. Grad., Gymnasium, Leipzig, Germany, 1930. Trainee wholesale bus. Leipzig, 1930-32, sales agt., 1933-38; tech. writer Radio H.Mende GmbH, Dresden, Germany, 1938-39; freelance journalist Emden, Germany, 1946-53, Hamburg, Germany, 1953-56; editor-in-chief Franzis-Verlag, Munich, Funkschau, 1956-80, Publ. Office for Electronics, Icking, Germany, 1981—; hon. prof. Freie U., Berlin, 1976. Oberleutnant German Navy, 1939-45. Recipient Badge of Honor Bayerischer Rundfunk, 1985, Badge of Honor Messe Berlin, 1999. Mem. Union Internat. de la Presse Electronique (pres. 1968-85, pres. (hon.) 1986—), Gesellschaft der Freunde der Gerschichte des Funkwesens (hon.), Bayerischer Journalistenverband. Home and Office: Kammerlbreite 12, D-82057 Icking Germany

TEUSCHER, ARTHUR, diabetologist; b. Bern, Switzerland. Degree, Ecole de Médecine, Paris, 1949; MD, U. Bern, 1951. chief dept. diabetes U. Bern Med. Sch., 1966-91, hon. prof., 1982. Author: Diagnosis of Diabetes, 1982, Manual for the Diabetes Team, 1995, 97, Diabetes Nutrition, 1996. Bd. dirs. Internat. Physicians for Prevention of Nuc. War, Switzerland, 1991. Mem. Swiss Patient Orgn. Natural Insulin (pres. 1988-2000), Insulin Forum Switzerland, European Diabetes Assn. (pres. diabetes epidemiology 1986-89, founding mem.). E-mail: arthur.leuscher@diab.ch.

TEUSCHER, EBERHARD, pharmacist; b. Halle, Germany, Dec. 9, 1934; s. Wolfram and Maria (Henke) T.; m. Gisela Hempel, July 30, 1964; 1 child, Franka. Degree in apothecary, U. Halle, 1958, dr. rer. nat., 1960; dr. habil., U. Greifswald, Germany, 1965. Lic. pharmacist. Asst. dept. pharmacognosy U. Halle, 1959-61; head asst. dept. botany U. Greifswald, 1962-68, asst. prof. dept. pharmacy, 1968-71, prof., 1971-96; sci. advisor pharmacy, author, 1996—; dean faculty natural scis. U. Greifswald, 1975-90. Author: Pharmacognosy, 1970, 78, 83, 88, 90, 97, Natural Toxins, 1988, 94. Mem. Soc. Med. Plant Rsch., Am. Soc. Pharmacognosy, German Pharm. Soc., N.Y. Acad. Sci.

TEVZADZE, GURAM, philosopher educator; b. Tbilisi, Georgian SSR, Jan. 30, 1932; s. Benjamin and Elene (Jivladze) T.; m. Rusudan Enukidze Tevzadze, Apr. 24, 1965; children: Gela, Gigi. Diploma in Philosophy, Tbilisi State U., 1954; philosophy candidate, 1958, PhD, 1963. Jr. scientist Inst. Philosophy, Georgia, 1957-59; sr. scientist, 1959-68; prof., head of chair History of Philosophy Tbilisi State U., Georgia, 1968—; academician-sec. Dept. Social Scis., Acad. Scis. Georgia, 1993—; v.p. Philos. Soc. Georgia, Tbilisi, Georgia, 1986—. Author: Theory of Knowledge of German Neokantianism, 1963, Critique of the Ontology of N. Hartmann, 1967, Immanuel Kant, 1979, The Ancient Philosophy, 1995, A History of Medieval Philosophy, 1996. Speaker of the Citizens Union of Georgia, 1994-99, Tbilisi, 1994—. Mem. Philos. Soc. Georgia, Internat. Goethe Soc. Avocation: gardening. Home: Tamarashvili St 9 Apt 5, Tbilisi 380062, Georgia Office: I Javakhishvili Tbilisi State U, Ilya Chavchavadze Av 1, Tbilisi 380028, Georgia

TEWARI, ASHUTOSH, urologist, oncologist; b. Kanpur, India, Aug. 17, 1960; s. Satyendra and Shakuntala T.; m. Mamta; children: Apporva, Akash. MCh, 1991. Sr. registrar in urology Royal Liverpool U. Hosp., Eng., 1992-93; fellow in renal and pancreatic transplant Royal Liverpool U. Hosp., 1992-93; fellow in urologic-oncology U. Fla., 1998; fellow in urology U. Calif. and VA Med. Ctr., San Francisco, 1994; scholar Henry Ford Hosp. and Med. Ctr., Henry Ford Health Sys., Detroit; Lectr. in field. Contbr. numerous articles to profl. jours., chpts. to books. Pfizer scholar, 1999, Josephine Ford scholar Josephine Ford Cancer Ctr. and Dept. Urology; grantee NIH, 1995-98, 99, DOD, others; recipient 3rd prize Am. Urol. Assn. CIRCON ACMI, 1997, 2nd prize Montague Boyd Essay Contest Am. Urol. Assn., 1997. Mem. Am. Urol. Assn. (3rd prize CIRCON ACMI 1997, 2nd prize Montague Boyd Essay Contest 1997, southeastern sect., north ctrl. sect.), Brit. Transplant Soc., Brit. Immunology Soc., Indian Soc. Organ Transplantiation, Internat. Soc. Urology, Mich. Prostate Cancer Consortium, Mich. Urology Soc., Soc. Minimally Invasive Therapy. Home: 4410 Charing Way Bloomfield Hills MI 48304-3003 Office: 1 Ford Pl # 5-c Detroit MI 48202-3450

TEWARI, HARISH CHANDRA, earth scientist; b. Almora, India, Jan. 8, 1943; s. Bhagwan Ballabh and Haripriya (Pande) T.; m. Rama Joshi, Dec. 6, 1970; children: Manik, Smita. BSc, Agra U., 1962, MSc, 1964; PhD, Indian Sch. of Mines, 1989. Sr. geophys. asst. Oil and Natural Gas Commn., Dehradon, India, 1965-73; scientist B Nat. Geophys. Rsch. Inst., Hyderabad, India, 1973-78, scientist C, 1978-84, scientist E-I, 1984-88, scientist E-II, 1988-93, scientist F, 1993—; head planning NGRI, Hyderabad, 1997—, party leader seismic group, 1982-84, 86-88, 92-94, 99—, mgmt. counsil, 1994-97, sec. rsch. coun., 1998—, mgmt. rep. ISO and modernization program. Editor: Deep Seismic Sounding and Crustal Tectonics, 1985; contbr. articles to profl. jours. Sec. NGRI Club, Hyderabad, 1986-88, v.p. 1992-94. Fellow Geol. Soc. India, Indian Geophys. Union; mem. Assn. of Exploration Geophysicist. Avocations: music, sports. Home: 5-82 St No 8 Habsiguda, 500 007 Hyderabad India Office: NGRI, Uppal Road, 500 007 Hyderabad India

TEWARI, RANJAN, company executive; b. Ambala, Haryana, India, Dec. 13, 1958; s. Surendra Nath and Sudarshan (Sangar) T.; m. Bharti Sharma, Oct. 20, 1985; children: Bhaskar and Ajit. B Tech. in Mech., Delhi U., 1980. Site engr. Utility Engrs. (I) Ltd., Bangladesh, 1980-84; project mgr. Sanvik Engrs. (I) Pvt. Ltd., Delhi, 1984-87; proprietor Ventac Engrs., Delhi, 1987-92; mng. dir. Ventac Overseas Pvt. Ltd., Delhi, 1992—. Mem. ASHRAE, Indian Soc. Heating, Refrigeration and Air Conditioning Engrs. (life). Avocations: travel, reading, music, cooking, trekking. Home: D-741 Saraswati Vihar, New Delhi 110034, India Office: Ventac Overseas Pvt Ltd, K-62 Green Park, New Delhi 110016, India

TEWARI, VINDHYA PRASAD, forester; b. Gonda, U Pradesh, India, May 31, 1960; s. Sant Ram Tewari and Sita Devi; m. Vijaya Dubey, June 22, 1991; children: Pulkit, Riya. BSc, Avadh U., Faizabad, India, 1979, MSc, 1981; DPhil, Allahabad U., India, 1984. Sr. rsch. fellow Coun. of Sci. and Indsl. Rsch., New Delhi, 1983-85, rsch. assoc., 1985-90; pool officer Coun. of Scientific Rsch. and Edn., New Delhi, 1992; scientist SD Indian Coun. of Forestry Rsch. and Edn., Dehradun, 1992-98; scientist SE Indian Coun. of Forestry Rsch. and Edn., New Delhi, 1999—; FAO fellow Inst. of Forest Mgmt. and Yield Sci., U. Goettingen, Germany, 1995-96. Contbr. articles to profl. jours. and publs. Recipient Chancellor's gold medal Avadh u., Faizabad, 1981, award Rifacimento Internat., New Delhi, 1991, Brandis prize, 1998. Mem. U.P. Rsch. Assn. (sec. 1983-84), AFRI Scientist Assn. (sec. 1997-98, joint sec. 1996-97, exec. mem. 1998-99), Assn. of India. Avocations: music, sports, reading, writing. E-mail: uptewari@yahoo.com. Home: Near Congress Office, 123 Raja Mohalla, Gonda 271001, India Office: Forest Resource Mgmt Econs, Arid Forest Rsch Inst/New Pali Rd, Jodhpur/Rajashan 342005, India

TEWES, R. SCOTT, lawyer; b. Chgo., Mar. 23, 1956; s. Raymond Henry and Vivian Marie Tewes; m. Marcia Anne King, June 5, 1981; children: Benjamin Scott, Matthew Philip, Madeline Anne Marie, Carrie Elizabeth. BS, Bob Jones U., 1978, MS, 1980; JD, U. S.C., 1983. Bar: S.C. 1983, D.C. 1985, Ga. 1987, U.S. Supreme Ct. Assoc. Brown & Hagins, Greenville, S.C., 1983-86; law clk. to Hon. Jean Galloway Bissell U.S. Ct. Appeals Fed. Cir., Washington, 1986-87; assoc., ptnr. Kilpatrick Stockton, Atlanta, 1987—. Articles editor S.C. Law Rev., 1982-83; contbr. articles to profl. jours. Active Greenville (S.C.) County Alcohol and Drug Abuse Commn., 1985-86; trustee Killian Hill Baptist Ch., Lilburn, Ga., 1994—. Mem. S.C. Bar (practice and procedure com., bar ethics adv. com. 1985-86), Am. Intellectual Property Law Assn., Christian Legal Soc., Federalist Soc., Lic. Execs. Soc., Order of Barristers. Avocations: running, biking, skiing. Office: Kilpatrick Stockton 1100 Peachtree St NE Ste 2800 Atlanta GA 30309-4530

TEWKSBURY, RUSSELL BAIRD, Internet strategist and new media consultant, educator; b. Ft. Lauderdale, Fla., 1961; s. Michael King and Barbara T. BS in Bus., U. South Fla., 1986. Mktg. cons., Tampa, Fla., 1988-90; pres. Baird Advt., Tampa, 1990-93, Marketworks Corp., Tampa, Fla., 1993-98; dir. mktg. Angel Flight, Tampa, 1989-94, also bd. dirs.; mem. mktg. and steering com. Paint Your Heart Out Tampa, 1989-93; lectr. Am. Mktg. Assn., 1996; spkr. INET'98 - the Internet Summit, Geneva, 1998, Caribbean Assn. Nat. Telecoms. Orgns., Aruba, 1999, 2000, Internat. Inst. Comm., 2000; exec. prodr. Eye of the Storm in assn. with NASA and The Discovery Channel. Columnist CANCION (quar. publ. CANTO). Mem. mktg. advance Sen. Paul Tsongas Presdl. Campaign, Tampa, 1992. Mem. Internet Soc., Internat. Inst. Comms., Fla. Motion Picture Assn. (lectr. 1996), Nat. Assn. TV Program Execs. Avocations: travel, music, sailing, scuba diving. Office: 7039 Bonaventure Dr Tampa FL 33607-5813

TEZANOS, JOSE FELIX, sociology educator; b. Santander, Cantabria, Spain, Aug. 8, 1946; s. Felix Tezanos and Francisca Tortajada; m. Pilar Vazquez; children: Susana, Sergio, Cesar. D Polit. Scis. and Sociology, U. Complutense, Madrid. Dir. Inst. Social Studies, Madrid, 1968-70; acad. dir. Inst. Social Techniques, Madrid, 1971-78; dir. Fundacion Sistema, Madrid, 1981—; prof. sociology Universidad Nacional de Educacion a Distancia, Madrid; dean Faculty Polit. Scis. and Sociology UNED, Madrid, 1986-88, dir. dept. sociology, 1994—; coord. internat. meetings on socialism of future, 1985—; pres. Fundacion Jaime Vera, 1989-94; sec. Internat. Rev. Socialism of Future, 1990-94. Author: Alienacion, Dialectica y Libertad, 1977, Estructura de Clases y Conflictos de Poder en la España Post-Franquista, 1978, La Democratizacion del tis bajo, 1987, Historie Ilustrada del Socialismo Español, 1993, La Explicacion Sociologica, 1996, Tendencias de Futuro en la Sociedad Española, 1997; editor Sistema. Revista Ciencias Sociales, 1973—. Mem. Madrid regional com. Spanish Socialist Workers Party, 1978-81, sec. sec. of exec. com., 1988-94, mem. nat. com., 1994—. Home: UNED, C/ Obispo Trejo s/n, 28040 Madrid Spain Office: Fundacion Sistema, Fuencarral No 127-1o izda, 28010 Madrid Spain

TEZCAN, SEMIH SALIH, civil engineering educator, consultant; b. Istanbul, Turkey, May 3, 1936; s. Sadik and Müveddet Fatma (Karacik) T.; m. Tomris Erbatur, July 20, 1961 (div. Mar. 1963); 1 child, Kamer; m. Özlem Saadet Öktemus, Aug. 15, 1984; children: Okan, Volkan. MSc and BS, Tech. U., Istanbul, Turkey, 1954, PhD, 1960. Cert. prof. engr. B.C., Can. Asst. prof. civil engring. U. B.C., Vancouver, 1961-64, assoc. prof. civil engring., 1964-67; prof. civil engring. Robert Coll., Istanbul, 1967—; dir. Computer Ctr., Bogazici U., 1974-79; dir. Earthquake Engring. Rsch. inst., Istanbul, 1976-79; rector Bogazici U., 1979-82; ad personam mem. exec. com., Coun. Univ. Rectors and Presidents of Europe, 1979-84. Editor Jour. Engring. Structures; project dir. environ. study, Golden Horn, Istanbul, 1977 (UN Environ. Program Best Project of Yr., 1977). Hon. consul gen. in Istanbul for Republic of Indonesia, 1984—. Lt., Turkish Armed Forces, 1957-59, Ankara. Recipient Gzowski Gold medal Engring. Inst. Can., Vancouver, 1966, Best Paper award Prefabrication Union, Turkey, 1989. Mem. ASCE, Am. Concrete Inst., Turkish Chinese Cultural Assn. (founding mem.), Turkish Earthquake Found. (v.p. 1993—), Turkish Higher Edn. Rsch. Found. (pres. 1982—), Bogazici U. Alumni Assn. (hon.). Moslem. Avocation: tennis. Home: Bogazici Sitesi 1/5, Arnavutkoy Istanbul Turkey Office: Bogazici U, Bebek, 80815 Istanbul Turkey

TEZE, ANDRE GUY, chemist, educator; b. Pontoise, France, Jan. 28, 1938; s. Rene and Elise (Aubin) T.; m. Madeleine Duverger, June 24, 1961; children: Bernard, Laurent. Lic. phys. scis., Sorbonne U., Paris, 1960, agregation, 1962; D degree, U. Pierre and Marie Curie, Paris, 1973. Tchr. INSCIR, Rouen, 1962-70; maitre de confs. U. Pierre and Marie Curie, Paris, 1971-91; prof. U. Paris Sud, Orsay, 1992-94, U. Versailles, 1994-2000; lectr. CNAM, Rouen, 1964-69, ENS Cachan, 1972-88; vis. prof. U. Waterloo, 1988, Georgetown U., Washington, U. Oreg., Eugene, 1989. Contbr. articles to profl. jours. including Jour. Am. Chem. Soc., Inorganic Syntheses, among others.

TEZLA, ALBERT, English educator; b. S. Bend, Ind., Dec. 13, 1915; s. Mihály and Lucza (Szénási) T.; m. olive Anna Fox, July 26, 1941; children: Michael William, Kathy Elaine. BA, U. Chgo., 1941, MA, 1947, PhD, 1952. Instr. Ind. U. Ext., S. Bend, 1946-48; from instr. to assoc. prof. U. Minn., Duluth, 1949-61, prof., 1961-82, prof. emeritus, 1982—; vis. prof. Hungarian lit. Columbia U., N.Y.C., 1966, cons., 1967-71, 77-81, vis. scholar, 1975; cons. U. Minn., Mpls., 1968-83; project reviewer NEH, Washington, 1979-82; vis. prof. Hungarian lit. U. Minn., Duluth, 1998. Author: An Introductory Bibliography to the Study of Hungarian Literature, 1964, Hungarian Authors: A Bibliographical Handbook, 1970, The Hazardous Quest: Hungarian Immigrants in the United States, 1895-1920, 1993; co-author: Academic American Encyclopedia, 1980, World Authors, 1975-80, 1985, Benét's Readers Encyclopedia, 1987, World Authors, 1980-85, 1991; editor, contbg. translator: Ocean at the Window: Hungarian Prose and Poetry since 1945, 1980, Three Contemporary Hungarian Plays, 1992; contbg. translator: Hungarian Short Stories, 1983, The Kiss: 20th Century Hungarian Short Stories, 1993; translator: God in the Wagon: Ten Short Stories (Ferenc Sánta), 1985 (Hungarian Pubs. award 1985), The Fifth Seal (Ferenc Sánta), 1986 (Hungarian Pubs. award 1986), On the Balcony: Selected Short Stories (Iván Mándy), 1988 (Hungarian Pubs. award 1988), Hungary: A Brief History (István Lázár), 1990, An Illustrated History of Hungary (István Lázár), 1992, Memoir of Hungary, 1944-48 (Sándor Márai), 1996, Once There Was a Central Europe: Selected Short Stories and Other Writings (Miklós Mészöly), 1997, A Wartime Memoir, Hungary, 1944-45 (Alaine Polcz), 1998; editl. cons. Holmes and Meier Pubs., 1998. Lt. (s.g.) USN, 1942-46, PTO. Recipient Abraham Lincoln award Am. Hungarian Found., 1998; Fulbright Rsch. fellow Associated Bd. Rsch. Coun., 1959-60, Rsch. fellow Internat. Coun. Traveling Grants, 1963-64, Rsch. fellow Internat. Rsch. and Exchs. Bd., 1978; Rsch. grantee Am. Coun. Learned Socs., 1961, 68, NEH, 1978-82. Mem. Internat. Assn. Hungarian Studies (mem. exec. com. 1978-83, John Lotz Meml. award 1986), Am. Hungarian Educators' Assn., Fulbright Assn. Democrat. Avocations: gardening, physical fitness, reading, classical films. Home: 5412 London Rd Duluth MN 55804-2511

THACHER, BARBARA AUCHINCLOSS, history educator; b. Oyster Bay, N.Y., July 27, 1918; d. Hugh and Frances Coverdale (Newlands) Auchincloss; m. Thomas Thacher, Aug. 4, 1942; children: Barbara Burrall Thacher Plimpton, Elizabeth Coverdale Thacher Hawn, Thomas Day II, Hugh Auchincloss, Peter Anthony, Andrew. BA cum laude, Bryn Mawr Coll., 1940; MA in History, Columbia U., 1965. Editl. rschr. Newsweek, N.Y.C., 1940-41, 44; writer N.Y. Times Sunday Mag., News of Week Rev., N.Y.C., 1941-43; co-editor Christmas Booklist for Children Harper's Mag., N.Y.C., 1957-59; asst. history dept. Barnard Coll., N.Y.C., 1964-65; rsch. asst. Ctr. Urban Edn., N.Y.C., 1966. Bd. dirs. Bryn Mawr Coll., 1966-88, chair bd. trustees, 1980-87, emeritus, 1988—, City Univ. of N.Y., trustee, 1970-73, WNET-TV-Channel 13, trustee, 1978-88; active Sheltering Arms Children's Svc., Istanbul Women's Coll., Leake & Watts Children's Home Svcs., Yonkers and N.Y.C., 1961-83, emeritus, 1983—, N.Y.C. Park Assn., Riverdale Girls Sch.; trustee Tchrs. Coll. Columbia U. Mem. Cosmopolitan Club (gov.), North Haven Casino. Democrat. Presbyterian. Home: 125 West Rd New Canaan CT 06840-3012

THACKARA, JAMES SHERMAN, writer; b. Los Angeles, Dec. 7, 1944; s. James Justin and Ellen Louise (Schmid) T.; m. Davina Laura Anne Millard, July 7, 1975; children: Leila Anne, Theresa Anne. BA, Harvard U., 1967. Film writer Bino Cicogna Rome, 1969-70, World Film Services, London, 1970-72, Costa Gavras, Paris, 1975-88. Author: America's Children, 1984, Ahab's Daughter, 1987, The Book of Kings, 1999. Activist Campaign Against Soviet Psychiat. Abuses for Polit. Purposes, 1975-79; organizer Nuclear Emergency Trust, 1986—; mem. com. 50 Dems. Abroad London, 1980-87; mem. European-Atlantic Group, 1986-87. Mem. Internat. PEN. Club.

THACKER, MARISE ANNE, retired anesthetist; b. Christchurch, New Zealand, Apr. 18, 1941; d. Walter Frederick William and Joyce (Burt) T. MB, BChir, 1966, diploma anaesthetics, 1968, FFA, 1978, RCSE, 1978. Ho. surgeon Timaru (New Zealand) Hosp., 1966-67; anesthetic ho. surgeon St. James, London, 1968-69; ho. surgeon dept. anesthetics St. Lukes, Guildford, Eng., 1970-71; registrar dept. anesthesics Christchurch Pub. Hosp., 1972-76, sr. ho. officer, 1977-78, specialist anesthetics, 1979-96. Anglican. Avocations: gardening, painting, walking, reading.

THACKER, PETER JAMES, banker; b. Solihull, U.K., Sept. 8, 1965; s. Ronald Walter and Barbara (Summerfield) T.; m. Brenda Burgess, June 7, 1997. BA, Selwyn Coll., 1987, MA, 1990. Mgr. corp. banking Lloyds Bank, London, 1990-92, derivatives trader, 1992-95, sr. mgr. derivatives trading, 1995-98; head short term interest rate trading Banque Paribas, London, 1998—. Mem. Chartered Inst. Bankers (assoc.), The Hawks Club. Avocations: rugby, restaurants, wine. Home: 3 Prebend Gardens, Chiswick,

London W4 1TN, England Office: Banque Paribas, 10 Harewood Ave, London NW1 6AA, England

THADANI, UDHO, physician, cardiologist; b. Hydedrabad, India, Apr. 1, 1941; came to U.S., 1980; s. Vensimal Mulchand and Gopi Thadani; m. Dorothy Ann Thadani, 1974; 1 child, Emma Sarala. MBBS, All India Inst. Med. Scis., New Delhi, 1964. Lic. physician, Okla., Md., Ont., Can., Eng., India; cert. internal medicine, U.K., Can.; cert. cardiology, Can.; diplomate Am. Bd. Internal Medicine, subspecialty cardiovascular diseases. Intern All India Inst. Med. Scis., New Delhi, 1964-65, house physician, surgeon, 1965-66; house physician in medicine Joyce Green Hosp., Dartford, Kent, Eng., 1966-67; sr. house physician in medicine Kingston Gen. Hosp., Hull, Eng., 1967-69, registrar, rsch. fellow in medicine and cardiology, 1969-71; registrar, rsch. fellow in medicine and cardiology U. Leeds (Eng.), The Gen. Infirmary at Leeds, 1971-75; sr. rsch. fellow, clin. asst. medicine Queen's U., Kingston Gen. Hosp., Ont., Can., 1975-78; asst. prof. medicine Queen's U., Kingston, 1978-80; staff physician Kingston Gen. Hosp., 1978-80; assoc. prof. medicine U. Okla. Health Scis. Ctr., Oklahoma City, 1980-83; prof. medicine Okla. U. Health Scis. Ctr., Oklahoma City, 1983—, mem. cardiology fellowship com., 1980-82; dir. clin. cardiology Okla. U. Health Scis. Ctr. and VA Med. Ctr., Oklahoma City, 1980-87, vice chief cardiovascular sect., 1981-99, dir. clin. rsch., 1987-99; vice chmn. rsch. and devel. com. VA Med. Ctr., Oklahoma City, 1989-92, chmn. physiology-pharmacology categorical rev. com., 1989-94, chmn. rsch. and devel. com., 1992-94; sr. rsch. fellow Ont. Heart Found., 1978-80, rsch. fellow, 1976-78; rsch. fellow dept. medicine Queen's U., Kingston, Ont., 1975-76; rsch. fellow U. Leeds, Pub. Health and Ciba Found., dept. medicine and cardiovascular sect. Leeds Gen. Infirmary, 1971-75. Editor: Medical Therapy of Ischemic Heart Disease, 1992, Nitrates Updated, 1996; contbr. over 100 articles to profl. jours., chpts. to books; mem. editl. bd. panel Cardiology Drug Facts and Comparison, 1989; contbg. rev. panel Drug Facts and Comparisons, 1989—; mem. editl. bd. Internat. Jour. Cardiology, 1987-93, Cardiovascular Drugs and Therapy, 1987—; reviewer Circulation, Jour. Am. Coll. Cardiology, Am. Jour. Cardiology, Brit. Heart Jour., Internat. Jour. Cardiology, Can. Jour. Cardiology, European Heart Jour., Annals of Internal Medicine, New Eng. Jour. Medicine, Archives of Internal Medicine, Cardiovascular Drugs and Therapy, Drugs, European Jour. Pharmacology, Clin. Pharmacology and Therapeutics. Fellow Royal Coll. Physicians (Can.), Royal Soc. Medicine London, Am. Coll. Cardiology (mem. cardiovascular drug com. 1990-94), Royal Coll. Physicians (London), Clin. Coun. Cardiology Am. Heart Assn. (coun. rep. Okla. 1989—), Royal Coll. Physicians and Surgeons Can., N.Y. Acad. Med. Scis.; mem. Royal Coll. Physicians (U.K.), AAAS, Can. Cardiovascular Soc., Am. Fedn. Clin. Rsch., Phi Kappa Phi (mem. FDA cardiovascular and renal drugs adv. com. 1995—). Avocations: gardening, tennis, travel. Office: Okla U Health Sci Ctr Cardiology Sect 920 SL Young WP 3120 Oklahoma City OK 73104

THAIN, JOHN, investment bank executive. CFO Goldman, Sachs & Co., N.Y.C. Office: Goldman Sachs & Co 85 Broad St New York NY 10004-2456

THAJEB, PETERUS (TAI TAU-EN), neurologist; b. Medan, Indonesia, June 18, 1957; s. Ishak (Tai Tjioe Tjuan) and Lily (Lie Li Ching); m. Shew-Tze Chang, June 26, 1982; children: Daniel Dailo, Maria D., Samuel D., David D. Grad. in Accordion, Medan Accordion Inst., Medan, Indonesia, 1973; MD, Taipei Med. Coll., Taiwan, 1982. Diplomate Taiwan Bd. Neurology. Intern Changhua Christian Hosp., Taiwan, 1981-82; family practice Mennonite Christian Hosp., Hwalien, Taiwan, 1982-84; resident in neurology Chang Gung Meml. Hosp., Taipei, 1984-87; vis. trainee in neuropathology U. Wash., Seattle, 1986; neurology fellowship Chang Gung Meml. Hosp., Taipei, 1987-88; attending physician, staff neurologist Cathay Gen. Hosp., Taipei, 1988-99; dir. dept. neurology Mackay Meml. Hosp., Taipei, 1999—; chmn. 7th Asian and Oceanian Congress of Neurology, Bali, Indonesia, 1987; vis. rschr. neurol. sci. Rush -Presbyn.-St. Luke's Med. Ctr., Chgo., 1995-96. Contbr. articles to profl. jours. Recipient award Exec. Yuan, Taiwan, 1976. Fellow Internat. Coll. Angiology, Am. Heart Assn., Am. Soc. Neural Transplantation and Repair, Am. Coll. Angiology, Royal Soc. Medicine London; mem. N.Y. Acad. Sci. (inaugural mem. Charles Darwin Assocs.), Am. Acad. Neurology (assoc.), Neurol. Soc. Republic of China, Internat. Soc. Cerebral Blood Flow and Metabolism, Movement Disorder Soc. Avocations: musical instrumental performance (accordion, piano, violin), musical composition, swimming. Office: Makay Meml Hosp Dept Neurology, PO Box Nei-hu 6-030, Taipei Taiwan

THAKUR, SHASHI SJELJER, career officer; b. Shillong, Meghalaya, India, Oct. 8, 1955; s. Chandra Shekher Nunu and Usha (Rani) T.; m. Kanchan Thakur, June 30, 1979; children: Avinash, Deepika. BS in Chemistry, St. Anthony's coll., Shillong, 1975; MS in Def. Studies, Madras (India) U., 1991. Electronic warfare officer INS Godavari, Bombay, 1986-88; signal command officer INS Vindhyagiri, Bombay, 1988-89; exec. officer INS Dunagiri, Bombay, 1989-91; commdg. officer CGS Rajkamal, Bombay, 1991-92, DET Thopputhurai, Tamilnadu, India, 1992-94; staff officer telecom. SNC Hdqs., Kochi, India, 1994—; project mgr. Datapro, Kochi, 1995-96; master fng. going ship Govt. India, Bombay, 1997—. Project Mgr. NGO Citizens Peace, Mumbai, India, 1992. Mem. Kerala Counsellor's Forum, Homeopathic Med. Mission, N.Y. Acad. Scis. Hindu. Avocations: yoga, swimming, sailing, reading, writing. Home: Sannathi St, Kochi 682004, India Office: INS Garuda, Naval Base, Kochi 682004, India

THALACKER, ARBIE ROBERT, lawyer; b. Marquette, Mich., Apr. 17, 1935; s. Arbie Otto and Jeanne (Emmett) T.; m. Rita Annette Skaaren, Sept. 11, 1956 (div. July 1992); children: Marc Emmett, Christopher Paul, Robert Skaaren; m. Deborah B. Garrett, Jan. 10, 1998. AB, Princeton U., 1957; JD, U. Mich., 1960. Bar: N.Y. 1961, U.S. Ct. Appeals (2d cir.) 1962. Assoc. Shearman & Sterling, N.Y.C., 1960-68, ptnr., 1968—; dir. Detrex Corp., Detroit, 1981—, chmn. bd., 1993-96. Leader Rep. Dist. Com., 1966-68; v.p., trustee Greenwich Village Soc. for Hist. Preservation; trustee Naropa Univ.; bd. dirs. Meredith Monk House Found., Shambhala Internat. Mem. ABA, N.Y. Bar Assn., Assn. Bar City N.Y. (securities regulatory commn. 1975-78), Wine and Food Soc. (bd. dirs. 1976-78, 85-93, 94—), Chevaliers du Tastevin, Commanderie de Bordeaux, Siwanoy Country Club (bd. govs. 1976-79), Derby Club, Links Club, Verbank Hunting and Fishing Club. Home: 17 Commerce St New York NY 10014-3763 Office: Shearman & Sterling 599 Lexington Ave Fl C2 New York NY 10022-6069

THALACKER, VICTOR PAUL, research scientist; b. Muscatine, Iowa, Apr. 21, 1941; s. Paul Albert and Eleanor Pauline Katherine (Lau) T.; m. Connie Lee Meininger, Apr. 25, 1970; children: Paul John, Jason Peter. BS in Chemistry, Wis. State U., 1963; PhD in Organic Chemistry, U. Ariz., 1967. From rsch. chemist to process rsch. mgr. 3M Co., St. Paul, 1967-84, lab. mgr., 1985—. Commr. St. Croix Valley Athletic Assn., Stillwater, Minn., 1983-90. Mem. Am. Chem. Soc., Soc. Plastics Engrs. Avocations: nursery and landscaping, tennis, golf. Home: 5151 Muir Ave N Stillwater MN 55082-1059 Office: 3M Co 3M Center # 3M Saint Paul MN 55144-1001

THALASSINOS, ELEFTHERIOS, maritime studies educator; b. Iraklion, Greece, Aug. 19, 1954; s. Ioannis and Maria (Kambouridou) T.; m. Sotiria Fragouli, May 1, 1977; children: Ioannis, Pantelis. BA, U. Athens, 1976; MBA, DePaul U., 1978; PhD, U. Ill., 1982. From lectr. econs. dept. to chair dept. maritime studies U. Piraeus, Greece, 1983—; mgr. internat. banking Piraeus Bank, Athens, 1997-99, head strategic planning unit, 1992-97; gen. dir. Bank of Greece, Athens, 1986-88; councellor to the minister Min. Nat. Economy, Athens, 1984-85. Author: Introduction to Econometrics, 1992, Business Statistics: Theory and Applications, 1996, International Economics, 1998. Home: 2 Narkissou and Ortasias St, 14565 Athens Greece Office: U Piraeus, 40 Karaoli & Dimitriou Str, 18532 Piraeus Greece

THALDEN, BARRY R., architect; b. Chgo., July 5, 1942; s. Joseph and Sibyl (Goodwin) Hechtenthal; m. Irene L. Mittleman, June 23, 1966 (div. 1989); 1 child, Stacey; m. Kathyn McKnight, Sept. 1996. BArch, U. Ill., 1965; M in Land Architecture, U. Mich., 1969. Landscape architect Hellmuth, Obata, Kassebaum, St. Louis, 1969-70; dir. landscape architecture PGAV Architects, St. Louis, 1970-71; pres. Thalden Corp. Architects, St. Louis, 1971—. Prin. works include Rock Hill Park, 1975 (AIA award 1977), Wilson Residence, 1983 (AIA award), Nat. Bowling Hall of Fame, 1983 (St. Louis RCGA award 1984), Village Bogey Hills (Home Builders award 1985, St. L. ASLA award 1994), St. Louis U. Campus Mall (St. L. ASLA award 1989), Horizon Casino Resort, Lake Tahoe, Nev., St. Louis Airport's Radisson Hotel, Lady Luck, Treasure Bay, Palace Casinos, Biloxi, Miss., Boomtown Casino, New Orleans, Pres. Casino on the Admiral, St. Louis, Plaza of Champions, Busch Stadium, St. Louis, Ho Chunk Casino, Wisconsin Dells, Potowatomi Casino, Milw. Terrible's Casino, Las Vegas. Bd. dirs. St. Louis Open Space Coun., 1973-83, Las Vegas Art Mus., St. Louis Art, Ednl. Counc.; apptd. Mo. Lands Architect Coun., 1990-94.. Named Architect of Yr. Builder Architect mag., 1986. Fellow Am. Soc. Landscape Architects (nat. v.p. 1979-81, pres. St. Louis chpt. 1975, trustee 1976-79, nat. conv. chair 1991); mem. AIA, World Future Soc. (pres. St. Louis chpt. 1984-94, keynote conf. spkr. 1995). Avocations: painting, gardening, tennis, guitar. Home: 8 Edgewater Is Saint Louis MO 63105 Office: Thalden Corp 7777 Bonhomme Ave Ste 2200 Saint Louis MO 63105-1911

THALÉN, INGELA, Swedish government official; b. Göteborg, Sweden, Oct. 1, 1943. Shop asst. Social Dem. Party Youth League, Göteborg, 1959-74; organizing sec. Social Dem. Party, Göteborg, 1975-78; mcpl. commr. Jörfölla, 1979-87; min. of labour Swedish Govt., Stockholm, 1987-90, min. health and social affairs, 1990-91, chmn. Parliamentary Com. on Labour Market, 1991-94, min. health and social affairs, 1994-96; sec. gen. Social Dem. Party, Stockholm, 1996-99, minister for Social Security, 1999—. Office: Ministry Health Soc Affairs, S-105 60 Stockholm Sweden

THALER, PAUL SANDERS, lawyer, mediator; b. Washington, May 4, 1961; s. Martin S. Thaler and Barbara (Friedman) Mishkin; m. Melinda Ann Frostic, Oct. 12, 1991; children: Rachel Leigh, Daniel Martin. AB, Vassar Coll., 1983; JD, Georgetown U., 1987. Bar: Md. 1987, D.C. 1988, U.S. Ct. Appeals (D.C. and 4th cirs.) 1988, U.S. Dist. Ct. Md. 1988, U.S. Ct. Appeals (fed. cir.) 1989, U.S. Dist. Ct. D.C. 1989, U.S. Ct. Internat. Trade 1990, U.S. Supreme Ct. 1992. Assoc. Cooter & Gell, Washington, 1987-93; ptnr. The Robinson Law Firm, Washington, 1993-96, Thaler Liebeler Machado & Rasmussen, LLP, 1996—; guest lectr. negotiations mediation George Washington U. Law Sch., 1996—; adj. prof. Kogod Sch. Bus., Am. U. Bus. Ethics, Bus. Law, 1999—. Treas. Montgomery Highlands Estates Homeowners Assn., Silver Spring, Md., 1990-99; mediator Superior Ct. of D.C., 1991—; mem. adv. com. Vassar Coll. Fund, 1996-99; trustee Nat. Child Rsch. Ctr., Washington, 1998—. Mem. ABA (sect. dispute resolution, vice chmn. ethics 1994-98), D.C. Bar Assn., Md. Bar Assn., Soc. Profls. in Dispute Resolution, Acad. Family Mediators. Home: 9429 Locust Hill Rd Bethesda MD 20814-3939 Office: Thaler Liebeler Machado & Rasmussen LLP Hamilton Sq 600 14th St NW Ste 600 Washington DC 20005-2028

THALER, RICHARD WINSTON, JR., investment banker; b. Boston, Apr. 9, 1951; s. Richard Winston and Victoria Louise (Sears) T.; m. Mary Alice Gast, June 28, 1980; children: Julia Davis, Sarah Sears, Hannah Warren. BA in Am. Polit. History cum laude, Princeton U., 1973; MBA, Harvard U., 1978. Salesman Media Networks, N.Y.C., 1973-74; banker Bank of Boston, Rio De Janeiro, Brazil, 1975-77, Boston, 1978-80; mng. dir. investment banking Lehman Bros., N.Y.C., 1980-96, Deutsche Banc Alex Brown, N.Y.C., 1996—. Spl. gifts solicitor Princeton U. Ann. Giving, N.Y.C., 1987-88, 97-98, class agt., 1988-93; del. Dem. Nat. Conv., 1996; trustee Daily Princetonian, 1989—, Episc. Divinity Sch., Cambridge, Mass., 1995—; mem. vestry Chapel of St. James the Fisherman, Wellfleet, Mass.; trustee at large Plimouth Plantation, Plymouth, Mass., 1995—; del. Dem. Nat. Conv., 1996, Dem. Leadership Coun. Mem. Mass. Soc. Mayflower Descendants, Princeton Club, Siwanoy Country Club, University Cottage Club, Bond Club of N.Y. Democrat. Episcopalian. Avocations: gardening, sailing, Am. polit. hist., exotic travel. Office: Deutsche Bank Alex Brown 130 Liberty St New York NY 10006-1105

THALLER, GEORGE ERWIN, quality assurance professional, consultant; b. Nuremberg, Bavaria, Germany, Nov. 5, 1947; s. Alois and Betty (Friedlein) T. Diploma engring., Tech. Acad. Berlin, 1971. Gen. mgr. Alois Thaller, Nuremberg, 1971-74; tech. specialist, EDP Eriag, Ingolstadt, Germany, 1974-79; test engr. software Triumph Adler AG, Nuremberg, 1979-85; mgr. software ammunition divsn. Diehl, Roethenbach, 1985; quality assurance rep. Diehl, Orlando, Fla., 1986-88; mgr. software quality assurance NATO project Diehl, Orlando, and Roethenbach, 1985-93. Author: Software-Quality: Engineering, Test, Assurance, 1990, Sternenzigeuner, 1992, Optimizing Software Quality: The Capability Maturity Model, 1993, Computer Security: Protecting Hard and Software, 1993, Software Metrics, 1994, 2nd edit., Software Documents, 1995, Systems Engineering, 1996, ISO 9001: Making it Work in Software Engineering, 1996, 2nd edit., The Individual Software Process, 1997, Software Engineering for Real-Time and Embedded Systems, 1997, The Year 2000 Problem, 1998, SPICE: The Future of ISO 9001 in Software Engineering, 1998, Satellites in Earth Orbit, 1999, The Global Positioning System, 1999, Spy Satellites, 1999, Communications and TV Satellites, 2000, Software Quality-The Way to Top Performance, 2000, Software Design and Implementation, 2000, Software Test Verification and Validation, 2000, Wireless Telephones Worldwide, 2000; author crime stories for children; contbr. articles to profl. jours. Recipient award for metal work Metal Work Guild Nuernberg, 1969, Metal Work Guild Bavaria, 1969, 2d prize award for metal work Metal Work Guild Fed. Republic of Germany, 1969. Mem. AIAA, IEEE (assoc.), Assn. for Computing Machinery (voting mem.), Soc. for Computer Simulation, Planetary Soc., Nat. Geog. Soc., N.Y. Acad. Scis. Lutheran. Avocations: photography, science fiction, African art. Home and Office: Kreutzerstr 44, 90439 Nuremberg Germany

THALMANN, JÖRG (ARTHUR), retired journalist; b. Horgen, Zurich, Switzerland, June 23, 1934; arrived in Belgium, 1967; s. Arthur and Olga (Stäubli) T. PhD, U. Zurich, 1967. Apprentice Neue Zürcher Zeitung, Zurich, 1962-63; collaborator Swiss Confedn. Adminstrn., 1963; editor Basler Nachrichten, Switzerland, 1964-67; press corr. Basler Zeitung, Brussels, 1967-97, ret., 1997—; radio corr. Swiss Radio DRS, Berne, 1967-82. Author: Wege zu Kafka, 1964, 1992—Was Tun?, 1988; co-author: Das Schweizer EWG—Handbuch, 1972, Helvetische Alternativen, 1971. Mem. Fed. Commn. for Constitutional Reform, 1973-77.

THAMM, JOCHEN WALTER, library director; b. Magdeburg, Germany, Jan. 11, 1952; s. Walter and Anna (Goldmann) T.; m. Gabriele Neumann, Apr. 16, 1977; children: Ute, Stephan, Anna. Diplom in math., Tech. U., Merseburg, German Dem. Republic, 1974; Fachbibliothekar, U. Berlin, German Dem. Republic, 1985. Mathematician various cos., 1974-83; dir. libr. Deutsche Akademie der Naturforscher Leopoldina, Halle, 1985—. Office: Dt Akademie Naturforscher, Bibliothek A-Bebel-Str 50a, D 06108 Halle Sachsen-Anhalt, Germany

THAMPI, MOHAN VARGHESE, environmental health and civil engineer; b. Kuching, Sarawak, Malaysia, Mar. 25, 1960; s. Padmanabha Ramachandran and Sosamma (Varghese) T. Gen. Cert. Edn., Cambridge U., 1976; B in Tech. with honors, Indian Inst. Tech., Kharagpur, India, 1983; MS in Engring., U. Tex., 1985; DSc (hon.), London Inst. Applied Rsch., 1992. Registered profl. engr., Tex., Fla., registered environ. mgr.; cert. safety tng. OSHA; cert. Nat. Coun. Examiners for Engrs. and Surveyors. Assoc. engr. Brown & Caldwell, Dallas, 1985-87; project mgr. Brown & Caldwell, Orlando, 1987-88, Stottler Stagg & Assocs., Cape Canaveral, Fla., 1988-91; sr. project engr. Chastain-Skillman, Inc., Lakeland, Fla., 1991-93; project mgr. Glace & Radcliffe, Inc., Winter Park, Fla., 1993-94; mgr. FDEP, West Palm Beach, Fla., 1995-96; project mgr. Office of Capital Projects Mgmt., Naples, Fla., 1996—. Author: Ultraviolet Disinfection Studies in a Teflon-Tube Reactor, 1985; contbr. articles to profl. jours. Active Rep. Pres.'s Citizens Adv. Commn., 1992. Recipient Cert. of Cont. Profl. Devel. award Fla. Engring. Soc., 1992. Mem. NRA, NSPE, ASCE (assoc.), Project Mgmt. Inst., Internat. Assn. Water Pollution Rsch. and Control, Am. Mensa, Am. Water Works Assn., Water Pollution Control Fedn. (com. for preparing design practice manuals 1989—), Internat. Freelance Photographers Assn., Internat. Platform Assn., Internat. Assn. Air Travel Couriers, Am. Mgmt. Assn., Am. Smokers Alliance, Smithsonian Instn., Nat. Geog. Soc., Nat. Registry Environ. Professionals, U. Tex. Ex-Students Assn., Wine Soc. Am., Nat. Family Opinion, Internat. Deep Purple Appreciation Soc., Wilson Ctr. Assocs., I.I.T. Kharagpur Tech. Found., NASA Tech Briefs Reader Opinion Panel, Chemical Engring. Jour. Product Rsch. Panel, Nat. Rifle Assn., Plant Engring. Editl. Quality Panel, Kharagpur Tech. Alumni Found., N.Am. Hunting Club, Knight Order of Templars (Jerusalem), PC Bug Computer Club. Mar Thoma Syrian Christian. Avocations: photography, music, travel, sports. Home: PO Box 11954 Naples FL 34101-2954

THAN, GABOR NANDOR, obstetrician and gynecologist, researcher; b. Pecs, Hungary, Oct. 26, 1941; s. Nandor and Nandorne Adel Krasznai T; m. Gaborne Maria Erdelyi, Apr. 13, 1971; children: Gabor Nandor, Alexandra Katalin, Mark Marcell. PhD, Univ. Med. Sch., Pecs, Hungary, 1977, DAcad, 1990, DMedHabil, 1993. Diplomate in medicine, obstetrics and gynecology. Asst. dept. ob-gyn. U. Pecs, 1965-69, sr. asst., 1969-77, asst. prof., 1977-86, assoc. prof., 1986-95, prof. ob-gyn., 1995—. Author: Advances in Pregnancy Related Protein Research, 1993; editor: (yearbook) Annual Report Dept. Obstetrics and Gynecology Pecs, 1975-85; contbr. more than 120 articles to jours. including The Lancet, Internat. Jour. Infertility, Human Reprodn., Am. Jour. Ob-Gyn., others. Grantee Hungarian Acad. Sci., 1978-81, Hungarian Sci. Polit. Com., 1981-84, Hungarian Nat. Rsch. Fund, 1991-95, 94-97, 99—, Sci. Health Coun./Hungarian Ministry Health, 1994-96, 98-99, Hungarian Rsch. Fund Higher Edn., 1998, 99—. Mem. Nat. Soc. Ob-Gyn. (coord. com. 1978-93), Hungarian Sci. Acad. (commn. human reprodn. sys. 1990—), N.Y. Acad. Sci. Roman Catholic. Home: Suranyi str-12/A B-lepcso, 7625 Pécs Hungary Office: U Pécs Dept Ob-Gyn, Edesanyak u 17, 7624 Pécs Hungary

THANARAK, PIMONPAN, English educator; b. Chonburi, Thailand, May 26, 1952; d. Cherd and Louis (Kaewsuma) Pindikanit; m. Issarachai Thanarak, Mar. 19, 1978; 3 children. BEd in English, Srinakarinwirot U., Thailand, 1974; diploma in applied linguistics, RELC, Singapore, 1989; MA in Linguistics, KMITT, Thailand, 1992; diploma in TESOL, U. Tech., Sydney, Australia, 1994. Tchr. Inst. Tech., Ayutthaya, Thailand, 1974—, head English dept., 1997, head Sall ctr., 1997—. Avocations: reading, gardening. Home: 19/48 U-Thong Rd, Ayutthaya 13000, Thailand Office: Rajamangala Inst Tech, 19 U-Thong Rd, Ayutthaya 13000, Thailand

THANAWALL, KHURSHED MEHERWANIT, textile company executive; b. Mumbai, India, Dec. 24, 1942; s. Heherwanji Cursetji and Jex (Jussawalla) T. B in Commerce, Bombay U., 1963. Dep. mng. dir. Kisumu Cotton Mills Ltd., Kenya, 1965-82; mng. dir. Barmag India Pvt. Ltd., Mumbai, 1986—; commr. P.T. Tubantia Kudus, Indonesia, 1978-83, P.T. Sumatex Subur, Indonesia, 1979-84; dir. Lakshmi Synthetic Machinery Mfrs. Ltd., Coimbatore; mem. Kenya Govt. Textile Industry Standards Com., 1975-82, Man Made Fibre Processing Machinery sectional com. Bur. of Indian Standards, 1988—; rep. to Internat. Standards Orgn. com. on textile machinery, 1989. Mem. Kenya Assn. Mfrs. (exec. com. 1973-82), Fedn. of Kenya Employers (mgmt. bd. 1970-82), Textile Mfrs. Assn. Kenya (exec. com. 1969-82), Textile Machinery Mfrs. Assn. India (exec. coun. 1987—), chmn. synthetic fibre machinery cell 1989—). Office: Barmag India Pvt Ltd Narima, Pt 306-309 Delamal Tower, Mumbai 400 021, India

THANGARAJ, MANUEL AMIRTHAVASAGAM, college administrator, higher education consultant; b. Erode, India, July 11, 1918; s. Amirthavasagam and Navaneetham T.; m. Mary Monica Coelho, Dec. 29, 1948; 1 child, Arun Joseph. BS with honors, Annamalai U., India, 1939, MA, 1941; PhD, Toronto U., 1948. Lectr. in physics Madras Christian Coll., 1939-48, prof., head dept. physics, 1948-67; prof., prin. Am. Coll., Madurai, India, 1967-79; gen. sec. All India Assn. for Christian Higher Edn., New Delhi, 1979-82; dir., founder Anbagam Instn. Mentally Handicapped Children, Madurai, India, 1970—; dir. S.B.T. Tchr. Tng. Coll. in Spl. Edn., Madurai, India, 1990—; hon. dir. Christian Mission Hosp., Madurai, 1982-85; mem. governing bd. Lady Doak Coll., Madurai, 1986—, chmn., 1999—; mem. governing bd. Internat. Sch., Kodaikanal, 1985-97; chmn. India program United Bd. for Christian Higher Edn. in Asia, 1991-97; mem. exec. and gov. bd. Christian Med. Coll. and Hosp., Vellore, 1968-97, chmn., 1971-78. Author: Modern Physics, 1961, Conquest of Space, 1973, Electronics, 1979, Life Giving Sun, 1963, Rays Visible and INvisible, 1965, Energy from the Atom, 1968, Space Travel, 1971. Treas. Diocese of Madurai-Ramnad, Madurai, 1982-85; examiner Govt. India Pub. Svc. Commn., New Delhi, 1958-61. Recipient Nat. Pioneer award for ednl. innovation All India Assn. for Christian Higher Edn., New Delhi, 2000; Hon. fellow Christian Med. Coll., Vellore, 1997; Vincent Massey scholar Can. High Commn. in India, 1942, Rhodes scholar, Oxford, 1945; grantee World Coun. Churches, Geneva, 1969. Mem. Ch. of South India. Avocations: tennis, music, reading, writing. Home and Office: Anbagam Extension, DRO Colony, Madurai 625 007, India

THANGARAJ, VENU, educator, researcher, probabilist; b. Madras, India, Mar. 25, 1952; s. Vadivel Venu and Venu Saraswathi; m. Shantha Thangaraj; children: Kirubhakar, Thagadi, Thangaraj. BSc, U. Madras, 1973; MSc, Annamalai U., India, 1975, PhD, 1983. Lectr. Regional Engring. Coll., Trichy, India, 1983-85; lectr. Ramanujan Inst., U. Madras, 1985-90, reader, 1991-96, prof., 1997—; vis. rschr. ICTP, Italy. Editor procs. CSIR jr. rsch. fellow, New Delhi, 1976, UGC sr. rsch. fellow, 1980. Mem. Indian Soc. Probability and Stats. (life, sec. 2000-2002), Ramanujan Math. Soc. (life, sec. 2000—), Assn. Math. Tchrs. India (life). Home: Sri Raghavendra Apts, 7 Kandasamy St, Chennai 600004, India Office: U Madras, Advanced Study in Math, Madras 600005, India

THANGAVELU, SELLAPPAN, physician, orthopaedic surgeon; b. Coimbatore, Madras, India, Oct. 1, 1943; s. Gounder and Lakshmi (Bakiam) S. MBBS, Kilpauk Med. Sch., Madras, 1969; MS, Madurai (India) Med. Sch., 1971. Diplomate in medicine. Dir. Sendil XRay Hosp., Pollachi, India, 1992-93; registrar North Manchester (Eng.) Hosp., 1993-94, Gen. Infirmary, Leeds, Eng., 1994-95; sr. resident Southend Gen. Hosp., Eng., 1995-96; sr. resident Chase Farm Hosp., London, 1996-97; staff surgeon Princess Royal Hosp., Eng., 1998—; vis. dir. XRay Inst., Pollachi, 1997-99; cons. The Surgery, London, 1996-97. Vol. ophthalmic cmty. svc. Eye Hosp., Madras, 1985-86. Recipient Mensa Merit award, 1995, CliniQuiz award Update Group Ltd., 1985. Fellow Royal Coll. Surgeons Edinburgh; mem. AAAS, Brit. Med. Assn., N.Y. Acad. Scis. Avocations: cycling, tennis, rare science book collection. Home: 56 Western Ave, London W3 7TY, England

THANIKACHALAM, MOHAN, surgeon; b. Madras, Tamilnadu, India, Feb. 25, 1967; s. Sadagopan and Chandra Thanikachalam. B Medicine B Surgery, Kasturba Med. Coll., Manipal, India, 1991; MD, U.S. Med. Licensure Exam., 1992. Transitional intern Carney Hosp./Boston U., 1993-94; surg. intern St. Elizabeth Med. Ctr./Tufts U., Boston, 1994-95, surg. resident, 1995-98, surg. chief resident, 1998-99, postdoctoral assoc., 1999—. Contbr. articles to profl. jours. Rep. Student Coun. Mangalore U., Manipal, India, 1989. Recipient Thoracic Surgery Rsch. Fellowship award Thoracic Surgery Found. award, 2000—, Fellowship award Am. Heart Assn., 2000—. Fellow ACS (assoc.); mem. Internat. Soc. Heart and Lung Transplantation. E-mail: mthanika@med-miami.edu. Home: 300 Galen Dr Apt 302 Key Biscayne FL 33149-2149 Office: U Miami Dept Cardiothoracic Surgtery ET 3072 1161 NW 12th Ave Miami FL 33136

THANOPOULOU, GEORGIA GINA G., counseling psychologist; b. Athens, Greece, Sept. 1, 1966; d. George A. and Joanna S. (Yannopoulou) T. BA Psychology and History with highest distinction, Am. Coll. Greece, Athens, 1988; MA in Theater Edn. and Drama Therapy, Emerson Coll., 1992; MEd in Psychoedn. Cons., Harvard U., 1994. Cert. therapist, drama therapy specialist, counseling psychologist, family therapist, adolescent therapist. Psychoednl. counselor Pierce Coll., Athens, 1994-97; prof. U. Indianapolis, Athens, 1997-98; postgrad. rsch. fellow in human devel. and psychology Harvard U., Cambridge, Mass.; dir. Ctr. for Counseling and Career Svcs. Tasis Hellenic Internat. Sch., Kifissia, Greece, 1998—; mem. exec. com. Tasis Hellenic Internat. Sch., 1998. Contbr. articles to profl. publs. Mem. Internat. Family Therapy Assn., European Counseling Assn. (mem. exec. com. 1996), Greek Assn. Counseling (mem. exec. coun.), Alumni Assn. Harvard U., Harvard Club Greece (mem. exec. bd. 1998). Avocations: theater, dance, art, cultural events, travel. Fax: 301-6233160. E-mail: ginath@tasis.edu.gr. Home: 4 SG Iordanidi St, P Phychico, 154 52 Athens Greece Office: Tasis Hellenic Internat Sch, Xenias I Artemidos Strs, 145 10 Kifissia Kefalari, Greece

THAN SHWE, prime minister of Burma, military officer; b. Kyaykse, Feb. 2, 1933. Dep. comdr.-in-chief Defense Svcs., 1990-92; dep. chmn. State Law and Order Restoration Coun., 1990-92, chmn., 1988—; prime min., min. def. Govt. of Burma, Yangon, 1992—; chair State Law and Order Restoration

Coun., 1992—. Office: Office of Prime Min, 16 Zawgyi Rd, Yangon Myanmar*

THAPA, KISHOR JUNG, military attache; b. Kathmandu, Nepal, Jan. 15, 1954; came to U.S., 1999; s. Gahendra Jung and Dumber Kumari Thapa; m. Jharna Thapa, Apr. 15, 1983; children: Karun Jung, Shasank Jung. BA, Trichandra, Kathmandu, 1983. 2d lt. Royal Nepalese Army, Kathmandu, 1973-74, lt., 1974-76, capt., 1977-82, maj., 1983-93, lt. col., 1994—. Avocations: travel, hunting. Home: 1607 Simmons Dr Mc Lean VA 22101-5157 Office: Royal Nepalese Embassy 2131 Leroy Pl NW Washington DC 20008-1848

THAPAR, ANITA, psychiatry educator, physician; b. Caerphilly, Wales, Sept. 9, 1962; d. B.N. and B. Datta; m. Ajay Thapar, June 28, 1986; children: Kirin, Arjun. B Medicine B Surgery, U. Wales, 1985, PhD, 1995. Jr. med. officer various hosps., Wales, 1985-91; Med. Rsch. Coun. rsch. tng. fellow U. Wales Coll. Medicine, Cardiff, 1991-95, rsch. fellow, 1995, prof. child and adolescent psychiatry, 1999—; sr. lectr., cons. in child and adolescent psychiatry U. Manchester, U.K., 1996-99. Contbr. articles to profl. jours., chpt. to book. Mem. Royal Coll. Psychiatrists (Laughlin prize 1989). Office: U Wales Dept Psychiatry, Child/Adolescent Psychiat, Heath Park Cardiff CF14 4XN, Wales

THAPPA, DEVINDER MOHAN, physician; b. Jammu, Jak State, India, Mar. 9, 1961; s. Om Parkash and Kaushalya (Devi) T.; m. Nirmal Kumari, Dec. 9, 1990; 1 child, Harsh Avinash. BSc, Jak State Bd, Jammu, 1979; MBBS, U. Jammu, 1984; MD, Pgimer, Chandigarh, India, 1989; D in Health Care Adminstrn., Inst. Health Care Adminstrn., 1994. Sr. resident Lady Hardinge Med. Coll., New Delhi, 1989-92; dermatologist Ctrl. Govt. Health Scheme, Jaipur, India, 1992-94; asst. prof. dermatology & sexually transmitted diseases JIPMER, Pondicherry, India, 1994-96; assoc. prof. dermatology and sexually transmitted diseases Jipmer, Pondicherry, India, 1996—; head dept. dermatology and STD, Jipmer, Pondicherry, 1996—. Editor: Textbook of Dermatology, Venereology and Leprology, 2000; co-editor: Clinical Leprosy, 1993; contbr. articles to profl. jours. Mem. Indian Assn. Dermatologists, Venereologists and Leprologists (sec. 1995-98, joint sec. nat. exec. 1998), Indian Leprosy Assn., Indian Assn. Study Sexually Transmitted Diseases, CHS Officers Welfare Assn. (v.p. 1997-98, pres. 1998-99), JIPMER Sci. Soc. (sec. 1998-99). Avocations: watching TV. Office: Dept Dermatology, Jipmer, Pondicherry 605006, India

THARAKAD, SARASWATHI SUBRAMANIUM, child development educator; b. Wyanaad, Kerala, India, May 23, 1939; d. Subramanium Subramanium and Sundarambal Sundaram Tharakad. BA with honours, Madras (India) U., 1959, MA, 1960; PhD, Iowa State U., 1972. Lectr. psychology Avinashillingam Home Sci. Coll., Coimbatore, India, 1960-65; asst. lectr. child devel. Maharaja Sayajirao U. Baroda, Gujarat, India, 1966-67, lectr., 1967-76, assoc. prof., 1976-83, prof., 1983—. Author: Invisible Boundaries: Grooming for Adult Roles, 1988; co-editor: New Directions in Human Development and Family Studies, 1993, Handbook of Cross-Cultural Psychology, 2d edit., 1997; editor: Culture, Socialization and Human Development, 1999. Recipient Johann Jacobs awards Jacobs Found., Zurich, 1994-96; Fulbright postdoctoral fellow, 1983-84, Rockefeller Found. resident fellow, Bellagio, Italy, 1991-92. Mem. Internat. Soc. Studies in Behavioral Devel., Internat. Assn. Cross-Cultural Psychology, Internat. Assn. Pre-Sch. Edn. Home: 203 Janardan House, 14 Pratapgunj, Gujarat Vadodara 390 002, India Office: Maharaja Sayajirao U Baroda, Dept Human Devel, Gujarat Vadodara 390 002, India

THARIN NIMMANHEMIN, Thai government official; b. Oct. 29, 1945. BA, Harvard U., 1968; MBA, Stanford U., 1970. With First Nat. City Bank of N.Y., Manila, 1970; v.p. First Nat. City Devel. Finance Corp., 1971; head credit and corporate planning Siam Comml. Bank, 1974-84, pres., CEO, 1984; min. fin. Govt. of Thailand, Bangkok, 1992-95, 97—. Office: Ministry of Finance, Rama VI Road, Bangkok 10400, Thailand*

THARP, DAVID WAYNE, association executive; b. Indpls., Jan. 6, 1956; s. Donald E. and Willa J. Tharp; m. Connie M. Durbala, May 17, 1980. BS in Bus. Adminstrn., Drake U., 1987. CPA, Iowa. Office mgr. Coco & Ermels, CPAs, West Des Moines, Iowa, 1988-92; dir. finance and adminstrn. Internat. Assn. Milk, Food and Environ. Sanitarians, Des Moines, 1993-96; exec. dir. Internat. Assoc. for Food Protection, Des Moines, 1997—. Mem. AICPA, Am. Soc. Assn. Execs. (cert. exec.), Iowa Soc. CPA's (continuing edn. com. 1995-98). Avocations: golf, bicycling, rollerblading. Fax: 515-276-8655. E-mail: dtharp@foodprotection.org. Office: Internat Assn for Food Protection 6200 Aurora Ave Ste 200W Des Moines IA 50322-2863

THASE, GUNTER HERMANN, marketing executive; b. Bremen, Germany, Apr. 11, 1939; arrived in Can., 1963; s. Hermann and Elizabeth (Schroeder) T.; m. Ursula Widmer, Oct. 9, 1965; children: Philip, Monica. Mgr. internat. mktg. Brit. Metal Can., Toronto, 1973-78; gen. mgr. mktg. devel. Brit. Metal Can. & Amalgamet Can., Toronto, 1978-82, sr. v.p., 1982-88; pres. Brit. Metal Can., Amalgamet Can. and Preussag Can., Toronto, 1988—; dir. Premetalco Inc., 1988—. Former chmn. Christ the King Dietrich Bonnhoefer Luth. Ch. Lt. German Army, 1961. Mem. Internat. Magnesium Assn., Nat. Club, Rotary. Office: Amalgamet Can, 418-111 Richmond St W, Toronto, ON Canada M5H 2G4

THATCHER, ADRIAN, theology educator; b. Bridgnorth, Shropshire, U.K., Apr. 28, 1944; s. Arthur Edgar and Rose Elsie (Dickinson) T.; m. Grace Dyer Ellis, Nov. 26, 1966; 1 child, John. BA, Oxford U., 1966, MA, 1969, PhD, 1973. Min. Bapt. Ch., Southmead, Bristol, U.K., 1966-69, Abingdon, Oxon, U.K., 1969-74; lectr. religious studies St. Paul's Coll., Cheltenham, U.K., 1974-77; lectr., head theology dept. U. Coll. St. Mark and St. John, Plymouth, U.K., 1977-95; prof. applied theology U. Coll. St. Mark and St. John, Plymouth, 1995—. Author: Marriage After Modernity, Christian Marriage in Postmodern Times, 1999, Liberating Sex: A Christian Sexual Theology, 1993, Truly a Person, Truly God, A Post-Mythical View of Jesus, 1990, The Ontology of Paul Tillich, 1978; co-author (with E. Stuart) People of Passion-What the Churches Teach about Sex, 1997; co-editor: Christian Perspectives on Sexuality and Gender, 1996, Christian Perspectives for Education, A Reader in the Theology of Education, 1990; editor: Spirituality and the Curriculum, 1999; contbr. chpts. in books, articles to profl. jours. Alan Richardson fellow Durham U., 1997. Mem. Soc. Study Theology, Soc. Study Christian Ethics, Ctr. Study Christianity and Sexuality. Mem. Labour Party. Anglican. Avocations: tennis, squash, running, swimming. Home: 29 Oak Tree Park, Plymouth Devon PL6 7JZ, United Kingdom Office: Univ Coll St Mark & St John, Derriford Rd, Devon Plymouth PL6 8BH, United Kingdom

THATCHER, MARGARET HILDA, former prime minister of United Kingdom; b. Oct. 13, 1925; d. Alfred Roberts; m. Denis Thatcher, 1951; 1 son and 1 dau. (twins). M.A., B.Sc., Somerville Coll., Oxford (Eng.) U. Research chemist, 1947-51, called to the Bar, Lincoln's Inn, 1953, hon. bencher, 1975, M.P., 1959-92; joint parliamentary sec. Ministry of Pensions and Nat. Ins., 1961-64; sec. of state for edn. and sci. Govt. of U.K., 1970-74; leader Opposition, 1975-79, prime min. of U.K., 1st lord of Treasury, 1979-90; chancellor U. Birmingham, Buckingham, Eng., 1992—. Author: In Defence of Freedom, 1986, The Downing Street Years, 1993, The Path to Power, 1995. Mem. Worshipful Co. of Glovers, 1983. Decorated Order of Merit, 1990, Most Hon. Order of Garter, Her Majesty The Queen, 1995; fellow Royal Soc., 1983; recipient Donovan award, 1981, Freedom of Royal Borough of Kensington and Chelsea, 1979, Falkland Islands, 1983, Freedom of City of London, 1989, Medal of Freedom, 1991; named Hon. Chancellor of the Coll. of William and Mary, Williamsburg, Va., 1993—. Address: House of Lords, London SW1A 0PW, England*

THATHACHAR, MANDAYAM A.L., electrical engineering educator; b. Mysore, India, May 20, 1939; s. Parthasarathy M.A. and Rukmini (Aravinda) M.; m. Yadugiri Chakravarthy, July 5, 1968; children: Malini, Jayanth. B of Elec. Engring., U. Mysore, 1959, M of Engring., Indian Inst. Sci., 1961, PhD, 1968. Lectr. Indian Inst. Tech., Madras, 1961-64; lectr. Indian Inst. Scis., Bangalore, 1964-68, asst. prof., 1968-73, assoc. prof., 1973-78, prof., 1978—; chmn. dept. elec. engring. Indian Inst. Scis., 1983-88, chmn. divsn. elec. scis., 92-97, chmn. senate curriculum com., 1990-92, Tatachem chaired prof., 1991-94; vis. prof. Yale U., Mich. State U., Concordia U., Nat. U. of Singapore. Co-author: Learning Automata, 1989; contbr. articles to profl. jours. Recipient Bowen Meml. prize U. Mysore, 1959, Alumni award Excellence in Rsch., Indian Inst. Sci., 1992, Nehru Nat. award, 1993. Fellow IEEE (chmn. Bangalore sect. 1990-91), Indian Nat. Sci. Acad., Indian Nat. Acad. Engring., Indian Acad. Sci. Avocations: reading, chess, videos, philosophical discussions. Home: 23 10th Cross Swimng Pl Ext, Malleswaram, Bangalore 560 003, India Office: Indian Inst Sci, Dept Elec Engring, Bangalore 560 012, India

THATHONG, SURIYANT, military officer; b. Det Udom Dist., Thailand, Sept. 3, 1952; s. Noosint and Noi Thathong; m. Naphaporn Somphong, July 29, 1978; children: Atcharee, Sarawanee, Chongphop. Cert., Air Tech. Tng., Don Muang, Thailand, 1970; cert. high edn. tchr. pranakhorn, Tchg. Coll., Bangkhen, 1974; EdB in History, Srinakarinvirot U., Bangkhen, 1977. Staff expert in material Head Quarter Master Supply, Don Muang, 1971-75, tchr. Air Tech. Tng. Sch., 1974; intelligence officer in operation Dir. of Intelligence, 1977-80, intelligence officer in targeting analyst, 1981-83, intelligence officer in tactical intelligence, 1984-86; intelligence officer squadron freedom Thai-Malaysia Thai-Laosborder, 1987-89; intelligence officer Internal Security and Polit. Dept., Bangkok, 1990; intelligence officer combined air operation ctr. COBRA Gold Dir. Intelligence, 1990-97; intelligence staff-officer supreme command hdqs. Army, Navy, Air Force, Police, Civilian, 2000—. Lt. col. Mil. Orgn., 1992-2000. Buddhist. Avocations: helping the poor, gardening, singing, animals. Home: 171/1975 Paholyothin Rd, Bangkok 10220, Thailand Office: Directorate Intelligence, Plan & Policy Don Muang, Bangkok 10210, Thailand

THATTE, URMILA MUKUND, pharmacology educator; b. Mumbai, India, July 12, 1958; d. Vasant R. and Meera Vasant Rao; m. Mukund Ramchandra Thatte, Oct. 30, 1982; children: Mohit, Nikhil. MB, BChir, Seth GS Med. Coll., Mumbai, 1980, MD, 1984; grad., Delhi Nat. Bd., 1987; PhD in Pharmacology, 1999. Lectr. pharmacology Seth Gordhandas Sunderdas Med. Coll., 1982-89, assoc. prof., 1990—. Author: Ayurveda Revisited, 1989, Green Solace, 1994, Ayurveda Unraveled, 1995. Recipient Gold medal U. Bombay, 1979, 80. Mem. Indian Pharm. Soc. (Achari prize 1987), Indian Soc. for Clin. Pharmacology and Therapeutics. Office: Seth GS Med Coll, Parel, Dept Pharmacology, Mumbai 400012, India

THAUER, RUDOLF KURT, microbiologist and researcher; b. Frankfurt, Hessen, Germany, Oct. 5, 1939; s. Rudolf and Charlotte (Kalberlah) T.; m. Helga Krebel, July 20, 1968; children: Kattrin, Jenny, Christian. Diploma in Biochemistry, U. Tübingen, Germany, 1966; Dr.rer.nat., U. Freiburg, Germany, 1968. Asst. prof. U. Freiburg, 1971-72; guest scientist U. Cleve., 1972; assoc. prof. U. Bochum, Germany, 1972-76; prof. U. Marburg, Germany, 1976—, dir. Max-Planck Inst. for Terrestric Microbiology, 1991—; v.p. Deutsche Forschungsgemeinschaft Bonn, Germany, 1983-87; Shimizu vis. prof. Stanford U., 1999; Wellcome vis. prof. Burroughs Wellcome Fund, U. Wis., Madison, 2000. Contbr. over 350 sci. papers to profl. jours. Recipient Otto-Warburg-Medaille, Gesellschaft fü Biologische Chemie, 1984, Gottfried-Wilhelm-Leibniz prize Deutsche Forschungsgemeinschaft, Bonn, 1986, Carus prize and medal Leopoldina, Schweinfurt, Germany, 1993. Named A.J. Kluyver Meml. lectr., U. Delft, 1995, Albert Neuberger lectr. in tetrapyrrole Sci. Queen Mary and Westfield Coll., 1997, Marjory Stephenson prize lectr., 1998. Mem. Deutsche Akademie der Naturforscher Leopoldina, Academia Europaea, Academie der Wissenschaften (Dannie-Heinemann prize 1986), Rehin, Westf. Akademie der Wissenschaften (corres. mem.). Office: Max-Planck Inst Terrestrish, Karl-von-Frisch-Strasse, Marburg D-35043, Germany

THAWAIT, SURENDRA KUMAR, mechanical engineer, researcher; b. Bilaspur, Vidya Nagar, India, Apr. 15, 1964; s. Daulat Ram and Ganesh Kumari T.; m. Vicky Nishma. BSME with honors, Govt. Eng. Coll., Bilaspur, India, 1986. Trainee mech. engr. BEC Fertilizers, Bilaspur, India, 1987; jr. exec. trainee South Eastern Coalfields Ltd., Korba, India, 1987-88, engr., 1988-92, exec. engr., 1992-93; exec. engr. South Eastern Coalfields Ltd., Bilaspur, India, 1993-98, sr. exec. engr., 1998-99; sr. exec. engr. South Eastern Coalfields Ltd., Korba, India, 1999—. Inventor design of knitting machine, 1998. Organizer Barai Chourasia Samaj, Bilaspur, India, 1998, 2000; exec. com. mem. Akhil Bharitiya Chourasia Samaj, Bhopal, India, 1999-2000. Mem. Loss Prevention Assn. of India, Bombay Productivity Coun., Inst. of Engrs., Inst. Mech. Engrs.; assoc. mem. Inst. of Valuers. Avocations: cricket, research work, social work, reading technical books, helping poor people. Home: Vidya Nagar, 495-004 Bilaspur Madhya Pradesh, India Office: South Ea Coalfields Ltd, Sub Area Mgr, 495-454 Korba Kusmunda Colliery, India

THAWLEY, MICHAEL, diplomat; b. Eng., 1950; arrived in Australia; m. Deborah Thawley; children: Cosimo, Tom, Sam. Student, Australian Nat. U.; postgrad. diploma in Russian, Surrey (Eng.) U. Joined Australian Fgn. Svc., 1972, first asst. sec. Prime Mins. Dept., 1993-96; nat. security advisor Prime Min. Australia Australian Fgn. Svc., Washington, 1996; dep. sec. dept. fgn. affairs and trade Australian Fgn. Svc.; amb. to the U.S. Govt. Australia, Washington, 2000—. Avocations: reading, music, gardening. Fax: 202-797-3168. Office: Embassy of Australia 1601 Massachusetts Ave NW Washington DC 20036-2273

THAWONMAS, RUCK, computer scientist, educator; b. Nakhonsithammrat, Thailand, Dec. 19, 1965; s. Dumri and Somsri Thawonmas; m. Ornouma Chuchaiya, Aug. 3, 1990; children, Ramita, Ran. BEng, Chulalongkorn U., Bangkok, Thailand, 1987; MEng, Ibaraki U., Hitachi, Japan, 1990; DEng, Tohoku U., Sendai, Japan, 1994. Vis. rschr. Hitachi Rsch. Lab./Hitachi Ltd., 1994-96, Riken, Wako, Japan, 1996-97, 98-99; asst. prof. U. Aizu, Aizu-Wakamatsu, Japan, 1997-98; assoc. prof. Kochi U. Tech., Tosayamada-cho, Kochi, Japan, 1999—; reviewing referee IEEE Trans. Fuzzy Sys., 1995—, IEEE Trans. Sys., Man and Cybernetics, 1997—, IEEE Trans. Neural Networks, 1998—, Jour. Acoustical Soc. Am., 1998—. Contbr. articles to profl. jours. Rsch. fellow Tohoku Kaihatsu Meml. Found., 1993-94, Riken, 1996-97; Monbusho scholar Japanese Govt., 1987-93. Mem. ACM, IEEE (sr.). Buddhist. Avocations: reading, movies, badminton, disc golf. Office: Dept Info Sys Engring, Kochi Univ Tech, Tosayamada-cho Kochi 782-8502, Japan

THAYER, EDNA LOUISE, medical facility administrator, nurse; b. Madelia, Minn., May 21, 1936; d. Walter William Arthur and Hilda Engel Emily Ann (Geistfeld) Wilke; m. David LeRoy Thayer, Aug. 30, 1958; children: Scott, Tamara, Brenda. Diploma in nursing, Bethesda Luth., 1956; BS in Nursing Edn., U. Minn., 1960; MSN, Washington U., St. Louis, 1966; MS in Counseling, Mankato (Minn.) State U., 1972. Cert. nursing adminstr. advanced ANA. Nurse Bethesda Luth. Hosp., St. Paul, 1956-58, U. Minn. Hosp., Mpls., 1958; from nurse to asst. head nurse supr., edn. dir. Fairmont (Minn.) Community Hosp., 1959-63; instr. Alton (Ill.) Meml. Hosp., 1963-66; from nursing instr. to assoc. prof. and dean Sch. Nursing Mankato State U., 1966-77; asst. adminstr. Rice County Dist. One Hosp., Faribault, Minn., 1977-89; RN, adminstrv. supr. St. Peter (Minn.) Regional Treatment Ctr., 1990-96; spkr., 1996—; nurse surveyor Minn. Dept. Tech. Edn., St. Paul, 1980-93; mem. adv. co. LPN and MA programs Tech. Inst., Faribault, 1977—. Mem. Rice County Ext. Bd., Faribault, 1986-91, adult leader 4-H Club, Rice County and St. Paul, 1971-97; advisor Med. Explorers, Faribault, 1977-89; mem. Rep. Rodosovich Health Com., Faribault, 1984-94; coun. mem. Our Savior's Luth. Ch., Faribault, 1984-87; mem. Rep. Boudreau Health Care Adv. Com., 1996—. Recipient alumni award Nat. 4-H Club, 1983, Disting. Friend of Nursing award Mankato State U., 1995. Mem. Minn. Orgn. Nurse Execs. (bd. dirs. 1987-89), Dist. F Nursing Svc. Adminstrs. (pres. 1980-82), Minn. Nurses Assn. (bd. dirs. 1982-87, Pres.'s award 1983, pres. 5th dist. 1974, 75, pres. 13th dist. 1984-86), AAUW, Sigma Theta Tau, Delta Kappa Gamma (pres. Pi chptr. 1982-84, Woman of Achievement award 1985), Hosp. Aux. Republican. Avocations: crafts, volunteer work, theater, plays. Home: RR 1 Box 7B Elysian MN 56028-9731

THAYER, KEITH BAYARD, engineering company executive; b. Phoenix, Nov. 6, 1927; s. Ezra Weld and Claire (Pile) T.; m. Ruth O'Bryan, Oct. 6, 1951; children: Jane, John, Joe, Joan, Julie, Jill, Jim, Jacque. BSME with honors, Kans. State U., 1950. Registered engr. Tex., Okla., La., Kans., Miss. Machinist's helper MK&T Railroad, Parsons, Kans., 1943-45; assembler Douglas Aircraft, Santa Monica, Calif., 1946-47; engr. Phillips Petroleum Co., Bartlesville, Okla., 1950-51; piping design engr. Foster Wheeler, Houston, 1951-53; chmn. bd., pres. CDI Stubbs Overbeck, Houston, 1953-96; pres., CEO Garuda U.S., Inc., Houston, 1996—. Mem. industry adv. com. Tex. A&M U., Galveston, 1994-96; industry adv. coun. mech. and nuclear engring. dept. Kans. State U., Manhattan, 1999—; examiner Malcolm Baldridge Quality award, 1999—; pres. Sharpstown Save Our Park com., Houston, 1973-80; liturgy com. St. Francis de Sales Ch., Houston, 1978-81. With USNR, 1945-47. Recipient Frank L. Evans award Energy Sources Tech. Conf. & Exhbn., New Orleans, 1991. Fellow ASME Internat. (life; internat. pres. 1997-98, Andy Lewis award petroleum divsn. 1987, Thayer Best Mech. Achievement award 1996); mem. Soc. Piping Engrs. and Designers (dir. 1985-90), Asia Soc., Sharpstown Civic Assn. (dir. 1997—), Greater Houston Partnership (CEO roundtable 1994—), River Bend Country Club. Roman Catholic. Avocations: painting, woodworking, knifemaking, golf, hunting. E-mail: kbthayer@aol.com. Office: Garuda US Inc 6200 Savoy Dr Ste 733 Houston TX 77036-3324

THAYER, WALTER RAYMOND, internist; b. Providence, R.I., Apr. 16, 1929; s. Walter Raymond and Esther Veronica (Hulme) T.; children: Walter, Ida Marie, Peter; m. Meredith Marks, 1998. Intern R.I. Hosp., Providence, 1955-57; sr. asst. surgeon USPHS/NIH, Bethesda, Md., 1956-58; resident Georgetown U. Hosp., Washington, 1958-59; fellow in gastroenterology Yale U. Sch. Medicine, New Haven, 1959-61, rsch. fellow in internal medicine, 1961; from instr. to asst. prof. medicine Yale U., New Haven, 1960-65; from assoc. prof. to prof. medicine Brown U. Sch. Medicine, Providence, R.I., 1965—; nat. scientific adv. bd. Crohn's and Colitis Found., Inc., 1978-83, rsch. and tng. awards com., 1978-85, chmn., 1980-85, chmn. med. adv. bd. R.I. chpt., 1983; adv. bd. Nat. Coop. Crohn's Disease Study Group, 1981-83; mem. Cancer Control Bd. R.I., 1976-77. Editl. reviewer Gastroenterology, Digestive Disease and Scis.; contbr. articles to profl. jours. Sr. asst. surgeon USPHS, 1956-58. NSF fellow, 1972. Fellow Am. Coll. Physicians, Am. Coll. Gastroenterology (gov. for R.I. 1996-98); mem. Am. Gastroenterol. Assn. (Clinician of Yr. award 1999), Am. Fedn. Clin. Rsch., R.I. Med. Soc., R.I. Gastroenterology Soc., Providence Med. Soc. Avocations: cross country skiing, birdwatching, gardening. Home: 65 Bullocks Point Ave Riverside RI 02915-5318 Office: RIH Med Found 2 Dudley St Ste 370 Providence RI 02905-3248

THEEDE, HANS JOHANNES, marine zoologist, researcher; b. Lohe, Germany, Dec. 17, 1934; s. Johannes and Marie (Lichtenstein) T.; m. Gisela Glüsing, May 16, 1967; 1 child, Edda. D Natural Scis., Kiel (Germany) U., 1962, Habilitation, 1971, Apl. Prof., 1974; D honoris causa, U. Agr., Szczecin, Poland, 1991. Postdoctoral fellow Inst. Marine Rsch. Kiel U., 1962-64, sci. asst., 1964-71, sr. scientist, 1971-73, lectr., 1973-89; prof. marine zoology Bremen U., Bremerhaven, Germany, 1989-94; marine zoologist Kiel U., Germany, 1994-99; prof. sci. soc., 1968-97. Editor: Die Ostee, Natur und Kulturraum, 1985; contbr. over 100 articles on ecology and physiology of marine animals to profl. publs. Recipient SETAC Environ. Edn. award 1999, Univ. medal Gdansk U., 1999. Mem. Baltic Marine Biologists (com., pres. 1968-97). Avocation: gardening. Home: Brückenstrasse 1, 24220 Flintbek Germany Office: Inst Marine Rsch Zoology Dept, Duesternbrooker Weg 20, D 24105 Kiel Germany

THEETRANONT, CHOTI, academic administrator. Pres. Chang Mai U., Thailand. Office: Chang Mai U, 239 Huay Kaew Rd, Chiang Mai 50200, Thailand*

THEILE, BURKHARD, physicist; b. Soemmerda, Thuringa, Germany, July 16, 1940; s. Hans U. and Rose E. (Kuszmink) T.; m. Dagmar Guenster, 1966 (div. Oct. 1978); children: Gudrun, Ulrike; m. Heide Luise Mueller, 1983. Diplom-physiker, Tech. U., Braunschweig, Germany, 1968, Dr.rer.nat, 1971. From asst. to assoc. prof. Tech. U., Braunschweig, 1970-80; program mgr. Dornier System, Friedrichshafen, Germany, 1981-83, Dornier GmbH, Neuilly, France, 1983-85; exec. v.p. Dornier of N.Am., Arlington, Va., 1986-90; gen. mgr. STN Atlas Electronic, Bremen, Germany, 1991-98, dir. future sys., 1998-99; head corp. strategy and tech. Rheinmetall DeTec AG, Ratingen, Germany, 2000—; advisor for space programs German Ministry for Sci., Bonn, 1974-79; chmn. tech. com. European Def. Industry Group, 1995-2000. Contbr. 45 articles to profl. jours. Mem. AIAA, Deutsche Gesellschaft fur Luft-u. Raumfahrt, Aircraft Owners and Pilots Assn. Office: Rheinmetall DeTec AG, D-40880 Ratingen Germany

THEIMER, WOLFGANG MICHAEL, telecommunications engineer; b. Bochum, N. Rhine, Germany, Feb. 25, 1965; s. Heinz Wolfgang and Christel T.; m. Ute Maria Stachelhaus, July 22, 1994; 1 child, Jule Marie. Dipl.-Ing., Ruhr-U. Bochum (Germany), 1990, Dr.-Ing., 1995. Rsch. asst. Ruhr-U. Bochum, 1990-95; R & D engr. Nokia Mobile Phones, Bochum, 1995-97, project mgr., 1997—. Cusanus scholar Cusanuswerk, 1986-89, scholar Deutscher Ahademischer Austauschdienst, 1987-88. Mem. IEEE. Roman Catholic. Avocations: playing piano, historical books. Office: Nokia Mobile Phones, Meesmannstr 103, Bochum 44807, Germany

THEIS, PAUL ANTHONY, publishing executive; b. Ft. Wayne, Ind., Feb. 14, 1923; s. Albert Peter and Josephine Mary (Kinn) T.; m. Nancy Ann Wilbur, Aug. 21, 1971; children: Mitchell A. BA in Journalism, U. Notre Dame, Ind., 1948; BS in Fgn. Svc., Georgetown U., 1949; postgrad., Am U., 1949-52. Reporter Army Times & Fairchild Pubs., Washington, 1950-53; corres. Newsweek Mag., Washington, 1953-54; adminstrv. asst. to U.S. Congressman, Washington, 1955-57; radio-TV dir. Nat. Rep. Congl. Com., Washington, 1957-60; dir. pub. rels. Nat. Rep. Congl. Com., 1960-74; exec. editor to Pres. The White House, 1974-76; dep. undersec. Dept. Agr., Washington, 1976-77; staff cons. U.S. Ho. of Reps., Washington, 1977-81; pres. Headliner Editorial Svc., Washington, 1981—; pub. rels. officer Pres. Eisenhower's Inaugural, Washington, 1957; vice chmn. publicity Pres. Nixon's Inaugural Com., 1969. Co-author: All About Politics, 1972; co-inventor game Hat in the Ring, 1965; co-editor Who's Who in Am. Politics, 1965-75. Alt. del. rep. Nat. Conv., Dallas, 1984, del., New Orleans, 1988, Houston, 1992; mem. D.C. Rep. Com., 1980-99. With U.S. Army Air Corps, 1943-46, ETO; maj. USAFR, Ret. Mem. Nat. Press Club, Capitol Hill Club, Cosmos Club. Roman Catholic. Home: 2903 Garfield St NW Washington DC 20008-3504

THEIS, STEVEN THOMAS, executive safety director; b. Trenton, N.J., June 16, 1959; s. Thomas Donald and Pauline (Ciko) T.; m. Mary L. Crane; children: Christopher William, Nicholas Thomas. BS, U. So. Calif., L.A., 1981; Cert. German Lang., Johann Wolfgang Goethe U., Frankfurt am Main, Germany, 1983; postgrad., Friedrich Alexander U., Erlangen, Germany, 1983-84; MS, U. Pa., 1999. Cert. safety profl., cert. hazardous materials mgr., EMT, N.J. With Henkels & McCoy, Inc., various locations, 1978—; constrn. coord. Henkels & McCoy, Inc., Phoenix, 1982; project mgr. Henkels & McCoy, Inc., Burlington, N.J., 1985-87; safety dir. N.J. div. Henkels & McCoy, Inc., Burlington, 1987-92; staff support coord. corp. office Henkels & McCoy, Blue Bell, Pa., 1992—, corp. dir. safety, 1992—; bd. dirs. Henkels & McCoy, Inc., 1996; safety and health instr. ARC, Woodbury, N.J., 1984—, safety and health instr., trainer, 1990—; basic instr. OSHA constrn. ind. stds. U.S. Dept. Labor, Chgo., 1987—; chairperson safety and health com. Gloucester County ARC, Woodbury, 1991—. Patentee in field. 1st lt. West Deptford Emergency Squad, Thorofare, N.J., 1987-88, capt., 1989-90, hon. mem. 1991—; vice chmn. West Deptford Twp. Bd. Health, 1989-90, v.p. West Deptford Vol. Fire and Ambulance Assn., 1989-90; emergency med. spl. coord. West Deptford Office Emergency Mtmg., 1989-90. Named Mem. of the Yr. West Deptford Emergency Squad, 1988; recipient Cameron award Nat. Safety Coun., 1992-93, 93-94. Mem. ASTM (membership sec. 1994, rec. sec. 1998-99), Am. Soc. Safety Engrs., Am. Welding Soc., Nat. Safety Coun., Am. Mgmt. Assn., Am. Nat. Stds. Inst., Nat. Safety Coun. (pub. utilities divn.), Nat. Electric Safety Code. Republican. Roman Catholic. Avocations: antiques, classical music, model building, fishing. Office: Henkels & McCoy Inc 985 Jolly Rd Blue Bell PA 19422-1958

THEIS, WERNER R., physics educator; b. Hamburg, Germany, Oct. 3, 1926; s. Walther L. and Paula (Busse) T.; m. Edith W. Hilgert, Mar. 22, 1963; children: Wolfgang, Karsten, Georg. Abitur, Realgymnasium, Hamburg, 1944; diploma in physics, U. Hamburg, Hamburg, 1952, D Natural Scis., 1954. Sci. asst. U. Hamburg, Hamburg, 1952-56, lectr., 1956-

63; ordentlicher prof. physics Free U., Berlin, 1963—. Author: Grundzüge der Quantentheorie mit exemplarischen Anwendungen, 1985. Mem. Berlin Sci. Soc. Lutheran. Home: Marienbader Str 12, 14199 Berlin Germany Office: Free U Berlin, Arnimallee 14, 14195 Berlin Germany

THEIS, WILLIAM HAROLD, lawyer, educator; b. Chgo., Nov. 8, 1945; s. Clarence M. and Marion K. (McLendon) T.; m. Maria Luisa Belfiore, Dec. 5, 1973; children: Catherine, Elizabeth. AB, Loyola U., Chgo., 1967; JD, Northwestern U., 1970; LLM, Columbia U., 1977, JSD, 1982. Bar: Ill. 1970, D.C. 1971, Wis. 1998, U.S. Ct. Appeals (7th cir.) 1971, U.S. Supreme Ct. 1974, Wis. 1998. Assoc. prof. La. State U. Law Ctr., 1972-78, Loyola U. Law Sch., Chgo., 1978-81; practiced in Chgo., 1981-99; pvt. practice Winnetka, Ill., 1999—; part-time lectr. admiralty Northwestern Sch. Law, Chgo. Contbr. articles to legal jours. Lt. USNR, 1970-72. Mem. Am. Law Inst. Office: 841 Foxdale Ave Winnetka IL 60093-1909

THEISEN, HENRY WILLIAM, lawyer; b. N.Y.C., Feb. 21, 1939; s. Charles and Jennie J. (Callahan) T.; m. Kathleen Anne Brennan, Jan. 23, 1966 (div. Oct. 1992); children: Gordon H., Anne, Maureen R., William R.; m. Deborah S. Lynch, June 11, 1994. BBA, Manhattan Coll., 1961; JD, Fordham U., 1966. Bar: N.Y. 1967, U.S. Dist. Ct. (no. dist.) N.Y. 1968, U.S. Ct. Appeals (2d cir.) 1971, U.S. Supreme Ct. 1974. Acct. Patterson & Ridgway, CPAs, N.Y.C., 1961-64; ptnr. Adams, Theisen & May, Ithaca, N.Y., 1967—; prosecutor City of Ithaca, 1969; estate tax atty. N.Y. State, Albany, 1976-90; county atty. Tompkins County, Ithaca, 1994—; examining counsel Ticor Title Guaranty Co., Monroe Title Ins. Corp.; corp. sec., bd. dirs. Paleontol. Rsch. Instn., Ithaca; lectr. wills and trusts adult edn. program Bd. Coop. Ednl. Svcs., Tompkins County, N.Y., 1995—. Author: (fin. and estate planning) Financial and Estate Planning Records, 1996. Pres. Ithaca Cmty. Music Sch., 1970; bd. reps. Tompkins County, Ithaca, 1976-81; bd. dirs. Tompkins Cmty. Hosp., 1980-83, Ctr. for Arts at Ithaca, Inc. (Hangar Theatre), 1989-92, Suicide Prevention Found. Tompkins County, 1996—; race dir. Finger Lakes Marathon, 1992-96; bd. dirs. Spl. Children's Ctr., 1969-74, pres., 1973-74; bd. dirs. Tompkins County SPCA, 1973-76, pres., 1976; chmn. task force orgn. Ithaca Pub. Edn. Initiative Inc., 1995-96; panel mem. Jud. Candidate Rating Panel, Binghamton, N.Y., 1993-94; candidate Supreme Ct. Justice, N.Y., 1992;. Mem. Tompkins County Bar Assn. (pres. 1990), Tompkins County C. of C. (pres. 1993), Estate Planning Coun. Tompkins County (co-founder, pres. 1985), Ithaca Rotary Club. Democrat. Roman Catholic. Avocations: watercolor painting, long distance running. Office: Adams Theisen & May 301 The Clinton House 103 W Seneca St Ste 304 Ithaca NY 14850-4191

THEISSEN, GERD, New Testament educator; b. Mönchengladbach, Germany, Apr. 24, 1943; s. Albert and Else (Finken) T.; m. Christa Schaible, Aug. 30, 1968; children: Oliver, Gunnar. D Theology, U. Bonn, Germany, 1968, Habilitation, 1973; D honoris causa, U. Neuchâtel, Switzerland, 1989, U. Glasgow, Scotland, 1990, U. St. Andrews, 1997. Lic. ch. svc., tchr. Asst. U. Göttingen, Germany, 1968-69; asst. U. Bonn, Germany, 1969-73, pvt. docent, 1973-78; tchr. secondary sch. Bonn, 1976-78; prof. U. Copenhagen, 1978-80; prof. N.T. U. Heidelberg, Germany, 1980—. Author numerous books, including: The Shadow of the Galilean, 1987, The Gospels in Context, 1991, The Open Door, 1991, Social Reality and Early Christians, 1992, The Sign Language of Faith, 1995, (with A. Merz) The Historical Jesus, 1997, Theory of Primitive Christian Religion, 1999. Recipient Prix des libraires religieuses, Paris, 1989, Sexauer Gemeindepreis, Sexau, 1993. Mem. Soc. Novi Testamenti Studiorum. Home: Max-Josef-Str 54/1, 69126 Heidelberg Germany

THELIN, PETER CARL, economist, educator; b. Wellsley, Mass., June 26, 1945; s. George Willard and Rosalia (Komarec) T.; m. Gail Patricia Thelin, July 28, 1968 (div. Apr. 1985); children: Adam Carl Thelin, Dina Lyn Perkins. BS in Natural Resource Econs., U. Calif., Berkeley, 1968, MS in Natural Resource Econs., 1970, postgrad., 1974-80. Instr. in econs. West Valley Coll., Saratoga, Calif., 1970—. Editor: A Commons Problem, 1993. Active Surfriders Found., Seabright Neighborhood Assn. Mem. Acad. Martial Arts (student 1994—), Coll. Traditional Korean Healing arts (student 1999—). Avocations: Tai Chi, bodysurfing, kayaking, reading, writing poetry. Home: 307 Mott Ave Santa Cruz CA 95062-3732 Office: West Valley Coll 14000 Fruitvale Ave Saratoga CA 95070-5640

THENG, BENNY KIAN GOAN, clay-organic chemist; b. Bandung, Indonesia, Sept. 19, 1934; arrived in New Zealand, 1970; s. Hoay Tek and Giok Nio (Tan) T.; m. Judith Helen Wells, May 9, 1964; children: Monica, Andrew, Tjun Wie. BS in Agriculture, U. Adelaide, Australia, 1961, PhD, 1965. Rsch. assoc. U. Leuven, Belgium, 1966-68; rsch. scientist CSIRO, Melbourne, Australia, 1968-70; scientist DSIR, Lower Hutt, New Zealand, 1970-92; program leader Landcare Rsch., Palmerston North, New Zealand, 1992—; cons. and lectr. in field. Author: (reference books) The Chemistry of Clay-Organic Reactions, 1974 (Adam Hilger prize 1974), Formation and Properties of Clay-Polymer Complexes, 1979, Soils with Variable Charge, 1980. Convener Uniting Parish, Upper Hutt, 1986-92. Rsch. fellow U. Western Australia, Perth, Australia, 1964-66; recipient Overseas Specialist award Sci. & Tech. Agy. Japan, Tokyo, 1992, Travel award New Zealand/Germany Coop. Agreement, Wellington, 1995. Fellow New Zealand Inst. Chemistry, Royal Soc. New Zealand, New Zealand Soc. Soil Sci. Avocations: contract bridge, reading. Home: 3 Guernsey Pl, Palmerston North New Zealand Office: Landcare Rsch Massey U, Pvt Bag 11 052, Palmerston North New Zealand

THEO, MILTON COSTA, lawyer; b. Johannesburg, South Africa, June 9, 1945; s. Costa John and Irene Theodora (Loukidis) T.; m. Mary Catherine Macrides, Nov. 28, 1970; children: Costa, Lara, Regina. B in Commerce, U. of the Witwatersrand, Johannesburg, 1967; LLB with honors, U. London, 1969. Editorial asst. area newspapers, Harare, Zimbabwe, 1960-76; ptnr. Surgey Pittman & Kerswell, Harare, 1969-77; asst. group sec. ACE (Liberia) Inc., Athens, Greece, 1978-80; assoc. Dr. M.H. Hoshan Law Office, Riyadh, Saudi Arabia, 1980-84; pvt. practice Internat. Legal Assocs., Riyadh, 1984—; bd. dirs. various cos.; atty. High Ct. of Zimbabwe, Harare, 1969—, other cts. worldwide, 1985—. Sec. Hellenic Club, Harare, 1969-74, chmn., 1975-76. Office: Ikarou 7 Nea Kifisia, 14564 Athens Greece

THEOBALD, HOLGER, physician, researcher; b. Stockholm, May 8, 1955; s. Herman Theodor and Helga Helena (Schmidt) T.; m. Ursula Christina Engber, June 23, 1996. MD, Karolinska Inst., Sweden, 1980. Jr. physician Jonkoping Hosp., Sweden, 1980-82; physician Vasteras Hosp., Sweden, 1983-86; head physician Dalen Health Ctr., Stockholm, 1987-94; cmty. health physician Karolinska Inst., Sweden, 1990—, clin. instr., 1992—, rsch. physician dept. family medicine, 1994—. Treas. Acad. Folkdans Group, Stockholm, 1997—. Mem. Swedish Physician Assn., Swedish Assn. Gen. Practitioners. Avocations: travel, dancing, ham-radio, gardening, cars. Office: Karolinska Inst, Divsn Family Med, Novum, 14157 Huddinge Sweden

THEOCARAKIS, BASIL, entrepeneur; b. Piraeus, Greece, Oct. 18, 1930; s. Nicholas Theocarakis and Anna (Tsoumas) Kontogeorgiou; m. Marina Alexandri, Jan. 15, 1961; children—Anna-Maria, Despina. J.D., Athens U., 1955. Pres., mng. dir. Theocarakis Group of Cos., 1980—. Served as officer Greek Army. Mem. Chamber Fine Arts. Avocation: oil painting. Home: 6 Ath Diakou Str, 152 37 Filothei Athens Greece Office: 169 Leoforos Athinon, 10447 Athens Greece

THEODORATOS, ATHANASIOS, business executive, consultant; b. Athens, Greece, June 3, 1967; s. Nickolas and Helen (Androuli) T.; m. Christina Kaltsidi, June 3, 1971. BSc in Bus. Adminstrn., Deree Coll., Athens, Greece, 1992; MBA, Keele U., Staffordshire, Eng., 1995. V.p. Tesco SA, Athens, 1989—; country rep. Elopak AG, Zurich, 1992—. With Hellenic Navy, 1987-89. Christian-Orthodox. Home: 12C Ag Georgiou St, 15236 Athens Greece Office: Tesco SA, 10 Paradisou St, 15125 Athens Greece

THEODORE, ARES NICHOLAS, research chemist; b. Kalamata, Greece, Oct. 28, 1933; came to U.S., 1954; s. Nicholas A. and Angeliki (Myseros) Theodoracopulos; m. Peggy Salvarakis, Sept. 3, 1961; children: Nicholas A., Angie A. BA cum laude, Westminster Coll., Salt Lake City, 1958; MS, U. Utah, 1961; postgrad., Case Western Res. U., 1967-68. Asst. prof. chemistry Westminster Coll., 1961-64; sr. rsch. chemist Diamond Shamrock Corp., Cleve., 1964-69; rsch. scientist Ford Motor Co., Detroit, 1969-73, sr. rsch. scientist, 1973-84, prin. rsch. scientist, 1984—. Contbr. articles to profl. jours.; patentee in field (59). Mem. ch. bd. Holy Cross Greek Orthodox Ch., Farmington Hills, Mich., 1986-88; campaigner Farmington Hills Dem. Com., 1986-88; mem. bus. coun. Boston Dem. Com., 1988—, Nat. Dem. Com., 1988—. U. Utah fellow, 1958-61, NSF fellow, 1964. Mem. Am. Chem. Soc. (treas. 1967), Ahepa (bd. govs. Dearborn, Mich. 1985-86). Avocations: swimming, golf, photography. Home: 34974 Valley Forge Dr Farmington Hills MI 48331-3210

THEODORE, EUSTACE D., educational advancement consultant; b. Marietta, Ohio, Aug. 4, 1941; s. Demetrios E. and Nicoletta D. T.; m. Carol Nagy, June 13, 1964; children: Kyle James, Graham Clark. B.A., Yale U., 1963; M.A., Cornell U., 1965, Ph.D., 1967. Mem. faculty Hollins Coll., Roanoke, Va., 1967-71, Mt. Holyoke Coll., South Hadley, Mass., 1971-72; dean Calhoun Coll., Yale U., New Haven, 1972-81; exec. dir. Assn. Yale Alumni, 1981-97; pres. Coun. for Advancement and Support of Edn., Washington, 1997-2000; prin. eAdvancement.org, 2000—; mgmt. and ednl. cons., 1965—. Contbr. articles to jours. Mem. Coun. Alumni Assn. Execs. (bd. dirs. 1991-97, pres. 1995-96), Coun. for Advancement and Support Edn. (trustee 1993-97, chair internat. task force 1994-97), CASE (Europe) (trustee 1995-2000), Commn. on Alumni Rels. (chair 1992-96). Office: eAdvancement.org 1301 21st St NW Washington DC 20036-1503

THEODORIDIS, GEORGE CONSTANTIN, biomedical engineering educator, researcher; b. Braila, Romania, Dec. 3, 1935; came to U.S., 1959; s. Constantin George and Anastasia (Haritopoulos) T.; m. Lilly Kate Hyman, Sept. 20, 1975; 1 child, Alexander. BS in Mechanical and Elec. Engring., Nat. Tech. U. Athens, 1959; DSc, MIT, Cambridge, Mass., 1964. Rsch. assoc. MIT, Cambridge, Mass., 1964; sr. scientist Am. Sci. Engring., Cambridge, Mass., 1964-68; assoc. prof. in residence U. Calif., Berkeley, 1968-70; biomedical engring. U. Va., Charlottesville, 1970—; prof. elec. engring. U. Patras, Greece, 1976-83; cons. Food and Drug Adminstrn., Washington, 1975-76, Applied Physics Lab, Columbia, Md., 1978-79. Author: Applied Math, 1983; contbr. articles to profl. jours. Den leader Boy Scouts Am., Charlottesville, Va., 1984-85. Fulbright fellow U.S. Govt., MIT, 1959-60; Nato fellow NATO, MIT, 1961-64; Spl. fellow NIH, U. Calif., 1968-70; recipient teaching award GE, MIT, 1963. Mem. Inst. Elec. and Electronics Engrs., Sigma Xi. Greek Orthodox. Avocations: history, travel. Home: 1817 Fendall Ave Charlottesville VA 22903-1613 Office: U Va Dept Biomed Engring PO Box 377 Charlottesville VA 22902-0377

THEODOROU, DOROS NICOLAS, chemical engineering educator, researcher; b. Athens, Greece, Oct. 29, 1957; s. Nicolas T. and Despina N. (Grigorakis) T.; m. Fani C. Ilia, Nov. 9, 1997; 1 child, Nicolas. Diploma in Chem. Engring., Nat. Tech. U., Athens, 1982; MSChemE, MIT, 1983, PhD in Chem. Engring., 1985. Lic. chem. engr., Greece. Asst. prof. U. Calif., Berkeley, 1986-90, assoc. prof., 1990-94, prof., 1994-95; assoc. faculty Lawrence Berkeley Lab., 1986-95; prof. U. Patras, Greece, 1994—; collaborating rschr. Nat. Rsch. Ctr. for Phys. Scis. Demokritos, Athens, 1993—; project leader Lawrence Berkeley Lab., 1986-95; cons. E.I. duPont de Nemours & Co., 1989-95; dir. Molecular Modeling of Materials Lab., NRCPS Demokritos, 1993—, Lab. Statis. Thermodynamics and Macromolecules, U. Patras, 1994—; sci. advisor Molecular Simulations, Inc., 1999—. Contbr. articles to profl. jours. Nat. rep. of Greece, TMR com. DGXII of European Commn., Brussels, 1995-98. With Hellenic Naval Acad., 1985-86. Recipient Presdl. Young Investigator award NSF, 1988-92, Robert W. Vaughan lectureship Calif. Inst. Tech., 1994, Sci. award Bodossakis Found., Athens, 1996. Mem. AIChE, Am. Chem. Soc., Tech. Chamber of Greece. Avocations: playing piano, travelling, hiking, literature. Office: Univ Patras, Dept Chem Engring, GR-26500 Patras Greece

THEODOROU, JOHN SPERO, orthodontist, researcher; b. Oak Park, Ill., May 8, 1927; arrived in Greece, 1976; s. Spero Nickolas and Amelia (Patratos) T.; m. Maria Navarro, June 1, 1962; children: Amelia, Spero, Peter. DDS, Loyola U., Chgo., 1951, MS in Oral Biology, 1967. Cert. Nat. Bd. Dental Examiners. Pvt. practice Chgo., 1951-65, sr. ptnr., 1967-75; pvt. practice Athens, Greece, 1975—; instr., lectr. in field. Founder Mission Dental Clinic, Chgo. Christian Indsl. League. With M.C., U.S. Army, 1945-47, Korea. Fellow Royal Soc. Health; mem. ADA, World Fedn. Orthodontists, Fedn. Dentaire Internat., Am. Assn. Orthodontics, Am. Orthodontic Soc., Am. Acad. Occlusodontia, Am. Acad. Nutritional Rsch., European Orthodontic Soc., Greek Assn. Orthodontics, Greek Dental Soc., Stomatologic Soc. Greece, the Jarabek Found. Orthodontic Rsch. Avocations: bible study, writing, antique cars, diet-nutrition, running. Home: Filias 45, N Filothei-Marousi, Filothei, 151 23 Athens Greece Office: Kapodistriou 52, 151 23 Filothei-Marousi, 151 23 Athens Greece

THEODOROU, PETROS, economist, consultant, researcher; b. Constantinople, Turkey, June 11, 1968; arrived in Greece, 1971; s. Theodoros and Georganou (Heleni) T. BSc, Aristotle U., Thessaloniki, Greece, 1992; PhD, U. Macedonia, Thessaloniki, 1997. Sr. mgr. Computer Logic, Thessaloniki, 1992-93; mgr. R&D dept. Astron Indsl. C.A., Thessaloniki, 1994-95; rsch. asst. U. Maceconia, 1993-97; postdoctoral rschr. Aristotle U., 1998; asst. prof. Tech. Ednl. Instn., 1998—. Contbr. articles to profl. jours. With Greek Army, 1997-98. Scholar State Scholarship Found., Greece, 1988-91, 1999. Mem. Mgmt. Tech. Orgn., N.Y. Acad. Scis. Greek Orthodox. Avocations: guitar, diving. Home: 25 Mayrokordatou St, 54645 Thessaloniki Greece Office: Aristotle U Dept Econs, Divsn Bus Adminstrn, 54006 Thessaloniki Greece

THEODORSSON, PALL, physics scientist; b. Reykjavik, Iceland, July 4, 1928; m. Svandis Skuladottir; children: Floki, Sigrun, Skuli, Bera. Student, U. Iceland, 1947-50, U. Copenhagen, 1950-55. Rsch. scientist Danish Atomic Energy Commn., Denmark, 1955-58, U. Iceland, 1958-61; dir. devel. Electronic Ltd., Iceland, 1961-63; rsch. scientist U. Iceland, 1964—. Author: Measurement of Weak Radioactivity, 1996. Achievements include development of various low level radioactivity measurement systems. Home: Braedratunga 25, 200 Kopavogur Iceland Office: Sci Inst Univ Iceland, Dunhaga 3, 107 Reykjavik Iceland

THEODORU, STEFAN GHEORGHE, civil engineer, writer; b. Braila, Romania, June 11, 1921; came to U.S., 1965; s. Alexandru and Georgeta (Iovitz) T.; m. Nina Bogos, Jan. 31, 1945; children: Anexander, Radu. Civil engineering degree, Politech. Inst., Bucharest, Romania, 1947. Civil engr. Romanian Govt., Bucharest, 1947-64, Rella et Co., Vienna, Austria, 1964-65, Hydrotech. Corp., N.Y.C., 1965-66, Leon Selzer Assoc. P.E.C.P., N.Y.C., 1966-76, pvt. practice, Long Island City, N.Y.C., 1976—. Author: Fata fara glas, 1993, Teatru Vol. I, 1993, Meeting in the Twilight, 1994, The Bag of Stars, 1995, Doamna, Teatru Vol. II, 1995, Transylvania, 1995, (haiku) Centum, 1997; author, editor: Versuri Vol. I, 1973, A Wallachian Flag, 1977, Versuri Vol. II, La Lumina, 1993, Odiseea unui cuget, 1993, Un Milionar nebun, 1996, Genius, 1996, Născută în castelul lui Dracula, 1997, Duninica la ora sase, Teatru Vol. III, 1997, Mărul din poveste, 1998, Adam si sotiile sale, 1998, Cersetorul, Teatru vol. 4, 1998, Iac'asa, 1999, Drapelul de Margine, 1999, Antologies: A Vision, a Verse, Vol. II, 1979, Dreams, 1963, 1980, Haiku World, 76, 1996, Numar Antologic 24, 1996, O Suta de Catarge, 92, 1997, Lumina Zorilor, 107-130, 1997, International Poetry and Art, 81, 88, 1997, Haiku Sans Frontières, 400, 1998, Light and Shadow, 36, 1998, Caligrafiile Clipei, 76-81, 1999, Culegatorii de Roua, 22, 1999, Almanah Origini, 75-84, 2000, Luna in Tandari, 2000, Dimensiuni din Lumina Spiritului, 71-74, 2000, Poetii Romani de Haiku, 58, 2000, Internet: Antologie de Haiku, 1997; contbr. various works to profl. anthologies; co-inventor Patern Recognition System, 1979. Mem. Am. Romanian Relief Found., N.Y. Acad. Scis., Romanian Gen. Engring. Assn. (ct. tech. expert 1948, 64), Profl. Internat. Journalists Union Romania, Internat. Writers Assn. Ohio, Internat. Assn. Romanian Writers & Artists Ga., Am. Legion, Romanian Vexilologic Soc. Home: 28-18 29th St Long Island City NY 11102

THEODOSSIADOU, EVANGELIA KONSTANTINOS, internal medicine physician; b. Athens, Greece, Jan. 6, 1961; d. Konstantinos and Rea-Aikaterini (Oikonomou) T. MD, U. Athens, 1985. Registrar ippoczation dept. Hosp. U. Athens; physician Athens, 1995—. Contbr. articles to med. jours. Home: Tertseti 7 str, GR-11141 Athens Greece

THEODOSSIOU, IOANNIS, economist, educator; b. Athens, Greece, July 3, 1954; s. Kyriakos and Maria (Zagouraki) T.; children: Maria-Adamandia, Kyriakos-Kimon. MA, U. Piraeus, Greece, 1980; MPhil, U. Glasgow, Scotland, 1983, PhD, 1988. With Nat. Bank of Greece, Athens, 1976-80; fellow U. Aberdeen, Scotland, 1987-90, lectr., 1990-95, sr. lectr., 1995-98, reader, 1998-99, prof., 1999—, also dir. Ctr. for European Labour Market Rsch. Author: (monograph) Wage Inflation and the Two-Tier Labour Market, 1992; editor (with R. Asplund and P.J. Sloane): Low Pay and Earnings Mobility in Europe, 1998; contbr. articles to profl. jours., including Econ. Jour., Economica, Applied Econs., Oxford Econ. Papers, Oxford Bull. Econ. Stats., J. Post Keynesian Econs., others. Grantee Econ. and Social Rsch. Coun., 1991, European Union, 1995. Fellow Royal Statis. Soc.; mem. Royal Econ. Soc., European Assn. Labour Economists. Avocations: squash, judo, music, hillwalking. Office: U Aberdeen Dept Econs, Dunbar St, Aberdeen AB24 3QY, Scotland

THEOFANOUS, THEO G., engineering educator, consultant; b. Athens, Greece, May 21, 1942; s. George T. and Smaro (Voudouris) T.; m. Danae P. Kembe, May 15, 1969; children: George, Lydia. BS in Chem. Engring., Nat. Tech. U., Athens, Greece, 1965; PhD in Chem. Engring., U. Minn., 1969; D in Laaperanta (hon.), U. Finland, 1999. Instr. in chem. engring. U. Minn., Mpls., 1968-69; asst. prof. chem. engring. Purdue U., West Lafayette, Ind., 1969-73, assoc. prof. chem. engring., 1973-74, assoc. prof. nuc. engring., 1974-76, prof. nuc. engring., 1976-85; prof. chem. and nuc. engring. U. Calif., Santa Barbara, 1985—, dir. Ctr. for Risk Studies and Safety, 1985—, prof. mech. and environ. engring., 1994—; v.p. Fauske, Grolmes, Henry & Theofanous, Ltd., Hinsdale, Ill., 1979-81; pres. Theofanous & Co., Inc., Santa Barbara, 1981—; cons. in field. Recipient Ernest Orlando Lawrence Meml. award U.S. Dept. of Energy, 1996. Fellow Am. Nuc. Soc.; mem. AIChE, AAAS. Achievements include finding the mechanism that caused the Sevesco accident; invented a methodology for risk assessment and mgmt. of high-consequence hazzards; contbr. in risk analyses of nuc. reactors and in mitigating the consequence of severe accidents. Office: U Calif Dept Chem Engring Santa Barbara CA 93106-5080

THEOFYLACTOS, CONSTANTINOS, energy engineer; b. Athens, Attica, Greece, Sept. 5, 1957; s. Grigorios and Sofronia (Beza) T. Diploma Mech. Engring., Middlesex Polytechnic, London, 1982; BS Mech. Engring., U. Evansville, 1985, MS Mech. Engring., 1986. Postgrad. asst. in mech. engring. U. Evansville, Ind., 1985-86; asst. researcher Hellenic Nat. Def. Gen. Staff, Athens, 1987-88; sr. cons./engr. C.G. Theofycactos/Cons. Engrs., Athens, 1988—; lectr. Inst. for Tech. Applications, Athens, 1989—, Cen. Instn. for Energy Efficiency Edn., Athens, 1993—, Tech. Chamber of Greece, Athens, 1989—; scientific advisor Inst. for Tech. Applications, Athens, 1991-94; project mgr. ITE's EEC Program "Save", Athens, 1993; cons. physics dept. U. Athens, 1994—; invited chmn. Orgn. Com. of World Congress of Ises, Kobe, Japan, 1989. Author: Energy Conservation in Industry, 1995; co-author: Energy Conservation in Office Buildings, 1995, Energy Conservation Strategies for Sports Centers - EEC Program SAVE, 1996; editl. bd. mem. Sun at Work in Europe Jour., Athens, 1992-94. With Greek mil., 1987-88. Fellow U. Evansville, 1985-87, Inst. Intern Edn., U. Stanford, 1986. Mem. Tech. Chamber of Greece, Internatl Solar Energy Soc., Hellenic Assn. of Cogeneration Heat and Power (pres.-elect 1999—), ASHRAE (assoc., founder Hellenic sect.), ASME (assoc.). Avocations: soccer, basketball, theatre, music/jazz and rock. Office: CG Theofylactos & Assocs, 7 Ioustinianou Str, Athens 11473, Greece

THEOHARIDES, THEOHARIS CONSTANTIN, pharmacologist, physician, educator; b. Thessaloniki, Macedonia, Greece, Feb. 11, 1950; s. Constantin A. and Marika (Krava) T.; m. Efthalia I. Triarhou, July 10, 1981; children: Niove, Konstantinos. Diploma with honors, Anatolia Coll., 1968; BA in Biology, History of Sci. and Med., Yale U., 1972, MS in Immunology, 1975, MPhil in Endocrinology, 1975, PhD in Pharmacology, 1978, MD, 1983; postgrad., Harvard U. Asst. in rsch. biology Yale U., New Haven, 1968-71; asst. in rsch. pharmacology Yale U., 1973-78, spl. instr. modern Greek, 1974, 77, exec. sec. univ. senate, 1976-78, rsch. assoc. faculty clin. immunology, 1978-83; asst. prof. biochemistry and pharmacology Tufts U., 1983-88, co-dir. med. pharmacology curriculum, 1983-85; co-dir. med. pharmacology curriculum, 1983-85, dir. med. pharmacology, 1985-93, assoc. prof. pharmacology, biochemistry and psychiatry, 1989-94, dir. grad. pharmacology, 1994—, prof. pharmacology and internal medicine, 1995—; vis. faculty Aristotelian U. Sch. Medicine, Thessaloniki, 1979; trustee Anatolia Coll., 1984-85; clin. pharmacologist Commonwealth Mass. Drug Formulary Commn., 1985—; co-chmn. neuro-immunology 2d and 3d World Conf. on Inflammation, Monte Carlo, 1986, 89; mem. internat. adv. bd. 4th, 5th, 6th and 7th World Conf. on Inflammation, Geneva, 1991, 93, 95, 97; spl. cons. Min. of Health, Greece, 1993-95; mem. supreme spl. sci. health coun. Hellenic Republic, 1998—; chmn. Internat. Com. to Upgrade Med. Edn. in Greece, 1994; bd. dirs., spl. cons. Inst. Pharm. Rsch. & Tech., Athens, 1994—; mem. supreme health bd. Hellenic Inst. Social Welfare, 1999—. Author books on pharmacology; mem. editorial bd. numerous jours.; contbr. articles to profl. jours.; patentee in field. bd. dirs., v.p. for rels. with Greece, Krikos, 1978-79; sec. Assn. Greeks to Yale, 1974-79, pres., 1982-83. Recipient Theodore Cuyler award Yale U., 1972, George Papanicoalou Grad. award, 1977, Med. award Hellenic Med. Soc. N.Y., 1979, 83, M.C. Winternitz prize in pathology Yale U., 1980, Disting. Svc. award Tufts U Alumni Assn., 1986, Spl. Faculty Recognition award Tufts U. Med. Sch., 1987, 88, Archon of Ecumenical Patriarchate of Christian Orthodox Ch., 2000. Mem. AMA, AAUP, AAAS, Hellenic Biochem. and Biophys. Soc., N.Y. Acad. Scis., Am. Inst. History Pharmacy, Soc. Health and Human Values, Am. Assn. History Medicine, Am. Soc. Cell Biology, Soc. Neurosci., Am. Fedn. Clin. Rsch., Conn. Acad. Arts and Scis., Am. Soc. Pharmacology and Exptl. Therapeutics, Hellenic Soc. Cancer Rsch., Hellenic Soc. Med. Chemistry, Internat. Soc. Immunopharmacology, Am. Soc. Microbiology, Am. Assn. Immunologists, Internat. Soc. History of Medicine, Mass. Med. Soc., N.E. Hellenic Med. Soc. (sec. 1984-85, v.p. 1985-86, 94-96, pres. 1986-87), Hellenic Sci. Assn. Boston (bd. dirs. 1985), Internat. Anatolia Alumni Assn. (sec. 1984-85), Alpha Omega Alpha, Sigma Xi. Achievements include research on mechanisms of release of secretory products: immunopharmacology membrane functions of polyamines; pathophysiology of mast cells in neuroimmunoendocrine diseases exacerbated by stress such as irritable bowel syndrome, interstitial cystitis, migraines and multiple sclerosis. Home: 14 Parkman St Apt 2 Brookline MA 02446-3802 Office: Tufts U Sch Med 136 Harrison Ave Boston MA 02111-1817

THEOPHANIDES, THEOPHILOS, chemistry educator, consultant; b. Platamon, Kavala, Greece, Mar. 12, 1932; arrived in Can., 1958; s. Michael and Sophia (Chatzicharalampidou) T.; m. Jacqueline Elizabeth Ballmer, July 2, 1934 (div. May 1994); children: Sheila, Mike. Dottore, U. Bologna, Italy, 1957; MA, U. Toronto, 1961, PhD, 1963; Dr honoris causa, U. Reims, France, 1994. Chemist SEKE, Athens, 1957-58, Knowl View Farms, toronto, 1958-60; teaching asst. U. Toronto, 1960-63; rsch. assoc. Howard U., Washington, 1963-65; asst. prof. U. N.B., Fredericton, Can., 1965-66; assoc. prof. chemistry U. Montreal, 1966-89, prof., 1977-89; dir. Nat. Hellenique Rsch. Found., Athens, 1976-78; prof. Nat. Tech. U. Athens, 1983—. Author: Elements de Transition, 1968; editor: Infrared and Raman Spectra of Biological Molecules, 1978, Fourier Transform Spectroscopy, 1984, Spectroscopy of Biological Molecules, 1984, Spectroscopy of Inorganic Bioactivators, 1988, Chemistry of Biological Systems and Molecular Chemical Engineering, 1990, 2nd International Symposium on Metal Cousin Biology and Medicine, 1992, Chemistry of Biological Systems and Molecular Chemical Engineering, 1992, European Conference on Spectroscopy of Biological Molecules, 1993, Biomolecular Structure and Dynamics, 1996, International Symposium on Magnesium, 1997; contbr. numerous articles to profl. jours. Recipient Silver medal French Acad. Medicine, 1984, Univ. medal U. Bologna, 1986, Univ. medal U. Ferrara, 1995, Golden medal Soc. Letters Athens, medal City of Lisbon, Portugal, 1996. Fellow Chem. Inst. Can.; mem. Greek Chamber Engrs. Greek Orthodox. Avocations: cycling, music, basket, travel, fishing. Home: Semelis 12, 11528 Athens Attiki, Greece

THEOPHILUS, MICHAELA JULITA PATRICIA, quality management consultant; b. Choiseul, St. Lucia, W.I., Sept. 30, 1954; d. Patrick Gillaume and Clara Simonese (Alfred) Joseph; m. Denison Laurent Theophilus, Jan. 7, 1989; children: Denise, Patrice. AA, Acad. Pacific Bus. Coll., 1987; MBA, U. W.I., 1999. Flight attendant LIAT, Antigua, 1972-80; sta. mgr. Montserrat Aviation, Antigua, 1980-86; adminstrv. exec. New Port Mgmt., An-

tigua, 1988-89; quality dir. Tropical Shipping, Nassau, 1991-92, quality/personal dir., 1992-95, sales, quality and human resource dir., 1995-98; prin., owner Michaela Theophilus & Assocs., Nassau, 1998—; quality mgmt. cons. Solomon Bros., Nassau, 1994, City Markets Ltd., Nassau, 1995, Grand Bahama Foods, Freeport, 1995, B.V.I. Hotel & Commerce Assn., Tortola, 1996; keynote spkr. Rotary Club, Nassau, 1994, B.V.I. Hotel & Commerce Assn., 1996; advisor quality project Students of Coll. of The Bahamas, Nassau, 1995-96. Contbr. articles to profl. jours. including Caribbean Quality Leadership Forum (Cert. of Merit 1993, 94, 95), Tropical Topics, Nat. Quality Congress (Silver award 1996). Dir. Bahamas Quality Coun., 1996—. Recipient Pres.'s award Container Terminals Ltd., 1995. Mem. ASTD, Am. Mgmt. Assn., Alpha Beta Kappa. Roman Catholic. Avocations: reading, creative writing, swimming, weight-training, gourmet cooking. Home: PO Box CB-11848, Nassau Bahamas Office: Michaela Theophilus Assocs, PO Box CB 11848, Nassau Bahamas

THEOTOKOGLOU, EFSTATHIOS ELEFTHERIOS, civil engineering educator; b. Athens, Greece, Jan. 19, 1956; s. Eleftherios Efstathios and Sofia Ioannis Theotokoglou. MSc, Nat. Tech. U. Athens, 1979, PhD, 1984. Diplomate civil engring. Rsch. scholar Nat. Tech. U. Athens, 1979-82, rsch. and tchg. assoc., 1987-88, lectr., 1988-92, asst. prof., 1992-99, assoc. prof., 1999—; postdoctoral fellow Norges Tekniske Hogskole-Dept. Marine Structures, Trondheim, Norway, 1989-91, vis. asst. prof., 1993-95; vis. asst. prof. dept. mech. engring. Fla. Atlantic U., Boca Raton, 1995. Author: Finite Element Method, 1994; contbr. articles to profl. jours. Mem. Internat. Assn. for Computational Mechanics, Hellenic Soc. Theoretical Applied Mechanics, Tech. Champer of Greece. Office: Nat Tech Univ Athens, 5 Heroes Polytechnion Ave, 15773 Athens Greece

THERBORN, GÖRAN ARNE AXEL, social scientist; b. Kalmar, Sweden, Sept. 23, 1941; s. Ragnar Ture Axel and Karin Otilia (Nilsson) T.; m. Sonia Isabel Pina, Aug. 12, 1982; children by former marriage: Thomas, Anna. PhD, Lund (Sweden) U., 1974. Assoc. prof. Gothenburg (Sweden) U., 1975, prof. sociology, 1987—; acting prof. sociology Umea (Sweden) U., 1976; assoc. prof. Lund U., 1975-81; prof. polit. sci. Cath. U., Nijmegen, The Netherlands, 1981-87; dir. Swedish Collegium for Advanced Study in Social Scis., 1996—; chmn. Nat. Rsch. Com. on Global Processes, 1995—; sci. evaluator Office of Prime Min., Belgium, 1996, Inter-U. Coun., The Netherlands, 1992-93, Sci. Found., Estonia, 1991; vis. prof. and fellow numerous univs. throughout the world. Author: Globalizations and Modernities, 1999, European Modernity and Beyond, 1995, Peripecias de la modernidad, 1991, Teorias Contemporaneas del Estado, 1990, Why Some Peoples are More Unemployed Than Others, 1986, The Ideology of Power and the Power of Ideology, 1980, What Does the Ruling Class Do When It Rules?, 1978, Science, Class and Society, 1976; columnist Dagens Nyheter, Stockholm, 1989. Active Sci. Coun. Swedish Labour Market Bd., 1992-96, Govt. Coun. on Rsch., 1989-91; cons. Swedish Fgn. Office, 1996, European chair Social Policy in Budapest, 1996. Fellow Inst. f. Hohere Studien zu Wien, 1991, Simon Sr. Rsch. fellow Manchester U., 1985; grantee Swedish Rsch. Couns. Mem. Internat. Sociol. Assn. (exec. com. 1994—), European Sociol. Assn. (exec. com. 1995-97), Scandinavian Sociol. Assn. (pres. 1992-94). Avocations: travel, skiing, arts. Office: Swedish Collegium Advanced, Gotavagen 4, 75236 Uppsala Sweden

THERNLUND, GUNILLA MARGARETHE, child/adolescent psychiatrist; b. Stockholm, Mar. 15, 1942; d. Carl Arvid and Astrid Rut (Wallin) T.; m. Sune Gösta Mattsson, Feb. 8, 1973 (div. Dec. 1981); children: Per, Ingrid. MD, Karolinska Inst., Stockholm, 1968; PhD, U. Lund, Sweden, 1996. Lic. psychotherapist. Intern psychiatry, pediats. Univ. Hosp., Stockholm, 1969-74; cons. child/adolescent psychiatry, dept. pediats. Univ. Hosp., Huddinge, Sweden, 1975-83; sr. psychiatrist Univ. Hosp., Lund, 1983-85, sr. child/adolescent psychiatrst, 1985-88, 91—; sr. child/adolescent psychiatrst Univ. Hosp., Malmo, Sweden, 1988-91. Contbr. articles to profl. jours. Mem. Swedish Assn. Child and Adolescent Psychiatry, Swedish Assn. Behavioral Medicine, Swedish Assn. Physicians. Home: Kungsg 28, S-21149 Malmo Sweden Office: Univ Hosp Lund, Ornv 28B, S-22732 Lund Sweden

THEROND, DOMINIQUE, publisher; b. Neuilly, France, Feb. 6, 1942; s. Paul and Suzanne (Revillon) T.; m. Francine Claes, May 7, 1966; children: Virginie, Nicolas, Louise, Chloe. Degree, trade sch., Paris. Dir. Les Editions de L'Epargne, Paris, 1979—; pres. pubs. of law French Syndicat Pubs., 1993-96. Named Chevalier des Arts et Lettres, Ministry of Culture, 1997. Avocation: golf. Office: Les Editions de L'Epargne, 12 Villa de Lourcine, 75014 Paris France

THEROUX, PAUL EDWARD, author; b. Medford, Mass., Apr. 10, 1941; s. Albert Eugene and Anne (Dittami) T.; m. Anne Castle, Dec. 4, 1967 (div. 1993); children: Marcel, Louis; m. Sheila Donnelly, Nov. 18, 1995. BA, U. Mass., Amherst, DLitt, 1988; DLitt, Trinity Coll., Washington, 1980, Tufts U., 1980. Lectr. U. Urbino, Italy, 1963, Soche Hill Coll., Malawi, 1963-65; mem. faculty English dept. Makerere U., Uganda, 1965-68, U. Singapore, 1968-71; vis. lectr. U. Va., 1972-73. Author: (fiction) Waldo, 1967, Fong and the Indians, 1968, Girls at Play, 1969, Murder in Mt. Holly, 1969, Jungle Lovers, 1971, Sinning with Annie, 1972, Saint Jack, 1973, The Black House, 1974, The Family Arsenal, 1976, The Consul's File, 1977, Picture Palace, 1978 (Whitbread prize for fiction), A Christmas Card, 1978, London Snow, 1980, World's End, 1980, The Mosquito Coast, 1981, The London Embassy, 1982, Half Moon Street, 1984, O-Zone, 1986, My Secret History, 1988, Chicago Loop, 1990, Millroy and the Magician, 1993, My Other Life, 1996, Kowloon Tong, 1997, Collected Stories, 1997, Collected Short Novels, 1998, (nonfiction) V.S. Naipaul, 1973, The Great Railway Bazaar, 1975, The Old Patagonian Express, 1979, The Kingdom by the Sea, 1983, Sailing Through China, 1983, Sunrise with Sea Monsters, 1985, The White Man's Burden, 1987, Riding the Iron Rooster, 1988, The Happy Isles of Oceania, 1992, The Pillars of Hercules, 1995, Sir Vidia's Shadow, 1998, Fresh Air Fiend, 2000, (film script) Saint Jack, 1979, Chinese Box, 1998. Recipient Editorial award Playboy mag., 1972, 76, 77, 79, Lit. award AAAL, 1977, James Tait Black award, 1982, Yorkshire Post Best Novel award, 1982, Thomas Cook Travel Book prize, 1989. Fellow Royal Soc. Lit., Royal Geog. Soc.; mem. AAAL.

THESLEFF, B. HOLGER, retired philology educator; b. Helsinki, Finland, Dec. 4, 1924; s. Claudius and Maggie (Wikman) T.; m. Andrea Edgren, May 27, 1950; children: Thomas, Ulrika. MA, U. Helsinki, 1948, PhD, 1954. Docent U. Helsinki, 1955-68, prof. Greek philology, 1968-88; docent Abo Akademi, Turku, 1958-75; rsch. work Acad. Finland, Helsinki, 1963-68. Author: Farewell Windjammer, 1951, Studies on Intensification, 1954, An Introduction to the Pythagorean Writings, 1961, Studies in Platonic Chronology, 1982, Roual Danish Acad. Studies in Plato's Two-Level Model, 1999; contbr. articles to profl. jours. Mem. Soc. Scientiarum Fennica, Royal Danish Acad. Scis. & Letters. Home: Bergmansgatan 3,, 00140 Helsinki, Finland

THEUNISSEN, MICHAEL HEINRICH, philosophy educator; b. Berlin, Oct. 11, 1932; s. Gert H. and Frieda Theunissen; m. Anneliese Stolz, Mar. 7, 1962; children: Viola, Oliver. Dr.phil., U. Freiburg, 1955; Dr.phil.habil., Free U. Berlin, 1964. Prof. philosophy U. Bern (Switzerland), 1967-71, U. Heidelberg (Fed. Republic Germany), 1971-80, Free U. Berlin, 1980-95; prof. theology U. Copenhagen, Denmark, 1995—. Author: Der Andere, 1965 (pub. in English as The Other, 1984), Sein und Schein, 1978, Negative Theologie der Zeit, 1991, Der Begriff Verzweiflung, 1993, Vorentwürfe von Moderne, 1996, Pindar L. Menschenlos und Wende der Zeit, 2000. Home: Beerenstrasse 50, D-1000 Berlin Germany Office: Free U Berlin, Habelschwerdter Alle 30, D-1000 Berlin Germany

THEVENOT, MAUDE TRAVIS, retired home economist; b. Many, La., Dec. 31, 1914; d. Rennie L. and Fairy D. (Minter) Travis; m. Aubrey J. Thevenot, July 4, 1952 (dec. Sept. 1981); 1 stepchild, Peter A. BA, Northwestern State U., 1939; MS, La. State U., 1963. Tchr. home econs. Bienville Parish High Sch., Jamestown, La., 1940-41; parish home mgmt. supr. Farmers Home Adminstrn., USDA, Natchitoches, Oak Grove, Winnefield, La., 1942-47; state home mgmt. supr. Farmers Home Adminstrn., USDA, Alexandria, La., 1948-52; social worker La. Dept. Pub. Welfare, New Roads, Alexandria, Marksville, La., 1952-56; home economist La. State U.-La. Coop. Extension Svc., Makrsville, Alexandria, 1957-74; specialist expanded food & nutrition edn. program La. State U.-La. Coop. Extension Svc., Baton Rouge, 1975-79; co-advisor in home econs. Ptnrs. of Am. La./El Savador and La. Home Econs., 1975. Author: Central District Louisiana Home Economics Association, 1984 Louisiana Federation of Chapters of the National Association of Retired Federal Workers, 1989; co-author: A Taste of Yesterday, 1988. Mem. Kent Plantation House, Inc., Alexandria, 1970—, com. mem. for orgn., 1970, exec. bd., 1985-88, cookbook chmn., 1985-90; mem. Friendship House-Adult Day Care Ctr., Alexandria, 1982-90, exec. bd., 1982-88, organizer, pres. vol. orgn., 1978-90; advisor Anchors as Pilot Club of Alexandria Outreach Com., Anchor Club of Pineville (La.) High Sch., 1978-90; mem. La. Avoyelles & Rapides Parish Farm Bur., Marksville, Alexandria, 1967-90, Avoyelles & Rapides Cowbelles, Alexandria, Marksville, 1967-70; mem. Calvary Bapt. Ch., leader Sunday Sch. class, mem. sr. group decoration com. for monthly luncheons, leader Dottie Hayes Bible Study Group. Recipient Plaque for Svc. Rapides Parish Coun. on Aging, Alexandria, 1971, Plaque for Outstanding Leadership & Svc., Rapides Parish Homemakers Coun., Alexandria, 1974, Plaque of Appreciation as Coord., Expanded Food and Nutrition Ednl. Program La. State U., Baton Rouge, 1978, 11 Certs. of Appreciation, Anchor Club of Pineville High Sch., 1980-90, Cert. of Recognition (3) Friendship House-Day Care for Adults, 1983, 84, 85, Plaque for Outstanding Svc., Rapides Coun. on Aging 20th Ann., 1967-87. Mem. Internat. Fedn. Home Econs., Am. Assn. Family and Consumer Sci., La. Home Econs. Assn. (v.p. 1972-73, Disting. Home Economist 1979-80), Am. Assn. Family and Consumer Svcs. (Wiley-Berger award 1995), Cen. Dist. Home Econs. (pres. 1972-73, Disting. Svc. award 1967, hon. mem. 1985), Nat. Assn. Extension Home Economist, La. Assn. Extension Home Economist, AAUW, La. Assn. Nat. Assn. Retired Fed. Employees (past pres., v.p. region VI, Meritorious Svc. plaque and cert. of citation 1988-89, Meritorious Svc. award 1992-93, life), CENLA (past pres.), Am. Assn. Retired Persons, La. State U. Alumni, La. State U. Home Econs. Retiree, Northwestern State U. Alumni, La. Retired Tchrs. Assn. (life), Pilot Club Internat., Epsilon Sigma Phi (life), Gamma Sigma Delta (Extension award of merit 1978). Democrat. Avocations: traveling, voluntary activities. Home: 507 Tanglewood Dr Alexandria LA 71303-3354

THEVIK, HAAVARD JAN, materials scientist, researcher, consultant; b. Kristiansund, Norway, Apr. 9, 1964; s. Knut O.T. and Signe J. (Valen) T.; m. Hanne Bjornes; children: Karl-Henrik, Herman, Kristian. MS in Physics, Norwegian Inst. Tech., Trondheim, 1989; PhD in Applied and Indsl. Math., U. Oslo, 1996. Cons. Andersen Consulting, Oslo, 1989-91; rsch. scientist Inst. Energy Tech., Kjeller, Norway, 1991-93, SINTEF Materials Tech., Oslo, 1996-98, Det Norske Veritas, Høvik, Norway, 1998—; chmn. bd. dirs. Convergence Group AS, Asker, Norway, 1995—. Contbr. articles to profl. jours. Mem. Norwegian Soc. Chartered Engrs., Minerals, Metals & Materials Soc. Fax: 47-6757 9911. E-mail: havard.thevik@dnv.com. Home: Undelstadveien 135, N-1370 Asker Norway Office: Det Norske Veritas, Veritasvn 1, N-1322 Høvik Norway

THEVOZ, MICHEL, art history educator, curator; b. Lausanne, Switzerland, July 15, 1936; s. Edmond and Maria (Thurler) T.; m. Emilienne Farny, Sept. 19, 1973; 1 child, Melody. Licence en lettres, U. Lausanne, 1959; diplome, Sch. of the Louvre, Paris, 1970; doctor, U. Lausanne, 1974. Curator Mus. Fine Art, Lausanne, 1966-75; dir. Ctr. de la tapisserie, Lausanne, 1970-75; curator Collection de l'art brut, Lausanne, 1975—; prof. art history U. Lausanne, 1980—. Author: Art Brut, 1974, Louis Soutter ou L'ecriture du desir, 1974, Le Langage de la rupture, 1978, L'Academisme et ses fantasmes, 1980, The Painted Body, 1984, Dubuffet, 1986, Jean Lecoultre, 1989, Detournement d'ecriture, 1989, Le Theatre du crime: Essai sur la peinture de David, 1989, Art Psychose et Mediumnite, 1990, Manifeste pour une mort douce, 1992, Requiem pour la folie, 1995, Le miroir infidele, 1996, Plaidoyer pour l'infamie, 2000. Avocation: jazz guitar. Home: 24 Chemin du Levant, CH-1005 Lausanne Switzerland Office: Collection de l'Art Brut, 11 Ave des Bergieres, Lausanne CH 1004, Switzerland

THE WHITE WITCHDOCTOR See TROUSSIER, PHILIPPE

THEYS, PHILIPPE PAUL, data quality professional; b. Lille, France, Feb. 20, 1949; came to U.S., 1994; s. Maurice and Paulette Theys; m. Odile Marie-Paule Theys, July 15, 1972; children: Sophie, Cedric, Alban, Alice. Diploma in Engring., Ecole Centrale De Paris, 1971; Lic., Scis. Econs., Assas, France, 1971; grad. in Plasma Physics, U. Paris-Orsay, France, 1972. Rsch. engr. French Atomic Commn., 1971-72; geophys. field engr. Schlumberger, France, Sweden, Germany, U.S., Australia, 1972-77; country mgr. Schlumberger, Taiwan, 1978-79; interpretation devel. mgr. Schlumberger, Ea. Hemisphere, 1980-81; mktg. mgr. Schlumberger, United Arab Emirates, Indonesia, Norway, 1982-89; quality mgr. Schlumberger, Worldwide, 1990-94, data quality mgr., 1994—; vice chmn. Log Characterization Consortium, 1997-99. Author: Log Data Acquisition and Quality Control, 1991; editor (mag.) The Log Analyst, 1994—. Lt. French Army, 1971-72. Mem. Soc. Profl. Well Log Analysts (v.p. edn. 1997-98, v.p. tech. 1998-99, pres. 2000—), Am. Soc. for Quality, Soc. Petroleum Engrs. Roman Catholic. Avocations: skydiving, long distance running, photography. E-mail: theys5@slb.com. Office: Sugarland Product Ctr 110 Schlumberger Dr Sugar Land TX 77478

THEYSE, LARS FREDERIK HERMAN, veterinary orthopedic surgeon, researcher; b. Nijmegen, Gelderland, The Netherlands, Feb. 10, 1963; s. Henny W. and Truke M. (Jansen) T.; m. Marsja Marina Vis, Feb. 13, 1962; children: Thymen, Basse. DVM, Utrecht U., The Netherlands, 1989. Diplomate European Coll. Vet. Surgeons. Resident Utrecht U., 1990-94, asst. prof., 1994—. Office: Dept Clin Scis Comp Animals, Yalelaan 8 PO Box 80154, NL3508TD Utrecht The Netherlands

THIAGARAJAN, MCDONALDS THULASILINGAM, business management educator; b. McDonald's Choultry, India, Oct. 26, 1936; s. McDonalds Srirangam and Rajamani (Jegannatham) Thulasilingam; m. Mahalakshmi Veerappa, Feb. 17, 1957; children: Rooparani, Arun, Amarnath. BME, U. Madras, 1956; dr.ing., Tech. U., Dresden, 1963. Rsch. assoc. Tech. U., 1960-63; head of indsl. engring. Tube Investments, Madras, 1963-69; prof., head of mgmt. PSG Coll. of Tech., Coimbatore, India, 1969-78; chief of R&D Textool Co. Ltd., Coimbatore, 1978-85; prof. mgmt. Bharathiar U., Coimbatore, 1985-86, prof. sch. mgmt., 1998—; dean Sch. of Mgmt. Pondicherry U., India, 1986-96, dir. Ctr. for Entrepreneur Tng., 1996-98; sr. cons. Productivity Coun., Coimbatore, 1969-74; R&D divsn. founder Textool Co., Ltd., 1978-85; founder, dean Sch. Mgmt. Pondicherry U., 1986-96, founder, dir. Ctr. for Entrepreneur Tng., Pondicherry U., 1996-98; vis. prof. Coker Coll., U. S.C., 1997. Governing mem. Productivity Coun., v.p., 1970s. Recipient Vijaya Shree award Indian Internat. Friendship Soc., 1995. Fellow Inst. of Materials Mgmt. U.K., Instn. of Engrs. India, Indian Instn. of Indsl. Engring. Avocations: study of Indian, British and American histories, classical and pop music, study of German, British and American literature. Home: 19 First St Bharathi Nagar, Coimbatore 641 004, India Office: Bharathiar Sch Mgmt, Bharathiar Univ, Coimbatore 641 046, India

THIAGARAJAN, TANGAVELU, science attache, researcher; b. Kuala Lumpur, Malaysia, Mar. 26, 1953; m. Pavany Thiagarajan, Apr. 22, 1981; children: Rathi, Thiba. B Tech. in Chem. Engring., U. Bradford, Eng., 1978, PhD in Total Quality Mgmt., 1996. Cert. lead assessor ISO. Process negr. Felda Oil Products, Johor, Malaysia, 1978-84; prodn. exec. Beechams Malaysia, Selangor, 1984-85; prin. rsch. officer Palm Oil Rsch. Inst. of Malaysia, Selangor, 1985—; regional mgr. Porim Americas, Washington, 1998—; sci. attache Embassy of Malaysia, Washington, 1998—; assessor quality sys. Malaysia palm oil industry, 1985-87; mem. adv. bd. Quality Network, Malaysia, 1996-97. Contbr. articles to profl. publs.; author procs. in field. Avocations: reading, golf.

THIANDOUM, HYACINTHE CARDINAL, archbishop; b. Poponguine, Senegal, Feb. 2, 1921; s. François Fari and Anne Ndiémé Sène; student Sem. Dakar, 1936-49; B.A. in Dogmatics and Social Scis., U. Propaganda, Gregorian U., Rome, 1955. Ordained priest Roman Catholic Ch., 1949; parish vicar, dir. works, Dakar, 1955-60; curate-dean cathedral, gen. vicar Dakar, 1960-62; archbishop of Dakar, 1962—; elevated to Sacred Coll. Cardinals, 1976; mem. Congregation of the Doctrine of the Faith, Rome, 5 yrs.; pres. Conf. Bishops of Senegal and Mauritania, 1962-87, Symposium of Bishops Conf. Africa and Madagascar, 1978-81; pres.-del. Synod of Bishops, 1977; gen. reporter Synod Bishops, 1987, African Synod, 1994; mem. post-African Synod Counsel; mem. permanent com. Conf. Francophone West African Bishops; mem. Bishops Commn. Mass Media, Papal Commn. Social Communications Media, Congregation People Evangelization, Congregation Clergy; formerly mem. council Gen. Secretariat of Roman Synod Bishops. Decorated grand cross Nat. Order Lion, 1976; comdr. Ordre National Français de la Légion d'Honneur, 1980; hon. chaplain Monastic Grand Cross Sovereign Order Malta, 1972. Mem. Consecrated Life Insts. and Apostolic Life Socs. Office: Archevêché, BP 1908 Villa Les Badamiers, Dakar-Fann21233861 Senegal*

THIBAUDEAU, MARY FRANCES, cultural organization administrator; b. Anaconda, Mont., Dec. 6, 1943; d. Frank Albert and Mary (May) T.; m. Alex W. Wells, Jr.; 1 child, Christopher. BA magna cum laude, U. Wash., Seattle, 1969. Therapist, counselor Thibaudeau and Assocs., Atlanta, 1976-88; chmn. Vietnam Reconciliation Bus. Group, Atlanta, 1988—; cons. Ga. Vets. Leadership Program, Atlanta, 1994. Exec. prodr. (documentaries) Vietnam: POWs Return—The Final Healing, 2000, TET '68: Healing Wounds of War. . .30 Years After, 1998, TET Vietnam Reconciliation Documentary; co-author, editor (screenplay) Perfume River, 2000. Exch. dir. Friendship Force Internat., Atlanta, 1993-94; co-founder, chmn. Tet Vietnam Reconciliation Found., 2000. Named Ga. Outstanding Citizen, Ga. Sec. State, 1994. Mem. Atlanta Vets. Assn. (hon.). Avocations: travel, reading, languages, hiking, photography. Home and Office: PO Box 767722 Roswell GA 30076-7722

THIBAULT, PAUL JOHN, linguistics educator; b. Newcastle, NSW, Australia, July 1, 1953; arrived in Italy, 1984; s. Philip Jan and Sylvia Katherine (Lovell) T.; m. Vincenza Andrisano, May 24, 1984 (div.); 1 child, Ilaria. BA with honors class 1, U. Newcastle, 1976; PhD, U. Sydney, Australia, 1985. Tutor Murdoch U., Perth, Australia, 1982-83; postdoctoral fellow U. Bologna, Italy, 1984-85; lectr. U. Sydney, 1986-89; vis. prof. U. Verona, Italy, 1989; assoc. prof. U. Padova, Italy, 1992-95, U. Venice, Italy, 1995—; found. faculty, course tchr. Cyber Semiotics Inst., 1996—; sci. advisor Ency. Semiotics and Cultural Studies, 1994-97, Systemic-Functional Congress, 1997. Author: Social Semiotics as Praxis, 1991, Re-reading Saussure, The Dynamics of Signs in Social Life, 1997; mem. editl. adv. bd. TEXT, 1998; contbr. chpts. to books and articles to profl. jours. Mem. Pegasus Project (Europe): Children and the Media, 1998. Recipient Vis. Scholar award U. Helsinki, 1995, Northrop Frye fellowship U. Toronto, 1996. Home: Via Oblach 8, 40141 Bologna Italy Office: U Venice Dept Linguistics, Dorsoduro 1405, 30122 Venice Italy

THIBEAULT, GEORGE WALTER, lawyer; b. Cambridge, Mass., Sept. 21, 1941; s. George Walter and Josephine (Maraggia) T.; m. Antoinette Miller, June 30, 1963; children—Robin M., Holly Ann. B.S., Northeastern U., 1964; M.B.A., Boston Coll., 1966, J.D., 1969. Bar: Mass. 1969. Assoc. Gaston & Snow, Boston, 1969-73; ptnr. Testa, Hurwitz & Thibeault, Boston, 1973—. Mem. ABA, Mass. Bar Assn., Am. Arbitration Assn. Home: 181 Caterina Hts Concord MA 01742-4773 Office: Testa Hurwitz & Thibeault High St Tower 125 High St Fl 22 Boston MA 02110-2704

THIBIER, MICHEL F., veterinary medicine educator; b. Vernon, France, Dec. 19, 1944; s. Jean Thibier and Anne Marie Sellier; m. Catherine Fouchet, Sept. 1975. DVM, Sch. Maisons-Alfort, France, 1967; DSc, U. Paris, 1977. Asst. prof. U. Paris INADG, 1969-78, 79-83, U. Miami, Fla., 1978-79; dir. Lab. Nat. Rsch. Animal Reproduction, France, 1983-94; dir. gen. CNEVA, France, 1994—; past mem. sci. coun. INRA; past pres. European Embryo Transfer Assn., 1988-94, Internat. Embryo Transfer Soc., 1996-97. Mem. editl. bd. Theriogenology, 1990-96; contbr. articles to profl. jours. Named Officier, Mérite Agenciele, France, 1995, Chevalier, Ordre Nat. du Mérite, 1995, Palmes Académiques, 1998, French Legion d'honneur, France, 1999. Mem. French Vet. Acad., Royal Swedish Acad. Aguailline and Forestry. Office: CNEVA, 23 Ave Gen Gaulle, 94701 Maisons Alfort France

THIEBAULD, CHARLES MARIE, physician; b. Brussels, Belgium, Aug. 12, 1937; s. Emmanuel and Julienne (Ugeux) T.; m. Jacqueline Hermand; children: Anne, Emmanuel, Sandrine, Laurent. MD with distinction, U. Louvain, Belgium, 1963; postgrad., U. Brussels. Diplomate in sports medicine and electrocardiography. Asst. in surgery Clinique Ste. Anne, Brussels, 1963-66; pres. Commn. Medico-Sportive Fed. Belge Tennis, 1970-82; chief dept. sports medicine Hopital d'Ixelles, 1983-86; advisor dept. clin. rsch. Omnichem Pharm., Louvain, 1975-81; conseiller dept. clin. rsch. Nippon Zoki Pharm., Osaka, Japan, 1984-91; pres. Centre Medecine Avancée, Brussels, 1983—; pres. Mission Medicale Belge, Paris-Dakar, 1983, Internat. Meeting Crescendo, 1993, 95, 96, 97. Editor: L'Enfant et Le Sport, 1997; contbr. articles to The Lancet, Clin. Chemistry, Fundamental Clin. Pharmacology, Methods and Findings, others; patentee in field. Named Hon. Citizen, State of Okla., 1971. Fellow Am. Coll. Sports Medicine; mem. European Coll. Sport Sci., N.Y. Acad. Sci. Avocations: jogging, tennis, skiing, sailing. Office: Centre de Medecine, et d'Etudes, Victor Allard 120, 1180 Brussels Belgium

THIÉBAUX, H. JEAN, mathematical statistician, researcher; b. Washington, Aug. 17, 1935; d. Clark and Helen (Griffin) Tibbitts; m. Martial Leon Thiebeaux, Jr., June 16, 1962 (div. Dec. 1985); children: Tamara, Michael, Aaron, Raananna, Laadan. AB, Reed Coll., 1957; MA, U. Oreg., 1960; PhD, Stanford U., 1964. Rsch. asst. Stanford (Calif.) U., 1963-64; asst. prof. U. Conn., Storrs, 1964-65, U. Mass., Amherst, 1965-71; from assoc. prof. to prof. Dalhousie U., Halifax, N.S., Can., 1975-87; program dir. NSF, Arlington, Va., 1992-94; rsch. scientist Nat. Ctrs. for Environ. Prediction (NCEP), Washington, 1987—; cons., vis. scientist NCAR, Boulder, Colo., 1972-74; vis. prof. McGill U., Montreal, Que., 1981-82, Pa. State U., State College, 1989-90; vis. scientist Nat. Meteorol. Ctr., Washington, 1985-87; cons. Can. Atmospheric Environment Svc., Toronto, 1977-87, NASA-Goddard and Langley, 1978-85; organizer 6th and 7th Internat. Meetings on Statis. Climatology, 1995, 98, Am. Geophys. Union, 1998; grant reviewer NSF; manuscript reviewer SIAM, Jour. Climate, JABES, Environ. and Ecol. Statistics, Atmosphere-Ocean, Weather and Forecasting. Author: Spatial Objective Analysis with Applications to Atmospheric Science, 1987, Statistical Data Analysis for Ocean and Atmospheric Sciences, 1994; contbr. articles to profl. jours. Jour. Climate, Tellus, EOS, Monthly Weather Rev., Jour. Royal Meteorol. Soc., Jour. Applied Meteorology, Can. Jour. Statistics, Nova Math, Applied Math Notes, Atmosphere-Ocean, Biometrika, also others. Bd. dirs. Davies Meml. Unitarian Universalist Ch., 1996-98. Fellow Royal Meteorol. Soc.; mem. Am. Geophys. Union, Internat. EnvironMetrics Soc., Washington Ethical Soc. (fin. com. 1990-93), Toastmasters Internat. (officer NOAA Sci. Ctr. chpt. 1990-92), Zonta. Democrat. Achievements include initiated and chaired the committee to establish a library in the World Weather Building; initiated and coordinated summer student research programs at the NOAA Science Center; coordinated the Analysis Forum; negotiated establishment of an interactive-video-telecommunication graduate studies program for NOAA employees with U. Maryland, College Park; inspired creation of the Geophysical Statistics Project at NCAR. Avocations: training ponies, gardening, travel, sports, photography. E-mail: Jean.Thiebaux@noaa.gov. Home: 9708 Old Allentown Rd Fort Washington MD 20744-3925 Office: Nat Ctrs Environ Prediction/USD Commerce 5200 Auth Rd Suitland MD 20746-4304

THIEDE, ANDREAS ALFRED, information technology engineer; b. Berlin, Apr. 24, 1961; s. Ulrich and Ruth (Sommer) T.; m. Karin Teichmann, Aug. 11, 1984; children: André, Anja. Diploma Ing., Dresden U. Technology, Germany, 1986, Dr. Ing., 1990. Sci. asst. Dresden U. Technology, 1986-90; sci. employee FhG-IAF, Freiburg, Germany, 1991-94, group mgr., 1995-99; prof. high frequency electronics U. Paderborn, 1999—. Patentee in field; contbr. articles to profl. jours. Mem. IEEE (sr.). Avocations: photography, stamps, hiking, swimming, fishing. Office: U Paderborn FB14, Warburger Str 100, 33095 Paderborn Germany

THIEDE, JORN, paleoceanographer; b. Berlin, Apr. 14, 1941; s. Klaus and Clotildis (Fieber) T.; m. Sigrid S. Dietrich; children: Rasmus Christoph, Hannes Kristian, Carl Fridtjof, Morten Lavrans. MS, U. Kiel, Fed. Republic of Germany, 1967, PhD, 1971. Assoc. prof. geol. oceanography Oreg. State U., 1974-77; prof., chmn. hist. geology U. Oslo, 1977-82; prof. paleontology and hist. geology Kiel U., 1982-87; prof. paleoceanology GEOMAR Rsch. Ctr. for Marine Geoscis., Kiel, 1987—; dir. Alfred-Wegener-Inst. for Polar & Marine Scis., Bremerhaven, Germany, 1997—. Recipient

Steno medal Danish Geol. Soc., 1984, Leibniz prize German Rsch. Found., 1988, Murchison medal Geol. Soc. London, 1994, Grand Prix d'Oceanographic, Rainer de Monaco, 1998. Fellow AAAS, Geol. Soc. Am., Am. Geophys. Union; mem. Geol. Union, Royal Norwegian Acad. Sci., Mainz Acad. Sci. and Lit., Russian Acad. Nat. Sci., Royal Danish Acad. Sci. Office: AWI, Columbusstrasse, D-27568 Bremerhaven Germany

THIEDE, WALTHER, researcher, publisher, consultant; b. Berlin, Dec. 18, 1931; s.Walther and Elisabeth (Nickel) T.; m. Ulrike Schumacher, Aug. 18, 1962. Pharmacist, U. Frankfurt, Germany, 1959; DSc, U. Bonn, Germany, 1964. Sci. del. Far East Asta-Werke AG, Bielefeld, Germany, 1966-68, Kobe/Osaka, Japan, 1968-73; med. dir. Lipha Arzneimittel, Essen, Germany, 1973-75; dir. mktg. and sales Kettelhack Riker Pharma GmbH, Borken, Germany, 1976-79; CEO UCB Chemie GmbH, Kerpen, Germany, 1979-87; dir. sales and med. sci. Weimer Pharm. GmbH, Rastatt, Germany, 1988-94; pvt. rschr. Cologne, 1994—. Author: BLV Nature Guide Birds, 16 edits., 13 fgn. edits., 1976-99, BLV Nature Guide Waterbirds-Coastal Birds, 5 edits., 6 fgn. edits., 1979-97, BLV Nature Guide-Birds of Prey and Owls, 1999, Bird-Life in County Oberbergisches Land, 1965, Birds of Prey, 3 edits., 1986-97; translator: Bird Migration, 1969, BLV Bird Guide; The Audubon European Guide, 2 edits., 1982, Animal Tracks, 2000; co-editor Ornithologische Mitteilungen, 1984-97, pub. 1998—; mem. editl. bd. Blätter aus dem Naumann-Museum, 1996—, Beiträge zur Gefiederkunde und Morphologie der Vögel, 1997—; contbr. articles to profl. jours. Mem. History of Sci. Soc., other sci. ornithol. scos. Lutheran. Home and Office: An der Ronne 184, D-50859 Cologne Germany

THIEL, ECKHARD, internist, educator; b. Tuebingen, Germany, Apr. 30, 1944; s. Otto and Ruth (Singer) T.; m. Annett Ines, July 30, 1986; children: Julia, Mira, Larissa. MD, Tuebingen U., 1968; diploma, U. Vienna, 1965. Intern, resident Univ. Munich, 1971-77, sr. asst., sr. lectr. dept. oncology and hematology, 1977-81; physician, head dept. hematology/oncology med. clin. City Ctr. U., Munich, 1981; assoc. prof. U. Munich (Germany), 1985-88; prof. internal medicine, head dept. hematology/oncology Free Univ., Berlin, 1988—; chmn. dept. internal medicine Univ. Med. Ctr., Steglitz, 1991—. Editor: Thiel and Therfelder Leukemia, 1984, Thiel and Ludwig Leukemia, 1993; contbr. over 400 articles to profl. jours. Recipient Vincenz Cerny award for oncology, 1979, Albert-Knoll award 1981, Nat. Cancer award of German Cancer Soc., 1989, Award of Poland Republic by Lech Walesa, 1994. Home: Sven Hedin Str 39, 14163 Berlin Germany Office: Frei U Berlin U Klinikum, Hindenburgdamm 30, 12200 Berlin Germany

THIEL, MANFRED, philosopher, poet, publisher; b. Görlitz, Germany; s. Helmut and Else (von Martin) T.; 1 chld. Bärbel. DrPhil, U. Heidelberg, Germany. Editor Studium Generale, 1946-65; pub. Elpis Verlag GmbH, 1977—; scientist, philosopher, poet Heidelberg, 1948—. Author: The Changing of the style of science and the crisis of world, 1958, Poetry and Experience, 1977, Heidegger, 1977, Nietzsche, 1980, Lenin Stalin, 1982, James Dewey, 1983, Bergson Rickert, 1984, Bertrand Russell, 1984, Karl Jaspers (two vol.), 1986, The Nihilism: Heidegger and the Sophistry, 1986, Encounter with East Asia, 1986, Sartre, 1987, Prolegomena to a Philosophy of Immediacy (two vol.) 1988, J.G. Herder, 1991, Fries, 1991, Hegel (two vol.), 1992, Schelling, 1993, The Book about Fortune and Bliss (two vol.) 1993, God, 1997, Kant (two vol.), 1997, Plotin, 1999, Philosophy-An Autobiography, 2000; author numerous poems; contbr. numerous essays and articles to profl. jours. Home: Rohrbacherstr 20, 69115 Heidelberg Germany

THIEL, WALTER, chemistry educator, researcher; b. Treysa, Hessen, Germany, Mar. 7, 1949; s. Karl and Erika (Seega) T.; m. Elisabeth Dünweg, July 1, 1983; children: Thomas, Sonja. MS, U. Marburg, Germany, 1971, PhD, 1973. Rsch. assoc. U. Tex., Austin, 1973-75, U. Marburg, 1975-82; prof. U. Wuppertal, 1983-92, U. Zürich, 1992-99; dir. Max Planck Inst. for Kohlenforschung, Mülheim, 1999—; vis. prof. U. Calif., Berkeley, 1987. Contbr. more than 180 articles to profl. jours. Heisenberg fellow DFG, 1982; recipient Alfred-Krupp-Förderpreis, Krupp-Stiftung, 1988. Home: Leonhard-Stinnes Str 52, D-45470 Mülheim Germany Office: Max Planck Inst fur Kohlenf, Kaiser Wilhelm Platz 1, D-45470 Mülheim Germany

THIEL, WALTER, anatomy educator; b. Wetzwalde, CSR, Oct. 13, 1919; s. Hermann and Elsa (Kunze) T.; m. Iris Kertecz, Dec. 20, 1971. MD, U. Graz, Austria, 1947, Univ. Lectr., 1957, Univ. Prof., 1960. Med. diplomate. Univ. asst. in anatomy U. Graz, Austria, 1947-60, head of Inst. of Anatomy, 1960-90. Editor/author: (book) Lehrbuch der Topographischen Anatomie, 1969; co-author: (book) Radiologische Diagnostik d. Harnorgane, 1974; author: (book) Photographic Atlas of Practical Anatomy I, 1997, Photographic Atlas of Practical Anatomy II, 1999. Recipient awards in field, 1989-90. Mem. Wiss. Gesellschaft d.Arzte in der Stmk, Anatomische Gesellschaft Lubeck. Home: Hugo-Wolf-Gasse 7, A-8010 Graz Styria Austria Office: Inst Anatomy, Harrachgasse 21, A-8010 Graz Styria Austria

THIELE, DETLEF FERDINAND, microbiologist; b. Billerbeck, Westfalen, Germany, May 8, 1959; s. Klaus Dieter and Roswitha (Sellhorst) T.; m. Andrea Gabriele Haage, Apr. 15, 1988; children: Saskia, Vivienne. DVM, U. Giessen, Germany, 1986, habilitation, 1995, privatdozent, 1996. Sci. asst. U. Giessen, 1986-88, rsch. project mgr., 1988-96; mgr. sci. svcs. IDEXX, 1996-97; sci. dir. Transia GmbH, Ober-Moerlen, Germany, 1997—. Avocations: computer, hifi, mountain biking, motorcycle, animals. Home: Ringstr 1, 35781 Weilburg Ahausen Hessen, Germany

THIELEN, PETER GERRIT, history educator; b. Berlin, 1924; s. Hans Peter and Frieda (Erdmann) T.; m. Gisela Freiin von Bischoffshausen, 1956; children: Peter-Christian, Askan. Phd, U. Bonn., Göttingen, Fed. Republic of Germany, 1952, habilitation, 1959. Univ. lectr. U. Bonn, 1959-64, prof., 1980—; prof. Pädagogische Hochschule, Bonn, 1964-80. Author medieval and modern history textbooks.

THIELHEIM, KLAUS OSWALD, physicist; b. Danzig, Feb. 27, 1932. PhD, U. Munich, Hamburg, Kiel, Fed. Republic of Germany. Prof. physics U. Kiel (Germany), 1979-97; dean of faculty Inst. Pure & Applied Nuclear Physics, Kiel, 1971-72, chmn., 1977-82, 88-90, 92-94, 96-97, also bd. dirs., ret. Author: (with H. Engel) Kernenergie-Technik, 1960; editor: Primary Energy, 1982; contbr. numerous articles to profl. jours. E-mail: thielheim@email.uni-kiel.de. Address: Postfach 51 51, 24 063 Kiel Germany

THIEMANN, WOLFRAM HANS-PETER, chemist; b. Oppeln, Germany, Jan. 29, 1938; s. Max and Margot (Glatzel) T.; m. Isabella Paul (div. 1991); children: Corinna, Sonja; m. Que Wen Thiemann. MSc, Free U. Berlin, 1963; PhD, Tech. U. Berlin, 1966; postgrad., Wesleyan U. Asst. Hahn Meitner Inst., Berlin, 1963-68; sr. scientist Nuclear Rsch. Ctr., Julich, Germany, 1968-76; prof. physical chemistry, environ. sci. U. Bremen, Germany, 1986—; hon. prof. YIT, China, PUC, Rio de Janeiro, El Miniya U., Egypt, U. Pune, India, U. Md. Contbr. articles in water rsch. & extraterrestrial chemistry to profl. publs. Mem. Internat. Soc. Study of Origins of Life, Soc. German Chemists. Avocations: bicycling, tennis, travel. Home: Hartungstr 20, D28203 Bremen Germany Office: U Bremen Dept Chemistry, PO Box 330 440, D 28334 Bremen Germany

THIENPONT, LOUIS ACHILES, surgical pathologist, cytologist; b. Ghent, Belgium, June 5, 1943; s. Gerard and Sonneville T.; m. Riet De Baets; children: Eva, Astrid. MD, State U. Ghent, 1969; grad. in Pathology, State U. Hosp. Ghent, 1974. Pathologist Ctrl. Lab., Antwerp, Belgium, 1975-77; surg. pathologist histopath and cytopath labs OLV Ziekenhuis, Aalst, Belgium, 1977—, head dept. surg. pathology and cytology, 1990—. Internat. Acad. of Pathology, Internat. Acad. of Cytology, Belgian Soc. of Clin. Cytology (pres. 1995-97, treas. 1997—), Belgian Soc. Pathology (bd. dirs. 1996—), European Fedn. Cytology Socs. (mem. com. on quality assurance, edn. and tng, sci. programme com.). Home: Onderbergen 63, B 9000 Ghent Belgium Office: OLV Ziekenhuis, Moorselbaan 164, B 9300 Aalst Belgium

THIERBACH, STEPHEN A., lawyer; b. N.Y.C., Dec. 17, 1961; arrived in Eng., 1990; s. Alfred W. and Priscilla E. (Childers) T. BA, U. Va., 1984; JD, Harvard U., 1987. Bar: N.Y. 1988. Assoc. Sullivan & Cromwell, N.Y.C., London, 1987-94; ptnr. Linklaters, London, 1995—. Republican. Avocations: golf, skiing, wine collecting. Office: Linklaters, One Silk St, London EC2Y 8HQ, England

THIERFELDER, TOMAS KARL ERNST, science educator; b. Karlshamn, Sweden, Dec. 18, 1955; s. Karl Theodor and Ursula Babette (Thielsch) T; m. Maria Margareta Kyhlback, Dec. 20, 1998; 1 child, Emelie. BS, Linkoping U., Sweden, 1989; PhD, Uppsala U., Sweden, 1998. Lectr. Uppsala U., Sweden, 1993-98, assoc. prof., 1998—; mng. dir. ECO-GIS, Uppsala, 1989—; sr. cons. Golder Assocs., Uppsala, 1998-99; lectr., cons. in field. Author: The Hydrodynamics of Nearshore Oceans, 1995, An Inductive Approach to the Modeling of Lake Water Quality, 1998; contbr. articles to profl. jours. Alice & Knut Wallenberg Found. scholar, 1995, Wenner-Gren Found. scholar, 1999. Mem. European Geophys. Soc., Internat. Assn. Sediment Water Sci. Avocations: orintology, history, gastronomy, philosophy. Office: Uppsala U Dept Math, PO Box 480, 45106 Uppsala Sweden

THIERRY, BERNARD, ethologist, researcher; b. Mostaganem, Algeria, Jan. 28, 1956; s. Robert and Monique (Pujol) T.; m. Viviane Pallage; 1 child, Florence. DVM, Paul Sabatier U., Toulouse, France, 1982; DSc in Ethology and Primatology, Louis Pasteur U., Strasbourg, France, 1984, Rsch. Habilitation, 1997. Rsch. dir. Nat. Ctr. Sci. Rsch., Strasbourg, 1986—; dir. rsch., mem. sci. com. sci. and citizens meetings Nat. Ctr. Sci. Rsch., aros, 1992-95; mem. sci. com. Oeuvre pour la Protection des Animaux de Laboratoire Found., Paris, 1994—. Author: Destins de Singes, 1990, (film) The Social World of Macaques, 1991; editor: Current Primatology, 1994; contbr. numerous articles to profl. jours. Mem. French Soc. for Study Animal Behavior (pres.), Assn. for Study Animal Behaviour, Internat. Primatological Soc., Francophone Soc. Primatology, Am. Soc. Primatologists. Office: U Louis Pasteur Lab Ethol, 7 rue de l'Université, 67000 Strasbourg France

THIERRY, FOUQUET, opera administrator; b. Paris, May 3, 1951; s. Jean and Eliane (Poussin) F. Student, Lycee Louis-Le-Grand, Paris, 1966-71, Ecole Poly., 1971-74. Adjoint de direction Opera de Paris, 1974-77, adminstr. du ballet, 1977-80, 83-85, charge de mission, 1980-83; dir. programs Paris Opera, 1987-89; dir. Opera Comique, Paris, 1989-94; dir. adj. Opera de Paris, 1994-96; dir. Opera Bordeaux, France, 1995—. With French Navy, 1973-74. Roman Catholic. Home: 4 cours Xavier Arnozan, 33000 Bordeaux France Office: Grand Théatre, BP 95, 33025 Bordeaux France

THIES, JULIE ANN, music educator; b. Janesville, Wis., Apr. 28, 1960; d. Allen Junior and Marion Luella (Hoeft) Pudleiner; m. Thomas Earl Thies, Aug. 28, 1982. MusB cum laude, U. Wis., 1982. Instr. piano Suzuki Music Acad. Chgo., 1983-84, Suzuki Piano Studio, Hazel Crest, Ill., 1985—. Mem. Music Tchrs. Nat. Assn. (nat. cert.), Suzuki Assn. of Ams., Ill. State Music Tchrs. Assn. (2nd v.p. membership 1995-99, rec. sec. 1993-95), South Suburban Music Tchrs. Assn. (pres. 1992-94, v.p. 1990-92, treas. 1988-90, Mem. of Yr. 1999). Avocations: bicycling, hiking, in-line skating. E-mail: jtthies@earthlink.net. Home: 1825 Olive Rd Homewood IL 60430-2316 Office: Suzuki Piano Studio 3000 W 170th Pl Hazel Crest IL 60429-1174

THIES, TIMOTHY R., artist, gallery owner; b. Boone, Iowa, Feb. 19, 1954; s. Ivan Russell and Janice Louise Thies; m. Kristen T. Thies, Dec. 17, 1980. AA, Colo. Inst. of Art, Denver, 1976; student, Ctrl. U. Iowa, 1972-73, U. Iowa, 1974, Nat. Acad. design, 1981. rep. by Christina Gallery, Martha's Vineyard, Mass., Greenhouse Gallery of Fine Art, San Antonio, West Wind Fine Art, Manchester Center, Vt. One man shows at Smith-Klein Gallery, Boulder, Colo., 1998, So. Vt. Art Ctr., Manchester, 2000; exhibited in group shows at Nat. Acad. Design, N.Y.C., 1981, Veerhoff Gallery, Washington, 1986, Pastel Soc. Am., N.Y.C., 1986, Midwest Pastel Soc./Pallette and Chisel Club, Chgo., 1987, Cape Cod Art Assn., Barnstable, Mass., 1988, Salmagundi 11th Ann. Art Exhibit, N.Y.C., 1988, Mystic Maritime Gallery, 1989, Nat. Arts Club, N.Y.C., 1989, The Copley Soc., 1991, 92, Cahoon Mus. of Am. Art, Cape Cod, Cotuit, Mass., 1992, Prince Gallery, Chgo., 1993, Cummaquid (Mass.) Fine Arts Gallery, 1993, Scottsdale (Ariz.) Artist's Sch., 1994, Copley Soc., 1995, Gov.'s Invitational exhbn., Loveland, Colo., 1995, Merrill Gallery, Denver, 1996, The Greenhouse Gallery, Tex., 1996, Copley Soc., 1997, Smith-Klein Gallery, 1997, DeMott Gallery of Fine Art, Vail, Colo., 1997, Oil Painters of Am. Nat. Juried Show, Park City, Utah, 1997, Attleboro (Mass.) Mus., 1998, So. Vt. Art Ctr., Manchester, 1999, Scottsdale Artist's sch., 1999, West Wind Fine Art, Manchester Center, 1999, Harvard Club of Boston, 1999; represented in permanent collections at Cape Cod Mus. of Fine Art, dennis, Mass., Chrysler Corp., N.Y.C., Raytheon Corp., Marlborough, Mass., W.L. Gore & Assocs., Newark, Del., S.W. Gore and Assocs., fairfield, Iowa, Data Gen., Paris, Bio-Electric Co., Mont., Kansas City (Mo.) Star, Pioneer Bank, Longmount, Colo., Computer Solutions, Bethesda, Md., The Hollister Corp., Ill., Foster Design, Boulder; contbr. articles to profl. jours. Recipient Grand prize Am. Artist Mag., 1999. Mem. Pastel Soc. Am., Copley Soc. of Boston (Copley Artist 1995), Oil Painters of Am., Soc. of Gilders. Office: West Wind Fine Art 7352 Main St Manchester Center VT 05255

THIESS, ALFRED MICHAEL, occupational medicine physician, toxicologist; b. Grossau, Sibiu, Romania, Oct. 3, 1921; s. Michael and Sofia T.; m. Gisela Helwert, Aug. 20, 1949; children: Andrea, Michael. MD, J.W. Goethe U., Germany, 1951, MD habil., 1968; MD honoris causa, U. Cluj-Napoca, Romania, 1995. Physician BASF, Ludwigshafen, Germany, 1951-63, med. dir., 1963-86; founder Medichem, Ludwigshafen, Germany, 1972; chmn. Medichem, Ludwigshafen, 1972-86; hon. pres. Medichem, 1986—; prof. U. Heidelberg, 1973—; lectr. Acads. Occupational Medicine Berlin, Munich, Ulm; mem. expert adv. com. on occupational health WHO, 1975-85. Contbr. more than 300 sci. papers on occupational health to profl. jours. and sci. confs. With German Army, 1943-45. Decorated Grand Order of Merit, German Fed. Rep., 1986; recipient Koelsh award German Assn. Occupational and Environ. Health. Fellow Soc. Argentina, da Trabalho, Brazil (corr.); mem. Occup. Health Assn. Germany (bd. dirs. 6 yrs.), Am. Occ. Medicine Assn., Am. Acad. Occupational Medicine, Conseille Europen Federation Industry Chemique, Brussels, Internat. Commn. Occupl. Health (hon.), Rotary Club (pres. Ludwigshafen 1972-73, First Saphir 1997, Paul Harris fellow 1990, Svc. Above Self award 1995). Avocations: sports, classical music. Home: Weimarer Str 73, 67071 Ludwigshafen Germany

THIESSEN, GORDON GEORGE, banker; b. South Porcupine, Ont., Can., Aug. 14, 1938; m. Annette Margaret Hillyar, Oct. 3, 1964; 2 children. BA with honours, U. Sask., 1960, MA, 1961; PhD in Econs., London Sch. Econs., 1972. Lectr. U. Sask., Saskatoon, Can., 1961-62; Economist Bank of Can., Ottawa, Ont., 1963-73; chief monetary and fin. analysis dept. Bank of Can., Ottawa, 1975-79, adviser, 1979-84, dep. gov., 1984-87, sr. dep. gov., 1987-94; gov. Bank of Can., Ottawa, Ont., 1994—; also chmn. bd. dirs. Bank of Can., Ottawa; vis. economist Res. Bank Australia, Sydney, 1973-75. Avocations: sailing; skiing.

THIGPEN, JAMES TATE, physician, oncology educator; b. Columbia, Miss., June 6, 1944; m. Louisa Berdie Kessler, June 14, 1969; children: Monroe Tate, James Howard, Samuel Calvin, Richard Allen, David Albert. BS, U. Miss., 1964, MD, 1969. Intern Strong Meml. Hosp., U. Rochester, N.Y., 1969-70; resident U. Miss. Sch. Medicine, 1970-71, fellow div. hematology/oncology dept. medicine, 1971-73, prof., dir. div. med. oncology dept. internal medicine, 1973—, also asst. prof. ob-gyn.; nat. med. del. from Miss. Am. Cancer Soc., 1983-85, mem. nat. pub. issues com., 1983-85; mem. cancer clin. investigations rev. com. Nat. Cancer Inst., 1990-95, chmn., 1993-95. Nat. bd. govs. ARC, 1981-87. Fellow ACP; mem. AMA, Miss. Med. Assn., Central Med. Soc., Jackson Acad. Medicine, Miss. Acad. Scis., SW Oncology Group, Gynecologic Oncology Group (group vice chmn. for sci. 1988—), Am. Fedn. Clin. Rsch., Am. Assn. Cancer Edn., Am. Soc. Clin. Oncology, Am. Assn. Cancer Rsch., Am. Soc. Hematology, Soc. Gynecologic Oncologists, So. Assn. for Oncology (pres. 1988-90), Am. Radium Soc. Baptist (deacon 1978—, Sunday sch. tchr. 1979-85). Club: Optimist (internat. v.p. 1983-84, internat. pres. 1990-91). Home: 3601 Kings Hwy Jackson MS 39216-3322 Office: Miss Oncology Assocs 2500 N State St Jackson MS 39216-4500

THIGPEN, MARY CECELIA, city official, consultant; b. L.A., Jan. 27, 1949; d. Tom Allen and Inell Theresa (Evans) Johnson; m. Willie Edward Thigpen, Apr. 30, 1971; children: Sonna Aminata, Monifa Ayodele. BA, Xavier U., New Orleans, 1971; MS in Urban Planning, U. New Orleans, 1979. Planner Urban Systems, Inc., New Orleans, 1977-79, Grimball/Garrandon/Savoy Engrs. and Architects, New Orleans, 1979-80; planner, cons. Mayor's Office, City of New Orleans, 1979; grants program evaluator Pinellas County Manpower Council, Clearwater, Fla., 1980-81; personnel mgmt. specialist Pinellas County Personnel Dept., Clearwater, 1981-83; adminstrv. analyst U. Calif., San Diego, 1983-85; sr. and personnel analyst City of Chula Vista, Calif., 1985—; planning cons. Mayor's office, New Orleans, 1979; b.p. bd. dirs. Cajon Valley Ednl. Found., El Cajon, Calif., 1988—; v.p. personnel commn. City of El Cajon, 2000—. Writer poetry. Named Woman of Distinction, San Diego County Women, Inc., 1990; named Mother of Yr., Delta Sigma Theta of San Diego County, 1996. Mem. Nat. Med. Assn. Aux. (v.p. 1986—), Jack and Jill Am, Calif. Women in Govt., Internat. Pers. Mgmt. Assn., Am. Planning Assn., Altrusa Club of Chula Vista, Nat. Coalition of 100 Black Women, Inc. Roman Catholic. Avocations: fashion design, arts promotion, handcrafts, writing poetry and plays. Home: 1551 Heron Ave El Cajon CA 92020-8810

THIM, HARTWIG WOLFGANG, engineering educator; b. Wels, Austria, Mar. 18, 1935; s. Karl and Wilhelmine (Stockhammer) T.; m. Friederike Desbalmes, Apr. 8, 1942; children: Norbert, Silvia, Julia. Engring. Diploma, Tech. U. Vienna, 1960, Dr. Tech., 1964. Asst. prof. Tech. U. Vienna, 1960-64, prof. and head of inst., 1974-85; mem. tech. staff Bell Labs., Murray Hill, N.J., 1964-69; supr. Fraunhofer Inst. Applied Solid State Physics, Freiburg, Germany, 1969-74; prof. microelectronics U. Linz, Austria, 1985—, head microelectronics, 1985—, dean tech. faculty, 1991-93. Editor: Proc. of GaAs-Symposium Inst. of Physics, 1980; contbr. over 70 articles to profl. jours.; patentee in field; inventor transferred electron amplifier. Mem. IEEE (sr.). Roman Catholic. Avocations: music, tennis, soccer, hiking. Home: Linzerstrasse 25A, A-4040 Linz Austria Office: Univ of Linz, Altenbergerstrasse 69, A-4040 Linz Austria

THIMIAN, HORST JULIUS, architect, engineer, researcher; b. Gleschendorf, Germany, Feb. 5, 1949; s. Bruno Leo and Hildegard (Werner) T.; m. Brigitte M.D. Jabusch, Sept. 30, 1970 (div. 1982); 1 child, Tabea O. Rothbart; m. Sylvia D. Freytag, Jan. 15, 1995. Diploma, U. Stuttgart, Germany, 1979. Pvt. practice, 1979-89; project developer Arch Office, Hamburg, Germany, 1989-95; project dir. Arch Office, Germany, 1997—. Author: Wohnen in Hamburg, 1989. Rschr. town planning Tech. U., Hamburg, 1984-86. Mem. Oxford Club, Highlander. Avocations: photography, diving, sailing.

THIMMIG, DIANA M., lawyer; b. Germany, May 5, 1959. BA cum laude, John Carroll U., 1980; JD, Cleve. State U., 1982. Bar: Ohio 1983, U.S. Dist. Ct. (no. dist.) Ohio 1983, U.S. Ct. Appeals (6th cir.) 1983, U.S. Supreme Ct. 1983, U.S. Ct. Appeals (3d cir. 1996); cert. Am. Bankruptcy Bd. for Consumer and Bus. Bankruptcy. Ptnr. Arter & Hadden, Cleve. Contbr. articles to profl. jours. Hon. consul of Germany, 1988—; trustee Geauga United Way Svcs. Coun., 1992-96, Altenheim, 1992-97, Legal Aid Soc., 1998—, Internat. Svcs. Ctr., 1998—, Cuyahoga County Bar Assn., 1995—. Mem. Women's City Club Cleve. (pres. 1995-97). Office: Arter & Hadden 1100 Huntington Bldg 925 Euclid Ave Ste 1100 Cleveland OH 44115-1475

THIMOTHEOSE, KADAKAMPALLIL GEORGE, psychologist; b. Karipuza, India, Feb. 11, 1938; came to the U.S., 1976; s. K.G. and Mariamma Varghese; m. Mariamma Thimotheose, May 20, 1968 (div.); children: Geebee, Sonia. MA in Psychology, ME.D 1st class & rank, Kerala U., India, 1967, B in Edn., 1960, MA in Sociology, 1969, MA in History, Kerala U., 1975, PhD in Psychology, 1975; D Therapeutic Philosophy (hon.), World U., 1989. Lic. psychologist, marriage and family therapist, Mich.; diplomate Am. Bd. Med. Psychotherapists, Am. Bd. Psychotherapy, Am. Bd. Sexology, Am. Bd. Forensic Examiners, Am. Bd. Forensic Medicine, Am. Bd. Psychol. Specialities. Lectr., head dept. ednl. psychology S.N. Tchrs. Coll., Trivandrum, India; clin./adminstrv. dir. Alexandrine House, Inc., Detroit, 1976-81; chief exec. officer Cen. Therapeutic Svcs., Inc., Southfield, Mich., 1981—; adv. bd. Trivandrum Med. Coll. Hosps., 1969-75; edn. faculty mem. U. Calicut, Kerala, India, 1969-75; v.p. forum ednl. rsch. and studies Kerala U., 1969-73. Author: Educational Psychology for B.Ed. Students, 1970; editor: Kerala University Journal of Education, 1969-73. Fellow Am. Bd. Med. Psychotherapists, Am. Acad. Clin. Sexologists. Am. Coll. Forensic Examiners, Am. Coll. Advanced Practice Psychologists; mem. APA, Am. Coll. Sexologists (sexologist), Am. Bd. Sexology (clin. supr.), World U. Round Table (hon. cultural doctorate in therapeutic philosophy), diplomate Am. Bd. Psychological Specialities. Republican. Avocations: photography, travel, reading, sightseeing. Home: 3048 Brewster West Bloomfield MI 48322-2471 Office: Cen Therapeutic Svcs Inc 17600 W 8 Mile Rd Ste 7 Southfield MI 48075-4316

THIND, SUKHPAL SINGH, publishing company executive, investment executive; b. Ludhiana, Punjab, India, Jan. 1, 1954; came to Eng., 1965; s. Gurcharan Singh and Harbajhan Kaur (Gill) T.; m. Jaswinder Kaur Johal, Feb. 20, 1984; children: Kieran, Amrit, Simran. BSc, U. East Anglia, Norwich, Eng., 1977, MSc, 1978, PhD, 1980. Sr. scientist 3M, St. Paul, 1980-84; sr. chemist Uniroyal Chem., Middlebury, 1984-85; assoc. Merrill Lynch, London, 1985-86; mgr. Deutsche Bank, London, 1986-89; exec. dir. Bank of Tokyo, London, 1989-92; head arbitrage UBS, Zurich, 1992-93; CEO Capital Market Advisors Ag, Zurich, 1993-2000, Arkat Found., Zurich, 1999; mem. control bd. www.arkat.org, 1999; contbr. articles to profl. jours. Family supporter edn. in India, 1965—. Mem. Sikh. Avocations: writing, travel, reading, promoting science education in less developed countries. Home: Hollanderstrasse 54, Uetikon am See, 8707 Zurich Switzerland Office: Arkat Found, Schanzeneggstrasse 1, 8002 Zurich Switzerland

THINKHAMROP, JADSADA, obstetrician-gynecologist; b. Khon Kean, Thailand, June 27, 1962; d. Haiseing and Kuieng (Saebae) Anansuwanchai; m. Bandit Thinkhamrop, Dec. 28, 1995; 1 child, Prinn. MD, Khon Kean U., 1987; MSc, Chulalongkorn U., Bangkok, 1995. Staff mem. faculty medicine Khon Kaen U., 1991—, asst. prof. faculty medicine, 1995—, staff mem. clin. epidemiology unit, 1995—, mem. rsch. com., 1998—. Contbr. articles to profl. jours. Mem. Royal Thai Coll. Ob-gyn. (rsch. com. 1996—), Thai Med. Assn. Home: 528/207 Maliwan Rd, Khon Kaen 40000, Thailand Office: Dept Ob-gyn Fac Medicine, Friendship Hwy, Khon Kaen 40002, Thailand

THIRIEZ, HERVE M., management consultant, educator; b. Loos, France, May 10, 1944; s. Gérard P. Thiriez and Mariette M. Poissonnier; m. Marie-Joëlle Bérard; children: Emmanuel, Valérie, Sylvain, Patrice. Diploma Engring., IMAG, Grenoble, 1966; PhD in Ops. Rsch., MIT, Boston, 1969. Asst. prof. MIT, 1969-70; prof. Groupe HEC, Jouy, France, 1970—; CEO Logma S.A., Versailles, France, 1980—, Edits. MEV, Versailles, 1980—; cons. Am. and European bus. in fields of strategy, modeling, micro-computers and computers, 1969—. Author 24 books, including: Jeux, Cultures et Strategie, 1995, Comprendre et Utiliser les Modeles en Gestion, Le Macintosh Professionnel, Initiation au Calcul Economique, also others; co-author: Multiple Criteria Decision-Making; contbr. numerous articles to profl. jours. and publs. Avocations: skiing, sailing, strategic games. Office: Groupe HEC, 78350 Jouy en Josas France

THIRLWALL, ANTHONY PHILIP, economist, educator; b. Workington, Eng., Apr. 21, 1941; s. Isaac and Ivy (Ticehurst) T.; m. Gianna Paoletti, Mar. 25, 1966 (div. 1986); children: Lawrence, Alexander. BA, U. Leeds, 1962, PhD, 1967; MA, Clark U., 1963. Asst. lectr. U. Leeds (Eng.), 1964-66; lectr., reader, prof. econs. U. Kent, Canterbury, Eng., 1966—; econ. adviser Labour Govt., 1968-70; vis. prof. Princeton (N.J.) U., 1971-72, Melbourne (Australia) U., 1981, 88, La Trobe (Australia), 1994; cons. Pacific Islands Devel. Program, 1989, 96, African Devel. Bank, 1994, 99. Author 12 books; editor 12 books; mem. editorial bd. Jour. Devel. Studies, Jour. of Past Keynesion Economics, African Devel. Rev.; contbr. over 160 articles to profl. jours. Mem. Nat. Inst. Econ. and Social Rsch. (bd. govs. 1979—), Royal Econ. Soc. (coun. 1979-89). Avocations: running, tennis. E-mail: a.p. thirlwall & ukc. ac.uk. Office: U Kent Keynes Coll, Canterbury England

THIRSK, (IRENE) JOAN, historian; b. London, June 19, 1922; d. William Henry and Daisy (Frayer) Watkins; m. James Wood, Sept. 12, 1945; children: Martin David, Jane Freya. B.A. with honors, Westfield Coll., U. London, 1947, Ph.D., 1950; D.Litt (hon.), U. Leicester, 1985, East Anglia

U., 1990, Kent U., 1993, Sussex U., 1994, Southampton U., 1999; D, Open U., 1991; D.Agric. (hon.), Wageningen U., 1993. Asst. lectr. sociology London U. Sch. Econs., 1950-51; sr. rsch. fellow agrarian history, dept. English local history Leicester U., Eng., 1951-65; reader econ. history U. Oxford, Eng., 1965-83; gen. editor Agrarian History Eng. and Wales, 1975-2000. Author: Economic Policy and Projects, 1978, Alternative Agriculture: A History From the Black Death to the Present Day, 1997; editor, contbr. The Agrarian History of England and Wales, vol. IV 1500-1640, 1967, vol. V 1640-1750, 1985, The English Rural Landscape, 2000. Mem. Royal Commn. on Hist. Monuments, 1977-86. Served with Brit. Army, 1942-45. Hon. fellow Queen Mary and Westfield Coll., London U., 1997, Kellogg Coll., Oxford, 1998. Fellow Royal Hist. Soc., Brit. Acad.; mem. Am. Philos. Soc. (fgn.), Colonial Soc. Mass. (corr.), Edmonton Hundred Hist. Soc. (pres. 1978-96), Brit Assn. for Local History (pres. 1986-92), Brit. Agrl. History Soc. (editor Jour. 1964-72, pres. 1983-86, 95-98), Past and Present (editl. bd. 1956-92), Econ. History Soc. (council 1955-83). Avocations: gardening, sewing, machine knitting. Home: 1 Hadlow Castle, Hadlow, Kent Tonbridge TN11 0EG, England

THIRTLE, MICHAEL ROBERT, community activist, consultant; b. Milw., Dec. 10, 1967; s. Robert Michael and Sandra Lee Thirtle; m. Denise Marie Domanico, June 10, 1990; children: Natalie Brooke, Jackson Ryan. BS, USAF Acad., 1990; MBA, Wright State U., 1993, MS, 1994; MPhil, Rand Grad. Sch., Santa Monica, Calif., 1997, PhD, 1999. Commd. 2d lt. USAF, Dayton, Ohio, 1990, advanced through grades to capt., 1994, ret., 1995; economist Rand Corp., Santa Monica, Calif., 1995-98; sr. cons. Pricewaterhouse Coopers, L.A., 1998-99; consulting dir. Nat. Data Corp., Chgo., 1999—; adj. faculty fin. Cardean U. Author: The Predator ACTD, 1997, Seeing the Lighthouse, 1999; contbr. articles to profl. jours. Bd. dirs. Acad. Selection Com., Ill. 8th Dist., 1999; liaison officer USAF Acad., Dayton, 1992-95; v.p. Ch. Coun., L.A., 1997-99; sch. tutor Santa Monica (Calif.) H.S., 1995-97. Capt. USAFR, 1995—. Mem. Air Force Acad. Assn. Grads., Am. Legion. Republican. Lutheran. Home: 1970 Marigold Ln Round Lake IL 60073-9540 Office: Nat Data Corp Health Info Svcs 500 Lake Cook Rd Ste 210 Deerfield IL 60015-4937

THISAYAKORN, CHAVALIT, engineering executive; b. Bangkok, Feb. 18, 1949; s. Thavee Ting and Vipar (Chen) T.; m. Kanya Jirapayoongchai, May 27, 1985; children: Don, Paul. B in Engring., Chulalongkorn U., Thailand, 1970; M in Engring., Tex. A&M U., 1971, PhD, 1975. Rsch. asst. dept. elec. engring. Tex. A&M U., 1971-75; asst. mktg. mgr. Unisys Dept. Yip In Tsoi & Co., Bangkok, 1976-80; mgr. paper mill Hiang Seng Fibre Container Co., Ltd., 1980-87; dep. mng. dir. Panjapol Paper Industry Public Co. Ltd., 1989-91; mng. dir. IWB-Siamtec Co. Ltd., 1991—. Contbr. more than 70 articles to profl. jours. Bd. dirs. digital remote sensing steering sub-com. Nat. Rsch. Coun. Thailand, 1976-98. Fellow Engring. Inst. Thailand (life); mem. IEEE (sr., dir. CAS Thailand chpt.), NSPE (sr.), Thailand Mgmt. Assn. (life), Computer Assn. Thailand (life), Nat. Energy Mgrs. Club (founding chmn., bd. dirs.), Tech. Assn. Pulp and Paper Industry, Chulalongkorn U. Alumni Assn. (life), Assumption Alumni Assn. (life), N.Y. Acad. Scis. Avocations: reading technical journals, swimming, badminton. Fax: (02) 982-9096. E-mail: ctk@a-net.net.th. Home: 96/68 Muang Thong 3/4, Jaeng Wattana Rd, Nonthaburi 11120, Thailand

THISSELL, JAMES DENNIS, physicist; b. Lincoln County, S.D., June 1, 1935; s. Oscar H. and Bernice G.J. (Olbertson) T. BA cum laude, Augustana Coll., 1957; MS, U. Iowa, 1963. Rsch. physicist U. Iowa, Iowa City, 1958-64; engr. McDonnell Douglas, St. Louis, 1965-66; scientist E.G. & G., Inc., Las Vegas, Nev., 1967-68; engr. Bendix Field Engring. Corp. Ames Rsch. Ctr., Moffett Field, Calif., 1970-77, Lockheed Missiles and Space Co., Sunnyvale, Calif., 1978—. Mem. AIAA, IEEE, Am. Phys. Soc., Am. Geophys. Soc., Sigma Xi. Republican. Lutheran. Home: 38475 Jacaranda Dr Newark CA 94560-4727 Office: LMTO 0/28-0/28-12 B158 FAC 1 PO Box 61687 Sunnyvale CA 94088-1687

THØGERSEN, HENNING, chemist, researcher; b. Viborg, Denmark, Aug. 12, 1953; s. Christian and Kathrine (Eriksen) T.; m. Bente Møller, Aug. 18, 1984; children: Martin, Peter. MSc, Tech. U. Denmark, 1977, PhD, 1980. Postdoctoral fellow U. Alberta, Edmonton, Canada, 1980-81; chemist N. Foss Electric, Hillerod, Denmark, 1981-82; prin. scientist Novo Nordisk A/S, Bagsvaerd, Denmark, 1982—. Contbr. articles to profl. jours. Mem. AAAS, Am. Pept. Soc., European Pept. Soc. Avocations: tennis, travelling, nature, gardening. Home: Gregersmindevej 8, DK-3520 Farum Denmark Office: Novo Nordisk, Novo Nordisk Park, DK-2760 Maaloev Denmark

THOMA, ELMAR HERBERT, mathematician; b. Baden-Baden, Fed. Republic Germany, Sept. 10, 1926; s. Hubert Ambros and Friederike K. (Meyer) T.; m. Helga Christine Hagemann; children: Markus, Sebastian. PhD, U. Erlangen, Fed. Republic Germany, 1952. Asst. U. Munich, 1954-57, reader, 1957-59; vis. prof. U. Wash., Seattle, 1959-61; assoc. prof. U. Heidelberg, Fed. Republic Germany, 1961-64; full prof. U. Münster, Fed. Republic Germany, 1964-70, Tech. U. Münich, 1970—; dean Faculty Math. and Nat. Sci., U. Münster, 1968-69; dean Gen. Faculty of Nat. Scis., Tech. U. München, 1973-75. Co-editor Math. Annalen, 1974-90. Mem. Deutsche Math. Vereiningung, Am. Math. Soc. Home: Lustheimstrasse 2, D-81247 Munich Bavaria, Germany Office: Tech U Munchen Math Inst, Arcisstrasse 21, D-80333 Munich Germany

THOMA, KALLIRROE-ANDRIANE THEODOROU, physics educator; b. Patras, Greece, Nov. 30, 1945; d. Theodoros Constantinou and Eleni Elia (Dimitropoulou) T.; m. Alexandros Antoniou Uradis, Jan. 13, 1970; children: Stella, Antonis, Eleni. BSc, U. Athens, Greece, 1968; MSc in Electronics, U. Kent, Canterbury, Eng., 1975, PhD, 1981. Physics tchr. Arsakeion High Sch., Patras, Greece, 1968-69; lab. asst. U. Patras, 1969-82, lectr., 1982-90; vis. rsch. fellow U. Kent, Canterbury, 1984-86; asst. prof. U. Patras, 1990—; mem. sci. com. S.S. Ionics Euroconferences, 1994—. Contbr. articles to profl. jours. Grantee State Scholarship Found., 1964, 73-76, Travel grants British Coun. Mem. Soc. of Greek Physicists, Internat. Soc. of S.S. Ionics, Friends of Classical Music. Avocations: cooking, traveling, going to the cinema and theatre. Home: Thessalonikis 38, 26441 Patras Greece Office: Univ Patras, Physics Dept, 26500 Patras Greece

THOMA, MANFRED HUBERT, electrical engineering educator; b. Neumarkt, Germany, Feb. 24, 1929; s. Hubert and Friederike (Meyer) T.; m. Elisabeth Franczok, 1955; children: Robert, Eberhard, Susanne. Engr., OHM Poly., Nürnberg, Germany, 1954; diploma in engring., U. Darmstadt, Germany, 1957, DEng, 1963; DSc (hon.), City U., London, 1991; DEng (hon.), U. Bochum, 1992, U. Helsinki, 1998. Sci. asst. U. Darmstadt, 1957-64, lectr., 1965-67; vis. prof. Purdue U., Lafayette, Ind., 1964-65; prof. elec. engring. U. Hannover, Germany, 1967—, dept. head, 1969-71, dean engring., 1971-72; vis. prof. Kyoto (Japan) U., 1977, 85; bd. dirs. BIOTECHNICA (world biggest fair in biotech.), Hannover. Author: Theory of Linear Control Systems, 1973; editor book series in comm. and control; also articles. Pres. Internat. Fedn. Automatic Control, Geneva, 1984-87. Recipient Internat. Corp. award WISITEX Found. (exhibition on indsl. electronics and mfg. tech.), Bombay, 1990, Outstanding Svc. award Internat. Fedn. Automatic Control, 1990. Mem. Braunschweig Sci. Soc., Ukrainian Acad. Sci., Hungarian Acad. Sci., Russian Acad. Sci. Office: U Hannover, Appelstrasse 11, D-30167 Hannover Germany

THOMALSKE, R.E. GÜNTHER, neurosurgeon, educator; b. Hohkirch, Silesia, June 8, 1925; s. Paul E.M. and Eleonore O.E. (Pletz) T.; m. Anne This, July 11, 1958; children: Christine, Catherine. Student, U. Berlin, 1943, U. Freiburg, Germany, 1943-44, U. Prague, Czechoslovakia, 1944-45; MD, U. Marburg, Fed. Republic Germany, 1949. Asst. in Bacteriologic Inst. U. Marburg, 1949; with Psychiat. Hosp., Marburg, 1949-50; asst. in gen. surgery Town Hosp., Delmenhorst, Fed. Republic Germany, 1950-51, asst. in ob-gyn., 1951-52; asst. surg. U. Hosp., Mainz, Fed. Republic Germany, 1952; asst. neurosurgeon Pasteur Hosp., Colmar, France, 1952-58; resident neurosurgeon U. Frankfurt (Fed. Republic Germany) Main Hosp., 1958-64, head neurosurgeon, 1964-68, lectr. neurosurgery, 1969-72, prof., 1972—, dir. dept. functional neurosurgery, 1973-90. Author: (with Münzenberg) Leg Pain, 1976, (with Tilscher) Back and Low Back Pain, 1990; editor: Series Pain, VCH, 1986—, Pain Conference, 1984—, Non Pharmacological Treatment of Pain, 1990. Mem. Internat. Assn. Study of Pain (v.p. German chpt. 1978-93), German Pain Soc. (hon.), German Soc. Neurosurgery, French Lang. Soc. Neurosurgery, German Soc. Neuroradiology, German Soc. Neurology, German EEG Soc., French Soc. EEG, Soc. Luso Epagnola Neurocir. (corr.), French Soc. Neuroradiology (corr.), Swiss Soc. Neurosurgery (corr.). Home: Tulpenstr 12, D-63263 Neu-Isenburg Germany Office: Aerztehaus, D-63263 Neu-Isenburg Germany

THOMAN, CHARLES JAMES, chemistry educator; b. Wilkes-Barre, Pa., Nov. 4, 1928; s. Charles James Thoman and Anne Calistos Conway; m. Grace Ursula Garrett, May 28, 1983. BS in Chemistry, MA in Philosphy, Spring Hill Coll., 1953; MS in Chemistry, Fordham U., 1956; B of Sacred Theology, Woodstock Coll., 1959, M of Sacred Theology, 1960; PhD in Chemistry, U. Mass., 1966. Prof. U. Scranton, Pa., 1953-55, 66-82, 1984-87; prof. Stephen F. Austin State U., Nacogdoches, Tex., 1987-89, U. Scis. Phila., Phila., 1989—; rsch. assoc. La. State U. Sch. Medicine, Shreveport, 1982-83; vis. prof. U. Ala., Tuscaloosa, 1983-84. Pres. Pa. Regional Tissue & Transplant Bank, Scranton, 1978-82. Mem. Am. Chem. Soc. (chmn. Phila. sect. 1995). Roman Catholic. Avocations: basketball, history of the Mafia. Home: 402 Lark Dr Mount Laurel NJ 08054-4426 Office: U Scis Phila 600 S 43d St Philadelphia PA 19104

THOMANECK, JURGEN KARL ALBERT, German language educator; b. Stettin, Germany, June 12, 1941; arrived in U.K., 1966; s. Paul and Margarete (Steinkopf) T.; m. Guinevere Ronald, Aug. 3, 1964; children: Yasmin, Naomi. MEd, Aberdeen (Scotland) U., 1969; PhD, Kiel U., 1969. From asst. to prof. Aberdeen U., U.K., 1968—, head dept., 1984-97. Avocations: football, reading, traveling. Office: U Aberdeen Dept German, Kings Coll, Aberdeen AB9 2UB, Scotland

THOMANN, KLAUS-DIETER, orthopaedic surgeon; b. Redewisch, Germany, Apr. 6, 1951; s. Klaus and Ursula (Leonhardt) T.; m. Cornelia Honscha, May 9, 1975; children: Christian, Tanja, Kirsten. MD, Johann-Wolfgang-Goethe U., Frankfurt, Germany, 1978. Med. diplomate. Pvt. practice Frankfurt, 1993—; asst. prof. Johann Wolfgang Goethe-Universitat, Frankfurt, 1991—, Johannes Gutenberg U., Mainz, 1993-99; prof. U. Mainz, 1999—; cons. physician Clinic Weisses Haus, Bad Soden, Germany, 1991-96. Author 10 books; contbr. articles to profl. jours. Robert Bosch Found. grantee, 1989-92. Home: Hammarskjoldring 141, 60439 Frankfurt M 50 Germany Office: 353 Eschersheimer Landstrasse, 60320 Frankfurt Germany

THOMAS, AKOT VARGHESE, chemicals executive, consultant; b. Kuzhikala, Kerala, India, Oct. 25, 1925; s. Thundiath Thomas Varghese and Puthupparampil Mary Koshy; m. Ruby Joseph David, Nov. 19, 1953; children: Albert V., Robert J. Diploma in engring., Victorial Jubilee Tech. Inst., Bombay, 1950. Cert. elec. engr. Elec. engr. Tata Chems., Mithapur, India, 1951-58, chief elec. engr., 1958-72, power mgr., 1972-78, v.p., 1978-84, pres., 1984-91, dir. projects, 1986-99, sr. cons., 1991-98; dir. ACC-Babcock, Bombay, 1984-92. Trustee Ctrl. Sch., Port Okha, India, 1985—, Tata Chems. Golden Jubilee Found., Bomba, 1989—, Tata Chems. Rural Devel., Mithapur, 1989—; hon. pres. K. P. Sch., Mithapur, 1995—. Mem. N.Y. Acad. Scis., Overseas Club. Avocations: hunting, driving, outdoor games, swimming, photography. Home: Ruby Villa, Albo Farm, Albo Farm Rd, 361345 Mithapur India Office: Tata Chems Ltd, Mithapur, Gujarat 361345, India

THOMAS, ALFRED BRUCE, retired lawyer, social services administrator; b. Nashville, July 14, 1933; s. Bruce Thomas and Gertrude A. Stammers; m. Louise Potts, June 2, 1961; children: Bruce, Jeffrey, Jennifer. BS in Metall. Engring., Case Western Res. U., 1956; JD, Cleve. State U., 1968. Rsch. engr. DuPont, Aiken, S.C., 1952-53; engr. Westinghouse, Pitts., 1953-59; world tour engr. Westinghouse, Cheswick, Pa., 1959-60; plant engr. Clevite Corp., Cleve., 1962-68; product atty. Huck Mfg. Co., Detroit, 1968-70; solo practice Grosse Point, Mich., 1970-72; county atty. Wayne County, Detroit, 1972-92; ret., 1992. Pres. Grosse Pointe Park Found., 1993; pres. Circumnavigators, Detroit, 1996; pres. Svcs. for Older Citizens, Grosse Point, 1997—. Recipient Peacemaker of Yr. award Grosse Point MEml. Ch., 1992. Presbyterian. E-mail: abt881@hotmail.com. Home: 881 Pemberton Rd Grosse Pointe MI 48230-1729

THOMAS, ANN VAN WYNEN, law educator; b. The Netherlands, May 27, 1919; came to U.S., 1921, naturalized, 1926; d. Cornelius and Cora Jacoba (Daansen) Van Wynen; m. A.J. Thomas Jr., Sept. 10, 1948. AB with distinction, U. Rochester, 1940; JD, U. Tex., 1943; post doctoral degree, So. Meth. U., 1952. U.S. fgn. svc. officer Johannesburg, South Africa, London, The Hague, The Netherlands, 1943-47; rsch. atty. Southwestern Legal Found., Sch. Law So. Meth. U., Dallas, 1952-67; asst. prof. polit. sci. So. Meth. U. Sch. Law, Dallas, 1968-73, assoc. prof., 1973-76, prof., 1976-85, prof. emeritus, 1985—. Author: Communism versus International Law, 1953, (with A.J. Thomas Jr.) International Treaties, 1950, Non-Intervention—The Law and its Import in the Americas, 1956, OAS: The Organization of American States, 1962, International Legal Aspects of Civil War in Spain, 1936-1939, 1967, Legal Limitations on Chemical and Biological Weapons, 1970, The Concept of Aggression, 1972, Presidential War Making Power: Constitutional and International Law Aspects, 1981, An International Rule of Law—Problems and Prospects, 1974. Chmn. time capsule com. Grayson County Commn. on Tex. Sesquicentennial, 1986-88; co-chmn. Grayson County Commn. on Bicentennial U.S. Constn., 1988-93; co-chmn. com. Grayson County Sesquicentennial, 1994-97; co-chmn. Grayson County Commn. on the Millenium, 1997—. Recipient Am. medal Nat. DAR Soc., 1992. Mem. Tex. Bar Assn., Am. Soc. Internat. Law, Grayson County Bar Assn. Home: Spaniel Hall 374 Coffee Cir Pottsboro TX 75076-3164

THOMAS, ANNE MOREAU, newspaper owner; b. Trenton, N.J., May 23, 1930; d. Daniel Howard and Lillis Dale (Simmonds) Moreau; m. Henry Seely Thomas, Jr., June 14, 1952 (dec. Aug. 1994); children: Catherine, John Martin II, Howard Moreau. BA, Middlebury Coll., 1951; DHL, Rutgers U., 1999. Tchr. North Hunterdon H.S., Annandale, N.J., 1951-52, Hunterdon Adult Sch., Flemington, N.J., 1953-70; home and food editor Hunterdon County Democrat, Flemington, 1954-99, owner, bd. sec., 1985-94, owner, chmn. bd., 1994—. Trustee Rutgers U., New Brunswick, N.J., 1985—, bd. govs., 1991—, chmn. bd. govs., 1995-98; mem. N.J. Commn. Higher Edn., Trenton, 1995-98. Recipient N.J. Food Communicator of Yr. award N.J. Dept. Agr., 1981, Golden award for cmty. svc. Hunterdon County C. of C., 1990, Eagle Leadership award Ctr./Urban cmty. Leadership, 1996, Hunterdon Disting. Citizen award Ctrl. N.J. Coun. Boy Scouts Am., 1999-2000; named Woman of Yr., Hunterdon County YMCA, 1997. Mem. N.J. Press Assn. (bd. dirs. 1977-85, pres. 1984, chmn. 1985), Hunterdon-Princeton Chaine des Rotisseurs, DAR, Copper Hill Country Club, N.J. Mus. Agr. (trustee), Hunterdon County Hist. Soc. (trustee), Friends of Rutgers Librs. (chmn.). Republican. Presbyterian. Avocations: restoration of circa 1750 Cape Cod family homestead, gardening, skiing, cooking. Home: 38 Pennsylvania Ave Flemington NJ 08822-1222 Office: Hunterdon County Democrat 18 Minneakoning Rd Flemington NJ 08822-5725

THOMAS, BARBARA ANN, medical sciences consultant; b. Stoke-on-Trent, Stafford, Eng., May 5, 1935; d. John and Annie (Jackson) Lockley; m. Michael Thomas, June 16, 1962; children: Karen Elizabeth, Christopher James. BA in Natural Scis., Tripos U., 1955, 56; MA, Newnham Coll., Cambridge, Eng., 1959; MB B, Middlesex Hosp. Med. Sch., London, 1959. Royal Coll. Radiologists, Royal Coll. Ob-Gyn. House officer Middlesex Hosp., 1959, casualty med. officer, 1960; gen. practice London, 1962-67; med. officer of health Harrow then Ealing, London, 1965-74; clin. med. officer Surrey, Eng., 1974-78; clin. coordinator Guildford (Eng.) Breast Screening Project, 1978-88; clin. dir. Jarvis Screening Ctr., Guildford, Eng., 1988-97; trainer Nat. Breast Cancer Tng. Ctr., Guildford, 1988—; mem. edn. com. Marie Curie Cancer Care; breast screening program evaluation com. Nat. Health Svc., 1983-87; advisor, breast disease, Women's Nat. Cancer Control Campaign, Eng., 1987—. Advisor, interviewee: (video) Ray of Hope, 1988, Only the Best Will Do, 1991, Think Pink, 1998; contbr. articles to profl. jours. Recipient grants Dept. Health, 1979, Travel fellowship, Council of Europe, 1984, 89; named Officer Brit. Empire, 1998. Mem. European Group for Breast Cancer Screening (sec. 1986-88). Avocations: antiquarian books, cartography, photography, walking, archaeology. Home: Copsen Knoll Rd, Frith Hill Godalming, Surrey GU7 2EL, England Office: Jarvis Screening Ctr, Stoughton Rd, Guildford GUI 1LJ, England

THOMAS, BERTRAM DAVID, retired chemical engineer; b. Renton, Wash., May 5, 1903; s. David and Minnie Belle (Custer) T.; m. Dorothy Glorian Butler, Dec. 21, 1928 (dec. 1986); children: Preston David, Nancy Glorian, Lawrence Eldon. BS, U. Wash., 1929, PhD in Chemistry, 1933. Registered profl. engr., Ohio. Rsch. engr. Battelle Meml. Inst., Columbus, Ohio, 1934-40, asst. dir., 1940-56, pres., 1956-68; ret.; mem. adv. com. on environment, Santa Barbara, Calif., 1970-73. Patentee ore dressing and coal preparation methods; contbr. articles to sci. publs. Trustee Columbus Mus. Art, 1962-67, Ohio State U., Columbus, 1965-68, Santa Barbara Mus. Art, 1973—; trustee, pres. Santa Barbara Botanic Garden, 1974-82. Recipient Order Civil Merit 1st Class, Republic of Korea, 1965; DEng. (hon.), Mich. Coll. Mining and Tech., 1957; DSci (hon.) Ohio State U., 1963, Otterbein Coll., Westerville, Ohio, 1965, Cleve. State U., 1968. Fellow AAAS; mem. Chemists Club N.Y., Am. Che. Soc., Sigma Xi. Home: 300 Hot Springs Rd Apt 21 Santa Barbara CA 93108-2043

THOMAS, BEVERLY IRENE, special education educator; b. Del Rio, Tex., Nov. 12, 1939; d. Clyde Louis and Eve Naomi (Avant) Whistler; m. James Henry Thomas, Jan. 28, 1972; children: Kenneth (dec.), Wade, Robert, Darcy, Betty Kay, James III, Debra, Brenda, Michael. BM summa cum laude, Sul Ross State U., 1972, MEd, 1976, MEd in Counseling, 1992, MEd in Mid. Mgmt., 1996. Cert. music, elem. edn., music edn., learning disabilities, spl. edn. generic, ednl. diagnosis, ednl. counseling, spl. edn. counseling and mid. mgmt. Tchr. Pecos-Barstow-Toyah Ind. Sch. Dist., 1974-92, 99—; edn. diagnostician West Tex. State Sch., Tex. Youth Commn., ret., 1999; tchr. Pecos-Barstow-Toyal Ind. Sch. Dist., 1999-2000; youth counselor Tex. Workforce Ctr., Pecos, 2000—. Mem. AAUW, ASCD, NEA, MENSA, Assn. for Children with Learning Disabilities (local sec. 1974), Tex. State Tchrs. Assn. (treas. 1991-94), Tex. Ednl. Diagnosticians Assn., Tex. Profl. Ednl. Diagnosticians, Reeves County Assn. of Children with Learning Disabilities, Nat. Coun. Tchrs. of Maths., Nat. Coun. Tchrs. English, Learning Disabilities Assn., Learning Disabilities Assoc., Tex., Coun. for Exceptional Children, Tex. Counseling Assn., Alpha Chi, Kappa Delta Pi. Home: PO Box 128 Pecos TX 79772-0128

THOMAS, CLAUDEWELL SIDNEY, psychiatry educator; b. N.Y.C., Oct. 5, 1932; s. Humphrey Sidney and Frances Elizabeth (Collins) T.; m. Carolyn Pauline Rozansky, Sept. 6, 1958; children: Jeffrey Evan, Julie-Anne Elizabeth, Jessica Edith. BA, Columbia U., 1952; MD, SUNY, Downstate Med. Ctr., 1956; MPH, Yale U., 1964. Diplomate Nat. Bd. Med. Examiners, Am. Bd. Psychiatry, Am. Bd. Forensic Medicine, Am. Bd. Psychological Splties. From instr. to assoc. prof. Yale U., New Haven, 1963-68, dir. Yale tng. program in social community psychiatry, 1967-70; dir. div. mental health service programs NIMH, Washington, 1970-73; chmn. dept. psychiatry U.M.D.N.J., Newark, 1973-83; prof. dept. psychiatry Drew Med. Sch., 1983—, chmn. dept. psychiatry, 1983-93; prof. dept. psychiatry UCLA, 1983-94, vice chmn. dept. psychiatry, 1983-93, prof. emeritus dept. psychiatry, 1994—; med. dir. Tokanui Hosp., TeAwamutu, N.Z., 1996; cons. A.K. Rice Inst., Washington, 1978-80, SAMSA/PHS Cons., 1991—; mem. L.A. County Superior Ct. Psych. Panel, 1991-97. Author: (with R. Bergen) Issues and Problems in Social Psychiatry, 1966; editor (with R. Bryce LaPorte) Alienation in Contemporary Society, 1976, (with J. Lindenthal) Psychiatry and Mental Health Science Handbook; mem. editorial bd. Internat. Jour. Mental Health, Adminstrn. In Mental Health. Bd. dirs. Bay Area Found., 1987—. Served to capt. USAF, 1959-61. Fellow APHA, Am. Psychoanalytic Assn. (hon.), Am. Psychiat. Assn. (life), Royal Soc. Health, N.Y. Acad. Sci., N.Y. Acad. Medicine; mem. Am. Sociol. Assn., Am. Coll. Mental Health Adminstrs., Am. Coll. Forensic Examiners, L.A. Acad. Med., Sigma Xi. Avocations: tennis, racquetball, violin, piano. Home and Office: 30676 Palos Verdes Dr E Palos Verdes Peninsula CA 90275-6354

THOMAS, COLIN GORDON, JR., surgeon, medical educator; b. Iowa City, July 25, 1918; s. Colin Gordon and Eloise Kinzer (Brainerd) T.; m. Shirley Forbes, Sept. 14, 1946; children: Karen, Barbara, James G., John F. BS., U. Chgo., 1940, M.D., 1943. Diplomate Am. Bd. Surgery. Intern U. Iowa Hosp., 1943-44, resident surgery, 1944-45, 47-50; assoc. in surgery U. Iowa Med. Sch., 1950-51, asst. prof., 1951-52; mem. faculty U. N.C. Med. Sch., Chapel Hill, 1952—, prof. surgery, 1961—, Byah Thomason Doxey-Sanford Doxey prof. surgery, 1982—, chmn. dept., 1966-84, chief div. gen. surg., 1984-89, part-time prof., 1991—. Contbr. surg. texts, numerous articles to med. jours. Served to capt., M.C. AUS, 1945-47. Recipient Prof. award U. N.C. Sch. Medicine, 1964, Disting. Svc. award U. Chgo., 1982, Med. Alumni Disting. faculty award U. N.C., 1984; Berryhill lectr. U. N.C., 1989; recipient Fleming Fuller award U. N.C. Hosps., 1994. Mem. AMA, ACS (Disting. Leadership award N.C. chpt. 1990), AAUP, Am. Thyroid Assn., Am. Assn. Cancer Research, Am. Assn. Endocrine Surgeons (pres. 1989-90), Soc. Univ. Surgeons, So. Surg. Assn. (v.p. 1989-90), N.Y. Acad. Scis., Halsted Soc., Ga. Surg. Soc., Soc. Exptl. Biology and Medicine, Am. Surg. Assn., Womack Surg. Soc. (pres. 1981-83), Soc. Internationale de Chirurgie, Soc. Surgery Alimentary Tract, N.C. Surg. Assn., Internat. Assn. Endocrine Surgeons, Alpha Omega Alpha. Episcopalian (warden 1961-62). Home: 408 Morgan Creek Rd Chapel Hill NC 27514-4934

THOMAS, CYNTHIA ELIZABETH, advanced practice nurse; b. Highland, Ind., Sept. 3, 1958; d. James William and Naomi Elizabeth (Rice) T. BS in Animal Sci., Purdue U., 1980; ADN, Purdue U. Calumet, 1986, BSN, 1988, MSN, 1990. RN, Ind.; cert. adult nurse practitioner, family nurse practitioner, clin. specialist in med.-surg. nursing. Med.-surg. open heart ICU/CCU staff nurse, charge nurse Porter Meml. Hosp., Valparaiso, Ind., 1986-94; med.-surg. clin. instr. Purdue U., Westville, Ind., 1993-94; advanced practice nurse Cmty. Health Ctrs. Koontz Lake, LaCrosse, North Judson, Starke Meml. Hosp., Ind., 1994-95; nurse practitioner/office coord. Hanna Family Med. Ctr., LaPorte Hosp./Lakeland Area Health Svcs., 1995-96; nurse practitioner Arnett Clinic, Lafayette, Ind., 1996-99; advanced practice nurse Purdue U., West Lafayette, Ind., 1999—; nursing instr. Bethel Coll., Mishawaka, Ind., 1995-96. Mem. AACN, Am. Acad. Nurse Practitioners, Alpha Zeta.

THOMAS, DALE, film producer; b. Pampa, Tex., July 6, 1951; s. Olan E. and Claudine (Sparlin) T. BA, Dallas Bapt. U., 1973; MEd, U. S.C., 1976. Coord. media svcs. U. S.C., Columbia, 1975-77; mgr. media svcs. Lexington Med. Ctr., Columbia, 1977-85; exec. producer, mgr. LexCom Prodns., Columbia, 1985-91; nat., internat. accounts mgr. Telemation, Denver, 1992-93; exec. v.p. Videosmith, Inc., Phila., 1993-94; mgr. creative svcs. Coors Brewing Co., Golden, Colo., 1994—. Prodr. mktg./sales/promotion and tng. programs including Bag It Right, 1988, 89 (Silver Reel awards 1988, Gold Addy 1990), Totally Satisfied, 1990 (Gold Addy 1990), MayDay, 1988, 89 (Silver Reel of Excellence 1988, CINE Golden Eagle 1989), Teenage Suicide Prevention, 1988 (CINE Golden Eagle 1987). Bd. dirs. Palmetto Mastersingers, Columbia, 1988-91, performer, 1987-91. Named 1st Disting. Alumnus U. S.C. Media Arts, 1983. Mem. Internat. TV Assn. (nat. bd. dirs. 1993-99, nat. v.p. 1990-91, nat. pres. 1992-93, chair festival adv. bd. 1989, chair internat. video festival 1988, regional v.p. 1985-87, chpt. pres. 1982-85, Chuck Weble award 2000), S.C. Affiliate of Nat. Soc. to Prevent Blindness (chmn. bd. 1989-90, Robert Scott Meml. award 1984).

THOMAS, DANA FIFE, journalist, educator; b. Washington, Feb. 3, 1964; d. Charles H. and Susie (Strackbein) T.; m. Hervé M.J. d'Halluin, Oct. 3, 1992. BA in Comm., Am. U., Washington, 1988. Staff asst. Rep. Richard T. Schulze, Washington, 1986; editl. asst. The Washington Post, 1988-92; freelance journalist Paris, 1992—; spl. corr. Paris bur. Newsweek mag., 1995—; adj. prof. Am. U. Paris, 1996-99. Recipient Ellis Haller award for outstanding achievement in journalism Sigma Delta Chi, 1987-88; scholar Sigma Delta Chi Found., 1987-88. Mem. Assn. de la Press Etranger, Anglo-Am. Press Assn. Home: 1 Rue de Narbonne, 75007 Paris France Office: Newsweek, 162 rue Faubourg St-Honore, 75008 Paris France

THOMAS, DANIEL FRENCH, lawyer; b. Balt., Sept. 9, 1937; s. William Daniel and Lillian Hanway (Thompson) T.; m. Sandra Jean Ailiff, Dec. 20, 1996. BA, Loyola Coll., Balt., 1959; JD, U. Md., 1962. Bar: Md. 1962, U.S. Dist. Ct. Md. 1963. Law clk. to Hon. William M. Horney Ct. of Appeals of Md., Annapolis, 1962-63; atty. Bregel & Bregel, Balt., 1963-70, Thomas & Kalichman, Balt., 1971—; lectr. Md. Inst. for Continuing Profl. Edn. of Lawyers, Balt., 1980—. Editor: Maryland Divorce and Separation Law, 1987, 92, 96; contbr. articles to profl. jours. Home: 1101 Saint Paul St

Apt 2104 Baltimore MD 21202-2673 Office: Thomas & Kalichman 7 Saint Paul St Ste 950 Baltimore MD 21202-1673

THOMAS, DANIEL JEAN, biologist, researcher; b. La Crau, Var, France, May 17, 1947; s. Pierre Alain and Georgette (Férec) T.; m. Maryvonne Jacqueline Chalm, June 29, 1974; children: Yann, Rozenn. Licence, U. Brest, France, 1969; Doctorat de 3d Cycle, U. Rennes, France, 1972, DSc, 1981. Attaché rsch. CNRS, Rennes, 1976-82, chargé rsch., 1984-91, dir. rsch., 1991—, sous-dir. lab., 1987-91; vis. assoc. NIH, Bethesda, Md., 1982-84, vis. scientist, summer 1989, guest rschr., summer 1995. Contbr. articles to profl. jours. Pres. Enterprise Com., Rennes, 1989-91. With inf. French Army 1974-75. Mem. Soc. Française de Biophysique Paris, Soc. Française de Minoscopies (v.p. 1999-2000, pres. 2000—). Avocations: movies, music, jogging, travel. Home: Le Chénais, 35690 Acigné Brittany France Office: U Rennes, Campus de Beaulieu, 35042 Rennes Cedex, France

THOMAS, DAVID JEFFREY, physicist, mathematician, researcher, editor, financier; b. Sunderland, Eng., Aug. 4, 1957; s. Jeffrey John and Greta Victoria (Gibson) T. BA, Cambridge (Eng.) U., 1978, MA, 1981, PhD, 1983. Chartered mathematician; chartered physicist. Rsch. fellow, Bye fellow Peterhouse, Cambridge U., 1981-86; staff scientist MRC Lab. Molecular Biology, Cambridge, 1984-88; rsch. scientist Nimbus Records Ltd., Monmouth, Eng., 1988-89, EMBL, Heidelberg, Germany, 1989-98; freelance scientific editor, 1999—, comml. fin. broker, 2000—; cons. BV Enraf-Nonius, Delft, Netherlands, 1981-87. Contbr. more than 35 articles to profl. jours. Fellow Inst. Math. and Its Applications, Inst. Physics. Anglican. Avocations: singing, cooking, photography, design (electronic, mechanical and graphic), producing compact discs, karate. Home: 10 St Lukes Rd, Birmingham B5 7DA, England

THOMAS, DWAYNE ALLEN, composer, publisher; b. Jamaica, N.Y., July 29, 1974. Student, U. Ky., 1993; AS in Fine and Performing Arts, Queensborough C.C., 1997. Intern promotions and publicity Uptown/MCA Entertainment, N.Y.C., 1994-95; pres. WORDZ: Inc. Creative Svcs., Jamaica, N.Y., 1995-99; v.p. promotions and publicity Tear-A-Wrist Records, Jamaica, 1997-98; mem. bookstore security York Coll., Jamaica, 1999; owner, maintainer web site, Jamaica, 1999—; sect. leader Queensborough Chorus, Bayside, N.Y., 1994-97; profl. actor and musician, 1997-2000. Author of poetry. Coach Jamaica Ctrl. Little League; vol. tutor, 2000—. Avocations: baseball, basketball, piano, chess, singing.

THOMAS, EDWARD DONNALL, physician, researcher; b. Mart, Tex., Mar. 15, 1920; married; 3 children. BA, U. Tex., 1941, MA, 1943; MD, Harvard U., 1946; MD (hon.), U. Cagliari, Sardinia, 1981, U. Verona, Italy, 1991, U. Parma, Italy, 1992, U. Barcelona, Spain, 1994, U. Warsaw, Poland, 1996, U. Jagiellonski, Cracow, Poland, 1996. Lic. physician Mass., N.Y., Wash.; diplomate Am. Bd. Internal Medicine. Intern in medicine Peter Bent Brigham Hosp., Boston, 1946-47, rsch. fellow hematology, 1947-48; NRC postdoctoral fellow in medicine dept. biology MIT, Cambridge, 1950-51; chief med. resident, sr. asst. resident Peter Bent Brigham Hosp., 1951-53, hematologist, 1953-55; instr. medicine Harvard Med. Sch., Boston, 1953-55; rsch. assoc. Cancer Rsch. Found. Children's Med. Ctr., Boston, 1953-55; physician-in-chief Mary Imogene Bassett Hosp., Cooperstown, N.Y., 1955-63; assoc. clin. prof. medicine Coll. Physicians and Surgeons Columbia U., N.Y.C., 1955-63; attending physician U. Wash. Hosp., Seattle, 1963-90; prof. medicine Sch. Medicine U. Wash., Seattle, 1963-90, head divsn. oncology Sch. Medicine, 1963-85, prof. emeritus medicine Sch. Medicine, 1990—; dir. med. oncology Fred Hutchinson Cancer Rsch. Ctr., Seattle, 1974-89, assoc. dir. clin. rsch. programs, 1982-89, mem., 1974—; mem. hematology study sect. NIH, 1965-69; mem. bd. trustees and med. sci. adv. com. Leukemia Soc. Am., Inc., 1969-73; mem. clin. cancer investigation review com. Nat. Cancer Inst., 1970-74; 1st ann. Eugene C. Eppinger lectr. Peter Bent Brigham Hosp. and Harvard Med. Sch., 1974; Lilly lectr. Royal Coll. Physicians, London, 1977; Stratton lectr. Internation Soc. Hematology, 1982; Paul Aggeler lectr. U. Calif., San Francisco, 1982; 65th Mellon lectr. U. Pitts. Sch. Medicine, 1984; Stanley Wright Meml. lectr. Western Soc. Pediatric Rsch., 1985; Adolfo Ferrata lectr. Italian Soc. Hematology, Verona, Italy, 1991. Mem. editl. bd. Blood, 1962-75, 77-82, Transplantation, 1970-76, Proc. of Soc. for Exptl. Biology and Medicine, 1974-81, Leukemia Rsch., 1977-87, Hematological Oncology, 1982-87, Jour. Clin. Immunology, 1982-87, Am. Jour. Hematology, 1985—, Bone Marrow Transplantation, 1986—. With U.S. Army, 1948-50. Recipient A. Ross McIntyre award U. Nebr. Med. Ctr., 1975, Philip Levine award Am. Soc. Clin. Pathologists, 1979, Disting. Svc. in Basic Rsch. award Am. Cancer Soc., 1980, Kettering prize Gen. Motors Cancer Rsch. Found., 1981, Spl. Keynote Address award Am. Soc. Therapeutic Radiologists, 1981, Robert Roesler de Villiers award Leukemia Soc. Am., 1983, Karl Landsteiner Meml. award Am. Assn. Blood Banks, 1987, Terry Fox award Can., 1990, Internat. award Gairdner Found., 1990, N.Am. Med. Assn. Hong Kong prize, 1990, Nobel prize in medicine, 1990, Presdl. medal of sci. NSF, 1990,. Mem. NAS, Am. Assn. Cancer Rsch., Am. Assn. Physicians (Kober medal 1992), Am. Fedn. Clin. Rsch., Am. Soc. Clin. Oncology (David A. Karnoksky Meml. lectr. 1983), Am. Soc. Clin. Investigation, Am. Soc. Hematology (pres. 1987-88, Henry M. Stratton lectr. 1975), Internat. Soc. Exptl. Hematology, Internat. Soc. Hematology, Academie Royale de Medicine de Belgique (corresponding mem.), Swedish Soc. Hematology (hon.), Swiss Soc. Hematology, Royal Coll. Physicians and Surgeons Can. (hon.), Western Assn. Physicians, Soc. Exptl. Biology and Medicine, Transplantation Soc., Nat. Acad. Medicine Mexico (hon.). Office: Fred Hutchinson Cancer Ctr 1100 Fairview Ave N D5-100 PO Box 19024 Seattle WA 98109-1024

THOMAS, EDWARD JOHN, physicist, educator; b. Plymouth, Devon, Eng., Nov. 25, 1937; s. John Henry and Lily Elizabeth Jane (Stephens) T.; married, 1964; children; Katherine Grace, Gerard William. MA, U. Oxford, 1967; MSc, U. London, 1964; PhD, U. Manchester, 1968. Chartered physicist. Rsch. scientist GEC Ltd., London, 1962-64; lectr. U. Manchester, 1964-68; staff tutor U. Bristol, 1968-80, sr. lectr., 1980-81, dir. continuing edn., 1981-93, prof. continuing edn., 1981—. Author: Type II Superconductivity, 1969, From Quarks to Quasars, 1977. Fellow Royal Soc. Arts; mem. Inst. Physics, U. Coun. for Adult and Continuing Edn. (treas. 1987-93), European Univs. Continuing Edn. Network (sec. gen. 1992—). Avocations: reading, writing, walking, eating. Office: U Bristol, Grad Sch Edn, Bristol BS8 1HH, England

THOMAS, ELLA COOPER, lawyer; b. Ft. Totten, N.Y.; d. Avery John and Ona Caroline (Gibson) C.; m. Robert Edward Lee Thomas, Nov. 22, 1938 (dec. Jan. 1985); 1 child, Robert Edward Lee Jr. Student, Vassar Coll., 1932-34, U. Hawaii, 1934-35, George Washington U., 1935-36; JD, George Washington U., 1940. Bar: U.S. Dist. Ct. D.C. 1942, U.S. Ct. Appeals (D.C. cir.) 1943, U.S. Supreme Ct. 1947, U.S. Tax Ct. 1973. Secret maps custodian U.S. Dist. Engrs., Honolulu, 1941-42; contbg. editor Labor Rels. Reporter, Washington, 1942; assoc. Smith, Ristig & Smith, Washington, 1942-45; law libr. George Washington Law Sch., Washington, 1946-53; reporter of decisions U.S. Tax Ct., Washington, 1953-75. Author: Law of Libel and Slander, 1949. Mem. Inter-Am. Bar Assn. (coun. mem. 1973-99), D.C. Bar Assn. Avocations: physical fitness, crostics, mote marine lab. vol. computer.

THOMAS, ELLEN LOUISE, private school administrator; b. Doylestown, Pa., Nov. 30, 1940; d. Edward Martin and Evelyn Graham (Axenroth) Happ; m. Eugene Greene Leffever, June 30, 1963 (dec. Nov. 1978); children: Eugene Greene II, Jeanette Ellen Dellaripa; m. William Dewey Thomas, Sept. 15, 1981; 1 child, Jeremiah David. BA in Edn., Immaculata (Pa.) Coll., 1962; postgrad., Pa. State U., 1962-67. Pvt. practice tutor Doylestown, 1958-65; tchr. Cen. Bucks Sch. System, Doylestown, 1962-65; adminstr. The Curiosity Shoppe, Doylestown, 1965—, The Toddler Ctr., Doylestown, 1979—; exec. dir. Camp Curiosity, Doylestown, 1984—, Thomas Lea Equestrian Ctr., Doylestown, 1988—; tchr. trainer Confortunity of Christian Doctrine, Doylestown, 1965-78; cons. early childhood Am. Sch. in Hong Kong, 1981-84; lectr. in early childhood Bucks County Community Ctr., Newtown, Pa., 1978-90; workshop facilitator Head Start, Phila., 1990; cons. day care Cen. Bucks C. of C., Doylestown, 1989-90; ednl. coord. Forest Grove Presbyn. Ch., 1984-90. Mem. U.S. C. of C., Washington, Bucks County C. of C., Doylestown, Nat. Fedn. of Ind. Bus., Washington; children's ministry coord. Jesus Focus Ministry, 1995—; trainer Pa. Child Care, 1995—; pres. Pa. Day Camp Assn., 1998—. Mem. ASCD, Assn. for Childhood Edn. Internat., United Pvt. Acad. Schs. Assn., Bucks County Assn. Edn. Young Children (pres. 1974-78). Office: The Curiosity Shoppe 4425 Landisville Rd Doylestown PA 18901-1134

THOMAS, ELLIOTT G., former bishop; b. Pittsburgh, PA, July 15, 1926. ordained priest June 6, 1986. Bishop Diocese of St. Thomas in the Virgin Islands, 1993-99. Office: PO Box 301825 Charlotte Amalie VI 00803-1825*

THOMAS, EUGENE C., lawyer; b. Idaho Falls, Idaho, Feb. 8, 1931; s. C.E. Thomas; m. Jody Raber; children: Michael E., Stephen R. A.B., Columbia U., 1952, J.D., 1954, LLD (hon.) Univ. Idaho, 1986, LLD (hon.), Coll. of Idaho, 1987. Bar: Idaho, 1954, U.S. Dist. Ct. Idaho 1957, US Ct. Appeals (9th cir.) 1958, U.S. Supreme Ct. 1970. Pros. atty. Ada County, Boise, Idaho, 1955-57; founding ptnr. Moffatt, Thomas, Barrett, Rock & Fields, Boise, 19578—; bd. dirs. Shore Lodge, Inc., McCall, Idaho, Nelson-Ball Paper Products, Inc., Longview, Wash., Peregrine Industries, Inc., Boise. Bd. editors ABA Jour., 1980-87. Bd. dirs. St. Luke's Regional Med. Ctr. and Mountain States Tumor Inst., Boise, 1963—, pres., chmn. bd. 1972-79; trustee Coll. of Idaho, 1980—, mem. exec. com., 1982—; trustee Associated Taxpayers of Idaho, 1983—, chmn., 1988-90. trustee Boise Futures Found., 1973—, bd. dirs., 1981—, bd. dirs. Univ./Community Health Scis. Assn., 1981—; chmn. Mayor's Select Com. on Downtown Devel., 1982-83. Named Exec. of Yr., Boise chpt. Nat. Secs. Assn., 1978, John Price lectr. 1987 ann. conf. Nat. Coll. Dist. Attys.; recipient disting. svc. award Idaho Pros. Attys., 1985, disting. svc. award Chgo. Vol. Legal Svc. Found., 1986. Fellow Internat. Acad. Trial Lawyers, Am. Bar Found. (trustee 1980-82, 86-87), Am. Law Inst.; mem. ABA (ho. of dels. 1971—, chmn. ho. of dels. 1980-82, bd. govs. 1980-82, pres. 1986-87, chmn. spl. com. on internat. affairs 1987-88), Idaho State Bar (pres. 1971-72, disting. lawyer award 1980, 86), Def. Research Inst. (state chmn. Pacific region 1978—), Idaho Assn. Def. Counsel (trustee 1966-69, pres. 1967-68), Internat. Assn. Ins. Counsel, Am. Bd. Trial Advocates, Fourth Dist. Bar Assn. (pres. 1962-63), Internat. Bar Assn. (chmn. biennial conf., governing coun. 1985-86), Conference of Pres. Union Internat. des Avocats (pres.), Nat. Conf. Bar Pres. (trustee 1974-76), Law Soc. Eng. and Wales (hon.), La Barra Mexicana (hon.), New Zealand Law Soc. (hon.), Can. Bar Assn. (hon.), Integrated Bar of the Philippines (hon.), Rocky Mountain Oil and Gas Assn. (chmn. Idaho legal com. 1978—). Clubs: Arid (dir. 1977-79), Hillcrest Country (bd. dirs. 1969-72) (Boise). Office: Moffatt Thomas Barrett Rock & Fields PO Box 829 Boise ID 83701-0829*

THOMAS, FRANK EDWARD, professional baseball player; b. Columbus, Ga., May 27, 1968. Student, Auburn U. With Chgo. White Sox, 1990—. Named to Sporting News All-Star Coll. All Am. team, 1989; Sporting News All-Star team, 1991, 93-94; recipient Silver Slugger award, 1991, 93, 94; mem. Am. League All-Star Team, 1993-95; recipient Am. League MVP award, 1994; named Major League Player of Yr., Sporting News, 1993. Office: Chgo White Sox Comiskey Park 333 W 35th St Chicago IL 60616-3651

THOMAS, FRANKLIN ROSBOROUGH, retired animator; b. Santa Monica, Calif., Sept. 5, 1912; s. Frank Waters and Ina Marcella (Gregg) T.; m. Jeanette Armentrout, Feb. 16, 1946; children: Ann Winfield, Gregg Franklin, Theodore William, Douglas Craig. Student, Fresno State Coll., 1929-31; AB magna cum laude, Stanford U., 1933; postgrad., Chouinard Art Sch., 1933-34, Walt Disney Studio, 1934. Directing animator Walt Disney Co., Burbank, Calif., 1934-78; ret., 1978; lectr., spkr. in field; chmn. jury N.Y. Internat. Animated Film Festival, 1975. Animator for numerous films, including Show White and the Seven Dwarfs, 1937, Pinocchio, 1940, Bambi, 1942, The Three Caballeros, 1945, The Many Adventures of Winnie the Pooh, 1977; directing animator The Adventures of Ichabod and Mr. Toad, 1949, Cinderella, 1950, Alice in Wonderland, 1951, Peter Pan, 1953, Lady and the Tramp, 1955, Sleeping Beauty, 1959, 101 Dalmatians, 1961, Sword in the Stone, 1963, Mary Poppins, 1964, The Jungle Book, 1967, The Aristocats, 1970, Robin Hood, 1973, The Rescuers, 1977; supervising animator: The Fox and the Hound, 1981; also animator for numerous shorts; co-author: Disney Animation -- The Illusion of Life, 1981, Too Funny for Words, 1987, Bambi-The Story and the Film, 1990, Jungle Book Portfolio, 1993, Disney Villains, English edit., 1993, French edit., 1995; contbr. editor to sketch book series; Dixieland jazz pianist Firehouse Five Plus 2, 1949-68, appearing on radio and TV programs The Bing Crosby Show, The Milton Berle Show, Ed Wynn TV Shows, others; subject of documentary Frank and Ollie; exhibited drawings in Whitney Mus., N.Y.C., 1981. Guest spkr. Russian Govt. and Soyuzmultfilm and other East European countries, 1976, U.S. Info. Agy. Cultural Exch. Program, 1986. With USAF, 1942-45. Recipient numerous awards, including Annie award Internat. Animated Film Soc., 9 Old Men award Hon. Cinema Soc. Mem. Phi Beta Kappa. Address: 758 Flintridge Ave Flintridge CA 91011-4027

THOMAS, GALE DENISE, psychologist; b. Atlanta. BA, Shaw U., 1978; MEd, N.C. State U., 1981; EdS, Ga. State U., 1986, PhD, 1992. Cert. sch. psychologist, Ga. Spl. edn. tchr. DeKalb County Sch. Sys., Decatur, Ga., 1981-82; sch. psychologist DeKalb County Sch. Sys., Decatur, 1985-90, lead psychologist, 1990-94, coord. psychol. svcs., 1994—; profl. tutor, co-owner The Tutorage, Atlanta, 1982-85. Active Jr. League DeKalb, Decatur, Leadership DeKalb Class 2000, Decatur. Named Individual of Yr. Dogwood chpt. Coun. Exceptional Children, Decatur, 1989. Mem. APA, Ga. Assn. Sch. Psychologists (regional rep. 1996-98, pres. 1998-99, past pres. 1999-2000), Delta Sigma Theta Sorority, Inc., Alphi Chi. E-mail: gdthomas@onebox.com and gdt7874@dcss.dekalb.k12.ga.us. Fax: 404-298-0007. Home: 934 Lake Drive Ct Stone Mountain GA 30088-2340 Office: Psychol Svcs 5839 Memorial Dr Stone Mountain GA 30083-3486

THOMAS, GLANFFRWD POWELL, mathematician, computer scientist, educator; b. Swansea, Wales, U.K., Dec. 1, 1949; s. David Glanffrwd and Ethel (Powell) T.; m. Mary Bernadette Grew, Aug. 1, 1979; children: Glanffrwd Patrick, Clare Finola. BA, Oxford (Eng.) U., 1971, MA, 1975; PhD, U. Wales, 1975. Chartered mathematician; chartered engr. Sys. analyst Arthur Andersen and Co., London and Chgo., 1974-76; rsch. fellow U. Wales, Aberystwyth, 1976-77; lectr. U. Coll. Cork, U.K., 1977-80; sr. prodr., editor BBC, London and Milton Keynes, 1980-88; course dir. U. London, Eng., 1988-92; head decision scis. Westminster U., London, 1992-95; prof. math. Luton U., Eng., 1995—; cons. Govt. of Kenya, Nairobi, 1986; advisor Brit. Govt., London, 1988-92, 96—, Hong Kong U., 1992—, Singapore Inst. Mgmt., 1992—, Open Learning Inst. Hong Kong, 1993—; dir. Grew Thomas, London, 1989—. Author books; contbr. articles to profl. jours.; prodr., writer, presenter, expert contbr. TV, radio and audio programs. Grantee Brit. Govt., London, 1982-88, Nairobi, 1988, Hong Kong Govt., 1994. Fellow Inst. Math. and Its Applications; mem. Brit. Computer Soc. Avocations: squash, computer games, fine wine, travel. E-mail: gpt@mac.com. Home: 66 Shakespeare Rd, Bedford MK40 2DJ, England

THOMAS, HELEN LEE, linguistics educator; b. Seymour, Ind., Feb. 4, 1951; d. Frank Walter and Virginia Ann (Kieffer) Voss; m. James Mitchell Thomas, Sept. 11, 1981 (div. 1989); children: Kyle, Kieffer. AB, Ind. U., 1973, MS, 1978, PhD in Linguistics, 1987. Dir. Intensive Edn. Lang. Ctr. U. Nev., Reno, 1982-88, dir. internat. programs, 1988-93, asst. prof., 1994-2000, assoc. prof., 2000—. Author: The English Language: An Owner's Manual, 1999; contbr. articles to profl. jours. including Modern Lang. Jour., English Jour. Fulbright Assn. scholar. Mem. Am. Assn. Applied Linguistics, Linguistic Soc. Am., Fulbright Assn., TESOL, Internat. Assn. World Englishes, Amnesty Internat. Avocations: skiing, hiking, sailing. Office: U Nev Reno English Dept 098 Reno NV 89509

THOMAS, HELMUT JAKOB, biochemist, educator, researcher; b. Ahrweiler, Germany, Aug. 20, 1929; s. Matthias and Anna Josefine (Peters) T.; m. Elke Moehler, Oct. 16, 1981; children: Christine, Annette. MD, U. Bonn, 1959. Univ. lectr. U. Bonn, Germany, 1966-70; assoc. prof. U. Ulm, Germany, 1970-75, prof., 1976; head dept. of physiol. chemistry U. Ulm, Germany, 1976, dean of faculty of theoretical medicine, 1972-73, v.p., 1976-79, emeritus, 1997. Co-author: Methods of Hormone Analysis, 1976, Fermente, Hormone, Vitamine, 1982; contbr. articles to profl. jours. Mem. German Soc. of Biol. Chemistry, German Soc. of Endrocinology, N.Y. Acad. Scis. Office: U Ulm Dept Physiologische, Albert Einstein Allee 11, 89081 Ulm Germany

THOMAS, HUGH (LORD THOMAS OF SWYNNERTON), historian; b. Windsor, Eng., Oct. 21, 1931; s. Hugh Whitelegge and Margery Angelo Augusta (Swynnerton) T.; m. Vanessa Mary Jebb, May 5, 1962; children: Inigo, Isambard, Isabella. Prof. history U. Reading, London, 1966-76, chmn. Centre Policy Studies, 1979-91; life peer, 1981—; King Juan Carlos I prof. of Spanish civilization, N.Y.C., 1995-96; prof. U. Boston, 1996—. Author: The Spanish Civil War, 1961, The Suez Affair, 1968, Cuba or the Pursuit of Freedom, 1971, An Unfinished History of the World, 1979, Havannah, 1984, Armed Truce, 1986, Madrid, A Traveller's Companion, 1988, Klara, 1988, Ever Closer Union, 1991, The Conquest of Mexico, 1993 (U.S. edit. titled Conquest), The Slave Trade, 1997, The Future of Europe, 1997. Recipient Somerset Maugham prize, 1962; Nat. Arts Council Book award, 1980; named to the Order of Isabel the Catholic Spain, 1987, Order of Aztec Eagle Mex., 1994. Mem. Royal Acad. History Spain. Office: House of Lords, London SW1, England*

THOMAS, JACQUELYN MAY, librarian; b. Mechanicsburg, Pa., Jan. 26, 1932; d. William John and Gladys Elizabeth (Warren) Harvey; m. David Edward Thomas, Aug. 28, 1954; children: Lesley J., Courtenay J., Hilary A. BA summa cum laude, Gettysburg Coll., 1954; student, U. N.C., 1969; MEd, U. N.H., 1971. Libr. Phillips Exeter Acad., Exeter, N.H., 1971-77, acad. libr., 1977—; chair governing bd. Child Care Ctr., 1987-91; chair Com. to Enhance Status of Women, Exeter, 1981-84; chair Loewenstein Com., Exeter, 1982—; pres. Cum Laude Soc., Exeter, 1984-86; James H. Ottaway Jr. prof., 1990—; mem. bldg. com. Exeter Pub. Libr., 1986-88; chair No. New Eng., Coun. for Women in Ind. Schs., 1985-87; chmn. Lamont Poetry Program, Exeter, 1984-86. Editor: The Design of the Library: A Guide to Sources of Information, 1981, Rarities of Our Time: The Special Collections of the Phillips Exeter Academy Library. Libr. trustee, treas. Exeter Day Sch., 1965-69; bd. Exeter Hosp. Vols., 1954-59; mem. Exeter Hosp. Corp., 1978—; bd. dirs. Greater Portsmouth Cmty. Found., 1990—; active AAC&U, On Campus with Women, Wellesley Coll. Ctr. for Rsch. on Women; mem. People to People Amb. Program, sch. and youth svcs. libr. del. to People's Rep. China, 1998. Grantee N.H. Coun. for Humanties, 1981-82, NEH, 1982; recipient Lillian Radford trust award, 1989. Mem. ALA, Internat. Assn. Sch. Librs., New Eng. Libr. Assn., N.J., Ednl. Media Assn., New Eng. Assn. Ind. Sch. Librs., Am. Assn. Sch. Librs. (chmn. non-pub. sch. sect.), Phi Beta Kappa. Fax: 603-777-4389. E-mail: jthomas@exeter.edu. Home: 16 Elm St Exeter NH 03833-2704 Office: Acad Libr Phillips Exeter Acad 20 Main St Exeter NH 03833-2438

THOMAS, JAMES ARTHUR, retired government official, electrical engineer; b. Meridian, Miss., Sept. 4, 1934; s. Walter James and Gladys Clarice (Harper) T.; m. Lily Juanita Purvis, Aug. 31, 1956; children: Karen Thomas Andrews, Chuck, Wendy Thomas Marks. BSEE, Miss. State U., 1962; MBA, Fla. State U., 1973. Sys. engr. NASA-Kennedy Space Ctr., Fla., 1962-74, engr. Orbiter project, 1974-82, engr. shuttle project, 1982-84; launch dir. of shuttle NASA-Kennedy Space Ctr., 1985-87, dir. safety, reliability and quality assurance, 1987-90, dep. ctr. dir., 1990-97. Mem. Nat. Space Club, Rocket Pioneers Club. Baptist. Avocations: reading, writing, swimming. Home: 355 Pine Blvd Merritt Island FL 32952-5004

THOMAS, JAMES EDWARD, accountant; b. Darlington, S.C., Oct. 18, 1944; s. Willie Thomas and Cleola (Sawyer) T.; m. Joan Yvette Grant, Mar. 15, 1945; 1 child, James E. II. BS in Acctg., Johnson C. Smith Coll., Charlotte, N.C., 1966; MA in Fin., C.W. Post Coll., Greenvale, N.Y., 1980; PhD in Edn., Fordham U., 1995; MBA, Pace U., 1976. Cert. paralegal. Asst. mgr. Mfrs. Hanover Trust, N.Y.C., 1970-78, Met. Savs. Bank, N.Y.C., 1978-81; auditor N.Y. State Dept. Social Svcs., N.Y.C., 1981-83; acct. N.Y.C. Bd. Edn., 1983-86; acct., agt. IRS, N.Y.C., 1987-99; dir. fin. N.Y.C Dept. Design and Constrn., Long Island City, 1999—; instr. Katherine L. Gibbs, Inc., N.Y.C., 1987-89. Mem. Assn. MBA Execs., Am. Mgmt. Assn., Internat. Platform Assn., Nat. Soc. Pub. Accts., Sigma Rho Sigma. Avocations: woodworking, basketball, basebell, track, reading. Home: 99-72 66th Md # 3R Rego Park NY 11374

THOMAS, JAMES EDWARD, JR., brokerage house executive; b. Atlanta, Apr. 23, 1950; s. James Edward and Dortha Jean (White) Thomas; m. Leslie Ann Stagmaier, Sept. 6, 1975; children: Steele Stagmaier, Katherine Mills. BA magna cum laude, U. Ga., 1972, JD cum laude, 1975. Mgr. Genuine Parts Co., Atlanta, 1975-77; v.p. Robinson Humphrey Co., Atlanta, 1977-94; ptnr. J.C. Bradford and Co., Atlanta, 1994—; bd. dirs. Enstar Comm. Corp., The Kinston Group, Inc., Atlanta, Tophat Soccer Club, Atlanta, Hall's Boathouse, Inc., Lakemont, Ga., Vista Environ. Info., Inc., San Diego. Pres. Castlewood Civic Orgn., Inc., Atlanta; mem. Lake Rabun Homeowners Assn., Lakemont, Ga.; mem. bd. advisors U. Ga., Habitat for Humanity. Mem. Internat. Platform Assn., Ga. Bar Assn., La Societe des Tetes Grandes, Capital City Club, U. Ga. LEADS Adv. Bd. Republican. Episcopalian. Avocations: boating, tennis, golf.

THOMAS, JEFF ALAN, educator; b. Oklahoma City, Sept. 8, 1967; s. Don C. and Lana L. (Hobbs) T.; m. Andrea M. Thomas; MEd, Southwestern Okla. State U., 1992; MS, PhD, U. So. Miss., 1999. Tchr. Univ. Mil. Sch. Wright, Mobile, Ala., 1996—. Outstanding Future Tchr. scholar Okla. Dept. Edn. Mem. Nat. Sci. Tchrs. Assn., Nat. Assn. for Rsch. in Sci. Tchg. Baptist. Avocation: sports. Office: U Mil Sch Wright 65 N Mobile St Mobile AL 36607-3120

THOMAS, JOHN, mechanical engineer, research and development; b. Tiruvalla, Kerala, India, Jan. 2, 1946; came to U.S., 1974; s. Munnencheril Varghese and Rachel (Mathai) T.; m. Mary Parapat Varghese, Apr. 28, 1975; children: Joel George, Sayana Rachel. BSc in Mech. Engring., Birla Inst. Tech., Ranchi, India, 1969; MA Sc in Mech. Engring., U. Waterloo, Ont., Can., 1974. Registered profl. engr., Wis. Lectr. mech. engring. U. Kerala, India, 1970-71; design engr. Combustion Engring., Inc., Springfield, Ohio, 1974-76; mech. engr. Ingersoll-Rand Co., Painted Post, N.Y., 1977-80; engr. Allis-Chalmers Corp., Milw., 1980-82; pvt. practice engring. cons. Milw., 1982-84; sr. tech. devel. engr. Cross & Trecker divsn. Kearney & Trecker Corp., Milw., 1984-87; prin. John Thomas & Assocs., Brookfield, Wis., 1988-90; sr. product engr. N.W. Water Group, Pub. Ltd. Corp., Waukesha, Wis., 1989-94; pres. Thomas Products Co., Brookfield, Wis., 1995—; staff engr. Milsco Mfg. Co. unit of Jason Inc., Milw., 1997—. Patentee in field. Mem. Am. Soc. Mech. Engrs., U. Waterloo Alumni Assn. Mem. Mar Thoma Syrian Ch. of Malabar. Avocation: photography. Home: 18330 Benington Brookfield WI 53045-5419 Office: Thomas Products Co PO Box 401 Brookfield WI 53008-0401

THOMAS, JOHN DAVID, musician, composer, arranger, photographer, recording engineer, producer; b. Muncie, Ind., Mar. 30, 1951; s. John Charles and Phyllis Lorraine (Wear) T.; m. Rosalie Faith Baldwin, July 27, 1974 (div. 1991); children: Bethany Carol, Mark David. Student, Purdue U., 1969-71, Jordan Coll. of Music, Indpls., 1961-65; BS in Music Theory and Composition, Ball State U., 1976. Musician, composer, 1955—; cellist The Howe String Quartet (with Ann Pinney, Mary Ann Tilford, Anne Wuster), Indpls., 1967-68; keyboardist, vocalist, cellist Fire and The Rebel Kind rock bands, Indpls., 1967-69, Good Conduct rock band, Muncie, Ind., 1972-73; pianist The Pavillion at Olde Towne, Los Gatos, Calif., 1969; radio announcer John David's Late Night Rock Show WCCR-AM, West Lafayette, Ind., 1969-70; photographer Indpls., 1964-84, 91—; budget analyst Office of Comptr. USAFAC, Indpls., 1976-84; co-leader, keyboardist, composer, arranger, vocalist, sound technician Jetstream band, Carmel, Indpls., Kokomo, Columbus, Bloomington, Ind., 1979-83; co-leader, keyboardist, vocalist, sound technician The Thomas Bros., King's Crown Inn, Kokomo, 1979; sound/audio visual technician Valley Cathedral Ch., Phoenix, 1987; pianist, synthesist Paul Thomas and Night and Day, The Tim Barnett Band, Indpls. Mus. Art, 1992, Radisson Hotel and Broadmoor Country Club, Indpls., 1991, Highland Country Club, Indpls., The Ritz Charles Hotel and Summertrace, Carmel, Ind., Stonehenge Resort, Bedford, Ind., 1991; solo pianist Terranova Mansion, Paradise Valley, Ariz., 1987, Wrigley Mansion, Phoenix, 1988, Boulders Resort, Carefree, Ariz., 1987, Clarion Inn/McCormick's Ranch Resort, Scottsdale, Ariz., 1986, China Gate, Phoenix, 1988, Victor's, Phoenix, 1988, Cascade Club, Everett, Wash., 1990; keyboardist, synthesist, key bassist, The Gulch Gang, Pinnacle Peak Patio, Scottsdale, 1984, Dee Dee Ryan, The Longhorn Saloon, Apache Junction, Ariz., 1984-86, The Last Straw Band, Country City saloon, Mesa, Ariz., 1986; keyboardist, pianist, vocalist with Peter, Paul and John, Anderson (Ind.) Coll., 1977; CEO, com-

poser, arranger, prodr., musician, engr. John David Thomas Prodns., Indpls., 1993—; CEO JD Thomas Music Co., 1999—, Monolith Records, 1999—; rec. artist CD label mp3.com., 2000—. Composer, lyricist of over 150 classical, religious, comml., rock, jazz, popular and avante garde/futuristic compositions, including Infinity, 1970-71, Death of Rock and Roll, 1970, Night Visions, 1972, First Things First, 1972, Two Nudes and a Fire Hydrant, 1972-73, Zeitgeist: The Spirit of the Time, 1974, The Little Prince, 1973, When We Dead Awaken, 1973, Pray, 1972, Apogee, 1974, Chinese Baby, 1973, Alabama DA (Top Forty recording), 1973, Angel, 1974, Music for French Horn, Cello, and Piano, 1976, Cruising Beyond, 1979, Jetstream Theme, 1979, Chrissy, 1979, Love Theme in B Minor, 1979, In Your Heart, 1983, Future Music, 1987, The Recurrent New Millenium Orchestral Olympic Disco Festival Dance, 1989, Jubilee in F, 1989, Praise Him, The King Liveth, 1989, Love Flowers: Reflections and Meditations on Beauty and Truth, 1990, Sheena's Theme, 1992, I Want You Forever You're My Miracle, 1992, My Pseudo-Erotic, Sensual, Exotic Musical Fantasy and Romance for Our Heavenly Nocturnal Starry-Skied Carpet Ride to Paradise in Istanbul and Constantinople, 1992, I'm in Love with Someone Beautiful, 1992, Improvisations for Sheena, 1992, Music for Baritone Vocal and String Orch., 1995, Meditations for Pipe Organ and Male Choir, 1996, Trumpet Voluntary in F, 1996, Pathway to Love, 1996, Majestic Brass Music in F#, 1997, J.D.'s Theme, 1998, Love Theme in D, 1972, 98, The Road to Tomorrow, 1999; (albums) The Journey of Life, Destiny's Calling: Improvisations, 1994, Musical Essences, 1995, (cd's) The Seen and the Unseen, 2000, Potpourri: Music for the World, 2000, Music for the World, vol. 2, 2000, (broadcast) Hometown Hour, Sta. WFBQ-FM, Indpls., 1979-80; performed orginal composition, Someday, WFBM-TV, Indpls., 1969; designer automotive concepts and popular fashions; recordings of over 45 original songs and compositions, Ind., Ariz., Wash., 1970— including Love Theme in D, 1972, 98, Majestic Brass Music in F# for Bethany and Mark, 1997, J.D.'s Theme, 1998; author (poetry with others) Mind, 1993, 96. Musician, vocalist, composer Downey Ave. Christian Ch., Indpls., 1961-69, Univ. Presbyn. Ch., West Lafayette, Ind., 1969-71, Castleview Bapt. Ch., Indpls., 1974-84, Valley Cathedral Ch., Phoenix, 1986-87, Edmonds (Wash.) Christian Ch., 1988-90, Edmonds United Meth. Ch., 1989-90; page to speaker Ho. of Reps. Ind. State Legislature, 1963; active All Souls Unitarian Ch., Indpls., 1994-96. GM scholar Purdue U., 1969-70, Hoosier scholar, 1969, Palmer Meml. Music scholar Ball State U., 1971-74; named to Ind. All-State Orch. (cellist), 1968; recipient 1st place award (cellist) Ind. State Music Contest, 1968, God and Country award, 1965, Outstanding Musician award Irvington Music Club, Indpls., 1969, Purdue U. Symphonette, 1970, Hometown Hour award WFBQ-FM Radio Sta., Indpls., 1979. Mem. ASCAP, NARAS, Audio Engring. Soc., Mensa. Avocations: reading, cd's, listening to music, dining, photography. Fax: 317-574-0580. E-mail: johndavidthomas@hotmail.com. Home and Office: 2704 Central Ct Indianapolis IN 46280-1930

THOMAS, JOSEPH WINAND, lawyer; b. New Orleans, Aug. 2, 1940; s. Gerald Henry and Edith Louise (Winand) T.; m. Claudette Condoll, Aug. 2, 1960 (div. Nov. 1985); children: Jeffery J., Anthony W.; m. Shawn B. Watkins, May 26, 1986 (div. June 1989); children: Adelle, Anne; m. Sandra J. Green, May 17, 1992; children: Winand, Elizabeth, Alice, Shepard, Julia. BS, Loyola U., Chgo., 1967; JD, Loyola U., New Orleans, 1973; MBA, Tulane U., 1984. Bar: La. 1973, U.S. Dist. Ct. (ea. dist.) La. 1973, U.S. Ct. Appeals (5th cir.) 1973, U.S. Supreme Ct. 1976, D.C. 1980. Staff atty. New Orleans Legal Assistance Corp., 1973-74; asst. atty. gen. State of La., 1974-80; pvt. practice New Orleans, 1980—; Pres., bd. dirs. New Orleans Legal Assistance Corp. Active NAACP, New Orleans, 1987-89; bd. dirs. Urban League, New Orleans. Mem. ABA, Louis Martinet Legal Soc., New Orleans Bar Assn., La. Bar Assn. Democrat. Roman Catholic. Office: 2 Canal St New Orleans LA 70130-1408

THOMAS, KEITH VIVIAN, historian, former college president; b. Wick, Glamorgan, U.K., Jan. 2, 1933; s. Vivian Jones and Hilda Janet Eirene (Davies) T.; m. Valerie June Little, Aug. 16, 1961; children: Emily Joanna, Edmund Vivian. MA, Oxford (Eng.) U., 1959; LLD (hon.), Williams Coll., 1988, Oglethorpe U., 1996; DLitt (hon.), U. Kent, 1983, U. Wales, 1987, U. Sheffield, 1992, U. Cambridge, U. Hull, 1995, U. Leicester, 1996, U. Sussex, 1996. Fellow All Souls Coll., Oxford, 1955-57; fellow and tutor St. John's Coll., Oxford, 1957-85; reader in modern history U. Oxford, U.K., 1978-85, prof. modern history, 1986; pres. Corpus Christi Coll., Oxford, 1986-2000; pro vice-chancellor Oxford U., 1988-2000; del. Oxford U. Press, 1980-2000, chmn. fin. com., 1988-2000; cons. editor Dictionary of National Biography 1986-90. Author: Religion and the Decline of Magic, 1971 (Wolfson prize 1972), Rule and Misrule in the Schools of Early Modern England, 1976, Age and Authority in Early Modern England, 1976, Man and the Natural World, 1983, The Perception of the Past in Early Modern England, 1984, History and Literature, 1989; editor: (with Donald Pennington) Puritans and Revolutionaries, 1978, Opus Books, Past Masters series, The Oxford Book of Work, 1999; mem. editl. bd. Past and Present, Ecumene, Prometeo; contbr. chpts. to books, articles to profl. jours. Mem. Econ. and Sci. Rsch. Coun., London, 1985-90; mem. rev. com. Export of Works of Art, 1989-92; trustee The Nat. Gallery, London, 1991-98, The Brit. Mus., 1999—; mem. Royal Commn. Hist. Manuscripts, 1992—. Served Royal Welch Fusiliers, 1950-52. Decorated knight bachelor (Eng.), cavaliere officiale Ordine al Merito della Repubblica Italiana; hon. fellow Balliol Coll., Oxford U., 1984—, St. Johns Coll., 1986—. Fellow Brit. Acad. (pres. 1993-97), Royal Hist. Soc. (literary dir. 1970-74, v.p. 1980-84); mem. Am. Acad. Arts and Scis. (fgn. hon. mem.), Academia Europaea (trustee). Avocation: visiting secondhand bookshops. Office: Corpus Christi Coll, Oxford OX1 4JF, England

THOMAS, KERRY-ANNE ABIGAIL, investment executive; b. Newport, Gwent, Wales, Dec. 23, 1970; d. Keith Edward and Patricia Sydney Ann (Cocks) T. Degree in law, U. Ctrl. Eng., Birmingham, 1992. Mgr. Kim's Legal Svcs., Birmingham, 1992-94; co. sec. Hambros Bank Ltd., London, 1994-98; dep. group sec. Investec Group, London, 1998—. Mem. Inst. Chartered Secs. and Adminstrs. Avocations: music, theatre, classics. Office: Investec Group, 2 Gresham St, London EC2V 7QP, England

THOMAS, KEVIN JOHN, business executive; b. Five Dock, NSW, Australia, Jan. 25, 1941; s. Arthur James Thomas and Nellie (Bayliss) T.; m. Rhonda Therese Elliott, Nov. 17, 1966 (div. Apr. 1994); children: Kym Joanne, Jeremy John; m. Helen Joyce Keighley, Nov. 7, 1999. Trade cert., Sydney (Australia) Tech. Sch., 1960. Cert. lithographer. Apprentice Gadsden-Hughes, Five Dock, 1956-62; lithographer various orgns., Australia, 1962-67; mgr. pre-press sect. Amalgamated Colour, Lewisham, Australia, 1967-70; nat. tech. mgr. F.T. Wimble, Rydalmere, Australia, 1970-76; gen. mgr. A.E. Hudson Proprietary Ltd., Newtown, Australia, 1976-84; mng. dir. Seaga Proprietary Ltd., Granville, Australia, 1984—; bd. dirs. Australian Graphic Arts Coun., Sydney, Amaco Proprietary Ltd., St. Leonards, Australia. Fellow Lithographic Inst. Australia (fed. v.p. 1995-97, bd. dirs. 1992—, apprentice chmn. 1986—, fed. pres. 1997-99), Graphic Arts Merchants Assn. Australia; mem. Sydney Rowing Club. Avocations: music, films. Office: Seaga Proprietary Ltd, 20 Wentworth St, NSW Granville 2142, Australia

THOMAS, MARILYN JANE, insurance agent, agency owner; b. Fremont, Ohio, Dec. 11, 1944; d. Myron Elwood and Elvira Evelyn (Plagman) Magsig; m. William E. Thomas, Jr., Nov. 7, 1992; stepchildren: Dana Lauren Thomas. BS in Edn., Capital U., Columbus, 1966; postgrad., U. Calif., Irvine, Fullerton, 1969-70. Tchr. pub. schs., Ohio, Calif., La., 1966-71; underwriter Tenn. Life Ins. Co., Houston, Tex., 1971-73; supr., mgr. contracts adminstrn. Phila. Life Ins. Co. (merger with Tenn. Life Ins. Co.), Houston, 1973-80; systems analyst Phila. Life Ins. Co., Houston, 1980-84; dir. market research/product devel. Phila. Am. Life Ins. Co. (merger Phila. Life Ins. Co.), Houston, 1984-87; 2d v.p. mktg. Phila. Am. Life Ins./New Era Life, Houston, 1987-97; owner Marilyn Thomas & Assocs., Houston, 1998—. Vol. Spl. Olympics, Houston; tchr. Project Business, 1981. Recipient Outstanding Woman award, Houston YWCA, 1984. Mem. Am. Bus. Women's Assn. (chmn. edn. com. 1987-88), Soc. Group Contract Analysts (chmn. com. 1977-80), Houston Assn. Health Underwriters, Toastmasters Internat. Republican. Lutheran. Avocation: cooking. Office: Ste 155 South 16800 Greenspoint Park Houston TX 77060-2304

THOMAS, MARTIN VINCENT, scientific research company executive; b. Dorking, Surrey, Eng., June 3, 1950; s. Albert Vincent and Ivy Doreen (Agate) T. BA, Cambridge (Eng.) U., 1971, MA, 1975, PhD, 1975. Rsch. assoc. Boston U. Med. Sch., 1975-77, asst. prof., 1977-78; univ. demonstrator Oxford (Eng.) U., 1978-79; rsch. scientist Shell Rsch. Ltd., Sittingbourne, Eng., 1979-84, sr. scientist, 1984-89; mng. dir. Cairn Rsch. Ltd., Sittingbourne, 1989—; cons. Musical Fidelity Ltd., London, 1983-85; rsch. fellow Leicester (Eng.) Biocentre, 1985-87, Marine Biol. Lab., Plymouth, Eng., 1989—. Author: Techniques in Calcium Research; contbr. articles to profl. jours. Named for Best Power Amplifier Design, Fedn. of Brit. Audio, London, 1984. Mem. Physiol. Soc., Biochem. Soc. Avocations: photography, hill walking. Office: Cairn Rsch Ltd, Ste 3G, Brents Indsl Estate, Faversham ME13 7DZ, England

THOMAS, MARY AUGUSTA, library administrator; b. Washington, Mar. 15, 1951; d. Abram Henry and Mary Agnes Rosenfeld; m. George D. Thomas Jr., Nov. 9, 1991. AB cum laude, Mt. Holyoke Coll., 1973; MSLS, Cath. U., Washington, 1978. From rare book libr. to mgr. planning and adminstrn. Smithsonian Librs., Washington, 1976-91, asst. dir., 1991—. Editor: Information Imagineering, 1998; contbr. articles to popular mags. Mem. ALA (chair editl. adv. bd. LA & M, 1998—, councilor 1999—), D.C. Libr. Assn. (pres. 1999), Fed. Librs. and Info. Ctrs. (adv. bd. 1997-99), Libr. Adminstrn. and Mgmt. Assn. (chair bus. and fiscal officer discussion group 1998-2000), Beta Phi Mu. Avocations: cooking, writing. Office: Smithsonian Librs Nhb 22 Washington DC 20560-0001

THOMAS, MICHAEL JAMES, business educator; b. Birmingham, Eng., July 15; s. James Henry and Marguerite Dinah (Hughes) T.; m. Nancy Yeoman, Aug. 23, 1958; children: Helen, Huw. BS, U. Coll. London, 1956; MBA, Ind. U., 1957. Chartered marketer, Eng. Mkt. rsch. mgr. Metal Box Co., London, 1957-60; rschr., asst. prof. Syracuse (N.Y.) U., 1960-72; vis. prof. Lancaster U., Eng., 1969-70, sr. lectr., 1972-85; prof. Strathclyde U., Glasgow, 1985—. Author: Pocket Guide to Marketing, 1990, Marketing Handbook, 1992; co-author: CIM Handbook of Strategic Marketing, 1998, International Marketing, 1998 (3 edits.). Bd. dirs. Alliance Univs. for Democracy, 1992—. Lt. Brit. Army, 1951-53. Decorated Order of Merit, Republic of Poland, 1995, Officer of Brit. Empire, 1999. Fellow Chartered Inst. of Mktg. (chmn. 1995), Royal Soc. of Arts; mem. Mkt. Rsch. Soc. (pres. 1999—). Avocation: ornithology. E-Mail: michael.thomas@Mi8.com. Home: 81 Miller St, APTG1 Canada Ct, Glasgow G1 1EB, Scotland Office: Strathclyde Univ, 173 Cathedral St, Glasgow G4 0RQ, Scotland

THOMAS, MITCHELL, JR., aerospace company executive; b. Terre Haute, Ind., Nov. 25, 1936; s. Mitchell and Carolyn Amalia (Wolff) T.; m. Helen Steimle, June 28, 1970; children: Sheri Helen, Deborah Michal, Mitchell III. AB cum laude, Harvard U., 1958; MS, U. Ill., 1959; PhD, Calif. Inst. Tech., 1964. With McDonnell Douglas, Santa Monica, Calif., 1959-64, group leader launch vehicles, 1964-65, sect. chief ablation and applied rsch. sect., 1965-67; br. chief thermophysics lab. McDonnell Douglas, Huntington Beach, Calif., 1969-75; dir. rsch. and devel. L'Garde Inc., Newport Beach, Calif., 1975-76, pres., 1976-96; pres. Thomas Dynamics Modeling, Inc., Villa Park, Calif., 1996—; mem. adv. com. on Gossamer structures NASA, 1981. Contbr. articles to profl. jours. Mem. AAAS, AIAA (assoc. fellow thermophysics com., tech. program chmn. for 8th thermophysics conf.). Office: TDM Inc 9691 Villa Woods Dr Villa Park CA 92861-3114

THOMAS, MOLLY, clinical pharmacologist; b. Kottayam, India, Oct. 6, 1938; d. Palathunkal and Mariamma (Mathen) Kurien; m. Thomas Sen Bhanu, Dec. 27, 1962; children: Maya, Deepa, Thomas. BSc, Madras Christian Coll., 1956; MBBS, Christian Med. Coll., Vellore, India, 1961, MD, 1968, PhD, 1980. From lectr. to prof. Christian Med. Coll., 1968—; coord. continuing med. edn. Christian Med. Coll., 1985-89, 92-97, vice dean, 1981-85, 91-98. Co-author: Emerging Infections, 1997, Paediatrics for Developing Countries, 1998, Basic Principles of Pharmacology—A Tropical Approach, 1998; contbr. articles to profl. jours. Fellow Royal Coll. Physicians Edinburgh; mem. Br. Pharmacol. Soc., Australasian Soc. Clin. & Exptl. Pharmacology & Therapeutics, Indian Pharmacol. Soc. Avocations: reading, painting, cooking, gardening.

THOMAS, NIHAL JACOB, endocrinologist, physician, researcher; b. Bangalore, Karnataka, India, June 23, 1964; s. Thomas Joshua and Molly Elizabeth (Jacob) T.; m. Maya Mary Mathew, June 1, 1991; 1 child, Rishi Thomas Joshua. Degree, St. Joseph's Coll., Bangalore, India, 1982; MBBS, Christian Med. Coll. Hosp., Vellore, India, 1986, MD in Internal Medicine, 1994. Tutor in medicine Christian Med. Coll., Vellore, India, 1993-94, lectr. endocrine, 1994-97; registrar in endocrine Royal Adelaide (Australia) Hosp., 1997-98; registrar in endocrinology Prince of Wales Hosp., Sydney, 1998—, rsch. assoc. pancreatic transplantation. Contbr. articles to med. jours. Recipient Best Presentation Assn. Physicians India, 1995. Fellow Royal Australasian Coll. Physicians. Avocations: poetry, piano, choreography, directing plays, teaching. Home: Christian Med Coll Hosp, Dept Endocrinology, Vellore 632004, India

THOMAS, NORMAN, education educator; b. Edmonton/London, June 1, 1921; s. Bowen and Ada (Redding) T.; m. Rose Matilda Henshaw, Dec. 24, 1942; children: Jill Evelyn, Paul Blodwyn. Hon. fellow, Coll. of Preceptors, U.K., 1988; DLitt (hon.), U. Hertfordshire, 1998. Cert. tchr. Various posts in commerce and industry London, 1937-47; primary sch. tchr. London, Hertfordshire, 1948-56; head tchr. Longmeadow Primary Sch., Stevenage, Eng., 1956-61; HM inspector of schs. HM Inspectorate, Eng., 1962-69, staff inspector, 1969-73, chief inspector, primary schs., 1973-81; chmn. com. of inquiry, primary edn., Inner London, 1984-85; specialist adviser House of Commons, Select Com. on Edn., U.K., 1984-86, 93-97; external examiner Bishop Grosseteste Coll., U. Surrey, Open U., 1982-84, 86-90, 93-96; vis. prof. East London Polytechnic, Univ. Warwick, Nottingham, Hertfordshire, 1984-88, 88-90,. Author: Primary Education From Plowden to the 1990s, 1990, The Aims of Primary Education in Handbook of Primary Education in Europe, 1989; author articles and profl. papers; contbr. book chpts. to books in field. Comdr. Brit. Empire, HM The Queen, U.K., 1980. Mem. Nat. Assn. for Primary Edn. (life). Avocations: reading, computing, photography. Home: 19 Langley Way, Herts WD1 3EJ Watford WD17 3EJ, England

THOMAS, NORMAN OSCAR, lawyer; b. Bridgetown, Barbados, June 12, 1942; s. Charles Christopher and Iris (King) T.; m. Ira Coralie Chase, Sept. 1965; children: Malcolm Andrew, Susan Coralie, Mark Mitchell. BL, London U., London, 1970; Diploma in Civil Law, City of London Coll., London, 1970; cert. legal edn., Hugh Wooding Law Sch., Trinidad, 1980; ML, London U., 1986. bd. dirs. Rothscarmon Corp., Barbados, Newstead Chambers, Barbados; sec. Royal Bank Trust Co., Bridgetown, 1975-78. Bus conductor London (Eng.) Transport, 1962-63; postman Gen. Post Office, London, 1963-64, postal clk., 1964-66; examiner Inland Revenue, London, 1966-70; asst. mgr. Royal Bank Trust Co., Bridgetown, 1970-78; atty. in pvt. practice Bridgetown, 1980—. Mem. ABA, N.Y. State Bar Assn., Internat. Bar Assn., Barbados Bar Assn. Mem. Dem. Labor Party. Anglican. Avocations: football, cricket, computers. Office: Newstead Chambers, Pinfold St, Bridgetown Barbados

THOMAS, OUIDA POWER, music educator; b. Louisville, Miss., Nov. 25, 1939; d. Robert Alvin and Mavis (Simpson) Power; m. Charles Victor Thomas, Aug. 4, 1962; children: Karla Victoria, Sylvia Katharine Thomas White, Charles Gregory. BS in Bus. Edn. with highest honors, Miss. State U., Starkville, 1963; M Music Edn., Delta State U., 1993; postgrad., U. Memphis, 1996—. Nat. cert. tchr. of music. Ind. music tchr. piano and organ, Grenada, Miss., 1963—; classroom gen. music tchr. Kirk Acad., Grenada, 1977-87; adjudicator auditions Federated Music Clubs, Oxford, Miss., 1990—. Accompanist musical prodns. Grenada Fine Arts Playhouse, 1979-81; organist, choirmaster All Saints' Episcopal Ch., Grenada, 1977—; mem. music and liturgy com. Episcopal Diocese of Miss., 1996-99. Mem. Am. Guild Organists, Nat. Guild Piano Tchrs. (chmn. local auditions 1977—, adjudicator auditions 1993—), Music Tchrs. Nat. Assn. (cert. in piano and organ), Miss. Music Tchrs. Assn. (cert. in piano and organ, exec. bd. 1993-94, state chair pre-coll. student activities 1995-96, chair state cert. 1999—, adjudicator auditions 1993—), Grenada Area Music Tchrs. Assn. (v.p. 1995—). Avocations: gardening, needlework. Home: 1985 Wooded Dr Grenada MS 38901-4073

THOMAS, PATRICIA GOODNOW, journalist; b. Framingham, Mass., Dec. 28, 1924; d. Charles Frederick and Dorothy (Eaton) G.; m. Roy Condit Thomas, Oct. 7, 1961. BS, Simmons Coll., 1946; MAT, Rollins Coll., 1971. News reporter-writer Radio Station WCOP, Boston, 1946-52; editorial specialist Central Intelligence Agy., Washington, 1952-54; asst. editor Hood Milk Corp., Boston, 1954-55; sr. writer/editor Voice of America, Washington, 1955-61; writer Orlando Mag., Orlando, Fla., 1964-72; tchr. French, Eng. Oviedo (Fla.) H.S., 1965-66; prof. of journalism Seminole Cmty. Coll., Sanford, Fla., 1972-88; freelance writer Blairsville, Ga., 1988—. Editor: From Sky to Sea, 1993; contbr. articles to profl. jours. Mem. Fla. Freelance Writers Assn., Kappa Delta Pi.

THOMAS, PAUL LINDSLEY, composer, organist, music director; b. N.Y.C., Mar. 18, 1929; s. Richard Banks and Virginia Bartholomew (Carrington) T.; m. Joyce Robertshaw, Sept. 3, 1955; 1 child, Craig Carrington. BA, Trinity Coll., Hartford, Conn., 1950; diploma, Am. Conservatory, Fontainbleau, France, 1954; MusB, Yale U., 1957, MusM, 1958; D of Musical Arts, U. North Tex., 1979. Organist, choirmaster St. George's-by-the-River, Rumson, N.J., 1950-55, St. James Episcopal Ch., West Hartford, Conn., 1955-60; organist Wesleyan U., Middletown, Conn., 1958-60; dir. Apollo Glee Club, Yale U., New Haven, 1958-60; instr. in organ So. Meth. U., Dallas, 1960-65; music dir., organist St. Michael and All Angels Ch., Dallas, 1960-97, composer in residence, music dir. emeritus, 1997—; music dir. Trinity Epis. Ch., Dallas, 1998—; chmn. liturgy and music commn. Episcopal Diocese of Dallas, 1995—. Composer (opera) Everyman, 1986; composer ch. anthems and organ music. Named Canon of Ch. Music, Episcopal Diocese of Dallas, 1980; recording grantee Stemmons Found., Dallas, 1995; Joyce and Paul Thomas Music Wing named in his honor St. Michael and All Angels, Dallas, 1994. Fellow Am. Guild Organists (dean Dallas chpt. 1967-69, gen. chmn. nat. conv. 1972, nat. coun. 1972-75); mem. Assn. Anglican Musicians, Am. Choral Dirs. Assn. Republican. Episcopalian. Home: 6822 Northwood Rd Dallas TX 75225-2538 Office: Trinity Episcopal Ch 12727 Hillcrest Rd Dallas TX 75230-2007

THOMAS, PAULETTE SUZANNE, holistic health practitioner, physician assistant; b. Lowell, Mass., Aug. 29, 1948; d. Armand Avila and Lucienne Adrienne (Lanseigne) Sawyer; Philip Edward Thomas Jr., June 9, 1979. AN, No. Essex C.C., Haverhill, Mass., 1972; cert. cardiac care nurse, Merrimack Coll., 1975; student, Boston Coll., 1976, Northeastern U., 1976-78, John A. Burns Sch. Medicine, 1981; D of Naturology, PhD in Naturology, Am. Inst. Holistic Theology, 1997. RN, Mass., Maine, Hawaii, Fla.; registered hypnotherapist; cert. hypnotherapist; diplomate naturopathic physician Am. Naturopathic Med. Cert. & Accreditation Bd. Head nurse insvc. and daycare Solomon Mental Health Ctr., Lowell, 1972-73; charge nurse ICU Las Olas Gen. Hosp., Ft. Lauderdale, Fla., 1973-74, Lemuel Shattuck Hosp., Jamaica Plain, Mass., 1975-76; charge nurse cardiac care unit Bon Secours Hosp., Methuen, Mass., 1974-75; supr., medicare coord. Oxford Manor, Haverhill, 1978-79, 84; physician asst. to chief internal medicine Straub Clinic and Hosp., Honolulu, 1980-82; owner managed elderly housing, Haverhill, 1982-87; physician asst. employee/occupl. health Lawrence (Mass.) Gen. Hosp., 1984-87; owner Tuckaway Shores Cabins and Restaurant, Jackman, Maine, 1987—; nursing educator cert. nursing asst. course Kennebec Valley Vocat. Tech. Inst., Fairfield, Maine, 1990-94; mem. profl. policies com., mem. safety com. Northland Living Ctr., Jackman, 1990-92. Author, editor, pub. Hawaiian Acad. Physician Assts. Newsletter, 1980-82; contbr. biweekly health column to Jackman/Moose River Chronicle, 1988-89. Bd. dirs. Tuckaway Assn., Nottingham, N.H., 1985-87; mem. Conservation Commn., Jackman, 1989; chmn. Main St. '90, Jackman and Moose River, 1989-90; originator, coord. Wellcome Wagon, Jackman and Moose River, 1990-92; mem. Town of Jackman Budget Com., 1991—. Mem. Am. Acad. Physician Assts. (pres. Hawaii chpt. 1980-82), First Nations Coun., Am. Naturopathic Med. Assn., Inst. Holistic Studies, Jackman/Moose River C. of C. Avocations: hiking, dancing, hand-crafts, music, boating. Home and Office: HC 64 Box 44 Jackman ME 04945-9602

THOMAS, PETER KYNASTON, neurologist; b. Swansea, Wales, U.K., June 28, 1926; s. Heber Lesley and Beatrice Ida (Couch) T.; m. Sawanthana Ponsford, Aug. 7, 1999. BSc, U. Coll., London, 1947; MB B of Surgery, U. Coll. Hosp. Med. Sch., London, 1950, MD, 1957, DSc, 1971; D (hon.), Mil. Med. Acad., Lodz, 1991. Asst. prof. neurology McGill U., Montreal, Can., 1961-62; cons. neurologist Royal Free Hosp., London, 1962-74, Nat. Hosp. for Neurology and Neurosurgery, London, 1963-74; prof. neurology emeritus U. London, 1974—. Joint editor: Peripheral Neuropathy, 3rd edit., 1993, Diabetic Neuropathy, 2d edit., 1999. Capt. Royal Army Med. Corps., 1952-54. Named Comdr. of the British Empire U.K. Govt. Mem. European Neurol. Soc. (past pres.), Assn. of British Neurologists (past pres.), Am. Neurol. Assn. Avocations: skiing, mountain trekking, contemporary music. Office: Inst. Neurology, Queen Sq, London WC1N 3BG, England

THOMAS, RENÉ FRANÇOIS, bank executive; b. Brest, Jan. 13, 1929; s. François and Jeanne Milbé0; 2 children. Degree in law and polit. sci. Inspector of fin., 1955; with Ministry of Fin., Morocco, 1960, Pub. Enterprises Accts. Verification Com., 1960; with Banque Nationale de Paris (formerly Comptoir Nat. d'Escompte de Paris), 1962—, ctrl. dir., 1972—, dep. dir. gen., 1979, chmn., CEO, 1982-93; hon. chmn. Banque Nationale de Paris Inter-continentale; dir. Vivendi, BNP, Chargeurs Internat., Vivendi, Pathe, Essilor, Usinor-Sacilor. Decorated Comdr. of Legion of Honour, 1995, comdr. Nat. Order of Merit. Office: Banque Nat de Paris, 16 blvd des Italiens, F-75009 Paris France also: 59 blvd d'Inkermann, 92200 Neuilly-sur-Seine France

THOMAS, ROBERT KEMEYS, chemistry educator, researcher; b. Harpenden, Eng., Sept. 25, 1941; s. Herbert Samuel Griffith and Agnes Paterson (McLaren) T.; m. Pamela Havas Woods, June 16, 1944; children: Emily, Anna, Nicholas. BA, U. Oxford, Eng., 1964, PhD, 1968. Rsch. asst. U. Oxford, 1968-78, lectr., 1978—; tutor U. Coll., Oxford, 1978—. Contbr. articles to profl. jours. Fellow Royal Soc. Chemistry, Inst. Physics. Home: 22 Lathbury Rd, Oxford OX2 7AV, England Office: Phys and Theoret Chem Lab, South Parks Rd, Oxford 0X1 3Q2, England

THOMAS, SAMUEL, company executive; b. Cheppad, Kerala, India, Sept. 9, 1945; s. Puthenveetil Abraham and Aley (Samuel) T.; m. Susan JAcob, Dec. 27, 1973; children: Thomas Samuel, Jacob Samuel. B Tech. with honors in Mech. Engring., Indian Inst. Tech., Kharagpur, 1967; MBA, U. Rochester, N.Y., 1971. Quality control engr. Shriram Refrigeration Industries, Hyderabad, 1967-69; accounts officer, stores officer Tata Engring. & Locomotive Co., Jamshedpur, India, 1972-76; asst. prof. Xavier Inst., Jamshedpur, 1977-81; divsn. acct., mgr. material planning & control, mgmt. acct. API Aurangabad, Mumbai, India, 1981-82; prin. cum gen. mgr. Agnel Tech. Complex, Mumbai, 1982-84; dir. Madras C. of C., Employer's Fedn. So. India Edn. Trust, Chennai, 1984-88; faculty mem., gen. mgr. Steel Authority India Ltd., Ranchi/Bhilai, 1988—; cons. Bihar State Mineral Devel. Corp., Ranchi, 1978. Author: Finance for Non Financial Managers, 1982. Recipient merit scholarship Indian Inst. Tech., Kharagpur, 1963, tuition scholarship U. Rochester, 1969. Avocation: reading management books. Home: D-44 Hospital Sector, Bhilai 490009, India Office: Steel Authority India Ltd, Bhilai 490001, India

THOMAS, TARQUIN CRAIG, computer scientist, writer; b. Haslemere, Surrey, Eng., May 7, 1966; s. Leicester Craig and Margaret Lina T. Systems analyst Multisoft Systems Ltd., Alton, Eng., 1984-85; cons. Migration Techs. Ltd., Windsor, Eng., 1987; prin. tech. mgr. TIS Ltd., Bourne End, Eng., 1988-94; cons. Barclays Global Investors, San Francisco, 1995—; cons. MISYS P.L.C., Eng., 1994. Author: (CD-Rom) EJW-CDR, 1994; contr. articles to profl. jours. Recipient Barclays Chmn.'s award for Cmty. Involvement. Mem. Inst. Data Processing Mgmt., Brit. Mensa. Avocations: art, advocacy child rights and welfare.

THOMAS, TERENCE PATRICK, writer, researcher, electronics design engineer; b. Concord, Ky., Sept. 16, 1942; s. Charles Edwin Thomas and Daisy Merle (Wolfe) Minger. Tchr. Freespace Alternate U., N.Y.C., 1977, The Mannes Coll. Music, N.Y.C., 1978-79, New Sch. for Social Rsch., N.Y.C., 1978; head design engr. NYU, N.Y.C., 1978-80; rschr. Thomas Enterprises, Venice, Fla., 1984—. Author: Sound Synthesis (Analog and Digital Techniques), 1990; contbr. to Robotics column Radio/Electronics Mag., Farmingdale, N.Y., 1986. Mem. N.Y. Acad. Scis. Achievements

include design of computer-controlled high-speed laser beam modulator; with use of conductive vinyl, development of robotic sensors to enable hand devices to sense slippage and apply only the amount of pressure necessary to lift an object, thus preserving delicate samples. Avocations: tennis, chess, science fiction, music composition, football. Home: 336 Warfield Ave S Venice FL 34292-2657

THOMAS, TERESA ANN, microbiologist, educator; b. Wilkes-Barre, Pa., Oct. 17, 1939; d. Sam Charles and Edna Grace T. BS cum laude, Coll. Misericordia, 1961; MS in Biology, Am. U., Beirut, 1965; MS in Microbiology, U. So. Calif., 1973; cert. in ednl. tech., U. Calif., San Diego, 1998. Tchr., sci. supr., curriculum coord. Meyers High Sch., Wilkes-Barre, 1962-64, Wilkes-Barre Area Public Schs., 1961-66; rsch. assoc. Proctor Found. Rsch. in Ophthalmology U. Calif. Med. Ctr., San Francisco, 1966-68; instr. Robert Coll. of Istanbul (Turkey), 1968-71, Am. Edn. in Luxembourg, 1971-72, Bosco Tech. Inst., Rosemead, Calif., 1973-74, San Diego C.C. Dist., 1974-80; prof. microbiology and ecology Sch. Math Scis. and Engring. Southwestern Coll., Chula Vista, Calif., 1980—; mem. Vecinos Baja Studies EcoMundo team internat. program Southwestern Coll.; pres. acad. senate, 1984-85, del., 1986-89; chmn., coord., steering com. project Cultural Rsch. Ednl. and Trade Exch., 1991-2000, Southwestern Coll.-Shanghai Inst. Fgn. Trade; coord. Southwestern Coll. Great Teaching Seminar, 1987, 88, 89, coord. scholars program, 1988-90; mem. steering com. Southwestern Coll.; mem. exec. com. Acad. Senate for Calif. C.C.s, 1985-86, Chancellor of Calif. C.C.s Adv. and Rev. Coun. Fund for Instrnl. Improvement, 1984-86; co-project dir. statewide, coord. So. Calif. Biotech. Edn. Consortium, 1993-95, steering com., 1993-98; adj. asst. prof. Chapman Coll., San Diego, 1974-83, San Diego State U., 1977-79; chmn. Am. Colls. Istanbul Sci. Week, 1969-71; mem. adv. bd. Chapman Coll. Cmty. Ctr., 1979-80; cons. sci. curriculum Calif. Dept. Edn., 1986-89; pres. Internat. Rels. Club, 1959-61; mem. San Francisco World Affairs Coun., 1966-68, San Diego World Affairs Coun., 1992—; v.p. Palomar Palace Estates Home Owners Assn., 1983-85, pres., 1994-99, v.p., 1999—; presenter in field; mem. Rsch. Conf. on Undergrad. Microbiology Edn., Conn. Coll., 1999. Mem. editl. rev. bd. Jour. Coll. Sci. Teaching, NSTA, 1988-92; bd. dirs. San Diego-Leon Sister Cities Soc., 1991-94. Mem. Chula Vista Nature Interpretive Ctr. (life), Internat. Friendship Commn., Chula Vista, 1985-95, vice chmn., 1989-90, chmn., 1990-92, Chula Vista, Calif., 1987-95; mem. U.S.-Mex. Sister Cities Assn., nat. bd. dirs., 1992-94, gen. chair 30th nat. conv., 1993; mem. City of Chula Vista Resource Conservation Commn., 1996—; mem. Chula Vista Bd. Ethics, 1999-2000; co-organizer Chula Vista People-to-People Sister City Dels. to Odawara City, Japan, 1991, 94, 99; cmty. adv. com. San Diego Mus. Man, 2000—; mem. County San Diego Solid Waste Hearing Panel, 2000—. NSF fellow, 1965; USPHS fellow, 1972-73; recipient Nat. Tchg. Excellence award Nat. Inst. Staff and Orgnl. Devel., 1989; recognized at Internat. Conf. Tchg. Excellence, Austin, 1989; Pa. Heart Assn. rsch. grantee, 1962; named Southwestern Coll. Woman of Distinction, 1987. Mem. NIH (steering com., mentor Bridge to Future program Southwestern Coll. and San Diego State U. 1993-98), NEA, Am. Soc. Microbiology (So. Calif. Microbe Discovery Team 1995-99), Nat. Sci. Tchrs. Assn. (life, internat. com., coord. internat. honors exch. lectr. competition sponsored with Assn. Sci. Educators Gt. Britain, 1986), Nat. Assn. Biology Tchrs. (life), Soc. Coll. Sci. Tchrs., S.D. Zool. Soc., Calif. Tchrs. Assn., Am. Assn. Cmty. and Jr. Colls., Giraffes, Am.-Lebanese Assn. San Diego (chmn. scholarship com., pres. 1988-93), Am. U. of Beirut Alumni and Friends of San Diego (1st v.p. 1984-91), Calif. Sci. Tchrs. Assn. (life), Lions Internat. (bull. editor 1991-93, best bull. award 1992, 93, 2nd v.p. 1992-93, 1st v.p. 1993-94, editor Roaring Times Newsletter 1993-94, chmn. dist. internat. rels. and cooperations com. 1993-95, with pub. rels. 1997-98, pres. SW San Diego County chpt. 1994-95, Sweetwater Zone chmn. dist. 4-L6 1996-97, pub. rels. 1997-98), Japan Soc. San Diego and Tijuana, Chula Vista-Odawara (Japan) Sister Cities Assn. (founding pres. 1994—), Kappa Gamma Pi (pres. Wilkes-Barre chpt. 1963-64, San Francisco chpt. 1967-68), Sigma Phi Sigma, Phi Theta Kappa, Alpha Pi Epsilon (hon. life mem., founder, advisor Southwestern Coll. chpt. 1989-90), Am. Lebanese Syrian Ladies Club (pres. 1982-83).

THOMAS, VIRGINIA VAUDALINE, retired educator; b. Sweetwater, Tex., Feb. 22, 1916; d. Claude and Marguerite Rogers; m. T.T. Thomas, July 24, 1934; children: James, Toby, Mondelene. BA, Hardin-Simmons Coll., 1950; MEd, Tex. Tech U., 1984. Cert. tchr., Tex. Elem. tchr. Plum Creek Sch., Sweetwater, 1934-36, Longworth Sch., Sweetwater, 1948-50, Sweetwater Sch., 1950-64, Divide Sch., North Nolon, Tex., 1950, Roosevelt Sch., Lubbock, Tex., 1964-66, Crosbyton (Tex.) Sch., 1966-74, O'Donnell (Tex.) Schs., 1974-78. Author: Plum Creek Memorabilia, 1976, Stories From My Past, 1986, Life, A Professional of Faith, 1998, Why We Bieleve The Bible, 1998, Out of Left Field, 1998; (poems) Spirit of a West Texas Poet, 1996, Inspirational Poetry, 1998; (dictionary) Texas Related to the Exceptional, numerous others; contbr. Sweetwater Reporter News, 1997. Vol. County-City Libr., Sweetwater, 1996-97, Nolan County Mental Health Assn., Sweetwater, 1997—. Named Sweetwater's Very Spl. Woman, 1999. Mem. Internat. Soc. Poets (Disting. Mem., Internat. Poet of Merit 1996), Kiwanis (publicity chmn., bd. dirs.). Mem. Ch. of Christ. Home: 1115 Josephine St Sweetwater TX 79556-3416

THOMAS, WILLIAM ERNEST GHINN, consulting surgeon, health facility administrator; b. London, Feb. 13, 1948; s. Kenneth Dawson and Monica Isobel (Markham) T.; m. Grace Violet Samways, June 30, 1973; children: Nicola Barbara Ghinn, Christopher William Ghinn, Jacqueline Monica Ghinn, Hannah Margaret Ghinn, Benjamin Alan Ghinn. Student, Dulwich Coll., London, 1959-66; BSc, London U., 1969, MS, 1980; MB BS, St. George's Hosp. Med. Sch., 1972. Cert. Higher Surg. Tng., 1983. House surgeon St. George's Hosp., London, 1973-74; sr. house officer St. Helier Hosp., Carshalton, Eng., 1974-75; surg. registrar Addenbrooke's Hosp., Cambridge, 1975-77; rsch. fellow Royal Coll. Surgeons, London, 1977-78; sr. surg. registrar Bristol (Eng.) Royal Infirmary, 1979-85; cons. surgeon Royal Hallamshire Hosp., Sheffield, Eng., 1986—; clin. dir. Ctrl. Sheffield U. Hosps. Trust, 1990—; mem. panel examiners Intercollegiate Splty. Bd., 1995—, mem. internat. faculty, gastrointestinal workshop, 1997; Hunterian prof., 1986-87, Arris and Gale lectr., 1981-82. Author: Nuclear Medicine, Applications To Surgery, 1988, Colour Guide to Surg. Pathology, 1992, Basic Surgical Skills, 1996, 99, Preparation and Revision for M.R.C.S., 1999; exec. editor, chmn.: Internat. Rev. Jour., 1988-97. Nat. pres. Gideons Internat. Brit. Isles, 1987-90, 96-99, v.p., 1994-96, internat. trustee, 2000—; mem. gen. com. Christian Med. Fellowship, 1980-86, 89-95; ch. warden Christchurch Fulwood Sheffield. Recipient Award and Testimonial for Bravery Royal Humane Soc., 1974, Dr. of Yr. Brit. United Provident Assn. Med. Found., 1985, Med. Mgr. of Yr. Brit. Assn. Med. Mgrs., 1995. Fellow Royal Coll. Surgeons (surg. skills tutor 1995—, mem. ct. examiners 1991—), Assn. Surgeons (Moynihan fellow 1982); mem. Brit. Soc. Gastroenterology (State of Arts lectr. 1986), Surg. Rsch. Soc. (travel fellow Brit. Jour. Surgery 1982), Royal Soc. Medicine (pres. surg. sect. 2000—). Avocations: skiing, photography, oil painting. Home: Ash Lodge, 65 Whirlow Park Rd, N Yorks Sheffield S11 9NN, England Office: Royal Hallamshire Hosp, Glossop Rd, S Yorks Sheffield S10 2JF, England

THOMAS, WILLIAM JOHN, chemical engineer, researcher; b. Swansea, Wales; s. Trevor Roylance and Gwendoline Novello (Williams) T.; m. Pamela Heather Rees, July 21, 1955; children: Mark Gareth, Clare Heather. BSc, U. Wales, Swansea, 1951, DSc, 1972; PhD, Imperial Coll., London, 1954. Mem. R&D dept. Internat. Nickel Co., Swansea, 1954-56; asst. lectr. U. Coll., Swansea, 1956-59; sr. sci. officer Atomic Rsch. Rsch. Estab., Harwell, 1959-61; chem. engring. lectr. U. Coll., Swansea, 1961-68; prof. chem. engirng. U. Bath, 1968-87, pro-vice chancellor, 1987-93, emeritus prof., 1994—; lectr. in field. Author: Heterogenous Catalysis: Principles and Practice, 1996, Adsorption Technology and Design, 1998; contbr. more than 60 articles to profl. jours. Asst. organist Bathampton Ch. Fellow Instn. Chem. Engrs., Royal Acad. Engring. Office: U Bath, Claverton Down, Bath BA2 7AY, England

THOMASCHEWSKI, DIETER, chemicals executive; b. Weissenburg, Alsace, France, Mar. 24, 1944; s. Arthur and Franziska (Betzer) T.; 1 child from a previous marriage, Joerg; m. Barbara Birk, Apr. 3, 1992. Diploma Kaufmann-bus. adminstrn., U. Saarbrücken, 1969. Jr. cons. BASF-Aktiengesellschaft, Germany, 1969-73, mgr. strategic planning forecast, 1974-75, sr. mgr. cons. dept mktg., 1976-80, sr. mkgt. mgr. chems., plastics, 1980-86; pres. BASF-Venezolana, Venezuela, 1987-89; group v.p. BASF-Info. Sys. U.S.A., 1990-91; exec. v.p., pres. fertilizer divsn. BASF AS, 1992-98, exec. v.p., pres. reg. divsn., 1998—; bd. dirs. Kali v. Salz, Germany, BASF-France, Belgium, et al. Contbr. articles to profl. jours. Fellow Schmalenbach Soc.; mem. European Fertilizer Mfrs. Assn. (pres. 1997-98), Internat. Fertilizer Assn. (v.p. West Europe 1995-98), Lions. Roman Catholic. Avocations: sports, music, travel, languages. Home: Pegauer Str 12, 67157 Wachenheim Rheinland Pfalz, Germany Office: BASF-Aktiengesellschaft, Carl Bosch Str 38, 67056 Ludwigshafen Rheinland Pfalz, Germany

THOMAS-COTE, NANCY DENECE, former office products manufacturing company executive, vacation rental executive; b. Long Beach, Calif., Feb. 20, 1959; d. Alan Thomas and Barbara Jean (Rush) Tuthill; m. Gary Cote. V.p. BTE, Inc., Long Beach, 1978-88; gen. mgr. BTE, Inc., Huntington Beach, Calif., 1982-88, pres., 1988-95, CEO, 1995-99; pres. Omni Label, Inc., Huntington Beach, 1985-90; co-owner LeMac Leasing, La Canada, Calif., 1985-90; owner Dayspring Wedding Cons., Long Beach, 1991-93, Rent the Beach!, 1999—. V.p. Long Beach Spl. Charities, Inc., 1987; pres. Long Beach Spl. Charities, Inc., 1988, Naples Bayside Acad. PTA, 2000—; mem. Long Beach Sch.-to-Career Coalition, 1997; bd. dirs. Girl Scout Coun. Greater Long Beach, 1999—. Mem. Assn. Women Bus. Owners (bd. dirs. L.A. chpt. 1995-96), An Income of Her Own, Best Broads. Office: Rent the Beach PMB 770 5318 E 2d St Long Beach CA 90803

THOMASHOW, STEVEN ROY, military officer, intelligence officer; b. Bronx, N.Y., Jan. 27, 1957; s. Isaac Tom and Dorothy (Cuillino Bodsky) T. Accredited, U.S. Mil. Acad. Commd. United States of the World, adm., with spl. ops., 1988—; served with Israeli War USN, served with Gulf War. Recipient Pres. Nat. Medal of Patriotism, Am. Police Hall of Fame, 1996. Fellow Nat. Law Enforcement Acad. (hon.); mem. Am. Fedn. Police. Avocations: karate, Torah studies, boxing, reading. Fax: 561 640-4359. Home and Office: 4644 Myrtle Ln West Palm Beach FL 33417-5316

THOMAS OF SWYNNERTON, LORD See THOMAS, HUGH

THOMASON, HARRY JACK LEE, JR., mechanical engineer; b. Washington, Apr. 12, 1953; s. Harry Emmitte and Annie Jeffreys aka Hattie Cornelia (Davis) T.; m. Ema Jean Bulaon, Dec. 15, 1974. AA, Prince Georges C.C., 1973; BS, U. Md., 1975. Cons. Thomason Solar Homes Inc., Ft. Washington, Md., 1975-79, v.p. engring., 1979-84; mech. engr. Naval Surface Weapons Ctr., Dahlgren, Va., 1984-86, White Oak, Md., 1986-87; energy conservation engr., asst. chief ops. Walter Reed Army Med. Ctr., Washington, DC, 1987-88; sr. mech. engr. Armed Forces Inst. of Pathology, 1988-90; mech. engr. U.S. Naval Acad., Annapolis, Md., 1990-95; instr. solar house heating and cooling, George Washington U., Washington, 1974-75. Contbr. articles to profl. jours. Patentee in field of solar energy; recipient 1st place environ. award Isaac Walton League, 1971, spl. awards Washington Soc. Engrs., 1971, IEEE, 1971, Solar Hall of Fame award, 1992, Internat. Man of Yr. award, 1991-92, named World Intellectual of 1993, named to Millennium Hall of Fame, 1998, named among 2,000 Outstanding Scientists of the 20th Century, 2,000 Outstanding Intellectuals of the 20th Century. Mem. ASME, Wash. Soc. Engrs.

THOMASON, PETER FRANK, materials scientist, educator, researcher; b. Horwich, Eng., Oct. 22, 1937; s. Joseph Alfred and Edna (Penwarden) T.; m. Pauline Helen Guest, Sept. 9, 1985. PhD, U. Salford, Eng., 1966, DSc, 1988. Rsch. fellow U. Salford, Eng., 1966-69, lectr., 1969-74, reader, 1974—; vis. prof. U. Calif., Berkeley, 1987-88; vis. scholar U. Cambridge, Eng, 1995-98; Matthias vis. fellow Los Alamos Nat. Lab., 1998; vis. scholar Materials Sci. Ctr., U. Manchester, Eng., 1999—. Author: Ductile Fracture of Metals, 1990; contbr. articles to profl. jours. Mem. Inst. Materials, Metals Minerals Materials Soc. Avocations: opera, classical music, cricket. Home: 11 The Green Handforth, Wilmslow SK9 3AG, England Office: U Manchester Materials Sci, Ctr., Grosvenor St, Manchester M1 7HS, England

THOMASSEN, LARS ALLAN, advertising executive; b. Copenhagen, Nov. 3, 1953; s. Kaj and Lone Thomassen; m. Christina Obel, June 24, 1989; children: Sophie, Cecilie, Clara, Johan. Grad., Copenhagen Bus. Sch., Denmark, 1975. Acct. handler Ted Bates & Ptnrs., Copenhagen, 1976-78; acct. dir. Lund & Lommer, Copenhagen, 1978-79; mng. dir. Batton, Barton, Ourstine & Osborne (formerly Henriksen & Sieling), Copenhagen, 1979-98; v.p. BBDO Europe, 1998—; chmn. Dansk Markedsfoeringsforbund, 1993-97, BBDO A/S, 1998—, NOS/BBDO Warzawa, Skandinavisk Film Kompagni A/S, Morgen YTV A/S Copenhagen; bd. dirs. C. Clausen Co. A/S, Sepia A/S, BBDO Bus. Comm. Adminstrn., Weco Transport A/S, Birger Christensen Gen. Trading Co. A/S, HLR&BBDO Sweden, BBDO/Helsinki, BBDO Myres Oslo, BBDO/Budapest, BBDO Europe London, BBDO Worldwide N.Y., OMD Europe London, BBDO Austria, Mark BBDO Prag, Graffiti BBDO Romania, BBDO Moscow. Home: Skovroedgaard, Kongevejen 16, DK-3460 Birkeroed Denmark Office: BBDO A/S, Store Kongensgade 72, DK1264 Copenhagen Denmark

THOMASSEN, PAULINE FRANCES, medical and surgical nurse; b. Cleve., Jan. 19, 1939; d. Henry Clifford and Mabel Pauline (Hill) Nichols; m. Ruben Thomassen, Nov. 10, 1979; children: Rhonda, Terry, Diana, Philipp, Jody, Barbara. AA in Nursing, So. Colo. State Coll., 1974, BA in Psychology with distinction, 1975; BSN magna cum laude, Seattle Pacific U., 1986. RN, Wash. Staff nurse III orthopedic unit, clin. spine educator Swedish Hosp. Med. Ctr., Seattle, 1975—, preceptor orientation of RNs and student RNs, 1975—, clin. spine educator, 2000—; mem. planning task force and faculty National Nurses Conference, The Nurse and Spinal Surgery, Cleve.; lectr. Coll. of Nursing Raleigh Fitkin Meml. Hosp., Manzini, Swaziland, South Africa, 1999; mem. med. mission to assist in clinic for street children, Satipo, Peru, 2000. Author: Spinal Disease and Surgical Interventions, 1995; contbg. author: Making Sense of Minimally Invasive Spine Surgery, 1998. Mem. Nat. Assn. Orthop. Nurses. Office: Swedish Health Center 747 Broadway Seattle WA 98122-4379

THOME, JOHANNES ULRICH VINZENZ, psychiatrist researcher; b. Saarbruecken, Saarland, Germany, Oct. 8, 1967; s. Hans and Gisela (Schwan) T.; m. Barbara Anne Steimer, Oct. 18, 1997. MD, U. Saarland, Homburg, Germany, 1993; PhD, U. Saarland, Saarbruecken, Germany, 1994. Med. tng. Necker, Paris, 1986, Charles U., Prague, 1989, U. Hosp., Nancy, France, 1992; resident Psychiat. and Neurol. Clinic, U. Wuerzburg, Germany, 1992-97; scientist lab. for clin. neurochemistry U. Wuerzburg, Germany, 1994-97; scientist divsn. molecular psychiatry Yale U., New Haven, 1997-99; scientist, psychiatrist Ctrl. Inst. for Mental Health, Mannheim, Germany, 1999—. Author: Psychotherapeutische Aspekte in der Philosophie Platons, 1995; co-editor: Alzheimer-Krankheit, 1997; contbr. articles to profl. jours. Erasmus grantee, 1992, grantee German Rsch. Coun., 1997; recipient Friedrich Von Klinggraeff medal, 1995. Mem. Soc. for Neurosci., German Soc. Biol. Psychiatry, German Soc. Psychiatry and Psychotherapy, Alzheimer Soc. Wuerzburg, Am. Soc. Philosophy, Counseling and Psychotherapy, Corps Frankonia Prag. Roman Catholic. Avocations: philosophy, music, horses. Home: Pastor-Vogt Strasse 21, 66571 Eppelborn Germany Office: Central Inst Mental Health J5, D-68159 Mannheim Germany

THOMFORD, WILLIAM EMIL, engineer, consultant; b. San Francisco, Mar. 15, 1927; s. Emil George and Anna Marie (Robohm) T.; m. Irene Shapoff, Mar. 21, 1948; children: Elaine Margaret, John William. AA, City Coll. San Francisco, 1949; BA, U. Calif., Berkeley, 1951; postgrad., Stanford U., 1967. Registered profl. engr., Calif. Various engring. positions So. Pacific Transp. Co., San Francisco, 1951-80, mgr. research and test, 1981-83; prin. Transp. Cons. Services, Millbrae, Calif., 1983—; tech. cons. Nippon Sharyo USA, Inc., N.Y.C., 1987—, Assn. Am. R.R.s, 1986—, Transp. Systems Ctr., U.S. Dept. Transp., 1989. Designer Hydra-Cushion, 1954 (Henderson medal Franklin Inst. 1964), Vert-A Pac rail car for 30 autos (Best Design in Steel award Am. Iron and Steel Inst. 1971), double stack car for 10 Internat. Standards Orgn. containers, 1980, fiberglas covered hopper car, 1982. Served with USN, 1944-46. Fellow ASME (rail transp. engring. achievement A. Stucki award 1991); mem. NSPE, Assn. Am. Railroads, Car Dept Officers' Assn. Lutheran. Club: Engrs. (San Francisco), Pacific Railway (San Francisco). Avocation: golf, fishing. Home and Office: 1176 Glenwood Dr Millbrae CA 94030-1014

THOMM, MICHAEL WOLFGANG, microbiologist; b. Bad Reichenhall Bayern, Oberbayern, Germany, Jan. 29, 1951; s. Friedrich and Elisabeth Maria (Schöller) T. Diploma biology, U. Munich, 1980; PhD, U. Regensburg (Germany), 1983. Postdoctoral fellow U. Regensburg, 1983-88, dozent, 1988-91; prof. microbiology U. Kiel, Germany, 1991—. Mem. AAAS, Vereinigung Allgemeine und Angewandte Mikrobiologie, Am. Soc. Microbiology. Office: U Kiel, Am Botanischen Garten 1-9, Schleswig-Holstein Kiel 24118, Germany

THOMPSON, ALAN ERIC, economics educator; b. Sept. 16, 1924; s. Eric Joseph and Florence T.; m. Mary Heather Long, 1960; 4 children. M.A., U. Edinburgh, 1949, M.A. with 1st class honors, 1951, Ph.D., 1953. Asst. in polit. econ. U. Edinburgh, 1952-53, lectr. econs., 1953-59, 64-71; prof. econs. of govt. Heriot-Watt U., Edinburgh, 1972—; adviser to Scottish TV, 1966-76; Scottish gov. BBC, 1976-79; vis. prof. Grad. Sch. Bus., Stanford U. (Calif.), 1966, 68; chmn. adv. bd. econs. edn. Esmee Fairbairn Rsch. Project, 1970-76. Bd. dirs. Scottish AIDS Rsch. Found., 1992; adv. Robert Burns Meml. Trust, 1995—. Author: (with others) Development of Economic Doctrine, 1980; contbr. articles to profl. jours. M.P. Labour party, Dunfermline, 1959-64; mem. Scottish Com. Pub. Schs. Commn., 1969-70; mem. Joint Mil. Edn. Com. Edinburgh and Heriot-Watt Univs., 1975—, local govt. boundary commn. for Scotland, 1975-82; chmn. Northern Offshore Resources Study, 1974-84; chmn. bd. govs. Newbattle Abbey Coll., 1980-82; bd. govs. Leigh Nautical Coll., 1981-87; trustee Bell's Nautical Trust, 1981-87; parliamentary adviser Pharm. Gen. Coun., 1985—; advisor Robert Burns Meml. Trust, 1995—. With Brit. Army, World War II. Carnegie Rsch. scholar, 1951-52. Fellow Royal Soc. Arts, Soc. Antiquaries (Scotland); mem. Assn. Nazi War Camp Survivors (v.p. 1960—), Edinburgh Amenity and Transport Assn. (pres. 1970-75). Clubs: New, Edinburgh Univ. Staff; Loch Earn Sailing.

THOMPSON, ALISON, administrator; b. Bournemouth, Eng., Jan. 11, 1963; m. Ian Brent Thompson, Oct. 2, 1988; children: Rachel Hannah, Luke Timothy Samuel. BA (hons.), Oxford Univ., 1985; MBA, Bradford U., 1988. Tech. Coates Industrial Finishes, Witney, Oxon, Eng., 1985-87; cons. Whiteleys Paper, West Yorks, Eng., 1989; report mgr. Hazleton, Harrogate, Eng., 1989-92; resource mgr. Assn. Chief Officers Probation, London, 1992—. Mem. Royal Soc. Chemistry.

THOMPSON, ANA CALZADA, secondary education educator, mathematician; b. Sanderson, Tex., Nov. 29, 1940; d. Leopoldo G. and Maria Deo Gracia (Sandoval) Calzada; m. Tommy Salinas Thompson, July 1, 1962; children: Tommy Michael, Anthony Jude, Ana Marie. BS, Sul Ross State U., Alpine, Tex., 1966; MEd, S.W. Tex. State U., 1980. Tchr. Poteet (Tex.) Ind. Sch. Dist., 1965-67, Northside Ind. Sch. Dist., San Antonio, 1967-68; tchr. math. N.E. Ind. Sch. Dist., San Antonio, 1968-97, chmn. dept., 1976-97; prof. math. St. Philips Coll., San Antonio, 1986—; mem. Region 20 Tchr. Ctr., San Antonio, 1978-82; pres. S.W. Tchr. Ctr., San Marcos, Tex., 1970-82. Contbg. author: Graphing Power, 1995. Sec., La Vernia (Tex.) Ind. Sch. Dist., 1977-87, mem. bd., 1978-87; del. Tex. Dem. Conv., Houston, 1988, Ft. Worth, 1992, Dallas, 1996; del. Guadalupe County Dem. Com., Seguin, Tex., 1988, 92, 96. Mem. NEA, Nat. Coun. Tchrs. Math., Tex. Tchrs. Assn., Alamo Dist. Coun. Tchrs. Math. Roman Catholic. Avocations: reading, knitting, travel, gardening.

THOMPSON, ANNIE LAURA ANNE, foreign language educator; b. Henderson, Tenn., July 8, 1937; d. Wesley Sylvester and Letha Irene (Jones) T.; m. Edward L. Patterson, June 7, 1980. BA, U. Ala., 1959; MA, Duke U., 1961; PhD, Tulane U., 1973. Instr. Spanish lang. U. Miss., Oxford, 1960-64; instr. Auburn (Ala.) U., 1964-66; tchg. asst. Tulane U., New Orleans, 1966-70; prof. Spanish lang. Delgado C.C., New Orleans, 1970—; instr. Spanish for Physicians and Med. Persons Tulane U., La. State U. Med. Eye Ctr., Ochsner Clinic and Hosp. Author: Religious Elements in the Quijote, 1960, The Attempt of Spanish Intellectuals to Create a New Spain, 1930-36, 1973, The Generation of 1898: Intellectual Politicians; asst. editor The Crusader, 1961-64. Rep. candidate for gov. State of La., 1991, 95, for 1st Dist. U.S. Congress, 1992; alt. mem. La. Coastal Commn., 1984—; del. Women's State Rep. Conv., 1987, La. State Rep. Conv., 1990, 93, La. Coastal Adv. Coun., 1988, Pan Am. Commn., 1992-95; v.p. pub. rels. Alliance for Good Govt., 1990; candidate State Senate La., 1994. Recipient Outstanding Tchr. award Delgado Coll. Student Govt. Assn., 1974; Woodoow Wilson fellow, 1959-60, NDEA fellow, 1968-69. Mem. AAUP, DAR, Pachyderm Club, Women's Rep. Club, Phi Beta Kappa, Phi Alpha Theta, Sigma Delta Pi. Republican. Mem. Ch. of Christ. Home: PO Box 24399 New Orleans LA 70184-4399

THOMPSON, BARNABY DAVID, film producer; b. London, Mar. 29, 1961; s. John Brian and Sally Gough (Waterhouse) T.; m. Christina Robert, Feb. 1, 1991; children: Preston, Esme. BA with honors, Regent's Park Coll., Oxford, 1983. Mng. dir. World's End Prodns., London, 1986-90; v.p. Broadway Pictures, N.Y.C., L.A., 1990-96; founder Fragile Films, London, 1996—. Prodr.: (films) Spiceworld, 1998, An Ideal Husband, 1999, Kevin and Perry, 1999; co-prodr.: Wayne's World I and II, 1992-93. Office: Fragile Films, 97-99 Dean St, London W1V 5RA, England

THOMPSON, BERTHA BOYA, retired education educator, antique dealer and appraiser; b. New Castle, Pa., Jan. 31, 1917; d. Frank L. and Kathryn Belle (Park) Boya; m. John L. Thompson, Mar. 27, 1942; children: Kay Lynn Thompson Koolage, Scott McClain. BS in Elem. & Secondary Edn., Slippery Rock State Coll., 1940; MA in Geography and History, Miami U., 1954; EdD, Ind. U., 1961. Cert. elem. and secondary edn. tchr. Elem. tchr., reading specialist New Castle (Pa.) Sch. System, 1940-45; tchr., chmn. social studies Talawanda Sch. System, Oxford, Ohio, 1954-63; assoc. prof. psychology and geography, chair edn. dept. Western Coll. for Women, Oxford, 1963-74; assoc. prof. edn., reading clinic Miami U., Oxford, 1974-78, prof. emeritus, 1978—; pvt. antique dealer, appraiser Oxford, 1978—. Contbr. articles to profl. jours. Mem. folk art com. Miami U. Art Mus., Oxford, 1974-76; mem. adv. com. Smith libr., Oxford Pub. Libr., 1978-81. Mem. AAUP, Nat. Coun. Geographic Edn. (exec. bd. dirs. 1966-69), Nat. Soc. for Study Edn., Assn. Am. Geographers, Soc. Women Geographers, Nat. Coun. for the Social Studies, Pi Lambda Theta, Zeta Tau Alpha, Pi Gamma Mu, Gamma Theta Upsilon, Kappa Delta Pi. Avocations: antique collecting, reading, travel, tennis. Home: 6073 Contreras Rd Oxford OH 45056-9708

THOMPSON, BYRON GREGORY, neurosurgeon, researcher; b. Kansas City, Mo., Sept. 28, 1959; s. Byron Gregory and Jeanne (Collins) T.; m. Ramona Gatschet; children: Byron Gregory III, Kelsey Anne, Molly Jeanne, Theresa Marie. AB, Harvard U., 1982; MD, U. Kans., 1986. Diplomate Am. Bd. Neurol. Surgery. Resident in neurosurgery U. Pitts., 1986-90, chief resident neurosurgery, 1992-93; rsch. fellow NIH, Bethesda, Md., 1990-92; fellow in skull base and neurovascular surgery Phoenix, 1993-94; chief neurovascular surgery dept. neurol. surgery U. Utah Sch. Medicine, Salt Lake City, 1994-98; chief neurovascular surgery U. Mich. Sch. Medicine, Ann Arbor, 1998—. Contbr. articles to profl. jours. Recipient Stroke Young Investigator award Am. Heart Assn., Phoenix, 1992, Galbraith award in cerebrovascular surgery Joint Sect. of Cerebrovascular Surgery, 1992. Mem. AMA, Am. Assn. Neurol. Surgeons (chmn. young neurosurgeons sect. 1999—, bd. dirs. 1999—), Congress Neurol. Surgeons. Avocations: hiking, skiing, cycling. Office: U Mich Dept Neurosurgery Taubman Health Care Ctr 2128 1500 E Medical Center Dr Ann Arbor MI 48109-0005

THOMPSON, CRAIG SNOVER, corporate communications executive; b. Bklyn., May 24, 1932; s. Craig F. and Edith (Williams) T.; m. Masae Sugizaki, Feb. 21, 1957; children: Lee Anne, Jane Laura. Grad., Valley Forge Mil. Acad., 1951; B.A., Johns Hopkins U., 1954. Newspaper and radio reporter Easton (Pa.) Express, 1954-55, 57-59, Wall St. Jour., 1959-60; account exec. Moore, Meldrum & Assocs., 1960; mgr. pub. relations Cen. Nat. Bank of Cleve., 1961-62; account exec. Edward Howard & Co., Cleve., 1962-67; v.p. Edward Howard & Co., 1967-69, sr. v.p., 1969-71; dir. pub. relations White Motor Corp., Cleve., 1971-76; v.p. pub. relations No. Telecom Inc., Nashville, 1976-77, White Motor Corp., Farmington Hills, Mich., 1977-80; v.p. corp. communications White Motor Corp., 1980-81; dir. exec. communications Rockwell Internat. Corp., Pitts., 1981-86, El Segundo, Calif., 1986-91; dir. exec. communications Rockwell Internat. Corp., Seal Beach, Calif., 1992-97, sr. communications exec., 1997; pres. Craig S.

Thompson. Inc., 1997—. Bd. dirs. Shaker Lakes Regional Nature Center, 1970-73. Served to 1st lt., inf. U.S. Army, 1955-57. Mem. Pub. Rels. Soc. Am. (accredited), Alumni Assn. Valley Forge Mil. Acad. (bd. dirs. 1988-94).

THOMPSON, DANNY CHARLES, advertising executive; b. Lamesa, Tex., June 30, 1956; s. Charles Richard and Mary Elizabeth (Dennis) T.; m. Sharol Kayleen Cooper, Mar. 15, 1974 (div. Apr. 1980); children: Charles Scott Thompson, Logan Jennings Thompson. AA in Adminstrn., Community Coll. Air Force, Randolph AFB, Tex., 1980; BS of Occupational Edn. in Bus. Adminstrn., Wayland Bapt. U., 1980; MA in Mgmt., Webster U., 1983. Enlisted USAF, 1974, advanced through grades to tech. sgt., 1982, resigned, 1983; dir. EDS, Dallas, 1983-85; constrn. mgr. Gemcraft Homes, Dallas, 1985-88; project mgr. D.R. Horton Homes, Inc., Ft. Worth, 1988-89; v.p. Mission Balloons, Inc., Lewisville, Tex., 1989-92; pres., owner Comml. Promotions & Balloons, Inc., Ft. Worth; lectr. City Colls. Chgo., Diyarbakir, Turkey, 1981. Dir. Help Line, Biloxi, Miss., 1975-78; vol. Big Bros., Raleigh, N.C., 1984-85; fund raiser PBS Channel 13, Dallas, 1987-88, Tex. Girld Choir, 1991-95. Sr. Master Sgt. USNG, 1986-97. Republican. Mem. Ch. of Christ. Avocations: water skiing, horseback riding, reading, tennis. Home: 7304 Chapman Dr North Richland Hills TX 76180

THOMPSON, DAVID ALFRED, industrial engineer; b. Chgo., Sept. 9, 1929; s. Clifford James and Christobel Eliza (Sawin) T.; children: Nancy, Brooke, Lynda, Diane, Kristy. B.M.E., U. Va., 1951; B.S. in Indsl. Engring, U. Fla., 1955, M.S. in Engring, 1956; Ph.D., Stanford U., 1961. Registered profl. engr., Calif; cert. profl. ergonomist. Research asst. U. Fla. Engring. and Industries Exptl. Sta., Gainesville, 1955-56; instr. indsl. engring. Stanford U., 1956-58, acting asst. prof., 1958-61, asst. prof., 1961-64, asso. prof., 1964-72, prof., 1972-83, prof., asso. chmn. dept. indsl. engring., 1972-73, prof. emeritus, 1983—; mem. clin. faculty occupational medicine U. Calif. Med. Sch., San Francisco, 1985—; pres., chief scientist Portola Assocs., Palo Alto, Calif., 1965—, Incline Village, Nev., 1965—; prin. investigator NASA Ames Rsch. Ctr., Moffatt Field, Calif., 1974-77; 0ons. Dept. State, Fed. EEO Commn., maj. U.S. and fgn. cos.; cons. emergency commn. ctr. design Santa Clara County Criminal Justice Bd., 1974, Bay Area Rapid Transit Control Ctr., 1977, Govt. of Mex., 1978, Amadahl Corp., 1978-79, Kerr-McGee Corp., 1979, Chase Manhattan Bank, 1980, St. Regis Paper Co., 1980-82, Pacific Gas & Electric, 1983-85, Pacific Bell, 1984-86, 89-93, IBM, 1988-91, Hewlett-Packard, 1990-91, 98-99, Reuter's News Svc., 1990-92, Safeway Corp., 1992-94, New United Motors Mfg., 1993-95, Sun Microsys., 1993-94, Microsoft, 1995-00; mem. com. for office computers Calif. OSHA. Dir., editor: documentary film Rapid Answers for Rapid Transit, Dept. Transp., 1974; mem. editorial adv. bd. Computers and Graphics, 1970-85; reviewer Indsl. Engring. and IEEE Transactions, 1972-86; contbr. articles to profl. jours. Served to lt. USNR, 1951-58. HEW grantee, 1967-70. Mem. IEEE, Am. Inst. Indsl. Engrs., Human Factors and Ergonomics Soc. E-mail: overjoy@pyramid.net. Home: PO Box 6685 Incline Village NV 89450-6685 Address: PO Box 6088 Incline Village NV 89450-6088

THOMPSON, DAVID B., bishop. Ordained priest, 1950; consecrated bishop, 1989. Coadjutor bishop Diocese of Charleston, S.C., 1989-90, bishop, 1990—. Office: Bishop of Charleston 119 Broad St Charleston SC 29401-2435

THOMPSON, DAVID GEORGE, gastroenterologist, educator; b. London, May 4, 1948; s. George David and Margaret (Lewington) T.; m. Hilary Harrison, Nov. 26, 1972; children: Toby, Catherine. BSc, London Hosp., 1969, MB, BS with honors, 1972; MD, London U., 1980. House officer London Hosp., 1973, lectr., 1975-82, sr. lectr., 1982-86; house officer Whittington (Eng.) Hosp., 1974, Hammersmith Hosp., Eng., 1975; rsch. fellow Mayo Clinic, Rochester, Minn., 1980-81; sr. lectr. U. Manchester, Eng., 1987-96, prof. gastroenterology, 1996—; asst. prof. U. N.C., 1980—; cons. physician Home Hosp., Salford, Eng. Mem. Brit. Soc. Gastroenterology (sec. 1990-92, rsch. medalist 1988, chmn. rsch. com. 1994—), Am. Gastroenterology Assn. Avocations: sports, cello. Home: Belmont Rd, Hale WA15 9PT, England Office: Hope Hosp, Dept Medicine, Salford M6 8HD, England

THOMPSON, DAVID MICHAEL, historian, educator; b. Leicester, England, Sept. 23, 1942; s. David and Alice (Beckett) T.; m. Margaret Clague, Aug. 16, 1969; three children. BA, U. Cambridge, 1964, MA, 1968, PhD, 1969, B of Divinity, 1986. Coll. lectr. history U. Cambridge, 1966-70, univ. lectr. modern ch. history, 1970—; dir. ctr. for advanced religious and theol. studies U. Cambridge, 1995—. author: Nonconformity in the Nineteenth Century, 1972, Let Sects and Parties Fall, 1980; editor: Stating the Gospel, 1990. Moderator Gen. Assembly United Reformed Ch., 1996-97. Fellow Royal Hist. Soc. Home: 7 Sherlock Rd, CB3 0HR Cambridge England

THOMPSON, DAVID THOMAS, consulting chemist, researcher; b. Luton, Eng., July 4, 1934; s. William Thomas and May Mary (Kempton) T.; m. Barbara Clare Waters, July 13, 1963; children: Clare, Vanessa, Adrian. BSc, Imperial Coll., London, 1955, PhD, 1958. Postdoctoral fellow UCLA, 1958-59; sr. DSIR fellow Imperial Coll., London, 1960-61; tech. officer, rsch. specialist ICI Plc, Runcorn, Eng., 1962-74; mgr. catalyst dept. Johnson Matthey Plc, Reading, Eng., 1974-78, mgr.new tech., 1978-91; cons. chemist, advisor on univ./industry rsch. collaboration Reading, 1991—. Editor, author: Insights into Speciality Inorganic Chemicals, 1995; co-author: Universities and Industrial Research, 1995; editor: The Company of the Future, 1999; tech. editor Gold Bull., 1996—, Special Interest in Catalysis by Gold. Fellow Royal Soc. Chemistry. Liberal Democrat. Baptist. Avocation: orchestral music. Home: Newlands, The Village, Whitchurch Hill, Reading RG8 7PN, England

THOMPSON, DAYLE ANN, aerospace company executive; b. Grand Forks, N.D., Jan. 6, 1954; d. Duane Theodore and Anna Mae (Desautel) T.; m. Michael Gary Sciulla, Aug. 6, 1977 (div. Sept. 1980); m. Manfred Hans von Ehrenfried II, June 11, 1982. Secretarial degree, Aaker's Bus. Coll., Grand Forks, 1973; Masters Cert. in Project Mgmt., George Washington U., 1995. Receptionist U.S. Rep. Norman F. Lent U.S. Ho. of Reps., Washington, 1973-74; office mgr., personal sec. U.S. Rep. Les AuCoin, U.S. Ho. of Reps., Washington, 1975-78; bus. mgr., bookkeeper Virgin Islands POST, St.Thomas, USVI, 1978; office and pers. mgr. Internat. Energy Assocs. Ltd., Washington, 1978-82; program support mgr. MSI Svcs. Inc., Washington, 1982-84; pres., treas., chief exec. officer Tech. and Adminstrv. Svcs. Corp., Washington, 1984—; Hosp. vol. ARC, Arlington, Va., 1987. Recipient Group Achievement award NASA, 1984, 93, Commendation Letter, NASA, 1985, 87, 88, 91, 93, 94, Small Bus. Prime Contractor of Yr. award Small Bus. Adminstrn. Region 3, 1994. Mem. Washington Space Bus. Roundtable (sponsor-benefactor 1990-92). Republican. Roman Catholic. Avocations: boating, fishing, reading. Home: 4200 42d Ave S Saint Petersburg FL 33711-4231

THOMPSON, DIDI CASTLE (MARY BENNETT), writer, editor; b. Terre Haute, Ind., Feb. 7, 1918; d. Robert Langley Bennett and Marjorie Rose (Tyler) Castle; student U. Ill., Champaign, 1935-36, U. Ky., 1936-39; m. Jamie Campbell Thompson, Jr., June 24, 1939; children—Jamie III, Julia King Balko, Langley Stewart Ruede. News editor Glen-Echoes, Glencoe, Ill., 1930; columnist Ky. Kernel, U. Ky., Lexington, 1937-39; radio script writer Modern Am. Music, 1940-42; asst. pub. relations dir. Salem Coll., Winston-Salem, N.C., 1945; pub. relations chmn. Barrington (Ill.) Horse Show, 1959-67; staff writer, columnist Barrington Press Newspapers, 1958-84; editor ECHO, Defenders of the Fox River, Inc. newsletter, 1970-80; travel editor Barrington Press Newspapers, 1973-84; columnist The Daily Herald, Paddock Publs., 1984-86; columnist Rapid City (S.D.) Journal, 1990-95; freelance writer, 1943—. Past bd. mem. Barrington chpt. Lyric Opera Guild Chgo., Barrington Sr. Center, Infant Welfare Soc. Chgo., Art Inst. Chgo., Barrington Assos.; elected trustee Village of Barrington Hills, 1969-73, health, pub. relations chmn., 1969-73; mem. Barrington Hills Plan Commn., 1986. Mem. DAR, Women in Communications (past dir.), Citizens for Conservation (past dir.), Barrington Countryside Assn. (past dir.), Barrington Hist. Soc., Spring Creek Basset Hounds Club, Barrington Hills Riding Club (past dir.), Pan Hellenic Coun., Gulf Shore Lit. Soc., Conservancy S.W. Fla. (Naples), Chgo. Press Club, Chi Omega. Episcopalian. Address: 1827 Princess Ct Naples FL 34110-1001

THOMPSON, EMMA, actress; b. London, Apr. 15, 1959; d. Eric Thompson and Phyllida Law; m. Kenneth Branaugh, Aug. 1989. Student of English, Cambridge U., Eng. Performances include: (films) Henry V, 1989, The Tall Guy, 1989, Dead Again, 1991, Impromptu, 1991, Howard's End, 1992 (Acad. award for best actress 1993), Peter's Friends, 1992, Much Ado About Nothing, 1993, The Remains of the Day, 1993 (Acad. award nominee for best actress 1993), In the Name of the Father, 1993 (Acad. award nominee for best supporting actress 1993), My Father, the Hero, 1994, Junior, 1994, Carrington, 1995 (Best Actress award Nat. Bd. Rev. 1995), Sense and Sensibility, 1995 (Golden Globe award nominee for best actress in film 1996, Acad. award nominee for best actress 1996), Winter Guest, 1996, Primary Colors, 1998, Judas Kiss, 1998, Maybe Baby, 2000; (TV in Eng.) Al Fresco, Up For Grabs (a.k.a. Sexually Transmitted), Tutti Frutti, (miniseries) Fortunes of War, Thompson; (TV in Am.) Fortunes of War, Cheers, 1991; (London stage) Me and My Girl, Look Back in Anger; also writer screen adaptation: Sense and Sensibility (Jane Austin), 1995 (Best Screenplay award N.Y. Film Critics 1995, L.A. Film Critics 1995, Boston Film Critics 1995, Golden Globe award for best adapted screenplay 1996, Acad. award for best adapted screenplay 1996, BAFTA Best Actress award 1996). Active in Footlights Theatrical Group, Cambridge, Eng. Office: William Morris Agy 151 S El Camino Dr Beverly Hills CA 90212-2775

THOMPSON, ERNEST VICTOR, writer; b. London, July 14, 1931; s. Ernest Arthur and Victoria Elizabeth (Harrup) T.; m. Elizabeth Spiller, Dec. 6, 1952 (div. 1972); children: Carol Elizabeth Ann, Virginia Louise; m. Celia Carole Burton, Sept. 11, 1972; children: Nathan Wyatt, Luke Adam. Telegraphist Royal Navy, 1947-56; police officer Bristol (Eng.) City Police, 1956-63; security investigator B.O.A.C., London, 1963-64; chief of security Civil Aviation, Zimbabwe, 1964-70, Mayfair Hotel, London, 1970-72; freelance writer Cornwall, 1973—. Author: Chase the Wind, 1975 (Best Hist. Novel award Macmillan London/Pan/Coward, McCann and Geoghegan, U.S.A., 1975), 26 novels. Mem. Royal Soc. Lit., West Country Writers Assn. (v.p. 1993), Cornwall Drama Assn. (pres.), Riding for the Disabled Assn. (reg. v.p.), Cornish Writer's Guild (pres.). Anglican. Avocations: travel, history, research, public speaking, broadcasting. Home: Parc Franton Pentewan, Cornwall PL26 6EH, England

THOMPSON, G. KENNEDY, financial services company executive; b. Rocky Mount, N.C., Nov. 25, 1950. BA in Am. Studies, U. N.C.; MBA, Wake Forest Fu. With 1st Union Corp., Charlotte, N.C., 1976—, head S.E. divsn., mgr. mid. market dept., 1999—, mgr. N.Y. loan prodn. office, pres. 1st Union-Ga., sr. v.p., head human resources, pres. 1st Union-Fla., vice chmn. corp., head global capital markets, until 1999, pres., CEO, 1999—; bd. dirs. Fla. Rock Industries, Inc., VISA Internat.; mem. fin. svcs. roundtable Fin. Svcs. Forum. Bd. visitors U. N.C., Chapel Hill, Babcock Grad. Sch. Mgmt., Wake Forest U.; bd. dirs. N.C. Blumenthal Performing Arts Ctr., Charlotte Latin Sch., so. region Boy Scouts Am., United Way, Charlotte; mem. met. bd. YMCA, Charlotte. Morehead scholar U. N.C. Office: First Union Corp 1 First Union CTR Charlotte NC 28288

THOMPSON, GARY G., sales trainer; b. Douglasville, Ga., Apr. 21, 1941; s. Douglas O and Katie Elizabeth (Carr) T. M in salaes engring., Univ. Hawaii, 1961. Sales trainer Nat. PreSchool Assn.; nat. sales dir. Thompson Assocs.; dir. Achicar Unlimited, West Palm Beach, Fla.; adv. bd. Achicar Unlimted. With U.S. Army, 1958-61. Recipient Egypt Firing Range U.S. Army, 1959. Mem. Lions Club. Republican. Avocations: reading, traveling, working with kids. E-mail: Gthomp2800@aol.com.

THOMPSON, GEOFFREY STUART, physician, consultant; b. Oldham, U.K., June 26, 1926; s. Frank Vincent and Maud Partington (Hague) T.; m. Angela Mary Stewart Brown, Apr. 28, 1962; children: Jonathan Richard, Jane Elizabeth. MB BChir, Trinity Coll., Cambridge, Eng., 1951, MA, 1954, MD, 1965. House surgeon U. Coll. Hosp., London, 1951-52; house physician, sr. registrar Liverpool Teaching Hosps., Eng., 1954-65; cons. physician South Manchester Hosps., Eng., 1965-91, hon. cons. physician, 1991-96. Contbr. articles to profl. jours. Flight lt. RAF Med. Br., 1952-54. Fellow Royal Coll. Physicians London, Manchester Med. Soc.; mem. Brit. Med. Assn., Brit. Diabetic Assn. Avocations: walking, swimming, football.

THOMPSON, GEORGE BRIAN, psychologist, educator; b. Invercargill, New Zealand, Apr. 1, 1938; s. Peter George and Jessie (Buck) T.; m. Margaret Jean Daley, May 4, 1974; children: Derek Adrian, Rona Louise. BA, U. New Zealand, Christchurch, 1960; MA, U. Canterbury, Christchurch, 1962; dip.edu.psych., U. Auckland, New Zealand, 1968; PhD, Monash U., Melbourne, Australia, 1980. Registered psychologist. Psychologist Lintas Pty., Ltd., Wellington, New Zealand, 1962-65, Psychol. Svcs., Dept. Edn., Napier, New Zealand, 1968-74; sr. tchg. fellow Faculty Edn., Monash U., Melbourne, Australia, 1974-78; vis. fellow dept. psychology U. Coll., London, 1984; sr. lectr. Sch. Edn., Victoria U., Wellington, New Zealand, 1978—; hon. cons. New Zealand Coun. for Ednl. Rsch., Wellington, 1980-2000; hon. rsch. project advisor New Zealand Bus. Roundtable, Wellington, 1994-96; rsch. cons. rsch. divsn. Ministry of Edn., Wellington, 1998; mem. literacy experts group Ministry of Edn., Wellington, 1998-99. Editor, author with others: Reading Acquisition Processes, 1993, Learning to Read: Beyond Phonics and Whole Language, 1999; contbr. articles to profl. jours. Fellow British Psychol. Soc. (assoc.), New Zealand Psychol. Soc. (assoc., Golden Jubilee Spl. award 1998); mem. Internat. Reading Assn. (pres. Wellington Coun. 1983-84), Soc. for the Scientific Study of Reading (bd. mem. 2000—). Avocations: piano playing, gardening, bush walking. Office: Edn Victoria U Wellington, Kelburn Pde PO Box 600, Wellington New Zealand

THOMPSON, GEORGE EDWARD, corrosion science and engineering educator; b. Liverpool, Eng., Mar. 7, 1946; s. John Henry and Elsie May (Serridge) T.; m. Marilyn Judith Wright, Apr. 17, 1971; children: James Robert, Sarah Louise. BSc, U. Nottingham, Eng., 1967, PhD, 1970, DSc, 1988. Postdoctoral fellow U. Nottingham, 1970-73; sect. leader Howson-Algraphy, Eng., 1973-74, prin. scientist, 1975-78; lectr. U. Manchester (Eng.) Inst. Sci. and Tech., 1978-83, sr. lectr., 1983-88, reader, 1988-90, prof. corrosion sci. and engring., 1990, head corrosion and protection ctr., 1990-93, 96—, univ. prof., 1994—. Contbr. over 500 articles to profl. jours. in anodizing and anodic processes, uniform and localized corrosion, atmospheric corrosion, corrosion inhibition, stone/monument degradation and conservation. Decorated Order Brit. Empire; recipient Beilby medal and prize Royal Soc. Chemistry/Inst. of Metals/Soc. Chem. Industry, 1987, T.P. Hoard award and prize, 1997, U.R. Evans award Inst. Corrosion, 2000. Fellow Inst. Metal Finishing, Royal Acad. Engring.; mem. Inst. Corrosion, Electrochem. Soc., Inst. Materials. Office: U Manchester Inst Sci/Tech Corrosion/Protection Centre, Sackville St PO Box 88, Manchester M60 1QD, England

THOMPSON, GEORGE FREDERICK, JR., public management educator; b. Anderson, Ind., Oct. 29, 1942; s. George Frederick and Ellen Leah (Reuter) T.; m. Sharon O'Rand, Sept. 8, 1968 (div. Nov. 1978); children: MacKendree and Kyrie' O'Rand; m. Ruth Ann Crowley, June 20, 1980; 1 child, Jonathan Crowley. BA, Pomona Coll., 1964; PhD, Claremont Grad. Sch., 1972. Asst. to sr. analyst Dept. Fin. State of Calif., Sacramento, 1972-75; assoc. dep. dir. for fin. and capital outlay planning Calif. Postsecondary Edn. Commn., Sacramento, 1975-76; vis. asst./assoc. prof. U. British Columbia faculty commerce and bus. adminstrn., 1976-77; sr. rsch economist Econ. Coun. Can., Ottawa, Ont., 1978-79; vis. assoc. prof., acting chmn. Grad. Sch. Mgmt. Pub. and Not for Profit Mgmt. Group UCLA, 1981; assoc. prof. Columbia U. Sch. Internat. and Pub. Affairs MPA Program, N.Y.C., 1980-85; Grace and Elmer Goudy Prof. Pub. Mgmt. and Policy Analysis Atkinson Grad. Sch. Mgmt. Willamette U., Salem, Oreg., 1985—; bd. dirs. Fin. Pub., Inc.; mem. task force on state budgeting Nat. Ctr. for Higher edn. Mgmt. Systems, Boulder, Colo., 1975-76, adv. com. Calif. State Senate Judiciary Com. subcom. on Consumr Affairs, 1980-81, Gov.'s Task Force on Sch. Fin. Reform, Oreg., 1988-89, adv. com. on Tax Reform, Oreg., 1990, Govt. Standards and Practices Commn., Oreg., 1995—; cons. House of Commons Can., on Regulatory Reform, Pub. Svcs. Commn. N.Y. Atty. Gen.'s Office of Consumer Affairs, Defense Sec.'s Commn. on Base Realignment and Closure, Senate Armed Svcs. subcom. on mil. constrn., others. Co-author: (with W.T. Stanbury) Regulatory Reform in Canada, 1982, (with L.R. Jones) Regulatory Policy and Practices: Regulating Better and Regulating Less, 1982, Reinventing the Pentagon, 1994, Public Management: Institutional Renewal for the 21st Century, 1999; translator (with Ruth Crowley) F. Scharpf's Crisis and Choice in European Social Democracy, 1991; editor: Regulatory Regimes in Conflict, 1984; co-editor: (with LeRoy Gramer) Reforming Social Regulation, 1982, (with W.T. Stanbury) Managing Public Enterprises, 1982; editor Internat. Pub. Mgmt. Jour.; contbr. numerous articles, notes, essays, book revs. to profl. jours. Mem. acad. adv. bd. Cascade Policy Inst. Recipient Clara Ihrig Linhardt Traveling fellowship, Mexico, Cen. Am., 1970-71, Mayr Found. Essay award, Lincoln Inst. Pub. Fin., Claremont Grad. Sch., 1973; nominated for Koopman prize of ORSA spl. interest group of defense analysis, 1987. Mem. Assn. for Pub. Policy and Mgmt., ASPA (exec. coun. sect. on pub. budgeting and fin. 1991-97, pres. 1998, sect. on rsch. and theory 1996—, Mosher award 1994, NASPAA/ASPA Disting Rsch. award 2000), Am. Soc. Mil. Controllers (Gold medal 1994), Oreg. Acad. Scis. Home: 540 Tillman Ave SE Salem OR 97302-3786 Office: Willamette Univ Atkinson Grad Sch Mgmt Salem OR 97301

THOMPSON, GEORGE LEE, consulting company executive; b. Denver, June 12, 1933; s. George H. and Frances M. (Murphy) T.; m. Patricia M. MacKenzie, Sept. 25, 1993; children: Shannon, Tracy, Bradley. BS in Bus., U. Colo., 1957; AMP in advanced mgmt., NYU, 1969. With GTE Sylvania, Danvers, Mass., 1957-65, nat. sales mgr., 1965-67, mktg. mgr., 1967-68; v.p. sales entertainment products Batavia, N.Y., 1968-73; dir. corp. mktg. Stamford, Conn., 1973-74; v.p. mktg. Servomation Corp., N.Y.C., 1974-76, exec. v.p., 1976-78; exec. v.p. Singer Co., Edison, N.J., 1978-81, pres., 1981-83; pres. consumer products SCM Corp., N.Y.C., 1983-86; pres., CEO Smith-Corona Corp., New Canaan, Conn., 1986-89, chmn., CEO, 1989-95; chmn. Mackenzie-Thompson Assocs., Palm City, Fla., 1995—; bd. dirs. Vol. Products, Inc.; chair Sweet P's, Essex, Conn., 1998—. Bd. dirs. Internat. Tennis Hall of Fame, Am. Jr. Golf Found., United Way of New Canaan, 1989-93; chmn. EC-92 Standards Com. U.S. Dept. Commerce; mem. bus. alumni adv. coun. U. Colo., 1989-94; mem. bd. overseers Sch. Bus. U. Conn., 1993-96; mem. Pres.'s Export Coun., 1991-93; mem. bd. advisors Jr. league. Recipient Disting. Bus. Alumni award U. Colo., 1990. Mem. Computer and Bus. Equipment Mfg. Assn. (bd. dirs. 1992-94), Sales and Mktg. Execs. Internat. (trustee), Am. Mgmt. Assn. (bd. trustees, exec. com. chmn., gen. mgmt. coun. 1989-99), St. John Assn. (bd. dirs., pres. 1983-93), New Canaan Field Club, Woodway Country Club, Club at Seabrook Island, Wilton Riding Club (bd. govs. 1980-83), Navesink Country Club (bd. govs. 1983-86), Harbour Ridge Yacht and Country Club, Essex Yacht Club, Fox Hopyard Club, Chi Psi. Episcopalian. Office: Mackenzie Thompson Assocs 51 Main St Essex CT 06426-1150 also: Sweep P's LLC Griswold Sq Essex CT 06426

THOMPSON, GILBERT RICHARD, physician, educator; b. Poona, India, Nov. 20, 1932; s. Richard Louis and Violet Mary (Harrison) T.; m. Sheila Jacqueline Deurvorst, June 14, 1958; children: Anna, Mark, Philip, Jennifer. MB BS, St. Thomas Hosp. Med. Sch., 1956; MD, U. London, 1963. Intern St. Mary's Hosp., Portsmouth and Southhampton Gen. Hosp., 1956-57; resident, registrar, sr. registrar Hammersmith Hosp., London, 1963-66; med. rsch. coun. travelling fellow Mass. Gen. Hosp., Boston, 1966-67; hon. cons. physician Hammersmith Hosp., London, 1967—; hon. sr. lectr. Royal Postgrad. Me d. Sch., 1967-95; prof Royal Post grad. med. sch., 1996-98; emeritus prof. Imperial Coll. Sch. Medicine, 1999—; asst. prof. Baylor U. Coll. Medicine, Houston, 1972-73; vis. prof. McGill U., Montreal, Que., Can., 1981-82. Author: A Handbook of Hyperlipidaemia; past editor Current Opinion in Lipidology; contbr. numerous sci. articles to profl. jours. Capt. M.C. Brit. Army, 1957-63. Recipient Lucian award McGill U. Royal Victoria Hosp., 1982. Fellow Royal Coll. Physicians, Am. Heart Assn. (coun. on arteriosclerosis); mem. European Atherosclerosis Soc., Brit. Atherosclerosis Soc. (past chmn.), Brit. Hyperlipidaemia Assn. (past chmn.). Roman Catholic. Avocations: fly fishing, running, skiing. Home: 3 Queen Anne's Gardens, London W4 1TU, England Office: Imperial Coll Sch Medicine, Divsn Investigative Sci/Hammersmith Hp, London W12 ONN, England

THOMPSON, GRAHAM, building material executive; b. Harrow, England, Oct. 25, 1938; s. Leslie Arnold and Alice Elizabeth (Rhodes) T.; m. Gillian Margaret Rose, June 16, 1962; 1 child, Mark Andrew. BSc in Mech. Engring. with hons., U. Leeds, England, 1961. Chartered mech. engr. Devel. mgr. Butterley Brick Co. Ltd., Derby, Eng., 1963-66; prodn. mgr. Westbrick Ltd., Exeter, Eng., 1966-69; mng. dir. Westbrick Ltd., Exeter, 1969-75, chmn., 1975-77; mng. dir. Beazer Bldg. Materials, Exeter, 1983-84; chief exec. Tarmac Bricks and Tiles, Exeter, 1987-93; mng. dir. Hawkins Tiles Ltd., Cannock, Eng., 1984-93, Severn Valley Brick Co. Ltd., Avonmouth, 1988-93. Fellow Inst. Energy, Inst. Materials; mem. Inst. Mech. Engrs., Brick Devel. Assn. (chmn. 1982-84, 86-88), Nat. Fedn. Clay Industries (pres. 1987-89), Brit. Masonry Soc. (pres. 1989-90). Home: 1 Higher Hoopern Ln, Exeter EX4 6DS, England

THOMPSON, GUY ALLEN, JR., biology educator; b. Rosedale, Miss., May 31, 1931; s. Guy Allen and Mona Louise (Chaney) T.; m. Eileen Mary Wood, Sept. 24, 1960; children: Sarah Marie Macklin, Gillian Louise Thompson, Jeremy James Thompson. BS, Miss. State U., 1953; PhD, Calif. Inst. Technology, Pasadena, 1959. Instr. dept. biochemistry U. Wash., Seattle, 1962-63, asst. prof., 1963-67; assoc. prof., dept. botany U. Tex., Austin, 1967-74, prof., dept. botany, 1974—, chmn. dept. botany, 1996-99; mem. rev. panels for grants NIH, Bethesda, Md., 1980, NSF, Washington, 1982-86, USDA, Washington, 1987, DOE, Washington, 1993. Contbr. numerous articles to profl. jours. and publs. 1st lt. USAF, 1953-55, Japan. Fellow AAAS; mem. Am. Chem. Soc., Soc. of Protozool. (nominating com.), Am. Soc. Plant Physiologists, Am. Soc. Biochemistry and Molecular Biology. Methodist. Avocations: hiking, gardening. Office: Sect Mol Cell & Devel Biol Univ of Tex Austin TX 78712

THOMPSON, HOLLEY MARKER, lawyer, association develepment and relations executive; b. Jamestown, N.Y., Jan. 30, 1947; d. Burdette James and Mary (Novitske) Marker; children: Jennifer Kristen Simos, Kendra Elise Blair, Jennifer Lynn, Stephanie Lynn; m. Lawrence D. Thompson. AAS, Jamestown C.C., 1966; BS, Ohio U., 1969; MA, W.Va. U., 1974, JD, 1980. Bar: W.Va. 1980, U.S. Dist. Ct. (so. dist.) W.Va. 1980, Pa. 1982, U.S. Dist. Ct. (we. dist.) Pa. 1982. Tchr. math. various pub. schs., Santa Ana (Calif.), Lakewood (N.Y.) and Morgantown (W.Va.), 1970-77; atty. for students W.Va. U., Morgantown, 1980; assoc. libr., lectr. W.Va. U. Coll. Law, Morgantown, 1980-83; assoc., libr. Jackson, Kelly, Holt & O'Farrell, Charleston, W.Va., 1983-86; cons. Hildebrandt, Inc., Somerville, N.J., 1986-94; v.p. assn. devel. & rels. LEXIS-NEXIS, Dayton, Ohio, 1994—; speaker at regional, nat. and internat. legal confs. Contbr. articles to profl. jours. Mem. ABA, Spl. Libr. Assn., Am. Assn. Law Libs., N.J. Assn. Law Libs., Legal Mktg. Assn., Phi Delta Phi. Office: LEXIS NEXIS 9443 Springboro Pike Miamisburg OH 45342

THOMPSON, JAN NEWSTROM, art historian, educator; b. Buffalo, Mar. 19, 1947; d. Marvin William and Nadene (Newstrom) T.; m. Paul L. Goldstein, Aug. 28, 1977; 1 child, Elizabeth Esther. BFA, SUNY, Buffalo, 1968, MA, 1971; MA, Rutgers U., New Brunswick, N.J., 1974, PhD, 1980. Instr. art history Canisius Coll., Buffalo, 1973-74; instr. art history, studio art Union Coll., Cranford, N.J., 1974-77; instr. art history Santa Clara (Calif.) U., 1977-94, San Jose (Calif.) U., 1988—, San Francisco Museum of Modern Art, 1987. Author: Frank Duveneck: Lost Paintings Found, 1987, Theodore Wores: An American Artist in Meiji, Japan, 1993. Mem. adv. bd. No. Calif. Coun. of Nat. Museum of Women in the Arts, 1995—; trustee Triton Museum of Art, Santa Clara, 1980-90. Mem. Coll. Art Assn. Am. Avocations; equestrianism, dressage. Office: San Jose Stat U Dept of Art and Design 1 Washington Sq San Jose CA 95192-0001

THOMPSON, JENNY, Olympic athlete. Silver medalist 100 Meter Freestyle, Barcelona, Spain, 1992; gold medalist 4 x 100 Medley Relay, Barcelona, 1992, 4 x 100m freestyle, Sydney, 2000, 4 x 100m medley, Sydney, 2000, 4 x 200m medley, Sydney, 2000. Address: care US Olympic Com 1750 E Boulder St Colorado Springs CO 80909-5724

THOMPSON, JOEL ERIK, lawyer; b. Summit, N.J., Sept. 15, 1940; s. Maurice Eugene and Charlotte Ruth (Harrington) T.; m. Bonnie Gay Ransa, June 15, 1963 (div. Dec. 1980); m. Deborah Ann Korp, Dec. 24, 1980 (div. Jan. 1987); children: Janice Santiesteban, Amber. Student, Va. Poly. Inst., 1958, Carnegie Inst. Tech., 1960-61; BSME cum laude, Newark Coll. Engr-

ing., 1966; JD, Seton Hall, 1970. Bar: N.J. 1970, Ariz. 1975, U.S. Tax Ct. 1972, U.S. Ct. Claims 1972, U.S. Customs Ct., 1972, U.S. Ct. Mil. Appeals, 1972, U.S. Ct. Customs and Patent Appeals 1972, U.S. Dist. Ct. N.J. 1970, Ariz. 1975, U.S. Ct. Appeals (9th cir.) 1975, U.S. Supreme Ct. 1975; cert. specialist criminal law Ariz. Bd. Legal Specialization; lic. profl. engr., N.J. Sr. technician Bell Tel. Labs., Inc., Murray Hill, N.J., 1965-67; patent agent Bell Tel. Labs., Inc., Murray Hill, 1967-70, staff atty., 1970-73; sr. trial atty. N.J. Pub. Defender's Office, Elizabeth, N.J., 1973-74; assoc. Cahill, Sutton and Thomas, Phoenix, 1974-76; trial lawyer Maricopa County Pub. Defender's Office, Phoenix, 1976-80; trial lawyer, criminal law specialist Henry J. Florence, Ltd., Phoenix, 1980-86; pvt. practice Phoenix, 1987—; judge Superior Ct. Ariz., Phoenix, 1987-95; instr. Phoenix Regional Police Acad., 1976-80, Glendale C.C., 1977, Ariz. State U. Sch. of Law, 1978, Am. Inst., 1990; pres., CEO Eagle Master Corp., Phoenix, 1995—; pres. Joel Erik Thompson, Ltd., Phoenix, 1987—; bd. dirs. Am. Loans, Inc.; presenter in field. Contbr. articles to profl. jours. Mem. planning com. Cammelback East Village, Phoenix, 1992-98, chmn., 1993-96; mayor's select com., Phoenix, 1997, blue ribbon com. Maricopa Assn. Govs., 1996-97. Mem. Ariz. Bar Assn., Nat. Assn. Criminal Def. Lawyers, Ariz. Attys. Criminal Justice (charter), Ariz. Assn. Pvt. Investigators (hon.), Internat. Assn. Identification (hon.), Tau Beta Pi, Pi Tau Sigma. Office: 3104 E Camelback Rd # 521 Phoenix AZ 85016-4502

THOMPSON, JOHN ALBERT, JR., dermatologist; b. Austin, Tex., June 5, 1942; s. J. Albert Sr. and Elizabeth (Brady) T. BA, Georgetown U., 1963; MD, Bowman Gray Sch. Medicine, 1967; Dermatology Fellowship, U. N.C., 1971-73. Diplomate Am. Bd. Dermatology. Resident in internal medicine N.C. Baptist Hosp., Winston-Salem, N.C., 1967-69; resident in dermatology N.C. Meml. Hosp., Chapel Hill, N.C., 1971-73; pvt. practice Charlotte, N.C., 1974—; clin. prof. dermatology Dept. Dermatology, U. N.C. Sch. Medicine, Chapel Hill, 1974—. Author profl. papers. Lt. comdr. USNR, 1969-71, Vietnam. Mem. Am. Acad. Dermatology (chmn. subcom. for sch. health edn. 1976-79, task force--nat. health ins.), Carolinas-Va. Dermatology Assn. (adv. bd. council rep. 1976-79), Charlotte Dermatology Assn., Mecklenburg County Med. Soc., N.C. Med. Soc., North Am. Clin. Dermatology Soc. Southern Med. Assn., Southeastern Consortium for Continuing Dermatol. Edn. (steering com. 1983—), South Cen. Dermatol. Congress (organizing com. 1982-86), Am. Soc. Dermatol. Surgery, Am. Dermatol. Soc. Allergy and Immunology, Am. Soc. Laser Medicine and Surgery, Inc. Democrat. Episcopalian. Home: 2633 Richardson Dr Apt 8A Charlotte NC 28211-3346 Office: Dermatol Laser Ctr Dermatologic Laser Ctr 2310 Randolph Rd Charlotte NC 28207-1526

THOMPSON, JOHN DOUGLAS, financier; b. Montreal, Que., Can., Sept. 28, 1934; s. William Douglas and Anne F. (Whebby) T.; children: Jacqueline, Catherine, Peter, Anne Marie, Francois. BEng, McGill U., 1957; MBA, U. Western Ont., 1960. Dep. chmn. bd. Montreal Trustco Inc.; past chmn. bd. dirs. Trust Cos. Assn. of Can., bd. dirs. Domtar Inc., Montrusco Assocs. Inc., Air Transat, Capital d'Amérique CDPQ Inc., Benvest Capital Inc., Shermag Inc., Manitex Capital Inc., Nat. Trust Co., Scotia Mortgage Corp., Scotia Life Ins. Co., Scotia Gen. Ins. Co., The Bank of Nova Scotia Trust Co., The Mortgage Ins. Co. of Can., Victoria and Grey Corp. Bd. dirs. MacDonald Stewart Found., Windsor Found., Salvation Army, chmn. Montreal adv. bd.; chmn. Montreal YMCA Found.; mem. audit com. McGill U.; past pres. St. Mary's Hosp. Found.; gov., past pres. St. Mary's Hosp. Ctr. Mem. Assn. Profl. Engrs., Que. and Ont., Mt. Royal Club (Montreal), Royal Montreal Golf Club, Mt. Bruno Country Club Inc., The Forest and Stream Club. Roman Catholic. Office: Montreal Trust, 1800 McGill College Ave 4th Fl, Montreal, PQ Canada H3A 3K9

THOMPSON, JOHN MICHAEL, chemist; b. Sacramento, Calif., Mar. 26, 1946; s. Farold Laverne and Mable (Bane) T.; m. Barbara Lee Pybrum, Mar. 25, 1972; children: Stacy Aileen, Jeremy Eric, Julie Elaine. BS in Chemistry, U. Calif., Davis, 1968; MS in Chemistry, Calif. State U., Sacramento, 1974. Phys. sci. aid, technician U.S. Geol. Survey, Sacramento, 1965-68, 70-71; rsch. chemist U.S. Geol. Survey, Menlo Park, Calif., 1972-95; chemist Air Liquide Electronic, 1998—; part-time faculty Calif. State U., Sacramento, 1971-72, 74. Sr. author: Chemical and Isotopic Compositions of Waters from Crater Lake, 1990; contbr. articles to profl. jours. and numerous reports on chemistry of Yellowstone Nat. Park Hot Springs. Chmn. Menlo Park Transp. Commn., 1983-90, Menlo Park Planning Commn., 1990-93. With USMC, 1968-70. Fellow Geol. Survey of Japan, 1989. Mem. AAAS, ACS, Am. Geophys. Union, Geothermal Resources Coun. Office: Air Liquide Electronic 3990 Fairview Indsl Dr Salem OR 97302

THOMPSON, JUDITH KASTRUP, nursing researcher; b. Marstal, Denmark, Oct. 1, 1933; came to the U.S., 1951; d. Edward Kastrup and Anna Hansa (Knudsen) Pedersen; m. Richard Frederick Thompson, May 22, 1960; children: Kathryn Marr, Elizabeth Kastrup, Virginia St. Claire. BS, RN, U. Oreg., 1958, MSN, 1963. RN, Calif., Oreg. Staff nurse U. Oreg. Med. Sch., Eugene, 1957-58; staff nurse U. Oreg. Med. Sch., Portland, 1958-61, head staff nurse, 1960-61; instr. psychiat. nursing U. Oreg. Sch. Nursing, Portland, 1963-64; rsch. asst. U. Oreg. Med. Sch., Portland, 1964-65, U. Calif., Irvine, 1971-72; rsch. assoc. Stanford (Calif.) U., 1982-87; rsch. asst. Harvard U., Cambridge, Mass., 1973-74; rsch. assoc. U. So. Calif., L.A., 1987—. Contbg. author: Behavioral Control and Role of Sensory Biofeedback, 1976; contbr. articles to profl. jours. Treas. LWV, Newport Beach, Calif., 1970-74; scout leader Girl Scouts Am., Newport Beach, 1970-78. Named Citizen of Yr. State of Oreg., 1966. Mem. Soc. for Neurosci., Am. Psychol. Soc. (charter), ANA, Oreg. Nurses Assn. Republican. Lutheran. Avocations: art collecting, travel, tennis. Home: 28 Sky Sail Dr Corona Del Mar CA 92625-1436 Office: U So Calif University Park Los Angeles CA 90089-0001

THOMPSON, JUUL HAROLD, lawyer, educator; b. Chgo., May 3, 1945; s. Jules Harold and Ruth Edith (Pudark) T.; m. Elizabeth Jean Bohler, Sept. 20, 1975 (div. 1990); children: Michael, Erin, David, Margaret, Joseph. BA in History, U. Chgo., 1967; JD, U. Ill., 1973. Bar: Ill. 1973. Asst. states atty. Kane County, Ill., 1974-76; ptnr. Beck and Thompson, Batavia, Ill., 1976-82; sole practice, Batavia, 1983—; counsel Batavia Council on Aging, 1979—; counsel Batavia Social Services Com., 1983-86; counsel Uni Quality Inc., 1993—; counsel Alwin/Komtek Inc., 1993—; instr. law Elgin Community Coll., Ill., 1981-84, Harper Community Coll., Palatine, Ill., 1981-83, Waubonsee Community Coll., Sugar Grove, Ill., 1982, Person Wollinsky CPA Rev. Course, Downers Grove, Ill., 1984. Mem. Holy Cross Cath. Ch. Parish Council, 1985-86; pres. A.G.S. PTO, 1986-88. Served as 1st lt. U.S. Army, 1969-71, Vietnam. Decorated Bronze Star (2). Mem. VFW (Batavia comdr. 1979-80, trustee 1985-86), Holy Cross Players. Republican. Lodge: K.C. (4th degree). Avocations: reading, woodworking, writing. Home and Office: 105 Hamlet St Batavia IL 60510-2147

THOMPSON, KEITH BRUCE, retired university administrator; b. London, Sept. 13, 1932; s. Charles Bruce and Eva Elizabeth (Vidler) T.; m. Kathleen Anne Reeves, Aug. 17, 1956; children: Bruce, Fiona. Diploma in edn., Oxford U., 1956, MA, 1959; MEd, Bristol U., 1968. Schoolmaster City of Bath (Eng.) Boys Sch., 1956-62; lectr. Newton Park Coll., Bath, 1962-67; head dept. Philippa Fawcett Coll., London, 1967-72; prin. Madeley Coll., Staffordshire, Eng., 1972-78; dep. dir. North Staffordshire Poly. (Staffordshire Poly. 1988—), Stafford, Eng., 1978-86, dir., 1986-92; univ. adminstr. Staffordshire U., 1992-95; chmn. Poly. Cen. Admissions System, Eng. and Wales, 1989-93. Author: Education and Philosophy, 1972; joint author: Curriculum Development, 1975; contbr. articles on edn., philosophy and phys. edn. to profl. jours. Avocations: music, sports.

THOMPSON, KEVIN PAUL, optical engineer; b. Minneapolis, Minn., Oct. 5, 1954; s. Clyde Warren and Virginia T.; m. Therese Ann, Jul. 19, 1974. BS in astrophysics, Univ. Minn., 1976, BS in physics, 1976; MS in optics, Optical Scis. Ctr. Univ. Ariz., 1979, PhD, 1980. Rsch. assoc. Optical Scis. Ctr. Univ. Ariz., Tuscon, 1976-80; optical engr. Perkin-Elmer, Danbury, Conn., 1980-86; v.p. optical engring. Optical Rsch. Assocs., Pasadena, Calif., 1986—. Inventor in field. Mem. Optical Soc. Am. (chmn. lens design group 1996-98), SPIE. E-mail: kthompson@opticalres.com. Fax: 626-795-9102. Office: Optical Rsch Assocs 3280 E Foothill Blvd Ste 300 Pasadena CA 91107-3188

THOMPSON, LARRY ANGELO, producer, lawyer, personal manager; b. Clarksdale, Miss., Aug. 1, 1944; s. Angelo and Anne (Tuminello) T.; m. Kelly Ann LeBlanc, 1999. BBA, U. Miss., 1966, JD, 1968. Bar: Miss. 1968, Calif. 1970. In-house counsel Capitol Records, Hollywood, Calif., 1969-71; sr. ptnr. in entertainment law Thompson, Shankman and Bond, Beverly Hills, Calif., 1971-77; pres. Larry A. Thompson Orgn., Inc., 1977—; co-owner New World Pictures, 1983-85; lectr. entertainment bus. UCLA, U. So. Calif., Southwestern U. Law Sch. Author: How to Make a Record Deal and Have Your Songs Recorded, 1975, Prime Time Crime, 1982; producer (TV) Jim Nabors Show, 1977 (Emmy nominee), Mickey Spillane's Margin for Murder, 1981, Bring 'Em Back Alive, 1982, Mickey Spillane's Murder Me, Murder You, 1982, The Other Lover, 1985, Convicted, 1986, Intimate Encounters, 1986, The Woman He Loved, 1988 (Emmy nominee, Golden Globe nominee), Original Sin, 1989, Class Cruise, 1989, Little White Lies, 1989, Lucy and Desi: Before The Laughter, 1990 (Emmy nominee), Broken Promises, 1993, Separated By Murder, 1994, Face of Evil, 1996, Replacing Dad, 1998, The Beat Goes On: The Sonny and Cher Story, 1999 (Emmy nominee), Murder in the Mirror, 2000; (motion pictures) Crimes of Passion, 1984, Fraternity Vacation, 1985, Quiet Cool, 1987, My Demon Lover, 1987, Breaking the Rules, 1992. Co-chmn. Rep. Nat. Entertainment Com.; apptd. by Gov. of Calif. to Calif. Entertainment Commn.; mem. Inauguration of Thompson Ctr. for Fine Arts in Clarksdale, 1986. Served with JAGC, U.S. Army, 1966-72. Recipient Show Bus. Atty. of Yr. award Capitol Records, 1971, Vision award, 1993; named Showman of Yr., U.S. TV Fan Assn., 1997. Mem. ABA, Miss. Bar Assn., Calif. Bar Assn., Inter-Am. Bar Assn., Hon. Order Ky. Cols., Am. Film Inst., Nat. Acad. Rec. Arts and Scis., Acad. TV Arts and Scis. Republican. Roman Catholic. Home: 9451 Hidden Valley Pl Beverly Hills CA 90210-1310 Office: Larry A Thompson Orgn 9663 Santa Monica Blvd Ste 801 Beverly Hills CA 90210-4303

THOMPSON, LARRY JAMES, gifted education educator; b. Savannah, Ga., May 14, 1948; s. James Howell and Dorothy (Hendley) T. BA, Armstrong Atlantic State U., 1970; MAT, Tulane U., 1974; EdD, U. Ga., 1986. Cert. tchr., instrnl. supr., adminstr., Ga. Tchr. social studies Chatham County Bd. Edn., Savannah, 1970-71, 75-87, adminstrv. coord. social studies, 1987-97, gifted, talented educator, 1997—. With USNR, 1971-73. Mem. Nat. Coun. Social Studies, Ga. Coun. Social Studies, Profl. Assn. Ga. Educators, Ga. Hist. Soc., Nat. Trust for Hist. Preservation, Phi Delta Kappa. Home: 18 E Deerwood Rd Savannah GA 31410-3171

THOMPSON, LEROY, JR., radio engineer, military reserve officer; b. Tulsa, July 7, 1913; s. LeRoy and Mary (McMurrain) T.; B.S. in Elec. Engring., Ala. Poly Inst., 1936; m. Ola Dell Tedder, Dec. 31, 1941; 1 son, Bartow McMurrain. Commd. 2d lt. U.S. Amy Res., 1935, advanced through grades to col., 1963; signal officer CCC, 1936-40; radio engr. Officer Hdqrs. 4th C A., 1941; with signal sect. Hdqrs. Western Def. command and 4th Army, San Francisco, 1942, comdg. officer 234th Signal Ops. Co., 1942; asst. chief, chief signal corps ROTC U. Calif., Berkeley, 1942-43; radio engring. officer O.C. SigO War Dept., Washington, 1943; radio engring officer Hdqrs. 3105th Signal Service Co. Hdqrs. CBI, New Delhi, 1944; signal officer Hdqrs. Northern Combat Area Command, Burma, 1944; signal officer Hdqrs. OSS Det 101, Burma, 1945; signal officer Hdqrs. OSS, China, 1945, radio engr., tech. liaison officer, Central Intelligence Group, CIA, 1945-50; chief radio br. Hdqrs. FEC, Tokyo, 1950-53, chief radio engring br. Signal C Plant Engring. Agy., 1953-55; radio cons. to asst. dir. def. research and engring. communications, 1960-62; ret., 1973; pvt. research and devel. on communication and related problems, 1963—; owner Thompson Research Exptl. Devel. Lab. Lic. profl. radio engr., Ga. Mem. IEEE (life sr.), NRA, Vet. Wireless Operators Assn., Am. Radio Relay League, Mil. Order World Wars, Res. Officers Assn., Am. Motorcycle Assn., Nat. Wildlife Fedn. Baptist. Home: 6450 Overlook Dr Alexandria VA 22312-1327

THOMPSON, LORING MOORE, retired college administrator, writer; b. Newton, Mass., Feb. 17, 1918; s. Henry E. and Ella (Gould) T.; m. Pearl E. Judiesch, Dec. 30, 1949; children—Bruce C., Douglas P. (dec.). B.S. in Indsl. Engring, Northeastern U., 1940; M.S., U. R.I., 1947; Ph.D., U. Chgo., 1956. Instr. U. R.I., 1946; asst. to pres. Assn. Colls. Upper N.Y., 1947-49; assoc. prof. U. Toledo, 1952-59, asst. dean acad. adminstrn., 1958-59; dir. univ. planning Northeastern U., Boston, 1959-63; dean adult programs Northeastern U., 1964-66, v.p. planning, 1967-80, emeritus, 1980—; faculty assoc. continuing edn. Ariz. State U., 1982-84; cons. in field. Author: (with others) Business Communication, 1949; contbr. (with others) articles to profl. publs. Bd. dirs. Back Bay Assn., Boston, 1961-63, v.p., 1963; trustee Huntington Gen. Hosp., Boston, 1970-80; mem. Fenway Project Area Com., 1973-76; mem. Mass. conf. ch. and edn. com. United Ch. of Christ, 1972-78, chairperson, 1973-74, mem. task force on ch. growth, 1978-80; mem. Chandler Area Coun., 1988-89; sec. Interfaith Coun. Greater Sun Lakes, 1993-96. Lt. USNR, 1942-45. Mem. Inst. Noetic Scis., Tau Beta Pi. Home: 25408 S Sedona Dr Sun Lakes AZ 85248-6636

THOMPSON, MAGGIE QUIXOTE, rheumatological herbalist; b. Cobalt, W.Va., July 29, 1947; d. William and Hieronymus (Wilson) T.; m. William Wilson Thompson, Jul. 19, 1969; children: Sartre, Kafka. BA, L.I.City Coll., Queens, N.Y., 1969; MD, Granada Univ., 1974. Intern, residency Granda Medical Ctr., Kingston, Granada, 1974-77; arthritis rsch. Nat. Inst. Health, Washington, 1977-81; doctors without borders Sorbonne Medical Inst., Paris, 1981-85; chief of rheumatology Grandad Medical Ctr., 1985-90; ECO Herbs for Long Life, Inc., N.Y., 1990—; bd. dirs. Herbs for Long Life, Inc., N.Y., 1990—. Contbr. articles to profl. jours. Activist Leonora Fwlani Pres. Campaign, N.Y., 1992. Mem. Univ. Club, Croatian Survivors Assn. Avocation: motorcycling.

THOMPSON, MARGARET KNOWLES, opera singer; b. Glen Cove, N.Y., Aug. 26, 1962; d. William James and Margaret Adele (Faris) T. BMus, U. Del., 1985. Mezzo-soprano City Theater, Pforzheim, Germany, 1991-95, Bielefeld, Germany, 1995-98, Krefeld, Monchengladbach, Germany, 1998—; mezzo-soprano Spoleto Festival, 1999; guest mezzo-soprano Leipzig, Wiesbaden, Karlsruhe. Recordings include Die Burgschaft (Kurt Weill), 2000. Avocations: baking, sculpting. Home: Koenigstrasse 30, D-41236 Moenchengladbach Germany

THOMPSON, MARTHA PARRISH, researcher, educator; b. Atlanta, Apr. 2, 1966; d. Harry Bruckner and Eleanor (Ashcraft) T.; m. Jeffrey Brooks Kingree, Oct. 1, 1994. BA, Ga. State U., 1989, PhD, 1995. Rsch. asst. Ga. State U., Atlanta, 1990-95, nat. rsch. svc. postdoctoral fellow, 1994-95; nat. rsch. svc. postdoctoral fellow Emory U. Sch. Medicine, Atlanta, 1995-97; epidemic intelligence svc. Ctrs. for Disease Control and Prevention, Atlanta, 1997-99, sr. svc. fellow, 1999—; adj. asst. prof. Emory U. Sch. Medicine, 1997—, Emory U. Sch. Pub. Health, 1999—. Contbr. articles to profl. jours. Recipient Nat. Rsch. Svc. award NIMH, 1994-95, 95-97; grantee Harland Found., Ga. State U., 1994, Soc. for Psychological Study of Social Issues, Emory U., 1997. Mem. Internat. Soc. Traumatic Stress, Am. Psychological Assn., Soc. Cmty. Rsch. and Action. Avocations: hiking, swimming, reading. E-mail: mgt8@cdc.gov. Home: 1184 Amsterdam Ave NE Atlanta GA 30306-2562

THOMPSON, MARY KOLETA, sculptor, non-profit organization director; b. Portsmouth, Va., Dec. 27, 1938; m. James Burton Thompson, May 5, 1957; children: Burt, Suzan, Kate, Jon. BFA, U. Tex., 1982; postgrad., Boston U., St. Mary's U. Minn., 1999; MA in Philanthropy and Devel., St. Mary's U. Minn., 1999. Cert. fund raising exec., non-profit mgmt. Pres., CEO The Planning Resource People, Lampasas, Tex., 1990—; Tex. fin. devel. specialist ARC Tex., 1994-98; devel. dir. Very Spl. Arts Tex., 1991-92; dir. devel. ARC, Austin, 1992-94; pub. affairs adminstr. Pink Palace Mus. and Memphis Mus. Inc., Memphis, 1998; CEO Lamapasas C. of C., Lampasas, TX, 1998-99; pres., CEO Assn. Non-Profit Orgns., 1998—, Tex. Assn. Bed and Breakfast Innkeepers, 1998; CEO Lampasas County C. of C., 1998-99; pres. A Little Cottage B&B, 1999—; owner Heritage Sta. Antiques, 1999—; dir. Tex. Children's Mus., Fredericksburg, 1987-88, Internat. Hdqrs. SHAPE Command Arts and Crafts Ctr., 1985-86; com. chmn. Symposium for Encouragement Women in Math. and Natural Sci., U. Tex., Austin, 1990. Sculptor portrait busts. Bd. dirs. Teenage Parent Coun., Austin, 1990-92, ARC. Named U.S. Vol. of Yr., Belgium, 1986; grantee NEA, 1988. Mem. AAUW (life, pres. 1990-92), Women in Comm. (co-chmn. S.W. regional conf.), U. Tex. Ex-Student Assn. (life), Tex. Hist. Found. (life), Leadership Tex. (life), Leadership Tex. Alumnae Assn. (bd. dirs.), Raleigh Tavern Soc. (founder), Austin Antiques Forum (founder), Lometa Lions Club. Avocations: writing, lecturing, meeting and strategic planning. Office: Resource Ctr PO Box 948 206 E 1st St Lampasas TX 76550-2813

THOMPSON, NICOLAS DE LA MARE, publisher; b. London, June 4, 1928; s. Rupert Spens and Florence Elizabeth (de la Mare) T.; previous marriage: Erica Pennell, Sept. 13, 1956; children: Sarah, Rupert, Simon; m. Caroline Middleton Graham, 1997. Higher Sch. Cert., Eton Coll., Eng., 1946; MA, Oxford U., 1949. Mng. dir. Weidenfeld and Nicolson, Ltd., London, 1956-70; pub. dir. Pitman plc, London, 1970-85; mng. dir. Heinemann Group of Pubs. Ltd., 1985-87; dir. Octopus Pub. Group Plc., 1985-90, Reed Internat. Books, 1990-93.

THOMPSON, PAUL DOUGLAS, management, hotel and club executive; b. Melfort, Sask., Can., Aug. 17, 1948; arrived in Bahamas, 1981; s. John Henry and Grace Elizabeth (Arbogast) T.; m. Brenda A. Cathrea, Aug. 24, 1974 (div. 1982); m. Sharyn Cynthia Leonard, June 15, 1990; 1 child, Christiane Thompson; 1 stepchild, Christopher L. Leonard. Diploma in wine and spirits, Ryerson Polytech., Toronto, Ont., Can.; cert., Innkeepers Mgmt. Holiday Inn, Memphis. Cert. hotel adminstr. Asst. gen. mgr. Sheraton Cavalier Hotels Ltd., Saskaton, Can., 1970-75; asst. food and beverage dir. Sutton Pl. Hotels Ltd., Toronto, Can., 1975-76; asst. gen. mgr. Wardair Hotels, Jamaica, 1976-77, Commonwealth Holiday Inn of Can., Ltd., Toronto, 1977-81; deputy mng. dir. Lyford Cay Club, Nassau, Bahamas, 1981-83, mng. dir., 1983—; dir. Bahamas Hotel Employers Assn., Nassau, 1984—; vice conseiller culinare Chaine des Rotisseur Nassau, 1991-96; dir. Bahamas Hotel Assn., Nassau, 1992-93; l'ordre mondial Chaine des Rotisseur, Nassau, 1995—. chmn. Red Cross Fair Com., Nassau, 1989-93; co-chmn. subcom. Commn. on the Family, Nassau, 1989-93; dir. adv. com. Coll. of Bahamas, Nassau, 1992; dir. Bahamas Red Cross Soc., Nassau, 1992—. Mem. Rotary (West Nassau chpt., dir. fund raising 1985-86). Avocations: sailing, photography, golf. Office: Lyford Cay Club, PO Box N-7776, Nassau Bahamas

THOMPSON, PAUL GEORGE, lawyer; b. Des Moines, Nov. 17, 1963. BBA, U. Iowa, 1985; JD, U. Mich., 1989. Bar: Colo. 1989, D.C. 1990. Assoc. atty. Fried Frank Harris Shriver, Washington, 1989-90, Holme Roberts & Owen, Denver, 1990-95; ptnr. Holme Roberts & Owen, London, 1996—. Co-author: Securities Regulation in the Russian Federation, 1996; contbr. articles to profl. jours. Mem. ABA, Internat. Bar Assn., D.C. Bar, Colo. Bar Assn., Denver Bar Assn.

THOMPSON, PAULINE ANNE, charity administrator; b. Leeds, Yorkshire, Eng., June 1, 1950; d. George Leonard and Constance (Webb) T. Social worker Notts County Coun., 1969-74; regional dir. Mencap East Midlands, 1974-79; dir. Disablement Income Group, London, 1979—; vice-chmn. trustees Ind. Living Fund U.K., 1988-93; mem. Dept. Health Tech. Adv. Group on Direct Payments, 1995-98; mem. reference group Royal Commn. Long-Term Care, 1998; tng. cons. to Govt. Benefits Agy., 1999—. Author: Not the OPCS: Being Disabled Costs More Than They Said, 1989, Short Changed by Disability, 1990, A Home of My Own?, 1991, Cause for Concern: What Directors of Social Services Think About the Impact of the Changes to the Independent Living Fund, 1993, There May Be Trouble Ahead: Why Occupational Pensions and Permanent Health Insurance Are No Substitutes for a Disability Income Scheme, 1995. Mem. Order Brit. Empire, 1995. Mem. Royal Hort. Soc. (life). Avocations: Cavalier King Charles spaniels, music, gardening, history. Office: Disablement Income Group, PO Box 5743, Firchingfield CM7 4PW, England

THOMPSON, PETER ALLAN, science educator, researcher; b. Vancouver, B.C., Canada, Jan. 16, 1956; arrived in Australia, 1993; s. John Edgar and Shirley Madaline (Carruthers) T.; m. Elizabeth Anne Chepesuik, Aug. 19, 1978; children: Michael, Andrew, Katharine. BSc, U. B.C., 1977, PhD, 1991; MMSt, U. Toronto, Canada, 1983. Scientist DFO, Canada, 1991-93; sr. scientist CSIRO, Australia, 1993-96; lectr. U. Tasmania, Australia, 1996—. Contbr. more than 40 articles to profl. jours. Office: Aquaculture U Tasmania, PO Box 1214, Launceston 7250, Australia

THOMPSON, RICHARD PAUL HEPWORTH, physician, consultant; b. Esher, U.K., Apr. 14, 1940; s. Stanley Henry and Winifred Lilian (Collier) H.; m. Eleanor Mary Hughes, 1974. BA, Oxford (Eng.) U., U.K., 1961; MA, Oxford (Eng.) U., 1964, BM, 1964, DM, 1971. Rsch. fellow Mayo Clinic, Rochester, 1969-71; lectr. Kings Coll. Hosp., London, 1968-72; cons., physician St. Thomas Hosp., London, 1972—; chmn. grants com. King Edward VII Fund, London, 1992-96. Author: Physical Signs in Medicine, 1980, Lecture Notes on the Liver, 1985. Fellow Royal Coll. Physicians. Home: 36 Dealtry Rd, London SW15 6NL, England Office: St Thomas Hospital, London SE1 7EH, England

THOMPSON, ROBERT CHARLES, lawyer; b. Council, Idaho, Apr. 20, 1942; s. Ernest Lavelle and Evangeline Montgomery (Carlson) T.; m. Marilyn Anne Wilcox, Jan. 17, 1960 (dec. Mar. 1962); m. Patricia Joan Price, June 1, 1963 (div. 1969); m. Jan Nesbitt, June 29, 1973 (dec. May 1998); m. Shari Lewis, Feb. 7, 1999; children: Tanya, Carrie, Christopher, Eric. AB, Harvard U., 1963, LLB, 1967. Bar: Mass. 1967, Calif. 1983, U.S. Dist. Ct. (ea. dist.) Mass. 1975, U.S. Ct. Appeals (1st cir.) 1976, U.S. Ct. Appeals (9th cir.) 1984, U.S. Dist. Ct. (no. dist.) Calif. 1983, U.S. Dist. Ct. (ea. dist.) Calif., 1996. Assoc. Choate, Hall & Stewart, Boston, 1967-73; asst. regional counsel EPA, Boston, 1973-75, regional counsel, 1975-82, assoc. gen. counsel, 1979-82; regional counsel EPA, San Francisco, 1982-84; ptnr. Graham & James, San Francisco, 1984-91, LeBoeuf, Lamb, Greene & MacRae, San Francisco, 1992—. Contbr. articles to profl. jours. Bd. dirs. Peninsula Indsl. and Bus. Assn., Palo Alto, Calif., 1986-98, chmn. Cambridge (Mass.) Conservation Commn., 1972-74; co-chmn. The Clift Confs. on Environ. Law, 1983-98; assoc. mem. Ban Conservation and Development Commission, 1998-. John Russell Shaw traveling fellow Harvard Coll., 1963-64; recipient Regional Adminstrs. Bronze medal EPA, 1976, 84. Mem. ABA (natural resources sect., com. on native Am. natural resources law, spl. com. on mktg.), Natural Resources Def. Coun., Sierra Club, Commonwealth Club, Phi Beta Kappa. Democrat. Episcopalian. Avocations: personal computers, yoga, antiques, wines, cooking. Office: LeBoeuf Lamb Greene & MacRae One Embarcadero Ctr San Francisco CA 94111

THOMPSON, ROBERT FRANK, JR., career officer; b. Durham, N.C., Sept. 25, 1959; s. Robert Frank Sr. and Betty Ross (Connelly) T.; m. Vickie Marie Fjone, Nov. 17, 1979; children: Robert Frank III, Kimberly Anne. BA in English and History, Met. State Coll. Denver, 1993. Commd. 2d lt. U.S. Army Nat. Guard, 1989, advanced through grades to maj., 1998; stationed at Panama, Ft. Polk, La., 1983-87; rural rt. carrier U.S. Postal Svc., Brighton, Colo., 1988-93; adminstrv. officer Colo. Army Nat. Guard, Denver, 1993-98, state family program dir., 1999-2000; defense movement coord, 1998; master fitness trainer Colo. Army Nat. Guard, 1987, advisor work climate improvement program, 1995, facilitator increasing human effectiveness, 1996. Editor The Adv., 1990-91; founder Bob Thompson Freelance Writing and Editing Svcs., 2000; founder, gen. editor The Christian Fine Arts Revue, 2000. Deacon Crossroads Bapt. Ch., Northglenn, Colo., 1997-99. Decorated Army Commendation medal (6); recipient Exceptional Acad. Achievement award ROTC, 1989, V.P.'s Honor Roll (3). Mem. U.S. F.A. Assn. (Hon. Order St. Barbaras 1993), Nat. Guard Assn. U.S., Golden Key Nat. Honor Soc., Phi Alpha Theta, Pi Gammma Mu. Republican. Avocations: freelance writing, traveling, reading, sports. Home: 11305 Nome St Henderson CO 80640-9259

THOMPSON, ROBERT JAYE, minister; b. Coffeyville, Kans., Nov. 4, 1951; s. Julis Levi and Verna Belle (Hardrick) T.; m. Carolyn Robinson, Aug. 23, 1971; children: Montie Shannon, Monica Shea, Marquis Shane, Marissa Seana, Terry Dwight, Mycal Shanton, Montre Sean. AA in History, Coffeyville Cmty. Jr. Coll, 1971; BA in History, Pittsburg (Kans.) State U., 1973; MDiv cum laude, Memphis Theol. Sem., 1991. Ordained to ministry Bapt. Ch., 1983. Pastor Sweet Home Bapt. Ch., Dardanelle, Ark., 1983-88; assoc. pastor Springdale Bapt. Ch., Memphis, 1988-92; instr. Tenn. Sch. of Religion, Memphis, 1989-92; asst. dean Regular Ark. Bapt. Home and Fgn. Mission Conv., 1994—; chaplain intern Federal Correctional Institution, Memphis, 1990; instr. Nat. Bapt. Congress of Christian Edn., 1994—; supply pastor Greenfield Presbyn. Ch., Waterford, Miss., 1990-92; pastor New Prospect Bapt. Ch., Russellville, Ark., 1992-98, Barraque St. Bapt. Ch.,

Pine Bluff, Ark., 1998—; treas. Antioch Dist. Assn., Ft. Smith, Ark., 1987-88; instr. Antioch Dist. Congress of Christian Edn., 1993-98, youth min., 1987-89, 94-98; sec. Ft. Smith Interdenominational Assn., 1984-88; sgt. Guardsmark, Inc., Memphis, 1989-92; program coord. Russellville Area Ministerial Assn., 1994; bd. dirs. Help Network; mem. steering com. Nat. Day of Prayer, Russellville, 1994-95; instr. Regular Ark. Bapt. Congress Christian Edn., 1996—. Dir. gen. Antioch Congress of Christian Edn., 1993-96, instr., 1993-98; dir. gen. Ft. Smith, Ark. 2d v.p.; treas. Antioch Dist. Assn., Ft. Smith, 1995-98; pres.-elect Russellville Area Ministerial Assn., 1995, pres., 1996; chmn. Nat. Day of Prayer Russellville, 1995-96; block worker Am. Heart Assn., Memphis, 1991; student body pres. Memphis Theol. Sem., 1990-91; bd. dirs. Shelter of Sunshine, Russellville, 1995-98, pres.-elect, 1996-97, pres., 1997-98; mem. Bd. of Adjustment, Russellville, 1996-97, v.p. bd. adjustment, 1997; pres. Race Rels. Task Force, Russellville, 1995-98; historian Regular Ark. Bapt. Conv., 1995—; mem. Black christian Pastors' and Ministers' Fellowship, Multi-dist. Bapt. Ministers Conf., dist. com. Boy Scouts Am. Recipient Benjamin E. Mays fellowship Fund for Theol. Edn., N.Y.C., 1990-91, Disting. Mil. Grad. Pittsburg State U., 1973. Mem. Memphis Bapt. Ministers Assn., Russellville Area Ministerial Assn. (pres. 1996), Rotary Internat. Democrat. Home: 4001 King Richard Cir Pine Bluff AR 71603-6127 Office: 1800 W Pullen St Pine Bluff AR 71601-3352

THOMPSON, ROBERT L., JR., lawyer; b. St. Paul, Aug. 9, 1944; s. Robert L. and Dorothy R. (Bergstrom) T.; m. Carolyn H. Foss, Aug. 4, 1973; children: Sarah, Kathryn, Jill. BA, Macalester Coll., St. Paul, 1967; JD, U. Oreg., 1973; LLM, NYU, 1988. Bar: Minn. 1973, U.S. Dist. Ct. Minn. 1978, N.Y. 1984. Corp. counsel Northrup King Co., Mpls., 1974-84; assoc. gen. counsel Sandoz Corp., N.Y.C., 1984-88, v.p., gen. counsel, sec., 1989-96; exec. v.p., gen. counsel Novartis Corp., N.Y.C., 1997—; mem. adv. bd. FM Global Ins. Co., N.Y.C., 1990—; mem. bd. visitors U. Oreg. Law Sch., 1995—. 1st lt. U.S. Army, 1968-70. Mem. ABA, Am. Corp. Counsel Assn., Assn. Bar City N.Y. Republican. Presbyterian. Office: Novartis Corp 608 5th Ave Fl 10 New York NY 10020-2305

THOMPSON, SANDRA LEE, library administrator; b. Dover, Ohio, Jan. 23, 1968; d. Robert Leonard and Gwendolyn Ruth Stewart; m. Alan McKinney Thompson, Sept. 9, 1990; children: LeeAnna, Alisha, James. BS in Edn., Ohio U., 1989; M of Libr. Info. Sci., U. S.C., 1999. Tchr. Harrison Hills City Sch. Dist., Hopedale, Ohio, 1989-90; asst. dir. Puskarich Pub. Libr., Cadiz, Ohio, 1990-97, dir., 1998—; mem. Ohio Libr. Coun., Columbus, 1994—; tech. chairperson Southeastern Ohio Libr. Orgn., Caldwell, 1997—. E-mail: thompss2@oplin.lib.oh.us. Office: Puskarich Pub Libr 200 E Market St Cadiz OH 43907-1200

THOMPSON, TERRIE LEE, graphic designer; b. Myrtle Creek, Oreg., Apr. 22, 1960; d. Claud Willie and Blanche Bernice Thompson. Student, Umpqua C.C., 1983-84; BFA, Pacific N.W. Coll. Art, 1988. Freelance graphic designer Terrie Thompson Design, Portland, 1987-90; graphic designer Promotion Products Inc., Portland, 1989-90, L. Grafix Inc., Portland, 1990-91, Warn Industries, Milwaukie, Oreg., 1991-92; pres. Thompson Typographics Inc., Portland, 1990—; typography contractor Nike Inc., Beaverton, Oreg., 1992—; typography trainer for various design firms and agys., Portland, 1992-98, pres. Seeing Spots, Inc., 1998—. Work published in various design publs., including The Best in Catalogue Design, Comm. Arts Design Ann., How Mag. Computer Art and Design Ann.; creator cartoon character "Spot", 1989. Vol. graphic designer Washington Park Zoo, Portland, 1990; vol. art dir. Portland Mac Users Group, Portland, 1995; vol. beach clean-up crew Stop Oreg. Litter and Vandalism, 1990—. Recipient Bronze award Optima Design Awards, 1995, Digital Art and Design Ann. award Print Mag., 1997, Regional Design Ann. award Print Mag., 1997, Applied Arts Annual, 1997, 98, Good Neighbor award Forest Park Neighborhood Assn., 1999. Avocations: hiking, travel, camping, photography, music. Home and Office: Thompson Typographics Inc PO Box 83327 Portland OR 97283-0327

THOMPSON, THEODIS, retired healthcare executive, health management consultant; b. Palestine, Ark., Aug. 10, 1944; s. Percy and Grozellia Monroves (Weaver) T.; m. Patricia Holley, Sept. 16, 1964; children: Gwendolyn Ware, Theodis E., Omari P. BS, Tuskegee Inst., 1968; MPA, U. Mich., 1969, PhD, 1972. Asst. chemist John T. Stanley Co., N.Y.C., 1964-66; news announcer, disc jockey KATZ Radio Sta., St. Louis, 1966-67; sr. rsch. assoc. U. Mich., Ann Arbor, 1969-71; asst. prof., chmn. Howard U., Washington, 1973-78; assoc. prof., dir. health planning U. So. Calif., L.A., 1978-79; dir. planning and evaluation Memphis Health Ctr., 1979-87, chief operating officer, 1987-88; CEO Bklyn. Plaza Med. Ctr., 1988-99; asst. chemist John T. Stanley Co., 1964-66; cons. Charles Mathis Assocs., Yonkers, N.Y., 1991—, USPHS, Bethesda, Md., 1993—; mem. adv. bd. N.Y. Urban League, Bklyn., 1991-93; lectr. St. Joseph's Coll., Bklyn., 1998—. Author, editor: Health Policy and Planning, 1975; contbr. articles to profl. jours. Bd. dirs. CHCANYS, Inc., N.Y.C., 1994; vice chair Cmty. Assocs. Devel. Corp., Inc., Bklyn., 1989. Recipient Disting. Svc. award N.Y. State Assn. Black and Puerto Ricans, Inc., 1992; named Disting. Man of Yr., 18th Senatorial Dist., 1996. Mem. APHA. Office: Bklyn Plaza Med Ctr Inc PO Box 02-2871 Brooklyn NY 11202

THOMPSON, VENITA BRANT, nutritionist, diet technician; b. Washington, Pa., Oct. 7, 1936; d. Kenneth Vernon and Reta Iona (Stephens) Brant; m. Charles R. Blackhurst, Feb. 27, 1954 (div. Nov. 1973); children: Debra Ann Blackhurst Fleming, Terry Alan, Christopher Bryan; m. James Orlando Thompson, Feb. 11, 1989. AS in Bank Mgmt., Hillsborough Communnity Coll., 1962, AA, 1984; AS in Diet Tech., Pa. State U., 1986; BA in Gerontology, U. South Fla., Tampa, 1992; MS in Community Health Administrn. and Wellness, Calif. Coll. Health Scis. Registered diet technician. Asst. cashier Internat. Bank Tampa, 1955-65, asst. v.p., 1965-71; v.p., cashier Carrolwood State Bank, Tampa, 1971-73; dietetic technician St. Joseph Hosp., Tampa, 1977-86, nutritional ops. mgr., 1986-92, nutritional ops. mgr., purchasing mgr., 1992-95; food svc. dir. Carrollwood Care Ctr., Tampa, 1995-96; dir. clin. nutrition IHS, Brandon, Fla., 1996—. Mem. Am. Soc. for Hosp. Food Svc. Adminstrs., Am. Dietetic Assn., Tampa Dietetic Assn., Soroptimist Club, Order Rainbow Girls. Democrat. Presbyterian. Avocations: fishing, swimming, travel. Home: 401 W Paris St Tampa FL 33604-6652 Office: IHS of Brandon 702 S Kings Ave Brandon FL 33511-5925

THOMPSON, WADE FRANCIS BRUCE, manufacturing company executive; b. Wellington, New Zealand, July 23, 1940; came to U.S., 1961, naturalized, 1990.; m. Angela Ellen Barry, Jan. 20, 1967; children: Amanda and Charles (twins). B in Commerce, Cert. Acctg., Victoria U., Wellington, 1961; MSc, NYU, 1963. Dir. diversification Sperry & Hutchinson, N.Y.C., 1967-72; v.p. Textar Corp., N.Y.C., 1972-77; chmn. Hi-Lo Trailer Co., Butler, Ohio, 1977—; chmn., pres., chief exec. officer Thor Industries Inc., Jackson Center, Ohio, 1980—. Trustee Mystic Seaport Mus., Conn., 1984—; trustee Wade F.B. Thompson Charitable Found. Inc., 1985—. Mcpl. Art Soc., N.Y.C., 1993—, Seventh Regiment Armory Conservancy, N.Y.C., 1997—. Mem. Union Club, N.Y. Yacht Club (N.Y.C.). Avocations: tennis, collecting contemporary art. Office: Thor Industries Inc PO Box 629 Jackson Center OH 45334-0629

THOMPSON, WAITE, investment company executive, researcher; b. St. Louis, Nov. 5, 1940; s. Frank Charles Jr. and Jane (Waite) T. BA, Principia Coll., 1962. Polit. cons. Rep. Party of Calif., L.A., 1964-67, 72-74; traveling v.p. Club Universe, L.A., 1967-68, 69-72; comml. real estate investor Coldwell Banker, L.A., 1974-79; pres. Waite Thompson Inc., Santa Fe, 1979—. Author: The Santa Fe Guide, 1981—. Bd. trustees Hist. Santa Fe Found., 1989-94, Old Santa Fe Assn., 1994-96; mem. City of Santa Fe Hist. Design Review Bd., 1996-99; mem. coun. benefactors Santa Fe Cmty. Found., 1994—; mem. adv. bd. Rep. Nat. Com., Washington, 1964-67, 72-74. Mem. Santa Fe Opera Found., Mus. N.Mex. Found., Nat. Soc. Sons/Daughters of the Pilgrims, Nat. Soc. Sons of Am. Revolution. Republican. Mem. Christian Sci. Ch. Avocations: walking, swimming, reading, tennis, family history. Home and Office: 503 Johnson Ln Santa Fe NM 87501-2865

THOMPSON, WALTER DAVID, JR., systems analyst; b. Leakesville, N.C., Sept. 8, 1952; s. Walter David Sr. and Rachel Henderlite (Jones) T. Student, St. Andrews Coll., 1970-75. Beverage distributor N.Y. Seltzer, N.Y.C., 1975-76; restaurant mgr. Fountainhead Cafe, N.Y.C., 1976-77; newspaper delivery Greensboro (N.C.) Daily News, 1978-80; computer programmer Gary Brown Assocs., Greensboro, 1980-82; pvt. cons. Thompson Software Systems, Greensboro, 1982-86; asst. treas. corp. trust Bankers Trust, N.Y.C., 1987-88; computer analyst bond funds Merrill Lynch, N.Y.C., 1988; team leader, cons. corp. fin. Citibank, N.Y.C., 1988-89; v.p., sr. systems analyst Kidder, Peabody & Co., Inc., Manakin-Sabot, Va., 1989-94; dir. MIS James River Capital Corp., Manakin-Sabot, Va., 1995—. Rsch. grantee NSF, 1971. Mem. Am. Mensa Ltd. (membership coord. 1990-91). Home: 2236 Rockwater Ter Richmond VA 23233-3622 Office: James River Capital Corp 58 Broad Street Rd Manakin Sabot VA 23103-2213

THOMPSON, WAYNE WRAY, historian; b. Wichita, Jan. 30, 1945; s. Clarence William and Elaine Maxine (Wray) T. m. Lillian Evelyn Hurlburt, June 28, 1969. BA, Union Coll., Schenectady, 1967; student, U. St. Andrews, Scotland, 1965-66; PhD, U. Calif., San Diego, 1975. Historian USAF, 1975—, Checkmate Air Campaign Planning Group, 1990-91; sr. hist. advisor Gulf War Air Power Survey, 1991-93. Contbr. Congress Investigates (Arthur M. Schlesinger Jr. and Roger Bruns, editors), 1975; editor Air Leadership, 1986; contbr. War in the Pacific (Bernard Nalty, editor), 1991; contbr.: Winged Shield, Winged Sword, 1997. Served with AUS, 1971-72. Mem. Am. Hist. Assn., Orgn. Am. Historians, Air Force Hist. Found., Air Force Assn., Soc. Historians Am. Fgn. Rels., Soc. for Mil. History, U.S. Commn. on Mil. History, Inter-Univ. Seminar on Armed Forces, Assn. Asian Studies, Asia Soc., World History Assn., Phi Beta Kappa. Home: 9203 Saint Marks Pl Fairfax VA 22031-3045 Office: Hdqrs Usaf History Washington DC 20332-0001

THOMPSON, WILLIAM BENBOW, JR., obstetrician/gynecologist, educator; b. Detroit, July 26, 1923; s. William Benbow and Ruth Wood (Locke) T.; m. Constance Carter, July 30, 1947 (div. Feb. 1958); 1 child, William Benbow IV; m. Jane Gilliland, Mar. 12, 1958; children: Reese Ellison, Belinda Day. AB, U. So. Calif., 1947, MD, 1951. Diplomate Am. Bd. Ob-Gyn. Resident Gallinger Mun. Hosp., Washington, 1952-53, George Washington U. Hosp., Washington, 1953-55; asst. ob-gyn. La. State U., 1955-56; asst. clin. prof. UCLA, 1957-64; assoc. prof. U. Calif.-Irvine Sch. Med., Orange, 1964-92, dir. gynecology, 1977-92, prof. emeritus, 1993—, vice chmn. ob-gyn., 1978-89; assoc. dean U. Calif.-Irvine Coll. Med., Irvine, 1969-73. Inventor: Thompson Retractor, 1976; Thompson Manipulator, 1977. Bd. dirs. Monarch Bay Assn. Laguna Niguel, Calif. 1969-77, Monarch Summitt II A ssn. 1981-83. With U.S. Army, 1942-44, PTO. Fellow ACS, Am. Coll. Ob-Gyn. (life), L.A. Ob-Gyn. Soc. (life); mem. Orange County Gynecology and Obstetrics Soc. (hon.), Capistrano Bay Yacht Club (commodore 1975), Internat. Order Blue Gavel, Dana West Yacht Club. Avocation: boating. Office: UCI Med Ctr OB/GYN 101 The City Dr S Orange CA 92868-3201

THOMPSON, WILLIAM GRANT, management executive; b. Westville, N.S., Can., June 27, 1925; s. Harvey Alden and Jessie (MacGregor) T.; m. Margaret Jean Mackenzie, Sept. 24, 1952; children: Heather, Anne, Andrew, Carole. Degree in bus. edns., Maritime Bus. Coll., Halifax, N.S., 1943. Chartered acct., N.S. Treas. Maritime Steel and Foundries, Ltd., New Glasgow, N.S., 1951-58; v.p. gen. mgr. EMI Elecs. Can., Ltd., Halifax, 1958-69; ptnr. Price Waterhouse, Ltd., Halifax, 1970-87, v.p., 1977-87; pres. Revenue Mgmt., Ltd., Halifax, 1987—; pres. MacCulloch & Co., Ltd., Halifax, 1983-87, Oakwood Investments, Halifax, 1983-87. Mem. Commn. Food Prices Rev. Bd., Ottawa, Ont., 1974-77; chmn. fin. com. Waterfront Devel. Corp., Halifax, 1977-81; chmn. Pine Hill Div. Hall, Halifax, 1974-79, Atlantic Sch. Theology, Halifax, 1982-85, Maritime Bd. Trustees, Sackville, N.B., 1982-88; treas., chmn. investment com. Fin. Svcs. Maritime Conf., 1988—; chmn. Windsor Elms Srs. Home, Windsor, N.S., 1983-87. Fellow Inst. Chartered Accts. N.S., Inst. Chartered Secs. and Adminstrs.; mem. Soc. Mgmt. Accts. N.S., Inst. Mgmt. Cons. Atlantic Can., Can. Litigation Acctg. and Valuation Inst., Saraguay Club. Mem. United Ch. Can. Home: 2184 Connaught Ave, Halifax, NS Canada B3L 2Z3

THOMPSON, W(ILMER) LEIGH, pharmaceutical company executive, physician, pharmacologist; b. Shreveport, La., June 25, 1938; s. Wilmer Leigh and Mary Bissell (McIver) T.; m. Maurice Eugenie Horne, Mar. 29, 1957; 1 child, Mary Linton Bounetheau. BS, Coll. Charleston, 1958; MS in Pharmacology, Med U. S.C., 1960, PhD, 1963, ScD (hon.), 1994; MD, Johns Hopkins U., 1965. Diplomate Am. Bd. Internal Medicine. Intern Johns Hopkins Hosp., 1965-66, resident, 1966-67, 69-70; staff assoc. NIH, Bethesda, Md., 1967-69; asst. prof. medicine and pharmacology Johns Hopkins U., Balt., 1970-74, dir. critical care medicine and emergency medicine, 1974-82; prof. medicine, assoc. prof. pharmacology Case Western Res. U., Cleve., 1974-82, head critical care and clin. pharmacology, 1974-82; prof. medicine Ind. U., 1985-95; dir. Lilly Rsch. Labs., Eli Lilly & Co., Indpls., 1982, exec. dir., 1982-86, v.p., 1986-88, group v.p., 1988-91, exec. v.p., 1992-93, chief sci. officer, 1993-94; chmn., CEO Profound Quality Resources Cons., Charleston, 1995—; bd. dirs. BAS, Tanabe Rsch. Labs., Guilford Pharms., Depo Med, Inspire, Ontogeny, La Jolla Pharms., Maret Corp., Orphan Med., Medarex, Ophidian. Editor: Textbook of Critical Care Medicine, 1984, 89, State of the Art: Critical Care, 1980-83. Served to surgeon USPHS, 1967-69. Recipient Faculty Devel. award Pharm. Mfrs. Assn. Found.; named Disting. Alumnus, Med. U. S.C., 1999; Burroughs Wellcome Fund scholar, 1975-80. Fellow ACP, Am. Coll. Critical Care Medicine; mem. Soc. Critical Care Medicine (pres. 1981-82, hon. life mem. 1987), Ctrl. Soc. Clin. Rsch., Am. Soc. Pharmacology and Exptl. Therapeutics. Episcopalian and Huguenot. E-mail: electricpotato@jhu.edu. Office: Profound Quality Resources Consulting 54 King St Charleston SC 29401-2731

THOMPSON-CAGER-STRAND, CHEZIA, literature educator, writer, performance artist; b. St. Louis, Sept. 8, 1951. BA, Washington U., St. Louis, 1973, MA, 1975; ArtsD, Carnegie-Mellon U., 1984. Tchg. asst. Washington U., 1973-76; instr., asst. prof. St. Louis C.C., 1975-79; asst. prof. Clarion (Pa.) State U., 1980-82, U. Md., Catonsville, 1982-86; assoc. prof. Smith Coll., Northampton, Mass., 1986-89; vis. assoc. prof. Bowie (Md.) State U., 1989-90; sr. v.p. Park Heights Devel. Corp., Balt., 1990-92; cons. Balt. City Pub. Sch., Inst. Div., 1992-94; prof. lang. & lit. Md. Inst. Coll. Art, Balt., 1993—; Disting. scholar in residence U. Pa. Dept. Theatre, University Park, 1989; project dir. poetry enrichment program U. City Pub. Sch., 1972; performance artist Artscape, 1996, exhibit curator, 1997; curator In Celebration of Maryland Artists, Govt. House, Annapolis, 1998; exhibit curator Through The Fire To the Limit: African Am. Artists in Md. Govt. House, Annapolis, 1999, Eye of Carl Clark, Photographer Md. Art Place, 2000. Author: Jumpin' Rope on the Axis, 1986, Power Objects, 1996 (Artscape Poetry Competition award 1996), The Presence of Things Unseen, 1996, Praise Song for Katherine Dunham Artscape, 1996, numerous poems; dir. dramatic works including Narrator Vachel Lindsay's Congo Visits Langston Hughes, 1989, Jestina's Calypso, 1988, 7 Principles: or how I got ova, 1987, Tribute to Martin Luther King, 1985; contbr. poetry to Catch a Fire!!!: Across Generational Anthology of Contemporary African-American Poetry, 1998, Dark Eros: Black Erotic Writings, 1997, International Dimensions of Black Women's Writing—Vol. I, 1995; contbg. editor: Maryland Poetry Review, Baltimore Review, Word Wrights, LINK: A Jour. of the Arts in Balt. and Beyond; contbr. lit. criticisms, articles to profl. jours, freelance for St. Louis Am. News., Pitts. Courier News, Balt. Sun News. Mem. adv. bd. Sexual Assault Recovery Ctr., Balt., 1989-93; site proj. evaluator Nat. Endowment Arts, Washington, 1984; mem. Heritage Art panel Md. State Coun. Arts, 1990-94; cons. Balt. Arrabers Documentation Project, 1992; bd. dirs. Md. Art Place, 1990-2000. Recipient Paul Robeson Black Artist award Washington U., 1972, W.E.B. DuBois Svc. award, 1973, Merit for Poetry award Mo. State Coun. Arts, 1974, Mayor's Citizen Citation Poetry award, 1996, Resolution for Literacy award City Coun. Balt., 1996, Md. State Arts Coun. Individual Artist award in poetry, 1999, Disting. Black Marylander award, 2000; named Oyo Traditions Pan-African Cultural Innovator, 1996. Mem. Nat. Women Studies Assn., Nat. Assn. Tchrs. English, Nat. Black Theater Network, African Lit. Assn., Coll. Art Assn. Office: Md Inst Coll Art Dept Lang and Lit 1300 W Mount Royal Ave Baltimore MD 21217-4134

THOMSEN, OLE THYBO, mechanical engineer, educator; b. Copenhagen, Denmark, May 27, 1962; s. Yongdal and Kyeman (Lee) P.; m. Weasook Shim, Jan. 5, 1983; children: Jinhee, Hyunjoon. BS, Sung Kyun Kwan U., Seoul, Korea, 1980, MS, 1982; MS, Tex. Tech. U., Lubbock, 1987; PhD, U. S.C., 1991. Cert. pharmicist. Lectr. Yonset U., Seoul, Korea, 1982-83; rschr. Dae Woong Pharmaceutical Co., Seoul, 1983-84; rsch. assoc. N.Y.U., 1991-93; asst. prof. Sung Kyum Kwan U., Seoul, 1993-96, chmn., 1995-97; assoc. prof. Sung Kyum Kwan U., T, 1997—; cons. Biopharm Co., 1999—, Hae-Eun, Inc., 1998—. Author: (book) Microbiology, 1998; Assoc. Editor (jour.) Pharmacon, 1995-96. Sgt. Korean Army, 1975-78. Mem. Soc. Leukocyte Biology, Korean Soc. Immunology (dir.), Korean Soc. Pharmacy, Am. Assn. Immunologists. Avocations: swimming, golf, reading. Office: Sung Kyun Kwan U Jang An-gu, Chunchun-dong 300, 440-746 Suwon S Korea

THOMSEN, OLE THYBO, mechanical engineer, educator; b. Copenhagen, Denmark, May 27, 1962; s. Vagn Thybo and Johanne Jensen (Visby) T.; m. Sonja Thybo Laursen, Dec. 18, 1993; children: Kasper, Jakob. Artium in Math./Physics, Aarhus Katedralskole, Aarhus, Denmark, 1981; MS, Aalborg U., Aalborg, Denmark, 1986; PhD, Aalborg U., 1990. Post doctoral rschr. Aalborg U., Denmark, 1989-93; rsch. fellow European Space Agy., Noordwijk, The Netherlands, 1993-95; assoc. prof. Aalborg U., 1995—; vis. prof. U. Del., Newark, Del., 1999-2000. Author: (book) Insert Design Handbook, 1996; (book chpt.) An Introduction to Sandwich Construction, 1995, The Handbook of Sandwich Construction, 1997; contbr. articles to profl. jours. Chmn. Mech. Engr. Study Curriculum com., Aalborg U., 1986-97, Inst. Mech. Engring., Aalborg U., 1989-93, 99—. Recipient Dana Prize award, Kai Hansen Found., Copenhagen, 1997, Best Paper award Am. Soc. for Composites, 1999. Mem. Danish Engring. Soc., The Advanced Structural Materials Info. Exhcnage Group, Am. Soc. for Composites. Fax: 45 98151411. E-mail: ott@ime.auc.dk. Office: Aalborg U Inst Mech Engring, Pontoppidan Straede, DK-9220 Ålborg Denmark

THOMSEN, PER HOVE, psychiatry educator; b. Sonderborg, Denmark, Aug. 12, 1959; s. Jorn Hove and Aase Hove (Mandoe) T.; 1 child, Jonathan Hove Appel. MD, Aarhus U., 1987, DSc, 1996, Specialist Child/Adolescent Psychiatry, 1996. Med. intern Hosps. in Aarhus, Copenhagen, 1987-91; registrar Psychiat. Hosp./Children-Adolescent, Aarhus, 1991-93, sr. cons., 1994—; sr. registrar Dep. Child Psychiatry, Copenhagen, 1993-94; asst. prof. U. Aarhus, 1994-97, prof., 1998—; dir. of rsch. Rsch. Ctr., Aarhus, 1995—; bd. dirs. Danish Psychiat. Orgn. Author: (books) From Thoughts to Obsessions, 1966 (WPA-OCD-Sect. Info. award 1996), Children Who are Different, 1997; author/editor: (book) Child and Adolescent Psychiatry, 1998; contbr. articles to profl. jours. Avocations: horseback riding, reading. Office: Psych Hosp for Children, Harald Selmersvej 66, Risskov 8240 Århus Denmark

THOMSEN, RICHARD, hydrologist; b. Århus, Denmark, June 16, 1947; s. Hugo Alfred and Inger (Hanson) T.; m. Anne Sofie Rømer Sørensen, Apr. 2, 1981; children: Jakob, Kristine. Grad. in Sci., Århus (Denmark) U., 1974. Cert. profl. hydrologist, Am. Inst. Hydrology. Hydrologist Århus County, 1974-80, head sect., 1980-86, head dept., 1986—; assoc. prof. Geol. Inst., Århus, 1979-80; tech. advisor for environ. appeal bd. High Ct., Denmark, 1990—; mem. Danish Water Resources com. Mem. editl. bd. Vandteknik; contbr. articles to profl. jours. Mem. Am. Geophys. Union Hydrology, Danish Waterworks Assn. (Initiative prize 1992), Assn. Groundwater Scientists and Engrs., Internat. Assn. Hydrogeologist. Avocations: restoring old houses, antique water supply. Office: Århus County, Dept Groundwater, DK-8270 Højbjerg Denmark

THOMSON, ALISTAIR PETER JAMES, pediatrician, consultant; b. London, Sept. 26, 1952; s. J.L. Gordon and June K.P. T.; m. Anna Donna Lazurek, Nov. 17, 1979; children: Katherine Jane, James Jacob. BA, Cambridge (U.K.) U., 1970-73, MB, 1976, MD, MA, 1991. House officer, various other positions King's Coll. Hosp., London, 1976-79; registrar pediatrics Pembury Hosp., Kent, Eng., 1981-82; registrar pediatrics St. Thomas' Hosp., London, 1982-83, rsch. fellow, 1983-85; sr. registrar pediatrics Merseyside Rotation, Liverpool, Eng., 1985-90; cons. pediatrics Mid-Cheshire (U.K.) Hosps. Trust, 1990—; postgrad. clin. tutor Leighton Hosp., Crewe, U.K., 1991—; chmn. Mersey Perinatal Audit Steering Group, 1996-98. Author in field of meningococcal disease and meningitis. Chmn. local rsch. ethics com., 1992-95. Rsch. grantee The Meningitis Trust, 1989, 97. Fellow Royal Coll. Physicians, Royal Coll. Pediats. and Child Health (mem. acad. bd. and continuing med. edn. subcom. 1998—); mem. Nat. Assn. Clin. Tutors (coun. 1995—, hon. asst. sec. 1996-99, hon. sec. 1999—), Pediatric Rsch. Soc. (hon. sec. 1993-97), British Pediatric Assn., British Med. Assn., British Assn. Perinatal Medicine, Liverpool Pediatric Club (chmn. 1994-95). Avocations: jazz music, photography. Home: 2 The Avenue Alsager, Stoke-on-Trent ST7 2AN, England Office: Leighton Hosp Dept Pediatrics, Middlewich Rd, Crewe CW1 4QJ, England

THOMSON, CHRISTINE DUMONT, nutrition educator; b. Melbourne, Australia, Dec. 20, 1946; d. Eugene Dumont and Irene Eunice (Turner) Robins; m. Barry James Thomson, Jan. 19, 1972; children: Cara Wanda, Michael James. BHSc in Chemistry and Nutrition, U. Otago, Dunedin, 1968, MHSc in Nutrition, 1969, PhD in Human Nutrition, 1972. Registered nutritionist; accredited sports nutritionist. Sci. officer U. Otago, Dunedin, 1973-77, 79-81, rsch. officer, 1982-86, lectr., 1987-89, sr. lectr., 1990-97, assoc. prof., 1998—; vis. prof. Oreg. State U., Corvallis, 1992. Contbr. chpts. to books and articles to profl. jours. Mem. Royal Soc. New Zealand, Internat. Soc. Trace Elements Rsch. in Humans, Am. Inst. Nutrition, Am. Soc. Clin. Nutrition, Nutrition Soc. New Zealand, Sports Sci. New Zealand (exec. bd. 1996—), Sports Medicine New Zealand. Avocations: tennis, squash, judging gymnastics, springboard diving. Home: 18 Bayne Tce Macandrew Bay, Dunedin 9003, New Zealand Office: U Otago Dept Human Nutrn, PO Box 56, Dunedin New Zealand

THOMSON, DERICK SMITH, editor, educator, poet; b. Stornoway, Isle Lewis, Scotland, Aug. 5, 1921; s. James and Christina (Smith) T.; m. Carol M. Galbraith, 1952; 6 children. MA, U. Aberdeen, Scotland, 1947; BA, U. Cambridge, Eng., 1948; DLitt (hon.), U. Wales, 1987, U. Aberdeen, 1994. Asst. in Celtic U. Edinburgh, 1948-49; lectr. in Welsh U. Glasgow, 1949-56, prof. Celtic, 1963-91; reader in Celtic U. Aberdeen, 1956-63; chmn. Gaelic Books Coun., Scotland, 1968-91. Editor Gairm Quar., 1952—; author: An Introduction to Gaelic Poetry, 1974, 2d edit. 1990, The Companion to Gaelic Scotland, 1983, 3d edit. 1994, Creachadh Na Clarsaich/Plundering the Harp (collected poems), 1982 (Saltire Book of Yr. award), Meall Garbh/The Rugged Mountain, 1995, Alasdair Mac Mhaighstir Alasdair, Selected Poems, 1996; author/editor: The New English-Gaelic Dictionary, 1981. Fellow Royal Soc. Edinburgh, Brit. Acad.; mem. Scottish Gaelic Texts Soc. (pres. 1964-96). Scottish Nat. Party. Home: 15 Struan Rd, Cathcart Glasgow G44 3AT, Scotland Office: Gairm Publications, 29 Waterloo St, Glasgow G2, Scotland

THOMSON, GRAEME ARTHUR, hematologist; b. Kilmarnock, Scotland, June 24, 1959; s. Patrick J.M. Thomson and Isobel M. Nicholson. BSc in Immunology with honors, U. Glasgow, Scotland, 1981; MD, U. Amsterdam, 1990. Postdoctoral rsch. fellow U. Calif., San Francisco, 1986-88; co-asst. Acad. Med. Hosp., Amsterdam, 1988-90; SHO in hematology Charing Cross Hosp., London, 1990-91; registrar in hematology Exeter (Eng.) Hosp., 1991-93; registrar in blood transfusion North-East Scotland Blood Trransfusion Svc., Aberdeen, 1993-94; clin. lectr., sr. registrar in hematology Hammersmith Hosp., London, 1994-96; clin. asst. in hematology Chelsea and Westminster Hosp., London, 1996-2000, assoc. specialist, 2000—. Home: 24 Fairmount Rd, London SW2 2BL, England Office: Chelsea & Westminster Hosp, 369 Fulham Rd, London SW10 9NH, England

THOMSON, HEIDI, English literature educator; b. Ghent, Belgium, June 7, 1961; arrived in N.Z., 1990.; d. Jozef and Juliana (Dinnewet) Van de Veire; m. John Thomson, Feb. 19, 1997. Lic. Germanic Philology, U. Ghent, Belgium, 1983, Diploma in Tchg., 1984, MA, 1985; MA, U. Ill., 1986, PhD, 1990. Lectr. Victoria U. of Wellington, 1990-96, sr. lectr., 1996—. Editor: Works of Maria Edgeworth, Vol. 5, 1999, The Absentee by Maria Edgeworth; contbr. articles to profl. jours. Recipient All-Campus Tchg. award U. Ill., 1989; Fulbright grantee, 1984; U. Ill. fellow, 1989, Corpus Christi Coll. Vis. fellow, 1996. Mem. SHARP, Friends of ATL. Avocation: hiking. Office: Victoria Univ of Wellington, PO Box 600, Wellington New Zealand

THOMSON, HELEN LOUISE, artist; b. Lewiston, Ill., Nov. 28, 1928; d. Clyde Arthur Pomeroy and Myrtle Lynch Cluney; m. William Edward Thomson, 1950; children: Persephone Ann, Lucinda Renee, Cynthia Louise. Student, Western Ill. U., 1972, 78, 85, U. Ill., 1972; diploma, North Light Art Sch. Artist Table Grove, Ill., 1970—; adj. prof. Western Ill. U., Macomb, 1985-94; mem. spkrs. roster Spoon River Coll., Canton, Ill., 1986-94; exec. dir. Two Rivers Arts Coun., Macomb, 1985-94. Exhibited in numerous one woman and group exhbns.; contbr. art to calendars United Fed. Savs. & Loan, 1980, 86. Pres. Spoon River Coll. Found., Canton, Ill., 1979-85, Fulton County Arts Coun., Canton, 1973-83; bd. dirs. Regional Arts Adv. Coun., Western Ill. U., 1978-85; mem. adv. panel Ill. Arts Coun., Chgo., 1980-83; officer PTA, Table Grove, 1957-85. Recipient Ruth Watts Svc. award Performing Arts Soc., Western Ill. U., 1994, award Two Rivers Arts Coun., 1994; selected for feature stories on pub. TV sta. WMEC, 1997, Canton Dily Ledger, Macomb Jour., Peoria (Ill.) Jour. Mem. PEO Sisterhood (pres., sec., chpalain, v.p.), Ill. Art League (exhbn. awards), Ill. Watercolor Soc., Galesburg Civic Art Ctr. (exhbn. awards), Chgo. Art inst. Mem. United Ch. of Christ. Avocations: antiques, antique dolls, family history, travel. Home and Studio: 404 S Broadway St Table Grove IL 61482-9688

THOMSON, JENNIFER ANN, microbiology educator; b. Cape Town, South Africa, June 16, 1947; d. Harold John and Frances (Speight) T. BSc, U. Cape Town, 1967; MA, Cambridge (Eng.) U., 1969; PhD, Rhodes U., South Africa, 1974. Lectr. U. Witwatersrand, South Africa, 1977-80, assoc. prof., 1981-83; dir. Lab Molecular Biology, CSIR, South Africa, 1984-87; prof. U. Capetown, South Africa, 1988—. Author: Recombinant DNA and Bacterial Fermentation, 1988; contbr. articles to profl. jours. Mem. nat. coun. Dem. Party, South Africa, 1991-94. Named Outstanding Young South African, Jaycee, 1984, Woman Achiever of Yr., Women's Bur., 1988. Mem. South African Women in Sci. and Engring. (chair 1994—). Avocations: hiking, bird watching, gardening, music. Office: U Cape Town, Dept Microbiology Pvt Bag, Rondebosch 7701, South Africa

THOMSON, KENNETH R. (LORD THOMSON OF FLEET), publishing executive; b. Toronto, Ont., Can., Sept. 1, 1923; s. Lord Thomson of Fleet; m. Nora Marilyn Lavis, June 1956; children: David Kenneth Roy, Peter John, Taylor Lynne. Student, Upper Can. Coll., Toronto; BA, MA, U. Cambridge, Eng., 1947. With editorial dept. Timmins Daily Press, Eng., 1947; with advt. dept. Cambridge (Galt) Reporter, 1948-50, gen. mgr., 1950-53; owner Thomson Newspapers, Toronto, 1953—; chmn., bd. dirs. Thomson Corp., The Woodbridge Co. Ltd.; pres., bd. dirs. Thomson Works of Art Ltd. With RCAF, World War II. Mem. Granite Club, Hunt Club, National Club, Toronto Club, York Club, York Downs Club. Baptist. Avocations: collecting paintings and works of art, walking. Home: 8 Castle Frank Rd, Toronto, ON Canada M4W 2Z4 Office: Thomson Corp, 65 Queen St W, Toronto, ON Canada M5H 2M8

THOMSON, LOUIS MILLS, JR., arbitrator; b. Toledo, Mar. 8, 1927; s. Louis Mills Thomson Sr. and Frances Dorward Hay Smith; m. Rose Marie Reuss, June 26, 1953; children: Louis II, Kyle, Alison, Stuart, Amy. BS, U. Toledo, 1950, MS, 1952. Dir. City of Toledo, 1960-71, exec. dir., 1972-91. Master sgt. U.S. Army, 1945-47, PTO. Fellow Nat. Acad. Arbitrators. Lutheran. Avocation: golf. Home: 3326 Winston Blvd Toledo OH 43614-3850

THOMSON, MARJORIE BELLE ANDERSON, sociology educator, consultant; b. Topeka, Dec. 4, 1921; d. Roy John and Bessie Margaret (Knarr) Anderson; m. John Whitner Thomson, Jan. 4, 1952 (div. June 9, 1963); 1 child, John Coe. Diploma hostess, Trans World Airlines, 1945; diploma, U.Saltillo, Mex., 1945; BS, Butler U., 1957; MS, Ft. Hays Kans. State U., 1966; postgrad., U. Calif., Santa Barbara, 1968, Kans. State U., 1972-73, Kans. U., 1973. Cert. elem. tchr., Calif., Colo., Ind., Kans., jr. coll. tchr. Tech. libr. N.Am. Aviation, Dallas, 1944-45; flight attendant TWA, Kansas City, Mo., 1945-50; recreation dir. U.S. Govt., Ft. Carson, Colo., 1951-52; elem. tchr. Indpls. Pub. Schs., 1954-57; jr. high tchr. Cheyenne County Schs., Cheyenne Wells, Colo., 1958-59; elem. tchr. Sherman County Schs., Goodland, Kans., 1961-62; lectr. Calif. Luth. U., Thousand Oaks, 1967-69; instr. Ft. Hays Kans. State U., 1969-71; dir. HeadStart Kans. Coun. of Agrl. Workers and Low Income Families, Inc., Goodland, 1971-72; supr. U.S. Govt. Manpower Devel. Programs, Plainville, Kans., 1972-74; bilingual counselor Kans. Dept. Human Resources, Goodland, 1975-82; leader trainee Expt. in Internat. Living, Brattleboro, Vt., 1967-71; cons. M. Anderson & Co., Lakewood, Colo., 1982—; participant Internat. Peace Walk, Moscow to Archangel, Russia, 1991, N.Am. Conf. on Ecology and the Soviet Save Peace and Nature Ecol. Collective, Russia, 1992, Liberators-The Holocaust Awareness Inst., Denver, 1992; amb. internat. Friendship Force, Tiblisi, Republic of Georgia, 1991, Republic South Africa, 1995, Republic of Turkey, 1996, Republic of Egypt, 1999, Republic of Israel-Kfar Blum Kibbutz, 1999, Republic of Austria, 1999; presenter State Conv. AAUW, Aurora, Colo., 1992, presenter nat. conv. Am. Acad. Audiology, Denver, 1992; cons. Gov.'s Conf. in Libr. and Info. Svc., Vail, Colo., 1992; presenter annual conf. Nat. Emergency Number 911 Assn., Denver, 1996. Docent Colo. Gallery of the Arts, Littleton, 1989; spkr. Internat. Self Help for Hard of Hearing People, Inc., 1990—, mem. state recreation resource com. for Self Help for Hard of Hearing People Internat. Conv., Denver, 1991; mem. Denver Deaf and Hard of Hearing Access Com., 1991—; spkr. Ret. Sr. Vol. Program, Denver, 1992—; dir. Holiday Project, Denver, 1992; mem. Lakewood Access Com., 1994—, Arvada Ctr.'s Women's Voices com., 1995; participant women readers com. Rocky Mountain News, Denver, 1995; trustee Internat. Self Help for Hard of Hearing People, Inc., Bethesda, Md., 1995-98; Deaf Panel spkr. for Deaf Awareness Week, Denver, 1995-98; program co-chair Lakewood Woman's Club, 1996, 97; mem. access adv. com. Arvada Ctr. for Arts and Humanities, 1997; commr. Denver Commn. for People with Disabilities, 1997-98; mem. Colo. State Rehab. Adv. Coun., 1997—, 98, Gov.'s Adv. Coun. for People with Disabilities, 1998—; mem. Lakewood Citizen Police Acad. XIX, 1999; participant Funding Assistive Technology: Where to Turn in Colo. and When, Denver, 1999; mem. program Wisdom Keepers, Lakewood, 1999-2000; participant Aurora 5 States Assistive Tech. Conf. for Disabled, 1999; mem. Colo. Drug Abuse Task Force, 2000. Grantee NSF, 1970, 71; recipient Svc. award Mayor of Lakewood, 1995, Honorable Mention Four Who Dare, Colo. Bus. and Profl. Women and KCNC Channel 4, 1995, J.C. Penney Nat. Golden Rule award for cmty. vol. svc., 1996, Cmty. Svc. award Mayor Denver, 1996, City and County of Denver Proclamation for Marjorie Thomson Day, Mayor Wellington E. Webb, April 8, 1997, Svc. Recognition award Oticon Co., 1997, Worker of Yr., Recognition award Dickie Co., 1997; coll. scholarship presented in her name, 2000. Mem. AAUW (life; v.p., program chairperson Lakewood br. 1996, Trailblazer award Denver br. 1997, mem. diversity com. Colo. 1997-98), AARP (pres. Denver-Grandview chpt. 1994), VFW Aux. (life), Sociologists for Women in Soc. (participant Gullah Culture, Charleston, S.C. 1997), Bus. and Profl. Woman's Club, Internat. Peace Walkers, Spellbinders, Denver Press Club (Wheat Ridge Grange # 155 1993-98), Lakewood Woman's Club, TWA Internat. Clipped Wings (cert.), Mile High Wings, Order Ea. Star (life), Sons of Norway, UNESCO, Bus. and Profl. Women's Club (com. for Ms. Golden Bus. and Profl. Woman of Yr. 1999), Confederate Air Force (hon. col.), Toastmasters, PHAMALy, Pi Gamma Mu, Alpha Sigma Alpha (life, participant Centennial Conv., Alumni Star). Democrat. Presbyterian. Avocations: photography, traveling, whitewater rafting, storytelling, writing. Home: 6941 W 13th Ave Apt G Lakewood CO 80215-5259

THOMSON, OLIVER CAMPBELL, communications company executive; b. Birmingham, U.K., Feb. 28, 1936; s. Oliver James and Linda Marie (Kelly) T.; m. Jean Patricia Christie, Sept. 10, 1960; children: Calum, Iain, Margaret. MA, Cambridge U., U.K., 1959; diploma Cam, London Coll. Distbrs., 1960; PhD, Glasgow U., 1994. Copywriter J. Walter Thompson, London, 1960-62; assoc. dir. R.W. Advt., Glasgow, 1969-70; dir. McAllum Advt., 1971-74; mng. dir. Charles Barker, Scotland, 1975-85; mktg. dir. Holmes McDougall, Edinburgh, 1985-86; mng. dir. Levy McCallum Advt., 1986—; lectr. Glasgow U., 1966-86. Author: Mass Persuasion in History, 1978, History of Sin, 1991, Easily Led-History of Propaganda, 1999, The Great Feud: Campbells and MacDonalds, 2000. Chmn. Four Acres Charitable Trust, Glasgow, 1987-99, Scottish IPA, Edinburgh, 1980-83; dir. Films of Scotland, Edinburgh, 1978-82. Avocations: walking, sailing, corling. Home: 3 Kirklee Terr, Glasgow G12 0TQ, United Kingdom Office: 203 St Vincent St, Glasgow G12 OTQ, United Kingdom

THOMSON, RICHARD GEOFFREY, public health physician, researcher; b. Peterborough, Eng., May 2, 1958; s. Lesley Bambridge and Honor (Gooding) Thomson; m. Tracy Robson, Sept. 1, 1989; children: Laura, Amy. BA in Physiology, Oxford (Eng.) U., 1979, MB BChir, 1982; MD, Newcastle U., 1990. Clin. rsch. fellow U. Newcastle-upon-Tyne, Eng., 1985-88; cons. in pub. health medicine, dir. svc. quality and stds. No. Regional Health Authority, Newcastle-upon-Tyne, 1990-92, dir. health strategy, 1992; sr. lectr. in pub. health medicine Newcastle-upon-Tyne Med. Sch., Newcastle-upon-Tyne, 1992-99; prof. epidemiology and public health, 1999—; mem. Faculty Pub. Health Medicine, London, 1990; mgmt. bd. dirs. Inst. for Health of Elderly, Newcastle-upon-Tyne, 1995—; regional mgmt. bd. dirs. No. Regional Health Authority, Newcastle-upon-Tyne, 1990-92; dir. U.K. Quality Indicator Project, Newcastle-upon-Tyne, 1996—. Author: (book chpt.) Quality in Health Care, 1996; assoc. editor: (jour.) Quality in Health Care, 1991—; contbr. articles to profl. jours. Fellow Faculty of Pub. Health Medicine, 1996; open scholar St. Edmund Hall, Oxford U., 1976. Fellow Royal Coll. Physicians. Avocations: squash, association football, English literature, pike fishing. Office: Newcastle upon Tyne Med Sch Dept Epidemiology and Pub Health, Sch Health Scis Framlington Rd, Newcastle upon Tyne NE2 4HH, England

THOMSON, RICHARD MURRAY, retired banker; b. Winnipeg, Man., Can., Aug. 14, 1933; s. H.W. and Mary T. BASC in Engring., U. Toronto, 1955; MBA, Harvard U., 1957; fellow course in banking, Queen's U., 1958. With Toronto Dominion Bank, Ont., Can., 1957—, asst. to pres. head office, 1963-68, chief gen. mgr., 1968-71, v.p., chief gen. mgr., dir., 1971-72, pres., 1972-77, pres. and CEO, 1977-78, chmn., 1978-98; CEO Toronto Dominion Bank, 1978-97, also bd. dirs., chmn., 1977-98; bd. dirs. CGC Inc., S.C. Johnson & Son Inc., The Prudential Ins. Co. Am., The Thomson Corp., Inco Ltd., Can. Pension Plan Investment Bd., Ont. Power Generation Inc., Toronto Dominion Bank., Stuart Energy Sys. Inc., TrizecHahn Corp.; chmn. bd. dirs. Can. Occidental Petroleum Ltd. Bd. dirs. The Hosp. for Sick Children Found. Office: Toronto-Dominion Bank, 55 King St PO Box 1, Toronto, ON Canada M5K 1A2

THOMSON, STEVEN JAMES, research agricultural engineer; b. Washington, Sept. 24, 1957; s. James and Marie Thomson; m. Debra Ruth West, Aug. 24, 1985. BS in Agrl. Engring., U. Ga., 1979, MS in Agrl. Engring., 1981; PhD in Agrl. Engring., U. Fla., 1990. Rsch. engr. U. Ga. Coastal Plain Experiment Sta., Tifton, 1981-85; asst. prof. engring. fundamentals dept. Va. Poly. Inst. and State U., Blacksburg, 1990-96; rsch. engr. USDA/ARS, Stoneville, Miss., 1996—. Contbr. articles to profl. jours. Mem. Am. Soc. Agrl. Engrs., Am. Soc. Agromony, Sigma Xi, Alpha Epsilon, Alpha Zeta, Phi Kappa Phi, Gamma Sigma Delta. Republican. Office: USDA-ARS-APTRU 141 Experiment Station Rd Stoneville MS 38776

THOMSON OF FLEET, LORD See THOMSON, KENNETH R.

THONDHLANA, JULIET, linguist, educator, consultant; b. Mt. Darwin, Zimbabwe, Mar. 2, 1961; d. Misheck Cornelius and Petronella Grace (Zowa) Chikanza; m. Herbert Farai Thondhlana, Aug. 9, 1986; children: Kudakwashe, Nyasha, Anesu. BA, U. Zimbabwe, 1983; MA in Gen. Linguistics, U. Fla., 1986; MA in Applied Linguistics, U. Lancaster, Eng., 1988; PhD, U. Zimbabwe, 1994. Lectr. in linguistics U. Zimbabwe, 1988—; cons. Speciss Coll., Harare, Zimbabwe, 1990—, A.C.M., Harare, 1989—, Syracuse U. in Harare, 1995—. Author: Vakasiiwa Pachena, 1984; editor LASU Procs., 1991. Rank Xerox fellow, U.K., 1990. Mem. Zimbabwe Assemblies of God. Avocations: creative writing, music, swimming, netball. Home: 25 Dorchester Rd, Mabelreigh, Harare Zimbabwe Office: U Zimbabwe Dept Linguistics, PO Box MP167, Harare Zimbabwe

THONGSAK, VAJEEPRASEE THOMAS, business planning executive; b. Udonthani, Thailand, Feb. 10, 1935; came to U.S., 1970; s. Chanmar and Pee Vajeeprasee; m. Somchit; 1 child, Rosarine. BS in Sociology, BA in Philosophy, Mahamakut U., Bangkok, 1968; MA in Edn., Kean Coll. N.J., 1976; MA in Philosophy, NYU, 1989; PhD in Mgmt., AMA Mgmt. Inst., 1987. CCM. Tchr. Machimavas Sch., Udonthani, 1958-65; spl. instr. Chana Songkram Sch., Bangkok, 1965-68; tchrs. staff Thai Sripratoom U., Bangkok, 1968-70; salesman Met. Life of N.Y., 1974-76; rep. Mut. Life of N.Y., 1976-78; agt. Equitable Life Ins., N.Y.C., 1983-84; insp. IBI Security Svc. Inc., L.I., 1979-85; security police insp. Brandeis U., Waltham, Mass., 1985-86; U.S. chief legal investigator, pvt. investigator U.S. Legal Investigation, Inc., U.S. Bur.'s Security Agy., Boston, N.Y.C., Fresno, Calif., 1987—; chmn. Worldwide Bank Assocs. Investment, 2000—; advisor Thai N.E. Assn., N.Y.C., 1980—, Rep. Nat. Com., Washingotn, 1980—; state advisor U.S. Congl. Adv., Washington, 1980; assoc. mem. Nat. Security Ctr., Citizen's Adv. Coun., Washington, 1989; pres., chief security agt. U.S. Bur. Security Agy., 1991; mem. Pres. Pvt. Sector Survey on Cost Control, Washington, 1989—; adv. bd. Am. Security Coun., Washington, 1983-88. Mem. G.O.P. Republican Conservative Party (recommendation pres. Gerald R. Ford 1977), 1977—, Nat. Republican Congl. Com. Victory Fund, Washington, 1982—, Republican Presdl. Task Force and Comsn. (recommendation chmn. Nat. Republican Senatorial Com. 1982, 93), 1982—, Am. Security Coun. Found., 1978—, Defense Dept. Defense Inst., 1982—, Nat. Rep. Senatorial Com., Washington, Chiefs of Police Nat. Drug Task Force, 1982—, Nat. Law Enforcement Officers Meml. Fund, Washington, 1982—, Natl. Wildlife Fedn., 1982—; apptd. state adviser U.S. Congl. Adv. Bd., 1979, 93; priest asst. U.S.A. Buddhayaram Temple, Bronx, 1970—; pres. S.E. Asia Found., 1970; mem. Citizens Against Govt. Waste, Washington; mem. U.S. Def. Com., Washington, 1982-86; sec. Wat Buddhamonthol United Buddhist Meditation Ctr., 1992—. Recipient Presdl. Seal, Rep. Orgn., 1983, 84, Rep. Presdl. Legion of Merit highest level of Govts. for Lifetime, 1993. Mem. Internat. Assn. Chiefs of Police, President's Club, Senator's Club, Rep. Presdl. Legion of Merit.

'T HOOFT, GERARDUS, physics educator; b. Den Helder, The Netherlands, July 5, 1946; s. Hendrik and Margaretha Agnes (van Kampen) 't H.; m. Albertha Anje Schik, July 1, 1972; children: Saskia Anne, Ellen Marga. Candidaatsexamen, Rijksuniversiteit Utrecht, The Netherlands, 1966, doctoraalexamen Theoretical Physics, 1969, PhD, 1972; DSc (hon.), U. Chgo., 1981, U. Louvain, 1996, U. Bologna, 1998, Eurasian U., Astana, Kazakjstan. Fellow European Ctr. Nuclear Rsch., Geneva, 1972-74; lectr., asst. prof. physics Free U. Utrecht, The Netherlands, 1974-77, prof., 1977—; Loeb lectr. Harvard U., Cambridge, Mass., 1976; Fairchild disting. scholar Calif. Inst. Tech., Pasadena, 1981; assoc. étranger Acad. des Scis., Paris, 1995. Assoc. editor Nuclear Physics B; contbr. articles to profl. jours. Recipient numerous awards including Dannie Heineman prize Am. Physical Soc. and Am. Inst. Physics, N.Y.C., 1979, Wolf prize Wolf Found, Jersualem, 1981, Piou XI medal Pontificia Accademia delle Sci. John Paul II, Vatican City, 1983, Spinoza premium NWO, 1995, Franklin medal, Phila., 1995, Gian Carlo Wick comm. medal, Lausanne, 1997, HEP prize European Phys. Soc., 1999, Comdr. Orde Ned. Leeuw, 1999, Nobel Prize in Physics, 1999. Mem. Koninklijke Nederlandse Academie voor Wetenschappen (Lorentz medal 1986), Nat. Acad. Scis. U.S.A. (fgn. assoc.), Am. Acad. Arts and Scis. (fgn. hon.). Office: Spinoza Inst, PO Box 80 195, NL3508TD Utrecht The Netherlands

THORARINSSON, HJALTI, surgeon, educator; b. Hjaltabakki, Iceland, Mar. 23, 1920; s. Thorarinn and Sigridur (Thorvaldsdottir) Jonsson; MD, U. Iceland, 1948; m. Alma Anna Thorarinsson, Oct. 22, 1946; children: Thorarinn, Oddur, Sigridur, Hrolfur, Gunnlaug. Surg. tng. U. Hosp., Reykjavik, Iceland, 1950-52, U. Hosp., Madison, Wis., 1952-54; cons. thoracic surgeon U. Hosp., Reykjavik, 1954-57, deptl. surgeon, 1957-59, asst. chief surgeon, 1959-62, chief surgeon, 1963-72, head dept. surgery, 1972-90; lectr. Faculty Medicine, U. Iceland, 1959-62, asst. prof., 1963-72, prof. surgery, 1972-90, ret., 1990. Decorated Knight Icelandic Order Falcon. NATO sci. fellow, 1961, 63; Council Europe med. fellow, 1965; Brit. Council scholar, 1965; research grantee Icelandic Sci. Found. Mem. Icelandic Assn. Surgeons (chmn. 1964-66), Assn. Icelandic Heart Physicians, European Assn. Cancer Research, Scandinavian Assn. Thoracic and Cardiovascular Surgeons (exec. bd., pres. 1968), Scandinavian Assn. Surgeons (exec. bd.), Am. Coll. Chest Physicians (chmn. internat. com. on cancer 1968), Internat. Surg. Group (pres. 1987-88). Lutheran. Clubs: Lions (chmn. Reykjavik 1969-70), Grafarholt's Golf, Glaumbaer's Fishing, Badminton. Contbr. articles to profl. jours. Home: 36 Laugarasvegur,, 36 Laugarasvegur, Reykjavik 104, Iceland Office: 3 Egilsgata, Reykjavik 101,, Iceland

THORBECKE, WILLEM HENRY, international company executive, consultant; b. Paris, July 4, 1924; s. Willem Johan Rudolf and Madelaine (Salisbury) T.; m. Sonya Stokowski, June 8, 1946; children: Noel Evangeline, Johan Rudolf, Willem Leif, Christine Louise. BS in Engring., MIT, 1948, BSBA, 1948. Exec. Royal Dutch Shell, N.Y.C., London, Tokyo, 1948-60, Mobil Corp., N.Y.C., 1960-69; cons. various cos., N.Y.C., Chgo., Houston, others, 1969-75; pres. Dravo Internat., Pitts., 1975-82, W.H. Thorbecke Assocs., Sewickley, Pa., 1982—; chmn., chief exec. officer Energy Support Svcs. Inc., Coraopolis, Pa., 1982-87, dir., 1987-90; founder, chmn., CEO Thorbecke Enterprises, Inc., Sewickley, 1996—. Dir. World Affairs Coun., Pitts., 1978—; chmn. MIT Enterprise Forum, Pitts., 1987-89, 93-94. Flight lt. RAF. Named Tri-State Area Entrepreneur of Yr. Venture Mag., Ernst & Young, 1987. Mem. Am. Mgmt. Assn. (internat. coun. 1977-83), Nat. Assn. Corp. Dirs., Duquesne Club (Pitts.), Haagse Club (The Netherlands). Republican. Episcopalian. Home: Deer Haven Farm Stonedale Rd Sewickley PA 15143

THORDARSON, WILLIAM, retired hydrogeologist; b. N.Y.C., Mar. 14, 1929; s. William and Lillian (Hirsch) T. BA, Columbia U., 1950; postgrad., U. Kans., Lawrence, 1953-55; MA, U. Colo., 1987. Hydrogeologist U.S. Geol. Survey, Denver, 1955-94. Author: Perched Groundwater, Nevada, 1965, Hydrogeology of Test Wells, 1975, Hydrogeology of South-Central Great Basin, 1983, Hydrogeologic Monitoring, Nevada, 1985, Hydrogeology of Anhydrite, 1989. Served with U.S. Army, 1950-52. Mem. Nat. Geog. Soc., Colo. Ground Water Assn., Colo. Sci. Soc., Geol. Soc. Wash. Home: 10890 W Evans Ave Unit 2D Denver CO 80227-2070

THORGEIRSSON, GUDMUNDUR, physician, cardiologist; b. Djupavik, Strandasysla, Iceland, Mar. 14, 1946; s. Thorgeir Gestsson and Asa Gundmundsdottir; m. Bryndis Sigurjonsdottir, July 20, 1968; children: Thorgeir, Sigurjon Arni, Hjalti, Bogi, Asa Bryndis. MD, U. Iceland, 1973; PhD, Case Western Res. U., 1978. Diplomate Am. Bd. Internal Medicine, Am. Bd. Cardiovascular Disease. Intern., resident path. medicine U. Hosps., Cleve., 1974-80, teaching fellow in cardiology, 1980-82; cardiologist Landspitalinn U. Hosp., Reykjavik, Iceland, 1982; assoc. prof. U. Iceland, 1985-98, prof., 1998—; cons. Heart Prevention Clinic, Reykjavik, 1982—; bd. dirs. Icelandic Heart Assn., Reykjavik; chmn. Icelandic Nutrition Coun., 1990-98; mem. steering com. 4S; chmn. Icelandic Sci. Ethics Com., 1999. Editor Icelandic Med. Jour., 1983-91; contbr. articles to profl. jours. Icelandic Sci. Fund grantee, 1983-89, 1992-99. Fellow ACP, Am. Coll. Cardiology, Soc. Scientarum Islandica; mem. Icelandic Med. Assn., Icelandic Cardiol. Soc. (pres. 1985-87). Avocations: books, Icelandic medical history, skiing. Home: Klapparas 4, Reykjavik Iceland Office: Landspitalinn U Hosp, Reykjavik Iceland

THORKILDSEN, ÅSMUND, art institution director; b. Drammen, Norway, July 1, 1954; s. Reidar and Erna Marie (Strand) T.; m. Hege Johnsen, June 10, 1983; children: Ingrid, Arthur. Candidatus Magisterii, U. Oslo, 1977, Magister Artium, 1983. Ednl. sec. Aftenskolen Evening Sch., Drammen, 1983-85; inspector Baerum Mcpl. Evening Sch., Sandvika, 1985-88; dir. Kunstnernes Hus, Oslo, 1988—; curator for olympic collection Lillehammer Olympics Orgn. Com., 1992-94; art critic Drammens Tidende-Buskeruds Blad, Drammen, 1985—; chmn. com. for aquisitions Norwegian Cultural Coun., Oslo, 1993-95; assoc. prof. art theory Nat. Coll. Art, Craft and Design, Oslo, 1998—; dir. Astrup Fearnley Mus. Modern Art, Oslo, 1999—. Author: Network, 1994, Leonard Rickhard, 1995, Per Berntsen (photographs), 1995, Continúoús, 1997, Laying Low, 1997. Mem. Internat. Assn. Art Critics. Lutheran. Avocations: wildlife, gardening. Office: Kunstnernes Hus, Wergelandsveien 17, 0167 Oslo Norway

THORMAR, HALLDOR, microbiologist, educator; b. Mar. 9, 1929; s. Thorvardur and Olina Marta (Jonsdottir) T.; m. Lilja Asdis Asbjornsdottir, Dec. 25, 1962; children: Sigridur, Asdis Birna, Olina Marta. Mag. Scient., U. Copenhagen, 1956; Postgrad., U. Calif., Berkeley, 1957-58; PhD, U. Copenhagen, 1966. Rsch. scientist U. Iceland, Reykjavik, 1958-60, 62-67, State Seruminstitute, Copenhagen, 1960-62; investigator Inst. Venezolano Investigaciones Cientificas, Caracas, Venezuela, 1965-66; chief rsch. scientist N.Y. State Inst. Basic Rsch. Devel. Disability, S.I., 1967-86; prof. U. Iceland, Reykjavik, 1985-99; vis. scientist U. Cambridge, Eng., 1963, Cath. U. Leuven, Belgium, 1992, 95, 97, Chinese Acad. Med. Sci., 1992; vis. prof. Free U. Brussels, Belgium, 1975. Contbr. numerous articles to profl. jours. and chpts. to books. Recipient Gold medal U. Copenhagen, 1955. Mem. Am. Soc. Microbiology, Icelandic Acad. Sci. Office: Inst of Biology, Grensasvegur 12, 108 Reykjavik Iceland

THORN, PATRICK ARTHUR, retired physician, researcher; b. Harrow, Eng., Nov. 22, 1919; s. Harold Eustace and Beryl Beatrice (Robinson) T.; m. Joan Parton, Apr. 20, 1950; children: Diana Joan, Caroline Beryl. MBBS, Middlesex Hosp. Med. Sch., Eng., 1942; MD, London, 1947. Cons. physician Royal Hosp., Wolverhampton, 1955-84; pres. West Midlands Physicians Assn., 1982. Contbr. articles to profl. jours. Lt. surgeon Royal Navy, 1942-46. Fellow Royal Coll. Physicians; mem. Staffordshire and Worcestershire Canal Soc. Avocations: canal history, walking, gardening, photography. Home: Napton, Foxlands Dr, West Midlands WV4 5NA, United Kingdom

THORNBURGH, RICHARD E., bank executive. Chief fin. officer Credit Suisse Group, Zurich; vice chmn., exec. bd. Credit Suisse First Boston. Address: 11 Madison Ave New York NY 10010-3629*

THORNDAHL, JYTTE, curator, anthropologist; b. Arhus, Denmark, May 12, 1949; d. Knud and Kirsten Magrethe (Saxov) T.; m. Aksel Gunnar Lindballe; children: Jens Jacob, Jan Aslak. Student, Cornell U., 1974-75; magister konferens, U. Aarhus, Denmark, 1977. Asst. tchr. U. Aarhus, Arhus, 1977-78; rschr. Djurslans Mus., Grena, Denmark, 1978-79; asst. tchr., lectr. U. Århus, Denmark, 1979-85; exhibition cons. Moesgard Mus., Arhus, 1985-87; curator, v. dir. Danish Mus. Electricity, Denmark, 1988—; accountant Danish Soc. History of Tech., Denmark, 1994—. Author: Kolindsund, 1980, Elektricitetens Aarhund Rede, 1992; contbr. articles to profl. jours. Mem. Bd. of Music Sch., Gjern, Denmark, 1995—. The Kaufmann grantee Cornell U., U. Aarhus, 1974. Mem. ICOM, Limuset. Avocations: amateur musician, Danish folk music. Home: Johs Jensensuej 19, 8641 Sorring Denmark Office: Danish Museum Electricity, Bjerringbrovej 44, 8850 Bjerringbro Denmark

THORNE, COLIN REGINALD, geography educator, consultant; b. Hull, Eng., Sept. 30, 1952; s. Reginald and Mollie (Smith) T.; m. Eileen Margaret Shaw, Oct. 10, 1981; children: Katherine, Jonathan. BS, U. East Anglia, Norwich, Eng., 1974, PhD, 1978. Vis. scientist USDA, Oxford, Miss., 1979-80; postdoctoral rschr. UEA, Norwich, 1980-81; assoc. prof. Colo. State U., Ft. Collins, 1981-84; lectr. U. London, 1984-90; prof. U. Nottingham, Eng., 1990—; affiliate prof. Colo. State U., 1984—; cons. Sir William Halcrow & Ptnrs., Swindon, Eng., 1990—, U.K. Envirnoment Agy., 1997—. Author 7 books on fluvial geomorphology. Recipient Collingwood prize, 1986; grantee numerous orgns. in U.S. and Eng. Mem. ASCE (chair task com. on river width adjustment 1993-97), Brit. Geomorphol. Rsch. Group (exec. com. 1990-93, editl. bd.). Avocations: family activities. Office: Sch Geography, U Nottingham, Nottingham NG7 2RD, England

THORNELY-TAYLOR, RUPERT MAURICE, acoustical consultant; b. Whalton, Northumberland, Eng., May 21, 1946; s. Maurice Humphrey Taylor and Mary Patricia Stuart (Wood) Pearson; m. Alison Grant Saunders, June 17, 1964 (div. 1987); m. Frances Marion Linbird, May 21, 1988. Pvt. practice London, 1968—; expert witness Royal Commn. Environ. Pollution, select coms. House of Commons, House of Lords, 1970—; mem. U.K. Noise Adv. Coun., 1970-80; dep. chmn. Working Group Noise as Hazard to Health, 1976-80; chmn. Working Group Noise Monitoring, 1974; cons. Orgn. Econ. Co-operation and Devel., Paris, 1980, Brit. Mass Transit Cons., Taipei, Taiwan, 1987, Seventh Plan Urban and Regional Transport, Bangkok, 1991; cons. noise and vibration London Underground LTD, 1990—, London Docklands Devel. Corp., 1983—, Nat. Rivers Authority, Maidenhead, Eng., 1990—; noise cons. City of London, 1990—. Author: Noise, 1970, rev. edits., 1974, 79, Electricity, 1979; co-author: Handbook of Noise Assessment, 1978; author: Noise, 1970, rev. edit., 1979; editor: Noise Control Data, 1976; contbr. articles to profl. jours. Active Fairwarp Conservation Assn., East Sussex, Eng., 1991; leader Wealden Dist. Coun. Fellow

Winston Churchill Meml. Trust, 1972. Mem. Inst. Acoustics (hon. treas. 1971-79, fellow 1981), Assn. Noise Cons. (hon. treas. 1972-75), Acoustical Soc. Am., Inst. Noise Control Engring. (assoc.), Nat. Pony Soc. (hon. treas. 1991-97). Avocations: painting, gardening, British native ponies. Home: Spring Garden, Fairwarp, Uckfield East Sussex TN22 3BG, England

THORNHILL, ARTHUR HORACE, JR., retired book publisher; b. Boston, Jan. 1, 1924; s. Arthur Horace and Mary Josephine (Peterson) T.; m. Dorothy M. Matheis, Oct. 28, 1944; children: Sandra Susanne Thornhill Brushart, Arthur Horace. AB magna cum laude, Princeton U., 1948. With Little, Brown & Co., Inc., Boston, 1948-88; v.p. Little, Brown & Co., Inc., 1955-58, gen. mgr., 1960-87, chief exec. officer, pres., 1962-87, chmn. bd., 1970-87; chmn., pres., dir. Little, Brown & Co. (Can.), Ltd., 1955-84; v.p. Time, Inc., 1968-87; vice chmn. Time-Life Books, Inc., 1976-86; mem. adv. council history dept. Princeton U., 1964-85; trustee, treas. Princeton U. Press, 1972-85; chmn. N.Y. Graphic Soc., 1974-79. Trustee Bennington Coll., 1969-76; fellow emeritus Ctr. for Creative Photography U. Ariz.; bd. dirs. Am. Book Pubs. Council, 1964-67. Served to 1st lt. USAAF, World War II. Decorated Air medal; recipient Princeton U. Press medal, 1985, Disting. Alumni award Dwight-Englewood Sch., 1998. Mem. Assn. Am. Pubs. (bd. dirs. 1978-81), Edgartown Yacht Club, Edgartown Reading Room (pres. 1990-92), Union Club (N.Y.C.), Princeton Club (N.Y.C.), Century Club (N.Y.C.), Publs. Lunch Club (N.Y.C.), Union Club (Boston), St. Botolph (Boston). Home: 50 S School St Portsmouth NH 03801-5258

THORNLEY, DALE JONATHAN, financial services company director; b. Dartford, Kent, Eng., Mar. 9, 1957; s. Roy Desmond and Joy Violet (Warren) T.; m. Anne Marie Battle, Oct. 3, 1986; children: Jennifer Anne, Sean Michael, Sarah Michelle. CFP. Agy. adminstrn. mgr. Abbey Life, London, 1973-80; client svcs. mgr. Merchant Investors, Croydon, Eng., 1980-92; compliance stds. officer Lincoln Nat., London, 1992-94; co. dir. Tribune Ind. Fin. Mgmt. Ltd., London, 1994-98; mng. dir. Equus Ind. Fin. Mgmt. Ltd./The Equus Alliance Ltd., London, 1998—; cons. Broker Panel money mktg. newspaper, Eng., 1995—. Recipient Fin. Planner award Chartered Ins. Inst., 1995. Avocations: golf, tennis. Home: 3 Highbury Close, W Wickham BR4 9PA, England Office: The Equus Alliance Ltd, 1 Harley St, London W1N 10A, England

THORNS, DAVID CHRISTOPHER, sociology educator; b. Annfield Plain, Eng., Aug. 26, 1943; arrived in New Zealand, 1973; s. Walter Francis and Nellie (Hill) T.; m. Gloria Kathleen Corrigan, Aug. 6, 1966; children: Karen Louise, Joy Marie. BA in Econs., U. Sheffield, Eng., 1964; MA, U. Exeter, Eng., 1967; DLitt, U. Canterbury, Christchurch, New Zealand, 1982. Lectr. sociology U. Exeter, 1965-73; sr. lectr. U. Auckland, New Zealand, 1973-76; sr. lectr. U. Canterbury, Christchurch, 1977-78, reader, 1979-94, prof., 1995—. Author: Suburbia, 1974, Quest for Community, 1976, Cities Unlimited, 1978, (with L. Kilmartin) Eclipse of Equality, 1983, (with D. Pearson) Fragmenting Societies, 1992; editor: New Directions in Sociology, 1976; mem. editl. bd. Housing Studies, Urban Affairs Rev. Mem. Nat. Housing Commn., Wellington, New Zealand, 1985-88; convenor social scis. panel Marsden Fund, New Zealand, 1997—; mem. Marsden Com., 1997—. Fellow New Zealand Royal Soc.; mem. Internat. Sociol. Assn. (v.p., mem. rsch. com. on housing 1994—). Methodist. Avocations: walking, reading, listening to music. Office: Univ Canterbury Dept Sociol, Pvt Bag 4800, Christchurch New Zealand

THORNSBERRY, WILLIS LEE, JR., chemist; b. Sturgis, Ky., Aug. 10, 1940; s. Willis Lee and Jane (Hall) T.; m. Mary Elizabeth Gaswint, June 19, 1965; children: Brian, Michele. BS, Murray State U., 1963; MS, U. Ark., 1967; PhD, Tulane U., 1974. Rsch. chemist Freeport-McMoran Inc., Belle Chasse, La., 1967-74, sr. rsch. chemist, 1974-92; pres. Tech. Devel. Svcs. Inc., Sturgis, Ky., 1995—. Contbr. articles to profl. jours. Coach, leader for youth groups Jefferson Parish Playgrounds, Gretna, La., 1970-84, Boy Scouts Am., Gretna, 1975-82. 1st lt. U.S. Army, 1963-65. Mem. Am. Chem. Soc. (sect. chmn. 1982), Sigma Xi (nominating com. 1967—). Democrat. Achievements include numerous patents for process for uranium recovery from phosphoric acid, recovery of silica from hydrofluorosilicic acid, stabilization of gypsum for construction purposes, preparation and use of fertilizer additives. Office: 1024 N Main St Sturgis KY 42459-1245

THORNSBURY, MICHAEL, judge; b. Williamson, W.Va., July 6, 1956; s. John and Maggie Z. (Thocker) T.; m. Dreama K. Keith, June 25, 1977; children: Melissa, Matthew, Elizabeth Ann. BA, Pikeville (Ky.) Coll., 1977; JD summa cum laude, U. Ky., 1980. Bar: Ky. 1980, W.Va. 1980, U.S. Dist. Ct. (so. dist.) W.Va. 1980, U.S. Dist. Ct. (ea. dist.) Ky. 1980, U.S. Appeals 1988. Chief legal aid dept. Fed. Correctional Instn., Lexington, Ky., 1978-80; pvt. practice Williamson, 1980-96; city atty. Town of Gilbert, W.Va., 1985-90; cir. judge Mingo 30th Jud. Cir., Williamson, 1997-98; re-elected to eight-yr. term, 2000; asst. pros. atty. County of Mingo, Williamson, 1981-85; special justice W.Va. Supreme Ct. Appeals; bd. trustees Pikeville Coll, 2000—. Mem. Mingo County Dep. Sheriff's Civil Svc. Commn., 1983-85. Recipient Amb. award Belfry H.S., 2000, Delbarton 2000 Cmty. Svc. award; Presdl. scholar Pikeville Coll., 1974. Mem. Assn. Trial Lawyer Am., Ky. Bar Assn., W.Va. Bar Assn., W.Va. Trial Lawyers Assn., W.Va. Jud. Assn., Ky. Trial Lawyers Assn., Mingo County Trial Lawyers Assn. (pres. Williamson chpt. 1986-88), Pike Coll. Alumni Assn. (bd. dirs.), Moose, Tug Valley Shriners (pres. 1999-2000), Kiwanis (bd. dirs. 1997—, pres. 2000-01), O'Brien Lodge 101, Scottish Rite, Temple Aide Beni Kedem Temple. Democrat. Methodist. Home: 1717 W 4th Ave Williamson WV 25661-3014 Office: Mingo Cir Judge PO Box 1198 75 E 2d Ave Williamson WV 25661

THORNTON, CHARLES VICTOR, metals executive; b. Salt Lake City, Feb. 8, 1915; s. Charles Victor and Winnie May (Fitts) T.; m. Margaret Louise Wiggins, Apr. 17, 1937; children: Charles Victor III, Carolyn Louise (Mrs. John J. Moorhouse), David Frank. BS in Civil Engring., U. Utah, 1935; HHD, Ind. Inst. Tech., 1972. Registered profl. engr., Ohio, Tex. Engr. Truscon Steel Co., Youngstown, Ohio, 1935-37; dist. engr. Truscon Steel Co., Washington, 1937-40; chief engr. So. Iron Works, Inc., Alexandria, Va., 1940-45; pres. Thornton Industries, Inc., Ft. Worth, 1945-75; chmn. bd. Thornton Industries, Inc., 1975-88; bd. dirs. Bank Commerce and Comml. Fin. Corp.; chmn. bd. dirs. Southview Corp. Author: American Association of Private Railroad Car Owners Roster of Private R.R. Cars, 1991, Autobiography, 1993, Charlie, 1994, Winnie, 1994. Chmn. bd. Southview Corp., 1980—, chmn. emeritus Shriners Hosps. for Children; mem. nat. adv. coun. U. Utah, 1985-96; chmn. investment com. Longhorn coun. Boy Scouts Am., 1985-88; v.p. campaign chmn. Ft. Worth Arts United, 1989; v.p. Tarrant County Arts Coun., 1989; pres. Tarrant County Water Bd., 1984-88; mem. policy com. Dallas-Ft. Worth Railtran, 1991-98; pres. Ft. Worth chpt. Internat. Good Neighbor Coun., 1991-92; bd. dirs. Ft. Worth Opera, 1997—; mem. World Affairs Coun. Ft. Worth, 1996, bd. dirs., 1997—, treas., 1998. Recipient Salesman of Yr. award Ft. Worth Sales and Mktg. Execs., 1984, Good Neighbor of Yr. award Internat. Good Neighbor Coun., 1984, Merit of Honor award U. Utah, 1986; holder airplane speed record Dallas to Wichita, Kans., 1969. Mem. ASCE (life) (Tex. sect. Svc. to People award 1995), Tex. Assn. Bus. (life), Ft. Worth C. of C. (pres. 1960), Am. Assn. Pvt. R.R. Car Owners (pres. 1982-83), Petroleum Club, Fort Worth Club, City Club, Exch. Club of Fort Worth (past pres.), La Cima Club, Oxford Club, Grand Coun. (Fort Worth chpt. Confrerie Saint Etienne), Masons (33 degree s.r.), Shriners (past imperial potentate), Kiwanis (past pres.), Elks, Petroleum Club, Tau Beta Pi. Fax: 817-237-0100. Office: PO Box 136397 Fort Worth TX 76136-0397

THORNTON, EDMUND B., philanthropist; b. Chgo., Mar. 9, 1930; s. George A. and Suzanne W. Thornton; children from previous marriage: Thomas, Jonathan, Susan, Amanda; m. Susan Feldhaus; 1 child, Taylor. BA, Yale U., 1954. With No. Trust Co., Chgo., 1957-59; asst. sec., asst. treas. Ottawa (Ill.) Silica Co., 1959-61, v.p. corp. devel., 1961-62, pres., CEO, 1962-75, chmn. bd., CEO, 1975-83, chmn. bd., 1983-86; dir., v.p. Ottawa Nat. Bank. Author various articles on historic preservation, history and military subjects. Del. Rep. Nat. Conv., 1964-84, precinct committeeman, 1978-92; chmn. LaSalle County Rep. Ctrl. Com., 1980-92, Ill. and Mich. Canal Nat. Heritage Commn., 1985—; pres. Ottawa Silica Co. Found., Edmund B. Thornton Found., Ottawa, 1986—. Recipient Conservation Svc. award U.S. Dept. Interior, 1973. Mem. Nat. Assn. Mfrs., U.S. C. of C., Nat. Indsl. Sand Assn. (dir. 1968-73), Ill. Mfrs.' Assn. (dir. 1969-75, chmn. 1975), Ill. State C. of C. (dir. 1972-78), Explorers Club, Chgo. Racquet Club, U. Chgo., Elks. Republican. Congregationalist. Home: PO Box 1 Ottawa IL 61350-0001 Office: PO Box 949 Ottawa IL 61350-0949

THORNTON, HAZEL MARJORIE, retired irrigation company administrator; b. Caterham, Surrey, Eng., Mar. 26, 1934; d. George Edward Percy and Miriam Alice (Davis) Gaston; m. Lawrence Albert Thornton, July 13, 1957 (dec. April 6, 1995); children: Helen Miriam, Mark Gaston. Diploma in French grade II, Inst. of Linguists, London, 1973; preliminary nursing cert., Queen Mary's Children's Hosp., Carshalton, Surrey, 1953. Clk. Brit. & Gen. Tube Co., Slough, Eng., 1955-59; sec. Langley (Eng.) Alloys Ltd., 1959-62; asst. to office mgr. T.P. Bennett and Son, London, 1962-64; sec. London Chamber Orch. Soc., 1968, Slough Coll. of Tech., 1971-76; dir., co-sec. Perrot Irrigation Ltd., Colchester, Eng., 1978-93; dir., sec. Irritec Ltd., Colchester, 1990-98; ret., 1998—. Contbr. articles to med. and profl. jours. Chmn. Consumers' Adv. Group Clin. Trials, 1994-99; mem. breast cancer rev. group, Cochrane, 1995—, cancer network, 1996—, breast cancer commissioning group NHS, 1996-97, adv. grp. to Current Control Trials Ltd.; mem. adv. coun. Nat. Cancer Alliance, 1997. Recipient Art award Surrey County Coun., 1951. Mem. Brit. Oncol. Assn., The Nottage Inst., Wivenhoe and Rowhedge Yacht Owners Assn., Trinity Coll.-Cambridge Music Soc. (life); friend Colchester Choral Soc., mem. com., 1977-93. Avocations: music, walking, reading, gardening, rowing. E-mail: hazelcagct@aol.com. FAX: 440 1206 728911. Home: Saionara 31 Regent St, Rowhedge Colchester C05 7EA, England

THORNTON, JOHN WILLIAM, SR., lawyer; b. Toledo, July 3, 1928; s. Cletus Bernard and Mary Victoria (Carey) T.; m. Mary Feeley, Mar. 10, 1951; children: John W. Jr., Jane Thornton Mastrucci, Deborah Thornton Hasty, Michael; m. Gabriela Marin, 1994. AB magna cum laude, U. Notre Dame, 1950, LLB summa cum laude, 1956, JD, 1969. Bar: Fla. 1956, U.S. Dist. Ct. (no., mid. and so. dists.) Fla. 1956, U.S. Ct. Appeals (5th cir.) 1956, U.S. Ct. Appeals (11th cir.) 1982. Assoc. area def. firm, Miami, Fla.; ptnr. Dixon, DeJarnette, et al, 1956-67, Stephens, Demos, Magill & Thornton, Miami, 1968-76; pvt. practice Thornton & Mastrucci, P.A. and predecessor firm, Miami, 1976—; chairperson legis. com. Fla. Med. Malpractice Claims Coun., Inc., 1984—, legis. and adminstrv. code rep. on hosp. risk mgrs. qualifications, rules and liability and nursing home rules and liability, 1986—; lectr. Fla. tort ins. law hosp. and physician series on risk mgmt. Am. Inst. Med. Law; lectr. South Fla. Hosp. Risk Mgmt. Soc.; legis. atty. Fla. Sch. Bd. Assn.; presenter legal, healthcare and ins. industry confs. Contbr. articles to profl. publs. Mem. Dade County Sch. Bd., 1967—. Lt. USN, 1950-53, Korea. Mem. ABA (vice chmn. torts and ins. practice sect., active various coms.), Internat. Assn. Def. Counsel (chmn. med. malpractice com. 1975-76, chmn. profl. errors and omissions com. 1987—), Def. Rsch. Inst. (chmn. practice and procedure com. 1976-77), Fedn. Ins. and Corp. Counsel (chmn. auto and casualty ins. sect. 1987—, chmn. legis. com. 1984-88, vice chmn. ethics com. 1990-94), Fla. Def. Lawyers Assn. (bd. dirs. 1976), Internat. Assn. Ins. counsel (chmn. med. malpractice 1972-74, com. 1975-99, def. counsel com. 1976-91, reins. excess and surplus lines com. 1980-99), Dade County Def. Bar Assn., Fed. Ins. Corp. Counsel (casualty ins. law com. 1972-99, med. malpractice com. 1974-99, excess surplus and reins. com. 1976-99, publs. com. 1976-87), Maritime Law Assn. U.S., Fla. Def. Lawyers Assn. (bd. dirs., chmn. legis. com. 1974-77), Internat. Law Soc., Broward County Bar Assn., Am. Judicature Soc., Am. Health Care Assn., Coral Gables Club, Ocean Reef Club, Riviera Country Club, Sapphire Valley Country Club. Roman Catholic. Office: Thornton & Mastrucci PA 4699 Ponce De Leon Blvd Coral Gables FL 33146-2101

THORNTON, LARRY LEE, psychotherapist, author, educator, minister; b. Lake, Miss., Nov. 9, 1937; s. Harvey L. and Onzell (Goodson) T.; children: Matt Alan, Leigh Ann, Pamela; m. Helen Louise Thornton. BA, Miss. Coll., 1959; MDiv, New Orleans Bapt. Theol. Sem., 1963, MA, 1964; MS, U. So. Miss., 1966, PhD, 1969; postgrad., Harvard U., 1985. Dir. admissions Miss. Coll., Clinton, 1961; sr. prof. psychology Delta State U., Cleveland, Miss., 1968-99; prof. psychology emeritus Delta State U., 1999—; founder, dir. Lic. Profl. Counseling, Assocs., Cleveland, 1988-98; pvt. practice Jackson, Miss., 1999—; adj. prof. psychology Miss. Coll., Clinton, 1999—, New Orleans Bapt. Theol. Sem., 2000—; chmn. Miss. Bd. Lic. Profl. Counselors, 1992-93. Author: Insights into Human Development, 1978. Charter mem. Internat. Devel. Coun., Bapt. Theol. Sem., Rûschlikon, Zurich, Switzerland, 1992. Recipient Panhellenic Outstanding Faculty award, 1996, S.E. Kossman Outstanding Tchr. award, 1991. Mem. APA, ACA. Avocations: golf, tennis, walking. E-mail: thorntonlh@aol.com. Home and Office: PO Box 11 42 Autumn Park Jackson MS 39206-5092

THORNTON, ROBERT KELSEY ROUGHT, English language educator; b. Huddersfield, Yorkshire, Eng., Aug. 12, 1938; s. Harold and Mildred Rought (Brooks) T.; m. Sarah Griffiths, Aug. 3, 1963 (div. 1975); children: Jason, Ben; m. Eileen Valerie Davison, Sept. 22, 1989; children: Amy, Tom. BA, U. Manchester, Eng., 1960, MA, 1961, PhD, 1971. Lectr. U. Newcastle, Eng., 1965-75, sr. lectr., 1975-84, prof., 1984-89; prof. U. Birmingham, 1989—, head sch. of english, 1989-97; pres. Friends of the Dymock Pets, 1999—. Author: G.M. Hopkins The Poems, 1975, The Decadent Dilemma, 1984; editor: The Midsummer Cushion, 1978, Ivor Gurney War Letters, 1985, Ivor Gurney Severn and Somme and War's Embers, 1987, Ivor Gurney Collected Letters, 1991, Ivor Gurney Best Poems and the Book of Five Makings, 1995, Ivor Gurney 80 Poems or So, 1997. Chmn. John Clare Soc., 1986-89. Avocation: painting. Home: The Old Vicarage, Tibberton near Droitwich Worcs WR9 7NP, England Office: U Birmingham Sch English, Edgbaston, Birmingham B15 2TT, England

THORNTON, STEVEN RUPERT, patent examiner; b. Rochester, England, Aug. 31, 1968; s. Francis William and Christina Lorraine (Fulcher) T.; m. Tanja Kuhn, Sept. 4, 1998. BS, U. Nottingham, England, 1989, DPhil, 1993; postgrad., U. Geneva, 1993-95, U. Exeter, England, 1995. Scientific editor Georg Thieme Verlag, Stuttgart, Germany, 1996-97, sr. scientific editor, 1998; patent examiner European Patent Office, The Hague, Netherlands, 1998—. Contbr. articles to profl. jours. Mem. Royal Soc. Chemistry. Avocations: reading, writing. Office: European Patent Office, The Hague Netherlands

THORNTON, YVONNE SHIRLEY, physician, author, musician; b. N.Y.C., Nov. 21, 1947; d. Donald E. and Itasker F. (Edmonds) T.; m. Shearwood McClelland, June 8, 1974; children: Shearwood III, Kimberly Itaska. BS in Biology, Monmouth Coll., 1969; MD, Columbia U., 1973, MPH, 1996. Resident in ob-gyn Roosevelt Hosp., N.Y.C., 1973-77; fellow maternal-fetal medicine Columbia-Presbyn. Med. Center, N.Y.C., 1977-79; commd. lt. comdr. M.C. USN, 1979; asst. prof. ob-gyn Uniformed Svcs. U. Health Scis., 1979-82; assoc. prof. Cornell U. Med. Coll., N.Y.C., 1989-92; dir. clin. svcs. dept. ob-gyn N.Y. Hosp.-Cornell Med. Center, 1982-88; asst. attending N.Y. Lying-In Hosp., 1982-89; assoc. clin. prof. ob-gyn Columbia P&S, 1995-98, clin. prof. ob-gyn., 2000—; clin. prof. ob-gyn. U. Medicine and Dentistry N.J., 1998-2000; dir. Chorionic Villus Sampling Program, 1984-92; dir. perinatal diagnostic testing ctr. Morristown Meml. Hosp., 1992-2000, divsn. maternal-fetal medicine St. Luke's Roosevelt Hosp. Ctr., 2000—; staff Nat. Naval Med. Center, Bethesda, Md.; saxophonist Thornton Sisters ensemble, 1955-76; vis. assoc. physician The Rockefeller U. Hosp., 1986-96; Diplomate Am. Bd. Ob-Gyn, examiner 1997—. Author: The Ditchdigger's Daughters, 1995, (named best books for young adults ALA, Excellence in Lit. award, N.J. Edn. Assn.) Primary Care for the Obstetrician and Gynecologist, 1997, Woman to Woman, 1997. Recipient Excellence in Literature award, N.J. Edn. Assn., 1996, winner Daniel Webster Oratorical Competition, Internat. Platform Assn., 1996. Fellow ACS, Am. Coll. Obstetricians and Gynecologists; mem. AMA, N.Y. Acad. Medicine, Am. Soc. Human Genetics, Assn. Women Surgeons, Soc. Maternal-Fetal Med., Am. Fedn. Musicians, Am. Coll. Physician Exec. Democrat. Baptist. Office: 1000 10th Ave New York NY 10019-1147

THORPE, IAN, Olympic athlete; b. Sydney, Australia, Oct. 13, 1982. Set new world record for 200 and 400 Pan Pacific Championships, 1999; recipient Gold medal 4 x 100-meter freestyle, 4 x 200-meter freestyle, 400-meter freestyle Sydney Olympics, 2000; anchor 4 x 100-meter freestyle relay team. Office: Australian Swimming Inc, PO Box 940, Dickson ACT 2602, Australia*

THORPE, JOHN ALDEN, association executive, mathematician; b. Lewiston, Maine, Feb. 29, 1936; s. Clyde Francis and Thelma (Littlefield) T.; m. Marilyn Alice Austin, June 7, 1959; children: Kendall Richard, Steven Russell. BS, MIT, 1958; MA, Columbia U., 1959, PhD, 1963. C.L.E. Moore instr. MIT, Cambridge, Mass., 1963-65; asst. prof. Haverford (Pa.) Coll., 1965-68; assoc. prof. SUNY, Stony Brook, 1968-77, prof., 1977-87; vice provost undergrad. edn., dean undergraduate coll. SUNY, Buffalo, 1987-93; provost Queens Coll./CUNY, 1993-98; exec. dir. Nat. Coun. Tchrs. of Math., Reston, Va., 1998—; mem. Inst. Advanced Study, Princeton, N.J., 1967-68; cons. Mobil R&D Corp., Princeton, 1967-70; cons. editor Saunders Coll. Pub., Phila., 1981-86; program dir. NSF, Washington, 1984-86, dep. div. dir. 1986-87. Author: Elementary Topics in Differential Geometry, 1979; (with others) Lecture Notes on Elementary Topology and Geometry, 1967, Linear Algebra, 1983, Elementary Linear Algebra, 1984; contbr. articles to profl. jours. Mem. Nat. Coun. Tchrs. of Math. (exec. dir. 1998—), Am. Math. Soc., Math. Assn. Am. (bd. govs. 1984-87, chair sci. policy com. 1988-92). Home: 11560 Southington Ln Herndon VA 20170-2445 Office: Nat Coun Tchrs Math 1906 Association Dr Reston VA 20191-1502

THORPE, SAMUEL STANLEY, JR., artist; b. Stoneham, Mass., July 15, 1933; m. Louise Harwood Gove; children: Michael, Scott, Craig, Heidi. Student, Sch. of Mus. of Fine Art, Boston. Represented in permanent collections at MBNA Am. Banks Corp. Collections, Aubuchon Hardware Corp., Nashua Fed. Savs. Bank, Indianhead Bank, Gardner Savs. Bank, Pepperell Bus. Assn., USA Distbg., Attys. Watnik & Watnik, PC, numerous pvt. collections including Ambassador and Mrs. Wylie T. Buchanan and Pres. and Mrs. George H.W. Bush. Mem. So. Vt. Art Assn., Chaffee Art Ctr. (Rutland, Vt.), Artists Guild of the Kennebunks, Leominster Art Assn., New Haven Paint and Palette Club, Salmagundi Club (N.Y.C.), Copley Soc. (Boston). Home: 30 Elm Cir Townsend MA 01469-1236

THORSELL, JAMES WESTVICK, ecologist; b. Wetaskiwin, Alta., Can., Dec. 5, 1940; s. Arnold E. and Irene (Westvick) T. BSc, U. Alta., Edmonton, Can., 1962; MA, U. Western Ont., London, Can., 1968; PhD, U. B.C., Vancouver, Can., 1971. Planner Parks Can., 1966-68; pvt. cons. Banff, Can., 1971-76; asst. prof. U. Alta., Edmonton, 1977-79; planner Kenya Wildlife Dept., 1979-81; sr. lectr. Coll. African Wildlife Mgmt., Tanzania, 1982-83; head natural heritage, sr. advisor Internat. Union for Conservation Nature & Natural Resources, Switzerland, 1984—; instr. Banff Ctr., 1971-75; v.p. Storm Mt. Lodge Ltd., 1975-79; cons. East-West Ctr., Hawaii, 1984; bd. mem. Seychelles Islands Found., 1992—; cons. in field. Author: Managing Protected Areas in Eastern Africa, 1984; editor: Conserving Asia's Natural Heritage, 1985; co-author: Protected Areas in the Tropics, 1987; contbr. articles to profl. jours. Fellow Royal Geog. Soc. Avocations: skiing, hunting, horses, photography, hiking. Home: Rue de la Raviere, 1269 Bassins Switzerland

THORSEN, NANCY DAIN, real estate broker; b. Edwardsville, Ill., June 23, 1944; d. Clifford Earl and Suzanne Eleanor (Kribs) Dain; m. David Massie, 1968 (div. 1975); 1 child, Suzanne Dain Massie; m. James Hugh Thorsen, May 30, 1980. BSc in Mktg., So. Ill. U., 1968, MSc in Bus. Edn., 1975; grad., Realtor Inst., Idaho, 1983. Cert. resdl. and investment specialist, fin. instr.; designated real estate instr. State of Idaho; accredited buyer rep. Personnel officer J.H. Little & Co. Ltd., London, 1969-72; instr. in bus. edn. Spl. Sch. Dist. St. Louis, 1974-77; mgr. mktg./ops. Isis Foods, Inc., St. Louis, 1978-80; asst. mgr. store Stix, Baer & Fuller, St. Louis, 1980; assoc. broker Century 21 Sayer Realty, Inc., Idaho Falls, Idaho, 1981-88, RE/MAX Homestead Realty, 1989—; spkr. RE/MAX Internat. Conv., 1990, 94, RE/MAX Stars Cruise, 1993, RE/MAX Pacific N.W. Conv., 1994, Century 21, Austral-Asia, 1995, women's seminar Clemson U., 1996, 98; real estate fin. instr. State of Idaho Real Estate Commn., 1994; founder Nancy Thorsen Seminars, 1995. Bd. dirs. Idaho Vol., Boise, 1981-84, Idaho Falls Symphony, 1982; pres. Friends of Idaho Falls Libr., 1981-83; chmn. Idaho Falls Mayor's Com. for Vol. Coordination, 1981-84; power leader Power Program, 1995; mem. Mtn. River Valley Red Cross, chair capital campaign, cmty. gifts chair ARC. Recipient Idaho Gov.'s award, 1982, cert. appreciation City of Idaho Falls/Mayor Campbell, 1982, 87, Civitan Disting. Pres. award, 1990, Bus. Women of the Yr. award C. of C., 1998; named to Two Million Dollar Club, 1987, 88, Four Million Dollar Club, 1989, 90, Top Investment Sales Person for Eastern Idaho, 1985, Realtor of Yr. Idaho Falls Bd. Realtors, 1990, Outstanding Realtors Active in Politics, Mem. of Yr. Idaho Assn. Realtors, 1991, Women of Yr. Am. Biog. Inst., 1991, Profiles of Top Prodrs. award Real Estate Edn. Assn., Above the Crowd award 1997; named Western Region Power Leader, Darryl Davis Seminars. Mem. Nat. Spkrs. Assn., Idaho Falls Bd. Realtors (chmn. Orientation 1982-83, chmn. edn. 1983, chmn. legis. com. 1989, 95—, chmn. program com. 1990, 91), Idaho Assn. Realtors (pres. Million Dollar Club 1988—, edn. com. 1990-93), Women's Coun. Realtors, Am. Bus. Women's Assn., So. Ill. U. Alumni Assn., Idaho Falls C. of C. (Bus. Woman of the Yr.-Professions, 1997), newcomers Club, Civitan (pres. Idaho Falls chpt. 1988-89, Civitan of Yr. 1986, 97, Outstanding Pres. award 1990, Hall of Fame 1998), Real Estate Educators Assn. E-mail: thorsen@srv.net. Office: RE/MAX Homestead Inc 1301 E 17th St Ste 1 Idaho Falls ID 83404-6273

THORSEN, RUNE ASBJØRN, researcher; b. Rødovre, Denmark, July 5, 1967; arrived in Eng., 1999; s. Finn Evan and Solveig Birthe Edel (Jacobsen) T. MSc in Elec. Engring., Tech. U. Denmark, 1994, PhD, 1997. Cert. in bioengring. With R&D ASAH-Medico A/S, Denmark, 1994-97; indsl. fellow Tech. U. Denmark, 1994-97; postdoctoral fellow Fondazione don Gnocchi Politechnico, Milan, 1997-98, U. Twente, The Netherlands, 1998-99; rschr. Univ. Coll. London, 1999—. Contbr. articles to profl. jours.; patent pending in field. Com. mem. Resident's Assn., Brøndby, Denmark, 1992-94. Avocations: cycling, music, clarinet, piano. Office: Salisbury Dist Hosp, Med Phys Biomed Eng, Salisbury SP2 8BJ, England

THORSON, STEVEN GREG, lawyer; b. Van Nuys, Calif., Feb. 7, 1948; s. Robert G. and Ruth C. T.; m. Patricia Lynn LaPointe, Aug. 3, 1974; 1 child, Kai Johannes. BA, St. Olaf Coll., 1977; JD, Hamline U., 1980. Bar: Minn. 1980, U.S. Dist. Ct. Minn. 1980, U.S. Tax Ct. 1980, U.S. Ct. Appeals (8th cir.) 1980. Pres. Thorson & Berg, Maple Grove, Minn., 1990-99; with Barna, Guzy & Steffen, Ltd. Attys. at Law, Mpls., 1999—; lectr. continuing legal edn., 1986—; apptd. to Minn. State Bar Assn. Commn. on Unauthorized Practice of Law, 1990-92; atty. for Columbus Twp. (Anoka County), 1981-96; mem. residential real estate com. Minn. State Bar Assn., 1992—. Mem. ch. coun. Peace Luth. Ch. Named One of Minn. Top Lawyers, Mpls/St. Paul mag., 1998, 2000. Mem. ABA, Minn. State Bar Assn., Hennepin County Bar Assn. (chmn. purchase agreement com. 1986-88), Anoka County Bar Assn. (pres. real estate sect. 1988). Avocations: alpine and nordic skiing. Home: 12071 Norway St NW Minneapolis MN 55448-2243 Office: 400 Northtown Fin Plz 200 Coon Rapids Blvd NW Ste 400 Minneapolis MN 55433-5894

THORSTEINSSON, ADALBJÖRN, anesthesiologist; b. Holmavik, Iceland, Aug. 29, 1951; s. Thorsteinn Gudbjörnsson and Adalheidur Johanna Björnsdottir; m. Ingibjörg Sigtryggsdottir, Apr. 15, 1951; children: Sigtryggur, Stefan Ingi, Adalbjörg. MD, U. Iceland, Reykjavik, 1977. Speciality certification anesthesiology, Iceland and Sweden. Intern Akureyri Hosp., Iceland, 1977-78; gen. practice The Dist. of Holmavik, Iceland, 1978-80; resident in anesthesiology U. Hosp., Reykjvik, 1980-84, Lund, Sweden, 1984-86; attending anesthesiologist dept. anesthesia & intensive care U. Hosp., Lund, 1986-90, Landspitalinn U. Hosp., Reykjavik, 1990—. Contbr. articles to profl. jours. Mem. Scandinavian Soc. Anesthesiologists (bd. dirs. 1997—), Icelandic Soc. Anesthesiologists (chmn. 1996—), Icelandic Med. Assn., Swedish Med. Assn., N.Y. Acad. Sci. Home: Skipholt 60, 105 Reykjavik Iceland Office: Anesthesia/Intensive Care, Landspitalinn, 105 Reykjavik Iceland

THORSTEINSSON, LEIFUR, immunologist, researcher; b. Reykjavik, Iceland, Apr. 29, 1949; s. Thorsteinn Ketilsson and Gudrun Sveinsdottir; m. Sigridur Solveig Fridgeirsdottir, Dec. 28, 1975; children: Steinunn, Eymundur. BSc, U. Iceland, Reykjavik, 1973, BSc with honors, 1975; PhD, U. Oslo, 1981. Rsch. fellow Inst. Immunology and Rheumatology U. Hosp., Oslo, 1975-81; sr. rsch. fellow dept. med. genetics Univ. Hosp./The Blood Bank, Reykjavik, 1982—; immunologist U. Hosp. Reykjavik, 1994; hon. rsch. fellow dept. immunology Univ. Hosp. Liverpool, England, 1994.

Contbr. articles to profl. jours. Avocations: mountain hiking, swimming, cross country skiing, photography. Home: Raudalaek 38, IS-105 Reykjavik Iceland Office: U Hosp/The Blood Bank, DeCode Genetics, Lynghals 1, 110 Reykjavik Iceland

THORSTENSEN, KETIL, scientist; b. Narvik, Norway, May 20, 1957; s. Torbjørn Kåre and Inger (Wist) T.; m. Eli Ryeng, June 26, 1980; 1 child, Ingrid. MSc, Trondheim Tech. U., Norway, 1981; PhD, U. Trondheim, 1988. Cert. biochem. engr. Postdoctoral fellow Albert Einstein Coll. Medicine, N.Y.C., 1988-89, 94; scientist U. Trondheim Univ. Hosp., 1989-92; postdoctoral fellow Norwegian Rsch. Found., Trondheim, 1993-95; scientist Univ. Hosp., Trondheim, 1995-96, sr. scientist, 1996-97, sr. scientist, head R&D, 1998—. Bd. dirs. Malvik Wind Band, 1996-97, v.p., 1997—. Pvt. Norwegian Army, 1976-77. Office: Trondheim U Hosp, Dept Clin Chemistry, N-7006 Trondheim Norway

THOTTUPURAM, KURIAN CHERIAN, priest, college director, educator; b. Cherianad, Kerala, India; came to U.S., 1971; s. Cherian Koruth and Eliamma (Kandanavila) T.; m. Susan Grace Kompady, Dec. 29, 1969; children: Cherian, Kurian Jr., Theodore-George. BA, St. Joseph's Coll., India, 1964; grad. diploma in theology, Sem. of Lateran U., 1966; MA, Karnatak U., 1970, Mundelein Coll., Chgo., 1973; MEd, Loyola U., Chgo., 1979, PhD, 1981; DD, Notre Dame de Lafayette U., 1993. Ordained subdeacon, 1967, deacon, 1970, priest, 1970, chorbishop, 1986. Tchr. Mt. Tabor Monastery Coll., Pathanapuram, India, 1966-70; founder Malankarese Orthodox Syrian Ch., Chgo., 1971—; pastor St. John's Syrian Orthodox Ch., 1971-72; founder, pastor St. Thomas Orthodox Ch., 1972-80, St. Mary's Orthodox Ch., 1982—; counseling psychologist Incentives Inst., Des Plaines, Ill., 1974-76; dir. social svc. Millardogden Ctr., Chgo., 1976-77; ednl. adminstr. ednl. program Chgo. Housing Authority, 1977-81; ecumenical officer Malankarese Orthodox Diocese, Chgo., 1981-85; dir. program planning and devel. Malcolm X Coll., Chgo. City Coll. System, 1985-91; english faculty Truman Coll., 1991-92; exec. dir. International Edn. Cons. and Evaluators of Ill., 1992; dir. curriculum/instrn. S.E.A. Ctr., 1993-94; mem. philosophy faculty Daley Coll., 1993-95, Triton Coll., 1995—; pioneer Malankarese Orthodox Chs., 1971-81; adj. prof. philosophy Coll. of Lake County, 1995-96; pres. Am. Acad. Comparative-Internat. Edn., Chgo., 1993—; mem. Sch. Bd. Coun., 1991-93. Author: Dhyanamitram, 1966, Kalari, 1967, Perumpepadam, 1968, Foundations of Kerala Education, 1981, Bible Reading Guide of the Malankara Orthodox Church, Education and Social Change, 1987, The Mystery of Man, 1971, Personality of a Child: A Constant Process of Dualistic Eruption into Monism, 1972, Incarnation: A Theologico-mystical Study, 1981, Holy Spirit: The Life Giver, 1981, An Orthodox Introduction to Sacraments, 1983, The Book of Common Prayer of the Syrian Orthodox Ch., 1985, Book of Ordinations of the Syrian Orthodox Ch., 1987, Marriage After the Holy Priesthood, 1985, Contraception and Orthodox Theology, 1990, The Orthodox Christian Priesthood: An Anthology of Patristic Writings, 1995, Pre-British European Educational Activities in India, 1989; chief editor: Voice of Orthodoxy, 1986. Chmn. social action Diocese of Niraram, India, 1967-71; mem. Zonal coun. Diocese of Am., 1975-78, Diocesan Coun.; bd. regents Lafayette U., Aurora, Colo., 1989-95; exec. mem. Alleppey DT Kerala Congress, India, 1967-71; pres. Ecumenical Coun. Kerala Chs. Chgo., 1983-97; founder Voice of Orthodox Found., Chgo., 1995. Recipient Taylor award for High Achievement, Greek Orthodox Archdiocese, Schmitt Found. award, 1977, Pub. Svc. award Citizens Cultural Found., 1985. Mem. Am. Ednl. Studies Assn., Midwest History of Edn. Soc., Am. Assn. Biofeedback Clinicians, Internat. Assn. of Mission Studies, Germany. Mem. Eastern Orthodox Ch. Avocations: music, philanthropic work.

THRAENHARDT, DIETRICH JOACHIM, political science educator; b. Breslau, Silesia, Germany, May 31, 1941; s. Günther and Siegtraud Martha (Weigelt) T.; m. Anna M. Hesse, Aug. 18, 1944; children: Angela D., Bettina R., Fumiko S. Dr. Rer. Soc., U. Konstanz, Germany, 1971; Habilitation, U. Münster, Germany, 1975. Dean U. Münster, 1987-90. Author: Parteien und Wahlen in Bayern, 1973, Geschte der BRD, 1986, Einwanderung und Einbürgerung in Deutschland: Jahrbuch Migration, 1998, Internat. Migration and Liberal Democracies, 1999. Mem. Deutsche Vereinigungför Politische Wissenschaft. Office: U Münster, Platz der Weissen Rose, Münster 4400, Germany

THRANE, HENRIK CARL ALBERT, education educator; b. Hellerup, Denmark, Aug. 6, 1934; s. Albert and Gerda (Abildgaard) T.; m. Elisabeth Zwahlen Thrane; children: Lars Henrik, Karin, Niels Christian, Claudia. MA, U. Copenhagen, 1960; DrPhil, U. Aarhus, 1975. Rsch. scholar U. Copenhagen, 1962-64; asst. keeper National Mus., 1965-71; curator Prehistoric Funen, Odense, 1972-96; prof. prehistoric archaeology U. Aarhus, 1996—; vice chmn. State Rsch. Coun. Humanities, 1991-94; mem. Comite Executif, UISPP, 1991—; Kevorkian lectr. in Iranian archaeology, 1968; field dir. Danish Archaeol. Expdn. to Iran, 1964; bd. dirs. Nordic Inst. Asian Studies, 1994-97; coun. Discovery Programme, Dublin, 1999; regents lectr. U. Calif., Berkeley, 1999. Author: Europaeiske Forbindelser, 1975, Lusehoi ved Voldtofte, 1984, Guld, Guder & Godtfolk, 1993, Steppens Nomader-Skovens Bønder, 1994; contbr. articles to internat. jours.; exhbns. include Golden Age, 1988, Archaeology of Ukraine, 1994. Recipient Gold Medal Copenhagen U., 1957, Westerby prize, Westerby Fund, 1992. Mem. German Archaeol. Inst. (corr.), Royal Soc. Letters (Lund, Sweden). Avocations: gardening, research. Home: 54 Lupinvej, DK5210 Odense Denmark Office: Dept Prehist Archaeology, Moesgard, DK8270 Højbjerg Denmark

THRANERT, OLIVER, political scientist; b. Braunschweig, Saxony, Germany, Jan. 11, 1959; s. Adolf and Irmtraud (Kyrath) T. PhD, U. Braunschweig, Germany, 1986. Sr. rschr. Friedrich Ebert Found., Bonn, 1986—; guest prof. U. Darmstadt, 1990-93, Free U. Berlin, 2000—; vis. rschr. Queens U. Kingston, Ont., 1991. Editor: (book) Enhancing the Biological Weapons Convention, 1996; contbr. articles to profl. jours. Mem. German Soc. Fgn. Policy. Mem. Social Democrat Party of Germany. Avocations: playing drums, jazz, motorcycling. Office: Friedrich Ebert Found, Hiroshima St 17, 10785 Berlin Germany

THRASHER, ROSE MARIE, critical care and community health nurse; b. Urbana, Ohio, Jan. 19, 1948; d. Jesse and Anna Frances (Clark) T. Student, Mercy Med. Ctr. Sch. Med. Tech, 1966-67, Wittenberg U., 1969-70; BSN, Ohio State U., 1974, BA in Anthropology, 1994, BA in History of Art, 1997, postgrad., 1997—. RN, Ohio; cert. cmty. health nurse ANA; cert. provider BCLS and ACLS, Am. Heart Assn., CCRN, AACN; cert. asthma mgmt. edn. Am. Lung Assn. Ohio. Pub. health nurse Columbus (Ohio) Health Dept., 1977-78; critical care nurse VA Med. Ctr., San Francisco, 1981, Staff Builders Health Care Svc., Oakland, Calif., 1975-76, 81-85; supr., case mgr. home health nurse passport program and intermittent care program Interim Health Care (formerly Med. Pers. Pool), Columbus, 1976-77, 85—, chart reviewer, 1996-98; IRP nurse Ohio State U. Hosps. East, Columbus, 1999—; ind. home health nurse, provider med. svcs. State of Ohio Dept. Human Svcs., 1999—; chart reviewer Interim Health Care Support Svcs., Columbus, 1997. Acad. scholar Wittenberg U., Ohio State U. Mem. AACN, ANA (coun. cmty. health nursing), AAUW, AAAS, Internat. Union Anthropl. and Ethnol. Scis., N.Y. Acad. Scis., Ohio Nurses Assn., Intravenous Nurses Soc., Ohio State U. Alumni Assn., Am. Anthropol. Assn., Midwest Art History Soc., Coll. Art Assn., Nat. Mus. Women in Arts, Nat. Women's Hall of Fame, Ohio Acad. Sci., Ohio State U. Coll. of Nursing Alumni Soc.

THRIFT, ASHLEY ORMAND, lawyer; b. Charlotte, N.C., Aug. 29, 1946; s. William Johnson Thrift Sr. and Katherine Roberta Ormand; m. Julianne Fickling Still, Aug. 3, 1974; children: Lindsay Still Thrift, Laura Still Thrift. AB in History, U. N.C., 1968; JD, U. S.C., 1972. Acting dean campus rels. U. S.C., Columbia, 1971-72, asst. dean Law Sch., 1972-74, assoc. counsel, 1974-75; legis. counsel Rep. James R. Mann U.S. Ho. of Reps., Washington, 1976-77, assoc. counsel subcom. on criminal justice judiciary com., 1977; legis. dir., counsel Senator Ernest F. Hollings U.S. Senate, Washington, 1977-84, chief of staff, counsel Senator Ernest F. Hollings, 1984-92; of counsel Womble Carlyle Sandridge & Rice PLLC, Winston-Salem, N.C., 1992-94; ptnr. Womble Carlyle Sandridge & Rice PLLC, Winston-Salem, 1994—. Bd. visitors Winston-Salem State U., 1995—; chair bd. dirs. N.C. Partnership for Children, Raleigh, N.C., 1995—; vice-chair bd. trustees U. N.C. Ctr. for Pub. TV, Research Triangle Park, N.C., 1995-00, chair, 2000—; bd. dirs. Assn. Ams. Pub. TV Stas., 2000—; chair govt. affairs com. Lex Mundi, 1999—. With USAR, 1968-74. Mem. Soc. Internat. Bus. Fellows. Democrat. Presbyterian. E-mail: athrift@wcsr.com. Home: 723 S Main St Winston Salem NC 27101-5330 Office: Womble Carlyle Sandridge & Rice PLLC 200 W 2nd St Ste 1600 Winston Salem NC 27101-4048

THRIFT, NIGEL JOHN, geographer, educator; b. Bath, Eng., Oct. 12, 1949; s. Leonard John and Joyce Mary (Wakeley) T.; m. Lynda Jean Sharples, May 1979; children: Victoria Caroline, Jessica Abigail. BA with honors, U. Wales, 1971; PhD, U. Bristol, 1979, DSc, 1992. Rsch. officer U. Cambridge, Eng., 1976-78; rsch. fellow U. Leeds, Eng., 1978-79; sr. rsch. fellow Australian Nat. U., Canberra, 1980-84; reader U. Wales, Lampeter, 1984-87; reader dept. geography U. Bristol, 1987-90, prof. dept. geography, 1990—, head dept. geography, 1994-99, chair rsch. assessment panel, 1997—. Author: Times, Spaces and Places, 1980, The Price of War, 1986, Spatial Formation, 1996, Money/Space, 1997, Shopping, Place and Identity, 1998, Cities, 2000; mem. editl. bd. Soc. and Space, 1983—, Time and Soc., 1989—; co-editor, mng. editor: Environment and Planning, 1979—. Fellow Royal Geog. Soc.; mem. Acad. Learned Socs. for the Social Scis. (academician). Office: Univ Bristol, University Rd, Bristol BS8 1SS, England

THRING, MEREDITH WOOLDRIDGE, chemical engineer, educator; b. Melbourne, Victoria, Australia, Dec. 17, 1915; arrived in Eng., 1919; s. Walter Hugh and Dorothy (Wooldridge) T.; m. Alice Margaret Hooley, Dec. 14, 1940; children: Susan Margaret Thring Kalaugher, John Meredith, Robert Hugh. BA, Cambridge U., 1937, MA, 1941, ScD, 1964; Dr. (hon.), Open U., 1982. Head combustion lab. Brit. Coal Utilisation Rsch. Assn., London, 1937-46; head dept. physics Brit. Iron and Steel Rsch. Assn., London, 1946-53; prof., head fuel tech. and chem. engring. dept. Sheffield U., 1953-64; prof., head dept. mech. engring. Queen Mary Coll., London U., 1964-81, prof. emeritus, 1981—; gen. supt. Internat. Flame Rsch. Found., Ijmuiden, Holland, 1949-76; mng. dir. Thring Advanced Devels. Ltd., Eng., 1966-86; convenor African Adv. Group, 1998—. Author: The Science of Flames and Furnaces, 1952, 62, Man, Machines and Tomorrow, 1972, How To Invent, 1977, The Engineer's Conscience, 1980, Robots and Telechirs, 1983, Quotations from G.I. Gurdjieff's Teaching, 1998. Recipient Robert Hadfield medal Iron and Steel Inst., 1949. Fellow Royal Acad. Engring. (founder fellow), Inst. Energy (sr. fellow, pres. 1962-63), Inst. Physics, Instn. Elec. Engrs., Inst. Chem. Engrs., Athenaeum (London). Mem. Ch. of England. Avocations: forestry, wood carving. Home and Office: Bell Farm Brundish, Suffolk 1P13 8BL, England

THRUSH, BRIAN ARTHUR, physical chemist, educator; b. Hendon, Middlesex, Eng., July 23, 1928; s. Arthur Albert and Dorothy (Money) T.; m. Rosemary Catherine Terry, May 31, 1958; children: Basil, Felicity. BA, U. Cambridge, Eng., 1949, MA, 1953, PhD, 1953, ScD, 1965. Univ. demonstrator U. Cambridge, 1953-58, asst. dir. rsch., 1959-64, lectr. in phys. chemistry, 1964-69, reader in phys. chemistry, 1969-78, prof. in phys. chemistry, 1978-95; fellow Emmanuel Coll., Cambridge, 1960—; vis. prof. Chinese Acad. Scis., 1980—; mem. U.K. Natural Environ. Rsch. Coun., 1985-90; mem. Lawes Agrl. Trust Com., 1979-89. Contbr. over 200 articles to sci. jours. Pres. chemistry sect. Brit. Assn. for Advancement of Sci., 1986-87. Recipient Tilden Lectureship medal Chem. Soc., 1965, Rank Prize for Optoelectronics, Rank Found., 1991. Fellow Royal Soc., Royal Soc. Chemistry (Michael Polanyi medal 1980), Academia Europaea. Home: Brook Cottage Pemberton Ter, Cambridge CB2 1JA, England Office: Emmanuel Coll, Cambridge CB2 3EP, England

THUBRON, COLIN GERALD DRYDEN, author; b. London, June 14, 1939; s. Gerald Ernest and Evelyn Kate Mary (Dryden) T. Grad., Eton Coll., 1957. Apprentice, editorial asst. Hutchinson & Co., London, 1959-62; freelance film maker, Morocco, Turkey, Japan, 1963-64; prodn. editor Macmillan Co., N.Y.C., 1964-65; freelance writer, London, 1965—. Author: Mirror to Damascus, 1967, Jerusalem, 1969, Journey into Cyprus, 1975, Emperor, 1978, Among the Russians, 1983, A Cruel Madness, 1984 (Silver Pen award 1985), Behind the Wall, 1987 (Thomas Cook award 1988, Hawthornden prize 1988), Falling, 1989, Turning Back the Sun, 1991, The Lost Heart of Asia, 1994, Distance, 1996, In Siberia, 1999, others. Fellow Royal Soc. Lit. Home: 27 St Ann's Villas, London W11 4RT, England

THUE, ANNIKEN, museum director, art historian; b. Baerum, Akershaus, Norway, Jan. 11, 1944; d. Oskar Niels and Agnes Marie (Blom) T.; m. Hans-Jakob Brun. MA in Art History, U. Oslo, 1974. Curator Old Bergen (Norway) Mus., 1975-79; sr. curator hist. mus. U. Bergen, 1980-85; sr. curator West Norwegian Mus. Applied Art, Bergen, 1985-87; dir. Oslo Mus. Applied Art, 1987—. Author: Frida Hansen: En Europeer i Norsk Tekstilkunst omkring 1900, 1986; contbr. numerous articles to books and periodicals. Bd. dirs. Norwegian Cou. for Rsch. in Humanities, 1984-88, Internat. Mus. FEstival Bergen, 1978-88, Internat. Coun. Mus. Applied Art Com., 1989—, v.p., 1999—; mem. culture com. Lillehammer (Norway) Olympic Com. and several undercoms., 1989-94. Decorated chevalier Ordre des Artes et des Lettres. Mem. Internat. Coun. Mus., Internat. Assn. Art Critics, Norwegian Assn. Mus. (chmn. 1998-99), Oslo Rotary. Office: Oslo Mus Applied Arts, St Olavsgate 1, 0165 Oslo Norway

THUEME, WILLIAM HAROLD, educator; b. St. Clair, Mich., Sept. 4, 1945; s. Harold Arthur and Delphine Betty (Buhl) T.; divorced; children: Benjamin William, Rebecca Kathleen, Jeffrey William, Sarah Kathleen. Student, Port Huron Jr. Coll., 1963-64; BA, Mich. State U., 1967, MA, 1969; PhD in Counseling, Universal Life Ch., 1997; postgrad., Oakland U., 1971, U. Mich., 1970-77, San Francisco State U., 1975, U. Hawaii, 1975; student, Aquinais Coll., 1968. Cert. tchr., Mich. Tchr. pub. schs., Charlotte, Mich., 1967-69, Ann Arbor, Mich., 1969—; fgn. travel coord.-Ambs. Abroad Program, Amsterdam, The Netherlands, 1968—; regional driver coord. for Southeastern Mich. Avis Rent-a-Car, 1983—. Author: (poetry) The Ideal Teacher Should Posess, 1987. Active UN Children's Found., Mich. Sheriffs Ednl. Found., Woods Rd. Assn., Normal Pk. Neighborhood Assn., U.S. Legal Found., Found. for Nicaraguan Democracy, Nat. Coun. Better Edn., participant Skyhook II Project; elections coord. Eaton County (Mich.) Rep. Party, 1968, mem. nat. com., 1968—, mem. nat. senatorial com.; mem. troop com. Coun. Boy Scouts Am., Ypsilanti, counselor for reading, 1988-89; cub scout summer camp instr. Wolverne Coun., 1987, merit badge counselor, 1988-89; coach of the angels Ypsilanti Am. Little League, 1988; parent adv. bd. The Childrens Devel. Lab. Ea. Mich. U., 1988-89; active Mich. United Conservation Clubs, Big Bros. Am., Charlotte, Mich., Human Rights Watch, Nat. Security Caucus U.S., 1988—, Heritage Found., 1988—, ofcl. sponsor Mandate for Leadership III, Policy Strategies for 1990's Project, Project Save Our Schs., 1988—, Citizens United for Better Edn., World Awareness, Inc., Group 61 Amnesty Internat., Legal Affairs Coun., Coun. for Inter-Am. Security, Nicaraguan Resistance Edn. Found., Nat. Right to Work Legal Def. Found., Citizens Against Govt. Waste, Citizens Commn. for Ethics in Govt., Citizens for Decency Through Law, Inc., Participating Parents for Progress in Ypsilanti Pub. Schs.; parents adv. bd. Chapelle Elem. Sch., Ypsilanti, 1989-90, West Mid. Sch., Ypsilanti, 1991-92, Ypsilanti Pub. Schs., 1990—, Ypsilanti H.S.; charter sponsor Victory over Communism Project; nominated charter mem. Presdl. Task Force; participant The Imperial Congress: Crisis in the Separation of Powers Project, line-item veto project The Heritage Found., 1989, campaign to revise medicare catastrophic coverage law project Nat. Assn. Uniformed Svcs., 1989, repeal of catastrophic coverage act program Conservative Caucus Inc., 1989, Srs. Coal. Against the Tax, 1989; nat. adv. coun. Citizens Com. for Right to Bear Arms; jr. and sr. choir, Sunday sch. tchr. St. Paul's Luth. Ch., 1959-64 (Perfect Attendance award 8 yrs.), Marine city, Mich., 1960-63; youth Sunday sch. tchr., dir. youth min. coun. Lawrence Ave. Meth. Ch., Charlotte, Mich., 1967-69, life ELCA Evang. Luth. Ch. in Am., Treas. St. Paul's Luther League, 1960. Recipient Spl. Recognition award Richard Nixon, 1968-79, Gerald Ford, 1974-76, Ronald Reagan, 1971-88, George Bush, 1989—, Spl. Recognition award Reagan Presdl. Campaign, 1981, Bush Presdl. Campaign, 1988, Citizen of Yr. award Citizens Com. for Right to Bear Arms, 1988, cert. recognition U.S. Justice Found., 1991, Hale Found., Am. Security Coun. 30th Anniversary Spl. Recognition cert., cert. appreciation award 2d Amendment Found., 1988, Appreciation of Devoted and Valuable Svc. award Chapelle Elem. Sch., 1988-89, Merit Badge, Wolverine Coun.; named One of Most Outstanding People of 20th Century, IBC, Cambridge, Eng., 1997, Internat. Man of Yr., IBC, 1998. Mem. NEA, NRA (life, endowment), The Lincoln Inst. for Rsch. Edn., United Conservatives of Am. (participant citizens against the catastrophic health act tax 1989), Mich. Edn. Assn., Internat. Reading Assn., Mich. Sheriffs Assn. (assoc.), Police Marksmanship Assn., Washtenaw Reading Coun., Southeastern Mich. Reading Assn., Mich. Reading Assn., Mich. Assn. for Supervision and Curriculum Devel., Ann Arbor Edn. Assn., Am. Security Coun., Am. Def. Inst., Found. for Christian Living, Am. Family Assn., Nat. Geog. Soc., Am. Film Inst., Internat. Freelance Photographers Orgn. (life), Taxpayers Edn. Lobby, Gun Owners Am., Nat. Assn. Federally Lic. Firearms Dealers, Conservative Caucus, Inc., Ams. for Freedom, Tri-County Sportsman League, Mich. State U. Alumni Assn. (Blue Water chpt.), Mich. State U. Coll. Comm. Arts Alumni Assn., Mich. State U. Coll. Social Sci. Alumni Assn., Ft. Gratiot, Lions Club (v.p. 1998—), Lions Club Internat., Sigma Alpha Eta, Washtenaw Sportsmen's Club (Ypsilanti), Optimists (v.p., bd. dirs. 1975-78) (Ann Arbor), Port Huron Noon Optimist Club. Lutheran. Office: St Pauls Luth Ch 5330 Palms Rd Casco MI 48064-3906

THUEMMEL, HANS GEORG, theologian, educator; b. Goerlitz, Germany, Mar. 5, 1932; s. Johannes and Hertha (Scholz) T.; m. Mechthild Lorenz, Aug. 23, 1957; children: Ottfried, Egbert, Anselm, Adelheid. D in Theology, U. Greifswald, 1959; PhD, U. Marburg, 1992. From asst. to prof. U. Greifswald, Germany, 1956-97, prof. emeritus, 1997—. Author: Die Kirche des Ostens im 3. und 4. Jahrhundert, 1988, Bilderlehre and Bilderstreit, 1991, Die Fruehgeschichte der ostkirchlichen Bilderlehre, 1992, Die Memorien für Petrus und Paulus in Rom, 1999. Avocation: painting. Home: Robert Blum Str 11, D-17489 Greifswald Germany

THUESEN, ELISABETH, law educator; b. Esbjerg, Denmark, 1936; d. Alfred and Inger Thuesen. LLM, U. Copenhagen, Denmark, 1967; cert. in politics, Inst. D'Etudes Politiques, Bordeaux, France, 1968; docteur en droit, U. Bordeaux, 1972. Rsch. fellow Copenhagen Bus. Sch., 1968-72, assoc. prof., 1973-88, sr. assoc. prof., 1988—; jurist, linguist EC Coun. of Ministers, Belgium, 1972. Office: Copenhagen Bus Sch Law Dept, Julius Thomsens Plads 10, 1925 Frederiksberg Denmark

THULESIUS, KNUT OLAV, physiologist, researcher; b. Braunschweig, Germany, July 9, 1930; s. Daniel and Marta (Ringstrom) T.; m. Layla Al-Ugaily, Dec. 10, 1982; children: Hans, Kristian, Magnus, Marie. MD, U. Gothenburg, Sweden, 1959, PhD, 1962. Physician U. Hosp., Gothenburg, 1959-62; assoc. prof. Ind. U. Med. Sch., 1963-64; physician U. Hosp., Gothenburg, 1964-65; chief clin. physiology Ctrl. Hosp., Vaxjo, Sweden, 1966-77; prof. clin. physiology, chmn. U. Hosp., Trondheim, Norway, 1978-79; prof., chmn. dept. pharmacology faculty medicine Kuwait U., 1980-90, 90-95; vice-dean rsch., 1987-90, 95-96; prof., chmn. dept. pharmacology faculty medicine Kuwait U., 1996-98; clin. physiology U. Hosp., Linkoping, Sweden, 1990-95. Contbr. over 200 articles to profl. jours.; patentee in method for preventing thrombosis. Chmn. Med. Student Assn., Gothenburg, 1957, Clin. Physiology Assn. Sweden, 1973, Red Cross, Vaxjo, 1971-77. Recipient prize Swiss Angiological Soc., 1972, Faltin medal Finnish Med. Soc., 1973, Gold medal Med. Film, 1974. Mem. Brit. Pharmacological Soc., Am. Soc. Exptl. Pharmacology and Therapeutics, Swedish Med. Soc. Avocations: painting, writing. Home: Kaptensgatan 17C, S-58212 Linkoping Sweden Office: Faculty Medicine, PO Box 24923, 13110 Safat Kuwait

THULIN, INGRID, actress, director, writer; b. Solleftea, Sweden, Jan. 27, 1926; d. Adam and Nana T.; m. Harry Schein, Sept. 15, 1956. Grad., Royal Dramatic Theatre Sch., Stockholm, 1951. Actress in numerous modern and classical plays Royal Dramatic Theatre, Stockholm, mcpl. theatres Malmo and Stockholm until 1962; actress Broadway, Italian stage, U.S. TV; films include: When Love Comes to the Village, 1950; Wild Strawberries, 1957; So Close to Life, 1958 (Best Actress, Cannes Internat. Film Festival); The Face, 1958; The Judge, 1960; The Four Horsemen of the Apocalypse, 1961; Winter Light, 1962; The Silence, 1963; La Guerre est Finie, 1968; The Damned, 1970; Cries and Whispers, 1973; A Handful of Love, 1974; La Cage, 1975; Cassandra Crossing, 1976; Agnes Will Die, 1977; One and One, 1978; Broken Skies, 1982; The Rehearsal, 1983; Il Corsario, La Casa del Sorriso, 1991; writer, dir. Swedish feature film Broken Skyes, 1983; dir. (short film) Devotion, Autobiography Somebody I Knew, 1992. Recipient numerous awards for acting excellence in theatre and films; named Best New Dir., Chgo. Film Festival, 1983. Address: Kevingestrand 7B, 18231 Danderyd Sweden

THULIN, JAN EINAR, biologist; b. Uddevalla, Sweden, May 13, 1944; s. Einar and Greta (Norman) T.; m. A. Margareta Malmqvist, May 4, 1974; children: S. Katarina, J. Magnus. BS, Goteborg U., 1971, PhD, 1981; DSc, Uppsala U., 1987. Asst. lectr. dept. zoology Goteborg (Sweden) U., 1973-80; sr. rsch. scientist Swedish EPA, Oregrund, 1980-88, 89-91; sr. rsch. scientist inst. marine rsch. Nat. Bd. Fisheries, Lysekil, Sweden, 1991-94, dir., 1994-2000; prof. Goteborg U., 1993; coord. global environ. facility/Baltic sea regional project Internat. Coun. for Exploration of the Sea, Copenhagen, Denmark, 2000—; vis. prof. dept. zoology U. Auckland, New Zealand, 1988-89; gen. sec. European Fedn. Parasitologists, 1984-92; del. for Sweden Internat. Coun. for Exploration of the Sea, 1994-2000. Author: (with others) Fish Diseases in Coastal Waters of Sweden, 1989; contbr. articles to profl. jours. Fellow U. Auckland Found., 1988-89. Mem. Scandinavian Soc. Parasitology (v.p., bd. dirs. 1984-92), British Soc. Parasitology, Bulgarian Soc. Parasitology (hon.), Rotary (sec. 1994-95), Odd Fellows. Avocations: fishing, hunting, stamps, old books. Office: Intl Coun Exploration Sea, Palaegade 2-4, DK-1261 Copenhagen Denmark

THULIN, LARS INGEMAR, cardiac surgeon, researcher; b. Helsingborg, Sweden, July 4, 1956; m. Christina Anna Birde, Mar. 28, 1988; children: Michelle, Nadine, André. MD, Lund (Sweden) U., 1981, PhD, 1988. Sr. cons. in cardiac surgery Univ. Hosp of Lund, 1994—. Capt. Naval Res. Corps, 1992-97. Mem. European Club of Young Cardiac Surgeons (gen. sec. 1988—). Home: Korsbargatan 7, SE 21228 Malmoe Sweden Office: Dept Cardiovascular Surgery, Univ Hosp of Lund, SE 22185 Lund Sweden

THULLNER, MARTIN CHRISTIAN, physicist; b. Sibiu, Romania, May 25, 1971; arrived in Switzerland, 1997; m. Martin Erhard and Barbara Marie (Schmidt) T. MSc, U. Heidelberg, Germany, 1997. Student rsch. asst. U. Heidelberg, 1994-97; rsch. asst. Swiss Fed. Sch. Tech., Zurich, 1997—. Mem. European Geophys. Soc., Am. Geophys. Union. Office: Inst Terrestrial Ecology, Grabenstrasse 3, CH-8952 Schlieren Switzerland

THUMEREL, PIERRE JEAN-FRANCOIS, business executive, educator; b. Mazingarbe, France, Nov. 24, 1956; s. George and Anita (Lecocq) T.; m. Sylvie Marie Gabrielle, Vienot de Vaublanc, Aug. 13, 1983; children: Olivier, Nicolas, Anne-Lorraine, Francois, Martin. Diploma, U. Tech., Valenciennes, France; MBA, Inst. Sup. de Gestion, France. With Pains Jacquet, 1980-82; with Mobil Plastics Europe, 1982-95, br. dir., sales and mktg. mgr. for France and Portugal, 1991-92; mktg. dir. food packaging Europe and internat. Mobil Plastics Europe, Luxembourg, 1993-94, dir. logistics and bus. processes, 1994-95; dir. Asia Pacific bus. devel. Mobil Packaging Films Internat. Inc., Singapore, 1995-97; dir. Asia Pacific Sales and Mktg. Mobil Pkg. Film Internat., Inc., 1997-99, mng. dir. Asia Pacific, 1999—; mng. dir. Asia Pacific ExxonMobil Chem. Films Asia Pacific Inc. Contbr. numerous articles to profl. jours. Mem. Hollandse Club (Singapore), Hunting Clubs (France). Roman Catholic. E-mail: Pierre Thumerel@Email.Mobil.com. Fax: 65 356 76 82. Office: ExxonMobil Chem Films Asia, 101 Thomson Rd 08-02, United Square 307591, Singapore

THURAISINGHAM, RANJIT ARULNAYAGAM, research scientist; b. Colombo, Sri Lanka, Aug. 21, 1948; arrived in Australia, 1987; s. Robert Thillainayagam and Grace Ranee (Navaratnam) T.; m. Sashika Wijayanathan, May 7, 1977. BSc with 1st class honors, U. Ceylon, Colombo, 1971; PhD, U. Cambridge, Eng., 1975. Asst. lectr. U. Colombo, 1971-76, lectr., 1976-81, sr. lectr., 1982-83; rsch. assoc. U. Western Ont., Can., 1984-87; rsch. fellow Macquarie U., Australia, 1987-89; rsch. scientist Def. Sci. and Tech. Orgn., Pyrmont, NSW, Australia, 1989—; vis. lectr. U. Jaffna, Sri Lanka, 1978-83, U. Vidyodaya, Sri Lanka, 1979-82, Open U., Sri Lanka, 1982-83; examiner in chemistry Dept. Edn., Sri Lanka, 1977, 82-83. Co-author: (book chpt.) Lasers Molecules and Methods, 1989; contbr. articles and papers to profl. jours. Participant World Coun. of Chs., Mass., 1979. Rsch. scholar U. Ceylon, 1971, postgrad. scholar Colombo-Plan, U. Cambridge, 1972-75; rsch. fellow SUNY, 1981-82. Mem. Sri Lanka Assn. for Advancement of Sci. (asst. editor 1980, sec. phys. scis. 1977, 78). Avo-

cations: tennis, gardening, reading. Office: Def Sci and Tech Orgn, Maritime Ops Div PO Box 44, Pyrmont NSW 2009, Australia

THURAM, LILIAN, professional soccer player; b. Point-a-Pitre, France, Jan. 1, 1972. Defender Monaco Football Club, France, 1990—, Parma Football Club, Italy, 1996—. Achievements include scoring the two goals which carried France into the final with a win over Croatia. Office: Parma AC, Viale Parriciani d'Italia, 1-43100 Parma Italy also: 1 piazzale Risorgimento, I-43100 Parma Italy*

THURAU, KLAUS WALTHER CHRISTIAN, physiologist; b. Bautzen, Germany, June 14, 1928; s. Walther Thurau and Helene (Engel) Grüttner; m. Antje M. Wiese, Feb. 1, 1957; children: Stephan, Matthias. MD, U. Kiel, 1955; Dr. h.c. (hon.), Semmelweis U., Budapest, Hungary, 1985. Chmn. dept. physiology U. Munich, 1968-98; mem. exec. bd. Internat. Coun. Sci. Unions, Paris, 1989. Editor European Jour. Physiology, 1985. Recipient Homer Smith award Am. Soc. Nephrology, 1990, Volhard medal Ges. f. Nephrologie, 1997. Mem. Internat. Soc. Nephrology (pres. 1987, A.N. Richards award 1997), VERUM Found. (chmn. 1993), Heinz and Heide Durr Found., 1998, German Physiol. Soc. Home: Josef-Vötter-Strasse 6, 81545 Munich Germany Office: U Munich Dept Physiology, Pettenkoferstr 12, 80336 Munich Germany

THURDIN, ERIK KARL ALBERT, management consultant; b. Stockholm, Apr. 15, 1941; s. Otto E. and Inga (Andersson) T.; m. Kerstin G.M. Elfström, Mar. 13, 1971; children: Annna J.L., Jonas E.O. MSc, Royal Inst. Tech., Stockholm, 1964; postgrad., Internat. Inst. for Mgmt. Devel., Lausanne, Switzerland, 1977. Guide representing Sweden, N.Y. World's Fair, N.Y.C., 1965; mgmt. cons. Sevenco AB, Stockholm, 1966-71, sr. mgmt. cons., 1983; mgmt. officer WHO, Geneva, 1972-77; sr. mgmt. cons. Arthur D. Little, Brussels, 1977-82; mng. dir. Nominator AB, Stockholm, 1984—. Contbr. articles to mag. 2d lt. Swedish Air Force, 1963-64. Mem. Swedish Assn. Exec. Search Cons., Internat. Inst. for Mgmt. Devel. Alumni Assn. (pres. Swedish chpt. 1985-89). Avocations: golf, tennis, skiing.

THÜRER, GEORG, humanities educator; s. Paul and Nina (Accola) T.; m. Maria Elisabeth Tobler, Apr. 5, 1941; children: Maria Barbara, Georg Daniel, Martin Andreas, Annina. PhD, U. Zurich, 1932. Tchr. high sch., 1932-35; prof. U. St. Gall, 1940-78. Home: Eichenbuehl, 9053 Teufen Switzerland

THURIES, EDMOND EMILE, science administrator; b. Lyon, France, Mar. 5, 1934; s. Raymond Thuries and Clotilde Burdet; m. Chantal Fouqué, Dec. 10, 1960; children: François, Eric, Elisabeth. Degree in math., U. Lyon, France, 1959; degree in aeronautics engring., Nat. Sch. Aero. and Space, Paris, 1957. Cert. in elec. engring. Rsch. engr. CGE, Villeurbanne, France, 1960-65; prin. engr. Delle-Alsthom, Villeurbanne, 1965-70; chief engr. Alsthom, Villeurbanne, 1970-76, tech. dir., 1976-89; tech. dir. GEC Alsthom T & D, Villeurbanne, 1989-96, sci. dir., 1996-98; pres. electrotech. commn. GEC-Alsthom, Paris, 1989-97; adminstr. French com. Internat. Conf. Large High Voltage Electric Systmes, Paris, 1997. Patentee in field; contbr. articles to profl. publs. Maj. French Air Force, 1957-60. Decorated Croix de la valeur militaire avec Palme Armée de l'Air, 1960, Chevalier de l'ordre national du merite French Govt., 1981. Mem. IEEE (sr.), Internat. Electrotech. Commn. (mem. sector bd. 1995-97), French Soc. of Elec. and Electrotech. Engrs. (sr.). Roman Catholic. Avocations: piloting, painting, skiing, tennis. Home: 34 rue de Versailles, 69330 Pusignan France Office: E Thuries Cons, 34 rue Versailles, 69330 Pusignan France

THURM, ULRICH, zoology educator; b. Sorau, Lausitz, Germany, July 8, 1931; s. Walter and Gertrud (Steiner) T.; m. Adelheid Reeh, Aug. 22, 1964 (dec. Dec. 1972); children: Rüdiger, Agnes, Frauke; m. Barbara Althoff, Nov. 4, 1974; children: Henrike, Gundolf. Student zoology, physics and chemistry, U. Göttingen and U. Freiburg, Fed. Republic Germany, 1951-54, U. Würzburg, Fed. Republic Germany, 1954-58; D of Natural Scis., U. Würzburg, Fed. Republic Germany, 1962; student zoology, physics and chemistry, U. Munich, 1958-62. Rsch. assoc. Max-Planck-Inst. for Biol. Cybernetics, Tübingen, Fed. Republic Germany, 1962-70; prof. zoology U. Bochum, Fed. Republic Germany, 1971-74; prof., dir. dept. neurobiology U. Münster, Fed. Republic Germany, 1974-96, dean Faculty Natural Scis., 1977-78, dean biol. scis., 1982-83. Contbr. numerous articles to profl. jours. and textbooks. Mem. Rheinisch-Westfälische Akademie Wissenschaften, Soc. for Phys. Biology (chmn. 1979-81), also other zool., physiol., neurosci., and biophys. socs. Lutheran. Avocations: music, philosophy. Office: U Münster Neurobiology Inst, Badestrasse 9, D-48149 Münster Germany

THURMAN, MELBURN D., anthropologist, researcher, consultant; b. Redford, Mo., Oct. 31, 1941; s. Elva and Pearl (Pogue) T.; m. Barbara Fiedler Thurman, Sept. 20, 1964 (dec. May 1994); children: Tanya Eurydice, John A.P. AB, U. Chgo., 1965; MA, UCLA, 1968; PhD, U. Calif., Santa Barbara, 1973. Mem. excavations crew Smithsonian River Basin Surveys, Mobridge, S.D., 1962, Tex. Archaeol. Salvage Project, Comstock, 1962; field investigator Social Sci. Inst. Washington U., St. Louis, 1963; mem. excavations crew So. Ill. U.-Carbondale, Carlyle, Ill., 1963; field asst. U. Chgo.-Oriental Inst. Nubian Expedition, Wadi Halfa region, Sudan, 1963-64; asst. archaeologist Fla. Atlantic U., Ft. Center, Fla., 1966; asst. UCLA Solvieux Project, Perigord region, France, 1967; lectr., asst. prof. U. Md., College Park, 1970-74; vis. asst. prof. Purdue U., West Lafayette, Ind., 1974-75; lectr. Princeton (N.J.) U., 1975-78; exec. dir. Old Mo. Rsch. Inst., Sainte Genevieve, 1978-83; cons. Sainte Genevieve, 1983—; cons. Pa. State Mus., 1972, N.J. State Archael. Plan, N.J. State Mus., 1980, Newberry Libr., Chgo., 1991; rsch. specialist Winterthur Mus., 1972; Steiner meml. lectr., 1973; mem. Smithsonian Assocs. Resident Faculty, Smithsonian Instn., 1977; interdisciplinary participant Ctr. for Gt. Plains Study, U. Nebr., 1978, advanced seminar Sch. for Am. Rsch., Santa Fe, 1989; Soc. for Hist. Archaeology del. to 30th ann. joint conf. with Soc. for Post-Medieval Archaeology, 1997). Adv. editor: North American Archaeologist, 1977-87; contbr. articles to profl. jours. Grantee NSF, 1970, Am. Philos. Soc., 1973, Eli Lilly Found., 1975, Princeton U. Com. for Rsch. in Humanities and Social Scis., 1975-77, U.S. Heritage, Conservation and Recreation Svc., 1979, Harry Frank Guggenheim Found., 1989, 90; fellow Newberry Libr., Chgo., 1986. Mem. Am. Hist. Assn., Mid. Atlantic Archaeol. Conf. (past pres. 1978-79), Soc. for Hist. Archaeology (intersocietal rels. com. 1997—). Avocation: film study. Address: PO Box 391 Sainte Genevieve MO 63670-0391

THURMAN, VIRGIL LEON, voice educator; b. Knoxville, Tenn., Nov. 4, 1940; s. Virgil Lee and Marie Campbell T. BA, David Lipscomb Coll., Nashville, 1962; MS, U. Ill., Urban-Champagne, Ill., 1965, EdD, 1977. K-12 vocal music educator Harlan (Ky.) County Schs., 1962-64; 4-12 vocal music educator North Royalton (Ohio) City Schs., 1965-68; grad. teaching asst. U. Ill., Urbana-Champaign, Ill., 1968-70; chorister Norman Luboff Choir, N.Y.C., 1970-71; announcer WILL-AM & FM Pub. Radio, Urbana-Champaign, Ill., 1971-73, 76-78; asst. prof. voice, choral music, music edn. Yankton (S.D.) Coll., 1973-76; instr. voice and choral music MacPhail Ctr. for the Arts, Mpls., 1977-86; artist-in-residence Mpls. Pub. Schs., 1977-78; sole proprietor, ptnr., specialist voice educator The Voice Ctr., Mpls., 1986-95; specialist voice educator Fairview Voice Ctr. Fairview-Univ. Med. Ctr., Mpls., 1995—; bd. dirs., pres. Minn. chpt. Nat. Assn. Tchrs. of Singing, 1980-81, 84-86; assoc. dir. Interdisciplinary Voice Colloquium, U. Minn., Mpls., 1981-84' voice dept. asst. coord. MacPhail Ctr. for the Arts U. Minn., 1982-86; founder, bd. dirs., prin. faculty The VoiceCare Network, 1982—; mem. adv. bd. Ctr. Advanced Studies Music Edn., U. Surrey Roehampton, London; guest presenter, Am. Choral Dirs. Assn., Music Educators Nat. Conf., Internat. Soc. for Music Edn., The Choristers Guild, Voice Found. Am., N.Y.C., Alberta Music Conf., Assn. for Prenatal and Perinatal Psychology and Health, Am. Orff-Schulwerk Assn., Internat. Soc. for Prenatal and Perinatal Psychology and Medicine, Austria, 1986, European Coun. Internat. Schs., 1992, Internat. Conf. Music Perception and Cognition, 2000; vis. instr. U. Ill., Roosevelt U., Chgo., Queensland State Schs., Australia, 1988, Middle Tenn. State U., U. St. Thomas, St. Paul. Author, co-editor: Bodymind and Voice: Foundations of Voice Education, 1997, 2000; contbr. articles to profl. jours. Music dir., conductor Betty Marin Hobby Singers, Mpls., 1977-80, Skyway Singers, Mpls., 1983-87, Choral Soc. Tri-Cities, Cumberland, Benham, Lynch, Ky., 1962-64; dir., actor Royalton Players Cmty. Theatre, North Royalton, Ohio, 1965-68; chorister Cleve. Orchestra Chorus, 1965-67, Cleve. Orchestra Chamber Chorus, 1967. Mem. ASCD, AAAS, Actors Equity Assn., Am. Choral Dirs. Assn., Am. Choral Dirs. Assn. of Minn., Am. Guild of Musical Artists, Am. Fedn. TV and Radio Artists, Assn. Canadian Choral Conductors, Assn. for Prenatal and Perinatal Psychology and Health, European Soc. for Cognitive Scis. of Music, Internat. Music Soc. for Prenatal Devel., Internat. Soc. for Music Edn., Nat. Assn. of Tchrs. of Singing, Music Educators Nat. Conf., N.Y. Acad. Scis., The Schubert Club, Thursday Musical, Voice and Speech Trainers Assn., The VoiceCare Network. Avocations: walking, jogging. E-mail address: lthurma1@fairview.org. Office: Fairview Voice Ctr 2450 Riverside Ave Minneapolis MN 55454-1450

THURÓCZY, JULIANNA, veterinarian; b. Budapest, Hungary, July 17, 1967; d. Zoltán and Annamária (Németh) T.; m. Lajos Balogh, Aug. 8, 1992; 1 child, Gergely Akos Balogh. Veterinary dr., U. Vet. Sci., Budapest, 1991; economist specialist in med. field, U. Econs., Budapest, 2000. Veterinary diplomate. Asst. U. Vet. Sci., Budapest, 1992-93, rsch. worker, 1997—. Contbr. articles to profl. jours. Recipient Szent-Iványi award for young rschr. Hungarian Vet. Soc., 1997; grantee for clin. work Márkus Found., 1993, 99, PhD work grantee Soros Found., 1997. Mem. Hungarian Nuclear Medicine Assn., Hungarian Endocrinology and Metabolism Assn., European Soc. Small Animal Reproduction, Profl. Women's Assn. Office: U Veterinary Sci, István u 2, 1078 Budapest Hungary

THURSTON, JAMES KENDALL, lawyer; b. N.Y.C., July 1, 1962; s. David Wheeler and Frances Davis Thurston; m. Camille Nadia Khodadad, June 16, 1995; children: Taylor Frances, Isabel Jena. BA in Arch., U. Pa., 1984; postgrad., Yale U., 1988-89; JD magna cum laude, Marquette U., 1989. Assoc. Lord, Bissell & Brook, Chgo., 1989-92, Altheimer & Gray, Chgo., 1992-94, Peterson & Ross, Chgo., 1994-95; ptnr. Wilson, Elser, Moskowitz, Edelman & Dicker, Chgo., 1995—. Contbr. articles to legal jours. Mem. ABA. E-mail: thurstonj@wemed.com. Office: Wilson Elser et al 120 N Lasalle St Chicago IL 60602-2424

THURSTON, SIDNEY WALTER, III, marine scientist; b. Concord, N.H., Mar. 10, 1958; s. Sidney Walter Jr. and Cynthia Jane (Sylvia) T. BSEE, Va. Tech., 1981; MS in ocean engring., Fla. Inst. Tech., 1992, PhD in Oceanography, 1999. Systems engr. Rockwell Internat., Washington, 1981-95; vis. physical scientist Univ. Corp. Atmospheric Rsch., Boulder, Colo., 1996; marine scientist Japan Sci. & Tech. Agy., Tokyo, 1997—; guest editor, mem. Marine Tech. Soc. Jour., 1994—; adv. US Japan Coop. Agreement for Natural Resources, 1995—; asst. instr. Va. Tech. Engring. Cultures, 1997—. Contbr. articles to profl. jours. Instr. Kurihama Christian Ch. Eng. Conversation Class, Tokyo, 1997—; active Greater Washington Area Bd. of Trade, 1995-96; treas. Mayflower Square COnd. Assn., 1990; spl. events judge Internat. Sci. Fair, Toronto, 1995. Recipient Dean John A. Knauss Nat. Marine policy fellowship Nat. Oceanic and Atmospheric Adminstrn., 1995. Mem. Am. Geophysical Union, The Oceanographic Soc., IEEE, Marine Tech. Soc. (editorial bd. 1995—). Roman Catholic. Avocations: scuba, jogging, classical music. Fax: 81 468 44 1274. E-mail: thurston@ipc.phri.go.jp. Home: Lions Mansion 502, Kurihama 173, Yokosuka 239, Japan Office: Japan Sci & Tech Agy, 3 1 1 Nagase, Yokosuka 239, Japan

THURZO, MILAN HENRICH, physical anthropologist, researcher; b. Banská Bystrica, Slovakia, Slovak Republic, Sept. 10, 1942; s. Viliam and Mária Magdaléna (Rosivalová) T.; m. Dana Martisová, May 13, 1967; children: Zuzana, Martin. BS in Biology, Comenius U., Bratislava, Slovakia, 1965, RNDr, 1972, CSc, 1977. Rsch. asst. Slovak Acad. Scis., Nitra, Slovakia, 1965-66; prin. rsch. asst. Slovak Nat. Mus., Bratislava, 1966-72, sr. prin. rsch. asst., 1972-77, asst. rsch. worker, 1977-87, sr. prin. rsch. worker, 1987-90, temp. dir., 1990, dir. Natural History Mus., 1990-93, sr. prin. rsch. worker, 1993-97; head anthropol. dept. Natural Sci. Faculty Comenius U., Bratislava, 1997—; assoc. prof. Comenius U., 1991—; vice chmn. Czechoslovak Com. ICOM, Praha, 1990-93. Author: Million Years of Man, 1985; editor Acta Rer. Natural Mus. Nat. Slovaci, 1982-97, Bull. Slov. Anthrop. Soc., 1998—; contbr. over 50 articles to profl. jours. Recipient Hrdlička Commemorative medal Czechoslovak Anthrop. Soc., 1992. Mem. Slovak Anthrop. Soc. (vice chmn. 1989—), Brain Rsch. Found. (bd. dirs. 1993-96). Avocations: body building, jogging, photography, English translation. Home: Tvarozkova 13, 81103 Bratislava Slovakia Office: Anthropol Dept Comenius U, Mlynska dolina B 2, 842 15 Bratislava Slovakia

THWING, BONNIE J., retail executive, nurse; b. Passaic, N.J., Nov. 2, 1957; d. Bridget M. Ciorciari-Hung; m. Ismael I. Yepes, May 26, 1985 (div. July 1990); m. Robert R. Thwing, Sept. 4, 1992; children: Jennifer, Matthew, Michael. A, Passaic County C.C., Paterson, N.J., 1979; BS in Adminstrn., Felician Coll., 1982; BSN, Kean Coll., 1984. RN, N.J., N.Y., Pa. Buyer Steiker Industries, Elmwood Park, N.J., 1978-83; RN Overlook Hosp., Summit, N.J., 1984-90; pricing mgr. Top Gallant Group, Edison, N.J., 1987-90; drier bus. trade mgr. Troy Corp., Florham Park, N.J., 1990—. Republican. Roman Catholic. Avocations: swimming, horseback riding. Office: Troy Corp 8 Vreeland Rd Florham Park NJ 07932-1501

TIAN, XIUCHUN, research scientist; b. Beijing, Mar. 21, 1963; came to US, 1986; d. Zhentong Tian and Rongzhen Ma; m. Xiangzhong Yang, Jan. 5, 1986; 1 child, Andrew. BS, Beijing Agrl. U., 1985; MS, Cornell U., 1989, PhD, 1994. Postdoct. assoc. Cornell U., Ithaca, N.Y., 1995-96; rsch. assoc. U. Conn., Storrs, 1996—. Contbr. articles to scientific jours. Co-organizer U. Conn. Chinese Sch., Storrs, 1999. Overseas fellow Chinese Edn. Commn., 1985; rsch. grantee Conn. Invention, Inc., 1999; recipient Nat. Rsch. Svc. award NIH, 1995. Mem. Internat. Embryo Transfer Soc., N.Y. Acad. Scis., Phi Kappa Phi. Avocation: internat. travel. Office: U Conn 3636 Horsebarn Rd Ext Storrs Mansfield CT 06269

TIAN, ZENG MIN, neurosurgery educator, chief physician; b. Chang Chun, Ji Lin, China, Nov. 1, 1951; s. Wei Tian and Pei Lian Jiang; m. Shu Lan Shen; 1 child, Chun Yu. BS, Shanghai (China) Med. Coll., 1976; MS, Ji Lin Med. Coll., Chang Chun, China, 1979; MD, PhD, Beijing Postgrad. Med. Coll., 1986. Med. diplomate. Physician Chang Chun Hosp., 1976-77; fellow Ji Lin Med. Coll., 1978-79; rsch. fellow Xi An (China) Med. U., 1980-82, Beijing Postgrad. Med. Coll., 1983-86; assoc. prof. Yan Jing Med. Inst., 1987-93, prof., 1994—; vis. fellow U. Pitts., 1993; med. adviser Chinese Nat. Broadcast, Beijing, 1996—; vice dir. Beijing Congress Biomed. Engring., 1996—. Editor: Modern Stereotactic Neurosurgery, 1997; contbr. articles to profl. jours. Recipient 2d degree Mil. Sci. and Tech., Beijing, 1992, 94; 3rd degree Nat. Com. Sci. and Tech., Beijing, 1996, 2nd degree, 1999; Star, Nat. Ministry Medicine, 1996; named Outstanding Scientist, Nat. Ministry, 1999; Nat. Ministry grantee, 1997. Mem. World Fedn. Neurosurg. Socs., N.Y. Acad. Scis. Avocations: traveling, photography. E-mail: tianzm@public.sti.ac.en. Office: Yan Jing Med Inst, 6 Fu Cheng Rd, Beijing 100037, China

TIAN, ZHIYU, software and medical device engineer; b. Chengdu, Sichuan, China, Apr. 13, 1963; s. Lingjun Tian and Shihui Yang; m. Xiaomin Huang, Aug. 12, 1992; 1 child, Charlie Jinshaw. BS, Beijing U. Aeros.-Astronautics, 1983, MS, 1990; PhD in Engring., cert. lectr., Tsinghua U., Beijing, 1993. Sr. software engr. Stellartech Rsch. Corp., Sunnyvale, Calif., 1999—. Contbr. articles to profl. jours. Grantee Chinese NSF, 1993. Mem. IEEE (sr.). Fax: 408-331-3101. E-mail: zhiyu.tian@ieee.org. Home: 1265 N Capitol Ave Apt 41 San Jose CA 95132-2512 Office: 1346 Bordeaux Dr Sunnyvale CA 94089-1005

TIAN, ZONGSHU, mechanics and applied mathematics educator; b. Beijing, Mar. 25, 1937; d. Hongbin Tian and Shushi Zhao; m. Xiaoqian Zhang. B. U. Archtl. Sci. and Tech., Xi'an, China, 1957. Asst. U. Archtl. Sci. and Tech. of Xi'an, 1957-61, lectr., 1961-64; lectr. grad. sch. Chinese Acad. Scis., Beijing, 1978-79, assoc. prof., 1980-87, prof., 1988—; vis. scholar MIT, Boston, 1982-84; vis. prof. U. Tech. Aachen, Germany, 1990-91. Author: Solid Mechanics, 1963, Advanced Finite Element Methods, 1988; co-author: A Course in Architectural Mechanics, 1962, Problems in Strength of Materials, 1964, Strength of Materials, 1972, Structural Mechanics, 1973; contbr. over 95 articles to profl. jours. Recipient Natural Sci. award Chinese Acad. Scis., 1996, Sci. Progress award Chinese Edn. Ministry, 1999. Mem. Internat. Assn. Computational Mechanics, Chinese Soc. Theoretical and Applied Mechanics. Avocations: planting flowers, music. Office: Grad Sch Chinese Acad Scis, PO Box 2706, Beijing 100080, China

TIANTONG, THITICHAI, Thai army officer; b. Banmee, Lop Buri, Thailand, Oct. 11, 1964; s. Wichean and Mog (Meekrea) T. BS, Chulachomklao Royal Mil. Acad., Thailand, 1988; diploma, U.S. Army F.A. Sch., 1992, Royal Thai Army Command and Gen. Staff Coll., Bangkok, 1997, U.S. Army Commmand and Gen. Staff Coll., 1999. Commd. officer Royal Thai Army, 1988, advanced through grades to lt. col.; battery fire direction officer 711st F.A. Bn., 1988-90, battery exec. officer, 1990-92; battery comdr. 721st F.A. Bn., 1993-95; bn. ops. officer 722d F.A. Bn., 1995-96; instr. Royal Thai Army Command and Gen. Staff Coll., 1997—. Buddhist. Home: 5/1234 Soi 7, Bachacheon, Village, Samakkee Rd, NB Nokkret 11120, Thailand Office: RTA Command-Gen Staff Coll, Terddumri Rd, Dusit, Bangkok 10300, Thailand

TIAPANI, ALBERT KAKOU, minister of construction of Cote d'Ivoire; b. Dabou, Sept. 27, 1944; married; 4 children. Degree in engring., Nat. Inst. Pub. Works, Abidjan; diploma, Ctr. Econ. Studies Programs, Paris. Engr. pub. works, sec. gen. Autonomous Port Abidjan, 1978-93, dir. gen., 1993—; min. constrn. urban planning Govt. Cote d'Ivoire, 1993—, min. housing and urban planning. Office: Min Housing Urban Planning, Cite Adminstrn Tour D, Abidjan Cote d'Ivoire*

TIAVAASUE FALEFATU MAKA SAPOLU, judge. Chief justice Supreme Ct. Western Samoa, Apia. Office: Supreme Ct, Dept Justice, Apia Samoa*

TIBALDI, ALESSANDRO, geologist, educator; b. Milan, Italy, Jan. 26, 1961; s. Ariberto and Serena (Lombardo) T.; m. Eva Maria Graziotto, Sept. 15, 1991; children: Riccardo, Isabella. MS, U. Milan, 1986, PhD, 1990; postgrad., Nat. Inst. Geophysics, Rome, 1991-92. Profl. cons. Electroconsult, Milan, 1986, SGAI, Forli, Italy, 1987; rsch. fellowship Nat. Inst. of Geophysics, Rome, 1991-92; assoc. rschr. U. Milan, 1993-96, full rschr., 1996-98, prof., 1999—. Author: (books) Remote Sensing in Geology, 1995, Morphology of Volcanoes, 1997. Town councillor Lesa, Italy, 1995-99. Recipient E.A. Flinn award Internat. Union of Geodesy and Geophysics, Wienn, Austria, 1991. Fellow Inst. for Alpine Geodynamics; mem. Am. Geophys. Union, Nat. Group for Volcanology, Italian Geol. Soc. (Mario Oxilia award 1987-88). Avocations: climatology, photography, jazz and folk music, mountain sports. E-mail: alessandro.tibaldi@unimb.it. Office: Univ Milan/Dept Geol Sci, Piazza della Scienza 4, 20126 Milan Italy

TIBBALDS, FRANCIS ERIC, architect; b. Brighton, Eng., Oct. 16, 1941; s. William Eric and Elsie Agnes (Wood) T.; m. Janet Grace McDonald, Sept. 6, 1969; children: Adam Dominic, Benedict Malcolm. Diploma in Architecture with distinction, The Poly. Sch. Architecture, London, 1966; M of Philosophy in Arts, Town Planning, U. Coll. London, 1969. Sr. architect planner Llewelyn-Davies, Weeks, Forestier-Walker & Bor, London, 1969-70; prin. architect planner Westminster City Council, London, 1970-72; dep. chief planning officer London Borough Lambeth, 1972-74; joint project dir. Group Five (Nigeria), Ilorin, Nigeria, London, 1974-75; dir. planning Llewelyn-Davies, Weeks, London, Saudi Arabia, Oman, Iran, 1975-78; chmn. Tibbalds Mauro Ltd., London, Cardiff, 1978—; external examiner Newcastle U., Poly. Cen. London and Poly. South Bank; vis. prof. Bartlett Sch. Architecture and Planning, Univ. Coll. London; vis. lectr. various colls. Founding editor Urban Design Quar., 1978-84, Freeman of City of London; contbr. articles to profl. jours. Founder, chmn. Urban Design Group, London, 1978-86, pres., 1991—. Fellow Royal Soc. Arts, Faculty of Bldg., Royal Town Planning Inst. (pres. 1988, hon. sec. 1990), European Coun. Town Planners (sr. v.p. 1991-92); mem. Royal Inst. Brit. Architects, London U. Town Planning Soc. (pres. 1968), Worshipful Co. of Chartered Architects. Avocations: music, choral singing, literature, sketching. Office: 31 Earl St, London EC2A 2HR, England WC2H OAW

TIBBS, CHRISTOPHER STANLEY, banker; b. Berkeley, Calif., June 15, 1947; s. Stanley Jewell and Frances Maud (Shapland) T. BA, U. Wash., Seattle, MBA. V.p. fin. instns. Citibank, Tokyo, Japan, 1975-84; regional sr. officer North Africa Citibank, Athens, Greece, 1985-87; corp. fin. head Hong Kong Citibank, Hong Kong, 1987-89; corp. fin. head Central Am. Citibank, Miami, 1989-94; corp. fin. head China Citibank, Shanghai, 1994—. Major USMC, 1966-86. Avocations: sailing, rugby, tennis. Office: Citibank NA, 100 Yanan Road East, 200002 Shanghai China

TIBES, ULRICH, physiologist, educator, pharmacologist; b. Trier, Germany, Jan. 19, 1941; s. Wilhelm Matthias and Katharina (Görgen) T.; m. Monica Haitzinger, Dec. 29, 1967; children: Verena, Raoul. Grad. in medicine, U. Cologne (Germany), 1967, MD, 1969. Researcher, sr. researcher med. faculty Physiol. Inst. U. Cologne, Cologne, 1968-78; head pulmonary pharmacol. Boehringer-Ingelheim Ltd., Biberach, Germany, 1978-82; prof. medicine U. Tübingen (Germany), 1980—; head pharmacodynamics Hoffman-La Roche, Basel, Switzerland, 1985-86; head oncology rsch. unit Hoffman-La Roche, Mannheim, Germany, 1986—; vis. prof. applied physiology U. Medellin (Colombia), U. Sao Paulo (Brazil), 1972, 77. Author: Circulation and Ventilation in Exercise, 1981; patentee in field; contbr. 9285 articles to profl. jours. Mem. German Physiol. Soc., German Pharmacol. Soc., N.Y. Acad. Scis., Hessian Chamber of Physicians, Fedn. of Univs. Avocations: modern paintings, skiing, sailing, wind-surfing. Home: Am Sandberg 102, D-60599 Frankfurt Germany

TIBLIER, FERNAND JOSEPH, JR., municipal engineering administrator; b. New Orleans, Mar. 11, 1960; s. Fernand Joseph and Dorothy May (Bosworth) T.; m. Janine Therese Cousineau, Sept. 1, 1990; children: Amanda, Christine. BA in Chemistry, Biology, Drury Coll., 1982; MS in Environ. Engring., U. Cen. Fla., 1986. Registered profl. engr., Fla. Rsch. asst. U. Cen. Fla., Orlando, 1983-86; asst. city engr., then acting city engr. City of Longwood, Fla., 1986-92, city engr., 1992-94, dir. pub. works, city engr., 1994-96; city engr., dir. pub. works City of Deltona, Fla., 1996—; mem. road impact fee com. Seminole County Citizen Adviser, Sanford, Fla., 1988-89; mem. water resources task force Seminole County Tech. Adviser, Sanford, 1992; advisor Pub. Works Acad. Oak Ridge High Sch., Orlando, 1996—; mem. Dean of Engring. adv. coun. U. Cen. Fla.; mem. tech. adv. com. Volusian Water Alliance. Lector, youth minister Nativity Ch., Lake Mary, Fla., 1987—; team capt. City of Longwood March of Dimes, 1992; mem. City of Longwood Planning Agy., 1997-98. Mem. ASCE, NSPE, Fla. Engring. Soc., Volusia Assn. Mcpl. Engrs. Republican. Roman Catholic. Avocations: home improvement, photography, travel, cooking, reading. Home: 407 Parson Brown Way Longwood FL 32750-4020 Office: City of Deltona Pub Works 1691 Providence Blvd Deltona FL 32725-4928

TIBURCIO, ANTONIO FERNANDEZ, plant physiology educator, researcher; b. Terrassa, Barcelona, Spain, Dec. 9, 1952; s. Antonio Fernandez and Pura Tiburcio; 1 child, Alba Fernandez. Degree in Pharmacy, U. Barcelona, 1975, PhD in Pharmacy, 1980. Asst. prof. U. Barcelona, 1975-85, prof. titular, 1986—; postdoctoral assoc. Yale U., New Haven, conn., 1983-86; mem. life sci. working group European Space Agy., Paris, 1996-2000; project reviewer European Space Agy./NASA, Washington, 1997, Com. Interministerial de Ciencia y Technologia Spain, 1990—, Binat. Agrl. Rsch. and Devel. Fund, U.S. and Israel, 1990—, U.S. Dept. Energy. Contbr. articles to profl. jours. including Plant Physiology, Plant Jour., Trends in Plant Sci. and Planta. With Spanish Mil., 1976-77. Mem. Soc. Espanola de Fisiologia Vejetal/Fedn. of European Socs. of Plant Physiology, Am. Plant Physiologist Soc., Soc. Catalana Biologia (treas. 1996—). Avocations: sports, music, dance. Home: Masferrer 9, Entlo 1a, 08028 Barcelona Spain Office: U Barcelona Fisiologia Veg, Diagonal 643, 08028 Barcelona Spain

TICA, ALDO OSCAR, oil company process engineer; b. Rosario, Argentina, Mar. 7, 1943; s. Octavio Francisco and Antonia (Blando) T.; m. Susana Ofelia Playa, Jan. 6, 1973; children: Walter, Anibal, Evangelina, Cristina. Degree in elec. engring., Nat. Tech. U., Rosario, 1973. Drawing designer Ipsam S.A., Pto San Martin, Argentina, 1960-65, Delta S.A.j.c., Pto San Martin, 1965-67; sr. designer Swift, Rosario, 1967-69, Sulfacid S.A., Fray L. Beltran, Argentina, 1969-73; sr. designer and mounter Ceramica S. Lorenzo, S. Lorenzo, Argentina, 1973-75; optimization headman YPF S.A., Lujan De Cuyo, Argentina, 1975—; std norm ISO 9000 quality 14001 Environ. and British STD 8800 Security Audit, 1998—; tchr. E.Nat. No. 1, S. Lorenzo, 1974-84. Contbr. articles to profl. jours. V.p. Nation, Lujan de Cuyo, 1986. Reserve subofficer Naval Army, 1963-65. Mem. Electromechanical State. Baptist. Avocations: running, cycling, soccer, tennis.

Home: Nihvil No 58, 5507 Lujan De Cuyo De Cuyo, Argentina Office: YPF SA, CC No 4, 5507 Lujan De Cuyo De Cuyo, Argentina

TICE, BRADLEY SCOTT, humanities educator; b. Palo Alto, Calif., Oct. 6, 1959; s. Lilburn Trent and Paula Nanette (Osborne) T. AA, De Anza Coll., Cupertino, Calif., 1983; BA in History, San Jose State U., 1987; PhD in Chemistry, Fairfax U., Baton Rouge, 1996; Diploma in Ayurvedic Medicine, The Ayurvedic Inst.; Diploma in Stress therapy, Internat. Yoga Sch.; LittD in Tchg., St. Clements Univ., The Carribean, 1998; D of Religious Sci., 1999, M in Religion, 1999, D in Religion, 1999, DD (hon.), 1999. Cert. Cmty. Emergency Response Tng., Cupertino, Calif. Mem. staff Stanford Linear Accelerator Ctr., 1981-87; prof. Pacific Lang. Inst., Cupertino, Calif., 1992—; dir. rsch. Advanced Human Design, Cupertino, 1992—; CEO Tice Pharms., San Jose; intern Ames Rsch. Ctr. NASA, Moffett Field, Calif., 1997-98; substitute libr. Robert Crown Law Libr., Stanford U., 1989; founder Modern Lang. Inst., Cupertino, Calif., 1992—, West Coast Lang. Labs., Cupertino, 1992—. Editor Jour. Pacific Lang. Inst., 1995-96; mem. editl. bd. The Story of Life. Vol. De Young Mus., San Francisco, 1990, Mus. Modern Art, San Francisco, 1990, Calif. Acad. Scis., San Francisco, 1990; vol. guide Monterey Bay Aquarium, 1990; elected mem. Cupertino Pub. Safety Commn., 2000—. Recipient Pres.'s award Nat. Author's Registry, 1996, editor's choice award (3), The Nat. Libr. of Poetry, 1995, (2), 1996, Cert. Merit for essay, Pharmacia Biotech and Sci. prize for young scientists, 1997, Commemorative Medal Honor, Hallmark, 2000; elected Order of Internat. Ambs., 1999, Internat. Man of the Year (medal of hon.), 1996, 97, Man of the Year (commemorative medal award), 1997, Internat. Order Merit, 2000, Commemmorative medal of honor Hallmark, 2000. Mem. ACS, IEEE, AIAA, COSPAR (mem. com. space rsch.), Am. Physical Soc., N.Y. Acad. Scis., Assn. Computing Machinery, Am. Soc. Microbiology, Internat. Assn. Tchrs. English as a Fgn. Lang., Internat. Soc. Poets, Mars Soc. (found. mem.), Calif. Assn. for Health, Phys. Edn., Recreation and Dance (v.p. elect for recreation 1999). Avocations: weight training, fencing, bicycling, swimming, scuba diving. Office: Pacific Language Inst PO Box 2214 Cupertino CA 95015-2214

TICHENOR, CHARLES BECKHAM, II, food and beverage executive; b. Indpls.; s. Norman and Esther (Bremmer) B.; m. Dr. Helen S. Tichenor. BS, Duke U.; postgrad., Harvard U.; PhD, Berne U., 1996. V.p. Sealtest-Kraft; pres., chmn. Champale Sparkling Beverage Corp., Trenton, N.J.; bd. dirs. Doughtie's Foods, Inc., Balt., Motor Coils Mfg., Pitts., Angostura, Trinidad, U.S. Fed. Res. Bank of Charlotte, Yoo Hoo Chocolate Beverage Co., Carlstadt, N.J., N.Y. Packaging Corp., Jersey City, South Tex. Oil Drilling, San Antonio, Dinamic Embellages, Rombach, France, Essex Bank, Va., Weisz Graphics, Columbia, S.C.; disting. corp. chief exec., prof. bus. Gardner-Webb U. Trustee Rider U., Lawrenceville, N.J. Lt. (j.g.) USNR, China-Okinawa, WWII. Mem. Davis Cup Tennis Team, 1942-43; recipient 2 Gold and 1 Silver medal U.S. tennis and racquet sports; Nat. Master in U.S. contract bridge. Mem. Am. Mgmt. Assn., Nat. Assn. Corp. Dirs., Merion Cricket Club (Phila.), Cleveland Country Club (Shelby, N.C.), Cosmos Club (Washington), Rotary Internat. Home: 137 Westfield Rd Shelby NC 28150-4856

TICHENOR, CHARLES BECKHAM, III, operations research analyst; b. Balt., Mar. 10, 1950; s. Charles Beckham II and Suzanne Nelson (Stevens) T.; m. Alison P. Walton, May 29, 1971; 1 child, Charles Beckham IV. BSBA, Ohio State U., 1972; MBA, Va. Tech., 1990; PhD in Bus., Berne U., 1999. Asst. prodn. supr. Champale Products, Norfolk, Va., 1977-80; ops. rsch. analyst IRS, Washington, 1989-93, tech. adv. info. sys. performance mgmt. office; adj. asst. prof. bus. Strayer U., Balt. Lt. col. USAR, ret. Mem. Mensa. Roman Catholic. Avocations: Tae Kwon Do (black belt), amateur astronomer. Home: 6207 Cardinal Brook Ct Springfield VA 22152-1516 Office: Def Security Coop Agy Jefferson Davis Hwy Ste 203 Alexandria VA 22301 also: Devel Support Ctr Inc 1625 Lindhurst Dr Ste 100 Elm Grove WI 53122-1749

TICHY, JOSEF, chemistry educator, researcher; b. Námêst na Hane, Czech Republic, June 25, 1936; s. František and Anna (Gatêková) T.; m. Eva Skálová, Feb. 24, 1968 (dec. 1990); children: Jiří, Alice. Engr., U. Chem. Tech., Pardubice, Czech Republic, 1961; PhD in Chem. Engring., Czech Acad. Scis., Prague, 1965; DSc, U. Pardubice, 1990. Assoc. prof. U. Pardubice, 1990-92, prof. chemistry, 1992—, vice rector, 1993-96, head dept. chemistry, 1997—. Author: (textbook) Chemical Kinetics, 1988; contbr. articles to profl. jours. and conf. procs. Mem. EFCATS, Czech Chem. Soc., Czech Soc. Chem. Engring. Roman Catholic. Avocations: history, philosophy, travel, culture. Home: Chemiku 132, 530 09 Pardubice Czech Republic Office: U Pardubice, nám. Čs. legií 565, 523 10 Pardubice Czech Republic

TICHY, MILIK OTAKAR, civil engineering educator, consultant, researcher; b. Naples, Italy, Dec. 5, 1929; s. Otakar Vladimir and Zdenka (Vosatkova) T.; m. Bela Bata, Dec. 21, 1952 (div. 1980); 1 child, Sarka Claudia Leff; m. Libuse Pavla Hlavsova, July 30, 1980. Civil Engr., Tech. U. Prague, 1953; CandSci, Acad. Sci., Prague, 1957; D of Engring. Sci., Acad. Sci., Czechoslovakia, 1967. Designer Kovoprojekta, Prague, 1951-53; rschr. Acad. Sci., Prague, 1957-67; sr. scientist Acad. Sci., 1967-91; prof. civil engring. Tech. U. Prague, 1988—; pvt. cons. Prague, 1991—; chmn. Standing Com. for Structural Concrete, Prague, 1973-88; forensic expert, Prague, 1967—; chartered arbitrator, 2000—; exec. mgr., dir. Brehova Ltd., 1994—; project mgr. Thomas J. Bata, Toronto, 1991—. Author: Statistical Theory of Concrete Structures, 1972, Plastic Analysis of Concrete Frames, 1977, Applied Methods of Structural Reliability, 1994; author, editor: Manual on Structural Loads, 1986. Mem. Czech Soc. Civil Engrs., Czech Soc. for Prevention of Risk (chmn.1997—). Avocation: writing science fiction stories for kids. Home: Dominova 11/2465, 158 00 Praha 5, Czech Republic

TICHY, MILOŠ ANTONÍN, biochemist, educator; b. Brno, Moravia, Czech Republic, Aug. 16, 1941; s. Antonín and Ludmila (Podešvová) T.; m. Eva Ruzena Maršíková, April 20, 1968; children: Veronika Ludmila, Markéta Helena. RNDr, Comenius U., Bratislava, Czechoslovakia, 1970; PhD, Charles U., Praha, Czechoslovakia, 1977. Clin. biochemist Mil. Med. Acad., Hradec Králové, Czech Republic, 1963—. Author: (with Z. Hrnčíř) Atlas of Monoclonal Immunoglobulins, 1981; (with A. Sakalová) Multiple Myeloma and Paraproteinemias, 1995; Laboratory Analysis of Paraproteins, 1997. Lt. Czech mil., 1963-64. Recipient awards Czech Soc. Clin. Biochemistry, 1982, Czech Soc. Clin. Chemistry, 1993, 98. Roman Catholic. Home: K Sokolovně, 503 41 Hradec Králové Czech Republic Office: 2nd Dept Internal Medicine, Pospíšilova tr 365, Hradec Králové Czech Republic

TICHY, ROBERT FRANZ, mathematician, researcher; b. Vienna, Austria, Sept. 30, 1957; s. Richard and Maria (Pazdernik) T.; m. Gabriele T. Stranzinger, 1988; children:Philipp, Sophie. PhD, U. Vienna, 1979. Math. educator U. Agr., Vienna, 1979-80; asst. Tech. U. Vienna, 1980-82, dozent, 1983-90; prof. Tech. U. Graz, 1990—; vis. prof. U. Salzburg, 1986, U. Marseille, 1991, 93, 95, 97, Tata Inst., Bombay, 1992, U. Debrecen, 1997, U. Ill., Urbana-Champaign, 2000; life ins. cons. Contbr. articles to profl. jours. Mem. Austrian Math. Soc. (Foerderungspreis 1985), Austrian Actuarial Assn., German Math. Assn., London Math. Soc., Am. Math. Soc. Roman Catholic. Avocations: modern art, travel, mountain climbing. Home: Ferdinand v. Saarweg 1, A-8042 Graz Austria Office: Tech U Graz Inst Math, Steyrergasse 30, A-8010 Graz Austria

TICHY, WALTER FRANZ, computer science educator; b. Bad Reichenhall, Germany, Apr. 22, 1952; s. Karl and Elisabeth Tichy; m. Ingrid M. Tichy, June 8, 1977; children: Evelyn M., Thomas F., Raphael O, Karl B. MS, Carnegie-Mellon U., 1976, PhD, 1980. Rsch. asst. Carnegie-Mellon U., Pitts., 1974-80; asst. prof. Purdue U., West Lafayette, Ind., 1980-85; sr. scientist Carnegie-Group, Inc., Pitts., 1985-86; prof. U. Karlsruhe, Germany, 1986—; asst. dean U. Karlsruhe, 1993-95. Editor: Configuration Management, 1994; contbr. articles to profl. jours. Mem. Assn. Computing Machinery, IEEE Computer Soc., Gesellschaft fur Informatik. Office: Univ Karlsruhe, Am Fasanengarten 5, D-76128 Karlsruhe Germany

TICKELL, SIR CRISPIN, environmentalist; b. Aug. 25, 1930; m. Chloe Gunn, 1954 (dissolved 1976); 3 children; m. Penelope Thorne Thorne, 1977. Student, Westminster Sch.; grad. with 1st class honors, Oxford (Eng.) U., 1952; D (honoris causa), Acad. Mex. Derecho Internat., 1989, U. Stirling, 1990; LLD (hon.), U. Mass., 1990, U. Birmingham, 1991, U. Bristol, 1991; DSc (hon.), U. East Anglia, 1990, U. Sussex, 1991, Cranfield U., 1992, Loughborough U., 1995, Exater U., 1999; ChD, Kent U., 1996; ChD (hon.), Sheffield U., 1996, East London U., 1998. With fgn. office Brit. Diplomatic Svc., 1954-55; with Brit. Embassy, The Hague, The Netherlands, 1955-58, Mex., 1958-61; mem. planning staff fgn. office Brit. Embassy, 1961-64; with Brit. Embassy, Paris, 1964-70; Brit. ambassador to Mex. Brit. Embassy, 1981-83; pvt. sec. Chancellors of Duchy of Lancaster, 1970-72; head western orgn. dept. FCO, 1972-75; dep. under-sec. of state Fgn. and Commonwealth Office, 1983-84; permanent sec. Overseas Devel. Adminstrn., 1984-87; Brit. permanent rep. Security Coun. UN, 1987-90; chmn. Internat. Inst. for Environ. and Devel., 1990-94; warden Green Coll., Oxford, 1990-97; chancellor U. Kent, Canterbury, Eng., 1996—; chmn. Climate Inst., Washington, 1990—; dir. Ctr. for Environ. Policy and Understanding Green Coll., 1992—; pres. Earth Ctr., South Yorkshire, Eng., 1996—; convenor Govt. Panel on Sustainable Devel., 1994—; chmn. Adv. Com. on Darwin Initiative for Survival of Species, 1992-99; chmn. Earthwatch Europe, 1991-97; mem. adv. com. on environ. Internat. Coun. for Sci., 1996—, chmn., 1998—; bd. dirs. Govett Enhanced Income Investment Trust. Author: Climatic Change and world Affairs, 1977, rev. edit., 1986; contbr. articles to profl. jours. Trustee BaringGounf., 1992—, Brit. Mus. Natural History, 1992—, World Wide Fund for Nature, U.K., 1993-99, Royal Bot. Garden, Edinburgh, Scotland, 1997—; gov. Ditchley Found.; sr. advisor Global Environ. Facility; v.p. Population Concern; mem. China Coun. for Internat. Coop. in Environ. and Devel., 1991—; mem. coun. St. George's House, Windsor, Eng., 1992-99; mem. Com. for Pub. Understanding of Sci., 1991-94; mem. environ. adv. coun. European Band for Reconstruction and Devel., 1991-94; overseer Thomas J. Watson Jr. Inst. for Internat. Studies, Brown U., Providence. King's scholar, Hinchliffe & Hon. scholar Oxford U.; named Officer Order of Orange Nassau, 1958; hon. fellow St. Edmund's Coll., Cambridge, 1995, Green Coll., 1997, Westminster Sch., 1993; named Disting. Lectr. Brit. Geol. Survey, 1994; Centennial Lectr., Ariz. State U., 1995; recipient Kelvin medal Royal Philos. Soc. Glasgow, 1996, 1st Happold medal Nat. Constrn. Industry Coun., 1998. Fellow Chartered Instn. Water and Environ. Mgmt. (hon.), Royal Scottish Geog. Soc.; mem. Marine Biol. Assn. (pres. 1990—), Gaia Soc. (pres. 1998—), Nat. Soc. for Clean Air and Environ. Protection (pres. 1997-99); fellow Ctr. Internat. Affairs, Harvard U., 1975-76; chef de cabinet to pres. Commn. of European Union, 1977-81; vis. fellow All Souls Coll., Oxford, 1981;. Office: Ablington Old Barn, Ablington Gloucester GL7 5NU, England

TIDBALL, JANE ALISON, judge; b. Helena, Mont.; Bar: Colo. 1984, U.S. Dist. Ct. Colo. 1987, U.S. Dist. Ct. Ariz. 1992.; d. Eugene Clayton and Marcia Ann Tidball; m. Dan A. Sciullo, Aug. 22, 1987; children: Jordan Lee Tidball-Sciullo, Cameron James Tidball-Sciullo. BA, U. Colo., 1980, JD, 1984. Law clerk Hon. Aurel Kelly, Colo. Ct. Appeals, Golden, Colo., 1984-85; pvt. practice Denver, 1985-91; lawyer FDIC/RTC, Denver, 1991-95; magistrate 20th Jud. Dist., Boulder, 1995-99; dist. ct. judge 1st Jud. Dist., Denver, Colo., 1999—. Mem. Phi Beta Kappa.

TIDWELL, GEOFFREY MORGAN, medical company executive; b. San Diego, Aug. 16, 1958; s. Morgan Alfred and Dorothy (Doolittle) T. BA in Psychology, U.S. Internat. U., 1991; MBA in Health Care Adminstrn., Nat. U., 1996. Rsch. asst. San Marcos (Calif.) Clinic, 1988-91; area svc. mgr. Nat. Med. Sys., Frederick, Md., 1993-94, Life Med. Svcs., San Diego, 1994-95; intern San Diego County Med. Soc., 1995-96; adminstrn. resident dept. interventional radiology U. Calif., San Diego, 1995-96; v.p., dir. clin. svcs. M&G Med. Svc., San Diego, 1995—; vis. scholar U. Calif. Sch. Medicine, San Diego, 1996, 97, 98; radio personality Sta. KOWF, Escondido, Calif., 1989-90, Sta. KKYY, San Diego, 1990-91, Sta. KRMX, San Diego, 1990-91, Sta. KGB, San Diego, 1991-97; clin. svcs., v.p. sales and mktg. M&G Med. Svc., San Diego, 1995—; dir. client svcs. Calif. Anti-Aging Inst., Encinitas, Calif., 1999—. Co-author chpts. Podiatry Today, vol. 10 # 7, 1997. Vol. telethon Muscular Dystrophy Assn., San Diego, 1991, Easter Seals, San Diego, 1991. Mem. Am. Coll. Healthcare Execs. (assoc.), Med. Group Mgmt. Assn. (assoc.), Emergency Med. Assembly (assoc.), Healthcare Coalition San Diego County (assoc.), Psi Chi. Republican. Methodist. Avocations: fitness training, horseback riding, target shooting, reading, guitar. Office: M&G Med Svcs 4198 Convoy St San Diego CA 92111-3702

TIDWELL, PAULA MARCELLA, business educator; b. Seattle, July 30, 1962; arrived in Australia, 1992; d. Eddy Tidwell and Ramona (Hopping) Kechelen; children: Jasmine Rebecca, Danielle Violet. BS, Memphis State U., 1985, MS, 1989, PhD, 1993. Course instr. Memphis State U., 1989-91; vis. lectr. CSU, Bathurst, N.S.W., Australia, 1992-93, tenured lectr., 1993-95, sr. lectr., 1995-97; assoc. prof., acting dean Faculty Bus. USQ, Toowoomba, Australia, 1997-98; prof., deputy dean UniSA, Whyalla Norrie, South Australia, 1998—; counselor Lakeside, Memphis, 1984-86; account exec., rsch. analyst K & A, Memphis, 1986-89; cons. Bathurst, 1993-96, Toowoomba, 1996—. Author: Consumer Behavior in Australia and New Zealand, 1996; contbr. numerous articles to profl. jours. and conf. procs. Mem. OES, Bathurst, 1982. Fellow AMI (chpt. pres. 1995-96); mem. ACR, MRSA, AMS, APS, SCP, APA, Sigma Xi. Avocations: golf, skydiving, white water rafting, computer programming. Fax: (61) 8-8647-6088.

TIEDE, TOM ROBERT, journalist; b. Huron, S.D., Feb. 24, 1937; s. Leslie Albert and Rose (Allen) T.; children: Kristina Anne, Thomas Patrick. BA in Journalism, Wash. State U., 1959. Mem. staff Kalispell (Mont.) Daily Interlake, 1960-61, Daytona Beach (Fla.) News Jour., 1961-63; war corr. Newspaper Enterprise Assn., N.Y.C., 1964—; lectr. in field., 1965—. Author: Your Men at War, 1965, Coward, 1968, Calley: Soldier or Killer?, 1971, Welcome to Washington, Mr. Witherspoon, 1979, The Great Whale Rescue, 1986, American Tapestry: Eye Witness Accounts of the 1900's, 1988, The Man Who Discovered Pluto, 1990, Fosser, 1994, Self Help Nation, 2000. Served as lt., inf. AUS, 1960. Recipient Ernie Pyle Meml. award, 1965; Freedoms Found. award, 1966; George Washington medal, 1972. Mem. Internat. Platform Assn., Sigma Delta Chi, Lambda Chi Alpha. Roman Catholic. Clubs: Overseas Press, National Press, Nat. Headliners (award 1966 Atlantic City). Achievements include work collected by Boston U. Library. Office: NEA 1090 Vermont Ave NW Washington DC 20005-4905 also: PO Box 1783 Charlottesville VA 22902-1783

TIEDEMANN, ALBERT WILLIAM, JR., retired chemist; b. Balt., Nov. 7, 1924; s. Albert William and Catherine (Madigan) T.; m. Mary Therese Sellmayer, Apr. 6, 1953; children: Marie Therese, Donna Elise, Albert William III, David Lawrence. BS, Loyola Coll., Balt., 1947; MS, NYU, 1949; PhD, Georgetown U., 1958. Tchg. fellow NYU, 1947-50; instr. chemistry Mt. St. Agnes Coll., 1950-55; chief chemist Emerson Drug div. Warner Lambert Pharm. Co., Balt., 1955-60; analytical supr. Hercules Powder Co., Allegany Ballistics Lab., Cumberland, Md., 1960-68; tech. svc. supt. Hercules Inc., Radford, Va., 1968-72; dir. Va. Div. Consol. Labs., Richmond, 1972-78; vice-chmn. Va. Toxic Substances Adv. Council, 1978-92; dep. dir. for labs. Va. Dept. Gen. Svcs., 1978-92, cons. 1992-98; ret . Mem. sci. adv. com. Longwood Coll., 1983-90. Served to lt. (j.g.) USNR, 1943-46; capt. Res., 1946—. Fellow Am. Inst. Chemists, Soc. Advancement Mgmt. (chpt. v.p. 1983-84, chpt. pres. 1984-85), Am. Soc. Quality Control (chmn. Richmond sect. 1975-76, councilor biomed. divsn. 1978-80), U.S. Naval Inst., Naval Res. Assn. (dist. pres. 1954-57; nat. v.p. 1962-63, 65-69; nat. chmn. Navy Sabbath Program 1969-75, Nat. Meritorious Svc. award 1971, Twice a Citizen award 1978), Cen. Atlantic States Assn. Food & Drug Ofcls. (exec. bd. 1977-84, v.p. 1981-82, pres. 1982-83, CASA award 1986), Nat. Assn. Food & Drug Ofcls. (chmn. sci. and tech. com. 1981-85, sec.-treas. 1985-87), Internat. Assn. Ofcl. Analytical Chemists (editl. bd. 1986-88, bd. dirs. 1987-90), Analytical Lab. Mgrs. Assn., Royal Acad. Pharmacy (elected acad. fgn. mem. Barcelona, Spain 1989—). Home: 10511 Cherokee Rd Richmond VA 23235-1008

TIEDEMANN, HENRIK, financial executive, consultant; b. Frederiksberg, Denmark, Apr. 24, 1946; s. Elith and Karen (Hansen) T.; m. Eva Dagil, Jan. 29, 1972; children: Pernille, Christian. Student, Copenhagen Bus. Sch., 1971, Inst. of Bankers, Cambridge, 1977, Cedep-Gen. Mgmt., Fontainebleau, France, 1981. Mgr. Scandinavian Bank, London, 1972-74; mktg. mgr. Den Danske Bank, Copenhagen, 1979-80, mgr. internat., 1980-86; investment mgr. Danske Securities, Copenhagen, 1986-88; dir. Hafnia Mcht. Bank, Copenhagen, 1988-91, Fin. Advisers, Copenhagen, 1991—; chmn. Deres Design, Copenhagen, 1995—; bd. dirs. OneSeal Denmark; chmn. Rich Andersen Eftf af 1911, Denmark, 1996—. Co-editor: Managerial Education Perspectives, 1976-1986, 1986. Mem. Ctr. Européan Éducation Permanente Alumni Assn., Holte Tennis Club (pres.). Lutheran. Avocations: art, tennis, golf. Office: Fin Advisers, Frederiksberggade 19, DK 1459 Copenhagen Denmark

TIEDERLE, VIKTOR CHRIS, physicist, microelectronic technician; b. Oberstdorf, Germany, Nov. 9, 1954; s. Viktor and Anna (Kirchner) T.; m. Ursula Seeger, Feb. 16, 1978; children: Tobias, Simon, Benjamin, Daniel. Intermediate Diploma, Tech. U. Munich, 1977; diploma in physics, Tech. U. Stuttgart, Germany, 1981; D in Prodn. Technique, Tech. U. Berlin, 1999. Electronic devel. Aerocontakt, Plochingen, Germany, 1981-82; microelectronic engr. MBB, Kirchheim, Germany, 1983-92; project mgr. assembly/interconnection TEMIC-MBB Microsysteme, Kircheim, Germany, 1992-99; mgr. process engring. Mannesmam VDO AG, Karben, Germany, 1999—; asst. prof. Profl. Sch. Esslingen, Germany, 1990-98. Contbr. articles to profl. jours. Served with German Army, 1974-75. Mem. Internat. Soc. for Hybrid Mfg., mem. German Welding Inst. Achievements include patent in microsoldering with laser, assembly of accelaration sensor. Avocations: family, work in Christian congregation. Office: Mannesmam VDO AG, Dieselstr 6-20, 61184 Karben Germany

TIEFENBRUN, JONATHAN, vascular surgeon; b. N.Y.C., Feb. 5, 1943; s. Joseph and Helen (Henkin) T.; m. Susan Kissil, June 19, 1966; children: Michele, Jeremy, Gregory. MD, SUNY, Bklyn., 1966. Diplomate Am. Bd. Surgery. Med. intern Kings County Hosp., Bklyn., 1966-67; resident in surgery Mt. Sinai Hosp., N.Y.C., 1967-73, chief resident in surgery, 1972-73, attending surgeon, 1973—; attending surgeon Beth Israel Hosp., N.Y.C., 1981—; sr. attending surgeon St. Luke's Roosevelt Hosp., N.Y.C., 1981—; asst. prof. Mt. Sinai Sch. Medicine, N.Y.C., 1973—. Contbr. articles to profl. jours. on medical ethics; inventor, patentee in field. NIH fellow, 1968-70. Fellow ACS, Am. Coll. Surgeons; mem. N.Y. Cardiovascular Soc. Avocation: classical guitar. Office: 67 W 55th St New York NY 10019-4902

TIELEMANS, PETER F.J., management consultant, researcher; b. Geldrop, The Netherlands, Oct. 16, 1968; s. P.A.W. and J.P.Th. (V.D. Berk) T. MSc, Utrecht U., 1992; PhD, Erasmus U., Rotterdam, 1996. Rschr. Erasmus U., Rotterdam, 1992-96; mgmt. cons. Ernst & Young, Utrecht, 1996—. Author: Lead Time Performance in Manufacturing Systems, 1996; contbr. articles to profl. jours. including Internat. Jour. Prodn. Econs. and European Jour. Operational Rsch. Mem. Dutch Soc. Logistics. Avocation: music. Home: Meidoorn 44, NL-566AS Geldrop The Netherlands Office: Ernst & Young Cons, Varrolaan 100, 3502 GC Utrecht The Netherlands

TIEN, CHANG-LIN, engineering educator; b. Wuhan, China, July 24, 1935; came to U.S., 1956, naturalized, 1969; s. Yun Chien and Yun Di (Lee) T.; m. Di-Hwa Liu, July 25, 1959; children: Norman Chihnan, Phyllis Chihping, Christine Chihyih. BS, Nat. Taiwan U., 1955; MME, U. Louisville, 1957; MA, PhD, Princeton U., 1959; PhD (hon.), U. Louisville, 1991, U. Notre Dame, 1992, Hong Kong U. Sci. and Tech., 1993, U. Conn., 1994, U. Waterloo, Can., 1995, U. Ill., 1995, Ohio State U., 1996, Hong Kong Bapt. U., 1996, Ariz. State U., 1996, Mills Coll., 1997, SUNY, Stony Brook, 1998. Acting asst. prof. dept. mech. engring. U. Calif., Berkeley, 1959-60, asst. prof., 1960-64, assoc. prof., 1964-68, prof., 1968-88, 90—, A. Martin Berlin chair prof., 1987-88, 90-97; Disting. prof. U. Calif., Irvine, 1988-90, NEC Disting. prof. engring, 1997—; chmn. divsn. thermal sys. U. Calif., Berkeley, 1969-71, also vice chancellor for research, 1983-85, chair dept. mech. engring., 1974-81; exec. vice chancellor U. Calif., Irvine, 1988-90; chancellor U. Calif., Berkeley, 1990-97; councillor Nat. Acad. Engring., 1998—; chair exec. com. Internat. Ctr. for Heat and Mass Transfer, 1980-82; hon. prof., dir. Xi'an Jiaotong U. Engring. Thermodynamics Rsch. Inst., 1987—; mem. adv. bd. Hong Kong U. Sci. and Tech., 1991—; chair internat. adv. panel Nat. U. Singapore, 1993—, U. Tokyo Inst. Indsl. Sci., 1995; tech. cons. Lockheed Missiles and Space Co., GE; gov. bd. dirs. Com. of 100, 1991—; bd. dirs. Wells Fargo Bank, Raychem Corp., 1996, Kaiser Permanente, AirTouch Comm., Chevron Corp., 1997; mem. coun. Fgn. Rels., 1996; active Aspen Inst. Domestic Strategy Group, 1992-97; chmn. Bay Area Econ. Forum, 1997—, Chief Exec.'s Commn. Innovation and Tech., Hong Kong, 1998-99, Asia Found. Bd. Trustees, 1999—; cons. in field. Author one book; editor Internat. Commn. Heat and Mass Transfer, 1981—, Internat. Jour. of Heat and Mass Transfer, 1981—; editor-in-chief Exptl. Heat Transfer, 1987—, Microscale Thermophysical Engineering, 1997—, ; editor twelve vols.; contbr. articles to profl. jours. Bd. dirs. Com. 100, 1991—; trustee Chiang Indsl. Charity Found., Ltd., Hong Kong, 1991—, Princeton U., 1991-95, U.S. Com. Econ. Devel., 1994—, Carnegie Found. Advancement Tchg., 1994-97; trustee Asia Found., 1993—, chmn., 1998—. John Simon Guggenheim fellow, 1965, Sr. U.S. Sci. fellow Japan Soc. for Promotion of Sci., 1980; recipient Sr. U.S. Sci. award Alexander von Humboldt Found., 1979, Pi Tau Sigma award for Excellence in Tchg., 1972 ; named Most Disting. Chinese scholar, Soc. Hong Kong Scholars, 1989, Li Ka Shing Disting. Lectr., U. Hong Kong, 1994, Gordon Wu Disting. Lectr., Princeton U., 1995, Martin Martel Lectr., Brown U., 1996. Fellow AAAS (bd. dirs. 1992—), ASME (hon., chair exec. com. heat transfer divsn. 1980-81, v.p. basic engring. 1988-90, Heat Transfer Meml. award 1974, Gustus L. Larson Meml. award 1975, AIChE/ASME Max Jakob Meml. award 1981, Disting. Lectr. award 1987-91), AIAA (Thermophysics award 1977), Am. Acad. Arts and Scis. (hon. 1991), Academia Sinica (hon., Taiwan 1988); mem. NAE (mem. internat. affairs adv. com. 1987-90, chair mech. engring. peer com. 1989-90, councillor 1998—), Am. Soc. Engring. Edn. (mem. nat. adv. coun. 1993—), Heat Transfer Soc. Japan (hon. 1995), Chinese Acad. Scis. (fgn. mem., Hon. Prof., Inst. Thermophysics 1981—). Office: U Calif Dept Mech Engring 6101 Etcheverry Hall # 1740 Berkeley CA 94720-1741

TIEN, CHENG, physicist, educator; b. Taipei, Taiwan, Mar. 31, 1948; s. Jia-Jen and Tzuu-Hwa (Wang) T.; m. Zan-Ping Ma, June 2, 1976; children: Tzyh-chyang, Tzyh-Hwa, Tzyh-Yang. BS, Nat. Cheng Kung U., Tainan, Taiwan, 1971; MS, Nat. Cheng Kung U., 1977; PhD, U. Calif., Riverside, 1986. Asst. prof. Temple U., Phila., 1986-87; assoc. prof. physics Nat. Cheng Kung U., Tainan, 1987-91, prof., 1991—. Contbr. articles to profl. jours. Named Hon. resident, City of Riverside, 1986. Mem. Am. Phys. Soc., Chinese Phys. Soc., N.Y. Acad. Sci., Phi Tau Phi, Phi beta Kappa. E-mail: chentien@mail.ncku.edu.tw. Home: 40 Alley 21 Lane 99, Pei-Yuang St, Tainan Taiwan Office: National Cheng Kung Univ, Dept Physics, Tainan Taiwan

TIEN, PO, virologist, biotechnologist; b. Huantai, Shandong, Peoples Republic of China, Dec. 25, 1931; s. Jun-yi and Sun-shi Tian; m. Meiyun Pei, Jan. 2, 1957 (dec. 1989); children: Yupei, Changpei; m. Jingyi Zhang, Apr. 4, 1991. Grad., Beijing Agr. U., 1954. Trainee prof. China Acad Scis., Beijing, 1954-61, asst. prof., 1962-77, assoc. prof., 1979-85; assoc. prof. Inst. Microbiology, China Acad. Scis., Beijing, 1985—; Disting. schoalr Adelaide (Australia) U., 1981; vis. prof. Dusseldorf (Germany) U., 1985; vis. scholar U. Md., College Park, 1990, SCRI, Dundee, Scotland, 1993, John Innes Inst., Norwich, Eng., 1993. Contbr. articles to profl. jours.; patentee in field. Recipient numerous sci. awards. Mem. Chinese Acad. Scis. (life), Am. Soc. Virology, Indian Virological Soc. (life). Home: 943A 601 Zhong Guancun, Beijing 100080, China Office: Inst Microbiology, CAS, Zhong Guancun, 100080 Beijing China

TIENARI, PEKKA JOHANNES, psychiatrist, educator; b. Pernio, Finland, May 27, 1931; s. Matti and Aino (Maatta) T.; m. Helena Rauhala, Apr. 29, 1954; children: Jukka Pekka, Janne Pekka. Lic. Medicine, U. Helsinki, Finland, 1957; MD, U. Helsinki, 1964. Resident Halikon Piirisairaala, 1953-55, Hesperia Hosp., 1955-59; resident U. Helsinki dept. psychiatry, 1959-61, asst. chief, 1961-65; prof., chmn. dept. psychiatry U. Oulu, Finland, 1965—; dean med. faculty U. Oulu, 1971-75; cons. psychiatrist Inst. Occupational Health, Helsinki, 1958-65, Out-Patient Clinic for Alcoholics, Helsinki, 1958-60, Clinic Marriage Guidance, Helsinki, 1958-59; lectr. psychiatry Social Coll., Helsinki, 1958-60; vis. prof. U. Rochester, N.Y., 1982. Author (with K.A. Achte and Y.O. Alanen) Textbook of Psychiatry, 1971; contbr. articles to profl. jours. NIH postdoctoral fellow NIMH, Bethesda, Md., 1967-68; WHO fellow, Eng., 1969. Mem. Finnish Psychiat. Assn. (pres. 1970-76), Scandinavian Assn. Psychiatrists (pres. 1978-82). Lodge: Rotary. Avocations: golf, music. Home: Rantakatu 13 B 3, 90100 Oulu Finland Office: Univ Ctrl Hosp, Peltolantie 5, 90210 Oulu Finland

TIENG, QUANG MINH, engineering researcher; b. Saigon, Vietnam, Nov. 14, 1960; s. Nhut Minh and Thuy Nguyet (Phan) T. BME, U. Polytechnic, Saigon, 1982; B of Elec./Computer Engring. with honors, Queensland U. of Tech., 1991, PhD, 1996, M of Info. Tech., 1998. Mech. engr. Binh Minh 7, Ho chi Minh City, Vietnam, 1982-85; lab. asst. Analabs, Brisbane, 1986-88; asst. engr. Met. South Area Office, Queensland Electricity Commn., Brisbane, 1988; tutor Sch. Elec. and Electronic Systems Engring. Queensland U. of Tech., Brisbane, 1992-95, rsch. asst. Space Ctr. for Satellite Navigation, 1995, postdoctoral rsch. fellow Ctr. Statis. Sci./Indsl. Maths., 1996-98; postdoctoral rsch. fellow Info. Security Rsch. Ctr., 1999; sr. rsch. officer Ctr. for Magnetic Resonance, 1999—. Contbr. articles to profl. publs. Recipient Rsch. award Australian Govt., 1992-95, Microwave Radar Undergrad. prize DSTO, 1992; Travel scholarship ANZIIS '93, ICASSP, 1994. Mem. IEEE, The Instn. of Engrs. Fax: 61-7-3365-3833. E-mail: tieng@cmr.ug.edu.au. Home: U Queensland, Ctr for Magnetic Resonance, Brisbane QLD 4072, Australia

TIERNEY, MICHAEL EDWARD, lawyer; b. N.Y., July 16, 1948; s. Michael Francis and Margaret Mary (Creamer) T.; m. Alicia Mary Boldt, June 6, 1981; children: Colin, Madeleine. BA, St. Louis U., 1970, MBA, 1978, JD, 1978. Bar: Mo. Assoc., law clk. Wayne L. Millsap, P.C., St. Louis, 1977-80; staff atty. Interco. Inc., St. Louis, 1980-83; textile divsn. counsel Chromalloy Am. Corp., St. Louis, 1984-87; v.p., sec. P.N. Hirsch & Co., St. Louis, 1983-84; sr. counsel, asst. sec. Jefferson Smurfit Corp., St. Louis, 1987-92, v.p., gen. counsel, sec., 1993-99; v.p., gen. counsel, sec. Morriss Holdings L.L.C., St. Louis, 1999—. Mem. adv. bd. St. Louis Area Food Bank, 1980—. U.S. Army Security Agy., 1970-73. Mem. Racquet Club St. Louis, Old Warson Country Club. Republican. Roman Catholic. Avocations: sailing, squash. Home: 10 Twin Springs Ln Saint Louis MO 63124-1139 Address: Witan Management 18500 Edison Ave Chesterfield MO 63005-3629

TIERNEY, ROBERT, artist, textile and graphic designer; b. Plymouth, Eng., Aug. 9, 1936; s. Cyril Fortesque and Hilda T.; student Plymouth Coll. Art, 1954-56; diploma in Art, Central Sch., London, 1956, postgrad., 1956-58; student Atelier Clay, Paris, 1959-60. Painter in watercolors, oil, design colors; textile/graphic designer cos. in U.K., Paris, Zurich, Vienna, also Denmark, Finland, Italy, Australia, Can., U.S., Japan, 1958—. Exhbn. debuts, London and Paris, 1958, N.Y.C. and Toronto, 1959; exhibited Can., 1979, Vienna, 1964—; works exhibited cities in U.S., Europe, Far East, 1982, 83, 84, 85, 86; touring exhbns., Japan, 1977-81, U.S., 1982, 5 other works accepted by Victoria and Albert Mus., U.K., 1986 . Designer Tickenham Rugby Centenary scarf, U.K., 1971, scarf Mus. Fine Arts, Boston, 1979; work exhibited annually London Design Centre, Manchester, Paris, 1959—, European Tour, 1989; paintings represented in permanent and pvt. collections; design works in pub. and govt. bldgs., pvt. residences, also archives Design Centre U.K., Victoria and Albert Mus., Boston Mus. Fine Arts; designed Royal Bouquet silk screen scarf to commemorate wedding of Prince of Wales, 1981. Registered Council Indsl. Design. Home: Modbury Club, 31 Church St, Modbury Ivybridge PL21 0QR, England Office: care Council Industrial Design, The Design Ctr Haymarket, London SW1, England

TIERNEY, WILLIAM MICHAEL, internist, educator; b. Detroit, July 2, 1951; s. Thomas John and Joan Rosemary (Lynch) Tierney; m. Mary Menzies, Aug. 12, 1972; children: Ryan Menzies, Adam Taylor. BA, Ind. U., 1973, MD, 1976, postgrad., 1976-79. Chief resident internal medicine Wishard Meml. Hosp., Ind. U. Med. Ctr., Indpls., 1979-80; fellow Regenstrief Inst. Health Care, 1980-82; asst. prof. dept. medicine Ind. U. Sch. Medicine, Indpls., 1980-86, assoc. prof., 1986-91, prof., 1991—; chmn. divsn. gen. internal medicine and geriatrics Ind. U. Med. Ctr., Indpls., 2000—; assoc. dir. computer sci. rsch. sect. Regenstrief Inst., 1987-93, dir. quality assessment and improvement sect., 1993—, dir. Regenstrief-Moi (Kenya) Informatics Fellowship, 1998—; mem. divsn. gen. internal medicine Roudebush VA Med. Ctr., 1996—, assoc. dir. health svcs. rsch. program, 1996—, dir. ambulatory care fellowship program., 1997—; chair large-scale database task force Nat. Heart Attack Alert Program, 1997—; mem. steering com. ambulatory quality improvement program Dept. Vets. Affairs, 1997-99, mem. steering com. vets. health study, 1995-97, mem. health svcs. rsch. large grants rev. bd., 1993; mem. steering Federated Coun. for Internal Medicine, 1997-98; expert witness Office of Hearing and Appeals, Social Security Adminstrn., 1981-92; mem. spl. study sect. NIH, 1989; med. malpractice reviewer Ind. Atty. Gen.'s Office, 1991-93. Contbr. articles to profl. jours. Founder, dir. med. support team Wishard Meml. Hosp., 1982-90; chmn. med. manpower com. Pan Am. Games, Indpls., 1985-87, sports medicine officer, 1987; vol. physician Indpls. Horizon House Ctr. for Homeless Persons, 1993-98; mem. Ind. Alliance for Preventive Health, Ind. State Dept. Health, 1993-96; co-founder Parents for Acad. Challenge, 1994-95; mem. coord. com. cmty. health access project Marion County Dept. Health; mem. Ind. Commn. on Health Care for the Working Poor, 1995-98; mem. steering com. Ind. U. Parents Fund, 1996—; mem. clin. performance team Clarian Health Care, mem. data repository subcom. info. sys. com., 1997; mem. evaluation subcom. Ind. Children's Health Care Ins. Program, 1998. Recipient Vitae bonae award for outstanding contbns. in fitness and health awareness Senator Richard Lugar, 1987; grantee NCHSR, PHS, NIH, AHCPR, Glaxo Pharms., Indpls. Found., Indpls. Health Found., Regenstrief Inst., Ind. State Dept. Health, Boehringer-Mannheim Pharms. Corp., Caremark, Inc., Eli Lilly Co., Dept. Vets. Affairs, NLM, NIH/Fogarty Internat. Ctr., Dept. Vets. Affairs, Ind. U., Electronic Data Sys., Clarian Health Ptnrs., CDC, Am. Lung Assn., Bristol-Myers-Squibb, NIMH. Fellow ACP (mem. med. informatics com. 1991-92), Am. Coll. Med. Informatics, Am. Med. Informatics Assn. (founding fellow, chair ambulatory health care area nat. symposium 1993, bd. dirs. 1996-99, nominations com. 1998); mem. APHA (co-editor Med. Care, med. nat. leadership med. care sect. 1997—), Soc. Gen. Internal Medicine (pres., membership chair midwestern region 1987, program chair nat. meeting 1989, fin. com. 1989-93, chair fin. com. 1991-92, mem. com. 1989-93, chair mgmt. com. 1991-92, nominating com. midwestern region 1990, nat. sec.-treas. 1991-92, nat. coun. mem. 1990-93, 95-97, mem. ethics com. 1992-94, chair ethics com. 1993-94, long-range planning com. 1993-96, edn. com. 1994-96, Glaser award com. 1995, pres. 1996-97, devel. com. 1997-99, chair devel. com. 1997-98, comms. com. 1998—, rsch. awards com. 1998—), Am. Fedn. Med. Rsch., Ctrl. Soc. Clin. Rsch., Soc. Med. Decision Making, Assn. Health Svcs. Rsch., Assn. for Better Care for Dying. Avocations: running, tennis. E-mail: wtierney@i-upui.edu.

TIETJEN, SCOTT PHILLIPS, computer programmer, analyst; b. West Haven, Conn., May 14, 1960; s. Henry Louis and Ruth Evelyn (Haupt) T. BS in Applied Math. and Computer Sci., Carnegie-Mellon U., 1982; MS in Computer Sci., Marist Coll., 1991. Staff programmer IBM Corp., Poughkeepsie, N.Y., 1982-93; cons. personal computer technician Aerotek, Inc., N.Y.C., 1993; cons. programmer/analyst Data-Based Devel. Sys., East Providence, R.I., 1994; cons. data security analyst Atlantic Search Group, Inc., Stamford, Conn., 1994-95; cons. programmer/analyst Maxim Group, Shelton, Conn., 1995; sr. cons., programmer/analyst Keane, Inc., Danbury and Rocky Hill, Conn., 1996—. Treas. Aid Assn. for Luths. Br. 6981. Mem. IEEE (computer soc.), Assn. Computing Machinery, Tall Clubs Internat. (club del.), Tri-County Talls of N.Y. and Conn. (newsletter editor), Rivercity High Soc. (Evansville, Ind.), Atlanta Sky-Hi Club, Atlantic Tall Club. Republican. Lutheran. Avocations: theatrical and architectural lighting design. Office: Keane Inc 100 Corporate Pl Rocky Hill CT 06067-1803

TIETMEYER, HANS, banker, former government official; b. Metelen, Westphalia, Germany, Aug. 18, 1931. Dipl. in Econs., U. Cologne, 1958, Dr.rer.pol., 1960; hon. doctorate, Westfälische Wilhelms U., Münster, Germany, 1994, U. Md., 1997. With Fed. Ministry for Economy, Fed. Republic Germany, Bonn, 1962-68, ministerial dir., 1972-82; mng. dir. Found. Cusanuswerk, Bonn, 1959-62, officer divsn. basic issues of econ. sys. and policy, 1962-67, head directorate European Common Market/rels. with 3d world, 1970-72, head directorate basic issues of econ., bus. cycle, growth, 1972-73, head directorate gen. I, 1973-82; permanent sec. Ministry of Fin., Fed. Republic Germany, Bonn, 1982-89; v.p. Deutsche Bundesbank, 1991-93, pres., bd. dirs., 1993-99; chmn. G-10 Ctrl. Bank Govs., 1994-99, German Gov. to IMF; pres. econ. policy com. EEC, Brussels, 1974-76, pres. monetary com., 1985; pres. group for positive adjustment policies OECD, Paris, 1977-78, chmn.; hon. prof. econs. Faculty Econ. Scis. Martin-Luther-U. Halle-Wittenberg, 1996; chmn. EC Economic Policy Com., EC Monetary Com.; bd. dirs. Ctrl. Bank Coun. Author books and articles. Chmn. bd. dirs. Deutsche Bundesstiftung Umwelt. Decorated grand cross Order of Merit (Germany). Mem. Pontifical Acad. Social Scis., Rotary Club Bonn. Avocation: sports. Office: Deutsche Bundesbank, Wilhelm-Epstein-Strasse 14, 60431 Frankfurt am Main, Germany

TIETZ, DIETMAR JUERGEN, computer Web engineer, scientist; b. Berlin, Jan. 19, 1951; s. Alfred Georg Paul and Gertrud Klara (Schulz) T. m. Angelina (Osorio Ugalde). PhD, Hamburg U., 1982. Lectr. U. Hamburg, 1977-82; sr. scientist macromolecular analysis NIH, Bethesda, Md., 1983-93; pres., CEO, chmn. mktg. Forty Plus Greater Washington, 1992-93; sci. project mgr. dept. biostats. Justus-Liebig U., Giessen, Germany, 1993-95; web engring. team lead, software arch. Aerotek Md., NASA EOSDIS govt. project Raytheon Systems, 1996-99; dir. product devel. Dynamic Diagrams subs. Cadmus Profl. Comm., 1999—. Editor: Nucleic Acid Electrophoresis Lab Manual, 1998; mem. editl. bd. Electrophoresis Jour., VCH Weinheim, Germany, 1994-96. Mem. Am. Chem. Soc., Assn. German Naturforscher and Aerzte. Lutheran. Avocations: nature, computers, photography, electronic keyboard. E-mail: djt@his.com. Office: Cadmus Profl Comm 940 Elkridge Landing Rd Linthicum MD 21090-2917

TIETZ, REINHARD, economics educator; b. Frankfurt am Main, Fed. Republic Germany, July 28, 1928; s. Edwin and Gerda (Broesel) T.; m. Ursula Naujoks, 1964; children: Christiane, Susanne. Student, U. Mainz, 1958-59; U. Muenchen, 1959-60, U. Frankfurt, 1960-63; diploma in bus., U. Frankfurt, 1963, D. in Polit. Sci., 1971. Lab. technician, sales engr. chem., paper, printing industry, 1951-58; univ. asst. U. Frankfurt, 1963-73, lectr. computer programming, 1970-73, asst. prof. econs., 1973-74, prof. econs., 1974-95; cons. OECD, 1973-74. Author: Anspruchsanpassungsorientiertes Wachstums-und Konjunkturmodell, 1973; editor: Wert-und Praeferenzprobleme in den Sozialwissenschaften, 1981, Aspiration Levels in Bargaining and Economic Decision Making, 1983; co-editor: Sozialwissenschaften im Studium des Rechts, 1977, Bounded Rational Behavior in Experimental Games and Markets, 1988; mem. editorial bd. Jour. Behavioral Decision Making. Mem. Am. Econ. Assn., Internat. Assn. for Rsch. in Econ. Psychology, Verein für Socialpolitik (chmn. com. for social scis. 1976-81), Gesellschaft fuer experimentelle Wirtschaftsforschung (chmn. 1982-95—), Gesellschaft fuer Wirtschafts- undSozialkybernetik. E-mail: tietz@wiwi.unifrankfurt.de. Home: Steinhausenstrasse 23, D 60599 Frankfurt am Main Germany

TIETZE, KLAUS DIETER, physicist; b. Lipine, Silesia, Germany (now Poland), Aug. 31, 1943; s. Günther Ernst and Erna Maria (Wrzeciona); m. Irmeli Tuulikki Suojanen, Aug. 1, 1970; 1 child, Tuuli Katharina. Diploma in Physics, Tech. U. Brunswick, Germany, 1970; Dr.rer.nat., U. Kiel, Germany, 1978. Rschr. Fed. Inst. Physics and Metrology, Brunswick, 1966-70; rsch. scientist Fed. Inst. Geoscis. and Natural Resources, Hanover, Germany, 1970-78, sr. rsch. scientist, 1978-88; sr. rsch. scientist Joint Geosci. Rsch. Inst., Hanover, 1989—; expedition leader Rsch. Expedition to Lake Kivu, Zaire, Rwanda, 1974, 75, Rsch. Expedition to Lake Tanganyika, Zaire, Burundi, Tanzania, 1981, Rsch. Expedition to Lake Nyos, Cameroon, 1986; cons. UNESCO, Yaounde, Cameroon, 1987; founder, main assoc., dir. PDT Gmbh-Physik Design Technik-Sensorik & Consulting, Celle, Germany, 1989—; mem. adv. com. Nyos-Monoun Degassing Project, 1997—. Contbr. numerous articles to profl. jours., chpts. to books. Mem. Internat. Assn. Volcanism and Chemistry of the Earth's Interior (mem. steering com. commn. on volcanic lakes 1987—), Am. Assn. Advancement Sci., Am. Geophys. Union, Internat. Assn. Theoretical and Applied Limnology, Geochem. Soc. Japan, Geophys. Soc. Finland, German Phys. Soc., German Aero Club, Nat. Geog. Soc., NY Acad. Sci., The Planetary Soc. Roman Catholic. Avocations: gliding, horseriding, photography, dancing, writing. E-mail: klaus.tietze@tietze-research.de. Home: Postweg 6A, D-29227 Celle Germany

TIETZE, WOLF RUDOLF, geographer, editor, researcher, consultant; b. Chemnitz, Saxony, Germany, Oct. 8, 1924; s. Rudolf Wilhelm and Johanna (Patzer) T.; m. Gretel Behrend, June 7, 1951 (div. Mar. 1980); children: Gunnar, Holger, Karen; m. Marie-Luise Steinmann, Apr. 28, 1980. D Natural Scis., U. Mainz, Germany, 11958. Editor, mng. dir. Georg Westermann Pubs., Braunschweig, Germany, 1951-67; prof. UCLA and Calif. State Coll., L.A., 1967-68; mem. faculty various univs., Germany, Hungary, Sweden, Switzerland, 1969-78, China, 1987; ind. editor, 1969-95; historian Commn. of Lower Saxony, History Soc. of Chemnitz. Author, editor, translator 160 books pub. in 12 countries, 1954—; founder editor Geoforum, 1970—, GeoJour., 1977—; editor: Westermann Lexikon d. Geographie 5 vols., 1968-72, also subsequent edits.; contbr. over 165 articles to sci. jours. in numerous countries. With German Armed Forces, 1942-45. Mem. German Cartographic Assn. (hon.), Hungarian Geog. Soc. (hon.), Geog. Soc. Finland (corr.). Home and Office: Magdeburger Strasse 17, 38350 Helmstedt Germany

TIEW, DANIEL, controller; b. Kuala, Lumpur, Malaysia, Apr. 9, 1960. B in Acctg. with honors, U. Malaya, 1984; LLB with honors, U. Wolverhampton, 1995. CPA, Australia, Malaysia, Hong Kong Soc. Accountants. Auditor Authur Andersen, Kuala, Lumpar, 1984-88; supr. in tng. Ernst & Young, Hong Kong, 1989-90; reg. fin. mgr. Walt Disney, 1990-92; fin. contr. Reebok Tng., Far East, Hong Kong, 1992-95; reg. fin. dir. Asia Pacific Reebok Trading Far East Ltd., 1995—. Avocations: travel, reading, scuba diving. Office: Reebok Internat Ltd, 25 Canton Rd Ste 1303-1312, Tsimshatsui Hong Kong

TIGERE, PATRICK, lawyer; b. Marondera, Zimbabwe, Sept. 13, 1968; s. Joel Tigere and Irene Nyika Mutomgbwera; m. Tsitsi Makona; children: Michelle, Irene. BSc with honours, U. Zimbabwe, Harare, 1990; diploma in pub. rels., Zimbabwe Inst. Pub. Rels., Harare, 1990; LLM, U. Lund, Sweden, 1992. Voters roll officer town clk.'s dept. City of Harare, 1991; assoc. protection and legal officer UN High Commr. for Refugees, Monrovia, Liberia, 1994-96; protection and legal officer UN High Commr. for Refugees, Dar es Salaam, Tanzania, 1996-99; legal advisor Standards and Legal Advice Sect. Dept. Internat. Protection. UNHCR Hdqs., Geneva, Switzerland, 2000—. Contbr. articles to publs., including Zimbabwe Legal Forum, African Jour. Internat. and Comparative Law. Nat. vice chmn. Zimbabwe Orgn. for Nuclear Edn., Harara, 1987-89; mem. Harare Jr. City Coun., 1987-88; chmn. univ. br. Zimbabwe African Nat. Union, Harare, 1989-90. Mem. African Soc. Internat. and Comparative Law, African Assn. Polit. Sci. (exec. coun. Zimbabwe chpt. 1990-92). Avocation: pursuing justice in all spheres of life. Home: 6 rue du Vieux-Billard, 1205 Geneva Switzerland Office: UNHCR Hdqs, 94 rue du Montbrillant, 1202 Geneva Switzerland

TIGGES, JOHN THOMAS, writer, musician, lecturer; b. Dubuque, Iowa, May 16, 1932; s. John George and Madonna Josephine (Heiberger) T.; m. Kathryn Elizabeth Johnson, Apr. 22, 1954; children: Juliana, John, Timothy, Teresa, Jay. Student, Loras Coll., 1950-54, 57, U. Dubuque, 1960. Night club entertainer, 1950-52; clk. John Deere Tractor Works, Dubuque, 1957-61; agt. Penn Mut. Life Ins. co., Dubuque, 1961-97; bus. mgr., bd. dirs. Dubuque Symphony Orch., 1960-68, 71-74; v.p., sec. Olson Toy and Hobby, Inc., 1964-66; pres. JKT, Inc., 1978-82; rsch. specialist Electronic Media Svcs. (Scripp-Howard), 1983-85; violinist; tchr. continuing edn. creative writing N.E. Iowa C.C., 1975-98; tchr. writing U. Wis. Outreach Program's Ednl. Teleconf. Network, summer writing workshop U. Iowa; tchr. Rhinelander Sch. of the Arts, 1997-98; mem. faculty S.W. Writers Workshop, 1998; co-founder Dubuque Symphony Orch., 1960; founder Julien Strings, 1972, Dubuque Sch. of Novel, 1978, N.E. Iowa Writers Workshop, 1981; co-host Big Broadcast Radio Program, WDBQ Radio, 1979-82; founder Sinipee Writers Workshop, 1985, dir. emeritus, 1997; founder Sinipee Critiquing/Editl. Svcs., 1988; faculty Southwest Writers Workshop, 1998. Author: (novels) The Legend of Jean Marie Cardinal, 1976, Garden of the Incubus, 1982, Unto the Altar, 1985, Kiss Not the Child, 1985, Evil Dreams, 1986, The Immortal, 1986, Hands of Lucifer, 1987, As Evil Does, 1987, Pack, 1987, Venom, 1988, Vessel, 1988, Slime, 1988, Book of the Dead, 1989, From Below, 1989, Comes the Wraith, 1990, Breed, 1990, Mountain Massacre, 1990, Blood on the Rails, 1990, One Man Jury, 1991, The Curse, 1993, Monster, 1995 (book of short stories) Nightales, 1990, (plays) No More-No Less, 1982, We Who Are About to Die, 1983, Remember When...?, 1997; contbg. author: Murder for Father, 1994, The New Amazons, 1997; (radio plays) Valley of Deceit, 1978, Rockville Horror, 1979, The Timid, 1982, All Bets are Down, 1991, 20th Century in Review, 2000; TV drama: An Evening with George Wallace Jones, 1983; biographies: George Wallace Jones, 1983, John Plumbe Jr., 1983; prodr. TV series: The Loneliest Job, 1989; co-author: (non-fiction) The Milwaukee Road Narrow Gauge: The Bellevue, Cascade & Western, Iowa's Slim Princess, 1985, They Came from Dubuque, 1983, Milwaukee Road Steam Power, 1994, Dubuque in the 19th Century, 2000, Dubuque in the 20th Century, 2000, Dubuque-Then and Now, 2000, Father of the Waters, 2000; co-author, editor: A Cup anda Half of Coffee, 1977; editl. asst. Julien's Jour.; contbg. editor Over 49 News and Views; interviewer, spl. reporter Editl. Assocs., 1982-84; columnist Memory Lane, What's the Difference, Telegraph Herald; syndicated columnist Tough Trivia Tidbits, Remember When...?, The 20th Century in Review; author 2,300 articles. Founder, bus. mgr. Dubuque Pops Orch., 1957; founder Better Quality Writing Pubs., 1996. Recipient Nat. Quality award, 1966-70, Carnegie-Stout Libr. World of Lit. honors award, 1981; John Tigges Writing contest named in his honor, John T. (and Kathryn E.) Tigges endowment scholarship for Writing Majors named in his honor, Loras Coll., Dubuque. Fellow World Lit. Acad.; mem. Horror Writers Am., Western Writers Am., Iowa Authors, Internat. Platform Assn., Toy Train Collectors Club, Dubuque Rails Model Railroad (co-founder 1987). Roman Catholic. Home: 2240 Coates St Dubuque IA 52003-7108

TIGHE-MOORE, BARBARA JEANNE, electronics executive; b. Wadsworth, Ohio, Jan. 12, 1961; d. Norton Raymond and Laura Alida (Frank) Tighe; m. Derek William Moore, June 26, 1982. Student, Hocking Tech. Coll., 1981, Sinclair Coll., 1986; BBA Honors Coll. magna cum laude, Kent State U., 1988. Lic. amateur radio operator. Tech. writer computer dept. Sinclair Coll., Dayton, Ohio, 1983; project mgr. O'Neil & Assocs., Dayton, 1983-84; biomed., bio-acoustic real-time flight simulation tempest developer Systems Rsch. Labs., Dayton, 1984-86; computer specialist Kent State U. Press, 1987-88; mgmt. analyst Electronic Warfare Frontier Engring. Inc., 1988-89; supr. small computer tech. svcs. Frontier Engring., Inc., 1989-90, project engr., 1990-92; ptnr., bd. dirs. MKCC, Dayton, 1990—, SDCC, Dayton, 1992—; regional mgr. User Tech. Assocs., Dayton, 1993-96; pres., owner Lida Ray Techs., Dayton, 1978—; mem. graphics steering com., mem. sanctioned UNIX software adv. team Aero. Sys. Divsn.; program chair IEEE Internat. Wireless LAN Conf.; mem. Engring. Application Support Environ. Security Working Group, pres., 2000; proceedings chmn. Nat. Aerospace & Electronics Conf., 1995, 96, 97, bd. dirs., pres., 2000; bd. dirs. MKCC, Dayton, 1993—, SDCC; pres. bd. dirs. NAECON, 2000; spkr. Govt. Land Mobile Commn. Conf., 1993, Internat. Engring. Mgmt. Cons., 1994, Wireless '93, Calgary, Alta., Nat. Aerospace & Electronics Conf., 1995, 96, 97. Author: Job Search Strategies for the 90's, 1993, Through the Glass Ceiling, 1997; co-author: Women on a Wire, 1996; editor: Graphics Directions, 1990-91; pub. Team Advisor, SDCC Cleaning Times, IEEE Update; contbr. poetry to mags. and anthologies; contbr. papers, articles to profl. jours. Counselor Kwam's Kinder Kamp; tchr. Bible Sch.; cook Meals on Wheels; organizer/cook funeral Svcs. Dinners. Recipient Vol. Citizen award Wadsworth C. of C, 1979, Ohio Essayist award, 1979, Virginia Perryman award, 1979, Disting. Leadership award, 1990, 91. Mem. IEEE (former treas., sec. Dayton sect., bd. dirs. 1995-97, chmn. bd. dirs. Dayton sect. 1999, region 2 chpt. coord. 2000—), Computer Soc. of IEEE (sec. 1991-92, vice chmn. 1992-93, chmn. 1994-95), Engring. Mgmt. Soc. of IEEE, Tech. and Soc. of IEEE, Data Processing Mgmt. Assn., Assn. Computer Machinery, Def. Planning Analysis Soc. (exec. bd.), Assn. Internat. Students Econs. & Commerce (pres. 1986-87), Internat. Film Soc. (pres. 1986-88), Armed Forces Comms. and Electronics Assn. (judge sci. fair western dist. 1992—), Equestrian Team (point rider 1977-87), Fencing Club, Phi Theta Kappa, Mortar Bd., Omicron Delta Kappa, Beta Gamma Sigma. Avocations: travel, investing, equestrian show jumping, soccer. Home: 729 Kyle Dr Tipp City OH 45371-1435

TIGYI, JOZSEF, biophysicist; b. Kaposvar, Hungary, Mar. 19, 1926; s. Andras and Julianna (Matrai) T.; m. Anna Sebes, Aug. 10, 1952; children: Gabor, Zoltan. MD, Med. U., 1950; PhD, Hungarian Acad. Sci., 1954, DSc, 1964. Rsch. assoc. Inst. Med. Biology, Berlin, 1952, Inst. Physiology, Shanghai, 1960, Inst. di Radiologie, Rome, 1962, Harvard Med. Sch., Boston, 1964-65; vis. prof. Inst. Biophysics, Moscow, 1971; prof., dir. Biophys. Inst. Med. U., Pecs, 1971—, rector, 1973-79. Author: Application of Radioactive Isotopes in Experimental Medicine, 1965, Biophysics, 1977. Mem. exec. bd. WHO, Geneva, 1972-75. Recipient Gold medal of Order of Labour, Coun. of Ministers, Budapest, 1970, 79. Mem. Am. Biophys. Soc., Hungarian Acad. Scis. (pres. biol. sect. 1980-88, nat. v.p. 1989—), Biophys. Soc. Hungary (pres. 1970-91, hon. pres. 1991—), Royal Soc. Medicine, N.Y. Acad. Scis., European Acad. Arts Scis. Humanities., Internat. Coun. Sci. Unions, Internat. Union for Pure and Applied Biophysics (sec. gen. 1984-93). Home: Fogaras U3, 7624 Pecs Hungary Office: Biophys Inst Medical U, Szigeti ut 12, 7643 Pecs Hungary

TIIHONEN, JARI ARTO TAPANI, forensic psychiatry educator; b. Säyneinen, Finland, Nov. 27, 1960; s. Aarne and Katri (Pitkänen) T.; m. Elina Juntunen, May 2, 1986; children: Jaakko, Laura, Ilkka. Licentiate in medicine, U. Kuopio, Finland, 1985, DMS, 1990, specialist in psychiatry, 1994, specialist in forensic psychiatry, 1994. Resident in psychiatry Niuvanniemi Hosp., Kuopio, 1985-93, chief psychiatrist, 1993-94; resident in psychiatry Kuopio U. Hosp., 1985-93; assoc. prof. U. Oulu, Finland, 1995; acting prof. forensic psychiatry U. Kuopio, 1995-97, prof., chmn., 1997—; cons. physician Ctrl. Prison, Riihimäki, 1987-89. Mem. Finnish Coll. Physicians, Finnish Med. Assn., No. Savolax Med. Soc. Office: U Kuopio Niuvanniemi Hosp, Dept Forensic Psychiatry, 70240 Kuopio Finland

TIILI, VIRPI, judge; b. 1942. LLD, U. Helsinki, Finland. Asst. lectr. civil and comml. law U. Helsinki, 1968-78; dir. legal affairs and comml. policy Ctrl. C. of C. of Findland, 1978-90; dir. gen. Office for Consumer Protection, Finland, 1990-94; judge Ct. of First Instance of European Communities, Luxembourg, 1995—. Office: Ct of Justice of Europ Cmty, Blvd Konrad Adenauer, Kirchberg L-2925, Luxembourg*

TIJMANN, WILLEM BERT, civil engineer, consultant; b. Semarang, Java, Indonesia, Oct. 19, 1929; came to the U.S., 1956; s. Johan Hendrik and Alida Catharina (Deylius) T.; m. Martha Vanderlaan, Oct. 21, 1958 (div. 1986); children: Sonya Maria, John (dec.); m. Mirna Aeschlimann, Aug. 18, 1991. BS, Poly. Coll., Amsterdam, The Netherlands, 1953, M in Civil Engring., 1955. Registered profl. engr., Europe. Sr. hydraulics engr. Olarte, Ospina Arias y Payan Ltda, Civil Engrs., Bogotá, Colombia, 1955-56; soils and materials engr. Fay Spofford, Boston, 1956-62; sr. project engr. Dames & Moore, San Francisco, 1962-76; v.p. Slope Indicator Co., Seattle, 1976-87; pres. E&T Instrumentation, Stoneham, Mass., 1987—, W.B.T. Cons., Edmonds, Wash., 1987—. Inventor: holds 4 patents in U.S. and Can. Mem. ASCE (hon.), ASTM (sr.), Internat. Soc. Soil Mechanics and Engring. Found., Assn. Engring. Geologists (affiliate). Avocations: certified professional diver, diving, sailing, tennis, hiking. E-mail: tijmann 70@yahoo.com. Home: 101A Pond St Stoneham MA 02180-2804 Office: PO Box 2367 Woburn MA 01888-0667

TIKAL, KAMIL JOSEF, psychiatrist, psychopharmacologist; b. Benešov, Prague, Czech Republic, Apr. 11, 1938; s. Josef and Jiřina (Nováková) T.; m. Zdenka Ludmila Hadravová, Dec. 18, 1982. MD, Charles U. Med. Faculty, Hradec Králové, Czech Republic, 1961; PhD, Slovac Acad. Scis., Bratislava, Slovak Republic, 1970. Jr. asst. Charles U. Med. Faculty, 1961-64; rsch. fellow Palacky U. Med. Faculty, Olomouc, Czech Republic, 1964-68, sci. worker, 1968-70; sr. lectr. Charles U. Med. Fculty of Hygiene, Prague, 1970-77, asst. prof., 1977-92; clin. pharmacologist, psychiatrist, head dept. Psychiat. Hosp., Kosmonosy, Czech Republic, 1992—; forensic expert in pharmacology Mcpl. Ct., Prague, 1994, forensic expert in physiology, 1994, forensic expert in psychiatry, 1997. Author: (textbook) Introduction into Pharmacology, 1985; contbr. articles to profl. jours. Mem. Internat. Brain Rsch. Orgn., European Coll. Neuropsychopharmacology, Med. Soc. J. E. Purkyně. Avocations: reading, walking. Home: Štorkánova 2805/4, 150 00 Prague 5, Czech Republic Office: Psychiat Hosp, 293 06 Kosmonosy Czech Republic

TIKHONOV, NIKOLAI IVANOVICH, computer design educator; b. Mariyevka Village, Russia, Mar. 3, 1949; s. Ivan Karpovich and Alexandra Ivanovna (Osipova) T.; m. Valentina Ivanovna Klinkova, Sept. 2, 1970; 1 child, Natali. MS in mfg. engring., Penza Polytech. Inst., Penza, Russia,

1972; PhD of engring., Moscow Automechanical Inst., Moscow, 1976; cert., Moscow State Tech. Univ., Moscow, 1984, Novgorod Training Inst., Novgorod, Russia, 1988, European Sch. Edn., Belgorod, Russia, 1995. Jr. rsch. scientist Novgorod Polytech. Inst., Novgorod, Russia, 1977, asst. prof. engr. mechanics, 1977-80, sr. lectr. of mfg. engr., 1980-83; assoc. prof. CAD system Novgorod State Univ., Novgorod, Russia, 1983-90, vice dean of engring. faculty, 1990-98; sr. rsch. assoc. NRC, Air Force Rsch. Lab., Ohio, 1998-99, assoc. prof. info. tech. and CAD sys., 1999—; chmn. of rsch. coun. of students Novgorod State Univ., 1980—, prin. rsch. of CAD system, 1983—, head of expert coun. of engr. faculty, 1992-93, rsch. adv. of predoctoral fellow, 1990—, mem. ednl. methodical bd. 1994—. Contbr. numerous articles to profl. jours.; mem. editorial bd. Politechnik, 1984-88. Mem. Bd. Flexible Mfg. System and Robotics, Novgorod, 1984-88; mem. organizing com. Internat. Conf. of Actual Problems of Strength adn V. Likhachev, Novgorod, 1997-98. Recipient Rsch. Training Edn. Ministry for Outstanding Engring. Students Moscow Automechanical Inst., 1972-73, NRC award AFRL, 1998; fellow Moscow Automechanical Inst., 1973-76. Mem. AAAI, Scientific Coun. of Engring. (sec. 1994-98). Avocations: hiking, planing of vegetables and fruits, internet, cinema. E-mail: tikhonov@info.novsu.ac.ru. Home: 2 Ul Mendeleyeva kv 45, 173016 Novgorod Russia Office: Novgorod State Univ, 41 B St Petersburg St, 173003 Novgorod Russia

TIKHONOV, NIKOLAY GAVRILOVICH, medical researcher; b. Balakovo, Saratov, Russia, May 6, 1946; s. Gavril Vasilievich and Galina Ferdorovna (Balashova) T.; m. Tatjana Alexandrovna Mushenkova, Oct. 6, 1967; children: Sergey Tikhonov and Natalja Tikhonova (twins). Candidate First Degree, Med. Inst., Saratov, Russia, 1973; MD, Saratov U., Russia, 1988. Cert. med. doctor. Asst. Med. Inst., Saratov, Russia, 1972-73; jr. rsch. assoc. Plague Rsch. Inst., Saratov, Russia, 1973-79, sr. rsch. assoc., 1979-81, lab. chief, 1981-85; dir. Plague Rsch. Inst., Volgograd, Russia, 1985—. Author rsch. papers. Mem. Russian Acad. Natural Scis. (v.p. 1995), Scis. Ecol. Acad. 3, N.Y. Acad. Scis., Volgograd Club of Doctors. Avocations: hunting, fishing. Home: Lenin's Ave 10-52, 400066 Volgograd Russia Office: Plague Rsch Inst, Golubinskaya St 7, 400131 Volgograd Russia

TIKHONOV, VADIM SEMENOVICH, mechanical engineer, researcher; b. Moscow, Jan. 13, 1949; s. Semen Iosifovich and Maria Nikolaevna (Arbuzova) T. Degree in electromech. engring., Moscow Aviation Inst., 1972, D Engring., 1977; postgrad., U. Ednl. Skill, Moscow, 1976. Engr., sr. engr. Moscow Aviation Inst., 1972-74, sr. sci. rschr., 1977-83; sr. sci. rschr., head dept. All-Union Inst. Mineral Resources, Moscow, 1983-87; leading sci. rschr. Ctrl. Rsch. Inst. Geol. Prospecting Base & Precious Metals, Moscow, 1988-99; gen. project rschr. Aquatic Co., Moscow, 1999—; sci. cons. All-Union Inst. Ocean Machine-Bldg., Dnepropetrovsk, USSR, 1986-89, All-Union Inst. Drilling Engring., Moscow, 1988-91, All-Union Inst. Pipeline Constrn., Moscow, 1993-95, Aquatic Co., Moscow, 1994-99. Contbr. articles to profl. jours. Avocations: mountaineering, collecting postage stamps, table tennis. Fax: 7-095-235-12-65. Office: Aquatic Co, 7-9 Letnikovskaya St, 113114 Moscow Russia

TIKHONOV, VILEN NIKOLAY, geneticist, researcher, educator; b. Kiev, Ukraine, USSR, May 28, 1925; s. Nikolay and Cecilia Tikhonov; m. Zoya Konstantin Burlak, Feb. 12, 1949; 1 child, Alex. MSc, MD, Moscow Agrl. Acad., 1947; D Agrl. Sci., USSR Inst. Animal Genetics, 1950; D in Biol. Scis., USSR, 1967. Head lab. Regional Inst. Animal Breeding, Saratov, Russia, 1950-52; sr. sci. worker Inst. Zool.-Tech. of Latvian Acad. Scis., Riga, 1952-59; sr. sci. worker Inst. Cytology and Genetics USSR Acad. Scis., Novosibirsk, 1959-64, head lab. immunogenetics Inst. Cytology and Genetics, 1965-86, rsch. leader, 1986—; prof. animal genetics Novosibirsk State Agrl. U., 1970-96; mem. acad. bds. Inst. Cytology and Genetics Russian Acad. Scis. Author/co-author over 350 sci. books and publs. in field, including Blood Group of Animals in Selection Process, 1967, Genetics of Mini-Pigs, 1990, Biochemical Polymorphism of Wild and Domestic Pigs, 1991; developer hybrid pigs and minipigs from wild boars for xenotransplantation with alteration karyotypes. Regional dir. Siberia of World Info. Transfer, N.Y. Mem. N.Y. Acad. Scis. Avocations: breeding dogs, collecting pig figures, recreational activities. E-mail: Tikhonov@CGI.NSK.su. Office: Inst Cytology and Genetics, Russian Acad Scis, 630090 Novosibirsk Russia

TIKHONOV, YURYI VLADIMIROVICH, biochemist; b. Moscow, Oct. 11, 1951; s. Tikhonov Vladimir and Zoy Fedorovna Tikhonov; m. Zoy Fedorovna Kokorina, July 11, 1992; 1 child, Dmitryi. Dipl Biochemist, State 2d Med. Inst., Moscow, 1975, DrBiochemistry, 1982; DSc, State Med. U., Moscow, 1992. Sci. rschr. State Med. U., Moscow, 1975—; cons. State Inst. of Skin, Moscow, 1997—. Contbr. articles to profl. jours. Mem. N.Y. Acad. Scis. Christian Orthodox.

TIKKAKOSKI, TAPANI ANTERO, radiologist, neuroradiologist; b. Kokkola, Finland, Apr. 18, 1959; s. Tauno Johannes and Eeva Liisa (Piilola) T.; m. Riitta Irmeli Saarinen, 1984; children: Mikko, Elina, Katri. MD, Oulu U., 1983, PhD, 1990. Radiologist Keski-P Ctrl. Hosp., Finland, 1987-89, 91—, Oulu (Finland) U., 1989-91, 95-97; with dept. radiology Keski-P Ctrl. Hosp., 1997—. Contbr. articles to profl. jours. 2d lt. Finland Med. Corps, 1985-86. Recipient Xenia Forselliana, Acta Radiologica, 1994. Mem. Am. Inst. Ultrasound Medicine, Radiol. Soc. N.Am., Finnish Assn. Radiologists, European Soc. Neuroradiology. Home: Salmentie 24, 67700 Fin-Kokkola Finland

TIKKANEN, ESA, hockey player; b. Helsinki, Finland, Jan. 25, 1965; married. Hockey player Edmonton, 1984-93, N.Y. Rangers, 1992-93, 93-94, 1996-97, 98-99; hockey player St. Louis, 1994-95, 95-96, N.J., 1995-96, Vancouver, 1995-96, 96-97, Fla. Panthers, 1997-98, Wash., 1997-98. Recipient ice hockey Bronze medal Olympic Games, Nagano, Japan, 1998. Achievements include member of Finland team during three World Jr. Championships, 1983-85, and three World Championships, 1985, 89, 93, member of six Stanley Cup winning teams. Avocations: golf, tennis. Office: NY Rangers Madison Square Garden 2 Penn Plaza New York NY 10121*

TIKKANEN, TUOMO AARNE JUHANI, psychologist; b. Helsinki, Finland, Mar. 4, 1951; s. Aarne J. and Synnöve K. (Niku-Paavo) T.; m. Auli M. Rissanen, Oct. 10, 1975; children: Anna, Tommi. MPhil, Helsinki U., Finland, 1980; Licentiate of Psychology, Jyväskylä U., Finland, 2000. Lic. Psychologist; registered psychotherapist. Youth counselor Helsinki Child Protection Bureau, Finland, 1976-77; psychologist Children's Castle Hosp., Helsinki, Finland, 1978-79; pvt. practice Helsinki, Finland, 1980—; psychologist Helsinki Sch. & Social Svcs., 1980-84; chief psychologist Helsinki City Sch. Bureau, 1985—; v.p. Finnish Assn. for Child and Youth Psychotherapy, 1996-2000. Mem. Finnish Psychol. Assn. (pres. 1994—), European Fedn. of Profl. Psychologists Assns. (pres.). Avocations: music, nature, sea, traveling. Office: Finnish Psychol Assn, Bulevardi 30 B3, 00120 Helsinki Finland

TIKOSH, MARK AXENTE, lawyer; b. Arad, Banat, Romania, Aug. 17, 1955; came to U.S., 1981; s. Axente and Elena Ticosh; m. Mary Victoria Rotarescu, Sept. 10, 1979. BBA in Acctg. summa cum laude, Calif. State U., Fullerton, 1989; JD, U. of the Pacific, 1992, LLM, 1993. Bar: Calif. 1993. Acct., auditor II Orange County Probation Dept., 1984-88; pvt. practice Sacramento, Calif., 1993-94, Long Beach, Calif., 1994—; cons. U. Banat Acad. Found., Timisoara, Romania, 1997—. Editor The Transnational Lawyer, 1991. Scholarship McGeorge Legal Edn. Endowment Found., 1989-90, Dana Found., 1992-93. Mem. Calif. State Bar Assn. (estate planning trust and probate law sect.), L.A. County Bar Assn. (litigation sect.), Beta Gamma Sigma. Republican. Avocations: travel, history, philosophy. Office: 800 E Ocean Blvd Ste 100 Long Beach CA 90802-5463

TIKTOPOULOS, ALEXANDROS, steel company executive, engineer; b. Sevastopol, Greek, Sept. 3, 1934; s. Thrasyvoulos and Irene (Stilidou) T.; m. Argyro Androulakis, May 2, 1962; children: Andreas, Irene. MS, Tech. U., Athens, Greece, 1957. Registered profl. engr., Greece. Asst. prof. electric machines Tech. U., Athens, Greece, 1958-60; project mgr. Techniki Enossis S.A./Constrn., Crete, Greece, 1960-62; project mgr. Viokat S.A./Erection, Ptolemais, Greece, 1962-64, Thessaloniki, Greece, 1964-66; chief engr. head office Viokat S.A./Erection, Athens, 1966-67; with Hellenic Steel Co., S.A., Thessaloniki, 1968-84, dep. mng. dir., 1980-86; mng. dir., chief exec. officer Hellenic Steel Co., S.A., Athens, 1986-94; bus. cons., 1994-98; pres., dir. Gen. Hellenic Steelmakers Union, Athens, 1999—; mem. Com. for Tech. Rsch. European Communities, Brussels, Consultative Com. of European Coal and Steel Community. Contbr. articles to profl. jours. With Greek Navy, 1957-60. Mem. Assn. Industries Northern Greece (sec. gen. 1973-75, v.p. 1975-81), Thessaloniki C. of C. and Industry (bd. dirs. 1982-85), Fedn. Greek Industries (v.p. 1986-88), Assn. Greek Metal Industries (bd. dirs., trustee 1971-94). Office: 39 Panepistimiou St, 10564 Athens Greece

TILAAR, HENRY A.R., social planner educator; b. Tondano, Indonesia, June 16, 1932; s. Kilala and Engelien (Mamuaya) T.; m. Martha Handana, Jan. 12, 1964; children: Bryan, Pingkan, Wulan, Kilala. MA in Edn., U. Indonesia, Jakarta, 1961; MSc in Edn., Ind. U., 1967, EdD, 1969. Prof. State U. of Tchrs. Coll., Jakarta, 1969-97; asst. min. Nat. Devel. Office (Bappenas), Jakarta, 1986-93; prof. U. Jakarta, 1987-98, prof. emeritus, 1997—; dir. Inst. Ednl. Mgmt. Devel., Jakarta, 1991—; cons. in field. Author: Education in National Development, 1990, National Education Management, 1992, Indonesian Education Development, 1945-1995, A Policy Study, 1995, Human Resources Development, Vision and Mission for 2020, 1997, Agenda for Education Reform for 21st Century, 1998, Education, Culture, and Civil Society, 1999. Chmn. bd. advisors Cath. U., Jakarta, 1995—; mem. bd. advisors Acad. Mgmt., Jakarta, 1996. Recipient Grand medal of merit Republic of Indonesia, 1998. Mem. Nat. Rsch. Coun., Indonesian Edn. Assn., Indonesian Soc. for Advancement of Social Scis., Indonesian Lectrs. Assn. Mem. Democratic Party. Roman Catholic. Avocations: gardening, jogging, watching soccer. Home: Jl Patra Kuningan Utara, Blok L-VII No 4, Jakarta Indonesia Office: LPMP State U Jakarta, Jl Rawamangun Muka, Jakarta DKI, Indonesia

TILBURY, RODNEY NEIL, chemistry educator; b. Perth, Australia, Mar. 6, 1960; arrived in New Zealand, 1991; s. Louis George and Mavis Rosina (Gannaway) T.; m. Farida Elizabeth Fozdar, Apr. 4, 1982; children: Ella Shirin, Dylan Reid, Elliott Yurikobanyal. BSc in Chemistry with honors, U. Western Australia, Perth, 1982, PhD, 1988. Rsch. asst. U. Western Australia, Perth, 1986, tutor, 1987-88; lectr. U. Papua New Guinea, Port Moresby, 1988-91, assoc. dean, 1990; lectr. Victoria U. Wellington, New Zealand, 1991-96, sr. lectr., 1997—. Editor (proceedings) 6th Congress of the Papua New Guinea Inst. of Chemistry, 1991; contbr. articles to sci. jours. Recipient Commonwealth Postgrad. award Australian Govt., 1982-86, Travel award Royal Soc. New Zealand, 1994. Mem. Am. Soc. for Photobiology, N.Y. Acad. Scis., Assn. Sci. Edn., New Zealand Inst. Chemistry, Assn. Women into Sci. Baha'i. Avocation: philately. Home: 51B Cornford St Karori, Wellington New Zealand Office: Victoria U Chemistry Dept, PO Box 600, Wellington New Zealand

TILBY, MICHAEL JOHN, French language and literature educator; b. Harrow-on-the-Hill, Eng., Apr. 16, 1949; s. Edward James and Winifred Joan (Trist) T.; m. Susan Elizabeth Wharton. BA, Cambridge (Eng.) U., 1971, MA, 1975; PhD, Ecole Normal Supérieure, Paris, 1976. Tutorial asst. U. Hull, Eng., 1975-76; lectr. comparative lit. U. East Anglia, 1976-77; fellow, lectr. French Selwyn Coll. U. Cambridge, 1977—, dir. studies in modern lang., 1980—, praelector, 1979-83, librarian, 1983-86, tutor, 1987—, tutor for admissions, 1987-92; sr. tutor, 1992—; editor Selwyn Coll. Calendar, 1980-88; gov. Ipswich Sch., 1992-2000, Watford Grammar Sch. for Boys, 1992—; mem. coun. Malvern Coll., 1995—. Author: A. Gide: Les Faux-Monnayeurs, Beyond the Nouveau Roman, Balzac; editor: Nouvelles Choisies de P. Mérimée, P. Lainé, La Dentellière; contbr. articles to profl. jours. and collaborative vols. French Govt. scholar, 1973-74. Mem. Modern Humanities Rsch. Assn., Soc. for French Studies (publicity officer, mem. exec. com. 1984-92), Soc. d'Histoire Littéraire de la France (Brit. corr. 1992—). Anglican. Avocations: cooking, opera, wine, Italy. Home: High Trees Church St, Hemingford Grey, Huntingdon Cambridgeshire PE28 9DF, England Office: Selwyn Coll, Cambridge CB3 9DQ, England

TILDEN, RALPH FULTON, retired music educator, organist; b. High Point, N.C., Feb. 10, 1930; s. Thomas Alphonso and Ruth Eugenia (Fulton) T. BMus, Cin. Conservatory Music, 1952, MMus, 1954. Tchr., Fla. Prof. organ Cin. Conservatory Music, 1954-60; tchr. music, theology Cathedral Sch., Orlando, 1960-65; prof. Edison C.C., Ft. Myers, Fla., 1966-95; organist, choirmaster Calvary Ch., Cin., 1954-60, St. Luke's Cathedral, Orlando, 1960-65, St. Luke's Ch., Ft. Myers, 1965-95; organ recitalist, U.S.A., France, Eng. Composer (choral works) Come, Holy Spirit, Come, 1987, His Voice as the Sound, 1997, Assumpta Est Maria, 2000. Vol., activist ACLU, 1960—, Nat. Gay & Lesbian Task Force, 1960—, Mtn. AIDS Support Coun., Boone, N.C., 1999. Mem. Am. Guild Organists (dean), Assn. Anglican Musicians, Organ Hist. Soc., Liturgy & Music Commn., Diocese of Western N.C. Democrat. Episcopal. Avocations: antique collecting, gardening. Home: 960 Meadow Ave Banner Elk NC 28604-9401

TILDEN, WESLEY RODERICK, writer, retired computer programmer; b. Saint Joseph, Mo., Jan. 19, 1922; s. Harry William and Grace Alida (Kinnaman) T.; m. Lorraine Henrietta Frederick, June 20, 1948 (dec. Mar. 1999). Grad., Navy Supply Corps Sch., 1945; BS, UCLA, 1948; BA, Park Coll., Mo., 1990. Purchasing agent Vortox Co., Claremont, Calif., 1951-61; lang. lab. dir. Mount San Antonio Coll., Walnut, Calif., 1962-65; computer programmer, operator General Dynamics, Pomona, Calif., 1967-70; ret., 1970. Author: (book) Scota, The Egyptian Princess, 1994, Merit-Sekhet: Foster Mother of Moses?, 1996; photographer, textbooks, mags., newspaper, catalogs. Historian Claremont Sister City Assn., 1963-66. Lt. USNR, 1942-46 PTO. Recipient with Lorraine Tilden People to People award Reader's Digest Found., 1963-64, 1964-65; named Hon. Citizen Guanajuato, Mexico, 1963. Mem. Soc. Mayflower Descendants, Scottish Clans, UCLA Alumni Assn., Park Coll. Alumni Assn., Univ. Club of Claremont, The Scituate (Mass.) Hist. Soc. Republican. Avocations: history, genealogy, photography, gardening. Home: 351 Oakdale Dr Claremont CA 91711-5039

TILEY, JOHN, law educator; b. Leamington Spa, Eng., Feb. 25, 1941; s. William Arthur and Audrey Ellen (Burton) T.; m. Jillinda Millicent Draper, Dec. 27, 1942; children: Nicholas John, Christopher George, Mary Isobel. BA, Oxford U., 1962, BCL, 1963, MA, 1967; MA, Cambridge U., 1967, LLD, 1995. Lectr. Lincoln Coll., Oxford, 1963-64; lectr-in-law U. Birmingham, U.K., 1964-67; fellow Queen's Coll., Cambridge, 1967—; lectr., asst. lectr. U. Cambridge, U.K., 1967-87, reader in tax law, 1987-90, prof. tax law, 1990—; recorder Lord Chancellors Dept., U.K., 1988-98; chmn. Faculty Bd. and Law, 1992-95; v.p. Queen's Coll., Cambridge, 1988-96; hon. bencher Inner Temple, London, 1993—; vis. prof. various law schs. in various countries. Author: Revenue Law, 4th edit., 2000; author, editor: Tiley's Collison's U.K. Tax Guide, 1999—; contbr. articles to profl. jours. Mem. Soc. Pub. Tchrs. of Law (pres. 1995-96). Home: Westchester Hungtingdon Rd, Cambridge CB3 OLG, England Office: Queens Coll, Cambridge CB3 9ET, England

TILGNER, SIEGFRIED JOHANN, biologist, ophthalmologist; b. Deschnei, Sudeten, Germany, June 16, 1929; s. Siegfried and Emilia (Zeipelt) T.; m. Anneliese Johanna Peter, Nov. 12, 1954; 1 child, Peter Siegfried. Diploma in biology, U. Halle, Fed. Republic Germany, 1954, Dr.rer.nat, 1957, Dr.rer.nat.habil., 1967. Asst. U. Halle, 1954-57, 57-58; fellow Stazione Zoologica, Naples, Italy, 1957; rsch. asst. U. Jena, Fed. Republic Germany, 1959-61, head rsch. lab., 1961-93, vice dir. dept. ophthalmology, 1968-86, assoc. prof., 1993-95, ret., 1995; cons. U. Jena, 1959—. Contbr. over 100 articles to profl. jours. Recipient Hufeland medal Ministry of Health, 1989. Mem. N.Y. Acad. Scis. (life.). Home: Saalweg 10, D-07747 Jena Thuringia Germany Office: U Jena Dept Ophthalmology, Bachstrasse 18, D-07740 Jena Thuringia Germany

TILIACOS, MICHAEL APOSTOLOS, physician; b. Kalymnos, Greece, Mar. 17, 1917; s. Apostolos and Afroditi (Skylla) T.; m. Mary, Aug. 30, 1956; 1 child, Kalliopi. MD, Athens U., 1946. Intern Evangelismos Hosp., Athens, 1941-45, registrar, 1945-50; hon registrar London Hosp., 1951-52; lectr. Evangelismos Hosp., 1953-55; dir. med. dept. Spiliopoulion Hosp., Athens, 1955-74; dir. med. dept. Evangelismos Hosp., 1974-87, prof. medicine. Author, editor: Lecturer of Social Interest, 1999; contbr. articles to profl. jours. With Greek Mil., 1941-42. Min. Health scholar, Brit. Council, London, 1950-52. Mem. Med. Soc. Athens, Med. Soc. Cardiology, Brit. Royal Soc., N.Y. Acad. Scis. Home: 27 Parthenonos St, 11742 Athens Greece Office: 28 Academias St, 10671 Athens Greece

TILININ, IGOR STANISLAVOVICH, physicist, educator; b. Vladivistock, Russia, Dec. 2, 1952; came to U.S., 1996; s. Stanislav Vladislavovich and Elena Andreevna Tilinin; m. Nadezhda Nikolaevna Yaroshuk, Aug. 7, 1980. MSc with distinction, Moscow Inst. Physics/Engring., 1976, PhD, 1981, DSc, 1994. Engr. Moscow Inst. for Physics and Engring., 1976-78, 81-83, asst. prof., 1983-90; rsch. fellow Inst. Phys. Chemistry, Polish Acad. Scis., Warsaw, 1994-96, docent, 1996; vis. scientist Lawrence Berkeley Nat. Lab., Berkeley, Calif., 1996-98; software engr. D.W. Smith & Assocs., San Mateo, Calif., 1998-2000; cons. DHL Sys., Inc., Burlingame, Calif., 2000—; vis. scientist Odense (Denmark) U., 1994, 95; guest prof. Charles U., Prague, Czech Republic, 1995; guest prof., vis. scientist U. Tech., Vienna, 1992-93. Author: Qualitative Problems on Atomic Physics with Solutions, 1990; co-author: Surface Analysis by Particle Backscattering, 1985. Recipient 2nd prize for best sci. paper Inst. Phys. Chemistry, Warsaw, 1995, 2nd prize for best rsch. work Moscow Inst. for Physics and Engring., 1982, 1st prize for best sci. paper Inst. Phy. Chemistry, Warsaw, 1997. Mem. AAAS, European Microbeam Analysis Soc., N.Y. Acad. Scis., Am. Phys. Soc. Christian. Home: 3135 Campus Dr Apt 320 San Mateo CA 94403-3138 Office: DHL Sys Ste 300 700 Airport Blvd Burlingame CA 94010

TILLEMA, HERBERT KENDALL, political science educator; b. Washington, Apr. 23, 1942; s. John A. and Ruth M. (Kendall) T.; m. Susan H. Murphy, July 11, 1966; children: Anne M., Marie K. BA, Hope Coll., Holland, Mich., 1964; PhD, Harvard U., 1969. Asst. prof. polit. sci. U. Houston, 1968-71; from asst. prof. to prof. polit. sci. U. Mo., Columbia, 1971—; mem. State of Mo. Peace Officer Stds. and Tng. Commn., Jefferson City, 1992-94. Author: Appeal to Force, 1973, International Armed Conflict Since 1945, 1991. Mem. Am. Polit. Sci. Assn., Internat. Studies Assn., Sierra Club (chair Osage Group 1973-74). Home: 306 Westridge Dr Columbia MO 65203-1774 Office: U Mo Dept Polit Sci Columbia MO 65211

TILLETT, GRACE MONTANA, ophthalmologist, real estate developer; b. Malone, N.Y., Dec. 5, 1924; d. Everett Reed and Althea Adela (Manson) Montana; m. Charles W. Tillett, Aug. 9, 1952; children—Charles, James, Avery. B.A., Syracuse U., 1946, M.D., 1949. Diplomate Am. Bd. Radiology, Am. Bd. Ophthalmology. Intern, Balt. City Hosps., 1949-50, resident, 1950-51; resident Johns Hopkins Hosp., Balt., 1951-53; practice medicine specializing in ophthalmology, Charlotte, N.C., 1957—; v.p. Prof. Optical Service, Charlotte, 1959—; pres. 2200 E. Seventh St. Real Estate Corp., Charlotte, 1965—; mem. staff Presbyn., Mercy, Charlotte Meml. hosps. Bd. dirs. Heart Assn. Charlotte, 1971-73, Dance Charlotte, 1978-79. Mem. Bus. and Profl. Women's Assn., Am. Acad. Ophthalmology, Am. Acad. Radiology, AMA, N.C. Med. Soc., Mecklenburg County Med. Soc., Charlotte Ophthalmol. Soc. Republican. Club: Charlotte Country. Office: 2130 Sharon Ln Charlotte NC 28211-3736

TILLIE, WILLY, archivist, educator; b. Poperinge, Belgium, June 14, 1942; m. Marie Louise Mahieu; children: An, Els, Jan. Historian, Geschiedenisleraar, Belgium, 1963. Tchr. VTI, Poperinge, 1963-97; archivist City of Poperinge. Author: Poperinge Historische gevels en gebouwen, 1975, Religieuze kunst in het Hoppeland, 1979, 150 jaar muziekleven in de Hoppestad, 1982, Terugblik Oude stadsgezichten in de Hoppestad, 1983, De Kroniek van Groot-Poperinge, 1987, De oorlog achter het front, 1987, reprint, 1999, Vlaamse haardtegels met slibversiering, 1987, Van alle markten thuis 800 jaar vrijdagmarkt - Poperinge, 1988, Poperinge in puin, 1990, Poperinge ondersteboven, 1990, Spreekwoorden en zegswijzen in de Westhoek, 1992, Scatologische spreekwoorden en zegswijzen in de Westhoek, 1993, Groeten uit het Hoppeland, 1993, 1970 Poperinge in woord en beeld, 1995. Avocations: travel, folklore, local history. E-mail: willy.tillie@online.be. Office: Aan de Schreve Kring, Korte Werf 3, 8970 Poperinge Belgium

TILLIETTE, XAVIER, philosophy educator, priest; b. Corbie, Picardy, France, July 23, 1921; s. Henri Tilliette and Yvonne Le Ker. License lit., U. Grenoble, France, 1942; license German, U. Lyon, France, 1946; license theology, Theol. Faculty, Lyon-Fourviere, 1953; PhD, U. Sorbonne, Paris, 1970; PhD in Theology (hon.), Theol. Faculty S. Luigi, Naples, Italy, 1993; PhD (hon.), U. Urbino, Italy, 1998. Entered Soc. of Jesus, 1938, ordained priest, 1951. Tchr. philosophy Coll. St. Louis, Paris, 1947-49, 54-57; writer Review Etudes, Paris, 1957-70; prof. modern philosophy Cath. U., Paris, 1969-88; vis. prof. Pontificial U. Gregoriana, Rome, 1972-96, prof. emeritus, 1996—; sec. redaction Rev. Archives Philosophy, Paris, 1961-71. Author: Schelling une Philosophie en Devenir, 2 vol., 1970 (medal of CNRS 1971), Schelling im Spiegel Seiner Zeitgenossen, 4 vols., 1974-96, L'Absolu et la Philosophie, 1986 (prize V. Delbos 1987), Le Christ de la Philosophie, 1990 (prize Montyon 1991), Le Christ des philosophes, 1993, L'intuition intellectuelle de Kant à Hegel, 1995, Schelling. Une biographie, 1999, La Mémoire et l'Invisible, 2000. Mem. Schelling Soc. (mem. of honor), Paul Claudel Soc. (dir. com.), Gabriel Marcel Soc. (chief com.). Home: 42 rue de Grenelle, 75343 Paris 07 France

TILLIL, HARTMUT HERMANN LUDWIG, internist; b. Stadtoldendorf, Germany, Sept. 12, 1956; s. Florenz Ludwig Karl August and Irmgard Elfriede (Hubrig) T.; m. Christiane Frees, Dec. 15, 1995. MD, U. Goettingen, Germany, 1982. Rsch. assoc. U. Goettingen, 1982-84, resident, 1984-85; rsch. assoc. U. Chgo., 1986-87; resident Klinikum Wuppertal GmbH, Germany, 1988-90, fellow, 1990-95, attending, 1996-2000; mem. staff Hosp. of U. Witten/Herdecke; privatdozent U . Duesseldorf, Germany, 1996; attending Klinikum E.V., Bergmann, Potsdam. Co-editor Diabetes Mellitus, 1996, Medizinische Klinik, 1997. Physician German Red Cross, Wuppertal, 1981—. Recipient Jr. Sci. award German Diabetes Soc., 1982, German Preclinical Emergency Medicine award Kuratorium Zur Foerderung Der Praeklinischen Notfallmedizin, 1990, AOK Health award AOK Health Ins., 1992, Juehling award U. Duesseldorf, 1997. Mem. German Soc. Internal Medicine (sci. congress sec. 1996-97), Am. Fedn. Med. Rsch., Am. Diabetes Assn., N.Y. Acad. Sci. Lutheran. Avocations: tennis, opera. Office: Klinikum EV Bergmann, Charlotten str 72, 14467 Potsdam Germany

TILLMAN, ANDREW R., law educator; b. Tahlequah, Okla., Nov. 10, 1951; s. Andrew Russel and Allene Ethel Tillman; m. Claudia Coffey, Dec. 12, 1975; 1 child, Andi Marie. JD, U. Tenn., 1989. Bar: Tenn. 1990, U.S. Dist. Ct. (ea. dist.) Tenn. 1990, U.S. Ct. Appeals (6th cir.) 1990. Law clk. to Hon. H. Ted Milburn 6th cir. Cin., 1989-91; assoc. Paine, Swiney, Tarwater, Knoxville, Tenn., 1991-97; adj. prof. law sch. U. Tenn., Knoxville, 1994, 95, 98, 2000; ptnr. Paine, Tarwater, Bickers, Tillman LLP, Knoxville, 1997—. Mem. Tenn. Bar Assn. Avocations: fishing, hunting, farming, welding, excavating. Home: 403 Lowe Rd Huntsville TN 37756-5501 Office: Paine Tarwater Bickers & Tillman LLP 1100 First Tenn Plz Knoxville TN 37929

TILLMAN, ELIZABETH CARLOTTA, nurse, educator; b. Md., Aug. 31, 1929; d. Walter Monroe and Mozelle Virginia (Shugars) Brown; m. Lloyd A. Tillman, Apr. 16, 1949; children: Lloyd A. Jr., William L., Susan E. Tillman Chaires. Diploma, Md. Gen. Hosp. Sch. Nursing, 1950; student, Towson State U., U. Md., Loyola Coll., Balt., Howard C.C. RN. Psychiatric nurse Spring Grove Hosp. Ctr., Catonsville, Md., 1950; pvt. duty home health nurse Md., 1951-60; dir., tchr., nurse Doughoregan Manor Day Sch., Ellicott City, Md., 1960-80; med.-surg. nurse Woman's Hosp., Balt., 1964, Md. Gen. Hosp., Balt., 1980; nursing instr. Howard County Dept. Edn., Ellicott City, 1981-91; nursing educator Howard County Sch. Tech., 1981-91, Howard County Gen. Hosp., 1981-91; geriatric nurse Lorien Columbia (Md.) Nursing & Rehab. Ctr., 1981-91; home health nurse Md., 1992—. Mem. NEA, Md. State Tchrs. Assn., Md. Gen. Hosp. Alumni Assn., Am. Vocat. Assn., Health Occupations Educators, Md. Vocat. Assn., Phi Eta Sigma, Iota Lambda Sigma. Home: 10002 Reed Ln Ellicott City MD 21042-2238

TILLMAN, JOSEPH NATHANIEL, engineering executive; b. Augusta, Ga., Aug. 1, 1926; s. Leroy and Canarie (Kelly) T.; m. Alice Lavonia Walton, Sept. 5, 1950 (dec. 1983); children: Alice Lavonia, Robert Bertram; m. Areerat Usahaviriyakit, Nov. 24, 1986. BA magna cum laude, Paine Coll., 1948; MS, Northrop U., 1975, MBA, 1976; DBA, Nova U., 1989. Dir. Rockwell Internat., Anaheim, Calif., 1958-84; pres. Tillman Enterprises, Corona, Calif., 1985—; guest lectr. UCLA, 1980-85. Contbr. articles to profl. jours. Capt. USAF, 1948-57, Korea. Recipient Presdl. Citation Nat.

Assn. for Equal Opportunity in Higher Edn., 1986. Mem. Acad. Mgmt. (chmn. 1985-86), Soc. Logistics Engrs. (pres. 1985-86), Paine Coll. Alumni Assn. (v.p. 1976—), NAACP (pres. 1984-88). Avocations: duplicate bridge, travel, swimming, skiing, hiking. Office: Tillman Enterprises 1550 S Rimpau Ave Spc 45 Corona CA 92881-3206

TILLMAN, MARY NORMAN, urban affairs consultant; b. Atlanta, Jan. 31, 1926; d. Mary Nellie Shehee; B.A., Morris Brown Coll., 1947; postgrad. U. Minn., 1964, Old Dominion U., 1975—; m. James A. Tillman, Jr., Apr. 11, 1952; children—James A., Gina G. Asst. bus. mgr. Morris Brown Coll., Atlanta, 1947-53; race relations and urban affairs cons. Tillman Assos. Cons. Social Engrs., Atlanta and Syracuse, N.Y., 1963—, sr. ptnr., treas., from 1965, now pres.; bd. dirs. The Tillman Inst. of Human Rels., Inc.; clin. prof. United Theol. Sem., New Brighton, Minn.; adj. prof. Gordon-Conwell Theol. Sem., South Hamilton, Mass. Mem. adv. council to urban ministries dept. So. Bapt. Conv., Community Relations Commission, Atlanta; bd. dirs. Christian Council Met. Atlanta, Tillman Inst. Human Relations. Mem. Tidewater Assn. Public Adminstrs. (dir.), Am. Acad. Consultants, Nat. Black Writers Consortium (v.p.), Joint Ctr. for Polit. Studies. Author: What is Your Racism Quotient?, 1964; (with James A. Tillman, Jr.) Why America Needs Racism and Poverty, 1972; (with J.A. Tillman, Jr.) Black Intellectuals, White Liberals and Race Relations: An Analytic Overview, 1973; What Is Your Exclusivity Quotient, 1978; also articles. Office: 1765 Glenview Dr SW Atlanta GA 30331-2307

TILLMAN, MASSIE MONROE, federal judge; b. Corpus Christi, Tex., Aug. 15, 1937; s. Clarence and Artie Lee (Stewart) T.; m. Karen Wright, July 2, 1993; children: Jeffrey Monroe, Holly. BBA, Baylor U., 1959, LLB, 1961. Bar: Tex. 1961, U.S. Dist. Ct. (no. dist.) Tex. 1961, U.S. Ct. Appeals (5th cir.) 1969, U.S. Supreme Ct. 1969; bd. cert. Personal Injury Trial Law, Tex. Ptnr. Herrick & Tillman, Ft. Worth, 1961-66; pvt. practice, Ft. Worth, 1966-70, 79-87; ptnr. Brown, Herman et al, Ft. Worth, 1970-78, Street, Swift et al, Ft. Worth, 1978-79; U.S. bankruptcy judge Ft. Worth divsn. No. Dist. Tex., 1987—. Author: Tillman's Trial Guide, 1970; comments editor, case notes editor; mem. editl. bd. Baylor Law Rev., 1960-61. Mem. Ft. Worth Symphony League. Fellow Am. Bd. Trial Advocates, Tex. Bar Found.; mem. Ft. Worth/Tarrant County Bar (bd. dirs. 1969-70, v.p. 1970-71), Trial Attys.'s of Am., Nat. Conf. of Bankruptcy Judges, Am. Bankruptcy Inst. Republican. Baptist. Avocations: competition shotgun shooting, quail hunting. Office: US Bankruptcy Ct US Courthouse 501 W 10th St Fort Worth TX 76102-3637

TILLMANN, ULRIKE LUISE, mathematician; b. Rhede, Fed. Republic Germany, Dec. 12, 1962; d. Ewald August and Marie-Luise (Demming) T. BA, Brandeis U., 1985; MA, Stanford U., 1987, PhD, 1990. Rsch. asst. Cambridge (Eng.) U., 1990—; lectr. Oxford (Eng.) U., 1992—; advanced fellow Engring. and Phys. Scis. Rsch. Coun., 1997—, prof. math., 2000—; vis. Sonderforschungs Bereich Bielefeld (Fed. Rep. Germany) U., 1989; postdoctoral rsch. asst. Math. Scis. Rsch. Inst., U. Calif., Berkeley, 1991; rsch. fellow Claire Hall, 1990-92; fellow, tutor Merton Coll., 1992—. Wien Internat. scholar, 1982-85; Sloan Found. fellow, 1989. Mem. Am. Math. Soc., London Math. Soc., German Math. Soc. Avocations: singing, volleyball. Office: Math Inst, 24-29 St Giles, Oxford OX1 3LB, England

TILMA, RENZE, software company executive; b. Ferwerd, The Netherlands, June 19, 1955; s. Bauke and Gerbentje (Westra) T.; m. Hishe Maria Zeinstra, June 22, 1979; children: Catrien, Bauhe, Ignas, Sierd, Jan, Lubbert, Paulus. Network controller KLIM, Amsterdam, The Netherlands, 1979-80; field engr. Raytheon, The Netherlands, 1981-84, software engr., 1984-86; software engr. Telex, The Netherlands, 1986-88; software team leader Memorex-Telex, The Netherlands, 1988-89; software devel. mgr. Mokia Data, The Netherlands, 1990-92; software devel. mgr. ICL, The Netherlands, 1992-95, product mgr., 1995-99; gen. mgr. TravSys, Maarssen, The Netherlands, 1999—; comml. dir. Travsys BU, Maarssen, 2000—. Sgt., Dutch Army, 1977-79. Roman Catholic. Avocation: sculpturing. Home: Lelystraat 12, NL3601BV Maarssen The Netherlands

TILQUIN, BERNARD, chemistry educator; b. Couvin, Wallonie, Belgium, Feb. 12, 1943; s. Desire Tilquin and Irma Jaemart; m. Francoise P.E.R. Haesendonck, Aug. 24, 1964; children: Christophe, Isabelle. BS, Cath. U. Louvain, Belgium, 1965, PhD, 1970. Cert. in chem. analysis of drugs. Asst. prof. chemistry Cath. U. Louvain, 1966-84; prof. U. Louvain, 1985—; prof. U. Nat. Zaire (UNAZA), 1980-83, U. Nagoya, Japan, 1988. Editor Biol. Actions Gamma Rays, 1988—; inventor radical mechanism. Office: U Louvain, Ave Mounier 72, 1200 Brussels Belgium

TILSON, JOE CHARLES, artist, sculptor; b. London, Aug. 24, 1928; s. Frederick Arthur Edward and Ethel Stapeley Louise (Saunders) T.; m. Joslyn Morton; children: Jake, Anna, Sophy. Student, St. Martins Sch. Art, London, 1949-52, Royal Coll. Art, London, 1952-55, Brit. Sch. at Rome, 1955-57. Represented by Marlborough Gallery, London, 1960-77, Waddington Galleries, London, 1977—. With RAF, 1946-49. Mem. Royal Acad. Art (Royal Acadamician-elect), Royal Coll. Art (assoc.). Home: 93 Bourne St, London SW1W 8HF, England

TILSON THOMAS, MICHAEL, symphony conductor; b. L.A., 1944; s. Ted and Roberta T. Studies with, Ingolf Dahl, U. So. Calif., others; student conducting, Berkshire Music Festival, Tanglewood, Mass.; student conducting (Koussevitsky prize 1968); LL.D., Hamilton Coll.; L.H.D. (hon.), D'Youville Coll., 1976. Asst. condr. Boston Symphony Orch., 1969, assoc. condr., 1970-72, prin. guest condr., 1972-74; also Berkshire Music Festival, summer 1970, 74; music dir., condr. Buffalo Philharmonic Orch., 1971-79; music dir., prin. condr. Great Woods Ctr. for Performing Arts, 1985-88; prin. condr. London Symphony Orch., 1988-95; artistic dir. New World Symphony, Fla., 1988—; prin. guest condr. London Symphony Orch., 1995—; music dir. San Francisco Symphony, 1995—. Condr., dir., N.Y. Philharmonic Young People's Concerts, CBS-TV, 1971-77; vis. condr. numerous orchs., U.S., Europe, Japan; chief condr. Ojai Festival, 1967, dir., 1972-77; opera debut, Cin., 1975; condr.: Am. premiere Lulu (Alban Berg), Santa Fe Opera, summer 1979; prin. guest condr., L.A. Philharm., 1981-85, Am. premiere Desert Music (Steve Reich), 1984; prin. condr. Gershwin festival London Symphony Orch., Barbcan Ctr., 1987; composer: Grace (A Song for Leonard Bernstein), 1988, Street Song (for Empire Brass Quintet), 1988, From the Diary of Anne Frank (for orchestra and narrator Audrey Hepburn and New World Symphony), 1990; commd. by UNICEF for Concerts for Life's European premiere, 1991; recording artist Sony Classical/CBS Masterworks, 1973—; co-artistic dir. Pacific Music Festival, 1990—, with Leonard Bernstein 1st ann. Pacific Music Festival, Sapporo, Japan, 1990; co-artistic dir. 2d ann. Pacific Music festival, 1991, Salzburg Festival, 1991; conducted Mozart Requiem. Named Musician of Year, Musical Am. 1970; recipient Koussevitsky prize, 1968, Grammy award for Carmina Burana with Cleve. Orch., 1976, for Gershwin Live with Los Angeles Philharm., 1983, Grammy nomination, Best Classical Album - Debussy: Le Martyre de Saint Sebastien (with the London Symphony Orchestra), 1994. Office: 888 7th Ave Fl 37 New York NY 10106-3799 also: San Francisco Symphony Davies Symphony Hall 201 Van Ness Ave San Francisco CA 94102-4595

TILY, STEPHEN BROMLEY, III, bank executive; b. Phila., July 7, 1937; s. Stephen Bromley Jr. and Edith Helen (Straub) T.; m. Janet Anita Walz, July 10, 1965; children: Deborah Powell, Stephen Bromley IV, James Charles II. BS in Econs., Washington and Jefferson Coll., 1960; postgrad., Temple U. Sch. Law, 1963. Trust officer Indsl. Valley Bank & Trust Co., Phila., 1968-71; v.p. Farmers Bank of Delaware, Wilmington, 1971-77; exec. officer G&T, Inc., Ltd., Wilmington, 1977-80; pres., COO DCG&T Co., Wilmington, 1977-91, chmn., CEO, 1991-93, chmn. emeritus, 1993—; chmn. The Declaration Group, Conshohocken, Pa., 1985-97; trustee Declaration Fund, 1988-99; tchr. Am. Inst. Banking, 1970-79. Capt. USAR, 1960-61. Mem. Fin. Analysts of Phila., Barnegat Light Yacht Club (commodore 1988-89, trustee 1989-92), Kimberton Fish and Game Assn., Waynesborough Country Club, John's Island Golf Club, Merion Golf Club, Ducks Unltd. Republican. Episcopalian.

TIMBERLAKE, MARSHALL, lawyer; b. Birmingham, Ala., July 25, 1939; s. Landon and Mary (Perry) T.; m. Rebecca Ann Griffin, Aug. 22, 1987; children: Sumner Timberlake Starling, Jane Ellison. BA, Washington and Lee U., 1961; JD, U. Ala., 1970. Bar: Ala. 1970, Ala. Supreme Ct. 1970, U.S. Dist. Ct. (no., so. and mid. dists.) Ala. 1970, U.S. Supreme Ct. 1976, U.S. Ct. Appeals (11th and 5th cirs.) 1981, U.S. Ct. Appeals (D.C. cir.) 1991. Assoc. Balch & Bingham Law Firm, Birmingham, 1970-76, ptnr., 1976—; pres. Legal Aid Soc., Birmingham, 1980-81; chmn. Ala. Supreme Ct. Commn. on Dispute Resolution, 1994-96, commr., 1996—; trustee Ala. Dispute Resolution Found., 1995—, vice chmn., 1997—. Pres. Ala. Alcohol and Drug Abuse Coun., 1994-95, dir., 1989—; v.p. Assn. Atty. Mediators, 1994-97; co-chair Gov.'s Task Force on State Agy. Alternative Dispute Resolution, 1998—; bd. dirs. Partnership Assistance to the Homeless, 1998—, chmn. endowment fund com., 1999—. Capt. U.S. Army, 1962-66, Vietnam. Recipient Ann. award Dispute Resolution Inst., 1998. Fellow Ala. Law Found.; mem. ABA, Ala. State Bar (chmn. corp. banking and bus. law sect. 1981-82, chmn. state bar task force on alternative dispute resolution 1992-94, State Bar Merit award 1995, co-chmn. state bar com. on ADR 1996-97, mem. state bar task force on jud. selection 1996-98), Birmingham Bar Assn. (mem. and co-chmn. grievance com. 1972-74, chmn. ethics com. 1975-76, chmn. unauthorized practice of law com. 1976-77, chmn. spl. projects com. 1994-95, co-chmn. com. on jud. and legal reform 1996-97, chmn. com. on jud. and legal reform 1997-98), Ala. Acad. Atty. Mediators (co-founder), Redstone Club (bd. govs. 1977 -78), Rotary (Birmingham chpt., chmn. civic club found. 1984), Beaux Arts Krewe, Mountain Brook Club. Republican. Presbyterian. Avocations: tennis, thoroughbred racing, photography. Office: Balch & Bingham 1901 6th Ave N Birmingham AL 35203-2618 Home: 3349 Brookwood Rd Birmingham AL 35223-2020

TIMCENKO, LYDIA TEODORA, biochemist, chemist; b. Beograd, Yugoslavia, July 4, 1951; came to U.S., 1975; d. Teodor Pavle and Branislava (Spasojevic) T.; m. Ghazi Youssef, June 16, 1980 (div. Oct. 1989); children: Ali Alexander, Kareem Misha; m. Peter Porzio, Mar. 11, 1996. BS in Chemistry, U. Belgrade, Yugoslavia, 1975; MS, Wayne State U., 1977, PhD, 1984. Grad. asst. Wayne State U., Detroit, 1976-78, 81-84, rsch. assoc., 1986-88, lectr. in chemistry, 1989; postdoctoral fellow Mich. Cancer Found., Detroit, 1985; postdoctoral fellow Sch. Medicine Wayne State U., 1986-88; lectr. in chemistry Lawrence Tech. U., Southfield, Mich., 1989, 90-91; biochemist Strohtech, Inc., Detroit, 1990-91; prof. chemistry Sussex County Coll., Newton, N.J., 1997-98; asst. prof. chemistry N.Y. Techol. Coll., City U. Bklyn., 1999—; prin. investigator, rsch. scientist ICN Galenika Inst., Clin. Ctr. Serbia, Belgrade, 1991-96; rsch. scientist, mktg. cons. Huet Biol., Birmingham, Mich., 1987-91; adj. prof. chemistry Kean Coll..; adj. prof. dept. chemistry and chem. biology Stevens Inst. Tech., Castle Point on Hudson, Hoboken, N.J. Contbr. articles to FEMS Letters, Biochemistry, Jour. Biol. Chemistry, Analytical. Mem. choir 1st Presbyn. Ch., Blairstown, N.J., elder; mem. Blair Women Assn., Blairstown Area Rep. Club. Fellow Am. Inst. Chemists; mem. AAAS, Am. Soc. Microbiology, Am. Chem. Soc., Phi Lambda Upsilon. Achievements include shigella toxin in shigella and E. coli, mitoch GPO in advenal cortex, liberation of labile sufur from ferredoxins, adhesion shigella to HCTH and HELA, localization of GST and GP in adrenal. Home: 306 State Route 94 Columbia NJ 07832-2771

TIMI, JORGE RIBAS, surgeon; b. Curitiba, Brazil, Nov. 11, 1957; s. Aziz and Circe (Ribas) T.; m. Melania Ribas, Sept. 4, 1984; children: Rochana, Eduardo. MD, U. Parana, 1980, MS in Surgery, 1992, PhD in surgery, 1997—. Cert. vascular surgeon. Vascular surgeon N.S. Gracas Hosp., Curitiba, Brazil, 1983—, U. Parana, 1998—; dir. dept. biol. and health scis. Positivo Univ. Ctr., 1999; vascular surgeon Cajuru Hosp., Curitiba, 1986—; dir. Pro-Circulation Fund, Curitiba, 1987-97. Editor: Brazilian Index of Vascular Surgery, 1995; assoc. editor Revista Cirurgia Vascular, 1993-95, mem. editl. bd., 1996—. Pres. Vascular Soc. Parana, 1991-93. Recipient L.E. Puech Award Best Paper Panamerican Congress of Phebology, 1998, Paraná Award in vascular surgery Brazilian Soc. Vasc. Surgery, 2000. Mem. Internat. Soc. Cardiovasc. Surgery, Brazilian Coll. Surgeons, Brazilian Soc. Vascular Surgery (dir. 1993-95). Avocation: theater. Office: 369 Bruno Filgueira St, 80240000 Curitiba Brazil

TIMM, VOLKER, engineer; b. Itzehoe, Germany, May 31, 1941; s. Hans and Herta (Boll) T.; m. Karla Bourwieg, May 31, 1968; 1 child, Eike Hermann. Abitur, Kaiser Karlschule, Itzehoe, 1961; diploma in engring., Tech. U., Braunschweig, Fed. Republic of Germany, 1968, PhD in Engring., 1978. Registered profl. engr., Fed. Republic of Germany. Devel. engr. Olympia Werke, Braunschweig, 1968-69; asst. engr. Tech. U., Braunschweig, 1969-78; engring. mgr. Philips Semiconductors Roehren-und Halbleiterwerke, Hamburg, Fed. Republic of Germany, 1978—; design mgr. Philips, Hamburg, 1978-94, sr. engr., 1994—. Contbr. articles to profl. jours. Mem. Computer Soc. of IEEE. Avocations: family, photography, personal computers. Office: Philips, Stresmannallee 101, D-22502 Hamburg Germany

TIMMER, BARBARA, lawyer; b. Holland, Mich., Dec. 13, 1946; d. John Norman and Barbara Dee (Folensbee) T. BA, Hope Coll., Holland, Mich., 1969; JD, U. Mich., 1975. Bar: Mich. 1975, U.S. Supreme Ct., 1995. Assoc. McCrosky, Libner, VanLeuven, Muskegon, Mich., 1975-78; apptd. to Mich. Women Commn. by Gov., 1976-79; staff counsel subcom. commerce, consumer & monetary affairs Ho. Govt. Ops. Com., U.S. Ho. of Reps., 1979-82, 85-86; exec. v.p. NOW, 1982-84; legis. asst. to Rep. Geraldine Ferraro, 1984; atty. Office Gen. Counsel Fed. Home Loan Bank Bd., 1986-89; gen. counsel Com. on Banking, Fin. and Urban affairs U.S. Ho. of Reps., Washington, 1989-92; asst. gen. counsel, dir. govt. affairs ITT Corp., Washington, 1992-96; ptnr. Alliance Capitol, Washington, 1994—; sr. v.p., dir. govt. rels. Home Savs. of Am., Irwindale, Calif., 1996-99; ptnr. Manatt, Phelps & Phillips, Washington, 1999—; gen. counsel MyPrimeTime, Inc., San Francisco, 2000—. Editor: Compliance With Lobbying Laws and Gift Rule Guide, 1996. Recipient Affordable Housing award Nat. Assn. Real Estate Brokers, 1990, Acad. of Women Achievers, YWCA, 1993. Mem. ABA (bus. law sect., electronic fin. svcs. subcom.), FBA (chair, exec. coun. banking law com., Exchequer Club, bd. dirs. Women in Housing and Fin., 1992-94, gen. counsel 1994-98), Supreme Ct. Bar Assn., Supreme Ct. Hist. Soc., Mich. Bar Assn., Bar of Dist. Columbia. Episcopalian. E-mail: btimmerdc@earthlink.net. Fax: 415-615-9017. Office: MyPrimeTime 410 Jessie St Ste 300 San Francisco CA 94103-1835

TIMMER, CORNELIS JOHANNES, chemist, researcher; b. Amsterdam, The Netherlands, Dec. 23, 1944; s. Cornelis and Willemina Christina (Veenhuizen) T.; m. Cornelia Anna Maria Horsten, Aug. 28, 1968; children: Saskia Erica. BSc, U. Amsterdam, 1968. Rsch. scientist Dutch Cancer Inst., Amsterdam, 1968-71; dir. clin. pharmacokinetics N.V. Organon, Oss, Netherlands, 1971—. Editor, reviewer Jour. Pharmacokinetics and Biopharmaceutics, 1977-80; contbr. articles to profl. jours. Avocations: classical music, chess. Home: Jachtslot 2, 5346 WK Oss The Netherlands Office: NV Organon, PO Box 20, 5340 BH Oss The Netherlands

TIMMER, MARIANNE, speed skater; b. Sappemeer, The Netherlands, Oct. 3, 1974. Speed skater, 1988—. Recipient Gold medal women's speed skating 1000 meters, Olympic Games, Nagano, Japan, 1998, Gold medal women's speed skating 1500 meters, 1998. Avocations: working on family sheep farm. Office: Dutch Olympic Com, PO Box 302, 6800 AH Arnhem The Netherlands*

TIMMERMANN, CLAUS CHRISTIAN, electrical engineering educator; b. Hannover, Germany, Aug. 20, 1947; s. Günter and Elisabeth (Zentgraf) T.; m. Renate Ricarda Borth, Aug. 27, 1976; children: Dirk, Jens. Diploma in engring., Tech. U., Braunschweig, Germany, 1971, D in Elec. Engring., 1975. Rsch. asst. for light wave guides Tech. U., Braunschweig, 1971-75; project leader studio quality fiber optic TV transmission Robert Bosch GmbH, Darmstadt, Germany, 1975-79; prof. U. Applied Scis., Mannheim, Germany, 1979; head Inst. for High Frequency Techniques & Optical Comm. U. Applied Scis., Mannheim, 1985—; lectr. for fiber optics German Army, Wehrakademie, Mannheim, 1981-95; cons., mgr. indsl. projects Steinbeisstiftung für Wirtschaftsfoerderung Stuttgart, 1982—. Author: Lichtwellenleiter, 1981 Lichtwellenleiterkomponenten und Systeme, 1984; author, editor: Hochfrequenzelektronik mit CAD vol. 1, 1997, vol. 2, 1998; contbr. articles to profl. jours.; patentee in field. Mem. IEEE, N.Y. Acad. Scis. Avocations: history, photography, cooking. Home: Duererstrasse 35, 68723 Plankstadt Germany Office: Univ Applied Sci, Windeckstrasse 110, 68163 Mannheim Germany

TIMMERMANS, JACQUES, pharmacist, researcher; b. Brussels, Dec. 18, 1956; s. Georges and Lucienne (Eeckhout) T.; m. Viviane Lievin; children: Dorian, Johanne. PhD in Pharm. Scis., U. Libre Brussels, 1991. Hosp. pharmacist U. Libre de Bruxelles, ERASME, Brussels, 1981-90, con. pharmacol. supr., 1987-88; pharmacovigilance expert Commn. European Cmtys., Com. Proprietary Medicinal Products, Brussels, 1990; head preformulation Union Chimique Belge Pharma., Braine-L'Alleud, Belgium, 1991—. Inventor resultant weight apparatus and method. Sci. fellow U. Brussels, 1991—; recipient 1st prize Royal Acad. Medicine, 1991. Mem. Belgium Soc. Pharm. Scis., Belgium Industry Pharmacist Union. Avocation: music. Home: Rue Cardinal Mercier 66, B-1460 Virginal-Ittre Belgium Office: UCB, Chemin Du Foriest, B-1420 Braine-l'Alleud Belgium

TIMMONS, EVELYN DEERING, pharmacist; b. Durango, Colo., Sept. 29, 1926; d. Claude Elliot and Evelyn Allen (Gooch) Deering; m. Richard Palmer Timmons, Oct. 4, 1952 (div. 1968); children: Roderick Deering, Steven Palmer. BS in Chemistry and Pharmacy cum laude, U. Colo., 1948. Chief pharmacist Meml. Hosp., Phoenix, 1950-54; med. lit. rsch. librarian Hoffman-LaRoche, Inc., Nutley, N.J., 1956-57; staff pharmacist St. Joseph's Hosp., Phoenix, 1958-60; relief mgr. various ind. apothecaries, Phoenix, 1960-68; asst. then mgr., dir. compounding Profl. Pharmacies, Inc., Phoenix, 1968-72; mgr. Mt. View Pharmacy, 1972-76, owner/mgr., 1976—; pres. Ariz. Apothecaries, Ltd., 1976—; mem. profl. adv. bd., bereavement counselor Hospice of Valley, 1983-96; mem. profl. adv. bd. Upjohn Health Care and Svcs., Phoenix, 1984-86; bd. dirs. Am. coun. on Pharm. Edn., Chgo., 1986-92, v.p., 1988, 89, treas., 1990-91; mem. expert adv. bd. compounding pharms. U.S. Pharmacoepial Conv., 1992—; preceptor U. Ariz., 1965—, Midwestern Coll. Pharmacy, Ariz. Campus, 1998—; lectr. on NHRT. Author poetry; contbr. articles to profl. jours. Mem. Scottsdale (Ariz.) Fedn. Rep. Women, 1963-68; various other offices Rep. Fedn.; mem. platform com. State of Ariz., Nat. Rep. Conv., 1964; asst. sec. Young Rep. Nat. Fedn., 1963-65; active county and state Rep. coms.; adv. bd. Internat. Jour. of Pharm. Compounding, 1996—; fin. chmn. Internat. Leadership Symposium: Women in Pharmacy, London, 1987; treas. Leadership Internat. Women Pharmacy, 1991—; mem. founders circle Gladys Taylor McGarey Med. Found., 1996—. Named Outstanding Young Rep. of Yr., Nat. Fedn. Young Reps., 1965, Preceptor of Yr., U. Ariz./Syntex, 1984; recipient Disting. Pub. Svc. award Maricopa County Med. Soc., 1962, Disting. Alumni award Wasatch Acad., 1982, Career Achievement award Kappa Epsilon, 1983, Leadership and Achievement award Upjohn Labs., 1985-86, Outstanding Achievement in Profession award Merck, Sharp & Dohme, 1986, award of Merit Kappa Epsilon, 1988, Disting. Coloradoan award U. Colo., 1989, Vanguard award Kappa Epsilon, 1991, Unicorn award Kappa Epsilon, 1993, Compounding Pharmacist of the Yr. award Profl. Compounding Corp. of Am., 1994, 96, Healing Heart award Gladys Taylor McGarey Found., 1998. Fellow Am. Coll. of Apothecaries (v.p. 1982-83, pres. elect 1983-84, pres. 1984-85, chmn. bd. dirs. 1985-86, adv. coun. 1986-92, Chmn. of Yr. 1980-81, Victor H. Morganroth award 1985, J. Leon Lascoff award 1990), Internat. Acad. of Compounding Pharmacists (bd. dirs. 1993-2000); mem. Ariz. Soc. of Hosp. Pharmacists, Am. Pharm. Assn. (Daniel B. Smith award 1990), Ariz. Pharmacy Assn. (Svc. to Pharmacy award 1976, Pharmacist of Yr. 1981, Bowl of Hygeia 1989, 1st Innovative Pharmacy award 1994), Maricopa County Pharmacy Assn. (pres. 1977, Svc. to Pharmacy award 1977), Am. Soc. of Hosp. Pharmacists, Am. Aircraft Owners and Pilots Assn., Air Safety Found., Nat. Assn. of Registered Parliamentarians, Civinettes (pres. Scottsdale chpt. 1960-61), Kappa Epsilon (recipient Career Achievement award 1986, Vanguard award 1991, Unicorn award 1993). Avocations: flying, skiing, swimming, hiking, writing. Office: Mt View Pharmacy 10565 N Tatum Blvd Ste B-118 Scottsdale AZ 85253-1095

TIMMONS, GERALD DEAN, pediatric neurologist; b. Rensselaer, Ind., June 1, 1931; s. Homer Timmons and Tamma Mildred (Spall) Rodgers; m. Lynne Rita Matrisciano, May 29, 1982; 1 child, Deanna Lynne; children from previous marriage: Jane Christina Timmons Mitchell, Ann Elizabeth, Mary Catherine. AB, Ind. U., 1953, MD, 1956. Diplomate Am. Bd. Psychiatry and Neurology. Intern Lima (Ohio) Meml. Hosp., 1956-57; resident Ind. U. Hosp., Indpls., 1957-59, 61-62; instr. neurology dept. Ind. U., Indpls., 1962-64; practice medicine specializing in psychiatry and neurology Indpls., 1962-64; practice medicine specializing in pediatric neurology Akron, Ohio, 1964—; chief pediatric neurology Children's Hosp. Med. Ctr., Akron, 1964—; chmn. neurology subcouncil Coll. Medicine Northeastern Ohio Univs., Rootstown, 1978-99; sr. examiner Am. Bd. Neurology and Psychiatry. Contbr. articles to profl. and scholarly jours. Served to capt. USAF, 1959-61. Mem. Summit County Med. Soc., Ohio Med. Soc., AMA, Am. Acad. Pediatrics, Am. Acad. Neurology (practice com. 1980-86), Child Neurology Soc. (chmn. honors and awards com. 1978-88), Am. Soc. Internal Medicine, Am. Electroencephalographic Soc. Republican. Methodist. Office: Akron Pediatric Neurology 300 Locust St Ste 460 Akron OH 44302-1804

TIMMONS, GORDON DAVID, economics educator; b. Elbert, Tex., May 21, 1919; s. Walter James and Ella Mae (McCarson) T.; m. Jean Betty Kulhanek, Feb. 11, 1947; children: Kathy, Linda, Scott, Jim, Tamara, Dallas, Timothy, Kelly, Susanna. Student, U. Tex., 1937-40, U. Mont., 1961-64; BS, Utah State U., 1955; MS, Mont. State U., 1958. Enlisted USAF, 1939, advanced through grades to col., ret., 1961; instr. Columbia Basin Coll., Pasco, Wash., 1966-86; pres. Assn. Higher Edn., 1969-72. Decorated Legion of Merit, Croix de Guerre (France). Mem. Acad. Polit. Sci., N.W. Econ. Conf. Democrat. Avocation: horse breeding. Home and Office: Star Rte Box 39-A Olney TX 76374-0039

TIMMS, RICHARD BRIAN, education consultant; b. London, May 2, 1936; arrived in South Africa, 1991; s. Leslie George and Ethel May (Woolford) T.; m. Anne-Karin Berg, Aug. 15, 1964 (dec. Nov. 1988); m. Julienne Bronwen Earle, Dec. 31, 1993. BA in Botany, Oxford (Eng.) U., 1960, MA, 1963. Schoolmaster Westminster Sch., London, 1960-68; asst. rep. British Coun., Dar Es Salaam, Tanzania, 1968-72; regional dir. British Coun., Istanbul, Turkey, 1972-76; cultural attaché British Coun., Bucharest, Romania, 1976-78; dir. tng. British Coun., London, 1978-83; dir. British Coun., Lusaka, Zambia, 1983-87; dep. controller Africa and Middle East divsn. British Coun., London, 1987-91; dir. British Coun., Johannesburg, 1991-94; edn. mgmt. cons. Cape Town, 1996—. With Royal Artillery, 1954-56. Recipient Order of Brit. Empire Her Majesty the Queen, 1994; Paul Harris fellow Rotary Internat., 1987. Avocations: choral music, travelling, walking, horticulture, cabinet-making. E-mail: timmsrb@zsd.co.za. Home: 6 Leeuloop, Klein Leeukop, Estate, Hout Bay, Cape Town 7806, South Africa

TIMOFEEV, ANDREI VICTOROVITCH, virologist; b. Moscow, Aug. 17, 1953; s. Victor Iakovlevitch Neigoldberg and Margarita Iakovlevna Timofeeva; m. Elena Victorovna Karpova, July 23, 1994. MD, MSc, 2d Med. Inst., Moscow, 1976; PhD, Inst. Devel. Biology, Moscow, 1982. Jr. rsch. fellow Inst. Devel. Biology, 1976-85; sr. rsch. fellow Chumakov Inst. Poliomyelitis and Viral Encephalitides Russia, Moscow, 1985-91, leading rsch. fellow, 1993-96, head of unit, 1996—; head of unit Vet. Acad., Moscow, 1991-92; postdoctoral fellow Inst. Biologie Physico-Chimique, Paris, 1992-93; cons. prodn. unit Chumakov Inst. Poliomyelitis and Viral Encephalitides, 1996—; expert INTAS, Brussels, 1999—. Contbr. articles to profl. jours. Fellow The Royal Soc., Eng., 1993-94; collaborative grantee The Wellcome Trust, Eng., 1994-98, rsch. grantee RFFS, Russia, 1999—. Avocation: poetry. Home: Molodezhnaya 4-318, 117296 Moscow Russia Office: IPVE RAMS, P/O Inst Poliomyelitis, 142782 Moscow Russia

TIMOFEEV, MIKHAIL FEODOROVICH, research center administrator; b. Moscow, Oct. 17, 1945; s. Feodor Mikhajlovich and Nadegda Ivanovna Timofeeva; m. Svetlana Leonidovna, Oct. 14, 1989; children: Dinah, Feodor, Serafima, Vasilissa, Sophia. 1st degree, Med. Inst. Sechenov, Moscow, 1970; 2d degree, Med. Inst. Pyrogov, Moscow, 1972; 3d degree, Med. Inst. Semashko, Moscow, 1975. Physician, asst. prof., sr. rsch. officer; dir. Rsch. Practical Ctr. for Reflexotherapy for Alcholism; cons. Red Cross; lectr. in field. Author: (book) Acupuncture and Alcoholism, 1999; contbr. articles to profl. jours. Mem. European Assn. Acupuncture, Nat. Acupuncture Detoxification Assn., N.Y. Acad. Scis. Avocation: spending time with family. Home: Malenkovskaja St H28 # 33, 107113 Moscow Russia

TIMOFEEV, OLEG YAKOULEVICH, science educator, researcher; b. Rakvere, USSR, Feb. 28, 1957; s. Yakov Mikhailovich Timofeev and Galina

Lukilianovna Kutovay; m. Elena Pavlovna Boryshmikova, Oct. 6, 1979 (div. June 1986); 1 child, Igor; m. Irina Nikolaevna Bogatova, Oct. 23, 1986; children: Alexey, Autonina. Degree in engring. and math. with honors, Leningrad Shipbuilding Inst., St. Petersburg, Russia, 1980, postgrad., 1983. Asst. prof. St. Petersburg States Marine Tech. U., 1983-86, sr. lectr., 1986-92, assoc. prof., 1992—; rschr. West Design Buro, St. Petersburg, 1980-88, 24th Navy Inst., St. Petersburg, 1990-96; sr. rschr. Arctic and Antarctic Rsch. Inst., St. Petersburg, 1992—. Author: Marine Encyclopedically Dictionary, 1993, Environmental Conditions of Baydaratzkay Bay, 1997, (requirements) Rules of Ice Strengthening for Icegoing Ships and Ice Breakers, 1992-96, (software) Computer Aided Design of Floating Dock Structure, 1985 (diploma Sci. Soc. Shipbuilding Industry 1986). Grantee Russian Transport Acad., 1994, 97-98, Russian Found. Basic Rsch., 1997-98, INTAS, 1999. Mem. N.Y. Acad. Scis. Avocations: sports, travel. E-mail: edtimoy@spb.cityline.ru. Home: Marshal Kozakov 40-68, 198332 Saint Petersburg Russia Office: State Marine Tech U, Lotzmanskay 3, 190008 Saint Petersburg Russia

TIMOFEEVSKI, SERGEI LEONIDOVICH, biochemistry and chemistry researcher; b. Novosibirsk, Russia, June 22, 1966; came to the U.S., 1994; s. Leonid Sergeyevich and Lyudmila Alexandrovna Timofeevski; m. Olga Gennadievna Timofeevski; 1 child, Nicole. BS, Leningrad State U., St. Petersburg, Russia, 1988; PhD, Russian Acad. Sci., St. Petersburg, Russia, 1994, Utah State U., 1999. Rsch. technician Inst. Macromolecular Compounds, Russian Acad. Scis., St. Petersburg, 1987-88, rsch. trainee, 1988-90, rsch. assoc., 1990-94; grad. rsch. asst. Utah State U., Logan, 1995-99; rsch. fellow Vanderbilt U., Nashville, 1999—. Contbr. articles to profl. jours. Photographer dept. newspaper Leningrad State U., St. Petersburg, 1983-87; counsellor Children's Camp Brigantina, Losevo, Leningrad, 1986-91. Recipient All-Union Students' Olympiad award Ministry of Edn. Kyrgyzstan, Frunze, 1981, Ministry Edn. Estonia, Tallinn, 1982, Ministry Edn. Georgia, Tbilisi, 1983; scholar Leningrad State U., St. Petersburg, 1983-88. Mem. Am. Soc. for Microbiology, All-Union Mendeleev Chem. Soc., Sigma Xi. Achievements include patent for water-soluble copolymers of N-vinyl-2-pyrrolidone and crotonic acid derivatives containing dexamethasone or hydrocortisone residues having glucocorticoid activity and process for preparation of these copolymers. Avocations: photography, hiking, fishing, competitive sports. E-mail: sltim@hotmail.com and sergei@toxicology.mc.vanderbilt.edu. Fax: 615-343-7534. Home: 315 Erin Ln Nashville TN 37221-2213 Office: Vanderbilt Univ Dept Biochemistry Light Hall 607 Nashville TN 37232-0001

TIMOFEI, SIMONA LUMINITA, chemical engineer, researcher; b. Timisoara, Timis, Romania, Dec. 31, 1958; d. Ion and Caterina (Antoniuc) T. Diploma in chem. engring., Tech. U., Timisoara, 1983; MA in English Lang., Western U., Timisoara, 1988, PhD in Theoretical Chemistry, 1995. Probationer engr. Fertilizer Enterprise, Arad, Romania, 1983-84, Azur, Timisoara, 1984-85; chem. engr. Inst. Chemistry Romanian Acad., Timisoara, 1985-88, rschr., 1988-95, sr. rschr., 1995—; researcher Ctr. Environ. Rsch., Dept. Chem. Ecotoxicology, Leipzig, Germany, 1998, ETH-Zentrum, Lab. Tech. Chemistry, Zürich, Switzerland, 1999. Contbr. articles to sci. jours., including Dyes and Pigments, Jour. Molecular Structure, Quantitative Struct.-Activity Relationship, Jour. Chem. Info. and Computer Scis.; editor: (with Chiriac, D. Ciubotariu and Z. Simon) Quantitative Relationships Betweem Chemical Structure and Biological Activity, The MTD method, 1996. Sci. grantee Japan Soc. for Promotion Sci., 1996. Mem. Qsar and Quantum Chemistry Group, Internat. Chemometrics Soc., Internat. Qsar and Modelling Soc. Avocations: classical and pop music, fashion. Fax: 40-56-191824. E-mail: stimofei@icht.sorostm.ro. Home: Take Ionescu 28 Apt 13, 1900 Timisoara Timis, Romania Office: Romanian Acad Inst Chem, Bul. Mihai Viteazul 24, 1900 Timisoara Timis, Romania

TIMONEN, KIRSI LIISA, epidemiologist, researcher; b. Kuopio, Finland, Mar. 10, 1964. MD, U. Kuopio, 1989, PhD, 1997. Asst. physician Kainuu Ctrl. Hosp., Kajaani, Finland, 1991-92; acting sr. lectr. dept. physiology U. Kuopio, 1992-93; rschr. unit environ. epidemiology Nat. Pub. Health Inst., Kuopio, 1994—. Chmn. cross-country skiing unit Puijo Ski Club, Kuopio, 1995-98. Avocations: cross-country skiing, aerobics, sports, music. Office: Nat Pub Health Inst Unit Environ Epidemiology, PO Box 95, 70701 Kuopio Finland

TIMONEN, PERTTI AARRE SULEVI, educational administrator; b. Lieksa, Finland, Jan. 2, 1943; s. Otto Edvard Timonen and Lempi Mirjami Oinonen Heinänen; m. Kaisa Marjatta Vihanta, June 5, 1971; children: Tuomo, Hannu. M Social Sci., U. Tampere, Finland, 1967, Lic. in Social Sci., 1972, D Social Sci., 1976, D Polit. Sci., 1980. Asst., rsch. asst., asst. prof. polit. sci. U. Tampere, 1968-85; dir. Inst. Extension Studies U. Lapland, Finland, 1985-86; dir. Adult Edn. Ctr., Tampere, 1986—. Contbr. articles to profl. jours., columns to newspapers. 2d lt. Finnish Armed Forces, 1962-63. Mem. Orgn. Adult Edn. Ctrs. Finland (vice chmn. 1995—). Social Democrat. Avocations: tennis, writing columns, social issues. Home: Sudenkatu 16 B, 33530 Tampere Finland Office: Adult Edn Ctr Tampere, Sammonkatu 2, 33540 Tampere Finland

TIMONIN, JURY ALEXANDROVICH, information science researcher; b. Leningrad, Russia, Aug. 7, 1945; s. Alexander Mitrophanovich and Nadezhda Ivanovna (Aleshina) T.; m. Tatjana Lavrentevna Kazmerchuk, Mar. 1, 1970; 1 child, Alexander. Specialist, Electrotechnical Inst., Leningrad, 1970; Candidate Tech. Scis., Inst. Civil Aviation Engring., Kiev, Ukraine, 1976. Cert. engring. Engr. Electroizmeritel, Zhytomyr, Ukraine, 1970-72; lab. chief Electroizmeritel, Zhytomyr, 1972-80, CAD dept. chief, 1980-96; faculty chief Inst. Entrepreneurship and Modern Techs., Zhytomyr, 1996—; CAD-sys. tchr. Kiev Poly. Inst., Kiev, 1986-97; rschr. project analytical controlling Can.-Ukrainian joint venture MTK, Zhytomyr, 1992-95, rschr. project analytical bus., 1996-99; rschr. project bus. engring. Inst. Entrepreneurship and Modern Techs., Zhytomyr, 1999—; mgmt. info. sys. lectr. Inst. Entrepreneurship and Modern Techs., Zhytomyr, 1993—. Author: (with G.N. Maslakov) Development of Active Filters, 1982, Methods of Adaptive Treatment of Non-Stationary Casual Signals, 1985; contbr. articles to profl. jours.; inventor in field. Recipient medal The Inventor USSR, 1981, medal Participant of Nat. Economy Reaching Exhbn. USSR, 1983. Avocations: landscape architecture. Office: Inst Entrepreneurship, 44 Puskinskaya St, 10008 Zhytomyr Ukraine

TIMOTHY, DAVID HARRY, biology educator; b. Pitts., June 9, 1928; s. David Edgar and Harriett P. (Stein) T.; m. Marian Claire Whiteley, Sept. 5, 1953; children: Marjory J., M. Elisabeth, David W. BS, Pa. State U., 1952, MS, 1955; PhD, U. Minn., 1956. Asst. geneticist Rockefeller Found., Bogota, Colombia, 1956-58; assoc. geneticist Rockefeller Found., Bogota, 1958-61; assoc. prof. N.C. State U., Raleigh, 1961-66, prof., 1966-93, prof. emeritus, 1993—; cons. to fgn. and U.S. govts., also U.S. and internat. sci. orgns.; mem. USDA crop adv. com. on grasses, 1983-87, mem. policy adv. com., sci. and edn. grants program, 1982-84, chief scientist USDA Sci. and Edn. Competetive Rsch. Grants Office, 1985, 86; with Nat. Plant Genetic Resources Bd., 1984-91, vice chmn., 1991; bd. dirs., treas. Genetic Resources Comms. Sys., Inc., 1985-91, pres., 1991-93; mem. bd. on agr. NAS-NRC, work group on U.S. Nat. Plant Germplasm Sys., 1987-89. Co-author monographs, also author articles. With AUS, 1946-48, PTO. Grantee NSF, 1965, 78, Rockefeller Found., 1968, 69, Pioneer Hi-Bred Internat., 1982, 83. Fellow AAAS (electorate nominating com., sect. O, Agr. 1988-90), Am. Soc. Agronomy, Crop Sci. Soc. Am. (editl. bd. 1982-84, assoc. editor Crop Sci. 1982-84, Frank N. Meyer medal for plant genetic resources 1994). Home: 13 Furches St Raleigh NC 27607-7048

TIMPKA, TOOMAS, computer scientist, physician, educator; b. Stockholm, Nov. 29, 1957; s. Leo and Sylvia (Rosenberg) T.; m. Carina Wennergreh, May 15, 1986 (div. 1990); children: Simon, Jonathan. MD, Karolinska Inst., Stockholm, 1983; PhD, Linkoping (Sweden) U., 1989. Jr. physician Univ. Hosp., Linkoping, 1983-87, physician dept. social medicine, 1987-93, cons. physician, 1994—, assoc. prof. dept. social medicine, 1992-97; prof. dept. social medicine, 1998—; asst. prof. dept. computer sci. Linkoping U., 1989-91, assoc. prof., dir. rsch. lab., 1989—. Author: Design of Decision Support for General Practitioners, 1989; contbr. articles to profl. jours. Recipient Annual award Swedish Assn. for Med. Informatics, 1986, 89, Gold Medal best scientific paper World Conf. Med. Informatics, 1998. Avocations: sports, literature, art, music. Office: Linkoping U Dept Computer, Sci, Linkoping Sweden

TIMS, ROBERT AUSTIN, data processing official, pilot; b. Seattle, Dec. 21, 1942; s. Robert Mitchell Tims and Winifred Eileen (Dorgan) Bristol; m. Jane Moore, June 6, 1980. Student, Pacific Union Coll., 1960-61, Alpha Aviation Sch., 1976-77; BS in Computer Info. Sys. with honors, Ark. State U., 1998. Lic. comml. and instrument pilot; cert. flight instr. Engring. technician Tex. Instruments, Inc., Ridgecrest, Calif., 1966-67, various projects, Conn., N.Y. and N.J., 1967-70; homesteader Leslie, Ark., 1970-77; chief pilot/flight instr. Sharp Aviation Co., Jonesboro, Ark., 1977-79; chief pilot Pizza Inn of Ark., Jonesboro, 1979-83; data processing mgr., chief pilot Realty Assocs. Brokerage, Inc., Jonesboro, 1983-91, microanalyst, 1991-94; pres., owner ABS Logic, Inc., computers and programming cons., Jonesboro, 1985—; programmer Jimco Lamp Mfg., Bono, Ark., 1998-99; programmer, analyst Maxim Group, Memphis, 2000—. Served with USN, 1962-66. Recipient Nat. Collegiate Bus. Merit award. Mem. CAP (squadron comdr. Jonesboro 1986-93), Am. Philatelic Soc., Planetary Soc., Nat. Space Soc., SETI Inst., Beta Gamma Sigma. Avocation: philately. Home and Office: 1616 Alonzo St Jonesboro AR 72401-4802

TIMUS, CLEMENTINA ALEXANDRINA, physicist; b. Ciacova, Timis, Romania, Aug. 31, 1946; d. Longin Andrei and Maria Eva (Benteu) Corutiu; m. Dan Timus, July 19, 1972. PhD, Inst. of Atomic Physics, 1992. Physicist Electrofar Factory, Bucharest, 1969-71; prin. physicist Inst. for Atomic Physics, Bucharest, 1971-88, scientist, 1988-90, sr. rsch. scientist III degree, 1990-93, sr. rsch. scientist II degree laser dept., 1993—; assoc. prof. U. Bucharest, 1992-99; expert evaluator European Commn., Brussels, 1999—. Contbr. articles to profl. publs. Mem. Communist Party, 1966-89; pres. European Integration and NATO Commn., IAP, 1997-98. Mem. Nat. Geographic Soc., Romanian Soc. of Physics, Soc. Photo-Optical Instrumentation Engring. (treas.), European Optical Soc. Greek Catholic. Avocations: classical music, phylately, history, skiing and hiking. Home: Crisana St Ap 22, 70782 Bucharest Romania Office: Nat Inst LP&R Physics, Atomistilor 1 PO Box MG-6, 76900 Bucharest Romania

TINAGLIA, MICHAEL LEE, lawyer; b. Chgo., Dec. 21, 1952; s. Michael Leo and Josephine (Esposito) T.; m. Lucia Yolando Guzzo, Oct. 14, 1978; children: Laura, Lisa, Elena. BA, Northwestern U., 1974; JD, DePaul U., 1977. Bar: Ill. 1977, U.S. Dist. Ct. (no. dist.) Ill. 1978, U.S. Dist. Ct. (ea. dist.) Wis. 1986. Assoc. Arnold & Kadjan, Chgo., 1977-79; ptnr. Leader & Tinaglia, Chgo., 1979-86; assoc. Laser, Schostok, Kolman & Frank, Chgo., 1987-92; prin. Law Office of Michael Lee Tinaglia Ltd., Chgo., 1992-93, 2000—; equity ptnr. DiMonte & Lizak, Park Ridge, Ill., 1994-99; v.p., corp. counsel Tiara Med. Sys., Inc., Oak Forest, Ill. Contbr. articles to profl. jours. Alderman City Coun., Park Ridge, 1997—, mem. pub. safety com., 1997—, mem. procedures and regulations com. Mem. Ill. Bar Assn., Chgo. Bar Assn. Roman Catholic. Avocations: skiing, guitar. Office: Law Offices of Michael Lee Tinaglia 161 N Clark St Ste 2550 Chicago IL 60601-3246

TINAUT, FRANCISCO V., engineering educator; b. Valencia, Spain, May 29, 1958; s. Vicente Tinaut and M. Dolores Fluixa; m. Marta Rodriguez, Oct. 12, 1985; children: Francisco, Carmen, Marma, Santiago. Degree in indsl. engring., Poly. U. Valencia, 1981; MSME, Carnegie Mellon U., 1985; D of Indsl. Engring., Poly. U. Valencia, 1986. Assoc. prof. U. Valladolid, Spain, 1987-92; prof. U. Valladolid, 1992—, dean Engring. Sch., 1992-96; dir. sect. Ctr. for Automotive R & D, Valladolid. Contbr. papers to profl. jours. Ministry of Edn. scholar for rsch. tng. Spanish Ministry of Edn., 1983-86, Fulbright scholar, 1984-85. Mem. Soc. Automotive Engring., Spanish Assn. Automotive Profls., Spanish Soc. Mech. Engring., Sigma Xi. Roman Catholic. Avocation: sailing. Fax: 34 983 42 33 63. E-mail: tinaut@eis.uva.es. Office: U Valladolid Sch Engring, Paseo del Cauce s/n, 47011 Valladolid Spain

TINDLE, CHARLES DWIGHT WOOD, broadcasting company executive; b. Bryn Mawr, Pa., Jan. 13, 1950; s. Charles Wood and Nancy (Sapp) T. Student, Kenyon Coll., 1968-71. Pres. Dwight Karma Broadcasting, Mesa, Ariz., 1971-76, Natural Broadcasting System, Mesa, 1976-79; producer, fellow Am. Film Inst. Ctr. for Advanced Film Studies, 1979-81; pres. Network 30, Scottsdale, Ariz., 1985—; owner Sta. KDKB-AM-FM, Mesa, Sta. KSML-FM, Lake Tahoe, Calif., Sta. KNOT-AM-FM, Prescott, Ariz., Sta. KBWA, Williams, Ariz. Recipient Peabody award U. Ga., 1976. Republican. Seventh Day Adventist. Home: 4445 E Flower St Phoenix AZ 85018-6452 Office: 644 N Country Club Dr Mesa AZ 85201-4948

TING, JAMES H., electronics company executive. BSc, U. Toronto, 1977, MSc, 1979. Registered profl. engr., Ont. Profl. engr. officer U. Toronto, 1977-78; sr. design engr. Owl Instruments, Ltd., 1978-79; co-founder Andicom Tech. Products, 1979-81; co-founder Semi-Tech Microelectronics Corp., 1981-83, chmn. bd., pres., CEO, 1983—. Avocation: classical music, reading, travel, sculpture. Office: 2800 14th Ave Ste 511, Markham, ON Canada L3R 0E4*

TING, JOSEPH K., mechanical engineer; b. Manila, Jan. 23, 1950; s. Manuel and Lourdes (Co) T.; m. Monique Crenn, Sept. 2, 1978; children: Audrey Adrienne, William Alexander. BS in Mech. Engring., De La Salle U., Manila, 1972; MSc, MIT, 1974; MBA, U. Ottawa, Ont., Can., 1986. Registered profl. engr., N.Y., Mass., Ont., Can. Product engr. Brier Mfg. Co., Providence, R.I., 1974-75; plant mgr. Nemo Brier Ltd., Hull, Que., Can., 1975; assoc. engr., asst. rsch. officer Nat. Rsch. Coun., Ont., 1975-86; sr. mech. engr., supr. Dormitory Authority/State of N.Y., Delmar, 1986—; adj. prof. Rensselaer Polytechnic Inst., Troy, N.Y., 1992—; ednl. counselor MIT Admissions, Cambridge, Mass., 1993—. Contbg. author: Canadian Financial Managment, 1983, Essentials of Engineering Economics, 1983, Computer Aided Design Drafting, 1987, ASHRAE Std. 15-1992, 1992; developer Rolls-Royce RB211 jet engine into a gas pumping engine. Pres. Chinese Am. Comm. Ctr., Albany, N.Y., 1993-94, bd. dirs. 1993—, chmn. facility devel. and mgmt. com., 1997-2000; bd. dirs. Habitat for Humanity, 2000—. Grantee E.I. DuPont Co.; recipient Disting. Svc. award Chinese Am. Comm. Ctr., 1991, Outstanding Svcs., 1996. Mem. ASHRAE (chpt. pres. 1991-92, chmn. refrigeration com. 1993-94, regional chmn. northeastern U.S. 1994-97, bd. dirs. Atlanta 1994-97, asst. regional chmn. 1992-94, 2000—, nominating com. 1997-98, 2000—, regional vice chmn. rsch. promotion 1998-99, govtl. affairs mem. tech., energy and govtl. activities com. 1999-2000, hist. com. 2000—, Black Ink award 1990, Golden Gavel award 1992, Disting. Svc. award 1997, Regional award of Merit 1998), MIT Alumni Club (pres. 1992-94, bd. dirs. 1992-2000, fin. dir. 1996-98), Gen. Soc. Mechanics and Tradesmen. Roman Catholic. Avocations: tennis, swimming, organizing seminars and confs., martial arts. Home: PO Box 234 Delmar NY 12054-0234 Office: Dormitory Authority State of NY 515 Broadway Albany NY 12207-2964

TING, PAUL WAI-TAI, auditor; b. Hong Kong, July 9, 1942; s. Fong-Ho and Sam-Pao (Tu) T.; m. Elaine Oi-Lan Law, Oct. 1, 1968; children: Vicky, Vivian. HK Sch. Commerce, 1974. Cert. practising acct., fin. svcs. auditor, quality analyst; chartered info. sys. practitioner, sec. Mgr. Hong Kong & Shanghai Banking Corp., Hong Kong, 1961-70; controller WMS Capital Corp. Ltd., Hong Kong, 1970-73; Asia Pacific area audit mgr. Chase Manhattan Bank N.A., Hong Kong, 1973-87; gen. auditor Chase AMP Bank, Sydney, Australia, 1987-90; chief internal auditor Advance Bank, Sydney, Australia, 1990-97; chief auditor, v.p. 1st Pacific Bank, Hong Kong, 1997-98; chief internal auditor, v.p. Hong Kong Mortgage Corp.Ltd., 1998—; lectr. on internal audit topics Hong Kong Mgmt. Assn., 1980-87, Macau Mgmt. Assn., 1980-87, Hong Kong Productivity Ctr., 1980-87, Chinese Banker's Club, 1980-87; chmn. examination and membership com. Inst. Internal Auditors, 1980-87. Justice of the Peace, NSW, Australia. Fellow Australian Soc. Cert. Practising Accts., Australian Inst. Banking and Fin., Inst. Chartered Secs. and Adminstrs., Australian Inst. Internal Auditors, Brit. Inst. Mgmt.; mem. Brit. Computer Soc., EDP Auditors Assn. Avocations: reading, jogging, bush walking, swimming. Office: Hong Kong Mortgage Corp Ltd, 7F Gloucester Twr 11 Pedder St, Central Hong Kong

TING, SAMUEL CHAO CHUNG, physicist, educator; b. Ann Arbor, Mich., Jan. 27, 1936; s. Kuan H. and Jeanne (Wong) T.; m. Susan Carol Marks, Apr. 28, 1985; children: Jeanne Min, Amy Min, Christopher M. BS in Engring., U. Mich., 1959, MS, 1960, PhD in Physics, 1962, ScD (hon.), 1978; ScD (hon.), Chinese U. Hong Kong, 1987, U. Bologna, Italy, 1988, Columbia U., 1990, U. Sci. and Tech., China, 1990, Moscow State U., 1991, U. Bucharest, Romania, 1993. Ford Found. fellow CERN (European Orgn. Nuc. Rsch.), Geneva, 1963; instr. physics Columbia U., 1964, asst. prof., 1965-67; group leader Deutsches Elektronen-Synchrotron, Hamburg, W.Ger., 1966; assoc. prof. physics MIT, Cambridge, 1967-68, prof., 1969—; Thomas Dudley Cabot Inst. prof. M.I.T., 1977—; program cons. divsn. particles and fields Am. Phys. Soc., 1970; hon. prof. Beijing Normal Coll., 1987, Jiatong U., Shanghai, 1987, U. Bologna, Italy, 1988. Assoc. editor: Nuclear Physics B, 1970; mem. editl. bd. Nuc. Instruments and Methods, Mathematical Modeling; contbr. articles to profl. jours. Recipient Nobel prize in Physics, 1976, De Gasperi prize in Sci., Italian Republic, 1988, Ernest Orlando Lawrence award U.S. Govt., 1976, Eringen medal Soc. Engring. Sci., 1977, Gold medal in Sci. City of Brescia, Italy, 1988, Golden Leopard award Town of Taormina, 1988, Forum Engelberg prize, 1996; Am. Acad. Arts and Sci. fellow, 1975. Mem. NAS; mem. Pakistani Acad. Sci., Acad. Sinica, Russian Acad. Sci., Hungarian Acad. Sci., Deutsche Acad. Naturforscher Leopoldina. Office: MIT Dept Physics 51 Vassar St Cambridge MA 02139-4308

TING, WAI, political science educator; b. Hong Kong, Mar. 30, 1954; s. Shau Ling Ting and Kwai Ying Hui; m. See Wai Charlotte Kwok, Sept. 21, 1992; children: Ying, Jun. BSSc with honors, Chinese U. of Hong Kong, 1976; maîtrise ès-lettres, U. Paris X, 1978, D Polit. Sci., 1984. Rsch. fellow Inst. S.E. Asian Studies, Singapore, 1985-86; lectr. dept. comm. Hong Kong Bapt. U., 1986-94, lectr. dept. govt. and internat. studies, 1994-95, assoc. prof. govt. and internat. studies, 1995—, course leader China studies, 1994-95. Contbr. numerous articles to profl. jours., books, mags., newspapers. Mem. exec. com. U. of Democracy, Hong Kong, 1989—. Robert Schuman scholar European Parliament, 1984; internat. visitor U.S. Dept. of State, 1994, European Union Visitor program, 1996. Mem. Internat. Studies Assn., Assn. for Asian Studies, Inst. Français des Rels. Internat., Am. Polit. Sci. Assn. Avocations: hiking, travel, music, fine arts. Office: Hong Kong Bapt U, Dept Govt/Internat Studies, Kowloon Tong Hong Kong

TINGA, BENIAMINA, Kiribati government official. Min. fin. and econ. planning Govt. Kiribati, Tarawa Atoll, mem. parliament Nikunau; chmn. pub. accounts com., auditor gen., sec. for fin. and econ. planning, contr. customs and excise. Office: Ministry Fin & Econ Planning, P O Box 67, Bairiki Tarawa Kiribati*

TINGGREN, JUERGEN, management consulting executive; b. Ab, Enskede, Sweden, Feb. 12, 1958; m. Denise Isabelle Buchser, 1984. MBA, Stockholm U. Econs., 1981, NYU, 1981. Sr. assoc. Booz Allen & Hamilton, Dusseldorf, Germany, 1981-85; regional mgr. Sika Finanz AG, U.S., 1985-97; exec. v.p. Schindler Mgmt. AG, Switzerland, 1997-98; pres. Asia-Pacific Schindler Mgmt. A/P Ltd., Hong Kong, 1999—. Avocations: opera, travel, art exhibitions, tennis, skiing. Office: Schindler Mgmt A/P Ltd, 29/Fl Top Glory Tower, Hong Kong China

TINGSANCHALI, TAWATCHAI, engineering educator; b. Bangkok, Thailand, Feb. 2, 1947; s. Kenter and Surang T.; m. Nuasom Pornlert, May 27, 1976; children: Chedha, Tharntip. B of Mech. Engring., Chulalongkorn U., 1968; M in Hydraulic Engring., Asian Inst. Tech., 1970, D of Water Resource Engring., 1974. Asst. prof. Asian Inst. Tech., Bangkok, Thailand, 1975-78, assoc. prof., 1979-88, prof., 1988—, chmn. water resources engring. divsn., 1987-88; forum chmn. Sch. of Civil Engring., 1998—. Contbr. articles to profl. jours. Recipient Outstanding Rsch. award Nat. Rsch. Coun., Bangkok, 1980, Top Honor award Indian Assn. Hydrologists, 1995; rsch. fellow Alexander Von Humboldt, 1983-84. Fellow ASCE, Internat. Water Resources Assn. (chmn. Thailand chpt. 1991—), Engring. Inst. Thailand (mem. governing bd. 1992—), Indian Assn. Hydrologists; mem. Internat. Assn. Hydraulic Rsch. Avocations: jogging, swimming, reading, amateur radio, touring. Office: Asian Inst Tech, PO Box 4 Klong Luang, Pathum Thani 12120, Thailand

TINTLE, CARMEL JOSEPH, public relations executive; b. Paterson, N.J., Sept. 25, 1924; s. Herbert J. and Agnes (Merna) T.; m. Alice M. Hayes, Sept. 1, 1948; children: Joseph, Alice Maureen. BS, Fordham U., 1951; postgrad., NYU. Editl. asst. Newsweek mag., N.Y.C., 1946-50; news editor Beverage Retailer Weekly, N.Y.C., 1950-52; city editor Paterson Sunday Eagle, 1950-52; staff writer Carl Byoir & Assocs., Inc., N.Y.C., 1952-59, asst. account exec., 1959-64, assoc. account exec., 1964; account supr. Grey Pub. Rels., Inc., N.Y.C., 1964; v.p. Schenley Affiliated Brands Corp., subs. Schenley Industries, N.Y.C., 1964-72, sr. v.p., 1972-74; v.p. corp. affairs Am. Distilling Co., 1975-80; v.p. Banfi Vintners, Old Brookville, N.Y., 1980-90; CEO Vinum Comm., Inc., Old Brookville, 1980-90; cons. corp. comm. Banfi Vinters, Old Brookville, 1990—. Ensign U.S. Maritime Svc., 1943-46. Mem. N.Y. Press Club, SAR, KC, St. Patrick Guard of Honor N.J., U.S. Mcht. Marine Vets. Home and Office: Winding Way East Convent Station NJ 07960

TIN TUN, Burmese government official. Prime min., min. planning and fin. Govt. of Burma (now Myanmar), Rangoon, 1988, min. for transport and communications, 1989-91, min. for constrn., 1989, min. for social welfare and labor, 1989-92, min. transport, min. labor and social welfare, 1992, now dep. min. energy, dep. prime min., 1992—, dep. prime min.; mem. State Law and Order Restoration Coun. Office: Office Dep Prime Min, Yangon Myanmar*

TINTURIN, NOËLLE COMPINSKY, pianist, music educator; b. L.A., Feb. 20, 1948; d. Manuel and Dorothy Marie (Atwood) Compinsky; m. Charles Douglas Russell, June 21, 1969 (div. Sept. 1976); 1 child, Celine Reneé Russell; m. Glenn Tinturin, Apr. 25, 1987. Student, U. So. Calif., 1964, Calif. State U., Northridge, 1969, Mt. St. Mary's Coll., L.A., 1972. Pvt. instr. piano L.A., 1967-93, Lake Arrowhead, Calif., 1993—; owner Tinturin Music Studio, 1993—; mem. numerous chamber music ensembles, 1967—; mem. (with Glenn Tinturin) Tinturin Duo (piano and guitar), 1990—; mem. chamber music faculty Idyllwild Sch. Music and Arts, U. So. Calif., 1967; oboist Mt. St. Mary's Cmty. Orch., L.A., 1964-69; founding mem. Am. Youth Symphony, L.A., 1965-69; accompanist for various choruses, vocalists, instrumentalists, 1970—. Piano soloist compact disc Romantic Miniatures, 1999; performer Tinturin Duo compact disc Romancero Gitano, 1994; arranger 14 classical works for Tinturin Duo; prodr. Mountain Musicales concert series, Lake Arrowhead, Calif., 1994—. Dir. classical music festival Arrowhead Arts Assn., Lake Arrowhead, 1998-99, bd. dirs., 1998—. Mem. ASCAP, Music Tchr.'s Nat. Assn., Music Tchr.'s Assn. Calif., Musician's Union (local 47, L.A.), Lake Arrowhead C. of C. Avocations: dancing, concerts, sailing, boating. E-mail: n.tinturin@gte.net. Home: PO Box 1773 Lake Arrowhead CA 92352-1773

TIONG, KWONG-KAU, electrical engineer, educator; b. Sibu, Sarawak, Malaysia, Nov. 26, 1957; s. Han-Liong Tiong and Suok-Mee Tong; m. Hsing-Ju Chen, Jan. 29, 1994; children: Ming-Chian, Je-Ya. BS, Reading (Eng.) U., 1979; MA, Bklyn. Coll., 1983; PhD, Poly. U., 1989. Assoc. prof. Nat. Taiwan Ocean U., Keelung, 1989-2000, prof., 2000—. Recipient Rsch. awards Nat. Sci. Coun., 1990, 91; rsch. grantee Nat. Sci. Coun., 1997. Mem. IEEE, Sigma Xi. Avocation: badminton. Office: Taiwan Ocean Univ, 2 Peining Rd, Keelung 202, Taiwan

TIONGSON-MAGNO, ESTRELLA TANJUTCO, psychologist, educator; b. Bagong Bayan, Bulacan, Philippines, Mar. 17, 1942; d. Teodoro (Tomacruz) and Sofia (del Rosario) Tanjutco; M. Antonio Santamaria Tiongson (div.); children: Corrinna, Carrissa; m. Joselito Bautista Magno; children: Erika Maia, Estrella Angela. Student, Coll. Mt. St. Vincent, N.Y., 1957-59; AB, Maryknoll Coll., Quezon City, Philippines, 1961; MA, Ateneo de Manila U., Quezon City, 1979, PhD, 1997. Educator Ateneo de Manila U., Quezon City, 1961-62; pers. staff ESSO Philippines, Manila, 1962-63; educator Internat. Sch., Makati, Philippines, 1963-85; pvt. practice counselor/therapist Quezon City, 1986—; psychologist Dayan Psychol. Clinic, Mandaluyong, Philippines, 1994-96; educator Ateneo Grad. Sch., Quezon City, 1994-95; presenter various psychol. convs. Contbr. articles to nat. publs. Vol. therapist Philippine Govt.: Help Cabanatuan Earthquake Victims, 1990, Crisis Line, Manila, 1988—, Armed Forces of Philippines Med. Ctr., Quezon City, 1988-90. Recipient award of appreciation Internat. Sch., Makati, Philippines, 1984, Apolinario Mabini rehab. award Philippine Found. Rehab. of Disabled Inc., Office of Pres. Malacanang Palace, 1990,

rsch. grant de la Salle U., Manila, 1994. Fellow Psychol. Assn. Philippines; mem. APA, Internat. Coun. Psychologists. Roman Catholic. Avocations: interior decorating, aerobics, malling. Home: 100-A Scout Delgado, 1103 Quezon City Philippines Office: Eagle Star Condominum, 25 F de la Rosa, 1108 Loyola Heights Philippines

TIPIKIN, DMITRIY SERGEEVICH, research scientist, secondary education educator; b. Redkino, Tver, Russia, May 21, 1968; s. Sergey Konstantinovich Tipikin and Margarita Petrovna Kulabukhova; d. Ol'ga Nikolaevna Istomina, Sept. 18, 1994 (div. Dec. 1998); 1 child, Alexandr Dmitrievich. MS, Moscow Inst. Physics & Tech., Dolgoprudny, Russia, 1991, PhD in Phys. and Math. Scis., 1994. Engr. Inst. Chem. Physics, Moscow, 1991-94, rschr., 1994-95, sr. rschr., 1997-99; vis. scientist Cornell U., Ithaca, N.Y., 1995-96; Humboldt fellow Tubingen (Germany) U., 1996-97; rschr. Inst. Problems Chem. Physics, Chernogolovka, Russia, 1999—; H.S. tchr. Moscow Inst. Fine Chem. Tech., 1998. Contbr. articles to profl. jours. Recipient Russian State Stipendship for Young Scientists, Russian Acad. Scis., Moscow, 1995; grantee Soros Sci. Found., Moscow, 1993. Mem. Humbold Club Moscow. Avocations: reading, jogging. E-mail: tipiki@cat.icp.ac.ru. Fax: 7 096 5764009. Office: Inst Problems Chem Physics, Institutskaya St, 142432 Chernogolovka Moscow, Russia

TIPLER, FRANK JENNINGS, III, physicist; b. Andalusia, Ala., Feb. 1, 1947; s. Frank Jennings Jr. and Anne (Kearley) T.; m. Jolanta Rokicka; children: Allison Anne, Caroline Nicole. S.B., MIT, 1969; PhD, U. Md., 1976. Rsch. mathematician U. Calif., Berkeley, 1976-79; sr. rsch. fellow Oxford (Eng.) U., 1979; rsch. assoc. U. Tex., Austin, 1979-81; assoc. prof. physics and math. Tulane U., New Orleans, 1981-87, prof., 1987—; vis. sr. scientist Max-Planck Inst. Astrophysics, Munich, 1987; vis. fellow U. Sussex, Brighton, Eng., 1987; vis. prof. Inst. Astrophysics, Liege, Belgium, 1988, U. Bern, Switzerland, 1988, U. Vienna, Austria, 1992. Author: l'Homme et le Cosmos, 1984, The Anthropic Cosmological Principle, 1986, The Physics of Immortality, 1994; editor: Essays in General Relativity, 1980; contbr. articles to profl. jour. Rsch. grantee NSF, 1984, 86. Libertarian. Office: Tulane U Dept Physics New Orleans LA 70118

TIPPLE, ALLAN GRAHAM, town planning researcher; b. Harrogate, Eng., Feb. 17, 1949; s. Arthur Dawson Tipple and Agnes Barclay (Lazenby) Scholey; m. Susan Patricia Thirlwall, Sept. 5, 1970; children: Matthew, Eleanor, David, Nicholas. BA in Town Planning, U. Sheffield, Eng., 1970, MA in Town Planning, 1972; PhD, U. Newcastle, 1984. Town planner Kitwe (Zambia) City Council, 1972-75; sr. asst. planner North Yorkshire County Council, Northallerton, Eng., 1975-78; lectr. U. Sci. and Tech., Kumasi, Ghana, 1978-82, U. Newcastle upon Tyne, Eng., 1982-83; dir. Ctr. for Archtl. Rsch. and Devel. Overseas, 1983—; planner Nat. Housing Authority, Lusaka, Zambia, 1972-73; cons. World Bank, Washington, 1985-88, Habitat, Nairobi, 1993—; lectr. Ghana, Nigeria, Egypt, India, Malaysia, Indonesia, Saudi Arabia, South Africa, Zambia. Author: Extending Themselves: User-initiated Transformations of Government-built Housing in Developing Countries, 2000; contbr. numerous articles on urban issues in Africa to profl. jours. Lay preacher Meth. Ch. Mem. Royal Town Planning Inst., Full Gospel Businessmen's Fellowship Internat. Avocation: Christian witnessing. Home: 9 Woodburn Sq, Whitley Bay NE26 3JE, England Office: U Newcastle upon Tyne, Ctr Archtl Rsch and Devel, Newcastle NE1 7RU, England

TIRADO, FELIPE SEGURA, dean; b. Mexico City, Apr. 18, 1948; s. Adalberto Arroyave Tirado and Mercedes Arroyave Segura; m. Maria Reyna Larrazolo, May 22, 1977; 1 child, Maria Emilia. Licence, Nat. U., Mexico, 1977; Master Degree, Leicester (U.K.) U., 1981; Doctoral Degree, Awaschlientes U., Mexico, 1997. Cert. psychologist. Rschr. Nat. U., Tlalngpantla, Mexico, 1976-95; dean Nat. U., Campus/Ztacala, 1995—. Contbr. articles to profl. jours. Named Nat. Rschr., 1987. Mem. Mexican Acad. Scis. Fax: 55657275. E-mail: ftlrado@servidor unam.mx. Office: Nat Univ Campus/Ztaclla, Av do los Barrios S/N, 54090 Tlalnepantla Mexico

TIRAO, JUAN ALFREDO, mathematician, educator; b. Córdoba, Argentina, Feb. 3, 1942; s. Juan Felipe and Amelia (Dumont) T.; m. María Cristina Nannini, Dec. 17, 1966; children: Paulo Andrés, Germán Alfredo, Eugenia Cristina, Marcos Agustin. Lic. in Math., U. de Córdoba, 1964; MS, U. Calif., Berkeley, 1969, PhD, 1970. Teaching asst. U. Calif., Berkeley, 1969; instr. Rutgers U., N.J., 1970; prof. U. de Córdoba, 1972—; vis. prof. U. Buenos Aires, 1972, U. Brazilia, Brazil, 1976; vis. scholar MIT, Cambridge, Mass., 1983, vis. prof. U. Mass., Amherst, 1992; dir. Inst. Math., Astronomy, Physics, U. de Córdoba, 1977-83, Ctr. of Investigation and Studies in Math., Córdoba, 1983—. Named Guggenheim fellow Guggenheim Found., N.Y., 1973, Joven Sobresaliente Camara Jr. de Buenos Aires, 1979, 1st Premio de Math., Coca-Cola En Las Artes & Las Ciencias, Buenos Aires, 1981. Fellow Acad. Nat. Scis., Buenos Aires, Acad. Nat. Scis. Córdoba; mem. Union Math. Argentina, Am. Math. Soc., Internat. Ctr. for Theoretical Physics (assoc.), Third World Acad. Scis., Nat. Rsch. Coun. Argentina (v.p. 1998—). Office: U de Córdoba, Physics Astronomy Math Dept, Valparaiso y R Martinez, 5000 Córdoba Argentina

TIRELLI, NICOLA, chemistry researcher; b. Rome, Italy, May 15, 1968; arrived in Switzerland, 1995; s. Vito Domenico and Matilde (Carli) Tirelli. MS, U. PISA, Italy, 1992, PhD, 1995. Qualified Chemist. Guest rschr. Procter & Gamble, Frankfurt, Germany, 1993; tchg. asst. U. Pisa, Pisa, 1992-95; rsch. and tchg. asst. Polytechic Zürich, Switzerland, 1995-97; rsch. asst. Polytechnic of Lausanne, Switzerland, 1998; lectr. Polytechnic of Zurich, Switzerland, 1998—; chemist restorator Italian Monumental Protection Assn., Pisa. Contbr. articles to profl. jours. Civil Alternative Service, Italy, 1993-96. Fellow Student Fellowships, Enichem, 1988-90. Mem. Am. Chem. Soc., Swiss Polymer Group, Italian Assn. Macromolecules. Roman Catholic. Avocations: science, philosophy, history, photography. Office: ETH Zurich, Moussonstr 18, 8044 Zurich Switzerland

TISCHENDORF, FRANK WALTER, internist, clinical chemist, immunologist; b. Gera, Thuringia, Germany, Oct. 12, 1936; s. Walter and Claire (Grimm) T.; children: Sven, Jens James. MD, U. Goettingen, Germany, 1963; Habil., U. Tuebingen, Germany, 1976, Diploma in Internal Medicine, 1972, Diploma in Lab. Medicine, 1979. Rsch. fellow Columbia U., N.Y.C., 1965-67; sci. asst. in internal medicine U. Tuebingen, 1967-77; sr. physician Mcpl. Hosp. Esslingen of U. Tuebingen, 1977-80; head, physician in chief dept. clin. chemistry Bernhard Nocht-Inst. for Tropical Medicine, Hamburg, Germany, 1980—; docent Tech. Acad. Esslingen, 1975-80, U. Tuebingen, 1976-85, U. Hamburg, 1986—; dir. tropical medicine course Bernhard Nocht Inst., 1988-89; mem. standardization com. on immunoglobulins of Internat. Union Immunol. Socs., 1977; mem. expert adv. panel on clin. chemistry Mcpl. Hosps. of Hamburg, 1980—; cons. Harbour Hosp., Hamburg, 1980-97; mem. expert adv. panel on lab. medicine Baden-Wüerttemberg Assn. Practitioners, 1976-86. Author: (atlas) Prima Vista Diagnosis, 1995, 2d edit., 2000; editor: External Manifestations of Disease, 1973, 6th edit., 1998; co-editor: The Eye in Systemic Diseases (with C. Meyer), 2000; assoc. editor Jour. Die Internistische Welt, 1976-86; editl. bds. Haemostaseologie, 1992—, Natur-und Ganzheitsmedizin, 1993-94, Die Medizinische Welt, 1987—, Tieraerztliche Praxis, 1998-99; contbr. numerous articles to profl. jours. and books. Mem. German Soc. Tropical Medicine, N.Y. Acad. Scis. Achievements include large scale crystallization of human fetal oxyhemoglobin and original contributions to immunochemistry and clinical significance of monoclonal immunoglobulins and lysosomal proteins of neutrophil and eosinophil granulocytes. Avocations: jazz, art, literature, skiing. Home: Kuulsbarg 17, 22587 Hamburg-Blankenese Germany Office: Tropical Inst, Bernhard Nocht-Strasse 74, 20359 Hamburg Germany

TISDALE, GREGORY BROKAW, artist; b. Newark, May 8, 1946; s. Lawrence Tisdale and Nancy Johanna Smith; m. Kathy Maschmeyer, July 20, 1991. Student, Ctr. for Creative Studies, Detroit, 1965-69. Comml. artist various advt. agys., Detroit, 1965-69; graphic artist Smith Henchman Grills, Detroit, 1974-75; art dir. Klock Advt., Detroit, 1975-84; freelance artist Detroit, 1984—; lectr. in field. Paintings featured in publs. including Best of Watercolor, 1995, In Watercolor Places, 1996, Dictionary of Sea Painters, 1997, Painting in Light and Shadow, 1997; painting of Edmund Fitzgerald declared only ofcl. painting by Mariners Ch.; State of Mich. Senate Resolutions No. 191 for artistic contrbns. to the cmty., 1987. Staff sgt. USAF, 1969-73. Mem. Internat. Guild Fine Artists (v.p. 1996—), Am. Soc. Marine Artists (artist mem.), Grosse Pointe Boat Club (commodore 1995). Avocations: sailboat racing, skiing, scuba diving, motorcycles, cruising boats. Home: 35 Briarwood Pl Grosse Pointe MI 48236-3773

TISDALE, JAMES EDWARD, pharmacy educator, pharmacotherapy researcher; b. Winnipeg, Man., Can., Apr. 23, 1960; came to U.S., 1986; s. Charles Edward Murray and Helen Joan (Millar) T. BSc in Pharmacy, U. Man., 1983; PharmD, SUNY, Buffalo, 1988. Bd. cert. pharmacotherapy specialist. Pharmacist Health Scis. Ctr., Winnipeg, 1984-86; fellow cardiovascular therapeutics Hartford (Conn.) Hosp., 1988-90; clin. asst. prof. U. Conn., Storrs, 1988-90; adj. clin. instr. Mass. Coll. Pharmacy and Allied Health Scis., Springfield, 1988-90; asst. prof. Coll. Pharmacy Wayne State U., Detroit, 1990-96, assoc. prof. Coll. Pharmacy, 1996—; coord. edn. and tng. dept. pharmacy Henry Ford Hosp., Detroit, 1990—; mem. cardiology item writing panel Specialty Coun. Bd. Pharm. Specialties, 1994-98; mem. expert panel Am. Soc. Health Sys. Pharmacists, 1994-96. Author 4 book chpts.; contbr. articles to profl. jours. Mem. Am. Coll. Clin. Pharmacy (chmn. publs. com. 1993-94, chmn. rsch. affairs com. 1995-97, chmn. ann. meeting program com. 1997-99, chmn. constn. and bylaws com. 1999—), Am. Heart Assn. Mich. (chmn. profl. edn. com. 1993-95, mem. clin. cardiology coun. 1994—), Am. Soc. Clin. Pharmacology and Therapeutics, Am. Pharm. Assn., Am. Soc. Health-Sys. Pharmacists. Achievements include research in area of antiarrhythmic drug pharmacokinetics and pharmacutherapy, drug therapy of atrial fibrillation and cardiac arrhythmias induced by drugs, including cocaine and haloperidol. Avocations: guitar, music, sports, travel, football officiating. Office: Wayne State U Coll Pharmacy 230 Shapero Hall Detroit MI 48202

TISDALE, MICHAEL JOHN, biochemistry educator; b. Mar. 25, 1945; s. Thomas and Gertrude May (Llewellyn) T.; m. Susan Pamela Whiting, Jan. 22, 1972; 1 child, Joanna Claire. BSc in Chemistry with 1st class honors, U. Hull (Eng.), 1967; PhD in Chemistry, Inst. Cancer Rsch., London, 1970; DSc in Cancer Biochemistry, U. London, 1983. Fellow Inst. of Cancer Rsch., London, 1970-71; sci. officer Rothamstead Exptl. Sta., Harpenden Herts, Eng., 1971-72; lectr. med. sch. St. Thomas Hosp., London, 1972-81; sr. rsch. fellow CRC exptl. chem. group Aston U., Birmingham, Eng., 1981-84, reader dept. pharm. sci., 1984-89, prof. cancer biochemistry, 1989—, head dept. pharm. and biol. scis., 1992-95. Author (book chpt.) New Approaches to Cancer Treatment, 1994. Avocation: breeding long horn cattle. Office: Aston U, Aston Triangle, Birmingham B4 7ET, England

TISDALE, PHEBE ALDEN, cryptographer. AB, Radcliffe/Harvard, 1932. Author: CAMEL-OT, 1998, Sparrowgrass Treasury of Religious Poetry, 2000, Connections, 2000. Mem. AAAS, N.Y. Acad. Scis. Home: 15 Jefferson Rd Winchester MA 01890-3116

TISELIUS, HANS GÖRAN, urology educator; b. Stockholm, Apr. 11, 1945; s. Eric H.G. and Maud K.V. (Asplund) T.; m. Ingrid M. Nilsson, June 3, 1972. Med. candidate, Karolinska Inst., Stockholm, 1966; MD, U. Lund, Sweden, 1972; PhD, U. Göteborg, Sweden, 1974. Med. diplomate. First asst. dept. med. chemistry U. Lund, Sweden, 1967-70; resident dept. surgery Linköping Univ. Hosp., Sweden, 1973-77, resident dept. urology, 1977-81, assoc. prof., 1981-91; prof. Linköping Univ. Hosp., 1992-98; prof. urology Stockholm (Sweden) Karolinska Inst., 1999—; pres. Adv. Bd. of European Urolithiasis Rsch., 1997-98. Mng. editor Scandinavian Jour. Urology and Nephrology, 1989-92. Recipient Fernström award Urolithiasis Rsch., 1984, Curt Engelhorn award, 1998. Mem. European Assn. Urology, Scandinavian Assn. Urology, Endourological Soc., European Urolithiasis Rsch. (pres. adv. bd. 1997-99), Internat. Soc. Urolithiais, Am. Urol. Assn. Avocation: painting. Home: Gulsippevägen 22, S-589 35 Linköping Sweden Office: Huddinge Univ Hosp, Dept Urology, SE-14186 Stockholm Sweden

TISHKOV, ALEXANDER ARKADEVICH, chemist; b. Moscow, Feb. 2, 1979; s. Arkady Alexandrovich and Natalya Yurevna (Ratnikova) T. Diploma, Moscow Chem. Lyceum, 1995; postgrad., Higher Chem. Coll., Moscow, 1995-2000, Inst. Organic Chemistry, 2000—. Asst. N.D. Zelinsky Inst. Organic Chemistry RAS, Moscow, 1995—. Contbr. articles to profl. jours. Recipient 4 Soros grants, 1995-2000, medal of Russian Acad. Scis., 1999. Home: Nizhegorodskaya 72/2 63, 109052 Moscow Russia Office: N.D.Zelinsky Inst Organic, Leninsky prop 47, 117913 Moscow Russia

TISMA, MARIJA STEVAN, artist; b. Indjija, Serbia, Yugoslavia, Aug. 22, 1950; s. Stevan Ilija and Djurdjinka Steva (Tubic) T.; m. Nenad Ante Rukavina, May 24, 1989; 1 child, Dane. BArch, Belgrade U., 1983. pres. ARDIUM.com, BBS for Art & Architecture, Belgrade, 1995—. One-man shows at Libertas Gallery, Dubrovnik, Croatia, 1977, Mostar RU Gallery, Bosnia-Hercegovina, 1980, Can. Embassy Gallery, Belgrade, Yugoslavia, 1987, Lazar Vozarevic Gallery, Yugoslavia, 1988, City Mus., Kraljevo, Yugoslavia, 1988, Singidunum Gallery, Belgrade, 1993, others; group shows include Oct. Salon, Belgrade, 1976-87, May Salon, Belgrade, 1977-87, Serbian Contemporary, Brussels, 1978; included in collections at Hotels Intercontinental, Belgrade, McDonald's Corp., Novi Sad, Yugoslavia. Yugoslav Ministry of Edn. grantee, 1978. Fellow Yugoslav Inst. Artists (Grand prize 1979, Great prize 1989); mem. Yugoslav Inst. Architects. Avocations: travel, books. Home: 15 Excelsior Pl Butler NJ 07405-1511

TISMANEANU, VLADIMIR, political science educator, researcher; b. Brasov, Romania, July 4, 1951; s. Leonte and Hermina Tismaneanu; m. Mary Frances Sladek, Nov. 22, 1991; 1 child, Adam Volo. PhD, U. Buchares, Romania, 1980. Rsch. assoc. Fgn. Policy Rsch. Inst., Phila., 1983-90; lectr. U. Pa., Phila., 1985-90; sr. asst. prof. U. Md., Coll. Pk., 1990-92, assoc. prof., 1992-97, prof., 1997—; mem. E. Europe com. Am. Coun. Learned Socs., N.Y.C., 1997—. Author: Crisis of Marxist Ideology in Eastern Europe, 1988, Reinventing Politics, 1992, Fantasies of Salvation, 1998; editor: Revolutions of 1989, 1999; mem. Jour. Democracy, 1996—; editor UC Press, 1998—. Bd. dirs. Internat. Forum Dem. Studies, Washington, 1997—. Recipient Vis. Disting. Lectr. award U.S. Dept. State, 1994. Mem. Am. Assn. Advancement Slavic Studies, Am. Polit. Sci. Assn. Fax: 202-686-5131. Office: U Md Dept Govt & Politics Tydings Hall College Park MD 20742

TISSERAND, JEAN-PAUL PHILIPPE (JEAN HAUTEPIERRE), bank executive; b. Lille, Nord, France, Mar. 28, 1967; s. Jean-Louis Fernand and Paulette (Ducatel) T. Diploma, Inst. d'etudes politiques, Paris, 1988, degree in demographic econs., 1990; degree in comml. law, Nanterre (France) U., 1991. Exec. econ. studies Unilever-CNF, Paris, 1992; exec., chief of legal unit Paris Town Hall, 1992; exec. econ. studies Cen. Bank France, Paris, 1993-97; sr. analyst credit instns. Comite des Etablissements de Credit, 1997—; occasional lectr. econ. U. Nancy and Aix, 1994-97. Chief editor quar. poetry jour. La lettre de Jean Hautepierre; contbr. poetry to anthologies. With French Navy, 1990-92. Mem. French Poetry Soc. Avocation: walking. Home: 5 rue Corneille, 75006 Paris France Office: Banque de France, 39 Croix-des-Petits-Champs, 75049 Paris France

TISSOT, JEAN-LOUIS ANTOINE, banker; b. Berkane, Morocco, Aug. 18, 1956; arrived in France, 1974; s. Emile Louis and Gabrielle (Alfonsi) T.; m. Erika Louise Rodriguez-Axtmayer, Feb. 13, 1964; children: Victoria, Marianne. MS in Engring., U. Caen, France, 1981, MBA, 1981; MA, Columbia U., 1985. Mgr. Socgen Capital Markets, Paris, 1986-88; fund mgr. Societe Generale, Paris, 1988-93; head internat. equity mgmt. Credit Lyonnais, France, 1993-98; mng. dir. Barclays Bank Europe, Paris, 1998—; dir. Barclays Internat. Funds, London, 1999, Barclays Internat. Funds Group; chmn., CEO Barclays Asset Mgmt., France, 1999—; dir. Banco Privado, Lisbon, Portugal, 1995-97, Slivinter Sicav, Paris, 1995-98. Avocations: foreign languages, opera. Home: 35 Rue de L'Arcade, 75008 Paris France Office: Barclays Asset Mgmt Europe, 45 Boulevard Haussmann, 75008 Paris France

TISYAKORN, LERS, food products and automotive chemicals executive; b. Bangkok, Dec. 30, 1951; s. Thawee and Vipa T.; m. Sylvia Widjaja, Aug. 15, 1974; children: John, James. Degree in Bus. Adminstrn., Western Australia Inst. Tech., Perth, 1971; MDiv, Bapt. Sem., Bangkok, 1992. Mgr. United Cold Storage Co. Ltd., Bangkok, 1971—; CEO Siam Automotive Chem. Co. Ltd., Bangkok, 1999—; pastor Hope of Bangkok Ch., Prapradaeng, 1986-90, Tabernacle Ch., Bangkok, 1991-98, Nam Pra Tai Ch., Pakkret, 1999—. E-mail: unitedco@a-net.net.th. Home: 69/5 Suksawad 70/11, 10130 Prapradaeng Thailand Address: United Cold Storage Co Ltd, 7 Soi Wat Kru-Nai Suk Sawas, 10130 Samut Prakarn Thailand

TISZA, MIKLOS, mechanical engineering educator, researcher; b. Debrecen, Hajdu, Hungary, Jan. 2, 1949; s. Miklos and Julianna (Racz) T.; m. Anna Katalin Nemeth, June 20, 1950; children: Beata, Miklos, Viktoria. MSc, U. Miskolc, 1972, PhD, 1977; CSc, Acad. Scis., Budapest, 1980, DSc, 1995. Asst. lectr. U. Miskolc, 1972-76, sr. lectr., 1977-80, assoc. prof., 1981-93, prof., 1994—, head sci. mgmt. dept., 1986-89, head mech. engring. dept., 1990—, pro-rector R&D, 2000—; project mgr. World Bank, Miskolc, 1991—. Author: Metal Forming, 1981, Metallography, 1985, Metal Forming: Theory of Plasticity, 1986, Materials Science for Mechanical Engineers, 1998; editor: Metal Forming: Theory and Practice, 1989. Recipient Order for Higher Edn. Coun. of Mins., 1977, Order of Labour, Pres. of Rep., 1981. Mem. Hungarian Soc. Mech. Engrs., Am. Soc. Materials, Internat. Deep-Drawing Rsch. Group (nat. sec. 1989—, v.p. 1995—), N.Y. Acad. Scis. Avocations: music, computers, swimming, tennis. Home: Balough Adam u 47, H-3529 Miskolc Hungary Office: U Miskolc, Miskolc-Egyetemvaros, H-3515 Miskolc Borsod, Hungary

TISZLAVICZ, LASZLO ISTVAN, physician, pathologist; b. Sajoszentpeter, Borsod, Hungary, Feb. 10, 1956; s. Lajos and Maria (Pap) T.; m. Bugyi Gyorgyi, Mar. 28, 1981; children: Lilla, Zoltan, Noemi, Adam. MD, Med. U. Szeged, Hungary, 1983; PhD, Albert Szent-Gyorgyi Med. U., 1996. Med. diplomate; cert. pathologist. Intern Martin Luther Univ., Halle, Germany, 1985-87, Medizinische Hochschule, Hannover, Germany, 1987-89; resident Albert Ludwigs Univ., Freiburg, Germany, 1989-94; sr. pathologist dept. pathology Albert Szent-Gyorgyi Med. U., Szeged, 1983—; cons. pathologist Town Hosp., Mako, Hungary, 1990—; med. cons. Soc. UFO Researches, Szeged, 1995. Mem. Soc. Hungarian Pathologists, N.Y. Acad. Scis. Avocations: football, table tennis. Home: Szegedi u 43, H-6900 Mako Hungary Office: Albert Szent-Gyorgyi Med U, Dept Path/PO Box 401, H-6701 Szeged Hungary

TITLYANOVA, ARGENTA ANTONINOVNA, ecologist, researcher; b. Blagovestchensk, USSR, Aug. 14, 1929; s. Antonin Andreevich and Eugenia Grigrievna (Lebedeva) T.; m. Nicolai Michailovich Makarov, June 10, 1953; children: Elena, Dimitri. PhD, Inst. Biology Applied Sci., Sverdlovsk, USSR, 1962; DSc, Inst. Soil Sci. and Agrochem, Novosibirsk, USSR, 1978. Jr. rsch. USSR Acad. Sci., Ural Branch, Lab. Biophysics, Sverdlovsk, USSR, 1952-63; assoc. prof., dean dep. faculty of natural scis. Novosibirsk State U., USSR, 1967-72; sr. rschr. Inst. Soil Sci. and Agrochemistry, Novosibirsk, 1972-74, head lab. biogeocenology, 1974-96, chief rschr., 1996—; prof. Novosibirsk State U., 1994—. Editl. bd. Jour. Vegetation Sci., 1985-95, Siberian Ecol. Jour., 1995—; author: (in russian) Carbon in Grasslands, 1977, Nitrogen and ACH Elements Cycling in Grasslands, 1979, Below-Ground Plant Organs in Grasslands, 1996. Project dir. sr. Social Ecology Charitable NGO, Novosibirsk, 1997-99. Mem. Internat. Soc. Soil Sci., Internat. Assn. Vegetation Sci., Internat. Soc. Root Rsch. E-mail: argenta@issa.nsc.ru. Office: Inst Soil Sci & Agrochem, Sovetskaya St 18, 630099 Novosibirsk Russia

TITO, TEBURORO, president of Kiribati; b. Aug. 25, 1953; married; 1 child. Attended, St. Joseph's Coll., Abaiang, Kiribati, U. South Pacific. Leader of opposition Maneaban te Mauri, 1987-91, dep. leader of opposition, 1991-94; pres. Govt. of Kiribati, Tarawa Atoll, 1994—. Office: Office of Pres, PO Box 68, Bairiki Tarawa Kiribati*

TITOV, ALEXANDER IVANOVICH, physicist, researcher; b. Tashkent, Russia, Jan. 23, 1947; s. Ivan Efimovich and Nina Petrovna (Grudistova) T.; m. Elena Vladimirovna Ivanenko, Apr. 11, 1986; children: Ivan, Tatiana, Maria. MS, Alma Ata State U., 1970; PhD, Jt. Inst. Nuclear Rsch., 1974, DSc, 1985. Jr. rsch. staff mem. Jt. Inst. Nuclear Rsch., Dubna, Russia, now lead rsch. staff mem.; vis. prof., univs. in Taiwan, Japan, Germany, 1990-99. Contbr. more than 200 articles to sci. and profl. jours. Mem. Russian Acad. Natural Sci. (corr.),. Home: Bogolivbov Str 15-539, 141980 Dubna Russia Office: Jt Inst Nuclear Rsch Bogoli, Lab Theoretical Physics, 141980 Dubna Russia

TITOV, ALEXANDRE NICKOLAYEVICH, physicist, researcher; b. Barnaul, Altay, USSR, Feb. 16, 1943; s. Nickolay Ivanovich and Elena Onisiforovna (Shehovceva) T.; m. Ludmila Veniaminovna Makhnova, Oct. 14, 1967 (div. Sept., 1997); children: Sergey, Maria; m. Madlen Erin, Oct. 17, 1996; children: Alexandre Erin, Nickolay Erin. Engr., Phys.-Tech. Inst. Moscow, 1966, PhD in Physics, 1971. Diploma Supreme State Cert. Com. Researcher Inst. Phys.-Tech. Measures, Moscow, 1969-72, sr. researcher, 1972-93; con. Nat. Metrology Lab., Turkey, 1993-96; vis. scientist Nat. Metrology Labs., Brazil, 1996—; UN Indslj. Devel. Orgn. expert, 1991—. Home: Leopoldo Miguez 25 apt 601, Rio de Janeiro Brazil Office: INMETRO DIDPT, Av N S das Graças 50 Xerém, Duque de Caxias Rio de Janeiro 25250020, Brazil

TITOV, VALENTIN ALEXANDROVICH, physical chemist, researcher; b. Odessa, Ukraine, Feb. 10, 1949; s. Alexander Alexandrovich and Anna Grigorievna (Varsanova) T.; m. Lubov Vasilievna Jaroshenko, Feb. 23, 1973; children: Egor Valentinovich, Maxim Valentinovich. Chem. Diplomate, Leningrad (Russia) State U., 1971; PhD, Inst. Inorganic Chemistry, Novosibirsk, Russia, 1980, DrSci, 1995. Jr. rschr. Inst. Inorganic Chemistry, Russian Acad. Sci., Novosibirsk, 1971-83, rschr., 1983-85, head of lab., 1985—; vis. rschr. Inst. Solid State Physics, Dresden, East Germany, 1975; sr. rschr. Novosibirsk State U., 1984-85; mem. nat. groups on thermodynamics and properties of electronics materials CODATA. Author several series of articles; editor: Direct and Inverst Tasks on Physical Chemistry, 1990. Mem Russian Acad. Sci. (coun. on semicondr. chemistry, coun. on pure substances). Russian Orthodox. Home: Demakov 12-53, Novosibirsk Russia 630128 Office: Inst INorganic Chemistry, Lavrentiev Ave 3, Novosibirsk Russia 630090

TITRUD, OLIVER GEORGE, retired medical educator; b. Clarissa, Minn., May 11, 1926; s. Geroge Marius Titrud and Gunda Gjerstad; m. Dorothy Selma Lindborg, Oct. 9, 1949; children: Kermit Oliver, Cheryll Lu, Douglas Glenn, Bethine Joy, Debrah Lynn, Timothy Craig, Howard George, Rebecca Ann. BS, Bemidji (Minn.) State U., 1948; MS, U. Denver, 1951; MEdn, Macalester Coll., 1958; D of Chiropractic, L.A. Coll. Chiropractic, 1963; cert. advanced studies, No. Ill. U., 1972. Assoc. prof. Northwestern Coll., Roseville, Minn., 1952-57, Pasadena (Calif.) Coll., 1957-60; prof. biology Azusa (Calif.) Pacific U., 1960-63, Warner Pacific Coll., Portland, Oreg., 1963-69; prof. anatomy Nat. Coll. Chiropractic, Lombard, Ill., 1969-72; mem. faculty Can. Meml. Chiropractic Coll., Toronto, Ont., 1972-73; acad. dean, prof. anatomy Western States Chiropractic Coll., Portland, 1973-79; mem. faculty Palmer Coll. Chiropractic, San Jose, Calif., 1979-89; prof. Naturopathic Coll., Portland, 1989-93; chmn. test com. Nat. Bd. Chiropractic Examiners, Denver, 1975-78. Author: Titrud's Method of Human Dissection, 1977. With USN, 1944-46. Grantee Western Mich. U., 1960. Avocations: studying languages, public speaking. Home: 1991 Santiam Dr Woodburn OR 97071-3037

TITTMANN, KARSTEN, physicist; b. Halle, Germany, Oct. 22, 1969; s. Peter and Anke (Weiss) T. Diploma, U. Magdeburg, Germany, 1993, D, 1997. Rsch. asst. U. Magdeburg, Germany, 1995-98, Inst. Fire Dept. Governing Doctoral Degree, 1997-98; with Bayer AG, Leverkusen, Germany, 1998—. Mem. AIAA. Avocations: computers, skiing, volleyball, biking. Office: Bayer AG, IM-KSB-FCR, EGO, D-51368 Leverkusen Germany

TITULAER, URBAAN MARIA, physics educator; b. Venlo, Limburg, The Netherlands, July 11, 1941; arrived in Austria, 1984; s. Hendrik J.A. and Lambertina J.J. (Ewalds) T. MS, Rijksuniversiteit, Utrecht, 1964, D in Natural Scis., 1973. Rsch. assoc. Harvard U., 1965; asst. Rijksuniversiteit, Utrecht, 1965-73; rsch. assoc. MIT, 1973-75; asst. Rheinisch-Westfälische Technische Hochschule, Aachen, 1975-84; prof. Essen U., 1980, Johannes Kepler U., Linz, Austria, 1984—; dean Johannes Kepler U., Linz, 1993-96; guest prof. Tokyo Inst. Tech., 1985, 97. Contbr. articles to profl. jours.

Mem. Austrian Phys. Soc. (bd. mem. 1986-94, pres. 1991-92), German Phys. Soc. Office: Johannes Kepler U, Altenberger Strasse 69, A4040 Linz Austria

TIUECO, RUBEN ARIAS, sales professional; b. Iriga City, The Philippines, Aug. 11, 1958; s. Soccoro (Arias) T. BS in Bus. Adminstrn., U. Northeastern Philippines, Iriga City, 1982, MBA, 1988. Data encoder Chowking Food Corp., Manila, 1987-88; sales rep. A-Z Mktg., Makati, The Philippines, 1987—. Home: Zone 2, #70 Hwy San Isidro, San Nicolas Iriga City 4431, The Philippines Office: A-Z Sales & Distribution Corp, 723 Bymatay St, Mandaluyong The Philippines

TIUNOV, MIKHAIL PETROVITCH, mammalogist; b. Hemniz, Germany, May 19, 1949; s. Petr Georgievitch and Nina Dmitrievna (Kadakova) T.; m. Tatjana Mikhailovna Omelko, Sept. 18, 1974; children: Jana, Ivan. MSc, U. Perm, Russia, 1972; PhD, U. Vladivostok, Russia, 1980, DSc, 1996. Cert. zoologist. Sr. lab. asst. Inst. Biology and Soil Sci., Vladivostok, 1974-76, engr., 1976-80, jr. rschr., 1980-85, rschr., 1985-91, sr. rschr., 1991-96, leading scientist, 1996—. Author: Chiroptera of the Far East of Russia, 1997; contbr. articles to profl. jours. Mem. N.Y. Acad. Scis., Russian Theriology Soc., Geog. Soc. Russia. Avocations: speleology, sport rafting. Home: Kaplunova 8-173, 690013 Vladivostok Russia Office: Inst Biol and Soil Sci, Prospect 100-Letia 159, 690022 Vladivostok Russia

TIURI, MARTTI EELIS, member Parliament of Finland, scientist; b. Koski, Finland, Nov. 13, 1925; s. Eeli Albert and Rauha Maria (Tammikoski) T.; m. Eila Orvokki Suvanto, Dec. 10, 1917; children: Ulpu, Markku, Seija. Diploma in engring., Helsinki U. Tech., Espoo, Finland, 1950, Dr. Exam., 1960; MS, Stanford U., 1956. Rsch. engr. State Ctr. for Tech. Rsch., Helsinki, 1950-61; prof. radio engring. Helsinki U. Tech., 1962-89; mem. Parliament of Finland, Helsinki, 1983—; vis. prof. elec. engring. radio obs. Ohio State U., Columbus, 1961-62. Author: Future Begins Now, 1984, Finland on the Way to the Future, 1986, Possibilities of the Earth, 1990, The Future is Different, 1999; contbr. Radio Astronomy (J.D. Kraus), 1964; patentee in field of electronics. Mem. Finn del. Parliamentary Assembly of Coun. of Europe, Strasbourg, France, 1989—; chmn. com. for Future at Parliament of Finland. Sgt. inf. Finn mil., 1944. Named to Lion Order Finland, 1970, Nordstjärna Sweden, 1985. Fellow IEEE; mem. Internat. Acad. Astronautics, Finnish Acad. Tech. Sci., Finnish Acad. Sci. and Letters, Assn. Electronics Engrs. Finland (hon.). Mem. Nat. Coalition Party. Avocations: video filming, nature. Home: Takojantie 1F, SF-02130 Espoo Finland Office: Parliament House, SF-00102 Helsinki Finland

TIWARI, GOPAL NATH, engineering educator; b. Ballia, India, July 1, 1951; s. Bashisht and Bhagirathi Tiwari; m. Kamalawathi Mishra, Dec. 1, 1955; children: Balgovind, Arvind, Ghanshyam, Gopika. BSc, Banaras Hindu U., Varanasi, 1970, MSc, 1972, PhD, 1976. Rsch. assoc. Indian Inst. Tech. Delhi, New Delhi, 1977-79, lectr., 1979-81, asst. prof., 1981-97, prof., 1997—; sr. lectr. U. Papua New Guinea, 1987-89; European fellow U. Ulster, No. Ireland, 1993. Author: Solar Distillation, 1982, Applied Solar Thermal Energy Devices, 1985, Thermal Control in Passive Solar Buildings, 1988, Solar Thermal Engineering System, 1997, Greenhouse Technology, 1998; contbr. articles to profl. jours. Chmn. Faculty Forum, Indian Inst. Tech. Delhi, 1983-85, 95-99; pres. Hari Sat Sang Sabha, Indian Inst. Tech., Delhi, 1998-2000. Recipient Hari Om Ashram Prerit S S Bhatnager award Govt. India, Bhavnager, 1982. Mem. Solar Energy Soc. India (life), Internat. Ctr. for Theoretical Physics (life Indian chpt.). Hindu. Avocation: music. Home: Adarsh Nager, Sagerpali Ballia, India Office: IIT Dehli, Ctr for Energy Studies, New Delhi 110016, India

TIWARI, SWAMI DWARKA NATH, public relations executive; b. Hatta, MP, India, Feb. 24, 1926; s. Swami Ramsevak and Swami Gomti (Adjaria) T.; m. Shakuntala Rani Tiwari, Feb. 19, 1960; 1 child, Sangita. BA, U. Sagar, 1948; MA, U. Nagpur, 1951; postgrad. in journalism, U. Jabalpur, 1972. Lectr. Damoh Arts Coll. U. Sagar, Jabadpur, India, 1951-53; subeditor Rashtra Doot, Nagpur, India, 1954-55; field investigator Directorate Econs. and Stats., Durg, India, 1955-57; info. compilor, asst. Hindustan Steel Ltd., Bhilai, India, 1958-66; info. and pub. rels. officer Jawaharlal Nehru Krishi Vishwa Vidyalaya, Jabalpur, 1966-86, cons., 1984; project implementation mem. Parikrama Environ. Edn. Inst., Jabalpur, 1997—; cons. Pratibha-Pavan Pharm., Bhopal, India, 1970—, Herbal Medicinists, Jabalpur, 1975—; mem. rsch. adv. group Tropical Forest Rsch. Inst. Indian Coun. Forestry and Edn., Govt. India, Jabalpur, 1997; asst. dir. and incharge medicinal plants cultivation tng. program Parikrama Environ. Edn. Inst., Jabalpur, 1999. Contbr. articles to profl. jours. Mem. Soc. for Conservation Tropical Biodiversity, Tropical Forest Rsch. Inst., Rotary Internat. (hon.). Home: Friends House, JP Nagar Adhartal, Jabalpur 482 004, India Office: SDN Tiwari, JPN Jabalpur 482004, India

TIWARY, KAPIL MUNI, English educator; b. Bihar, India, Feb. 1, 1932; s. Ram Kabilas Tiwary and Dhanwanti (Mishra) Devi; m. Jonhi Pandey; 1 child, Usha. BA, Bihar U., Patna, India, 1952; MA, Patna U., 1954, U. Pa., 1967; PhD, U. Pa., 1968. Lectr. Patna U., 1955-73, reader, 1973-79, prof., 1979-92; prof. Taiz (Yemen) U., 1993—; chmn. dept. English Patna U., 1990-92, dean faculty of humanities, 1991-92. Author: Panini's Description of Nominal Compounds, 1985, Language of the Socially Disadvantaged, 1990; editor: Language and Theme, 1980, Aspects of English Prose, 1986. Fulbright scholar, India, 1964. Avocations: language, learning. Home: Rd No 14 Shahdeo Path, Patel Nagar, Patna 800023, India

TIZANI, WALID M.K., civil engineer, researcher; b. Tripoli, Lebanon, Feb. 27, 1959; s. Khaled and Arwa (Akil) T. BSc, U. Mosul, Iraq, 1984; MSc, U. Leeds, Eng., 1987; PhD, U. Bradford, 1991. Rschr. U. Leeds, 1991-92; rschr. U. Nottingham, 1992-94, lectr., 1994—. Contbr. more than 25 articles to profl. jours. including Design Studies, Computational Structures Tech., among others. Grantee Engring. and Phys. Rsch. Coun., 1994, 97, 99, Dept. Environment, 1997. Achievements include devel. of software for specialist design task in structural steel; research in integrated design sys. and artificial intelligence. Office: Nottingham U Dept Civil Engring, University Pk, Nottingham NG7 2RD, England

TIZARD, BARBARA, education and child development researcher; b. London, Apr. 16, 1926; d. Herbert and Elsie (Kirk) Parker; m. Jack Tizard, Dec. 20, 1947 (dec. Aug. 1979); children: Bill, John (dec.), Jenny, Martin (dec.), Lucy. BA with honors, Oxford (Eng.) U., 1948; PhD in Psychology, U. London, 1957. Ednl. psychologist Child Guidance Clinic, London Hosp., 1957-60; lectr. dept. exptl. neurology Inst. Psychiatry U. London, 1963-67, research officer dept. child devel. Inst. Edn., 1967-71, sr. rsch. fellow, 1971-77, reader in edn., 1978-80, prof. edn., 1980—; dir. Thomas Coram rsch. unit Inst. Edn., 1980-90; cons. WHO, 1984—. Author: Early Childhood Education, 1975, Adoption: A Second Chance, 1977, (with others) Involving Parents in Nursery and Infant Schools, 1981, Young Children Learning, 1984, Young Children at School in the Inner City, 1988, Black, White or Mixed Race, 1993; co-editor: The Biology of Play, 1977; mem. editl. bd. Jour. Child Psychology and Psychiatry, 1979-90, Social Devel., 1990—; contbr. numerous articles to profl. jours. Fellow Brit. Psychol. Soc., Brit. Acad. (sr.). Office: U London Thomas Coram Research, 27 Woburn Square, London WC1N OAA, England

TIZARD, DAME CATHERINE (ANNE), association executive; b. Apr. 4, 1931; d. Neil Maclean and Helen Montgomery Maclean; m. Robert James Tizard, 1951 (div. 1983); 4 children. Grad., Matamata Coll., New Zealand, U. of Auckland, New Zealand. Tutor in zoology U. of Auckland, 1967-84; mayor City of Auckland, 1983-90; Gov.-Gen. of New Zealand, 1990-96; chmn. New Zealand World-Wide Fund for Nature, 1996-99, New Zealand Historic Places Trust, 1996—; mem. Auckland City Coun., 1971-83, Auckland Regional Authority, 1980-83. Avocations: music, reading, drama, scuba diving. Address: 12A Wallace St, Herne Bay Auckland 1002, New Zealand

TIZIANO, JEAN-PAUL, plastic surgeon, researcher; b. Marseille, France, Feb. 11, 1945; s. Victor and Helene Louise (Bompart) T.; m. Denise Jacqueline Porropane, Dec. 6, 1975; children: Muriel, Sandie. Grad. in Literary and Mathematics, Lycée Perier-Marseille, 1962; MD, Marseille Med. U., 1976. Jr. resident Pub. Hosps., Marseille, 1968-72, sr. resident, 1972-77, asst., 1977-79; pvt. practice plastic surgeon Marseille, 1979-92, West Indies, 1992-93, Kuwait City, 1995; anatomy instr. Med. Sch., Marseille, 1972-75; maxillo-facial cons. Hosps., Marseille, 1979-82, plastic cons., 1978-80. Author: Dermography, 1990, Manuel Pratique de Medecine Esthetique, 1993; contbr. articles to profl. jours. Mil. surgeon French Navy, 1969-70. Named Nat. Winner New Tech., Paris, 1999. Mem. French Plastic Surgery Soc., French Aesthetic Medicine and Dermatologic Surgery, French Assn. Maxillo-Facial Surgeons. Home: 27 Blvd des Joncs, 13008 Marseille France Office: Biotic Phocea, 12 Impasse des Roseaux, 13008 Marseille France

TIZZIO, THOMAS RALPH, brokerage executive; b. Elmont, N.Y., Jan. 9, 1938; s. Anthony Thomas and Ann Marie (Pascale) T.; m. Mary Ann Gentile, Aug. 26, 1962; children: Anthony, Vincent, Thomas. BBA, Bklyn. Coll., 1962. Underwriter W.J. Roberts & Co., N.Y.C., 1957-65; sr. underwriter Atlantic Mut. Ins. Co., 1965-67; various positions AIG Am. Home Assurance Co., N.Y.C., 1967-74, sr. v.p. property underwriting, 1974-78; exec. v.p. AIG Transatlantic Reins. Co., N.Y.C., 1978-80, pres., bd. dirs., 1980-82; sr. v.p. reins. Am. Internat. Group, Inc., N.Y.C., 1982-85, pres. domestic brokerage divsn., 1985-91, pres. Brokerage divsn., 1986-91, pres., 1991-97, sr. vice chmn., 1997—. Mem. Am. Inst. for Property and Liability Underwriters (trustee), Ins. Inst. Am. (trustee). Office: Am Internat Group Inc 175 Water St New York NY 10038-4918

TJANDRA, JOE JANWAR, surgeon, educator; b. Palembang, Indonesia, Feb. 5, 1957; arrived in Australia, 1975; s. Hasan N. and Tini (Lim) T.; m. Yvonne Lai Wan Pun, Jan. 18, 1986; children: Douglas, Bradley. MB BS, U. Melbourne, Australia, 1981, MD, 1989. Surg. registrar, rsch. fellow Royal Melbourne Hosp., 1986-90; assoc. surgeon Queen Mary Hosp., Hong Kong, 1990; colorectal fellow Cleve. Clinic, 1990-91, assoc. surgeon, 1991-92; colorectal surgeon Unif. Hosp. Wales, Cardiff, 1992-93, Royal Melbourne Hosp., Melbourne, 1993—; chmn. gastrointestinal trials subcom. Anti Cancer Coun. Victoria, Melbourne, 1995-97; mem. exec. com. Australasian GI Trials Group, Australia, 1996-97. Contbr. Monoclonal immunoscintigraphy, 1988 (D.R. Leslie prize 1988), papers to profl. jours. Fellow Royal Coll. Surgeons Eng., Royal Australasian Coll. Surgeons (traveling fellow), Royal Coll. Physicians and Surgeons Glasgow; mem. Colorectal Surg. Soc. Australia, Am. Soc. Colon and Rectal Surgeons, Assn. Coloproctology of Gt. Britain and Ireland. Avocations: swimming, golf. Office: Royal Melbourne Hosp Pvt Med Ctr, Royal Parade Ste 15, 3050 Parkville Victoria, Australia

TJIPILICA, PAULO, Angolan government official; b. Dec. 21, 1939. BA in Law, Lisbon Law Faculty, 1976. Legal counselor Coun. of Ministers, Portugal, 1976-92; lawyer Bar of Lisbon, 1978-92; mem. cen. com. UNITA, 1979-91; founder Movement for Democratization in Angola; min. of justice Republic of Angola, 1992—. Office: Ministry of Justice, Rua 17 de Setembro CP 2250, Luanda Angola*

TJIRIANGE, NGARIKUTUKE ERNEST, Namibian government official, lawyer; b. Windhoek, Namibia, July 12, 1943; m. Juley Tjiriange; 3 children. LLM, Kiev State U., PhD. Sec. Windhoek br. South West African People's Orgn., 1963-64, dep. sec. legal and econ. affairs, 1970-76, sec. legal affairs, 1976—, sec. secretariat, 1978-82, head legal svcs., directorate election during independence, 1990; mem. Constituent Assembly, 1989—; min. justice Govt. of Namibia, Windhoek, 1990—; participant process leading adoption UN Resolution 435; rep. South West African People's Orgn. at various confs. including Vienna Conf. on Law Treaties, UN Gen. Assembly, Security Coun., 3d UN Law of the Sea Conf., Diplomatic Conf. on Reaffirmation and Devel. Internat. Humanitarian Law; lectr. law UN Inst. Namibia, 1977-82. Contbr. articles to profl. jours. Recipient Labor Rels. cert. Internat. Inst. Labor Studies, Human Rights cert. Internat. Inst. Human Rights, 1975. Mem. African Assn. Internat. Law (founder), Internat. Assn. Dem. Lawyers (mem. bur.). Office: Office Ministry of Justice, Independence Ave/PBag 13302, Windhoek Namibia*

TJOFLAT, GERALD BARD, federal judge; b. Pitts., Dec. 6, 1929; s. Gerald Benjamin and Sarita (Romero-Hermoso) T.; m. Sarah Marie Pfohl, July 27, 1957 (dec.); children: Gerald Bard, Marie Elizabeth; m. Marcia Penman Parker, Feb. 21, 1998. Student, U. Va., 1947-50, U. Cin., 1950-52; LL.B., Duke U., 1957; D.C.L. (hon.), Jacksonville U., 1978; LLD (hon.), William Mitchell Coll. Law, 1993. Bar: Fla. 1957. Individual practice law Jacksonville, Fla., 1957-68; judge 4th Jud. Cir. Ct. Fla., 1968-70, U.S. Dist. Ct. for Middle Dist. Fla., Jacksonville, 1970-75, U.S. Ct. Appeals, 5th Cir., Jacksonville, 1975-81; judge U.S. Ct. Appeals, 11th Cir., Jacksonville, 1996—, chief judge, 1989-96; mem. Adv. Corrections Coun. U.S., 1975-87, Jud. Conf. of U.S., 1989—, Fed. Jud. Ctr. Com. on Sentencing, Probation and Pretrial Svcs., 1988-90; mem. com. adminstrn. probation system Jud. Conf. of U.S., 1972-87, chmn., 1978-87; U.S. del. 6th and 7th UN Congress for Prevention of Crime and Treatment of Offenders. Hon. life mem., bd. visitors Duke U. Law Sch.; pres. North Fla. coun. Boy Scouts Am., 1976-85, chmn., 1985-90; trustee Jacksonville Marine Inst., 1976-90, Episc. H.S., Jacksonville, 1975-90; mem. vestry St. Johns Cathedral, Jacksonville, 1969-71, 73-75, 77-79, 81-83, 85-87, 93, 95-96, sr. warden, 1975, 83, 87, 91, 92. Served with AUS, 1953-55. Recipient Merit award Duke U., 1990, Fordham-Stein prize, 1996. Mem. ABA, Fla. Bar Assn., Am. Law Inst., Am. Judicature Soc. Episcopalian. Office: US Ct Appeals US Courthouse PO Box 960 311 W Monroe St Rm 539 Jacksonville FL 32201

TJORNELUND, JETTE, scientist; b. Ribe, Denmark, Apr. 6, 1963; p. Aksel Bech and Karen Marie (Sorensen) T.; m. Egon Christensen, Sept. 11, 1993; children: Helena Tjornelund Christensen, Laerke Tjornelund Christensen. M in Pharmacy, Royal Danish Sch. Pharmacy, Copenhagen, 1987, PhD in Analytical Chemistry, 1991. Cert. analytical chemistry. Asst. prof. dept. organic chemistry Royal Danish Sch. Pharmacy, Copenhagen, 1991-95, assoc. prof. dept. analytical and pharm. chemistry, 1995—. Fax: 45 35 306010. E-mail: jt@mail.dfh.dk. Home: Valorevejen 37, 4130 Viby Sj Denmark Office: Royal Danish Sch Pharmacy, Universitetsparken 2, DK-2100 Copenhagen Denmark

TJOSVOLD, DEAN WILLIAM, university administrator, educator; b. Sheboygan, Wis., Feb. 12, 1945; arrived in Hong Kong, 1994; s. Dale Sylvester and Margaret Caroline (Williams) T.; m. Jenny Shuet Chee Cheung; children: Jason, Wesley, Lena, Colleen. BA, Princeton U., 1967; MA, PhD, U. Minn., 1972. Sr. fellow Nat. U., Singapore, 1983-84; assoc. prof. Simon Fraser U., 1979-84, prof., 1984—; chair prof. Lingnan Coll., Hong Kong, 1996—; vis. prof. State U. Groningen, The Netherlands, 1991-92, Hong Kong U. Sci. & Tech., 1994-95. Author: (books) The Emerging Leader, 1993, Learning to Manage Conflict, 1993, Psychology for Leaders, 1995. Mem. Internat. Assn. Conflict Mgmt. (pres. 1992-94). Office: Lingnan U, Dept Mgmt, Tuen Mun Hong Kong China

TJURIN, VLADIMIR ALEXANDROVICH, physics educator; b. Kazan, Russia, June 7, 1951; s. Alexander Fjodorovich and Valentina Ivanovna (Ignatjeva) T.; m. Natalia Yevgenjevna Yegorova, Mar. 27, 1981; 1 child. Cand. Sci. in Radiophysics, State U., Kazan, 1990. Engr. State U., Kazan, 1973, asst., 1987-94, assoc. prof., 1994—; chmn. Coun. of Young Scientists of Physics, 1982-84, dean's dep. of physic's faculty, 1991-92. Contbr. articles to profl. jours. Avocations: swimming, skiing. Office: Fac Physics/State Univ, 18 Kremlevskaja str, 420008 Kazan/Tatarstan Russia

TJUVAJEV, JURI, surgery educator, researcher; b. Tbilisi, Georgia, Jan. 31, 1964; s. George Michael Guelovani and Alla Tihon Tjuvajev; m. Rasa Sirevichute Spudene, Nov. 11, 1983 (div. Sept. 1987); m. Irini Nozdrachov, Apr. 18, 1988; children: George, David, Daniel, Devin. MD, U. Tartu, Estonia, USSR, 1986, PhD in Neurosurgery and Neurology, 1989. Neurosurgeon, physician Tartu U. Hosp., 1986-91; sr. rsch. fellow dept. neurology Meml. Sloan Kettering Cancer Ctr., N.Y.C., 1991-95, asst. prof., 1995-98, assoc. prof., 1998—; cons. Neurobiol. Techs., Inc., San Francisco, 1986—. Mem. editl. bd. Neoplasia, 1998—. Grantee NIH, Bethesda, Md., 1998, 2000. Mem. Am. Assn. for Cancer Rsch., Am. Soc. for Gene Therapy, Internat. Soc. for Studies on Cerebral Blood Flow and Metabolism, N.Y. Acad. Scis. Avocations: fishing, woodcrafting, martial arts. Fax: 212-639-2721. E-mail: tjuvajev@neurol.mskcc.org. Home: 11 Chatham Hill Rd Stroudsburg PA 18360-8348 Office: Meml Sloan Kettering Cancer Ctr 1275 York Ave New York NY 10021-6094

TKACH, VOLODIMIR, physicist, educator; b. Vladivostok, Russia, July 24, 1943; s. Ivan and Vera Tkach; m. Lidia Marsheva-Tkach, Mar. 2, 1974; 1 child, Natalia. MSc, Kharkov (Russia) State U., 1965; PhD, Phys. Inst. P. Lebedev, Moscow, 1973; ScD, Joint Inst. for Nuc. Rsch., Dubna, Russia, 1987. Rsch. fellow, then sr. rsch. fellow Kharkov Inst. Physics and Tech., 1966-89, prof., 1989-94; prof. Mid. East U., Ankara, Turkey, 1994-95, U. Guanajuato, Leon, Mex., 1995—. Contbr. articles to profl. jours. Office: U Guanajuato Inst Physics, Lomas del Bosque # 103, 37150 León Guanajua, Mexico

TKACHENKO, NIKOLAI VLADIMIROVICH, physicist; b. Zelinograd, Russia, Jan. 7, 1957; s. Vladimir Nikolaevich and Zinaida Andreevna (Anikieva) T.; m. Natalia Nikolaevna Kuznetsova, Aug. 27, 1980; children: Evgenia, Vladimir. MSc, Gen. Physics Inst., 1980, PhD, 1989. Rschr. Physics Inst. Acad. Sci. Moscow, 1980-82, rsch. scientist Gen. Physics Inst., 1982-91; rsch. scientist U. Helsinki, Finland, 1991-95, Tampere (Finland) U. Tech., 1995—. Contbr. articles to profl. jours. Office: Inst Materials Chemistry, Tampere U Tech PO Box 541, 33101 Tampere Finland

TKACHENKO, OLEKSANDR M., government official; b. Shpola, Cherkasy Region, Ukraine, Mar. 7, 1939. Grad., Bila Tserkva Agrl. Inst. Past. dep. of the chmn. of Coun. Ministers Ukraine, then state minister Agrarian Policy and Food, minister agr. Govt. of Ukraine, since 1991, v.p. cabinet mins. Ukraine, 1985-92, past 1st dep. spkr., vice-chmn. Verchovna Rada parliament, 1994-98, chmn. Verchovna Rada parliament, 1998—; prof. econ. sci. Brussel Acad Sci. Mem. Russian-Ukrainian Acad. Sci. E-mail: selpu@rada.gov.ua. Office: vul Sadova 3, 010019 Kiev Ukraine

TKACHENKO, YEVGENIY ALEXANDROVICH, engineering company administrator; b. Kiev, Ukraine, May 22, 1968; came to U.S., 1990; s. Alexander Michailovich and Irina (Vladimirovna) T.; m. Elena Tkachenko, Aug. 5, 1988; 1 child, Elizabeth. BSEE, Lehigh U., 1991; MSEE, Kiev (Ukraine) Poly. Inst., 1993, Lehigh U., 1993; PhD in Elec. Engring., Lehigh U., 1995. Sr. engr. Alpha Industries, Woburn, Mass., 1995-96, prin. engr., 1996-97, engring. mgr., 1997—. Contbr. articles to profl. jours. Recipient fellowship Taylor Found., 1991-95, Sherman Fairchild fellowship Lehigh U., 1992-95. Mem. IEEE Microwave Theory and Techs. Soc., IEEE Electron Device Soc., IMAPS Soc., ARFTG Soc., Phi Beta Delta. Russian Orthodox. Avocations: checkers (Champion of Ukraine 1988), soccer, volleyball, tennis, travel. E-mail: gtkachenko@alphaind.com. Office: Alpha Industries Inc 20 Sylvan Rd Woburn MA 01801-1885

TKACHUK, ZENOVIY YURIYOVYCH, biochemist, consultant; b. Kolomya, Ukraine, Jan. 19, 1948; s. Uriy Urievych and Maria Vasylivna (Huculak) T.; m. Larysa Volodymyrivna Khotyan, Mar. 10, 1973; children: Bohdana, Volodymyr. M in Biochemistry, Chernivtsy U., 1970; PhD, Acad. Sci. Ukraine, Kyiv, 1974. Rschr. Inst. Molecular Biology and Genetics, Kyiv, 1973-86, sr. rschr., 1986-92, head lab., 1992—; adviser Prime Minister Ukraine, Kyiv, 1992, 96, Pres. Ukraine, Kyiv, 1993-94. Author: Foundaments of General Genetics, 1995, Ukrainian Dream, 1996; patentee in field. Greek Catholic. Fax: 229 81 06. Home: Apt 51, Klovsky Uzviz 17, 252021 Kyiv Ukraine

TKADLEC, JOSEF, mathematics educator; b. Vsetín, Czechoslovakia, Mar. 10, 1960; s. Josef and Anastázie (Dlouhá) T.; m. Marcela Novotná, Jan. 9, 1987; children: Markéta, Josef. Diploma in math., Charles U., Prague, Czech Republic, 1984, D in Natural Scis., 1984; diploma univ. pedagogue, Inst. Tech. Studies, Prague, Czech Republic, 1989; Candidate of Scis., Czech Tech. U., Prague, Czech Republic, 1991. Rsch. asst. Charles U., Prague, 1981-84; grad. rsch. assoc. Czech Tech. U., Prague, 1985-87, asst. prof., 1987-98; assoc. prof. Czech Tech. U., 1999—. Contbr. articles to profl. jours. Com. mem. Turistic Club of Czech Tech. U., Prague, 1987-90; fin. mgr. Orienteering Club of Czech Tech. U., Prague, 1992—. 2nd lt. Czechoslovakian Army, 1984-85. Fellow German Acads. Scis., Greifswald, 1994-95; grantee Aktion Austria-Czech Republic, Vienna, 1995, Ministry of Edn. of Czech Republic, 1998. mem. Union Czech Mathematicians and Physicists (grantee 1987), Internat. Quantum Structures Assn., Am. Math. Soc. Avocations: science fiction, orienteering. Office: Czech Tech U Fac Elec Engr, Zikova 4, 166 27 Prague Czech Republic

TLASKAL, TOMAS, pediatric cardiac surgeon; b. Prague, Czech Republic, Apr. 2, 1950; s. Jaromir and Kveta (Prochazkova) T.; m. Kveta Laurinova, Dec. 16, 1977; 1 child, Kveta. MD, U. Charles, Prague, 1974. Diplomate European Bd. Thoracic and Cardiovascular Surgery. Houseman dept. surgery Hosp. Novy Bydzov, Czech Republic, 1974-76; houseman divsn. cardiovascular surgery Univ. Hosp. Motol, Prague, 1976-84, cardiac surgeon divsn. cardiovascular surgery Kardiocentrum, 1985—, cons. cardiac surgeon, 1990—, dep. chief divsn. cardiovascular surgery, 1991—, assoc. prof. surgery, 1997—; expert in pediat. cardiac surgery Hosp. William Soler, Havana, Cuba, 1987-88; cons. Inst. Care for Mother and Child, Prague, 1998—; tchr. 2d Med. Faculty, U. Charles, 1992—, Inst. Postgrad. Edn. in Medicine, Prague; rschr. Internat. Govt. Agy., Ministry of Health, Prague, 1999; presenter in field pediat. cardiac surgery. Mem. editl. bd. Cardiovascular Engring.; contbr. articles to profl. jours. Fellow European Assn. Cardio-Thoracic Surgery; mem. Internat. Soc. Cardio-Thoracic Surgeons, Assn. European Pediat. Cardiology, Cardio-Thoracic Surgery Net, Czech Med. Assn., Czech Soc. Cardiovascular Surgery, Czech Soc. Cardiology. Avocations: family, travel, nature, arts, photography. E-Mail: tomas.haskal@ifmotol.cuni.cz. Home: Nad Palatou 3, 15000 Prague 5, Czech Republic Office: U Hosp Motol Kardiocentrum, Uvalu 84, 150 06 Prague 5, Czech Republic

TLASKALOVA-HOGENOVA, HELENA, immunologist; b. Prague, Czech Republic, Dec. 29, 1938; d. Hynek and Marie (Trousilova) Hogen; m. Vlastimil Tlaskal, July 24, 1964; children: Jiri, Helena. MD, Charles U., 1962; PhD, Inst. Microbiology, Czech Acad. Sci., Prague, 1968. Clinician Hosp. Usti nad Labem, Czech Republic, 1962-64; from scientific worker to head divsn. immunology Inst. Microbiology Czech Acad. Sci., 1964—. Author: Chapter in: Fetal and Neonatal Infection, 1991; editor: Advances in Mucosal Immunology, 1995; contbr. articles to profl. jours. Mem. Czech Immunol. Soc. (pres.), Internat. Soc. Mucosal Immunology, European Biomed. Rsch. Assn., Internat. Union of Immunol. Socs. (mem. coun.). Avocations: swimming, fishing, gardening. Office: Inst Microbiology Czech Acad Sci, Videnska 1083, 142 20 Prague 4, Czech Republic

TLASS, MUSTAFA ABDUL-KADER, government official, military officer; b. Al-Rastan, Syria, May 11, 1932; s. Abdulkader Muhammad and Fatma Ahmad (Bakeer) T.; m. Lamiaa Hasan Al-Jabiry, 1958; children: Nahed, Firas, Manaf, Saria. Student, Mil. Coll., Homs, Syria, 1954; diploma, Acad. K.E. Voroshilov, Moscow, 1972, PhD in Mil. Sci. (hon.), 1980; PhD in History Scis., Inst. of Mil. History, Moscow, 1990; MSc in Engring., Armour Acad., Moscow, 1990; D (hon.), Humanitarian Acad. Soviet Armed Forces, 1992. Tchr. Al-Qraiya Sch., Al-Suwayda, Syria, 1950-52; 2d lt. armour weaponry Mil. Acad., Homs and elsewhere, Syria, 1954; advanced through grades to maj. gen. Gen. Staff, Damascus, Syria, 1968; chief Nat. Security Ct., Homs, 1965; pres. emergency mil. ct. Ministry of Def., Damascus, 1966, dep. comdr.-in-chief, 1970, min., 1972—, head mil. party com., gen. staff, 1977—, dep. minister, chief gen. staff, 1968; prof. mil. scis. Gen. Staff Acad., 1993; now also dep. prime min. Damascus; appointed dep. chief supreme council Syrian and Egyptian forces 1973 war, Cairo and Damascus, 1973; mem. People's Assembly Syrian Parliament, 1971—; dep. of commander-in-chief, dep. of prime minister Min. of Def., 1972—; founder Dar Tlass forRsch., Translation, and Pub., 1983. Author numerous books on mil. and hist. writings; also poetry. Pres. Com. Geographic Encyclopedia; mem. regional command Al-Baa'th Arab Socialist Party, Damascus, 1965, mem. politbureau, 1969, mem. People's Assembly, 1971, mem. ctrl. com., 1980. Decorated Order of Anniversary of Established United Arab Republic, Order of Victory Token, Order Loyalty Third Degree, Order of Mar. 8th 1963, Order Long Svc. and Ideal Instance, Order of Courage of First Degree, Order Peace in Lebanon, Order of Morocan Mil. Merit, Order of Two Niles, Order Honour Star, others; recipient Solenzera Inst. prize, 1986, The Syrian, Moroccan and Palestinian, Orders of Merit, Badge Mil. Honour Class of Knight, Senegalese Order and Lebanese Cedar Order of Ranking Officer, Meml. medal of 20th Anniversary of Soviet Victory in World War II. Mem. Mil. Scis. Acad., United Syrian-Egyptian Polit. Leadership, Union Arab Writers, Arabic Lang. Acad. Damascus, Russian Acad. Natural Scis. (fgn.).

Muslim. Club: Photography Damacus. Avocations: reading, writing, photography, tennis, swimming. Home: Al-Rawda 58, Damascus Syria Office: Ministry of Defense Office Prime Minister, Shahbandar St, Damascus Syria also: Office of Prime Min, Shahbandar, Damascus Syrian Arab Republic*

TLOU, THOMAS, university vice-chancellor; b. Gwanda, Zimbabwe, June 1, 1932; s. Malapela Mabetha and Moloko (Nare) T.; m. Sheila Morake, 1977; 3 children. BA cum laude, Luther Coll., DLitt (hon.); MAT, Johns Hopkins U.; MA, PhD, U. Wis.; LLD (hon.), Ohio U., 1986. Head dept. history, dean humanities U. Botswana, Lesotho and Swaziland, 1973-76; prof. history U. Botswana, 1975—, dep. vice-chancellor, 1980-84; vice-chancellor U. Botswana, Gaborone, 1984-97; prof. history, 1998—; founding dir. Nat. Rsch. Inst., 1975-76; amb. of Botswana to UN, 1977-80; rep. from Govt. of Botswana to UN Coun. Namibia; mem. various UN delegations and coms.; mem. Oral Data Com., 1971-73; mem. Bur. Non-Aligned Movement, 1978-80; mem. rev. com. U. Botswana; mem. Namibia Presdl. Com. High Edn., 1991; chair nat. archives adv. coun. Ea. and So. African Univs.; bd. dirs. Botswana Savs. Bank, Botswana Tech. Ctr.; mem. Nat. Employment Manpower Incomes Coun., 1993—; mem., dep. mem. Botswana Inst. of Devel. Policy Analysis, 1996—; mem. Luth. World Fedn. Study Group on African Religion, 1998—, Luth. World Fedn. Found., Bd., 1998—; mem. SADC Cons. on Human Resources Devel., 1997—, Botswana Nat. AIDS Coun., 1994-2000, U. Namibia Coun., 2000—; vice-chmn. Botswana Inst. Devel. Policy Analysis, 1999, chmn., 1999—; chmn. Botswana Nat. Coun. on Edn., 1999—. Author: History of Botswana, 1984, 2d edit., 1997, A History of Ngamiland, 1985, Biography of Sir Seretse Khama, First President of the Republic of Botswana, 1995; contbr. chpts. to books and articles to profl. jours. Mem. Nat. Archives Adv. Coun., Nat. Employment Manpower & Incomes Coun., Botswana Presdl. Com. Incomes Policy, 1989-90, ACU Coun., 1992—; mem. coun. Botswana Confederation Industry & Manpower, 1991—; chair SADCC Consultancy Human Resources Devel., 1991; mem. Consultancy on Protocol on Cooperation in Edn., SADC region, 1996-97; mem. exec. bd. UNESCO, 1992-95; bd. dirs. Botswana Nat. Mus. & Art Gallery; trustee Newspapers Trust Botswana. Named Chevalier dans l'Ordre des Palmes Académiques, 1982, Presdl. Order of Honour, 1994. Mem. Assn. African Univs. (mem. exec. bd. 1993—), African Studies Assn., Internat. Assn. Univs. (alt. mem. adminstrn. bd. 1985-90), Botswana Soc. (life), History Assn. Botswana, U.S.A. African Studies Assn., Assn. Commonwealth Univs. (chair 1993-94), Assn. Ea. and So. African Univs. (chair 1992-95). Avocations: reading, music, swimming. Office: PO Box 1004, Gaborone Botswana

TOACSE, GEORGE RADU, electrical engineering educator, researcher; b. Copacel, Fagaras, Romania, Jan. 24, 1941; s. Radu N. and Maria (Maga) T.; m. Ana Maria Harabagiu, Aug. 1, 1980; 1 child, Radu. Grad. in Elec. Engring., Tech. U., Timisoara, Romania, 1963; PhD (hon.), Transilvania U., Brasov, Romania, 1976. Asst. prof. Tech. U., Timisoara, 1963-66; asst. prof. Transilvania U., 1966-70, lectr., 1970-90, assoc. prof., 1990-91, prof., 1991—; dir. Rsch. Inst. for Computer Techniques, Brasov, 1984-90; coord. Tempus Programme SJEP-08180-94, Brasov, 1994-97, SJEP-13394-98, SJEP-13559-98, Brasov, 1998-00; establisher, coord. new dept. electronics and computer, Transylvania U., Brasov, 1990—. Inventor celerator for stepping motor (Brasov Invention Salon medal 1978). Mem. IEEE Romania. Avocations: reading, hiking, traveling. Home: Str Verii No 1 Apt 16, 2200 Brasov Romania Office: Transilvania Univ, Bul Eroilor No 29, 2200 Brasov Romania

TOADER, IOAN HOREA IOSIF, civil engineer; b. Maguri, Cluj, Romania, Sept. 24, 1943; came to U.S., 1998; s. Ioan and Agaftea (Todea) Toader; m. Veronica Mitrofan, June 27, 1969; children: Florin, Ioana, Vlad, Dana. MS, Cluj Polytech. Inst., Romania, 1967, PhD, 1981. Asst. prof. Cluj Polytechnic Inst., Romania, 1967-89, assoc. prof., 1990-94; civil engr. Zwick and Assocs., Inc., Olmsted Twp., Ohio, 1995-96; structural engr. O.E. Olsen and Assocs., Inc., St. Petersburg, Fla., 1999—; cons. Cluj Polytech. Inst., 1970-90. Author: (book) Steel Structures, 1983; contbr. articles to profl. jours. Grantee DAAD, Tech. U., Darmstadt, Germany, 1973-74. Mem. ASCE, Structural Engring. Inst. Avocations: classical music, fine arts, opera, tennis, baseball. Home: 169 Dauntless Dr Penn Hills PA 15235-3032 Office: OE Olsen and Assocs Inc 3342 Tyrone Blvd N Saint Petersburg FL 33710-2340

TOBAJAS-BRÚ, FRANCISCO JAVIER, insurance executive; b. Barcelona, Catalonia, Spain, May 16, 1948; s. Jose and Victoria (Tobajas) Bru; children: Mireia, Natalia, Roger, Anna; m. Mariona, Apr. 27, 1997. Electronics Engr., U. Politechnics, Barcelona, 1969; computers diplomate, U. Madrid, 1970; diploma in bus. adminstrn., U. Navarra, Spain, 1977. Engring.-bus. diplomate. Asst. acct. La Suisse Ins., Barcelona, 1962-66; systems analyst Enher Energy, Barcelona, 1966-69; project mgr. Cematica Software, Barcelona, 1969-71, Centro Calculo Sabadell Software, Sabadell, Spain, 1971-73; CEO Centro Calculo Ausona Software, Vic, Spain, 1973-78, Mutua Penedes Ins., VilaFranca, Spain, 1978-89; subdir. gen. Mutua Universal Ins., Barcelona, 1989—; consejero-delegado Osonaserveis Software, Vic, 1977-89; vice-chmn. Union Mutuas Aseguradoras Ins., Barcelona, 1985-93; cons. Mutua Penedes Ins., VillaFranc, 1989-93, Secyprosa Software, Barcelona, 1989-92. Vice major Govt. Town-Vilafranca del Penedes, Spain, 1983-87. Mem. Instituto Estudio Superiores de la Empresa - U. Navarra, Inst. Internal Auditors, Assn. de Tecnicos de Informatica, Jr. Chamber (vice chmn. 1974-77). Socialist. E-mail: tobajas@att.global.net. Office: Mutua Universal Matepss 10, Balmes 17-19, 08007 Barcelona Spain

TOBEY, MARTIN ALAN, cardiologist; b. Dallas, Tex., Sept. 24, 1947; s. Nathan Gene and Rose Marcus T.; m. Judith Helane Ross, Mar. 10, 1974; children: Daniel, Rachel. BS with highest distinction, Pa. State U., 1968; MD, Jefferson Med. Coll., 1970. Diplomate Am. Bd. Internal Medicine, Am. Bd. Cardiovascular Diseases, Am. Bd. Interventional Cardiology. Intern Phila. Gen. Hosp., 1970-71; resident in internal medicine Parkland Meml. Hosp., Dallas, 1971-74; fellow in cardiology U. Tex. Southwestern Med. Sch., Dallas, 1976-78; cardiologist Cardiology Assocs. of Fort Worth, Tex., 1978—; mem. med. bd. Harris Hosp. Meth., Ft. Worth, 1988-90, chmn. cardiology divsn., 1988-90. Author (software) Workshops in Coronary Angioplasty, 1984. Major U.S. Army, 1974-76. Fellow Am. Coll. Cardiology (regional rep. Tex. chpt. 1996—), Am. Heart Assn., Alpha Omega Alpha. Avocations: classical music, bicycling, computers. Office: Cardiology Assocs Ft Worth 1300 W Rosedale St Fort Worth TX 76104-2802

TOBIAS, JEFFREY STEWART, radiotherapist consultant; b. London, Apr. 12, 1946; s. Gerald Joseph and Sylvia (Pearlberg) T.; m. Gabriela J. Tobias, Nov. 16, 1973; children: Katharine Deborah, Benjamin Alexander, Max William Solomon. MA, Cambridge U., Eng., 1968, MD, 1971. House phycician St. Bartholomew's Hosp., London, 1971; house surgeon Whittington Hosp., London, 1972; sr. house officer Univ. Coll. Hosp., London, 1973, Hammersmith Hosp., London, 1974; rsch. fellow Sidney Farber Cancer Inst., Boston, 1975, St. Bartholomew's Hosp., London, 1976; lectr. radiotherapy and oncology Royal Marsden Hosp., London, 1977-80; now cons. radiotherapy & oncology, dir. of dept. U. Coll. Hosp. and Middlesex Hosp., London; mem. coun. Royal Coll. Radiologists London; chmn. U.K. Coordinating Com. Cancer Rsch. Head and Neck Working Group; mem. med. rsch. coun. Working Party in Gynaecological and Brain Tumors; mem. cancer rsch. campaign Breast Cancer Working Party; chmn. edn. com. Cancer Rsch. Campaign, U.K. Author: Primary Management of Breast Cancer, 1985, Cancer and Its Management, 1986, Cancer A Colour Atlas, 1990; editor: Current Radiation Oncology. Fellow Royal Coll. Physicians, Royal Coll. Radiologists; mem. Am. Soc. Therapeutic Radiology and Oncology, European Soc. for Therapeutic Radiology and Oncology, Brit. Oncological Assn. (past hon. sec.). Fax: 020 7 637 1201. E-mail: j.tobias@uclh.org. Home: 48 Northchurch Rd, London N1, England Office: Gower St, U Coll Hosp, London WC1, England also: Meyerstein Inst Oncology, Middlesex Hosp Mortimer St, London W1N 8AA, England

TOBIAS, KEVIN RICHARD, borough manager; b. Reading, Pa., Oct. 12; s. Frank Theodore and Stella Catherine Tobias; m. Elizabeth Ann Tobias, Oct. 12, 1991; children: Emma, Patrick. BA in Telecom., Pa. State U., 1986; MPA, Kutztown U. Pa., 1996. Cmty. devel. specialist City of Reading, 1987-97; mgr. Borough of Topton, Pa., 1997—. Mem. Pa. State U. Berks/Lehigh Valley Coll. Alumni Assn. (pres. 1999-00). Avocations: running, reading, woodworking. Office: Topton Borough 205 S Callowhill St Topton PA 19562-1750

TOBIAS, PHILLIP VALLENTINE, anthropologist, anatomist, educator; b. Durban, Union South Africa, Oct. 14, 1925; s. Joseph Tobias and Fanny (Rosendorff) Norden. BSc, U. Witwatersrand, Johannesburg, South Africa, 1946, BSc with honors, 1947, MBB Ch., 1950, PhD, 1953, DSc, 1967; DSc (hon.), U. Natal, 1980, U. Western Ont., 1986, U. Alta, 1987, U. Cape Town, 1988, Cambridge U., 1988, U. Guelph, 1990, U. South Africa, 1990, U. Durban, Westville, 1993, U. Pa., 1994, U. Witwatersrand, 1994, Museum Nat. d'Histoire Naturelle, Paris, 1996, U. Barcelona, 1997, U. Turin, 1998, Charles U., Prague, 1999, U. Stellenbosch, 1999. Lectr. in anatomy U. Witwatersrand, 1951-52, sr. lectr., 1953-58, prof., 1959-93, prof. emeritus, 1994—, head dept., 1959-90; hon. prof. palaeoanthropology Bernard Price Inst. Palaeontol. Rsch., 1977—, hon. prof. zoology, 1981—; dir. Palaeoanthropology Rsch. Unit, 1979-96; dir. Sterkfontein Rsch. Unit, 1999—, hon. professorial rsch. fellow, 1994—, dean Sch. Medicine, 1980-82; vis. prof. anthropology Cambridge U., 1964, U. Pa., 1992, 93, 94, U. Florence, 1996, Andrew D. White prof.-at-large Cornell U., 1996—. Author: The African in the Universities, 1951, Chromosomes, Sex-Cells and Evolution, 1956, The Meaning of Race, 1961, Man's Anatomy, 1963, 4th edit., 1989, Olduvai George, Vol. 2, 1967, vols. 4A and 4B, 1991, The Brain in Hominid Evolution, 1971, The Bushmen, 1978 (Anisfield-Wolf award Cleveland Found.), Man the Tottering Biped, 1982, Evolution of Human Brain, Intellect and Spirit, 1981, Dart, Taung and the "Missing Link", 1984, Hominid Evolution: Past, Present and Future, 1985, Images of Humanity, 1991, Il Bipede Barcollante, 1992, Paleoantropologia, 1992; editor (with K. Omoto) The Origins and Past of Modern Humans: Towards Reconciliation, 1998; contbr. over 900 articles to profl. jours. Pres. non-racial Nat. Union South African Students, 1948-51, Edn. League of South Africa, 1952-57; chmn. So. African nat. commn. UNESCO, 1998-2000; founding mem. Nat. Edn. Union of South Africa, 1980—; mem. coun. South African Inst. Race Rels., 1974-75. Recipient Internat. Balzan Found. prize, Berne, 1987, Achievement award Inst. Human Origins, 1989, L.S.B. Leakey prize, 1991, Carmel Merit award U. Haifa, 1992, Order of Meritorious Svc. Gold class Co. Africa, 1992, Huxley Meml. medal Royal Anthrop. Inst. Gt. Britain and Ireland, 1996, Charles Darwin Lifetime Achievement award Am. Assn. Phys. Anthropologists, 1997, commdr. Nat. Order of Merit, France and Italy, 1998, Order of Southern Cross class II, 1999, Ales Hrdlicka medal Humpolec, 1999, Gold medal of Charles Un, Prague, 1999, Gold medal Simon van der Stel Found., 1999, Wood Jones medal Royal Coll. Surgeons, London, 1997, commdt. Order of Merit Italy, 2000. Fellow AAAS (hon.), Royal Soc. South Africa (hon.), Royal Soc. London, Coll. Medicine South Africa (hon.); mem. NAS (fgn. assoc.), Am. Philos. Soc., Austrian Acad. Sci. (fgn. corr. mem.), Inst. for Study of Man in Africa (founding pres. 1961-68, 84-85), Anatomical Soc. of South Africa (founding pres.), South African Archaeol. Soc. (pres.), Geol. Soc. So. Africa (hon.), Assn. Sci. Writers South Africa (pres.), Internat. U. Anthropol. and Ethnol. Scis. (hon. life), Internat. Assn. Human Biologists (pres. 1994-98), Am. Acad. Arts and Scis. (hon.), Am. Assn. Anatomists (hon.), Can. Assn. Anatomists (hon.), Israel Assn. Anatomists (hon.), Royal Coll. Physicians (hon.), Anatomical Soc. Gt. Brit. and Ireland (hon.), Mexican Assn. Biol. Anthropology (hon.), Geog. Soc. Lisbon (hon.), Rotary (Paul Harris fellow, Sapphire Pin award 1981, 91). Office: U Witwatersrand Med Sch Anat Sci, 7 York Rd Parktown, Johannesburg 2193, South Africa

TOBIAS-JONES, BRIAN, oil field technology company executive; b. Newport, South Wales, Mar. 12, 1936; s. Arthur Rowland and Elizabeth May (Hayes) Tobias-Jones; m. Shirley Yvonne Swenson, Sept. 1963 (div. Aug. 1992); 1 son, Heath Meirion; m. Sheila Mary Wilde, Feb. 1996 (dec. Dec. 1998). Grad., Newport Tech. Coll.; BBA, Pacific Western U., 1983. Field engring. mgr. AMF Overseas Corp., Kuwait, 1973-75, mgr. Mid East, 1975-76, mgr. Africa and Mid East, 1976-77; mgr. Eastern Hemisphere AMF Overseas Corp., London, 1980-82; pres. Petro Industries, Inc., Dallas, 1983—, Amtex, Investments Inc., London, Paris, Dallas, 1987—; ptnr., pres. Coastal Petroleum, Inc., Coastal Securities Inc.; chmn. bd. dirs. Amtex Petroleum Inc., 1990; CEO, pres. Amtex Fin. Inc., Dallas, London, Paris, 1990, Tobias Enterprises Inc., Dallas, 1991; bd. dirs. internat. affairs Olympian Investment Co., Inc.; tchr.

TOBIN, DENNIS MICHAEL, lawyer; b. Chgo., June 3, 1948; s. Thomas Arthur and Lois (O'Connor) T.; m. Sue Wynn Henslee, June 14, 1969 (div. 1977); m. Karen Thompson, Oct. 11, 1980; children: Kyle James, Daniel Patrick. BA with honors, U. Ill., 1971; JD, Loyola U., Chgo., 1976. Bar: Ill. 1976, U.S. Dist. Ct (no. dist.) Ill. 1976, U.S. Ct. Appeals (7th cir.) 1985, U.S. Supreme Ct. 1985, Wis. 1989. Trial atty. Cook County Homicide Task Force, Chgo., 1976-84; prin. Dennis M. Tobin & Assocs., Chgo., 1984—; gen. counsel Forest Health Systems and Found., Ill., Miss., Hawaii, 1986—, Manages Behavioral Care Inc., Psychiat. Ins. Co. Am. Dir. Forest Health Systems Found.; mem. Chgo. Coun. on Fgn. Rels. Mem. ABA (forum on health law), Nat. Assn. Criminal Def. Attys., Chgo. Bar Assn. (com. on health law), Am. Soc. Law and Medicine, Ill. Assn. Criminal Def. Attys. (v.p. 1984-87), Ill. Attys. for Criminal Justice, Wis. Bar Assn., Ill. Assn. Hosp. Attys., Nat. Health Lawyers Assn., U.S. Sporting Clays Assn., Nat. Sporting Clays Assn., Gateway Gun Club. Roman Catholic. Office: 18-3 E Dundee Rd Barrington IL 60010-5292

TOBIN, JAMES, economics educator; b. Champaign, Ill., Mar. 5, 1918; s. Louis Michael and Margaret (Edgerton) T.; m. Elizabeth Fay Ringo, Sept. 14, 1946; children: Margaret Ringo, Louis Michael, Hugh Ringo, Roger Gill. AB summa cum laude, Harvard U., 1939, MA, 1940, PhD, 1947, LLD, 1995; LLD (hon.), Syracuse U., 1967, U. Ill., 1969, Dartmouth Coll., 1970, Swarthmore Coll., 1980, New Sch. Social Research, 1982, NYU, 1982, Colgate U., 1984, Western Md. Coll., 1984, Harvard U., 1995, U. Wis., 1996; D in Econs. (hon.), New U. Lisbon, 1980; D in Econs. and Bus. (hon.), Athens U., 1992; LHD (hon.), Bates Coll., 1982, Gustavus Adolphus Coll., 1986; LLD (hon.), U. Hartford, 1984, U. New Haven, 1986; LHD (hon.), Hofstra U., 1983, Sacred Heart U., 1990, Bard Coll., 1995, Beloit Coll., 1996; D in Social Scis. honoris causa, U. Helsinki, 1986. Assoc. economist OPA, WPB, Washington, 1941-42; tchg. fellow econs. Harvard U., Cambridge, Mass., 1946-47, with Soc. Fellows, 1947-50; assoc. prof. econs. Yale U., New Haven, 1950-55, prof., 1955—, Sterling prof. econs., 1957-88, prof. emeritus, 1988—; mem. Council Econ. Advisers, 1961-62, Nat. Acad. Scis. Author: National Economic Policy, 1966, Essays in Economics-Macroeconomics, vol. 1, 1972, The New Economics One Decade Older, 1974, Consumption and Econometrics, vol. 2, 1975, Asset Accumulation and Economic Activity, 1980, Theory and Policy, vol. 3, 1982, Policies for Prosperity, 1987; co-author: Two Revolutions in Economic Policy, 1987, National and International, 1996, Full Employment and Growth, 1966, Money, Credit, and Capital, 1997. With USNR, 1942-46. Recipient Nobel prize in econs., 1981; Social Sci. Research Council faculty fellow, 1951-54; Grand cordon Order of the Sacred Treasure, Japan, 1988; Centennial medal Harvard Grad. Sch., 1989, Disting. Pub. Svc. award Conn. Bar Assn. Fellow Am. Acad. Arts and Scis., Econometric Soc. (pres. 1958), Am. Statis. Assn., Brit. Acad. (corr.); mem. Am. Philos. Soc., Am. Econ. Assn. (John Bates Clark medal 1955, v.p. 1964, pres. 1971), Acad. Scis. Portugal (fgn. assoc.), Phi Beta Kappa. Home: 117 Alden Ave New Haven CT 06515-2109 Office: Yale U Dept Econs Box 208281 New Haven CT 06520-8281

TOBIN, JAMES ROBERT, biomedical device manufacturing company executive; b. Lima, Ohio, Aug. 12, 1944; s. J. Robert and Doris L. (Hunt) T.; m. Janet Trafton, Dec. 30, 1971; children: James Robert III, Amanda Trafton. BA in Govt., Harvard U., 1966, MBA, 1968. Fin. analyst Baxter Internat., Inc., Deerfield, Ill., 1972-73, internat. contr., 1973-75; mng. dir. Japan Baxter Internat., Inc., 1975-77, mng. dir. Spain, 1977-80; pres. IV Sys. Divsn. Baxter Internat. Inc., 1981-84; group v.p. Baxter Internat., Inc., 1984-88; exec. v.p. Baxter Internat., Inc., Deerfield, 1988-92, pres., COO, 1992-94; pres., COO Biogen, 1994-97, pres., CEO, 1997-98; pres., CEO Boston Sci. Corp., 1999—, also bd. dirs.; bd. dirs. Creative Biomolecules, Pathogenesis, PE Corp. Bd. dirs. Beth Israel Deaconess Hosp. Lt. USN, 1968-72. Republican. Home: 33 Huckleberry Hill Rd Lincoln MA 01773-3508

TOCA, ANGEL, educator; b. Mexico City, Mex., Feb. 22, 1959; arrived in Spain, 1973; s. Angel T. and Regina Otero; m. Elsa De Miguel; children: Javier, Laura. Grad., Valladolid, 1985. Chemist Santa Barbara Explosives Plant, Valladolid, Spain, 1983-87; tchr. secondary sch. Junta Galicia, Coruna, Spain, 1987-88, Lugo, Spain, 1988-92; tchr. secondary sch. Spanish Edn. Dept., Cantabria, Spain, 1992-98, Cantabria's Edn. Dept., 1999—. Author: International Academy of History of Science. Mem. History Sci. Soc., Soc. History Tech., Soc. Catalana hist. Sci. Home: PO Box 161, 39300 Torrelavega Spain

TOCANTINS, PAULO, trading company executive; b. Lundiai, Sao Paulo, Brazil, July 27, 1940; s. Alipio and Marisa Amelia Tocantins; m. Mathilde Henriques, Mar. 21, 1964; children: Renato Henriques, Patricia Henriques, Rodrigo Henriques. Engr., EPUC, Rio de Janeiro, 1965, MS, 1967; PhD in Econ. Engring., Nat. Sch., Rio de Janeiro, 1968. Trainee Alfa Romeo, Rio de Janeiro, 1963-65, engr., 1965-68; engr. Cia. Hecânica brasileira, Rio de Janeiro, 1968-69, Cia. Vale do Rio Doce, Rio de Janeiro, 1969-71; gen. dir. Nordon, Rio de Janeiro, 1971-72; pres., owner Consultev Internat. Trading Co., Rio de Janeiro, 1972—; cons. Pechiney, France, Plesser & Thruaca, Austria, KHD, Germany, Rheinbraun, Germany. Avocation: paintings.

TOCCHETTI, ANDREA, transportation engineering educator, researcher; b. Napoli, Campania, Italy, Feb. 16, 1936; s. Luigi and Rita (Maffezzoli) T.; m. Clorinda Pisapia, Dec. 21, 1961; children: Paolo, Michele, Luigi, Alessandro. Grad. in Transp. Engring., U. Degli Studi Di Napoli, 1961. Asst. U. Degli Studi Di Napoli, 1962-75, prof., 1975—; prof. U. Di Roma 2, Italy, 1987—; mem. Italian Railways Engrs. Com., 1975—, Italian Road Tunnels Com., 1972-79; pres. Workgroup on Sustainable Road Transport, Italy, 1991-94; cons. Code 1357 European Econ. Commn., Europe, 1997—. Author: Infrastrutture Ed Impianti Aeroportuali, 1983, La Capacità Di Traffico Degli Aeroporti, 1989. Councillar responsible Comune Di Formia, Italy, 1995-97. Avocations: athletics, music. Home: Via Posillipo 38A, 80123 Napoli Italy Office: Dept Ingegneria Trasporti, Via Claudio 21, 80125 Napoli Italy

TOCHIKURA, TATSUROKURO, applied microbiologist, home economics educator; b. Nagaoka, Niigata, Japan, Nov. 15, 1927; s. Tatsujiro and Fuji (Sato) T.; m. Kano Takako, Nov. 8, 1953; children: Momoyo, Tadafumi. BS in Agrl. Chemistry, Kyoto (Japan) U., 1951, PhD, 1960. Cert. indsl. microbiology and microbial biochemistry. Rsch. assoc. dept. agrl. chemistry Kyoto (Japan) U., 1956-61, assoc. prof. dept. agrl. chemistry, 1961-68, prof. dept. food sci. and tech., 1968-91, prof. emeritus, 1991; prof. home econs. Kobe (Japan) Women's U., 1991—; vis. asst. prof. Oreg. State U., 1964-65. Co-author: Microbial Production of Nucleic Acid-Related Substances, 1976, Methods in Carbohydrate Chemistry, 1980, Bioconversion of Waste Materials to Industrial Products, 1991. Mem. Am. Soc. Microbiology, Japan Bioindustry Assn., Japan Soc. for Fermentation and Bioengring., Japan Soc. for Bioscience Biotech. and Agrochemistry. Office: Kobe Womens Univ, 2-1 Aoyama Higashi-Suma, Kobe 654-8585, Japan

TOCKLIN, ADRIAN MARTHA, insurance company executive, lawyer; b. 1951; m. Gary Michael Tocklin, 1974. BA, George Washington U., 1972; JD, Seton Hall U., 1994. Regional claim examiner Interstate Nat. Corp., St. Petersburg, Fla., 1973-74; br. supt. Underwriter's Adjusting Co. subs. Continental Corp., Tampa, Fla., 1974-77; asst. regional mgr. adminstrn. ops. Livingston, N.J., 1977-78; br. mgr. Paramus, N.J., 1978-80; sr. v.p. mktg. N.Y.C., Piscataway, N.J., 1980-84; regional v.p., mgr. Livingston, N.J., 1984-86, exec. v.p., 1986-88, also bd. dirs.; sr. v.p. Continental Corp., 1988-92, exec. v.p., 1992-94; pres. Continental Corp., N.Y.C., 1994-95; pres. diversified ops. CNA Ins., Chgo., 1995-98; CEO, pres. Tocklin & Assocs., 1998—; pres. bd. dirs. U.S. Protection Indemnity Agy., Inc., N.Y.C.; bd. dirs. Underwriters Adjusting Co., Arbitration Forums, Inc., Tarrytown, N.Y., Continental Ins. Co., Sonat Corp., 1st Ins. Co. of Hawaii; dir. CNA Surety, 1997—, El Paso Energy Corp., 1999—. Editor-in-chief Profl. Ins. Bulletin Update, N.Y.C., 1977-79. Named Ins. Women of Yr. APIW, 1998. Mem. YWCA Acad. Women Achievers, Nat. Assn. Ins. Women (Oustanding Ins. Woman in N.Y.C.), NOW. Democrat. Lutheran.

TOD, APRIL, writer; b. London, Apr. 24, 1948; d. Malcolm Maxwell Tod and Pamala Burrows Littledale. Student, London U., 1964-68. Interpreter Conf. Svcs., London, 1971-78. freelance journalist, writer contbg. to nat. newspapers, mags. on sports related subjects; stringer for Sports Illustrated; contbg. editor: Tennis. Mem. Women's Motor Racing Club, Brit. Women's Tennis Assn., Kandahar Club, Queen's Club. Avocations: tennis, skiing, music, travel, people. Home and Office: 46 Waldemar Ave Mansions, 2 Clatworthy House, Cleeve Way London SW15 4DD, England

TODA, SUSUMU, structural researcher; b. Obanazawa, Japan, Dec. 1, 1940; s. Tetsuo and Tosuo (Okuyama) T.; m. Sahoko Miwa, Nov. 2, 1969; 2 children. B of Engring., Waseda U., Tokyo, 1964, M of Engring., 1966, D of Engring., 1980; Aero. Engr., Calif. Inst. Tech., 1975. Sr. rschr. Nat. Aerospace Lab., Tokyo, 1975-82, head of airframe structural lab., 1983-84; sr. engr. Nat. Space Devel. Agy., Tokyo, 1985-88; head structural dynamics lab. Nat. Aerospace Lab., Tokyo, 1988-95, dir. structural mechanics divsn., 1995-96, dir. space tech. rsch. group, 1996-97, dep. dir. gen., 1998-99, dir.-gen., 1999—; cons. Nat. Space Devel. Agy., 1988—; mem. com. on space debris NRC, Washington, 1993. Contbr. articles to profl. jours. Recipient Disting. Rsch. award Min. Sci. and Tech., Tokyo, 1996; STA scholar, 1974. Fellow AIAA (assoc.); mem. Japan Soc. for Aero. and Space Scis. (dir. acctg. 1989-91, 93-95, dir. editl. 1997-98, v.p. 1998-99, chmn. space debris study group 1991—, pres. 2000—), Soc. for Exptl. Mechanics, The Planetary Soc. Achievements include effects of the cutouts on buckling behavior of shells; structural development of the Japanese Earth Resources Satellite; space debris hypervelocity impacts on space structures. Fax: 81-422-40-3016. E-mail: toda@nal.go.jp. Home: 1-4-6 Sekimae Musashino-shi, Tokyo 180-0014, Japan Office: Nat Aerospace Lab, 7-44-1 Jindaijihigashi-machi, Chofu Tokyo 182-8522, Japan

TODA, TATSUSHI, molecular geneticist, researcher, educator; b. Gifu City, Japan, Aug. 14, 1960; s. Shuji and Sadako (Ikawa) T.; m. Takako Nagashima, Dec. 17, 1989. MD, U. Tokyo, 1985, PhD, 1993. Med. dr. dept. neurology U. Tokyo, 1985-91; rsch. scientist dept. biochemistry Cancer Inst., Tokyo, 1992-93; asst. prof. dept. human genetics U. Tokyo, 1994-96, assoc. prof. Inst. Med. Sci., 1996—. Contbr. articles to profl. jours. including Stroke, Nature Genetics, Am. Jour. Human Genetics, Annals of Neurology. Rsch. grantee Japanese Ministry Health and Welfare, 1993—, grantee for sci. rsch. Japanese Ministry Edn., Sci. and Culture, 1995—, grantee for sci. rsch. on priority areas, 1995—. Mem. Japanese Soc. Neurology, Japanese Soc. Child Neurology, Japanese Soc. Human Genetics. Avocations: listening to music, tennis, piano. Home: 4-1-23-604 Shibuya, Shibuya-ku, Tokyo 150-0002, Japan Office: Osaka U Dvsn Clin Genetics, 2-2-B9 Yamadaoka Suita Bio Med Rsch Ctr, Osaka 565-0871, Japan

TODD, IAN PELHAM, retired surgeon, consultant; b. London, Mar. 23, 1921; s. Alan Herapath and Constance Alice Payne (Edwards) T.; m. Jean Audrey Ann Noble, July 25, 1945; children: Neil, Jocelyn, Jane, Caroline, Steuart. Student, Sherborne, Dorset, Eng., 1935-38; MD, U. Toronto, 1943; Diploma Child Health, U. London, 1945; MS, Toronto (Can.) U., 1956. Surgeon St. Bartholomew's Hosp., London, 1958-81, St. Marks Hosp., London, 1954-86; hon. cons. surgeon King Edward VII's Hosp. for Officers, 1965-87; civilian cons. Royal Navy, 1970-86. Author, editor: Intestinal Stomas, 1978, Operative Surgery Vol. 3, 1982. V.p. Imperial Cancer Rsch. Fund, Eng., 1986-90; mem. Brit. Red Cross, London. Maj. RAMC, 1944-47. Named hon. fellow surgery France, Belgium, Greece, India, Malaysia, Brazil; Wellcome Rsch. fellow London, Toronto, 1955-56, Knight of Brit. Empire, 1989; recipient Lister prize in surgery Toronto U., Star of Jordan, 1973. Fellow ACS (hon.), Royal Coll. Surgeons Eng. (coun. 1975-86, pres. 1986-89, Hunterian lectr. 1953, Zachary Cope lectr. 1985), Royal Coll. Surgeons Can. (hon.), Royal Coll. Physicians and Surgeons Glasgow (hon.), Coll. Physicians and Surgeons Bangladesh (hon.), Royal Australasian Coll. Surgeons (hon.), Am. Soc. Colorectal Surgeons (hon.), Coll. Surgeons South Africa (hon.), Med. Soc. London (pres. 1984-85). Avocations: travel, music, skiing. Home: 4 Longmead Close, Norton St Philip Bath BA3 6NS, England

TODD, MALCOLM, Roman literature and language educator; b. Durham, Eng., Nov. 27, 1939; s. Wilfrid and Rose (Evelyn) Johnson T.; m. Molly Tanner, Sept. 2, 1964; children: Katharine Grace, Malcolm Richard. BA, U. Wales, 1961, DLitt, 1983; MA, Oxford (Eng.) U., 1984. Asst. to dir. Landesmuseum, Bonn, Germany, 1963-65; lectr. Nottingham (Eng.) U.,

1965-77, reader, 1977-79; prof. Exeter (Eng.) U., 1979-96; prin. Trevelyan Coll., Durham (Eng.) U., 1996—; vis. fellow All Souls Coll., Oxford, 1984, Brasenose Coll., Oxford, 1990. Author: The Northern Barbarians, 1975, 2d edit., 1987, Roman Britain, 1981, The Early Germans, 1992; editor: Research on Roman Britain, 1989, Fermani, 1998, 2000. Sr. rsch. fellow British Acad., 1990. Fellow Soc. Antiquaries. Avocations: book collecting, writing, walking, traveling. Office: Trevelyan College, Trevelyan Coll, U Durham, Devon Durham DH1 3LN, England

TODD, MARY KING, university educator; b. Ballymena, Northern Ireland; d. David and Anne King (Walkinshaw) Johnston; m. John Todd, Aug. 22, 1983. BA, Univ. Arts, Belfast, 1964; MA, Coleraine, 1979, DPhil, 1990. Lectr. Ballymena Coll., N. Ireland, 1965-75, ABE organizer, 1975-89, head of section adult edn., 1989-90, head of dept. liberal studies, 1990-92, head of adult edn., 1992-94; course tutor higher degrees Open Univ., N. Ireland, 1995—; info. officer Christian Endeavour, Ireland, 1993—, editor, 1986—; dir. modern lang. project Ballymena Coll., 1992-93; mem. tng. adv. panel NICOD, Belfast, 1994-98. Contbr. articles to profl. jours. Pres. Irish Christian Endeavour, 1990-91; youth leader Christian Endeavour, Eskylane, 1971—, award scheme adv., 1990—; pres. Brit. Christian Endeavour Union, 1998-99; bible class leader Presby. Ch., Eskylane, 1969—; mem. Coun. Leprosy Mission, 1999—. Avocations: gardening, walking, travel. Home and Office: 4 Chapeltown Rd, BT412LD Antrim Northern Ireland

TODD, SHIRLEY ANN, school system administrator; b. Botetourt County, Va., May 23, 1935; d. William Leonard and Margaret Judy (Simmons) Brown; m. Thomas Byron Todd, July 7, 1962 (dec. July 1977). B.S. in Edn., Madison Coll., 1956; M.Ed., U. Va., 1971. Cert. tchr., Va. Elem. tchr. Fairfax County Sch. Bd., Fairfax, Va., 1956-66, 8th grade history tchr., 1966-71, guidance counselor James F. Cooper Mid. Sch., McLean, Va., 1971-88, dir. guidance, 1988-96; chmn. mktg. Lake Anne Joint Venture, Falls Church, Va., 1979-82, mng. ptnr., 1980-82. Del. Fairfax County Republican Conv., 1985, 96. Fellow Fairfax Edn. Assn. (mem. profl. rights and responsibilities commn. 1970-72, bd. dirs. 1968-70), Va. Edn. Assn. (mem. state com. on local assns. and urban affairs 1969-70), NEA, No. Va. Counselors Assn. (hospitality and social chmn., exec. bd. 1982-83), Va. Counselors Assn. (exec. com. 1987), Va. Sch. Counselors Assn., Am. Assn. for Counseling and Devel., Women's Golf Assn. (pres. 1997-98), Chantilly Nat. Golf and Country Club (v.p. social 1981-82, Centreville, Va.). Baptist. Avocations: golf, tennis. Home: 6543 Bay Tree Ct Falls Church VA 22041-1001

TODD, ZANE GREY, retired utilities executive; b. Hanson, Ky., Feb. 3, 1924; s. Marshall Elvin and Kate (McCormick) T.; m. Marysnow Stone, Feb. 8, 1950 (dec. 1983); m. Frances Z. Anderson, Jan. 6, 1984. Student, Evansville Coll., 1947-49; BS summa cum laude, Purdue U., 1951, DEng (hon.), 1979; postgrad., U. Mich., 1965; DHL, U. Indpls., 1993. Fingerprint classifier FBI, 1942-43; electric system planning engr. Indpls. Power & Light Co., 1951-56, spl. assignments supr., 1956-60, head elec. system planning, 1960-65, head substation design div., 1965-68, head distbn. engring. dept., 1968-70, asst. to v.p., 1970-72, v.p., 1972-74, exec. v.p., 1974-75, pres., 1975-81, chmn., chief exec. officer, 1976-89, dir., chmn. exec. com., 1989-94, chief exec. officer, 1981-89; chmn., pres. IPALCO Enterprises, Inc., Indpls., 1983-89, dir., chmn. exec. com., 1989-94; chmn. bd., chief exec. officer Mid-Am. Capital Resources, Inc. subs. IPALCO Enterprises, Inc., Indpls., 1984-89, also bd. dirs., 1984-94; gen. mgr. Mooresville (Ind.) Pub. Svc. Co., Inc., 1956-60; bd. dirs. Nat. City Bank Ind. (formerly Mchts. Nat. Corp.), 1975-94, Am. States Ins. Co., 1976-94; hon. dir. 500 Festival Assocs., Inc., pres. 1987. Originator probability analysis of power system reliability; contbr. articles to tech. jours. and mags. Past pres. adv. bd. St. Vincent Hosp.; bd. dirs. Commn. for Downtown, YMCA Found., Crime Stoppers Cen. Ind., Corp. Community Coun.; past chmn., bd. trustees Ind. Cen. U. (now U. Indpls.); Nat. and Greater Indpls. adv. bds. Salvation Army, 1984-96; bd. govs. Associated Colls. of Ind., 1979-92. Sgt. AUS, 1943-47. Recipient William Booth award Salvation Army, 1994; named Disting. Engring. Alumnus Purdue U., 1976, Outstanding Elec. Engr. Purdue U., 1992, Knight of Malta, Order of St. John of Jerusalem, 1986. Fellow IEEE (past chmn. power sys. engring. com.); mem. ASME, NSPE, Power Engring. Soc., Ind. Fiscal Policy Inst. (bd. govs.), Ind. C. of C., Indpls. C. of C., Mooresville C. of C. (past pres.), PGA Nat. Country Club, Ulen Country Club, Columbia Club, Indpls. Athletic Club (past bd. dirs.), Meridian Hills Country Club (past bd. dirs.), Skyline Club (bd. govs.), Newcomen Soc. (past chmn. Ind.), Rotary, Lions (past pres.), Eta Kappa Nu, Tau Beta Pi. Home: 7645 Randue Ct Indianapolis IN 46278-1565

TODDYWALLA, VILLI SAM, medical biologist, researcher; b. Bombay, India, Oct. 11, 1942; d. Maneck Cawasji and Piroja Maneck (Dordi) Barisvala; m. Sam Phirozshah Toddywalla, Dec. 15, 1973; 1 child, Phiroze. BSc, Bombay U., 1964, MSc, 1966, PhD, 1973. Rsch. asst. Indian Coun. Med. Rsch., Bombay, 1967-71, asst. rsch. officer, 1971-74, rsch. officer, 1974-80, sr. rsch. officer, 1980-87, asst. dir., 1987-93, dep. dir., 1993-98, sr. dep. dir., 1998—; rsch. trainee Karolinska Inst., Stockholm, 1980-81; adj. prof. Pharm. Sch. U., Kans., 1989; vis. scientist U. Colo. Health Sci. Ctr., 1994-95. Recipient Rsch. Tng. grantee WHO, 1980. Mem. Internat. Soc. Rsch. in Human Milk & Lactation, Indian Soc. Study Reproduction & Fertility. Avocations: interior decoration, reading, visiting historical places. Office: Indian Coun Med Rsch, J M Street Parel, 400012 Bombay India

TODINOV, MICHAEL TODOROV, materials scientist, researcher; b. Stara Zagora, Bulgaria, Feb. 12, 1960; s. Todor Todinov Rousev and Marina Vuleva Genova; m. Proletsena Ananieva, July 29, 01988; 1 child, Marin Mihaylov. MSc, Tech. U. Sofia, Bulgaria, 1987, engr. specialilst in applied math., 1988, engr. specialist in computer sci.; PhD Sch. Metallurgy and Materials, U. Birmingham, Eng., 1999. Rsch. fellow dept. materials sci. and engring. Tech. U. Sofia, 1988-94; rsch. fellow Sch. Metallurgy and Materials U. Birmingham, 1994—, statistician, 1998—. Contbr. articles to sci. publs. Soldier Bulgarian Army, 1981-83, Zvezdets. Mem. Am. Soc. Metals, N.Y. Acad. Scis. Orthodox. Avocations: chess, swimming, badminton, jogging, cycling. E-mail: m.t.todinov@bham.ac.uk. Office: U Birmingham, Sch Metallurgy & Materials, Birmingham B15 2TT, England

TODONAI, ROBERT PAUL, artist; b. Port Augusta, Australia, Apr. 11, 1963; s. Steve Istvan and Margreta Marianne (Jaeger) T. Diploma in sci. and art, Sci.-Art Rsch. Ctr., Berri, Australia, 1984. Rsch. asst. Sci.-Art Rsch. Ctr., Berri, 1984-89; dir. Bonum Rsch. Ctr. Pty. Ltd., Barham, 1989—; treas., dir. Sci.-Art Rsch. Ctr. Australia, Inc., 1995—. Author: Robert Todonai, 1983; co-author: Two Bobs Worth, 1989. Named Artist to the Town of Loxton Dist. Coun. Loxton, 1988; recipient award for artistic excellence Thalians Hollywood Walk of Fame, 1999. Mem. N.Y. Acad. Scis. Avocations: building stone studios, landscape gardening, chess. Home: PO Box 733, Murwillumbah NSW 2484, Australia

TODOROV, NICKOLA STEFANOV, physicist; b. Novo Selo, Haskovo, Bulgaria, Jan. 3, 1943; s. Stefan Nickolov and Krustina (Stefanova) T.; 2 children. MS, Faculty Physics and Math., Sofia, Bulgaria, 1968. Physicist Inst. Physics, Sofia, 1968-72; rsch. assoc. III Inst. Solid State Physics, Sofia, 1972-77, rsch. assoc. II, 1977-81, rsch. assoc. I, 1981—; referee sci. papers in internat. jours. Contbr. numerous articles to profl. jours. Recipient Award of Excellence, Pres. of Bulgarian Acad. Scis., 1989. Avocations: hiking, history, geography, psychology. Home: 193 GS Rakovski Str 2, 1000 Sofia Bulgaria Office: Georgi Nadjakov Inst, Soldi State Physics, 1784 BU Sofia Bulgaria

TODOROV, TODOR STOILOV, theory mechanisms and machines educator, mayor; b. Sofia, Bulgaria, Feb. 20, 1957; s. Stoil Bojanov and Elena Stoimenova (Doychinova) T. MSc, Tech. U., Sofia, 1983, U. Sunderland, U.K., 1995. Diplomate mech. engring. Designer Tech. U., Sofia, 1984-87, rschr., 1987-88, prof., 1988—; mayor Town Coun. Vladaya, City of Sofia, 1996-99; tchr. U. Forestry, Sofia, 1984. Author: Design of Electro-mechanical Devices, 1996, Manual of Theory of Mechanisms and Machines, 1996; inventor machine for producing non-woven coverings, 1992. Mem. Union Dem. Forces. Avocation: guitar playing. Home: 3 Belibreg St, 1641 Sofia Vladaya, Bulgaria Office: Tech U Sofia, 1156 Sofia Bulgaria

TODOROV, VASIL VELICHKOV, nephrologist, educator; b. Sofia, Bulgaria, Oct. 15, 1953; s. Velichko Vasilev Todorov and Gena Penova Chatalska; m. Maia Christova Donova, June 4, 1978; children: Christo, Gergana. MD, Med. Acad., Sofia, 1979, diploma in internal medicine, 1984, diploma in nephrology, 1986; PhD, Nat. Attestation Com., Sofia, 1990. Physician Emergency Ctr., Pleven, Bulgaria, 1979-80; physician, tchg. asst. Med. U., Pleven, 1980-88, sr. tchg. asst., 1988-95, assoc. prof., 1995—; head clinic Med. U., Pleven, 1995—, chief dept. internal medicine. Mem. European Dialysis and Transplant Assn., N.Y. Acad. Scis., Balcan Assn. Nephrology, Dialysis, Transplantation and Artificial Organs. Avocations: fishing, hunting. Home: St Karadja 23 B Apt 13, 5800 Pleven Bulgaria Office: Med U Clinic Nephrology, G Kochev 8 Str, 5800 Pleven Bulgaria

TODOROVIC, ALEKSANDAR, broadcasting educator; b. Belgrade, Yugoslavia, Dec. 23, 1938; s. Svetislav and Natalija (Dinic) T.; m. Ksenija Manojlovic, Jan. 25, 1969; 1 child, Jelena. BSc, U. Belgrade, 1964; D honoris causa, Shiller Internat. U., 1996. From dep. tech. mgr. to editor-in-chief TV Belgrade, 1971-88; dir. rsch. & devel. Radio TV Belgrade, 1988-89; mng. dir. Yugoslav Radio TV, 1989-93; dir., dean Internat. Acad. Broadcasting, Montreux, Switzerland, 1993—; bd. editors RTV.TP Belgrade, 1979-92; vice chmn. SG 11 Internat. Telecomm. Union, 1984-89; chmn. Tech. Com. European Broadcast Union, 1989-91. Author: Broadcast Video Tape Recording Technology, 1984, 85; co-author: Digital Television, 1989; contbr. articles to profl. jours. Recipient award Internat. Broadcasting Conv., Brighton, U.K., 1986, Doctor Honoris Causa, Schiller U., 1996. Fellow Soc. Motion Picture and TV Engrs.; mem. Royal TV Soc., European Assn. Internat. Educators. Avocations: music, literature. Office: Internat Acad Broadcasting, 11 Ave de Florimont, 1820 Montreux Switzerland

TODOROW, MARKO MARKOW, Bulgarian government official; b. Munich, Feb. 26, 1944; arrived in Bulgaria, 1946; s. Marko Markow and Gertrud (Probst) T.; m. Svilena Vassileva Nedeva, Aug. 30, 1970; 1 child, Ventzislav. Diploma in engring., U. Rostock, Germany, 1968; PhD in Engring., U. Megdeburg, Germany, 1978. Head computing machinery dept. Tech. U. Rousse, Bulgaria, 1979-81; assoc. prof. Tech. U. Russe, Bulgaria, 1981—, dir. state computing ctr., 1981-85, head tech. mechanics dept., 1990-93, rector, vice-chancellor, 1993; now head univ. computer ctr. U. Russe; mem. Parliament, 1990-91; min. sci. and edn. Sofia, Bulgaria, 1993-95; mcpl. councillor Rousse, 1995—. Chmn. Coordinational Dem. Forces Com. of Union, Rousse, 1989-90; founder Bulgarian Liberal Party. Corp. Bulgarian Army, 1961-63. Mem. Union Bulgarian Scientists, Hiker Union Bulgaria, Open Soc. Club Rousse, Lions. Mem. Ea. Orthodox Ch. E-mail: mtodorov@mech.ru.acad.bg. Home: Tzar Oswoboditel 86/D, 7012 Rousse Bulgaria Office: U Rousse Dept Tech Mechanics, Studentska 8, 7017 Rousse Bulgaria

TODSEN, DANA ROGNAR, health care executive; b. St. Petersburg, Oct. 8, 1947; s. Birger Rognar and Elsie (Ewing) T.; m. Janis Hellman, June 13, 1970; children: Matthew Kristian, Jennifer Alana. BA, U. South Fla., 1970, MA, 1976. Assoc. dir. So. Health Found., Tampa, Fla., 1976-78; dir. U. Tampa, 1978-82; mng. dir. St. Anthony's Health Care Found., St. Petersburg, 1982-85; dir. devel. Moffitt Cancer Ctr., Tampa, 1985-91; CEO Meml. Health Trust, 1991-98; found. cons. Quorum Health Resources, Brentwood, Tenn., 1997—; pres., CEO Bapt. Health Found., Birmingham, Ala., 1998—; pres. Todsen & Assocs., Savannah, Ga., 1997—; adj. instr. Hillsborogh C.C., 1978, U. South Fla., 1980; keynote spkr. in field. Contbr. articles to profl. jours. Bd. trustees Cmty. Found. Greater Tampa; bd. dirs. Savannah Maritime Festival, 1991-98, Ga. Nonprofit Resource Ctr. Ala., 1998—, Ga. Med. Soc. Growing Health Partnership, 1996-98, Pres.'s Summit for Am.'s Future, The Alliance for Youth, 1997-98, Ptnrs. for Cmty. Health, 1996-98, Ronald McDonald House Charities of the Coastal Empire, 1992-98, St. Andrew's Prep. Sch., 1993-96, United Way of the Coastal Empire, 1993, Centennial Olympic Games Yachting Com., 1993-96, Children's Home Soc., 1983-91, Leadership, Tampa Bay, 1987—, bd. dirs., 1987-91, pres., 1990-91; mem. Leadership Tampa, 1981—; cons. Coffeeville (Kans.) Health Found., Monroe Health Found., Monroeville, Ala., Hubbard Regional Hosp., Webster, Mass., Gibson Meml. Hosp., Gibson City, Ill., Jordan Health Sys., Plymouth, Mass., Hickory (N.C.) Day Sch., Beaufort (S.C.) Acad., Spring of Tampa Bay, McLaughlin Rsch. Inst., Great Falls, Mont., Big Bros./Big Sisters Tampa, Met. Ministries, Tampa Cmty. Health Ctr., Suicide and Crisis Ctr., Exec. Svc. Corp. Tampa. Fellow AHA Health Forum, 2000. Mem. Am. Coll. Healthcare Execs., Nat. Soc. Fund Raising Execs. (cert., bd. dirs. 1992—, pres. 1992—), Assn. Am. Med. Coll., Nat. Ctr. for Nonprofit Bd., Acad. for Health Svc. Mktg., Am. Mktg. Assn., Assn. for Healthcare Philanthropy (cert.), Am. Coll. Healthcare Mktg., Sales & Mktg. Execs. Internat., Mil. Affairs Coun., Coun. for Advancement and Support Edn., Philanthropic Action Coun., Savannah Area C. of C. (mil. and civilian affairs coun.), Greater Tampa C. of C., Tampa Tiger Bay, Greystone Country Club, Summit Club, Savannah Yacht Club, Chatham Club, First City Club, Rotary Club Birmingham, Alpha Tau Omega. Democrat. Methodist. Home: 3705 Wyngate Cv Birmingham AL 35242-4218 Office: Bapt Health Found PO Box 830605 Birmingham AL 35283-0605

TOENNIES, JAN PETER, research chemical physicist; b. Phila., May 3, 1930; arrived in Fed. Republic Germany, 1957; s. Gerrit and Dita (Jebens) T.; m. Monika Elisabeth Zelesnick; children: Susanne, Annette. BA, Amherst (Mass.) Coll., 1952; PhD in Chemistry, Brown U., Providence, 1957; D (hon.), U. Gothenburg, 2000. Rsch. asst. Bonn (Fed. Republic Germany) U., 1957-65, dozent, 1965-68; dir., sci. mem. Max Planck Inst. Fluid Mechanics, Göttingen, Fed. Republic Germany, 1969—; adj. prof. Bonn U., 1971—; assoc. prof. Göttingen U., 1971—; cons. Uranit GmbH, Jülich, Fed. Republic Germany, 1977-89. Author: Chemical Reactions in Shock Waves, 1964; adv. editor Jour. Chem. Physics, 1973—; editor monograph series, Springer Series in Chem. Physics, 1979—. Recipient Gold Heyrovsky medal Czechoslovak Acad. Scis., 1991, Alumni citation Brown U., 1988, Hewlett-Packard Europhysics prize for outstanding achievement in condensed matter rsch., 1992. Fellow Am. Phys. Soc.; mem. German Phys. Soc. (sect. chmn. 1977-80), Göttingen Acad. Scis. (corr., Physics award 1964), Deutsche Akademie der Naturforscher Leopoldina. Home: Ewaldstrasse 7, D-37085 Göttingen Germany Office: Max Planck Inst, Stromunsforschung Bunsenstr, D-37073 Gottingen Germany

TOEPLITZ, GIDEON, symphony society executive; b. Tel Aviv, Nov. 18, 1944; s. Erich and Ruth (Loeb) T.; m. Gail Ransom, Sept. 2, 1978. B.A., Hebrew U., Jerusalem, 1969; M.B.A., UCLA, 1973. Flutist, Israel Philharm. Orch., 1969-71; asst. mgr. Rochester Philharm., 1973-75; asst. mgr. Boston Symphony, 1975-79, orch. mgr., 1979-81; exec. dir. Houston Symphony Soc., 1981-87, exec. v.p., mng. dir. Pitts. Symph. Orch., 1987—; active Am. Symphony Orchestra League. Mem. Nat. Acad. Rec. Arts and Scis., Am. Jewish Com. (bd. dirs.), Penn S.W. Assn. (bd. dirs.). Home: 2087 Beechwood Blvd Pittsburgh PA 15217-1705

TOEPPE, WILLIAM JOSEPH, JR., retired aerospace engineer; b. Buffton, Ohio, Feb. 27, 1931; s. William Joseph Sr. and Ruth May (Hipple) T. BSEE, Rose-Hulman Inst. Tech., Terre Haute, Ind., 1953. Engr. Electronics divsn. Ralph M. Parsons Co., Pasadena, Calif., 1953-55; pvt. practice cons. Orange, Calif., 1961-62; engring. supr. Lockheed Electronics Co., City of Commerce, Calif., 1962-64; staff engr. Interstate Electronics Corp., Anaheim, Calif., 1957-61; engring. supr. Interstate Electronics Corp., Anaheim, 1964-89, ret., 1989. Author: Finding Your German Village, 1990, Gazetteers and Maps of France for Genealogical Research, 1990, German Geneal. Soc. Am. Library User's Guide, 1995, Sandusky County, Ohio, Births, Infant-Name Soundex Index, 1997, Osnabrück Farm Histories, 1999, GCSA Libr. Shelf List Catalog, 1999. Pres. Golden Cir. Home Owners' Assn., Orange, 1989-95. With U.S. Army, 1955-57. Mem. Ohio Geneal. Soc. (life), So. Calif. Geneal. Soc., German Geneal. Soc. Am. (bd. dirs. 1993-97). Avocations: genealogy, music. Home: 700 E Taft Ave Apt 19 Orange CA 92865-4400

TOERSTAD, ELISABETH HEGGELUND, engineer; b. Oslo, Sept. 28, 1965; d. Bjorn Torris and Audny (Hegerberg) H.; m. Eirik Toerstad, Dec. 31, 1992; children: Vegard, Eivind. Grad., Oslo Engring. Sch., 1985, Norwegian Sch. Mgmt., Oslo, 1986, U. Bergen, Norway, 1990; cand. mag. physics-math./orgnl. psyc., U. Oslo, 1991, MSc in Structural Physics, 1994. Engr. Selmer Furuholmen AS, Oslo, 1986-88, Advanced Building Methods Norge AS, Drammen, Norway, 1988-89, H. Eeg Henriksen AS, Oslo, 1989; rschr. U. Oslo, 1992-95; project engr. Det Norske Veritas, Hovik, Norway, 1995-96, sr. engr., 1996—; mem. Nat. Com. Approval of Bldg. Contractors, Oslo, 1987-97. Contbr. articles to profl. jours. Bd. dirs. Bredde Vel, Lorenskog, 1996—, Sorli Nursery Sch., Lorenskog, 1998—. Mem. Norsk Fysisk Selskap, Polyteknisk Forening. Avocations: hiking, cross country skiing, dancing, literature. Office: Det Norske Veritas, Veritasvn 1, 1322 Hovik Norway

TOFF, MAXINE, adult educator, business consultant; b. London, July 4, 1936; d. Alfred and Helena (Stanton) Gee; m. Stuart Ridgeway Toff, Marc. 5, 1959; children: Borah-Anne, Lisa-Claire, Zachary David. Diploma in advanced ednl. studies, Southampton U., 1988. Tutor Presch. Playgroups Assn., London, 1979-81, Sussex, Eng., 1981-89; adult educator B.D.E.G., Hove, Eng., 1989-93, multicultural advisor, 1988—; multicultural advisor Acorns Day Nursery, Seven Oaks, Kent, Eng., 1989. Contbr. articles to mags. Organizer Stoneham Park Action Group, Sussex, 1983-89; euphonium player Orch. 2000. Avocations: sky diving, swimming, yoga, cycling. Office: Company Child Care, 50 Sackville Gardens, Hove BN3 4GH, England

TOFIAS, ALLAN, accountant; b. Boston, Apr. 13, 1930; s. George I. and Anna (Seidel) T.; m. Arlene Shube, Aug. 30, 1981; children: Bradley Neil, Laura Jean Silver. BA, Colgate U., 1951; MBA, Harvard U., 1956. CPA, Mass. Sr. acct. Peat, Marwick, Mitchell & Co., Boston, 1956-60; mng. ptnr. Tofias, Fleishman, Shapiro & Co., P.C., Boston, 1960-96; chmn. bd., 1996-97; bd. dirs. Rowe Cos., One Price Clothing Stores, Inc.; trustee Gannett, Welch & Kotler Mut. Funds. Mem. Brookline (Mass.) Town Meeting, 1970-77, mem. fin. adv. bd., 1975-81; mem. New Eng. Bapt. Health Care Corp., 1985—, trustee, chmn. fin. com., 1998—; bd. dirs. West Newton YMCA, 1986-89; mem. exec. com. Boston Aid to Blind, bd. dirs., 1988-97, pres., 1993-94. Lt. USNR, 1951-54. Mem. AICPA (coun. 1995-99), Mass. Soc. CPA's (pres. 1995-96), Nat. CPA Group (exec. com. 1983-88, vice chmn. 1985-88), BKR Internat. (world bd. dirs. 1988-97, chmn. 1994-96), Wightman Tennis Club (treas. 1974-76), Newton Squash and Tennis Club (bd. dirs. 1996-99), Masons. Home: 59 Monadnock Rd Wellesley MA 02481-1334 Office: 2044 Beacon St Waban MA 02468-1445

TOGASAKI, SHINOBU, computer scientist; b. San Francisco, Aug. 17, 1932; s. Kikumatsu and Sugi (Hida) T.; m. Toshiko Kawaguchi, Nov. 24, 1959; children: John Shinobu, Ann Mariko. BS in Math., Duke U., 1954; postgrad., Stanford U., 1954-56. Math. programmer IBM, 1956-69; sr. programmer IBM, Palo Alto, 1970-87; mgr. applications devel. Service Bur. Corp., Palo Alto, 1961-64, sr. analyst, 1964-68; systems architect devel. lab. Service Bur. Corp., San Jose, Calif., 1968-70; chief fin. officer Robin Hood Ranch, Inc., 1976-86; mgr. architecture & strategy Hewlett Packard Corp., Cupertino, Calif., 1987-89, mgr. strategic planning, 1989-93; chief architect MFA Hewlett Packard, 1993—. Mem. Am. Mgmt. Assn., AAAS, Am. Statis. Assn., Assn. Computing Machinery, Inst. Mgmt. Sci., Sigma Pi Sigma. Home: 2367 Booksin Ave San Jose CA 95125-4705 Office: 19447 Pruneridge Ave Cupertino CA 95014-0609

TOGHILL, PETER JAMES, medical association administrator, physician; b. Bushey, Eng., June 16, 1932; s. John Walter and Lena Mary (Jow) T.; m. Rosemary Anne Cash, Apr. 25, 1964; children: Claire Elizabeth, Helen Louise, Joanna Mary. Student, Univ. Coll., London, 1950-52; MB, BS, Univ. Coll. Hosp., 1955; MD, U. London, 1966. Med. registrar, rsch. fellow Univ. Coll. Hosp., London, 1960-64; sr. med. registrar King's Coll. Hosp., London, 1964-68; cons. physician Queen's Med. Ctr., Nottingham, Eng., 1968-94; dir. continuing med. edn. Royal Coll. Physicians, London, 1993-98; vis. cons. physician, Falkland Islands, 1980; instr. medicine U. Nottingham, 1968-94, clin. sub-dean, 1978-82. Editor: Examining Patients, 2d edit., 1995, Essential Medical Procedures, 1996, Introduction to the Symptoms and Signs of Clinical Medicine, 2000; contbr. numerous articles to med. jours., chpts. to books. Capt. Royal Army M.C., 1956-58. Rsch. fellow Brit. Empire Cancer Camp, 1962-63. Fellow Royal Coll. Physicians (London) (procensor and censor 1990-92), Royal Coll. Physicians (Edinburgh); mem. Assn. Physicians U.K. and Ireland. Avocations: cricket, painting, cycling.

TOGO, HISATAKE, research institute administrator; b. Tokyo, Jan. 3, 1931; s. Yoshitora and Noriko (Obayashi) T.; m. Teiko Namba, Feb. 27, 1960; 2 children. BA, Gakushuin U., Tokyo, 1953; Dr.Engring., Tokyo U., 1990. Dir. rsch. Tokyo Met. Govt., 1978-80, dir. comprehensive planning, 1980-85, dep. dir.-gen. urban planning, 1985-87, dir.-gen. pers. commn., 1987-90; exec. dir. Tokyo Inst. Mcpl. Rsch., 1990—; mem. exec. com. World Conf. Met. Governance, Tokyo, 1992-93; lectr., Internat. Christian U., 1993-98; vice chmn. exec. com. 3d Conf. World Capitals, Tokyo, 1992-93; mem. organizing com. Metropolis '96 of World Assn. of Major Metropolises, Tokyo, 1995-96; vis. prof. Seigakuin U., 1998—. Author: The Development of Urban Policies, 1986, Tracing Urban Reform Plan of Tokyo, 1993; co-author: The Government of World Cities, 1995; editor: 50 Years of Tokyo Metropolitan Administration, 1995. Mem. City Planning Inst. Japan; mem. world conf. internat. cooperation cities and citizens (tech. comm.), 1997-98. Avocation: classical music. Home: 7-6-2 Kinuta Setagaya-ku, Tokyo 157-0073, Japan Office: Tokyo Inst Mcpl Rsch, 1-3 Hibiya Pk, Tokyo 100-0012, Japan

TOH, CHAI, information science educator; b. Singapore, Singapore, Dec. 19, 1965. Diploma in Elec. Engring., Singapore Poly., 1986; B in Engring., Manchester (Eng.) U., 1991; PhD, Cambridge U., 1996. Network specialist Archive Singapore, Singapore, 1991-92; tech. staff/project leader Info. Tech. Inst., Nat. Computer, Singapore, 1992-93; lab. supr. Cambridge U., Cambridge, Eng., 1993-96; project leader Hughes Rsch. Labs., Malibu, Calif., 1996-98; prof. Ga. Tech. U., Atlanta, 1998—; tech. bd. mem. Convergence Corp., Norcross, Ga., EBA Systems, San Francisco. Author, editor: Wireless Computer Networks, IEEE Network Mag., 1996-99; feature editor: Mobile Comm. & Computing, ACM Mobile Computing and Comm. Rev., 1996—; editor: Computer Sci., Personal Techs. Jour., 1996—; patentee in field. Hon. Cambridge Commonwealth Trust scholar, 1993-96; fellow Cambridge Commonwealth Soc., 1993; fellow Cambridge Philos. Soc., 1994; prin. investigator NSF, 1999. Mem. IEEE (sr.; tech. chmn. Conf. on Broadband Wireless, 1999, tech. co-chmn. Workshop on Ad Hoc Mobile Networking, 1999, guest editor Jour. on Selected Areas in Comm., 1999), Sigma Xi. Office: Ga Tech U Sch Elec and Computer Engrg 777 Atlantic Dr Atlanta GA 30332-0001

TOH, KOK-AUN, science educator; b. Penang, Malaysia, Aug. 24, 1943; arrived in Singapore, 1977; s. Choo-Geok and Kim-Lee (Png) T.; m. Swee-Har Lee, Dec. 8, 1968; 1 child, Sheryl. BSc with honors, U. Malaya, Malaysia, 1966; AM, Stanford U., 1983; DPhil, Oxford (Eng.) U., 1990. Fed. insp. of schs. Ministry of Edn., Malaysia, 1973-77; lectr. dept. sci. edn. Inst. Edn., Singapore, Singapore, 1977-84, head dept. sci. edn., 1984-87, 90-91; head divsn. physics Nat. Inst. Edn., Singapore, 1991-92, dep. head Ctr. for Ednl. Rsch., 1995-2000, head dept. sci. and tech. edn., 2000—; assoc. prof. Nanyang Technol. U., Singapore, 1994—. Exec. editor Singapore Jour. Edn., 1991-95, Asia Pacific Jour. Edn., 1996-98; contbr. articles to profl. publs. Mem. Assn. for Sci. and Math. Edn. (pres. 1975-77), Ednl. Rsch. Assn. (life, hon. sec. 1991-93, v.p. 1993-97, pres. 1997-99). Avocations: jogging, bicycling, swimming, chess, Internet surfing. Office: Nanyang Tech U Nat Inst Edn, 469 Bukit Timah Rd, Singapore 259756, Singapore

TOH, SOON HUAT, executive; b. Singapore, June 30, 1960; s. Kim Tian and Char Bor (Lim) T.; m. Kek Choo Lee; children: Wen Hui, Yan Hui David, Xin Hui, Ke Hui. DPhil, So. Calif. U., 1999. Mng. dir. Novena Furnishing Ctr., Singapore, 1985—, Castilla Design, Singapore, 1994—, Novena Holdings, Singapore, 1993—, The White Collection, Singapore, 1999—, Suzhou Novena Furniture, China, 1994—, Shenzhen Calo Novena Furniture, China, 1996—. Mem. mgmt. com. Boon Lay Cmty. Ctr., Singapore, 1992—. Mem. Lions. Buddhist. Avocation: reading. Office: Novena Holdings, 47 Sungei Kadut Ave, Singapore 729670, Singapore

TOHMON, RYOICHI, optical engineer; b. Toyonaka, Osaka, Japan, Aug. 11, 1960; s. Shinzo and Teruko (Nishizawa) T.; m. Kumiko Adachi, Oct. 31, 1992; children: Miri, Rei. BSEE, Waseda U., Tokyo, 1983, MSEE, 1987, D of Engring., 1990. Cert. in engring. Engr. Minolta Camera Co., Tokyo, 1983-85; rsch. assoc. Waseda U., Tokyo, 1989-90; engr. Eastman Kodak Japan, Yokohama, 1990-93, Anritsu Corp., Atsugi, Japan, 1993—. Patentee in field; contbr. articles to profl. jours. Mem. Soc. Photo-Optical Instrumentation Engrs., Optical Soc. Am.

TOHNO, YOSHIYUKI, cell biologist, educator; b. Higashi Osaka, Japan, Mar. 29, 1944; s. Suetaroh and Misao (Yamanaka) T.; m. Setsuko Saitoh, July 15, 1970; children: Machiko, Hiroyuki. MD, Nara Med. U., 1963. Assoc. Nara Med. U., Kashihara, Japan, 1969-77, lectr., 1977-84, assoc. prof., 1984-96, prof., 1996—; lectr. in field. Contbr. articles to profl. jours. Mem. World Soc. Cellular and Molecular Biology, Internat. Assn. Bioinorganic Scis., N.Y. Acad. Scis. Home: Yao, Osaka 581-0866, Japan Office: Nara Med U Lab Cell Biology, Dept Anatomy, Kashihara, Nara 634-8521, Japan

TOHVER, BERIT INGRID ELSA, pianist, educator; b. Malmö, Sweden, Sept. 12, 1933; d. Sverre Nils Hartvig and Elsa Maria (Winell) Nilsson; m. Gustav Tohver, Apr. 10, 1954; children: Matts Gustav, Annika Mari. Degree, Music High Sch., Stockholm, 1953; PhD in Musicology, Gothenburg U., Sweden, 1998. Piano tchr. Malmö City Sch., 1953-63, Music Konservatorium, Lund, Sweden, 1961-63, Mcpl. Inst., Örebro, Sweden, 1963-70; piano tours Scandinavia, 1969—; asst. prof. Sch. Music and Musicology, U. Gothenburg, 1973-98. Debut concert Stockholms Concert Hall, 1961; debut with orch. in Malmö, 1956; soloist in Swedish radio and TV, 1962—; concerts and lectr. Sibelius Acad. Helsinki, Norges Music H.S., Oslo, Music H.S., Coepnhagen. Mem. Swedish Piano Tchrs. Assn., European Piano Tchrs. Assn. Avocations: literature, gardening, walking in the woods. Home and Office: Linnégatan 43, SE-41308 Göteborg Sweden

TOIVANEN, AULI MARJAANA, internal medicine educator; b. Helsinki, Mar. 1, 1938; d. Hannes Iisakki and Emma Matilda (Karo) Pirilä; m. Paavo Uuras Toivanen, Nov. 3, 1961; children: Laura, Otto, Pekka, Hannes, Suoma. MD, Turku (Finland) U., 1962, D Med. Sci., 1969. Rsch. fellow dept. medicine and pathology U. Minn., Mpls., 1969-71; asst. physician dept. physiology U. Turku, 1961-62, asst. physician dept. med. microbiology, 1962-65, asst. physician dept. medicine, 1965-68, lectr. medicine, 1971-77, assoc. prof., 1977-88, prof., 1988—; mem. Basel (Switzerland) Inst. for Immunology, 1979-80; head dept. medicine Turku U. Hosp., 1988—. Editor: (with Paavo Toivanen) Avian Immunology, Basis and Practice, Vols. I-II, 1987, Reactive Arthritis, 1988; contbr. over 250 articles to sci. jours. Mem. Finnish Med. Assn. Duodecim (coun. 1983—, chmn. coun. 1989-91, bd. dirs. 1985-87), Finnish Soc. for Internal Medicine (bd. dirs. 1979-82, pres. 1993-95). Home: Kaskenkatu 2 A 2, 20700 Turku Finland Office: U Turku, Dept Medicine, 20520 Turku Finland

TOIVANEN, HELLI MARIA, psycho-physiology educator; b. Ilmajoki, Finland, Feb. 8, 1939; d. Mauri Johannes Makela and Rauha Kerttu Siltaloppi; m. Topi Antero; children: Hannu, Sami. BS, U. Helsinki, Finland, 1963, MS, 1989, PhD, 1994. Tchr. various schs., colls. and univs., Finland, 1964—; rschr. U. Kuopio, Finland, 1989—; cons. on stress-mgmt., orgnl. devel., leadership, human relationships and relaxation therapy. Developed comprehensive stress theory; contbr. articles to mags. and profl. jours. Grantee Finnish Govt., 1989-95, Gyllenberg Found., 1989-95. Home: Kirkkokatu 17 A 7, 70100 Kuopio Finland Office: Ctr Tng & Devel U Kuopio, PO Box 1627, 70211 Kuopio Finland

TOIVANEN, PAAVO UURAS, immunologist, microbiologist, educator; b. Tuupovaara, Finland, June 14, 1937; s. Vilho Pekka and Suoma Helena (Silvennoinen) T.; m. Auli Marjaana Pirilä, Nov 3, 1961; children: Laura, Otto, Pekka, Hannes, Suoma. BS, Turku (Finland) U., 1958, MD, 1962, D Med. Scis., 1966. Asst. physician Dept. Med. Microbiology Turku U., 1961-69, docent, 1968-69, assoc. prof., 1969-78, prof. bacteriology, serology, 1978—; mem. Basel Inst. for Immunology, 1979-80, mem. internat. adv. bd., 1991-95, chmn. internat. adv. bd., 1994-95. Editor: Avian Immunology, Basis and Practice, 1987, Reactive Arthritis, 1988. Mem. Finnish Soc. Immunology (pres. 1979-82), Am. Assn. Immunologists, Am. Soc. Microbiology, Transplantation Soc., Finnish Soc. Pathology, Finnish Soc. Hematology, Scandinavian Soc. Immunology (treas. 1978-82). Lutheran. Office: Turku U Dept Microbiolo, Kiinamyllynkatu 13, FIN20520 Turku Finland

TOIVOLA, YRJÖ ILMARI, corporate chairman; b. Viipuri, Finland, Sept. 15, 1927; s. Uuno Ilmari and Karin Sofia (Vuorio) T.; m. Kerttu Maija Lehtiö, Mar. 31, 1956; children: Sinikka, Jyrki, Tiina. MS in Tech., Helsinki U. Tech., 1955; PhD (hon.), U. Helsinki, 1986; D in Tech. (hon.), U. Tech., Helsinki, 1988. Engr. Vaisala Oy, Vantaa, Finland, 1955-58, dir. R&D, 1958-61, asst. mng. dir., 1963-69, pres., 1969-91, chmn., 1992-93; mng. dir. Vaisala Sudamericana S.A., Buenos Aires, 1961-63; bd. dirs. Fedn. Finnish Metal and Engring. Industries, Helsinki, 1981-93, Confedn. Finnish Industries, Helsinki, 1983-85, Finnish Fgn. Trade Assn., Helsinki, 1985-96; vice chmn. Tech. Devel. Ctr., Helsinki, 1983-89. Contbr. numerous articles to profl. jours. Chmn. Fund for Advancement Tech., Helsinki, 1978-90; adv. coun. Helsinki U. Tech., 1979-97, U. Helsinki, 1991-93; bd. dirs. Sci. and Tech. Policy Coun. State, Helsinki, 1985-96; chmn. Finnish Space Com., 1992-95; chief del. of Finland Coun. European Space Agy.; chmn. Innopoli Sci. Ctr., 1992—; chmn. Mentor Programme, 1992—; chmn. in several technology cos., 1991—. Named Councellor of Industry Pres. Finland, 1982; recipient Golden Medal Merit U. Tech., 1954, Medal Merit, 1983, Fedn. Finnish Electronics and Elect. Industries, 1981. Mem. Finnish Engring. Soc., Geophys. Soc., Applied Arts Assn. (bd. dirs. 1986—), European Cultural Found., Finnish Acad. Tech. (bd. dirs. 1987-90, vice chmn. 1990-93, Medal Merit 1982). Lutheran. Avocations: reading, art, international affairs. Home: Fredrik 28B13, FIN-00120 Helsinki Finland Office: Vaisala Oy, Innopoli Oy, Teknukantie 12, FIN02150 Espoo Finland

TOIVONEN, JARKKO KALEVI, telecommunication executive; b. Turku, Finland, Jan. 2, 1962; s. Aaro Kalevi and Maire Sinikka (Iltanen) T.; m. Pirjo Marita Lamminen, May 20, 1984; 1 child. BS, Tech. Coll., Turku, Finland, 1987; MS, Tech. U., Tampere, Finland, 1997. Mfg. mgr. Logistic Mgr. Micronas Semiconductor SA, Switzerland, 1997-98; area mgr. Telemecanique, Finland, 1987-89; sourcing contractor Nokia Mobira, Finland, 1989-91; chief buyer Nokia Consumer Elecs., Germany, 1991-93; materials mgr. Nokia Mobile Phones, Finland, 1993-94, mgr. materials & prodn. planning, 1994-95, mfg. mgr., 1995-97; sr. cons. Pi-Cons., Uantaa, Finland, 1999—. Mem. Soc. Telecom. Engrs. (founder 1986). Avocations: aquarium, audio engineering. Home: Jyrkkalankatu 2 A 560, FIN20210 Turku Finland Office: Pi-Cons, F1-01600 Uantaa Switzerland

TOKAEV, KASYMZHOMART KEMEL-ULY, government official; b. Almaty, Kazakstan, May 17, 1953; s. Kemel Tokaev and Turar Shabarbaeva; m. Nadezhda Poznanskaya, Aug. 12, 1983; 1 child, Timur. Grad., Inst. Internat. Rels., Moscow, 1975; student, Beijing Inst. Chinese Lang., 1983-84. With Ministry of Fgn. Affairs, Moscow, 1975, Embassy of the USSR, Singapore, 1975-79; 3d, 2d sec. Min. Fgn. Affairs, 1979-83, 2d sec., 1984-85; sec. Embassy of the USSR, China, 1985-91; trainee Diplomatic Acad. Fgn. Ministry, Moscow, 1991-92; dep. min. Diplomatic Acad. Fgn. Ministry, Almaty, Kazakstan, 1992-93; first dep. min. Diplomatic Acad. Fgn. Ministry, Almaty, 1993-94, min., 1994—; prime min. Govt. Kazakhstan, Almaty. Author: Chronic of the Student's Manifestation in Beijing, May 1989, 1993, 50 Years Serving for Peace, 1995. Address: 10 Beibetshilik St, 473000 Astana Kazakstan Office: Ministry Fgn Affairs, Aiteke bi 65, 480091 Almaty Kazakhstan*

TOKAR, MIKHAIL, physicist, theoretician; b. Tomsk, USSR, Sept. 25, 1953; s. Zel'man T. and Ksenia Tikhonova; m. Larissa Klepikova, Sept. 2, 1978; children: Anton, Oleg. M, Moscow Phys. Tech. Inst., 1976, PhD, 1979; DSc, Kurchatov Inst., 1990. Researcher Inst. for High Temperatures of Acad. of Scis., Moscow, 1979-88, sr. researcher, 1988-90, leading researcher, 1990—; guest scientist IPP, Julich, Germany, 1993-94, mem. scientific staff, 1995—. Contbr. articles to profl. jours. Fellow Humboldt Found. IPP, Julich, Germany, 1991-92.

TOKARCZYK, ROMAN ANDRZEJ, law and philosophy researcher and educator; b. Grudki, Lublin, Poland, Mar. 16, 1942; s. Andrzej Jan and Karolina Rozalia (Dubiel) T.; m. Czestawa Paulina Malec, Apr. 30, 1942; 1 childe Malgorzata. LLM, Mariae Curie Sktodowska U., Lublin, 1966, PhD in Law, 1970. From asst. to prof. Mariae Curie Sktodowska U., Lublin, 1966-96, prof., 1996—; rsch. assoc. prof. Notre Dame U., 1974; vis. assoc. prof. Harvard U., 1974, 93; dir. dept. faculty law and adminstrn. Mariae Curie Sktodowska U., Lublin, 1979—; dean faculty law and economy Studium Generale Sandomiriense, Sandomierz, Poland, 1996—. Author: Contemporary Political Doctrines, 1971, 10th edit., 2000 (Min. Edn. award 1973), Laws of Birth, Life and Death, 1984, 6th edit., 2000 (Min. Edn. award 1985), An Introduction to Comparative Law, 1989, 6th edit., 2000, Philosophy of Law, 1993, 6th edit., 2000, An Introduction to American Law, 1996, 5th edit., 2000, History Philosophy of Law, 1988, 1993,3rd edit., 2000, 6th edit., 2000, Contemporary Law Cultures, 2000. Mem. Tribunale of State, Warsaw, Poland, 1994. Internat. Rsch. Exch. Bd. scholar, 1974, NATO scholar, 1993; recipient awards Polish Min. Higher Edn., 1973, 77, 83, others. Mem. Internat. Communal Studies Assn. Israel, U.S. (bd. dirs.), Polish Acad. Medicine, Internat. Soc. Philosophy Law Social Philosophy. Roman Catholic. Avocations: skiing, dancing, photography. Home: Dudzinskiego 16, 20 815 Lublin Poland Office: Pl Marii Curie Sktodowskiej 5, 20-031 Lublin Poland

TOKAREV, VADIM IVANOVICH, aviation civics educator; b. Kyiv, Ukraine, May 25, 1939; s. Ivan Kuzmich Tokarev and Larisa Ivanovna Cherkasova; m. Irina Pavlovna Zyatkevich, July 7, 1966; 1 child, Sergei. Degree in engring., Kyiv Poly. Inst., 1962, DSc, 1968. From asst. to prof. Kyiv Internat. U. Civil Aviation, 1965—. Co-author: Standardization and Noise Abatement for Airplanes and Helicopters, 1980, Civil Aviation and Environmental Protection, 1984, Decreasing of Noise of Inboard Air Conditioning System, 1986, Noise Abatement for Passenger Airplanes in Operation, 1990. Mem. Ukrainian Assn. Acousticians. Office: KIUCA, 1 Kosmonavta Komarova Av, 252058 Kyiv Ukraine

TOKARSKAYA, ZOYA BORISOVNA, radiobiologist, researcher; b. Borovichi, Novgorod, Russia, June 16, 1924; d. Boris Antonovich and Polina Semenovna (Kudryavtseva) Tokarsky; m. Vitalii Petrovitch Gartsev; 1 child, Evgenii. MD, Med. Inst., St. Petersburg, 1951, postgrad., 1954; degree in radiobiology, Roentgen Radiol. Inst., St. Petersburg, 1957; MD (hon.), Biophysics Inst., Moscow, 1979. Med. radiology lectr. Inst. Physician Continuing Edn., Kharkov, Ukraine, 1957-59; scientist br. No. 1 Biophysics Inst., Ozyorsk, 1959-63, sr. scientist br. No. 1, 1963—. Contbr. articles to profl. jours. including Jour. Health Physivcs, Jour. Voprosy Oncologii, among others. Mem. Trade Union Engring. Industry Worker, Ozyorsk. Recipient Excellent Worker of Pub. Health badge Pub. Health Ministry, 1968. Mem. Russian Radiol. Soc., Russian Biochem. Soc., Nuclear Soc. Internat. Avocations: reading, travel. Home: Sverdlova St 16-21, 456780 Ozyorsk Russia Office: Biophysics Inst Br No 1, Ozyorsk Rd 19, 456780 Ozyorsk Russia

TOKATLIDIS, IOANNIS, agricultural sciences educator; b. Kozani, Dihimarros, Greece, Jan. 17, 1959; s. Stilianos and Melania (Anastasiadou) T.; m. Despina Parasoglou, May 6, 1989; 1 child, Stilianos. Degree in Agrl. Scis., Aristotelian U., Thessaloniki, Greece, 1982, MSc, 1991, PhD in Agr. and Plant Breeding, 1997. Extension officer Ministry Agr., Kozani, 1986-88, Thessaloniki, 1988-90; tchr. high sch., Serres, Greece, 1990-92, Veria, Greece, 1992-94; prof. agrl. scis. Tech. Edn. Inst. West Macedonia, Florina, Greece, 1994—. Contbr. articles to sci. jours., including Maydica, Jour. Agrl. Sci., Geoponika. Sublt. Greek Army, 1983-85. Scholar Aristotelian U., 1979, 81. Mem. Greek Plant Breeding Soc., Agriculturists Assn. Madeconia-Thraki. Orthodox. Avocations: skiing, basketball, music. Home: Florinis 15, 565 32 Thessaloniki Polihni, Greece Office: Tech Edn Inst W Macedonia, Terma Kontopoulou, 531 00 Florina Greece

TOKCAN, ÖMER ÇETIN, consumer products company executive; b. Istanbul, Turkey, Aug. 24, 1934; s. Mecit and Hacer Nurten (Yumak) T.; m. Türkan Usbuğ, Mar. 18, 1964; children: Sebnem, Elif, Gül, Yunuscan, Menekse. BS in Econs., Istanbul U., 1958; with Internat. Tchrs. Program, Harvard U., 1961; spl. student, Ind. U., 1959-60; cert., IMEDE, Lausanne, Switzerland, 1970. Asst. fin. Istanbul U., 1961-62; head rsch. dept. Prime Ministry State Planning Orgn., Ankara, Turkey, 1963-67; gen. mgr. Eczacibasi Ceramic Factory, Istanbul, 1967-70, Eczacibasi Holding Co., 1970-82, Toprak Paper Mill, Istanbul, 1982-89; mem. exec. com. Evyap Soap Co., Istanbul, 1990-99; ceo Evyap Egypt Inc., 2000—. Contbr. articles to profl. jours. 1st lt., 1st Army Transp. Corps, 1961-63, Istanbul. Home: Sültas Evleri #23, 80630 Levent/Istanbul Turkey Office: Evyap Soap Factory, Cendere Yolu #10, 80670 Istanbul Turkey

TOKE, FREDERICK K. J., social services executive, clergyman, psychologist; b. Singapore, June 29, 1960; s. Kee See and Soo Ah (Lau) T.; m. Agnes S.I. Kor, June 17, 1989; children: Matthew, Tiffany. BA in Theology, St. George U., U.K., 1988, MA in Counselling Psychology, 1993. Ordained to ministry Ch. of God (Cleve.), Singapore Republic, 1997. Sales dir. Tiff, Mattheson & Assocs., Singapore, 1983-86; dir. Tiff, Mattheson & Assocs., 1983—; pastor Ch. of Singapore, 1989-94, Ch. of Praise, Singapore, 1994-96; pastor, pres. Mt. Olives Ch. of God, Singapore, 1996—; exec. dir. Family Life Ctr., Singapore, 1996—; cons. Praise Kindergarten, Singapore, 1999—. Editor, author: Life Skills, 1999. With Singapore Armed Forces, 1978-80. Mem. APA, ACA.

TÖKE, LÁSZLÓ, chemistry educator; b. Vönöck, Vas, Hungary, May 3, 1933; s. Sándor and Mária (Berecz) T.; children: Eva, László. Cand. Sci., Tech. U., Budapest, 1957, PhD, 1962, ScD, 1974. Cert. chem. engr. Asst. prof. Tech. U., Budapest, 1957-69, assoc. prof., 1969-75, prof. organic chemistry, 1975—. Author: Medicinal Chemistry; contbr. over 200 articles to profl. jours.; patentee (66) in field. Recipient State prize Hungarian Govt., Budapest, 1975. Mem. Hungarian Acad. Scis. (head rsch. group 1989—, v.p. chem. divsn. 1996—). Office: Tech Univ budapest, Dept Organic Chem Tech, 1521 Budapest Hungary

TOKERUD, ROBERT EUGENE, electrical engineer; b. Great Falls, Mont., Aug. 30, 1936; s. Fred Eugene Tokerud and Helen A. (Tadevich) Thomas; m. Marsha Kay Tokerud; children: Pamela, Torri, Marc, Camille, Corinne, David, Jeramie, Autumn, Melanie. BSEE, U. Calif., Berkeley, 1959; cert. Inst. Mgmt., Northwestern U., 1975. Sr. project engr. Sperry Utah Co., Salt Lake City, 1959-65; mgr. infosystems Lockheed Electronics Co., Houston, 1965-69; mgr. earth resources Lockheed Engring. and Sci. Co., Houston, 1969-74, asst. dir. sci. and applications, 1974-79, dir. bus. devel., 1980-87; life sci. program mgr. Lockheed Engring. and Sci. Co., Washington, 1987-89; pres. Lockheed Martin Logistics Mgmt., Arlington, Tex., 1989-97; v.p. Lockheed Corp., 1993-97; exec. v.p. Lockheed Martin Aircraft and Logistic Ctrs., 1997; ret., 1997; cons. Aerospace, 1997-2000; CEO Operational Techs., 2000—. Author conf. procs., other profl. publs. Bd. dirs. El Lago (Tex.) Water and Waste Mgmt. Dist., 1974; commr. Tex. Strategic Mil. Planning Commn., 1997—. Mem. Air Force Assn., Army Aviation Assn. Am. Fax: 210-731-0008. E-mail: btokerud@otcorp.com. Office: 4100 NW Loop 410 San Antonio TX 78229-4251

TOKHEIM, ROBERT EDWARD, physicist; b. Eastport, Maine, Apr. 25, 1936; s. Edward George and Ruth Lillian (Koenig) T.; m. Diane Alice Green, July 1, 1962; children: Shirley Diane, William Robert, David Eric, Heidi Jean. BSEE, Calif. Inst. Tech., 1958, MSEE, 1959; Degree of Engr., Stanford U., 1962, PhD in Elec. Engring., 1965. Rsch. asst. Hansen Labs Physics Stanford (Calif.) U., 1960-65; microwave engr. Watkins-Johnson Co., Palo Alto, Calif., 1965-73, staff scientist, head ferrimagnetic R&D dept., 1966-69; sr. physicist SRI Internat., Menlo Park, Calif., 1973—. Co-author: Tutorial Handbook on X-ray Effects on Materials and Structures, 1992; contbr. articles to Jour. Applied Physics, IEEE Transactions on Magnetics, conf. proceedings on shock compression, and others. Mem. IEEE (sr. mem.), Am. Phys. Soc., Toastmasters, Tau Beta Pi, Sigma Xi. Achievements include discovery of nonreciprocal line-coupled microwave ferrimagnetic filters, optimum thermal compensation axes in YIG and GaYIG ferrimagnetic spheres, development of various shock wave equation-of-state computational models and computational debris modeling for large laser machines. Office: SRI International 333 Ravenswood Ave Menlo Park CA 94025-3453

TOKIMOTO, KEISUKE, mycologist; b. Takino-cho, Hyogo, Japan, Apr. 29, 1945; s. Kiyoshi and Shigeno (Kataoka) T.; m. Kyoko Kaneda, Dec. 4, 1952; children: Sanae, Nobu. Dr.Agr., Nagoya (Japan) U., 1985. Sr. rschr. Tottori (Japan) Mycol. Inst., 1971—, chief breeding sect., 1991—, head rschr., 1998—; guest prof. Tottori U., 1999—, Kobe U., 2000—. Author: The Biology and Cultivation of Edible Mushrooms, 1978; contbr. articles to profl. jours. Mem. World Soc. for Mushroom Biology and Mushroom Products. Avocation: taking pictures. Office: Tottori Mycological Inst, Kokoge-211, Tottori-shi 689-1125, Japan

TOKIN, IVAN B., biologist, researcher; b. Moscow, June 5, 1932; s. Boris P. Tokin and Agnessa G. Filatova; m. Galina F. Filimonova, Sept. 22, 1967; children: Ivan, Anna. PhD, State U., Leningrad, Russia, 1954; D of Biology, Inst. Morphology Acad. Sci., Moscow, 1960; DSc, Inst. Devel. Biol. Acad. Sci., Moscow, 1973. Cert. excellent biol. diplomate. Scientist State U., Leningrad, 1959-63; head lab. electron microscopy Inst. Radiation Hygiene, Leningrad, 1963-72; dir. Inst. Marine Biology, Acad. Sci. USSR, Murmansk, 1972-80; head, prof. dept. math. biology State U., St. Petersburg, 1980—. Author: (books) Electron Microscopy of Germ and Somatic Cells of P. Equorum, 1961, Problems of Radiation Cytology, 1974, (with V. M. Schubik) Action of Radiation on Immunology Processes, 1972 (premium of Ministry of Health 1974), (with G. F. Filimonova) Intestinal Epithelium: Proliferation, Regulation, Apoptosis, 1997; mem., chief sec., editl. coun. Jour. Anatomy, Histology, and Embryology, 1964-74. Dep. Chamber of Deps., Severomorsk, 1973. Recipient medal Soc. Anatomists of Italy, 1968; grantee Internat. Sci. Found., 1994, German Radiation Rsch. Soc., 1995. Mem. Soc. Anatomists, Histologists, and Embryologists (mem. supreme coun. 1969-73), Soc. Ecology and Ecotoxicology (pres. 1996—), Bodega Marine Sci. Assn. Avocations: chess, painting. Fax: 7-812-4284677. Office: State U Fac Applied Math, Library Sq 2, Saint Petersburg 198904, Russia

TOKOLA, TIMO ERKKI, management consultant; b. Turku, Finland, June 5, 1963; s. Esko Erkki and Sanna-Liisa (Mantymaa) T.; m. Auli Helena Sookari, Dec. 23, 1987. Dr.Sci., U. Joensun, Finland, 1998, Lic. Sci. Agr./Forestry, 1991; MS, U. Joensun, 1988. Jr. profl. officer Jaakko Poyry Cons., Kathmandu, Nepal, 1991-93; lectr. U. Joensuu, Finland, 1993-95; project mgr. Enso Forest, Jakarta, Indonesia, 1995-97; lectr. U. Joensuu, 1997-98, docent, 1999—; project mgr. Soil and Water, Ltd., JP Group, Helsinki, 1998—. Contbr. articles to profl. jours. Lt. Finnish Army, 1984—. Mem. Finnish Soc. Forest Sci., Finnish Soc. Photogrammery and Remote Sensing. Avocations: sport exercise, trekking. Office: Soil & Water LTO, PO Box 50 Jaakonkatu 3, 01621 Vantaa Finland

TOKOUSBALIDES, PARASKEVAS T., chemist; b. Piraeus, Attica, Greece, Mar. 10, 1934; s. Timoleon and Helen Tokousbalides; m. Maria Chrysagi, Jan. 15, 1977; children: Timoloeon, Alexis. BSc in Chemistry, U. Athens, 1958; PhD in Phys. Chemistry, U. Toledo, 1975. Mgf. chemist MANOS Edible Oils, Piraeus, Greece, 1961-64, A.I. Lt., Aba, Freetown, Tema, Nigeria, Sierra Leone, Ghana, 1964-69; tchg. asst. dept. chemistry U. Toledo, 1969-75; postdoctoral fellow dept. chemistry U. Tenn., Knoxville, 1975-77; faculty rsch. assoc. dept. chemistry U. Md., College Park, 1977-78; mgf. chemist Victory/Cosmetics, Athens, 1979-81; mfg. dir. Minerva/Edible Oils, Athens, 1981-98, external rels. dir., 1998—. Contbr. articles to sci. jours. Mem. SEVITEL Assn. Greek Olive Oil Industries (pres. 1994—), FEDOLIVE Fedn. European Olive Oil Assns. (pres. 1999-01), Am. Oil Chemist Soc., Nat. Union Greek Chemists. Fax: 01 2849837. E-mail: ptokou@minerva.com.gr. Home: 27 Pleiadon Str, Kifisa 145 61, Greece Office: MINERVA, 31 Valaoritou Str, 144 52 Metamorphosis Greece

TOKUDA, HARUHIKO, endocrinologist, educator; b. Nagoya, Aichi, Japan, Mar. 21, 1960. MD, Jichi Med. Sch., Minamikawachi-machi, Japan, 1984; degree in physiolgy, Nagoya U., 1991. Clin. resident Nagoya 2nd Red Cross Hosp., 1984-86; clinician Toei (Japan) Hosp., 1986-89; physician Nagoya U., 1989-92; chief internal medicine Shinshiro (Japan) City Hosp., 1992-95, Chubu Nat. Hosp., Obu, Japan, 1995—. Contbr. articles to profl. jours. Office: Chubu Nat Hosp, 36-3 Gengo Morioka, Obu 474-8511, Japan

TOKUMASU, KOJI, medical educator; b. Tokyo, Oct. 24, 1931; s. Tadaaki and Kichiko (Yamuachi) T.; m. Mieko Seii, Nov. 23, 1957; children: Mayumi Morita, Shinya. MD, Tokyo U., 1956, Tokyo U., 1961. Asst. dept. ear-nose-throat Tokyo U., 1961-66; rsch. fellow dept. neurology Mt. Sinai Hosp., N.Y., 1963-64; lectr. Tokyo U. Hosp., 1967-71; assoc. prof. dept. ear-nose-throat Kitasato U., Sagamihara, Japan, 1972-84, prof. dept. ear-nose-throat, 1984-97, prof. emeritus Sch. Medicine, 1997—. Author: Textbook of Oto-rhino-laryngology, 1978; author, editor: Clinical Medicine Series for Nursing No. 11 Oto-rhino-laryngology, Head and Neck Surgery, 1968; contbr. articles to profl. jours. Fulbright scholar, 1963-64; physiol. study grantee Standing Dept. Edn. Japan, 1992-93, Elderly Employment Promoting Assn., 1994-95. Mem. Barany Soc., Equilibrium Rsch. Assn. (councillor 1965—, bd. dirs. 1991-96), Oto-rhino-laryngol. Soc. of Japan (councilor 1996—). Liberal. Buddhist. Avocations: travel, painting. Home: 1-5-4 Minamikugahara Ota-ku, Tokyo 146-0084, Japan

TOKUNAGA, EMIKO, dancer; b. San Francisco, Sept. 28, 1939; d. Shigao and Utako (Seiki) T. BFA, U. Utah, 1961; MA, NYU, 1966. Co-dir. Tokunaga Dance Ko, N.Y.C., 1967—; faculty Boston Conservatory, 1971—, Harvard and Radcliff, Cambridge, Mass., 1986-92; dance program coord. Radcliffe Coll., 1995-98; Over 40 residencies in U.S., Japan and Norway. Choreographer 60 modern and Japanese dances; dancer: over 2000 performances in theaters and ednl. instns. in U.S., Norway and Japan. Nat. Endowment for the Arts grantee, Japan-U.S. Friendship Commission, N.Y.C. Dept. of Cultural Affairs; adminstrn. fellow Harvard U., 1995-96. Office: Tokunaga Dance Ko 1 Sheridan Sq New York NY 10014-6825

TOKURA, NOBUYUKI, electrical engineer, researcher; b. Marugame, Kagawa, Japan, Oct. 11, 1947; s. Noboru and Setsuko (Fujioka) T.; m. Kazumi Takimoto, Apr. 29, 1973; children: Hitomi, Miyuki. BS, Tokushima (Japan) U., 1970, MS, 1972; D in Engring., Tokyo Inst. Tech., 1997. Engr. Nippon Telegraph & Telephone Yokosuka Electorial Comm. Lab., Japan, 1972-82, staff engr., 1982-84; rsch. engr. Nippon Telegraph & Telephone Yokosuka Electorial Comm. Lab., Yokosuka, 1984-87; exec. engr. Network Sys. Devel. Ctr. Nippon Telegraph & Telephone, Tokyo, 1987-88; supr. NTT Optical Network Sys. Labs., Yokosuka, 1988-97, Optowave Lab., Inc., 1997—. Contbg. author: Advance in Local Area Networks, 1987, Optoelectronic Technology and Lightwave Communications Systems, 1989; patentee in field. Mem. IEEE, Inst. Electronics, Info. and Comm. Engrs. (reviewer 1986—). Avocations: woodcraft, jigsaw puzzles, reading science fiction, walking, gardening. Home: 1-20-1 Maborikaigan, Yokosuka 239-0801, Japan Office: Optowave Lab Inc, 3-1 Hikari no Oka, Kanagawa Yokosuka 239-0847, Japan

TOKURA, YOSHIKI, dermatologist, educator; b. Fukuroi, Shizuoka, Japan, July 17, 1954; s. Shouichi and Keiko (Honma) T.; m. Miyako Tsuda, May 1, 1981; children: Kotaro, Chihiro, Ryoji, Izumi. MD, Hamamatsu (Japan) U., 1982, PhD, 1989. Med. diplomate of dermatology. Intern and resident Sch. Medicine Hamamatsu U., 1982-84, asst. instr. dermatology, 1984-89, asst. prof., 1993-00, assoc. prof., 2000—; vis. scientist Sch. Medicine Yale U., New Haven, 1989-91; chief dermatologist Shizuoka City Hosp., 1991-92. Rsch. grantee Lydia O'Leary Meml. Found., Tokyo, 1994, Cosmetology Rsch. Found., Tokyo, 1994, Shiseido Basic Rsch. Found., Tokyo, 1995. Mem. Soc. for Investigative Dermatology, Japanese Dermatol. Assn. (mem. bd. councillors 1999—), Japanese Soc. for Investigative Dermatology (mem. bd. councillors 1995—). Avocation: classical music. Home: 552-205 Aritama Nishimachi, Shizuoka Hamamatsu 431-3123, Japan Office: Hamamatsu Univ Sch Medicine, 3600 Handa-cho Dept Dermat, Shizuoka Hamamatsu 431-3192, Japan

TOLAND, JOHN WILLARD, historian, writer; b. La Crosse, Wis., June 29, 1912; s. Ralph and Helen Chandler (Snow) T.; m. Toshiko Matsumura, Mar. 12, 1960; 1 dau., Tamiko; children by previous marriage: Diana Toland Netzer, Marcia. B.A., Williams Coll., 1936; student, Yale Drama Sch., 1936-37; L.H.D., Williams Coll., 1968, U. Alaska, 1977, Western Conn. U., 1986. Mem. adv. council Nat. Archives. Author: Ships in the Sky, 1957, Battle: The Story of the Bulge, 1959, But Not in Shame, 1961 (Best Book Fgn. Affairs award Overseas Press Club), The Dillinger Days, 1963, The Flying Tigers, 1963, The Last 100 Days, 1966 (Best Book Fgn. Affairs citation Overseas Press Club), The Battle of the Bulge, 1966, The Rising Sun, 1970 (Van Wyck Brooks award for non-fiction, Best Book Fgn. Affairs award Overseas Press Club, Pulitzer prize for non-fiction), Adolf Hitler, 1976 (Best Book Fgn. Affairs award Overseas Press Club, Gold Medal Nat. Soc. Arts and Letters), Hitler, The Pictorial Documentary of His Life, 1978, No Man's Land, 1980 (Best Book Fgn. Affairs citation Overseas Press Club), Infamy, 1982, In Mortal Combat, 1991; (novels) Gods of War, 1985, Oc-

cupation, 1987, In Mortal Combat, 1991, Captured by History, 1997; author short stories. Served to capt. USAAF, 1942-46, 1947-49. Mem. Authors Guild, Accademia del Mediterraneo., Western Front Assn. (hon. v.p.). Home: 101 Long Ridge Rd Danbury CT 06810-8434*

TOLBERT, CLINTON JAME, army officer, machinist; b. Auburn, Ala., Dec. 22, 1953; s. Clinton and Rosia Love (Fillmore) T.; m. Gloria Jean Fitzpatrick, Sept. 23, 1974; children: Christopher, Mark, Marcella. BS, Tukegee U., 1983; MBA, Troy State U., 1987, MS, 1990; AS in Applied Sci., So. U., Opelika, Ala., 1996. EMT U.S. Army, Fort Benning, Ga., 1972-75; machine operator West Point Pepperll, Inc., Valley, Ala., 1975-82; 1st lt. Army Nat. Guard, Roanoke, Ala., 1982-86; capt. Army Nat. Guard, Roanoke, 1986-92; major Army Nat. Guard, Montgomery, Ala., 1992-96; machinist Falk Corp., Auburn, Ala, 1996—. Elder Methodist Ch., Auburn, Ala., 1996—. Named All- Am. Scholar, U.S. Achievement Acad., Lexington, Ky., 1996; recipient Minority Leadership award, U.S. Achievement Acad., Lexington, 1996. Mem. Nat. Guard Assn. Democrat. Avocations: reading, golf. Home: 989 Fitzpatric Rd Auburn AL 36830

TOLEDANO, ALICIA Y., statistician, educator; b. Fredericksburg, Va., May 1, 1965; d. Stuartand Carole Anne T.; m. Lee Russell Shekter, Mar 31, 1996; children: Jacob Samuel, Dylan Harry. BS, Cornell U., 1987; MS, Harvard U. Sch. Pub. Health, 1991, DSc, 1993. Asst. prof. U. Chgo., 1993-99, Brown U., Providence, R.I., 2000—; advisory panelist U.S. FDA, 1999—. Mem. Am. Statis. Assn., Internat. Biometric Soc., Soc. Clin. Trials. Office: Ctr Statis Scis Brown U Box G-H Providence RI 02912

TOLEDO, ANGELES, sales executive; b. Mexico City, Mar. 13, 1958; d. Jorge Toledo and Angeles Diaz Rubin; m. Enrique Ortiga, May 27, 1988; 1 child, Paulina Ortiga. BA, U. Mexico, 1980; cert., U. Americas, 1981, Cinematography Ctr., Mexico City, 1983. Dir. Nat. Gallery Mexico, 1980-82; asst. to the dir. Nat. Mus. of Modern Art, 1983, curator, 1983-84; co-dir. Artmart Gallery, N.Y.C., 1984-87; imports mgr. Zona, Inc., N.Y.C., 1988-92; dir. gen. Galeon Primero S.A., Mexico, 1992-99. Author art critic publs. Mem. Assn. Women Entrepreneurs. Office: Galeon Primero SA de CV, Cuernavaca # 152 Condesa, 06140 Mexico City Mexico

TOLEDO, FREDERICO GRANCHI STEIDEL, physiologist; b. Rio de Janeiro, Brazil, Jan. 21, 1972; s. Jose Augusto Toledo and Francisca Granchi. MD, U. Fed. Rio de Janeiro, 1996. Rsch. trainee Universidade Fed. do Rio de Janeiro, 1990-93; spl. project assoc. Mayo Clinic, Rochester, Minn., 1994, postdoctoral rsch. fellow, 1996-98. Mem. Planetary Soc. Avocations: computers, movies, art. Office: 1200 West Ave Apt 523 Miami FL 33139-4314

TOLERA, ADUGNA, agricultural studies educator, researcher; b. Shamboo, Ethiopia, Nov. 28, 1959; s. Tolera Yadeta and Barbare Darasu; m. Shashitu Dhaba, Jan. 1, 1987; children: Hanwi, Abdi, Gadise, Lalise. BSc, Alemaya Coll. Agr., Ethiopia, 1983; MSc, Agrl. U. of Norway, Ås, 1990, PhD, 1999. Grad. asst. Addis Ababa U., Awassa, Ethiopia, 1983-84; asst. lectr. Addis Ababa U./Awassa Coll. Agr., 1984-86, lectr., 1986-93; asst. prof. Awassa Coll. Agr., 1994—; head dept. animal sci. Addis Ababa U./Awassa Coll. Agr., 1991-93. Fellow Norwegian Internat. Devel. Agy., Norway, 1987, Norwegian Univs. Com. for Devel. Rsch. and Edn., Norway, 1994. Office: Awassa Coll Agr, PO Box 5, Awassa Sidama, Ethiopia

TOLF, ROBERT WALTER, writer; b. Chgo., Aug. 3, 1929; s. Carl Oscar and Margaret Emilia (Zeltner) T.; m. Nancy Ellen List, Aug. 9, 1952; 1 child, Carolyn Anne. BA cum laude, Harvard U., 1951; PhD, U. Rochester, 1957. Attache, 2d sec. U.S. Dept. State, various locations, 1957-70; editor Fla. Trend, St. Petersburg, 1973—; columnist, critic Sun-Sentinel, Ft. Lauderdale, Fla., 1975—; exec. dir. Phileas Soc., Ft. Lauderdale, 1988—; producer, writer, narrator Columbus Documentaries, Ft. Lauderdale, 1989-92. Author: The Russian Rockefellers, 1976, Addison Mizner, 1983, Chicago Sketch Book, 1988, Paris Sketch Book, 1990, Discover Florida, 1982, Country Inns of the Old South, 1978, 83, Country Inns of New York State, 1984, Country Inns of the Mid-Atlantic, 1986, Florida Weekends, 1990, 94, Florida's Best Beach Vacations, 1992, Florida Country Inns, 1993, 96, Destination Florida--Sanibel and Captiva, 1993, Destination Florida--South Beach Miami, 1993, 14 Florida Restaurant Guides, 1973-96, Trumpy, 1996, others; editor: Columbus Documents, 1992; author, prodr., narrator 15 videos in The Great Explorers Series. Lt. U.S. Army, 1954-57. Mem. Harvard Varsity Club, Fox Club, Harvard Club Broward County. Office: 3100 S Ocean Blvd Apt 422 Highland Bch FL 33487-2503

TOLIDIS, KOSMAS-THEODORE, dentist, educator; b. Thessaloniki, Greece, July 15, 1964; s. Theodore and Maria Tolidis; m. Georgia Zachou, Sept. 4, 1999. Degree in dentistry, U. Thessaloniki, 1989, degree, 1997; MS, Bristol Dental Sch., England, 1993. Pvt. practice Thessaloniki, 1990—; cons. dental surgury for children U. Thessaloniki, 1993-97; lectr. U. Thessaloniki, 1998—. Exec. editor Cosmos of Dentistry, 1999—, Anavathmos, 1999—; presentor in field. Gen. sec. ASKOTH Dental Polit. Union, Thessaloniki, 1998—; mem. Prefectural Polit. Coun. Nea Dimokratia, 1999—; candidate in Prefectural elections, Thessaloniki, 1998; commentator CosmoTV, Thessaloniki, 1996—. With Med. Corps, Hellenic Army, 1990-91. Fellow Bristol Dental Sch., 1996—, U. Thessaloniki, 1989-97. Mem. Dental Soc. Thessaloniki (head dental prevention com. 1999—, exec. sec. 1999—), Hellenic Dental Assn. (cert., rsch. award 1995), Orgn. Dental Continuing Edn. (head sci. com. 1999—), European Acad. Pediat. Dentistry. Greek Orthodox. Avocations: reading, travelling, athletics, internet. E-mail: ktolidis@dent.auth.gr. Office: Dental Clinic, 51 Tsimiski, GR 54623 Thessaloniki Greece

TOLINS-KAUFMAN, SELMA L., psychologist; b. Flushing, N.Y., Aug. 6, 1930; d. Emanuel Leifer and Sally Lillian Weinstock; m. David B. Tolins, Jr., May 30, 1951 (div. June 1984); children: Madeline Tolins-Schlitt, Andrew M.; m. David Kaufman, July 28, 1984. BA, Queens Coll., 1952; MEd, Temple U., 1967. Lic. psychologist, Pa. Tchr. East Meadow (N.Y.) Sch. Dist., 1952-55, Tchr. Tng. Sch. P.S. 201, Flushing, 1955-56, Centennial Sch. Dist., Warminster, Pa., 1962-63; guidance counselor Centennial Sch. Dist., Warminster, 1963-66, psychologist, 1966-70; dir. guidance and psychology Upper Moreland Sch. Dist., Willow Grove, Pa., 1970-78; dir. pupil pers. svcs. Methacton Sch. Dist., Fairview Village, Pa., 1978-90; pvt. practice consulting psychologist Maple Glen, Pa., 1975—. Author children's plays. Mem. Nat. Assn. Pupil Svcs., Pa. Pupil Svcs. Assn., Pa. Psychol. Assn., Spl. Edn. Assn. Avocations: tennis, bridge, travel, opera, theatre. Home: 1881 Dillon Rd Maple Glen PA 19002-3104

TOLIVER, LEE, mechanical engineer; b. Wildhorse, Okla., Oct. 3, 1921; s. Clinton Leslie and Mary (O'Neall) T.; m. Barbara Anne O'Reilly, Jan. 24, 1942 (dec. Jan. 1999); children: Margaret Anne, Michael Edward. BSME, U. Okla., 1942. Registered profl. engr., Ohio. Engr. Douglas Aircraft Co., Santa Monica, Calif., 1942, Oklahoma City, 1942-44; engr. Los Alamos (N.Mex.) Sci. Lab., 1946; instr. mech. engring. Ohio State U., Columbus, 1946-47; engr. Sandia Nat. Labs., Albuquerque, 1947-82; instr. computer sci. and math. U. N.Mex., Valencia County, 1982-84; number theory researcher Belen, N.Mex., 1982—. Author: (computer manuals with G. Carli, AF. Schkade) Experience with an Intelligent Remote Batch Terminal, 1972; (with C.R. Borgman, T.I. Ristine) Transmitting Data from PDP-10 to Precision Graphics, 1973, Data Transmission-PDP-10/Sykes/Precision Graphics, 1975; Relations Between Prime and Relatively Prime Integers, 1998. With Manhattan Project (Atomic Bomb) U.S. Army, 1944-46. Mem. Math. Assn. Am., Am. Math. Soc. Achievements include devel. of 44 computer programs with manuals. Home: 206 Howell St Belen NM 87002-6225

TOLIVIA, DELIO RUBEN, cell biologist, researcher; b. Gijon, Asturias, Spain, Aug. 6, 1944; s. Celedonio Evaristo and Teresa Elvira (Fernandez) T.; m. Adelina Cadrecha, Aug. 8, 1970; 1 child, Delio Ruben. BS, U. Complutense, Madrid, 1969; PhD in Biol. Scis., U. Oviedo, Spain, 1975. Assoc. prof. biol. scis. U. Oviedo, 1969-75, asst. prof. biol. scis. (temp.), 1975-79, asst. prof. biol. scis., 1979—. Dir. numerous doctoral theses and investigation projects; contbd. over 50 articles to profl. jours. Mem. N.Y. Acad. Scis. Office: Univ Oviedo Faculty Med, c/ Julian Claveria s/n, 33006 Oviedo Asturias, Spain

TOLL, JOHN SAMPSON, university president, physics educator; b. Denver, Oct. 25, 1923; s. Oliver Wolcott and Merle d'Aubigne (Sampson) T.; m. Deborah Ann Taintor, Oct. 24, 1970; children: Dacia Merle Sampson, Caroline Taintor. BS with honors, Yale U., 1944; AM, Princeton U., 1948, PhD, 1952; DSc (hon.), U. Md., 1973, U. Wroclaw, Poland, 1975; LLD (hon.), Adelphi U., 1978; PhD (hon.), Fudan U., Peoples Republic China, 1987; LHD (hon.), SUNY, Stony Brook, 1990; LLD (hon.), U. Md., Eastern Shore, 1993. Mng. editor, acting chmn. Yale Sci. mag., 1943-44; with Princeton U., 1946-49, proctor fellow, 1948-49; Friends of Elementary Particle Theory Research grantee for study in France, 1950; theoretical physicist Los Alamos Sci. Lab., 1950-51; staff mem., assoc. dir. Project Matterhorn, Forrestal Rsch. Ctr., Princeton U., 1951-53; prof., chmn. physics and astronomy U. Md., 1953-65; pres., prof. physics SUNY, Stony Brook, 1965-78; pres., prof. physics U. Md., 1978-88, chancellor, 1988-89, chancellor emeritus, prof. physics, 1989—; pres. Univs. Rsch. Assn., Washington, 1989-94, Washington Coll., Chestertown, Md., 1995—; 1st dir. SUNY Chancellor's Panel on Univ. Purposes, 1970; physics cons. to editl. staff Nat. Sci. Tchrs. Assn., 1957-61; U.S. del., head sci., secretariat Internat. Conf. on High Energy Physics, 1960; mem.-at-large U.S. Nat. Com. for Internat. Union of Pure and Applied Physics, 1960-63; chmn. rsch. adv. com. on electrophysics to NASA, 1961-65; mem. gov. Md. Sci. Resources Adv. bd., 1963-65; mem., chmn. NSF adv. panel for physics, 1964-67; mem. N.Y. Gov.'s Adv. Com. Atomic Energy, 1966-70; mem. commn. plans and objectives higher edn. Am. Coun. Edn., 1966-69; mem. Hall of Records Commn., 1979-88; mem., chmn. adv. coun. Princeton Plasma Physics Lab, 1979-85; mem. Adv. Coun. of Pres.'s, Assn. of Governing Bds., 1980-88, So. Regional Edn. Bd., 1980-90; mem. exec. com. Washington/Balt. Regional Assn., 1980-89, Nat. Assn. State Univs. and Land Grant Colls., 1980-88, Ctr. for the Study of the Presidency, 1983-84; mem. univ. programs panel of energy rsch. bd. Dept. Energy, 1982-83; mem. SBHE Adv. Com., 1983-89, Md. Gov.'s Chesapeake Bay Coun., 1985; mem. resource com. State Trade Policy Coun. Gov.'s High Tech Roundtable Md. Dept. Econ. Devel., 1986-89; marine divsn. chmn. NASULGC, 1986; bd. trustees Aspen Inst. for Humanities, 1987-89; mem. Commn. on Higher Edn. Middle States Assn. Colls. and Schs., 1987; chmn. adv. panel on tech. risks and opportunities for U.S. energy supply and demand U.S. Office Tech. Assessment, 1987-91; chmn. adv. panel on internat. collaboration in def. tech., U.S. Office Tech. Assessment, 1989-91; mem. Sea Grant Rev. Panel U.S. Dept. Commerce, 1992—, chair, 1996-97, Com. on Financing Higher Edn. Nat. Assn. Independent Colls. Univs., 1996-98; bd. govs. Chesapeake Bay Maritime Mus., 1996—; dir. Hodson Scholarship Found., 1996—; mem. Md. Gov.'s Blue Ribbon Citizens Pfiesteria Action Commn., 1997; mem. governing coun. Wye Faculty Seminar, 1997—; dir. Eastern Shore Assn. Coll. Pres., 1998—, mem. bd. dirs. Md. Ctr. Agroecology, Inc., 1999—; vis. prof. Nordic Inst. Theoretical Physics, Niels Bohr Inst., Denmark, U. Lund, Sweden, 1975-76; mem. Math. Scis. Edn. Bd. NAS, 1991-93; hon. bd. mem. Radcliffe Creek Sch., 2000—. Contbr. articles to profl. jours. Mem. Adv. Coun. Boy Scouts Am. De-Mar-Va Coun., 1999. Recipient Benjamin Barge prize in math. Yale U., 1943, George Beckwith medal for Proficiency in Astronomy, 1944, Outstanding Citizen award City of Denver, 1958, Outstanding Tchr. award U. Md. Men's League, 1965, Copernicus award govt. of Poland, 1973, Stony Brook Found. award for disting. contbns. to edn., 1979, Disting. Svc. award State of Md., 1981, Silver medal Sci. U. Tokyo, 1994, Internat. Landmark award U. Md., 1994, first recipient Lifetime Achievement award Md. Assn. for Higher Edn., 2000, Chief Exec. Leadership award Coun. for Advancement and Support Edn., 2000; named Washingtonian of Yr., 1985, Citizen of Yr. Chestertown Optimist Club, 1997; John Simon Guggenheim Meml. Found. fellow Inst. Theoretical Physics U. Copenhagen, U. Lund, Sweden, 1958-59. Fellow Am. Phys. Soc., Washington Acad. Scis. (pres. 1995-96), N.Y. Acad. Scis.; mem. NSTA, Am. Coun. Edn. (bd. dirs. 1986-89, NAACP (life), Am. Assn. Physics Tchrs., Fedn. Am. Scientists (chmn. 1961-62), Philos. Soc. Washington, Assn. Higher Edn., Yale U. Sci. and Engring. Assn. (award for disting. contbns. 1996), Cosmos Club, Hamilton St. Club, Baltimore, Univ. Club (Washington and N.Y.), Phi Beta Kappa, Sigma Xi (Sci. Achievement award 1965), Phi Kappa Phi (disting.), Omicron Delta Kappa (hon.), Sigma Pi Sigma. Achievements include research on elementary particle theory, scattering. Office: U Md Dept Physics College Park MD 20742-0001 also: Washington Coll Pres's Office Chestertown MD 21620

TOLLAN, ARNE, water and environmental management executive; b. Kristiansund, Norway, June 19, 1938. MS, Oslo U., 1962; postgrad., Norwegian Def. Coll., 1990-91. Asst. dir. Norwegian Inst. for Water Rsch., Oslo, 1982-86; chief air pollution unit UN Econ. Commn. for Europe, Geneva, 1983-85; dir. Norwegian Water Resources and Energy Adminstrn., 1986-98. Author: Vann-en naturressurs, 1977. Mem. Nordic Hydrol. Soc., Norwegian Geophys. Soc. (pres. 1991-92). Office: Norwegian Water Resources-, Energy Directorate Box 5091, 0301 Oslo Norway

TOLLE, HENNING, control theory and robotics educator; b. Berlin, May 23, 1932; m. Gertraude Schäfer, Apr. 26, 1963; children: Ines, Janna, Nicola. Diploma in engring., Tech. U. Berlin, 1955, D Natural Scis., 1956. Sci. asst. Inst. Applied Math., Tech. U. Braunschweig (Fed. Republic Germany), 1955-57; expert advisor German Fed. Agy. for Social Ins. Supervision, Berlin, 1958-61; head astrodynamics, projects and satellite programs ERNO Raumfahrt GmbH, Bremen, 1961-73; prof. emeritus control theory and robotics Tech. U. Darmstadt (Fed. Republic Germany), 1973-98. Author: Optimierungsverfahren, 1971, Optimization Techniques, 1975, Mehrgrössen-Regelkreissynthese, Vol. I, 1983, Vol. II, 1985, (with E. Ersu) Neurocontrol, 1992; mem. editl. bd. Aerospace Sci. & Tech. Mem. Gesellschaft fuer Mess- und Automatisierungstechnik, Deutsche Gesellschaft fuer Luft- und Raumfahrt. Home: Heinrich Heine Strasse 8, D-64380 Rossdorf Germany

TOLLE, MELINDA EDITH, engineer, scientist; b. N.Y., Aug. 8, 1964; d. Robert Dale and Mildred Elva Tolle. BS in Physics, U. Utah, 1986, BS in Geophysics, 1986, MS in Mech. Engring., 1988. Cert. quality engr. Am. Soc. for Quality; cert. quality mgr. Engr. assoc. Alcoa, Brigham City, Utah, 1987-88; sr. engr. assoc. Thiokol, Brigham City, Utah, 1988-90, engr., 1990-92, sr. scientist, sr. engr., 1992-98, prin. scientist, prin. engr., 1998-2000, sr. prin. engr., 2000—; adj. instr. Weber State U., Ogden, Utah, 1996—. Mem. AIAA (sect. chair 1999—, regional dep. dir. Meb 2000—), Am. Soc. for Quality (sect. chair 1997-98, mem. chair 1995-96, vice chair 1996-97, deputy regional dir. for membership 2000—, strategic mgmt. plan chair 2000—), Am. Nuc. Soc., Utah Engring. Coun. (bd. dirs. 1998—), Alpha Nu Sigma (pres. 1988). Office: Thiokol PO Box 707 Brigham City UT 84302-0707

TOLLEMAR, JAN GUSTAV, surgeon, researcher; b. Stockholm, Dec. 26, 1957; s. Carl Gustav and Siv Ingrid (Berglund) T.; m. Marie Kerstin Wilmenius; children: Carl Victor, Per Ludvig. MD, Karolinska Inst., Stockholm, 1985, PhD, 1991. Qualified gen. surgery Swedish nat. bd. health. Fellow dept. transplantation surgery and clin. immunology Karolinska Inst./Huddinge Hosp., Stockholm, 1985-90; resident dept. otorhinolaryngology Huddinge Hosp.and Södertälje Hosp., Stockholm and Södertälje, 1985-86; intern dept. surgery, internal medicine, anesthesiology, psychiat., gen. medicine Huddige Hosp., Stockholm, 1990-92; resident gen. surgery dept. surgery Nacka Hosp., Stockholm, 1992-94; resident anesthesiology Huddinge Hosp., Stockholm, 1994-95, resident thoracic surgery, 1995; attending surgeon, asst. dir. Karolinska Inst./Huddinge Hosp., Stockholm, 1995—, assoc. prof. in transplantation immunology; cons. Nat. Bd. of Health, Uppsala, Sweden, 1994. Contbr. articles to profl. jours. Active Boy Scouts, Mälarhöjden, Sweden, 1964—. Lt. Swedish Army, 1978-79. Recipient Jansen Mycology award Jansen Pharms., Sweden, 1988; rsch. grantee Children's Cancer Found., 1989—, Jenny Found., 1991-97, Karolinska Inst., 1988—. Mem. Swedish Med. Assn., Scandinavian Transplantation Soc., European Soc. Organ Transplantation, The Transplantation Soc., European Bone Marrow Transplantation Group, Internat. Soc. for Human and Animal Mycology, Swedish Transplantation Soc., Nordic Bone Marrow Transplantation Group, European Orgn. for Rsch. and Treatment of Cancer. Avocations: golf, skiing, sailing, hunting. Home: Färgstigen 3, 141 31 Huddinge Sweden

TOLLENAERE, LAWRENCE ROBERT, retired industrial products company executive; b. Berwyn, Ill., Nov. 19, 1922; s. Cyrille and Modesta (Van Damme) T.; m. Mary Elizabeth Hansen, Aug. 14, 1948; children: Elizabeth, Homer, Stephanie, Caswell, Mary Jennifer. BS in Engring., Iowa State U., 1944, MS in Engring., 1949; MBA, U. So. Calif., 1969; LLD (hon.), Claremont Grad. Sch., 1977. Specification engr. Aluminum Co. Am., Vernon, Calif., 1946-47; asst. prof. indsl. engring. Iowa State U., Ames, 1947-50; sales rep. Am. Pipe and Constrn. Co. (now AMERON), South Gate, Calif., 1950-53; spl. rep. Am. Pipe and Constrn. Co. (now AMERON), S.Am., 1952-54; 2nd v.p., mgr. Columbian divsn. Am. Pipe and Constrn. Co. (now AMERON), Bogota, S.Am., 1955-57; divsn. v.p., mgr. Am. Pipe and Constrn. Co. (now AMERON), Calif., 1957-63; v.p. concrete pipe ops. Am. Pipe and Constrn. Co. (now AMERON), Monterey Park, Calif., 1963-65, pres. corp. hdqrs., 1965-67; pres., CEO Ameron Inc., Monterrey Park, Calif., 1967-89; CEO, pres. Ameron Inc., Pasadena, 1989-93, chmn. bd. dirs., 1989-94, ret., 1994. Trustee The Huntington Library, Art Gallery and Bot. Gardens; emeritus mem. bd. fellows Claremont U. Ctr.; bd. gov.'s Iowa State U. Found. Mem. Newcomen Soc. N.Am., Calif. C. of C. (bd. dirs. 1977-92), Calif. Club (past pres.), Jonathan Club, Bohemian Club, San Francisco Club, Commanderie de Bordeaux Club, L.A. Confrerie des Chevaliers du Tastevin Club, Twilight Club, Lincoln Club, Beavers Club (past pres., hon. dir.), Valley of Montecito Club, Alpha Tau Omega. Republican. Avocations: fishing, hunting, equestrian, philately. Home: 1400 Milan Ave South Pasadena CA 91030-3930 Office: 750 E Green St Ste 301 Pasadena CA 91101-2134

TOLLETT, KENNETH SCRUGS, education educator; b. Wash., July 14, 1931; s. Harrel E. and Hattie Mae (Scruggs) T.; m. Jacqueline Scott, June 1953 (div. 1974); children: Erica, Nicola; Queen Wiggs (div. June 1995); 1 child, Kenneth S. AB, U. Chgo., 1952, MA, 1958, JD, 1955. Bar: Tex. 1961, U.S. Dist. Ct. (no. dist.) Ill. 1955. Legal aide, atty. Sheriff Joseph Lohman Cook County, Chgo., 1955-57; acting dean, prof. Tex. So. U., Houston, 1958-62, dean Sch. Law, 1963-70; vis. fellow Ctr. for study of Dem. Instns., Santa Barbara, Calif., 1970, 71; dir. Inst. Study Ednl. Policy Howard U., Wash., 1974-85; disting. prof. higher edn. Howard U., 1971—; vis. prof. Sch. Law U. Colo., Boulder, 1970-71; cons., writer Pres. bd. advisors Hist. Black Colls. and U., Wash., 1992; dir., supr. prodn. ISEP various publs. Author: Affirmative Action: Sound Advocacy, Full Data and Debate Can Save it, 2000; contbr. articles to profl. jours. Recipient C. Francis Stodford award Nat. Bar Assn., 1968, U. Chgo. Alumni Assocs. Profl. Achievement award, 1972; grantee Howard U., 1971—. Mem. Am. Assn. U. Profs. (com. govt. rels. 1992—, cons. com. minority edn. 1991-94), Nat. Coun. Educating Black Children, Senate Coun. Howard U. (faculty), Internat. Assn. Philosophy Law and Social Philosophy (Am. sect., 1972—), Carnegie Commn. Future Higher Edn., Tex. Constl. Revision Commn., Supreme Ct. Hist. Soc. (program com. 1994—). Avocations: reading, art appreciation, history, fitness. Office: Howard U Grad Sch A&S 4th Coll Sts NW Annex I Washington DC 20059-0001

TOLLEY, JOHN PATRICK, machinery and valve manufacturing company executive; b. Oxford, Eng., Sept. 11, 1941; s. Leslie John and Margaret (Butterfield) T.; m. Nancy Louise Pierson, Aug. 13, 1966; children: Christopher John, Geoffrey Pierson. BA in Natural Sci., Cambridge U., 1963; MBA, London Bus. Sch., 1971. Engr. Westinghouse Electric Corp., Pitts., 1963-69; prodn. mgr. John Holroyd and Co. Ltd., Milnrow, Eng., 1972-75, plant mgr., 1975-77; mng. dir. Holcroft Castings and Forgings Ltd., Rochdale, Eng., 1977-83, Sagar-Richards Ltd., Halifax, Eng., 1983-88, Rabone Chesterman Ltd., Birmingham, Eng., 1988-90; chief exec. Excelsior Indsl. Holdings Ltd., Ashton-under-Lyne, Lancashire, Eng., 1990-91; chmn. Briarcroft Ltd., Manchester, Eng. Fellow British Inst. Mgmt. (chmn. Manchester br. 1985-88). Home and Office: 7 Forest Pl Cross in Hand, Heathfield, East Sussex TN21 0TG, England

TOLLIFSON, THOMAS GERALD, retired art education consultant, teacher; b. Albert Lea, Minn., Feb. 4, 1925; s. Virgil Irving and Lucile Katherine Tollifson; m. Jeannine May Dill, Aug. 10, 1952. BS in Art Edn., U. Minn., 1950; MA in Art Edn., Ohio State U., 1952. Art tchr. Columbus (Ohio) State Sch. for Mentally Retarded, 1951-52; art helping tchr. Arlington (Va.) Elem. Schs., 1952-54; art tchr. Washington Lee H.S., Arlington, 1954-56; art edn. instr. Am. U., Washington, 1953-54; art tchr. Jones Jr. H.S., Upper Arlington, Ohio, 1956-66; state art edn. cons. Ohio Dept. Edn., Columbus, 1966-94; ret., 1994; art edn. instr. Ohio State U., 1950-51, 59-60, U. Va., Arlington, 1954-55—. Author (art edn. TV series guides) Images and Things, Nat. Instrn. TV, 1971, The Big A, 1986, In Touch, Tollifson's Art Attack Sta. KCTS-TV, Seattle; co-author, actor (TV program) What's an Art Curriculum for Anyway?", 1980; editor (art curriculum guide) Planning a Balanced Comprehensive Art Curriculum, Ohio Dept. Edn., 1970, 87, 92; co-prodr.: (ednl. TV program) Making Connections, 1995; co-author: Comprehensive Arts Education Curriculum Framework for Ohio Schools, 1991, Ohio Plan for Comprehensive Arts in Education, 1978; art exhbn. Fitton Art Ctr., Hamilton, Ohio, 1997. Founder Ohio Gov.'s Youth Art Exhbn., Columbus, 1969—, Ohio Alliance for Arts Edn., 1974, Ohio Youth Art Month, 1973, Ohio Arts Criticism Invitational and Open, 1989; advisor Getty Ctr. for Arts in Edn., L.A., 1987, Joint Coun. State Bd. Regents and State Bd. Edn., 1999—, Coalition for Equity and Adequacy, Columbus, 1999—. Sgt., U.S. Army Inf., 1943-45, ETO. Named Gov.'s Arts Educator of Yr., Ohio Arts Coun., 2000; recipient Grand Nat. Youth Art Month award, 1974; Jerry Tollifson Ohio Mid. Sch. Art Criticism Open Contest named in his honor, 2000. Fellow Ohio Art Edn. Assn. (advisor Ohio arts edn., adv. com. 1994—, Outstanding Ohio Art Educator of Yr. 1984); mem. Nat. Art Edn. Assn. (nat. art adminstr./supr. award 1995, Disting. Svc. award 1990), Nat. Assn. State Dirs. Art Edn. (founder, chmn. 1967-70). Avocations: drawing, painting, sculpture, architecture, landscape design. Home: PO Box 24352 Columbus OH 43224-0352

TOLLIT, DOMINIC JOHN, marine biologist, researcher; b. London, Jan. 29, 1965; s. Michael Federick and Jacqueline Anne T. BSc, Aberystwyth (Wales) U., 1986; PhD, Aberdeen U., Cromarty, Scotland, 1996. Rschr. Royal Postgrad. Med. Sch., London, 1990-91, U. Aberdeen, 1991-96, Royal Soc. London, Sabah, Borneo, 1997, Australian Antarctic Divsn., Hobart, Australia, 1997, Nat. Trust Fiji, Suva, 1999; cons. British Petroleum, Scotland, 1994. Contbr. articles to sci. jours. including Can. Jour. Zoology, Molecular Ecology, others. Mem. British Sub-Aqua Club. Avocations: scuba diving, hiking, music, travel. Home: 40 Midford Lane, Wiltshr Bath BA3 6JS, England

TOLMAN, RICHARD ROBINS, zoology educator; b. Ogden, Utah, Dec. 1, 1937; s. Dale Richards and Dorothy (Robins) T.; m. Bonnie Bjornn, Aug. 18, 1964; children: David, Alicia, Brett, Matthew. BS, U. Utah, 1963, MSEd, 1964; PhD, Oreg. State U., 1969. Tchr. sci. Davis County Sch. Dist., Bountiful, Utah, 1964-66; instr. Mt. Hood C.C., Gresham, Oreg., 1968-69; staff assoc., project dir. Biol. Scis. Curriculum Study, Boulder, Colo., 1969-82; prof. zoology Brigham Young U., Provo, Utah, 1982—, chair dept. of zoology, 1994-98; assoc. dean Coll. Biology and Agrl. Brigham Young U., Provo, 1998—. Contbr. articles to profl. jours. Scoutmaster Boy Scouts Am., Orem, Utah, 1992. With USAR, 1956-63. Alcuin fellow Brigham Young U., 1991. Mem. Nat. Sci. Tchrs. Assn., Utah Sci. Tchrs. Assn. (exec. sec. 1991—), Nat. Assn. for Rsch. in Sci. Teaching, Nat. Assn. of Biology Tchrs. Mem. Ch. of LDS. Avocations: whitewater rafting, hunting, fishing, hiking. Home: 174 E 1825 S Orem UT 84058-7836 Office: Brigham Young Univ Dept Zoology Provo UT 84602

TOLMAN, VLADIMÍR BŘETISLAV, chemist, researcher; b. Prague, Mar. 21, 1935; s. Vladimír Břetislav Jan Josef and Vlasta (Lichtenbergová) T.; m. Helena Huňková, June 22, 1959 (div. Nov. 7, 1984); 1 child, Vladimír. Ing. chemistry, Inst. Chem. Tech., Prague, 1958; PhD, Charles U., Prague, 1967. Jr. rschr. Inst. Biology Czechoslovak Acad. Sci., Prague, 1959-61, rschr. Inst. microbiology, 1962-66, sr. rschr. Isotope Lab., 1966-85, sr. rschr. Inst. Nuclear Biology and Radiochemistry, 1986-93; head sci. coun. Inst. Nuc. Biology and Radiochemistry, Prague, 1990-92; sr. rschr. Inst. Chem. Tech., Prague, 1993-96; sr. rschr. Inst. Exptl. Botany Czech Acad. Sci., Prague, 1996—; guest researcher Va. Poly. Inst. State U., Blacksburg, Va., 1975; diploma thesis supr. Charles U., Prague, 1973, 76, 93, cons. Faculty of Pharmacology, 1995—. Co-author: Fluorine-Containing Amino Acids, 1995; patentee in field. Mem. Czech Chem. Soc., Am. Chem. Soc. (divsn. fluorine chemistry), Union of Pure and Applied Chemistry (affiliate), Czechoslovak Entomol. Soc. Avocations: music, entomology, philately. Home: U zastávky 1, 14300 Prague 4, Czech Republic Office: Inst Exptl Botany, Acad Sci Vídenska 1083, 142 20 Prague 4, Czech Republic

TOLMIE, DONALD FRANCOIS, religious studies educator; b. Keetmanshoop, Nambia, Nov. 11, 1959; s. Donald and Wilhelmina (Bethal) T.; m. Sara Johanna Steyl, Mar. 23, 1985; 3 children. BA, U. Free State,

Bloemfontein, Rural South Africa, 1980, BA in Greek, 1981, MA in Greek, 1984, BTh, 1984, DTh, 1992. Reverend D.R. Ch., Walvis Bay, Rural South Africa, 1989-90; assoc. prof. Faculty of Theology U. of the Free State, Bloemfontein, South Africa, 1990—. Author: Jesus' Farewell to the Disciples, 1995, Narratology and Biblical Narratives: A Practical Guide, 1999. Mem. Studiorum Novi Testamenti Societas, Soc. Bibl. Lit., New Testament Soc. South Africa, South African Acad. Sci. and Art.

TOLSTOGUZOV, VLADIMIR BORISOVICH, chemistry researcher; b. Moscow, Russia, Apr. 22, 1937. BSc in Chemistry, Inst. Chem. Technol., Moscow, 1959, PhD in Phys. Chemistry, 1962; DSc in Phys. Chemistry, USSR Acad. Scis., 1975. Researcher, asst. prof. Inst. Chem. Technol., Moscow, 1959-63; researcher Inst. of Organoelement Compounds, USSR Acad. Scis., Moscow, 1963-66, sr. researcher, 1966-75, lab. head, 1975-93; lab. head Inst. Food Substance, USSR Acad. Scis., Moscow, 1993—; prof. sr. scientist Nestlé Rsch. Ctr., Lausanne, Switzerland; mem. editorial bd. Food-Die Nahrung, Berlin, Germany, 1987—, Food Hydrocolloids, Oxford, Eng., 1986—, Carbohydrate Polymers, London, 1981—, Jour. of Sci. and Food and Agriculture, London, 1987—. Author: Inorganic Polymers, 1968, Artificial Foodstuffs, 1978, Novel Forms of Protein Foods, 1987, Food Production Economics, 1986. Avocations: history and econ. aspects of food prodn. Office: Nestec Ltd Rsch Ctr, Vers-chez-les Blanc Box 44, CH-1000 Lausanne 26, Switzerland

TOLSTORUKOV, MICHAEL Y., biophysicist; b. Atbasar, Akmolinsky, Kazakhstan, Jan. 6, 1971; s. Eugene I. and Eugeniya S. (Belotserkovskaya) T.; m. Svetlana V. Boriskina, July 22, 1995. BSc in Biophysics, Kharkov (Ukraine) State U., 1993, MSc in Biophysics, 1995, PhD in Physics and Math., 1999; MSc in Patentology and Informatics, Kharkov Poly. U., 1995. Jr. rschr. Kharkov State U., 1999, assoc. prof., 1999—; vis. fellow Nat. Cancer Inst., NIH, Bethesda, Md., 2000—. Contbr. articles to profl. jours. Postgrad. scholar Internat. Sci. and Ednl. Program Found., Switzerland and Ukraine, 1996-97; travel grantee Civil R & D Found., U.S., 1997; travel fellow Internat. Union for Pure and Applied Biophysics/UNESCO/Internat. Coun. Sci., 1999. Avocations: pets, travel. Office: Nat Cancer Inst NIH 12 South Dr Bethesda MD 20892-0001

TOLSTOY, NIKOLAJ THEODORSSON, civil engineer; s. Theodor and Ulla (Key) T.; m. Gunnel De Geer, Sept. 19, 1975; children: Theodor, Georg. MS in Civil Engring., Chalmers U. Tech., Gothenburg, Sweden, 1973; PhD, Royal Inst. Tech., Stockholm, 1994. Site rschr. Inst. Testing Materials and Products, Stockholm, 1973-75; info. engr. Bldg. Centre, Gothenburg, 1975-78; rschr. Swedish Inst. Bldg. Rsch., Gavle, 1978-94; bldg. cons. AB Jacobson & Widmark, Lidingo, Sweden, 1994—. Capt. Swedish Navy, 1966-69. Mem. CIB Bldg. Pathology. Avocations: sailing, reading, skiing. Office: AB Jacobson & Widmark, Arenavägen 7, 121 88 Stockholm-Globen Sweden

TOM, C. F. JOSEPH, economics educator; b. Guangzhou, Guang Dong, People's Republic of China, May 30, 1922; came to U.S., 1939; s. Y.S. Tom and K.H. Chan; m. Grace Moy, Feb. 14, 1948. BA, Hastings Coll., 1944; MA, U. Chgo., 1947, PhD, 1963. Instr. econs. Beloit (Wis.) Coll., 1948-54; asst. prof. Lebanon Valley Coll., Annville, Pa., 1954-64, assoc. prof., 1964-67, chmn. dept. econs. and bus. adminstrn., 1964-74, prof., 1967-89, prof. emeritus, 1989—. Author: The Entrepot Trade and the Monetary Standards of Hong Kong, 1964, Monetary Problems of an Entrepot: The Hong Kong Experience, 1989. Econs.-in-Action grantee Republic Steel Corp., Case Western Res. U., Cleve., 1953; Ford Found. faculty grantee U. Pa., summer 1960; Gen. Electric Found. faculty grantee U. Va., summer 1963, UCLA, summer 1969; Econs. Seminar grantee Stel Industry, U. Chgo., 1975. Mem. Am. Econ. Assn., Hong Kong Econ. Assn. Avocations: travel, chess, golf, reading, music. Home: PO Box 125 Cornwall PA 17016-0125 Office: Lebanon Valley Coll Annville PA 17003

TOMA, SEITA, author; b. Hiroshima-Shi, Japan, May 16, 1913; s. Yochachiro and Matsu (Kawamoto) T.; m. Fusako Miyazaki, July 22, 1942; children: Satoko, Hiroko, Kazuko. BA, Waseda U., Tokyo, 1936. Head Inst. Fgn. Affairs Kumamoto Gakuen U., Kumamoto-shi, Japan, 1972-75, prof., 1971-87. Author: The Ancient State of Japan, 1946, The Formation of the Ancient East Asian World, 1966, The Formation of the Modern East Asian World, 1977, The Rebellion of the Troops in Soul, 1882 and the Realization of the Modern East Asian World, 1987. Mem. Rekisigaku Kenkyu Kai, Kokogaku Kenkyu Kai, Toyoshi-Kenkyu-Kai. Home and Office: 2127-164 Sakae Koushi-Machi, Kikuchi-Gun Kumamoto 861-1113, Japan

TOMAIUOLO, NICHOLAS GREGORY, librarian, educator; b. Hartford, Conn., June 30, 1955; s. Carmen Peter and Victoria Lucy (DeLuca) T.; children: Benjamin David, Kristin Elizabeth. BS, U. Conn., 1977; MLS, So. Conn. State U., 1988. Cert. tchr. secondary English, Conn. Electronic resources libr. U. Conn. Health Ctr. Libr., Farmington, 1988-94; libr., bibliographic instr., assoc. libr. reference dept. Ctrl. Conn. State U., New Britain, 1994—; instr. adult edn. Town of Wethersfield, Conn., 1995—; world wide web and bibliographic database search cons. Co-editor newsletter Elihu Burritt Libr., Ctrl. Conn. State U., 1994—. Contbr. articles to profl. publs. Mem. Conn. Libr. Assn. (at large), Beta Phi Mu (life). Republican. Roman Catholic. Home: 11 Buckland Rd Wethersfield CT 06109-1204 Office: Ctrl Conn State Univ Elihu Burritt Libr Stanley St New Britain CT 06050

TOMALTY, DEREK JAMES, writer; b. Potsdam, N.Y., June 15, 1969; s. Melvin David and Sandra Jean Tomalty. Student, SUNY, Binghamton, 1987-89; BA, Potsdam Coll., 1995. Movie projectionist The Roxy, Potsdam, 1988; salesperson Radio Shack/Tandy Co., Inc., Ogdensburg, N.Y., 1989, Household Merit, Gouverneur, N.Y., 1989-90; food svc. staff Potsdam Coll., 1994-95; with Confidential Svc., Canton, N.Y., 1997, No. Border Indsl., Ogdensburg, 1999—; writer The Transition box, Ogdensburg, 1999—. Mem. World Federalist Assn., Nat. Alliance for the Mentally Ill, St. Lawrence Valley; vol./mentor North Country Self-Help, 1999. Unitarian Universalist. Avocations: walking, classical music, philosophy.

TOMAN, RUDOLF LUDOVIT, biochemist, researcher; b. Bratislava, Slovak Republic, Nov. 4, 1944; s. Emil and Klára (Lukoviny) T.; m. Elena Havránková, Dec. 21, 1969; 1 child, Katarina. MS in Biotech., Slovak Tech. U., Bratislava, Slovakia, 1968; PhD in Organic Chemistry, Slovak Acad. Scis., Bratislava, 1973, DSc in Microbiology, 1995. Registered engr. Rsch. asst. Inst. Chemistry, Slovak Acad. Scis., Bratislava, 1969-73, postdoctoral rsch. assoc. Inst. Chemistry, 1973-76, sr. rsch. scientist I, 1983-89; postdoctoral rsch. assoc. dept. chemistry Ohio State U., Columbus, 1976-77; sr. rsch. leading scientist Inst. Virology, Slovak Acad. Scis., Bratislava, 1992—, head dept. rickettsiology and chlamydiology, 1995—, head sci. bd., 1995-98; cons. UN/UNIDO, Vienna, 1988—; mem. bd. scientists Slovak Acad. Scis., Bratislava; vis. prof. U. Ga., Athens, 1992-93. mem. editl. bd. Chem. Papers, 1987-91, 2000—, Acta Virologica, 1992-93; contbr. articles to profl. jours.; patentee in field. Recipient gold medal for merits Czecho-Slovak Sci. Tech. Soc., Bratislava, Slovakia, 1987, silver medal Akita (Japan) U. Sch. Medicine, 1996, gold medal Ain Shams U., Cairo, 1997. Mem. Czechoslovak Sci. Tech. Soc. Inst. Chemistry (pres. 1979-88, silver medal for merits 1984), Soc. Indsl. Chemistry (v.p. 1985-89), Slovak Soc. Scientists (silver medal for merits 1994), Slovak Soc. Scientists and Rsch. Workers (v.p. 1990—), Slovak Sci. Tech. Soc. (mem. bd. 1990-98). Avocations: tennis, skiing, swimming, mountaineering. Office: Slovak Acad Scis Inst Virol, Dúbravská cesta 9, Bratislava 84245, Slovakia

TOMAN, WALTER KARL, psychologist, educator; b. Vienna, Austria, Mar. 15, 1920; s. Karl A. and Paula (Hradil) T.; m. Eleonore L. Gruener; children: Christina E., Adrienne V. PhD in Psychology, U. Vienna, 1944; Psychoanalysis Lic., Inst. Psychoanalysis, Vienna, 1951. Asst. lectr. U. Vienna, 1945-50, lectr., 1951; lectr. Harvard U., Cambridge, Mass., 1951-54; prof. psychology Brandeis U., Waltham, Mass., 1954-64, U. Erlangen, Fed. Republic Germany, 1964-86; prof. emeritus U. Erlangen, 1986—; scientific cons. Inst. Advanced Studies, Vienna, 1963—, dir., 1966-67. Author: Psychoanalytic Theory of Motivation, 1960, Family Constellation, 1961, Motivation, Personality, Environment, 1968, Introduction to General Psychology, 1973, Depth Psychology, 1978, Family Therapy, 1988, Psychotherapy in Everyday Life, 1991, Emergency Calls, 1994; editor: Psychotherapy Handbook, 1985. Recipient psychology award City of Vienna, 1953, family rsch. award Georgetown U., Washington, 1980. Mem. Internat. Psychoanalytical Assn., Austrian Pen Club, German Psychol. Assn., Am. Family Therapy Assn. Office: Dept Psychology, Bismarckstrasse 1, D-91054 Erlangen Bavaria, Germany

TOMA-REDNIC, CARMEN DORINA, physician, researcher; b. Tighina, Basarabia, Romania, Aug. 19, 1939; d. Titus and Ioana (Postea) Rednic; m. Jenica Florea, Aug. 1, 1969 (div. May 1966); children: Florea, Diana, Carmen, Michaela; m. Liviu Augustin Toma, Sept. 25, 1968. MD, Faculty Medicine, Cluj, Romania, 1974. Generalist physician Unified Hosp., Cugir, Romania, 1962-67; rschr. U. Medicine, Cluj, 1967-76; lab. specialist physician Children Hosp., Cluj, 1976-90, lab. primar physician, 1990—, head labs., 1992—. Contbr. articles to profl. jours. Active Viva la musica choir, 1976-78. Avocation: music. Home: Petru Maior nr 7, Cluj Romania Office: Cl Pediatrie III, Campeni nr 4, 3400 Cluj Romania

TOMASELLI, MICHELE, chemist; b. Napoli, Italy, Sept. 28, 1939; d. Roberto and Ada (Cevoli) T.; m. Luigia Burlin, Nov. 12, 1969; children: Simona, Roberto. Student, Naples U., 1966. Asst. Stazione Sperimentale Pelli, Naples, 1968-75, rschr., 1975-89, first rschr., 1989—; quality system inspector I.C.E.C., Milan, 1995; acting dir. Italian Leather Rsch. Inst., 1997—. Author: Leather Clothing-Tanning Technology, Cleaning and Maintenance, 1991; contbr. articles to profl. jours. With Army, 1966-67. Mem. Assn. Italiana Chimici Cuoio (dir. coun. mem. 1996), Societa Chimica Italiana.

TOMASELLI, SYLVANA PALMA, academic fellow; b. Placentia, Nfld., Can., May 28, 1957. BA, U. B.C., Can., 1977; MA, York U., Can., 1978, Cambridge U., 2000. Rsch. fellow Newnham Coll., Cambridge, Eng., 1985-88, Hughes Hall, Cambridge, 1996—; affiliated lectr. history faculty Cambridge, 1998—; coll. lectr. St. John's Coll., Cambridge, 2000—. Co-editor: Rape, 1986, The Dialectics of Friendship, 1989, Mary Wollstonecraft's Vindications, 1995, The Philosophical Canon, 1996. Roman Catholic. Office: St Johns Coll, Cambridge CB2 1TP, England

TÓMASSON, TÓMAS ÁRMANN, ambassador; b. Reykjavik, Iceland, Jan. 1, 1929; s. Tómas and Gudrun (Thorgrímsdóttir) T.; children: Jón, Ingibörg, Tómas, Árni. BA, U. Ill., 1952; MA, Fletcher Sch. Law & Diplomacy, 1953; postgrad., Russian INst., Columbia, 1953-54. Icelandic fgn. svc. officer, 1954; sec. of Embassy Moscow, 1954-58; officer Ministry Fgn. Affairs, Reykjavik, 1958-60; 1st sec., counsellor of Embassy Paris, 1960-66; dep. permanent rep. of Iceland to NATO and OECD, 1960-66; chief of divsn. Ministry Fgn. Affairs, 1966-69, chmn. def. com., dep. sec. gen., 1970-71; permanent rep. of Iceland on North Atlantic Coun., amb. to Belgium and EC, 1971-77; permanent rep. to UN, 1977-82; amb. to France and permanent rep. to OECD and UNESCO, also accredited to Spain, Portugal, Cabo Verde, 1982-84; amb. to Belgium and EC, Icelandic permanent rep. to NATO, 1984-86, amb. to the USSR, 1987-90; amb. to U.S. Washington, 1990-93; accredited to Can., Mex., Brazil, Venezuela, Argentina; amb., head of del. to disarmament negotiations, Vienna, 1990; permanent rep. to UN, 1993-94; with Ministry Fgn. Affairs, Rewkjavik, Iceland, 1995—. Decorated Grand knight Order of Falcon, Iceland and Belgian, French, Luxembourg, Portuguese and Swedish orders. Mem. Cercle Royal Gaulois Artistique et Ltteraire. Home: Espigerdi 4/9H, 108 Reykjavik Iceland Office: Ministry Fgn Affairs, 150 Reykjavik Iceland

TOMASSONI, MARIA-LETIZIA, pathologist, researcher; b. Narni, Terni, Italy, Mar. 23, 1967; d. Romano Tomassoni and Clara Bartolucci; m. Marco Boccolini, Oct. 21, 1990; 1 child, Marianna. MD, U. Perugia, Italy, 1994, specialization in clin. pathology, 1999. Med. diplomate. Resident in clin. pathology Med. U. Perugia, 1994—, Ctr. Neurochemistry, Strasbourg, France, 1998-99. Contbr. articles to sci. jours. ERASMUS fellow, 1991, fellow Italian Soc. Biochemistry and Molecular Biology, 1998, fellow Fedn. European Biochem. Socs., 1999. Mem. Italian Group Biomembranes and Bioenergetics, Italian Soc. Biochemistry and Molecular Biology, Italian Soc. Clin. Biochem., Italian Soc. Lab. Medicine. E-mail: tomassoni@narni.it. Fax: +39-075-5720592. Office: Inst Gen Path Med Univ, PO Box 58 Succ 3, 06100 Perugia PG, Italy

TOMASZ, PALEWSKI, physics educator, researcher; b. Logiszyn, Russia, Aug. 17, 1941; arrived in Poland, 1945; s. Józef and Maria (Czeczotko) P.; m. Krystyna Kozlowska, July 1, 1972; 1 child, Katarzyna. MGR, Tech. U., Wrocław, Poland, 1964, D, 1972, D Habilitation, 1993. Asst. Tech. U., 1964-72, adj., 1972-84, head trade union, 1974-80, vice dir. inst., 1976-84; adj. Internat. Lab., Wrocław, 1984-93, asst. prof. physics, 1993—, vice dir., 1985—. Avocation: hunting. Office: Internat Lab, Gajowicka 95, 53-421 Wrocław Poland

TOMASZEWSKI, JEREMIASZ JERZY, biochemist; b. Lublin, Poland, Apr. 18, 1930; s. Wladyslaw and Genowefa (Jargiello) T.; m. Halina Elzbieta Wloch, Jan. 1, 1950; children: Tatiana, Tomasz. M in Chemistry, Slodowska-Curie U., Lublin, 1961; D in Natural Sci., U. Lublin, 1966; D in Med. Sci., Med. Acad., Lublin, 1973. Dep. dir. Ctrl. Clin. Lab., Lublin, 1961-66; head rsch. ctr. Med. Acad., Lublin, 1967-79, head dept. clin. biochemistry environ. and toxicology, 1980—; mem. Nat. Specialist Bd. of Lab. Diagnostic, Warsaw, 1978-91; v.p. Nat. Commn. for Lab. Equipment, Warsaw, 1979—; head commn. attestation Polish Coll. Lab. Medicine, 1993-98; v.p. commn. prophyl. Polish Cardiac Soc., 1991-98. Contbr. numerous articles in field to profl. jours. Mem. Internat. Fedn. Clin. Chemistry, World Assn. Pathol. Soc., Polish Soc. Lab. Diagnostics (mem. exec. bd. 1972-78), Commn. in Clin. Pathol. Com. Polish Acad. Sci. Roman Catholic. Office: Dept Clin Biochem & Env Tox, Jaczewskiego 8, 20-950 Lublin Poland

TOMASZEWSKI, JERZY, history educator; b. Radomsko, Poland, Oct. 8, 1930; s. Dyonizy and Irena (Podgórska) T.; m. Zofia Teresa Antosiak, Apr. 21, 1957; 1 child, Agata. M in Econs., Szkoła G. Planowania, Warsaw, 1954, D in Econs., 1960. Asst. SGPIS, Warsaw, 1950-54, lectr., 1956-65; asst. prof. Szkoła Główna Gospodarstwa Wiejskiego, Warsaw, 1965-70; asst. prof. U. Warsaw, 1970-72, prof., 1972—; prof. Inst. Political Sciences, 1972-90, Historical Inst., 1990—; mem. bd. dirs. Zydowski Inst. Historyczny, Warsaw, 1970—. Author of over 30 books in field. Mem. Polskie Towarzystwo Historyczne, Czechoslovak History Conf., World Union Jewish Studies. Home: Czarnieckiego 52, 01-548 Warsaw Poland Office: U Warsaw, Krakow Przedmiescie 26/28, 00-325 Warsaw Poland

TOMASZEWSKI, PIOTR, pharmacist, biochemist researcher, educator; b. Brno, Morava, Czechoslovakia, Dec. 31, 1968; s. Jerzy and Bozenna (Walentukanis) T. MPharm, Med. U. Warsaw, 1992. Asst. Med. U. Warsaw, 1992—. Author: Hepatodiagnostic Parameters in Monitoring Therapy of Liver Diseases, 1996 (with others) Arterial Blood Ketone Bodies Concentrations as Indicator of Metabolic State of Liver After Hepatectomy, 1993; contbr. articles to profl. jours. including Polish Jour. Soc. Mem. Polish Pharm. Soc. (bd. coun. Warsaw br. 1994-2001). Roman Catholic. Avocations: mountaineering, trekking, ethnology, photography. Office: Banacha 1 Str, PL-02097 Warsaw Poland

TOMAT, DARIO CLAUDE, manufacturing consultant; b. Trieste, Italy, Apr. 14, 1952; arrived in Australia, 1956; s. Guido and Nerina (Ferluga) T.; m. Christine Mary Wood, Jan. 6, 1978; children: Julia Patricia, Richard David, Gillian Laura. B in Engring., Tasmania U., 1975; BBA, Tasmania Inst. Tech., 1988; Co. dirs. Diploma, U. New England, 1992; MBA, Deakin U., 1995. Registered profl. engr. Profl. engr. W.E. Bassett and Ptnrs., Hobart, Australia, 1976-78; project mgr. Westwill Pty Ltd., Launceston, Australia, 1978-82; cons. Energy Mgmt. Ctr., Hobart, 1982-85; sr. energy planner Hydro-Electric Commn., Hobart, 1985-88; contracts engr. HEC Enterprises Corp., Hobart, 1988-90; gen. mgr. Ctr. for Precision Tech., Hobart, 1990-96; dir. Edn. and Devel. Svcs., Hobart, 1997—; dir. Whetstone Pty. Ltd., Edn. & Tng. for Profls., Engring. & Tech. Placements. Comdr. Royal Australian Navy Res., 1984—. Recipient Prince of Wales award Citizen in Support of Res. Forces, 1994, Australia Day medal Australia Day Coun., 1989. Fellow Instn. Engrs. Australia (dep. chair nat. com. mfg. 1996—); mem. Assn. Profl. Engrs., Scientists and Mgrs. (fed. councillor 1990—), Soc. Mfg. Engrs. Home: 12 Lachlan Dr, Mount Nelson 7007, Australia

TOMAŽEVIČ, MIHA, civil engineer, educator; b. Ljubljana, Slovenia, Sept. 19, 1942; s. Blaž and Heda (Derganc) T.; m. Natasa Verdaj, Apr. 23, 1969; 1 child, Jernej. BSc in Civil Engring., U. Ljubljana, 1966, PhD in Tech. Scis., 1985; MSc in Earthquake Engring., U. Kiril & Metodij, Skopje, Macedonia, 1977. Cert. engr. Head sect. Inst. Testing and Rsch. in Materials and Structures, Ljubljana, 1976-88, head dept., 1988-94; asst. dir., head dept. Slovenian Nat. Bldg. and Civil Engring. Inst., Ljubljana, 1994-96, dir., 1996—; cons. Gruppo Interdisciplinare Centrale, Udine, Italy, 1977-81; mem. Fed. Expert Commn. for evaluation of damage to bldgs. after earthquake of Montenegro, Yugoslavia, 1979-81; mem. Yugoslav Bur. Stds. working group for preparation of Yugoslav Seismic Code, 1979-81; mem. Yugoslav Bur. Stds. working group for prepration of Yugoslav Code for repair and strenghtening of earthquake damaged bldgs. and revitalizaiton, 1982-85; mem. CIB Commn. W23-A subcom., 1982-87; regional cons. UN Devel. Program/UN Indsl. Devel. Orgn., Thessaloniki, Greece, 1983-84; mem. Yugoslav Govt. Expert Mission to Ciudad de Mexico, 1985; assoc. prof. earthquake engring. and masonry structures U. Ljubljana, 1986, prof., 1991; vis. prof. U. Trento, Italy, 1988; mem. Yugoslav Bur. Stds. working group for preparation Yugoslav Code Masonry Structures, 1988-91; invited lectr. series of seminars Masonry Soc. and U. Tex., Arlington, 1989; vis. prof. U. Chile, Santiago, 1991; mem. CIB Commn. W23 for wall structures, 1992—; mem. Mexican Govt. Internat. Expert Commn. on rehab. of Mexico City Met. Cathedral, 1992; mem. tech. com. for bldg. structures, working group for reinforced-concrete and masonry structures, constrn. of bldgs. in seismic zones Slovenian Inst. Stds. and Metrology, 1993—; cons. The World Bank, Maharashtra Emergency Earthquake Reconstrn. Project, Bombay, 1994-95; chmn. rsch. coun. protection against natural and other disasters Ministry Sci. and Tech., Republic of Slovenia, 1995—, mem. sci. and rsch. titles electory com., 1995—; vis. prof. U. Padue, 1999, 2000. Co-author: Building Construction Under Seismic Conditions in the Balkan Region, Volume 3: Design and Construction of Stone and Brick-Masonry Buildings, 1984, Earthquake Engineering - Building Structures, 1990; author: Masonry Buildings in Seismic Regions, 1987, Diseno sismico de estructuras de albanileria, 1991, Introduction to Experimental Analysis of Civil Engineering Structures, 1991, Assessment of Damage and Usability of Earthquake Damaged Structures, 1998, Earthquake-Resistant Design of Masonry Buildings, 1999, contbr. articles to profl. jours., chpts. to books. Recipient award for rsch. achievements Boris Kidrič Found., Ljubljana, Slovenia, 1986, award Commune of Bežigrad, City of Ljubljana, 1987, award Office Civil Def., Secretariat of Def., Slovenia, 1988, Best Paper award Tehnika Jour., Belgrade, Yugoslavia, 1989, award Yugoslav Assn. Testing and Rsch. in Materials and Structures, Belgrade, 1990, Silver medal Ministry of Def., Ljubljana, 1993. Mem. Earthquake Engring. Rsch. Inst., Masonry Soc. (bd. dirs. 1994-95, outstanding paper award 1993), Slovenian Acad. Engrs., Soc. Civil Engrs. Slovenia, Slovenian Assn. Earthquake Engring, European Assn. Earthquake Engring. (exec. com. 1999—). Achievements include computer programs "POR" and "SREMB", seismic resistance of masonry buildings. Home: Kvedrova 1, 1000 Ljubljana Slovenia Office: Slovenian Nat Bldg & Civil Engring Inst, Dimičeva 12, 1000 Ljubljana Slovenia

TOMAZI, GEORGE DONALD, retired electrical engineer; b. St. Louis, Dec. 27, 1935; s. George and Sophia (Bogovich) T.; m. Lois Marie Partenheimer, Feb. 1, 1958; children: Keith, Kent. BSEE, U. Mo., Rolla, 1958, Profl. EE (hon.), 1970; MBA, St. Louis U., 1965, MSEE, 1971. Registered profl. engr., Mo., Ill., Wash., Ohio, Calif. Project engr. Union Electric Co., 1958-66; dir. corp. planning Gen. Steel Industries, 1966-70; exec. v.p. St. Louis Research Council, 1970-74; exec. v.p. Hercules Constrn. Co., St. Louis, 1974-75; dir. design and constrn. div. Mallinckrodt, Inc., St. Louis, 1975-93; ret., 1993. Author: P-Science: The Role of Science in Society, 1972, The Link of Science and Religion, 1973. Active Nat. Kidney Found.; bd. dirs. U. Mo. Devel. Council, St. Louis Artists Coalition, Citizens for Modern Transit; elder Luth. Ch.; v.p. Coun. Luth. Chs., St. Louis; mem. adv. com. grad. sch. U. Mo., Columbia, mem. pres's. role and scope commn.; dir. Coun. Luth. Chs. Greater St. Louis; mem. bldg. com. Humane Soc. Mo.; v.p. coun. Luth. Ch. of the Living Christ. Served with U.S. Army, 1959-61. Recipient award Acad. Elec. Engrs., U. Mo., Rolla, Achievement award Humane Soc. of Mo., special award 1998. Mem. NSPE, IEEE (chmn. state govt. activities com. 1990-93), Japan-Am. Soc., AAAS, AIChE, Profl. Engrs. in Industry, Mo. Soc. Profl. Engrs. (Profl. Engr. in Industry 1989, pres. St. Louis chpt.), Profl. Engrs. and Land Surveyors (chmn. Mo. bd. for architects 1989-95), Am. Def. Preparedness Assn., U. Mo. Alumni Assn. (bd. dirs. 1972-78), Engrs. Club (pres. 1985-86), Mo. Athletic Club, Rotary, Sigma Pi. Office: 12723 Stoneridge Dr Florissant MO 63033-4620

TOMB, MYRON HAY, lawyer; b. Indiana, Pa., Mar. 1, 1947; s. Myron Hay and Gertrude (Mangan) T.; children: Devin Elizabeth, Jordan Hay. BA in Econs., Indiana U. Pa., 1969; JD, U. Pitts., 1972. Bar: Pa., U.S. Supreme Ct. Assoc. Tomb & Tomb, Indiana, 1972-82; ptnr. Carmella & Tomb, Indiana, 1983-93, Tomb, Mack and Kauffman, Indiana, Pa., 1993—; instr. bus. law Ind. U., Pa., 1975-76, instr. constl. law, 1976-77. Author: (catalog) The Art of the Pattisons, 1987. Del. Dem. Nat. Conv., N.Y.C., 1980, mem. rules com., 1984; pres., bd. dirs. Indiana U. Pa. U. Mus., 1989-96; chair investment com. Found. for Indiana U. Pa., 1987—; mem. Pa. Coun. on the Arts, 1992—, exec. com., chmn. lit. art in edn. and visual arts panels; bd. trustees, v.p. So. Allegheny Mus. Art, 1992—. Mem. ATLA, Indiana County Bar Assn. (pres. 1995), Pa. Bar Assn., Nat. Sch. Bd. Assn., Coun. Sch. Attys. Avocations: tennis, skiing, collecting art and antiques. Home: 1536 Indian Springs Rd Indiana PA 15701-3223 Office: Tomb Mack & Kauffman McCreary Town House 52 S 9th St Indiana PA 15701-2664

TOMBÁCZ, ETELKA, chemist, educator; b. Szeged, Hungary, Feb. 14, 1952; d. Ferenc Tombácz and Etelka Arany; m. Miklós Csáki, Jan. 16, 1971; 1 child, László. Chemist, Attila József U., Szeged, 1975, D Univ., 1977; PhD, Hungarian Acad. Scis., Budapest, 1986. From rsch. asst. to asst. prof. chemistry Attila József U., 1975-88, assoc. prof. chemistry, 1988—. Contbr. articles to profl. jours. Recipient A. Buzágh prize Hungarian Acad. Scis., 1982. Fellow Internat. Humic Substances Soc. (Hungarian coord. 1997—); mem. Internat. Assn. Colloid and Interface Scientists, Colloid Com. Hungarian Acad. Scis. Home: Tisza Lajos u. 57, H-6725 Szeged Hungary Office: SZTE Dept Colloid Chemistry, Aradi Vt. 1, H-6720 Szeged Hungary

TOMBAUGH, DOROTHY ELVE, retired secondary school educator, author, lecturer; b. Newark, N.Y., Mar. 19, 1917; d. John E. and Edith Deming Elve; m. Roy Wilson Tombaugh, Aug. 10, 1940; children: Sandra Tombaugh Ehrman, Karen Tombaugh Dean. BS, Alfred U., 1938, DSc, 1983; MAT, Siena Heights U., 1965, DHL (hon.), 1982. Cert. med. technologist, Am. Soc. Clin. Pathologists. Med. technologist Rochester (N.Y.) Gen. Hosp., 1938-39, Sage Meml. Hosp., Ganado, Ariz., 1940, Cedars of Lebanon Hosp., L.A., 1941; spectographer, rsch. asst. Applied Rsch. Labs., Glendale, Calif., 1942-44; tchr. chemistry and biology Euclid (Ohio) H.S., 1963-79; lectr. NSF Grant, 1979-81; judge for state and internat. sci. fairs N.E. Ohio, So. Ariz., 1965-98; lectr. NSF Chatauqua for Coll. Tchrs., 1977-80; lectr. in field. Author: Biology for the Blind, 1973; contbr. articles to profl. jours. Troop leader Girl Scouts, Eagle Rock, Calif., 1943-44, Bethel Park, Pa., 1954-55, Dayton, Ohio, 1957-59; deacon Presbyn. Ch., North Elmonte, Calif., 1947-50, Tucson, 1990-93; fin. com. YWCA, Pitts., 1954-56. Named Outstanding Biology Tchr., Nat. Assn. Biology Tchrs., Ohio, 1975. Presbyterian. Avocations: greenhouse and gardening, raising hatchling tortoises. Home: 2341 S Circle X Pl Tucson AZ 85713-6703

TOMBAUGH, RICHARD L., financial aid consultant; b. Warsaw, Ind., Aug. 16, 1938; s. Wayne Hurst and Trella Marie (Kuhn) T.; m. Phyllis Cook, 1960 (div. 1967); children: Brian, Bradley; m. C. Jeannie Tombaugh, Apr. 10, 1976; children: Randall, Meagan. B of Phys. Edn., Purdue U., 1960, MS in Edn., 1961; postgrad. in higher edn., Mich. State U., 1965. Asst. unit mgr. residence halls U. Wis., Madison, 1961-63; asst. dir. admissions, dir. student loans and fin. aid Purdue U., West Lafayette, Ind., 1965-72; from assoc. dir. to dir. fin. aid George Washington U., Washington, 1972-74; exec. sec. Nat. Assn. Student Fin. Aid Adminstrs., Washington, 1972-75; exec. dir. Nat. Inst. Fin. Aid Adminstrn., Washington, 1972-75; pres. Ednl. Methods, Inc., Denver and Washington, 1975-79; v.p. mktg. Sys. Rsch. Inc., Washington and L.A., 1979-80; dir. student fin. assistance tng. program Nat. Assn. Student Fin. Aid Adminstrs., others, 1980-82; sr. program analyst Advanced Tech., Inc., Reston, Va., 1983-84; coord. market devel., mgr. ednl. svcs. Nat. Computer Sys., Inc., Englewood, Colo., 1984-88; cons., dir. need analysis svcs., dir. mktg. CSX Comml. Svcs., Jacksonville,

Fla., 1989-92; pres., CEO, Edn. Fin. Cons. Group, Jacksonville, 1992—. Contbr. articles to profl. publs. Scoutmaster Boy Scouts Am., 1956-60. Mem. Nat. Assn. Student Fin. Aid Adminstrs. (nat. coun. 1968-70, 70-75, Hall of Honor inductee, Disting. Svc. award 1975), Midwest Assn. Student Fin. Aid Adminstrs. (Disting. Svc. award 1975), DC/Del./Md. Assn. Student Fin. Aid Adminstrs. (life), Fla. Assn. Student Fin. Aid Adminstrs. E-mail: rltefcg@sprynet.com. Home: 2311 Barefoot Trce Atlantic Bch FL 32233-6604 Office: Edn Fin Cons Group Inc 6440 Southpoint Pkwy Ste 280 Jacksonville FL 32216-8003

TOMCZUK, BRONISLAW ZBIGNIEW, electrical engineering educator and researcher; b. Prudnik, Poland, Aug. 25, 1953; s. Michal and Adela (Siekierka) T.; m. Elzbieta Lipinska, July 4, 1977; 1 child, Izabela. Engr., Elec. Engring. Tech. Sch., Opole, 1972; MSc, Tech. U. Opole, 1977; PhD, Tech. U. Lodz, Poland, 1985, DSc, 1995. Rsch. and tchg. asst. Opole Poly. Inst., 1978-85; asst. prof. Tech. U. Opole, 1986-95, prof., 1995—, assoc. chmn. elec. engring. and automatic control dept., 1996-99, head elec. engring. group, 1997—. Co-author: Investigations of Electrical Machines and Driving Systems, 1985; contbr. articles to profl. jours.; patentee in field. Mem. N.Y. Acad. Scis., Polish Acad. Scis. (Electronic Commn. of Silesia Dept.), Assn. Polish Elec. Engrs. Avocations: cycling, gardening, travel. Home: Bytnara Rudego 18c/6, 45-265 Opole Silesia, Poland Office: Tech U Opole/Elec Engring, Luboszycka, PL-45036 Opole Poland

TOMCZYK, ANDRZEJ, aviation engineer, educator; b. Koszalin, Poland, Dec. 1, 1945; s. Jan and Karolina (Hylinska) T.; m. Grazyna Grabik; children: Emilia, Krzysztof, Barbara. MSc, Warsaw U. Technology, 1970; PhD, Polish Acad. Sci., 1976; DS, Mil. Acad. Tech., Warsaw, 2000. Designer Aircraft Rsch. & Devel. Ctr., Mielec, Poland, 1970-72; rschr. Polish Acad. Sci., Warsaw, 1972-75; design mgr. Aircraft Rsch. & Devel. Ctr., 1975-76; prof. Rzeszow U. Technology, Poland, 1976—. Author: Digital Flight Control Systems, 1999. Home: Mikolajczyka 12/33, 35-209 Rzeszów Poland

TOMÉ, WOLFGANG AXEL, physicist, researcher, educator; b. Ludwigsburg, Fed. Republic Germany, May 15, 1962; came to U.S., 1987, permanent resident, 1999; s. Kurt Wolfgang and Monika Else (Bub) T.; m. Marie-Jacqueline Lamoth, Aug. 24, 1990; 1 child, Anne-Sophie. Vordiplom in Physik, Eberhard-Karls U., Tuebingen, Fed. Republic of Germany, 1986; MS in Physics, U. Denver, 1989; PhD in Physics, U Fla., 1995. Diplomate Am. Bd. Radiology, Am. Bd. Therapeutic Radiol. Physics. Grad. teaching asst. U. Denver, 1987-89, grad. rsch. asst., 1988; grad. rsch. asst. U. Fla., Gainesville, 1989-95, postdoctoral assoc. in med. physics, 1995-98, asst. prof. Human Oncology, 1998—. Author: Path Integrals on Group Manifolds, 1998; contbr. articles to Founds. of Physics, Jour. Math. Physics, Acta Physics Polonica, Annales Inst. Henri Poincaré, Med. Physics, Internat. Jour. Radiation Oncology, Biology and Physics, others. Doctoral fellow Studienstiftung des deutschen Volkes, 1992; fellow Studienstiftung des deutschen Volkes, 1986. Mem. Am. Soc. for Therapeutic Radiology and Oncology, Am. Assn. Physicists in Medicine, Internat. Assn. Math. Physics, Am. Coll. Med. Physics, Sigma Xi Rsch. Soc., Alpha Nu Sigma, Pi Mu Epsilon, Phi Beta Delta. E-mail: wtomc@facstaff.wisc.edu. Office: U Wis Dept Human Oncology Madison WI 53706

TOMER, GITIT, pediatrician; b. Petach-Tikva, Israel, July 29, 1967; d. Elias and Anna Rosenbach; m. Yaron Tomer, Feb. 7, 1991; children: Nir, Danielle. MD, Tel-Aviv U., 1995. Clin. analyst Israel Def. Forces, 1985-87; resident in pediatrics NYU Med. Ctr., 1995-98, teaching asst. dept. pediatrics, 1997-98; fellow pediatric gastroenterology Mount Sinai Med. Ctr., N.Y.C., 1998—; rsch. fellow The Sambur Ctr. for Pediatric Hematology-Oncology, The Children's Hosp., Petach-Tikva, Israel, 1992-94, Pediatric Liver Rsch. Lab., Mount Sinai Med. Ctr., N.Y.C., 1999—. Contbr. articles to profl. jours. Named dean's list, Technion Sch. of Medicine, Haifa, Israel, 1987-89. Mem. AMA, Am. Acad. Pediatrics, Am. Gastroenterological Assn., N.Am. Soc. for Pediatric Gastroenterology and Nutrition. E-mail: gitit.tomer@mssm.edu. Fax: 212-212-876-5631. Office: Divsn of Pediatric Gastroenterology Mount Sinai Med Ctr One Gustave L Levy Pl New York NY 10029

TOMESCU, IOAN, mathematician, educator; b. Ploiesti, Romania, Nov. 5, 1942; s. Ioan and Virginia (Constantinescu) T.; m. Marioara Dumitru, Nov. 17, 1973; children: Mihaela, Alexandru-Ioan. BA in Computer Sci., U. Bucharest (Romania), 1965, PhD in Computer Sci., 1971. Asst. prof. Faculty of Math., Bucharest, 1965-71, assoc. prof., 1971-90, prof., 1990—, head computer sci. dept., 1990—; sec. commn. exact scis. Nat. Coun. Acad. Accreditation, Bucharest, 1994—; mem. Nat. Commn. for Attestation of U. Degrees and Positions, Bucharest, 1996—; pres. Nat. Com. Mathemat. Olympiads, 1990-94. Author: Introduction to Combinatorics, 1975. Recipient Prize for Applied Maths. First Balkan Math Competition, 1971, prize Romanian Acad. Scis., 1975. Mem. Romanian Soc. Mathemat. Scis. (v.p. 1995-2000), Romanian Mathemat. Soc., Am. Mathemat. Soc., Assn. Computing Machinery. Avocations: mathematical competitions for high school students in Romania. Home: Sos Colentina Nr 4, SC B Apt 64, 72262 Bucharest Romania Office: Facultatea Matematica, Str Academiei 14, 70109 Bucharest Romania

TOMICH, LILLIAN, lawyer; b. L.A.; d. Peter S. and Yovanka P. (Ivanovic) T. AA, Pasadena City Coll., 1954; BA in Polit. Sci., UCLA, 1956, cert. secondary tchg., 1957, MA, 1958; JD, U. So. Calif., 1961. Bar: Calif., U.S. Ct. Appeals (9th Cir.) 1978. Sole practice, 1961-66; house counsel Mfrs. Bank, L.A., 1966; assoc. Hurley, Shaw & Tomich, San Marino, Calif., 1968-76, Driscoll & Tomich, San Marino, 1976—; dir. Continental Culture Specialists Inc., Glendale, Calif. Trustee St. Sava Serbian Orthodox Ch., San Gabriel, Calif. Recipient Episcopal Gramata award Serbian Orthodox Met. of Midwestern Am., 1993, Episcopal Gramata award Serbian Orthodox Bishop of Western Am., 1996; Charles Fletcher Scott fellow, 1957; U. So. Calif. Law Sch. scholar, 1958. Mem. ABA, Calif. Bar Assn., Los Angeles County Bar Assn., Women Lawyers Assn., San Marino C. of C., UCLA Alumni Assn., Town Hall and World Affairs Coun., Order Mast and Dagger, Iota Tau Tau, Alpha Gamma Sigma, Pi Kappa Delta. Office: 2460 Huntington Dr San Marino CA 91108-2643

TOMICH-BOLOGNESI, VERA, educator; b. L.A.; d. Peter S. and Yovanka (Ivanovich) T.; m. Gino Bolognesi, July 12, 1969. AA, John Muir Jr. Coll., Pasadena, Calif., 1951; BA in Polit. Sci., UCLA, 1953, MEd, 1955, EdD, 1960. Cert. secondary tchr., Calif.; cert. secondary sch. adminstrn., Calif.; cert. jr. coll. tchr., Calif. Tchg. asst. dept. edn. UCLA, 1956; tchr., dept. chmn. Culver City (Calif.) Unified Sch. Dist., 1956-91; rschr., writer U.S. Dept. Edn., Washington, 1961, del. to Yugoslavia, 1965; co-owner, exec. Metrocolor Engring., San Gabriel, Calif., 1973—; cons., Continental Culture Specialists, Inc., Glendale, Calif., 1985-92; rsch. asst. Law Firm of Driscoll & Tomich, San Marino, Calif., 1989—. Author: Education in Yugoslavia and the New Reform, 1963, Higher Education and Teacher Training in Yugoslavia, 1967; screenplay editor 1996—. Bd. trustees St. Sava Serbian Orthodox Ch., San Gabriel, 1975-95, mem., 1960—. Recipient Episcopal Gramata, Serbian Orthodox Ch. of Western Am., 1996; named in Outstanding Young Women of Am., 1966. Mem. NEA (life), Calif. Tchrs. Assn., UCLA Alumni Assn., Alpha Gamma Sigma, Pi Lambda Theta. Home: 100 E Roses Rd San Gabriel CA 91775-2343 Office: Metrocolor Engring 5110 Walnut Grove Ave San Gabriel CA 91776-2026

TOMILOV, ANDREY PETROVICH, electrochemist, consultant; b. Kirov, Russia, Apr. 24, 1926; s. Petr Andreevich and Elizaveta Mikhailovna (Lihanova) T.; m. Taisiya Vasilevna Gladicheva, Sept. 3, 1954; children: Tatiana, Natalia. Grad., Coll. Airplane Constrn., Kirov, Russia, 1947; Engr., Mendeleevs Inst. Chemical Tech., Moscow, 1952; D Tech. Sci., Moscow, 1966. Scientist State Rsch. Inst. Organic Chemistry and Tech., Moscow, 1952-60; head of lab. Inst. Organic Chemistry and Tech., Moscow, 1960-92, main sci. worker, 1992—; cons. to industry, Ufa, Volgograd, Dzerzhinsk, Russia, 1960-90. Co-author: The Electrochemistry of Organic Compounds, 1968, The Electrochemical Synthesis of Organic Substances, 1972, Electrochemistry of Elementoorganic Organic Compounds I, II, 1985, 86; contbr. articles to sci. jours. Named Honored Chemist, Ministry of Chemistry, 1976; recipient Lenin Prize, 1971. Mem. Sciential Soviet Electrochemistry, Russian Acad. Scis. (mem. presidium coun. on electrochemistry organic compounds), Internat. Slovonic Acad. Orthodox Chrisitian. Office: Inst Organic Chemistry/Tech, sh Entuziastov 23, 111024 Moscow Russia

TOMINAGA, SHIN-ICHI, biochemist, educator; b. Yokohama, Kanagawa, Japan, Dec. 13, 1951; s. Hiroyuki and Noriko T.; m. Kazue Yamagata, Oct. 10, 1978; children: Naoko, Kei-ichiro, Tomokazu. MD, U. Tokyo, 1976, PhD, 1982. Physician Jichi Med. Sch. Hosp., Tochigi, Japan, 1976-78; asst. prof. Inst. Med. Sci., U. Tokyo, 1982-83; assoc. rsch. scientist Yale U., New Haven, 1983-85; sr. rsch. scientist Okinaka Meml. Inst. Med. Rsch., Tokyo, 1986-90; assoc. prof. biochemistry Jichi Med. Sch., Tochigi, 1990-96, prof. and chmn. dept. biochemistry, 1996—. Mem. Japanese Biochem. Soc., Japan Soc. for Cell Biology, Internat. Soc. for Interferon and Cytokine Rsch., N.Y. Acad. Sci. Office: Jichi Med Sch, 3311-1 Yakushiji, Minamikawachi-machi Kawachi-gun Tochigi 329-0498, Japan

TOMIOKA, NOBORU, molecular biologist, researcher; b. Ko-chi City, Japan, Dec. 22, 1949; s. Ryoutaro and Tokiko Tomioka; m. Junko Mita, June 12, 1983; children: Naoko, Hirotsugu, Ryou. BSc, U. Hiroshima, Japan, 1974, MSc, 1976, PhD, 1982. Cert. H.S. sci. tchr. Rsch. scientist Mitsui-Toatsu Chem. Inc., Yokohama, Japan, 1981-85; sr. rsch. scientist Mitsui-Toatsu Chem. Inc., Mobara, Japan, 1985-86, Mitsui Chems., Inc., Mobara, Japan, 1997—; rsch. fellow Nat. Inst. Genetics, Mishima, Japan, 1980-82, City of Hope, Duarte, Calif., 1983-84, Inst. Med. Sci., Tokyo U., 1991-93. Contbr. articles to profl. jours. Mem. AAAS, Japanese Soc. Hematology, Molecular Biology Soc. Japan. Avocations: skiing, baseball. Office: Mitsui Chems Inc, Life Sci Lab, 1144 Togo, Mobara City 297-0017, Japan

TOMITA, AKIHIKO, astronomer; b. Osaka, Japan, Nov. 7, 1967; m. Yuko T. Hanba. DSc, Kyoto (Japan) U., 1996. Rsch. fellow Kyoto (Japan) U. Dept. Astronomy, 1995-96, U. Tokyo Inst. Astronomy, 1996-97; asst. prof. Wakayama (Japan) U., 1997-99, assoc. prof., 1999—. Contbr. articles to profl. jours. Mem. Astron. Soc. Japan, Astron. Soc. Pacific. Office: Wakayama U, 930 Sakaedani, Wakayama 640-8510, Japan

TOMIYA, TOMOAKI, internist, gastroenterologist, medical educator; b. Tokyo, Aug. 22, 1959; s. Isamu and Emiko (Inoue) T. MD, U. Tokyo, 1984, PhD, 1997. Resident U. Tokyo Hosp., 1984-85; med. staff Toshiba Hosp., Tokyo, 1985-86; resident Nat. Oji Hosp., Tokyo, 1986-87; sr. resident assocs. U. Tokyo Hosp., 1987-93; physician, dept. gastroenterology Nat. Med. Ctr. Japan, Tokyo, 1993-94; assoc., 1st dept. internal medicine U. Tokyo, 1994—. Contbr. articles to med. jours. Avocations: golf, skiing, travel.

TOMJANOVICH, RUDOLPH, professional athletic coach; b. Hamtramck, Mich., Nov. 24, 1948. Scout Houston Rockets, 1981-83, asst. coach, 1983-92, head coach, 1992—. Named to Sporting News All-Am. first team, 1970; coach NBA championship team, 1994-95. Office: Houston Rockets Two Greenway Plz Ste 400 Houston TX 77046-3865

TOMKA, PETER, Slovakian diplomat; b. Banská, Bystrica, Slovakia, June 1, 1956; s. Ján and Kornélia (Plai) T.; m. Zuzana Halgasová, June 30, 1990. Grad., Charles U., Prague, Czechoslovakia, 1979; PhD in Internat. Law, Charles U., 1985. Lectr. Law Sch., Charles U., Prague, 1980-86, assoc. lectr. in internat. law, 1986-91; asst. legal advisor Fed. Ministry of Fgn. Affairs, Czechoslovakia, 1986-90, head pub. internat. law divsn., 1990-91; counsellor, legal advisor Permanent Mission to UN, N.Y.C., 1991-92, amb., dep. permanent rep. of Slovakia, 1993-97, charge d'affaires, 1994-97; legal advisor Ministry Fgn. Affairs, Bratislava, Slovakia, 1997-98, dir. gen. legal and consular affairs, 1998-99; permanent rep. of Slovakia to UN, N.Y.C., 1999—; agt. of Slovakia Internat. Ct. of Justice in Gabcikovo-Nagymaros Project Case, Hungary/Slovakia; mem. Permanent Ct. Arbitration, 1995; chmn. UN Legal Com., 1997; vice chair com. legal advisors Coun. of Europe, 1998-99; mem. UN Internat. Law Commn., 1999—, vice chmn., 2000. Office: Perm Mission of Slovakia UN 866 U N Plz Rm 494 New York NY 10017-1822

TOMKINSON, ROBERT CHARLES, financial executive; b. Belfast, No. Ireland, July 14, 1941; s. William Robert and Helen Mary (Blane) T.; m. Joanna Sally Hastings, June 15, 1968; children: James Robert, Simon William. Grad., Oxford U., 1963. Chartered acct. Articled clk. Ball Baker Deed & Co., London, 1963-66; mgr. Peat Marwick Mitchell & Co., London, 1966-75; dep. mng. dir. Scrimgeour Hardcastle & Co. Ltd., London, 1975-79, Overseas Coal Devels. Ltd., London, 1979-8l; fin. dir. Intercontinental Fuels Ltd., London, 1979-8l, Automotive Products Plc, Leamington, Eng., 1982-86, Electro Components Plc, London, 1986-97; chmn. Pitards Plc, 1997—; deputy chmn. Lloyd Thompson, London, 1987—; chmn. coun. U. Buckingham, 1997—. Fellow Inst. Chartered Accts in Eng. and Wales, Corp. Treas. Inst., Boodles Club. Mem. Conservative Party. Mem. Ch. of England. Avocations: fishing, riding, skiing. Home and Office: Home Farm, Wappenham, Towcester NN12 8SJ, England

TOMKO, JOZEF CARDINAL, archbishop; b. Udavské, Slovak Republic, Mar. 11, 1924. STD, Lateran U., Rome, 1951, JCD, 1962; ScSocD, Gregorian U., Rome, 1955; PhD, Fu Yen U., Taipeh, Taiwan. Ordained priest Roman Cath. Ch., 1949. Consecrated archbishop Titular See Doclea, 1979; proclaimed cardinal, 1985; prefect congregation for Evangelization of Peoples. Address: Villa Betania, Via Urbano VIII 16, 00165 Rome Italy Address: Via della Conciliazione 44, 00193 Rome Italy*

TOMKOS, IOANNIS, research scientist, communications educator; b. Athens, Greece, Mar. 15, 1973; s. Vagelis and Despina (Tsivitzi) T. BSc in Physics, U. Parma, Greece, 1994; MSc, U. Athens, 1996, postgrad., 1998—. Rschr. U. Paris, 1996; prof. Tech. Sch., Athens, 1996—; rschr. U. Athens, 1996—; cons. in field. Contbr. articles to profl. jours. Hellenic Nat. Inst. Scholarships grant, 1991-93. Mem. IEEE, Greek Physicist Union. Greek Orthodox.

TOMKOW, GWEN ADELLE, artist; b. Detroit, May 16, 1932; d. Galen A. and Edythe Christine (Barr) Roberts; m. Michael Tomkow, Nov. 14, 1953; children: Eric Michael, Thomas Edward, Nikola Christine, Kit Adair. A of Bus., Detroit Bus. Inst., 1952; student, Birmingham Bloomfield Art Assn., Assn., Mich., 1985-87, Visual Art Assn., Livonia, Mich., 1984-89. Tchr. watercolor Visual Art Assn., Livonia, 1989-2000; tchr. workshop Ella Sharp Mus. Jackson Civic Art, Mich., 1996; tchr. watercolor workshop Village Fine Art Assn., Milford, Mich., 1996; slide lectr. Livonia Artist Club, 1995, Palette and Brush Club, Southfield, Mich., 1995, Pontiac (Mich.) Oakland Artists, 1995, Ea. Mich. U. Watercolor Soc., 1994; tchr. watercolor workshop Ann Arbor Women Painters U. Mich. Art Sch., 1997; slide lectr. Western Ohio Water Color Soc., 1999; artist-in-residence Farmington Art Commn., Farmington Hills, 1988; slide lectr. Springfield (Ohio) Art Mus. Contbr. articles and photos to books, including: The Artistic Touch, 1994-95, The Artistic Touch 2, 1996, The Artistic Touch, 1999, Splash 3, 1994-95, Splash 4, 1996, Exploring Color, (by Nita Leland) 1998; also Watercolor edit., Am. Artist Mag., 1991; exhbns. include Cary Gallery, 1995, 97, Joppich's Bay St. of Northport, 1988-98, 2000, Art Corridor, 1998; represented in permanent collections E. Carothers Dunnegan Gallery of Art Mus. Recipient Purchase awards U.S.A. Springfield (Mo.) Art Mus., 1990, 93, 94, Watercolor U.S.A., 1999, 1st prize Helen de Roy Competition, Oakland C.C., Farmington, Mich., 1988, 92, Grumbacher Gold medal Farmington Artists Club, Farmington Hills, Mich., 1995, 98. Mem. Nat. Watercolor Soc. (signature, Alex Nepote Meml. award 1998), Mich. Watercolor Soc. (Meml. award 1992), Farmington Art Assn. (pres. 1987-89), Detroit Soc. Women Painters Sculptors (sec. 1994-95, award 1999), Palette and Brush (v.p. 1982-83), Founders Soc. Detroit Inst. Arts, Nat. Mus. Women in the Arts. Presbyterian. Avocations: tennis, golf, choir singer, theater.

TOMLINSON, JAMES LAWRENCE, mechanical engineer; b. Detroit, Sept. 12, 1935; s. James Emmet and Ethel Pearl (Williams) T.; m. Marilyn Joyce Peterson, Aug. 24, 1957; children: James, Mary, Robert, Susan. BSME, Mich. Tech., 1957. Registered profl. engr., Mich. Design engr. Buick Motor div. GMC, Flint, Mich., 1960-61, project engr., 1961-66, sr. project engr., 1966-71; staff analysis engr. GM Corp., Warren, Mich., 1971-82, sr. staff analysis engr., 1983-88; pres. Eastport (Mich.) Engring., 1989—. Mayor City of Grand Blanc, 1985-89, city councilman, 1969-84, police liaison/commr., 1971-82, planning adv. bd., 1978-80, planning commn., 1985-89; nat. coun. mem. Boy Scouts Am., 1979-90, 93—, regional bd. mem., 1995—, coun. commr., 1979-84, coun. v.p., 1984—, nat. camp sch. staff, 1986-88, regional camp inspector/accreditation team, 1988—; vice chmn. Genesee County Sml. Cities and Villages Assn., 1986, chmn., 1987; bd. dirs. Three Lakes Assn., Inc., 1997—. Capt. USAF, 1958-60. Recipient Silver Beaver Tall Pine coun. Boy Scouts Am., 1980, Silver Antelope Ctrl. region, 1996. Mem. NSPE (treas. Flint chpt. 1968-72, Engr. of the Yr. Flint chpt. 1990), SAE (mem. com. 1992-94, 96-98), ASME (exec. bd. Saginaw Valley chpt. 1968-70), Friends of Torch Lake Twp., Inc. (pres. 1994—). Mem. Congl. Ch. Home: PO Box 25 Eastport MI 49627-0025

TOMLINSON, MARGARET LYNCH, lawyer; b. Cleve., June 21, 1929; d. John Joseph and Margaret (Stevenson) Lynch; m. Alexander C. Tomlinson. AB, Smith Coll., 1950; JD, N.Y. Law Sch., 1963. Bar: N.Y. 1963, D.C. 1971, U.S Ct. Appeals (D.C. cir.) 1971. Staff officer Dept. of State, 1950-55; U.S. Del. UN Gen. Assembly, N.Y.C., 1964-68; asst. legal adviser U.S. Mission to the UN, 1963-69; asst. to Sen. Claiborne Pell, Washington, 1969-71; sr. adviser U.S. Del. to the Law of the Sea Conf., 1972-78; ptnr. Dickey, Roadman & Dickey, Washington, 1978-82; cons. office gen. counsel CIA, Washington, 1987-93; cons. Law of the Sea; bd. dirs. Coun. Ocean Law, Washington, 1984—, vice-chmn., 1994—; U.S. del. spl. session UN Gen. Assembly, 1994. Contbr. articles to profl. jours. Mem. ABA (internat. law sect., chmn. law of the sea com.), Am. Soc. Internat. Law, Internat. Law Assn., D.C. Bar Assn., Nat. Press Club, Sulgrave Club. Home: 3314 P St NW Washington DC 20007-2701

TOMLINSON, MICHAEL JOHN, British education official; b. Rotherham, Yorkshire, Eng., Oct. 17, 1942; s. Jack and Edith (Cresswell) T.; m. Maureen Janet Tupling, July 17, 1965; children: Philip John, Jane Louise. BS, Durham (Eng.) U., 1964; postgrad. cert. in edn., Nottingham (Eng.) U., 1965. Chemistry tchr. Henry Mellish Grammar Sch., Nottingham, Eng., 1965-69; head chemistry Ashby Grammar Sch., Leicestershire, Eng., 1969-77; insp. schs. Her Majesty's Govt., Eng., 1978-92; dep. dir. inspection Office for Stds. in Edn., London, 1992-94, dir. inspection, 1995—. Recipient Queen's Silver Jubilee medal, 1977, Chem. Edn. medal Royal Soc. Chemistry; Comdr. Order Br. Empire, 1997. Avocations: gardening, food, drink. Office: Office for Stds in Edn, Alexandra Ho 33 Kingsway, London WC2B 6SE, England

TOMMASINO, CONCEZIONE, anesthesiologist; b. Sessa Aurunca, Italy, Oct. 18, 1950; d. Virginio and Elisabetta (Rea) T.; m. Piero Picozzi, Sept. 10, 1986; children: Valentina, Michele. MD, U. Naples, 1975. Rschr. U. Naples, Italy, 1980-88; assoc. rschr. U. San Diego, 1980-84; asst. prof. U. Milan, Italy, 1988—. Roman Catholic. Avocations: opera, classical music, skiing, travel. Office: San Raffaele U Hosp, Via Olgettina 60, 20132 Milan Italy

TOMODA, HIROSHI, educational administrator, researcher; b. Kanazawa, Japan, Jan. 6, 1955; s. Yoshio and Kimiko (Ishida) Horiuchi; m. Atsuko Kimita, Oct. 25, 1980; 1 child, Yosuke. B, U. Tokyo, 1978, M, 1980, PhD, 1983. Rschr. The Kitasato Inst., Tokyo, 1983-85, 1985-97; chief rschr. postdoctoral Johns Hopkins U., Balt., 1987-89; dir. The Kitasato Inst., 1997—; assoc. prof. Kitasato U., 1997—. Inventor, patentee in field. Recipient Sumiki-Umezawa prize Japan Antibiotics Assn., Tokyo, 1997. Mem. Johns Hopkins Soc. Scholars. Avocations: baseball, tennis. Home: 3-71-11-211 Shimoishihara, Chofu, Tokyo 182-0034, Japan Office: The Kitasato Inst, 5-9-1 Shirokane, Tokyo 108-8642, Japan

TOMOEDA, CHERYL KUNIKO, academic researcher; b. Honolulu, Sept. 24, 1958; d. Charles Kunio and Doris Masue (Takehara) T. BS, U. Hawaii, 1980; MS, U. Ariz., 1982. Cert. speech-lang. pathology. Speech pathologist Amphitheater Pub. Schs., Tucson, 1983-84; rsch. asst. U. Ariz., Tucson, 1982-83, rsch. asst. II, 1984-86, rsch. coord., 1985-91, sr. rsch. specialist, 1991—. Author: (test) Ariz. Battery for Comm. Disorders of Dementia, 1991, The Functional Linguistic Communication Inventory, 1994, (book) The ABC/s of Dementia, 1993, Improving Function in Dementia, 1997; prodr. videoconf. series Telerounds. Recipient U. Ariz. Asian Am. Faculty, Staff and Alumni Assn. award, 1999, Cert. of Recognition for spl. contbns. in multicultural affairs Am. Speech-Lang.-Hearing Assn., 2000. Mem. Acad. Neurologic Communication Disorders and Scis. (acting sec. 1991, sec. 1992-93), Internat. Neuropsychol. Soc., Am. Speech-Lang.-Hearing Assn. Office: U Ariz Nat Ctr Neurogenic Comm Disorders Dept Speech & Hearing Scis Tucson AZ 85721-0001

TOMOMATSU, ATSUNOBU, international development specialist, educator, consultant; b. Nagoya, Aichi, Japan, Nov. 21, 1948; s. Chiyoichi and Haruko (Mizutani) T.; m. Hideka Tanaka, Feb. 8, 1987; children: Masae, Kiyo, Satoe. BS, Saitama U., Urawa, Japan, 1973; MS, Nagoya (Japan) U., 1975, D in Agr., 1980. Rsch. assoc. Japan Sci. Promotion Soc., Tokyo, 1979-80; asst. prof. Nagoya U., 1980-81; tech. cooperation expert Japan Internat. Cooperation Agency, Bogor, Indonesia, 1980-83; agrl. devel. specialist Japan Internat. Cooperation Agency, Tokyo, 1984-91; rsch. fellow Internat. Food Policy Rsch. Inst., Washington, 1986-88; assoc. prof. Utsunomiya (Japan) U., 1991-94, prof., 1994—. Author, editor: International Cooperation for Agricultural Development in Developing Countries, 1994; contbr. articles to profl. jours. Bd. trustees Soc. Agrl. Edn. Rsch. Devel. Abroad, Tokyo, 1995; councilor Japanese Soc. Regional and Agrl. Devel., Tokyo, 1995. Mem. Tropical Agr. Rsch. Assn. Japan, Japan Soc. Internat. Devel., Soc. Internat. Devel. Fax: 028-649-5193. Office: Utsunomiya Univ, Mine Machi 350, Utsunomiya Tochigi 321 8505, Japan

TOMOMATSU, HIDEO, chemist; b. Tokyo, June 8, 1929; came to U.S., 1959; s. Shinsai Nasu and Suma T.; m. Yuko Ito, Nov. 12, 1967; 1 child, Tadao. BSChemE., Waseda U., 1952; MS in Chemistry, U. of the Pacific, 1960; PhD in Chemistry, Ohio State U., 1964. Registered profl. engr., Tex., U.S. patent agt. Chem. Hodogaya Chem. Co., Tokyo, 1952-59, Texaco Chems. Co., Austin, Tex., 1964-72; Quaker fellow Quaker Oats Co., Barrington, Ill., 1972-96; cons. Functional Food Resources, Inc., Escondido, Calif., 1996—. Contbr. articles to profl. jours.; patentee in field. Mem. Am. Chem. Soc., Am. Assn. Cereal Chemists, Inst. Food Technologists. Home: 2555 Seascape Gln Escondido CA 92026-3862

TOMONAGA, SUSUMU, anatomy educator; b. Yamaguchi, Japan, Feb. 14, 1939; s. Nobuichi and Tomiko Tomonaga; m. Hideko Tomonaga, May 17, 1966; children: Atsuko, Junko, Izumi. BS, Yamaguchi (Japan) U., 1962, DMS, 1973. Asst. prof. Yamaguchi U., 1966-69, lectr., 1969-76, assoc. prof., 1976-81, prof., 1981—; rsch. fellow Australian Nat. U., Canberra, 1973-75. Recipient Nakamura award Yamaguchi U. Sch. Medicine, Ube, 1980. Mem. Internat. Soc. Devel. and Comparative Immunology, Histochem. Soc. (U.S.), N.Y. Acad. Scis., Japanese Assn. for Devel. and Comparative Immunology. Home: 2-16-9 Minami-Obayama, Ube, Yamaguchi 755-0083, Japan Office: Yamaguchi U, Sch Allied Health Scis, 1-1-1 Minami-Kogushi, Yamaguchi 775-8554, Japan

TOMOV, BORIS IVANOV, rector, mechanical engineer, educator; b. Rousse, Bulgaria, Apr. 1, 1940; s. Ivan Tomov and Iordanka Tzoneva (Karaivanova) Doncheva; m. Stefka Petkova Stefanova, Sept. 11, 1971; children: Ivan, Tzveta. M in Engring., Tech. U., Rousse, 1965; PhD, Tech. U., Warsaw, 1973. Designer P. Karaminchev Plant, Rousse, 1966-68; asst. U. Rousse, 1968-83, assoc. prof., 1983—, pro-dean, 1987-89, dean faculty, 1989-93, pro-rector, 1993, rector, 1993—. Recipient Golden Badge, Com. Sci. Tech., 1976. Mem. Bulgarian Scientific Soc., Polish Soc. Material Sci. Office: U Rousse, 8 Studentska Str, 7017 Rousse Bulgaria

TOMOVIC, MILETA MILOS, mechanical engineer, educator; b. Belgrade, Yugoslavia, Dec. 29, 1955; came to U.S., 1979; naturalized, 1995; s. Milos Nedeljko and Danica Dane (Lemaic) T.; m. Cynthia Lou Bell, Apr. 15, 1994; children: Adriane, Milos, Senja. BS, U. Belgrade, 1979; MS, MIT, 1981; PhD, U. Mich., 1991. Rsch. asst. MIT, Cambridge, Mass., 1979-81, 83-85; design engr. Foundry Belgrade, 1982-83; sys. engr. Energoproject, Belgrade, 1985-86; assoc. prof. Purdue U., West Lafayette, Ind., 1991—; v.p. Metalcasting Engring., Inc., 1996—; cons. Tech. Assistance Program, 1993—; mem. adv. bd. Engineered Casting Solutions. Assoc. editor Foundry, 1995—, also conf. procs. in field; author textbook on materials and mfg. processes. Grantee Purdue Rsch. Found., 1994, 95; named Key prof. Foundry Edn. Found., 1991—. Mem. ASME (chpt. bd. dirs. 1993-95), Am. Soc. Metals (chpt. chmn. 1994-95), Am. Soc. Engring. Educators, Am.

Foundrymen Soc. (chpt. bd. dirs. 1995—). Christian Orthodox. Achievements include patents in areas of metalcasting refiner plates for pulp and paper industry, mill balls for cement and metal extraction industry; research on wear and impact resistant materials, new metalcasting technologies, welding processes. Avocations: tennis, skiing, swimming. Home: 3344 Dubois St West Lafayette IN 47906-1199 Office: Purdue U MET Dept Knoy Hall West Lafayette IN 47907

TOMPA, GABOR, theatre director; b. Tirgu Mures, Romania, Aug. 8, 1957; s. Miklos and Gabriella (Mende) T.; children: Eszter, Abel. Dir. Hungarian Theatre, Cluj, Romania, 1981-90; assoc. prof. Theatre Acad., Tirgu Mures, 1990-94; full prof. Theatre Acad. Cluj, 1991—; artistic dir. Hungarian Theatre, 1990—.

TOMPERT, JAMES EMIL, lawyer; b. Battle Creek, Mich., July 21, 1954; s. James Russell and Marjorie Mary (Storkan) T. BA, Duke U., 1976; JD, U. Mich., 1981. Bar: D.C. 1981, Md. 1985, Va. 1986. Legis. asst. to congressman U.S. Ho. of Reps., Washington, 1977-78; assoc. Baker & Hostetler, Washington, 1981-84; assoc. Cooter & Gell, Washington, 1984-86, ptnr., 1987-94; ptnr. Cooter Mangold Tompert & Wayson PLLC, Washington, 1995—. Mem. Arts Club Washington, 1989—, Univ. Club of Washington, 1997—. Mem. ABA, D.C. Bar Assn. Office: Cooter Mangold Tompert & Wayson PLLC 5301 Wisconsin Ave NW Washington DC 20015-2015

TOMPKINS, CURTIS JOHNSTON, university president; b. Roanoke, Va., July 14, 1942; s. Joseph Buford and Rebecca (Johnston) T.; m. Mary Katherine Hasle, Sept. 5, 1964; children: Robert, Joseph, Rebecca. BS, Va. Poly. Inst., 1965, MS, 1967; PhD, Ga. Inst. Tech., 1971. Indsl. engr. E.I. DuPont de Nemours, Richmond, Va., 1965-67; instr. Sch. Indsl. and Systems Engring., Ga. Inst. Tech., Atlanta, 1968-71; assoc. prof. Colgate Darden Grad. Sch. Bus. Adminstrn., U. Va., Charlottesville, 1971-77; prof., chmn. dept. indsl. engring. W.Va. U., Morgantown, 1977-80, dean Coll. Engring., 1980-91; pres. Mich. Technol. U., Houghton, 1991—, also bd. dirs.; mem. engring. accreditation commn. Accreditation Bd. for Engring. and Tech., 1981-86; mem. exec. bd. Engring. Deans Coun., 1985-89, vice chmn., 1987-89; mem. engring. adv. com., chmn. of planning com. NSF, 1988-91, chm. Mich. Univs. pres. coun., 1996-98; bd. dirs. Oak Ridge Assoc. Univs., 1996-99, Mich. Technologies, Inc., 1998-99; Pres. Coun. Assn. Governing bds. 1996—, Gov's. Workforce Commn., 1996-99; mem. engring. adv. bd. U. Cin., 1996—. Author: (with L.E. Grayson) Management of Public Sector and Nonprofit Organizations, 1983, (with others) Maynard's Industrial Engineering Handbook, 1992; contbr. chpt. to Ency. of Profl. Mgmt, 1978, 83. Co-chmn. W.Va. Gov.'s Coun. on Econ. Devel.; bd. dirs. Pub. Land Corp. W.Va., 1980-89; mem. faculty Nat. Acad. Voluntarism, United Way Am., 1976-91; mem. Morgantown Water Commn., 1981-87, Morgantown Utility Bd., 1987-91; mem. steering com. W.Va. Conf. on Environ., 1985-89; chmn. Monogalia County United Way, 1989-90; campaign chmn. Copper Country United Way, 1995-96. Named to Com. of 100 Va. Tech. Coll., Disting. Alumni Acad. dept. indsl. engring; recipient Frank and Lillian Gilbreth Indsl. Engring. award Inst. Indsl. Engrs., 1998. Fellow Inst. Indsl. Engrs. (life mem., trustee 1983-90, pres. 1988-89), Am. Soc. Engring. Edn. (pres. 1990-91), Mich. Soc. Profl. Engrs.; mem. Am. Assn. Engring. Soc. (bd. govs. 1987-90, exec. com. 1987-90, sec.-treas. 1989-90), Jr. Engring. Tech. Soc. (bd. dirs. 1988-91), Nat. Soc. for Sci., Tech. and Society (bd. dirs. 1991-94), Internat. Hall of Fame of Sci. and Engring. (hon. trustee), Ga. Tech. Coll. Engring. Disting. Alumni Acad., Ga. Tech. Sch. Indsl. and Sys. Engring. Disting. Alumni Acad., W.Va. U. Dept. Indsl. Engring. Disting. Alumni Acad. (hon.), Mich. C. of C. (bd. dirs 1997—), Blue Key (hon.), Sigma Xi, Phi Kappa Phi, Tau Beta Pi, Alpha Pi Mu. Methodist. Home: 2 Woodland Rd Houghton MI 49931-9746 Office: Mich Technol U 1400 Townsend Dr Houghton MI 49931-1200

TOMPKINS, RAYMOND EDGAR, lawyer; b. Oklahoma City, July 13, 1934; s. Charles Edgar and Eva Mae (Hodges) T.; m. Sue Anne Sharpe, June 10, 1963; children: Matthew Stephen, Christopher T., Katherine Anne. BS, Okla. State U., 1956; JD, U. Okla., 1963. Bar: Okla. 1963, U.S. Dist. Ct. (no. dist.) Okla. 1963, U.S. Dist. Ct. (we. dist.) Okla. 1964, U.S. Ct. Appeals (10th cir.) 1965, U.S. Supreme Ct. 1968, U.S. dist. Ct. (ea. dist.) Okla. 1969, U.S. Ct. Appeals (9th cir.) 1981, U.S. Ct. Appeals (4th cir.) 1986. Adminstrv. asst. U.S. Congress, 1966-68; ptnr. Linn & Helms, Oklahoma City, 1980-90, Daughery, Bradford, Haught & Tompkins, P.C., Oklahoma City, 1990-94; shareholder Conner & Winters, P.C., Oklahoma City, 1994—; mediator and arbitrator Nat. Assn. Securities Dealers. Past chmn. bd. trustees Okla. Ann. Methodist Conf., St. Luke's United Meth. Ch.; past chmn. adminstrv. bd.; mem. Okla. Bur. Investigation Commn., past chmn.; past gen. counsel Rep. State com., Interstate Oil Compact. Maj. USAR. Recipient award of Honor Oklahoma City Bi-Centennial Commn., 1976. Master William S. Holliway Am. Inns of Ct. (emeritus, pres.), Robert J. Turner Am. Inn of Ct.; mem. ABA, Okla. County Bar Assn. (Pres.'s award 1988), Okla. Bar Assn. (chmn. bench & bar com. 1995-97, Law Day award), Am. Arbitration Assn. (mediator/arbitrator), NASD (mediator, arbitrator), Am. Judicature Soc., Assn. Atty.-Mediators (pres. Okla. chpt., panel mem.), Blue Key, Lions (pres. Oklahoma City chpt.). Home: 329 NW 40th St Oklahoma City OK 73118-8419 Office: 211 N Robinson Ave Ste 1700 Oklahoma City OK 73102-7136

TOMS, KATHLEEN MOORE, nurse; b. San Francisco, Dec. 31, 1943; d. William Moore and Phyllis Josephine (Barry) Stewart; m. Benjamin Peskoff; children from previous marriage: Kathleen Marie Toms Myers, Kelly Therese Shaver. AA, City Coll., San Francisco, 1963; BPS in Nursing Edn., Elizabethtown (Pa.) Coll., 1973; MS in Edn., Temple U., 1977; MS in Nursing, Gwynedd Mercy Coll., 1988; grad., U.S. Army War Coll., 1999. RN, Calif. Med.-surg. nurse St. Joseph Hosp., Fairbanks, Alaska, 1963-65; emergency rm. nurse St. Joseph Hosp., Lancaster, Pa., 1965-69, blood, plasma and components nurse, 1969-71; pres. F.E. Barry Co., Lancaster, 1971—; dir. insvc. edn. Lancaster Osteo. Hosp., 1971-75; coord. practical nursing program Vocat. Tech. Sch., Coatesville, Pa., 1976-77; dir. nursing Pocopson Home, West Chester, Pa., 1978-80, Riverside Hosp., Wilmington, Del., 1980-83; assoc. Coatesville VA Hosp., 1983-89, chief nurse, 1984-89; with VA Ctrl. Office; supr. psychiat. nursing Martinez (Calif.) VA Med. Ctr., 1989-94; assoc. chief nursing svc. edn. VA Ho. Calif. Sys. Clinics, Pleasant Hill, 1994—; nurse mgr. VA Ctr. Rehab. and Extended Care, Martinez, 1996—; trainee assoc. chief Nursing Home Care Unit, Washington; mem. Pa. Gov.'s Coun. on Alcoholism and Drug Abuse, 1974-76; mem. Del. Health Coun. Med.-Surg. Task Force, 1981-83; dir. Lancaster Cmty. Health Ctr., 1973-76; lectr. in field. Col. Nurse Corps, USAR. Decorated Army Commendation medals (5), Meritorious Svc. medals (2); recipient Cmty. Svc. award Citizens United for Better Pub. Rels., 1974; award Sertoma, Lancaster, 1974; Outstanding Citizen award Sta. WGAL-TV, 1975; U.S. Army Achievement award, 1983. Mem. Elizabethtown U. Alumni Assn., Temple U. Alumni Assn., Pa. Nurses Assn. (bd. dirs. 1972-76), Sigma Theta Tau, Beta Gamma. Achievements include invention of auto-infuser for blood or blood components. Home: 208 Sea Mist Dr Vallejo CA 94591-7748 Office: VA No Calif Sys of Clinics 2350 Contra Costa Blvd Pleasant Hill CA 94523-3930 also: VA No Calif Health Care Sys Ctr Rehab & Extended Care 150 Muir Rd Martinez CA 94553-4668

TOMS, MICHAEL ANTHONY, broadcast journalist, editor, writer, producer; b. Washington, June 7, 1940; s. Austin Herman Toms and Margaret Dorothy (Pitcher) Slavinsky; m. Justine Willis, Dec. 16, 1972; children: Michael Anthony, Robert Welch. Student, U. Miami, 1959-60, U. Va. Extension, 1961-63; postgrad., Calif. Inst. Integral Studies, San Francisco, 1973-75; DrTheology, Sem. St. Basil the Great, Sydney, Australia, 1981; DHL (hon.), U. Humanistic Studies, San Diego, 1983. Field govt. rep. VariTyper Corp., Washington, 1960-64; sales mgr. VariTyper Corp., San Francisco, 1964-67; regional sales mgr. VariTyper Corp., San Bernardino, 1967-68; pres. Creative Mktg. Assocs., San Francisco, 1968-73; chmn. bd. The Response Mktg. Group, San Francisco, 1971-73; CEO Michael A. Toms & Assocs., San Francisco, 1973-76; pres. New Dimensions Found., San Francisco, 1973—; sr. acquisitions editor Harper Collins, San Francisco, 1989-95; exec. prodr., host nat. pub. radio interview series New Dimensions, 1980—, on-line radio series Spirit of the Times, 1999—; chmn. bd. emeritus Calif. Inst. Integral Studies, San Francisco, 1979-83; exec. dir. Audio Inds., Inc., San Francisco, 1981-83; adj. prof. Marylhurst Coll. Grad. Sch. of Bus., 1993—, Union Grad. Sch., 1994—; founder, CEO New Dimensions Broadcasting Network, 1994—; exec. editor New Dimensions Book Series, 1993—; mem. bd. dirs. KQED, Inc., San Francisco, 1980-83, Green Earth Found., 1989-95, KZYX-FM, Mendocino County, Calif., 1989-91; mem. bd. adv. The Great Round, 1989-95. Author: Worlds Beyond, 1978, The New Healers, 1980, An Open Life, 1988, At The Leading Edge, 1991, Wise Words, 1997, The Power of Meditation and Prayer, 1997, The Well of Creativity, 1997, The Soul of Business, 1997, Roots of Healing, 1997, Money, Money, Money, 1998, Buddhism in the West, 1998; co-author: True Work, 1998; exec. prodr.: Spirit of the Times, Deep Ecology for the 21st Century; editor The Inner Edge newsletter, 1997—. Mem. Task Force to Promote Self Esteem and Personal and Social Responsibility, Mendocino County, Calif., 1988-89; mem. internat. adv. bd. Radio for Peace Internat., 1988—; bd. dirs. Human Potential Audio Found., 1994-97; mem. adv. bd. New Road Map Found., 1991—. Mem. Internat. Assn. for Socially Responsible Radio (founding dir. 1991—). Avocations: travel, writing, reading, birdwatching. Home: PO Box 1029 Ukiah CA 95482-1029 Office: New Dimensions Found PO Box 569 Ukiah CA 95482-0569

TOMSETT, ALAN JEFFREY, retired accountant; b. London, May 3, 1922; s. Maurice Jeffrey and Edith Sarah (Mackelworth) Tomsett; m. Joyce May Hill, Sept. 11, 1948; children: Ann Sara, Ian Hugh. B.Com, U. London, 1952. With Hodgson, Harris & Co. Chartered Accts., London, 1938, R.A.F., 1941-46; mgr. Smallfield, Rawlins & Co., 1951; acct. Northern Mercantile & Investment Corp., 1955, William Baird & Co. Ltd., 1962-63; chief acct. British Transport Docks Bd., 1964-73, fin. dir., 1974-83; fin. dir. Assoc. British Ports Holdings PLC, 1983-87, dir., 1983-92. Churchwarden St. John's Shirley, 1988-92. Officer Order of Brit. Empire. Fellow Inst. Chartered Accts., Chartered Inst. Mgmt. Accts., Chartered Inst. Pub. Fin. and Accountancy, Joint Diploma Mgmt. Acctg. Svcs., Inst. Chartered Sec. and Adminstrs., Chartered Inst. Transp. (v.p. 1981-82, hon. treas. 1982-88), Royal Soc. Arts. Avocation: gardening. Home and Office: 102 Ballards Way, Croydon CRO 5RG, England

TOMSON, GORAN BENGT, public health scientist; b. Stockholm, Dec. 24, 1947; s. Bengt and Margret (Gustafsson) T.; m. Ylva Tomson (div.); children: Klara, Artur, Axel; m. Tanja Tomson. MD, Karolinska Inst., 1973, PhD, 1990. Intern. cons. dept. pediat. Huddinje U., Stockholm, 1975-81; head Flemingsbergs Health Ctr., Stockholm, 1982-84; cons., rschr. divsn. internat. health Karolinska Inst., Stockholm, 1984-94, assoc. prof., sr. lectr. divsn. internat. health, 1994-95, acting prof. divsn. internat. health, 1995-96, assoc. prof. divsn. internat. health, 1997—; sr. pub. health specialist World Bank, Washington, 1996; mem. Oxford Rsch. Forum, 1998—, WHO Expert Adv. Panel Drug Policy and Mgmt., 1995—; project leader, dir. Sida supported Lao Nat. Drug Policy Project, 1993—. Editor: Essential Drug Information, 1992. Chair Göran Sterky Found., Sweden, 1997—. Many rsch. grants. Office: Divsn Internat Health IHCAR, Karolinska Inst, SE 17176 Stockholm Sweden

TOMSON, ILMAR NICOLAEVICH, geologist researcher; b. Tbilisi, Georgia, Russia, Feb. 21, 1927; s. Nicolay Martinovich and Muza Sergeevna (Lebedianski) T.; m. Lidia Ivanovna Lazareva, Oct. 20, 1951. Degree in Mine Engring., Moscow Inst. Nonferrous Metals, 1948; Candidate of Scis., Acad. of Scis., Moscow, 1954, DSc, 1973. Geologist Mine Verhny, Dalnegorsk, Russia, 1948-51; aspirant Inst. Geology of Ore Deposits, Moscow, 1951-54, sr. rschr., 1955-70, chief lab., 1970—, chief. sci. counsel, 1975—. Author: (book) Metallogeny of Ore District, 1988, Global Regularity of Distribution Giant Ore Deposits, 1974; mem. editl. bd. Geology of Ore Deposits. Mem. N.Y. Acad. Scis., Acad. Scis. of Russia, Commn. on Tektonic of Ore Deposits (v.p. 1974). Avocation: drawing. Home: Profsouznaia st, 43 K2 Apt 696, 117420 Moscow Russia Office: Inst. Geology Ore Deposits, Staromonteynyi Per 35, 109017 Moscow Russia

TOMUSCHAT, HANS CHRISTIAN ULRICH, lawyer, educator; b. Stettin, Germany, July 23, 1936; s. Ernst and Erica (Schoder) T.; m. Heide E. Mohr (div. 1986); children: Julia, Philipp. BA, U. Heidelberg, Fed. Republic Germany, 1959, JD, 1964, PhD, 1970. Prof., dir. inst. internat. and European law Humboldt U., Berlin, Fed. Republic Germany, 1995. Author books in field constl. pub. internat. law; contbr. articles to profl. jours. Mem. UN Human Rights Com., N.Y.C., Geneva, 1977-86, UN Internat. Law Commn., Geneva, 1985-96; judge adminstrv. tribunal InterAm. Devel. Bank, Washington, 1995-97, African Devel. Bank, Abidjan, 1999—; coord. Commn. for Hist. Clarification, Guatemala, 1997-99. Recipient prize Legatum Visserianum, Netherlands, 1964. Mem. Internat. Commn. Jurists, German Assn. Internat. Law (coun., pres. 1993-97), Assn. German Tchrs. Constnl. Law (bd. dirs. 1986-87), Inst. de Droit Internat. (assoc.). Avocations: tennis, jogging, swimming. Office: Inst Völker/Europarecht, Unter den Linden 6, D-10099 Berlin Germany

TONCHEV, SVETLEN HRISTOV, physicist, scientist, researcher; b. V. Turnovo, Bulgaria, Aug. 24, 1954; s. Hristo Delchev and Krustina Stoyanova (Andreeva) T.; m. Rossitsa Naidenova, Aug. 21, 1983; children: Hristo Svetlenov, Ognjan Svetlenov. MA, U. Sofia, Bulgaria, 1979; PhD, Bulgarian Acad. Sci., Sofia, 1985. Lic. physicist. Physicist Inst. Solid State Physics, Bulgarian Acad. Scis., Sofia, 1980-82, rsch. assoc., 1985-95, assoc. prof., 1995—. Contbr. articles to profl. jours. Recipient Gold Integral, Nat. Com. Sci. and Tech. Progress, 1983. Mem. SPIE (Bulgarian sect.), Bulgarian Phys. Union, Bulgarian Scientist's Union. Orthodox. Avocation: jeweler. Home: Bl.404, Entr 3, Apt 72, Compl Drouzhba 2, 1582 Sofia Bulgaria Office: Bulgarian Acad Scis Inst Solid State Physics, 72 Tzarigradsko Chaussee Bd, 1784 Sofia Bulgaria

TONDL, ALEŠ, retired engineering researcher; b. Znojmo, Moravia, Czech Republic, July 31, 1925; s. Ladislav and Milada (Šlechtová) T.; m. Henrieta Lieblova, June 16, 1953; 1 child, Vladimir. 31719ring., Tech. U. Brno, Czech Republic, 1950, PhD, 1950; Cand. Sci., Tech. U. Prague, Czech Republic, 1955, DSc, 1967; Dr. (h.c.), Tech. U., Brno, Czech Republic, 1999. Asst. prof. Tech. U. Brno, 1949-50; scientist Nat. Rsch. Inst. for Machine Design, Prague, 1950-55; sr. scientist Slovak Acad. Scis., Bratislava, 1956, Nat. Rsch. Inst. for Machine Design, Prague, 1957-90; ret.; vis. prof. Tech. U. Vienna; lectr. in field various univs. in Austria, Eng., France, Germany, Italy, Lithuania, The Netherlands. Author: Some Problems of Rotor Dynamics, 1965, Quenching of Self-Excited Vibrations, 1991; co-author: Non-Linear Vibrations, 1986, Autoparametric Resonance in Mechanical Systems, 2000; contbr. over 200 articles to profl. jours.; editl. bd. Jour. Sound and Vibration, Jour. for Machinery; adv. bd. Nonlinear Dynamics, Chaos, Solitons and Fractals. Recipient Nat. Prize for Rsch. work in Rotor Dynamics, Czech Govt., 1963. Mem. Soc. for Mechanics at Czech Acad. Scis., Gesellschaft für angewandte Mathematik und Mechanik, Internat. Fedn. Theory of Machines and Mechanisms (hon.). Roman Catholic. Avocation: gardening. Home: Zborovska 41, CZ 15000 Prague Czech Republic

TONDOWIDJOJO, JOHN VINCENT, communication educator, priest; b. Ngawi, Indonesia, Sept. 27, 1934; s. Kanjeng Raden Mas Tumenggung Tondowidjojo and Raden Ayu Soetiretno. BPhil, Inst. Philosophy, Surabaya, Indonesia, 1958; strata II theology, Coll. Brignole Sale, Genoa, Italy, 1963; bacc-strata III, Pontificia U. Urbaniana, Rome, 1988. Specialization in composition & dirigent Centro Della Cultura, Venice, Italy, 1961, comm., art & media Trinity & All Saints Coll., U.K., 1979, pub. rels. & interpersonal comm. Niagara U., 1985, mgmt. for mgrs. U. Minn., 1985. Lectr. Cath. U., Surabaya, 1963-85, Inst. Theology & Philosophy, Malang, Indonesia, 1980—; dir. nat. comm. tng. ctr. Sanggar Bina Tama, Surabaya, 1979—; lectr. Cath. U. Atma Jaya, Yogyakarta, Indonesia, 1998—; chmn. Found. Widya Sasana Inst., Malang, 1989-93, Found. Widya Yuwana Inst., Madiun, Indonesia, 1994—, Catechetical Commn. Diocese, Surabaya, 1974084, Social Comm. Commn. Diocese, Surabaya, 1976—, Interreligious Commn. Diocese, Surabaya, 1988-96; dir. diocese Pastoral Tng. Ctr., Madiun, 1997—; moderator Diocese Cath. Profls., Surabaya, 1979—; inventor in field. Editor, author books & bull. Sanggar Bina Tama Comm. Tng. Ctr.; author: Menapak Jejak Misionaris Lazaris 5 vols., 1995, Ethnology in Indonesia 5 vols., 1993, Pertumbuhan dan perkembangan St. Cornelius, Madiun, 1897-1998, 1998, Sejarah perkembangan Keuskupan Surabaya, 1800-2000, 5 vols. Recipient CTC Sanggar Bina Tama appreciation award Pontifical Commn. Comm. Social, The Vatican, 1982, Man of Yr. award, 1998; named Outstanding Man of 20th Century, 2000. Mem. ASTD, IFTDO, IPRA, UCIP (amb. journalism), WACC, AMIC, Inst. Tng. Devel., Ctr. Bus. Ethics. Roman Catholic. Avocations: music, public relations, writing. Fax: 62-31-33-81-66. Home and Office: Jalan Residen Sudirman No 3, Surabaya 60136, Indonesia

TONE, PHILIP WILLIS, retired lawyer, former federal judge; b. Chgo., Apr. 9, 1923; s. Elmer James and Frances (Willis) T.; m. Gretchen Altfillisch, Mar. 10, 1945; children: Michael P., Jeffrey R., Susan A. BA, U. Iowa, 1943, JD, 1948. Bar: Iowa 1948, Ill. 1950, D.C. 1950. Law clk. Justice Wiley B. Rutledge, Supreme Ct. U.S., Washington, 1948-49; assoc. firm Covington & Burling, Washington, 1949-50; assoc., ptnr. firm Jenner & Block, Chgo., 1950-72, 80-97; judge U.S. Dist. Ct., Chgo., 1972-74, U.S. Ct. Appeals (7th cir.), Chgo., 1974-80; spl. counsel Nat. Commn. on Causes and Prevention of Violence, 1968-69, U.S. Senate subcom. to investigate individuals representing interests of fgn. govts., 1980; Chmn. Ill. Supreme Ct. Rules Com., 1968-71, sec., 1963-68; mem. Com. on Jud. Br. of Jud. Conf. of U.S., 1987-91; gen. counsel U.S. Golf Assn., 1988-92; mem. Fed. Jud. Fellows Commn., 1986-92; chmn. Fed. Jud. Ctr. Found. Contbr. articles to legal periodicals. With AUS, 1943-46. Grad. fellow Law Sch. Yale U., 1948. Fellow Am. Coll. Trial Lawyers (regent 1984-87, pres. 1988-89); mem. ABA, Am. Bar Found., Am. Law Inst., Ill. Bar Assn. (bd. govs. 1960-64), Chgo. Bar Assn. (bd. mgrs. 1966-69), Am. Judicature Soc., Law Club Chgo. (pres. 1979-80), Legal Club Chgo.

TONEGAWA, SUSUMU, biology educator; b. Nagoya, Japan, Sept. 5, 1939; came to U.S., 1963; s. Tsutomu and Miyoko (Masuko) T.; m. Mayumi Yoshinari, Sept. 28, 1985; children: Hidde, Hanna, Satto. BS, Kyoto U., Japan, 1963; PhD, U. Calif., San Diego, 1968. Rsch. asst. U. Calif., San Diego, 1963-64, teaching asst., 1964-68; mem. Basel (Switzerland) Inst. Immunology, 1971-81; prof. biology MIT, Cambridge, 1981—; investigator Howard Hughes Med. Inst., 1988—; dir. MIT Ctr. for Learning and Memory, 1994; professorship Amgen, Inc., 1994. Mem. editl. bd. Immunity. Decorated Order of Culture, Emperor of Japan; recipient Cloetta prize, 1978, Avery Landsteiner prize Gesselschaft für Immunologie, 1981, Louisa Gross Horwitz prize Columbia U., 1982, award Gardiner Found. Internat., Toronto, Ont., Can., 1983, Robert Koch Found. prize, Bonn., Fed. Republic Germany, 1986, co-recipient Albert Lasker Med. Rsch. award, 1987, Nobel prize in Physiology or Medicine, 1987; named Person with Cultural Merit Japanese Govt., 1983. Mem. NAS (fgn. assoc.), Am. Assn. Immunologists (hon.), Scandinavian Soc. Immunology (hon.). Office: MIT 77 Massachusetts Ave Cambridge MA 02139-4307*

TONELLO, LUIS, judge. Pres. Supreme Ct., Uruguay. Office: Gutierrez Ruiz 1310, 11100 Montevideo Uruguay*

TONG, ALEX WAIMING, immunologist; b. Hong Kong, Apr. 8, 1952; came to U.S., 1970; s. Robert S. and Agnes M. (Cheng) T.; m. Susan J. Radtke, May 23, 1980 (div. Mar. 1988); 1 child, Nicole L.; m. S. Quay Mercer, May 13, 1995; children: Alexander C., Caitlyn Y. BA in Biology, U. Oreg., 1973; PhD in Microbiology and Immunology, Oreg. Health Scis. U., 1980. Undergrad. teaching asst. biology dept. U. Oreg., Eugene, 1972-73; rsch. asst. dept. microbiology and immunology Oreg. Health Scis. U., Portland, 1975-80, teaching asst. Sch. Medicine, 1977-78, rsch. assoc. dept. micrology and immunology, 1981-82; postdoctoral fellow Surg. Rsch. Lab. Portland VA Med. Ctr., 1980-82; rsch. assoc. in immunology Charles A. Sammons Cancer Ctr., Baylor U. Med. Ctr., Dallas, 1982-86; assoc. dir. immunology lab. Baylor U. Med. Ctr., Dallas, Tex., 1986—; asst. prof. Inst. Biomed. Studies, Baylor U., Waco, 1988-97, assoc. prof., 1997—; prin. investigator Nat. Cancer Inst., Bethesda, Md., 1994—; adj. faculty immunology grad. studies program U. Tex. Southwestern Med. Ctr., Dallas, 1982—. Contbr. articles to profl. jours. Tatar rsch. fellow Med. Rsch. Found. Oreg., Portland, 1981-83. Mem. Am. Assn. Immunologists, Am. Assn. Cancer Rsch., Am. Soc. Hematology, Clin. Immunology Soc., Japan Karate Assn. Dallas (dir.), Internat. Traditional Karate Fedn. (cert. coach 1990—, cert. referee 1988—), Am. Amateur Karate Fedn. (dir. S.W. region). Democrat. Avocations: traditional karate, alpine skiing, scuba diving. Office: Baylor U Med Ctr Cancer Immunology Rsch Lab 3500 Gaston Ave Dallas TX 75246-2096

TONG, GOH CHOK, government executive; b. Singapore, May 20, 1941; married; 2 children. BA in Econs., U. Singapore, 1964; MA in Devel. Econs., Williams Coll., 1967. Adminstrv. officer Min. Fin., 1964, mgr. planning & projects, 1969-73, mng. dir., 1973-77; elected MP, 1976—; sr. min. State for Fin., 1977; min. trade and industry, 1979, 81, min. health, 1981, 2d min. defense, 1981, min. defense, 2d min. health, 1982, 1st deputy prime min., min. defense, 1985, prime min., 1991—; sec. gen. PAP, 1992—. Office: Office of Prime Min, Istana Annese Orchard Rd, Singapore 238823, Singapore*

TONG, MIRIAM, lawyer; b. Hong Kong, June 4, 1970; d. Ronnie and Rita (Chan) T. BA in Econs. and Polit. Sci., U. Toronto, 1993; profl. certificate of laws, U. Hong Kong, 1995. cert. atty. Hong Kong, Eng., Wales. Assoc. corp. dept. Paul, Weiss, Rifkind, Wharton & Garrison, Hong Kong, 1998—, mem. coms. and technology practice group, mem. corp. group, assoc. corp. dept., 1998-2000; v.p. AdSociety Ltd., Hong Kong, 2000—. Mem. Law Soc. Hong Kong, Law Soc. England and Wales, Am. C. of C. Avocations: scuba diving, travel, rollerblading, reading. Office: units 2509-11 25th Fl, Citibank Plz 3 Garden Plz, City Bank Tower Central Hong Kong

TONG, RONNY KA WAH, barrister; b. Hong Kong, Aug. 28, 1950; s. Chi Fan and Shuk Ying (Chan) T.; m. Daisy Wai Lan Yeung, Sept. 27, 1948; 1 child, Justin Wai Hin. Student, Queens Coll., Hong Kong; LLB with 1st class honors, Hong Kong U., 1972; BCL with honors, Oxford (Eng.) U., 1974. Bar: Eng., 1974, Hong Kong, 1975, Barrister and Solicitor Supreme Ct. of Victoria, Australia, 1983, Advocate and Solicitor Supreme Ct. Republic of Singapore, 1986, N.Y. 1988. Barrister-at-law Hong Kong, 1975—; dep. judge Supreme Ct. of Hong Kong, 1992; Her Majesty's counsel Parliament, 1990; chmn. Hong Kong Bar Assn., 1999—; external examiner comml. law and practice paper postgrad. cert. laws courses Polytech. Hong Kong, 1994-94, U. Hong Kong, 1991-94, course cons. comml. law and practice PCLL course, 1994—, dep. chmn. panel securities and futures appeals, 1994-99, dep. chmn. com. takeovers appeal, 1994-99, dep. chmn. bd. rev., 1995—; adjudicator Registration Persons Tribunal, 1996—; bd. dirs. Urban Svcs. Appeals, Regional Svcs. Appeals, others. Winter-Williams scholar Oxford U., 1972-74; recipient Grad. award Rotary Internat., 1973-74, Lloyd Stott Mem. prize, 1974, J.B. Montagu Pupillage prize, 1974, Middle Temple Ct. Honour prize, 1974. Mem. Hong Kong Bar Assn. (rep. supreme ct. rules com. 1978, 79, rep. Hong Kong dist. ct. rules com. 1979-90, com. inquiry in investigation of alleged misconduct of a barrister 1986, 87, 89, working party on dist. ct. rules 1988, standing com. on legal aid 1988-93, criminal and law enforcement injuries compensation bds. 1989-95, among others), Gen. Coun. Bar of Eng., N.Y. State Bar Assn. Avocations: golf, tennis, swimming. Office: Temple Chambers 16th Fl, One Pacific Pl 88 Queensway, Hong Kong China

TONG, SIU WING, computer programmer; b. Hong Kong, May 20, 1950; came to U.S., 1968; BA, U. Calif., Berkeley, 1972; PhD, Harvard U., 1979; MS, U. Lowell, 1984. Rsch. assoc. Brookhaven Nat. Lab., Upton, N.Y., 1979-83; software engr. Honeywell Info. Systems, Billerica, Mass., 1984-85; sr. programmer, analyst Hui Computer Cons., Berkeley, Calif., 1985-88; sr. v.p. devel., chief fin. officer Surgicenter Info. Systems, Inc., Orinda, Calif., 1989-94; sr. sys. specialist Info. Sys. Divsn. Contra Costa County Health Svcs., Martinez, Calif., 1995-97; info. tech. supr. Info. Sys. Divsn. Contra Costa County Health Svcs., Martinez, 1997—. Vol. tchr. Boston Chinatown Saturday Adult Edn. Program of Tufts Med. Sch., 1977-79. Muscular Dystrophy Assn. fellow, 1980-82. Mem. AAAS, IEEE, Assn. Computing Machinery, N.Y. Acad. Scis. Home: 17 Beaconsfield Ct Orinda CA 94563-4203 Office: Contra Costa County Health Svcs 595 Center Ave Ste 210 Martinez CA 94553-4634

TONG, TANJUN, biochemist, educator; b. Ningbo, Zhejiang, China, Aug. 15, 1934; s. Rui Quan and Xiao (Huang) T.; m. Zong-yu Zhang, July 17, 1963; children: Bei, Zheng. MD, Beijing Med. Coll., 1959, PhD, 1964. Faculty dept. biochemistry Beijing Med. Coll., 1964-78, sr. instr., 1978-85; assoc. prof. dept. biochemistry Beijing Med. U., 1985-88, prof., 1988—, vice chmn., 1985-95, dir., 1995—; prof. Peking U. Health Sci. Ctr., 2000—; vis. scholar Johns Hopkins U., Balt., 1979-80; vis. assoc. prof. U. Calif.-Davis, 1986-87; vis. scientist NYU, 1987-88; dep. dir. Beijing Med. Coll., 1982-85;

prof. Peking U., Beijing, 1995-98; staff mem. peer rev. sys. Nat. Sci. Found. of China, 1996—. Editor-in-chief, 1st author: Medical Gerontology, 1995 (Chinese Health Min. award 1998). Recipient Outstanding Contbn. for Med. and Health Devel. award State Coun. of People's Republic of China, 1992, 20th Century Award for Achievement, Internat. Biog. Ctr., Cambridge, Eng., 1994, Gen. Higher Edn. award Beijing Municipality, 1993; NIH fellow, 1980-81, Min. of Edn. Internat. Rsch. fellow, 1978-80. Mem. Chinese rsch. Soc. of Elderly Health, Chinese Soc. Biochemistry and Molecular Biology. Achievements include research in molecular mechanisms of cellular aging, cancer-suppressive activity of biological fluids, nuclear mechanisms of peptide growth factor action; avocations: reading, mountain climbing. Office: Peking U Health Sci Ctr, 38 Xue-yuan Rd, Beijing 100083, People's Republic of China

TONG, ZHI SHEN, physics educator; b. Zhenjiang, China, Apr. 8, 1932; s. Long Quan and Yu Lian (Yang) T.; m. Mei Zhen Wu, Aug. 16, 1957; children: Jue, Lu. Grad., Fudan U., Shanghai, China, 1953; postgrad., Beijing (Peking) U., 1953-56. Lectr. Lanzhou U., China, 1957-80, assoc. prof., 1981-85, prof., 1986; prof. Shanghai Coll. Mechs., China, 1987, China Textile U., Shanghai, 1988—. Contbr. articles to profl. jours. Mem. Shanghai Assn. Physics, Shanghai Assn. Corrosion Sci. & Tech. Home: An Shun Rd 401 Rm 30 Bldg, 220 Ln, Shanghai 200051, China Office: Donghua U Dept Physics, Yan An West Rd 1882, Shanghai 200051, China

TONGE, DAVID SEYMOUR, management company executive; b. Bournemouth, Eng., May 20, 1942; arrived in Istanbul, 1984; s. Arthur Seymour and Joan Mary (Clements) T.; m. Sally Wilson, June 1968 (div. 1976); 1 child, Oliver; m. Iffet Renda, May 1978 (div. 1986); m. Emine Usakligil. BA, Magdalene Coll., Cambridge, Eng., 1963. Mgmt. trainee Mfrs. Hanover Trust, N.Y.C., London, 1963-64; rschr. Economist Intelligence Unit, London, 1964-66; rep. Economist Intelligence Unit, Istanbul, Ankara, Turkey, 1966-69; corr. BBC, Observer, Guardian, Athens, Greece, 1969-77; diplomatic corr. Fin. Times, London, 1978-84; founder, chief exec. IBS Rsch. & Consultancy, Istanbul, 1984—. Author, editor: Doing Business in Turkey, 1989—. Mem. British C. of C. (bd. dirs. 1988-97). Avocations: gardening, surfing, walking. Office: IBS Rsch Consultancy, Abdi Ipekci Cad 59/6 Macka, 80200 Istanbul Turkey

TONI, ALDEMARO, publishing executive; b. Florence, Italy, Sept. 14, 1935; s. Bruno and Quinta (Bartolini) T.; m. Claudia Costagli; children: Benedetto, Paola. Diploma in Italian lit., U. Florence, 1976. Pub. Erba d'Arno Rev., Florence, 1980—; sub-editor Erba d'Arno Quar. Rev., Florence, 1980-96, editor, 1996—; pub. Edizioni dell'Erba, Florence, 1982—. Author: La Canonica, 1991, many novels. Office: Edizioni dell'Erba, Piazza Garibaldi 3, Fucecch, 50054 Florence Italy

TONINI, ERSILIO CARDINAL, archbishop; b. Centovera de San Giorgio Piacentino, July 20, 1914. Archbishop emeritus of Ravenna Cervia, Italy; elevated to cardinal Roman Cath. Ch., 1994—. Office: Via Santa Teresa 8, 48100 Ravenna Italy*

TONKENS, SOLVIN WILLIAM, retired physician; b. Milw., Dec. 31, 1919; s. William and Fanny (Maltz) T.; m. Muriel Ann Schandorf, Oct. 21, 1956 (dec. Aug. 1986); m. Rebecca Ann McAfee, Dec. 22, 1986; stepchildren: Terri, Toni. DO, U. of Health Scis., Kansas City, Mo., 1946. Cert. in emergency medicine. Intern Manhattan Gen. Hosp., N.Y.C., 1946-47; resident Bklyn. Women's Hosp., 1947; family practice Kansas City, Mo., 1948-71; physician emergency medicine Kansas City, Kans., Mo., 1971-84; dir. med. program and med. affairs, plant physician Ford Assembly Plant, Claycomo, Mo., 1984—; dir. emergency medicine Am. Med. Svcs., Lees Summit, Mo., 1978-84. Mem. Masons. Jewish. Avocations: gardening, travel, grandchildren. Home: 12861 Cambridge Ter Shawnee Mission KS 66209-1634

TONKIN, HUMPHREY RICHARD, academic administrator, educator; b. Truro, Cornwall, Eng., Dec. 2, 1939; came to U.S., 1962; s. George Leslie and Lorna Winifred (Sandry) T.; m. Sandra Julie Winberg, Mar. 9, 1968 (div. 1981); m. Jane Spencer Edwards, Oct. 1, 1983; 1 child, Sebastian George. BA, St. John's Coll., Cambridge, Eng., 1962, MA, 1966; AM, Harvard U., 1966, PhD, 1966; DLitt (hon.), U. Hartford, 1999. Asst. prof. English U. Pa., Phila., 1966-71, assoc. prof., 1971-80, prof., 1980-83, vice-provost undergrad. studies, 1971-75, coord. internat. programs, 1977-83, master Stouffer Coll. House, 1980-83; pres. State Univ. Coll., Potsdam, N.Y., 1983-88, U. Hartford, Conn., 1989-98; prof. humanities, pres. emeritus U. Hartford, 1998—; vis. fellow Whitney Humanities Ctr. Yale U., 1998-99; vis. prof. English Columbia U., N.Y.C., 1980-81; exec. dir. Ctr. Rsch. and Documentation on World Lang. Problems, Rotterdam and Hartford, 1974—. N.Am. editor: Lang. Problems and Lang. Planning; author: (bibliography) Sir Walter Raleigh, 1971, Esperanto and International Language Problems, 4th edit., 1977, Spenser's Courteous Pastoral, 1972, (with Jane Edwards) The World in the Curriculum, 1981, The Faerie Queene, 1989, (with Allison Keef) Language in Religion, 1989, Esperanto: Language, Literature and Community, 1993; Esperanto, Interlinguistics and Planned Language, 1997, contbr. articles, studies, revs. to profl. jours. Pres. Pa. Coun. Internat. Edn., 1980-81; bd. dirs. World Affairs Coun. Phila., 1979-83, Zamenhof Found., 1987-94, Hartford Symphony Orch., 1989-98, World Affairs Coun. Conn., 1989—, Greater Hartford Arts Coun., 1989-99, Can.-U.S. Found. Ednl. Exchange, 1997—, chmn. 1999—; bd. dirs. World Learning, 1998—; chmn. Coun. Internat. Exch. Scholars, 1988-94, Esperantic Studies Found., 1991—, Partnership for Svc.-Learning, 1991-96; bd. dirs. Am. Forum, 1985—, chmn., 1998—. Recipient Lindback award for disting. teaching, 1970; Frank Knox fellow Harvard U., 1962-66; Guggenheim fellow, 1974. Fellow Acad. Esperanto; mem. Universal Esperanto Assn. (pres. 1974-80, 86-89, rep. to UN 1974-83, hon. com. 1995—), Spenser Soc. (pres. 1983-84, former dir.), Internat. Acad. Scis. San Marino, Conn. Acad. Arts and Scis., Cosmos Club. Home: 279 Ridgewood Rd West Hartford CT 06107-3542 Office: U Hartford Mortensen Libr 200 Bloomfield Ave Hartford CT 06117-1545

TONKIN, INA LYNN DYER, cardiovascular radiologist, educator; b. Louisville, Apr. 26, 1944; d. Robert S. and Nancy E. (Camp) Dyer; m. Allen K. Tonkin, June 29, 1968; children: Allison Elizabeth-Ann, Kieth Allen. BA, DePauw U., 1966; MD, U. Louisville, 1970. Diplomate Am. Bd. Radiology, Am. Bd. Vasc. Interventional Radiology, Am. Bd. Pediatric Radiology. Intern U. Fla., Gainesville, 1970-71, resident in radiology, 1971-73, fellow in cardiovascular radiology, 1974-75; asst. prof. U. Ariz. Health Sci. Ctr., Tucson, 1975-77, U. Ala.-Birmingham, 1977-79; assoc. prof. radiology U. Tenn., Memphis, 1979-84, prof., 1984—, prof. pediatrics, 1985—; exec. com. LeBonheur Children's Med. Ctr., Memphis, 1981-85, chief of med. staff, 1987; disting. scientist Armed Forces Inst. of Radiologic Pathology, Washington, 1992-93. Editor: (book) Pediatric Cardiovascular Imaging, 1992; contbr. chpts. to books, rsch. articles to profl. jours. Recipient Disting. Alumnus award U. Louisville Med. Sch., 1999. Fellow Am. Heart Assn. (exec. com. Coun. Cardiovascular Radiology 1980—), Soc. Cardiovascular and Interventional Radiology, Am. Coll. Radiology; mem. Soc. Pediatric Radiology (treas.), Jour. Rev. Club of Memphis (sec. 1984, pres. 1985). Methodist. Home: 3415 Chambers Chapel Rd Lakeland TN 38002-9573 Office: LeBonheur Children's Med Ctr 50 S Dunlap St Memphis TN 38103-4909

TONKOPII, VALERII DMITRIEVITCH, toxicologist, researcher; b. Donetsk, Russia, May 2, 1939; s. Dmitriy Denisovitch and Anastasija Ivanovna (Schurenok) T.; m. Inna Semenovna Gendelman, June 15, 1965; 1 child, Dmitrii. B.Med.Sci., Med. Inst. Donetsk, Russia, 1962; PhD, Mil. Medicine Rsch. Inst., Leningrad, Russia, 1969, MD, 1982. Physician Mil. Unit, Vilnius, Russia, 1962-69; scientist Mil. Med. Acad., Leningrad, 1969-70; scientist Mil. Medicine Rsch. Inst., Leningrad, 1970-72, sr. scientist, 1972-74, dep. chief, 1974-76, chief of dept., 1976-89; chief of dept. Inst. for Lake Rsch., St. Petersburg, Russia, 1989—. Author: Treatment of Poisonings by Hyperbaric Oxygenation, 1982; editl. bd. Jour. Ecol. Chemistry, 1993—. Col. Mil. Med. Svc., 1962-89. Recipient State Prize Laureate, Gold Medal, 1982; Pres.'s State Sci. grantee, 1994-97, 97—, INTAS grantee, 1996—. Mem. N.Y. Acad. Sci., Internat. Soc. Study of Xenobiotics, Soc. Environ. Toxicology and Chemistry. Avocations: tourism, gardening, fishing. Home: Ordinarnaya str 20 app 87, 197136 Saint Petersburg Russia Office: Inst Lake Rsch, Sevastyanova str 9, 196199 Saint Petersburg Russia

TONN, ELVERNE MERYL, pediatric dentist, dental benefits consultant, forensic odontologist; b. Stockton, Calif., Dec. 10, 1929; s. Emanuel M. and Lorna Darlene (Bryant) T.; m. Ann G. Richardson, Oct. 28, 1951; children: James Edward, Susan Elaine Tonn Adams. AA, La Sierra U., Riverside, Calif., 1949; DDS, U. So. Calif., 1955; BS, Regents Coll., U. State N.Y., 1984. Lic. dentist; diplomate Am. Bd. Forensic Dentistry, Am. Bd. Quality Assurance and Utilization Rev. Physicians; cert. dental benefits cons. Pediatric dentist, assoc. Walker Dental Group, Long Beach, Calif., 1957-59, Children's Dental Clinic, Sunnyvale, Calif., 1959-61; pediatric dentist in pvt. practice Mountain View, Calif., 1961-72; pediatric dentist, ptrn. Pediatric Dentistry Assocs., Los Altos, Calif., 1972-83; pediatric dentist, ptnr. Valley Oak Dental Group, Manteca, Calif., 1987—; from clin. instr. to assoc. prof. U. Pacific, San Francisco, 1964-84; assoc. prof. U. Calif., San Francisco, Calif., 1984-86; ; pediatric dental cons. Delta Dental Plan, San Francisco, 1985—; chief dental staff El Camino Hosp., Mountain View, 1964-65, 84-85; lectr. in field. Weekly columnist Manteca Bull., 1987-92; producer 2 teaching videos, 1986; contbr. articles to profl. jours. Lectr. to elem. students on dental health Manteca Unified Sch. Dist., 1982—; dental health screener Elem. Schs., San Joaquin County Pub. Health, 1989-92; dental cons. Interplast program Stanford U. Sch. Medicine. Capt. U.S. Army, 1955-57. Fellow Am. Coll. Dentists, Internat. Coll. Dentists, Am. Acad. Pediatric Dentistry, Royal Soc. Health (Eng.), Acad. of Dentistry for Handicapped, Pierre Fauchard Acad., Acad. Dental Materials, Am. Soc. Dentistry for Children; mem. ADA, Internat. Assn. Pediatric Dentistry, Internat. Assn. Dental Rsch., Fedn. Dentaire Internationale, Am. Assn. Dental Cons., Calif. Dental Assn., Calif. Soc. Dentistry for Children (pres. 1968), Calif. Soc. Pediatric Dentists, N.Y. Acad. Scis., Calif. Acad. Sci., Rotary Internat., Nat. Assn. for Healthcare Quality, Am. Coll. Med. Quality. Republican. Avocations: photography, travel, medieval history. Home: 374 Laurelwood Cir Manteca CA 95336-7122 Office: Valley Oak Dental Group Inc 1507 W Yosemite Ave Manteca CA 95337-5182

TONNELLIER, MICHEL ANDRE, art educator, architect, painter, engraver; b. Paris, Feb. 21, 1942; s. Maurice Louis and Paulette (Payen) T. Cert. Art Tchr., Ville de Paris, 1963; degree in Architecture, Ecole des Beaux Arts, Paris, 1979. Art tchr. Ville de Paris, 1963-67, Nat. Edn., Caen, France, 1967—, U. Caen, 1991—; acrhitect Council House, Clinchamps sur Orne, France, 1985, Tourist Reception Office, La Souleuvre, France, 1992, Rural Gite, Beny Bocage, France, 1997; cons. P.R.O.M.O.C.A., Caen Roven, France, 1983-85; estate agt. O. P.A.C. Calvados, Caen, France, 1984-95. Art exhbns. include Salon De La Gravure, Bayeux, France, 1971, (paintings) Glatbach, Germany, 1989, Hotel D'Escoville, Caen, France, 1991. Recipient 1st prize Engraving, Anthony, France, 1964, Architectural OCntest Place de La Republique, Caen, France, 1983. Mem. Ordre des Architects. Office: Architecte, 11 Rue Belvedere, 14000 Caen France

TØNNESSON, STEIN DORENFELDT, historian; b. Copenhagen, Denmark, Dec. 2, 1953; arrived in Norway, 1955; s. Kåre Dorenfeldt and Birgit (Hansen) T.; m. Lise Elinor Watz, Aug. 19, 1977 (div. Mar. 1984); 1 child, Erik Watz; m. Bodil Stenseth, Aug. 3, 1984. CandMag, U. Oslo, 1982, CandPhilol, 1982, DrPh, 1991. Historian Norwegian Assn. Sports, 1983-85; rsch. fellow Inst. Def. Studies, Norway, 1985-88, Internat. Peace Rsch. Inst., Oslo, 1988-92; rsch. prof. Nordic Inst. Asian Studies, Denmark, 1992-95, sr. rsch. fellow, 1995-98; prof. Ctr. for Devel. and Environment, U. Oslo, 1997—. Author: The Vietnamese Revolution of 1945, 1991, History of Norwegian Sports, 1986, 1946: Outbreak of the Indochina War, 1987; editor: Asian Forms of the Nation, 1996. Home: Jacob Aalls Gt 13, 0368 Oslo Norway Office: U Oslo/Environ Devel Ctr, Blindern PO Box 1116, 0317 Oslo Norway

TONNISSON, TEOFILUS, optics scientist, physicist; b. Türi, Paide, Estonia, May 29, 1952; s. Arnold and Marianne (Viilup) T.; m. m. Liidia Velliste, Mar. 7, 1973 (div. 1982); children: Rene, Kristiina; m. Maimu Haug, Dec. 23, 1982; children: Ninell, Aleksander. MS, Tartu U., 1975, PhD, 1980. Jr. rsch. scientist Tartu Obs., 1975-82, sr. rsch. scientist, 1982-89; dir. rsch. and devel. Tech. Ctr. VEMO, Tartu, 1989-91; of Estonian Acad. Sci., Tartu, 1991—. Co-author: Investigations of the Atmospheric Optical Phenomena Aboard the Scientific Station Salyut-4, 1979, Remote Sensing of Atmosphere from Space Station Salyut-7, 1989; contbr. over 15 articles to profl. jours.; patentee in field. Recipient Silver prize Soviet Cosmonautix Exhibition, 1985. Avocations: philosophy, music, sports, literature, frontier sciences. Home: Obs 2-11, 61602 Toravere Tartu, Estonia Office: Interspectrum Ou, 185 A Riia St, 51014 Tartu Estonia

TONNOS, ANTHONY, bishop; b. Port Colborne, Ont., Can., Aug. 1, 1935. Ordained priest Roman Cath. Ch., 1961. Bishop Diocese of Hamilton, Ont., Can., 1984—. Office: Roman Catholic Church-Canada, 700 King St W, Hamilton, ON Canada L8P 1C7

TONOUKOUIN, LUCIEN, diplomat; m. Justine Tonoukouin. Amb. of Benin to U.S. Govt. of Benin, Washington, 1994—. Office: Embassy of the Republic of Benin 2124 Kalorama Rd NW Washington DC 20008*

TÖNSHOFF, BURKHARD, pediatrician, nephrologist; b. Wuppertal, Germany, Mar. 4, 1958; s. Paul Rolf and Hildegard (Neuhaus) T.; m. Christianne Senghaas, May 27, 1989; 1 child, Sebastian. Degree, U. Freiburg, Germany, 1983, MD, 1984. Intern Univ. Children's Hosp., Freiburg, 1983-84; resident in pediatrics, pediatric nephrology fellow Univ. Children's Hosp., Heidelberg, Germany, 1985-92, asst. prof. pediatrics and pediatric nephrology, 1995—; instr. pediatric nephrology and physiology SUNY, Stony Brook, 1992-94. Contbr. numerous articles, revs. to profl. publs., chpts. to books. Scholar German Govt., 1978, Deutsche Akademische Austauschdienst, 1979; Feodor-Lynen rsch. grantee Alexander von Humboldt Found., 1992, rsch. grantee Am. Heart Assn., 1993, Nat. Kidney Found., 1994. Home: Weberstr 14, 69120 Heidelberg Germany Office: Kinderklinik, Im Neuenheimer Feld 150, D-69120 Heidelberg Germany

TÖNSHOFF, HANS KURT, mechanical engineering educator; b. Bochum, Germany, May 14, 1934; s. Kurt and Margarete (Maas) T.; children: Roman, Silke, Till. Diploma Engring., Tech. U., Hannover, Germany, 1959, D Engring., 1965; D Engring. (hon.), U. Erlangen, 1992, U. Thessaloniki, 1998. Designer NAMCO, Cleve., 1961-62; dir. design and devel. Tönshoff & Co., Dortmund, Germany, 1965-68, v.p., 1968-70; prof. prodn. engring. U. Hannover, 1970—, dean faculty mech. engring., 1972-74; commr. rsch. and tech. State of Lower Saxony, 1984-86; dir. Laser Ctr. Hannover, 1987, Inst. Integrated Prodn., Hannover, 1988; mem. Internat. Instn. for Prodn. Engring. Rsch. (CIRP), 1975—. Contbr. articles on prodn. engring. to nat. and internat. jours. Mem. Sci. Coun., Germany, 1980-84; curator Volkswagen Found., Hannover, 1982-87; v.p. German Rsch. Coun., Bonn, 1989-95. Recipient Cross of Merit Fed. Republic Germany, 1988, Fredrick W. Taylor Research medal Soc. of Manufacturing Engineers, 1994. Mem. German Acad. Soc. Prodn. Engring., Internat. Instn. Prodn. Engring. Rsch., Soc. Mfg. Engrs. (Taylor award 1994), Rotary Club Hannover-Ballhof. Roman Catholic. Avocations: hiking, baroc music, bowling. Office: Inst Prodn Engring & Machine Tools, Schlosswender Strasse 5, 30159 Hannover Germany

TOOHEY, EDWARD JOSEPH, financial services company executive; b. Jersey City, Jan. 15, 1930; s. John Joseph and Estelle Anita (Hudson) T.; B.A., Yale U., 1953; m. Ruth Phyllis Scheidecker, Mar. 13, 1948; 1 dau., Phyllis Karen. With Merrill Lynch, Pierce, Fenner & Smith, Inc., N.Y.C., 1956—, mgmt. devel. program exec., 1966-68, v.p. resident mgr., N.Y.C., 1968-77, Washington, 1977-80, v.p., regional dir., N.Y.C., 1980-90, first v.p., 1990-94, mng. dir. instl. nat. sales, 1994—; pres. Bunbury Co., N.Y.C. Trustee Windham Found., Grafton, Vt., 1978—; vice chmn. Peddie Sch., Hightstown, N.J., 1981—, trustee, 1976—; bd. dirs. N.Y.C. Ballet, 1983-96, emeritus, 1996—. Served to maj. USMC, 1953-55. Clubs: Canoe Brook Country (Summit, N.J.); Yale, Sky, Univ. (N.Y.C.); Georgetown (Washington). Home: 1 Gracie Ter New York NY 10028-7955 Office: World Fin Ctr New York NY 10080-0001

TOOKES, JAMES NELSON, real estate investment company executive; b. Tallahassee, Sept. 16, 1934; BS, Fla. A&M U., 1955, MEd, 1956; m. Hortense Latricia James, June 22, 1958; 1 child, Gerald Ray. Tchr., Griffin Elem. Sch., Tallahassee, 1957-58, Douglas Elem. Sch., Wabasso, Fla., 1958-59; tchr. Barrow Hill Sch., Tallahassee, 1959-60, prin., 1960-67; summer sch. math. tchr. various sch. centers Leon County Dist., Tallahassee, 1960-65; prin. Pineview Elem. Sch., Tallahassee, 1967-73; pres. Geray Petroleum, Inc., Tallahassee, 1980—, J.N.T. Properties, Inc., Tallahassee, 1973-77; broker Tookes Realty, Tallahassee, 1973-85; adv. bd. Barnett Bank of Tallahassee, 1977-79. Bd. dirs. Marine State Bank, Tallahassee Youth Center, 1952-54, Tallahassee Meml. Regional Med. Center, 1977-82; chmn. div. United Fund campaign, 1962; trustee Tallahassee C.C., 1974-82, chmn. bd., 1976-77. Recipient Sch. Adminstr. Service award Pineview Elem. Sch. Student Coun., 1967-73; commendation award Bert Roger's Sch. Real Estate, 1973; Contbns. to Cmty. award Phi Beta Lambda, 1974; named 1 of 5 Most Outstanding Black Businessmen in State of Fla., Fla. A&M U. Sch. Bus. and Industry, 1974. Mem. Phi Delta Kappa, Kappa Alpha Psi (Man of Yr. 1973). Home: 925 E Magnolia Dr Apt 5C Tallahassee FL 32301-6606 Office: JNT Properties Inc 116 E 3rd Ave Tallahassee FL 32303-6117

TOOLE, JAMES FRANCIS, medical educator; b. Atlanta, Mar. 22, 1925; s. Walter O'Brien and Helen (Whitehurst) T.; m. Patricia Anne Wooldridge, Oct. 25, 1952; children: William, Anne, James, Douglas Sean. BA, Princeton U., 1947; MD, Cornell U., 1949; LLB, LaSalle Extension U., 1962. Intern, then resident internal medicine and neurology U. Pa. Hosp., Nat. Hosp., London, Eng., 1953-58; mem. faculty U. Pa. Sch. Medicine, 1958-62; prof. neurology, chmn. dept. Bowman Gray Sch. Medicine Wake Forest U., 1962-83; vis. prof. neurosci. U. Calif. at San Diego, 1969-70; vis. scholar Oxford U., 1989; mem. Nat. Bd. Med. Examiners, 1970-76; mem. task force arteriosclerosis Nat. Heart Lung & Blood Inst., 1970-81; chmn. 6th and 7th Princeton confs. cerebrovascular diseases; cons. epidemiology WHO, Japan, 1971, 73, 93, USSR, 1968, Ivory Coast, 1977, Japan, 1993; mem. Lasker Awards com., 1976-77; chmn. neuropharmacologic drugs com. FDA, 1979; chair Commn. on Presdl. Disability, 1994-97; cons. NASA, 1966. Author: Cerebrovascular Diseases, 5th edit., 1999; editor: Current Concepts in Cerebrovascular Disease, 1969-73, Jour. Neurol. Sci., 1990-97; mem. editorial bd. Annals Internal Medicine, 1968-75, Stroke, 1972-91, Jour. AMA, 1975-77, Ann. Neurology, 1980-86, Jour. of Neurology, 1985-89. Pres. N.C. Heart Assn., 1976-77. Served with AUS, 1950-51; flight surgeon USNR, 1951-53. Decorated Bronze Star with V, Combat Med. badge. Fellow ACP (life), AAAS (life), Royal Coll. Physicians; mem. AMA, Am. Clin. and Climatol Assn. (life), Am. Heart Assn. (chmn. com. ethics 1970-75), Am. Physiol. Soc., Am. Neurol. Assn. (sec.-treas. 1978-82, pres. 1984-85, archivist, historian 1988—), World Fedn. Neurology (sec.-treas. 1982-89, mgmt. com. 1990-98, pres. 1998—), Am. Acad. Neurology, Am. Soc. Neuroimaging (pres. 1992-94), Internat. Stroke Soc. (exec. com. 1989-97, program chmn. 1992, pres. 2000), Nat. Stroke Assn. (bd. dirs. 1993—, exec. com. 1994—, chmn. Commn. on U.S. Presdl. Disability 1994—), N.C. Stroke Assn. (pres. 1999—); hon. mem. Assn. Brit. Neurologists, German Neurol. Soc., Austrian Soc. Neurology, Irish Neurol. Assn., Russian Acad. Neurology. Home: 1836 Virginia Rd Winston Salem NC 27104-2316

TOOLEY, TERRY L(EE), software company executive; b. Tulsa, Feb. 23, 1948; s. Floyd Arthur and Thelma Francis (Patton) T.; m. Jennifer Gaye Brigham, Jan. 18, 1969. BS, Okla. State U., 1972; MBA, U. Okla., 1982. Commd. 2d lt. USAF, 1972, advanced through grades to capt., 1976, resigned, 1982; dir. domestic bus. devel. United Techs. Norden Sys., Norwalk, Conn., 1982-95; dir. Washington ops. United Techs. Norden Sys., Norwalk, 1992-95; sr. industry dir. Oracle Corp., Redwood Shores, Calif., 1996-2000, sr. dir. travel, transp. and hospitality sector, 2000—. Named Outstanding Young Man of Am., U.S. Jaycees, 1979. Mem. Air Force Assn. (treas. chpt. 1984-86), Phi Kappa Tau. Avocations: sailing, personal computers. Home: 1313 Kings Brook Ct Southlake TX 76092-7809 Office: Oracle Corp 222 Las Colinas Blvd W Ste 1000 Irving TX 75039-5445

TOOMAJIAN, WILLIAM MARTIN, lawyer; b. Troy, N.Y., Sept. 26, 1943; s. Leo R. and Elizabeth (Gundrum) T.; children: Andrew, Philip. AB, Hamilton Coll., 1965; JD, U. Mich., 1968; LLM, N.Y.U., 1975. Bar: N.Y. 1968, Ohio 1978. Mem. firm Cadwalader, Wickersham & Taft, N.Y.C., 1971-77, Baker & Hostetler, Cleve., 1977—. Served to lt. USCG, 1968-71. Mem. ABA, Ohio Bar Assn., Cleve. Bar Assn., Cleve. Tax Club. Home: 3582 Lytle Rd Cleveland OH 44122-4908 Office: Baker & Hostetler 3200 National City Ctr 1900 E 9th St Ste 3200 Cleveland OH 44114-3475

TOOMES, HEIKKI, thoracic surgeon, educator; b. Viljandi, Estonia, June 15, 1941; s. Aadu and Sinaida (Kalle) T.; m. Ann-Sofie Björk, July 5, 1969; children: Linda Miriam, Matti Vilhelm. MD, U. Lund, Sweden, 1970; PhD, U. Tübingen, Germany, 1987. Resident dept. thoracic and cardiovasc. surgery U. Lund, 1970-74; sr. thoracic surgeon Clinic for Thoracic Medicine, Heidelberg, Germany, 1975-84; head dept. thoracic surgery Schillerhoehe Hosp., Gerlingen, Germany, 1985—; mem. faculty U. Heidelberg, 1980-93, U. Tübingen, 1996—; numerous lectures and presentations at nat. and internat. congresses, 1977—. Assoc. editor Thoracic and Cardiovasc. Surgeon, 1988; contbr. numerous articles to med. jours. Recipient Curt-Adam prize Soc. for Med. Edn., Berlin, 1983. Mem. German Soc. for Thoracic Surgery (founding, pres. 1993-95), European Soc. Thoracic Surgeons (founding, pres. 2000-01), European Bd. Thoracic and Cardiovasc. Surgeons. Avocations: horseback riding, skiing. Office: Schillerhoehe Hosp, Solitudestrasse 18, D-70839 Gerlingen Baden-W, Germany

TOOMEY, JEANNE ELIZABETH, animal activist; b. N.Y.C., Aug. 22, 1921; d. Edward Aloysius and Anna Margaret (O'Grady) Toomey; m. Peter Terranova, Sept. 28, 1951 (dec. 1968); children: Peter Terranova, Sheila Terranova Beasley. Student, Hofstra U., 1938-40; student law sch., Fordham U., 1940-41; BA, Southampton Coll., 1976; postgrad., Monmouth Coll., 1978-79. Reporter, columnist Bklyn. Daily Eagle, 1943-52; with The Fitzgeralds, NBC Radio, N.Y.C., 1952-53; reporter, writer King Features Syndicate, N.Y.C., 1953-55; reporter, columnist N.Y. Jour.-Am., N.Y.C., 1955-61; newsman AP, N.Y.C., 1963-64; stringer; columnist News Tribune, Woodbridge, N.J., 1976-86; editor Calexico (Calif.) Chronicle, 1987-88; editor community sect. Asbury Park (N.J.) Press, 1988; pres., dir. Last Post Animal Sanctuary, Falls Village, Conn., 1989—. Author: Murder in the Hamptons, 1994, Assignment Homicide, 1998. Named Woman of the Yr. N.Y. Women's Press Club, 1960. Mem. Newswomen's Club of N.Y., Overseas Press Club, N.Y. Press Club, Sylurians. Roman Catholic. Address: PO Box 259 Falls Village CT 06031-0259

TOOMING, HEINO ÜLO, agrometeorologist, researcher; b. Mustvee, Tartumaa, Estonia, Oct. 22, 1930; s. Gustav and Amanda (Kadak) T.; m. Ilje Born, July 27, 1957 (div. 1971); children: Tõnis, Reet; m. Aili Maare Lauringson, June 7, 1976. Diploma in Geophysics, Tartu (Estonia) U., USSR, 1954, Candidate Phys. Math., 1961, DSc in Biology, 1972. Sr. rsch. scientist in geophysics Diploma, 1967; prof. meteorology, agrometeorology, climatology Diploma, 1990. Fellow Inst. Physics & Astronomy Estonian Acad. Scis., Tartu, USSR, 1954-74; fellow Eston Agrometeorol. Lab. Main Geophys. Observatory, Leningrad, USSR, 1974-76; fellow Estonian Agrometeorol. Lab. Inst. Exptl. Meteorology, Obninsk, USSR, 1976-77, Inst. Agrl. Meteorology, Obninsk, USSR, 1977-91; chief researcher Estonian Meteorol. and Hydrol. Inst., Tallinn, Estonia, 1991-99; sr. rsch. assoc. Estonian Nat. Def. and Pub. Svc. Acad., Tallinn, 1999—, prof. applied meteorology, 1995—; mem. coun. ecology Acad. Scis., Moscow, 1971-76, yield programming Acad. Agrl. Scis., 1974-91. Author: (with B.I. Guljaev) Methods of Measurements of Photosynthetically Active Radiation, 1967, Japanese edit., 1971, Solar Radiation and Yield Formation, 1977, Japanese edit., 1982, Ecological Principles of Maximum Crops Productivity, 1984; editor: Meteorology in Estonia in Johannes Letzmann's Times and Today, 1995; mem. editl. bd. Agrometeorology of the Hydrometeorological Pub. House, Leningrad, 1974-91; contbr. articles to profl. jours. Mem. Estonian Geograph. Soc., Estonian Ecol. Coun., Russian Soc. Plant Physiology (hon. corr.), Estonian Naturalists Soc. (hon., chair sec. exact sci. 1963-71), European and African Region Internat. Assn. Wind Engring. (Estonian contact 1995—). Avocations: essayistics, chess, philately. E-mail: tooming@research.emhi.ee. Home: Paekaare 68-6, 13611 Tallinn Estonia Office: Estonian Meteorol & Hydrol Inst, Teaduse 2, 75501 Saku Harjumaa, Estonia

TOOMPERE, MARIKA, philologist; b. Tallinn, Estonia, Dec. 22, 1950; d. Voldemar and Reet (Koplik) Erik; m. Peter Toompere (div. 1995); children: Henri, Kristine, Helene. Philologist of German pedagogical, U. Tallinn, 1973; nurse, Med. Sch., 1975; qualify for informatics, Tech. U., 1986. Tchr. High Sch., Tallinn, 1973-78; engr. Periodical Distbn., Tallinn, 1978-85; mng.

dir. Ministry of Post and Comm., Estonia, 1985-91; head internat. rels. SE Estonian Post, Estonia, 1991-98; prodn. dir. Estonian Post Ltd., Estonia, 1998—. Author: Catalogue of Estonian Newspapers and Magazines. Avocations: foreign languages, needlework. Home: Kalevipoja põik 10-22, Tallinn 13614, Estonia Office: Estonian Post, Narva Road 1, Tallinn 19090, Estonia

TOORABALLY, NAEEM SALAHUDDIN, import-export company executive; b. Baroda, Gujarat, India, Sept. 26, 1942; arrived in Japan, 1951; s. Haji Salahuddin and Rafia (Mohibi) T.; m. Falaknaaz Muljibhoy, Mar. 18, 1971; children: Nasreen, Nazeem. B in Commerce, M.S. U. Baroda, 1964. Dir. V.H. Toorabally & Co. Ltd., Osaka, Japan, 1965—; v.p. C.L. India (Pvt) Ltd., New Delhi. Avocation: gardening. Home: 6-17 Yamate Cho, Ashiya 659, Japan Office: VH Toorabally & Co Ltd, 4-12 Koraibashi 4-chome, Osaka 541-0043, Japan

TOPALIAN, NAOMI GETSOYAN, writer; b. Beirut, Lebanon, Jan. 26, 1928; came to the U.S., 1953; d. Avedis S. and Zarouhi T. (Yezegelian) G.; m. Paul G. Topalian, Sept. 18, 1954; children: Andrew P., Janet Z. Topalian Moffatt. Diploma, Am. U. Hosp. Sch. Nursing, Beirut, 1952; BS, Boston U., 1967. RN, Mass. Pediat. nurse Children Med. Ctr., Boston, 1954-55; inservice edn. supr. Winchester (Mass.) Hosp., 1967-70; tchr. nursing Northeastern Vocat. H.S., Wakefield, Mass., 1970-72; med. and surg. nurse various tchg. hosps., Boston, 1973-87. Author: Dust to Destiny, 1986, People, Places and Moultonborough, 1989, Legacy of Honor, 1995; contbr. Personality and Presidency: A Scientific Inquirey, 1998, Breaking the Rock of Tradition, 2000; contbr. articles to profl. jours. Supt. primary divsn., Sunday sch. tchr., mem. pulpit com., co-pres. couples club Armenian Meml. Ch., Watertown, Mass.; Armenian lang. tchr. First Armenian Ch. of Belmont; active Belmont Coun. Chs., chair religious edn. com.; pres. Armenian Women's Edn. Club. Mem. Armenian Internat. Womens Assn. Avocations: needle work, knitting, counseling the bereaved. Home: 46 Circle Rd Lexington MA 02420-2926

TOPEL, HELGA, scientific writer, scientific translator; b. Danzig, Poland, Mar. 22, 1924; d. Fritz Johannes Julius and Hertha Paula Johanna (Blech) T. PhD, U. Bonn, Fed. Republic of Germany, 1950. Freelance author various radio stas. and jours. West Germany, 1952-56, 59-61; asst. dir. Lyceum Alpinum Zuoz, Switzerland, 1957-58; sci. translator Deutscher Normenausschuss, Stuttgart, 1961-67; writer, translator various orgns., 1968-75; translator, rsch. libr. Rsch. Ctr. Maxhütte, Sulzbach-Rosenberg, Fed. Republic of Germany, 1975-84; freelance author Addictions Rsch., Sulzbach-Rosenberg, Fed. Republic of Germany, 1978—; cons. various therapeutic instns., East and West Germany, 1985—. Author: Biomedical Basis of Alcoholism, 1985, Endogene Opioide und Opiatrezeptoren im Alkoholismus, 1990, Euphorie und Dysphorie, 1991, Die Lebensqualität im Gehirn, 1994, Die Zeit der Idole, 1998. Recipient postgrad. scholarship German Rsch. Found., 1951. Mem. N.Y. Acad. Scis. Avocations: classical Russian literature, active in protection of bears. Home and Office: Adolf Kolping Strasse 7, Sulzbach Rosenberg 92237, Germany

TOPERVERG, BORIS P., physicist; b. Sevastopol, Russia, Apr. 7, 1948; s. Pavel M. and Evdokiya P. (Kulish) T.; m. Irina A. Brodskaya, Aug. 8, 1972; 1 child, Olga B. BS, Mcpl. Sch., Krasnodar, USSR, 1965; MS in Physics, Rostov State U., Rostov-on-Don, USSR, 1970; PhD in Physics, LNPI, Leningrad, USSR, 1980. Assoc. rschr. Leningrad Nuclear Physics Inst., Acad. Scis. USSR, Gatchina, 1972-86; sr. rsch. scientist Petersburg Nuclear Physics Inst., Russian Acad. Scis., Gatchina, 1986—; sr. rsch. scientist PNPI, St. Petersburg, Russia, 1980-86; gastwissenschaftler GKSS-Forschungszentrum, Geestchacht, Germany, 1990-91, Max-Planck-Inst., Stuttgart, Germany, 1998; dir. rsch. Lab. Leon Brillouin CEA-CNRS, Saclay, France, 1991-92; guest scientist Interfacultair Reactor Inst., Delft, The Netherlands, 1993, 97; physicist Inst. Laue Langevin, Grenoble, France, 1994-96, sci. collaborator, 1999—. Mem. European Phys. Soc., Neutron Scattering Soc. Am. Avocation: violin. Fax: ō76882416. E-mail: boristop@ill.fr. Home: Tuchkov 1-31, 199053 Saint Petersburg Russia Office: Inst Laue Langevin, av des Martyrs, 38042 Grenoble Cedex 9, France

TOPFER, FRANK-RAINER, lawyer, arbitrator; b. Leipzig, Saxony, Germany, Nov. 23, 1955; s. Manfred Arno and Gerda T.; m. Marion Carmen Spanier, Oct. 5, 1979; children: Tobias, Thomas. Dipl.Juris., Martin-Luther U., Halle-Wittenberg, Germany, 1982; JD, U. Economics, Berlin, 1985. Lectr., rsch. asst. U. Economics, Berlin, 1982-90; ptnr. Baker & McKenzie, Berlin, 1990—; arbitrator Berlin Ct. Arbitration, 1989—. Author: Law in the Trade with the German Democratic Republic, 1989, Market Guide to Eastern Germany, 1990, Practice of Mining Law, 1996. Mem. Berlin Bar, Soc. for Promotion of Arbitration (bd. mem.). Avocations: swimming, jogging. Home: Weinbergsweg 4, D-10119 Berlin Germany Office: Baker & McKenzie, Friedrichstr 79-80, 10117 Berlin Germany

TOPHØJ, LAURITS, NATO official; b. Sønderborg, Denmark, June 30, 1940; Married Else Tophøj; 2 children: Else, Trine. Student in flight schs., Denmark and Can., 1960-62; grad., Royal Danish Air Force Acad., 1967, Danish Armed Force Staff Coll., 1975. Commd. 2d lt. Danish Armed Forces, 1962, advanced through grades to lt. gen., 1997, pilot Air Def. squadron, 1962-69, pilot tactical fighter squadron, 1970-72; dep. ops. officer Danish Armed Forces, Air Sta. Aalborg, 1973-74; squadron comdr. transport squadron Danish Armed Forces, 1975-82, staff officer procurement br., Hdqrs. chief of def., 1982-84, ops. officer Air Sta. Aalborg, 1984-87, br. chief plans & resources Hdqrs. chief of def., 1987-88, base comdr. Air Sta. Karup, 1989-90, chief of staff Tactical Air Command of Denmark, 1990-94, comdr. Tactical Air Command of Denmark, 1994-97; Danish mil. rep. to NATO Hdqrs. Danish Armed Forces, Brussels, 1997—. Decorated Disting. Flying Cross. Named to Comdr. 1st class Order of Dannebørg. Office: NATO Hdqrs, Blvd Leopold III, 1110 Brussels Belgium*

TOPKAYA, YAVUZ ALI, metallurgy educator; b. Sivrihisar, Eskisehir, Turkey, Sept. 6, 1947; s. Mehmet and Halise (Bayar) T.; m. Fatma Ilhan Durusu, Feb. 20, 1975; children: Cem, Pinar. B in Metallurgy, Sheffield (Eng.) U., 1969; PhD, McMaster U., Hamilton, Ont., Can., 1974. Head metallurgy sect. Mineral Rsch. and Exploration Inst. Turkey, Ankara, Turkey, 1975-79; prof. Mid. East Tech. U., Ankara, 1979—, asst. head dept. metall. and materials engring., 1982-90, 97—; joint rschr. U.S. Bur. Mines, Salt Lake City, 1986-89, U. Liége, Belgium, 1988-90; vis. prof. Coun. for Mineral Tech., Johannesburg, South Africa, 1990. Contbr. articles to profl. jours. Com. mem. State Planning Orgn., Ankara, 1977. Scholar Turkish Govt., Eng./Can., 1964-74. Mem. Nat. Geog. Assn., Turkish Chamber Metall. Engring. Avocations: traveling, reading, listening to music, cinema, painting. Home: Bilkent Camlik Sitesi, Kugu Cikmazi Sokak 104, 06530 Bilkent Ankara Turkey Office: Dept Metall & Mat Engring, Middle East Tech Univ, 06531 Ankara Turkey

TOPLIN, ROBERT BRENT, history educator, television producer; b. Phila., Sept. 26, 1940; s. Maurice Cunningham and Janet Rachel (Belsinger) T.; m. Karin Bendel, Dec. 26, 1996; children: Cassandra, Jennifer. BS, Pa. State U., 1962; MA, Rutgers U., 1965, PhD, 1968. Asst. prof. Denison U., Granville, Ohio, 1968-74; assoc. prof. Denison U., Granville, 1976-78; assoc. prof. and program dir. U. Houston-Clear Lake City, 1974-76; assoc. prof. U. N.C. at Wilmington, 1978-80, prof. history, 1980; vis. prof. U. N.C.-Chapel Hill, 1983; media advisor NEH; lectr. in field. Project dir.: A House Divided (TV series) U.S.A.; A Television history, Pres.'s in Crisis, The Am. Frontier; author: The Abolition of Slavery in Brazil, 1972, Unchallenged Violence: An American Ordeal, 1975, Freedom and Prejudice: The Legacy of Slavery in the United States and Brazil, 1982, History By Hollywood: The use and Abuse of the American Past, 1996; editor: Slavery and Race Relations in Latin America, 1974; editor anthology: American History Through Film, 1983, Ken Burns's The Civil War: Historians Respond, 1996, Oliver Stone's USA: Film, History and Controversy, 2000; contbg. editor: Jour. Am. History, 1986—; contbr. articles to hist. jours.; book reviewer various jours.; project dir. Denmark Vesey's Rebellion (PBS TV), 1982, Solomon Northup's Odyssey (PBS TV), 1984; Charlotte Forten's Mission (PBS TV), 1985; (films) The War to End All Wars, 1985, Lincoln and the War Within, 1992. Pres. Williston Jr. H.S. PTA; v.p. New Hanover County PTA, New Hanover County Bd. Edn. Grantee or fellow Ford Found., 1967, NEH, 1970, 77-80, 82-89, 90-91, Am. Philos. Soc., 1970m 81, Denison U. Rsch. Found., 1972, Annenberg/Corp. for Pub. Broadcasting, 1983-84; grantee Ill. Humanities Coun., 1991; fellow Am. Coun. Learned Soc., 1991. Mem. Am. Hist. Assn. (tchg. com. 1990-93), Orgn. Am. Historians (mem. com. on radio, TV, film media 1978-80, Erik Barnouw prize 1985, 87-89), Conf. on Latin Am. History (com. on tchg. materials 1978), Erik Barnouw prize com. 1987-88. Democrat. Jewish. E-mail: Toplinrb@uncwil.edu. Office: U NC at Wilmington Dept History Wilmington NC 28403

TOPLISS, DUNCAN JAKE, endocrinologist; b. Burton-on-Trent, Eng., Nov. 14, 1950; arrived in Australia, 1957; s. Joseph William and Elsa (Wright) T.; m. Marian Heather Miller, July 19, 1986; 1 child, Jessica Elizabeth. MB BS, Monash U., Melbourne, Australia, 1973, MD, 1989. Med. officer Alfred Hosp., Melbourne, 1974-79; rsch. fellow dept. medicine U. Toronto, Can., 1979-81; rsch. assoc. dept. medicine U. Minn., Mpls., 1981-82; dep. dir. endocrinology and diabetes Alfred Hosp., Melbourne, 1982-96, dir. endocrinology and diabetes, 1996—; assoc. prof. medicine Monash U., Melbourne, 1993—; plenary lectr. Internat. Thyroid Congress, 1995. Contbr. numerous articles to med. jours. Fellow Royal Australasian Coll. Physicians, Am. Coll. Endocrinology; mem. Endocrine Soc. Australia (treas. 1992-96, pres. 1996-98), Asia and Oceania Thyroid Assn. (councillor 1991—, Otsuka prize 1995), Endocrine Soc. (U.S.), Am. Thyroid Assn., Assn. Monash Med. Grads. (pres. 1992—). Office: Alfred Hosp, Dept Endocrinology/Diabetes, 3181 Melbourne Australia

TOPOL, CHAIM, actor, producer, director; b. Tel Aviv, Sept. 9, 1935; s. Jacob and Rela (Goldman) T. BSC; m. Galia Finkelstein, 1956; 3 children. Founder Green Onion, satirical theatre, 1956, Mcpl. Theatre of Haifa (Israel), 1959; star London stage prodn. Fiddler on the Roof, U.S. stage prodn., 1989, Israeli tour, 1997-98, Melbourne, Australia, 1998; actor, producer, dir. Genesis Project, filming the Bible, N.Y.C.; films include Cast a Giant Shadow, 1965, Sallah, 1966, Before Winter Comes, 1969, A Talent for Loving, Fiddler on the Roof, 1971, The Public Eye, Flash Gordon, Follow Me, 1972, Galileo, 1974, For Your Eyes Only, 1980, Left Luggage, 1997, The House on Garibaldi Street, 1979; TV miniseries include: The Winds of War, 1983, Queenie, 1987, War and Remembrance, 1988. Recipient Best Actor Golden Globe award, David di Donatello award, Golden Gate award; nominated Acad. award, Tony award, 1991. Author: (autobiography) Topol by Topol, 1981, To Life, 1994, Topol's Treasury of Jewish Humour, Wit and Wisdom, 1995. Address: 3 Dov Hoz St, Tel Aviv 63564, Israel

TOPOLSKI, JERZY, historian, educator; b. Poznan, Poland, Sept. 20, 1928; s. Wladyslaw Topolski and Halina (Pietrzynska) Topolska-Cychnerska; m. Zofia Kulejewska, Apr. 21, 1954 (div. 1958); m. 2d Maria Barbara Antczak, Sept. 9, 1961 (div. 1978); m. 3d Maria Danuta Labedzka, July 29, 1978. M.Polit. Economy, U. Poznan, 1950; Ph.D., U. Torun (Poland), 1951. Asst., U. Poznan, 1951; fellow Acad. Social Scis., Warsaw, 1951-54; prof. asst. Polish Acad. Scis., 1954-56, docent Polish Acad. Scis.-U. Poznan, 1956-61; prof. U. Poznan, 1961—, also vice dir. Inst. History, 1968-81, dir. inst., 1981-89. Author: Birth of Capitalism in Europe, 1965, 2d edit., 1976, Methodology of History (State award 1969), 1968, Theory of Historical Knowledge, 1983, The Manorial Economy in Early Modern East-Central Europe, 1994, Poland in Early Modern Period, 1994; co-author, editor: History of Poland (State award 1978), 1976. Judge, State Tribunal, Warsaw, 1982, 90; pres. Polish Com. of Hist. Scis., 1984-91. Decorated Comdr.'s Cross Order Polonia Restituta (Poland); prof. Contemporary Philosphy of History, Institute of History. Office: U Poznań Inst History, SW Marcin 78, 61-809 Poznań Poland*

TOPP, SUSAN HLYWA, lawyer; b. Detroit, Oct. 9, 1956; d. Michael Leo and Lucy Stella (Rusak) Hlywa; m. Robert Elwin Topp, July 25, 1985; children: Matthew, Sarah, Michael and Jamie (triplets). BS in Edn. cum laude, Ctrl. Mich. U., 1978; JD cum laude, Wayne State U., Detroit, 1991. Bar: Mich. 1992, U.S. Dist. Ct. (ea. dist.) Mich. 1992. Conservation officer Mich. Dept. Natural Resources, Pontiac, 1980-88; environ. conservation officer Mich. Dept. Natural Resources, Livonia, 1988-93; pvt. practice Gaylord, Mich., 1993; ptnr. Rolinski & Topp, PLC, Gaylord, 1993; assoc. Plunkett & Cooney, PC, Gaylord, 1993—; adj. faculty Audubon Internat. Active Rocky Mountain Mineral Law Found., Urban Land Inst. Recipient Am. Jurisprudence award Wayne State U., 1987, Trial Advocacy award, 1988. Mem. ABA (nat. resources and environ. law com.), AAUW, Mich. State Bar Assn. (environ. law sect. coun. mem. 1999), Mich. C. of C. Roman Catholic. Avocations: backpacking, skiing, scuba diving, back-country camping, canoeing. Office: Plunkett & Cooney PC 123 W Main St Gaylord MI 49735-1397

TORASHIMA, KAZUO, federal official. Dir. gen. Japan Def., Tokyo. Office: 9-7-45 Akasaka, Minato-ku, Tokyo 107-8513, Japan*

TORCHÉ, MARK DAVID, physics educator; b. Syracuse, N.Y., Feb. 9, 1957; s. Robert Samuel Torché and Anita May (Knowlton) Timmel; m. Kelly Elizabeth Schumaci, Oct. 30, 1982. BS in Physics, SUNY, New Paltz, 1986, MS in Sci. Edn., 1992. Cert. pub. sch. tchr., N.Y. Avionics instr. USAF, Biloxi, Miss., 1977-79; physics tchr. Highland Falls (N.Y.) High Sch., 1988-89, New Paltz High Sch., 1989—; ednl. cons. IBM, Atlanta, 1992—, Ulster County Bd. Cooperative Ednl. Svcs., New Paltz, 1993—. V.p. New Paltz United Tchrs., 1993—. Named Master Tchr., WNYT-Texaco Nat. Tchr. Tng. Inst., 1993-94; fellow Partnership in Edn. and Industry, 1991. Mem. ASCD, Am. Assn. Physics Tchrs., Sci. Tchrs. Assn. N.Y. State. Avocations: model rocketry, R-C airplanes, model making, underwater photography. Office: New Paltz HS Physics Dept 196 Main St New Paltz NY 12561-1200

TORCHYNSKA, TETYANA VICTORIVNA, physicist; b. Dnipropetrovsk, Ukraine, Oct. 31, 1950; s. Victor Trofimovich and Elvina Stepanovna (Koorochkina) T.; m. Georgiy Prokofierich; m. Georgiy Prokofievich Polupan, Oct. 7, 1972; 1 child, Oleg Georgievich. MS, Nat Tech U, Kiev, Ukraine, 1973; PhD, Inst. of Semiconductors, Kiev, Ukraine, 1978, DSc, 1991, Sr. Scientists, 1991, Investigator, 1992. Engr. Nat. Tech. U., Kiev, 1973-74; postgrad. student Inst. Semiconductors, Kiev, 1974-77, scientist investigator, 1977-84, sr. scientist, 1984-90, head of dept., 1990—; full prof. Nat. Inst. Polytechnic Illepieo, 1999—; mem. gen. scientific counsel Inst. Semiconductor for Physics, Kiev, 1997—, mem. specialised qualification counsel of doctor degree award, 1995—; mem. of counsel space gelioenergetics Nat. Space Agy., Kiev, 1993—; mem. counsel application physics Min. of Scis. and Tech., Kiev, 1997—. Author: (book) Mechanism of Degradation of III-V Semiconductor LEDs and Lasers, 1997; author inventions in field; contbr. articles to profl. jours. Mem. Women of Ukraine, 1998—, Space Fedn. of Ukraine, 1992—. Recipient State Ukrainian prize Pres. of Ukraine, Kiev, 1995, medal "In Memory of 1500th Anniversary of Kiev," Presidium of Supreme Soviet, Moscow, 1983, medal "Innovator USSR," Cabinet of Min. of Nat. Acad. of Scis., Moscow medal, 1988, 98, others. Mem. Am. Physics Soc., N.Y. Acad. Scis., SPIE Ukraine Soc., Am. Material Rsch. Soc. Avocation: painting. Office: Nat Poly Inst Material Sci, Facutly Physics and Maths, 07738 Mexico City Mexico

TORELLA, LUCIO, editor; b. Napoli, Italy, May 28, 1929; s. Amedeo and Maria (Dolcetti) T.; 1 child, Anna Luisa. Diploma in accountancy, U. Napoli, 1949. Reporter Corriere Lombardo, Milan, 1949-54, Autoclub/VIA, Milan, 1954-62; editor Notiziario Motoristico Catalogo Motoristico, 1962-96; pres. Expomotor, Milan, 1973-75; dir. Milano Centro Notizie, 1994—; reporter Il Leonardo, 1994-95; dir. Milano Centro Notizie; pres. Expomotor, Milan, 1973-75. Mem. Lions Club Leonardo Da Vinci (pres. 1996, treas. 1994, 95, 97, Melvyn Jones award 1997). Home: Vie Lombardia 18, 20131 Milan Italy Office: ACI Edizioni Motoristiche, Via B Crespi 30/2, 20159 Milan Italy

TORFFVIT, OLE JOHN, physician, researcher; b. Naestved, Denmark, Nov. 11, 1951; s. Jens Carl William and Annelise (Kristansen) Jensen; m. Annette Britta Petersen, Nov. 27, 1971 (div. Oct. 1991); children: Kasper, Nana; m. Eva Kerstin Maria Persson, Feb. 17, 1996; children: Felicia, Simon. MD, U. Copenhagen, 1977; diploma in internal and renal medicine, Sweden, 1985, diploma in endocrinology, 1998; PhD, U. Lund, Sweden, 1991. Resident Hosp., Halmstad, Sweden, 1977-82; resident Univ. Hosp., Lund, 1982-85, specialist, 1985—, tchr., 1988-91, splst. in internal and renal medicine, 1985—, assoc. prof., 1995, specialist in endocrinology, 1998—. Author: Diabetic Nephropathy, 1991; contbr. articles to profl. jours. Mem. European Assn. for the Study of Diabetes (hon. sec. 2000—), European Diabetic Nephropathy Study Group. Office: Dept Internal Medicine, Univ Hosp, 221 85 Lund Sweden

TORFOSS, DAG, physician; b. Oslo, Apr. 9, 1952; s. Jan and Vanja Evelyn (Larsson) T.; m. Gerd Hilda Tanke, Aug. 2, 1977; 1 child, Irene. Cand.med., U. Oslo, 1986. Lic. specialist infectious diseases, Norway; lic. specialist in medicine, Norway; bd. cert. internal medicine. Resident Cmty. Hosp., Norway, 1986-89, VAMC, Boise, Idaho, 1989-90, UHIMRP, Honolulu, 1991-93, Ulleval U. Hosp., Oslo, 1994-96, Rikshispitalet U. Hosp., Oslo, 1996-98, 98-00; attending physician infectious diseases Det Norske Radiumhospital, 2000. Fellow U. Hawaii Integrated Med. Residency Program, 1993-94. Mem. The Norwegian Med. Assn., Am. Coll. Physicians.

TORFS, DIRK EDDY, automation executive; b. Leuven, Belgium, Nov. 6, 1965; m. Godelieve Notre, Dec. 12, 1992. Diploma in mech. engring., Cath. U. Leuven, 1989, PhD, 1995, degree in bus. adminstrn., 1998. Rschr. Cath. U. Leuven, 1989-95; projects and engring. mgr. Trasys, Zaventem, Belgium, 1995-96, divsn. head, 1996-98; project and engring. mgr. ABB Belgium, 1998-2000; vice-CEO Begaux Imtech & Imtech Automation, Wommelgem, Belgium, 2000—, also bd. dirs. Contbr. articles to profl. jours. Mem. IEEE, BIRA (Best Engr. Thesis award 1989), KVIV. Avocations: soccer, travel. Home: Grote Baan, B-3150 Wespelaar Belgium Officw: Imtech, Koralenhoeve 9, B-2160 Wommelgem Belgium

TORI, CARLOS A., pediatrician; b. Lima, Peru, July 17, 1940; s. Antonio and Alicia Arena Tori; m. Mariana H. Fernandez, June 6, 1966; children: Patricia, Ursula, Alvaro. MD, U. Peruna Cayetano Heredia, Lima, 1966. Diplomate Am. Bd. Pediats. Jr. resident Hosp. for Sick Children, Toronto, Ont., Can., 1966-67, sr. resident, 1967-68; sr. asst. resident Johns Hopkins Hosp., Balt., 1968-69; fellow in neonatology N.Y. Hosp., Cornell Med. Ctr., N.Y.C., 1969-70; pediatrician Air Force Hosp., Lima, 1970-72, Clinica San Felipe, Lima, 1970—; invited prof. pediats. U. Peruana Cayetano Heredia, Lima; pediatrician Clinica Medica Cayetano Heredia, Lima, 1993—, Clinica San Felipe, Lima, 1971—. Mem. Los Inkas Country Club (mem. qualifying bd. 1998—). Roman Catholic. Avocations: tennis, golf, river ganotaje, ham radio. Office: Gregorio Escobedo 650, Office 404, L-11 Jesus Maria Peru

TORII, KIYOSHI, English literature educator; b. Osaka, Japan, May 28, 1935; s. Seihei and Shizu (Shimizu) T.; m. Tsuyako Kishimoto, Aug. 1, 1965; children: Manabu, Mariko. BA, Osaka City U., 1963, MA, 1970. English tchr. Tezukayama H.S., Nara City, 1963-68; lectr. English lit. Osaka Seikei Jr. Coll., Osaka City, 1970-73, asst. prof., 1973-81; assoc. prof. Osaka Shoin Women's Coll., Higashi-osaka City, 1981-83, prof., 1983—, chmn. dept. English, 1990-96, dean of admissions, 1996-2000, dean Faculty of Liberal Arts, 2000—; dean of students Osaka Shoin Women's Coll., 1986-90, councilor of bd. trustees Osaka Shoin Ednl. Inst., Higashi-osaka City, 1986-90, 94—. Author: A Genealogy of Gull-Catcher in Shakespeare, 2000; co-author: English Language and Literature, 1981, Surface and Depth of Britain, 1987, Studies in English Language and Literature, 1988. Mem. planning com. for Citizen's Conf. Higashi-osaka City, 1987—. Recipient Award of the Contbn. to Mcpl. Activities Mayor of Higashi-osaka City, 1988, 1997. Mem. Young Men Christian Assn. Osaka. Office: Osaka Shoin Womens Univ, 4-2-26 Hishiya-nishi, Higashi-osaka 577-8550, Japan

TORII, SHUICHI, mechanical engineer, educator, researcher; b. Asakura, Fukuoka, Japan, Jan. 27, 1960; s. Osamu and Hiroko (Tokoshima) T.; m. Naomi Yasutake, Dec. 11, 1988; children: Shunichiro, Yasutaka. BS, Kagoshima (Japan) U., 1983; MS, Kyushu U., Fukuoka, Japan, 1985, Dr.Engring., 1989. Rsch. assoc. Kyushu U., Fukuoka, 1985-89; rsch. assoc. Kagoshima (Japan) U., 1989-93, assoc. prof., 1993—; vis. scholar U. Mich., Ann Arbor, 1990-91. Editor Jour. Soc. Mech. Engrs.. Tokyo, 1994—; contbr. articles to profl. jours. Mem. AIAA, ASME, Japan Soc. Mech. Engrs., Atomic Energy Soc. Japan, Heat Transfer Soc. Japan.

TORII, SHUKO, psychology educator; b. Toyohashi, Aichi-ken, Japan, Apr. 5, 1930; m. Toshiko Mochizuki, June 19, 1975. BA, U. Tokyo, 1954, MA, 1956, PhD, 1964. Rsch. asst. Tokyo Inst. Tech., 1959-61, U. Tokyo, 1961-65; assoc. prof. Tokyo U. Agr. Tech., 1965-70; rsch. assoc. U. Mich., Ann Arbor, 1966-68; rsch. assoc. Inst. Molecular Biophysics Fla. State U., 1968-69; from assoc. prof. to prof. psychology U. Tokyo, 1970-91; prof. U. Sacred Heart, Tokyo, 1991-2000, prof. emeritus, 2000—. Author: The World of Vision, 1979, Psychology of Vision, 1982, Visual Perception in the Congenitally or Early Blinded after Surgery, 1992, 2nd edit., 1997; author, editor: Perception, 1983, Visually Handicapped and Technology of Sensory Substitution, 1984, The Visually Handicapped and Their Cognitive Activity, 1993. Mem. Japanese Psychonomic Soc. (assoc. editor 1981-88, editor 1988-96, pres. 1996-99), Japanese Psychol. Assn. (mem. editorial com. 1987-89, editor 1989-92), Optical Soc. Am., Assn. Rsch. in Vision and Ophthalmology. Home: 2-17-26-204 Takada, Toshima, Tokyo 171-0033, Japan

TORII, TETSUYA, retired science educator; b. Takao, Taiwan, May 14, 1918; s. Nobuhei Torii and Masako Suzuki; m. Noriko; children: Tohru, Mari Tanaka, Nobuya. MS, Univ. Tokyo, 1943, DSc (hon.), 1956. Chem. lectr. Kanagawa U., Yokohama, Japan, 1952-55; assoc. prof. chem. Chiba U., Japan, 1955-62, prof. chem., 1962-63; prof. chem. Chiba Inst. Tech., 1963-90; exec. dir. The Japan Polar Rsch. Assn., Tokyo, 1964-94; pres. Japan Polar Rsch. Assn., Tokyo, 1995—; dir. Japan Chem. Analysis Ctr., Chiba, 1980-90. Editor: pictorial book Antarctica 1970 (adapted to put into the time capsule); discoverer: new mineral in Antarctica antarcticite 1965. Officer Japanese Navy, 1943-45. Recipient Silver Cup, Prime Minister of Japan, 1962, citation Ministry of Edn., Sci. and Culture, 1977, prize Geochem. Rsch. Assn., 1977. Mem. Am. Geophys. Union, Geochem. Soc. Japan, Balneological Soc. Japan (pres. 1988), Explorer Club (U.S.A.). Avocation: mountaineering. Home: 4 18 18 Ogikubo, Suginami-ku, Tokyo 167-0051, Japan Office: The Japan Polar Rsch Assn, 2-3-4 Hirakawa-cho, Tokyo Chiyoda 102-0093, Japan

TORIIZUKA, KAZUO, research scientist, pharmacist; b. Tokyo, Minato-ku, Japan, Jan. 12, 1954; s. Kiyoshi and Nao (Kurita) T.; m. Yoshie Kojima, Nov. 10, 1979; children: Yosuke, Shozo, Tomoyo. BS in Pharm. Scis., Chiba (Japan) U., 1977, MS, 1979; PhD, Toyama Med. & Pharm. U., 1987. Rschr. SS Pharm. Co., Ltd., Chiba, 1979-80; pharmacist Toyama Med. & Pharm. U., 1980-86, lectr., 1983-88, asst. prof., 1988-92; vice dir., chief lab. Oriental Medicine Rsch. Ctr. Kitasato Inst., Tokyo, 1992-2000; assoc. prof. Showa U., Tokyo, 2000—; vis. asst. prof. U. Tex. Health Sci. Ctr., San Antonio, 1988-90, adj. assoc. prof., 1993-96, adj. prof., 1996—; lectr. Showa U., Tokyo, 1995-2000. Author: Basic Skills in Clinical Pharmacy Practice, 1985, Pharmacology of Japanese Traditional Kampo Medicine, 1997, Recent Advances in Pharmacological Research on Traditional Herbal Medicine, 1999; mem. editl. bd. Japanese Jour. Oriental Medicine, 1997—. Grantee Uehara Meml. Found., 1994, Rsch. Encouragement award Isukura Kampo Medicine, 1995, Min. Health and Welfare Japan, 1993-98. Mem. Japan Soc. for Oriental Medicine, Med. and Pharm. Soc. for Wakan-Yaku (bd. dirs. 1992—). Avocations: reading books, mountaineering. Office: Sch Pharm Scis/Showa Univ, 1-5-8 Hatanodai, Shinagawa, Tokyo 142-8555, Japan

TORIO, MELANIO SARUCA, government official; b. Tayug, Pangasinan, Philippines, Oct. 22, 1948; s. Miguel Silvestre and Soledad B. (Saruca) T.; m. Sonja Franco Alameda, July 16, 1969; children: Nicollo A., Cromwell A. AB in Polit. Sci. U. Philippines, 1969, postgrad., 1990-92; MBA Candidate, Ateneo de Manila, Philippines, 1995. Acting supt. printing Nat. Printing Office, Quezon City, Philippines, 1993-96, acting supt., 1993-98, supt. printing, 1998, asst. dir., 1998, dir. IV, 1998—; mem. Cmposite Adv. Group, Philippines, 1996; treas. Printing Industry Bd. Philippines, 1992-94, dep. chmn., 1992-98; chmn. Printing Industry Bd. Found., Philippines, 1999—; interim pres. Philippine Assn. Govt. Printing Instns., 1999. With Philippine mil., 1998-99. Named Outstanding Citizen of Las Pinas City, City Govt. of Las Pinas, 1998. Mem. Rotary of Las Pinas-Central, Philippines (dir. 1986-87), Kiwanis of Las Pinas (v.p. 1987), Toastmasters Club of Las Pinas (v.p. 1988), Printing Industry Bd. Found., Inc. (chmn. 1998-99), Philippine Assn. Govt. Printing Instns. (chmn. 1998-99). Mem. Ch. of Jesus Christ of Latter Day Saints. Avocations: swimming, hiking, reading. Home: Lt 3 Blk 7 Gloria Diaz St, BF Resort Village, Las Pinas City Philippines

Office: Nat Printing Office, EDSA cor NIA Northside Rd, Diliman Quezon City 1104, Philippines

TORIUMI, IWAO, trading company executive; b. Feb. 22, 1933; m. Toshiko Toriumi; children: Manami and Ayumi. Degree, Hitotsubashi U., Tokyo, 1956. Dir. Marubeni Corp., 1986—, exec. v.p., 1991-92, pres., 1992—, CEO, chmn. Mem. Japan Fedn. Econ. Orgns. (acting chmn. com. on fgn. trade 1994-96, chmn. Japan-Myanmar econ. com. 1995—), Japan Fgn. Trade Coun., Inc. (v.p. 1994—), Japan Assn. Corp. Execs. (vice chmn. com. on N.Am.-Japan rels. 1993-95, chmn. com. on Oceania-Japan rels. 1995-97, chmn. on aging and declining birth rate 1997—), Japan Textile Importers Assn. (pres. 1994-96), Japan-U.S. Bus. Coun. (exec. com. mem. 1994-97), Japan-Qatar Friendship Assn. (pres. 1994—), Japan Fedn. of Importers' Orgn. (pres. 1995-96), Tokyo C. of C. and Industry (com. on internat. econ. affairs 1997—). Office: Marubeni Corp, 1-4-2 Ohtemachi, 1-chome, Chiyoda-ku Tokyo 100-8088, Japan*

TORKELSSON, ULF JOAKIM, astronomer; b. Örkelljunga, Sweden, June 12, 1966; s. Erik Herbert and Kerstin Margareta (Johnsson) T. BSc, U. Lund, Sweden, 1989, PhD, 1994. Postdoctoral fellow U. Utrecht, Netherlands, 1994-95; postdoctoral fellow Inst. of Astronomy Cambridge (Eng.) U., 1995-98; lectr. Göteborg U., 1998—. Contbr. articles to sci. jours., including Astronomy and Astrophysics, Astrophys. Jour., Chaos, Solitons and Fractals, Monthly Notices Royal Astron. Soc. Office: Chalmers U Tech/ Goteborg U, Dept Theoretical Physics, S-412 96 Göteborg Sweden

TORKELUND, KAY ROBERT, financial executive; b. Roedovre, Copenhagen, Denmark, Apr. 16, 1959; arrived in Germany, 1987; s. Kaj August and Eileen Ruth (Chapman) T.; m. Jytte Friis, Sept. 5, 1961 (div. Jan. 2000); children: Madeleine, Marc. B.Com., U. Copenhagen, 1986. With Forstaedernes Bank, Copenhagen, 1982-84; salesman Siemens, Copenhagen, 1984-87; deposit broker Exco, Frankfurt, Germany, 1987-91; sales mgr. Flemings, Luxemburg, Frankfurt, 1991-94; mng. dir. Mercury Vertrieb SG, Frankfurt, 1994-97; European sales dir. Threadneedle Investments, London, 1997—; bd. dirs. Mercury Asset Mgmt. SA, Luxembourg, Threadneedle Investment Fund Mgrs. S.A., Luxembourg, Threadneedle Global Assets SicAv, Luxembourg. Mem. Royal Danish Businessmen's Club. Avocations: family, windsurfing. Fax: (352) 471341. Home: 18 Elm Grove Rd, L-6858 London SW13 0BT, England

TORKORNOO, GERTRUDE ARABA ESAABA, lawyer; b. Cape Coast, Ghana, Sept. 11, 1962; d. Abraham Kofi and Comfort Aba Sackey; m. Francis Kofi Torkornoo, Nov. 1989; children: Matita, Edem, Seyiram, Selasi. BA, U. Ghana, Accra, 1984; B Law, Ghana Sch. of Law, 1986. Legal aid asst. FIDA (Ghana), Accra, 1986-87; assoc. Fugar & Co., Accra, 1987-93, dir., 1993-96; assoc. Nabarro Nathanson, London, 1989-90, 91; sr. ptnr. Sozo Law Consult, Accra, 1997—; cons. Productivity Inst. Mgmt. Devel., Accra, 1992—; cons. Ministry Rds. & Hwys., Accra, 1994; exec. mem. Ghana Inst. Bldg., Accra, 1994. Contbr. articles to profl. jours. Legal aid officer Int. Fedn. Women Lawyers, 1987-90; v.p Women Aglow Fellowship Internat., Sakumono, 1996; assoc. mem. Ghana Inst. Bldg., 1995. Mem. Ghana Bar Assn., Internat. Bar Assn., Internat. Constrn. Contracts Com. Coun. Charismatic Chs. Avocations: teaching, lecturing, tennis. Office: Sozo Law Consult, PO Box C2108, PO Box Accra Ghana

TÖRMÄLÄ, PERTTI OLAVI, engineering educator, inventor; b. Tampere, Finland, Nov. 26, 1945; s. Matti Olavi and Elma (Kaarina) T.; m. Mirja Leena. MSc, U. Helsinki, 1970, B.Md.Sci., 1973, PhD, 1974, MD hc, 2000. Asst. prof. non-metallic materials Inst. Materials Sci. Tampere U. Tech., 1975-82, prof. textile tech. and inst. chmn., 1983-85, temp. occupant of professorship plastics tech., 1984-85, prof. plastics tech. and inst. chmn., 1985-98; rsch. prof. Acad. of Finland, Tampere, 1986-91, acad. prof. of Finland, 1995—; bd. dirs. Bionx Implants Inc. Contbr. over 600 articles to profl. jours.; author 8 textbooks. Recipient Inventor award Ministry of Trade and Industry, 1987, Finnish Engring. Work award, 1988, Tech. award of Nordic Coun., 1988, award Tampere U. Tech., 1993. Achievements include 200 international patents. Office: Tampere Univ of Tech, PO Box 589, FIN33101 Tampere Finland

TORMEN, GIUSEPPE, astrophysicist; b. Belluno, Italy, Jan. 2, 1962; s. Ferruccio and Rosa (Morra) T.; m. Francesca Ravagni, Jan. 1, 1992. Laurea in Physics, U. Padua, Italy, 1987, PhD in Astronomy, 1994. Visitor Ariz. State U. and MIT, Cambridge, Mass., 1992-93; rsch. fellow Inst. Astrophysics, Paris, 1994-95, U. Cambridge, Eng., 1995-96, Max Plack Inst. for Astrophysics, Munich, 1996-98, U. Padova, Italy, 1998—. Contbr. articles to profl. jours. Roman Catholic. Avocations: music, photography, cycling, chess. Home: Via G Segusini 13, 32100 Belluno Italy Office: U Padua Dept Astronomy, Vicolo dell'Osservatorio 5, 35122 Padua Italy

TÖRN, AIMO ALF, computer science educator; b. Lovisa, Finland, June 29, 1938; s. Ilmari Lauri and Helga Karin Sofia (Kronfelt) T.; m. Annamaija Rautiainen, June 1967; children: Niklas Petri, Tomas Matti. MS, Abo Akademi U., Finland, 1961; PhD, Abo Akadermi U., Finland, 1963, DS, 1974. Asst. prof. math. Abo Akademi U., Finland, 1972-74, assoc. prof. Sch. of Econs. and Bus. Adminstrn., 1974-80, assoc. prof. adminstrv. data processing, 1980-90, prof. computer sci., 1990—; vice rector AA Sch. of Econs. and BA, Finland, 1978-80; chmn. AA Computer Ctr. Bd., 1980—, Abo Scientific Bd. of Mil. Def., 1990—. Editor: Noak '77 Proceedings, 1977; author: (books) Programming From Problem to Documentation, 1981, Global Optimization, 1989, Simulation Modelling, 1991. Chmn. Swedish People's Party, Abo, 1987-91. Mem. Assn. Computing Machinery, IEEE. Achievements include clustering approach to global optimization. Office: Abo AkademiDept, Dept Computer Sci, FIN20520 Abo Finland

TORNABENE, PHILLIP A.A., real estate investor; b. Innisfail, Queensland, Australia, Oct. 22, 1939; s. Ross Tornabene and Ida (Lizzio) Garozzo; m. Noeline Briskie, Aug. 28, 1963; children: Victoria, Mariesa. H.S. Diploma, St. Augustine's, Cairns, Australia, 1957. Various sales positions, 1960-85; mng. dir. Lake Group Australia Pty. Ltd., 1985-92, H.M.S. Australia Pty. Ltd., Brisbane, Australia, 1993-98; residential property trader, networking builder PNT Consulting Pty Ltd. representing Morinda International, 1998—. Mem. Tattersals Club.

TORNATORE, GIUSEPPE, film director; b. Bagheria, Palermo, Italy, May 27, 1956. Dir., screenwriter: (films) Il Camorrista, 1986, Cinema Paradiso, 1988 (Acad. award for fgn. lang. film 1989, Brit. Acad. Film and TV Arts awards for best fgn. lang. film and best original screenplay 1990, Golden Globe award for best fgn. film 1990, Cannes Internat. Film Festival Grand Prize), Everybody's Fine, 1990, A Pure Formality, 1994, The Star Maker, 1995; co-dir. La Domenica Specialmente, 1991, (film anthology) Lo Schermo a Tre Punte, 1995; Dir., Legend of the Pianiston the Ocean, 1998. Malena, 2000. Home: via Santamaura 7, Rome Italy Office: Dirs Guild Am 7920 W Sunset Blvd Los Angeles CA 90046-3300*

TORNBERG, CLAES EGMONT, university administrator; b. Vaesteraas, Sweden, Feb. 10, 1936; s. Egmont Lars and Aina (Setterborg) T.; m. Ann-Charlotte Elisabeth von Hofsten, June 19, 1959; children: Caroline, Catharina, Richard, Peter. Grad., SW War Coll., 1966, SW War Coll., 1968; M in Strategy, Mgmt. and Naval Scis., U.S. Naval War Coll., 1977; grad., U.S. Postgrad. Sch., 1989. Comdg. officer; head planning and policy dept. Naval Staff, 1979-83; comdr. Swedish Fleet, 1983-90; commandant SW War Coll./Def. Coll., 1990-98; mgmt. cons.; chmn. Krisineberg Rsch. Sta., Gothenburg U. Contbr. articles to profl. jours. Rear adm. Swedish Navy, 1985. Fellow Swedish Inst. Internat. Efforts; mem. Royal Acad. Naval Scis. (pres. 1991—), Royal Acad. Mil. Scis., The Swedish Maritime League (pres. 1999—). Lutheran. Home: Strandstigen 11, 18134 Lidingoe Sweden

TORNHAGE, CARL-JOHAN ANDERS, pediatrician; b. Joncoping, Sweden, Sept. 12, 1953; s. Harald Karl-Olof and Ingegerd Tora (Thorman) T.; m. Ewy Barbro Nystrom, Mar. 3, 1984; children: Hanna, Emmma, Linnea, Robert, Elina. MD, U. Gothenburg, Sweden, 1980; PhD in Medicine, U. Umea, Sweden, 1997. Pvt. practice pediatrics, Umea, 1988—, pvt. practice neonatology,, 1995—. Home: Boterstena Post Box 1188, 54294 Mariestad Sweden Office: Nuclear Hosp, 54185 Skövde Sweden

TÖRNQVIST, RUNAR OLOF, program manager; b. Stockholm, Sweden, Dec. 18, 1952; arrived in Finland, 1956; s. Gunnar Olof and Berit Ingar (Stenberg) T.; m. Carola Christina Nyman, Jan. 20, 1990; children: Jannika, Jockum, Jerker. MS in Physics, Helsinki U. Tech., 1977, D of Technology in Physics, 1983; MS in Econs., Helsinki Swedish Sch. Econs., 1986. Teaching and rsch. asst. Helsinki U. Tech., Espoo, Finland, 1979-80; sr. scientist Lohja Corp., Espoo, Finland, 1981-83, project mgr., 1984-85, yield analyst, 1986, mgr. ale devel., 1987, mgr. ale and el devel., 1988, mgr. color el. devel., 1989-90; mgr. color el. devel. Planar Internat., Espoo, Finland, 1991-98; dir. product engring. Planar Internat., Espoo, 1998-99; vis. rschr. U. Pasteur, Strasbourg, France, 1978. Contbr. articles to profl. jours. Chmn. Pro-Strömsby, Kirkonummi, Finland, 1989, 90. Recipient 1st prize Nat. Physics Competition Math. and Sci. Tchrs. Assn., Helsinki, 1972. Achievements include 2 patents. Avocations: Sailing, Scandinavian history. Office: Planar Internat, Olarinluoma 9, Espoo FIN-02200, Finland

TORNQVIST, STEFAN, program manager; b. Arboga, Sweden, Mar. 7, 1968; s. Sture and Kerstin (Holmgren) T. MSocSc, Uppsala U., Sweden, 1994. Rsch. officer FOA-Defense Rsch. Establishment, Stockholm, 1994—; officer res., 1992—. Avocations: cooking, riding, reading. Office: FOA Defense Rsch, SE 17290 Stockholm Sweden

TORNSTROM, ROBERT ERNEST, lawyer, oil company executive; b. St. Paul, Jan. 17, 1946; s. Clifford H. and Janet (Hale) T.; m. Betty Jane Hermann, Aug. 5, 1978; children: Carter, Gunnar, Katherine. BA, U. Colo., 1968, JD, 1974; diploma grad. sch. mgmt. exec. program, UCLA, 1990. Bar: Colo. 1974, U.S. Dist. Ct. Colo. 1974, Calif. 1975, U.S. Dist. Ct. (cen. dist.) Calif. 1975. Atty. Union Oil Co. of Calif., Los Angeles, 1974-76, counsel internat. div., 1977-78; regional counsel Union Oil Co. of Calif., Singapore, 1976-77; sr. atty. Occidental Internat. Exploration and Prodn. Co., Bakersfield, Calif., 1978-81, mng. counsel, 1981-85, v.p., assoc. gen. counsel, 1985-88, v.p., regional ops. mgr., 1988-91; pres. Occidental Argentina, Buenos Aires, 1991-93, Occidental of Russia, Moscow, 1993-94; dir. comml. negotiations Occidental Internat., 1994-96; chmn. of bd. Sullivan Petroleum Co., 1997—; bd. dirs., chmn. bd. Parmaneft Joint Venture, Vanyogannef JV, Moscow; bd. dirs. Calif. Land and Cattle Co., King City, 602 Operating Corp.; exec. bd. Cmty. House, Bakersfield; legal cons. Island Creek Coal Co., Lexington, Ky. Served to capt. U.S. Army, 1968-71, Vietnam. Decorated Bronze Star. Recipient Am. Jurisprudence award Bancroft-Whitney Co., 1974; named Eagle Scout, Boy Scouts Am. Mem. Am. Soc. Internat. Law, Am. Corp. Counsel Assn., Soc. Mayflower Descendants, Moscow Country Club, Stockdale Country Club. Republican. Episcopalian. Avocations: skiing, tennis, golf, riding, collecting classic automobiles. Home: 310 Mount Lowe Dr Bakersfield CA 93309-2468 Office: 14800 Sunnybank Ave Bakersfield CA 93312-8702

TÖRNUDD, KLAUS MATTIAS, diplomat, educator; b. Helsinki, Finland, Dec. 26, 1931; s. Allan Victor Törnudd and Helene Margareta Niininen; m. Mirja Liisa Siirala, Aug. 19, 1960; children: Nina, Martin. M. Pol. Sc., U. Helsinki, 1956, Lic. Pol. Sc., 1959, Dr. Pol. Sc., 1961. Diplomatic officer Finnish Fgn. Svc., Helsinki, N.Y.C., Cairo, Moscow and Geneva, 1958-67, 71-74; prof. internat. politics U. Tampere, Finland, 1967-71; dep. dir. Finnish Min. Fgn. Affairs, Helsinki, 1974-77, dir. polit. affairs, 1977-81, under sec. state, 1983-88; permanent rep. Finnish mission UN, N.Y.C., 1988-91; amb. to France Paris, 1993-96; faculty mem. Geneva Ctr. Security Policy, 1997-98; vis. prof. Nat. Def. Coll., 1998—. Author: Electoral System of Finland, 1968, Finland and the International Norms of Human Rights, 1986. Office: Nat Defense Coll Dept Strat Def Stds, PO Box 266, 00171 Helsinki Finland

TORO, HERNAN, communications educator; b. Tulua, Colombia, Jan. 31, 1948; s. Enrique and Berenice (Patino) T.; m. Patricia Calonje, Aug. 23, 1971; children: Calonje, Alejandra. Licenciado en Letras, Univ. del Valle, Cali, Colombia, 1973; Maestria den Lit., Paris VIII, 1977; DEA, Paris IV/ Paris VIII, 1979. Corrs. person Revista Cromos, Paris, 1977-81; creative dir. Comm. Group, Cali, 1981-82; editor Univ. del Valle, 1982-84, with comm. dept., 1984-87, prof. Sch. of Social Comm., 1987-94, dean Faculty of Artes, 1995—. Author: (books) Ajuste de cuentas, 1985, La ilusion informativa, 1993, A velas abiertas, 1993, Revista Universidad del Valle, 1995, Los Animales Solo Vivon en el Presente, 1997. Office: U del Valle Fac De Artes Integrada, Ciudad Univ de Melendez, Cali Colombia

TÖRÖK, BÉLA, surgeon; b. Gige, Somogy, Hungary, Nov. 25, 1925; s. Béla Ödön and Rozalia (Nagy) T.; m. Teréz Mária Erdélyi, Nov. 14, 1953; children: Béla Jr., Attila. MD, U. Sch. Medicine, Pécs, Hungary, 1953; PhD, Hungarian Acad. Sci., Budapest, 1963, DSc, 1972. Asst. U. Sch. Medicine, Pécs, 1953-63, assoc. prof., 1963-72, prof., dir., 1972-92; rschr. Humboldt Found., Munich, 1965, Roche Found., Zürich, Switzerland, 1967-68; pres. clin. sect. Hungarian Acad. Sci., Pécs, 1975-85; pres. exptl. sect. Hungarian Soc. Surgeons, Budapest, 1985-92; prorector for tchg. and sci. Univ. Sch. Medicine, Pécs, 1976-82, prorector for internat. rels., 1991-93; guest prof. U. Tubingen, Germany, 1993. Mem. editl. bd. Magyar Sebészet, 1976-92, Basic Rsch. in Cardiology, 1993-96; contbr. articles to profl. jours. Recipient Silver plaque U. Tubingen, 1989; named hon. citizen Tucson, Ariz., 1992. Mem. Czechoslovakian Soc. Surgeons (hon.), N.Y. Acad. Scis. Avocation: travel. Office: Ctr Rsch Lab Univ Sch Med, PO Box 99, H-7643 Pécs Hungary

TÖRÖK, ISTVÁN, physicist, researcher; b. Pápa, Hungary, Feb. 22, 1939; s. István and Etelka (Pongrácz) T.; m. Anna Palatinszky, Jan. 27, 1972 (div. 1983); children: Imre, Tamás. Student, Fazekas M. Gimnázium, Debrecen, Hungary, 1953-57, Kossuth L. Tud. Egy., Debrecen, Hungary, 1957-62; PhD, Kossuth L. Tud. Egy., Debrecen, Hungary, 1977; CSc, Hungarian Acad. Sci., Budapest, 1996. Physicist Cen. Rsch. Inst. for Physics, Budapest, Hungary, 1962-63, ATOMKI-Inst. Nuclear Rsch., Debrecen, 1963—. Mem. Trade Union, Debrecen, 1962—. Mem. Eötvös R. Phys. Soc., J. Neumann Computer Sci. Soc., Hungarian Friends of Minerals, Hungarian Friends of Maps. Avocations: orienteering, maps, minerals, photography. Office: ATOMKI-Inst Nuclear Rsch, Bem-Tér 18/c Pf 51, H-4001 Debrecen Hungary

TOROK, MARGARET LOUISE, insurance company executive; b. Detroit, June 22, 1922; d. Perl Edward Ensor and Mary (Seggie) Armstrong; m. Leslie A. Torok, Aug. 14, 1952; 1 child, Margaret Mary Ryan. Lic. Ins. Agy. From ins. agt. to corp. officer Grendel-Wittbold Ins., Southgate, Mich., 1961-72; pres. of corp. Grendel-Wittbold Ins., Southgate, 1972—; bd. dirs. Ind. Ins. Agts. of Mich., Lansing, 1984-92, Ind. Ins. Agts. of Wayne County, Dearborn, 1967—, pres. 1978. Bd. dirs. So. Wayne County C. of C., Taylor, 1975—, CEO, chmn. bd. dirs., 1997-98; bd. dirs. City of Southgate Tax. Increment Fin. Authority Dist. and Econ. Devel. Commn., 1987—; bd. dirs. YMCA, Wyandotte, 1980—, leadership chmn., 1990-94; leadership chmn. Downriver Cmty. Alliance; lay chmn. Cath. Svc. Appeal for Archdiocese of Detroit, 1989; co-chair fundraiser Sacred Heart Ch.; mem. bd. MESC Employers Com., 1991-95; mem. com., bd. New Workforce Devel. Com. (gov. appt., charter mem.). Recipient Capital award Ind. Ins. Agts. of Mich., 1988, Lifetime Achievement award, Amb. award, 1994, Woman of Yr. AAUW, 1994, Salute to Excellence award Downriver Coun. of Arts, 1993-94, Chmn. of Yr. award MESC Job. Svc. Employers Com., 1991, Robert Stewart award Wyandotte Svc. Club Coun., 1994, Info. Ctr.-Partnership award, 1996, W.O. Hildebrand award Mich. Assn. Ins. Agts., 1997; named to Ins. Hall of Fame, Olivet Coll., 1998. Mem. Wyandotte Yacht Club, Grosse Ile Golf and Country Club, Soroptimist Club of Wyandotte Southgate Taylor (pres. 1984-86, Advancing Status Women award 1988, Soroptimist of Yr. award 1993-94), Mich. Assn. Ins. Agts. Roman Catholic. Office: Grendel Wittbold Agy Inc 12850 Eureka Rd Southgate MI 48195-1344

TORO-LABBE, ALEJANDRO MIGUEL, chemist, educator, researcher; b. Porvenir, Magallanes, Chile, July 5, 1954; s. Luis Hernando Toro and Ema Rosa Labbe; m., 1979 (div. 1991); children: Daniel Alejandro, Barbara Patricia. Lic. in chemistry, U. Chile, Santiago, 1979; diploma in chemistry, U. Paris, 1981, DSc, 1984. Rsch. asst. U. Chile, Santiago, 1977-85, asst. prof., 1985-89, assoc. prof., 1989-97, full prof., 1997-98; full prof. Pontifica U. Catolica de Chile, Santiago, 1998—; postdoctoral staff Pa. State U., 1987-88; guest prof. Nat. Ctr. Scientific Rsch., Paris, Madrid, 1991—, U. Autonoma Met., Mexico City, 1998—, Nat. Sci. Agy., Argentina, 1999—; vis. prof. U. Paris, 1994. Editor Jour. Molecular Structure, 1998 (Rsch. award 1999); contbr. articles to profl. jours. Named Presdl. Chair Scis. Presidency of Chile, 1998; rsch. grantee Nat. Sci. & Engring. Rsch. Coun. Canada, 1992; Marie Curie fellow European Econ. Cmty., 1991. Mem. Am. Chem. Soc., Chilean Soc. Chemistry. Roman Catholic. Avocations: music, traveling, reading, horse riding. Office: Pontificia U Cath Chile, Facultad Quimica V Mackenna 4860, Santiago Chile

TORP, ARNE, educator; b. Holt, Norway, Oct. 14, 1942; s. Knut and Gudrun (Skaali) T.; m. Berit Helene Dahl; children: Ane, Asne Helene. Instr. Gudbrandsdal Gymnas, Norway, 1967-68, Luther Coll., Decorah, Iowa, 1970-71; lectr. U. Oslo, Norway, 1971-77, Telemark Dist. Coll., Norway, 1977-79; sr. lectr. U. Oslo, 1979—. Author: Norsk og nordisk for og naa, 1982, Nordiske spraak i nordisk og germansk perspektiv, 1998; co-author: Spraaklinjer, 1991, Hovuddrag i norsk spraakhistorie, 1993. Mem. Norwegian Lang. Coun. Home: Baerumsveien 144A, N-1358 Jar Norway Office: U Oslo, PO Box 1013, N-0315 Oslo Norway

TORPEY, ROBIN LEE, computer science and information systems educator; b. Cuba, N.Y., Oct. 30, 1958; s. Charles E. and Betty L. Torpey; m. Laurie Ann Alaimo, Nov. 23, 1979; children: Gwendolyn, Megan. AAS in Avionics Tech., C.C. of Air Force, 1984; AS in Office Mgmt., Park Coll., 1991; BS in Interdisciplinary Studies, SUNY, Alfred, 1995. Cert. in microcomputer tech. Asst. prof. computer sci. and computer info. sys. SUNY Alfred State Coll., 1991—; cons. Cuba Circulating Libr. Staff sgt. USAF, 1981-84. Mem. ALA. Methodist. Avocations: travel, photography. Fax: 978-334-5587. E-mail: torpeyrl@alfredtech.edu. Office: SUNY Alfred State Coll 222 EJ Brown Hall Alfred NY 14802

TORRADES CARNÉ, FRANCESC, chemist, researcher, educator; b. Monistrol de Montserrat, Spain, Feb. 14, 1959; s. Amado and Teresa Torrades. B in Chemistry, Autonoma U. Barcelona, Bellaterra, Spain, 1981, D in Chemsitry, 1992. From. asst. to assoc. prof. Poly. U. Catalonia, Terrassa, Spain, 1982-89, sr. lectr., 1990—. Contbr. articles to profl. jours. Avocations: skiing, tennis, football. Home: C Font 2, E-08691 Monistrol Montserrat Spain Office: Poly Univ Catalonia, C Colom 11, E-08222 Terrassa Spain

TORRANCE, SAM, professional golfer; b. Aug. 24, 1953; m. Suzanne Danielle; children: Daniel, Phoebe, Anouska. Winner Under-25 Match Play tournament Radici Open, 1972; winner Zambian Open, 1975, Martini Internat., 1976, Scottish PGA Championship, 1978, 80, 85, 91, 93, 95, Columbian Open, 1979, Australian PGA Championship, 1980, Irish Open, 1981, 95, Spanish Open, 1982, Portuguese Open, 1982, 83, Scandanavian Open, 1983, Tunisian Open, 1984, Benson & Hedges Internat., 1984, Sanyo Open, 1984, Monte Carlo Open, 1985, Italian Open, 1987, 95, German Masters, 1990, Jersey Open, 1991, Kronenborg Open, 1993, Catalan Open, 1993, Honda Open, 1993, British Masters, 1995, Anderson Consulting Match Play, 1996, French Open, 1998; mem. Double Diamond Team, 1973 (winners), 76, 77, Alpha Dunhill Cup Team, 1985, 86, 87, 89, 90, 91, 93, 95, (winners), 99, Henessy Cognac Cup Team, 1976 (winners), 78, 80 (winners), 82 (winners), 88, World Cup Team, 1976, 78, 82, 84, 85, 87, 89, 90, 91, 93, 95, Ryder Cup Team, 1981, 83, 85 (winners), 87, 89, 91, 93, 95 (winners), 99 (vice capt.), Asahi Glass Four Tours Team, 1985, 91 (capt., winners). Mem. British Empire, 1995. *

TORRA REVENTÓS, VICENC, computer scientist, educator; b. Barcelona, Spain, Aug. 15, 1968; s. Vicenc Torra and Rosa Maria Reventós; m. Monica Merin; 1 child, Marti. Degree in computer sci., Facultat D'Informatica, Barcelona, 1991, MSc, 1992, PhD, 1994. Asst. prof. U. Barcelona, Lleida, Spain, 1991-92, U. Lleida, 1992; asst. prof. U. Rovira i Virgili, Tarragona, Spain, 1992-94, permanent asst. prof., 1994-97, prof. computer sci., 1997-99; rsch. inst. d'Investigació en Intelligencia Artificial IIIA-CSIC, 1999—; subdir. Escola Tecnica Superior D'Enginyeria, Tarragona, Spain, 1994; organizer Catalan Conf. on Artificial Intelligence, 1998. Contbr. articles to profl. jours. Mem. IEEE, Internat. Fuzzy Sets Assn., Catalan Assn. Artificial Intelligence, European Soc. for Fuzzy Logic and Technologies. Office: Inst d'Investigació en, Intell Artificial Campus UAB, 08193 Bellaterra Spain

TORRAS, JOSEPH HILL, pulp and paper company executive; b. Americus, Ga., Nov. 14, 1924; s. Fernando Joseph and Nell Wilson (Hill) T.; m. Mary Ravenel Robertson, Sept. 20, 1952; children: Mary Martin, Fernanda Maria, Joseph Hill. S.B., Yale U., 1948; M.B.A., Harvard U., 1950; D in Bus. Adminstrn., Piedmont Coll., 1997. Asst. to fin. v.p. Seatrian Lines, Inc., 1950-51; with St. Regis Paper Co., 1951-60, sales mgr. printing papers div., 1956-60; exec. v.p. Brown Co., Boston, 1960-64; pres., chmn. bd. Premoid Corp., West Springfield, Mass., 1964-87; pres. Precon, Inc., Ludlow, 1967-87, Astro Tissue Co., Battleboro, Vt., 1968-72; chmn. bd. Whitman Products, Ltd., West Warwick, R.I., 1976-89; pres., CEO, Preco Corp., Amherst, Mass., 1976—; chmn., CEO Lincoln Pulp & Paper Co., Lincoln, Maine, 1968—, Eastern Fine Paper, Inc., Brewer, Maine, 1989—, Eastern Pulp & Paper Corp., 1995—; CEO, Shelburne Corp., 1999—; bd. dirs. Bay Banks, Inc., Boston; adv. dir. Liberty Mut. Ins. Mem. Mass. Gov.'s Bus. Adv. Coun., 1985-89, devel. bd. Yale U., 1989—; bd. govs. Mass. Gen. Hosp.; bd. dirs. Mass. Taxpayers Assn., 1976-86; trustee Hist. Deerfield, 1990—, Piedmont Coll., Ga., 1991-99. Lt. (j.g.), aviator USNR, 1943-46. Mem. Tissue Paper Mfrs. Assn. (dir. 1963-64), Am. Pulp and Paper Mill Supts. Assn., Salesman's Assn. Paper Industry, NAM (dir. 1981-85), Colony Club. Independent. Office: Shelburne Corp 100 University Dr Amherst MA 01002-2275

TORRENCE, GWEN, Olympic athlete; b. Atlanta, June 12, 1965; m. Manley Waller Jr.; 1 child, Manley Waller III. BA, U. Ga., Decatur, Ga., 1987. 2d place NCAA 100, 1985; 7th place USA/Mobil 100, 1985; 5th place USA/Mobil 200, 1985; champion NCAA 100, 1987, NCAA 200, 1987; 5th place U.S. World Championships 200; winner of sprints World Univ. Games; winner Pan Am. Games 200, 1987; 3rd place in both 100 and 200 Olympic Trials, 1988; 2d place USA/Mobil 100, 1991; winner USA/Mobil 200, 1991; gold medalist 200 Meter, Barcelona, Spain, 1992; winner Mobil Grand Prix 100 meters, 1993; gold medalist 100 meters World Track & Field Championships, Gutenborg, Sweden, 1995; bronze medalist 100 meters Olympic Games, Atlanta, 1996, gold medalist 4x100 meters relay, 1996. Winner 100 meters, 200 meters USA/Mobil Track & Field Championships, 1995, 100 meters World Athletic Championships, 1995, Gold medal 100 meters, 200 meters Goodwill Games, 1995, Gold medal 4 x 100 meter relay Atlanta Olympics, 1996, Bronze medal 100 meters. Achievements include 5th place world ranking at 200 meters Track & Field News, 1987, ranked number 3 sprinter in the world, 1991, ranked 3rd place in world in the 100, 1993, ranked 2d place in world in the 200, 1993, ranked 4th place in world in the 400, 1993. Address: US Track & Field 1 RCA Dome Ste 140 Indianapolis IN 46225-1023

TORRENCE-THOMPSON, JUANITA LEE, public relations executive; b. Brockton, Mass., Nov. 8; d. James Lee Torrence and Zylpha Odyselle Mapp-Robinson; m. Hugh Warren Thompson, Dec. 19, 1965; 1 child, Derek Rush. BS in Bus. & Comm., SUNY, Old Westbury, 1983; MA in Comm., Fordham U., 1989. Newsletter editor UN Internat. Sch., 1976-77; pub. rels., editl. asst. Nat. Assn. Theatre Owners, 1979-80; asst. acct. exec. Richard Weiner, Inc., 1984; newsletter editor SUNY Empire State Coll., 1985-87; editor Dorf & Stanton Comm., Inc., 1987-88; pub. rels. exec. pvt. practice, 1988—; adj. prof. pub. rels. Coll. New Rochelle, N.Y., 1997. Author: Spanning The Years, Wings Span to Eternity; contbr. articles, poems, short stories, essays to mags., newspapers & newsletters. Bd. dirs. So. Queens Park Assn., Jamaica, N.Y., 1988-91; mem. parent faculty soc. UN Internat. Sch., N.Y.C., 1976-80; pub. rels. cons. UN Coll. Fund, N.Y.C., 1994. Recipient Feature Article award Writers Digest, 1985, Meritorious Svc. award United Negro Coll. Fund, 1994, Editors Choice award Nashville Newsletter, 1994, Robins Nest Mag., 1996, First prize N.Y. Pub. Libr. Contest, 1996, Outstanding Achievement award SUNY, Empire State Coll., Old Westbury, honoree SUNY, Margaret A. Walker Short Story Competition award 1999, others. Mem. AAUW, Nat. Assn. Black Journalists, Pub. Rels. Soc. Am., Poetry Soc. Am., Acad. Am. Poets, Native Am. Journalists Assn., Black Pub. Rels. Soc., Black Women in Pub., Poets & Writers,. Avocations: travel, theatre, films, poetry, concerts. Office: PO Box 751205 Forest Hills NY 11375-8805

TORRENS, FRANCISCO, physical chemistry educator; b. Valencia, Spain, July 26, 1961; s. Francisco Torrens and María Pilar Zaragozá; m. Gloria María Castellano, Oct. 9, 1992. BS, U. Valencia, 1984, MS, 1987, PhD, 1990; PhD, U. Valencia, 1991. Rsch. officer Nat. Ctr. Sci. Rsch., Nancy, France, 1991; asst. prof. U. Valencia, 1990-95, lectr. phys. chemistry, 1995—. Author: Molecular Associations in Azines and Macrocycles, 1991; contbr. articles to profl. jours. including Jour. Molecular Graphics and Modelling, Jour. Computational Chemistry, others. Doctoral Rsch. scholar Gen. Valencia, 1987-91. Mem. Quantitative Structure-Activity Relationships and Modelling Soc., Molecular Graphics and Modelling Soc. Roman Catholic. Avocations: music, cinema, literature, art, cookery. Office: U Valencia Dept Phys Chem, Dr Moliner 50, E 46100 Burjassot Valencia, Spain

TORRENS, MICHAEL JOHN, neurosurgeon, medical researcher; b. Taunton, Eng., June 25, 1942; arrived in Greece, 1990; s. Richard Michael and Freda Edith (Bray) T.; children: Anna Lucy, Sorcha Kate, Michail Papageorgiou. BSc, London U., U.K., 1963, M Phil, 1967, MB, BS, 1967; ChM, Bristol U., U.K., 1976. Diplomate Royal Coll. Surgeons of Eng. Rsch. fellow U. Bristol, 1973; registrar neurosurgery Radcliffe Infirmary, Oxford, U.K., 1974; sr. registrar Frenchay Hosp., Bristol, 1975-76, cons. neurosurgeon, 1977-90; cons. neurosurgeon Hygeia Hosp., Athens, 1991—, chmn. sect. neurosurgery, 1995—, head of clin., 1997—. Author: Urodynamics, 1983, Physiology of Lower Urinary Tract, 1987, Operative Spinal Surgery, 1991, Operative Skull Base Surgery, 1996; founder, editor British Jour. Neurosurgery, 1987-91. Chmn. Internat. Continence Soc. Recipient Duke U. scholar, 1967. Mem. Soc. British Neurosurgeons, Cervical Spine Soc., N.Y. Acad. Sci. Avocations: writing, painting, traveling. Home and Office: Dionysou 10, Halandri Athens 15234, Greece

TORRES, ALBERTO MANUEL, physician; b. Jaen, Spain, Oct. 31, 1958; s. Manuel Torres and Natividad Cantero; m. Carmen Martinez, May 15, 1998; 1 child, Adrian. MD, Med. Sch., Granada, Spain, 1982; M in Pub. Health, Harvard U., 1986, D in Pub. Health, 1991. Pub. health worker Andalusian Health Svc., Jaen, Spain, 1982-84; med. inspector Min. of Health, 1984-85; lectr. U. Geneva, 1992-93; prof., chmn. Nat. Sch. Pub. Health, Madrid, Spain, 1994-98; assoc. prof. dept. pub. health faculty medicine U. Miguel Hernandez, 1998—; med. officer WHO, Geneva, 1992-94, cons., 1995—, head collaborating ctr., 1996—; cons. European Commn. Humanitarian Office, Brussels, 1995—; coord. European Masters Internat. Health, Madrid, 1996—. Author: (chpt.) Disease Control Priorities in Developing Countries, 1992; contbr. articles to profl. jours. Fulbright scholar, 1986-90, Fondo Investigaciones Sanitarias, 1985-86; Rsch. fellow Harvard U., 1988-90. Mem. Spanish Soc. Epidemiology, European Pub. Health Assn., Spanish Soc. Internat. Health Tropical Medicine (founding), Doctors Without Borders, Action Against Hunger, Fulbright Assn. Avocations: classical music, theater, literature, swimming, skiing. Home: San Vincente 105, 03560 Alicante Spain Office: U Miguel Hernandez Facult de Med, Ctra Alicante-Valencia Km 87, Alicante San Juan 03550, Spain

TORRES, ARTURO, physician; b. Mexico City, Oct. 22, 1961; s. Martin and Amelia Torres; m. Clara Elba Rosas, Oct. 26, 1990; children: Amelia, Clara Elba, Jose Arturo. MD, U. Nac. Autonoma de Mexico, Mexico City, 1989. Cert. Mexican Bd. Internal Medicine. Intern Hosp. Regional 20 de Noviembre; resident Hosp. Espanol de Mexico Sociedad de Beneficencia Espanola; clin. rsch. coord. Bayer de Mexico SA de CV, Mexico City, 1993-95, med. dir., 1995—. Mem. editl. bds. Bibliografia Medica Mexicana, 1991-93, Medicina Hoy y Manana, 1996—. Recipient disting. visitor diploma Varacruz City Coun., 1996, 99, disting. visitor recognition Boca del Rio City Coun., 1996, 99. Mem. Assn. Internal Medicine Mexico, Am. Heart Assn. (circulation, clin. cardiology and high blood pressure coun.), Am. Soc. Hypertension, Am. Soc. Microbiology, Internat. Diabetes Fedn., AAAS, N.Y. Acad. Sci., Latin Am. Assn. Diabetes, Latin Am. Soc. Internal Medicine. Roman Catholic. Avocations: soccer, football, baseball. Home: No 16, 1a Cda Concepcion Beistegui, 03100 Mexico City DF, Mexico Office: Bayer de Mexico, SA de CV, Calz Mexico-Xochimilco No 77, 14370 Mexico City DF, Mexico

TORRES, DARA, Olympic athlete; b. Beverly Hills, Calif., Apr. 15, 1967. Degree in broadcasting, U. Fla. Intern CNN and NBC Sports; commentator TV sports NBC, ESPN, TNT, Fox News, Fox Sports; spokesperson Tae Bo workout tapes. Host sci. and tech. show Discovery Channel. Recipient Gold medal (2) 4 x 100-meter freestyle, 4 x 100-meter medley (team) Sydney Olympics, 2000, Gold medal 100-meter freestyle, 4 x 100-meter freestyle, 4 x 100-meter relay (team) Pan Pacific Championships, 1987, Gold medal 4 x 100-meter freestyle relay (team) L.A. Games, 1984, Bronze medal 4 x 100-meter freestyle relay (team), Silver medal 4 x 100-meter medley (team), 1988, Gold medal 4 x 100-meter free relay (team) Barcelona Olympics, 1992; 12-time nat. champion; former world-record holder 50-meter freestyle, Am.-record holder 100-meter freestyle. Office: USA Swimming 1 Olympic Plz Colorado Springs CO 80909-5746*

TORRES, KENNETH LAWRENCE, pump manufacturing company executive; b. Bombay, India, June 7, 1944; s. Cecil Lawrence and Florence (Rogers) T.; m. Jean Rogers, July 27, 1968; children—Dawn Torres, Ashley. B.Sc. in Engring., Sheffield U., 1964. Mng. dir. Torres Engring. & Pumps Ltd., Sheffield, Eng., 1981—. Patentee pump design. Office: Torres Engring & Pumps Ltd, 28 Sanderson St, Sheffield S9 2TW, England

TORRES, TERRY TEROL, mechanical engineer, general contractor; b. N.Y.C., Apr. 27, 1946; s. Angel M. and Flor E. (Lozada) T.; 1 child, Tuesday Lee; m. Mary Hunter Stevens, July 4, 1980; children: Laura Diana, Anna Maria. BS in Mech. Engring., Va. Poly. Inst. and State U., 1969. State cert. gen. contractor, lic. real estate broker, Fla. Tech. sales engr. Westinghouse Elec., N.Y.C., 1969-70; project engr. Southern Bell AT&T, Miami, 1970-75; supervising engr. Am. Bell, Inc., San Juan, P.R., 1975-76; chmn., CEO Atlantic Aluminum Dist., Ft. Pierce, Fla., 1977-82, Cosmos Developing Assn., Vero Beach, Fla., 1976—; pres., CEO Cosmos Contracting Corp., Vero Beach, Fla., 1981—, Watershed Environ. Technologies, Inc., Vero Beach, Fla., 1995—; tech. cons. P.R. Telephone Co., San Juan, 1975-76; solar engring. and design, MIT, Cambridge, Mass., 1975; chmn. govt. affairs Indian River Co. Bd. Realtors, Vero Beach, 1990; environ. cons. Vero Beach, 1995-96. Designer and contractor vent-skin walls with radiant barrier for bldg. constrn., 1986, high-performance homes and bldgs., 1986—; designer and developer ventilation systems for indoor firing ranges, Ft. Benning, Ga., 1972; designer, chief engr. bomb disposal trailers and portable units, Miami, 1973-74. Project supr. and contractor Habitat for Humanity, Very Beach, 1996. Lt. U.S. army Inf., 1970-72. Recipient Five-Star Energy award City of Vero Beach, 1988, Energy Efficiency award Fla. Power and Light Co., Ft. Pierce, 1987, cert. achievement Indian River Bd. Realtors, 1989. Mem. Nat. Assn. Realtors, Nat. Geographic Soc., Aircraft Owners and Pilots Assn., Fla. Assn. Realtors. Republican. Episcopalian. Office: Watershed Environ Techs Inc PO Box 3808 Vero Beach FL 32964

TORRES, VANESSA DE MACEDO, chemical and minerals engineer, researcher; b. Ipatinga, Brazil, Sept. 19, 1969; d. Jose Geraldo and Virginia De Macedo (Mortimer Macedo) T. BSChemE, Fed. U. Minas Gerais, Belo Horizonte, Brazil, 1992; MSc in Minerals Engring., U. Sao Paulo, Brazil, 1996, PhD in Minerals Engring., 1999. Registered profl. engr., Brazil. Jr. engr. Cia Vale do Rio Doce, Belo Horizonte, 1992-93, engr., 1993-99, sr. rsch. engr., 1999—; vis. scholar U. B.C., Vancouver, Can., 1998. Contbg. author: Latin American Perspectives, 1998; author software for expert sys. for gold ore process design Intelligold, 2000. Mem. Soc. Mining Engrs. of AIME (Robert Peele Meml. award 1999), Can. Inst. Mining. Roman Catholic. Achievements include patentee on production of gold and PGM's using pressure cyanidation. Home: R Sta Rita Durao 1194-902, 30140111 Belo Horizonte M Gerais, Brazil Office: Cia Vale do Rio Doce, PO Box 9, 33030970 Santa Luzia M Gerais, Brazil

TORRES-LABAWLD, JOSE DIMAS, institutional research director, service company executive, educator; b. Luquillo, P.R., Mar. 25, 1932; s. Antonio Torres Herrera and Maria S. (Labawld) Torres; m. Patricia Ann Zaccaria, Apr. 18, 1959; children: Peter, Michelle, Mary E., Patrick, David, Gwendolyn, Christopher. BA cum laude, Inter-Am. U., San German, P.R., 1957; MPA, Syracuse U., 1959; postgrad., U. Notre Dame, 1961-62; PhD, Ohio State U., 1973; postgrad., Dartmouth Coll., 1995-96. Mgmt. ofcl., adminstr. U.S. state dept. Point IV program Office of Pers., Office of Gov., San Juan, P.R., 1959-61; lectr. Ind. U., South Bend, 1963-64; lectr. NDEA Knox Coll., Galesburg, Ill., 1965; instr. Ohio U., Athens, 1965-69; rsch. assoc. Mershon Ctr. Ohio State U., Columbus, 1970-71; dir. dept. gen. studies Hocking Coll., Nelsonville, Ohio, 1973-75, dir. instl. rsch., 1975—; pres. IMSA, Inc., Athens, 1981—; bus. cons. IMSA, Inc., 1981—. Coord. youth for understanding internat. exchg. program U.S. State Dept., 1966-70; cand. Athens County Cen. Com. Dem., 1974; chmn. fin. com. Ohio U. Christ the King Parish, 1992—; dir. Transnational Bus. Program, U.S., Mexico, Can., 1995—. Cpl. U.S. Army, Korea, 1951-53. Commonwealth of P.R. fellow Syracuse U., 1959; Hocking Coll. scholar, 1990. Mem. Am. Arbitration Assn., Assn. for Instnl. Rsch., U.S. Hispanic C. of C., World Trade Club, Columbus Area C. of C., VFW, Lions (pres. Athens chpt. 1984), Am. Legion, Phi Alpha Theta. Roman Catholic. Avocations: tennis, golf, piano, painting, chess. Home: 15 Grand Park Blvd Athens OH 45701-1438

TORRETTI, ROBERTO, retired philosophy educator, editor; b. Santiago, Chile, Jan. 16, 1930; came to U.S., 1970; s. Roberto and Valentina (Edwards) T.; m. Carla Cordua, July 11, 1953. Degree in law and philosophy, U. Chile, 1952; PhD, U. Freiburg, 1954. Lic. tchr., Chile. Mem. staff, translator UN Secretariat, N.Y.C., 1955-58; lectr. in social sci. U. P.R., San Juan, 1958-61; prof. philosophy U. Concepcion, 1961-64, U. Chile, Santiago, 1964-70; prof. philosophy U. P.R., San Juan, 1970-95, prof. emeritus, 1995—, dir. Seminario de Filosofia, 1977-87. Author: Manuel Kant, 1967, Philosophy of Geometry from Riemann to Poincare, 1978, Relativity and Geometry, 1983, Creative Understanding, 1990, El Paraiso de Cantor, 1998, The Philosophy of Physics, 1999; editor Dialogos, 1972-95. Grantee Alexander von Humboldt Stiftung, 1965; fellow John Simon Guggenheim Meml. Found., 1975-76, 80-81, Pitts. Ctr. Philosophy of Sci., 1983-84. Mem. Inst. Internat. de Philosophie, Acad. Internat. de Philosophie des Scis., Philosophy Sci. Assn., Brit. Soc. for the Philosophy of Sci. Avocations: classical Greek, desktop publishing. E-Mail: cordua@rdc.cl. Home: Casilla 20017, Correo 20, Santiago Chile

TORREY, CLAUDIA OLIVIA, lawyer; b. Nashville, June 10, 1958; d. Claude Adolphus and Rubye Mayette (Prigmore) T. BA in Econ., Syracuse U., 1980; JD, N.Y. Law Sch., 1985. Bar: N.Y. State 1988. Legal intern Costello, Cooney & Fearon, Syracuse, N.Y., 1979; legal clk. First Am. Corp., Nashville, 1981; legal asst. James I. Meyerson, N.Y.C., 1982-85; jud. law clk. N.Y. State Supreme Ct., N.Y.C., 1985; interim project supr., legal asst. CUNY Ctrl. Office, 1985-86; legal analyst Rosenman & Colin Law Firm, N.Y.C., 1986-87; asst. counsel N.Y. State Legis., Albany, 1988-90; atty., cons. pvt. practice, Nashville, Cookeville, Tenn., 1991—; bd. mem. Children's Corner Day Care Ctr., Albany, N.Y., 1989-90. Ch. rep. FOCUS exec. coun. Westminster Presbyn. Ch., Albany, 1990; v.p. dormitory coun., flr. rep. Syracuse U., 1977-79. Mem. ABA (young lawyers divsn. liaison to ABA forum on health law 1994-96), Internat. Platform Assn., N.Y. State Bar Assn. (chmn. health law sect. study group on health info., privacy and confidentiality 1998-99), Alpha Kappa Alpha. Avocations: singing, reading, harp, travel, art. Home and Office: PO Box 150234 Nashville TN 37215-0234

TORRING, OVE, endocrinologist; b. Naestved, Denmark, Feb. 29, 1948; s. Andreas and Carla (Jensen) T.; m. Ruth Kahr Jensen, Oct. 25, 1969; children: Anders, Anna Louise. MD, Arhus (Denmark) U., 1974; Dr. Med. Sci., Karolinska Inst., Stockholm, 1985. Assoc. prof. endocrinology Karolinska Inst., Stockholm, 1992; intern So. Hosp., Stockholm, 1974-76, resident in internal medicine, 1976-79; resident in endocrinology Karolinska Hosp., 1979-83, cons., 1990-95; guest scientist Mayo Clinic, Rochester, Minn., 1987, 89-90; chief physician, cons. Nat. Univ. Hosp., Copenhagen, 1995-99; cons. R&D geriats. Huddinge (Sweden) U. Hosp., 1999—; sr. rsch. adviser Karobio, Sweden, 1989; chief thyroid sect. Instn. Molecular Medicine Karolinska Inst., 1993-96; invited lectr. Yale U., Harvard Med. Sch., 1993, Nat. Ctr. Health Statistics, Washington, 1996; Forest vis. prof. Loma Linda U., 1993; chmn. organizers, scientific com. of 2d Baltic Bone Conf., Bornholm, 1997, 3d Baltic Bone Conf., 1999; faculty opponent Copenhagen U., Aarhus U., Denmark, Oulu U., Helsinki U., Finland, Melbourne U., Australia. Contbr. articles to profl. jours. and chpts. to books; referee profl. jours.: Endocrinology, European Jour. Endocrinology, Acta Pediatrica, Scand. Clin. Lab Invest., Nephrology Dialysis Transplantation, others. Mem. N.Y. Acad. Sci., Mayo Alumni Assn., Am. Soc. Bone Mineral Related Rsch., Swedish Soc. Endocrinology, European Thyroid Assn., Stockholm Bone Soc. (co-founder, chmn. 1993-95), Danish Med. Assn. and Soc., Danish Endocrine Soc., Danish Bone Soc. (mem. sci. com., bd. dirs.). Avocation: jazz trumpet. Fax: 46 8 58586436. E-mail: ovetorring@swipnet.se. Office: Huddinge Univ Hosp, Dept Geriats B:56, 141 86 Huddinge Sweden

TORSHEN, JEROME HAROLD, lawyer; b. Chgo., Nov. 27, 1929; s. Jack and Lillian (Futterman) T.; m. Kay Pomerance, June 19, 1966; children: Jonathan, Jacqueline. BS, Northwestern U., 1951; JD, Harvard U., 1955. Bar: Ill. 1955, U.S. Dist. Ct. (no. dist.) Ill. 1955, U.S. Ct. Appeals (7th cir.) 1958, (8th cir.) 1961, (9th and D.C. cirs.) 1972, U.S. Supreme Ct. 1972. Assoc. Clausen, Hirsh & Miller, Chgo., 1955-62; pres. Jerome H. Torshen, Ltd., Chgo., 1963-87, Torshen, Schoenfield & Spreyer, Ltd., Chgo., 1987-94, Torshen, Spreyer, Ltd., Chgo., 1994, Torshen, Spreyer & Garmisa, Ltd., Chgo., 1994-97, Torshen, Spreyer, Garmisa & Slobig, Ltd., Chgo., 1997—; spl. asst. atty. gen. Ill., 1965-70; assoc. counsel Spl. Commn. Ill. Supreme Ct., 1969; counsel Ill. Legis. Redistricting Commn., 1971-72; spl. state's atty. Cook County, Ill., 1979-81, 83-86; spl. counsel Met. San. Dist. Greater Chgo., 1977-81, 84-88. Contbr. articles to profl. jours. Counsel Cook County Dem. Cen. Com., Chgo., 1982-87; bd. dirs. Jewish Family and Community Svc., Parents' Coun. Washington U., St. Louis, 1988-92; mem. collectors' group Mus. Contemporary Art; sustaining fellow Art Inst. Chgo. Served with U.S. Army, 1951-52. Recipient Torch of Learning award Am. Friends of Hebrew U., 1985, Outstanding Civic Duty award, Union League Club of Chgo., 1967. Fellow Am. Coll. Trial Lawyers; mem. ABA, Chgo. Bar Assn. (commn. on jud. evaluation 1986-90), Bar Assn. 7th Cir. Appellate Lawyers Assn. (founder, pres. 1976-77), Decalogue Soc., Standard Club, Sixty Club of Chgo., Union League Club of Chgo. Office: 105 W Adams St Ste 3200 Chicago IL 60603-4109

TORSTENDAHL, ROLF, history educator; b. Jönköping, Sweden, Jan. 9, 1936; s. Torsten Vilhelm and Ragnhild (Abrahamsson) T.; m. Anna-Maria Ljung, July 16, 1960 (dec. Dec. 1987); children: Stefan, Peter; m. Tamara Alekseevna Salycheva, June 17, 1996. Lic., Uppsala (Sweden) U., 1961, PHD, 1964. Lectr. dept. history Uppsala U., 1964-67, assoc. prof., 1968-78, prof., 1981—, head dept. history, 1993-97, dean Faculty of Arts, 1994-99; Sven Warburg Prof. History U. Stockholm, 1978-80; dir. Swedish Collegium for Advanced Study in Social Scis., 1985-90. Author: Bureaucratisation in Northwestern Europe, 1991; editor: The Formation of the Professions, 1990, State Theory and State History, 1992, History-Making, 1996. Mem. Acad. Europaea, Norwegian Acad. Sci. and Letters, Russian Acad. Sci. (hon. mem. Ural divsn.), Swedish Soc. Sci., Royal Soc. Scholarship, Royal Acad. Letters, History and Antiquities. Home: St Olofsgatan 4, S-75312 Uppsala Sweden Office: Uppsala U Dept History, St Larsgatan 2, S-75310 Uppsala Sweden

TORTAROLO, EDOARDO, historian, educator; b. Torino, Italy, Sept. 14, 1956; s. Ezio and Irmgard (Wolf) T.; m. Michela Garda, Mar. 5, 1983; children: Alessandro, Dora. MA, U. Torino, 1980, PhD, 1987. Prof. U. Torino, 1992—; Leibniz prof. U. Leipzig, Germany, 1997. Author: la Ragione Sulla Sprea, 1989 (Chabod award 1990); editor Storia Della Storiografia. Rsch. fellow John Carter Brown Libr., 1982, Inst. für Europäische Geschichte, 1985, A. Von Humboldt Stiftung, 1989-91. Mem. Gen. Comm. Internat. D'Histoire de L'Historiographie (sec. 1996), Internat. Soc. Intellectual History (steering com.). Avocation: jogging. Home: Via Balbo 39, 10124 Torino Italy Office: Univ Torino Dept Storia, Via S Ottavio 20, 10124 Torino Italy

TORTELLO, ENZO, quality assurance professional; b. Genoa, Ligury, Italy, July 9, 1946; s. Giovanni Battista and Consolina (Traverso) T.; m. Marina Maria Bellinazzo, Sept. 20, 1973; 1 child, Stefano. Engr., U. Genoa, 1971. From rotating machinery designer to mgr. strategic planning Ansaldo Energia, Genoa, 1973-93, mgr. quality control, 1993—; prof. electrotech. U. Sardinia, 1978-80. Patentee in field; contbr. articles to profl. jours. 2d lt. Italian Armed Forces, 1971-72. Mem. Cigré (convenor), Power Gen. Europe (program com.). Roman Catholic. Avocations: soccer, reading, art, movies, walking. Office: Ansaldo Energia, via M Lorenzi 8, 16152 Genoa Ligury, Italy

TORTORA, CIRO, manufacturing executive; b. Naples, Italy, Jan. 27, 1945; s. Antonio and Maria (Pasinati) T.; m. Raffaelina Gargiulo, July 10, 1972; 1 child, Chiara. D in Engring., U. Naples, 1969. Reg. engr., Naples. Rsch. and devel. supr. CGA, Naples, 1970-86, product devel. mgr., 1991—; tech. mgr. Sige Group, Caserta, 1986-89; sales, purchasing mgr. Elettromeccanica Lucana, Potenza, Italy, 1990-91; cons. U. Naples, 1989-90. Contbr. articles to profl. jours.; patentee in field. With Italian Army, 1969-70. Avocations: bicycling. Office: Compagnia Gen Accumulatori, Via Benevento 40, 80013 Casalnuovo Di Napoli Italy

TORU, EGUCHI, microbiologist, researcher; b. Neyagawa, Osaka, Japan, Sept. 16, 1958; s. Haruo and Teruko E.; m. Emi Kameyama; children: Yui, Fumi. B in environ. health, Azabu U., 1982. Rschr. SLC Inc., Hamamastu, Japan, 1982; rschr. SUNSTAR Inc., Osaka, 1982-93; sr. rschr. SUNSTAR Inc., 1993—; guest rschr. Osaka U. Faculty of Tech., 1985-87. Contbr. articles to profl. jours. Patentee in field. Avocation: fishing. Office: SUNSTAR Inc, 3 1 Asahi machi, Tatatsuki 569 1195, Japan

TORVI, KAI ANTERO, economist; b. Kokkola, Finland, Jan. 3, 1954; s. Eino Asari and Ruut Elsa (Tarmo) T.; m. Tuula Margit Wikholm, July 3, 1984. MA in Econs., U. Helsinki, Finland, 1976. Rsch. asst. Acad. of Finland, Helsinki, 1976-78, Helsinki City Mus., 1978-79; spl. planning officer Econ. Planning Centre, Helsinki, 1979-84; sr. fellow Ctr. for Finnish Bus. and Policy Studies, Helsinki, 1985—. Author: Metsateollisuustuotteiden hintaproblematiikka, 1980, (with others) International Commodity Agreements For Minerals, 1982; co-editor Finnish Econ. Jour., 1982-88. Chmn. Finnish Statis. Assn., Helsinki, 1985-86. Mem. Finnish Yacht Club (sec. 1991-95, vice-commodore 2000—). Avocations: sailing, skiing. Office: Ctr Finnish Bus. and Policy Studies, Hyrjonkatu 13A, FIN00120 Helsinki Finland

TORVILL, JAYNE, ice dancer; b. Oct. 7, 1957; d. George and Betty (Smart) T.; m. Philip Christensen, 1990. MA (hon.), Nottingham Trent U., 1994. Ins. clk., 1974-80. Decorated Mem. Brit. Empire, 1981, Order Brit. Empire, 2000; recipient (all with Christopher Dean) Personality of Yr. award BBC Sportsview, 1983-84, Gold medal ice dancing Olympic Games, 1984, Bronze medal ice dancing Olympic Games, 1994; named (with Michael Hutchinson) Brit. Pair Skating Champion, 1971, (all with Christopher Dean) Brit. Ice Dance Champion, 1978-83, 94, European Ice Dance Champion, 1981, 82, 84, 94, World Ice Dance Champion, 1981-84, World Profl. Ice Dance Champion, 1984, 85, 90, 95, 96; inductee (with Christopher Dean) Figure Skating Hall of Fame, 1989. Office: c/o Sue Young, PO Box 32 Heathfield, East Sussex TN21 OBW, United Kingdom

TOŠ, IGOR PEGAN, architect; b. Beograd, Yugoslavia, Mar. 26, 1943; arrived in Slovenia 1946, Croatia, 1959; s. Stanko Omerza and Zdenka Spangher (Pegan) T.; m. Neva Ursic, May 11, 1974. Diploma in archtl. engring., U. Zagreb, Croatia, 1967; postgrad., U. Hannover, Germany, 1972-73, U. Ljubljana, Slovenia, 1984—. Urban planner Atelier d'Architecture Henry Collomb, Lausanne, Switzerland, 1967; architect Ingradinvest, Zagreb, 1969-72; rschr. U. Hannover, 1972-73; authorized architect archtl. firms, Zagreb, 1973-79; gen. mgr. Sistemprojekt, Zagreb, 1979-87, rschr., mgr., 1987—. Designer various bldgs., 1967-97; rsch. and devel. projects in architecture, 1972-97; contbr. articles to profl. jours. Bd. dirs. Croatian-German Soc., Zagreb, 1995—; vice chmn. Croatian DAAD Club, Zagreb, 1998. Recipient jury award in competition for momument-mus.-Belvedere on Petrova Gora, 1971, graphical design jury award, Zagreb, 1970. Mem. Assn. Croatian Architects (ctrl. bd. 1976—), Croatian Soc. Designers (co-founder), Croatian Systems Soc. (bd. dirs. 1993-96). Avocations: fine, musical and theatrical arts, philosophy. Office: Sistemprojekt, Kruziceva 4, HR 10000 Zagreb Croatia

TOS, MIRKO, physician, educator; b. Vitomarci, Ptuj, Slovenia, Oct. 3, 1931; s. Thomas and Genovefa (Peklar) T.; m. Nives Pavsic, July 1957; children: Miriam, Vivian, Tina. Grad., Med. Sch., Ljubljana, Slovenia, 1957, Med. Sch., Copenhagen, 1960; ENT spls., PhD, Med. Sch., Copenhagen, 1966. Physician Hosp., Ptuj, Slovenia, 1957, Veile, Denmark, 1957-59, Helsingor, Denmark, 1959-60; physician Riegshosp., Copenhagen, 1960-61; physician Glostrup, Copenhagen, 1961-67, assoc. chmn. ENT dept., 1967-71; assoc. chmn. ENT dept. Gentofte Hosp., Copenhagen, 1971-79, chmn. ENT dept., 1979—; assoc. prof. U. Copenhagen, 1975-79; prof., 1979—; Pres., organizer 3rd Cholesteatoma Conf., Copenhagen, 1989, 1st Internat. Conf. on Acoustic Neuroma, Copenhagen, 1991, 15th European Rhinol. Soc. Congress and 13th Internat. Symposium on Infection and Allergy of Nose, European Rhinological Soc. Internat. Symposium Infection and Allergy of Nose, Copenhagen, 1994, Copenhagen Otitis Media Conf., 1997; organizer yearly typanoplasty courses for Scandinavian otologists; organizer, chmn. 4 internat. courses in acoustic neuroma surgery. Author: Manual of Middle Ear Surgery, Vols. 1, 1993, Vol. 2, 1995, Vol. 3, 1995, 97, Surgical Solutions in Conductive Hearing Loss, 2000; co-author: Manual of Translabyrinthine Surgery for Acoustic Neuroma, 1990; editor: Cholesteatoma, 1990, Acoustic Neuroma, 1992, Rhinology, State of the Art, 1995, Nasal Polyps, 1995, Otitis Media Today, 1998; contbr. about 610 articles to med. jours. Wilhelm Meyer grantee, 1982. Mem. Am. Assn. Rsch. Otology, Am. ENT Soc. (hon.), Italian ENT Soc. (hon.), German ENT Soc. (hon.), French ENT Soc. (hon.), Danish ENT Soc. (hon.), Internat. Skull Base Soc., European Skull Base Soc., European Fedn. Otolaryngol. Socs. (pres. exec. com.), Collegium Oto-Rhino-Laryngologicum Amicitiae Sacrum, Politzer Soc. (bd. dirs.), European Rhinol. Soc. (past pres.), European Acad. Otology and Neuro-Otology (past pres.), Scandinavian Otolaryngol. Soc. (pres.). Avocations: tennis, skiing, surfing. Home: Hesseltoften 14, 2900 Hellerup Copenhagen Denmark Office: Gentofte Hosp, ENT Dept, 2900 Hellerup Copenhagen Denmark

TOSCANO, MAURO, company executive; b. Milan, Nov. 19, 1959. Degree in Account Mgmt. Mktg., L. Bocconi U., Milan, 1983. Account exec. Needham Harper Worldwide, Chgo., 1983-84; client dir. P&T/P&T Co., Milan, 1985-93; founder, CEO Materia Advt., Milan, 1994-98; ptnr., CEO Conquest Materia, Milan, 1998—. E-mail: mauro toscano@conquest-group.com. Fax: 02/782126. Office: Conquest Materia, C so Europa 13, 20122 Milan Italy

TOSCHI, ROMANO, thermonuclear fusion expert, engineering educator; b. Bologna, Italy, July 18, 1929; arrived in Germany, 1994; m. Agnese Nobiloni, Feb. 24, 1946; children: Nicola, Natalia. D of Elec. Engring., U. Bologna, Bologna, 1954; prof. elec. engring., U. Rome, 1984. Dir. Energia Ambiente Energy Conversion Lab., Frascati, Italy, 1963-70, Energia Ambiente Fusion Lab., Frascati, 1971-77, Energia Ambiente Rsch. Ctr., Frascati, 1978-83; leader European Fusion Exptl. Reactor, Garching, Germany, 1984-91; European leader Internat. Thermonuclear Exptl. Reactor, Garching, 1992—. Contbr. numerous articles to profl. jours. Office: Max Planck Inst Plasmaphys, Boltzmannstr 2, 85748 Garching Germany

TOSHACH, CLARICE OVERSBY, real estate developer, former computer executive; b. Firbank, Westmoreland, Eng., Nov. 21, 1928; came to U.S., 1955; d. Oliver and Nora (Brown) Oversby; m. Daniel Wilkie Toshach, July 30, 1965 (dec. Aug. 1992); 1 child, Duncan Oversby Toshach; 1 child from previous marriage, Paul Anthony Beard. Textile designer Storeys of Lancaster, Eng., 1949-55; owner, operator Broadway Lane, Saginaw, Mich., 1956-70; pres., owner Clarissa Jane Inc., Saginaw, 1962-70, Over-Tosh Computers, Inc. dba Computerland, Saginaw and Flint, Mich., 1983-95; mgr., ptnr. Mich. Comml. Devel. L.L.C., Saginaw, 1995—. Trustee Saginaw Gen. Hosp., 1977-83, Home for the Aged, 1978-80; bd. dirs. Vis. Nurse Assn., pres., 1981-83; bd. dirs. Hospice of Saginaw, Inc., v.p., 1981-83; mem. long range planning com. United Way of Saginaw, 1982-83; cmty. advisor Jr. League of Saginaw, 1982-83; pres. Saginaw Gen. Hosp. Aux., 1972-82, pres., 1976-77.

TOSHEFF, JULIJ GOSPODINOFF, psychiatrist; b. Svishtov, Bulgaria, July 3, 1925; came to U.S., 1968; s. Gospodin P. and Mara A. (Karaivanova) T.; m. Finnie I. Kancheva, Feb. 10, 1927; 1 child, Deana. MD, Higher Med. Inst., Sofia, Bulgaria, 1952. Resident Higher Inst. Specialization of

Physicians, Sofia, Bulgaria, 1953-56, 59-62, staff physician, 1957-59, staff psychiatrist clinic psychiatry, 1962-67; staff internist Gen. City Hosp., Tetovo, Yugoslavia, 1967; rsch. assoc. dept. psychiatry Johns Hopkins U. Sch. Medicine, Balt., 1968-69, instr. behavioral biology, dept. psychiatry, 1969-72; intern South Baltimore Gen. Hosp., 1972-73; resident L.I. Jewish Med. Ctr., Hillside Hosp., Glen Oaks, N.Y., 1973-76, staff psychiatrist, 1976—. Contbr. articles to profl. jours. Lt. Bulgarian Army. Mem. APA. Avocations: classical music, opera, reading. Office: 45 N Station Plz Great Neck NY 11021-5011

TOŠOVSKY, JOSEF, bank official; b. Náchod, Czechoslovakia, Sept. 28, 1950; m. Bohunka Světlíková; 2 children. Grad., Sch. Econs., Prague, Czechoslovakia, 1973. Banker Czechoslovakia State Bank, Prague, 1973—, dep. dir., 1978-84; pres. Czech Nat. Bank, Prague, 1989-92; gov. Czechoslovakia State Bank, Prague, 1993-97, 98—; chief economist Živnobanka, London, 1984-85, dep. dir., 1989; cons. to bank chair Czechoslovakia State Bank, Prague, 1986-89; prime min. Czech Republic, 1997-98; gov. IMF, 1990—; lectr. in field. Contbr. articles to profl. jours. Recipient Karel Englis prize Masaryk U., Brno, 1994; named European Mgr. of the Yr., European Bus. Press Fedn., 1994, European Banker of the Yr., Group 20+1, 1996. Office: Ceska narodni banka, Na Prikope 28, 115 03 Prague 1, Czech Republic

TOSTE, ANTHONY PAIM, chemistry educator, researcher; b. Mountain View, Calif., June 26, 1948; s. Antonio Paim and Natalia (Silveira) T.; m. Janet Miyoko Akaike, June 21, 1975; children: Eriko Maria Akaike-Toste, Emiko Natalia Akaike-Toste. BS in Chemistry with honors, Santa Clara (Calif.) U., 1970; PhD in Biochemistry and Chemistry, U. Calif., Berkeley, 1976. Rsch. fellow Cardiovascular Rsch. Inst., San Francisco, 1977-79; rsch. scientist Battelle Meml. Inst. Pacific N.W. Nat. Lab., Richland, Wash., 1980-88; asst. prof. S.W. Mo. State U., Springfield, 1988-94, assoc. prof., 1994-99, full prof., 1999—; cons. Mitsubishi Metal Corp., Tokyo, 1984-87, Dow Chem., Tex., 1994-96; presenter in field. Contbr. articles to jours. in field, cmty. svc. presentations. Bd. dirs. Mid Columbia Arts Coun., Richland, 1987-88, Bot. Soc. of s.w. Mo., Springfield, 1997—; pres. bd. dirs. Springfield Sister Cities Assn., 1993-96; co-founder, leader Internat. Friendship Study Tours to Japan, 1996, 99. Rsch./equipment grantee NSF, 1990; recipient Diverse Cmty. award Sister Cities Internat., Boston, 1996. Mem. Am. Chem. Soc. (treas. 1989-91), Am. Nuc. Soc. (Best Poster award 1987), Assn. Official Analytical Chemists (program chair 1986, 90), Mo. Acad. Sci. (program chair 1997). Avocations: picture framing, collecting fine art, woodworking, reading, cinema. Home: 2113 E Woodhaven Pl Springfield MO 65804-6767 Office: S W Mo State U Dept Chemistry 901 S National Ave Springfield MO 65804-0088

TOSTI, DONALD THOMAS, psychologist, consultant; b. Kansas City, Mo., Dec. 6, 1935; s. Joseph T. Tosti and Elizabeth M. (Parsons) Tosti Addison; m. Carol J. Curless, Jan. 31, 1957 (dec. 1980); children: Rene, Alicia, Roxanna, Brett, Tabitha, Todd Marcus; m. Annette Brewer, Dec. 29, 1989. BSEE, U. N.Mex., 1957, MS in Psychology, 1962, PhD in Psychology, 1967. Chief editor Tchg. Machines, Inc., Albuquerque, 1960-64; divsn. mgr. Westinghouse Learning Corp., Albuquerque, 1964-70; founder, sr. v.p. Ind. Learning Sys., San Raphael, Calif., 1970-74; pres. Ind. Learning Sys., San Raphael, 1974-76; chmn. bd. Omega Performance, San Francisco, 1976-77; pres. Operants, Inc., San Rafael, 1978-81; v.p. Forum Corp., San Rafael, 1981-83; mng. ptnr. Vanguard Cons. Group, San Francisco, 1983—. Author: Basic Electricity, Advanced Algebra, Fundamentals of Calculus, TMI Programmed Series, 1960-63, Behavior Technology, 1970, A Guide to Child Development, Tactics of Communication, 1973; co-author: Learning Is Getting Easier, 1973, Indtroductory Psychology, 1981, Usibility Factors in Hardware and Software Design, 1982, Comparative Usibility, 1983, Performance Based Management, Positive Leadership, 1986, Strategic Alliances, 1990, The Professional Manager, 1995, Power and Governance, 1996, Global Fluency, 1999, Organizational Alignment, 2000, Internal Branding, 2000. Mem. APA, Internat. Soc. for Performance Improvement (v.p. rsch. 1983-85, treas. 1997-99, Outstanding Mem. award 1984, Life Membership award 1984, Outstanding product award 1974). Home: 41 Marinita Ave San Rafael CA 94901-3443

TOSTI, SILVANO, chemical engineer, researcher; b. Frascati, Italy, June 28, 1959; s. Sanzio Tosti and Margherita De Simoni; m. Bruna Brunelli, Oct. 4, 1986; children: Emma, Camilla. Degree in chem. engring., La Sapienza, Rome, 1983. Rschr. ENEA, Rome, 1985-92, ENEA-Euratom, Frascati, 1993—. Contbr. articles to profl. jours. Roman Catholic. Avocations: chess, reading. Home: Via Della Sorgente 6, 00044 Frascati Italy Office: ENEA, Via E Fermi 27, 00044 Frascati Italy

TOSTO, SEBASTIANO, materials scientist; b. Corciano, Perugia, Italy, Aug. 10, 1944; s. Giuseppe and Carmela (Gravagno) T.; m. Elena Gelmini, May 10, 1979; 1 child, Giuseppe. DSc in Chemistry, U. Rome, 1968, DSc in Physics, 1971. Rschr. Fiat, Turin, Italy, 1972-85, ENEA, Rome, 1985—. Contbr. articles to profl. jours.; patentee in field. Mem. Materials Rsch. Soc., Am. Phys. Soc., Italian Phys. Soc. Avocation: music. Office: ENEA Inst New Technologies Energy & Environ, Via Anguillarese 301, 00060 Rome Italy

TÓTH, IMRE, chemist, researcher; b. Kiskunfélegyháza, Hungary, Jan. 13, 1958; arrived in The Netherlands, 1991; s. Imre Tóth and Anna Szemerédi. MSc, U. Veszprém, Hungary, 1982, PhD, 1985. Grad rsch. asst. U. Veszprém, Hungary, 1982-85, asst. prof., 1985-88; postdoctoral rsch. assoc. Va. Tech., 1988-90; sci. rsch. fellow U. Amsterdam, The Netherlands, 1991-93; sr. rsch. chemist DSM Rsch., The Netherlands, 1993—. Inventor hydroformylation of internal olefins, carbonylation of butadiene, immobilization of homogeneous catalysts, mechanistic studies; contbr. articles to profl. jours. Mem. N.Y. Acad. Scis. Avocations: astronomy, tennis. Office: PO Box 18 DSM Rsch, 6160MD Geleen The Netherlands

TOTH, ISTVAN, medicinal organic chemistry educator; b. Szilagysomlyo, Hungary, Apr. 25, 1946; arrived in Australia, 1998; s. Ferenc and Maria (Kincses) T.; m. Krisitina Nora Medveczky, Apr. 14, 1977; children: Adrienne, Alexandra, Bettina. PhD, Tech. U., Budapest, Hungary, 1972; DSc, Hungarian Acad. Sci., Budapest, Hungary, 1994. Lectr. Tech. U., Budapest, Hungary, 1969-77; sr. rsch. fellow Ctrl. Inst. Chemistry, Hungarian Acad. Sci., Budapest, Hungary, 1977-82, scientific group leader, 1982-87; Glaxo sr. lectr. U. London, Sch. Pharmacy, 1987-95, reader, 1995—; sci. advisor Chinoin Chem., Budapest, 1977-87, Alchemia Ltd., Brisbane, Australia, 1995—; prof. U. Qland, Brisbane, 1999—; prin. scientist Alchemia Pty. Ltd.; vis. prof. U. London. Contbr. chpts. to books and articles to profl. jours.; patentee in field. Recipient Acad. award Hungarian Acad. Sci., 1980, Inventor Gold medal Ministry Industry, 1986. Roman Catholic. Avocations: skiing, windsurfing, horseback riding. Office: Univ Qld Sch Pharmacy, Steele Bldg, Brisbane 4072, Australia

TÓTH, JÁNOS, applied mathematician; b. Budapest, Hungary, June 9, 1947; s. János and Jánosné (Fekete Vilma) T.; m. Mária Szórád; children: Ágnes Veronika, Ádám, János Pál. MSc in Probability Theory, L. Eötvös U., Budapest, 1971; PhD in Math. Sci., Hungarian Acad. Sci., Budapest, 1986. Predoctoral fellow Inst. Med. Chemistry, Semmelweis U. Med. Sch., Budapest, 1971-73, rsch. fellow computing group, 1973-81; sr. rsch. fellow Computer and Automation Inst. Hungarian Acad. Sci., Budapest, 1981-89; sr. rsch. fellow Inst. Technol. Chemistry, Hungarian Acad. Sci., Veszprém, 1989-90; head dept. computer sci. Agrl. U., Gödöllő, Hungary, 1991-99; instr. dept. analysis Budapest U. Tech. and Econs., 1998—; instr. dept. applied analysis L. Eötvös U., 1976—. Co-author: (in Hungarian) Mathematics and Mathematica, 1996, (in English) Mathematical Models of Chemical Reactions, 1989; co-editor: (collected papers) Theory, Models, Tradition, 1992, (in Hungarian) Research and Publication in Science, 1999. Recipient Farkas Gyula prize János Bolyai Math. Soc., Budapest, 1981, Széchenyi Professorship, Ministry for Edn. and Culture, 1998—. Mem. N.Y. Acad. Scis., Hungarian Acad. Sci. (com. reaction kinetics and photochemistry). Avocations: music, reading, excursions, mathematics. Office: BUTE dept analysis, Müegyetem rkp 3-9, H-1111 Budapest Hungary

TOTH, JÓZSEF, diplomat; b. Budapest, Hungary, Apr. 10, 1961; s. József and Józsefné Toth; m. Mária Urbánzki, July 20, 1985; children: Anita, Agnes. MBA, U. Econs., Budapest, 1985. Desk officer Germany Ministry Fgn. Affairs, Budapest, 1985-89; diplomat Embassy of Hungary, London, 1989-94; head office of polit. state sec. Ministry Fgn. Affairs, Budapest, 1994-97; min., DCM Embassy of Hungary, Washington, 1997—. E-mail: hembwegy@aol.com. Office: Embassy of Hungary 3910 Shoemaker St NW Washington DC 20008

TOTH, KALMAN, cardiologist; b. Pecs, Hungary, June 20, 1959; s. Kalman and Ibolya (Stampfer) T.; m. Judit Vekasi Toth, Sept. 24, 1983; 1 child, Andras. MD, Med. U. Pecs, Hungary, 1983; PhD, Hungarian Acad. Scis., Budapest, 1992. Med. diplomate. Resident Med. U. Pecs, Hungary, 1983-87, asst. prof., 1987-90; rsch. scholar USC, L.A., 1990-91; asst. prof. Med. U. Pecs, Hungary, 1992-94, assoc. prof., chief cardiology, 1994-95, prof., 1995—; pres. Heart Found. at Pecs, Hungary, 1994—. Contbr. papers in field. Mem. Hungarian Soc. Cardiology, Hungarian Soc. Hemorheology (sec. gen. 1993-97, pres. 2000—), European Soc. Clin. Hemorheology, Internat. Soc. Clin. Hemorheology (pres. 1995-99). E-mail: tothk@clinics.pote.hu. Home: Urogi 32, Pécs 7634, Hungary Office: U Med Sch Pecs, Ifjusag 13, Pécs 7643, Hungary

TOTH, PAL, anatomist, educator, neuroscientist; b. Pecs, Hungary, Sept. 28, 1953; s. Pal Toth and Maria Pandur; m. Gabriella Gabor, July 26, 1975; children: Daniel, Bence, Panna. MD, U. Med. Sch. Pecs, 1978, PhD. Demonstrator in anatomy U. Med. Sch., Pecs, 1974-78, jr. lectr., 1978-83, lectr., 1983-93, reader in anatomy, 1993—; vis. rsch. fellow Flinders U., Adelaide, Australia, 1987-89; vis. rsch. fellow Ctr. Nat. de la Rsch. Sci., Gif Sur Yvette, France, 1985, 93, Marseille, 1991, Consejo Superior de Investigaciones Cientificas Inst., Cajal, Madrid, 1994. Contbr. articles to profl. jours. Mem. Internat. Brain Rsch. Orgn., European Neurosci. Assn. Roman Catholic. Avocations: photography, tourism, music, painting. Office: U Med Sch Dept Anatomy, Med Fac U Pecs Dept Anatomy, Szigeti Ut 12, 7643 Pecs Hungary

TOTHFALUSI, ANDRAS, finance company executive, consultant; b. Budapest, Hungary, Apr. 10, 1945; s. Laszlo Tothfalusi and Klara Vigh; m. Ildiko Csakany, Nov. 30, 1974; 1 child, Tamas. BA, Coll. for Horticulture, Nyiregyhaza, Hungary, 1966; MA, Budapest U. of Econs., 1976. Cert. economist Univ. Coun.; cert. agrl. engr. Coll. Coun. Rsch. assoc. Ctr. for Statis. and Econ. Analysis, Budapest, 1968-73; rsch. fellow Inst. Econs. Hungarian Acad. Scis., Budapest, 1973-91; mng. dir. MAP Anglo-Hungarian Fin. Ltd., Budapest, 1991-99, ECHO Consulting Ltd., Budapest, 1987—; vis. rsch. fellow Ecole des Hautes Etudes Sociales, Paris, 1982, 84, 87, U. Libre de Brussels, 1988; corr. Ea. European Energy Rev., Hartsdale, 1992-98. Editor: (books) Motor Industry in Eastern Europe, 1991, 93, Pulp and Paper in Eastern Europe, 1994, Hungary: The Electrical Power Infrastructure, 1994. Co. sgt.-maj. Hungarian Army, 1966-68. Mem. Hungarian Assn. Mgmt. Cons. Avocations: reading, traveling, films, music. Fax: 36 1 385 2312. E-mail: tothfalusi@echo.hu. Office: ECHO Consulting Ltd, Bartok Bela ut 19, H-1112 Budapest Hungary

TOTOEV, YURI ZAREVICH, civil engineering educator; b. Kiev, Ukraine, Mar. 30, 1960; arrived in Australia, 1992; s. Zarya Iraklievich and Emma Semionovna (Agapieva) T.; m. Luba Vladimirovna Kraevskaya, Feb. 12, 1983; children: Anastacia and Ksenia. MSc, Kiev Civil Engring. Inst., 1982, PhD, 1987. Engr. State Constrn. Co., Ukraine, 1982-84; part-time tutor Kiev Civil Engring. Inst., Ukraine, 1984-87, rsch. officer, 1987-91; dir. Bur. for Implementation of New Technologies, Kiev, 1991-92; rsch. assoc. U. Newcastle, Callaghan, Australia, 1993-94, assoc. lectr. civil engring., 1994-99, lectr., 1999—. Home: 40 Paterson Close, Whitebridge NSW 2290, Australia Office: U Newcastle Dept Civ Engrin, University Dr, Callaghan 2308, Australia

TOTSKY, ALEXANDER VLADIMIROVICH, engineering educator, researcher; b. Kharkov, Ukraine, May 1, 1952; s. Vladimir Isifovich and Anna (Vasilyevna) T.; m. Liudmila Rostislavna Orlova, Aug. 3, 1974; 1 child, Olga. Engr. Degree, Kharkov State U., 1974; PhD in Engring., Aviation Inst., Kharkov, 1981. Rschr. Physics Engring. Rsch. Inst., Soukhumi, USSR, 1974-77; sr. rschr. Kharkov Aviation Inst., USSR, 1977-82, jr. lectr., 1982-87; prof. State Aerospace U., Kharkov, Ukraine, 1987-99. Contbr. articles to profl. jours. George Soros Found. grantee, 1993. Avocations: tennis, skiing, driving. E-mail: lukin@xai.kharkov.ua. Home: dpt 202, ul Akademika Pavlova 311, Kharkov Ukraine 310168 Office: State Aerospace U, ul Chkalova 17 dpt 505, Kharkov Ukraine 310071

TOTTEN, GEORGE OAKLEY, III, political science educator; b. Washington, July 21, 1922; K George Oakley Totten Jr. and Vicken (von Post) Börjesson Totten Barrois; m. Astrid Maria Anderson, June 26, 1948 (dec. Apr. 26, 1975); children: Vicken Yuriko, Linnea Catherine; m. Lilia Huiying Li, July 1, 1976; 1 child, Blanche Maluk Lemes. Cert., U. Mich., 1943; AB, Columbia U., 1946, AM, 1949; MA, Yale U., 1950, PhD, 1954; docentur i japanologi, U. Stockholm, 1977. Lectr. Columbia U., N.Y.C., 1954-55; asst. prof. MIT, Cambridge, 1958-59, Boston U., 1959-61; assoc. prof. U. R.I., Kingston, 1961-64; assoc. prof. polit. sci. U. So. Calif., L.A., 1965-68, prof., 1968-92, chmn. dept., 1980-86, prof. emeritus, 1992—; dir., founder Calif. Pvt. Univs. and Colls. Yr.-in-Japan program Weseda U., 1967-73; dir. East Asian Studies Ctr., 1974-77; 1st dir. USC-UCLA Joint East Asian Studies Ctr., 1976-77; sr. affiliated scholar Ctr. for Multiethnic and Transnat. Studies, 1993-98; chair USC Korea Project, 1998—; vis. prof. U. Stockholm, 1977-79, 1st dir. Ctr. Pacific Asia Studies, 1985-89, sr. counselor bd. dirs., 1989—; hon. pres. Huaxiu Pvt. Sch., Anyang City, Henan Province, China, 1999—. Author: Social Democratic Movement in Prewar Japan, 1966, Chinese edit., 1987, Korean edit., 1997; co-author: Socialist Parties in Postwar Japan, 1966, Japan and the New Ocean Regime, 1984; editor: Helen Snow's Song of Ariran, 1973, Korean edit., 1991, Chinese edit., 1993, Kim Dae-jung's A New Beginning, 1996, Lee Hee-ho's (Mrs. Kim Dae-jung's) Praying for Tomorrow: Letters to My Husband in Prison, 1999; author, co-editor: Developing Nations: Quest for a Model, 1970, Japanese edit., 1975, China's Economic Reform: Administering the Introduction of the Market Mechanism, 1992, Community in Crisis: The Korean American Community After the Los Angeles Civil Unrest of April 1992, 1994; co-translator: Ch'ien Mu's Traditional Government in Imperial China, 1982; contbr. The Politics of Divided Nations, 1991, Chinese edit., 1995, Japanese edit., 1997; editl. bd. Koreanicus, 1997—. Mem. U.S.-China People's Friendship Assn., Washington, 1974—, World Feds., 1962—; mem. Com. on U.S.-China Relations, N.Y.C., 1975—; chmn. L.A.-Pusan Sister City Assn., L.A., 1976-77; bd. dirs. L.A.-Guangzhou Sister City Assn., 1990—, mem. bd. dirs., Japan-Am. Soc. of Calif., 1990-94; bd. dirs. Japan-Am. Soc. So. Calif., 1980—; mem. nat. adv. com. Japan Am. Student Conf., 1984—, Assn. of Korean Pol. Studies in N.Am., 1992—, v.p. 1996-98; bd. mem. Assn. for the Study of Korean Culture and Identity, Korea, 1999—; coun. mem. China Soc. for People's Friendship Studies, Beijing, 1991—. 1st lt. AUS, 1942-46, PTO. Recipient Plaque for program on Korean studies Consulate Gen. of Republic of Korea, 1975, Disting. Emeritus award U. So. Calif., 1996; Social Sci. Rsch. Coun. fellow, 1952-53; Ford Found. grantee, 1955-58, NSF grantee, 1979-81, Korea Found. grantee, 1993, Rebuild L.A. grantee, 1993, Philippine Liberation medal, 1994. Mem. Assn. Asian Studies, Am. Polit. Sci. Assn., Asia Soc., Internat. Polit. Sci. Assn., Internat. Studies Assn., Japanese Polit. Sci. Assn., European Assn. Japanese Studies, U. So. Calif. Faculty Ctr., Phi Beta Delta (founding mem. Beta Kappa chpt. 1993—). Episcopalian. Home: 5129 Village Green Los Angeles CA 90016-5205 Office: USC Korea Project Dept Polit Sci Vkc 327 Los Angeles CA 90089-0001

TOTTY, BARBARA ANN, health services administrator; b. Stamford, Eng., Nov. 15, 1951; d. Fred and Marjory Alice (Bell) Archer; 1 child, Christina Louise. Sr. MLSO in liver pathology Royal Free Hosp., London, 1976-81; chief MLSO Hosp. for Sick Children, London, 1981-85; MLSO Addenbrooke's Hosp., Cambridge, Eng., 1970-76; chief technologist in histopathology Addenbrooke's Hosp., Cambridge, 1985-93, prin. technologist, 1993—; course leader Anglia U., Cambridge, 1992—; assessor U.K. NEQAS Immunocytochemistry Scheme, London, 1994—; insp. Clin. Pathology Accreditation (U.K.) Ltd., 1993—; presenter Histochemistry Meeting, 1982; rep. CPA (EQA) Ltd., 1998—; specialist subject reviewer Quality Assurance Agy., 1998—. Mem. adv. bd. Jour. Cellular Pathology, 1996—. Recipient Viviane Maggi prize, 1982. Fellow Inst. Biomed. Sci. (chief examiner in cellular pathology 1994—, mem. sci. adv. panel 1996—); mem. Nat. Soc. Histotech., Path. Soc. Home: 39 Barton Rd, Cambs Cambridge CB3 7LL, England Office: Addenbrooke's NHS Trust Box 235, Hills Rd, Dept Histopathol, Cambridge CB2 2QQ, England

TOU, STEPHEN KWOK WOON, science educator; b. China, Sept. 13, 1950; s. Siu Tong Tou and Suk Ching Au; m. Josephine Fong Chun Wong, Mar. 3, 1985; 1 child, Samuel Yu Heng. B of Applied Sci., Queen's U., Kingston, Ont., Can., 1972; M of Engring., Concordia U., Montreal, Que., Can., 1975; PhD, City U., London, 1984. Chartered engr. Inst. Mech. Engrs. U.K. Aerodynamicist United Aircraft, Montreal, Que., 1972-74; mech. engr. Ont. Hydro, Toronto, 1974-78; sr. lectr. Hong Kong Poly. U., 1978-84; sr. rsch. engr. Norton Christensen, Salt Lake City, 1985-86; assoc. prof. Nanyang Technol. U., Singapore, 1986—; cons. Mass Transit Sys., Hong Kong; rschr. Ministry of Def., Singapore; rsch. grant assessor Hong Kong City U., 1995; external examiner U. Malaysia, 1993. Contbr. papers to profl. jours.; patentee in field; reviewer profl. jours. W.W. King scholar Queen's U., 1970; rsch. grantee Hong Kong Poly. U., 1983, Nanyang Technol. U., 1990, 93, 96. Mem. ASME, Inst. Mech. Engrs. Avocations: computer, music. Fax: 65 4678202. E-mail: mkwtou@ntu.edu.sg. Office: Nanyang Technol U, Sch Mech & Prodn Engring, Singapore Singapore

TOUATI, CHARLES, religious studies educator; b. Tlemcen, Algeria, Feb. 1, 1925; arrived in France, 1945; s. Haim and Rose (Sultan) T.; m. Madeleine Meyer, Aug. 10, 1949 (dec. July 1993); children: Pierre-Yves, Joël, Laurent. Rabbi, Jewish Sem. of France, Paris, 1948; Dr. in History of Philosophy, Sorbonne, Paris, 1965, Dr d'Etat Lettres, 1971. Asst. prof. Ecole Pratique Hautes Etudes, Paris, 1967-72, full prof., 1972-94; prof. Jewish Sem. of France, Paris, 1950-88; mem. Comite Nat. de Recherche Scientifique, Langues et Civilisations Orientales, 1971-75; dir. Revue des etudes Juives, Paris, 1981-97; dir. Collection de la Revue des Etudes Juives, Louvain, 1981—. Author: La Pensée de Gersonide, 1973, 2d edit., 1992, Prophètes, Talmudistes, Philosophes, 1990 (Couronné par Acad. des Scis. Morales et Politiques 1991), Juda Hallévi; Le Kuzari, 1994; contbr. articles to profl. jours. Decorated chevalier de la Légion d'Honneur. Mem. Mekisey Nirdamim Acad. Jerusalem, Acad. Jewish Philosophy (hon. fellow), Soc. des Etudes Juives (pres. 1970-72, v.p. 1972—), Assn. French Rabbis (hon. pres. 1999—). Avocations: reading, languages. Home: 49 rue Archereau, 75019 Paris France Office: Ecole Prat Hautes Etudes, Sorbonne/45 rue des Ecoles, 75005 Paris France

TOUBORG, MARGARET EARLEY BOWERS, non-profit executive; b. Rome, N.Y., Aug. 12, 1941; d. George Thomas and Margaret Earley (Brown) Bowers; m. Jens Touborg, Sept. 9, 1961 (div. 1985); children: Margaret Earley Touborg-Jebsen, Anne Touborg Zimmer, Sarah, Peter Nicolai. AB magna cum laude, Radcliffe Coll., 1965; MEd, Harvard U., 1984. Asst. to pres. Radcliffe Coll., Cambridge, Mass., 1984-86, exec. asst. to pres., 1986-87, dir. corp. and found. relations, 1988-89; pres. U. Cape Town Fund, Inc., N.Y.C., 1989—; sr. project dir. Open Soc. Scholars Fund, N.Y.C., 1989—. Trustee The Trinity Sch., N.Y.C., 1994—, Bemis Lectr. Series, Lincoln, Mass., 1982-85; nat. cons. Schlesinger Libr. on History of Women in Am., 1995-95; assoc. chmn. edn. div. United Way Mass., 1986. Mem. Harvard Club N.Y.C., Phi Beta Kappa (Iota chpt. chmn. com. hon. membership 1976-94), Cosmpolitan Club (N.Y.C.). Episcopalian.

TOUBY, RICHARD, lawyer; b. Sioux City, Iowa, Nov. 17, 1924; s. Louis and Rebecca (Keck) T.; m. Marion Lascher, Aug. 6, 1949; children: Jill Diane, Kim Paula. LLB, U. Miami, 1948; LLM, Duke U., 1950. Bar: Fla. 1948. Faculty U. Miami, Coral Gables, Fla., 1948-63; mem. 8th Air Force Meml. Assn., 305 Bomb Group (H) Assn., 1994—. 1st Lt. USAF, 1943-45. Office: 19 W Flagler St Ste 907 Miami FL 33130-4407

TOUCHY, DEBORAH K.P., lawyer, accountant; b. Pasadena, Tex., Dec. 9, 1957; d. Donald Carl and Bobbie Jo (Jackson) Putzka; m. Harry Roy Touchy, Jr., Feb. 23, 1980. BBA, Baylor U., 1979; JD, U. Houston, 1988. Bar: Tex. 1989; CPA, Tex.; cert. in estate planning and probate law Tex. Bd. Legal Specialization. Sr. mgr. tax KMPG Peat Marwick, Houston, 1980-86; assoc. Fizer Beck Webster & Bentley, Houston, 1989-90; pvt. practice law Houston, 1990—; chmn. spl. events Jr. League Houston, 1997-98. Editor Houston Law Rev., 1988-89. Chmn. ticket sales incentives Chi Omega, Houston, 1985; active ticket sales Mus. Fine Arts, Houston, 1984; facilities chmn. Woodland Trails West Civic Orgn., Houston, 1982-83; pres. Women Attys. in Tax & Probate, 1994-95. Recipient Outstanding Alumi award Beta Alpha Psi, 1997. Mem. ABA (estate-probate sect. 1989—, vice chmn. commn. property com. 1994—), AICPA (taxation sect., estate and gift tax com. 1992-95, 1998—), Tex. Soc. CPAs (bd. dirs. 1995—, chmn. tax inst. com. 1996-97, estate planning com. 1990-94, 96—), Houston Chpt. CPAs (chmn. taxpayer edn. 1985-86, chmn. membership com. 1992-93, v.p. 1993-94, 96-97, chmn. tax forums 1994-95, long range planning com. 1995-96, treas.-elect 1997-98, chmn. leadership devel. 1997-98, treas. 1998-99, chmn. ann. charity event 1999-2000, bd. dirs. 1999-2000, pres.-elect 2000—), Houston Bar Assn. (estate-probate sect. 1989—), State Bar Tex. (estate-probate sect. 1989—, mem. elder law com. 1991-97), Houston Estate and Fin. Forum, Baylor U. Women's Assn. (treas. 1993-94, chmn. fin. com. 1994-95, parliamentarian 1995-96, sec. 1996-97, pres. 1997-98, chmn. audit com. 1999-2000), Chief Justice-Advocates, Tex. Bd. Legal Specializations (cert. estate planning, probate law 1994), Order of Coif, Omicron Delta Kappa, Phi Delta Phi, Beta Alpha Psi (Outstanding Alumni 1997). Office: 2932 Plumb St Houston TX 77005-3058

TOUFAR, PAVEL, writer; b. Prague, Czechoslovakia, July 13, 1948; s. František and Anna (Krčmová) T.; m. Jaroslava Houdková, June 8, 1979; 1 child, Martina. MA, Charles U., Prague, 1972. Cert. in internat. space law. Freelance writer Prague, 1972—; space reporter Czech TV, Prague, 1980—; editor: Panorama Pub. House, Prague, 1982-83; rschr., cons. Space Rsch. Stress Lab., Czechoslovakia, 1978-88, 98—. Author: Desire for Stars, 1976, Voyagers to Space, 1976, 78, Document, 1977, The Realization of Phantasy, 1978, An Experiment, 1980, 95, Great Voyagers through the Space, 1989, The Death Is Lurking in Space, 1996, Space Scandals, 1999, Meeling with Mystery (1-4), 2000; chief editor: Signál, 1991-92. Recipient award for popularization of sci. Czech Acad. Sci., 1986, Gold medal of Intercosmos. Mem. Czech Union of Writers, Club of Nonfiction Authors (com. mem. 1992—), Internat. Inst. Space Law. Home: U Staré Školy 2/115, 110 00 Prague 1, Czech Republic

TOUNGUI, PAUL, Gabonese government official. Min. fin. Ministry of Fin., 1990-94; min. mines, energy and water resources Ministry of Mines, Energy and Oil, Libreville, Gabon, 1994—. Office: Ministry Mines Energy & Oil, BP 576-874, Libreville Gabon*

TOURAINE MOULIN, FRANÇOISE, scientific attache; b. Lyon, France, May 3, 1944; came to U.S., 1997; d. Paul Marius Moulin and Marcelle Anne Marie Franceries; m. Jean François Touraine, Sept. 7, 1968 (div. June 1996); children: Laure Agnès, Alexia Marjorie. PharmD, U. Claude Bernard, 1966, PhD in Immunology, 1972, M in Med. Ethics and Philosophy, 1993. Cert. pharmacist, clin. biologist. Biologist, dir. dept. clin. immunology Hospices Civils de Lyon, 1976—; co-dir. of Rsch. INSERM 433 Faculté de Médécine Lacnnec-Lyon 1, 1992—; scientific attache Embassy of France to the U.S., Washington, 1997—; cons. for biomed. ethics and biotech. French Ministry of Health, Paris, 1993-95. Co-author: Transplantation and Clinical Immunology, 1980-92; contbr. articles to profl. jours. Chargé de Mission, bioethics Ministry of Rsch. and Tech., Paris, 1995-97. Chevalier de l'Ordre de Merite, 1997. Mem. Assn. for Ethics in AIDS (pres. treatment in developing countries 1995—), Soc. Françciase d'Immunologie, Internat. Soc. for Neuro Immuno Modulation, Assn. for Women and HIV (v.p. 1996—), European Acad. of Arts, Scis. and Letters. Roman Catholic. Avocations: reading, writing, antique collecting. E-mail: ftm@amb.wash.fr. Office: Embassy of France Scientific Svc 4101 Reservoir Rd NW Washington DC 20007-2170

TOURET, JACQUES LEON ROBERT, geology educator; b. Fumay, France, Jan. 2, 1936; arrived in The Netherlands, 1980; s. Martial Charles and Suzanne (Gouilly) T.; m. Christiane Poinsignon, Oct. 7, 1960 (div. 1974); children: Olivier, Mathilde, Cécile; m. Lydia Ben Mohammed, May 15, 1975; 1 child, Anne Cindy. Lic. in scis., Nancy (France) U., 1958, DSc, 1969; geology engr., Nancy Sch. Engrs., 1958. Assoc. prof. Nancy U., 1969-74, Paris U., 1974-80; prof. geology Free U., Amsterdam, 1980—. Editor and assoc. editor various sci. jours. Capt. Corps of Engrs., French Mil., 1962-64.

Recipient Carriere prize French Acad. Scis., 1970, André Dumont medal Belgium Geol. Soc., 1992, Van Waterschoot van der Gracht medal Dutch Geol. Soc., 1996. Mem. Royal Dutch Acad. Arts and Scis., Acad. Europea, Norwegian Acad. Scis. and Letters. Socialist. Avocation: violin. Office: Vrije U Dept Petrology, De Boelelaan 1085, 1081HV Amsterdam The Netherlands

TOURNIER, MICHEL, writer; b. Paris, Dec. 19, 1924; s. Alphonse and Marie-Madeleine (Fournier) T. Ed., U. Paris, Sorbonne, U. Tubingen; dr honoris causa, London Univ. Coll. In radio and TV prodn., 1949-54; press attaché, Europe, 1955-58; head lit. services Editions Plon, 1958-68. Author: Vendredi ou les limbes du Pacifique, 1967, Le Roi des Aulnes, 1970, Les meteores, 1975, Le vent paraclet, 1977, Le coq de bruyere, 1978, Des clefs et des serrures, 1979, Gaspard, Melchoir et Balthazar, 1980, La Goutte d'Or, 1986, La Médianoche Amoureux, 1990, Le Crépuscule des Masques, 1992, Le Miroir des Idées Eleazar, 1996, The Erl King. Decorated officier Légion d'Honneur; recipient grand prix du Roma Acad. Française, 1967; prix Goncourt, 1970, Goethe medaille. Mem. Academie Goncourt.

TOURTELLOTTE, MILLS CHARLTON, mechanical and electrical engineer; b. Great Falls, Mont., Dec. 16, 1922; s. Nathaniel Mills and Frances Victoria (Charlton) T.; m. Dorothy Elsie Gray, Sept. 16, 1947 (dec. 1994); children: Jane Tourtellotte Collins, Kathryn Tourtellotte Bauman, Thomas; m. Linda M. Merritt, July 1, 1995. BS, Ill. Inst. Tech., 1947, MS, 1952. Registered profl. engr., Ill., Mich., Tex. Engr. Automatic Electric Co., Chgo., 1947-49, Inland Steel Co., East chicago, Ind., 1952-56; sr. project engr. Gulf States Tube divsn. Vision Metals, Rosenberg, Tex., 1956—; fallout shelter analyst Fed. Emergency mgmt., Washington, 1970—; dealer Amsoil, 1977—. Contbr. articles to profl. jours.; patentee mech. and elec. devices. Election judge Ft. Bend County Republican party, 1965; chmn. 4H Adult Leaders Assn., 1968. Named Friend of 4H, Ft. Bend County Extension Svc., 1968. Mem. NSPE, ASME (life), Tex. Soc. Profl. Engrs. (edn. chmn. 1969), Fluid Power Soc., Am. Soc. for Engring. Edn. (industry chmn. 1969), Assn. Iron and Steel Engrs. (life), Mich. Soc. Profl. Engrs., Ill. Soc. Profl. Engrs., VFW (life, quartermaster 1984), Am. Legion, Houston Inventors Assn., Handyman Club Am. Office: Vision Metals Gulf State Tube Divsn PO Box 952 Rosenberg TX 77471-0952

TOURTET, CHRISTIANE ANDRÉE, writer, human rights activist, photo journalist; b. Grenoble, France, June 18, 1945; came to U.S., 1965; d. André and Maria Tourtet. Cert. completion humanistic psychology, Fla. Jr. Coll., Jacksonville, 1969, AS with high honors, 1973, AA with high honors, 1974; BA, Jacksonville U., 1975. Hostess interpreter-translator Credit Lyonnais, Grenoble, 1963-65; instr. French Albany (N.Y.) Acad. for Girls, 1965-66; instr. French, asst. lang. lab. Coll. of St. Rose, Albany, 1966-67; instr. French Bartram Sch., Jacksonville, 1970; instr. French and modeling Fla. Jr. Coll., Jacksonville, 1971-74; producer-dir., radio personality ednl. French program Sta. WFAM FM radio, Jacksonville, 1977-79; interpreter, translator French Lang. Bank, Jacksonville, 1980-83; tutor pvt. and small group classes in French; model for publicity ads, brochures in major mags., newspapers; lectr. in field. Author: Fruits of Life (Silver medal Arts Scis. Letter, Paris, 1977); editor, contbr. publs. New Leaf News, Fla. Flambeau, Back to School Mag.; editor, pub., contbr. Environ. Med. and Disability Corner, Tallahassee Area Ch. News, FSView, AARP Newsletter, Tallahassee Alliance with Disabilities Newsletter; recs. Flamingo Studios, Tallahassee, Fla., 1986-87; paintings exhibited in France, Monte Carlo and U.S.; photography exhibited in galleries, pub. in mags. including Today's Photographer; participant in over 28 TV commls. Pres. Le Cercle Francais, Albany, 1965. Recipient 1st prize Solfege Artistic Competition, 1957, 1st prize Accordian Acad. Grenoble, 1958; Gold medal Cup of France, 1959, Cup of Europe, 1959, 2d prize Singing Competition City of Grenoble, 1961, medal of City of Grenoble, France, 1977, medal of Dauphine County, 1977, medal of Chevalier of Order of Merit, Paris, 1976, medal of Chevalier of French Courtesy, Paris, 1977, medal of Nat. Merit, Paris, 1976; crowned twice by Romanian Prince Paltin Sturdza, Princess Cornelia Sturdza and Prince Michael Sturdza. Mem. NAFE, APHA, Am. Acad. Environ. Medicine (assoc.), Environ. Illness Assn. Tallahassee (founder, pres. 1989—), Nat. Ctr. Environ. Strategies, Share, Care, Prayers, H.E.A.L., Am. Med. Writers Assn., Internat. Platform Assn., Nat. Assn. Sci. Writers, Freelance Media Svcs., India Assn. Tallahassee (publicity officer), Internat. Freelance Photographers Orgn., Am. Image Press, Phi Theta Kappa. Address: PO Box 20517 Tallahassee FL 32316-0517

TOURTILLOTT, ELEANOR ALICE, nurse, educational consultant; b. North Hampton, N.H., Mar. 28, 1909; d. Herbert Shaw and Sarah (Fife) T. Diploma, Melrose Hosp. Sch. Nursing, Melrose, Mass., 19830; BS, Columbia State U., 1962. RN. Gen. pvt. duty nurse Melrose, Mass., 1930-35; obstet. supr. Samaritan Hosp., Troy, N.Y., 1935-36, Meml. Hosp., Niagara Falls, N.Y., 1937-38, Lawrence Meml. Hosp., New London, Conn., 1939-42, New Eng. Hosp. Women and Children, Boston, 1942-43; dir. H. W. Smith Sch. Practical Nursing, Syracuse, N.Y., 1949-53; founder, dir. assoc. degree nursing program Henry Ford C.C., Dearborn, Mich., 1953-74; dir. pioneering use of learning gtechs. visa mixed media USPHS, 1966-71; prin. cons. initial coord. Wayne State U. Coll. Nursing, Detroit, 1975-78; condr. numerous workshops on curriculum design, 1966—; charter mem. Women in Mil. Svc. for Am., 1993—; mem. Mich. Bd. Nursing, 1966-73, chmn., 1970-72, mem. rev. com. for constrn. nurse tng. facilitates, divsn. nursing USPHS, 1967-70, mem. nat. adv. coun. on nurse tng., Dept. Health Edn. and Welfare, 1972-76. Author: Commitment-A Lost Characteristic, 1982; contbg. co-author: Patient Assessment-History and Physical Examination, 1975-78; contbr. chpts., articles, speeches to profl. publs. Capt. Nurse Corps U.S. Army, 1943-45, U.S., ETO. Recipient Disting. Alumnae award Tchrs. Coll. Columbia U., 1974, Spl. Tribute 77th Legis. Mich., 1974, Disting. Alumnae award Wayne State U., 1975, Disting. Svc. award Henry Forde C.C., 1982; established and endowed Eleanor Tourtillott Outstanding Student Nurse of Yr. award at Henry Ford C.C., 1993; inducted to Nursing Hall of Fame Tchrs. Coll. Columbia U., 1999. Mem. DAR, ANA, Nat. League Nursing (chmn. steering com., dept. assoc. degree programs 1965-67, bd. dirs. 1965-67, 71-73, mem. assembly constituent leagues 1971-73, coun. asoc degree programs citation 1974, Mildred Montag Excellence in Leadership award coun. asoc. degree programs 1994(), Mich. League Nursing (pres. 1969-71), Mich. Acad. Sci., Arts and Letters, Am. Legion, Tchrs. Coll. Alumnae Assn., Wayne State U. Alumnae Assn., Phi Lambda Theta, Kappa Delta Pi. Address: 4860 S Johnson St Littleton CO 80123-2118

TOUS, SOZAN SHAWKY, pharmaceutics educator; b. Assiut, El-Kossia, Egypt, Aug. 19, 1947; d. Michael Shawky and Wadeda Basta (Makar) T.; m. Mamdoh-Magdie Nashed Gayed, July 28, 1974; children: Moheb, Mariam, Margo. B in Pharmacy, U. Assiut, 1970, PhD, 1981. Hosp. pharmacist Ministry of Public Health, Assiut, Egypt, 1970-71; demonstrator in pharms. Assiut U., 1971-77, asst. lectr. pharms., 1977-81, asst. prof., 1981-86, assoc. prof., 1986-92, prof., 1992—; supr. for postgrad. students Assiut U., 1981—; sci. coord. Assiut U. and U. D'Aix-Marseille, France; mem. adminstrv. coun. Red Crescent Soc. Assuit Ctr. Contbr. articles to profl. jours. Postdoctoral scholarship Paris Sud (France) U., 1993. Mem. Pharm. Assn. Avocations: stories, sewing clothes, drawing. Office: Faculty of Pharmacy, Assiut Univ, Assiut Egypt

TOUS DE TORRES, LUZ M., banker; b. San Juan, P.R., Apr. 23, 1944; d. Rafael Tous Cortes and Iris Fernos; m. Manuel A. de Torres, Jr., Feb. 17, 1967; children: Rosa Iris, Lara Sofia. BBA magna cum laude, U. P.R., 1965; MBA summa cum laude, Interam. U., 1976; also P.R. Sch. Banking, 1976. With Banco Popular, San Juan, 1965—, sr. v.p. corp. real estate adminstrn., 1987—. Co-founder P.R. Indsl. Editors Assn., pres., 1970-72; dir. bank's blood program for ARC, 1972—, dir. bank's personnel donors program United Fund, 1981—; trustee BPPR Found., 1986-87; dir. Greater San Juan Com., 1993, pres. 2000. Recipient Outstanding Acad. Achievement award Interam. U., 1976. Mem. NAFE, Soc. Human Resources Mgmt. (accredited profl. in human resources), Internat. Facility Mgmt. Assn. (cert. facility mgr.), Internat. Assn. Corp. Real Estate Execs., Bldg. Owners Mgmt. Assn., Urban Land Inst., Met. Mus. of Art (N.Y.), Mus. Contemporary Art, P.R. Mus. of Art, Corp. Devel. Hato Rey Fin. Ctr., Puerto Rico, Rotary (sec. 2000). Office: PO Box 362708 San Juan PR 00936-2708

TOUSEY, ROBERT RYAN, lawyer; b. L.I., N.Y., May 31, 1958; s. Fred Lester and Alice Marie (Ryan) T.; m. Betty Grivakis, Nov. 20, 1988 (div. June 1994); children: Christopher, Stephanie. BS, U. Md., 1984; JD, U. Balt., 1989. Bar: Md. 1989, U.S. Dist. Ct. Md. 1990, U.S. Ct. Appeals (4th cir.) 1991, U.S. Tax Ct. 1991, U.S. Supreme Ct. 1992. Sr. tax cons. Ernst & Young, Balt., 1989-91; trial atty. Owens, Robertson & Parler, Balt., 1991-94, Law Office of Stephen L. Miles, Balt., 1994-99, Goodman, Meagher & Enoch, LLP, Balt., 1999—; law sch. rep. ABA Law Student Divsn., Balt., 1987-88. Sr. editor U. Balt. Law Forum, 1986 (Exceptional Svc. award 1988). Past mem. Howard County Drug Abuse Adv. Bd., Ellicott City, Md., 1993-95; Congl.candidate, 3d Dist. Md., 1994; active, religious edn. tchr. St. Augustine's Roman Cath. Ch.; past internat. bd. mem. Parents Without Ptnrs.; Md. state pub. policy chair Am. Cancer Soc. Sgt. USAF, 1978-82. Recipient Outstanding Svc. award County Exec. Ecker, Ellicott City, 1995, Spl. Congl. Recognition cert., 1997. Mem. Md. State Bar Assn., Am. Cancer Soc. (divsn. dir., pub. policy chair, past pres. Howard County unit 1990-92), Parents Without Ptnrs. (Mid Atlantic Regional coun. pres.). Republican. Avocations: public service, baseball, movies, travel. Home: 3133 Normandy Woods Dr Apt H Ellicott City MD 21043-4585 Office: 111 N Charles St Ste 700 Baltimore MD 21201-3803

TOUSSAINT, PATRICK, materials engineering researcher; b. Ixelles, Belgium, Jan. 30, 1969; s. Janine Caryn. Engr. civil metallurgiste, Free U. Brussels, 1992, PhD, 1997. Rschr. U. Libre Brussels, 1992-98; industrialization engr. and metall. quality stainless steels USINOR Industeel, Charleroi, Belgium, 1998—; mem. Coun. of the Faculty of Applied Scis., U. Libre Brussels, 1995-98. Contbr. articles to profl. jours. Mem. Assn. Royale Des Ingenieurs Free U. Brussels (orgn. com. 1992-96), Union des Anciens Etudiants Free U. Brussels, Fedn. European Materials Socs. Avocations: simulation games, foreign languages. Office: USINOR Industeel Belgium, Rue de Chatelet 266, B-6030 Marchienne au Pont Belgium

TOUT, CHRISTOPHER ADAM, astronomer, consultant; b. Billericay, Essex, Eng., Apr. 25, 1964; s. Kenneth William Alexander and Eleanor Jane (Coleman) T.; m. Eniko Regos, Sept. 25, 1992. BA, U. Cambridge, Eng., 1985, MA, 1989, PhD, 1989. Sci. officer Royal Greenwich Obs., Herstmonceux, U.K., 1982-83; NATO fellow Lick Obs., Santa Cruz, Calif., 1990-91; Particle Physics and Astronomy Rsch. Coun. advanced fellow U. Cambridge, Eng., 1993-2000; fellow and coll. lectr. math. Churchill Coll., Cambridge, 2000—; regent Emmanuel Coll. Monarchist League, 1988-89, 93—; rsch. fellow Sidney Sussex Coll., Cambridge, Eng., 1992-94, Space Telescope Sci. Inst., Balt., 1995-96; Royal Soc. exch. fellow Konkoly Obs., Budapest, Hungary, 1996-97; vis. astronomer Monash U., Melbourne, Australia, 1997. Editor: Evolutionary Processes in Binary Stars, 1996; contbr. articles to profl. jours. Fellow Royal Astronomical Soc. Anglican. Catholic. Avocations: bird watching, cycling. E-mail: cat@ast.cam.ac.uk. Fax: 44 1223 337523. Home: 58 Hurrell Rd, Cambridge CB4 3RH, England Office: Inst Astronomy U Cambridge, Madingley Rd, Cambridge CB3 0HA, England

TOUW, GEERT HENK, manufacturing company executive; b. Eindhoven, The Netherlands, Dec. 21, 1945; s. Hendrik Jan Touw and Corry Willy Tempelmans Plat; 1 child from previous marriage, Sascha Caroline; m. Deborah Ann Del Balso, Aug. 11, 1979; 1 child, Jason Alexander. BS in Econs., U. London, 1968. With N.V. Philip's Gloeilampenfabrieken, Eindhoven, The Netherlands, 1968-69, Marston Radiators Ltd., Leeds, U.K., 1969-70; shareholder, dir. Malta Radiators Ltd., Zebbug, Malta, 1970-74; mgr. internat. ops. perfex divsn. McQuay Inc., Mpls., 1975-81, v.p. internat. ops. perfex divsn., 1981-82, v.p. internat. and aftermarket ops. perfex divsn., 1982-83, v.p., gen. mgr. energy systems and svcs. divsn., 1983-84; v.p., gen. mgr. internat. group Snyder Gen. Corp., Dallas, 1984-86; mng. dir. Donaldson Europe NV (Donaldson Co. Inc.), Belgium, 1986-2000; v.p., gen. mgr. Donaldson Co. Inc., Europe, Africa, Middle East, 2000—; bd. dirs. Am. C.of C., Brussels, Belgium. Trustee United Fund for Belgium a.s.b.l./v.z.w. Fellow Inst. Dirs. U.K., Inst. Mgmt. U.K.; mem. Chartered Inst. Mktg. U.K., Assn. MBA Execs. USA, East India Club U.K. Anglican. Avocations: art, international affairs, participative sports. Office: Donaldson Europe NV Rsch Pk, Zone 1 Interleuvenlaan 1, B-3001 Leuven Belgium also: Donaldson Co Inc PO Box 1299 Minneapolis MN 55440-1299

TOUWAIDE, ALAIN JACQUES ANDRÉ, science educator, researcher; b. Brussels, Sept. 19, 1953; arrived in Spain, 1993; s. Henry and Simone (Lenelle) T. Degree in classics, Cath. U. Louvain, Belgium, 1975, degree in Oriental studies, 1978, PhD, 1981; Habil, U. Toulouse, 1997. Asst. U. Louvain, 1982-83, sr. rsch. fellow, 1983-85; assoc. prof. U. Nice, France, 1992-93; vis. prof. U. Provence, France, 1989-90, Cen. U., Barcelona, Spain, 1993-94, Consejo Superior de Investigaciones Cientificas, 1997-98; cons. in field, 1990— ; freelance journalist, 1985—. Author: Farmacopea Araba Medievale, 4 vols., 1992-93, La tossicologia antica a Bisanzio, 1993, Nicandro, Theriaka y Alexipharmaka, 1998, Une histoire du médicament en Occident (Prix d'Histoire de la Médecine/Acad. Belgium 1996), Therapeutics, an Anthology, 1998. Fellow Linnean Soc. (London); mem. Internat. Acad. History of Pharmacy. E-mail: atouwaide@hotmail.com. Home: Apartado de Correos 14587, 28080 Madrid Spain Office: U Okla Dept History of Sci 601 Elm Ave Rm 622 Norman OK 73019-3111

TOUYZ, STEPHEN WILLIAM, clinical psychologist, educator; b. Cape Town, Republic of South Africa, Aug. 29, 1950; s. Harry and Tilly (Woolfowitz) T.; m. Rennette Dawn Elk, Jan. 18, 1976; children: Justin Lawrence, Lauren Marissa. BS, U. Cape Town, 1972, PhD, 1976; BS with honors, U. Witwatersrand, 1974. Tutor U. Witwatersrand, 1974; sr. tutor U. Cape Town, 1974-75; sr. rsch. asst. Groote Schuur Hosp., Cape Town, 1974-75, intern clin. psychologist, 1976-78; staff psychologist Royal Prince Alfred Hosp., Sydney, Australia, 1978-80; clin. lectr. U. Sydney, 1979-91, clin. assoc. prof. psychiatry, 1991-94, clin. prof. psychiatry, 1994-96; dir. Ctr. for Study and Treatment of Dieting Disorders, 1994-95; prof., chmn. dept. psychology U. Sydney, 1996-98, prof. clin. psychology, 1999—; head clin. psychology unit Royal Prince Alfred Hosp., Sydney, 1980-88; cons. psychologist anorexia nervosa unit Northside Clinic, Sydney, 1979-84, Royal Prince Alfred Hosp., 1983-88, Lynton Pvt. Hosp., 1984-97; head dept. med. psychology Westmead Hsop., 1988-96; hon. assoc. dept. psychology U. Sydney, 1979-96, prof.; hon. clin. assoc. dept. psychology Macquarie U., 1990—; dep. chmn. divsn. psychol. medicine Westmead Hosp., 1993-94; NSW advisor on health psychol. dept. of vets affairs Commonwealth of Australia, 1994—; mem. Westmead Hosps. Sci. Coun., 1988-96; cons. practice guidelines com. for eating disorders APA, 1990-93. Author: Grune and Stratton, 1984, Williams and Wilkins, 1985; rsch. grantee South African Coun. for Sci. and Indsl. Rsch., 1973-76, Nat. Health and Med. Rsch. Coun. Australia, 1983-87, 95—, Ramaciotti Found., 1983-84, Elli Lilly, 1991-93. Fellow Internat. Coll. Psychosomatic Medicine (v.p. Australia and New Zealand chpt. 1993-99); mem. Australian Psychol. Soc., Australian Behaviour Modification Assn., Australian Soc., Psychiat. Rsch., Am. Psychol. Assn. (affiliate), Internat. Acad. Sci., Australian Sleep Rsch. Assn., Australian Soc. Study Brain Impairment, Inc. Office: U Sydney, Dept Psychology, Sydney New South Wales 2006, Australia

TOUZEAU, OLIVIER JEAN-MARC THIERRY, ophthalmologist, clinical researcher; b. Paris, France, Dec. 15, 1965; s. Max Jean-Louis Etienne and Yvette Genevieve (Houdin) T. MD, U. Paris 6, 1991. Fellow in ophthalmology Hopitaux de Paris, 1991-96; asst. in anatomy U. Paris 6, 1996-98; ophthalmologist Hopital Saint Antoine, Paris, 1996—, Hopital Quinze-Vingts, Nat. Ctr. Ophthalmology, Paris, 1998—. Mem. French Soc. Ophthalmology, Am. Acad. Ophthalmology. Home: 10 rue Vergniaud, 75013 Paris France Office: Hop St Antoine Dept Oph, 184 rue Faubourt St Antoine, 75012 Paris France

TOUZENIS-BENDECK, GEORGE, director; b. Athens, Greece, May 18, 1947; s. Konstantin and Julia (Bendeck) Touzenis. Diploma in fine arts, Ecole Nat. Supr. Beaux Arts, Paris, 1974. Hon. attaché Royal Greek Embassy, Copenhagen, 1969-72; prof. Acad. Fine Arts, St. Etienne, France, 1974-79; rector Acad. Fine Arts, Nantes, France, 1979-87, Marseilles, France, 1987-90; inspector gen. Min. Culture, Paris, 1990-93; dir. Manufacture Nat. de Sevres, Paris, 1993—; trustee Internat. Festival Arles, France, 1990-93, Ctr. Nat. des Arts, Paris, 1995—; mem. High Com. Art Edn., Paris, 1992—; cons. Internat. Media Comm., London, 1994—. Author: Mulley Mulloch, 1992, Art Since 1945, 1994, The Art of Claire Aumaitre, 1991. Lt. Royal Greek Army, 1967-69. Decorated knight Ordre St. Mark Alexandria (Greece), knight Order of Jerusalem (Greece), chevalier Ordre Arts et Letters (France), King's Messanger Royal Greek Household (Greece). Fellow Royal Soc. Genealogists; mem. Royal Heraldists Soc., French Porcelain Soc., Internat. Churchill Soc., Acad. de Versailles, Soc. Histoire de l'Art Francais, Athenaeum Club, Reform Club. Greek Orthodox. Avocations: collecting prints and objects, bibliophile, travel, cooking. Home: 4 Grande rue Pavillon, 92310 Sevres France Office: Manufacture Nat Sevres, Place de la Manufacture, 92310 Sevres France

TOVEY, FRANK IVOR, retired surgeon; b. Bath, Somerset, England, Sept. 1, 1921; s. Ernest and Ellen Louise Tovey; m. Winifred Ethel Hill, Dec. 11, 1947; children: Rosemary, Jennifer, John, David. B of Surgery and Medicine, U. Bristol, 1944; M of Surgery, U. Liverpool, 1961. Surgeon Meth. Hosp. Chaotung, S. W. China, 1947-49, Holdsworth Meml. Hosp., Mysore, S. India, 1951-67; cons. surgeon Basingstoke (England) Dist. Hosp., 1968-86, ret., 1986; rsch. fellow U. Coll. Hosp., London, 1968—. Contbr. articles to profl. jours. Officer of the Order of the British Empire, 1966. Fellow Royal Soc. Medicine, Assn. Surgeons of Great Britain, Royal Coll. Surgeons; mem. British Soc. Gastroenterology. Mem. United Reformed Ch. Home: S Crossborough Hall, Basingstoke RG21 4AG, England

TOWELL, TIMOTHY LATHROP, foreign service officer; b. Cleve., Jan. 31, 1934; s. Bernard A. and Eleanor (Assmus) T.; m. Dane Anderson Nichols, Nov. 1, 1969; children: Timothy Nichols, Dane Billings. BA, Yale U., 1957; MA, Case-Western Res. U., 1962. Commd. fgn. svc. officer Dept. State; vice consul U.S. Consulate, Valencia, Spain, 1963-65; spl. asst. to ambassador Am. embassy, Madrid, 1965-66; U.S. Consul, Am. embassy, Asuncion, Paraguay, 1966-67; 1st sec. Am. Embassy, La Paz, Bolivia, 1967-68; Bolivian desk officer Dept. State, Washington, 1968-70, Spanish desk officer, 1970-72; U.S. consul U.S. Consulate, Porto Alegre, Brazil, 1972-75; 1st sec. Am. Embassy, Brussels, Belgium, 1975-79; dep. chief of mission, U.S. Mission, Havana, Cuba, 1979-80; congl. liaison officer Europe, Dept. State, Washington, 1980-83; dep. chief of protocol of U.S., Washington, 1983-88; ambassador to Paraguay, 1988-91; regional dir. Africa The Peace Corps, Washington, 1991-92; pres. fgn. policy group, 1992—. Mem. Met. Club (Washington), Tavern Club (Cleve.).

TOWERS, BERNARD LEONARD, medical educator; b. Preston, Eng., Aug. 20, 1922; s. Thomas Francis and Isabella Ellen (Dobson) T.; m. Carole Ilene Lieberman (div. 1992); 1 child, Tiffany Sabrina; children from previous marriage: Helena Marianne, Celia Marguerite, Julie Carole. M.B., Ch.B., U. Liverpool, 1947; M.A., U. Cambridge, 1954. House surgeon Royal Infirmary, Liverpool, 1947; lectr. U. Bristol, 1949-50, U. Wales, 1950-54, Cambridge U., 1954-70; fellow Jesus Coll., 1957-70, steward, 1961-64, tutor, 1964-69; dir. med. studies, 1964-70; prof. pediatrics UCLA, 1971-84, prof. anatomy, 1971-91, prof. psychiatry, 1983-91, prof. emeritus anatomy and psychiatry, 1991—, convenor, moderator medicine and soc. forum, 1974-89; pvt. practice integrative medicine, 1991-98, ret., 1998; co-dir. Program in Medicine, Law and Human Values, 1977-84; cons. Inst. Human Values in Medicine, 1971-84; adv. bd. Am. Teilhard Assn. for Future of Man, 1971-98; v.p. Teilhard Centre for Future Man, London, 1974-98. Author: Teilhard de Chardin, 1966, Naked Ape or Homo Sapiens?, 1969, Concerning Teilhard, 1969; also articles, chpts. on sci. and philosophy.; Editor anat. sect.: Brit. Abstracts Med. Scis, 1954-56, Teilhard Study Library, 1966-70; adv. bd.: Jour. Medicine and Philosophy, 1974-84. Served to capt. RAMC, 1947-49. NIH grantee, 1974-78; NEH grantee, 1977-83. Fellow Cambridge Philos. Soc., Royal Soc. Medicine; mem. Brit. Soc. History of Medicine, Soc. Health and Human Values (pres. 1977-78), Anat. Soc. G.B., Worshipful Soc. Apothecaries London, Am. Assn. for Study Mental Imagery, Western Assn. Physicians, Societe Europeene de Culture Venise. Home: 15340 Albright St Unit 310 Pacific Palisades CA 90272-2522

TOWERY, CURTIS KENT, judge; b. Hugoton, Kans., Jan. 29, 1954; s. Clyde D. and Jo June (Curtis) T. BA, Trinity U., 1976; JD, U. Okla., 1979; LLM in Taxation, Boston U., 1989. Mem. Curtis & Blanton, Pauls Valley, Okla., 1980-81; lawyer land and legal dept. Trigg Drilling Co., Oklahoma City, 1981-82; adminstrv. law judge Okla. Corp. Commn., Oklahoma City, 1982-85; counsel Curtis & Blanton, Pauls Valley, Okla., 1985-88; adminstrv. law judge Okla. Dept. Mines, Oklahoma City, 1985-88, assoc. gen. counsel, 1989-92; contracts and purchasing adminstr., atty. Okla. Turnpike Authority, Oklahoma City, 1992-93; asst. gen. counsel Okla. Corp. Commn., 1993-97; spl. judge City of Oklahoma City, 1997—; adminstrv. law judge Okla. Dept. of Labor, 1998; v.p., trust officer Bank One Trust, Oklahoma City, 1998—; bd. dirs. First Nat. Bank Pauls Valley, 1983-88. Assoc. bd. Okla. Mus. Art, 1985-88, Okla. Symphony Orch., 1987-92; assoc. bd. Ballet Okla., 1987-92, sec., 1990-91, v.p., 1988-89; mem. Oklahoma City Estate Planning Coun., Ruth Bader Ginsburg Am. Inn of Ct., 1999—. Mem. ABA, Tex. Bar Assn., Okla. Bar Assn., Faculty House, Rotary, Elks, Phi Alpha Delta, Sigma Nu. Democrat. Presbyterian. Avocations: flying, golf, traveling, investment analysis. Home: PO Box 14891 Oklahoma City OK 73113-0891 Office: 1200 NW 63d St Ste 200 Oklahoma City OK 73116

TOWEY, CARROLL FRANCIS, senior education specialist; b. Boston, Jan. 30, 1932; s. Thomas Patrick and Marietta V. (Alcock) T.; m. Marie Elizabeth Linehan, Aug 24, 1957 (dec. Apr., 1992); children Mary Ellen Roth, Michael Carroll, Kevin James; m. Miriam A. Quinlan, Sept. 4, 1993. BS in Edn., Salem State Coll., 1953; MEd, Boston U., 1957, cert. advanced grad. study (adult edn.), 1967; EdD, U. Mass., 1973. Sr. supr. Mass. Dept. Edn., Boston, 1965-67; sr. program advisor U.S. Dept. Edn., Washington, 1967—; mem. Met. Wash. Assn. for Adult and Continuing Edn., Washington, 1981-85, pres. 1983-84; author: reports to U.S. Dept. Edn. on model programs, evaluation of adult education, and compliance by states to federal regulations; bd. dirs. Northern Va. Chpt. Retired Officers Assn., 1997. Mem. Mass. Soc. Washington, D.C., 1982—, v.p. 1993-95, pres. 1995-96, treas., 1996-97. With U.S. Army, 1955-57, Korea. Recipient Appreciation certs. Nat. Defense U., 1990, Nev. Dept. Edn., 1991, Pima County, Ariz., 1992. Mem. Fed. Vocat. Edn. Assn. (pres. 1993-94), Am. Assn. Adult and Continuing Edn. (founding mem., pres. Met. Washington 1983-84, Appreciation cert. 1988), Ret. Officers Assn. (bd. dirs. Nova Troa 1997, 2d v.p. 1998-99, 1st v.p. 2000), Phi Delta Kappa Boston U. Democrat. Roman Catholic. Avocations: gardening, reading, financial management, sports. Home: 1016 S Wayne St Apt 309 Arlington VA 22204-4435 Office: US Dept Edn 400 Maryland Ave SW # Wdc Washington DC 20202-0001

TOWGHI, NASSER M., mathematician; b. Karachi, Pakistan, May 1, 1962; came to U.S., 1976; s. Malek Mohammad and Hasineh Towghi. MS, Mich. State U., 1980; PhD, U. Conn., 1993. Vis. instr. U. Ariz., Tucson, 1993-96; rsch. asst. dept. elec. and sys. engring. U. Conn., Storrs, 1996—. Home: 1121 Palmer Ln East Lansing MI 48823-5234 Office: U Conn Dept Elec and Sys Engring U 157 Storrs Mansfield CT 06269

TOWL, GRAHAM JOHN, forensic psychologist, educator; b. Redcar, England, Aug. 13, 1961; s. John Bruce and Barbara (Moore) T.; m. Jackie Walton, Nov. 16, 1993. BA, U. Durham, Eng., 1988; MSc, U. London, 1990. Psychiat. nurse Nat. Health Svc., Eng., 1982-85; psychologist Prison Svc., Eng., 1988-91, head of unit HMP Highpoint, 1991-95; area forensic psychologist Prison Svc., Suffolk, Eng., 1995—; vis. scholar U. Cambridge, Eng., 1995-98; vis. lectr. U. Kent, Eng., 1997-98; vis. dir. studies Anglia Poly. U., Cambridge, 1995-98. Co-author: The Handbook of Psychology for Forensic Practitioners, 1996; editor: Suicide and Self-Injury in Prisons, 1997, Group Work in Prisons, 1995; co-funding editor: Forensic Update, 1995; co-founder, editor Brit. Jour. Forensic Practice, 1998; contbr. numerous articles to profl. jours. Mem. Brit. Psychol. Soc. (chartered forensic psychologist, chair divsn. criminol. and legal psychology 1998-99, chair working group on ethics 1996-97). Office: Rm 421 Cleland House, Page St, Page St London SW1P 4LN, England

TOWLE, TONY, poet, editor; b. N.Y.C., June 13, 1939; s. Erwin Weible and Mary Rigg T.; children: M. Scott, Rachel L. Student, Georgetown U., 1957-58, NYU, 1962, Columbia U., 1963. Adminstrv. asst. Universal Ltd. Art Editions, West Islip, N.Y., 1964-81; editor, adminstr. asst. Ctr. Entrepreneurial Mgmt., N.Y.C., 1982-85; copy editor Arts Mag., N.Y.C., 1988-92; sr. staff writer Nat. Found. Tchg. Entrepreneurship, N.Y.C., 1986—. Author: (poetry books) North, 1970 (Frank O'Hara award 1970), New and Selected Poems, 1983, Some Musical Episodes, 1992. Fellow N.Y. State Coun. Arts, 1975, NEA, 1979, Ingram-Merrill Found., 1982; recipient Avant-Garde poetry prize Gotham Book Mart, 1963, Frank O'Hara award.

Avocation: history, making postcards. Home: 75 Hudson St Apt 2 New York NY 10013-2865

TOWLER, GARY, psychology educator; b. Nottingham, Eng., Mar. 6, 1961; s. Barry Towler and Iris Ann Marshall. BSc, North East London Poly., 1985; MSc, Reading (Eng.) U., 1987; PhD, U. East Anglia, Eng., 1991. Sci. officer Agrl. & Food Rsch. Coun. Inst. Food Rsch., Norwich, Eng., 1987-89; sr. rsch. assoc. U. East Anglia, Norwich, Eng., 1990-91, rsch. mgr., 1991-93; sr. lectr. U. Derby, Eng., 1993—; bd. dirs. Intellectual Property Worldwide, Ltd., Eng., G.B. Property Svcs. Ltd., Eng. Contbr. articles to profl. jours. Avocations: tennis, squash, kayaking. Office: Univ Derby, Michleover, Derby DE3 5GX, England

TOWNE, EDGAR ARTHUR, theologian, educator; b. Albany, N.Y., Feb. 27, 1928; s. Arthur Bethuel and Margaret (Shug) T.; m. Sara Jean Wright, June 14, 1952 (div. 1961); children: Mary Michal, Jonathan Wright, Nathan Arthur; m. Marian Kleinsasser, Dec. 18, 1961; 1 child, Stephen Edgar. BA, Coll. Wooster, 1949; BD, Pitts. Theol. Sem., 1952; MA, U. Chgo., 1962, PhD, 1967. Ordained to ministry Presbyn. Ch. (USA), 1952. Assoc. prof. systematic theology Winebrenner Theol. Sem., Findlay, Ohio, 1962-67; prof. philosophy and religion Findlay Coll., 1967-70; min. Hyde Park Union Ch., Chgo., 1971-75; prof. theology Christian Theol. Sem., Indpls., 1975-93, prof. theology emeritus, 1993—; vis. prof. theology Christian Theol. Sem., Indpls., 1970-71; vis. scholar Grad. Theol. Union, Berkeley, Calif., 1981-82, Pitts. Theol. Sem., 1988-89; co-moderator com. on pub. ministry Synod of Lincoln Trails, Ind., Ill., 1986-88. Author: Two Types of New Theism: Knowledge of God in the Thought of Paul Tillich and Charles Hartshorne, 1997. Mem. ethics com. Meth. Hosp. Ind., Indpls., 1985-90. Mem. Am. Theol. Soc. (pres. Midwest div. 1986-87), Am. Acad. Religion, Ctr. Process Studies, Soc. Christian Ethics, Highlands Inst. for Am. Religious and Philos. Thought. Democrat. Home: 5129 N Illinois St Indianapolis IN 46208-2613

TOWNEND, JAMES BARRIE STANLEY, barrister; b. Deal, Kent, Eng., Feb. 21, 1938; s. Frederick Stanley and Marjorie Elizabeth (Arnold) T.; m. Airelle Claire Nies, June 20, 1970; 1 child, Pascale Jehanne Lucie. MA with honours, Oxford U., 1960. Barrister-at-law, 1962; apptd. Queen's Counsel, 1978. Recorder Crown Ct., 1979—; bencher Middle Temple, 1986—; head of chambers, King's Bench Walk, Temple, 1982-99; mem. Bar Coun., 1984-88; chmn. Family Law Bar Assn., 1986-88. Mem. Kingston and Esher DHA, 1983-86. Lt. Royal Artillery, 1955-57. Avocations: sailing, fishing, writing verse. Home: 28 Coombe Lane West, Surrey, KT2 7BX Kingston Upon Thames England Office: 1 Kings Bench Walk/Temple, London EC4Y 7DB, England

TOWNES, CHARLES HARD, physics educator; b. Greenville, S.C., July 28, 1915; s. Henry Keith and Ellen Sumter (Hard) T.; m. Frances H. Brown, May 4, 1941; children: Linda Lewis, Ellen Screven, Carla Keith, Holly Robinson. B.A., B.S., Furman U., 1935; M.A., Duke U., 1937; Ph.D., Calif. Inst. Tech., 1939. Mem. tech. staff Bell Telephone Lab., 1939-47; assoc. prof. physics Columbia U., 1948-50, prof. physics, 1950-61; exec. dir. Columbia Radiation Lab., 1950-52, chmn. physics dept., 1952-55; provost and prof. physics MIT, 1961-66, Inst. prof., 1966-67; v.p., dir. research Inst. Def. Analyses, Washington, 1959-61; prof. physics U. Calif., Berkeley, 1967-86, 94, prof. physics emeritus, 1986-94, prof. grad. sch., 1994—; Guggenheim fellow, 1955-56; Fulbright lectr. U. Paris, 1955-56, U. Tokyo, 1956; dir. Enrico Fermi Internat. Sch. Physics, 1963; Richtmeyer lectr. Am. Phys. Soc., 1959; Scott lectr. U. Cambridge, 1963; Centennial lectr. U. Toronto, 1967; Lincoln lectr., 1972-73, Halley lectr., 1976, Krishnan lectr., 1992, Nishina lectr., 1992; Weinberg lectr. Oak Ridge (Tenn.) Nat. Lab., 1997, Rajiv Gandhi lectr., 1997, Henry Norris Russell lectr. Am. Astron. Soc., 1998; dir. Gen. Motors Corp., 1973-86, Perkin-Elmer Corp., 1966-85; mem. Pres.'s Sci. Adv. Com., 1966-69, vice chmn., 1967-69; chmn. sci. and tech. adv. com. for manned space flight NASA, 1964-70; mem. Pres.'s Com. on Sci. and Tech., 1976; rschr. on nuclear and molecular structure, quantum electronics, interstellar molecules, radio and infrared astrophysics. Author: (with A.L. Schawlow) Microwave Spectroscopy, 1955, Making Waves, 1996, How the Laser Happened. Adventures of a Scientist, 1999; author, co-editor: Quantum Electronics, 1960, Quantum Electronics and Coherent Light, 1964; editorial bd. Rev. Sci. Instruments, 1950-52, Phys. Rev., 1951-53, Jour. Molecular Spectroscopy, 1957-60, Procs. Nat. Acad. Scis., 1978-84, Can. Jour. Physics, 1995—; contbr. articles to sci. publs.; patentee masers and lasers. Trustee Calif. Inst. Tech., Carnegie Instn. of Washington, Grad. Theol. Union, Calif. Acad. Scis.; mem. corp. Woods Hole Oceanographic Instn. Decorated officier Légion d'Honneur (France); recipient numerous hon. degrees and awards including Nobel prize for physics, 1964; Stuart Ballantine medal Franklin Inst., 1959, 62; Thomas Young medal and prize Inst. Physics and Phys. Soc., Eng., 1963; Disting. Public Service medal NASA, 1969; Wilhelm Exner award Austria, 1970; Niels Bohr Internat. Gold medal, 1979; Nat. Sci. medal, 1982, Berkeley citation U. Calif., 1986; Common Wealth award, 1993, ADION medal Obs. Nice, 1995; Mendel award Villanova U; Frank Annunzio award Christopher Columbus Fellowship Found., 1999; Rabindranath Tagore Birth Centenary plaque Asiatic Soc., 1999; named to Nat. Inventors Hall of Fame, 1976, Engring. and Sci. Hall of Fame, 1983. Fellow IEEE (life, Medal of Honor 1967), Am. Phys. Soc. (pres. 1967, Plyler prize 1977), Optical Soc. Am. (hon., Mees medal 1968, Frederick Ives medal 1996), Indian Nat. Sci. Acad., Calif. Acad. Scis.; mem. NAS (coun. 1968-72, 78-81, chmn. space sci. bd. 1970-73, Comstock award 1959, Carty medal 1962), Am. Philos. Soc., Am. Astron. Soc., Am. Acad. Arts and Scis., Royal Soc. (fgn. mem.), Russian Acad. Scis. (fgn. mem.), Pontifical Acad. Scis., Max-Planck Inst. for Physics and Astrophysics (fgn. mem.), N.Y. Acad. Scis. (hon. life); elected to NAE 1998. Office: U Calif Dept Physics 366 Leconte # 7200 Berkeley CA 94720-0001

TOWNLEY, JULIE B., high school counselor; b. Nov. 20, 1942. BSc, U. Oregon, 1967; M in Counseling, Ariz. State U., 1984. Prin., owner Vogue Fitness Ctrs., Napa, Calif., 1978-82; lectr. Ariz. State U., Tempe, 1982-85; judicial educator Ctr. for Judicial Edn. and Rsch., San Francisco, 1989-95; coll. counselor De LaSalle High Sch., Concord, Calif., 1996—. Editor U. Calif. Sch. Medicine, Davis, 1972-78. With acting co. Oreg. Shakespearean Festival, Ashland, Oreg., 1962. Office: De LaSalle High School 1130 Winton Dr Concord CA 94518-3599

TOWNSEND, BARBARA, actress; b. Oakland, Calif.; d. Charles Edward Townsend and Anna Woodworth Kalkman; m. John Jackson Shaffer III, June 25, 1938 (dec. 1944); 1 child, Sandra Shaffer Van Doren; m. William Louis Wheeler Jr., May 27, 1958 (dec. 1969). BA, U. Calif., Berkeley; student, Am. Acad. Dramatic Arts, N.Y.C. tchr. Sch. of Drama, Nairobi, Kenya, 1970-75. Actress appearing in feature films Hard to Kill, Say Anything, Motel Vacancy, Good Cop, (TV shows) Star Trek, Divorce Court, Nikki and Alexander, After Mash, Murder She Wrote, Aaron's Way, Hunter, St. Elsewhere, Mr. Belvedere, Highway to Heaven, Remington Steele, Little House on the Prairie, Streets of San Francisco, As the World Turns, Guiding Light, Quantum Leap, Civil Wars, Northern Exposure, Sisters, (Broadway shows) The Rose Tatoo, Best of Spirits, As You Like It, (theatre) Children's World Theatre, Am. Theatre Wing, Orpheus Descending, Ann of Green Gables, Nairobi, Talk Back Taper II, L.A. Vol. recorder Braille Inst., L.A., 1978-94; vol. Bedside Network, N.Y.C., 1960-69; reader to Headstart children, handicapped adults in retirement home, 1994—; rschr. Spl. Women's Aux. of Navy, Washington, 1941-44; mentor for reading in elem. sch., 1996—. Mem. Actors Equity Assn., Screen Actors Guild, Am. Fedn. Radio and TV Artists. Democrat. Avocations: attending opera, symphony, ballet, reading. Office: Artists Group Inc 10100 Santa Monica Blvd Los Angeles CA 90067-4003

TOWNSEND, JAMES WILLIS, computer scientist; b. Evansville, Ind., Sept. 9, 1936; s. James Franklin and Elma Elizabeth (Galloway) T.; m. Leona Jean York, Apr. 20, 1958; 1 child, Eric Wayne. BS in Arts and Scis., Ball State U., 1962; PhD, Iowa State U., 1970. Rsch. technologist Neuromuscular div. Mead Johnson, Evansville, 1957-60; chief instr. Zoology dept. Iowa State U., Ames, 1965-67; asst. prof. Ind. State U., Evansville, 1967-72; cons. electron microscopy Mead Johnson Rsch. Ctr., Evansville, 1971-73; mgr. neurosci. Neurosci. Lab., Kans. State U., Manhattan, 1974-76; head electron microscopy Nat. Ctr. for Toxicology Rsch., Jefferson, Ark., 1976-82; dir. electron microscopy U. Ark. Med. Sci., Little Rock, 1982-87; dir. computer ops. pathology dept. Univ. Hosp., Little Rock, 1987-99, sr. analyst clin. info. sys., 1999—; workshop presenter Am. Soc. Clin. Pathology, 1980-81, Nat. Soc. Histotechnologists, 1984-88. With USAF, 1957. Contbr. articles to profl. jours.; reviewer Scanning Electron Microscopy, 1977-78. Nat. Def. fellowship NDEA, Iowa State U., 1962-65; recipient Chgo. Tribune award Chicago Tribune, 1955. Mem. Sigma Xi, Sigma Zeta. Baptist. Avocations: genealogy, American Civil War, scuba. Home: 4 Breeds Hill Ct Little Rock AR 72211-2514 Office: Univ Ark for Med Sci CIS Slot 637 4301 W Markham St Little Rock AR 72205-7101

TOWNSEND, KENNETH ROSS, retired priest; b. Holly Grove, Ala., Oct. 31, 1927; s. James Ernest and Mary H. (Jordan) T.; m. Irene Fogleman, Mar. 18, 1951; children; Marietta, Martha, Kenneth Ross, Elizabeth. AB, Birmingham South Coll., 1956; postgrad., Union Theol. Sem., 1960-63; MDiv, Va. Theol. Sem., 1964. Ordained priest Episcopal Ch., 1965. Pastor meth. chs. N.C. and Va. Confs., 1954-63; priest Bath Priest Parish, Dinwiddie, Va., 1964-69, St. Paul's Ch., Vanceboro, N.C., 1969-89; ret., 1989; lectr. philosophy Richard Bland Coll. of Coll. William and Mary, Williamsburg, Va., 1966-68; del. to synod Province IV, 1973; mem. liturgical com. Episcopal Diocese of East Carolina, Wilmington, N.C., 1971-82, mem. prison commn., 1984; occasional supply priest Olivet Ch., Franconia, Va., 1995—. Writer, painter. With USNR, 1945-46. Mem. Delta Sigma Phi. Home: 2521 Paxton St Lake Ridge Woodbridge VA 22192

TOWNSEND, MILES AVERILL, aerospace and mechanical engineering educator; b. Buffalo, N.Y., Apr. 16, 1935; s. Francis Devere and Sylvia (Wolpa) T.; children: Kathleen Townsend Hastings, Melissa, Stephen, Joel, Philip. BA, Stanford U., 1955; BS MechE, U. Mich., 1958; advanced cert., U. Ill., 1963, MS in Theoretical and Applied Mechanics, 1967; PhD, U. Wis., 1971. Registered profl. engr., Ill., Wis., Tenn., Ont. Project engr. Sundstrand, Rockford, Ill., 1959-63, Twin Disc Inc., Rockford, 1963-65, 67-68; sr. engr. Westinghouse Electric Corp., Sunnyvale, Calif., 1965-67; instr., fellow U. Wis., Madison, 1968-71; assoc. prof. U. Toronto, Ont., Can., 1971-74; prof. mech. engring. Vanderbilt U., Nashville, 1974-81; Wilson prof. mech. and aerospace engring. U. Va., Charlottesville, 1981—, chmn. dept., 1981-91; ptnr., v.p. Endev Ltd., Can. and U.S., 1972—; cons. in field. Contbr. numerous articles on dynamics, design dynamical systems, controls and optimization to profl. jours.; 7 patents in field. Recipient numerous research grants and contracts. Fellow ASME, AAAS; mem. N.Y. Acad. Scis., Sigma Xi, Phi Kappa Phi, Pi Tau Sigma. Avocations: running, reading, music. Home: 212 Alderman Rd Charlottesville VA 22903-1704 Office: U Va Dept Mech and Aerospace Engring Thornton Hall Charlottesville VA 22903-2442

TOWNSEND, PETER DAVID, physicist, educator; b. Wokingham, Berks, U.K., May 14, 1937; s. Stanley George and Elsie Eleanor (Smith) T.; m. Parthina Susan Randall, June 29, 1963 (deceased); children: Janet, Sarah. BS, Reading U., 1958, PhD, 1961, DSc, 1976; hon. doctoris causa, U. Autonoma Madrid, 1998. Vis. scientist Brookhaven Nat. Lab., 1961-66; lectr., reader, prof. U. Sussex, U.K., 1966—; vis. scientist U. New South Wales, Australia, 1970, Autonoma U. de Madrid, 1988, CENG, France, 1977-78; vis. prof. Chinese U. Hong Kong, 1992; cons. Societa Italiana Vetra, 1988-96. Author: Thermoluminescence Dosimetry Materials, 1995, Optical Effects of Ion Implantation, 1994, Point Defects in Materials, 1988; contbr. over 400 articles to profl. jours. Avocations: fencing, violin. Office: U Sussex, Sch Engring, Sussex Brighton BN1 9QH, England

TOWNSEND, SUSAN ELAINE, religious organization officer; b. Phila., Sept. 5, 1946; d. William Harrison and Eleanor Irene (Fox) Rogers; m. John Holt Townsend, May 1, 1976. BS in Secondary Edn., West Chester State U., 1968; MBA, Nat. U., 1978; PhD in Human Behavior, La Jolla U., 1984. Biology tchr. Methacton Sch. Dist., Fairview Village, Pa., 1968-70; bus. mgr., analyst profl. La Jolla Research Corp., San Diego, 1977-79; pastoral asst. Christ Ctr. Bible Therapy, San Diego, 1980-82, also bd. dirs.; v.p., pub. relations World Outreach Ctr. of Faith, San Diego, 1981-82, also bd. dirs.; owner, pres., cons. Townsend Research Inst., San Diego, 1983-89; teaching assoc. La Jolla U. Continuing Edn., 1985-86, adminstr., assoc. registrar, adj. faculty, 1990. Author: Hostage Survival-Resisting the Dynamics of Captivity, 1983; contbr. articles to profl. jours. Instr. USN Advanced Survival Evasion Resistance Escape Sch., 1986-89; security officer Shield Security, San Diego, 1991-92; COO Matthew 25:34-40 Ministries, San Diego, 2000—; bd. dirs. Christ Fellowship Ch. of San Diego, 1987-96, music dir., 1992—; religious vol. Met. Correctional Ctr., San Diego, 1983-89; vol. San Diego County Jail Ministries, 1978-2000, scheduling coord., 1993-99, sec., 1998-2000. Comdr. USN, 1970-76, USNR, 1976-93. Mem. Naval Res. Assn. (life), Res. Officers Assn.(outstanding Jr. Officer of Yr. Calif. chpt. 1982), Navy League U.S. (life), West Chester U. Alumni Assn., Nat. U. Alumni Assn. (life), La Jolla U. Alumni Assn., Gen. Fedn. Women's Club (pres. Peninsula Women's Club 1983-85, 94-96, pres. Parlimentary Law Club 1984-86, 96-98, rec. sec. Past Pres.' Assn. 1994-96, pres. 2000-02), Calif. Fedn. Women's Clubs (v.p.-at-large San Diego dist. 25 1982-84, rec. sec. 1994-96, 1st v.p./dean of chmn. 1996-98, pres. 1998-2000).

TOWNSEND, TERRY, publishing executive; b. Camden, N.J., Dec. 14, 1920; d. Anthony and Rose DeMarco; m. Paul Brorstrom Townsend, Dec. 8, 1961; 1 child, Kim. BA, Duke U., 1942; LHD (hon.), Dowling Coll., 1991. Pub. rels. dir. North Shore U. Hosp., Manhasset, N.Y., 1956-68; pres. Theatre Soc., L.I., 1967-70, Townsend Comm. Bur., L.I., 1970-98; ptnr. L.I. Communicating Svc., Bellport, 1977—; pub. L.I. Bus. News, 1979-98; v.p. ParrMeadows Racetrack, Yaphank, N.Y., 1977. Columnist, writer L.I./Bus., Ronkonkoma, 1970-75. Assoc. trustee North Shore U. Hosp., 1968—; bd. govs. Adelphi U. Friends Fin. Edn., 1978-85; chmn. ann. archtl. awards competition N.Y. Inst. Tech., 1970-83; trustee Dowling Coll., 1984-2000, hon. life trustee, 1996—; trustee L.I. Fine Arts Mus., 1984-85; pub. broadcasting PBS Sta. WLIW TV, Garden City, L.I., N.Y., 1990-93; bd. dirs. Family Svc. Assn. Nassau County, 1982-92; dinner chmn. L.I. 400 Ball, 1987; trustee Mus. at Stony Brook, 1994—. Recipient Media award 110 Ctr. Bus. & Profl. Women, 1977, Enterprise award Friends of Fin. Edn., 1981, L.I. Loves Bus. Showcase Salute, 1982, Cmty. Svc. award N.Y. Diabetes Assn., 1983, Disting. Long Islander in Comm. award L.I. United Epilepsy Assn., 1984, Spl. award Dowling Coll. Spring Tribute, 1989, Disting. Svc. award Episcopal Health Svcs., 1989, Disting. Citizen award Dowling Coll., 1991, Gilbert Tilles award Nat. Assn. Fundraising Execs., 1994, Hadassah Cmty. Svc. award, 1996, Golden rule award Little Village Sch., 1997, Lifetime Achievement award L.I. Assn., 1998, Promote L.I. Achievement award, 1998, Lifetime Achievement award Advancement for Commerce & Industry, 1999; named 1st Lady of L.I., L.I. Pub. Rels. Assn., 1973, L.I. Woman of Yr. L.I. Assn. Action Com., 1989. Office: LI Communicating Svcs PO Box 915 Bellport NY 11713-0915

TOWNSEND, THOMAS PERKINS, former mining company executive; b. Bryn Mawr, Pa., Mar. 28, 1917; s. John and Mildred (Perkins) T.; m. Laura M. Trench, Sept. 14, 1940; children: Joanne Townsend Taber, Hunter, Elizabeth Macdonald. B.S. in Econs., U. Pa., 1939; postgrad., Harvard U., 1944. C.P.A., Pa. Sr. acct. Price Waterhouse & Co., 1945-48; treas., dir. Fox Products Co., 1948-53, Wilcolator Co., 1953-55; staff acct. Tex. Gulf Sulphur Co., N.Y.C., 1955-57; asst. treas. Tex. Gulf Sulphur Co., 1958-61, v.p., controller, 1961-62, v.p., treas., 1962-64, v.p. internat. ops., 1964-68; exec. v.p. Bosco Middle East Oil Corp., Greenwich, Conn., 1968-69; pres. Conn. Real Estate Corp., Greenwich, 1969-70, also bd. dirs., 1969—; v.p. finance Rosaria Resources Corp., N.Y.C., 1970-81; treas. Unidyne Corp., 1984-85; cons. AMAX, Inc., 1981-85; bd. dirs. Thermal Exploration Corp., Carlin Gold Co. Chmn. nat. com. for employment youth Nat. Child Labor Com., 1968-70; trustee, pres. South Kent Sch.; trustee Soc. to Advance Retarded, Norwalk, Conn.; bd. dirs. United Way of Tri-State, Denison Pequotsegos Nature Ctr.; mem. New Canaan Bd. Fin., Conn., 1985-89 . Served to lt. (s.g.) Supply Corps, USNR, World War II. Mem. Am. Inst. Accts., N.Y. State Soc. CPAs, Fin. Execs. Inst., Mason's Island Yacht Club, Off Soundings Club. Episcopalian (treas., vestryman 1960-72, 87-95). Home: 9 Kensington Ct Mystic CT 06355-3116

TOWPIK, ANDRZEJ, Polish diplomat, NATO official; married; 2 children. Grad., Main of Fgn. Svc., Poland, 1961; postgrad., Columbia U., 1963-64; LLD, Jagiellonian U., Cracow, 1969. With Polish Ministry of Fgn. Affairs, 1975—; 1st sec. of Embassy of Poland Madrid, 1977-81; dep. dir. of policy planning dept., 1981-86; counsellor-minister Polish Mission to UN Office in Gen., 1986-90; dir. of dept. of European Instn., 1990-93, ambassador, 1993-94; polit. dir. Ministry of Fgn. Affairs, Poland, 1994, undersec. of state, 1994-97; amb., head of Polish Mission to NATO and Western European Union, Brussels, 1997—. Office: NATO Hdqrs, Blvd Leopold III, 1110 Brussels Belgium*

TOWRY, ELISA ROBINSON, electronics engineer; b. Huntsville, Ala., Sept. 12, 1961; d. Ellis Walter and Claudine (Hayes) R.; m. Thomas Rex Towry, Nov. 5, 1988. BSEE, U. Ala, Huntsville, 1983. Electronic technician U.S. Army Missile Command, Redstone Arsenal, Ala., 1982-83, electronic engr., 1983—; tested over 3500 semi-active laser (SAL) seekers; test dir. Automated Laser Seeker Performance Evaluation System facility, 1987—. Contbr. more than 250 tech. reports to profl. publs. Mem. Soc. Photo-Optical Instrumentation Engrs. (assoc.). Achievements include patent for background illumination/sun in field of view simulator, SAL expert. Office: US Army Aviation and Missile Command AMSAM-RD-MG-SD Redstone Arsenal AL 35898

TOY, JOHN, priest; b. London, Nov. 25, 1930; s. Sidney and Violet Mary (Doudney) T.; m. Mollie Tilbury, Sept. 28, 1962; children: Paul B.J., Katherine V. BA with 1st class honours in Theology, Durham (Eng.) U., 1953, MA, 1962; PhD, Leeds (Eng.) U., 1982. Ordained priest Anglican Ch., 1956. Curate St. Paul's Newington Ch., London, 1955-58; travelling sec. Student Christian Movement, Eng., 1958-60; chaplain, lectr. Ely Theol. Coll., Eng., 1960-65; chaplain St. Andrew's Ch., Gothenburg, Sweden, 1965-69; lectr., sr. lectr., prin. lectr. Coll. of Ripon & York St. John, 1969-83; chancellor York (Eng.) Minster, 1983-99; selector ordination candidates, Eng., 1980-99; bishops' insp. of theol. colls., Eng., 1985—; vice chmn. bd. govs. Manor Sch., York, 1994-99. Author: Jesus, Man for God, 1988; also various cathedral booklets, 1983—. Avocations: history, architecture, travel. Home: 11 Westhorpe, Southwell NG24 0ND, England

TOYA, MASAYUKI, mechanical engineer, educator; b. Sapporo, Japan, Feb. 15, 1946; s. Tomiyuki and Miyoko (Hanamura) T.; m. Taka Kusunoki, Mar. 23, 1971; children: Nobuyuki, Akiko. B in Engring., Kyoto U., 1968, M in Engring., 1970, D in Engring., 1979. Instr. Kyoto U., Japan, 1971-86; from assoc. prof. to prof. Kagoshima U., Japan, 1986—. Co-author: Stress Intensity Factors Handbook, 1987; contbr. articles to profl. jours. Mem. Japan Soc. Mech. Engrs., Soc. Materials Sci. Japan, Japan Soc. Aeronautical & Space Scis. Avocation: fishing. Office: Kagoshima U Dept Mech Engr, Korimoto 1-21-40, 890-0065 Kagoshima Japan

TOYAMA, HIDEO, biotechnologist; b. Miyazaki, Japan, Nov. 22, 1954; s. Nobuo and Keiko Toyama; m. Akiko Ohtsubo, Aug. 4, 1985; children: Akira, Makoto. BS, Miyazaki U., 1978, MS, 1980; PhD, Osaka (Japan) U., 1984. Engr. Orgn. for Promotion of Indsl. Tech., Miyazaki, 1984-85; engr. Info. Ctr. of Indsl. Tech, Miyazaki, 1985-88, chief engr., 1988-89; lectr. Minamikyushu U., Miyazaki, 1989-92, asst. prof., 1992-2000, prof., 2000—. Contbr. articles to profl. jours. Mem. Soc. for Biosci. and Bioengring., Japan Soc. Biosci., Biotech. and Agrochemistry, Soc. for Antibacterial and Antifungal Agts. Japan. Achievements include breeding of cellulase hyper-producing mutants of fungus. Avocations: reading, thinking. E-mail: wonder@iris.dti.ne.jp. Fax: 81-983-22-6616. Phone: 81-983-22-6616. Home: Maruyama 2-235, Miyazaki 880-0052, Japan

TOYODA, SHOICHIRO, automobile company executive; b. Nagoya, Japan, Feb. 27, 1925; s. Kiichiro and Hatako Toyoda; m. Hiroko Mitsui, Nov. 30, 1952; children: Atuko, Akio. B in Engring., Nagoya U., 1947, D in Engring., 1955. Dir. Toyota (Japan) Motor Co., Ltd., 1952-61, mng. dir., 1961-67, sr. mng. dir., 1967-72, exec. v.p., 1972-81; pres. Toyota Motor Sales Co., Ltd., 1981-82; pres. Toyota Motor Corp., 1982-92, chmn., 1992-99, hon. chmn., 1999—; bd. dirs. Denso Co., Ltd., Nagoya Broadcasting Network; chmn. bd. dirs. Inst. Internat. Econ. Studies. Chmn. Keidanren, Tokyo, 1994-98; consul gen. Honorario de Costa Rica, Nagoya, 1984—. Recipient Medal with Dark-Blue Ribbon, Govt. of Japan, 1972, The Deming Prize, 1980, Medal with Blue Ribbon, Govt. of Japan, 1984, Grand Decoration of Honor in Gold with star, Austria, medal of Isabel la Catolica, King of Spain, 2000; named Knight Comdr. of the Most Noble Order of the Crown, Thailand, 1990, Gran Cruz de la Order Nacional al Merit, Colombia, 1991, Knight Comdr. of British Empire, Govt. of U.K., 1995, Grand Cordon of the Order of the Sacred Treasure, Govt. of Japan, 1995, Order Francisco de Miranda First Class, Venezuela, 1995, Ordem Nat. do Cruzeiro do Sul, Govt. of Brazil, 1996, Order of Merit, Govt. of Turkey, 1998, Legion D'Honneur, Commandeur Govt. of France, 1998, Grande Ufficiale, Govt. of Italy, 1998, Hon. Companion, the Gen. Divsn. of the Order of Australia, 1999. Office: Toyota Motor Corp, 1 Toyota-cho, Toyota Aichi Pref 471, Japan

TOYODA, TATSURO, automobile company executive; b. June 1, 1929; m. Ayako Toyoda. Ed., Tokyo U. With Toyota Motor Corp., 1953—, exec. v.p. in charge internat. ops., 1988-92, pres., 1992-95, vice chmn., 1995-96, sr. advisor, 1996—; former pres. Nummi jt. venture with GM, 1984-86. Decorated grand cordon Order of Sacred Treasure. Office: Toyota Motor Corp, 1 Toyota-cho, Toyota 471-8571, Japan

TOYODA, TETSUYA, virologist, educator; b. Toyokawa, Aichi, Japan, Feb. 2, 1958; s. Tsuneo and Chizuko Toyoda; m. Michiko Nishimura, Mar. 29,1987; 2 children. MD, Nagoya (Japan) U., 1982, D Med. Sci., 1987. Rsch. assoc. Nagoya U., 1987-92; asst. prof. Nat. Inst. Genetics, Mishima, Japan, 1992-95; prof., chmn. dept. virology Kurume (Japan) U., 1995—. Office: Kurume U Dept Virology, 67 Asahimachi, Kurume Fukuoka 830-0011, Japan

TOYONAGA, AKIRA, English educator; b. Kobe, Hyogo Pref, Japan, Mar. 14, 1930; s. Hiroshi and Kinu (Nakamura) T.; m. T. Keiko (dec. Aug., 1987); m. Chieko Katayama, Nov. 6, 1988. BA, Kansai U., Osaka, Japan, 1959, MA, 1961. Tchr. of English Osaka Prefecture Bd. Edn., 1961-70; lectr. Kansai U., Suita, Japan, 1970-73; asst. prof. Kansai U., Suita, 1973-80, prof., 1980—. Author: Dialects in American Literature, 1998; co-author: (books) Appreciation of English and American Literature, 1975, Tributes to English Language and Literature. Commr. Dept. Welfare Ikoma City, 1982-84. Mem. English Linguistics Soc. Japan, Soc. of English Grammar and Usage Kyoto, Japan. Avocations: fishing, Japanese chess. Home: 2 chome 8-12 Myoken-higashi, Osaka Katano 576-0012, Japan Office: Kansai U, 3-3 Yamate-cho 3 chome, Osaka Suita 564-80, Japan

TOYOSHIMA, NOBORU, virtual world researcher; b. Omiya, Saitama, Japan, Aug. 10, 1960. BA, Sophia U., Tokyo, 1984; MA, Stanford (Calif.) U., 1994. Editor LOGIN mag. ASCII Corp., Tokyo, 1982-84; rschr. ASCII HighTech Lab., Tokyo, 1984-86; rschr. and planner HighTech Lab. Japan, Inc., Tokyo, 1986-87; v.p., rsch. fellow Den'no Shokai, Tokyo, 1987-97; rschr. Open Loop Inc., Sapporo, Japan, 1998—; content mgr. eBaY Inc., San Jose, Calif., 1999-2000. Author: Introduction to Personal Tele-Computing, 1987, Foundations of Multimedia, 1992. Mem. Assn. for Computing Machinery, Cognitive Sci. Soc. U.S.A., Cognitive Sci. Soc. Japan, Japanese Soc. Social Psychology, Am. Anthropol. Assn. Avocations: photography, musicals, ham, aerobics. Office: Open Loop Inc, 2-3-2-1 Kitano Kiyota-ku, Sapporo 040-0867, Japan

TOYOTA, NAOKI, physicist; b. Onomichi, Japan, Oct. 15, 1948; s. Mitsuji Tenma and Sanae T.; m. Kimie Satoh, Oct. 30, 1977; children: Mihoko, Naochika, Daiju. BS, Tohoku U., Sendai, Japan, 1972; MS, Tohoku U., 1974, PhD, 1977. Rsch. assoc. Tohoku U., Sendai, Japan, 1977-85; assoc. prof. Tohoku U., 1985-93; prof. Osaka Pref. U., Japan, 1993-98, Tohoku U., Sendai, Japan, 1998—; visiting prof. U. Leiden, The Netherlands, 1988, U. Alberta, Canada, 1980. Mem. Am. Physical Soc., Japanese Physical Soc. Avocations: cooking, fishing, reading. Office: Physics Dept Tohoku U, Aramaki Aobaward, Sendai Miyagi 9808578, Japan.

TOZAWA, YOSHIO, management consultant; b. Sapporo, Hokkaido, Japan, Feb. 15, 1952; s. Tadashi and Keiko (Susuki) T.; m. Yumiko Nakamoto, Nov. 12, 1983; 1 child, Yoriko. BS, U. Tokyo, 1974, MS, 1976. Rschr. Tokyo Sci. Ctr., IBM, 1979-84, T.J. Watson Rsch. Ctr., IBM, Yorktown, N.Y., 1984-85; rschr. Tokyo Rsch. Lab., IBM, 1985-86, rsch. mgr., 1986-92; mgmt. cons., IBM Japan Ltd., Tokyo, 1992-94; info. tech. cons. Tokyo, 1994—; councillor Japanese Soc. Artificial Intelligence, 1988-92. Patentee in image processing. Recipient Best Paper award Japanese Soc. Artificial Intelligence, 1991. Home: 1-13-5-902 Mukougaoka, Bunkyo-ku

Tokyo 113-0023, Japan Office: IBM Japan Ltd, 19-21 Nihonbashi-Hakozaki, Chuo-ku Tokyo 103-8510, Japan

TOZAWA, YUMIKO, medical researcher; b. Kamakura, Kanagawa, Japan, Nov. 13, 1956; d. Fujishige and Teruko (Horiuchi) Nakamoto; m. Yoshzo Tozawa, Nov. 12, 1983; 1 child, Yuriko. Bachelor's degree, U. Kyoto, 1980, Master's degree, 1982; PhD, U. Tokyo, 1998. Cert. med. dr., lectr. Lectr. Coll. for Nursing, Osaka, Japan, 1982-83, Saitama Sch. Medicine, 1998—; guest rschr. Sch. Medicine, U. Tokyo, 1998—. Author: (book) The Health and the Rise of Civilization. Home: 1-13-5-905 Mukogaoka, 113-0023 Bunkyo-ku Tokyo, Japan Office: U Tokyo, 3-28-6 Mejirodai Bunkyo-ku, 112-8688 Tokyo Japan

TOZZER, JACK CARL, civil engineer, surveyor; b. Marion, Ohio, Jan. 5, 1922; s. Carl Henry and Henrietta (Schellenbaum) T.; children: Brent Jack, Hal Jack; m. Aleta C. Lehner, July 14, 1974. BCE, Ohio No. U., 1944. Registered profl. engr., Ohio, Fla., registered surveyor, Ohio. Pres. firm Tozzer & Assocs. Inc., Marion, 1948-85; county engr. Marion County, Ohio, 1964—; city engr. Marion, 1959, Galion, Ohio, 1960-85; cons. civil engr. Mem. cons. bd. Coll. Engring. Ohio No. U., 1970; v.p. Marion Community Improvement Corp.; mem. Marion County Regional Planning Commn. Served with USNR, 1944-46. Recipient Order of Engr. Coll. Engring. Ohio No. U., 1971. Fellow ASCE; mem. NSPE, Marion C. of C., Cons. Engrs. Ohio, Profl. Land Surveyors Ohio, Ohio Hist. Soc., Marion County Hist. Soc. (past dir.), Elks, Delta Sigma Phi. Lutheran. Home: 307 Forest Lawn Blvd Marion OH 43302-5523 Office: Courthouse # 1 Marion OH 43302

TRAAVIK, INGEMAR TERJE, virology educator, consultant; b. Oslo, Dec. 5, 1943; s. Ingemar Maxwell and Linda Amunda (Schröder) T.; m. Francis Sophia Maria Mennen, May 23, 1980; children: Stig, Dag, Joakim, Jannik, Sebastian. DVM, Norwegian Coll. Vet. Medicine, Oslo, 1969; PhD, U. Tromsø, Norway, 1979. Pvt. practice veterinarian Vega, Norway, 1969-70; virologist Nat. Inst. Pub. Health, Oslo, 1970-76; asst. prof. U. Tromsø, 1977-82, prof., 1983—; cons. virologist Regional Hosp., Tromsø, 1977—; chmn. Inst. Med. Biology, U. Tromsø, 1981-83, dep. dean Sch. Medicine, 1981-83, mem. univ. bd., 1989—; vis. prof. U. Oxford, Eng., 1983-84, U. Calif., San Diego, 1988-89, U. Calif., Irvine, 1994-95; chmn. Nat. Rsch. Program on Environ. Effects of Biotech., 1991-94. Co-author, actor in stageplay Gene Reply, 1993-94; contbr. chpts. to books, articles to internat. profl. jours. Mem. bd. tech. affairs City of Tromsö, 1988-92, City Coun., 1988-92; mem. Govtl. Biotech. Adv. Bd., 1993—. Recipient prize for excellent cancer rsch. Erna and Olav Aakre Found., 1992; grantee NRC, 1979—, Nat. Cancer Soc., 1984—. Mem. Norwegian Biochem. Soc. (chmn. regional br. 1979-81, bd. dirs. 1979-81), Norwegian Microbiol. Soc., Am. Soc. Microbiology, European Assn. Cancer Rsch., N.Y. Acad. Scis., Norwegian Soc. Virology (founder, bd. dirs. 1992—), Nordic Soc. Virology (Denmark, Finland, Sweden, Norway, Iceland; chmn. 1993-95); co-founder, scientific dir. Norwegian Inst. Gene Ecology, 1998—. Mem. Venstre Party. Avocations: sports, hiking. Home: Synnavinden 19, N-9015 Tromsø Norway Office: U Tromsö, Inst Med Biology, N-9037 Tromsø Norway

TRABANT, JUERGEN, linguistics educator; b. Frankfurt am Main, Germany, Oct. 25, 1942; s. August and Dora (Weiler) T.; m. Christiane Rommel; children: Bettina, Daniela. PhD, U. Tuebingen, Germany, 1969. Asst. U. Tuebingen, 1969-72; lectr. U. Bari, Rome, 1969-71; asst. prof. U. Hamburg, Germany, 1972-75; prof. Paedagogische Hochschule, Berlin, 1975-80, Freie U., Berlin, 1980—; guest prof. Stanford U., 1988-89, U. Calif., Davis, 1997. Author: Zur Semiologie des Literarischen Kunstwerks, 1970, Elemente der Semiotik, 1975, Apeliotes oder Der Sinn der Sprache, 1986, Traditionen Humboldts, 1990, Neue Wissenschaft von alten Zeichen, 1994, Sprache Denken, 1995, Artikulationen, 1998. Decorated officier l'Ordre National du Merite; recipient Habilitationsstipendium, Deutsche Forschungsgemeinschaft, 1975, Akademiestipendium, Volkswagenstiftung, 1985; fellow Collegium Budapest, 1994-95. Mem. Berlin Brandenburgische Akademie der Wissenschaften. Office: Freie Univ FB17, Habelschwerdter Allee 45, 14195 Berlin Germany

TRABITZ, EUGENE LEONARD, aerospace company executive; b. Cleve., Aug. 13, 1937; s. Emanuel and Anna (Berman) T.; m. Caryl Lee Rine, Dec. 22, 1963 (div. Aug. 1981); children: Claire Marie, Honey Caryl; m. Kathryn Lynn Bates, Sept. 24, 1983; 1 stepchild, Paul Francis Rager. BA, Ohio State U., 1965. Enlisted USAF, 1954, advanced through grades to maj.; served as crew commdr. 91st Stragetic Missile Div., Minot, S.D., 1968-70; intelligence officer Fgn. Tech. Div., Dayton, Ohio, 1970-73; dir. external affairs Aero Systems Div., Dayton, 1973-75; program mgr. Air Force Armament Div., Valparaiso, Fla., 1975-80; dir. ship ops. Air Force Ea. Test Range, Satellite Beach, Fla., 1980-83; dep. program mgr. Air Force Satellite Text Ctr., Sunnyvale, Calif., 1983-84; ret., 1984; sr. staff engr. Ultrasystems Inc., 1984-86; pres. TAWD Systems Inc., Palo Alto, Calif., 1986-92, Am. Telenetics Co., San Mateo, Calif., 1992—; cons. Space Applications Corp., Sunnyvale, 1986-87, Litton Computer Svcs., Mountain View, Calif., 1987-91, Battelle Meml. Inst. Columbus, 1993—. V.p. Bd. County Mental Health Clinic, Ft. Walton Beach, Fla., 1973-75. Decorated Bronze Star. Mem. DAV (life), World Affairs Coun., U.S. Space Found. (charter), Air Force Assn. (life), Assn. Old Crows, Nat. Sojourners, Commonwealth Club Calif., Masons (32 degree). Avocations: golf, tennis, racketball, sailing, bridge. Home: 425 Anchor Rd Apt 317 San Mateo CA 94404-1058

TRACEY, ANDREW TRAVIS NORMAN, ethnomusicologist, musician; b. Durban, Natal, South Africa, May 5, 1936; s. Hugh Travers and Ursula (Campbell) T.; m. Heather Mary Beard, May 22, 1966; children: Mary Clare, Geoffrey. MA, Oxford (Eng.) U., 1963; D of Music, U. Natal, 1995. Mus. dir. South African mus. show Wait a Minim, worldwide, 1962-69; staff musicologist Internat. Libr. African Music, Roodepoort, South Africa, 1969-78; dir. Internat. Libr. African Music, Grahamstown, South Africa, 1978—. Author: (booklet) How to Play the Mbira, 1970; editor symposia procs.; filmmaker 2 series on Chopi and Shona music, 1970-80. Avocations: making and playing musical instruments, playing in steel band. Office: Internat Libr African Music, Rhodes U, Grahamstown 6140, South Africa

TRACEY, IRENE MARY CARMEL, neuroscientist; b. Oxford, Eng., Oct. 30, 1966; d. James Michael and Irene Beech (Bell) T.; m. Myles Robert Allen, Sept. 10, 1994; 1 child, Colette Phoebe. BA in Biochemistry 1st Class, Oxford U., 1989, PhD in Biochemistry, 1993, MA (hon.), 1995. Domus sr. scholar Merton Coll., Oxford U., 1990-93; rsch. fellow Harvard Med. Sch., Mass. Gen. Hosp., Boston, 1994-96; Florey rsch. fellow clin. neurology Oxford U., 1996-97, jr. rsch. fellow sci. and math. Corpus Christi Coll., 1996—; neuroscientist, head applications and pain group Oxford U. Ctr. Functional Magnetic Resonance Imaging Brain, 1997—; univ. rsch. lectr. Oxford U., 2000—; lectr. Trinity Coll. Oxford U. Contbr. articles to profl. jours.; reviewer jour. articles. Internat. fgn. scholar Am. Acad. Neurology, 1993.

TRACHE APOSTOL, ANDREEA, physicist; b. Bucharest, Romania, May 30, 1967; d. Gheorghe and Beatrice Apostol; m. Livius-Marian Trache. BS, U. Bucharest, 1989; PhD, Inst. Atomic Physics, Bucharest, 1996. Sci. rschr. Inst. Atomic Physics, Bucharest, 1990-96, sr. rschr. III, 1996—, head thin film group, 1993-99; rsch. assoc. Rice U., 1999—; sr. thin film engr. Denton Vacuum, 1999—. Contbr. articles to profl. jours. Mem. Romanian Phys. Soc., Optical Soc. Am., SPIE. Avocations: books, music, sports. Home: 2810 Pueblo Ct N College Station TX 77845-7711 Office: Tex A&M U College Station TX 77843

TRACHTENBERG, MATTHEW J., bank holding company executive; b. N.Y.C., June 20, 1958; s. Mark Trachtenberg and Joanne Horne. BA magna cum laude, NYU, 1974; JD, Bklyn. Law Sch., 1977; MBA in Fin., Fordham U., 1982. Bar: N.Y. 1979. Mgmt. trainee Mfrs. Hanover Trust Co., N.Y.C., 1977-78, credit analyst, 1978-79, corp. banking rep., 1979-80, asst. sec., 1980-82, asst. v.p., 1982, v.p., 1982-86, v.p., corp. sec., 1987-92; v.p., corp. sec. Mfrs. Hanover Corp., N.Y.C., 1987-92; dir. Mfrs. Hanover Found., 1987-92; v.p., sec. regional bd. Chem. Bank, N.Y.C., 1992-96; v.p., dep. corp. sec. Chem. Banking Corp., N.Y.C., 1992-96, Chem. Bank, 1992-96; sec. Chem. Bank Regional Bd., 1992-96; v.p. Chem. Bank, 1992-96, Chem. Banking Corp., 1992-96; v.p. asst. corp. sec. Chase Manhattan Corp., N.Y.C., 1996-98, Chase Manhattan Bank, N.Y.C., 1996-98; v.p. PNC Bank, N.Y.C., 1999—, sr. pvt. banker, 1999—; sec. Chase Manhattan Regional bd., 1996-98; v.p. PNC Bank, N.Y.C., 1999—, sr. pvt. banker, 1999—. Bd. dirs., pres. Nat. Orch. Assn.; bd. dirs., treas. N.Y. Eye and Ear Infirmary; pres. U.S.O. of Met. N.Y.; mem. adv. edn. com. Lighthouse for the Blind. N.Y. State Regents scholar. Mem. N.Y. State Bar Assn., Am. Soc. Corp. Secs., Phi Beta Kappa, Pi Sigma Alpha. Avocations: music, fishing, painting, writing. Office: PNC Bank 345 Park Ave Fl 29 New York NY 10154-0004*

TRACHTENBERG, STEPHEN JOEL, university president; b. Bklyn., Dec. 14, 1937; s. Oscar M. and Shoshana G. (Weinstock) T.; m. Francine Zorn, June 24, 1971; children: Adam Maccabee, Ben-Lev. BA, Columbia U., 1959; JD, Yale U., 1962; M in Pub. Adminstrn., Harvard U., 1966; LHD (hon.), Trinity Coll., 1986; HHD (hon.), U. Hartford, 1989; LLD (hon.), Hanyang U., Seoul, 1990; DPA (hon.), Kyonggi U., Seoul, 1994; LLD (hon.), Richmond Coll., London, 1995; MD (hon.), Odessa State Med. U., Ukraine, 1996; LLD (hon.), Mount Vernon Coll., 1997; LHD (hon.), Boston U., 1999, Gratz Coll., 1999. Bar: N.Y. 1964, U.S. Supreme Ct. 1967. Atty. AEC, 1962-65; legis. asst. to Congressman John Brademas of Ind., Washington, 1965; tutor law Harvard Coll., also; teaching fellow edn. and pub. policy J.F. Kennedy Grad. Sch. Govt., Harvard U., 1965-66; spl. asst. to U.S. edn. commr. Office of Edn., HEW, Washington, 1966-68; assoc. prof. polit. sci. Boston U., 1969-77, assoc. dean, 1969-70, dean, 1970-74, assoc. v.p., co-counsel, 1974-76, v.p. acad. services, 1976-77; pres., prof. pub. adminstrn. U. Hartford, Conn., 1977-88, George Washington U., Washington, 1988—; mem. adv. bd. The Presidency; bd. dirs. Consortium of Univs. Washington Met. Area; mem. Fed. City Coun.; bd. dirs. Riggs Bank, Greater Washington Bd. Trade, Nat. Edn. Telecom. Orgn., Washington Rsch. Libr. Consortium, DC Com.to Promote Washington; life mem. Newcomen Soc. U.S.; assoc. mem. Am. Coun. Learned Soc.; exec. adv. coun. SCT Edn. Systems. Contbr. articles to profl. jours. Bd. dirs. Urban League, Washington; mem. D.C. Mayor's Bus. Adv. Coun.; mem. exec. panel Chief Naval Ops.; bd. overseers List Coll. Jewish Theol. Sem. Am. Winston Churchill fellow Eng., 1969, Hon. Wolcott fellow, 1999; named Outstanding Young Person, Boston Jr. C. of C., 1970, One of 100 Young Leaders, Acad. Am. Council Learning, 1978, Alumnus of Yr. James Madison High Sch., Bklyn., 1982, one of Fifty Outstanding Alumni Problem Solvers Harvard's John F. Kennedy Sch. Government, 1987; recipient Myrtle Wreath award Hadassah, 1982, Scopus award Am. Friends of Hebrew U., 1984, fellow Morse Coll. Yale U., Human Rels. award NCCJ, 1987, award NAACP, 1988, citation Conn. Bar Assn., 1988, Univ. medal of highest honor Kyung Hee U., Seoul, Korea, 1990, Martin Luther King, Jr. Internat. Salute award, 1992, Hannah G. Solomon award Nat. Coun. Jewish Women, 1992, Father of Yr. award Washington Urban League, 1993, Univ. Pres. medal Kyonggi U., Seoul, 1993, Am. Czech and Slovak Assn. Merit award, 1993, John Jay award Columbia U., 1995, Spirit of Democracy award Am. Jewish Congress, 1995, Newcomen Soc. award, 1995, Disting. Achievement medal Greenberg Ctr. for Judaic Studies U. Hartford, 1995, Disting. Pub. Svc. award U.S. Dept. of State Sec.'s Open Forum, 1997, Tree of Life award Jewish Nat. Fund, 1999; Jan. 22, 1998 declared Stephen Joel Trachtenberg Day in Washington D.C. by D.C. City Council, Feb. 2, 1999 proclaimed Stephen Joel Trachtenberg Day in San Francisco by Mayor of San Francisco. Mem. Am. Assn. Univ. Adminstrs. (pres. 1999-2000, Disting. Svc. award 1996, B'nai B'rith Humanitarian award 1996, chair Md./DC selection com. 1998, 99, Rhodes scholarships), N.Y. Acad. Scis., Internat. Assn. Univ. Pres. (N.Am. coun.), Coun. Fgn. Rels., Sr. Soc. Sachems, Ind. Retail Cattleman's Assn. (adv. coun.), Masons (Grand Cross award), Scottish Rite Freemasonry (33d degree), Harvard Club (N.Y.C.), Tumble Brook Country Club (Bloomfield, Conn.), Cosmos Club (Washington), Univ. Club (Washington), Nat. Press Club, George Washington U. Club, Hannibal Club, Phi Beta Kappa. Office: George Washington U Office Of President Washington DC 20052-0001

TRACI, DONALD PHILIP, retired lawyer; b. Cleve., Mar. 13, 1927; m. Lillian Traci Calafiore; 11 children. BS cum laude, Coll. of the Holy Cross, Worcester, Mass., 1950; JD magna cum laude, Cleve. State U., 1955; LLD (hon.), U. Urbino, Italy, 1989. Bar: Ohio 1955, U.S. Dist. Ct. (no. and so. dists.) Ohio 1955, U.S. Ct. Appeals (3d, 6th and 7th cirs.), U.S. Dist. Ct. (we. and ea. dists.) Pa., U.S. Supreme Ct. 1965. Ptnr. Spangenberg, Shibley, Traci, Lancione & Liber, Cleve., 1955-94; ret., 1994—; lectr. York U., Toronto, Ont., Can., Case Western Res. U., Cleve. Marshall Law Sch., U. Mich., Akron U., U. Cin., Ohio No. U., Harvard U. Trustee Cath. Charities Diocese of Cleve.; past pres. Bd. Cath. Edn.; former chmn. bd. regents St. Ignatius H.S., Cleve.; mem. pres.'s coun. Coll. of Holy Cross; Eucharist min. St. Rose of Lima Ch. With USN, 1945-46. Fellow Am. Coll. Trial Lawyers, Internat. Acad. Trial Lawyers (past pres.), Am. Bd. Trial Advocacy; mem. ABA, ATLA (trustee Lambert Chair Found., lectr. trial practice), Ohio State Bar Assn. (lectr. trial practice), Ohio Acad. Trial Lawyers (past chmn. rules seminar, lectr. trial practice), Cuyahoga County Bar Assn. (lectr. trial practice), Cleve. Acad. Trial Lawyers (lectr. trial practice), Trial Lawyers for Pub. Justice (sustaining founder), Cleve. Bar Assn. (chmn. Advocacy Inst., trustee, CLE com., jud. selection com., spl. justice ctr. com., fed. ct., common pleas ct. and ct. appeals com., pres. 1986), Jud. Conf. U.S. 6th Cir. Ct. (life), Jud. Conf. 8th Jud. Dist. Ohio (life), Knights of Malta, Knights of Holu Sepulchre of Jerusalem, Delta Theta Phi. Home: 12700 Lake Ave Apt 505 Lakewood OH 44107-1547

TRACT, MARC MITCHELL, lawyer; b. N.Y.C., Sept. 20, 1959; s. Harold Michael and Natalie Ann (Meyerowitz) T.; m. Sharon Beth Widrow; children: Melissa Hope, Harrison Michael, Sarah Michelle. BA in Biology, Ithaca Coll., 1981; JD, Pepperdine U., 1984. Bar: N.Y. 1985, N.J. 1985, D.C. 1986. Assoc. Kroll & Tract, N.Y.C., 1985-90, ptnr., 1990-94; ptnr. Rosenman & Colin LLP, N.Y.C., 1994—; bd. dirs. Sorema N.Am. Reinsurance Co., N.Y.C., Navigators Group Inc., N.Y.C., MAPFRE Reinsurance Corp., San Francisco, C.A., AXA Nordstern Art Ins. Corp. Am., N.Y.C., Fortress Ins. Co., Rosemont, Ill., N.Y.C., Oriska Ins. Co., Oriskany, N.Y. Bd. dirs. Italian Acad. Found. Mem. ABA, Assn. of Bar of City of N.Y., N.Y. State Bar Assn., N.J. State Bar Assn., N.Y. County Lawyers Assn., Am. Coun. Germany, Old Westbury Golf and Country Club, Met. Club, Econ. Club N.Y. Republican. Office: Rosenman & Colin LLP 575 Madison Ave Fl 11 New York NY 10022-2511

TRACY, SUSANNE MARY, nurse educator; b. Rochester, N.Y., June 9, 1945; d. Edward and Ann (Bihun) Koszalka; m. Daniel A. Tracy, III, June 17, 1967; children: Lisa, Michael, Scott, Erin. BSN, Niagara Univ., 1967; MN, Univ. S.C., 1975; postgrad., Univ. R.I., 1996—. Registered nurse, N.H., Mass. Navy nurse U.S. Navy, Niagara Falls/Pensacola, N.Y./Fla., 1966-68; instr. of nursing Columbus State Univ., Columbus, Ga., 1975-77; asst. prof. nursing Jefferson Cmty. Coll., Watertown, N.Y., 1977-81; asst. head nurse of rehab. Penrose Hosp., Colorado Springs, Colo., 1981-82; edn. cons. Penrose & St. Mary Corwin Hosp., Colorado Springs, Pueblo, Colo., 1982-85; asst. prof. nursing Rivier Coll., Nashua, N.H., 1985-91, assoc. prof. nursing, 1991—. Contbr. articles to profl. jours. Decorated Nat. Svc. medal U.S. Navy, 1967; named Outstanding Young Women of Am. Nat. Awards Program, 1977. Mem. Eastern Nursing Rsch. Soc., Nursing Info. System Coun. of New Eng., New Eng. Edn. Assessment Network (bd. dirs. 1995—), Am. Assn. Higher Edn. Avocations: research, travel. E-mail: olsldr@aol.com.

TRACY, TRACY FAIRCLOTH, special education educator; b. Washington, Aug. 22, 1961; d. James Claybert and Esther (Harrell) Faircloth; m. Charles Randall Tracy, Aug. 16, 1986; children: James Wren, Corissa Estelle. BS in Spl. Edn.-Mental Retardation, Old Dominion U., 1983. Tchr. Newport News (Va.) Pub. Schs., 1983—, community-based instruction specialist, 1992—. Leader Camp Fire, Inc., Newport News, 1983-92; vol. Newport News Spl. Olympics, 1984—, treas., 1987—; mem. Va. PTA, Nat. PTA. Recipient Award for Outstanding Svc. Newport News Spl. Olympics, 1986, 88, 90, Citizenship award Denbigh Kiwanis, 1988, Appreciation award Hampton-Newport News Cmty. Svcs. Bd., 1989; named Outstanding Young Women Am., 1988. Mem. Assn. for Retarded Citizens, Coun. for Exceptional Children, Student Coun. for Exceptional Children (pres. 1982-83), Kappa Delta Pi (No Va. chpt.), Alpha Chi. Democrat. Methodist. Avocations: arts and crafts, swimming, walking. Home: 4708 Harlequin Way Chesapeake VA 23321-1247 Office: Enterprise Acad 813 Diligence Dr Ste 110 Newport News VA 23606-4237

TRACZYK, ZDZISŁAWA, hematologist, consultant; b. Witowice, Cracow, Poland, May 5, 1930; d. Edward Jacenty and Julianna (Patej) Andrysik; m. Władysław Zygmunt Traczyk, Dec. 7, 1954; 1 child Zdzisław Władysław. Physician, 1st Med. Inst., Moscow, 1956; MD, PhD, Med. U., Warsaw, Poland, 1964; assoc. prof., Med. Acad., Warsaw, Poland, 1969. Diplomate in Internal Medicine and in Hematology. From jr. to sr. rsch. fellow Dept. of Hematology Inst. of Hematology, Warsaw, 1957-70; head Cytomorphology and Tissue Culture Lab., Warsaw, 1970-77, IV Divisn. of Internal Medicine, Ctrl. Clin. Hosp., Warsaw, 1977-92, Outpatient Clinic of Hematology and Chemotherapy, Warsaw, 1992-97; hematology cons. Ctrl. Clin. Hosp., Warsaw, 1977-97, head AIDS problem com., 1987-97, Inst. of Hematology and Transfusiology, Warsaw, 1997—. Author: (book) Manual of Hematology for Practitioner, 1978, 2d rev. edition, 1984; mem. editorial bd. (jour.) Medical Problems (Polish). Mem. Ethics Com. Ministry of Health, Warsaw, 1976-78. Decorated Knight Polonia Restituta Order, Pres. State Coun., Warsaw, 1986; recipient Gold Cross of Merit, Pres. State Coun., Warsaw, 1979, award Ministry of Nat. Edn., Warsaw, 1994. Fellow Internat. Soc. Hematology, N.Y. Acad. Sci., Polish Soc. Hematology (chmn. Warsaw br. 1995-99), Polish Soc. Oncology, Polish Med. Soc., Assn. Combatants Polish Rep. Expolit. Prisoners. Avocations: music, painting. Office: Inst Hematology and Transfusiology, ul Chocimska 5, 00-957 Warsaw Poland

TRAEGER, CLAUS, literature educator; b. Leipzig, Germany, Feb. 4, 1927; s. Gerhard Karl and Elly Gertrud (Rieffel) T.; m. Yvonne Edith Lenz (dec. Aug. 1972); children: Petra, Katja; m. Christine Fischer. Dr. phil., U. Leipzig, 1958; PhD, U. Greifswald, 1964. Rschr. worker German Acad. Scis., Berlin, 1955-64; prof. German lit. U. Leipzig, 1965-69, chmn., prof. gen. and comparative lit., 1969-92, ret., 1992—; dir. German dept. U. Leipzig, 1967-69, dir. sect. cultural scis. and lit., 1969-74, 85-87. Editor, author: Dictionary of Literary Sciences, 1986, 2d edit., 1989; author: Studies in Theory and History of Literature (3 vols.), 1970, 72, 81; editor: French Revolution and German Literature, 1972, 2d edit., 1979, 3d edit., 1988); editor Zeitschrift fuer Germanistik, 1980-90; contbr. articles to profl. jours. Recipient Lessing award G.D.R., 1974, Nat. award, 1984, Goethe Schiller Plaque Weimar, 1977. Mem. Saxon Acad. of Scis., N.Y. Acad. Scis., Senat Internat. Assn. German Langs. and Lits. Home: Heinrich von Kleist St 19, D-04416 Markkleeberg Germany

TRAFIMOW, DAVID A., psychology educator; b. Ft. Campbell, Ky., May 12, 1962; s. Jordan H. and Alice Trafimow; m. Sabine C. Trafimow, June 14, 1987. BA, U. Ill., 1984, PhD, 1993; MA, Ind. U., 1988. Asst. prof. Va. Tech., Blacksburg, 1992-94; asst. prof. N.Mex. State U., Las Cruces, 1994-98, assoc. prof., 1998—. Contbr. articles to profl. jours. Mentor McNair Program, New Mex. State U., 1997, 98, 99. Named one of Outstanding Young Men of Am., 1998. Mem. Social Psychol. Attitude Rschrs. Avocations: reading, opera, running, travel. Office: N Mex State U Dept Psychology MSC 3452 PO Box 30001 Las Cruces NM 88003-8001

TRAFIMOW, JORDAN HERMAN, orthopedist; b. Chgo., Nov. 4, 1935; s. Jack and Florence (Silver) Trafimow; m. Alice Emma Lewis, July 11, 1959; children: David, Alan, Janet. BS in Med., U. Ill., 1957, MD, 1958. Orthopedic surgeon Permanente Med. Group, L.A., 1966-69, Elmhurst (Ill.) Clin., 1969-86; asst. prof. Rush St. Luke Presbyn. Med. Ctr., Chgo., 1986—. Contbr. articles to profl. jours. Capt. U.S. Army, 1960-62. Fellow Am. Acad. Orthopedic Surgeons, N.Am. Spine Soc. Jewish. Avocation: chess. Office: Neurodiagnostics 640 E Saint Charles Rd Ste 202 Carol Stream IL 60188-2600

TRAGEN, IRVING GLENNE, consultant; b. May 18, 1922; m. Eleanor May Dodspn, Aug. 7, 1947. AB, U. Calif., Berkeley, 1943; LLM, U. Chile, Santiago, 1946; JD, U. Calif., 1945. Personnel officer Mex.-U.S. Commn. Eradicate Foot & Mouth Disease, Mex., 1948-49, WHO/Pan Am. Sanitary Bur., Washington, 1950-53; with U.S. Dept. State & AID, El Salvador, Chile, Peru, Venezuela, Washington, Calif., 1953-63; dir. L.Am. bur. instl. devel. AID, Washington, 1963-65; dir. AID Mission, La Paz, Bolivia, 1965-68; country dir. Argentina, Paraguay, Uruguay U.S. Dept. State, Washington, 1969-71; v.p. Inter-Am. Found., Rosslyn, Va., 1971-73; chief Ctrl. Am. Regional Office U.S. Dept. State & AID, Guatemala, 1973-75; dir. USAID & econ. counselor U.S. Embassy U.S. Dept. State & AID, Panama, 1975-77; deputy U.S. rep. U.S. Mission fo OAS, U.S. Dept. State, Washington, 1977-80; exec. dir. Inter-Am. ECOSOC, Washington, 1980-84; exec. sec. Inter-Am. Drug Abuse Control Commn., Washington, 1984-94; prin. advisor Regional C.Am. Legal Devel., San Jose, Costa Rica, 1995-97; cons., prin. advisor L.Am./European Orgns., Hanford, Calif., 1995—; mem. adv. bd. U. Pacific, Stockton, Calif., 2000. Mem. editl. bd. (Spanish edit.) Money Laundering Alert Internat., 2000. Trustee emeritus Museo de las Americas, Denver, 2000. Home and office: 925 Greenfield Ave Hanford CA 93230-3506

TRÄGER, FRANK REINER, physics, educator; b. Meerane, Saxony, Germany, June 4, 1948; s. Max Erich and Irmgard Träger; m. Christel Margarete Markstahler, Mar. 21, 1974; 1 child, Jens. Physics diploma, U. Heidelberg, Germany, 1973, PhD, 1976, habilitation, 1981. chmn. Internat. Symposium on Metal Clusters, Heidelberg, 1986, German Russian Symposium Laser Physics, Kassel, 1994, Internat. Symposium Surface Studies by Nonlinear Laser Spectroscopies, Kassel, 1994. Rsch. asst. U. Heidelberg, Germany, 1976-81; vis. scientist IBM Almaden Rsch. Ctr., San Jose, Calif., 1982-83; sr. scientist U. Heidelberg, Germany, 1984-86, asst. prof., 1986-89; full prof. U. Kassel, Germany, 1990—, head dept. physics, 1995-96. Editor: Metal Clusters, 1986, Surface Studies by Nonlinear Laser Spectroscopies, 1995, Atomic Physics Methods in Modern Research, 1997, Nonlinear Optics at Interfaces, 1999; editor-in-chief Applied Physics B-Lasers and Optics, 1996—; contbr. articles to profl. jours. Mem. Am. Phys. Soc., German Phys. Soc., Soc. German Natural Scientists and Physicians, N.Y. Acad. Scis. Office: U Kassell Fac Physics, Heinrich-Plett-Strasse 40, D-34132 Kassel Germany

TRAGER, GARY ALAN, endocrinologist, diabetologist; b. N.Y.C., July 30, 1950; s. Jacob Morris and Elena (Tanzer) T.; m. Marie-Christine Nicole Lachal, Dec. 26, 1976; children: Ashley Audrey, Brendon Alden. BA in Biology and Anthropology, SUNY, Binghamton, 1972; MD, U. Cen. del Este, Dominican Republic, 1980. Subintern-rotating Jamaica (N.Y.) Hosp., 1979-80; intern and resident medicine Bklyn.-Cumberland Med. Ctr., 1980-83; fellow endocrinology SUNY, Stony Brook, 1983-85, clin. asst. instr., 1983-85; asst. attending Huntington (N.Y.) Hosp., 1985-90, assoc. attending, 1990-97, sr. attending, 1997—; adv. bd. Sankyo-Park Davis, Merck & Co., Bayer Pharms., Hoechst Marion Roussel, Boehringer Mannheim, Eli Lilly & Co., Park Davis, Pratt Pharms., Upjohn, Johnson and Johnson, Pfizer, Inc. and Roerig Divsn.; nat. adv. bd., nat. speaker bureaus Parke Davis, Novodisc, Sherring-Plough, spkr. Forest Pharms., Ciba Geisy, Knoll; mem. nutrition com. Huntington Hosp., 1987—, dir. diabetes club, 1985—; mem. Nassau-Suffolk Hosp. Coun. on Diabetes, with Nat. Diabetes Ednl. Initiative, lab com. H.H., 1997—, pharm. and therapy com., 1998—. Mem. profl. edn. com. Am. Diabetes Assn., Long Island, Melville, N.Y., 1985—; mem. Am. Diabetic Assn. Fund, Long Island, N.Y., 1989—; ad hoc mem. Eaton's Neck Emergency Squad, Long Island, 1985-89; I.P.R.O. Nassau-Suffolk Counties, 1998—. Mem. AMA, Am. Fertility Soc., Am. Diabetes Assn., Am. Soc. Internal Medicine, Am. Soc. Andrology, Am. Assn. Clin. Endocrinologists, Peripheral Neuropathy Inst., An. Soc. Hypertension, Adrenal Soc. Office: 158 E Main St Huntington NY 11743-2988

TRAGER, MICHAEL DAVID, lawyer; b. N.Y.C., Feb. 15, 1959; s. Philip and Ina (Shulkin) T.; m. Mariella Gonzalez, Sept. 12, 1987; children: Nicholas, Alexander. BA, Wesleyan U., Middletown, Conn., 1981; JD, Boston U., 1985. Bar: Mass. 1985, Conn. 1986, Fla. 1988, D.C. 1989. Staff atty. enforcement divsn. Securities & Exchange Com., Washington, 1985-87; assoc. Morgan, Lewis & Bockius, Miami, Fla., 1987-88; participating assoc. Fulbright & Jaworski, Washington, 1989-92; ptnr. Trager & Trager, Washington, 1992-93; of counsel Fulbright & Jaworski, Washington, 1993-94, ptnr., 1995—, co-head litigation dept. securities practice group. Bd. dirs. Jewish Nat. Fund-Mid-Atlantic Region, 1993-97; officer Horace Mann PTA, 1997-99. Mem. ABA (bus. law sect. fed. regulation securities com. and civil litigation and SEC enforcement matters subcom., litigation sect. securities litigation com. and SEC enforcement subcom., class action and derivative litigation com. and securities litigation subcom., task force on SEC's insider trading and selective disclosure rules, bd. market), Assn. SEC Alumni, Securities Industry Assn. (legal and compliance divsn.), D.C. Bar (corp., fin. and securities law sect. corp. counsel and planning group for broker-dealer

programs 1992-94, broker-dealer regulation com., task force on SEC's proposed insider trading and selective disclosure rules), Mass. Bar, Fla. Bar., Conn. Bar., Bond Market Assn. (litigation adv. com.). Office: Fulbright & Jaworski 801 Pennsylvania Ave NW Fl 3-5 Washington DC 20004-2623

TRAINA, PAUL JOSEPH, environmental engineer; b. N.Y.C., Mar. 8, 1934; s. Peter and Mary (Panepinto) T.; m. Mary Ann Delehanty, Oct. 8, 1955; children: Peter F., Kenneth P., Jean Marie, Julie Ann, Marie L. BCE, Manhattan Coll., 1955; M in San. Engring., U. Mich., 1960. Registered profl. engr., Ga. Chief water resources USPHS, Atlanta, 1960-63, dep. dir. S.E. com. Water Pollution Control project, 1963-67; dir. tech. svcs. Fed. Water Pollution Control Adminstrn., Athens, Ga., 1967-70; dir. enforcement div. EPA, Atlanta, 1972-79, dir. water div., 1979-85; sr. cons. Camp Dresser McKee, Cambridge, Mass., 1985—. Mem. Am. Acad. Environ. Engring. (diplomate), Am. Pub. Works Assn., Water Environ. Fedn. Home: 2366 Woodcreek Ct Tucker GA 30084-3301

TRAINER, FREDERICK EDWARD, economics educator; b. Sydney, Australia, Mar. 5, 1941; s. Frederick Arthur and Ada (Thornton) T.; m. Sandra May Norris; 1 child, Jamie. BA with honors, Sydney U., 1963, MA with honors, 1968, PhD, 1972. Tutor dept. of edn. Sydney U., 1964-72; lectr. Sch. of Edn. U. NSW, 1972-90, lectr. Sch. Social Work, 1990—; lectr. in field. Author: (books) Abandon Affluence, 1985, Developed to Death, 1989, The Conserver Society, 1995, Towards a Sustainable Economy, 1995, Saving the Environment: What It Will Take, 1998; contbr. numerous articles to profl. jours. Developer, operator Pigface Point alt. lifestyle ednl. ctr., Sydney, 1985—.

TRALLE, ALEKSY, mathematician; b. Minsk, Belarus, Apr. 21, 1958; arrived in Poland, 1990; s. Eugeniusz and Irena (Kuncewicz) T.; m. Irena Morocka, Dec. 9, 1988; children: Leon, Eugeniusz, Wojciech. Diploma in math., Belarus U., Minsk, 1980; PhD in Differential Geometry, Belarus U., 1984; habilitation in differential geometry, Wroclaw (Poland) U. Lectr. Belarus U., Minsk, 1985-88; asst. prof. Belarus U., 1988-90; asst. prof. Szczecin (Poland) U., 1990-93, assoc. prof., 1993-96; assoc. prof. Polish Acad. Scis., Warsaw, 1996—, Wroclaw (Poland) U., 1996—; dir. Inst. Math. Szczecin U., 1994-96, head dept. geometry, 1993-96. Author: (with John Oprea) (monograph) Symplectic Manifolds with no Kähler Structure, 1997; contbr. articles to profl. jours. Grantee Polish Rsch. Com., Warsaw, 1993-95, 95—, German Acad. Exch. Svc., Bonn, 1995, rsch. in pairs grantee Volkswagen-Stiftung, Oberwolfach, Germany, 1996, grantee Max Planck Inst. for Math., Bonn, 1998. Mem. Am. Math. Soc., Polish Math. Soc. Mem. Solidarity Party. Roman Catholic. Avocations: sports, swimming. Home: Sikorskiego 7/14A, 70-323 Szczecin Poland Office: Wroclaw U, Pl Grundwaldzki 2/4, 50-384 Wroclaw Poland

TRAN, DANH XUAN, mechanical engineer, educator; b. Thua-Thien, Vietnam, Aug. 20, 1943; parents Than Tran and Van Thi Nguyen; m. Kim Anh Tong, May 12, 1971; children: Tu-Anh, Tung, Tu-Chan, Bach. B in Engring. with honors, U. Canterbury, 1967, BSc, 1969, PhD, 1971. Lectr., vice dean U. Hue, Vietnam, 1971-77; lectr. U. Technology, Hochiminh City, Vietnam, 1977-89; from lectr. to sr. lectr. Victoria U., Australia, 1991—. 2d lt. South Vietnamese army, 1972-75. Mem. Australasian Assn. Engring. Edn., Soc. Exptl. Mechs. Avocations: tennis, table tennis, gardening. Office: Victoria U, PO Box 14428, Melbourne 8001, Australia

TRAN, DUONG HIEN, computational numerician; b. Hanoi, Vietnam, Dec. 31, 1946; s. Xuan Tieu and Thi Luong (Duong) T.; Bich Hien Nguyen, Aug. 15, 1975; children: Due, Duy. MSc, Tech. U. of Hanoi, 1967; PhD, Polish Acad. Scis., 1981. Rschr. Inst. of Mechanics, Nat. Ctr. for Scientific Rsch. Vietnam, Hanoi, 1968-78, Inst. of Fundamental Technol. Rsch., Polish Acad. Scis., Warsaw, 1978-95; prof. Tech. U. Szczecin, 1995—. Author: (with M. Kleiber) The Stochastic Finite Element Method, 1992, (with M. Kleiber, P.Kowalczyk, H. Antunez) Parameter Sensitivity in Nonlinear Mechanics, 1997; contbr. articles to profl. jours. Avocation: computer programming. E-Mail: tdhien@man.szczecin.pl. Fax: 48-91-4340946. Home: Bohaterow Warszawy 55m50, 71-070 Szczecin Poland Office: Tech U of Szczecin, Piastow 41, 71-065 Szczecin Poland

TRAN, HENRY BANG Q., social work case manager; b. Binh Dinh, Vietnam, Dec. 28, 1952; came to U.S., 1975; s. Mau Dinh and Ho Thi Tran; m. Thuhong T. Ngo; children: John, Michael, Robert, Richard, Jennifer. BA, Northeastern Ill. U., 1977, MA, 1978. Cert. social worker, real estate broker. Social worker Tex. Dept. Human Svcs., Houston, 1980-96; founder, pres. Texo Properties, Inc., Houston, 1984-85; pres. N.E.W.S. Properties, Houston, 1985—; case mgr. Tex. Workforce Commn., 1996—; instr. math. City Colls. Chgo., 1977, Vietnamese lang. U. Houston, 1985. V.p. Buddhist Assn. for Services of Humanity in Am., Houston, 1985—; pres. Quang Trung Mut. Assistance Assn., Houston, 1984—. Fellow U. Miami, 1979. Mem. Nat. Assn. Realtors, Tex. Pub. Employee Assn., Dalat U. Alumni Assn., Asia Soc., Houston Vietnam Lions Club (pres. 1991). Avocations: tennis, soccer, jogging.

TRAN, JACK NHUAN NGOC, gas and oil reservoir engineer; b. Quang Binh, Vietnam, Sept. 21, 1933; came to U.S., 1975; s. Dieu Ngoc and Ly Thi (Nguyen) T.; m. Christine Quang Huynh; children: Quoc Dung, Ann Nga Huyen, Ephram Anh Dung, John Hung Dung. BS, U. San Francisco, 1977, MBA, 1978. With Republic of Vietnam Mil., 1952-67; cadet Rep. Vietnam Mil. Acad., Dalat, 1952-53; 1st lt., co. comdr. 1st Republic of Vietnam Bn., South Vietnam, 1953-54; editor-in-chief Republic of Vietnam Revs., Saigon, 1955-57; commandant Republic of Vietnam Aerial Photo Ctr., Saigon, 1958-61, Republic of Vietnam Mil. Intelligence Sch., Caymai and Saigon, 1962-67; mem. Republic of Vietnam Senate, 1967-73; v.p. The Meteco Corp., Saigon, Vietnam, 1971-72; pres., chmn. bd. Meteco-Vinaseco Co., Saigon, 1972-75; air photo analyst Std. Oil Co., San Francisco, 1975-79; gas and oil engr. Chevron Oil Co., San Francisco, 1980—; col. U.S. Intelligence, Calif., 1980-90. Author: Flower in the Battle Field, 1956, Geological Survey of the Kndu, CA, 1982, Beluga River Oil Development, 1984, The Military Life, 1992; editor-in-chief Chien-Si Quoc-Gia Mag. Recipient Hon. Key of the City, City of Omaha, Nebr., 1989, Hon. Citizen City of Fayetteville, N.C., 1969; Resolution of Recognition, Senate of State of Hawaii, 1969, Senate of State of Tex., 1969. Mem. The U. of San Francisco Alumni Assn., Rotary Internat. Roman Catholic. Avocations: swimming, music, reading, traveling. Home: 1418 Lundy Ave San Jose CA 95131-3310

TRAN, MINH SON, physician; b. Cholon, South Vietnam, June 12, 1938; s. Hoi Van and Xuan-thi (Nguyen) T.; m. Pauline Anne Vanty Nguyen; children: Jacques Minh-Son, Pierre Minh-Son. Cert. in phys. and biol., Faculty of Scis., Saigon, Vietnam, 1959; MD, Saigon U., 1967. Lt., MD 43d Regiment 18th Div. Army Republic South Vietnam, 1967-68; capt., surgeon Ban Me Thuot (South Vietnam) Mil. Hosp., 1968-69, Hosp. for Paralytic, Vung Tau, South Vietnam, 1969-70, Gen. Republic Hosp. Saigon, 1970-75; physician Paris U., 1978—, Dispensary Pasteur, Bondy, France, 1981—. Prisoner-of-war Saigon, 1975-76; polit. refugee in Paris, 1978—. Mem. Sci. Assn. Acupuncturist Med. Drs. France. Roman Catholic. Avocations: swimming, ping-pong. Home and Office: 3 Valentina Terechkova, 93270 Sevran France

TRÂN, QUANG HAI, ethnomusicologist; b. Linh Dong Xa, Vietnam, May 13, 1944; s. Van Khe and Thi Suong (Nguyen) T.; m. Bach Yen, June 17, 1978; 1 dau., Thi Minh Lam. Diploma, Nat. Conservatory Music, Saigon, Vietnam, 1961, Cambridge (Eng.) U., 1965; diploma Ctr. d'Etudes Musique Orientale, Inst. de Musicologie, Paris, 1969; MusD (hon.), Internat. U. Found., 1987; Ecole Pratique des Hautes Etudes; Cultural Doctorate, World U., 1988; diploma d'Etat de Professeur de Musique Traditionnelle, Ministry of Culture, France, 1989; PhD (hon.), Albert Einstein Internat. Acad. Found., 1989. Tchr. Centre Studies for Oriental Music, Paris, 1970-75; ethnomusicologist Musèe de l'Homme, Paris, 1968—, Musée Nat. des Arts et Traditions Populaires, Paris, 1968-87; instr. U. Nanterre, Paris X, 1987; mem. sci. coun. Internat. Ctr., Khoomei, Tuva, Russia, 1995; pres. Jury of 2d World Khoomei Festival, 1995. Author: Am Nhac Viet Nam (Music of Viet Nam), 1989, Musiques du Monde (Musics of the World), 1993, Music of the World, 1994, Musiques et Danses Traditionnelles d'Europe, 1995, Musikallerder Welt, 1996, Musicas del Mundo, 1998, Tuyên tâp 50 cakhuc, 1999; contbr. numerous articles to music publs. including New Grove Dictionary of Music and Musicians, Encyclopedia Universalis, Voices of the World (3 CD and booklet collection CNRS/Musee de l'Homme), 1996, Vietnam: Musics of the Montagnards (2 CD, booklet collection CNRS/Musee de l'Homme), 1997; composer: Nho mién thuong du (Nostalgia of the Highlands) (for 16-stringed zither), 1971, Xuan Ve (The Spring is Coming Back) (for 16-stringed zither), 1971, Ao thanh (Magic Sound), 1973, Ve Nguon (Return to the Sources) (in cooperation with Nguyen Van Tuong) (electroacoustical music), 1975, Shaman, 1982, Hat haigiong, 1982, Tieng hat dan moi Mong, 1982, Nui Ngu Song Houng (for monochord), 1983, Nam Bac Mot Nha (for 16 string zither), 1984, Voyage chamanique (for voice), 1986, Tro ve nguon col, 1988, Solo Thai (for 16 string zither), 1989, Tambours 89 (for percussions and tape rec. Bicentennial of French Revolution), 1989, Envol (for overtones), 1989, (for 16 stringed zither) Vinh Ha Long, 1993, Cuu Long Giang ihan Yeu, 1993, Hon Vietnam, 1993, (for Jew's harp) Paysage des Hauts Plateaux, 1997, Nostalgie au Pays Mong, 1997, Vietnam mon Pays, 1997, Tuva! Tuva!, 1997, Le Saut des Crapauds, 1997, Harmonie des Guimbardes, 1997, L'univers Harmonique, 1997, others; also numerous songs; performer on 15 LPs and 8 CDs; composer film music for Long Van Khanh Hoi, 1980, La Rencontre du Dragon et du Coq, 1997; co-author, actor, composer film Le Chant des Harmoniques (The Song of Harmonics), 1989 (Spl. prize Acad. of Scis. 1990, Grand prize 4th Visual Anthropology Film Festival, Estonia 1990, Prix Spl. pour la Recherche, 6th Internat. Film Festival of Sci. Film, Palaiseau, France 1990, Grand prize No. Telecom 2nd Internat. Festival of Sci. Film, Montreal, Can. 1991); author, performer on Vietnamese music including (CD) Vietnam/Dreams and Reality, 1988, Vietnam Zither, 1993, Jew's Harps of the World, 1997, Landscape of the Highlands, 1997; author and performer of videofilms including Music of Vietnam/Trân Quang Hai and Bach Yen, 1988, Trân Quang Hai, Vietnamese Musician, 1988, Vietnamese Dan Tranh Zither by Trân Quang Hai, 1993. Recipient Grand prize for Vietnam/Tran Quang Hai and Bach Yen, Record Acad. Charles Cros, 1983, medaille d'Or de la musique Academie Culturelle Asiatique, 1986, Alfred Nobel medal Albert Einstein Internat. Acad. Found., 1991, Grand Amb. Achievement award, 1991, Van Laurens award Brit. Voice Assn. and Ferens Inst., London, 1991, Medaille de Cristal du Ctr. Nat. de la Rsch. Sci., Paris, 1996. Mem. Soc. Ethnomusicology, Asian Music Soc., Internat. Folk Music Coun. (liaison officer rep. of France), Internat. Musicological Soc., Internat. Assn. Sound Archives, UNESCO Internat. Coun. Museums and Collections of Mus. Instruments, European Sem. Ethnomusicology (founding mem.), Soc. Musicology, Centre d'Etudes de Musique Orientale, Assn. FranÇaise des Archives Sonores, Sociètè des Auteurs des Compositeurs et des Editeurs de la Musique, Nat. Ctr. for Sci. Rsch. (rsch. team), French Soc. Ethnomusicology (founding mem.), French Assn. Rsch. in S.E. Asia (founding mem.), Assn. FranÇaise de Recherche sur l'Asie du Sud Est, Ctr. Internat. d'Etudes Vietnamiennes, Assn. Preserving and Developing Vietnamese Songs, Asia/Pacific Soc. for Ethnomusicology, Assn. Vietnamese Artists and Writers in Europe, Am. Biol. Inst. and Rsch. Assn. (dep. gov. 1987—), Internat. Biol. Assn. (dep. dir. gen. 1987, dep. dir. 1987—), Vietnamese Profls. Sci. Soc. Toronto (hon.). Home: 12 rue Gutenberg, F-94450 Limeil Brevannes France Office: Musee de l'Homme Dept d'Ethnomusicologie, 17 Place Du Trocadero, 75116 Paris France

TRAN, QUOC TRANG CONG HOANG, business consulting company executive; b. Ho Chi Minh City, Vietnam, June 15, 1956; s. Tam Cong Tran and Sau Thi Nguyen; m. Phuong Thi Tran, 1977; children: Hoang Tu Cong, Thao Nguyen Thi. BA in Lit., Tong Hop U., Ho Chi Minh City, 1988, BA in Econs., 1989; MA, Social Sci. Inst., Ho Chi Minh City, 1990; PhD in Econs., Nat. Econ. U., Vietnam, 1996. Econ. specialist, reporter Ho Chi Minh City, 1975-83; econ. specialist Vietnamese Communist Party, Ho Chi Minh City, 1983-87; dir. 3.2 Co., Ho Chi Minh City, 1987-90; gen. dir. Cholifac Co., Ho Chi Minh City, 1990-92; v.p., CEO Cholimex Co., Ho Chi Minh City, 1992-95; pres. Vietco Holding Ltd., Ho Chi Minh City, 1995—; CEO Vietnam Plastics Mfrs. Assn., 1996-97, v.p., CEO, 1997—; dir. Fgn. Trade Tng. Lang. Coll., 1992-96; chmn. The He Pvt. U., Vungtau, Vietnam; CEO Vietnam Plastic Housing Nat. Project, 2000, CEO Vietnam BOPP Film Joint Stock Co., 2000; pres. Vietnam Plastic Housing Co., Ltd. Dep. editor Vietnam Plastic mag., 1995. Mem. Vietnam-Saigon Plastic Assn. (vice-chmn. 1990-96, pres. 1998—), Vietnam-Sweden Bus. Coun. (mem. com.), Orgn. Asian Plastic Fedn. Industries, Pacific Asia Travel Assn. (Vietnam chpt., tng. dir.), Asean Fedn. Plastics Industries (coun. mem. 1995-97, 98—), Vietnam Rubber Plastic Dirs. Club (chmn.), Asia Plastic Forum Orgn. (coun. mem.), Asean Fedn. Plastics Industries (counc. mem. 1995—, vice chmn., 1999—), Fedn. Scientific and Technological Assn., HCMC counc. mem.). Communist. Buddhist. Avocations: golf, tennis, chess. Office: VIETCO Holding Ltd, 192 Phung Hung, Dist 5, Ho Chi Minh City Vietnam

TRAN, TRUNG VAN, mathematics educator, researcher; b. Khanh-Binh-Tay, An-Xuyen, Vietnam, Mar. 3, 1947; arrived in Germany, 1970; s. Quan van Tran and Thi Hien Dam; m. thi Cam Anh Nguyen, Oct. 13, 1975; 1 child, Minh Chau. Sci. lic., U. Saigon (Vietnam), 1970; diploma in math., U. Heidelberg (Germany), 1974, PhD in Math., 1976, habil. and venia, 1988. Rsch. assoc. U. Heidelberg, 1977-83, asst. prof., 1983-88, prof., 1989-90; prof. U. Essen (Germany), 1990—; vis. assoc. prof. U. Nebr., Lincoln, 1988-89. Grantee Deutsche Forschungsgemeinschaft, 1977-79, 80, 92—, Sonderforschungsbereich, 1985-88. Mem. Am. Math. Soc., Internat. Assn. Cryptol. Rsch. Avocations: playing classical music. Office: Inst for Exptl Math U Essen, Ellernstrasse 29, 45326 Essen Germany

TRANCHIMAND, HENRI-MICHEL FRANÇOIS, investment banking executive; b. Pertuis, Vaucluse, France, Nov. 6, 1950; s. Gabriel Alphonse and Marie-Magdeleine Jeanne (Silvy) T.; m. Claire Marie-Laure Durant, June 22, 1974; children: Antoine, Vincent, Marie. MS, Ecole Ctrl. de Lyon, 1973; BA in Econs., U. Lyon, France, 1974; MBA, Carnegie Mellon U., 1975. V.p. J.P. Morgan, Paris, 1985-88; mng. dir. J.P. Morgan, Madrid, 1989-90, Brussels, 1991-92, London, 1993-94; asst. gen. mgr. CPR, Paris, 1995-96; CEO CPR (USA) Inc., Jersey City, 1997-98, Banque CPR, Paris, 1997-98, Dexia Asset Mgmt. France, Paris, 1999—. Home: 9 Rue Huysmans, 75006 Paris France Office: Dexia AMF, 40 rue Washington, 75008 Paris France

TRANDABURU, TIBERIU, endocrinologist, researcher; b. Bucharest, Romania, Aug. 6, 1941; s. Tiberiu Gheorghe and Maria (Dorobantu) T.; m. Viorica Rodica Manolache, June 15, 1966 (div. Sept. 1982); 1 child, Iulian Alexandru; m. Ioana Vulpe, July 29, 1984; children: Tiberiu Andrei, Ana Maria. MD, U. Bucharest, 1964; D in Animal Physiology, U. Cluj-Napoca, Romania, 1974. Probation rschr. Inst. Biology, Bucharest, 1964-67, testified rschr., 1967-75, sr. rschr. III, 1975-90, sr. rschr. II, 1990-92, sr. rschr. I, 1992—, chief dept., 1982—; prof. histology faculty of dentistry U. Buzău, Romania, 1992-94. Contbr. articles to profl. jours. Active Forum for Sci. and Reform, Bucharest, 1997. Scholar Alexander von Humboldt Found., Germany, 1970, Internat. Rsch. and Exchs. Bd., N.J., 1991, Deutscher Akad. Austauschdienst, Germany, 1994. Mem. Romanian Soc. Cell Biology, Humboldt Club. Mem. Romanian Christian Dem. Party. Christian Orthodox. Avocations: reading, jogging. Home: Apt 20, Banu Manta St 26 bloc 19A, 78162 Bucharest Romania Office: Inst Biology, Spl Independentei 296, 79651 Bucharest Romania

TRÄNKMANN, GERT JOACHIM, orthodontist, educator; b. Chemnitz, Sachsen, Germany, Oct. 23, 1935; s. Werner Gert and Anna Elfriede Irma Tränkmann; m. Maria Magdalena Margarete Else von Lilienfeld-Toal, July 26, 1962; children: Konstantin, Christopher, Alexander. Dental degree, U. Heidelberg, 1958, DDS, 1960; degree in orthodontia, U. Kiel, 1966. Pvt. practice Mudau, Germany, 1959; asst. dentist Clin. for Dental Surgery, Schwäbisch-Hall, Germany, 1959; asst. dentist clinic for dental surgery U. Kiel, Germany, 1960-62, asst. dentist clinic for orthodontics, 1963-66; asst. dentist clinic for orthodontics U. Saarland, Germany, 1967, tchr. in orthodontics, 1968-69, asst. dir., 1970-71, dir., 1971-73; univ. prof. med. sch., dir. clinic for orthodontics U. Hannover, Germany, 1973—. Author: Die Plattenapparatur in der Kieferothopädie, 1985; co-author: Die zahnärztliche Versorgung behinderter Patienten, 1985, Kleines Lehrbuch der Angle-Klasse II, 1, 1996, Effektivität der Myofunktionellen Therapie bei einzelnen Dysgnathien, 1999, Entwicklung der Dentition und Okklusion, 1999, Behandlung mit Plattenapparaturen, 2000; contbr. articles to profl. jours. Mem. senate Med. Sch. Hannover, 1976-79, pres. bd. for DDS examinations, 1987—; pres. bd. for dental examination Govt. of Niedersachsen, Germany, 1987—. Mem. Deutsche Gesellschaft Zahn-Mund-und Kieferheilkunde, Deutsche Gesellschaft Kieferorthopädie, Vereinigung der Hochschullehrer Zahn, Mund-und Kieferheilkunde, Arbeitskreis Myofunktionelle Therapie/Gesellschaft orofaziale Dyskinesien, Gesellschaft Kieferorthopädische Zahntechnik. Avocation: hockey. Office: Medizinische Hochschule, Carl-Neuberg-Str 1, D-30625 Hannover Germany

TRANQUE GARNELO, RAFAEL, company executive; b. Ponferrada, Leon, Spain, Apr. 1, 1962; s. Rafael Tranque Perez and Anunciacion Garnelo Garcia. Lic. in Econs., Valladolid State U., Spain; audit cert. course, Coll. Econs. Valladolid; MBA, Inst. Empresa, Madrid. Fin. and orgn. cons. in internat. environments Palencia, Spain. Home and Office: Av Rep Argentina No 6, 34002 Palencia Spain

TRANQUILINO, FRANCISCO PASCUAL, internist, cardiologist; b. Manila, July 6, 1966; s. Jose Castro and Josefina (Pascual) T.; m. Edna May Desquitado, Dec. 20, 1995; children: Kathryn Angela, Lorenzo Miguel. BS in Zoology, U. of The Philippines, Los Baños, 1987; MD, U. East Ramon Magsaysay Meml. Med. Ctr., Manila, 1991; advanced course in cardiology, Epworth Hosp., Melbourne, Australia, 1997; postgrad., U. of The Philippines, Manila, 1998—. Diplomate Philippine Specialty Bd. Internal Medicine. Consul-gen. U. of The Philippines Los Baños Zool. Soc., 1986-87; scribe Alpha Sigma Phi, Manila, 1990-91; pres. U. of East Ramon Magsaysay Meml. Med. Ctr., Manila, 1991; resident coord. outpatient svcs. dept. medicine U. of The Philippines Gen. Hosp., Manila, 1993-94, resident coord. adult maj. med. unit dept. medicine, 1994-95, asst. chief fellow sect. cardiology, 1996-97; mem. editl. staff 2d Pacific Rim Conf. on Hypertension, Manila, 1997; cons. Cavite (Philippines) Med. Ctr., 1997—, Bautista Hosp., Cavite, 1997—, Cardiac Care Ctr., Manila, 1999—, Healthway Med. Clinics, Alabang, The Philippines, 1999—; lectr. in field. Contbr. rsch. articles to profl. jours. Mem. U. of The Philippines Dept. Medicine Found., Manila, 1995. Fellow Philippine Coll. Physicians, Philippine Heart Assn. (assoc.); mem. Cavite Med. Soc. Avocations: writing prose and poetry, swimming, tennis. Office: Cardiac Care Ctr, 1344 Taft Ave Rm 215, 1000 Ermita Manila, The Philippines

TRAN-VIET, TU, cardiovascular and thoracic surgeon; b. Hue, Binh-Tri-Thien, Vietnam, Apr. 26, 1949; s. Yen Tran-Viet and Ngoc Hat Ho Thi; m. Thu-Huong Le, July 23, 1976; children: Chi, Thi. MD, Med. Sch. of Tours, France, 1974. Intern Centre Hospitalier, St. Brieuc, France, 1973-75; asst. Clinique du Val d'Or, St. Cloud, France, 1976-78; asst. Hopital Laennec, Paris, 1978-83, cardiovascular and thoracic surgeon, 1981—; vis. asst., 1981-83, asst. prof., 1984—. Author: Tetralogie de Fallot, 1981; editor: (video jour.) Communication Medicale, 1983; contbr. articles to profl. jours. Mem. Societe de Chirurgie Thoracique et Cardio Vasculaire de Langue Francaise, Societe Europenne de Cardiologie, Societe de Pathologie Exotique, European Soc. for Vasc. Soc. Home: Chateau de Chancenay, 20 Route de Bar le Duc, 52100 Chancenay France Office: Clinique La Renaissance, Vitry-le-Francois, Clinique Francois 1 Saint Dizier France

TRAORE, MAURICE MÉLÉGUÉ, Burkina Faso government official; b. Kankalaba, Comoe, Burkina Faso, 1951; m.; 3 children. DES in Diplomacy and Internat. Orgn., PhD in Polit. Sci. Adviser Minister Fgn. Affairs., Ouagadougou, Burkina Faso, 1981-82; 1st counselor Burkina Faso Embassy, Washington, 1983; chargé d' affaires USSR, Czechoslovakia, Hungary, E. Germany, Bulgaria, Poland, Moscow, 1984-86; advisor Planning Group for Fgn. Affairs, Ouagadougo, 1988-91; dep. Nat. Assembly Burkina Faso, Ouagadougo, 1992—; min. secondary, higher edn. and sci. rsch. Burkina Faso Govt., Ouagadougo, from 1992; now pres. Assembly People's Deps., Ouagadougo. Office: 01 BP 6482, Ouagadougou 01, Burkina Faso

TRAPE, JEAN-FRANÇOIS, parasitologist, entomologist; b. Algiers, Algeria, July 13, 1949; s. Robert and Suzanne (Fourest) T.; m. Martine Jamar, Oct. 14, 1975; children: Sandrine, Sebastien. MD, U. Paris V, 1975; CES in Parasitology, U. Paris VII, 1977; DEA in Entomology, U. Paris XI, 1980, ScD, 1986. Attaché de biology Hosp. Pitie-Salpetriere, Paris, 1978-79; rsch. scientist Orstom, Brazzaville, Congo, 1980-84; head med. entomology Inst. Pasteur, Cayenne, French Guyana, 1984-86; head malarialogy lab. Orstom, Dakar, Senegal, 1986—; mem. malaria commn. Ministry of Coop., France, 1992—, malaria control program com. Ministry of Health, Senegal, 1994—, steering com. vaccines for malaria WHO, Geneva, 1996-97; adv. panel Malaria Control Initiative, World Bank/WHO, 1996—; mem. WHO expert panel for malaria, 1999—. Author: (booklet) Malaria and Urbanization in Central Africa, 1987; contbr. articles to profl. jours. Fellow Royal Soc. Tropical Medicine and Hygiene (sec. for Senegal 1996—), West African Soc. Parasitology, Am. Soc. Tropical Medicine and Hygiene. Avocations: fishing, diving. Office: ORSTOM, BP 1386, Dakar Senegal

TRAPP, JOSEPH BURNEY, classics educator; b. Carterton, New Zealand, July 16, 1925; came to Eng., 1951; s. Henry Mansfield Burney and Frances Melanie (Wolters) T.; m. Elayne Margaret Falla, June 9, 1953; children: Michael Burney, James Stephen. MA, U. New Zealand, 1947. Asst. librarian Alexander Turnbull Libr., Wellington, New Zealand, 1946-50; asst. lectr. Victoria U., Wellington, 1950-51, U. Reading, Eng., 1951-53; asst. librarian, librarian Warburg Inst., U. London, 1953-76, prof., dir. inst., 1976-90, hon. fellow, 1990—. Author: Erasmus, Colet and More: The Early Tudor Humanists and their Books, 1991, Essays on the Renissance and the Classical Tradition, 1990; editor: The Apology of Sir Thomas More, 1979, The King's Good Servant: Sir Thomas More (exhbn. catalogue), 1977, Medieval English Literature, 1974, The Cambridge History of the Book in Britain, 1400-1557, 1999; contbr. articles to learned jours. Fellow Brit. Acad. (v.p. 1983-85, fgn. sec. 1988-95), Soc. Antiquaries, Royal Swedish Acad. of History, Antiquities and Letters (fgn. mem.). Office: U London Warburg Inst, Woburn Sq, London WC1H 0AB, England

TRAPPE, PAUL, sociologist; b. Trier, Germany, Dec. 12, 1931; s. Johannes and Ottilie (Kaess) T.; m. Margrith Diemand, Mar. 4, 1966; children: Luzius, Simon, Sonia. Student, U. Innsbruck, 1951-52, U. Paris, 1952, U. Freiburg, 1953, U. Frankfurt, 1953-55; PhD, U. Mainz, West Germany, 1959; habilitation, U. Bern, Switzerland, 1964. Asst. U. Mainz, 1959-61; asst. U. Bern, 1961-63, docent, 1964-66; docent Freiburg U., West Germany, 1965-66; prof., dir. Inst. Sociology, U. Kiel, West Germany, 1966-69; dir. Inst. Sociology, U. Basle, Switzerland, 1968—. Author books; contbr. numerous articles to profl. jours.; editor Social Strategies, 1975—. Recipient Triennial Jubilee prize Internat. Coop. Alliance, 1970. Mem. Soc. Advancement of Sci., N.Y. Acad. Scis., Internat. Sociol. Assn., Soc. Internat. Devel., Soc. Study of Internat. Problems (pres. 1967-81), Internat. Assn. Philosophy of Law and Social Philosophy (pres. 1979-83), Soc. Econ. Devel. (chairperson interdisciplinary rsch. unit 1994-2000), European Faculty Land Use and Devel. (pres. 1999—). Office: Basel U Inst Sociology, Petersgraben 27, CH-4051 Basel Switzerland

TRASI, DILIP SUDHAKAR, electronic company executive, researcher, consultant; b. Bombay, Sept. 17, 1950; s. Sudhakar Shivrao and Nalini Sudhakar (Bantwal) T.; m. Anjali Vasant Betrabet, Apr. 17, 1980; children: Akshay, Aditi. B of Engring., V.J.T. Inst., Bombay, 1973; M of Tech., IIT, Bombay, 1975. Design exec. Nelco, Bombay, 1975-81; propr. Kem-Sai Corp., Bombay, 1981—; ptnr. Aksai Rsch., Bombay, 1987—; cons. Meltron, India, 1983-88, Meltron Semiconductors Ltd., Nasik, India, 1987-92, PLA Electroappliances Pvt. Ltd., 1998—, Aura Electrochem Batteries Pvt. Ltd., 1999—. Patentee in field; contbr. articles to profl. jours. Avocations: chess, swimming, photography, psychic healing. Home: 206 Navinasha DP Rd, 400014 Bombay India

TRASI, GIAMPAOLO, financial analyst, head of equity strategy; b. Rome, June 27, 1960; s. Renato and Wanda (Glinni) T.; m. Vivica Boden, May 21, 1994; children: Cecilia, Raffaella, Valentina. Degree in Econs. magna cum laude, U. Rome, 1983; MBA, S.A.A., Turin, Italy, 1987. CPA. Fin. analyst IMI, Rome, 1984-87; fin. analyst SIGE, Milan, Italy, 1987-89, head of equity rsch., 1989-93; head strategy and markets SIGECO, Milan, 1994-95; head rsch., strategist Banca IMI Group, Milan, 1995—; expert in EVA applications; spkr. in field. Author in field, speaker in several confs. on EVA. Winner, Investment Dartboard, Wall St. Jour., 1993, 94. Mem. Italian Fin. Analysts Assn. (bd. dirs., mem. editl. com. Rivista). Avocations: reading, guitar playing. Office: IMI Banca Intermediazione Mobiliare, Corso Matteotti 4/6, 20121 Milan Italy

TRASKOS, SABRINA, business development director; b. L.A., Dec. 23, 1970; d. Michael John Traskos and Yen Pham. BA, U. Calif., Berkeley,

1992, JD, 1995; JD (hon.), U. Rio de Janeiro, 1994. Assoc. UNRWA, Cairo, 1995-96; dir. content mgmt. Frost & Sullivan, Mountain View, Calif., 1996-2000; spkr. in field. Recipient Black Belt Hawang Kwan, 2000. Avocations: running, sailing, Tae Kwondo. Office: eSpoke com 2109 14th Ave San Francisco CA 94116-1862

TRASLER, GORDON BLAIR, criminologist, psychology educator; b. Bournemouth, Eng., Mar. 7, 1929; s. Frank Ferrier and Marian (Blair) T.; m. Kathleen Patricia Fegan, Sept. 19, 1953. BS, U. London, 1952, PhD, 1955; MA, U. Exeter, Eng., 1960. Chartered psychologist. Psychologist HM Prisons, Wandsworth, Winchester, Eng., 1955-57; lectr. U. Southampton, Eng., 1957-64, prof. psychology, 1964-94, emeritus prof., 1994—; Leverhulme rsch. fellow, 1995-98; chmn. Inst. for Study and Treatment of Delinquency, Eng., 1981-89, v.p., 1989—; mem. Adv. Com. Penal Sys., Eng., 1968-74. Author: In Place of Parents—A Study of Foster Care, 1960, The Explanation of Criminality, 1962; co-author: The Formative Years, 1968; co-editor: Behaviour Modification with Offenders, 1980; editor: Brit. Jour. Criminology, 1980-85; contbr. numerous articles to profl. jours. Justice of the Peace, Southampton, 1978—; chief scientist's advisor Dept. Health, 1977-85; mem. Winchester Health Authority, Eng., 1981-87. Fellow Brit. Psychol. Soc. (chmn. divsn. criminol. and legal psychology 1980-83); mem. Am. Soc. Criminology (Sellin-Glueck award 1990). Home: Fox Croft Old Kennels Ln, So22 4JT Winchester England Office: U Southampton, Dept Psychology, S017 1BJ Southampton England

TRAUB, J(OSEPH) F(REDERICK), computer scientist, educator; b. June 24, 1932; m. Pamela Ann McCorduck, Dec. 6, 1969; children: Claudia Renee, Hillary Anne. BS, CCNY, 1954; PhD, Columbia U., 1959. Tech. staff Bell Labs., Murray Hill, N.J., 1959-70; prof. computer sci. and math., head dept. computer sci. Carnegie-Mellon U., Pitts., 1971-79; Edwin Howard Armstrong prof. computer sci., chmn. dept., prof. math. Columbia U., 1979-86; prof. computer sci. Princeton (N.J.) U., 1986-87; pres. John Von Neumann Nat. Supercomputer Ctr., Consortium for Sci. Computing, Princeton, 1986-87; Edwin Howard Armstrong prof., chmn. dept. computer sci., prof. math. Columbia U., N.Y.C., 1987-89, Edwin Howard Armstrong prof. computer sci., math., 1989—; external prof. Santa Fe Inst., 1995-98; fellow Biosgroup, 1998—; dir. N.Y. State Ctr. Computers and Info. Systems, 1982-88; disting. lectr. MIT, 1977; vis. Mackay prof. U. Calif., Berkeley, 1978-79; cons. Hewlett-Packard, 1982, IBM, 1984, Schlumberger, 1986, Signet Bank, 1994, Lucent Techs., 1996, Bios Group, 1998—; mem. pres.'s adv. com. computer sci. Stanford U., 1972-75, chmn., 1975-76; adv. com. Fed. Jud. Center; mem. sci. council I.R.I.A., Paris, 1976-80; central steering com., computing sci. and engring. research study NSF, also liaison to panel on theoretical computer sci. and panel on numerical comp., 1974-80; mem. adv. com. Carnegie-Mellon Inst. Research, 1978-79; mem. applied math. div. rev. com. Argonne Nat. Lab., 1973-75; mem. adv. com. math. and computer sci. NSF, 1978-80; chmn. computer sci. and tech. bd. NRC, 1986-90; chmn. computer sci. and telecommunications bd. NRC, 1990-92; trustee Columbia U. Press, 1983-85; founding chair Spl. Interest Group on Numerical Math., 1965-71. Author: Iterative Methods for the Solution of Equations, 1964, Russian edit., 1985; (with H. Wozniakowski) A General Theory of Optimal Algorithms, 1980, Russian edit., 1983, Chelsea, 1998; (with G. Wasilkowski and H. Wozniakowski) Information, Uncertainty, Complexity, 1983, Information-Based Complexity, 1988; (with A.G. Werschulz) Complexity and Information, 1998; editor: Complexity of Sequential and Parallel Numerical Algorithms, 1973, Analytic Computational Complexity, 1976, Algorithms and Complexity: New Directions and Recent Results, 1976, Jour. Assn. Computing Machinery, 1970-76, Transactions on Math. Software, 1974-76, Jour. Computer and Sys. Scis., 1973-86, Internat. Jour. on Computers and Math. with Applications, 1974—, Cohabiting With Computers, 1985; (with P. Hut and D. Ruelle) Fundamental Sources of Unpredictability, 1997; founding editor Jour. Complexity, 1985—, Ann. Rev. Computer Sci., 1986-92; assoc. editor Complexity, 1995—. Sherman Fairchild Disting. scholar Calif. Inst. Tech., 1991, 92; recipient Award for Disting. Svc. to Computing Rsch. Computer Rsch. Assn., 1992, Lezione Lincee Acad. Nazionale dei Lincei, 1993, Sr. Scientist award Alexander Von Humboldt Found., 1992-98, City of N.Y. Mayor's award for excellence in sci. and tech., 1999. Fellow AAAS (coun. 1971-74), ACM (chmn. award com. 1974-76), N.Y. Acad. Scis.; mem. IEEE (Emanuel R. Piore Gold medal 1991), NAE (membership com. for computer sci., elec. engring. and control 1986-87, membership com. for computer sci. and engring. 1987-91, presdl. search com. 1993-94), Conf. Bd. Math. Scis. (coun. 1971-74), Soc. Indsl. and Applied Math., Am. Math. Soc. E-mail: traub@cs.columbia.edu. Office: Columbia University Dept Computer Sci 1214 Amsterdam Ave #MC0401 New York NY 10027-7003

TRAUB, LANCE WAYNE, research engineer, lecturer; b. Johannesburg, South Africa, May 11, 1968; came to U.S., 1994; m. Angela Amber Traub, Aug. 8, 1998. BSc, U. Witwatersrand, South Africa, 1989, MSc, 1992; PhD, Tex. A&M U., 1999. Rsch. engr. U. Witwatersrand, Johannesburg, 1992-94; rsch. asst. Tex. A&M U., College Station, 1994-98, rsch. assoc., lectr., 1999—; cons. Drytech Pty. Ltd., Johannesburg, 1980-94. Contbr. articles to profl. jours. Regents Grad. fellow Tex. A&M U., 1994-95; grantee U. Witwatersrand, 1989-92, Found. for R&D, 1989-92. Mem. AIAA, Royal Aero. Soc. Avocations: archery, plastic modelling. E-mail: LWT3904@vms.tamu.edu. Home: 1508 Arctic Cir College Station TX 77840-4443 Office: Tex A&M U 701 Hr Bright Bldg College Station TX 77843-0001

TRAUBE, CHARLES, internist, cardiologist; b. Bklyn., Oct. 18, 1950; s. Abraham and Helen (Halpern) T.; m. Shoshana Gerstner, June 3, 1973; children: Chani, Elie, Adeena. BS in Math. summa cum laude, Bklyn. Coll., 1972; MD, Albert Einstein Coll. of Medicine, 1975. Diplomate in internal medicine, cardiology, geriatrics Am. Bd. Internal Medicine. Intern Brookdale Hosp. Med. Ctr., Bklyn., 1975-76, resident, 1976-78, resident in internal medicine, 1977-78, resident in cardiology, 1978-79, fellow in cardiology, 1979-80, asst. dir. med. ICU, attending cardiologist; asst. clin. prof. SUNY, Bklyn. Contbr. articles to profl. jours. Fellow N.Y. Cardiol. Soc.; mem. AMA, ACP. Democrat. Jewish. Address: 2270 Kimball St Ste 210 Brooklyn NY 11234-5139 Home: 11 Rolling Hill Ln Lawrence NY 11559-1507

TRAUE, JAMES EDWARD, library science educator; b. Auckland, New Zealand, Feb. 10, 1932; s. Albert and Evelin (Webb) T.; m. Julia Margaret Bergen, Apr. 19, 1973. MA, U. New Zealand, 1956. Libr. Nat. Libr. Svc., New Zealand, 1957-61; from reference libr. to asst. chief libr. Gen. Assembly Libr., New Zealand, 1962-71; chief libr. Dept. Scientific & Indsl. Rsch., New Zealand, 1971-73, Alexander Turnbull Libr., New Zealand, 1973-90; tchg. fellow Victoria U. Wellington, New Zealand, 1990-98, sr. assoc., 1998—; fgn. specialist Legis. Reference Svc., Libr. Congress, Washington, 1965-66. Author: New Zealand Studies: A Guide to Bibliographic Resources, 1985, Committed to Print, 1991; editor: Who's Who in New Zealand, 1978. Convener Friends of Wellington Pub. Libr., 1996—. Fellow New Zealand Libr. Assn. Office: Victoria U Sch Comms Info, Mgmt PO Box 600, Wellington 6001, New Zealand

TRAUNG, JAN-OLOF, naval architect; b. Goteborg, Bohuslan, Sweden, Apr. 8, 1919; s. Olof Sven Teodor and Ellen Katarina Hogstrom T.; m. Annastina Vilhelmina Borglund, Nov. 27, 1943 (wid. Oct. 1980); 1 child, Anna; m. Evelyn Marianne Lindgren, Aug. 10, 1985. Diploma, Ingenieurschule Mittweida, Germany, 1939. Chartered engr. Brit. Coun. Engring. Instns. Naval architect, tech. mgr. AB Sverre, 1939-50; chief naval architect and fleet mgr. FAO/UN, 1950-76; sr. ptnr. Traung & Assocs./Marine Cons. HB, 1976—; mem. fisheries adv. com. Swedish Internat. Devel. Authority, 1976-82; chmn. Swedish Fedn. of Boat Surveyors, 1987-90, dir. 1991-96. Editor: Fishing Boats of the World, Vols. 1-3; contbr. numerous articles to profl. jours. and publs. Bd. dirs. Nordic Assn. Former Internat. Civil Servants, Copenhagen, Denmark, 1994-97. Mem. Royal Instn. Naval Architects, Soc. Naval Architects and Marine Engrs., Swedish Engrs. Assn., Swedish Fedn. of Yacht Surveyors, Royal Goteborg Yacht Club, Swedish Cruising Assn. Avocation: sailing. Home: Nonnensgatan 3C, S-412 72 Göteborg Bohuslan, Sweden

TRAUPE, HEIKO, dermatologist, educator; b. Nordhorn, Germany, Aug. 20, 1951; s. August Friedrich and Marie Auguste (Eicke) T. MD, Sch. Medicine, Muenster, Germany, 1978. Bd. cert. dermatologist Chamber of Physicians, Westphalia and Lippe. Resident U. Muenster, 1978-84, dermatologist, 1984-88, assoc. prof., 1992—; bd. dirs. European Soc. Pediat. Dermatology, 1987-96, Arbeits Gemeinschaft Paediatric Dermatologie, 1992—. Author: The Ichthyoses, 1989 (Springer), Paediatrische Dermatologie, 1999 (Springer); mem. adv. bd. Dermatology, 1992—. Heisenberg fellow German Rsch. Coun., 1988-92; recipient Gottron Just Scientific award U. Ulm and City of Ulm, 1987. Mem. Am. Soc. Human Genetics, German Dermatol. Soc., German Soc. Human Genetics. Avocations: theater, travel. E-mail: traupeh@uni-muenster.de. Office: U Muenster Dept Dermatology, Von Esmarch Str 56, 48149 Münster Germany

TRAUTMAN, DONALD W., bishop; b. Buffalo, June 24, 1936. Ed., Our Lady of Angels Sem., Niagara Falls, N.Y., Theology Faculty, Innsbruck, Austria, Pontifical Biblical Inst., Rome, Cath. U., St. Thomas Aquinas U., Rome. Ordained priest Roman Cath. Ch., 1962, consecrated bishop, 1985. Titular bishop of Sassura and aux. bishop Diocese of Buffalo, 1985; bishop Erie, Pa., 1990—; episc. moderator Diocesan Fiscal Mgmt. Conf.; mem. com. for review of scripture translations; past mem. Prolife com. doctrine and migration Nat. Conf. Cath. Bishops; past chmn. Bishop's Liturgy Com. Home: 205 W 9th St Erie PA 16501-1304 Address: St Mark's Ctr PO Box 10397 Erie PA 16514-0397

TRAUTMANN, NORBERT GÜNTER, chemist; b. Straubing, Bavaria, Germany, Aug. 5, 1939; s. Nikolaus Michael and Emma (Sauer) T.; m. Ute Peter, May 16, 1968; children: Petra Christine, Karin Ingrid. Diploma, U. Mainz, Fed. Republic Germany, 1964, D in Nat. Scis., 1968. Sci. asst. U. Mainz, 1965-70, dep. mgr., 1971-90, mgr., 1991—; postdoctoral fellow Lawrence Berkeley (Calif.) Lab., 1970-71. Contbr. articles to profl. jours. Recipient Fritz-Strassmann award German Chem. Soc., 1984, Helmholtz award Physikalisch-Technische Bundesanstalt, 1990, Otto-Hahn award City of Frankfurt, 1998. Avocation: wine tasting. Home: Carl Orff Strasse 31, D-55127 Mainz Germany Office: U Inst Kernchemie, Fritz Strassmann Weg 2, D-55128 Mainz Germany

TRAUTWEIN, ALFRED XAVER, biophysics educator; b. Neu-Ulm, Bavaria, Germany, Nov. 5, 1940; s. Franz Xaver and Franziska T.; m. Hildegard Gertrude Kunkelmann, Aug., 1988; children: Hanno Franz-Georg, Florian. Diploma in Physics, Tech. U., Munich, Germany, 1967, PhD in Physics, 1969. Prof. physics U. Saarbrücken, Germany, 1973-80; prof. physics Med. U. Lübeck, Germany, 1980—, vice-rector, 1996—; sec. German Biophys. Soc., 1995—. Recipient (with R. Weiss) Max Planck prize A.v. Humboldt Found., 1994, Gay-Lussac prize French Nat. Ministry for Edn., Rsch. and Tech., 1999. Mem. Soc. Biol. Inorganic Chemistry (pres. 2000—), Rotary. Office: Inst Physik Medizinische U, Ratzeburger Allee 160, D-23538 Lübeck Germany

TRAVAGLINI, JOSEPH, educational consultant; b. Phila., Sept. 17, 1932; m. Marilyn Irene Gordon, Dec. 26, 1956; children: Mark D., David H. BSBA, Drexel U., 1955; M of Govtl. Adminstrn., U. Pa., 1960; PhD, U. Md., 1974. Dir. personnel svcs. Antioch Coll., Yellow Springs, Ohio, 1960-65; mgr. adminstrv. svcs. U. Chgo., 1965-66; asst. bur. chief Pa. State Dept. Edn., Harrisburg, 1966-67; asst. to pres. Essex C.C., Baltimore County, Md., 1967-75; program mgr. individualized degree programs Ctrl. Mich. U., Mt. Pleasant, 1975-88; dean grad. and external programs Coll. Santa Fe, 1988-89; assoc. dean, dir. The Union Inst., San Diego Ctr., Cin., 1989-92; ednl. cons. San Diego, 1993—; co-chair accreditation study Essex C.C., 1969-70; team leader program learning seminar U. Mich., Ann Arbor, 1982; reviewer Calif. Postsecondary Edn. Commn., Sacramento, 1990-91; cons. to pres. La Jolla U., San Diego, 1993. Author: (chpt.) Personalized Instruction in Education Today, 1970; co-author: (chpt.) The University and the Inner City, 1980. Pres. Joppatowne (Md.) Civic Assoc., 1969-74; county coun. candidate Harford County, Bel Air, Md., 1974; alumni amb. Drexel U., Phila., 1997—; vol. auditor Balboa Pk. Japanese Friendship Garden, San Diego, 1995—. With U.S. Army, 1955-57. Recipient Samuel S. Fels scholarship U. Pa., 1958-60, fellowship U. Colo., 1968. Mem. Wharton Alumni Club So. Calif., Sierra Club, World Wildlife Fund, Nature Conservancy, Phi Delta Kappa (emeritus). Democrat. Avocations: environment, international travel, jogging, music, politics. Home: 3375 Date St San Diego CA 92102-1635

TRAVELSTEAD, CHESTER COLEMAN, former educational administrator; b. Franklin, Ky., Sept. 25, 1911; s. Conley and Nelle (Gooch) T.; m. Marita Hawley, Aug. 1, 1936; children—Coleman, Jimmie. A.B., Western Ky. State Coll., Bowling Green, 1933; M.Music, Northwestern U., 1947; Ph.D., U. Ky., 1950; D.Hum., Morehead (Ky.) State U., 1975; Ph.D., John F. Kennedy U., Buenos Aires, 1975; LHD, U. N.Mex., 1980. Tchr., prin. rural and consol. schs. Mecklenberg County, Va., 1931-32, 33-35; tchr. gen. sci., math., music Picadome High Sch., Lexington, Ky., 1935-37; dir. music Henry Clay High Sch., Lexington, 1937-42; personnel supr. Lexington Signal Dept., Dept. War, 1942-43; supr. music Lexington pub. schs., 1945-47; rep. Investors Diversified Services, Inc., 1947-48; coordinator in-service tchr. edn. Ky. Dept. Edn., 1950-51; asst. prof. edn., asst. dean Coll. Edn., U. Ga., Athens, 1951-53; dean Sch. Edn., U. S.C., Columbia, 1953-56; dean Coll. Edn. U. N.Mex., Albuquerque, 1956-68; v.p. acad. affairs U. N.Mex., 1968-76, provost, 1976-77; Mem. Nat. Council Accreditation Tchr. Edn., 1960-66, chmn., 1963-65. Author books; contbr. articles in field to profl. jours. Pres. bd. dirs. N.Mex. Symphony Orch., 1977-78, 84-85; treas. U.S. Senator Jeff Bingaman's re-election campaign, 1988-93; mem. N.Mex. Jud. Stds. Commn., 1995-96. With USNR, 1943-45; PTO. Mem. AAUP, NEA, Nat. Soc. Study Edn., Soc. Advancement Edn., Phi Kappa Phi, Phi Delta Kappa., Kappa Delta Pi. Home: Montebello # 128 10500 Academy Rd NE Albuquerque NM 87111-7306

TRAVERS, NOEL JOSEPH, lawyer, lecturer, legal advisor; b. Dublin, Ireland, Aug. 25, 1967; arrived in Luxembourg, 1995; m. Elizabeth Theodora McCullagh, Sept. 4, 1992. BCL, Univ. Coll., Dublin, 1987, LLM, 1989; M in Advanced European Legal Studies, Bruges, Belgium, 1990; Barrister of Law degree, Kings Inns, Dublin, 1991. Bar: Ireland, Trinity term 1991. Lectr. law Univ. Coll. Dublin, 1990-95, assoc. dean Faculty Law, 1992-95; legal adviser (referendaire) to Adv. Gen. Fennelly Ct. of Justice of European Cmty., Luxembourg City, Luxembourg, 1995—; corr. European Law Rev., Sweet & Maxwell, Eng., 1995—. Cons. editor Irish Competition Law Reports, Baikonur, 1995—; contbr. articles and revs. to profl. publs. Mem. Bar of Ireland. Avocations: tennis, reading, jogging. Office: Ct of Justice of Euro Cmty, Chambers Adv Gen Fennelly, L-2925 Luxembourg Luxembourg

TRAVERS, VINCENT MARIE GEORGES, surgeon; b. Clermont, Ferrand, France, Aug. 13, 1957; s. Georges and Yvette (Tremblin) T.; m. Nicole Rosenstrauch, Oct. 17, 1980 (div. Nov. 1999); children: Camille, Thibault. MD, Necker U., Paris, 1986. Intern Hopitaux de Paris, 1980-86; chef de clinique St. Antoine Hosp., Paris, 1986-89; rsch. mgr. Health Ministry, Hiroshima, Japan, 1986; orthopedic surgeon Clinique du Parc, Lyon, France, 1989—; chmn. Performing Art Med. Ctr., Lyon, 1995—; pres. Internat. Congress on Art and Medicine, Lyon, 1996. Mem. Municipality of Lyon, 1995—. Officer French Mil., W.I., 1983-84. Mem. French Hand Surgery Soc., European Soc. for Shoulder and Elbow Surgery, Group for Study of Orthopaedic Surgery, N.Y. Acad. Scis. Avocation: piano. Office: Clinique du Parc, 86 Blvd des Belges, 69006 Lyon France

TRAVIESO, LISSETTE, chemical engineer, researcher; b. La Habana, Cuba, Apr. 8, 1950; d. Felix J. and Abigail (Cordoba) Travieso; m. Jose Manuel Astudillo, July 14, 1972; 1 child, Annette; m. Enrique Pablo Sanchez, May 5, 1990. Chem.Engr., Polytech. Superior Inst. "Jose A. Echevarria", La Habana, 1973; MSc, B.C. U., Vancouver, Can., 1978; PhD, Superior Sch., Prague, Czech Republic, 1983. Head microalgae lab. Divsn. Environ. Pollution Studies-Nat. Ctr. Sci. Rsch., La Habana, 1974—; tech. Ctr. Advanced Studies and Rsch., Mexico City, 1985-95; advisor various orgns. and ministries, Cuba, 1978—; cons. cons. Environ. Consulting Divsn., Inversiones Gamma S.A., 1999—. Contbr. articles to profl. jours.; patentee in field. Fellow N.Y. Acad. Scis.; mem. InterAm. Assn. Sanitary Engrs. Avocation: swimming. Home and Office: Calle 23 No 802, Esq B Vedado, Havana Cuba

TRAVIS, ALICE DIMERY, journalist; b. Kingstree, S.C., Sept. 23, 1943; d. Virgil Cornelius Dimery and Mary Agnes (Fassitt) Dimery-Murphy; m. William Daniel Travis, Sept. 9, 1967 (div. July 1973); m. Antonio Maugeri, Oct. 30, 1980; 1 child, Alexander Virgil. AB in Sociology, Immaculata Coll., 1965; postgrad., U. Pa., 1965-66, Temple U., 1966-69. Staff technician, mgmt. trainee Bell Telephone Co. of Pa., Phila., 1965-68; dir. tng. comprehensive health svcs. Temple U., Phila., 1968-70; co-host Panorama Metromedia TV, Washington, 1970-73; co-host AM New York ABC TV/WABC, N.Y.C., 1973-75; rsch. cons. Paterson, Michael, Jones, London, 1975-76; host Gerber Carter Comm., N.Y.C., 1977-78; comm. cons. Alice Travis, Inc., N.Y.C., 1976-88; rsch. journalist Mahopac Falls, N.Y., 1988—; comm. cons. J. Ray McDermott, Bell Labs., 1977—; tng. analyst Ciba Geigy, Hooker Chem., 1988. Author: Cognitive Evolution: The Biological Imprint of Applied Intelligence, 1995; moderator 26 programs, You series, U.S. Dept. HEW, 1972, 73; host, creator spl. programming People, 1973. Recipient Annie E. Gorman award in sociology Immaculata Coll., 1965, Comm. award Inst. Fgn. Svc., U.S. Dept. State, 1971, media awards Fed. Editors Assn., 1973, Am. Women in Radio and TV, 1973, AAUW, 1975; named Media Woman of the Yr., Nat. Assn. Media Women, 1978, numerous others; keys to cities of Savannah, Ga., West Orange, N.J. Roman Catholic. Avocations: fashion designing, real estate development. Office: PO Box 365 Mahopac Falls NY 10542-0365

TRAVIS, JOYCE MARIE, real estate executive; b. Lamar, Colo., Jan. 29, 1947; d. Morris Eugene and Mildred Marie (Neary) T.; m. Richard d. Copess, Sept. 19, 1970 (divorced). BA in Tech. Journalism, Colo. State U., 1969; postgrad., U. No. Colo., 1969-72, Ill. State U., 1976-81. Editor, mgr. State Farm Ins., Bloomington, Ill., 1972-82; staff v.p. Inst. Real Estate Mgmt., Chgo., 1982—. Mem. ASTD, Am. Soc. Assn. Execs., Pub. Rels. Soc. Am. Office: Inst Real Estate Mgmt 430 N Michigan Ave Chicago IL 60611-4011

TRAVIS, SIMON P.L., gastroenterologist; b. Harford, Devon, Eng., Mar. 27, 1958. MB, BS, St. Thomas Hosp., London, 1981; DPhil, Oxford (Eng.) U., 1992. Resident St. Thomas Hosp., London, 1981-82; lectr. Oxford U., Oxford, 1988-91; sr. registrar John Radcliffe Hosp., Oxford, 1991-94; cons. Derriford Hosp., Plymouth, Eng., 1994—; jr. rsch. fellow Linacre Coll., Oxford, 1989. Author: Gastroenterology, 1992, 2d edit., 1998; contbr. articles to profl. jours. Lt. comdr. Royal Navy, 1982-87. Fellow Royal Coll. Physicians. Avocations: mountaineering, sailing, family.

TRAWINSKI, DAVID LEE, aerospace engineer; b. Balt., Mar. 25, 1959; s. Leon Stanislaus and Mildred Trawinski; m. Janice Diane Conigliaro, Oct. 2, 1982 (div.); m. Elizabeth Marie Ford, July 2, 1994. BS in Chemistry, Towson State U., 1982; M in Engring. Sci., Loyola Coll., Balt., 1985, exec. MBA fellow, 1990. Various engring. positions Martin Marietta, Balt., 1981-85, corp. tech. ops. intern, 1985-86, sr. group engr., 1986-87, mgr. material and process engrs., 1987-91; mgr. comml. aero structures programs Martin Marietta, 1991-95; F-22 Materials and Processes engring. mgr. Lockheed Martin Aeronautical Systems, Marietta, Ga. Contbr. articles to profl. jours. Mem. AIAA, Soc. Advanced Materials and Process Engrs. (sec. Balt., Washington chpt. 1987-88, treas. 1988-89, vice chair 1989-90, chmn. 1990-92, ATL chpt. 1998), Materials Engrs. Assocs. (pres. 1990-91), Group Nine Videography (pres. 1990-98). Republican. Roman Catholic. Avocations: videography, golf, rugby, tennis. Home: 4192 Gramercy Main Kennesaw GA 30144-6170 Office: Lockheed Martin Aeronautical Svcs Co 86 S Cobb Dr Marietta GA 30063-0001

TRAYHURN, PAUL, research biologist, educator; b. Exeter, England, May 6, 1948; s. William and Eileen (Morphew) T.; m. Deborah Gigg; four children. BSc, U. Reading, Eng., 1969; DPhil, U. Oxford, Eng., 1972, DSc, 1995. Rsch. staff Med. Rsch. Coun., Cambridge, Eng., 1975-86; prof., heritage scholar U. Alta., Edmonton, Can., 1986-88; head divsn. biochem. scis. Rowett Rsch. Inst., Aberdeen, 1988-97, asst. dir. acad. affairs, 1997-2000; prof. U. Aberdeen, 1992-2000; prof. Inst. Nutrition Rsch., U. Oslo, Norway, 2000—. Co-editor: Brown Adipose Tissue, 1986; editor-in-chief Brit. Jour. Nutrition, 1999—; contbr. articles to profl. jours. Fellow Royal Soc. Edinburgh; mem. AAAS, Biochem. Soc., Nutrition Soc., Physiol. Soc. Office: PO Box 1046 Inst Nutr Rsch, U Oslo, N 0316 Oslo Norway

TRAYLOR, DONALD REGINALD, mathematics educator; b. Shreveport, La., Aug. 14, 1937; s. Guy Kirby and Eva (Hunt) T.; m. Jacqueline Rose Pearson, June 4, 1959; children: Chapman Parker, Kirby Russell, Pearson Hunt. BA, U. Tex., 1959; MS, Auburn U., 1960, PhD, 1962. Asst. prof. Auburn (Ala.) U., 1962-63; asst. prof. U. Houston, 1963-66, assoc. prof., 1966-71; pres., prof. U. Houston, Victoria, 1972-77; fellow Am. Coun. on Edn., Washington, 1971-72; pres. Traylor Products & Svcs., San Antonio, 1977-90; prof. math. U. of the Incarnate Word, San Antonio, 1990—, interim v.p. acad. affairs, 1993-95, acting dean Sch. Math., Nursing and Sci., 1995-96, dean Sch. Grad. Studies and Rsch., 1996—, v.p. for extended acad. programs, 1999—; mem. adv. coun. Auburn U., 1966-96, St. Mary's U., San Antonio, 1978-85. Author: Advanced Calculus, 1970, Creative Teaching: Heritage of R.L. moore, 1972; editor: Proceedings of Topology Conference, 1968; inventor tactile drawing and writing device. Grantee NASA, 1964, NSF, 1965-67, NIH, 1985-89, NSF and Eisenhower, 1992—. Office: U of the Incarnate Word 4301 Broadway St San Antonio TX 78209-6318

TRAYLOR, ROBERT ARTHUR, lawyer; b. Syracuse, N.Y., Jan. 15, 1949; s. Robert Arthur and Julia Elizabeth (McNulty) T.; m. Bonita Lynn Schmidt, Nov. 26, 1977. BS, LeMoyne Coll., 1970; JD cum laude, Syracuse U., 1975. Bar: N.Y., U.S. Dist. Ct. (no. dist.) N.Y., U.S. Tax Ct. Assoc. Love, Balducci & Scaccia, Syracuse, N.Y., 1976-77; estate tax atty. IRS, Syracuse, 1977-81; assoc. Scaccia Law Firm, Syracuse, 1981—. Contbr. articles to profl. jours. Of counsel St. Ann Sch., Syracuse, 1981—, mem. coordinating com. Vision 2000 1994—, mem. bd., 1998—. With U.S. Army, 1970-72. Mem. ABA, Onondaga County Bar Assn. (vol. lawyer program 1993—, Vol. Lawyer of Month 1994), World Wildlife Fedn. Republican. Roman Catholic. Avocations: motorsports, military history, Catholic education. Home: 112 Knowland Dr Liverpool NY 13090-3130 Office: Scaccia Law Firm State Tower Bldg Ste 402 Syracuse NY 13202-1798

TRAYLOR, WILLIAM ROBERT, publisher; b. Texarkana, Ark., May 21, 1921; s. Clarence Edington and Seba Ann (Talley) T.; m. Elvirez Sigler, Oct. 9, 1945; children: Kenneth Warren, Gary Robert, Mark Daniel, Timothy Ryan. Student, U. Houston, 1945-46, U. Omaha, 1947-48. Div. mgr. Lily-Tulip Cup Corp., N.Y.C., 1948-61; asst. to pres. Johnson & Johnson, New Brunswick, N.J., 1961-63; mgr. western region Rexall Drug & Chem. subs. Dart Industries, L.A., 1963-67; pres. Prudential Pub. Co., Diamonds Springs, Calif., 1967—; cons. to printing industry, 1976-98; syndicated writer (under pseudonym)s. Bill Friday's Bus. Bull., 1989—. Author: Instant Printing, 1976 (transl. into Japanese), Successful Management, 1979, Quick Printing Encyclopedia, 1982, 8th edit., 1998, How to Sell Your Product Through (Not to) Wholesalers, 1980; pubr. Professional Estimator and Management Software for Printing Industry, 1997, Small Press Printing Encyclopedia, 1994. With USCG, 1942-45. Named Man of Yr. Quick Printing Mag., 1987. Mem. Nat. Assn. Quick Printers (hon. lifetime), C. of C., Kiwanis, Toastmasters. Democrat. Avocations: snow skiing, boating.

TRAYNELIS, STEPHEN FRANCIS, neuroscientist, educator; b. South Bend, Ind., Mar. 3, 1962; s. Vincent John and Elaine Anne T.; m. Janice Faye Jernigan, Nov. 26, 1988; children: Joshua Laine, Ruth Anne, James Vincent. BS in Chemistry summa cum laude, W.Va. U., 1984; PhD in Pharmacology, U. N.C., 1988. Postdoct. rsch. dept. pharmacology U. Coll. London, 1989-91; postdoct. rsch. molecular neurobiology lab. Salk Inst., La Jolla, Calif., 1992-94; asst. prof. dept. pharmacology Emory U., Atlanta, 1994—; mem. grant rev. bds., ad hoc grant revs. including Civilian Rsch. and Def. Found., 1996-97, pvt. and English granting agys., 1996; lectr., seminars SFB Kolloquium, Goettingen, 1995, Ciba-Geigy, Basel, Switzerland, 1995, SIBIA, Inc., La Jolla, 1995, Rush U., Chgo., 1995, NIH, 1996, NYU, 1996, U. Minn., 1997, Cornell U., Yale U., 1999, Agora for Biosys., Sigtuna, Sweden, 1999, CNRS Caen France, Montpelier, France, 2000, L'Ecole Normale Supieure, France, 2000, other univs., corps. Mem. editl. bd. Molecular Pharmacology; ontbr. numerous manuscripts, abstracts, articles to scientific jours.; developer Modified Diffusional analysis softwared, 1988, Synaptic Analysis Software, 1991-94, Ion Channel Kinetic Modeling Software, 1996—, Synaptic/single channel modeling-Analysis Software "NPM", 1996—. Recipient Nat. Rsch. Svc. award NIH, 1989, 90, 92; predoctoral fellow NSF, 1984, fellow Am. Epilepsy Soc., 1993, John Merck Fund, 1995-99, Emory U. Tchg. Fund, 1997, John Merck scholar, 1995, John Moore Chemistry scholar, 1980, W.Va. Achievement scholar, 1980;

grantee Univ. Rsch. Com., 1994, 99, Epilepsy Found. Am., 1995, NIH-NINDS, 1995, 96, 98, 2000, Emory U. Rsch. Com., 1995; recipient travel awards Wellcome Trust, Brain Trust Am. Epilepsy Soc., 1990-94, Burroughs-Wellcome travel award, 1998, Ind. Investigators award, NARSAD. Mem. AAAS, Am. Soc. Pharmacology and Exptl. Therapeutics, Biophys. Soc., Soc. Neurosci. (councilor exec. com. Atlanta chpt. 1995-96, pres. Atlanta chpt. 1997), A.S.P.E.T., Phi Beta Kappa, Phi Kappa Phi, Golden Key. Office: Emroy U Dept Pharmacology 1510 Clifton Rd NE Atlanta GA 30322-4218

TRAYNOR, JOHN MICHAEL, lawyer; b. Oakland, Calif., Oct. 25, 1934; s. Roger J. and Madeleine (Lackmann) T.; m. Shirley Williams, Feb. 11, 1956; children: Kathleen Traynor Millard, Elizabeth Traynor Fowler, Thomas. BA, U. Calif., Berkeley, 1955; JD, Harvard U., 1960. Bar: Calif. 1961, U.S. Supreme Ct. 1966. Dep. atty. gen. State of Calif., San Francisco, 1961-63; spl. counsel Calif. Senate Com. on Local Govt., Sacramento, 1963; assoc. firm Cooley Godward, LLP, San Francisco, 1963-69, ptnr., 1969—; adviser 3d Restatement of Unfair Competition, 1988-95, 3d Restatement of Torts; Products Liability, 1992-97, Apportionment, 1994-99, 1988 Revs. 2d Restatement of Conflict of Laws, 3rd Restatement of Restitution, 1997—; lectr. U. Calif. Boalt Hall Sch. Law, Berkeley, 1982-89, 1996-98; chmn. EarthJustice Legal Def. Fund (formerly Sierra Club Legal Defense Fund), 1989-91, pres. 1991-92, trustee, 1974-96. Mem. bd. overseers Inst. for Civil Justice The RAND Corp., 1991-97; bd. dirs. Environ. Law Inst., 1991-97, 00—, Sierra Legal Def. Fund (Can.), 1990-96. Served to 1st lt. USMC, 1955-57. Fellow AAAS, Am. Bar Found. (life); mem. Am. Law Inst. (coun. 1985—, 2d v.p. 1993-98, 1st v.p. 1998—, pres. designate, 1999—), Bar Assn. San Francisco (pres. 1973). Home: 3131 Eton Ave Berkeley CA 94705-2713 Office: Cooley Godward LLP 1 Maritime Plz Ste 2000 San Francisco CA 94111-3510

TRBOJEVIC, VLADIMIR MILAN, risk analyst and safety engineer; b. Belgrade, Yugoslavia, Mar. 21, 1944; s. Milan Dane and Krunica (Pantic) T.; m. Dusanka Djuric, June 16, 1977; children: Ana, Milan. Dipl.Ing., Faculty of Mech. Engring., Belgrade, 1967; DIC, MSc, Imperial Coll., London, 1970, PhD, 1976. Rsch. asst. Imperial Coll., London, 1970-71; teaching asst. Faculty of Mech. Engring., Belgrade, 1971-78; rsch. analyst Atkins Rsch. & Devel., Epsom, U.K., 1978-79; sr. engr. Dames & Moore, London, 1979; sr. engr. Principia Mechanica Ltd., London, 1980-81, dir., 1981-85; prin. engr. Technica Ltd., London, 1985-89; dir. Four Elements Ltd., London, 1989-98, EQE Internat., London, 1998—. Contbr. articles to profl. jours. Mem. ASME. Avocations: tennis, skiing. Home: 88 Kingwood Rd, London SW6 6SS, England Office: Four Elements Ltd, EQE Internat Ltd, 18 Mansell St, London E1 8AA, England

TREACY, SANDRA JOANNE PRATT, art educator, artist; b. New Haven, Aug. 5, 1934; d. Willis Hadley Jr. and Gladys May (Gell) P.; m. Gillette van Nuyse, Aug. 27, 1955; 1 child, Jonathan Todd. BFA, R.I. Sch. Design, 1956; student, William Paterson Coll., 1973-74. Cert. elem. and secondary tchr., N.J. Tchr. art and music Pkwy. Christian Ch., Ft. Lauderdale, Fla., 1964-66; developer Pequannock Twp. Bd. of Edn., Pompton Plains, N.J., 1970-72, tchr. art, 1972-76; vol. art tchr. Person County Bd. of Edn., Roxboro, N.C., 1978-80, tchr. art, 1980-91; tchr. art So. Jr. High Sch., Roxboro, 1989-91, Woodland Elem. Sch., Roxboro, 1989-93; tchr. Helena Elem. Sch., Timberlake, N.C., 1991-93; tchr. elem. art Bethel Hill Sch., Roxboro, 1974-79, vol. art tchr., 1979-80; tchr. basic art, vol. all elem. schs. Person County, Roxboro, 1977-80; tchr. arts and crafts, summers 1981-882; tchr. art home sch. So. Mid. Sch., 1993—, Person H.S., 1993-94. Artist, illustrator. Mem. Roxboro EMTs, 1979-81; bd. dirs. Person County Arts Coun., 1980--81, 93-95, pres., 1981-82; piano and organ choir accompanist Concord United Meth. Ch., 1981—; leader Morgan Trotters, 1992-94, asst. dir., 1993-96, bd. dirs.; mem. Roxboro Cmty. Choir, 1994—; coach, horseback riding for handicapped. Mem. NEA, Nat. Mus. of Women in the Arts (continuing charter), Smithsonian Assocs., N.C. Assn. Arts Edn., N.C. Assn. Educators, N.C. Art Soc. Mus. of Art, Internat. Platform Assn., Womans Club (tchr. Pompton Plains chpt. 1974-79), Person County Saddle Club (rec. sec. 1981-84), Puddingston Pony Club (dist. sec. 1974-75), Roxboro Garden Club (continuing, commr. 1980-82, pres. 1982-84, 87—, sec. 1993-94, 97-98, v.p. 1993-95, pres. 1995—), Roxboro Woman's Club (arts dept.). Republican. Avocations: horseback riding, swimming, sailing, reading, playing piano and organ. Home: 1345 Kelly Brewer Rd Leasburg NC 27291-9622

TREACY, WILLIAM JOSEPH, electrical and environmental engineer; b. N.Y.C., Jan. 16, 1959; s. William Joseph and Angela Bridget (Keane) T.; m. Tamra Jeanne Ackerman, Dec. 7, 1985; 1 child, Denise Marie. BSEE, Manhattan Coll., 1981; M in Aero. Sci., Embry-Riddle U., 1987. Registered profl. engr., N.Y. Commd. 2d lt. USAF, 1981, advanced through grades to capt.; project mgr. USAF, Victorville, Calif., 1981-84; dept. chief Netherlands GLCM program office USAF, Ramstein, Germany, 1984-88; chief engr. USAF, Soesterberg, The Netherlands, 1988-91; heavy repair supt. USAF, Plattsburgh, 1991-92; CFO USAF, Plattsburgh, N.Y., 1992-94, chief environ. engr., 1994-95; bldg. systems supr. Plattsburgh Airbase Redevel. Corp., 1995—; computer technician, Plattsburgh, 1992—. Active Red Cross, Plattsburgh, 1992. Decorated Meritorious Svc. medal, Air Force Commendation medal with one oak leaf cluster, others; USAF ROTC Program Acad. scholar, 1978. Mem. IEEE, ASHRAE, NSPE, Nat. Fire Protection Assn., Internat. Assn. Elec. Insps., Assn. for Facilities Engring., Aircraft Owners and Pilots Assn., Friends of Ft. Ticonderoga, Am. Legion. Republican. Roman Catholic. Avocations: flying, star trek memorabilia, cross-country skiing. Home: 60 Leonard Ave Plattsburgh NY 12901-2565 Office: Plattsburgh Airbase Redevel Corp 426 Us Oval Ste 1000 Plattsburgh NY 12903-3976

TREADWELL, ELIZABETH LORENE, writer, editor, educator; b. Oakland, Calif., May 9, 1967; d. Donald Duncan and Lujuana (Wolfe) T.; m. Paul Albert Jackson, June 5, 2000. BA, U. Calif., Berkeley, 1991; MFA, San Francisco State U., 1997. Editor, publ. Outlet mag., Double Lucy Books, Berkeley, 1997—; instr. Peralta C.C., San Francisco Bay Area, Calif., 1998—. Author: Eleanor Ramsey: The Queen of Cups, 1997, Eve Doe, 1997, The Erratix and Other Stories, 1998, Populace, 1999; contbr. stories, poems and criticism to numerous mags. Exec. dir. Small Press Traffic Lit. Arts Ctr., San Francisco, 2000—. Recipient Elizabeth Mills Crothers award U. Calif., Berkeley, 1991, Michael Rubin award San Francisco State U., 1997. Home: #B 1712 Martin Luther King Way Berkeley CA 94709 also: PO Box 9013 Berkeley CA 94709-0013

TREASURER, JAMES WATT, fish biologist; b. Aberdeen, Scotland, Dec. 19, 1951; s. John and Elsie Ann (Watt) T.; m. Wilma Gairn Sutherland, Aug. 28, 1974; children: Claire Marie, David James. BSc in Zoology with honors, U. Aberdeen, Scotland, 1974, PhD in Reproductive Biology, 1980; MPhil, Open U., Milton Keynes, U.K., 1990. Sci. asst. Dept. Agrl. Fisheries for Scotland, Aberdeen, 1974; health svcs. mgr. Nat. Health Svc., Aberdeen, 1978-89; dep. rsch. mgr. Marine Harvest, Lochailort, Scotland, 1989-93; fish health mgr. Marine Harvest Mcconnell, Lochailort, 1993—. Editor: Wrasse: Biology and Use in Aquaculture, 1986; contbr. over 70 publs. to profl. jours. Mem. Fisheries Soc. of Brit. Isles, Freshwater Biol. Assn., European Assn. Fish Pathologists. Avocations: coaching athletics and hockey, angling. Office: Marine Harvest, Lochailort PH38 4LZ, Scotland

TREBER, SALVADOR, economist, educator; b. Villa Libertad, Argentina, Apr. 4, 1931; s. Abraham and Sara (Fingerman) T.; m. Rosa Reznichenco, June 6, 1953; children: Graciela Ines, Adriana Alicia, Gabriela Liliana. Degree in econs. sci., U. Nacional Córdoba, Argentina, 1954. CPA. Adj. prof. econs. U. Nacional Córdoba, 1958-61, commd. prof. econs., 1961-70, prof. econs., 1971-93; prof. econs. U. Córdoba, 1995-2000, prof. post-grad.; cons. Consejo Fed. de Inversiones, Buenos Aires, 1969-73, to pres. Banco Ctrl., Buenos Aries, 1983-85, dir., 1985-86; v.p. Inst. Economia Fed. Coll. Econs., Buenos Aires, 1980, 81-91, 93; exec. Jornadas de Finanzas Publicas, Córdoba, 1968-75; coord. Comisión Est. Económica Col. Grad., Córdoba, 1976-83; prof. econs. U. Buenos Aires, 1983-85, Instituto Nacional Pub. Adminstrn., Buenos Aries, 1984-86; economist Estudio Treber, Córdoba. Author: La Empresa Esetatal Argentina, 1968, La Economia Argentina, 1977, La Economia Argentine Actual, 1988, Vida y Pasión d/P. Cavallo, 1992, 3 others; contbr. many articles to profl. publs. Recipient 1st prize Cámara Argentine Soc. Anónimas, 1971, Assn. Rosarina de Pöblicas, 1974. Home and Studio: Fragueiro 215 Piso 1, 5000 Cordoba Argentina

TREBICHAVSKY, ILJA, immunologist; b. Bratislava, Slovakia, May 22, 1942. Dr rer. nat., Charles U., Prague, Czechoslovakia, 1964; PhD, Acad. Scis., Prague, 1976. Head of lab. of immune regulations Inst. Microbiology, Prague, 1991—; tutor postdoctoral studies Charles U., Prague, 1990—; mem. com. Grant Agy., Prague, 1996. Contbr. chpts. to books and textbooks; articles to profl. jours. Mem. Czech Immunol. Soc. Avocation: mountaineering. Home: Skuherského 588, 51773 Opočno Czech Republic Office: Inst Microbiology, Vídeňská 1083, 14220 Prague Czech Republic

TREBING, DAVID MARTIN, financial executive; b. Lincoln, Nebr., June 2, 1961; s. Harry Martin and Joyce Alice (Christie) T. BA in Mktg., Mich. State U., 1984; MBA in Fin., Wake Forest U., 1986. Project mgr. mktg.-sales Gilbarco div. Exxon Corp., Greensboro, N.C., 1984-86; cash mgmt. analyst Chrysler Fin. Corp., Troy, Mich., 1986-87; sr. corp. fin. specialist Chrysler Corp., Auburn Hills, Mich., 1987-92; mgr. activity-based costing implementation Chrysler Corp., Detroit, Mich., 1993-96, mgr. Asia-Pacific Sales Fin., 1996-98; v.p. fin. and adminstrn. Daimler Chrysler Taiwan Co. Ltd., 1998—. Mem. Internat. Armed Forces Coun., Detroit, 1987-92, Detroit Hist. Soc., Jr. Coun./Detroit Inst. Arts, St. George's Soc. N.Y., N.Y.C.; mem. exec. com., bd. dirs. Meadow Brook Theatre and Festival; Chgo. com. Coun. on Fgn. Rels.; bd. dirs. devel. fund Mich. State U. Lt. (j.g.) USNR, 1987-90. Inst. fellow Inst. Pub. Utilities, 1983. Mem. Am. C. of C. (mem. Taiwan transp. com., tax com.), Econ. Club Detroit, Army and Navy Club, Detroit Athletic Club, Church Club of N.Y., Vet. Corps Arty. State N.Y., SAR (pres. Detroit chpt. 1987-89), Soc. War 1812, Soc. Colonial Wars (chmn. grants and awards com., dep. gov. gen. Mich. Soc.), English-Speaking Union, Pres. Club Mich. State U., Colonial Order of Acorn, Chgo. Yacht Club. Avocations: skiing, tennis, travel, skeet/trap shooting. Office: Daimler Chrysler Corp CIMS 896-00-00 1000 Chrysler Dr Auburn Hills MI 48326-2766

TREBLE, FREDERICK CHRISTOPHER, electrical engineer, consultant; b. Aldershot, Hampshire, U.K., Feb. 20, 1916; s. Michael Frederick and Edith Ellen (Drysdale) T.; m. Elnora Jones, Mar. 9, 1940 (dec. Feb. 1991); children: Paul, Anne, John, Frances. BSc with honours, U. London, 1937. Chartered engr. Sci. officer Ministry of Aircraft Prodn., London, 1940-46; sr. sci. officer Ministry of Supply, London, 1946-57; sr. sci. officer Royal Aircraft Establishment, Farnborough, Eng., 1957-63, prin. sci. officer, 1963-77; consulting engr. photovoltaic solar energy Farnborough, 1977—; cons. PV stds. com. Internat. Electrotech. Commn., Geneva, 1983-90; sec. U.K. sect. Internat. Solar Energy Soc., 1979-90, 99—. Author: Solar Electricity-A Lay Guide, 1993, 2d edit., 1999; editor, contbg. author: Generating Electricity from the Sun, 1991; contbg. author: Energy-Present & Future Options, 1984; contbr. articles to conf. procs. Mem. Inst. Elec. Engrs., Solar Energy Soc. Achievements include early studies of effects of radiation damage in space solar cells; developed photovoltaic performance measurement techniques; developed large, lightweight deployable solar arrays for spacecraft. Home and Office: 43 Pierrefondes Ave, Farnborough GU14 8PA, England

TRECEK, TIMOTHY SCOTT, lawyer; b. Racine, Wis., Sept. 26, 1968; s. Robert Thomas and Mona Marie Trecek; m. Karyn Marie Kwiatkowski, Aug. 27, 1994; children: Gabrielle Grace, Danielle Terese. BS in Polit. Sci., Marquette U., 1990, JD, 1993. Bar: Wis. 1993, U.S. Dist. Ct. (ea. dist.) Wis. 1993. Atty. Kasdorf, Lewis & Swietlik, Milw., 1993-95, Habush, Habush, Davis & Rottier, Milw., 1995—. Mem. ABA, Wis. Acad. of Trial Lawyers (com. mem. bd. attys. profl. responsibility), Wis. State Bar Assn., Assn. of Trial Lawyers of Am. Roman Catholic. Avocations: golfing, family. Office: Habush Habush Davis & Rottier 777 E Wisconsin Ave 2300 Milwaukee WI 53202-5381

TRECHSEL, STEFAN, law educator; b. Berne, Switzerland, June 25, 1937; s. Manfred F. and Stefanie E. (Friedlaender) T.; m. Franca J. Kinsbergen, Aug. 18, 1967; children: Charlotte Stefanie, Anna Cristina. BA, Berne U., 1963, JD, 1966; PhD (hon.), N.Y. Law Sch., 1975. Dist. atty. Berne, 1971-75; guest prof. U. Fribourg, Switzerland, 1975-77; prof. U. St. Gallen, Switzerland, 1979-99, U. Zurich, 1999—. Author: The Reason for Punishing Participants in Crime, 1967, The European Convention of Human Rights, Its Protection of Personal Liberty and the Swiss Codes on Criminal Procedure, 1974, Swiss Penal Code Short Commentary, 1989, 2d edit. 1997; contbr. articles to profl. jours. Active European Commn. Human Rights, Strasbourg, 1975-99, 2nd v.p., 1987-94, pres. 1995-99. Major Swiss mil. Mem. Internat. Penal Law Assn. (bd. dirs. 1984 , pres. Swiss nat. group 1980), Max Planck Inst. Penal Law (bd. dirs. 1984-96), Austrian Inst. Human Rights (bd. dirs. 1987), Internat. Law Assn. Avocations: playing cello, bicycling, literature. Office: St Gallen U, Wilfriedstr 6, CH-8032 Zurich Switzerland

TREECE, JOSEPH CHARLES, insurance broker; b. Loma Linda, Calif., Sept. 1, 1934; s. Roy G. and Jeane L. (Reade) T.; m. Sandra Larkins; children: Debbie, Mike, David. BA, Chapman Coll., 1956. Cert. Ins. Counselor, Assoc. in Risk Mgmt. Comml. banker Security Pacific Nat. Bank, Hemet, Calif., 1959-72; ins. broker H.I.S./Kent & Hamilton, Hemet, 1972-89, Russell & Kaufmann, Hemet, 1989-96, Sawyer, Cook & Co., Redlands, Calif., 1996—. Dir. YMCA, Hemet. Lt. USN, 1956-59. Recipient Associate Achievement award Am. Assn. Mng. Gen. Agts., 1991, Disting. Svc. award Cert. Profl. Ins. Agents Soc., 1995. Mem. Ramona Pageant Assn. (life, chmn.-supr. 1962), Profl. Ins. Assn. (state dir. 1988-91), Profl. Ins. Agts. (pres. Riverside and San Bernardino, Calif. 1989-90), Joint Ins. Assn. (pres. Riverside and San Bernardino 1991), Ind. Ins. Agts. (pres.), Cert. Profl. Ins. Agts. (nat. pres. 1992, Disting. Svc. award 1995), Hemet C. of C. (pres. 1970), Kiwanis Club (life, Hemet chpt. pres. 1971, lt. gov. divsn. 6 Cal-Na-Ha 1972). Avocations: golf, camping, fishing, canoeing. Home: 839 Don Dr Hemet CA 92543-3729 Office: Sawyer Cook & Co 1 E State St Redlands CA 92373-4729

TREFTS, JOAN LANDENBERGER, retired educator, administrator; b. Pitts., Jan. 31, 1930; d. William Henry III and Eleanore (Campbell) Landenberger;m. Albert Sharpe Trefts Sr., June 20, 1952; children: Dorothy, Albert Jr., William, Deborah Elizabeth. AB, Western Coll. for Women, 1952; M., John Carroll U., 1982, John Carroll U., 1984. Lic. and cert. home economist, cert. prin., N.Y., Ohio, supr., biol. sci., econs., vocat. edn., prekindergarten edn. Summer sch. prin. John Adams High Sch., Cleve., 1972-95; cons. Cleve. Partnership Program. Trustee Presley Assn. of Chautauqua, N.Y. Named Tchr. of Yr., Cleve., 1994. Mem. Nat. Officers Colonial Clergy (nat. officer, chancellor), Colonial Dames Am. (pres. chpt., nat. officer ct. honor), Daus. Am. Colonists (state officer), DAR, U.S. Duas. of 1812, Colonial Daus. of 17th Century (nat. officer), Colonial Dames of XVII Century (state officer), Dames of Ct. of Honor (nat. officer), Am. Home Econ. Assn., Ohio Vocat. Assn. (bd. dirs.), Am. Vocat. Assn. (nat. com.), Union Clubs, Cleveland Skating Club, Clearwater Country Club, Presbyn. Assn. (trustee). Republican. Presbyterian. Avocations: curling, rug hooking, needlepoint. Home: 20101 Malvern Rd Shaker Hts OH 44122-2825

TREFZGER, RICHARD CHARLES, surgeon; b. Peoria, Ill., Jan. 27, 1948; s. John Dennis and Marilyn Lestilie (Wilson) T.; m. Nancy Ellen Guy, Dec. 19, 1971; children: Emily Jean, Michael Guy. BS, U. Ill., 1970, MD, 1973. Diplomate Am. Bd. Surgery. Intern in surgery Med. Coll. Wis., Milw., 1973-74, resident in surgery, 1974-75; resident in surgery Presbyn.-St. Luke's Hosp., Chgo., 1975-78; instr. surgery Rush Med. Coll., Chgo., 1977-78; med. dir. Westminster Village Retirement Ctr., Bloomington, Ill., 1980-84, St. Joseph's Trauma Ctr., Bloomington, 1986-96, BroMenn Regional Trauma Ctr., Normal, Ill., 1994-96; chief surgery Bromenn Regional Med. Ctr., Normal, Ill., 1987-88, 94-96; chief surgery St. Joseph's Med. Ctr., Bloomington, 1989-91, pres. med. staff, 1991-92; clin. instr. U. Ill. Coll. Medicine, 1980—; chmn. bd. dirs. BroMenn Physician Hosp. Orgn., 1995-96, pres. med. staff 2000; sec. med. staff BroMenn Regional Med. Ctr., 1998, v.p., 1999, bd. dirs., 1999—. Mem. Ill. State U. Civic Chorale, Normal, 1991-98; bd. dirs. Barton Stone Christian Home, Jacksonville, Ill., 1979-82, Cmty. Cancer Ctr., Bloomington, 1996—, pres. 2000; sec., 1998, v.p., 1999; v.p. ofcl. bd. First Christian Ch., Bloomington, 1981, 99—, elder, 1980—. Fellow ACS (councilor Ill chpt. 1986-88, mem. Ill. chpt. com. on trauma 1996—); mem. AMA, Ill. Surg. Soc. (gov. 1990-94, v.p. elect 1997, v.p. 1998, pres. elect 1999, pres. 2000), Rotary (dir. 1982-85, 94-99, sec. 1995-96, v.p. 1996-97, pres. 1997-98, Paul Harris fellow 1989, band-saxophone), Masons, Scottish Rite, Danvers (Ill.) Cmty. Band-saxaphone, Alpha Omega Alpha. Mem. Christian Ch. Avocations: marathon running, skiing, music, travel. Home: 41 Pendleton Way Bloomington IL 61704-6243 Office: Surg Assocs 1404 Eastland Dr Bloomington IL 61701-3532

TREGENZA, NORMAN HUGHSON, investment banker; b. Morristown, N.J., Feb. 1, 1937; s. Norman J. and Marion Esther (Hughson) T.; m. Alyce Virginia Bruene, Aug. 27, 1966; children: Norman Arthur, Suzanne Carol. BA, St. Lawrence U., 1959; MBA, NYU, 1963. Sr. investment officer Tchrs. Ins. and Annuity Assn., N.Y.C., 1960-71; sr. v.p. Republic Funding Corp., N.Y.C., 1971-82; pres. Convent Capital Corp., 1982—; bd. dirs. Powertrusion 2000 Internat., Inc., Scottsdale, Ariz. Chmn. stewardship com. Presbyn. Ch., Morristown, 1978, ruling elder, 1979, pres. bd. trustees, 1982; trustee St. Lawrence U., Canton, N.Y., 1983-95, Gill/St. Bernards Sch. (hon.), The Morris Mus., Morristown. Mem. St. Lawrence U. Alumni Assn. N.J. (pres. 1970-72), Nat. Coun. USS Constitution Mus. Club: Baltusrol Golf, Park Ave., Indian Mound Golf. Home and Office: West Shore Dr Silver Lake NH 03875

TREGLE, LINDA MARIE, dance educator; b. Fort Sill, Okla., Sept. 8, 1947; d. Franklin and Helen Marie (Diggs) T. BA, Mills Coll., Stockton, Calif., 1970, MA, 1974; life credential, U. Calif., 1974. founder, dir., choreographer Internat. Studios, Inc., Stockton, 1970—; dance instr. San Joaquin Delta Coll., Stockton, 1970—; program cons., choreographer Alpha Kappa Alpha, Stockton, 1984—, choreographer SDW Motion Pictures, Stockton, 1983—; advisor Internat. Dance Club San Joaquin, 1970—; founder, dir. Tregles Internat. Dance Co., 1970—; mem. Ruth Beckford's Dance Studio. Directed and choreographed numerous dance prodn. videos. Mem. NAACP, Black Employment Trends (community rep. 1988—), Calif. Tchrs. Assn., Alpha Kappa Alpha. Avocations: creative writing, table sports, drama, arts, dance. Home: 2411 Arden Ln Stockton CA 95210-3256 Office: San Joaquin Delta Coll 5151 Pacific Ave Stockton CA 95207-6304

TREGLOWN, JEREMY DICKINSON, writer, editor, educator; b. May 24, 1946; s. Geoffrey and Beryl Treglown; m. Rona Bower, 1970 (div. 1982); 3 children; m. Holly Eley Urquhart, 1984. MA, BLitt, Oxford (Eng.) U.; PhD, U. London. Lectr. Lincoln Coll., Oxford U., 1974-77, Univ. Coll. London, 1977-80; asst. editor The Times Literary Supplement, London, 1980-82; editor The Times Literary Supplement, 1982-90; hon. rsch. fellow Univ. Coll. London, 1991—; Ferris prof. Princeton U., 1992; prof. English and comparative lit. U. Warwick, 1993—; vis. fellow All Souls Coll., 1986; Mellon vis. assoc. Calif. Inst. Tech., 1988; Jackson Bros. fellow Beinecke Libr., Yale, 1999. Author: Roald Dahl, A Biography, 1994; gen. editor Plays in Performance series, 1981-85; editor: The Letters of John Wilmot, Earl of Rochester, 1980, Spirit of Wit: Reconsiderations of Rochester, 1982, The Lantern-Bearers and other Essays by Robert Louis Stevenson, 1988, (with B. Bennett) Grub Street and the Ivory Tower: Literary Journalism and Literary Scholarship from Fielding to the Internet, 1998; contbr. to The Guardian, Observer, Sunday Times, Ind. on Sunday, N.Y.; mem. editl. bd. Liber, A European Rev. of Books, 1988-90; contbg. editor Grand St., 1990-98; contbr. articles on poetry, drama and literary history to acad. jours. Fellow Royal Soc. Lit. (mem. coun. 1989-95), Royal Soc. Arts.

TREHERNE, KATHERINE THAMER, painter, illustrator; b. L.A., Mar. 27, 1955; arrived in Eng., 1986; d. Donald Chapman and Hillary Helen (Fitzpatrick) Thamer; m. Patrick John Treherne, Mar. 8, 1986; children: Mary Agnes, Thomas Michael Justin, Joseph Patrick Ciaran, Peter Edmund Gabriel. BA in Studio Arts, U. Calif., U.S.A., 1977. Cert. tchr. Calif. 1977. Illustrator: (book) Song of Solomon, 1979, The Red Shoes, 1980, The Black Horse, 1984 (Parent's Choice Illustration award 1984), The Light Princess, 1987, The Little Mermaid (Red Book Illustration award, 1989), Tatsinda, 1990; art exhbns. include Chgo. Art Internat. Expo., SUNY, Albany, Calif. State U., Dominguez Hills, and others. Roman Catholic.

TREIBER, HUBERT, administrative sciences educator; b. Geislingen, Baden-Württemberg, Germany, July 30, 1942; s. Hugo and Elisabeth (Grün) T.; m. Ulrike Hildbrand, Sept. 11, 1970. MA, U. Freiburg, Fed. Republic of Germany, 1969; lic., U. Konstanz, Fed. Republic of Germany, 1972, HHD, 1973. Prof. law faculty U. Hannover, Fed. Republic of Germany, 1976—; hon. fellow Law Sch. U. Wis., Madison, 1981-82; Jean Monnet fellow European U. Inst., Florence, Italy, 1986-87; Beinecke Libr. fellow Yale U., New Haven, 1991; corr. editor Theory and Soc. Jour., St. Louis, 1991—. Author 15 books and 4 TV movies; contbr. numerous articles to profl. jours. 1st lt. German Air Force, 1961-64. Recipient Christa-Hoffmann-Riem award, 2000. Roman Catholic. Office: U Hannover, Koenigsworther Platz 1, 30167 Hannover Germany

TREICHEL, JÜRGEN KLAUS, radiologist; b. Berlin, Germany, May 29, 1937. MD, Med. Acad. Dusseldorf, 1965. Intern, then resident Free U., Berlin, radiologist, 1970-74, asst. prof., 1974-77, radiologist, prof., 1977—; chief Klinikum Ludwigsburg, Fed. Republic of Germany, 1979—. Author: Double Contrast Examination of the Stomach, 1982; contbr. articles to profl. jours. Mem. German Soc. RAdiology (Hermann Holthusen award 1979), European Soc. Gastrointestinal Radiology. Office: Klinikum Ludwigsburg, Posilipostr 49, D 71640 Ludwigsburg Germany

TREIMAN, REBECCA ANN, psychologist; b. Princeton, N.J., Nov. 5, 1954; d. Sam Bard and Joan (Little) T.; m. Charles A. McGibbon, Aug. 11, 1981; children: Joseph, Robert. BA, Yale U., 1976; PhD, U. Pa., 1980. Asst. prof. Ind. U., Bloomington, 1980-84; prof. dept. psychology Wayne State U., Detroit, 1984—; mem., chair mental health perception and cognition rev. com. NIMH, Washington, 1991-95. Author: Learning to Spell: A Study of First-Grade Children, 1993; editor Jour. of Memory and Lang., 1997-2000; contbr. articles to profl. jours. Recipient Bd. of Govs. Faculty Recognition award Wayne State U., 1995; grantee NSF, NFS, NIH, others, 1981—. Fellow APA; mem. Soc. for Rsch. in Child Devel., Soc. for the Sci. Study of Reading (bd. dirs. 1997-2000), Midwestern Psychol. Assn. (program com. chair 1990-91, exec. coun. 1992-94), Psychosomatic Soc. Office: Wayne State Univ 71 W Warren Ave Detroit MI 48201-1305

TREITEL, SIR GUENTER HEINZ, law educator, writer; b. Berlin, Oct. 26, 1928; s. Theodor and Hanna Lilli (Levy) T.; m. Phyllis Margaret Cook, Jan. 1, 1957; children: Richard James, Henry Marcus. BA, Oxford U., 1949, BCL, 1951, MA, 1953, DCL, 1976. Barrister, Queen's Counsel. Asst. lectr. LSE, London, 1951-53; lectr. U. Coll., Oxford, Eng., 1953-54; fellow Magdalen Coll., Oxford, 1954-79; All Souls readership in English law Oxford U., 1964-79, Vinerian Chair of English law, 1979-96; fellow All Souls Coll., Oxford, 1979-96; vis. prof. numerous univs. in U.S. and elsewhere. Author: The Law of Contract, 1962, 10th edit., 1999, An Outline of the Law of Contract, 1975, 5th edit., 1995, Remedies for Breach of Contract: a Comparative Account, 1988, Unmöglichlkeit, Impracticability und Frustration im anglo-amerikanischen Recht, 1991, Frustration and Force Majeure, 1994; contbr. sect. on overseas sales Benjamin's State of Goods, 1974, 5th edit., 1997. Trustee Brit. Mus., London, 1983-98; mem. coun. Nat. Trust, London, 1984-93. Hon. bencher Gray's Inn. Fellow Brit. Acad. Avocations: music, reading. Office: All Souls Coll, Oxford OX1 4AL, England

TREJOS, FRANKLIN ANTHONY, physician assistant; b. Spokane, Wash., July 6, 1955; s. Frank Trejos and Lloydene Louise (Small) Mielbrecht; m. Denise Lynn Mortimer, Aug. 25, 1979 (div. 1986); m. Felicia Jo Cote, May 27, 1994; children: Cerena, Cebrena, Alyssa. Student in med. assistance, Western Coll. Med. Dental Asst, 1978; grad. physician asst., U. Utah Coll. Medicine, 1984. Advanced EMT Kootenai County Emergency Med. Rescue Svc., Coeur d'alene, Idaho, 1980-82; phys. asst. Franklin Park Minor Emergency Ctr., Spokane, Wash., 1984-85; phys. asst. family practice Cigna Health Plan, Mesa, Ariz., 1985-87; phys. asst. gen.surgery, orthoped. surgery, and neursurgery Mayo Clinic Scottsdale, Ariz., 1987-97; faculty physician asst. program Midwestern U., Glendale, Ariz., 1997—. Fellow Am. Acad. Physician Assts. Avocations: waterskiing, mountain biking, astronomy, photography. Home: 2122 E Behrend Dr Phoenix AZ 85024-1256 Office: Midwestern U Physician Asst Program 19555 N 59th Ave Glendale AZ 85308-6813

TRELEA, IOAN-CRISTIAN, control engineer, researcher; b. Iasi, Romania, Jan. 2, 1968; s. Antonie and Natalia (Paghida) T.; m. Sabine Sandrine Lucas, Sept. 6, 1997. Degree in control engring., Tech. U. Iasi, Romania, 1992;

MS, Inst. Nat. Poly. Grenoble, Grenoble, France, 1993; PhD, Ecole Nat. Sup. Ind. Aliment., Massy, France, 1997. Asst. prof. Tech. U. Iasi, 1993-94; rschr. Danone, Le Plessis Robinson, France, 1997; assoc. prof. Institut Nat. Agronomique Paris Grignon, Paris, 1998—. Contbr. articles to profl. jours. including Jour. Food Process Engring., Jour. Process Control, and Drying Tech. Office: INAPG, LGMPA, 78850 Thivervalgrignon France

TRELLES, LUIS ANTONIO, neurology educator; b. Lima, Peru, Sept. 3, 1942; s. Julio Oscar and Maria (Montero) T.; m. Cecilia Thorne; children: Maria Veronica, Maria Del Pilar, Maria Del Carmen. Medicine, Cayetano Heredia U., Lima, 1968; MD, Cayetano Heredia U., 1977. Med. diplomate. Resident St. Toribio Neurol. Hosp., Lima, 1968-70; fellowship Born-Bunge Inst. Anvers, Belgium, 1970-71; resident Paris (France) Hosp., Hosp. de la Salpetriere, 1971-73; asst., neurology prof. Lhermitte Hosp. Salpetriere, Paris, 1973-75; asst. in neuroanatomy Faculty Medicine Broussais-Hotel Dieu, Paris, 1971-75; neurologist Sto. Toribio Neurol. Hosp., Lima, 1976—; prof. neurol. scis. Cath. U., Lima, 1976—; head rsch. dept. Nat. Inst. Neurol. Sci., Lima, 1983-90, dir., 1990-93; prof. neurology U. Cayetano Heredia, Lima, 1991—; bd. dirs. Revista de Neuropsiquiatria, Lima, editor, 1977—; bd. dirs. Clinica Santa Clara S.C.R. Ltd., Lima, Magnetic Resonance, 1993. Vice min. Pub. Health, Peru, 1985. Recipient Leignel Lavastine prix U. Paris, 1975, Gran Cruz Hipolito Unanue, Peruvian, 1985, Gran Cruz Daniel Alcides Carrion, Peruvian, 1985. Mem. Soc. Francaise Neurology, Am. Acad. of Neurology, Am. Acad. Sci., Societe Francaise, Soc. Peruana Neurologia, Royal Soc. of Medicine, Internat. Soc. for Magnetic Resonance in Medicine. E-mail: ltrelle@pucp.edu.pe. Office: Resomasa, Javier Prado Este 1180, 0027 Lima 1977, Peru

TREMBLY, CRISTY, television executive; b. Oakland, Md., July 11, 1958; d. Charles Dee and Mary Louise (Cassidy) T. BA in Russian, German and Linguistics cum laude, W.Va. U., 1978, BS in Journalism, 1978, MS in Broadcast Journalism, 1979; advanced cert. travel, West L.A. Coll., 1982; advanced cert. recording engring., Soundmaster Schs., North Hollywood, Calif., 1985. Videotape engr. Sta. WWVU-TV, Morgantown, W.Va., 1976-80; announcer, engr. Sta. WVVW Radio, Grafton, W.Va., 1979; tech. dir., videotape supr. Sta. KMEX-TV, L.A., 1980-85; broadcast supr. Sta. KADY-TV, Oxnard, Calif., 1988-89; news tech. dir. Sta. KVEA-TV, Glendale, Calif., 1985-89; asst. editor, videotape technician CBS TV Network, Hollywood, Calif., 1989-90; videotape supr. Sta. KCBS-TV, Hollywood, 1990-91, mgr. electronic news gathering ops., 1991-92; studio mgr., engr.-in-charge CBS TV Network, Hollywood, 1992—; radio operator KJ6BX Malibu Disaster Comm., 1987—; coun. mem. L.A. World Affairs 2000—. Prodr. (TV show) The Mountain Scene, 1976-78. Sr. orgn. pres. Children of the Am. Revolution, Malibu, Calif., 1992—; chmn. adminstrv. coun. Malibu United Meth. Ch., 1993—, choir 1995—; sec., mem. adv. com. Tamassee (S.C.) Sch., 1992—; vol. Ch. Coun., L.A. Riot Rebldg., Homeless shelter work, VA Hosps., Mus. docent; sponsor 3 overseas foster children; mem. internat. vis. coun. Outstanding Program Resource; mem. L.A. World Affairs Coun., 2000—. Named one of Outstanding Young Women of Am., 1988, Internat. Vis. Coun. Outstanding Pvt. Resource, L.A. County; recipient Asst. editor Emmy award Young and the Restless, 1989-90, Golden Mike award Radio/TV News Assn., 1991, 92, Pub. Svc. commendation, County of L.A., 1999, cert. leadership, USIA, cert. commendation, City of L.A., 1999. Mem. ATAS (gov. 2000—, mem. exec. com. on electronic prodn. 1992—, mem. awards com. 1994-96, 97-98, engring. awards com. 1997-98, judge local and nat. Emmys 1991—, mem. membership com. 1994-96), DAR (state chair jr. membership 1987-88, state chair scholarships 1992-94, state chmn. jr. contest 1994-96, others, Malibu organizing regent 1991, state chair motion pictures radio and TV Calif. 1988-90, Mex. 1990—, Nat. Outstanding Jr. 1993, nat. vice-chair broadcast media 1995-98, state chair pub. rels. 1996-99, organizing regent Baja Calif. chpt., 1999—, nat. vice-chair units overseas Mex. 1998—, organizing regent Baja Calif. 1999), Am. Women in Radio and TV (So. Calif. bd. 1984-85, 93—, pres.-elect 1995-96, pres. 1996-97, dist. dir. 1997-98), Women in Film - Internat. (com. mem. 1999—), Soc. Profl. Journalists, Women in Comms., Travelers Century Club (program chair 1987—), Soc. Broadcast Engrs. (1995—), Mensa (life), Soc. Motion Picture/TV Engrs. (pres. 1995-97), Beta Sigma Phi. Democrat. Methodist. Avocations: singing, cooking, travel, genealogy, languages. Home: 2901 Searidge St Malibu CA 90265-2969 Office: CBS TV City 7800 Beverly Blvd Los Angeles CA 90036-2188

TREMMEL, FRITZ ALOIS, lawyer; b. Speyer, Germany, Jan. 24, 1950; s. Robert and Katharina Tremmel; m. Sonja Hörner, Apr. 24, 1987. MBA, U. Applied Sci., Ludwigshafen, Germany, 1974; LLM, U. Heidelberg, Germany, 1979. Qualified lawyer, mgmt. expert. Adminstrn. trainee Ins. Co., Speyer, Germany, 1964-67, adminstrn. official, 1967-71; lawyer Wellensiek & Ptnr., Heidelberg, 1983—. Mem. Profl. Assn. Lawyers, Local Assn. Lawyers, Study Group for Insolvency. Avocations: bicycle riding, history, literature. Home: Mönchbergsteige 7, 69120 Heidelberg Germany Office: Wellensiek & Ptnr, Blumenstr 17, 69115 Heidelberg Germany

TRENCH, WILLIAM FREDERICK, mathematics educator; b. Trenton, N.J., July 31, 1931; s. George Daniel and Anna Elizabeth (Taylor) T.; m. Lucille Ann Marasco, Dec. 26, 1954 (div. Dec. 1978); children: Joseph William, Randolph Clifford, John Frederick, Gina Margaret; m. Beverly Joan Busenshut, Nov. 22, 1980. BA in Math., Lehigh U., 1953; AM, U. Pa., 1955, PhD, 1958. Applied mathematician Moore Sch. Elec. Engring., U. Pa., 1953-56; with GE Corp., Phila., 1956-57, Philco Corp., Phila., 1957-59, RCA, Moorestown, N.J., 1957-64; assoc. prof. math. Drexel U., Phila., 1964-67, prof., 1967-86; Andrew G. Cowles disting. prof. math. Trinity U., San Antonio, 1986-97, prof. emeritus, 1997—. Author: Advanced Calculus, 1978; co-author: (with Bernard Kolman) Elementary Multivariable Calculus, 1971, Multivariable Calculus with Linear Algebra and Series, 1972, Elementary Differential Equations, 2000; contbr. rsch. articles in numerical analysis, ordinary differential equations, smoothing, prediction and spl. functions to profl. jours. Mem. Am. Math. Soc., Soc. Indsl. and Applied Math., Internat. Linear Algebra Soc., Phi Beta Kappa, Eta Kappa Nu, Pi Mu Epsilon. Achievements include development of Trench's Algorithm for inversion of finite Toeplitz matrices, of fast algorithms for computing eigenvalues of structured matrices, of asymptotic theory of solutions of nonlinear functional differential equations under mild integral smallness conditions. Home: 95 Pine Ln Woodland Park CO 80863-9535

TRENOGIN, VLADILEN ALEXANDROVICH, mathematician, educator; b. Kyshtym, Russia, Aug. 11, 1931; s. Alexandr Trenogin and Eugenia (Mikhaleva) Kondor; m. Vera Kuzretzova, Dec. 30, 1960; two children. MSc, Moscow State U., 1955, PhD, 1960, DSc, 1969. From asst. to full prof. Moscow Physics Tech. Inst., 1955-72; head maths. dept., prof., prin. rschr. Moscow Steel Alloys Inst., Moscow, 1972—; lectr. in field. Author: Functional Analysis, 1980; co-author: Theory of Branching of Solutions of Non-linear Equations, 1969, Math Encyclopedia, 1985 (hon. badges, awards), Problems and Exercises in Functional Analysis, 1984; contbr. articles to profl. jours. Named Hon. Scientist of Russia. Mem. GAMM, Russian Nat. Acad. Applied Sci., Coun. Math. Russian Edn. Minister, pers. mem. GAMM and ISAAC (sect. of applied math and mech.). Office: Moscow Steel & Alloys Inst, Leninsky Prospekt 4, 117 936 Moscow Russia

TRENT, JOHN THOMAS, JR., lawyer; b. Hammond, Ind., Mar. 11, 1954; s. John Thomas and Sally (Ritter) T.; m. Laura Marie Nelson, Aug. 5, 1978; children: Lauren, Valerie, Alex. AB, Wabash Coll., 1976; JD, Vanderbilt U., 1979. Bar: Tenn. 1979, U.S. Dist. Ct. (mid. dist.) Tenn. Mng. dir. Boult, Cummings, Conners & Berry P.L.C., Nashville, 1979—; spkr., panelist real estate and other groups. Chmn. adminstrv. bd. and other coms. and offices West End United Meth. Ch., Nashville, 1983—99; bd. dirs. Cumberland Sci. Mus., 1997—, Jr. Achievement Middle Tenn. Fellow Nashville Bar; mem. ABA, Nat. Assn. Indsl. and Office Parks (past bd. dirs. Nashville chpt.), Tenn. Bar Assn., Nashville Bar Assn., Nat. Assn. Bond Lawyers, Assn. Attys. and Execs. in Corp. Real Estate. Office: Boult Cummings Connors & Berry PLC 414 Union St Ste 1600 Nashville TN 37219-1744

TRESGUERRES, JESUS A.F., endocrinologist, edcator; b. Lugo, Spain, Nov. 29, 1948; s. Jesus A.F. and Flor (Hernandez) T.; m. Carmen Centeno, Aug. 30, 1974; children: Ana, Alberto. MD, Medicine Complutense, Madrid, 1971, PhD, 1976. Asst. prof. Med. Sch., Madrid, 1972-74; rsch. asst. Med. Sch., Hamburg, Germany, 1974-76; asst. prof. Med. Sch., Madrid, 1977-78, assoc. prof., 1978-90, prof., 1990—; cons. Serono Labs., Madrid, 1982—; mem. European Space Orgn., Paris, 1990—; sec. Hormonal Steroids Com., 1986—. Author, editor: Human Physiology, 1992, 2d edit., 1999, Endocrine Physiology, 1989, Growth Retardation, 1992, 2nd edit., 1996. Mem. Royal Nat. Acad. Medicine, Spanish Soc. Endocrinology (Lilly award 1995), Am. Endocrine Soc., European Neuroendocrine Assn. Avocations: tennis, skiing, hunting. Office: U Complutense Med Sch, Dept Physiology, 28040 Madrid Spain

TRESKA, VLADISLAV, surgeon; b. Plzen, Czech Republic, Nov. 13, 1957; s. Vladislav and Kvetuse (Krejcova) T.; m. Lenka Valdmanova, Dec. 19, 1981; children: Inka, Aneta. Grad. med. sch., Charles U., Plzen, Czech Republic, 1981. Resident Charles U., Dept. Surgery, Plzen, Czech Republic, 1981-84, sr. resident, 1984-87, asst. prof., 1987-91, assoc. prof., 1991-99, prof., head dept. surgery, 1999, head transplant ctr., 1999; cons. in field. Author: Abdominal Aortic Aneurysms, 1999, Cytokines in Vascular and Transplantation Surgery, 1999; co-author: Diabetic Foot, 1999, Arterial Aneurysms, 1999. Sen. Charles U., Prague, 1998—, Plzen, 1995-95, 98—. Mem. Soc. Cardiovascular Surgery London, Internat. Union Angiology, European Soc. Organ Transplantation. Avocations: tennis, skiing, history, music, travel. Home: U Ceskeho dvora 11, 317 02 Plzen Czech Republic Office: Charles U Hosp Dept Surgery, Alej svobody 80, 304 60 Plzen Czech Republic

TRETIAKOV, ALEKSEI ANATOLIY, mathematician; b. Moscow, Jan. 27, 1957; s. Tretiakov and Anastasia (Rosikhina) A.; m. Olga Georgiy Antokhina, Feb. 12, 1976 (dec. Feb. 1988); 1 child, Olga; m. Tatiana Alaksey Alekseeva, Mar. 11, 1989. MS, Moscow U., 1979, PhD, 1984. Rschr. Moscow U., 1979-85; full prof. Russian Acad., Moscow, 1985—. Author: Factor-Analysis of Nonlinear Map, 1994; editor: Modelling in Operation Research, 1996. Home: Festivalnaia St #5 Ap 46, 125565 Moscow Russia

TRETINNIKOV, OLEG NIKOLAYEVICH, physicist; b. Pinsk, USSR, Apr. 6, 1958; s. Nikolay Anufrievich and Olga Ivanovna (Khot'ko) T.; m. Galina Kazimirovna Dubbovskaya, May 17, 1980; children: Olga, Artyem. MS, Belarussian State U., USSR, 1980; PhD, Inst. of Physics/Acad. Sci., Belarus, 1988. Rsch. asst. Inst. of Physics Belarus, Minsk, 1980-82, jr. rsch. assoc., 1982-88; sr. rsch. assoc. B.I. Stepanov Inst. Physics, Minsk, 1989-90, sr. scientist, 1991—; rsch. fellow Osaka Nat. Rsch. Inst., Japan, 1993-94. Contbr. articles to profl. jours. Office: BI Stepanov Inst of Physics, 70 Prospekt F Skariny, 220072 Minsk Belarus

TRETTIN, ROSEMARY ELIZABETH, fraternal organization administrator; b. Appleton, Wis.; d. August W. and Elizabeth C. (Etten) T. BA, Mt. Mary Coll., Milw., 1945. Tchr., forensic coach Pulaski (Wis.) High Sch., 1947-51, Freedom (Wis.) High Sch., 1951-60, St. Mary Cen. High Sch., Menasha, Wis., 1960-79; forensic coach Xavier High Sch., Appleton, 1979-86; pres. St. Mary Ct. Nat. Catholic Soc. Foresters, Appleton, 1953-86, 91—, nat. dir., 1974-78, nat. v.p., 1978-86, pres., 1986-90; sec. Green Bay (Wis.) Diocesan Assn., 1974-78, pres., 1978-86; Mem. Nat. Cath. Communications Found., N.Y.C., nat. dir., 1986-89, exec. v.p., 1989-90; dir. Wis. Fraternal Congress, 1982-83, Ill. Fraternal Congress, 1989-90; co-leader Fish Community Svc., Civic Leaders Am. Eucharistic min. St. Mary Ch., coord. leisure club. Named to Hall of Fame, Wis. Forensic Coaches Assn., 1994. Mem. Nat. Cath. Forensic League (sec., pres.), Nat. Forensic League (Double Diamond Key award 1983), Cath. Daus. Am., Outagamie County Hist. Soc., Monté Alverno Retreat Guild (treas. and pres.), Optimist (Appleton Noon Club), St. Joseph Fraternity of Secular Franciscans (sec.), Christ Child Soc. Roman Catholic. Avocations: gardening and travelling.

TRETZ, CHRISTOPHE ROBERT, electrical engineer; b. Strasbourg, France, Mar. 22, 1968; came to the U.S., 1991; s. Philippe and Liliane (Gué) T. Diplôme d'Ingénieur, Ecole Nationale Supérieure d'Electronique, d'Electrotechnique, d'Informatique, d'Hydraulique de Toulouse, Toulouse, France, 1991; MS, Columbia U., 1992, PhD, 1997. Rsch. asst. Columbia U., N.Y.C., 1992-97; adv. engr. IBM Rsch., Yorktown Heights, N.Y., 1997-2000; mem. tech. staff design engr. Advanced Micro Devices, Sunnyvale, Calif., 2000—; rsch. mentor Semiconductor Rsch. Corp., Durham, N.C., 1997—. Mem. IEEE (tech. com. internat. soi conf. 1998—). Roman Catholic. Achievements include inventor reduction of hysteresis in soi cmos circuits, method and system to tune integrated circuit, method and system for selecting sizes of components for integrated circuits. Avocations: skiing, golf, wine-tasting, gourmet cooking. E-mail: christophe.tretz@amd.com. Home: 235 Briar Ridge Dr San Jose CA 95123-2667 Office: Advanced Micro Devices One AMD Pl MS 365 PO Box 3453 Sunnyvale CA 94088-3453

TREVES, VANNI EMANUELE, lawyer, company director; b. Florence, Italy, Nov. 3, 1940; m. Angela Veronica Fyffe, Jan. 8, 1972; children: Alexander, William, Louise. MA, Oxford (Eng.) U., 1961; LLM, U. Ill., 1962. Solicitor of Supreme Ct. of Eng. Vis. atty. White & Case, N.Y.C., 1969-70; assoc. Macfarlanes, London, 1965-69, ptnr., 1970-87, sr. ptnr., 1987-99; chmn. Channel Four Corp., 1998—; chmn. BBA Group Plc, London, 1989—, McKechnie Plc, London, 1991—, Fledgeling Equity and Bon Funds, 1994, Dennis Corp., 1996-99. Chmn. devel. bd. Nat. Portrait Gallery, London, 1993-99; gov. London Bus. Sch., 1996, chmn., 1998—; mem. devel. bd. London Bus. Sch., 1993, gov., 1996; gov. Coll. of Law, 1999. Office: Macfarlanes, 10 Norwich St, London EC4A 1BD, England

TREVIJANO, RAMON, theology educator; b. San Sebastián, Spain, Aug. 13, 1932; s. Fernando Trevijano and Manuela Etcheverría. Lic. in philosophy, Gregorian U., Rome, 1954, ThD, 1959; lic. in Holy Scriptures, Pont. Biblical Inst., Rome, 1961; lic. in history, U. Zaragoza, Spain, 1964. Prof. Theol. Inst. Cordoba, Argentina, 1964-66, Theol. Faculty of the Nord of Spain, Burgos, 1967-77, Theol. Faculty Buenos Aires, 1968-74; prof. Theol. Faculty Salamanca, Spain, 1978—, dean, 1981-84; dir. Theol. Inst. Cordoba, 1965-66; dir. rev. Salmanticensis, 1978—; dir. collection Plenitudo Temporis, 1994—. Author: Comienzo del Evangelio. Estudio sobre el prólogo de San Marcos, 1971, Orígenes del Cristianismo. El Trasfondo Judío del Cristianismo Primitivo , 2d edit., 1996, PatrologÚa, 3d edit., 1998, Estudios sobre el Evangelio de Tomás, 1997. Mem. Soc. Biblical Lit., Assn. Internat. d'Etudes Patristiques. Home: Francisco de Vitoria 19 2 B, 37008 Salamanca Spain Office: U Pontificia, Compañía 5, 37002 Salamanca Spain

TREVINO, LEE BUCK, professional golfer; b. Dallas, Dec. 1, 1939; s. Joe and Juanita (Barrett) T.; m. Claudia Bove; children: Richard Lee, Lesley Ann, Tony Lee, Troy Liana, Olivia Leigh, Daniel Lee. Ed. pub. schs. Head profl. Hardy's Driving Range, Dallas, 1961-65; asst. profl. Horizon Hills Country Club, El Paso, Tex., 1966-67; chmn. bd. Lee Trevino Enterprises, Inc., 1967—; joined PGA Tour, 1967, PGA Sr. Tour, 1989. Hon. chmn. Christmas Seal campaign, 1969-72, sports ambassador, 1971; mem. Pres.'s Conf. on Phys. Fitness and Sports; grand marshal Sun Carnival Parade, 1969-70, 71-72; mem. sports com. Nat. Multiple Sclerosis Soc. Served with USMCR, 1956-60. Recipient Hickok Belt award, 1971; named Golf Rookie of Yr., 1967, PGA Player of Yr., 1971, Tex. Pro Athlete of Yr., 1970, Gold Tee award, 1971, AP Pro Athlete of Yr., 1971, Player of Yr. Golf Mag., 1971, Sportsman of Yr. Sports Illustrated, 1971, PGA Sr. Tour Players of Yr., 1990, 92, 94, Internat. Sports Personality of Yr. Brit. Broadcasting Assn., 1971, Rookie and Player of Yr., Sr. PGA Tour, 1990; mem. Tex. Hall of Fame, Am. Gulf Hall of Fame, World Golf Hall of Fame. Achievements include Tournament winner Tex. Open, 1965, 66, N.Mex. Open, 1966, U.S. Open, 1968, 71, Amana Open, 1968, 69, Hawaiian Open, 1968, Tucson Open, 1969, 70, World Cup, 1969, 71, Nat. Airlines Open, 1970, Brit. Open, 1971, 72, Canadian Open 1971, 77, 79, Can. PGA, 1979, Danny Thomas-Memphis Classic, 1971, 72, 80, Tallahassee Open, 1971, Sahara Invitational, 1971, St. Louis Classic, 1972, Hartford Open, 1972, Jackie Gleason Classic, 1973, Doral-Eastern Open, 1973, Mexican Open, 1973, 75, Chrysler Classic, Australia, 1973, PGA Championship, 1974, 84, World Series Golf, 1974, Greater New Orleans Open, 1974, Fla. Citrus Open, 1975, Colonial Nat. Invitational, 1976, 78, Colgate Mixed Team Matches, 1979, Brit. Masters, 1985, U.S. Sr. Open, 1990; King Hassan Moroccan trophy II, 1977; Lancome trophy Benson & Hedges, 1978, 80; 1st golfer to have scored four sub-par rounds in U.S. Open Competition, 1968; leading Money winner, 1970, 2d pl. money winner 1971, 1972; Vardon trophy winner, 1970 1972, 74, 80; Can. PGA, 1983; PGA Seniors Championship, 1994; capt. Ryder Cup Matches, 1985; first golfer to have scored 4 sub-par rounds in PGA competition. Office: Assured Mgmt Co 1901 W 47th Pl Ste 200 Westwood KS 66205-1834

TREVINO, MATEO A., mechanical engineer; b. Mexico City, Oct. 28, 1945; s. Mateo and Ma De La Paz (Gaspari) T.; m. Cristina Heres; children: Paula, Sofia, Mateo. BSME, Esime IPN, Mexico, 1969. Subdir. ops. ININ, Mexico City, 1981-83; gen. dir. Clemex, Mexico City, 1981-87, Concarril, Mexico City, 1987-88, FIDE, Mexico City, 1989—. Avocations: reading, classical music, theatre, cinema, travel.

TREVOR, BRONSON, economist; b. N.Y.C., Nov. 12, 1910; s. John Bond and Caroline Murray (Wilmerding) T.; A.B., Columbia Coll., 1931; m. Eleanor Darlington Fisher, Nov. 8, 1946; children—Eleanor, Bronson, Caroline. Own bus., 1931—; dir., asst. sec. Northwestern Terminal R.R., 1952-58; chmn. bd. Texinia Corp., 1959-92. Former dir. chmn. fin. com. Gen. Hosp. of Saranac Lake mem. Council for Agrl. and Chemurgic Research, Am. Forestry Assn. Mem. Republican County Com. of N.Y. County, 1937-39; leader in primary election campaigns N.Y. County, 1937, 38, 39 to free local Rep. party orgn. from leftwing affiliations. Served with U.S. Army, 1942, World War II. Mem. S.A.R., Soc. Colonial Wars. Clubs: Union, Knickerbocker, Racquet and Tennis, Piping Rock, Bath and Tennis. Author: (pamphlet) The United States Gold Purchase Program, 1941; also numerous articles on econ. subjects. Home: Heron Ln Paul Smiths NY 12970 Office: PO Box 182 Oyster Bay NY 11771-0182

TREVOR-ROPER, H(UGH) R(EDWALD) (BARON DACRE OF GLANTON), historian, author, educator; b. Jan. 15, 1914; s. Bertie William Edward and Kathleen (Davison) Trevor-Roper; m. Alexandra Howard-Johnston, 1954 (dec. Aug. 1997). Educated Charterhouse, Christ Ch., Oxford. Rsch. fellow Merton Coll., Oxford, 1937-39, student, Christ Ch., 1945-57, censor, 1947-52; Regius prof. modern history, fellow Oriel Coll. Oxford U., 1957-80; master of Peterhouse, Cambridge, Eng., 1980-87; dir. Times Newspapers Ltd., 1974-88. Author: Archbishop Laud, 1573-1645, 1940, The Last Days of Hitler, 1947, Hitler's Secret Conversations, 1941-44, 1953, The Gentry 1540-1640, 1953, Men and Events: Historical Essays, 1957, The Rise of Christian Europe, 1965, George Buchanan and the Ancient Scottish Constitution, 1966, Religion, the Reformation and Social Change, and Other Essays, 1967, The Philby Affair, 1968, The European Witch-Craze of the 16th and 17th Centuries, 1970, A Hidden Life: The Enigma of Sir Edmund Backhouse, 1976, Princes and Artists: Patronage and Ideology at Four Habsburg Courts, 1517-1633, 1976, Renaissance Essays 1985, Catholics, Anglicans and Puritans, 1987, From Counter-Reformation to Glorious Revolution, 1992; editor: The Bormann Letters, 1954, Gibbon, The Decline and Fall of the Roman Empire, 1963, Blitzkrieg to Defeat: Hitler's War Directives, 1939-1945, 1964, Essays in British History, 1964, The Age of Expansion: Europe and the World, 1559-1660, 1968, Macaulay, The History of England, 1968, Final Entries 1945: The Diaries of Joseph Goebbels, 1978. Office: Old Rectory, Didcot Oxon OX11 7EB, England

TREXLER, THOMAS W., research scientist; b. Evansville, Ind., Mar. 15, 1968; s. Frederic T. and Jean L. T.; m. Suzanne M. Trexler, May 19, 1990; 1 child, Sierra. AA, Goldenwest Coll., Huntington Beach, Calif., 1995; BA, U. So. Calif., L.A., 1997; MS, Yale U., 1999. Aircraft mechanic, engring. liaison McDonnell Douglas Aircraft Corp. (now Boeing), Long Beach, Calif., 1989-95; rsch. asst. U. So. Calif., L.A., 1995-97, Yale U., New Haven, Conn., 1997-99, U. Calif., Santa Barbara, 1999—; presenter confs. in field. Pres. Student Action for the Environ., U. So. Calif.; vol. Big Bro./Big Sisters of Orange County, Huntington Beach, Calif., 1995—. Recipient Sea Grant internship Yale U., New Haven, 1999, Outstanding Vol. award U. So. Calif., 1997, Tyler prize scholarship for excellence, 1996. Mem. Am. Geophys. Union, Am. Water Resources Assn., Assn. Am. Geographers. Office: U Calif Santa Barbara 4670 Physical Scis North Santa Barbara CA 93106-5131

TREYZ, JOSEPH HENRY, librarian; b. Binghamton, N.Y., Nov. 23, 1926; s. Joseph Henry and Edna Belle (Leonard) T. B.A., Oberlin Coll., 1950; postgrad., Harvard U., 1951; M.L.S., Columbia U., 1952. Circulation asst. N.Y. Acad. Medicine Library, 1950-51; cataloger Columbia Libraries, N.Y.C., 1951-53, Stevens Inst. Tech., Hoboken, N.J., 1953-54; adminstrv. asst. Yale Library, 1955, asst. head catalogue dept., 1955-61; head new campuses program U. Calif., La Jolla, 1961-65; asst. dir. U. Mich. Library, Ann Arbor, 1965-71; dir. libraries U. Wis., Madison, 1971-83, asst. to chancellor, 1983-85; sec.-treas. L.D. Repos, Inc., 1985-87, pres., 1987—; univ. rep. Consumer Reaction Project for Catalog Card Reprodn. Study, 1961; condr. survey tech. services Fordham U. Libraries, 1967-69, Brandeis U. Libraries, 1970-71; mem. Wis. Gov.'s Com. on Library Devel., 1973-81, Wis. com. Library Services and Constrn. Act, 1979-81; del. U.S. Mission to China on Libraries, 1979. Author: Books for College Libraries, 1967; also articles. Bd. dirs. Wis. Center for Theatre Research. Served with AUS, 1945-46. Mem. Universal Serials and Book Exchange (v.p. 1976, pres., chmn. bd. dirs. 1977), ALA (councilor 1970-74, 77-81, chmn. various coms. 1967-69, recipient Melvil Dewey medal 1970), Assn. Research Libraries (commn. orgn. materials, dir. 1975-78), Midlnet (v.p. 1978-79, pres. 1979-80), Assn. Coll. and Research Libraries (chmn. editorial bd. Choice 1968-70), Wis. Library Consortium (pres. 1975-76), Wis. Assn. Acad. Libraries (chmn. 1973-74), Council U. Wis. Librarians (chmn. 1975-76, 79-80, 81-83), Wis. Library Assn. (bd. dirs. 1973-74, mem. White House Conf. com. 1977-78), Madison Area Library Council (v.p. 1973-74), Mich. Library Assn. (chmn. tech. services sect. 1968-69), N.Y. Tech. Services Librarians (pres. 1959-60). Methodist. Home: 801 N Venetian Dr Miami FL 33139-1031

TRICHET, JEAN-CLAUDE, banker; b. Lyons, Dec. 20, 1942; married; children: Pierre-Alexis, Jean-Nicolas. Mining engr., Licencié Scis. Economiques; grad., Inst. d'Etudes Politiques, 1971. Rsch. engr., 1966-70, dep. inspector fin., 1971-73, gen. inspectorate of fin., 1974, seconded to the treasury, 1975; gen. sec. Comité Interministerial pour l'Amenagment Industrie, 1976-77; econ. advisor to the min. for econ. affairs and fin. René Monory, 1978; advisor to the pres. of the republic Valéry Giscad D'Estaing, 1978-80; head of the office for devel. aid of the treasury, 1981, dep. dir. of bilateral affairs, treasury, 1981-84, head of internat. affairs, treasury, 1985-86; chief of staff, min. econ. affairs, fin. and privatization Edouard Balladur, 1986-87; undersec. of the treasury, censor Banque de France, 1987-93, gov., chmn. Monetary Policy Coun.., 1993—; cons. industry, energy, rsch. and microecons., sovereign debt rescheduling; dir. Bank for Internat. Settlements and the European Ctrl. Bank; chmn. European Monetary Com., 1992-93, Paris Club, 1985-93; alternate gov. Internat. Monetary Fund. Decorated chevalier Ordre Nat. de la Légion d'Honneur, officer Ordre National du Mérite, Grand Crix Orders, Brazil, Yugoslavia, Comdr. Orders Austria, Argentina, Ecuador. Office: Banque de France, 07-1050 Relations Avec Le Public, 75049 Paris Cedex 01, France*

TRICOLI, VINCENZO, chemical engineer; b. Napoli, Italy, Sept. 4, 1964; s. Guido and Wanda Maria (Leto) T. MSChemE, U Pisa, 1990, PhD in Chem. Engring., 1994. Vis. scholar U. Minn., Mpls., 1992-93, postdoctoral fellow, 1994-95; asst. prof. U. Pisa, Italy, 1996—. Contbr. articles to profl. jours. Mem. European Colloid and Interface Soc., Electrochem. Soc. Avocations: swimming, reading.

TRIEBEL, JOACHIM, hotel executive; b. Berlin, Germany, July 4, 1938; s. Fritz and Elise (Schafer) T. MBA, 1984. Hotel gen. mgr. Hilton Internat.; gen. mgr. Holiday Inns, Sheraton Hotels. Created 1st internat. cruise ship in Philippines, 1975, 1st internat. beach resort in northern Cebu, Philippines, 1979, 1st internat. 5-star hotel in N.E. China, 1988, 1st internat. joint-venture hotel in Vietnam, 1992. Mem. Global Hoteliers Club, Rotary Internat., Internat. Skal Club, Chaine des Rotisseurs, Internat. Hotel Assn., Am. Hotel and Motel Assn., Six Continents Club, World Globetrotters Club, HCIMA and Minister. Avocations: golfing, horseback riding, car racing, flying, swimming. Office: Eurasia, PO Box 3, 5000 Iloilo The Philippines

TRIER, ELSE, humanities educator; b. Gentofte, Copenhagen, Denmark, Oct. 27, 1950; d. Gajus and Jytte (Hannov) T.; children: Kasper Trier-Poulsen, Ditte Trier-Poulsen. Cand.mag. in History/Danish, U. Copenhagen, 1980; Cand.mag. in Data Processing, U. Roskilde, 1990. Student prof. U. Copenhagen, 1976-78; prof. dept. history VUC Vest, Copenhagen, 1980—; lectr., cons. in field. Author: Høje-Taastrup, Past and Present, 1993 (Culture award 1994), Ishøj - Past and Present, 1998, (booklets) The History of Blaakildegård, 1992, The History of Thorshøjgård, 1995; contbr. articles to profl. jours. Bd. dirs. History assn. of Høje Taastrup, 1990. Recipient Cultural award Høje-Taastrup City, 1994. Home: Sek-

skanten Bl, 2630 Taastrup Denmark Office: VUC Vest, Gymnasievej 10, 2620 Albertslund Denmark

TRIER, OIVIND THORVALD DUE, software engineer; b. Oslo, Norway, May 3, 1966; s. Oivind and Ellinor (Glomsaas) T. MS, Norwegian Inst. Technology, Trondheim, 1991; PhD, U. Oslo, 1996. Rsch. asst. Norwegian Inst. Technology, 1990-91; rschr. Norwegian Def. Rsch. Establishment, Kjeller, 1991-92; software engr. Sysdeco Innovation, Kongsberg, Norway, 1992-96; sr. software engr. Sysdeco GIS, Kongsberg, 1997-2000, tech. mgr., 2000—. Mem. IEEE. Avocations: skiing, orienteering, running, rock climbing. Office: Sysdeco GIS, Dyrmyrgata 47 PO Box 433, N-3604 Kongsberg Norway

TRIFONOVA, EMILIA PETROVA, educator, researcher; b. Berkovitsa, Bulgaria, Sept. 30, 1939; d. Peter and Tsvetana (Doitcheva) T.; m. Serafim Ivanov Kamenov, Jan. 5, 1964 (dec. Mar. 1997); children: Kamen, Tsvetana. MS, St. Kliment Ohridski Univ., Sofia, Bulgaria, 1964; PhD, St. Petersburg State Univ., St. Petersburg, Russia, 1973. Researcher St. Kliment Ohridski Univ., Sofia, 1966-76, lectr. in semiconductor chem., 1976-92, assoc. prof., 1992—; invited researcher A.F. Ioffe Physical Tech. Inst. Acad. Scis., St. Petersburg, Russia, 1968; expert Inst. of Inventions & Rationalizations, 1978-80. Contbr. articles to profl. jours.; inventor in field. Recipient rsch. grant Bath Univ. Tech., U.K., 1974. Mem. Union of Scientists of Bulgaria, Orgn. of Bulgarian Physicists. Avocations: music, literature. E-mail: ept@phys.uni-sofia.bg. Office: St Kl Ohridski Univ, 5 J Bourchier Blvd, Sofia 1164, Bulgaria

TRIFTSHÄUSER, WERNER, physics educator; b. Selb, Bavaria, Germany, Mar. 22, 1938; s. Hans and Lina (Ziegler) T.; m. Eva-Lucia Hrncirik, Nov. 13, 1981; children: Germar, Caroline, Natalie. Diploma in physics, Tech. U., Munich, 1962, D. in Natural Scis., 1965. Rsch. assoc. U. N.C., Chapel Hill, 1967-68, Queen's U., Kingston, Can., 1968-70; dir. rsch. group Nuclear Rsch. Ctr., Jülich, Fed. Republic Germany, 1970-75; prof. U. der Bundeswehr, München, 1975—; hon. prof. U. Wuhan, 1994. Mem. Am. Phys. Soc., Deutscher Hochschulverband, Internat. Adv. Com. on Positron Annihilation, N.Y. Acad. Scis. Home: Ringelnatzweg 3, 85521 Ottobrunn Germany Office: U der Bundeswehr München, Werner-Heisenberg-Weg 39, 85577 Neubiberg Germany

TRIGEAUD, JEAN-MARC DANIEL, educator, author; b. Bordeaux, France, Dec. 28, 1951; s. André François Marie and Marguerite Fernande (Peyramayou) T.; m. Marie-Catherine Lea Genevieve Bergey, Oct. 1, 1977; children: Sophie-Héléne, Laurent, Béatrice. Prof. Dr. Philosophy of Law, U. Paris, 1979; postgrad., State U. Bordeaux, 1980. Charge cours faculty law State U. Paris XI, 1975-77, State U Picardie, Amiens, France, 1977-79; asst. faculty law State U. Haute, Normandie, France, 1979-80; maître asst. State U., Bordeaux, France, 1980-83, maître conférences, 1983-92, prof., 1992—. Contbr. articles to profl. jours.; author 14 books including La possession des biens, 1981, Humanisme de la liberté I, 1985, II, 1990, Essais de philosophie du droit, 1987, Philosophie juridique européenne, 1988, Rosmini, 1992, Persona ou la justice au double visage, 1990, Introduction à la philosophie du droit, 1992, Éléments d'une philosophie politique, 1993, Métaphysique et éthique au fondement du droit, 1995, Justice et tolérance, 1997, L'homme coupable, 1999. Mem. Sci. Inst. Paris, Sci. Acad. Genoa, Sci. Acad. Modena, Sci. Acad. Cordoba-Argentina. Roman Catholic. Avocations: archeology, literature. Office: State U Law Bordeaux-Montesquieu, Av L Duguit, 33608 Pessac Cedex, France

TRIGG, DAVID, business management educator; b. Warragul, Australia, Dec. 16, 1942; s. Robert Thomas and Elfriede Cecile (Wittenburg) T.; m. Marie Catherine Glen, Mar. 30, 1968; children: Juanita Marie, Glen David. BA, U. N.E., Armidale, Australia, 1976; MBA, Monash U., Melbourne, 1989, PhD, 1997. Chartered mem. Australian Human Resources Inst. Comdr. Royal Australian Navy, 1964-86; mgr. Dept. Def., Australia, 1986-90; acad. Phillip Inst., Australia, 1991-92, Royal Melbourne Inst. Tech., 1992—; dir. Carpetwool Marketers Ltd., Geelong, Australia, 1990—; ptnr. Davmar Consultancy Group, Melbourne, 1990—; prin. Latrobe Cattle Sta., Wandong, Australia, 1975—; prin. Glenview Dairy Enterprise. Contbr.: Best Management Practices, 1994, Comparative Management Practices, 1995; contbr. articles to profl. jours. Bd. dirs. Kilmore Dist. Hosp., 1992-2000. Mitsui Bank grantee, 1992. Mem. Assn. for Global Bus., Australian New Zealand Acad. Mgmt., Naval and Mil. Club, RAN Ski Club.

TRIGG, TIMOTHY ELLIOT, biotechnology executive; b. Sydney, Australia, Dec. 10; s. Frank Elliot and Margaret Joan (Waterhouse) T.; m. Paula Briggs-Bury, Dec. 30, 1972; children: Angus, Robert. B Rural Sci., U. New Eng., Armidale, Australia, 1968; MSc, U. Aberdeen, Scotland, 1971; PhD, U. Aberdeen, 1974. Scientist Ministry of Agr., Hamilton, New Zealand, 1975-80; leader animal prodn. rsch. Victorian Dept. Agr., Australia, 1980-86; dir. vet. bus. Peptide Tech. Ltd., Sydney, 1987-95; mng. dir. Peptech Animal Health, Sydney, 1995—; sr. cons. ACIL, Lahore, Pakistan, 1985. Editor: Silage in the 80's; contbr. numerous articles to profl. jours.; inventor in field. Trimble Rsch. fellow Govt. New Zealand, 1979. Mem. Australian Inst. Agrl. Sci., Nutrition Soc., Australian Soc. of Animal Prodn., Australian Club, Royal Sydney Yacht Squadron. Avocations: sailing, oenology, music, reading. Home: 8 Yosefa Ave, Warrawee NSW 2074, Australia Office: Peptech Animal Health, Peptech Ltd, 35-41 Waterloo Rd, North Ryde NSW 2113, Australia

TRIGGS, TEAL ANN, design educator, historian; b. Austin, Tex., Apr. 6, 1957; arrived in Eng., 1986; d. Edward Elmer and Rae Janice (Richardson) T.; m. Walter E. Boettcher, Apr. 5, 1980 (div.). BFA in Graphic Design with honors, U. Tex., 1979, MA in Art History, 1983; MA in Design History, Middlesex Poly., London, 1990. Freelance designer, photographer Austin, 1976-86; book designer U. Tex. Press, 1983-86; course leader graphic design Ravensbourne Coll. Design and Comm., London, 1990-96; lectr., course dir. MA, Typo/graphic Studies London Coll. Printing, 1996—; vis. tutor Epsom (Eng.) Sch. Art and Design, 1990, Ctrl. St. Martins, London, 1991-92; external examiner Gwent (Eng.) Coll. Higher Edn., 1993-96, Southampton (Eng.) Inst., 1996-2000, Middlesex U., 1997-2000. Editor: Communicating Design: Essays in Visual Communication, 1995; co-editor: (with R. Sabin) Below Critical Radar: Fanzines and Alternative Comics From 1976 to the Present Day, 2000; contbr. articles to profl. publs. Cofounder Women's Design Rsch. Unit, London, 1995—. Ford Found. grantee in photography, Austin, 1979; rsch. grantee Royal Female Sch. of Art Found., London, 1997; travel grantee Brit. Coun., Israel, U.S., 1996, 97, London Inst. rsch. grants, 1998,99, 2000, Arts and Humanities Rsch. Bd. rsch. grant, 1999. Fellow Soc. Typographic Designers; mem. Coll. Art Assn., Internat. Coun. Graphic Design Assns. Avocation: writing. Office: London Coll Printing, Elephant and Castle, London SE1 6SB, England

TRIGUNAYAT, GOVIND CHANDRA, physics educator; b. Aligarh, India, Apr. 18, 1936; s. Gokul Chandra and Ram Devi Sharma; m. Shachi Rani Trigunayat, May 9, 1960; children: Alok, Neelima, Ajay. BS, Agra U., Aligarh, India, 1953; MS, Aligarh U., 1955; PhD, Delhi U., 1960. Jr. rsch. fellow C.S.I.R., Delhi, 1956-58; sr. rsch. fellow C.S.I.R., 1958-59; lectr. U. Delhi, 1959-68, reader, 1968-79, prof., 1979—; Mem. Nat. Com. Crystallography, Acad. Coun. U. Delhi; lectr. in field. Pres. Maurice Nagar Assn.; founder/chmn. Professors Forum, Delhi U., 1990-91. Mem. Soc. Scientific Values. Avocation: photography. Home: C-13 Maurice Nagar, Delhi 110007, India Office: Dept Physics/Astrophysics, U Delhi, Delhi 110007, Delhi

TRIIPAN, MAIVE, library director; b. Virumaa County, Estonia, Jan. 4, 1942; d. Osvald and Minna (Olesk) Triipan; m. Kalle Dobkevich, Mar. 6, 1971 (div. June 4, 1974); 1 child, Raul. B. of Librarianship, Tartu U., 1967. Rsch. mgmt. asst. Libr. of Estonian Acad. Scis., Tallinn, 1967-74, asst. dir. rsch. work, 1974-84, dir., 1984—; mem. State Libr. Coun., Tallinn, 1974-87, State Libr. Coun. at Dept. of Culture and Edn., Tallinn, 1989—, Tech. U. Coun., Tallinn, 1993—, Estonian Nat. Libr. Coun., Tallinn, 1994—; fin. mgr. Merelaug, 1998-99; project mgmt. Scis. Dept. Estonian Inst. Pub. Adminstrn. Editl. bd. Estonian Retrospective, 1975; mng. pub. National Bibliography 1525-1940, 1993. Mem. Estonian Librs. Assn. Avocations: literature, music, art. Address: Acad Scis, Ravala Ave 10, EE0100 Tallinn Estonia*

TRIKAMJEE, ASHWIN HIRJEE, lawyer; b. Durban, Kwazulu, South Africa, Nov. 29, 1944; s. Hirjee and Jumna (Thanki) T.; m. Mridula Mackenjee, Nov. 29, 1973; children: Shaylen, Thulja. JD, U. South Africa, 1974. Pres. South African Soccer Fedn. Profl. League, 1978-91; chmn. Nat. Soccer League, South Africa, 1992-94, Soccer City, South Africa, 1992-94; pres., dir. South African Post Office, 1992-94; dir. Masters Internat., South Africa, 1995-96, Fasic Ltd., South Africa, 1997—, Lion Match Ltd., South Africa, 1999—; pres. South African Mindu Mahasagha, 1998—; atty. Carlicke & Bousfield, Inc., Durban. Vice pres. Natal Indian Congress, South Africa, 1971-73; treas. South African Students Orgn., 1972; founder mem. Black People's conv., 1971; trustee Steve Biko Meml. Trust, 1985. Mem. South African Football Assn. (v.p. 1992-94), Durban Legal Ctr. (pres. 1981-83), Natal Law Soc. (pres. 1992-94), Assn. of Law Socs. South Africa (pres. 1997-98). Hindu. Avocations: squash, gym, running. Office: Carlicke & Bousfield Inc, 333 Smith St 22d Flr, 4001 Durban Natal, Republic of South Africa

TRIKHA, AJIT, psychiatrist; b. Madras, India, Oct. 14, 1952. MB BS, Armed Forces Coll. Poona U., 1974. Diplomate Am. Bd. Psychiatry and Neurology, Geriatric Psychiatry, Am. Bd. Forensic Medicine. Intern Montefiore Med. Ctr.-Albert Einstein Coll. Medicine, Bronx, N.Y., 1988-89; resident psychiatry Goodmayes-St. Bartholomew's-The Royal London Hosps., 1982-86, Watford Gen. Hosp., Hertfordshire, Eng., 1986-87; fellow psychiatry Washington U., St. Louis, 1987-88; med. dir. Mid-America Behavioral Healthcare, Inc., Belleville, Ill., 1992-98, Rock Creek Partial Hospitalization Program, Cahokia, Ill., 1996-98; mgr. St. Mary's Partial Hospitalization Program, Cahokia, Ill., 1998-00; med. dir. Counseling Ctr., Belleville, 1998-2000. Mem. AMA, Am. Psychiat. Assn. Office: 6915 W Main St Belleville IL 62223-3029

TRILL, PAULINE MAUD, investment and financial planning executive; b. London, June 13, 1946; d. Walter Robert and Edith Dorothy (Morris) Franklin; m. David Trill; children: Graham, Rachel, Elizabeth. Cert. fin. planner. Investment and fin. planning mgr. David Roberts and Ptns. Ltd., Lancs. Vol. Cancer Rsch. Mem. Life Ins. Assn. (by diploma). Avocations: walking, swimming, reading, cooking. Home: 4 Bellaby Park, Nawton York YO62 yRA, England

TRILLO, FEDERICO, federal official. Min. of def. Spain. Office: Ministry of Def, Paseo de la Castellana 109, 28016 Madrid Spain*

TRIMBLE, DAVID, first minister designate of Northern Ireland; b. Bangor, Co Down, North Ireland, Oct. 15, 1944; m. Daphne Elizabeth Orr, 1978; children: Richard, Victoria, Nicholas, Sarah. Lectr. in law Queen's U., Belfast, Northern Ireland, 1968; mem. Vanguard Unionist Party, 1973, Ulster Unionist Party, 1978; mem. parliament for Upper Bann, 1990; leader Ulster Unionist Party Govt. of Ireland, 1995—, first min., 1998—. Co-recipient Nobel Peace prize, 1998. Avocations: classical music, opera, history, reading. Office: Ulster Unionist Party, 3 Glengall St, Belfast BT12 5AE, Northern Ireland*

TRIMECHE, ABDESSELEM, veterinarian researcher; b. Monastir, Tunisia, Mar. 18, 1964; s. Neji and Fatma (Aguir) T.; m. Sonia Ben Younes; 1 child, Nada. DVM, Vet. Sch., Tunisia, 1990; M for Animal Prodn., I.S.P.A., Rennes, France, 1994; PhD, U. Rennes, 1996. Med. Diplomate. Vetinarian Vet. Sch., Nantz, France, 1990-96; postdoctoral INRA, Nouzilly, France, 1996-98; rschr. Inst. de la Recherche, Tunis, Tunisia, 1998—; prof. asst. Vet. Sch., Tunisia. Author: (book) Thriogenology, 1996, Cryobiology, 1997; inventor of Medium for Equine Spermatozoa Cryopreservation, 1996, Theriogenology, 1998, 99. Office: Vet Sch, 2020 Sidi Thabet, 1006 Tunis Tunisia

TRINAJSTIĆ, NENAD, research scientist; b. Zagreb, Croatian, Oct. 26, 1936; s. Cvijetko and Regina (Pavić) T.; m. Judita Juričev, Mar. 26, 1960; children: Regina, Dean. BTech, U. Zagreb, 1960, MSc, 1966, PhD, 1967. Rsch. asst. Inst. R. Bošković, Zagreb, 1962-67, dozent, 1967-71, assoc. prof., 1971-77, prof., 1977—. Author: Chemical Graph Theory, 1983, 2d edit., 1992; editor Croatica Chem. Acta, 1994—. Recipient award City of Zagreb City Coun., 1973, State Sci. award State Coun., 1982. Mem. Matrix Croatica, Croatian Acad., Knights of Croatian Dragon, P.E.N. Club Zagreb. Achievements include being one of founders of mathematical chemistry. Avocations: movies, sports, walking, reading. Home: Zorkovačka 4 Apt 911, HR10000 Zagreb Croatia

TRINCO, ORNELLA MARIA, publishing executive; b. Johannesburg, South Africa, Jan. 11, 1956; d. Adelino and Anna Trinico. Grad., Wits U., Johannesburg, 1978. With African Bus. Pty. Ltd., South Africa, 1981-88; publ. Dictum Publs. Pty. Ltd., Gardenview, South Africa, 1988—, also bd. dirs. Mem. Inst. Adminstrn. and Commerce. Avocations: reading, gardening.

TRINDADE, ARMANDO, archbishop; b. Goa, Oct. 25, 1927; arrived in Pakistan, 1927; s. Athanasius Crispin and Olinda (D'Souza) T. M in Philosophy, Papal U., Kandy, Sri Lanka, 1946, M in Theology, 1950; MA with honors, Oxford (Eng.) U., 1960; MA in Edn., U. Notre Dame, 1963; PhD in Edn., Stanford U., 1971. Consecrated bishop, 1973. Asst. prin., prin. in various schs. Pakistan, 1951-70; variouis pastoral assignments Eng., Scotland, U.S.A., 1951-73; bishop Lahore, Pakistan, 1973-93, archbishop, 1994—. Home and Office: Archbishop of Lahore, 1 Lawrence Rd PO Box 909, Lahore 54000, Pakistan

TRINGALE, ANTHONY ROSARIO, insurance executive; b. Syracuse, N.Y., Apr. 20, 1942; s. Anthony and Susan Marie Tringale; children: Anthony William, Michael Paul, Mark David, Amber Marie. BSFS, Georgetown U., 1967; CLU, Am. Coll. Life Underwriters, 1973. CLU,. Office mgr. trainee N.Y. Life Ins. Co. No. Va., 1965-66; office mgr. N.Y. Life Ins. Co. No. Va., Fairfax, Va., 1966, field underwriter, 1966-68; mgmt. asst. home office N.Y. Life Ins. Co., N.Y.C., 1973; gen mgr. N.Y. Life Ins. Co., Pitts., 1973-76; gen. mgr. Acacia Mut. Life Ins. Co., Annandale, Va., 1976-83; fin. and ins. planner, mgmt. and mktg. cons. Acacia Mut. Life Ins. Co., Annandale, 1983-86; from field rep. to mktg. com. Acacia Mut. Life, Anandale, Va., 1983-86; pres. Benefits By Design, Fairfax, Va., 1986—, Acacia Prodn. Clubs, 1984, 86; lectr. estate and employee and exec. fringe benefit plans and retirement programs, bus. ins. and comm.; mem. steering com. Entrepreneurship Forum, Washington, 1980—; nat. adv. bd. Entrepreurship Inst., Columbus, Ohio, 1985—; mem., chmn. Mktg. Edn. Adv. Coun., Commonwealth of Va. Supts. Bus. and Industry Adv. Coun., 1989—; mem. Mktg Edn. Adv. Bd. Fairfax County Pub. Schs., 1980—; chmn. 1983-84, 90-91. Contbr. articles in field of personal and bus. fin. strategies to Md. Bus. Observer, Washington Bus. Jour., NALU's Life Assoc. News; 4 yr. radio host Basically Bus. Sta. WGMS-FM, Washington. Trustee SME-1 Accreditation Inst. U. Memphis, 1990-99; trustee GSSMM SME1 Syracuse U., 1995-99, past liason rep. Am. Soc. CLUs, Bryn Mawr, Pa. 1988-98, bd. dirs., v.p. exec. com., chmn. grants com. No. Va. Cmty. Found.; founding vice chmn. Fairfax Orgn. Christians/Jews United in Service; arbitrator Fairfax County Dept Consumer Affairs; lector, extraordinay minister Basilica Nat. Shrine Immaculate Conception, 19806; bd. dirs. Summer Opera Theater Co., 1996-98; past chmn. planned giving com. ARC; v.p., sec., bd. dirs., exec. com. The Jeane Dixon Children to Children Found.; chmn. VIP panel D.C. and No. Va., 1988-92, pres. 1992-94; mem. adv. bd. D.C. Fairfax County Salvation Army Corps; bd. dirs. Nat. Cath. Cmty. Found., 1996-97; bd. dirs. Birch Pond Homeowners Assn., pres., 1998-2000; past pres., bd. dirs., exec. com. United Cerebral Palsy of D.C. and No. Va., 1985—. Mem. No. Va. Soc. CLUs (past pres.), Am. Soc. CLUs, No. Va. Assn. Life Underwriters (treas. 1972, nat. com. 1997-99, Pres.' Cup 1991-92), Assn. Advanced Life Underwriting, Sales and Mktg. Execs. Met. Washington (pres. 1979-80, 95-97, treas. 1989-92, bd. dirs. 1990—, sr. v.p. profl. devel. 1993-95), Nat. Assn. Life Underwriters (nat. agent award Gen. Agts. and Mgrs. Conf. 1976-83, exec. com. 1984-85, life qualifying), No. Va. Estate Planning Coun. (exec. com. 1985-92, pres. 1990-91), Internat. Platform Assn. (trustee, bd. govs. 1990-2000), No. Va. Gen. Agts. and Mgrs. Assn. (pres. 1980-81, dir. 1982-83), Greater Washington Area Health Underwriters, Fairfax County C. of C. (dir. small bus. 1989-90, dir. membership 1990-91, exec. com. dir. at large 1991-92, Small Bus. Adv. of Yr. award 1990), Nat. Christopher Columbus Quincentary Jubilee Adv. Bd. (dir. at large 1995—), Nat. Italian-Am. Found. Coun. of 1000 and Italian Am. Leaders Com. Venture Clinic (chmn., pres. 1989-94, TV interviewer, host The Venture Game), Million Dollar Round Table (life, qualified), John Carroll Soc. Ins. Club Washington (pres. 1997-98), Birch Pond Homeowners Assn. (pres. bd. dirs. 1998-2000). Office: Ins Cons Group 12813 Dogwood Hills #222 Fairfax VA 22033-3249

TRINGER, LÁSZLÓ, psychiatrist, educator; b. Györszentmárton, Györ, Hungary, Apr. 2, 1939; s. Márton and Mártonné (Fridrich Róza) T.; m. Katalin Mariházi, sept. 5, 1965; children: T. Ágoston, T. Zoltón, Dóra. MD, Semmelweis U., Budapest, 1963. Intern, resident psychiat. clinic Semmelweis U.; asst. Semmelweis U., Budapest, 1963-65, rsch. asst. psychiat. dept., 1965-70, head divsn. psychiatry, 1970-89, prof., 1989—, dir. tchg. hosp., 1992-94, dir., head dept. psychiatry, 1994—, head ednl. com., 1991—. Author: Clinical behavior therapy, 1985, Therapeutic Conversation, 1991, Anxiety and Anxiety Disorders, 1996, Textbook of Psychiatry, 1999,. Mem. Hungarian Assn. Psychiatry (gen. sec. 1980-89), Hungarian Assn. Cognitive Behavior Therapy, European Assn. Cognitive Behavior therapy (pres. 1995-96). Roman Catholic. Avocations: gardening, handwork, music. Office: Semmelweis Univ, Balassa 6, H-1083 Budapest Hungary

TRINH, CAM-TU T., chemist; b. Saigon, Vietnam, Feb. 16, 1972; s. Cuong Quoc Trinh and Hoa Kim Lam; m. Tai Huu Nguyen, Aug. 2, 1998. AS, Kapiolani C.C., Honolulu, 1994; BS, U. Hawaii, 1996. Immigrant worker Pacific Gateway Ctr., Honolulu, 1997—; home hosp. tutor Dept. Edn., Honolulu, 1998—; rschr. NSF, U. Hawaii, 1995. Club advisor Vietnamese Club McKinley H.S., 1997—. Mem. Am. Chemistry Soc. (treas. 1995-96). Avocations: playing Vienamese folk instrument, crafting, collecting stamps, gardening. Fax: 808-842-1962. Home: 736 Lukepane Ave Honolulu HI 96816-1013 Office: Pacific Gateway Ctr 720 N King St Honolulu HI 96817-4511

TRIPATHI, PRABODH CHANDRA, manufacturing company executive; b. Deoria, India, Jan. 1, 1944; s. Arjun and Gandhari T.; m. Dipti Sharma, June 6, 1973. BS, BHU, Banaras, India, 1965; M Tech, IIT, Bombay, 1967; ME, Nova Scotia Tech. U., Halifax, Can., 1968. Assoc. prof. dept. elec. engring. Pant U., Nainital, India, 1971-74; sr. engr., dep. mgr., mgr. Bharat Heavy Elecs. Ltd., Hardwar/New Delhi, 1974-85; sr. mgr., head elec. Bharat Heavy Elecs. Ltd., New Delhi, 1986-88, dep. gen. mgr., sr. dy. gen. mgr. head elec., 1989-94, additional gen. mgr., head elec., 1995-96, gen. mgr., 1997—; assoc. prof. elec. engring. Pant U., Nainital, 1971-74; project engr. BHEL, New Delhi, 1975-88, elec. engring. mgr., 1989-95, mgr. of engring., info. tech. and procurement, 1996—. Contbr. articles to profl. jours.; mem. editl. com. BHEL Feedback Jour., 1994—. Fellow Instn. Engrs./India; mem. IEEE (sr.), Computer Soc. of India, IEEE (Commendation for Notable Svcs. 1988). Avocation: reading. Home: E-2114 Palam Vihar, Gurgaon/Haryana India Office: Bharat Heavy Elec Ltd, BHEL House/Sirifort, New Delhi 110 049, India

TRIPATHI, SHRI KANT, ecologist, researcher; b. Varanasi, India, Jan. 1, 1964; s. Radhey Shyam and Sabitri (Mishra) T.; m. Durgawati Pandey, May 31, 1985; children: Saurabh, Shivam. BSc, Gorakhpur (India) U., 1983; MSc, Kumaum U., Nainital, India, 1985; PhD, Banaras Hindu U., Varanasi, India, 1992. Jr. rsch. fellow Banaras Hindu U., Varanasi, 1986-89, sr. rsch. fellow, 1989-92, rsch. assoc., 1993-98, scientist, 1999—. session chmn. VI Internat. Congress, Manchester, Eng., 1994; chmn. Ctr. Environment and Rural Devel., Varanasi, 1997—. Fellow Tropical Ecology; mem. Rsch. Assocs. Assn. (mem. gov. body 1997—), Internat. Assn. for Ecology, Indian Sci. Congress Assn., Current Sci. Assn. Home: K 53/53 Madhyameshwar, Varanasi 221001, India Office: Banaras Hindu U, Varanasi India

TRIPATHI, YAMINI BHUSAN, biochemist, educator, researcher; b. Varanasi, India, Apr. 30, 1957; s. Surendra Narain and Radha (Upadhyay) T.; m. Pratibha Shukla; children: Deepshikha, Suyash, Bharat Bhusan. BS, Banaras Hindu U., Varanasi, 1977, MS in Biochemistry, 1979, PhD in Biochemistry, 1983. Rsch. asst. Banaras Hindu U., 1979-81, demonstrator, 1981-84, lectr., 1981-89, sr. lectr., 1989-93, reader, 1993—; postdoctoral fellow Tubingen U., Germany, 1983; vis. scientist Indian Inst. of Science, Bangalore, India, 1989-90, Mo. U., 1990-91, Temple U., Pa., 1996, UCLA; gen. sec. Young Scientists Assn., Banaras Hindu U., 1981-83, pres., 1982-85, pres. ABVP, 1981-83, head dept. medicinal chemistry, 1993-96, gen. sec. Tchrs. Assn., 1995. Editor: Medical Systejms with Holistic Approach. Pres. SNT Meml. Found., Varanasi, 1992—. With Nat. Cadet Corp., 1976-78. Recipient grant DRDO Ministry of Def. 1998, Univ. Grants Commn., 1985, 91, grant Ministry of Health, 1997, Univ. Grant Commn. Career award, Young Scientist award., Nat. Biotechnology award, Molecular Biology award, Malaviya Medal; grantee Dept. Biotechnology, 1999. Mem. Soc. Biol. Chemistry (life), Indian Sci. Congress Assn. (life), Prof. S.N. Tripathi Meml. Found. Radiation Biology (life). Hindu. Avocations: populization of science, health practices and moral ethos through lectures, exhibitions and publications. E-mail: yamini@banares.ernet.in. Home: 71 Krishna Bagh Nagwa, Varanasi 221 005, India Office: Banaras Hindu U Inst Med Scis, Dept Medicinal Chemistry, Varanasi 221 005, India

TRIPP, JOHN HOWARD, pediatrician, consultant, educator; b. Dartford, Kent, England, Nov. 16, 1944; s. George Frederic and Ann (Buckingham) T.; m. Judy Margaret Peskett; children: Melanie Ruth, Esther Anne. BSc, Guy's Hosp., London, 1965; MBBS, Guys Hosp., London, 1969; MD, U. London, London. House officer Guy's Hosp., London, 1968-69; sr. house officer Great Ormond St. Children's Hosp., London, 1971; registrar Hosp. for Sick Children, London, 1971-73, sr. registrar, 1977-80; rsch. fellow Inst. Child Health, London, 1973-76; cons. pediatrician Royal Devon & Exeter (England) Hosp., 1980—; sr. lectr. U. Exeter, 1984—. Editor: Manual of Pediatric Gastroenterology & Nutrition, 1992, Guidelines on the Practice of Ethics Committees in Medical Research Involving Human Subjects, 1996; contbr. articles to profl. jours. Rsch. grantee Joseph Rountree Found., 1990, 92, NHS Exec. Fellow Royal Coll. Physicians of Eng., Royal Coll. Paediatrics and Child Health of Eng. Avocations: sailing, farming, skiing. Home: Pixie Cottage Alphington, EX2 8TD Exeter Devon, England Office: U Exeter Hosp Dept Child Health, Church Rd Heavitree, EX2 5SQ Exeter Devon, England

TRIPP, KAREN BRYANT, lawyer; b. Rocky Mount, N.C., Sept. 2, 1955; d. Bryant and Katherine Rebecca (Watkins) Tripp; m. Robert Mark Burleson, June 25, 1977 (div. 1997); 1 child, Hamilton Chase Tripp Barnett. BA, U. N.C., 1976; JD, U. Ala., 1981. Bar: Tex. 1981, U.S. Dist. Ct. (so. dist.) Tex. 1982, U.S. Ct. Appeals (fed. cir.) 1983, U.S. Dist. Ct. (ea. dist.) Tex. 1991, U.S. Supreme Ct. 1994, U.S. Dist. Ct. (no. dist.) Tex. 1998, U.S. Ct. Appeals (5th cir.) 2000. Law clk. Tucker, Gray & Espy, Tuscaloosa, Ala., 1978-81; law clk. to presiding justice Ala. Supreme Ct., Montgomery, summer 1980; atty. Exxon Prodn. Rsch. Co., Houston, 1981-86, coord. tech. transfer, 1986-87; assoc. Arnold, white and Durkee, Houston, 1988-93, shareholder, 1994-98; shareholder Winstead, Sechrest & Minick, Attys. at Law, Houston, 1998; pres. Blake Barnett & Co., 1996—; pvt. practice, 1999—; Creator, program planner, master of ceremonies 1st and 2d intellectual property law confs. for women corp. counsels. Editor Intellectual Property Law Rev., 1995-00; contbr. articles to profl. jours. Chair U. Houston Fall CLE Inst., 2000. Mem. ABA (intellectual property law sect., ethics com. 1992-96), Houston Bar Assn. (interprofl. rels. com. 1988-90), Houston Intellectual Property Law Assn. (outstanding inventor com. 1982-84, chmn. 1994-95, sec. 1987-88, treas. 1991-92, bd. dirs. 1992-94, 98-2000, nominations com. 1993, 96, chmn. fall CLE Inst.), Tex. Bar Assn. (antitrust law com. 1984-85, chmn. internat. law com. intellectual property law sect. 1987-88, internat. transfer tech. com. 1983-84), Tex. Exec. Women, Women's Fin. Exch., Am. Intellectual Property Lawyers Assn. (patent law com. 1995), Women in Tech. (founder), Lil Eli's Club (founder), Phi Alpha Delta. Democrat. Episcopalian. Office: 1100 Louisiana St Ste 2690 Houston TX 77002-5216

TRISI, PAOLO, dental researcher; b. Pescata, Italy, Dec. 26, 1964; s. Mario and Maria Luisa (Retrosi) T.; m. Irene Agrestini, Mar. 13, 1986; children: Valeria, Alessio, Francesco. Degree in dentistry, U. Chieti, Italy, 1988; PhD, U. Rome, 1994. Asst. prof. U. Chieti, 1988-94; sci. dir. Biomaterials Clin. Rsch. Assn., Pescara, Italy, 1995-97, Pescara, 1997—. Home: Via San Silvestro 163/3, 65132 Pescara Italy Office: Biomaterials Clin Rsch Assn, Via San Silvestro 163/1, 65132 Pescara Italy

TRISTO, GASTONE, chemist; b. Padua, Italy, Feb. 24, 1947; s. Pietro and Norma (Camprese) T.; m. Francesca Lucia Pilon, Apr. 27, 1975. Degree in Chemistry, U. Padua, 1971. Asst. U. Padua, 1972-73; asst. Istituto Zooprofilattico, Padua, 1974-82, head of lab., 1982-88, head dept. chemistry, 1988—. Contbr. articles to profl. jours. Pres. Assn. Reg. Mutilati della Voce, Padua, 1995. Avocations: television, playing guitar, music. Home: Via G Crivellari 19, Rio di Ponte San Nic, 35020 Veneto Italy Office: Inst Zooprofilattico Speri, delle Venezie Strada Romea n. 14/a, Agripolis 35020 Legnaro Veneto, Italy

TRITLE, LAWRENCE ALAN, history educator; b. Glendale, Calif., Oct. 13, 1946; s. Robert Charles Jr. and Dorothy (Brown) T.; m. Margaret Burlington, Jan. 31, 1970. BA, UCLA, 1968; MA, U. S. Fla., 1972; PhD, U. Chgo., 1978. Prof. Loyola Marymount U., L.A., 1978—, Marie Chilton chair humanities, 1988; vis. prof. Loyola U. Chgo., 1981-82, 90-91, UCLA, 1992. Author: Phocion the Good, 1988, From Melos to My Lai. War & Survival, 2000; editor: The Greek World in the Fourth Century BC, 1997, Balkan Currents, 1998, Text and Tradition: Studies in Greek History & Histiography, 1999. Lt. U.S. Army, 1968-71, Vietnam. NEH fellow U. Pa., 1979. Mem. Am. Philol. Assn. (chair com. ancient history 1997-99), Am. Hist. Assn., Assn. Ancient Historians, Soc. Mayflower Descendants (So. Calif. chpt.). Democrat. Home: 7222 W 78th St Los Angeles CA 90045-2516 Office: Loyola Marymount U 7900 Loyola Blvd Ste 1 Los Angeles CA 90045-2699

TRITT, LINCOLN C., writer, educator, musician; b. Salmon River, Alaska, Oct. 18, 1946; s. Isaac Albert and Naomi (Peter) T. Grad., Mt. Edgecombe H.S., 1966; student, U. Alaska, 1972, 84-87; student electricity and electronics, Naval Tng. Ctr., 1967, student radioman class A sch., 1967; studied with traditional tchrs. Exploration worker, driver, driller asst. Kandik Oil Field Parker Exploration, Fairbanks, Alaska, 1977; negotiator Venetie (Alaska) Tribal Govt., 1980, heavy equipment operator, 1982; phone survey rep. Mental Health Program and U. Alaska, 1984; curriculum developer Yukon Flats (Alaska) Sch. Dist., 1985; laborer Peter Kewitt and sons, Deadhorse, Alaska, 1985; bookkeeper Tanana Chiefs Conf., Inc., on-site supr., 1985; translator fed. Indian law Fed. Indian Law workshop, Venetie, Alaska, 1986; grant contract negotiator with fed. agys., 1987; grant adminstr., overall project dir. Arctic Village Traditional Coun., 1988-89; liaison, coord. U.S. Geophys. Inst./U. Alaska, Fairbanks, 1989; instr. rural coll. U. Alaska, 1990; tribal adminstr. Native Vill. Venetie (Alaska), 1994-95; carpenter Bur. Indian Affairs Sch., Arctic Vill., Alaska, 1970; postal clk. U.S. Postal Svc., Fairbanks, Alaska, 1971, substitute postmaster, 1984—; tchr. Gwich'in lang., 1974; store mgr. Midnight Sun Native Store, Arctic Village, Alaska, 1975. Author screenplay on Native Am. alcohol experience; contbr. essays, stories to Raven Tells Stories: An Anthology of Alaska Native Writings, Coyote Bark, Alaska Mag., Alaskan Epiphany, All Alaska Weekly, Talking Leaves, Tundra Times, The Turtle Quarterly, The Council, Nimrod; columnist Fairbanks Daily News Miner, Northland News; composer (song) Belief; mem. of cast: Earth and the Great Weather, 1993, 95, 97; performed at Athabascan Old-Time Fiddling Festival, Summer Folk Festival, Fairbanks Folk Festival, Plate and Palate Restaurant, Native Village at Alaskaland; cons. (videos, films) Wisdom of the Elders, Caribou People. Firefighter Dept. Natural Resource, Fairbanks, Alaska, 1984; lobbyist Gwich'in People, 1986-87; mem. restructuring com. Howard Luke Alternative Sch., 1993, 94; Rural Campuses U. Alaska, 1990; coord. first Gwich'in Gathering in Arctic Village, Alaska, 1988; mem. coun. Native Village of Venetie (Alaska) Govt., 1974-86; mem. Arctic Village Traditional Coun., 1973-89, chief, 1987-89; mem. sch. bd. Arctic Village, 1974-76. Served with USN, 1966-70, Vietnam. Mem. Native Writers Circle of Ams., Internat. Conf. Higher Edn. Indigenous People, Internat. Conf. Hunting and Gathering Socs., Alaska Native Viet Nam Vets, Fairbanks Folk Fest. Avocations: music, photography, recording, space science, history. Home: PO Box 22016 Arctic Village AK 99722-0016

TRITT-GOC, JADWIGA, physicist, researcher; b. Poznań, Poland, July 27, 1953; d. Władysław and Aniela (Nowostawska) T.; m. Roman Goc, Mar. 10, 1939; 1 child, Michał. MSc, A. Mickiewicz U., Poznań, Poland, 1977; PhD in Molecular Physics, Polish Acad. Sci., Poznań, Poland, 1985, Habilitation, 1996. Rsch. worker Inst. Molecular Physics, Polish Acad. Sci., Poznań, Poland, 1980-84, asst. prof., 1990—; vis. rsch. assoc. U. Ill., Chgo. 1985-86, vis. asst. prof., 1988-90; assoc. prof. Inst. Molecular Physics, Polish Acad. Sci., 1997—. Contbr. over 40 articles to profl. jours. State Com. for Sci. Rsch. grantee Inst. Molecular Physics, Polish Acad. Sci., Poznań, 1995-96. Roman Catholic. Avocations: books, politics, music. Home: Odolanowska 38, 60-161 Poznan Poland Office: Polish Acad Sci, Smoluchowskiego 17, 60-179 Poznan Poland

TRITTIN, JUERGEN, government official. Min. European and fed. affairs Lower Saxony, Germany, 1990-94; min. conservation and nuclear safety Govt. of Germany, min. of environment. Office: Ministry of Environment, Alexanderplatz 6, 11055 Berlin Germany*

TRIVEDI, HITESH K., research scientist. BSME, Sardar Petel U., India, 1984; MSMAE, Ill. Inst. Tech., 1990. Lectr. Birla Vishwakarma Mahavidyalaya Eng. Coll., Vallabh-Vidyanagar Nagar, India, 1984-88; rsch. asst. IIT, Chgo., 1988-90; program mgr. UES, Inc, Dayton, Ohio, 1991—. Contbr. articles to profl. jours. Mem. ASME, Soc. Tribology & Lubrication Engrs. (chmn. aerospace coun. 1996, chmn. Dayton chpt. 1997, Capt. Alfred Hunt award 1999), Soc. Automotive Engrs. Office: UES Inc 4401 Dayton Xenia Rd Dayton OH 45432-1805

TRIVEDI, NIKUNJ MANIKANT, homeopath, researcher; b. Botad, Gujarat, India, June 18, 1959; s. Manikant Gaurishanker and Chandrika Manikant/Naradlal Trivedi; m. Amita Nikunj Janardan Bhatt, Dec. 14, 1985; children: Arti Nikunj, Parth Nikunj. Diploma in homeo. medicine and surgery, Homeopathic Med. Coll., Anand, India, 1980. Cons. homeopath Arti Clinic, Anand. Contbr. rsch. articles to profl. jours. Ex-project chmn. Slum-Medi-Aids, Gujrat, 1983-86; pres. Rotaract Club, Anand-Gujarat, 1984-85, mem. adv. bd. blood donation, 1983-84; mem. Jaycees, Vallabh, Vidyanagar, 1981-82. Named Best Dr., Jaycees, 1981-82, Best Project Chmn., Rotaract, 1983-86. Mem. Soc. Homeopaths (Eng.: overseas mem.), Brit. Homeopathic Assn., Homeopathic Med. Assn. India (life), Anand Homeopathic Med. Assn. (life). Avocations: traveling, wildlife, music-ghazals, writing poetry ghazals. Fax: 59271. Home: Arti Clinic Arti Complex, 388 120 V V Nagar Gujarat, India Office: Arti Clinic, Shanti-Niketan I P Rd, 388 001 Anand Gujarat, India

TRIVEDY, CHETAN RAMESCHANDRA, head and neck oncologist, researcher; b. Nairobi, Kenya, June 10, 1969; s. Rameschandra Himatlal Trivedy and Mradulagauri Bhanushankar Raval. B of Dental Surgery, U. Liverpool, Eng., 1993; postgrad., King's Coll., London, 1995—. Cert., Gen. Dental Coun. House officer in dentistry U. Liverpool, 1993; sr. house officer in oral and maxillofacial surgery Mt. Vernon Hosp., London, 1993-95; hon. rsch. fellow Royal Coll. Surgeons dept. dental scis. King's Coll. Dental Inst., London, 1995—; part-time assoc. specialist in oral surgery Northwick Park Hosp., London, 1996-99; part-time assoc. oral/dental surgeon, London; part-time non-resident emergency dental surgeon King's Coll. Hosp., London, 1996—; adviser, founder King's Areca Nut Rsch. Group, London; dir., founder Brahmin Millennium Health Project, London. Contbr. articles to profl. jours. Health promoter, adviser to Indian cmty. in London; fund raiser King's Brainwave Appeal, 1999. Recipient Oral and Dental Rsch. Trust award, 1997, Cert. of Merit, Dental divsn. Royal Soc. Medicine, 1997, Dental Rschr. of Yr. award Faculty of Gen. Dental Practitioners, 1999. Fellow Royal Coll. Surgeons Eng.; mem. Brit. Assn. Head and Neck Oncologists (traveling fellow 1997), Indian Med. Assn. Hindu. Avocations: trekking/climbing, wildlife, fund raising, Indian semi-classical music. E-mail: c.trivedy@kcl.ac.uk. Home: 45 Scarle Rd, Wembley HAO 4SR, England Office: RCS Dental Scis, Caldecot Rd, London SE5 9RW, England

TRIVELPIECE, ALVIN WILLIAM, physicist, educator, consultant; b. Stockton, Calif., Mar. 15, 1931; s. Alvin Stevens and Mae (Hughes) T.; m. Shirley Ann Ross, Mar. 23, 1953; children: Craig Evan, Steve Edward, Keith Eric. BS, Calif. Poly. Coll., San Luis Obispo, 1953; MS, Calif. Inst. Tech., 1955, PhD, 1958. Fulbright scholar Delft (Netherlands) U., 1958-59; asst. prof., then asso. prof. U. Calif. at Berkeley, 1959-66; prof. physics U. Md., 1966-76; on leave as asst. dir. for research div. controlled thermonuclear

research AEC, Washington, 1973-75; v.p. Maxwell Labs. Inc., San Diego, 1976-78; corp. v.p. Sci. Applications, Inc., La Jolla, Calif., 1978-81; dir. Office of Energy Research, U.S. Dept. Energy, Washington, 1981-87; exec. officer AAAS, Washington, 1987-88; dir. Oak Ridge (Tenn.) Nat. Lab. 1989-2000; v.p. Martin Marietta Energy Systems, 1989-95, Lockheed Martin Energy Systems, 1995; pres. Lockheed Martin Energy Rsch. Corp., 1996-2000; pvt. cons. Oak Ridge, 2000—; head del. joint NAS and Soviet Acad. Scis. mtg. and conf. on energy and global ecol. problems, USSR, 1989; chmn. math. scis. ednl. bd. NAS, 1990-93; chmn. coordinating coun. for edn. NRC, 1991-93, mem. Commn. on Phys. Scis., Math. and Applications, 1993-96; bd. dirs. Bausch & Lomb, Inc., Rochester, N.Y., 1989—; mem. Tenn. Sci. and Tech. Adv. Commn., 1993-96, chmn., 1996-99; adv. com. Federal Networking Coun., 1992-96; chmn. and pres. Tenn. Tech. Devel. Corp. 1998-2000. Author: Slow Wave Propagation in Plasma Wave Guides, 1966, Principles of Plasma Physics, 1973; also articles. Named Disting. Alumnus, Calif. Poly. State U., 1978, Calif. Inst. Tech., Pasadena, Calif., 1987; recipient U.S. Sec. of Energy's Gold medal for Disting. Svc., 1986, Disting. Assoc. award, 2000, Tenn. Outstanding Svc. Commendation, Senate Joint Resolution #530, 2000; Guggenheim fellow, 1966. Fellow AAAS, IEEE (Outstanding Engr. award region 3 1995), Am. Phys. Soc.; mem. AAUP, NAE, Am. Nuclear Soc., Am. Assn. Physics Tchrs., Capital Hill Club, Nat. Press Club, Sigma Xi, Tau Beta Pi. Achievements include patents in field. Home and Office: 8 Rivers Run Way Oak Ridge TN 37830-9004

TRKAL, VIKTOR, physical chemist, researcher; b. Praha, Czechoslovakia, Mar. 13, 1929; s. Viktor and Maria (Baštecká) T.; m. Miroslava Fendrichová, Mar. 26, 1955; 1 child, Michaela. MA, Charles U., Praha, Czech Republic, 1952, PhD, 1958. Asst. Charles U., 1951-52; rschr. Rsch. Inst. Physics, Praha, 1953-55, Inst. Radio Engring. and Elec. Acad. Sci. Czech Republic, Praha, 1995-2000; dir. Inst. Raido Engring. and Elec. Acad. Sci. Czech Republic, Praha, 1990-94, rschr., 1995—. Author 4 books in field; contbr. over 70 articles to profl. jours. Lt. Czechoslovak Army, 1953-56. Mem. European Phys. Soc., Czech Phys. Soc., Czech Chem. Soc. Home: Vršni 39, CZ 18200 Praha 8, Czech Republic Office: Acad Sci Czech Republic, Chaberská 57, 182 51 Praha 8, Czech Republic

TRKANJEC, ZLATKO, physician, consultant; b. Virovitica, Croatia, Dec. 17, 1958; s. Mirko and Barica (Trefil) T.; m. Jasna Tekavec, Mar. 6, 1982; 1 child, Luka. MD, Zagreb Sch. Medicine, Croatia, 1982, MS, 1992, PhD, 1999. Splst. neurology, 1983. Intern Clin. Hosp. Ctr., Zagreb, Croatia, 1983; physician Health Ctrs., Zabok and Poreč, Croatia, 1984; physician Klenovnik (Croatia) Hosp., 1986-96, head dept. alcoholism and tb, 1989-92; resident in neurology KB Sestre Milosrolnice U. Hosp., 1996—; prof. neurology Zagreb Nursing Sch., 1996-99; physician dept. clin. neurology Sestre Milosrdnice U. Hosp., Zagreb, 1999—; assoc. prof. neurology Zagreb U., 1999—; sec. organizing com. 2nd Croatian Congress Neurology, Zagreb, 1997. Author, editor: Klenovik-750 Yrs., 1995; editor: Proceedings 2nd Croatian Congress Neurology, 1994—, Proceedings 1st Congress Croation Soc. Stroke Prevention, 1999; contbr. articles to med. jours. Pres. organizing com. celebration 750th Yr. Klenovnik, 1994; mem. Klenovnik Mcpl. Govt., 1992. Commandant med. unit Ivanec's Bn., 1992. Fellow Croatian Med. Assn. (Acknowledgement 1995), Croatian Neurologic Soc. (Acknowledgement 1997), N.Y. Acad. Scis., Am. Acad. Neurology. Avocations: sports. Office: Sestre Milosrdnice U Hosp, Neurology Vinogradska 29, HR 10000 Zagreb Croatia

TROBIAN, HELEN R., retired college administrator, consultant; b. Hillsboro, Ill., Aug. 28, 1918; d. Charles Ethan Reed and Susannah B. Good; m. Albert Lori Trobian, Aug. 17, 1947 (dec. Oct. 1996). BS in Edn., N.W. Mo. State U., 1940; MA, Columbia U., 1947, EdD, 1950. Cert. Inst. for Women in Higher Edn. Adminstrn., Bryn Mawr Coll. Tchr. music and social studies Sharpsburg (Iowa) H.S., 1940-41; prof. music edn. Salem (W.Va.) Coll., 1950-51; dir. nat. film discussion project Nat. YWCA, Ford Found. Grant, N,Y.C., 1952-53; prof. instrumental music Wiley Coll., Marshall, Tex., 1959-63; adj. faculty music Milligan Coll., Tenn., 1993-96, cons. proposals; dir. humanities summer sch. Bennett Coll., Greensboro, N.C., 1965-68, writer fed. proposals, 1969-89. Author: (books) Instrumental Ensemble, 1963, Chosen, 1999; contbr. articles to acad. and rsch. publs. Condr. Chamber Orch., Belpre, Ohio, 1954-56; choir dir. Congl. Ch., Belpre, 1954-56; dir. adult beginners orch. Nat. Bd. YWCA, N,Y.C., 1952-53; curriculum rsch. project Inst. for Svcs. to Edn., Boston, summers 1972-74; participant Graz (Austria) Ctr., Piedmont Univ. Ctr., Winston-Salem, N.C., 1969. Sgt. U.S. Army, 1942-45. Mem. Am. Assn. Ret. Persons, Tubists Universal Brotherhood Assn. Avocations: playing wind instruments, reading novels, writing memoirs. Home: 1390 Milligan Hwy Johnson City TN 37601-5520

TROCEWICZ, JERZY, chemistry educator; b. Perkowice, Poland, July 12, 1948; s. Czeslaw and Marianna (Tomczyk) T.; m. Krystyna Ewa Pisarska, Aug. 5, 1973; children: Wojciech, Jacek, Jakub. MS, Maria Curie-Sklodowska U., Lublin, Poland, 1971, DSc, 1987. Asst. Maria Curie-Sklodowska U. Lublin, 1972-80, 81-88; rsch. fellow Tokyo Inst. Tech., 1980-81, Southwestern Med. U., Dallas, 1988-90, Lund (Sweden) U., 1992. Patentee in field; contbr. articles to profl. jours. Del. Alliance Two Hearts, Manila, 1994. Recipient 3rd Degree award Ministry High Edn. and Scis., Warsaw, 1980, 1st Degree award Gen. Tech. Orgn., Lublin, 1980. Mem. N.Y. Acad. Scis., Am. Friends Vatican Libr. Roman Catholic. Avocations: travel, languages, music, movies. Home: Samsonowicza 7 m 4, 20485 Lublin Poland Office: Maria Curie-Sklodowska U, Faculty Chemistry, 20-031 Lublin Poland

TROCH, PETER, civil engineer, researcher; b. Aalst, Belgium, Jan. 24, 1968; s. Herman Troch and Diane Callebaut; m. Benedikte Blindeman, June 18, 1994; 1 child, Vincent. Degree in Civil Engring., U. Ghent, Belgium, 1991; PhD in Civil Engring., U. Ghent, 2000. Project engr. Aquafin, Antwerp, Belgium, 1992-93; rsch. asst. U. Ghent, 1993—; presenter in field. Contbr. articles to profl. jours. Mem. Royal Flemish Soc. Engrs. Office: U Ghent Dept Civil Engring, Technologiepark 9, B-9052 Ghent Belgium

TROCKEL, WALTER, mathematics and economics educator; b. Essen, Germany, Mar. 18, 1944; s. Walter and Gertrud (Walden) T.; m. Monika Trockel Krämer, Jan. 16, 1970; children: Stefan, Jan, Tobias, Daniel. Diploma in Maths., U. Bonn (Germany), 1971, D in Econs., 1974, Habil., 1983. Cert. Math. Econs. Rsch. asst. Dept. Econs., Bonn, 1971-84; full prof. Inst. Math. Econs., Bielefeld, Germany, 1985—; vice-rector Bielefeld U., 1996-98; vis. prof. Inst. Math. Econs., Bielfeld, 1984-85, U. Calif., San Diego, 1988-89, U. Ariz., Tucson, 1994-95, UCLA, 1998-99; mem. adv. bd. Ctr. for Interdisciplinary Rsch., Bielefeld, 1991-93. Mng. editor: Springer Lecture Notes in Economics and Mathematical Systems, 1992—; mem. editl. bd. Econ. Theory, Jour. Math. Econ., Rev. Econ. Design; contbr. articles to profl. jours. Grantee Deutsche Forschungsgemeinschaft, Bonn, 1982. Mem. Deutsche Mathematiker Vereinigung, Econometric Soc., Theoretischer Ausschuss des Vereins für Socialpolitik, Soc. for Advancement of Econ. Theory, European Econ. Assn.; Game Theory Soc., Soc. for Econ. Design. Avocations: tennis, soccer, precolumbian art. E-mail: imwt@wiwi.uni-bielefeld.de. Home: Am Brinkhof 12, 33813 Oerlinghausen NRW, Germany Office: IMW Univ Bielefeld, Universitätsstr 25, 33615 Bielefeld NRW, Germany

TROCKI, LINDA KATHERINE, geoscientist, natural resource economist; b. Erie, Pa., Oct. 7, 1952; d. Bernard Joseph and Catherine Frances (Manczka) T. BS in Geology with highest honors, N.Mex. Inst. Mining and Tech., 1976; MS in Geochemistry, Pa. State U., 1983, PhD in Mineral Econs., 1985. Staff mem. Los Alamos (N.Mex.) Nat. Lab., 1976-78, 83-90; geologist Internat. Atomic Energy Agy., Vienna, Austria, 1978-80; grad. rsch. asst. Los Alamos (N.Mex.) Nat. Lab., 1981-83, dep. group leader, 1990-92, dep. program dir., 1992-93, program dir., 1993-95; asst. to pres. Chevron Petroleum Tech. Co., Houston, Tex., 1995-96; v.p. and mgr. Advanced Technology, Bechtel Nat. Inc., 1996-98; dep. gen. mgr. Bechtel Nevada, Las Vegas, 1999—; spl. asst. to dep. sec. U.S. Dept. Energy, 1994-95; com. Global Found., Coral Gables, Fla., 1988-94; mem. Chief of Naval Ops. Task Force on Energy, Alexandria, Va., 1990-91. Contbr. to profl. publs. Pres. Vista Encantada Neighborhood Assn., Santa Fe, 1988-89. Fellow East West Ctr., Honolulu, 1988. Mem. AAAS, Internat. Assn. Energy Economists, Mineral Econs. and Mgmt. Soc. (pres. 1994-95). Office: Bechtel Nevada PO Box 98521 Las Vegas NV 89193-8521

TROEMEL, MARTIN, retired chemistry educator; b. Berlin, Oct. 31, 1934; s. Werner and Emma (Hemme) T.; m. Christiane Lehmann, Aug. 11, 1960; children: Christian, Maria, Bernhard, Anna. Diplom-Chemiker, U. Frankfurt, Germany, 1960; Dr.phil.nat., U. Frankfurt, 1963. Asst. U. Frankfurt, 1963-70, lectr., 1969-70, prof. inorganic chemistry, 1971-2000, dean dept. chemistry, 1974-75, 89-90; ret., 2000. Contbr. articles to profl. jours. including Jour. Solid State Chemistry, Acta Crystallographica, Zeitschrift für Kristallographie. Roman Catholic. Avocations: philosophy of science, history of science and technology. Office: Inst fü Anorganische Che, Marie-Curie-Str 11, Frankfurt 60439, Germany

TROFIMOV, VLADIMOR ISAKOVICH, physicist, researcher; b. Sokol, Russia, July 24, 1941. Student, Leningrad State U., 1963; D in Phys. & Maths. Sci., Kharkov State U., 1992. Leading scientist Electromechanics Rsch. Inst., Moscow, 1970-94, Inst. Radioengineering and Electronics, Moscow, 1994—. Author: (monograph) Growth and Morphology of Thin Films, 1993; contbr. papers in field. Fax: 095-203-8414. E-mail: trof@mail.cpline.ru. Home: 159 Lenin Str 33, 143400 Krasnogorsk Moscow, Russia Office: Inst Radioenring & Elec, 11 Mokhovaya, 103907 Moscow Russia

TROFIMOVA, NATALIA NIKOLAEVNA, chemist, researcher; b. Yakutsk, Russia, Aug. 9, 1963; d. Nikolai Vasilievich and Galina Gavrilievna (Panaeva) Yegorov; m. Valeriy Nilovich Trofimov, Apr. 19, 1989; children: Anastasia Valerievna, Taisia Valerievna. B in Chemistry, Yakutsk State U., 1986; PhD, Irkutsk (Russia) State U., 1999. Lab. asst. Irkutsk Inst. Chemistry, 1991-93, rsch. chemist, 1993-99, sr. rschr., 2000—. Contbr. articles to profl. jours. Grantee Russian Found. for Basic Rsch., Moscow. Avocations: travel, growing vegetables and flowers. Office: Irkutsk Inst Chem RAS, Favorskogo Str 1, 664033 Irkutsk Russia

TROILO, MICHELE, engineering educator, consultant; b. Genoa, Italy, July 19, 1942; s. Luigi and Maria (Dellacá) T.; m. Ida Freschi; children: Cristina, Matteo, Daniele. Laurea in Ingegneria, U. Genoa, 1965. Prof. engring. Dept. Machine Sys. Energetics & Transport U. Genoa, 1980—. Mem. Ordine degli Ingegneri (sec. 1995—). Avocations: music, bridge. Office: U Genoa DIMSET, Via Montallegro 1, I-16145 Genoa Italy

TROITSKI, YURI VLADIMIROVICH, physicist, researcher; b. Semipalatinsk, USSR, July 10, 1928; s. Vladimir Mikhailovich and Zinaida Fedorovna (Lapshina) T.; m. Galina Stepanovna Rodyukova, June 22, 1955; children: Sergei, Dmitri. MSc, State U. Nizhni Novgorod, Russia, 1952; DSc, USSR Acad. Scis., Novosibirsk, 1972. Postgrad. rschr. Russian Acad. Scis., Novosibirsk, 1955-60, head lab. Inst. Semiconductor Physics, Siberian Divsn., 1963-69, head lab. Inst. Automation and Electrometry., 1973-98, prof., 1990—. Author: Single Frequency Gas Lasers, 1975, Mulitple Beam Reflection Interferometers, 1985; contbr. over 190 articles to sci. publs. Grantee Internat. Sci. Found., N.Y., 1993, Ministry of Sci. of Russian Fedn., Moscow, 1994—. Mem. N.Y. Acad. Scis. Fax: 7-383-2-333863. Office: Inst Automation Electromet, Acad Koptyug Ave 1, 630090 Novosibirsk Russia

TROITZSCH, DIRK, biomedical engineer; b. Dessau, Germany, Sept. 25, 1966; s. Guenter Gisela Brigitte (Christall) T. MS, Univ. Dresden, 1992. Registrar Univ. Hosp., Leipzig, 1988, cardiovascular surgery, 1988-91, neurosurgery, 1991—. Co-author: Cerebral Protection in Cerebrovascular and Aortic Surgery, 1997; co-editor: Molecularbiological Methods and Approaches in Transplantation Medicine, 1996; contbr. articles to profl. jours.; mem. editl. staff Jour. Cardiovascular Engring. Mem. European Soc. Engring. & medicine, European Soc. Organ Transplantation, European Soc. Extra Corporeal Tech., Internat. Soc. Heart & Lung Transplantation, Internat. Soc. Applied Cardiovascular Biology. Avocations: sports, swimming, skin-diving, literature. Office: Univ Leipzig, Ruhrstrasse 38, D 06846 Dessau Germany

TROITZSCH, KLAUS GERHARD, social science informatics educator; b. Oberg, Lower Saxony, Germany, Nov. 28, 1946; s. Helmut and Lea Margarete (Haslböck) T.; m. Ingrid Maria Kalab, Aug. 18, 1972. Diplom-Politologe, U. Hamburg (Germany), 1972, PhD, 1979; PhD habilitation, Koblenz-Landau U., Germany, 1985. Asst. Liberal Party Group State Legis., Hamburg, Germany, 1972-74; chief whip Liberal Party Group State Legis., Hamburg, 1974-78; researcher Koblenz-Landau U., Koblenz, Germany, 1979-85; prof. Koblenz-Landau U., Koblenz, 1986—; chair bd. advs. InformationsZentrum Sozialwissenschaften, Bonn, Germany, 1996—; Interuniv. Expertise Ctr. ProGAMMA, Groningen, The Netherlands, 1997—. Author: Modellbildung und Simulation in den Sozialwissenschaften, 1990; co-author: Simulation for the Social Scientist, 1999; co-editor, contbr. Computer Aided Sociological Research, 1990, Social Science Simulation from a Philosophy of Science Point of View, 1996, Social Science Microsimulation, 1996, Tools and Techniques for Social Science Simulation, 2000. Mem. state legislature Bürgerschaft der Freien und Hansestadt Hamburg, Germany 1974-78. Lt. Signal Corps German Army, 1965-68. Mem. Liberal Party. Lutheran. Home: Schenkendorfstrasse 16, D-56068 Koblenz Rhineland-Palatinate, Germany Office: Koblenz-Landau U, Rheinau 1, D-56075 Koblenz Rhineland-Palatinate, Germany

TROITZSCH, ULRIKE, geologist, mineralogist, researcher; b. Bochum, Germany, Nov. 8, 1969; d. Ulrich and Barbara (Mäder) T. Diploma in geology, Tech. U., Darmstadt, 1995; postgrad., ANU, Canberra, Australia, 1996—. Contbr. articles to profl. jours. Mem. Mineralogical Soc. of Am. Avocations: outdoor activities, classical music, piano. Home: 43 Maitland St, Hackett ACT 2602, Australia Office: ANU Geology Dept, Canberra ACT 0200, Australia

TROJAN, STANISLAV, neurophysiologist, educator; b. Prague, Aug. 16, 1934; s. Stanislav Trojan and Marie (Seegerova) Trojanova; m. Miroslava Peliskova, Jan. 18, 1964; children: Marie, Stanislav. MD, Charles U., Prague, 1958, PhD, 1964; DS, Masaryk U., Brno, Czech Republic, 1978. Med. diplomate. Rsch. student Faculty of Medicine/Charles U., Prague, 1957-58, asst. prof., 1958-69, assoc. prof., 1969-81, prof., 1981—; bd. dirs. Inst. Physiology, Charles U. Author: Adaptation to Hypoxia and Anoxia During Ontogenesis, 1978, Physiology and Rehabilitation of the Motor System, 1996, 2d edit. 2000; editor: Ontogenesis of the Brain, Vols. I-V, 1968, 74, 80, 86, 92, Medical Physiology, 1994, 96, 99. Mem. Czech Physiol. Soc. (pres. 1992-99), Internat. Brain Rsch. Orgn., N.Y. Acad. Sci. Office: First Faculty of Medicine, Albertov 5/Inst Physiology, 128 00 Prague 2, Czech Republic

TROJANOWSKI, FORD ALEXANDER, college adminstrator; b. Wantagh, N.Y., Aug. 25, 1962; s. Thedore Trojanowski and Grace Porter. BA in Psychology, VIIlanova U., 1984, BA in Philosophy, 1984, BA in Sociology, 1984; MS in Edn., L.I. U., 1992. Area coord. SUNY, Old Westbury, N.Y., 1988-92; asst. dir. housing CUNY Hunter Coll., N.Y.C., 1992-98; dir. residence life CUNY Grad. Ctr., N.Y.C. 1998—. Author: Jesus Las Vegas, 1989, (screenplay) Tryst, 1997. Mem. Nat. Assn. Student Personnell Adminstrs., N.E. Assn. Coll. Housing Officers, Internat. Order Ordinary (pres. 1999-2000). Avocations: golf, photography, writing, cooking. E-mail: ftrojanowski@hotmail.com. Home: 41-41 43d St Apt C-15 Sunnyside NY 11104

TROJE, HANS ERICH, legal educator; b. Göttingen, Germany, Apr. 28, 1934; s. Kurt and Emmy (Weiss) T.; m. Elisabeth Luise Heimpel, June 11, 1935; children: Nikolaus, Christian, Dorothee, Konstantin. Dr.jur., U. Freiburg im Breisgau, 1961; habilitation, U. Frankfurt am Main, Germany, 1969. Rsch. fellow Max Planck Inst. Europäische Rechtsgeschichte, Frankfurt am Main, 1964-71; prof. U. Frankfurt am Main, 1971—. Author: Graeca leguntur, 1971, Europa und griechisches Recht, 1971, Juristenausbildung heute, 1979, Gestohlene Liebe. Zum Problem der Rettung der Ehe, 1988, Humanistische Jurisprudenz, 1993, Das Unfassbare der Frau. Von der Einzigartigkeit des Michelangelo Antonioni, 1994, Archeologia del matrimonio, 1996. Avocations: music, literature, visual arts. Home: Am Berg 1, D 65779 Kelkheim im Taunus Germany Office: Johann Wolfgang Goethe U, Senckenberganlage 31, D 60054 Frankfurt am Main Germany

TROJER, LENA, chemist, gender researcher; b. Langbro, Sweden, Aug. 24, 1951; d. Uno and Ing-Britt (Freeman) Månsson; m. Magnus Trojer; 3 children. PhD, U. Lund, 1981; degree, U. Linkoping, 1988, docent, Tech. U.

Lulea, 1995. Rsch. asst. U. Lund, Sweden, 1974-81; tchr. non formal edn. Folk High Sch., Jamshog, Sweden, 1984-94; sr. lectr. Tech. U. Lulea, Sweden, 1992-98, acting prof., 1994-98; prof. U. Karlskrona/Ronneby, Ronneby, Sweden, 1998—; dir. Ctr. for Women's Studies, Lulea, 1993-96, Grad. Sch. for Women Tech. Faculty, Lulea, 1994-98. Editor: Feminist Voices on Gender, Technology and Ethics, 1994, Natural Science Seen Through Feminist Theory of Science, 1995; author: Crossing Boarders and Carrying Norms, 1996, Competence for Leadership in Research Organizations, 1999, The Encounter Between Rhetoric and Realities, 1999; editor: Wanderings, 1996. Mem. Swedish Coun. for Planning and Coord. of Rsch. (bd. dirs. 1995—). Office: U Karlskrona/Ronneby, Divsn Gender Rsch, S-372 25 Ronneby Sweden

TROMBOLD, WALTER STEVENSON, supply company executive; b. Chanute, Kans., June 21, 1910; s. George John and Margaret (Stevenson) T.; m. Charlotte Elizabeth Kaufman, Dec. 28, 1941; children: Joan Benjamin, Lynn Oliphant, Walter Steven, David George, Charles Phillip. AA, Iola Jr. Coll., 1930; BS in Bus., U. Kans., 1932; spl. degree Balliol Coll., Oxford U., 1943. Pers. worker with evangelist Billy Sunday, 1928; asst. mgr. S.H. Kress & Co., 1932-38; counsel Penn. Mut. Life Ins. Co., 1938-40; field mgr. Travelers Ins. Co., Kansas City, 1940-41; with Reid Supply Co. Wichita, Kans., Kansas City, Mo., Topeka, 1946-86; pres., chmn. bd. Reid Supply Co., Inc., 1954-86; chmn. bd. Trombold Consultation Svc., 1986—; bd. dirs., v.p. Nat. Distbrs. Coun.; active amateur photographer, 1924—. Bd. dirs., officer YMCA, 1920—; merit badge councilor Boy Scouts Am.; bd. dirs. Wesley Hosp. Assocs., 1972-82, Camp Fire Girls, Salvation Army, mem. adv. bd., 1988—, Salvation Army Rehab. Ctr., 1988—; life mem. PTA, 1953—, pres., 1952; chmn. pers. adv. bd. City of Wichita, Kans., 1956-86; commr. Gen. Assembly Presbyn. Ch. USA, past deacon, elder, trustee; commr. Synods of Mid-Am., Presbytery of So. Kans.; assoc. chmn. Nat. Laymen's Bible Week, 1972-86; mem. Super Sr. Tennis, 1970-98; area chmn. Neighbor Watch, 1990—; ofcl. photographer U. Kans. Relays. Lt. comdr. USN, 1942-46. Recipient award Nat. Jr. C. of C., Wichita Jr. C. of C., Laundry and Cleaners Allied Trades, Old Timer Club Nat., Nat. Distributors Coun., Sr. Men's Tennis Assn., U. Kans. RElays, Kans. State H.S. Assn., Wichita Swim Club, Am. Athletic Union, YMCA, Salvation Army, Rotary, Boy Scouts. Am., Camp Fire Girls, Sr. Men's Swimming, City of Wichita. Mem. Textile Allied Trades Assn. (bd. dirs., dist. chmn. Hon. Man 1976), Kans. LST Assn. (charter pres. 1990), Kans. U. Alumni Assn. (life), Kans. C. of C., Wichita C. of C., Sales and Mktg. Execs. (bd. dirs., v.p.), Old Timer Club (sec., treas. 1964-86, Hon. Man of Yr. 1977), Wichita Racquet Club, Knife and Fork Internat. Club (bd. dirs., v.p.), Univ. Club (chmn. bd. dirs., v.p.), Rotary (bd. dirs., ofcl. photographer, historian, Disting. Svc. award 1989, 96), Masons (32 degree), Alpha Tau Omega. Republican. Presbyterian. Home: 1401 W River Blvd Wichita KS 67203-3355

TROMMER, GERT FRANZ, engineering educator; b. Coburg, Germany, Dec. 27, 1952; s. Franz and Ilsagerth (Schramm) T.; m. Monika Ritter. Engrng. diploma, Tech. U., Munich, 1977, PhD, 1982. Asst. prof. Tech. U., Munich, 1981-87; devel. engr. MBB, Munich, 1987-91; dept. head inertial and sensor technics Deutsche Aerospace, 1991-95, project mgr. Asraam sensor unit, 1995-96; dir. missile system components Daimler Benz Aerospace, 1996-98; dir. flight control sys. Daimler Chrysler Aerospace, 1998-99; prof., dir. Inst. Theory & Sys. Optimization in Elec. Engr. U. Karlsruhe, 1999—. Author: Dielectric Waveguides, 1989, others; contbr. articles to profl. jours. Mem. Deutscher Hochschulverband, Sierra Club, Optical Soc. of Am., Greenpeace, Inst. Navigation. Achievements include 51 patents; inventor of passive fiber optic gyroscope; design of integrated optics and fiber optic devices, integrated navigation systems; leadership in design of navigation sys. and IR seekers. Home: Virchowstr 18, D-76133 Karlsruhe Germany Office: U Karlsruhe, Kaiserstr 12, D-76128 Karlsruhe Germany

TROMMSDORFF, GISELA, social sciences educator; b. Munster, Germany, Dec. 24, 1941; d. Fro Helge and Irmgard (Eckert) T. Student, U. Gottingen, Germany, 1963-64, U. N.C., 1964-65; diploma, U. Mannheim, Germany, 1967, Dr. phil., 1970, venia legendi, 1975. Rsch. asst. in sociology and social psychology New Sch. Social Rsch., N.Y., 1967-68; project dir. Sonderforschungsbereich, 1968-78; guest prof. U. Giessen, Germany, 1972, U. Hohenheim, 1973-74; prof. Tech. U., Aachen, Germany, 1978-87, U. Konstanz, 1987—; mem. sci. adv. bd. Rural Youth Acad., Frede , 1992—, Socio-Econ. Panel, Berlin, 1993—, Ministry Family, Sr. Citizens, Women and Adolescents, Bonn, 1995—, Hamburg U., 1995-97, Social Sci. Rsch. in Japan, 1996—. Author: Gruppeneinflusse, 1978, Erziehung f.d. Zukunft, 1978; editor: Erziehungsziele, 1984, Kindheit und Jugend in Verschiedenen Kulturen, Entwicklung und Sozialisation, Sozialisation und Entwicklung von Kindern vor und nach der Vereiningung, 1996, (with H.J. Kornadt) Deutsch-japanische Begegnungen in den Sozialwissenschaften, 1993, (with others) Individuelle Entwicklung, Bildung und Berufsverläufe; co-editor Zeitschrift für Sozialisationsforschung und Erziehungssoziologie, 1990—, Zeitschrift für Entwicklungspsychologie und Pädagogische Psychologie, 1996—; consultative editor Psychologie in Erziehung und Unterricht, 1993-98; mem. editl. bd. Culture & Psychology, 1995—; co-editor Commn. Rsch. on Social and Polit. Trnasformation in the New Fed. States of Germany,, 1991-99; contbr. articles to profl. jours. Rep. for Germany Econ. and Social Rsch. Coun. Commn. European Communities, Brussels, 1994. Rsch. scholar Keio U., 88, 89, 91. Mem. German-Japanese Soc. Social Sci. (v.p. 1989—), Deutsche Gesellschaft für Soziologie, Deutsche Gesellschaft für Asienkunde, European Assn. Exptl. Social Psychology, Internat. Soc. Study of Behavioral Devel. Home: PF 227, 6705 Deidesheim Rheinland-Pfalz, Germany

TROMP, EMSLEY D., bank executive. Pres., dir. Bank Van de Nederlandse Antillen, Curaçao. Office: Bank Nederlandse Antillen, Breedestraat 1, Willemstad Curacao, Netherlands Antilles

TROMPETER, RICHARD SIMON, pediatrician; b. London, Jan. 27, 1946; s. Nysen and Betty (Rubin) T.; m. Barbara Ann Blum, Mar. 26, 1978; children: Sara, Alexander, Nicholas, Rebecca. MB BS, Guys Hosp., London, 1970. Sr. house officer Various Hosps., London, 1971-74; registrar Hosps. for Sick Children, Great Ormond St., London, 1975-78; sr. registrar Guys Hosp., London, 1978-83; cons., pediatrician Royal Free Hosp., London, 1983-89; cons., pediatrician, pediatric nephrologist Hosp. for Sick Children, London, 1989—. Contbr. articles to profl. jours. Fellow Royal Coll. Physicians, Royal Coll. Paediats. and Child Health. Office: Hosp for Children, Great Ormond St, London WC1 3JH, England

TRONCHETTI PROVERA, MARCO, business executive; b. Milan, 1948; 3 children. Degree in bus. and adminstrn., Bocconi U. Milan, 1971. Founder maritime transp. holding co., 1973-86; ptnr. Pirelli & C., 1986; mng. dir., gen. mgr. Soc. Internat. Pirelli S.A., Basel, Switzerland, 1988-92; mng. dir., gen. mgr. fin., adminstrn. and gen. affairs Pirelli SpA, Milan, 1991-92, exec. dep. chmn., mng. dir., 1992-96; dep. chmn. Pirelli & Co., Milan, 1995—; chmn., CEO Pirelli SpA, Milan, 1996—, joint vice chmn. Office: Pirelli SpA, Viale Sarca 222, 20126 Milan Italy*

TRONE, JACQUELYN LEE, artist; b. York, Pa., Apr. 16, 1941; d. John and Bernice (Garvick) Trone; m. Thomas D. White; children: Theodore Trone Butera, John Andrew Butera. BA in Interior Design, Pa. State U., 1963. Antiques dealer Colonial Yard, Audubon, Pa., 1971-97. Artist 18th, 19th century style oils, watercolors, bride's boxes, 19th century style dolls; solo shows at Mus. of Am. Folk Art, N.Y., Sturbridge Village Mus., Mass., Mercer (Pa.) Mus., Landis Valley Mus., Pa., Gallery Americana, Tex., Eldred Wheeler, Houston; exhibited in group shows at Am. Craftsmen, Wilton, Conn., Historic Waterford Found., Va., Designer Craftsman, Pa., Winter at Colonial Yard, Pa., 1992—, Spring at Colonial Yard, 1990—, The Highlands, Blue Bell, Pa., 1997, Williamsburg Designer show Williamsburg, Va., 1989-96, Home and Garden TV Network "Country at Home" series, 1997-98, Country Living Mag., 1995, 96; work in permanent pvt. collections; contbr. articles to profl. jours. Pres. Audubon Women's Club, 1978; active mem. Lower Providence Twp. Libr. Mem. The Herb Gatherers (com. head 1990-94), Nat. Assn. Artisans and Craftsmen (bd. dirs. 1991-98). Avocations: herb gardening, gourmet cooking, antiques, antique dolls, garden design. Home and Studio: 500 S Park Ave Audubon PA 19403-1921

TROOST, SEIJER, chemical company executive; b. Hoogeveen, The Netherlands, May 13, 1940; s. Jan R. and Dina (Kikkert) T.; m. Alby Poll, May 30, 1963; children: Ina, Sjoukje, Jan Jaap, Saskia. MSc, U. Groningen, 1964, PhD, 1969; grad., Christ Coll., Cambridge U., 1991. Rsch. chemist Unilever Ltd., Vlaardingen, The Netherlands, 1964-70, KNZ CR, Hengelo, The Netherlands, 1970-74; chief chemist Chlorine Tech Ltd., Sydney, 1974-75; gen. mgr. Akzo Nobel, Amervsfoort/Hemgelo, 1976—; mem. Raad Voor Milieu Hygiene, Den Haag, The Netherlands, 1990-94, Waterschap R&D, Almelo, The Netherlands, 1982—; cons. CEFIC/EUROCHLOR, Brussels, 1988—, VNO-NCW, Den Haag, 1982—. Contbr. articles to profl. jours.; patentee in field. City coun. mem. Oldenzaal, 1972-76, Overijssel, 1982-87, 95-99; mem. Regional Dist. Coun., Twente, 1978-82... Fellow De Groote Soc., Multatuli Soc. Avocations: antiquarian and rare books, photography, local history, swimming, skating. Fax: 35.541 533456. E-mail: stroost@worldonline.nl. Home: Pastorie Straat 22, 7571BW Oldenzaal The Netherlands Office: Akzo Nobel Chem, PO Box 25, 7550 GC Hengelo The Netherlands

TROPAREVSKY, ALEJANDRO, paint company executive; b. Buenos Aires, May 10, 1936; s. Pedro and Amalia (Puchalsky) T.; m. María Lydia Pisarello Adorni, Oct. 20, 1958; children: María Silvia, María Inés, Mariía Gabriela, María Claudia. D in Chemistry, U. Buenos Aires, 1959. Chemist rsch. lab. S.A. ALBA, Buenos Aires, 1958-61, chemist indsl. paint labs., 1961-64, chief devel. lab., 1964-75, mgr. new product devel. lab., 1975-90; tech. coord. devel. labs. Bunge Paints, Buenos Aires, 1990—. Fellow Oil and Colour Chemists' Assn.; mem. Argentine Chem. Soc. Home: 3726 Catamarca, 1636 La Lucila Argentina Office: S A ALBA, 362 25 de Mayo, 1002 Buenos Aires Argentina

TROPER, MICHEL, law educator; b. Paris, Sept. 8, 1938; s. Philippe and Amalia (Kiesler) T.; m. Mathilda Friedman, May 31, 1980; 1 child, Deborah. Diploma, Inst. Polit. Studies, Paris, 1959; MBA, European Inst. Bus. Adminstrn., Fountainebleau, France, 1960; LLD, U. Paris, 1967. Prof. law U. Rouen, 1969-80, U. Paris X, Nanterre, 1978—. Author: La séparation des pouvoirs et l'histoire constitutionnelle française, 1973, (with Grzegrorczyk and Michaut) Le positivisme juridique, 1993, (with Jaume) 1789 et l'invention de la constitution, 1994, Pour und Théorie juridique de l'Etat, 1994, (with Burdeau and Hamon) Droit constitutionnel, 25th edit., 1997; editor: (with Karlsson) Law, Justice and the State II. The Nation, the State and Democracy, 1995. Office: U Paris X, 200 Ave de la Republique, 92001 Nanterre France

TROSBORG, ANNA, English and linguistics educator; b. Brande, Jutland, Denmark, Nov. 13, 1937; d. Niels and Nielsine (Larsen) Arevad; m. Arne Trosborg, Sept. 17, 1960. BA, U. Aarhus, Denmark, 1974, MA, 1976; PhD, U. Aarhus, 1982; D Ling. Merc., Aarhus Sch. Bus., 1995. Lectr. dept. English, U. Aarhus, 1976-87; assoc. prof. English and linguistics Aarhus Sch. Bus., 1987-89, prof., 1989—; vis. scholar U. Edinburgh, Scotland, spring 1979; vis. prof. City U. Hong Kong, autumn 1996; presenter at numerous confs. Author: Rhetorical Strategies in Legal Discourse. Statutes and Contracts, 1997, Interlanguage Pragmatics: Requests, Complaints and Apologies, 1995; editor spl. issue Jour. Pragmatics, 1994, Text Typology and Translation, 1997, Analysing Professional Genres, 2000; contbr. articles to profl. jours., including Jour. Child Lang., Finning Jour. Lang. Learning and Lang. Tchg., Italian Rev. Applied Linguistics, Jour. Pragmatics, Hermes. Grantee Rsch. Coun. for Humanities, Copenhagen, 1978-80, 90, NorFA, Oslo, 1993-98. Mem. AILA, ADLA. Avocations: family life, nature, travel, cooking. E-mail: AT@asb.dk. Home: Ternevej 12, 8382 Hinnerup Denmark Office: Aarhus Sch Bus, Fuglesangs Alle 4, 8210 Århus Denmark

TROSHIN, SERGEY MIKHAILOVICH, research scientist, educator; b. Alexin, Tula, Russia, Nov. 27, 1950; s. Mikhail and Tatiana (Eugenievna (Venkova) T.; m. Vera Vasilievna Kobzeva, Mar. 11, 1978; 1 child, Anton. Physicist, Moscow State U., 1974; PhD, Inst High Energy Physics, Protvino, Russia, 1978, D Phys. & Math. Scis., 1987. Jr. rschr. Inst. High Energy Physics, Protvino, 1977-85, sr. rschr., 1985-90, leading rschr., 1990-95, chief rschr., 1995—. Author: Spin Phenomena in Particle Interactions, 1994; contbr. articles to profl. jours. E-mail: troshin@mx.ihep.su. Home: 12 Lenin St, 144282 Protvino Moscow, Russia Office: Divsn Theoretical Physics, Inst High Energy Physics, 142284 Protvino Moscow, Russia

TROTMAN, ALEXANDER J., retired automobile manufacturing company executive; b. Middlesex, Eng., July 22, 1933; married. MBA, Mich. State U., 1972. Various positions Ford Motor Co., 1951—, Ford of Britain, 1955-67; dir. car prodn. planning office Ford of Europe, 1967-69; spl. assignment advanced car prodn. planning dept. Ford USA, 1969-70, mgr. product planning dept. Lincoln-Mercury divsn., 1970-71, dir. mktg. staff sales planning office, 1971-72, exec. dir. product planning, product planning and rsch., 1972-75, chief car planning mgr., car prodn. devel. group, 1975-77, exec. dir. ops. planning, 1977-78, asst. gen. mgr. truck and recreational products ops., 1978-79; v.p. truck ops. Ford of Europe, 1979-83; pres. Ford Asia-Pacific Inc., 1983-84, Ford of Europe, Inc., 1984-88; exec. v.p. N.Am. Auto Ops., 1988-93; pres. Ford Auto Group, 1993; bd. dirs. Ford Motor Co., IBM Corp., Armonk, N.Y., Imperial Chem. Industries, London, N.Y. Stock Exch., N.Y.C.; adv. com. mem. Chase Internat. Knighted by Queen of Eng., 1996. Officer RAF, 1951-55. Mem. Am.-China Soc., U.S. China Bus. Coun., U.S.-Japan Bus. Coun., Bus. Roundtable, Bus. Coun. Office: Ford Motor Co One American Rd Dearborn MI 48126-2798*

TROTSENKO, ALEXANDER VLADIMIROVYCH, thermophysicist, researcher; b. Odessa, Ukraine, Nov. 17, 1946; s. Vladimir Eugenievych and Evdokia Afanasievna (Frolova) T.; m. Nina Michailovna Zabolotnaya, July 4, 1973; children: Oksana, Vladimir. Engr., U. Odessa, Ukraine, 1969; D in Engrng., Odessa Tech. Inst., Ukraine, 1975. Engr. Rsch. Inst. Odessa, Ukraine, 1969-71; post-grad. studies Odessa Inst., Ukraine, 1971-75, rschr., 1975-79, vice prof., 1979-99. Contbr. articles to profl. jours. Office: State Acad Refrigeration, 1/3 Dvoryanskaya Str., 65026 Odessa Ukraine

TROTT, EDWARD ASHLEY, reproductive endocrinologist; b. Apr. 6, 1961; s. Edward Wilbur and Patricia Dorothy (White) T.; m. Andrea Marie Steede, June 21, 1986; children: Kiley Edward, Kory Ashley. BS with honors, U. Calif., 1983; MD, Jefferson Med. Coll., 1990. Diplomate Nat. Bd. Med. Examiners. Intern Hahnemann U. Hosp., Phila., 1990-91; resident Med. Ctr. of Del., Newark, 1991-94; fellow, instr. Med. Coll. of Ga., Augusta, 1994-96; dir. Del. Inst. for Reproductive Medicine, Newark, 1996—; cons. Univ. Hosp., Augusta, 1994-96; ad hoc reviewer Fertility and Sterility, Rochester, 1996; surg. skills instr. Med. Coll. of Ga., 1994-96. Author: Handbook for Primary Care in Ob/Gyn., 1996; contbr. articles to profl. jours. Recipient Tap Pharms. Resident award Tap Pharms., 1992. Mem. AMA, ACS, Nat. Med. Assn., Med. Assn. of Ga., Am. Soc. of Reproductive Medicine, Phi Beta Sigma, Phi Zeta Kappa. Methodist. Avocations: soccer, fishing, kite flying. Office: Del Inst for Reproductive Medicine 556 S Dupont Blvd Ste H Milford DE 19963-1706

TROTT, JOHN FRANCIS HENRY, investment banker; b. Croydon, Surrey, Eng., Jan. 23, 1938; m. Averil Margaret Trott, Apr. 24, 1965; children: Christopher John, Nicola Margaret, Jeremy Charles. Dir. Kleinwort Benson Ltd., London, 1972-86; chmn. bd. Kleinwort Benson Internat. Investment, London, 1986-92; exec. v.p. Bessemer Trust Co. N.A., London, 1992-98; chmn. Standard Life Assurance Co., Edinburgh, Brunner Investment Trust. Home: Odstock Castle Square, Bletchingley RH1 4LB, England

TROTT, JUSTINA A., physician, medical association administrator, internist, medical educator; b. Bridgeport, Conn., Jan. 22, 1948; d. Dominick and Irene Trott; 1 child, Arianna. BA, N.Y. U., 1970; MD, Med. Coll. Pa., 1974. Cert. med. doctor. Mem. Am. Coll. Physicians, Am. Coll. Women's Health Physicians (bd. dirs. 1999—). Avocations: music, hiking, traveling, cooking. Home: 7506B Old Santa Fe Trl Santa Fe NM 87505-9358

TROTTA, VINCENZO, gynecologist; b. Foggia, Italy, Oct. 15, 1939; s. Umberto and Antonietta (De Biase) T.; m. Sept. 27, 1969 (div. Dec. 30, 1992); children: Antonella, Valeria. B Medicine, B Surgery, U. Federico II, Naples, Italy, 1963; specialist ob-gyn., U. Parma, Italy, 1968; surgeon, U. Bologna, Italy, 1972. Tchr. Red Cross Italy, Salerno, 1963-67, 71-72; pres. Associazione Italiana Educazione Demografica, Salerno, 1974-87; v.p. Lotta Contro i Tumori, Salerno, 1981—; dir. Conservazione Gameti, Salerno, 1985-96, Human Fertilization Ctr., Salerno, 1991—; asst. physician, gynecologist Regional Hosp., Salerno, 1964-73, dep. physician, gynecologist, 1973-84, head physician, gynecologist, 1984-86; head physician Nat. Qualification Surgery, Italy, 1976. Contbr. over 60 sci. publs. to nat. revs. Mem. Societa Italiana di Ginecologia e Ostetricia, Am. Fertility Soc., Società Italiana Fertilità E Sterilità, Internat. Soc. for Impotence Rsch., Alpha Scientists in Reproductive Medicine, European Soc. Human Reproduction and Embryology. Avocations: tennis, study of history. Home: Via Delle Ginestre 55, 84134 Salerno Italy Office: Human Fertilization Ctr, Via Roma 28, 84121 Salerno Italy

TROUILLARD, LAURENT, radiologist; b. Niort, France, May 28, 1950; s. Michel and Paulette (Leonard) T.; m. Isabelle Marianne Chatelain, July 9, 1976. MD, U. Paris, 1975, radiologist, 1978; diploma of senology, Strasbourg, France, 1982; diploma of RMN, Paris, 1999. Col. Terre. Mem. Rotary. Avocations: computers, travel. E-mail: Laurent Trouillard@wanadoo.fr. Home: 10 rue Yver, 79000 Niort France Office: Cabinet de Radiologie, 42 rue Burgonce, 79000 Niort France

TROUILLAS, PAUL, medical educator; b. Lyon, France, Dec. 19, 1943; s. Louis and Emilie (Rochedix) T.; m. Jacqueline Bonhomme, Sept. 18, 1971; children: Christophe, Sebastien, Alexis. PhD, Faculty Scis., Paris, 1966; MD, Faculty Medicine, Lyon, 1971; grad., Pasteur Inst., Paris, 1968. Intern Lyon (France) Hosps., Hospices Civils de Lyon, 1967-71; asst. prof. Hospices Civils de Lyon, France, 1971-78; prof. neurology, asst. chief svc. Hospices Civils de Lyon and Claude Bernard U., Lyon, 1978-84, prof. neurology and chief svc., 1984-93; chmn. Neurology Coll. Claude Bernard U., Lyon, 1990-93, prof. neurology, 1993—; chmn. neuropharmacology rsch. com. Ataxia Rsch. Group, World Fedn. Neurology, 1993—. Author: Le Complexe de Marianne, 1988; editor: Serotonin, The Cerebellum and Ataxia, 1993. Expert Commissariat Gen. du Plan, Paris, 1978-80; town clk. and assoc. mayor City of Lyon, 1983-89. Recipient Nat. Hospitalization prize Ministry of Health, Lion's Club, Paris, 1991, Chevalier Nat. Order of Merit. Mem. N.Y. Acad. Sci., Am. Heart Assn. (stroke coun.). Avocations: art appreciation, historical documents. Office: 59 Boulevard Pinel, 69003 Lyon France

TROUP, MALCOLM, music educator, concert pianist; b. Toronto, Can., Feb. 22, 1930; s. William John and Wendela Mary (Seymour-Conway) T.; m. Carmen Lamarca Subercaseaux, Feb. 24, 1962; 1 child, Wendela Colomba Troup Lumley. Assoc. degree, Royal Conservatory of Music, Toronto, 1948; fellow, Guildhall Sch. of Music & Drama, London, 1952; PhD in Music, U. York, Eng., 1968; prof. (hon.), U. Chile, 1966; LLD (hon.), Meml. U. Newfoundland, 1985; MusD (hon.), City Univ., London, 1995. Concert pianist worldwide, 1954-70; dir. music Guildhall Sch. of Music & Drama, 1970-75; prof. music City U., London, 1975-95, head dept., 1975-93, emeritus prof. music, 1995—; gov. Music Therapy Charity Trust, 1979—; juror Chopin Competition of Australia, 1988, 1st Dvorak Internat. Piano competition Czech Republic, Rome, 1997, 1st EPTA Internat. Piano competition Zagreb, 1998, Young Musicians of Yr., CBC Nat. Talent Competition, Eckhard-Grammate Piano Competition, Can. Coun. Internat. Jury; v.p. World Piano Competition, London; leader internat. delegation of piano tchrs. Citizen Ambassador Program People to People, People's Republic of China, 1995; bd. mgmt. London Internat. String Quartet Competition. Author: Serial Strawinsky in 20th Century Music, 1968; contbg. author: The Messiaen Companion, 1995; editor Piano Jour., 1987—; appeared in festivals including Prague, Berlin, York, Belfast, Montreal Expo, CBC Toronto, Halifax, Commonwealth Arts Festival London; played with leading orchs. including LSO, Hallé, Hamburg, Berliner-Sinfonie, Bucharest, Warsaw, Oslo Philharmonic, Bergen Harmonien, Toronto, Winnipeg, Sao Paulo, Lima, Santiago; numerous recordings; contbr. articles to profl. jours. Mem. exec. com. Anglo-Chilean Soc., London, 1990—; freeman City of London, 1971—; trustee Jewish Music Inst., 1991—. Recipient Commonwealth medal Harriet Cohen Internat. Awards, 1955, Liszt medal Am. Liszt Soc., 1998. Fellow Royal Soc. Arts.; mem. Royal Soc. Musicians, Worshipful Co. of Musicians (liveryman, mem. ct. assts. 1973—, master 1999), European Piano Tchrs. Assn. (chmn. 1978—), Beethoven Piano Soc. Europe (chmn. 1991—). Office: City Univ Dept Music, Northampton Square, London EC1VOHB, England

TROUPE, BONNIE LEE, college program coordinator, educator; b. Quincy, Mass., Mar. 22, 1966; d. Stanley G. and Penelope J. (Erikson) T.; 1 child, Emma Elizabeth. BA in English and Secondary Edn., Salve Regina Coll., Newport, R.I., 1988; MA in English, Bridgewater State Coll., 1992. Cert. secondary tchr., R.I. ESL tchr. Hampton Sch. English, Tokyo, 1988-89; grad. asst. Bridgewater (Mass.) State Coll., 1990-92; staff assoc. office of grants and sponsored projects Bridgewater State Coll., 1992-95, coord. office of grants and sponsored projects, 1995—; journalism tchr. Project Contemporary Competitiveness, Bridgewater, 1986—; proposal reviewer U.S. Dept. Edn., Washington, 1994; instr. Bridgewater State Coll., 1995—; mem. Russian-Am. Spl. Edn. Collaborative, 1992—. Mem. bd. Mass. Soc. Prevention of Cruelty to Children, S.E. region, Brockton, 1992—. O'Donnell scholar, Trinity and All Saints Coll., Leeds, Eng., 1986-87, grad. scholar Wadham Coll., Oxford (Eng.) U., 1991; recipient Sarah Brown Sullivan award, Salve Regina Coll., 1988. Mem. AAUW, Nat. Coun. Univ. Rsch. Adminstrs., Profl. and Orgnl. Devel., Rsch. Adminstrs. Discussion Group, Soc. Rsch. Adminstrs., Mass. Women in Pub. Higher Edn. Avocations: art appreciation, travel. Home: 195 Twin Lakes Dr Halifax MA 02338-2213 Office: Office Grants and Sponsored Projects Bridgewater State Coll Bridgewater MA 02325-0001

TROUPE, WILLIAM HAROLD, lawyer; b. Quincy, Mass., Aug. 7, 1945; s. George Harold and Elizabeth (Harvey) T.; m. Linda M. Corbett, July 19, 1970; children: Allyson Leigh, Adam Jeremy. BBA, U. Mass., 1967; JD, Suffolk U., 1972. Bar: Mass. 1972, U.S. Dist. Ct. Mass. 1975, U.S. Ct. Appeals (1st cir.) 1975, U.S. Supreme Ct., 1991. New Eng. claims mgr. Greater N.Y. Ins. Co., Boston, 1972-73; ptnr. Lawrence Locke & Assocs., Boston, 1973-84, Wynn & Wynn PC, Boston, 1984-89, Hislop Carney & Troupe, Boston, 1990-98; founding ptnr. Carney & Troupe, Boston, 1999—; spkr. continuing legal edn. programs. Contbr. numerous articles on worker's compensation to legal jours. Mem. Mass. Bar Assn. (chmn. worker's compensaton com. 1985-87), Boston Bar Assn. Office: Carney & Troupe 5th Fl 10 High St Fl 5 Boston MA 02110-1605

TROUSSIER, PHILIPPE (THE WHITE WITCHDOCTOR), professional soccer coach. Coach ASEC Abidjan Football Club, Kaizer Chiefs Football Club, South Africa, Ivory Coast Nat. Team, Nigeria Nat. Team, Burkina Faso Nat. Team, South Africa Nat. Team, Japan Nat. Team. *

TROUT, MAURICE ELMORE, foreign service officer; b. Clifton Hill, Mo., Sept. 17, 1917; s. David McCamel and Charlotte Temple (Woods) T.; m. Margie Marie Mueller, Aug. 24, 1943; children—Richard Willis, Babette Yvonne. B.A., Hillsdale Coll., 1939; M.A. in Pub. Adminstrn, St. Louis U., 1948, Ph.D. in Polit. Sci, 1950. Joined U.S. Fgn. Service, 1950; assigned Paris, France, 1950-52, Vienna, Austria, 1952-55, London, Eng., 1955-59, Vientiane, Laos, 1959-61; with Office Exec. Dir. Bur. Far Eastern Affairs, Dept. State, Washington, 1961-65; Am. consulate gen. Munich, Germany, 1965-69; 1st sec., consul Am. embassy, Bangkok, Thailand, 1969-72; dep. office dir. Bur. Politico-Mil. Affairs, Dept. State, Washington, 1972-75; Dept. State advisor Armed Forces Staff Coll., Norfolk, Va., 1975-77. Bd. dirs. Internat. Sch., Bangkok, 1970-72. Served with USCG, 1939-45; capt. USAFR, 1951-55. Recipient Achievement award diplomacy and internat. affairs Hillsdale Coll., 1962. Mem. Am. Fgn. Service Assn., Diplomatic and Consular Officers Ret., Delta Tau Delta, Delta Theta Phi, Pi Gamma Mu. Home: 6203 Hardy Dr Mc Lean VA 22101-3114

TROUVÉ, RENAUD THEODORE, medical company executive, anesthesiology educator; b. Ham, Somme, France, June 23, 1954; s. Michel Albert and Colette Marie (Guilbert) T.; divorced; children: Helene, Claire, Vincent. B in Biochemistry, U. Paris, 1980, MS in Physiology, Human Biology, 1980, PhD in Toxicology, 1982, DSc in Biophysics, 1984, PhD in Pharmacology, 1991. Rsch. asst. U. Paris Toxicology Lab., 1980-82; rsch. assoc. U. Paris Biophysics, 1982-84; rsch. scientist Inst. Nat. de la Santé et de la Recherche Médicale, Paris, 1984-86; asst. prof. Columbia U., N.Y.C., 1986-89; sr. project leader Ctr. Nat. de Transfusion Sanguine, Paris, 1989-91, dir. rsch., 1989-92; assoc. prof. anesthesiology U. Tex., Houston, 1991—; directing mgr. Transonic Sys. France, Angers, 1992-96; pres. and CEO Biocerom, Angers, France, 1992-97; cons. pharmacology ASERC, Paris, 1983-92, cons. Rhône Poulenc, Paris, 1984-86; consulting scientist Nat. Inst. Drug

Abuse, Balt., 1986-87; assoc. prof. Univ. Angers, 1994—, cons. in quality and health, 1998—; dir. R&D Virtual Functions Sys., Palos Verdes, Calif., 1998; founder, adminstr. Serendi Internat. Cons., Luxembourg, 1999. Author: (book) Toxicomanies, 1989; contbr. to publs. Proceedings Soc. Exptl. Biology and Medicine, 1983—; inventor antidotes to cocaine toxicity, 1986, antiaggregant properties of activated protein C, 1992. Gen. sec. Nat. League Against Toxicomania, Paris, 1992-96, Ctr. on Drugs, Paris, 1993-96; pres. French Rsch. Inst. on Toxicomania; v.p. Internat. League Against Toxicomania, 1996—; adminstr. Fedn. Nationale Assns. Prevention Toxicomanie. Recipient Nat. Laureate French Assn. Ins. Cos., Paris, 1989, Nat. Laureate (for Biocerom) L'usine Nouvelle, Nantes, France, 1995. Mem. Am. Soc. Pharmacology and Exptl. Therapeutics, Am. Heart Assn., N.Y. Acad. Scis., Brit. Pharm. Soc., European Soc. Microcirculation, French Toxicologists Soc. (Nat. Laureate award 1986). Achievements include patents for antidotes to cocaine toxicity, antiaggregant properties of activated protein C, calcium channels inhibitors in parasympathetic syndromes, amino acids carriers in newborns, improvement of cardiac ischemia using hemodilution, antidotes to organophosphoreous compounds, true flow measurement in .250 mm or micrometer vessels by a transit time technique. Office: Inst Theoretical Biology, 10 Rue Bocquel, F-49100 Angers Anjou, France

TROVOADA, MIGUEL, Sao Tome and Principe president; b. Dec. 27, 1936. Formerly dir. fgn. rels. São Tome and Príncipe Liberation Movement; former mem. Polit. Bur.; sec. gen. external rels., 1972; min. def., min. fgn. affairs Govt. of São Tomé and Príncipe, 1975, min. econ. coordination, cooperation and tourism, 1975-79, prime min., 1975-79; min. trade, industry and fisheries São Tomé and Príncipe, 1978-79; imprisoned, 1979-81, exiled in Portugal, 1981-91; pres., comdr.-in-chief Armed Forces Govt. of São Tomé and Príncipe, 1991-95, pres., 1995—. Office: Office of Pres, Praga do Povo, São Tome São Tome and Príncipe*

TROW, GEORGE FREDERICK, college administrator; b. Saltburn, Yorkshire, Eng., July 28, 1956; s. Frederick George and Dorothy (Bassindale) T.; m. Lorna May Downie, Oct. 29, 1983; children: David Thomas, Ruth Kristina. MBA, Leicester (Eng.) U., 1994. Mgr./chef in catering industry, 1972-82; lectr. Bournville Coll., Birmingham, Eng., 1982-85; lectr. II Halton Coll., Widnes, Eng., 1985-87; sr. lectr. Northampton (Eng.) Coll., 1987-91, asst. head dept., 1991-94; head dept. Henley Coll., Coventry, Eng., 1994—. Mem. Nat. Assn. Heads of Catering (vice chair 1999—), Midlands Assn. Heads of Catering (chair 1999—). Avocations: walking, football, wines. Home: 9 Villiers Rd, Kenilworth, Warwickshire England CV8 2JB Office: Henley Coll Coventry, Menley Rd, Bell Green, Coventry England CV2 1ED

TROWBRIDGE, CHARLES WILLIAM, physicist, engineer, researcher; b. Totton, Hampshire, Eng., July 10, 1930; s. Maurice Cecil and Constance Winifred (Sherrell) T.; m. Rita May Creed, June 19, 1954; children: Dinah Mary, Simon Albert. BS in Physics, U. London, 1962, DSc in Engring., 1995; DSc (hon.), Tech. U. Graz, Austria, 1996. Chartered engr. Physicist Atomic Energy Establishment, Harwell, Eng., 1957-61; physicist Rutherford Appleton Lab., Oxford, Eng., 1961-71, group leader, 1961-71; chmn. Vector Fields Ltd., Oxford, 1984—; pres. Vector Fields Inc., Chgo., 1987—; vis. prof. Imperial Coll., London, 1986-89, Kings Coll., London, 1989—, U. Genoa, Italy, 1988, 96; chmn. indsl. liaison com. U. Southampton, 1995—. Co-author: (book) The Analytical and Numerical Solution of Electric and Magnetic Fields, 1992, (software packages) GFUN: 3-D integral equation for magnet design, 1972, TOSCA: 3D Finite Element package for static fields, 1979 (Queens award for Tech. 1992), ELEKTRA: 3D Finite Element package for electromagnetic fields, 1986. Officer Mercantile Marine, 1948-56. Decorated Officer of Brit. Empire, Her Majesty Queen Elizabeth II, 1993. Fellow Instn. Elec. Engrs. (Innovation medal 1993); mem. IEEE (sr.), Internat. Compumag Soc. (pres. 1993—), Royal Netherlands Acad. Arts and Scis. (elected fgn. mem.). Avocations: genealogy, literature, mathematics, mountaineering, music. Home: D'Arcy's Field Ford Ln, Frilford Oxford OX13 5NS, England Office: Vector Fields Ltd, 24 Bankside, Kidlington OX5 1JE Oxford, England

TROWBRIDGE, THOMAS, JR., mortgage banking company executive; b. Troy, N.Y., June 28, 1938; s. of Thomas and Elberta (Wood) T.; m. Delinda Bryan, July 3, 1965; children: Elisabeth Tacy, Wendy Bryan. BA, Yale U., 1960; MBA, Harvard U., 1965. V.p. James W. Rouse & Co., Balt., 1965-66, Washington, 1966-68, San Francisco, 1968-73, 76-78; pres. Rouse Investing Co., Columbia, Md., 1973-76; pres. Trowbridge, Kieselhorst & Co., San Francisco, 1978-97, CEO, chmn., 1997-2000; ret., 2000. Bd. dirs. Columbia Assn., 1975-76; trustee, treas. The Head-Royce Sch., Oakland, Calif., 1980-84; trustee, pres. Gen. Alumni Assn. Phillips Exeter Acad., 1984-90. Lt. USNR, 1960-63. Mem. Urban Land Inst., Calif. Mortgage Bankers Assn. (bd. dirs. 1991-98, pres. 1996-97), Mortgage Bankers Assn. Am. (bd. govs. 1993-2000), Olympic Club, Pacific Union Club, Lambda Alpha Internat. Republican. Presbyterian. Avocation: golf. Home: 4 Ridge Ln Orinda CA 94563-1318

TROWSDALE, JOHN, research scientist; b. Hull, England, Feb. 8, 1949; s. Roy Robinson and Doris (Graham) T.; m. Susan Price, July 17, 1971. BSc, U. Birmingham, England, 1970, PhD, 1973. Rschr. Imperial Cancer Rsch. Fund, London, 1980-97; prof. U. Cambridge, England, 1997—. Fellow Acad. of Med. Scis. Avocation: music.

TROXEL, KENT M., engineering consultant, computer consultant; b. Gary, Ind., July 26, 1958; s. Timothy A. and Joan C. (Lee) T.; children: Grant, Megan. BS in Mech. Engring., Purdue U., 1980, postgrad., 1982-84; postgrad., Ill. U., 1985-86. Registered profl. engr., Ind. Engr. Inland Steel, East Chicago, Ind., 1978-85; staff tech. rep. Inland Steel, East Chicago, 1987-88; pres. K.T. Design, Inc., Highland, Ind., 1981—; engring. supr. WCI Machine Tool, Belvidere, Ill., 1985-87; dir. sales and engring. Roll Ctr. Inc., Gary, 1988-90; cons. Inland Steel, East Chicago, 1989—, Raycon, Ann Arbor, Mich., 1990—, Star Tool, Chicago Hgts., 1990—. Inventor anti-friction drive, retracting shade. Cub master Boy Scouts Am., Highland, 1990—. Mem. ASME, Assn. Iron and Steel Engrs., Soc. Mfg. Engrs. (sr.), Soc. Automotive Engrs. Avocations: sailing, hunting, fishing, golf. Office: K T Design Inc 2645 Ridge Rd Highland IN 46322-1663

TROXELL, LUCY DAVIS, consulting firm executive; b. Cambridge, Mass., Apr. 25, 1932; d. Ellsworth and Mildred (Enneking) Davis; m. Charles DeGroat Bader, June 13, 1952 (div. Aug. 1974); children: Christie P. Walker, Mary Ellsworth Bader, Charles D. Bader Jr., Davis Bradford Bader; m. Victor Daniel Shirer Troxell, Aug. 1974. BA, Smith Coll., Northampton, Mass., 1952. Cert. paralegal, employee benefit specialist, assoc. in risk mgmt. Paralegal O'Melveny & Myers, L.A., 1976-77; acct. exec. Olanie Hurst & Hemrich, L.A., 1977-78; asst. to trustee Oxford Ins. Mgmt., L.A., 1978-80; dir. corp. svcs., asst. corp. sec. Consolidated Elec. Distbrs., Inc., Westlake Village, Calif., 1980-93; pres. MONMAK LDT, Westlake Village, 1993—. Sustaining mem., bd. dirs. Jr. League, Hartford, Conn., L.A., 1952—; clk. St. Mathew's Parish Vestry, Pacific Palisades, Calif., 1988, sr. warden, 1989-90; bd. dirs. Smith Coll. Club, Hartford, L.A., 1952—, Nat. Charity League, L.A., 1964-68; lic. lay eucharistic minister Episcopal Ch.; vol. ARC; bd. dirs., treas. HOA Lakeshore Cmty. Assn., 1999. Sophia Smith scholar. Fellow Internat. Soc. Cert. Employee Benefit Specialists (charter mem., bd. dirs., sec., treas. 1988-89, pres. 1989-90, edn. chmn. 1986-88 L.A. chpt.), Risk and Ins. Mgmt. Soc. (program chmn. L.A. chpt. 1985-86), Theatre Palisades (bd. dirs. 1960-74). Republican. Avocations: finance, acting, music appreciation, art. Home: 450 Puerto Del Mar Pacific Palisades CA 90272-4233 Office: MONMAK LDT 31220 La Baya Dr # 322 Westlake Vlg CA 91362-4008

TROXELL, MARY THERESA (TERRY TROXELL), geriatrics services professional; b. Syracuse, N.Y., Aug. 29, 1950; d. Henry and Mary (McDermott) Flynn; 1 child, Melissa Lee. BSN, U. Pa., 1971. Cert. quality improvement specialsit; cert. gerontol. nurse specialist; cert. case mgr. Supr. neonatal ICU St. Joe's, Syracuse, 1976-79; dir. nursing Hillhaven, Phoenix, 1979-81; quality assurance nurse long term care Maricopa County, Phoenix, 1981-83; dir. nursing Desert Haven Nursing Home, Phoenix, 1983-84; team leader, surveyor health care licensure State of Ariz., Phoenix, 1985-87, program mgr. long term care licensure and certification, 1987-89, program mgr. enforcement and compliance licensure and cert., 1989-91; dir. profl. svcs. Unison Healthcare, Phoenix, 1991-94; v.p. clin. ops. SunQuest Healthcare, Phoenix, 1994-96; sr. v.p. clin. and ancillary ops. Unison Healthcare, 1996-98, exec. v.p. opers., 1998—. Author: (manuals) Licensure Procedures, 1990, Quality Improvement, Restorative Nursing: A Key to Quality, 1992, Director of Nursing Manual, 1996, Clinical Operations Series, 1997. Developer legislation for adult care homes, health care licensure laws State of Ariz., 1990. Mem. Ariz. Health Care Assn. (chair legis. com. 1992-94, chair devel./revision nursing facility laws 1992-94), Am. Health Care Assn. (nat. facility stds. com. 1992-96, nat. multifacility com. 1993-96, LTC nurses coun. 1995, nat. quality com. 1996-97, regional v.p. region XI, adv. com.), Quality Improvement Nurses Assn., Gerontol. Nurses Assn., Am. Health Care (v.p. region XI). Home: 10224 E Sahavro Scottsdale AZ 85260-6331 Office: Unison Health Care Ste 245 8800 N Garney Center Dr Scottsdale AZ 85258

TROY, JOSEPH FREED, lawyer; b. Wilkes-Barre, Pa., Aug. 16, 1938; s. Sergei and Shirley Jean T.; m. Brigitta Ann Balos, June 9, 1962; children: Darcy Kendall, Austin Remy. BA, Yale U., 1960; LLB, Harvard U., 1963. Bar: Calif. 1964, D.C. 1979. Assoc. Hindin, McKittrick & Marsh, Beverly Hills, Calif., 1964-68, ptnr., 1968-70; pres. Troy & Gould, Los Angeles, 1970—; lectr. Calif. Continuing Edn. of Bar, 1972-80, 94; dir. Amerigon Inc., 1993-96, Movie Gallery, Inc., 1994—, Digital Video Systems, Inc., 1996-98, Argoquest, Inc., 2000—. Author: Let's Go: A Student Guide to Europe, 1962, Accountability of Corporate Management; co-author: Protecting Corporate Officers and Directors from Liability, 1994. Pres. L.A. Chamber Orch. Soc., 1968-75, chmn. bd. dirs., 1975-78, vice chmn. bd. dirs., 1978-81; bd. dirs. L.A. Opera, 1972—, v.p., mem. exec. com., 1987—; hon.consul of Tunisia, L.A., 1984-88; pres. Internat. Festival Soc.; bd. dirs. Brentwood Pk. Property Owners Assn., 1988-93. Reid Hall fellow U. Paris, 1958. Mem. ABA, Calif. State Bar Assn. (chmn. task force on complex litigation 1997-99), D.C. Bar Assn., L.A. County Bar Assn. (chmn. bus. and corp. law sect. 1977-78), French Am. C. of C. U.S. (exec. v.p. 1983-85), French Am. C. of C. L.A. (chmn. 1982-84), Wine and Food Soc. So. Calif. Inc. (bd. dirs.), Beach Club, Calif. Club. Office: 1801 Century Park E Ste 1600 Los Angeles CA 90067-2318

TROYER, ALVAH FORREST, agriculture executive, plant breeder; b. LaFontaine, Ind., May 30, 1929; s. Alvah Forrest and Lottie (Waggoner) T.; m. Joyce Ann Wigner, Sept. 22, 1950; children: Anne, Barbara, Catherine, Daniel (dec.). B.S., Purdue U., 1954; M.S., U. Ill., 1956; Ph.D., U. Minn., 1964. Rsch. assoc. U. Ill., Urbana, 1955-56; rsch. fellow U. Minn., St. Paul, 1956-58; rsch. sta. mgr. Pioneer Hi-Bred Internat., Inc., Mankato, Minn., 1958-65, rsch. coord., 1965-77; dir. R & D, Pfizer Genetics, St. Louis, 1977-81, v.p. and dir. R & D,, 1981-82; v.p. R & D, DeKalb (Ill.) Plant Genetics, 1982-93; cons. Hybrid Seed divsn. Cargill, Mpls., 1993-98; adj. prof. crop sci. dept. U. Ill., 1998—; rschr. corn breeding, econ. botany, crop physiology, increasing genetic diversity, recent corn evolution. Contbr. articles to numerous publs.; developer of popular corn inbred lines and hybrids. Master sgt. U.S. Army, 1951-53, Korea. Decorated Bronze star; recipient Nat. Coun. Comml. Plant Breeders Genetics and Plant Breeding award, 1992, Outstanding Achievement award U. Minn., 1998. Fellow AAAS, Am. Soc. Agronomy, Crop Sci. Soc. Am.; mem. Am. Genetic Assn., Genetic Soc. Am., N.Y. Acad. Scis., CAST, VFW, Masons, Sigma Xi, Gamma Sigma Delta (Award of Merit 1996), Alpha Zeta, Lambda Chi Alpha, Gamma Alpha. Methodist. Home: 611 Joanne Ln Dekalb IL 60115-1862

TROYJO, MARCOS PRADO, diplomat; b. São Paulo, July 4, 1966; s. Mario and Troyjo and Antonia Vital Do Prado. B Econs., São Paulo Sch. Econs., 1991; B Sociology and Politics, Sã Paulo Sch. Sociology, 1991; M Sociology, U. Sã Paulo, 1994; degree in diplomacy, Inst. Rio Branco, 1994. Chief of staff dept. sci. and tech. Ministry of External Rels. of Brazil, 1994-97; press sec. Permanent Mission of Brazil to UN, N.Y.C., 1997—; mem. Hildegerst Seminars, N.Y.C., 1998—. Mem. Forum of the Ams. E-mail: mtroyjo@delbrasonu.org.

TROZZOLO, ANTHONY MARION, chemistry educator; b. Chgo., Jan. 11, 1930; s. Pasquale and Francesca (Vercillo) T.; m. Doris C. Stoffregen, Oct. 8, 1955; children: Thomas, Susan, Patricia, Michael, Lisa, Laura. BS, Ill. Inst. Tech., 1950; MS, U. Chgo., 1957, PhD, 1960. Asst. chemist Chgo. Midway Labs., 1952-53; assoc. chemist Armour Rsch. Found., Chgo., 1953-56; tech. staff Bell Labs., Murray Hill, N.J., 1959-75; Charles L. Huisking prof. chemistry U. Notre Dame, 1975-92, Charles L. Huisking prof. emeritus, 1992—; asst. dean U. Notre Dame Coll. Sci., 1993-98; P.C. Reilly lectr. U. Notre Dame, 1972, Hesburgh Alumni lectr., 1986, Disting. lectr. sci., 1986; vis. prof. Columbia U., N.Y.C., 1971, U. Colo., 1981, Katholieke U. Leuven, Belgium, 1983, Max Planck Inst. für Strahlenchemie, Mülheim/Ruhr, Fed. Republic Germany, 1990; vis. lectr. Academia Sinica, 1984, 85; Phillips lectr. U. Okla., 1971; C.L. Brown lectr. Rutgers U., 1975; Sigma Xi lectr. Bowling Green U., 1976, Abbott Labs., 1978; M. Faraday lectr. No. Ill. U., 1976; F.O. Butler lectr. S.D. State U., 1978; Chevron lectr. U. Nev., Reno, 1983; J. Crano lectr. U. Akron, 2000; plenary lectr. various internat. confs.; founder, chmn. Gordon Conf. on Organic Photochemistry, 1964; trustee Gordon Rsch. Confs., 1988-92; cons. in field. Assoc. editor Jour. Am. Chem. Soc., 1975-76; editor Chem. Revs., 1977-84; editorial adv. bd. Accounts of Chem. Rsch., 1977-85; cons. editor Encyclopedia of Science and Technology, 1982-92; contbr. articles to profl. jours.; patentee in field. Fellow AEC, 1951, NSF, 1957-59; named Hon. Citizen of Castrolibero, Italy, 1997; recipient Pietro Bucci prize U. Calabria/Italian Chem. Soc., 1997. Fellow AAAS, Am. Inst. Chemists (Student award 1950), N.Y. Acad. Scis. (chmn. chem. scis. sect. 1969-70, Halpern award in photochemistry 1980), Inter-Am. Photochemical Soc.; mem. AAUP, Am. Chem. Soc. (Disting. Svc. award St. Joseph Valley sect. 1979, Tex. lectr. 1975, Pacific Coast lectr. 1981, Coronado lectr. 1980, 93, 98, N.Y. state lectr. 1993, Hoosier lectr. 1995, Ozark lectr. 1995, Rocky Mountain lectr. 1996, Tex. Coast lectr. 1996, Osage lectr. 1998), Sigma Xi. Roman Catholic. Home: 1329 E Washington St South Bend IN 46617-3340 Office: U Notre Dame Dept Chemistry-Biochemistry Notre Dame IN 46556-5670

TRSIC, MILAN, chemistry educator, researcher; b. Belgrad, Serbia, Yugoslavia, Nov. 15, 1937; arrived in Brazil, 1978; s. Welizar and Sika Trsic; m. Liliana Espinos, Sept. 15, 1964; 1 child, Carmina Mara Veronica; m. Maria Eugenia Pinochet, Nov. 24, 1978; children: Marcos Pinochet, Manuel Pinochet. BSc, U. Chile, Santiago, 1960, grad. in pharm. chemistry, 1961; PhD, U. Paris, 1966. Lectr., rschr. U. Chile, 1961-63, 67-72; postdoctoral fellow U. Uppsala, 1972-73; rsch. assoc. U. Calgary, Alta., Can., 1974-78; vis. prof. chemistry U. Frankfurt am Main, Germany, 1978-79; vis. prof. chemistry U. Sao Paulo, Brazil, 1979-83, assoc. prof., 1983-91, prof., 1991—, head dept., 1993-97; dean inst., 1998—. Contbg. author: Applied Quantum Chemistry, 1986; co-editor: Quasar: Structure Activity Relationships of Analgesics, Narcotic Antagonists and Hallucinogens, 1978, Procs. 3d Brazilian Symposium on Theoretical Chemistry, 1985; contbr. articles to sci. jours., including Molecular Physics. Recipient rsch. award Brazilian Sci. Found., 1982-99. Mem. Brazilian Chem. Soc. Orthodox Catholic. Avocations: reading, music. Office: U Sao Paulo Inst Chemistry, PO Box 780, 13560970 São Carlos SP, Brazil

TRUBETSKOV, MICHAEL KIRILLOVICH, researcher; b. Moscow, Dec. 30, 1958; s. Kirill Mikhailovich and Rosa Ivanovna Trubetskov; m. Marina Dmitrievna Levukova, Nov. 16, 1990; 1 child, Michael. MS, Moscow State U., 1982, PhD, 1986. Cert. in physics. Rschr. physics dept. Moscow State U., 1985-92, sr. rschr. Rsch. Computing Ctr., 1992-97, leading rschr. Rsch. Computing Ctr., 1997—; tchr. Physics Dept., Moscow, 1983-92; mem. sci. coun. Rsch. Computing Ctr., Moscow State U., 1993—. Author: OptiLayer Thin Film Software, 1991, (book) Conformal Mapping with Computer-Aided Visualization, 1995; contbr. articles to sci. jours. Mem. Internat. Soc. for Optical Engring. Avocations: jazz and classical music, fishing, water touring. Fax: 7-095-938-2136. E-mail: miket@trub.srcc.msu.su. Home: Valdaiskii pr 15-13, Moscow 125445, Russia Office: Moscow State U, Vorob'evy Gory, Moscow 119899, Russia

TRUBETSKOY, VLADIMIR SERGEEVICH, polymer chemist; b. Moscow, Oct. 13, 1957; s. Sergey V. and Nina V. Trubetskoy; m. Olga V. Merzlikine, Feb. 9, 1984; children: Sergey, Vassily, Ivan. M in Chemistry summa cum laude, Moscow State U., 1974, MS, 1979; PhD in Biochemistry, USSR Acad. Med. Scis., Moscow, 1984. Sr. rsch. fellow Inst. Exptl. Cardiology, Moscow, 1984-90; postdoctoral fellow dept. biochemistry U. Tenn., Knoxville, 1990-91; asst. in chemistry Ctr. Imaging and Pharm. Rsch., Mass. Gen. Hosp., Boston, 1991-93; assoc. chemist dept. radiology Med. Sch. Harvard U., Ctr. Imaging and Pharm. Rsch., Mass. Gen. Hosp., Boston, 1993-96; sr. chemist Mirus Corp., Madison, Wis., 1996—. Co-contbr. articles, contbr. rev. to profl. jours. Radiol. Soc. N.Am. Seed grantee, 1996; Small Bus. Innovation rsch. grantee NIH, 1998; recipient Outstanding Pharm. Paper award Controlled Release Soc., 1993. Mem. Am. Chem. Soc., Am. Soc. for Gene Therapy. Eastern Orthodox. Fax: 608-441-2849. E-mail: vladimirt@genetransfer.com. Office: Mirus Corp 505 S Rosa Rd Madison WI 53719-1262

TRUBITSYN, MICHAEL, physicist, educator; b. Alma-Ata, Kazakstan, Sept. 11, 1962; arrived in Ukraine, 1963; s. Pavel Trubitsyn and Mariya Shevchenko; m. Nataliya Medvedeva, Sept. 28, 1986 (div.); 1 child, Iliya; m. Nataliya Falina, Mar. 1, 1996; 1 child, Anna. Student, State U., Dniepropetrovsk, Ukraine, 1979-84, postgrad., 1984-87, 99—; PhD in Solid State Physics, Voronezh Poly. Inst., Russia, 1989. Cert. physicist, educator. From jr. rschr. to rschr. State U., Dniepropetrovsk, 1987-90, asst. prof., 1990-92, sr. rschr., 1992-99. Contbr. sci. articles. to profl. jours. Travel grantee various orgns. Avocations: aquariums, flower growing. Office: State U Phys Dept, per Nauchnyi 13, 49625 Dniepropetrovsk Ukraine

TRUBKO, SERGEY VLADIMIR, optical designer, researcher; b. St. Petersburg, Russia, Sept. 26, 1948; came to U.S., 1994; s. Vladimir F. Trubko and Polina L. Chornaya; m. Yelizaveta Asinovskaya, Oct. 31, 1987; children: Raisa, Tim. BS, U. Fine Mechanics and Optics, St. Petersburg, 1971, MS with honors, 1973, PhD, 1977. From scientist to sr. scientist Metrology Inst., State Optical Inst., St. Petersburg, 1977-94; cons. Bklyn., 1995; sr. optical engr. Symbol Tech., Inc., Holtsville, N.Y., 1996-98; chief scientist CycloVision Tech., Inc., N.Y.C., 1998-2000; v.p. Remote Reality, Inc., N.Y.C., 2000—. Author: Design of Cemented Doublets, 1984; contbr. articles to profl. jours. Mem. Internat. Soc. Optical Engring. Achievements include invention of three-mirror off-axis system and catadioptric panoramic imaging system; holds 7 patents. Office: Remote Reality Inc 4 Technology Dr Westborough MA 01581-1727

TRUCHE, PIERRE, French federal judge; b. Lyon, France, Nov. 1, 1929. Dir. etudes École Nat. de la Magistrature, 1974-77, dep. dir., 1977; atty. gen. Douai, Grenoble, France, 1978-82; procurator Marseilles, 1982-84; procurator gen. Lyon, 1984-88, Paris, 1988-92; procurator gen. Cour de Cassation, 1992-96, pres., 1996-99; pres. Commision Nationale Consultative des Droits de l'Homme, Paris, 1999—. Office: Cour de Cassation, 5 Quai de l'Horloge, 75055 Paris RP, France Office: Commision Nationale Cons, 35 rue Saint Dominique, 75007 Paris France

TRUDNAK, STEPHEN JOSEPH, landscape architect; b. Nanticoke, Pa., Feb. 25, 1947; s. Stephen Adam and Marcella (Levulis) T.; m. Arden Batchelder Weill, Sept. 6, 1980. BS in Landscape Arch., Pa. State U., 1970. Jr. landscape arch. Kling Partnership, Phila., 1970-72; mem. landscape arch. firm Keith French Assocs., Washington, 1972-73; head dept. landscape arch. Linganore Ctr. Design, Frederick, Md., 1973-74, Toups and Loiederman, Rockville, Md., 1974-76; project landscape arch. Kaiser Transit Group, So. Calif. Rapid Transit Dist., Dade County Transit Improvement Program, Metro Rail Transit Cons.; v.p. Harry Weese & Assocs., Ltd., Miami, Fla., 1976-84; v.p. landscape arch. Canin Assocs., Orlando, Fla., 1984-87; dir. planning and design Bonita Bay Properties, Inc., Bonita Springs, Fla., 1987-91; prin. Stephne J. Trudnak, P.A. Landscape Arch. and Land Planning, 1991—. Bd. dirs., v.p. Koreshan State Hist. Site, 1989-94; mem. 'not for profit' com. Bonita Springs Cmty. Redevel. Agy., 1994-97; v.p. Bonita Springs Mainstreet Program, 1996, 2000, pres., 1997-98; del. for Congressman Porter Goss, Congl. Small Bus. Summit, 1998, 2000, del. representing Fla. state rep. Carol Green Fla. Small Bus. Summit, 1999; bd. dirs. Bonita Springs YMCA, 1999—; mem. Leadership Bonita, 2000. Fellow Am. Soc. Landscape Archs. (pres. Fla. chpt. 1983, chpt. adv. bd. 1984-85, elections task force 1986, publs. task force 1987, trustee 1987-89, membership task force, chmn. 1989-90, nat. v.p. chpt. and mem. svcs. 1992-94, nondues revenue task force 1994-95, ASLA On-Line task force 1997—, chair 1999, specifications task force 1998-99), Nat. Xeriscape Coun. (Fla. steering com.), Nat. Speleol. Soc. SCARAB; mem. Bonita Springs C. of C. (chair beautification com. 1991-92, 94-95, bd. dirs. 1995—, v.p. edn. divsn. 1996-98, vice chmn. cmty. devel. divsn. 1998-99, Affiliate of Yr. 1997, Citizen of Yr. 1999, Charter Class Leadership Grad. 2000). Home: 554 104th Ave N Naples FL 34108-3225 Office: 3461 Bonita Bay Blvd Bonita Springs FL 34134-4384

TRUE, HANS CHRISTIAN GODSKESEN, applied mathematics educator; b. Copenhagen, June 8, 1936; s. Soeren Peter and Wanda Agnete (Godskesen) T.; m. Bozena Maria Duda, Mar. 24, 1973; children: Peter, Martin Philip, Daniel Patrick, Christian Dennis. MSME, Tech. U. of Denmark, 1960, PhD in Applied Math., 1964; MS in Applied Math., Harvard U., 1967. Rsch. assoc. Tech. U. of Denmark, 1960-61, asst. prof., 1967-69, assoc. prof., 1969—; sr. engr. ES-Consult, Denmark, 1992-96; dir. True Consult, 1997—; sr. engr. Scan Rail Consult, 1997-98; guest tchr. Yale U., 1964-65; guest prof. U. Leeds, Eng., 1985; guest rschr. Pa. State U., Calif. Inst. Tech., 1974-75, Northwestern U., Clemson U., 1987-88; cons. Danish State Rys., 1991—; sondergutachter Deutsche Forschungsgemeinschaft and Alexander von Humboldt Stiftung, Germany, 1995—; conf. chmn. 3d European Nonlinear Oscillations Conf. (3rd ENOC), 17th Internat. Assn. of Vehicle Systems Dynamics Symposium; referee Alexander von Humboldt Found. and scientific jours. Assoc. editor Jour. of Math. in Industry, 1986—; contbr. numerous articles to profl. publs. Pvt. Danish Home Def., 1960-61. Recipient Anniversary medal Mining U. Cracow, 1989; Fulbright fellow, 1964-67, Alexander von Humboldt fellow U. Freiburg, 1970-71. Mem. IAVSD (trustee 1995—, 2d v.p. 1999—), ASME, Internat. Consortium of Indsl. and Applied Math., European Mechanics Coun. (mem. conf. coun. 1999—), Ingeniøoforeningeni Denmark, NRHS, ISIMM, Internat. Union Theoretical and Applied Mechanics (working party dynamics 1997—), Danish Alexander von Humboldt Club (co-founder 1999). Lutheran. Avocations: hiking, skiing, model railways and railways. Home: Dalstroeget 18, DK-2860 Soeborg Denmark Office: Tech U Denmark, Bldg 321 Dept Math Modelling, DK-2800 Lyngby Denmark

TRUE, LELAND BEYER, civil engineer, consultant; b. Cheyenne, Wyo., Aug. 20, 1921; s. James Beaman and Mary Laura (Beyer) T.; m. Janet R. Hill (dec. Aug. 1976); 1 child, Patricia Ann; m. Alef Collins, May 8, 1977. BSCE, U. Wyo., 1943. Hydrographic field asst. U.S. Geol. Survey, Cheyenne and Laramie, Wyo., 1942-43; engr. P.1 Boysen Dam U.S. Bur. Reclamation, Thermopolis, Wyo., 1946-52; with Morrison-Knudsen Co., Inc., 1952-70, 77-86; project mgr. Greer's Ferry Dam Morrison-Knudsen Co., Inc., Heber Springs, Ark., 1961-63; project mgr. Blue Ridge Dam Morrison-Knudsen Co., Inc., Payson, Ariz., 1963-65; project mgr., estimator home office Morrison-Knudsen Co., Inc., Boise, Idaho, 1965-69; project mgr. Toa Vaca Dam Morrison-Knudsen Co., Inc., Villalba, P.R., 1969-70; resident area engr. metro subway A.A. Mathews, Inc., Washington, 1970-77; asst. chief engr. Morrison-Knudsen Co., Inc., Boise, 1977-86; pvt. practice constrn. cons. Boise, 1986—. Staff sgt. U.S. Army Corps Engrs., 1943-46. Mem. ASCE (life). Avocations: fishing, hunting, golf, rocks, RV travel. Home and Office: 6055 N Crewe Ave Boise ID 83703-2066

TRUEB, BEAT, biochemist, researcher; b. Zurich, Switzerland, Oct. 21, 1954; s. Hansrudolf and Heidi P. (Philipp) T.; m. Judith M. Köppel, Sept. 13, 1989; children: Roman, Flavia. MSc, ETH Zurich, 1978, PhD, 1981, Habilitation in biochemistry, 1991. Postdoctoral researcher U. Wash., Seattle, 1983, Fred Hutchinson Cancer Rsch. Ctr., Seattle, 1984; asst. prof. ETH Zurich, 1985-94; assoc. head M.E. Müller-Inst.for Biomechs., Bern, Switzerland, 1995—. Contbr. articles to profl. jours.; editor Jour. Biochim. Biophys. Acta, 1996—. Recipient Jucker Cancer award U. Zurich, 1992, Töndury award Swiss Soc. for Anatomy, Histology and Embryology, 1993, START career devel. award Swiss Nat. Sci. Found., 1987. Mem. Swiss Soc. for Biochemistry (sec. 1995—), Swiss Connective Tissue Soc. (chmn. 1996—). Office: ME Müller Inst, PO Box 30, CH-3010 Bern Switzerland

TRUEBA, FERNANDO, film director and producer, screenwriter; b. Madrid, Jan. 18, 1955; s. Maximo Rodriguez and Palmira Trueba; m. Cristina Huete, Oct. 8, 1982; 1 child, Jonas-Groucho. Film critic El Pais, newspaper, Madrid, 1976-79; editor, dir. Casablanca, film mag., Madrid, 1981-83; film dir., prodr., screenwriter Creative Artists Agy., Beverly Hills, Calif. Dir., screenwriter Opera Prima, 1980 (Silver Hugo award Chgo. Film Festival 1980), Mientras el Cuerpo Aguante, 1982, Sal Gorda, 1983, Se Infiel y No

Mires con Quien, 1985, El Año de Las Luces, 1986 (Silver Bear award Berlin Film Festival 1987), The Mad Monkey, 1989, Belle époque, 1992 (Academy Award, Best Foreign Language Film, 1993), Two Much, 1996; producer, screenwriter A Contratiempo, 1981, De Tripas Corazon, 1984, La Mujer de tu Vida, 1988-89; producer Lulu de Noche, 1985, El Juego Mas Divertido, 1987, Earth Magicians, 1989—, Amo tu cama rica, 1991, Alas de mariposa, 1991 (Concha of Gold award San Sebastian Film Festival 1991), Sublet, 1992, La Buena Vida, 1996; dir. La Nina de Tos Ojos, 1998, also dir. short films. Mem. Acad. Motion Pictures Spain (pres. 1988). Home: Bueso Pineda 29, 28043 Madrid Spain Office: CAA c/o Emanuel Nunez 9830 Wilshire Blvd Beverly Hills CA 90212-1804

TRUELLE, JEAN LUC, neurologist, educator; b. Paris, July 6, 1939; s. Jean Georges and Jeanne Marie Therese (Davous) T.; m. Michele Montrwvil; children: Philippe, Olivier, Jean Marie. MD in Neurology, Paris, 1969. Sr. resident La Salpêtriére, Paris, 1970-72; prof. neurology U. Angers, France, 1976; dean's assessor U. Angers, 1982-84, head dept. neurology, 1984-86; head dept. neurology Hosp. Foch, Suresnes, France, 1986—; founder ARCEAU rehab. ctr. for traumatic brain injured, 1984. Co-author: Pratique Neurologique, 1983. With French Navy, 1964-65. Mem. French Soc. Neurology, European Brain Injury Soc. (past pres. 1989, 93), Rotary Club Paris (v.p. 1997). Roman Catholic. Avocations: running (marathons), skiing, reading, classical music. Home: 15 Villa Paul Verlaine, 75019 Paris France Office: Hosp Foch, 40 Rue Worth, 92151 Suresnes France

TRUESDALE, GEOFFREY ASHWORTH, former environmental chemist; b. Birmingham, Eng., Mar. 16, 1927; s. Reginald and Ellen (Ashworth) T.; m. Beryl Hathaway, May 5, 1951; children: David Geoffrey, Carolyn Pamela. BS in Chemistry, U. London, 1950. Tech. officer Water Pollution Rsch. Lab., Stevenage, Eng., 1947-68; chem. inspector Dept. of the Environment, London, 1968-70; ptnr. Balfours, Cons. Engrs., London, 1970-88; dir., chmn. Consultants in Environ. Scis. Ltd., London, 1982-92; ret., 1993-94; cons. Balfour-Maunsell, Cons. Engrs., London, 1988-92. Contbr. articles to profl. jours. Pres. Inst. Water Pollution Control, U.K., 1978-79, European Water Pollution Control Assn., 1984-87. Named Freeman of City of London, 1989, Order of Brit. Empire, 1995. Fellow Inst. Water and Environ. Mgmt. (coun. mem. 1987-91, pres. 1988-89); mem. Co. of Water Conservators (City of London, master 1991-92). Home: Bracebridge Oast Rd, Oxted RH8 9DX, England

TRUESDELL, WALTER GEORGE, minister, librarian; b. N.Y.C., Oct. 22, 1919; s. George Anson and Hattie (Evans) T.; m. Mary Schurok, June 10, 1944; children: Walter George, Susan Hattie. AB, Columbia U. Columbia Coll., 1941; MA, Columbia U. Tchrs. Coll., 1975; MDiv, Theol. Sem. of the Ref. Episcopal Ch., Phila., 1944; BLS, Pratt Inst., 1950. Ordained to ministry Ref. Episcopal Ch., 1944. Asst. min. First Ref. Episcopal Ch., N.Y.C., 1944-54, sr. assoc. min., 1989—; rector Ch. of the Redemption, Bklyn., 1956—; lectr. apologetics and English Bible Theol. Sem. Ref. Episcopal Ch., Phila., 1945-48; libr. Theol. Sem. Ref. Episcopal Ch., Phila. (relocated to Blue Bell, Pa., Sept. 2000), 1964-93, Shelton Coll., 1951-69; libr. Cummins Meml. Theol. Sem. Reformed Episcopal, Summerville, S.C., 1996—; chmn. com. on state of ch. Ref. Episcopal Ch., 1960-87, mem., 1987-96, mem. gen. com. 1978-96; real estate broker, 1979—. Editor Episcopal Recorder, 1980-90. Mem. ALA (life), Pa. Libr. Assn., Assn. Statisticians Am. Religious Bodies. Home and Office: 306 E 90th St New York NY 10128-5121 Office: Cummins Meml Theol Sem 705 S Main St Summerville SC 29483-5911

TRUINI PALOMBA, MARIA GIUSEPPINA, supreme court lawyer, judge; b. Borbona, Ri-Latium, Italy, Aug. 25, 1935; d. Costanzo and Ezia (Giorgi) Truini; m. Emilio Palomba, Jan. 11, 1964; children: Francesco Maria, Giovanna Palomba. Degree in Law, State U. Rome, 1960. Tchr. State High Sch., Rieti, Italy, 1955-84; local magistrate Rieti, Italy, 1974-86; judge Fiscal Commn., Rieti, Italy, 1974—, Fiscal Commn. Reg. Rome v.p., 1996—. Author: La Cucina Sabina, 1991; contbr. articles to profl. jours. Mem. drug Prevention Assn., L'Aquila, 1979—; hon. guard Nat. Inst. Royal Tombs of Pantheon, Rome, 1980—. Decorated Cavalier of the Merit of the Italian Rep., 1984, Lady of the Order of Chivalry of the Holy Sepulchre of Jerusalem, Grand Master Cardinal, 1990, Lady of the Sovereign and Military Order of the Temple of Jerusalem, 1998; mem. Italian Red cross, 1986—, patroness, 1978; vol. UNICEF. Mem. Nat. Civil Lawyers Union (dist. pres. Rieti, nat. councillor 1990—), Italian Women Jurists Assn. (dist. pres. Rieti and nat. councillor 1990—), Internat. Assn. of Lawyers, Eurojuris Internat. Geie, Italian Acad. Cooking (nat. cons. 1974, dist. del.), Italian Women's Mgmt. Assn., Italian Women's Nat. Coun., Amnesty Internat. Lawyers, Aeroclub (pres. 1992-93), Rotary (councillor 1994-95, pres., 1996-97), v.p. FILDIS-IFUW, Rome, 2000—. Avocations: travel, cinema, theatre, cooking, volleyball. Home and Office: A Gherardi 70, 02100 Rieti Italy

TRUITT, CHARLOTTE FRANCES, clergywoman; b. Newark, Ohio, Feb. 8, 1922; d. Frank Wilson and Charlotte (Hook) T.; m. Robert Kennedy Carter, Mar. 17, 1946 (div. 1972); children: Mary Elizabeth Carter O'Brien, Robert Truitt Carter; m. Robert Harold Bonthius Sr., Apr. 29, 1977. Student, Ohio State U., 1941-46; MA in Christian Edn., Meth. Theol. Sch., Delaware, Ohio, 1976, MDiv, 1977. Ordained to ministry United Ch. of Christ, 1979. Asst. dir. youth program YWCA, Columbus, Ohio, 1965-68, dir. youth program, 1968-70, dir. family life and racial justice programs, 1970-72; mission coord. and youth minister First Cmty. Ch., Columbus, 1972-75; min. Christian edn. Broad St. United Meth. Ch., Columbus, 1975-76; cons., trainer Action Tng. Network, Ohio and Maine, 1976-90; pres. bd. Family Life and Sex Edn. Coun., Columbus, 1971-72; bd. dirs. Ohio Coun. Chs., Columbus, 1973-74; del. United Ch. of Christ, Nicaragua, 1983, and co-founder Nat. Witness for Peace, 1983. Contbr. articles to religious jours. and publs. Pres. bd. dirs. North Ctrl. Mental Health Ctr., Columbus, 1973-74; mem. Columbus Urban League Edn. Commn., 1965-67, Hancock Comprehensive Plan Commn., Hancock, Maine, 1990; chair scholarship bd. Thorsen Scholarship Fund, Hancock, 1988-89; bd. dirs., fin. chair The Next Step Domestic Violence Project, Ellsworth, Maine, 1993-94; bd. dirs. Witness for Peace, pers. chair, 1983-85, chair, 1994-95. Recipient Martin Luther King Jr. award NAACP, Portland, Maine, 1989, Disting. Svc. award The Next Step Domestic Violence Project, Ellsworth, 1994. Mem. AAUW, Hancock-Waldo Clergy Assn., Friends Taunton Bay, Natural Resources Coun. of Maine, Peace Action, Religious Coalition for Reproductive Choice, United Ch. of Christ Christians for Justice Action, Witness for Peace, Ctr. for Sci. in Pub. Interest, Americans United for Separation Ch. and State. Mem. United Ch. of Christ. Avocations: flower gardening, bird watching, reading, nature walks, drawing. Home and Office: HC 64 Box 270-51 Blue Hill ME 04614-9608

TRUJILLO-CUTHRELL, LORETTA MARIE, chemical engineer; b. Santa Fe, N.Mex., May 22, 1959; d. Jose E.F. and Irene D. (Fernandez) Trujillo; m. Robert Blair Cuthrell, May 16, 1987. BSChemE, U. N.Mex., 1988. Process engr. Kerr McGee Chem., Trona, Calif., 1989-91; chem. engr. N.Am. Chem. Co., Trona, 1991—, quality coord., 1992-98; quality coord. IMC Chem., Trona, Calif., 1998—; with lab. Gen. Tech., Albuquerque. Mem. AICE (vice-chair 1995—), Women in Mining. Office: Argus Facility Gen Tech Albuquerque NM 87107

TRULEAR, HAROLD DEAN, minister, theological educator, social researcher; b. Phila., Oct. 4, 1954; s. Harold Holland and Elizabeth C. (Dean) T.; m. Vickie Lynette Butler, June 27, 1981; children: Harold Butler, Jared Morgan, Frances Elizabeth. BA, Morehouse Coll., 1975; MPhil, Drew U., 1979, PhD, 1983. Club dir. Youth for Christ, Paterson, N.J., 1977-83; assoc. prof. ch. and society Drew U., Madison, N.J., 1978-87; dir. black ch. studies Ea. Bapt. Theol. Sem., Phila., 1987-90; dean 1st profl. programs N.Y. Theol. Sem., N.Y.C., 1990-96, prof. ch. and society, 1990-98; v.p. Pub./Pvt. Ventures, Phila., 1998—; assoc. pastor Cmty. Bapt. Ch., Paterson, 1981-87, 91-97; pastor Mt. Zion Bapt. Ch., Phila., 1987-90; assoc. min. Zion Bapt. Ch., Ardmore, Pa.; clergy assoc. St. Mary's Episcopal Ch., Ardmore; cons. Christian Coll. Consortium, 1990, Vanderbilt U. Div. Sch., Nashville, 1995; mem. adv. bd. Phila. Project for Youth Ministry, 1995-97; bd. dirs. N.Y. Christian Higher Edn. Consortium, N.Y.C. Guest editor The Pastor Scholar, 1997; contbr. chpts. to books. Bd. dirs. Paterson Clergy Assn., 1977-83, Opportunities Industrialization Ctr., Paterson, 1981-87, Inter Varsity Christian Fellowship, Madison, Wis., 1995—, Inndwelling, World Impact, Chester, Pa. Grantee N.J. Hist. Commn., 1984, Assn. Theol. Schs., 1984, Ford Found., 1994-95. Fellow Partnership for Rsch. on Religion and At Risk Youth; mem. Am. Acad. Religion, Soc. for the Study Black Religion, Soc. for Pentecostal Studies, Bapt. Mins. Conf., Am. Bapt. Chs. N.J. (mins. coun.), Phi Beta Kappa. Republican. Achievements include research on youth, young adults, religion and public policy. Avocations: collecting baseball cards, travel, railroading. Home: 912 Church Ln Yeadon PA 19050-3717 Office: Pub Pvt Ventures 2005 Market St Ste 900 Philadelphia PA 19103-7060

TRULLI, JARNO, race car driver; b. Pescara, Italy, July 13, 1974. Race car driver, 1995—. 2-time karting world champion, 4-time Italian champion, European champion, N.Am. champion, 2-time winner Meml. Sienna Kart World Cup, 1994-95, champion German Formula 3, 1996. Office: Prost Grand Prix, 7 Ave Eugene Freyssenet, 78286 Guyancourt Frankreich, France*

TRULSEN, KARSTEN, wave hydrodynamicist, researcher; b. Oslo, Norway, Sept. 24, 1964; s. Jan Karsten and Gerd Nina (Iversen) T. BSc, U. Tromso, Norway, 1987, MSc, 1989; PhD, MIT, 1995. Post doctoral U. Bergen, Norway, 1995-97, U. Complutense de Madrid, Spain, 1997-98; rsch. scientist Sintef Applied Math., Blindern, Norway, 1999—. Contbr. articles to profl. jours. Office: Sintef Applied Math, PO Box 124, N-0314 Blindern Norway

TRUMBULL, STEPHEN MICHAEL, entrepreneur; b. Columbus, Ohio, Sept. 18, 1954; s. Clyde Austin and Patricia Ann (Ranck) T. MusB in Voice Performance and Choral Edn., DePauw U., Greencastle, Ind., 1977; postgrad., Ohio State U., 1982-85. Cert. profl. music educator, Ohio; cert. broker/dealer. Dir. vocal music Columbus City Schs., 1978-87; pres., owner Columbus Music Studios, 1984—; pres. The Trumbull Pub. Co., Washington, 1986—, Stephen M. Trumbull, Inc., Columbus, 1986—, Goldmark Securities Corp., Columbus, 1987-90; exec. v.p. Hamilton Capital Corp., Columbus, 1988-90, also bd. dirs., corp. v.p., sec., bd. dirs., 1987-90; v.p. Hamilton Mktg. Corp., Columbus, 1988-90, Kaiser Enterprises, Columbus, 1988-90; pres. Shelter One Group Corp., Columbus, 1988-90, also bd. dirs.; chmn. bd., chief exec. officer Ascona Communications, Inc., L.A., 1990-92; chief exec. officer Recording Industry Sourcebook, L.A., 1990-92; mng. ptnr. SRS Pub. Co., 1991-95; pres., CEO Music Bus. Registry, Inc., L.A., 1995—; soloist First Cmty. Ch., Columbus, 1982-90, Bay Shore Cmty. Ch., Long Beach, 1999—; mktg. cons. Beckenhorst Press, Inc., Columbus, 1986-87; exec. producer Wake Up and Dream, L.A., 1990-92; cons. The Source Group, Toronto, 1986—. Adviser Lambda Chi Alpha, Ohio State U., chmn. alumni adv. bd., 1982-87; pres. Friends of Neoteric Dance Theatre, Columbus, 1986-88; coord. nat. competition Jr. Achievement Nat. Conf., Bloomington, Ind., 1973-95; bd. dirs. Neoteric Dance Theatre, 1986-88, Reach for the Stars, Inc., L.A., Susan Van Pelt Dance Ensemble, 1989-92, Reach for the Stars, Inc., L.A., 1990-92, The Awareness Found., L.A., 1992-93; bus.-mktg. com. Jr. Achievement Ctrl. Ohio, Inc., 1987-92; cons. Nat. Hockey League Awards, Toronto, 1990—. Named Outstanding Alumni, Lambda Chi Alpha, 1984. Mem. Columbus Edn. Assn. Lodge: Optimist. Avocations: swimming, traveling, sailing. Home: 1906 Birkdale Dr Columbus OH 43232-3022 Office: 7510 W Sunset Blvd Ste 1041 Los Angeles CA 90046-3408

TRUNKOVSKY, EVGENIJ MARKOVICH, astronomer, researcher; b. Kandalaksha, Murmansk, Russia, Oct. 1, 1952; s. Mark Karlovich and Alexandra Georgievna (Gusel'nikova) T.; 1 child, Natalya Evgenjevna. Grad., Russian Secondary Sch., Kandalaksha, 1969; degree in astronomy, Moscow State U., 1976, PhD, 1988. Cert. in astronomy and physical and math. sci. Worker Aluminium plant, Kandalaksha, Russia, 1969-70; jr. rschr. Inst. Physics Atmosphere Russian Acad. Sci., Moscow, 1976-79; sr. lab. asst. Sternberg Astron. Inst. Moscow State U., 1980, sci. rschr. Sternberg Astron. Inst., 1987—. Physics and Astronomy tchr. A.N.Kolmogorov' Specialized Sch., 1990—, engr. Sci. Computer Ctr., 1980; lectr. Moscow Planetarium, 1984-87; leader of commn. Euro-Asian Astron. Soc., 1990-93. Contbr. articles to profl. jours. Grantee European So. Obs., 1993-95, H.Chretien Internat. Rsch. grantee, Am. Astron. Soc., 1995, Leading Sci. Schs. grantee, Russian Found. Basic Rsch., 1996, 2000. Mem. Euro-Asian Astron. Soc., Internat. Occultation Timing Assoc. (regional coord.), European Astron. Soc. Russian Orthodox. Avocations: music, literature, philosophy, art, photography. Fax #: (7-095) 932-88-41. E-mail: tem@sai.msu.ru. Home: Sci Sta p/o Shikhovo, 143092 Zvenigorod Russia Office: Sternberg Astron Inst, Universitetskij Prospect 13, 119899 Moscow Russia

TRUNZ, ERICH, humanities educator; b. Königsberg, Germany, June 13, 1905; s. August and Helene (Fähser) T.; widowed 1983; 1 child: Hermann. PhD, U. Berlin, 1931; Habilitation, U. Freiburg, Germany, 1937. Prof. German U., Prague, 1940-45, U. Münster, Germany, 1950-57, U. Kiel, Germany, 1957-70. Author: J.M. Meyfart, 17th Century Theologian and Author, 1987, A Day in Goethe's Life, 1990, Thought and Poetry in Baroque Germany, 1992, Thought and Literature of the Age of Goethe, 1993; editor: Goethe's Works, Hamburg edit., 14 vols. 1948-60, 15th revised edit., 1993; contbr. articles to profl. jours. Home: Struckbrook 18, D-24161 Altenholz bei Kiel Germany

TRUONG, KHUONG TRONG, biologist, researcher; b. N.Y.C., Nov. 2, 1970; arrived in France, 1992; s. Tuong Trong and Quy Kim (Tran) T. BS, U. Tours, France, 1994; MS, U. Paris 6, 1995, PhD, 1999. Tchg. asst. U. Cergy-, Pontoise, France, 1995-99; rschr. Inst. Curie, Paris, 1999—. Contbr. articles to profl. jours.; patentee in field. Mem. Internat. Soc. Analytical Cytology. Home: 125 rue de la Glaciere, 75013 Paris France Office: Inst Curie Rsch Section, UMR147 26 rue D'Ulm, 75248 Paris Cedex 05 France

TRUONG, THANH NGUYEN, chemistry educator, researcher; b. Qui-Nhon, Binh-Dinh, Vietnam, Apr. 17, 1962; came to U.S., 1980; s. Sanh Hanh Truong and Lang Thi Nguyen; divorced; children: Taki N., Takara E. BS, N.D. State U., 1985; PhD, U. Minn., 1990. NSF postdoctoral fellow U. Houston, 1990-92; prof. U. Utah, Salt Lake City, 1992—; cons. Dow Chem., 1998—. Contbr. articles to profl. jours. Founder Vietnam Assn. Utah, Salt Lake City, 1993. Recipient Young Investigator award NSF, 1993-98. Mem. AIChE, Am. Chem. Soc., Am. Phys. Soc. Avocations: ballroom dancing, yoga, hiking. Office: U Utah Dept Chemistry 315 S 1400 E Rm 2020 Salt Lake City UT 84112-0850

TRUONG, TUONG NGOC, engineering educator, researcher; b. Ho Chi Minh City, Vietnam, Jan. 25, 1958; s. Trach Ngoc Truong and Tot Thi Pham; m. Dung Phuong Tran, Feb. 4, 1985; 1 child, Ngoc Anh Tuan. B in Engring., Ho Chi Minh City Poly. U., 1981; M in Engring., Asian Inst. Tech., Bangkok, 1993, D in Engring., 1999. Lectr. Ho Chi Minh City Poly. U., 1981-91; rsch. assoc. Asian Inst. Tech., Bangkok, 1993-99, rsch. engr., 1999—. Mem. N.Y. Acad. Scis. Home: Dist 1, 387/1 Nguyen Trai St, Ho Chi Minh City Vietnam Office: Asian Inst Tech KM 42, Phaholyothin Kwy PO Box 4, Klongluang 12120, Thailand

TRUONG, VAN-TAN, materials scientist; b. Sadec, Vietnam, Dec. 5, 1950; arrived in Australia, 1977; s. Hung Chanh and Ha Thanh (Luu) T.; m. Setsuko Takahashi, Dec. 16, 1977; children: Takuya, Kumica. B in Engring., Tokyo Inst. Tech., 1975, M in Engring., 1977; PhD, U. Adelaide, Australia, 1981. Polymer scientist Sola Internat., Adelaide, Australia, 1980-85; materials scientist Australian Dept. Health, Melbourne, Victoria, 1985-87; sr. rsch. scientist aeronautical & maritime rsch. lab. Def. Sci. and Tech. Orgn., Maribyrnong, Victoria, 1987—. Inventor/European patentee disposable contact lenses, microwave absorber; contbr. articles to profl. publs. and conf. procs., chpts. to books. Recipient best rsch. award Australasia Corrosion Assn., 1999; Outstanding Overseas Student scholar Japanese Economy Fedn., Tokyo, 1975-77; PhD scholar U. Adelaide, 1977-80. Mem. Royal Australian Chem. Inst., Soc. Polymer Sci. (Japan), Materials Rsch. Soc. (U.S.A.). Office: Def Sci Tech Orgn Aero Maritime, Rsch Lab Cordite Ave, Maribyrnong Victoria 3032, Australia

TRUPO, FRANK JOHN, plastic surgeon; b. N.Y.C., Oct. 15, 1957; s. Frank and Rose T.; m. Gail Stringer, May 22, 1987; children: Stephanie, Thomas, Joseph. BS, Bethany Coll., 1979; MD, W.Va. U., 1984. Diplomate Nat. Bd. Med. Examiners, Am. Bd. Plastic Surgery. Resident gen. surgery Charleston (W.Va.) Area Med. Ctr., 1984-87; resident plastic, reconstructive, cosmetic, maxillofacial and head and neck surgery Kans. U. Med. Ctr., Kansas City, 1987-89; pvt. practice plastic surgery Charleston, W.Va., 1990—; chief sect. plastic surgery St. Francis Hosp., Charleston, 1993—, chmn. credentials com., 1996, 97—, med. adv., peer reviewer, 1994—; med. advisor, peer reviewer W.Va. Med. Inst., Mountain State BC/BS. Fellow ACS, Am. Soc. Lasers in Medicine and Surgery; mem. Am. Soc. Aesthetic Plastic Surgery, So. Med. Assn., Kanawha Med. Soc. (pres. 1997), Am. Soc. Plastic and Reconstructive Surgeons. Office: 331 Laidley St Ste 510 Charleston WV 25301-1682

TRUSHINSKY, ZDISLAV KAZIMIROWITCH, internist, educator; b. Vyshkovo, Grodno, Byelorussia, June 18, 1933; s. Kazimir Joseph and Valeria Joseph (Kuzmitch) T.; m. Henrietta Nikolai Jovner, Sept. 25, 1960 (div. Oct. 1974); 1 child, Sveta; m. Tatiana Nikolai Pushkin, Dec. 18, 1974; 1 child, Eugeny. MD, Med. Inst. Minsk, Byelorussia, 1955; Candidate Med. Scis., Russian State Med. U., Moscow, 1961, DM, 1970. Family physician rural hosp., Dvorets, Byelorussia, 1955-58; asst. prof. Russian State Med. U., Moscow, 1961-70; assoc. prof. State Stom Inst., Moscow, 1970-71; prof. internal medicine State Stomatological Inst., Moscow, 1971-88; prof., head dept. internal medicine Ivanovo (Russia) Med. Acad., 1988—; cons. prof. Moscow Railway Hosp., 1971-88; chief editor sci. publ. Moscow State Stom Inst., 1982-86; chief cons. cardiologist Autocrane Factory Hosp., Ivanovo, Russia, 1989—, Obolsunovo sanatorium, Ivanovo, 1995—. Author: Microfocal Myocardial Infarction, 1989, Prophylaxis and Treatment of Myocardial Infarction, 1992, Main Mechanisms of Human Adaption, 1993, Treatment of Arterial Hypertension, 1994. Mem. Assn. Physicians Moscow, Assn. Cardiologists Russia, N.Y. Acad. Scis. Avocations: reading fiction, pop music, picking mushrooms, swimming. Home: Otradny proyezd, House N9 Fl N10, 127273 Moscow Russia Office: Ivanovo State Med Acad, 8 Engels Ave, 153462 Ivanovo Russia

TRUSINA, PAVEL, translator, interpreter; b. Celadna, Czechoslovakia, Aug. 28, 1959; s. Jan and Marta (Chlevistanova) T.; m. Lubica Vecanova Trusinova, June 22, 1984; children: Jan, Daniel, Anna. Student, Charles U., Czechoslovakia, 1982. Diplomate in translating and interpreting, Charles U., Prague, Czechoslovakia. Translator CZ Press Agy., Prague, Czechoslovakia, 1982-83; translator, interpretor TESLA, Czechoslovakia, 1983-93, pvt. practice, 1993—. Author: Czech-English and English-Czech Dictionary, 1983. E-mail: pt@telecom.cz.

TRUSLOW, MARION ARCHER, secondary education educator; b. Gainesville, Ga., June 8, 1945; s. Marion Archer Truslow and Mattie Ruth Manus; m. Carolyn Frances Lanier, Sept. 5, 1991. BA in History, Ga. State U., 1967; postgrad., Ga. Tech., 1963-66, U. Va., 1969-71, Drew U., 1976-77; MA in History, Vanderbilt U., 1969; PhD in History, NYU, 1994. Instr. evenings Essex County Coll., Newark, 1972-82; admission chmn. Grad. Sch. Arts and Scis. NYU, 1974-76; chair dept. history The Calhoun Sch., N.Y.C., 1984-91; instr. evenings Ga. State U., Atlanta, 1990-94; instr. Woodward Acad., College Park, Ga., 1991-94, St. Timothy's Sch., Stevenson, Md., 1994-96; chair dept. history The Covenant Sch., Charlottesville, Va., 1996-99; instr. Rabun Gap (Ga.) Nacoochee Sch., 1999—; cons. AP European History exam. The Coll. Bd., Princeton, N.J. Author: Peasants into Patriots, 1994 (O'Connor award N.Y. Irish History Roundtable 1994-95). Adult educator Monticello Area Cmty. Action Agy., Charlottesville, Va., 1970. Fellow The Curriculum Initiative, Bronfman Found., Princeton, N.J., 2000, AP World History Inst., Kennesaw (Ga.) State U., 2000; George C. Marshall fellow Va. Mil. Inst., Lexington, 1999; fellow NEH, U. Bonn and U. Va., 1997; Fulbright scholar USIA, The Netherlands, 1992. Mem. Am. Hist. Assn., Phi Alpha Theta (founder Mu Tau chpt., treas. 1965-67). Roman Catholic. Avocations: walking in woods, reading philosophy, fly fishing, reading history. Home: PO Box 590 Rabun Gap GA 30568-0590 Office: Rabun Gap Nacoochee Sch 339 Nacoochee Dr Rabun Gap GA 30568-2200

TRUSS, JOHN KENNETH, mathematics educator; b. Watford, Eng., Apr. 19, 1947; s. Clifford Owers and Joyce Mary (Birtwistle) T.; m. Priscilla Mary Grasby, Sept. 6, 1969; children: Mary Elizabeth, Christopher William, Patrick Andrew, Francis Peter. BA, Cambridge (Eng.) U., 1968; PhD, Leeds (Eng.) U., 1973. Lectr. Oxford (Eng.) U., 1972-76, Paisley (Scotland) Coll. Tech., 1979-85; vis. fellow Polish Acad. Scis., Warsaw, 1976-77; tchr. King Charles' I High Sch., Kidderminster, Eng., 1977-79; lectr. math. Leeds (Eng.) U., 1985-91, reader math., 1992-98, prof., 1998—; vis. assoc. prof. Simon Fraser U., Burnaby, B.C., Can., 1987-88. Author: Discrete Mathematics for Computer Scientists, 1991, 2d edit., 1998, Foundations of Mathematical Analysis, OUP, 1997; editor: Logic Colloquium 86, 1986; also articles. Jr. rsch. fellow Univ. Coll., Oxford, Eng., 1973-75. Mem. Brit. Logic Colloquium (treas. 1990-98), London Math. Soc., Royal Acad. Music (licentiate), Royal Coll. Organists (assoc.). Avocations: piano, violin. Office: U Leeds, Dept Pure Math, Leeds LS2 9JT, England

TRUTTER, JOHN THOMAS, consulting company executive; b. Springfield, Ill., Apr. 18, 1920; s. Frank Louis and Frances (Mischler) T.; m. Edith English Woods II, June 17, 1950 (dec.); children: Edith English II, Jonathan Woods. BA, U. Ill., 1942; postgrad., Northwestern U., 1947-50, U. Chgo., 1947-50; LHD (hon.), Lincoln Coll., 1986. Various positions Ill. Bell, Chgo., 1946-58, gen. traffic mgr., from asst. v.p. pub. rels. to gen. mgr., 1958-69, v.p. pub. rels., 1969-71, v.p. operator svcs., 1971-80, v.p. community affairs, 1980-85; mem. hdqs. staff AT&T, N.Y.C., 1955-57; pres. John T. Trutter Co., Inc., Chgo., 1985—; pres., CEO Chgo. Conv. and Visitors Bur., 1985-88; pres. Chgo. Tourism Coun., 1988-90; v.p. Profl. Impressions Media Group, Inc., 1998—; mem. adv. bd. The Alford Group, Chgo., 1984—, Bozell-Worldwide, Chgo., 1994-96; chancellor Lincoln Acad. of Ill., 1985—. Co-author: Handling Barriers in Communication, 1957, The Governor Takes a Bride, 1977. Past chmn., life trustee Jane Addams Hull House Assn.; chmn. United Cerebral Palsy Assn. Greater Chgo., 1967-95, hon. chmn., 1995—, chmn. Canal Corridor Assn., 1991-99; bd. dirs. Chgo. Crime Commn., Abraham Lincoln Assn., Lyric Opera Chgo.; v.p. English Speaking Union, 1989-91, bd. govs., 1980—; chmn. bd. City Colls. Chgo. Found., 1987-91; past chmn. Children's Home and Aid Soc. Ill.; v.p. City Club Chgo.; treas. Chgo. United, 1970-85; mem. Ill. Econ. Devel. Commn., 1985; past presiding co-chmn. NCCJ; numerous others; bd. govs. Northwestern U. Libr. Coun., 1984—; trustee Lincoln (Ill.) Coll., 1987-90, Mundelein Coll., 1988-91; mem. sch. problems coun. State Ill. Assembly, 1985-91, spl. commn. on adminstrn. of justice in Cook County, 1986-92; founding chmn. adv. coun. Evanston Hist. Soc., 1995-98. Lt. col. U.S. Army, 1945. Decorated Legion of Merit; recipient Laureate award State of Ill., 1980, Outstanding Exec. Leader award Am. Soc. Fundraisers, Humanitarian of Yr. award, Jane Addams award The Hull House Assn., 1991, Nat. Infinitec award for individual leadership in assistive technology for disabled people, 1997, Jack Brickhouse award for outstanding svcs., 2000. Mem. Pub. Rels. Soc. Am., Sangamon County Hist. Soc. (founder, past pres.), Ill. State Hist. Soc. (pres. 1985-87), Coun. on Ill. History (chmn. 1991—), U. Ill. Alumni Assn. (bd. dirs. 1990-94), Tavern Club, Econ. Club, Mid-Am. Club, Alpha Sigma Phi (Nat. Merit Achievement award 1994), Phi Delta Phi. Fax: 847-441-0582.

TRUVE, ERKKI, molecular biologist; b. Tallinn, Estonia, Feb. 23, 1965; s. Rando and Urve (Tamm) T.; m. Katrin Kaelas, Apr. 21, 1990; children: Liis, Mikk. Diploma in biology cum laude, Tartu (Estonia) U., 1988, PhD, 1996. Sr. engr. Inst. Chem. Physics and Biophysics, Tallinn, Estonia, 1988, jr. rsch. scientist, sr. rsch. scientist, 1996—; prin. lectr. Tallinn Pedagogical U., 1997-98; prof., head Ctr. for Gene Tech. Tallinn Tech. Univ., 1997—; vis. scientist Inst. Biotech. U. Helsinki, 1989, 91, 93, 95, Norwegian Plant Protection Inst., Ås, 1993, Inst. Molecular Biology and Biotech., Heraklion, Greece, 1994. Contbr. articles to profl. jours.; patentee in field. Recipient award for young Baltic scholars Academia Europae, 1996. Mem. Am. Soc. Virology, Am. Soc. Biochem. and Molecular Biology, Internat. Soc. for Molecular Plant-Microbe Interactions, Estonian Biochem. Soc., Estonian Soc. Genetics, Soc. for Gen. Microbiology, Assn. for Plant Tissue Culture (intern), Estonian Soc. Human Genetics, Estonian Gene Technology Com. Lutheran. Avocations: hiking, basketball. Home: Madala 5-47, EE10311 Tallinn Estonia Office: Inst Chem Physics/Biophysic, Akadeemia Tee 23, EE12618 Tallinn Estonia

TRYBA, MICHAEL, anesthesiologist, researcher; b. Walsum, Germany, July 21, 1950; s. Bernhard and Johanna Tryba; m. Jacoba Sperschneider, Dec. 31, 1975; children: Christiane, Carmen, Phillip. MD, U. Hannover,

1977. Resident U. Hannover, 1977-83, sr. physician, 1983-84, oberarzt, 1985-86, lectr., 1984-86; vice chmn. U. Hosp. Bergmannsheil, Bochum, 1987-96; chmn. Klinikum Kassel, 1997—; lectr. Ruhr U., Bochum, 1987-90, prof., 1990—. Author: Prevention of Stress Bleeding--A New Concept, 1988; contbr. articles to profl. jours. Mem. European Acad. Anesthesiologists, European Soc. Anesthesiologists (Brussels, bd. dirs.), European Soc. Regional Anesthesia (Hans Killian award 1987, bd. dirs.), Am. Soc. Regional Anesthesia, European Soc. Intensive Care Medicine (Brussels), Internat. Assn. of the Study of Pain, Sertuerner Soc. (bd. dirs.). Roman Catholic. Avocations: music, enamel crafts, sports. Home: Vor der Prinzenquelle 17, D-34130 Kassel Germany Office: Klinikum, Moenchebergstr 41-43, D-34125 Kassel Germany

TRYBA, TED NICKOLAS, professional golfer; b. Wilkes-Barre, Pa., Jan. 15, 1967. Mktg. Degree, Ohio State U., 1989. Profl. golfer, 1989—; winner Gateway Open, 1990, Utah Open, 1991, Shreveport Open, 1992; finished in top ten United Airlines Hawaiian Open, AT&T Pebble Beach Nat. Pro-Am; 2d pl. Walt Disney World/Oldsmobile Classic; PGA Tour title Anheuser-Busch Golf Classic, 1995; finished in top ten Meml. Tournament, 1998; PGA Tour title FedEx St. Jude Classic, 1999. Avocation: basketball. Office: N Fla Sect of PGA 200 Forest Lake Blvd Ste 3 Daytona Beach FL 32119-8108*

TRYBAN, ESTHER ELIZABETH, lawyer; b. Chgo., Aug. 14, 1958; d. Chester Joseph and Lottie Elizabeth (Napora) T. AAS with honors, Elgin (Ill.) C.C., 1977, AS with honors, 1982; BS with honors, Roosevelt U., Chgo., 1986; JD, U. Chgo., 1989. Bar: Ill. 1989, U.S. Dist. Ct. (no. dist.) Ill. 1989, U.S. Ct. Appeals (7th cir.) 1990, U.S. Supreme Ct., 1996. Supr. adminstrv. svcs. law dept. Motorola, Inc., Schaumburg, Ill., 1977-86; staff law clk. U.S. Bankruptcy Ct., No. Dist. Ill., Chgo., 1989-90; asst. corp. counsel City of Chgo., 1990—. Mem. ABA, Nat. Lawyers Guild, Assn. Former Bankruptcy Law Clks, Ill. State Bar Assn., Chgo. Bar Assn. (chair govt. svc. com. 1996-97). Roman Catholic. Avocations: reading, football, traveling. Office: City Chgo Dept Law 30 N Lasalle St Ste 900 Chicago IL 60602-2503

TRYBUL, THEODORE NICHOLAS, education educator; b. Chgo., Apr. 12, 1935; s. Theodore and Sophie Trybul; children: Adrienne, Barbie, Cathy, Diane, Elizabeth, Teddy. BS, U. Ill., 1957; MS, U. N.Mex., 1963; DSc, George Washington U., 1976. Registered profl. engr., D.C. Dir. Sr. Exec. Svc., ES-IV Fed. Govt., Washington, 1966-83; prof. George Washington U., Washington, 1983-94, Tex. Grad. Sch., Corpus Christi, Tex., 1994—; adv. bd. NSF, Nat. Acad. Engring., NIH, Surgeon Gens. Office. Contbr. articles to profl. jours. Officer Corpus Christi C. of C., Neuces Club, Millionaires Club, CC Town Club. Col. U.S. Army, 1957. Fellow ASME, Soc. for Computer Simulation, Health Care Execs., Sir Isaac Walton, Audubonn Soc., Sierra Club; mem. Pi Tau Sigma, Phi Betta Kappa, Kappa Mu Epsilon, Sigma Xi. Avocations: golf, tennis, fishing, mountain climbing. Fax: (916) 855-4398. E-mail: ttrybul@hotmail.com. Office: 9320 Tech Center Dr Sacramento CA 95826-2558

TRYLAND, MORTEN, veterinary virologist, researcher; b. Lørenskog, Norway, June 17, 1961; s. Tor Sigmund and Aase Margrethe (Ryen) T.; m. Torill Mørk, June 30, 1995; children: Mattis, Simen. DVM, Norwegian Coll. Vet. Medicine, Oslo, 1991; PhD, Tromsø (Norway) U., 1996. Vet. practitioner Vesteraalen, Norway, 1991-92; project rschr. Ctr. Vet. Medicine, Tromsø, 1992-93; assoc. prof. vet. medicine Norwegian Coll. Vet. Medicine, Tromsø, 1996-97; rschr. Nat. Vet. Inst., Oslo, 1998-99; assoc. prof. vet. medicine Norwegian Sch. of Vet. Sci., Tromsø, 1999—. Contbr. articles to profl. jours. Office: Norwegian Sch Vet Sci, Dept Arctic Vet Medicine, N-9292 Tromsø Norway

TRZECIAK, HENRYK IRENEUSZ, pharmacologist, educator; b. Ruda Śl—ska, Poland, May 28, 1938; s. Bronisław and Magdalena (Opiełka) T.; m. Jadwiga Teresa Dubicka, Apr. 19, 1969; 1 child, Hanna Małgorzata. MSChE, Poly. High Sch., Gdansk, 1961; MD, Silesian Acad. Medicine, 1968, DSc, 1968, PhD, 1980. Asst. pharmacologist Silesian Acad. Medicine, Katowice, Poland, 1961-62, asst. lectr., 1962-68, lectr., 1968-80, asst. prof., 1968-85, assoc. prof., 1985—; prof. Silesian Med. U., 1996—. Mem. Polish Pharmacol. Soc. (pres. Silesian divsn. 1993; pres. 1998-2001). Roman Catholic. Home: Robotnicza 14, 40689 Katowice Piotrowice, Poland Office: Silesian Med U Dept Pharm, Medykow 18, 40752 Katowice-Ligota Poland

TRZYNADLOWSKI, ANDRZEJ MARIA, electrical engineering educator; b. Lvov, Poland, June 14, 1941; came to U.S., 1983; s. Jan and Izabela Trzynadlowski; m. Elzbieta Bramowicz, May 27, 1967 (div. Mar. 1979); 1 child, Andrzej; m. Dorota Malgorzata Maszewska, July 17, 1979; children: Bart, Nicole. MSEE, Tech. U. Wroclaw, Poland, 1964, MS in Electronics, 1969, PhDEE, 1974. Tchg. asst., lectr. Tech. U. Wroclaw, 1966-79; vis. assoc. prof. U. Salahuddin, Arbil, Iraq, 1980-82; vis. asst. prof. U. Tex., Arlington, 1983-84; asst. prof. U. Wyo., Laramie, 1984-87; assoc. prof., then prof. U. Nev., Reno, 1987—; Danfoss vis. prof. Aalborg (Denmark) U., 1997. Author: The Field Orientation Principle in Control of Induction Motors, 1994, Introduction to Modern Power Electronics, 1998, Control of Induction Motors, 2000; also articles; patentee in field. Cell vice chmn. Solidarity party, Wroclaw, 1980-81. Fellow IEEE (assoc. editor IEEE Transactions on Indsl. Electronics, IEEE Transactions on Power Electronics 1997—); mem. Industry Applications Soc. of IEEE (mem. indsl. drives com., indsl. power converters com. 1987—, Myron Zucker student-faculty grantee 1992), Eta Kappa Nu. Democrat. Roman Catholic. Avocations: travel, reading, walking. E-mail: chin@ee.unr.edu. Home: 4075 Twin Falls Dr Reno NV 89511-6067 Office: Univ Nev Elec Engring 260 Reno NV 89507

TSAHALIS, DEMOSTHENES THEODOROS, engineering educator; b. Anavriti, Greece, Mar. 20, 1948; s. Theodoros Dimitrios and Rallitsa (Koparanidou) T.; m. Vassiliki Baraboutis, July 17, 1971; children: Harry, Jason. Diploma in mech. and elec. engring., Nat. Tech. U. Greece, Athens, 1971; MS in Aerospace Engring., Va. Poly. Inst. & State U., 1972, PhD in Engring. Mechanics, 1974. Registered engr. Tech. Chamber of Greece. Staff rsch. engr. Shell Devel. Co., Houston, 1974-86, 86-88, sr. rsch. engr., 1979-84; search head Shell Rsch. Shell Devel. Co., Rijswijk, The Netherlands, 1984-88; prof. U. Patras, Greece, 1988—, dir. lab. fluid mechanics and energy; cons. to oil cos., U.S. and Europe, 1980—; cons. European Commn., Brussels, 1990—. Contbr. sci. and engring. articles to profl. jours. Mem. ASME (editor conf. procs. 5th Internat. Offshore Mechanics and Arctic Engring. Conf. Tokyo 1986), EUROSOLAR (founding mem., bd. dirs. 1994—), Hellenic Soc. Theoretical and Applied Mechanics, Greek Assn. Computation Mechanics, Biopolitics Internat., Hellenic Acoustic Soc., Hellenic Evaluation and Tech., Assessment Soc., European Biog. Directory. Avocations: travel, music, fishing. Office: U Patras Lab Fluid Mechs & Energy, PO Box 1400, 26500 Patras Greece

TSAI, CHING-PIAO, civil engineering educator, researcher; b. Kaohsiung, Taiwan, Republic of China, Sept. 4, 1957; s. Chien-Chang and Yueh-Neu (Chung) T.; m. Li-Shu Tsai, Dec. 31, 1983; children: Richard Yu-Ting, Allen Yu-Chun. BS, Nat. Cheng-Kung U., Taiwan, 1979, PhD, 1988; MS, Nat. Taiwan U., 1981. Lectr. Nat. Chung-Hsing U., 1984-88, assoc. prof., 1988-95, prof., 1995—, dir. divsn. careers adv. svc., 1995—. Editor in charge Jour. Chinese Inst. of Civil and Hydraulic Engring.; mem. editl. bd. Jour. Engring., Jour. Harbor Tech.; contbr. articles to profl. jous. including ASCE Jours., Applied Ocean Rsch., Ocean Engring., Internat. Jour. Offshore and Polar Engring., Internat. Jour. Numerical and Analytical Methods in Geomechs. 2d lt. Army of Republic of China, 1981-83. Mem. ASCE, ASME, Chinese Inst. Civil and Hydraulic Engring. (Best Paper award 1993), Chinese Soc. Mechanics, Internat. Soc. Offshore and Polar Engrs., N.Y. Acad. Scis. Mem. Soka Gakki Internat. Avocation: performing on the Chinese cheng, swimming, Chinese classical music, orchestral music, reading. Office: Nat Chung-Hsing U, Dept Civil Engring, 402 Taichung 402, Taiwan

TSAI, CHONG-SHIEN, engineering educator, consultant; b. Putai, Chiayi, Taiwan, Dec. 23, 1953; came to U.S., 1983; s. Po-Cheng and Liang (Shaw) T.; m. Min-Whei Tsai, Apr. 26, 1980; 1 child, Ie-San. BS, Nat. Cheng-Kung U., Tainan, Taiwan, 1977; MS, Nat. Taiwan U., 1979; PhD, SUNY, buffalo, 1987. Engr. CTCI, Inc., Taiwan, 1979-83; cons. Hong-Chyau Cosntrn., Inc., Taiwan, 1979-83; rsch. asst. SUNY, 1983-87; rsch. asst. SUNY, Buffalo, 1987-90, rsch. asst. prof. dept. civil engring., 1991-96; cons. Earthquake Hazard Prevention, Inc., N.Y. State, 1995—; assoc. prof. Feng Chia U., Taichung, Taiwan, 1996—. Author: NSAT User's Manual, 1996; author computer program. Recipient 1st prize for paper competition Internat. Bridge Conf., 1986. Mem. ASCE, Am. Soc. for Computational Mechanics, Internat. Soc. for Computational Mechanics, United Univ. Profs. (Excellence award 1990). Democrat. Achievements include obtaining exact-time domain radiation conditions for the fluid-structure interactions during earthquakes. Avocations: football, music, swimming, reading, basketball. Home: 76 Summerview Rd Williamsville NY 14221-1310 Office: Feng Chia U, Dept Civil Engring, Taichung Taiwan

TSAI, DIANA HWEI-AN, economics educator; b. Kaohsiung, Taiwan, July 28, 1959; d. Chao-Tsao Tsai and Shu-Ing Liu; m. Charles Tak-Ming Choi, Aug. 15, 1992. BA, Nat. Cheng-Chi U., Taiwan, 1980, MBA, 1982; MA, Ohio State U., 1987; PhD, Rensselaer Poly. Inst., N.Y., 1991; postgrad., U. Toronto, Can., 1992. Sr. rsch. analyst MOEA Energy Com., Taiwan, 1982-84; asst. prof. Clarkson U., N.Y., 1991-92; asst. prof. econs. Concordia U., Montreal, Que., Can., 1993-95; assoc. prof. econs. Nat. Sun Yat-Sen U., Kaohsiung, 1995—; cons. N.Y. State Pub. Svc. Commn., N.Y., 1991-93. Author: Macroeconomic Policy as Implicit Industrial Policy: Its Industry and Enterprise Effects, 1998; contbr. articles to profl. jours. Recipient rsch. award Nat. Sci. Coun., Taiwan, 1996-99; rsch. grantee Mackay Grant, Can. Coun., 1994, 98. Mem. Am. Econ. Assn., Taiwan Econ. Assn., Internat. Telecomm. Assn., European Assn. Rsch. in Indsl. Econs. Office: Nat Sun Yat-Sen Univ, Grad Inst Economics, Kaohsiung Taiwan

TSAI, FENG-PO, health facility administrator; b. Po-Tzu, Chai-Yi, Taiwan, Jan. 16, 1958; m. Chao-Wen Chen, Jan. 11, 1995. MD, China Med. Coll., Taichung, Taiwan, 1989. Cert. ob-gyn., infertility splst. Ob-gyn. Chang Gung Meml. Hosp., Taipei, Taiwan, 1989-93; infertility splst. Chang Gung Meml. Hosp., Taipei, 1993-95; supt. Tsai and Dr. Chen's Women Hosp., Chang Chun, Taiwan, 1995—; TV program host Infertility Dr. Chang Ghua TV, Chang Che, 1998-99, Dr. Tsai's Time, 1998-99; moderator 4th World Congress Endoscopic Surgery, Japan, 1993. Author: Birth Control: The Comprehensive Guide, 1998, Man and Woman Sex Talk, 1998, Be A Healthy Woman Within Modern Living, 1999, Guide to RU486, 1999, booklets on pregnancy and gynecologic disease; contbr. articles to profl. jours. Recipient Best Laparoscopic Surgery Video award TAOCE, 1993. Mem. AAAS, Am. Soc. Reproductive Medicine, Taiwan Soc. Reproductive Medicine, Taiwan Soc. Perinatology, Taiwan Assn. Gyn. Endoscopist (Best Laparoscopic Surgery Video award 1993), Soc. Ultrasound Medicine, N.Y. Acad. Scis. Avocations: reading, writing, travel, tennis, table tennis.

TSAI, HSUAN SAN See CAI, XUAN SAN

TSAI, JINGPHA (JEFFREY TSAI), computer scientist, educator; b. Cha-I, Taiwan; m. Fuh-Te Tsai; children: Edward, Christina. MS, Northwestern U., 1983, PhD, 1985. Prof. U. Ill., 1997—. Author 5 books; co-editor-in-chief: Artificial Intelligence Tools, 1994; contbr. more than 130 articles to profl. jours. Recipient Univ. scholar award U. Ill., Tech. Achievement award IEEE Computer Soc. Fellow IEEE, AAAS, Soc. for Design and Process Sci. Office: MCI 154 EECS Dept 851 S Morgan St Chicago IL 60607-7042

TSAI, LI FELLÄNDER, orthopaedist, educator; b. Boo, Sweden, June 16, 1965; d. John and Helve (Säinas) T.; m. Göran Fredrik Felländer, Oct. 9, 1993; children: Shannon, Philippa, Mac. MD, Karolinska Inst., Sweden, 1991, PhD, 1992. Assoc. prof. orthopedics Karolinska Inst., 1996—; cons. orthopedics, study dir. Huddinge (Sweden) U. Hosp. Contbr. chpt. to book Andrology, 1994. Winner in Acad. Leadership, Jr. Chamber, Sweden, 1998. Mem. Swedish Med. Assn., Swedish Soc. Medicine, Swedish Orthopedic Assn. Avocations: skiing, golf. Office: Huddinge U Hosp K54, Dept Orthopedics, S 14186 Huddinge Sweden

TSAI, SHANG-YING, psychiatrist; b. Tainan, Taiwan, Aug. 9; s. Shu-Shang and Yuy-Bi (Chen) T.; m. Shu-Fen Lin, Sept. 3, 1994; children: Mu-Yun, Keng-Heng. MD, Taipei (Taiwan) Med. Coll., 1989. Cert. psychiatrist, Taiwan. Resident in psychiatry Taipei City Psychiat. Ctr., 1989-92; chief resident Taipei Med. Coll. Hosp., 1992-93, attending psychiatrist, 1993—; chief psychiat. dept., assoc. prof. Taipei Med. Coll., 1994—; vis. prof. U. Cin., 1999. Contbr. articles to profl. jours. Rsch. grantee Nat. Sci. Coun., Taiwan, 1996, 98—, Dept. Health, Taiwan, 1998-2000; recipient Rsch. award Nat. Sci. Coun., 1999-2000. Mem. Am. Psychiat. Assn., Taiwanese Psychiat. Assn., Taiwanese Med. Assn. Avocations: photography, judo, travel, playing piano. Office: Taipei Med Coll Hosp, 252 Wu-Hsing St, 110 Taipei Taiwan

TSAI, SHENG-YI, physics educator, researcher; b. Kobe, Hyogo, Japan, Oct. 9, 1937; m. Aimei Lin, Aug. 6, 1962; 1 child, Meisui. BSc, Osaka (Japan) U., 1960, MSc, 1964, DSc, 1967. Assoc. mem. Atomic Energy Rsch. Inst. Nihon U., Chiyoda, Japan, 1966-68; asst. Coll. Sci. Tech. Nihon U., Tokyo, 1968-78, lectr., 1978-81, assoc. prof., 1981-86, prof. physics, 1986—; lectr. Kobe U., Japan, 1973, Waseda U., Japan, 1977-89, Chuo U., Japan, 1986—; vis. scientist Dalhousie U., Can., 1974-75. Contbr. articles to profl. publs. Rsch. grantee Japan Ministry of Edn., 1978. Mem. Phys. Soc. Japan, N.Y. Acad. Scis. Office: Nihon U Coll Sci Tech, Kanda-Surugadai 1-8, Chiyoda-ku Tokyo 101-8308, Japan

TSAI, SHIH-CHUAN, nuclear medicine physician; b. Kaohsiung, Taiwan, Oct. 31, 1968; s. Yun-Lung and Li (Chiang) T. B in Medicine, China Med. Coll., 1994. Resident in nuclear medicine Taichung (Taiwan) Vets. Gen. Hosp., 1994-99. Avocations: reading, movies, table tennis. Office: Show Chwan Meml. Hosp., 542 Sec 1 Chung-Shan R, Changhua 500, China

TSAI, TSU-MIN, surgeon; b. Taipei, Taiwan, Dec. 15, 1936; arrived in U.S., 1976; m. Fu-Mei Tsai; children: Yi-Yi Tsai, Ring-Ring Tsai Tien, Berlin Tsai. MD, Taiwan U., 1961. Diplomate Am. Bd. Orthopedic Surgeons with added qualifications in surgery of the hand. Intern Nat. Taiwan U. Hosp., China, 1961-62, resident in urology, surgery and orthopedics, 1964-70; intern U. Louisville, 1976-77, resident in orthopedics, 1977-79; Christine Kleinert fellow in hand surgery U. Louisville Affiliated Hosps., 1976; clin. prof. orthopaedic surg., dir. divsn. hand surgery Louisville Sch. Medicine, 1980—; presenter in field, including Oxmoor Ctr., Louisville, Shanghai, China, Dublin, Ireland, U. Ky., Lexington, Nara, Japan, Med. Coll. Ohio, Toledo, ASSH Ann. Meeting, Cin. (all 1994), Internat. Congress European Soc. Biomechs., Cologne, Germany, Chang Gung Meml. Hosp., Taipei, Taiwan, Shriner's Hosps. for Crippled Children, Lexington, Ky., IFSSH, Helsinki, Finland, French Surg. Soc., Paris, Harkess Soc., Nashville, Tenn., Hand Forum, Sea Island, Ga., 1st Internat. Workshop for Reconstructive Microsurgery, Inst. Plastic Surgery, Mexico City (all 1995), Mini symposium on Pediatric Hand and Microsurgery, Taipei, Taiwan, Internat. Soc. Reconstructive Microsurgery, Singapore, JSSH/ASSH Combined Meeting, Maui, Hawaii, European Congress Hand Surgery, Paris, Japanese Soc. Surgery of the Hand, Okinawa, Hiroshima (Japan) U. Hand Club, Keio U., Tokyo, Internat. Microsurg. Soc., Montreal, Que., Can., Christine M. Kleinert Inst., Louisville, Hand Forum, Sedona, Ariz., ASSH Ann. Meeting, Nashville, Assn. Argentina Orthopedia y Traumatologia, Buenos Aires (all 1996), Am. Soc. Reconstructive Microsurgery, Boca Raton, Fla., Bombay Hand Soc., Am. Soc. Orthop. Surgeons, San Francisco, Hong Kong Soc. Surgery of the Hand, Madras Hand Inst., India, others (all 1997), Japanese Soc. Surgery of the Hand, Osaka, Japanese Orthop. Assn., Yokohama, Am. Assn. Orthop. Surgeons, New Orleans, Flap course, Focus on Anatomy course, Christine M. Kleinert Inst., Louisville, others (all 1998); Disting. Vis. Prof. Divsn. Plastic and Reconstructive Surgery, Washington Hosp. Ctr., 1990, others. Contbr. articles to profl. jours. and publs. Fellow Am. Coll. Surgeons, Am. Acad. Orthopedic Surgeons; mem. Jefferson Count Med. Soc., Jefferson County Orthopaedic Soc., Ky. Orthopaedic Soc., Ky. Med. Soc., Ky. Pediat. Soc., AMA, Internat. Soc. Reconstructive Microsurgery, Am. Soc. Reconstructive Microsurgery, Western Pacific Orthopedic Assn., Am. Soc. Surgery of the Hand, Hand Forum, Clin. Orthopedic Soc., Japanese Orthopaedic Assn. SICOT Soc. Avocations: fishing, tennis. Office: Kleinert Kutz & Assocs 225 Abraham Flexner Way Louisville KY 40202-1846

TSAI, TUNG-HU, pharmacologist, researcher, educator; b. Kaohsiung City, Taiwan, Aug. 21, 1957; s. Yu-Fang and Bi-Liang T.; m. Hsueh-Chin Huang; children: Yi-Lin, Yi-Wen. BSc, Taipei (Taiwan) Med. Coll., 1987; MSc, Nat. Yang-Ming U., Taipei, 1989, PhD, 1995. Lectr. Nat. Yang-Ming U., Taipei, 1989-96, assoc. prof., 1996—; rsch. fellow Nat. Rsch. Inst. Chinese Medicine, Taipei, 1999—; assoc. investigator Nat. Rsch. Inst. Chinese Medicine, Taipei, 1994-99. Contbr. articles to profl. jours. Postdoc. fellow Cambridge (Eng.) U., 1996-97. Mem. Pharm. Soc. Taiwan, Pharmacology Soc. Taiwan. Avocations: swimming, football. Home: 6 F 570 Pei-An Rd, Taipai 104, Taiwan Office: Nat Rsch Inst Chinese Med, 155-1 Sect 2 Li-Nong St, Taipei 112, Taiwan

TSAI, WU-FU, ophthalmologist, educator; b. Taipei, Taiwan, Sept. 28, 1939; s. Chin-Chung and Mei-Yue Tsai; m. Diana Tsai, Oct. 10, 1963; 4 children. Doctor, Nat. Taiwan U., 1965. Diplomate Bd. Ophthalmology, China. Instr. Nat. Taiwan U., 1970-74, assoc. prof., 1974-85, clin. prof., 1985—; clin. prof. Nat. Chen-Kung U., Taiwan, 1990—; prof. Nat. Cheng-Kung U., Taiwan, 1988-90; chief Chi-Mei Hosp., Taiwan, 1990—; cons. Taipei Myopia-Prevention Found., 1985-88. Contbr. articles to profl. jours. Recipient medal Nat. Dept. Edn., Taipei, 1984; Nat. Sci. Devel. Com. grantee, 1974. Fellow Internat. Coll. Surgeons; mem. Internat. Schepen's Soc., Am. Acad. Ophthalmology. Avocation: collecting antiques. Office: Chi-Mei Found Hosp, 901 Chung Hwa Rd, Yung Kang Tainan Taiwan

TSAI, YI HUNG, pharmacist; b. Pintong Hsien, Taiwan, Republic of China, June 5, 1943; s. Tsai Kuei and Hsiu Yueh (Lin) T.; m. Yen Yen Wang, Dec. 18, 1970; 2 children. BA, Kaohsiung Med. Coll., Republic of China, 1967; PhD, Kyoto Pharm. U., Japan, 1987. From asst. to assoc. prof. Kaohsiung Med. Coll., 1969-82, prof., 1982—; dean of students Kaohsiung Med. Coll., 1982-86, dir. hosp. pharmacy, 1987-99, dean grad. inst. pharm. scis., 1994-2000, dean sch. pharmacy, 1994-2000. Contbr. articles to profl. jours. Recipient Svc. medal Exec. Yuan, 1987, Adminstrv. medal, 1990, Excellence Tchg. medal Ministry Edn., 1989. Mem. Pharm. Soc. China, Clin. Pharmacy Assn. China, Chinese Chem. Soc. Avocations: fishing, swimming. Office: Kaohsiung Med Univ, 100 Shih Chen 1st Rd, Kaohsiung 807, Taiwan

TSAI, YUNG-CHIEH, gynecologist, educator; b. Tainan, Taiwan, June 13, 1963; s. Si-Chan Tsai and A-Chu Chen; m. Mei-Chiung Hsu; children: Pochien, Lancet, Pasteur. MD, China Med. Coll., Taichung, Taiwan, 1989. Gynecologic splst.; birth control splst.; splst. reproductive medicine and infertility. Rsch. fellow Chang Gung Meml. Hosp., Kaohsiung, Taiwan, 1993-94, attending physician, 1995-97; rsch. fellow U. Hosp. Cin., 1994-95; lectr. China Inst. Tech., Tainan, 1997-99; assoc. prof. Chian Nan Coll. Pharmacy and Sci., Tainan, 1999—; dir. Ctr. Reproductive Medicien Chimei Found. Hosp., Tainan, 1997—; commr. China roup Meml. Hosp., Kaohsiung, 1995-97, Chimei Resource Ctrl. Com., Tainan, 1998; advisor The Mananger Grow Mag., 1995. Contbr. articles to profl. jours. Commr. Yung-Fu Elem. Sch., Tainan, 1997. Mem. Taiwanese Fertility Soc., Am. Soc. Reproductive Medicine, Chimei Assn. Infertile Couple (founder), European Soc. Human Reproduction and Embryology. Avocations: computers, music, swimming, travel, studying. Office: Ctr Reproductive Medicine, 901 Zhung Hwa Rd, 700 Tainan Taiwan

TSAKALOS, STRATOS VASILIOS, pharmaceutical company executive; b. Fities, Agriniou, Greece, Nov. 11, 1948; s. John and Angeliki (Agelouli) T.; married; children: John, Angelica. BS, U. Salonica, Greece, 1972; MS, U. London, 1975. Dir. fin. F. Hoffmal La Roche Co., Athens, Greece, 1978-80; asst. gen. mgr. Smith Kline and French Hellas S.A., Athens, 1980-83; gen. mgr. Smith Kline and French Labs S.A., Athens, 1983-90; mng. dir. Kite Hellas Ltd., Athens, 1991—; adj. lectr. Inst. Mktg., Athens, 1978-85. Home: 11A R Ferraiou St, 151 21 Peuki Attica, Greece

TSAKIROGLOU, CHRISTOS, chemical engineer, researcher; b. Veria, Imathia, Greece, Apr. 18, 1961; s. Dimitrios and Sofia (Organtzoglou) T.; m. Maria Theodoropoulou, Sept. 20, 1997. Chem. engring. diploma, U. Thessaloniki, Greece, 1985; PhD in Chem. Engring., U. Patras, Greece, 1990. Postdoctoral fellow ICE/HT-FORTH, Patras, 1992-93, rsch. assoc., 1995-98, assoc. rschr., 1998—; postdoctoral fellow IFP, Paris, 1994-95. Contbr. articles to profl. jours. With inf. Greek Army, 1991-92. Mem. Tech. Chamber Greece, Combustion Inst., Soc. Petroleum Engrs. Home: Athinon 81, GR-26441 Patras Greece Office: ICE/HT-FORTH, Stadiou St Platani POB 1414, GR-26500 Patras Greece Address: Inst Chem Engr/High TempChe, POB 1414, 265 00 Patras Greece

TSAKNIS, JOHN PANAGIOTIS, food science educator; b. Karpenisi, Evritania, Greece, Jan. 31, 1955; s. Panagiotis and Alice (Dioti) T.; m. Aggeliki Kourtis, Nov. 6, 1982; children: (twins) Alice and Yolanda. BSc in Food Tech., Technol. Edn. Instn. Athens, Greece, 1980; BSc in Pedagogical, Pedagogic Tech. Sch., Athens, 1983; MA, U. Humberside, U.K., 1992; PhD, U. Lincolnshire, U.K., 1996. Chartered chemist Royal Soc. Chemistry. Quality control inspector Eleourgiki, Athens, 1980-84; prof. Technol. Ednl. Instn., Athens, 1984—. Author: Quality Assurance, 1997, Food Analysis, 1997; contbr. articles to profl. jours. Mem. N.Y. Acad. Scis. Home: 62 Katsantoni St, 18546 Piraeus Attiki, Greece Office: Dept Food Tech TEI Athens, Ag Spyridonos St, 12910 Athens Attiki, Greece

TSAKOS, NIKOLAS PANAGIOTIS, shipping company executive; b. Athens, Attika, Greece, June 5, 1963; s. Panayiotis N. and Irene G. (Saroglou) T. Student, Columbia U., 1985; MS in Shipping, Trade and Fin., London City U., 1987. Pres. M.I.F. Ltd., Oslo, 1993—; dir. Burren Energy PLC, Am. Bur. Shipping, N.Y.C., Greek Cooperation Com., London, Bur. Veritas, Paris, Internat. Tanker Assn., Oslo, Hellenic Shipping War Risks Ins. S.A. Vice chmn. Hellenic Marine Environ. Protection. With Greek Navy, 1987-88. Named Young Businessman of Yr., Athens U., 1994, Businessman of Yr., Athens Acad., 1997. Mem. Athens Yacht Club (dir.), Athens Aviation Soc. (dir.), Classic Car Soc. Christian Orthodox. Avocations: skiing, tennis, yachting, flying, soccer. Office: Tsakos Shipping & Trading, Megaron Makedonias Syngroy, 17564 P Faliron Athens, Greece

TSALOLIKHIN, SEMYON IAKOVLEVICH, biologist, zoologist, researcher; b. Leningrad, Russia, Dec. 2, 1944; s. Iakov Samuilovich and Elena Iakovlevna (Novikova) T.; m. Irina Akovovna Gamaley, Nov. 25, 1966 (div. 1970); 1 child, Anastasya Gamaley; m. Tatiana Georgievna Kashitskaya, Apr. 14, 1972; 1 child, Artemy. Grad., State U. St. Petersburg, Russia, 1969, PhD (hon.), 1976, DSc (hon.), 1987. Lab. asst. Zool. Inst., St. Petersburg, 1967-72, 74-76; jr. rsch. asst. Inst. Fish Rsch., St. Petersburg, 1972-74; jr. rsch. asst. Zool. Inst., 1976-86, sr. rsch. asst., 1986-92, chief rsch. asst., 1992—. Author: Free Living Nematodes of Baikal Lake, 1980, Nematodes from Families Tobrilidae and Tripylidae of All World Fauna, 1983, Nematodes of Fresh and Brackish Waters of Mongolia, 1985; author, editor: Key to Freshwater Invertebrates of Russia and Adjacent Lands, vol. 1-4, 1994-99. With Russian Army, 1969-70. Avocation: philately. Office: Zool Inst Russian Acad Scis, Univ Embankment 1, 199034 Saint Petersburg Russia

TSAMBAOS, DIONYSIOS, dermatologist, educator; b. Athens, Greece, Sept. 12, 1948; s. George and Mary (Schick) T. MD, U. Athens, 1973; PhD, U. Berlin, 1984. Registrar dept. dermatology U. Düsseldorf, Germany, 1977-78; sr. registrar dept. dermatology U. Göttingen, Germany, 1978-79; asst. prof. dept. dermatology U. Berlin, 1979-84; prof., chmn. dept. dermatology U. Patras, Greece, 1985—. Contbr. articles to profl. jours. Mem. 18 sci. socs. Avocations: photography, music, travelling. Office: Univ Patras, Dept Dermatology, 26500 Rio Patras Greece

TSAMOPOULOS, JOHN, chemical engineer, educator; b. Athens, Greece, Dec. 9, 1956; s. Abraham and Angela (Agiakli) T. Diploma, Chem. Engring., Athens, Greece, 1979; MS, MIT, 1981, PhD, 1985. Asst. prof., assoc. prof., prof. SUNY, Buffalo, 1985—; prof. U. Patras, Greece, 1993—; cons. IBM, N.Y., 1990-91. Contbr. over 45 articles to profl. jours. Recipient Rsch. Initiation, NSF, 1987, Engring. Rsch. award, 1992, Electronic Materials Process award IBM, 1990, Bubble Interactions award, NASA, 1994. Mem. AIChE, Soc. Rheology, Tech. Chamber Greece, Hellenic Soc. Rheology. Important achievements have been made while researching forces between interacting bubbles, drops or deformable bodies in various flow fields, dynamics of spin coating with viscoelastic fluids, flow instabilities in

polymer processing, dynamics of liquid bridges and their breakup, two-phase flow in fixed beds and oil pipelines. Office: Univ Patras, 26500 Patras Greece

TSANG, CHI FO, chemist, researcher; b. Hong Kong, Feb. 17, 1967; s. Chi Y. Tsang and Yu Y. Szeto; m. Catherine Yuet M. Lee, Apr. 22, 2000. BS, Chinese U. Hong Kong, 1989; PhD, U. Houston, 1995. Postdoctoral fellow in materials sci. & engring. U. Tex., Austin, 1995-96; rsch. engr. Inst. Microelectronics, Singapore, 1996-97, sr. rsch. engr., 1997—. Contbr. articles to profl. jours. and process devel./tech. integration semiconductor industry. Mem. Am. Chem. Soc., N.Am. Thermal Analysis Soc. Home: Blk 665 Chu Kang Crescent, Singapore 680665, Singapore Office: Inst Microelectronics, 11 Science Park Rd, Singapore 117685, Singapore

TSANG, DONALD, government official; b. Hong Kong, 1944; married; two sons. MA in Pub. Adminstrn., Harvard U. Joined Hong Kong Govt., 1967, dep. sec. gen. duties, 1985, dir. gen. of trade, 1991-93, sec. for Treasury, 1993-95, fin. sec., 1995—. Office: Govt Sec, Lower Albert Rd, Hong Kong Hong Kong

TSANG, REGINALD C., pediatrician; b. Hong Kong, Sept. 20, 1940; married; 2 children. MBBS, Hong Kong U. MEd. Sch., 1964. Intern Hong Kong U., Queen Mary Hosp., 1964-66, Michael Reese Hosp., Chgo., 1966-67; resident Hong Kong Hosp., 1965, Michael Reese Hosp., 1967-69; instr. pediatrics U. Cin., 1969-70, asst. prof. pediatrics, 1971-75, assoc. prof. pediatrics, obs.-gyn., 1975-77, prof., 1979—; clin. chief dept. pediatrics U. Hosp., 1979-97; attending pediatrician Children's Hosp., Cin., 1971—, Cin. Gen. Hosp., Univ. Hosp., 1971—, Jewish Hosp., Cin., 1979-97, Good Samaritan Hosp., 1986—, Bethesda Hosp., 1988-97, Christ Hosp., 1989—; assoc. chmn. pediatrics U. Hosp., 1994-97, vice chmn. rsch. and univ.affairs, 1990-93, vice chmn. pediatrics univ. and affiliated programs, 1988-90, David G. and Priscilla R. Gamble prof. neonatology, 1986-97; cons. and speaker in field. Contbr. 380 articles to profl. jours. Grantee NIH, 1972-97, many others. Fellow Am. Coll. Nutrition (chmn. coun. nutrition and perinatology 1979-82, pres. 1989-91); mem. Midwest Soc. Pediatric Rsch. (pres. 1978-79), Am. Fedn. Clin. Rsch., Soc. Pediatric Rsch., Endocrine Soc., Am. Soc. Clin. Nutrition, Am. Pediatric Soc. (coun. 1993—), Am. Men and Women of Sci., Ctrl. Soc. Clin. Rsch., Perinatal Rsch. Soc. (coun. 1989—), Am. Soc. Bone Mineral Rsch., Nat. Perinatal Assn. Office: UCMC Pediats Ctr Bone Rsch and Health PO Box 670541 Cincinnati OH 45267-0001

TSANGARIS, GEORGE MICHAEL, physicist, educator, researcher; b. Dimitsana, Arkadia, Greece, June 3, 1939; s. Michael John and Katerina George (Pijania) T.; m. Vasha Nazou, Sept. 4, 1969; children: Michael, John. Diploma in physics, U. Athens, Greece, 1966; PhD in Polymer Physics, U. Liverpool, Eng., 1981. Asst. Nat. Tech. U., Athens, 1972-79, from lectr. to asst. prof., 1981-91, assoc. prof., 1992—; rsch. fellow U. Liverpool, 1979-81; vis. rsch. fellow Cranfield (Eng.) U., 1991-92. Author 6 books; co-author: Atomic and Molecular Structure, 1989; contbr. articles to profl. jours. Lt. Greek Army, 1966-68. Mem. Hellenic Assn. Physicists, Dielectric Soc. (Eng.), Soc. Environ. Toxicology and Chemistry-Europe. Greek Orthodox. Avocations: fishing, swimming, literature, classical music, philosophy of sciences. Fax: 30-1-7723139. Home: 8, M. Asias str., 151 21 Athens Greece Office: Nat Tech U, 9, Iroon Polytechniou Str., 157 80 Athens Greece

TSANGARIS, JOHN MICHAEL, chemistry educator; b. Athens, Greece, Sept. 7, 1933; s. Michael and Catherine (Pisanias) T.; m. Amersia Hadziharalambidou, Jan. 5, 1965; children: Catherine, Michael. Diploma in chemistry, U. Athens, 1956; MS, U. Va., Charlottesville, 1962, PhD, 1967. Instr. in chemistry Nat. Tech. U., Athens, 1963-65, 67-70; sr. rsch. scientist Nat. Hellenic Rsch. Inst., Athens, 1970-72; asst. prof. chemistry Nat. Tech. U., Athens, 1972-74; rsch. assoc. dept. chemistry U. Liverpool (Eng.), 1975, U. Patras (Greece), 1976; prof. chemistry U. Ioannina (Greece), 1977—; vis. prof. dept. chemistry U. Liverpool, 1983-84, Harvard U., Cambridge, Mass., 1989, Free U., Brussels, 1993; vice-rector U. Ioannina, 1986-87. Authors: Agricultural Chemistry, 1973, Inorganic Chemistry of Transition Elements, 2 vols., 1980, 85, Inorganic Chemistry of Representative Elements, 1983; co-author: Fundamental Principles of Atomic and Molecular Structure, 1987; contbr. over 140 articles to profl. jours. Corp. Greek Army, 1957-58. Mem. Greek Chemist Assn., Hellenic Sci. Orgn. for Protection of the Environment, Alpha Chi Sigma, Sigma Xi (assoc.). Greek Orthodox. Avocations: philately, literature, gardening. Home: 19 Viziinou St, 11141 Athens Greece Office: Univ Ioannina, Dept Chemistry, 45110 Ioannina Greece

TSAO, CHI-YUAN ALBERT, engineering educator; b. Taipei, Taiwan, Republic of China, June 3, 1956; s. Ke-Liang Tsao and Mao-Lun Ma; m. Shih-Min Chang, Feb. 9, 1980; children: Stephanie, Angela. BS, Nat. Cheng Kung U., Tainan, Taiwan, 1978; MS, U. Mo., Rolla, 1982; PhD, MIT, 1990. Asst. engr. Pacific Electric Wire and Cable Co., Taipei, 1978-80; advanced devel. engr. GTE Products Corp., Warren, Pa., 1983-85; sr. rsch. engr. Caterpillar Inc., Peoria, Ill., 1990-91; assoc. prof. Nat. Cheng Kung U., Tainan, 1991-98, prof., 1998—; adj. prof. Bradley U., Peoria, 1990; tech. assessment com. Metal Powder Industries Fedn., 1990-92. Inventor in field. Bd. dirs. Faculty Union of Nat. Cheng Kung U., 1995—, univ. bridge team; pres. The Republic of China student assn. MIT, 1988-89. IBM fellowship IBM, 1982-83; recipient Young Engr. award Chinese Inst. of Engrs., 1996. Mem. ASM Internat., Am. Powder Metallurgy Inst. Internat., The Minerals, Metals and Materials Soc., Alpha Sigma Mu. Avocations: bridge, chess, swimming, guitar, tennis. Office: Nat Cheng Kung U, Dept Materials Sci/ Engring, Tainan Taiwan, Republic of China

TSAO, JIIN-WEN, psychologist, counselor; b. Taipei, Taiwan, Aug. 14, 1968; d. Teng-Fang and Shu-Chen (Wen) T.; m. Chi-Huang Chen, Sept. 19, 1999. BS, Chung Yuan Christian U., Chunghi, Taiwan, 1990; MS in Edn., U. Wis., River Falls, 1995. Asst. counselor Soochow U., Taiwan, 1990-93; counseling specialist Ctr. for Human Devel., Taipei, 1993-94; sch. counselor Nat. Taipei Tchrs. Coll., 1995—; psychologist, supr. China Airlines, Taipei, 1996—; vol. counselor Taipei Mcpl. Family Edn. Svc. ctr., 1989-93. Mem. APA (assoc.), Chinese Guidance Assn., Mental Health Assn. Taiwan.

TSAO, SHYH-LIN, electrical engineering educator; b. Taipei, Taiwan, Mar. 10, 1965; s. Tai-Kuo and Kue-Funn (Lin) T.; m. Mei-Ling Kuo; children: Chin-Yu Tsao, Chin-Ann Tsao. BS in Physics, Fu-Jen U., Taipei, Taiwan, 1987; MS, Inst. Optical Sci., Taiwan, 1989; PhD in Elec. Engring., Nat. Taiwan U., Taipei, 1995. Cert. electronic, opto-electronics, optical engr., physicist. Lectr. Tawkang U., Taipei, Taiwan, 1994, Fu-Jen U., Taipei, Taiwan, 1994-95; assoc. prof. St. John's & St. Mary's Inst. Tech., Taipei, Taiwan, 1995-97, Yuan-Ze U., Chung-Li, Taiwan, 1997—; cons. Po-Hsin Co., Taipei, 1994. 2d lt. Taiwan Army, 1989-91. Named 1st in class Fu-Jen U., Taipei, 1984, 85, 86, 87; scholar Ministry of Edn., 1988, 92-93, rsch. scholar Nat. Sci. Coun., 1994. Mem. AAAS, IEEE, SPIE, Optical Soc. Am., Optical Engring. Soc. Rep. China. Avocations: amateur harmonic player, harmonic teacher, table tennis. Home: Hsing Chuang, PO Box 1-236, Taipei Taiwan Office: Yuan Ze U Dept Elec Engring, 135 Yuan-Tung Rd, Nei Li Chung-Li Taiwan

TSAPENKO, NIKOLAI EVGENIEVICH, mathematician, educator; b. Nizhniy Novgorod, Russia, May 22, 1953; s. Evgeniy Fedorovich and Laresa Ivanovna (Ivanova) T.; m. Evgenia Viktorovna Patskevich Mar. 1991 (div. June 1996); 1 child, Evgeniy. MS in Radio Physics, Power Engring. Inst., Moscow, 1976; PhD in Math. Physics, Belarusian Acad. Scis., Minsk, 1992. Rsch. assoc. Radio Engring. and Electronics Inst. Acad. Scis., Moscow, 1977-79; postdoctoral Mining Inst., Moscow, 1979-84; asst. prof. Acad. Water-Transport, Moscow, 1985-91; assoc. prof. Power Engring. Inst., Tech. U., Moscow, 1992-95; lectr. State Tech. U., Moscow, 1995—. Author: Analytical Functions and Integral Transformations, 1996; contbr. articles to profl. jours. Mem. Dem. Choice Russia, 1994. Recipient medal Defender of Free Russia, 1994. Mem. N.Y. Acad. Scis. Avocations: sport, poetry. Home: Malysheva St 26 Bldg 1, Apt 25, 109263 Moscow Russia

TSATSARONIS, GEORGE, mechanical engineering educator, researcher; b. Thessaloniki, Greece, Sept. 22, 1949; came to U.S., 1982; s. Asterios and Chrysoula (Ioannidou) T. Diploma in mech. engring., Nat. Tech. U., Athens, Greece, 1972; MBA, Tech. U. Aachen, Germany, 1976, PhD in Mech. Engring., 1977, Habilitation in Thermoeconomics, 1985. From rsch. assoc. to lectr. to sr. staff mem. Inst. of Thermodynamics, Aachen, 1972-82; rsch. prof. Energy & Environ. Engring. Ctr. Desert Rsch. Inst., Reno, Nev., 1982-86; prof. mech. engring. Ctr. for Electric Power, Tenn. Technol. U., Cookeville, 1986-94; prof. energy conversion and protection of environ. Tech. U. Berlin, 1994—, dir. Inst. for Energy Engring., 1996—; reviewer in field; hon. prof. North China Electric Power U., 1997. Author: (with A. Bejan and M. Moran) Thermal Design and Optimization, 1996; assoc. editor Energy, The Internat. Jour., 1986—, Jour. Energy Resources Tech., 1988-95, Energy Conversion and Mgmt., 1995—, Internat. Jour. Applied Thermodynamics, 1998—; co-editor 17 bound vols.; contbr. numerous articles to profl. jours. Chmn. exec. com. Internat. Ctr. for Applied Thermodynamics, 1998—. Recipient Borchers award Tech. U. Aachen, 1977, E.F. Obert Best Paper award ASME, 1994, 98, James Harry Potter Gold medal ASME, 1998. Fellow ASME (chmn. systems analysis com. 1987-90, mem. exec. com. advanced energy sys. div. 1993-97); mem. AIChE, Greek Soc. Engrs., German Assn. Univ. Profs. Greek Orthodox. Home: Weissdornweg 15, 12205 Berlin Germany Office: Tech U Berlin, Marchstr 18, 10587 Berlin Germany

TSATURYAN, ANDREY KIMOVICH, researcher; b. Moscow, Mar. 17, 1952; s. Kim Tigranovich and Rada Lvovna (Babina) T.; m. Olga Ivanovna Pivovarova (div. July 1988); children: Anna, Karen; m. Irina Viktorovna Ostrovskaya, Jan. 14, 1989; 1 child, Anastasia. MS, M.V. Lomonosov Moscow U., 1974, PhD, 1983. Jr. rsch. scientist Bakulev Inst. for Cardiovasc. Surgery, Moscow, 1974-77; jr. rsch. scientist Inst. Mechanics, M.V. Lomonosov Moscow U., 1977-86, sr. rsch. scientist, 1986—. Contbr. articles to profl. jours. Rsch. grantee Internat. Sci. Found., N.Y.C., 1995; Internat. Rsch. fellow The Wellcome Trust, U.K., 1991, Go-West fellow, rsch. grantee Internat. Assn. for Promoting Collaboration With Scientists from Ind. States of Former USSR, Brussel, 1994, 96, 97, 98; Internat. Rsch. scholar Howard Hughes Med. Inst., 19995. Mem. Russian Nat. Com. for Theoretical and Applied Mechanics, Russian Acad. Scis. (rsch. coun. for biophysics, rsch. coun. for biomechanics). E-mail: tsat@inmech.msu.su. Fax: 7 095 9390165. Office: Inst Mechanics Moscow Univ, 1 Mitchurinsky Prospect, 119899 Moscow Russia

TSCHACHER, WOLFGANG, psychologist, researcher; b. Hohengehren, Germany, June 29, 1956; s. Hans-Dieter and Maria (Weber) T.; m. Daniela Praxedis Hofmann, Oct. 31, 1986; children: Julian, Nikolai, David. Diploma in psychology, U. Tübingen, Germany, 1984, D in Psychology, 1990; privatdozent, U. Bern, Switzerland, 1996. Cert. psychologist and family therapist. Rsch. asst. German Inst. Distance Studies, Tübingen, 1987-92; family therapist Alcohol Counseling Ctr., Tübingen, 1990-92; head rsch. Social-Psychiatric U. Hosp., Bern, 1992-95, U. Psychiatric Svcs., Bern, 1996—; organizer Herbstakademie symposia, 1990—. Author: (monograph) Interaktion in selbstorganisierten Systemen, 1990, Prozessgestalten, 1997; editor: Self-Organization and Clinical Psychology, 1992; contbr. articles to profl. jours. First-aid attendant German Red Cross, Esslingen, 1979-80. Mem. Deutsche Gesellschaft für Psychologie, Soc. Psychotherapy Rsch. Avocations: literature and poetry, photography, Alpine trekking. Office: Univ Psychiatric Svcs, Laupenstrasse 49, CH-3010 Bern Switzerland

TSCHALAER, CHRISTOPH, physicist, researcher; b. Zurich, Switzerland, July 25, 1938; came to U.S., 1989; s. Adolf Arnold and Klara Alina Tschalaer; m. Joan Irene Smith, July 17, 1965; children: Ronald Paul, Elisabeth Ann. Diploma in exptl. physics, Fed. Inst. Tech., Zurich, 1962; PhD in Nuclear Physics, U. So. Calif., L.A., 1967. Sr. sci. officer Rutherford High Energy Lab., Chilton, Eng., 1966-69; target group leader Swiss Inst. Nuclear Rsch., Villigen, Switzerland, 1969-72, exptl. facilities sect. leader, 1972-77, engring. and exptl. facilities divsn. leader, 1978-87; enring. dept. leader Paul Scherrer Inst., Villigen, 1987-89; sr. rsch. scientist MIT/Bates, Middleton, Mass., 1989-91, assoc. dir. ops., 1991—; cons. dist. heating Town Coun. Energy Commn., Endingen, Switzerland, 1980-84; guest scientist Los Alamos (N.Mex.) Nat. Lab./LAMPF Divsn., 1977, 85, reviewer LAMPF ops., 1987, reviewer MLNSC Target upgrade, 1996, reviewer LANSCE upgrade, 1996, mem. LANCSE Divsn. Rev. Com., 1997, 99, reviewer LDRD program, 1999; cons. CEBAF constrn. Jefferson Lab., Newport News, Va., 1992; reviewer accelerator product of tritium MIT, Cambridge, 1994, reviewer accelerator driven transmutation of waste, 1998. Contbr. articles to profl. jours.; inventor proton polarisation analiser, 1970, Beam Extraction System, 1986. Hon. mem. Men's Choir, Endingen, 1978-89. Mem. Am. Phys. Soc., Sandy Bay Yacht Club. Avocations: hiking, sailing, singing. E-Mail: Chris@bates.mit.edu. Office: MIT Bates Linear Accelerat 21 Manning Ave Middleton MA 01949-1526

TSCHARNTKE, TEJA, ecologist, educator; b. Harsum, Germany, July 13, 1952; s. Günter and Rut (Burchardt) T.; m. Susanne Asche, Oct. 25, 1991. Diploma in sociology, U. Marburg (Germany), 1978, diploma in biology, 1981; PhD in Biology, U. Hamburg (Germany), 1986. Prof., dir. dept. agroecology U. Göttingen (Germany), 1993—. Contbr. articles to profl. jours. Avocations: sports, politics. Home: Weinbrennerstr 58, D-76185 Karlsruhe Germany Office: U Goettingen, Waldweg 26, D-37073 Göttingen Germany

TSCHERMAK-WOESS, ELISABETH, botany educator; b. Znaim, Austria, Jan. 28, 1917; d. Leo and Philippine (Zwolenski) Tschermak; m. Friedrich Woess, July 29, 1944; children—Ulrike, Wolfgang. Doktorat, U. Wien, 1941. Mem. Bot. Inst., U. Wien, Austria, 1941—, prof. botany, 1967—; prof. emeritus, 1985—. Author: Strukturtypen der Ru-K., 1963. Contbr. articles to profl. jours. Mem. Zool. Bot. Ges. Wien, Deutsche Bot. Gesellschaft, Internat. Assn. Lichenology. Office: U Vienna Inst fur Botanik, Rennweg 14, A1030 Vienna Austria

TSCHESCHE, HARALD, chemist, scientist, educator; b. Gottingen, Germany, June 7, 1935; s. Rudolf Reinhold Bruno and Annemarie (Hirsche) T.; m. Wulfhild Natorp, Mar. 21, 1969 (dec. 1977); children: Frank, Anja; m. Monika Wellpott, Nov. 1994. Diploma, U. Bonn, Germany, 1960, U. Heidelberg, Germany, 1960; Dr.rer.nat., U. Heidelberg, Germany, 1962; habilitation, Tech. U. Munich, Germany, 1970. Rsch. assoc. MIT, Cambridge, England, 1962-63; asst. Tech. U. Munich, Germany, 1963-72, dozent, 1972-74, wissenschaft rat, divsn. head, 1974-76; offered chair organic chemistry Tech. U. Braunschweig, Germany, 1976—; prof. biochemistry U. Bielefeld, Germany, 1976—; bd. dirs. Soc. for Promotion of Rsch. and Tech. Transfer, U. Bielefeld; chmn. exec. com. Inst. Innovation Transfer, Bielefeld. Co-editor, editor numerous books (in English); assoc. editor: Jour. Protein Chemistry; contbr. over 325 articles to profl. jours. Mem. Gesellschaft Deutscher Chemiker, Gesellschaft Biologische Chemie, Gesellschaft Deutscher Naturforscher Arzte, Max Bergman Kreis, Deutsche Gesellschaft Bindegewebsforschung, N.Y. Acad. Scis. (Max Bergman medal 1994). Home: Cranachstrasse 18, D-33615 Bielefeld Germany Office: U Bielefeld, Universitatstrasse, D-33615 Bielefeld Germany

TSCHIEDEL, HANS JÜRGEN, classical educator; b. Warnsdorf, Germany, Apr. 19, 1941. Dphil, U. Erlangen-Nürnberg, Germany, 1969, Dr.phil.habil., 1976. Pvt. dozent U. Erlangen-Nürnberg, Germany, 1976-82; prof. classical philology Katholische U., Eichstätt, Germany, 1982—. Author: Phaedra und Hippolytus, 1970, Caesars Anticato, 1981; co-editor: Ratis omnia vincet. Untersuchungen zu den Argonautica des Valerius Flaccus, 1991; contbr. articles to profl. jours. Office: Katholische U Eichstätt, Universitätsaee 1, D-85071 Eichstätt Bavaria, Germany

TSCHOEPE, DIETHELM, physician, consultant; b. Bonn, Germany, Oct. 31, 1958; m. Susanne Tschoepe, Sept. 10, 1987. MD, Ludwigs-Maximilians U., 1984. Registrar Diabetes Rsch. Inst. Heinrich-Heine U., 1984-90, sr. registrar, 1990-94, cons., 1994—. Editor: Acute Coronary Syndromes, 1999; editor European Heart Jour. Supplement, 1999, Diabetes Metabolism Reviews, 1998, Diabetes, 1996. Recipient Anna Juehling-Wunderlich AW U. Duesseldorf, 1993. Mem. Lions Club (pres. 1996-97), Am. Diabetes Assn., European Atherosclerosis Soc., German Soc. for Cardiology (chair heart and metabolic syndrome working group 1997—), German Diabetes Assn. (chair diabetes and the heart working group 1997—, Ferdinand Bertram AW 1998). Avocations: paintings, photography. E-mail: Tschoepe@uni-duesseldorf.de. Office: Diabetes Rsch Inst, Auf'm Hennekamp 65, D-40225 Düsseldorf Germany

TSCHUDIN, HEINZ, information services company executive; b. Zofingen, Aargau, Switzerland, Mar. 26, 1938; s. Fritz and Lilly (Erismann) T.; m. Pia Hool, Mar. 14, 1964; children: Matthias, Stefan, Johannes. BS, Engring. Coll., Luzern, Switzerland, 1963; postgrad., U. St. Gallen, Switzerland, 1974-75. Training mgr. Sperry Univac, Zurich, Switzerland, 1970-72, dir. customer svc., 1972-88; gen. mgr. Unisys Complex Systems, Zurich, 1988-90, Unisys UBS Ops., Zurich, 1990-92; mng. prin. Unisys Info. Systems Group, Austria, Switzerland, 1992-95; mgmt. cons. Unisys Computer Systems Group, London, 1996-98; mgmt. cons. Y2K Del., Switzerland, 1998-99, free mgmt. cons., 1999—; pres. info. processing com. Swiss Nat. Sports Coun., Bern, Switzerland, 1978-84. Co-author: Psychology in Economy and Government, 1982; contbr. articles to profl. jours. Commr. Boy Scouts Switzerland, 1960-72; mem. Nat. Sports Coun., Switzerland, 1974-84; v.p. Internat. Orienteering Fedn., Sweden, 1982-88, pres., 1988-94. Capt. infantry Swiss Army, 1958-96. Named Grand Officer, Internat. Mil. Sports Coun., 1990. mem. Swiss Informaticians Soc., Panathlon. Avocations: orienteering, endurance sports, literature, classic music. Home: Pfadhagstrasse 21, CH-8304 Wallisellen Switzerland

TSCHUGG, MICHAEL WERNER, public relations professional; b. Mannheim, Germany, Nov. 10, 1954; s. Ernst and Margot (Caspari) T. M in Econs., U. Mannheim, Germany, 1980; MBA, U. Lincolnshire and Humberside, Eng., 1998. Editor LTI Pub., Heppenheim, Germany, 1981-83; group head pub. rels. WOB Advt., Viernheim, Germany, 1983-88; group head, prin. Burson-Marsteller, Frankfurt, Germany, 1988-91; head pub. rels. Degussa AG, Frankfurt, 1992-97; sr. mng. dir. Gavin Anderson & Co., Frankfurt, 1997-98; mng. ptnr. Kohtes Klewes Frankfurt GmbH, Frankfurt, 1998—. Author: Encyclopedia of Public Relations, 1989. Cpl. German Mil. Police, 1973-75. Mem. German Assn. Pub. Rels., Frankfurt Press Club, Mannheim Press Club (bd. mem. 1989). Avocations: saxophone, Aikido. Office: Kohtes Klewes Frankfurt Gmb, Windmuehl str 1, 60329 Frankfurt Germany

TSE, CHARLES YUNG CHANG, drug company executive; b. Shanghai, China, Mar. 22, 1926; s. Kung Chao and Say Ying (Chen) T.; m. Vivian Chang, Apr. 25, 1955; 1 dau., Roberta. BA in Econs, St. John's U., Shanghai, 1949; MS in Acctg, U. Ill., 1950; JD, N.Y. Law Sch., 1990. Asst. to controller Am. Internat. Group, N.Y.C., 1950-54; asst. mgr. Am. Internat. Group, Singapore-Malaysia, 1955-57; with Warner-Lambert Co., Morris Plains, N.J., 1957-86; area mgr. S.E. Asia Warner-Lambert Co., 1966-68, regional dir. S.E. Asia, 1968-69, v.p. Australasia, 1970-71, pres. Western Hemisphere Group, 1971-72, pres. Pan Am. Mgmt. Center, 1972-76, pres. European Mgmt. Center, 1976-78, pres. Internat. Group, 1979-86, sr. v.p. corp., 1980-83, exec. v.p. corp., 1984-85, vice chmn., 1985-86; dir. Foster Wheeler Corp., Livingston, N.J., 1984-98, Superior Telecom., Inc., 1996—, Com. of 100; mem. faculty bus. adminstrn. dept. Fairleigh Dickinson U., 1961-64; pres. Cancer Rsch. Inst., Inc., N.Y.C., 1991-92. Bd. visitors CCNY, 1974-78; trustee Morristown Meml. Hosp. (N.J.), 1982-86; bd. dirs. Bus. Council for Internat. Understanding, 1984-87. Mem. NAM (dir. 1984-86), Assn. of the Bar of the City of N.Y. (mem. Asian affairs com. 1991—). Office: 300 Park Ave Fl 17 New York NY 10022-7402

TSE, CHI-WAI DANIEL, university president; b. Macao, Oct. 28, 1934; m. Toa-Kit Ng, May 30, 1960; 1 child, Benita. BS in Math., Baylor U., 1960, MS in Physics, 1962; PhD in Physics, U. Pitts., 1965; LLD (hon.), Baylor U., 1981; DSc (hon.), Chinese U. Hong Kong, 1986; PhD (hon.), hon. professorship, Shanghai U. Tech., 1990; D (hon.), U. Strathclyde, 1994; LLD (hon.), Hong Kong U. Sci. & Tech., 1997, U. Western Sydney, 1999. Head dept. physics Hong Kong Bapt. Coll., 1968-71, asst. v.p., acting pres., 1970-71, pres., 1971—; bd. overseers Insts. Biotech., 1989-97; mem. Ct. of Univ. of Hong Kong, 1985-97, consultative com. Bus. and Profls. Fedn. Hong Kong, 1992—, adv. group Hong Kong Forum on Asia and Pacific, 1984—; hon. adviser Hong Kong Fedn. Students, 1985—, Hong Kong Assn. Bus. Edn., 1985—, Hong Kong Assn. Advancement Sci. and Tech., 1989—, Hong Kong Ednl. Rsch. Assn., 1992-94, The Friends of the Country Parks, 1993—, Lions Nature Edn. Centre, Internat. Assn. Lions Club, 1991—, Beijing-Hong Kong Acad. Exch. Ctr., 1985—; adviser Hong Kong Fedn. Edn. Workers, 1985—, Hong Kong Soc. Asia and Pacific 21 Ltd., 1987—; chmn. bd. dirs. World Vision Hong Kong, 1991—; hon. gov. Hong Kong Inst. Promotion of Chinese Culture Ltd., 1985—; bd. govs. Centre for Hong Kong-Am. Ednl. Exch., 1993—; Hong Kong affairs advisor, 1993-97; mem. prep. com. for Hong Kong Spl. Adminstrv. region Nat. People's Congress, 1996; chmn. Prep. Com. on Chinese Medicine, 1995-99, Standing Com. on Lang. Edn. and Rsch., 1996—; cons. prof. Beijing Tsinghua U., 1997; mem. Chinese People's Polit. Consultative Conf., 1998—; chmn. Chinese Medicine Coun. Hong Kong, 1999—, Adv. Com. on Food and Environmental Hygiene, 1999—; mem. Com. on Bilingual Legal Sys., 1998—. Mem. editorial bd. Jour. Ch. and State, Baylor U., 1983—. Apptd. mem. Kowloon City Dist. Bd., 1985-94; chmn. Com. on Promotion of Civic Edn., 1988-95, Bilingual Laws Adv. Com., 1988-97; bd. trustees Hong Kong Bapt. Theol. Sem., 1990—; mem. Stats. Adv. Bd., 1986, Hong Kong Exam. Authority, 1977-87, Basic Law Consultation Com., 1985-90, exec. coun., 1986-91, legis. coun., 1985-91; dir. Bapt. Conv., Hong Kong, 1990—; exec. mem. Bapt. Oi Kwan Social Svc., 1982—; hon. dir. Hong Kong Chinese Christian Chs. Union, 1990—; convenor ICAC Pub. Edn. Sub-com. and Cmty. Rels. Com., 1973-83. Decorated officer Brit. Empire OBE, 1986, comdr. Brit. Empire CBE, 1991; recipient Justice of Peace award The Queen, U.K., 1977, Gold Bauhinia star Hong Kong Spl. Adminstrv. Region Govt., 1998; named Disting. Alumni Baylor Alumni Assn., 1995. Mem. Am. Phys. Soc., Royal Soc. Arts, Royal HK Jockey Club, Royal Golf Club. Avocation: golf. Office: Hong Kong Bapt U, Kowloon Tong, Kowloon Hong Kong

TSE, DAVID KWAI-CHE, international business educator, consultant; b. Hong Kong, July 15, 1953; s. Ho-Fun and Sup-Nui (Lee) T.; m. Diana Lai-Ha Chan, May 30, 1980; children: Daniel H., Caleb H. BBA, Chinese U. Hong Kong, 1977; MBA, U. Calif., Berkeley, 1978, PhD, 1984. From asst. to assoc. rpf. U. B.C., Vancouver, Can., 1984-93; dep. head Hong Kong U. Sci. and Tech., 1993-94; prof. internat. bus. City U., Hong Kong, 1994-98; dir. Chinese Mgmt. Ctr., Hong Kong, 1995—; prof. internat. mtkg. Hong Kong U., 1998—; cons. Hong Kong Bank, 1995, Elec and Eltek Internat. Holdings, Hong Kong, 1996—, All China Market Rsch., 1997; dir. Market-tInfor Ltd., Hong Kong, 1997—. Editor: China's Industrial Market Yearbook, 1997; contbr. articles to profl. jours. Mem. Asia Acad. Mgmt. (founding v.p.), Acad. Internat. Bus. (mem. editl. bd. 1995—). Avocations: soccer, running, squash, reading. Office: Univ Hong Kong Bus Sch, Pokfulam, Hong Kong Hong Kong

TSE, HARLEY Y., immunologist, educator; b. China, July 17, 1947; s. Ton-cheuk and Hou-Ying (Choy) T.; m. Kwai-Fong Chui, Jan. 13, 1979; children—Kevin Y., Alan C., Leslie W. B.S. with honors, Calif. Inst. Tech., 1972; Ph.D., U. Calif.-San Diego, 1977; M.B.A., Rutgers U., 1986. Fellow Arthritis Found., NIH, Bethesda, Md., 1977-80; sr. research immunologist Merck Sharp & Dohme Research Lab., Rahway, N.J., 1980-83, research fellow, 1983-86; adj. asst. prof. Columbia U., 1981-84 ; assoc. prof. Wayne State U. Sch. Medicine, 1986—. Contbr. articles to profl. jours. Bd. dirs. Chinese Social Service Center, San Diego, 1975. Recipient NIH Rsch. Career Devel. award, 1992-97; Calif. Biochem. Research fellow, 1975, Arthritis Found. fellow, 1977-80; NIH grantee, Nat. Multiple Sclerosis Soc. grantee, 1988—. Mem. Am. Assn. Immunologists,, NIH Immunological Sci. Study Sec., 1995-99, Chinese Student Assn. (pres. 1974-76)., Soc. Chinese Bioscientist in Am., Detroit Immunological Soc. (pres. 1989-91). Roman Catholic. Home: 5393 Tequesta Dr West Bloomfield MI 48323-2351 Office: Wayne State U Sch Medicine 540 E Canfield St Detroit MI 48201-1928

TSE, KA KUEN, engineering executive; b. Hong Kong, 1962; s. W. Tse and W. Kan; m. Amy Chan; m. Jenkin, Jerome. Cert. in mgmt. svc., Hong Kong Poly. U., 1988; MBA, U. Hull, U.K., 1998; MS, U. Warwick, U.K., 1997. Sr. engr. Philips H.K. Ltd., Hong Kong, 1986-91; engring. dir. Supreme Dragon Ltd., Hong Kong, 1991-96, Hyper-tech Computers, Toronto, Ont., Can., 1996-98; cons. Kinrome Hong Kong Ltd., 1998—; bd. dirs. Comportisics Investment, Hong Kong, Kinrome Can. Supplies. Mem. IEEE, IIE, IEE (England), N.Y. Acad. Scis. Avocations: music, computers, reading. Home: PO Box 71388, Kowloon Hong Kong

TSE, MAN-CHUN MARINA, special education educator; b. Kai-Ping, China, Dec. 14, 1948; came to U.S., 1972; d. Sun-Poo and Su-ling Cheung;

m. Richard Anderson. BA in English, U. Chinese Culture, Taipei, Taiwan, 1970; MS in Spl. Edn., U. So. Calif., 1974. Cert. tchr., spl. edn. tchr., Calif. Rsch. asst. lit. U. Chinese Culture, 1970-72; English tchr. Tang-Suede Mid. Sch., Taiwan, 1970-72; instr. Willing Workers, Adult Handicapped Program L.A. Sch. Dist., 1976-77; instr. ESL Evans Adult Sch., L.A., 1977-82; instr. ESL, polit. sci. Lincoln Adult Sch., L.A., 1986-94; spl. edn. tchr. Duarte (Calif.) Unified Sch. Dist., 1977—; commr., program co-chair Calif. Spl. Edn. Adv. Commn., Sacramento, 1994-96; mem. Calif. State Bd. Edn., 1996-99; mem. Calif. State Summer Sch. for the Arts, 1998-99; coun. mem. L.A. County Children Planning Coun., 1995—; com. mem. L.A. County Sci. & Engring. Fair Com., 1993—; hon. adv. bd. Asian Youth Ctr., San Gabriel City, Calif., 1992—; mem. exec. bd. Pres. Com. on Employment of People with Disabilities (U.S.), 1997—; com. mem. tchr. devel. project Nat. Assn. State Bd. Edn., 1977—; mem. Calif. State Supts. Art Task Force, 1997—, Calif. Supt. Pre-Sch. Task Force, 1997—; advisor Calif. Coun. Tech., 1996—; mem. Calif. Rehab. Coun. Appeared on numerous TV and radio programs. Bd. trustee Bruggemeyer Libr., Monterey Park, Calif., 1993-99; pres. L.A. County Coun. Reps., 1994—; mem. Calif. Statewide Focus Group Diversity, Sacramento, 1995-97; chair Chinese Am. Edn. Assn., 1993—; co-chair, co-founder Multi-Cultural Cmty. Assn., 1992—; bd. dirs. Rosemead-Taipei Sister City, 1993—, San Gabriel Valley Charity Night Com., 1992—; chmn. Los Angeles County-Taipei County Friendship Com., 1996—. Recipient Recognition cert. Duarte Edn. Found., 1990, cert. Valley View Sch., 1991, award State Calif., 1991, Appreciation award City Rosemead, 1992, Commendation cert. Alhambra Sch. Dist., 1992-93, Edn. award Asian Youth Ctr., 1992, 1992, Commendation cert. City L.A., 1992, commendation County L.A., 1992, award U.S. Congress, 1993, Recognition cert. Calif. Legis. Assembly, 1993, Proclamation City Alhambra, 1993, Chinese Am. PTA award, 1993, John Anson Ford award L.A. County Human Rels. Com., 1993, Appreciation cert. Chinese Consolidated Benevolent Assn., 1994, Recognition cert. Calif. State Senate, 1994, Appreciation cert. City Monterey Park, 1995, Spl. Achievement award Calif. Spl. Edn. Adv. Commn., 1997, Outstanding Comm. Svc. award City of Duarte, Calif., 1997, Spl. Achievement award Duarte United Edn. Ctr., 1997, Disting. Woman of Yr. award Calif. 24th Dist. Sen.'s Office, 1997, Svc. award Calif. Fedn. Exceptional Children Coun., 1998, Calif. Sanitorial award, 1999, L.A. County Bd. Suprs. Outstanding Svc. award, 1999. Monterey Park City award, 1999. Mem. Calif. Tchr. Assn., Chinese Edn. Assn., Internat. Platform Assn., Nat. Assn. State Bds. Edn. Office: Duarte Unified Sch Dist 1620 Huntington Dr Duarte CA 91010-2534

TSEESNIEX, MODRIS, mechanical engineer; b. Latvia, July 5, 1938; s. Ernest and Veronica (Dishler) T. Diploma in Mech. Engring., Tech. U., Riga, Latvia, 1966. Chief mechanic Old Riga Restoration Orgn., 1988-89; energy engr. State Publ. House, Riga, 1989-90; dep. dir. Sci. Infoctr., Riga, 1991-92; lectr. Tech. Coll., Olaine, Latvia, 1994-95; exec. Augstceltne Co., Riga, 1995-96; bd. sec. Latvian Farmers Forests, Riga, 1996-98; supt. State Security Svc., 1998. Del. People's nat. Front I Congress, Riga, 1988. With Latvian Nat. Guard, 1994-2000. Avocations: tennis, yachting, water and mountain skiing, mountaineering.

TSEITLIN, MARK ARONOVICH, metallurgical company manager, consultant; b. Dnepropetrovsk, Ukraine, June 24, 1934; s. Aron Yakovlevich and Tamara Yakovlevna (Slavina) T.; m. Valeriya Alexandrovna Kozhakina, Apr. 8, 1956; 1 child, Alexander Markovich. Diploma, State Moscow Inst. of Steel and Ferro-Alloys, 1951-56, DSc post grad course, 1967. Master, foreman of shift in blast furnace shop Serovski Metall. Plant, Serov, Russia, 1956-58; shift forman in blast furnace shop Kosogorskij Metall. Plant, Tula, Russia, 1958-63; head ctrl. rsch. lab. Novotulskij Metall. Plant, Tula, 1963-83; head blast furnace shop Tulachermet, Tula, 1983-85, head tech. and devel. dept., 1985-92; mktg. dir. Joint Stock Co. Tulachermet, Tula, 1992—; chmn. bd. dirs. JSC Tulachermet, Tula, 1996—; bd. dirs. Tulskij Promishlennik Bank, Tula. Contbr. over 120 articles to profl. jours.; patentee in field. Recipient Laureate of State award Russian Govt., Moscow, 1981, Silver medal for achievements in metallurgy, 1984, badge of honor, Parliament, Moscow, 1986; named to Order of Friendship between Nations of Russian Fedn., Moscow, 1995. Mem. Internat. Pig Iron Secretariat, N.Y. Acad. Scis., Tula C. of C. and Industry (bd. dirs. 1995—). Avocations: sports, travel. Home: Demonstratsii St 38-6, 300034 Tula Russia Office: JSC Tulachermet, Novotulskaya 1, 300017 Tula Russia

TSEKERIDOU, SOFIA, electrical engineer; b. Lagadas, Greece, Jan. 6, 1973; d. Ioannis and Kiriaki (Savidou) T. Diploma in elec. engring., U. Thessaloniki, Greece, 1996, postgrad., 1996-2000. Trainee U. Des Saarlandes, Saarbruecken, Germany, 1994; rschr. Aristotle U. Thessaloniki, Greece, 1996—, teaching asst., 1996—; vis. rschr. Tampere U. Tech., Finland, 1998, 99. Nat. Scholar Found. grantee, Thessaloniki, 1991. Mem. IEEE, SPIE, ACM, Tech. Chamber Greece. Home: Ipirou 6, 54639 Thessaloniki Greece Office: Aristotle U Thessaloniki, Dept Informatics, 54006 Thessaloniki Greece

TSEKOV, ROUMEN TSVETANOV, chemistry educator; b. Rousse, Bulgaria, Jan. 18, 1963; s. Tsvetan Ivanov and Stefanka Velikova T. MS, U. Sofia, Bulgaria, 1988, PhD, 1993; postgrad., SUNY, Buffalo, 1994. Asst. prof. U. Sofia, Bulgaria, 1988-91, sr. asst. prof., 1991-95, main asst. prof., 1995—; bd. govs. EcoHorizons Found., Silistra, Bulgaria, 1995—. Contbr. articles to profl. jours. Humboldt fellow MPI-KGF, Freiberg, Germany, 1997; recipient Bronze medal XIIi Internat. Chem. Olympiad, Bourgas, Bulgaria, 1981, Gold medal Bulgarian Ministry Edn., 1981, Bulgarian Ministry Sci. and Edn., 1987, Bulgarian NSF award, 1996. Office: U Sofia, 1 James Bourchier Ave, 1126 Sofia Bulgaria also: MPI-KGF, Chemnitzer Str 40, 09599 Freiberg Germany

TSELEPI-MITRELIAS, MARINA, physicist, researcher; b. Ioannina, Greece, Feb. 12, 1969; d. Ioannis and Frideriki (Zerva) TSelepi; m. Thanos Mitrelias, Feb. 25, 1997. BSc in Physics, U. Ioannina, 1992; MSc in Materials Sci., U. Liverpool, Eng., 1994; PhD in Physics, Cambridge (Eng.) U., 1999. Rsch. asst. Cambridge U., 1997—. Contbr. articles to internat. jours. Avocations: travel, reading books, cinema. Home: 4 York St, Cambridge CB1 2PY, England

TSELUTIN, VLADIMIROVICH KONSTANTIN, agriculturist, researcher; b. Kharkov, Ukraine, Oct. 30, 1954; s. Vladimir and Nina (Churkina) T.; m. Janna Korchinova, Aug. 29, 1976; 1 child, Konstantin. D Biol. Scis., Rsch. Inst. Farm Animal Breed, St. Petersburg, 1984; postgrad., Acad. Mgmt. and Agribus., St. Petersburg, 1993-95. Engr. Tech. Inst., Kharkov, Ukraine, 1978-79; rschr. Rsch. Inst. Farm. Animal Breeding and Genetics, St. Petersburg, 1979—. Contbr. articles to profl. jours. With Ukraine mil., 1976-77. E-mail: tsk@piter.net. Home: 19 Komunarov St, 40 Flat, 189623 Saint Petersburg Pavlovsk, Russia Office: Rsch Inst Farm Animal, Moskovskoe Shosse 55A, 189620 Saint Petersburg Russia

TSENDIN, KONSTANTIN DAMDIN, physicist, researcher; b. Ulan Bator, Mongolia, Sept. 15, 1942; arrived in Russia, 1959; s. Damdin-Suren and Zevina Lvbov (Vladimir) T.; m. Noemi Wolf Heifetz, Dec. 11, 1965; children: Alexandr, Ilia. M. U. Leningrad (Russia), 1965; PhD, State Optical Inst., 1978; DSc, A.F. Ioffe Inst., St. Petersburg, 1993. Engr. Inst. Magnetodielectrics, Leningrad, 1965-68; researcher A.F. Ioffe Inst., Leningrad, 1968-91; sr. researcher A.F. Ioffe Inst., St. Petersburg, 1991-95, leading researcher, 1995—; asst. prof. Tech. U., St. Petersburg, 1992-95, prof., 1995—. Co-author, editor: Electronic Phenomena in Chalcogenide Glassy Semiconductors, 1996; co-author: Physics and Applications of Non-Crystalline Semiconductors in Optoelectronics, 1997. Home: Prof Popov St 43 Ap 2, 197022 Saint Petersburg Russia Office: AF Ioffe Phys Tech Inst, Politechnicheskaya 26, 194021 Saint Petersburg Russia

TSENG, AMPERE AN-PEI, mechanical engineer, educator, administrator; b. Kiangsi, China, Jan. 21, 1946; came to U.S., 1971, naturalized, 1982; s. Chi-Kung and Ai-Chung; m. Maggie Shih-Ying Yang, Aug. 9, 1975; children: Claire, Karen, Miles. MS, U. Ill, 1974; PhD, Ga. Inst. Tech., 1978. Mech. engr. Taitan (Taiwan) Industries Pty. Ltd., 1968-71; devel. engr. Westinghouse Electric Corp., Tampa, Fla., 1977-79; staff engr. Martin Marietta Labs., Balt., 1979-84; tech. staff, project leader RCA Labs., Princeton, N.J., 1984-85; assoc. prof. Drexel U., Phila., 1985-91, prof., 1991-96; dir. Ctr. for Automation Mfg., 1990-94; prof., dir. Mfg. Inst., Ariz. State U., Tempe, 1996—. Mem. editl. bd. Adv. Mfg. Processes, 1986-88, Jour. Engring. Materials and Tech., 1987-93, Mfg. Rev., 1991-93, Jour. Materials Processing and Mfg. Sci., 1992—, Advances in Polymer Tech., 1995—, Jour. Chinese Mech. Engring., 1997—. Recipient Cert. of Appreciation, Aluminium Assn., 1984, award for superior performance Martin Marietta Labs., 1979-84; grantee NSF, Nat. Inst. Stds. and Tech., Dept. Energy, Dept. Def. Mem. ASME (chair materials divsn.). Home: 4946 E Cheery Lynn Rd Phoenix AZ 85018-6550 Office: Ariz State U Mech Engring PO Box 876106 Tempe AZ 85287-6106

TSENG, CHENG KUI, marine biologist; b. Xiamen, China, June 18, 1909; s. Bi Cong and Sui Qing (Lin) T.; m. N. Y. Ye June 15, 1931 (div. Sept. 1952); m. Yi Fan Zhang, May 15, 1954; children: Yun Peng, Zhen Li, William Yun Chi, Lillian S.L. Wang. BSc, Xiamen U., 1931; MSc, Lingnan U., 1934; DSc, U. Mich., 1942. Botany asst. and instr. Xiamen U., China, 1930-35; assoc. prof. Shandong U., Qingdao, China, 1935-38, Lingnan U., Guangzhou and Hong Kong, 1938-40; postdoctoral fellow U. Mich., 1942-43; rsch. assoc. Scripps Inst. Oceanography, La Jolla, Calif., 1943-46; prof. Shandong U., 1946-52; rsch. prof., asst. dir., dir., then dir. emeritus Inst. Oceanology, Qingdao, China, 1950—. Author: Common Seaweeds of China, 1983, Oceanology of China, 1994; editor: Manual of Laminaria Cultivation, 1962, Chinese Economic Seaweeds, 1962, Encyclopedia Sinicarum--Atmospheric, Oceanological and Hydrological Sciences, 1987; contbr. articles to profl. jours. Mem. AAAS, Chinese Soc. Oceanology & Limnology (pres. 1979-88, pres. emeritus), Internat. Seaweed Assn. (coun. mem. 1980-92), Internat. Phycological Soc. (pres. 1986-87), Chinese Soc. Botany, Chinese Oceanography Soc. (pres. emeritus), Chinese Phycological Soc. (hon. life, pres. 1979-91, pres. emeritus 1991—), World Aquaculture Soc., N.Y. Acad. Scis., Chinese Acad. Scis., 3d World Acad. Scis. Avocation: music. Home: 5 Qihe Rd, 266003 Qingdao China Office: Inst Oceanology, 7 Nanhai Rd, Qingdao 266071, China

TSENG, CHING SHIOW, mechanical engineer, educator; b. Taiwan, Sept. 4, 1955; s. Fu Tseng and Chu Chou; m. Cathy Yu; children: Grace, Janet. BS, Nat. Chengkung U., 1978; MS, U. Fla., 1985, PhD, 1987. Engr. Industry Tech. Rsch. Inst., Hsinchu, Taiwan, 1979-80, Chun San Inst. Tech. and Sci., Taoyan, Taiwan, 1988-95; from assoc. prof. to prof. Nat. Ctrl. U., Chungli, Taiwan, 1988—. Mem. IEEE. Avocation: tennis, swimming, jogging. Office: Nat Ctrl U, Dept Mech Engring, 320 Chung-Li Taiwan

TSENG, CHIN-HSIAO, internist, diabetologist, medical educator; b. Phnom-Penh, Cambodia, Aug. 4, 1958; arrived in Taiwan, 1973; s. Sung-Jung Tseng and Hsiu-O (Wen) T.; m. Choon-Khim Chong, Feb. 14, 1988; children: Sharon, Shelly. MD, Nat. Taiwan U., Taipei, 1986, PhD, 1996. Cert. acupuncturist; cert. fluoroscopy operator. Resident dept. internal medicine Nat. Taiwan U. Hosp., Taipei, 1986-89, chief resident, 1989-90, fellow divsn. metabolism dept. internal medicine, 1989-91, attending physician dept. internal medicine, 1991—, lectr. Med. Coll., 1993—; assoc. prof. Sch. Pub. Health Taipei Med. Coll., 1996—; reviewer rsch. grants Nat. Sci. Coun., Taipei, 1994—. Contbr. articles to profl. jours. Recipient Excellent Rsch. award Laser Medicine Soc., Taipei, 1997, Nat. Sci. Coun. Rsch. award 1997, 98. Fellow Am. Coll. Angiology; mem. Am. Diabetes Assn., European Soc. Microcirculation, Diabetes Assn. (Taiwan) (dep. sec. gen. 1998—, Prof. Fang-Wu Chen Outstanding Rsch. award 1991, Harvester award 1991, 92, 93, Novo-Nordisk Rsch. award 1996, Merck, Sharpe and Dohme award 1995, 98), Formosan Med. Assn. (reviewer jour. 1992—), Taiwan Soc. Atherosclerosis and Vascular Diseases (Med. Rsch. award 1997). Avocations: reading, music, jogging, travel. Office: Nat Taiwan U Hosp, 7 Chung-Shan South Rd, Taipei Taiwan

TSENG, CHUEN-CHYI, periodontist, educator; b. Ping-Tung, Taiwan, Feb. 23, 1955; s. Shiing-Jiaw and Lai-Hao (Lin); m. Lily Yeh, Jan. 3, 1982; children: Samuel, Lisa, Tina. DDS, Nat. Taiwan U., 1979; MS, U. Minn., 1988, cert. of periodontics, 1988. Diplomate Periodontics, Taiwan. Resident Nat. Taiwan U., 1981-84; clin. instr. U. Minn., 1986-88; from asst. to assoc. prof. Nat. Cheng Kung U., Taiwan, 1988—; chief periodontics Nat. Cheng Kung U. Hosps., 1988—, chmn. dental dept., 1992-97; dep. chmn. dental dept. Chi Mei Found. Hosp., Yung Kang City, Taiwan, 1997—. Contbr. articles to profl. jours. including Jour. Clin. Periodontology, Australian Dental Jour. Med. officer Taiwan Army, 1979-81. Recipient rsch. award Nat. Sci. Coun., 1992, 93, 94. Mem. Chinese Assn. Dental Rsch., Formosan Med. Assn., Am. Acad. Periodontology, Tainan Dental Assn. (bd. dirs. 1989—), Acad. Periodontology (bd. dirs. 1989—), Oral Implantology (bd. dirs. 1995—). Avocations: swimming, jogging, table tennis. Office: 901 Chung-Hwa Rd, Yung Kang City, Yng Kang City Tainan 710, Taiwan

TSENG, KING-JET, engineering educator, research scientist; b. Singapore, Mar. 26, 1963; s. Shian-Chung and Yeow-Choo (Khoo) T.; m. Mona Poh-Gek Chew, Nov. 8, 1994; children: Felix Jia-yuan, Felicia Hui-juan. B in Engring., Nat. U. Singapore, 1988, M in Engring., 1990; PhD, Cambridge (Eng.) U., 1994. Chartered engr., U.K. Lectr. Ngee Ann Poly., Singapore, 1989-90; prof. Nanyang Tech. U., Singapore, 1993—, supr. Power Electronics and Drives Lab. Contbr. articles to profl. jours. including IEE Proceedings, Microprocessors and Microsys., IEEE Transactions on Power Electronics, among others. Recipient Swan Premium award Instn. Elec. Engrs., 1996. Fellow Cambridge Philos. Soc., Cambridge Commonwealth Soc.; mem. IEEE (sr., chmn. indsl. applications Singapore chpt. 1988—, millenium medal 2000), IEE (chartered). Avocations: travel, photography. Office: Nanyang Tech U Sch Elec Eng, Blk S2 Nanyang Ave, Singapore 639798, Singapore

TSENG, TIEN-JIUNN, physics educator; b. Hankow, Hu Pei, China, Nov. 21, 1938; s. Tong-yuan and Yue-ying (Tao) T.; m. So-Lan Lem Tseng, Aug. 14, 1971; children: Lin-con, Lin-haw. BSc, Chung Yuan Christian U., Taiwan, Republic of China, 1962; PhD, U. N.B., Fredericton, Can., 1973. Assoc. prof. Chung Yuan Christin U., Chung Li, 1973-76, dean of students, 1975-78, prof., 1976—, dir. R&D, 1980-81, dean of sci., 1980-83; dir. libr. Chung Yuan Christian U., Chung Li, 1987-89, dir. chaplain's office, 1989-92, dean of students, 1992—; pres. Christ's Coll., 1997—; vis. scientist McGill U., Montreal, Que., Can., 1978-80, vis. prof., 1983-84; councillor in natural scis. Nat. Sci. Coun., Taipei, Republic of China, 1990—. Editorial bd. mem. of dictionary/mechanics Nat. Inst. for Compilation & Translation, Taipei, 1989—; contbr. articles to profl. jours. Chancillor (group) Kuo-Ming Tang polit. party, Chung Li; chmn. com. of elders and deacons/ch., Taipei, 1988—; elder The Holy Word Ch., Taipei, 1989—; mem. bd. China Evang. Mission, Taipei, 1989—; bd. chmn. Chona Evang. Mission, 1996—. Recipient annual award/rsch. works Nat. Sci. Coun., 1984-92. Mem. Phys. Soc. of Republic of China (bd. dirs. 1984-90, 92—), N.Y. Acad. Scis., Am. Physics Soc., Phys. Edn. Soc., Sigma Xi, Phi Tao Phi. Avocations: ping-pong, reading. Office: Christ s Coll Office Pres, 51 Tzu Chiang Rd Tanshui, Taipei 320, Taiwan

TSENG, TSEUNG-YUEN, engineering educator, researcher; b. Hong Kong, Jan. 8, 1953; arrived in Taiwan, 1959; s. F.C. and F.S. (Hsu) T.; m. Mei-Li Chen, Dec. 25, 1978; children: Amy, Nick. Diploma, Taipei Inst. Tech., 1973; MS, Purdue U., 1978, PhD, 1982. Postdoctoral fellow U. Fla., Gainesville, 1982-83; assoc. prof. Chiao-Tung U., Hsinchu, 1983-86, prof., 1986—; dir. Electronic Ceramics Lab., 1986—. Editor Chinese Jour. Materials Sci.; contbr. articles to profl. jours. 2d lt. Taiwan Marines, 1973-75. Recipient Disting. Alumni award Taipei Inst. Tech., 1991, Excellence Rsch. award, Nat. Science Coun. of Republic of China, 1987-92, Young Scientists award Chinese Ceramic Soc., 1988, Disting. Rsch. award Nat. Sci. Coun. of Republic of China, 1995-98, Ceramic medal Chinese Ceramic Soc., 1999. Fellow Am. Ceramic Soc.; mem. IEEE (sr.), N.Y. Acad. Scis. Home: 14F-3 No 31, Chien Chung First Rd, Hsinchu Taiwan Office: Chiao-Tung U Dept Electronics Engring, Dah-Hsueh Rd, Hsinchu Taiwan

TSENOGLOU, CHRISTOS, chemical engineer, educator; b. Athens, Greece, July 26, 1954; came to U.S., 1978; s. Ioannis and Angela (Kahramanos) T. Diploma, Nat. Tech. U., Athens, 1978; MS, Northwestern U., 1981, PhD, 1985. Asst. prof. Stevens Inst. Tech., Hoboken, N.J., 1985-92, assoc. rsch. prof., 1992-95; rsch. assoc., prof. dept. indsl. chemistry/polymers U. Athens, Greece, 1996-97; vis. prof. dept. chem. engring., polymer tech. lab. Nat. Technical U. Athens, 1998—; cons. Johnson and Johnson Dental Products, East Windsor, N.J., 1986—, Werner and Pfleiderer, Ramsey, N.J., 1987 —, Polymer Processing Inst., Hoboken, 1991-95, Nat. Starch and Chem. Co., Bridgewater, N.J., 1992—, Kerr/Sybron, L.A., 1998—, Highly Filled Materials Inst., Hoboken, N.J., 1998—; chmn. polymer rheology symposium 23rd Am. Chem. Soc. Mid. Atlantic Regional Meeting, Madison, N.J., 1990. Author: (with others) New Trends in Physics and Physical Chemistry of Polymers, 1989; contbr. articles to Jour. of Polymer Sci., Physics Edn., Macromolecules, Jour. of Rheology, Rheologica Acta, Polymer Engring. and Sci. Grantee Office Naval Rsch., 1986-89, NSF, 1993-96. Mem. AAAS, AIChE, Am. Chem. Soc., Am. Physical Soc., Soc. of Rheology, Brit. Soc. of Rheology, N.Y. Acad. Scis. (vice-chair polymer sci. divsn. 1991-92). Achievements include development of molecular blending laws for polymer mixtures and composites, general rubber elasticity theory; study on the effects of fractal aggregation in suspension rheology; research on rheology of polymer melts, solutions, blends and suspensions, structure/property relationships in polymer fluids and elastomers, non-Newtonian fluid mechanics in polymer processing and mixing, molecular theories of viscoelasticity and diffusion in polymers. Home: 49 Fokinos Negri St, 113-61 Athens Greece Office: Nat Tech U Athens Dept Chem Engring, Polymer Tech Lab, 157-80 Zografou Greece

TSERENPILYN, GOMBOSUREN, former Mongolian government official; b. Uburhangai, Mongolia, Jan. 5, 1943; s. Tserenpil Tudeviin and Handjav Onoltyn; m. Surenkhorloo Dembereliin, Feb. 20, 1970; children: Gombosurengiin Erdenebayar, G. Biligsaikhan, G. Amartuvshin. Diploma in Printing Engring., Printing Inst., Moscow, 1966; diploma of higher polit. edn., Higher Party Sch., Moscow, 1974-76. Engr., technologist State Printing House, Ulaanbaatar, Mongolia, 1967-70, chief of sect., 1970-74; head of dept. Ministry Fgn. Affairs, Ulaanbaatar, 1976-82, dep. min., 1982-84; min.-counsellor Embassy of the Mongolian People's Republic, Moscow, USSR, 1984-87; alt. mem. Ctrl. Com. Mongolian People's Revolutionary Party, Ulaanbaatar, 1986, dep. head fgn. rels. dept. Ctrl. Com., 1987-88; min. Ministry Fgn. Affairs, Ulaanbaatar, 1988-90, min. fgn. rels., 1990-96; mem. Politburo Mongolian People's Revolutionary Party, Ulaanbaatar, 1990-91; mem. State Great Hural (Parliament), 1992-96, Leadership Counsel Mongolian People's Revolutionary Party, 1996-97; chmn. bd. Mongolian Nat. Security Printing Co., 1997—. Contbr. articles to newspapers and mags. Decorated Order of the Polar Star (Mongolian People's Republic), Order of Gwanghwa (ROK), Sukhbaatar Order. Avocation: literary translation from Russian.

TSERING, UGYEN, diplomat. Fgn. sec. Bhutan Rep. UN, 1998—, chmn. 3rd com. social, humanitarian, cultural. Office: UN 28th Fl 2 United Nations Plaza New York NY 10017*

TSETSKHLADZE, GOCHA REVAZI, archaeologist, educator; b. Likhauri, Georgia, USSR, Jan. 18, 1963; arrived in Eng., 1990; s. Revazi E. and Nanuli (Trapaidze) E. MPhil, Kharkov (Ukraine) U., 1988; PhD in Archaeology and Ancient History, Russian Acad. Scis., 1993; PhD in Classical Archaeology, U. Oxford, 1998. Excavation team mem. Russian Acad. Scis., Moscow/Kiev/Tbilisi, 1978-88; rsch. asst. Rsch. Inst., Batumi, Georgia, 1988; Soros vis. scholar, Linacre Coll. Oxford (Eng.) U., 1990-91, Dervorguilla scholar, Balliol Coll., 1991-94; Jubilee rsch. fellow Royal Holloway and Bedford New Coll., London, 1994-95, Brit. Acad. instnl. rsch. fellow, 1996—; dir. U. London excavation in South Russia; gen. sec. Internat. Pontic Congresses, London, 1994—; Brit. acad. rep. Eurasia Antiqua, Berlin, 1996—; mem. Copenhagen Polis Ctr., 1995—; extensive internat. lectr. numerous instns., including Ashmolean Mus., U. Oxford, 1994, Inst. Classical Studies, U. London, 1994, Al. I. Cuza U., Iasi, Romania, 1995, Hist. Mus., Piatra Neamt, 1995, Inst. Thracology, Bucharest, 1995, Univs. Barcelona and Zaragoza, Spain, 1995, Inst. Archaeology and Ethnology, Copenhagen U., 1996, others including Am. Us. such as NYU, Yale U., Princeton U., Chicago U., Pa. U., Boston U., Montreal U.; mem. bd. examiners for masters degree courses U. London, 1995—, for PhD in archaeology, 1996—; vis. prof. Copenhagen U. Inst. Archaeology and Ethnology, 1998. Founder and gen. editor (series of publs. on the Black Sea) Colloquia Pontica, 1993; author: Die Griechen in der Kolchis, 1998, Pichvnari and its Environs, 1999; mem. editl. com. jour. Il Mar Nero, Bucharest, 1994—, 98—; contbr. chpts. to books, numerous articles and book revs. to profl. jours. and conf. procs.; co-editor: Archaeology of Greek Colonisation, 1994, Economy and Society of Colchis (6th-1st cc BC), (in German) 2000, Periplous Papers to Sir John Boardman, 2000, Greek Settlements in the Eastern Mediterranean and the Black Sea, 2000; editor: Greek and Roman Settlments on the Black Sea Coast-Proceedings of a workshop held at the 95th Annual Meeting of the Archaeological Institute of America, Washington DC, December 1993, 1994, The Archaeology of Greek Colonisation, 1994, The Greek Colonisation of the Black Sea. Historical Interpretation of Archaeology, Historia-Einz 121, 1998, North Pontic Archaeology, 2001, New Studies on the Black Sea Littoral, 1996, Ancient Greeks West and East, 1999. Mem. Classical Assn. Russia, Societas Caucasologica Europeaa, Soc. Study of Caucasia (U.S.), Inst. Classical Studies (London), Assn. Study of Rels. between Georgia and European Countries (hon.), Soc. Promotion of Hellenic Studies (London), Royal Holloway Classical Soc., Archaeol. Inst. Am., others. Office: Royal Holloway & Bedford, New Coll Dept Classics U London, Egham Surrey TW20 0EX, England

TSHERING, UGYEN, Bhutan diplomat; b. Thimphu, Bhutan, Aug. 8, 1954; married. Grad., U. Calif., Berkeley. Joined Govt. Planning Commn., Bhutan, 1978, coord. bilateral and multilateral assistance to govt., 1983-89, project coord. Computer Support Ctr., 1984, sec. computerization com., 1983-89, dir. planning commn., 1986-89; permanent rep. of Bhutan to UN, N.Y.C., from 1989; chmn. 3d Com. (Social, Humanitarian, Cultural), Bhutan; chair Asian Devel. Bank, World Bank Projects Implementation Com., 1986—; chair tech. com. on rural devel. S.E. Asian Assn. Regional Cooperation, 1988-89. Office: Permanent Mission of Bhutan to UN 2 UN Plz 27th Fl New York NY 10017-4403*

TSHWETE, STEVE, South African government official; b. Springs, Transvaal, South Africa. Law clk. King William's Town, 1983; min. of sport and recreation Govt. of South Africa, 1994—; min. safety and security. Address: Wachthuis 7th Fl, 231 Pretorius St, Bldg X463 Pretoria 0001, South Africa*

TSIAMIS, ATHANASSIOS, psychologist; b. Athens, Apr. 26, 1957; s. Constantinos and Calomera Tsiamis; m. Evangelia Goulandris, Dec. 27, 1989; children: Contantinos, Aristides. MA in Ednl. Psychology, McGill U., Montreal, Que., Can., 1986; BA in Psychology, Deree Coll., Athens, 1983. Instr. Greek Pedagogical Inst., Xinis Ednl. Orgn., Athens, 1987-90, dir. studies, 1990-92; ednl. psychologist I.M. Panagiotopoulos Sch., Athens, 1992—; ednl. psychologist Cargacos Sch., Athens, 1988-90; part-time instr. Deree Coll., Athens, 1990—, U. LaVerne, Athens, 1997—; cons. Ekentro, Tutorial Sch. Secondary Edn., Athens, 1999. Pres. Deree Coll. Students Union, Athens, 1981-82. Mem. APA (fgn. affiliate), European Coun. for High Ability, Assn. Greek Psychologists. E-mail: tsiamisa@otenet.gr. Fax: 7480913. Home: 18 Daskalaki St, 11526 Attica Greece Office: IM Panagiotopoulos Sch, 14 N Litra, 15452 Athens Attica, Greece

TSIDILKOVSKI, ISAAC MICHAILOVICH, physicist; b. Rakitno, Kiev, Russia, May 21, 1923; s. Mikhail and Polina Zinovievna (Khaichenko) T.; m. Ludmila Moiseievna Sheinis, June 13, 1951; children: Vladislav, Edward. Student, Poly. Inst., Kiev, 1941, U. Kiev, 1951; Candidate Sci., U. Leningrad, 1956, PhD, 1959. Lic. physicist. Lectr. Tchrs. Tng. Inst., Melitopol, Russia, 1951-52; scientist Dagestan br. Acad. Scis. USSR, Makhachkala, 1952-57; prof. Inst. Metal Physics, Sverdlovsk, 1958-60, head lab., 1961-95; counsillor Russian Acad. Scis., Ekaterinburg, Russia, 1995—. Author: Thermomagnetic Effects in Semiconductors, 1960, Electrons and Holes in Semiconductors, 1972 (Loffe prize 1978), Band Structure of Semiconductors, 1982, Electron Spectrum of Gapless Semiconductors, 1997, Half A Century with Semiconductors, 1999, Effective Mass Conception, 1999, Metal-Insulator Transitions in Magnetic Field, 2000; contbr. articles to profl. jours. Maj. Russian Inf., 1941-45. Recipient USSR State prize, 1982, Lomonosov prize, 1994. Mem. Russian Acad. Scis. Avocations: reading fiction especially historical novels, memoirs. E-mail: tsidil@imp.uran.ru. Home: Dekabristov 85-24, 620144 Ekaterinburg Russia Office: Inst Metal Physics, S Kovalevskoj 18, 620219 Ekaterinburg Russia

TSIEN, JOE Z., neurobiologist, educator; b. Wuxi, Jiangsu, China, Oct. 8, 1962; came to US, 1986.; s. Weirao Qian and Xiaoqin Huang; m. Xueying Cao, Aug. 20, 1987; children: Ted, Philip. BS, East China Normal U., 1984; PhD, U. Minn., 1990. Postdoct. fellow Columbia U., N.Y.C., 1990-93; rsch. assoc. MIT, Cambridge, Mass., 1993-97; prof. Princeton (N.J.) U., 1997—. Contbr. articles to profl. jours.; discovered memory gene "Nature", 1999, created "smart" mice, developed brain-region-specicif gene knockout

technology. Recipient Bacaner Rsch. award Minn. Med. Found., 1990, Beckman Young Investigator award Beckman Found., 1997, Scientific Achievement award Orgn. Chinese Ams., 1999. Avocations: tennis, running, biking. Office: Princeton U Dept Molecular Biology Washington Rd Princeton NJ 08544-0001

TSILINGIRIS, PANAYOTIS THEODORE, mechanical engineer, electrical engineer, researcher, energy engineering consultant, educator; b. Athens, Greece, Oct. 12, 1952; s. Theodore and Euridice (Peioglou) T.; m. Fotini Karassava, May 8, 1982; children: Euridice, Dimitri. Diploma, Nat. Tech. U. of Athens, 1976; PhD, U. Reading, Eng., 1985. R & D engr. Greek Army, Athens, 1977-79; cons. engr. Comml. Bank of Greece, Athens, 1979—; prof. heat transfer and thermodynamics Higher Tech. Instn. Athens, 1998—; dir. rsch. programs Coun. Tech. Rsch., Athens, 1987-90; vis. prof. Nat. Tech. U. Athens, 1986-91, Loughborough (Eng.) U. Tech., 1994; sr. rschr. Ctr. for Renewable Energy Sources, Athens, dir. active solar systems dept., 1992-95; sr. energy cons. Comml. Bank of Greece, Athens, 1995-98; lectr. Gen. Sec. Youth, Athens, 1988-92, Nat. Productivity Ctr., Athens, 1988-89, prof., Higher Technol. Inst. Athens, 1998—. Contbr. articles to profl. jours. Lt. Greek Corps of Engrs., 1976-79. Undergrad. scholar Greek State Scholarships Found., 1971, postgrad. scholar, 1981, 83. Fellow Diplarios Coll.; mem. ASME (assoc.), Tech. Chamber of Greece, Greek Instn. Mech. Engrs., Internat. Solar Energy Soc., Eletilen/ISES (Greek sect.), N.Y. Acad. Scis. Avocations: painting, athletics, handicrafts. Home: 14 Th Kairi St, 17122 Athens Greece

TSINDOS, SPERO PERRY, naturopathic physician, writer; b. Melbourne, Australia, July 9, 1954; s. Constantine Eustace and Mary Zoy (Morris) T.; m. Tess Nagorka, Mar. 20, 1983; children: Jessica, Aaron Constantie. Degree in naturopathy, NSW Coll., Sydney, Australia, 1987; degree in homeopathy, Australian Inst. Homoepathy, Sydney, Australia, 1988. Dir. Holistic Health Clinic, Washington, 1987-89, Doncaster (Australia) Naturopath Clinic, 1989-98; lectr. Southern Sch. Natural Therapies, Melbourne, Australia, 1994-98, Australian Coll. Natural Medicine, Melbourne, 1995-98; dir. TRM Pub. Pty. Ltd., Melbourne, 1997-98. Author: (reference text) Therapeutic Reference Manual of Complementary Medicines, 1997. Mem. Australian Naturopathic Practioners Assn. Avocations: electronics, gardening, woodcarving. Office: TRM Pub Pty Ltd, 1 Fromhold Dr, Doncaster 3108, Australia

TSIPENYUK, DMITRY YURIEVICH, physicist, inventor; b. Kiev, Russia, Sept. 13, 1962; s. Yuri Mikhailovich and Evgenia Alexandrouna (Pronevich) T. MSc in Engring., Phys. Tech. Inst., Moscow, 1985; PhD, Gen. Physics Inst., Moscow, 1992. Engr. Gen. Physics Inst., 1985-87, jr. rschr., 1987-90, rschr., 1990-93, sr. rschr., 1993—. Contbr. articles to profl. jours. Recipient award Am. Phys. Soc., 1991, grant Internat. Space U., 1995, grant Internat. Soc. Photogrammetry and Remote Sensing, 1996. Avocations: tennis, table tennis, surfing, inventor. Office: Gen Physics Inst, Vavilova Str 38, 117333 Moscow Russia

TSIPENYUK, YURI MIKHAILOVICH, physicist, educator; b. Kiev, Ukraine, Apr. 12, 1938; s. Mikhail Isaakovich and Rosalia Iosifovna (Turovskaya) T.; m. Eugeniya Aleksandrovna Pronevich, Sept. 13, 1962; 1 child, Tsipenyuk Dmitri. Engr., Moscow Inst. Physics & Tech., Moscow, 1962; Candidate Sci., Inst. for Phys. Problems, Moscow, 1969; DSc, Joint Inst. Nuclear Rschrs., Dubna, Russia, 1979. Engr., jr. scientist, sr. scientist, leading scientist Inst. Phys. Problems, Russian Acad. Sci., Moscow, 1962—; Soros prof., Moscow, 1997. Author: Principles and Methods of Nuclear Physics, 1993, Nuclear Methods in Science and Technology, 1997; co-discoverer quadrupole photofission, 1965; contbr. articles to profl. jours. Avocation: tennis. Home: Udaltsova 4-79, 117415 Moscow Russia Office: PL Kapitza Inst Phys Probs, Russian Acad Sci Kosygina 2, 117334 Moscow Russia

TSIPIS, KOSTA MICHAEL, science educator; b. Athens, Greece, Feb. 12, 1934; s. Michael Kosta and Zoe (Alexiou) T.; m. Judith Ebel, Dec. 20, 1970; children: Mikael, Andreas, Yanni. BSc, Rutgers U., 1958, MSc, 1960; PhD, Columbia U., 1966. From asst. prof. to sr. rsch. sci. MIT, Cambridge, 1966—; dir. program in sci. and tech. internat. security. Author: Tactical and Strategic Antisubmarine Warfare, 1974, Arsenal-Understanding Weapons in the Nuclear Age, 1985, Kosta Tsipis on the Arms Race-A Collection of Critical Essays, 1987, New Technologies, Defense Policy and Arms Control, 1989; editor: The Future of the Sea-Based Deterrent, 1973, Military R&D., 1977, Tutorials on Nuclear Weapons, 1983, Annual Review of Military Research and Development, 1983, Reason Enough to Hope, 1998, and others; contbr. articles to profl. jours. and chpts. in books. Fellow Am. Physical Soc. (Szilard award 1983), AAAS, N.Y. Acad. Scis. Office: MIT 77 Massachusetts Ave Cambridge MA 02139-4307

TSIRKUNOV, YURY MIKHAILOVICH, mechanical engineer, fluid mechanics specialist, researcher; b. Leningrad, USSR, June 20, 1949; s. Mikhail Arkhipovich Rozhin and Nina Avraamovna Tsirkunov; m. Nellie Dmitrievna Pavlenko, Jan. 20, 1972; 1 child Evgeny (dec.). MS in Mech. Engring., Leningrad (USSR) Mech. Inst., 1972, PhD in Fluid Mechanics, 1976; ABA in Sociology and Social Psychology, Two-year Humanitarian U., Leningrad, USSR, 1982. Jr. rschr. Leningrad Mech. Inst., 1975-78, sr. rschr., 1978-89; head Two Phase Flows Rsch. Group Baltic State Tech. U., St. Petersburg, Russia, 1989—; assoc. prof. Baltic State Tech. U., St. Petersburg, 1993—; cons. Spl. Sci. Prodn. Corp., Leningrad, USSR, 1978-85; participant EUROMECH Conf., 1994, 97. Contbr. over 52 publs. to profl. and acad. jours. Grantee Russian Fedn. Ministry of Higher Edn., Moscow, 1994-95, 96-97, Russian Found. for Basic Rsch., Moscow, 1994, 96-98, 99—, Internat. Sci. Found., N.Y., U.S.A., 1994; (joint grant) Internat. Sci. Found. and Govt. of Russia, N.Y. and Moscow, 1995. Mem. N.Y. Acad. Sci., European Mechanics Soc. Avocations: classic lit., classical music. Fax: 7-812-316-2409. Home: Apt 125, Bldg 2, 33 Tikhoretsky pr, 195427 Saint Petersburg Russia Office: Baltic State Tech U, 1 1-ya Krasnoarmeiskaya, 198005 Saint Petersburg Russia

TSIRPANLIS, ZACHARIAS, humanities educator; b. Kos, Greece, June 13, 1938; s. Nicolas Tsirpanlis and Kalliopi Klutsi, m. Cathy Sivva, Oct. 23, 1978; children: Kalliopi, Evangelia. MA, U. Thessaloniki, Greece, 1961, PhD, 1968. Asst. prof. U. Thessaloniki, 1965-70, keeper hist. archives, 1970-72; assoc. prof. U. Ioannina, Greece, 1972-75, prof., 1975-99; prof. humanities U. Thessaloniki, 1999—. Author: Cardinal Bessarion's Bequest, 1967, The Macedonian Students in Rome, 1971, Documents from Vatican Archives, 1973, The Greek College in Rome, 1980, Register of the Venetian Candia, 1985, Rhodes and the South-East Aegean Islands from the Archives of the Order of St. John, 1995, The Dodecanese under the Italians 1912-1943, 1998. Mem. Soc. Macedonian Studies, Soc. Slavic Studies, Soc. Greek Historians, Cyprus Research Ctr., Inst. for Balkan Studies. Home: Mitropoleos 26, 546 24 Thessaloniki Greece Office: U Thessaloniki, PO Box 10190, 54110 Thessaloniki Greece

TSITOLOVSKY, LEV, neurobiologist, researcher; b. Sevastopol, USSR, May 23, 1941; arrived in Israel, 1992; s. Efim Tsitolovsky and Emilia Kaminsky; m. Natalia Shalomeeva, May 20, 1966 (div. 1969); m. Ludmila Kiseleva, Dec. 1, 1969; 1 child, Katrine. MS, Moscow Phys.-Tech. Inst., 1966; PhD, Lomonosov State U., Moscow, 1971; prof., Inst. Radio Engring., 1985. Sr. rsch. scientist Lomonosov State U., 1966-74; scientist Inst. Normal Physiology, Moscow, 1975-83; head Lab. Informatics, Inst. Radio Engring., Moscow, 1983-92; head Neurocomputers Lab., SOFTARMAT, Ltd., Moscow, 1991-92; sr. scientist Bar-Ilan U., Ramat-Gan, Israel, 1993—. Contbr. articles to profl. jours.; sci. editor Pavlov's Jour. Higher Neural Activity, 1985-92. Grantee Israel Ministry of Sci., 1994, USSR Ministry of Edn., 1989. Mem. Physiol. Soc. Israel, Physiol. Soc. USSR. Achievements include discovery of the selective form of excitable membrane plasticity and damage of neural cells by means of motivational excitation. Avocations: journalism of popular science, writing short stories. Home: HaRav Maimon 1/5, 77353 Ashdod Israel Office: Bar Ilan U, Dept Life Scis, 52900 Ramat Gan Israel

TSITOURAS, KONSTANTINOS, chemical engineer, educator, economist; b. Apr. 7, 1957; s. Dimitrios and Panagiota (Tzoura) T. Diploma in Chem. Engring., Nat. Tech. U., Athens, Greece, 1980; MSc in Advanced Chem. Engring., Imperial Coll., London, 1984; BS in Bus. Adminstrn., Grad. Sch. Econs. & Bus. Admin, Athens, Greece, 1986; vacation student, Brit. Petroleum, Surrey, Eng., 1978. With military svc. instruments divsn. Calibration Svc. Air Force, 1980-82; with Hellenic Fertilizers, Athens, 1985-91; with prodn., rsch. and devel. divsn. Analytical Instruments SA, Athens, 1992; with MSE Consulting, 1993-94; with prodn., rsch. and devel. divsn. Corinth Refineries, Athens, 1995; strategic planner gas supply depts. DEPA S.A., Athens, 1995—. Contbr. articles to various publs. Scholar State scholarship Found., 1980. Mem. Greek Assn. Chem. Engrs., Tech. Chamber of Greece. Avocations: photography, languages. Home: 4 Pallikaridou,, Hymittos 17237, Greece

TSITSOS, STELIOS, telecommunications engineer; b. Kariotissa, Greece, Oct. 26, 1966; s. Polidoros and Anastasia (Papadopoulou) T. Diploma in Elec. Engring., U. Thrace, Xanthi, Greece, 1989; M in Comm. Engring., U. Manchester Inst. Sci./Tech., Eng., 1991, PhD in Comm. Engring., 1994. Rsch. asst. UMIST, Manchester, 1991-94, rsch. assoc., 1996-99; sr. telecomm. engr. Greek Telecoms, Athens, Greece, 1999—; cons. TDK Corp., Europe-Japan, 1996-99. Recipient undergrad. fellowship Nat. Inst. of Scholarships, Greece, 1989, postgrad. scholarship Onassis Found., Greece, 1991, tuition fees award EPSRC, U.K., 1991. Mem. IEEE, Inst. Elec. Engrs. (assoc.), Tech. Chamber Greece. Avocations: athletics, driving, reading. Home: 93 Egnatias St, GR-58001 Kariotissa Greece Office: Greek Telecoms Network Dept, 99 Kifissias Ave, GR-15181 Maroussi, Athens Greece

TSITVERBLIT, NAFTALI ANATOL, fluid mechanics researcher; b. Kiev, Ukraine, Oct. 29, 1963; arrived in Israel, 1987; s. Isaac Avraham and Zoya (Beletsky) T. MSc, Kiev Poly. Inst., 1981-87; PhD, Tel-Aviv U., 1995. Engr. Scientific Rsch. Inst. Robotics, Kiev, 1985-87; postdoc. fellow Lamont-Doherty Earth Obs. Columbia U., Palisades, N.Y., 1995-97; tchg. asst., instr. mech. engring. Tel-Aviv U., 1988-94, vis., 1997—; vis. scientist Cornell U., 1994. Co-author: (chpt.) Nonlinear Instability of Nonparallel Flows, 1994; contbr. papers to profl. jours. Woods Hole Oceanographic Inst. fellow, 1996. Mem. AAAS, N.Y. Acad. Sci., Am. Phys. Soc., Am. Geophys. Union. Achievements include research in multiplicity of the equilibrium states in laterally heated stably stratified fluid systems and its role in explaining diversity of previous observations in such systems; discovery of a new mechanism for steady convection in double-component fluid systems, resulting from the different boundary conditions, and identification of this mechanism and its role in various fluid mechanical configurations, in particular discovery of finite-amplitude flows arising from this convective mechanism that are disconnected from the conduction state; clarification of the nature of the oscillatory instability in confined vortex flows with vortex breakdown and formulation of a general method for identification of the nature of complex instability mechanisms. Email: naftali@eng.tau.ac.il or tsit@rosie.ldgo.columbia.edu. Home: 1 Yanosh Korchak St Apt 6, Netanya 42495, Israel

TSO, MARK ON-MAN, ophthalmologist; b. Hong Kong, Oct. 19, 1936; s. Paul and Amy (Ho) T.; m. Petrina Chan, Dec. 19, 1964. MBBS, U. Hong Kong, 1961, DSc, 1995. Diplomate Am. Bd. Ophthalmology. Staff ophthalmologist Armed Forces Inst. of Pathology, Washington, 1969-71, rsch. assoc., 1971-76; prof. of ophthalmology U. Ill., Chgo., 1976-94, dir. of Georgiana Theobald Ophthalmic Path. Lab., 1976-94, med. dir. Lions of Ill. Eye Bank, 1989-94; prof., chmn. dept. ophthalmology and visual scis. Chinese U. of Hong Kong, 1994-99; chair XI Acad. Ophthalmologica Internationalis, 1997—; pres. Coll. of Ophthalmologists of Hong Kong, 1997-99; v.p. Internat. Coun. of Ophthalmology, 1998—; prof. ophthalmology and pathology John Hopkins U., Balt., 1999—. Author: Retinal Diseases, 1988. Sr. univ. scholar U. Ill., 1985-88, De Ocampo lectr. The Asia Pacific Acad. of Ophthalmology, 1995; recipient Friedenwald award and lectr. Assn. for Rsch. in Vision and Ophthalmology, 1989. Fellow Royal Coll. Surgeons (Edinburgh). Office: John Hopkins U 600 N Wolfe St Baltimore MD 21287-0005

TSOCHAS, CONSTANTINOS, physician; b. Thessaloniki, Greece, Sept. 18, 1933; s. Athanasios and Katina Tsochas; m. Elisabeth Mavridou, Sept. 27, 1959; children: Tsocha, Katerina. MD, Aristotelian U. Thessaloniki, 1959, Specialist in Internal Medicine, 1963, PhD, 1968; Specialist in Pneumonology & Physiology, Ctr. Chest Diseases, Thessaloniki, 1964. Lic. physician. Intern in internal medicine AHEPA Hosp., Thessaloniki, 1959-60; resident Hosp. Chest Diseases of North Greece, Thessaloniki, 1961-63; asst. dir. Clinics Internal Medicine Hosp. Mental Diseases, Thessaloniki, 1964-65; asst. dir. Gen. Ctrl. Hosp., Thessaloniki, 1966; dir. St. George Clinic, Athens, Greece, 1972-79; prof. Higher Tech. Edn. Ctr., Athens, 1973-83, head Sch. Paramed. Professions, 1973-76, 82-83; pres. Tech. Ednl. Instn., Athens, 1983-87; prof. faculty health and caring Professions of Tech. Ednl. Instn., Athens, 1983—; med. dir. Faran S.A. Pharmaceutics, Athens, 1971-72, Eaton Pharms. S.A., Athens, 1972-74. Author: On the C-Reactive Protein Content of the Cerebrospinal Fluid, 1967, The Water and the Electrolytes, 1969, Deontological Issues in Medical and Paramedical Professions, 1975, Public Health Laws, 1976, Nosology, 1987, First Aid, 1986, Clinical Pharmacology, 1996, Optical Pharmacology, 1997; author, editor: The Medicine of the Work, 1970, others; contbr. articles to profl. jours. Vice dir. Greek Red Cross Youth Orgn., Thessaloniki, 1970; cons. Red Cross br. Ctrl. Macedonia, 1970. Maj. Greek Army, 1960-62. Recipient Silver Medal Cross, Internat. Red Cross, 1968, Hon. Distinction, Greek Samaritans, 1968, hon. diploma Orgn. for Prevention of Accidents, 1969. Fellow Royal Soc. Health; mem. Athens Med. Assn. Socialist. Christian Orthodox. Avocation: painting. Home: 12 Laskaratou St, GR-11141 Athens Greece Office: Tech Edn Instn Athens, Ag Spiridonos St, GR-12210 Athens Egaleo, Greece

TSOCHATZIDIS, NIKOLAOS A., chemical engineer, researcher; b. Serres, Greece, June 29, 1965; s. Anastassios and Artemis (Zouridaki) T.; m. Chryssanthi B. Palazi, Nov. 18, 1995; 1 child, Anastassios. Diploma in chem. engring., Aristotle U. Thessaloniki, Greece, 1989, PhD in Chem. Engring., 1994. Rschr. Chem. Process Engring. Rsch. Inst., Thessaloniki, 1989-96; pvt. practice cons. Thessaloniki, 1989-96; rschr. Ecole Nat. Superiore Inst. Genie Chimique, Toulouse, France, 1996-97; chem. engr. Pub. Gas Corp. Greece, Serres, 1997—; assoc. prof. Tech. Ednl. Inst., Serres, 1995—. Contbr. articles to sci. jours.; patentee in field. Cpl. Greek Army, 1995-96. Postdoctoral rsch. fellow Bodosakis Found., Greece, 1990, European Union, France, 1996. Mem. Chem. Engring. Assn. Greece, Gas Engring. Assn. Greece, Tech. Chamber Greece. Christian Orthodox. Avocations: chess, fishing. Home: Ag Ioannis, GR 62100 Serres Greece Office: DEPA SA, BMS Sidirokastro, GR 62300 Sidirokastro Greece

TSODIKOV, ALEXANDER DAVID, biostatistician, educator; b. St. Petersburg, Russia, Dec. 20, 1964; arrived in Germany, 1994; s. David Isac and Vera Semion (Fidelman) T.; m. Elena Sergei Serbina, Oct. 7, 1999; 1 child, Anna. MS in Applied Math., St. Petersburg Tech. U., 1988, PhD in Math., 1991; diploma in epidemiology and biostats., Karolinska Inst., Sweden, 1992. Engr. St. Petersburg Tech. U., 1988-90, rsch. fellow, 1990-92, sr. rsch. fellow, 1992-93; postdoctoral fellow Inst. Curie, Paris, 1993-94; rsch. scientist U. Leipzig, Germany, 1995-97; rsch. asst. prof. U. Utah, Salt Lake City, 1997—. Author: Statistical Models, 1996; contbr. more than 40 articles to profl. jours. including Math. Biosci., Biometrics, Proc. U.S. Nat. Acad. Scis., Statis. Med., among others. Grantee Ministry of Sci. (France), 1993, Internat. Union Against Cancer (Switzerland), 1992, German Rsch. Found., 1995. Achievements include rsch. in cancer models, optimal screening schedules, and statis. methods in cancer. Home: 5562 Brookridge Dr Apt 14J Salt Lake City UT 84107-6844

TSOLAS, ORESTES EROFILOS, biological chemistry educator; b. Istanbul, Turkey, Dec. 5, 1933; arrived in Greece, 1978; BSc, Robert Coll., Istanbul, 1954; BA, Cambridge (Eng.) U., 1957, MA, 1961; PhD, Yeshiva U., 1967. Accredited clin. chemist., Nat. Registry in Clin. Chemistry. Biochemist Hippocration and Aghia Olga Hosps., Athens, Greece, 1959-61; rsch. asst. Albert Einstein Coll. Medicine and NYU, N.Y.C., 1961-67; rsch. assoc. Albert Einstein Coll. Medicine, 1967-70, asst. prof., 1970-72; asst. mem. Roche Inst. Molecular Biology, Nutley, N.J., 1972-78; founding prof. biol. chemistry and head lab. Med Sch., Greece, 1978—; dean U. Ioannina Med. Sch., 1980-83, dir. sect. functional scis., 1984-85, pres. biochemistry degree programme, 1998—; dir. gen. Inst. Pasteur Hellenique, Athens, 1995; founding dir., U. clin. biochemistry lab. Regional Gen. Hosp. Ioannina "G. Hatzikosta", 1983-91; dir. clin. biochemistry lab Regional U. Gen. Hosp., Ioannina, 1989—; dir. Ioannina Biomed . Rsch. Inst., 1998—; panel mem. selective activation of molecules NATO Sci. Affairs Divsn., Brussels, 1987-88; vis. scientist, disting. vis. scientist Roche Inst. Molecular Biology, 1988-89, 94; vis. prof. U. Sao Paulo, Brazil, Rutgers U., Newark, N.J., U. San Marcos, Lima, Peru, others; mem. advanced courses com. Fedn. European Biochemical Socs., 1995-98; mem. conseil scientifique Inst. Pasteur Hellenique; mem. Nat. Adv. Rsch. Coun., Athens. Collaborative rsch. grantee NATO, grantee Gen. Secretariat Sci. and Tech. Mem. Am. Soc. Biochemistry and Molecular Biology, Biochemical Soc. (Great Britain), Hellenic Biochemical and Biophysical Soc. (v.p., pres. 1992-93), Nat. Acad. of Clin. Biochemistry., Balkan Clin. Lab. Fedn. (pres. 1996-99). Achievements include research on enzymology, protein chemistry, carbohydrate metabolism and immunoactive peptides. Home: Roma 20, Ioannina Greece 45221 Office: U Ioannina Med Sch, Lab Biological Chemistry, GR-451 10 Ioannina Greece

TSOTSOROS, STATHIS, economist, management executive; b. Nafpactos, Greece, Apr. 22, 1949; s. Nicolaos and Julia (Mandelos) T.; m. Helen Harissis, Feb. 24, 1974; children: Nicolaos, Dimitris. MS in Elec. Engring., Nat. Tech. U., Athens, 1972; BS in Econs., U. Athens, 1978; PhD in Econs., Pantios Sch. Polit. Scis., AThens, 1982. Registered profl. engr. Dist. engr. Pub. Power Corp., Arcadia, Greece, 1974-75, head tech. sector, 1975-76; dist. dir. Pub. Power Corp., Arcadia-Argolis, 1976-81; dir. by gov. Pub. Power Corp., Athens, 1983-84; cons. Ministry of Energy, Greece, 1981-83; v.p. and governing council in charge Econ. Affairs Fin. and Mining Trust, Athens, 1984-85; v.p. and mng. dir. Bus. Reconstrn. Orgn., Athens, 1984-86; v.p. exec. com., dir. gen. Orgn. for Planning and Environ. Protection of Athens, 1986-88; pres., mng. dir. Effective Thesis Cons. SA, Athens, Greece, 1993-96; gen. mgr. radio and telecomm. ops. Sky 100.4 Hellenic Satellite TV SA, Athens, Greece, 1997-98; pres., mng. dir. ALPHA Satellite TV SA, Athens, 1998—; cons. Hellenic Agy. for Local Govt. and Devel., Athens, 1987-88, feasibility studies and property value, ops. assessment, for indsl. enterprises, 1988-91; cons., pres. Tech. Chamber of Greece, 1991-94; mng. dir. Indomin, S.A., Athens, 1991-93; chmn. 5-yr. plan formulation com. Ministry of Energy and Natural Resources, Greece, 1982-87, chmn. 5-yr. plan formulation com. of Ministry of Nat. Economy, Attica Region, 1988-89; guest researcher evolution of Greek Indsl. Enterprises, Ctr. for Neohellenic Rsch. Nat. Rsch. Found., 1987-93; cons. to mayor of Athens, 1991-92; pres. Hellenic Govt. Com. for agreement planning and contractual devel., 1994-95; sec. Inst. Strategic Devel. Studies, 1995—; prof. polit. econs. Pantio U., Athens, 1993—. Author: Economic and Social Mechanisms in the Highland Regions (1715-1828), Problematic (financially unstable) Industrial Enterprises and Public Law N. 1386/83, Industrial Capital Accumulation in Greece 1897-1939 Part I, 1993, Part II, 1994, Energy Development in the Post War Era, 1995; contbr. articles to profl. jours. Cpl. Army, Greece, 1972-73. Grantee Comml. Bank of Greece, 1984, Nat. Bank of Greece, 1987. Mem. Panhellenic Soc. Mech. and Elec. Engrs., Tech. Chamber of Greece, Econ. Chamber of Greece. Hellenic Socialist Party. Greek Orthodox. Avocations: music, swimming. Home: 1 Syrou St Holargos, 15562 Athens Greece Office: ALPHA Satellite TV SA, 201 Pireaus St, 11853 Athens Greece

TSOULOS, GEORGE VASILIOS, electrical and electronics engineer; b. Kalamata, Messinia, Greece, May 15, 1968; arrived in the U.K., 1993; s. Vasilios and Niki Tsoulou; m. Georgia Athanasiadou, 1998. MS, Nat. Tech. U. Athens, 1992; PhD, U. Bristol, Eng., 1996. Cert. elec. engr. Rsch. asst. Nat. Tech. U. Athens, 1992-93; rsch. assoc. U. Bristol, 1994-96, 96-98, rsch. fellow, 1998, cons., 1996—; expert COST 231, Europe, 1996-97, COST 259, Europe, 1998—; dir. Smart Cell Solutions Ltd., Bristol, 1999; with PA Consulting Group, Cambridge, U.K., 1999—. Contbr. articles to profl. jours. Recipient Spl. Scientist award Greek Army, 1998, PhD scholarship U. Bristol, 1994. Mem. IEEE, Internat. Communications Soc., Tech. Chamber of Greece. E-mail: gtsoulos@hotmail.com. Home: 140 Woodhead Dr, Cambridge CB4 1YX, United Kingdom

TSOUROS, CONSTANTIN CLAUDE, computer science educator; b. Alexandria, Egypt, Dec. 15, 1945; arrived in Greece, 1964; s. Paul Tsouros and Gladys Adelaide (Luttrel) Breitung; m. Glykeria Thoukididou, Aug. 13, 1969 (div. 1990); children: Paul, Michael; m. Glykeria Kalfakakou, Aug. 19, 1992; 1 child, Demosthenes. Bachelor in Math., Aristotle U., Thessaloniki, Greece, 1972, DEng, 1981. Instr. Sch. Engring.-Aristotle U., 1975-80, asst. prof., 1980-86; prof. computing U. Macedonia, Thessaloniki, 1986—, vice rector, 1988-91, head dept. informatics, 1996—. Author: Algorithms and programs, 1990, Elements of Graph Theory, 1993, Analysis of Algorithms, 1994; contbr. articles to profl. jours. Mem. Hellenic Operational Rsch. Soc. (pres. 1996—), Greek Math. Soc., Internat. Soc. Inventory Rsch. Greek Orthodox. Avocations: tennis, classical music, basketball, table tennis. Home: 32 Ydras Str, 546 38 Thessaloniki Macedon, Greece Office: U Macedonia, 156 Egnatia Str, 540 06 Thessaloniki Greece

TSUBOMURA, HIROSHI, chemistry educator; b. Nara, Japan, Aug. 12, 1927; s. Akira and Masae Tsubomura; m. Michi Tsuzuki, May 12, 1957; children: Taro, Kenji, Yosuke. BSc, U. Tokyo, 1950, DSc, 1957. Rsch. assoc. U. Tokyo, 1955-60, asst. prof., 1960-62; prof. chemistry Osaka U., Toyonaka, Japan, 1962-91; prof. chemistry Kobe (Japan) Gakuin U., 1993-98, retired, 1998. Author: Chemistry of Excited States, 1967, Structural Physical Chemistry, 1971, Photoelectrochemistry and Energy Conversion, 1980, New Physical Chemistry, 1994. Recipient Matsunaga award Matsunaga Found., 1971, award Chem. Soc. Japan, 1981, purple ribbon medal Govt. of Japan, 1993. Avocation: golf. Home: 8-19-38 Mino, Mino 562-0001, Japan

TSUBOTA, TOSHIO, veterinary science educator; b. Osaka, Japan, Feb. 9, 1961; s. Isamu and Masumi Tsubota; m. Ayumi Takaya; children: Hanayo, Kurino, Nanami, Suzune. MS, Hokkaido U., Sapporo, Japan, 1985, PhD, 1988. Asst. prof. Gifu (Japan) U., 1988-95, assoc. prof., 1995—. Author: Physiology of Mammals, 1998; contbr. articles to profl. jours. Recipient Shimamura award Japanese Soc. Animal Reprodn., 1990. Mem. Japanese Soc. Zoo and Wildlife Medicine (sec. 1995—). Avocations: jogging, swimming. Home: 981-1 Ishigai, Gifu 501-1106, Japan Office: Gifu U, 1-1 Yanagido, Gifu 501-1193, Japan

TSUCHI, RYUICHI, geoscientist, researcher; b. Taipei, Taiwan, China (Japan at that time), Jan. 23, 1929; s. Tadao and Yukiko (Otuka) T.; m. Kohko Hanaoka, Jan. 27, 1962; children: Kazuhiro, Hidetaka, Hiroshi, Yoriko. Degree, U. Tokyo, 1951, DSc, 1961. Rsch. assoc. Shizuoka U., Shizuoka, Japan, 1951-63; lectr. Shizuoka U., 1963-64, assoc. prof., 1964-70, prof., 1970-92, prof. emeritus, 1992—; project leader IGCP-246, 1986-92; chmn. reg. com. Pacific Neogene Stratigraphy, SNS. IUGS, 1991—, IGCP Nat. Com. Japan, 1992—; vice chmn. subcom. Neogene Stratigraphy, 1996—. Home: Izumi 2-40-28 Suginami, 168-0063 Tokyo Japan Office: Miyatake 1-9-24, 422-8035 Shizuoka Japan

TSUCHIHASHI, TATSUHIKO (JACK TSUCHIHASHI), shipping company executive; b. Kyoto, Japan, Feb. 4, 1940; m. Yoshimi Yoshioka, May 21, 1966; children: Chigusa, Chiaki, Akiro. BA, Kyoto U., 1963. With Kawasaki Kisen Kaisha (K line), Tokyo, 1963—; traffic mgr. K-Line-Kerr Corp. (K-Line), San Francisco, 1975-80; gen. mgr. liner dept. Kawasaki Kisen Kaisha (K line), Tokyo, 1987-90, dir., gen. mgr. energy dept., 1992-94, mng. dir., 1994-97; exec. v.p. K Line Am., Inc., Murray Hill, N.J., 1990-92; mng. dir. terminal bus. dept. Daito Corp., Tokyo, 1997-2000, pres., 2000—. Avocations: painting, soccer, hiking. Office: Daito Corp 2-1-13, Shibaura, Minato-ku, Tokyo 105-0014, Japan

TSUCHIYA, MASAHIKO, chemist; b. Tokyo, Dec. 25, 1931; s. Saburo and Matsue (Nagashima) T.; m. Etsuko Aoki, Nov. 8, 1959; children: Emiko, Toshihiko. B, U. Tokyo, 1953, M, 1955, D of Engring., 1958. Asst. U. Tokyo, 1959-62, lectr., 1962-65, assoc. prof., 1965-87, prof., 1987-88; prof. Yokohama U., Japan, 1987-97, prof. emeritus, 1997—; lectr. Hosei U., Tokyo, 1998—. Author, editor: Recent Development in Mass Spectrometry, 1988; editor-in-chief Mass Spectroscopy, 1978-92; inventor in field. Mem. Mass Spectrometry Soc. Japan, European Mass Spectrometry Soc. Avocations: golf, singing, travel. Home: 4-37-27 Kugayama, Tokyo 168-0082, Japan

TSUCHIYA, TETSU SATORU, humanities educator; b. Wakayama, Japan, Sept. 19, 1923; s. Hiroyoshi and Hana (Okada) T.; m. Haruko Muramatsu, Apr. 2, 1955; children: Eiko Okada, Michiko Narita. B of Arts and Letters,

Tokyo U., 1950, MA, 1955. Asst. prof. Yamanashi U., Kōfu, Japan, 1957-60; asst. prof. Meiji U., Tokyo, 1960-65, prof., 1965-94, emeritus prof., 1994—, dep. dean student affairs, 1969-72, dean acad. affairs, 1981-83; vis. rsch. fellow U. Ibadan, Nigeria,1973; vis. prof. U. Nairobi, Kenya, 1987, hon. prof., 1988—; vis. prof. Soka U., 1994-96. Author: Modernization and Africa, 1978, Literature of the Commonwealth, 1983, The Mind of the African, 1989, Embracing Africa-Its Culture and Anti-Apartheid Movement, 1990, Writers' Africa-Modern African Literature, 1994, Beyond Albion, 1994, My Life, My Dream for Africa, 1998; translator: Inside Africa (John Gunther), 1956, The Buried Day (C. Day Lewis), 1962, The Congo Since Independence (Catherine Hoskyns), 1966, The Palm-Wine Drinkard (Amos Tutuola), 1970, The Scotch (J.K. Galbraith), 1972, Emergency (Richard Rive), 1975, The Black Interpreters (Nadine Gordimer), 1975, Modern African Short Stories, 3 vols., 1977, Emperor Shaka The Great (Mazisi Kunene), 1979, East African Why (How, When) Stories (Pamela Kola), 1981, The Witch-Herbalist of the Remote Town (Amos Tutuola), 1983, A Soldier's Embrace & Other Short Stories (Nadine Gordimer), 1985, Father Come Home (Eskia Mphahlele), 1987, Cultural Exchange between Africa and Japan; contbr. articles and book revs. to profl. jours. 2d lt. Japanese mil., 1943-47. Mem. African Soc. in Japan (mem. working com. African fund 1980—), Royal African Soc., Kenya Oral Lit. Assn., Japan Pen Club. Avocation: traveling. Home: 1-32-27 Tsukushino Machida-shi, 194-0001 Tokyo Japan

TSUDA, ICHIRO, physicist, mathematician; b. Kume-Gun, Okayama, Japan, June 4, 1953; s. Takatomi and Kinko (Oomachi) T.; m. Atsuko Kubota, Apr. 8, 1984; children: Kiwako, Ayako. BS, Osaka U., Toyonaka, Japan, 1977; MS, Kyoto U., Japan, 1979, DSc in Physics, 1982. Rsch. scientist Rsch. Devel. Corp. Japan, Tokyo, 1982-83, group leader, 1983-88; assoc. prof. Kyushu Inst. Tech., Iizuka, Japan, 1988-93; prof. applied math. Hokkaido U., Sapporo, Japan, 1993—; sec. Japanese Neural Network Soc., Tokyo, 1988-91, mem. prize com., 1995, bd. dirs., 1997—; bd. dirs. Fuzzy Logic Systems Inst., Iizuka, 1992—. Author: Chaos Aspects of Brain (in Japanese), 1990, Chaos Scenarios of Complex Systems (in Japanese), 1996; editor Internat. Neural Network Soc., 1994—; patentee in field. Grantee-in-aid Ministry of Edn., Tokyo, 1988—. Mem. AAAS, Phys. Soc. Japan, Math. Soc. Japan, Japanese Neural Network Soc. Office: Hokkaido U Grad Sci Dept Math, Kita-10, Nishi-8, Kita-ku, Sapporo Hokkaido 060, Japan

TSUDA, TORU, communications engineering educator; b. Nagoya, Aichi, Japan, Feb. 11, 1934; m. Yuriko Shimane, Nov. 10, 1962; children: Yoko, Yasuko. BS, Chiba (Japan) U., 1958; DEng, Osaka (Japan) U., 1984. Section mgr. Fujitsu Labs., Kawasaki, Japan, 1971-73, mgr., 1973-82, dep. gen. mgr., 1982-86; gen. mgr. Fujitsu Ltd., Kawasaki, Japan, 1986-92; prof. Wakayama (Japan) U., 1992-99, Kogakkan (Japan) U., 1999—; part-time lectr. Tokyo Inst. Tech., 1976-85; v.chmn. Telecomm. Tech. Com., Tokyo, 1989-91; mem. exec. com. Ministry Post & Telecomm., Asian ISDN Coun., 1988-92, councilor, 1988; advisor Wakayama Rsch. Lab., Kainan, Japan, 1993-99; councilor Wakayama Indsl. Tech. Ctr., 1994-99. Author: ISDN Transmission and Signaling, 1992; contbr. articles to profl. jours.; patentee in field. Mem. IEEE, IEICE of Japan, NY Acad. Scis. Avocations: golf, music, reading, arts. Home: 2193-51 Kawawacho, Tsuzukiku Yokohama 224-0057, Japan Office: Kogakkan U Social Welfare, 7-1 Kasugaoka Nabari, Mie 518-0498, Japan

TSUDA, YOSHIKAZU, quality management specialist; b. Kobe, Japan, Oct. 9, 1935; s. Syojiro and Ishino (Kasai) T.; m. Rumiko Hosokura, July 13, 1963; 1 child, Akiko. BS, Osaka City U., 1960. Rsch. asst. Atomic Bomb Casualty Commn., Nagasaki, Japan, 1960-61; rsch. fellow Nihon U., Tokyo, 1961-65, Tokyo Met. U., 1965-68; asst. prof. Rikkyo U., Tokyo, 1968-72, assoc. prof., 1972-81, prof., 1981-97; advisor, lectr. in pvt. practice Tokyo, 1997—; lectr., councillor Union Japanese Scientists and Engrs., Tokyo, 1975—; chief lectr., course organizer Assn. Overseas Tech. Scholarship, Tokyo, 1982—. Co-editor: A Dictionary of Total Quality, 1985; author, supervisory editor: Total Quality Management in Multi-Natioal Deployment of Production, 1988. Mem. Japanese Soc. Quality Control, Am. Soc. Quality Control, Soc. Applied Statistics. Avocations: opera, playing oboe, skiing, swimming, travel. Office: 6-37-9-1902 Minamisenju, Arakawa Tokyo 116, Japan

TSUGE, KENYA, retired medical educator, social service executive; b. Okayama City, Japan, Nov. 25, 1921; s. Satokichi and Sugako (Urakani) T.; m. Ihoe Kan, Apt. 29, 1949; children: Akiko, Hiroko. MD, Okayama Med. Sch., Japan, 1945, grad., 1949. Asst. prof. Okayama U., 1954-64; prof. Hiroshima U., Japan, 1964-85; chmn. Hiroshima Prefectural Rehab. Ctr., Higashi-Hiroshima, Japan, 1985-94, cons., 1994—; pioneer in field of hand surgery Internat. Fedn. Socs. for Surgery of Hand, Paris, 1992. Author: Principles and Practices of Hand Surgery, 1965, Comprehensive Atlas of Hand Surgery, 1984, Approach the Elbow, 1991. Mem. Japanese Soc. Surgery Hand (hon.pres. 1968-69), Japanese Soc. Rheumatism and Joint Surgery (hon., pres. 1982-83), Japanese Orthopaedic Assn. (hon.). Home: A-810 1-9-26 Ujina Miyuki, Hiroshima 734-0015, Japan Office: Hiroshima Hand MicoSurg Ct, 9-5 Nakajima-cho Naka-ku, Hiroshima 730-0811, Japan

TSUI, ALEC YIU WA, stock exchange executive; b. Hong Kong, May 28, 1949; s. Robert and May (Young) T.; m. Mimi Lai; 1 child, Caine. BS, U. Tenn., 1975, M in Engring., 1976; postgrad., Harvard U., 1993. Mgr. fin. planning and analysis China Light & Power Co. Ltd., Hong Kong, 1986-88; gen. mgr. fin. and info. tech. SFC, Hong Kong, 1989-90, gen. mgr. fin., tech. and human resources, 1990-92, gen. mgr. commn. resources and licensing, 1992; asst. dir. licensing, gen. mgr. human resources Securities & Futures Commn., Hong Kong, 1992-93; dep. chief exec. The Stock Exch. of Hong Kong Ltd., 1996, CEO, 1997-2000; COO Hong Kong Exch. & Clearing Ltd., 2000; CEO Regent Group Ltd., 2000—; mem. Standing Com. on Co. Law Reform; mem. fin. svcs. adv. com. Hong Kong Trade Devel. Coun.; mem. banking and fin. industry tng. bd. Vocat. Tng. Bd. of Hong Kong. Active mem. investment sub-com. of gov. com. Beat Drugs Fund Assn. Office: Regent Group Ltd, Citicbank Plz, 3 Garden Rd, Central Hong Kong China

TSUI, DANIEL C., electrical engineering educator. PhD in Physics, U. Chgo., 1967. Rsch. assoc. U. Chgo., 1967-68; mem. technical staff Bell Labs., Murray Hill, N.J., 1968-82; Arthur LeGrand Doty prof. dept. elec. engring. Princeton (N.J.) U., 1982—. Contbr. articles to profl. jours. Recipient Buckley prize for Condensed Matter Physics, 1984, Benjamin Franklin medal in Physics, 1998, Nobel prize in Physics, 1998. Fellow AAAS, Am. Phys. Soc.; mem. NAS, Acad. Sinica. Fax: 609-258-6279. E-mail: tsui@ee.princeton.edu. Office: Princeton U Dept Elec Engring Rm B 426 Princeton NJ 08544-0001

TSUI, KAN-MING, clinical geneticist; b. Hong Kong, Oct. 23, 1963; s. Kam-Yeung Tsui and Yee-Ying To; m. Siu-Kuen Lam, Oct. 11, 1996. MBChB, Chinese U. Hong Kong, 1988. Mem. Royal Coll. Physicians (U.K.), DCH (Ireland), Fellow Hong Kong Acad. Medicine (Pediat.), Fellow Hong Kong Coll. Paediat. Med. officer Kwai Chung Hosp., Hong Kong, 1989, Princess Margaret Hosp., Dept. Orthopedics, Hong Kong, 1990, Hong Kong Govt. Dept. Health, Clin. Genetic Svc., 1991-93; vis. scholar U. Wales, 1993-94; clin. geneticist Hong Kong Dept. Health, Clin. Genetic Svc., 1994-97; pvt. practice Hong Kong, 1997—; hon. sec. organizing com. 2d Asian Pacific Regional Meeting Internat. Soc. Neonatal Screening, 1995; hon. sec. organizing com. 1st Hong Kong Med. Genetics Conf., 1996. Contbr. articles to med. jours. Recipient performance pledge Dir. Health Commendation, Hong Kong Dept. Health, 1996. Fellow Hong Kong Coll. Paediatricians. Office: Shop 110 Pierhead Plaza, Pierhead Garden Tuen Mun, Hong Kong China

TSUJI, AKIHIRO, finance company executive. CEO Tomen Corp., Osaka, Japan. Fax: 81-03-3588-9980. Office: Tomen Corp, 1-6-7 Kawara-machi, Chuo-ku Osaka 530-8622, Japan*

TSUJI, FUMIO, pharmacologist; b. Hyogo, Japan, Dec. 21, 1965; s. Tamotsu and Kayo (Nakamura) T. BS, Gifu Pharm. U., Japan, 1990. Rsch. scientist Santen Pharm. Co. Ltd., Osaka, Japan, 1990—; rsch. scientist Juntendo U. Sch. Medicine, Tokyo, 1994-97. Contbr. articles to profl. jours. Mem. AAAS, N.Y. Acad. Scis. Avocations: chorus, tennis. Home: 1-4-7-601 Yariyamachi, Osaka 540-0027, Japan OFfice: Santen Pharm Co, 3-9-19 Shimoshinjo, Osaka 533-8651, Japan

TSUJI, KOH, radiation oncologist; b. Kozagawa, Wakayama, Japan, Jan. 18, 1958; s. Sohta and Misao (Nagano) T.; m. Keiko Misaki, Jan. 22, 1989. Diploma, Wakayama Med. U., 1982. Staff radiologist, radiation oncologist Wakayama Med. U. Hosp., 1989-92, intern, 1982-83; resident radiologist Osaka City Med. U. Hosp., 1983-84; radiologist Nat. Wakayama Hosp., Mihama, 1985-87; staff researcher Fukui Med. U., Matsuoka, 1987-89; chief radiologist, radiation oncologist Minami-Wakayama Nat. Hosp., Tanabe, 1993—. Recipient rsch. grants Ministry Edn., Culture and Sci., 1991, Ministry Health and Welfare, 1995, 96, 97. Mem. Japan Radiol. Soc., Japan Radiation Rsch. Soc., Japanese Soc. for Therapeutic Radiology, Japan Soc. for Cancer Therapy. Avocations: playing flute, classical music. Office: Minami-Wakayama Nat Hosp, 27-1 Takinai, Tanabe Wakayama 646-8558, Japan

TSUJI, SHINGO, physician; b. Osaka, Japan, Mar. 16, 1957; s. Jun-ichi and Tomoe T.; m. Hitomi Hashimoto, Mar. 16, 1991; 1 child, Momoka. MD, Osaka U., Japan, 1981, PhD, 1994. Intern Osaka U. Hosp., Japan, 1981-82; physician Kansai Rohsai Hosp., Amagasaki, Japan, 1982-85, Osaka U. Hosp., 1986—; asst. prof. Osaka U. Grad. Sch. Medicine, 1997—. Author: Gastroenterologic Endoscopy, 2d edit.; inventor in field. Rsch. fellow U. Ala., Birmingham, 1988-90, Vanderbilt U., Nashville, 1992. Mem. Am. Gastroen. Assn., Japanese Soc. Gastroen. Endscopy, Japanese Soc. Gastroen., Japanese Soc. Exptl. Ulcer, Kanae Rsch. Found. Office: Osaka U, Dept Medicine, Osaka 565-0871, Japan

TSUJI, SHUICHI, physician, health facility administrator; b. Tokyo, May 23, 1961; s. Kimiyoshi and Haruko (Miki) T.; m. Yukari Watanabe, June, 1989; children: R isako, Asako. MD, Hokkaido U., Sapporo, Japan, 1986. Resident Keio U. Hosp., Tokyo, 1986-92; rschr. Keio U. Sports Medicine Rsch. Ctr., Yokahama, Japan, 1992-97; mem. med. staff Kitasato Inst. Hosp., Tokyo, 1997-98; owner Eminecross Medicine Ctr., Tokyo, 1999—; med. cons. Snow Bland Co., Tokyo, 1990—, Japan Basketball Assn., Tokyo, 1991—, Runessance Sports & Fitness Club, Tokyo, 1999—, Kidbics Assocs., Tokyo, 2000—. Author: Exercise, Nutrition and Stress, 1995, Mental Training in Slum Dunk, 1999; translator: Sports Nutrition, 1997, Body Wise Woman, 1997. Mem. Am. Coll. Sports Medicine, Melpomene Inst. Avocations: basketball, traveling. Office: Eminecross Med Ctr, 1-23-14-1F Minami Aoyama, Minato Tokyo 107 0062, Japan

TSUJI, TADAO, economics educator; b. Hikone, Shiga, Japan, May 30, 1926; s. Chuzabro and Hisako (Nakamura) T.; m. Keiko Okada, May 1, 1965; children: Kaoruko, Yasuaki. M in Econs., Doshisha U., Kyoto, Japan, 1957. Chief rschr. Nat. Planning Assn., Tokyo, 1959-66; lectr. Chiba Comml. Coll., Ichikawa, 1966-69; prof. econs. Doshisha U., Kyoto, 1969-97, prof. emeritus, 1997—. Author: International Capital Movements and Bank Rate, 1967, Capital Accumulation and Capital Investment Abroad, 1978, States and World Economies, 1987, Long Waves in the World Economy, 1995, International Economies in 21st Century, 1997. Buddhist. Avocations: fine arts, travel. Home: Higashi 2-12-13, Kami-o-oka Konanku, Yokohama 233-0001, Japan

TSUJI, TOHRU, company executive; b. Oita, Japan, Feb. 10, 1939; married; two sons. LLB, U. Tokyo, 1961. Joined Marubeni, 1961; various positions Marubeni Group Cos., apptd. gen. mgr. pulp dept., 1986, dep. gen. mgr. forest products divsn., 1989, gen. mgr. forest products divsn., 1991; mng. dir., 1995, sr. mng. dir., 1997, pres., 1999, exec. officer constrn., forest products and gen. merchandise, 1996; pres., CEO Marubeni Corp.; dir. Japan Paper Exporters Assn.; mem. subcom. on forest resources and subcom on pulp and paper Japan-Russian Bus. Coop. Com.; chmn. Japan Rubber Importers Assn., Japan Paper Importers Assn.; mem. Japan-New Zealand Businessmen's Conf.; mem. land and housing policies com., relocation of capital functions com. Japan Fedn. Econ. Orgns. Office: 5-7 Honmachi 2-chome, Chuo-ku Osaka 541-8588, Japan*

TSUJI, TOSHIZO, hospital administrator, educator; b. Kyoto, Japan, Jan. 2, 1932; s. Yasujiro and Yuki (Nakamura) T.; m. Yoshiko Taniguchi, Mar. 21, 1977; children: Mari, Toshifumi. MD, Kyoto Prefectural U. Medicine, 1957, DSc, 1964. Intern Kyoto 1st Red Cross Hosp., 1957-58; clin. fellow Kyoto Prefectural U. Medicine, 1959-60, asst. prof., 1971-74, assoc. prof., 1974-97; clin. fellow U. Ala. Med. Ctr., Birmingham, 1964-67, instr. medicine, 1967-68; postdoctoral fellow in molecular biology U. Edinburgh, Scotland, 1968-70; v.p. Kyoto Prefectural Yosanoumi Hosp., Iwataki, 1983—; pres. Kyoto Prefectural Yosanoumi Blood Ctr., Iwataki, 1974-83; prin. Kyoto Prefectural Nursing Sch., Iwataki, 1988-94; pres., med. juridical person Ohtha Found. Ohta Hosp., Kyoto, 1997—; mem. WHO, Kyoto, Japan, 1983—. Contbr. articles to profl. jours. Recipient med. diploma Japanese Ministry Health and Welfare, 1958; fellow NIH, 1965, European Molecular Biology Orgn., 1968. Fellow Japanese Soc. Internal Medicine, Japanese Soc. Gastroenterology, Japanese Soc. Hepatology (West Dist.); mem. AAAS, N.Y. Acad. Scis. Avocations: golf, tennis, stamps, gardening, classical music. Home: 988 Uoya, Miyazu Kyoto, Japan

TSUJII, KAORU, consumer products executive; b. Sakai, Osaka, Japan, Mar. 22, 1945; s. Uichi and Shizuko (Haji) T.; m. Yukiko Maruyama, Feb. 3, 1974; 2 children. MS, Osaka U., 1970, PhD, 1983. Dir. Tokyo 1st Rsch. Labs. Kao Corp., Tokyo, 1988-89, dir. Inst. for Fundamental Rsch., 1990-94, prin. rsch. Inst. for Fundmental Rsch., 1994-96; rsch. fellow Tokyo Rsch. Ctr. Kao Corp., 1996-98; team leader Japan Marine Sci. and Tech. Ctr., 1998—; vis. prof. Chiba (Japan) U., 1996-97; mem. evaluation com. Tokyo U. of Agrl. and Tech., Tokyo, 1996. Author: (with others) Organized Solutions, 1992; author: Surface Activity and Applications, 1995, Surface Activity, 1998; author, editor (series) Colloid Science, 1996. Recipient Outstanding Paper Presentation Am. Oil Chem. Soc., 1993, most valuable paper awrd Assn. Oil and Fat Industry Japan, 1997. Mem. Japan Chem. Soc. (Divsnl. award 1998), Japan Oil Chem. Soc. (Progress award 1982), Polymer Soc. Japan. Avocations: walking, reading books. Home: 3-9-26 Shodo, Sakae-ku, Yokohama 247-0022, Japan Office: Japan Marine Sci & Tech Ctr, 2-15 Natsushima-cho, Yokosuka 237-0061, Japan

TSUKADA, YUTAKA, medical educator, researcher; b. Sapporo, Hokkaido, Japan, May 27, 1938; s. Takumi and Minae Tsukada; m. Keiko Fujii, May 10, 1969; children: Takako, Mikiko, Seiko. MD, Hokkaido U., Sapporo, 1964, PhD, 1969. Asst. prof. Hokkaido U., Sapporo, 1971-74, assoc. prof., 1974-88; dir. rsch. divsn. SRL Inc., Tokyo, 1988—; vis. prof. Kyolin U., Tokyo, 1990—; councillor Japanese Cancer Assn., Tokyo, 1984—. Author: (with F.G. Lehman) Carcinoembyonic Proteins, 1979, (with C.W. Chu) Tumor Markers, 1981, (with H. Peeters) Protides of Biological Fluids, 1984, (with H. Hirai) Cell Differentiation, 1988, (with T. Kawai) Gene Diagnosis Manual, 1995. Recipient rsch. prize Cancer Rsch. Fund, 1983, prize for Nobel Cancer Treatment, Japan Med. Soc., 1986. Mem. Am. Assn. Cancer Rsch., Japanese Biochem. Assn. (councillor 1992—), Japanese Electrophysiology Assn. (councillor 1993—), Japanese Drug Delivery Sys. Assn. (councillor 1990—), Japanese Tumor Marker Assn. (mgr. 1986—), Japanese Cancer Assn. (councillor 1984—), Japanese Biomed. Assn. (councillor 1995—), Japanese Soc. for Gene Diagnosis and Therapy (mgr. 1995—), Japanees Soc. for Cancer Chemotherapy (councillor 1996), N.Y. Acad. Scis. Office: SRL Inc, 51 Komiya-cho Hachioji-shi, Tokyo 192, Japan

TSUKAMOTO, KATSUICHI, administrator Japanese research association; b. Itami City, Hyogo P., Japan, Sept. 19, 1921; s. Syukichi and Shizu (Koga) T.; m. Yoshiko Inoue, Aug. 19, 1945; children: Yasuko, Ikuko. Commd., Mil. Acad., Tokyo, 1940; grad., Imperial Army War Coll., Tokyo, 1945; student, Staff Coll., Camberley, Eng., 1960. Officer Japanese Army, 1940-45, Ground Self-Defense Force, Japan, 1951-78; editl. writer Sankei Newspaper Co., Tokyo, 1978-86; gen. sec. Rsch. Inst. for Peace and Security, Tokyo, 1986-96, pres., 1996-98, dir., advisr, 1998—. Author: (books) Korean Peninsula and Japanese Security, 1978, People's Armed Forces, North Korea, 1988. Lt. gen. cmmdr. Western Army, Kumamoto City, Japan, 1976-78. Decorated for Amity Promotion, Pres. Republic of Korea, 1971, Order of Merit, Prime Minister Japan, 1991. Avocations: reading, golf. Home: No 8-9-10 Tamagawa-Gakuen, Machida Tokyo 194-0041, Japan Office: Rsch Inst Peace & Security, No 6-1-20 Roppongi, Minatoku Tokyo 1060032, Japan

TSUKAMOTO, OSAMU, meteorologist, educator; b. Fukuyama, Hiroshima, Japan, Nov. 22, 1949. BS, Tohoku U., Sendai, Japan, 1972; MS, Kyoto (Japan) U., 1974, DSc, 1986. Rsch. assoc. Kyoto (Japan) U., 1974-84; assoc. prof. Okayama (Japan) U., 1984-96, prof., 1996—. Author: Recent Studies of Turbulent Phenomena, 1986; contbr. articles to scientific jours. Office: Okayama U, Tsushima-naka 3-1-1, 700 Okayama Japan

TSUKIJI, RICHARD ISAO, international marketing and financial services consultant; b. Salt Lake City, Jan. 31, 1946; s. Isamu and Mitsuie (Hayashi) T.; children: Angela Jo, Richard Michael. Grad. Sacramento City Coll., 1966; AA, U. Pacific, McGeorge Sch. Law, 1970-72. Grocery mgr. Food Mart, Inc., Sacramento, 1963-65; agy. supr. Takehara Ins. Agy., Sacramento, 1965-68; sales rep. Kraft Foods Co., Sacramento, 1969-71; sales mgr. Olivetti Corp., Sacramento, 1972-73; co-founder Mktg. Devel. and Mgmt. Coll., Sacramento, 1973, pres., 1973-74; pres. Richard Tsukiji Corp., Sacramento, 1974-77; CEO, chmn. bd. Assocs. Investment Group, Sacramento, 1978-82 ; chmn. bd. RichColor Corp. Sacramento, 1978-83, E.J. Sub Factories, Inc., Elk Grove, Calif., 1978-81; gen. agt. Comml. Bankers Life Ins. Co., 1974-82; chmn. bd. Phoenix Industries, Inc., Carson City, Nev., 1981-84, Databank, Inc., Roseburg, Oreg., 1982-83; pres. Computers, Etc. Corp., Carson City, 1982-84; regional v.p. U.S. BankCard Group, Salem, Oreg., 1993-95; pres. Richard Tsukiji Comm., Inc., Sacramento, 1993—; CEO RTC Wireless,Inc., 1994—, Bonaventure Group, Inc., Wilmington, Del., 1995—; bd. dirs. Michton, Inc., Pontiac, Mich., Hunt & Johnson, Inc., Phoenix Group, Melbourne, A.N.D. Corp., New Orleans, ET World Travel, Salt Lake City, Utah, Bonaventure Group, Inc., Wilmington, Del., Royal Am. Bank, Cayman Islands; exec. v.p. Edco Corp., Glide, Oreg., 1982-94; chmn. bd. Computer Edn. Resource Ctr., 1983-90, Bonaventure, Inc., Roseburg, 1984-91, RTC Wireless Group, Inc., Oakland, Calif., 1995—, RTC Wireless Group, Inc., San Jose, Calif.; editor ST World, Melrose, Oreg., 1985-88, publisher, 1988-91; editor ST World Reseller, 1988-91. Mem. Yolo County Oral Rev. Bd., 1975-76; bd. dirs. Valley Area Constrn. Opportunity Program, 1972-76, chmn., 1976-77; bd. dirs. Douglas County Citizens Community Involvement, 1980-82; bd. dirs. Computer Edn. Found., Sacramento, 1983-93, Access Sacramento Cable Television, 1993, Heart to Heart Found., 1993; chmn. pub. rels. Sacramento Asian Pacific C. of C., 1993—; bd. dirs. Chinese Am. Coun. Sacramento, 1994—; mem. Asian Cmty. Ctr., 1994—, Sacramento Chinese Cmty. Svc. Ctr., 1994—; bd. dirs. ARC Sacramento-Sierra chpt., 1995—, ARC Nat. Disaster Team, 1996—, Commr. Sacramento City Coun., Human Rels. and Fair Housing Commn., 1996—, No. Calif. Asian Peace Officers Assn., 1995—, Sacramento Chinese Cmty. Svc. Ctr., 1995—, Japanese Am. Citizens League, 1995—; democratic precinct committeeman, Melrose, Oreg., 1982-86; appt. mem. adv. coun. Sacramento City Minority/Women Bus. Enterprise, 1995; bd. dirs., v.p. Orgn. Chinese Ams., Inc., 1996; commr. Sacramento City/County Human Rights Commn., 1996—. Served with U.S. Army, 1962-63. Recipient Commendation, Calif. Senate, 1978. Mem. Internat. Assn. Fin. Planners, Associated Gen. Contractors, VIC-20 Users Group (pres. Roseburg 1983-84), Atari Computer Enthusiasts (pres. Sacramento 1983-85), U.S. Commodore Council (pres. Natl. 1984-85), Sacramento Jaycees (dir. 1977-78), Orgn. Chinese Ams. (v.p. Sacramento chpt. 1995—), Asian Alliance, Japanese Am. Citizens League, Sacramento Urban League. Democrat. Roman Catholic. Address: 905 K St Sacramento CA 95814-3511

TSUMBA, LEONARD LADISLAS, banker; b. Harare, Zimbabwe, Africa, June 27, 1943. BA in Bus. Adminstrn., Georgetown U., 1969; MA in Econs., Howard U., 1970; PhD in Econs., Va. Poly. Inst., 1975. Instr. econs. Hampton Inst., 1970-72; asst. prof. econs. Trinity Coll., Hartford, Conn., 1975-77; from internat. economist to monetary economist, v.p. Citibank NA, 1977-81; from exec. asst. to gov. to dep. gov. Res. Bank of Zimbabwe, Harare, 1981-87; mng. dir., group chief exec. Finhold, Harare, 1987-93; gov. Res. Bank of Zimbabwe, Harare, 1993—; cons. money and fin. divsn. UN Commn. on Trade and Devel., Switzerland, 1979. Omirron Delta Epsilon, Intl. Hon. Soc. in Econs., 1972; Beta Gamma Sigma, Hon. Soc. of Colleges, 1976. Fellow Inst. Dirs. (U.K.), Inst. Bankers (Zimbabwe, pres. 1990-91); mem. Omicron Delta Epsilon, Beta Gamma Sigma. Office: Res Bank Zimbabwe, 80 Samora Machel Ave, Harare Zimbabwe

TSUNASHIMA, YOSHISUKE, physical chemist, researcher, educator; b. Tokyo, Dec. 16, 1939; s. Ryohtaro and Kiyoko (Inoue) T.; m. Hiroko Iwata, Feb. 14, 1971. B, Waseda U., Tokyo, 1964; M, Tokyo Inst. Tech., 1966; PhD, Kyoto U., Japan, 1972. Asst. instr. Inst. Chem. Rsch. Kyoto U., Uji, Japan, 1970-87, asst. prof., 1987-93, prof., 1993—; rsch. instr. indsl. chemistry Kyoto (Japan) U., 1995—; rsch. fellow chemistry SUNY, Stony Brook, 1976-78; cons. Fuji Photo Film Co., Ashigara, Japan, 1996—; vis. lectr. phys. engring. Fukui U., Japan, 1997. Author: Polymer Solutions, 1993, (with others) Polymer Handbook, 4th edit., 1999; contbr. articles to profl. jours., chpts. to books. Mem. Soc. Polymer Sci., Cellulose Soc. Japan. Avocations: tennis, trekking, painting, carving. Office: Inst Chem Rsch, Kyoto U, Uji Kyoto 611-0011, Japan

TSUNEKAWA, YOSHIKI, engineering educator; b. Matsumoto, Nagano, Japan, June 23, 1945; m. Hiroe Kobayashi, Jan. 27, 1973; children: Tohko, Takehiro. BS, Nagoya (Japan) U., 1968, MS, 1970; PhD, Rutgers The State U., 1973. Rschr. Rutgers The State U., 1973-74; engr. Toyota Motor, Japan, 1974-81; assoc. prof. Toyota Tech. Inst., Nagoya, Japan, 1981-91, prof., 1991—; vis. assoc. prof. MIT, Cambridge, 1987. Contbr. articles to profl. jours. Fellow Japan Foundry Engring. Soc., Japan Thermal Spray Soc., Am. Soc. Metals Internat. Avocations: fishing, golf. Office: Toyota Tech Inst, 2-12 Hisakata, Tempaku, Nagoya 468-8511, Japan

TSUNEMATSU, KEN, lawyer; b. Kumamoto City, Japan, Mar. 30, 1932; s. Hikojiro and Toyo (Yamamoto) Ueda; m. Hiroko Ujiie, Mar. 3, 1973. BS in Law, U. Tokyo, 1955; M.Comparative Law, Columbia U., 1963. Qualified atty., Japan. Clk. Toshiba Corp., Kawasaki City, Japan, 1955-63; assoc. Sullivan & Cromwell, N.Y.C., 1963-64; assoc. Blakemore & Mitsuki, Tokyo, 1964-73, ptnr., 1973-87; ptnr. Tsunematsu Yanase & Sekine, Tokyo, 1987-99; of counsel Nagashima Ohno & Tsunematsu, Tokyo, 2000—; auditor SECOM Sci. Tech. Found., Tokyo, 1980—, Murata Sci. Found., Nagaokakyo City, Japan, 1985—; mem. adv. bd. on model law on secured transaction EBRD, London, 1992. Author: International Financial Law (Euromoney), 1983, Acquisition of Shares in a Foreign Country, Substantive Law and Legal Opinions, 1993; co-editor: International Securities Regulations (Oceana). Mem. bd. visitors Columbia U. Sch. of Law, N.Y.C., 1996—. Mem. Harlan Fisk Stone Fellowship (life). Home: 25-21-202 Hongo 1-chome, Bunkyo Tokyo 113-0033, Japan Office: Nagashima Ohno & Tsunematsu, 3-12 Kioicho Chiyoda-ku, Tokyo 102-0094, Japan

TSUNEMATSU, MASAO, English educator; b. Hirata-shi, Japan, Nov. 12, 1930; s. Takeo and Tsuruno (Araki) T.; m. Yoko Toyota, Jan. 28, 1959; 1 child, Yoshie Hirose. BE, Shimane U., Matsue, Japan, 1953; ME, Kent State U., 1958. English tchr. Izumo Indsl., Izumo-shi, Japan, 1953-56; from asst. to prof. English Shimane U., Matsue, 1956-90; prof. English Konan U., Kobe, Japan, 1990-99, Otemae U., Nishinomiya, Japan, 1999—; dean of students Shimane U., Matsue, 1982-84; dir. grad. divsn. Konan U., Kobe, 1995-97. Fulbright grant Kent State U., 1956-57, ACLS Am. studies grant U. Va., 1975-76, 81-82. Home: 1-1-8 Koshibara, 690-0012 Matsue Japan Office: Otemae Univ, 6-42 Ochayasho-cho, 662-8552 Nishinomiya Japan

TSUNEOKA, YUTAKA, molecular geneticist; b. Nabari, Mie, Japan, Apr. 15, 1959; s. Tadao and Shuu (Higuchi) T.; m. Yumi Teraoka, Mar. 9, 1986; children: Yu, Ei. BA, Tokyo U. Fgn. Studies, 1984; MD, Kagawa Med. U., 1990, PhD, 1994. Lic. physician, Japan. Rsch. assoc. Nat. Def. Med. Coll., Tokorozawa, Japan, 1994-96, 1998; postdoctoral asst. U. Cin., 1996-98; staff physician Onaga Hosp., Tokorozawa, 1998-99, Kaishindoh Hosp., Tokyo, 1999; postdoctoral asst. U. Cin., 2000—. Mem. AAAS. Avocations: tennis, skiing, baseball, cycling, basketball. Home: 8115 Village Dr Cincinnati OH 45242-4317 Office: U Cincinnati Dept Environ Health PO Box 670056 Cincinnati OH 45267-0056

TSUNEYUKI, TOSHIO, economics educator, translator; b. Kisarazu-city, Japan, June 23, 1947; s. Tadao and Hatsu (Kuzuta) T.; m. Chiyoko Miwatashi, Oct. 30, 1947; children: Fumiko, Miwako. Bachelor's, Internat. Christian U., Tokyo, 1972; Master's, Senshu U., Tokyo, 1974. Asst. Senshu U., Tokyo, 1974-78; lectr. Sanshu U., Tokyo, 1978-83; asst. prof. Senshu U., Tokyo, 1983-90, prof., 1990—; rsch. fellow Leicester (Eng.) U., 1980. Author: The English Society on the Eve of the Puritan Revoloution, 1990, Economics in the News, 2 vols., 1998; translator: The Culure of Capitalism,

1992. Mem. The Socio-Econ. History Assn., The Japanese Assn. Studies in English Comm., Japan Soc. Internat. Econs. Home: 4-3-16 Nozaki, Mitaka-city 181-0014, Japan Office: Senshu U Faculty Econs, 2-1-1 Higashi Mita Tama-ku, Kawasaki-city 214-0033, Japan

TSUNEZUKA, YOSHIO, surgeon; b. Maizuru-City, Kyoto, Japan, Dec. 18, 1965; s. Toshiro and Sumii (Saito) T.; m. Atsuko Tobita; 1 child, Haruka. MD, Kanazawa U., 1984, PhD, 1990. Dr. Kanazawa (Japan) U. Surgery (I), 1992-93, Koseiren Hosp., Takaoka, Japan, 1993-94; prof. dept. oncology and virology Kanazawa U. Cancer Rsch. Inst., 1994-95; dr. Nat. Shizuoka (Japan) Hosp., 1995-96; head physician Ishikawa Prefecture Ctr. Hosp., Kanazawa, 1997-98; instr. thoracic surgery Ishikawa Prefecture Cen. Hosp., Kanazawa, 1998—. Contbr. articles to profl. jours. Fellow Kanazawa U. Sch. Medicine, 1996-97. Mem. Japanese Assn. for Thoracic Surgery, Japan Surg. Soc. Avocation: scuba diving. Home: Taiyogaoka 13-7, 920-1154 Kanazawa Ishikawa, Japan Office: Ishikawa Prefect Cen Hosp, Dept Thoracic Surgery, 920-8530 Kanazawa Ishikawa, Japan

TSUNG, FUGEE, engineering educator, researcher; b. Taipei, Taiwan, 1967. BS, Nat. Taiwan U., Taipei, 1990; MS, U. Mich., 1993, PhD, 1997. Cert. quality engr.-in-tng. Asst. prof. dept. indsl. engrng. & engrng. mgmt. Hong Kong U. Sci. and Tech.; rsch. engr. Ford Motor Co., Mich. Contbr. articles to sci. jours.; guest editor spl. issue Indsl. Engrng. Rsch. Competitive Earmarked Rsch. grantee Govt. Rsch. Coun. Hong Kong, 1998-2000; rsch. fellow Chrysler, Mich., Rockwell Automotive Mfg. fellow Rockwell Internat., 1994. Mem. Am. Soc. Quality, Inst. Indsl. Engrng., Inst. Ops. Fax: 030852-23580062. E-mail: season@ust.hk.

TSUNO, KATSUSHIGE, electron optics researcher; b. Niigata, Japan, July 23, 1945; s. Teruo and Mie (Osawa) T.; m. Shoko Sato, May 6, 1972; children: Satoko, Takuya, Ryo. M Engrng., Tohoku U., Sendai, Japan, 1965, DEng, 1981. With JEOL Ltd., Tokyo, 1965—, mgr., 1986—; sr. researcher, 1996—; vis. rschr. Cambridge (Eng.) U., 1984-86; part-time lectr. Poly. U., Kanagawa, Japan, 1990—, Muroran (Hokkaido, Japan) Inst. Tech., 1993-96; mem. sci. adv. com. 5th Internat. Conf. on Charged Particle Optics; mem. program com. SPIE Charged Particle Optics. Exec. editor: J. Electron Microscopy. Patentee in field (Japan); contbr. articles to sci. publs. Mem. Am. Microscopical Soc., Electron Microscopical Soc. Japan (Seto award 1998). Home: 2-10-11 Mihori, Akishima 196, Japan Office: JEOL Ltd, 1-2 Musashino 3-chome, Akishima Tokyo 196, Japan

TSUNODA, HAJIME, obstetrician-gynecologist; b. Iwakuni, Yamaguchi, Japan, Jan. 4, 1956; s. Mamiko Yamamoto, Mar. 20, 1983; children: Aiko, Maiko, Yu. MD, U. Tsukuba, Ibaraki, Japan, 1981, PhD, 1989. Cert. in ob-gyn. Resident U. Tsukuba Hosp., 1981-87; asst. prof. U. Tsukuba, 1987—. Contbr. articles to profl. jours. Mem. N.Y. Acad. Sci. E-mail: htsunoda@md.tsukuba.ac.jp Fax: 81-298-53-3072. Home: Azuma 4-13-39, Tsukuba Ibaraki 305-0031, Japan Office: U Tsukuba Inst Clin Med, Tennoudai 1-1-1, Tsukuba Ibaraki 305-8575, Japan

TSUNOGAE, HIROSHI, education educator, administrator; b. Shimizu, Shizuoka, Japan, Apr. 19, 1935; s. Tokio and Yoshi (Nakamura) T.; m. Yoshiko Kawamura, Mar. 29, 1964; children: Yumiko Matsunaga, Hiroki. BEd, Tokyo Kyouiku U., 1958, MEd, 1960. Asst. Shizuoka (Japan) U., 1964-66, lectr., 1966-68, assoc. prof., 1968-77, prof., 1977-99, prof. emeritus, 1999—, dean dept. edn., 1996—; prof. Gakuen (Japan) U., 1999—; vis. prof. Leeds (Eng.) U., 1983-84; chmn. Coun. Life-Long Learning, Shizuoka Prefecture, 1994—. Author: Law and School Management, 1975, Powers Around Schools, 1988, Management of Institutions for Life-Long Learning, 1989, Administration of Life-Long Learning, 1996, An Introduction to the Study of Lifelong Learning, 1999. Recipient Min. of Edn. award Ministry of Edn., 1993. Mem. Japanese Assn. Life-Long Edn. (bd. dirs. 1980—), Japanese Assn. Sch. Edn. (bd. dirs. 1996—). Home: 2-2 Sakuragaoka-cho, Shimizu-shi Shizuoka 424-0836, Japan Office: Tokoha Gakuen U Dept Edn, 1-22-1 Sena, Shizuoka 420-0911, Japan

TSUNOGAI, SHIZUO, marine/atmospheric geochemistry educator/research; b. Shizuoka City, Japan, Aug. 2, 1938; s. Haruo and Mme (Honda) T.; m. Rei Utsue Kubota, Mar. 24, 1967; children: Urumu, Maki. BS, Tokyo Kyoiku U., 1961, MS, 1963, DSc, 1966. Asst. prof. faculty fisheries Hokkaido U., Hakodate, Japan, 1966-71, assoc. prof. faculty fisheries, 1971-81, prof. faculty fisheries, 1981-94; prof. environ. earth scis. Hokkaido U., Sapporo, Japan, 1994—; vice-chmn. internat. biosphere-geosphere program Internat. Coun. of Sci. Unions, 1992-95, v.p. sci. com. oceanic rsch., 1998—. Author: Marine Chemistry, 1983; contr. articles to profl. jours. Mem. AAAS, Am. Geophys. Union, Oceanography Soc. E-mail: mag-hu@ees.hokudai.ac.jp. Home: Kita 10 Nishi 1, Grand Heights 203, Sapporo Hokkaido 001 0010, Japan Office: Grad Sch Environ Earth Sci, Hokkaido U Kita 10 Nishi 5, Sapporo Hokkaido 060-0810, Japan

TSURUMI, YUKIO, cardiologist; b. Tokyo, Oct. 25, 1958; s. Norio and Mitsu Tsurumi; m. Setsuko Kodaka, Dec. 1, 1985; children: Tokuma, Yuka. MD, Gunma U., Maebashi, Japan, 1985; PhD, Tokyo Women's Med. U., 1996. Intern Gunma U., 1985-87; resident Tokyo Women's Med. U., 1987-90; dir. cardiology Honda Meml. Tohoku Cardiovasc. Ctr., Koriyama, Japan, 1992-94; chief interventional cardiology Tokyo's Women's Med. U., 1996—, dir. Cardiac Catheterization Lab., 1996—; advisor Japanese Soc. Intracardiovasc. Imaging, Tokyo, 1998, Japanese Soc. Interventional Cardiology, 1999. Contbr. articles to profl. jours. Mem. Japanese Soc. Interventional Cardiology. Fax: 81-3-3356-0441. Office: Tokyo Womens Med U, 8-1 Kawada-Cho, Shinjuku Tokyo 162-8666, Japan

TSURUTA, KIYOHARU, communications company executive, consultant; b. Shimoda, Shizuoka, Japan, Oct. 27, 1925; s. Yasujiro and Toyoko (Takano) T.; m. Kimiko Hirose, Mar. 16, 1954; children: Naoyuki, Jiro. BS, Waseda U., Tokyo, 1950. Bd. dirs. IBM Japan, Tokyo, 1984-86; sr. exec. v.p. NI&C Internat., Tokyo, 1988-90, pres., 1990-92; exec. advisor InfoCom Rsch., Tokyo, 1991-94; statutory auditor Cresco, Tokyo, 1992-97; exec. advisor Molex Japan, Tokyo, 1992-97; cons. Telecomm. Tech. Coun., Tokyo, 1985-87, Industry Structure Coun., Tokyo, 1987-88; pres., chmn. Pacific Telecomm. Coun., Honolulu, 1987-91. Mem. Info. Processing Soc. Japan (bd. dirs. 1984-86). Avocations: earthenware, chorus, travel. Home: 2-12-5 Zengyo, Fujisawa Kanagawa 251-0871, Japan

TSURUTA, TAKUHIKO, publishing executive. Pres., CEO Nihon Kezai Shimbun, Inc., Nikkei, Japan. Office: Nihon Keizai Shimbum Inc, 1-9-5 Otemachi Chiyoda-ku, Tokyo 100-8066, Japan*

TSUSHIMA, TOSHIO, endocrinologist, researcher, medical educator; b. Tokyo, Mar. 13, 1937; s. Ichiro and Hisae Tsushima; m. Setsuko Katahira, June 6, 1967; children: Yuko, Taro, Jiro. MD, U. Tokyo, 1963, PhD, 1971. Intern U. Tokyo, 1963-64, resident, 1964-71; rsch. fellow McGill U., Montreal, Can., 1972-73, U. Manitoba, Winnipeg, Can., 1973-74; asst. prof. U. Tokyo, 1975-78; assoc. prof. Tokyo Women's Coll., 1978-81, prof. medicine, 1981—; chief investigator Inst. Growth Sci., Tokyo, 1981-96. Mem. editl. bd. Endocrine Jour., 1985; contbr. more than 180 articles to profl. jours. Recipient award Japan Med. Rsch. Found., 1980; grantee Japanese Govt., 1975-98. Mem. Japan Endocrine Soc. (bd. dirs. 1975), Japan Thyroid Soc. (bd. dirs. 1983, pres. 1999—), Am. Endocrine Soc., N.Y. Acad. Scis. Office: Tokyo Womens Med U, Kawadacho 8-1, Shinjuku-ku Tokyo 162, Japan

TSUSHIMA, YUKO, novelist; b. Tokyo, Mar. 30, 1947; d. Shuji and Michiko T.; 2 children. BA, Shirayuri Women's Coll., 1968, MA, 1969. Author novels: Dōji no kage, 1973, Mugura no haha, 1975, yorokobi no shima, 1978, Chōji, 1978 (Women's Lit. award 1978), Hikari no ryōbun, 1979 (Noma award for New Writers 1979), Yama o hashiru onna, 1980, Moeru Kaze, 1980, Suifu, 1982, Hi no Kawa no hotori de, 1983, Danmariichi, 1984, Ōma monogatari, 1984, Yoru no hikari ni owarete, 1986, Mahiru e, 1988, Yume no Kiroku, 1988, The Shooting Gallery and Other Stories, 1988, Kusamura: jisen tanpenshu, 1989, Oinaru yume yo hikari-yo, 1991, Kagayaku Mizu no jidai, 1994, Kaze-yo Sorao kakeru Kaze-yo, 1995, Hinoyama-Yamazaruki, 1998, Watashi, 1999. Recipient Izumi Kyōka prize, 1977, Kawabata Yasunari prize, 1983, Yomiuri prize, 1987, Tanizaki prize, 1998, Noma prize, 1998. Mem. Japan Writer's Assn., Lit. Women's Assn. Office: Sakai Lit Agy, 1-7.12 Kanda-Jinbo-cho, Chiyoda-ku Tokyo 106, Japan

TSUTAKAWA, EDWARD MASAO, management consultant; b. Seattle, May 15, 1921; s. Jin and Michiko (Oka) T.; m. Hide Kunugi, Aug. 11, 1949; children: Nancy Joyce, Margaret Ann Langston, Mark Edward. Student, U. Wash., 1941, Wash. State U., 1949. Free-lance comml. artist Spokane, 1943-47; artist Maag & Porter Comml. Printers, Spokane, 1947-54; organizer Litho Art Printers, Inc., Spokane, 1954—, gen. mgr., pres., 1965-80; charter organizer, dir. Am. Comml. Bank, 1965-80; prin. E.M. Tsutakawa Co., bus. cons. U.S., Japan Trade Negotiator, 1980-89; v.p., operation officer, dir. Mukogawa Ft. Wright Inst. Pres. emeritus Spokane-Nishinomiya Sister City Soc., Sister Cities Assn. of Spokane; mem. Eastern Wash. State Hist. Soc.; bd. dirs. Spokane Regional Internat. Trade Alliance, Leadership Spokane. Recipient Disting. Svc. medal Boy Scouts of Japan, 1967, Cultural medal in Edn., Japan, 1985, Disting. Svc. award City of Nishinomiya, 1971, Disting. Svc. to Expo '74 State of Wash., 1974, Book of Golden Deeds award Exch. Club, 1978, Disting. Cmty. Svc. award UN Assn., 1979, Whitworth Coll., 1987, Svc. to Youth award Spokane YMCA, 1988, Silver Hawk medal Boy Scouts Japan, 1997, Internat. Rels. and Trade Pioneer Recognition, Spokane Area C. of C., 1998; decorated Order of Sacred Treasure medal Govt. of Japan, 1984. Mem. Japanese Am. Citizens League, Japan Am. Soc. Wash. State (pres.'s award 1991), Kiwanis (Spokane). Methodist. Home: 4116 S Madelia St Spokane WA 99203-4229

TSUTANI, KIICHIRO, clinical pharmacologist, physician; b. Kanazu-machi, Fukui-ken, Japan, Mar. 5, 1950; s. Seiichi Tsutani and Fumiko Shimakawa; m. Yoshiko Kudo; children: Yuri, Mari, Eri. BA, Tokyo Inst. Tech., 1972; MD, Tokyo Med. and Dental U., 1979, PhD, 1983. Cert. tchg. expert Kampo (Japanese herbal). Physician Oriental Medicine Rsch. Ctr., Kitasato Inst., Tokyo, 1979-81; med. officer traditional medicine WHO Regional Office for We. Pacific, Manila, 1984-90; rsch. fellow Takami program in internat. health Harvard Sch. Pub. Health, Boston, 1990-91; assoc. prof. Tokyo Med. and Dental U., 1992—; vis. dir. Kitasato Inst., Tokyo, 1992—; dir. internat. affairs dept. Japan Soc. Acupuncture, 1994—; mem. working group ICH M1, Tokyo, 1995—; chmn. Japanese Informal Network for Cochrane Collaboration, 1995—. Mem. editl. bd. Am. Jour. Chinese Medicine, 1993—; mem. internat. adv. bd. Bd. Complimentary Therapies in Medicine, 1993—. Recipient Takami Rsch. Encouragement award Inst. Seijon and Life Scis., 1992, 32d Japan Translation Culture award Japan Translators Assn., 1995, 9th Acad. Encouragement award Japan Soc. Oriental Medcine, 1995. Shinto-Buddhist. Avocations: Oriental art, visiting hot springs. Home: 6-15-14-705 Shirogane, Minatoku Tokyo 108-0072, Japan Office: Tokyo Med Dent U Clin Pharm, 2-3-10 Kanda-surugadai, Cl Pharm Chiyoda-ku, Tokyo 101-0062, Japan

TSUTANI, MOTOHIRO, accounting educator; b. Handa, Aichi, Japan, Dec. 22, 1935; s. Hideichi and Fusano Tsutani; m. Chiyo Suzuki, Apr. 1, 1960; children: Yoko, Takako. BA in Commerce, Nagoya U. Commerce, Nagoya, Japan, 1958; MA in Commerce, Meijo U., 1960. Asst. commerce and bus. admindtrn. Nagoya U. Commerce and Bus. Adminstrn., 1960-61; instr. Nagoya U., 1961-67, assoc. prof., 1967-74, prof., 1974—; chmn. student com. Nagoya U. Commerce and Bus. Adminstrn., 1984-91. Author: Structure of E. Walb's Balance Sheet, 1963, Increase & Decrease Bookkeeping, 1983, Structure of Double-entry Bookkeeping, 1985, Development of Chinese Accounting, 1988, The World History of National Auditing, 1993, The Chinese Accounting History, 1998. Chief of a ward Yoshizumiku Miyoshicho Aichi, Miyoicho, Japan, 1964; mem. Socio Ednl. Com., Miyoshicho, 1966-70. Mem. Gen. Assn. Japan Indsl. and Edn. (pres. 1980-90, hon. mem. 1990—), Japan Acctg. Assn., Am. Acctg. Assn., Japan Auditing Assn., Japan Acctg. History Assn., Internat. Acctg. Computerization Conf. (mem. preparation com. 1991-92, bd. dirs. 1992—). Home: 2003 Takashima 1 chome, Tenpakuku, Nagoya 468-0022, Japan Office: Nagoya U Commerce Bus Admin, 4 Sagamine, Komenoki, Nissinshi Aichi 470-0193, Japan

TSUTSUI, KAZUYOSHI, medical educator; b. Hiroshima, Japan, Sept. 30, 1952; s. Giro and Haruko (Saga) T.; m. Hiroko Teranishi, Aug. 1, 1987. BS, Waseda U., Tokyo, 1976, ScD, 1981. Vis. scientist U. So. Calif., 1988-89; asst. prof. Kobe U. Sch. Medicine, 1990-91; assoc. prof. Hiroshima U., 1992-95, prof. brain sci., 1996—; mem. internat. joint rsch. project with U.K., 1997—, project for integrated brain rsch., Japan, 1999—. Editor Zool. Sci., 1998—; editl. advisor Neuroendocrinology Letters, 1999—. Recipient Okuma award Waseda U., 1981. Shinto. Avocation: pictures. Home: 2-4-5 Hatsukaichi-chi, Hiroshima 739, Japan Office: Hiroshima Univ, Fac Integrated Arts/Scis, Higashi Hiroshima 739-8521, Japan

TSUTSUI, YOSHIRO, educator; b. Tokyo, Mar. 8, 1950; s. Toshihiro and Tamiko (Fujita) T.; m. Hiroko Kataiwa; 4 children. BS, Tokyo Univ. Edn., 1974; BA, Osaka City (Japan) U., 1979; MA in Econs., Osaka U., 1981, PhD in Econs., 1989. Rsch. assoc. Osaka U., 1982-83, assoc. prof., 1991-93, prof., 1993—; rsch. assoc. Nagoya (Japan) City Univ., 1983-84, asst. prof., 1984-87, assoc. prof., 1987-91; vis. fellow Yale U., New Haven, 1986-88; spl. rschr. Inst. for Posts & Telecomm. Policy, Tokyo, 1990-92; vis. scholar U. Calif., San Diego, 2000—. Author: Financial Markets and Banking Industry, 1988 (Nikkei Economics Book prize 1988); editor: Japanese Capital Markets, 1996; assoc. editor Econ. Studies Quarterly, Tokyo, 1994-95, editor: Rev. Monetary and Fin. Studies, Tokyo, 1996-99; contbr. articles to profl. jours. Fellow Japan Soc. Monetary Econs., Japan Fin. Econs. Assn., Stock Price Evaluation Com. (vice-chmn.). Avocation: badminton.

TSUTSUMI, OSAMU, chemist; b. Nagasaki, Japan, Dec. 3, 1970; s. Yutaka and Machiko Tsutsumi; m. Shizuka Douzono, June 22, 1997; 1 child, Erika. BS, Kumamoto U., 1993; MS, Tokyo Inst. Tech., 1995, PhD, 1998. Rsch. fellow Japan Soc. for Promotion Sci., 1997-99; fellow Calif. Inst. Tech., 1998-99; rsch. assoc. U. Ariz., 1999; asst. prof. Tokyo Inst. Tech., 1999—. Office: Tokyo Inst Tech Chem Resources Lab, 4259 Nagatsuta Midori-ku, Yokohama 226-8503, Japan

TSUTSUMI, YOSHIAKI, transportation executive; s. Yasujiro T.; married; 3 children. Owner Seibu Lions Baseball Team, 1979—; chmn. Seibu Rlwy. Co. Ltd., Tokyo, Kokudo Corp., Tokyo; chmn. bd. dirs. Seibu Rlwy. Co. Ltd., Tokyo. Avocations: skiing, photography. Office: 1-11-1 Kusunokidai, Tokorozawa City Saitama PR 359, Japan*

TSUYUMU, SHINJI, molecular plant pathologist; b. Shanghai, China, July 6, 1944; parents Masashi and Tomiko (Kawada) T.; m. Masako Yamaji, June 22, 1969; four children. BA, Shizuoka U., 1967; MA, U. Calif. Davis 1970; PhD, U. Hawaii, 1973. Postdoctoral researcher Purdue U., West Lafayette, Ind., 1973-74; assoc. prof. Shizuoka U., 1974-94, prof., 1994—, dir. Inst. for Molecular Biology and Biotech., 1998—; vis. prof. Kans. State U., Manhattan, 1982-83. Author: Encyclopedia for Plant Pathology, 1995; contbr. articles to profl. jours. Grantee Japan Min. Edn., 1997—; recipient award Saito-Shorei Found., Shizuoka, 1984, Sapporo Biosci. Found., 1989. Recipient award Japanese Soc. Plant Pathology, 1998. Fellow Plant Pathol. Soc. Japan; mem. AAAS, Am. Soc. Microbiology, Molecular Biology Soc. Japan. Roman Catholic. Avocations: modern jazz, baseball. Office: Shizuoka U Faculty Agr, 836 Ohya, Shizuoka 422, Japan

TSUZAWA, MASAMI, association administrator; b. Changchun, Kirin, China, Jan. 18, 1923; s. Yoshihiko and Harue (Nishikawa) T.; m. Teruko Arai, Oct. 17, 1952; 1 child, Genich. B of Engrng., Tokyo U., 1944. Prof. Police Comms. Sch. Nat. Police Agy., Tokyo, 1950-58, chief radio comm. divsn. Comm. Bur., 1964-73, dir. Comm. Bur., 1973-78; exec. dir. Japan Traffic Mgmt. Tech. Assn., Tokyo, 1979-92, v.p., 1992-99, pres., 2000—; spl. mem. Nomination Com. for Superior Govt. Ofcls., Tokyo, 1960-64; rep. for Japan gen. meeting Internat. Criminal Police Orgn., Paris, 1967, chmn. com. meeting Asia region, Tokyo, 1974; commr. Radio Tech. Coun., Ministry of Posts and Telecomms., Tokyo, 1973-78. Author: Theory and Practice on VHF Vehicular Radio Communications, 1961, Security and Electronics, 1994; author, editor: UHF SSB Multi-directions and Multi-Channels Radio System, 1971. Mem. IEEE (life, sr. mem.), Inst. Electronics, Info. and Comm. Engrs. (Tech. medal 1978), Nippon Club (councillor 1997—), Sagami Country Club. Mem. Liberal Democratic Party. Buddhist. Avocations: golf, contract bridge, go, haiku, cruising. Home: 4-14-15 Minami Tsukushino, Machida Tokyo 194-0002, Japan Office: Japan Traffic Mgmt Tech Asn, 6 Ichigaya-Tamachi 2-Chome, Shinjuku-ku Tokyo 162-0843, Japan

TSVETKOV, OLEG BORIS, themophysicist, researcher; b. Leningrad, Russia, Sept. 7, 1939; s. Boris Iacov and Alexandra Ivan (Sutiaginskaia) T.; m. Marianna Konstantin Utkina, Oct. 17, 1938; children: Svetlana, Alexandra. Diploma in engring., Tech. Inst. of Refrigeration, Leningrad, 1961, PhD, 1965, DSc, 1983; postgrad., Northwestern U., Evanston, Ill., 1979-80, U. Md., 1987-88. Rsch. asst. prof. Tech. Inst. of Refrigeration, Leningrad, 1964-68, acting dir. rsch. dept., 1970-79, postdoctoral fellow, 1980-83, pro rector rsch., 1983-99; assoc. prof. Royal U., Phnom-Penh, Cambodia, 1968-70; vis. scholar Northwestern U., Evanston, 1979-80; vice chmn. 14th World Congress of Refrigeration, Moscow, 1975; head of dept. State Acad. Refrigeration and Food Tech. (formerly Tech. Inst. Refrigeration), St. Petersburg, 1991—; mem. nat. com. thermophysics of Russian Acad. Scis., Moscow, 1997—. Author: Thermal Conductivity of Refrigerants, 1984; mem. editl. bd. Refrigeration Bus., 1995—; inventor in field. Recipient Excellence in Tchg. and Rsch. medal USSR Ministry of Higher Edn., Moscow, 1981, award for Excellence in Higher Edn. Russia, 1999; rsch. grantee Internat. Sci. Found., 1994. Mem. Internat. Union of Pure and Applied Chemistry, Internat. Acad. Refrigeration (bd. govs., chmn.), Internat. Acad. Refrigeration (bd. govs., chmn., v.p. 1999—), Internat. Inst. Refrigeration (v.p. com. B1 1995—), Internat. Acad. Scis. in Higher Edn., Sci. and Tech. Soc. of Food Industry (pres. 1990—), Assn. Pro Rectors, Acad. Engring., N.Y. Acad. Scis. Avocations: travel, gardening, photography, poetry, theater. Home: 31 Moika Embankment Apt 54, 191186 St Petersburg Russia Office: State Acad Refrigeration & Food Tech, 9 Lomonosov St, 191002 St Petersburg Russia

TSYBAKOV, BORIS SOLOMON, information theory researcher, educator; b. Moscow, May 14, 1934; s. Solomon Mark and Evdokia Tikhon (Tsybakova) Pinsker; m. Lidia Sergey Tsybakova, Oct. 14, 1956; 1 child, Alexander. D of Sci. in Engring., Moscow Inst. of Physics/Tech. Jr. rschr. Inst. for Radio and Electronic Engring., Moscow, 1958-63, sr. rschr., 1963-77; head of lab. Inst. for Info. Transmission Problems, Moscow, 1977—; prin. engr. Qualcomm, Inc., San Diego, 1999—; prof. Moscow Inst. of Physics and Tech., 1965-93. Assoc. editor, editl. bd. Problems of Info. Transmission jour., 1965—; editor Wireless Personal Comms., An Internat. jour., 1992—, Jour. Comms. and Networks, 1999—; contbr. articles to profl. publs. Recipient Prominent Comm. Profl. of Russia award Pres. of Russia, 1996. Mem. IEEE, Russian Acad. Sci. Club. Avocation: lawn tennis. Office: Qualcomm Inc 5775 Morehouse Dr Rm L400G San Diego CA 92121-1714

TSYFANSKY, SEMYON LYEV, mechanical engineer, educator, consultant; b. Vasilkov, Ukraine, Aug. 16, 1932; s. Solomon and Mariya Lazar (Kaminskaya) T.; m. Nadezda Alfons Kistenis, Sept. 5, 1958; children: Vadim, Yuliya. Mech. Engr., Aviation Engrng. Sch., Kharkov, Ukraine, 1955; Cand.Sc.Eng., Air Force Acad., Leningrad, Russia, 1965; Dr.Sc.Eng., Higher Commn. Moscow, 1970; Dr.Habil.Sc.Eng., Coum. of Sci., Riga, 1992. Assoc. prof. Mil. Engrng. Sch., Perm, Russia, 1965-70, chief dept. mil. engrng., 1970-75; prof. Polytech. Inst., Riga, 1975-86; chief rschr. Tech. U., Riga, 1986-91, chief of lab., 1991—; cons. VNDT Nondestructive Testing, Carmiel, Israel, 1997—. Author: Oscillations of Vibromachines, 1991; contbr. articles to profl. jours. Col. Russian Air Force, 1950-75. Recipient Laureate of State Prize, Govt. Lativa, 1990, Laureate, Exhbn. of the USSR, Moscow, 1984, Internat. Exhbn. "Expo-85", Plovdiv, Bulgaria, 1985.n. Mem. Nat. Com. in Mechanics, N.Y. Acad. Scis. Avocation: woodcarving. Office: Riga Technical Univ, 1 Kalku St, LV-1658 Riga Latvia

TSYMBALENKO, VLADIMIR LEONIDOVICH, experimental physicist, researcher, consultant; b. Vinnitsa, Ukraine, USSR, May 19, 1949; s. Leonid Vladimirovich and Natalya Ivanovna (Raketskaya) T.; m. Elena Evgen'evna Gukova, Jan. 20, 1979; 1 child, Natalya. Red diploma in physics and engrng., Moscow Phys.-Tech. Inst., 1972; PhD, Inst. for Phys. Problems, Moscow, 1974, postgrad., 1974-77. Rschr. Inst. Solid State Physics, Chernogolovka, USSR, 1977-79; rschr. Inst. Atomic Energy, Moscow, 1979-85, sr. rschr., 1985—. Contbr. articles to sci. jours., including Phys. Letters. Recipient Kurchatov prize in Quantum nucleation, 1996. Avocations: experimental physics, mountaineering. Home: Isaakovskii b2-1-125, 123181 Moscow Russia Office: RRC Kurchatov Inst, sq Kurchatov 1, 123182 Moscow Russia

TSYPLAKOV, OLEG GEORGIEVICH, engineering educator, consultant; b. St. Petersburg, Russia, Apr. 9, 1933; s. Georgy Nikonovich and Olga Nikolaevna (Kopytina) T.; m. Rajsa Alexeevha Kabanova, June 24, 1954; children: Georgy, Olga. Diploma in mech. engring., Leningrad's Mech. Inst., St. Petersburg, 1958, PhD, 1963, DSc, 1970. Cert. engr. Head workshop Plant Mech. Equipment, St. Petersburg, 1957-58; lectr. Coll. Metallurgy, St. Petersburg, 1958-64; head tech. dept. Izhorsky Zavod, St. Petersburg, 1958-60; lectr. Leningrad Mech. Inst., St. Petersburg, 1960-64, asst. prof., 1964-88; prof. Baltic State U. Tech., St. Petersburg, 1988—; lectr. Profl. Tng. Inst., St. Petersburg, 1960-82; rsch. supr., 1965; rsch. cons., 1974-84; mem. state evaluation commn., St. Petersburg, 1990—. Author: Principles of Forming Fiber Glass Shells, 1958, Scientific Principles of Technology of Composite Materials, 1975, Technological Design of Products of Composite Materials, 1984, Technological Priniciples and Experience of Creation of Products of Composite Materials, 1993. Named Honored Inventor Russian Govt., 1984; recipient Golden award Expo Ctr., 1972-80. Mem. Internat. Acad. Informatization (chmn. coun. inventors 1983). Avocations: poetry, opera, gardening, hunting. Office: Baltic State U Tech, 1st Krasnoarmeiskaya, 1, 198005 Saint Petersburg Russia

TU, CHENCHIANG, environmental services administrator; b. Taoyuan, Taiwan, Republic of China, Mar. 4, 1966; s. Hsi-Ling and Yueh-Chung (Chiu) T.; m. Huai-Hsuan Peng. BA, Nat. Taipei Inst. Tech., 1986; MS, Marquette U., 1992. Cert. hazardous waste treatment technician. Project mgr. Waste Minimization Tech. Inc., Taipei, Taiwan, 1992-96; asst. mgr. ERM-Taiwan, Taipei, 1996-97; project mgr. CECL-Taiwan, Taipei, 1997—; rsch. asst. Marquette U., Milw., 1991-92. Contbr. articles to profl. jours. Pres. Chinese Student Assn. Marquette U., 1991-92. Corporal Mil. Police of the Army, 1986-88. Avocations: traveling, hiking. Home: 8F No 49 Lane 30, Chengkung Rd Sec 4, Taipei 114 ROC, Taiwan Office: China Environ Cons Ltd, 14F No 2 Fu Hsing North Rd, Taipei 104 ROC, Taiwan

TU, CHUANYI, space physics educator, researcher; b. Beijing, July 24, 1940; s. Yugong Tu and Nonghua Xiao; m. Jinhua Xiao; children: Fangqiu, Ronghui. Grad., Peking U., Beijing, 1964. Asst. prof. Peking U., Beijing, 1972-78, instr., 1978-92, full prof., 1992—; prin. investigator rsch. Nat. Natural Sci. Found. China, 1985—. Author: Solar-Terrestrial Space Physics, 1988; first author: MHD Structures, Waves and Turbulence in the Solar Wind, 1995; assoc. editor Jour. Geophys. Rsch.-Space Physics, Am. Geophys. Union, 1990-92. Recipient award of Chinese natural sci., Nat. Sci. and Tech. Com., Beijing, 1989, Wong Dan Ping Sci. prize Com. of Wong Dan Ping Sci. Prize, Beijing and Hong Kong, 1992, Vikram Sarabhei medal Com. on Space Rsch. Internat. Coun. Sci. Unions, 1992; rsch. fellow dept. mech. engring., Catholic U. of Am., 1980-81, fellow Max-Planck-Inst. für Aeronomie, Katlenberg-Lindau, Germany, 1988-90. Mem. Chinese Soc. Space Sci., Am. Geophys. Union. Fax: 10-62564095. E-mail: cytu@public3.bta.net.cn. Office: Dept Geophysics, Peking Univ, Beijing 100871, China

TU, GUANGNAN, ethnologist; b. Huangpi, Hubei, China, Jan. 10, 1928; s. Yuntan Tu and Yan Ying; m. Demian Xu, Oct. 11, 1959; children: Jie, Xin. BA, Macalester Coll., 1950; diploma, The Sch. Diplomacy, Beijing, 1957. Brit. sect. mem. dept. Europe and Africa Ministry Fgn. Affairs, Beijing, 1950-55; rsch. fellow Inst. Internat. Studies, Beijing, 1959-61; com. mem. acad. com. Chinese Acad. Social Scis.-Inst. L.Am. Studies, Beijing, 1980-88, dep. dir. info. divsn., 1981-83, dep. dir. divsn. L.Am. history and politics, 1983-85; advisor to Chinese Assn. for Global Ethnic Studies, Beijing, 1997—; mem. coun. Western Returned Scholars Assn., Beijing, 1950-66; chmn. br. com. of the revolutionary com. Chinese Kuomintang, CASS, Beijing, 1993-99. Contbg. author: Ethnography Vol. of Ency. China, 1986; translator: Marx and the Third World, 1981 (Inst.'s First Hon. award 1989), The Political Economy of Development and Underdevelopment, 1984 (Inst.'s Second Hon. award 1989); assoc. editor in chief: Global Ethnological Dictionary, 1993. Active Revolutionary Com. of the Chinese Kuomintang.

Recipient hon. cert. for outstanding contbn. in social scis. Chinese State Coun., 1992. Mem. Am. Returned Scholars Assn. (coun. mem. 1994—), L.Am. Returned Students Assn. (advisor 1995—), Xuan Wu Dist. Joint Friendship Union of Overseas Compatriots and Friends (mem. standing coun. 1994—). Avocations: shadow boxing, social dancing, playing Chinese chess and volleyball. Home: Xuan Wu Dist, Yaziqiao Nanli 2-1-301, Beijing 100055, China Office: Inst Latin Am Studies CASS, PO Box 1104, Beijing 100007, China

TU, GUI YI, surgeon; b. Shanghai, China, Feb. 3, 1928; m. Yun Lin Hong, Apr. 25, 1955; 1 child, Jun Patrick. Grad., St. John's U., 1952, Shanghai Second Med. Coll., 1953. Resident, attending surgeon Dept. Otolaryngology, Peking Union Med. Coll., 1953-62; attending surgeon dept. surg. oncology Cancer Hosp., Chinese Acad. of Med. Scis., Beijing, 1963-79, assoc. prof., dep. head dept. surg. oncology, 1980-85, prof., 1985, vice and acting pres., 1984-88, chmn. dept. head and neck surgery, 1985-92; prof. Coll. of Oncology Peking Union Med. U., Beijing, 1995; vis. prof. dept. surgery Royal Price Alfred Hosp., St. Vincent's Hosp., Royal North Shore Hosp., Sydney, Australia; acad. com. Chinese Acad. of Med. Scis., 1993. Editl. bd. Chinese Jour. of Oncology, 1985; dep. editor-in-chief Chinese Jour. of Otorhinolaryngology, 1992; chief editor Chinese Archives in Ororhinolaryngology and Head and Neck Surgery, 1993; contbr. numerous articles to profl. jours. Recipient First Grade award Ministry of Pub. Health, 1995, 3rd grade award, 1995, 2d grade award, 1997, Nat. Com. on Advancement of Sci. and Tech., 1996. Fellow ACS (hon.), Am. Trilogical Soc. (hon.), Am. Soc. for Head and Neck Surgery (corr.); mem. Am. Rhinological Soc. (hon.), Am. Laryngological Assn. (corr.), Chinese Soc. of Head and Neck Surgery, Anti-Cancer Assn. (dep. chmn. 1988). Avocations: reading, swimming. Home: PO Box 2258, Beijing 100021, China Office: Dept Head and Neck Surgery, Cancer Hosp CAMS, Beijing 100021, China

TU, JI-YUAN, fluid mechanics engineer; b. Ninbao, Zhajian, China, July 7, 1958; arrived in Australia, 1992; s. Wei-Ming Tu and Wan Zhen Liu; m. Xue-Qin Shi, Nov. 8, 1986; 1 child, Tian-Yi. BE, Northeast U., Shenyang, China, 1982, MSc, 1984; lic. engr., Royal Inst. Tech., Stockholm, 1991, PhD, 1992. Lectr. Fudan U., Shanghai, China, 1984-89; rsch. asst. Royal Inst. Tech., Stockholm, 1989-92; rsch. assoc. U. Sydney, Australia, 1992-93; rsch. fellow U. NSW, Sydney, 1993-95; sr. computational scientist Australian Nuc. Sci. and Tech. Orgn., Sydney, 1996—; leader computational modelling and verification Australian Nuclear Sci. and Tech. Orgn., Sydney, 1996—; adj. assoc. prof. U. NSW, 1999—; cons. CAF Consulting Firm, Sydney, 1995—; session chair ASME-FED, San Diego, 1996; invited lectr. German Rsch. Found., Mersebury, 1996. Contbr. articles to scientific jours., chpts. to books; patentee in field. Fellow Japanese Soc. for Promotion of Sci., Australian Acad. Sci.; mem. ASME, Austrlian Engr. Assn., Modelling and Simulation Soc. Australia, Nuc. Sci. and Tech. Soc. Australia, N.Y. Acad. Scis. Avocations: sports, travel. Office: Australian Nuc Sci Tech, Bldg 40 Pvt Mail Bag 1, Menai NSW 2234, Australia

TU, SHAN-TUNG, science educator; b. Yongding, Fujian, China, Nov. 4, 1961; parents Xiangsheng Tu and Chunying Zeng; m. Lining Liang, Mar. 19, 1998. Bachelor's degree, Nanjing Inst. Chem. Tech., 1982, Master's degree, 1985, D of Engring., 1988. Postdoctoral rschr. Southwestern Jiaotong U., Chengdu, 1989-90; guest scientist Royal Inst. Tech., Stockholm, 1990-93; assoc. prof. Nanjing Inst. Tech., 1993-94, prof., 1994—; v.p. Nanjing U. Chem. Tech., 1997—, prof., v.p.; chief engr. Sinopec Equipment Failure Analysis and Prevention Ctr., Nanjing, 1996; 1st vice-chmn. high temperature materials and strength com. Chinese Mech. Engring. Soc. Contbr. numerous rsch. articles to profl. jours. (China Youth Sci. and Tech. award 1990, 1st prize Sci. and Tech. Progress Award 1995, 2d prize Natural Sci. Award of Nat. Petrochem. Bur. 1998, 2d prize Nat. Sci. and Tech. Progress Award 1999). Named one of Top Ten Excellent Young Tchrs., Jiangsu Province Govt., 1985. Avocations: painting, martial art. Fax: 86 25 3600956. E-mail: sttu.njuct.edu.cn. Office: Nanjing U Chem Tech, # 5 Xin Mo Fan Rd, Nanjing Jiangsu 210009, China

TU, SHIH-TIEN TIM, metal products executive, consultant; b. Taipei, China, July 3, 1956; s. Ching-Tao and Shu-Ching (Hsin) T.; m. Hua Becky Yu; 3 children. BS in Engring., Nat. Taiwan U., Taipei, 1978; PhD, Purdue U., 1985. Tchg. asst. Purdue U., West Lafayette, Ind., 1983-85; from devel. engr. to sr. devel. engr. BASF Narmco, Anaheim, Calif., 1985-89; from. mgr. tech. products to v.p. United Metals Enterprise Co., Ltd., Taipei, 1989-92, pres., 1992—; dir. Grand Heat, Taichung, Taiwan, 1993—; cons. Cytec, Anaheim, 1991; organizer Alcoa's Amazing Maze; spkr., moderator in field. Dir. Taiwan AL Recycling Found., Taipei, 1991-95, Australia and N.Z. Bus. Assn., ROC-Australia Bus. Coun., Taipei, 1990—. Mem. Soc. Advanced Material Process Engring., Am. Club in China. Office: United Metals Enterprise Co, United Metals Enterprise Co, 10F #80 Sung Chiang Rd, Taipei Taiwan China

TU, SUSAN, retired librarian; b. Taipei, Taiwan, Republic of China, June 10, 1923; arrived in U.S., 1961, naturalized, 1976; d. Tsungming Tu and Sonsui Lin; children: Helene Lin, Andy Lin, Jean Lin, Charlyn Lin. Student, Surugadai Girl's Jr. Coll., Tokyo, 1942, Taihoku Imperial U., Taiwan, 1944, U. Calif., Berkeley, 1961; BA, Utah State U., 1965; MA, U. Utah, 1971; MSLS, La. State U., 1973, cert. of med. librarianship, 1975, MEd, 1977, postgrad., 1976-77. Tchr. Taipei (Taiwan) Mcpl. Girls' High Sch., 1958-61; chief libr. Saints Coll., Lexington, Miss., 1974-76; hosp. libr. U.S. Army, Ft. Polk, La., 1977-79; dist. libr. Rock Island (Ill.) dist. U.S. Army Corps Engrs., 1979-83; div. libr. North Atlantic div. U.S. Army Corps Engrs., N.Y.C., 1984-88; dist. libr. N.Y. Dist., N.Y.C., 1988-90. Co-producer various videos, slide prodns., TV program. Mem. adv. bd. The Formosa Chamber Music Soc., Inc. Mem. Spl. Librs. Assn., Chinese-Am. Librs. Assn., Photographic Soc. Am. Avocations: photography, travel, beauty appreciation, literature, music.

TU, YAQING, engineering educator, researcher; b. Chongqing, China, June 18, 1963; s. Tianchang Tu and Wenlan Zhu; m. Wei Wang, June 22, 1988; 1 child, Wangshu. BS in Engring., Chengdu U. Sci. and Tech., China, 1984; MS, Chongqing U., 1991, PhD, 1994. From asst. to prof. Logistical Engring. U., Chongqing, 1984—. Contbr. over 100 sci. articles to profl. jours. and confs. including Optical Engring., ACTA Automatica Sinica, China Civil Engring. Jour. Recipient Nat. Sci. and Tech. Progress prize, China, 1988, 91, 96, 97, 98, Outstanding Young People award China Assn. Sci. and Tech., 1998. Mem. Internat. Soc. Optical Engring. Achievements include patents about fiber optic sensing and ultrasonic wave, an expert system approach to the Computer Aided Design of Intelligent Controller, a novel fiber optic array sensing approach and its signal processing algorithms using neural networks; research in fiberoptic sensing and intelligent structure and in artificial intelligence and intelligent control. Office: Logistical Engring U, No 174 Changjiang Rd Two, Chongqing 400016, China

TUBA, ZOLTÁN, botanist, educator; b. Sátoraljaújhely, Hungary, May 16, 1951; s. Zoltán and Gizella (Buróczy) T.; m. Ildikó Madas; children: Zoltán, Koppány. BSc, Tchrs. Tng. Coll., Hungary, 1978; MSc, József Attila U., 1982, dr. rer. nat., 1983; PhD, Hungarian Acad. Scis., 1985, DSc, 1998. Asst., rsch. fellow Ecology and Botany Rsch. Inst., Vácrátót, Hungary, 1978-85; assoc. prof. Agrl. U., Gödöllő, Hungary, 1985-92; prof. Agrl. U., Gödöllő, 1992—, head dept. botany and plant physiology, 1997—; vis. prof. U. Karlsruhe, Germany, 1992-93, U. Edinburgh, Scotland, 1993-94, U. Exeter, Eng., 1994-95; pres. Plant Physiology sect. Hungarian Biol. Soc., 1986-89; sec. Hungarian Commn. IGBP; founder Hungarian Global Climate Change and Plant Rsch. Sta., 1994. Co-author: Bioindication of Environmental Pollution, 1986 (prize 1987); author: Aquatic Plants, 1987, 2d edit., 1995; author, editor: Bryoecology, 1987, Grassland Ecology Under Elevated Carbon Dioxide, 1997; mem. editl. bd. Botanikai Közlemenyek, Acta Botany Hungary, 1992—; contbr. articles to internat. sci. jours. Recipient Acad. prize, 1992; named project mgr. European Union, 1993. Mem. COST Action 619 (mgmt. com.), Hungarian Plant Physiol. Soc. (mem. governing body 1990—), N.Y. Acad. Scis. Avocations: aquatic plants, water sports, fishing, squash, tennis. Office: Botany Department, Agricultural Univ, H-2100 Gödöllö Hungary

TUBBS, EDWARD LANE, banker; b. Delmar, Iowa, Apr. 17, 1920; s. Clifton Marvin and Mary Ellen (Lane) T.; m. Grace Barbara Dyer, Nov. 27, 1941; children: Steven, Alan, William. BS, Iowa State U., 1941; postgrad., U. Wis. Grad. Sch. Banking. With Iowa State U. Agrl. Ext. Svc., Newton, 1942; instr. vets. on-farm DeWitt (Iowa) Schs., 1957-58; v.p., dir. Jackson State Bank, Maquoketa State Bank, 1959-66; chmn., pres., dir., trust officer Maquoketa State Bank, 1966—; pres., dir. Onward Bancshares, Inc.; chmn., dir. 1st Ctrl. State Bank, DeWitt; dir. Tri-County Bank & Trust; pres., dir. Mabsco Agrl. Svcs., Inc., 1982-87; supt. banking State of Iowa, 1987-89; bd. dirs. Iowa Bus. Growth Corp.; lectr. banking schs.; exeh. del. USSR, 1959, 85; banking indsutry del. Baltic Countries, 1993; state dir. Conf. State Bank Supts., 1988-89. Contbr. articles in field. Pres. Elwood (Iowa) Sch. Bd., 1956-62; treas. City of Maquoketa, 1975-81; mem. People to People; trustee Sharar Found., Clinton Coll., 1983-86; v.p., bd. dirs. Timber City Indsl. Devel. Corp.; treas. Maquoketa Cmty. Svcs., 1967-80; trustee Iowa 4-H Found., 1987-91, Hoover Presdl. Libr. Assn. Inc., truatee, 1987—; gov. Iowa State U. Found., 1989—; trustee CCFA Found., 1990-94; elder, moderator United Ch. of Christ. With AUS, 1942-43. Recipient 4-H Club Alumni award, 1962, Century Farm award Iowa Dept. Agr., 1976, Disting. Pub. Svcs. award Jackson County, 1990, Gold Clover award Iowa 4-H Club, Heart of Gold award, 1996, Iowa Agrl. Ext. Assn. award, 1982, Floyd Andre award for disting. svc. to agr., 1985; named Jaycee Boss of Yr., 1970; named to Iowa Agrl. Hall of Fame, 1985; Hall of Fame, Clinton Fair, 1999. Mem. Bank Adminstrn. Inst., Am. Bankers Assn. (dir., coun. 1984-86, Ag Banker award 2000), Iowa Bankers Assn. (treas. 1978-79, pres. 1980-81), Am. Legion, Isaac Walton League, Iowa State U. Alumni Assn. (dir. 1980-86), Maquoketa C. of C. (dir. 1966-69), Order of Knoll (founders club Iowa State U.), Iowa Friends of Agr. (exec. com. 1987—), Rotary (Paul Harris fellow), Gamma Sigma Delta (Alumni Achievement award 1989), Alpha Zeta. Home: 1605 Blair Ct Maquoketa IA 52060-3301 Office: 203 N Main St Maquoketa IA 52060-2204

TUBIELLO, FRANCESCO NICOLA, research scientist; b. Novara, Italy, Sept. 18, 1963; arrived in U.S., 1990; p. Giuseppe Tubiello and Maria Pannuzzo. MS in Physics, U. Torino, Italy, 1989; MS in Energetics, NYU, 1992, PhD in Earth Sys. Sci., 1995. Dir. agroforestry Biosphere 2, Tucson, 1996-98; assoc. rsch. scientist Columbia U., N.Y.C., 1996—; cons. Harvard U., Boston, Ministry Environment, Rome. Rsch. grantee Ministry of the Environment, Rome, 1996—, Environ. Def. Fund, N.Y.C., 1999—, USDA, Washington, 1999. Mem. Am. Soc. Agronomy (acting chair climate change group). E-mail: franci@giss.nasa.gov.

TUCAPSKY, ANTONIN, composer, conductor, educator; b. Opatovice, Czechoslovakia, Mar. 27, 1928; s. Vaclav and Josefa (Sirkova) T.; student Janacek Acad. Music, Brno, 1950-51; student Masaryk U., Brno, 1947-51, Ph.D., 1969; m. Beryl Musgrave, Oct. 13, 1972. Prof. music, Tchrs. Tng. Coll., Novy Jicin, 1955-59; lectr. music pedagogical faculty Ostrava U., 1959-73; condr. Moravian Tchrs. Choir, Czechoslovakia, 1964-73; lectr. music theory and composition Trinity Coll. Music, London, 1975—; compositions include: In Honorem Vitae, Lauds (choral), 1977, The Time of Christmas, Before Trees Stir, (choral), 1978, The Sacrifice cantata, 1977, Missa Serena oratorio, 1979, Pocket Music-Wind Quintet, Four Dialogues clarinet and piano, 1979, Comoedia Cantata, 1982, Suite for Oboe and Piano, 1983, Sonata for Classical Guitar, 1984. Sonata per Violino Solo, 1985, Kohelet cantata, 1994, Veni, Sancte Spiritus (choral), 1985, The Undertaker opera, 1987, Stabat Mater oratorio, 1989, Triptychor for Symphony Orch., 1990, Concerto for Violin and Orch., 1993, Concerto for Clarinet and Orch., 1999, String Quartet, 1993, Toccata e Canzone for Organ and Piano, 1993, Divertimento for Oboe, Clarinet and Bassoon, 1995, Concerto for Viola and Orch., 1996, Eclogues-Piano Trio, 1996, Oboe-Quintet, 1997. Mem. Composers Guild Gt. Britain, Royal Soc. Musicians Gt. Britain, Czechoslovak Soc. Arts and Scis., Assn. of Czechoslovakia Composers, Prague. Author: Janacek's Male Choruses, 1971; recording artist: Supraphon, 1969, Bedivere Records Ltd., 1979, SOMM-CD Records. Home: 50 Birchen Grove, London NW9 8SA, England

TUCCARI, GIOVANNI, pathologist, educator; b. Messina, Italy, Aug. 9, 1955; s. Emanuele and Caterina (Donato) T.; m. Maria Silvestri, Oct. 14, 1985; children: Emanuele, Salvatore, Francesca. MD, U. Pisa, Italy, 1979. Fellow in pathology Inst. Pathology, Messina, 1979-83, specialist in pathology, 1983-86, asst. prof., 1987-90; cont. asst. prof. dept. pathology Polyclinico U., Messina, 1990-99, prof. dept. human pathology, 2000—. Mem. Agnor Euopean Com., Italian Soc. Histochemistry, Italian Soc. Pathology. Avocations: basket making, travel, books. Office: Dept Human Pathol Policlin, Via Consolare Valeria, 98125 Messina Italy

TUCCI, ALBERT WILLIAM, retired human resources executive, consultant; b. Canastota, N.Y., Nov. 14, 1938; s. Samuel and Anna (Penna) T.; m. Mary Katherine Moseley, Mar. 25, 1961; children: Anne Elizabeth, Katherine Lynn. BS, St. Lawrence U., 1960; MS, Western Conn. U., 1971; PhD, U. Md., 1984. Advanced profl. certificate in math., pers. adminstrn. and supervision. Math. tchr. Long Beach, Huntington Beach (Calif.) Pub. Schs., 1960-63; supr. pers. Columbia Broadcasting System, N.Y.C., 1963-65; math. tchr. Chappaqua (N.Y.) Pub. Schs., 1965-71; from pers. asst. to mgr. human resources Howard County Pub. Schs., Ellicott City, Md., 1971-96; pvt. practice human resources cons.; speaker colls. and univs., 1973—; assessor Md. Ctr. Progressive Assessments, Balt., 1974—. Author: Teacher Satisfaction, 1984, (manual) The Supervisor Interview, 1991; contbr. numerous articles to profl. publs. Mem. adv. bd. Johns Hopkins U., Balt., U. Md., College Park, 1985-96; fundraiser Am. Heart Assn., 1985, 86, United Way, 1980-83; coach, dir. Howard County Youth Program, Ellicott City, 1976-82; bd. dirs. Md. Youth Symphony Orch., 1997. NDEA grantee, 1969; recipient rsch. award U. Md., 1985, award of excellence Nat. Assn. Secondary Sch. Prins., 1987. Mem. Middle Atlantic Assn. Schs., Colls. and Univs. (emeritus 1996), Mensa, Phi Delta Kappa. Roman Catholic. Avocations: music, theatre, skiing, golf, writing. Home: 10124 Bell Inn Ln Ellicott City MD 21042-5651

TUCCI, GERALD FRANK, manufacturing company executive; b. N.Y.C., Sept. 9, 1926; s. Frank and Mary (Fattizzi) T.; m. Eva G. Gyllander, May 14, 1968; children: Francis Henrik, Michael Fredrik, Amy Christina. Student, Dartmouth Coll., 1944; BSc in Naval Sci., Brown U., 1946, BSME, 1948; MBA with distinction, Harvard U., 1950. Mfg. trainee Am. Can Co., Jersey City, 1950-51; asst. v.p., plant mgr. Artcraft Hosiery Mills, Inc., Darby, Pa., 1951-53; v.p. Leach & Garner, Co., Attleboro, Mass., 1953-63, Gen. Findings, Inc., Attleboro, Mass., 1953-63; pres. Micro Contacts, Inc., Hicksville, Mass., 1963—, Micro Pneumatic Logic, Inc., Ft. Lauderdale, Fla., 1973—. Lt. (s.g.) USNR, 1944-47. Mem. ASME, Am. Soc. Mfrs., North Hempstead Country Club, Met. Club (N.Y.), Harvard Bus. Sch. Club N.Y., Frenchman's Creek Country Club, Beta Theta Pi. Republican. Roman Catholic. Office: 62 Alpha Plz Hicksville NY 11801-2618

TUCEK, STANISLAV, neurochemist; b. Pardubice, Czechoslovakia, Apr. 18, 1932; s. Frantisek and Vlasta (Vozkova) T.; m. Dana Pechackova, 1962; children: Martin, Lenka. MD, State Med. Inst., Kharkov, Ukraine, 1957; PhD, Charles U., 1964; DSc, Czechoslovak Acad. Scis., 1978. Assoc. prof. Charles U. Sch. Medicine, Prague, Czechoslovakia, 1966-70; head dept. neurochemistry Inst. Physiology Czech Acad. Scis., Prague, 1972—; hon. prof. Kazan Med. U., Russia, 1993—; chmn. Scientific Coun. of Inst. Physiology Czech Acad. Scis., Prague, 1997—; Quastel vis. prof. Hebrew U. Jerusalem, 1997. Author: Acetylcholine Synthesis in Neurons, 1978; editor: The Cholinergic Synapse, 1979, Synaptic Transmitters and Receptors, 1987, Metabolism and Development of the Nervous System, 1987; contbr. articles to profl. jours. Mem. European Soc. Neurochemistry (pres. 1984-88), Internat. Brain Rsch. Orgn. (governing coun. 1985-92), Czechoslovak Acad. Scis. (corr.). Office: Inst Physiology Acad Scis, Videnska 1083, 14220 Prague Czech Republic

TUCK, EDWARD FENTON, venture capitalist; b. Memphis, July 5, 1931; s. Edward Fenton and Jane Florence (Lewis) T.; m. Janet Allene Barber, July 6, 1957; children: Jean, Ann. BSEE, Mo. Sch. Mines, 1953; elec. engr. (hon.), U. Mo., 1980, D Engring. (hon.), 1997. Registered profl. engr., Calif. Various engring. and mfg. mgmt. positions Lenkurt Elec. Co. divsn. GTE, San Carlos, Calif., 1957-62; v.p., co-founder Kebby Microwave Corp., San Carlos, 1962-64; asst. tech. dir. ITT Computers, 1964-67; v.p., tech. dir. N.Am. Telecomms. Group ITT, 1967-72; gen. mgr., pres. Tel-Tone Corp., Kirkland, Wash., 1972-74; v.p. mktg. and engring. Am. Telecomm. Corp., El Monte, Calif., 1975-79; pres. Edward Tuck & Co. Inc., West Covina, Calif., 1979-86; gen. ptnr. The Boundary Fund, West Covina, 1986-95; with Kinship Ptnrs. II, 1990—; prin. Falcon Fund, 1982—; TriQuint Semiconductors, Beaverton, Oreg.; chmn. Endgate Corp., Sunnyvale, Calif., High Tower Software, Irvine, Calif.; bd. dirs. Teledesic Corp., Kirkland, Wash. Contbr. articles to profl. jours. Trustee U. Mo., Rolla; mem. jet propulsion lab. comml. adv. com. Named mem. Acad. Elec. Engring. U. Mo. Fellow Instn. Radio, Elec. and Electronic Engrs. Australia; mem. IEEE (sr., 1st prize for article 1962), AAAS, Assn. Profl. Cons. (pres., bd. dirs. 1979-86). Democrat. Office: Kinship Partners II 1900 W Garvey Ave S Ste 200 West Covina CA 91790-2653

TUCK, MARY BETH, nutritionist, retired educator; b. Point, Tex., Dec. 9, 1930; d. Basil Barney and Daisy (Morris) Rabb; children: Karen, Kenny (dec.). BS, East Tex. State U., 1952, MEd, 1966; PhD, Tex. Woman's U., 1970. Tchr. Longview (Tex.) Pub. Schs., 1952-64; instr. nutrition Stephen F. Austin U., Nacogdoches, Tex., 1966-69; assoc. prof. East Tex. State U., Commerce, Tex., 1970-96; ret., 1996; cons. Women, Infants and Children Program, Hunt County, Tex., 1989, East Tex. State U. Wellness Program, Commerce, 1989-93, nutritionist Selvaggi Med. Clinic, Commerce, 1989-93; nutrition del. People to People Citizen Amb. Program, USSR, 1990; lectr. in field. Reviewer, editor textbooks; contbr. articles to profl. jours. Bd. dirs. commerce div. Am. Heart Assn., 1994-97; mem. Meth. Mission Work/Study Team, Israel, 1996, 98, Commerce Leadership Inst., 1997; mem. missions com. 1st United Meth. Ch., mem SPRC com., 1996-99, choir, chmn. assoc. pastor parsonage com., 1996—; mem. sr. adult ministries, 1997—; bd. dirs. NorthEast Tex. Symphony, sec., 1998—; mem. Commerce Symphony League, 1998—; mem., supporter plan/devel. amphitheater South Sulphur River Devel. Assn., 1998—. Recipient Gold Blazer award East Tex. State U. Alumni Assn., 1995. Mem. N.E. Tex. Ret. Tchrs. Assn. (v.p. 1996-97, pres. 1999—), Afflatus Culture Club (pres. 1988-91), Louise Drake Garden Club (v.p. 1991-92, pres. 1992-93, 97-98), Commerce Area Alumni Assn. (1st v.p. 1993-94), Delta Kappa Gamma (sec. 1988-92, 94-96).

TUCKER, ALLAN MARC, mastering engineer; b. Bklyn., May 26, 1949. BA, CUNY, 1971. Rec. engr. Bell Sound Studios, N.Y.C., 1971-73, Platinum/Chess Records, Englewood, N.J., 1975-77, Vanguard Records, N.Y.C., 1977-80, Foothill Sound, N.Y.C., 1971-88; pres., chief mastering engr. Foothill Digital, N.Y.C., 1988—; rec. engr. Malcolm Addey Recorders, N.Y.C., 1972-87; ops. mgr. Nat. Video and Rec. Studios, N.Y.C., 1979-83; freelance studio engr., 1971-88. Mastering engr. over 2,000 albums/CDs. Recipient 2 Visionary awards 3M Corp.; selected Beta/Co-developer by Sonic Solutions, 1988-91; winner Emmy, TEC and Grammy awards. Mem. Nat. Acad. Rec. Arts and Scis., Audio Engring. Soc., Sonic Solutions DVD-Audio Developers Group. Office: Foothill Digital Inc 215 W 91st St New York NY 10024-1321

TUCKER, ALVIN LEROY, retired government official; b. Bklyn., Sept. 7, 1938; s. Alvin Leroy Jr. and Alveria (Klune) T.; m. Jacqueline Twiggs, Aug. 27, 1966; children: Hazel, Pluma, Jacqueline, Alvin. BS, U. Md., 1965. CPA, Md.; cert. internal auditor, govt. fin. mgr.; cert. def. fin. mgr. Auditor Dept. Army, Washington, 1965-67; dep. insp. gen. HUD, Washington, 1986-89; auditor Dept. Def., Washington, 1967-72, budget analyst, 1972-79, dir. tng. and edn., 1979-83, dep. asst. insp. gen., 1983-86, dep. comptr., 1989-94, dep. CFO, 1991-97, chmn. concessions com., 1989-97; sr. mgr. Grant Thornton, Vienna, Va., 1997—; mem. steering com. Joint Fin. Mgmt. Improvement Program, 1990-93; mem. CFO's Coun., 1989-97, chmn. fin. sys. com., 1989-97; mem. Fed. Acctg. Stds. Adv. Bd., 1991-97. With U.S. Army, 1958-61. Recipient Defense medal for disting. civilian svc. with Bronze Palm, meritorious sr. exec. medal. Mem. AICPA, Am. Soc. Mil. Comptrs., Assn. Govt. Accts. (nat. exec. com. 1993-94), Kiwanis (club pres. 1981-82, 86-87). Avocation: genealogy. Office: Grant Thornton 1900 M St NW Ste 300 Washington DC 20036-3531

TUCKER, BOWEN HAYWARD, lawyer; b. Providence, Apr. 13, 1938; s. Stuart Hayward and Ardelle Chase (Drabble) T.; m. Jan Louise Brown, Aug. 26, 1961; children: Stefan Kendric Slade, Catherine Kendra Gordon. AB in Math., Brown U., 1959; JD, U. Mich., 1962. Bar: R.I. 1963, Ill. 1967, U.S. Supreme Ct. 1970. Assoc. Hinckley & Allen, Providence, 1962-66; sr. atty. Caterpillar, Inc., Peoria, Ill., 1966-72; counsel FMC Corp., Chgo., 1972-82, sr. litigation counsel, 1982-95, assoc. gen. counsel, 1995—. Chmn. legal process task force Chgo. Residential Sch. Study Com., 1973-74, mem. Commn. on Children, 1983-85, Ill. Com. on Rights of Minors, 1974-77, Com. on Youth and the Law, 1977-79; mem. White House Conf. on Children, ednl. svcs. subcom., 1979-80; chairperson Youth Employment Task Force, 1982-83; mem. citizens com. on Juvenile Ct. (Cook County), 1978-94, chmn. detention subcom., 1982-94; mem. econ. effects adv. com. Rand Inst. Civil Justice, 1990-92; bd. dirs. Voices Ill. Children, 1998—. 1st lt. U.S. Army, 1962-69. Mem. ABA, Am. Law Inst., Ill. State Bar Assn., R.I. Bar Assn., Chgo. (chmn. com. on juvenile law, 1976-77), Engine Mfrs. Assn. (chmn. legal com. 1972), Chgo. Lincoln Inn of Ct. (sec., treas. 1996-98), Constrn. Industry Mfrs. Assn. (exec. com. of Lawyers' Coun. 1972, 1975-79, vice chmn. 1977, chmn. 1978-79), Mfrs. Alliance (products liability coun. 1974-95, vice chmn. 1981-83, chmn. 1983-85), Product Liability Adv. Coun. (bd. dirs. 1986—, exec. com. 1990-97, vice chmn. 1991-93, chmn. 1993-95), ACLU (bd. dirs. Ill. div. 1970-79, exec. com. 1973-79, sec. 1975-77), Am. Arbitration Assn. (mem panel of arbitrators 1985-96), Phi Alph Delta. Club: Brown Univ. of Chgo. (nat. alumni schs. program 1973-85, v.p. 1980-81, pres. 1981-86), Law Club of City of Chicago. Home: 107 W Noyes St Arlington Heights IL 60005-3747 Office: 200 E Randolph St Ste 6700 Chicago IL 60601-6436

TUCKER, EDWIN WALLACE, law educator; b. N.Y.C., Feb. 25, 1927; s. Benjamin and May Tucker; m. Gladys Lipschutz, Sept. 14, 1952; children: Sherwin M., Pamela A. BA, NYU, 1948; LLB, Harvard U., 1951; LLM, N.Y. Law Sch., 1963, JSD, 1964; MA, Trinity Coll., Hartford, Conn., 1967. Bar: N.Y. 1955, U.S. Dist. Ct. (ea. and so. dists.) N.Y. 1958, U.S. Ct. Appeals (2d cir.) 1958, U.S. Supreme Ct. 1960. Pvt. practice, N.Y.C., 1955-63; Disting. Alumni prof. and prof. bus. law U. Conn., Storrs, 1963—, mem. bd. editors occasional paper and monograph series, 1966-70. Author: Adjudication of Social Issues, 1971, 2d edit., 1977, Legal Regulation of the Environment, 1972, Administrative Agencies, Regulation of Enterprise, and Individual Liberties, 1975, CPA Law Review, 1985; co-author: The Legal and Ethical Environment of Business, 1992; book rev. editor Am. Bus. Law Jour., 1964-65, adv. editor, 1974—; co-editor Am. Bus. Jour., 1965-73; mem. editl. bd. Am. Jour. Small Bus., 1979-86; editor Jour. Legal Studies Edn., 1983-85, editor-in-chief, 1985-87, adv. editor, 1987—; mem. bd. editors North Atlantic Regional Bus. Law Rev., 1984—. With USAF, 1951-55. Recipient medal of excellence Am. Bus. Law Assn., 1979. Mem. Acad. Legal Studies in Bus., North Atlantic Regional Bus. Law Assn. Home: 11 Eastwood Rd Storrs Mansfield CT 06268-2401

TUCKER, GARY WILSON, nursing educator; b. Oct. 2, 1956; s. Clayton Wilson Jr. and Jewell (Shelton) T. AAS, Cleveland (Tenn.) State Community Coll., 1980; BSW, Lamar U., Beaumont, Tex., 1991; MPH, U. Tex. Sch. Pub. Health, 1996; BSN, Lamar U., 1999. CCRN, ACLS. Nurse, relief shift supr. Moccasin Bend Mental Health Inst., Chattanooga, 1980-81; staff nurse pediat. ICU Thompson Childrens', Chattanooga, 1981-83; nurse, cons. King Fahad Hosp., Riyadh, Saudi Arabia, 1983; staff nurse ICU/ CCU Beaumont (Tex.) Med.-Surg. Hosp., 1984-88; charge nurse CCU, hemodialysis Bapt. Hosp., Beaumont, 1988-93, cardio-vascular nurse educator, 1993-96, dept. head, staff devel. and continuing edn. nurse, 1996-99; rsch. technican U. Tex., Houston Health Sci. Ctr., 1998-99; nursing instr. Lamar U., Beaumont, Tex., 1999—. Mem. AACN, ANA, Tex. Nurses Assn. Home: 601 22nd St Beaumont TX 77706-4915 Office: Lamar U Dept Nursing PO Box 10081 Beaumont TX 77710-0081

TUCKER, HOWARD MCKELDIN, investment banker, consultant; b. Washington, Apr. 1, 1930; s. Howard Newell and Bessie Draper (McKeldin) T.; m. Julia Spencer Merrell, Feb. 1, 1952 (div. 1975); children: Deborah, Mark, Alexander, H. David; m. Megan Evans, Aug. 17, 1979. BA, U. Va., 1954; MBA, NYU, 1956. CFA. With pension investment dept. J.P. Morgan & Co., 1954-61; reg. rep.-analyst Mackall & Coe, Washington, 1962-69; dir. internat. dept., analyst Legg Mason Wood Walker & Co., Washington, 1969-79; with Govt. Rsch. Corp./Nat. Jour., 1979-82, Potomac Asset Mgmt., 1982-91; ptnr., mng. dir. Capital Insights Group, Washington, 1992—; mem. task force balance-of-payments U.S. Dept. Treasury, 1967-70; cons. County

Natwest (Washinton Analysis Corp.), 1985-90; bd. dirs. Monarch Enterprises, Inc., Uniflight, Inc., Sci. Mgmt. Assocs., Inc., Jeffrey Bigelow Assocs. Author: Literature in Medicine, In Memoriam, Michael Halberstam, M.D., 1984; book reviewer Washington Post; contbr. articles to profl. jours. Dir. Washington Area Coun. Chs., 1962-65; vestryman Christ Episcopal Ch., Georgetown, 1962-65; mem. chpt. Washington Nat. Cathedral, 1966-72; del. Va. Republican Conv., 1968; trustee Nat. Cathedral Sch. for Girls, 1972-78; chmn. Missionary Devel. Fund Episcopal Diocese D.C., 1974; co-dir. Andover-Exeter Washington Intern Program, 1976-86; co-organizer U.S.-Ger. Parliamentary Exchange, 1980-82; observer OECD, 1980-82; spl. overseas visitor Australian Govt., 1982; patron West Europe program Woodrow Wilson Ctr., 1985-86. With USNR, 1950-56. Mem. Am. Hort. Soc. (bd. dirs. 1999—), Nat. Economists Club, Washington Soc. Investment Analysts, Cogswell Soc., Naval and Mil. Club London, Nat. Press Club, Yale Club, Georgetown Visitation Tennis Club, Saints and Sinners Club, Dumplings Yacht Club, Wodehouse Soc., Beta Theta Pi. Home: 4 Potomac Ct Alexandria VA 22314-3821

TUCKER, JAMES, writer; b. Cardiff, Wales, Aug. 15, 1929; s. William Arthur and Violet Irene (Bushen) T.; m. Marian Roberta Craig, July 17, 1954; children: Patrick James, Catherine Marian, Guy William, David Craig. BA, U. Wales, 1951, MA, 1974. part-time tutor U. Wales, 1968—. Author: Criticism: The Novels of Anthony Powell, 1975; author numerous crime novels under pen names of Bill James: You'd Better Believe It, 1985, Top Banana, 1996, Lovely Mover, 1998, Eton Crop, 1999, Kill Me, 2000, as David Craig: The Alias Man, 1968, Whose Little Girl Are You?, 1974 (filmed as The Squeeze), The Tattooed Detective, 1998, Bay City, 2000, as James Tucker: Equal Partners, 1960, Blaze of Riot, 1979, as Judith: Jones: Baby Talk, 1998, After Melissa, 1999; journalist contbg. to newspapers, mags., TV and radio. With RAF, 1951-53. Mem. Soc. Authors, Crime Writers assn., Mystery Writers of Am. Avocation: walking. Office: Curtis Brown, 28/9 Haymarket, London SW1, England

TUCKER, JOHN ROBERT, financial executive, author; b. West Palm Beach, Fla., Jan. 27, 1931; s. William Herman Tucker Sr. and Jessie Brasselle Tucker Massingale; m. Charlotte Ann Kause, Oct. 10, 1959; children: Helene Ann, Thomas Kenneth. BA in Arts and Humanities, U. Md., 1951; M Internat. and Pub. Affairs, Columbia U., 1955, cert. East Asian Inst., 1955; diploma, Indsl. Coll. Armed Forces, 1957. Asst. to pres. Govt. Employees Ins. Co., Washington, 1956-62; pres., CEO Tucker Corp., Potomac, Md., 1963-80; sr. fellow Pres.'s Pvt. Sector Survey on Cost Control, Washington, 1981-84; CEO Icon Corp., Washington, 1985—. Author: The Bicentennial Tragedy, 1975, The Megapower, 1995. Capt. USAF, 1951-53. Recipient Gov.'s Cup from Gov. of Md., 1951. Mem. U. Md. College Park Alumni Assn. (life), Harvard U. Grad. Sch. Arts and Scis. Alumni Assn., George Washington U. Gen. Alumni Assn., Nat. Press Club, Nat. Economists Club, Pres. Club U. Md., Harvard Club (Washington), Columbia U. Club of Washington, Columbia Club of N.Y. Republican. Episcopalian. Avocations: photography, gardening, travel. Home: 3450 Terrace Ct # 1042 Alexandria VA 22302-1244

TUCKER, MATTHEW D., controller, systems administrator; b. St. Louis, Aug. 7, 1977; s. Joseph D. Tucker and Yvonne Marie Pfeil; m. Karen Lee Hentchel, Aug. 8, 1997; 1 child, Kaitlyn Anne. BSBA, Truman State U., 1999; postgrad., So. Ill. U., 1999—. Cert. acctg. specialist. Crew leader Hardee's, House Springs, Mo., 1994-95; washdown crew Six Flags Over Mid-Am., Eureka, Mo., 1995-96; short order cook Too Talls Two Eatery & Spirits, Kirksville, Mo., 1996-97; comm. rep. Northeast Regional Med. Ctr., Kirksville, Mo., 1997-98; pub. rels. intern Kirksville Coll. Osteopathic Medicine, 1998-99; webmaster AFWC Inc., Sauget, Ill., 1999, comptr., 1999—; former advisor DonCo Enterprises Inc., Sauget. Mem. bus. adv. bd. N.W. R1 Sch. Dist., House Springs, 2000; competitive event judge Distributive Edn. Clubs Am., St. Louis, 2000. Mem. Am. Subcontractors Assn. (midwest coun.). Avocations: outdoors, computers, reading, sports.

TUCKER, RICHARD BLACKBURN, III, lawyer; b. Pitts., Oct. 28, 1943; s. Richard B. Jr. and Alice (Reed) T.; m. Dorothy Dohoney, Aug. 24, 1974; 1 child, R. Wade. BA, U. Va., 1965; JD, Columbia U., 1968. Bar: Pa. 1970, R.I. 1971, U.S. Supreme Ct. 1984. Vista vol. Greater Kansas City (Mo.) Legal Aid & Defender Soc., 1968-69; atty. R.I. Legal Svcs., Providence, 1970-76, Tucker Arensberg, P.C., Pitts., 1976—. Active western Pa. chpt. Nat. Hemophilia Found., Pitts., 1976-82. Mem. Pa. Bar Assn., Allegheny County Bar Assn. (vice-chmn. appellate practice com. 1994-95, chmn., 1996-97). Democrat. Episcopalian. Avocations: tennis, skiing. Home: 217 Edgeworth Ln Sewickley PA 15143-1052 Office: Tucker Arensberg PC 1 PPG Pl Pittsburgh PA 15222-5413

TUCKER, SAM MICHAEL, pediatrician; b. Benoni, Transvaal, South Africa, Oct. 15, 1926; arrived in the U.K., 1955; s. Harry and Rachel (Goldstein) T.; m. Barbara Helen Kaplan; children: Dana, Mark, Trevor. MB BChir, U. Witwatersrand, South Africa, 1952. Cons. pediatrician Nat. Health Svc., United Kingdom, 1965-90; prof. pediatric audiology Brunel U., London, 1988. Contbr. articles to profl. jours. Trustee Friends of Russian Children, 1988—, Centre Acad., London. Lt. South African Air Force, 1944-46. Fellow Royal Coll. Physicians London and Edinburgh, Royal Soc. Medicine (treas. 1985-96, sr. hon. treas. 1999, com. mem. 1996), Roual Coll. Pediatrics and Child Health. Avocations: sports, travel. Home: 65 Uphill Rd Mill Hill, London NW74PT, United Kingdom Office: 152 Harley St, London WIN 1HH, England

TUCKER, WILLIAM MORRIS, psychiatric educator; b. St. Louis, June 5, 1941; s. Joseph Louis and Jean (Sapin) T.; m. Susan Brown, June 2, 1968 (div. June 3, 1983); children: Zachary, Jed; m. Sheila May Troyan, Apr. 12, 1986. AB, Harvard U., 1962; MA, Yale U., 1965; MD, Columbia U., 1969. Intern (rotating) Roosevelt Hosp., N.Y.C., 1969-70; resident N.Y. State Psychiat. Inst., 1970-72, Albert Einstein Coll. Medicine, 1972-73; staff psychiatrist Bronx (N.Y.) State Hosp., 1973-75; coord. residency tng. Beth Israel Hosp., N.Y.C., 1975-77; dir. residency tng. St. Luke's-Roosevelt Hosp., N.Y.C., 1977-89; dir. psychiat. svcs. N.Y. State Office Mental Health, Albany, 1990-2000, dep. chief med. officer, 2000—; liason N.Y. State Psychiat. Assn., 1990—. Fulbright scholar, 1963. Fellow Am. Psychiat. Assn. (pres. NYCDB 1997-98); mem. Med. Soc. State N.Y. (advisor to com. on psychiat. medicine 1990—). Democrat. Jewish. Avocations: sailing, skiing, windsurfing. Home: 150 Columbus Ave Apt 24A New York NY 10023-5971 Office: NY State Office Mental Health 44 Holland Ave Albany NY 12208-3411

TUCKMAN, FRED AUGUSTUS, management consultant; b. Magdeburg, Germany, June 9, 1922; arrived in U.K., 1939; s. Otto and Amy Tina (Adler) T.; m. Patricia Caroline Myers, July 24, 1966; children: Michael David, Jane Tina, Jeremy Francis Henry. BSc in Econs., London Sch. Econs., 1949. Dept. mgr. Marks & Spencer plc, London, 1950-54; sec., pers. mgr. B.I.A. Ltd., London, 1955-63; asst. sec. Temple Press Ltd., London, 1963-65; ptnr. Hay Assocs., various locations, 1965-85; mem. European Parliament for Leicester, 1979-89; mgmt. cons. London, 1989—. Mem. Camden Borough Coun., London, 1965-71; mem., hon. sec. The Bow Group, 1955-85; pres. Anglo-Jewish Assn., London, 1989-95. Flight sgt. RAF, 1942-46. Decorated Officer of the Brit. Empire, 1990, Comdrs. Cross of the Order of Merit of Germany, 1990. Fellow Chartered Inst. Secs., Chartered Inst. Pers. and Devel., Chartered Inst. Mgmt.; mem. Inst. Mktg., Inst. Pers. Mgmt. (regional chmn. 1968-70), Carlton Club, The Athenaeum. Conservative Party. Jewish. Avocations: family, music, reading.

TUDDENHAM, EDWARD GEORGE, pathologist; b. Porthcawl, Glamorgan, Wales, May 8, 1944; s. Edward Peter and Sybil Kathleen (Cooper) T.; m. Helen Kaye Little, Sept. 13, 1969 (div. 1996); children: Laurence M., James E.; m. Michelle Tanya Hudson, Oct. 18, 1997. MB BChir, Westminster Hosp. Med. Sch., London, 1968; MD, U. London, London, 1985. Sr. house officer, registrar United Liverpool (Eng.) Hosps., 1969-71; lectr. in hematology Welsh Nat. Sch. Medicine U. Hosp. Wales, Cardiff, 1972-75; rsch. assoc. dept. medicine divsn. hematology U. Conn. Sch. Medicine, Farmington, 1976-77; sr. lectr. hematology Royal Free Hosp. Sch. Medicine, 1978-86, dir. Katharine Dormandy Hemophilia Ctr. and Hemostasis Unit, 1978-86; dir. hemostasis rsch. group MRC Clin. Rsch. Ctr., Harrow, 1986-94; mem. MRC clin. sci. staff, prof. hemostasis Imperial Coll. Sch. of Med. Author 3 books, including Molecular Genetics of Haemostasis, 1994; contbr. numerous chpts., revs., articles, and editls. to profl. publs. Chmn. Flor del Bosque Forest Conservative Trust, 1990—; activist Friends of the Earth, London. Recipient medal French Haemophilia Soc., 1983, Macfarlane medal Haemophilia Soc. U.K., 1984, Murray Thelin award Nat. Hemophilia Found., 1989. Fellow Royal Coll. Physicians U.K., Royal Coll. Pathologists U.K., Royal Coll. Physicians Edinburgh. Avocations: mycology, green woodworking, tropical forest conservation. Office: Haemostasis Rsch Group, Du Cane Rd, London W12 ONN, England

TUDOR, JOHN COLIN, ophthalmic surgeon; b. St. Albans, Herts, Eng., Sept. 3, 1941; s. Colin Ewert and Alma Frances (Service) T.; m. Sandra Tudor; children: Catharine, Alison, John William. MA, St. Catharine's Coll., Cambridge, Eng., 1963; MB, BChir, St. Bartholomews Hosp., London, 1966. Intern opthalmology St. Bartholomews Hosp., London, 1967; registrar opthalmology Bristol Eye Hosp., 1968; sr. registrar opthalmology Southampton Eye Hosp., 1973; cons. ophthalmic surgeon Queen Alexandra Hosp., Cosham, Hants, Eng., 1977—; hon. tutor Southampton U., 1977—. Fellow Royal Coll. Surgeons Eng., Royal Coll. Surgeons Edinburgh, Royal Coll. Ophthalmologists, Hayling Island Lodge (sec.); mem. Hosp. Conss. and Splst. Assn. (Hampshire chmn.). Home: Winton House, Portsdown Hill Rd, Portsmouth PO6 1BE, England Office: 38 Saint Edward Rd Hants, Portsmouth PO5 3DJ, England

TUDZYNSKI, PAUL, biologist; b. Fluorn, Fed. Republic Germany, Jan. 28, 1951; m. Bettina; children: Melanie, Tobias, Joachim, Christoph. Dr.rer.nat., U. Bochum, 1978, Habilitation, 1983. Wissenschaftlicher asst. Lehrstuhl fur Allgemeine Botanik, Ruhr Univ., Bochum, 1976-83; privatdozent Lehrstuhl fur Allgemeine Botanik, Ruhr Univ., 1983-86; prof. microbiology U. Düsseldorf, 1986-88; prof. and dir. Inst. f. Botanik and Bot. Garten Westfälische Wilhelms U., Münster, Fed. Republic Germany, 1988—. Editor Applied Microbiology and Biotech., Molecular Plant Pathology; contbr. articles to profl. jours. Recipient Sandoz prize, Internat. Assn. Gerontology, 1985. Mem. German Soc. for Genetics, German Bot. Soc., Vereinigung für Allgemeine und Angewandte Mikrobiologie, Internat. Soc. Plant Microbe Internat. Office: Inst f Botanik, Schlossgarten 3, D-48149 Münster Germany

TUERK, HELMUT, diplomat; b. Linz, Austria, Apr. 24, 1941; m. Monika Tuerk; 3 children. JD, U. Vienna, 1963; postgrad., Coll. Europe, Bruges, Belgium, 1963-64. Del. UN Gen. Assembly, 1966, 74-76, 82-92; with internat. law dept. Fed. Ministry Fgn. Affairs, 1965-67, 72-78; min.-counselor Austrian Embassy, Bonn, Germany, 1978-82, legal advisor, 1982-93; dep. sec. gen. fgn. affairs Washington, 1991-93, Austrian amb. to U.S., 1993-99; dir. gen. Office of the Fed. Pres. of the Republic of Austria, Vienna; del. UN Conf. Succession States in Respect of State Property, Archives and Debts, 1983, 2d World Conf. to Combat Racism and Racial Discrimination, 1983; led Austrian delegation to Human Rights Commn. UN, 1987, 89; head Austrian delegation, 1989; chmn. 6th com. 44th UN Gen. Assembly; agt. European Commn. Human Rights and European Ct. for Human Rights Austrian Fed. Govt., 1982-93; mem. Permanent Ct. Arbitration, the Hague, 1986—. Contbr. articles to profl. jours. Office: Office Fed Pres, Republic Austria Hofburg, 1014 Vienna Austria

TUESTA, IGNACIO DIAZ, cardiac surgeon, computer consultant; b. Cadiz, Andalucia, Spain, May 8, 1964; s. Jose Antonio Diaz Tuesta and Maria del Pilar Revilla; m. Arancha Revuelto, Sept. 11, 1999. MD, U. Madrid, 1988, degree in aerospace physiology, 1989. Visual Flight Regulations and Instrumental Flight Regulations pilot lic. Intern in thoracic surgery 12 Octubre Hosp., Madrid, 1989, resident in cardiac surgery, 1990-94, resident, 1991-95; rschr. Nat. Rsch. Coun., Madrid, 1989; cons. cardiac surgery Hosp U. de Canarias, Tenerife, 1995—, Hosp. U. de Canarias, Tenerife, 1995—; dir. Medisoft, Inc., Madrid, 1988—. Author: Postoperative Care in Cardiac Surgery, 1995, Controversies in Cardiac Surgery, 1996; contbr. articles to profl. jours. including Circulation and Transplantation. Lt. Spanish Army Med. Br., 1989-90. Recipient Holland award Phillips Internat., 1984, Nat. Environ. award Environ. Coun., 1985, Logical award Simo, 1985, Ramon y Cajal award, 1988, Honor Grad. award Sch. Medicine, 1988, 1st award among honored grads. U. Complutense, 1989. Mem. Astron. Assn. (Pleyades award 1985), Spanish Soc. Cardiology (finalist award 1994), Spanish Soc. Cardiovasc. Surgery, Canary Soc. Cardiovasc. Surgery (sec. Tenerife chpt. 1996). Roman Catholic. Avocations: computers, astronomy, electronics, flying. E-mail: tuesta@usa.net. Office: Hosp U de Canarias, Cirugia Cardiaca, 38320 La Lafuna Tenerife, Spain

TUETING, SARAH, professional hockey player; b. Winnetka, Ill., Apr. 26, 1976. Degree in neurobiology, Dartmouth Coll. Goal keeper U.S. Nat. Women's Hockey Team, 1996—. Recipient ice hockey Gold medal Olympic Games, Nagano, Japan, 1998. Avocations: soccer, tennis, playing piano and cello. Office: c/o USA Hockey 1775 Bob Johnson Dr Colorado Springs CO 80906*

TUFAILE, ALBERTO, physicist, researcher; b. São Paulo, Brazil, Mar. 25, 1967; s. Jamil Maumed and Alaide Andrade Tufaile; m. Adriana Pedrosa Biscaia, Dec. 21, 1991. BSc, U. São Paulo, 1995, MSc, 1996, postgrad. Designer Compania de Sistemas e Projetos Engenharia, São Paulo, 1985-86; technician Petroquímica União, Santo André, Brazil, 1986-89; rschr. CNPq, São Paulo, 1995—. Recipient Golden Pound award Lab. de Fenômenos Não-Lineares, 1999. Mem. Soc. Brasileira de Física. Avocation: painting. E-mail: tufaile@yahoo.com and tufaile@if.usp.br. Fax: 813-3443. Home: Av Eng Heitor A E Garcia, 05580000 São Paulo Brazil Office: Univ de São Paulo, Inst Fisica Caixa 66318, 05315970 Sao Paulo Brazil

TUFTE, THOMAS, communications researcher, educator; b. Copenhagen, Dec. 21, 1964; s. Svein Roald and Birgitte (Ryge) T.; m. Pernille Juul Tufte, Aug. 10, 1991; children: Anna Linnea, Laura Marie. BA in cultural sociology, U. Copenhagen, 1986, MA in Sociology, 1989, PhD in Comm., 1995. Fundraiser Dansk AFS, Copenhagen, 1985-86; intern UNESCO, Paris, 1990; youth coord. Danchurchaid, Copenhagen, 1990-93; jr. profl. officer UNDP, Asuncion, Paraguay, 1994-96; postdoctoral rschr. U. Copenhagen, 1996-99, assoc. prof., 1999—; coord. Acad. Comm. Network, Europe/L.Am., 1996—; cons. Danish Trade Union Movement, Copenhagen, 1989-92. Author: Democracy on the Move, 1991, Living With the Rubbish Queen, 2000; author/dir.: Youth in the Middle East, 1993; co-editor: Television and Video in Latin America, 1993; editl. bd. INTERCOM, Sao Paulo, 1995—; co-editor Danish Jour. Comm., 1996—. Bd. dirs. Dansk AFS, 1987-88, Luna, Denmark, 1987-90, Danish Com. of European Coun. N/S Campaign, 1988. Danish Coun. for Devel. Rsch. fellow, 1993-94, Danish Coun. for Humanities fellow, 1996—. Mem. SMID, INTERCOM, IAMCR, ORBICOM (assoc.). Avocations: photography, hiking, film. Home: Soenderengen 95A, 2860 Soeborg Denmark Office: Univ of Copenhagen Dpt Film, Njalsgade 80, 2300 Copenhagen S, Denmark

TUGBIYELE, EMMANUEL AKANDE, education consultant; b. Igbajo, Osun, Nigeria, Apr. 22, 1923; s. Abraham Dada and Comfort Ige Tugbiyele; m. Dorcas Yetunde Bamigboye, Oct. 28, 1951 (div. Dec. 1959); 1 child, Abiodun; m. Wuraola Caroline Elutilo, May 5, 1960; children: Bolanle, Aduke, Olusegun, Titilola. BA, Va. Union U., 1954; MA in Tchg., Harvard U., 1955. Registered accredited mgmt. trainer, Nigeria. Tchr. Bapt. Mission, Igbajo, Nigeria, 1945-47, Abeokuta, Nigeria, 1948-52; vice prin. Bapt. Mission, Agbor, Nigeria, 1955-57; from lectr. to sr. lectr. U. Ibadan, Nigeria, 1957-68; from assoc. prof. to prof. U. Lagos, Nigeria, 1968-76; dir. tng. Dunlop Nigeria, Lagos, 1976-79; CEO Tawabat Consultancies Ltd., Lagos, 1979—. Author: Yoruba Conundrums, 1948, The Emergence of Nationalism and Federalism in Nigeria, 1956, The Educational System—Philosophy, Form and Content, 1976, An Introductory History of Igbajo, 1986, My Reminiscences, 1993; co-author: Igbajo—Citadel of the Brave, 1995, The Nigerian Baptist Convention in the 21st Century, 1999; contbr. articles to profl. jours. Counselor Action Group Party, Nigeria, 1958-60, 76-79; mem. Assets Investigation Tribunal, Western Nigeria, 1967-68, Constituent Assembly of Nigeria, Lagos, 1977-78; chmn. tech. com. Oyo State U. of Tech., Ibadan, 1990. Fellow City of Nairobi, 1972. Fellow Nigerian Inst. Training and Devel., Nigerian Inst. Mgmt., Inst. Pers. Mgmt. Nigeria; mem. Inst. Mgmt. Cons. Nigeria. Mem. Nigerian Baptist Convention. Avocations: playing the organ, listening to radio, reading newspapers and magazines. Home: Aguda-Surulere, 19 Jadeshola Oshodi St, Lagos Nigeria Office: Tawabat Consultancies Ltd, 360 Herbert Macaulay St, Akoka-Yaba Lagos Nigeria

TUGENDHAT, BARON LORD CHRISTOPHER SAMUEL, finance company executive; b. Feb. 23, 1937; s. Georg T.; m. Julia Lissant Dobson, 1967; 2 children. Grad., Gonville and Caius Coll., U. Cambridge, U.K. Leader, feature writer Fin. Times, London, 1960-70; M.P. from City of London and Westminster South Ho. of Commons, London, 1974-76; mem. EEC Commn., 1977-85, v.p., 1981-85; dir. The BOC Group, 1985—, LWT plc, 1991-94, Eurotunnel plc, 1991—; chmn. Abbey Nat. plc, 1991—, Royal Inst. of Internat. Affairs, 1985-95. Author: Oil: the Biggest Business, 1968, The Multinationals, 1971 (McKinsey Found. Book award, 1971), Making Sense of Europe, 1986, (with William Wallace) Options for British Foreign Policy in the 1990s, 1988; contbr. articles to profl. jours. Gov. Coun. of Ditchley Found., 1986—; v.p. Coun. Brit. Lung Found., 1986—. Mem. Buck's Club, Royal Anglo-Belgian Club. Avocation: reading. Office: Abbey Nat PLC, Abbey House Baker St, London NW1 6XL, England Home: 35 Westbourne Park Rd, London W2 5QD, England*

TUĞRUL, BERIL ASIYE, science administrator, educator; b. Bursa, Turkey, Mar. 29, 1952; d. Sehabettin Selcuk and Perihan (Aydoğdu) Üçyiğit; m. Hasan Tahsin Tuğrul, June 30, 1974; 1 child, Pelin. Degree in Mech. Engring., Istanbul (Turkey) Tech. U., 1973, MSc, 1975, PhD, 1984. Engr. Nuc. Rsch. Ctr., Istanbul, 1974-75; head group nuc. safety licensing Turkish Atomic Energy Commn., Ankara, 1975-77; univ. mem. Inst. for Nuc. Energy Istanbul Tech. U., 1977—, dep. dir. Inst. for Nuc. Energy, 1988-99, head nuc. applications divsn. Inst. for Nuc. Energy, 1997—; expert Turkish Standardization Orgn. NDT Com., 1990; expert rschr. Turkish Sci. and Tech. Rsch. Coun. Unit Archaeol. Orgn., 1990; cons. Turkish Airlines, Istanbul, 1993-95; v.p. Turkish Atomic Energy Authority Nuc. Safety and Licencing Com., 1998—. Art and regional editor Archaeology Tech. Abstract, 1988—; contbr. articles to profl. jours. Mem. Am. Nuc. Soc., Am. Soc. for Nondestructive Testing, Soc. for Archaeol. Scis. E-mail: tugrul@nuklees.itu.edu.tr. Home: Ihlamur Cad, 81600 Istanbul Turkey Office: Inst Nuc Energy, Istanbul Tech Univ, 80626 Istanbul Turkey

TUGULEA, ANDREI, science educator; b. Untesti, Moldova, Romania, Aug. 19, 1928; s. Teodosie and Ana Tugulea; m. Tatiana Tureanu, Jan. 30, 1955; children: Alexandru, Cezar-Adrian. D of Elec. Engring., Poly. Inst. Bucharest, Romania, 1951, PhD, 1958, D Docent, 1974. Cert. in engring. electrotechnics. Asst. U. Poly., Bucharest, 1951-57, lectr., 1957-64, prof., 1964—, head of chair for electrotech., 1968-76, dean Faculty Electrotechnics, 1976-84, head dept. engring. scis., 1995-99. Author: Electromagnetic Field, 1983, 94; contbr. over 100 articles to profl. publs. Sec. of state Romanian Govt., 1990-91; sen. Romanian Senate, Bucharest, 1992-96. Mem. IEEE, Romanian Acad. (sec. gen. 1999, Traian Vuia prize 1964). Democrat. Orthodox. Avocation: classical music. E-mail: andrei@acad.ro. Home: Str Dimitrie Orbescu 11, 70252 Bucharest Romania Office: Academia Romana, Cala Victorei 215, 71102 Bucharest Romania

TUHÁČKOVÁ, ZDENA, biochemist, researcher; b. Prague, Czech Republic, Feb. 10, 1943; d. Václav and Bozena (Koudelová) Soudek; m. Borivoj Tuháček, Mar. 29, 1965. D in Natural Scis., Charles U., Prague, 1976; PhD, Acad. Scis., Prague, 1980. Med. asst. Oncol. Inst., Prague, 1964-75, rschr., 1976-85; sr. rschr. Inst. Tuberculosis, Prague, 1986-90; sr. rsch. scientist Inst. Molecular Genetics Acad. Scis., Prague, 1991—. Contbr. articles to profl. jours. including Biochem. Jour., Biochemica Biophysica Acta, European Jour. Biochemistry, Internat. Jour. Cancer. Dep. local parliament, Prague, 1990-94. Grantee Acad. Sci. Czech Republic, 1992, Ministry Health Czech Republic, 1995, Agy. Czech Republic, 1999. Mem. Biochem. Molecular Biology Soc., European Assn. Cancer Rsch. Roman Catholic. Avocations: music, history of art, traveling. Office: Acad Scis Czech Republic, Flemingovo nam 2, 166 37 Prague 6, Czech Republic

TUHKANEN, SAKARI MARTTI, educator; b. Helsinki, Finland, Feb. 4, 1952; s. Lauri Artturi and Karin Elisabet (Lanaeus) T. PhD, Univ. Helsinki, 1984. Instr. Univ. Helsinki, 1976-88; jr. researcher Acad. of Finland, 1988-90; prof. Univ. Turku, 1990—. Contbr. articles to profl. jours. Mem. Geographical Soc. Finland, Finnish Soc. Devel. Studies (chmn. 1991-97, vice chmn. 1997-98). Avocations: nature, gardening. Home: Tavastilankatu 1 Residence 13, FIN20610 Turku Finland Office: Univ Turku Dept Geography, FIN20014 Turku Finland

TUILA'EPA SAILELE MALIELEGAOI, Western Samoan government official; b. Apr. 14, 1945; m. Gillian Meredith; 6 children. Attended, St. Joseph's Coll., Apia, St. Paul's Sch., Auckland; B Commerce, MA Commerce, Auckland U., 1969. Mem. Parliament, 1978, re-elected, 1982, assoc. min. finance, 1982, min. finance, 1984-85, 88—, min. commerce, trade and ind., min. treas., inland revenue and customs; investigating officer, 1970, dep. dir. econ. devel., 1971, dep. to the fin. sec., 1982, min. fin., prime min., min. commerce, min. fgn. affairs. Avocations: rugby, cricket. Office: Dept Finance, PO Box 3017, Apia Western Samoa*

TU'IPELEHAKE, PRINCE FATAFEHI, Tongan government official; b. Nuku' alofa, Tonga, Jan. 7, 1922; s. Vilame Tungi and Salote Tupou III; m. Princess Melenaite Tupou Moheofo; children: Mele Siuilikutapu Kalanivalu-Fotofili, Elisiva Fusipala Hahano Vahái, Sione Ngu Uluvalu Takeivulai Tukuaho, Lavinia Mataotaone Maafu, Ofeina'e he Langi Tuku' aho, Viliami Tupoumalohi Mailefihi Tuku' aho. Ed., Newington Coll., Sydney, Australia, Catton Agr. Coll., Queensland, Australia. Vis. agrl. officer 1944-49; gov. Vava'u, 1949-55, Ha' apai, 1955; minister of lands, 1953; former prime minister of Tonga, also minister for agr., min. of marine affairs; chmn. Tonga Commodities Bd. Decorated comdr. Order Brit. Empire. Address: Ministry Marine Affairs, PO Box 14, Nuku'alofa Tonga*

TUIVAGA, SIR TIMOCI (ULUIBUROTU), judge; b. Oct. 21, 1931; s. Isimeili Siga and Jessie (Hill) T.; m. Vilimaina Leba Parrott, 1958; 4 children. Grad., U. Auckland. Bar: 1964. Native magistrate Fiji, 1958-61; with Crown Coun., 1965-68; prin. legal officer, 1968-70, Puisne judge, 1972, acting chief justice, 1974; chief justice Fiji, 1980-87, 1988—. Avocations: golf, gardening. Office: PO Box 2215, 228 Ratu Sukuna Rd, Suva Fiji*

TULBA, ABDALLAH, Syrian government official. Former min. justice Govt. of Syria, Damascus; now min. state Govt. of Syria. Office: Office of Prime Minister, Shahbandar St, Damascus Syria*

TULETA, MAREK, physicist, educator, researcher; b. Cracow, Poland, Apr. 25, 1950; s. Juliusz and Stanisława (Rogala) T.; m. Dorota Pluta, Mar. 26, 1978; 1 child, Izabela. MS Inst. Physics, Siliesian U., Katowice, Poland, 1975; PhD Inst. Physics, Jagellonian U., Cracow, 1985. Lectr. Inst. Physics, Tech. U. Cracow, 1975-85, sr. lectr., 1985—; rsch. assoc. Inst. Physics, Jagellonian U., 1977—, Pa. State U., Univeristy Park, 1988-89. Contbr. articles to sci. publs., including Jour. of Physics, Vacuum, others. Roman Catholic. Avocations: chess, travel. Home: Siewna 21D/6, 31 231 Cracow Poland Office: Tech U Cracow Inst Physics, Podchorazych 1, 30 084 Cracow Poland

TULISZKA, EDMUND, combustion engineering researcher; b. Leszno, Poland, Oct. 18, 1920; s. Roman and Elzbieta (Kazmierowska) T.; m. Janina Teresa Kawka, Dec. 6, 1951; children: Roman, Sznitko Ewa. Degree in engring., U. Lodz, Poland, 1949; D Tech. Sci., Tech. U. Lodz, Poland, 1960. Asst. prof. Tech. U. Lodz, 1955-62; dir. Inst. Heat Engring. and Combustion Engines Tech. U. Poznan, 1962-81, chief, 1981-91, prof. emeritus, 1991—, vice rector, 1972-75, rector, 1981-82; prof. Tech. U. Poznan, Poland, 1966—; chmn. sci. coun. Devel. Rsch. Ctr. Combustion Engines of Poznan, 1972-82. Author: Compressors, Blowers and Fans, 1969, rev. edit. 1976, Steam and Gas Turbines, 1973; contbr. articles to profl. jours. Mem. Polish Acad. Scis. (various cosm. 1966-90). Mem. Solidarity. Achievements include development of same theoretical problems. Avocations: sports, travel. Home: Rolna 46a/4, 61-487 Poznań Poland Office: Tech U Poznań, ul Piotvowo 3, 60-965 Poznań Poland

TULL, WILLIS CLAYTON, JR., librarian; b. Crisfield, Md., Feb. 22, 1931; s. Willis Clayton and Agnes Virginia (Milbourne) T.; m. Taeko Itoi, Dec. 18, 1952. Student, U. Balt., 1948, Johns Hopkins U., 1956; BS, Towson (Md.)

State Coll., 1957; MLS, Rutgers U., 1962; postgrad., Miami U., Oxford, Ohio, 1979. Editl. clk. 500th Mil. Intelligence Svc. Group, 1952-53; tchr. Hereford Jr.-Sr. H.S., Parkton, Md., 1957-59; aide Enoch Pratt Free Libr., Balt., 1959-61, profl. asst., 1962-64; coord. adult svcs. Washington County Free Libr., Hagerstown, Md., 1964-67; asst. regional libr. Eastern Shore Regional Libr., Salisbury, Md., 1967; br. libr. Balt. County Pub. Libr., Pikesville, Md., 1968-71; asst. area br. libr. Balt. County Pub. Libr., Essex, Md., 1971-72; sr. info. specialist Balt. County Pub. Libr., Catonsville, Md., 1972-87; on-line supr. Balt. County Pub. Libr., Towson, Md., 1988-89; sr. info. specialist Balt. County Pub. Libr., Reisterstown, Md., 1989-90; exec. dir. Milbourne and Tull Rsch. Ctr., 1991—. Contbr. to profl. and geneal. jours. Mem. Rep. Ctrl. Com. Baltimore County, 1971-72. With U.S. Army, 1949-52. Fellow Nat. Congress Patriotic Orgns.; mem. Freedom To Read Found., Md. Libr. Assn. (chmn. intellectual freedom com. 1969-70), Friends Johns Hopkins U. Librs., Libr. of Congress Assocs., Md. Assn. for Adult Edn. (coord. Western Md. region 1965-67), Am. Coun. Trustees and Alumni, Am. Acad. Religion, Metaphys. Soc. Am., Nat. Assn. Scholars, Woodrow Wilson Internat. Ctr. for Scholars, Assn. for Asian Studies, World Future Soc., Freedom House, Internat. Rescue Com., Nature Conservancy, Unitarian and Universalist Geneal. Soc. (founder, bd. dirs. 1971-87), Md. Geneal. Soc., Royal Soc. St. George, Sons and Daus. Pilgrims, Descs. Early Quakers, SAR, Soc. War of 1812, Ancient and Hon. Mech. Co. Balt., Kappa Delta Pi. Home and Office: 10605 Lakespring Way Hunt Valley MD 21030-2818

TULLIO, GIUSEPPE, economist, researcher; b. Rome, Mar. 30, 1948; s. Pietro Tullio and Elisabetta De Vecchis; m. Dominique Marie Korsmeier, Nov. 15, 1975 (div. 1986). Laurea in Stats., U. Rome, 1970; MA in Econs., U. Chgo., 1973, PhD in Econs., 1977. Economist Banca d'Italia, Rome, 1974-77, dep. dir. rsch., 1988-89; economist Internat. Monetary Fund, Washington, 1978-80; econ. advisor Ministry of the Budget, Rome, 1981-83, European Commn., Brussels, 1984-87; prof. econs. U. Cagliari, Italy, 1990-94, U. Brescia, Italy, 1995—; econ. adv. Russian Govt., Moscow, 1996-98; lectr. Luiss U., Rome, 1981-83; vis. fellow Inst. Internat. Econ. Studies U. Stockholm, 1983-84; vis. prof. U. Berlin, 1991, Fundacao Getulio Vargas, Rio de Janeiro, 1993, U. Campinas, Brazil, 1995, U. La Plata, Argentina, 1996, U. Paris, 1999. Author: The Monetary Approach to External Adjustment: A Case Study of Italy, 1981, Essays in Monetary and Fiscal Policy in Italy, 1983, German Macro-Economic History: 1880-1979: A Study of the Effects of Economic Policy on Inflation, Currency Depreciation and Growth, 1987, Inflation and Wage Behaviour in Europe, 1996; contbr. numerous articles to newspapers and profl. jours.; spkr. in field. Avocations: traveling, history and political science, restoring family-owned medieval towers in cen. Italy. Office: U Degli Studi Brescia, Via San Faustino 74/B, 25122 Brescia Italy

TULLY, DANIEL PATRICK, financial services executive; b. 1932; m. Grace Tully; children: Daniel G., Eileen, Elizabeth, Timothy. BBA, St. Johns U., 1953. With Merrill Lynch, Pierce, Fenner & Smith, N.Y.C., 1955—, mem. acctg. dept., 1955-59, acct. exec. trainee, 1959-63, asst. to mgr. Stamford, Conn. office, 1963-70, mgr., 1970-71, v.p., 1971-79, dir. individual sales, 1976-79, exec. v.p., 1979-82, pres. individual services group, 1982-84, pres. consumer mktg., from 1984; pres., COO Merrill Lynch & Co., Inc., N.Y.C., 1985; former exec. v.p. Merrill Lynch & Co. (parent), N.Y.C., 1979, CEO, 1992-96, chmn., 1993-97; chmn. emeritus Merrill Lynch & Co. (parent). Served U.S. Army, 1953-55. Office: Merrill Lynch & Co Inc 301 Tresser Blvd Fl 10 Stamford CT 06901-3239

TULU, DERARTU, Olympic athlete. Winner Gold medal 10,000 meters Sydney, 2000. Office: Ethiopian Athletic Fedn, PO Box 3241, Addis Adaba Stadium Addis Adaba Ethiopia*

TULUB, ALEXANDER ALEXANDROVICH, physicist, researcher, educator; b. St. Petersburg, Russia, Apr. 17, 1955; s. Alexander Vladimirovich and Tatiana Petrovna (Grigorieff) T. M in Chemistry, St. Petersburg U., 1977, M in Math., 1990, PhD in Phys. Chemistry, 1982, D Physics and Math., 1999. Rschr. Faculty of Chemistry, St. Petersburg State U., 1977-85; rschr. Acad. Pharmacy and Chemistry, St. Petersburg, 1985-94; sr. rschr. St. Petersburg U., 1994—, assoc. prof., 1994—. Author: Molecular Mechanisms of Binding of Antitemor Platimun Complexes with DNA and Cytoskeletal Proteins, 1999 (Mendeleyev award 1999), also articles. Capt. Russian Army, 1976-78. Mem. N.Y. Acad. Sci., City Tennis Club. Home: Zheleznovodskaya St 31-25, 199155 St Petersburg Russia Office: St Petersburg State U, Univ Naberezhaya 7/9, 197034 St Petersburg Russia

TULUN, VAHDET Y. ALI, insurance company executive; b. Istanbul, Turkey, Oct. 1, 1956; s. Vasfi Mustafa Tulun and Aysegul Buyukaksoy Kaytaz; m. Muzeyyen Onec, May 5, 1982; 1 child, Ugur. Grad., Istanbul U., 1979. Cert. economist, specialist on mgmt. and mktg. Prodn. planner Monosan A.S., Istanbul, 1980-81; mgmt. trainee Sark Sigorta A.S., Istanbul, 1981-82, asst. supt., 1982-87, supt. fire ins. dept., 1987-88, mktg. mgr., 1988-90; asst. gen. mgr. mktg. Emek Sigorta A.S., Istanbul, 1990-95, gen. mgr., 1995-96; gen. mgr. Demir Hayat Sigorta A.S., Istanbul, 1996—. Bd. mem. Found. for Children, Istanbul, 1991—. Mem. Istanbul Chess Club. Avocations: reading, surfing the Internet, playing chess, photography, traveling. Office: Demir Hayat Sigorta AS, Buyukdere Cd 122/B, 80280 Istanbul Turkey

TULYAKOVA, TATYANA VLADIMIROVNA, biotechnologist, researcher; b. Moscow, May 25, 1944; d. Vladimir Ilich and Elena Vladimirovna (Shteinbrecht) Burlakova; m. Andrei Sergeevich Tulyakov, June 25, 1966 (dec. 1977); 1 child. Diploma with honors, Tech. U., 1966; student, Acad. of Food Prodn., 1977. Engr. Inst. of Automatization, Moscow, 1967-69; sr. engr. PCB-12, Moscow, 1969-72; scientific rschr. Inst. of Bakery, Moscow, 1972-85; head of dept. Inst. of Food Biotech., Moscow, 1985-96; head of lab. JSC Derbenevka, Moscow, 1996—; head of projects Tech. U., Moscow, 1985-96, cons. candidate dissertation, 1996—; chmn. scientific bd. Inst. of Food Biotech. Orgn., Moscow, 1985-96; mem. scientific bd. Acad. of Agrl. Sci. Orgn., Moscow, 1987-96; corr. Acad. of Technol. Sci. of RF Orgn., Moscow, 1994-99. Author: Control and Automatization of Yeast Production, 1984, Cycle of Works on Yeast Biotechnology, 1972-87 (State award 1987); patentee in field. Chmn. bd. dirs. JSC Derbenevka, 1997. Avocations: skiing, swimming. Home: Alabayana 11-49, 125057 Moscow Russia Office: JSC Derbenevka, Derbenevka, 114114 Moscow Russia

TULYA-MUHIKA, SAM, statistician, consultant; b. Kabale, Kigezi, Uganda, Nov. 24, 1939; s. Zefania and Tezira (Tibakaba) Tibigambwa; m. Edrida Charity Lushaya, Dec. 15, 1973; 5 children. BS, U. East Africa, Uganda, 1967; PhD, U. Sheffield, U.K., 1972. Lectr. Makerere U., Uganda, 1970-73, sr. lectr., 1973-80, assoc. prof., 1980-83, prof., 1983—; dir. Inst. Stats. and Applied Econs., Uganda, 1972-89; v.p. Internat. Statis. Inst., The Hague, 1977-79; dir. Ctrl. Bank Uganda, 1974-86; chmn. Uganda Airlines, 1986-88, Uganda Revenue Authority, 1991-97, Fedn. Ugandan Cons., 1994—, Gen. Concrete Products Internat. Corp., 1996—. Author: The Rise and Fall and Rise Again of the East African Community, 2000; co-author, editor-in-chief: Global Lessons From the Rise and Fall of the East African Community, 1995; contbg. author: East African Short Plays, 1968, Teaching of Statistics in Schools Throughout the World, 1982; contbr. articles to profl. jours. Chmn. Pub. Svc. Salaries Review Commn., Uganda, 1980-82, East African Co-operation Forum, Nairobi, 1993—, Uganda Nat. Immigrants Devel. Agy., 1994—; mem. Pub. Svc. Review and Re-orgn. Commn., Uganda, 1989-91. Fellow Econ. Devel. Inst. World Bank, Royal Statis. Soc. U.K., Inst. Statisticians U.K.; mem. Internat. Statis. Inst. (v.p. 1977-79), African Statis. Soc., Uganda Statis. Soc. Mem. Ch. of Eng. Avocations: classical music, chess, soccer, lawn tennis.

TUMAKOV, VLADIMIR LEONIDOVICH, physicist, researcher; b. Rustavi, Georgia, USSR, Feb. 16, 1957; arrived in Russia, 1974; s. Leonid Grigorievich and Galina Prokofievna (Karpenko) T.; m. Tatiana Pavlovna Gordeeva, June 2, 1977; children: Katerina, Pavel. PhD in Physics and Math., Inst. High Energy Physics, Protvino, Russia, 1996. Lab. asst. Inst. High Energy Physics, 1980-81, jr. rschr., 1981-87, rschr., 1987-97, sr. rschr., 1997-98; rschr. U. Calif., Irvine, 1999—; fellow high energy rsch. orgn. KEK, Japan, 1997-98. Internat. Sci. Found. grantee, 1994. Office: U Calif Dept Physics And Astronomy Irvine CA 92697-0001

TUMANI, HAYRETTIN, physician, neuroscientist; b. Antakya, Turkey, May 1, 1964; arrived in Germany, 1972; s. Mehmet and Edibe (Yarimay) T.; m. Visal Ayabakan Tumani. MD, U. Gottingen, Germany, 1991. Resident dpet. neurology U. Gottingen, Germany, 1992-94; rsch. scientist Splty. Labs Santa Monica, Calif., 1994-95; physician, scientist, lectr. dept. neurology U. Gottingen, Germany, 1995—; dir. neurochemistry lab., dept. neurology U. Ulm, Germany, 1999, cons. neurologist, scientist, asst. dir. dept. neurology, 1999—. Author: Multiple Sclerosis: Clinical and Pathological Basis, 1997; contbr. articles to profl. jours. Fellow Friedrich-Ebert Found.; mem. World Fedn. Neurology, Internat. Soc. Neurochemistry, German Soc. Neurology, German Soc., Neurosci., Soc. Sports Medicine, European Neurol. Soc. Office: U Ulm Dept Neurology RKU, Oberer Eselsberg 45, 89081 Ulm Germany

TUMI, CHRISTIAN WIYGHAN CARDINAL, bishop; b. Kikaikelaki, Cameroon, Oct. 15, 1930. Ordained priest Roman Cath. Ch., 1966. Elected to Yagoua, 1979, consecrated bishop, 1980, coadjutor bishop Garoua, 1982-84, diocesan bishop Garoua, 1984-91, archbishop of Douala, 1991—, created cardinal,, 1988. Address: Archvêché, BP 179, Douala Cameroon*

TUMMINELLI, ROBERTO VITTORIO R., educator, author; b. Milan, Italy, Dec. 28, 1937; s. Michele Maria Tumminelli and Maria Lucilla Evangelista; m. Maria Adelaide Lancia, July 31, 1964 (div. May 1972); 1 child, Roberta; m. Roberta Origgi, Oct. 30, 1991; 1 child, Nicola Pietro Alessandro. Gen. cert. edn., Istituto de Amicis, Milan, 1958; degree in polit. sci., U. Pavia, Milan, 1963. Tchr. Unione Professori, Milan, 1964-67, asst. mgr., 1967-70, headmaster, 1970-72, chmn., 1972—; asst. mgr. Istituto de Amicis, Milan, 1973-78, adminstr., 1979—; prof. history of polit. thought Universita Degli Studi, Milan. Translator, editor: Voyage En Carie, 1981; author: Ilsangue e la Ragione, 1987, A History of Utopias, 1992, the Body of the Night, 1997, others. Rep. Anti-Fascist Movement, Italy, 1968-80; founder Anti-Fascist Com. Milan, 1974. Mem. Knights of Malta. Roman Catholic. Avocations: charity, tennis, bass playing. E-mail: VRTumminelli@iol.it. Home: V Lamarmora 36, 20122 Milan Italy Office: Istituto de Amicis, V Lamarmora 34, 20122 Milan Italy

TUMOVÁ, BELA, retired microbiologist, virologist, educator; b. Prague, Czechoslovakia, Aug. 2, 1929; s. Josef and Angela (Hruskova) T.; m. Augustin Stumpa, Oct. 19, 1962. Biologist, Charles U., 1952, dr. rer. nat., 1953, DSc, 1984; PhD, Acad. Scis. Prague, 1963. Rschr. Pub. Health Inst., Prague, 1953-62; head influenza ctr. Inst. Epidemiology and Microbiology, Prague, 1963-68; vis. prof. U. Wis., Madison, 1968-72; head influenza ctr. Inst. Hygiene and Epidemiology, Prague, 1972-99; ret., 1999, advisor, lectr., 2000—; head dept. virus respiratory infections Nat. Inst. Pub. Health, Prague, 1986—; lectr. Charles U. Med. Sch., Prague, 1990-95, Postgrad. Med. Sch., Prague, 1990—. Co-author chpts. in books. WHO fellow Nat. Inst. Med. Rsch., London, 1963-64; recipient Pub. Health award Sci. Coun. Ministry Health, 1974, Nat. prize Czech Republic, 1982. Mem. European Sci. Work Group on Influenza (v.p. 1993—), European Group for Rapid Viral Diagnosis, European Group for Clin. Virology, Soc. Epidemiology and Microbiology (hon.), Czech Med. Assn., N.Y. Acad. Scis. Avocations: fine arts, paintings, history. Home: Pod Trebesinem 2361, 100 00 Prague 10 Czech Republic Office: Nat Inst Pub Health, Srobarova 48, 100 42 Prague Czech Republic

TUN, ZAW, forensic medicine researcher; b. Rangoon, Burma, Mar. 14, 1961; s. Than Htut and Tin Tin Yee; m. Khin Thuzar Oo, Mar. 15, 1993; children: Norman, Steven. M.B.B.S., Inst. Medicine I, Yangon, 1985; PhD, Osaka (Japan) U. Med. Sch., 1999. House surgeon Mandalay (Myanmar) Gen. Hosp., 1985-86, asst. surgeon, 1989-92; demonstrator Dept. Anatomy IM(1), Yangon, 1992-93, Dept. Forensic Medicine IM(1), Yangon, 1993-94; asst. police surgeon Yangon Gen. Hosp., 1993-94; tchg. and rsch. asst. Osaka U. Med. Sch., 1999—. Contbr. articles to profl. jours. Min. of Edn. scholar, 1994-99. Mem. Assn. Japanese DNA Polymorphism, Medico-Legal Soc. Japan, N.Y. Acad. Sci. Avocations: reading, music, computers, tennis, table tennis. Home: Syuku no Syo 854-2, Ibaraki, Osaka 567-0051, Japan

TUNAY-UNSAL, NURAN, geological engineer, researcher; b. Igdir, Turkey, Dec. 26, 1956; came to U.S., 1995; d. Kamil and Feride (Gunay) Tunay; m. Ilhan Unsal, Oct. 28, 1979; 1 child, Volkan. Diploma in Geol. Engring., Earth Sci. Geol. Engring., Turkey, 1982; cert. in Civil Engring., Min. of Pub. Works, Ankara, Turkey, 1985. Geol. engr. Gen. Directorate of Bank of Provinces, Konya-Ankara, Turkey, 1982-84, Gen. Directorate of Hwy., Kayseri-Ankara, Turkey, 1984-89, Adminstrn. Pub. Works, Manisa, Turkey, 1989-95; cons. Pub. Works, Manisa, Turkey, 1989-95; adv. bds. Pub. Works, Municipality, Civil Cts., Manisa, Turkey, 1992-94. Inventor: Adaptation of Stabilized Hydrated Lime, Publication of the Chamber of Geol. Engring. of Turkey, 1993. Recipient of presentations 46th Congress of Geology of Turkey, Ankara, 1993. Fellow Geol. Assn. Can.; mem. Geol. Soc. Am., Chamber of Geol. Engrs. of Turkey. Achievements include the soil improvement with hydrated lime stabilization; applied in the area of Manisa Teachers House Buildings, was one of the first applications in Turkey. Home: 8655 Bay Pkwy Apt A4 Brooklyn NY 11214-4122

TUNBRIDGE, WILLIAM MICHAEL GREGG, physician, consultant; b. Leeds, Yorkshire, Eng., June 13, 1940; s. Ronald Ernest and Dorothy (Gregg) T.; m. Felicity Katherine E. Parrish, Aug. 28, 1965; children: Clare Katherine, Anne Jacqueline. BA, Cambridge (Eng.) U., 1961, MB, BCh, 1964, MD, 1977. House physician, house surgeon U. Coll. Hosp., London, 1964-65; sr. house officer Mpilo Hosp., Bulawayo, Zimbabwe, 1965-66; sr. house officer Manchester (Eng.) Royal Infirmary, 1967-68, tutor in medicine, 1970-72; registrar Hammersmith Hosp., London, 1970-72; rsch. fellow U. Newcastle upon Tyne, Eng., 1972-75, U. Liege, Belgium, 1976-77; sr. registrar Newcastle U. Hosps., 1975-77; cons. physician Newcastle Gen. Hosp., 1977-94; dir. postgrad. med. edn. and tng. Oxford U., England, 1994—; cons. physician John Radcliffe Hosp., Oxford, 1994—. Author: (with R.S. Bayliss) Thyroid Disease, The Facts, 3rd edit., 1998. Fellow Royal Coll. Physicians of London; mem. European Thyroid Assn. (com. 1980-84). Avocation: walking. Office: Oxford U Med Sch Dept Postgrad Med Edn, The Triangle Roosevelt Dr, Oxford 0X3 7XP, England

TUNC, MUSTAFA, pathologist; b. Serik, Antalya, Turkey, Feb. 27, 1964; s. Ismail Hakki and Hatice Gulten (Unver) T.; m. Demet Sehlikoglu, Aug. 15, 1994; 1 child, Lara. Grad., Hacettepe Med. Sch., Ankara, Turkey, 1988. Med. doctor diplomate. Resident faculty pathology Ankara U. Med., 1988-93; specialist in pathology State Hosp., Denizli, Turkey, 1993-95; instr. Akdeniz U. Med. Sch., Antalya, 1995-96; specialist Antalya Pvt. Pathology Ctr., 1996—; observer, rschr. Inst. Ortopedico Rizzoly, Bologna, Italy, 1992. Contbr. articles to profl. jours. Pvt. doctor Turkish Health Orgn., 1992. Mem. Turkish Struggle for Erosion of Ground, Hacettepe Univ. Grad. Club. Avocations: golf, music, Internet, tennis. Home: C blok No 5/9, Eski Lara Cad Alpek 1 sit, 07100 Antalya Turkey Office: Antalya Patoloji Merkezi, 100yil bulv. Pinireis 28/6, 07050 Antalya Turkey

TUNCER, A. MURAT, physician; b. Aydin/Nazilli, Jan. 14, 1957; s. Mehmet Isfendiyar and Sevinc Yapraktasir; m. Safyye Ozgunes, Jan. 4, 1983; children: Aslihan, Mehmet. MD, Istanbul U., 1980; postgrad., Hacettepe U., Ankara, Turkey, 1989. Pediatric resident Hacettepe U. Children's Hosp., Ankara, 1980-84, acad. mem., 1987-92, dir., 1992—. Editor: Turkish Jour. of Pediatrics, Pediatric Jour. Compulsory Mil. Svc., 1984-85. Recipient Turkish Nat. Scientific Commn. award, 1997, Cihat Tahsin Gursoy Sci. award, 1980. Mem. Turkish Nat. Pediatric Soc. (gen. sec. 1997—), Nat. Pediatric Soc., Am. Soc. of Hematology, Internat. Soc. for Exptl. Hematology. Islam. Avocations: jogging, swimming, chess, tennis. Fax: 90-312-3105700. E-mail: mtuncer@usa.net. Home: Dicle Caddesi No 14, Ankara 06380, Turkey Office: Hacettepe U Childrens Hosp, Sihhiye, Ankara 06100, Turkey

TUNCER, MERAL, pharmacologist, educator, pharmacist; b. Ladik, Samsun, Turkey, May 25, 1943; d. Abdulhalim and Emine (Eminağaoğlu) Suner; m. Hasan Hadi Tuncer, Nov. 15, 1968. Degree in Pharmacy, Ankara (Turkey) U., 1966, MD, 1972; PhD in Pharmacology, Hacettepe U., Ankara, 1976. Asst., instr. Hacettepe U., Ankara, Turkey, 1973-76-82; asst. prof. Hacettepe U., Ankara, 1982-89, prof., 1989—; vis. scientist Mayo Clinic, Rochester, Minn., 1987-88. Office: Hacettepe U Dept Pharmacol, Faculty Medicine, 06100 Sihhiye Ankara Turkey

TUNE, JAMES FULCHER, lawyer; b. Danville, Va., May 13, 1942; s. William Orrin and Susan Agnes (Fulcher) T.; m. Katherine Del Mickey, Aug. 2, 1969; children: Katherine Winslow, Jeffrey Bricker. BA, U. Va., 1964; MA, Stanford U., 1970, JD, 1974. Bar: Wash. 1974, U.S. Dist. Ct. (we. dist.) Wash. 1974. Assoc. Bogle & Gates, Seattle, 1974-79, ptnr., 1980-99, head comml./banking dept., 1985-93, mng. ptnr., 1986-93, chmn., 1994-99; ptnr. Dorsey & Whitney LLP, Seattle, 1999—; bd. dirs. BIEC Internat. Inc., Kalama, Wash., BHP Steel Ams. Inc., Long Beach, Calif., Nichirei Foods, Inc., Seattle, Passport Cuisine Internat., Inc., Seattle; chmn. Seattle-King City Econ. Devel. Coun., 1992. Chmn. Seattle Repertory Theatre, 1995. Lt. USN, 1964-69, Vietnam. Woodrow Wilson fellow, 1964, Danforth Found. fellow, 1964. Mem. ABA, Wash. State Bar Assn. (lectr. CLE 1976, 78, 84), Seattle-King County Bar Assn., Seattle C. of C. (vice chmn. City Budget Task Force 1980-82), Phi Beta Kappa, Ranier Club, Seattle Tennis Club. Presbyterian. Office: Dorsey & Whitney LLP US Bank Bldg Ctr 1420 5th Ave Ste 3400 Seattle WA 98101-4010

TUNE, TOMMY (THOMAS JAMES TUNE), musical theater director, dancer, choreographer, actor; b. Wichita Falls, Tex., Feb. 28, 1939; s. Jim P. and Eva Mae (Clark) T. Student, Lon Morris Jr. Coll., 1958-59; BFA, U. Tex., 1962; postgrad., U. Houston, 1962-63. Dancer, choreographer, dir. various prodns., N.Y.C., 1963—. Dancer (Broadway prodns.): Baker Street, 1965, A Joyful Noise, 1966, How Now Dow Jones, 1967, Seesaw, 1973 (Tony award Best Featured Actor musical 1974), (films): Hello Dolly, 1968, The Boyfriend, 1971; dir., choreographer Broadway prodns.: The Best Little Whorehouse in Texas, 1978 (Tony award nominations Best Dir. musical 1979, Best Choreography 1979, Drama Desk award Best Dir. musical 1979), A Day in Hollywood/A Night in the Ukraine, 1980 (Tony award Best Choreography 1980, Tony award nomination Best Dir. musical 1980, Drama Desk awards Best Musical Staging, 1980, Best Choreography 1980), Nine, 1982 (Drama Desk award Best Dir. musical 1982, Tony award Best Dir. musical 1982, Tony award nomination Best Choreography 1982), Grand Hotel, 1989 (Tony awards Best Choreography 1990, Best Dir. 1990, Drama Desk awards Best Choreography 1990, Best Dir. musical 1990); dir., actor, choreographer My One and Only, 1983 (Tony awards Best Actor musical 1983, Best Choreography 1983, Tony award nomination Best Dir. musical 1983, Drama Desk award Outstanding Choreography 1983), The Will Rogers Follies, 1990 (Tony awards Best Choreography 1991, Best Dir. 1991, Drama Desk award Best Choreography 1991); tour Bye, Bye Birdie, 1991-92; dir. Broadway prodn.: Stepping Out, 1987; dir. Off-Broadway prodns.: The Club, 1976 (Obie award 1977), Sunset, 1977, Cloud 9, 1981 (Drama Desk award Best Dir. 1982, Obie award Disting. Direction 1982); performed in the USSR, 1988; actor: BuskerAlley. Recipient Drama League Musical Achievement award, 1990; inducted into Theatre Hall of Fame, 1991. Mem. Dirs. Guild Am., Stage Soc. Dirs. and Choreographers, Actors Equity Assn. Office: care Internat Creative Mgmt 40 W 57th St New York NY 10019-4001 also: Tommy Tune Inc 50 E 89th St New York NY 10128-1225

TUNG, JEFFREY CHAO-HUI, linguist, educator; b. Kaohsiung, Taiwan, Oct. 21, 1931; s. Chih Tung and Shun Chen; m. Wendy Chi-yuan Huang, Nov. 23, 1956; children: Thih-yuen Tung, Sophia Tung. BA, Taiwan U., Taipei, 1954; MA, Taiwan Normal U., Taipei, 1959, U. Tex., Austin, 1964; postgrad., U. Calif., Berkeley, 1966-67. Instr. Taiwan Normal U., 1960-66; translator Nippon Koei Tsengwen Reservoir Team, Taipei, 1967-73; assoc. prof. English Taiwan Normal U., 1971-83, prof. English, 1983-96; vis. prof. linguistics Keio U., Tokyo, 1989-91, inst. assoc., 1991—; editor China Post, Taipei, 1959-61, China News, Taipei, 1962-63; cons. Student Book Co., Taipei, 1976—, Edn. Ministry, Taipei, 1985—. Author: The Present Perfect and Related Matters, (in Chinese) 1982, Chinese Syllables and English Syllables, (in English) 1983, Time Frames of English Sentences, (in English) 1985. 2d lt. Taiwan Army, 1954-56. Recipient Outstanding Coll. Tchg. award Edn. Ministry, Taipei, 1993. Mem. Linguistic Soc. Am., Linguistic Soc. Japan, English Linguistic Soc. Japan. Avocations: haiku, singing, swimming, hiking, train travel. Home: (10F-2) 335 Roosevelt Rd 3, Taipei 106, Taiwan Office: Taiwan Normal U English Dep, 162 Hoping East Rd (Sec 1), Taipei 106, Taiwan

TUNG, PHAM DINH (PAUL JOSEPH PHAM DINH TUNG), Roman Catholic cardinal; b. Ninh Binh, Viet Nam, May 20, 1919; s. Pham Van Hien and Nguyen Thi Bong. Student, Major Sem., Hanoi, Viet Nam, 1940-46. Priest Hanoi, 1949; bishop Bac ninh, Viet Nam, 1963-90; apostolic adminstr. Hanoi, 1990-94, archbishop, 1994—, elevated to Cardinal, 1994; mem. Propaganda Fide, The Vatican, 1995, mem. Cor Unum, 1995. Author: Spirituality, 1962, (poetry) The Life of Christ, 1969, (predication) Homelies-Years ABC, 1989. Avocations: football, volleyball. Home and Office: Toa Tong Giam Muc, 40 Pho Nha Chung, Ha Noi Vietnam

TUNG, SAMUEL SHUI-LIANG, economics and business educator; b. Sinyan, Pingtung, Republic of China, Sept. 27, 1946; s. Cheuh and Hsiu-Ing (Chen) T. B in Commerce, Nat. Chengchi U., Taipei, Republic of China, 1969, M in Commerce, 1972; PhD in Econs., U. Hawaii, 1979; PhD in Bus., U. Wis., 1987. CPA, Md. Rsch. assoc. Dirctorate-Gen. of Budget, Acctg. and Statistics, Taipei, 1972-74; sr. economist, chief Econ. Rsch. Ctr., Guam, 1978-81; asst. prof. econs. Baruch Coll. CUNY, 1987—; vis. scholar U. N.C., Chapel Hill, 1981-83. Contbr. articles to profl. jours. Lt. Army Republic of China, 1969-70. Recipient Profl. Assoc. award East-West Ctr., Honolulu, 1979, Grad. Degree Study award, 1974-78; fellow Ernst & Whinney Found., 1986. Mem. Am. Acctg. Assn., Am. Fin. Assn. Democrat. Avocations: tennis, jogging, photography. Office: U Hong Kong Bapt U, Dept Acctg and Law, Hong Kong Hong Kong

TUNG, YEISHIN, research scientist; b. Taipei, Taiwan, Aug. 27, 1962; came to U.S., 1987; s. Wei and Kuoing (Wu) T. BSChemE, Chung Yuan U., Chun Li, Taiwan, 1984; MS in Materials Sci., Rutgers U., 1989, PhD in Materials Sci., 1993. Rsch. asst. Rutgers U., New Brunswick, N.J., 1989-93; rsch. assoc. Fisk U., Nashville, 1994-97, rsch. asst. prof., 1997-98; staff analyst accelerator techiques group Charles Evans & Assocs., Redwood City, Calif., 1998—. Author: (book chpt.) Hyphenated Techniques in Polymer Characterization, 1994. 2d lt. Taiwan infantry, 1984-86. Recipient Coblentz Soc. award Coblentz Soc., 1993. Mem. Am. Phys. Soc., Am. Vacuum Soc., Materials Rsch. Soc., Am. Chem. Soc. Achievements include observation of surface phonon mode of semiconductor quantum dots; measurement of sublimation rates of high explosives.

TUNGSANGA, KRAI, civil engineer, engineering company executive; b. Bangkok, Thailand, Oct. 28, 1952; s. Krui and Lek (Tayanithi) T.; 1 child. BCE, Kasetsart U., Bangkok, 1974; MSCE, Ohio State U., 1977. Civil engr. Royal Irrigation Dept., Bangkok, 1974; project engr. Ohio Dept. Transp. Bur. of Bridges, Columbus, Ohio, 1977-78, found. engr., 1979-89; project engr. Asian Engring. Cons., Bangkok, 1977-78, project mgr., 1989-90; mng. dir. Pyramid Devel. Internat. Corp., Ltd., Bangkok, 1990—. Named Alumnus of the Yr., Coll. Engring., Kasetsart U., 1995. Mem. ASCE, Engring. Inst. Thailand (bd. dirs. 1995—), Rotary Club of Chareonnakorn (pres. 1996-97). Office: 28 Soi Mahatharadol, Narathiwat Rajchanakarin Rd, Sathorn Bangkok 10120, Thailand

TUNINSKAYA, GALINA M., chemist; b. Lutsk, Volinskiy, Ukraine; came to U.S., 1993; d. Michael and Faina (Metushanska) T.; m. Mark Rokhfeld, Dec. 30, 1979; children: Marianna, Dmitriy. BS, Leningrad Inst. Chem. Engring., Russia, 1975, MS, 1977. Engr., chemist Linen Mfg., Zhitomir, Ukraine, 1977-80; from. prof. to rsch. chemist Pedagogical Inst., Zhitomir, Ukraine, 1980-93; from rsch. chemist to chief chemist Applied Consumer Svcs., Miami, 1993-97, tech. dir., 1997—. Active Russian Outreach Program, Miami, 1995—. Mem. AAAS, Am. Chem. Soc. Office: Applied Consumers Svcs 9500 NW 77th Ave Ste 5 Hialeah Gardens FL 33016

TUNITSKAYA, VERA LEONIDOVNA, chemist, researcher; b. Moscow, USSR, Feb. 24, 1951; d. Leonid Nikolaevich and Vera Fridrikhovna (Eihman) T.; m. Alexander Veniaminovich Itkes, Aug. 22, 1980; 1 child, Alexander. Degree in chem. engring., Moscow Inst. Fine Chem. Tech., 1974; PhD, Inst. Organic Chemistry, Moscow, 1980. Chemist Inst. Organic Chemistry, Moscow, 1974-80, rschr., 1980-83; rschr. Moscow State U., 1983-87; sr. rschr. Inst. Molecular Biology, 1987—. Home: Volginstr 31, Bldg 3 Apt 205, 117437 Moscow Russia Office: Inst Mol Biol Rus Acad Scis, Vavilovstr 32, 117987 Moscow Russia

TUNNER, WILLIAM SAMS, urological surgeon; b. San Antonio, Nov. 14, 1933; s. William Henry and Sarah Margaret (Sams) T.; m. Sallie Berry Woodul, Dec. 4, 1965; children: William Woodul, Jonathan Sams. Student, Washington and Lee U., 1952-55; MD, U. Va., 1960. Diplomate Am. Bd. Urology. Intern in surgery, then asst. surg. resident Duke Hosp., 1960-62; fellow cancer surgery Cancer Inst. NIH, Bethesda, Md., 1962-64; resident in urol. surgery Cornell-N.Y. Hosp., 1964-68, fellow transplantation, dialysis and biochemistry, instr., 1968-70; asst. prof. urol. surgery U. Tex. Med. Sch., San Antonio, 1970-72; pvt. practice Richmond, Va., 1972—; mem. staff Henrico County St. Marys Hosp., Chippenham, Johnston-Willis hosps.; asst. clin. prof. urology Med. Coll. Va., 1972—. Contbr. articles to med. jours., films. Fellow ACS (past pres. Va. chpt., past gov. at large), Am. Acad. Pediatrics (affiliate); mem. AMA, Soc. Internat. Urologiè, Transplantation Soc., Soc. Pediatric Urology, Am. Urol. Assn., Am. Nephrology Assn., SR, Country Club Va., Alpha Epsilon Delta, Beta Theta Pi. Episcopalian. Avocation: equestrian activities. Home: Braedon Farm 1240 Shallow Well Rd Manakin Sabot VA 23103-2300 Office: St Mary's Hosp Profl Bldg 5855 Bremo Rd Richmond VA 23226-1926

TUN-PE, immunologist; b. Rangoon, Burma, Aug. 8, 1942; s. U-Kyin and Nyunt-Yi; m. Sann-Mya, Oct. 23, 1976; two children. MBBS, Inst. Medicine Rangoon, 1964; PhD, U. London, 1975. Postgrad. fellow Hammersmith Hosp., London, 1970-71; rsch. fellow St. Mary's Med. Sch., London, 1971-75; asst. lectr. Inst. Medicine, Rangoon, 1975-81; from head immunology to dir. rsch. Dept. Med. Rsch., Rangoon, 1981—. Fellow Internat. Soc. Toxicology, Royal Coll. Tropical Medicine & Hygiene, Royal Coll. Physicians. Home: 25 Pyithayar Rd, 11082 Rangoon Burma

TUOMIOJA, ERKKI SAKARI, Finnish government official; b. Helsinki, July 1, 1946; s. Sakari and Vappu T.; m. Marja-Helena Rajala. BS in Econs., Helsinki Sch. Econs., 1973; Lic. Polit. Sci., U. Helsinki, 1980, PhD, 1996. Mem. Parliament of Finland, 1970-79, 91—; dep. mayor City of Helsinki, 1979-91; min. trade and industry Finnish Ministry Trade and Industry, Helsinki, 1999-2000; min. fgn. affairs Ministry Fgn. Affairs, Helsinki, 2000—; chmn. supervisory bd. Elanto, Helsinki, 1982-95. Contbr. articles to profl. jours. Mem. Finnish Olympic Com., Helsinki, 1980—. Social Democrat. Office: Parliament of Finland, SF-00102 Helsinki Finland

TUORI, TIMO KUSTAA, engineering executive; b. Pori, Satakunta, Finland, Nov. 24, 1955; s. Yrjö Gustaf and Lea Rakel (Nieminen) T.; m. Taru Kirsti Sinikka Orre, Mar. 7, 1982; children: Anna, Tomi, Jussi, Ville. MSc, U. Jyväskylä, Finland, 1987; PhD, U. Loughborough, U.K., 1998, U. Exeter, Eng., 1993-94. Rsch. scientist Tech. Rsch. Ctr. of Finland, Jyväskylä, 1987-95, product mgr., 1995—; coord. European Commn., 1996—, nat. expert, 1998—, sci. officer, 2000—; lectr. in field. Patentee in field. With Finish Mil., 1978-79. Mem. IEEE, ASA, ASJ, AAAS. Evangelical Luth. Ch. Avocations: slalom, cross-country skiing, sailing, tennis. Home: Ave des Milles Metres 84, 1150 Woluwe-Saint-Pierre Brussels, Belgium Office: EC Directorate Rsch, Rue Montoyer 75, B-1050 Brussels Belgium

TUOVINEN, JUSSI J.A., laboratory director; b. Helsinki, Finland, Sept. 18, 1960; s. Jouko J. and Eeva (Malmi) T.; m. Leena K. Niemela, May 26, 1984; children: Emilia, Susanna, Stella. Diploma Engr., Helsinki U. Tech., Espoo, Finland, 1986, Licenciate of Tech., 1989, Dr of Tech., 1991. Tchg. asst. Helsinki U. Tech., Espoo, 1984-87, rsch. asst., 1985-86, study mgr., 1989-90, rsch. engr., 1986-91; sr. postdoctoral rsch. asst. U. Mass., Amherst, 1991-94; project mgr. Helsinki U. Tech., 1994-95; lab. dir. Millilab, Espoo, 1996—; rsch. prof. VTT Info. Tech., Espoo, 1999—; Exch. Vis. fellow Acad. of Finland, 1991. Author more than 80 articles. European Space Agy. fellow, 1992-94. Mem. IEEE (sec. Finland sect.). Achievemements include patent in field. Avocation: flying. Home: Neljaskuja 5, 02620 Espoo Finland Office: Millilab, Otakaari 7B, Espoo 02044, Finland

TUPAMAKI, OLAVI, construction consultant, financial adviser; b. Petajavesi, Finland, Oct. 21, 1944; s. Kauko Kalervo and Anja Ilona Tupamaki; m. Ulla Angela Lindholm, Feb. 29, 1980. MSCE, U. Tech., Helsinki, 1968. Chartered realtor, Finland. Chief engr. Pha Rung Shipyard Project, Hanoi, Vietnam, 1976-77; mktg. mgr. Perusyhtyma Nigeria Ltd., Lagos, 1977-80, gen. mgr., 1981-82; mgr. internat. bus. devel. Perusyhtyma Ltd., Helsinki, 1983; area mgr. Partek Group Cos., Riyadh, Saudi Arabia, 1984-87; mng. dir. Saudi Vetonit Co. Ltd., Riyadh, 1984-87; gen. mgr. Partek Concrete Ltd./A-Factories, Lohja, Finland, 1987-89; dir. R & D, Partek Concrete Ltd., Helsinki, 1989-95; sec.-gen. ENCORD, Brussels, 1997-99; mng. dir. Villa Real Ltd., Espoo, 1995—; chmn. bd. Villa Real Ltd., Espoo, Finland, 1988—, FutureConstruct, Amsterdam, 1995—, Quality in Constrn., Helsinki, 1993-94, Robotic Tech. Sys. Plc., London, 1997—; bd. dirs. Merita Fund Mgmt. Ltd., Rakennuslehti Ltd., Helsinki, Machine Vision, Helsinki, Intelligent Mfg. Systems, Brussels, Europa-Huis, Hamburg. Author: RTD Strategies for European Construction, 1997, Construction Can!, 1998, European RTD on Concrete, 2000; contbr. articles on component system bldg. and constrn. to internat. jours., chpts. to books; inventor methods for better concrete, mfg. systems and products. Mem. Parliament Finland, Helsinki, 1970-75; cabinet mem. Nordic Coun., 1970-75, Town Coun. Petajavesi, Finland, 1968-76. Ensign Finnish Army, 1970-71. Mem. Assn. Finnish Civil Engrs. (bd. dirs. 1990-92), Internat. Real Estate Inst., Internat. Coun. for Bldg. Rsch., Coun. on Tall Bldgs. and Urban Habitat, Assn. Finnish Mut. Funds, Am. Concrete Inst., Concrete Assn. Finland, Internat. Union Labs. for Materials and Structures (sr.), Finnish Soc. of Automation. Avocations: motor sports, classic cars, golf. Office: Villa Real Ltd, PO Box 100, 02321 Espoo Finland also: Ave Louise 65, 1050 Brussels Belgium

TUPOU, HIS MAJESTY TAUFA'AHAU, IV, King of Tonga; b. July 4, 1918; eldest son of Viliami Tungi and Queen Salote Tupou III; m. Princess Mata'aho, 1947; children: Tupouto'a, Pilolevu, 'Alaivahamama'o, 'Aho'eitu. Ed., Newington Coll., Sydney U., B.A., LL.B., 1942. Former min. of edn., 1943; minister of health, 1944-49, premier of Tonga, Fgn. Affairs, minister of Agr., 1949-65; king of Tonga, 1965—; revised Tongan Alphabet, 1949, established teacher's tng. coll., 1944, high sch., 1947, broadcasting sta., 1961, govt. newspaper, 1964. First Chancellor U. South Pacific, 1970-73. Decorated knight Order Brit. Empire, Kreuzes Des Vedienstordens, Fed. Republic of Germany, 1979, Comdr. Brit. Empire, 1952, Knight Comdr. St. Michael and St. George, 1968, Grand Cross Victorian Order, 1970, Grand Cross St. Micheal and St. George. Address: Office of H.M. the King, PO Box 6, Nuku'alofa Tonga*

TUPOU, TEVITA, Tongan government official; b. July 27, 1941; m. Saane Tupou, 1968; 4 children. LLB, U. Auckland, New Zealand; postgrad., Oxford U. Lic. lawyer, Tonga. 1st sec. Tonga High Commn., London, 1969-72; crown solicitor Tonga, 1973-85, solicitor gen., 1986-88; atty. gen., min. justice Govt. of Tonga, Nuku'alofa, 1988—; mem. Legis. Assembly, 1988—; barrister and solicitor High Ct. New Zealand. Pres. Amateur Sports Assn., Nat. Olympic Com.; mem. Oceania Nat. Olympic Com. Office: Office of Attorney General, PO Box 130, Nuku'alofa Tonga

TUPOUTO'A, PRINCE, Crown Prince of Tonga, government official; b. Nuku'alofa, Tonga, May 4, 1948; s. Taufa'ahau Tupou IV and Halaevalu Mata'aho. Ed. public schs., Tonga, New Zealand, Switzerland; grad., Royal Mil. Acad., Sandhurst, Eng. Joined Ministry Fgn. Affairs Govt. of Tonga, 1970, minister of fgn. affairs and def., 1979-99; Crown Prince of Tonga. Commd. col.-in-chief Tonga Def. Services and Royal Guards, 1969. Office: Ministry Fgn Affairs, Office of HM The King PO Box 62, Nuku'alofa Tonga*

TUR, ANATOLI, research physicist; b. Petropavlovsk, Kazhkhstan, USSR, July 19, 1949; arrived in France, 1991; s. Valentine and Olga (Young) T.; m. Tatiana Akhiezer, May 22, 1987; 1 child, Boris. Grad. in physics, Kharkov (USSR) State U., 1972; CandSci, Space Rsch. Inst. Moscow, 1978, DSc, 1988. Scientist Inst. Physics and Tech., Kharkov, 1972-82; sr. scientist Space Rsch. Inst. Moscow, 1982-88, head dept., 1988-91; assoc. dir. rsch. U. Nancy, France, 1992-93; assoc. dir. rsch. Obs. Midi-Pyrenees, Nat. Ctr. Sci. Rsch., Toulouse, France, 1993-94, dir. rsch., 1994—. Contbr. articles to Physics Letters A, Jour. Fluid Mechanics, Physics of Plasmas. Mem. Planetary Soc., N.Y. Acad. Scis. Home: 16 Pl St Georges, 31000 Toulouse France Office: Obs Midi-Pyrenees, 14 ave Edouard Belin, 31400 Toulouse France

TURAEV, VLADIMIR GEORGIEVITCH, mathematician, researcher; b. Leningrad, Russia, Oct. 17, 1954; Immigrated to France, 1990; s. Georgij and Helena (Volodarskaja) T.; m. Anna Pavlova, May 7, 1979 (div. Dec. 1987); 1 child, Dmitrij; m. Muriel Laville, Mar. 2, 1996; children: Marie-Catherine, Marc. MSc, Univ., Leningrad, 1975; PhD, Steklov Math. Inst., Moscow, 1979, DSc Physics and Math., 1988. Sci. rschr. Leningrad Dept. Steklov Math. Inst., Leningrad, 1976-90; dir. rsch. Cntre National de Recherche Scientifique, Strasbourg, France, 1990—; tchr. math. Phys.-Math. Sch. No. 45, Leningrad, 1972-76; prof. math. Pedagogical Inst., Leningrad, 1979-82; vis. prof. Stanford U., Palo Alto, Calif., 1992, Yale U., New Haven, 1994, U. Geneva, 1996-97, Max-Planck Inst. Math., Bonn, 2000—. Author: (book) Quantum Invariants of Knots and 3-Manifolds, 1994, (with C. Kassel and M. Rosso) Quantum Groups and Knot Invariants, 1997. Office: IRMA, 7 Rue Rene Descartes, 67084 Strasbourg France

TURAKAINEN, PAAVO KALEVI, mathematics educator; b. Saari, Finland, Feb. 8, 1942; s. Sirkka Marketta Yli-Hakula, Feb. 3, 1963; children: Pekka, Ville-Veikko. MS, U. Turku, 1965, Lic. Philosophy, 1967, PhD, 1968. Asst. math. U. Turku, 1965-69; assoc. prof. computer sci. U. Helsinki, 1969-70, acting prof. applied math., 1970-71; prof. computer sci. U. Jyvaskyla, Finland, 1970; prof. math. U. Oulu, Finland, 1971—; vis. prof. math. U. Fla., Gainesville, 1973-74; docent in math. U. Turku, 1970—; head dept. math. U. Oulu, 1988-97, mem. coun. faculty of sci., 1988-94. Contbr. articles to profl. jours. and publs. Sr. scientist grantee Acad. Finland, 1980, 86-87, 93-94; decorated Knight 1st Class, White Rose of Finland, 1993. Mem. European Assn. Theoretical Computer Sci. (mem. coun. 1988-94). Home: Mustasuontie 19, Oulu 90560, Finland Office: U Oulu Dept Math, Linnanmaa, Oulu SF-90014, Finland

TURAN, ILTER ADIL, political science educator; b. Istanbul, Turkey, Mar. 28, 1941; s. Sait M. and Semahat E. (Evrensel) T.; m. Gul Gunver, July 26, 1970; 1 child, Belkis. BA, Oberlin (Ohio) Coll., 1962; MA, Columbia U., 1964; PhD, Istanbul U., 1966. Asst. prof. Istanbul U., 1966-70, assoc. prof., 1970-76, prof., 1976-93, chair dept. internat. rels., 1989-93; prof. Koç U., Istanbul, 1993-98, Istanbul Bilgi U., 1998—; pres. Istanbul Bilgi U., Istanbul, 1998—; bd. dirs. SEV Found. Contbr. articles to profl. jours. Founding mem. Çekül, Istanbul, 1991—, ÇEV, Istanbul, 1994—, EGV, Istanbul, 1995—; founding mem.fTESEV, Istanbul, 1993, bd. mem. 3d It. Turkish mil., 1972-74. Mem. Turkish Polit. Sci. Assn. (v.p. 1991—), Internat. Polit. Sci. Assn., Am. Polit. Sci. Assn. Avocation: newspaper column. Home: Susam Sok 4/5 Cihangir, 80060 Istanbul Turkey Office: Istanbul Bilgi U, Kustepe, 80310 Sisli, Istanbul Turkey

TURANEK, JAROSLAV, biochemist; b. Dacice, Czech Republic, Aug. 18, 1958; s. Jaroslav and Zdena (Slaba) T.; children: Jan, Vojtech. Rerum Naturale Dr, U. Masaryk, Brno, Czech Republic, 1982, PhD, 1987. Scientist Inst. Vertebrate Zoology, Brno, Czech Republic, 1988; scientist Vet. Rsch. Inst., Brno, Czech Republic, 1988-94, prin.investigator, 1994—. Author: Vodnikvety Sinic, 1996; contbr. articles to profl. jours. Avocations: tennis, swimming,literature, music. Office: Vet Rsch Inst, Hudcova 70, 620 32 Brno Czech Republic

TURBIN, RICHARD, lawyer; b. N.Y.C., Dec. 25, 1944; s. William and Ruth (Fiedler) T.; m. Rai Saint Chu-Turbin, June 12, 1976; children: Laurel Mei, Derek Andrew. BA magna cum laude, Cornell U., 1966; JD, Harvard U., 1969. Bar: Hawaii 1971, U.S. Dist. Ct. Hawaii 1971. Asst. atty. gen. Western Samoa, Apia, 1969-70; dep. pub. defender Pub. Defender's Office, Honolulu, 1970-74; dir. Legal Aid Soc. Hawaii, Kaneohe, 1974-75; sr. atty., pres. Law Offices Richard Turbin, Honolulu, 1975—; legal counsel Hawaii Crime Commn., 1980-81. Co-author: Pacific; author: Medical Malpractice, Handling Emergency Medical Cases, 1991; editor Harvard Civil Rights-Civil Liberties Law Rev., 1969. Legal counsel Dem. Party, Honolulu County, 1981-82; elected Neighborhood Bd., 1985, elected chair, 1990-97; bd. dirs. Hawaii chpt. ACLU, 1974-78, East-West Ctr. grantee, 1971, 72. Mem. ATLA, ABA (chair internat. torts and ins. law and practice com., mem. governing coun., chair tort and ins. practice sect. 1999-2000, chair-elect 1998-99), Hawaii Bar Assn., Hawaii Trial Lawyers Assn. (bd. govs.), Hawaii Jaycees (legal counsel 1981-82), Chinese Jaycees Honolulu (legal counsel 1980-81), Honolulu Tennis League (undefeated player 1983), Hawaii Harlequin Rugby Club (sec., legal counsel 1978-82), Pacific Club, Outrigger Canoe Club. Jewish. Home: 4817 Kahala Ave Honolulu HI 96816-5231

TURCAN, ROBERT ALAIN, archaeology educator, historian; b. Paris, June 22, 1929; s. Pierre Joseph Marie and Yvonne Georgette (Bayle) T.; m. Marie Jeanne Marguerite Deleani, Dec. 28, 1956; children: Isabelle, Pierre, Anne Marie. Student, Lycee Louis le Grand, Paris, 1949-52; lic. agregation (hon.), Ecole Normale Superieure, Paris, 1952-53, 54-55. With Ecole Francaise de Rome, 1955-57, prof. Latin lit., 1963-74, prof. Roman and Gallo-Roman archaeology, 1974-87; prof. Roman and Gallo-Roman archaeology U. Paris IV, 1987—; dir. antiquities Rhône-Alpes, Lyon, 1975-76; dir. research Ctr. d'Etudes Romaines et Gallo-Romaines, Lyon, 1975-84. Author: Sarcophages romains a representations dionysiaques, (Reinach award 1967), 1966, Religions de l'Asie, 1972, Mithras Platonicus, 1975, Mithra et le mithriacisme (Saintour 1982), 1981, Firmicus Maternus, L'erreur des religions palennes, 1982, Numismatique romaine du culte metroaque, 1983, Heliogabale et le sacre du soleil, 1985, Vivre a la cour des Cesars, 1987, Religion romaine: Iconography of Religions XVII, 1988, Les cultes orientaux dans le monde romain, 1989, L'art romain dans l'histoire, 1995, Rome et ses dieux, 1998, Messages d'outre-tombe, 1999. Recipient Jean-bernat award Inst. de France, Acad. des Inscriptions et Belles Lettres, 1959. Corr. mem. Deutsches Archaeologisches Inst. zu Berlin, Inst. de France, Ctrl. European Acad. Sci. and Art. Roman Catholic. Home: 3 Residence du Tourillon, 69290 Craponne France Office: U Paris IV Inst Art/Archeol, 3 Rue Michelet, 75006 Paris France also: Inst de France, 23 quai de Conti, 75006 Paris France

TURCAT, ANDRÉ, former test pilot, consultant, educator; b. Marseille, France, Oct. 23, 1921; s. Emile Turcat and Claire Fleury; m. Elisabeth Borelli, May 8, 1945 (dec.); children: Rémi, Benoit, Philippe (dec.). Degree in engrng., Ecole Poly., France, 1942; D of History of Art, U. Toulouse, France, 1990. Cert. test pilot, airline pilot. Dir. Flying P Test Sch., Brétigny, France, 1952-53; chief test pilot Nord Aviation, France, 1954-61; dep., then dir. Flight Test Aerospatiale, France, 1962-76; dir. Concorde Flight Test Programme, 1969-76. Author: Mecanique du vol des Avions, 1962, Concorde, Essais et Batailles, 1977, Etienne Jamet (Esteban Jamete) Sculpteur Francais de la Renaissance en Espagne, 1994. Dep.-mayor Toulouse, 1971-77; rep. European Parliament, Strasbourg, 1980-81. Col. French Air Force, 1945-53. Decorated Comdr. of Legion d'Honneur and of Brit. Empire, 1970; recipient Harmon Internat. trophy, 1959, 72, Iven Kincheloe award Soc. Exptl. Test Pilots, Elmer Sperry award, 1983. Mem. Acad. Jeux Floraux, Nat. Acad. Air and Space (founder, hon.). Roman Catholic. Home: Rte du Tholonet, 13100 Beaurecueil France

TURCHI, PETER JOHN, aerospace and electrical engineer, physicist, educator; b. N.Y.C., Dec. 30, 1946; s. Charles Orlando and Fay Florence (Bregla) T.; m. Judith Ann Radogna, June 13, 1967; children: Janita Nicole, Rebecca Lenore. BSE in Aerospace and Mech. Sci./Physics, Princeton U., 1967, MA, 1969, PhD, 1970. Rsch. assoc. Plasma Propulsion Lab., Princeton (N.J.) U., 1963-70; plasma physicist Air Force Weapons Lab., Kirtland AFB, N.Mex., 1970-72; rsch. physicist Naval Rsch. Lab., Washington, 1972-77, chief Plasma Tech. br., 1977-80; scientist R&D Assocs., Arlington, Va., 1980-81; dir. RDA Washington Rsch. Lab., Alexandria, Va., 1981-89; prof. aerospace engrng. Ohio State U., Columbus, 1989-99; leader hydrodynamics and pulsed power sci. Los Alamos (N.Mex.) Nat. Lab., 1999—; chmn. Megagauss Inst., Inc., Alexandria, 1979-89, bd. dirs., 1989—; chmn. mech. and aero. engrng. adv. coun. Princeton U., 1988-92, mem. engrng. sch. adv. coun., 1988-92, dean's leadership coun., 1992-93; resident/collateral faculty Ohio Aerospace Inst., 1989-95; lab. cons. Los Alamos (N.Mex.) Nat. Lab., 1989-99; intergovtl. sr. rsch. scientist USAF Phillips Lab. and Air Force Rsch. Lab., Kirtland AFB, 1990—, vis. chief scientist Advanced Weapons and Survivability, 1996-97; lectr. George Washington U., 1987-89, Air Force Pulsed Power Lecture Program, 1979-81, Internat. Space U., 1998; cons. on pulsed power tech.; chmn. 2d Internat. Conf. on Megagauss Fields, Arlington, 1979; chmn. Spl. Conf. on Prime-Power for High Energy Space Systems, Norfolk, Va., 1982; mem. internat. organizing com. Megagauss Magnetic Field Confs., 1979—; adj. prof. aerospace engrng. Ohio State U., Columbus, 1988, 89—. Editor: Space Propulsion, Propulsion Techniques: Action and Reaction, 1998, Megagauss Physics and Tech., 1980; assoc. editor Jour. Propulsion and Power, 1990-93; guest editor IEEE Transactions on Plasma Sci., 1997-98; contbr. chpts. to books and articles to profl. jours.; patentee in field. Pres. Collingwood (Va.) Civic Assn., 1980-81; rep. Mt. Vernon (Va.) Coun., Mt. Vernon Dist., Fairfax County; pres. Pulsed Power Conf. Inc., Albuquerque, 1985-87, bd. dirs., 1983—. 1st lt. USAF, 1970-72. NSF Grad. fellow, 1967-70; recipient Invention award USAF, 1972, Rsch. Publ. award Naval Rsch. Lab., 1976, USN and Air Force Invention awards, 1978-83. Fellow AIAA (assoc., internat. chmn. 18th, 19th, 21st and 22d elec. propulsion confs. 1985-91, mem. tech. com. plasmadynamics and lasers, 1983-86, mem. elec. propulsion com. 1987-93, 97—, chmn. 1991-93, mem. standing com. acad. affairs 1997—, mem. editl. adv. bd. 1998—, Nat. Student award 1967), IEEE (tech. com. chmn. 5th and gen. chmn. 6th pulsed power confs. 1985-87, plasma sci. and applications exec. com. 1987-89, pulsed power sci. and tech. standing com. 1995—, chmn. 2000—, Erwin Marx award for pulsed power tech. 1999); mem. Am. Phys. Soc., Elec. Rocket Propulsion Soc. (pres. 1994—), Planetary Soc., Va. Ki Soc., Albuquerque Aikido Soc., Sigma Xi, Tau Beta Pi. Clubs: Princeton Campus. Achievements include research in electromagnetic implosion soft x-ray source, high energy x-ray generation by ultrahigh speed plasma flows, plasma flow switch for magnetic energy delivery above 10 megamperes; stabilized liner implosion system for controlled thermonuclear fusion. Office: Los Alamos Nat Lab P-22 Mail Stop D410 Los Alamos NM 87545-0001

TURCO, LIVIA, Italian government official; b. Cuneo, Feb. 13, 1955. Mem. Mcpl. Coun. Turin, Regional Coun. Piedmont; mem. chamber deps. Italian Communist Party, 1987, mem. justice commn., coord. shadow cabinet; mem. pub. & pvt. employment commn. Chamber Deps.; mem. nat. secretariat Dem. Party Left; mem. Parliament Govt. Italy, Rome, 1987—, min. for social solidarity, 1996—. Office: Social Affaris Dept, Piazza Colonna 370, 00100 Rome Italy*

TURCOTTE, JEAN-CLAUDE CARDINAL, archbishop; b. Montreal, Que., Can., June 26, 1936; s. Paul-Émile and Rita (Gravel) T. Attended, U. Catholique de Lille, France; DD (hon.), McGill U. Grand Seminaire of Montreal Lic. Theology, ordained priest Roman Catholic Ch., consecrated bishop. Aux. bishop Diocese of Montreal, Que., Can., 1982-90, archbishop, 1990—; cardinal Diocese of Montreal, Que., Can., 1994. Office: 1071 Rue de la Cathedrale, Montreal, PQ Canada H2B 2V4*

TURCU, ION CRISTIAN EDMOND, physicist; b. Bucharest, Romania, Oct. 15, 1951; arrived in Eng., 1984, naturalized, 1993; s. Ionel and Maria (Crivat) T.; m. Monica Luminita Ivan, Apr. 17, 1976; 1 child, Jacqueline Sandra Maria. BSc, London U., 1974, PhD, 1997. Tchr. physics C.A. Rossetti Lyceum, Bucharest, 1974-79; asst. prof. physics Bucharest Tech. U., 1979-84; sr. rsch. assoc. Rutherford Appleton Lab., Oxfordshire, Eng., 1985-88; higher sci. officer Rutherford Appleton Lab., Oxford, England, 1988-93, sr. sci. officer, and mgr. of the laser-plasma X-Ray source facility, 1993-98; dir. Ed Tex Ltd., Oxford, England, 1994—; chief scientist JMAR Rsch., Inc., San Diego, 1998—; vis. lectr. King's Coll., U. London, 1992-95; vis. scientist plasma rsch. Inst. Atomic Physics, Bucharest, 1974-84; founding chmn. Harwell Bicycle User Group, Eng., 1995-98. Author: Energia, Incotro?, 1978, X-Rays from Laser-Plasmas: Generation and Applications, 1998; contbr. more than 80 articles to profl. jours. Mem. Wantage (Eng.) Town Coun., 1995-98. Recipient rsch. award EUREKA, 1988, U.S. Advanced Rsch. Project Agy., 1994; Brit. Coun. and Romanian Govt. scholar, 1971-74. Mem. IEEE, Inst. Physics London, Soc. Photo-Optical Instrumentation Engrng., Optical Soc. Am., Royal Coll. Sci. Assn., Royal Instn., Brit. Assn. for the Advancement Sci. Achievements include patents and inventions in field; research and development of first high average power plasma source of x-ray radiation at 1 nm wavelength; many world firsts in new field of applications of 1 nm x-rays. Avocations: history, politics, travel, swimming, basketball. Office: JMAR Rsch Inc 3956 Sorrento Valley Blvd San Diego CA 92121-1427

TURENKO, ANATOLIY NIKOLAIYEVITCH, academic administrator; b. Kamenka, Ukraine, Feb. 24, 1940; s. Nikolay Yemelyanovitch Turenko and Galina Denisovna Pitchkur; m. Yevgeniya Alyokhina, Jan. 25, 1964; children: Igor, Aleksandr. Diploma in engrng., Auto.-Hwy. Inst., Kharkiv, Ukraine, 1967, Candidate of Scis., 1973, DSc, 1998; postgrad., Transport Acad., Kiev, Ukraine, 1993. Fitter Kamenka, Ukraine, 1959; asst. Auto.-Hwy. Inst., 1967-69, lectr., 1972-76, dean, 1976-81, pro-rector, 1981-92, rector, 1992—, hon. prof., 1997; hon. prof. Sian Auto U., China, 1994; v.p. Transport Acad., Kiev, 1990—; mem. State Prize Com., Kiev, 1994—; academician N.Y. Acad. Scis., 1999—. Author monograph in field; contbr. articles to profl. jours.; 20 patents in field. Coord. coun. mem. Zlagoda, Kiev, 1999. Recipient medal for virgin soil devel. USSR Supreme Soviet, 1964, medal and title of labor vet. USSR Supreme Soviet, 1988, State and Engrng. prize Ukraine State Prize Com., 1998, Honored Scientist award Pres. of Ukraine, 1998. Avocations: hunting, volleyball, driving, billiards. Office: State Auto-Hwy Tech U, 25 Petrovsky St, 310078 Kharkiv Ukraine

TURETSKY, JUDITH, librarian, researcher; b. Bklyn., Jan. 19, 1944; d. Samuel and Ruth (Moskowitz) Turetsky. BS, Boston U., 1965; MS, Long Island U., 1969. Tchr. Trumbull (Conn.) Bd. Edn., 1965-66; libr. Darien (Conn.) Bd. Edn., 1968-69, Albert Einstein Coll., Bronx, 1969-74; researcher Koskoff, Koskoff & Bieder, Bridgeport, Conn., 1977-86. Author:(book and micro film), The History and Development of the D. Samuel Gottesman Library of Albert Einstein College of Medicine. Mem. Med. Libr. Assn., Hadassah U. Women's Orgn. (life mem.), Yeshiva U. Women's Orgn. (life mem.). Democrat. Avocations: reading, classical music, crocheting, doll collecting. Home and Office: 62 Gate Ridge Rd Fairfield CT 06432-1164

TURGEON, PIERRE, professional hockey player; b. Rouyn, Quebec, Aug. 29, 1969. With N.Y. Islanders, 1992-95, Montreal Canadiens NHL, 1995-97, St. Louis Blues NHL, 1997—; played in NHL All-Star Game, 1990, 93, 94. Recipient Michel Bergeron Trophy, 1985-86, Michael Bossy Trophy, 1986-87, Lady Byng Meml. Trophy, 1992-93. Office: c/o St Louis Blues 1401 Clark Ave Saint Louis MO 63103

TURK, ESIN C., public relations educator; b. Ankara, Turkey, Dec. 8, 1947; came to U.S., 1970; d. Emin and Feriha Kamuran Cakirogu; m. Idris Koksal Turk, Oct. 16, 1969; 1 child, Elif Bughan. BS, Ankara U., 1969; MA, Syracuse U., 1973; PhD, U. So. Miss., 2000. Prof. Miss. Valley State U., Itta Bena, Miss., 1982—. Author: Pembe Duvar, 1962. Mem. Nat. Comm. Assn., So. States Comm. Assn., Miss. Comm. Assn., Am. Cancer Soc. Avocations: reading, travel, writing. Office: Miss Valley State U Itta Bena MS 38941

TÜRK, HIKMET SAMI, federal official; b. Trabzon, Turkey, 1935; s. Süleyman and Ayse Sultan T. Law degree, Istanbul U., Turkey, 1958; LLD, U. Cologne, Germany. Asst. prof. comml. law U. Ankara (Turkey), Turkey, 1960-76; assoc. prof. U. Ankara (Turkey), 1977-97, prof., 1998—; min. of justice Turkish Govt., Turkey, 1995—. Author 7 books; contbr. more than 70 articles to profl. jours. Recipient Great Prize of Social and Human Scis., Bus. Bank of Turkey, 1990. Office: Min of Justice Adalef, Bakanligi, Bakanliklar Ankara 06100, Turkey

TURK, JAMES CLINTON, JR., lawyer; b. Radford, Va., Oct. 27, 1956; s. James Clinton and Barbara (Duncan) T.; m. Allison Blanding, Oct. 16, 1993; children: Lindsey Leigh, Katherine Alexandra, Alana Rae. BA in Econs., Roanoke Coll., 1979; JD, Samford U., 1984. Bar: Va. 1984, U.S. Dist. Ct. (ea. and we. dists.) Va. 1984, U.S. Bankruptcy Ct. 1985, U.S. Ct. Appeals (4th cir.) 1985, U.S. Supreme Ct. 1988; cert. specialist in civil and criminal trial advocacy Nat. Bd. Trial Advocacy. Ptnr. Stone, Harrison & Turk, Radford, 1985—; adj. prof. criminal justice dept. Radford U. Sec. Radford Rep. Com., 1984—; fundraising chmn. Am. Heart Assn., Radford, 1986—; bd. dirs. New River Valley Workshop, Inc., v.p., 1990-92, pres., 1992-93; bd. dirs. new River C.C. Ednl. Found.; apptd. chmn. and dir. Va. Student Assistance Authorities by Gov. George Allen, 1994—; escheator City of Radford and Pulaski County; rep. western dist. CJA Panel Attys., Va.; mem. 4th Cir. Jud. Conf. Mem. ATLA (sustaining, fellow Coll. of Advocacy), ABA, Am. Bd. Trial Advs., Va. Bar Assn. (civil litigation sect. coun. 1991—, criminal litigation sect. coun. 1994—), Nat. Assn. Criminal Def. Lawyers (life; death penalty com. and indigent def. com.), Va. Trial Lawyers Assn.,

Jaycees, Rotary. Republican. Roman Catholic. Avocations: weightlifting, skiing, travel, flying, scuba diving. Home: 460 Quailwood Dr Blacksburg VA 24060-6724 Office: Stone Harrison Turk PC PO Box 2968 Radford VA 24143-2968

TURK, ROBERT LOUIS, radiologist; b. Lima, Ohio, Oct. 30, 1940; s. Herman Matthew and Daphne Carol (Stout) T.; m. Penelope Bryant, Mar. 25, 1964 (dec.); children: Marjorie Carol Turk Desmond, Susan Elizabeth Turk Charles. BA, Stanford U., 1962; MD, UCLA, 1966. Diplomate Am. Bd. Radiology, Am. Bd. Nuclear Medicine. Rotating intern U. Iowa, Iowa City, 1966-67; resident in radiology Harbor Gen.-UCLA Hosp., Torrance, Calif., 1967-70; radiologist, chief staff, vice chief, head radiology El Cajon (Calif.) Valley Hosp., 1972-83; pvt. practice, El Cajon, 1983—. Elder Presbyn. Ch., 1966—. Maj. M.C., USAR, 1970-72, Vietnam. Mem. Am. Coll. Radiology, Radiol. Soc. N.Am., Calif. Radiol. Soc., San Diego Radiol. Soc. (pres. 1990-91, past treas., rep.). Democrat. Avocations: tennis, sailing. Home: 1760 Key Ln El Cajon CA 92021-1507 Office: El Cajon X-Ray Imaging 1663 Greenfield Dr El Cajon CA 92021-3599

TÜRKÇAPAR, MEHMET HAKAN, psychiatrist; b. K Maras, Turkey, Feb. 5, 1966; s. Tahsin and Suna (Ustun) T.; m. figen Özyurt, June 27, 1992; 1 child, Merd. MD, Hacettepe U., Ankara, 1990. Lic. psychiatrist, Turkey. Resident in psychiatry SSK Ankara Hosp., 1990-95; psychiatrist Mevki Mil. Hosp., Ankara, 1998-99, SSK Ankara Hosp., 1999—; cons. psychiatrist SSK Ankara Residency Tng. Hosp., 1999—. Author: Freud, 1993; contbr. articles to sci. and profl. jours. Mem. Turkish Assn. for Cognitive and Behavioral Psychotherapies (gen. sec. 1998—), Turkish Assn. of Psychiatry. Office: Compos Mentis, Billur S 5/3, Ankara Turkey

TURKI, ABD EL-MOHSEN MOHAMED, physical chemistry educator, researcher; b. Ashmun, Menofia, Egypt, Oct. 3, 1958; s. Mohamed Abd El-Hameed T.; m. Nadia Abd El-Razik Farag, July 1977 (div. 1982); 1 child, Sherehan; m. Safa Abd El-Monem Mohamed, Sept. 5, 1993; children: Mohamed, Marwa. BS with honors, Suez Canal U., Ismailia, Egypt, 1981, MSc, 1987; PhD, Petroleum Acad. Baku, Moscow, 1993. Demonstrator faculty sci. Suez Canal U., 1981-87, asst. lect. faculty sci., 1987-88; fellowship mem. Petroleum Acad. Baku, 1988-93; lectr. faculty sci. Suez Canal U., 1993—. Contbr. articles to profl. jours. Office: Suez Canal Univ, Dept Chemistry Faculty Sci, Ismailia Egypt

TURKOVÁ, HELGA, library director; b. Prague, Czech, Apr. 20, 1942; d. Johann Turek and Anna (Kusbachová) Turková. Grad., Charles U., Prague, Czech, 1964, PhD, 1969. Diploma in librarianship. Libr. Czechoslovak Acad. of Scis., Prague, Czech, 1964-65, Prague Info. Svc., Prague, Czech, 1965-67; ind. spez. libr. Dept. of Hist. Castles Libr. Nat. Mus. Libr., Prague, Czech, 1967-90, dir., 1990—. Co-author: (book) Rilke and Kraus and Vrchotovy J., 1985, (catalogue) Catalog incunabula in Castles Libraries, 1992; editor: Sborník Národního muzea-řada C-literární historie, 1990—. Mem. of coun. Friends of Old Prague, 1963—, Soc. of R.M. Rilke, 1992—. Mem. Assn. of Librs., Společnost Národního muzea, Literary Sci. Soc. of Sci. Acad. of Czech Rep. Roman Catholic. Avocations: history of Prague, history, art. E-mail: helga.turkova@nm.cz. Office: Knihovna Národni muzeum, Václavské náměstí 68, 115 79 Prague 1, Czech Republic

TURKOVÁ, VLADIMÍRA, editor-in-chief, consultant; b. Prague, Czech Republic, June 14, 1954; d. Milan Vebr and Pavla (Roubíčková) Marešová; m. Václev Turek, July 5, 1974; 1 child, Pavel Turek. PhD, Charles U., Prague, 1977. Head of methodic dept. Nat. Gallery, Prague, 1978-91; head of pub. rels. Franz Kafka Soc., Prague, 1992-93; editor-in-chief Orbis, Prague, 1993-98; pub. rels. cons. Olympus, Prague, 1992; guide Prague Info. Svc., 1993—. Editor-in-chief: (mag.) The Lands of the Czech Crown, 1994-98; spl. editor Czech Tourist Authority, 1999—; editor: A Guide to the Czech Republic—Prague and the Tourist Treasure of the Czech Republic, Moravia at the Turn of a New Millenium. Home: Na Zvonici 113, 250 65 Libeznice Czech Republic Office: Czech Tourist Authority, Vinohradská 46, 120 41 Prague 2, Czech Republic

TURKULIN, BRANKA, librarian; b. Zagreb, Croatia, Sept. 23, 1955; d. Kresimir and Zorka T. BA, U. Zagreb, 1982, BSc, 1983, MSc, 1998. Head libr. Faculty Sci. Dept. Maths., Zagreb, 1984-88; libr. head Inst. Tourism, Zagreb, 1989—. Mem. Croatian Libr. Assn., European Assn. Sci. Editors. Office: Inst Tourism, Vrhovec 5, Zagreb Croatia 10000

TURLEY, WILLIAM STEPHEN, political scientist, educator; b. Wallace, Idaho, Apr. 6, 1943; s. Abel George and Gertrude Dyke (Gnaedinger) T.; m. Clarisse Zimra, Nov. 22, 1971; 1 child, Olivia. BA, Whitman Coll., 1965; MA, U. Wash., 1967, PhD, 1972. Prof. So. Ill. U., Carbondale, 1971—. Author: The Second Indochina War, 1985; editor: Reinventing Vietnamese Communism, 1993. Mem. Internat. Studies Assn., Assn. for Asian Studies. Office: So Ill U Dept Polit Sci Carbondale IL 62901

TURLIK, IWONA, communication executive; b. Poznan, Poland, May 18, 1951; d. Mieczyslaw and Anna (Rymaszewska) Lemanczyk; m. Marian Turlik, Aug. 25, 1973; 1 child, Daniel. MSEE, Tech. U. Wroclaw, 1973, PhD, 1977. Faculty Tech. U. Wroclaw, Poland, 1977-81; from tech. staff to program mgr. Bell No. Rsch., Research Triangle Park, N.C., 1981-89; prof. U. N.C., Charlotte, 1990-94; v.p., dir. Motorola Advanced Technology Ctr., Schaumburg, Ill., 1994—. Author: Multichip Module Handbook, 1997, Multichip Module Technology Handbook, 1997. Fellow IEEE. Office: Motorola Advanced Technology Ctr 1301 E Algonquin Rd Schaumburg IL 60196-1078

TURLINGTON, CHRISTY, model; b. Walnut Creek, Calif., Jan. 2, 1969; d. Dwain and Elizabeth T. With Ford Models, Inc., 1985; model Calvin Klein, 1986; face of Calvin Klein's Eternity Fragrance, 1988—; with Maybelline Cosmetics, 1992; rep. (abroad) Ford Models, Paris; beauty spread with Vogue, 1987; has worked with Herb Ritts, Patrick Demarchelier, Steven Meisel; has worked for Anne Klein, Michael Kors, Chanel, Perry Ellis; appeared in George Michael's "Freedom" video. Office: United Talent Agy 9560 Wilshire Blvd Ste 500 Beverly Hills CA 90212-2427 also: 344 E 59th St New York NY 10022-1513

TUR-MARI, JOSEP ANTONI, physiologist; b. Palma de Mallorca, Spain, Mar. 9, 1957; s. Juan Tur-Bonet and Margarita Mari-Maestre; m. Margalida Bujosa-Sastre, Dec. 26, 1981; children: Neus, Aina. Degree in pharmacy, U. Barcelona, 1979, PhD, 1983; diploma in lab. animals mgmt., U. Autonomous Barcelona, 1987. From fellow in physiology to prof. physiology U. Balearic Islands, Palma de Mallorca, 1980—; cons. Found. la Caixa, Palma de Mallorca, 1994—; chmn. ICLAS-FELASA joint meeting, 1999. Author: The Pain: A Concept in Constant Evolution, 1988; editor, author: Evolution of Pithyusic Cookery in XXth Century, 1995; editor: Ency. of Eivissa and Formentera, 1995, Water and Lyfe, 1997; contbr. articles to profl. jours. Grantee Balearic Island Regional Govt., 1979, Min. Edn. and Sci., Spain, 1980-83, Min. Health, Spain, 1993-94, 98—. Mem. European Soc. for Comparative Biochemistry and Physiology, Spanish Soc. for Lab. Animal Sci., N.Y. Acad. Scis. Avocation: singing tenor in local chorus. Home: Avinguda de L'Argentina 87, E-07011 Palma de Mallorca Spain Office: U Balearic Islands, Dept Biology & Health Scis, E-07071 Palma de Mallorca Spain

TURMOV, GENNADY PETROVICH, academic administrator; b. Voronezhskaya area, USSR, Aug. 28, 1941; s. Peter Sergeevich and Anna Yosifovna (Ovcharenko) T.; m. Svetlana Ivanovna Potopyak, Dec. 20, 1963; 1 child, Elena Gennadyevna. Engr., Far-Ea. Poly. Inst., Vladivostok, USSR, 1966, PhD, 1974; D Tech. Scis., Higher Naval Engring. Acad., Leningrad, USSR, 1986; prof., Pacific Ocean Higher Naval Coll., Vladivostok, 1989. Naval arch., engr. Commd. 1st grade lt. Navy, USSR, 1969, advanced through grades to capt. 1st rank (col.), 1988; v.p. scientific work Far-Ea. State Tech. U., Vladivostok, Russia, 1991-92; pres. Far-Ea. State Tech. U., Vladivostok, 1992—; vice-chmn. Rector's Soviet, Vladivostok, Russia, 1992—. Author: Ships and Vessels Design, 1982, Technology of Ship Hull Repair, 1984, Russian Fleet: History and Modernity, 5 vols., 1995-96, The Basis of Calculated Projecting of Ship Hull Design, 1997. Dep. Region Duma, Vladivostok, Russia, 1993; pres. Anticrisis Mgmt. Assn., Vladivostok, 1997. Recipient Vologdin prize laureate Acad. Coun. Far-Eastern State Tech. U., 1996, Peter the Great medal Assn. Petronauka, 1997; named Honored Sci. and Engring. Worker Russia, 1995. Mem. Internat. Assn. U. Pres., Internat. Soc. Engring. Edn., Prof.'s Club, Rotary Club. Avocation: books. Office: Far-Ea State Tech U, 10 Pushkinskaya St, 690600 Vladivostok Russia

TURNBULL, ALAN, corrosion scientist, researcher; b. Glasgow, Scotland, Sept. 4, 1949; s. Alexander Stewart and Mary Margaret (Ewing) T.; m. Ruth Jane Bolton, Feb. 26, 1971; children: Joanna, Karina. BSc with 1st class honours in Chemistry, U. Strathclyde, Scotland, 1970; PhD, U. Bristol, Eng., 1974. Fellow Nat. Phys. Lab., Teddington, Eng., 1973—, head aqueous corrosion group, mgr. nat. corrosion svc., 1973—; vis. scientist nuclear engring. dept. MIT, Cmbridge, 1989; mem. corrosion working party on environ.-assisted cracking European Fedn.; mem. corrosion metals and alloys com. Internat. Stds. Orgn., convenor working group on stress corrosion cracking; mem. working party on fracture mechanics approach to corrosion assisted cracking European Structural Integrity Soc.; keynote spkr. numerous internat. meetings. Editor: Corrosion Chemistry within Pits, Cervices and Cracks, 1987, Hydrogen Transport and Cracking in Metals, 1996; contbr. over 100 articles to profl. publs. Recipient Bengough prize and medal Inst. Materials, 1994; Carnegie scholar Carnegie Trust for Univs. Scotland, 1970. Fellow Inst. Materials (chartered engr.), Inst. Corrosion (T.P. Hoar prize 1987); mem. Nat. Assn. Corrosion Engrs., Electrochem. Soc. Avocations: soccer, golf, running. Office: Nat Phys Lab, Queen's Rd, Teddington TW11 0LW, England

TURNBULL, E. R. (NED TURNBULL), state judge; b. Lexington, Ky., Feb. 13, 1961; s. E.R. Turnbull and Nancy (McBryde) Unger; m. Leslee Allison King, July 22, 1988; children: Rand, King, Sid. BA, So. Meth. U., 1984; JD, U. Tulsa, 1990. Bar: Okla. 1990. Asst. dist. atty. major crimes divsn. Tulsa County Dist. Atty.'s Office, Tulsa, 1990-94; state dist. judge Dist. Ct. of State of Okla., Tulsa, 1995—, chief judge criminal divsn., 1998—; revised Okla. criminal felony murder statute and Tulsa County criinal ct. rules; mem. rules com. Okla. Ct. Criminal Appeals, 1996, mem. emergency appellate divsn., 1996. Bd. dirs. Youth Svcs. Tulsa, 1992—, Tri-County Coun. for Aging, Tulsa, 1994-97. Named Outstanding Young Oklahoman, Okla. Jr. C. of C., 1996, gov.'s commendation and exec. dept. proclamation State of Okla., 1996. Mem. Okla. Bar Assn., Okla. Trial Judges Assn., Tulsa County Bar Assn., Rotary. Presbyterian. Avocations: exercise, reading, child rearing.

TURNBULL, GORDON JAMES, psychiatrist; b. Edinburgh, Scotland, Dec. 22, 1948; s. James William and Constance Barker (Inglis) T.; m. Alison Grey Fisher, Oct. 22, 1977; children: Iain, Stuart, Robert. BSc, Edinburgh U., 1970, MBChB, 1973. Physician RAF, 1970-93; house physician Jersey Gen. Hosp., Channel Islands, 1973; house surgeon Bangour (Scotland) Gen. Hosp., 1974; sr. house officer accident and emergency Westminster Hosp., London, 1975; clin. dir. traumatic stress unit Ticehurst House Hosp., East Sussex, Eng., 1993—; hon. sr. lectr. psychiatry U. Kent, Canterbury. Author: (chpt.) Psychological Reactions in Post-Traumatic Stress Disorder, , 1993, Sensory Deprivation in Hostages, 1993, Acute Treatments in Post-Traumatic Stress Disorder, 1995, Classification of Post-Traumatic Stress Disorder, 1996. With RAF, 1990. Winston Churchill fellow, 1976, Nat. Ctr. for PTSO, Palo Alto; recipient RAF Aviation Medicine prize, 1991, People of Yr. award Royal Assn. for Disability and Rehab., 1993. Fellow Royal Coll. Physicians, Royal Coll. Psychiatrists, Royal Geog. Soc., Royal Soc. Arts. Avocations: reading, dog-walking, golf. Office: Ticehurst House Hosp, Ticehurst England

TURNBULL, VERNONA HARMSEN, retired residence counselor, education educator; b. Teeds Grove, Iowa, Dec. 6, 1916; d. Henry Ferdinand and Ida Amelia (Dohrmann) Harmsen; m. Alexander Turnbull, Oct. 12, 1961. BA, Cornell Coll., Mt. Vernon, Iowa, 1939; MEd, U. Colo., Boulder, 1947, profl. cert. edn., 1955. Cert. secondary and h.s. tchr. Tchr. English, Latin and phys. edn. Winslow (Ill.) H.S., 1939-45; dir. women's activities, instr. Trinidad (Colo.) State Jr. Coll., 1947-53; counselor women, assoc. prof. edn. Western State Coll., Gunnison, Colo., 1953-54; instr., residence counselor Stephens Coll., Columbia, Mo., 1955-61; ret., 1961. Active Salvation Army Aux. Mem. AAUW, Am. Assn. Ret. Persons (corr. sec. 1986-87), Kena Kampers Camping Club. Avocations: photography, camping, art, dancing, baking.

TURNER, ALAN GORDON, urological surgeon; b. Croydon, Eng., Oct. 3, 1943; s. William Leslie and Marjorie Alice (Thompson) T.; m. Anthea Jean Mosley, Mar. 28, 1971; children: Matthew, Caroline, Katheryn. MB BS, U. London, 1968. House physician Mt. Vernon Hosp.; house surgeon, professorial surg. unit Charing Cross Hosp., 1969, casualty officer, 1970, registrar in urology, 1973; registrar in surgery Bedford Hosp., 1971; rsch. fellow Inst. Career Rsch., London, 1974-75; lectr. in urology Royal Marsdon Hosp., London, 1975-77; lectr. urology and renal transplantation Charing Cross Hosp., London, 1977-80; cons. urologist Petersborough Dist. Hosp., Eng., 1980-90; chief med. officer, Royal Heritage Life Assurance, Peterborough, 1987—; med. dir. Peterborough Hosps. NHS Trust. Dep. lord lt. County of Cambridgeshire. Fellow Royal Coll. Surgeons Edinburgh, Royal Coll. Surgeons Eng., Royal Soc. Medicine; mem. Brit. Assn. Urol. Surgeons, Med. Rsch. Coun. London (mem. urol. rsch. group). Office: Edith Cavell Hosp, Dept Urology, Bretton Gate, Peterborough PE3 6GZ, England

TURNER, ANNE MARGUERITE, medical geneticist; b. Newcastle, Australia, Oct. 28, 1952; d. Jack and Mary Isobel (Allan) T.; m. David paul Wolski; children: Lara Jane, Robert James. MB, BChir (hons.), U. New South Wales, Sydney, 1977. Trainee in pediat. Prince of Wales Children's Hosp., Randwick, 1977-82; cons. pediatrician, 1983-89; fellow in med. genetics Prince of Wales Children's Hosp., Randwick, 1992, clin. rsch. asst., 1993; clin. geneticist New Children's Hosp., Camerdown, 1994; lectr. sch. pediatrics U. of New South Wales, 1994—; clin. geneticist Sydney Children's Hosp., 1995-98, head dept. med. genetics, 1998—. Contbr. articles to profl. jours., chpts. to books. Grantee Ophthalmol. Rsch. Inst. Australia, 1998, Australian Retinitis Assn., 1998-99, Sydney Children's Hosp. Found., 1999. Fellow Royal Australian Coll. of Physicians (pediats.); mem. Human Genetics Soc. Australia (cert. clin. geneticist). Office: Dept Med Genetics Randwick, Sydney Children's Hosp, Sydney 2031, Australia

TURNER, ANTHONY PETER FRANCIS, biotechnologist, educator; b. London, June 5, 1950; s. Thomas F.W. and Juliette M. (Frasca) T.; m. Elizabeth Caroline Bellamy, May 23, 1984; children: Ellen Katherine, Daniel Anthony John. BSc (hon.), U. East London; postgrad. cert. in edn., Christchurch Coll., 1973; MSc, U. Kent, Canterbury, Eng., 1977; PhD, Portsmouth U., Eng., 1980. Lectr. South Kent Coll. Tech., Folkstone, 1974-76; rsch. asst. U. Kent, 1976-77, rsch. fellow, 1980-81; rsch. asst. Portsmouth U., 1977-80; sr. fellow Cranfield (Eng.) U., 1981-89; project dir. MediSense, Inc., Mass., 1983-84; rsch. dir. Pena Biotech. Ltd., U.K., 1987-89; prof. Cranfield (Eng.) U., 1989—, head biotech. ctr., 1992—, head inst., 1996, head, 1999; bus. dir. Cranfield Biotech. Ltd., 1989-91; project leader European Concerted Action, Brussels, 1988—; vis. prof. Tokyo Inst. Tech., 1989, U. Florence, 1993; bd. dirs. Can. Bioconcepts, Nat. Applied Scis.; chmn. bd. Real Time Sense (Europe); mng. dir. Cranfield Diagnostics; presenter in field. Acad. editor Elsevier Applied Sci., London, 1986—; editor: Biosensors: Fundamentals and Applications, 1987, 89, Advances in Biosensors, 1991, 92, 93, 95, 98; editor-in-chief jour. Biosensors and Bioelectronics, 1986—; editor Jour. of Instrumentation and Analytical Methods, 1995; mem. editl. bd. Jour. Anaerobe, 1994; contbr. over 400 papers to profl. publs. Recipient Energy prize Brit. Petroleum, 1982, Pers. Investigation award Royal Soc., London, 1982, Best Paper award Eurosensors, 1991, prize for measurement sci. Nat. Phys. Lab., 1994, Hewlett Packard award, 1995, ATB Milano award, 1995, Mid Bedfordshire Innovation award, 1998; Brit. Diabetic Assn. sr. fellow, 1982. Fellow Royal Soc. Chemistry, Inst. Biology; mem. European Biosensor Group (founder, chmn. 1987), European Soc. for Engring. and Medicine, Romanian Soc. Clin. Engring. and Medicine (hon.), U.K. Sensor Group (exec. 1991). Achievements include some 30 patents in elucidation and application of mediated electrochemistry in biosensors; co-development of biosensor for blood glucose. Office: Cranfield U, Cranfield U at Silsoe, Cranfield MK45 4DT, England

TURNER, BRIAN (LINDSAY), poet; b. New Zealand, 1944. Customs officer New Zealand Customs Dept., Dunedin, 1962-64, Christchurch, 1964-66; trade and univ. sales rep., editor Oxford Univ. Press., Wellington, New Zealand, 1968-74; radio journalist Radio Otago, Dunedin, 1974; mng. editor John McIndoe Ltd., Dunedin, 1975-83, 85-86; writer-in-residence U. Canterbury, New Zealand, 1997. Writings include: (poetry) Ladders of Rain, 1978, Ancestors, 1981, Listening to the River, 1983, Bones, 1985, All That Blue Can Be, 1989, Beyond, 1992, Timeless Land, 1995; (other writings) Images of Coastal Otago, 1982; (editor) The Guide to Trout Fishing in Otago, 1994, New Zealand High Country: Four Seasons, 1983, (with Glenn Turner) Opening Up, 1987, The Last River's Song, 1989 (with Glenn Turner) Lifting the Covers, 1998, (with Josh Kronfeld) On the Loose, 1999. Robert Burns fellow U. Otago, 1984; recipient Commonwealth Poetry prize, 1978, John Cowie Reid Meml. prize, 1985, New Zealand Book award for poetry, 1993, Scholarship in Letters, 1994. Office: Main Rd, Oturehua Ctrl Otago New Zealand

TURNER, DAVID LOWERY, system safety engineer; b. Atlanta, Feb. 2, 1936; s. Albert Olson Sr. and Ella May (Waldrop) T.; m. Sharon Kay Brewer, May 26, 1972 (div. 1978); children: Angela Kay, Jacqueline Kay; m. Rita M. Robertson, Aug. 25, 1993. Student, Samford U., 1958-60, U. Ala., 1960-62, U. Houston, 1977-79; BS in Safety Engring., Kennedy-Western U., 1991. Registered profl. safety engr.; lic. claims adjuster, Tex., real estate agt., Tex. Safety engr. USF&G, Birmingham, Ala., 1963-69, Parker Bros. Co. Inc., Houston, 1969-80; safety dir. MGF Oil Corp./MGF Drilling Co., Houston, 1980-84; safety mgr. Creole Prodn. Svcs. Inc., Houston, 1985-86; safety div. mgr. Mason Chamberlain Inc., Stennis Space Center, Miss., 1986-91; sys. safety engr. Raytheon Engrs. and Constructors, A Raytheon Co., Johnston Island, 1991—; cons. Fullbright and Jaworski Law Firm, Houston, 1980-81. Vol. West Meml. Vol. Fire Dept., Katy, Tex., 1979-80. With USAF, 1954-58. Mem. Am. Soc. Safety Engrs. (profl.), Nat. Safety Coun., Sys. Safety Soc., Tex. Safety Assn., Nat. Ready Mix Concrete Assn., Internat. Assn. Drilling Contractors, NASA Safety Coun., Gulf Coast Safety Coun., MCI Exec. Safety Coun. (co-chmn. 1986-91). Republican. Baptist. Avocations: hunting, fishing, golf, tennis, bowling. Home: PO Box 098 APO AP 96558 Office: Raytheon Engrs & Constructors A Raytheon Co Johnston Island APO AP 96558

TURNER, DAVID ROBERT, pathology educator, consultant histopathologist; b. Barnehurst, Eng., Feb. 26, 1939; s. Harry James and Vera (Jackson) T.; m. Doreen Mary Duncombe (div. 1980); children: Karen Mary, Ian Keith, Sarah Ann, Judith Dawn; m. Juliet Mary Heaton, Dec. 22, 1980; children: Mark John, Nils Alexander. B of Medicine, BS, Guy's Hosp., 1962, PhD, 1969. Lectr. in anatomy Guy's Hosp., London, 1963-69, lectr. in pathology, 1969-72, sr. lectr. in pathology, 1972-75, reader in pathology, 1975-80, prof. histopathology, 1980-81; cons. histopathologist Musgrove Park Hosp., Taunton, Eng., 1981-82; prof. pathology Nottingham (Eng.) U., 1983-97, prof. emeritus, 1998—; vice dean Nottingham Med. Sch., 1984-87; cons. histopathologist Univ. Hosp., Nottingham, 1983-97, St. George's Hosp., London; com. on classification of Glomerula Diseases WHO, 1976—. Author: An Atlas of Renal Pathology, 1980; author sci. papers on glomerulonephritis and metalloproteinases and their inhibitors in tumor invasiveness. Fellow Royal Coll. Pathologists; mem. Assn. Profs. Pathology (sec. 1988-91, chmn. 1991-94), Fedn. Assns. of Clin. Profs. (chmn. 1994-98). Anglican. Avocations: long distance running, collecting books, woodwork, managing a small holding. Office: St George's Hosp, Dept Histopathology, London SW17 OQT, England

TURNER, ELVIN L., retired educational administrator; b. Springfield, Ohio, Jan. 9, 1938; s. Willie and Jinada (Lawson) T.; m. Betty Jo Breckinridge, June 11, 1966 (div. Jan. 1972); 1 child, Anthony; m. Carrie Johnson, Aug. 3, 1972; 1 child, Brenetta Bell. BS in Biology and Chemistry, Knoxville (Tenn.) Coll., 1962; MEd, U. Cin., 1968; postgrad., Nova U., Ft. Lauderdale, Fla., 1973, Kensington U., Glendale, Calif., 1993—. Cert. secondary prin., tchr., Ohio. Spl. edn. tchr. Cin. Pub. Schs., 1965-69, coord. spl. edn., 1969-72, asst. prin., 1972-78, prin., 1978-90, asst. prin., 1990-93; part-time adj. prof. Mt. St. Joseph (Ohio) Coll., 1987-88; mem. adv. com. Millcreek Psychiat. Ctr. for Children, Cin., 1988-89; bus driver Bristol Village Retirement Cmty., 1997-99; ombudsman Pro-Srs., Cin., 1993-96, Waverly, Ohio, 1997—; sec. Bristol Village Residents Assn., 1997. Bd. dirs. Big Bros./Big Sisters, Cin., 1973; mem. bd. deacons New Hope Bapt. Ch., Hamilton, Ohio, 1993; Sunday sch. tchr. Bethel AME Ch., Lebanon, Ohio, 1996; elected sec. exec. adv. coun. Bristol Village Nat. Ch. Residencies, Waverly, Columbus, Ohio, 1997. Recipient plaques and grants. Mem. Nat. Assn. for Secondary Sch. Prins., Ohio Assn. for Secondary Sch. Prins., Knoxville Coll. Alumni Assn., Phi Delta Kappa, Alpha Phi Alpha. Avocations: bowling, golf, reading, travel. Home: 1269 Park Plaza Dr Columbus OH 43213-2650

TURNER, FREDERICK CLAIR, political science educator; b. Cambridge, Mass., Oct. 3, 1938; s. Clair Elsmere and Naomi (Cocke) T.; m. Caroline Craven, Aug. 26, 1960 (div. 1976); children: Frederick Clair, Elizabeth Wingate, Caroline Truxtun; m. Leslie Anne Wenc, July 9, 1993; 1 child, Matthew Leslie. AB magna cum laude, Harvard U., 1961; MA, Tufts U., 1962, MALD, 1963, PhD, 1965. Asst. dir. Latin Am. studies Harvard U., Cambridge, 1963-65; asst. prof. polit. sci. U. Conn., Storrs, 1965-68, assoc. prof., 1968-70, prof. polit. sci., 1970-97; prof. polit. sci. U. San Andrés, Victoria, Argentina, 1997—; Designated mem. adv. com. Latin Barometer, Berlin, 1994; designated counselor for L.Am. to steering com. World Values Study, Madrid, 1993; lectr. in field. Author: Catholicism and Political Development in Latin America, 1971, The Dynamic of Mexican Nationalism, 1968; editor: Juan Perón and the Reshaping of Argentina, 1983 (Book prize New Eng. Coun. on L.Am. Studies 1983), Social Mobility and Political Attitudes: Comparative Perspectives, 1992, Elecciones y opinión pública en América, 2000, Opinião Pública, Brazil, 2000—; contbr. numerous articles to profl. jours., chpts. to books; mem. editl. bd. Este País (Mex.), 1991—, Internat. Jour. Pub. Opinion Rsch., 1988—, Can. Rev. Studies in Nationalism, 1986-94. Grantee U. Conn. Rsch. Found., 1966, 68, 73, 76, NEH, 1972-73, NSF, 1972-76, UNESCO and Social Sci. Rsch. Coun., 1981, U.S. Dept. Edn., 1987-89, U. Affiliations Program of U.S. Info. Agy., 1991-96, 93-98. Mem. World Assn. for Pub. Opinion Rsch. (pres. 1988-90), New Eng. Coun. for L.Am. Studies (pres. 1978-79), Internat. Polit. Sci. Assn. (chmn. rsch. com. 1981-98), Internat. Sociol. Assn. (sec. rsch. com. 1991—), Internat. Social Sci. Coun. (v.p. 1994-98), Am. Assn. for Pub. Opinion Rsch., Am. Polit. Sci. Assn., L.Am. Studies Assn., Centro de los Oficiales de las Fuerzas Armadas (Buenos Aires), El Consejo Argentino para las Relaciones Internacionales (Buenos Aires), Internat. House of Japan, Harvard Club Boston, Harvard Club of N.Y.C., Sigma Phi Epsilon. Home: Ayacucho 2171 PB 1, 1112 Buenos Aires Argentina Office: U San Andrés, Vito Dumas 284, 1644 Victoria Argentina

TURNER, GLORIA TOWNSEND BURKE, social services association executive; b. Lumberton, N.C., Nov. 16, 1938; d. John B. and Alice (Haite) Townsend; m. James Rae Burke, June 3, 1957 (dec. 1974); children: William H., Sonya Kyle; m. Robert R. Turner,June 23, 1977. Student, U. S.C., 1974; degree in nursing, York Tech. Coll./U. S.C., 1976. RN, S.C. Staff nurse, head nurse York Gen. Hosp., Rock Hill, S.C., 1976-78; head med. dept., indsl. nursing J.P. Stevens Plant, Rock Hill, 1976-78; hsop., nursing home auditor S.C. Med. Found., Columbia, 1978-79; exec. dir. Kershaw County Coun. on Aging, Camden, S.C., 1979-93; dir. med.-surg. units Conway (S.C.) Hosp., 1993-98; house supervisor Scotland Meml. Hosp., Laurinburg, N.C., 1998—; adminstr. Active Nursing Svc., Myrtle Beach, S.C., 2000—; bd. dirs. S.C. Fedn. Older Ams., 1988-95; mem. state adv. com. on Alzheimers, Columbia, 1984—; trustee Kershaw County Meml. Hosp., Camden, 1989-93. Mem. Camden C. of C., Rotary. Methodist. Avocations: reading, watching football and basketball, travel. Home: 147 Dusty Trail Ln Surfside Beach SC 29575-8852

TURNER, HENRY BROWN, finance executive; b. N.Y.C., Sept. 3, 1936; s. Henry Brown III and Gertrude (Adams) T.; m. Sarah Jean Thomas, June 7, 1958 (div.); children: Laura Eleanor, Steven Bristow, Nancy Carolyn. A.B., Duke U., 1958; M.B.A., Harvard U., 1962. Controller Fin. Corp. of Ariz., Phoenix, 1962-64; treas., dir. corporate planning Star-Kist Foods, Terminal Island, Calif., 1964-67; dir., 1st v.p. Mitchum, Jones & Templeton, Los Angeles, 1967-73; asst. sec. Dept. Commerce, Washington, 1973-74; v.p. fin. N-Ren Corp., Cin., 1975-76; v.p. Oppenheimer & Co., N.Y.C., 1976-78; exec. v.p., mng. dir. corporate fin. Shearson Hayden Stone Inc., N.Y.C., 1978-79; sr. mng. dir. Ardshiel Inc., 1980-81, pres., 1981-93, chmn. emeritus, 1994—;

vis. lectr. U. Va. Sch. of Bus.; bd. dirs. MacDonald & Co., Pembrook Mgmt., Inc., Golden State Vitners, Inc., Cellu-Tissue Corp., Wrangler Stewart Ranch, Cave Creek, Ariz. Sponsor Jr. Achievement, 1964-67. Served to lt. USNR, 1958-60. Coll. Men's Club scholar Westfield, N.J., 1954-55. Mem. Fed. Govt. Accountants Assn. (hon.), Duke Washington Club, Omicron Delta Kappa.

TURNER, HUGH JOSEPH, JR., lawyer; b. Paterson, N.J., Oct. 5, 1945; s. Hugh Joseph and Louise (Sullivan) T.; m. Charlene Chiappetta, Feb. 11, 1983. BS, Boston U., 1967; JD, U. Miami, Coral Gables, Fla., 1975. Bar: Fla. 1975, U.S. Dist. Ct. (so., no. and mid. dists.) Fla. 1975, U.S. Ct. Appeals (11th cir.) 1981, U.S. Supreme Ct. 1984. Tchr. Browne & Nichols, Cambridge, Mass., 1968-72; ptnr. Smathers & Thompson, Miami, Fla., 1981-87, Kelley Drye & Warren, Miami, 1987-93, English, McCaughan & O'Bryan, Ft. Lauderdale, 1993—; chmn. Fla. Bar internat. law sect., 1988-89. Contbg. author book on internat. dispute resolution Fla. Bar, 1989; contbr. articles to profl. jours. Bd. dirs. Japan Soc. South Fla., Miami, 1989-97; mem. Sea Ranch Lakes Village Coun., 1997-2000; mayor Sea Ranch Lakes, 2000—. Mem. ABA, Def. Rsch. Inst. Avocation: running. Office: English McCaughan O'Bryan 100 NE 3rd Ave Ste 1100 Fort Lauderdale FL 33301-1144

TURNER, JAMES DANIEL, computer company executive; b. Chevely, Md., Dec. 16, 1950; s. Allen Ephrem and Mary Lynn (Thompson) T.; m. Hari Kertonadi, Nov. 20, 1978; children: Melinda Lee, Imelda Rose. BS in Physics, George Mason U., Fairfax, Va., 1974; ME in Engring. Physics, U. Va., 1976; PhD in Engring. Sci. and Mechanics, Va. Poly. Inst. and State U., Blacksburg, 1980. Dynamics sect. chief Charles Stark Draper Lab., Cambridge, Mass., 1979-84; dynamics and control group leader Photon Rsch. Assocs., Cambridge, 1984-92, divsn. mgr., 1992; v.p. Moldyn (PRA Subs.), Cambridge, 1991-92; pres. Amdyen Systems, Cambridge, 1992—; assoc. dir. NSF Industry & Univ. Coop. Rsch. Ctr. Virtual Proving Ground, Nat. Advanced Driving Simulation, U. Iowa, Iowa City, 1996—; exec. bd. Electricore, Indpls., 1996—; cons. in field. Author: Optimal Spacecraft Rotational Maneuvers, 1986; contbr. chpts. to books. Recipient Rsch. award Sigma Xi, 1981, grants from govt. and industry. Mem. AIAA, Assn. Astronautical Sci., Am. Chem. Soc. Republican. Methodist. Achievements include patents for molecular dynamics simulation method and apparatus, demonstration of applications of advanced multibody dynamics modelling techniques for atomic systems for drug design. Office: NADS Simulation Ctr 2401 Oakdale Blvd Iowa City IA 52242-5003

TURNER, JOHN ANDREW, economist; b. Chgo., July 9, 1949; s. Henry Andrew and Mary Margaret (Tilton) T.; m. Kathleen King Peery, June 21, 1975; 1 child, Sarah. BA, Pomona Coll., Claremont, Calif., 1971; MA, Stanford U., 1972; PhD, U. Chgo., 1977. Rsch. econ. SSA, Washington, 1976-80, U.S. Dept. Labor, Washington, 1980-96, ILO, Geneva, 1996-98; rsch. econ. Office of Sec. U.S. Dept. Labor, 1999—; cons. OECD, Paris, 1989, IMF, 1995, AFL-CIO, 1996; chmn. Internat. Pension Conf., U.S. Dept. Labor, Washington, 1990; adj. prof. George Washington U., 1994-96. Author: Pension Policy for a Mobile Labor Force, 1993; editor: Trends in Pensions, 1989 (transl. into Japanese 1991), Pension Policy: An International Perspective, 1991, Trends in Health Benefits, 1993, Private Pension Policies in Industrialized Countries, 1995, Securing Employer-Based Pensions, 1996, Social Security: Development and Reform, 2000. Fulbright scholar Institut de Recherches Economiques et Sociales, France, 1994. Mem. Am. Econ. Assn. Methodist. Avocation: tennis. Home and Office: 3713 Chesapeake St NW Washington DC 20016-1813 Also: Internat Labor Office, Geneva Switzerland

TURNER, JOHN FREELAND, non-profit administrator, former federal agency administrator, former state senator; b. Jackson, Wyo., Mar. 3, 1942; s. John Charles and Mary Louise (Mapes) T.; m. Mary Kay Brady, 1969; children: John Francis, Kathy Mapes, Mark Freeland. BS in Biology, U. Notre Dame, 1964; postgrad., U. Innsbruck, 1964-65, U. Utah, 1965-66; MS in Ecology, U. Mich., 1968. Rancher, outfitter Triangle X Ranch, Moose, Wyo.; chmn. bd. dirs. Bank of Jackson Hole, 1985-89; photo-journalist; mem. Wyo. Ho. of Reps., 1970-74; mem. Wyo. Senate, 1974-89, pres., 1987-89; dir. Fish and Wildlife Svc. Dept. Interior, Washington, 1989-93; pres. Conservation Fund, Arlington, Va., 1993—; chmn. bd. dirs. Inst. Environ. and Natural Resources, U. Wyo., Laramie; exec. adv. Hancock Timber Resource Group, 1993—; bd. dirs. Land Trust Alliance, 1994—, vice chmn.; bd. dirs. N.E. Utilities; mem. Nat. Coal Coun., 1995—, Teton Sci. Sch. Bd., Nat. Wetland Forum, 1983, 87; mem. exec. com. Coun. of State Govts.; chmn. Pride in Jackson Hole Campaign, 1986; bd. dirs. Wyo. Waterfowl Trust; chmn. steering com. of UN conv. on Wetlands of Internat. Importance, 1990—; head U.S. delegation to Conv. on Internat. Trade Endangered Species. Author: The Magnificent Bald Eagle: Our National Bird, 1971. Named Citizen of Yr. County of Teton, 1984; recipient Nat. Conservation Achievement award Nat. Wildlife Fedn., 1984, Sheldon Coleman Great Outdoors award, 1990, Pres.'s Pub. Svc. award The Nature Conservatory, 1990, Stewardship award Audobon Soc., 1992, Nat. Wetland Achievement award Ducks Unlimited, 1993, Chevron/Times-Mirror Nat. Conservation Leadership award, 1995. Mem. Nat. Wildlife Refuge Assn. (bd. dirs.), Boone & Crocket Club (profl. mem.). Republican. Roman Catholic.

TURNER, JOHN NAPIER, former prime minister of Canada, legislator; b. Richmond, Eng., June 7, 1929; s. Leonard and Phyllis (Gregory) T.; m. Geills McCrae Kilgour, May 11, 1963; children: Elizabeth, Michael, David, Andrew. BA with honors in Polit. Sci., U. B.C., Can., 1949; BA, Oxford U., Eng., 1951, BCL, 1952; MA, Oxford U., 1957; postgrad., U. Paris, 1952-53; LLD, U. N.B., 1968, York U., Toronto, 1969, U. B.C., 1994, U. Toronto, 1996; D. of Civil Law (hon.), Mt. Allison U., N.B., 1980. Bar: Eng. 1953, Que. 1954, Ont. 1968, B.C. 1969, Y.T. 1969, N.W.T. 1969, Barbados 1969, Trinidad 1969. With Stikeman, Elliot, Tamaki, Mercier and Turner, Montreal, Que., 1953-65, McMillan Binch, Toronto, 1976-84; M.P. for St. Lawrence-St. George Montreal, 1962-68, Ottawa-Carleton, 1968-76; parliamentary sec. to Minister of Northern Affairs and Nat. Resources, 1963-65; minister without portfolio, 1965-67; registrar-gen. Govt. of Can., 1967-68, minister of consumer and corp. affairs, 1968, solicitor-gen., 1968, minister of justice and atty.-gen. of Can., 1968-72, minister of fin., 1972-75, prime minister of Can., 1984; leader Liberal Party Can., 1984-90; mem. parliament Vancouver Quadra, 1984-93; with Miller Thomson, Toronto, 1990—; created Queen's Counsel, Ontario and Quebec, 1968; former positions include minister without portfolio, registrar gen., minister consumer and corp. affairs, solicitor gen., minister justice and atty. gen., minister fin. Author: Senate of Canada, 1961, Politics of Purpose, 1968. Can. Track Field Champion, 1948; mem. English Track and Field Team, 1950-51. Appointed Companion of Order of Can., 1995. Mem. Eng. Bar Assn., Grey's Inn London, Bar. Assns. of Ont., Que., B.C., Barbados, Trinidad, Mt. Royal Club, Montreal Racquet Club, Queen's Club, Badminton and Racquet Club, York Club, The Vancouver Club, Nat. Club. Liberal. Roman Catholic. Avocations: tennis, canoeing, skiing. Home: 59 Oriole Rd, Toronto, ON Canada M4V 2E9 Office: Miller Thomson, 20 Queen St Box 27 Ste 2500, Toronto, ON Canada M5H 3S1

TURNER, JOHN SIDNEY, JR., otolaryngologist, educator; b. Bainbridge, Ga., July 25, 1930; s. John Sidney and Rose Lee (Rogers) T.; m. Betty Jane Tigner, June 5, 1955 (dec.); children: Elizabeth, Rebecca, Jan Marie; m. Nina Jones, June 16, 1999. BS, Emory U., 1952, MD, 1955. Diplomate Am. Bd. Otolaryngology. Intern U. Va. Hosp., 1955-56; resident in otolaryngology Duke U. Med. Ctr., 1958-61; prof. otolaryngology Emory U., Atlanta, 1961-95, chmn. dept., 1961-95, prof. emeritus; cons. Healthcare Partnership Cons., Atlanta, 1995—; ear specialist, chief otolaryngology Emory Clinic, 1961-95; area cons. in field U.S. 3d Army, 1962-69; assoc. dir. heart disease control program Fla. Bd. Health, 1956-58; Ga. state chmn. Deafness Rsch. Found., 1968-95; v.p. Clifton Casualty Ins. Co., Atlanta, 1975-95. Mem. internat. editl. bd. Drugs Jour., 1982—, Ethicals in Med. Progress, 1982—, Dialogue Jour., 1988-95; mem. editl. bd. Otolaryngolog—Head and Neck Surgery, 1991; contbr. chpts. to books, articles to profl. jours. With USPHS, 1956-58. Recipient Appreciation award Children of Fulton County and Fulton County Health Dept., 1975, Citation for Disting. Svc., Fla. divsn. Am. Cancer Soc., 1957, Lester A. Brown award Ga. Soc. Otolaryngology—Head and Neck Surgery, 1995. Mem. AMA, So. Med. Assn. (chmn. otolaryngology sect. 1974, cert. of appreciation 1974), Am. Acad. Otolaryngology--Head and Neck Surgery (Honor award 1994), Triological Soc. (v.p., chmn. so. sect. 1991—), Am. Acad. Otolaryngic Allergy, Ga. Soc. Otolaryngology (pres. 1973), Med. Assn. Ga., Med. Assn. Atlanta, Assn. Acad. Depts. Otolaryngology, Optimists (pres. Atlanta 1975), Alpha Omega Alpha. Democrat. Methodist. Home: 3451 Marina Crest Dr Gainesville GA 30506-1061

TURNER, KELLEY BAILEY, volunteer program administrator; b. Houston, Mar. 17, 1962; d. Myron Edgar Bailey and Georgia Numsen (Reynolds) White; m. Mark Edward Turner, May 21, 1994. BA in Art History and Comms. cum laude, U. St. Thomas, 1993. Lic. FCC. Coord. sch. svcs., asst dir. vis. svcs. Houston Mus. Natural Sci., Edn. Sch. Svcs., Houston, 1991-94; coord. vol. svcs. and comty. partnerships Hermann Hosp., Houston, 1996-98; adminstr. Vols. in Pub. Schs. Cmty. Partnerships Houston Ind. Sch. Dist., 1998—; presenter Internat. Conf. on Vol. Adminstrn., Chgo., 1999—; instr. Vol. Mgmt. Acad., Houston C.C. Cen. Mem. Jr. League of Houston, Inc., 1990-94; floor presenter Mus. Natural Sci., 1991-94; vol. Houston SPCA; mem. adv. bd. Houston Internat. Festival, 1992-93, chmn. curriculum guide, 1992-93, chmn. curriculum guide com.; bd. dirs. country selection com. Chrysalis Repertory Dance Co., 1995-97; bd. dirs., membership chair Houston Assn. Vol. Adminstrs., 1998-2000; mem. adv. coun. Ret. Srs. vol. Program, Interfaith Ministries of Greater Houston, 1999-2000; vol. team capt. Houston Mayor's Summit on Women, 1999; mem. com. Internat. Yr. of Vols., 2000—; mem. bd. advocates Planned Parenthood Houston and Southeast Tex., 2000—. Named Vol. of Yr. Jr. League Houston, 1991. Fax: 713-892-6015. Home: 1923 Vassar St Houston TX 77098-5429 Office: Houston Ind Sch Dist 3830 Richmond Ave Houston TX 77027-5802

TURNER, LESTER NATHAN, lawyer, international trade consultant; b. Colmar, Ky., July 11, 1933; s. Clifford G. and Minnie G. (Ensor) T.; m. Sandra B. Ward, July 3, 1976; children: Kimberly L., Michele M., Renee S., Mark L., Jeffrey S., Derek Kyle. BS, Lincoln Meml. U., 1955; JD, U. Mich., 1959. Bar: Mich. 1960, U.S. Dist. Ct. (ea. and we. dist.) Mich., U.S. Ct. Appeals (6th cir.), U.S. Supreme Ct. 1982. Law clk. to presiding justice, research atty. Mich. Supreme Ct., Lansing, 1960-62; ptnr. Sinas, Dramis, Brake & Turner, Lansing, 1960-78; sole law practice, internat. cons. bus. law and primarily in Mid. East Countries emphasis on Palestine Nat. Authority, Lansing, Harbor Springs, Mich., 1978—; prin., CEO Palestinian Tourism Co. Ltd., Palestinian Co. Transp. Ltd., North Bay Ltd.; Mem. std. jury instrn. com. Mich. Supreme Ct., Lansing, 1963-73; cons. higher commn. investment and fin. Palestinian Pres., 1997—. Mem. Mich. State Bar Assn., Mich. Trial Lawyers Assn. (bd. dirs. 1963-74, vice pres. 1974). Methodist. E-mail: tcb@freeway.net Fax: 616-526-0922. Home and Office: PO Box 499 Harbor Springs MI 49740-0499

TURNER, MALCOLM ELIJAH, biomathematician, educator; b. Atlanta, May 27, 1929; s. Malcolm Elijah and Margaret (Parker) T.; m. Ann Clay Bowers, Sept. 16, 1948; children: Malcolm Elijah IV, Allison Ann, Clay Shumate, Margaret Jean; m. Rachel Patricia Farmer, Feb. 1, 1968; children: Aleta van Riper, Leila Samantha, Alexis St. John, Walter McCamy. Student, Emory U., 1947-48; B.A., Duke U., 1952; M.Exptl. Stats., N.C. State U., 1955, Ph.D., 1959. Analytical statistician Communicable Disease Center, USPHS, Atlanta, 1953; rsch. assoc. U. Cin., 1955, asst. prof., 1955-58; asst. statistician N.C. State U., Raleigh, 1957-58; assoc. prof. Med. Coll. Va., Richmond, 1958-63, chmn. div. biometry, 1959-63; prof., chmn. dept. statistics and biometry Emory U., Atlanta, 1963-69; chmn. dept. biomath., prof. biostats. and biomath. U. Ala., Birmingham, 1970-82, prof. biostats. and biomath., 1982—; prof. emeritus biostats. U. Ala., 1998—; instr. summers Yale U., 1966, U. Calif. at Berkeley, 1971, Vanderbilt U., 1975; prof. U. Kans., 1968-69; vis. prof. Atlanta U., 1969; cons. to industry. Mem. editorial bd. So. Med. Jour., 1990—; contbr. articles to profl. jours. Fellow Ala. Acad. Sci., Am. Statis. Assn. (hon.), AAAS (hon.); mem. AAUP, AMA (affiliate), Biometrics Soc. (mng. editor Biometrics 1962-69), Soc. for Indsl. and Applied Math., Mensa, Sigma Xi, Phi Kappa Phi, Phi Delta Theta, Phi Sigma. E-mail: malcolmt@scientist.com. Home: 1734 Tecumseh Trl Pelham AL 35124-1012

TURNER, MARVIN WENTZ, insurance company executive; b. Lower Marion, Pa., Oct. 17, 1959; s. Gilbert Jr. and Frances (McAlister) T.; m. Julia (Davis) Turner. BBA, Howard U., 1981; postgrad., Temple U., 1984-86; MBA, George Washington U., 1988; JD, Georgetown U., 1998. Registered investment advisor; cert. fund specialist. Claim advisor Prudential Ins., Fort Washington, Pa., 1982-84; ptnr. Mgmt. Enterprise, Phila., 1984-86; analyst CNA Fin. Group, Washington, 1986-88; fin. analyst Bell Atlantic, Arlington, Va., 1988-93; CFO Local Govt. Ins. Trust, Columbia, Md., 1993—; mng. dir. Hopkins Turner Wharton, Inc., Bethesda, Md., 1995—; adv. bd. mem. Access Washington; ptnr. Target Group Investors, Upper Marlsboro, Md., 1990—; fin. advisor Turner Mgmt. Group, Watkins Park, Md., 1991. Ptnr. The Tucker Group, Cheverly, Md., 1990. Recipient Elizabeth B. Adams Meml. award George Washington U., 1988, minority fellowship, 1987. Mem. Nat. Black MBA Assn. (exec. bd. D.C. chpt., treas. 1988-90, v.p. 1992-94), Fin. Exec. Inst. Home: 13300 Burleigh St Uppr Marlboro MD 20774-1960 Office: Fin Assets Capital LLC 1201 Pennsylvania Ave NW Washington DC 20004-2401

TURNER, MARY JANE, educational administrator; b. Colorado Springs, Colo., June 1, 1923; d. David Edward and Ina Mabel (Campbell) Nickelson; m. Harold Adair Turner, Feb. 15, 1945 (dec.); children: Mary Ann, Harold Adair III. BA in Polit. Sci., U. Colo., 1947, MPA in Pub. Adminstrn., 1968, PhD in Polit. Sci., 1978. Secondary tchr. Canon City (Colo.) Sch. Dist., 1950-53; tchr. assoc. in polit. sci. U. Colo., Denver, 1968-70, Boulder, 1970-71; rsch. asst. Social Sci. Edn. Consortium, Boulder, 1971, staff assoc., 1972-77; dir. Colo. Legal Edn. Program, Boulder, 1977-84; assoc. dir. Ctr. for Civic Edn., Calabasas, Calif., 1984-88; dir. Close Up Found., Alexandria, Va., 1988-92; sr. edn. advisor Close Up Found., Arlington, Va., 1992—. Author: Political Science in the New Social Studies, 1972; co-author: American Government: Principles and Practices, 1983, 4th edit., 1996, Law in the Classroom, 1984, Civics: Citizens in Action, 1986, 2d edit., 1991, U.S. Government Resource Book, 1989; contbg. author: Internat. Ency. Dictionary of Edn., 2000. Recipient Isadore Starr award for spl. achievement in law-related edn. ABA, 1997. Mem. Nat. Coun. for Social Studies (chair nominations 1983-84, chair bicentennial com. 1986), Social Sci. Edn. Consortium (pres. 1986-87, bd. dirs. 1984-87, 99—), Pi Lambda Theta, Pi Sigma Alpha. Democrat. Presbyterian. Office: Close Up Found 44 Canal Center Plz Alexandria VA 22314-1592

TURNER, NEIL CLIFFORD, agricultural scientist, research scientist; b. Preston, Lancashire, Eng., Mar. 13, 1940; arrived in Australia, 1974; s. William and Etty (Ashworth) T.; m. Jennifer Ruth Gibson, Mar. 2, 1968; children: Matthew Stuart, Calvin Mark, Kirk Edward. BS, U. Reading (Eng.), 1962; DS, 1983; PhD, Adelaide (Australia) U., 1968. practising agriculturalist. Plant physiologist Conn. Agrl. Expt. Station, New Haven, 1967-74; rsch. scientist Commonwealth Scientific & Indsl. Rsch. Orgn. Plant Industry, Canberra, Australia, 1974-83; rsch. leader Commonwealth Scientific & Indsl. Rsch. Orgn. Plant Industry, Perth, Australia, 1984-95, chief rsch. scientist, 1995—; vis. scientist U. Bayreuth (Germany), 1982, Internat. Rice Rsch. Inst., Los Baños, Philippines, 1983, U. Wuerzburg, Germany, 1993; sub program leader Ctr. for Legumes in Mediterranean Agr., Perth, Australia, 1994-2000; bd. trustees Internat. Ctr. Rsch. Agroforestry, Kenya, 1994-2000; adj. prof. U. Western Australia, 1998—. Editor: Adaptation of Plants to Water and High Temperature Stress, 1980, Plant Growth, Drought and Salinity, 1986, Crop Production on Duplex Soils, 1992. Alexander Von Humboldt rsch. fellow, 1982, 93. Fellow Australian Inst. Agrl. Sci. (medal 1993), Australian Acad. Technol. Sci. and Engring., Am. Soc. Agronomy, Crop Sci. Soc. Am. Mem. Ch. of Christ. Avocations: swimming, gardening, travel. Office: CSIRO Plant Industry, Pvt Bag #5, Wembley WA 6913, Australia

TURNER, PETER JOHN, naval architect, marine engineer; b. Leicester, Eng., Apr. 8, 1959; s. Geoffrey Holt and Phyllis Joyce (Cotter) T. Student, Stroud Coll., 1975-77, Stroud Coll., 1975-77, Bath (Eng.) Coll., 1977-81; BS in Ship Sci., Southampton (Eng.) U., 1985. Apprentice technician Ministry of Def. Navy, Bath, Eng., 1977-81; profl. tech. officer Goddess, Bath, 1981-85; profl. and tech. officer Logistic Support Section, Bath, 1985-91, Goddess Section, Bath, 1991-93, Drawing Office Control Sect., Bath, 1993-97, Tech. Publs. Sect., Bath, 1997-98, Gen. Engring. Sect., Bath, 1998—; assoc. mem. Inst. of Dirs., London, 1994-95, Inst. of Mgmt., London, 1993—. Contbr. over 248 articles to profl. jours. Ch. server St. James Parish Ch., Dursley, 1974—. Midshipman Royal Navy Res. Unit, , 1981-84. Recipient Nobel Peace Prize, 1996; recipient numerous Certs. of Achievement including Cert. of Thanks from The Samaritans, 1999, Internat. Fund for Animal Welfare, 1998, Whale and Dolphin Conservation Soc., Royal Soc. for Protection of Birds Ramsey Island, Guild of Wealth, World Wide Fund-UK Rhino Appeal, 1999, Adopt a Whale Project, David Shephard Conservation Found., Age Concern. Fellow Instn. Diagnostic Engrs.; mem. Soc. Naval Archs. and Marine Engrs., Royal Instn. Naval Architects (grad. mem.), Nautical Inst. (companion mem.), Royal Nat. Lifeboat Inst. (life gov.), Soc. Profl. Engrs. (charitable trustee), Union Internat. des Ingenieurs Profls, Assn. of Royal Navy Officers, Royal United Svcs. Inst., Ecclesiological Soc., N.Y. Acad. Sci., Nat. Geog. Soc., Assn. Ind. Entrepreneurs. Mem. Ch. of England. Avocations: sailing, rowing, canoeing, gardening, reading, television. Home: 8 Stanthill Dr Dursley, Gloucestershire GL11 4PP, England Office: Ministry Def Navy Rm 149, Spur 10 Crescent Ensleigh, Bath BA1 5AB, England

TURNER, RALPH VERNON, historian educator; b. Forrest City, Ark., Aug. 27, 1935; s. Vernon Oliver and Thelma Tipton (Smith) T. BA, U. Ark., Fayetteville, 1957, MA, 1958; PhD, Johns Hopkins U., Balt., 1962. Asst. prof. Fla. State U., Tallahassee, 1962-66; asst. prof., assoc. prof. Ohio U., Athens, 1966-70; assoc. prof. Fla. State U., Tallahassee, 1970-73, prof., 1973-94, disting. rsch. prof., 1994-99; retired, 1999. Author: The King and His Courts, 1968, The English Judiciary in the Age of Glanvill and Bracton, 1985, Man Raised from the Dust, 1988, King John, 1994, Judges, Administrations and the Common Law, 1994, The Reign of Richard Lionheart, 2000; contbr. articles to profl. jours. Recipient Fulbright Scholarship, U. Poitiers, 1957-58. Fellow Royal Hist. Soc.; mem. Charles Homer Haskins Soc., Am. Hist. Assn., Med. Acad. Am., Pipe Roll Soc., Phi Beta Kappa. Episcopalian. Avocations: art collecting, travel, cooking; E-mail address: rvtu1066@aol.com.

TURNER, RICHARD L., retired computer software engineer; b. Kniman, Ind., Jan. 2, 1938; s. Lewis Lee and Amy T.; m. Judith A. Turner, Dec. 14, 1963; children: John, Nora. BS, Purdue U., 1960; MBA, U. Chgo., 1965. Industl. engr. U.S. Steel, Gary, Ind., 1960-63; computer system analyst U.S. Steel, Pitts., 1963-68; compute software engr. Goodyear T. & R., Akron, Ohio, 1968-87; engr. mgr. Goodyear T. & R., Luxembourg, 1987-88; info. tech. regional engr. N.Am. Goodyear T. & R., 1988-00; retired, 2000. Contbr. articles to profl. jours. Member MENSA (editor 1995—, recipient 6 publication awards), Intertel. Avocation: RV travel, reading. Home: 889 Martindale Dr Tallmadge OH 44278-2974

TURNER, RICHARD TIMMIS, marketing executive; b. Nantwich, Cheshire, U.K., Aug. 17, 1942; s. John Richard Timmis and Alison Elizabeth (Bythell) T.; m. Margaret Corbett, Sept. 11, 1982; children: Catherine, Rebecca. BA in Polit. and Modern History (hons.), U. Manchester, U.K., 1965. With Rolls-Royce plc, various locations, 1965-85; comml. dir. civil engines Rolls-Royce plc, Derby, U.K., 1985-88; group mktg. dir. Rolls-Royce plc, London, 1991—, also dir.; group mktg. dir., bd. dirs. STC plc, London, 1988-91; non-exec. dir. Corus Group plc, London, 1994—, Senior plc., 1996—; bd. dirs. British Trade Internat., 1999—, chmn. sectors group. Decorated O.B.E., 1978. Fellow Royal Aero. Soc.; mem. Inst. Dirs., Soc. Brit. Aerospace Cos. (pres. 1994-95), Athenaeum, British Bus. Coun. (dep. U.K. chmn. Singapore 1997—). Avocations: farming, rugby football, music, opera. Office: Rolls-Royce plc, 65 Buckingham Gate, London SW1E 6AT, United Kingdom

TURNER, ROBERT, physicist, researcher; b. Daventry, Eng., Feb. 18, 1946; s. Victor Witter and Edith Lucy Brocklesby (Davis) T.; m. Jean Kitty Pattenden, Sept. 11, 1965 (div. Feb. 1975); 1 child, Paul; m. Charlotte Elizabeth (Dupré), June 21, 1975; children: John Frederick, Lucy Jacqueline. BA, Cornell U., 1968; PhD, Simon Fraser U., Vancouver, B.C., Can., 1972; diploma, Univ. Coll. London, 1977. Rsch. asst. Cavendish Lab., Cambridge, Eng., 1972-75; rsch. fellow U. Edinburgh, Scotland, 1977-80; lectr. in physics Napier Coll., Edinburgh, Scotland, 1980-84, U. Nottingham, Eng., 1984-88; vis. scientist NIH, Bethesda, Md., 1988-93; reader Inst. Neurology, London, 1993-96, prof., 1996—; dir. Lothian Energy Group, Edinburgh, 1980-88; mem. adv. bd. Biomed. MR Unit, Brussels, 1992-96. Mem. editl. bd. Physiol. Measurement, Bristol, Eng., 1993—, Magnetic Resonance in Medicine, Balt., 1995—, NeuroImage, L.A., 1995—; U.S. patentee in field; contbr. over 90 articles to profl. jours., chpts. to books. Nat. Rsch. Coun. Can. studentship, 1970-72; fellow Sci. Rsch. Coun., Cambridge, 1972; prin. fellow Wellcome Trust, 1993. Roman Catholic. Avocations: choral singing, skiing, hiking, travel. Home: 2 Sandringham Gardens, London N8 9HU, England Office: Inst Neurology, Queen Square, WC1N 3BG London WC1N 3BG, England

TURNER, ROBERT STANLEY, orthopaedic surgeon, bioethicist; b. Waterloo, Iowa, Nov. 24, 1928; s. Henry George Turner and Ruby Lydia McMillin; m. Dorothy Lavonne Burgess, Sept. 5, 1953 (dec.); children: Bruce, Ann, Kent; m. Karen Lou Howard, May 19, 1990; children: Rebecca, Geoffrey, Strom. BA, State u. Iowa, 1952, MD, 1954. Diplomate Am. Bd. Orthopaedic Surgery. Intern Meml. and Maricopa County Hosps., Phoenix, 1954-55; med. officer USPHS Hosp., Tahlequah, Okla., 1955-57; orthopaedic res. USPHS Hosp., San Francisco, 1957-60, Shriner's Hosp. Crippled Children, Phila., 1960-61; orthopaedic surgeon Lovelace Clinic Med. Ctr., Albuquerque, 1961-95, chmn. orthopaedic surgery dept., 1966-93; clin. assoc. prof. to clin. prof. orthopaedic surgery U. N.Mex., Albuquerque, 1965—; contract orthopaedic surgeon Lovelace Clinic Med. Ctr., 1995—. Founder Dorothy Turner Meml. Ecumenical Seminars, 1987—; bd. govs. Lovelace Clinic Med. Ctr., 1968-81; trustee Lovelace Med. Found., 1972-93; mem. adv. bd. Carrie Tingley Hosp. for Children, Albuquerque, 1989-95; mem. bd. N.Mex. Mus. Natural History Found., Albuquerque, 1989-95, Black River Ctr. for Learning, Carlsbad, N.Mex., 2000—; mem. coun. trustees Lovelace Respiratory Rsch. Inst., 1997-00; moderator ch. bd. Monte Vista Christian Ch., Albuquerque, 1996-97, bd. mem. Tres Rios Area Christian Chs., Carlsbad, N.Mex., 1998-00. Sr. surgeon, USPHS, 1961-95. Recipient Ecumenical Svc. award Tres Rios Area Christian Ch., 1987, Svc. award Carrie Tingley Hosp. for Children, 1995, Meritorious Svc. award N.Mex. Orthopaedic Assn., 1994. Fellow ACS, Am. Acad. Ortho. Surgeons; mem. Clin. Orthopaedic Soc., We. Orthopaedic Assn., Gtr. Albuquerque Med. Assn., N.Mex. Med. Soc., Hibbs Soc. (co-pres. 1984-85). Disciple of Christ. Republican. Avocations: bio-ethical events, family, world travel, gardening, investments. E-mail: rst560NM@aol.com. Home: 560 Black Bear Pl NE Albuquerque NM 87122-1821

TURNER, SHAWN DENNIS, lawyer; b. Salt Lake City, Apr. 19, 1959; s. Gerald Lewis and Cynthia Sue Turner; m. Pamela M. Morgan, May 31, 1985; children: Erin K., Jessica L. BS, U. Utah, 1984; MBA, Cornell U., 1986; JD, Brigham Young U., 1990. Bar: Utah 1990, U.S. Dist. Ct. Utah 1992, U.S. Ct. Appeals (10th cir.) 1992, U.S. Tax Ct. 1992, U.S. Ct. Claims 1993. Law clk. Utah Atty. Gen.'s Office, Salt Lake City, 1988-89; aasoc. McKay Burton & Thurman, Salt Lake City, 1990-91; shareholder Brown, Larson, Jenkins & Halliday, Salt Lake City, 1991-96; ptnr. Larson, Turner, Fairbanks & Dalby, L.C., Salt Lake City, 1996—; tax cons. Deloitte Haskins & Sells, Salt Lake City, 1986-87; agt. Attys. Title, Salt Lake City, 1996—; mem. Advantage Title Co., Salt Lake City, 1997—. Mem. Utah State Bar Assn. (tax sect., litig. sect., estate planning sect.), U.S. Chess Fed. Office: Larson Turner Fairbanks & Dolby L C 4516 S 700 E Ste 100 Salt Lake City UT 84107-8319

TURNER, STUART WILLIAM, psychiatrist, consultant; b. Sheffield, Eng.; s. Bill and Margery Turner; m. Morag J. Brocklehurst; children: Eve, Laurence. MA, Cambridge U., Eng., 1977, MB BChir, 1976, MD, 1987. Lectr. in psychiatry Kings Coll. Sch. Medicine and Dentistry/Inst. Psychiatry, London, 1983-87; sr. lectr. in psychiatry Middlesex Hosp. Med. Sch., London, 1987-93; vice dean Univ. Coll., London Med. Sch., 1996-98; dir. Traumatic Stress Clinic, London, 1991—, Internat. Soc. for Traumatic Stress Studies, 1995-97; med. dir. Camden & Islington CHS NHS Trust, London, 1993-98; pres. European Soc. for Traumatic Stress Studies, 1995-97, bd. dirs.; trustee Redress, 1997—; chair U.K. Trauma Group, 1996—. Author of pub. jours., chpts. cons. on traumatic stress, homelessness, refugees, schizophrenia. Dir. rsch. & devel. North Ctrl. London Cmty. Rsch. Con-

storium, 1997—. Fellow Royal Coll. Psychiatry, Royal Coll. Physicians. Office: Traumatic Stress Clinic, 73 Charlotte St, London W1P 1LB, England

TURNER, TED (ROBERT EDWARD TURNER), television executive; b. Cin., Nov. 19, 1938; s. Robert Edward and Florence (Rooney) T.; m. Judy Nye (div.), m. Jane Shirley Smith, June 1965 (div. 1988); children: Beau, Rhett, Jennie; children by previous marriage: Laura Lee, Robert Edward IV; m. Jane Fonda, Dec. 21, 1991. Grad. in classics, Brown U.; DSc in Commerce (hon.), Drexel U., 1982; LLD (hon.), Samford U., 1982, Atlanta U., 1984; D Entrepreneurial Sci. (hon.), Cen. New Eng. Coll. Tech., 1983; D in Pub. Adminstrn. (hon.), Mass. Maritime Acad., 1984; D in Bus. Adminstrn. (hon.), U. Charleston, 1985. Account exec. Turner Advt. Co., Atlanta, 1961-63, pres., chief oper. officer, 1963-70; pres., chmn. bd. Turner Broadcasting System, Inc., Atlanta, 1970-96; vice chmn. Time Warner Inc. (merger Turner Broadcasting System), 1996—; bd. dirs. Atlanta Hawks; owner Atlanta Braves. Bd. dirs. Martin Luther King Ctr., Atlanta. Won America's Cup in his yacht Courageous, 1977; named Yachtsman of Yr. 4 times.Recipient Outstanding Entrepreneur of Yr. award Sales Mktg. and Mgmt. Mag., 1979, Salesman of Yr. award Sales and Mktg. Execs., 1980, Pvt. Enterprise Exemplar medal, Freedoms Found. at Valley Forge, 1980, Communicator of Yr. award Pub. Rels. Soc. Am., 1981, Communicator of Yr. award N.Y. Broadcasters, 1981, Internat. Communicator of Yr. award Sales and Mktg. Execs., 1981, Nat. News Media award VFW, 1981, Disting. Svc. in Telecommunications award Ohio U. Coll. Communication, 1982, Carr Van Anda award Ohio U. Sch. Journalism, 1982, Spl. award Edinburgh Internat. TV Festival, Scotland, 1982, Media Awareness award United Vietnam Vets. Orgn., 1983, Bd. Govs. award Atlanta chpt. NATAS, 1982, Spl. Olympics award Spl. Olympics Com., 1983, Dinner of Champions award Ga. chpt., Multiple Sclerosis Soc., 1983, Praca Spl. Merit award N.Y. Puerto Rican Assn. for Community Affairs, 1983, World Telecommunications Pioneer award, N.Y. State Broadcasters Assn., 1984, Golden Plate award Am. Acad. Achievement, 1984, Outstanding Supporter Boy Scouting award Nat. Boy Scout Coun., 1984, Silver Satellite award Am. Women in Radio and TV, Lifetime Achievement award N.Y. Internat. Film and TV Festival, 1984, Corp. Star of Yr. award Nat. Leukemia Soc., 1985, Disting. Achievement award U. Georgia, 1985, Tree of Life award Jewish Nat. Fund, 1985, Bus. Exec. of Yr. award Ga. Security Dealers Assn., 1985, Life Achievement award Popular Culture Assn., 1986, George Washingtonn Disting. Patriot award S.R., 1986, Mo. Honor medal Sch. Journalism, U. Mo., 1987, Golden Ace award Nat. Cable TV Acad., 1987 Sol Taishoff award Nat. Press Found., 1988, Citizen Diplomat award Ctr. for Soviet-Am. Dialogue, 1988, Chmn.'s award Cable Advt. Bur., 1988, Directorate award NATAS, 1989, Paul White award Radio and TV News Dirs. Assn., 1989 Bus. Marketer of Yr. Am. Mktg. Assn., 1989, Disting. Svc. award Simon Wiesenthal Ctr., 1990, Glasnost award Vols. Am. and Soviet Life mag., 1990, numerous others; inducted into Hall of Fame, Promotion and Mktg. Assn., 1980, Dubuque (Iowa) Bus. Hall of Fame, 1983, Nat. Assn. for Sport and Phys. Edn. Hall of Fame, 1986. Mem. Nat. Cable TV Assn. (Pres.'s award 1979, 89, Ace Spl. Recognition award 1980), NAACP (life, bd. dirs. Atlanta chpt., Regional Employer of Yr. award 1976), Nat. Audubon Soc., Cousteau Soc., Bay Area Cable Club (hon.). Avocations: sailing, fishing. Office: Turner Broadcasting 1 CNN Ctr PO Box 105366 Atlanta GA 30348-5366

TURNER, THOMAS BOURNE, retired microbiology educator; b. Prince Frederick, Md., Jan. 28, 1902; s. George Dorsey and Virginia (Lyles) T.; m. Anne Parran Somervell, Oct. 22, 1927 (dec. Feb. 1960); children: Anne Turner Pope, Pattie Bourne Turner Walker; m. Lorna Caithness Levy, Sept. 16, 1961 (dec. 1982). BS, St. John's Coll., Annapolis, 1921; MD, U. Md., 1925, ScD (hon.), 1966; LHD (hon.), Johns Hopkins U., 1991. Jacques Loeb fellow, instr., assoc. in medicine Johns Hopkins U., Balt., 1927-32, prof. microbiology Sch. Hygiene and Pub. Health, 1939-57, prof. microbiology, dean med. faculty Sch. Medicine, 1957-68, dean emeritus, 1968—, archivist, 1968-82, archivist emeritus, 1982—; staff mem. internat. health divsn. Rockefeller Found., N.Y.C., 1932-39; dir. venereal disease control divsn., dir. civil pub. health divsn. Office Surgeon Gen.; cons. to surgeon gen. U.S. Army. Author: Biology of the Treponematoses, 1957, Fundamentals of Medical Education, 1963, Heritage of Excellence: The Johns Hopkins Medical Institutions, 1974, Part of Medicine, Part of Me, 1981, (with V.L. Bennett) Forward Together-Industry and Academia, 1993; contbr. articles to profl. jours. Mem. gen. adv. com., vice chmn. com. on virus rsch. and epidemiology Nat. Found.; mem. bd. visitors and govs. St. John's Coll.; pres. Alcoholic Beverage Med. Rsch. Found., 1981-90. Col. U.S. Army, 1942-46. Decorated Legion of Merit; Thomas B. Turner Auditorium, Johns Hopkins Sch. Medicine named in honor. Mem. Assn. Am. Med. Colls. (pres.), Assn. Am. Physicians, Am. Soc. Clin. Investigation, Harvey Soc., Gibson Island Club, West Hamilton St. Club, Mt. Vernon Club (courtesy), Phi Beta Kappa, Kappa Alpha. Home: 1426 Park Ave Baltimore MD 21217-4230 Office: Johns Hopkins U Sch Medicine 1830 E Monument St Ste 2-301 Baltimore MD 21287-0003

TURNER, WILFRED, diplomat; b. Littleborough, Lancashire, Eng., Oct. 10, 1921; s. Allen and Eliza (Leach) T.; m. June Gladys Tite, Mar. 26, 1947; children: Nicholas Hugh, Matthew Julian, Harriet Louise Macrae. BSc, London U., 1942. Exec. Ministry Labour and Nat. Svc., Rochdale and Cambridge, Eng., 1938-42, 47-55; sr. inspector Ministry Labour and Nat. Svc., Birmingham, Eng., 1959-60; labor adviser Brit. High Commn., New Delhi, 1955-59; prin. Ministry of Health, London, 1960-63; sec., chief exec. Com. on Safety of Drugs, London, 1963-66; 1st sec. Her Majesty Diplomatic Svc., Nigeria and Malaysia, 1966-73; counselor Her Majesty Diplomatic Svc., Accra, Ghana, 1973-76; high commr. Brit. High Commn. Botswana., Gaberone, 1977-81; dir., chief exec. Southern Africa Assn., London, 1983-88; non-exec. dir. Transmark Ltd., London, 1986-90. Mem. Twickenham (Eng.) Town Com., 1993-98; chmn. Strawberry Hill Residents Assn., Twickenham, 1993-98. Capt. Brit. Army, 1942-47. Named Companion Order of St. Michael and St. George Her Majesty the Queen, 1977, Comdr. Royal Victorian Order Her Majesty the Queen, 1979. Mem. Royal Inst. Internat. Affairs, Royal Africa Soc. Avocations: international affairs, hill walking, travel. Home: 44 Tower Rd, Twickenham TW1 4PE, England

TURNER, WILLIAM COCHRANE, international management consultant; b. Red Oak, Iowa, May 27, 1929; s. James Lyman and Josephine (Cochrane) T.; m. Cynthia Dunbar, July 16, 1955; children: Scott Christopher, Craig Dunbar, Douglas Gordon. BS, Northwestern U., 1952; LLD (hon.), Am. Grad. Sch. Internat. Mgmt., 1993. Pres., chmn. bd. dirs. Western Mgmt. Cons., Inc., Phoenix, 1955-74, Western Mgmt. Cons. Europe, S.A., Brussels, 1968-74; U.S. amb., permanent rep. OECD, Paris, 1974-77, vice chmn. exec. com., 1976-77, U.S. rep. Energy Policy Com., 1976-77, mem. U.S. dels. internat. meetings, 1974-77; chmn., CEO Argyle Atlantic Corp., Phoenix, 1977—; mem. western internat. trade group U.S. Dept. Commerce, 1972-74; U.S. Rep. Consultative Group parent orgn. Coord. Com. (COCOM) Multilateral Export Controls Communist Nations, Paris, 1974-77; chmn. European adv. coun., 1981-88, Asia Pacific adv. coun. AT&T Internat., 1981-88; mem. U.S.-Japan Bus. Coun., Washington, 1987-93, European adv. coun. IBM World Trade Europe/Mid. East/Africa Corp., 1977-80; mem. Asia Pacific adv. coun. Am. Can Co., Greenwich, Conn., 1981-85, GE of Brazil adv. coun. GE Co., Coral Gables, Fla., 1979-81, Caterpillar of Brazil adv. coun. Caterpillar Tractor Co., Peoria, Ill., 1979-84, Caterpillar Asia Pacific Adv. Coun., 1984-90, U.S. adv. com. Trade Negotiations, 1982-84; bd. dirs. Goodyear Tire & Rubber Co., Akron, Ohio, Rural/Metro Corp., Microtest, Inc., Phoenix; founding mem. Pacific Coun. Internat. Policy, L.A., 1995—; chmn. internat. adv. coun. Avon Products, Inc., N.Y.C., 1985-98; mem. Spencer Stuart adv. coun. Spencer Stuart and Assocs., N.Y.C., 1984-90; chmn., mem. internat. adv. coun. Advanced Semiconductor Materials Internat. NV, Bilthoven, The Netherlands, 1985-88; bd. dirs. The Atlantic Coun. of U.S., Washington, 1977-92; co-chmn. internat. adv. bd. Univ. of Nations, Kona, Hawaii, 1985—; bd. dirs. World Wildlife Fund/U.S., 1983-85, World Wildlife Fund/The Conservation Found., 1985-89, Nat. Coun., 1989-95, 96—; bd. govs. Joseph H. Lauder Inst. Mgmt. and Internat. Studies, U. Pa., 1983—; trustee Heard Mus., Phoenix, 1983-86, mem. nat. adv. bd., 1986-93;. trustee Am. Grad. Sch. Internat. Mgmt., 1972—, chmn. bd. trustees, 1987-89; bd. govs. Atlantic Inst. Internat. Affairs, Paris, 1977-88; adv. bd. Ctr. Strategic and Internat. Studies, Georgetown U., 1977-81; dir. Pullman, Inc., Chgo., 1977-80, Nabisco Brands, Inc., Parsippany, N.J., 1977-85, Salomon, Inc., N.Y.C., 1980-93, AT&T Internat., Inc., Basking Ridge, N.J., 1980-84, Atlantic Inst. Found., Inc., N.Y.C., 1984-90; mem. European Cmty.-U.S. Businessmen's Coun., 1978-79; bd. govs. Am. Hosp. of Paris, 1974-77; nat. trustee Nat. Symphony Orch. Assn., Washington, 1973-83, Am. Sch., Paris, 1976-77, Orme Sch., Mayer, Ariz., 1970-74, Phoenix Country Day Sch., 1971-74; mem. nat. coun. Salk Inst., 1978-82; mem. U.S. Adv. Com. Internat. Edn. and Cultural Affairs, 1969-74; nat. rev. bd. Ctr. Cultural and Tech. Interchange Between East and West, 1970-74; mem. vestry Am. Cathedral, Paris, 1976-77; pres., bd. dirs. Phoenix Symphony Assn., 1969-70; chmn. Ariz. Joint Econ. Devel. Com., 1967-68; exec. com., bd. dirs. Ariz. Dept. Econ. Planning and Devel., 1968-70; chmn. bd. Ariz. Crippled Children's Svcs., 1964-65; treas. Ariz. Rep. Com., 1956-57; chmn. Ariz. Young Rep. League, 1955-56; chmn. bd. Mercy Ships Internat., Inc., A Ministry of Youth With A Mission, Lindale, Tex., 1985-2000; mem. trade and environ. com. Nat. Adv. Coun. for Environ. Policy and Tech.-U.S. EPA, Washington, 1991-95; dir. exec. com., chmn. internat. com. Ariz. Econ. Coun., Phoenix, 1989-93; dir. exec. com. Orgn. for Free Trade and Devel., Phoenix, 1991-93; chmn. Internat. Adv. Coun. Plasma Tech., Inc., Santa Fe, 1992-97. Recipient East-West Ctr. Disting. Svc. award, 1977. Mem. U.S. Coun. Internat. Bus. (trustee, exec. com.), Coun. Fgn. Rels., Coun. Am. Ambs. (vice chmn. bd.), Nat. Adv. Coun. on Bus. Edn., Coun. Internat. Edn. Exch., Met. Club, Links Club (N.Y.C.), Paradise Valley (Ariz.) Country Club, Bohemian Club (San Francisco). Episcopalian. Fax: 480-948-4674. E-mail: wct-aac@mindspring.com.

TURNER-WARWICK, MARGARET, physician, educator; b. Nov. 19, 1924; d. William Harvey and Maud Kirkdale (Baden-Powell) Moore; m. Richard Trevor Turner-Warwick, Jan. 21, 1950; children: Gillian, Lynne. MA, BM, BCh, Oxford (Eng.) U., 1950, DM, 1956; PhD, London U., 1961; DSc (hon.), NYU, 1985, Exeter U., 1990, U. London, 1990, Hull U., 1991, U. Sussex, 1992, U. Oxford, 1992, U. Cambridge, 1993, U. Leicester, 1997. Clin. tng. U. Coll. Hosp., Brompton Hosp., 1950-61; cons. physician Elizabeth Ganett Anderson Hosp., 1961-67, Brompton and London Chest Hosps., 1967-72; prof. medicine Brompton and Cardio Thoracic Inst., London, 1972-87; dean Cardiothoracic Inst., London, 1984-87; pres. Royal Coll. Physicians, London, 1989-92; chmn. UKCCCR, London. Author: (book) Immunology of Lung, 1979. Non-exec. mem. Royal Brompton Governing Body, London; chmn. Royal Deven. Exel. Healthcare Trust, 1992-95. Named Dame Comdr. Brit. Empire, 1991; recipient Osler medal Oxford, 1996, Pres. award European Respiratory Soc., 1997. Fellow ACP (hon.), Faculty Occupl. Medicine, Royal Australian Coll. Physicians, Faculty Pub. Health Medicine, Royal Coll. Physicians Edinburgh, Royal Coll. Physicians and Surgeons Glasgow, Royal Coll. Gen. Practitioners (ad eundum), U. Coll. London, Royal Coll. Physicians Ireland, Royal Coll. Physicians and Surgeons Can. (hon.), Royal Coll. Anaesthetists (hon.), Coll. Medicine South Africa (hon.), Royal Coll. Pathologists (hon.), Royal Coll. Radiology, Bencher Middle Temple (hon.), Lady Margaret Hall Oxford (hon.), Girton Coll. Cambridge (hon.), Green Coll. Oxford (hon.), Imperial Coll., London (hon.); mem. Assn. Physicians Gt. Britain and Ireland (hon.), Acad. Malaysia, South German and Australasian Thoracic Socs. (hon.), Brit. Thoracic Soc. (pres. 1982, President's medal 1999), Alpha Omega Alpha. Avocations: gardening, violin, country life, watercolor painting. Home: Pynes House Thorverton Nr Exeter, Devon EX5 5LT, England

TURNEY, ALAN HARRY, retired state official; b. London, Aug. 20, 1932; s. Harry Landry and Alice Theresa (Bailey) T.; m. Ann Mary Dollimore, June 22, 1957. BSc, London Sch. Econ., 1961. Asst. pvt. sec. Sec. of State, London, 1962-65; prin. in police, prison, criminal justice and fire depts. London, 1965-76; asst. sec. broadcasting, rev. forensic sci., prison dept., 1976-86, head fire and emergency planning dept., 1986-92. Sec. Hertfordshire Rugby Football Union, 1969-78. Decorated Companion of Most Honourable Order of the Bath, Her Majesty The Queen, 1990. Mem. Ch. of Eng. Avocations: rugby football, freemasonry. Home: Brookfield Cottage Bury End, Nuthampstead Roylston Hertfordshire SG8 8NG, England

TURNIDGE, GREGORY ELLIOTT, finance company executive; b. Sydney, Australia, Mar. 26, 1953; s. Douglas Norman and Amy Ellis (Rannard) T.; m. Dagmar Erica Uhl, Jan. 11, 1975; children: Alia, Alexandra. BA with honors, Macquarie U., Sydney, 1975, MEcons with honors, 1979. Rsch. officer Res. Bank of Australia, Sydney, 1974-77; mgr. rsch. Victorian Chamber of Manufactures, Melbourne, 1978-80, gen. mgr., 1981-82, 84; mem. Office of Mgmt. and Budget Task Force, Govt. of Victoria, Melbourne, 1982-83; mng. dir. Aluminium Smelters of Victoria Pty Ltd., Melbourne, 1984-98, Galen Investment Pty Ltd., Melbourne, 1998—; chmn., bd. dirs. Nat. Inst. for Econ. and Industry Rsch., Melbourne, 1989-95; chmn. Aluvic Asia Pty. Ltd., Hong Kong, 1988-98, Aluvic, Hitchcock Internat. Inc., Mpls., 1995-98, Aluvic Aerospace Pty. Ltd., 1999—; bd. dirs. Aluvic Europe, Auxerre, France; bd. dirs. Kidson Collins Pty. Ltd., Creative Learning Cons. Pty. Ltd.; mem. economists group Confedn. of Australian Industry, Canberra, 1978-81; advisor to bd. dirs. Dacar S.A., Auxerre, 1999—. Author: (publ. series) Victorian Chamber of Manufactures Econ. Rsch. Series, 1979, 80, 81. Industry rep. Victorian Inst. Secondary Edn., Econ. Studies, Melbourne, 1979-80; pres. Auburn Sch. Coun., Melbourne, 1987-93; trustee Com. for Econ. Devel. of Australia, Melbourne, 1993-99, mem. Victorian adv. com., 1997—. Fellow Australian Inst. Co. Dirs.; mem. Australian Aluminium Coun. (bd. dirs. 1991-98). Avocations: jogging, wine appreciation, reading.

TURNOVEC, FRANTIŠEK, economist, educator; b. Prague, Czech Republic, Jan. 6, 1941; s. František and Jiřina (Hromádková) T.; m. Akkul Keperová, May 1, 1939; children: Marie, František. MSc, Leningrad U., 1964; PhD in Math., Charles U., 1982; PhD in Econs., Econs. U., Bratislava, 1990. Asst. prof. Econs. U., Bratislava, Slovakia, 1964-70, assoc. prof., 1989-92; systems analyst Rsch. Comp. Ctr., Bratislava, 1970-89; assoc. prof. Agrl. U., Nitra, Slovakia, 1992-93; sr. rschr. Econ. Inst. of Acad. Scis., Czech Republic, 1993—; assoc. prof. Charles U., Prague, 1993-98, prof., 1998—; dir. CERGE of Charles U., Prague, 1994-99; vis. rschr. Princeton U., 1993, Pitts. U., 1994; vis. prof. Inst. for Advanced Studies, Vienna, 1996-97, Fern U., Hagen, Germany, 1991; mem. Acad. Bd. of Faculty of Social Scis., Charles U., 1995—, Acad. Bd. of Masaryk U., Brno, 1998—. Author: Arithmetics of Voting and Calculus of Power, 1998, Political Economy of European Integration, 2000; co-author: The Theory of Games, 1966, The Theory of Games and Decision Making, 1991; editor Ctrl. European Jour. for Ops. Rsch. and Econs., Vienna, 1993—; contbr. articles to profl. jours. Action for Cooperation in Econs. fellowship Commn. of European Union, 1996-97; rsch. grant Grant Agy. of the Czech Rep., 1998—. Mem. European Public Choice Soc, Internat. Input-Output Soc., Czech Econ. Soc., Czech Soc. for Ops. Rsch. Home: Krhanice 123, 257 42 Krhanice Czech Republic Office: Charles U, Opletalova 26, 110 00 Prague Czech Republic

TURNPENNY, PETER DOUGLAS, clinical geneticist; b. London, Mar. 30, 1953; s. Douglas Walter and Doreen Ada (Webb) T.; m. Alison Mary Douglas, Sept. 24, 1977; 4 daughters. BSc, Edinburgh (Scotland) U., 1974, MBChB, 1977; diploma in child health, Royal Coll. Ob-Gyns., London. Pediatrician Nazareth (Israel) Hosp., 1983-90; sr. registrar in clin. genetics Aberdeen (Scotland) Royal Hosps. NHS Trust, 1990-93; cons. clin. geneticist Royal Devon and Exeter (Eng.) Healthcare NHS Trust, 1993—; med. adviser to Nat. Fetal Anti-Convulsant Syndrome Assn. Editor, contbr. 3 chpts.: Secrets in the Genes: Adoption, Inheritance, and Genetic Disease, 1995; contbr. articles to Jour. Med. Genetics and (jour.) Clin. Dysmorphology. Awarded Hilda Lewis Meml. lecture Brit. Agys. for Adoption and Fostering, U.K., 1994. Fellow Royal Coll. Pediatrics and Child Health, Royal Coll. Physicians; mem. Brit. Soc. Human Genetics. Office: Royal Devon and Exeter Hosp, Barrack Rd, Devon Exeter EX2 5DW, England

TURNQUEST, ORVILLE A., Bahamian governor general; b. Grants Town, New Providence, July 19, 1929; s. Robert and Gwendolyn Turnquest; m. Edith Louise Thompson, 1955; 3 children. Student, U. London. Counsel, atty. Supreme Ct., Bahamas; pvt. practice Bahamas, 1953-92; atty. gen. Govt. of Bahamas, Nassau, 1992-94, min. justice, 1992-93, min. fgn. affairs, 1992-94, dep. prime min., 1993-94, gov.-gen., 1995—; stipendiary and circuit magistrate and coronor, 1959; law tutor, mem. examining bd. Bahamas Bar, 1965-92; pres. Bahamas Bar Assn.; chair Bahamas Bar Coun., 1970-72; sec.-gen. Progressive Liberal Party, 1960-62; mem. Parliament, 1962-67, 82-94; del. Bahamas Constitutional Conf., London, 1963, Bahamas Independence Conf., London, 1972; pres. COmmonwealth Parliamentary Assn., 1992-93. Patron Bahamas Games; chancellor Diocese Nasau and The Bahamas; mem. Anglican Ctrl. Ednl. Authority, Nat. Com. World Colls.; bd. govs. St. John's Coll., St. Anne's H.S. Avocations: tennis, swimming, music, reading. Office: Office of Governor General, Govt Hill PO Box N-3301, Nassau Bahamas*

TURNWALD, GERHARD, mathematician; b. Vienna, Austria, June 1, 1960; arrived in Germany, 1986; s. Otto and Gerti (Benischek) T. Diploma, Tech. Univ. of Vienna, 1983, PhD, 1984. Asst. prof. Tech. U. of Vienna, 1985-86; asst. prof. U. Tuebingen, Germany, 1986-96, dozent, 1990—. Editor Finite Fields and Their Applications, 1993—; co-author: Dickson Polynomials, 1993; contbr. articles to profl. jours. Office: U Tuebingen Math Inst, Auf der Morgenstelle 10, D-72076 Tuebingen Germany

TURO, RON, lawyer; b. Fort Wayne, Ind., Apr. 2, 1955; s. John B. and Joan L. (Gluntz) T.; m. Claire Teresa Fetterman T., May 24, 1980; children: Andrew Jacob, Patricia Erin, Dominic Earl. BA in History with honors, Pa. State U., 1978; JD, Dickinson Sch. Law, 1981. Bar: Pa. 1981, U.S. Dist. (mid. dist.) Pa. 1982, U.S. Supreme Ct. 1987, U.S. Ct. Appeals (3d cir.) 1989. Ast. pub. defender Cumberland County, Carlisle, Pa., 1981-84; ptnr. Griffie & Turo, Carlisle, 1984-89; pvt. practice Carlisle, 1989—; lectr. Dickinson Sch. Law, 1996—, Weidener U. Sch. Law, 2000—. Founder West Shore Police Recognition Dinner, Camp Hill, Pa., 1985—; mem. Nat. Cath. Com. on Scouting, 1988—; chmn. Region III, Pa., N.J., 1993-95, parliamentarian and legal coun., 1991—, advisor religious act, 1998-2000; bd. dirs. AHEDD, Inc., 1993-94, vice chmn. 1994-95, chmn., 1995—; trustee David E. Baker Scholarship Trust, 1997—; bd. dirs. Pa. Assn. for the Blind, 1998—, exec. search com., 1999-2000; bd. dirs. Common Sense Adoption Svcs. Inc., 1998—. Recipient St. George Emblem Boy Scouts Am., 1983, Eagle Scout 1969, Golden AAD Emblem, 1989. Mem. Nat. Lawyer's Assn., Nat. Assn. Criminal Def. Lawyers, Pa. Bar Assn., Pa. Assn. Criminal Def. Lawyers, Cumberland County Bar Assn. (social chmn. 1985-98, pub. rels. com. 1998—, nominating com. 1999—, membership chmn. 2000—), St. Thomas More Soc. (v.p. 1996-98, treas. 1998—), Mensa (local sec. 1990-92, editor 1992-95, ombudsman 2000—), KC (pres. Capital area chpt. 1989, Knight of Yr. 1981, grand knight 1985-87, 93-95, fin. sec. 1996—, dist. dep. 1998—). Republican. Roman Catholic. Avocations: scouting, scuba diving, travel. Home: 539 Baltimore Pike Mount Holly Springs PA 17065-1028 Office: 28 S Pitt St Carlisle PA 17013-3211

TUROCK, BETTY JANE, library and information science educator; b. Scranton, Pa., June 12; d. David and Ruth Carolyn (Sweetser) Argust; m. Frank M. Turock, June 16, 1956; children: David L., B. Drew. BA magna cum laude (Charles Weston scholar), Syracuse U., 1955; postgrad. (scholar), U. Pa., 1956; MLS, Rutgers U., 1970, PhD, 1981. Library and materials coordinator Holmdel (N.J.) Public Schs., 1963-65; story-teller Wheaton (Ill.) Public Library, 1965-67; ednl. media specialist Alhambra Public Sch., Phoenix, 1967-70; br. librarian, area librarian, head extension service Forsyth County Public Library System, Winston-Salem, N.C., 1970-73; asst. dir. Montclair (N.J.) Public Library, 1973-75, Monroe County Library System, Rochester, N.Y., 1978-81; asst. prof. Rutgers U. Grad. Sch. Comms., Info. and and Libr. Studies, Rochester, N.Y., 1981-87; assoc. prof. Rutgers U. Grad. Sch. Communications Info and Libr. Studies, 1987-93, prof., 1994—, dept. chair, 1989-95, dir. MLS program, 1990-95; dir. MLS program Rutgers U. Grad. Sch. Comm., Info. and Libr. Studies, 1990-95; vis. prof. Rutgers U. Grad. Sch. Library and Info. Studies, 1980-81; adviser U.S. Dept. Edn. Office of Libr. Programs, 1988-89. Author: Serving Older Adults, 1983, Creating a Financial Plan, 1992; editor: The Bottom Line, 1984-90; contbr. articles to profl. jours. Trustee Raritan Twp. (N.J.) Public Library, 1961-62, Keystone Coll., 1991—, Freedom to Read Found., 1994-97, Librs. for the Future, 1994-97, Fund for Am.'s Librs., 1995; Trustee Bd. Am. Libr., Paris, 1999—; mem. Bd. Edn. Raritan Twp., 1962-66; ALA coord. Task Force on Women, 1978-80; mem. action coun.; treas. Social Responsibilities Round Table, 1978-82. Charles Weston scholar Syracuse U., 1955; recipient N.J. Libr. Leadership award, 1994; named Woman of Yr. Raritan-Holmdel Woman's Club, 1975. Mem. AAUP, Am. Soc. Info. Sci., Assn. Libr. and Info. Sci Edn., Am. Libr. Assn. (pres. 1995-96, pres.-elect 1994-95, exec. bd. 1991-97, coun. 1988-97, equality award 1998), Rutgers U. Grad. Sch. Library and Info. Studies Alumni Assn. (pres. 1977-78, Disting. Alumni award 1994), Phi Theta Kappa, Psi Chi, Beta Phi Mu, Pi Beta Phi. Unitarian. Home: 39 Highwood Rd Somerset NJ 08873-1834 Office: Rutgers U 4 Huntington St New Brunswick NJ 08901-1071

TUROVETS, SERGEI IVANOVITCH, laser physicist; b. Lyadets, Belarus, USSR, May 14, 1961; s. Ivan Ivanovitch and Elena Mikhailovna (Sharstuk) T.; m. Nina Dmitrievna Dranets, Feb. 1, 1980 (div. Nov. 1992); 1 child, Lilya. Dipl. physics, Moscow State U., 1983; PhD Inst. Physics, Acad. of Sci., Minsk, Belarus, 1992. Engr., rschr. Kamsky Automobilnyi Zavod, Naber Chelny, Russia, 1983-84; sci. worker Inst. Physics, Minsk, USSR, 1987-89; sci. sec. Acad. Scis., Minsk, 1990-92, sr. sci. worker Inst. Physics, 1993-2000; sr. photonic device simulation sci. SIROS Tech., Inc., San Jose, Calif., 2000—; lectr. Kama Politech. Inst., Naber Chelny, 1983-84, dept. theoretical physics Belarus State U., Minsk, 1992-98; vis. rschr. dept. biophysics Stockholm U., 1995, Bath U., U.K., 1994-95, Göttingen U., Germany, 1995-96; bd. dirs. Byelorussian Assn. Young Scientists, Minsk, 1990-93; vis. scientist Cantabria U., Spain, 1999-2000. Contbr. articles to profl. jours. Grantee Am. Phys. Soc., 1993, Internat. Sci. Found., 1993, Ministry Edn. Sci., 1998; recipient Gold medal USSR Govt., 1977, prize Belorussian YCL Com., 1990, Royal Soc. London award, 1995, Royal Soc. Stockholm award, 1995; Royal Soc. London fellow U. Wales, Bangor, 1995-96. Avocations: classical music, cinema. Office: SIROS Tech Inc 1010 Daggett Dr San Jose CA 95134

TUROVSKA, BAIBA, chemist, researcher; b. Talsi, Latvia, Feb. 12, 1952; d. Alberts and Pārsla (Grinvalde) Medins; m. Ivars Turovskis, June 19, 1986. Bsc, Latvian U., Riga, 1975; D in Chemistry, Latvian Inst Organic Synthesis, Riga, 1989. Tchr. Riga (Latvia) 59th Middle Sch., 1975-78; rsch. fellow Latvian Inst. Organic Synthesis, Riga, 1978—. Contbr. articles to profl. jours. Mem. Popular Front of Latvia, Riga, 1988-99. Grantee Internat. Sci. Found., 1994-95, Danish Rsch. Coun., 1994-96. Mem. N.Y. Acad. Scis., Electrochem. Soc., Internat. Soc. Electrochemistry. Home: Salaspils 18/4-118, LV 1057 Riga Latvia Office: Latvian Inst Organic Synth, 21 Aizkraukles St, LV 1006 Riga Latvia

TURPIN, CALVIN COOLIDGE, retired university administrator, educator; b. Granite City, Ill., Nov. 8, 1924; s. Golden and Gertrude (West) T.; m. Eudell Coody, June 29, 1944; children: Susan Turpin Jones, John Thomas. BA, Baylor U., 1949, MA, 1952; BD, So. Bapt. Theol. Sem., 1955, M of Religious Edn., 1958; MA, Vanderbilt U., 1962; MDiv, So. Bapt. Theol. Sem., 1973; DSc in Theology, Golden Gate Bapt. Theol. Sem., 1967. Prof. history and Greek Jacksonville Coll., Tex., 1950-52; prof. religion Belmont Coll., Nashville, 1955-56, Austin-Peay State U., Clarksville, Tenn., 1956-57; assoc. libr. Inst. of Old Testament Golden Gate Bapt. Theol. Sem., Mill Valley, Calif., 1961-66; dir. librs., prof. libr. sci. Minot (N.D.) State Coll., 1966-67; dir. librs., prof. religion Judson Coll., Marion, Ala., 1967-70; prof. religion, dir. librs. Hardin-Simmons U., Abilene, Tex., 1970-77; vis. prof. Tex. Woman's U., Denton, 1974-75. Author: Beyond My Dreams: Memories and Interpretations, 1992, Writings and a Selected Bibliography of Calvin C. Turpin, 1995, 50 Years of Ministry: Challenges and Changes, 1997; co-author: Rupert N. Richardson: The Man and His Works, 1971, History of the First Baptist Church, Gilroy, California, 1995; contbr. numerous articles to profl. publs. Nat. dep. chief chaplains CAP-USAF Aux., 1990-92; Calif. dept. chaplain Am. Legion, San Francisco, 1990-92, 94-95; vets. pk. commr. San Benito County, Hollister, Calif., 1990-92; rent control commr. City of Hollister, 1993-95. Brigadier gen. USSC, 1992—. Lilly Endowment scholar Lilly Found., 1962. Mem. Rotary Club, Lions Club, Beta Phi Mu, Phi Delta Kappa, Gamma Iota. Republican. Baptist. Avocations: volunteer chaplaincy, writing, authentic cowboy cooking. Home: 188 Elm Dr Hollister CA 95023-3430

TURPIN, JOSEPH OVILA, counselor, educator; b. Rockford, Ill., July 11, 1943; s. D. John and Mona Belle (Albright) T.; m. Hester R. Thompson, June 26, 1969; children: Matthew, Michael. AB in Sociology, Ind. U., 1965, MS in Mental Retardation, 1966, postgrad., 1966-67; PhD in Rehab. Psychology, U. Wis., 1986. Rsch. assoc. Ind. U., Bloomington, 1966-67; instr. U. Wis. Parkside Extension, Kenosha, 1967-71; tchr. Kenosha Unified Sch. Dist., 1967-71; coord. Racine area Gov.'s Com. on Spl. Learning State of Wis. Dept. Adminstrn., 1971-73; dir. Racine County Comprehensive Mental Health, Mental Retardation, Alcohol and Other Drug Abuse Svcs. Bd, 1973-78; vocat. cons., counselor supr. Industrial Injury Clinic, Neenah, Wis., 1978-83; owner, vocat. expert Vocat. Counseling Svc., Inc., Madison, Wis., 1983-88; teaching intern, counseling supr., student tchr. supr. U. Wis.,

Madison, 1983-86; asst. prof. rehab. counselor edn. Ohio U., Athens, 1986-89; assoc. prof. rehab. counseling program Calif. State U., San Bernardino, 1989-94, prof. rehab. counseling program, 1994—, coord. rehab. counseling program, 1990-94; mem. sch. psychologist exam. com. Dept. Edn. State of Ohio, 1989; rschr., presenter, cons. in field. Contbr. articles to profl. publs. Bd. dirs. United Cerebral Palsy of Racine County, 1969-73, Children's House, Inc., Racine, 1971-73, Ctrl. Ohio Regional Coun. on Alcoholism, 1987-89, Ctr. for Cmty. Counseling and Edn., 1993-99, pres., 1998; bd. dirs. Inland Caregivers Resource Ctr., 1993-99, Health and Hosp. Planning Com. of Racine County, 1976; treas. Cub Scout Pack # 68, Boy Scouts Am., Neenah, 1981-83, Whitcomb Village Assn., Inc., 1984; bd. dirs. Aquinas H.S., 1992-94, pres. 1994; H.S. liaison West Point Parents Club of Inland Empire, 1992-94; budget rev. com. United Fund Racine County, 1975. Grantee Rehab. Svcs. Adminstrn., 1985-88, Ohio U., 1987-88, Ohio U. Coll. Osteo. Medicine and Coll. Edn., 1989, Office Spl. Edn. and Rehab., 1989-92, Inland Reg. Ctr., 1999. Mem. ACA (pub. policy and legis. com. 1992-94, various subcoms.), APA, Assn. Counselor Educators and Suprs. (we. region legis. chair 1996-98), Am. Rehab. Counseling Assn. (exec. coun. 1992-94, ethics com. 1990-91, chair coun. on profl. preparation and stds. 1992-94), Nat. Rehab. Counseling Assn. (bd. dirs. 1993-94, chmn. grievance com., pres. 1997), Nat. Rehab. Assn. (bd. dirs. 1998), Alliance Rehab. Counseling (bd. dirs. 1996-98, co-chair 1998). Office: Calif State U 5500 University Pkwy San Bernardino CA 92407-2318

TURRNBERG, BENGT LENNART, nautical engineer; b. Soffle, Sweden, Aug. 26, 1951; m. Hanna Elzbieta Waligor, Feb. 3, 1989; children: Daniel, Therese. Degree in engring., Naval Tech. Sch., Karlskrona, Sweden, 1972; grad., Armed Forces Joint Coll., Stockholm, 1991. From petty officer to lt. comdr. Royal Swedish Navy, Stockholm, 1970-92; prin. tech. officer Swedish Def. Materiel Adminstrn., Stockholm, 1992—. Home: Vinggatan 10, Skarpndck SE-12836, Sweden

TURTIAINEN, ARI PETRI, marketing professional; b. Helsinki, Finland, Jan. 22, 1958; s. Armas Eemil and Siiri (Tuomi) T.; m. Eija Marjo Kullberg-Turtiainen, June 26, 1978. MS in Engring., Tampere U., Finland, 1982. Sales support engr. Oy Grönblom Ab, Helsinki, 1982-84, Computervision, Helsinki, 1985; product mgr. Computervision, Brussels, 1985-86; product mgr. Oy DAVA Ab, Helsinki, 1986, dept. mgr., 1987, mktg. mgr., 1987-89; mktg. mgr. Computervision Nordic, 1989-93; sales and mktg. dir. Optimi-Ohjelmistot, 1993-1995; country mgr. Data Gen. Finland, 1997-2000; mng. dir. Corus Tech., Finland, 2000—. Author: NC in CADCAM Systems, 1982; also articles. Club: Blebeijit (Tampere). Home: Rajakuja 3, FIN04260 Tuusula Finland Office: Corus Tedhnologies, 00180 Helsinki Finland

TURTOI, DUMITRU, science educator; b. Bucharest, Romania, May 24, 1936; s. Mihail and Niculina (Rogozea) T.; m. Adriana Demayo, May 21, 1962; children: Petrosanu Dana-Mihaela, Calinov Irina Ana. Chemist engr., Inst. Technol. Chemistry D.I. Medeleev, Moscow, 1961; PhD, U. Poly., Bucharest, 1982. Cert. prof. dr. engr. in inorganic technol. chemistry. Chief lab. U. Poly., Bucharest, 1961-63, univ. asst., 1963-76, univ. lectr., 1976-90, reader, 1990-95, prof., 1995—; dir. contractual rsch. Inst. Chem. and Pharm. Rsch., Bucharest, 1975-90, Inst. Chem. Rsch., Bucharest, 1975-99, Rm. Valcea, 1975-99, Inst. Leather Rsch., Bucharest, 1975-99. Author: Pure and Ultrapure Inorganic Substances, 1979, Environmental Chemistry, 1997; contbr. papers to profl. jours.; patentee in field. Named Expert of Nat. Com. for Fine Chems. in Coun. Mutual Econ. Assistance, Min. of Chem. Industry, 1973. Avocations: mountain tourism, artistic photography, lumenophilly. Office: Poly U of Bucharest, Gh Polizu St 1, 78126 Bucharest Romania

TURTOLA, RISTO PEKKA, architect; b. Marttila, Finland, Jan. 6, 1934; s. Viljo Abel and Irma Silvia (Lindstrom) T.; Architect, Polytech. U. Helsinki, 1964; m. Anja Marita Roos, June 5, 1960. Designing architect Olli Kivinen, Helsinki, 1964-68; leading architect Kauria-Turtola, Helsinki, 1965—; teaching asst. Poly. U. Helsinki, 1971-72, specialized tchr., 1976. Served with Pioneers, 1961-62. Recipient 1st prize Kokkola, Koivuhaka City Planning Competition, 1964, Tampere, Pispala Nordic City Planning Competition, 1968; 3d prize Turku, Univ. and City Planning Competition, 1976. Mem. Assn. Finnish Architects. Home: 8 Pohjoisranta, 00170 Helsinki Finland Office: 2 Rauhankatu, 00170 Helsinki Finland

TURTURRO, JOHN, actor; b. Brooklyn, Feb. 28, 1957; s. Nicholas and Katherine Turturro; m. Katherine Borowitz; 1 child, Amedeo. Grad., SUNY (New Paltz), 1978; student, Yale Drama Sch. Worked in regional theater and off-Broadway in Danny and the Deep Blue Sea (Obie award 1985), Men Without Dates, Tooth of the Crime, La Puta Vida, Chaos and Hard Times, The Bald Soprano, Of Mice and Men, The Resistable Rise of Arturo Ui, 1991, Waiting for Godot; appeared in Broadway prodn. Death of a Salesman, 1984; appeared in films Raging Bull, 1980, The Flamingo Kid, 1984, To Live and Die in L.A., 1985, Desperately Seeking Susan, 1985, Hannah and Her Sisters, 1986, Gung Ho, 1986, Offbeat, 1986, The Color of Money, 1986, The Sicilian, 1987, Five Corners, 1988, Do the Right Thing, 1989, Miller's Crossing, 1990, Men of Respect, Mo Better Blues, 1990, Jungle Fever, 1991, Barton Fink, 1991 (winner best actor award, Cannes Film Festival, 1991, David Donatello award Montreal Film Festival-Best Actor), Backtrack, 1991, Brain Donors, 1992, Fearless, 1993, Being Human, 1994, Quiz Show, 1994, Grace of My Heart, 1994, Search and Destroy, 1995, Unstrung Heroes, 1995, Clockers, 1995, Box of Moonlight, 1996, Girl 6, 1996, The Big Lebowski, 1997, Animals, 1997, The Truce, 1998, Lesser Prophets, 1998, Rounders, 1998, He Got Game, 1998, The Source, 1999, The Cradle Will Rock, 1999, Company Man, 1999, Two Thousand and None, 1999, Oh Brother, Where Art Thou?, 1999, The Man Who Cried, 1999, The Luzhin Defense, 1999; film dir. (debut) Mac (Camera d'Or award Cannes Film Festival, 1992), Illuminata, 1998. Office: care ICM 40 W 57th St New York NY 10019-4001 also: 16 N Oak St 2 A Ventura CA 93001-5620

TUSCAI, SHAWNNA SUZANNE, transportation executive; b. Florissant, Mo., Apr. 7, 1970; d. Robert F. and Susan M. Bronner; m. T.J. Tuscai, Nov. 21, 1998. BS in Fin., Pa. State U., 1992; MBA in Mktg., Villanova U., 1998. Acct. Matlack, Inc., Wilmington, Del., 1992-94; logistics analyst Transport Internat. Pool, Devon, Pa., 1994-95; opers. analyst Transport Internat. Pool, Devon, 1995-96, acct. mgr., 1996-98; European mktg. mgr. Transport Internat. Pool, Amsterdam, 1999—. Avocations: fitness, travel, reading.

TUSENIUS, ROBERT RENÉ, company director, consultant; b. The Hague, The Netherlands, Aug. 9, 1923; arrived in S. Africa, 1949; s. Bernhard J. and Corrie A. (Jurgens) T.; m. Madelon Wesseling, Jan. 8, 1949; children: Madelon Louise, Micheline Renée. BA, U. Pretoria, South Africa, 1952; B in Commerce, U. Pretoria, 1952, MBA, 1954, M in Commerce cum laude, 1956; DComm, U. Pretoria (S. Africa), 1957. Mgmt. trainee Shell, The Netherlands, 1947-49, S. African Iron and Steel Corp., 1950-53; with Coun. Scientific & Indsl. Rsch., 1953-59; ind. profl. mgr., bus. adv., dir. numerous orgns., S. Africa, 1959-72; prof., dir. Grad. Sch. Bus. Stellenbosch U., 1972-82; founder, chmn. Operational Improvement Mgmt., 1982—; first dir. GSB's Inst. Entrepreneurship amd Mgmt., 1975-76; founder, chmn. Internat. Investment and Mgmt. Co., 1995. Contbr. numerous articles to profl. jours. Founder, chmn. Action S. Africa, 1974, Youth Leadership Forum, 1978, Trust for Peace and Prosperity in S. and So. Africa, 1982, Found. for Peace and Prosperity in Africa, 1996. Lt. Netherlands E. Indian Army, 1944-46. Decorated Cross of Merit for Work in Resistance Queen of The Netherlands, 1943, Cert. of Merit Nat. African C. of C. and Industry, 1978. Home: 186 Helderberg Village, 7130 Somerset West Cape, South Africa Office: OIM (Ply) Ltd, PO Box 322, 7129 Somerset West Cape, South Africa

TUSKA, JON, author, publisher; b. South Milwaukee, Wis., Apr. 30, 1942; s. Andrew and Florence Catherine (Tommet) T.; m. Vicki Piekarski, May 24, 1980; 1 child, Jennifer Lee. BA, Marquette U., 1965. Owner Pers. Cons., Milw., 1969-74; editor, pub. Views & Revs. mag., 1969-75; freelance writer, 1975--91; co-owner, agt. Golden West Literary Agy., Portland, Oreg., 1992—; mem. adj. faculty MA and tchg. program and undergrads. Lewis and Clark Coll., 1979-88' staff music critic Ovation mag., 1987-89, Fanfare mag., 1989-95; spl. film. cons. Images of Indians, PBS, 1980, Images of Appalachia, PBS, 1984, Mommy, Who's Winning Now? The Cold War in America, Turner, 1986, Say It with Music: Irving Berlin's America, PBS, 1986, Broadway's Eternal Romantics: Lerner and Loewe, PBS, 1988, John Wayne: Standing Tall, PBS, 1989, Big Guns Talk, Turner, 1997; prodr. classical music programs, art and news features and interviews with musicians and motion picture personalities, and film revs. for radio stas. Oreg. Pub. Broadcasting. Author: Philo Vance: The Life and Times of S.S. Van Dine, 1973, The Films of Mae West, 1973, The Filming of the West, 1976, The Detective in Hollywood, 1978, The Vanishing Legion: A History of Mascot Pictures 1927-35, 1982, 2d edit., 1986, Billy the Kid: A Bio/Bibliography, 1983, Dark Cinema: American Film Noir in Cultural Perspective, 1984, The American West in Film: Critical Approaches to the Western, 1985, In Manors and Alleys: A Case-Book on the American Detective Film, 1988, A Variable Harvest: Essays and Reviews in Literature and Film, 1989, Encounters with Filmmakers: Eight Career Studies, 1991, The Complete Films of Mae West, 1992, Billy the Kid: His Life and Legend, 1994, (with Vicki Piekarski) The Frontier Experience: A Reader's Guide to the Life and Literature of the American West, 1984; editor-in-chief (with Piekarski) Ency. of Frontier and Western Fiction, 1983; editor: The Western Story: A chronological Treasury 1894-1994, 1994, Shadow of the Lariat, 1995, Star Western: Twenty-Two Western Stories from the Golden Age, 1995, The Big Book of Western Action Stories, 1995, (with Piekarski) The Morrow Anthology of Great Western Stort Stories, 1997, The First Five Star Westen Corral, 2000, Five Star Westerns. Avocations: reading, classical music, film history, book collecting. Home and Office: 2327 SE Salmon St Portland OR 97214-3943

TÜSKÉS, GÁBOR, literary historian, researcher; b. Pécs, Hungary, Sept. 13, 1955; s. Tibor and Anna (Szemes) T.; m. Éva Knapp, Dec. 3, 1980; 1 child, Anna. PhD, Loránd Eötvös U., Budapest, Hungary, 1985; post-doctoral studies, Hungarian Acad. Sci., Budapest, 1987. Contractural rschr. Inst. for Ethnology Hungarian Acad. Scis., Budapest, 1980-82; rsch. fellow Soros-Hungarian Acad. Scis.-Found., Budapest, 1987-89, Alexander von Humboldt-Found., Würzburg, Germany, 1989-91; rschr. Inst. for Literary Studies Hungarian Acad. Scis., Budapest, 1991-92, sr. rschr., 1992-99, head dept., 2000—; cons. Acad. Scis., Göttingen, Germany, Inst. of Mariology, Regensburg, Germany, 1988-94, Nat. Ctr. for Sci. Rsch., Paris, 1990—. Author: (book) Baroque Pilgrimage in Hungary on the Basis of the Miracle Literature, 1993 (in Hungarian), European Relations of the Narrative Religious Literature in the 17th Century, 1997 (in Hungarian), Andras Osze, 1998 (in Hungarian); co-author: Baroque Popular Graphics About Places of Pilgrimage in Hungary, 1987 (in Hungarian), Popular Piety in Hungary: Studies on Comparative Literature & Cultural History, 1996 (in German); editor: Studies on the History of Popular Piety in Hungary, 1986, Lajos Hopp, Kelemen Mikes: Biography and Start of Literary Career, 2000 (in Hungarian); co-editor: Literature, History, Folklore, Papers of the Budapest Conference on the Third Centenary of Kelemen Mikes' Birth, 1992 (in Hungarian), The Meditations of Prince Francis Rakoczi II, 1997 (in Latin, French, and Hungarian); contbr. articles to internat. profl. jours. Named Hon. assoc. Nat. Ctr. Sci. Rsch., Paris, 1993; recipient fellowshp Mellon Found., Wolfenbüttel, 1994; grantee British Acad., London, 1996, 98. Mem. Internat. Soc. for Eighteenth Century Studies, Oxford, Internat. Soc. for Folk Narrative Rsch., Bergen, Internat. Soc. of Ethnology and Folklore, Paris, Soc. for Hungarian Literary History, Budapest. Office: Inst Lit Studies Acad Scis, Ménesi ut 11-13, H-1118 Budapest Hungary

TUTEJA, RENU, biologist; b. Dehradun, India, Apr. 30, 1957; d. Charan and Vidya Devi Pahwa; m. Narendra Tuteja, Dec. 10, 1982; children: Gaurav, Dhruva. BSc, Lucknow U., 1975, MSc, 1977; PhD, Kanpur U., 1983. Postdoctoral fellow NIH, Bethesda, Md., 1983-86; postgraduate rschr. UCLA, 1986-88; scientist ICGEB, Trieste, Italy, 1988-95; scientist ICGEB, New Delhi, 1995-99, cons., 1999—. Author: Artificial DNA; contbr. articles to profl. jours. Avocations: writing, research, listening to music. Home: B-1/1581 Vasant Kunj, 110070 New Delhi India Office: ICGEB PO Box 10504, Aruna Asaf Ari Marg, 110067 New Delhi India

TÜTEM, ESMA, chemist, educator; b. Istanbul, Marmara, Turkey, Dec. 27, 1955; d. Hasan and Zihniye (Gakan) T. MSc, Istanbul U., 1978, PhD, 1985. Cert. chem. engr. Rsch. asst. Istanbul U. for Pharmacy, 1979-82; rsch. asst. Istanbul U. Faculty Engring., 1982-89, asst. prof., 1989-92, assoc. prof., 1992-97, prof., 1997—. Contbr. articles to profl. jours. Mem. Internat. Water Assn., Turkish Chem. Soc. Avocations: music, swimming, traveling. Office: Istanbul U Fac Engr Chem, Avcilar, 34850 Istanbul Turkey

TUTHILL, L. LEE, economist; b. Champaign, Ill., June 11, 1956; d. Dean and Stacy E. (Johnson) T.; m. Colin G. Agostini; children: Gabriel, Natalie. BA, U. Md., 1978; M in Internat. Affairs, Columbia U., 1980. Internat. affairs U.S. Internat. Trade Commn., Washington, 1983-89; counsellor telecomms. trade policy World Trade Commn., Washington, 1990—. Office: World Trade Orgn, Rue de Lausanne 154, CH-1211 Geneva 21 Switzerland

TUTIN, DOROTHY, actress; b. London, Apr. 8, 1930; m. Derek Waring, 1963; 2 children. Ed., Royal Acad. Dramatic Art, London. Appeared at Stratford Festival, 1958, 60; took part in Shakespeare's Meml. Theatre tour of Russia, 1958, Shakespeare recital before Pope, Vatican, 1964; prin. roles: Rose, The Living Room; Katherine, Henry V; Sally Bowles, I am a Camera; St. Joan, The Lark; Catherine, The Gates of Summer; Hedwig, The Wild Duck; Viola, Twelfth Night; Ophelia, Hamlet; Dolly, Once More, with Feeling; Portia, The Merchant of Venice; Cressida, Troilus and Cressida; Sister Jeanne, The Devils, 1961, 62; Juliet, Romeo and Juliet; Desdemona, Othello; Varya, The Cherry Orchard, 1961; Prioress, The Devils, Edinburgh, 1962; Polly Peachum, The Beggar's Opera, 1963; Queen Victoria, Portrait of a Queen, 1965, N.Y., 1968; Rosalind, As You Like It, 1967; Old Times, 1971; Peter Pan, 1971; A Month in the Country, 1974, 76; Cleopatra, Antony and Cleopatra, 1977; Lady Pliant: Double Dealer, 1978; Genia. Undiscovered Country, 1986; Miss Madrigal in Chalk Garden, 1986, Madam Ravanskaya in The Cherry Orchard, Thursdays Ladies, 1987, Harlequinade and The Browning Version, 1988, Desirèe in a Little Night Music, 1989, Queen Katherine in Henry VIII, 1991, Party Time, 1991, The Seagull, 1992, Getting Married, 1993, After October, 1997, The Gin Game, 1999; films include: The Beggar's Opera, The Importance of Being Earnest, A Tale of Two Cities, Cromwell, Savage Messiah, The Shooting Party, Great Moments in Aviation; TV appearances include: Henry VIII Anne Boleyn, 1974, South Riding, 1976, The Double Dearler, 1980, The Eavesdropper, 1981, The Combination, 1981, Life After Death, 1981, La Ronde, 1982, King Lear, 1982, Landscape, 1982, The Father, 1986, A Kind of Alaska, Murder with Mirrors, The Demon Lover, Evensong, 1986, Yellow Wallpaper, 1990, Anglo Saxon Attitudes: Young Lady, 1992, Scarlett, 1994, Great Kandinsky, 1995, Jake's Progress, 1995, Indian Summer, 1996, Maybe This Time Will be the Last Time, 1998. Recipient Evening Standard award as best actress, 1960; Variety Club of G.B. award for best film actress, 1972; Soc. of West End Theatre award for actress of the year in a revival, 1976, 78. Office: care Michael Whitehall, 125 Gloucester Rd, London SW7 WTE, England

TUTINS, ANTONS, electronics and audio engineer; b. Ludza, Latvia, May 2, 1933; s. Francis and Veronika (Seipulniks) Tutins; came to U.S., 1950, naturalized, 1963; student U. Minn., 1951-55; BS in Elec. Engring., Ill. Inst. Tech., 1970; MBA, U. Chgo., 1974; m. Raita Snebergs, July 8, 1961; 1 child, Robert. With Motorola Communications div., Chgo., 1964-73; product engring. mgr. Knowles Electronics, Inc., Franklin Park, Ill., 1973-81; dir. quality assurance and mfg. engring. Perma Power Electronics Inc., Chgo., 1982-95; pres. AT Systems, Des Plaines, Ill., 1995—; tech. cons. Accord, Inc., Westchester, Ill., 1995—. Bd. dirs. Spl. Interest Group of Object Oriented Tech., 1995—. With USN, 1955-57. Mem. IEEE, Acoustical Soc. Am., Chgo. Acoustical and Audio Group (pres. 1977-78), Audio Engring. Soc,, Midwest Acoustics Conf. (exec. com., pres. 1980), Latvian Cath. Student Assn. Dzintars (pres. 1979-81), Am. Latvian Cath. Assn. (registered agt. 1978—, v.p. 1985), Baltic Info. Exch. (v.p. 1991—), Motorola Engring. Club (pres. 1970-71). Roman Catholic. Home: 1338 Briar Ct Des Plaines IL 60018-2146 Office: 10301 W Roosevelt Rd Westchester IL 60154-2575

TUTSCHKE, WOLFGANG, mathematician; b. Görlitz, Germany, Sept. 28, 1934; s. Walter and Margarete (Seifert) T.; m. Gudrun Schiel, May 21, 1960; 1 child, Mary. Diploma in math., U. Leipzig, Germany, 1958, D in Natural Scis., 1959; Habilitation, U. Berlin, 1965. Collaborator Acad. of Scis., 1958-67; prof. math. U. Halle, Germany, 1967-92, Tech. U. Graz, 1995—; vis. prof. math. Tech. U. Graz, 1992-93, 94, Mining U. Leoben, U. Graz, 1993-94, Chandigarh, 1995, 96. Author textbooks on real and complex analysis, 1967—; contbr. over 100 articles to profl. jours.

TUTT, SYLVIA IRENE MAUD, business consultant, educator; b. London; d. Charles Leslie and Emily Ditcham (Wiseman) T. Sr. ptnr. Clems Assocs., London, 1966—. Author: Private Pension Scheme Finance, 1970, Pensions and Employee Benefits, 1973, Pension Law and Taxation, 1981, Financial Aspects of Pension Business, 1985, Financial Aspects of Life Business, 1987, A Mastership of a Livery Company, 1988, Financial Aspects of Long Term Business, 1991, Pensions Law, Administration and Taxation, 1998; contbr. articles to profl. jours. Fellow Royal Soc. Arts, Royal Statist. Soc., Inst. Chartered Co. Secs. and Adminstrs. (edn. com. 1980-82, pres. women's soc. 1975-76, chairperson London br. 1984-85, coun. 1975-76, 80-82); mem. Co. Chartered Co. Secs. and Adminstrs. (mng. trustee 1976—, mem. fin. and gen. purpose com. 1995—), Chartered Insce. Inst. (sr. examiner 1975—), Soc. Fin. Advisers (sr. examiner 1992—), City Livery Club (mem. coun. 1986—), Royal Overseas League, Worshipful Co. Scriveners (ct. asst. 1999—), Worshipful Co. Chartered Co. Secs. and Adminstrs. (master 1983-84), Soroptimist, United Wards' Club City of London (pres. 1998—). Anglican. First woman in 800 years of livery history to become a Master of a City of London Livery Company. Home: 19 Forest Hall, Brockenhurst Hampshire SO42 7QQ, England Office: Clems Assocs, 21 Sandilands, Croydon CR0 5DF, England

TUTTLE, WILLIAM G(ILBERT) T(OWNSEND), JR., research executive; b. Portsmouth, Va., Nov. 26, 1935; s. William Gilbert and Edith Inez (Ritter) T.; m. Helen Lynn Warren, Dec. 27, 1959; children: Lynn, Robert, Jonathan. B.S., U.S. Mil. Acad., 1958; M.B.A., Harvard U., 1963. Commd. 2d lt. U.S. Army, 1958, advanced through grades to gen., 1989; dir. combat service support (Office Combat Devels., Hdqrs. Tng. and Doctrine Command), Ft. Monroe, Va., 1976-77; comdr. 3d Armored Div. Support Command Frankfurt, W. Ger., 1977-79; comdr. Mil. Traffic Mgmt. Command Eastern Area Bayonne, N.J., 1979-81; dir. force mgmt. Hdqrs. Dept. Army, Washington, 1981-82; chief policy and programs br. Supreme Hdqrs. Allied Powers Europe, 1982-84; comdr. U.S. Army Operational Test and Evaluation Agy., 1984-86; dep. comdg. gen. Logistics, Tng. and Doctrine Command and comdg. gen. U.S. Army Logistics Ctr., Ft. Lee, Va., 1986-89; comdg. gen. U.S. Army Materiel Command, Alexandria, Va., 1989-92; ret., 1992; pres., CEO, bd. trustees Logistics Mgmt. Inst., McLean, Va., 1993—; U.S. Army Kermit Roosevelt lectr., 1991; bd. dirs. Procurement Round Table; mem. bd. advisors Nat. Contract Mgmt. Assn.; cons. to Def. Sci. Bd., Nat. Rsch. Coun. Prin., Coun. on Excellence in Govt.; nat. councillor Atlantic Coun. Decorated D.S.M. (3), Bronze Star (3), Legion of Merit. Mem. Nat. Def. Transp. Assn., Nat. Def. Indsl. Assn. (Logistician Emeritus award 1998), Assn. U.S. Army (Pres.'s award 1992). Lutheran. Office: Logistics Mgmt Inst 2000 Corporate Rdg Mc Lean VA 22102-7805

TUTU, DESMOND MPILO, retired archbishop; b. Klerksdorp, Republic of South Africa, Oct. 7, 1931; m. Leah Nomalizo Shenxane; children: Trevor Thamsanqa, Theresa Thandeka, Naomi Nontombi, Mpho Andrea. Diploma in teaching, Pretoria (Republic of South Africa) Bantu Normal Coll., 1953; BA, U. South Africa, 1954; licentiate in theology, St. Peter's Theol. Coll., Republic of South Africa, 1960; postgrad, King's Coll., U. London; DD (hon.), Gen. Theol. Sem., N.Y., 1978, Aberdeen U., Scotland, 1984, Trinity Luth. Sem., 1985, Trinity Coll., Hartford, Conn., 1986, Chgo. Theol. Sem., 1986, U. West Indies, Trinidad and Tobago, 1986, Oberlin Coll., 1986, U. of the South, 1988, Emory U., 1988, Wesleyan U., 1990, Lincoln U., Pa., 1990, Oxford U., Eng., 1990; DCL (hon.), Kent (Eng.) U., 1978; LLD (hon.), Harvard U., 1979, Claremont Grad. Sch., 1984, Temple U., 1985, 86, Mt. Allison U., Sackville, N.B., Can., 1988, Northeastern U., 1988; ThD (hon.), Ruhr U., 1981; STD (hon.), Columbia U., 1982, Dickinson Coll., 1984; LHD (hon.), St. Paul's Coll., 1984, Howard U., 1984, Morehouse Coll., 1986, Cen. U., 1986, CUNY, 1986; HHD (hon.), Wilberforce U., 1985; PhD (hon.), U. Rio, Rio de Janiero, 1986; hon. doctorate, U. Strasbourg, France, 1988, Wesleyan U., 1990, Lincoln U., 1990, U. Mo., 1990, U. New Rochelle, 1990, 1990, Brown U., 1990, Seton Hall U., 1990, U. P.R., 1990, others. Ordained priest Anglican Ch., 1961. Schoolmaster, 1954-57, parish priest, 1960—; lectr. Fed. Theol. Sem., 1967-69, UBLS Roma, Lesotho, 1970-72; assoc. dir. theol. edn. fund World Coun. Chs., Bromley, Kent, Eng., 1972-75; dean of Johannesburg Republic of South Africa, 1975-76; bishop of Lesotho, 1976-78, bishop of Johannesburg, 1985-86; archbishop of Cape Town Republic of South Africa, 1986-96; archbishop emeritus City of Capetown, 1996—; chairperson Truth and Reconciliation Commn., 1996—; sec.-gen. South African Council Chs., 1978-85; vis. prof. Anglican Studies, N.Y. Gen. Theol. Sem., 1984; pres. All Africa Conf. of Chs., 1987-97; chancellor U. Western Cape, Republic of South Africa, 1988—. Author: (collections of sermons and addresses) Crying in the Wilderness, 1982, Hope and Suffering, 1983, The Rainbow People of God: The Making of a Peaceful Revolution, 1994, An African Prayer Book, 1995, No Future Without Forgiveness, 1999. Vice chmn. Internat. Alert, 1986; mem. disbursements adv. com. Fund for Edn. in South Africa, N.Y.C., 1988; mem. com. of honor for meml. to Imre Nagy and companions Hungarian Human Rights League, 1988; mem. hon. com. Spl. Fund for Health in Africa, 1990. Recipient Prix d'Athene Onassis Found., 1980, Family of Man gold medallion, 1983, Martin Luther King Jr. Humanitarian award Ann. Black Am. Hero and Heroines Day, 1984; Nobel prize for peace, 1984, Martin Luther King Jr. Peace award, 1986, Internat. Integrity award John-Roger Found., 1986, Pres. award Glassboro State Coll., 1986, World Pub. Forum award City of San Rafael, Calif., 1986, Order of So. Cross Govt. of Brazil, 1987, Order of Merit Govt. of Brazil, 1987, Pacem in Terris award Quad Cities, 1987, Albert Schweitzer Humanitarian award Emmanuel Coll., 1988, Freedom of the City Florence, Italy, 1985, Methyr Tydfil, U.K., 1986, Durham, Eng., 1987, Hull, Eng., 1988, Disting. Peace Leadership award Nuclear Age Peace Found., 1990, Pres.'s medal Claremont Grad. Sch., U.S., 1990, Freedom of the Borough of Lewisham, U.K., 1990, Freedom of the City of Kinshasa, 1990, Grand Officier de la Légion d'Honneur, Pres. Chirac of France, 1998; co-recipient Third World prize, 1989; King's Coll. fellow, 1978. Mem. NAACP (life), World Council Global Co-operation. Address: 9th Fl Old Mutual Bldg, 106 Adderley St PO Box 3162, Cape Town 80001, South Africa

TÜTÜNCÜOGLU, SARENUR, pediatrician, educator; b. Manisa, Turkey, Sept. 30, 1957; parents Mehmet and Gülten (Çipiloğlu) Gökben; m. Erhan Mehmet T., Aug. 6, 1983; children: Berke, Bilge. MD, Ege U., 1980, pediatrics degree, 1985, pediatrics neurology degree, 1991. Resident Ege U. Hosp., Izmir, Turkey, 1980-85; pediatrician Inegül State Hosp., Bursa, Turkey, 1985-87; pediatrician Ege U. Hosp., Izmir, 1987-90, assoc. prof., 1990-97, prof., 1997—. Author: (booklet) Pediatric Neurology Notes, 1995, Management of Cerebral Palsy, 1996, Nonepileptic Paroxysmal Phenomena, 1995. Grantee Nestle Co., 1991-92. Mem. Internat. Child Neurology Assn., Çocuk Nürolojisi Derneği, Milli Pediatri Derneği, European Pediatric Neurology Soc. Home: 6355 Sok No 9/12 Bostanli, 35540 Izmir Turkey Office: Ege Univ Hosp, Bornova, 35100 Izmir Turkey

TUUL, JOHANNES, physics educator, researcher; b. Tarvastu, Viljandi, Estonia, May 23, 1922; came to U.S., 1956, naturalized, 1962; s. Johan and Emilie (Tulf) T.; m. Marjatta Murtoniemi, July 14, 1957 (div. Aug. 1971); children: Melinda, Melissa; m. Sonia Esmeralda Manosalva, Sept. 15, 1976; 1 child, Johannes. Elem. Tchg. Credential, Tartu Normal Sch., Estonia, 1941; diploma in Elec. Engring., Stockholm Tech. Inst., 1947; BS, U. Stockholm, 1955, MA, 1956; ScM, Brown U., 1957, PhD, 1960. Tchr. Valuste Elem. Sch., 1941-43; escaped to Finland December, 1943; after Finland surrendered to Russia escaped to Sweden, 1944; instr. Stockholm Tech. Inst., 1947-49; lab. engr. Electrical Prospecting Co., Stockholm, 1949-53; elec. engr. LM Ericsson Telephone Co., Stockholm, 1954-55; rsch. physicist Am. Cyanamid Co., Stamford, Conn., 1960-62; sr. rsch. physicist Bell & Howell Rsch. Ctr., Pasadena, Calif., 1962-65; from asst. to assoc. prof. Calif. State Poly. U., Pomona, 1965-68; chmn. physics and earth scis. dept. Calif. State Poly. U., 1971-75, prof. physics, 1975-91; prof. emeritus, 1992—; vis. prof. Pahlavi U., Shiraz, Iran, 1968-70; cons. Bell & Howell Rsch. Ctr., Pasadena, Calif., 1965, Teledyne Co., Pasadena, Calif., 1968; guest researcher Naval Weapons Ctr., China Lake, Calif., 1967, 72; resident dir. Calif. State U. Internat. Programs in Sweden and Denmark, 1977-78. Author: Physics Made Easy, 1974; contbr. articles to profl. jours. Pres. Group Against Smoking Pollution, Pomona Valley, Calif., 1976; foster parent Foster Parents Plan, Inc., Warwick, R.I., 1964—; block capt. Neighborhood Watch, West Covina, Calif., 1982-84; citizen amb. People to People Internat., 1990—; mem. Physics Edn. Del. to Peoples Rep. China, 1990; mem. Baltic Assist Delegation, 1992. Fellow Brown U., 1957-58; rsch. grantee U. Namur (Belgium), 1978, Ctr. Nat. Recherche Scientifique, France, 1979; recipient Humanitarian Fellowship award Save the Children Fedn., 1968, spl. award Travelers' Cen-

tury Club, 1998. Mem. AAAS (life), N.Y. Acad. Scis., Am. Phys. Soc. Republican. Roman Catholic. Achievements include research in energy conservation and new energy technologies.

TUULIK, VIIU, neurologist, educator, researcher; b. Tartu, Estonia, Apr. 29, 1939; d. Oskar-Eduard Hendrik and Helene Anton (Oidram) Eomois; m. Vello Villem Tuulik, Nov. 28, 1938; children: Vahur, Varje Riin. MD, Tartu U., 1974, PhD, 1994. Intern, resident dept. neurology and neurosurgery Clinicum of Tartu U.; head dept. Haapsalu Hosp. Neurology and Orthopedy, Estonia, 1963-71; neurologist Clinic of Occupl. Diseases, Tallinn, Estonia, 1971-72; sr. rschr. Estonian Inst. Exptl. and Clin. Medicine, Tallinn, 1972—; asst. prof. biomedicine Tallinn Tech. U., 1994—. Contbr. articles to profl. jours. Mem. Physicians Assoc. Soc. of Neurologists, German-Baltic Physicians Assn. (sec. 1994-97), Med. Women's Internat. Assn., European Soc. for Engring. and Medicine, N.Y. Acad. Scis. E-mail: vtu@hot.ee. Home: Sytiste 34-58, EE 0034 Tallinn Estonia Office: Estonian Inst Exptl Med, Hiiu 42, EE 0016 Tallinn Estonia

TUUNDE, STEPHEN WASIBANI, surgeon, consultant; b. Mbale, Uganda, July 22, 1945; d. Zadoki Gallimu and Asinansi Wajje (Mugala) W.; m. Kevin Ndaula Nabulya, Nov. 27, 1949; 6 children. MB, BChir, Makerere Coll., Urganda, 1972, M in Med. Surgery, 1980. Gen. med. officer Min. Health, Uganda, 1972-76, specialist surgeon, 1980-87, cons. surgeon, 1987-95; dist. med. officer Kabale, Uganda, 1976-77; sr. house officer Mulago, Uganda, 1977-80; sr. cons. surgeon Mbale Hosp., Uganda, 1995—; med. supt. St. Anthony's Hosp., Uganda, 1984—; head dept. cmty. practice Makerere U., 1994—; med. coord. Salem, Uganda, 1996—. Inventor in field. Can. Internat. Devel. Agy. fellow, McGill U., Montreal, 1993. Fellow Assn. Surgeons of East and So. Africa; mem. Assn. of Surgeons Uganda, Uganda Med. Assn. Avocation: badminton. Home: Nabweya Village, PO Box 1158, Mbale Uganda Office: Mbale Hosp, PO Box 921, Mbale Uganda

TVERSKOY, GREGORY NAFTOLY, medical units company executive; b. Leningrad, Russia, Apr. 12, 1931; s. Naftoly Gersh and Maria (Braverman) T.; m. Mara Mendel Grinshpun, Oct. 18, 1938 (dec. Sept. 1993); 1 child, Olga. Engr., Inst. Mechanics & Optics, Leningrad, 1955; PhD, Inst. Automatic, Leningrad, 1969. Sr. and PhD electronic diplomate, Russia. Engr. Sci. Rsch. Inst., Moscow, 1955-56; sr. engr. Inst. Radio Tech., Leningrad, 1956-61; leading engr. Inst. of Automatic, Leningrad, 1961-69, sr. rsch. worker, 1969-71, chief of lab., 1971-90; dir. Med.-Tech. Ctr., Leningrad, 1990-91; mgr. Antennas Arad. Ltd. Co., Arad, Israel, 1993-95; gen. dir. Med. Units Ltd. Co., Arad, 1995—. Author: Radar's Signal Simulation, 1974; contbr. articles to profl. jours.; inventor in radar and med. tech. Head sci. coun. Inst. Advanced Studies, Arad, 1991—, Scientists' Union, Israel, 1993—. Avocations: travel, chess. Home: 5/17 Ben Yair St, 89021 Arad Israel Office: Medical Units Ltd Co, PO Box 1244, 89058 Arad Negev, Israel

TWARDOWSKI, ANDRZEJ, physics educator, researcher; b. Warsaw, Poland, July 17, 1955. MSc, Warsaw U., 1978, PhD, 1982, DSc, 1990. Assoc. prof. Warsaw U., 1990-94, prof. physics, 1995—; rschr. in solid state physics, semiconductors and magnetics. Contbr. over 150 articles to jours. in field. Office: Inst Exptl Physics, Warsaw U HOZA69, 00681 Warsaw Poland

TWEATS, DAVID JOHN, preclinical safety sciences director; b. Crewe, Eng., Feb. 4, 1950; s. Eric and Pauline Joan (Lewis) T.; m. Gwyneth Mary Stallard, July 3, 1971; children: Sarah Elizabeth, James Alexander Charles. BS in Genetics and Microbiology, U. Sheffield, Eng., 1968-71; PhD, U. London, 1975. Cert. biologist; accredited toxicologist. Rsch. demonstrator U. Coll. Swansea, Eng., 1974-76; unit head Mutagenicity Glaxo, Harefield, Eng., 1976-81; sect. head Genetic Toxicology, 1981-85, dept. head Toxicology, 1985-95; internat. head Toxicology Glaxo Wellcome, Ware, Eng., 1995-96; dir. Preclinical Safety Scis., 1997—; sec. U.K. Environ. Mutagen Soc., 1984-90; v.p., 1992-94, pres., 1994-96 UKEMS; chmn. Genotoxicology Working Party European Fedn. Pharmaceutical Industry Assns., Brussels, Belgium, 1992—; genotoxicology expert; PhD examiner U. Swansea, Bath, and Sussex; vis. prof. Sch. Biol. Scis., U. Wales, Swansea, 2000—. Ch. sec. Leaside Meth./URC Ch., Ware, U.K., 1981-83; circuit steward Waltham Abbey and Hertford Meth. Circuit, U.K., 1992-98. Fellow U.K. Inst. Biology, U.K. Royal Coll. Pathology. Methodist. Avocations: angling, astronomy, piano, badminton, lecturing on biology.

TWIDALE, C(HARLES) R(OWLAND), geomorphologist, educator; b. Lincolnshire, Eng., Apr. 5, 1930; s. George Wilfred and Gladys May (West) T.; m. Kathleen Mary Gargini, Apr. 21, 1956; children: Nicholas, Richard Jonathan, Amanda Elizabeth. Ed., Wintringham Grammar Sch., Grimsby; BSc, U. Bristol, 1951, MSc, 1953, DSc, 1977; PhD, McGill U., 1957; D. Honoris Causa, U. Complutense, Madrid, 1991. Rsch. officer, divsn. land rsch. Commonwealth Sci. and Indsl. Rsch. Orgn., Canberra, 1952-57; mem. faculty dept. geography, geology U. Adelaide, 1958—; vis. prof. geology and geophysics U. Calif., Berkeley, 1971; vis. prof. geology U. Tex., Austin, 1979. Nuffield Commonwealth bursary, 1965; NSF sr. fgn. scientist fellow, 1965-66, also vis. prof. Rensselaer Poly. Inst., Troy, N.Y., vis. rsch. prof. U. Coruña, 2000; mem. engring. and earth scis. panel Australian Rsch. Coun., 1992-97. Author: Geomorphology, 1968, Structural Landforms, 1971, Analysis of Landforms, 1976, Granite Landforms, 1982, (with E. M. Campbell) Australian Landforms, 1993, (with J. R. Vidal Romani) Formas y Paisajes Graniticos, 1998; contbr. articles to profl. jours. Recipient Mueller medal Australian and New Zealand Assn. Advancement Sci., 1993. Fellow Royal Soc. South Australia (pres. 1975-76, Verco medal 1977), (hon.) Sociedad Española de Geomorfologia. Home: 7 Brecon Rd, Aldgate SA 5154, Australia Office: U Adelaide, Dept Geology & Geophysics, Adelaide SA 5005, Australia

TWIDELL, JOHN WILLIAM, energy educator, consultant; b. Windsor, Berkshire, Eng., Apr. 4, 1939; s. William and Joan Alma (Turner) T.; m. Mary Beckingham, May 21, 1966; children: Mark, Sara, Adam. BSc, U. Oxford, Eng., 1960, MA, 1963, DPhil, 1963. Lectr. U. Khartoum, Sudan, 1964-68; rsch. fellow U. Essex, Eng., 1968-70; reader U. Strathclyde, Glasgow, Scotland, 1970-93; prof., dir. AMSET Ctr. and Lincoln Renewable Energy Ctr., De Montfort U., 1993-94; bd. dirs. Orkney Sustainable Energy Ltd., Scotland, Brit. Wind Energy Assn., AMSET Ctr. Ltd. Co-author: Renewable Energy Resources, 1986, rev. edit., 1990, Sunrise on Sustainability, 1996; editor: Energy for Rural and Island Communities, 4 vols., 1982, 83, 85, 86, Guidebook for Small Island Turbines, 1987, Jour. Inland Engring. Mem. Brit. Wind Energy Assn. (tech. award 1996, pioneer 1995), U.K. Solar Energy Soc. Liberal Democrat. Anglican. Avocations: hill walking, hockey. Home: AMSET Ctr, Bridgford House, Horninghold LE168DH, England

TWIG, JACK See BRANCH, JOHN WELLS

TWILLEY, JOSHUA MARION, lawyer; b. Dover, Del., Mar. 23, 1928; s. Joshua Marion and Alice Hunn (Dunn) T.; m. Rebecca Jane Buchanan, Dec. 27, 1952; children—Stephanie, Jeffrey, Linda, Edgar, Joshua; m. 2d, Rosemary Miller, Dec. 1, 1972. B.A. cum laude, Harvard U., 1950, J.D., 1953. Bar: Del. 1953, U.S. dist. ct. Del. 1960, U.S. Sup. Ct. 1976. Sole practice, Dover, 1955-72; sr. ptnr. Twilley, Jones & Feliceangeli, Dover, 1972-88; Twilley, Street & Brayerman, 1988-95, Twilley & Street, 1995—; pres. Del. Indsl. Enterprises, Inc.; chmn. Incorporating Svcs. Ltd., Del. Incorporating Svcs. Ltd.; bd. dirs. First Nat. Bank Wyo.; sec. Sunshine Builders, Inc. mem. Del. Pub. Service Commn., 1975—, vice chmn. 1995—; pres. Kent County levy ct., 1970-75. Mem. exec. com. Del. Democratic Com., 1970-93; pres. Elizabeth Murphey Sch., 1957—. Served with U.S. Army, 1953-55. Mem. ABA, Del. Bar Assn., Kent County Bar Assn. Democrat. Lutheran. Avocations: gardening, landscape architecture. Home: 124 Meadow Glen Dr Dover DE 19901-5544 Office: 426 S State St Dover DE 19901-6724

TWINING, CHARLES HAILE, ambassador; b. Balt., Nov. 1, 1940; s. Charles Haile and Martha R. (Caples) T.; m. Irene Verann Metz, May 30, 1972; children: Daniel, Steven. BA, U. Va., 1962; MA, Johns Hopkins U., 1964; postgrad., Cornell U., 1977-78. Joined Fgn. Svc., Dept. State, Washington, 1964; with Am. Embassy, Tananarive, 1964-66, Cords Dalat, Vietnam, 1966-68; desk officer Ivory Coast, Upper Volta, Nigeria; with Dept. of State, Washington, 1970-72; with Am. Embassy, Abidjan, 1972-74, Bangkok, 1975-77; dep. office dir. for Australia and New Zealand Dept. of State, Washington, 1978-80, with East Asian pers., 1980-82; former charge d'affaires Am. Embassy, Cotonou, 1982-83; former prin. officer Am. Con Gen, Douala, 1983-85; former dep. chief of mission Am. Embassy, Ouagadougou, Burkina Faso, 1985-88; former dir. Office of Vietnam, Laos and Cambodia Dept. State, Washington; spl. rep., amb. to Cambodia Phnom Penh, 1991-95; amb. to Cameroon and Equatorial Guinea Dept. State, Yaounde, 1996-98; fgn. policy advisor USCINCPAC; Contbr.: Cambodia: 1975-78, 1990. Office: Fgn Policy Advisor HQ USCINCPAC PO Box 64028 Camp H M Smith HI 96861-4028

TWISS, ROBERT MANNING, prosecutor; b. Worcester, Mass., Aug. 2, 1948; s. Robert Sullivan Jr. and Marion (Manning) T.; m. Joan Marie Callahan, Aug. 4, 1979. BA, U. Mass., 1970; JD, U. San Francisco, 1975; MA in Criminal Justice, Wichita State U., 1979; LLM, Georgetown U., 1981. Bar: Mass. 1976, Calif., 1988, U.S. Ct. Mil. Appeals 1976, U.S. Dist. Ct. Mass. 1976, U.S. Ct. Appeals (1st cir.) 1976, U.S. Ct. Appeals (5th cir.) 1986, U.S. Ct. Appeals (9th cir.) 1988, U.S. Dist. Ct. (ea. and cen. dist.) Calif. 1989. Atty. office chief counsel IRS, Washington, 1980-86; trial atty. criminal div. U.S. Dept. Justice, Washington, 1986-87; asst. U.S. atty. U.S. Dept. Justice, Sacramento, 1987-93, 94—, chief organized crime and narcotics, 1991-92, 1st asst. U.S. atty., 1992-93, U.S. atty., 1993, exec. assst. U.S. atty., 1994. Contbr. articles to profl. jours. Capt. JAGC, U.S. Army, 1976-80. Named to McAuliffe Honor Soc. U. San Francisco, 1975; recipient Markham award Office Chief Counsel IRS, Washington, 1985. Avocation: athletics. Office: Office US Atty 501 I St 10th Fl Sacramento CA 95814-7306

TWITCHELL, E(RVIN) EUGENE, lawyer; b. Salt Lake City, Mar. 4, 1932; s. Irvin A. and E. Alberta (Davis) T.; m. Joyce A. Newey, Aug. 9, 1957 (div. May 1989); children: Robert R., Lauren E., David J., Michael S.; m. Linda Sue Wilson, 1991; children: Bonnie Wilson, Jimmy Wilson, Benjamin Wilson, Stefanie Wilson. Student, Brigham Young U., 1954-55; BA, Calif. State U., Long Beach, 1959; JD, UCLA, 1966. Bar: Mich. 1977, U.S. Dist. Ct. (ea. dist.) Mich., U.S. Supreme Ct. 1987. Contract adminstr. Rockwell No. Am. Aviation, Seal Beach, Calif., 1966-68; sr. contracts adminstr. McDonnell Douglas Corp., Long Beach, Calif., 1968-73; in-house counsel Albert C. Martin & Assocs., L.A., 1973-77; instr. bus. law Golden West Coll., Huntington Beach, 1973-74; corp. counsel, corp. sec. Barton Malow Co., Southfield, Mich., 1977-97, ret., 1997; mem. Detroit EEO Forum, 1983-87; arbitrating and cons., 1997—. Pres. Corona (Calif.) Musical Theater, 1975-76; dist. chmn. Boy Scouts of Am.-North Trails, Oakland County, Mich., 1978-80; treas. Barton Malow PAC, Southfield, 1983-97. Sgt. USAF, 1950-52. Mem. ABA, Mich. Bar Assn., Am. Arbitration Assn. (arbitrator Detroit, Ala., Ga., and Fla. areas 1985-97, arbitrator Ala.-Ga. area 1997—), Am. Corp. Counsel Assn. (v.p., dir. 1983-97). Republican. Mem. LDS Ch. Avocations: cartooning, painting, karate, music, theatre, writing. Home and Office: 142 Gammage Rd Eufaula AL 36027-5874

TWOHY, CYNTHIA HOWARD, research scientist; b. Long Beach, Calif., Jan. 5, 1960; d. Richardson James Twohy and Virginia Lee Hall; m. James E. Ragni, Dec. 30, 1989. BS summa cum laude, U. Calif., Davis, 1981; MS, U. Wash., 1988, PhD, 1992. Sr. food technologist Case-Swayne Co., Inc., Santa Ana, Calif., 1981-85; grad. rsch./tchg. asst. U. Wash., Seattle, 1985-88; atmospheric scientist Nat. Ctr. for Atmospheric Rsch., Boulder, Colo., 1988-99; asst. prof., sr. rsch. Oreg. State U., Corvallis, 1997-99; rev. of jour. publs., 1990-99. Contbr. articles to profl. jours. Math. tutor United Way, Lafayette, Colo., 1992; sci. fair judge Kohl Elem. Sch., Broomfield, Colo., 1996-98; pet visitation for srs. Elm's Haven Care Ctr., Thornton, Colo., 1995-97; master gardener Colo. State U. Cooperative Ext., Adams County, Colo., 1997. postdoctoral fellow Nat. Ctr. for Atmospheric Rsch., Boulder, 1992-94; rsch. grant In-Situ Measurement of Cirrus Cloud Properties, NASA, 1995-96; rsch. grantee NSF, 1999-2001, others. Mem. Am. Assn. Aerosol Rsch. (vice-chair atmospheric aerosols 1999-2001), Prytanean Women's Honor Soc., Am. Geophys. Union, Phi Kappa Phi. Avocations: horseback riding, gardening, genealogy, mosaic. E-mail: twohy@oce.orst.edu. Office: Oreg State Univ Oceanography Admin 104 Corvallis OR 97331

TWOMBLY, JEAN SAWYER, musician, educator; b. Bethlehem, Pa., Feb. 12, 1946; d. Edwin A. and Elizabeth (Stempel) Sawyer; m. Stephen Doane Twombly, Dec. 29, 1979. BS in Music Edn. magna cum laude, Susquehanna U., 1968; MMus in Early Music Performance, Longy Sch. Music, Cambridge, Mass., 1994. Artistic dir. Ensemble Soleil, N.H., 1995—; adj. asst. prof. Colby-Sawyer Coll., New London, N.H., 1986—; pvt. music tchr., New London, 1983—. Grantee N.H. Humanities Coun., 1997-99, N.H. State Coun. on Arts, 1998, 99. Mem. Am. String Tchrs., Boston Musician's Assn., Early Music Am., Viola da Gamba Soc. New Eng. (bd. dirs. 1999—). Avocations: stained glass and wood lanterns, poetry, skiing, sailing. Office: Ensemble Soleil PO Box 933 New London NH 03257-0933

TWOMEY, THOMAS A., JR., lawyer; b. N.Y.C., Dec. 8, 1945; s. Thomas A. and Mary (Maloney) T.; m. Judith Hope Twomey, Dec. 15, 1979; stepchildren: Erling Hope, Nisse Hope. BA, Manhattan Coll., 1967; postgrad., U.Va., 1967-68; JD, Columbia U., 1970. Bar: N.Y. 1972, U.S. Tax Ct. 1974. Asst. town atty. Town of Southampton N.Y., 1973-74; spl. asst. dist. atty. Suffolk County, N.Y., 1973-74; pvt. practice law Riverhead, N.Y., 1974-75; ptnr. Hubbard & Twomey, Riverhead, 1976-79, Twomey, Latham, Shea & Kelley, Riverhead, 1980—; chair N.Y. State East End Econ. and Environ. Task Force, 1993; mem. deans coun. Stonybrook Sch. Medicine, 1991—; adj. prof. environ. law Southampton Coll., 1977-78. Bd. dirs. East End Arts Coun., Riverhead, 1983, Guild Hall East Hampton, 1993—; bd. dirs. East Hampton Libr., 1994—, pres., 1998—; trustee L.I. Power Authority, 1989-94; town historian, Town of East Hampton, 1999, editor town history. Recipient Environ. award, U.S. EPA, 1980. Mem. ABA, Suffolk County Bar Assn., State Energy Coun., N.Y. State Fresh Water Wetlands Appeals Bd. Democrat. Home: PO Box 398 Riverhead NY 11901-0203 Office: Twomey Latham Shea & Kelley 33 W 2nd St Riverhead NY 11901-2701

TWORUSCHKA, UDO, religious historian; b. Seesen, Germany, Feb. 12, 1949; s. Alfred and Charlotte (Köppe) T.; m. Monika Funke, Dec. 23, 1975; children: Miriam, Christopher, Sarah, Ronja. DPhil, Bonn U., Germany, 1972. Instr. comparative religion U. Cologne, Germany, 1984-93; prof. comparative religion U. Jenz; dir. Interdisciplinary Inst. History of Religions, Bad Münstereifel, 1982; mem. steering group internat. project Islam in Textbooks, 1989—. Author: Die Einsamkeit, 1974, Methodische Zugänge zu den Weitreligionen, 1982, Die vielen Namen Gottes, 1985, Analyse der evangelischen Religionsbücher zum Thema Islam, 1986, (with Monika Tworischka) Vorlesebuch Fremde Religionen, 2 vols., 1988; Sucher, Pilger, Himmelsstürmer, 1991, (with A. Falaturi) Islam im Interricht, 1991; editor: (with Minika Tworuschke) Religionen der Welt, 1992, (with Michael Klöcker) Handbuch der Religionen, 1997. Pres. Bund fur Freies Christentum, 1986-94. Mem. Deutsche Gesellschaft Missionswissenschaft, Internat. Assn. History Religions, Deutsche Vereinigung Religionsgeschichte, Wissenschaftliche Gesellschaft Theologie. Avocations: swimming, activity in mass media. Office: U Jena, Fünstengralen 1, D-07743 Jena Germany

TWYCROSS, ROBERT GEOFFREY, medical educator; b. West Bridgeford, U.K., Jan. 29, 1941; s. Jervis and Irene Margaret (Dell) T.; m. Deirdre Maeve Campbell, Mar. 28, 1964; children: Alison, Judith, Fiona, John, David. BA in Physiology with honors, Oxford (Eng.) U., 1962, BM BCh, 1965, MA, 1965, DM, 1977. House physician and surgeon Radcliffe Infirmary, Oxford, 1966; sr. house physician Lancaster (U.K.) Royal Infirmary, 1967; med. registrar Epsom (U.K.) Dist. Hosp., 1968-70; med. registrar dept. cardiology Manchester (U.K.) Royal Infirmary, 1970-71; rsch. fellow St. Christopher's Hospice, London, 1971-76; vis. med. officer St. Joseph's Hospice, London, 1971-76; cons. physician Sir Michael Sobell House, Oxford, 1976—; Macmillan clin. reader in palliative medicine U. Oxford, 1988—; prof. palliative medicine (hon.) U. del Salvador, Buenos Aires, 1999—; sr. rsch. fellow St. Peter's Coll., Oxford, 1987—; mem. expert adv. panel on cancer WHO, 1985—, dir. collaborating ctr. for palliative cancer care, 1988—; dir. Oxford Internat. Ctr. for Palliative Care. Author: Pain Relief in Advanced Cancer, 1994, Introducing Palliative Care, 1995, 3d edit., 1999, Symptom Management in Advanced Cancer, 1995; co-author: (with Wilcock A., Thorp S.) Palliative Care Formulary, 1998; co-editor: (with Todd J., Jenns K.) Lymphoedema, 2000; contbr. over 200 articles to profl. publs., chpts. in books. Bd. dirs. Pallium Found., The Netherlands, 1993-99. Recipient Aid and Cooperation medal Polish Ministry of Health and Social Care, 1993, Founder's award Nat. Hospice Orgn., 1994, Serturner award, Germany, 1995. Fellow Royal Coll. Physicians, Royal Coll. Radiologists, Royal Soc. Medicine; mem. Internat. Assn. for Study of Pain (founding), Assn. for Palliative Medicine (founding), Brit. Lymphology Soc. (founding), European Assn. for Palliative Care (founding), Palliative Care Rsch. Forum (founding). Avocations: gardening, walking, reading, theater. Home: Tewsfield Netherwoods Rd, Oxford OX3 8HF, England Office: Sir Michael Sobell House, Churchill Hosp, Oxford OX3 7LJ, England

TYAGANANDA, SWAMI, religious educator; b. Belgaum, Karnataka, India, Sept. 19, 1956; s. Ramchandra Gopal and Vatsala Vishnu (Kamat) Tilve. BSc, Bombay (India) U., 1976. Monk Ramakrishna Order, India, 1976—; assoc. minister Ramakrishna Vedanta Soc., Boston, 1998—; chaplain MIT and Harvard U. Editor: (books) Monasticism: Ideal and Traditions, 1991, Service: Ideal and Aspects, 1993, Values: The Key to a Meaningful Life, 1996, Healthy Mind, Healthy Body, 1997; translator: (book) The Essence of the Gita, 2000. Avocations: reading, discussing, writing, hiking. Home and Office: 58 Deerfield St Boston MA 02215-1803

TYAGI, ANAND K., materials scientist; b. Meerut, India, July 5, 1963; s. RAmniwas and Snehlata T.; m. Deosuta, Mar. 11, 1986; three children. MSc, Meerut U., 1985, MPhil, 1989; M in Technology, Indian Inst. Technology, Kanpur, 1990; PhD, Meerut U., 1995. Scientist Nat. Coun. Cements & Bldg. Materials, New Delhi, 1986-91; faculty G.N.D. Univ., Amritsar, India, 1991-95; asst. prof. S.B.S. Coll. Engring. & Tech., Ferozepur, India, 1995—, head dept. materials engring., in charge acad. affairs; coord. materials sci. in engring. program Panjab's Tech. U., Jalandhar, India. Mem. Materials Rsch. Soc. India, Indian Thermal Analysis Soc., Indian Ceramic Soc., Catalysis Soc. India. Fax: 01632-44012. Office: SBS Coll Engring, Moga Rd PB No 20, Ferozepur 152001, India

TYAGI, SOM DEV, physicist, educator; b. New Delhi, July 26, 1947; came to U.S. 1968, naturalized, 1979; s. Chander Bal and Vidya (Hanso) T.; m. Andrée Parenteau, Nov. 25, 1995. B.Sc. with honors, Delhi U., 1967, M.Sc., 1969; M.S., Lowell U., 1972; Ph.D., Brigham Young U., 1976. Postdoctoral assoc. Drexel U., Phila., 1976-79, asst. prof. physics, 1979-84, assoc. prof., 1984-90, prof., 1990—. Contbr. articles to profl. jours. Grantee U.S. Navy, U.S. Army, EPA, 1980—. Mem. Soc. Physics Students, Am. Phys. Soc., Sigma Xi, Sigma Pi Sigma. Home: 3649 Marian Dr Boothwyn PA 19061-1617 Office: Drexel U Dept Physics 32nd and Chestnut Sts Philadelphia PA 19104

TYKKYLÄINEN, MARKKU JUHANI, geography educator; b. Eno, N. Karelia, Finland, May 13, 1952; s. Aukusti Sakari and Maire Siviä (Saartola) T.; m. Eija Irene Lipponen, Sept. 10, 1973; children: Laura, Noora. BSc, U. Joensuu, Finland, 1975, MSc, 1977, lic. sci., 1980, DSc, 1988. Docent U. Joensuu, 1989. Rsch. assoc. Acad. Finland, 1978-83; lectr. U. Joensuu, Finland, 1984-86, 87-89; rschr. Helsinki Sch. of Econs. and Bus. Adminstrn., Mikkeli, Finland, 1987; sr. asst. prof. U. Joensuu, Finland, 1990-92, 93-95; sr. rsch. assoc. Acad. Finland, 1992-93, sr. fellow, 1996-98, prof., 1998—; head Inst. Rural Studies, Joensuu, Finland, 1990, 93-95; prof. U. Joensuu, 1998—. Editor, author: (books) Coping with Closure: An International Comparison of Mine Town Experiences, 1992, Local Economic Development, A Geographical Comparison of Rural Community Restructuring, 1998; editor: (books) Development Issues and Strategies in the New Europe, 1992, Local and Regional Development During the 1990s Transition in Eastern Europe, 1995. Mem. European Regional Sci. Assn., Am. Geog. Soc., Geography Soc. Finland (exec. com. 1997-2000, chmn. 2000—). Avocation: aviation. Fax: 358-13-251-3454. E-mail: markku.tykkylainen@joensuu.fi. Office: U Joensuu, PO Box 111, Fin80101 Joensuu Finland

TYLER, ANNE (MRS. TAGHI M. MODARRESSI), author; b. Mpls., Oct. 25, 1941; d. Lloyd Parry and Phyllis (Mahon) T.; m. Taghi M. Modarressi, May 3, 1963 (dec. Apr. 1997); children: Tezh, Mitra. BA, Duke U., 1961; postgrad., Columbia U., 1962. Author: If Morning Ever Comes, 1964, The Tin Can Tree, 1965, A Slipping-Down Life, 1970, The Clock Winder, 1972, Celestial Navigation, 1974, Searching for Caleb, 1976, Earthly Possessions, 1977, Morgan's Passing, 1980, Dinner at the Homesick Restaurant, 1982, The Accidental Tourist, 1985, Breathing Lessons, 1988 (Pulitzer Prize for fiction 1989), Saint Maybe, 1991, (juvenile) Tumble Tower, 1993, Ladder of Years, 1995, A Patchwork Planet, 1998; contbr. short stories to nat. mags. Home: 222 Tunbridge Rd Baltimore MD 21212-3422

TYLER, JOHN EDWARD, III, lawyer; b. Kansas City, Mo.. BA, U. Notre Dame, 1986, JD, 1989. From assoc. to ptnr. Lathrop & Gage L.C., Kansas City, 1989-99; gen. counsel, sec. Ewing Marion Kauffman Found., Kansas City, 1999—; adj. prof. Rockhurst U., Kansas City, 2000—. Contbr. articles to profl. jours. Pres. Genesis Sch., Kansas City, 1995-96, 96-97; pres. Archbishop O'Hara H.S., Kansas City, 1994-95, 95-96, 96-97; chair tax increment fin. commn. city of Raytown, Mo., 1997-99; bd. dirs. Ctr. for Mgmt. Assistance, Kansas City, pres., 1999—. Named Man of Yr. Leukemia Soc., Kansas City, 1998, Bernie Hoffman award for cmty. svc. Cmty. Svc. Awards Found., 1997. Mem. ABA, Mo. Bar Assn. (Thomas D. Cochran award for cmty. svc. 1995), Kans. Bar Assn., Kansas City Metro. Bar Assn. (young lawyer of yr. 1998). Home: 2420 SW Wintercreek Ct Lees Summit MO 64081-4085 Office: Ewing Marion Kauffman Found 4801 Rockhill Rd Kansas City MO 64110-2046

TYLER, MAURICE STANLEY, language educator; b. Heston, England, Nov. 23, 1935; s. Stanley Frank and Doris Freda (Robinson) T.; m. Annette Butterworth, Apr. 1, 1961; children: Amanda, Christopher, Julia. BA, St. John's Coll., Cambridge, 1957, MA, 1959. Tchr. French, German King Edward VI Grammar Sch., Aston, England, 1959-62, Wallington County Sch for Boys, Sutton, England, 1962-65; head fgn. langs. Royal Latin Sch., Buckingham, England, 1965-94; part-time tchr. French Sponne Sch., Towcester, England, 1994-95; part-time tchr. German Kingsbrook Sch., Milton Keynes, England, 1995-96; part-time tchr. German, French Bury Lawn Sch., Milton Keynes, 1997—; tchr.-gov. Royal Latin Sch., 1985-89, 93-94; examiner Delegacy Local Examinations, Oxford, England, 1991-97, O.C.R., Cambridge, 1997—; mem. joint adv. & cons. group County Coun. Edn. Com., Buckinghamshire, England, 1990-94; mem. county com. Assn. Tchrs. & Lects., Buckinghamshire, 1969-94. Editor Jour. of France and Colonies Philatelic Soc., 1994—. Joint sec. Buckingham Twinning Com., 1968-75; chmn. Buckingham Judo Club, 1973-82; sec. Buckingham Film Soc., 1971-74. Avocations: philately, notaphily, bridge, photography, theatre. Home: 56 Mortons Fork Blue Bridge, Milton Keynes MK13 0LA, England

TYLER, RICHARD, fashion designer; b. Sunshine, Australia, Sept. 22, 1950; m. Doris Taylor (div.); 1 child, Sheridan; m. Lisa Trafficante, 1989; 1 child, Edward Charles. Prin. Zippity-doo-dah, Melbourne, Australia, 1968-80, Tyler-Trafficante, L.A., 1988—; design dir. Anne Klein Collection, N.Y.C., 1993-94, 99; fashion dir. owner Tyler Trafficante, Inc., 1999—. Designer Richard Tyler Couture introduced for Women, 1989, Richard Tyler Collection debut for Men, April 1997, Richard Tyler Shoes for Women, 1996, Richard Tyler Collection for Women, 1997, Richard Tyler Shoes for Men, 1997. Recipient New Fashion Talent Perry Ellis award Coun. Fashion Designers Am., 1993, Womenswear Designer of Yr. award, 1994, Perry Ellis award for new fashion talent in menswear, 1995.

TYLER, RICHARD JAMES, personal and professional development educator; b. Warwick, R.I., June 16, 1957; s. Virginia (Campanella) Tyler. Gen. mgr. Gem Exch., Charlotte, N.C., 1977; nat. sales mgr. So. Merchandising, Charlotte, 1978; pres. Direct Import Distributing, New Orleans, 1981; nat. territorty dir. TV Fanfare Pub., 1982; v.p. ARC Pub., New Orleans, 1983; exec. v.p., gen. mgr. Superior Bedrooms, Inc., 1984; CEO Richard Tyler Internat., Inc., Houston, Internat. Bus. Inst., Inc., Houston, Tyler Internat. Rsch. Inst., Inc., Houston, Shopportunities, Houston, Richard Tyler Investments Ltd., 2000, Richard Tyler Investments LLC; mem. adv. bd. Sales and Mktg. Mag., N.Y.C., 1991—; founder Leadership of Tomorrow program; profl. speaker, cons. in field. Author: Creating Excellence in Quality and Service, 1991, The Science and Art of Excellent Selling, 1993, Richard Tyler's Guide to Entrepreneurial Excellence, 1993, Richard Tyler's Smart Business Strategies. The Guide to Small Business Marketing Excel-

lence, 1996; pub. newsletter Richard Tyler's Excellence Edge, 1992; contbr. articles to profl. publs. Mem. Rep.-Senatorial Inner Cir., Washington, 1991. Mem. ASTD, Soc. Human Resource Mgmt., Nat. Speakers Assn., Internat. Platform Assn., Internat. Assn. Entrepreneurs. Avocations: sports, theater, deep sea fishing, amateur wrestling.

TYLEVICH, ALEXANDER V., sculptor, architect, educator; b. Minsk, Belarus, Sept. 12, 1947; came to U.S., 1989; s. Wulf Tylevich and Asia Klebanova; m. Poline M. Dvorkin, Jan. 22, 1981; children: Alexei, Katherine. BA in Arch., Minsk Archtl. Inst., 1965; MA in Arch., Byelorussian Poly. Inst., Minsk, 1971. Prin., sr. arch. Minskprojekt, 1971-84; artist, arch. Fine Arts Found., Minsk, 1984-89; sculptor-arch. Tylevich Arts, St. Paul, 1989—. Prin. works include Vincentian Letter sculpture DePaul U., Chgo., Montessori's Vision: Through the Eyes of a Child, Lake Country Sch., Mpls., Tree of Life, U. Minn., Mpls., Sculpture Anoka Ramsey C.C., Coon Rapids, Minn. (suspended recognition), Resurrection, Ch. of St. Stephen, Anoka, Minn., Madonna and Child, The Ch. of St. Mary, Alexandria, Minn., Gateway to Belief/Point of Belief, St. Mary's U., Winona, Minn., Thomas Becket, The Cath. Cmty. of Thomas Becket, Eagan, Minn., Tribute to Erich Mendelsohn, FORECAST Pub. Artwork, St. Paul, Zenon Possis, North Meml. Hosp., Mpls., Winona Tech. Coll. Aviation Facility (Minn. Percent for Art in Pub. Pls. program), North Shore Synagogue, Syosset, N.Y., Mt. Zion Temple, St. Paul, St. Paul Sem., St. Joseph Abbey, St. Benedict, La., Mepkin Abbey, S.C., master plan for Ctr. of Minsk, Minsk City Govt. Bldg., Subway Sta., Minsk, pvt. collections; exhibited in group shows at Monumental Art of Byelorussia, Minsk, 1989, Sacred Image, Sacred Text, Nat. Jewish Mus., Washington, 1993, Harvard U. Grad. Sch. Design New Eng., 1993, St. John's U., Collegeville, Minn. Grantee Minn. Met. Regional Arts Coun., 1991, Howard B. Brin Arts Endowment, 1991, FORECAST Pub. Artworks, 1993. Fellow Archtl. Assn. USSR. Home: 1937 Highland Pkwy Saint Paul MN 55116-1350

TYLLIA, FRANK MICHAEL, university official, educator; b. Rossland, B.C., Can., Dec. 1, 1942; came to U.S., 1942; s. Alex J. and Lenora M. (Janni) T.; m. Kathryn A. McWalter, Mar. 21, 1970. BBA, Gonzaga U., 1965, BA in Edn., 1967; MA in Edn., Seattle U., 1972. Tchr. pub. schs., Seattle, 1967-72, prin., 1972-78; prin. Edmonds Sch. Dist., Lynnwood, Wash., 1978-97; field supr. M Tchg. City U., Bellevue, Wash., 1997—; adj. prof. Seattle Pacific U., 1990—. Active alumni mentoring program Gonzaga U., Seattle, 1993—; active Kirkland conf. com. King County Juvenile Justice, 1997—, mem. King County Diversion Adv. Bd., 1998—. Mem. ASCD, Assn. Wash. Sch. Prins. (various coms.), Washington Athletic Club, Phi Delta Kappa. Home and Office: 4527 103d Ln NE Kirkland WA 98033-7639

TYMAN, ADAM STEFAN, electrical engineer, educator; b. Sambor, Lwow, Poland, Apr. 4, 1946; s. Adam and Maria (Pawlikowska) T.; m. Teresa Jadwiga Dziurzynska, June 27, 1970; children: Eva, Barbara. MSc, Tech. U. Wroclaw, 1971, PhD, 1977. Asst. Tech. U. Wroclaw, Poland, 1971-78, asst. prof., 1978—, vice mgr. sci. matter Inst. Elec. Engring. Fundamentals, 1999—. Mem. Polish Elec. Engrs. (sec. elec. materials com. 1988-95). Avocations: gardening, tennis. Home: Zielinskiego 71/4, 53-533 Wroclaw Poland Office: Tech Univ Wroclaw I-7, Wroclaw U Tech I-7, Wybrzeze Wyspianskiego 27, 50-370 Wroclaw Poland

TYMAN, JOHN HENRY PAUL, chemistry educator; b. London, Nov. 9, 1923; s. Thomas John and Rebecca (Colbran) T.; m. Norah Whittingham, Sept. 23, 1946 (div.); m. Barbara Eveline Hood Phillips, Oct. 31, 1970; children: Robert, Philip. BSc, U. London, 1943, PhD, 1960, DSc, 1982. Chartered chemist. Works, devel. chemist May and Baker (now Rhone Poulenc Rorer), London, 1943-45; rsch. chemist, sr. scientist Unilever, Port Sunlight, Wirral, 1945-57; rsch. devel. mgr. Proprietary Perfumes Ltd. (now Quest Internat. Ltd.), London, Kent, Eng., 1957-62; lectr. in chemistry Brunel U., Eng., 1962-82, reader in chemistry, 1982-89; cons. European Colour, London, 1984-95, Cardolite Corp., N.J., 1993—. Editor, author 5 books; patentee in field; presenter Internat. Union of Pure and Applied Chemistry Symposium; contbr. articles and papers to numerous jours. Sch. gov. London Borough of Richmond on Thames, 1975-85; mem. editl. bd. Mountaineering, Jour. Brit. Mountaineering Coun., 1959-75. Recipient numerous rsch. grants from industry and rsch. couns. Fellow Royal Chem. Soc.; mem. Soc. Chem. Industry, Lipid Group Royal Soc. Chemistry (chmn. 1992-95). Avocations: painting, playing music, fgn. travel, mountaineering. Home and Office: 150 Palewell Park, London SW14 8JH, England

TYNDALL, JAY MARK, lawyer; b. Indpls., Feb. 29, 1964; s. William Mark and Jewetta Corine (Main) T.; m. Yuko Shigetomi, Feb. 14, 1991; children: Saige Mark, Hanna. BA, Earlham Coll., 1986; JD, U. Dayton, 1991. Bar: Wash. 1992. Fgn. law advisor Kitahama Law Office, Osaka, 1994-96; assoc. Adachi, Henderson, Miyatake & Fujita, Tokyo, 1996-98; contract atty. Seattle, 1999; pvt. practice Puget Sound Area, 2000—; presenter profl. seminars. Mem. ABA, Wash. State Bar Assn.

TYRER, HUGH, engineering metallurgist, consultant; b. Richmond, Surrey, Eng., Mar. 2, 1926; s. Edward George and Gladys Amelia (Kayes) T.; m. Olwen May Blakemore, Feb. 19, 1953 (div. Jan. 1979); 1 child, Wendy; m. Joanna Margaret Child, Feb. 24, 1979. Student, Vickers Apprentice Sch., Weybridge, Eng., 1942-46. Chartered engr. Lab. technician Vickers Armstrongs Ltd., Weybridge, 1942-46, group leader materials, 1947-56; asst. lab. mgr. Brit. Aircraft Corp., Weybridge, 1966-80; tech. cons. Brit. Aerospace, Weybridge, 1980-87; propr. HT Cons., Aldershot, Eng., 1987—; lectr. Surrey County Coun., Weybridge, 1947-64; specialist lectr. Cranfield (Eng.) Coll. Aeronautics, 1991-99; adviser London Ins. Market. Mem. Royal Aeronautical Soc., Inst. of Materials (assoc.). Conservative. Anglican. Avocations: photography, Medieval metallurgy, forensic metallurgy. Office: HT Cons, 35 Southlands Close Ash, Aldershot Surrey GU12 6NH, England

TYRL, PAUL, mathematics educator, researcher, consultant; b. Prague, Czech Rep., Dec. 24, 1951; came to U.S., 1970, naturalized, 1978; s. Vladimir Tyrl and Marta Kocian. BA with honors, N.J. City U., 1977, MA, 1980; EdD, Rutgers U., 1987. Cert. tchr. secondary edn., higher edn. N.J. quality controller Agfa-Perutz, Munich, 1969-70; technician AT&T, Kearny, N.J., 1970-73; acquisition librarian N.J. City U., 1973-74, post office supr., 1974-76, dir. math. lab., instr. math., 1976-80; instr. math. Hudson County C.C., N.J., 1980-82, assoc. prof., coord. math., 1982-84; prof., chmn. math., acad. coord., curriculum dir. Sch. New Resources-New Rochelle Coll., N.Y.C., 1984—; rschr. Rutgers U., New Brunswick, N.J., 1980—; cons. Jersey City Bd. Edn., N.J., 1982—. Contbr. articles to profl. jours. Recipient Commemorative medal of honor, 1986. Mem. AAAS, ASCD, Nat. Coun. Tchrs. Math. (reviewer and referee), N.Y. Acad. Scis., Am. Ednl. Rsch. Assn., Math. Assn. Am., Am. Math. Assn. 2-Yr. Colls., Am. Math. Soc., Am. Mus. Natural History, Nat. Geog. Soc., Nat. Wildlife Fedn., Smithsonian Instn. Roman Catholic. Achievements include research in mathematics anxiety and mathematics problem solving.

TYRRELL, ALAN RUPERT, barrister; b. Bolobo, Zaire, June 27, 1933; s. Trevor Graham Rupert and Winifred Alice (Mackenzie) T.; m. Elaine Eleanor Ware, Mar. 26, 1960; children: Alison, Simon. LLB, London Sch. Econs., 1954. Called to English Bar, 1956. Pvt. practice London, 1956—; recorder, Eng., 1972—, Queen's Counsel, 1976—; master of the bench Grays Inn, 1986—; dep. high ct. judge, 1990—; mem. European Parliament, 1979-84. Author: A Student's Guide to Europe, 1983; author, editor: The Legal Professions in the New Europe, 1993, 2d edit., 1996; editor: Moores Practical Agreements, 1965, Public Procurement and Remedies, 1997. Bd. dirs. Med. Protection Soc., U.K., 1990-98, Papworth Hosp. NHS Trust, Cambridge, Criminal Injuries Corp.; arbitrator Internat. C. of C., 1999—. Fellow Chartered Inst. Arbitrators. Mem. Conservative Party. Avocation: bridge. Home: 15 Willifield Way, London NW11 7XU, England Office: Temple, Francis Taylor Bldg, London EC4 7BY, England

TYRRELL, DAVID ARTHUR JOHN, retired virologist; b. Ashford, U.K., June 19, 1925; s. Sidney Charles and Agnes Kate (Blewett) T.; m. Betty Moyra Wylie, Apr. 15, 1950; children: Frances E., Susan C., Stephen A.J. (dec.). MB, BChir with honors, Sheffield U., U.K., 1948, MD, 1953. House physician United Sheffield Hosps., Eng., 1948; rsch. registrar Royal Hosp., Sheffield, 1950-51; house physician City Gen. Hosp., Eng., 1948-49; jr. registrar Royal Infirmary, Sheffield, 1949-51; asst. physician Rockefeller Inst. Hosp., N.Y.C., 1951-54; external sci. staff Med. Rsch. Coun. Gt. Britain, Sheffield, 1954-57; MRC sci. staff common cold unit Salisbury Wilts, 1957-90; head divsn. communicable diseases, dep. dir. Clin. Rsch. Ctr., London, 1967-83; ret., 1990; chmn. biologicals subcom. Com. Safety Medicines, 1989-92, chmn. adv. com. on dangerous pathogens, 1982-91, chmn. spongiform encephalopathy adv. com., 1989-95, chmn. nat. task force on chronic fatigue syndrome, 1992-99. Contbr. articles to profl. jours. Fellow Royal Coll. Physicians, Royal Coll. Pathologists, Royal Soc.; mem. Infectious Disease Soc. Am. (hon.), Internat. Soc. for Interferon Rsch. (hon.), Australasian Soc. Infectious Diseases (hon., life), Am. Assn. Physicians (hon.). Mem. Ch. of Eng. Avocations: gardening, music, walking, history of 20th century medical science. Home: Ash Lodge, Dean Ln Whiteparish, Salisbury Wiltshire SP5 2RN, England

TYRRELL, PATRICK JOHN, career military officer; b. Sheffield, Yorkshire, Eng., Jan. 18, 1950; s. Val and Shelagh (Straw) T.; m. Glynis Morris, Oct. 21, 1972; 1 child, Jessica; m. Debra Anne Gross. MA in Chemistry, Jesus Coll., Oxford, 1972; LLB, U. London, 1982, diploma of mgmt. studies, 1974; diploma of mgmt. studies, Royal Coll. Def. Studies, 1996. Staff officer Supreme Hdqrs. Allied Powers Europe MONS, Belgium, 1988-91; staff officer def. policy Ministry of Defence, London, 1991-93, asst. dir. CIS policy, 1993-96; commandant Defence Intelligence and Security Sch., Chicksands, Eng., 1997-99; dep. CEO, Defence Comm. Svcs. Agy., Corsham, Eng., 1999—. Order of the British Empire, Her Majesty the Queen, 1991. Avocations: house renovation, philosophy of information, walking. E-mail: PatrickTyrrellRN@cs.com. Home: Vale House, Cornwall Ponsanooth TR3 7JB, England Office: DCSA, Basil Hill, Corsham Wiltshire SN13 9NR, England

TYSCHENKO, IDA, physicist; b. Selionaja Roshcha, Russia, Mar. 9, 1961; d. Evgenij and Tamara (Eide) T.; m. Vladimir Popov, Sept. 11, 1997; 1 child, Itor'. Degree in engring. and physics, Electro-Tech. Inst., Novosibirsk, Russia, 1983, PhD, 1992. Engr. Inst. Semicondr. Physics, Russian Acad. Scis., Novisbirsk, 1986-89, rsch. asst., 1989-93, sci. worker, 1993-98, sr. rsch. scientist, 1998—. Contbr. articles to profl. jours. Scholar German Acad. Exch. Svc., 1994-95; grantee Ministry Sci. and Art of Saxony, Germany, 1995, 96, 97, 98, Am. Phys. Soc. Avocation: family. E-mail: tys@isp.nsc.ru. Home: Demakova 12/1 132, 630128 Novosibirsk Russia Office: Inst Semicondr Physics RAS, Pr Lavrenjava 13, 630090 Novosibirsk Russia

TYSON, JOHN, II, engineering executive; b. Bryn Mawr, Pa., Apr. 15, 1958; s. Noel Jon Tyson and Patricia Jane (Peterson) Tyson Stroud McCurdy; m. Holly Hoch, Oct. 6, 1990; children: Julia Hudson, Patricia Noel, John III. BSME, Duke U., 1981. Profl. engr., Pa. Field engr. Schlumberger Offshore Svcs., Lafayette, La., 1981-82; dir. engring. Measurement Systems, Inc., Norristown, Pa., 1982-84; v.p., founder Teletrac Corp., Norristown, Pa., 1984-92; engring. mgr. Laser Tech., Inc., Norristown, Pa., 1984-86, v.p., 1986-98; v.p., founder, dir. Tech. Devel. Corp., Norristown, Pa., 1986-98; pres., founder Trilion Quality Sys. LLC, Southeastern, Pa., 1998—. Contbr. articles to profl. jours. Patentee in field. Mem. St. David's Ch., Wayne, Pa., 1958—. Mem. ASME, Soc. Experimental Mechanics, Soc. Automotive Engrs., Am. Soc. Nondestructive Testing (chmn. laser methods group). Avocations: sailing, scuba, tennis, flyfishing. E-mail: tyson@trilion.com. Home: 241 Atlee Rd Wayne PA 19087-3835 Office: Trilion Quality Sys PO Box 102 Southeastern PA 19399-0102

TYSON, LAURA D'ANDREA, dean, economist, educator; b. Bayonne, N.J., June 28, 1947. BA, Smith Coll., 1969; PhD, MIT, 1974. Prof. econ. and bus. adminstrn. U. Calif., Berkeley, 1978-98, BankAmerica dean Haas Sch. Bus., 1998—; chmn. Pres.'s Coun. Econ. Advisors, Washington, 1993-95; nat. econ. advisor to Pres. U.S. Nat. Econ. Coun., Washington, 1995-96. Editor: (with John Zysman) American Industry in International Competition, 1983, (with Ellen Comisso) Power, Purpose and Collective Choice: Economic Strategy in Socialist States, 1986, (with William Dickens and John Zysman) The Dynamics of Trade and Employment, 1988, (with Chalmers Johnson and John Zysman) Politics and Productivity: The Real Story of How Japan Works, 1989, Who's Bashing Whom? Trade Conflict in High Technology Industries, 1992. Office: Haas Sch Bus 545 Student Srvs # 1900 Berkeley CA 94720-0001*

TYSON, LUCILLE R., administrator; b. North Wales, Pa., Feb. 14, 1939; d. Edwin Shelly and Marion (Wenhold) Rosenberger; m. Ronald Saylor Tyson, June 29, 1963; children: Bryan, Bruce. AS, Middlesex County Coll.; BA, Wheaton Coll.; MSW, Rutgers U. Cert. gerontol. nurse; lic. social worker; RN. Dir. N.J. Parkinson Info. & Referral Ctr. Robert Wood Johnson U. Hosp., New Brunswick, N.J.; human svcs. planner Middlesex County Dept. Human Svcs., New Brunswick; dir., right to know regulations Roosevelt Hosp., Edison, N.J.; dir., quality assurance Cen. N.J. Jewish Home for Aged, Somerset, N.J. Mem. Piscataway (N.J.) Twp. Coun., 1990—; mem. rev./appeals com. Middlesex County Dept. Human Svcs., 1992—; bd. dirs. Metlar Ho. Found.; mcpl. dir. Piscataway Rep. Orgn., 1995—; county committeewoman Middlesex County Rep. Orgn., 1995—. Mem. ANA, NASW, Nat. Soc. DAR, N.J. Nurses Assn., Assn. Quality Assurance Profls. N.J., Geriatric Inst. N.J.

TYSZER, JERZY STANISŁAW, engineering educator, researcher; b. Sroda Wlkp., Poland, Oct. 1, 1958; s. Marian and Eugenia (Piekarska) T.; m. Ewa Branicka Tyszer, Oct. 2, 1982; 1 child, Katarzyna. M in Engring., Poznan (Poland) U. Tech., 1981, PhD, 1987; Dr. Habilis, Tech. U. Gdansk, 1994. Asst. prof. Poznan (Poland) U. Tech., 1982-89; post-doctoral fellow McGill U., Montreal, Can., 1990-91; adjunct prof., 1992-96; prof. The Franco-Polish Sch. of New Info. and Comm. Tech., Poznan, Poland, 1995-96, Poznan (Poland) U. Tech., 1998—; cons. Bell-Northern Rsch., Ottawa, Can., 1992-96, Inst. Comm. and Info. Tech., Poznan, Poland, 1996—, Mentor Graphics Corp., Portland, Oreg., 1996; vis. prof. The Franco-Polish Sch. New Info. and Comm. Tech., Poznan, Poland, 1994-95. Author: Object-Oriented Computer Simulation of Discrete-Event Systems, 1999, Arithmetic Built-In Self-Test for Embedded Systems, 1997, Computer Simulation, 1990; contbr. articles to profl. jours. Recipient Coop. Rsch. and Devel. grantee, NSERC, Can., 1993-96. Mem. IEEE (sr.), IEEE Computer Soc., Polish Data Processing Soc. Avocations: music, hiking. Office: Poznan University of Technology, Ul Piotrowo 3A, 60-965 Poznan Poland

TYSZKOWSKI, ROBERT, business executive, cell biologist; b. Boston, May 25, 1961; s. Walter and Nora Francis (Lange) T.; m. Patricia Anne McArdle, Dec. 30, 1995. BA, U. Mass., 1983; BS, U. N.H., 1985; postgrad., Harvard U., 1985-87, 90-93. Lic. cons. Mass. Dept. Pub. Health. Rsch. asst. Ritzman Rsch. Lab., Durham, N.H., 1984-85; clin. pathology intern Brigham & Women's Hosp., Harvard Med. Sch., Boston, 1985-87; clin. rschr., cell biologist Mass. Gen. Hosp., Harvard Med. Sch., Boston, 1987—; CEO Lange Internat., Boston, 1987—; dir. ops. Renal Rsch. Unit, Boston, 1989—, radiation safety officer, 1990—; exec. dir. Radiation Safety Svcs., Inc., Boston, 1996—; sr. ptnr. P.M.T. Assoc., Inc., Boston, 1996—; sr. v.p. Evidaunt Investigations, Inc., N.Y.C., 1997—; vice-chmn. bd. Evidaunt Investigations, Inc., Boston, 1997—; chmn. bd. Ea. Equine Assocs., Inc., Hamilton, Mass., 1985—, Lange Internat., Boston, 1987—, Radiation Safety Svcs., Inc., Boston, 1996—, Armser Corp., 1999—; mem. adv. com. U.S. Combined Tng. Assn., 1986-90, Ptnrs. Healthcare Sys., 1997—; mem. adv. bd. P.M.T. Assocs. Inc., Boston, 1996—. Contbr. numerous articles to profl. jours. Co-chmn. organizing com. Harvard-Yale Benefit Polo, Hamilton, 1990, U. N.H. Fund Raising Event, Boston, 1991; mem. organizing com. U. N.H. Equestrian Events, 1983-85, Ledyard Three-day Event, Wenham, Mass., 1987-88, 90, U. Mass. Fund Raising Drive, Amherst, 1980-81. Dana fellow, 1981-82, fellow Harvard U., 1987-89. Mem. AAAS, Am. Coll. Forensic Examiners, Am. Nuc. Soc., Admiral Nimitz Found., N.Y. Acad. Scis., Assn. of Offcl. Analytical Chemists Internat., Boston Athenaeum (life), Health Physics Soc., Inst. of Early Am. History and Culture, New Eng. Hist. Geneal. Soc., Nat. Assn. Investigative Specialists, Mus. Fine Arts/Boston, Redwood Libr. and Athenaeum, Nimitz Mus. Pacific War, Tex. State Archives, Manhattan C. of C., U.S. Ct. Tennis Assn., U.S. Golf Assn., U.S. Polo Assn., Faculty Club, Nat. Tennis Club (Newport, R.I.), Myopia Polo Club, Tennis and Racquet Club, Union Club, Univ. Club. Republican. Episcopalian. Avocation: equestrian sports, royal tennis. Office: Lange Internat PO Box 5669 Boston MA 02114-0011 Also: Evidaunt Investigations Inc 60 State St Ste 700 Boston MA 02109-1803

TYURKYAN, RAFFI ARMENAKOVICH, mining executive; b. Poti, Georgia, Apr. 3, 1929; arrived in Ukraine, 1951; s. Armenak A. and Russana M. (Karapetyan) T.; m. Liana G. Aristakesyan, Sept. 1954; 1 child, Karine. Diploma in engring., Inst. Tech., Tbilisi, Georgia, 1951; cand. of sci., Mining Inst., Moscow, 1965, DSc, 1989. Exec. dir. mine bldg. Donetsk, 1953-55; dir. vertical mine tunnel bldg. Ukrainian Mining Arch. Trust Donetskshakhoprokhodka, 1955-76; gen. dir. Ukrainian Ministry Mining Bldg., 1976-87, Orthekhshakhtostrov Project Inst., Donetsk, 1987—; prof. Donetsk U. Tech., 1991—; tech. supr. bldg. of underground sect. of hull Chernobil (Ukraine) Atomic Sta., 1986. Author: Technic and Technology of Building of Vertical Mines Tunnels, 1970, Building and Digging of Vertical Mines Shafts, 1982, Work of Miners in Chernobil for Liquidation of Accident in Chernobil Atomic Station, 1996; contbr. chpts. to books, articles to profl. jours.; 45 patents in field. Recipient Lenin Premium award Cabinet of Mins., Moscow, 1957, Order for Participation in liquidation of accident in Chernobil Atomic Sta., Supreme Coun., USSR, 1986, 2 Orders of Lenin medals, 15 others, 1955-85. Mem. Ukrainian Acad. Mining Sci., Ukrainian Acad. Mining Arch., N.Y. Acad. Scis. Avocations: philosophy, history, travel. Home: Str Kobozeva 68/11, 340000 Donetsk Ukraine Office: Orgtekhshakhtostroy Inst, Blvd Shevchenko 133, 340052 Donetsk Ukraine

TYUTYUNNIK, VYACHESLAV MIKHAJLOVICH, information scientist; b. Kupyansk, Kharkov, Ukraine, Oct. 4, 1949; arrived in Russia, 1955; s. Mikhail Ivanovich and Svetlana Stepanovna (Yurkova) T.; 1 child from previous marriage, Aleksej Vyacheslavovich; m. Elvira Anatoljevna Topilskaya, Sept. 24, 1996. Mech. engr., Inst. Chem. Engrs., Tambov, Russia, 1972; D in Chemistry, Mendeleev Inst. Chem. Tech., Moscow, 1977; Sr. Doctorate in Info. Scis., All-Russian Inst. Sci. Tech. Info., Moscow, 1998. Registered profl. engr. Engr. Inst. Chem. Engrs., 1972, jr. rsch. worker, 1973, sr. rsch. worker, 1973-81; head chair info. systems Tambov State U., 1995—; head chair informatics Inst. Culture, Tambov, 1981-95, prof. informatics, 1992—; pres., exec. dir. Itnernat. Info. Nobel Centre, Tambov, 1992—; chief Informatics, Ltd., Tambov, 1989-92. Author: Atom's Biography, 1984, 2d edit., 1985 (Best Book award 1986), A. Nobel and Nobel Prizes, 1988, 2d edit., 1991 (Best Book award 1989), Nobel Prize Winners in Literature, 1991 (Best Book award 1992), Nobel Prize Winners in Chemistry, 1989, 2d edit., 1991, 3d edit., 1993. Chief Regional Coun. Young Scientists, Tambov, 1978-86. Recipient Honor prize Russian Ministry of Culture, 1989, 92, W. Nernst medal Portuguese Electrochem. Soc., 1991, J. Soros prize Internat. Fund Cultural Initiative, 1993; Nobel Found. grantee, 1991. Mem. Russian Chem. Soc. (contbg. editor jour. 1992), Internat. Assn. Survey Statisticians. Mem. Radical Party. Avocations: collecting scientific-popular literature, stamps, coins, and Nobel information. Home: 30-6 Pervomajskaya Pl, 392002 Tambov Russia Office: Internat Infor Nobel Centre, 6 Soviet St, 392002 Tambov Russia

TYYSTJÄRVI, ESA, plant scientist; b. Helsinki, Finland, June 2, 1957; s. Pentti and Raija (Sarkkinen) T.; m. Eija Koivukoski, 1981 (div. 1992); children: Joonas, Maria, Venla; m. Taina Kallio, 1993; children: Sofia, Topias. MPh in Plant Physiology, U. Turku, Finland, 1987, D Plant Physiology, 1993. Rschr. photosynthesis U. Turku, 1987-94, 96—, docent in plant physiology and biophysics, 1995—; mng. dir. QA-Data Oy, 1995—. Author: (computer program) FIP-Fluorescence Induction Program, 1989, 90, 91, 92, 93, 94, 95; co-contbr. chpt. to: Techniques and New Developments in Photosynthesis Research, 1989, (2 chpts.) Current Research in Photosynthesis, Vo. II, 1990, research in Photosynthesis, Vol. II, 1992, (2 chpts.) Research in Photosynthesis Vol. IV, 1992, (2 chpts.) Photosynthesis: from Light to Biosphere, 1995 (3 chpts.) Photosynthesis: Mechanisms and Effects, 1998; contbr. articles to sci. jours. Mem. Scandinavian Soc. Plant Physiology (treas. 1997—). Achievements include inventor/patentee of method for the identification of chlorophyll-containing organisms. Home: Mestarinkatu 15 as 28, FIN20810 Turku Finland Office: U Turku, Dept Biology, FIN20014 Turku Finland

TZADUA, PAULOS CARDINAL, archbishop; b. Addifinni, Ethiopia, Aug. 25, 1921; s. Tzadua and Tensaye (Hailu) Asgeda. Dr. Polit. Sci., Cath. U. Milan, 1957, Dr. Law, 1958. Ordained priest Roman Cath. Ch., 1944. Elected bishop, 1973; appointed archbishop of Addis Ababa, Ethiopia, 1977; elevated to Sacred Coll. of Cardinals, 1985. Translator: The Fetha Nagast (The Law of the Kings). Contbr. articles to profl. jours.*

TZAFESTAS, SPYROS GEORGIOU, robotics and control educator, researcher; b. Corfu, Greece, Dec. 3, 1939; s. George and Elpida Tzafestas; m. Niki C. Kalliamvakos, Oct. 4, 1965; children: Elpida, Costas. BS in Physics, U. Athens, Greece, 1963, diploma in Electronics, 1964; diploma in Elec. Engring., Imperial Coll., London, 1967; MS in Control Engring., London U., 1967; PhD in Systems and Control, Southampton (Eng.) U., 1969, DSc, 1978; DSc (hon.), Internat. U. Found., Madrid, 1989; D. in Engring. (hon.), Munich Tech. U., 1997. Rsch. asst. NRC Demokritos, Athens, 1963-64, rsch. dir., 1969-73; prof. control Patras (Greece) U., 1973-84; prof. robotics and control Nat. Tech. U. Athens, 1985—; organizer, chmn., co-chmn. numerous internat. confs.; leader several nat. and European R&D projects on robotics and mfg. syss. Author 17 books; editor 40 rsch. books; editor-in-chief Jour. Intelligent and Robotic Systems, (book series) Microprocessor-Based and Intelligent Systems Engineering; assoc. editor 15 internat. tech. jours.; contbr. over 500 articles to profl. jours. Recipient Hon. award Greek Soc. Writers, 1995. Fellow IEEE, Inst. Elec. Engrs. London; mem. ASME, Internat. Assn. Maths. and Computers in Simulation, Soc. Intelligent Robotics and Expert Systems, N.Y. Acad. Scis. Fax: 30-1-7722490. Home: 91 E Venizelou Str, Holargos Athens 15561, Greece Office: Nat Tech U Athens Dept Elec & Comp Engr, Intell Robotics & Autom Lab, Zografou Athens 15773, Greece

TZALLAS, NIOVE, painter; b. Jannina, Greece, Jan. 26, 1938; d. George and Kaliroi (Papastergiou) Georgopoulos; m. Neocosmos Tzallas, Aug. 21, 1959. Student, Athens Sch. Beaux Arts, 1955-58, Atelier Andre Lhote, France, 1958-59, Cen. Sch. Arts and Crafts, Eng., 1959-61. One-woman shows at Paris, 1962, Rome, 1963, Gallery Royal Soc. Painters, London, 1964, Gallery du Damier, Paris, 1968, Gallery U. Paris, 1969, 72, Mus. de Havre, France, 1971, Galerie Vallombreuse, Biarritz, France, 1974, Gallery Mouffe, Paris, 1975, Gallery Bernheim-Jeune, Paris, 1982, BH Corner Gallery, London, 1985, 86, Everarts Galerie, Paris, 1988, 90, 93, Montserrat Gallery, N.Y., 1994, Galerie Art Present, Paris, 1996; exhibited in floating exhbns. aboard S.S. Pegassos, S.S. Semiramis, 1966, S.S. Olympia, 1967; exhibited in group shows at Salon des Independents, Grand Palais des Champs Elysees, 1973-98, Grand Prix Internat. de la Baie des Anges, Nice, France, Galerie Riviera, Nice, 1974, Galerie Blaise St. Maurice, Paris, 1974-77, Galerie l'Arthotèque, Monte Carlo, 1975, Salon Populiste, Paris, 1975, Maison de la Culture à Ville-neuve-la Garenne, 1976-77,, Ctr. Cultural de Mussidan, Dordogne, France, 1977, The Breakers Gallery, Palm Beach, Fla., 1976-78, Ctr. European Delobbe à Olloy Sur Viroin, Belgium, 1978, Galerie la Roue, Paris, 1978-79, Salon de l'Art Libre, Paris, 1978-79, Festival d'Art Graphique d'Osaka, Japan, 1983-84, Metropolis Galerie Internat. D'Art, Geneva, 1984, Mus. Luxembourg, Paris, L'Union des Femmes Peintres et Sculpteurs, 1981, 82, Galerie Hautefeuille, Paris, 1988-9, Galerie, Quincampoix, Paris, 1989, Espace Delpha, Paris, 1989, Espace Laser, Paris, 1989, Galerie Jules Salles, Nimes, France, 1993, Salon de Academie Culturelle Internat. des Artistes de France de la ville de Gimont, 1993, Salon Internat. d'Art Contemporain. Home: 15 Ekalis St, 145 61 Kifissia, Attica Greece Studio: 13 Pericleous Stavrou str, 115 24 Athens Greece

TZANAKOS, GEORGE STEFANOS, physicist, educator; b. Myrsini, Laconia, Greece, Aug. 22, 1940; s. Stefanos G. and Stamatiki A. (Antonakos) T.; m. Evangelia Michelis, July 24, 1969. BSc in Physics, U. Athens, Greece, 1964; MSc in Physics, Syracuse U., 1974, MSc in Computer Sci., 1977, PhD in Physics, 1976. Rsch. assoc. physics dept. Syracuse (N.Y.) U., 1975-80, asst. prof. physics dept., 1980-81; asst. prof. physics dept. Columbia U., N.Y.C., 1981-87, assoc. rsch. scientist Nevis labs., 1987-89; assoc. prof. physics U. Athens, 1989—; vis. prof. dept. biomed. engring. Rutgers U., Piscataway, N.J., 1987-93, vis. prof., 1993—. Contbr. articles to profl. jours. NSF fellow, 1969-72. Mem. IEEE, AAAS, Am. Phys. Soc., Assn. Computing Machinery, N.Y. Acad. Scis., Sigma Xi. Achievements include discovery of tau-neutrino. Avocations: composition and conducting music. Office: U Athens Dept Physics, Nuclear & Particle Physics Divsn, 15771 Athens Greece

TZANNETAKIS, TZANNIS, Greek government official; b. Gytheion, Greece, 1927; married; 2 children. Commd. officer, advanced through grades to comdr. Greek Navy, resigned after mil. coup, 1967; arrested and imprisoned 9 mos., exiled 1 yr.; sec.-gen. Greek Nat. Tourist Orgn., Athens; M.P., 1977—; min. pub. works Govt. of Greece, 1980-81; supr. local govt. affairs New Democracy Party, 1982-86, prime min., min. fgn. affairs, 1989, min. nat. def., 1989-90, vice premier, min. culture, 1990-91, dep. prime min., 1992-93. Author: The Greek Agora Public Political Science, 1994, India-Another Way of Life, 1994; translator: Upanishads, 1961, Mani, 1973. Decorated Honor Grand Cross of Greece, Grand Cross Of Luxembourg. Home: Odos Pefkon 25 Kifissia, Athens Greece Office: Omirou 54, Athens Greece

TZARDIS, PERICLIS JOSEPH, surgeon; b. Athens, Greece, Apr. 29, 1956; s. Joseph and Athina (Chrysocheris) T.; m. Constantina Paravantis, Jan. 28, 1981; two children. MD, Athens U., 1980, PhD, 1987. Med. officer 404 Mil. Hosp., Larissa, Greece, 1980-81; sr. house officer Gen. Hosp. Argos, Greece, 1981-82; registrar Hippocration Gen. Hosp., Athens, 1983-88; rsch. fellow U. Minn., Mpls., 1988-90; from attending surgeon to sr. attending surgeon Red Cross Hosp., Athens, 1990—. Co-author: Malignant Tumors of the Gastrointestinal Tract, 1991; contbr. articles to profl. jours. Mem. Internat. Soc. Univ. Colon & Rectal Surgeons, European Assn. Endoscopic Surgery, Internat. Soc. Surgery. Avocations: scuba diving, tennis, gardening, cooking. Home: 4 Krvstalli St, 15452 Athens Greece

TZARTOS, SOCRATES, biochemist; b. Athens, Greece, July 13, 1945; s. John and Stiliani (Perili) T.; m. Elisabeth Perdiki, Sept. 12, 1971; 1 child, John. BSc in Natural Scis., U. Athens, 1970, PhD in Biology, 1976. Predoctoral rschr. Nat. Hellenic Rsch. Found., Athens, 1973-76; postdoctoral fellow U. Cambridge, Eng., 1976-78; rsch. assoc. Salk Inst., San Diego, 1978-81, Inst. Pasteur, Paris, 1981-83; head dept. biochemistry Hellenic Pasteur Inst., Athens, 1983—, rsch. dir., 1989-2000; prof. immunobiology U. Patras, 2000—. Contbr. more than 190 articles to internat. sci. jours. Sub-lt. Greek Army, 1970-72. EMBO fellow, 1976-78, 81-83, 93; grantee Muscular Dystrophy Assn., European Union, NATO, Assn. Français de Myopathies. Mem. EMBO, Neurosci. Soc., Greek Biochem. and Biophys. Soc. (treas.). Achievements include identification of the main immunogenic region of the AChR; in depth elucidation of its structure and role in myasthenia gravis; production and extensive characterization of 150 anti-AChR monoclonal antibodies. Fax: 30-1-6478842. E-mail: tzartos@mail.pasteur.gr. Home: 147 Formionos St, 16121 Athens Greece Office: Hellenic Pasteur Inst, 127 Vas Sofias Ave, Athens 11521, Greece

TZEKOV, TZEKOV CHRISTO, neurosurgeon, educator, consultant; b. Vratza, Bulgaria, Oct. 22, 1950; s. Tzeko Christov Tzekov and Vatza Mihaylova Vekova; m. Valentina Radkova Tomova, Mar. 6, 1983; children: Vanya, Asen. Diploma, Med. Acad., Sofia, Bulgaria, 1974, qualification, 1979; qualification, Med. Acad., Sofia, Bulgaria, 1983. Surgeon Dist. Hosp., Vratza, 1974-79; neurosurgeon Higher Med. Inst., Sofia, 1979-96; asst. prof.; cons. Nat. Emergency Ctr., Sofia, 1989-98. Co-author: Tumors of CNS in Childhood, 1987, Pediatric Neurosurgery, 1989; contbr. articles to profl. jours.; inventor in field. Mem. European Assn. Neurosurgery, European Assn. Pediat. Neurosurgery, Nat. Geog. Soc., N.Y. Acad. Scis. Avocations: philately, hiking. Home: Lomsko Chaussee Bl 272 E137, 1220 Sofia Bulgaria Office: Higher Med Sch Neurosurgery, 1 G Sofiiski St, 1431 Sofia Bulgaria

TZELGOV, JOSEPH, psychologist, scientist; b. Zgierz, Poland, May 24, 1946; s. Israel and Eugenia (Berholtz) T.; m. Margalith Levin, May 5, 1946; children: Eran, Eitan. BA, Ben Gurion U., Berr Sheva, Israel, 1970; MA, The Hebrew U., Jerusalem, 1974, PhD, 1981. Rsch. psychologist Israeli Def. Forces, 1970-73; instr. Ben Gurion U., 1974-81, lectr., 1982-85, sr. lectr., 1985-91, assoc. prof., 1991-97, prof., 1997—; vis. scientist MIT, 1981-82; mem. sci. com. Nat. Inst. Testing and Evaluation, Jersalem. Mem. editl. bd. Israeli Jour. Social Scis., 1993. Rsch. grantee U.S.-Israeli Binat. Sci. Found., 1985, 87, Israeli Acad. Scis., 1986, 2000, Nat. Coun. Rsch. and Devel., Israel, 1987. Mem. APA, Psychonomic Soc., European Soc. Cognitive Psychology, Human Factors Soc. Avocation: swimming. E-mail: tzelgov@bgumail.bgu.ac.il. Fax: 972-7-6472932. Office: Dept Behavioral Sciences, Ben Gurion U, 84105 Beer Sheva Israel

TZEN, TZE-CHENG JASON, biotechnology educator; b. Kaohsiung, Taiwan, Feb. 3, 1964; s. Wen-Lee and Yu-Chun (Chuang) T.; m. Mei-Chi Wang, Mar. 31, 1999. BS, Tsing-Hua U., Hsin-chu, Taiwan, 1986; PhD, U. Calif., Riverside, 1993. Rsch assoc. Okla. State U., Stillwater, 1993-94; assoc. prof. Chung Hsing U., Taichung, Taiwan, 1994-99, prof., 1999—; cons. Ming-Wei Enterprise Assn., Taichung, Taiwan, 1994—, Kuoeh Tsuan Sci. Co., 1999—. Contbr. articles to profl. jours including: Plant Physiology, Proceedings Nat. Acad. Sci. USA, Jour. Cell Biology, Jour. Biolog. Chemistry, Botanical Bull. Acad. Sinica, Jour. Biochemistry, Plant Cell Physiology, Jour. Agri. Food Chem. Recipient Outstanding Rsch. award Nat. Sci. Coun. Rep. of China, 1999. Mem. Japanese Soc. Plant Physiologists, N.Y. Acad. Scis. Avocation: table tennis. Office: Grad Inst Agrl Biotech, Chung Hsing U, T'aichung Taiwan

TZENG, CHII-RUEY, obstetrician, gynecologist; b. Ping-Tung, Taiwan, China, Aug. 1, 1951; s. Yung-Hsiang and Chu (Chiao) T.; m. Yuh-Huey Charng, Jan. 11, 1987; children: Wan-Tin, Shang-Yu (Jeffery). MD, Taipei Med. Coll., 1976; MPH in Maternal and Child Health, Harvard U., 1981. Lectr. and sr. physician sect. infertility Dept. Ob/Gyn., Va. Gen. Hosp., Norfolk, 1982; dir. Lab. of In Vitro Fertilization and Embryo Transfer Vets. Gen. Hosp., Dept. Ob-Gyn., Taiwan, 1984-90; assoc. prof. sect. infertility/reproductive endocrinology Nat. Yang-Ming Med. Coll., Dept. Ob-Gyn., Taipei, Taiwan, 1987-91; chief divsn. family planning, dept. ob-gyn. Taipei Med. Coll., Taipei, 1991-93; dir. dept. ob-gyn. Taipei Med. Coll. Hosp., Taipei, 1991-93, vice-supt., head, assoc. prof. dept. ob-gyn., 1993—, dir. Ctr. Reproductive Medicine and Scis., 1994—; ofcl. rep. World Congress on Endometriosis, Salvador, Bahia, Brazil, 1994. Contbr. articles to profl. jours.; inventor in field. 2nd lt. Chinese Air Force, 1976-78. Named Best Doctor in Clin. Work, Vets. Gen. Hosp., China, 1985, The Best Rsch. Achievement/Lectureship/Scholarship in ARTA, Internat. Conf. for MC Chang Festschrift, 1992. Mem. Endocrine Soc. The Republic of China, Am. Fertility Soc. (mem. IVF spl. interest group), Mass. Med. Soc., Assn. ob Ob/Gyn of China, Chinese Soc. Genetics (bd. dirs. 1993—), Soc. for Implantation and Early Pregnancy in Humans (internat. adv. com. 1992), Chinese Fertility Soc. (pres. 1996—, v.p. 1994-96), Taiwan Fertility Soc. (pres. 1996-98). Avocations: music, painting, reading, travel. Home: 3F, 60 Tien-Mou West Rd, Taipei Taiwan Office: Taipei Med Coll Hosp, 252 Wu Hsing St, Taipei Taiwan

TZENG, PEI-YUAN, aeronautical engineering educator, researcher; b. Taichung, Taiwan, Republic of China, Jan. 1, 1951; s. Mu-Tsuan and Sheu-Tsun (Huang) T.; m. Chiu-Hsiang Wang, Dec. 17, 1978; children: Yih-Hwei, Yun-Hsin, Yun-Fang. BS in Aero. Engring., Chung Cheng Inst. Tech., Taoyuan, Republic of China, 1973; MS in Aero. Astro., Stanford U., 1977, engr. degree in aero. astro., 1978; PhD in Aero. Engring., U. Mich., 1985. Tchr. asst. Chung Cheng Inst. Tech., Taoyuan, 1973-75, lectr., 1978-81, assoc. prof., 1986-96, chmn. dept. mech. engr., 1987-89, chmn. dept. aero. engring., 1989-92, dean Grad. Sch., 1992-94, prof., 1996—; assoc. rschr. Chung Shan Inst. Sci. Tech., Lungtan, 1986-91; patent referee Ctrl. Std. Bur., Taipei, 1990-93; examiner Ministry of Nat. Exam., Taipei, 1987, 92, 96. Assoc. editor-in-chief Transaction of Aero. and Astro. Soc. of Republic of China, 1987-89; editor-in-chief Jour. Chung Cheng Inst. Tech., 1992-94; editor Transaction of Aero. & Astro. Soc. of Republic of China, 1994—; contbr. articles to profl. jours. including Jour. Physics of Fluids, AIAA Jour., Jour. Numerical Heat Transfer, Internat. Jour. Numerical Methods for Heat and Fluid Flow, Can. Jour. Chem. Engring., among others. Hon. officer Bay Area Chinese Student Assn., San Francisco, 1977; vice chmn. Mich. Republic of China Student Club, Ann Arbor, 1984. Recipient Model Student award Taichung City Govt., 1965, Outstanding Instr. award Ministry of Nat. Def., 1988, 97, Rsch. award Nat. Sci. Coun., 1997, 99, 2000, Model Alumni award Chung Cheng Inst. Tech., 1998; grantee Nat. Sci. Coun., Taipei, 1987, 89, 90, 92, 93, 95-99, 2000. Mem. Aero. and Astro. Soc. (bd. dirs. 1989—), U. Mich. Alumni Assn. (bd. dirs. Taiwan chpt. 1993—), Soc. Theoretical and Applied Mechanics of Republic of China, Chinese Soc. Mech. Engrs., Combustion Inst. of the Republic of China. Avocations: playing clarinet, swimming, Chinese calligraphy. Home: 7F 317 San-Kuang Rd, Chung-Li 320, Taiwan Office: Chung Cheng Inst Tech Tahsi, Dept Aero Engring, Taoyuan 33509, Taiwan

TZORTZAKAKIS, EMMANUEL A., agriculturalist; b. Heraklion, Crete, Greece, June 18, 1965; s. Antonios E. Tzortzakakis and Tarsia A. Tzortzakaki. BSc, Agrl. U., Athens, 1988; PhD, U. Reading, England, 1993. Rschr. Nat. Agrl. Rsch. Found., Heraklion, 1994—. Contbr. articles to profl. jours. Mem. N.Y. Acad. Scis., European Soc. Nematologists, Soc. Nematologists. Office: NAGREF Plant ProtectionInst, PO Box 1802, 71110 Heraklion Crete, Greece

TZURIEL, DAVID, psychologist, educator; b. Tel Aviv, Sept. 23, 1946; s. Yitzchack and Lea Subbari; m. Yona Roizenblit, Aug. 13, 1969; children: Karen, Sheera, Erez, Hadas, Na'ama, Tehia. BA, Bar-Ilan U., Ramat-Gan, Israel, 1970, MA, 1974; PhD, Vanderbilt U., 1977. Lic. clin. psychologist, ednl. psychologist. Prof. Bar-Ilan U., Ramat-Gan, 1977—; sr. psychologist intern Inst. for Enhancement of Learning Potential, Jerusalem, 1980-95; chair Spl. Edn. Program, Israel. Author: (books) Cognitive Modifiability, 1998, Dynamic Assessment of Young Children, 2000; editor: (books) Interactive Assessment, 1992, Mediated Learning Experience, 1999. Mem. APA, Internat. Assn. for Cognitive Edn. (pres. 1999-01), Israeli Psychol. Assn. Mem. Nat. Religious Party. Jewish. Office: Bar-Ilan U, Sch Edn, Ramat-Gan Israel

UAHWATANASAKUL, YONG, physician; b. Bangkok, Thailand, June 24, 1937; s. U. Chu Liang and Tan Liang Enah; m. Jeamjit Sethbhakdi, June 8, 1963; children: Suchart Kenneth, Kesara, Kuntida, Kalaya. BA in Chemistry cum laude, Harvard Coll., 1959; MD, Harvard U., 1963. Diplomate Am. Bd. Internal Medicine, Thai Bd. of Internal Medicine, Thai Bd. Endocrinology. Intern Newton-Wellesley Hosp., Newton Lower Falls, Mass., 1963-64; asst. resident New England Deaconess Hosp., Boston, 1964-66; fellow Joslin Clinic, Boston, 1965-66; clin. fellow in endocrinology Mass. Gen. Hosp., Boston, 1966-67; rsch. fellow in medicine Harvard Med. Sch., Boston, 1966-67; lectr. in medicine Chulalongkorn U., Bangkok, Thailand, 1968-97; chmn., bd. dirs. CMB Packaging, Thailand, 1984-94; vice chmn., bd. dirs. Bangkok Met. Bank, 1974-97; chmn., exec. com. Hwa Chiew Gen. Hosp., Bangkok, 1981-92. Author: (with others) World Book of Diabetes in Practice, 1982, Diabetes Melitus in General Medicine, 1983. Bd. trustees Pok Tek Tung Found., Bangkok, 1981—, U. Chu Liang Found., Bangkok, 1974-99, Chulalongkorn Med. Sch. Found., Bangkok, 1980-84. Fellow Royal Coll. of Physicians (Thailand); mem. Am. Diabetes Assn., The Royal Thai Sports Club (life), Thai Mgmt. Assn. (life), Harvard Club of Thailand (life mem.). Avocation: photography. Home: 204 Soi Srinakorn, Linchee Rd, Bangkok 10120, Thailand Office: Medi-Clinic Regent Ho 5 Fl, 183 Rajdamri Rd, Bangkok 10330, Thailand

UBAIZ, MAMEDE ALI, physician; b. Barretos, Sao Paulo, Brazil, July 27, 1935; s. Ubaiz S'alim Ali and Fauzia Rage (Ubaiz; m. Nadir Cassiano, May 29, 1965; children: Samir, Soraya, Sandro, Sergio. MD, U. Sao Paulo, 1993. Diplomate in medicine. Med. asst. St. Marcelina Hosp., Sao Paulo, 1963-69, House of Mercy, Sao Paulo, 1969; physician Med. Ctr., Sao Paulo, 1969—. Author: Arabic Language Grammatical Study, 1980. Served to lt. Brazilian Res. Mem. Union Siria. Islamic. Avocation: astronomy. Home: Av 21 No 389 Barretos, São Paulo 14780, Brazil Office: Med Ctr, Av 21 No 389, Barretos São Paulo 14780, Brazil

UBBINK, JOHAN BERNARD, research scientist, laboratory administrator; b. Utrecht, The Netherlands, July 8, 1968; arrived in Switzerland, 1998; Student, Zernike Coll., Groningen, The Netherlands, 1980-86; MSc in Chemistry, U. Leiden, The Netherlands, 1991; PhD in Chem. Engring., Delft U. Tech., The Netherlands, 1997. Rsch. asst. U. Bristol, U.K., 1990-91; rsch. scientist TNO Prins Maurits Lab., Rijswijk, The Netherlands, 1991-92; sr. scientist Givaudan Roure Rsch. Ltd., Dubendorf, Switzerland, 1998-99; rsch. scientist Nestlé Rsch. Ctr., Lausanne, Switzerland, 1999—; vis. scientist. Moscow State U., 1996-97. Contbr. rsch. papers to profl. jours. 2d lt. Royal Netherlands Army, 1991-92. Travel grantee Netherlands Orgn. for Sci. Rsch., Moscow, 1996. Mem. Royal Dutch Chem. Soc., Am. Chem. Soc., Controlled Release Soc. Home: Rte Vers-chez-les-Blanc 2, CH-1073 Savigny Switzerland Office: Nestlé Rsch Ctr, Vers-Chez-Les-Blancs, CH-1000 Lausanne Switzerland

UBELIS, ARNOLDS, physicist; b. Preili dist., Latvia, May 13, 1943; s. Peteris and Alma (Vevere) U.; children: Ieva, Andzs, Darta, Alma-Anna, Arnolds-Visvaldis; m. Regina Skila, Aug. 16, 1996. MSc, U. Latvia, 1969; PhD, U. St. Petersburg, 1983. From rschr. to sr. rschr., lect. U. Latvia, Riga, 1969—; expert cons. in field. Editor: Radiative and Collisional Characteristics of Atoms and Molecules Tellurium, 1989; contbr. articles to profl. jours. Fellow Union Latvian Scientists, Internat. Network Engring. & Scientists, N.Y. Acad. Scis.

UBEROI, MAHINDER SINGH, aerospace engineering educator; b. Delhi, India, Mar. 13, 1924; came to U.S., 1945, naturalized, 1960; s. Kirpal Singh and Sulaksha (Kochar) U. B.S., Punjab U., Lahore, India, 1944; M.S., Calif. Inst. Tech., 1946; D.Eng., Johns Hopkins U., 1952. Registered profl. engr. Mem. faculty U. Mich., Ann Arbor, 1953-63, prof. aeros., 1959-63, vis. prof., 1963-64; prof. aerospace engring. U. Colo., Boulder, 1963—, chmn. dept. aerospace engring., 1963-75; fellow F. Joint Inst. for Lab. Astrophysics, Boulder, 1963-74; hon. rsch. fellow Harvard U., 1975-76; invited prof. U. Que., Can., 1972-74; vis. scientist Max Planck Inst. for Astrophysics, Munich, 1974. Author numerous rsch. publs. on dynamics of ionized and neutral gases and liquids with and without chem. reactions, gravity and electromagnetic fields; editor Cosmic Gas Dynamics, 1974. Council mem. Ednl. TV Channel 6, Inc., Denver, 1963-66. Guggenheim fellow Royal Inst. Tech., Stockholm, Sweden, 1958; exchange scientist U.S. Nat. Acad. Scis.; exchange scientist Soviet Acad. Scis., 1966. Mem. Am. Phys. Soc., Tau Beta Pi. Home: 819 6th St Boulder CO 80302-7418

UBUKA, TOSHIHIKO, biochemistry educator, dean; b. Kagaminocho, Okayama, Japan, Jan. 31, 1934; s. Yoshio and Shigeko (Hashimoto) U.; m. Satoko Iwamiya, Oct. 18, 1960; children: Takayoshi, Hiromi, Atsue. MD, Okayama U., 1959, PhD, 1964. With Okayama U., 1964-73, asst. prof., 1973-80, assoc. prof. Med. Sch., 1980-81, prof. Med. Sch., 1981-99, dean Med. Sch., 1997-99, prof. emeritus, 1999—; prof., dean Kawasaki U of Med Welfare, 1999—; rsch. assoc. Med. Coll. Cornell U., N.Y.C., 1968-71. Co-author: Methods in Enzymology, vol. 143, 1987; editor Acta Med Okayama, 1980-99, Physiol Chem Phys and Med NMR, 1982—, Amino Acids, 1991—; chief editor Acta Med Okayama, 1987-90. Fellow Japanese Biochem. Soc., Japanese Soc. Nutrition and Food Sci.; mem. AAAS, N.Y. Acad. Scis., Internat. Soc. Amino Acid Rsch., Soc. Study Inborn Errors Metabolism, The Protein Soc. Achievements include research in sulfur biochemistry, sulfur nutrition, cysteine metabolism in mammals, protein modification with mixed disulfides, inborn errors of cysteine metabolism. Home: 527-1 Nishikarakawa, Okayama 701-1213, Japan Office: Okayama U Med Sch Dept Biochem Kawasaki U Med Welfare, 288 Matsushima Kurashiki, Okayama 701-0193, Japan

UCAN, OSMAN NURI, electrical engineer, educator; b. Kars, Turkey, Jan. 1, 1960; s. Haci and Nermin (Firat) U.; m. Birsen Bayar, May 30, 1988; children: Bahadir, Bengisu. BS, Istanbul Tech. U., 1985, MSc, 1988, DSc, 1995. From asst. to assoc. prof. Istanbul U., 1986—. Mem. IEEE. Office: Istanbul U Engring Fac, Elec & Electronic Dept, 34850 Avcilar Istanbul, Turkey

UÇAR, BIRSEN KESKIN, pediatrics educator; b. Gaziantep, Turkey, Oct. 12, 1962; d. Mehmet Yasar and Remziye (Töret) Keskin; m. Ali Yalçin Uçar, Aug. 18, 1989; children: Müge, Zeynep. MD, U. Istanbul. Resident in pediatrics Karadeniz Tech. U. Faculty of Medicine, Trabzon, Turkey; assoc. prof. pediat. U. Osmangazi Faculty Medicine, Eskisehir, Turkey, 1999—. Mem. Turkish Nat. Pediatric Soc., UNICEF Turkish Nat. Com. Soc. Avocations: reading books, listening to music, swimming. Office: U Osmangazi Faculty Med, Dept Pediatrics, TR-26480 Eskisehir Turkey

UCHIDA, HIROHISA, engineering educator; b. Tokyo, Nov. 25, 1949; s. Hideo and Hisako (Takahashi) U.; m. Susanne Dagmar, Weilert, July 6, 1979; children: Helmut-Takahiro, Herman-Hideyuki, Herbert-Akihito. B Engring., Tokai U., Tokyo, 1973, M Engring., 1975; DS, U. Stuttgart, Germany, 1977. Cert. tech. H.S. tchr., Japan Ministry of Edn. Rschr. Max-Planck-Inst. for Metals Rsch., Stuttgart, 1975-81; asst. prof. Tokai U., Hiratsuka, 1981-84, assoc. prof., 1984-90, prof., 1990—; supermagnetic materials rsch. project leader Kanagawa Acad. Sci. and Tech., Kawasaki, Japan, 1990-94; energy materials rsch. project leader Gen. Rsch. Orgn. Tokai Edn. Sys., Tokyo, 1994—; exec. dir. divsn. rsch. Tokai U., Hiratsuka, 1997—; project leader R&D of Magnetic Materials for Space Tech., Nat. Space Devel. Agy., 1995—; chmn. Coun. Eco-Energy City Network Sys., New Energy & Indsl. Tech. Devel. Orgn., 1997—; mem. Coun. Indsl. Tech., Ministry Internat. Trade & Industry, 1998—; mem. Univ.-Industry Collaboration com. UNESCO, 2000—; lectr. in field. Editor, chmn. conf. procs. Jour. Alloys & Compounds, 1995, 97; mem. editl. bd. Internat. Jour. Hydrogen Energy, 1999—; internat. adv. bd. Jour. Advanced Engring. Materials, 1999—; editl. bd. Internat. Jour. Hydrogen Energy; internat. adv. bd. Jour. Advanced Engring. Materials, 1999—; contbr. over 150 articles to papers and books and profl. publs.; columnist Nikkei Sangyo Newspaper, 1995—. Bd. dirs. German-Japan Assn., Stuttgart, 1977-81; councilor Assn. of State Bagen-Wuerttemberg, Germany, Tokyo, 1995—, Honda Found., Tokyo, 1991—. Recipient Japan Rare Earth Soc. award, 1997, Japanese Min. Edn. award, Inst. Applied Energy award, Internat. Assn. Hydrogen Energy award, 1998, Future Tech. award 98 World Solar Car Rallye, 1998. Mem. Japan Hydrogen Energy Assn. (v.p. 1996—); Internat. Assn. Hydrogen Energy ((mem. adv. bd. and Permanent Working Sci. Com. on Hydrogen Treatment of Materials, 1998—). Avocations: overseas travel, mountain hiking, driving. E-mail:huchida@keyaki.cc.u-tokai.ac.jp. Fax: 463-58-1812. Office: Tokai U Sch Engring, 1117 Kita-Kaname, Hiratsuka Kanagawa 259-1292, Japan

UCHIDA, MITSUKO, pianist; b. Dec. 20, 1948; d. Fujio and Yasuko Uchida. Student, Hochschule für Musik, Vienna, Austria. First recital at age 14, Vienna; performs regularly with Berlin Philharm., Vienna Philharm., Cleve. Orch., others; performed complete Mozart sonatas London, 1982, Tokyo, 1983, N.Y.C., 1991; Schubert and Schönberg recitals Salzberg, Austria, London, Vienna, Tokyo, others, 1994-96; recs. include complete piano sonatas and concertos of Mozart, Beethoven's piano concertos, Debuey's Etudes, Schumann's Carnaval. Recipient 1st prize Beethoven Competition, Vienna, 1968, 2d pl. award competition, Warsaw, Poland, 1969, others. Avocation: listening to music. Address: Van Walsum Mgmt Ltd, 4 Addison Bridge Pl, London W14 8XP, England

UCHIDA, TATSUO, science educator; b. Kosai-shi, Japan, Nov. 21, 1947; s. Yasutaro and Tomie (Ohta) U.; m. Kayo Yoshida, Apr. 27, 1984; 3 children. BS, Tohoku U., Sendai, Japan, 1970, MS, 1972, PhD, 1975. From rsch. assoc. to assoc. prof. Tohoku U., Sendai, 1975-89, prof., 1989—. Inventor color liquid crystal display (Spl. Recognition award Soc. for Info. Display 1988). Recipient Sci. and Tech. Agy. award, 1986, Ichimura Sci. award Rsch. Devel. Found., 1993. Fellow Soc. for Info. Display, 1994. Home: Miyagino-ku, 2-1-11 Takasago, 983-0014 Sendai Japan Office: Tohoku U Grad Sch Engring, Dept Elecs Aramaki Aoba-ku, 980-8579 Sendai Japan

UCHIDA, TSUNEKO, biochemist, researcher, educator; b. Aioi, Hyogo, Japan, Mar. 15, 1932; d. Yukichi and Yuku (Arata) Tsujimura; m. Tadashi Uchida, Mar. 27, 1956; children: Yuko, Keiko. BS in Chemistry, Nagoya (Japan) U., 1954, MS in Biochemistry, 1956; PhD, U. Tokyo, 1966. Rschr. Inst. Infectious Diseases, U. Tokyo, Faculty Sci., 1956-61, lectr. dept. biophysics and biochemistry, 1961-71; chief Lab. Biochemistry, Mitsubishi Kasei Inst. Life Scis., Tokyo, 1971-81, dir. dept. rschr. on active substances, 1981-87, dir. dept. biomolecular rsch., 1987-92, emeritus rschr., 1992-97; reviewer Jour. Biochemistry, 1977-79, 80-82; lectr. Tokyo Inst. Tech., 1991, Meiji U., Tokyo, 1993—, Tokyo U. Agr., 1995—; organizer Recent Aspects of Alzheimer's Disease Symposium, 1995; mem. invited staf Nat. Chem. Lab. for Industry, Ministry Internat. Trade and Industry, 1981; mem. rsch. promoting com. Sci. and tech. Agy., 1981-84. Author: The Enzymes, Vol. IV, 1971, CRC Handbook of Microbiology, Vol. III, 1973, Vol. VIII, 1987; editor, author: From Biochemistry to the Life Sciences, 1985. Rsch. grantee Naito Found., 1969; grantee Japan Ministry Edn., Sci. and Culture, 1989-93. Mem. Japanese Biochem. Soc. (coun.), Molecular Biology Soc. Japan, Japanese Soc. Neurochemistry. Achievements include research on microbial RNases (T1, T2, U1, U2, also others) and nucleic acid-related enzymes; function and structue of RNase H domain of reverse transcriptase; mechanism of formation of PHF in Alzheimer's disease and involvement of tau protein kinases in AD(TPK1/GSK3 beta and TPKII/CDK5+p23). Home: 5-33-6-305 Kamikitazawa, Tokyo 156-0057, Japan

UCHIGATA, YASUKO, physician; b. Nanatsuka-machi, Ishikawa, Japan, May 22, 1951; d. Jinji and Mitsuko Uchigata. MD, Kanazawa (Japan) U., 1977, PhD, 1981. Specialist in pediatrics, endocrinology, diabetes. Vis. fellow NIH, Bethesda, Md., 1983-87; vis. assoc. NIH, Bethesda, 1987; asst. Diabetes Ctr., Tokyo Women's Med. Coll., 1987-92, lectr., 1992-96, assoc. prof., 1996—; rsch. assoc. dept. biochemistry Toyama Med. and Pharm. U., 1981-83. Recipient award Uehara Meml. Life Sci. Found., Tokyo, 1990, award Naito Meml. Found., Tokyo, 1990, Shionogi Lilly prize, 1992, Yayoi Yoshioka prize Japanese Women's Doctor Soc., 1997; grantee Ministry Edn., Sci. and Culture, Japan, 1994—. Mem. Japan Endocrine Soc., Japan Diabetes Soc., Am. Diabetes Assn. Avocations: art appreciation, music appreciation. Home: Shinjuku 1-35-3-1304, Shnjuku-ku, Tokyo 160, Japan

UCHINO, KENJI, electrical engineer; b. Tokyo, Apr. 3, 1950; came to U.S., 1991; s. Yutaka and Akie (Hamazaki) U.; m. Michiko Uchino. BSc, Tokyo Inst. Tech., 1973, MS, 1975, PhD, 1981. Rsch. assoc. Tokyo Inst. Tech., 1976-85; assoc. prof. Sophia U., Tokyo, 1985-93; prof. Pa. State U., University Park, 1991—; dir. Internat. Ctr. for Actuators & Transducers, Pa. State U., 1992—; v.p. NF Elec. Instruments, Inc., 1992-94; exec. assoc. editor Kluwer Academic, Boston, 1994—; profl. com. mem. Space Shuttle Utilizing Com., Tokyo, 1986-88; standing auditor Tokyo Savor Elec. Co., Ltd., 1986-91. Author: Piezoelectric/Electrostrictive Actuators, 1986, Piezoelectric Actuators — Problem Solving, 1991, Piezoelectric Actuators and Ultrasonic Motors, 1997; editor (video) Piezoelectric Actuators, 1991. Recipient Best Paper award Japan Soc. Oil/Air Pressure Control, 1987, Best Movie Meml. award Japan Sci. Movie Fesitval, 1989. Fellow Am. Ceramics Soc.; mem. IEEE, Japanese Soc. Applied Physics, Smart Actuators/Sensors Soc. (chmn.), Japan Tech. Transfer Assn. Achievements include patents for multiple ceramic actuator designs. Office: Pa State U 134 Materials Research Lab University Park PA 16802-4800

UCHINO, TAKASHI, research scientist; b. Osaka, Japan, Dec. 14, 1962; s. Tadayoshi and Akemi (Inada) U.; m. Yasuko Kurosu, Apr. 4, 1993; children: Natsumi, Ayumi, Wataru. B in Engring., Kyoto (Japan) U., 1987, M in Engring., 1989, PhD, 1993. Rschr. Nippon Sheet Glass Co. Ltd., Hyogo, Japan, 1992-95; instr. Kyoto U., 1995-99, assoc. prof., 1999—. Contbr. articles to profl. jours. Mem. AAAS, Am. Phys. Soc. Office: Inst Chem Rsch Kyoto Univ, Gokasho Uji, Kyoto 611-0011, Japan

UCHIYAMA, ICHIRO, psychology educator; b. Nagoya, Japan, July 29, 1956; s. Michiaki and Tomiko Uchiyama; m. Junko Suzuki, Mar. 16, 1991; 1 child, Motoharu. BA, Doshisha U., Kyoto, Japan, 1980; MA, Nagoya U., 1983, postgrad., 1987. Asst. prof. U. Shizuoka, Hamamatsu, Japan, 1988-94; asst. prof. Doshisha U., Kyoto, 1994-95, assoc. prof., 1995—. Editor: Social Psychology, 1996; author: Emotions: In Psychology for Human Understanding, 1995. Mem. com. for traffic safety Japan Automobile Fedn., Nagoya, 1988—; mgr. Osaka Traffic Sci., 1997—. Mem. Japanese Soc. Devel. Psychology (dir. 1999—), Japanese Soc. Rsch. in Emotion (dir. 1994—), Japanese Assn. Behavioral Sci. (dir. 1994—), Tokai Assn. Psychosomatic Medicine (councilor 1987—). Avocation: igo. Home: 2-25-3 Maeyama, Showa, Nagoya 466, Japan Office: Doshisha U Dept Psychology, Karasuma-Imadegawa, Kyoto 602-8580, Japan

UCHIYAMA, KATSUMI, scientist, educator; b. Tokyo, Nov. 27, 1956; s. Toshio and Sui (Shinohara) U.; m. Reiko Kobayashi; children: Miho, Yuki. M, Hoshi U., Tokyo, 1982, D, 1987. Rsch. assoc. Hoshi U., Tokyo, 1982-93, asst. prof., 1993-95; assoc. prof. Tokyo Met. U., 1995—; vis. prof. Mt. Sinai Sch. Medicine, N.Y.C., 1995. Author: Encyclopedia for Chemistry, 1989, analytical Principle and Technology, 1997. Commr. Min. Intenat. Trade and Industry, Tokyo, 1999. Recipient The Ohtani Inst. prize,

Tokyo, 1985, Excellence Poster prize Japan Chem. Soc., Tokyo, 1999; rsch. grantee JSPS, Tokyo, 1995—. Avocations: fishing, camping. Office: Tokyo Met U, Dept Applied Chem, Tokyo 192 0397, Japan

UCHRIN, CHRISTOPHER GEORGE, environmental engineer and scientist; b. South Amboy, N.J., Oct. 27, 1950; s. George Christopher and Annette Rose Marie (Skokan) U.; m. Lisa C. Ferguson, July 31, 1998; 1 child, George Henry. B in Civil Engrng., Manhattan Coll., 1972, M. in Environ. Engrng., 1974; PhD in Environ. Engrng., U. Mich., 1980. Registered profl. engrng. N.Y. Environ. engr. U.S. EPA, N.Y.C., 1972-77; Rackham fellow U. Mich., Ann Arbor, Mich., 1977-78, rsch. asst., 1978-80; asst. prof. Rutgers U., New Brunswick, N.J., 1980-86, assoc. prof., 1986-90, prof. environ. sci., 1990—; chair dept. environ. sci. Rutgers U., New Brunswick, 1991-94, dir. grad. program in environ. sci., 1986-91; co-dir. Joint PhD Program in Exposure Assessment, Rutgers U. & UMDNJ/Robert Wood Johnson Med. Sch., 1991—, coord. undergrad. curriculum in bioresource engrng., 1999—. Mem. ASCE, Am. Chem. Soc., Water Environment Fedn., Am. Soc. for Materials, Soc. Environ. Toxicology and Chemistry, N.J. Acad. Sci. (pres. 1991-92). Office: Rutgers U Dept Environ Sci PO Box 231 New Brunswick NJ 08903-0231

ÜCISIK, AHMET HIKMET, engineering educator; b. Istanbul, Turkey, Feb. 14, 1945; s. Ahmet Mekki and Afife Ücisik. MSc, Istanbul Tech. U., 1967, PhD, 1972; postdoctoral, MIT, 1973, UCLA, 1974, U. Pa., 1976. Vis. prof. McGill U., Can., 1979, U. Pa., 1980, 81, 82, Osaka U., 1986; dir. Marmara Rsch. Ctr., Gebze, Turkey, 1988-90; pres. Inst. for Advanced Tech., Gebze, 1992-93; head Inst. of Biomed. Engrng., Bogazici U., Istanbul, 1987—; mem. Turkish Std. Inst., Ankara, 1993—; pres. Inst. for Advanced Tech., 1992-93; dir. Tubitak's Marmara Rsch. Ctr., Gebze, 1988-90. Recipient award Japan Soc. for Promotion Sci., 1986, Turkish Sci. and Tech. Rsch. Coun., 1984, 90, Am. Soc. for Non Destructive Testing, 1974. Mem. Am. Ceramic Soc., Am. Soc. for Metals, Orthop. Rsch. Soc., Material Rsch. Soc., Soc. Japanese Biomed. Engrng., Japan Soc. Dental Materials, N.Y. Acad. Scis. Avocations: photography, history of technology. E-mail: ucisile@hotmail.com. Fax: 90-212-2277934. Office: Bogazici U, Inst of Biomed Engring, Bebek 80815, Turkey

UDA, MASASHI, personal care industry executive; b. Kawanoe, Ehime, Japan, Apr. 4, 1948; d. Naomasa and Fumiko (Takahashi) U.; m. Yoko Yamada; 3 children. BL, Waseda UC, Japan, 1971. With pers. dept. Nagase Co., Ltd., Japan, 1971-77; with sales dept. Toyo Eizai Corp., Osaka, Japan, 1977-83, dir., 1983-86, mng. dir., 1986-88, pres., 1988—. Mem. Rotary Club. Avocations: listen to music, watching pictures, Wondervogel. Office: Toyo Eizai Corp, 1-4-11 Kawaramachi Chuo-ku, 541-0048 Osaka Japan

UDAGAWA, TAKESHI, physicist, educator; b. Tokyo, May 3, 1932; came to U.S., 1970; s. Saheiji Udagawa and Teruko (Yamazaki) Urayama; m. Yukiko Amano, Mar. 20, 1960 (dec. Oct. 1989); children: Yoichi, Taturo; m. Mami Eto, Apr. 15, 1991. BS, Tokyo Inst. Sci., 1957; MS, Tokyo U. of Edn., 1959, PhD, 1962. Instr. Tokyo Inst. Tech., 1962-64; rsch. assoc. Fla. State U., Tallahassee, 1964-66; rsch. fellow Niels Bohn Inst., Copenhagen, 1966-68; assoc. prof. Kyoto (Japan) U., 1968-70; prof. dept. physics U. Tex., Austin, 1970—; rsch. fellow Kernforschungsanlage, Juelich, Germany, 1981-95. Contbr. articles to profl. jours. Rsch. grantee Dept. Energy, Washington, 1970-96. Mem. Am. Phys. Soc., Japanese Phys. Soc. Achievements include contbns. to various aspects of nuclear reaction theories. Home: 4018 Amy Cir Austin TX 78759-8146 Office: U Tex Dept Physics Austin TX 78712

UDALOV, YURI BORISOVITCH, physicist; b. Yuzhno-Sakhalinsk, Russia, Jan. 29, 1955; s. Boris V. and Judwiga I. (Lasitskaya) U.; m. Elena N. Kislova, Jan. 30, 1981; children: Alexander, Nickolai. Diploma phycisist, cum laude, Engrng. Physics Inst., 1978; PhD, P.N. LeBedev Physics Inst., 1984. Rsch. assoc. LeBedev Physics Inst., Moscow, 1978-90, U. Twente, Enschede, The Netherlands, 1990-99, Netherlands Centrum for Laser Rsch., 1999—; CIO Detexxion B.V., 1999—; Triz cons. IDEA Found., Euschede, 1995—. Author: Control of Spectra of Molecular Lasers, 1996; patentee in field. NWO fellowship Dutch Scientific Orgn., 1994. Office: U Twente, Drienerlolaan 23 POB 217, 7500AE Enschede The Netherlands

UDASHEN, ROBERT NATHAN, lawyer; b. Amarillo, Tex., June 10, 1953; s. Leo Joe and Esther K. (Klugsberg) U.; m. Dale Lynn Sandgarten, Aug. 15, 1976. BA with high honors, U. Tex., 1974, JD, 1977. Bar: Tex. 1977, U.S. Ct. Appeals (5th cir.) 1978, U.S. Dist. Ct. (no. and so. dists.) Tex. 1978, U.S. Ct. Appeals (11th cir.) 1981, U.S. Supreme Ct. 1981, U.S. Dist. Ct. (ea. dist.) Tex. 1989, U.S. Dist. Ct. (we. dist.) Tex. 1991. Staff atty. Staff Counsel for Inmates, Huntsville, Tex., 1977-79; assoc., ptnr. Crowder, Mattox & Udashen, Dallas, 1979-85; ptnr. Udashen & Goldstucker, Dallas, 1985-87; pvt. practice, 1987-94; ptnr. Milner, Lobel, Goranson, Sorrels, Udashen & Wells, Dallas, 1995-2000, Milner, Goranson, Sorrels, Udashen & Wells, Dallas, 2000—; bd. dirs. Open, Inc., Dallas; instr. trial advocacy Sch. Law So. Meth. U., 1993-95; adj. prof. criminal procedure Sch. Law So. Meth. U., 1998-99. Contbr. articles to profl. jours. Adv. bd. Coalition for Safer Dallas, 1994. Mem. State Bar Tex. (penal code com. 1992-93), Nat. Assn. Criminal Def. Lawyers, Tex. Criminal Def. Lawyers Assn., Dallas Criminal Def. Lawyers Assn. Office: Milner Goranson Sorrels Udashen & Wells 2515 Mckinney Ave Ste 1500 Dallas TX 75201-7604

UDEH, KENNETH OGBONNA, food biotechnologist, researcher; b. Owerri, Nigeria, May 26, 1959; arrived in Poland, 1990; s. Cyril Okechukwu and Regina Uba (Nnodim) U.; m. Zofia Urszula Skrzydlewska, Apr. 1, 1989; children: Paulina, Diana. Diploma in cold storage tech., Coll. Food Tech., Sandomierz, Poland, 1981; MSc, Lublin (Poland) Agrl. U., 1986, PhD in Food Biotech., 1996. Rsch. fellow Lublin Agrl. U., 1996—; dep. dir. gen. Internat. Biog. Ctr., Cambridge, Eng.-Poland, 1999—. Contbr. articles to profl. jours.; patentee in field. Grantee Polish Sci. Com., 1991-94. Mem. Polish Food Technologists' Soc. (Lublin sect.), N.Y. Acad. Scis. Avocations: football, table tennis, music (pop and classical). Office: Lublin Agrl U Dept Food Tech, Akademicka 13, 20-950 Lublin Poland

UDEM, THOMAS, physicist; b. Bayreuth, Germany, Sept. 25, 1962; s. Eberhard and Ingrid (Deyerling) U.; 1 child, Hannah Frank. Diploma, U. Giessen, Germany, 1993; PhD, Ludwig-Maximilians-U., Munich, Germany, 1997. With Max Planck Inst. for Quantum Optics, Garching, Germany. Co-recipient Philip Morris Rsch. award, 1998. Office: Max Planck Inst Quantenoptk, Hans Kopfermann Str 1, 85748 Garching Germany

UDINA, IRINA GENNAD'EVNA, geneticist; b. Leonidovo, Russia, May 18, 1955; d. Gennadii Nickolaevich and Raisa Nickiforovna (Sivakova) U.; m. Andrei Viktonovich Vereshchetin, July 13, 1985 (div. Sept. 1989); 1 child, Anna Vereshchetina. Degree in biol. scis., IOGEN, Russian Acad. Scis., Moscow, 1990. Rschr. IOGEN, Russian Acad. Scis., 1978-94, sr. rschr., 1994—; dep. chief comparative animal genetics lab. IOGEN, 1996-99; tchr. biology gymnasia of Acad. Slavic Culture, 1993-95. Author: Bovine Major Histocompatability Complex, 1993, Human Gene Therapy of the Former USSR Territory, Vol. 1, 2000; translator Genetika, Moscow, 1996-98; contbr. articles to sck. publs. Fellow in biodiversity Soros, 1992-93, 94-95; grantee Russian Human Genome Project, 1993, 95, Russian Fund for Fundamental Rschrs., 1996-98. Mem. HUGO. Avocations: swimming, travel, photography. Office: Vavilov Gen Genet Inst RAS, Gubkin 3, 117809 Moscow Russia

UDJO, ERIC OGHENERIOBORORUE, federal agency administrator; b. Abraka, Nigeria, Mar. 20, 1954; arrived in South Africa, 1996; s. Alexson Majemite and Mary (Igun) U.; m. Eugenia Nasibagha Jumbo, Mar. 20, 1987; children: Okeroghene, Oghenevwogaga. BSc in Sociology, U. Ibadan, Nigeria, 1978; MSc in Med. Demography, U. London, 1981, PhD in Med. Demography, 1985. Tchr. Ogbavweni Grammar Sch., Usiefrun, Nigeria, 1973-75; tutor Sch. of Nursing, Bauchi, Nigeria, 1978-79; grad. asst. to sr. lectr. U. Maisuauri, Nigeria, 1979-90; postdoctoral fellow Population Coun. Am., Harare, Zimbabwe, 1990-92; sr. lectr. U. Botswana, Gaborone, 1992-96; dir. Stats. South Africa, Pretoria, 1997—; cons. UN, N.Y.C., 1992, Ministry of Fin., Gaborone, 1995-96, Botswana Govt., 1996; assoc. Ctr. Population Studies U. Pretoria, 1998—. Contbr. articles to profl. jours. Vice-sec. Botswana Shukokai Karate Union, Gaborone, 1994-96; asst. instr. Botswana Sukokai Karate Sch., Gaborone, 1994-96. Rsch. grantee U. Maiduguri, 1982, The Rockefeller Found., 1989. Mem. N.Y. Acad. Scis., Internat. Union Sci. Study of Population, Demographic Assn. So. Africa. Avocations: tennis, table tennis, squash, swimming, karate. Office: Stats South Africa, 274 Schoeman St Pvt Bag X44, 0001 Pretoria South Africa

UDOEV, YURI PAVLOVICH, physicist, educator; b. Moscow, Nov. 22, 1937; s. Pavel Trofimovich and Lidiya Nikolaevna (Smirnova) U. Engr.-physicist, Poly. Inst., Leningrad, USSR, 1961, PhD, 1974. Sr. scientist Supreme Cert. Com. USSR. Sr. engr. Poly. Inst., Leningrad, 1965-70, sr. scientific worker, 1971-93; scientific supr., cons. students' graduation works Poly. Inst. (now State Tech. U.), 1971—; docent State Tech. U., St. Petersburg, Russia, 1994—. Contbr. articles to profl. jours.; inventor in field. Grantee Internat. Sci. Found., 1993; scholar Russian Ministry Edn., 1998—. Mem. Internat. Soc. Optical Engrng. Office: State Tech U, 29 Polytechnicheskaya Str, 195251 Saint Petersburg Russia

UDOLPH, JÜRGEN, linguist, educator; b. Berlin, Feb. 6, 1943; s. Georg and Charlotte (Knappek) U.; m. Maria Woitalla, June 11, 1971; children: Susanne, Martin, Anja, Katja. MA, U. Göttingen, Germany, 1971, PhD, 1978. Sci. asst. U. Göttingen, 1972-79; sci. employee Acad. Sci. at Mainz, Mainz and Göttingen, Germany, 1979-2000; prof. onomastics Inst. for Slavic Langs. and Lit., Leipzig, Germany, 2000—. Author: Studies in Slavic River-Names, 1979, Investigations in Slavic and Indoeuropean Toponymics, 1975—, Onomastic Studies About the Origin of the Germanic Tribes, 1994, L. Easter The History of a Word, 1999. Henning-Kaufmann grantee, 1983. Mem. Internat. Commn. for Slavic Onomastics. Home: Steinbreite 9, D37124 Sieboldshausen Germany Office: Inst Slavic Langs and Lit, Brühl 34-50, D-04109 Leipzig Germany

UDRISTE, CONSTANTIN NICOLAE, mathematics educator; b. Turceni, Gorj, Romania, Jan. 22, 1940; s. Nicolae C. and Dumitra (Iordache) U.; m. Aneta Anghel, Aug. 21, 1965; children: Daniel Ion, Sorin Adrian. Diploma, U. Timisoara, Romania, 1963; D of Math., Babes-Bolyai U., Cluj-Napoca, 1971. Tchr. math. high sch., Bucharest, Romania, 1963-64; asst. prof. math. Poly. U. Bucharest, 1964-70, lectr., 1970-76; prof. Poly. Inst., Bucharest, 1976—. Author: Problems and....., 1980, Minima and Maxima, 1980, Algebra, Geometry and Differential Equations, 1982, Convex Functions and Optimization Methods on Riemannian Manifolds, 1994, Geometric Dynamics, 2000; rev. U. Mich. Math. Revs., 1986—, Zentralblatt für Mathematik, Berlin, 1973—; editorial bd. Math. Gazette, Bucharest, 1978-86; editor-in-chief Balkan Jour. Geometry and Its Applications, 1995—; contbr. over 100 articles to math. jours. Dep. Popular Council Nicolae Bâlcescu, Bucharest, 1965-70. Recipient Dragomir Hurmuzescu prize Acad. of R.S.R., 1985, award for disting. didectic and sci. activity Ministry Edn., Romania, 1988; corr. mem. Accademia Pelontana dei Pericolanti, Italy, 1997—; mem. rsch. bd. advisors ABF, 1999—. Mem. Soc. Math. Scis. Romania, Tensor Soc. Japan, Profs.' Council Transport Faculty, Am. Math. Soc., Balkan Soc. Geometers (v.p. 1994—). Office: Poly U Bucharest, Splaiul Independentei 313, 77206 Bucharest Romania

UDUPA, K. MANJUNATHA, aerospace structural design engineer; b. Khambadakone, India, Jan. 12, 1950; s. K. Krishna and Saraswathi Udupa; m. M.V. Vijayalakshmi, Mar. 15, 1979; childre: K. Shubha, K. Sahana. BE, KREC Surathkal, India; ME, Indian Inst. Tech., Bangalore; PhD, Indian Inst. Tech., Madras, 1990. Aero. engr. Hindustan Aeronautics Ltd., Bangalore, India, 1973-77, dep. design engr., 1977-84, mgr. design, 1984-86, sr. mgr. design, 1986-91, chief mgr. design, 1991-98, gen. mgr., 1998—. Mem. Aeronautical Soc. India. Avocations: gardening, repairing, reading, teaching. Office: Helicopter Design Bur, 560017 Bangalore India

UDUPA, NAYANABHIRAMA, pharmaceutical science educator; b. Kinnigoli, Karnataka, India, July 15, 1953; s. Sri K. Anantha Padmanabha and Kamalakshi Udupa; m. Vijayalaxmi K. Rao, Feb. 12, 1979; children: Pavithra, Shravan Kumar. B in Pharm., Banaras Hindu U., Varanasi, India, 1974, PharmM, 1976, PhD, 1987. Product devel. scientist Indian Drugs and Pharms. Ltd., Rishikesh and Gurgaon, 1976-81; product devel. exec. Citadel Fine Pharms. Ltd., Madras, India, 1981-84; lectr. pharmaceutics Banaras Hindu U., Varanasi, India, 1984-87; reader in pharmacy Coll. Pharmacy K.M.C., Manipal, India, 1987-89, prof., 1989—, prin., 1997—; convenor and organizer symposium and workshop on drug delivery, Manipal, 1991, 95, 96, 2000; prin. investigator rsch. projects on niosome encapsulated anticancer drugs CSIR, New Delhi, 1990, 95, controlled release preparations UGC, New Delhi, U. Saskatchewan (Can.), 1990—, new drug delivery systems, Dr. T.M.A. Pai Found., 1991-99; lectr. in field. Author: Selected Topics in Industrial Pharmacy, 1990, Progress in Drug Delivery-Manipal Experience, 1995, Battle Against Cancer with Pharmaceutical Weapon, 1998, others; editor Pharmag Quarterly Rsch. Jour., 1989—; mem. editl. bd. Indian Jour. Pharm. Sci., Pharm. Today; contbr. over 200 rsch. papers, 70 reviews to internat. profl. jours. Joint sec. 42d Indian Pharm. Congress, Manipal, 1990. Recipient Best Paper award, 1996; Japanese Drug Delivery Soc. fellow, Kyoto, 1993, FIP fellow, The Netherlands, 1994, AICTE and Dr. T.M.A. Pai Found. fellow, New Delhi, 1995; rsch. grantee Dandiya Endowment Trust, 1997, numerous others. Mem. Indian Pharm. Assn. (pres. 1995—, sec. Manipal br. 1987-93), Indian Inst. Indsl. Engrng. Home: Flat 2/4 KMC Quarters, Manipal Karnataka 576119, India Office: Coll Pharmacy KMC Manipal, Coll Pharm Scis, Manipal Karnataka 576119, India

UDUT, VLADIMIR VASIL'EVICH, laboratory administrator; b. Tomsk, Russia, Apr. 29, 1952; s. Udut Vasiliy Semenovich and Maria Stepanovna Galibina; m. Galina Konstantinovna Baigulova, July 27, 1974; children: Elena, Asia. Student, Med. Inst., Tomsk, 1969-76; Candidate in Med. Sci., RAMS Inst. Oncology, Tomsk, 1986; DMS, RAMS Inst. Pharmacology, Tomsk, 1994. Cert. in gen. medicine. Gynecologist Maternity Hosp., Tomsk, 1977-79; jr. sci. worker dept. anesthesiology and reanimatology Inst. Oncology, Tomsk, 1979-86, sr. sci. worker dept. tumor prophylactic & early diagnostic, 1986-87, leader tumor prophylactic and early diagnostic dept., 1986-87; mgr. clinic pharmacology lab. Inst. Pharmacology, Tomsk, 1992-97, vice-dir. clinic work, 1997—; expert of care Pub. Health Regional Dept. for Rsch. Electrophysiol. Methods, Tomsk, 1978—. Author 3 books; patentee in field. Mem. Sci. Soviet Inst. Pharmacology, Soviet Inst. Oncology, Soviet Inst. Pharmacology. Avocations: work, sports. E-mail: amd@pharm.tsu.ru. Office: RAMS Inst Pharmacology, Nakhimova St 1a, Tomsk 634028, Russia

UE, MAKOTO, chemist, researcher; b. Kihou, Mie, Japan, Sept. 21, 1956; s. Kazuya and Isao (Nishi) U.; m. Akemi Ishigami, Nov. 23, 1982; children: Nozomi, Tsubasa, Aoi, Akane. BS, Tokyo U. Agr. and Tech., 1979; MS, U. Tokyo, 1981, PhD, 1995. Rsch. chemist Mitsubishi Petrochem. Co., Tokyo, 1981-94; vis. scientist U. Pitts., 1988-89, Lawrence Berkeley Lab., Berkeley, Calif., 1989-90; sr. rsch. scientist Mitsubishi Chem. Corp., Tokyo, 1994—; part time tchr. various univs., 1999—; sec. Anodizing Rsch. Soc. in the Surface Finishing Soc. of Japan, Tokyo, 1994—. Mem. editl. bd. Electrochem. Soc. Japan, 1993-95, 97-99 (ECSJ Paper award 1994, IBA-ITE Rsch. award 1997), Surface Sci. Soc., Japan, 1999—; contbr. articles to profl. jours.; patentee in field. Mem. Am. Chem. Soc., Electrochem. Soc., Internat. Soc. Electrochemistry. Avocations: computers, tennis, running. Home: 7-14-12 Chuo Ami Inashiki, Ibaraki 300-0332, Japan Office: Mitsubishi Chem Corp, 8-3-1 Chuo-Ami Inashiki, Ibaraki 300-0332, Japan

UEDA, KENICHI, journalism educator; b. Akita, Japan, Feb. 2, 1927; s. Ichirou Ueda and Yuki Fukuchi; m. Kikuko Ueda, Sept. 10; children: Yuichi, Naoto. LLB, Waseda U., Tokyo, 1951; M Journalism, Tokyo U., 1953. Washington D.C. bur. chief The Mainichi Newspapers, Tokyo, 1968-71, polit. news editor, 1971-72, editorial chief, 1977-79, mng. editor, 1979-81, editor in chief, 1981-83; newscaster Tokyo Broadcasting System, 1983-88; prof. Tohogakuen U., 1988—. Author: Japanese Journalism, 1986. Chmn. Bd. Edn. Minato-Ku, Tokyo, 1983, 87, 90, 93, Bd. Edn. Assn., Tokyo, 1983-84; v.p. Japan Soc. Baseball League, Tokyo, 1978-83; dir. Japan Essayst Club, Tokyo, 1984—, Minato Unesco Assn., Tokyo, 1983—. Recipient Prize, Japan Newspaper Assn., Tokyo, 1979-82. Mem. Japan Journalist Club (dir. 1980-83). Buddhist. Avocations: golf, reading, playing piano, travel. Home and Office: 3-24-9 Nishiazabu, Minato-ku, Tokyo Japan

UEDA, MASAHIRO, electronics educator; b. Sabae, Fukui, Japan, July 12, 1943; s. Kinya Takashima and Chieko Ueda; m. Sachiyo Tomita, Apr. 29, 1971; children: Yasuhiro, Hiromi, Naokazu. B of Engring., Osaka (Japan) Prefectural U., 1966, M of Engring., 1968, D of Engring., 1971. Asst. prof. Ehime U., Matsuyama, Japan, 1971-75; assoc. prof. Fukui (Japan) U., 1975-83, prof., 1983—. Contbr. articles to profl. jours.; inventor in field. Office: Fukui U Edn Faculty, Bunkyo 3-9-1, 910-0017 Fukui Japan

UEDA, REED TAKASHI, historian, educator; b. Honolulu, Sept. 14, 1949; s. Goro and Mildred (Yoshimoto) U.; m. Peggy Lynn Rubin, Aug. 9, 1970; children: Katya, Alyona. BA, UCLA, 1970; MA, U. Chgo., 1973, Harvard U., 1976; PhD, Harvard U., 1981. Rsch. editor Harvard Encyclopedia of Am. Ethnic Grups, Cambridge, Mass., 1977-79; instr. Harvard U., Cambridge, Mass., 1980-81; prof. Tufts U., Medford, Mass., 1981—; vis. prof. Brandeis U., Waltham, Mass., 1986, Harvard U., 1987-89, 96; academic developer TV series Immigration, 1992; mem. steering group com. on internat. migration MIT; mem. Boston History Collaborative, 1998—; staff historian Dreams of Freedom Immigration Mus., Boston, 1999—; mem. planning com. immigration and urban history seminar Mass. Hist. Soc., 1999—. Author: Avenues to Adulthood, 1987, Postwar Immigrant America, 1994; assoc.-editor: Jour. of Interdisciplinary History, 1996—; mem. editl. bd. Harvard Educational Review, 1977-78, Am. Quar., 1993, Mass. Hist. Rev., 2000. Mem. Gov.'s Edn. Reform Rev. Commn., Commonwealth of Mass. Fellow Am. Coun. Learned Soc., Woodrow Wilson Internat. Ctr., NEH, Charles Warren Ctr. Mem. Mass. Hist. Soc., St. Botolph Club. Office: Tufts U Dept History Medford MA 02155

UEDA, SATOSHI, rehabilitation medicine physician, educator; b. Iwaki, Fukushima, Japan, Jan. 3, 1932; s. Kosaku and Yae (Suzuki) U.; m. Reiko Horie, Dec. 3, 1961; children: Hiroshi, Yaeko. MD, U. Tokyo, 1956, DMS, 1963. Med. diplomate, Japan; specialist in rehab. medicine, Japan. Prof. U. Tokyo, 1984-92, Teikyo U., Ichihara, Japan, 1992-97, Teikyo Heisei U., Ichihara, 1997-99, Japan Coll. Social Work, Tokyo, 1999—. Author: (books) Rehabilitation Medicine Illustrated, 1971, 2d edit., 1994, Philosophy of Rehabilitation, 1983. Chmn. Coun. for Phys. and Occupl. Therapists, 1994—. Mem. Internat. Phys. Rehab. Medicine (pres. 1997-99), Japanese Assn. Rehab. Medicine (exec. bd. dirs. 1984-2000, pres. 1986-87), Japanese Soc. for Rehab. of Persons with Disabilities (v.p. 1992—), Rehab. Internat. (nat. sec. for Japan 1983—). Avocations: classical music, arts, novels. Home: 3-77-20 Nakazato, Kiyose 204-0003, Japan

UEDA, WASA, medical educator; b. Osaka, Japan, Oct. 26, 1943; s. Kasaburo and Fumiko (Fukuo) U.; m. Kazuko Akamatu, Mar. 3, 1972; children: Kennichi, Yasuko. Med. degree, Okayama (Japan) Univ., 1969. Intern USAF Hosp., Tachikawa Tokyo, Japan, 1970-71; jr. staff Okayama (Japan) Univ. Hosp., 1971-72, asst. prof., 1976-80; resident U. Vt., Burlington, 1972-74, asst. prof., 1974; dept. head Kochi Prefectural Hosp., Kochi, Japan, 1974-76; vis. prof. U. Iowa, Iowa City, 1980-81; assoc. prof. Kochi Med. Sch., 1981-2000, prof., 2000—. Mem. Japan Soc. Anesthesiology, Am. Soc. Anesthesiologists. Avocations: tennis, mechanics. Office: Kochi Med Sch, Nankoku, Kochi 783-8505, Japan

UEDA, YOSHISUKE, education educator; b. Kobe, Hyogo, Japan, Dec. 23, 1936; s. Shun-Ichi and Hatsue (Kan-Nae) U.; m. Miyoko Nishijima, Mar. 11, 1962; children: Hirokazu, Masatoshi, Tatsuya. B degree, Kyoto U., 1959, M degree, 1961, Doctorate, 1965. Instr. Kyoto U., Japan, 1964-67, lectr., 1967-71, assoc. prof., 1971-85, prof., 1985-2000; prof. emeritus Kyoto U., 2000—; prof. Future U.-Hakodate, Japan, 2000—; dir. The Inst. of Elec. Engrs. of Japan, 1992-93, v.p. 1993-94. Mem. adv. bd. An Interdisciplinary Jour. of Nonlinear Sci. Chaos, 1991-95, 98—, An Internat. Jour. of Nonlinear Dynamics and Chaos in Engring. Sys. Nonlinear Dynamics, 1995—; hon. editor An Interdisciplinary Jour. of Nonlinear Sci., Chaos, Solitons and Fractals, 1991—; mem. editl. bd. Internat. Jour. Bifurcation and Chaos, 1991—; author: (monograph) The Road to Chaos, 1992. Avocations: driving, travel, reading. Office: Dept Complex Sys, Future Univ-Hakodate, Hokkaido 041-8655, Japan

UEDA, YUICHI, surgeon; b. Ikoma, Nara, Japan, Nov. 14, 1951; s. Shoei Matsuda and Teruko U.; m. Keiko Kumaki, Nov. 25, 1979; two children. MD, Kobe U. Sch. Medicine, Japan, 1976; PhD, Kyoto U., 1994. Jr. resident Tenri Hosp., Japan, 1976-78, sr. resident, 1978-82, staff surgeon, 1982-85; staff surgeon Tenri Hosp., 1986-91; registrar Nat. Heart Hosp., London, 1985-86; vice-dir. cardiovasc. surgery Tenri Hosp., 1992-95, dir. cardiovasc. surgery, 1996-99; prof., chmn. dept. cardiothoracic surgery Nagoya U., Japan, 1999—. Contbr. articles to profl. jours. Fellow Am. Coll. Chest Physicans; mem. Soc. Thoracic Surgeons, European Assn. Cardio-Thoracic Surgery. Office: Nagoya U Sch Medicine, 65 Tsurumai Showa-ku, Nagoya 466-8550, Japan

UEDING, GERT, humanities educator; b. Bunzlau, Germany, Nov. 22, 1942. Grad., Univ. Tübingen, Germany, 1970; habilitation, Univ. Tübingen, Hannover, Germany, 1973. Acad. asst. Univ., Hannover, Germany, 1970-74; prof. Univ., Oldenburg, Germany, 1974-83; prof. Univ. Tübingen, Germany, 1983—, dir. seminar for gen. rhetoric, 1988—. Author: Wilhelm Busch, 1977, Hoffmann und Campe, 1981, Klassik und Romantik, 1988, Friedrich Schiller, 1990; editor: Historisches Wörterbuch der Rhetorik, 1992, Aufklärung über Rhetorik, 1992, Jean Paul, 1993, Grundr der Rhetorik, 1994, Klassische Rhetorik, 2000, Moderne Rhetorik, 2000. Mem. Schiller-Gesellschaft, Karl-May-Gesellschaft, Lichtenberg-Gesellschaft, Ernst-Bloch-Gesellschaft. Office: Seminar Allgemeine Rhetorik, Wilhelmstrasse 50, 72074 Tübingen Germany

UEHA, SADAYUKI, engineering educator; b. Tango-cho, Kyoto, Japan, Feb. 28, 1943; m. Sachiko Minami; children: Mayu, Satoshi. B Engring., Nagoya (Japan) Inst. Tech., 1965; M Engring., Tokyo Inst. Tech., 1967, D Engring., 1970. Rsch. assoc. Tokyo Inst. Tech., 1970-80, assoc. prof., 1980-91, prof., 1992—; chmn. World Congress on Ultrasonics, 1997-99. Recipient Best Paper award Japan Soc. Applied Physics, 1997, Inst. Electronic, Info. and Comm. Engrs., 1999. Fellow Acoustical Soc. Am., Japan Soc. Ultrasonics in Medicine, Acoustical Soc. Japan (v.p. 1993-95, pres. 1997-99, Satoh Paper award 1985). Office: Tokyo Inst Tech, 4259 Nagatsuta Midoriku, Yokohama Kanagawa 226-8503, Japan

UEHLEKE, HARTMUT, retired pharmacology and toxicology educator; b. Holzminden, Germany, Aug. 17, 1924; s. Rudolf and Paula Uehleke; m. Inge Patzke, Apr. 16, 1955; children: Bernhard, Marianne, Rainer. MD, U. Marburg, Germany, 1953; PhD, U. Munich, Germany, 1958. Rsch. asst. Max-Planck-Inst. Psychiatry, Munich, 1954-56, Max-Planck-Inst. Cellular Chemistry, Munich, 1957-58; sci. asst. Inst. Pharmacology U. Tübingen, 1958-62, lectr., 1962-68, prof., 1969-74; chief dir. toxicology Fed. German Health Office, Berlin, 1975-88. Editor Arch. Toxicol., 1966-75; mem. editl. bd. Toxicology, 1974-98, Xenobiotica, 1972-82, Res. Com. Chem. Path. Pharmacol, 1970-92, Eur.J. Drug Metab. Pharmacokin., 1976; contbr. more than 200 articles to profl. jours. Recipient E. Merck award E. Merck Darmstadt Germany, 1965, Golden Merit award Italian Soc. Toxicology, 1972, Svc. award U. Ghent, 1972; WHO cancer fellow, 1967-68. Mem. N.Y. Acad. Sci. Evangelical-Lutheran. Avocations: tennis, hiking, music, sailing. Home: Karwendelstr 13, 12203 Berlin Germany

UEHLING, BARBARA STANER, educational administrator; b. Wichita, Kans., June 12, 1932; d. Roy W. and Mary Elizabeth (Hilt) Staner; children: Jeffrey Steven, David Edward. B.A., U. Wichita, 1954; M.A., Northwestern U., 1956, Ph.D., 1958; hon. degree, Drury Coll., 1978; LLD (hon.), Ohio State U., 1980. Mem. psychology faculty Oglethorpe U., Atlanta, 1959-64, Emory U., Atlanta, 1966-69; adj. prof. U. R.I., Kingston, 1970-72; dean Roger Williams Coll., Bristol, R.I., 1972-74; dean arts scis. Ill. State U., Normal, 1974-76; provost U. Okla., Norman, 1976-78; chancellor U. Mo.-Columbia, 1978-86, U. Calif., Santa Barbara, 1987-94; sr. vis. fellow Am. Council Edn., 1987; mem. Pacific Rim Pub. U. Pres. Conf., 1990-92; exec. dir. Bus. and Higher Edn. Forum, Washington, 1995-97; cons. North Ctr. Accreditation Assn., 1974-86; mem. nat. educator adv. com. to Compt. Gen. of U.S., 1978-79; mem. Commn. on Mil.-Higher Edn. Rels., 1978-79, Am.Coun. on Edn., bd. dirs. 1979-83, treas., 1982-83, mem. Bus.-Higher Edn. Forum, 1980-94, exec. com. 1991-94; Commn. on Internat. Edn., 1992-94, vice chair 1993; bd. dirs. Coun. of Postsecondary Edn., 1986-87, 90-93, Meredith Corp., 1980-99; mem. Transatlantic Dialogue, PEW Found., 1991-93. Author: Women in Academe: Steps to Greater Equality, 1979; editorial bd. Jour. Higher Edn. Mgmt., 1986-95; contbr. articles to profl. jours. Bd.

dirs., chmn. Nat. Ctr. Higher Edn. Mgmt. Sys., 1977-80; trustee Carnegie Found. for Advancement of Teaching, 1980-86, Santa Barbara Med. Found. Clinic, 1989-94; bd. dirs. Resources for the Future, 1985-94; mem. select com. on athletics NCAA, 1983-84, also mem. presdl. commn.; mem. Nat. Coun. on Edn. Rsch., 1980-82. Social Sci. Research Council fellow, 1954-55; NSF fellow, 1956-57; NIMH postdoctoral research fellow, 1964-67; named one of 100 Young Leaders of Acad. Change Mag. and ACE, 1978; recipient Alumni Achievement award Wichita State U., 1978, Alumnae award Northwestern U., 1985, Excellence in Edn. award Pi Lambda Theta, 1989. Mem. Am. Assn. Higher Edn. (bd. dirs. 1974-77, pres. 1977-78), Western Coll. Assn. (pres.-elect 1988-89,k pres. 1990-92), Golden Key, Sigma Xi.

UEHLING, JUDITH OLSON, artist, painter, printmaker, sculptor; b. Chgo., Apr. 3, 1935; d. Raymond and Virginia (Ericsson) Olson; m. David Theodore Uehling, June 19, 1959 (div. Nov. 1983); children: Mark David, Greta Lynn, Mary Birgit. BA, Smith Coll., 1957; postgrad., Sch. Art Inst., Chgo., 1957-58. vis. artist Peacock Printmakers, Aberdeen, Scotland, 1982; hon. sec. Printmakers Coun., London, 1985-91, exhbn. commr., Valetta, Malta, 1991; lectr. in field. One-woman shows include Fanny Garver Gallery, 1976, 79, 81, Ripon (Wis.) Coll., 1978, Novi Sad Art Gallery, Yugoslavia, 1983-84, Am. Ctr. U.S. Internat. Comm. Agency, Belgrade, 1983-84, Meml. Union, U. Wis., Madison, 1984, Peacock Printmakers, Aberdeen, 1984, Galerie Bremer, Berlin, 1988, A.I.R. Gallery, N.Y.C., 1999; group exhbns. include Lemon Geranium Gallery, N.Y.C., 1973, Hansen Galleries, N.Y.C., 1975, Internat. Exhbn. Graphic Art, Frechen, Germany, 1976, Internat. Biella (Italy) Prize for Prints, 1976, Invitational Bicentennial Art Competition, Milw., 1976, Grafik aus Amerika, Leverkusen, Germany, 1976, 77, 3d Norwegian Internat. Print Biennial, Fredrikstad, Norway, 1976, 4th, 1978, Gallery Marronier, Kyoto, Japan, 1979, Utubo Gallery, Osaka, Japan, 1979, State Capitol Bldg., Madison, Wis., 1982, Royal Scottish Acad., Edinburgh, 1983; 11th, 12th, 14th, and 15th Internat. Biennial of Graphic Art, Ljubljana, Yugoslavia, Parrish Art Mus., Southampton, N.Y., 1999; exhibited in galleries at Anderson O'Day, London, Anna Bornholt Gallery, London, Bremer Gallery, Berlin; exhibited in numerous juried shows; represented in numerous permanent collections including Mus. of City of N.Y., Gallery of Yugoslav Portrait, Tuzla, Yugoslavia, Graves Art Gallery, Sheffield, Eng., Lovell, White, Durrant, Eng., Victoria and Albert Mus., Eng., Whitworth Art Gallery, Manchester, Eng., Wiltshire County Museums, Eng., Bank of Am., U. Wis., Madison, Columbus (Ga.) Mus., Washington County Mus. of Fine Arts, Maryland, Continental Bank, Chgo.; commns. include Wis. Telephone Co., 1977, Affiliated Bank Madison, 1978, Lovell, White Durrant, London, 1990, Allied Dunbar, 1991, Eagle Ins., London, 1993; contbr. articles to profl. jours. Vol. Artists Talk on Art, N.Y.C., 1995—. Recipient Fellowship award Hereward Lester Cooke Found., 1976, Chmn. Action grant Wis. Arts Bd., 1982, Acquisition prize 10th Internat. Exhbn. of Original Drawings, Rijeka, Yugoslavia, 1986, Artist by Appt. grant Frans Masereel Centrum, Belgium, 1987-89, Best of Show award 18th Ann. Metro Show, City Without Walls, Newark, N.J., 1999, numerous purchase awards. Mem. Chelsea Arts Club (London), Internat. Sculpture Ctr., Print Europe Orgn., Coll. Art Assn. Avocations: studying German language, walking, playing recorder. Home and Office: 152 Wooster St New York NY 10012-5330

UEKI, MASANORI, materials scientist; b. Fukuoka, Japan, Mar. 21, 1949; s. Narutaka and Hatsuko (Shimura) U.; m. Mamiko Ota, Sept. 3, 1983 (dec. June 1993); children: Mao, Tadamasa. M of Engring., Tokyo Inst. Tech., 1973, D of Engring., 1976. Registered profl. engr., 1997. Rsch. assoc. Kumamoto (Japan) U., 1976-79; postdoctoral rschr. Northwestern U., Evanston, Ill., 1977-79; R&D mgr. CBMM Internat. Ltd., Tokyo, 1979-81; assoc. prof. Kanazawa (Japan) Inst. Tech., 1982-87; sr. rschr. advanced tech. rsch. lab. Nippon Steel Co., Kawasaki, Japan, 1987-92, chief rschr. advanced tech. rsch. lab., 1992-97; prof. Kanazawa Inst. Tech., 1997—; lectr. Yokohama (Japan) Nat. U., 1989-96, Tokyo Inst. Tech., 1991-92. Author: High Temperature Plastic Deformation of Metals and Alloys, 1984; editor Bulletin of JSME, 1988-90, Bulletin of Japan Ceramic Soc., 1990-92. Postdoctoral fellow Nat. Sci. Found., 1978, 79; recipient Best Paper award Jour. Ceramic Soc. Japan, 1997. Mem. Japan Cons. Engrs. Assn., N.Y. Acad. Sci. Avocations: baseball, swimming, climbing. Home: Nakai 2 Chome 27-17, Shinjuku 161-0035, Japan Office: Kanazawa Inst Tech-Tokyo, Akasaka Lab 8-7 Akasaka 6-chome, Minato 107-0052, Japan

UEMATSU, KUNIHIKO, nuclear energy agency executive; b. Kochi, Japan, May 4, 1931; s. Takeo and Mitsue Uematsu; m. Setsuko Tsukuda, Jan. 18, 1962; children: Hirohiko, Yoshihiko, Mari Marianne. Degree, Kyoto U., Japan, postgrad.; D of Nuclear Engring., MIT, 1961. Head fuel and materials devel. Power Reactor and Nuclear Fuel Devel. Corp., Japan, 1968-82, dir. fuel devel. divsn., 1982-83, exec. dir., 1983-88; dir.-gen. nuclear energy agy. OECD, Paris, 1988-95; exec. v.p. PNC, Japan, 1996—; spl. tech. adviser Japan Nuclear Cycle Devel. Inst., 1996-98. Avocations: golfing, walking. Office: PNC, 1-9-13, Akasaka Minato-ku, Tokyo Japan*

UEMOTO, MICHIHISA, chemistry educator, researcher; b. Kyoto, Japan, Feb. 21, 1958; s. Hiroshi and Setsuko (Tatehana) U.; m. Kyoko Iwasaki, Dec. 10, 1989; children: Yoshihisa, Haruka, Mio. BA, Tokyo U. of Agrl. & Tech., Fuchu, Tokyo, 1980, MA, 1982; PhD, Gakushuin U., Toshima, Tokyo, 1985. Rsch. assoc. Gakushuin U., Toshima, Tokyo, 1985-87; postdoctoral fellow Riken Inst. Phys. and Chem. Rsch., Wako, Saitama, Japan, 1985-87; rsch. worker Tokyo Met. Indsl. Rsch. Inst., Kita, Tokyo, 1987—; adj. lectr. Tokyo Univ. Agrl., and Tech., Fuchu, Tokyo, 1991-97; mem. com. Japanese Nat. Examination, 1999—; adminstrv. mem. of analytical chemistry Liaison Coun. Govtl. and Prefectual Indsl. Rsch. Inst. Japan, 1996—. Contbr. articles to profl. jours. Vol. officer Assn. Residents Asaka, Saitama, 1992—. Mem. AAAS, Chem. Soc. Japan, Soc. for Solution Chemistry of Japan, Japan Soc. for Analytical Chemistry, Japan Welding Soc. (analytical com. sect. precious brazing filler metals). Avocations: participant sports, sauntering, spas. Office: Tokyo Met Indsl Rsch Inst, Nishigaoka Kita-ku, Tokyo 115-8586, Japan

UEMURA, HIDEKI, physician, surgeon; b. Tokyo, Apr. 12, 1961; s. Satoshi and Yoshiko (Yamakawa) U.; m. Noriko Yashiro, June 29, 1991 (div. June 1997); m. Tomoko Kodama, July 8, 1997. MD, U. Tokyo, 1986; MPhil, U. London, 1997. Med. trainee U. Tokyo, 1986-88; resident Nt. Cardiovasc. Ctr., Osaka, 1988-91, staff surgeon, 1991-95, cons. surgeon, 1995—; sr. rschr. Nat. Heart & Lung Inst., London, 1993-95; lectr. U. Tokyo, 1997—. Autho: Advances in Cardiac Surgery, Vol. 7, 1996, Annual of Cardiac Surgery, 10th edit., 1997, Journal of Thoracic Cardiovascular Surgery, 1995, The Annals of Thoracic Surgery, 1995; mem. editl. bd. Cardiology in the Young, 1997—. Mem. European Assn. for Cardio-Thoracic Surgery (London), European Soc. of Cardiology (Leiden), Japan Assn. for Thoracic Surgery. Avocations: classical music, violin playing, cooking, mixing drinks. Office: Nat Cardiovasc Ctr, 5-7-1 Fujishirodai Suita, Osaka 565-8565, Japan

UEMURA, TOSHIO, economist, educator; b. Anjo-City, Aichi-Pref, Japan, Jan. 6, 1951; s. Jiro and Yukie (Nakashima) U.; m. Shigemi Asahara, Mar. 16, 1986; 3 children. BA, Yokohama City U., 1973; MA, Waseda U., Tokyo, 1978; Dr. Econs., Chuo U., Tokyo, 1985. Lectr. Asia U., Tokyo, 1985-88, assoc. prof. econs., 1988—. Co-author: The Economics of Quality, 1980, Japanese Industrial Organizations, 1995, The Economics of Institutions, 1995; co-editor: Various Aspects of Economics, 1998; contbr.: (book) Scritti in onore di Alberto Mortara, 1990. Mem. Japan Soc. Rsch. and Info. on Pub. and Coop. Economy (sec. 1985-96), Japan Econ. Policy Assn. (sec. 1989—), Japan Soc. of Pub. Utility Econs. (councilor 1995—). Avocations: Igo, Shogi. Office: Asian U Faculty of Econs, 5-24-10 Sakai, Musashino 180-0022, Japan

UENG, STEVE WEN-NENG, orthopedic surgeon; b. Taipei, Taiwan, Dec. 12, 1950; s. Ueng Chin-Gee and Lin Fon-Zau U.; m. Lin Mei-Ling, June 4, 1977; children: Ruey-Shiuan, Lih-Shuoh. MD, Taipei Med. Coll., 1977. From resident in surgery to attending orthopedist Chang Gung Meml. Hosp., Taiwan, Republic of China, 1979—; chief dept. orthopedics Chang Gung Meml. Hosp., 1994-97, chief hyperbaric oxygen ctr., 1994-97; assoc. prof. Chang Gung U., 1994-99, prof., 1999—, vice supt., 1997, supt., 1999—. Grantee Nat. Sci. Coun. Republic of China, 1993, 95, 96, 97, 98, 99, 2000. Mem. Orthopedic Assn. Republic of China, Undersea and Hyperbaric Med. Soc., European Soc. Bone and Joint Infection. Avocations: tennis, golf, painting. Office: Chang Gung Meml Hosp, #5 Fu-Hsing St Kweishan, T'aoyuüan Taiwan

UENO, EDWARD ISAO, environmental scientist; b. Numazu-shi, Japan, Nov. 28, 1938; s. Hirokichi and Sei (Sajiki) Saito; m. Taeko Ueno, Apr. 8, 1970; children: Mikako, Masanobu. BSc, Tokai U., 1961; MSc, Meiji U., 1963, PhD, 1966. Ednl. official Ministry of Edn., Tokyo, 1966-99; vis. prof. Tech. U., Braunschweig, Germany, 1975-78, Tex. Tech. U., Lubbock, 1980; res. R&D group of intense neutron source U. Tokyo, 1980-89, rep. of fusion sci. group, 1989—; sec. for policy Ho. of Reps., Tokyo, 1999—; vis. prof. FM Tokyo Broadcasting Sta., 1981; adviser policy planning com. Japanese Govt., 1994, Hitoyoshi City, 1994. Author: Energy and Resources, 1992, 93, Waste and Resource, 1994, 95, 96, 97, 98, 99, 00, Ekoshisutemu Noho no Kiseki (The Miracle based on Agricultural Method of Microbiological Ecosystems), 1995, The Human Beings Perish from the Earth in Eighty Years, 2000, Twentieth Century Achievement Award of Five Hundred Leaders of Influence, 1996; contbr. numerous articles to profl. jours. Dozenten fellow Alexander von Humboldt Found., 1975; spl. rsch. grant Ministry of Edn., 1980, grants-in-aid for scientific rsch., 1981. Mem. Inst. for Ecosystem Agr. (chief sec. 1992-95), Soc. for the Study to Design Water (dir. 1993-96), Soc. of Waste and Resource Rsch. (mgr. 1994—), The Inst. for Eco and Economy System (pres. 1995—), Order Internat. Fellowship, Internat. Order Merit (Eng.), Club of Fusion Sci. (chief dir. 1983—), Vereinigung der Humboldtlaner in Japan, The Nat. Geographic Soc., The Inst. for Eco and Economy System Inc. (pres. 1999—). Avocations: go, karate, traveling, reading, writing. Office: Inst Econ and Economy Sys, 5-22-8-5F Higoshiogu, Arakawa-ku Tokyo 116-0012, Japan

UENO, EI, surgeon; b. Kumanogawa, Japan, Sept. 29, 1950; s. Tamehaya and Takako (Miyamae) U.; m. Keiko Yokoyama, Apr. 23, 1977; 1 child, Fuyo. MD, Tokyo Med. Coll., 1976; PhD, U. Tsukuba, 1995. Jr. resident Jichi Med. Sch., Minamikawachi, Japan, 1976-78, sr. resident, 1978-81, asst., 1981-82; asst. prof. U. Tsukuba, Japan, 1983—; adv. bd. Internat. Breast Ultrasound Sch.; guest assoc. prof. Tokyo Med. U., 1998—; pres. Breast Cancer Conf., 1999—. Author, editor: Breast Ultrasound, 1991, Atlas of Breast Surgery, 1993, rev. edit., 1998; author: Mastologia Dinamica, 1995, Ultrasound of Superficial Structures, 1995. Fellow Japan Surg. Soc., Japan Soc. of Ultrasound in Medicine (councillor 2000—); mem. Japanese Breast Cancer Soc. (councillor 1992—), Ibaraki Soc. of Breast Disease (pres. 1995—), Internat. Assn. of Breast Ultrasound (organizing com. 1989—), Japanese Assn. Breast amd Thyroid Sonology (pres. 1998—), Breast Cancer Conf. (pres. 1999—), World Soc. Breast Health (com. 2000—). Avocations: swimming, skiing, surfing, spear fishing. E-mail: ei-ueno@md.tsukuba.ac.jp. Home: 2-2-15 Sengen, Tsukuba 305-0047, Japan Office: Inst Clin Med U Tsukuba, 1-1-1 Tennoudai, Tsukuba 305-8575, Japan

UENO, KAZUE, college president, microbiologist, researcher; b. Seki, Japan, July 24, 1929; s. Hachiro Horibe and Taka Ueno; m. Kazuko Katino, Apr. 10, 1955; 3 children. DVM, Gifu (Japan) U., 1950, PhD, 1958. Assoc. rschr. NIH, Tokyo, 1950-55; asst. prof. Gifu U. Sch. Medicine, 1955-71, assoc. prof., 1971-72; assoc. rschr. UCLA, 1971-72; prof. Gifu U. Sch. Medicine, 1978-94, prof. emeritus, 1994—; pres. Gifu Coll. Med. Tech., Seki, Japan, 1995—; cons. Calpis Lab., Tokyo, 1994—. Author: Anaerobes and Anaerobic Infections, 1968, Clinical Microbiology, 1977, Mixed Surgical Infections, 1986, Drug Susceptibility for Clinical Isolates in Southeast Asian Countries, 1992. Recipient Pres. Kojima's award Kojima Found., 1971, Lifetime Achievement award Anaerobe Soc. Ams., 1994; fellow freeman City of Salamanca, Spain, 1975, others. Fellow Infectious Diseases Soc. Am.; mem. N.Y. Acad. Scis. Avocation: golf. Office: Gifu Coll Med Tech, 795-1 Nagamine Ichihiraga, Seki Gifu 501-3892, Japan

UEOKA, RYUICHI, chemistry educator; b. Ozu Town (Kumamoto), Japan, Oct. 10, 1946; s. Seiichi and Teruko (Noguchi) U.; m. Toshiko Hokazono, June 16, 1974; children: Kana, Hidetsugu. BS, Kumamoto (Japan) U., 1969, PharmD, 1989; MS, Kyushu U., Fukuoka, Japan, 1975, PhD in Engring., 1982. Assoc. prof. chemistry Sojo U. (formerly Kumamoto Inst. Tech.), 1977-91, prof., 1991—, chmn., 1995—, dept. life sci. head prof., 2000—. Author: Supramolecular Chemistry, 1996; contbr. articles to profl. jours.; patentee in field. Recipient Encouragement award Soc. Synthetic Chemistry Japan, 1987, Young Scholar Lecture award The Chem. Soc. Japan, 1986. Avocations: fishing, painting. Home: Izumi 3-9-1, Kumamoto 862-0941, Japan Office: Sojo Univ, Ikeda 4-22-1, Kumamoto 860-0082, Japan

UESHIMA, SHIGEJI, investment company executive. CEO Mitsui & Co. Ltd., Tokyo. Office: Mitsui & Co Ltd, 1-2-1 Ohtemachi Chiyoda, Tokyo 100, Japan*

UETTWILLER, JEAN-JACQUES, solicitor; b. Paris, Aug. 1, 1945; s. Robert and Jacqueline (Millou) U.; m. Jeannine Chapelle, Feb. 18, 1966; children: Olivier, Sophie. Law grad., U. Paris, 1972. Bar: Paris 1986, Brussels 1991. Legal mgr. St. Nancéienne & Varin Bernier, Paris, 1970-74; legal dir. Revillon Group, Paris, 1975-82, Bongrain Group, Paris, 1982-86; ptnr. Berlioz & Co., Paris, 1986-92; ptnr., co-founder UGGC, Brussels, 1993—; lectr. Ecole Supérieure Libre des Sciences Commerciales Appliquées, Paris, 1989—. Author: Les prix de transfert Intra-groupe, 1995, les dangers des LBO, 1996; co-author: Guide de Rédaction des Statuts de SAS, 1995; contbr. articles to profl. publs. Mem. French Assn. Tax Lawyers, Union Internationale des Avocats (pres. fgn. investment com.), Assn. des Avocates Conseils d'entreprises (pres.). Home: 3 Avenue Paul Doumer, 75116 Paris France Office: UGGC, 47 Rue de Monceuv, 75008 Paris France

UEYAMA, KEISHI, cardiovascular surgeon; b. Kanazawa, Japan, July 1, 1960; s. Takeshi and Tokii (Sanbai) U.; m. Yuki Iozaki, Jan. 16, 1994. MD, Hokkaido U., Sapporo, Japan, 1987; PhD, Kanazawa U., Japan, 1992. Staff Fukui Cardiovascular Ctr., Japan, 1992-94, 96-97; instr. Baylor Coll. Medicine, Houston, 1994-96; dir. Maizuru Mut. Hosp., Japan, 1997—. Mem. Japan Surg. Soc., Japanese Assn. Thoracic Surgery, Japanese Circulation Soc. Home: Momoyama cho 1-1 #A-6, Kyoto 625-0060, Japan Office: Maizuru Mut Hosp, Hama 1035, Kyoto 625-8585, Japan

UFFNER, MICHAEL S., retail automotive executive; b. Phila., July 18, 1945; s. Ray and Shirley A. (Block) U.; m. Marilyn A. Ursomarso; 1 child, Lauren R. BA, MA, U. Pa., 1971. V.p. Union Park Pontiac, BMW, Honda, Wilmington, Del., 1972-82; pres. Del. Motor Sales Inc., Wilmington, 1982—; mem. manpower tng. adv. com. Gen. Motors Corp., pres. dealer adv. coun., 1985; mem. Gen. Motors Dealer policy bd., 1990-91. Mem. New Castle County Small Bus. Commn., 1993—, Wilmington Police Bus. Adv. Coun., 1991—; bd. dirs., mem. exec. com. BBB Del., 1992—, chmn., 1998-2000; bd. dirs. Am. Heart Assn., Del. chpt., 1985-86, pres., 1986-87, chmn. Recipient numerous awards, including Time Mag. Quality Dealer award, 1997, Gold Heart award Am. Heart Assn., 1989. Mem. Cadillac Motor Car Divsn. Nat. Dealers Coun. (vice chmn. 1989-90, chmn. 1990-91, chmn. DeVille brand com. 1995-97), Am. Heart Assn. (v.p., bd. dirs. Nat. Ctr. 1987-90), Am. Econ. Assn., Del. Automobile and Truck Dealers Assn. (bd. dirs., v.p. 1992-93, pres. 1994-95), U. Pa. Alumni Assn. (v.p. Del. chpt. 1978-80, pres. 1980-81), Del. C. of C. (chmn. small bus. com. 1991-95, vice chmn. bd. dirs. 1996-99, bd. dirs. 1993—, mem. exec. com. 1995—, chmn. small bus. alliance 1995-96, chmn. bd. dirs. 2000—), U.S. C. of C. (bd. dirs. 1998—), Fieldstone Golf Club, Hercules Country Club, Ocean City Yacht Club, Univ. Whist Club, Tavistock Civic Assn. (pres. 1976-77). Office: 1606 Pennsylvania Ave Wilmington DE 19806-4018

UGAJIN, RYUICHI, physicist, inventor; b. Tokyo, June 17, 1963; s. Shoji and Yoko (Mizuno) U. PhB, U. Tokyo, 1988, MSc, 1990, PhD, 1997. Rsch. scientist Sony Corp. Rsch. Ctr., Yokohama, Japan, 1990-99, Frontie Sci Labs. (divsn. Sony Corp.), Yokohama, 1999—; sr. rsch. scientist, mgr. Bio/Complex Lab. Sony Corp., Yokohama, 2000—. Contbr. articles to sci. jours., including Phys. Rev. Letters, Applied Physics Letters, Phys. Rev. B., Jour. Applied Physics. Mem. Phys. Soc. Japan. Avocations: music, travel. E-mail: Ryuichi.Ugajin@jp.sony.com. Office: Frontier Sci Labs Sony Corp, 134 Goudo-cho Hodogaya-ku, Yokohama 240-0005, Japan

UGAROV, MICHAEL V., physics researcher; b. Moscow, Dec. 8, 1970. MS in Physics, Moscow Inst. Physics and Tech., 1994; PhD in Physics, Gen. Physics Inst., Moscow, 1999. Rsch. scientist Gen. Physics Inst., 1994-99; postdoctoral fellow U. Houston, 1999—. Contbr. articles to profl. jours. Young Investigator Rsch. Opportunities grantee Civil Rsch. and Devel. Found., 1998. Avocations: music, astronomy, soccer, foreign languages.

UGGEN, CHRISTOPHER, sociologist, criminologist; b. St. Paul, May 29, 1964; s. Kermit Stanley and Nancy Lee Uggen; m. Rhonda Marie Breakfield, Aug. 2, 1986; children: Tor Stanley, Hope Kathryn. BA, U. Wis., 1986, MS, 1990, PhD, 1995. Asst. prof. U. Minn., Mpls., 1995—. Editl. adv. bd. Jour. Criminal Law and Criminology; contbr. articles to profl. jours. Grantee Nat. Inst. Justice, 1998, NSF, 1999, Soros Found., 2000; scholar Internat. Soc. Criminology, 1998. Mem. Am. Soc. Criminology (nat. policy com. 1998-99, Cavan awadr for outstanding scholarly contbns. 2000), Am. Sociol. Assn. Avocations: running, playing guitar, reading fiction. E-mail: uggen@atlas.socsci.umn.edu.

UGODCHIKOV, ANDREY GRIGORYEVICH, science educator; b. Vetluga, Russia, Nov. 3, 1920; s. Grigory Afanasyevich Ugodchikov and Marya Yulianovna Sosnovskaya; m. Irina Nikolayevna Blokhina, July 2, 1941; children: Nikolay Andreyevich, Grigory Andreyevich. Degree in mech. engring., Indsl. Inst., Nizhny Novgorod, Russia, 1943; Cand. Tech. Sci., Sea Transport Inst., Nizhny Novgorod, Russia, 1950; D of Tech. Sci., Math. Inst., Kiev, Ukraine, 1958. Sr. engr. Yekaterinburg (Russia) factory, 1943-46; grad. student lectr. Sea Transport Inst., Nizhny Novgorod, 1946-51; from asst. prof. to prof. Civil Engring. Inst., Nizhny Novgorod, 1951-59, dept. head, 1959-67; dept. head State U., Nizhny Novgorod, 1967-77, rector, 1969-88, prof. dept. elasticity and plasticity, 1988—; dir. Rsch. Inst. of Mechanics, Nizhny Novgorod, 1975-88; com. mem. Com. of State Prizes in Sci. and Tech., Coun. Mins., Moscow, 1987-91. Author: Construction of Conformly Representing Functions, 1966; co-author: Optimization of Elastic Systems, 1981, Boundary Element Method in the Mechanics of Deformed Solids, 1986, Three-Dimensional Complex Potentials and Their Application to the Theory of Elasticity, 1995; contbr. articles and monographs to profl. jours. Dep. Regional Soviet, Nizhny Novgorod, 1973-88. Decorated Order of Red Banner of Labour, Presidium of Supreme Soviet of USSR, 1971, 80; recipient Badge of Honor, Presidium of Supreme Soviet of USSR, 1976, medals Presidium of Supreme Soviet of USSR, 1945, 67, 70, 76, 88, 95. Mem. Russian Nat. Com. on Theoretical and Applied Mechanics, Academic Internat. Acad. Scis. Higher Sch. Home: Genkina St 21 Apt 18, Nizhni Novgorod 603115, Russia Office: State U Nizhny Novgorod, Gagarin Ave 23, Nizhni Novgorod 603022, Russia

UGREKHELIDZE, MINDIA, judge. Chmn. Supreme Ct. Georgia. Office: Supreme Ct, Zubalashvili St 32, Chavchavadze Tbilisi Georgia*

UGROZOV, VALERY VYCHESLAVOVICH, physical chemist, mathematics educator; b. Moscow, May 27, 1954; s. Vycheslav Vasilyevich and Antonina Vasilyevna (Capitanova) U.; m. Irina Victorovna Mosckina, Apr. 12, 1980; 1 child. Student, Moscow State U., 1977. Cert. physicist. Engr. Inst. Physico-Chem. USSR, Moscow, 1977-82, postgrad., 1980-82; sr. rsch. worker Inst. Chromatography, Moscow, 1982-87, Inst. Physico-Chem. Ly Karpov, Moscow, 1987-98; prof. dept. food industry math. Moscow State U., 1998—. Patentee in field. Avocations: running, swimming, body building, skiing, music. Home: Leninsky pz 129 kop 1 583, 117513 Moscow Russia Office: Moscow State U Food Industry, Math Dept Volokolamskoy Str 11, 125080 Moscow Russia

UGUR, HALIL, ambassador; b. Ankara, Turkey, 1950; married; one daughter. Degree Electronics Engring., Mid. East Tech. U., 1972; postgrad., Harvard Bus. Sch., 1984. Amb. E. and P. of Turkmenistan to U.S., 1994—. Avocations: horseback riding, folk arts, all cultures. Office: Embassy of Turkmenistan 2207 Massachusetts Ave NW Washington DC 20008-2848

UHDE, LARRY JACKSON, joint apprentice administrator; b. Marshalltown, Iowa, June 2, 1939; s. Harold Clarence and Rexine Elizabeth (Clemens) U.; m. Linda-Lee Betty Best, Nov. 19, 1960; children: Mark Harold, Brian Raymon. Student, Sacramento City Coll., 1966, Am. River Coll., Sacramento, 1975. Equipment supr. Granite Constrn., Sacramento, 1962-69; truck driver Iowa Wholesale, Marshalltown, Iowa, 1969-70; mgr. Reedy & Essex, Inc., Sacramento, 1970-71; dispatcher Operating Engrs. Local Union 3, Sacramento, 1971-73; tng. coord. Operating Engrs. Joint Apprenticeship Com., Sacramento, 1973-83, apprenticeship div. mgr., 1983-87, adminstr., 1987-95; ret., 1995; instr. asst. advanced transp. tech. Sacremento City Coll., 1996—; chmn. First Women in Apprenticeship Seminar, 1972, Calif. Apprentice Coun., 1992, chair Blue Ribbon com.; com. mem. Sacramento Gen. Joint Apprenticeship Com., 1973-74; rep. Sacramento Sierra's Bldg. and Constrn. Trades Coun., 1973-75; com. mem. Valley Area Constrn. Opportunity Program, 1974-77; commr. State of Calif. Dept. Indsl. Rels., Calif. Apprenticeship Coun., chmn. 1992; mem. Apprenticeship Adv. Com. Internat. Union Oper. Engrs. Contbr. articles to trade papers. Mgr., v.p. Little League, 1971-75; co-chmn. Fall Festival St. Roberts Ch., 1973-75; v.p. Navy League Youth Program, 1978-81; instr. ARC, 1978-87; counselor United Way 1980—; bd. mem. County CETA Bd., 1981-82; coun. mem. Calif. Balance of State Pvt. Industry Coun., 1982-83, Sacramento Pvt. Industry Coun., 1982-83; coord. Acholic Recovery Program, 1984—. With USN, 1956-60. Inducted into Calif. Apprenticeship Hall of Fame, 1996. Mem. Western Apprenticeship Coords. Assn. (statewide dir. 1987—), U.S. Apprenticeship Assn., Sacramento Valley Apprenticeship Tng. Coords. Assn. (rep.), Rancho Murieta County, U.S. Golf Assn., Bing Maloney Golf Club. Democrat. Roman Catholic. Avocations: golf, archery, bowling, hunting, camping, dancing.

UHITIL, SUNČICA, microbiologist, researcher; b. Slavonski Brod, Croatia, Mar. 14, 1958; d. Zdenko and Eva (Klaić) U.; m. Ivo Poluta, Dec. 9, 1989; 1 child, Vlaho. Veterinarian, Vet. Faculty, Zagreb, Croatia, 1983, MS, 1987, PhD, 1993. Sci. trainee Vet. Faculty, Zagreb, 1983-87; food microbiologist Vet. Sta., Zagreb, 1987—. Author: Food—Like Poison or Drug, 1999; contbr. rsch. articles to profl. jours. Mem. HMD, FEMS. Home: Draškovićeva 10, 10000 Zagreb Croatia Office: Vet Sta Zagreb, Heinzelova 68, 10000 Zagreb Croatia

UHLEMANN, JENS, chemical engineer; b. Mainz, Germany, May 7, 1964; s. Hans and Irene Ursel U.; m. Olga Rajonhson, May 16, 1992; children: Annkathrin Mirana, Jan-Philip Rado. Diploma in Chem. Engring., TU Clausthal, Germany, 1988; Degree in Engring., E.N.S.I.G.C., Toulouse, France, 1989; Doctorate I.N.P., Toulouse, 1992. Postdoctoral fellow U. Calif., Berkeley, 1992-93; R&D engr. Bayer AG, Leverkusen, Germany, 1993-97; dir. flavor technology Haarmann & Reimer GmbH, 1997—. Recipient Rsch. fellow Procope/DAAD, 1988, Doctoral fellow Program Science/EC, 1989-91; Postdoctoral fellow NATO/DAAD, Berkeley, 1992-93. Mem. Toenissteiner Kreis, DAAD-Freundeskreis. Home: Moltkestrasse 2a, D-37603 Holzminden Germany

UHLENBROCK, STEFAN, musicologist, editor; b. Nuremberg, Germany, Aug. 20, 1964; s. Walter and Ursula (Herrndoerfer) Frisch; m. Gabi Uhlenbrock, Mar. 23, 1968; children: Lisa, Lea. MA, Friedrich-Alexander-U., Erlangen, Germany, 1993. Sales mgr. Edition Hage, Germany, 1990-93; freelance writer Germany, 1991—; libr. Kirchenchorverband, Bayern, Germany, 1995—; editor Gottesdienst & Kirchenmusik, Bayern, 1996—. Author: Hans Sachs—Geschichten und Gedichte, 1994. Office: Kirchenchorverband, Weiltinger Str 15, 90238 Nuremberg Bayern, Germany

UHLENBROOK, STEFAN, hydrologist; b. Neubechum, Germany, May 8, 1969; s. Reiner and Ellen (Kortling) U.; m. Silke Musch, June 5, 1998; children: Sina, Yael. MS, U. Freiburg, Germany, 1995, PhD, 1999. Rschr. U. Freiburg, Germany, 1996—. Author: (book) Investigation of Fast Runoff Components, 1995, Runoff Determination During Floods, 1997, Investigation and Modeling of Runoff Generation Processes in a Sneso Scale Catchment, 1999. Recipient Tison award 2000; grantee in hydrology, Friedrich-Ebert-Stiftang, Bonn, Germany, 1992-95. Mem. Internat. Assn. Hydrological Scis., European Geophysical Union, Am. Geophysical Union. Office: Inst Hydrology U Freiburg, Fahnenbergplatz, 79098 Freiburg Germany

UHLENDORF, VOLKMAR HANS FRIEDRICH, research physicist; b. Gudensberg, Hessen, Germany, Oct. 10, 1951. Diploma in physics, U.

Goettingen, Germany, 1978, PhD in Physics, 1982. Postdoctoral rschr. Max-Planck-Inst., Goettingen, 1982-84; scientist U. Konstanz, Germany, 1984-87, Schering AG, Berlin, 1987-2000; sr. scientist Schering AG, 2000—. Patentee in field. Mem. IEEE, Acoustical Soc. Am. (assoc.), German Alpine Club. Avocations: rock climbing, mountaineering, photography. Office: Schering AG, Muellerstrasse 170-178, 13342 Berlin Germany

UHLER, WALTER CHARLES, government official, writer, reviewer; b. Lebanon, Pa., Feb. 23, 1948; s. Victor Cornelius and Barbara Jean (Malin) U.; m. Judy Ann Sherk, Aug. 7, 1967 (div. 1984); children: Terry Allen, Matthew David. Life partner: Carol A. DePrisco. BA in Polit. Sci. cum laude, Pa. State U., 1973, BA in Russian cum laude, 1973, cert. Russian area, 1973, MPA, 1992. Tchg. asst. Pa. State U., University Park, 1975-76; procurement agt. Naval Aviation Supply Office, Phila., 1976-80; contracts adminstr. GSA, Phila., 1980-81; contracting officer Def. Logistics Agy., Phila., 1981-86, corp. contracting officer, 1986-94; chief fin. svcs., 1993—; regional cons. Def. Logistics Agy., L.A., 1985-86; nat. cons. Def. Logistics Agy., Cameron Station, Va., 1989-90; leader Testing Labs. Privatization Assessment Team Def. Logistics Agy., Ft. Belvoir, Va., 1997-98; participant Air Force Intelligence Conf. on Soviet Affairs, Arlington, Va., 1988, Venona Conf., Washington, 1996, Ballistic Missile Def. Conf., Washington, 1998, AP/Harriman Inst. Conf., N.Y.C., 1999; spkr. on contracts DOD Conf., Cleve., 1988, on restructuring costs, Memphis, 1994; chmn. Ann. Nat. Conf. Contracting Officers and Auditors, 1987-93; mem. Citizen Amb. Archivists' Del. to Russia and Poland, 1995, Citizen Amb. Del. to China, 1996, Russia and Finland, 1998; prodr., interviewer (with George Enteen) Sergei Vasilievich Utechin's Oral Reminiscences, 1997—. Contbr. articles to profl. jours. Baseball coach Valley Athletic Assn., Bensalem, Pa., 1979-88, basketball coach, 1980-85, coord., 1981; tutor Ctr. for Literacy, Phila., 1991-93, Project GIVE, Phila., 1995-98. Recipient Comdrs. Excellence award Defense Contract Mgmt. Area Ops., 1993. Mem. Am. Assn. for Advancement Slavic Studies, Soc. for Mil. History, Acad. Polit. Sci., Nat. Book Critics Cir., Am. Acad. of Polit. and Social Scis., Friends of the Free Libr. of Phila. Democrat. Avocations: history, literature, Pa. State U. football. Office: DCMC Phila DCMDE-GDTC PO Box 11427 Philadelphia PA 19111-0427

UHLIG, BIRGIT A., scientist, researcher; b. Herten, Germany, June 26, 1962. Diploma in agrarian engring., U. Bonn., Germany, 1987; D of Agr., 1993; PhD, CSIRO, Merbein, Australia, 1991. Sci. rsch. fellow Inst Obstbau und Gemüsebau U. Bonn, 1992-93, sci. rsch. fellow, editor jour. Inst. Fruit and Veg. Prodn., 1994-95; sci. asst. Inst. Vegetable and Fruit Sci. U. Hannover, Sarstedt, Germany, 1995—; spkr. in field. Author: (booklet) Renewable Resources, 1993; contbr. reports, papers, and articles to profl. jours. Mem. Internat. Soc. Horticultural Scis., European Fruit Rsch. Insts. Network, Fedn. European Socs. Plant Physiology, German Horticultural Soc., Am. Soc. Plant Physiologists, Soc. Exptl. Biology. E-mail: uhlig@obst.uni-hannover.de. Office: U Hannover, Am Steinberg 3, D-31157 Sarstedt Germany

UHLIG, EGON, chemistry educator; b. Neundorf, Saxonia, Germany, Nov. 8, 1929; s. Fritz and Ella (Wagler) U.; m. Christa Beyer, July 18, 1953; children: Wolfram, Ronald. Diploma, U. Leipzig, Fed. Republic of Germany, 1952, D in Natural Sci., 1955, D in Habilitation, 1960. Asst. U. Leipzig, 1952-60; prof. U. Jena, Germany, 1960-95, dean faculty natural sci., 1977-89, dean faculty of chemistry, 1990-93. Author: (textbook) Lehrwerk Chemie, vol. II, 1973, vol. 7, 1973. Lutheran. Home: Dietrichweg 22, D 07749 Jena Germany Office: Friedrich-Schiller U Jena, Furstengraben, D 07749 Jena Germany

UHLIG, HARALD F.H.V.S., economics educator, researcher; b. Bonn, Germany, Apr. 26, 1961; s. Sigmar and Elfriede Uhlig; m. Christine; children: Anjuli Sarah, Jan Peter. Diploma in math., Tech. U., Berlin, 1985; PhD in Econs., U. Minn., 1990. Asst. prof. Princeton (N.J.) U., 1990-94; rsch. prof. econs. Tilburg (The Netherlands) U., 1994—. Asst. editor Rev. Econ. Studies, Macroecon. Dynamics, Computational Econ.; editor European Econ. Rev.; contbr. articles to profl. jours. Named to Rev. Econ. Studies Tour, London, 1990; Sloan Dissertation fellow, Sloan Found., Boston, 1989-90; Studienstiftung des Deutschen Volkes study grantee, Bonn, Germany, 1982-85, Fulbright study grantee, Fulbright Commn., Bonn, 1985. Mem. CEPR, Econometric Soc., Am. Econ. Assn., Verein für Socialpolitik. Avocations: cello, Middle Eastern history, music. Home: Donkerstraat 3a, 5061 PD Oisterwijk The Netherlands Office: Humboldt U Dept Econs, Spandauer Str 1, 10178 Berlin Germany

UHRIK, CARL THOMAS, computer scientist, educator; b. Cedar Rapids, Iowa, Dec. 9, 1957; s. Richard Lee and Shirley Marie Uhrik; m. Michael W. Burkart, Sept. 1, 1999. BSEE, Tex. A&M U., 1980, MS in Computer Sci., 1981; MS, U. Ill., 1985, PhD, 1991. Asst. lab. mgr. Lab. for Informatic Engring. U. Trento, Italy, 1990-95; speech recognition engr. Berdy Med. Sys., Boulder, Colo., 1996-99; prof. U. Phoenix, Denver, 1996—; internationalization engr. Intl.com/Lionbridge, Boulder, 1999—. Fulbright scholar, 1986-87. Roman Catholic. Avocations: vegan vegetarian cooking, reading, films, outdoors, biking. E-mail: uhrik@hotmail.com. Home: 3725 Birchwood Dr Apt 23 Boulder CO 80304-1421

UICICH, RAUL EDUARDO, biochemist, researcher; b. Comodoro Rivadavia, Chubut, Argentina, Mar. 18, 1948; s. Felix Uicich and Elisa Crocce; m. Maria Lidia Grieco, May 16, 1981; children: Pablo Javier, Matias Raul. Licentiate clin. analyst, U. Buenos Aires, 1974, cert. biochemist, 1975. Fellow Infant Nutrition Rsch. Ctr., Buenos Aires, 1982-84, head lab., 1984—; head Nutrition and Metabolism Lab., Nat. Pediat. Hosp., Buenos Aires, 1990—; vis. fellow dept. pediat. U. Iowa Hosps. and Clins., Iowa City, 1989, Biochem. Clin. Inst., Barcelona, Spain, 1996. Contbr. over 20 articles to med. jours., including Nutrition Rsch., Infant Medicine. Recipient Bermberg Found. award, 1995, award Argentine Nutrition Soc., 1996, 1st Place award Am. Oil Chemist's Soc., 1999. Mem. Latin Am. Nutrition Soc. (treas. 1998-2000), Argentine Chemists' Assn. (mem. com.), Assn. Official Analytical Chemist, Latin Am. Pediat. Rsch. Soc. Roman Catholic. Avocations: football, volleyball, reading. Office: CESNI, Bdo de Irigoyen 240, 1072 Buenos Aires Argentina

UIKE, YASUYUKI, chemical engineer; b. Saga-City, Japan, Apr. 27, 1940; s. Shiro and Mitsu (Kuroda) U.; m. Marina Szczepaniak, July 11, 1971; children: Kyoko-Nadja, Shiro-Patrik.. B.Mech.Engring., Waseda U., Tokyo, 1964, B.Chem.Engring., 1972. Factory mgr. Rikon Nosan-Kako, Saga, Japan, 1964-65; chemist Sandoz-Wander, East Hanover, N.J., 1966-67, Sandoz Ltd., Basel, Switzerland, 1967-68, Sandoz Inc., East Hanover, 1973-78; engr./chemist Sandoz Ltd., Basel, 1978-97; engr.-chemist Novartis Pharma, Basel, 1997—. Patentee in field. Pres. Japanese Assn., Basel, 1990-97; mem. com. Friend of M. Baumont, Paris. Mem. Am. Inst. Chem. Engrs. Avocations: mechanics, carpentry, mountaineering, architecture, history. Home: Laerchenweg 2, CH-4225 Brislach BL, Switzerland Office: Novartis Pharma, S-145-764, CH-4002 Basel BS, Switzerland

UIMONEN, RISTO JUHANI, columnist; b. Oulu, Finland, Nov. 22, 1947; s. Kaarlo Johannes and Hilkka Orvokki (Arola) U.; m. Maija-Leena Kinnunen, Mar. 13, 1971; children: Tuire, Tuukka. M of Polit. Sci., U. Tampere, Finland, 1973. Journalist Kaleva Newspaper, Oulu, Finland, 1970-71, Turun Sanomat Newspaper, Turku, Finland, 1972-73, BBC World Svc., London, 1973-75, Turun Sanomat Newspaper, Helsinki, Finland, 1976-81; exec. producer MTV Television News, Helsinki, 1981-84, mng. editor, dep. editor, 1984-86; editl. writer Helsingin Sanomat Newspaper, Helsinki, 1986-98; editl. writer, dep. editor Helsinki Sanomat, 1998—. Author: Travelers London, 1979, Tough Game with the Pennies, 1984, Publicity Game, 1992, The Young Prime Minister, 1994, Wag the Dog-Finnish Democracy in Disorder 1983-200?; co-author: The World of Images, 1995, A Century of Finnish Bandy, 1996. Mem. Young Finnish Journalist Soc. Home: Haukiverkko 13 B 6, 02170 Espoo Finland Office: Helsingin Sanomat, PO Box 70, 00089 Sanomat Finland

UJIHARA, KIKUO, engineering educator; b. Ibaraki, Japan, Nov. 17, 1940; m. Mieko Yorioka, Apr. 26, 1969; children: Shumpo. Ushio. B in Engring., U. Tokyo, 1964, M in Engring., 1966, D of Engring., 1970. Lectr., assoc. prof. Univ. Electro-Comm., Chofu, Japan, 1969-86; prof. Univ. Electro-Comm., Chofu, 1986—. Achievements include finding a correction factor to Schawlow-Townes formula for a laser and proposal of the concept of effective area of a planar microcavity laser. Office: Univ Electro-Comm, 1-5-1 Chofugaoka, Chofu 182-8585, Japan

UJIIE, JUNICHI, investment company executive. Co-chmn. of bd., co-CEO Nomura Securities Internat., N.Y.C.; pres., CEO The Nomura Securities Co., Ltd., Tokyo. Office: Nomura Securities Internat, 9-1 1 Chome Nihonbashi, Chuo-ku Tokyo 103, Japan*

UKAEGBU, DAVID OKWUKANMANIHU, accountant, management consultant; b. Umuahia, Abia, Nigeria, Jan. 28, 1939; s. Amos Ukaegbu Iweha and Sussanah Ihejiaba Anyim-Ukaegbu; divorced. Attended, Kings Coll., Lagos, 1957-58; A level, U. Ibadan, Lagos, Nigeria, 1959; Cert.O/A level, Wolsey Hall Coll., Oxford (Eng.) U., 1960; attended, Inst. Taxation, London, 1961-64, H. Houlks Lynch London Tax. & Accountancy, 1961-68; Article of Clerkship, Inst. of Chartered Accts., 1967-70; attended, Inst. Chartered Accts. in England & Wales, 1967-70; postgrad., Calif. Coast U., 1982. Cert. fin. mgmt. cons. Chief clk. J.T. Leach and Chartered Accts., Lagos, 1956-60; asst. mgr. audits Banner Mounsey Chartered Accts., Lagos, 1960-64, B Harmood & Co. Chartered Accts., Eng., 1966-67; articled clk. Morris Gregory Chartered Acct., Eng., 1967-68, Harmood, Banner, Midgeley, Snelling & Barnes Chartered Accts., Lagos, 1969-70; acct., auditor Charter House Auditors, Lagos, 1971-74; reporting acct. Silver Shoes Mfg. Co. Ltd., Lagos, 1974-85, chief acct., cons., 1976—; edn. com. Inst. Adminstrv. Accts., Lagos, 1981; mgmt. cons. Lagos State Consultancy Bd., 1987—. Program convener YMCA, Lagos, 1965-66. Recipient Men of Achievement, 1995, Internat. Leadership Achievement, 1995. Fellow Inst. Fin. Accts. (launching com. 1990-93), Assn. Cost and Exec. Acctg.; mem. AAAS, Am. Mgmt. Assn., Brit. Inst. Mgmt., Brit. Inst. Securities Laws, Inst. Inc. Pub. Accts. (Dublin), Inst. Chartered Accts. (articled clk.), Inst. of Chartered Secs. and Adminstrs., Nigeria Employers Cons. Assn. (treas. Eal Frin 1990-93), Planetary Soc., N.Y. Acad. Scis. Avocations: reading, table tennis, lawn tennis. Office: Charter House, PO Box 998, Umuahia Abia State Nigeria

UKAI, YASUO, retired agronomy educator; b. Tokyo, Sept. 18, 1937; s. Manjiro and Iyo Ukai; m. Kiyoko Ban, July 25, 1941; children: Makoto, Megumi. M Agronomy, U. Tokyo, 1964, D Agronomy, 1966. Radioisotope mng. Researcher Inst. Radiation Breeding MAFF, Ibaraki, Japan, 1966-79, head of lab., 1979-86; head lab. Nat. Inst. Agro-Environ. Scis., Ibaraki, 1986-91; prof. U. Tokyo, 1991—; radioisotope mgr. Inst. Radiation Breeding, Ibaraki, Japan, 1979-86; dir. Exptl. Station for Landscape Plants, Chiba, Japan, 1994-97; mem. Com. Stats. of Agr., Tokyo, 1993-98; sci. writer, 1998—. Author: Principles of Plant Improvement, I, II, 1984, Crop Plants Which Changed the World, 1985, Improved Plants, 1985, Plant Breeding, I, II, 1992. Recipient Japanese Soc. Breeding, Ministry's prize Ministry of Agr., Forestry and Fishery, 1993. Avocations: Japanese chess, painting, wood sculpture. Home: 1994-9 Migimomi Tsuchiura, Ibaraki 300, Japan

UKERUN, SYLVESTER OHWEVWO, chemistry educator; b. Adagbrassa, Nigeria, Oct. 24, 1956; s. Anthony Okijirhie and Theresa Tiro (Oniore) U.; m. Francisca naa Akusia Codjoe, Mar. 21, 1986; children: Stephanie, Michael. BSc, Lagos U., 1978; PhD, UMIST, Manchester, Eng., 1984. Tutor Govt. State Sch., Donga, Nigeria, 1978-79; demonstrator Lagos (Nigeria) U., 1979-81; lectr. Adeyemi Coll., Ondo, Nigeria, 1984-85, Fed. U. Tech., Akure, Nigeria, 1985-92, U. Ghana, Acera, 1993-94; sr. lectr. Delta State U., Abraka, Nigeria, 1995—; project coord. Fed. u. Tech., Akure, 1985-92; head dept. chemistry Delta State U., Abraka, 1997. Editor Jour. Tchr. Edn.; contbr. articles to profl. jours.; guest writer Ghanaian Times, 1993-94. Census enumerator, Nat. Nigerian Census, 1973; examiner West Africa Exam Coun., Nigeria, 1991. Fellow Ronzoni Inst., Milan, 1992; scholar Ministry of Edn., Nigeria, 1976-78, Scholarship Com. of London, 1981-84. Mem. N.Y. Acad. Scis. Democrat. Roman Catholic. Avocations: music, fine art, jogging, travel, exploration. Home: PO Box MD 149 Madina, Accra Ghana Office: Delta State U, PO Box 75, Abraka Nigeria

UKSHE, ALEXANDER EVGENIEVICH, physicist, researcher; b. Berezniki, Russia, Aug. 6, 1956; s. Eugeniy Alexandrovich and Nina Sergeevna (Brylina) U. Grad., Latvijas U., Riga, Latvia, 1981; degree in physics and math. sci., Inst. Solid State Physics, Chernogolvoka, Russia, 1989. Technician computer ctr. Inst. Chem. Physics, Chernogolovka, 1973-74, engr., 1981-83, jr. scientist, 1983-86, scientist, 1986-90, sr. scientist, 1990—; engr., programmer Demos Co. Ltd., Moscow, 1991-93; tech. dir. Demos-Sherna Ltd., Chernogolovka, 1993—. Contbr. articles to profl. jours. Mem. Russian Internat. Soc. Solid State Ionics. Avocations: bicycling, mountain traveling, rock-n-roll dances, UHF amateur radio. Home: Institutski av 2 Apt 20, 142432 Chernogolovka Russia Office: Inst Problems Chem Physics, Russian Acad Scis, 142432 Chernogolovka Russia

ULEHLA, IVAN, physics educator; b. Skalica, Czechoslovakia, Oct. 17, 1921; s. Miloslav and Anna Marie (Tilschova) U.; m. Ludmila Ulehlova, Oct. 31, 1942 (div. 1966); children: Ivan, Josef, Katerina; m. Libuse Pouchla, Sept. 9, 1966; 1 child, Premysl. RNDr, Charles U., 1949. Asst. Charles U., Prague, Czechoslovakia, 1949-51, Komensky U., Bratislava, Czechoslovakia, 1951-54; sr. researcher Inst. Nuclear Physics, Prague, Czechoslovakia, 1954-60; asst. prof. physics Tech. U., Prague, Czechoslovakia, 1960-63, prof., 1963-67; dir. Nuclear Ctr. Charles U., Czechoslovakia, 1975-85, prof. physics, 1967—; vice-dir. Joint Inst. Nuclear Research, Dubna, USSR, 1964-67; sci. sec. 1st Conf. on Atomic Energy, Geneva, 1955, spl. asst. 2d Conf., 1958. Author book on nuclear physics, 1962, books on physics and philosophy, 1962, 82. Decorated Order of Labor (Czechoslovakia). Mem. European Phys. Soc., Czechoslovakian Acad. Scis. (corr.), Czechoslovakian Union Math. and Physics (pres. 1981-87). Home: Vavrenova 1169, 14200 Prague 4, Republic of Czech

ULFKOTTE, UDO KONSTANTIN, editor; b. Lippstadt, Germany, Jan. 20, 1960; s. Theo and Gertrud Ulfkotte; m. Doris Juliana Bergold, Nov. 2, 1989. MA, U. Freiburg, Germany, 1985, PhD, 1986. Mid. East editor Frankfurter Allgemeine Zeitung, Frankfurt, 1986—; polit. adviser African affairs Konrad-Adenauer Found., 2000—; tchr. econ. and econ. espionage Lueneburg U., 2000—. Author: (books) Middle East Politics, 1986, Know the Internet, 1999, Classified Information, 1997 (Bestseller of Yr. 1997), Market of Thieves, 1999 (Bestseller 1999). Mem. Havanna-Lounge Internat. Assn. Avocations: classical music, horse riding, gardening, architecture. E-mail: u.ulfkotte@faz.de. Office: Frankfurter Allgemeine Zeit, Hellerhofstreet 2-4, D-60267 Frankfurt Germany

ULFVES, BJÖRN OLAV, import company official; b. Helsinki, Finland, Apr. 4, 1929; s. Eugen Fridolf and Irma Celia (Jansson) U.; children: Patrik, Mikael, Kristian; m. Margareta Solveig Twerin, Feb. 24, 1990. Diploma, Tech. U., Helsinki, 1951. Sales engr. Gulf Oil, Helsinki, 1955-56, Tesla Oy, Helsinki, 1956-62; mng. dir. Oy Vestek Ab, Espoo, Finland, 1962-91, chmn. bd., 1991—. Mem. Nylandska Jaktklubben (hon.). Avocation: sailing. Home: Braxenv 4 C, 02170 Espoo Finland Office: Oy Vestek Ab, Martintie 3, 02270 Espoo Finland

ULGEN, KUTLU SEFIKA, chemical engineer, educator; b. Istanbul, Turkey, June 5, 1963; d. Muammer Kemal and Müzeyyen Ünsan (Orgun) Özergin; m. Osman Zeki Ulgen, Sept. 25, 1991; 1 child, Oguz. BSc, Boğaziçi U., Istanbul, 1987; MSc, Boğazigi U., Istanbul, 1989; PhD, U. Manchester, Eng., 1992. Instr. chem. engring. Boğaziçi U., Istanbul, 1992-94, asst. prof., 1994-96, assoc. prof., 1996—. Contbr. articles to profl. jours. Overseas Rsch. studentship UMIST, Manchester, 1989-91. Avocations: jazz, skiing, travel. Office: Boğaziçi Univ, Dept Chem Engring, 80815 Bebek Istanbul Turkey

ULGEN, MERT, pharmacologist; b. Istanbul, Turkey, Dec. 1, 1961; s. Suat and Ulkan (Yuca) U. B in Pharmacy, Marmara U., 1981, MSc, 1987; PhD, London U., 1992. From rsch. asst. to full prof. pharm. chemistry Marmara U., Istanbul, 1984—; vice dean faculty pharmacy Marmara U., 1999—. Author: Professional English for Pharmacists, 1997, Organic Nomenclature, 1999. Mem. Turkish Med. Chemistry Assn. Avocations: organ playing, computers, traveling, collecting doll.s. Home: Muderris Ziya Bey Sok, Osmanbey apt 34/3, Feneryolu Istanbul Turkey Office: Marmara U, Faculty Pharmacy, 81010 Istanbul Turkey

ULIJASZEK, STANLEY J., anthropologist; b. Nottingham, Eng., July 3, 1954; s. Michal and Anna Ulijaszek; m. Pauline Anne Scott; children: Michael, Alexandra, Peter. BS, U. Manchester, 1975; MS, U. London, 1978, PhD, 1987; MA, U. Cambridge, Eng., 1990, U. Oxford, 1999. Lectr. U. Cambridge, 1986-97, rschr., 1997—; lectr. U. Oxford, 1999—. Author: Human Energetics in Biological Anthropology, 1995; co-author: Nutritional Anthropology, Prospects and Perspectives, 1993; editor: Health Intervention in Less Developed Countries, 1995, co-editor: Cambridge Ency. of Human Growth and Development, 1998, Human Adaptability, Past, Present, and Future, 1997, Seasonality and Human Ecology, 1993. Mem. European Anthropol. Assn. (coun. mem. 1996—), N.Y. Acad. Sci. Avocations: painting, 20th century art history.

ULLAH, HABIB, chief executive officer; b. Panjpir, N.W.F.P., Pakistan, Apr. 1, 1962; s. Haji Mohammad and Amina Karim; m. Mus Tamina, July 17, 1990; children: Nazish, Ansa, Saqlain, Fahad. Chief exec. Bldg. Material Co., 1980—. Dist. counselor Awami Nat. Party Swabi. Awami Nat. Party. Muslim. Avocations: coin collecting, stamp collecting, gardening, building creating.

ULLÉN, FREDRIK, researcher, concert pianist; b. Västerås, Sweden, Apr. 13, 1968; s. Per Göran and Gunnel Linnéa (Norström) U.; m. Judit Adrienn Csatószegi, July 6, 1998; 1 child: Laura. B, Karolinska Inst., Stockholm, 1987, PhD, 1996; MA, Royal Acad. Music, Stockholm, 1990. Internat. concert pianist, 1991—; rschr. Karolinska Inst., Stockholm, 1996—. Mem. editl. bd. Nutida Musik; recordings include Ligeti (complete), Chopin transcr., Stockhausen, various Swedish compositions; contbr. articles to sci. jours. Recipient Diapason d'or, CHOC de Le Monde de la Musique, 1996. Mem. Soc. for Neurosci., Prometheus Soc. (pres. 1999—). Avocations: philosophy, literature, art. Office: Nobel Inst Neurophysiology, Karolinska Inst SE, 17177 Stockholm Sweden

ULLENDORFF, EDWARD, orientalist, educator; b. Jan. 25, 1920; s. Frederick and Cilli (Pulverman) U.; m. Dina Noack, Apr. 27, 1943. MA, U. Jerusalem, 1941; DPhil, Oxford U., 1951; MA (hon.), U. Manchester, Eng., 1962; DLitt (hon.), St. Andrews U., Scotland, 1972; PhD (hon.), Hamburg U., 1990. With Govt. Palestine, 1946-48; mem. faculty Oxford Inst. Colonial Studies, 1948-49; lectr., then reader Semitic langs. St. Andrews U., 1950-59; prof. Semitic langs. U. Manchester, 1959-64, prof. Ethiopian studies, 1964-82; prof. Semitic langs. U. London, 1979-82, emeritus prof., 1982—; cataloguer Ethiopian manuscripts Royal Libr. Windsor Castle, 1952; mem. adv. bd. Brit. Libr., 1975-83; Schweich lectr. Brit. Acad., 1967. Author: The Definite Article in the Semitic Languages, 1941, Exploration and Study of Abyssinia, 1945, Catalogue of Ethiopian Manuscripts in the Bodleian Library, Oxford, 1951, The Semitic Languages of Ethiopia, 1955, The Ethiopians, 1959, 3d edit., 1973, (with Stephen Wright) Catalogue of Ethiopian MSS in Cambridge University Library, 1961, Comparative Semitics in Linguistica Semitica, 1961, (with S. Moscati and others) Introduction to Comparative Grammar of Semitic Languages, 1964, An Amharic Chrestomathy, 1965, The Challenge of Amharic, 1965, Ethiopia and the Bible, 1968, (with J.B. Pritchard and others) Solomon and Sheba, 1974, Studies in Semitic Languages and Civilizations, 1977, (with M.A. Knibb) Book of Enoch, 1978, The Bawdy Bible, 1979; annotator/translator: Emperor Haile Selassie, My Life and Ethiopia's Progress, 1975, (with others) The Amharic Letters from Emperor Theodore of Ethiopia to Queen Victoria, 1979, (with C.F. Beckingham) The Hebrew Letters of Prester John, 1982, A Tigrinya Chrestomathy, 1985, Studia Aethiopica et Semitica, 1987, The Two Zions, 1988, From the Bible to Enrico Cerulli, 1990, H.J. Polotsky (1905-91), 1992, From Emperor Haile Sellassie to H.J. Polotsky, 1995; joint editor Studies in Honor of G.R. Driver, 1962, Ethiopian Studies, 1964; chmn. editl. bd. Bull. Sch. Oriental and African Studies, 1968-78; editor Jour. Semitic Studies, 1961-64; contbr. articles and revs. to scholarly jours. Served with Armed Forces, 1941-46, Eritrea and Ethiopia. Recipient Imperial Ethiopian Gold medallion, 1960, Haile Selassie Internat. prize for Ethiopian studies, 1972. Fellow Brit. Acad. (v.p. 1980-82), Accademia dei Lincei Rome, Oxford Hebrew Centre (hon.); mem. Anglo Ethiopian Soc. (chmn. 1965-68), Assn. Brit. Orientalists (chmn. 1963-64), Soc. O.T. Study (pres. 1971), Royal Asiatic Soc. (v.p. 1975-85). Home: 4 Bladon Close, Oxford OX2 8AD, England

ULLENS DE SCHOOTEN, GUY FRANCIS, executive; b. San Francisco, Jan. 31, 1935; s. Jean and Marie Therese (Wittouck) U.; m. Micheline Marie Franckx; children: Philippe, Brigitte, Yves, Nicolas. Degree in law, Leuven Univ., Belgium, 1958; MBA, Stanford Univ., 1960. CEO Eurocan Packaging Co., Mechelen, Belgium, 1965-73, Tiense Suikerraffinaderij, Tienen, Belgium, 1973-89, Artal Group SA, Luxembourg, 1989—. Bd. dirs. The SEI Ctr. for Advanced Studies in Mgmt. Avocations: traveling, reading, Chinese art collection. Office: Artal Group SA, 105 Grand Rue, L 1661 Luxembourg Luxembourg

ULLMANN, BERNARD FRANCOIS, journalist, author; b. Paris, Jan. 13, 1922; s. Claude Andre and Louise Rachel (Franck) U.; m. Pierrette Chauvet, Oct. 1957; children: Laurence, Pierre-Guillaume; m. Marie Berthe Gaborit De Montjou, July 1973; 1 child, Emmanuel. BA, U. Paris, 1939; Licence en Droit, Faculte de Droit, Paris, 1946. Program asst. R. Francaise, Paris, 1946-48, BBC-French Mag., London, 1948-49; reporter Agence France Presse, London, 1949-50; war correspondent Agence France Presse, Korea, 1951-52; bur. chief Agence France Presse, Australia, 1952-53; roving correspondent Agence France Presse, Saigon, 1954-55, Middle East, Algeria, 1955-59, Bangladesh,, Vietnam, U.S., China, Chile, 1967-74; bur. chief Agence France Presse, Peking, China, 1959-60, Moscow, 1962-66, Washington DC, 1973-77; sr. fgn. correspondent L'Express, Paris, 1977-86. Author: (book) The Big Red Sun, 1971, AFP-Une Histoire de l'agence France Presse, 1992, Jacques Soustelle, 1995; asst. editor Passages Paris, 1987—. 2d lt. French Air Force, 1942-45. Recipient Croix de G., French Ministry of Defense, 1945, Silver Star U.S. Govt., 1952, Chevalier de la Legion d'Honneur French Govt., 1973. Avocation: sailing. Home: 9 rue Marcelin Berthelot, 92130 Issy-les-Moulineaux France

ULLMANN, JULIAN RICHARD, computer science educator; b. London, June 21, 1936; s. Richard Edwin and Thelma Beatrice (Ford) U.; m. Margaret Evelyn Beeston, Nov. 7, 1964; children: David Ivan, Karen Margaret. BA, Cambridge (Eng.) U., 1959; PhD, London U., 1968. Chartered engr. Sci. officer Nat. Phys. Lab., Teddington, Eng., 1959-64, sr. and prin. sci. officer, 1968-75; sr. rsch. fellow Post Office, London, 1964-68; prof. Sheffield (Eng.) U., 1975-86; prof., head dept. computer sci. Royal Holloway Coll., London, 1986-89, King's Coll., London, 1989-96. Author: Pattern Recognition Techniques, 1973, Microcomputer Technology, 1982, A Pascal Database Book, 1986, Compiling in Modula-2, 1994. Pilot officer RAF, 1954-56. Fellow Brit. Computer Soc., Royal Soc. Arts. Avocations: classical music.

ULLMANN, UWE, microbiologist; b. Ludwigshafen, Germany, Nov. 10, 1939; s. Heinz and Marianne (Nieser) U.; m. Doris Ullmann; children: Sven, Arne. With Dept. Hygiene, Tübingen, Germany, 1968-74, cons., 1974-76, with, 1976-80; prof. med. microbiology Kiel, Germany, 1980—. Office: Dept Med Microbiology/Virology, Brunswiker Str 4, 24105 Kiel Germany

ULLRICH, DIETER, physician; b. Bergneustadt, Germany, Apr. 11, 1955; s. Hansjurgen and Friederike (Ertl) U.; m. Holle Bertl Schiefer, Aug., 1982; children: Katja, Franziska. Diploma in medicine, Gesamthochschule Essen, Germany, 1980, D, 1982. Resident in biochem. pharmacology U. Göttingen, 1980-82, resident in pediat., 1982-89, resident in clin. pharmacology, 1988-89, resident in ear, nose, throat clinic, 1989-93; pvt. practice, 1993—. Author: HNO-Erkrankungen im Kindesalter, 1994; contbg. author: Biochemical Basis of Carcinogenesis, 1984, Advances in Glucuronide Formation, 1985, Hepatic Encephalopathy, 1988, Head and Neck Cancer-Advances in Basic Research, 1996; contbr. articles to profl. jours. Avocations: sailing, running, golf, family activities. Office: Wedemarkstr 83, 30900 Wedemark Germany

ULLRICH, SÖREN, biologist, researcher; b. Kiel, Schleswig-Holstein, Germany, Mar. 15, 1961; s. Karl-Friedrich and Gudrun (Meier) U.; m. Brigitte Galda, July 6, 1989; children: Hanna, Nils. Diploma, U. Kiel, 1989, D, 1992. Researcher Inst. Meerskunde, Kiel, 1992—; opponent Åbo Akademie, Turku, Finland, 1994; project leader NIG-AQ 13 GKSS Rsch.

Ctr., Germany, 1992-94. Contbr. articles to profl. jours. Sgt. Navy, 1980-82. Grantee U. Kiel, 1989-91, Ministry Edn. and Rsch., 1995-96, 97-98. Mem. Am. Soc. Limnology and Oceanography, European Assn. Fish Pathologists, Baltic Marine Biologists. Avocations: beekeeping, sailing, string quartet. Office: Inst Meereskunde, Hohenbergstr 2, 24105 Kiel Germany

ULLSTEN, ROBERT STIG KARL, education administrator; b. Umeå, Vasterbotten, Sweden, July 31, 1937; s. Carl Augustinus and Stina Märta (Röstöm) U.; m. Ann-Maria Gunda Lundström, Apr. 19, 1962; children: Marika, Erik, Åsa. MA, U. Uppsala (Sweden), 1963. Adj. Tecnical Inst., Luleå, Sweden, 1963-65, Tchr. Tng. Coll., Luleå, 1964-65, Dragoskolan Upper Sec. H.S., Umeå, Sweden, 1966; dep. prin. Dragoskolan Upper Sec. H.S., Umeå, 1971-82; prin. Centrala Gymn, Umeå, 1982-92; prin. curriculum devel. Local Bd. Adminstrn., Umeå, 1992-96, project mgr. Learning in Info. Soc., 1996—. Sgt. Artillery, 1960-84. Mem. Folkpartiet. Mem. Swedish Protestant Ch. Avocations: golf, bridge. Office: Schs in Umeå, City Hall, S 907 84 Umeå Sweden

ULMANIS, GUNTIS, former President of Latvia; b. Riga, Latvia, Sept. 13, 1939; m. Aina Ulmane; children: Guntra, Alvils, Paula. Student, Latvian U. Economist, mcpl. employee Riga, Latvia, 1963-92; dep. Parliament, Riga, 1993; pres. of Latvia, 1993-99; hon. chmn. bd. Nat. LIbr. Support Found. Author: (autobiography) You are not Asked Much, (book of photographs) My Time as President. Active CPSU, 1965-89, Union of Farmers of Latvia, 1992—. Achievements include facilitating admission of Latvia to Coun. of Europe; declaring moratorium on the execution of the death penalty in Latvia. Avocations: reading historical and political memoirs, sports, nature. Office: Office of Pres, Pils Laukums 3, LV-1900 Riga Latvia

ULMAR, GERD, psychiatrist, educator; b. Tilsit, Germany, Sept. 24, 1941; s. Hugo and Frieda (Jaehrling) U.; m. Bärbel Marquardt, Jan. 29, 1969; children: Florian, Benjamin, Susanne. MD, diploma in psychology, U. Munich, 1969. Asst. Max Planck Inst., Heidelberg, Germany, 1970-72, Göttingen, Germany, 1973-75; asst. dept. psychiatry U. Freiburg, Germany, 1975-80, neuropsychiatrist, 1980; chief Mental Hosp., Marburg, Germany, 1980-84; lectr. U. Marburg, 1983, prof. psychiatry, 1989-96; dir. Mental Health Ctr., Wiesloch, Germany, 1985—; prof. psychiatry U. Heidelberg, 1997—. Co-editor: Persönlichkeitstörungen, 1990, Krankenhauspsychiatrie, 1990—; editor: Psychiatrische Versorgungsperspektiven, 1995. Mem. German Assn. Psychiatry, Psychotherapy and Nervous Medicine, German Soc. Biol. Psychiatry. Office: Psychiat Zentrum Nordbaden, Postfach 1420, D-69155 Wiesloch Germany

ULMER, PETER EUGEN, law educator, consultant; b. Heidelberg, Germany, Jan. 2, 1933; s. Eugen and Elisabeth (Linser) U.; m. Jorinde Heygster, Oct. 9, 1959; children: Hansgeorg, Marianne, Sibylle, Almut. JD, U. Heidelberg, 1959, Habilitation, 1968; M.C.L., U. Mich., 1959; Doctorate (hon.), U. Madrid, 1993, Montpellier U., 1995, Lleida U., 1998. Lawyer KPMG Deutsche Treuhand-Ges., Frankfurt, Fed. Republic of Germany, 1961-64; law cons. EEC Comm., Brussels, 1964-68; prof. Law Sch. U. Hamburg, 1969-75; prof. Law Sch. U. Heidelberg, 1975—, pres., 1991-97. Author numerous books; editor law reviews and commentaries, 1975—; contbr. articles to profl. publs. Mem. Rotary. Avocations: chamber music, hiking. Home: Albert-Ueberle Str 21, D-69120 Heidelberg Germany

ULMSCHNEIDER, PETER HERMANN, astrophysics educator; b. Manheim, Fed. Republic Germany, Sept. 2, 1938; s. Walter and Hilde (Dostmann) U.; m. Helgard Schättler, July 1, 1967; children: Katharina, Martin, Jakob. MS, Yale U., 1964, PhD, 1966. Sci. asst. U. Tübingen, Fed. Republic Germany, 1966-67; sci. asst. U. Würzburg, Fed. Republic Germany, 1967-73, lectr., 1973-79, prof., 1979-80; prof. U. Heidelberg, Fed. Republic Germany, 1980—. Fellow Am. Astron. Soc., German Astron. Soc.; mem. Lions. Roman Catholic. Home: Turnerstr 3, 69126 Heidelberg Germany Office: Inst for Theoret Astrophys, Tiergarten Str 15, 69121 Heidelberg Germany

ULRICH, ALFRED GEORG, neuropathologist; b. Zurich, Switzerland, Feb. 4, 1930; s. Alfred Alex and Lily Emma (Sautter) U.; m. Annakatharina Debrunner, June 8, 1958; children: Lili, Anna-Momika, Tom, Hans. MD, U. Zurich Sch. Medicine, 1955. Intern Inst. Histopathology, Zurich, 1955; resident in neurology U. Zurich, 1956-59, resident in psychiatry, 1959-60; resident Clin. Internal medicine, St. Gallen, Switzerland, 1961; trainee Inst. Neurology, London, 1962-63; sr. resident neuropathology U. Zurich, 1964-70; trainee Albert Einstein Coll. Medicine, N.Y.C., 1970-71; prof. neuropathology Faculty Medicine, Basel, Switzerland, 1972—. Mem. Swiss Assn. Neuropathoogy, Br. Neuropathology Soc., Am. Assn. Neuropathology, Internat. Soc. Neuropathology.

ULRICH, LIAN SUSAN GALBO, obstetrician, gynecologist, researcher, consultant; b. Copenhagen, Denmark, Jan. 17, 1952; d. Peter Thorvald Galbo and Clara (Hermann) Galbo; m. Jørgen Lennart Ulrich, June 25, 1977. MD, U. Copenhagen, Denmark, 1979; diploma in Pharm. Medicine, England, 1989. Cert. specialist in gynecology and obstetrics, Denmark. Med. registrar various hosp., Denmark, 1979-83; sr. registrar, surgery, ob./gyn. Frederikssund County Hosp., Denmark, 1983-86; mgr. Novo Nordisk A/S, Copenhagen, Denmark, 1986-89; med. dir. Novo Nordisk A/S, Copenhagen, 1989-93, sr. rsch. physician, 1993-95; gynecologist U. Hosp. Gentofte, Copenhagen, 1995—; cons. pharm. cos., Denmark, 1995—; speaker at internat. med. meetings, 1986—. Author: (with others) Lipids and Women's Health, 1991, (Chapter VI: "Metabolic Changes of Menopause"), Drug Development for Life Cycle Management in Women, 1998: (chapter XII: "Cardiovascular Disease"), (thesis) Advantages and Disadvantages of Long-Term Hormone Replacement Therapy of the Climacteric Syndrome, 1988 (Gold medal U. Copenhagen); contbr. articles to profl jours. including Lancet, Am. Jour. Obstetrics and Gynecology, Internat. Jour. Obstetrics and Gynecology , Circulation and numerous others, 1983—. Chmn. Young Doctors' W. Zealand County Com., Denmark, 1981-82; mem. Ct. Arbitration Frederiksborg County, Denmark, 1983-86; dep. mem. of Specialist Edn. Com., Danish Soc. Ob./Gyn., 1984-87. Mem. Faculty Pharm. Medicine, Royal Coll. of Physicians, London, Glasgow, Edinburg, 1990, Danish Assn. Physicians (mem. coun. 1980-84). Avocations: tennis, swimming, bridge, sailing, friends. Home: Skydebanevej 19 Veddelev, 4000 Roskilde Denmark Office: U Hosp Copenhagen Gentofte, Dept OBGYN Niels Andersensvej 65, 2900 Hellerup Denmark

ULRICH, MARIE-HELENE DEMOULIN, astrophysicist; b. Marseilles, France, Mar. 10, 1939; d. Henri and Renee (Salle) Demoulin; m. Bruce T. Ulrich, Sept. 26, 1970 (div. 1983); m. Halton C. Arp, Jan. 19, 1984; 1 child, Delina. PhD, U. Paris, 1969. Postdoctoral fellow U. Calif., San Diego, 1968-69; chargée de recherches U. Paris, 1969-71; rsch. scientist, asst. prof. U. Tex., Austin, 1971-77; sr. scientist European So. Observatory, Garching, Fed. Republic Germany, 1977—. Contbr. numerous articles to profl. jours. Mem. Internat. Astron. Union, Am. Astron. Soc., AAAS, Eurosci., European Astron. Soc. Office: European So Observatory, Karl Schwarzschild 2, 85748 Garching Germany

ULRICH, PAUL GRAHAM, lawyer, writer, editor; b. Spokane, Wash., Nov. 29, 1938; s. Donald Gunn and Kathryn (Vandercook) U.; m. Kathleen Nelson Smith, July 30, 1982; children—Kathleen Elizabeth, Marilee Rae, Michael Graham. BA with high honors, U. Mont., 1961; JD, Stanford U., 1964. Bar: Calif. 1965, Ariz. 1966, U.S. Supreme Ct. 1969, U.S. Ct. Appeals (9th cir.) 1965, U.S. Ct. Appeals (5th cir.) 1981. Law clk. judge U.S. Ct. Appeals, 9th Circuit, San Francisco, 1964-65; assoc. Lewis and Roca, Phoenix, 1965-70, ptnr., 1970-85; pres. Paul G. Ulrich P.C., Phoenix, 1985-92, Ulrich, Thompson & Kessler, P.C., Phoenix, 1992-94, Ulrich & Kessler, P.C., Phoenix, 1994-95, Ulrich, Kessler & Anger, P.C., Phoenix, 1995-2000, Ulrich & Anger, P.C., Phoenix, 2000—; owner Pathway Enterprises, 1985-91; judge pro tem divsn. 1, Ariz. Ct. Appeals, Phoenix, 1986; instr. Thunderbird Grad. Sch. Internat. Mgmt., 1968-69, Ariz. State U. Coll. Law, 1970-73, 78, Scottsdale C.C., 1975-77, also continuing legal edn. seminars. Author and pub.: Applying Management and Motivation Concepts to Law Offices, 1985; editor: Arizona Appellate Handbook, 1978-2000, Working With Legal Assistants, 1980, 81, Future Directions for Law Office Management, 1982, People in the Law Office, 1985-86; co-author, pub.: Arizona Healthcare Professional Liability Handbook, 1992, supplement, 1994, Arizona Healthcare Professional Liability Defense Manual, 1995, Arizona Healthcare Professional Liability Update Newsletter, 1992-99; co-author: Federal Appellate Practice Guide: Ninth Circuit, 1994, 2d edit., 1999, supp. 2000; contbg. editor Law Office Econs. and Mgmt., 1984-97, Life, Law and the Pursuit of Balance, 1996, 2d edit., 1997. Mem. Ariz. Supreme Ct. Task Force on Ct. Orgn. and Adminstrn., 1988-89; mem. com. on appellate cts. Ariz. Supreme Ct., 1990-91; bd. visitors Stanford U. Law Sch., 1974-77; adv. com. legal assisting program Phoenix Coll., 1985-95; atty. rep. 9th Cir. Jud. Conf., 1997-2000. With U.S. Army, 1956. Recipient continuing legal edn. award State Bar Ariz., 1978, 86, 90, Harrison Tweed spl. merit award Am. Law Inst./ABA, 1987. Fellow Ariz. Bar Found. (founding 1985—); mem. ABA (chmn. selection and utilization of staff pers. com., econs. of law sect. 1979-81, mem. standing com. legal assts. 1982-86, co-chmn. joint project on appellate handbooks 1983-85, co-chmn. fed. appellate handbook project 1985-88, chmn. com. on liaison with non-lawyers orgns. Econs. of Law Practice sect. 1985-86), Am. Acad. Appellate Lawyers, Am. Law Inst., Am. Judicature Soc. (Spl. Merit citation 1987), Ariz. Bar Assn. (chmn. econs. of law practice com. 1980-81, co-chmn. lower ct. improvement com. 1982-85, co-chmn. Ariz. appellate handbook project 1976-2000), Coll. Law Practice Mgmt., Maricopa County Bar Assn. (bd. dirs. 1994-96), Calif. Bar Assn., Phi Kappa Phi, Phi Alpha Delta, Sigma Phi Epsilon. Democrat. Home: 2529 E Lupine Ave Phoenix AZ 85028-1823 Office: Ste 250 3707 N 7th St Phoenix AZ 85014-5057

ULRICH, RADOMÍR, forester, educator; b. Plánice, Czech Republic, May 26, 1934; s. Frantisek and Ružena (Janská) U.; m. Marie Kotková, Aug. 3, 1963; 1 child, Radomira. MSc, U. Agr. Brno, Czech republic, 1957, PhD, 1980. Working plan officer Inst. Forest Mgmt., Karlovy Vary, Bohemia, 1957-64; forest dist. mgr. Forest Enterprise, Kynžvart, Bohemia, 1964-70; forest adminstr. KNV Plzeň, Bohemia, 1970-71; asst. prof. U. Agr. Brno, Moravia, 1971-88, assoc. prof., 1988-95, prof. forestry, 1995—. Contbr. articles to profl. jours.; patentee in field. Mem. Czech Forestry Soc. (head tech. sect. 1980-96). Avocation: game management. Home: Pšeník 1, 639 00 Brno Moravia, Czech Republic Office: Mendel Univ Agr & Forestry, Zemedelska 3, 613 00 Brno Moravia, Czech Republic

ULRICH, ROBERT J., retail discount chain stores executive; b. 1944. Grad., U. Minn., 1967, Stanford U., 1978. Chmn., chief exec. officer, dir. Dayton Hudson Corp.; with Dayton Hudson Corp. (now Target Corp.), Mpls., 1967—, exec. v.p. dept. stores divsn., 1981-84, pres. dept. stores divsn., 1984-87, chmn., CEO Target stores divsn., 1987-93, dir., 1993—, chmn, CEO, 1994—. Office: Target Corp 777 Nicollet Mall Minneapolis MN 55402-2004

ULRICH, ROLF, psychologist; b. Oberstdorf, Germany, Aug. 8, 1951; s. Reinhold and Helene (Reisinger) U.; m. Gabriele Huber, Mar. 1, 1977; children: Julika, Jens, Dominik, Alissa. Diploma in Psychology and Stats., U. Konstanz, Germany, 1978. Rsch. asst. U. Tübingen, Germany, 1979-84, asst. prof., 1984-89; prof. psychology U. Tübingen, 1999—; vis. scholar U. Calif., San Diego, 1990-91; prof. psychology U. Konstanz, 1991-94, U. Wuppertal, Germany, 1994-99. Heisenberg scholar German Rsch. Found., 1989. Mem. APA, Psychonomic Soc., Soc. Mathematical Psychology. Avocations: cycling, sailing, skiing, tennis. Office: U Tübingen, Friedrichstr 21, 72072 Tübingen Germany

ULRICH, RUSSELL DEAN, osteopathic physician; b. LaPorte, Ind., Apr. 15, 1947; s. Russell Denzel and Betty Faye (Higgins) U.; m. Evelyn Kay Gove, July 14, 1967; children: Tonya Kay, Nolan Dean, Bryce Alan. BA in Religion, Wesleyan Holiness Coll., 1970; BA in Psychology, U. Ariz., 1974; DO, Coll. Osteo. Medicine, 1978. Diplomate Am. Osteo. Bd. Family Physicians with qualification in geriatrice. Tchr. Montezuma Schs., Cottonwood, Ariz., 1970-72; intern William Beaumont Army Med. Ctr., 1978-79; gen. preactice medicine Piedmont Med. Clinic, Ala., 1982-85, Piedmont Family Practice Ctr., 1985—; asst. chief of staff Piedmont Hosp., 1983-84, chief of staff, 1984-92; bd. dirs. Jacksonville Hosp., 1996—. Med. advisor Piedmont Rescue Squad, 1982—; mem. Calhoun County Disaster Preparedness Com., Anniston, Ala., 1984—; bd. dirs. Dayspring Ministries. Served to capt. U.S. Army, 1978-82. Mem. AMA (Physician's Recognition award 1982, 85, 89, 92, 95, 98), Am. Osteo. Assn., Ala. Osteo. Med. Assn. (sec. treas. 1988—), PHO (pres. 1996—, Culhoun County chpt.). Republican. Methodist. Home: 845 Maple Ln Jacksonville AL 36265-6855 Office: Piedmont Family Practice Ctr PO Box 450 Piedmont AL 36272-0450

ULRICH, VOLKER, economist, researcher; b. Ludwigshafen, Germany, Aug. 5, 1958; s. Reinhold and Gisela (Reimer) U.; m. Gaby Stuhlfauth. MA, U. Mannheim, Germany, 1982; Dr.rer.pol., U. Mannheim, 1988. Asst. prof. econs. U. Mannheim, 1989-96; prof. econs. U. Greifswald, 1997—; lectr. Adminstrn. Acad., Wiesbaden, 1993—. Contbr. articles to profl. jours. Grantee Kariny-Islinger Found., 1984, 89, Ritter Found., 1998. Mem. Am. Econ. Assn., German Econ. Assn., Internat. Health Econ. Assn. Avocations: tennis, jogging, skiing. Office: U Greifswald Dept Law/Econs, 17487 Greifswald Germany

ULSAKER, GUNNAR ARNFINN, organic chemist, researcher; b. Lillehammer, Norway, Dec. 2, 1940; s. Thorleif and Helga (Saether) U.; m. Gabriella Hajagos, Dec. 17, 1974; children: Martin, Maria. Diploma in chemistry, U. Oslo, 1971. Rschr. Nycomed, 1971-74; lab. chemist Norwegian Medicines Control Authority, Oslo, 1974-80, sr. rschr., 1980—; censor organic chemistry U. Oslo, 1987-97; cons. Norwegian Fgn. Aid, Colombo, Sri Lanka, 1991; expert assessor European Pharmacopeia, Strasbourg, France, 1994-00; contact person European Network Official Medicines Control Labs., Norway, 1999—. Patentee in field; contbr. articles to profl. jours. Avocations: skiing, old cars, gardening. Home: Flataveien 24, 2050 Jessheim Norway Office: Norwegian Med Control Authority, Sven Oftedals vei 6, 0950 Oslo Norway

ULTES, ELIZABETH CUMMINGS BRUCE, artist, retired art historian and librarian; b. Urbana, Ohio, Mar. 27, 1909; d. William Mansfield and Helen Finnette (Cummings) B.; m. William Ultes, Jr., May 2, 1934 (dec. Oct. 1973); 1 child, Elizabeth Cummings Ultes Hoffman. BA in Econs., Hollins Coll., 1930; BFA in History of Art, Wittebberg U., 1979; student painting, Positano, Italy, 1960, San Miguel Allende, Mex., 1980. Instr. art history continuing edn. dept. Wittenberg U., Springfield, Ohio, 1959-80; warder, art libr. Springfield Pub. Libr., 1959-70; ret., 1970; former writer art critiques Springfield Daily News-Sun. Exhibited in 2 one-woman shows, Springfield, group shows in Dayton Art Mus., Springfield Fair, Springfield Mus.; 3 paintings in permanent collection Clark County Hist. Mus. Included in The Library and Rsch. Ctr., Nat. Mus. Women in the Arts, 1997. Avocations: painting, genealogy, reading, cooking. Home: 5155 N High St Columbus OH 43214-1525

ULUFA'ALU, BARTHOLOMEW, prime minister. Prime min. Embassy of Solomon Islands, Solomon Islands. Office: Office of Prime Min, PO Box G1 Honiara, Guadalcanal Solomon Islands*

ULUSOY, ÖZGÜR, engineering educator; b. Afyon, Turkey, Mar. 30, 1964; s. Ömer and Fatma U.; m. Sinem Bulakbasi, 1993; children: Emre, Erdem. BS, Middle East U., Ankara, Turkey, 1986; MS, Bilkent U., Ankara, Turkey, 1988; PhD, U. Ill., Urbana-Champaign, 1992. Assoc. prof. Bilkent U., Ankara, Turkey, 1993—. Editor: Current Trends in Database Technology, 1998; contbr. articles to profl. jours. Recipient Young Investigator award Parlar Found., 1994. Mem. IEEE, ACM. Office: Bilkent U, Dept Computer Engring, 06533 Bilkent-Ankara Turkey

ULVSKOG, MARITA, Swedish government official; b. Luleå, Sept. 4, 1951; married; 1 dau. Degree in journalism, U. Stockholm, 1973. Freelance journalist, journalist Norrländska Socialdemokraten, 1973-78; journalist Swedish Trade Union Confederation Newspaper, 1978-82; editor-in-chief Dala-Demokraten, 1990-94; press sec. to Ingvar Carlsson Cabinet Office Swedish Govt., 1982-90, min. pub. adminstrn., 1994-96, min. culture, 1996—. Mem. Social Democratic Party. Address: Fredsgatan 8, S-103 33 Stockholm Sweden Office: Min of Culture, Jakobsgt 26, 103 33 Stockholm Sweden*

ULYBYSHEV, YURI PETROVICH, aerospace engineer; b. Voronez, Russia, May 11, 1954; s. Petr Gerasimovich and Anna Georgievna (Sysoeva) U.; m. Anna Sergeevna Strelnikova, Dec. 19, 1958; children: Denis, Sergei. MS, Moscow High Tech. Sch., 1977; PhD, NPO Energia, 1990. Engr., group mgr., sr. scientist NPO Energia, Kaliningrad, Russia, 1977-92; prin. scientist RSC Energia, Korolev, Russia, 1992-99, head ballistics dept., 1999—. Contbr. articles to profl. jours. Mem. Am. Math. Soc., N.Y. Acad. Sci. Home: Gagarin Str 17 kv 5, 141070 Korolev Moscow, Russia Office: RSC Energia Space Ballistic, Lenin Str 4A, 141070 Korolev Moscow, Russia

UMALI, SIMPLICIO PINGUL, JR., food service executive; b. Caloocan City, The Philippines, Mar. 2, 1953; s. Simplicio Quito and Emiliana (Pingul) U.; m. Pureza Enriquez, Dec. 10, 1976; children: Jose Carlo, John Michael, Katherina Claire. BBA, U. Philippines, Metro Manila, 1974, MBA, 1979. Mktg. devel. mgr. Smith Bell & Co., The Philippines, 1975-76; asst. v.p. Bell Carpets, Inc., The Philippines, 1976-79; group product mgr. Smith Kline Corp., The Philippines, 1979-82; mktg. dir. Hoechst Far East Mktg. Corp., The Philippines, 1982-91; country mgr. Zuellig Phar. Corp., The Philippines, 1991-96; pres., CEO Dutchboy Philippines, Inc., The Philippines, 1996-99; gen. mgr. Gardenia Bakeries Philippines Inc., 1999—; asst. prof., lectr., De La Salle U., Philippines, 1983-96. Mem. Mktg. Execs. of the Pharm. Industry (pres. 1995), Rotary Club of Paranaque Ctrl., Philippines (pres. 1995-96). Roman Catholic. Avocations: photography, cycling, swimming, golf. Office: Gardenia Bakeries Philippines Inc, Star Ave Laguna Internat Indsl Park, Mamplasan Binan Laguna The Philippines

UMBEHOCKER, KENNETH SHELDON, priest; b. Mpls., Sept. 23, 1934; s. Kenneth and Mildred Adeline (Johnson) U. BA, Vanderbilt U., 1956; MDiv, Seabury-Western, Evanston, Ill., 1959, 2000; M Mgmt., U. Ga., 1974. Ordained to ministry Episcopal Ch., 1959. Priest-in-charge St. John's Ch., Hallock, Minn., 1959-62; rector St. Paul's Ch., Virginia, Minn., 1962-67; priest-in-charge Emmanuel Ch., Rushford, Minn., 1968-74; asst. to dean Gethsemane Cathedral, Fargo, N.D., 1974-86; priest-in-charge St. Peter's Ch., Warroad, Minn., 1986-90; rector Ch. of the Good Shepherd, Windom, Minn., 1990-94, St. John's by the Lake, Worthington, Minn., 1990-94, Holy Trinity, Luverne, Minn., 1990-94, Episcopal Parish of St. Mark and St. John, Jim Thorpe, Pa., 1995—; community developer, 1968-86; trustee Episcopal Diocese of Minn., Mpls., 1987-90, coun. mem., 1980-94; mem. standing com. Diocese of Bethlehem, 1998—. Field rep. Am. Cancer Soc., Mpls., 1965-67; dept. mgr. Rochester (Minn.) Area C. of C., 1967-74; exec. dir. Fargo Parking Authority and Downtown Assn., 1974-86; mem. standing com. Diocese of Bethlehem, 1998—. Seabury fellow Seabury-Western Sem., 1980; named Young Man of Yr. Rochester Jaycees, 1970; recipient Order of Purple Cross, York Rite Coll. North Am., 1988; Canterbury scholar Canterbury Cathedral of Canterbury, Eng., 1996. Mem. Am. Acad. Parish Clergy, Am. C. of C. Execs., Nat. Parking Assn. (v.p. 1983-86, Disting. Svc. award 1985), Union League Phila., Knights Templar (grand comdr. N.D. club 1985-86), Masons (grand chaplain Minn. club 1994), Seven Continents Club. Home: 32 Race St Jim Thorpe PA 18229-2004

UMEADI, ALBERT NKUNI, civil engineer, consultant; b. Lagos, Nigeria, Sept. 26, 1955; came to U.S., 1978; s. Michael Okoye and Mercy (Udezue) U.; m. Frances Chinwe Iloemezue, Apr. 1, 1995. BSc, U. Md., 1984. Registered profl. engr., Tex. Asst. project engr. IBM, Austin, Tex., 1985-94; project engr., cons. Profl. Svcs. Industries Inc., Austin, 1994-96, Raba-Kistner Cons. Inc., Austin, 1996—. Mem. ASCE (assoc.), Am. Concrete Inst. Avocations: tennis, traveling, dancing. Home: # 146 1901 E Anderson Ln Apt 148 Austin TX 78752-1908

UMEBAYASHI, CLYDE SATORU, lawyer; b. Honolulu, Sept. 2, 1947; s. Robert S. and Dorothy C. Umebayashi; m. Cheryl J. Much, June 27, 1975. BBA in Travel Industry Mgmt., U. Hawaii, 1969, JD, 1980. Spl. dept. atty. gen. Labor and Indsl. Rels. Appeals Bd., Honolulu, 1980-81; atty., dir., shareholder Kessner, Duca, Umebayashi, Bain & Matsunaga, Honolulu, 1981—; commr. Hawaii Criminal Justice Commn. Bd. dirs. Wesley Found., Honolulu, 1993-97. Mem. Hawaii State Bar Assn. Office: Kessner Duca Umebayashi Bain & Matsunaga 220 S King St Fl 19 Honolulu HI 96813-4526

UMECHUKWU, PANTALEON O. JACOB, philosophy of communication educator; b. Amesi, Aguata, Nigeria, Aug. 6, 1952; s. Jacob Nwankwo and Victoria Unamma (Onwuachu) U. Diploma in journalism, London Sch. of Journalism, London, 1977; BA in Philosophy with honors, Urban U., Rome, 1980, BD in Theology with honors, 1983; MA in Polit. Philosophy, U. Nigeria, Nsukka, 1990, MA in Mass Comm., 1992, PhD in Philosophy, 1994. Vice-rector Jr. Seminary, Anambra, Nigeria, 1983-84, rector, 1984-85; parish priest Awka Cath. Diocese, Anambra, 1986-89; head dept. mass comm. U. Nigeria, 1996-98. Author: The Press Coverage of Religious Violence in Nigeria, 1995, Mass Communication in Nigeria: A Student's Companion, 1995; co-author: The Nsukka Analyst, 1995; contbr. articles to profl. jours. Dir., chaplain Man of Order & Discipline Movement, Awka, 1987—. Mem. Internat. Cath. Union of the Press. Avocations: reading, writing, traveling, music, discussing current issues. Office: Dept Mass Comm, U Nigeria. PO Box 520, Nsukka Enugu, Nigeria

UMEDA, IWAO, English language educator; b. Yasaka-cho, Japan, Mar. 12, 1929; s. Gengo and Sugi U.; m. Fumiko Kotaki, Mar. 29, 1957. BA, Kyoto (Japan) U. Edn., 1953; postgrad., U. Tex., 1960-61; MA in Tchg., Ind. U., 1962. Prof. Kyoto Sangyo U., 1972-99, prof. emeritus, adv. coun., 1999—, dean Faculty Fgn. Langs., 1984-88, dir. Internat. Inst. Linguistic Scis., 1985-88, dir. Lang. Lab. Ctr., 1988-99; vis. assoc. prof. U. Ill., 1969-71. Author: A Comprehensive View of English Linguistics, 1984: translator: An Introduction to Language, 1980, International English: A Guide to Varieties of Standard English, 1986, Teaching and Learning Languages, 1986. Fulbright fellow, 1960-62. Mem. Japan Assn. Coll. English Tchrs. (mem. steering com. 1977-99), Lang. Lab. Assn. Japan (trustee 1992-99, v.p. Kansai chpt. 1994-98), English Linguistic Soc. Japan, Internat. Assn. Applied Linguistics. Avocations: tennis, gardening. Home: 14-2 Higashi Wakidaicho, Omiya Kita-ku, Kyoto 603-8431, Japan

UMEH, MARIE ARLENE, English language educator; b. Bklyn., Aug. 29, 1947; d. Rudolph Vasper and Erma Eunice (Hinds) Linton; m. Davidson C. Umeh, Jan. 7, 1976; children: Ikechukwu, Uchenna, Chizoba, Ugochukwu. BA, St. John's U., Jamaica, N.Y., 1970; MS, Syracuse U., 1972; MPS, Cornell U., 1977; MA, U. Wis., 1980, PhD, 1981. Instr. SUNY, Brockport, 1972-74, Oneonta, 1974-75; asst. instr. Cornell U., Ithaca, N.Y., 1976-77; prin. lectr. Anambra State Coll., Awka, Nigeria, 1982-89; substitute assoc. prof. Medgar Evers Coll., CUNY, Bklyn., 1989; adj. prof. Hostos C.C., CUNY, Bronx, 1990, Queens Coll., CUNY, Flushing, N.Y., 1990; assoc. prof. English John Jay Coll., CUNY, 1990—, faculty advisor, 1989—. Editor: Flora Nwapa, 1998, Buchi Emecheta, 1996; editor Rsch. in African Lit., 1995. Recipient Africademic award John Jay Coll. African Students Assn., 1996, Dominican Students' award, 1993; NEH fellow, 1991. Mem. AAUW, MLA (exec. com. African lit. 1996—), African Lit. Assn. Avocations: reading, writing, aerobics, jazz. Office: CUNY John Jay College Dept English 445 W 59th St New York NY 10019-1104

UMEHARA, MASAKATSU, physicist, researcher; b. Syuzenji-cho, Shizuoka, Japan, Dec. 4, 1944; s. Kyouhei and Rise (Kotouda) U.; m. Chikako Orihara, Nov. 23, 1978; children: Tomoyuki, Mayuko. BS, Shizuoka U., 1967; MS, Tohoku U., 1969, DSc, 1976. Rschr. Nat. Inst. Rsch. in Inorganic Materials, Tokyo, 1969-78; sr. rschr. Nat. Inst. Rsch. in Inorganic Materials, Tsukuba, 1978—; lectr. Tsukuba U., 1984-95, vis. rschr. Electrotechnical Lab., Tsukuba, 1991-94. Contbr. articles to profl. jours. Recipient Rsch. Achievement prize Sci. and Tech. Agy., 1995. Mem. Phys. Soc. Japan. Home: 3-11-30 Koyadai, Tsukuba 305-0074, Japan Office: Nat Inst for Rsch Inorg Mat, 1-1 Namiki, Tsukuba Ibaraki 305-0044, Japan

UMEKI, SHIGENOBU, physician, researcher; b. Arita, Wakayama, Japan, Sept. 23, 1951; s. Saichi and Katsuyo (Okamoto) U.; m. Yasuko Toshida, Feb. 11, 1980; children: Kazunori, Hirochika. Student, Gifu (Japan) Univ., 1971, postgrad., 1979. Jr. resident Gifu Univ. Sch. Med., 1977-79, asst. biochemistry, 1983-84; sr. resident internal medicine Kawasaki Med. Sch., Kurashiki, Japan, 1984-90, asst. prof., 1990-93; dir. internal medicine dept. Kumeda Hosp., Osaka, Japan, 1989-91, 93—. Fellow Japanese Coll. Physicians (award 1986), Internat. Coll. Angiology (award 1987), Am. Coll.

Chest Physicians (award 1989); mem. Japanese Soc. Internal Medicine, Japanese Biochem. Soc., AMA. Avocations: travel, tennis, reading, painting. Home: 655 3 Okayama Cho, Osaka Kishiwada 596-0814, Japan Office: Kumeda Hosp, 2944 Obu-Cho Kishiwada, Osaka 596, Japan

UMEMURA, TERUYOSHI, engineering educator; b. Okazaki, Aichi, Japan, Jan. 21, 1936; s. Kenji Takayama and Tai Umemura; m. Toyoko Ohwaki, Oct. 20, 1964; children: Akihiro, Kojiro. BEng, Nagoya (Japan) U., 1958; DEng, Tokyo U., 1978. Registered profl. engr. Prodn. engr. Toyota Body Co., Ltd., Kariya, Aichi, 1958-60; rsch. engr. Atomic Fuel Corp., Tokaimura, Ibaraki, Japan, 1960-65; assoc. prof. Saitama U., Urawa, japan, 1965-78; assoc. prof. Nagaoka U. Tech., Niigata, Japan, 1978-80, prof., 1980—, dir. tech. devel. ctr., 1992-98; guest prof. Nat. Inst. Polar Rsch., Tokyo, 1990-96. Contbr. articles to profl. jours. Gov. Found. for Applied Rsch. and Tech., Nagaoka, 1992-98, Niigata Engring. Co. 100th Anniversary Found., Niigata, 1993—. Mem. Japan Inst. Metals, Japan Soc. Mech. Engrs., Japan Foundrymen's Soc. (councillor 1984-87, 96-98, svc. award 1989, Kobayashi prize 1993, Iidaka prize 1994), Japan Soc. Snow and Ice (councillor 1989-94, tech. award 1995), Internat. Glaciological Soc., Nagaoka Acad. Engring. (pres. 1994—), N.Y. Acad. Scis. Avocations: fishing, skiing, listening to music. Home: Toyozume 212 14, Nagaoka 940-1142, Japan Office: Nagaoka U Tech, Kamitomiokamachi 1603-1, Nagaoka 940-2188, Japan

UMENWEKE, MESHACH OTUODICHUKWU, geologist, educator, consultant, researcher; b. Umuchu, Anambra, Nigeria, Apr. 20, 1948; s. Umenweke Umeononobi and Nwayiabia Lolo (Ikeako) U.; m. Bertha Echezona Orachusi, Aug. 3, 1969; children: Meshach Nnama, Emmanuel Ogochukwu, Ifeoma Chibuzo. BSc with honors, U. Nigeria, 1973; PhD, U. London, 1980. Jr. rsch. fellow U. Nigeria, Nsukka, Calabar Campus, Calabar, 1974-75; prodn. geologist Shell-BP, Lagos, 1979-80, Mobil Producing, Lagos, 1981-83; assoc. prof. Nnamdi Azikiwe U., Awka, 1984—, coord. gen. studies program, 1980-93, head dept. geology, 1990-94, postgrad. supr. MSc and PhD programs, 1990—; vis. sr. lectr. U. Nigeria, Nsukka, 1995-96, U. Windsor, Can., 1996. Editor Jour. Sci., Engring. Tech., 1993-98; contbr. articles to profl. jours. Bd. govs. Umuchu H.S., 1992-98; chmn. edn. com. Umuchu Improvement Union, 1990; patron Blind Students Assn. Anambra State, Awka, 1989-90; mem. Umuchu Improvement Union Rep. Assembly, 1992-98. Spl. Marshall, Rd. Traffic Control, Nigeria mil., 1990-98. Grantee Anambra State Govt., 1992, 94, Internat. Devel. Rsch. Coun. (Can.), 1992-96. Fellow Geol. Soc. Loondon; mem. Geol. Mining and Geosci. Soc., Nigerian Environ. Soc. Avocations: hockey, music, judo, lawn tennis. Home: St Thomas Anglican Ch, Umuchu Aguata Nigeria Office: Nnamdi Azikiwe U, Dept Geol Sci, PMB 5025 Awka Anambra, Nigeria

UMEYAMA, MOTOHIKO, educator; b. Hita, Japan, Mar. 27, 1955; s. Yoshio and Moto (Okano) U. BS, Tokyo U. Fisheries, 1978; MS, Tokyo Met. U., 1980; PhD, U. Hawaii, 1989. With Mitsui Cons. Co., Ltd., Tokyo, 1980-84; chief scientist CTI Sci. Systems Co., Ltd., Tokyo, 1991-94; assoc. prof. Tokyo Met. U., 1994—; vis. scientist Delft U. Tech., The Netherlands, 1989-90; rsch. asst. U. Hawaii, Honolulu, 1987-88; chief civil engr. Min. Pub. Works, Indonesia, 1992-93; asst. mgr. Office of Prime Min., Cook Islands, 1993-94. Asia Pacific scholar, State of Hawaii, Honolulu, 1984-87; Govtl. fellow, Netherlands Orgn. Internat. Coop. Higher Edn., 1989-90. Mem. Japan Soc. Civil Engrs., Oceanographic Soc. Japan. Baptist. Avocations: music, painting. Home: 2-22-17-202 Shimoyugi, Tokyo 192-0372, Japan Office: Tokyo Met U Dept Civil Engr, 1-1 Minamiohsawa, Tokyo 192-0397, Japan

UMEZU, TOYOSHI, behavioral scientist; b. Koyasu, Kanagawa, Japan, Apr. 15, 1961; s. Takeshi and Ayako (Ito) U. BS, U. Tsukuba, Japan, 1984, MS, 1986; PhD, Gunma U., Maebashi, Japan, 1990. Rschr. Nat. Inst. Environ. Studies, Tsukuba, 1990-94, sr. rschr., 1994—; postdoctoral fellow U. Va., 1995-97. Contbr. articles on behavioral pharmacology and toxicology and environ. sci. to sci. jours. Mem. AAAS (Internat. Order of Merit), N.Y. Acad. Sci., Japanese Pharmacol. Soc., Japanese Soc. Neuropsychopharmacology, Japan Assn. Indsl. Health. Avocations: listening to music, reading, eating delicious meals. Home: Takezono 3-303-214, Tsukuba 305-0032, Japan Office: Nat Inst Environ Studies, Nat Inst Environ Studies, Onogawa 16-2, Tsukuba 305-0053, Japan

UMIBE, FUJIO, management consultant; b. Nishinomiya, Hyogo, Japan, Feb. 28, 1926; s. Seijiro and Mitsuchiyo (Ito) U.; m. Emiko Goto, May 7, 1956; children: Hiroshi, Takeshi, Kiyoshi. B Engring., Univ. Tokyo, 1950; MS, Va. Polytechnic Inst., 1952. Engr. Tokyo Shibaura Elec. Co., Ltd., Kawasaki, Japan, 1950-63; mgr. indsl. engring. sect. Tokyo Shibaura Elec. Co., Ltd., Kawasaki, 1963-71, mgr. engring., JAL Cargo Terminal Div., 1971-72; mgr. JAL Cargo Terminal Div. Toshiba Corp. (formerly Tokyo Shibaura Elec. Co., Ltd.), Kawasaki, 1972-79, chief specialist, R&D Ctr., 1979-84; fellow Toshiba Rsch. Cons. Corp., Kawasaki, 1984-89, pres., 1989-91; cons. mgmt. engr.ng., tech. English Yokohama, Japan, 1991—; interpreter in field, 1953—; cons. in field; lectr. Univ. Shizuoka, Hamamatsu, Japan, Hosei U., Koganei, Japan, 1992-94. Contbg. editor/author: Mechanical Engineering Handbook, 1986; editor: Problem Solving Workbook, 1974; author tech. papers in field. Recipient Minister of Edn., Sci. and Culture award for first grade test, Soc. for Testing English Proficiency, Tokyo, 1968, Work Design Internat. Instr., The Work Design Soc. of Japan, Tokyo, 1968. Fellow Ops. Rsch. Soc. of Japan (v.p. 1985-86); mem. The Japan Inst. Indsl. Engring. (hon., Disting. Svc. award 1994), Japan Indsl. Mgmt. Assn., IEEE Engring. Mgmt. Soc. Avocations: music, gardening, travel, golf, games. Home: 21-12 Hirato 3 chome, Totsukaku Yokohama 244-0802, Japan

UMOINYANG, IMO EDET, mathematics educator, researcher; b. Ikot Mbon Ikono, Uyo Akwa Ibom States, Nigeria, June 20, 1963; s. Edet Etim and Esther Edet (Nsidibe) Inyang; m. Helen Imo Akpan, Apr. 8, 1991; children: Imo Ndoanie, Dat-Toyo, Ubokabasi Emekem. Cert. in edn., Coll. of Edn., Uyo, Nigeria, 1983; BS in Edn., U. Calabar, Nigeria, 1988, MEd, 1991; diploma in computer programming, 1994; PhD, U. Ibadan, 1999, BA in Theology, 1999. Tchr. Govt. Sch. Kachia, Nigeria, 1983-84, Comprehensive Secondary Sch. Ekori, Obubra, Nigeria, 1984-87, McIntire Secondary Cmty. Sch., Abak, Nigeria, 1987-89, Eastern Secondary Comml. Sch., Calabar, 1989-91, Edgerley Girls Secondary Sch., Calabar, 1991-92; lectr. U. Calabar, 1992—; examiner Nat. Tchrs. Inst., Kaduna, 1991-96; head sci. dept. Eastern Secondary Comml. Sch., 1990-91; exams officer Inst. of Edn., U. Calabar, 1992-95, 98—, project coord., 1993-95. Editor, author: Family: The Nucleus of the Society, 1994; contbr. articles to profl. jours.; editor Jour. of Cross River OMEP, 1995—; author: Research Methods in Enviromental Education, 1994, Techniques in Educational Measurement, 1999. Dir. youth evangelism AME Zion Ch., Nigeria, 1993-95, 94-96, 96-98, asst. pastor, 1992-94, presiding elder, 1997—; chmn. schs. sports com. Ministry of Edn., Abak, Nigeria, 1988-90. Grantee African Acad. Scis., 1995. Mem. Am. Edn. Rsch. Assn., Nat. Coun. on Measures in Edn., Sci. Tchrs. Assn. Nigeria, O.M.E.P. Nigeria, W.C.C.I. Sub-Saharan Africa. Avocations: preaching, reading, tennis, soccer, photography. Office: U Calabar Inst of Edn, PMB 1115, Calabar Nigeria

UMRIGAR, PURVEZ MANECK, human resources executive; b. Poona, India, Apr. 23, 1956; s. Maneck D. and Maneckbai M. (Masalawala) U.; m. Roshni Purvez Amaria Umrigar, Nov. 9, 1990; children: Urvaksh, Nirvana. Student, N. Wadia Coll. Master mariner F.G. class I. 2d navigating officer Shipping Corp. India, Bombay, 1977-78; chief officer S.C.I., Bombay, 1979; chief officer Wallem Shipmanagement, Hong Kong, 1980-84, master, 1984-86; site supt. Wallem Shipmanagement, Ulsan, South Korea, 1987-88; tech. supt. Wallem Shipmanagement, Hong Kong, 1988-89, marine human resources mgr., 1989—; com. mem., treas. Nautical Inst., Hong Kong, 1993—. Avocation: study of human sciences. Home: 1B Dragon Ct 30 Tai Hang Rd, Hong Kong Hong Kong Office: Wallem Shipmanagement, Hopewell Ctr 46th Fl 183 Queens Rd E, Hong Kong Hong Kong

UNBEHAUEN, HEINZ DIETRICH, electrical engineering educator; b. Stuttgart, Germany, Oct. 7, 1935; s. Leonhard and Margarete (Scheerer) U.; m. Elke Erbele, July 1967; children: Andreas, Regine, Manfred. Dipl.Ing., U. Stuttgart, 1961, Dr Ing., 1964, Habilitation, 1969. Sci. rsch. fellow U. Stuttgart, 1961-64, sci. asst., 1964-69, lectr., 1969-71, assoc. prof., 1971-75; prof. elec. engring. Ruhr U., Bochum, Germany, 1975—, dean, 1978-79; hon. prof. Tongji U., Shanghai, 1986; advisor of UNIDO and UNESCO. Author: Identification of Continuous Systems, 1987, Control Engineering I-III, 1982, 10th edit., 2000; hon. editor IEEE Procs.; assoc. editor IEEE-CAS, 1993-95, Automatica, C-TAT, 1984-95, OCAM, Adaptive Control and Signal Proc., Computers and Elec. Engring., Sys. Sci.; contbr. more than 400 articles to profl. jours. Recipient IBC-2000 Outstanding People award of the 20th Century, 1997, Man of Yr. award ABI, 1997; scholar Japanese Soc. for Promotion Sci., 1973, 97, German Acad. Exch. Soc., 1975, 82, 83, 89, 95, 96, VW Stiftung, 1990-91. Fellow IEEE (program chmn. Conf. Control Applications 1994); mem. Verein Deutscher Elektrotechniker (chmn. Verein Deutscher Ingenieure-Gesellschaft Mess Automatisierungstechnik adaptive sys. sect. Düsseldorf 1973-93). Office: Ruhr U, Universitässtrasse 150, 44780 Bochum Germany

UNCUTA, CORNELIA, chemist, researcher; b. Macedonia, Romania, Dec. 10, 1944; d. Petre and Virginia (Savin) U. PhD in chem. engring., Poly. Inst., Bucharest, Romania, 1966. Rschr. Inst. Atomic Physics, Bucharest, 1966-77; sr. rschr. Inst. Organic Chemistry, Bucharest, 1977—. Contbr. sci. articles to profl. jours. Recipient GH. Spacu award Romanian Acad., 1988. Mem. Romanian Chem. Soc. (gen. sec. 1993-97). Home: Aleea Poiana Cernei 4, 77321 Bucharest Romania Office: Inst Org Chem PO Box 15-254, Spl Independentei 202 B, 71141 Bucharest Romania

UNDERWEISER, IRWIN PHILIP, mining company executive, lawyer; b. N.Y.C., Jan. 3, 1929; s. Harry and Edith (Gladstein) U.; m. Beatrice J. Kortchmar, Aug. 17, 1959; children: Rosanne, Marian, Jeffrey. B.A., CCNY, 1950; LL.D., Fordham U., 1954; LL.M., NYU, 1961. Bar: N.Y. 1954. With firm Scribner & Miller, N.Y.C., 1951-54, 56-62; partner firm Feuerstein & Underweiser, 1962-73, Underweiser & Fuchs, 1973-77, Underweiser & Underweiser, 1977—; v.p., sec. Sunshine Mining Co., Kellogg, Idaho, 1965-70, chmn. bd., 1970-78, pres., 1971-74, 77, v.p., 1977-83; vice chmn., dir. Underwriters Bank and Trust Co., N.Y.C., 1969-73; sec., dir. Bus. Consortium Fund, 1994—, Triad Capital Corp. N.Y., 1994—; dir. Anchor Post Products, Inc. Bd. dirs. Silver Inst. Inc., vice chmn., 1998—; bd. dirs. Bronx Mus. of the Arts, 1993—, Sheltering the Homeless is Our Responsibility, 1993—; gen. counsel, mem. bus. council Friends City Center Music and Drama, N.Y.C., 1966-67; pres. W. Quaker Ridge Assn., 1969-70; treas. Scarsdale Neighborhood Assn. Presidents, 1970-71. Served with AUS, 1954-56. Mem. Am., N.Y. State bar assns., Bar Assn. City N.Y., Phi Beta Kappa, Phi Alpha Theta. Home: 7 Rural Dr Scarsdale NY 10583-7701 Office: 405 Park Ave New York NY 10022-4405

UNDERWOOD, GERALD TIMOTHY, business consultant; b. Nogales, Ariz., June 15, 1928; s. Timothy Irve and Ellen Christine (Rentzmann) U.; m. Marie Lois Steadman, Aug. 7, 1949; children: Lynn Gaye, Keri Ann Underwood Horrell. B in Engring., U. So. Calif., L.A., 1951. Mgr. factory sys. Deere & Co., Dubuque, Iowa, 1966-70, mgr. product engring. svcs., 1970-75; mgr. mgmt. devel. Deere & Co., Moline, Ill., 1975-77; factory mgr. Deere & Co., Monterrey, Mex., 1977-79; mgr. corp. engring. stds. Deere & Co., Moline, 1979-81, dir. engring. resource planning, 1981-84; dep. dir. internat. trade SBA, 1983; dir. metric program, dir. internat. programs E.A. divsn., U.S. Dept. Commerce, Washington, 1984-91; pres., cons. INTRX Assocs., Mo., 1991—; mgr. PC coord. Deere & Co. Europe, Mannheim, Germany, 1960-65, sys. analyst, Moline, 1958-60; sys. mgr./PC mgr. Beckman Instruments, Fullerton, Calif., 1954-58, Statham Labs., Santa Monica, Calif., 1951-54. Contbr. articles to profl. jours. Pres. Dubuque Cmty. Sch. Bd., 1974-75; steering com. YMCA of Washington, 1987; scout leader Boy Scouts Am., Fullerton, 1955. Recipient Bronze Medal award U.S. Dept. Commerce, Washington, 1989. Mem. ASTM, Soc. Automotive Engrs., Am. Soc. Agrl. Engrs., Am. Nat. Metric Coun. (pres. 1991-93, Presdl. award 1991), Am. Legion. Republican. Achievements include patent on hydraulic fitting protective device (closure). Avocations: hiking, investing, computer work, golf, fluent Spanish and German. Fax: (615) 673-8517.

UNDERWOOD, JOHN H., research engineer; b. Swampscott, Mass., Jan. 25, 1941; s. John Harvie Underwood and Esther F. (Butterfield) Charron; m. Margaret L. Paine, Dec. 26, 1964; children: Kristen Lee, John Harvie, Brian Thomas. BSME, U. Mass., 1962; MS in Metallurgy, NYU, 1965. Project engr. Bendix Corp., Teterboro, N.J., 1962-65; rsch. engr. Army Armament Rsch., Devel. and Engring. Ctr., Watervliet, N.Y., 1965—; vis. scientist Materials Rsch. Labs., Melbourne, Australia, 1987. Author, editor: Application of Fracture Mechanics for Selection of Metallic Structural Materials, 1982; editor: Chevon-Notched Specimens: Testing and Stress Analysis, 1984, Fracture Mechanics: Seventeenth Volume, 1986, Fatigue and Fracture Mechanics: 28th Vol., 1997; co-editor: Surface Crack Growth: Models, Experiments and Structures, 1990, Fracture Mechanics: 26th Edition, 1995. Chmn., bd. dirs. Cambridge (N.Y.) United Fund, 1967-69; pres. bd. edn. Cambridge Cen. Sch., 1973-74, 78-79. Recipient Outstanding Engring. Alumni award U. Mass., 1991. Fellow ASTM (mem. exec. com. E8 on fatigue and fracture 1980-95, chmn. symposium on fatigue and fracture mechanics 1996, chmn. symposium on fracture mechanics 1984, Irwin medal 1990, Wessel award 1999); mem. Soc. Exptl. Mechanics. Achievements include development of new methods for measurement of fracture and fatigue properties of metals and composites. Avocations: hiking, house construction, photography. Home: 193 Middle Rd Salem NY 12865-4517 Office: Army Armament Rsch Devel and Engring Ctr Bldg 115 Watervliet NY 12189

UNDERWOOD, RICHARD ALLAN, English language educator; b. Plymouth, Mich., Mar. 28, 1933; s. Harold Raymond and Yvonne Clara (Foster) U.; m. Sandra Jane Hayes, Nov. 17, 1962; 1 child, Eric Michael. BA, U. Mich., 1955, MA, 1967, PhD, 1970. Asst. prof. Clemson (S.C.) U., 1970-77, assoc. prof., 1977-84, prof. English, 1984—. Author: A Little Bit of Love, 1963, Shakespeare's "The Phoenix and Turtle": A Survey of Scholarship, 1974, Shakespeare on Love: The Poems and the Plays, 1985, The Two Noble Kinsmen and Its Beginnings, 1993; translator: En Smula Karlek, 1969, 81; editor: Phoenix with a Bayonet: A Journalist's Interim Report on the Greek Revolution (by Bayard Stockton), 1971. 1st lt. U.S. Army, 1955-57. Fellow Bread Loaf Writers Conf., 1963; vis. scholar Rackham Sch. Grad. Studies, U. Mich., 1983-85, 90-91, 91-92, 92-93, 93-94. Avocation: piano music. Home: 111 Lakeview Cir Clemson SC 29631-1019 Office: Clemson U 809 Strode Clemson SC 29631-1436

UNDERWOOD, ROBERT LEIGH, venture capitalist; b. Paducah, Ky., Dec. 31, 1944; s. Robert Humphreys and Nancy Wells (Jessup) U.; BS with gt. distinction (Alcoa scholar), Stanford U., 1965, MS (NASA fellow), 1966, PhD (NSF fellow), 1968; MBA, Santa Clara U., 1970; m. Susan Lynn Doscher, May 22, 1976; children: Elizabeth Leigh, Dana Whitney, George Gregory. Rsch. scientist, project leader Lockheed Missiles & Space Co., Sunnyvale, Calif., 1967-71; spl. asst. for engring. scis. Office Sec., Dept. Transp., Washington, 1971-73; sr. mgmt. assoc. Office Mgmt. and Budget, Exec. Office Pres., 1973; with TRW Inc., L.A., 1973-79, dir. retail nat. accounts, 1977-78, dir. product planning and devel., 1978-79; pres., CEO OMEX, Santa Clara, Calif., 1980-82; v.p. Heizer Corp., Chgo., 1979-85; v.p. No. Trust Co., pres. No. Capital Corp., Chgo., 1985-86; mng. ptnr. ISSS Ventures, 1986-88; exec. v.p. N.Am. Bus. Devel. Co., Chgo., 1988—; dir. various pvt. and pub. portfolio cos., MECC 1991-96; trustee Burridge Mut. Funds, 1996-98; mem. adv. com. indsl. innovation NSF, 1982-96; mem. sch. bd. Avoca Dist. 37, 1990-99, v.p., 1996-99; mem. adv. bd. Leavey Sch. Bus. and Adminstrn. Santa Clara U., 1995—. Mem. IEEE, Sigma Xi, Phi Beta Kappa, Tau Beta Pi, Beta Gamma Sigma. Elder, Presbyterian Ch., 1978-79. Clubs: Union League Chgo., Chgo. Club; Manasquan River Yacht (Brielle, N.J.); Indian Hill (Winnetka, Ill.). Contbr. articles to profl. jours. Home: 59 Woodley Rd Winnetka IL 60093-3748 Office: 135 S La Salle St Chicago IL 60603-4159

UNDERWOOD, STEVEN CLARK, publishing executive; b. Arlington Heights, Ill., Dec. 1, 1960; s. Donald William and Mary Frances (Clark) U. BBA, U. Tex., 1982, MBA, 1987; JD, So. Meth. U., 1985. Bar: Tex. 1985. Sr. fin. analyst CBS, Inc., N.Y.C., 1987-89; assoc. bus. mgr. Supplementary Edn. Group Simon & Schuster, Englewood Cliffs, N.J., 1989-90; bus. mgr. Fearon/Janus/Quercus divsn. Simon & Schuster, Belmont, Calif., 1990-92, pres. Fearon/Janus/Quercus divsn., 1992-93; pres. Globe Fearon divsn. Simon & Schuster, Upper Saddle River, N.J., 1993-96; v.p., dir. of bus. devel. Secondary Edn. Group, Simon and Schuster, Upper Saddle River, N.J., 1996-97; v.p. bus. devel. Simon and Schuster, Upper Saddle River, N.J., 1997-98; v.p. sch. markets Troll Comms., Mahwah, N.J., 1998—. Mem. ABA, Am. Mgmt. Assn. (pres.'s assn.), Assn. Am. Pubs., Nat. Eagle Scout Assn., Coll. Bus. Adminstrn. Found., Tex. Bar Assn., Tex. Alumni Assn., U. Tex. Century Club, Alpha Phi Omega, Beta Gamma Sigma, Phi Kappa Phi, Phi Eta Sigma, Golden Key. Republican. Methodist. Avocations: sailing, scuba diving, karate, camping, rafting. Home: 902 Somerset Ct Ramsey NJ 07446-2919

UNDEUTSCH, UDO HEINZ-HERMANN, psychology educator; b. Weimar, Germany, Dec. 22, 1917; s. Paul and Maria (Niggemeyer) U.; m. Hanna Bierfreund, Jan. 9, 1946; children: Klaus, Ursula, Barbara, Elisabeth, Inge. MA in Psychology, Fr. Schiller U.-Jena, 1942, Dr.rer.nat., 1941. Asst. prof. Fr. Schiller U., Jena, 1941-45; assoc. prof. psychology U. Mainz, 1946-51; prof. psychology U. Cologne, 1951—. Author: Psychologische Untersuchungen am Unfallort, 1962, Die psychische Entwicklung der heutigen Jugend, 1966, Sicherheit im Betrieb, 2d edit., 1965, Psychologische Impulse für die Verkehrsicherheit, 1977; editor: Forensische Psychologie, 1967. Pres. Com. Safety for the Child, 1972; mem. rsch. group Human Factor in Traffic Safety, Koln, 1968. Recipient Bundesverdienstkreuz 1st class (Fed. Republic Germany), Golden Diesel Ring, Assn. Motor Journalists, 1984, officer Order of King Leopold II (Belgium). Mem. Deutsche Gesellschaft für Psychologie, Berufsverband Deutscher Psychologen. Roman Catholic. Home: Farnweg 1, 50226 Frechen Germany

UNDY, ROGER, management educator, academic administrator; b. Nottingham, Eng., Nov. 2, 1938; s. Harold and Harriet (Holmes) U.; m. Kathleen Claire Stevenson, Sept. 19, 1959; children: Kim, Ruth. BA, Oxford (Eng.) U., 1972. Research assoc. Oxford U. Ctr. Mgmt. Studies, 1972-75, research fellow, 1975-77, fellow in indsl. relations, 1977-80, sr. tutor, 1980-83; fellow Templeton Coll. Templeton Coll. Oxford Ctr. Mgmt. Studies, 1983—, dir. Oxford Inst. Employee Relations, 1985—, dean, 1988, acting pres., 1990-92; cons. Eng. and Europe, 1977—. Author: Change in Trade Unions, 1981, Ballots and TU Democracy, 1984, Managing the Unions, 1996; contbr. articles to profl. jours. Labour Party candidate Parliament, Bridgwater, Eng., 1974. Mem. Assn. Univ. Tchrs. Mem. United Reformed Ch. Avocations: gardening, snooker. Home: 6 Feilden Grove, Headington, Oxford England Office: Oxford U Templeton Coll, Kennington, Oxford OX1 5NY, England

UNG, JANET W., marketing researcher; b. Seattle, May 2, 1970; d. Tom and May Ung. BA in Econs., BA in Sociology, U. Wash., 1993. Market rschr. Grubb & Ellis, Seattle, 1990-93; exec. asst. Kidder, Matthews & Segner, Seattle, 1993-94; project mgr. Asia Market Intelligence, Ltd., Taipei, Taiwan, 1994—; v.p. projects AIESEC, Seattle, 1992-93. Mem. Chinese Am. Profls. in Taiwan, Am. C. of C. E-mail: janet ung@ami-group.com. Office: Asia Market Intelligence, 133 Min Sheng E Rd 11th Fl, Taipei Taiwan

UNG, LIM ENG, physician; b. Ipoh, Perak, Malaysia, May 16, 1942; s. Cheow Khek Ung and Ean Phaik Khoo; m. Huang Sek Chang, Aug. 29, 1968; children: Casey, Coreen. MBBS, U. Singapore, 1967; MD (hon.), Open Internat. U., Colombo, 1993; diploma in practical dermatology, U. Wales, Cardiff, 1997. Cert. in aviation medicine. House officer Gen. Hosp., Kuala Lumpur, Malaysia, 1967-68; gen. practitioner Lahad Datu, Malaysia, 1971—; cons. Felda Sahabat, Lahad Datu, 1985—. Capt. Royal Malaysian AF, 1968-71. Mem. Malaysian Med. Assn., Malaysian Soc. Ultrasound in Medicine, Malaysian Soc. Hypnosis, Lahad Datu Golf and Country Club (pres. 1995—). Avocations: golf, jogging. Office: Ungenglim Health Svcs, PO Box 60291, 91112 Lahad Datu Sabah, Malaysia

UNGAR, GORAN, polymer scientist, chemistry educator; b. Zagreb, Yugoslavia, Croatia, June 12, 1948; arrived in Eng., 1984; s. Pavao and Sala (Kramer) U.; children: Natasha, Erika. D in Chemistry, U. Zagreb, 1972, M. in Macromolecular Sci., 1975; PhD in Physics, U. Bristol, Eng., 1979. Rsch. asst. Ruder Bokovic Inst., Zagreb, 1972-75, lab. head, 1979-84; rsch. asst. U. Bristol, Eng., 1975-79; rsch. assoc. U. Bristol, 1984-89; lectr. U. Sheffield, 1989-99, reader, 1999—; referee numerous internat. sci. jours., speaker numerous sci. confs. and seminars, cons. to internat. chem. cos. including BP Am., Cleve. Contbr. numerous articles to sci. jours., and chpts. to books. Mem. Inst. of Physics, British Liquid Crystal Soc. Avocations: mountaineering, canoeing, skiing, music. Home: 43 Winchester Crescent, Sheffield S10 4ED, England Office: Univ Sheffield-Dept Engring Mats, Mappin St, Sheffield S1 3JD, England

UNGARETTI, RICHARD ANTHONY, lawyer; b. Chgo., May 25, 1942; s. Dino Carl and Antoinette (Calvetti) U.; children: Joy A., Paul R. BS, DePaul U., 1964, JD, 1970. Bar: Ill. 1970, U.S. Dist. Ct. (no. dist.) Ill. 1970, U.S. Supreme Ct. 1980. Assoc. Kirkland & Ellis, Chgo., 1970-74; ptnr. Ungaretti & Harris, Chgo., 1974—. Mem. adv. coun. DePaul Coll. Law, Chgo., 1988. Mem. ABA, Chgo. Bar Assn., Ill. State Bar Assn., Internat. Coun. Shopping Ctrs., Am. Coll. Real Estate Lawyers, Justinian Soc., Urban Land Inst. (assoc.), Lamda Alpha. Avocations: golf, fishing, hunting. Office: Ungaretti & Harris 3500 Three First Nat Plz Chicago IL 60602

UNGARO, EMANUEL MATTEOTTI, fashion designer; b. Aix-en-Provence, France, Feb. 13, 1933; s. Cosimo and Concetta (Casalino) U.; m. Laura; 1 dau. Student, Lycée, Aix-en-Provence, 1943-50. Worked with father as tailor Aix-en-Provence, 1951-54; then for Camps Paris, 1955-57; with Cristobal Balenciaga, Paris, 1957-64, dir. Balenciaga br., Madrid, 1958-60; worked for André Courréges, Paris, 1964; ind. couturier, Paris, 1965. Designer of both couture and ready-to-wear men's and women's fashions; also fragrance designer since 1977. Office: 2 Ave Montaigne, F 75008 Paris France

UNGARO, MARIA REGINA, agronomist, researcher; b. Sao Paulo, Brazil, Nov. 15, 1951; d. Ernani R. Goncalves and Clelia Aparecida (Fray) Goncalves; m. Fernando Ungaro, Sept. 13, 1974; children: Gustavo, Eduardo, Mariana. BSc, U São Paulo, Piracicaba, Brazil, 1973, MSc, 1981, Dr, 1994. Sci. rschr. IAC, Campinas, Brazil, 1974-85, head oilseed dept., 1985-89, 90—, sci. rschr., 1997—; sci. adv. FAPESP, Sao Paulo, 1997—, CNPq, Brasilia, Brazil, 1995—; sci. adv. Jour. Pesquisa Agropecuaria Gaucha, 1996—. Contbr. articles to profl. jours. Recipient Honor award Sao Paulo State Govt., 1981. Mem. Internat. Sunflower Assn. (found. mem.), Lions Club Internat. Avocations: reading, hand work, cooking. E-mail: ungaro@cec.iac.br. Home: Rua Dr Socrates de Oliveira 99, Chacara Urbana, 13201838 Jundiai SP, Brazil Office: Inst Agronomico-CEGRAN, Avenida Barao Itapura 1481, 13020-97 Campinas, Sao Paulo Brazil

UNGE, PETER OTTO LENNART, physician; b. Vadstena, Ostergotland, Sweden, Mar. 31, 1951; s. Lennart Otto and Astrid Ella Mary (Karlsson) U. m. Maj-Britt Elisabeth Forsman, Oct. 4, 1975; children: Elin, Daniel, Staffan, Fredrik, Katrin. MD, Karolinska Inst., 1977. Cert. specialist in internal medicine. Trainee Gavle (Sweden) Hosp., 1976-82; sr. cons. Sandviken (Sweden) Hosp., 1982-92, head dept. internal medicine, 1992-97; head dept. internal medicine Lanssih Gavle Sandviken, 1997—; cons. to drug industry USA, Finland, Sweden, Japan, 1984—. Contbr. articles to profl. jours. Lt. Swedish Army, 1986. Mem. Swedish Soc. Gastroenterology and Gastrointestinal Endoscopy, Scandinavian Clinics for United Rsch., Sallskapet. Avocation: sailing. Home: ÄsvÄgen 27, 818 33 Valbo Sweden Office: Dept Medicine, Lanssjukhuset Gavle Sandviken, 801 87 Gävle Sweden

UNGER, FELIX, heart surgeon; b. Klagenfurt, Carinthia, Austria, Mar. 2, 1946; s. Carl and Maria Unger; m. Monika Von Fioreschy, 1971; children: Stephan, Matthaus. MD, U. Vienna, 1971; D (hon.), U. Budapest, 1994, U. Tokyo, 1997. Prof. U. Innsbruck, 1978-85; head of heart surgery Salzburg State Hosp., 1985—; intern Vienna, 1971; dir. European Heart Inst., Salzburg, 1990—. Author: Assisted Circulation, Vols. 1-5, 1979-97, Wucht des Ganzen, 1997; inventor ellipsoidheart. Mem. European Acad. Scis. and Arts (founder, pres. 1990—). Roman Catholic. Avocation: arts. Home: Schwimmschulstr 31, A-5020 Salzburg Austria Office: European Acad Scis and Arts, Waagplatz 3, A-5020 Salzburg Austria

UNGER, GARY ALLEN, recording industry executive, singer, lyricist; b. Clinton, Iowa, Aug. 14, 1947; s. Charles Elmer Unger and Lois Grace Haack. Grad. high sch., Ill., 1967. Internat. import-export mgr. G & U Enterprises, Clinton, 1968—; mgr., pres. Groove Song Music, Clinton,

1968—, Narrowroad Music, Clinton, 1968—; mgr., v.p. ACI, Clinton, 1978-79; mgr., pres. ECI Internat. Records, Clinton, 1980-96, GTM, Clinton, 1973, Aci Am. Comm. Ind. Corp., Nashville, 1976—; pres. Sugarvine Music (BMI); on Art Bell Radio Talk Show, Radio Network, 1996-97. Lyricist: Home, I Will Always Love You Part I and II, I Like It, I Love It, Thinkin About You, Give Them All to Jesus, (with G. Russen) My Coloring Book, 1955, God Bless the Service, (with D. Swanson) Please! Don't Tell Me No More Lies, Country Sunshine, 1965, Tennessee River, 1965, The Love in Her Soul, Heart to Heart, 1968, Fool for Your Love, God Bless You Jesus, 1967, God Bless the Service, Born in This U.S.A., 1967, Parts I, II, and III, I've Never Been to England, God Knows, If You're Not In It for Love, Real Love, Hey June and Darline, I Got Jesus on My Mind, God Bless the Service, Parts I and II, Heaven O Sweet Angel, The Love in Her Soul, Please Remember Me, Oh! Country Doll, Oh! Baby Doll, You Win My Love, Oh! Sweet Honey, Girl I Love You, Love is Like a Butterfly, Let Us Pray Together, My Coloring Book, Lost in the 50's Tonight, Kentucky Rain Blue I'm So Blue, All I Want Is a Life with You Jesus, On the 4th of July, Boot Scootin Boogie, Love Is (co-writer: Joan Brothers), Almost Like a Song, Why Can't Every Day Be Like Christmas, Resolution, Moody Blues, Third Rock From the Sun, God Bless Texas Too, Maybe You Can Drive my Car, Oh, My, My, Those Rock N Years, My Achin Breaken Heart, Born to Love You, We Were Meant for Each Other, Jesus OH! Jesus I Love You, Don't Worry Be Happy Like Happy, Please Don't Bump the Jukebox, I Like It I Love It, Hey It's a Small Town, God Bless the U.S.A. (Born in the USA), The Happiest Guy in the Whole USA, God Writes the Songs, When You Walked In, You Better Think Twice Again, My Coloring Book, On Independence Day, Together With Our Heartfelt Love, She's Gone Country, You Light Up My Life, Give Them All to Jesus, Was I Touched by a Holy Angel?, Almost Everywhere, No One Else on Earth, Praise the Lord, On American Bandstand, Love Is, If Tomorrow Never Comes, In My Life, The Long and Winding Roads, Please! Remember Me, Hello-Good-Buy, Oh! Country Doll, Creator of the Stars, others. Mem. RIAA, GNACMAI, Nat. Assn. Songwriters Internat., Nat. Music Found. Fax: 319-243-1334. Home: PO Box 852 Clinton IA 52733-0852

UNGER, GERE NATHAN, physician, lawyer; b. Monticello, N.Y., May 15, 1949; s. Jessie Aaron and Shirley (Rosenstein) U.; m. Alicen J. McGowan, July 21, 1990; children: Elijah, Breena, Ari, Sasha, Arlen. JD, Bernadean U., 1979; MD, Inst. Politecnico, Mexico City, 1986; D Phys. Medicine, Met. U., Mexico City, 1987; postgrad., Boston U., 1993, Harvard Law Sch., 1994-96; LLM in Med. Law, U. Glasgow, 2000. Dipomate Am. Bd. Forensic Examiners, Am. Bd. Med. Legal Analysis in Medicine and Surgery, Am. Bd. Forensic Medicine, Am. Bd. Risk Mgmt. Med. dir. Vietnam Vets. Post-Traumatic Stress Disorder Program, 1988-90; emergency rm. physician, cons. in medicaid fraud Bronx (N.Y.)-Lebanon Hosp., 1990—; clin. legal medicine Paladin Profl. Group, P.A., Palm Beach, Fla., 1992-98; pres. Albany Law Jour. Co., Inc., 1998—; jurisconsult Office of Gere Unger, M.D., J.D., 1999—; mediator, arbitrator World Bank, 2000—; mediator, arbitrator, negotiator World Intellectual Property Orgn., 1994; mem. peer rev. com. Nat. Inst. on Disability and Rehab. Rsch., Office Spl. Edn., U.S. Dept. Edn., 1993; mem. clin. ethics com. Inst. Medecine Legale et de Medecine Sociale, Strasbourg, France, 1994; mem. surg. critical care com. Am. Soc. Critical Care Medicine, 1992; N.Y. state capt. Am. Trial Lawyers Exch., 1992. Editl. rev. bd. Am. Bd. Forensic Examiners, 1993, Jour. Neurol. and Orthopaedic Medicine and Surgery, 1993. Commandant Broward County Marine Corps League, 1995—. With USMC, 1968-72. Diplomate Am. Bd. Disability Analysts; fellow Internat. Coll. Surgeons (mem. ethics com. 1994, mem. emergency response program Ea. region 1994), Am. Acad. Neurol. and Orthopaedic Surgeons, Am. Coll. Legal Medicine, Am. Coll. Forensic Examiners, Exec. Practice Mgmt.; mem. ABA, ATLA, FBA (mem. health com., rep. ABA 1994, chmn. med. malpractice/tort com. and FBA liaison to AMA), Nat. Coll. Advocacy, Internat. Bar Assn., Am. Coll. Physician Execs. (chair forum on law and med. mgmt. 1995), Kennedy Inst. Ethics, Am. Soc. of Laser Medicine and Surgery, Nat. Assn. of Forensic Econs., Am. Bd. Disability Analysts, Internat. Royal Soc. of Medicine (London). Avocations: flying, boating. Office: 8 Elk St Ste 3 Albany NY 12207-1010

UNGER, HERMANN, physicist, educator; b. Beilstein, Germany, May 8, 1934. Diploma in physics, U. Stuttgart, 1961, dr.-ing., 1967, prof., 1968. With Robert Bosch GmbH, Stuttgart, Germany, 1953-54; postgrad. rsch. fellow Argonne (Ill.) Nat. Lab., 1960-61; rsch. asst. U. Stuttgart, 1962-67, head project reactor safety and environment IKE, 1971-87; asst. prof. Northwestern U., Evanston, Ill., 1968-71; prof. U. Stuttgart, Germany, 1974-87, Ruhr-Univ. Bochum, Germany, 1987—. Editor: DPG-Arbeitskreis Energie Hauptvortraege des AKE Energie, 1992-93. Mem. Kerntechnische Gesellschaft, Deutsche Physikalische Ges., Verein Deutscher Ingenieure, Deutsche Gesellschaft für Luft- und Raumfahrt. Office: Ruhr-Universitat Bochum, Universitatsstr 150, D-44801 Bochum Germany

UNGER, HOWARD ALBERT, artist, photographer, educator; b. Mt. Vernon, N.Y., Oct. 13, 1944; s. Howard Albert and Florence A. (Peterson) U.; m. Anrita Abelow, Aug. 25, 1972; 1 son, Christopher Howard. Student, Art Students League, N.Y.C., 1960-61, Sch. Visual Arts, N.Y.C., 1975-76, N.Y. Inst. Holography, 1976; BFA, Kent State U., 1966, MA, 1968; MEd, Columbia U., 1972, EdD, 1975; MA, N.Y. Inst. Tech., 1994. Cert. open water diver, 1988, advanced scuba diver, 1989. Grad. tchg. fellow in photojournalism Kent State U., 1966-67, instr. in art, 1966-67, grad. teaching fellow in art, 1967-68; head program in art, tchr. art Kew-Forest Prep. Sch., Kew Gardens, N.Y., 1968-69; technician TV sta. Tchrs. Coll., Columbia U., 1971-72, instr. art and edn., 1972-75, instr. curriculum and tchg., 1976-82, instr. dept. comm., computing and tech. in edn., 1982—; asst. prof. visual comm. tech. dept. humanities Ocean County Coll., 1972-78, assoc. prof., 1979-82, prof., 1982—, gallery coord. Fine Arts Ctr., 1972—; part-time grad. instr. comm. arts N.Y. Inst. Tech., N.Y.C., 1994-95; instr. comm. and edn. Sch. Edn. NYU, 1973-74; design and photograph coord. RCA Records, N.Y.C., 1969-70; freelance designer, 1965—. Exhibitor photography in one-man shows, Photographis Societas Photographis, Columbia U., 1971, Ziegfeld Gallery, N.Y.C., 1972; group shows, Kent State U., 1965-68, Ocean County Coll., 1973-83, 14 Sculptor Gallery, N.Y.C., 1995; permanent collections, Internat. Ctr. Photography, N.Y.C., Mus. Holography, N.Y.C., Kent State U., Ocean County Coll., Tchrs. Coll., Columbia U., pvt. collections; lectr. in photography; co-author: (with William Maxwell) photog. illustrator Printmaking: A Beginner's Handbook, 1977; photog. illustrator: The Fourth R. Stewart Kranz, 1971; contbg. author: A Tour Through The Realm of Science Plus Art, 1974; photography critic: Village Voice, 1976-77; photography columnist Soho Weekly News, 1977-78. Recipient 1st place award Am. Greeting Card Competition, 1966; recipient honorarium dept. curriculum and teaching Tchrs. Coll., Columbia U., 1973. Mem. Soc. Photography Educators, NEA, Mus. Modern Art, NJ. Edn. Assn., Met. Mus. Art, Am. Mus. Natural History, Profl. Assn. Diving Instrs. (lic. advanced scuba diver), Nat. Assn. Underwater Instrs. (lic. advanced scuba diver). Republican. Home: 515 E 79th St New York NY 10021-0705 Office: Ocean County Coll College Dr Toms River NJ 08754-2001

UNGER, TANYA SHAWN, geologist, consultant; b. St. Louis, Aug. 14, 1975; d. J. Keith and Donna Jean (Means) U. BS cum laude, U. Vt., 1997. Geologist, consultant U.S. Geol. Survey, Woods Hole, Mass., 1997—. Mem. Am. Geophysical Union, Phi Beta Kappa. Avocations: hiking, camping, snowboarding, quilting, painting. Office: US Geol Survey Woods Hole Field Ctr 384 Woods Hole Rd Woods Hole MA 02543-1523

UNGERER, DIETRICH ALBRECHT, safety scientist, educator; b. Heilbronn, Germany, Jan. 27, 1933; s. Gottlieb and Bertha (Stein) U.; m. Elke Regina Ehlert, Feb. 2, 1968; children: Kristina, Jörn, Meike. Diploma, U. Heidelberg, Germany, 1956. Cert. safety sci. Rsch. asst. U. GÖttingen, Germany, 1956-57, U. Heidelberg, 1957-67; dir. Tech. U., Berlin, 1967-74; full prof. U. Bremen, Germany, 1974—. Author: Theory of Sensorimotor Learning, 1977; co-author: Safety Programm Bus Driver, 1994 (1st prize Internat. Social Security Assn. 1994), Stress and Leadership in Action, 1997, Stress and Stress Coping in Action, 1999; editor: Communication and Prevention, 1983. Mem. Am. Soc. for Cybernetics, European Assn. for Accident (pres.), German Soc. for Aeronautics and Astronautics.

UNGERER, HORST, international economist, lecturer, writer; b. Stuttgart, Germany, Dec. 14, 1930; came to U.S., 1970; s. Max and Elisabeth Ungerer; m. Rajka Ungerer, Sept. 30, 1970; 1 stepchild, Daniel Kolak. Diploma in Econs., U. Tuebingen, Germany, 1956, D in Econs., 1959. Tchg. asst. U. Tuebingen, 1956-59; sect. chief Deutsche Bundesbank, Frankfurt, Germany, 1959-65; alt. exec. dir. Internat. Monetary Fund, Washington, 1965-68; dept. head Deutsche Bundesbank, 1968-70; divsn. chief Internat. Monetary Fund, 1970-73, advisor, 1973-80, asst. dir., 1980-91; mem. monetary com. European Cmty., Brussels, 1968-70; guest prof. Bundeswehr U., Hamburg, Germany, 1992, Duke U., Durham, N.C., 1993, U. Saarbruecken, Germany, 1994. Author: A Concise History of European Monetary Integration, 1997; contbr. numerous articles to profl. jours. Avocations: piano and harpsichord, classical music and jazz, history of art, travelling, photography. Home: 8314 Westmont Ter Bethesda MD 20817-6819

UNGERER, MARTIN, physician, researcher; b. Munich, Germany, Mar. 12, 1965; s. Fritz and Gisela U.; m. Katharina Löhr, 1997. Degree, U. Nice, France, 1987; MD, U. Munich, 1997, D, 1991, Habil, 1999. Post doctorate Gene Ctr., Munich, 1991-92; rsch. fellow Med. Clinic, Munich, 1992—. Contbr. articles to profl. jours. Mem. German Soc. Heart Rsch. (award 1992).

UNGERLEIDER, ROBERT NORMAN, lawyer; b. Englewood, N.J.; s. Emil and Lillian Stone U.; m. Linda L. Salsman, Sept. 23, 1967; children: Michelle E. Ungerleider Friedman, Deborah E. Ungerleider Tight. BA, Rutgers U., 1962, LLB, 1965. Bar: N.J. 1965, Ill. 1975, U.S. Dist. Ct. (no. dist.) N.J. 1965, U.S. Dist. Ct. (no. dist.) Ill. 1975. Staff atty. Middlesex County Legal Svc. Corps., Perth Amboy, N.J., 1968-70; exec. dir. Perth Amboy Model Cities Adminstrn., 1970-72; sr. assoc. SPA/Redco, Inc., Chgo., 1972-74; assoc. Sheldon L. Baskin, Esq., Chgo., 1974-86; ptnr. Katz, Randall, Weinberg & Richmond, Chgo., 1986, 2000-01; mem. blue ribbon adv. bd. Cook County Recorder of Deeds, Chgo., Mcpl. Ct. adv. com., Chgo.; mem. blue ribbon devel. com. Nat. Ctr. on Poverty Law, Chgo., 2000; adj. prof. housing laws Northwestern Sch. Law, 2000-2001; adj. prof. Marshall Sch. Law, 1998-99. Co-editor Tenant-Landlord Handbook Illinois, 1976; exec. editor ABA Jour. on Affordable Housing and Cmty. Devel. Law., 1993—; contbr. articles to ABA Jour. Vol. Am. Peace Corps, Bombay, 1965-67; mem. Mental Health Nd, Middlesex County, N.J., 1969, New Brunswick, cmty. adv. bd. N.J. Pub. Broadcasting, Trenton, 1969; bd. dirs., pres. Chiavalle Montesorri Sch., Evanston, Ill., 1974-76. Recipient cert. of recognition Coun. for Jewish Elderly, 1978; named Advocate of Yr., Ray Graham Assn. for Physically Handicapped, 1978. Mem. ABA (governing com. Forum on Affordable Housing 1995-2002, chair forum on affordable housing and cmty. devel. law 2000-2001), Ill. State Bar Assn., Chgo. Bar Assn. Avocations: travel, sports, books, music. E-mail: rungerleider@krw.com. Home: 100 Williamsburg Rd Evanston IL 60203-1813 Office: Katz Randall Weinberg & Richmond 333 W Wacker Dr Ste 1800 Chicago IL 60606-1329

UNGLAUB, ERICH, philologist, institute administrator; b. Friedberg, Bavaria, Germany, Sept. 2, 1947. Dr phil, U. Munich, 1983. Lectr. U. Munich, 1982-95; dir. Inst. for German Philology, Flensburg, Germany, 1995—; prof. U. Flensburg, 1995—. Author: Das mit Fingern deutende Publicum, 1983; contbr. articles to profl. jours., including Recherches Germaniques, Orbis Litterarum, Neohelicon, Euphorion. E-mail: unglaub@t-online.de. Office: Inst for German Philology, Schützenkuhle 26, D-24937 Flensburg Germany

UNGUREAN, PAVEL VASILE, economist, educator; b. Reghin, Romania, June 5, 1966; s. Leonida and Ana (Logigan) U.; m. Gabriela Victoria Lingurean, May 9, 1991; 1 child, Tudor Marius. Economist, U. Cluj-Napoca, Romania, 1989, PhD, 1997. Credit inspector Nat. Bank Romania, Signisoara, Romania, 1989-90; prof. Econ. High Sch., Mures, 1990-91; prof. faculty econs. Babes-Bolyai U., Clubj-Napoca, 1991—. Co-author: Money and Credit, 1998, author: The Interest and Their Role in the Economy, 1998, the Interest Practic Guide, 1999. Cpl. Romanian mil., 1984-95. Mem. Internat. Fedn. Accts. Home: Muresului Nr 37/8, 3400 Cluj-Napoca Romania Office: Faculty Econs Fin Dept, St 21 Dec 1989 Nr 128, 3400 Cluj-Napoca Romania

UNGUREANU, ERNEST M., parasitology educator, consultant; b. Bistricioara, Romania, July 5, 1912; s. Mihai C. and Elena M. (Creanga) U.; m. Lucretia E. Cepreaga, Oct. 30, 1937; children: Steliana, Viorica. BS, Iasi (Romania) U., 1936, DSc, 1946. Entomologist Ministry of Health, Iasi, 1937-45, chief, malaria divsn., 1945-63; prof. parasitology Ministry of Edn., Iasi, 1946-75; cons. prof. U. Medicine, Iasi, 1975—; malaria advisor, WHO, Geneva, 1963-73, cons., 1973—; dir. Inst. Hygiene, Iasi, 1960-63. Contbr. articles to profl. jours. Fellow Romanian Soc. Tropical Medicine; mem. N.Y. Acad. Scis., Romanian Acad. Med. Scis. (emeritus), Romanian Acad. Scientists (hon.). Romanian Orthodox. Avocations: fishing, painting. Office: U Medicine and Pharmacy, Parasitology Lab, 6600 Iasi Romania

UNGVARI, GABOR SANDOR, psychiatrist, educator; b. Budapest, Hungary, May 2, 1948; arrived in New Zealand, 1987; s. Jozsef and Magdolna (Kalman) U.; m. Katalin Erzsebet Meggyes, Nov. 22, 1972; children: Peter, Daniel. MD, Med. Sch., 1972; PhD, Acad. of Sci., 1982. Assoc. prof. dept. psychiatry Med. Sch., Budapest, 1982-88; sr. lectr. dept. psychiatry U. Otago, Dunedin, New Zealand, 1988-95; assoc. prof. dept. psychiatry Chinese U. of Hong Kong, 1995—; cons. Prince Wales Hosp., 1992—. Editor: Recent Advances in Leonhardian Nosology, 1997; co-author: Troublesome Disguises, 1997; contbr. numerous articles to profl. jours. Fellowship Shaw Coll., 1995—. Fellow Australian and New Zealand Coll. of Psychiatrists, Hong Kong Coll. of Psychiatrists, Hong Kong Acad. of Medicine; mem. Internat. Wernicke-Kleist-Leonhard Soc. (sec.-treas. 1995—). Avocations: American fiction, swimming, long-distance running, movies. Home: 12 Melrose St, Dunedin New Zealand Office: Prince of Wales Hosp, Dept Psychiatry, Shatin Hong Kong NT, China

UNIKEL, EVA TAYLOR, interior designer; arrived in Can., 1956; came to U.S., 1967; d. Istvan Domolky and Lea Maria (Koszegi) Coan; m. Alan L. Unikel; 1 child, Renee Christine; m. June 26, 1993. BS, So. Ill. U., 1972. Dir. mktg. Lococo Design, St. Louis, 1982-83; project mgr., nat. dir. mktg. hosp. div. Hotel Restaurant Planners div. Profl. Interiors, St. Louis, 1983-87; founder Interior Solutions Inc., Hinsdale, Ill., 1987—. Mem. AIA (assoc.), Nat. Assn. Women Bus. Owners, Am. Soc. Interior Design (chairperson 1984-86), Nat. Assn. Indsl. Office Pks., Bldg. Owners and Mgrs. Assn., Internat. Interior Design Assn. Roman Catholic. Office: 500 E Ravine Rd Hinsdale IL 60521-2449

UNISON-PACE, WENDY JANE, nurse, critical care; b. Mar. 20, 1964; d. Harvey Charles and Bette Adele (Aimone) U. Student, Coll. DuPage, 1982-84; BS, No. Ill. U., 1988; BSN, Concordia U. & West Suburban Coll. Nursing, 1995; grad. in Nursing Adminstrn., Va. Commonwealth U., 2000—. Cert. Pediatric Advanced Life Support, Advanced Cardiac Life Support, Emergency Nursing Pediatric; RN, Va. Residential supr., instr. in sign lang. Mental Health & Deafness Resources Inc., Ctr. on Deafness, Des Plaines, Ill., 1989-95; RN oncology unit West Suburban Hosp. Med. Ctr., Oak Park, Ill., 1995; RN cardiac care unit and level 3 ER Raliegh Gen. Hosp., Beckley, W.Va., 1995-97; faculty mem. Coll. at W.Va., 1996-97; RN level 1 trauma ctr./ER, clin. nurse II Charleston Area Med. Ctr., Charleston, W.Va., 1997-98; RN level 1 trauma ctr./ER, EDNet clin. coord., clin. nurse II Med. Coll. Va. Hosps./Va. Commonwealth U., Richmond, Va., 1998—. Educator, instr., ARC, Lombard, Ill., 1986-98. Recipient award of Hon. 1st Place Addison Cultural Arts Devel. Commn., 1982, Vol. Educator Excellence awards ARC, 1987-91, Cmty. Health Edn. & Safety Svcs. award, ARC, 1988, Cert. Appreciation, 1992, Dr. Alma J. Labuski Leadership award Student Nurses Assn. Ill., 1994, Pres. Svc. award West Suburban Coll. of Nursing, 1995. Mem. Student Nurse's Assn. at Ill. (hon.)(v.p. 1994-95, programs com. chair 1994-95), Nat. League Nursing, Am. Nurses' Assn., AACN, Emergency Nurses' Assn., Va. Nurses' Assn., Sigma Lambda Sigma (v.p. 1985-86, pres. 1986-87). Republican. Lutheran. E-mail: WJaneU@aol.com. Home: PO Box 478 Powhatan VA 23139-0478

ÜNLÜ, SELCUK, German language and literature educator; b. Isparta, Turkey, Aug. 12, 1943; s. Mustafa Sevket and Gülsüm (Tuncel) Ü; m. Serife Sayin, July 7, 1966; children: Namik Kemal, Mutlu, Mustafa Sevket. Degree, Atatürk, Erzurum, Turkey, 1968, MS, 1970, DS, 1975. Doctorate Atatürk, 1975-81, lectr., 1981-86; prof. German lang. and lit. Selcuk U., Konya, Turkey, 1986—, vice dean, 1984-86, 87, vice rector, 1987-89, head Social Scis. Inst., 1990-93. Author: Palace in German Literature, 1998, Criminality in German Stories, 1992, New German Literature, 1996, German Literature in the 20th Century, 1998. 2d lt. arty. Turkish Armed Forces, 1975. Mem. Schiller Soc., W. Raabe Soc., Eichendorff Soc. Avocations: reading, jogging, travel, communication. Home: Havuzlu Sokak # 8/6, 42099 Konya Turkey Office: Selçuk Ülnü, Havuzlu Sokak nr 8/6, Meliksah Mah TR-42090, Turkey

UNNO, WASABURO, astrophysicist; b. Urawa, Japan, Oct. 2, 1925; s. Hiroshi and Mitsu (Takahashi) U.; m. Kikuko Nakamura, May 24, 1952. MSc, U. Tokyo, 1947, DSc, 1955. From asst. prof. to prof. U. Tokyo, 1952-83, prof. emeritus, 1983—; prof. Kinki U., Osaka, Japan, 1983-95; rsch. assoc. Princeton (N.J.) Univ. Obs., 1956-57, U. Mich. Obs., Ann Arbor, 1957-58; guest researcher Max-Planck-Inst. Physics, Munich, Germany, 1963-64, CSIRO, Sydney, Australia, 1968-69. Co-author: Nonradial Oscillations of Stars, 1979, 2d edit., 1989; contbr. articles to profl. jours. Mem. Internat. Astronomical Union, Astronomical Soc. Japan. Zen Buddhist. Avocations: fossil hunting, Go, ancient temple art. Home: Senjikan Inst Future Study, 4-15-12 Kichijoji Minami, Tokyo 180-0003, Japan Office: Tokyo U Astronomy Dept, 113 Bunkyo-ku, Tokyo 113, Japan

UNO, HISASHI, communications educator; b. Tokyo, Aug. 26, 1935; s. Ryosuke and Atsuko (Bunno) U.; m. Masako Kashiwaghi, Oct. 3, 1960; children: Yukiko, Yoshiki. BA, Tohoku U., Sendai, Japan, 1958. Reporter Mainichi Shimbun Newspapers, Tokyo, 1959-69; reporter, editor AP, Tokyo, Bangkok, 1969-72; info. officer UN, N.Y.C., 1972-73; dep. dir. info. ctr. UN, Tokyo, 1973-78; dir. info. ctr. UN, Manila, 1978-81, Dhaka, Bangladesh, 1981-85, Jakarta, Indonesia, 1985-90; editor in chief dept. pub. info. UN, N.Y.C., 1990-93; prof. Kansai Jogakuin Women's Coll., Miki, Japan, 1993-98, Kansai U. Internat. Studies, Miki, Japan, 1998—. Author: The Olympics: Tokyo for 1964, 1962, Random Thoughts of English, 1966, A World of Proverbs, East and West, 1967, Operation Advertising, 1969, Random Thoughts of Japanese, 2000; co-author: Challenges in Asia: Economic and Social Progress, 1983, Communication Age for a New Society, 1994, Living a Personal Life, 1996, Spring: A Collection of Ideas From 41 Leaders, 2000; contbg. editor: Current English Dictionary, rev. edit., 1965. Mem. Japan Assn. for Current English Studies, Smithsonian Inst., Am. Mus. Nat. History. Avocations: traveling, writing. Fax: 81 791 48 7592. E-mail: hisuno@webtv.ne.jp, hisuno@kuins.ac.jp. Home: 1322 317 Kizu, Ako 678 0165, Japan Office: Kansai U Internat Studies, 18 Aoyama 1-chome Shijimi, Miki 673 0521, Japan

UNO, IKUO, insurance company executive. CEO Nippon Life Ins. Co., Osaka, Japan. Office: Nippon Life Ins Co, 3-5-12 Imabashi Chuo-ku, Osaka 541-8501, Japan*

UNOSAWA, KAZUKO, English language educator; b. Tama, Tokyo, Japan, Nov. 8, 1955; d. Toshiro and Masako Gosho; m. Noboru Unosawa, Nov. 25, 1983; 1 child, Masahiro. Student, Keisen Jr. Coll., Tokyo, 1977; BA in Liberal Arts, Internat. Christian U., Tokyo, 1980; MA in Internat. Studies, Tsukuba U., Ibaragi, 1982; MA in Teaching English to Speakers Other Langs., Columbia U., Tokyo, 1989. Sec. editorial bd. Japanese Jour. Ethnology, Tokyo, 1983-86; instr. English program for returnee children Japan Overseas Ednl. Svcs., Tokyo, 1983-89, program coord., 1988-89; instr. English Kanda Inst. Fgn. Langs., Tokyo, 1984-88; lectr. English Tamagawa U., Tokyo, 1988-91; lectr. Toyo Eiwa Women's U., Kanagawa, Japan, 1990-91; asst. social scis. div. Internat. Christian U., 1991-93; lectr. English, Shukutoku Jr. Coll., Saitama, Japan, 1993-96; lectr. English Shukutoku U., Saitama, Japan, 1996—; lectr. English Tokyo Met. Inst. Tech., Tokyo, 1998—. Translator Bull. of Nat. Mus. History, Chiba, Japan, 1983-86; contbr. articles to profl. jours. Judge 16th ann. speech contest Yokohama (Japan) Mayor's Cup, 1989. Mem. Japanese Soc. Ethnology, Japan Assn. Lang. Tchrs., Assn. Intercultural Edn., Japan Assn. Coll. English Tchrs., Japan Assn. Current English Studies, Tchrs. English to Speakers Other Langs. Home: The Square A-1202, Sekido 1-1-5, Tama-shi, Tokyo Japan Office: Shukutoku U, Fujikubo 1150-1 Miyoshimachi, Iruma-Gun Saitama Saitama, Japan

UNSER, ALFRED, JR., professional race car driver; b. Apr. 19, 1962; s. Al Sr. U.; m. Shelley Unser (div.); children: Al, Cody, Shannon. Runner-up Indpls. 500, 1989. Winner Indianapolis 500 1992, 94, Indy Car Champion 1990, 94; 1981 SCCA Super Vee Champion, 1986 24 Hours of Daytona winner and IROC champion, 1987 24 Hours of Daytona winner, 1988 IROC champion, 1990 Driver of Yr.; named ABC's Wide World of Sports, 1994 Athlete of Yr.; recipient ESPN's ESPY award for Auto Racing Performer of the Yr., 1994; winner 8 out of 16 Indy car races, 1994, 31 car career victories and 7 career poles. Office: Team Penske 366 Penske Plaza Reading PA 19603 Address: PO Box 56696 Albuquerque NM 87187-6696

UNSER, GUENTHER, political science educator; b. Karlsruhe, Germany, June 19, 1936; s. Emil and Elisabeth (Beck) U.; m. Jutta Beyer, Aug. 31, 1968; 1 child, Isabel. Diploma in Econs., U. Freiburg, Germany, 1963; D Social Sci., Tech. U. Aachen, Germany, 1971. Personal asst. of Klaus Mehnert Tech. U. Aachen, 1965-73, lectr. polit. sci., 1974—. Author: Die Uno Aufgaben und Strukturen der Vereinten Nationen, 6th edit., 1997; contbr. articles to profl. jours. Mem. German Soc. Study of Ea Europe, German Soc. UN (exec. com.). Avocations: music, walking, tennis. Office: Inst Polit Sci, Ahornstrasse 55, D-52074 Aachen Germany

UNSWORTH, ANTHONY, engineering educator; b. Astley, Lancashire, Eng., Feb. 7, 1945; s. James and Annie (Halliwell) U.; m. Jill Chetwood, Dec. 22, 1967. BSc in Mech. Engring., Salford (Eng.) U., 1967; MSc in Mech. Engring., Leeds (Eng.) U., 1968, PhD in Bioengring., 1972, DEng, 1990. Chartered engr. Apprentice David Brown Corp., Huddersfield, Eng., 1961-67, rsch. engr., 1967-69; rsch. fellow Leeds U., 1969-71, lectr., 1971-76; lectr. Durham (Eng.) U., 1976-79, sr. lectr., 1979-84, reader, 1984-89, prof., 1989—, chmn. Sch. Engring., 1990-94, prof., dep. dean sci., 1994-97, dean of sci., 1997-2000, chmn. Sch. Engring., 2000—. Author over 170 rsch. papers in tribology and bioengring. Fellow Inst. Mech. Engrs. London (Tribology Silver medal 1972, Donald Julius Groen prize 1991), Royal Acad. of Engring.; mem. Brit. Orthopaedic Rsch. Soc. Avocation: singing. Office: U Durham Sch Engring, South Rd, Durham DH1 3LE, England

UNSWORTH, PHILIP FRANCIS, microbiologist, consultant; b. Oldham, Lancashire, Eng., Sept. 18, 1947; s. Stephen and Teresa (McElin) U. BS in Physiology with honors, U. Manchester (Eng.), 1968, MBChB, 1971. Accredited splst. med. microbiology. House physician Royal Infirmary, Manchester, Eng., 1971; house surgeon Royal Infirmary, Manchester, 1972; asst. lectr. Middlesex Hosp., London, 1972-73, temporary lectr., 1974-75; lectr. St. Thomas' Hosp., London, 1975-76; asst. microbiologist Ctrl. Pub. Health Lab. Pub. Health Lab. Svc., London, 1977-78; sr. microbiologist Pub. Health Lab. Svc., 1978-79; cons. microbiologist Tameside Gen. Hosp., Ashton-u-Lyne, Lancashire, Eng., 1979—. Contbr. articles to profl. jours. Asst. dir. Student Hall of Residence, Manchester, Eng., 1979-89, tutor, 1989—. Fellow Royal Coll. Pathologists; mem. Brit. Soc. Antimicrobial Chemotherapy, Am. Soc. Microbiology, Hosp. Infection Soc. Roman Catholic. Avocations: reading, sports, walking, music, languages.

UNTERMAN, EUGENE REX, aviation sales and manufacturing company executive; b. Mpls., Sept. 3, 1953; s. Melvin and Nancy (Wolfson) U.; m. Melanie Wells Munson, July 12, 1980 (div., Mar. 1997); children: H. Aaron, Jeffery Wells, Julie Ann; m. Patricia Joan Bishop, Oct. 11, 1998. Student, Loyola U., Chgo., 1971-73, Northwestern U., 1973-75. Trader Chgo. Mercantile Exchange, 1975-76; pres. Mid-West Aircraft Co., Sandwich, Ill., 1976-89, Heartland Aircraft Group Ltd., Geneva, Ill., 1990-96, Unterman Aviation Cons., Batavia, Ill., 1996—; computer cons. Chgo. Rawhide Corp., Elgin, Ill., 1983. Author: How to Buy A Used Aircraft Without Taking a Dive, 1989. Airport adv. bd. City of Geneva, Ill., 1983; alderman 2d ward City of Geneva, 1988-89. Mem. Jaycees (Jaycee of Yr. 1988, 89, 90, pres. 1988-89, 94-95), St. Charles (Ill.) Sportsman Club (treas. 1985-86, pres. 1987-88, 90—, bd. dirs. 1988-89). Jewish. Avocations: coaching youth hockey, refereeing hockey, old timers league. Office: Unterman Aviation Cons 201 Houston St Ste 234 Batavia IL 60510-1979

UNTRACHT, STEVEN HARRIS, surgeon; b. Bklyn., Jan. 30, 1955; s. Harry and Lillian (Barshatzky) U. BA summa cum laude, Boston U., 1975; PhD in Biophysics & Theoretical Biology, U. Chgo., 1980, MD, 1981. Diplomate Am. Bd. Surgery, Nat. Bd. Med. Examiners, Am. Bd. Forensic Examiners. Resident in surgery Mass. Gen. Hosp., Boston, 1981-86, clin. and rsch. fellow, 1986; hon. sr. registrar in thoracic surgery Wessex Cardiothoracic Ctr., Southampton, Eng., 1987; clin. fellow in surgery Harvard Med. Sch., Boston, 1981-87; asst. attending physician Morristown (N.J.) Meml. Hosp., 1987-88; active staff dept. of surgery West Jersey Health Sys., Camden, N.J., 1988-92; assoc. in gen. surgery Guthrie Med. Group, P.A., Corning, N.Y., 1992-94; attending surgeon U. Pitts. Med. Ctr.-Lee Regional & Conemaugh Meml. Med. Ctr., Johnstown, Pa., 1994—; tchg. attending, surg. residency Conemaugh Meml. Med. Ctr., Johnstown, 1994—; mem. profl. adv. bd. Lee Regional Hospice, Johnstown, 1995—; mem. Drs. Without Borders, 1996—, med. missionary Batticaloa, Sri Lanka, 1996, Vavuniya, Sri Lanka, 1997; clin. asst. prof. surgery Temple U., Phila., 1997—. Contbr. articles to profl. jours. Mem. Amnesty Internat. Recipient Med. Alumni award U. Chgo., 1981; joint recipient Nobel Peace prize, 1999. Fellow ACS (liaison physician commn. on cancer U. Pitts. Med. Ctr.-Lee Regional 1997—), Am. Coll. Forensic Examiners; mem. Soc. Critical Care Medicine, Phi Beta Kappa. E-mail: shuntracht@pol.net. Office: 321 Main St Ste 5J Johnstown PA 15901-1632

UNUMA, TATSUYUKI, patent lawyer; b. Tokyo, Jan. 16, 1931; s. Eiko Toriumi, Dec. 20, 1960; children: Tatsuya, Yukari. BSc, Tohoku U., Sendai, Japan, 1953. Cert. patent atty. Engr. Japan Radio Co., Ltd., Tokyo, 1953-56, Kawasaki Aircraft Co., Ltd., Kobe, Japan, 1956-64; associated patent atty. Nagai & Esaki, Tokyo, 1965-70; pres. Unuma & Ptnrs., Tokyo, 1970-97; sr. ptnr. Nissho & Co., Tokyo, 1998—. Exec. mem. Social Welfare Coun. Meeting for the Handicapped, Kawasaki, Japan, 1987—; CEO Social Welfare Facilities Corp., Kawasaki, 1996—. Recipient Meritorious Deed prize Min. Internat. Trade and Industry, 1985, Yellow Ribbon of Merit, Prime Min. of Japan, 1994. Mem. Japan Patent Attys. Assn. (v.p. 1975, vice chmn. coun. meeting 1970, 97, Meritorious Deed award 1979), Nat. Patent Attys. Cert. Com. (ofcl. mem. 1982-83), Patent Attys. Coop. Assn. Japan (pres. 1984-85), Asian Patent Attys. Assn., Assn. Internat. pour la protection de la Propriete Industrielle of Japan. Avocation: go, shogi, golf, kouta. Office: Nissho & Co, 7-22-27 Nishishinjuku, Shinjuku-ku, Tokyo 160-0023, Japan

ÜNVER, OLCAY ISMAIL HAKKI, government official, water resources engineer, planner; b. Erzurum, Turkey, Feb. 2, 1957; s. Ahmet and Meliha (Tekiner) Ü.; m. July 25, 1980 (div.); children: Alkim G., Erinç K. BS in Civil Engring. with honors, Middle-East Tech. U., Ankara, Turkey, 1979, MS in Civil Engring., 1981; PhD in Civil Engring., U. Tex., 1987. Design engr. City of Ankara, 1980-81; rsch. assoc. U. Tex., Austin, 1985-86; staff engr. Lower Colo. River Authority, Austin, 1986-88; specialist State Planning Orgn., Turkey, 1988-90; regional dir. Republic of Turkey Prime Ministry, GAP Regional Devel. Adminstrn., 1990-91; pres. Republic of Turkey Prime Ministry, GAP Regional Devel. Adminstrn., Ankara, 1991—; cons. in field; part-time lectr. Dicle U., Sanliurfa, 1989-91; cons., co-founder IRRISCO, Tex. and N.Mex., 1987-88; lectr. in field. Mem. editl. bd. Internat. Jour. Water Resources Devel., also guest editor; editl. bd. Hydro Rev. Worldwide; owner The GAP Mag.; contbr. articles to profl. jours. NATO Sci. fellow, 1981-84, Turkish Sci. and Tech. Rsch. Coun. fellow, 1981-87. Mem. ASCE, World Water Coun. (gov. 1996—), Internat. Hydropower Assn. (mem. coun. 1997—), Internat. Water Resources Assn., Am. Geophys. Union, Am. Water Resources Assn., Can. Water Resources Assn., Soil and Water Conservation Soc. of Am., World Assn. of Soil and Water Conservation, Ctr. for Irrigation Tech., Turkish Chamber of Civil Engrs. Home: Birlik Mah Balta Sitesi #30, Ankara Turkey Office: Prime Ministry GAP Adminstn, Willy Brandt Sokak 5, Cankaya Ankara Turkey

UNVERZAGT, JOHN GERALD, airline captain; b. New Orleans, Dec. 16, 1939; s. John Gustov and Marie U.; m. Kathryn Lorraine Luke; children: Mark Edward, Virginia Ann O'Meara, Steven Andrew, David Alexander, Laura Karlyn; stepchildren: Karyn Stephanie Chester, Ashley Dixon Acone. BA in Polit. Sci., Tulane U., 1961. Lic. pilot , flight engr. FAA. Pilot Delta Air Lines, Inc., Atlanta and New Orleans, 1965-72, flight instr., 1969, internat. capt., 1973—. Co-chmn. Coalition of Frats. and Sororities for Alcohol and Drug Edn., 1988-92; mem. adv. coun. Charter Peachford, 1988; pres. Young Reps., Metairie, La., 1969-70. Capt. USAF, 1961-65. Mem. Air Line Pilot's Assn. (chmn. pub. rels. com. MSY 1975-78, chmn. Delta Pilot Assistance com. MSY 1980-83, various offices 1965—), Kappa Sigma (dist. grand master 1985-89, asst. dist. grand master 1989-93, commr. alcohol and drug edn. commn. 1983—, alumni advisor 1971-77, awards 1976, 87, 88, Atlanta Kappa Sigma Alumni Man of Yr. 1989). Avocations: learning, travel, working with youth, investing. Home and Office: Eagle Landins Investments One Eagle Landing Erwin TN 37650

UNWIN, SIR (JAMES) BRIAN, bank executive; b. Sept. 21, 1935; s. Reginald and Winifred Annie (Walthall) U.; m. Diana Susan Scott, 1964; 3 children. MA, Oxford U., Yale U.; hon. fellow, New Coll., 1997. Asst. prin. CRO, 1960; pvt. sec. Brit. High Commr., Salisbury, Rhodesia, 1961-64; 1st sec. Brit. High Commn., Accra, 1964-65; with FCO, 1965-68; transferred to HM Treasury, 1968; pvt. sec. Chief Sec. to Treasury, 1970-72; asst. sec., 1972, under sec., 1976, seconded to Cabinet Office, 1981-83; dep. sec. HM Treasury, 1983-85, cabinet, 1985-87; chmn. Bd. HM Customs and Excise, 1987-93; pres. Customs Cooperation Coun., 1991-92; chmn. Civil Svc. Sports Coun., 1989-93; pres. European Investment Bank, Luxembourg, 1993-99, hon. pres., 2000—; chmn. supervisory bd. European Investment Fund, Luxembourg, 1994-99; gov. European Bank for Reconstruction and Devel., 1993-99; mem. adv. bd. IMPACT, 1990-93; bd. dirs. Ctr. d'Etudes Prospectives. Mem. bd. dirs. Found. Pierre Werner, English Nat. Opera, 2000—, Dexia, 2000—; mem. Reform Club, Kingswood Village Club (Surrey). Avocations: opera, bird watching, Wellingtoniana, cricket. Office: 25 Links Rd, Epsom Surrey KT173PP, United Kingdom

UOSUKAINEN, RIITTA MARIA, government official, educator; b. Jääski, Finland, June 18, 1942; m. Toivo Verneri Uosukainen, 1968. Licentiate in Philosophy. Tchr. Imatrankoski Upper Secondary Sch., 1969-71; provincial instr. Finnish Province of Kyme, Finland, 1976-83; M.P. Finnish Parliament, 1983—, speaker, 1994—; min. of edn. Govt. of Finland, 1991-94; lectr. didactics Joensuu U., Finland, 1976-77; chmn. Com. for Edn. and Culture, 1991-94; chmn. supervisory bd., Alko Ltd., 1994—. Mem. Imatra Mcpl. Coun., 1977-92, 1st vice-chmn., 1980-86; presdl. elector, 1982, 88; mem. supervisory bd. Finnish Nat. Opera, 1996—; mem. Nat. Bd. Econ. Def., 1996—. Mem. Assn. Carelians (vice-chmn. 1986-92). Address: Parliament of Finland, Eduskunta, FIN-00102 Helsinki Finland

UOTILA, LASSE JUHA, physician; b. Leppavirta, Finland, Aug. 1, 1946; s. Arvi and Aili (Taivalaho) U.; m. Marita T. Yli-Tokko, June 15, 1979; children: Martti, Suvi. MD, U. Helsinki, 1971, DrMedSci, 1974, docent's competence med. biochemistry, 1979, docent's competence clin. lab. medicine, 1986. Instr., sr. lectr. dept. med. chemistry U. Helsinki, 1972-82; acting specialist clin. chemistry, acting adminstrv. dep. Helsinki U. Ctrl. Hosp., 1982-90, dept. head lab., 1991—; clin. lab. med. intern Clin. Lab., Helsinki U. Ctrl. Hosp., 1975, 76-78; postdoctoral rsch. fellow dept. biochemistry U. Stockholm, 1975-76, U. Wis., Madison, 1979-81; cons. clin. chemistry Labquality Inc., Helsinki, 1988—. Contbr. articles to profl. jours. Recipient Gustaf Komppa prize Finnish Chem. Soc., 1975. Mem. Finnish Soc. Clin. Chemistry (former treas.), Societas Biochemica, Biophysica et Microbiologiae Fenniae, Finnish Med. Assn., Am. Assn. for Clin. Chemistry. Avocations: classical music, old steamships, computers. Office: Helsinki U Ctrl Hosp Clin Lab, Haartmaninkatu 4, 00290 Helsinki Finland

UOZUMI, TAKESHI, biotechnology researcher and educator; b. Inami-cho, Hyogo, Japan, Mar. 15, 1939; s. Motoichi and Mitsue (Iwasaki) U.; m. Fumiko Hori, Oct. 16, 1964; children: Hiroki, Gakuji, Mariko. BS, U. Tokyo, 1962, MS, 1964, PhD, 1967. Researcher Kanegafuchi Chem. Industry, Takasago, Hyogo, 1963-69; instr. U. Tokyo, 1969-78, assoc. prof., 1978-87, prof. biotech., 1987-99; prof. Meiji U., 1999—. Contbr. rsch. reports to profl. jours. Recipient Encouragement award Japanese Agrl. Chem. Soc., 1977, Kei Arima award Japan Bioindustry Assn., 1996. Mem. AAAS, Japan Soc. for Biosci., Biotech. and Agrochemistry (bd. dirs. 1993-97, dir. Kanto chpt. 1997-99, award 1998), Am. Soc. Microbiology, Japanese Biochem. Soc. Buddhist. Avocations: photography, driving, linguistics. Home: 4-32-8 Takashimadaira, Itabashi-ku Tokyo 175-0082, Japan Office: Meiji U Dept Life Scis, 1-1-1 Higashimita Tama-ku, Kawasaki 214-8571, Japan

UPADHYAY, LOKESH, endocrinologist; b. Faizabad, India, June 22, 1960; s. Anshuman and Urmila (Pandey) U.; m. Uma Dwivedi, June 14, 1994; children: Stuti, Vighnesh. BSc, Avadh U., Faizabad, India, 1981, MSc, 1983; cert. in Yoga Sci., Banaras Hindu U., Varanasi, India, 1988, PhD, 1990; DSc Complimentery Medicine, Internat. Open U., Colombo, Sri Lanka, 1996. Rsch. fellow Inst. Med. Scis., Varanasi, 1984-85, jr. rsch. fellow, 1985-87, sr. rsch. fellow, 1987-89, postdoctoral fellow, 1989-90, rsch. assoc., 1991-95, project officer, 1996-97, pool officer, 1998—; hon. dir. Chandramouli Gramudyog Inst., Gonda, India, 1993—; exec. mem. Cancer Rsch. Inst., Faizabad, 1993—; sec. V.A.S. Coll. Ayodhya, Faizabad, 1995—; assoc. editor Indian Jour. Cancer and Biol. Rsch., Faizabad, 1995—. Contbr. articles to profl. jours. Fellow U. Grants Commn., New Delhi, 1985, Dir. Gen. Health, 1989. Mem. All India Rsch. Assn. (sec. 1992), Bhu-Ra Assn. (convenor 1995), Gram Pradushan Control Soc. (advisor 1996), Endocrine Soc. India (life), Young Scientist Assn. Office: Dept Medicine Inst Med Scis, Banaras Hindu U, Varanasi 221005, India

UPADHYAY, PREM CHANDRA, oil company executive; b. Kanpur, India, Oct. 30, 1941; s. Hem Chandra Upadhyay and Kalindi Devi Dandotiya; m. Sneh Prabha Tewari, June 22, 1965; children: Deepak, Amal. BSc, U. Allahabad, India, 1959; B Mech. Engring., Birla inst. Tech. & Scis., Pilani, India, 1963. Regional ops. mgr. Hindustan Petroleum Corp. Ltd., New Delhi, 1976-80, Ahmedabad, India, 1980-83; sr. ops. mgr. All India H.O. Hindustan Petroleum Corp. Ltd., Bombay, 1983-89; editl. dir. Dubai (United Arab Emirates) Quality Group, 1984-86; quality assurance officer Emirates Petroleum Products Co., Dubai, 1992—; cons. in quality mgmt. sys. Editor: Middle East Quality Rev., 1996; chmn. editl. com. newsletter Quality Quill. Recipient Cert. of Appreciation, Econ. Dept. Govt. of Dubai, 1995, 96, 98. Mem. Dubai Quality Group (founder, mem. bd. dirs. tech. com. 1994-96). Avocations: reading.

UPADHYAYA, HIMANSHU P., psychiatrist, researcher; b. Mumbai, Maharashtra, India; s. Priyavadan Ramanlal and Kokila Priyavadan U.; m. Vidya Himanshu, June 4, 1992; 1 child, Malvika. MBBS in Medicine, U. Bombay, Mumbai, 1991; MS in Neuropharmacology, U. Tex., 1993. Diplomate Am. Bd. Psychiatry and Neurology, Am. Bd. Child and Adolescent Psychiatry. Resident med. officer Tata Meml. Hosp., Bombay, 1990; resident in psychiatry U. Cin., 1993-96; resident in child psychiatry Med. U. S.C., Charleston, 1996-98, asst. prof., 1998—; cons. psychiatrist VA Med. Ctr., Cin., 1995-96, Dorchester Mental Health Ctr., Summerville, S.C., 1997-98; mem. rsch. com. dept. psychiatry U. Cin., 1995-96. Contbr. articles to profl. jours. Vol. YMCA, 1990; founding mem. Bhagvat Gita Self Study Group, Charleston, 1997—. K-12 grantee Am. Acad. Child Psychiatry and NIH, 1998. Mem. AMA, Am. Acad. Child and Adolescent Psychiatry (Eli Lilly award 1997, mem. adolescent substance abuse com. 2000—), Am. Psychiat. Assn. (Rsch. Travel award 1998), S.C. Psychiat. Assn., S.C. Child and Adolescent Psychiat. Assn., India Assn. Greater Charleston, Phi Kappa Phi. Hindu. Avocations: playing guitar, movies, exercise, reading, tennis. E-mail: upadhyah@musc.edu. Office: Med U SC PO Box 250861 67 President St Charleston SC 29425

UPADHYE, MILIND DHUNDIRAJ, electronics engineer, educator; b. Pune, India, May 23, 1961; s. Dhundiraj Vithal and Kamala (Korde) U.; m. Neeta Mukund Pangarkar, May 29, 1988; 1 child, Chinmay. BSc, Bombay U., 1981, MSc, 1983. Cert. electronics engr. Technician Nehru Planetarium, Bombay, 1981-83; lectr. Elphinstone Coll., Bombay, 1983-85; mgr. R&D Onida TV, Bombay, 1985-90; digital circuit (CKT) designer Japan Victor Co. (JVC), Iwai, Japan, 1990-95; mng. dir. Asian Compusoft Ltd., Thane, India, 1995-99; FSE TeleCruz Tech. Inc., San Jose, Calif., 1999—. Mem. IEEE. Avocations: photography, astronomy. Home: Flat 105, Madhuban Bldg Raheja Twp, Malad Mumbai 400 097, India Office: 36B Solaris 1 Baji Pasalkar, Saki Vihar Andheri (E), Mumbai 400 072, India

UPDIKE, JOHN HOYER, writer; b. Shillington, Pa., Mar. 18, 1932; s. Wesley R. and Linda G. (Hoyer) U.; m. Mary E. Pennington, June 26, 1953 (div. 1976); children: Elizabeth, David, Michael, Miranda; m. Martha Bernhard, Sept. 30, 1977. AB, Harvard U., 1954; student, Ruskin Sch. Drawing and Fine Art, 1954-55. With New Yorker mag., N.Y.C., 1955-57. Author: (fiction) The Poorhouse Fair, 1959 (Richard and Hinda Rosenthal Found. award Am. Acad. and Nat. Inst. Arts and Letters 1960), The Same Door, 1959, Rabbit, Run, 1960, Pigeon Feathers, 1962, The Centaur, 1963 (Nat. Book award 1963, Prix Medicis Etranger 1966), Olinger Stories, 1964, Of the Farm, 1965, The Music School, 1966, Couples, 1968, Bech: A Book, 1970, Rabbit Redux, 1971, Museums and Women, 1972, Warm Wine, 1973, A Month of Sundays, 1975, Marry Me, 1976, Couples, 1976, The Coup, 1978, From the Journal of a Leper, 1978, Problems, 1979, Too Far to Go: The Maples Stories, 1979 (Am. Book award nomination 1980), Three Illuminations in the Life of an American Author, 1979, Your Lover Just Called: Stories of Joan and Richard Maple, 1980, The Chaste Planet, 1980, Rabbit Is Rich, 1981 (Pulitzer prize for fiction 1982, Nat. Book Critics Circle award 1982, Am. Book award 1982), Invasion of the Book Envelopes, 1981, Bech Is Back, 1982, The Beloved, 1982, The Witches of Eastwick, 1984, Confessions of a Wild Bore, 1984, Roger's Version, 1986 (Nat. Book Critics Circle award nomination 1986), Trust Me, 1987, More Stately Mansions, 1987, S., 1988, Rabbit at Rest, 1990 (Pulitzer prize for fiction 1991, Nat. Book Critics Circle award 1991), Memories of the Ford Administration, 1992, Brazil, 1994, The Afterlife, 1994, In the Beauty of the Lilies, 1996, Toward the End of Time, 1997, Bech at Bay, 1998, Gertrude and Claudius, 2000 (poetry) The Carpentered Hen and Other Tame Creatures, 1958, Telephone Poles, 1963, A Child's Calendar, 1965, The Angels, 1968, Bath after Sailing, 1968, Midpoint, 1969, Seventy Poems, 1972, Six Poems, 1973, Tossing and Turning, 1977, Sixteen Sonnets, 1979, Five Poems, 1980, Spring Trio, 1982, Jester's Dozen, 1984, Facing Nature, 1985, Collected Poems 1953-1993, 1993, A Helpful Alphabet of Friendly Objects, 1995, In the Cemetery High Above Shillington, 1996, (plays) Three Texts from Early Ipswich, 1968, Buchanan Dying, 1974, (non-fiction) Assorted Prose, 1965, On Meeting Authors, 1968, A Good Place, 1973, Picked-Up Pieces, 1975, Hub Fans Bid Kid Adieu, 1977, Talk from the Fifties, 1979, Ego and Art in Walt Whitman, 1980, Hawthorne's Creed, 1981, Hugging the Shore, 1983 (Nat. Book Critics Circle award 1984), Emersonianism, 1984, Just Looking, 1989, Self-Consciousness, 1989, Odd Jobs, 1991, Golf Dreams, 1996, More Matter, 1999; adapter: (librettos) The Magic Flute, 1962, The Ring, 1964, (plays) Bottom's Dream, 1969; author words and music: (with Gunther Schuller) The Fisherman and His Wife, 1970; editor: Pens and Needles, 1970, (with S. Ravenel) The Best American Short Stories 1984, 1984, A Century of Arts and Letters, 1998 (with K. Kenison) The Best Am. Short Stories of the Century, 1999. Recipient O. Henry First Short Story award, 1966, 91, MacDowell medal for literature, 1981, Medal of Honor for literature Nat. Arts Club, 1984, PEN/Malamud Meml. prize PEN/Faulker award Found., 1988, Nat. Medal of Arts, 1989, Harvard Arts medal, 1998, Nat. Book Found. award Lifetime Achievement, 1998; Guggenheim fellow, 1959. Mem. AAAL, Am. Acad. Arts. and Scis. Democrat. Episcopalian.

UPHILL, ERIC PARRINGTON, archaeologist, educator; b. Croydon, England, Sept. 15, 1929; s. Walter Eric and Ada Elizabeth (Prest) U.; m. Patricia Ann Read, 1980. BA, Emmanuel Coll., Cambridge, Eng., 1954, MA, 1957. Mem. inst. archaeology London U., 1952—, mem. Libr. User's Forum, 1995—; lectr. ctr. for extramural studies Birkbeck Coll., London, 1960-94, examiner, 1995—; hon. rsch. fellow dept. Egyptology Univ. Coll. London. Co-author: Who Was Who in Egyptology, 2d edit., 1972, 3d edit., 1995; author: The Temples of Per Ramesses, 1984, Egyptian Towns and Cities, 1988, 2d edit., 2001, Pharaoh's Gateway The Hawara Labyrinth of King Amenemhat III, 2000; contbr. chpts. and material to books including Great Tombs of the First Dynasty, III, 1958, MacDonald Library History Civilization from its Beginnings, 1962, Man, Settlement and Urbanism, 1972, The Fortress of Buhen: The Archeological Report, 1979, Macmillan Dictionary of Art, 1996. With Brit. Army, 1948-50. Mem. Egypt Exploration Soc. (mem. com. 1965-85). Anglican. Avocations: music, genealogy research. Office: U Coll London Dept Egyptology, Gower St, London WC1E 6BT, England

UPHOFF, KARIN MARGRET, nutritionist; b. Wetter, Westfalen, Germany, June 26, 1961; d. Walter and Eva (Pomplun) U.; m. Helmut Wagner; children: Tim, Kira, Tabitha, Robin, Kaya, Riko. Diploma, U. Germany, 1986, PhD, 1991. Project mgmt. dir. German Green Cross, Marburg. Author: computer program Erna, Erna MED, 1992, Darmvitalisierung, 1995; Chronische Verstopfung, 1995, Computer Program Davit, 1995; editor Zahnersatz Natürlich, 1993—, EFG, 1991—, Morbus Crohn, 1997, Ernahrungs report, 1993—, sgL, 1998—, FGH in Dialog, 2000—. Avocations: volleyball, tennis. Office: Deutsches Grünes Kreuz, Schuhmarkt 4, 35037 Marburg Germany

UPPOOR, RAJENDRA, pharmaceutical scientist, pharmacist, educator, researcher; b. Ripponpete, Karnataka, India, Feb. 11, 1960; came to U.S., 1989; s. Vittal Kamath and Suvarna (Vittal) U.; m. VenKata Ramana K. Sista, Oct. 31, 1995; 1 child, Vivek Vittal. B in Pharmacy, Govt. Coll. of Pharmacy, Bangalore, India, 1981, M in Pharmacy, 1984; diploma in pharmaceutical tech., State U. Ghent, Belgium, 1986; PhD, Med. U. of S.C., Charleston, 1995. Registered pharmacist Karnataka State Pharmacy Coun., India; lic. pharmacist, Md. Co-founder, prodn. mgr. Gururaj Micropulverizers, Bangalore, India, 1979-85; student trainee Burroughs Wellcome (India), Bombay, 1981; trainee supr. Eskaylab India, Bangalore, 1982; asst. prof. St. John's Pharmacy Coll., Bangalore, 1984-85; mktg. officer Associated Capsules, Bombay, 1985-87; devel. officer Sci. Tech. Ctr., Bombay, 1986-87; pharmacist Ministry of Health, Riyadh, Saudi Arabia, 1987-88; tchg. asst. Duquesne U. Sch. Pharmacy, Pitts., 1989; rsch. asst. Med. U. of S.C., Charleston, 1989-94; cons. Ohmeda PPD, Inc., Murray Hill, N.J., 1994; sr. scientist Ohmeda PPD, Inc., Murray Hill, 1994-96, lead scientist, 1996; review chemist Office New Drug Chemistry, Ctr. for Drug Evaluation and Rsch., FDA, Rockville, Md., 1996—, Anti-inflammatory, Analgesic and Ophthalmic Drug Products Team, 1996-98, Ophthalmic Drug Products Team, 1998-2000; with oncology drugproducts team Divsn. New Drug Chemistry I, 2000—; pharmacist CVS/Pharmacy, Montgomery County, Md., 1997—, Prince George's County, 1997—; mem. drug products tech. com. CDER/FDA, 1998—. Pres. Internat. Student Orgn. Med. Univ. S.C., Charleston, 1991-92; gen. sec. Pharm. Soc. The Govt. Coll. of Pharmacy, Bangalore, India. 1983-84; student rep. in Indian schs. and colls., 1966-84. Recipient Spl. Recognition award ONDC, 1999, Team Excellence award CDER, 1999; Nat. Merit scholar Govt. of India, 1975-81; Internat. fellow WHO, Geneva, State U. Ghent, Belgium, 1986; Univ. Grants Commn. scholar Govt. of India, 1982-84. Mem. Am. Assn. Pharm. Scientists, Vivekananda Kendra Yoga Therapy and Rsch. Ctr.(instr. 1981-82, life mem.), National Cadet Corps (Naval Wing 1972-77), Aircraft Owners and Pilots Assn., Pharmacy Honor Soc., TSS Flying Club, Montgomery County Airpark Assn., Rho Chi. Achievements include concentric coating technique/application for sustained release of drugs; application of glucose oxidase-catalase as an antioxidant system in pharmaceutical solutions; formulation, product development, scale-up and manufacturing of lipid emulsions for intravenous use, freeze drying of pharmaceuticals. Avocations: amateur pilot, philately, travel, history, photography. Home: 6 Beauvoir Ct Rockville MD 20855-1250 Office: HFD-810/150 Divsn New Drug Chemistry I/Oncology Team Woodmont Office Complex 2 1451 Rockville Pike Rockville MD 20852-1420

UPTON, FREDERICK STEPHEN, congressman; b. St. Joseph, Mich., Apr. 23, 1953; s. Stephen E. and Elizabeth Brooks (Vial) U.; m. Amey Richmond Rulon-Miller, Nov. 5, 1983; 2 children. BA in Journalism, U. Mich., 1975. Staff asst. to Congressman David A. Stockman, Washington, 1976-81; legis. asst. Office Mgmt. and Budget, Washington, 1981-83, dep. dir. legis. affairs, 1983-84, dir. legis. affairs, 1984-85; mem. 100th-106th Congresses from 4th (now 6th) Mich. dist., Washington, 1986—, mem. edn. and the workforce com.; mem. commerce com. Field mgr. Stockman for Congress, St. Joseph, 1975; campaign mgr. Globensky for Congress, St. Joseph, 1981. Republican. Office: US House of Reps 2333 Rayburn Hob Washington DC 20515-0001

UPTON, GRAHAM JOHN GILBERT, statistics educator; b. Edinburgh, Scotland, Jan. 22, 1944; s. Albert John and Doreen Elizabeth (Hobbs) U.; m. Susan Amy Joy Fisher, July 29, 1967 (div. sept. 1987); children: Robin, Christopher; m. Sandra Leslie Davies, Sept. 6, 1997. BSc, U. Leicester, Eng., 1965; MSc, U. Birmingham, Eng., 1966, PhD, 1970. Lectr. math. stats. U. Newcastle, Newcastle-upon-Tyne, Eng., 1968-73; lectr. math. U. Essex, Colchester, Eng., 1973-88, sr. lectr., 1988-93, reader, 1993—; vis. prof. U. Dokkyo, Saitama, Japan, 1986; chief examiner U. Cambridge (Eng.) Local Exam. Syndicate, 1984-89; vis. expert Orgn. for Econ. Co-operation and Devel., Paris, 1985-89. Author: Analysis of Cross-Tabulated Data, 1978, Spatial Data Analysis By Examplevol. 1, 1985, vol. 2, 1988, Understanding Statistics, 1996, Introducing Statistics, 1998. Recipient Leverhulme prize U. Leicester, 1965. Fellow Royal Statis. Soc.; mem. Biometric Soc. Avocation: making lists. Office: U Essex, Wivenhoe Park, Colchester CO4 3SQ, England

UPTON, KATHRYN ANN, emergency trauma nurse; b. Ft. Smith, Ark., Dec. 13, 1955; d. William A. and Kathryn (Derrickson) U. BSN, U. Tex., Arlington, 1986. Cert. CEN, ACLS, BLS, PALS, trauma nurse core certification. Commd. ensign USN, 1987-89, advanced through grades to lt., 1989-90; staff nurse med.-surg. USN San Diego Balboa, 1987-88, relief charge/staff emergency rm., 1988-90; staff nurse neonatal ICU USN Bethesda (Md.) Nat. Naval Med. Ctr., 1990-91; staff nurse burn ICU/emergency rm. USNS Comfort-Persian Gulf, 1990-91; asst. charge nurse USN Nat. Naval Med. Ctr., Bethesda, 1991-92; ret. USN, Ft. Lauderdale, Fla., 1992; trauma nurse Broward Gen. Trauma Ctr., Ft. Lauderdale, Fla., 1992-94; nurse mgr. ambulatory care Miami Vets. Adminstrn. Hosp., Miami, 1994-95; trauma nurse, pediats. emergency rm. Joe DiMaggio Children's Hosp., 1995-96; nurse mgr. emergency rm. Presbyn. Hosp., Dallas, 1996—. Decorated Meritorious Unit Commendation, Navy Commendation medal, Nat. Def. medal, SW Asia medal, Kuwati Liberation medal, Sea Svc. medal, Combat Action ribbon, Battle "E" ribbon. Avocations: teaching adults reading, swimming, interior design.

UPTON, MARTIN, agriculture educator; b. London, Nov. 28, 1933; s. Frank Harry and Rachel Amelia (Cain) U.; m. Veronica Mary Horton, June 27, 1964; children: Timothy Adetokunbo, Stephen Dominic, Rebecca Lucy, Ben. BSc in Agr., U. Reading, Eng., 1957, MSc in Rsch., 1963; P.G. Diploma, Leeds (Eng.) U., 1958. Rsch. asst. U. Reading, 1964-66, lectr., 1967-76, reader, 1976-86, prof. agrl. econs., 1986-99, ret., now prof. emeritus, 1999; lectr. U. Ibadan, Nigeria, 1960-66; economist Dept. Agr. for No. Ireland, Belfast, 1966-67; cons. FAO, Rome, 1970—, ODA, Kenya, 1980-90. Author: Farm Management in Africa, 1973, Agricultural Production Economics and Resource Use, 1976, Success in Farming, 1985, African Farm Management, 1986, The Economics of Tropical Farming Systems, 1996. Sgt. Edn. Corps, Royal Army, 1951-53. Mem. Agrl. Econs. Soc. Liberal Democrat. Anglican Ch. Avocations: swimming, music. Home: The Old Schoolhouse, Reading RG7 2EB, England Office: Univ of Reading, 4 Earley Gate, Reading RG6 6AR, England

UPTON, THOMAS VERNON, medical educator; b. Antigo, Wis., Apr. 27, 1948; s. Laverne Leo and Mildred Helen (Burmeister) U.; m. Teresa Anne Ugis, June 11, 1977; children: Mark, Paul, Catherine, Marie. BA, Cath. U. Am., MA, 1972, PhD, 1977. Assoc. prof. Gannon U., Erie, Pa., 1977-83, 84—; vis. prof. Cath. U. Am., Washington, 1983-84; cons. in field. Contbr. articles to profl. jours. Basselin Found. scholar, 1968-71; J.K. Ryan Found. fellow, 1974-77, NEH fellow, 1980, 83, 86, 88. Mem. Am. Philos. Assn., Cath. Philos. Assn. (bd. dirs. 1984-86), Soc. Ancien. Republican. Roman Catholic. Avocations: jogging, fishing, reading, exercising, golf. Office: Gannon U PO Box 3098 Erie PA 16508-0098

UPWARD, CHRISTOPHER, academic researcher, orthographer; b. London, Nov. 14, 1938; s. Edward Falaise and Hilda Maude (Percival) U.; m. Janet Hilary Hutcheon, July 30, 1963; children: Antony, Richard. BA, U. Cambridge, Eng., 1961; Cert. Edn., U. Bristol, Eng., 1962. Tchr. Bolton (Eng.) Sch., 1962-65; from lectr. to sr. lectr. Wolverhampton (Eng.) Poly., 1965-69; from lectr. to sr. lectr. Aston U., Birmingham, Eng., 1970-95, rschr., 1995—; translator Lawrence & Wishart, London, 1970-80. Author: Cut Spelling: A Handbook to the Simplification of Written English by Omission of Redundant Letters, 1992, 2d edit., 1996, (poetry) Apprehensions, 1982; translator: Karl Marx/Frederick Engels, Collected Works vol.

42, Letters 1864-68, 1987. Mem. Simplified Spelling Soc. (com. mem., editor-in-chief 1992). Avocations: languages, writing systems. Home: 61 Valentine Rd, Birmingham B14 7AJ, England Office: Aston U Aston Triangle, Sch Lang & European Studies, Birmingham B4 7ET, England

UPWARD, PAUL ANTHONY, chemist; b. Marston Magna, Somerset, England, May 29, 1953; s. Ronald Patrick and Jean Doreen (Cary) U.; m. Delia Mary Henry, Sept. 17, 1983; children: Kayleigh, Catrina. Lic. Plastics and Rubber Inst. Sr. techologist Larkhill Soling Co. Ltd., Yeovil, Somerset, England, 1971-89; chemist Astron Elastomerprodukte GmbH, Wien, Austria, 1989-95; sales mgr. Stemaco Raw Materials Ltd., Maidenhead, Berks., Eng., 1995—. Part time youth leader Dorset Edn. Com., 1974-78, Somerset Edn. Com., 1978-79. Mem. Inst. Materials, N.Y. Acad. Scis. Home: 44 Priors Way, Maidenhead Berks SL6 2EL, England Office: Stemaco Raw Materials Ltd, 57 Moorbridge Rd, Maidenhead Berks SL6 8LT, England

URABE, AKIO, hematologist, researcher; b. Japan, Apr. 1, 1946; s. Yoshio and Hideko (Kuninaka) U.; m. Hiroko Kato, May 6, 1973; children: Miyako, Akihiro. MD, U. Tokyo, 1973. Rsch. assoc. U. Tokyo Hosp., 1975-77; rsch. fellow Sloan-Kettering Inst., N.Y.C., 1977-79; assoc. physician Rockefeller U. Hosp., N.Y.C., 1978-79; instr. medicine U. Tokyo Hosp., 1979-87; asst. prof. medicine U. Tokyo, 1987-89; assoc. prof. Teikyo U., Tokyo, 1989-91; dir. div. hematology NTT Kanto Med. Ctr., Tokyo, 1991—; ct. physician to Crown Prince, Tokyo, 1987-91, to Emperor, 1989-91. Author: Erythropoietin, 1991; editor: Differentiation and Proliferation of Blood Cells, 1991, Hematopoietic Factors, 1993. Mem. N.Y. Acad. Scis., Japanese Soc. Hematology, Internat. Soc. for Exptl. Hematology, Am. Soc. Hematology. Avocations: golf, photography, tea ceremony. Office: NTT Kanto Med Ctr, 5-9-22 Higashi-Gotanda, Shngwaku Tokyo 141-8625, Japan

URABE, TOHSUKE, mathematics educator, researcher; b. Tokyo, Aug. 3, 1953; s. Syun-ichi and Mariko (Namikawa) U.; m. Yasuko Ichikawa, May 25, 1986; 1 child, Mika. BA, Kyoto (Japan) U., 1978, MA, 1980, PhD in Math., 1984. Sci. worker Max-Planck Inst. for Math., Bonn, Germany, 1987-89, 98-99; assoc. prof. math. Tokyo Met. U., 1981-87, 89-98; prof. math. Ibaraki (Japan) U., 1999—. Author: (with Heisuke Hironaka) Introduction to Analytic Spaces, 1981; Dynkin Graphs and Quadrilateral Singularities, 1993. Avocations: mountain climbing, personal computers. Office: Ibaraki U, Dept Math Scis, Mito Ibaraki 310-8512, Japan

URADE, YOSHIHIRO, molecular biologist, researcher; b. Kashihara, Japan, Oct. 26, 1953; s. Yoshitsugu and Isako U.; m. Reiko Izumo. PhD in Molecular Biology, Kyoto (Japan) U., 1983. Sr. scientist Hayaishi Bioinfo. Transfer Project, ERATO, Kyoto, 1983-87; sr. scientist, dept. enzyme and metabolism Osaka Biosci. Inst., Suita, Japan, 1987-88; vis. prof. Roche Inst. Molecular Biology, N.J., 1988-90; sr. scientist Ciba-Geigy Internat. Rsch. Labs., Takarazuka, Japan, 1990-93; vice-head, dept. molecular behavioral biology Osaka Biosci. Inst., 1993-98, head dept. molecular behavioral biology, 1998—; rsch. dir. Core Rsch. for Evolutional Sci. and Tech., Japan Sci. and Tech. Corp., 1997—; vis. prof. Grad. Sch. Medicine, Osaka U., Japan, 2000—. Named internat. hon. citizen New Orleans. Office: Osaka Bioscience Inst, 6-2-4 Furuedai, Osaka Suita 565, Japan

URAL, OKTAY, civil engineering educator. BA in Math., Trinity U., 1956; BS in Civil Engring., Tex. A&M U.; MSCE, U. Tenn., 1959; PhD in Civil Engring., N.C. State U., 1964; BSCE, 1958. Asst. prof. U. Mo., Rolla, 1967-69, assoc. prof., 1969-73, prof., 1973, founding dir. Inst. for Interdisciplinary Housing Studies; prof. Fla. Internat. U., Miami, 1973—, founding dir. constrn. div. Coll. Engring. and Applied Scis., dir. Inst. Housing and Bldg.; lectr. various univs.; chmn., dir., 30 nat. and internat. confs.; bd. dirs. Internat. Found. Earth Constrn., Internat. Coun. Bldg. Rsch. Studies and Documentation, Rotterdam, The Netherlands, 1978-80; mem. sci. adv. panel UN Disaster Relief Orgn.; pres. Turkish Housing Authorit, advisor to prime min. Turkish Republic, 1990-92. Author: Matrix Operations and Use of Computers in Structural Engineering, 1971, Finite Element Method: Basic Concepts and Applications, 1973, A Systematic Approach to Basic Utilities in Developing Countries, 1974, Construction of Lower-Cost Housing, 1980; editor-in-chief Internat. Jour. Housing Sci. and Its Applications, 1977—; editor 22 vols. of sci. congress procs.; contbr. articles to profl. jours. Grantee HUD, Washington, Com. on Banking and Currency, U.S. Ho. of Reps., NSF, Fla. Power and Light Co., Fla. Internat. U. Found., Inc., Dept. Edn., State Fla.; recipient Medail de Vermeil for Experts, Govt. France. Fellow ASCE (chmn. structures com. on electronic computation edn. com., urban planning and devel. div. housing com., control group, Harland Bartholomew award); mem. Internat. Assn. Housing Sci. (pres.), Am. Soc. Engring. Edn. (internat. com.), Sigma Xi, Tau Beta Pi, Phi Kappa Phi, Chi Epsilon. Home: 522 21st St NW Apt 407 Washington DC 20006-5017 Office: Fla Internat U Inst Housing & Bldg Dept Civil Engring Miami FL 33199-0001

URAM, GERALD ROBERT, lawyer; b. Newark, July 11, 1941; s. Arthur George and Mildred (Stein) U.; m. Melissa Gordon, May 27, 1995; children: Michael, Alison, Carolyn Gordon Lewis. BA, Dartmouth Coll., 1963; LLB, Yale U., 1967. Bar: N.Y. 1967. Assoc. Paul, Weiss, Rifkind, Wharton & Garrison, N.Y.C., 1967-74; v.p., corp. counsel Prudential Bldg. Maintenance Corp., N.Y.C., 1974; ptnr. Davis & Gilbert, N.Y.C., 1974—; lectr. N.Y. Law Sch. Bd. dirs. St. Francis Friends of Poor, Inc. Mem. ABA, N.Y. State Bar Assn., Assn. Bar City of N.Y. Contbr. to profl. publs. Office: 1740 Broadway Fl 3 New York NY 10019-4315

URATA, EIZO, mechanical engineering educator; b. Tokyo, Apr. 23, 1939; s. Hideo and Hideko (Ohtsubo) U.; m. Michiko Ohara, Mar. 26, 1972; children: Nobuyuki, Masahiro. BS, Tokyo Met. U., 1963; D of Engring., Tokyo Inst. Tech., 1972. Rsch. assoc. Tokyo Inst. Tech., 1975-76; scholarship researcher Alexander von Humboldt Stiftung, Aachen, Germany, 1963-81; assoc. prof. Kanagawa U., Yokohama, Japan, 1981-87, prof., 1987—; cons. Japan Soc. Promotion of Machine Industry, Tokyo, 1976—. Co-author: Oil Hydraulic control, 1977; contbr. articles to profl. jours; patentee in field. Mem. Japan Soc. Mech. Engrs., Japan Hydraulic and Pneumatic Soc., Soc. Instrument and Control Engrs. Avocations: Go, Shogi. Home: Ogawa 2-18-18, Machida 194-0003, Japan Office: Kanagawa U Faculty Engring, Rokkakubashi 3-27-1 Kanagawa, Yokohama 221-8686, Japan

URBAN, ALAN GENE, painter, art executive; b. Chgo., Apr. 12, 1948; s. Ernest Frank and Jean Barbara (Jenicek) U.; m. Katherine Ann Taylor, Apr. 17, 1982; children: Jennifer, Alexander. AA, Miami-Dade C.C., 1968; BA, U. South Fla., 1971. Art dir. St. Petersburg (Fla.) Times Pub. Co., 1972-75; pres., creative dir. Urban, Taylor and Assocs., Miami, 1975—; sr. ptnr. Fiddler and Urban, Inc., Miami, 1982—; cons. El Norte Pub. Co., Monterey, Mex., 1979-80, Columbus (Ohio) Dispatch Pub. Co., 1980-81, El Diaria De Nuevo Laredo (Mex.), 1982-84, Zocalo Pub. Co., Piedras Negras, Mex., 1985—, Ctr. for Fine Arts, Miami, 1993-95. Exhibited in group shows at Soc. Four Arts, 1979, 99, Nat. All Media Competition, Ridge Art Assn., 2000, Art 2000, Nathan D. Rosen Mus. Gallery, 2D/3D All Fla. Exhbn., Ft. Myers Alliance for the Arts, 2000, Spin-Nat. Theme Show (1st place award), Alan Urban, Paintings and Graphic Design (two-person show), Pensacola Jr. Coll. Gallery, 1999, All-Fla. Juried Competition and Exhbn. (Merit award), 1999, 2000, Print Regional Design Annual show, 1986 (2 certs. of excellecnce), Graphic Design: USA, 1986 (2 Desi awards), Printing Industry Am. show, 1986 (Best of Category award), Pensacola Jr. Coll. Art Gallery, 1999, Boca Raton Mus. Art, 2000; published in art and design mags. including Typograph 13 (Merit award) How Mag., Publish Mag., Design Ann. (2 Best in Category awards), Graphic Design Inspirations and Innovations, Prints Regional Design Anns., 90-92 (5 merit awards); patentee antenna device. Sustaining mem. Sta. WPBT Pub. Television, Miami, 1979; mem. Met. Mus. and Art Ctr., Miami, 1987. Recipient IMMY award Info. Industry Assn., 1985, Award of Merit, Boca Raton Mus., 1999; 9 awards of merit, Am. Inst. Graphic Arts, 1990, 11 awards of merit, 1992, award of merit, Graphis Design, 1993. Mem. Am. Adv. Fedn. (ADDY awards 1985—), Am. Inst. Graphic Artists, Graphic Arts Guild, Soc. Publ. Designers (Award of Merit 1985), Soc. Newspaper Design, Ft. Lauderdale Mus. of Art, Boca Raton Mus. of Art, Bakehouse Art Complex, Art Ctr./S. Fla., Lowe Art Mus., Mus. of Contemporary Art. Republican. Presbyterian. Office: Urban Taylor and Assocs 12250 SW 131st Ave Miami FL 33186-6402

URBAN, DONALD WAYNE, lawyer; b. Belleville, Ill., Oct. 9, 1953; s. Andrew Anthony and Eileen Marie (Tibbitt) U.; m. Mary Beth Evans, June 9, 1979 (div. Oct. 1994); m. Georgianna Dowling, Feb. 2, 1995; 1 child, Andrew Jared. BA, So. Ill. U., 1976; JD, Washington U., 1979. Assoc. Sprague & Sprague, Belleville, 1979-96; ptnr. Sprague & Urban, Belleville, 1996—; author, lectr. Ill. Inst. for CLE, Springfield. Author: Blasting & Subsidence Illinois Institute for Continuing Legal Education Handbook, 1983, vol. 2, 1986, vol. 3, 1989. Pres. Looking Glass Playhouse, Lebanon, Ill., 1988-90, 95-97; spokesman St. Clair County Bicentennial, Belleville, 1989. Mem. Gamma Theta Upsilon. Democrat. Avocation: community theatre. Home: 815 Belleville St Lebanon IL 62254-1312 Office: Sprague & Urban 26 E Washington St Belleville IL 62220-2101

URBAN, KLAUS KARL, psychology educator; b. Bärn, Sudeten, Germany, Apr. 27, 1944; s. Karl and Anna (Tandler) U.; m. Sigrid Renate Kipka, Nov. 2, 1966; 1 child, David. PhD, U. Osnabrück, Germany, 1976, Habilitation, 1988. Tchr. Cath. Volksschule, Hamburg, Germany, 1966-70; sci. asst. U. Osnabrück, 1970-79; prof. ednl. psychology U. Hannover, 1979-94, prof., 1994—; guest prof., rsch. fellow U. Melbourne, Australia, 1992; sci. dir. Model Project for gifted children, Hannover, 1984-87. Author: Verstehen Gesprochener Sprache, 1977, Besonders Begabte Kinder, 1990; (tests) Test for Creative Thinking, 1996; writer songs, lyrics, satirical texts (Hafiz award 1991, 92), Das Blaue vom Himmel, 1995; editor: Hochbegabte Kinder, 1982, Gluck, 1985, Giftedness, 1986, Begabungen Entwickeln, 1991. Mem. World Coun. for Gifted and Talented Children (exec. com. 1979-87, v.p. 1985-87, 97—, chmn. rsch. com. 1993-97, exec. com. 1995—), European Coun. for High Ability (mem. exec. com. 1990-94), Deutsche Gesellschaft Psychologie, Deutsche Gesellschaft Erziehungswissenschaft, Arbeitskreis Begabungsforschung (chmn. 1991-97). E-mail: klausurban@aol.com. Home: Winzenburg 7, 31552 Rodenberg Germany Office: Univ Hannover, Bismarckstr 2, 30173 Hannover Germany

URBAN, MARTIN, retired museum director; b. Liebemühl, Germany, Dec. 16, 1913; s. Julius Urban; ed. U. Königsberg, U. Bonn, U. Kiel; prom. Dr. phil., 1950; prof., 1980; m. Ruth Henneberg, 1942; children: Agnes, Dagmar, Petra, Gabriele. Asst., custodian Schleswig-Holsteinisches Landesmus., Schleswig, Schloss Gottorf, 1950-62; dir. Found. Seebüll Ada and Emil Nolde, Neukirchen, W. Ger., 1963-92; ret., 1992. Author papers on art in Middle Ages, 20th century, especially German expressionism and Emil Nolde, Catalogue Raisonne of Nolde's oil paintings. Address: Nolde Stiftung Seebüll, Sylt Zwisdelu den Hdigen 64, D-25980 Westerland Germany

URBAN, MIROSLAV, chemistry educator, researcher; b. Martin, Slovakia, June 6, 1942; s. Karol and Vlasta (Valentová) U.; m. Tatiana Plešková, July 11, 1964; children: Martin, Zuzana. M in Chemistry, Comenius U., Bratislava, Czechoslovakia, 1964; PhD in Chemistry, Charles U., Prague, Czechoslovakia, 1971; DSc, Slovak Tech. U., Bratislava, 1989. Asst. prof. faculty scis. Comenius U., 1966-78, assoc. prof., 1978-90, prof. dept. phys. chemistry, 1990—; rsch. assoc. U. Fla., Gainesville, 1984, 92; vis. scientist Max Planck Inst. Astrophysics, Garching, Germany, 1987—, U. Lund, Sweden, 1989—; chmn. Accreditation Commn., Slovakia, 1990-95. Author: (with P. Cársky) AB Initio Calculations: Methods and Applications in Chemistry, Lecture Notes in Chemistry, Vol. 16, 1980, (with others) Methods in Computational Chemistry, Vol. 1, 1987; contbr. articles to profl. jours. Recipient State award Govt. of Czechoslovakia, 1987. Roman Catholic. Avocations: classical music, sports. Home: H Meličkovej 22, 84105 Bratislava Slovakia Office: Comenius U Sci Phys Chem, Mlynská Dolina, 84215 Bratislava Slovakia

URBAN, VOLKER, neurosurgeon; b. Mainz, Germany, Oct. 10, 1958; s. Emil and Ilse (Bobeth) U. MD, U. Mainz, Germany, 1987. Intern U. Mainz, 1986-87, resident in neurosurgery, 1987-94, asst. physician neurosurgery, 1987-94; supr. physician neurosurgery Horst-Schmidt-Kliniken, Wiesbaden, Germany, 1995—. Inventor doctors teleconsultation unit based on ISDN, neuroendoscopic system, endoscop-based microroboter, URS universal surgical robot system. Mem. German Soc. Neuroendocopy & Neuronavigation (exec. com. 1993—), German Soc. Endoscopy, German Soc. Neurosurgery. Avocations: sailing, classic music. Office: Dr Horst Schmidt Kliniken, Ludwig Erhard St 100, 65199 Wiesbaden Germany

URBANEK, GUENTHER ERNST, retired marketing professional; b. Vienna, Mar. 26, 1933; s. Franz X. and Maria (Wimmer) U.; m. Friederike A. Michaeler, June 30, 1962; 1 child, Ulrike M. Dipl.Ing., U. Tech., Vienna, 1960, Dr.techn., 1968. Postgrad. asst. prof. U. Tech., Vienna, 1961-69; project engr. Radio Corp. Am./RCA-GB, Vienna, 1969-73; sales/mktg. mgr. Siemens Ag Oesterreich, Vienna, 1973-93, cons., 1993-99; ret.; cons. Oesterr. Bundeskanzleramt-Forschungsbeirt, Vienna, 1961-65, European Office of Aerospace Rsch., Brussels, 1965-69, IBM Rsch. Lab., Zurich, 1966-69. Contbr. articles to profl. jours. Mem. Acoustical Soc. Am. (emeritus).

URBANI, CARLO ENRICO, dermatologist; b. Milan, June 1, 1961; s. Stellio Urbani and Vittorina Lorini; m. Paola Quinteri, May 7, 1988 (separated). Degree in Medicine & Surgery summa cum laude, U. Milan, 1986, specialization in dermatology, 1989, specialization in chemotherapy, 1993. Resident dept. internal medicine H. Sacco, Milan, 1983-86; fellow resident dept. dermatology H. San Paolo, Milan, 1986-89; cons. dermatologist Sci. Inst. for Hospitalization-Treatment Hosp San Raffaele-Resnati, Milan, 1989—; cons. dermatologist Hosp. Ctr. Multimedica, Sesto S. Giovanni, Milan, 1998—; designated med. practitioner in immigation med. exams. of Can. health programs, 1990—; spkr. in field. Author: Accessory Mammary Tissue in Clinical Practice, 1996, (with others) Complementary Medicine in Dermatology, 1998; reviewer: (jour.) Dermatology; contbr. over 100 articles to med. jours. Recipient Disting. Leadership award in dermatology and human genetics, 2000. Fellow Am. Acad. Dermatology; mem. Internat. Soc. Dermatology, Dermatology Found., Italian Soc. Dermatology and Venereology, Italian Soc. Dermatologic Surgery and Oncology, Italian Med. Assn., Italian Soc. Chemotherapy, European Acad. Dermatology and Venereology, N.Y. Acad. Scis. Roman Catholic. Avocations: trekking, jogging, table tennis, swimming. Home: Via G Frua 11, 20146 Milan Italy Office: U Milan Dermatology Svc, Via Santa Croce 10/A, 20122 Milan Italy

URBANIAK, STANISLAW JOSEPH, physician; b. Leslie, Fife, Scotland, Jan. 26, 1945; s. Stanislaw and Jane Stuart (McFarlane) U.; m. Ann Howard Murison, Sept. 19, 1972; children: Suzanne, Kathryn. BSc with honors, U. Edinburgh, Scotland, 1967, MB, BChir, 1970, PhD, 1977. Sr. house officer Edinburgh Royal Infirmary, 1971-72, sr. registrar, 1974-77, cons., immunohaematologist, 1977-82; MRC rsch. fellow Clin. Endocrinology Unit, Edinburgh, 1972-74; regional dir. Scottish Nat. Blood Transfusion Svc., Aberdeen, Scotland, 1982-2000; hon. reader U. Aberdeen, 1994-99, prof. transfusion medicine, 1999—; mem. nat. panel of specialists Sec. of State for Scotland, 1982-86, 93—; mem. mgmt. bd. Scottish Nat. Blood Transfusion Svc., 1990—; inspector Clin. Pathology Accreditation Scheme, United Kingdom, 1993—; mem. exec. com. World Apheresis Assn., 1994—. Contbr. numerous articles to profl. jours. Recipient various grants in support of rsch. activities. Mem. British Soc. Immunology, British Blood Transfusion Soc. (founder, asst. sec. 1983-86), European Soc. Haemapheresis (pres. 1993-96). Avocations: game fishing, hill walking, restoration of historical buildings. Office: Aberdeen Royal Infirmary, Blood Transfusion Svc, Aberdeen AB9 2ZW, Scotland

URBASSEK, HERBERT MICHAEL, physicist; b. Kaiserslautern, Germany, Dec. 13, 1956. D Natural Sci., Tech. U., Braunschweig, Germany, 1983. Rsch. assoc. Tech. U., Braunschweig, 1984-90; Heisenberg fellow, lectr. U. Wuppertal, Germany, 1991-92; prof. U. Kaiserslautern, Germany, 1993—. Recipient Gaede award German Vacuum Soc., 1990. Office: Physics Dept U, Erwin-Schrödinger Str, D-67663 Kaiserslautern Germany

URBINA, FEBE GLORIA, elementary school principal; b. Nuevo Laredo, Tamaulipas, Mexico, Aug. 25, 1942; came to U.S., 1947; d. Manuel Urbina and Irene Salce de Urbina. BA, Howard Payne Coll., 1965; MEd, U. Houston, 1975. Cert. tchr., adminstr., biling. educator, spcl. edn., mid mgmt., ednl. diagnostician, Tex. Cashier Weingarten Grocery, Houston, 1960-64; social worker Neighborhood Ctrs. Assn., Houston, 1965-68; elem. sch. tchr. Houston Ind. Sch. Dist., 1968-70, curriculum coord., 1970-2000, prin., 1973—; adj. instr. Adult Edn. Houston C.C., 1965-71; mem. Legal United L.Am. Citizens Ednl. Adv. Bd., Houston, 1975-76; adj. English tchr. Harris County C.C., Pasadena, Tex., 1986-88; mem. supt.'s adv. bd. Houston Ind. Sch. Dist., 1990-97; presenter Conv. of Excellence, 1988, 90, 95, 98, Conv. Sch. External Funds, 1998, Lightspan Conv., 1998. Co-author: (book) Strategies for Bilingual/ESL Teachers, 1968. Sunday Sch. Tchr. Southmain Bapt. Ch., Houston, 1970-76; ch. pianist Heights Bapt. Temple, Houston, 1976-86; mem. Meadowbrook Civic Club, Houston, 1987-98. Recipient Mary Hill Davis award Home Mission Bd., Atlanta, 1961; named Hispanic Principal of Yr., Houston Ind. Sch. Dist. 1975, Principal of Yr. 1994. Mem. ASCD, Houston Assn. for Sch. Adminstrs. Avocations: travel, music, mission trips, translating, reading. Home: 899 Old Genoa Red Bluff Rd Houston TX 77034-4010 Office: Bonner Elem Sch 8100 Elrod St Houston TX 77017-5216

URBINA, MANUEL, II, legal research historian, history educator; b. Rodriguez, Nuevo Leon, Mex., Sept. 23, 1939; came to U.S., 1947; s. Manuel and Irene (Salce) de Urbina. BA, Howard Payne Coll., 1962; postgrad., Nat. Autonoma U. Mex., Mexico City, 1963-64; MA, U. Tex., 1967, PhD, 1976; postgrad., Cambridge (Eng.) U., 1982; JD, U. Houston, 1983. Prof. Latin Am. history Coll. of the Mainland, Texas City, Tex., 1967—; founder, curator Urbina Mus. History of Mex., Houston, 1990—; chmn., legal counsel Urbina Found., Houston, 1985—; chmn., CEO Urbina Pub. Co. Inc., Houston and Mexico City, 1985—. Author: (TV Series) The Mexican Side of the Texas Revolution, 1985, The Mexican Side of the Mexican War, 1985, The Battle of San Jacinto-A Mexican Viewpoint, 1985, The Battle of the Alamo-A Mexican Viewpoint, 1986, Relations Between the United States and Mexico, 1987, General Emiliano Zapata in North American Historiography, 1989, The Mexican War in International Law, 1995, The Mexican War in United States Constitutional Law, 1996, Efectos De La Independencia De Texas Sobre El Gobierno, La Politica, Y La Sociedad De México, 1996, Bilingual Dollars of the Bank of Texas (1835) in the Context of the Separation of Texas From Mexico, 1998, General Pancho Villa in International Law, 1999; editor, interviewer history videos, oral history interviews with participants in the Mexican Revolution; contbr. articles to newspapers and mags. including Houston Chronicle, Mexico City Novedades, San Antonio Light, Boletin Del Archivo General Del Estado de Nuevo León, Boletin de la Sociedad Numismatica de Mexico. Founder Cinco de Mayo Assn., Galveston County, Tex., 1976; founder, faculty sponsor Mex. Am. Student Assn., Coll. of Mainlan, 1974—. Named Hispanic of Yr. Galveston County League of United Latin Am. Citizens, 1982; NEH grantee, 1971-72; U.S. Dept. State scholar diplomat, 1979. Mem. League of United Latin Am. Citizens, Tex. State Hist. Assn., Howard Payne U. Alumni Assn., U. Houston Law Alumni Assn., U. Tex. Alumni Assn., Interam. C. of C., Soc. Numismatica Mex. Democrat. Baptist. Avocations: reading, research, travel, trumpet playing, volunteer work. Home: 889 Old Genoa Red Bluff Rd Houston TX 77034-4010

URCIUOLI, J. ARTHUR, investment executive; b. Syracuse, N.Y., Nov. 13, 1937; s. Joseph R. and Nicoletta Anne (Phillips) U.; m. Margaret Jane Forelli, Aug. 13, 1966; children: Caryn Sloan Jacoby, Christian J.A. B.S., St. Lawrence U., 1959; J.D., Georgetown U., 1966; grad. Advanced Mgmt. Program, Harvard Bus. Sch., 1982. Bar: N.Y. 1966. Atty. Brown, Wood, Fuller, Caldwell & Ivey, N.Y.C., 1966-69; internat. investment banker, dir. internat. fin. Merrill Lynch, N.Y.C., Paris, 1970-78; pres. Merrill Lynch Internat., 1978-82; chmn. Merrill Lynch Internat. Bank, London; dir. banking div. Merrill Lynch Capital Markets, 1980-84; dir. Merrill Lynch Bus. Fin. Services, Merrill Lynch Co., 1984-93; dir. mktg. group Merrill Lynch Pvt. Client, 1993-97; chmn. Internat. Pvt. Client Group Merrill Lynch Pvt. Client, N.Y.C., 1997-99, ret., 1999; chmn. Archer Corp., 1999—. Contbr. articles to profl. jours. Trustee St. Lawrence U., 1976-89, Bruce Mus., Greenwich, Conn., 1990-94; bd. dirs. United Way, Greenwich, 1978-81. Capt. USMC, 1959-63. Mem. Securities Assn. (chmn. sales and mktg. com. 1987-89), Forum for Investor Advice (chmn. 1996-98), River Club (N.Y.C.), N.Y. Yacht Club, Riverside (Conn.) Yacht Club, Rocky Point Club (Old Greenwich, Conn.), The Oaks Club (Sarasota, Fla.). Republican. Congregationalist.

URCULO, ENRIQUE, neurosurgeon; b. Bilbao, Vizcaya, Spain, Aug. 15, 1952; s. Enrique and Rosario (Bareño) U.; m. Marta de Miguel, Sept. 17, 1977; children: Marta, Enrique, Ignacio. MD, Complutense U., Madrid, 1976; Nuerosurgeon, Bilbao U., Spain, 1982; PhD in Medicine, U. Basque Country, 1990. Resident neurosurgery San Sebastian, Spain, 1977-82; asst. neurosurgeon Hosp. de Guipuzcoa, Spain, 1982-92, head neurosugery, 1992—; assoc. prof. U. Basque Country, 1982—. Co-author, contbr.: Neurologia Quirurgica, 1988; contbr. articles to profl. jours. Mem. Spanish-Portuguese Soc. Neurol. Surgery, European Skull Base Soc., Soc. Española de Abordajes Percutaneos Vertebrales. Roman Catholic. Avocations: playing tennis, reading. Home: Pasco de Beloke 3. 3o1, 20009 San Sebastian Spain Office: Hosp de Guipuzcoa, Pasco Dr Beguiristain 115, 20080 San Sebastian Spain

URDEA, JOHN, electromechanical engineer; b. Sercaia, Romania, Feb. 15, 1946; s. Nicolae and Maria U.; m. Elena Greserink, Oct. 27, 1979; 1 child, Alex. MSEE, Polytech. Inst., Romania, 1968. Jr. engr. TLHS/Constrn. Site, Bucharest, Romania, 1968-69; elec. engr. TLHS/Elec. Constrn., Bucharest, 1969-71; design engr. TLHS/Design Dept., Bucharest, 1971-75; chief energetical engr. TLHS Hdqtrs., Bucharest, 1975-82; v.p. electromech. Romagrimex, Raqqa, Syria, 1982-83; maintenance mgr. Aqua Spa, Oklahoma City, 1984-85, plant mgr., 1985-86; project mgr. Econowatt Corp., Pelham, N.Y., 1986-88; sys. engr., project mgr., shift mgr. Consol. Edison, N.Y.C., 1988—; shift mgr. Con Edison, N.Y.C.; cons. Fin. Square, Inc., N.Y.C., 1986-88. Mem. Rep. Nat. Com., Washington, 1990. Mem. IEEE, N.Y. Acad. Scis. Republican. Greek Orthodox. Avocations: music, skiing, soccer, auto repair. Home: 6 W Oak Hill Dr Oyster Bay NY 11771-3909

URHAUSEN, JAMES NICHOLAS, real estate developer, construction executive; b. Berwyn, Ill., Oct. 6, 1943; s. Jack Nicholas and Florence Frances (Stalzer) U.; m. Philomena Anne Malizia, July 16, 1966 (div. 1980); children: Kristen Anne, James Nicholas III; m. Anne Siegert, July 22, 1983; children: Bradley James, Samantha Elise. BA, St. Procopius Coll., Lisle, Ill., 1965. High sch. tchr. Nazareth Acad., LaGrange Park, Ill., 1965-66; asst. village mgr. Village of Hinsdale, Ill., 1966-69; village mgr. Village of Oak Brook, Ill., 1969-73; v.p., sec.-treas. Collins Devel. Corp., St. Charles, Ill., 1973-80; exec. v.p. Westway Constrn. Corp., St. Charles, Ill., 1980-84, pres., chief exec. officer, 1984—; guest lectr. No. Ill. U., Dekalb, 1976—; expert witness Ill. Dept. of Transp., Chgo., 1976—; dir. Harris Bank/St. Charles, Ill., 1992—. Chmn. Hotel Baker Bd. Gov.'s St. Charles, 1982-84, Bd. of Fire and Police Commmrs., St. Charles, 1986—; mem. 708 Comty. Mental Health Bd., St. Charles, 1986—, Kane County Selective Svc. Sys. Bd., St. Charles, 1981—, Kane County Solid Waste Adv. Com., Geneva, 1990—, Metra Citizen's Adv. Bd., 1993—; bd. dirs. Neighborhood Improvement Assn., St. Charles Twp., 1992—, pres., 1996—; bd. dirs. Delnor Cmty. Health Sys., 1993—, Glenwood Sch. for Boys, 1996—; chair tech. adv. com. Kane County Stormwater Mgmt. Com., 1996—. Mem. Home Bldrs. Assn. Greater Chgo. (dir. 1989—), Nat. Assn. Home Bldrs., No. Ill. Home Bldrs. Assn., Fox Valley Polit. Action Group, St. Charles C. of C. (amb. 1988, Community Devel. award 1989, Charlemagne award 1993, Sam Walton Bus. Leadership award 1996). Republican. Roman Catholic. Avocations: golf, rail photography, power boating, model trains. Home: 3103 Greenwood Ln Saint Charles IL 60175-5627 Office: Westway Constrn Corp 440 S 3rd St Saint Charles IL 60174-2854

URIARTE REBAUDI, LIA NOEMI, literature educator; b. Buenos Aires, Mar. 26, 1925; d. Roberto Uriarte Castro and Noemí Rebaudi Basavilbaso. Profesora en letras, Buenos Aires U., 1949, licenciada en letras, 1972. Cert. in lit. scis. Asst. prof. U. Católica, Buenos Aires, 1960-66; assoc. prof. U. Católica Argentina, 1966-69, prof., 1969—; dir. Medieval Spanish Lit. Internat. Congress, 1985, 87, 90, 93, 96, 99. Author: Canto elegiaco, 1986, Canto de alabanza, 1987; contbr. articles to profl. jours; songwriter for piano and orchestra; painter. Recipient Internat. Woman of Year award Internat. Biographical Ctr., Cambridge, Eng., 1992-93. Mem. Assn. Internacional de Hispanistas, San Fernando Club. Roman Catholic. Home: Carabobo 250, C1406DGP Buenos Aires Argentina Office: U

Cat332lica Argentina, Av Alicia Moreau de Justo, 1500 Buenos Aires 1107, Argentina

URIBE, JAVIER MIGUEL, investment executive; b. Baranquilla, Colombia, Sept. 4, 1941; s. Jose and Ofelia (Diaz-Granados) U.; m. Dena Rue Whitaker, Apr. 1, 1963 (div. Sept. 1987); children: Sandra J., Joseph J., Cristina; m. Diana L. Anglada, Dec. 4, 1987. BS in Indsl. Mgmt., Purdue U., 1967. With Citibank, N.A., 1967; resident v.p. Citibank, N.A., Bogota, Colombia, 1975-76; v.p. Citibank, N.A., Port of Spain, Trinidad, 1976-78, N.Y.C., 1978-80, San Juan, P.R., 1980-85; pres. Citicorp Fin. Svcs. Corp., San Juan, P.R., 1980-85; chmn., chief exec. officer Merrill Lynch Govt. Securities, San Juan, 1985-88; pres. San Juan Capital Corp., 1988—; advisor exec. program Ind. U., Bloomington, 1978-80; chmn. Trinfinance Leasing, Port of Spain, Trinidad, 1976-78, Met. Mortgage Co., San Juan, 1989—; trustee Ashford Presbyn. Community Hosp., San Juan, 1990-96. Bd. dirs. Maracaibo (Venezuela) Botannical Gardens Found., 1974-75. Mem. Securities Industry Assn. of P.R. (founder, treas. 1985-86), N.Am. Assn. (bd. dirs. Caracas, Venezuela chpt. 1973-74), Berwind Country Club, Centro Ecuestre de P.R. (pres. 1989-91), P.R. Equestrian Fedn., Ingenio Polo Club. Roman Catholic. Avocation: golf. E-mail: sjcc-jmu@worldnet.att.net. Home: PO Box 9023462 San Juan PR 00902-3462 Office: San Juan Capital Corp Tetuan 103 Ste One San Juan PR 00901

URIBE, MARTIN, economics educator; b. Cordoba, Argentina, Feb. 18, 1964; came to the U.S., 1989; s. Agustin Uribe and Delia Neuman; m. Stephanie Schmitt-Grohe, July 11, 1998; 1 child, Cristobal. MA, CEMA, Buenos Aires, 1988; PhD, U. Chgo., 1994. Economist Bd. Govs. Fed. Res. Sys., Washington, 1994-98; asst. prof. econs. U. Pa., Phila., 1998—; cons. World Bank, Washington, 1993. Assoc. editor Internat. Econ. Rev., 1999-2000. E-mail: uribe@econ.upenn.edu. Office: Univ Pa 3718 Locust Walk Philadelphia PA 19104-6209

URIBE ECHEVARRIA, JORGE, dentist; b. Cordoba, Argentina, Nov. 24; s. Juan and Alicia Forletti Uribe E.; m. Norma Gladys Nunez, July 3, 1965; children: Andrea Gladys, Leonardo Jorge, Diego Ignacio. Odontologia Diploma, U. Nat. Cordoba, 1964, D Odontologia, 1976. vis. prof. U. Mich., Ann Arbor, 1988. Dir. dept. rehab. U. Nat. de Cordoba, 1989-92, 1992-95, 1998-2000; prof. titular operatoria dental Fac. de Odontologia/U. Nat. de Cordoba, 1989-92, 1992-95, 1998-2000; pres. Divn. Argentina Internat. Assn. for Dental Rsch., 1993-94; chmn. Argentina chpt. Acad. Dentistry Internat., 1998; subsec. Investigation and Sci., U. Nat. Cordoba, 1998; assessor Commn. of Med. Sci., Conicor, 1996-98. Author: Operatoria Dental, 1992, Odontologia Clinica A Fines Del Milenio, 1997. Recipient award Cruz de Oficial de La Reina, isabel La Catolica, Espana, 1992, Premio Universidad, 1963, U. Nat. Cordoba, 1963. Fellow Pierre Fauchard Acad., Internat. Coll. Dentist, Acad. Dentistry Internat. Office: Centro Dental Privado, Montevideo 36, 5000 Cordoba Argentina

URIBE-RESTREPO, GUSTAVO, civil engineer; b. Bogota, Colombia, Jan. 8, 1958; s. Gustavo and Eleonora (Restrepo) U.; m. Monica Riano De Uribe, Dec. 6, 1986; children: Alejandra, Andres, Cristina. Degree in Civil Engring., U. Los Andes, Bogota, Colombia, 1980; MS in Water Resources, Stanford U., Palo Alto, 1982; MS in Transp. Engring., U. Calif. Berkeley, 1983. Cert. civil engr. Field engr. Restrepo y Uribe Ltd., Bogota, Colombia, 1980-81, main engr., 1983-84, project coord., 1984-86, project dir., 1987—, ptnr., 1987—; consulting Restrepo y Uribe Ltd., Bogota, Colombia, 1980-96. Contbr. articles to profl. jours. Mem. ASCE, Stanford Alumni Assn., Uniandinos. Home: Apt 403, Transversal 22 # 118-22, Bogota Colombia Office: Restrepo y Uribe Ltd, Calle 95 # 15-47 Piso 6, Bogota Colombia

URIBE VILLEGAS, OSCAR, sociologist; b. Toluca, Mex., Nov. 6, 1928; s. M. Rafael and Luz (Villegas) Uribe. BS, Nat. Prep. Sch., Mex., 1948; postgrad., Nat. Sch. Anthropology, Mex., 1949-52, Sch. Polit. and Social Scis., Mex., 1951-54, Coll. Mex., 1957-62; Govt. extra-mural studies, U. London, 1966-70. Researcher, coordinator Inst. Investigaciones Sociales Nat. U. Mex., Coyoacán, 1952-72; titular researcher Nat. U. Mex., 1972—, prof. sch. polit. and social scis., 1953-58; acad. dean Inst. of Soc. Rsch. Nat. Autonomous U. of Mexico, 1990—; cons. Consejo Nat. Turismo, 1964—. Author: Técnicas Estadísticas para Investigadores Sociales, 1958, La Matemática la Estadística y las Ciencias Sociales, 1963, Curvas Sociográficas, 1969, Causación Social y Vida Internacional, 1958, El A.B.C. de la Correlación, 1962, 25 Conceptos de Uso sociológico, 1965, El Mesías, aportación a su casuística cabeza de Piedra por Yashar Kemal, 1966, Sociolingüística Concreta, 1970, Los Elementos de la Estadística Social, 1971, Sociolingüística Doctrinaria, 1971, Situaciones de Multilingüismo en el Mundo, 1972, El Progreso, 1973, La Sociolingüística Actual, 1974, Las Disciplinas Sociolingüísticas, 1976, Imágenes del Hombre en la Rusia zarista y en la Unión Soviética, 1977, Issues in Sociolinguistics, 1977, Para una Sociología del Cercano Oriente, 1978, Koinoniología, 1979, En Pro de la Amistad Mexicano-Finesa, 1980, Progreso e Independencia, 1984, El Enfasis Sociológico en Socio-Lingüística, 1984, Una Iniciación a la Lingüística Otomiana, 1985, El Mexicano, Mentalidad Mexicana de Habla Castellana, 1987, De Rerum Humana Natura y la Universitas Mexicana, 1987, Ensayos Marginales, 1987, La Revuelta Contemporanea segun Camus, 1989, SociolingÜistica de los Indoamericanos, 1993, Reflexiones sobre una Socio-Politica del Lenguaje, 1994, Rasgos Identarios de India Asiática, 1995, 2d edit., 1999, La Identidad Nacional en México Mesoamericano y en las Neo-Humanidades, 1995, La Socioconstrucción en la Albania del Novecientos, 1996, A Book In the Making: On Mexico, 1996-97, Materiales para tratar de entender la problemática maya, 1997, Autenticidad, Identidad, Desarrollo y Evolución, 1997, La Locura, Necia imputación Mutua y Hábil Manipulación Hegemónica, 1998; Edición crítica traducción y adaptacion de Nikos Kazantzaki: El Yang-TSE(Bouddba) la Vida Avasalladora y la Humana Liberación, 1998, El Lenguaje, universal sociológico, diversificado en idiomas, 1999, La Nausée, the Jerk y el Anillo de Moebius, 1999-2000, Koinoniología 2d edit., 2000; Aux. editor Revista Mexicana de Sociologia, 1952-66; mem. editorial bd. Internat. Jour. Sociology Lang., Revista Interamericana de Sociología. Recipient Presea Presencia Estado Mex., 1984. Mem. Mex. Sociol. Assn., Internat. Sociol. Assn. (coun. 1966-70), Ctr. Rsch. Bilingualism U. Laval (corr.), Assn. Internat. Polit. Sci., Inst. Internat. Sociology, Soc. Linguistica Italiana, Soc. Lingua Portuguesa, Inst. Mex. Cultura, Consejo Cultura Estado Mex., Soc. Mex. Estudios Semioticos (pres.), Internat. Assn. Semiotic Studies. Fax: 5665 24-43. Home: 117 Palestina, 02080 Mexico City 16 Mexico Office: Inst Investigaciones Sociales, Circuito Mario de la Cueva, Coyoacan 04510, Mexico

URIBURU, IGNACIO JUAN FRANCISCO, surgeon; b. Buenos Aires, Argentina, Sept. 8, 1940; s. Marcelo Alberto and Ester (Bellouard) U.; m. Maria Teresa Quirno; children: Ignacio, Marcelo, Pablo. MD, Buenos Aires U., 1964; spl. fellow hand surgery, Harvard Med. Sch., 1970, Roosevelt Hosp., N.Y.C., 1971. Chief resident surgery Buenos Aires U. Med. Sch., 1968-69; chief hand surg. svc. Buenos Aires U. Hosp., 1974-86, Mater Dei Hosp., Buenos Aires, 1992—. Author: Medical and Surgical Emergencies, 1981; contbr. chpts. in books and articles to profl. jours. Recipient Luis Tamini award Argentinian Soc. Orthopaedic Surgery, 1976-77. Mem. J.W. Littler Soc. for Hand Surgery, E.A. Nalebuff Hand Club. Avocations: shooting, fly fishing, horseback riding, biking. Office: San Martin de Tours 2916, 1425 Buenos Aires Argentina

URICK, DEAN W., tax and financial planner; b. Omaha, May 19, 1964; s. John William Urick and Kathy Ann Leinemann; m. Michelle, Feb. 20, 1999; 1 child, Ashleigh Reese. Registered rep. series 24-gen. securities prin., Nat. Assn. Securities Dealers; cert. estate planner; registered investment advisor rep. Estate planner Global Financial Advisory, Sarasota, Fla., 1991-97, Wallace Planning Group, Sarasota, Fla., 1997—; spkr. in field. Youth counselor Faith Baptist Ch., Sarasota, 1994—. Mem. Internat. Assn. Financial Planning, Nat. Assn. Cert. Estate Planners, Nat. Assn. Securities Dealers, Million Dollar Round Table. E-mail: dwurick@wallaceplanning.com. Home: 5219 Box Turtle Cir Sarasota FL 34232-4300 Office: Wallace Planning Group 1800 2d St 882 Sarasota FL 34236

URIE, ROBERT GRAHAM, medical products executive; b. London, Jan. 12, 1946; s. Robert and Sylvia Urie; m. Christine Elizabeth Morgan, Mar. 23, 1944; children: Emma, James. Degree in indsl. chemistry, Loughborough (Eng.) U., 1968. Mgr. BOC, Eng., 1968-78; mktg. mgr. Volvo, Eng., 1978-82; mktg. dir. Franklin Med., 1982-86; mng. dir. Mediplus Ltd., High Wycombe, Eng., 1986—; cons. Strategic Innovations, Eng., 1988-91. Chmn. Round Table, Eng., 1985. Mem. Inst. Mgmt., Royal Inst. Mktg. (cert.), Royal Inst. Chemistry (chartered). Avocations: sailing, cooking, wine, theatre. Office: Mediplus Ltd, 37-39 Baker St, Bucks High Wycombe HP11 2RX, England

URQUHART, JOHN CAMERON, anesthesiologist; b. Aberdeen, Scotland, May 9, 1961; s. Gordon and Florence (Cameron) U.; m. Susan Jane Temperley, May 9, 1987; children: Alexander, Sally. MBBS, U. London, 1985. Anesthetist trainee, 1987-89; co. physician CEGA Air Ambulance, U.K., 1989-90; specialist Royal Army Med Corps, U.K., 1990-94; sr. registrar East Anglia, U.K., 1994-98; cons. anaesthesia, West Suffolk Hosp., 1998—. Author: The Anaesthetic Aide-Memoire, 1996, The Anaesthesia Viva: Volume 1, 1996, The Anaesthesia Viva: Volume 2, 1997; editor: Modern Obstetric Anaesthesia, 1999. Recipient Registrar's prize Trisvc. Anaesthesia Soc., 1993. Fellow Royal Coll. Anaesthetists. Mem. Ch. of Scotland. Avocations: trout fishing, model railways, rugby football. Office: W Suffolk Hospital, Dept Anaesthesia, Bury Saint Edmunds IP33 2QZ, England

URQUHART-HAY, DONALD, surgeon; b. Christchurch, New Zealand, May 24, 1929; s. Walter and Beryl Eunice (Robertson) Urquhart-Hay; m. Pamela Mary Bowden-Hennin, Feb. 12, 1960; children: Simon, Charlote, Timothy. MD, Otago U., Dunedin, New Zealand, 1954. Med. and surg. diplomate. House surgeon various hosps., New Zealand and Eng., 1955-58; house officer Royal Nat. Orthopedic, London, 1959-60; registrar Gen. Hosp., Southland, Eng., 1961-63; sr. registrar Inst. Urology, London, 1964-66; cons. urologist Capital Health, Wellington, New Zealand, 1966-94, MidCentral Health, Palmerston North, New Zealand, 1996-99; chief commr. Order St. John, New Zealand, 1980-86, prin. med. officer, 1986-92; cons. urologist Mil. Hosp., Taif, Saudi Arabia, 1992, Health Svcs., Dubai, United Arab Emeritus, 1993. Contbr. articles to med. jours. Aide de camp Govt. House, Wellington, 1972-75; pres. Medico-Legal Soc., Wellington, 1981-83. Comdr. Royal New Zealand Naval Res., 1966-86. Recipient awards Order St. John, 1972, 76, 80. Fellow RCS, Australian Coll. Surgeons; mem. British Urology Soc., Urol. Soc. Australia. Presbyterian. Avocations: clocks, carpentry, gardening, sailing, skiing. Home: Stone Farm, Totaranni Rd RD 1, Otaki New Zealand Office: Wakefiedl Spec Medical Ctr, Rintoul St, Wellington New Zealand

URRETS-ZAVALÍA, ALBERTO JERÓNIMO, ophthalmologist, researcher; b. Cordoba, Argentina, Sept. 30, 1920; s. Alberto and Matilde (Maldonado A.) U.-Z.; m. Susana Martinez Paz, Dec. 16, 1946; children: Susana Urrets-Zavalia de Aguirre, Cecilia Urrets-Zavalia de Giraudo. Grad. Physician, Surgeon, Nat. U. Cordoba, 1946, MD in Surgery, 1947. Prof. ophthalmology, Chief Ophthalmic Clinic Nat. U. Cordoba Med. Sch., 1956-86, prof. emeritus, 1992—; chair ophthalmology Found. of Seminar, Nat. U. Cordoba Med. Sch., 1956, creator Eye Bank, 1957; speaker lectrs. and confs. Author: Le Décollement de la rétine, 1968, Diabetic Retinopathy, 1977; editor: (with G. Blankenship) Current Concepts in Diagnosis and Treatment of Vitreoretinal Diseases, 1981. Recipient prize Soc. Oftalmologia del Litoral, Argentina, 1952, Gold medal Am. Jour. Ophthalmology, 1959, Gold Medal Castroviejo Lecture award Castroviejo Soc., 1983, Gradle Meml. Lecture and Gold Medal, 1987, Spl. prize and Gold medal XIII Argentine Congress of Ophthalmology, 1987, Hon. Mem. award Circulo Medico de Cordoba, 1988; named Hon. Prof., U. San Francisco Xavier, Chuquisaca, Bolivia, 1960; recognized by Latin Am. ophthalmolgists in recognition of sci. and tchg. work U. de Antioquia, Colombia, 1982. Fellow Am. Acad. Ophthalmology, Am. Coll. Surgeons, N.Y. Acad. Scis., Royal Coll. Ophthalmologists U.K.; mem. Nat. Acad. Ciencias Argentina, Med. Assn. Argentina, Nat. Acad. Medicine Argentina, Med. Acad. Cordoba, Acad. Ophthalmologic Internat. (charter), Consejo Internat. Oftalmologia, Internat. Assn. Ophthalmic Microsurgery, Club Jules Gonin (hon.), Inst. Barraquer (hon.), Hellenic Ophthal. Soc., Deutsche Ophthal. Gesellschaft, Deutsche Retinologische Gesellschaft, Internat. Ophthalmic Surgeons, Soc. Francaise d'Ophtalmologie, Soc. Belge d'Ophtalmologie, Soc. Española de Oftalmología. Achievements include establishing system of med. residencies approved by Nat. U. Cordoba Med. Sch.; creation of system of fellowships from which specialists have been favored; organized teaching of grads. in ophthalmology. Home: Av Hipolito Yrigoyen 370, Cordoba 5000, Argentina Office: Inst Urrets-Zavalia, Arquitecto Thays 75, Cordoba 5000, Argentina

URROZ ARANCIBIA, CARLOS, gallery director, consultant; b. Madrid, Oct. 2, 1966; s. Jose Angel Urroz and Maria Estibaliz Arancibia. Grad., ICADE, Madrid, 1990, Harvard U., 1991. Mktg. mgr. Agatha Ruiz de la Prada, Madrid, 1991-94; dep. dir. ARCO, Madrid, 1994-98; dir. Helga de Alvear Gallery, Madrid, 1998—; art cons. for pvt. collectors. Advisor Arconoticias Mag., 1995—. Active Reina Sofia Mus., Madrid, Guggenheim Mus., Bilbao, Friends of ARCO, Madrid. Avocations: visual arts, performing arts, gourmet tours, golf. Office: Galeria Helga de Alvear, Doctor Fourquet 12, 28012 Madrid Spain

URRUTIA, MIGUEL, banker. Pres. Ctrl. Bank Colombia. Office: Banco de la Republica, Carerra 7A No 14-78Apdo Aereo 3531, Bogota Colombia*

URSANO, ROBERT JOSEPH, psychiatrist; b. Heidelberg, Ger., May 26, 1947; s. James Joseph and Neoma Faye (Summers) U.; m. Diane T. Ursano; children: Amy, Anna. BS magna cum laude, U. Notre Dame, 1969; MD, Yale U., 1973; grad., Washington Psychoanalystic Ins, 1986. Diplomate Nat. Bd. Med. Examiners, Am. Bd. Psychiatry and Neurology; lic. physician N.Y., Tex., Md. Resident in psychiatry Wilford Hall USAF Med. Ctr., 1973-75; postdoctoral fellow in psychiatry Yale U./Yale Psychiat. Inst., 1975-77; staff psychiatrist USAF Sch. Aerospace Medicine, Brooks AFB, Tex., 1977-79; clin. asst. prof. U. Tex. Health Sci. Ctr., San Antonio, 1977-79; asst. prof. and dir. third yr. clerkships Dept. psychiatry, Uniformed Svcs. U. Health Scis., Bethesda, Md., 1979-81; assoc prof. and dir. 3rd yr. clerkships Dept. psychiatry, Uniformed Svcs. U. Health Scis., 1981-83, assoc. prof. and assoc. chmn. dept. psychiatry, 1983-86, prof. and assoc. chmn. dept. psychiatry, 1987-92; prof., chair dept. psychiatry Uniformed Svcs. U. Health Scis., Bethesda, Md., 1992—; examiner Am. Bd. Psychiatry and Neurology, 1984—; asst. prof. Nat. Naval Med. Ctr Dept. Psychiatry, Georgetown U. Sch. Medicine, Washington, 1980-84, assoc. prof., 1984-88, prof., 1988—. Author: Concise Guide to Psychodynamic Psychotherapy, 1990, Concise Guide to Principles and Practice of Psychodynamic Psychotherapy in the Era of Managed Care, 1998; editor: Individual and Community Responses to Trauma and Disaster: The Structure of Human Chaos, 1994, Emotional Aftermath of The Persian Gulf War: Veterans, Families, Communities and Nations, 1996, Acute and Chronic PTSD, 1997; reviewer Am. Jour. Psychiatry, Jour. Nervous and Mental Disease, Psychosomatics, Psychiatry, Jour. Applied Social Psychology, Archives of Gen. Psychiatry, Hosp. and Community Psychiatry, all 1986—, Jour. Neuropsychiatry and Clin. Neurosci., 1988—, Jour. Traumatic Stress, 1989—; editor-in-chief Psychiatry, 1999—; contbr. numerous articles to profl. jours., chpts. to books; editor-in-chief Psychiatry, 1999—. Decorated Air Force Commendation medal; recipient Dept. Def. Humanitarian Svc. medal, Dept. Def. Superior Svc. award, William C. Porter award Assn. Mil. Surgeons of U.S.; recipient Disting. Tchg. award Am. Soc. Psychoanalysts Physicians. Fellow Am. Psychiat. Assn., Am. Coll. Psychiatrists, Am. Coll. Psychoanalysts; mem. Am. Psychoanalytic Assn., Internat. Psychoanalytic Assn., Am. Psychosomatic Soc., Washington Psychiat. Soc., Washington Psychoanalytic Soc., Soc. of USAF Psychiatrists (v.p. 1981-82), Assn. for Acad. Psychiatry, Alpha Epsilon Delta, Phi Beta Kappa. Home: 3900 Cleveland St Kensington MD 20895-3804 Office: Uniformed Svcs U Health Sci 4301 Jones Bridge Rd Bethesda MD 20814-4712

URSIC, SREBRENKA, information technology researcher, manager, consultant; b. Zagreb, Croatia, Mar. 4, 1947; s. Ivo and Katarina Ursic; m. Damir Schoenauer Vuk. BSEE, U. Zagreb, 1970, MSEE, 1973. Product and software devel. specialist RIZ Semicondrs., Zagreb, 1970-80, asst. gen. mgr., 1980-82, bipolar integrated cir. researcher, 1982-84; application specific integrated cir. design group leader Rade Končar Inst., Zagreb, 1984-90; tech. cons., mgr. Sistemprojekt Group/Systemcom, Zagreb, 1990—; mem. working group for microelectronics UNESCO, Belgium, 1984; conf. chmn. Ex-Yugoslav Microelectronics Conf., 1988; del. Croatian Nat. Sci. Coun., Zagreb, 1982-84; invited spkr. at profl. confs. Contbr. articles to profl. jours. Recipient Annual award Croatian Info. Assn., 1999. Fellow MIDEM (exec. com. 1974-89); mem. IEEE, N.Y. Acad. Scis., Sodalitas Gymnasii Classici Zagrabiensis. Avocations: music, hatha yoga, holistic recuperation methods, tennis. Home: Kruziceva 4, 10000 Zagreb Croatia

URUSOV, VADIM SERGEEVICH, chemist, researcher; b. Moscow, June 3, 1936; s. Sergei P. Urusov and Bella S. Orlova; m. Marina A. Mordvinzeva, June 2, 1960 (div. May 1987); children: Olga, Alexander; m. Natalia R. Khisina, Mar. 6, 1994; 1 child, George V. Diploma, Moscow U., 1958; grad., Vernadsky Inst. Acad. Scis., Moscow, 1965, DSc in Chemistry, 1975. Rschr. Vernadsky Inst. Acad. Scis., 1958-69, sr. rschr., 1969-79, head of lab., 1979—, prof., 1983; head dept. Moscow U., 1984—. Author: Energetic Crystal Chemistry, 1975, Theory of Isomorphous Miscibility, 1977, Theoretical Crystal Chemistry, 1987, Solid State Geochemistry, 1997. Recipient Soros professorship award Internat. Sci. Found., 1994, 96. Mem. Russian Acad. Natural Scis., Russian Acad. Scis. (corr.). Avocations: classical music, history, mushroom-picking. Office: Moscow U, Vorobjevy Gori, 119899 Moscow Russia

URUSOVA, IRINA ARKADIEVNA, internist; b. St. Petersburg, Russia, Jan. 7, 1967; d. Arkadiy Urusov and Galina Krapivnik. MD, Pavlov State Med. U., 1990. Intern Semmelweis Med. U. Hosp., Budapest, 1993-94; resident N.Y. Hosp. Ctr. Queens, N.Y.C., 1995-98; attending physician Columbia Meml. Hosp., Hudson, N.Y., 1998—. Mem. Am. Coll. Physicians, Am. Soc. Internal Medicine, AMA. Office: Cairo Family Care Ctr 336 Main St Cairo NY 12413-3117

URUSOVSKII, IGOR ALEKSEEVICH, physicist, researcher; b. Ivanovo, Russia, May 10, 1930; s. Aleksei Fedorovich Urusovskii and Lyudmila Gavrilovna (Shakhova) Urusovskaya; m. Aida Aleksandrovna Rogunova, Aug. 24, 1950 (dec. June 2000). Student, State U., Gorkii, 1947-52; candidate in physics and math., Acoustics Inst., Moscow, 1963; PhD in physics and math., Acoustics Inst., 1993. Jr. rschr., Phys. Inst. Acad. Sci., Moscow, 1952-54; jr. rschr., Acoustics Inst. Acad. Sci., 1954-56, 58-66, aspirant, Acoustics Inst., 1956-58, sr. rschr., Acoustics Inst., 1966-96, leading rschr., Acoustics Inst., 1996—. Contbr. over 50 articles to profl. jours. Avocation: music. E-mail: mironov@akin.ru. Home: 18-3-48 Ostrovityanova St, 117321 Moscow Russia Office: N N Andreev Acoustics Inst, 4 Shvernik St, 117036 Moscow Russia

URYSON, ANNA, physicist; b. Moscow, Dec. 17, 1950; d. Vladimir Osip and Ira Faivel (Stupel) U. PhD in Physics, Moscow State U., 1974. Sci. rschr. Lebedev Physics Inst., Moscow, 1974—. Contbr. articles to profl. jours. Grantee Am. Astron. Soc., 1992, Am. Phys. Soc., 1993, ISF (Soros Found.), 1993. Office: Lebedev Physics Inst, Leninsky pr 53, 117924 Moscow Russia

URZICA, MARIUS, Olympic athlete. Winner Gold medal gymnastics - pommel horse Sydney, 2000. Office: Federatia Romana Gimnastica, Str Vasile Conta 16 Sector 11, 70139 Bucarest Romania*

USATYI, ALEXANDER FEODOROVICH, nuclear scientist; b. Saint Petersburg, Russia, Apr. 15, 1931; s. Feodor Yudovich Usatyi and Anna Filippovna (Katayeva) Usataya; m. Tatiana Ivanovna Rozhkova, Sept. 10, 1960 (div. 1963); m. Tina Valerianovna Metreveli, March 17, 1973; 1 child, Ekaterina. BS, Moscow U., 1954; candidate of sci., Kurchatov Inst. Atomic Energy, Moscow, 1966. Jr. rschr. Russian Rsch. Ctr. Kurchatov Inst., Moscow, 1955-64, rschr., 1965-77, sr. rschr., 1978-80; head lab. Atomenergoexp, Moscow, 1981-85; dir. Chernobyl Sci. Group Chernobyl Sci. Expedition, Ukraine, 1986-88; head lab. Russian Rsch. Ctr. Kurchatov Inst., Moscow, 1989—; mem. sci. bd. Inst. Molecular Genetics Russian Acad. Scis., Moscow, 1975-78, Atomenergoexp, Moscow, 1981-85, Chernobyl Sci. Expedition, 1986-90, Inst. Nuclear Reactor Russian Rsch. Ctr. Kurchatov Inst., Moscow, 1990—; mem. Invalids of Chernobyl Russian Rsch. Ctr., Kurchatov Inst., Moscow, 1999—. Contbr. articles to profl. jours. Recipient medal Vet. of Labor Russian Govt., 1985, medal Valour Russian Govt., 1998; cert. Chernobyl Repairing Works Russian Govt., 1987. Fellow Unity Chernobyl (medal 1996); mem. Internat. Electron Paramagnetic Resonance Soc., Nuclear Soc. Moscow, N.Y. Acad. Scis., Mountian Climbers Soc. (Edelweiss Order). Avocations: alpinism, tennis, stamps, violin, guitar. Home: Tallinnskaya Ul 2 531, 123458 Moscow Russia Office: Russian Rsch Ctr Kurchatov Inst, Kurchatov Square 1 OVE, 123182 Moscow Russia

USCHEEK, DAVID PETROVICH, chemist; b. University Heights, Ohio, July 9, 1937; s. Peter Ivanovich and Marie (Ocasek) U. BS, Case Western Res. U., 1959; PhD in Chem. Engring., LaSalle U., 1998. Chemist The Glidden Co., Cleve., 1963-67, Mobil Chem. Co., Cleve., 1967-71, Limbacher Coatings, Cleve., 1971-72; tech. dir. Continental Products, Euclid, Ohio, 1972-80; chemist Body Bros. Paint Corp., Bedford, Ohio, 1980-83, Harrison Paint Corp., Canton, Ohio, 1983-88, Akron (Ohio) Paint and Varnish, 1988-95, Ritrama Duramark, 1995-98, Mahoning Paint Corp., 1999—; cons. The Analyst, Chardon, Ohio, 1991—. Mem. Am. Chem. Soc., Internat. Union of Pure and Applied Chemists, N.Y. Acad. Scis. Fax: 440-354-5036. Home: 8602 Auburn Rd Chardon OH 44024-8711

USHAKOV, NIKOLAI MICHAILOVICH, physicist, researcher; b. Leningrad, Russia, Feb. 22, 1949; s. Michail Nikitovich and Maria Zynovjevna (Kudasova) U.; m. Olga Vladimirovna Materova; children: Kate, Mike. BSc, State U., Saratov, Russia, 1971, PhD, 1980; postgrad., State U. Doctor's Sch., Saratov, 1997—. Cert. radiophysicist including quantum radiophysics. Engr. Rsch. Inst. Mechanics/Physics, Saratov, 1971-73, jr. rsch. worker, 1973-76, sr. rsch. worker, 1976-84; sr. rsch. worker Inst Radioengring. & Elec., Russian Acad. Sci., Saratov, 1984-89, leader rsch. worker, 1989-97. Contbr. articles to profl. jours.; patentee in field. Recipient Silver medal Ctrl. State Exhbn., Moscow, 1988; named Inventor of USSR, 1978. Mem. SPIE. Avocations: jogging, anglering, gardening. Home: PO Box 3576, 410030 Saratov Russia

USHAKOV, VASILII, academic administrator; b. Semipalatinsk, USSR, Mar. 27; s. Yakov Ignatiyevich and Akulina Ignatiyevna (Ovchinnikova) U.; m. Emma Tikhonovna Shaburova, Oct. 2, 1962; 1 child, Elena Vasiliyevna. Engr., Tomsk Poly. U., 1962, PhD, 1966, lectr., 1967, DSc, 1974, prof., 1976. Asst., lectr., prof., chair high voltage engring. Tomsk Poly. U., 1965—, head of chair high voltage engring., 1974-81, dir. High Voltage Rsch. Inst., 1979-92, vice-rector on rsch., 1992—; mem., vice-head two Panels for Def. of Dissertations, 1974—; mem. sci. coun. Tomsk Poly. U., 1979—. Author: Electrical Breakdown in Liquids, 1979, Electrical Aging and Resource of Monolithic Polymeric, 1992, High Voltage Installation Insulation, 1994; co-author: Radiational Charge Storage in Solid Dielectrics and Methods of Its Diagnostics, 1991. Councillor on sci. Gov. Tomsk Region, 1996. Mem. Russian Engring. Acad. (academician), Russian Electrotechnical Acad. (academician). Avocations: skiing, table tennis, swimming, do market-gardening. E-mail: ushakov@tpu.ru. Fax: 7382 2 415 658. Home: Apt 14, 43 Lenin Ave, 634034 Tomsk Russia Office: Tomsk Poly Univ, 30 Lenin Ave, 634034 Tomsk Russia

USHAKOV, YURI VIKTOROVICH, diplomat; b. Moscow, Mar. 13, 1947; married; 1 daughter. Grad., Moscow State Inst. Internat. Relations, 1970; PhD in History, Diplomatic Acad. Joined Ministry Fgn. Affairs of the USSR, 1970, with Soviet Embassy in Denmark, 1970-86; dep. chief mission, min.-counsellor Embassy of the USSR/Russian Fedn., Denmark, 1986-92; head divsn. security and cooperation in Europe Ministry Fgn. Affairs Russian Fedn., 1992-93, dir. Directorate of All-European Cooperation, 1994-96; amb., permanent rep. Russian Fedn. to the Orgn. Security and Cooperation Europe, Vienna, Austria, 1996-98; dep. min. fgn. affairs Govt. Russian Fedn., 1998-99; amb. to the U.S. Govt. Russian Fedn., Washington, 2000—. Fax: 202-298-5749. Office: Embassy of the Russian Fedn 2650 Wisconsin Ave NW Washington DC 20007-4600

USHENKO, AUDREY ANDREYEVNA, painter, art historian, educator; b. Princeton, July 28, 1945; d. Andrew Pavlevitch and Fay (Hampton) U.; m. S.M. Harcaj; 1 child, Emily. Student, Sch. of Art Inst., 1963-64; BA, Ind. U., 1965; MA, Northwestern U., Evanston, Ill., 1967, PhD, 1979. Instr. Valparaiso (Ind.) U., 1968-73, asst. prof., 1978-79; instr. Alan R. Hite Inst.

U. Louisville, 1973-74; asst. prof. Northwestern U., Evanston, Ill., 1974-75; vis. faculty Columbia Coll., 1980-88; assoc. prof. Ind.-Purdue U., Ft. Wayne, Ind., 1988—. Gallery artist Gruen Gallery, Chgo., 1983—, Denise Bibro Gallery, N.Y.C., 1993—, Yvonne Rapp Gallery, Louisville, 1989—; artist oil paintings Bacchus & Ariadne III, 1987 (NAD Clark prize), Social Security, 1987 (Purchase prize 1989), Chgo. Art Expo, 1996, Marriage Project-Travelling Exhbn., 1996, Conviviality, 1997 (NAD Isidor Medal 1997), Fort Wayne Mus. of Art, 1998; curator exhbn., N.Y.C., 1998-99. Mem. AAUP (sec. local chpt. 1990—), NAD. Democrat. Orthodox. Avocations: reading, music. Home: 2519 East Dr Fort Wayne IN 46805-3612

USHERWOOD, PETER NORMAN RUSSELL, science educator; b. Gravesend, Kent, Eng., Oct. 7, 1936; s. Donald Mann and Elsie Daphne (Russell) U.; m. Gloria Marina Hopton, Sept. 27, 1958; children: Keri Andrew, Russell David, Stephen Paul, Lisa Jane. BS, U. Wales, 1958; PhD, U. Glasgow, 1962. From asst. lectr. to lectr. U. Glasgow, Scotland, 1960-68, sr. lectr., 1968-74; prof. U. Nottingham, Eng., 1974—; com. chmn. Sci. and Engring. Rsch. Coun., U.K., 1976-93; exec. editor Sheffield (Eng.) Acad. Press, 1994—; cons. Blackie & Sons Ltd., Glasgow, 1968-89, Pharmaceutic and Pesticide Ind. Worldwide, 1966-94. Author: Nervous Systems, 1973; editor: Simple Nervous Systems, 1975, Insect Muscle, 1975, Neurotox '84, 1985. Mem. Children's Panel, Scotland, 1972; mem. adv. com. Ministry Agr. and Fisheries, London, 1974. Fulbright fellow, Columbia U., 1963. Fellow Royal Soc. Edinburgh, Inst. Biology, Zool. Soc. London, Soc. for Exptl. Biology (pres. 1980), Brit. Pharmalogical Soc., Brit. Physiological Soc., Brit. Soc. for Chemistry Industry. Avocations: scientific research, association football, novel writing. Home: 35 Normanby Rd, Nottingham NG7 2RD, England Office: U Nottingham, University Park, Nottingham NG7 2RD, England

USHERWOOD, TIMOTHY PAUL, medical educator; b. Brighton, Sussex, Eng., Dec. 15, 1953; came to Australia, 1995; s. Francis and Daphne Usherwood; children: Kathryn, Frances, Samuel. BSc, London U., 1975, MBBS, 1978, MD, 1991. Gen. practitioner prin. Greenock, Eng., 1984-89; sr. lectr. gen. practice Sheffield (Eng.) U., 1989-95; prof. gen. practice U. Sydney, Australia, 1995—. Fellow Royal Coll. Gen. Practitioners, Royal Coll. Physicians (Glasgow). Office: U Sydney Dept Gen Practice, PO Box 154, Westmead NSW 2145, Australia

USHIKI, TATSUO, anatomist, researcher; b. Itoigawa, Niigata, Japan, July 5, 1957; s. Takeo Isogai and Yoshiko Ushiki; m. Hiroko Kato, Nov. 10, 1985; children: Tetsuro, Tomohiko, Nobuyuki. MD, Niigata U. Sch., 1982, PhD, 1986. Rsch. assoc. Iwate Med. U. Sch. Medicine, Morioka, Japan, 1986-88, lectr., 1989; assoc. prof. Hokkaido U. Sch. Medicine, Sapporo, Japan, 1990-95; prof. anatomy Niigata U. Sch. Medicine, 1995—. Exec. editor Jour. Electron Microscopy, 1995—; cons. editor Arch. Histol. Cytology, 1996—. Mem. Japanese Assn. Anatomists, Japanese Soc. Electron Microscopy. Office: Niigata U Sch Medicine, 1 Asahimachi-dori, 951 8510 Niigata Japan

USHIO, MASAO, engineering educator; b. Amagasaki, Hyogo, Japan, Jan. 21, 1942; s. Yoshihei and Kameyo (Taniguchi) U.; m. Tomi Yamaguchi, May 2, 1966; children: Watatsuna, Tomoo, Kazushi. B in Engring., Osaka U., 1964, M in Engring., 1969, D in Engring., 1975. Rschr. Sanyo Electric Co. Ltd., 1964-66; rsch. assoc. Osaka U., 1970-75, assoc. prof., 1976-90, prof., 1991—; vis. scientist MIT, 1979-80. Author, editor: Fundamentals and Application on Materials Processing by Thermal Plasma. Recipient Nishiyama-kinen award ISIJ, 1992. Mem. IIW (chmn. com. XII 1998—), Japan Welding Soc. (trustee 1994-98, chmn. com. welding processes 1992—, achievement award 1999, Best Paper of Yr. award 1988), Japan Inst. Welding (trustee 1996—), Sci. Coun. Japan (chmn. joining tech. com. 1998—). Avocations: classical music, golf. Office: Osaka U JWRI, Mihogaoka 11-1, Osaka Ibaraki 567-0047, Japan

USHIŌ, TETSUYA, computer engineer; b. Nagasaki, Japan, Aug. 26, 1955; s. Takeshi Ushiō and Kazukō Amanō; m. Yukō Fujihara, Feb. 28, 1987; children: Masatō, Sayaka, Lisa. B in Engring., U. Tokyo, 1979; MS, Stanford U., 1986. Engr. Info. Sys. Divsn. Hitachi, Ltd., Kawasaki, Japan, 1986-92, sr. engr. Info. Sys. Divsn., 1992-99, dept. mgr. bus. plnning Indsl. Sys. Divsn., 1999—. Mem. Info. Processing Soc. Japan, Assn. Computing Machinery. Home: 2-4-12-904 Hisamoto, Takatsu Kawasaki 213-0011, Japan Office: Hitachi Ltd, 6-23-15 Minami-Ohi, Shinagawa Tokyo 140-8570, Japan

USINGER, MARTHA PUTNAM, counselor, educator; b. Pitts., Dec. 10, 1912; d. Milo Boone and Christiana (Haberstroh) Putnam; m. Robert Leslie Usinger, June 24, 1938 (dec Oct. 1968); children: Roberta Christine (dec.), Richard Putnam. AB cum laude, U. Calif., Berkeley, 1934; postgrad., Oreg. State U., 1935, U. Ghana, 1970, Coll. Nairobi, 1970. Tchr. Oakland (Calif.) Pub. Schs., 1936-38; tchr. Berkeley (Calif.) Pub. Schs., 1954-57, dean West Campus, counselor, 1957-78; lectr., photographer in field. Author: Ration Books and Christmas Crackers, 1989; contbg. author Robert Leslie Usinger, Autobiography of an Entomologist, 1972. Mem. DAR, Berkeley Ret. Tchrs., U. Calif. Emeriti Assn., U. Calif. Alumnae Assn., Prytanean Alumnae Assn. (alumnae pres. 1952-54), Berkeley Camera Club, Mortar Bd., Am. Friends of Puttenham, P.E.O., Delta Kappa Gamma. Avocations: photography, slide shows and lectures, ethnic textiles, travel, geneology.

USOL'TSEVA, NADEJDA VASIL'EVNA, chemistry educator; b. Myshkin, Russia, July 19, 1944; d. Vasilii Michailovich and Valentina Alekseevna (Lipilina) U.; m. Boris Gennadievich Tabachnik, Oct. 14, 1967; children: Dmitri, Irina. MD, Med. Inst., Ivanovo, Russia, 1967, PhD, 1973; DSc in Phys. Chemistry, U. St. Petersburg, Russia, 1990. Physician-biochemist Dist. Main Hosp., Ivanovo, 1967-76; sr. rschr. U. Ivanovo, 1976-83, head of liquid crystal lab., 1983—, prof. chemistry, 1992—, v.p. internat. rels., 2000—; guest prof. U. Valladolid, Spain, 1995-96; head of sect. Technology Acad. Sci., Ivanovo, 1993—. Author: Lyotropic Liquid Crystals, 1994; contbr. articles to profl. jours. Mem. Univ. Sci. Coun., Ivanovo, 1983—. Rsch. grantee Pres. of Russia, 1994-96, European Union, Brussels, 1995-97, Russian Sci. Found. and DFG Programme, 1997-98. Mem. N.Y. Acad. Scis., Internat. Liquid Crystal Soc. (mem. bd. 1992—), German-Am. Women's Club (Berlin). Avocation: playing the piano. Office: Ivanovo State U, Ermaka Str 37/7, 153025 Ivanovo Russia

USOV, SERGEI VADIMOVICH, engineering company executive; b. Tula, Russia, June 16, 1952; s. Vadim Sergeevich Usov and Rozalia Nikolaevna (Safronova) Usova; m. Tatiana Evgenevna Maksakova; 1 child, Pavel. M. U. Tula, 1974, D, 1979; Prof. degree, Internat. U., Moscow, 1994; M, U. Pitts., 1995. Supr. Tulamashzavod JSC, Tula, 1974-75, engr., 1975-76, head lab., 1976-79, dep. head dept., 1979-84, head laser dept., 1984-94, dir. laser prodn., 1994—; academician Laser Acad. Sci., Russian Fedn. Active Otechestvo, Moscow, 1999. Recipient State Hon. laureate, 1989. Mem. Welding Soc., Internat. Soc. Optoelectronic Engrs. Office: Tulamashzavod JSC, Mosinst 2, 300002 Tula Russia

USTARAN, JUAN IGNACIO, chemist; b. Mexico City, Apr. 7, 1955; s. Ignacio and Rosa Maria (Cervantes) U.; m. Angelina Enrique, Dec. 2, 1978; children: Juan Salvador, Maria Paulina, Daniela. Degree in chemistry, U. Iberoamericana, Mexico City, 1978. Dir. gen. Labs. ABC Quimica Investigacion y Analysis S.A., 1979—; dir. gen. cen. control antidoping XII Campeonato Mundial Futbol Mexico, 1986; dir. gen. ABC Instrumentacion Analitica S.A., 1986-91; dir. gen., pres. consejo adminstrn. fecha ABC Estudios y Proyectos S.A., 1986-95; dir. gen. cen. control doping XVI Juegos Centroamericanos y Caribe, 1990; asesor control doping Confedn. Deportiva Mexicana, 1988-91; asesor control doping fecha Com. Olimpico Mexicano, 1988-91; dir. gen. fecha ABC Adminstrn. & Svcs. S.C., 1989; corp. pres. Grupo Corp. ABC, 1989-97; coord. cientifico Centro De Control Antidoping, La Habana, Cuba, 1991—; asespr Centro Nacional de Capacitacion e Investigacion Ambienlal, 1997—; mem. task force NARAP for Monitoring and Assessment of the Environ. Cooperation Commn., NAFTA. Contbr. articles to profl. jours. Mem. Am. Water Assn., Assn. Mexicana Contra Contaminacion Agua y Aire (vocal exec. 1988-90), Assn. Mexicana Biochem. Clinica, Water Pollution Control Fedn., Soc. Mexicana Engring. Sanitaria y Ambiental A.C., Soc. Mexicana Engring. Ambiental A.C., Assn. Mexicana Para Control Residuos Solidos y Peligrosos A.C., Assn. Mexicana de Labs. Analiticos del Mex. Ambiente A.C. (pres 1995—).

USTINOV, SIR PETER ALEXANDER, actor, director, writer; b. London, Apr. 16, 1921; s. Iona and Nadia (Benois) U.; m. Isolda Denham, 1940 (div.); 1 child, Tamara; m. Suzanne Cloutier, Feb. 15, 1954 (div. 1971); children: Pavla, Igor, Andrea; m. Hélène du Lau d'Allemans, 1972. Student, Westminster Sch., London, Mr. Gibbs Prep. Sch., London, London Theatre Sch.; D.Mus. (hon.), Cleve. Inst. Music, 1967; LL.D. (hon.), U. Dundee, 1969, LaSalle Coll. of Phila., 1971, U. Ottawa, 1991; Litt.D. (hon.), U. Lancaster, 1972; Doctorate (hon.), U. Toronto, 1984, 95; LHD (hon.), Georgetown U., 1988; Doctorate (hon.), Free U. Brussels, 1995. Stage appearances include The Wood Demon, 1938, The Bishop of Limpopoland, 1939, Madame Liselotte Beethoven-Fink, 1939, White Cargo, Rookery Nook, Laburnum Grove, Pygmalion, 1939, First Night, 1940, Swinging the Gate, 1940, Fishing For Shadows, 1940, Hermione Gingold Revue, 1940, Diversion No. 1 Revue, 1940, Squaring the Circle, 1941, Crime and Punishment, 1946, Frenzy, 1948, Love in Albania, 1949, The Love of Four Colonels, 1951-52 (N.Y. Critics award, Donaldson award), Romanoff and Juliet, 1956 (Evening Standard drama award), Photo Finish, 1962, 63, The Unknown Soldier and His Wife, 1968, 73, Who's Who in Hell, 1974, King Lear, 1979, 80, Beethoven's Tenth, 1983, 83-84, 87-88; currently appearing worldwide in An Evening with Peter Ustinov; film appearances include One of Our Aircraft Is Missing, 1941, The Way Ahead, 1944, Private Angelo, 1949, Odette, 1950, Quo Vadis (Acad. award nomination for Best Supporting Actor), 1950, Hotel Sahara, 1952, Beau Brummel, 1953-54, The Egyptian, 1954, We're No Angels, 1955, Lola Montez, 1955, The Spies, 1955, An Angel Flew Over Brooklyn, 1955, I Girovaghi, 1955, The Sundowners, 1960, Spartacus, 1960-61 (Acad. award for Best Supporting Actor), Romanoff and Juliet, 1961, Billy Budd, 1962, Topkapi, 1963, John Goldfarb, Please Come Home!, 1964, Blackbeard's Ghost, 1967, The Comedians, 1967, Hot Millions, 1968, Viva Max, 1969, Hammersmith Is Out, 1971, Big Truck and Poor Clare, 1971, One of Our Dinosaurs Is Missing, 1974, Logan's Run, 1975, Treasure of Matecumba, 1975, The Last Remake of Beau Geste, 1976, Purple Taxi, 1977, Death on the Nile, 1977, The Thief of Baghdad, 1978, Ashanti, 1979, Charlie Chan and the Curse of the Dragon Queen, 1980, Evil Under the Sun, 1981, Memed, My Hawk, 1982, Appointment With Death, 1988, The French Revolution, 1989, Lorenzo's Oil, 1992, The Phoenix and The Magic Carpet, 1993, Stiff Upper Lips, 1997, The Bachelor, 1999; dir.: (plays) Squaring the Circle, 1941, Love in Albania, 1949, No Sign of the Dove, 1952, A Fiddle at the Wedding, 1952, Romanoff and Juliet, 1956, Photo Finish, 1962, 64, Half Way Up the Tree, 1967, The Unknown Soldier and His Wife, 1968, 73, (operas) L'Heure Espagnole (Ravel), Covent Garden, 1962, Gianni Schicchi (Puccini), Covent Garden, 1962, Erwartung (Schoenberg), Covent Garden, 1962, The Magic Flute (Mozart), Hamburg Opera, 1968; dir., scenery and costume designer: Don Giovanni (Mozart), Edinburgh Festival, 1973; dir., producer, set and costume designer: Don Quichotte (Massenet), Paris Opera, 1973; dir., producer: The Brigands (Offenbach), The German Opera, Berlin, 1978; dir., writer libretto: The Marriage (Moussorgsky), Piccola Scala, 1981; dir.: Mavra and The Flood (Stravinsky), Piccola Scala, 1982, Katja Kabanowa (Janacek), Hamburg Opera, 1985, The Marriage of Figaro, Mozarteum and the Hamburg Opera, 1987, Jolanthe (Tchaikovsky) and Francesca da Rimini (Rachmaninoff), Dresden Opera, 1993, The Love of the Three Oranges (Prokofiev), Bolschoi, Moscow, 1997; appeared on radio, London (BBC), Germany, Belgium, Rome, Paris, N.Y.C., Hollywood; TV appearances include In All Directions (host, producer, co-star), BBC, History of Europe, BBC, Einstein's Universe, PBS and BBC, 1979, Barefoot in Athens (Emmy award), Storm in Summer (Emmy award), The American Revolution, CBS (George Peabody award), Omnibus (Emmy award), The Well Tempered Bach (Emmy award nomination), PBS, 1984, 13 at Dinner, CBS, 1985, Deadman's Folly, CBS, 1985, Peter Ustinov's Russia, 1985, Appointment with Death, 1987, Around the World in Eighty Days, NBC, 1988-89, Secret Identity of Jack the Ripper, 1989-90, Monet: Legacy of Light, 1990, Ustinov Aboard the Orient Express, 1991-92, Ustinov Meets Pavarotti, 1993, Inside the Vatican, 1994, The Old Curiosity Shop, 1995, Haydn Gala, 1995, documentaries on Thailand and Hong Kong, 1995, an Evening with Sir Peter Ustinov, 1995, Russia Now, 1995, Paths of the Gods, 1996, Following the Equator, 1998, occasional political commentaries, BBC; recordings include Mock Mozart, The Grand Prix of Gibralter, Peter and the Wolf (directed by Herbert Von Karajan), Nutcracker Suite, The Soldier's Tale (Stravinsky) (with Jean Cocteau), Hary Janos (Kodaly), London Symphony Orch., The Little Prince (St. Exupéry), (narration) Grandpa, Babar and Father Christmas, The Old Man of Lochnagar, Grandpa, Peter Ustinov Reads the Orchestra; author: (plays) Fishing for Shadows, 1940, House of Regrets, 1942, Blow Your Own Trumpet, 1943, Beyond, 1943, The Banbury Nose, 1944, The Tragedy of Good Intentions, 1945, The Indifferent Shepherd, 1948, Frenzy, 1948, The Man in the Raincoat, 1949, The Moment of Truth, 1951, The Love of Four Colonels, 1951, High Balcony, 1952, No Sign of the Dove, 1953, Romanoff and Juliet, 1956, The Empty Chair, 1956, Paris Not So Gay, 1958, Photo Finish, 1962, The Life in My Hands, 1964, The Unknown Soldier and His Wife, 1967, Halfway Up the Tree, 1967, Who's Who in Hell, 1974, Overheard, 1981, Beethoven's Tenth, 1983, 87-88, others, (films) The Way Ahead (with Eric Ambler), 1942-43, School for Secrets, 1946, Vice Versa, 1947, Private Angelo, 1949, Romanoff and Juliet, 1961, Billy Budd (with DeWitt Bodeen), 1962-63, The Lady L (with Ira Wallach), 1964, Hot Millions (with Ira Wallach), 1968, Memed, My Hawk, 1982, (cartoon) We Were Only Human, 1960, (short stories) Add a Dash of Pity, 1960, Frontiers of the Sea, 1966, (novels) The Loser, 1961, Krumnagel, 1971, The Disinformer, 1989, The Old Man and Mr. Smith, 1991, (autobiography) Dear Me, 1977, My Russia, 1983, Ustinov in Russia, 1987, Ustinov at Large, 1991, Still at Large, 1993, Quotable Ustinov, 1995; (TV) Alice in Wonderland, 1999; (TV voice) Animal Farm, 1999. Chancellor U. Durham, 1992; pres. World Federalist Movement, 1992. With Brit. Army, 1942-46. Decorated Comdr. Order of Brit. Empire, 1975, Commandeur des Arts et Lettres, 1985, Knight of the Realm, 1990; recipient Disting. Svc. award UNICEF, 1978, Prix de la Butte, 1978, Best Actor award Variety Club Gt. Britain, 1979, medal of Honor Charles U. (Prague), 1991, Britannia award, 1992, Critic's Circle award, 1993, German Cultural award, 1994, German Bambi, 1994, Internat. Child Survival award, 1995, Rudolph Valentino award, 1995, Norman Cousins Global Governance award, 1995, German Video prize for life-time achievement, 1997; named rector U. Dundee, 1971-73; elected to Acad. Fine Arts Paris, 1988. Office: care William Morris Agy, 31/32 Soho Sq GB, London W1V 5DG, England

USTINOV, VLADIMIR VASILIEVICH, physicist; b. Nizhny Tagil, Russia, Sept. 9, 1949; s. Vasilii Konstantinovich and Lubov Kalistratovna (Nekazakova) U.; m. Larisa Pavlovna Alekseeva; children: Svetlana, Julya; m. Tatyana Pavlovna Krinitsina. Magister, Ural State U., Ekaterinburg, Russia, 1971; CandPhysMathSc, Inst. Metal Physics, Ekaterinburg, 1975, D of Physics and Math. Scis., 1986. Jr. scientist Inst. Metal Physics, Ural divsn. Russian Acad. Scis., Ekaterinburg, 1974-79, sr. scientist, 1979-86, head of lab, vice dir., 1986-98, dir., 1998—; prof. Ural State Tech. U., 1995—; Contbr. more than 120 articles to sci. jours. Mem. City Coun., Ekaterinburg, 1982-89. Mem. Am. Phys. Soc., Material Rsch. Soc., Russian Acad. Sci. (corr.). Avocation: skiing. Office: Inst Metal Physics UD RAS, 18 S Kovalevskaya St, 620219 Ekaterinburg GSP-170, Russia

ÜSTÜNEL, ALI SÜLEYMAN, mathematician, researcher; b. Iznik, Turkey, July 13, 1950; arrived in France, 1974; s. Mehmet Salih and Rukiye Lemiye (Ünsel) Ü.; m. Jacqueline Marie-Françoise Quilleré, June 3, 1977. BSc in Physics, Mid. East Tech. U., Ankara, Turkey, 1971, MSc in Math., 1973; D degree, U. Paris, 1981. Asst. Mid. East Tech. U., Ankara, 1971-74; asst. U. Poitiers, France, 1977-79, maitre de conf., 1979-81; rschr. Centre Nat. d'Etudes de Telecomm., Paris, 1981-87; prof. Ecole Nat. Supérieure de Telecomm., Paris, 1987—; mem. professorial com. U. Oslo, Norway, 1993—. Contbr. articles to profl. jours. Lt. Turkish mil., 1985. Grantee French Ministry of Fgn. Affairs, 1974-77. Avocations: running, painting, bridge. Office: Ecole Nat Supérieure Telecomm, 46 rue Barrault, 75634 Paris France

USUBOV, RAMIL IDRIS OGLY, government official; b. Khodzhaly, Azerbaijan, 1948; married; 3 children. Grad., Policy Acad., 1980]. Lawyer, with various police depts.; min. of interior Nakhichevan Autonomous Republic, 1987-89; head passports, visa, pers., criminal investigation depts. Ministry of Internal Affairs, 1989-93; minister of interior Nakhichevan Autonomous republic, 1993-94; min. interior Govt. of Azerbaijan, Baku, 1994—. Office: Ministry of Internal Affair, Hussi Hajiyeva Kuc 7, Baku 370005, Azerbaijan*

USUI, NORIYUKI, finance educator; b. Koga, Ibaraki, Japan, Mar. 30, 1940; m. Huang Meng-Feng; 1 child, Aiya. BA, Doshisha U., Kyoto, Japan, 1963; MA, Meiji U., Tokyo, 1967. Prof. dept. commerce Tokyo Internat. U., 1982—; vis. prof. coll. law and commerce, Nat. Chung Hsing U., Taiwan, 1986-88. Office: Tokyo Internat U, 1-13-1 Matobakita, Kawagoe 350-1197, Japan

USUKI, SATOSHI, physician, educator; b. Ehime, Japan, July 2, 1944; s. Wataru and Chieko (Doi) U.; m. Yoshie Inage, Aug. 8, 1974; children: Hiromune, Yoshimune, Chiemi. MD, Yokohama (Japan) City U., 1971, U. Tokyo, 1981. Ednl. asst. U. Tokyo, 1971-78; asst. prof. U. Tsukuba, Japan, 1978-93, assoc. prof., 1993—; fellow, prof. of distinction Inst. Advanced Rsch. in Asian Sci. and Medicine, WHO, Hempstead, N.Y., 1990-91; lectr. Hüddinge U. Hosp., Karolinska Inst., Sweden, 1992-94, U. Libr. Ctr. Med. Sci., Ibaraki Prefectural U. Health Scis., 1999—; councilor The Japan Endocrine Soc., The Japan Soc. for the Study of Toxemia of Pregnancy, The Japan Soc. of Fertility and Sterility, The Japan Menopause Soc., The Japan Soc. for Comparative Endocrinology, The Japan Soc. of Obstetrics and Gynecology. Promoter East Asian Econ. Caucus; trustee Minamiuwakai; mem. Japan-North Am. Med. Exch. Found., 1987, Internat. Human Resources Inst. Network. Recipient Japan-China Med. Assn. award, 1988, Li Shi Zhen Outstanding Manuscript award Hong Kong Inst. Promotion Chinese Culture, 1990-93. Fellow Inst. Advanced Rsch.; mem. AAAS, APA, N.Y. Acad. Sci., Inter-Am. Sci. Hypertension, Fallopius Internat. Soc., Am. Inst. Ultrasound in Medicine, Internat. Soc. Gynecol. Endocrinology, Am. Assn. Gynecol. Laparoscopists, Inst. Growth Sci. Assn. (assoc., Japan), Am. Roentgen Ray Soc., Internat. Soc. Amino Acid Rsch., Am. Physiol. Soc., Am. Soc. Hypertension, Internat. Study Group for Steroid Hormones, Internat. Soc. Cardiovascular Pharmacotherapy, Internat. Menopause Soc., Internat. Soc. Infectious Diseases, The Growth Hormone Rsch. Soc., The Soc. Behavioral Neuroendocrinology, Internat. Neuropeptide Soc., Am. Soc. Bone and Mineral Rsch., The Pituitary Soc., The European Soc. for Comparative Endocrinology, Internat. Soc. of Neuroendocrinology, Soc. for Endocrinology, The Endocrine Soc., Planetary Soc., Nat. Geographic Soc., Internat. Soc. Outer Space Law, Am. Physiol. Soc. Avocations: Japanese fencing (Renshi 6 Dan), Japanese military arts, Kashima Shinryu (Shomokurokuden), Iai (2 Dan), tea ceremony. Home: Kurakake 725-3, Tsukuba Ibaraki 305-0024, Japan Office: U Tsukuba Inst Clin Medicine, Tennodai 1-1-1, Tsukuba Ibaraki 305-8575, Japan

USUKI, YOSHIE, ophthalmologist, educator; b. Sumida, Tokyo, May 30, 1949; d. Koichi and Miyoko Inage. MD, Tokyo Women's Med. Coll., 1975, PhD, MD, DSc, 1979. Ednl. asst. Tokyo Women's Med. Coll., 1979-80; asst. prof. ophthalmology Inst. Clin. Medicine U. Tsukuba (Japan), 1979-97; asst. prof. tech. div. for visually impaired Coll. Tsukuba, 1990—; dir. Ninomiya Ophthalmic Hosp., Ibaraki, Japan, 1997—. Contbr. numerous articles to profl. jours. Recipient Gold prize 46th Ophthal. Photoexhibn. Japan Soc. Clin. Ophthalmology, 1992. Mem. The Japan Soc. Ophthalmology. Avocations: flower arrangements, traveling, reading. Home: Takezono 2-808-103 Tsukuba, Ibaraki 305-0032, Japan Office: Ninomiya Ophthalmic Hosp, Matsunoki 26-2 Tsukuba-shi, Ibaraki 305-0006, Japan

USYNIN, IVAN FEDOROVICH, biochemist, researcher; b. Nizhneangarsk, Russia, Dec. 13, 1954; s. Feodor Timopheevich and Ekaterina Dmitrievna (Zubkova) U.; m. Olga Vladimirovna Bykova, Apr. 2, 1981; children: Elizaveta Ivanovna, Dmitry Ivanovich. Diploma in biology, Tomsk (Russia) State U., 1977; PhD, Inst. Internal Medicine, Novosibirsk, Russia, 1987. Scientific worker Inst. Biology and Biophysics, Tomsk, 1977-78, Inst. Clin. and Exptl. Medicine, Novosibirsk, 1978-86; sr. rschr. Inst. Biochemistry, Novosibirsk, 1987—; cons. Inst. Physiology, Novosibirsk, 1995—. Inventor in field; contbr. articles to profl. jours. Named Disting. Scientist of Russia, Russian Acad. Scis., 1997. Mem. Biochem. Soc. Novosibirsk. Avocations: tennis, swimming. Home: Ekvatornaj St 15/16, 630060 Novosibirsk Russia Office: Inst Biochemistry, Ul Acad Timakova, 2, 630117 Novosibirsk Russia

UTAKAPAN, CHUKIAT, publishing executive, editor; b. Narathiwas, Thailand, May 10, 1942; s. Rath and Rareab (Nathalang) U.; m. Metta Sengpanich, 1975; children: Rarin, Rapee. BA, Chulalongkorn U., Bangkok, 1965. Editl. staff Thaiwattana Panich Co., Ltd., Bangkok, 1965-72; head pub. rels. divsn. Housing Authority Thailand, Bangkok, 1972-76; mgr. Amarin Press Ltd., Bangkok, 1976-87; mng. dir. Amarin Printing and Pub. Co., Bangkok, 1987-91, pres., mng. dir., 1991-97, pres., 1997—. Editor Alternative Healthcare and Holistic Lifestyles Mag. Recipient Asian Tokyo Fashion Assoc. award, Japan, 1990, Grand Companion decoration His Majesty the King of Thailand, Bangkok, 1999. Mem. Gen. Wisdom of the Land Found. (sec.). Avocation: reading. Home: 13/3 Arunamarin Rd, Bangkok-Noi 10700, Thailand Office: Amarin Printing Pub Co Ltd, 65/16 Chaiyapruk Rd, Taling-Chan 10170, Thailand

UTAMURA, MOTOAKI, manufacturing executive; b. Hofu, Yamaguchi, Japan, Feb. 24, 1948; s. Masaaki and Koh Utamura; m. Mitsu Emoto, Apr. 8, 1973; children: Tetsuya, Shinobu, Hanae. Diploma in liberal arts, U. Tokyo, 1969, B in Nuc. Engring., 1971, PhD, 1985. Rschr. Hitachi (Japan) Ltd., 1971-78, sr. rschr. Energy Rsch. Lab., 1979-92, sr. engr. Hitachi Works, 1993-97, asst. to gen. mgr. Hitachi Works, 1998-2000; chmn. internat. conf. Internat. Gas Turbine Inst., Atlanta. Author: Numerical Simulation in Science and Technology. Avocations: museums, classic mathematics. Fax: 81294241591. Home: 3-13-15 Takasuzu-cho, Hitachi 317-0066, Japan Office: Hitachi Works Hitachi Ltd, 3-1-1 Saiwai-cho, Hitachi 317-8511, Japan

UTEEM, CASSAM, president of Republic of Mauritius; b. Mar. 22, 1941; married; 3 children. Student, Royal Coll., Port Louis; Diploma in Social Work, U Mauritius; Maitrise-es-Science, U. Paris; DCL (hon.), U. Mauritius, U. Aix Marseilles III, Acad. Nat. Malgache. Officer, supr. Cable and Wireless; pers. mgr. Currimjee Jeewanjee & Co., Ltd., 1969; mcpl. councillor City of Port Louis, 1977-79, 86-88, lord mayor, 1986; min. social security and nat. solidarity, 1982-83, dep. prime minister and min. industry and indsl. tech., 1990-92; pres. Republic of Mauritius, 1992—. Mem. Legis. Assembly, 1976-92. Named Grand Comdr. of the Order of the Star and Key of the Indian Ocean. Mem. L'Academie Nat. Malgache (hon.). Office: Office of The President, Government Ctr, Port Louis Mauritius*

UTENS, ELISABETH MARIA W. J., psychologist; b. Rysbergen, N Brabant, The Netherlands, Dec. 25, 1959; d. Albertus Johannes M. Schotel; children: Thom, Marlon. MS, Cath. U. Brabant, The Netherlands, 1983; PhD, Erasmus U., Rotterdam, Netherlands, 1989. Cert. clin. psychologist, child psychologist, health psychologist. Rschr., clin. psychologist Sophia Children's Hosp., Rotterdam, 1989—. Contbr. articles to profl. jours. Mem. Netherlands Inst. of Psychologists in Amsterdam. Avocation: playing saxophone. Office: Sophia Childrens U Hosp, Dr Molewaterplein 60, 3015 GJ Rotterdam Zuid, The Netherlands

UTERMANN, ANDREAS ERNST FERNDINAND, fund investment manager; b. Brussels, Belgium, Jan. 23, 1966; arrived in England, 1986; s. Jurgen Karl Ernst and Brigitte Elisabeth (Häberle) U.; m. Claudia S. Dorsch, July 25, 1998. BSc in Econs., London Sch. Econs., 1989; MA in Econs., Katholieke U., Leuven, Belgium, 1990. Trainee Deutsche Bank Dortmund, Germany, 1984-86; dir. Mercury Asset Mgmt., London, 1990-97; mng. dir. Merrill Lynch Mercury, London, 1998—; adv. bd. Money Trader Investment, 1992—. Author: The ERM: Impact on Inflation and Exchange Rates, 1990. Chmn. Hampstead Liberal Democrats, London, 1996—. Mem. Assn. Investment Mgmt. Rsch., Securities Inst. Protestant. Avocations: tennis, skiing, scuba. Office: Merrill Lynch Mercury, 33 King William St, EC4R 9AS London England

UTHOFF, DETLEF, ophthalmology surgeon, educator; b. Mülheim an der Ruhr, Germany, May 7, 1942; m. Anke Uthoff; children: Philipp, Nicolas, Daniel, Moritz, Antonia. Grad. with recognition, U. Kiel, Germany, 1971. With U. Kiel, 1967-69; med. asst. St. Elisabeth Clinic, Kiel, 1967-69; med. asst. Rsch. Inst. Borstel, 1967-69, sci. asst., 1969-71; locum med. leader gen. sect. Dist.-Clinic Heide, 1971-72; pvt. practice, 1972; med. asst. clinic ophthalmology U. Kiel, 1975-79; sr. cons. eye sect. Flechsig Kiel Clinic, 1980-85; med. dir. Eye Hosp. Kiel-Bellevue, 1985—; prof. ophthalmology U. Tel Aviv Sackler Sch. Medicine, 1995—; rschr. micro-surgery and plastic

surgery fields of ophthalmology Manhatten Eye Hosp., N.Y.C., 1979-80, Pollack Eye Hosp., Gainsville, 1979-80, Iliff Eye Hosp., Balt., 1979-80; chmn. bd. Inst. for Systemrsch. Health World Healthiness Orgn., 1985-86; habilitation, prof. U. Tel-Aviv.; adj. prof. several German and fgn. univs. Contbr. numerous articles to profl. jours. German Rsch. Cmty. scholar U. Kiel, 1972-75. Fellow Internat. Eye Found. Am.; mem. AAAS, Am. Intraocular Implant Soc., Am. Soc. Cataract and Refractive Surgery, German Ophthalmology Soc., Profl. Orgn. Ophthalmologists in Germany (mem. Internat. Ophthalmic Microsurgery Study Group), German Soc. Plastic and Recovering Surgery, German Soc. for Intraocularlens Implantation, Geman Soc. for Socialpädiatry, N.Y. Acad. Scis., European Refractice Surgery Soc., Internat. Soc. Ocular Surgeons, Soc. for Immunology (sci. advisor), Retinologic Soc., Julius Hirschberg Soc., Soc. Francaise d'Ophtalmologie, Inst. for Health Investigation (chmn. bd.), Internat. Assn. of Ocular Surgeons. Office: Augenklinik Kiel-Bellevue, Lindenallee 21, 24105 Kiel Germany

UTKIN, ALEXANDER VASILIEVICH, physicist; b. Sovetsk, Russia, Nov. 9, 1953; s. Vasilii Iliich and Tatyana Grigorievna (Sidorenkova) U.; m. Tatyana Bobryakova, Dec. 17, 1977; 1 child, Ekaterina. Diploma, Moscow Inst. Physics and Tech., 1977, PhD, 1980. Jr. scientist Inst. of Chem. Russian Acad. Scis., Chernogolovka, Russia, 1980-89, sr. scientist, 1989—. Contbr. articles to profl. jours. Russian Found. Basic Rsch. grantee, 1996-98, 2000—. Office: Inst Chem Physics, Russian Acad Scis, 142 432 Chernogolovka Russia

UTKUSEVEN, MUSTAFA, lawyer, consultant; b. Manisa, Turkey, May 31, 1969; s. Hüseyih and Rasida (Soriöglu) U. Law, Istanbul (Turkey) U., 1992. Lawyer Overseas Rsch. & Cons., Ltd., Istanbul, 1993—. Mem. Assn. Am. Internat. Property, Inter-Pacific Bar Assn., Istanbul Law Assn. Avocations: books, music, photography. Office: Overseas Rsch & Cons Ltd, Halaskargazi Cad 357/4 Belka Apt, 34260 Sisli Istanbul, Turkey

UTLEY, F. KNOWLTON, library director, educator; b. Northampton, Mass., May 4, 1935; s. Frederick K. and Florence E. (Moore) U.; m. Faith E. Green, July 2, 1960; children: Richard F., Stephen R., David E. BS, Castleton State Coll., 1960; MA, U. Conn., 1967; EdD, Boston U., 1979; MLS, U. Ala., 1983. Tchr. indsl. arts Montpelier (Vt.) High Sch., 1960-61, Southwick (Mass.) High Sch., 1961-63; tchr., drafting instr. Putnam (Conn.) High Sch., 1963-68; media specialist Cen. Conn. State U., New Britain, 1968-69, dir. media svcs., 1969-72; doctoral teaching fellow Boston U., 1972-73; dir. libr., media svcs. Manchester (Mass.) Pub. Schs., 1973-79; assoc. prof. libr. scis. U. Maine, Farmington, 1979-80; dir. grad. program libr. media Livingston (Ala.) U., 1980-83; dir. libr. media svcs. Am. Internat. Coll., Springfield, Mass., 1983—; pres. C/W Mars-Cen. and Western Mass. Auto Res., 1987-88; chmn. bd. dirs. Cooperating Librs. of Great Springfield, 1988-89, Western Mass. Media Coun., 1991-93; founder, headmaster Hampshire Christian Acad., South Hadley, Mass., 1996—. Mem. Belchertown Housing Authority, 2000—. Mem. ALA, Am. Christian Schs. Internat., Assn./Edn. Comm. and Tech. New Eng. Edn. Media Assn., New Eng. Libr. Assn., Mass. Sch. Libr. Media Assn., Mass. Libr. Assn., Phi Delta Kappa. Home: 11 Canal Dr Belchertown MA 01007-9224 Office: Am Internat Coll 1000 State St Springfield MA 01109-3151

UTLEY, JANE BESON, poet; b. Houston, Dec. 14, 1954; d. John Mark and Frances Ester (Rupert) Beson; m. Ronald Gene Utley, June 29, 1985. Asst. mgr. McCoy Devel. Corp., Houston, 1978-81; with accounts receivable dept. Arpco Office Supply, Houston, 1981; payroll analyst Toshiba Internat., Houston, 1981-86; songwriter Jeff Roberts Pub., 1996-97. Contbr. poems to Best Poems of the 90's, 1996, American Poetry Annual, 1997, Word Weaver, 1997, Treasure the Moment, vol. X, 1997, A Celebration of Poets, 1997, (audio tape) Internat. Libr.'s The Sound of Poetry, anthologies; pub. comml. song Majestic Records and Countrywine Pubs. Mem. Top RecordsSongwriters Assn. Avocations: writing, fishing, gardening, reading. Office: Flooring Cons PO Box 1610 Brookshire TX 77423-1610

UTLEY, JON BASIL, think tank director, journalist; b. Moscow, Mar. 10, 1934; came to U.S., 1939, naturalized, 1952; s. Arcadi and Freda (Utley) Berdichevsky; m. Ana Maria Hijar, 1968. BS, Georgetown U., 1956; student, U. Munich, 1952, Alliance Française, Paris, 1956. Mgr. Am. Internat. Underwriters, Cali, Colombia, 1959-60; editor, pub. Bogotá Bull., 1960-61; v.p. Universal Investors Svcs., Nassau, 1962-67; real estate developer Washington, 1968—; mng. gen. ptnr. Kimwill Oil Assocs., Warren, Pa., 1978-86; pres. Ocean McLean Corp., 1989-97, Needle in a Haystack, Washington, 1990-98, Needle Express, 1993-98; fgn. corr. Jour. Commerce, Internat. Reports, S. Am., 1969-74; columnist Times of the Ams., 1974-92, assoc. editor, 1981-92; columnist Washington Inquirer, 1981-90, Washington Times, 1981-82; contbg. editor Conservative Digest, 1984-89; mem. editl. adv. bd. Internat. Reports, 1981-91; lectr. Accuracy in Media, treas.; Ukraine, 1997, Cyprus, 1999, Freedoms Found. Valley Forge; commentator Voice of Am., 1985-2000; Jamestown Found. observer Russian elections, 2000. Contbr. articles to Washington Post, Harvard Bus. Rev., Nat. Rev., Human Events, Miami Herald, Lincoln Rev., N.Y.C. Tribune, Am. Legion mag., El Salvador Gazette, Lima Times, others. Observer Guatemalan elections Georgetown U. Ctr. Strategic Studies, 1985, Romanian elections, 1990, Fussian elections, 2000; trustee Ctr. Internat. Rels., adv. com. Solidarity Endowment; co-founder Com. to Avert a Mideast Holocaust, 1990-94. Assoc. scholar Competitive Enterprise Inst., 1995-98; Robert A. Taft fellow Ludwig Von Mises Inst., 1998—. Mem. Coun. Inter-Am. Security (bd. dirs. 1988-93), United Srs. Assn. (bd. dirs. 1993—), World English Lang. Newspaper Assn. (pres. 1996), Hispanic Am. Ctr. Econ. Rsch. (bd. dirs. 1997—), Ams. Against Bombing/Ams. Against World Empire (chmn. 1998—), Nat. Press Club, Phila. Soc., John Randolph Club, Coun. Nat. Policy. E-mail: Jutly@aol.com. Office: 910 17th St NW Ste 422 Washington DC 20006-2605

UTSUNOMIYA, HIROSHI, materials scientist; b. Anjyo, Aichi, Japan, Aug. 26, 1965; s. Nobuaki and Ikuko (Shimaoka) U. B Engring., Osaka U., Suita, Japan, 1988, M Engring., 1990, PhD, 1993. Rsch. fellow Osaka U., Suita, 1993-2000, lectr., 2000—; rsch. visitor U. Birmingham, Eng., 1995-96. Recipient paper prize Japanese Soc. Tech. Plasticity, Tokyo, 1994, Young Rschr. prize Japanese Soc. Tech. Plasticity, Tokyo, 1995; Kusumoto award Osaka U., 1988, Young Researcher Japan Inst. Metals, Sendai, 1997. Home: 6-1-2 Minamimukonosou, Amagasaki 661-0033, Japan Office: Osaka U Dept Materials Sci & Engring, 2-1 Yamada Oka, Suita 565-0871, Japan

UTSUNOMIYA, TOSHIO, medical equipment association professional; b. Zentusji, Kagawa, Japan, Nov. 20, 1921; s. Jiemon and Mine (Iwatani) U.; m. Kikuko Saito, Apr. 19, 1955. B of Engring., U. Tokyo, 1943, D of Engring., 1961. Asst. prof. U. Tokyo, 1948-61, prof., 1961-82; vis. asst. prof. Columbia U., N.Y.C., 1959-61; prof. Sci. U. of Tokyo, Noda, Japan, 1982-97; pres. Japan Assn. for Advancement of Med. Equipment, Tokyo, 1985-93, chmn., 1993—; cons. Sumitomo Electric Industries, Osaka, 1982-93; chmn. med. and welfare equipment R&D com. Ministry of Internat. Trade and Industry, 1984—. Editor, author (with others) Bio-Control and Bio-Information System, 1978; editor-in-chief The Inst. of Electronic and Comm. Engrs. of Japan, 1985; contbr. articles to profl. jours. Decorated Order of the Sacred Treasure The Prime Minister's Office, 1997; recipient Broadcast Culture prize NHK, 1989, Disting. Svc. on Sci. and Tech. Gov. of Tokyo, 1980. Fellow IEEE (chmn. Tokyo sect. 1989-92); mem. The Inst. of TV Engrs. (hon.), Japan Soc. for Med. and Biol. Engring. (hon.), Japan Electronic Industry Devel. Assn. (com. for accessibility of info. processing equipment 1984-99). Avocations: Japanese chess, personal computers, gardening. Fax: 81-44-951-2330. E-mail: utsumiya@pp.iij4u.or.jp. Home: 2800-6 Ozenji Asao, Kawasaki 215-0013, Japan

UTTINGER, HANS WALTER, retired federal administrator; b. Lucerne, Switzerland, Aug. 31, 1929; s. Hans Karl and Josefine (Rimensberger) U.; m. Wanda Pileri, April 10, 1965 (div. Oct. 1976); m. Hilde Keckeis, Aug. 12, 1977. BIM, N.W. Polytech., London, 1961; MBA, U. Santa Clara, 1962; PhD, U. de Fribourg, Switzerland, 1963. Head export sales Furrer-Jacot Jewel Mfrs., Schaffhausen, Switzerland, 1967-69; head distribution Landis & Gyr, Zug, Switzerland, 1969-72, dep. export mgr. elec. meter divsn., 1975-77; project leader Sodeco SA, Geneva, 1972-73; sr. advisor Pakistan Design Inst., Karachi, 1977-79; direktionsadjunkt Defence Dept., Berne, Switzerland, 1979-92, retired, 1992—. Author: A Swiss Family in the Services of Savoy, France and The Netherlands, 1977. Major Swiss Signal Corps., 1982-90. Named to Knighthood King of Italy, 1979. Fax: 0039-0421-22.06.63.

UTVIK, TORIL INGA RØE, research scientist, environmental chemist; b. Oslo, May 12, 1967; d. Oystein and Edel (Berre) Røe; m. Ole Harald Utvik, Oct. 31, 1998; 1 child, Emelie. MSc, Norwegian U. Sci. and Tech., Trondheim, 1991, PhD, 1998. Rsch. scientist Norsk Hydro Rsch. Ctr., Porsgrunn, Norway, 1991-98, sr. rsch. scientist, 1998—. Home: Sandslibakken 27, 5253 Sandsli Norway Office: Norsk Hydro E&P Ops, Environ Sect, 5020 Bergen Norway

UTZ, KARL-HEINZ, dentist, educator; b. Solingen, Germany, Oct. 20, 1950; s. Karl and Ingeborg (Baudler) U.; m. Barbara Matischewski, July 25, 1980; two children. D Med. Dentistry, U. Zahnklinik, Bonn, Germany, 1982, Priv.-Doz., 1991; Prof., Universitaet, Bonn, Germany, 1996. Asst. U. Zahnklinik, Bonn, 1977-79; pvt. practice, Moers, Germany, 1980-81; asst. U. Bonn, 1981-84, asst. prof., 1984-96, prof., 1996—. Contbr. chpts. to books. Gefreiter, Sanitaetsdienst, 1970-71. Mem. Soc. Oral Physiology, Study Group of Restorative Dentistry. Office: Poliklinik Zahnaerztliche Prothetik, Welschnonnenstrasse 17, 53111 Bonn Germany

UUSITALO, ARJA LEENA TUULIA, medical researcher; b. Tampere, Finland, Aug. 16, 1965; d. Esko Erkki Kustaa and Leena Annikki (Makinen) U.; m. Mika Juhani Koskinen, Aug. 17, 1996; children: Santtu Mikael Koskinen, Veikka Samuel Koskinen. MD, U. Tampere, 1990, PhD, 1998. Physician in surgery/radiology Ctrl. Hosp., Scinäjoki, Finland, 1990; physician Rehab. Ctr., Ikaalinen, Finland, 1991; jr. rschr. Rsch. Inst. for Olympic Sports, Jyvaskyla, Finland, 1991-94; physician in dept. of clin. psysiology Ctrl. Hosp. Jyvaskyla, 1994-95, U. Hosp., Tampere, Finland, 1995; rschr. Rsch. Inst. for Olympic Sports, Jyvaskyla, 1996-98; physician rehab. ctr. Reuma Hosp., Heinola, Finland, 1998—; physician dept. clin. physiology and nuc. medicine Kuopio U. Hosp., 1999—. Author: The Way to Win, 1995; contbr. articles to profl. jours. Mem. Finnish Soc. of Sports Medicine (sec. 1995—). Avocations: sports, running, music. E-mail: arja.uusitalo-koshinen@kuh.fi. Home: Aittolammentie 5C9, 70780 Kuopio Finland Office: Kuopio U Hosp, PO Box 1777, FIN70211 Kuopio Finland

UUSITALO, MIKKO ALEKSI, research scientist; b. Helsinki, Finland, July 28, 1970; s. Seppo Juhani and Aino Laina (Hämäläinen) U. MS, Helsinki U. Tech., 1993, PhD, 1997. Rschr. low temp. lab. Helsinki U. Tech., Espoo, 1992-97; physics rschr. Picker Nordstar Inc., Helsinki, 1997-99; rsch. & devel. expert Nat. Tech. Agy. (TEKES), Helsinki, 1999—; bd. dirs. Low Temp. Lab., Espoo, 1994-95. Contbr. articles to profl. jours. With Finnish Air Force, 1991. Grantee The Helsingin Sanomat Centenary Found., 1997, The Vilho, Yrjo and Kalle Vaisala found., 1995, Magnus Ehrnrooth Found., 1994. Mem. Finnish Phys. Soc. (organizing com. for ann. meeting 1996). Avocations: sailplaines, Tae Kwon Do. Office: Nat Tech Agy, PO Box 69, FIN00101 Helsinki Finland

UWAH, EDET JOHNNIE, science educator; b. Obo Atai, Uyo, Nigeria, Feb. 4, 1950; s. Johnnie Uwah Udo-Udo and Arit William Udo; m. Ikamaise Edet Udo; children: Dongesit, Kufreabasi, Mfen, Martha, Emmanuel. BSc, Obatemi Awolowo U., Ife, Nigeria, 1975, MSc, 1978; PhD, Ahmadu Bello U., Zaria, Nigeria, 1984. Cert. applied nuclear physics environ. sci. Grad. asst. Obatemi Awolowo U., Ile-Ife, 1976-78; lectr. U. Uyo, Nigeria, 1978-85; lectr. I Nigerian Def. Acad., Kaduna, Nigeria, 1985-88; sr. lectr. U. Calabar, Nigeria, 1988-92; assoc. prof. U. Calabar, 1992-95, prof., 1995—; Environ. sci. cons. U. Calabar, 1991—. Author: (book) Advanced Lab Physics, 1999; mem. editl. bd. Nigerian Jour. Physics, 1988—, Tropical Jour. Sci., Jour. Geosci. Pastor Apostolic Ch., Calabar, 1997—; sec. Nigerian U. Physics Series, 1995—; chmn. TAC Bible Coll., Ufo, 1993-98; mem. Sch. Bd., Obo Ata, 1992—. Mem. Nigerian Inst. Physics, Nigerian Environ. Soc., Nigerian Geosci. Soc. Mem. Apostolic Ch. Avocations: football, singing, swimming, long jump. Office: U Calabar, Dept Physics PMB 1115, Calabar Nigeria

UY, HARVEY SIY, ophthalmologist; b. Manila, The Philippines, Sept. 22, 1964; s. Antonio Lao and Chia Ti (Siy) U.; m. Pik Sha Ting Chan, July 11, 1999. BS in Biology magna cum laude, U. Philippines, Quezon City, 1986; MD, U. Philippines, Manila, 1991. Med. diplomate Philippines and Am. bds.; diplomate Philippine Bd. Ophthalmology; cert. U.S. Ednl. Commn. for Fgn. Med. Grads. Ophthalmology resident Philippine Gen. Hosp., Manila, 1992-94; med. and surg. retina fellow St. Luke's Med. Ctr., Quezon City, 1995-96; ocular immunology and uveitis fellow Mass. Eye and Ear Infirmary, Boston, 1997-98; assoc. clin. prof. dept. ophthalmology Philippine Gen. Hosp., Manila, 1998—; ptnr. Allied Ophthalmic Cons., Manila, 1998—; active cons. Inst. Ophthalmology, St. Luke's Med Ctr., Quezon City, 1998—, rschr. Inst. Rsch. and Biotech., 1998—. Contbg. author: (textbook) Uveitis, 2000; editor: Philippine Jour. Ophthalmology, 1998—; contbr. articles to profl. jours. Named Outstanding Physician, City of Malabon, 1999. Mem. Manila Med. Soc., Am. Acad. Ophthalmology, Assn. for Rsch. in Visual Scis. and Ophthalmology, Philippine Acad. Ophthalmology, Philippine Ocular Inflammation Soc., Vitreo-Retinal Soc. of The Philippines. Avocations: mountain biking, badminton, photography. Office: St Lukes Med Ctr S-611, E Rodriguez Sr Blvd, Quezon City The Philippines

UYAMA, YOSHIKIMI, chemist, educator; b. Hyogo, Japan, Sept. 3, 1945; s. Yoshihiro and Mikiko (Kajino) U.; m. Emiko Mihara, May 24, 1974; children: Kumi, Yumi, Mika, Yoshinori. BS, Kyoto U., 1970, PhD, 1993. Inst. phys. chemistry Sch. Osaka Prefecture, Japan, 1970-91; lectr. rsch. ctr. for biomed. engring. Kyoto U., 1993-98, lectr. Inst. Frontier Med. Scis., 1998—; researcher Kyoto U., 1973-76, 83-90, 90-93; chief dir. Universe Co., Ltd., Osaka, Uyama Seiboh Co., Ltd., Osaka, 1991—, Uyama (Thailand) Co., Bangkok. Author: Lubricating Polymer Surfaces, 1993; contbr. articles to profl. jours. Mem. AAAS. Avocations: Shogi, karate. Home: 2-11 Tamatsukuri Motomachi, Tennojiku, Osaka 543-0014, Japan Office: 53 Kawahara-cho Shogoin, Sakyo-ku Kyoto 606, Japan

UYANIK, NURSELI, chemistry educator; b. Istanbul, Turkey, Sept. 6, 1952; d. Hayri Hasan and Meliha Fatma (Okan) Aksoy; m. Ömer Lüfti Uyanik, Aug. 11, 1977; children: Nese, Hayri Ugur. BSc, Istanbul Tech. U., 1973, PhD, 1986; MSc, Middle East Tech. U., Ankara, Turkey, 1977. Asst. Inönü U., Malatya, Turkey, 1977-80; asst. Istanbul Tech. U., 1980-86, dr. asst., 1986-88, asst. prof., 1988-91, assoc. prof., 1991-2000, prof., 2000—. Author/co-author 4 books; contbr. 30 articles to profl. jours.; 50 presentations in field. Orgn. com. mem. NSF-Tübitak Joint workshop, Istanbul, 1994, 35th IUPAC Internat. Congress, Istanbul, 1995, Polymer Symposium Turkic Congress, Tashkent, 1995, sci. sec. 1996; asst. dir. NATO-ASI Polymer Recycling, Antalya, 1997. Mem. Am. Chem. Soc., IUPAC, Turkish Chem. Soc., Turkish Rubber Assn., Turkish Polymer Sci. & Tech. Soc. Avocations: painting, photography, reading. Office: Istanbul Tech U, Dept Chemistry, 80626 Istanbul Turkey

UYEDA, SEIYA, geophysics educator; b. Tokyo, Nov. 28, 1929; s. Seiichi and Hatsuo (Okino) U.; m. Mutsuko Kosaka, July 6, 1952; children: Taro, Makiko, Naoko. BS, U. Tokyo, 1952, DSc, 1958; DSc (hon.), U. Athens, Greece, 1996. Rsch. assoc. Earthquake Rsch. Inst. U. Tokyo, 1957-64, assoc. prof. Geophys. Inst., 1964-69, prof. Earthquake Rsch. Inst., 1969-90; prof. dept. marine sci. and tech. Tokai U., Shimizu, Japan, 1990-94, dir. earthquake prediction rsch. ctr., 1995-96; prof. Tex. A&M U., College Station, 1990-95; dir. Internat. Frontier Program on Earthquake Rsch. Riken, 1996—. Author: Debate About the Earth, 1966, Island Arcs, 1973, The New View of the Earth, 1978. Recipient Tanakadate prize Soc. Terrestrial Magnetism and Electricity, 1955, G.P. Woollard award Geol. Soc. Am., 1989, Matsumae Prize for Academic Accomplishment, Tokai Univ., 1992. Fellow AAAS (hon.), Nat. Acad. Sci. (fgn. assoc., A Agassiz medal 1972), Russian Acad. Scis. (fgn.), Geol. Soc. London (hon.), European Union Geoscis. (hon.), Am. Geophys. Union (Walter Bucher medal 1991); mem. Am. Acad. Arts and Scis. (fgn.), Soc. Geology France (assoc.), Japan Acad. (Acad. prize 1987). Home: 2-39-6 Daizawa Setagaya-ku, Tokyo 155-0032, Japan Office: Tokai U, 3-20-1 Orido, Shimizu 424, Japan

UYEHARA, CATHERINE FAY TAKAKO (YAMAUCHI), physiologist, educator, pharmacologist; b. Honolulu, Dec. 20, 1959; d. Thomas Takashi and Eiko (Haraguchi) Uyehara; m. Alan Hisao Yamauchi, Feb. 17, 1990. BS, Yale U., 1981; PhD in Physiology, U. Hawaii, Honolulu, 1987. Postdoctoral fellow SmithKline Beecham Pharms., King of Prussia, Pa., 1987-89; mem. grad. faculty in pediatrics U. Hawaii John Burns Sch. Medicine, Honolulu, 1991—; rsch. pharmacologist Kapiolani Med. Ctr. for Women and Children, Honolulu, 1990-91; statis. cons. Tripler Army Med. Ctr., Honolulu, 1984-87, 89—, chief rsch. pharmacology , 1991—, dir. collaborative rsch. program, 1995—; mem. grad. faculty in pharmacology U. Hawaii John A. Burns Sch. Medicine, 1993—; grad. faculty Interdisciplinary Biomed. Sci. program, 1995-98, Cell and Molecular Biology program, 1998—, mem. grad. faculty in physiology, 1999—. Contbr. articles to profl. jours. Mem. Am. Fedn. for Med. Rsch., Am. Physiol. Soc., Soc. Uniformed Endocrinologists, Endocrine Soc., We. Soc. Pediatric Rsch., N.Y. Acad. Scis., Hawaiian Acad. Sci., Sigma Xi. Democrat. Mem. Christian Ch. Avocations: swimming, diving, crafts, horticulture, music. Office: 1 Jarrett White Rd Bldg 40 Tripler Amc HI 96859-5000

UYENO, TAKASHI, oil shipping company executive; b. Yokohama, Kanagawa, Japan, Dec. 10, 1944; s. Yutaka and Misao (Ishizawa) U.; m. Junko Wada, Oct. 3, 1970; children: Miki, Gen. BA in Econs., Keio U., Tokyo, 1967; diploma in social studies, Oxford (Eng.) U., 1970. Mem. staff Uyeno Unyu Shokai, Yokohama, Japan, 1967-72, v.p., 1972-75; v.p. K.K. Uyeno Unyu Shokai, Yokohama, 1975-87, pres., CEO, 1987-98; pres., CEO Uyeno Transtech Ltd., Yokohama, 1998—. Bd. dirs. Tamagawa U., 1996—; chmn. Young Pres. Orgn., Yokohama U., 1994; ; hon. consul Republic of Venezuela, 1997—, hon. regent Cal. Luth. Univ., 1999—; mem. Linacre Devel. com., 1999—. Mem. All Japan Coastal Shipping Assn. (v.p. 1997—), All Japan Tank-Truck Assn. (v.p. 1984—), Yokohama C. of C. and Industry, Rotary (sec. R.I. dist. 2590 1998-99, gov.-elect 2000-01). Avocations: mountain climbing, reading, Noh singing, golf, music. Home: 898 Nikaido, Kamakura Kanagawa 248-0002, Japan Office: Uyeno Transtech Ltd, 70-3 Yamashita-Cho Naka-Ku, Yokohama Kanagawa 231-0023, Japan

UYGUR, MEHMET CEMIL, urology educator; b. Icel, Turkey, Aug. 14, 1962; cons. Nefromed, Ankara, 1995—, Gorkem, Ankara, 1996—.; s. Cavit and Zehra U.; m. Dilek Sahin, May 6, 1994. MD, Hecettepe U., Ankara, Turkey, 1986. Dr. Ministry of Health, Erzincan, Turkey, 1986-87; urologist Ministry of Health, Artvin, Turkey, 1993-94; resident dept. urology Med. Sch. Hacettepe U., Ankara, 1988-93; attendant urologist Ministry of Health Ankara Hosp., 1994-98, assoc. prof. urology dept. urology, 1998—. Mem. Ataturkcu Dusunce Dernegi, Ankara, 1998—. Mem. Ankara Urologists Assn., Ankara Urol. Group, European Assn. Urology, N.Y. Acad. Scis. Avocations: sports, music, computer, NGO's. Home: 33 Cadde 42-27, ISCI Bloklari Mahallesi, Ankara 06520, Turkey Office: Urol Dept Ministry Health, Ulucanlar Caddesi, Ankara 06340, Turkey

UZAN, BERNARD, artistic director; b. Tunis, Tunisia, Dec. 5, 1944; arrived in Can., 1988; s. Henri and Elise Gabrielle (Pansieri) U.; m. Diana Soviero, Nov. 9, 1984. PhD, Paris U., 1968. Gen. & artistic dir. Théâtre français d'Amérique, Boston, 1973-83, Tulsa Opera, 1987-88, L'Opéra de Montreal, Que., Can., 1988—; adminstr., exec. dir. Alliance français de Boston, 1974-83; stage dir.: U.S.: San Francisco, Fla., Phila., New Orleans, Portland, Dallas, others; Can.: Montreal, Toronto, Vancouver, Ottawa, Quebec City, Edmonton, Calgary, Winnipeg; Europe: Monte-Carlo, Zurich, Palermo, Turin, others; in charge internat. affairs Eurolyrica, 1997—; bd. dirs. Opera Am., 1998—. Office: L'Opéra de Montréal, 260 de Maisonneuve W, Montreal, PQ Canada H2X 1Y9

UZAWA, KIYOSHI, oil company executive, mechanical engineer; b. Honolulu, Aug. 9, 1916; s. Takashi and Ren (Naruse) U.; m. Kyoko Sakurai, Nov. 30, 1944; children: Yoshiko, Mihoko, Etsuko. Degree in mech. engring., Nippon U., 1939. Asst. to dir. Mobil Sekiyu K.K., Tokyo, 1976-81; cons. Mass. Port Authority, Tokyo, 1985-95; writer, translator Tokyo, 1995—; mktg. exec. Mobil Sekiyu K.K., Tokyo, 1972-81; mktg. engr., 1951-61, tech. translator, 1951-71; machine, plant design Tohendo Kaihatsu, Tunghua, China, 1939-40. Corporal Imperial Japanese Army, 1940-43. Home: 19-18 Maruyama, 2 Chome Nakano Ku, Tokyo 165-0021, Japan

UZDENSKY, ANATOLY BORISOVICH, biophysics researcher, educator; b. Pinsk, USSR, July 8, 1947; s. Boris Solomonovich and Nehama Mihelevna (Shulman) U.; m. Valentina Nikolaevna Alekseeva, Oct. 13, 1969; children: Dmitry, Irina. Phys. engr., Leningrad (Russia) Polytech., Inst., 1971; PhD in Physiology, Rostov U., Rostov-on-Don, Russia, 1980. Cert. in biophysics. From jr. to sr. rschr. Rostov U., Rostov-on-Don, 1971-95, assoc. prof., 1995—. Inventor mode of fish resistance enhancement, 1983, mode of fish eggs viability enhancement, 1986, molecular monoelectronic tunnel element, 1989. Mem. Soc. for Photooptical Engring., Biomed. Optics Soc., European Soc. for Photobiology, Am. Soc. for Photobiology. E-mail: uzd@krinc.ru. Office: Rostov U Dept Biophysics, 194/1 Stachky Ave, Rostov-on-Don 344090, Russia

UZLOV, IVAN GERASIMOVIC, metallurgist, researcher; b. Kriviy Rig, Ukraine, Aug. 14, 1923; s. Gerasim Polikarpovich and Sidorovna (Lukerya) U.; m. Svetlana Victorovna Kulbitskya, Dec. 16, 1948; children: Vladimir Ivanovich, Konstantin Ivanovich. BS, Inst. Ferrous Metals, Dnepropetrovsk, Ukraine, 1949, PhD, 1958, ScD, 1971. Registered engr., Ukraine. Main engr. Inst. Ferrous Metals, 1950-59, sci. sec., 1959-62, v.p., 1962-72, dir. dept., 1972-78, 88—, pres., dir. state program, 1978-88. Author: Heating of Rolled Products, 1970, Railroad Wheel Steel, 1985, High Strength Fitting Steel, 1985, Heat Treatment of Rolled Products, 1981; editor dept. Sci. Tech. Jour., Dnepropetrovsk, 1992-00. Mem. presidium Ctrl. Sci. T.F.M., Moscow, 1978-90,. Recipient award State prize of USSR, 1975, Min. of USSR, 1985; named hon. scientist of Ukraine, 1983. Mem. Ctrl. Sci. Tech. Soc. Ukraine (presidium 1965-00), Engrs. Acad. Ukraine, N.Y. Acad. Scis. Avocation: green thumb. Fax: 380567768562. E-mail: uzlov@mailexcite.com. Office: Inst Ferrous Metals, Starodubova Sq 1, 49050 Dnepropetrovsk Ukraine

UZOMAH, TIMOTHY CHUKWUMA, polymer scientist, researcher; b. Isu, Imo State, Nigeria, Nov. 30, 1946; s. Ambrose Ohakwe and Catherine Orianu (Ekeocha) U.; m. Stella Dibuloma Agunwah, Oct. 3, 1982; children: Chinonye, Chizitere, Chiamaka. BSc with honors, U. Ibadan, Nigeria, 1977; MEd, SUNY, Buffalo, 1981; MSc, U. Port Harcourt, Nigeria, 1988; PhD, Fed. U. Tech., Owevri, Nigeria, 1996. Tchr. Nat. Youth Svc. Corps, Calabar, Nigeria, 1977-78, Alvan Ikoku Coll. Edn., Owerri, Nigeria, 1978—; vis. tchr. Fed. U. Tech., Minna, Nigeria, 1997-98. Author sch. sci. review; contbr. articles to profl. jours. Scholar Senate, U. Ibadan, 1975-77, Imo State Govt., 1975-77. Mem. Chem. Soc. Nigeria, Polymer Inst. Nigeria. Avocations: reading, football, lawn tennis. Office: Alvan Ikoku Coll Edn, Chemistry Dept, Owerri Imo State Nigeria

UZU, TAKASHI, internist, nephrologist, researcher; b. Kobe, Hyogo, Japan, Nov. 10, 1962; s. Hisashi and Akemi (Furuta) U.; m. Midori Okumura, Mar. 9, 1987; children: Asami, Tomoki, Kayo. MD, Shiga U. Med. Sci., Otsu, Japan, 1988, PhD, 1994. Trainee 3d dept. medicine Shiga U. Hosp., 1988-93; mem. staff Kashiwara (Japan) City Hosp., 1993-94, Nat. Cardiovasc. Ctr. Hosp., Suita, Japan, 1994-99, Osaka Rosai Hosp., Sakai, Japan, 1999—. Contbr. articles to med. jours., including Hypertension, Lancet, Circulation. Mem. Japanese Soc. Nephrology (Oshima award 1999). Home: 3-13-60 Ogata, Osaka Kashiwara 582-0018, Japan Office: Osaka Rosai Hosp Div Neph, 1179-3 Nagasone-cho, Osaka Sakai 591-8025, Japan

UZUNIDIS, DIMITRI NICOLAS, economist, journalist, sociologist; b. Alexandropolis, Greece, May 24, 1960; s. Nicolas Dimitri and Domna (Christidis) U.; m. Sophie Marguerite Boutillier Uzunidis; children: Antigone, Alexandre. Diploma in journalism, Homer Sch., Athens, Greece, 1979; M in Sociology, U. Nanterre, 1985, PhD, 1987. Assoc. prof. Inst. Polit. Studies, Lille, France, 1991-96; asst. prof. U. Littoral, Dunkerque, France, 1992—; dir. rsch. unit Innovation and Indsl. Redeployment. Editor: Innovations, Economie et Innovation. Recipient Rsch. award Min. Industry, Athens, Greece, 1989, Min. Edn., Paris, 1999. Mem. AFSE, Obs. Globalization Paris. Avocations: photography, tennis. Office: Lab RII, 21 Quai de La Citadelle, F-59140 Dunkerque France

VAAHTONIEMI, LAURI HENRIKKI, dentist, researcher; b. Suomussalmi, Finland, July 25, 1961; s. Heikki and Sirkku (Säippä) V.; m. Armi Hannele Raatevaara, Sept. 6, 1986; children: Kaisa, Saara. DDS, U. Turku,

Finland, 1984; PhD, U. Oulu, Finland, 1998. Dentist Kokkolan (Finland) Health Ctr., 1986—; rschr. U. Oulu, Finland, 1992—. Contbr. articles to profl. jours. Vol. Dental Vol. for Israel. Evangelical Lutheran. Avocations: literature, outdoor activities. Office: Kokkola Health Ctr, Mariankatu 28, FIN67200 Kokkola Finland

VACCARO, ANTOINE, fundraising company executive; b. Favara, Agrigento, Italy, Nov. 2, 1955; arrived in France, 1962; s. MIchel and Girolama (Zambuto) V.; m. Catherine Francoise Bezsonoff, Nov. 4, 1960; children: Elena, Alexandra. Bachelor's degree, Dauphine U., Paris, 1977, Master's degree, 1979, PhD, 1986. Head fundraising svc. Found. de France, Paris, 1976-83; sales mgr. G. Cam, Paris, 1983-84; fundraising exec. Medecins du Monde, Paris, 1985-88; mgr. co. Excel SA, Paris, 1988—; lectr. CEP, Nanterre U., France, 1989—, Pantheon U., France, 1995—, Celsa Sorbonne, Paris, 1990—. Author: Communication et Collecte de Fonds, 1987, Donations et Legs, 1990; co-author: L'argent du Coeur, 1996, Medecine Humanitaire Flammarion, 1996. Adminstr. Atlas, Paris, 1995—. Recipient Grand Prix Strategie, Paris, 1995. Avocations: golf, painting, skiing. Home: 7 Rue de la Bluterie, 94370 Sucy en Brie France Office: Excel SA, 51 rue de l'echiquier, 75010 Paris France

VACCARO, JEROME VINCENT, psychiatrist, educator; b. Bklyn., Apr. 17, 1955; s. Louis Sylvio and Margaret Gertrude (Miller) V.; m. Andra M. Penbrook, Apr. 20, 1991; children: Alexandra, Hunter. BS, CUNY, 1977; MD, Albert Einstein U., 1981. Diplomate Am. Bd. Psychiatry. Chief resident Albert Einstein U., Bronx, N.Y., 1984-85; assoc. prof. U. Hawaii, Honolulu, 1985-89, UCLA, 1989—; med. dir. Pacificare Behavioral Health, 1996—. Editor: Community Psychiatry, 1995; contbr. articles to med. jours. including Hosp. and Comty. Psychiatry, Comty. Mental Health Jour. Mem. Am. Psychiat. Assn., Am. Assn. Comty. Psychiatrists (editor jour. 1984-93).. Office: Pacificare Behavioral Health 5990 Sepulveda Blvd Ste 400 Van Nuys CA 91411-2523

VACCARO, PABLO OSCAR, physicist, researcher; b. Buenos Aires, Jan. 6, 1964; arrived in Japan, 1991; s. Héctor Jorge Vaccaro and Lidia Clementina López. Student, Comahue Nat. U., Neuquén, Argentina, 1980-83; licenciado en fisica, Inst. Balseiro, Bariloche, Argentina, 1986, PhD in Physics, 1991; postgrad., Kyoto (Japan) U., 1993. Invited rschr. ATR-Optical and Radio Comm. Rsch. Lab., Seika-cho, Japan, 1993-96, ATR-Adaptive Comm. Rsch. Lab., Seika-cho, 1996—; invited prof. dept. applied physics Konan U., Kobe, Japan, 1998—; presenter in field. Contbr. articles to profl. jours. Scholar Comision Nacional de Energia Atomica, Bariloche, Argentina, 1983-86, 87-91; fellow Japanese Ministry Edn., Kyoto, 1991-93. Mem. IEEE, Am. Phys. Soc. E-mail: vaccaro@acr.atr.co.jp. Office: ATR-Adaptive Comm Rsch Lab, 2-2 Hikaridai Seika-cho, Soraku Kyoto 619-0288, Japan

VACEK, JAROSLAV, rector; b. Litostrov, Czech Republic, June 26, 1943. BA, Charles U., 1965, MPhil, 1967, PhD, 1972, Docent of Sanskrit and Tamil Philology, 1991. Asst. Oriental Studies Charles U., Prague, Czech Republic, 1967-91; dir. Inst. Indian Studies Charles U., Prague, 1993—, vice rector, 1994-97; founder, head Mongolian studies sect. Charles U., 1975-83, chair, 1989-90, chair dept. Near Eastern, African and Indian Studies, 1990-91, dep. chair, 1991-93; vis. lectr. Free U., Berlin, 1992. Co-author: Introduction to the Study of Indian Languages, vol. 1, 1971, vol. 2, 1975, A Tamil Reader Introducing Sangam Literature, 1989, Textbooks of Mongolian, 1979-90; mem. editl bd. Archiv Orientální, Prague, Pondicherry (India) Inst. Linguistics and Culture; contbr. chpts. in books and articles to profl. jours. Mem. sci. coun. Faculty Arts, Charles U., 1990-92, 94—, sci. coun., Charles U., 1993-97; mem. sci. coun. Oriental Inst., Acad. Scis., Prague, 1990-93, 94-96, 2000—. Mem. Czech Oriental Soc., Linguistic Assn., Linguistic Cir. of Prague, Friends of India Assn. (Prague). E-mail: jaroslav.vacek@ruk.cuni.cz Fax: 2449-1673. Office: Charles U Inst Indian Studies, Celetna 20, 116 42 Prague Czech Republic

VACEK, KAREL, physics educator; b. Havlíckův Brod, Czech Republic, Aug. 4, 1930; s. Karel and Annastazie (Čapková) V.; m. Zdenka Krupková (dec. Sept. 1973); 1 child, Karel; m. Světla Kubálková, May 29, 1976; children: Martin, Světla. MSc, Charles U., Prague, Czech Republic, 1953, PhD, 1958, DSc, 1972. Rsch. fellow U. Strasbourg, France, 1960, 68; sr. lectr. U. Khartoum, Sudan, 1962-64; prof. physics Charles U., 1965-90, prof. emeritus, 1990—; rsch. fellow U. Ill., Urbana, 1976. Author: Physics for Biology Students, 1986; co-editor Procs.. ICPE of Physicists, 1980; contbr. over 150 articles to sci. jours., including Nature, Solid State Physics, Phys. Letters, Photochemistry and Photobiology. Recipient nat. prize in physics Czech Republic, 1979, Silver medal of Charles U. Mem. Am. Optical Soc., European Phys. Soc., European Photochem. Assn. Avocations: touring, music. Home: Pocernická 512, 108 00 Prague 10, Czech Republic Office: Charles U Fac Math-Physics, Ke Karlovu 3, 121 16 Prague 2, Czech Republic also: JEPU Fac Pedagog, Ceském ladeze 8, Usti Czech Republic

VACH, HOLGER, physicist, educator; b. Wuppertal, NRW, Germany, Sept. 14, 1956; s. Werner Hans and Hannelore Auguste (Sohl) V.; m. Christiane Marie-Louise Lesage, Aug. 23, 1992. BS, Ruhr U., 1978; MS in Physics, U. Ariz., 1982, MS in Optical Sci., 1983; PhD, Ludwig Maximilians U., 1987. Tchg. asst. physics dept. U. Ariz., Tucson, 1981-83, rsch. asst. Optical Scis. Ctr., 1982-83; rsch. asst. Max Planck Inst. Quantenoptik, Munich, Germany, 1983-87; postdoctoral fellow optique quantique Ecole Polytech., Palaiseau, France, 1987-89; rschr. optique quantique Ecole Polytech., Palaiseau, 1989—; tchr., staff mem. physics dept. Ecole Polytech., Palaiseau, 1991—. Referee sci. jours, 1995—; contbr. more than 60 articles to profl. jours. With German Civil Svc., 1976-79. Mem. Am. Piano Found., U. Ariz. Alumni Assn. Avocations: music, tenor saxophone, swimming, hiking, travel. Office: Optique Quantique, Ecole Polytechnique, 91128 Palaiseau France

VACHLIOTIS, DIMITRIS GEORGE, chemistry educator; b. Patra Ahaia, Greece, May 25, 1965; came to U.S., 1995; s. George Chrissanthos and Helen Dimitris (Giannikopoulou) V.; m. Amy George Koulogeorgiou, June 29, 1991; 1 child, George. BS in Chemistry, Roosevelt U., Chgo., 1990; MSc in Chemistry, Pacific Western U., 1994, PhD in Chemistry, 1998. Chemist Kraft Gen. Foods, Glenview, Ill., 1990-92, Citgo Petroleum, Cicero, Ill., 1992-93; supr. chemist Xttrium Lab., Chgo., 1993-96; chemist Morton Grove (Ill.) Pharm., 1996-97; specialist nuclear magnetic resonance U. Patra, 1997—; instr. St. Athanasios Greek Sch., Aurora, Ill., 1993-97; instr. English, Axon Sch., Patra, 1997—. Author: The Chemistry of Drugs Today, 1998; editor: NMR Spectroscopic Metabolite Imaging, 1996. With Greek Army Air Force, 1995-96. Mem. Greek Chemist Club. Greek Orthodox. Avocations: tennis, chess, football, computer games. Home: Theodotou 14, TT 26442 Patra Agyia Greece Office: U Patra, Rio-Patra Univ Town, 26500 Rio Patra Ahaia Greece

VACHON, LOUIS-ALBERT CARDINAL, archbishop; b. St. Frederic, Que., Can., Feb. 4, 1912; s. Napoleon and Alexandrine (Gilbert) V. D.Ph., Laval U., 1947, hon. degree, 1982; D.Th., St. Thomas Aquinas U., Rome, 1949; hon. degrees, U. Montreal, McGill and Victoria, 1964, Guelph U., 1966, Moncton U., 1967, Bishop's, Queen's and Strasbourg U., 1968, U. Notre Dame, 1971, Carleton U., 1972, Laval U., 1982. Superior Grand Seminaire Québec, 1955-59; superior gen. Le Séminaire de Qué., 1960-77; prof. philosophy Laval U., 1941-47, prof. theology, 1949-55, vice-rector, 1959-60, rector, 1960-72; protonotary apostolic, 1963-77, aux. bishop of Que., 1977-81, archbishop of Que. and primate of Can., 1981-90, apptd. Cardinal with title St. Paul of the Cross, 1985; Past pres. Corp. Laval U. Med. Centre; mem. Sacred Congregation for Clergy, Vatican, 1986—; adminstrv. bd. Nat. Order of Qué., 1985—, Can. Conf. Cath. Bishops, 1981—. Author: Espérance et Présomption, 1958, Verité et Liberte, 1962, Unité de l'universite. 1962, Apostolat de l'universitaire catholique, 1963, Memorial, 1963, Communauté universitaire, 1963, Progres de l'universite et consentement populaire, 1964, Responsabilite collective des universitaires, 1964, Les humanites aujourd'hui, 1966, Excellence et loyauté des universitaires, 1969, Pastoral Letters, 1981—. Hon. pres. La Société des etudes grecques et latines du Québec; assoc. mem. bd. Quebec Symphony Orch.; bd. govs. Laval U. Found. Decorated officier de l'Ordre de la Fidelité française, companion Order of Can., du Conseil de langue française, Ordre nat. du Qué., officier de la Légion d'honneur, France. Fellow Royal Soc. Can.; mem. Canadian Assn. French Lang. Educators (pres. 1970-72), Assn. Univs. and Colls. Can. (pres. 1965-66), Conf. Rectors and Prins. Que. Univs. (pres. 1965-68), Internat. Assn. Univs. (dep. mem. adminstrv. bd. 1965-70), Assn. des universites partiellement ou entierement de langue française (adminstrv. bd. 1961-69), Internat. Fedn. Cath. Univs. (adminstrv. bd. 1963-70), Ordre des francophones d'Amérique.

VADGAMA, PANKAJ, physician; b. Nairobi, Kenya, Feb. 16, 1948; s. Maganlal V.; m. Dixa; children: Reena, Roosnin, Preeya. MB, BS, Newcastle U., 1971, BS, 1976, PhD, 1984. Demonstrator Newcastle U., U.K., 1972-73, dir. biosensor rsch. group, 1983-88; researcher Royal Victoria Infirmary, U.K., 1973-77; prof. clin. biochemistry Manchester U., U.K., 1988-2000; dir. of IRC in biomaterials Queen Mary and Westfield Coll./U. London, 2000—. Author revs. in field. Mem. Assn. Clin. Biochemists, Brit. Biophys. Soc. Avocations: reading, walking. Office: Manchester U, Stott Ln, Salford M68HD, England

VADLEJCH, JAN, nuclear engineer, consultant; b. Prague, Czechoslovakia, Apr. 27, 1944; came to U.S., 1979, naturalized, 1984; s. Judr Jan and Marie (Strakova) V.; m. Natalia Borodin, Dec. 28, 1969. MSME, Prague Tech. U., Czechoslovakia, 1969. Sr. rschr. Czechoslovak Acad. Scis. Inst. of Thermomechanics, Prague, Czechoslovakia, 1969-75; dir. rsch. Nuclear Rsch. Inst., Rez u Prahy, Czechoslovakia, 1975-77; sr. sci. programmer World Computer Corp., Paris, France, 1977-79; mgr. mech. engring. Quadrex Corp., Campbell, Calif., 1979-82; mgr. engring. Quadrex Internat. Corp., Mannheim, Fed. Republic of Germany, 1982-84, dir. SW Europe; cons. Nira and Ansaldo, Genova, Italy, 1984-87; cons. Interatom div. Siemens, Bergisch Gladbach, Fed. Republic Germany, 1988; sr. v.p. Quadrex Internat. Corp., Heidelberg, Federal Republic Germany, Paris, France, Rapallo, Italy, 1989-92; cons. Westinghouse Electric Corp., Prague, Czech Republic and Bratislava, Slovak Republic, 1993-98; v.p. Stone & Webster Internat. Corp., Boston, 1995; sr. v.p. Quadrex Internat. Corp., Heidelberg and Paris, 2000—. Contbr. articles to profl. jours. Mem. Am. Nuclear Soc., ASME, ANSI. Republican. Office: Quadrex Internat Corp, Luthersrasse 40, 69120 Heidelberg Germany Home: 220 Rue Saint Jacques, 75005 Paris France

VADON, GÁBOR PÁL, radiologist; b. Budapest, Hungary, Apr. 29, 1938. MS, State Med. Univ., Pecs, Hungary, 1962, MD Specialist, 1966; PhD, Hungarian Acad. Sci., 1982. Asst. prof. Med. Univ. of Pecs, Hungary, 1962-68, sr. asst. prof., 1968-86; prof., dept. dir. Med. Univ. Szeged, Hungary, 1986-92; prof., dir. Med. Imaging Ctr., Pecs, Hungary, 1992—; cons. Hungarian Nat. Health Ins., 1989—, Hungarian State Welfare Dept., 1993—. Author: (book) Percutan Interventions...Surgery, 1984, Gastrointestinal Angiography in Diagnostics & Therapy, 1985; contbr. over 94 articles to profl. med.-radiol. jours. Named Chmn. Honoris Causa, Internat. Danube Symposium, Vienna, 1993. Mem. N.Y. Acad. Sci., Hungarian Radiol. Soc. (Bela Alexander award 1992), Hungarian Radiologist's Collegium, Internat. Gastrosurg. Club. Avocations: amateur bicycle tourism. Office: Med Diagnostic Ctr, RET St 2, H 7624 Pécs Hungary

VADSTRUP, WIBEKE, gallery owner; b. Copenhagen, Dec. 6, 1943; d. Torben and Mildrid (Bojesen) Andersen; m. Steen Vadstrup, Aug. 6, 1966; children: Catherine, Nicolai. Cand. phil., U. Copenhagen, 1964; libr., Royal Libr. Sch., Copenhagen, 1970. Asst. libr. Frederiksberg Ctrl. Libr., Copenhagen, 1970-81, head libr., libr. events, 1982-87; owner Bie & Vadstrup Gallery, Copenhagen, 1988—; ptnr., dir. DCA Gallery, N.Y.C., 1994—. Editor and pub. (folder series) The Art of Seeing, 1992-96. Mem. Dansk Galleri Sammenslutning, Fedn. European Art Galleries Assn., Internat. Danish Galleries. Avocations: designing quilts, Modern Am. Lit. Office: Bie & Vadstrup Gallery, Store Strandstraede 19B, 1255 København Denmark

VADUS, GLORIA A., scientific document examiner; b. Forrestville, Pa.. Diploma, Cole Sch. Graphology, Calif., 1978; BA in Psychology Counseling, Columbia Pacific U., 1981, MA in Psychology, 1982; diploma handwriting expert, Edith Eisenberg, Bethesda, Md., 1991. Cert. Am. Acad. Graphology, Washington, 1978, instr. Coun. Graphological Socs., 1980; ct. qualified document examiner; registered graphologist, 1978; cert. behavioral profiling and cert. questioned documents, Am. Bd. Forensic Examiners. Pres., owner Graphinc, Inc., 1985—; accredited instr. graphology Montgomery County Schs., Md., 1978-79; instr. Psychogram Centre, 1978-85; testifier superior and probate cts.; pub. forum panelist, lectr. and writer in field; cons. graphologist. Developed Trilogy base for rsch. for Am. Handwriting Analysis Found.; author numerous studies and papers in field, also environ. papers. Chmn. Letter of Hope for POW's; vol. Montgomery County, 1987-88; bd. dirs., cmty. affairs chair East Gate I Civic Assn., Potomac, Md., 1985-87. Recipient Gold Nib Analyst of Yr. award Am. Handwriting Analysis Fedn., 1982, Dancing Fan award Marine Tech. Soc., Tokyo chpt., 1991, Spl. award U.S./Japan Marine Facilities Panel Valuable Contbns. Japanese Panel UJNR/MFP, 1978-94, Woman of the Yr. award Am. Biog. Inst., 1990, 93-96, Who's Who of the Yr., 1994, 98, Internat. Woman of the Yr. award Internat. Biog. Ctr. (Eng.), 1991-93, 95-96, 98, Outstanding Woman of 20th Century award Am. Biog. Inst. Bd. of Internat. Rsch., 1999, Profound Contbns. to Soc. to the Yr., 2000. Fellow Am. Bd. Forensic Examiners (diplomate; Meritorious award 1994, Outstanding Contbrn. cert.); mem. Am. Handwriting Analysis Found. (life, cert., pres. 1982-84, chmn. rsch. com., chmn. adv. bd. 1981-87, chmn. nominations com. 1985-86, officiator 1986, mem. policy planning and ethics com. 1986-91, ethics chmn. 1989-91, chmn., past pres. adv. bd. 1989-91, bd. dirs. 1981-91); mem. IEEE-Distaff (internat. chmn. 1969-72), Nat. Forensic Ctr., Nat. Assn. Document Examiners (ethics hearing bd. 1986, chmn. nominations com. 1987-88, elections chmn. 1988, parliamentarian 1988-92, bd. dirs. 1985-92), Internat. Platform Assn., Soc. Francaise de Graphologie for Am. Handwriting Analysis Found., Nat. Writers Club, Charles F. Menninger Soc., Soroptomist Internat. (internat. chair, v.p., Bethesda chpt. v.p. Montgomery County, bd. dirs. 1987-92), Henry Hicks Garden Club of the Westburys, N.Y. (v.p., judge, chair flower shows, bd. dirs. 1967-71), Sierra Club, Nat. Wildlife Fedn., Ratune Conservancy. Home: 8500 Timber Hill Ln Potomac MD 20854-4237

VAEA, BARON OF HOUMA, Tongan prime minister; b. Nuku'alofa, May 15, 1921. Gov. of Ha'apai, 1960-68; commr. and consul for Tonga London, 1969-70, high commr. and consul for Tonga, 1970-72; min. labor, commerce and industries Kingdom of Tonga, Nuku'alofa, 1973-1991, acting dep. prime min., 1989, min. agr. and forestry, min. fisheries, min.marine and ports, 1991, min. responsible for telecom., 1991—, min. responsible for women affairs, 1991—, prime min., 1991; chmn. Nat. Res. Bank of Tonga, Tonga Broadcasting Comm., Port Adminstrn. Com., Tonga Telecomms. Commns., Shipping Corp. of Polynesia, Tonga Investment, Ltd. Office: Office of Prime Minister, PO Box 61, Nuku'alofa Tonga*

VAEGAN, clinical visual electrophysiologist; b. Sydney, Australia, Oct. 10, 1943; s. Maurice and Betty (Fischer) Levy; children: Harris, Annabelle, Jo Roxy. BA, Sydney U., 1964; MSc, Monash U., 1967; PhD, U. New South Wales, 1977. Dir. Visiontest Australia, Sydney, 1976—; vis. fellow Smith Kettlewell Eye Rsch. Found., San Francisco, 1989—, U. Houston Sch. Optometry, 1982. Grantee Nat. Health & Med. Rsch. Coun., 1981-95. Mem. Internat. Soc. Clin. Electrophysiology and Vision, Assn. Rsch. into Vision & Ophthalmology, Physiol. Soc. U.K. Avocations: cycling, swimming, camping.

VAFIADES, PANDELIS, retired electrical engineering educator; b. Thessaloniki, Greece, June 1, 1932; s. Christos and Hellen (Kouides) V.; m. Aliki Handji, June 29, 1962; children: Hellen, Anna. BS, Air Acad. Greece, Athens, 1955; M in Engring., Tex. A&M U., 1964. Ret. tech. officer Hellenic Air Force, Greece, 1951-81; vis. prof. elec. engring. Calif. State U., Long Beach, 1982-85. Author: Modern Television, 1967, 6th edit., 1993, Satellite Television, 1987, A Control Systems Course, 1983, 2d edit., 1986, A Control Systems Course, Part 2, 1993, Electric Circuit Analysis, 1986, Logic Design of Digital Systems, with Computer Applications, 1991, Basic Theory of Transistors and Integrated Circuits, 1971, 2d edit., 1976, Analog-Digital Television and Video, 1997. Mem. IEEE (sr.). Christian Orthodox. Avocation: music. Home: 30 E Venizelou St, 14122 Iraclio Athens Greece

VAGELATOS, ARISTIDES TH, computer engineer; b. Argostoli, Kefalonia, Greece, Jan. 5, 1966; s. Theofrastos Ar. and Maria L. Vagelatos. B of Computer Engring., U. Patras, 1989, PhD in Natural Lang. Processing, 1998. Computer engr. Computer Tech. Inst., Patras, Greece, 1990-95, sr. rschr., 1997—. Served with Greek Navy, 1995-96. Avocations: windsurfing, basketball, reading, music, motor-bike riding. Office: CTI, Kolokotroni 3, GR26221 Patras Greece

VAGELOS, PINDAROS ROY, pharmaceutical company executive; b. Westfield, N.J., Oct. 8, 1929; s. Roy John and Marianthi (Lambrinides) V.; m. Diana Touliatos, July 10, 1955; children: Randall, Cynthia, Andrew, Ellen. AB, U. Pa., 1950; MD, Columbia U., 1954; DSc (hon.), Washington U., 1980, Brown U., 1982, U. Medicine and Dentistry of N.J., 1984, NYU, 1989, Columbia U., 1990; LLD (hon.), Princeton U., 1990; LHD (hon.), Rutgers U., 1991; DSc (hon.), N.J. Inst. Tech., 1992, SUNY, 1994. Intern medicine Mass. Gen. Hosp., 1954-55, asst. resident medicine, 1955-56; surgeon Lab. Cellular Physiology, NIH, 1956-59; surgeon Lab. Biochemistry, 1959-64, head sect. comparative biochemistry, 1964-66; prof. biochemistry, chmn. dept. biol. chemistry Washington U. Sch. Medicine, St. Louis, 1966-75; dir. divsn. biology and biomed. scis. Washington U. Sch. Medicine, 1973-75; sr. v.p. research Merck, Sharp & Dohme Research Labs., Rahway, N.J., 1975-76, pres., 1976-84; corp. sr. v.p. Merck & Co., Inc., Rahway, N.J., 1982-84, exec. v.p., 1984-85, CEO, 1985-86, chmn., CEO,, 1986-94, ret. chmn., CEO, 1994; chmn. Regeneron Pharms., Inc. (now called Merck Pharms. Inc.), Tarrytown, N.Y., 1995—; mem. Inst. Medicine, NAS, 1974—; chmn. sci. adv. bd. Ctr. for Advanced Biotech. and Medicine, 1985-94; bd. dirs. Estee Lauder, Prudential Ins. Co., PepsiCo, Inc. Trustee U. Pa., 1988—, chmn. bd., 1994—; trustee Rockefeller U., 1976-94, Danforth Found., 1978—; mem. President's Commn. on Environ. Quality, 1991-93, Adv. Com. Trade Policy and Negotiations, 1992-94, Bus. Coun., 1987-95; bd. mng. dirs. Met. Opera Assn., Inc., 1989-95; bd. dirs. N.J. Performing Arts Ctr., 1989—, co-chmn , 1992. Recipient award for chemistry in svc. to soc., NAS, 1995, Pupin medal, 1995. Mem. Am. Chem. Soc. (Enzyme Chemistry award 1967), Am. Soc. Biol. Chemists, Nat. Acad. Scis., Am. Acad. Arts and Scis., Am. Philosophical Soc., Bus. Roundtable (policy com. 1987-94). Avocations: jogging, tennis. Discoverer of acyl-carrier protein. Office: Merck Pharms Inc 1 Crossroads Dr Bldg A Bedminster NJ 07921-2688

VAGLIANO, ALEXANDER MARINO, banker; b. Paris, France, Mar. 15, 1927; came to U.S., 1940, naturalized, 1945; s. Andre M. and Barbara (Allen) V.; children: Barbara A., Andre M., Justin C. Grad., St. Paul's Sch., Concord, N.H., 1944; B.A., Harvard, 1949, LL.B. cum laude, 1952. Bar: N.Y. bar 1952. Asso. firm White & Case, N.Y.C., 1952-58; asst. treas. J.P. Morgan & Co., Inc., N.Y.C., 1959; v.p. Morgan Guaranty Trust Co., N.Y.C., 1959-62, 65-66; sr. v.p. Morgan Guaranty Trust Co., 1968-76, exec. v.p., 1976-81; chief exec. officer Banca Vonwiller, Milan, Italy, 1967-68; chmn. Morgan Guaranty Internat. Finance Corp., 1976-81, J.P. Morgan Overseas Capital Corp., 1976-81; ptnr. Price Waterhouse and Ptnrs., 1983-85; chmn. Sunset Ridge Farm, Inc., 1983—, Michelin Fin. Corp., Greenville, S.C., 1985-98; chmn. bd. advisors Equity Linked Investors, N.Y.C., 1985—; pres. The N.Y. Farmers, 1992-94; bd. dirs. Holographics, Inc., N.Y.; dir. office of capital devel. and fin. Near East and South Asia, AID, 1963-65; adviser Yale Econ. Growth Ctr., 1973-80, NYU Inst. French Studies, 1979-86; trustee Coun. for Excellence in Govt., 1990-93. Pres. Parks Council N.Y.C., 1971-73; bd. dirs. French Am. Found. , N.Y.C., 1986-93; gov. The Atlantic Inst. Internt. Affairs, 1986-90. Served with AUS, 1945-47. Mem. Council Fgn. Relations. Clubs: Brook (N.Y.C.); Travellers (Paris). Home and Office: Sunset Ridge Farm Inc Norfolk CT 06058

VAGNINI, LIVIO LEE, chemist, forensic consultant; b. North Bergen, N.J., Apr. 26, 1917; s. Frank S. and Margaret (Avondo) V.; m. Daniele Hogge, Sept. 29, 1949; children: Frank, Stephen, Eric. BS in Chemistry, Fordham U., 1938; postgrad., U. Md. Med. Sch., 1938-39. Diplomate Am. Bd. Forensic Examiners. Chemist H.A. Wilson Co. div. Englehard Industries, Inc., 1940-42; chief chemist U.S. Army Graves Registration, Liege, Belgium, 1946-48; chief forensic chemist U.S. Army Criminal Investigation Lab., Frankfurt, Fed. Republic Germany, 1948-60; sr. chemist FDA, Washington, 1960-62, CIA, Washington, 1963-73; project engr. Mitre Corp., McLean, Va., 1973-75; staff scientist Planning Research Corp., McLean, 1975-77; program dir. L. Miranda Assocs., Washington, 1978-81; forensic cons. Carmel, Calif., 1981—. Contbr. articles to profl. publs. Mem. Ft. Ord (Calif.) Retiree Coun., 1988, 89—; treas. Alliance Francaise Monterey Peninsula; adv. commn. Monterey County Commn. Vets. Svcs., 1990, 91, 92; Assn. Former Intelligence Officers, 1973—. Served with U.S. Army, 1942-46, lt. col. ret., 1975. Decorated Bronze Star. Fellow Am. Inst. Chemists, Am. Acad. Forensic Scis., Am. Chem. Soc.; mem. Nat. Assn. for Uniformd Svcs. (Monterey chpt.)Internat. Soc. Blood Transfusion, Internat. Soc. Forensic Toxicology, Ret. Officers Assn. (pres. Monterey County chpt. 1985), Sons in Retirement (pres. Pebble Beach br. 1986), Am.-Scandinavian Soc. (1st v.p., program dir. Monterey County 1989), Internat. Assn. of Forensic Sci., Am. Coll. of Forensic Examiners (diplomate). Roman Catholic. E-mail: liviaki@aol.com. Home: 26069 Mesa Dr Carmel CA 93923-8952

VAGO, PIERRE, architect; b. Budapest, Hungary, Aug. 30, 1910; arrived in France, 1927; s. Joseph and Ghita (Lenart) Vago; m. Nicole Cormier, Dec. 1968; children: Jean-Pierre, Florence, Michel, Catherine. Ed. Ecole Spec. Architecture, Paris, 1928-32; hon. degrees several univs. Practice architecture, Paris, 1934-85; designed many buildings in several countries; participant many internat. competitions; prof. at several univs. Writer many publs. in various countries. Lt. French Navy, 1939-45. Decorated chevalier Légion d'Honneur, médaille de la Resistance, commandeur of Arts and Lettres (France), St. Gregoire le Grand (Vatican); many others. Mem. Internat. Union Architects (hon. pres.), AIA (hon.), Royal Inst. Brit. Architects (hon.), Bund Deutscher Architekten (hon.), Paris Acad. d'Architecture, Berlin Akad. der Künste, Internat. Acad. Architecture (v.p.). Roman Catholic.

VAGUE, JEAN MARIE, physician; b. Draguignan, France, Nov. 25, 1911; s. Victor Francois and Marie (Voiron) V.; m. Denise Marie Jouve, Sept. 3, 1936; children: Philippe, Thierry, Irene (Mrs. Claude Juhan), Maurice. Baccalaureat, Cath. Coll., Aix en Provence, France, 1928; MD, Marseilles (France) U., 1935. Intern, Hotel Dieu Conception, Marseilles, 1930, resident, 1932-39; practice medicine specializing in endocrinology, Marseilles, 1943—; assoc. prof. Marseilles U., 1946-57, prof., clinic endocrinology, 1957—. Dir. Ctr. Alimentary Hygiene and Prophylaxis Nutrition Diseases Nat. Rys. Mediterranean region, 1958—; expert chronic degenerative diseases (diabetes) WHO, 1962—. Served to lt. French Army, 1939-40. Decorated Cross Legion Honor, Acad. Palms, knight pub. health, knight mil. merit, War Cross; recipient Willendorf Internat. award Internat. Assn. Study Obesity, 1990. Mem. Endocrine Soc. U.S., Am. Diabetes Assn., Royal Soc. Medicine (London), European Assn. for Study Diabetes, Spanish, Italian, French (past pres.) socs. endocrinology, French Acad. Medicine, Spanish Acad. Medicine, Italian Acad. Medicine, Belgian Acad. Medicine, French Lang. Diabetes Assn. (past pres.). Author: Human Sexual Differentiation, 1953, Notions of Endocrinology, 1965, Obesities, 1991, 98, Dawn on Iaboc's Ford, History of Man, History of Men, 1993, others. Achievements include first identification of the metabolic and vascular complications of android obesity and their mechanism; research in demonstration of diabetogenic and atherogenic power of obesity with topographic distbn. fat in upper and deep part of body, evolution of android diabetogenic obesity from 1st stage of efficacious hyperinsulinism to less efficacious hyperinsulinism and hypoinsulinism-neurogerminal degeneration, degenerative lesions of germinal epithelium and nervous system. Home: 6 Prado Parc, 411 Ave du Prado, 13008 Marseille France Office: Hopital U Timone Clin Endocrinologique, Blvd Jean-Moulin, 13385 Marseille France

VAGUE, PHILIPPE ANDRÉ, physician, biologist, educator; b. Marseille, France, Feb. 18, 1938; s. Jean and Denise (Joufe) V.; m. Véronique Lassmann, Dec. 13, 1982; children: Camille, Adrien; children from previous marriage: Bertrand, Sophie, Aymeric. MD, U. Marseille, 1966; PhD in Human Biology, U. Montpellier, France, 1978. Mem. staff, resident Univ. Hosp., Marseille, 1959, assoc. prof., physician, 1970-81, prof. internal medicine, nutrition, dir. lab. dietology, 1981, redactor in chief diabetes and metabolism, 1986-90. Assoc. editor Diabetologia, 1991-93; contbr. articles to profl. publs. Mem. French Sci. Soc., French Soc. Endocrinology, French Soc. Artifician Nutrition, Internat. Sci. Soc., French Lang. Assn. (pres.), French Lang. Soc. Nutrition and Dietetics, Internat. Diabetes Fedn., European Assn. for Study of Diabetes, Am. Diabetes Assn., Internat. Group Diabetes Treatment with Implantable Insulin Delivery Devices, Internat.

Diabetes Immunotherapy Group. Avocations: sports, sailing. Home: 90 Traverse Fort Fouque, 13012 Marseille France Office: Univ Hosp, Timone Bd Jean Moulin, 13385 Marseille France

VAHABOGLU, MUSTAFA HALUK, infectious diseases physician; b. Ankara, Turkey, Apr. 19, 1956; s. Omer and Guzin (Koselioglu) V.; m. Aliye Selma Erel, Apr. 25, 1987; 1 child, Deniz. BS, Samsun Coll., 1973; MD, Ankara U., 1983. Resident in infectious diseases and clin. microbiology Taksim Tchg. Hosp., Istanbul, 1991, sr. resident, 1991-94; head infectious disease, clin. microbiology dept. Kocaeli U., Turkey, 1994—. Office: Kou Tip Fakultesi, Sopali Ciftligi Derince, Kocaeli 41900, Turkey

VAHAVIOLOS, SOTIRIOS JOHN, electrical engineer, scientist, corporate executive; b. Mistra, Greece, Apr. 16, 1946; s. John Apostolos and Athanasia (Pavlakos) V.; m. Aspasia Felice Nessas, June 1, 1969; children: Athanasia, Athena, Kristy. BSEE, Fairleigh Dickinson U., 1970; MSEE, Columbia U., 1972, M in Philosophy, 1975, PhDEE, 1976. Mem. tech. staff Bell Telephone Labs., Princeton, N.J., 1970-75, supr., 1975-76, dept. head, 1976-78; founder, pres., CEO Phys. Acoustics Corp., Princeton, 1978—, MISTRAS Holdings Corp., Princeton, 1984—; adviser Greece Ministry Def., Athens, 1986-88; bd. dirs. Orthosonics, Inc., N.Y.C.; chmn. policy com. Internat. Com. of Nondestructive Testing. Contbr. more than 100 papers to profl. publs. 13 U.S. patents, 7 fgn. patentsin field. Bd. dirs. Holy Cross Greek Orthodox Sch. Theology, Boston, 1989—; pres. bd of trustees St. George Greek Orthodox Cmty., Trenton, N.J.; adv. bd. Trenton State Coll., N.J., 1983—; chmn. Princeton sect. United Fund, 1976-78. Recipient Spartan Merit award Spartan World Soc., 1987, Entrepreneur of Yr. award Arthur Young/Inc. Mag., N.J., 1989. Fellow IEEE (Centennial medal award 1984, Dr. Ing Eugene Mittlemen Achievement award 1993), Am. Soc. Nondestructive Testing (bus. and fin. com. 1984-87, 88—, bd. dirs. 1985, sec. 1989, treas. 1990, v.p. 1991, pres. 1992, chmn. bd. 1993, chmn. internat. com. nondestructive testing 1994—, chmn. internat. com. on nondestructive testing, editor handbook on Acoustic Emission 1988, Lester Honor award 1998), Acoustic Emission Working Group; mem. ASTM, IEEE Indsl. Electronics Soc. (sr. mem. adminstrv. com. 1988, founder, v.p. conf. 1974-78, 2d prize Student Paper Contest 1970, Outstanding Young Engr. award 1984, editor Trans. on Indsl. Electronics 1976-82), N.Y. Acad. Scis., Internat. Found. for Advancement of Nondestructive Testing (v.p.). Independent. Greek Orthodox. Avocations: bird hunting, soccer, technical writing, gardening. Home: 7 Ridgeview Rd Princeton NJ 08540-7601 Office: Phys Acoustics Corp PO Box 3135 Princeton NJ 08543-3135

VAHIDY, AHSAN AHMAD, genetics educator; b. Ludhiana, E Punjab, India, Jan. 21, 1942; arrived in Pakistan, 1947; s. Shaheer Basheer and Muqaddisa Nargis (Khatoon) V.; m. Rehana Faruqi, July 24, 1970; children: Hassaan S., Farhaan S. ISc, U. Karachi, Pakistan, 1959, BSc, 1961, MSc, 1963; PhD, U. Hawaii, 1969. Rsch. asst. horticulture U. Hawaii, Honolulu, 1969; asst. prof. horticulture U. Sulaimaniyah, Iraq, 1974-77; lectr. in botany U. Karachi, 1963-65, asst. prof. genetics, 1970-74, 77-79, assoc. prof., 1979-82, prof., 1982—; chmn. genetics U. Karachi, 1979-96, dir. Biol. Rsch. Centre, 1996—, mem. bd. advanced study and rsch., 1988-94; vis. scientist Mo. Bot. Garden, St. Louis, 1986;mem. fac. med. U. Karachi, 1991—, vis. prof. Baqai Med. U., Karachi, 1992—, Fed. Govt. Urdu Sci. Coll., Karachi, 1985-95, dept. biotech., Karachi, 1996—; mem. bd. grad. studies Aga Khan Med. U., 1997—; rsch. supr. more than 30 grad. students' theses. Mem. editl. bd. Jour. Sci., Biol. Rsch., Jour. of U. Karachi, 1980—, Med. Spectrum Jour. Pakistan Med. Assn., 1998—; contbr. over 75 articles to sci. publs. Warden boys' hostels, U. Karachi, 1977-79, pres. athletics club, 1978-80, chmn. landscape gardening coun., 1983—; mem. bd. govs. Rehan Coll. Edn., 1993—. East-West Ctr. scholar U.S. Govt. and U. Hawaii, 1965-69; NSF rsch. grantee U. Karachi, 1986-90; recipient Cert. Commendation and Nat. Book Found. award Ministry Edn. Govt. Pakistan, 1994, Outstanding Rsch. Publ. award U. Karachi, 1995, Plaque of NISHAN-E-ZAFAR, Kar U. Tchrs. Soc., 1997, Meritorious Rsch. award U. Karachi, 1997. Mem. Am. Soc. Hort. Sci., N.Y. Acad. Sci., East-West Ctr. Alumni Assn., Gamma Sigma Delta. Islamic. Avocations: computer programming, coin collecting, swimming, jogging. Home: C-99 Staff Town, U Karachi, Karachi 75270, Pakistan Office: U Karachi, MAHQ Biol Rsch Ctr, Karachi 75270, Pakistan

VAHIDY, REHANA FARUQI, immunologist, educator; b. Hirdui, India, Dec. 28, 1943; arrived in Pakistan, 1950; d. Abdul Razzaque and Hashmi (Begum) Faruqi; m. Ahsan Ahmad Vahidy, July 24, 1970; children: Hassaan, Farhaan. BSc with honors, U. Karachi, Pakistan, 1964, MSc, 1965; MS, U. Hawaii, Honolulu, 1968. Asst. lectr. microbiology U. Karachi, Pakistan, 1965-66, asst. prof. microbiology, 1970-93, assoc. prof. microbiology, 1993-96, prof. microbiology, 1996—; rsch. asst. dept. microbiology U. Hawaii, Honolulu, 1968-69; mem. bd. grad. studies in microbiology U. Karachi, 1982—, mem. acad. coun. Akhtar Eye Hosp., 1989, inspection team, 1996—, disciplinary com., 1997—. Contbr. over 25 articles to profl. jours. Rsch. grantee Nat. Sci. Rsch. Devel. Fund, Islamabad, Pakistan, 1990-94, U. Grnats Commn., Islamabad, 1991-92. Mem. Pakistan Soc. Scientists and Sci. Profls. (life), Pakistan Pharmocol. Soc. (life). Muslim. Avocations: interior decoration, dress design, reading, watching movies. Office: Dept Microbiology, U Karachi, Karachi 75270, Pakistan

VAHLIN, ANDERS, telecommunications engineer, research scientist; b. Selånger, Medelpad, Sweden, Feb. 11, 1964; arrived in Norway, 1992; m. Hilde Christine Meisingset, July 30, 1997. MS, Chalmers U. Tech., Gothenburg, Sweden, 1990; PhD, Norwegian Inst. Tech., Trondheim, 1995; Internat. Diploma, Imperial Coll., London, 1991. Design engr. AB Knight, Gothenburg, Sweden, 1985-86, Seatronics AB, Gothenburg, 1988-89, Enator AB, Gothenburg, 1990-92; tchg. asst. Norwegian Inst. Tech., Trondheim, 1992-95; rsch. scientist Nera ASA, Bergen, Norway, 1995-99; mgr. Nera Networks AS, Bergen, Norway, 1999—; cons. SINTEF, Trondheim, Norway, 1992. Contbr. articles to profl. jours., chpt. to book. Sgt. Swedish Army, 1984-85. Mem. IEEE, Norsig, Chalmers Soc. Grads. Office: Nera Networks AS, PO Box 7090, N-5020 Bergen Norway

VAIDHYANATHAN, BALASUBRAMANIAM, materials scientist; b. Salem, Tamilnadu, India, Apr. 6, 1969; s. Balasubramaniam and Babysaroja N. V.; m. Annapoorani Annapoorani, Nov. 19, 1999. BSc in Physics, Bharathiar U., Coimbatore, India, 1989, MSc in Applied Scis., 1991; PhD, Indian Inst. Scis., Bangalore, India, 1997. From jr. rsch. fellow to sr. project asst. Indian Inst. Scis., Bangalore, 1991-97; fellow Pa. State U., 1997-99; rsch. fellow Brunel U., Middlesex, U.K., 2000; rsch. assoc. Inst. Polymer Tech. and Materials Engring. Loughborough (U.K.) U., 2000—. Patentee in field; contbr. articles to profl. jours. Convener students group for interdisciplinary interactions Indian Inst. Sci., 1995-97. Sgt. Nat. Cadet Corps., 1989. Mem. Material Rsch. Soc. India, Am. Ceramic Soc. (jour. rev. com. mem.). Avocations: music, cricket, chess, carem, billiards. Home: Singanallur Post, 158 Kothari Nagar, 641005 Coimbatore India Office: Loughborough Univ, Inst Poly Tech & Mat Engr, Loughborough LE11 3TU, United Kingdom

VAIDYA, DURGESH SHIVRAM, chemical engineer, researcher; b. Mumbai, India, Apr. 15, 1969; came to U.S., 1991; s. Shivram Bhskar and Shailaja (Shivram) V. PhD in Chem. Engring., SUNY, Buffalo, 1997. Rsch. scientist Spectran Corp., Sturbridge, Mass., 1997—. Contbr. articles to profl. jours. Office: Spectran Corp 50 Hall Rd Sturbridge MA 01566-1299

VAIDYA, SADASHIV SATISH, electrical engineer; b. Chalisgaon, India, Oct. 13, 1961; s. Satish Barku and Shanta Bai (Wagh) V.; m. Pushpalata Sadashiv Lendait, Dec. 26, 1988; children: Neha, Nishant. BEE, Visvesvaraya Regional Coll., Nagpur, India, 1983. Sr. engr. Mazagon Dock Ltd., Bombay, 1983-91; design engr. Nat. Petroleum Constrn. Co.-Western India Enterprise Ltd., Abudhabi, United Arab Emirates, 1991; elec. engr. Abu Dhabi Marine Operating Co., Abudhabi, 1991—. Avocations: biographies, spiritual books, devotional singing, writing, voluntarism. Home: Chunabhatti Mumbai, 1/19 Trimurty Coop Hsg Scty, Bombay 22, India Office: ADMA-OPCO Engring Divsn W9, PO Box 303, Abu Dhabi United Arab Emirates

VAIDYAN, KURIAN VARGHESE, educator; b. Chettikulangara, Kerala, India, Mar. 6, 1947; s. Varghese Kurian and Kunjannamma Varghese; m. Mary Panchilazhikathu Alex, Oct. 18, 1976; 1 child, Ancy. BSc, U. Kerala, Trivandrum, India, 1965, MSc, 1967; PhD, Indian Inst. Tech., Madras, 1971. Lectr. U. Kerala, Trivandrum, 1971-78, reader, 1978-84, prof., 1984—. Contbr. articles to profl. jours. Sec., joint sec. Assn. Brit. Coun. Scholars, Trivandrum, 1988-93, 93-94; pres. Kerala U. Tchrs. Orgn., Trivandrum, 1992, 93. Recipient Commonwealth Acad. Staff Fellowship award Assn. Commonwealth Univs., London, 1993, Bharat Excellence award Friendship Forum India, New Delhi, 2000. Fellow Kerala Acad. Scis. (life, treas. 1990-92), United Writers' Assn. (life); mem. Indian Soc. for Nondestructive Testing (life, vice-chmn. 1991-93, 95-97), Materials Rsch. Soc. India (life). Avocations: reading, sight seeing. E-mail: vaidyank@md4.vsnl.net.in and dlcampus@md2.vsnl.net.in. Home: 562 Prasanth Nagar, Trivandrum Kerala 695 011, India Office: Univ Kerala, Kariavattom, Trivandrum Kerala 695 581, India

VAIDYANATHAN, SUBRAMANIAN, spinal cord medicine physician; b. Tiruchirapalli, Madras, India, Aug. 16, 1947; arrived in Eng., 1992; s. Vaidyanathan Subramanian and Ramanathan Sarada; m. Usha Natarajan, June 6, 1985. MBBS, U. Madras, 1970; M in Surgery, Postgrad. Inst. Med. Edn., Chandigarh, India, 1974, MCh, 1976, PhD, 1984. Diplomate in urology Nat. Bd. Examinations. Rsch. assoc. Indian Coun. of Med. Rsch., 1979-81; lectr. urology Postgrad. Inst. Med. Edn. and Rsch., 1981-86, asst. prof., 1986-87, assoc. prof., 1987-91, additional prof., 1991-92; registrar in spinal injuries Regional Spinal Injuries Ctr., Southport, Eng., 1992-97, trust physician in spinal cord injury, 1997—; vis. prof. U. Mass., 1994, Jawaharlal Inst. of Postgrad. Med. Edn. and Rsch., Pondicherry, India, 1986, U. Madras, 1987. Contbr. over 200 articles to internat. jours.; past mem. editl. bd. Indian Jour. of Urology; reviewer Spinal Cord, 1998—. Former mem. exec. com. Indian Assn. for Advancement of Med. Edn. Recipient prize Nat. Acad. Med. Scis., New Delhi. Achievements include research on neuropathic bladder (clinical, histopathological and molecular biological aspects) in spinal cord injury patients, study of symptomatic urinary infections in persons with spinal cord injury. Office: Rgnl Spinal Injuries Ctr, Town Lane, Southport, Merseyside Merseyside PR86PN, England

VAIKMÄE, REIN, palaeoclimatologist; b. Schleswig-Holstein, Germany, June 29, 1945; s. Arvo and Elma (Haidak) V.;m. Margot Seppel, July 30, 1966; 1 child, Ivar (dec.). Diploma engring., Tallinn Tech. U., 1969; PhD, USSR Acad. Scis., Moscow, 1981. Rsch. asst. Inst. Geology, Estonian Acad. Scis., Tallinn, 1973-81, sr. rsch. asst., 1981-87, head isotope geology lab., 1987-89, dir. inst., head isotope-palaeoclimatology lab., 1990-99; head of isotope-palaeoclimatology lab. Inst. Geology, Tallinn Tech. U., 1999—; head dept. sci. and univs. Ministry of Edn., Republic of Estonia, 1999—; chmn. Internat. Geosphere-Biosphere Program Estonian Nat. Com., Tallinn, 1993—. Mem. Academia Europaea, N.Y. Acad. Sci., Am. Geophys. Union, Internat. Glaciological Soc., Geochem. Soc. Avocations: jogging, singing in choir, reading. Office: Tallinn Tech U Inst Geology, 7 Estonia Ave, 10143 Tallinn Estonia

VAIL, FREDERICK WILLMOTT, business consultant; b. Omaha, Dec. 19, 1955; s. Hugh Beuglar and Leona Ann (Tierney) V.; m. Isobel Elizabeth Hamilton, June 27, 1985; 1 child, Jessika Elizabeth. Diploma in mgmt., Henley Mgmt. Coll., Henley-Upon-Thames, England, 1993; MBA with distinction, U. Hull, England, 1997. Telecomm. analyst SM&R Comm., St. Petersburg, Fla., 1979-82; info. tech. cons. Arabian Am. Oil Co., Dhahran, Saudi Arabia, 1982-88; mgr. cons. svcs. Price Waterhouse Mgmt. Cons., London, 1988-91; exec. dir. United Telesis LTd., Windsor, England, 1991-92; head enterprise comm. Saudi Arabian Oil Co., Dhahran, 1993-97, head of process improvement, 1997-2000; cons. continuing excellence, 2000—. Tech. advisor Dhahrabn Hills Sch. Tech. Bd., 1997. Avocations: sailing, skiing, reading, travel. E-mail: fwvail@yahoo.com.

VAIL, IRIS JENNINGS, civic worker; b. N.Y.C., July 2, 1928; d. Lawrence K. and Beatrice (Black) Jennings; grad. Miss Porters Sch., Farmington, Conn.; m. Thomas V.H. Vail, Sept. 15, 1951; children: Siri J., Thomas V.H. Jr., Lawrence J.W. Exec. com. Garden Club Cleve., 1962-93; mem. women's coun. Western Res. Hist. Soc., 1960—, Cleve. Mus. Art, 1953—; chmn. Childrens Garden Fair, 1966-75, Public Square Dinner, 1975; bd. dirs. Garden Center Greater Cleve., 1963-77; trustee Cleve. Zool. Soc., 1971—; mem. Ohio Arts Coun., 1974-76, pub. sq. com. Greater Cleve. Growth Assn., 1976-93, pub. sq. preservation and maintenance com. Cleve. Found., 1989-93, chmn. pub. sq. planting com., 1993. Recipient Amy Angell Collier Montague medal Garden Club Am., 1976, Ohio Gov.'s award, 1977. Chagrin Valley Hunt Club, Cypress Point Club, Kirtland Country Club, Colony Club, Women's City of Cleve. Club (Margaret A. Ireland award). Home: 14950 County Line Rd Chagrin Falls OH 44022-6800

VAIL, MARY BARBARA, publicist; b. Kingsville, Tex., Apr. 24, 1956; d. Fred G. and Nora J. (Smith) Leon; m. David L. Vail, Mar. 30, 1980; children: Sean Kristofer, Ashley Noel. Student, Tex. A&I U.; BS, U. Hawaii, 1982; postgrad., Hawaii Pacific U., 1991-92. Display specialist Linda's, Kingsville, 1986-87; mktg./membership dir. Malibu (Calif.) Riding and Tennis Club, 1990-91; mktg. dir. Pacific Aerospace Mus., Honolulu, 1991-93; pres. Vail Media, Inc. (Scarlett Mktg. & Promotions), Aiea, Hawaii, 1993-95; owner, sole propr. Mary B. Vail Publicist. Vol. fundraiser AOWC, Point Mugu, Calif., 1990-91; vol. Laguna Vista Elem. Sch., Camarillo, Calif., 1990, Barbers Point (Hawaii) Elem. Sch., 1992—; vol., mil. liaison 1st Night Honolulu, 1991; co-chmn. Aloha Family Festival, Pearl Harbor, Hawaii, 1991, Fly Thru Time, 1992, 93, 94, Mugu Air Show, Chinese C. of C. Fashion Show, 1994, Narcissus Festival; Ho'Okipa Aloha, HIA Hospitality Tng. Coun.; vol. numerous orgns. including Salvation Army, Spl. Olympics, Honolulu C. of C., Am. Diabetes Assn., Japanese C. of C., Muscular Dystrophy Assn., Juvenile Diabetes Assn., Children's Miracle Network, Susan G. Komen Breast Cancer Found., Las Vegas C. of C., Profl. Black Women's Alliance, Hadassah Jewish Women's Orgn. Decorated knight Order St. George, K.M. Mem. NAFE, Pub. Rels. Soc. Am., Pub. Rels. Soc. Hawaii, U. Hawaii Alumni Assn., Food Science and Numan Nutrition Alumni Assn., So. Nev. Homebuilders Assn. Avocations: jogging, crafts, sewing, landscaping, decorating.

VAIL, THOMAS VAN HUSEN, retired newspaper publisher and editor; b. Cleve., June 23, 1926; s. Herman Lansing and Delia (White) V.; m. Iris W. Jennings, Sept. 15, 1951; children: Siri Jennings, Thomas Van Husen, Jr. A.B. in Politics cum laude, Princeton U., 1948; H.H.D. (hon.), Wilberforce U., 1964; L.H.D., Kenyon Coll., 1969, Cleve. State U., 1973. Reporter Cleve. News, 1949-53, polit. editor, 1953-57; with Cleve. Plain Dealer, 1957-91, v.p., 1961-63, pub., editor, 1963-91, pres., 1970-91; dir. AP, 1968-74; ret., 1991. Bd. dirs. Greater Cleve. Growth Assn.; bd. dirs., past pres. Cleve. Conv. and Visitors Bur.; mem. Nat. Adv. Commn. on Health Manpower; presdl. apptd. to U.S. Adv. Commn. on Info., Pres.'s Commn. for Observance 25th Anniversay UN; trustee No. Ohio region NCCJ, Nat. Brotherhood Week chmn., 1969; trustee Cleve. Coun. World Affairs; fellow Cleve. Clinic Found.; former mem. Downtown Cleve. Corp.; former mem. distbn. com. Cleve. Found.; chmn., founder New Cleve. Campaign; trustee, founder Cleve. Tomorrow; former trustee Com. Econ. Devel.; former mem. Pres.'s Adv. Coun. on Pvt. Sector Initiatives; participant Nat. Conf. Christians and Jews. Lt. (j.g.) USNR, 1944-46. Recipient Nat. Human Relations award, 1970, Cleve. Man of Year award Sales and Mktg. Execs. Cleve., 1976, Ohio Gov.'s award, 1982, Downtown Bus. Council recognition award Greater Cleve. Growth Assn., 1983, award Nat. Conf. Christians and Jews, 1970, award Mt. Vernon Adv. Com., 1994. Mem. Nat. Assn. Profl. Journalists (Lifetime Hall of Fame), Am. Newspaper Pubs. Assn., Am. Soc. Newspaper Editors, Soc. Profl. Journalists, Kirtland Country Club (Willoughby, Ohio), Cypress Point Club (Pebble Beach, Calif.), Bohemian Club (San Francisco), Chagrin Valley Hunt Club (Gates Mills, Ohio), Links Club (N.Y.C.). Episcopalian. Home: L Ecurie 14950 County Line Rd Hunting Valley Chagrin Falls OH 44022 Office: 29225 Chagrin Blvd Ste 200 Beachwood OH 44122-4632

VAIL, VAN HORN, German language educator; b. Buffalo, Dec. 23, 1934; s. Curtis Churchill and Faith Newbrook (Ely) V.; m. Michele Juliette Edelstein, May 5, 1969; 1 son, Mark Curtis. B.A., U. Wash., 1956; M.A., Princeton U., 1961, Ph.D., 1964. Instr. Princeton U., 1962-65, asst. prof., 1965-66; asst. prof. German Middlebury (Vt.) Coll., 1966-69, assoc. prof., 1969-75, prof., 1975—; chmn. dept. Middlebury Coll., Vt., 1970-73, 87-88; dir. studies Middlebury Sch. in Germany Middlebury Coll., 1967-68, 70-71, 74-75, 85-86, 88-89, 92-93, 95-96; mem. nat. screening com. Fulbright Scholarships, 1979-81. Author: German in Review, 1967, 2d edit., 1986, 3d edit., 2000, Der Weg zum Lesen, 1967, 2d edit., 1974, 3d edit., 1986, Modern German, 1971, 2d edit., 1978, 3d edit., 1992, Tonio Kröger als Weg zur Literatur, 1974, Workbook for Modern German, 1992, Student Manual for 3d Edit. of German in Review, 2000. Served to 1st lt. M.I., U.S. Army, 1956-58. Fulbright scholar U. Heidelberg, 1958-59. Mem. MLA. Home: 352 Cider Mill Rd Middlebury VT 05753-9407 Office: Middlebury Coll Middlebury VT 05753

VAILE, MARK, administrator; b. Sydney, Australia, Apr. 18, 1956; married. Elected Ho. of Reps., New South Wales, Australia, 1993, nat. party whip, 1996-97; min. Dept. Transp. & Regional Devel., Australia, 1997-98, Dept. Agrl., Forests & Fisheries, Australia, 1998-2000, Dept. Trade, Australia, 2000—. Office: Dept Transp & Regional Dev, Parliament House Ste MF 26, Canberra ACT 2600, Australia*

VAINER, BEN, physician, researcher; b. Copenhagen, June 18, 1969; s. Gert and Beret (Levin) V.; m. Anette Fish, Oct. 29, 1989; children: Nadja, Noomi, Jonathan. MD, U. Copenhagen, 1995. Resident Herlev Hosp., Copenhagen, 1995-96; resident Glostrup Hosp., Copenhagen, 1996-97, rsch. fellow, 1997-2000, resident, 2000—. Contbr. articles to profl. jours. including Am. Jour. Gastroenterology, Digestive Diseases and Scis., Am. Jour. Surg. Pathology, Clin. and Exptl. Immunology, among others. Recipient gold medal U. Copenhagen, 1996. Mem. Danish Gastroent. Soc., European Inflammation Soc., Danish Soc. of Internal Medicine. Fax: 43-23-39-50. E-mail: ben.vainer@dadlnet.dk. Home: Toftekaersvej 12, DK-2820 Gentofte Denmark Office: Glostrup Hosp Dept Medicine, Ndr Ringvej, DK-2600 Glostrup Denmark

VAINSHTEIN, PETER, applied mathematics educator; b. Moscow, Sept. 9, 1944; arrived in Israel, 1991; s. Boris Vainshtein and Dora Pasvolsky; children: Dmitry, Yakov. MSc, Moscow U., 1966, PhD, 1972, DSc, 1989. Jr. rschr. Inst. Mechanics, Moscow, 1966-76, sr. rschr., 1976-89, group head, 1989-91; assoc. prof. Technion U., Haifa, Israel, 1991—. Contbr. articles to profl. jours. Office: Technion, Technion City Dept Mech Engring, 32000 Haifa Israel

VAIOS, CHRISTOS IOANNIS, systems engineer; b. Grevena, Macedonia, Greece, Feb. 14, 1961; s. Ioannis and Eugenia (Tzialla) V.; m. Nilda Collazo, Aug. 12, 1986; 1 child, Eugene. AS in Engring., No. Essex Coll., Haverhill, Mass., 1982; BSEE, U. Mass., 1985, MS in Systems Engring., 1987; MBA, U. Phoenix, 1995. Rsch. engr. Ctr. for Atmospheric Rsch., Lowell, Mass., 1984-87; systems engr. AT&T Bell Labs., Holmdel, N.J., 1987-96; MTS design supr. Lucent Technologies, Holmdel, 1996-97; mng. dir. advanced techs. Bus. Consulting Lucent Technologies, Holmdel, 1997-98; dir. strategic mktg. and bus. devel. GlobeSpan, Inc., Red Bank, N.J., 1998—; sr. mem. tech. staff AT&T Labs. Holmdel, N.J., 1995-96, mem. tech. staff, 1989-95, mem. tech. staff I, 1987-89; rsch. asst. Ctr. for Atmospheric Rsch., Lowell, 1984-87. Patentee in field. Mem. Aliockmon Soc. of Macedonians, N.Y.C., 1993, Homeless Soup Kitchen, Red Ban, N.J., 1992, The Concord Coalition, Washington, 1992. Mem. IEEE, N.Y. Acad. Scis., Delta Mu Delta, Zeta Iota, Eta Kappa Nu. Avocations: tennis, carpentry, classic luxury cars, mountain hiking. Home: 84 Garden Rd Shrewsbury NJ 07702-4474 Office: GlobeSpan Inc 100 Schulz Dr Red Bank NJ 07701

VAIREANU, DANUT IONEL, chemical engineer, educator; b. Costesti, Arges, Romania, 1963; s. Virgil and Filofteia Vaireanu; m. Cristiana Adriana Flamaropol, 1989; 1 child, Dan Costin. BSc, Polytech. Inst. Bucharest, 1988, MSc, 1988; MSc, U. Manchester, 1993; PhD, U. Manchester Inst. Sci Tech., 1995. Chem. engr., rsch. scientist DACIA S.A., Pitesti, Romania, 1988-90; head med. dept. Sintofarm S.A., Bucharest, Romania, 1990; rsch. and tchg. assoc. Polytech. Inst. Bucharest, 1990-91; rsch. scientist U. Manchester Inst. Sci. and Tech. Eng., 1991-95; sr. lectr. U. Polytech. Bucharest, 1995—; exec. dir. S.C. Dentismart S.R.L., Bucharest, 1996—; cons. OSIM Romanian Stds. and Authority, Bucharest, 1995—; auth. trans. by the Ministry of Justice, Bucharest, 1996—; vis. academic U. Manchester, 1997-98; mem. Acad. Coun. Faculty, 2000—. Editor: Electrochemical Technology Processes, 1991, Electrochemistry, Corrosion and Electrochemical Technology, 1999, Metallic Materials and Electrochemistry, 2000, Electrochemistry and Materials Science, 2000, Tehnology of Electrochemical Processes, 2000, Dictionary of Electrochemistry and Electrochemical Technology, 2000, Electrochemical Control and Treatment of Waste Water, 2000; contbr. articles to profl. jours. Lt. Romanian Army, 1982-83. Fellow NATO, 1997-98; recipient award Soros Found., 1991-92, ORS of London, 1993, 94, 95. Mem. Electrochem. Soc. USA, Royal Soc. Chemistry U.K. (chartered), Romanian Electrochem. Soc., Romanian Chem. Engring. Soc. Avocations: bridge, chess, Go, table tennis, swimming. Office: CP 39-C10 Sector 2, 73200 Bucharest Romania

VAIRIS, SHTRAUSS, polymer engineer, researcher; b. Sabile, Latvia, Dec. 3, 1946; s. David and Vilma (Tilberga) S.; m. Iveta Abolina, June 22, 1974; children: Maris, Uldis. Diploma in Engring., Riga (Latvia) Poly. Inst., 1970; Candidate Sci. Engring., Inst. Polymer Mechanics, Riga, 1978, DSc in Engring., 1992. Engr. Inst. Polymer Mechanics, 1969-72, rschr., 1972-80, prin. rschr., 1980—; head tech. com. Metrology of Latvian Nat. Accreditation Office, 1974—. Contbr. articles to profl. jours. Recipient Gold medal Leipzig Internat. Fair, 1988. Avocations: cinema, music, gardening. Office: Inst Polymer Mechanics, 23 Aizkraukles St, LV 1006 Riga Latvia

VAISBURD, SOLOMON EFIMOVICH, chemist; b. Khmelnitsky, Ukraine, Dec. 15, 1928; s. Yefim N. and Tsilya J. Vaisburd; m. Irene A. Rogova, Mar. 5, 1964; 1 child, Haim S. Chemist with honors, U. Leningrad, 1951; PhD, Technol. Inst., 1960; DSc, Mining Inst., 1970. Jr. rschr. Metallurgical Inst., Leningrad, 1951-56, sr. rschr., 1956-60, chief physico-chem. lab., 1960-90; rsch. fellow Technion, Haifa, Israel, 1991—; lectr. Mining Inst., Leningrad, Metall. Inst., Moscow, Metall. Inst., Tbilisi, Indsl. Inst., Norilsk, Politech. Inst., Sverdlovsk, Politech. Inst., Alma-Ata, U. Kiev, U. Krasnodar. Author: Physico-chemical Properties and Structure of Sulphide Melts, 1996; contbr. numerous articles to profl. publs.; patentee in field. Lectr. Inst. of Humanistic Judaism, 1993-96, Radio of Israel, 1992-96. Avocations: music, poetry, architecture, history of the science and religion. Home: 33/15 Dror St, Sh Amalya, 42369 Netanya Israel Office: Technion Materials Engring, Technion City, 32000 Haifa Israel

VAISEY, DAVID GEORGE, librarian, archivist; b. Tetbury, Eng., Mar. 15, 1935; s. William Thomas and Minnie (Payne) V.; m. Maureen Anne Mansell, Aug. 7, 1965; children: Katharine, Elizabeth. BA, Oxford U., Eng., 1959, MA, 1962. Archivist Staffordshire County Council, Stafford, Eng., 1960-63; from asst. librarian to sr. asst. librarian Bodleian Library, Oxford, Eng., 1963-75, keeper of western manuscripts, 1975-86, Bodley's librarian, 1986-96, Bodley's librarian emeritus, 1997—; dep. keeper Oxford U. Archives, 1966-75, keeper, 1995-2000; vis. prof. dept. library studies UCLA, 1985; commr. Royal Commn. Hist. Manuscripts, 1987-98; founding chmn. Nat. Coun. Archives, 1988-91. Served to 2d lt. Brit. Army, 1954-56. Fellow Exeter Coll., Oxford, 1975; hon. research fellow, Univ. Coll., London, 1987, hon. fellow Kellogg Coll., Oxford, 1996; named Encomienda of the Order of Isabel la Catolica (Spain), Comdr. of the Order of the Brit. Empire. Fellow Royal Hist. Soc., Soc. Antiquaries; mem. Brit. Records Assn. (v.p. 1998—), Soc. Archivists (pres. 1999—). Office: Bodleian Libr Oxford U Archives, Broad St, Oxford OX1 3BG, England

VAISHYA, JAGDISH SHARAN, physicist, researcher, consultant; b. Gwalior, India, Nov. 15, 1942; s. Govind Sahai and Basanti Devi Vijaywargi; m. Virbala Vaishya; children: Vijay Yogesh, Vijay Pratibha. BSc, Govt. Sci. Coll., Gwalior, 1961, MSc, 1963; PhD, Delhi (India) U., 1968. Rsch. assoc. Indian Inst. Tech., Kanpur, 1969-71; IAEA fellow Internat. Ctr. for Theoretical Physics (ICTP), Trieste, Italy, 1972; assoc. fellow Jawaharlal Nebru University (J.N.U.), Delhi, 1975-76; sr. sci. asst. Nat. Phys. Lab., Delhi, 1964-69, scientist, 1972-75, 76—. Contbr. over 50 articles to sci. jours., including Phys. Rev., Physics Letters, Nuovo Cimento, Solar Energy Optics Comm., Applied Optics, Jour. Modern Optics. Recipient award Indian Cryogenic Soc., 1976. Fellow Metrology Soc. India; mem. Optical Soc. India (life), Laser Soc. India (life). Achievements include experimental verification of phenomenon of spectral shift due to source correlation and its applications. Home: C1A/41B Janakpuri, New Delhi 110 058, India Office: Nat Phys Lab, Dr KS Krishnan Rd, New Delhi 110 012, India

VAISMAN, IZU, mathematics researcher, educator; b. Jassy, Romania, June 22, 1938; arrived in Israel, 1976; s. Strul and Etla (David) V.; m. Silvia Avram, May 8, 1969. MSc in Math., Jassy U., 1959, PhD in Math., 1965, D (h.c.), 1999. Asst. prof. math. Jassy U., 1964-69, assoc. prof. math., 1969-76; prof. math. U. Haifa, Israel, 1976—; chmn. dept. math., U. Haifa, 1982-84, 99—. Author: Cohomology and Differential Forms, 1973, Sympletic Geometry and Secondary Characteristic Classes, 1987, Lectures on the Geometry of Poisson Manifolds, 1994. Mem. Israel Math. Union. E-mail: vaisman@math.haifa.ac.il. Office: Univ Haifa, Dept Math, 31905 Haifa Israel

VAITIEKŪNAS, RAIMUNDAS PETRAS, marketing consultant, educator; b. Vilnius, Lithuania, Apr. 3, 1955; s. Algirdas and Birutė (Šablinskaitė) V.; m. Dijana Janina Pėžaitė, Apr. 30, 1976. BSc, Vilnius Pedagogical U., Lithuania, 1978; cert. in Mktg., AMU Gruppen, Sweden, 1993. History tchr. Secondary Sch. #7, Klaipeda, Lithuania, 1978-81; dept. head City of Klaipeda Komosol and Komunist systems, 1981-89; dept. head mktg. and info. Kertė (Bus. Cons. Firm), Klaipėeda, 1989—; mktg. instr. N Skuciene Pvt. Coll., 1994—. V.p., senator JCI NOM&LOM, Klaipeda, 1994, 95, 96. Mem. Lithuanian Bus. Info. Assn. (cons.). Avocations: coin and pin collecting, reading, yachting, music. E-mail: kerte@klaipeda.aiva.lt. Home: Alksnynes Str 5A-9, LT-5815 Klaipeda Lithuania Office: Kerte Bus Consulting, S Duakanto 2 (PO Box 69), Lt-5800 Klaipeda Lithuania

VAIZEY, MARINA, writer, lecturer; b. Jan. 16, 1938; d. Lyman and Ruth Stansky; m. Lord Vaizey, 1961 (dec. 1984); 3 children. BA in Medieval History and Lit., Harvard U.; BA, MA, Girton Coll., Cambridge. Art critic Fin. Times, 1970-74, Sunday Times, 1974-92; dance critic NOW!, 1979-81; editor Nat. Art Collections Fund Publs., 1991-94; cons. Nahanal Art Collections, 1994-98; lectr. cultural travel, 1997—. Author: 100 Masterpieces of Art, 1979, Andrew Wyeth, 1980, The Artist as Photographer, 1982, Peter Blake, 1985, Christiane Kubrick, 1990, Christo, 1990, Gillian Ayres, 1991, Sorensen, 1994, Picasso's Ladies, 1998, Sutton Taylor, 1999, (with C. Gere) Great Women Collectors, 1999; cons. editor: Art The Critics Choice, 1999; contbr. articles to profl. pubs. Gov. Camberwell Coll. of Arts and Crafts, 1971-82, Bath Acad. of Art, Corsham, 1978-81, South Bank Bd. 1993—; trustee Imperial War Mus., 1991—, Geffrye Mus., London, 1990—, Nat. Mus. and Galleries on Merseyside, 1986—; pres. Friends of NMGM, 1994—; mem. art working group Nat. Curriculum, Dept. Edn. and Sci., 1990-91; visual arts adv. com. British Coun., 1987—, Crafts Coun., 1988-94; mem. Arts Coun. 1976-79, mem. art panel, 1973-78, dep. chmn. 1976-79. Mem. 20th Century Soc. (com. 1995-98), Harvard Club London. Home: 24 Heathfield Terr, Chiswick London W4 4JE, England

VAJDA, JANOS, neurosurgeon; b. Budapest, May 6, 1946; s. Gyorgy and Julia (Freivogel) V.; m. Maria Bak, Sept. 1974; children: Julia, Vera. MD, U. Budapest, 1970. With Nat. Inst. Neurosurgery, Budapest, 1970—, mem. staff pediatric dept., 1970-73; head dept., 1990—; mem. Gough Cooper dept. neurol. surgery Inst. Neurology, U. London at Nat. Hosp., Eng., 1982; vis. prof. neurosurgery Nat. Inst. Neurology and Neurosurgery of Cuba, Havana, 1985; part-time sr. lectr. Rabin Med. Ctr., Tel Aviv U., Petah-Tiqva, Israel. Author: Neurosurgery, 1995. Named Eminent Physician, Hungarian Govt., 1984; Fogarty Internat. Sr. fellow in neurosci. Neuroclin. Trials Ctr., U. Va., Charlottesville, 1992-94, 2d prize for paper World Fedn. Neurosurg. Socs., 1981. Mem. Hungarian Neurosurg. Soc. (exec. com. 1988), European Assn. Neurosurg. Socs. (tng. com. 1991), Israel Neurol. Soc., Eurasian Neurosurg. Acad. Jewish. Home: Szt Istvan Park 17, H-1137 Budapest Hungary Office: Nat Inst Neurosurgery, Amerikai 57, 1426 Budapest Hungary

VAJDA, MIHÁLY, philosopher, educator; b. Budapest, Hungary, Feb. 10, 1935. Diploma, Eötvös L. U., Budapest, 1958; PhD, Acad. Scis., Budapest, 1967. Research fellow Acad. Scis., 1962-73; vis. prof. U. Bremen, Fed. Republic Germany, 1977-80; vis. fellow Columbia U., N.Y.C., 1985; vis. prof. New Sch. Social Research, N.Y.C., 1987, 89; Ashley Fellow Trent U., Pterborough, Ont., Can., 1988; prof. KLTE, Debrecen, Hungary, 1989—. Author: Bracketed Science, 1968, On Phenomenology, 1969, On Fascism, 1976, State and Socialism, 1981, Russian Socialism in Central Europe, 1989. Home: Duránci U 29, H-1116 Budapest Hungary Office: KLTE, Egytem Tér 1, H-4032 Debrecen Hungary

VAJDA, TAMAS, organic chemistry educator; b. Budapest, Aug. 4, 1928; s. Andor and Magda (Vass) V.; m. Erzsebet Mora, Oct. 6, 1962; children: Peter, Janos. Diploma in chemistry, Eötvös U., Budapest, 1951, PhD summa cum laude, 1959; DSc, Hungarian Acad. Scis., Budapest, 1990. Instr. in organic chemistry Eötvös U., Budapest, 1951-67, asst. prof., 1967-71, assoc. prof., 1971-93, prof., 1993—; postdoctoral fellow Fla. State U., Tallahassee, 1964-65. Contbr. more than 50 articles to profl. jours. Grantee Van't Hoff Found., 1960. Mem. Soc. Cryrobiology, Internat. Soc. Bioelec. Avocations: swimming, traveling. Office: Eötvös U Dept Organic Chemistry, PO Box 32, H-1518 Budapest 112, Hungary

VAJNER, LUDEK, educator; b. Prague, Czech Republic, Nov. 19, 1954; m. Olga; children: Olga, Petr. DVM, Sch. Vet. Medicine, Brno, Czech Republic, 1980, PhD, 1993. Rschr. Sch. Vet. Medicine, Brno, Czech Republic, 1980-82; chief animal breeder Agrl. Coop., Roven, Czech Republic, 1982-84; sr. rschr. dept. pathology Rsch. Inst. Pharmacy & Biochem., Rosice nad Labem, Czech Republic, 1984-92; sr. lectr. dept. histology & embryology Sch. Vet. Medicine, 1992-94, 2n Med. Faculty, Charles U., Prague, 1994—. Avocation: scouting. Office: Inst Histology & Embryology, V uvalu 84, CZ 15006 Prague 5, Czech Republic

VAJPAYEE, ATAL BIHARI, prime minister of India; b. Gwalior, India, Dec. 25, 1926; s. Krishna Bihari Vajpayee. Student, Victoria Coll., Gwalior, D.A.V. Coll., Kanpur, India; PhD (hon.), Kanpur U., 1993. Mem. Rashtriya Swayamsewak Sangh, 1941, Indian Nat. Congress, 1942-46; mem. Lok Sabha, 1957-62, 67-84, mem. for New Delhi, 1977-84, 91—; mem. Rajya Sabha, 1962-67; founding mem. Bharatiya Jana Sangh, 1951, parliamentary leader, 1957-77; pres. Bharatiya Janata Party, 1980-86, parliamentary leader, 1980-84, 86, min. external affairs, 1977-79; leader opposition Lok Sabha, 1993-98; prime min. India, 1998—; chair pub. accounts com. Com. Lok Sabha, 1969-70, 91-93; mem. Nat. Integration Coun., 1961—. Author: New Dimensions in Parliament, also collections of poems and articles. Recipient Bharat Ratna Pt. Govind Ballabh Pant award, 1994, Padma Vibhushan, Lokmanya Tilak Puruskar. Avocations: reading, writing, travel, cooking. Home: 6 Raisina Rd, New Delhi 110001, India Office: Office of Prime Minister, South Block, New Delhi 110011, India*

VAJRALA, KRISHNAIAH, communications company executive, consultant; b. Pathapally, India, Jan. 8, 1940; s. Venkaiah and Narayanamma (Puppala) V.; m. Pushpavathy Gubba, May 10, 1968; 1 child, Kiran Kumar. MTech, O.U., Hyderabad, India, 1985. Chartered Engr., Instn. Engrs. Jr. engr. Bharat Heavy Electricals Ltd., Hyderabad, 1965-67, foreman, 1967-71; asst. engr. Hindustan Cables Ltd., Hyderabad, 1971-75, exec. engr., 1975-81, asst. works mgr., 1981-83, project mgr., 1983-88, dep. gen. mgr., 1988-93, gen. mgr., 1993-97, sr. gen. mgr., 1997-98; dir. ops. M/S Surana Telecom, 1999—. Contbr. articles to profl. jours. Fellow Instn. Engrs. (India). Home: 32/B Santoshnagar Colony, (Old), Hyderabad 500 059, India Office: M/S Surana Telecom Ltd, #214, 215/A&215/D Phase II, Cherlapally 500 051, India

VAJTAY, STEPHEN MICHAEL, JR., lawyer; b. New Brunswick, N.J., Mar. 18, 1958; s. Stephen Michael and Veronica Gizella (Fehèr) V.; m. Gabriella Katherine Soltèsz, Aug. 5, 1989; children: Stephen, Andrew, Gregory, Daniel. BA, Rutgers U., 1980; JD, Georgetown U., 1983; LLM, NYU, 1989. Bar: N.J. 1984, U.S. Tax Ct. 1985. Assoc. McCarter and English, Newark, N.J., 1983-91, ptnr., 1991—; trustee Hungarian Scout Assn. in Exteris, Garfield, N.J., 1985—; trustee Partnership for a Drug-Free N.J., Inc., Montclair, 1993—; adj. prof. law Seton Hall U. Sch. Law, Newark, 1995—; spkr. at lectrs. and seminars, 1992—. Contbr. articles to profl. jours. Mem. Bd. of Adjustment, New Brunswick, N.J., 1993-98. Mem. ABA, N.J. Bar Assn. (chmn.-elect tax sect.), Essex County Bar Assn., Phi Beta Kappa. Roman Catholic. Office: McCarter and English Four Gateway Ctr 100 Mulberry St Newark NJ 07102

VAKS, VALENTIN GRIGOR'EVICH, physicist, theoretician, educator; b. Irkutsk, Russia, May 23, 1932; s. Grigory Isaacovich and Alexandra (Vasil'evna) V.; m. Iraida Ivanovna Pekova, Feb. 21, 1960; 1 child, Tat'yana Valentinovna Vaks Zabolotskaya. Grad. in Physics, Engr.-Phys. Inst., Moscow, 1956; Candidate of Physics, Inst. Theoretical and Exptl. Physics, Moscow, 1962; D of Physics, A.F. Ioffe Physico-Tech. Inst., Leningrad, Russia, 1968. Jr. rschr. Kurchatov Inst. Atomic Energy, Moscow, 1956-64, sr. rschr., 1964-89, leading rschr., 1989-92, prin. rschr., 1992—. Contbr. articles to profl. jours. Chmn. Ecol. Coun. Kurchatov Inst., Moscow, 1991-94. Named Soros prof. Internat. Soros Sci. Edn. Program, 1994. Mem. Moscow House of Scientists. Avocation: mountain tourism. Office: Russian Rsch Ctr, Kurchatov Square 1, 123182 Moscow Russia

VAKULENKO, MAKSYM OLEGHOVYCH, physicist; b. Kiev, Ukraine, Oct. 17, 1964; s. Olegh Vasyljovych and Dija Todorivna (Ghavrylenko) V.; m. Oljgha Mykolajivna Shelest, July 8, 1999; 1 child, Danylo. Disting. diploma, U. Kiev, 1986; PhD in Theoretical Physics, Inst. for Theoretical Physics, 1991; diploma, Dance Acad., Kiev, 1997. Jr. rschr. Inst. for Theoretical Physics, Kiev, 1991-92, rschr., 1992—; assoc. prof. Kiev State Linguistic U., 1999—; head coord. coun. State Lang. Inculcation, Kiev, 1997—; mem. Nat. Bd. Geographic Names, Ukraine, 1993—, Terminology Commn. of Nat. Scis., U. Kiev, 1992—, Press Ctr. of Higher Sch. Acad. Scis., 1997—. Author: Russian-Ukrainian Dictionary of the Physical Terminology, 1996; contbr. articles to profl. jours. Grantee Soros Found., 1992, Open Soc. Inst., 1996, Internat. Assn. for the Promotion of the Ind. States of the Former Soviet Union, 1995, 99. Mem. Ukrainian Physics Soc. Avocations: ballroom dancing, music, athletics. E-mail: vakul@phys.univ.kiev.ua. Home: 32-9, Prospekt Akad Ghlushkova, 03187 Kiev Ukraine Office: Inst Theoretical Physics, 14-b Metrologhichna, 03143 Kiev Ukraine

VAKULENKO, OLEGH VASYLJOVYCH, physics educator, scientific researcher; b. Kherson, Ukraine, Mar. 4, 1937; s. Vasylj Jonovych and Ksenija Serghijivna (Netudykhatka) V.; m. Dija Todorivna Ghavrylenko, Feb. 8, 1964; children: Maksym, Olesja. Grad., U. Kiev, Ukraine, 1960, PhD, 1966. Asst. Kiev U., 1963-66, sr. lectr., 1966-70, assoc. prof., 1970-86, prof. physics, 1986—; head physics sect. Terminol. Commn. Nat. Scis., U. Kiev, 1983—; academician Higher Sch. Acad. Scis., Ukraine, 1997—; mem. spl. coun. on theses Inst. of Semicondrs., Ukraine, 1998. Author: Optical Recharge of Impurities in Semiconductors, 1994; sci. editor: Russian-Ukrainian Dictionary of Physical Terminology, 1996; contbr. articles to profl. jours.; patentee in field. Grantee Open Soc. Inst., 1996, Internat. Assn. for the Promotion of the Ind. States of the Former Soviet Union, 1995. Mem. Internat. Optical Soc. Avocations: fishing, terminology. E-mail: vakul@phys.univ.kiev.ua. Home: 32-9, Prospekt Akad Ghlushkova, 03187 Kiev Ukraine Office: Kiev U Dept Physics, Prospekt Akad Ghlushkova 6, 03127 Kiev Ukraine

VAL, GEORGES ANTOINE, international financial development consultant, photographer; b. Garmisch, Bavaria, Germany, Mar. 6, 1945; arrived in France, 1949; s. Ferencz and Valeria (Kurucz) V. Cert. acct. Acct. Palmer Chartered Accts., Paris, 1966-67; mgr. C(ie) G(ale) de Geophysique, France, 1967-70; account mgr. Kilomoto Goldmines, Zaire, 1970-72, Dumez Nigeria Ming Ltd., Nigeria, 1972-84; gen. mgr. Rare Art Ltd., Eng., 1984-89; cons. Euro Project Paris, 1989—. Exhibited in solo shows at Africa Ctr., London, 1984, French and German Cultural Ctr., Lagos, Nigeria, 1985, Gröningen Mus., 1986, Free Dist. Montmartre, Paris, 1997, Paris Underground, 1998, UNESCO Paris, 1999; contbr. articles, photographes to prof. jours. Bd. dirs. Mus. Society, Nigeria, 1972-85, Societe de Geographie, Paris, 1994-2000; gen. sec. Free Dist. Montmartre, Paris, 1997. Mem. Lions Internat. (dir. internat. rels. Nigeria chpt. 1982-85). Achievements include fluency in French, English, Hungarian, German, Portuguese, Swahili, Pidgin; sailing down the Niger River in Nigeria in a dinghy solo. Avocations: studying and researching multicultural relations, traveling.

VALAGUSSA, ROBERTO PAOLO, publishing executive, consultant; b. Milan, Nov. 14, 1952; s. Aldo and Liliana (Tschuor) V. Degree in Sci. and Econs., U. Bocconi, Milan, 1975. Acct. Peat Marwick Mitchell & Co., Milan, 1975; export mgr. Standard Chartered Bank, London, Milan, 1976-78; internat. mng. dir. Gruppo Ed Fabbri, Milan, Paris, London, 1979—; consejero del. Ediciones Orbis, Barcelona, Spain, 1988—; gen. mgr. Edition Fabbri Paris, Fabbri Verlag, Hamburg, Fed. Republic of Germany, Fabbri Publs., London; bd. dirs. GE Ltd., London; pres. Fabbri USA, N.Y.C.; internat. exec. ptnr. H. Neumann Internat., Paris, 1990—; mng. ptnr. Search Ptnrs. Internat., Paris and Milan, 1993—. Avocations: sports, travel, reading. Home: Via Borgonuovo 5, 20121 Milan Italy also: 24 rue Clément Marot, 75008 Paris France

VÁLAS, GYÖRGY, information specialist; b. Budapest, Hungary, Jan. 18, 1937; s. József and Ilona (Bán) V.; m. Ágnes Gellei, Apr. 3, 1965; children: Péter, Judit. Diploma in Physics, Lorand Eötvös U., Budapest, 1961. Rsch. physicist Ctrl. Rsch. Inst. for Physics, Budapest, 1961-74; systems software engr. Ctrl. Statis. Office, Budapest, 1974-77, VBKM Works, Budapest, 1977-80; sr. info. cons. Nat. Tech. Info. Ctr. and Libr., Budapest, 1980-97; freelance info. cons. Budapest, 1997—. Mem. editl. bd. Annals of Improbable Rsch., 1996—; contbr. articles to profl. jours. Mem. John Neumann Computer Soc., Hungarian Astron. Soc. Avocations: swimming, travel, gardening, music, do-it-yourself projects. E-mail: valas@omk.omikk.hu. Office: c/o Nat Tech Info Ctr Libr, PO Box 12, H-1428 Budapest Hungary

VALASQUEZ, JOSEPH LOUIS, industrial engineer; b. Balt., Apr. 15, 1955; s. Jose Louis and Edith Rosabel (Saunders) V.; m. Nicole Diane Feldser, Sept. 4, 1983; children: Alexandra Nicole, Joseph Jr. AA, Essex Coll., 1977; BS in Indsl. Engring., U. Ariz., 1982; MBA in Fin., So. Ill. U., 1985. Registered profl. engr., Fla.; cert. quality engr.; cert. quality auditor; cert. quality mgr.; cert. project mgmt. profl.; cert. integrated resource mgmt.; pvt. pilots license. Machinist Bausch & Lomb, Balt., 1974-77; indsl. engr. IBM Corp., Tucson, 1980-81; sr. indsl. engr. Gen. Dynamics, San Diego, 1981-83; supr. engring. Avco Corp., Nashville, 1983-84; mgr. engring. Burroughs Corp., Coral Springs, Fla., 1984-85; dir. total quality mgmt. Lambda Novatronics, Inc., Pompano Beach, Fla., 1985—; pres. Woodland Properties; corp. mgt. continuous improvement Sensormatic Corp.; corp. dir. quality Sunbeam Corp., Delray Beach, Fla.; v.p. corp. quality Sunbeam Corp., Boca Raton, Fla.; computer cons., Margate, Fla., 1987; founder, owner E.P.I. Cons., Pompano Beach. Mem. Am. Inst. Indsl. Engrs., Fla. Engring. Soc. Republican. Roman Catholic. Avocations: real estate management, computer programming, mountain climbing, canoeing, private pilot. Home: PO Box 9821 Coral Springs FL 33075-0821

VALAVANIS, NIKITAS K., mechanical engineer; b. Larissa, Greece, May 29, 1968; s. Konstantinos and Sevasti (Parassidis) V. B in Mech. Engring., Cleve. State U., 1992; M in Indsl. Engring., U. Thessaly, Greece, 1998. Tech. dir. Valavanis Bros. Glassworks, 1992—. Mem. ASME, NSPE, Tech. Chamber Greece. Home: 4 K Parthenis, 41335 Larissa Greece Office: 109 Farsalon str, Larissa 41335, Greece

VALAVANIS, THEODORE BYRON, cardiologist; b. Drama, Greece, Aug. 19, 1957; s. Byron Theodore Valavanis and Chamaidi John Lagoualavanis; m. Sofia Christos Goutoudis, Sept. 28, 1991; 1 child, Philippa. Degree, U. Thessaloniki, Greece, 1985. Physician med. svc. rural regions Nikisiani, Greece, 1983-85; house officer dept. internal medicine Gen. Hosp. Drama, 1985-86, Health Ctr. Elefteroupolis, Greece, 1986-87; house officer, sr. house officer dept. cardiology Ika Hosp., Thessaloniki, 1987-89; chief cardiologist Railroad Multiclinic, Thessaloniki, 1992—; vis. cardiologist dept. haemodynamics St. Bartholomew's Hosp., London, 1990; vis. cardiologist Dept. Echocardiography and Doppler, Thessaloniki, 1991; cons. cardiologist 2d Ctr. for Elderly People, Thessaloniki, 1991—, YMCA Championship Athletic Teams, Thessaloniki, 1991—, Com. Pensions due to Mutilation of Comml. Ins., 1992—; cons. on hygiene Continent Comml. Hypermarket, Thessaloniki, 1992—, Carrefour Comml. Hypenuovlet, Thessalonike, 2000—; lectr. Congress Athletic Heart, Thessaloniki, 1989, Internat. Congress Cardiology, Thessaloniki, 1990; mem. Am. Coun. Cardiac Sonography, 1996—, Am. Coun. Interoperative Echocardiography, 1997—, Am. Coun. on Pediatric Echocardiography. Contbr. investigative rsch. articles to periodicals. Mem., donor Local Blood Giving Assn., Ahepa Hosp., Thessaloniki, 1982; active YMCA Adminstrv. Coun., Thessaloniki, 1990—, Local Table-Tennis Com., Thessaloniki, 1990—, Local Swimming Com., Thessaloniki, 1990—, Local Shooting Com., Thessaloniki, 1991—, Local Water-Polo Co., Thessaloniki, 1991—, Local Hand-Ball Com., Thessaloniki, 1992—. Recipient Diploma for Anti-Smoking Campaign, Nat. Anti-Smoking Assn., 1990, Medal and Diploma for exceptional blood donors Nat. Blood-Giving Assn., 1991. Mem. Greek Soc. Cardiology, No. Greece Soc. Cardiology, European Soc. Cardiology, Nat. Geog. Soc., Am. Heart Assn., N.Y. Acad. Scis., Am. Soc. Echocardiography, Am. Soc. Hypertension, Am. Soc. Heart Failure, Greek Aero. Med. Assn., Rotary. Avocations: amateur radio communications, photography, collecting stamps, astronomy, astrophysics, and modellism. Office: Papanostasiou str 48, 54639 Thessaloniki Greece

VALCAVI, UMBERTO, chemistry educator; b. Desenzano, Italy, Sept. 15, 1928; s. Giuseppe and Rosa (Bianchini) V.; m. Ines Scrocca, Sept. 17, 1960; children: Rosella, Giampaolo. Grad. Indsl. Chemistry, U. Milan, Italy, 1955; Libero docente in organic chemistry, State U. Italy, 1965. Rschr. Farmitalia S.P.A., Milan, 1955-59; dir. rsch. Istituto Biochimico Italiano SPA, 1959-76, sci. dir., 1977-80, gen. mgr., 1981-86, pres., exec. com., 1986-89; prof. organic and bio-organic chemistry U. Milan, 1964—, prof. biotechnology, 1997—; mem. sci. bd. Lorenzini Found., 1977—; bd. dirs. Italian Soc. Pharm. Scis., Chem. Italian Soc. Lombardia. Author: Advanced Organic Chemistry, 1980, Applied Organic Chemistry, 1983, Bioorganic Chemistry, 1992, Chemistry of Biotechnical Products, 1994, Steroids, 1997; contbr. 100 articles to Internat. Jour. Organic Chemistry, Internat. Jour. Pharm. Chemistry; holder 26 patents. Recipient Gran Cross Knight, Italian Rep., 1980, Order of Merit, Commdr. Italian Rep., 1982. Fellow N.Y. Acad. Sci.; mem. AAAS, Am. Chem. Soc., Rotary. Avocations: pre-history, origin of life. Fax: 0039-02-79-46-98. E-mail: valcavi@icil64.cilea.it. Home: 21 Viale Biancamaria, Milan 20122, Italy Office: Dept Biotech and Biosci, Plazza delle Scienze 2, 20126 Milan Italy

VALCHER, MARIA ELENA, mathematics educator; b. Bologna, Italy, Nov. 1, 1967; d. Sergio and Leda (Speranza) V. M, U. Padova, Italy, 1991; PhD, U. Padova, 1995. Asst. prof. U. Padova, 1994-98, assoc. prof., 1998—. Author: Modelli Dinamici Multidimensionali, 1994, Dispensa per il Corso di Sistemi Multivariabili, 1995; assoc. editor IEEE Transactions on Atomic Control. Office: U Lecce, Via Monteroni, I-7 3100 Lecce Italy

VALCKX, NICO, economics educator; b. Gent, Belgium, May 25, 1972; s. Guido and Vera (De Baets) V. MA in Econs., Ghent (Belgium) U., 1994; MSc in Econs. magna cum laude, Cath. U. Leuven, Belgium, 1997; PhD, U. Antwerpen, Belgium, 2000. Tchg. asst. Ghent U., 1994-95; rsch. fellow Ghent U./Belgian Nat. Fund for Sci. Rsch., 1996-99; rsch. assoc. U. Antwerpen, 2000—. Author: Investment Behavior in OECD Countries: Macro and Institutional Determinants, 1994, Macroeconomic Determinants of Stocks in OECD Countries, 1994, The Information Value of Asset Prices for Monetary Policy in the European Union, 1997, 2000. Mem. Am. Econ. Assn., Royal Econ. Soc. Avocations: tennis, windsurfing, opera, theatre. Home: Oude Gentweg 45, 9960 Assenede Belgium Office: U Antwerpen Econs, Prinsstraat 13, B-2000 Antwerpen Belgium

VALDERAS, SANTIAGO, NATO official, military officer; b. Larache, Morocco, Mar. 26, 1933; m. Maria Concepción López, May 26, 1963; children: Santiago, Concepción. Grad., Gen. Air Acad., 1957. Commd. 1st lt. Spanish Air Force, 1957, advanced through grades to gen., 1999, numerous positions with rescue squadron, various wings; comdr. wing #12 Spanish Air Force, Torrejón AFB; with air def. staff, air combat command staff, air staff, joint staff Spanish Air Force, comdr. NATO Coordination Group, dep. chief of Air Staff, 1992-93, Spanish mil. rep. to NATO Mil. Com., 1994—, chief of def. of Spain, 1996—. Decorated Medal of Royal and Mil. Order St. Hermenegildo, air medals, Medal of Merit of Civil Guard, others. Avocation: golf. Office: Def Staff Hdqrs, Calle Vitruvio 1, 28006 Madrid Spain

VALDERAS-CAÑESTRO, SANTIAGO, career officer; b. Larache, Morocco, Mar. 26, 1933; m. Concepción López Méndez; children: Santiago, Concepción. Joined Def. Staff, Madrid, chief. Gen. of air Air Force, Spain. Office: Estado Mayor Defensa, Vitruvio 1, 28071 Madrid Spain

VALDEZ, ARNOLD, dentist, lawyer; b. Mojave, Calif., June 27, 1954; s. Stephen Monarez Jr. and Mary Lou (Esparza) V.; m. Brandy Radovich, Dec. 31, 1994; children: Bayleigh, Briton, Barrington. BS in Biol. Sci., Calif. State U., Hayward, 1976; BS in Dental Sci. and DDS, U. Calif., San Francisco, 1982; MBA, Calif. State Poly. U., 1985; BS and JD cum laude, Pacific West Coll. Law, 1995. Bar: Mex., 1996; diplomate Am. Bd. Forensic Medicine, Am. Bd. Forensic Dentistry; cert. ind. med. examiner, qualified med. examiner, Calif. Pvt. practice specializing in temporomandibular joint and Myofascial Pain Dysfunction Disorders Pomona, Calif., 1982, Claremont, Calif., 1982—; CEO Valcom, 1994—; assoc. Marin, O'Connell & Meché, 1996; CEO Valcom-A Telecom. Corp.; network adminstr. Amiga and IBM compatibles; mem. adv. com. dental assisting program Chaffey Coll., Rancho Cucamonga, Calif., 1982—; mem. staff Pomona Valley Hosp. Med. Ctr.; ptnr. Marin, O'Connell & Meché. Vol. dentist San Antonio Hosp. Dental Clinic, Rancho Cucamonga, 1984—, Pomona Valley Assistance League Dental Clinic, 1986—; bd. dirs. Pacific West Coll. Law, 1993—, v.p. fgn. devel., 1996—, v.p. curriculum, 1998—. Fellow Am. Coll. Forensic Examiners, Acad. Gen. Dentistry (mastership 1994); mem. ADA, Am. Equilibration Soc., The Cranial Acad., Newport Harbor Acad. Dentistry, Calif. Dental Assn. (table clinic judge 1998—), Tri-County Dental Soc. (cochmn. mktg. 1986, chmn. sch. screening 1987, Golden Grin award), Acad. Gen. Dentistry, Acad. Computerized Dentistry, U. Calif.-San Francisco Alumni Assn., U. So. Calif. Sch. Dentistry Golden Century Club, Toastmasters, Psi Omega, Delta Theta Phi. Democrat. Roman Catholic. Avocations: skiing, gymnastics, kenpo karate (2d degree black belt), racquet sports, dancing. Home: 515 Seaward Rd Corona Del Mar CA 92625-2600 Office: 410 W Baseline Rd Claremont CA 91711-1607

VALDEZ, ERNESTO VENEGAS, pharmacology educator, medical consultant; b. Dagupan, The Philippines, Nov. 18, 1927; s. Juan Gutierrez Valdez and Juliana Estrella Venegas V.; m. Resurreccion Edillor Jamias, Apr. 16, 1958; children: Marylou, Ernesto, Eduardo, Rosalind, Eileen. AA, U. Philippines, Manila, 1948, MD, 1953. Instr. pharmacology U. Philippines Coll. Medicine, 1953-60; postdoctoral fellow pharmacology U. Calif. San Francisco Med. Ctr., 1960; postdoctoral fellow cardiovasc. rsch. Ga. Med. Coll., 1960; asst. prof. U. Philippines Coll. Medicine, 1961-65; postdoctoral fellow Kans. U. Med. Ctr., 1968; assoc. prof. U. Philippines Coll. Medicine, 1966-69, prof., 1969-92, prof. emeritus, 1992—, mem. adv. bds., cons., 1953—; med. dir. Johnson & Johnson, Manila, 1974-87, med. cons., 1987-95; mem. NRC of Philippines; lectr. pharmacology U. Calif. San Francisco Med. Ctr., 1959-60; vis. assoc. prof. pharmacology Kans. U. Med. Ctr., 1968; chmn. pharmacology U. Philippines Coll. Medicine, 1973-75, 88-91, asst. coll. sec., 1967-70, coll. sec., 1970-73. Assoc. editor: Physician's Drug Index, 1965, 67, Philippine Drug Reference, 1984, Philippine Med. Assn. Compendium, 1988, Philippine Nat. Drug Formulary, 1990. Recipient 1st prize for basic sci. rsch. Manila Med. Soc., 1954, 57, 1st prize for clin. rsch., 1962; Cultural Heritage award Govt. of The Philippines, 1963, Meritorious Svc. award Phi Kappa Phi, 1994; named Outstanding Educator Med. Alumni Soc., 1999. Fellow Philippine Soc. of Exptl. and Clin. Pharmacology, Philippine Soc. of Microbiology and Infectious Diseases, Philippine Coll. of Pharm. Medicine, Philippine Soc. for the Advancement of Sci. Roman Catholic. Avocations: tennis, bowling, classical music. Home: Monte Vista Subdivsn, 82 Guiho, Marikina 1800, The Philippines

VALDEZ, JESUS BALDOMERO, gastroenterologist, medical educator; b. Aplao, Castilla, Peru, June 15, 1945; s. Jesus Isaac and Rosa Victoria (Herrera) V.; m. Bertha Luz Duran, June 9, 1973; children: Saúl, Iné. MD, U. Fed. Dorio Grande Dosul, Porto Alegre, Brazil, 1967; PhD, U. Peruana Cayetano Heredia, Lima, 1976. Intern U. Rio Grande do Sul, Brazil, resident in gastroenterology and internal medicine; resident in gastroenterology and internal medicine Hosp. Gen. de Arequipa; chief of gastroenterology Hosp. Nat. del Sur Arequipa, 1974—; prof. prin. medicine U. Nat. de San Agustin Arequida, 1970—. Avocations: history, geography, photography, archeology, sports. Home: La Chacrita B-9 Cayma, Arequipa Peru Office: Ed Dou Mateo of 203, Calle Urubamba s/u Cayma, Arequipa Peru

VALDEZ, NORA, artist, educator; b. Mercedes, Argentina, Feb. 11, 1962; d. Juan Pablo and Augustina (Mana) de V.; m. Brian C.P. Connors, Apr. 12, 1986; 1 child, Stephanie. BFA, Coll. Fine Arts Mercedes, 1982. Instr. Elisabet Ney Sculpture Conservatory, Austin, Tex., 1998; vis. artist, instr. LaGuna Gloria-Austin Mus. Art, 1998; mentor Worcester (Mass.) Art Mus., 1995-98, 2000; resident artist Revolving Mus., Boston, 1992-96; artist Jekyll Island, Ga. Exhibited works at Inst. Contemporary Art, Boston, 1995, DeCordova Mus., Lincoln, Mass., 1995, Fuller Mus. Art, Brockton, Mass., 1996. Home and Office: 975 N Beachview Dr Jekyll Island GA 31527-0628

VALDEZ, STEVEN ANDREW, advertising executive; b. Port-of-Spain, Trinidad and Tobago, Jan. 5, 1962; s. Denis Albert and Marlene Ruth (Whitney) V.; m. Deborah Teresa Richards, Dec. 15, 1984; children: Stevie, Sasha, Christian. Student, St. Mary's Coll., Port-of-Spain, 1973-74, Fatima Coll., Mucurapo, Trinidad and Tobago, 1975-77. Graphic artist Inprint, Trinidad and Tobago, 1977; art dir. Uno Advt., Trinidad and Tobago, 1978-89; dir., gen. mgr. Aleong & Agostini Advt., Trinidad and Tobago, 1989-96; co-owner, mng. dir. Valdez & Torry, St. Clair, Trinidad and Tobago, 1996—. Designer logo for Pope John Paul II visit to Trinidad and Tobago; graphic design work for Hilton Hotel feature in Food and Beverage Trends mag., 1984. Pres. All Trinbagonians Against Crime, 1994. Recipient Illustration award Trinidad Art Soc., 1984, award for Best Supermarket Mktg. Program, Food Mktg. Inst., 1995, 96, Graphic Design award Trinidad Art Soc., 1987, award for photography Royal Bank of Trinidad and Tobago, Ltd., 1987. Mem. Advt. Agys. Assn. of Trinidad and Tobago (pres. 1995-96), Trinidad and Tobagp Chamber of Industry and Commerce (vice chmn., media sect. com. 1995-96), Trinidad Country Club, Trinidad Union Club. Avocations: reading, tennis, cricket, illustrating local culture. Fax: 622-7136. Home: 5 Hillock Pl Ext Blue Range, Diego Martin Trinidad and Tobago Office: Valdez & Torry Advt Ltd, 7 Alcazar St, Saint Clair Trinidad and Tobago

VALDIMARSSON, HELGI, immunologist; b. Reykjavik, Iceland, Sept. 16, 1936; s. Valdimar Jonsson and Filippia Kristjansdottir; m. Olöf Asgeirsdottir (div. 1962); children: Asgeir, Valdimar; m. Gudrun Agnarsdottir, June 2, 1964; children: Birna, Agnar, Kristjan. MD, Sch. Medicine, Reykjavik, 1964. Diplomate Iceland Bd. Medicine, Brit. Bd. Medicine. Lectr. Royal Postgrad. Med. Sch., London, 1971-75; sr. lectr., cons. St. Mary's Hosp., London, 1975-80; prof. U. Iceland, Reykjavik, 1980—; dean U. Iceland Med. Sch., Reykjavik, 1991-96; vis. prof. St. Mary's Imperial Sch. Medicine, 1980-96; chmn. coun. sci. U. Iceland, 1992-96. Editor Scandinavian Jour. Immunology, 1992—; contbr. over 150 articles to profl. jours. Pres. Scandinavian Soc. Immunology, 1992-97. Fellow Wellcome Found., 1971-75; Project grant Wellcome Found., 1975-80. Fellow. Royal Coll. Pathologist; mem. Icelandic Med. Assn. Avocations: skiing, swimming, music, chess. Office: Univ Hosp, Dept Immunology, 101 Reykjavik Iceland

VALDNA, VELLO, engineering researcher; b. Tallinn, Estonia, Nov. 5, 1937; s. Evald and Edla (Vanamolder) V.; m. Eve-Heidi Nurmsoo, Sept. 14, 1963; children: Eero, Tauno. Diploma in engring., Tallinn Tech. U., 1963; PhD, Ural Sci. Ctr., Sverdlovsk, Russia, 1984. Cert. engring. and technology of semiconductor materials and devices. Designer Design Office Giprozybflot, Tallinn, 1963-66; rsch. fellow Tallinn Tech. U., 1967-69, sr. rschr., 1970-89, 92—, chief rschr., 1989-92; cons. Estonian Radioelectrical Design Bur., Tallinn, 1967-71, Gorki's Sci. Inst. Measurement Instruments, Nizni-Novgorod, Russia, 1971-83, Biofarmavtomatika, Nizni-Novgorod, 1989-90, Siemens Analytical X-ray Sys., Inc., Madison, Wis., 1996-98, Bruker Analytical X-ray Sys., Inc., Madison, 1998—. Contbr. articles to profl. jours.; inventor in field. Recipient Estonian Sci. awards Govt. Soviet Estonia, Tallinn, 1985, 98; grantee Estonian Sci. Found., Tallinn, 1997, Siemens Analytical X-ray Sys., Inc., Madison, Wis., 1997, Deutsche Forschungsgemeinschaft, Stuttgart, 1998. Mem. Materials Rsch. Soc., Estonian Phys. Soc., Estonian Chem. Soc. Avocations: teaching, optoelectronics, music, swimming, skiing. Home: 64A-11 Akadeemia St, EE-0026 Tallinn Estonia Office: Tallinn Tech Univ, 5 Ehitajate Rd, EE-0026 Tallinn Estonia

VALE, PETER CHRISTOPHER JULIUS, humanities educator; b. Duiwelskloof, South Africa, July 8, 1947; s. Percy Alfred and Elizabeth Stilwell (McKay) V.; m. Louise Carol Peel, Oct. 27, 1982; children: Beth Nosiswe, Daniel Sibusiso. BA with honors, U. of the Witwatersrand, Johannesburg, South Africa, 1973; MA, U. Leicester, Eng., 1976, PhD, 1981. Asst. dir. South African Inst. Internat. Affairs, Johannesburg, 1973-75; rsch. assoc. Internat. Inst. for Strategic Studies, London, 1975-77; internat. rels. lectr. U. Witwatersrand, Johannesburg, 1977-80; dir. rsch. South African Inst. Internat. Affairs, Johannesburg, 1980-84; rsch. prof., dir. Inst. Social and Econ. Rsch. Rhodes U., Grahamstown, 1984-89; prof. So. African Studies Ctr. for So. African Studies U. Western Cape, Cape Town, 1989-98, vice rector acad. affairs, 1999—; UNESCO prof. African studies U. Utrecht, The Netherlands, 1996-97; vis. scholar Christian Michelsen Inst., Bergen, Norway, 1995. Author: South Africa & Southern Africa: Theory and Practice, Choices and Ritual, 1997, South Africa and Southern African Security: Of Lepers, Laagers, and Leanness, 1995; editor: (with Joachem Spanger) Bridges to the Future: Prospects for Peace and Security in Southern Africa, 1995, (with Larry A. Swatuk and Bertil Oden) Theory, Change and Southern Africa's Future, 2000. Trustee Inst. for Dem. in South Africa, 1987-98; advisor on fgn. policy African Nat. Congress, 1993-94. Seventh Bradlow fellow South African Inst. Internat. Affairs, 1989, hon. fellow Ctr. for African Studies Eduardo Mondane U., Mozambique, 1993; recipient Coun. award for the Humanities U. Witwatersrand, 1979. Mem. South African Polit. Sci. Assn. South Africa (pres. 1989-90), Internat. Studies Assn., South African Hist. Soc., Internat. Inst. for Strategic Studies. Avocations: reading, writing, running. Office: U of the Western Cape, Pvt Bag X17, Bellville, Cape 7535, South Africa

VALEIKA, VIRGILIJUS, chemistry educator, researcher; b. Jonava, Lithuania, Aug. 25, 1958; s. Anicetas Petras and Vanda (Urbonaitė) V.; m. Violeta Čyžaitė, Apr. 17, 1982; children: Vanda, Vita. Diploma Engr., Kaunas (Lithuania) U. Tech., 1980, PhD, 1997. Engr. Kaunas U. Tech., 1980-84, rschr., 1984-97, gen. asst., 1997-98, assoc. prof., 1998—; cons. to leather producing cos., Lithuania, 1986—. Contbr. articles to sci. jours., including Leather, Jour. Soc. Leather Technologists and Chemists, also conf. procs.; patentee in field in Lithuania and USSR. Grantee Lithuanian Fund Sci. and Study, 1997, 98, 2000. Roman Catholic. Avocations: computers, postage stamps, music. Office: Kaunas U Tech, Radvilenu pl 19, 3028 Kaunas Lithuania

VALENCIA, ANGEL ALEJANDRO, career officer; b. Riobamba, Chimborazo, Ecuador, Aug. 20, 1951; s. Jorge Enrique Valencia and Blanca Elena Vallejo; m. Julia de Lourdes Rigail, Sept. 29, 1976; children: Andrea Angelica, Julio Cesar. Grad. navy officer, Navy Sch., Salinas, 1974. Profl. estudy U.S. Marines, Quanticao Virotnia, 1976-77, U.S. Army, Fort Bragg, N.C., 1977, Brasilian Army, Rio de Janeiro, 1978; pres. adie de camp. Republic Pres., Quito, 1994-96; navy attache Embassy of Ecuador, Rome, 1998—, navy intelligence dir., 1999-2000. Editor books. Mem. Navy Club. Roman Catholic. Avocations: tennis, sports, ecology. Home: Norberto Salazar #2275, URB Santa Rosa, Tumbaco-Quito Pichincha, Ecuador Office: Ecuadorian Navy Exposicion, #208 y la Recoueta, Quito Pichincha, Ecuador

VALENCIA-RODRIGUEZ, LUIS, diplomat, lawyer; b. Quito, Ecuador, Mar. 5, 1926; s. Pedro Leonidas and Maria Guadalupe (Rodriguez) V.; m. Cleopatra Moreno Dec. 23, 1952; children: Luis Felipe, Alexis, Maria, Kirina, Maritza. B, Coll. Mejia, Quito, 1939-44; JD, Cen. U., Quito, 1944-50. Adminstr. sec. Ministry Foreign Affairs, Quito, Ecuador, 1944-52, mem. svc., 1952-94; amb. Ministry Foreign Affairs, Bolivia, Brasil, Peru, Venezuela, Argentina, 1969-91; permanent rep. to UN Ministry Fng. Affairs, Quito, 1994-99, minister fgn. affairs, 1965-66, 81-84. Author: (book) Fundamentos U.N., 1971, Principles U.N., 1972, Law of the Sea, 1977, Settlement Disputes, 1981, Short Stories, 1981. Avocations: reading, swimming. Home: Calle Agustin Mentoso 273, Quito Ecuador Office: Ministry Foreign Affairs, Av 10 de Agosto y Carrion, Quito Ecuador also: Permanent Mission Ecuador to UN 866 United Nations Plz Rm 516 New York NY 10017-1822

VALENČIČ, IVAN, psychologist, writer, art critic, counselor; b. Postojna, Slovenia, Jan. 19, 1958; s. Ivan and Avgusta (Kakež) V. BS in Psychology, U. Ljubljana (Slovenia), 1980, MS in Psychology, 1984. Counsellor Schs. in dist. Ilirska Bistrica, Slovenia, 1981—. Assoc. editor: Mreža Drog quarterly mag., 1995-97; contbr. articles to profl. jours., mags. Mem. Psychol. Assn. Slovenia. Home: Gregorčičeva 14, 6250 Ilirska Bistrica Slovenia

VALENTA, PAVEL, chemist, researcher; b. Pisek, Czech Republic, Apr. 5, 1921; arrived in Germany, 1970, naturalized, 1979; s. Joseph and Josepha (Pertlicek) V.; m. Eva Teplic, Mar. 28, 1948; children: Pavel, Hana, Eva. PhD, Charles U., 1951. Rschr. J. Heyrovsky's Polarographic Inst., Prague, Czech Republic, 1951-69, Lab. of Electrochemistry, CNRS, Paris, 1969-70; head dept. Inst. Applied Phys. Chemistry KFA, Juelich, Germany, 1970-86; cons. Inst. Applied Phys. Chemistry, KFA, 1986—; vis. prof. chemistry U. Concepcion, Chile, 1989, U. Extremadura, Badajoz, Spain, 1990-92, U. Guanajuato, Mex., 1993, U. Costa Rica, San Jose, 1993, 95. Author: Electric and Electronic Instruments in Chemical Laboratory, 1971; contbr. articles to profl. jours. Mem. IUPAC (analytical chem. divsn. 1989-95), Soc. German Chemists, Soc. Chemists of Costa Rica (hon.). Mem. Free Evangelic Ch. Avocations: music, history, jogging. Office: ICG-y, Rsch Ctr Julich (KFA) ICG-7, D-52425 Jülich Germany

VALENTE, JOHN FREDERICK, transplant surgeon; b. San Francisco, June 23, 1960; s. Joseph Louis and Sonja Fredericka (Zobel) V.; m. Suzanne Lynn Narce, May 29, 1987. BS in Biology, U. San Francisco, 1983; MD, U. Calif., San Francisco, 1987. Resident gen. surgery U. Ariz., Tucson, 1987-92; fellow trauma/critical care U. Cin., 1992-93, fellow transplantation surgery, 1993-95, asst. prof. surgery, 1996—; fellow rsch. Shriners Burns Inst., Cin., 1995-96; v.p. NovaCell Biotechs. Inc., Cin., 1996—. Contbr. articles to profl. jours., chpts. to books. ARCS scholar ARCS Found., 1981. Mem. AMA, ACS (candidate), Shock Soc., Surg. Infection Soc., Am. Soc. Transplant Surgeons (mem. edn. com. 1998—, Pharmacia-Upjohn award 1996), Alpha Sigma Nu. Republican. Roman Catholic. Achievements include patent pending on co-culturing bone marrow cells for immunomodulation, surg. dir. Legacy Transplant Svcs. Office: Good Samaritan Hosp Transplant Svcs NSC 430 1040 NW 22nd Ave Portland OR 97210-3057

VALENTE, PETER CHARLES, lawyer; b. N.Y.C., July 3, 1940; s. Francis Louis and Aurelia Emily (Cella) V.; m. Judith Kay Nemeroff, Feb. 19, 1966; children: Susan Lynn, David Marc. BA, Bowdoin Coll., 1962; LLB, Columbia U., 1966; LLM, NYU, 1971. Bar: N.Y. 1967. Assoc. Blank Rome Tenzer Greenblatt LLP, N.Y.C., 1967-73, ptnr., 1973—; ptnr. in charge tax and fiduciary dept., N.Y. office. Co-author column on wills, estates and surrogates's practice N.Y. Law Jour. Fellow Am. Coll. Trust and Estate Counsel; mem. ABA, N.Y. State Bar Assn. (lectr. on wills, trusts and estates), Assn. of Bar of City of N.Y., N.Y. County Lawyers' Assn. (former bd. dirs. and chmn. com. on surrogates' ct., lectr. on wills, trusts and estates), Phi Beta Kappa. Office: Blank Rome Tenzer Greenblatt LLP 405 Lexington Ave New York NY 10174-0002

VALENTI, FREDERICK ALAN, actor, screenwriter; b. Wiesbaden, Fed. Republic Germany, Feb. 24, 1967; s. Fred and Arietta Maxinne (Deline) V.; m. Melissa Ann Valenti. BA in Theater Arts, San Francisco State U., 1988; MA in Film History & Criticism, UCLA. Model Kim Dawson Agy., Dallas, 1982-84; actor, screenwriter I.C.M., San Francisco, 1992—; play dir. Children's Theater Workshop, San Francisco, 1987—. Actor: (films) This is Spinal Tap, 1984, Home Alone, 1990, Presumed Innocent, 1990, Silence of the Lambs, 1991, Groundhog Day, 1993, Clueless, 1995, The English Patient, 1997, The Sixth Sense, 1999, (play) Breaking New Ground, 1986 (Critics award 1986); screenwriter The Hip Guys, 1988; prodr. (stage) The Magic of D.R. Gibson, 1997, Chef Ken Takes the Cake, 1999; dir., playwright Pokie Cobb is Returning Home, 1998. Organizer San Francisco Youth for a Better Day rally, 1987; spokesman Just Say No to Drugs campaign, San Francisco, 1987, 88; chmn. Dallas Area Labor Day Telethon, 1990; chmn. Dallas chpt. AMFAR, 1992-95; founder Melissa Ann Valenti Found. for Benefit of Korean Adoptees, 1999. Recipient Youth in Film award Acad. Motion Picture Arts and Scis., 1984, Cauldron award Dallas Ctr. of Performing Arts, 1990, Emmy for The Longest Day, 1993; Cable Ace award for Dennis Miller Live, 1995, Emmy for writing Seinfeld, 1997. Fellow Screen Actors Guild, Actors Equity Assn.; mem. Internat. Brotherhood of Magicians. Democrat. Roman Catholic. Avocations: flying, auto racing, surfing, culinary arts, cycling. Home: 3704 Julienne Dr Plano TX 75023-7073 Office: Valenti Prodns 1708 Timberway Dr Richardson TX 75082-4530

VALENTIN, BEATE, freelance journalist, art market expert; b. Wernau (Neckar), Baden-W., Germany, Aug. 4, 1962; d. Johann and Rosalie (Steigerwald) Schneider; m. Claes Valentin, Oct. 1, 1988 (div. Dec. 1996); 1 child, Rebecca Sofie. MA in Art History, U. Bonn, Germany, 1989; postgrad., Georg von Holtzbrinck Sch. for Wirtschaftsjournalisten, Düsseldorf, Germany, 1989-91. Asst. Nihon Keizai Shimbun, Bonn, 1986-89; trainee Verlagsgruppe Handelsblatt, Düsseldorf, 1989-91; editor Handelsblatt, Düsseldorf, 1991-92; freelance journalist, art market cons., 1992—. Contbr. articles to profl. publs. Avocations: sailing, tennis, golf. Home and Office: PO Box 1344, D-73243 Wernau B-W, Germany

VALENTIN, JACK (KNUT JAKOB VALENTIN), nuclear energy researcher; b. Solna, Sweden, Dec. 7, 1944; s. I. F. Valter and Märta (Falk) V.; m. U. Katharina Lindström, Apr. 12, 1969 (div. Apr. 1981); m. G. M. Cecilia Levan Torudd, Mar. 28, 1985. BS in Biology, U. Stockholm, 1967, MS, 1968, PhD in Genetics, 1973. Asst. prof. dept. genetics U. Stockholm, 1971-72; assoc. prof. State Inst. Blood Group Serology, Stockholm, 1974-75; acting full prof. dept. genetics U. Göteborg, Sweden, 1976-77, assoc. prof. dept. genetics, 1978-83; head dept. gen. supervision Swedish Radiation Protection Inst., Stockholm, 1983-89, head dept. nuclear energy supervision, 1989-97; sec. Internat. Commn. on Radiation Protection, Stockholm, 1997—; com. mem. Internat. Commn. on Radiol. Protection, 1989-93, 93-97. Author: A Book about Radiation, 1987, others; translator: Watson, the Double Helix, 1968, others; author, compère TV series on genetics, 1980-81. Avocations: tinkering with old cars and airplanes. Office: Internat Commn Radiation Protection, S-17116 Stockholm Sweden

VALENTINE, ANDREW DOMINIC, English language consultant; b. London, July 8, 1956; s. Charles Vladimir and Joanna Wincott Valentine; m. Yasuko Ono, Oct. 7, 1994. BA with honours, Leicester (Eng.) Poly., 1978; MA, U. Western Cape, Cape Town, South Africa, 1991. Postgrad. cert. edn.; cert. to teach Eng. as fgn. lang.; tchg. credential, Calif. Tchr. history various high schs., L.A., 1981-86; English lang. cons. Beppu (Japan) U., 1986-87, Han Nam U., Taejon, Republic of Korea, 1993, Mitsu Chems., Iwakuni, Japan, 1994—. Author: Modern Historical Method, 1996. Avocations: cycling, reading history. Office: Mitsui Chem, Iwakuni-Ohtake 6-1-2, Waki, Yamaguchi ken 740, Japan

VALENTINE, BRIAN HARVEY, obstetric and gynecological surgeon; b. Isleworth, London, Feb. 23, 1942; s. Leslie Richard and Constance Clare Maud (Harvey) V.; m. Oili Margareta Karlsson, Dec. 10, 1966 (div. Feb. 1980); 1 child, Anna Katrina; m. Barbara Pauline Johnston, May 15, 1980; children: Richard, John. MBBS, Guys Hosp., London, 1966; Diploma in Ob-Gyn., Royal London Coll., 1973. Accredited Royal Coll. Ob/Gyn. Commd. 2nd Lt. Royal Army Med. Corp., 1964; advanced through ranks to Major, 1964-73; sr. obstetric house officer Louise Margaret Mil. Maternity Hosp., Aldershot, Eng., 1972-73; sr. gynecol. house officer Westminister Hosp., London, 1973-74; registrar Nottingham (Eng.) City Hosp., 1974-76; sr. registrar Nottingham City & Womens Hosp., 1976-81; cons. Eastbourne (Eng.) Dist. Gen. Hosp., 1981—. Founder Eastbourne Obstetrics and Gynecol. Ladies Laser Equipment Funds, East Sussex, 1982—; chmn. Assisted Conception Unit Com. Esperance Hosp., Gastbourne, Eng., 1991—. Major Active Res. Officers. Recipient Sir Ernest Finch Meml. prize Trent Regional Health Authority, 1977, Harold Malkin prize Royal Coll. Obstetricians; Kitchner Found. scholar, 1962-66. Fellow Royal Coll. Surgeons of Edinburgh, Royal Coll. Ob/Gyn.; mem. Brit. Soc. Colposcopy and Cervical Pathology, British Gynecol. Cancer Soc., Hosp. Cons. and Specialist Assn. (coun. 1986-93). Mem. Ch. of Eng. Avocations: swimming, gardening, antletics, golfing. Home: The Paddock, E Sussex Westham BN24 5LJ, England Office: Kent Lodge Clinic, 6 Trinity Trees, E Sussex Eastbourne BN21 3LD, England also: Eastbourne Dist Gen Hosp, Kings Dr, Eastbourne East Sussex BN22 2ND, U.K.

VALENTINE, GENE C., securities dealer; b. Washington, Pa., June 19, 1950; s. John N. and Jane S. Valentine. BS in Psychology, Bethany Coll., 1972; student, U. Vienna, Austria, 1971-72. Commd. ensign USN, 1972, advanced through grades to lt., 1987, hon. discharged, 1978; owner Horizon Realty, San Francisco, 1978-82; dir. land acquisitions Windfarms Ltd. subs. Chevron, U.S.A., San Francisco, 1980-82; v.p. mktg. Christopher Weil & Co., Sherman Oaks, Calif., 1982-85; chmn., CEO Pacific Asset Group Inc. (name now Fin. West Group, Inc.), Westlake Village, Calif., 1985—; bd. dirs. Fin. West Group, Inc., Paradox Holdings, Kennsington Holdings; founder, chmn., dir. Second Byte Found. Bd. trustees Bethany Coll., W.Va., 1998—; mem. Rep. Party, L.A. Mem. NASD, Internat. Assn. Fin. Planning (bd. dirs. L.A. chpt. 1982-87). Episcopalian. Avocations: equestrian, sailing, tennis, golf, running. Fax: 805-495-9935. E-mail: fw6inc@aol.com. Office: Fin West Group Inc Branch # 200 2663 Townsgate Rd Westlake Village CA 91361-2702

VALENTINE, MICHAEL ROBERT, banker, director; b. Cobham, Surrey, Eng., Jan. 16, 1928; s. Alfred Buyers and Violet Elise (Chegwidden) V.; m. Shirley Josephine Hall, Mar. 16, 1957; children: Josephine, Helen, James. MA, Corpus Christi Coll., Cambridge, Eng., 1949. Sr. mgr. Coopers & Lybrand, London, 1951-60; vice chmn. SG Warburg & Co., Ltd., London, 1960-88, cons., 1988-99, dir.; chmn. Croda Internat. plc, 1983-99; chmn. BNY Trust Co., Ltd. Lt. Royal Corps Signals, 1949-51. Anglican. Avocations: opera, vintage cars.

VALENTINE-THON, ELIZABETH ANNE, biologist; b. Worcester, Mass., Nov. 11, 1948; d. Lillian Elizabeth (Aalto) Valentine; divorced; 1 child, Michael. BA, Anna Maria Coll., 1971; MEd, Boston U., Heidelberg, Germany, 1974; MS, U. Wis., 1976; PhD, U. Essen, Germany, 1985. Lab technician Mason Rsch. Inst., Worcester, 1968-72, German Cancer Rsch. Ctr., Heidelberg, 1972-74; rsch. scientist Inst. Human Genetics, Essen, 1977-86, State Hygiene Inst., Bremen, Germany, 1987-90; head dept. molecular diagnostics Schiwara Practice Lab. Medicine, Bremen, 1990—; lectr. U. Bremen, 1988-90, Sch. Med. Tech., Bremen, 1990—; DAAD commn. to teach summer sch. for PCR and infectious diseases Makerere U., Kampala, Uganda, 1994. Translator from German to English, The HLA System, 1991; contbr. articles to profl. jours. Rsch. grantee German Nat. Rsch. Agy., Toenjes-Vagt-Agy. Mem. Am. Soc. Microbiology, German Soc. Virology, Internat. Com. of Jackson Lab., European Soc. for Clin. Virology, Alpha Mu Gamma, Delta Epsilon Sigma. Roman Catholic. Avocation: tennis. Home: Beim Kronskamp 12, D-28355 Bremen Germany Office: Schiwara Practice Lab Medicine, Haferwende 12, 28357 Bremen Germany

VALENTINI, GABRIELE, rheumatology educator; b. Portici, Napoli, Italy, Apr. 24, 1950; s. Antonio and Carmela (Guarra) V.; m. Delia Ferrazzani; 1 child, Massimo. MD, U. Naples, 1975. Asst. in medicine U. Naples, 1975-81, rschr., 1981-92, assoc. prof. medicine, 1992-95, assoc. prof. rheumatology, 1995—. Contbr. articles to profl. jours. Telese grant for rheumatology rsch., 1993. Mem. Soc. of Rheumatology, Italian Soc. of Internal Medicine. Avocations: tennis, antique dealing, history of Naples. Home: Rampe Brancaccio, 80132 Naples Italy Office: Second U of Naples, Via Pansini S, 80131 Naples Italy

VALENTINI, HANS-BURKHARD, physicist, researcher; b. Breslau, Silesia, Germany (now Poland), May 30, 1935; s. Hans Gustav and Gisela Mathilde (Heckmann) V.; m. Gerburg Irmgard Hennig, Oct. 19, 1963; children: Susanne, Henriette, Hildburg. Diploma in physics, U. Leipzig, East Germany, 1959; Dr. rer. nat., U. Jena, East Germany, 1967; Dr. sc. nat., U. Greifswald, East Germany, 1986, Dr. rer. nat. habil., 1991. Sci. coworker Inst. Magneto-Hydrodynamics, Jena, 1959-69, Ctrl. Inst. Electron Physics, Jena, 1970-81; sci. coworker, group head Phys. Tech. Inst., Jena, 1982-91; group head Inst. Phys. High Tech., Jena, 1992-94, U. Greifswald, 1995-97, U. Bochum, 1997-98, Inst. Phys. High Tech, Jena, 1999—. Contbr. numerous articles to sci. pubs. including Plasma Physics, Applied Physics, others. Grantee German Sci. Found., German Fed. Ministry Edn. and Rsch. Mem. AAAS, German Phys. Assn., German Assn. Plasma Tech., Inst. Physics London (affiliate). Avocations: walking, reading, travel, gardening. Office: Inst Phys High Tech Inc, Winzerlaer Str 10, D 07702 Jena Germany

VALENTINUZZI, MAX EUGENE, bioengineering and physiology educator, researcher; b. Buenos Aires, Argentina, Feb. 24, 1932; s. Maximo and Emma L. (Mazzulli) V.; m. Nilda Pontorno, May 16, 1957; children: Debora Fabiana, Veronica Sandra. BA, Colegio Nacional Buenos Aires, 1950; Degree in Elec. Engring., U. Buenos Aires, 1951-56; PhD in Physiology and Biophysics, Baylor Coll. Medicine, Houston, 1969. Technician Casalis Srl, Buenos Aires, 1954-55; elec. engr. Transradio Internat., Buenos Aires, 1955-60; rsch. assoc. Emory U., Atlanta, 1960-62; assoc. prof. U. del Sur, Bahia Blanca, Argentina, 1963-66; asst. prof. Baylor Coll. Medicine, Houston, 1969-73; prof. U. Tucuman, Argentina, 1973—; career investigator CONICET, Tucuman, 1977—; dir. Inst. Superior Investigaciones Biologicas, Tucuman, 1981-86. Contbr. articles to profl. jours. Recipient Nightingale prize Internat. Fedn. Med. and Biol. Engring., London, 1973, Houssay prize Argentine Soc. Biology, Buenos Aires, 1981, Catalina B. de Baron prize CORDIC, Buenos Aires, 1983-84, Golden Route prize Soc. Dist. Diarios, Buenos Aires, 1984, Career Achievement award IEEE/EMBS, 1996. Fellow IEEE; mem. Am. Physiol. Soc., Bioengring. Soc. Argentina, Med. Engring. and Physics Instn. London, Acad. Nat Ingenieria, Acad. Ciencias Medicas Cordoba. Avocation: music. Office: U Tucuman, C C 28, 4107 Yerba Buena Tucuman, Argentina

VALENTOVIC, MONICA A., pharmacologist, toxicologist. BS, Mich. Technol. U., 1978; MS, U. Toledo, 1980; PhD, U. Ky., 1983. Asst. prof. Marshall U. Sch. of Medicine, Hungtington, 1984-89, assoc. prof., 1989-94, prof., 1994—. Contbr. articles to profl. jours. Mem. Soc. of Toxicology, Am. Soc. Nephrology. E-mail: valentov@marshall.edu. Office: Marshall U Sch Medicine Dept Pharmacology 1542 Spring Valley Dr Huntington WV 25704-9588

VALERO-GARCES, MARIA CARMEN, language educator, translator, researcher; b. Teruel, Spain, July 2, 1958; d. Daniel and Primitiva (Garcés) Valero; m. Enrique Rodrigo, July 27, 1986; children: Ruben, Alba. BA in English Philology, U. Zaragoza, Spain, 1982, PhD, 1990; diploma in transl., Nat. Distance Edn. U., Spain, 1995. Cert. fgn. lang. tchr. English tchr. secondary sch. Guadalajara, Spain, 1982-89; assoc. tchr. U. Alcala, Madrid, 1990-91, asst. tchr., 1992-96, assoc. prof., 1997—; rschr. U. Alcala, Madrid, 1994-97, conf. organizer, 1994-97; translator, tchr. tng., U. Minn., Mpls., 1994-96, freelance translator, U. Minn., 1994-96. Author: Languages in Contact, 1995, Essays on Literary Translation, 1995, (course book on tech. texts) English-Spanish, 1997; editor procs., essays on 1st, 2d, 3d transl. confs., 1995, 96, 98. Fellow Ministry Edn., Madrid, 1989, U. Alcala, Madrid, 1995, 97. Mem. Spanish Assn. Applied Linguistics, Spanish Assn. Anglo-Am. Studies, Translator's Cir./Hermes Seville (Spain). Avocations: reading, translating, biking, outdoor activities. Home: Humanes de Mohernando 17, 19002 Guadalajara Spain Office: U Alcalá, Col San Jose de Caracciolos, 28801 Alcalá de Henares Spain

VALETTE, JEAN PAUL, writer; b. Paris, Oct. 21, 1937; s. Jean and Monique (Lavie) V.; m. Rebecca M. Valette, Aug. 6, 1959; children: Jean-Michel, Nathalie, Pierre. Baccalaureat, U. Poitiers, France, 1954; Diplome, Hautes Etudes Commls. de Paris, 1959; PhD, U. Colo., 1962. Acct. Arthur Andersen, 1964-66; rsch. economist Charles River Assocs., 1966-69. Author: Lisons, 1968, The Role of Transportation in Regional Economic Development, 1971, France, A Cultural Review Grammar, 1973, C'est comme ca, 1978, 86, Spanish for Mastery, 1980, 84, 88, 96, French for Mastery, 1975, 81, 86, 89, 90, Contacts: langue et culture francaises, 1976, 82, 85, 89, 94, 97, 2001, French for Fluency, 1985, Rencontres, 1985, Situaciones, 1988, 94, Discovering French, 1993, 94, 95, 97, 2000, Discovering French Interactive, 1994, A votre tour, 1995, Ventanas, 1998, Europak, 2000, Weaving the Dance, Navajo Yeibicei Textiles (1910-1950), 2000. Decorated Palmes Académiques (France). Mem. Am. Assn. Tchrs. French, Am. Coun. on Tchg. of Langs. Address: 16 Mount Alvernia Rd Chestnut Hill MA 02467-1019

VALIAVEETIL, GEORGE JOHN, psychiatrist; b. Mayvelloor, Kerala, India, Mar. 6, 1934; s. John Chacko and Mariamma (Kollanparambil) V.; m. Ammu George Mathiyazath, May 17, 1961; children: Likha, Paul George,

Lisha. Degree, St. Berchman's Coll., Kerala, India, 1952; B Medicine B Surgery, Med. Coll., Trivandrum, India, 1957, MD in Gen. Medicine, 1967. Med. officer Health Svcs., Kerala, 1960-75, civil surgeon, 1975-81, dist. med. officer, 1984-85; physician Dept. Health, Republic of Zambia, 1981-84; cons. physician various pvt. hosps., Kerala, 1985—. Mem. Indian Med. Assn. (pres. Pathanamthitta dist. bf. 1978-79). Home: 308/X Valiaveetil House, Pathanamthitta 689645, India Office: St Andrews Mission Hosp, Puthencavu, Chengannur Kerala 689123, India

VALIČ, FEDOR RUDOLF, environmental, occupational health educator; b. Zagreb, Croatia, June 26, 1923; s. Rudolf and Elza (Schultz) V.; m. Katarina Martinčič, 1952; 1 child, Darja. BSc in Chem. Engring., U. Zagreb, 1950, PhD, 1955. Chief unit Inst. Med. Rsch., Zagreb, 1951-56; adviser WHO, Alexandria, Egypt, 1956-60, 78-81, Hdqrs. WHO, Geneva, 1981-83; prof., dept. chief Andrija Stampar Sch. Pub. Health, Zagreb, 1961-93, asst. dean, dean, 1964-78; prof. Faculty Medicine, Zagreb, 1961-93; vice-rector U. Zagreb, 1988-93, prof. emeritus, 1994; mem. occupl. health expert panel WHO, 1984—. Contbr. more than 270 articles to environ./occupl. health profl. jours.; editor in field. V.p. Internat. Orgn. Occupl. Health, 1972-78; chmn. Internat. Com. Indsl. Hygiene, 1972-82; pres. Croatian Univ. Sports Fedn., Zagreb, 1992-96, Croatian Air Pollution Prevention Assn., Zagreb, 1994—. Recipient Life Achievement award Republic Croatia, 1992. Mem. Croatian Acad. Arts & Scis. (corr.), Croatian Acad. Med. Scis. (corr.), Egyptian Pub. Health Assn. (hon.), Occupl. Health Soc. Argentina (hon.). Avocations: tennis, skiing, swimming, mountaineering. Home: Savska 3, 10000 Zagreb Croatia Office: Andrija Stampar Sch, Rockefellerova 4, 10000 Zagreb Croatia

VALK, ROBERT EARL, corporate executive; b. Muskegon, Mich., Aug. 21, 1914; s. Allen and Lulu (Schuler) V.; m. Ann Parker, August 9, 1941 (div. July 1959); children: James A., Sara C.; m. Alice Melick, Dec. 29, 1960; children: Marie, Susan. B.S. in Mech. Engring, U. Mich., 1938. With Nat. Supply Co., 1938-55; plant mgr. Nat. Supply Co., Houston, 1945-48; works mgr. Nat. Supply Co., Toledo, Houston and Gainesville, Tex., 1949-55; asst. v.p. prodn. Electric Auto-Lite Co., Toledo, 1956, v.p., group exec. gen. products, 1956-60; gen. mgr. mfg. automotive div. Essex Internat., Inc., 1960-66, v.p. corp., gen. mgr. automotive div., 1966-74; pres. ITT Automotive Elec. Products Div., 1974-80; v.p. ITT N.Am. Automotive Ops. Worldwide, 1980-86; chmn. Chamberlin, Davis, Rutan & Valk, 1986—; trustee Henry Ford Health Care Sys., Detroit. Bd. dirs. Ecumenical Theological Ctr. Mem. Am. Soc. Naval Engrs., Soc. Automotive Engrs., Am. Ordnance Assn., Am. Mgmt. Assn., Air Force Assn., Am. Mfrs. Assn., Wire Assn., Nat. Elec. Mfrs. Assn., Engring. Soc. Detroit. Republican. Episcopalian. Clubs: Country (Detroit), Renaissance Club, Yondotega, Economics (Detroit); Grosse Pointe, Bay View Yacht; Little Harbor (Harbor Springs, Mich., Question Club. Home: 80 Renaud Rd Grosse Pointe MI 48236-1742 Office: 21 Kercheval Ave Ste 270 Grosse Pointe MI 48236-3633

VALKI, LASZLO, international lawyer, law educator; b. Budapest, July 1, 1941; s. Laszlo Valki and Jolan Arany; m. Katalin Gönczöl, Oct. 21, 1967. Degree in law, Eotvos U., Budapest, 1964, PhD in Legal Scis., 1975. Asst. prof. dept. internat. law Eotvos U., 1964-68, assoc. prof., 1968-85, prof., 1985—, dept. head, 1981—; dir. Ctr. for Security Studies, Budapest, 1982-98, NATO Info. and Rsch. Ctr., 1999—. Author: Decision Making in the Common Market, 1977, Social Nature of International Law, 1989; editor, co-author: Changing Threat Perceptions and Military Doctrines, 1992, NATO: History, Organization, Strategy, Enlargement, 1999, Kosovo: Anatomy of a Crisis, 2000. Mem. adv. com. Nemeth Govt., 1989-90, Govt. on Integration, 1996-99; sec.-gen. Hungarian Soc. Internat. Affairs, 1992—. Recipient Gold Medal of Labour Govt. of Hungary, 1987, Szent-Gyorgyi Albert award, 1993. Office: Eotvos U, Egyetem ter 1-3, 1364 Budapest Hungary

VALKO, KLARA LIVIA, pharmacist, researcher; b. Budapest, Hungary, Dec. 21, 1953; arrived in U.K., 1991; d. Bela Valko and Jolan Illes; m. Peter Janos Slegel (div. 1992); 1 child, Adam. BPharm, U. Budapest, 1977; PhD, Semmelweis U., Budapest, 1979; CSci, Hungarian Acad. Sci., 1985, DSc, 1995. Lectr. dept. pharm. chemistry Sch. Pharmacy, U. Budapest, 1977-81; rsch. assoc. Inst. Enzymology Hungarian Acad. Scis., Budapest, 1981-85, sr. rsch. assoc. Ctrl. Rsch. Inst. Chemistry, 1985-91; rsch. fellow U. London, 1991-93, hon. lectr., 1993—; rsch. sci. Glaxo Wellcome (formerly Wellcome Rsch. Lab.), Stevenage, Eng., 1993—; postdoctoral fellow Yale U., New Haven, 1984-85; cons. Wyeth-Ayerst Rsch., Princeton, N.J., 1988-90. Co-author: HPLC in Pharmaceutical Chemistry, 1999, Retention and Selectivity Studies in HPLC, 1994; contbr. articles to profl. jours. Mem. Hungarian Chem. Soc., Chromatographic Soc., N.Y. Acad. Scis. Office: Glaxo Wellcome Rsch Ctr, Dept Phys Sci, Stevenage SG1 2NY, England

VALKONEN, JARI PEKKA TAPANI, virology educator, researcher; b. Ristiina, Finland, June 17, 1964; arrived in Sweden, 1997; s. Tapani E. and Ritva A. (Haapiainen) V. MS Faculty Agr. and Forestry, U. Helsinki, 1989, D of Agr. and Forestry, 1993. Vis. scientist Rothamsted Experimental Sta., Harpenden, U.K., 1989-90, Internat. Potatoe Ctr., Lima, Peru, 1990-91; rschr. dept. crop prodn. U. Helsinki, 1991-93; rschr. Cornell U., Acad. Finland, 1993-94, rschr. U. Helsinki,, 1993-96; sr. fellow Acad. Finland-Inst. Biotech., Helsinki, 1996-97; prof. virology Swedish U. Agrl. Scis., Uppsala, Sweden, 1997—. Co-author textbook. Recipient Mikko Sillanpää award for agrl. rsch. Finnish Cultural Found., 1994. Lutheran. Avocation: music. Office: Swedish U Agrl Scis, Genetic Ctr Genetik Vagen 5, S 75007 Uppsala Sweden

VALKOVA, HANA, physical education educator, psychologist; b. Brno, Czech Republic, July 9, 1943; d. Leopold and Vlasta (Valova) Buchnickova; m. Drahomir Valek, Feb. 29, 1964; children: Stepan, Jakub. M in Phys. Edn., Palacky U., 1965, M in Russian Lang., 1966, MD in Psychology, 1977; MD in Spl. Edn., Faculty of Arts, 1991. Phys. edn. tchr. Regional Min. of Edn., Olomouc, Czech Republic, 1965-70; univ. phys. edn. tchr. Teacher's Tng. Coll., Olomouc, Czech Republic, 1970-81; univ. tchr. Palacky U., Olomouc, Czech Republic, 1997—; head dept. Palacky U., Olomouc, Czech Republic, 1975-89; key person of CR, EARAPA, Leuven, Belgium, 1993—; head dept. Adap. Phys. Activity, Palacky U. Olomouc, Czech Republic, 1995—; sports psychologist Basketball Team, Dukla, Olomouc, 1967-81. Editor: Czech Special Olympics Editorial. Vice dir. Czech Spl. Olympics, Prague, 1990—; global trainer Spl. Olympics Internat., 1997—. Mem. Czech Spl. Olympics, Czech Assn. Psychology. Avocations: sports, tourism, gardening, grandchildren.

VALKOVA, LARISA ALEXANDROVNA, physicist, researcher; b. Ivanovo, Russia, Nov. 18, 1953; d. Alexandr Mikhailovich and Klavdia Grigorjevna (Vlasova) Maiorov; m. Sergei Vladimirovich Valkov, Mar. 1, 1975; 1 child, Anton. Diploma with honors, State U. Ivanovo (Russia), 1975; PhD in Physics and Maths., Acad. Scis., Moscow, 1993; postdoc., U. Paris V, 1993-94. Sr. researcher. Tchr. h.s., Navoloki, USSR, 1975-77; engr. State U. Ivanovo, USSR, 1978-80, researcher, 1980-85; sr. researcher State U. Ivanovo, Russia, 1985-96; leading researcher State U. Ivanovo, 1997—. Contbr. articles to profl. jours. Supr. grant Russian Found. Moscow, 1996—. Postdoc. grantee Ministry Fgn. Affairs, France, 1993-94, grantee Soros Found., 1994, Russian Found. Fundamental Investigation, 1996-98, fellow U. Ancona, Italy, 1998. Mem. Russian Liquid Crystal Soc. Avocations: travel, languages, sports. Home: G Khlebnikov st 36 189, 153048 Ivanovo Russia Office: Ivanovo State U, Ermak st 39, 153025 Ivanovo Russia

VALKOVIC, VLADO, physicist, researcher; b. Draga Baška, Croatia, July 19, 1939; s. Josip and Anka (Dekanic) V.; m. Durda Lakatos, Dec. 29, 1962; children: Ozren, Marin. BA, U. Zagreb, Croatia, 1961; MSc, U. Zagreb (Yugoslavia), 1963, PhD, 1964. Rsch. assoc. Rice U., Houston, 1965-67, asst. prof. physics, 1970-71, assoc. prof., 1971-73, prof., 1977-79; head nuclear reaction lab. Inst. Ruder Bošković, Zagreb, 1968-70, head Lab. for Nuclear Microanalysis, 1980-89; head phys., chem. instrumentation lab. Internat. Atomic Energy Agy., Vienna, 1989-96; sci. advisor Institute Ruder Bošković, Zagreb, 1977—; adj. prof. Rice U., 1979—; vis. prof. Free U., Amsterdam, 1981-82. Author: Trace Elements, 1975, Nuclear Microanalysis, 1977, Trace Elements in Human Hair, 1977, Trace Elements in Petroleum, 1979, Spektroskopija Karakteristicnih X-Zraka, 1980, Analysis of Biological Materials for Trace Elements Using X-Ray Emission Spectroscopy, 1980, Trace Elements in Coal, Vol. I, II, 1983, Human Hair, Vol. I, Vol. II, 1988, Radioactivity in the Environment, 2000; mem. editorial bd. Jour. Trace and Microprobe Techniques, Physica Medica, Rome; mem. editorial adv. group CRC Press, Inc., Jour. Applied Cosmetology. R.A. Welch Found. research grantee, 1972-77; Elena Aizen de Moshinsky prof. physics Istituto de Fisica, U. Mex. Fellow Instituto Nazionale di Legnaro (guest scientist 1986-96), Am. Phys. Soc.; mem. European Phys. Soc. (adv. coms.), Soc. Mathematicians and Physicists of Croatia (sec. mgmt. bd. nuclear physicists sect. 1968), Soc. for Environ. Geochemistry and Health, N.Y. Acad. Scis., Internat. Soc. for Study of the Origin of Life. Home: Prilesje 4, 41000 Zagreb Croatia Office: Inst Rudjer Boskovic, Bijenicka C 54, Zagreb Croatia

VALKOVIC, ZVONIMIR, electrical engineer; b. Malinska, Croatia, Sept. 23, 1941; s. Josip and Katica (Fiorentin) V.; m. Radmila ZŽivkovic, June 17, 1967; children: Gordana, Tamara. BEE, U. Zagreb, 1965, MSc., 1970, D.Sc., 1975. Rsch. engr. in transformer electromagnetics Institut Rade Končar, Zagreb, Croatia, 1965-70; head rsch. & devel. group Institut Rade Končar, 1970-84, rsch. & devel. mgr., 1984-95, sr. rsch. engr., 1995—; prof. U. Zagreb. Editor Rade Končar-Str. Informacije; contbr. articles to profl. jours; patentee in field. Recipient Nat. award N. Tesla for Sci., Govt., Croatia, 1975. Mem. Internat. Conf. on Large High-Voltage Electric Systems, Croatian Assn. Engrs. Home: Tijardoviceva 2, 10000 Zagreb Croatia Office: Inst Konccar, Basstijanova BB, 10001 Zagreb Croatia

VALKOVITCH, ERNEST JAN, pathologist, medical administrator; b. Bialystok, Poland, Mar. 26, 1940; s. Jan Pavel Valkovitch and Eugenia Aleksandr Chodasevitch; m. Helena Anatol Olejnik, Oct. 11, 1989; children: Stanislaw, Aleksy. Diploma, State Med. Inst., Minsk, 1963; postgrad., Leningrad, USSR, 1968; PhD in Med. Scis., Leningrad, 1969, DMS, 1978. Pathologist Oncology Inst., Minsk, 1963-65; docent, chair pathology Pediat. Acad., Leningrad, 1976-79, prof., chair pathology, 1979-82; head of chair histology and embryology Pediat. Acad. St. Petersburg, 1982—; dean Pediat. Med. Acad., Leningrad, 1975-82. Author: General and Clinical Embriology, 1989, Foetus and Newborn's Histology, 1987; contbr. chpts. to books and articles to publs.; mem. editl. staff: (jour.) Morphology. Chmn. Polish Soc., St. Petersburg, 1992-97; mem. Presidium of Fedn. of Polish Med. Orgn. Abroad, 1987—. Capt. Army Med. Svc. Named Hon. Tchr. Higher Edn., Rusia, 1998—. Mem. St. Petersburg's Histologist and Embryologist Soc. (mem. adminstrn. 1982—). Home: 32 Marshal Kaakova St, 198332 Saint Petersburg Russia

VALLANCE, IAIN DAVID THOMAS, telecommunications executive; b. May 20, 1943; s. Edmund Thomas Vallance and Jane Wright Bell Ross Davidson; m. Elizabeth Mary McGonnigill, 1967; 2 children. Grad., Brasenose Coll., U. Oxford, U.K.; MSc, London Grad. Sch. Bus. Studies; ScD (hon.), U. Ulster, 1992; Dr. Tech. (hon.), Loughborough U. Tech., 1992; Dr. Bus. Adminstrn. (hon.), Kingston U., 1993; ScD (hon.), Napier U., 1994; Dr. Tech. (hon.), Robert Gordon U., 1994; Dr. Engring., Herriot Watt U., Edinburgh, 1995. Joined Post Office, 1966, dir. ctrl. fin., 1976-78, with telecomm. fin., 1978-79, with materials dept., 1979-81; bd. dirs. for orgn. and bus. sys. BT, London, 1981-83; mng. dir. local comm. svcs. divsn. Brit. Telecom, London, 1983-85, chief ops., 1985-86, chief exec., 1986-87, chmn., CEO, 1987—; mem. pres. com. Confedn. Brit. Industry, 1988—; mem. pres. com., adv. coun. BITC, 1988—; bd. dirs. Royal Bank of Scotland; mem. Listed Cos. Adv. Com. of London Stock Exch., 1993, European Adv. Com. of N.Y. Stock Exch., 1995. Trustee Police Found., 1989—, Monteverdi Trust; mem. pres.'s com. European Found. for Quality Mgmt., 1988; fellow London Bus. Sch., 1989; chmn. Princess Royal Trust for Carers, 1991—; liveryman of Worshipful Co. of Wheelwrights, freeman City of London. Hon. gov. Glasgow Acad., 1993. Mem. Am. C. of C. (mem. internat. adv. bd. 1991—). Avocations: hill walking, music. Office: Brit Telecom plc, 81 Newgate St, London EC1A 7AJ, England*

VALLANCE-OWEN, JOHN, medical educator; b. London, Oct. 31, 1920; s. Edwin Augustine and Julia May (Vallance) Owen; m. Renée Thornton, June 24, 1950; children: Andrew, Sarah, Catherine, Colin. MA, MD, Cambridge (Eng.) U., 1946. Med. 1st asst. to Sir Horace Evans The London Hosp., 1949-51; sr. med. registrar, med. tutor Royal Postgrad. Med. Sch. London, 1951-55, 56-58; cons. physician, lectr. medicine Royal Victoria Infirmary, Newcastle upom Tyne, England, 1958-64; cons. physician, reader medicine Royal Victoria Infirmary, 1964-66; cons. physician, prof. medicine Royal Victoria Hosp., Belfast, Northern Ireland, 1966-82; found. prof., chmn. dept. medicine Chinese U. Hong Kong, 1983-88, assoc. dean faculty medicine, 1984-88; hon. cons. medicine Hong Kong Govt. and Prince Wales Hosp., Shatin, 1984-88, Brit. Army, Hong Kong, 1985-88; vis. prof. Royal Postgrad. Med.Sch. Hammersmith Hosp., London, Imperial Coll. Sci., Tech. and Medicine, London; cons. physician London Ind. Hosp., Wellington Hosp., London, 2000; med. advisor on clin. complaints N. Thames Regional Hosp. Authority, 1989-99. Rockefeller Travel fellow Med. Rsch. Coun., 1955-56. Mem. India Inst. Diabetes Assn. Physicians Gt. Britain and Ireland, Brit. Di abetic Assn., Brit. Med. Assn., European Assn. Study Diabetes, Hong Kong Med. Assn., Internat. Soc. Internal Medicine, Med. Rsch. Soc., East India Club, United Svcs., Recreation Club (Hong Kong), Gog/Magog Golf Club. Home: 10 Spinney Dr, Great Shelford, Cambridge CB2 5LY, England Office: Regional Health Authority, Wellington Hosp, London NW8 9LE, England

VALLANCIEN, GUY, urologist, educator; b. Boulogne, France, Jan. 1, 1946; s. Bernard and Marguerite (Claudet) V.; m. Anne Vandange, July 28, 1970; children: Axelle, Olivier, Clemence. B, Lycee Janson, Paris, 1963. Resident Paris, 1973-76; chief resident La Pitie Hosp., Paris, 1979-82; urologist Porte de Choisy, Paris, 1982-94; chief urology dept. Inst. Montsouris, Paris, 1995—; prof. urology U. Paris VI, 1992. Mem. French Assn. Urology (sec. gen. 1986-92), European Assn. Urology (chmn. statutes com. 1995-96, mem. strategy planning com. 1997—), Soc. Internat. d'Urologie (treas. 1994-97), Club d'Urologie Pratique (pres. 1982—), Cercle du Bois de Boulogne. Avocations: music, sailing, skiing. Office: Institut Montsouris, 75014 Paris France

VALLARTA, JOSEFINA M., retired child neurologist; b. Manila, Philippines, June 23, 1935; came to U.S., 1966; d. Salvador Del Mundo and Josefa Gotauco; m. Leopoldo Vallarta, May 28, 1959; children: Jocelyn Devita, Vivien Temperani, Maria Vallarta, Paula Jurion. AA, U. Santo Tomas, Manila, 1953, MD magna cum laude, 1958; MSc in Neurology, McGill U., Montreal, Can., 1963. Diplomate Am. Bd. Pediatrics, Am. Bd. Psychiatry and Neurology. Resident, fellow Montreal Children's Hosp., 1959-62; fellow in neuropathology Montreal Neurol. Inst., 1962-63; child neurologist Rainier Sch., buckey, Wash., 1967-75, Children's Orthopedic Hosp., Seattle, 1967-75, Marybridge Children's Hosp., Tacoma, 1974-93, Neurology and Neurosurgery Assoc., Tacoma, 1975-90, Child Devel. and Mental Retardation Ctr., U. Wash., Seattle, 1976-89; pres. med. staff Marybridge Children's Hosp., Tacoma, 1980, med. dir. neurodevel. program, 1979-93; clin. instr., assoc. prof. pediatrics and neurology U. Wash., 1967—; ret., 1994; examiner Am. Bd. Neurology, San Diego, L.A. and Seattle, 1982, 85, 90, 91; bd. dirs. Am. Bd. Neurology; presenter in field; mem. pediat. ICU Marybridge Children's Hosp., 1976-90; mem. med. bd. Wash. Elks therapy Program, 1981-93. author: Caring for Our Special Children Early: Intervention Services, 1996; contbr. articles to med. jours. Winthrop scholar, 1957-58. Mem. Wash. State Med. Assn., Child Neurology Soc., S.W. Wash. Pediatric Soc., N.w. Pacific Soc. Neurology and Psychiatry, Soc. Devel. and Behavioral Pediatrics, Med. Soc. Pierce County (pub. sch. health com. 1981-83, ethics com. 1980-93). Avocations: travel, jazzercise, hiking, dancing, quilting. Home: 10408 SW 268th St Vashon WA 98070-8424 also: 22607 N Via De La Caballa Sun City West AZ 85375-2215

VALLCORBA, JAUME, publisher, editor, educator; b. Tarragona, Spain, Nov. 21, 1949; s. Jaume and Teresa (Plana) V. BA, Autonoma's U., Barcelona, Spain, 1974; PhD, U. Barcelona, 1983. Editor, pub. Quaderns Crema, Barcelona, 1979—; prof. U. Pompeu, Fabra, Spain, 1997—; dir. Quaderns Crema, 1979—. Author: Lectura De La Chanson De Roland, 1989, Noucentisme, Mediterraneisme: Classicisme, 1994; editor: (14 books) Critical Edition of J.V. Foix's Poetry, 1983-97, Critical Edition of J.M. Junoy's Poetry, 1984; editor, pub. El Acantilado, 1999. Mem. Plenari Del Milenari De Catalunya, Barcelona, 1988; senator Senat De Ciutadans, Barcelona, 1994, Barcelona 2004, 1997. Office: Quaderns Crema, Muntaner 462, 08006 Barcelona Spain

VALLDUVI, ENRIC, linguist; b. Reus, Catalonia, July 23, 1962; s. Enric and Maria-Rosa (Botet) V.; m. Blanca Cabre, July 14, 1995. BA, U. Barcelona, 1985; MA, U. Pa., 1987, PhD, 1990. Lectr. U. So. Calif., L.A., 1990-91; rsch. fellow U. Autonoma, Barcelona, 1991-92; rsch. assoc. U. Edinburgh, Scotland, 1993-95, U. Rovira i Virgili, Tarragona, Spain, 1995; assoc. prof. U. Pompeu Fabra, Barcelona, 1995—. Author: The Informational Component, 1992; editor: Studies in HPSG, 1996, The Tbilisi Symposium: Selected Papers, 1998; contbr. articles to profl. jours. Mem. Linguistic Soc. Am., Spanish Assn. Angloam. Studies, Internat. Soc. Linguistics. Office: U Pompeu Fabra, La Rambla 30-32, Barcelona 08002, Spain

VALLE, VICENTE, management consultant; b. Navarcles, Barcelona, Spain, May 8, 1926; came to U.S., 1944; s. Manuel and Carmen (Marti) V.; m. Maria Luisa Bencomo, Dec. 15, 1951; children: Carmen Alicia Valle Patel, Vicente Jr. SB, Harvard U., 1948. Mgr. human resources Exxon's Creole Petroleum Corp., Venezuela, 1948-61; asst. human resources mgr. internat. ops. Continental Oil Co. (Conoco), N.Y.C., 1961-64; mgr. human resources Exxon Corp. affiliates, Brazil, Argentina, 1964-72; dep. human resources mgr. Esso Inter-Am., Coral Gables, Fla., 1978-80; mem. compensation, orgn. and exec. devel. com. Exxon Corp., N.Y.C., 1978-80; corp. officer, sec. Esso Inter-Am., Inc., Rio de Janeiro and London, 1972-78; corp. officer, sec., mgr. human rels. Esso Inter-Am., Inc., Coral Gables, 1980-87; corp. officer, sec. Esso Africa, Rio de Janeiro and London, 1972-78; dir. ops. Internat. Exec. Svc. Corps, Stamford, Conn., Panama, Costa Rica, 1990-94; pres. Valle & Assocs., Inc., Longboat Key, Fla., 1994—; vol. bus. advisor, cons. to various local firms throughout L.Am., Internat. Exec. Svc. Corps, 1987-94. Republican. Roman Catholic. Home and Office: 3939 Walnut Ave Unit 338 Carmichael CA 95608-7330

VALLE-AGUILUZ, JORGE ENRIQUE, restaurateur, consultant, hotelier, businessman; b. San Pedro Sula, Cortéz, Honduras, Nov. 27, 1957; s. Jorge Augusto Valle-Castro and Virginia Marta (Aguiluz-Berlioz) De Valle. Grad. in bus. adminstrn., U. Honduras, 1984; grad. in hotel mgmt., Scuola Internat. Turistiche, Rome, 1985, Klessheim, Salzburg, Austria, 1986; Diploma in Hotel Mgmt. with merit. Owner, gen. mgr. Cafe Allegro Restaurant, Bars, Hostel, Tegucigalpa, Honduras, 1987-98, Casaerio Valuz, Hotel Campestre, Zambrano, Honduras, 1998—; cons. in field; key contact SERVAS, 1979-82. Author: (chpt. revision) Mexico and Central American Handbook, 1987—. Am. Field Svc. Internat. Intercultural Programs scholar, San Diego, 1975-76. Mem. Honduras Underwater Group, Alliance Francaise, Tegucigalpa Hash House Harriers (organizer 1984, 87-91). Mem. Liberal Party. Roman Catholic. Avocations: international relations, arts promotion, hiking, camping, travel. E-mail: caseriovaluz@hotmail.com. Home: 3A Avda 7A Calle, 2164 Colonia El Prado, Tegucigalpa Honduras

VALLÉE, PIERRE-GABRIEL, electronics executive, investment banker; b. Saint-Etienne, Loire, France, Nov. 16, 1941; s. Raymond and Solange (Broch) V.; m. Feliciana (Garayar-Escudero); 1 child, Isabelle. MS in Engring., Ecole Nat. Superieure Arts et Metiers, Paris, 1964; MBA in Econs., U. Paris, 1966. Engr. Pont-A-Mousson, Nancy, France, 1968-72; gen. counsel Socea-SFE, Rueil-Malmaison, France, 1972-74; contr. Thomson Visualisation Traitement, Paris, 1975-76; v.p. fin. and legal Co. Internat. Info., Paris, 1977-78; exec. officer Thomson-CSF, Paris, 1979-81; v.p. fin. and adminstrn. Thomson-CGR, Paris, 1983—; v.p. Gen. Electric CGR, Paris, 1988—; chmn. Opindus, 1991; CEO Innolion, Paris, 1994, Lion Expansion, Paris, 1997; gen. ptnr. ACE Mgmt. Paris, 2000. Contbr. articles to profl. jours. Mem. Nat. Acctg. Assn. Avocations: tennis, reading. Home: 29, Rue de la Cote, 92500 Rueil-Malmaison France Office: ACE Mgmt, 2 PP Rio de Janeiro, 75008 Paris France

VALLEE, RENE LOUIS, nuclear research engineer, consultant; b. Constantine, Algeria, France, May 21, 1926; s. Etienne Raoul Vallee and Julie Antoinette Vallee Geuman; m. Jeanine Anna Fabiano, Dec. 20, 1952; children: Frederique, Bernard, Frank. Grad., Supelec, Paris, 1951; expert's diploma in electronics, Orsay U., Paris, 1967. Registered profl. engr. Engr. Alsthom/Indsl. Electric Lab., Applied Electronics, Paris, 1953-58; researcher Commissariat a l'Energie Atomique - Ctr. Saclay, Paris, 1959-76; tutorial prof. French Thomson Co. Ltd., Paris, 1989—. Author: Mathematics Binary Logic, 1970, Electromagnetism, 1971; inventor Grand Unified Synergetics Theory (GUST). Recipient Silver medal Soc. D'Encouragement Pour la Recherche et L'Invention, 1974. Mem. Soc. Electriciens et Electroniciens, N.Y. Acad. Scis. Avocations: mathematics, literature, science, religious history. Achievements include application for taming nuclear power without polluting wastes, 1999. Home: 4 Allee des Copalms, 91380 Chilly-Mazarin Essonne, France

VALLÉE, ROBERT GILBERT, mathematician, educator; b. Poitiers, France, Oct. 5, 1922; s. Gustave and Marcelle (Rat) V.; m. Nicole Georges-Lévi, Nov. 26, 1969; children: Catherine, Brigitte, Geneviève. Ingénieur Diplomé, École Poly., Paris, 1946; DSc in Math., U. Paris, 1961; Dr honoris causa, U. Petrosani, Romania. Assoc. dir. Inst. Blaise Pascal, Paris, 1956-58; maître de conférences Ecole Poly., Paris, 1961-71; prof. math. U. Besançon, France, 1962-71; prof. U. Paris I, 1975-87; prof. U. Paris-Nord, Villetaneuse, 1971-87, prof. emeritus, 1987—; dir.-gen. Inst. Scis. Math. and Applied Econs., Paris, 1980-82, World Orgn. of Systems and Cybernetics, Paris, 1987—. Author: Cognition Et Système, 1995; editor-in-chief Revue Internationale De Systémique, 1986-88; contbr. articles to profl. jours. Recipient medal Coll. De Systémique of Afcet, 1987, Norbert Wiener Meml. Gold medal World Orgn. of Sys. and Cybernetics, 1990. Mem. Soc. Math. France (bd. dirs. 1964-67), Cybernetics Acad. Odobleja (v.p. 1994—), Assn. Internat. Cybernetics (bd. adminstrn. 1987—), Assn. Francaise de Biologie Théorique (bd. dirs. 1984-88), Cercle D'Etudes Cybernétiques (founder 1950), Acad. Francophone Engrs. Office: WOSC, 2 Rue de Vouillé, 75015 Paris France

VALLEGIO, GIUSEPPE EUGENIO, composer; b. Siquirres, Limón, Costa Rica, Dec. 16, 1949; s. Giuseppe Vittorio Emmanuele V. and Alizia (Salazarini) Romero; m. Ingrid Del Rosario Redondo, Jan. 2, 1971 (div. 1976). Bus. acct., Pan Am. Disfuser, N.Y.C.; bus. corrs., Internat. Sch. Latin Am., Ft. Lauderdale; grad., Biblical Sch. Emmaus, 1975. Diplomate gen. Formation. Staff mem. Costarica Com. Social Security, Puerto Limon, 1966, Costa Rica Airways, Puerto Limon, 1967; office asst. No. Railway Co., Puerto Limon, 1968-71; acct. asst. Felix Del Barco Store, Puerto Limon, 1974-76; escribient Law Power, Puerto Limon, 1976-77; seller The Provider Store, Puerto Limon, 1977; acct. Costa Rica Nat. Bank, Puerto Limon, 1977-87; translator Brown & Salazar, Puerto Limon, 1987; tchr., music Dept. Pub. Edn., Puerto Limon, 1989—; nursing asst. Com. Social Security, 1966; coin (bill) asst. Wall St. Stock Exch., 1971-74; preacher Christian Ch., Hatillo, San Jose, 1978-82; mailman Costa Rica Posts, Puerto Mohin, 1982. Author: The Redactions, 1963, The Princess, 1964, The Romanian, 1965, The Compositions, 1966, Favius, 1967. Active with Costa Rican Assn. Against Cancer, 1975, Ctr. Family Orientation, 1975, Com. Reahb. Alcohol Abuse, 1977, Costa Rician Musical Union, 1985. Fellow Nat. Inst. Ins. (hon. 1966), Am. Numismatic Assn., Costa Rician Philatelic Assn.; mem. Assn. Medicine Students (hon. 1972), Ctr. Formation and Youth Recreation, Assn. Second Level Tchrs., Young's Writers. Avocations: coin, bill, medal, post card and stamp collecting. Office: No Railway Co, PO Box 466, Puerto Limon 7300, Costa Rica

VALLEJO-MONSALVE, HERNANDO, management consultant, engineering consultant; b. Cali, Valle, Colombia, July 6, 1960; s. Carlos Alberto Vallejo-Gomez and Nohra Lucia (Vallejo) Monsalve; m. Adriana Martelo-Forero, Nov. 13, 1987; children: Daniel, Mauricio, Maria. B Degree, Calasanz, Pereira, Colombia, 1977; Civil Engr., Escuela Colombia Ingenieria, Bogota, 1984; DIC Engring., Imperial Coll., London, 1986; MS Engring. Rock Mechanics, U. London, 1986. Engring. aide Lopez Arango Ingenieros, Bogota, 1981-83, Consultoria Colombiana, Bogota, 1984; design engr. Ingetec, Bogota, 1987-88, prin. engr., 1988-91; coord. engr. Consultoria Colombiana, Bogota, 1992; cons. HIMAT/IICA, Bogota, 1992-93, subdir., 1993-94; ptnr. Ponce de Leon Assoc. Engrs., 1994-96, Odinsa SA, 1996-98, Autopistas del Cafe SA, 1998—; cons. engr. HDA Calabazas/Las Villas, Pereira, 1979-94, Soc. Colombian Engrs., Bogota, 1991, Imperial Coll., 1985-

86. Author publs. in field. Mem. Soc. Colombiana Ingenieros, Soc. Colombiana Geotecnia, Assn. Colombian Ciencias Hidricas, Internat. Soc. Rock Mechanics, Internat. Soc. Soil Mechanics and Found. Engring., Internat. Assn. Engring. Geology. Avocations: photography, lectrs., tennis, squash. Home and Office: AA 91601, Bogota ZP 0882, Colombia Office: Servicio Colombiano De, Biblioteca, C4600 Bogota Colombia

VALLES, ENRIQUE MARCELO, engineering educator; b. Bahía Blanca, Argentina, Jan. 12, 1946; s. Marcelo Victoriano Valles and Blanca Fermina Aramburu; m. Anahí Diana Lamana, June 18, 1974; children: Esteban, Ana Sofia, María Clara. Degree in chem. engring., U. Nat. del Sur, Argentina, 1971; PhD in Chem. Engring., U. Minn., 1978. Assoc. prof. U. Nacional del Sur, Bahía Blanca, Argentina, 1978-88, prof., 1989—; assoc. rschr. Nat. Rsch. Coun. Argentina, 1978-79, ind. rschr., 1980-87; prin. rschr. Nat. Rsch. Coun. Argentina, Bahía Blanca, 1987-2000, supr. rschr., 2000; vis. prof. U. Mass., Amherst, 1987-88; organizer 1st grad. program in chem. engring. in Argentina, U. Nat. del Sur, 1978-82, gen. sec. sci. and tech., 1981-83, 91-94; mem. adv. com. on chem. engring. Nat. Rsch. Coun. Argentina, 1985-86, 90-91, 92-95, 97, 99-2000; cons. Interam. Devel. Ban, World Bank, 1995—; dir. PLAPIQUI; mem. directorate Argentine Nat. Agy. Sci. and Tech., 1997-98. Contbr. articles to profl. jours.

VALLET-REGI, MARIA, chemistry educator, administrator; b. Las Palmas, Spain, Apr. 19, 1946; d. Juan Vallet de Goytisolo and Teresa Regi Rivas; m. Jose Ignacio Otamendi Pineda; children: Ignacio, Alvaro, Natalia. D in Chemistry, U. Complutense, Madrid. Prof. U. Complutense, dir. Dept. Inorganic and Biorganic Chemistry. Contbr. 300 articles in sci. jours. Fellow Inst. Magnetismo Aplicado; mem. AAAS, Royal Soc. Chemistry (mem. internat. adv. bd. Jour. Materials Chemistry), Spanish Royal Soc. Chemistry (v.p.), European Soc. Biomaterials, Am. Chem. Soc., Soc. for Biomaterials. Office: Univ Complutense, Dept Inorganic Chem, 28040 Madrid Spain

VALLIANT, JAMES STEVENS, lawyer; b. Glendale, Calif., Sept. 29, 1963; s. William Warren and Carol Dee (Heath) V.; m. Holly Lynne White. BA, NYU, 1984; JD, U. San Diego, 1989. Bar: Calif. 1989. Law instr. U. San Diego, 1988-89; dep. dist. atty. Dist. Atty.'s Office, San Diego, 1989—; host talk show WJM Prodns., Hollywood, Calif., 1996. Contbr. articles in objectivism and early Christianity. Recipient Citation of Appreciation MADD, 1993. Office: Dist Attys Office 330 W Broadway San Diego CA 92101-3825

VALLITTU, PEKKA KALEVI, dentist, researcher; b. Mikkeli, Finland, May 11, 1965; s. Seppo and Sinikka Mirja (Kärkkäinen) V.; m. Anna-Maija Kaislamäki, June 27, 1992. DDS, PhD, U. Kuopio, Finland, 1994; docent in prosthodontic material sci., U. Turku, Finland, 1995. Cert. dental technician. Lectr. Inst. Dental Tech., Kuopio, 1989-93; acting lectr. U. Kuopio, 1992, rsch. worker, 1993, lectr., 1994-96; vis. scientist Scandinavian Inst. Dental Meterials, Haslum, Norway, 1995—; pvt. practice, Kuopio, 1995-97—; asst. prof. U. Turku (Finland) Inst. Dentistry; reviewer Am. Jour. Orthodontics and Dentofacial Orthopaedics, 1996—, Jour. Prosthodontics, 1996—, Internat. Jour. Prosthodontics, 1997—, Acta Odontology Scandinavia, 2000—. Reviewer Finnish Dental Jour., 1995—, asst. editor in prosthodontics, 1995—; contbr. articles to profl. jours.; inventor in field. Mem. ADA, Finnish Dental Soc. (responsible for continuing edn. of prosthodontics 1995—), Internat. Assn. Student Clinicians, European Prosthodontic Assn., Internat. Assn. for Dental Rsch., Am. Acad. Dental Materials, Scandinavian Soc. for Prosthetic Dentistry, Internat. coll. Prosthodontists. Avocations: model aircrafts, photography. Office: U Turku Inst Dentistry, Lemminkaisenkatu 2, FIN20520 Turku Finland

VALLOTTON, MICHEL BERNARD, physician, endocrinologist, educator; b. Lausanne, Switzerland, Mar. 4, 1933; s. Maxime and Jeanne-Marie (Estoppey) V.; m. Marie-Claude Delachaux; children: Olivier, Nicolas, Dominique. MD, U. Lausanne, 1961. Cert. specialist in endocrinology. Intern, resident Univ. Hosp., Geneva-Zurich, Switzerland, 1958-62; rsch. fellow Inst. of Biochemistry, Zurich, 1962-6; clin. rsch. fellow Mass. Gen. Hosp./Harvard Med. Sch., Boston, 1964-67; chief Lab. for Clin. Investigation and divsn. endocrinology Univ. Hosp., Geneva, 1968-98, asst. prof., 1972-74, prof., 1974—, hon. prof. medicine, 1998—; cons. endocrinology Univ. Hosp., Geneva, 1970-98, acting chief divsn. endocrinology and diabetes, 1994-98; cons. Geriatric Hosp., Geneva, 1980-98; mem. sci. bd. Found. du Prix Marcel Benoist, Found. Carlos et Elsie de Reuter pour la Rechercher Médicale, Found. Prof. Dr. Med. Max Cloëtta, Krebsstiftung, Zürich, Appeal Ct. Internat. Orgn. for the Control Medicaments Switzerland. V.p. Found. Félix Vallotton; coun. mem. Found. du Grand Theatre Geneva. Recipient Bizot prize Faculty of Medicine, U. Geneva, 1974; Sandoz Found. fellow, 1966-67, NIH fellow, 1966-67. Fellow Royal Coll. Physicians; mem. Am. Endocrine Soc., Am. Soc. Hypertension, Royal Acad. Medicine Belgium, Med. Soc. Geneva, Swiss Soc. Biochemistry (Friedrich-Miescher prize 1972), Swiss Soc. Endocrinology (pres. 1973-75), Swiss Assn. against Arterial Hypertension (pres. 1989-90), Internat. Soc. Hypertension, Swiss Acad. Med. Scis. (pres. ctrl. ethics com. 1999). Avocations: literature and bibliophily, art galleries, mountain climbing. E-mail: michel.b.vallotton@hcuge.ch. Office: Univ Hosp, Div Endocrinology/Diabetol, CH-1211 Geneva Switzerland

VALLURUPALLI, SUBRAHMANYESWARA RAO, physician; b. Machilipatnam, India, Aug. 10, 1945; s. Veeraraghava Rao and Bhaskaramma (Yalamanchi) V.; m. Lakshmi Cherukuri, Mar. 15, 1968; children: Sunanda, Suneela, Srikanth. MBBS, Rangaraya Med. Coll., Kakinada, India, 1968. Cons. physician Srikaroth Nursing Home, Gudiwada, India, 1979-99. Mem. Indian Med. Assn., Lions. Avocations: stamp collecting, photography. Home and office: 1/19 Pamarru Rd, Gudiwada 521301, India

VALMAS, ANNE, library director; b. Estonia, Valga, Oct. 28, 1941; d. Herbert and Aini (Suudar) Suuder; m. Evraim Valmas, Oct. 29, 1966 (dec. Dec. 1974); children: Anu, Leho. MA, Tartu U., 1965. Head Keila City Libr., 1965-66; libr., head of dept. Libr. of Tallinn Tech. U., 1966-79; head of dept., dep. dir. Estonian Nat. Libr., 1979-89; head of dept. Estonian Acad. Libr., Tallinn, 1989-97, dir., 1998—. Contbr. 100 articles to profl. jours.; author 14 books; editl. bd. Jour. Raamatukogu, 1990—. Mem. cen. com. Estonian Book, 2000. Recipient Ann. award Cultural Fund of Estonia, 1993, Cultural Endowment of Estonia, 1997. Mem. Estonian Librs. Assn. (v.p.). Avocations: literature, music. Home: Tammsaare tee 107-89, Tallinn 12913, Estonia Office: Estonian Academic Library, Rävala Ave 10, Tallinn 15042, Estonia

VALNÍČEK, BORIS J., entrepreneur, astronomer; b. Jičín, Czech Republic, Apr. 11, 1927; s. Jan and Jekaterina (Bobrova) V.; m. Miluše Francová, June 17, 1950; children: Nadja, Igor. Degree, Charles U., Prague, Czech Republic, 1953; PhD, Acad. Scis., Prague, 1961, prof., 1980. Asst. Charles U., 1948-50; astronomer Acad. Scis., Ondrejov, Czech Republic, 1950-67, chief of dept., 1967-91; entrepreneur, dir. Optix, Ondrejov, 1991—. Author textbooks on astronomy; contbr. numerous articles to profl. and popular jours. Recipient State prize for astrophysics Govt. Rep., 1961, Award of Labor, Pres. of State, 1987. Mem. Internat. Astron. Union, Czech Astron. Soc. Avocations: hunting, history of art. Office: Optix, Na Horce 148, 25165 Ondrejov Czech Republic

VALPOTIĆ, IVO, immunologist; b. Zagreb, Croatia, June 4, 1946; s. Ivica and Helena (Brnčić) V.; m. Milka Birkić, July 3, 1976; children: Hrvoje, Gordan. BS, U. Zagreb, 1972, MSc, 1979, PhD, 1983. Rsch. fellow Tissue Typing Ctr., Zagreb, 1972-74; rschr. Inst. for Physiol. and Pathology of Animal Prodn., 1974-76; scientific adminstr. Ministry of Sci., Zagreb, 1976-83; scientific collaborator Pig-Breeding Ctr., Zagreb, 1983-87; vis. scientist Nat. Animal Disease Ctr., Ames, Iowa, 1988-89; scientific adviser Vet. Faculty, U. Zagreb, 1990—; rsch. leader Dept. Biology, Zagreb, 1991—; cooperative scientist Bayer, Leverkusen, Germany, 1996—. Assoc. editor Periodicum Biologorun, 1995—; contbr. numerous articles to profl. publs. Cochran scholarship USDA, 1987. Mem. Am. Assn. of Vet. Immunologists, Soc. for Mucosal Immunology, Croatian Immunol. Soc. Roman Catholic. Avocations: fishing, table tennis, music 60's & 70's, movies, car driving. Office: Dept Biology Vet Faculty, U Zagreb PO Box 190, 10000 Zagreb Croatia

VALSANGKAR, ANIL BHIMRAO, oceanographer, researcher; b. Valsang, Solapur, India, July 2, 1950; s. Bhimrao Narayan Valsangkar and Pushpa Bhimrao Sardeshmukh; m. Sulbha Mangesh Zarapkar, Oct. 25, 1985; children: Kshitija, Akash. BS, D.A.V. Coll., Solapur, 1972; MS, Indian Inst. Tech., Bombay, 1975, PhD, 1980. From sr. sci. asst. to scientist EI, Nat. Inst. Oceanography, Goa, India, 1980-97, scientist EII, 1997—. Mem. Am. Geophys. Union, Indian Geophys. Union. Avocations: dramatics, writing and studies, poems, trekking, social work. Fax: (0) 832-223340, 229102. E-mail: vals@csnio.ren.nic. Office: Nat Inst Oceanography, Dona Paula, Goa Goa 403004, India

VALSTAD, TOR NILS, survey engineering manager; b. Oslo, Nov. 1, 1943; s. Knut Magnus and Irene Synnøve Valstad; children from previous marriage: Anniken, Keino; 1 child, Jørgen. Student, Air Force Coll. Tech., Kristiansand, Norway, 1963-64, Coll. of Engring., Oslo, 1964-67. Land and quantity surveyor Fjellanger Widerøe, Trondheim, Oslo, 1965-86; chief surveyor Norconsult, Eldoret, Kenya, 1971-73, Bujumbura, Burundi, 1986; mgr. Aker, Oslo, 1986-91; chief survey engr. Veidekke, Oslo, 1991-93; mgr. Municipality of Oslo, 1993—; cons. Norconsult, Pt. Louis, Mauritius, 1981, Olavsfjord, Iceland, 1989, Nuuk Anlaeg, Godthåb, Greenland, 1990, Noremco, Moshi, Tanzania, 1990. Author: (jours.) Mountains of Uganda, 1973, Aerial Photography from Helicopters, 1983; prin. works include constrn. games arenas 1994 Winter Olympics; inventor three-dimensional cadastre, 1995-96. Mem. Norwegian Assn. of Cartography, Geodesy, Hydrography and Photogrammetry (map. com. 1980—), Norwegian FIG (Internat. Fedn. Surveyors) Com. (engring. survey com. 1993-2000, Spatial Info. Mgmt. 1996—), Nordic Soc. Astronomy, Norwegian Soc. Engrs., Oslo Orienteringskrets (mapping advisor 1989-2000). Avocations: maps, stamps, mountain climbing, orienteering, adventure. Home: Ulsrudveien 25, N-0690 Oslo Norway Office: Plan-og Bygningsetaten, Trondheimsveien 5, N-0560 Oslo Norway

VALTEROVA, IRENA, ecology chemist, researcher; b. Prague, Czechoslovakia, Oct. 15, 1952; d. Jaroslav Reichelt and Bedriska (Humlová) Reicheltová; m. Bohumir Valter, Oct. 22, 1977; 1 child, Marketa. MS, Charles Univ., Prague, 1977; PhD, Acad. of Sci., Prague, 1983. Study stay Charles Univ., Prague, 1977-78; postgrad. Inst. of Organic Chem. Biochem. Czech. Acad. Sci., Prague, 1979-83, researcher, 1984-90; postdoc. rsch. fellow Royal Inst. Tech., Stockholm, Sweden, 1990-92; sr. scientist Inst. Organic Chem. Biochem. Acad. Sci. Czech. Rep., Prague, 1992—; juror Internat. Students Competition Young Europeans' Environ. Rsch., 1996-97. Contbr. articles to profl. jours. Mem. Czech Chem. Soc. (com. for org. chem.), Internat. Soc. Chem. Ecol. Avocations: music, skiing, gardening. Office: Acad Sci Czech Republic, Flemingovo 2, 166 10 Prague Czech Republic

VALTERS, RAIMONDS EDUARDS, chemist, educator; b. Riga, Latvia, May 27, 1938; s. Eduards and Vilhelmina (Zabludovska) V.; m. Sarma Leimane, Sept. 8, 1962; children: Karlis, Andrejs. Candidate of Chem. Scis., Riga Poly. Inst., 1965; D of Chem. Scis., Latvian Acad. Scis., Riga, 1975. Jr. rsch. scientist Riga Poly. Inst., 1961-65, sr. rsch. scientist, 1966-76, head of rsch. group, 1976-86, chief rsch. scientist, 1986-88; prof. dept. organic chemistry Riga Tech. U., 1988—; chmn. dept. chemistry, biology and medicine Latvian Acad Scis., 1998—; lectr. in field; mem. habilitation coun. Riga Tech. U.; mem. adv. bd. Latvian Acad. Libr.; mem. emeritus professorship awards coun. Latvian Ministry Edn. Author: Ring-Chain Isomerism in Organic Chemistry, 1978 (J. Vanags award 1982), (with W. Flitsch) Ring-Chain Tautomerism, 1985. Mem. Internat. Soc. Heterocyclic Chemistry, Latvian Acad. Scis., Latvian Chem. Soc. (bd. dirs. 1990—). Avocation: tourism. Home: 46/48-43 Stabu St, LV-1011 Riga Latvia Office: Riga Tech U Dept Organic Chemistry, 14 Azenes Str, LV-1048 Riga Latvia

VALTONEN, SIMO, neurosurgeon; b. Helsinki, Finland, June 8, 1943; m. Gun Andersin, 1969; children: Anna, Maria. MD, U. Zurich, 1969; PhD, U. Helsinki, 1975. Resident dept. neurosurgery Helsinki U. Ctrl. Hosp., Helsinki, 1972-76; registrar Inst. of Neurol. Scis., Glasgow, 1976-77; sr. lectr. U. Helsinki, Finland, 1978-83; head dept. neurosurgery Turku U. Hosp., Finland, 1983—; expert reviewer for neurosurgery Finnish Med. Bd. Lt. Finnish Army, 1964-65. Mem. Scandinavian Neurosurg. Soc. (chmn. 1992-95), European Assn. of Neurosurg. Soc. (chmn. auditing com. 1995-99), Finnish Neurosurg. Soc. Home: Hippoksentie 3, 20720 Turku Finland Office: Turku U Hosp, 20520 Turku Finland

VALVERDE, LLORENC, computer science educator, researcher; b. Felanitx/Balearic Islands, Spain, Aug. 18, 1953; s. Ginés and Maria del Carmen (Garcia) V.; m. Antonia Albons, Jan. 6, 1976; 1 child, Joan Genis. Licenciado en Matematicas, U. Barcelona, 1979; PhD in Computer Sci., Poly. U. Catalunya, Barcelona, 1982. Asst. prof. Poly. U. Catalunya, 1976-82, assoc. prof., 1982-88, prof. computer sci., 1988-89; prof. computer sci. U. of the Balearic Islands, Palma de Mallorca, Spain, 1989—; head of dept. of math. and computer sci., 1995—. Editor: Uncertainty in Intelligent Systems, 1993, IMPU '92. Advanced Methods in Artificial Intelligence, 1993; contbr. articles to tech. jours. Recipient Barcelona award for rsch. in cognitive scis. and logic, 1985. Mem. IEEE, AAAI, N.Am. Assn. for Fuzzy Info. Processing, Assn. for Computing Machinery.

VAMOS, FLORENCE M., lawyer; b. N.Y.C., Apr. 9; d. Joseph Calabro and Louise Marie Horvath; m. Joseph S. Vamos. BA magna cum laude, U.Minn., 1974; JD, William Mitchell Coll. Law, St. Paul, 1978. Bar: Ind. 1978, Mich. 1982, U.S. Dist. Ct. (so. dist.) Ind. 1978, U.S. Dist. Ct. (no. dist.) Ind. 1979, U.S. Dist. Ct. (so. dist.) Mich. 1981, U.S. Dist. Ct (ea. dist.) Mich. 1982. Pvt. practice law South Bend, Ind., 1978-90, Mishawaka, Ind., 1990—. Mem. Ind. State Bar Assn., Mich. State Bar Assn., Cass County (Mich.) Bar Assn., St. Joseph County (Ind.) Bar Assn., Nat. Inst. Trial Advocacy.

VÁMOS, TIBOR, computer scientist, educator; b. Budapest, Hungary, June 1, 1926; s. Miklos and Ilona (Rausnitz) V.; 1 child, Peter; m. Maria Fekete (dec. Nov. 1985). MA, Budapest Tech. U., 1950; PhD, Hungarian Acad. Scis., 1958, DrSc, 1964; Dr. honoris causa, Tallin Tech. U., 1986. Elec. engring. leader of installation Inota (Hungary) Plant, 1950-52; head of installation Dunaujvaros (Hungary) Power Plant, 1952-54; rsch. fellow, head automation dept. Power Rsch. Inst., Budapest, 1958-64; dir. Computer and Automation Rsch. Inst. Hungarian Acad. Scis., Budapest, 1964-85, rsch. prof., chmn. bd., 1986—; Disting. vis. prof. George Mason U., Fairfax, Va., 1992-93, Disting. affil. prof., 1993—. Author: Computer Epistemology, 1991; co-author: The Handbook of Applied Expert Systems, 1997; co-editor: The Neumann Compendium, 1995; contbr. more than 270 articles to profl. jours. Recipient State prize Hungarian Govt., 1983, Chorafas prize Swiss Acads., Bern, 1994, IFAC medal, 1990, Order of the Hungurian Republic, 1996, Engrs. for peace and universal culture Grand Prize, Engrs. for Peace and Global Culture Found., Hungarian Acad. Scis. and Assn. Engring. and Natural Sci. Socs., 1996. Fellow IEEE; mem. Internat. Fedn. Automatic Control (pres. 1981-84, lifetime advisor), J. von Neumann Soc. for Computing Scis. (pres. 1975-85, hon. pres. 1986—), Austrian Computer Soc. (hon.), Austrian Soc. for Cybernetic Studies (hon.), Soc. Hongroise des Études Classiques (hon.). Achievements include research on uncertainty relations of control; pattern recognition and robot vision algorithms; pattern representation of knowledge; epistemological problems of information. Avocations: fine arts, mountaineering. Home: Karpat u 40, Budapest H-1133, Hungary Office: Hungarian Acad Sci Computer/Automation Rsch Inst, Lagymanyosi u 11, Budapest H-1111, Hungary

VÁMOS, YOURI ELEMÉR, choreographer, ballet director; b. Budapest, Hungary, Nov. 21, 1946; s. Elemer and Klara (Dubrovay) V. Dance artist diploma, Ballettschule Staatsoper, Budapest, 1967. Solo dancer State Opera, Budapest, 1967-72; first soloist Bavarian State Opera, Munich, Germany, 1972-86; guest dancer Jacob's Pillow, 1977-78; ballet dir., choreographer State Theater Dortmund, Germany, 1986-89, Opera Bonn, Germany, 1989-93, Basler Ballett, Basel, Switzerland, 1992-96; artistic dir. Ballett Deutsche Oper am Rhein, Düsseldorf, Germany, 1996—. Choreographer: (ballets) The Empress of New Foundland, 1979, Coppelia am Montmartre, 1981, Das zweite Gesicht, 1982, Lucidor, 1983, Theseus und Ariadne, 1984, Carmina Burana, 1985, Schwanensee, 1986, Undine, 1987, Der NuBknacker, 1988, Le rouge et Le Noir, 1988, Spartakus, 1989, Tschaikowsky, 1990, Spartakus, Julien Sorel, 1991, Vathek, 1991, Dornröschen die letzte Zarentochter, 1993, Der holzgeschnitzte Prinz und der wunderbare Mandarin, 1994, Ein Sommernachtstraum, 1995, Shannon Rose, 1996, Josephslegende, 1997, Romeo and Julia, Quasi una Fantasia, 1999, Der Fall Othello, 2000. Recipient Rose award Daily News, Munich, 1978, Hungarian Dance award, 1995; named Artist of Yr. Art Soc. Munich, 1980, Evening News Germany, 1993. Avocation: sailing. Office: Ballett Deutsche Oper am Rhein, Niederkasseler Kirchweg 36, D-40547 Düsseldorf Germany

VÁMOSSY, FERENC, architecture educator, art critic, editor; b. Szeged, Hungary, Oct. 30, 1930; s. Mihály and Klára Várallyay (Mihályné) V.; widowed, 1957; m. Mária Sváb, May 18, 1957; children: Ferenc, Zoltán, Mária, László, István, Erzsébet. M of Architecture, Tech. U. Budapest, Hungary, 1952, PhS, 1965; MA, Lorand Eotvos U. Sci., Budapest, 1968; D, Hungarian Acad. Scis., 1998. Architect Inst. Pub. Bldg., Budapest, 1952-57; rschr. Faculty Architecture Tech. U. Budapest, 1957-86, assoc. prof., 1986-89, prof., 1989—, vice dean, 1989-95, PhD program dir. Sci.'s Architecture, 1993—; lectr. Acad. Applied Art, Budapest, 1963-71, assoc. prof., 1971-93, prof., 1993—; lectr. in field. Author: Contemporary Architecture, 1974 (Finest Book Yr. award 1974), Theory of Architecture 1963-84, 1984 (Ybl Miklos prize 1984); chmn. editl. bd. Magyar Épitömüvészet, 1986-95; contbr. articles to profl. jours. Recipient Apáczai Csere János prize Min. Culture & Edn., 1994, Order Labour award Presdl. Coun. Hungarian People's Republic, 1985, rsch. awards Hungarian Acad. Scis., 1972, 75, Szechenyi prize, Pres. of Hungarian Republic, 1999. Mem. Assn. Hungarian Architects (bd., head com. theoretical criticism 1971-74, 78-89), Chamber & Assn. Hungarian Architects (v.p. 1991-94), Commn. History & Theory Architecture Hungarian Acad. Scis., Soc. Popularization Sci. Knowledge, mem. Hungarian Accreditation Comm., 1998—.

VAN AARTSEN, JOZIAS J., Dutch government official; b. The Hague, The Netherlands, Dec. 25, 1947. Grad., Amsterdam Free U. Supervisory dir. Govt. Computer Ctr., Dutch Govt. Printing Office; bd. mem. Expertise Ctr. for Employment Among Minorities; bd. chair Stella Youth Theatre Ctr.; editor Liberal Reveille; bd. chmn. Nat. Inst. Arts Edn.; employee Parliamentary People's Party for Freedom and Democracy, 1970-74, dir. Rsch. Orgn., 1974-79; head Office of Sec. Gen., 1979-83; Dep. Sec. Gen., 1983-85, Sec. Gen., 1985-94; coun. chmn. Bd. Sec. Gens. Ministry of Interior, 1994—; Min. Agr. and Fisheries Dutch Govt., 1994—, Min of Foreign Affairs. Office: Min Fgn Affairs, PO Box 20061, 2500 eb The Hague The Netherlands Address: PO Box 20061, Bezuidenhoutseweg 67, 2594AC The Hague The Netherlands*

VANACLOCHA, VICENTE, neurosurgeon, educator; b. Carlet, Valencia, Spain, June 12, 1958; s. Vicente and Carmen (Vanaclocha) V.; m. Nieves Saiz, Apr. 3, 1989; children: Nieves, Amaparo, Leyre. MD, Med. Sch., Valencia, 1981. Resident Hosp. Clinico, Valencia, 1983-87, Radcliffe Infirmary, Oxford, Eng., 1984; sr. resident Groote Schuur, Cape Town, South Africa, 1988-89; head divsn. neurosurgery Clinica Universitaria, Pamplona, Spain, 1989-99, Hosp. San Jaime, Torrevieja, Spain, 2000—; assoc. prof. neurosurgery U. Navarra, 1991-99. Contbr. book chpts., articles to profl. jours. Recipient prize on brain tumors San Francisco de Asis Found., 1996, 97, Spanish ENT Soc. prize, 1998, Spanish Neurosurgery Soc. prize, 1999; Brit. Coun. grantee Radcliffe Infirmary, 1984, Navarra Govt. grantee U. Frieburg, Germany, 1990, Anat. Inst. Würzburg, Germany, 1991, Red Cross Hosp., Cape Town, 1991, Echebano Found. grantee, 1991, Govt. of Navarra grantee, 1997, 98, 99. Roman Catholic. E-mail: vvanacloch@h-sanjaime.com.

VANAK, FAKHRUDDIN, marketing executive; b. Sidhpur, India, Mar. 25, 1935; s. Sk. Badruddin M. Abdulla and Fatima Jivajee; m. Mehfuza, July 4, 1940; children. MBA, Indian Inst. Mgmt., Ahmedabad, 1974. Sales asst. S. Vanak & Co., Calcutta, India, 1954-56; mgr. S. Vanak & Co., Patna, India, 1957-58, ptnr., 1958-60; ptnr. Vankos & Co., Patna, India, 1961-79, comml. CEO, 1962-73; mktg. CEO Vankos & Co., Patna, 1974-79; mng. dir. Vanjax Sales, Madras, India, 1980-87; chmn., mng. dir. Vanjax Sales, Chennai, India, 1988—. Author, pub.: Woh Jo Shaiyeri Ka Sabab Hua, 1976, Ethics of Statecraft, 1988. Mem. AIEMA, Nat. Confedn. Sm. Industries, Muslim Edn. Found., Rotary/Lions Internat. (sec. 1988, dir. 1996). Avocations: reading, writing, cricket, chess, cards. Fax: 0091 44 625772. E-mail: vanjax@vsnl.com. Office: Vanjax Sales Ltd, 343 Sidco Industrial Estate, 600 098 Chennai India

VAN AKEN, HUGO KAREL, anesthesiologist, educator; b. Mechelen, Belgium, Mar. 2, 1951; s. Albert and Elisa (Flies) Van A.; m. Grete Maria Gantenbrink; children: Pieter, Caroline, Margareta. MD, Cath. U., Leuven, Belgium, 1976, specialist in Anesthesiology, 1980; promotion, Med. Faculty U. Hosp., Münster, Germany, 1981; habilitation, U. Hosp., Münster, Germany, 1983, transfusion medicine specialist, 1986. Asst. dept. anesthesiology Cath. U., Leuven, 1976-78; asst. clinic anesthesiology and intensive care Westfälische Wilhelms U., Münster, 1979-80, sr. staff physician clinic anesthesiology and intensive care, 1980-83, pvt. tutor, 1983, dir. clinic, polyclinic for anesthesiology, intensive care, 1985—; ordinary prof. anesthesiology Cath. U., Leuven, Belgium; dir. Klinik und Poliklinik f. Anaesthesiologie/Op. Inten. Westfälische Wilhelms-Univ., Münster, 1995—. Editor: Neuro-Anesthetic Practice, 1995, Anesthesia and Analgesia; guest editor: Baillière's Clinical Anesthesiology, 1993, Anesthesia & Analgesia, 2000; editor-in-chief: Current Opinion in Anesthesiology. Fellow Royal Coll. of Anesthetists, European Acad. Anesthesiology (hon. senator, hon. sec., pres. 2000—), Polish Soc. Anesthesiology and Intensive Therapy (hon.), Assn. U. Anesthesiologists (hon., U.S.). Avocation: sailing. Office: Anesth Dept, Westfälische Wilhems U, 48129 Münster Germany

VAN ALLEN, KATRINA FRANCES (KATRINA FRANCES), painter; b. Phoenix, Feb. 18, 1933; d. Benjamin Cecile Sherrill and Magdalen Mary (Thomas) Adams; m. Ray C. Bennett II, Dec. 31, 1950 (div. 1955); m. William Allen Van Allen, Mar. 15, 1963 (dec. Mar. 1971); m. Donovan Wyatt Jacobs, Apr. 22, 1972; children: Ray Crawford Bennett III, Sherri Lou Bennett Maraney. Student, Stanford U., 1950, 51, 52, Torrance C.C., 1962, 63; MA, U. Tabriz, Iran, 1978; studied with Martin Lubner, Jerold, Burchman, John Leeper, L.A.; student, Otis Art Inst., Immaculate Heart Coll.; studied with the late Russa Graeme, 1968, 69, 70. Office mgr. H.P. Adams Constrn. Co., Yuma, Ariz., 1952-59; nurse Moss-Hathaway Med. Clin., Torrance, Calif., 1962-63; interviewer for various assns. N.Y.C., 1964-70. Solo shows include: Zella 9 Gallery, London, 1972, Hambleton Gallery, Maiden Newton, Eng., 1974, Intercontinental Gallery, Teheran, Iran, 1976, USIA Gallery, Teheran, 1977, 78, Tabriz, 1977, Mashad, 1978, Esfahan, 1978, Shiraz, 1978, Coos Art Mus., Coos Bay, Oreg., 1993; exhibited in group shows at La Cienega Gallery, L.A., 1970, 79, 80, 81, 82, Design Ctr. Gallery, Tucson, 1985, Coos Art Mus., 1992-97, 98, 99, 2000, Expressions West, 2000; represented in permanent collections at Bankers Trust Bd. Room, London, Mfrs. Hanover Bank, London, U. Iowa Med. Sch., Iowa City, Bank of Am., Leonard E. Blakesley Internat. Law Offices, Marina del Rey, Calif., and numerous pvt. collections. Bd. dirs. Inst. for Cancer and Leukemia Rsch., 1966-67, 68. Recipient Five City Tour and Honorarium, Iran Am. Soc., 1977. Mem. Nat. Women in the Arts, L.A. Art Assn., Bay Area Art Assn., Lower Umpqa Flycasters, Coos Country Club. Avocations: fly-fishing, hiking, bridge, golf, the arts. Fax: 541-888-5861. E-mail: vanallen33@yahoo.com. Home and Studio: 3693 Cape Arago Hwy Coos Bay OR 97420-9604

VAN ALLEN, PHILIP ANDREW, interactive development company executive, educator; b. Santa Monica, Calif., Jan. 15, 1958; s. William Allen and Dorothy (Wright) van A. BA in Exptl. Psychology highest honors, U. Calif., Santa Cruz, 1988. Freelance audio engr. L.A., 1975-81; programmer analyst Santa Monica Coll., 1981-83; sr. mktg. support analyst Prime Computer, Culver City, Calif., 1983-85; software developer PVA Rsch., Santa Cruz, 1985-88; sr. software engr., mgr. tech. design Philips Interactive Media, L.A., 1988-91, sr. producer, 1991-93; pres., founder Commotion New Media, Santa Monica, 1993—; prof. Interactive Media Santa Monica Coll., 1998—; tech. dir. Interval Rsch., Palo Alto, 1997-98; adj. prof. McGill U., Montreal, 1994-95; faculty Art Ctr. of Design, Pasadena, Calif., 2000—; mem. adv. bd. Acacia Launchpad, Pasadena, Calif., 1999—; cons. Acacia Rsch. Corp., Pasadena, Calif., 1999—; cons. Internet strategy. Prodr. CD-ROMs and web sites; inventor smart musical instruments; patentee on methods and systems for providing human/computer interfaces. Mem. Phi Beta Kappa. Democrat. Unitarian. Avocations: photography, bicycling, piano. Office:

Commotion New Media 12021 Wilshire Blvd # 815 Los Angeles CA 90025-1206 also: Santa Monica Coll 1900 Pico Blvd Santa Monica CA 90405-1628

VAN ALSTYNE, W. SCOTT, JR., lawyer, educator; b. East Syracuse, N.Y., Sept. 21, 1922; s. Walter Scott and Cecil Edna (Folmsbee) Van A.; m. Margaret Reed Hudson, June 23, 1949 (div.); children: Gretchen Anne, Hunter Scott; m. Marion Graham Walker, May 3, 1980. B.A., U. Buffalo, 1948; M.A., U. Wis., 1950, LL.B., 1953, S.J.D., 1954. Bar: Wis. 1953. Assoc. Shea & Hoyt, Milw., 1954-56; asst. prof. law U. Nebr., 1956-58; pvt. practice Madison, Wis., 1958-72; prof. law U. Fla., 1973-90, prof. emeritus, 1990—; lectr. law U. Wis., 1958-72; lectr. Cambridge-Warsaw Trade Program Cambridge U. (Eng.), 1976; vis. prof. law Cornell U., 1977, U. Leiden, The Netherlands, 1988, 91; spl. lectr. U. Utrecht, The Netherlands, 1991; vis. prof. Wake Forest U., 1997; spl. counsel Gov. of Wis., 1966-70; bd. dirs. non-resident divsn. State Bar Wis., 1981-96, pres., 1988-90, bd. govs. 1988-90. Prin. author: Goals and Missions of Law Schools, 1990; contbr. articles to profl. jours. Mem. Gov.'s Commn. on edn., Wis., 1969-71; cons. Wis. Commn. on Legal Edn., 1995-96. Served with AUS, 1942-45, 61-62; col. Res., ret. Decorated Legion of Merit. Mem. SR (N.Y.), Holland Soc. (N.Y.), Madison (Wis.) Club, Ft. Rensselaer (N.Y.) Club, Netherland Club (N.Y.C.), Order of Coif, Phi Beta Kappa, Omicron Delta Kappa, Phi Delta Phi. Republican. Presbyterian. Office: U Fla Holland Law Ctr Gainesville FL 32611

VAN ANDEL, TJEERD HENDRIK, earth history educator, global change researcher; b. Rotterdam, The Netherlands, Feb. 15, 1923; came to U.S., 1957, naturalized, 1962; s. Jacobus Cornelis and Olga Maria Louise (Ripke) van A.; m. Marjorie Louann Rojahn, Feb. 15, 1962 (div. Feb. 1988); m. Katharine Bridget Pretty, Feb. 12, 1988. PhD, Groningen (The Netherlands) U., 1950. Hon. prof. earth sci. Cambridge (Eng.) U., 1988—; sedimentologist Bataafse Petroleum Mij, Amsterdam, The Netherlands, 1950-53; geologist Cia Shell de Venezuela, Maracaibo, 1953-56; rsch. oceanographer Scripps Inst. Oceanography, La Jolla, Calif., 1957-68; prof. oceanography Oreg. State U., Corvallis, 1968-76; Loell prof. earth and ocean sci. Stanford (Calif.) U., 1976-88; mem. planning com. on ocean drilling, La Jolla, 1964-78; chief scientist French Am. Mid-ocean Survey, 1974-76; chief scientist Galapagos Ocean Hotspring Project, 1975-79; chmn. mgmt. bd. Godwin Inst. Quaternary Rsch., Cambridge, 1995—, also 60 other positions in nat. and internal ocean sci. mgmt. and police. Author: New Views on an Old Planet, 1965, 2d edit. 1995 (Best Scholarly Book in Phys. Scis. award 1985), Science at Sea, 1981, (with C.N. Runnels) Beyond the Acropolis—A Rural Greek Past, 1987, (with Runnels and M. Jameson) A Greek Countryside: The Southern Argolid from Prehistory to Present Day, 1995; contbr. over 200 articles and book revs. to sci. jours. Recipient Waterschoot medal Geol. Soc. Netherlands, 1984. Fellow Am. Geophys. Union, Royal Netherlands Acad. Scis., Geol. Soc. Am., Calif. Acad. Scis.; mem. Soc. Archaeol. Scis., also others. Democrat. Avocations: nature studies, gardening. Office: Cambridge U Dept Earth Scis, Downing St, Cambridge CB2 3EQ, England

VAN ANTWERPEN, FRANKLIN STUART, federal judge; b. Passaic, N.J., Oct. 23, 1941; s. Franklin John and Dorothy (Hoedemaker) Van A.; m. Kathleen Veronica O'Brien, Sept. 12, 1970; children: Joy, Franklin W., Virginia. BS in Engring. Physics, U. Maine, 1964; JD, Temple U., 1967; postgrad., Nat. Jud. Coll., 1980. Bar: Pa. 1969, U.S. Dist. Ct. (ea. dist.) Pa. 1971, U.S. Ct. Appeals (3d cir.) 1971, U.S. Supreme Ct. 1972. Corp. counsel Hazeltine, Corp., N.Y.C., 1967-70; chief counsel Northampton County Legal Aid Soc., Easton, Pa., 1970-71; assoc. Hemstreet & Smith, Easton, 1971-73; ptnr. Hemstreet & VanAntwerpen, Easton, 1973-79; judge Ct. Common Pleas of Northampton County (Pa.), 1979-87, U.S. Dist. Ct. (ea. dist.) Pa., Phila., 1987—; appointed to U.S. Sentencing Commn. Jud. Working Group, 1992-93, U.S. Jud. Conf. Com. on Defender Svcs., 1997; trial judge U.S. vs. Scarfo, 1988-89; adj. prof. Northampton County Area C.C., 1976-81; solicitor Palmer Twp., 1971-79; gen. counsel Fairview Savs. and Loan Assn., Easton, 1973-79. Contbr. article to Cardoza Law Review, 1967. Recipient Booster award Bus. Indsl. and Profl. Assn., 1979, George Palmer award Palmer Twp., 1980, Man of Yr. award, 1981, Law Enforcement Commendation medal Nat. Soc. SAR, 1990; named an Alumnus Who Has Made a Difference in the World, U. Maine, 1991. Mem. ABA (com. on jud. edn.), Fed. Bar Assn. (hon.), Pa. Bar Assn., Northampton County Bar Assn., Am. Judicature Soc., Fed. Judges Assn., Pomfret Club, Nat. Lawyers Club Washington, Union League Club, Pa. Soc. Club, Sigma Pi Sigma. Office: US Dist Ct Holmes Bldg 2nd and Ferry St Easton PA 18042

VAN APPLEDORN, E(LIZABETH) RUTH, writer; b. Holland, Mich., Dec. 19, 1918; d. John and Elizabeth (Rinck) van A. B of Music, Oberlin Coll., 1940; M of Music, Mich. State U., 1942. Prof. emeritus U. Minn., Duluth, 1946-82; lectr. in field, 1955-70; substitute Ch. organist, 1950-70. Contbr. prose poetry to religious publs. Recipient U. Svc. award, U. Minn., 1983; named Outstanding Educator of Am., 1975. Mem. Internat. Soc. Poets, Mu Phi Epsilon (life). Home: 5120 Norwood St Duluth MN 55804-1149

VAN APPLEDORN, MARY JEANNE, composer, music educator, pianist; b. Holland, Mich., Oct. 2, 1927; d. John and Elizabeth (Rinck) van A. MusB with distinction, Eastman Sch. Music, 1948, MusM, 1950, PhD in Music, 1966; postgrad., MIT, 1982. Chmn. music theory and music composition Tex. Tech. Univ., Lubbock, 1950—, chmn., founder symposium of contemporary music, 1951-82, chmn. grad. studies in music, 1970-81; Paul Whitfield Horn prof. Tex. Tech. Univ., 1989—; Mem. Ann. ASCAP Std. Panel Awards, 1980-2000. Author: Keyboard Singing and Dictation Manual, 1968; composer: Suite for Carillon, 1980 (1st prize World Carillon Fedn. 1980), Cacophony for Band (Va. Coll. Band Dirs. Nat. Assn. award 1981), Legend of Sankta Lucia, 1982, Liquid Gold for Saxophone and Tape, 1986 (Premio Ancona award 1986), Four Duos for Viola and Cello, 1987 (1st prize Tex. Composers Guild 1987), Set of Seven (N.Y.C. Ballet), 1988, Sonatine for Clarinet and Piano, Weill Recital Hall, N.Y.C., 1988, 7th World Congress Women in Music, Belgium, 1991, Concerto for Trumpet and Band, 1990, Festival a Kerkrade, Cantata: Rising Night After Night, 1990, also recorded by Vienna Modern Masters, Slovak Radio Orch. and Chorus, Bratislava, Czechoslovakia; Terrestrial Music, a double concerto for violin and piano with string orch., 1992, recorded Polish Radio Orch., 1997, Opus One CD173; Cycles of Moons and Tides for Symphonic Band, 1995, Passages (Brit. Trombone Assn. award 1996), Les Hommes vidés for unaccompanied chorus T.S. Eliot's The Hollow Men, (French trans. Pierre Leyris), Music of Enchantment for Native Am. flute, strings and percussion, 1997, Gestures for clarinet quartet, 1999, Miniatures for Trombone Quartet, 2000, Songs Without Words for 2 coloratura sopranos and piano, 2000, Meliora, fanfare for orchestra, 2000. Commd. for carillon work Skybells Crystal Cath. Carillon, 1991. Recipient Internat. Trumpet Guild Brass Trio Competition award for Trio Italiano, 1996, Rhapsody for Violin and Orch., 1996, Incantations for Oboe and Piano, 1998, Five Psalms for Trumpet, Tenor Voice and Piano, 1998, Galilean Galaxies for Flute, Bassoon and Piano, 1998, Symphony Percussion Orch., 2000; faculty rsch. grantee Tex. Tech. U ., 1982, MIT, 1982. Mem. ASCAP, Soc. Composers Inc., Internat. League Women Composers, Delta Kappa Gamma (internat. scholar 1959-60), Mu Phi Epsilon, Alpha Chi Omega, Kappa Kappa Psi, Tau Beta Sigma. Home: 1629 16th St Apt 216 Lubbock TX 79401-4703 Office: Tex Tech U PO Box 42033 Lubbock TX 79409-2033

VAN ARENDONK, JOHANNUS ANTONIUS MARIE, genetics educator, researcher; b. Nieuw Ginneken, The Netherlands, Sept. 13, 1958; m. Thea Maas. MS, Wageningen Agrl. U., The Netherlands, 1982, PhD, 1985. Asst. prof. Wagenigen Agrl. U., The Netherlands, 1985-89, assoc. prof., 1989-98, personal chair animal and breeding and genetics, 1998—. Contbr. articles to profl. jours. Office: Wageningen Agrl U, Wageningen U, PO Box 338, NL6700AH Wageningen The Netherlands

VAN ARNAM, MARK STEPHEN, manufacturing executive; b. Erie, Pa., Oct. 27, 1949; s. George Mark and Patricia Anne (Dunne) Van A.; m. Lisa O.; 1 child, Mark, Jr. Student, Geneseo State U., 1967-68, Daytona Beach Community Coll., 1971-73. EMT, Fla. Dir. ops. Emergency Med. Svcs., Daytona Beach, Fla., 1972-81; v.p. Wheeled Coach Industries, Orlando, Fla., 1982-91; pres. and CEO Am. Emergency Vehicles, Jefferson, N.C., 1991—, Am. Emergency VEH, 1991—, INTERFLEET, 1995—; exec. v.p. Halcore Group, 1998—; bd. dirs. Van Data Systems, Daytona Beach; mem. risk adv. bd. Azstar Casualty Co., Scottsdale, Ariz., 1989-92; lectr. U. Cen. Fla., 1987, Fleet Mgmt., 1989, EMS Safety, Cleve., 1991; instr. Tex. Tech U., 1991. Mem. Indsl. Devel. Bd., Orlando, 1984-86. With USN, 1967-71, Vietnam. Mem. Nat. Ambulance Mfrs. Assn. (pres. 1987-90), Am. Ambulance Assn., Calif. Ambulance Assn., Internat. Assn. Fire Chiefs (task force), Profl. Car Soc. Methodist. Avocations: golf, travel. Office: Am Emergency Vehicles One American Way Jefferson NC 28640-1059

VAN ARSDEL, THOMAS PAUL, architect, engineering consultant; b. Phila., July 7, 1923; s. William Campbell and Mabel Elizabeth V.; m. Carolyn Jean Beall; children: Thomas II, Peter Roland, Carolyn Sue, Richard. BS in Sci., Purdue U., 1943; degree in Elec. Engring., U.S. Army, 1944; JD cum laude, Bernadean U., 1983. Registered profl. engr., Ind., Ohio, Miss.; registered architect, Ohio. Chief structural engr. Fanning and Howey, Celina, Ohio, 1968-74; dir. pipeline safety divsn. Pub. Svc. Commn. State of Ind., Indpls., 1976-87; engr. Rundell-Ernstberger, Muncie, Ind., 1987-97; arch. City of Fortville, Ind., 1997; pvt. practice architect, engr. Fortville, 1997—; Patentee in field; expert witness in Mich., Ohio, Ind., 1987-99. World record holder Sr. Masters Divsn. 220# class bench press competition;. Mem. AAAS, AIA, Nat. Soc. Profl. Engrs., Bldg. Officials Code Adminstrs. Internat., Indpls. Scientific and Engring. Found. (chmn. of ops. com.), N.Y. Acad. Scis., Indpls. Scientech. Club, Scottish Rite Mason, Murat Shrine. Home and Office: PO Box 4 Fortville IN 46040-0004

VAN ASSELT, MARJOLEIN B. A., interdisciplinary researcher; b. Apeldoorn, The Netherlands, May 2, 1969; d. Ada (de Lange) van Asselt. Degree in computer sci., U. Twente, Enschede, The Netherlands, 1988, degree in engring., 1994, degree in philosophy and tech., 1994. Jr. rschr. Nat. Inst. for Pub. Health and Environment, Bilthoven, The Netherlands, 1993-96; mem. staff EAWAG, Human Ecology Group, Zurich, Switzerland, 1996-97; free-lance rschr. Amsterdam, 1997; mem. staff and dep. dir. Internat. Ctr. for Integrative Studies, Maastricht, The Netherlands, 1997—; dir. ICIS-BV. Pres. European Student Assn., 1989-90. Avocations: dance, literature, arts, hiking, cycling. E-mail: M.vanAsselt@icis.unimaas.nl. Office: Maastricht U Ctr Integrativ, Studies PO Box 616, NL6200MD Maastricht The Netherlands

VANATTA, JOHN CROTHERS, III, physiologist, physician, educator; b. Lafayette, Ind., Apr. 22, 1919; s. John Crothers and Ida Lahr (Raub) V.; m. Carol Lee Geisler, July 30, 1944; children: Lynn Ellen, Paul Richard. B.A., Ind. U., 1941, M.D., 1944. Intern Wayne County Gen. Hosp., Eloise, Mich., 1944-45, resident in internal medicine, 1946-47; fellow in physiology, pharmacology Southwestern Med. Coll., Dallas, 1947-48, fellow in exptl. and internal medicine, 1948-49; instr. physiology U. Tex. Southwestern Med. Sch., 1949-50, asst. prof., 1950-53, assoc. prof., 1953-57, prof. physiology, 1957—, Robert W. Lackey prof. physiology, 1987-89; prof. physiology So. Meth. U. Dallas, Dallas, 1969-80, Baylor Coll. Dentistry, Dallas, 1992—; mem. staff Parkland Meml. Hosp., Dallas, 1953-57, VA Hosp., Dallas, McKinney, Tex., 1956-58; cons. div. nuclear edn. tng. AEC, 1964-67. Author: Oxygen Transport, Hypoxia and Cyanosis, 1974, Fluid Balance - A Clinical Manual, 1988; contbr. articles to profl. jours. Scouter, Circle 10 council Boy Scouts Am., Dallas, 1963-78; v.p. Luth. Health Care Council N. Tex., 1975-80, pres., 1980-81. Served as lt. (j.g.) M.C., USNR, 1945-46, PTO. Mem. AMA, AAAS, Am. Physiol. Soc., Soc. Exptl. Biology and Medicine, Phi Beta Pi, Sigma Xi, Delta Tau Delta. Lutheran (councilman 1951-91, v.p. 1974-75). Home: 10416 Remington Ln Dallas TX 75229-5262

VAN BECKHOVEN, DIRK, design engineer; b. Mol, Belgium, May 2, 1954; s. Ben and Margareta (Vleugels) Van B.; m. Marleen Kahn, Dec. 29, 1978 (div. July 1988). Degree in tech. engring., Hoger Inst. der Kempen, Geel, Belgium, 1977. Asst. tech. mgr. Soc. Anonime d'Interconnection et de Telephonie, Antwerp, Belgium, 1977-78; design engr. Studiecentrum voor Kernenergie, Mol, 1978—. Avocations: skiing, mountain biking, computers. Home: Hezerpad 63, B-3920 Lommel Belgium Office: SCK, Boeretang 200, B-2400 Mol Belgium

VAN BEEK, EDWIN JACQUES RUDOLPH, radiologist, researcher; b. Rotterdam, The Netherlands, June 10, 1960; s. Adriaan and Helena Wilhelmina (Van Bree) Van B.; m. Miriam Dorothy Sneddon, Aug. 22, 1988; children: Andrew, Steven. MD, Erasmus U., Rotterdam, 1987; PhD, U. Amsterdam, The Netherlands, 1994. Sr. house officer Black Notley Hosp., Braintree, U.K., 1987, Colchester Dist. Gen. Hosp., U.K., 1987-89; resident surgery Acad. Med. Ctr., Amsterdam, 1989-90, rsch. fellow, 1990-94, registrar radiology, 1994-98; sr. clin. lectr., hon. cons. radiology U. Sheffield, Eng., 1999—; hon. lectr. U. Amsterdam, 1999—. Author: Epidemiology and Diagnosis of Pulmonary Embolism, 1994; co-author: Diagnostic Imaging in Suspected Scaphoid Fractures, 1992; co-editor: Pulmonary Embolism, 1999; contbr. numerous articles to profl. jours.; chpts. to books. Fellow Royal Coll. Radiologists; mem. Radiol. Soc. N.Am., Phi Kappa Epsilon. Avocations: sports, museums, travel. Home: 23 Hallamshire Rd, Fulwood Sheffield England Office: Royal Hallamshire Hosp, Glossop Rd Fl C Acad Radiol, Sheffield S10 2JF, England

VAN BEEK, URSULA JOLANTA, historian, researcher; b. Katowice, Silesia, Poland, July 12, 1949; d. Kazimiera Dabrowka Gidaszewska; m. Bruno Maksymilian, July 1, 1972 (div. May, 1988); 1 child, Bruno Robert; m. Johannes Theodorus Van Beek, Aug. 8, 1989. MA in History, U. Silesia, Katowice, Poland, 1976; PhD, U. South Africa, Pretoria, 1991. Jr. lectr. U. Silesia, Katowice, Poland, 1976-78; tchr. Nchanga Trust Sch., Chingola, Zambia, 1981-88; rsch. fellow U. Stellenbosch, S. Africa, 1995—; cons. Polish Embassy, Pretoria, S. Africa, 1996-98. Author: (book) Science Systems in Transition, 1997; editor: (book) South Africa and Poland in Transition , 1995; contbr. chpts to other books. Grantee Human Scis. Rsch. Coun., Pretoria, 1993, 98. Mem. Hist. Soc. of Cape Town, S. Africa Inst. of Internat. Affairs, Mensa S. Africa. Avocations: cryptic crossword puzzles, piano, classical music, cycling, walking. Home: Beach House, The Promenade, Cape Town, Hout Bay 7800, South Africa Office: U Stellenbosch Ctr Interdis Studies, Private Bag XI, Stellenbosch 7602, South Africa

VAN BELZEN, NICO, molecular cell biologist, consultant; b. Zeist, The Netherlands, Apr. 27, 1961; s. Johan and Elizabet (Van den Berg) Van B.; m. Merian Suzanne Adriana Wilhelmina Cornelia Van Broekhoven; 1 child, Ianthe Adriana Elisabeth Maria. MSc in Biology, U. Utrecht, The Netherlands, 1986, PhD in Biology, 1990. Postdoctoral staff U. Limburg, Maastricht, The Netherlands, 1990, Erasmus U., Rotterdam, The Netherlands, 1990-98, Nutrition Expertise Ctr., DMV Internat./Campina Melkunie, Veghel, The Netherlands, 1998—; cons. Polytechnic West-Brabant, Breda, The Netherlands, 1995—. Contbr. articles to profl. jours. Mem. Dutch Soc. for Cell Biology, Dutch Soc. for Microscopy, Dutch Soc. for Developmental Biology. Avocations: windsurfing, computer programming. Office: Ctr Expertise for Nutrition, PO Box 14, 6700 AA Waseningen The Netherlands

VAN BENTHEM, JOHAN FRANCISCUS ABRAHAM KAREL, philosophy, mathematics-computer science educator; b. Rijswijk, The Netherlands, June 12, 1949; came to U.S., 1991; s. Abraham K. and Janna M.G. (Eggermont) van B.; m. Alida T. Blom, July 22, 1977; children: Arthur A., Lucas L. B Physics, U. Amsterdam, The Netherlands, 1969, MPhil, 1972, MMath., 1973, PhD in Math., 1977; PhD (hon.), U. Liège, 1998. Asst. prof. dept. philosophy U. Amsterdam, 1972-77, prof. dept. math. and computer sci., 1986—; assoc. prof. U. Groningen, The Netherlands, 1977-86; prof. dept. philosophy Stanford (Calif.) U., 1991—, Bonsall prof. for disting. visitors in humanities, 1994—. Author: The Logic of Time, 1983, Modal Logic and Classical Logic, 1985, Essays in Logical Semantics, 1986, Language in Action, 1991, Exploring Logical Dynamics, 1996; editor: Handbook of Logic and Language, 1997; coord. editor Jour. Symbolic Logic, 1991-93. Recipient Spinoza award Dutch Rsch. Coun., 1997—. Mem. European Assn. for Logic, Lang. and Info. (chmn. exec. bd. 1991-95), Royal Dutch Acad. Scis., European Acad. Fax: 31 20 525 5206. E-mail: johan@wins.uva.nl. Office: Stanford U Dept Philosophy Stanford CA 94305 also: U Amsterdam Inst Logic Lan & Comp, Plantage Muidergracht 24, NL-1018 TV Amsterdam The Netherlands

VAN BEYLEN, MARCEL MAURICE, chemistry educator; b. Mechelen, Belgium, Aug. 2, 1937; s. Florent Raymond and Bertha Rosalia (Van Causbroeck) Van B.; m. Christiane Paule Riesterer, June 28, 1963; children: Filip, Erik. Candidate scis., Katholieke U., Leuven, Belgium, 1957, lic. scis., 1959, DSc, 1962; postdoctoral rsch. assoc., SUNY, Syracuse, 1963-65. Investigator Nat. Fund for Sci. Rsch. Katholieke U., Leuven, 1963-66, rsch. assoc., 1966-68, docent, 1968-72, prof., 1972-74, full prof., 1974—; vis. prof. U. Paris Nord, 1979, 85, Japanese Soc. Promotion Sci., 1979, Polish acad. Sci., 1980, 99, Soviet Acad. Sci., 1984, 89, Bulgarian Acad. Sci., 1986, Kansai U., Japan, 1995; pres. Belgian polymer rsch. contact group Belgium Sci. Foun., 1987-90; investigator various Belgium Sci. Found. projects; participant Concerted Actions programs. Co-author: Ionic Polymerization and Living Polymers, 1993; contbr. chpts. to books; author publs. on polymer chemistry in most internat. jours. on phys. and polymer chemsitry; mem. edit. bd. Makromolekulare Chemie, 1988-98. Lt. Belgian Army Res., 1962-63. Recipient Laureate Stas-Spring prize Acad. Brussels, 1962, Laureate P. Bruylants prize Katholieke U., 1963, Laureate Acad. Scis. Brussels, 1971, Japan Internat. award, Soc. Polymer Sci., 2000. Mem. Am. Chem. Soc. (mem. polymer divsn.), Royal Flemish Chemical Soc., N.Y. Acad. Scis., Groupe Francais d' etudes et d'application des Polyeres. E-mail: marcel.vanveylen@chem.kuleuven.ac.be. Home: Molenveldlaan 10, B-3010 Kessel-Lo Belgium Office: Katholieke U Lab Macromolecular and Phys Organic Chem, Dept Chem Celestijnenlaan 200 F, B-3001 Heverlee Belgium

VAN BLADEL, JEAN GEORGES, engineering educator, retired; b. Antwerp, Belgium, July 24, 1922; s. Georges Van Bladel and Alice Ciselet; m. Hjordis Pettersson, Aug. 10, 1954; children: Viveca Eric Sigrid. MSEE, Brussels U., 1947; PhD, U. Wis., 1950; PhD (hon.), U. Liege, 1987, Mons Inst. Tech., 2000, Inst. Tech. Mons, 2000. Head radar dept. Philips MBLE, Brussels, 1951-54; assoc. prof. elec. engring. Washington U., St. Louis, 1954-56; assoc. prof. elec. engring. U. Wis., Madison, 1956-60, prof. elec. engring., 1960-64; prof. elec. engring. U. Ghent, Belgium, 1964-87, dean of engring., 1976-78; prof. emeritus, retired U. Ghent, 1987—; sec. gen. Internat. Union of Radio Sci., 1979-93, hon. pres., 1999—; mem. Royal Acad. of Scis., Brussels, 1984—, pres. 1995, fgn. mem., Madrid, 1989—. Author: (books) Electromagnetic Fields, 1964, Relativity and Engineering, 1984, Singular Electromagnetic Fields and Sources, 1991; contbr. articles to profl. jours. Recipient Heinrich Hertz Gold medal IEEE, 1995, Disting. Achievement award, 1997, Internat. Montefiore prize Liege, Belgium, 1965. Mem. Univ. Club/Brussels. Roman Catholic. Home: G De Smet Laan 22, B9831 Sint Martens Latem Belgium

VAN BLERCK, MARIUS CLOETE, tax consultant; b. Langebaanweg, South Africa, Feb. 11, 1955; s. Victor George and Maria (Cloete) van B.; m. Pauline Manser Smith, Feb. 18, 1978; children: Timothy, Michelle, Claire. B in Commerce, U. Cape Town, South Africa, 1975, cert. in the theory of accountancy, 1976, B in Commerce in Taxation with honors, 1979, LLM, 1992. Chartered acct. South Africa. Tax cons. Arthur Young & Co., Cape Town, 1980-82; tax mgr. Arthur Andersen & Co., Cape Town, 1982, head tax divsn., 1983-86, tax ptnr., 1983-86; group tax cons. Anglo Am. Corp., Johannesburg, South Africa, 1986-94; sr. group tax cons. Anglo Am. Corp., Johannesburg, 1994-98; sr. v.p. tax. Anglo Am. PLC, London, 1999—; chmn. sci. com. South African Fiscal Assn., 1992—; chmn. South African Fiscal Think Tank, 1992—. Author: Mining Tax in South Africa, 1990; founding editor South African Tax Rev., 1988—, (electronic tax svc.) InfoTax, 1997; creator (Internet sites) Taxfax, 1995—, www.exexe.com, 2000—; contbr. articles to profl. jours. Advisor Com. on Mining Taxation, South Africa, 1988, Commn. of Inquiry into Taxation, South Africa, 1995—; mem. Income Tax Spl. Ct., South Africa, 1994—, Fin. and Fiscal Commn., South Africa, 1995—. Named Jr. Corp. Businessman of Yr., Afrikaans C. of C., South Africa, 1992. Mem. South African Fiscal Assn., Gauteng Soc. Chartered Accts. Avocations: drawing, painting, reading, writing. Office: Anglo Am Corp, 55 Marshall St, Johannesburg 2001, South Africa

VAN BOXEL, JOHN HENDRICUS, meteorologist, climatologist; b. Raamsdonk, The Netherlands, Dec. 23, 1955; s. Nico H. and Nellie (Oome) Van B.; m. Ruthmila S.F. Ogenia, May 26, 1989; children: Danique, Marouska. DR, Free U., Amsterdam, The Netherlands, 1986. Tchr., rschr. U. Amsterdam (The Netherlands), 1988—. Contbr. articles to profl. jours. Mem. Am. Meteorological Soc., Netherlands Soc. Meteorology. Avocations: family, volleyball, computers. Home: Pater Pirestroat 26, 1111 KR Diemen The Netherlands Office: U Amsterdam, Nieuwe Prinsengracht 130, 1018 VZ Amsterdam The Netherlands

VAN BREEDAM, ALEXIS ELIZABETH THEOPHIEL, management consultant, educator; b. Wilrijk, Antwerp, Belgium, Oct. 19, 1965; s. Jos R.M. and Stanislawa (Roszkiewicz) Van B.; m. Hilde B.W. Vanmechelen; children: Stephanie, Elise. Comml. Engr., U. Antwerp, 1988, PhD in Applied Econs., 1994; M Stats., U. Brussels, 1989. Cert. in prodn. and inventory mgmt. Asst. prof. U. Antwerp, 1989-95, prof., 1995—; prof. U. Limburg, Belgium, 1996—, U. Valenciennes, France, 1996—; dir. KPMG ORINOCO, Brussels, 1997-99; ptnr. KPMG Cons., Brussels, 1999-2000; mng. dir. Mobious Rsch. and Cons., Ghent-Antwerp, Belgium, 2000—. Contbr. articles to profl. jours. Mem. bd. univ., Antwerp, 1992-97. Recipient prize Belgian Ops. Rsch. Soc., 1988. Mem. Belgian Ops. Rsch. Soc. (Nat. Belgian Contbr. award IFORS 96 Congress). Avocations: cultural activities, basketball. Home: Groot Veld 16, 2550 Kontich Antwerp, Belgium

VAN BRUGGEN, COOSJE, artist; b. Groningen, The Netherlands, June 6, 1942; came to U.S., 1978, naturalized, 1993; f. J.A.R. Van Bruggen and A.M. Andriessen; m. Claes Oldenburg, July 22, 1977. DS in Art History, Rijks U. of Groningen, 1967; DFA (hon.), Calif. Coll. Art and Craft, 1996; DLitt (hon.), U. Teesside, Middlesbrough, Eng., 1999. Curator Stedelijk Mus., Amsterdam, The Netherlands, 1967-71; prof. Acad. Fine Arts, Enschede, The Netherlands, 1971-76; sr. critic dept. sculpture Yale U., New Haven, 1996-97; editor Catalogue Sonsbeek, 1971; mem. selection com. Documenta 7, Kassel, Germany, 1982; curator (with Dieter Koepplin) Bruce Nauman: Drawings, 1965-1986, Basel, Switzerland, 1986-88. Author: Bruce Nauman, 1989, John Baldessari, 1990, Frank O. Gehry Guggenheim Museum Bilbao, 1997, also essays; executed sculptures in Kansas City, Mo., Milan, Italy; ptnr. with Claes Oldenburg on large-scale sculptures. Mem. exec. dir.'s leadership coun. Artist's Call Against U.S. Intervention, Amnesty Internat. Recipient award for distinction in sculpture Sculpture Ctr., N.Y.C., 1994, Sculpture award Inst. Contemporary Art, Boston, 1996. E-mail: studio@oldenburgvanbruggen.com.

VAN BRUNT, EDMUND EWING, physician; b. Oakland, Calif., Apr. 28, 1926; s. Adrian W. and Kathryn Anne (Shattuck) Van B.; m. Claire Monod, Feb. 28, 1949; children: Karin, Deryk, Jahn. BA in Biophysics, U. Calif., Berkeley, 1952; MD, U. Calif., San Francisco, 1959; ScD (hon.), U. Toulouse, France, 1978. Postdoctoral fellow NIH, 1961-63; rsch. assoc. U. Calif., San Francisco, 1963-67; staff physician Kaiser Permanente Med. Ctr., San Francisco, 1964-91; dir. div. rsch. Kaiser Permanente Med. Program, Oakland, Calif., 1979-91; assoc. dir. Kaiser Found. Rsch. Inst., Oakland, 1985-91, sr. cons., 1991—; Kaiser Permanente Med. Program No. Calif. region; adj. prof. U. Calif., San Francisco, 1975-92; chmn. instnl. rev. bd. Kaiser Permanente No. Calif. region, 1986—; pres. bd. trustees French Found. Med. Rsch. and Edn., San Francisco, 1994-98. Contbr. articles to profl. books and jours. With U.S. Army, 1944-46. Fellow ACP, Am. Coll. Med. Informatics; mem. AAAS, Calif. Med. Assn., U. Calif. Emeritus Faculty Assn. Avocations: flying, photography, swimming.

VAN BULCK, HENDRIKUS EUGENIUS, accountant; b. Beek en Donk, The Netherlands, Dec. 13, 1950; came to U.S., 1972; s. Marcellus Maria and Josephina Theodora (Koelman) Van B.; m. Margaret West, Aug. 7, 1976; children: Marcel Allen, Sydney Josette. Grad., Nijenrode, The Netherlands, 1972; MBA, U. Ga., 1974, PhD in Bus. Adminstrn., 1979. CPA, S.C. Instr. U. S.C., Sumter, 1975-77; asst. prof. Clemson (S.C.) U., 1977-80; chmn. dept., assoc. prof. St. Andrew's Presbyn. Coll., Laurinburg, N.C., 1980-83; staff acct. L. Allen West, CPA, Sumter, 1983-84; ptnr. West & Van Bulck, CPAs, Sumter, 1984-88, Van Bulck & Co., Sumter, 1989—; part time instr. U. S.C., Sumter, 1983-85; cons. med. practice mgmt./bus. valuations. Contbr. articles to profl. jours. Chmn. Make-a-Wish Found., Midlands, S.C., 1983-90. Recipient Mktg. award Netherlands Ctr. of Dirs., 1972. Mem. AICPA (accredited in bus. valuation 1999), S.C. Assn. CPAs, Ga. Soc. CPAs, Physicians Viewpoint Network, Habitat for Humanity, Kiwanis (pres. Sumter chpt. 1996-97), Med. Group Mgmt. Assn., Beta Gamma Sigma. Presbyterian. Avocations: sailing, photography. Home: 234 Haynsworth PO Box 1327 Sumter SC 29151-1327 Office: Van Bulck & Co CPAs 15 Broad St Sumter SC 29150-4224

VAN BULCK, MARGARET WEST, accountant, financial planner, educator; b. Chgo., Nov. 25, 1955; d. Lee Allen and Margaret Ellen (Sauls) West; m. Hendrikus E.J.M.L. van Bulck, Aug. 7, 1976; children: Marcel Allen, Sydney Josette. BS in Mktg., U. S.C., 1978; MA in Econs., Clemson U., 1981. CPA, S.C. Econs. instr. St. Andrews Presbyn. Coll., Laurinburg, N.C., 1980-82; staff acct. L. Allen West, CPA, Sumter, S.C., 1982-84; ptnr. West & Van Bulck, CPAs, Sumter, 1984-88, Van Bulck & Co., CPA's, Sumter, 1989—; part time instr. U. S.C., Sumter, 1985-87, mem. full time faculty, 1989-92. Contbr. articles to profl. jours. Treas. Make-A-Wish Found., Sumter, 1985-87, wish granting chmn. 1987-88; edn. found. chmn. Laurinburg/Scotland County chpt. AAUW, 1981-83; treas. Friends Sumter County Library, 1986-88, Sumter Gallery of Art, 1989-91; mem. Jr. Welfare League, Sumter; Circle Bible leader, Sunday Sch. tchr., hospice vol., 1990-92; deacon First Presbyn. Ch., 1994-97; den leader pack 86 Boy Scouts of Am., 1992-95, troop com. mem., advancement chair, 1998—. Recipient Sirrine Found. award, Clemson U., 1978, 79; grantee U.S. Dept. Labor, 1979-80. Mem. AICPA, S.C. Assn. CPAs, Internat. Assn. Fin. Planning, Sumter Estate Planning Coun. (past treas.), Trian Club (treas. 1998—), Carolinian Club, Omicron Delta Epsilon. Presbyterian. Home: 234 Haynsworth St PO Box 1327 Sumter SC 29151-1327 Office: Van Bulck & Co CPAs PO Box 1327 Sumter SC 29151-1327

VAN CAILLIE-BERTRAND, MICHELINE, pediatrician, educator; b. Antwerp, Belgium, May 20, 1946; d. Fernand Bertrand and Dora Van Broeckhoven; m. Bernard Van Caillie; 1 child, Marie-Noemie. MD, U. Louvain, Belgium, 1970; PhD, Erasmus U., Rotterdam, The Netherlands, 1985. Bd. cert. pediatrician. Head pediat. gastroenterology and nutrition dept. Queen Paola Children's Hosp., Antwerp, 1981—; guest prof. dept. pharm. sci. Lab. Food Scis., U. Antwerp; founding mem. Belgian Group Pediat. Gastroenterology and Nutrition; mem. European Soc. Pediat. Gastroenterology and Nutrition Working Group on Acute Diarrhea. Mem. Med. Women Assn. Belgium (past pres.), European Soc. Pediat. Gastroenterology Hepatology and Nutrition, Soroptimist. Office: Queen Paola Children's Hosp, AZM OCMW Lindendreef 2, 2020 Antwerp Belgium

VAN CAMPEN, STEPHEN BERNARD, executive recruiter, consultant; b. East Stroudsburg, Pa., Oct. 1, 1941; s. Bernard Allen and Marion (Van Whye) Van C.; m. Ellen Baars, July 22, 1989; children: Brendon, Regan, Meghan, Taylor, Hannah. BS in Sci. and Pre-Veterinary Med., Pa. State U., 1959-64; postgrad. in indsl. rels., George Washington U. Grad. Sch, 1965-68; law student, U. Balt., 1966-68. With FDA, Balt., Washington, 1964-66; indsl. rels. officer Joseph E. Seagrams & Sons, Balt., N.Y.C., San Francisco, 1966-72; worldwide dir. exec. staffing RCA/Hertz Corp., N.Y.C., 1972-74; dir. internat. indsl. rels. Revlon Internat., N.Y.C., 1974; pres./owner/cons. Gilbert & Van Campen Exec. Search, Internat. (subs.: J.B. Gilbert Assocs., Inc., Amtrade Assocs., Internat., GVC Fin. Svcs.), N.Y.C., 1974—; owner, pres. Lillagaard Hotel Corp., Ocean Grove, N.J., 1992—; owner N.J. Profl. Meeting Planners Group, No. Shore Region Convention and Vis. Bur.; appointed to N.J. Gov.'s Commn. on Internat. Trade, 1992; Bush White House nominee to Nat. Parks Adv. Commn., Dept. Interior; chmn. internat. trade subcom. ad hoc N.J. Assembly Small Bus. Adv. Coun.; bd. dirs. N.J. SBDC, N.J. Shore Region Tourism Coun.; named to Commerce and Econ. Devel. Transition Team for Gov.-elect Christine Todd Whitman; chmn. Econ. Devel. Task Force, Warren County, N.J., 1994; participant 1st U.S.-Cuba Bus. Summit, 1998. Rep. fundraiser; active N.J. Rep. Gov.'s Club, N.J. State Fin. Com.; appointed to Congressman Zimmer's Warren County N.J. Fed. Adv. Com., Warren County Econ. Adv. Coun., N.J. Gov.'s appointee 1988— and chmn. fed. enacted Del. Water Gap Nat. Recreation Area citizens adv. com., Gov.-elect Christie Todd Whitman Transition Team-Commerce and Econ. Devel.; elected to Warren County Rep. Com.; chmn. adv. bd. Warren Presdl. Correctional Facility; chmn. Calno Cemetery Assn.; chmn. Warner County Econ. Devel. Blue Ribbon Task Force; vice chmn. bd. trustees Warren County C.C., 1983—, chmn. found. bd.; exec. bd. Tri-County Washington coun. and George Washington coun. Boy Scouts Am.; bd. dirs. N.J. Shore Regional Tourism Coun., N.Y. SBDC, N.J. Juvenile Justice Adv. Bd.; mem. 1st N.J. Trade Del. Soviet Union; mem. commerce and econ. devel. transition team Gov.-elect Christie Whitman, N.J., 1994; chmn. N.J. assembly bus. retention Com. of Task Force for Bus. Rentention, Attraction, Expansion and Internat. Trade; chmn. N.J. Gov.'s Conf. Travel and Tourism, Atlantic City, 1994; chmn. N.J. No. Shore Region CUB Allaire Airport Conv. Ctr.; pres.-elect Warren County Econ. Partnership. Recipient Medal of Honor, Ellis Island, 1994. Mem. ASTD, Am. Mgmt. Assns., Am. Coun. on Germany, U.S. C. of C., Nat. Fgn. Trade Coun., World Trade Inst., U.S.-USSR Trade and Econ. Coun., N.Y. C. of C. and Industry, N.J. C. of C., Commerce and Industry Assn. N.J., Am. C. of C.s and U.S. Bus. Couns. Abroad, Soc. Human Resource Mgmt., Nat. Assn. Corp. and Profl. Recruiters, Employment Mgmt. Assn., N.J. Hotel/Motel Assn. (bd. dirs., mem. exec. bd.), N.J. Travel Industry Assn. (bd. dirs., v.p. exec. bd.), N.Y. Pers. Mgmt. Assn., Soc. Plastics Engrs., Soc. Cosmetic Chemists, Small Bus. Adv. Coun., Ocean Grove C. of C. (vice chmn.). Republican. Methodist. Home: 37 Petersburg Rd Hackettstown NJ 07840-4903 Office: Gilbert & Van Campen Intl 420 Lexington Ave New York NY 10170-0002 also: Gilbert & Van Campen Intl Conference Ctr 99 Lake Dr Belvidere NJ 07823

VAN CAUWENBERGE, HENRI SERAPHIN, internal medicine educator; b. Liege, Belgium, May 24, 1923; s. Remi and Henriette Elisabeth (Tellings) Van C.; m. Martine Gisele Anne Ruhwiedel, Apr. 11, 1982; children: Isabelle, Philippe. MD, U. Liege. Asst. U. Liege, 1948-54; chief resident ULG, Liege, 1954-57, prof. agrégé dept. medicine, 1957-60, chief physician, 1960-63, prof. internal medicine, 1963-88, emeritus prof. medicine, 1988—, chmn. dept. medicine. Author: Water and Electrolytes, 1964, Pituitary Hormones, 1970; contbr. articles to sci. and med. jours. and revs. Mem. commn. of medicine, Belgium. Active med. res., Belgium. Decorated chevalier Legion of Honor (France), officer Ordre of Senegal, also Belgian decorations. Mem. Acad. Medicine France, Acad. Medicine Belgium, Lions. Avocation: music.

VANCE, ALASDAIR LAGHLANN ANGUS, psychiatrist, consultant, educator; b. Melbourne, Victoria, Australia, Oct. 25, 1965; s. Peter Walker Vance and Helen Bridges Webb; m. Janet Kay McGaw, Jan. 1, 1994. MD, Monash U., Melbourne, 1999; cert. accreditation in child psychiatry, Melbourne U./Monash U., 1999. Rsch. officer Mental Health Rsch. Inst. Victoria, Melbourne, 1996, rsch. fellow, 1997-98; fellow in child and adolescent psychiatry Moroondah Hosp., Melbourne, 1997, cons. psychiatrist, 1998, cons. in child and adolescent psychiatry, 1999—; lectr. Monash U., Melbourne, 1997—; dep. dir. Rsch. Maroondah Hosp., Melbourne, 1999; coord. ADMD Rsch. Program Maroondah Hosp., Melbourne, 1997—; coord. MRS study into first episode psychosis Mental Health Rsch. Inst. Victoria, Melbourne, 1997-98; dir. postgrad. child psychiatry rsch. tng. Melbourne U./Monash U., 1998—. Contbr. articles to profl. jours. Cmty. organizer TEAR, Melbourne, 1991—. Fellow Royal Australian New Zealand Coll. Psychiatrists (acad. jour. referee 1998-99). Avocations: natural philosophy, late 20th century composers, water sports, Australian poetry, gardening. Office: Ringwood East, 21 Ware Cres, 332 Melbourne Australia

VANCE, LESLIE EDWIN, multimedia technologist; b. Richland Center, Wis., Sept. 28, 1949; s. Leslie Williams Vance and Beata Ann (Harris) Elliott. BA, U. Wis., 1979, MA, 1981; PhD, Pa. State U., 1986. Announcer Sta. WRCO, Richland Center, Wis., 1966-68, Sta. WCOW, Sparta, Wis., 1968-69; news dir. Sta. WRJC, Mauston, Wis., 1969-72; photographer Richland Center, 1972-76; rsch. asst. Ctr. for Comm. Rsch., Madison, Wis., 1979-81; mgr. instrnl. support ctr. Pa. State U., State College, 1981-86; ednl. technologist Princeton (N.J.) Ctr. Edn., 1986-87; tech. architect Andersen Consulting, St. Charles, Ill., 1987—; cons. Rite Aid Corp., Camp Hill, Pa., Electronic Pub. Task Force, Motorola U., Schaumberg, Ill., U. Wis., Madison, Learning and Evaluation Assocs. Inc., State College, Pa.; exec. adv. bd., The Journal of Management Executive. Contbr. chpts. to books, articles to profl. jours.; presenter in field; producer (edu. video) The Wisconsin Sesquicentennial Coach Run; designer (courses) Object Technology Starter Kit, 1995, Spreadsheets for Educators, 1984; designer, co-designer computer programs on instrnl. devel. Mem. Acad. Mgmt., Assn. Computing Machinery, Am. Horse Publ. Avocations: carriage driving, equine photography. Home: 618 S 5th Ave # 2 Saint Charles IL 60174-2930 Office: Andersen Consulting 3755 E Main St Saint Charles IL 60174-2463

VANCE, MARY LEE, academic administrator; b. Seoul, Korea, Nov. 16, 1957; d. Irwin F. and Mae Hoeft; m. Eric J. Vance. BA, U. Wis., 1979, MA, 1983; PhD, Mich. State U., 1993. From advisor to coor. Mich. State U., East Lansing, 1984-93; coord. Holmes Scholars Holmes Group, East Lansing, 1993-94; dir. edn. student svcs. Iowa State U., Ames, 1994-97; dir. acad. support and advising svcs. George Mason U., Fairfax, Va., 1997—; adj. asst. prof. Iowa State U., 1994-97; cons. Southeastern Assn. Edn. Opportunity Program Personnel, Memphis, 1993-94. Contbr. articles to jours. Mem. strategic planning steering com. Ames Cmty. Sch. Dist., 1995-96; mem. Leadership Ames, 1995; bd. dirs. YWCA, Ames, 1996; mem. Make A Wish, 1998—. Recipient Outstanding Asian Pacific Am. Faculty/Staff awards, 1985-93, All U. Diversity Photo award, 1992, Outstanding Grad. Woman Spl. Merit award, 1992, Appreciation, Southeastern Assn. Ednl. Opportunity Program Pers., 1992, 93, 94, Office Supportive Svcs., 1993, Holmes Scholars, 1994, Holmes Group, 1994, Cert. of Achievement, Leadership Ames, 1995. Mem. Nat. Orgn. Acad. Advising Assn., Assn. Higher Edn. and Disability, Nat. Orientation Dirs. Assn., Asian Pacific Am. Women's Leadership Inst., Acad. Affairs Adminstrs. Bapt. Avocations: reading, gourmet cooking, eating, movies. Office: George Mason U MSN 2E6 4400 University Dr Fairfax VA 22030

VANCE, MICHAEL CHARLES, lawyer; b. Marshalltown, Iowa, May 31, 1951; s. Randall Scott and Irma Vance; m. Bonnie K. Becker, Jan. 1, 1995; children: Thomas Randall, Patrick Michael. BA in Polit. Sci. and Econs., U. Iowa, 1973, JD with distinction, 1976. Bar: Iowa 1976, U.S Dist. Ct. (so. dist.) Iowa 1976, U.S. Tax Ct. 1991. Sole practice Mt. Pleasant, Iowa, 1976—; atty. City of Wayland, Iowa, 1976—; instr. bus. law Iowa Wesleyan Coll., Mt. Pleasant, 1977-78; asst. county atty. Henry County, Mt. Pleasant, 1979-97, jud. magistrate, 1997—. Mem., bd. dirs. Community Mental Health of Henry, Louisa and Jefferson Counties, Mt. Pleasant, 1977-82; chairperson Henry County Dems., Mt. Pleasant, 1978-83; pres. Mt. Pleasant Sesquicentennial Assn., 1984-86, St. Alphonsus Ch. Parish Council (pres. 1983-85), Mt. Pleasant, 1985— (trustee). Mem. ABA, Iowa Bar Assn. (bd. govs. 1996—), Henry County Bar Assn. (sec.-treas. 1977-78, v.p. 1978-79, pres. 1979-80, 88-91), Iowa Trial Lawyers Assn., Iowa Conf. Bar Assn. Presidents (bd. dirs. 1979-81), Iowa Assn. Jud. Magistrates (bd. dirs. 1998—), Mt. Pleasant C. of C. (bd. dirs. 1991-93, named Citizen of Yr. 1985), Mt. Pleasant Jaycees (bd. dirs. 1978-83), Rotary, KC, Omicron Delta Kappa, Omicron Delta Epsilon. Roman Catholic. Home: 2005 Bittersweet Cir Mount Pleasant IA 52641-8301 Office: PO Box 469 101 N Jefferson St Mount Pleasant IA 52641-2039

VANCE, THOMAS RAY, engineer; b. Charleston, W.Va., Sept. 24, 1938; s. Bethel Raymond and Madolyn Elizabeth (Fisher) V.; m. Janice Lee Jordan, Dec. 23, 1958; children: Barbara Vance, Jeffrey Ross, Deborah. BSME, W.Va. U., 1960, MSTAM, 1966, PhD, 1968. Registered profl. engr., W.Va., Ohio. Devel. engr. The Babcock and Wilcox Co., Alliance, Ohio, 1960-63; staff engr. Los Alamos (N.Mex.) Scientific Lab., 1964-66; program mgr. Tech. divsn. IBM Corp., Hopewell Junction, N.Y., 1968-92; dir. W.Va. State Farm Mus., Point Pleasant, W.Va., 1994-97; prin. Vance & Assocs., Point Pleasant, 1992—; instr. coll. engring. W.Va. U., Morgantown, 1966-68; instr. evening divsn. Dutchess C.C., Poughkeepsie, N.Y., 1962-68; chmn. adv. com. Dept. Engring. Ohio State U., 1988-91; mem. Stevens Inst. of Tech., Alliance for Tech. Mgmt., Hoboken, N.J.. Contbr. articles to profl. jours. Vice chmn. Point Pleasant River Mus. Com., 1993-94; mem. Point Pleasant Hist. Dist. Com., 1993-94. Scholarship NASA. Mem. W.Va. Assn. of Profl. Engrs., Nat. Assn. of Profl. Engrs. Republican. Lutheran. Achievements include patent in repair of thin film lines. Home: 4 Main St Point Pleasant WV 25550-1026 Office: Vance and Assocs 329 Main St Point Pleasant WV 25550-1114

VANCLIEF, LYLE, federal official; b. Prince Edward County, Can.; m. Sharon Hall; children: Kurt, Vanessa. Student, Belleville Coll. Inst.; BS in Agr., U. Guelph, 1966. Mem. family-owned bus. Willowlee Farms Ltd., Prince Edward County; mem. parliament House of Commons, Prince Edward-Hastings, 1988—; parliamentary sec. to Minister of Agr. and Agri-food, 1993; mem. standing com. on Agr.; co-critic for agr., assoc. critic for pub. works, House of Commons, 1988-93; mem. Ont. Task Force Health and Safety in Agr., 1983-85; mem., chmn. several coms. for Minister of Agr.; speaker in field of agrl. econs. and politics. Past twp. councillor, chmn. planning bd. Prince Edward Hastings; mem. bd. edn. Prince Edward County, chmn. bd. dirs., chmn. salary negotiating com.; active United Ch., past chmn. bd. dirs. Rednersville Pastoral Charge. Mem. Ont. Inst. Agrologists, Agrl. Inst. of Can. Office: House of Commons, 207 Confederation Bldg, Ottawa, ON Canada K1A 0A6

VANDAME, JEAN-MARIE RICHARD, professional services company executive; b. Gien, France, Oct. 30, 1960; s. Marc and Antoinette (Dumouchel de Premare) V.; m. Chantal Geraldine de Blocquel de Croix de Wismes, Sept. 3, 1983; children: Thomas, Camille, Clemence, Alix. Degree in engring., Inst. Super. Electronique, Paris, 1982; MBA, Inst. Adminstrn. Entreprises, Paris, 1984. Product mktg. engr. Tex Instruments, Paris, 1983-84; field sales engr. Tex Instruments, Rennes, France, 1984-86; sr. mgr. Ernst & Young, Paris, 1986-92, assoc. dir., 1995-96, internat. ptnr., 1996—; pres. KnowledgeWare, Brussels, 1992-95. Home: 3725 N Magnolia Ave Chicago IL 60613 Office: CG Ernst & Young Sears Tower 233 S Wacker Dr Chicago IL 60606

VAN DAMME, ELS JEANINE, scientific researcher; b. Merchtem, Brabant, Belgium, June 10, 1964; d. Jozef A. and Irene J. (Van Buggenhout) Van D. M in Biology and Botany, Cath. U. Leuven, Belgium, 1986, PhD in Scis., 1991. Rsch. asst. Cath. U. Leuven, 1986-92, postdoctoral fellow, 1992—. Editor: Handbook of Plant Lectins, 1998; contbr. articles to profl. jours.; patentee in field. Recipient Laureate, Royal Acad. Scis., 1993. Home: Langdorpsesteenweg 268, 3201 Aarschot Brabant, Belgium Office: Cath U Leuven, W de Croylaan 42, 3001 Leuven Brabant, Belgium

VANDAMME, THIERRY FERDINAND, pharmacy educator; b. Mouscron, Hainaut, Belgium, May 6, 1964; s. Pierre and Daniele (Vandamme) Ackermans. Pharmacist, U. Liege, Belgium, 1988; Indsl. Pharmacist, Cath. U. of Louvain, Woluwe, Belgium, 1989, PhD in Pharmaceutics, 1994. Asst. Cath. U. of Louvain, 1990-94; assoc. prof. U. Strasbourg, France, 1996—; vis. prof. Advanced Polymer Systems, Redwood City, Calif., 1994-95; cons. pharm. cos., France, 1996—. Patentee in field; contbr. articles to profl. jours. Capt. Med. Svc., Belgian Mil., 1990—. Mem. Controlled Release Soc. Avocations: equitation, theater, opera, classical music. Office: Univ Strasbourg, Rte du Rhin 67, 67401 Illkirch-Graffenstaden Cedex, France

VAN DE GEER, SARA ANNA, mathematician, educator, researcher; b. Leiden, The Netherlands, May 7, 1958. MS, U. Leiden, 1982, DS, 1987, PhD, 1987. Rschr. U. Tilburg, The Netherlands, 1982-83, Ctr. for Math. and Computer Sci., Amsterdam, The Netherlands, 1983-87; asst. prof. U. Bristol, Eng., 1987-88; rschr. Ctr. for Math. and Computer Sci., 1988-89; asst. prof. U. Utrecht, The Netherlands, 1989-90, U. Paul Sabatier, 1997-98; asst. prof. math. U. Leiden, 1990-97, prof., 1999—. Author: Regression Analysis and Empirical Processes, 1987, Empirical Processes in M-Estimation, 2000; assoc. editor Statistica Neerlandica, 1995—, Annals Stats., 1998—; contbr. articles to profl. jours. Mem. Bernoulli, Internat. Statis. Inst. Office: Niels Bohrweg 1, PO Box 9512, 2300 RA Leiden The Netherlands

VAN DE GIESEN, NICK, hydrologist; b. Alkmaar, The Netherlands, Aug. 14, 1961; s. Nicolas C. and Anna H. (Smit) Van De G.; m. Martha A. LArson, Aug. 5, 1994. MS, Agrl. U., Wareningen, The Netherlands, 1986; PhD, Cornell U., 1992. Asst. rschr. Cornell U., Ithaca, N.Y., 1992-93; scientist West Africa Pice Devel. Asn., Couake, Ivory Coast, 1993-96; sr. scientist Bonn U., Germany, 1997—; cons. in field. Editor: Dambo Development Zimbabwe, 1995. Netherlands Assn. Sci. scholar, 1987. Mem. Am. Geophys. Union, Internat. Assn. Hydrological Sci., Phi Kappa Phi. Office: ZEF, Walter-Felex-Str 3, 53113 Bonn Germany

VANDEMAN, MICHAEL JOSEPH, computer programmer, environmental activist, writer; b. Columbus, Ohio, Mar. 2, 1943; s. Philip R. and Jacqueline Vandeman. BA in Math., U. Calif., Berkeley, 1966; MA in Math., Harvard U., 1968; PhD in Psychology, UCLA, 1973. Chair wildlife com. Sierra Club, 1996-00. Avocations: transportation activism, wildlife activism.

VAN DEMARK, RUTH ELAINE, lawyer; b. Santa Fe, N.Mex., May 16, 1944; d. Robert Eugene and Bertha Marie (Thompson) Van D.; m. Leland Wilkinson, June 23, 1967; children: Anne Marie, Caroline Cook. AB, Vassar Coll., 1966; MTS, Harvard U., 1969; JD with honors, U. Conn., 1976; MDiv, Luth Sch. Theology, Chgo., 1999. Bar: Conn. 1976, Ill. 1977, U.S. Dist. Ct. Conn. 1976, U.S. Dist. Ct. (no. dist.) Ill., U.S. Ct. Appeals (7th cir.) 1984, U.S. Supreme Ct. 1983; ordained to ministry, Luth Ch., 1999. Instr. legal rsch. and writing Loyola U. Sch. Law, Chgo., 1976-79; assoc. Wildman, Harrold, Allen & Dixon, Chgo., 1977-84, ptnr., 1985-94; prin. Law Offices of Ruth E. Van Demark, Chgo., 1995—; pastor Wicker Park Luth. Ch., Chgo., 1999—; mem. rules com. Ill. Supreme Ct., 1999—, chair appellate rules subcom., 1996—; mem. dist. ct. fund adv. com. U.S. Dist. Ct. (no. dist.) Ill., 1997—. Assoc. editor Conn. Law Rev., 1975-76. Mem. adv. bd. Horizon Hospice, Chgo., 1978—, YWCA Battered Women's Shelter, Evanston, Ill., 1982-86; del.-at-large White House Conf. on Families, L.A., 1980; mem. alumni coun. Harvard Divinity Sch., 1988-91; vol. atty. Pro Bono Advocates Chgo., 1982-92, bd. dirs., 1993-99, chair devel. com., 1993; bd. dirs. Friends of Pro Bono Advocates Orgn., 1987-89, New Voice Prodns., 1984-86, Byrne Piven Theater Workshop, 1987-90, Luth. Social Svcs. Ill., 1998—; founder, bd. dirs. Friends of Battered Women and Their Children, 1986-87; chair 175th Reunion Fund Harvard U. Div. Sch., 1992. Mem. ABA, Ill. Bar Assn., Conn. Bar Assn., Chgo. Bar Assn., Appellate Lawyers Assn. Ill. (bd. dirs. 1985-87, treas. 1989-90, sec. 1990-91, v.p. 1991-92, pres. 1992-93), Women's Bar Assn. Ill., Jr. League Evanston (chair State Pub. Affairs Com. 1987-88, Vol. of Yr. 1983-84), Chgo. Vassar Club (pres. 1979-81), Cosmopolitan Club (N.Y.C.). Home: 2046 W Pierce Ave Chicago IL 60622-1946 Office: 225 W Washington St Ste 2200 Chicago IL 60606-3408

VANDEN, HARRY EDWIN, political science educator; b. Wilmington, Del., Sept. 29, 1943; s. Harry Edwin Sr. and Rena Baker (Van Zandt) V.; m. Vera Esther Ballin, Sept. 3, 1967 (div. Feb. 1995); children: David Jeffrey, Jonathan Harry. Diploma, U. Madrid, 1965; BA, Albright Coll., 1966; MA, Syracuse U., 1969, cert. in L.Am. Studies, 1969; PhD, New Sch. Social Rsch., 1976. Field rsch. coord. Nat. Opinion Rsch. Ctr., N.Y.C., 1969-70; adj. asst. prof. Richmond Coll., CUNY, N.Y.C., 1971; Fulbright scholar U.S. Govt., Lima, Peru, 1973-74; tech. expert Inst. Nacional Administracion Publica, Lima, 1974-75; from asst. prof. to prof. U. South Fla., Tampa, 1975—, dir. Caribbean and L.Am. Ctr., 1993-97. Author: Mariátegui: influencias en su formación ideológica, 1975, National Marxism in Latin America, 1986, A Bibliography of Latin American Marxism, 1991; co-author: Democracy and Socialism in Sandinista Nicaragua, 1993; co-editor: The Undermining of the Sandinista Revolution, 1997; contbr. articles to profl. jours., chpts. to books. V.p. bd. dirs. WMNF Cmty. Radio, Tampa, 1990-96; bd. dirs. Hispanic Needs and Svcs., Tampa, 1996—. NEH grantee, 1980. Mem. Soc. for Iberian and L.Am. Thought (pres. 1983-85), Southeastern Coun. on L.Am. Studies (pres. 1988-89), L.Am. Studies Assn. (co-chair Ctrl. Am. sect. 1997-2000), Am. Polit. Sci. Assn., Am. Soc. Internat Law. Democrat. Avocations: judo, swimming, auto repair and restoration. Office: U South Fla Dept Govt 4202 E Fowler Ave Tampa FL 33620-8000

VAN DEN AKKER, HARRY E.A., chemical engineering educator; b. Vught, The Netherlands, May 11, 1950; s. Peter C. and Mary (Grooten) Van Den A.; m. Helen P. Vreede, June 21, 1975; children: Willemyn, Jeroen, Matthys, Robert-Jan. MS, Eindhoven U. Technology, The Netherlands, 1974, PhD, 1978. Rsch. engr. Shell Rsch., Amsterdam, 1977-84, 85-88; exch. scientist Shell Oil, Houston, 1984-85; prof. Delft (Netherlands) U. Tech., 1988—; dir. Kramers Lab v Fysische Tech.; course dir. of course turbulence/computational fluid dynamics, PAON, Leiden, The Netherlands, 1992, 93, 95; mem. bd. Nuclear Reactor Inst., Delft U. Tech., 1997—; mem. Scientific Coun. TNO Inst. Applied Physics, Delft, 1988—; mem. assembly of World Conf. on Experimental Heat Transfer, Fluid Dynamics and Thermodynamics, 1999—; chmn. 4th Internat. Conf. on Gas/Liquid and Gas/Liquid/Solid reactor Engring., Delft, The Netherlands, 1999. Contbr. articles to profl. jours. and publs.; patentee in field. Dir. church choir, organist local church, The Netherlands, 1982—. Mem. European Fedn. Chem. Engring. (del. to working party on mixing 1990—), Netherlands Royal Inst. Engrs. (bd. dirs. sect. applied physics 1998—), Dutch Phys. Soc. (bd. dirs. 1997—). Roman Catholic. Office: Kramers Lab v Fysische Tech, Prins Bernhardlaan 6, NL2628BW Delft The Netherlands

VANDENBERG, DONALD, retired education educator, philosopher; b. Milw., Wis., Aug. 4, 1931; arrived in Australia, 1976; s. Richard Albert and Elsie Eleanor Dorothy (Sheamann) V.; m. Erma Jean Pinkston, May 19, 1955; children: Marta, Donald Jr., Sara Ellen. BA cum laude, Maryville Coll., 1958; MA, U. Wis., 1961; PhD, U. Ill., 1966. Cert. high school English tchr., philosopher of edn. at tertiary level. English tchr. Whitehall (Mich.) Sr. H.S., 1960-62; philosopher of edn. U. Calgary, Alta., Can., 1965-68, 72-73, Pa. State U., State College, 1968-72, UCLA, 1973-76; reader in edn. U. Queensland, Brisbane, Australia, 1976-96, ret., 1996. Author: Being and Education, 1971, Human Rights in Education, 1983, Education as a Human Right, 1990; editor : Phenomenology and Educational Discourse, 1997; contbr. articles to profl. jours. With USN, 1949-53. Coe fellow in Am. studies, U. Wyoming, Laramie, 1958-59; recipient GTA award U. Ill., Urbana, 1962-65. Fellow Philosophy of Edn. Soc. (program com. 1971-72). Avocations: running, swimming, gardening, housekeeping. Home: 12 Salisbury St, Indooroopilly QLD 4068, Australia

VAN DEN BERG, HENK, entomologist; b. Ermelo, The Netherlands, July 24, 1962; s. Evert and Teunie (van Eck) van den B.; m. Martina Jasmin Voigt, May 20, 1994. BSc, Agrl. U. Wageningen, 1984, MSc, 1987, PhD, 1993. Entomologist CAB Internat., Nairobi, Kenya, 1987-91; IPM specialist FAO, Medan, Indonesia, 1992-93, CAB Internat., 1993-95, FAO, Jakarta, Indonesia, 1995-99; with FAO, Kandy, Colombo, Sri Lanka, 1999—. Office: FAO-IPM, PO Box 1505, Colombo 7, Sri Lanka

VAN DEN BERGH, JEROEN C.J.M., economics educator; b. Ossendrecht, Noord-B., The Netherlands, Aug. 1965; s. Livinus van den Bergh and Corrie Konings; m. Ada Ferrer Carbonell. M of Econometrics and Ops. Rsch., U. Tilburg, The Netherlands, 1988; PhD in Econs., Free U., Amsterdam, 1991. Asst. prof. environ. econs. Free U., 1990-91, postdoctoral rschr., 1992-96, sr. rschr., 1996-97, prof., 1997—; chmn. area econs. Nat. Sci. Found., 1999—, mem. land ocean interactions in the coastal zone com., 1998—. Author: Ecological Economics and Sustainable Development: Theory, Methods and Applications, 1996; co-author: Meta-analysis in Environmental Economics, 1997; editor: Handbook of Environmental and Resource Economics, 1999, (book series) Studies in Ecological Economics; co-editor: Recent Advances in Spatial Equilibrium Modelling, 1996, Theory versus Implementation of Sustainable Development Modelling, 1998, others; mem. editl. bd. Ecol. Econs., Regional Environ. Change, Internat. Jour. Global Environ. Issues, Internat. Jour. of Agnic Resources, Governance and Ecology. Vis. scholar Stockholm Sch. Econs., Royal Inst. Tech., Stockholm, Inst. Future Studies, Stockholm, Ctr. Econ. Rsch. and Grad. Edn., Prague, U. Venice, Rensselaer Poly. Inst., Troy, N.Y., Vienna U. of Econs. and Bus. Mgmt. Mem. Internat. Soc. Ecol. Econs. (bd. dirs. 2000—). Avocations: guitar, singing, badminton, movies. Office: Free Univ Dept Spatial Econ, De Boelelaan 1105, 1081 HV Amsterdam Noord-H, The Netherlands

VANDENBERGHE, LUC MARCEL ADHEMAR, psychologist; b. Bruges, Belgium, Oct. 12, 1962; s. Maurits and Hilda (Cools) V.; m. Sonia Maria Mello Neves, July 28, 1994; 1 child, Sofia. Degree in psychology, U. Ghent, 1988. Clin. psychologist Ad. Hosp., Soest, Germany, 1989-94; head social svcs. De Refuge, Bruges, Belgium, 1995; lect. U. Fed. Minas Gerais, Belo Horizonte, Brazil, 1996-97; vis. lectr. U. Catholic Goias, Brazil, 1997-98, lectr., rschr., 1998—. Mem. APA, Brasilian Psychol. Assn., Belgian Psychol. Soc. Roman Catholic. Avocations: painting, semiotics, philosophy. Home: SHIS QL 18 Conj 7 Casa 15, 71650075 Brasilia Brazil

VANDENBORRE, HUGO, solid state physicist, executive; b. Kampenhout, Brabant, Belgium, Mar. 18, 1944; m. Grete Van den Troost, Apr. 20, 1948; children: Bieke, Hans, Dorien. M in Physics, Cath. U., Leuven, Belgium, 1967, M in Nuc. Sci., 1968, PhD in Solid State Physics, 1971. Rschr. Belgium, 1971-75, project leader, 1976-85; mng. dir. Hydrogen Systems N.V., Turnhout, Belgium, 1985—, now pres., CEO; v.p. renewable energy

Internat. Energy Agy. Patentee in field (40). Mem. European Electrochem. Engrs. (pres. 1987-89). Fax: 32-14-412114. E-mail: h.vandenborre@hydrogensystems.be. Office: Hydrogen Systems NV, Brugstraat 45/1, B-2300 Turnhout Belgium

VAN DEN BRANDE, JAN, oncologist; b. Antwerp, Belgium, Jan. 12, 1965; s. Leon and Paula (Van den Bosch) Van den B. MD, Antwerp U., 1991; specialist in internal medicine, U. Hosp. Antwerp, 1996, med. oncologist, 1997. Pvt. practice Antwerp, 1991—. Mem. Am. Soc. Clin. Oncology, European Soc. Med. Oncology, Belgian Soc. Med. Oncology. E-mail: Jan.Van.den.Brande@uza.uia.ac.be. Home: Van Amstelstraat 88, Hoboken 2660, Belgium Office: Dept Med Oncology UZA, Wilrijkstraat 10, Edegem 2650, Belgium

VAN DEN BREG, ROBERT G. F., corporate executive; b. Rotterdam, Holland, July 22, 1947; m. Miriam Van Den Berg; 1 child, Christine. ME, Coll. of Advanced Tech., Dordrecht, Netherlands, BS in Econs.; JD, U. Leiden, Netherlands. Export dir. firefighting systems Ajax de Boer, Amsterdam. Office: Ajax de Boer, PO Box 4105, 1009 AC, Amsterdam Holland

VAN DEN BRINK, JEROEN, physicist; b. Arnhem, The Netherlands, Nov. 10, 1968; s. Arnold and Bep (Aarsman) Van den B. PhD, U. Groningen, The Netherlands, 1997. Rschr. Max-Planck Inst., Stuttgart, Germany, 1997—; active Univ. Coun., Groningen, 1990-91. Rsch. fellow Humboldt Found., Bonn, Germany, 1998. Mem. Am. Phys. Soc.

VANDEN-BROECK, JEAN-MARC, mathematician; b. Liege, Wallonie, Belgium, Sept. 11, 1951; s. Abel Vanden-Broeck and Marie-Claire Spiegels; m. Mirna Džamonja, Oct. 10, 1992. Ingenieur phys., U. Liege, 1974, licensed in oceanology, 1975; PhD in Applied Math., Adelaide (Australia) U., 1978. Rsch. assoc. scientist Courant Inst., N.Y.C., 1978-79; rsch. assoc. Stanford (Calif.) U., 1979-81; prof. U. Wis., Madison, 1981—; prof. Sch. Math., U. East Anglia, Norwich, Eng., 1998-2000; rsch. prof. N.J. Inst. Tech., Newark; Lady Davis prof. The Technion, Israel, 1994-95. Assoc. editor Jour. Australian Math. Soc., Quarterly Jour. Mechanics and Applied Math.; contbr. over 130 articles to sci. jours., including Jour. Fluid Mechanics, European Jour. Applied Math., others. Recipient Young Investigator award NSF, 1984. Mem. Am. Phys. Soc., Soc. Indsl. and Applied Math., London Math. Soc. Avocation: reading. Home: 16 Hedgemere, Thorpe Marriott NR8 6GG, England Office: Sch Math, U East Anglia, Norwich NR4 7TJ, England

VANDENBURG, KATHY HELEN, small business owner, career counselor; b. Clifton, N.J., Feb. 6, 1969; d. Milan and Helen (Derco) Suchanek; m. James Joseph Vandenburg III, Aug. 31, 1996. BA in Psychology, Montclair State U., 1991; MA in Edn., Seton Hall U., 1995; postgrad., Rider U., 1997-98. Admissions counselor William Paterson U., Wayne, N.J., 1995-96; career counselor New Brunswick (N.J.) Pub. Schs., 1996-2000; owner, mgr. Career Counseling and Ednl. Cons., Milford, N.J., 2000—; career counselor Cornerstone Relocation Group, Warren, NJ, 2000—. Mem. ACA, Nat. Resume Writers Assn., N.J. Career Devel. Assn., N.J. Counseling Assn. Avocations: swimming, travel, classical music, theatre, cooking.

VAN DEN EYNDE, JEAN JULES, executive search consultant; b. Antwerp, Belgium, Apr. 15, 1953; s. Adolphe Van den Eynde and Dory Convents; m. Elisabeth Hardt, Sept. 3, 1983; children: Laura, Sophie, Nicolas. Candidate law, U. Faculteiten St. Ignatius Antwerpen, Antwerp, 1973; license law, U. Antwerp, 1976; LLM, Harvard U., 1977, MPA, 1978. Bar: Brussels 1979. Asst. Sullivan & Cromwell, N.Y.C., 1978-79; assoc. De Bandt Van Hecke, Brussels, 1979-81; counsel Internat. Fin. Corp. (World Bank), Washington, 1981-83; sr. counsel IFC (World Bank), Washington, 1983-88; ptnr. Carre Orban, Brussels, 1988-93; mng. dir. Russell Reynolds Assocs., Brussels, 1993—. Editor Harvard Internat. Law Jour., 1976-78, The Internat. Lawyer, 1982-90; contbr. articles and book revs. to profl. jours. Chmn. Fulbright Found. Belgium, Brussels, 1996—. Harkness fellow Commonwealth Fund N.Y., 1976-78. Mem. Harvard Club Belgium (treas. 1990-99, chmn. 2000—), Harvard Law Sch. Assn. Europe (treas. 1991-94). Avocations: skiing, gardening, biking. Home: 34 Ave Victor Gilsoul, 1200 Brussels Belgium Office: Russell Reynolds Assocs, 27 Blvd St Michel, 1040 Brussels Belgium

VAN DEN HEEVER, DAWID JOHANNES, occupational hygienist; b. Nababeep, Western, South Africa, Apr. 2, 1965; s. Dawid Johannes and Hester Wilhelmina (Louw) Van den H. Nas Diploma, Cape Technikon, Cape Town, S. Africa, 1987, Nas Higher Diploma, 1988; M Tech, Technikon Free State, Bloemfontein, S. Africa, 1992, D Tech, 1997. Profl. occupl. hygienist. Lectr. Cape Technikon, S. Africa, 1988; environ. health officer Windhoek City Coun., Namibia, 1989; sr. lectr. Technikon Free State, Bloemfontein, S. Africa, 1990—; CEO VDH Indsl. Hygiene, Bleomfontein, 1992—; dir. Workmed Pty. Ltd., Bloemfontein, 1996—. Capt. SWA Territory Force, 1983-87. Fin. grantee Found. for Rsch. Devel., Pretoria, 1992-94, 96, 97, 98, 99. Mem. Am. Conf. of Govtl. Indsl. Hygienists, Inst. of Occupl. Hygienists of South Africa. Avocation: photography. Office: VDH Indsl Hygiene cc, 98 Zastron St PO Box 26792, Langenhoven Park Bloemfontein South Africa

VAN DEN HOEK, KEES, publisher; b. Lopik, Utrecht, The Netherlands, June 27, 1955; s. Jan and Emmy (Sluis) van den Hoek; m. Jessy Sluys; children: Cas, Just. MA, Erasmus U., Rotterdam, The Netherlands, 1981. Policymaker Royal Dutch Book Trade Orgn., Amsterdam, 1982-91; founder, owner Thoth Pubs., Bussum, The Netherlands, 1985—. Office: Thoth Publishers, Prins Hendriklaan 13, 1404 AS Bussum The Netherlands

VAN DEN HOOGENBAND, PETER, olympic athlete; b. Eindhoven, The Netherlands, Mar. 14, 1978. Mem. swim team The Netherlands; fourth pl. in 100 and 200 meter freestyle Olympics, Atlanta, 1996; winner gold in 100 and 200 meter freestyle Olympics, Sydney, Australia, 2000; fifth pl. in 100 meter freestyle European Championship, 1997; winner gold in 50, 100, and 200 meter freestyle European Championship, Istanbul, 1999, winner gold in 4x100 meter freestyle relay, 1999, winner gold in 4x100 meter medley relay, 1999, winner gold in non-Olympic 50 meter butterfly, 1999; winner bronze in 200 meter freestyle World Championship, 1998. Named one of three swimmers to earn six titles at a single European Championship, 1999. Office: Koninklijke Nederlandse Zwembond, Symfonielaan 13 PO 3438 EX, PO Box 7217 PO 3430 JE Nievwegein The Netherlands*

VAN DER AALSVOORT, GEERDINA MARIA, educational psychologist, researcher; b. Nistelrode, The Netherlands, June 8, 1952; d. Rudolphus Van der Aalsvoort and Martina Van der Stappen; m. Paulus Timotheus Godefroij. Degree in Teaching, 1973; MA, Catholic U., The Netherlands, 1982; PhD, Catholic U., 1994. Surgeon asst. Canisius/Wilhelmina Hosp., 1970-76; lectr. Catholic U., 1982-86; psychologist Pedological Inst., The Hague, 1986-89; lectr. Catholic U., 1989-94, U. Leiden, 1994—; psychologist Pedagogical Inst., 1997—. Contbr. articles to jours. in field. Recipient Travel scholarship, Utrecht, 1993. Mem. EARLI, YACE, NVO. Avocations: scuba diving. Office: U. Leiden, Wassenaarseweg 52, 2333 Leiden The Netherlands

VAN DER AUWERAER, MARK GERMAINE JOZEF, chemistry educator; b. Mechelen, Belgium, Oct. 1, 1955; s. André Leopold and Lucienne Remy (Maurissens) Van der A.; m. Lutgart Maria Elisabeth Minne, May 31, 1986; children: Veerle, Greet. B of Chemistry magna cum laude, Cath. U. Leuven, Belgium, 1975, lic. in chemistry summa cum laude, 1977, PhD in Sci. summa cum laude, 1981, habilitation, 1990. From sr. rsch. asst. to rsch. assoc. NFWO, Belgium, 1982-90; onderzoeksleider FKFO, Belgium, 1990-94; rsch. dir. FWO, Belgium, 1994—; prof. K.U. Leuven, 1993—; sec. exec. com. UPS6 Conf., Leuven, 1993, ECME96 Conf., Leuven, 1996; vis. prof. Ecole Normale Superior, Cachan, France, 1994; chmn. organizing com. Eurolights II, Hengelhoef, Belgium, 1995. Contbr. articles to profl. jours. 2d lt. Belgian Army, 1981-82, comdt., 1999. von Humboldt grantee Fritz Haber Inst., Germany, 1982-83; recipient Vlaamse Leergangen award, 1982, Grammatikakis-Neumann prize European Photochemistry Assn., Zurich, Switzerland, 1992. Roman Catholic. Home: Kapeldreef 22, 3001 Heverlee Belgium Office: KU Leuven Dept Scheikunde, Celestijnenlaan 200F, 3001 Heverlee Belgium

VAN DER BIJL, PIETER, dental and medical educator; b. Cape Town, South Africa, Aug. 6, 1946; s. Paulus and Maria Lysina (De Graaff) Van der B.; m. Anna Paula Salzberg, July 15, 1972; 1 child, Pieter. BSc, U. Cape Town, 1968, BSc with hons., 1969, PhD, 1971; B in Dental Surgery, U. Stellenbosch, South Africa, 1981; BSc with hons., U. Stellenbosch, 1985, DSc, 1998. Jr. lectr. U. Cape Town, 1970-72; rschr. U. Leiden, The Netherlands, 1972-75; sr. rschr. Med. Rsch. Coun., Tygerberg, South Africa, 1975-76; from lectr. to prof. U. Stellenbosch, 1976-90, prof., 1990—; cons. Medicine Control Coun. South Africa, 1986-92, Medicolegal, South Africa, 1987—; vis. scientist U. Iowa, Ames, 1995, 97. Contbr. over 160 articles to profl. jours. Elder Dutch Reformed Ch., Goodwood, South Africa, 1980-81; dep. chmn. PTA, Goodwood, 1989-90; instr. Karate Kai, Goodwood, 1986—. Capt. South African Anti-Aircraft Artillery, 1964-65. Alberta Heritage Found. Med. Rsch. fellow, 1997. Mem. Dental Assn. South Africa (J.C. Middleton Shaw fellow 1986, Julius Staz Rsch. award 1995), Internat. Assn. Dental Rsch. (treas. 1996—, keynote spkr. Perth, Australia 2000). Avocations: reading, travelling, nature photography, military history. Home: 110 Stewart St, Goodwood 7460, South Africa Office: Faculty Medicine, U Stellenbosch Pvt Bag X 1, Tygerberg 7505, South Africa

VANDERBILT, ARTHUR T., II, lawyer; b. Summit, N.J., Feb. 20, 1950; s. William Runyon and Jean (White) V. BA, Wesleyan U., Middletown, Conn., 1972; JD, U. Va., 1975. Bar: N.J. 1975, U.S. Dist. Ct. N.J. 1975, U.S. Supreme Ct. 1978. Jud. clk. to presiding justice N.J. Superior Ct., 1975-76, dep. atty. gen., 1976-78, asst. counsel to gov., 1978-79; ptnr. Carella, Byrne, Bain & Gilfillan, Roseland, N.J., 1979—; chmn. Supreme Ct. Ethics Com.; mem. Supreme Ct. Adv. Com. Profl. Ethics. Author: Changing Law 1976, Jersey Justice, 1978, Law School, 1981, Treasure Wreck, 1986, Fortune's Children, 1989 (Book of the Month Club, Readers Digest and fgn. edits.), New Jersey's Judicial Revolution, 1997, Golden Days, 1998, Jersey Jurists, 1998, The Making of a Bestseller, 1999. Fellow ABA Found.; mem. ABA (Scribes award 1976), N.J. Bar Assn., Am. Judicature Soc., Nat. Assn. Bond Lawyers, The Authors Guild, Inc., Nat. Writers Union. Republican. Presbyterian. Avocation: writing. Office: Carella Byrne Bain & Gilfillan 6 Becker Farm Rd Roseland NJ 07068-1735

VANDERBURG, PAUL STACEY, insurance executive, consultant; b. Detroit, Apr. 13, 1941; s. Harold Stacey and Alice Bertha (Lyle) V. Cert. in plastics tech., Oakland U., 1966; AS in Bus., C.S. Mott C.C., 1971; Casualty Claims Law Assoc., Am. Ednl. Inst., 1986; BA in Bus. Adminstrn. and Mgmt., Columbia Pacific U., 1990; cert. in human resource devel., U. South Fla., 1992; fraud claims law assoc., Am. Ednl. Inst., 1995. Lic. ins. adjuster, Mich., Fla. Ins. field claims adjuster Underwriters Adjusting Co., Pontiac, Mich., 1972-76; pres., CEO Sun Cycle, Inc., Drayton Plains, Mich., 1975-77; sr. ins. claims adjuster Kemper Ins. Group, Tampa, Fla., 1979-80; ins. field claims adjuster Auto-Owners Ins. Co., Lakeland, Fla., 1981-82; sr. recovery specialist CIGNA Corp., Tampa, 1984-85; ins. field claims adjuster Seaboard Adjustment Bur., Lakeland, 1985-87; sr. field claims ins. adjuster Hallmark Ins. Adjusters, Clearwater, Fla., 1987-88; pvt. practice Tampa, 1988—. Author: Insurance Subrogation Management, 1991. Apptd. law enforcement rep. Hillsborough County (Fla.) Human Rels. Bd., 1999—. Staff sgt. U.S. Army, 1963-69. Mem. Am. Security Coun. (nat. adv. bd.), Fla. Sheriffs Assn., Am. Legion, Ctr. for Internat. Security Studies, Assn. of Workers' Compensation Claims Profls., Soc. of Claims Law Assocs. Republican. Avocations: boating, fishing, photography. Home and Office: 6505 Dimarco Rd Tampa FL 33634-7311

VAN DER CRUYSSE, DIRK J.S., educator, researcher, writer; b. Bruges, Belgium, Mar. 25, 1939; s. Achille Van der Cruysse and Lia D'Hoore; m. Magda O.L. Coëme; children: Alexander H.A., Christopher A.L. BA, U. Louvain, Belgium, 1962; M, U. Ghent, Belgium, 1966; PhD, U. Poitiers, France, 1970. Asst. prof. U. Antwerp, Belgium, 1971-77, prof., 1977-84, full prof., 1984—; bd. dirs. Flanders Festival, Belgium, Royal Flemish Philharm. Orch. Author: Madame Palatine, 1988 (4 literary awards 1989), Louis XIV et le Siam, 1991, Choisy androgyne et mandarin, 1995, Chardin le Persan, 1998. Recipient Chevalier des Arts et des Lettres French Govt., 1996. Mem. Royal Acad. Belgium, Soc. Saint Simon (v.p. 1988—). Fax: 32-3-2204564. Home: Bredabaan 23, 2930 Brasschaat Belgium Office: U Antwerp, Prinsstraat 13, 2000 Antwerp Belgium

VAN DER DUSSEN, WILLEM JOHANNIS, philosophy educator; b. Bandung, Indonesia, Oct. 21, 1940; s. Jacob Johan and Johanna Arnolda (de Grave) van der D.; m. Azmenouhi Arda Boyadjian, May 18, 1968; children: Seta, Talien, Remco. MA in History, U. Leiden, The Netherlands, 1966, MA in Philosophy, 1970, PhD in Philosophy, 1980. Mem. staff Netherlands U. Found. for Internat. Cooperation, 1971-73; from asst. to assoc. prof. U. Nijmegen, The Netherlands, 1973-88; prof. philosophy Open U. The Netherlands, 1988—. Author: History as a Science. The Philosophy of R.G. Collingwood, 1981, Filosofie van de geschiedenis, 1986; editor: R.G. Collingwood, The Idea of History, 1993, (with W.H. Dray) R.G. Collingwood, The Principles of History and Other Writingsi n Philosophy of History, 1999. Mem. Heerlen (The Netherladns) City Coun., 1997—. Recipient prize Prince Bernhard Found., 1984. Mem. Maatschappij Nederlandse Letterkunde. Home: Molenberglaan 81, 6916 EL Heerlen The Netherlands

VAN DER ELST, NICOLE, author, consultant, educator; b. Paris, July 18, 1932; d. Luc and Suzanne (Deslandres) Van der E. Diploma, HEC-JF, Paris, 1953. Adminstrv. sec. French sect. Brussels World Fair, 1956-60; documentalist French Shipowners Com., Paris, 1960-64, pub. rels. officer, 1965-77; prof. bus. comm. ISIT, Paris, 1978-92; journalist Nat. Assn. for Profl. Edn., 1983-94; author, cons. Paris, 1979—; cons. ILO, Geneva, 1973; in charge of workshops CELSA, U. Paris IV, 1970-77. Author books, essays, and monographs; editor L'Opinion Repond, 1970; co-editor newsletter Democratie et Spiritualite, 1998-99; contbr. articles to profl. jours. Adminstr. CICF Info. Ctr. of Women Execs., Paris, 1966-67. Mem. French Assn. Pub. Rels. (v.p. 1975-81), Fedn. of European Pub. Rels. Assns. (v.p. 1978-79). Avocation: painting. Home: 110 rue de Rennes, 75006 Paris France

VANDERGRIFF, KENNETH LYNN, minister; b. Knoxville, Tenn., Nov. 12, 1954; s. Kenneth Charles and Dorothy Jean (Frazier) V.; m. Beth Foster, Aug. 6, 1976; children: Kenny, Jeananne. BS in English Edn., Fla. State U., 1976; MDiv, Southwestern Bapt. Seminary, Ft. Worth, 1981, PhD in Old Testament, 1988. Teaching fellow Southwestern Bapt. Theol. Seminary, 1984-87, adj. instr., 1989; min. of edn. Northwest Hills Bapt. Ch., San Antonio, 1989-95; instr. Inst. Christian Studies, Ft. Worth, 1983, 86, Wayland Bapt. U., San Antonio, 1988-95, Campbell U., N.C., 1996—. Recipient Stella Ross award in Old Testament studies Southwestern Bapt. Theol. Seminary, 1981. Mem. Soc. Bibl. Lit., Am. Acad. of Religion, Christians for Bibl. Equality. Democrat. Home: 212 Forest Brook Dr Apex NC 27502-5836

VAN DER HEM, KLAAS GJALT, hemato-oncologist; b. Groningen, Netherlands, Dec. 2, 1958; s. Gjalt Klaas and Janna Johanna (Hofstra) Van der H.; m. Henderika Hilda Stokroos, Aug. 8, 1986; children: Joost Gjalt Klaas, Peter Heere Jurgen, Laurens Lieuwe Sybolt. MD, State U. Groningen, 1986; PhD, Free U., Amsterdam, 1996. Physician Free Univ. Hosp., Amsterdam, 1986-91, hematologist, 1991-95; hemato-oncologist Hosp de Heel, Zaandam, Netherlands, 1995—. Mem. N.Y. Acad. Scis., European Hematology Assn. Home: Nieuwerhoek 28, 1081CB Amsterdam Netherlands Office: Hosp de Heel, Kon Julianaplein, 1052DV Zaandan Netherlands

VAN DER HEYDEN, ULRICH, historian, political scientist, journalist, editor; b. Ueckermünde, Germany, Sept. 7, 1954; s. Karl-Heinz and Ingeborg (Ramm) van der H.; children: Sylva, Verena. Student, Poly. Oberschule, Ueckermünde, 1971, Erweiterte Oberschule, Torgelow, East Germany, 1973; diploma in history, Humboldt U., Berlin, 1981, PhD, 1984, 97. Asst. internat. affairs Humboldt U., Berlin, 1984; fellow Inst. Econ. History Acad. Scis., Berlin, 1984-86, fellow Inst. World History, 1986-91; fellow Ctr. for Modern Oriental Studies, Berlin, 1992-95; fellow seminar of African studies Humboldt U., Berlin, 1996-99; dir. dept. Brandenburgische Kolonialgeschichte, Inst. for Devel. Policy, Potsdam, 1992. Author: Dictionary of North American Indians, 1992, 96, 97, The Discovery of America in Literature, 1994, History of African Studies in Germany, 1999; editor: (book series) Cognoscere, 1993—, The German Democratic Republic and the Third World, 1993—, Mission History Archive, 1996—. Lt. Peoples Army of German Dem. Republic, 1973-76. Mem. Berlin Soc. Mission History (vice chmn.), Soc. Brandenburg-Princes Town-One World (chmn.). Office: Humboldt-Univ Berlin Inst African Studies, Prenzlauer Promenade 149-152, 13189 Berlin Germany

VANDERHOEFT, PATRICK JEAN ROGER, retired surgeon, researcher; b. Brussels, Jan. 9, 1930; s. Roger Eugéne and Barbara Kathleen (Stapleton) V.; m. Marie Renée Jeanne Heilporn, Dec. 16, 1954; children: Claire, Anne. MD, U. Brussels, 1955. Surgical resident U. Hosp. St. Pierre, Brussels, 1955-69, thoracic surgeon, 1963-65, head thoracic surgery, 1966-77; rsch. assoc., fellow Mayo Clinic, Rochester, Minn., 1961-62; chief thoracic surgery Cliniques U. ERASME, Brussels, 1978-95, ret., 1995; vis. thoracic surgeon AK Sjukhuset Uppsala, Sweden, 1964. Author, editor: The Lung Is an Effector Not a Sensor in Mammalian Breathing, 2000; contbr. articles to profl. jours. Fellow at large Mayo Clinic Found., 1962—; grand officer de l'Ordre de la Couronne, 1966; grand officer de l'Ordre de Leopold, 1998. Commandant Belgium Reserves. Recipient Sci. NATO grant Mayo Clinic, 1961-92. Mem. Soc. Royal Belge de Chirurgie (hon., sec. 1966-70, gen. sec. 1971-75), Acad. Royale Medicine Belgium, Union des Anciens de l'ULB, Amnesty Internat., Sigma Xi. Avocations: gardening, photography. Performed the 21st world clin. lung transplantation, 1969. Home: Ave du Loriot 4, B 1640 Rhode St Genese Belgium Office: Svc Chirurgie Thoracic, Hosp ERASME rte Lennik 808, B 1070 Brussels Belgium

VANDERHOEK, SHERRY A., counselor; b. Chgo., July 20, 1956; d. John Albert and Stella Rose Troike; m. Herman Vanderhoek; stepchildren: Michiel, Martin. AAS, Prairie State Coll., 1992; BA, Govs. State U., 1994, MA, 1997. Lic. profl. counselor, Ill.; cert. counselor Nat. Bd. Cert. Counselors. Counselor South Suburban Coun. on Alcoholism, East Hazel Crest, Ill., 1990-93, South Suburban Family Shelter, Hazel Crest, Ill., 1996-97; facilitator Aunt Martha's Youth Svcs. Ctr., Inc., Park Forest, Ill., 1991-92; grad. asst. Govs. State U., University Park, Ill., 1995-97; pvt. practice counselor Matteson, Ill., 1998—. Mem. ACA, Ill. Counseling Assn. (founder Govs. State chpt., pres. 1996, regional gov. 1997-2000), Ill. Alcohol and Other Drug Profl. Cert. Assn., Ill. Counselor Educators and Suprs. (Outstanding Grad. Student award 1996), Internat. Assn. Addiction and Offender Counselors, Assn. for Counselor Edn. and Supervision (Outstanding Grad. Student Scholarship award 1997), Psi Chi (chpt. founder, pres. 1997), Chi Sigma Iota (chpt. sec. 1995). Avocations: stained glass, cross-stitch, cooking. Home and Office: 3707 215th St Matteson IL 60443-3706

VAN DER HOEVEN, CEES H., food products executive. CEO, chmn. bd. Koninklijke Ahold N.V., Zaandam, The Netherlands, chmn. bd.; pres., CEO Royal Ahold N.V. *

VANDERHOOFT, JAN ERIC, orthopedic surgeon, educator; b. Salt Lake City, May 16, 1962; s. Gerard F. and Else-Marie Vanderhooft; m. Sheryll Jo Vanderhooft, Mar. 25, 1984; children: Peter, Lauren. BS, Stanford (Calif.) U., 1984; MD, U. Utah, 1988. Cert. Am. Bd. Orthopaedic Surgeons, added qualification in hand surgery. Resident, fellow U. Wash., Seattle, 1988-94; attending physician Salt Lake Orthopedic Clinic, 1994—; clin. dir. orthop. rotation St. Mark's Hosp. U. Utah, 1998—; clin. dir. family medicine residency orthop. rotation Columbia St. Mark's, 1998—; clin. instr. U. Wash., 1993-94; asst. clin. prof. dept. orthopedics U. Utah. Contbr. articles to profl. jours. and chpts. to textbooks. Bd. dirs. Turn Cmty. Svcs., Salt Lake City, 1996—, chmn. bd., 2000—. Recipient: Family Medicine Res. award for excellene in tchg., 1995, 96, 98, 99. Fellow Am. Acad. Orthopaedic Surgeons; mem. Western Musculoskeletal Assn. (bd. dirs. 1995-96), Am. Soc. for Surgery of Hand, Utah Med. Assn., Western Orthop. Assn., Utah Orthopedic Soc. (sec.), Alpha Omega Alpha. Office: Salt Lake Orthopedic Clinic 1160 E 3900 S Ste 5000 Salt Lake City UT 84124-1275

VAN DER LEUN, JAN CORNELIS, biophysicist; b. Rotterdam, The Netherlands, June 14, 1928; s. Cornelis and Johanna (Kroon) van der L.; m. Jannie Florence Goedhart, Aug. 30, 1957; children: Cornelis Jan, Christine Florence, Joanne Pauline, Gera Elisabeth. BA in Math. and Physics, U. Utrecht, The Netherlands, 1948, MS in Exptl. Physics, 1955, PhD in Biophysics, 1966. Biophysicist, Inst. Dermatology U. Utrecht, 1953-66; asst. prof. physics in medicine Cornell U. Med. Coll. (N.Y.), 1966-67; photodermatologist U. Utrecht, 1967-80, prof. dermatology and biophysics, 1980-93, emeritus prof., 1993—; chmn. effects sessions coordinating com. on ozone layer UN Environ. Programme, 1980-86, chmn. internat. panel on environ. effects of ozone depletion, 1988—, editor reports, 1989, 91, 94, 98; chmn. Commn. on Risks ov UV Radiation, Health Coun. The Netherlands, 1984-86, 93-94; mem. The Netherlands Health Coun. Co-author: Ozone Depletion, 1989, Nonionizing Radiation Protection, 1989, Biological Responses to Ultraviolet A Radiation, 1992, Ultraviolet B Radiation and Ozone Depletion: Effects on Humans, Animals, Plants, Microorganisms and Materials, 1993, Environmental Ultraviolet Photobiology, 1993, Protecting the Ozone Layer: Lessons, Models and Prospects, 1998; mem. editl. bd. Photodermatology, Photoimmunology and Photomedicine, Global Change and Human Health; contbr. articles to profl. jours. 1st Lt. Meteorologist, Royal Dutch Air Force, 1949-51. Recipient Global Ozone award UN Environ. Program, 1995, Global 500 Roll of Honor, 1997. Mem. Assn. Internat. Photobiology (Finsen medal 1996), European Soc. for Photobiology, Am. Soc. for Photobiology, European Soc. for Dermatol. Rsch., Dutch Photobiology Group (chmn. 1986-93), Norwegian Dermatol Soc. (corr.). Mem. Dutch Reformed Ch. Home: Rhijnauwenselaan 6, NL3981HH Bunnik The Netherlands Office: U Hosp Utrecht Dermatology, Heidelberglaan 100, NL-3584 CX Utrecht The Netherlands

VANDERLINDEN, CAMILLA DENICE DUNN, telecommunications industry manager; b. Dayton, July 21, 1950; d. Joseph Stanley and Virginia Danley (Martin) Dunn; m. David Henry VanderLinden; Oct. 10, 1980; 1 child, Michael Christopher. Student, U. de Valencia, Spain, 1969; BA in Spanish and Secondary Edn. cum laude, U. Utah, 1972, MS in Human Resource Econs., 1985. Asst. dir. Davis County Community Action Program, Farmington, Utah, 1973-76; dir. South County Community Action, Midvale, Utah, 1976-79; supr. customer service Ideal Nat. Life Ins. Co., Salt Lake City, 1979-80; mgr. customer service Utah Farm Bur. Mutual Ins., Salt Lake City, 1980-82; quality assurance analyst Am. Express Co., Salt Lake City, 1983-86, quality assurance and human resource specialist, 1986-88; mgr. quality assurance and engrng. Am. Express Co., Denver, 1988-91; mgr. customer svc. Tel. Express Co., Colorado Springs, Colo., 1991-97; dir. Call Ctr. United Membership Mktg. Group, Lakewood, Colo., 1997-98; telesvcs. industry mgr. Piton Found., Denver, 1998—; customer care dir. SafeRent, 2000—; dir. Customer Care and Tng.@Saferent, LLC, Denver; mem. adj. faculty Westminster Coll., Salt Lake City, 1987-88, mem. adj. faculty, mem. quality adv. bd. Red Rocks C.C., 1990-91. Vol. translator Latin Am. community; vol. naturalist Roxborough State Park; internat. exch. coord. EF Fgn. Exch. Program. Mem. Internat. Customer Svc. Orgn. (officer call ctr. chpt.), Colo. Springs Customer Svc. Assn. (officer). Christian. Avocations: swimming, hosting fgn. exchange students. Home: 10857 Snow Cloud Trail Littleton CO 80125-9211

VAN DER LUGT, G. J. A., insurance company executive. CEO, ING Group N.V., Amsterdam, The Netherlands, now chmn. exec. bd. Office: ING Group, Strawinskylaan 2631, Amsterdam 1077, The Netherlands*

VAN DER MAELEN URIA, JUAN FRANCISCO, physical chemistry educator; b. Oviedo, Asturias, Spain, Oct. 12, 1959; s. Francisco Van Der Maelen and Amparo Uria; m. Maria Del Mar Alvarez-Zaragoza, July 28, 1990. BS, U. Oviedo, Spain, 1979, MS in Chemistry, 1983, PhD in Chemistry, 1991; MS in Physics, UNED, Madrid, 1991. Rsch. scientist U. Oviedo, 1982-88, asst. prof., 1989-90, assoc. prof., 1991-96, permanent prof., 1996-99, sr. lectr., 1999—; analyst, programmer Oviedo, 1984-88; postdoctoral student U. Göttingen, Germany, 1993. Co-editor: From Crystal Growth to Macro Molecular Crystallography, 1996; author article in books: New Trends in Crystallography, 1995, Crystallography Reviews, 1999; contbr. articles to profl. jours.; referee internat. edit. Anales de Quimica. Postdoctoral grantee U. Oviedo, U. Göttingen, 1993. Mem. Royal Soc. Spanish Chemists, Crystallography Spanish Group, Internat. Union Crystallography (mem. jour. referee's staff). Avocations: music, sports, swimming. Office: Quimica Fisica Y Analitica, Avda Julian Claveria 8, E-33006 Oviedo Spain

VAN DER MAST, MARC FRANCIS JEAN, cardiac surgeon; b. Essen, Antwerp, Belgium, Feb. 22, 1953; s. Edward Hendrik and Emilie (Smeulders) Van Der Mast; m. Anne De Wolf, Sept. 5, 1992; children: Julie, Anouk, Vincent, Margot, Jeroen. MD, Cath. U., Leuven, Belgium, 1978, Degree in Thoracic Surgery, 1985. Resident cardiac surgery U. Hosp., Antwerp, 1985-90, sr. resident cardiac surgery, 1990-92; head dept. cardiac surgery Heilig Hart Ziekenhuis, Roeselare, Belgium, 1992—; cons. mem. cardiac surgery U. Hosp. Antwerp, 1992-93; presenter in field. Contbr. articles to profl. jours. Mem. AAAS, European Soc. Artificial Organs, European Soc. for Cardiovascular Surgery, Europese Soc. Heart Transplantation, Eurotransplant, Belgische kon Genodschap Heelkunde, Belgian Soc. for Cardiothoracic Surgery. Home: Jacob Van Arteveldestr 14, 8800 Roeselare Belgium Office: Heilig Hart Ziekenhuis, Wilgenstraat 2, 8800 Roeselare Belgium

VAN DER MEER, JOS WILLEM MAARTEN, internist; b. The Hague, The Netherlands, Apr. 15, 1947; s. Maarten D.J. and Anna H.E. (Van Manen) Van der M.; m. Mechtilde Kever, Sept. 24, 1982; children: Helene A., Jonathan H.M. Degree, Hogere Burgerschool-Beeklan, The Hague, 1964; MD, U. Leiden, The Netherlands, 1971, PhD, 1982. Resident in internal medicine Bronovo Hosp., The Hague, 1971-73, Univ. Hosp., Leiden, The Netherlands, 1973-76; head outpatient clinic infectious disease Univ. Hosp., Leiden, 1977-88; prof. internal medicine Cath. U., Nijmegen, The Netherlands, 1988—; cons. Univ. Hosp., Leiden, 1976-88; vis. scientist Tufts-New Eng. Med. Ctr., Boston, 1987; head dept. gen. internal medicine Univ. Hosp., Nijmegen, 1992—; chmn. working party immunodeficiency, The Netherlands, 1993—. Recipient award Myalgic Encephalomyllitis Found., 1997. Fellow Infectious Disease Soc. Am., Royal Soc. Medicine, Royal Coll. Physicians (hon.); mem. Infectious Diseases Soc. of The Netherlands and Flanders (pres. 1992-97, Prof. WRO Goslings award 1983, Internat. ME award 1997, Marco de Vries award 1998). Avocations: drawing, painting, music. Home: Berg en Dalseweg 106, 6522 BS Nijmegen The Netherlands Office: Univ Hosp, Geert Grooteplein Zuid 8, 6525 GA Nijmegen The Netherlands

VAN DER MEER, SIMON, physicist; b. The Hague, The Netherlands, Nov. 24, 1925; s. Pieter and Jetske (Groeneveld) van der M.; m. Catharina M. Koopman, Apr. 26, 1966; children: Esther, Mathijs. Engring. degree in physics, Poly. U., Delft, The Netherlands, 1952; Dr. (hon.), U. Geneva, 1983, U. Amsterdam, The Netherlands, 1984, U. Genoa, Italy, 1985. Research engr. Philips Physics Lab., Eihdhoven, The Netherlands, 1952-55; sr. engr. CERN European Orgn. Nuclear Research, Geneva, 1956-90; ret., 1990. Co-recipient Nobel prize for physics, 1984. Mem. AAAS (fgn., hon.), Royal Netherlands Acad. Scis. (corr.).

VAN DER MEIJ, GOVERT PIETER, physics educator; b. Haarlem, The Netherlands, July 1, 1951; s. Govert and Phyllis (Hart) Van der M.; m. Florina Johanna Burger, Mar. 15, 1979; children: Maarten Arthur, Wouter Gesinus Stanley. DSc in Math. and Sci., U. Leiden, 1984. Lectr. physics Inst. Indsl. and Maritime Tech., Amsterdam, The Netherlands, 1985—; former guest scientist Netherlands Energy Rsch. Foun. Avocations: badminton, sailing. Home: Doorzwin 1128, Den Helder 1788 KB, The Netherlands Office: Hogeschool van Amsterdam, Weesperzyde 190, 1097 DX Amsterdam The Netherlands

VAN DER MEULEN, JOSEPH PIERRE, neurologist; b. Boston, Aug. 22, 1929; s. Edward Lawrence and Sarah Jane (Robertson) VanDer M.; m. Ann Irene Yadeno, June 18, 1960; children—Elisabeth, Suzanne, Janet. AB, Boston Coll., 1950; MD, Boston U., 1954. Diplomate: Am. Bd. Psychiatry and Neurology. Intern Cornell Med. div. Bellevue Hosp., N.Y.C., 1954-55; resident Cornell Med. div. Bellevue Hosp., 1955-56; resident Harvard U., Boston City Hosp., 1958-60, instr., fellow, 1962-66; assoc. Case Western Res. U., Cleve., 1966-67; asst. prof. Case Western Res. U., 1967-69, assoc. prof. neurology and biomed. engring., 1969-71; prof. neurology U. So. Calif., L.A., 1971—; also dir. dept. neurology Los Angeles County/U. So. Calif. Med. Center; chmn. dept. U. So. Calif., 1971-78, v.p. for health affairs, 1977—, dean Sch. Medicine, 1985-86, 95-97, vice dean med. affairs, 1995-97; dir. Ind. Health Professions, L.A., 1991—; vis. prof. Autonomous U. Guadalajara, Mex., 1974; pres. Norris Cancer Hosp. and Research Inst., 1983-98. Contbr. articles to profl. jours. Mem. med. adv. bd. Calif. chpt. Myasthenia Gravis Found., 1971-75, chmn., 1974-75, 77-78; med. adv. bd. Amyotrophic Lateral Sclerosis Found., Calif., 1973-75, chmn., 1974-75; mem. Com. to Combat Huntington's Disease, 1973—; bd. dirs. Calif. Hosp. Med. Ctr., Good Hope Med. Found., Doheny Eye Hosp., House Ear Inst., L.A. Hosp. Good Samaritan, Children's Hosp. of L.A., Phila. Health Edn. Corp., Barlow Respiratory Hosp., USC U. Hosp., chmn., 1991—; bd. govs. Thomas Aquinas Coll.; bd. dirs. Assn. Acad. Health Ctrs., chmn., 1991-92; pres. Scott Newman Ctr., 1987-89. Served to lt. M.C. USNR, 1956-58. Nobel Inst. fellow Karolinska Inst., Stockholm, 1960-62; NIH grantee, 1968-71. Mem. AMA, Am. Neurol. Assn., Am. Acad. Neurology, L.A. Soc. Neurology and Psychiatry (pres. 1977-78), L.A. Med. Assn., Mass. Med. Soc., Ohio Med. Soc., Calif. Med. Soc., L.A. Acad. Medicine, Alpha Omega Alpha (councillor 1992—), Phi Kappa Phi. Home: 39 Club View Ln Palos Verdes Peninsula CA 90274-4208 Office: U So Calif 1540 Alcazar St Los Angeles CA 90033-4500

VAN DER MEULEN, MICHAEL, electrical engineering educator; b. Tönisvorst, Germany, Sept. 13, 1960; s. Hans Günter and Maria Henriette (Küppers) van der M. Diploma in engring., Rheinisch-Westfälische, Technische Hochschule, Aachen, Germany, 1991. Cert. elec. engring. Planning engr. Städtische Werke, Krefeld, Germany, 1991-92; referendar Schule für Elektrotechnik, Essen, Germany, 1994-97; dozent Esta Bildungswerk, Mühlheim, Germany, 1997; acct. Opel Bank, Krefeld, Germany, 1998-99; sect. leader Metro MEM Energie Mgmt., Dusseldorf, Germany, 1999-2000; tchr. Berufskolleg Hilden, Germany, 2000—; rschr. in field. Contbr. articles to profl. jours. Active Tischtennis - Freunde Rhenania Königshof, Krefeld, 1973, Vorderlader-Schützen Krefeld, 1986. 1st lt. German Signal Corps, 1980-86. Mem. IEEE (antennas and propagation com. 1990), Intelligence History Study Group, Fernmeldering e.V. Avocations: technical history EW, cryptology, cryptanalysis. Home: Edmund Bungartz Weg 3, 47803 Krefeld Germany Office: Berafskolleg Hilden, Am Holterhoefchen 34, 40724 Hilden Germany

VAN DER MYE, WALTER STEPHEN, managing director; b. Sydney, NSW, Australia, May 24, 1948; s. Baardhout and Gwendyth Eldridge (Gee) van der M.; m. Lynette Anne McPhee, May 30, 1987; children: Katherine Louise, Lisa Anne. B of Comm. with honors, U. NSW, 1970, PhD, 1976; internat. sr. mgmt. program, Harvard U., 1993. Mgr. Banque Nationale de Paris, Sydney, 1979-84, chief mgr., 1984-87; 1st v.p. Capital Markets Banque Nationale de Paris, London, 1987-90; chief exec. Queensland Industry Devel. Corp., Brisbane, Australia, 1990-96; mng. dir. Nat. Electricity Market Mgmt. Co., Melbourne, Australia, 1997—; dir. Queensland Dairy Authority, Brisbane, 1994-95, QNI Ltd., Brisbane, 1995-98; dep. chancellor U. So. Queensland, Brisbane, 1995-96; dep. chmn. Austa Electric, Brisbane, 1995-96. Fellow AICD, AIM, CPA. Office: NEMMCO, Level 16 461 Bourke St, Melbourne 3000, Australia

VANDER NAALD EGENES, JOAN ELIZABETH, business owner, educator; b. Des Moines, Feb. 13, 1936; d. Bert and Cathryn Alice (Bunger) Vander Naald; m. David Iddings Grant, July 25, 1959 (div. Oct. 1984); children: Jeffrey, Pamela, Elizabeth, Jennifer. BA, U. Iowa, 1958. Cert. profl. in edn., Iowa, Colo.; cert. travel agt., Iowa. Instr. St. Katherine's Sch., Davenport, Iowa, 1958-59, Iowa Ctrl. C.C., Fort Dodge, 1959-61; city councilwoman Boone, 1980-86; instr. Des Moines Area C.C., Boone Campus, 1983; founder, owner, importer Global Ednl. Svcs., Des Moines, 1992-97; receptionist, sec. Automobile Club of So. Calif., West Los Angeles, 1997-2000; bd. mem. Iowa Psychology Bd. Examiners, Des Moines, 1984-93; rsch. interviewer Iowa State U., Ames, 1984; resource tchr., workshop presenter about Russia, 1988-94; freelance photographer, 1988—. Lifetime mem. Rep. Senatorial Inner Circle, Washington, 1987—; pres. Iowa 4th Dist. Rep. Women, 1990-91, Polk County (Iowa) Rep. Women, 1994; precinct chair 12, ward 01, Des Moines, 1995-97; pres. Des Moines Metro Opera Guild, 1996-97, coun. sec., 1995-97; extensive vol. activities, including various fundraising chairs. Recipient 1st prize Youth Projects, Iowa Devel. Commn., 1983, Women Helping Women award for volunteerism, Boone, 1983; named Entrepreneur of Yr. in Iowa award GE, 1995. Republican. Avocation: swimming. Home: 10650 Kinnard Ave Apt 312 Los Angeles CA 90024-5994

VANDERPAS, JEAN BAPTISTE, laboratory professional; b. Ixelles, Brabant, Belgium, July 2, 1953; s. Emile Vanderpas and Hélène Zahles; m. Maria Teresa Rivera; children: Gabriel, Marie-Béatrice, Nathalie. MD, Free U., Brussels, 1978, clin. pathologist, 1984, PhD in Clin. Medicine, 1991. Head of the field Cooperation, Zaire, 1978-81; postgrad. staff Hosp., St. Pierre, Belgium, 1981-84; resident Hosp. U., Erasme, Belgium, 1984-85; rsch. fellow NYU Med. Ctr., N.Y.C., 1985-86; asst. Clin. Louis Caty, Baudour, 1987-90; head Clin. Med. Lab., Belgium, 1990—. Author: Encyclopedia of Food Sciences and Nutrition, 1999. Mem. European Thyroid Assn. Roman Catholic. Home: Rue du Bois de La Haut 14, 7000 Mons Belgium Office: Ctr Hosp Univ, Ambroise Pare Bd Kennedy 2, 7000 Mons Belgium

VANDERPERRE, AXEL MAURICE, health products executive, consultant; b. Brussels, Aug. 23, 1959. B in Biomedical Engring., U. Brussels, 1982; MBA, Hoge Sch. Antewerp, Belguim, 1988. Product mgr. health care 3M Belgium, Brussels, 1984-98; sales & mktg. mgr. med. devices Cyanamid Benelux, Mont-St.-Guibert, Belgium, 1988-90; internat. product mgr. oncology, anesthesia Janssen Pharm., Beerse, Belgium, 1990-94, internat. mgr. prof. affairs & comm., 1994-97; CEO MedLi Internat., Brussels, 1997—. Editor: Cancer and the Puzzle of Pain, 1999. Mem. European Assn. Palliative Care (cons. 1999—, website cons. 1999), European Sch. Oncology (cons. 1997-98). Avocations: chess, reading, food. Fax: 32-2-532-26-12. Home: Avenue Emile Duray 68,B14, 1000 Brussels Belgium Office: MedLi Internat, Olmenlaan 6, 1750 Brussels Belgium

VAN DER PLAS, HENK CORNELIS, chemistry educator, researcher, administrator; b. Voorhout, The Netherlands, May 4, 1929; s. Henk Johannes and Alida Wilhelmina (van Velzen) van der P.; m. Wilhelmina Demmers, Jan. 19, 1957; children: Hein, Paul, Bob, Carolien, Dolf. Doctorandus, U. Amsterdam, The Netherlands, 1956, PhD, 1960; D (hon.), Akademia Medica, Warsaw, Poland, 1987; U. Leuven, Belgium, 1989; PhD (hon.), Agrl. U. Prague, Czech Republic, 1993, Tech. U. Cracow, Poland, 1995, Agrl. U. Gödöllő, Hungary, 1995, Timiryalev Agrl. Acad., Moscow, 1996. Mem. Russian Acad. Scis., Moscow, 1993. Asst. prof. chemistry Wageningen (The Netherlands) Agrl. U., 1958-60, assoc. prof. chemistry, 1963-71, full prof. chemistry, 1971-96, vice chancellor, 1977-81, 88-93; chmn. bd. dirs. Netherlands U. Found. Internat. Cooperation, 1984-88, found. Bilance, 1994—; Netherlands Inst. Social Studies, 1995—; pres. European Network Agrl. Univs., Belgium, 1994-97. Author: Ring Transformation of Heterocycles, 1973, 74 (award 1981); co-author (with O.N. Chupakhin and V.N. Charushin): Nucleophilic Substitution of Aromatic Hydrogen, 1995, Degenerate Ring Transformation of Heterocycls, 1999; co-editor: Bio-organic Heterocycles, 1984, 85, 86, 91, Agro-Biotechnology in the Netherlands, 1990, 93; contbr. over 400 articles to profl. publs. Recipient award Fedn. European Chem. Socs., 1986, Hiller award Organic Chem. Inst., Riga, Latvia, 1991. Mem. Royal Netherlands Chem. Soc. (pres. 1974-76), Internat. Soc. Heterocyclic Chemistry (pres. 1984-87, Heterocyclic Chemistry award 1981), Polish Chem. Soc. (hon.), Hungarian Chem. Soc. (hon.). Roman Catholic. Avocations: swimming, tennis, singing, music. Home: Kabeljauwallee 4A, 6865 BN Doorwerth The Netherlands

VANDERPOEL, JAMES ROBERT, lawyer; b. Harvey, Ill., Sept. 27, 1955; s. Waid Richard and Ruth (Silberman) V.; m. Deanne Czabaranek, May 1987; children: Jacqueline, Robert, Jennifer. BS in Fin., Ind. U., 1978; JD, Santa Clara U., 1982. Bar: Calif. 1982, U.S. Dist. Ct. (no. dist.) Calif. 1982. Group contracts mgr. Motorola Computer Group, Tempe, Ariz., 1984—. Avocations: basketball, hiking, golf, snorkeling, gardening. Office: Motorola Computer Group 2900 S Diablo Way Tempe AZ 85282-3214

VANDERPOOL, WARD MELVIN, management and marketing consultant; b. Oakland, Mo., Jan. 20, 1918; s. Oscar B. and Clara (McGuire) V.; m. Lee Kendall, July 7, 1939. MEE, Tulane U. V.p. charge sales Van Lang Brokerage, Los Angeles, 1934-38; mgr. agrl. div. Dayton Rubber Co., Chgo., 1939-48; pres., gen. mgr. Vee Mac Co., Rockford, Ill., 1948—; pres., dir. Zipout, Inc., Rockford, 1951—, Wife Saver Products, Inc., 1959—; chmn. bd. Zipout Internat., Kenvan Inc., 1952—, Shevan Corp., 1951—, Atlas Internat. Corp.; pres. Global Enterprises Ltd., Global Assos. Ltd.; chmn. bd. dirs. Am. Atlas Corp., Atlas Chem. Corp., Merzat Industries Ltd.; trustee Ice Crafter Trust, 1949—; bd. dirs. Atlas Chem. Internat. Ltd., Kenlee Internat., Ltd., Shrimp Tool Internat. Ltd.; mem. Toronto Bd. Trade; chmn. bd. dirs. Am. Atlas Corp., Am. Packaging Corp. Mem. adv. bd. Nat. Security Council, congl. adv. com. Heritage Found.; mem. Rep. Nat. Com., Presdl. Task Force, Congl. Adv. Com. Hon. mem. Internat. Swimming Hall of Fame. Mem. Nat. (dir. at large), Rock River (past pres.), sales execs., Sales and Mktg. Execs. Internat. (dir.), Am. Mgmt. Assn., Rockford Engring. Soc., Am. Tool Engrs., Internat. Acad. Aquatic Art (dir.), Am. Inst. Mgmt. (pres. council), Am. Ordnance Assn., Internat. Platform Assn., Heritage Found., Ill. C. of C., Jesters Club, IAA Swim Club, Elmcrest Country Club, Pyramid Club, Dolphin Club, Marlin Club, Univ. Club, Athletic Club, Oxford Club, Masons (consistory), Shriners, Elks. Home: 374 Parkland Dr SE Cedar Rapids IA 52403-2031 also: 40 Richview Rd # 308, Toronto, ON Canada M9A 5C1 also: 704 Park Center Dr Santa Ana CA 92705-3563 Office: PO Box 1972 Cedar Rapids IA 52406-1972 also: 111 Richmond St W Ste 318, Toronto, ON Canada M5H 1T1

VAN DER SAR, EDWIN, soccer player; b. Aug. 29, 1970. Goalkeeper Ajax Amsterdam, Netherlands, Juventus FC, Torino, Italy. Address: Juventus FC, Piazza Crimea 7, IT-10137 Torino Italy*

VANDER SLOTEN, JOS EDWARD AUGUST, biomechanical engineer, educator; b. Leuven, Belgium, Oct. 2, 1962; s. Myriam C. Gelaude, Jan. 16, 1988; children: Evelien, Tom. MSc in Engring., K.U. Leuven, Belgium, 1985, PhD, 1990. Rsch. assoc. Belgian Nat. Fund for Sci. Rsch., Leuven, 1986-90; sr. rsch. assoc. FWO, Leuven, 1990—, prof., 1997—; dep. sec.-gen. World Acad. of Biomed. Technologies, 1997—. Editor: Book of Abstracts, 1996, Computer Technology in Biomaterials Science and Engineering, 1999. Mem. European Soc. for Engring. and Medicine (sec.-gen. 1996—), European Soc. for Biomechanics, Internat. Fedn. for Med. and Biol. Engring. Avocations: designing, flying, radio-controlled model airplanes. Offic: KU Leuven-Biomechanics, Celestynenlaan 200 A, B-3001 Heverlee Belgium

VAN DER SLUIS, WIEBE, editor; b. Lippenhuizen, The Netherlands, Dec. 5, 1945; s. Aize and Klaske (Nijdam) V.; m. Joke Gesink, May 18, 1972; children: Rick, Nienke. ING, Agrl. Coll., Groningen, The Netherlands, 1964. Gen. sec. Farmers Youth Orgn., Arnhem, The Netherlands, 1964-72; editor pig farming Misset, Doetinchem, The Netherlands, 1972-80, editor sheep farming, 1976-84, editor Pluimveehoudery, 1980-84, editor World Flower Trade mag., 1984-86, editor Pigs, 1982-91, editor World Poultry, 1982—. Recipient DLG award in bronze German Agrl. Soc., 1990. Chmn. Internat. Club of Pig and Poultry Journalists. Avocations: stamp collecting, volleyball, tennis, golf, gardening. Fax: 31 (0)314 340515. E-mail: w.van.der.sluis@ebi.nl. Office: Elsevier Int Bus Info, PO Box 4, 7000 BA Doetinchem The Netherlands

VAN DER STRAATEN, JAN, leisure studies educator; b. De Werken en Sleeuwijk, The Netherlands, July 18, 1935; s. Jan Cornelis and Anna (Visser) V.; m. Maria Frederica Verhagen, Apr. 26, 1990. Master, Nederlandse Econom. Hogeschool, Rotterdam, 1971; Dr., Tilburg (The Netherlands) U., 1990. Dir. Strago-Electro B.V., Gorinchen, The Netherlands, 1953-67; dep. head dept. environ. stats. C.B.S., The Hague, The Netherlands, 1969-73; dep. head dept. econ. rsch. Municipality of Rotterdam, 1973-84; sr. lectr. dept. social econs. Tilburg U., 1984-90, asst. prof. dept. leisure studies, 1990—; sr. rschr. European Ctr. for Nature Conservation, The Netherlands, 1994-98. Mem. editl. bd. Environ. Politics, 1992-2000, Bus. Strategy and the Environment, 1993—, Milieu, 1993—, Jour. Sustainable Tourism, 1998—; editor: Tourism and the Environment, 1992-99, Towards Sustainable Development, 1994; contbr. articles to profl. jours. Chmn. SOVON, Beek/Ubbergen, The Netherlands, 1986-90, NMGA, Eindhoven, The Netherlands, 1990-95. European Union grantee, 1992-95, 94-96, 96-2000; fellow Free U. Brussels. Fellow European Assn. for Environ. Mgmt. Edn.; mem. European Assn. Evolutionary Polit. Economy (area coord. environ. economy 1992-95), European Soc. for Ecol. Econs. (v.p. 1996-98). Avocations: mountain climbing, skating, cross-country skiing, bird watching, photography. E-mail: saxifraga@ecnc.nl. Home: Bredaseweg 335, 5037 LC Tilburg The Netherlands Office: Tilburg University, Warandelaan 2 PO Box 90153, 5000 LE Tilburg The Netherlands

VAN DER VELDEN, ALEXANDER JACOBUS MARIA, aerospace engineer, aerospace company executive; b. Kruisland, The Netherlands, Nov. 23, 1961; came to the U.S., 1987; s. Jacques and Elisabeth (Veraart) Van der V.; m. Minami Yoda, June 16, 1995. Degree in engring., Delft U. Tech., The Netherlands, 1986; PhD, Stanford U., 1992. Rsch. asst. Stanford (Calif.) U., 1988-92; engr. in charge Daimler-Benz Aerospace, Bremen, Germany, 1992-95; pres. Synaps, Inc., Atlanta, 1995—, Synaps Ing-Gmbh, Bremen, 1998—. Co-author: New Design Concepts for High Speed Air Transport, 1997. Recipient Centennial Futurist award Honeywell, Munich, 1985, Dirs. Discretionary award NASA, Ames, Calif., 1989, Best of 1991 team award Popular Sci. Mag., 1991, Innovation Oblique Flying Wing, NASA, Ames, 1990, award for best contbn. to Daimler Chrysler Rawid Program, 1999. Mem. AIAA, ASME. Achievements include automated design system for supersonic and transonic wings; pointer design automation software. Home: 2071 Somervale Ct NE Atlanta GA 30329-1686 Office: Synaps Inc 2957 Clairmont Rd NE Ste 170 Atlanta GA 30329-1647

VAN DER VIJGH, WILLEM JAN FREDERIK, research laboratory administrator, educator; b. Amsterdam, The Netherlands, Aug. 4, 1941; s. Arnold B. and Janke (Boonstra) Van der V.; m. Elisabeth Van den Berg, Mar. 29, 1969; children: Ronald J.V., Caroline E. BS, Free U., Amsterdam, 1967, PhD, 1977. Instr. analytical chemistry Free U., 1963-66; tchr. chemistry Highschool Hilversum, Amsterdam, 1965-73; head clin. rsch. lab. Free U., Amsterdam, 1971—, prof. bioanalysis and pharmacokinetics, 1991—. Contbr. over 200 articles to profl. jours. Avocations: mountaineering, tennis, playing piano. Office: KRIGO Acad Ziekenhuis, Vrije Univ PO Box 7057, 1007 MB Amsterdam The Netherlands

VAN DER VOORT, PASCAL, chemistry educator, new materials researcher; b. Turnhout, Antwerp, Belgium, Feb. 21, 1967; s. Alphonsius Van der Voort and Maria Josephine Verhoeven; m. Ines De Ridder, Oct. 15, 1994; 1 child, Lali. MSc with greatest distinction, U. Antwerp, 1989, Aggregation in high sch. tchg., 1989, PhD in Scis. with greatest distinction, 1993. Rschr. Belgian Ministry Employment, 1993-94; tchg. asst. U. Antwerp, 1989-93, asst. prof. chemistry, 1994—; guest prof. Ga. Inst. Tech., 1996-97; chmn. XIV Chemistry at Interfaces, Belgium, 1996; reviewer Jour. Colloid Interface Sci., 1997—, Analytica Chimica Acta, 1998—, Energy and Fuels, 1998—, Chem. Com., 1999—, Jour. Material Chemistry, 1999—, Phys. Chemistry and Chem. Physics, 1999—, Jour. Phys. Chem., 1999—. Author: Characterization and Chemical Modification of the Silica Surface, 1995; contbr. over 50 articles to sci. jours., including Jour. Royal Soc.-Faraday Trans., Jour. Phys. Chemistry, Jour. Porous Materials. Named Outstanding Rschr. in Ceramics, Belgian Soc. Ceramics, 1997. Mem. Belgian Soc. Ceramics. Avocations: snooker, history, Latin language, gardening. Office: U Antwerp (UIA) Dept Chem, Universiteitsplein 1, B-2610 Wilrijk Antwerp, Belgium

VANDER VORST, ANDRÉ SYLVAIN JOSEPH, engineering educator; b. Brussels, Oct. 22, 1935; s. Guillaume and Marcelle (Allard) Vander V.; m. Josette Zeegers, Dec. 29, 1959 (dec. Jan. 1981); children: Claire, Pierre, Cécile, Catherine, Chantal. Student, U. Louvain, Louvain, Belgium, 1958; cert. in nuclear scis., U. Louvain, 1956, 57, D. in Applied Sci., 1965; M., MIT, 1965. Asst. U. Louvain, Louvain, 1958-62; prof. U. Louvain, 1962—, dean engring., 1972-75, v.p., 1973-75, pres. open faculty, 1973-87; vis. researcher MIT, Cambridge, Mass., 1964-65, Stanford (Calif.) U., 1965-66; chmn. and mem. various commns. on communications, microwaves, and edn., Belgium. Author: Electromagnetic Theory, 1980, Microwaves, 1981, Transmission Lines, 1982; contbr. articles to profl. jours. Recipient Meritorious Svc. award IEEE-MTT Soc., Millennium medal IEEE. Fellow IEEE; mem. SITEL (Prix SITEL), Academia Europaea, Electromagnetics Acad. (MIT). Avocation: conducting music. Office: U Louvain, Batiment Maxwell, B 1348 Louvain Belgium

VAN DER WAL, EELCO, foundation executive; b. Baarn, The Netherlands, Nov. 2, 1958; s. Peter and Kate Lisbeth (Einthoven) v.; life partner Ariane Leonore Moussault, Feb., 1995. Student, Kottenpark Coll., Enschede, The Netherlands, 1977; student in tech. mktg., CTO, Eindhoven, 1989; student in physics, U. Groningen, The Netherlands, 1986. Sr. sales cons. Philips NL, Eindhoven, 1986-89; product mgr. Philips IAS, Eindhoven, 1989-92, bus. mgr., 1992-93, mktg. mgr., 1993-95; dir. OTS Group, Zaltbommel, The Netherlands, 1995-97; CEO Forum Found., Zaltbommel, 1997—; mng. dir. PLCopemn, Zaltbommel, 1995—; chmn. PICMG Europe, Zaltbommel, 1997—. Contbr. articles to profl. jours. Mem. CTO Alumni Assn. Office: Forum Foundation, PO Box 2015, NL5300CA Zaltbommel The Netherlands

VAN DER WALT, BAREND JOHANNES, philosophy educator; b. Potchefstroom, South Africa, Apr. 12, 1939; s. Jeremia Jesaja and Catharina Elizabeth (Delport) Van Der W.; m. Johanna Magrieta Loock, June 28, 1964; children: Jeremia J., George C., Barend J., Marieta M. BA, Potchefstroom U., 1960, BA with honors, 1961, ThB, 1966, MA in Philosophy, 1968, DPhil, 1975. Student asst. Potchefsfstroom U., South Africa, 1964-68; prof. philosophy Potchesfstroom U., 1980—; scientific asst. Free U., Amsterdam, 1969-70; sr. lectr. philosophy U. Fort Hare, South Africa, 1970-74; dir. Inst. Reformational Studies, South Africa, 1974-99. Author: The Liberating Message: A Christian Worldview for South Africa, 1994 (award for Reformational Scholarship 1997), Leaders With a Vision: How Christian Leadership Can Tackle the African Crisis, 1995, Man and God: The Transforming Power of Biblical Religion, 1997, Afrocentric or Eurocentric? Our Task in a Multicultural South Africa, 1997; editor: (youth mag.) Die Bondsbode, 1963-68, (Xhosa periodical) Umthombo Wamandla, 1973-84, (circular) Orientation, 1975-99. Chmn. Christian Literature Com. for Africa, 1987-97. Grantee Free U., Amsterdam, Potchefstroom U., South Africa, 1968-70, rsch. grantee Human Scis. Rsch. Coun., 1974-82, travel grantee Human Scis. Rsch. Coun., 1972-97. Mem. Assn. Christian Scholarship (Australia), Internat. Assn. Promotion of Christian Higher Edn. (mem. coun.), Soc. Reformatorial Philosophy. Mem. Reformed Ch. South Africa. Avocations: gardening, hiking. Home: 7 Bezuidenhout St, 2530 Potchefstroom South Africa Office: Potchefstroom U, for Christian Higher Edn, 2520 Potchefstroom South Africa

VAN DER WALT, JOHANN GEORGE, veterinary physiologist, educator; b. Johannesburg, Republic of South Africa, Mar. 16, 1944; s. Johan George and Jacqueline (du Toit) van der W.; m. Alida Elizabeth van Domselaar, June 13, 1969; children: Ian, Eric. BSc with honors, U. Witwatersrand, Republic of South Africa, 1966, MSc, 1967; DSc, Pretoria U., Republic of South Africa, 1977. Registered animal scientist. Profl. officer Dept. Agr., Republic of South Africa, 1966-71, sr. profl. officer, 1971-77, chief profl. officer, 1977-81, head sect. ADSRI, 1981-87; assoc. prof. U. Pretoria, 1987-90, prof., head dept. vet. physiology, 1990—. Chief editor South African Jour. Animal Sci., 1987-99. Lt. South African Police Res. Force, 1982-93. Agrl. scholar Brit. Petroleum, 1979-80, Thomas Lawrence Pawlett scholar, 1985. Mem. Internat. Union Physiol. Scis. South Africa, Physiol. Soc. South Africa (mem. com. 1987-95), South African Soc. Animal Sci. (chief editor 1987—), South African Biochem. Soc., African Assn. Physiol. Scis. (coun. mem.). Avocations: scuba diving, speleology, photography. Home: 244 Anderson St Brooklyn, 0181 Pretoria Gauteng, South Africa Office: U Pretoria Dept Vet Physiol, Faculty Vet Sci, 0110 Onderstepoort South Africa

VAN DER WATEREN, JAN FLORIS, librarian, psychotherapist, consultant; b. Pretoria, South Africa, May 14, 1940; arrived in Eng., 1965; s. Jacob and Wilhelmina D. (Labuschagne) van der W. BA, Potchefstroom U., 1962, Potchefstroom U., 1963; MA, Potchefstroom U., 1966; postgrad. diploma in librarianship, Univ. Coll., London, 1969. Registered U.K. Coun. Psychotherapy. Dep. libr. Royal Inst. Brit. Archs., London, 1971-78; mng. libr. Brit. Archtl. Libr., London, 1978-83, dir., Sir Banister Fletcher libr., 1983-88; keeper, chief libr. Nat. Art Libr., London, 1988-2000; pvt. practice psychotherapy, 1983—; cons. for libr. bldgs. Contbr. numerous articles on art librarianship to profl. jours. Fellow Libr. Assn., Royal Soc. Art, Royal Inst. Brit. Archs. (hon.); mem. Architecture Club, Grolier Club (N.Y.C.). Avocation: 20th Century Japanese literature. E-mail: jan.vanderwateren@ukgateway.net. Home: 52 Blenheim Crescent, London W11 1NY, England

VAN DER WATT, JAN GABRIEL, religious studies educator; b. Germiston, Gauteng, South Africa, Nov. 5, 1952; s. Andre and Cornelia Jacoba Van der W.; m. Shireen Crous, July 16, 1977; 1 child: Nireen. MA in Greek, U. Pretoria (South Africa), 1979, DDiv in New Testament, 1986, DLitt in Greek, 1999. Ordained minister. Sr. lectr., head dept. New Testament U. Fort Hare, Alice, South Africa, 1980-86; prof. New Testament U. Pretoria, 1986—, head dept. New Testament, 1993—; guest prof. Theologiese U. Kampen (The Netherlands), 1994-95, Christian U. St. Petersburg (Russia), 1994-95, U. Vienna, 1998, Cath. Theol. U. and Rijksuniv. Utrecht (The Netherlands), 1999; vis. prof. U. Stellenbosch (South Africa), 1995. Author: What Makes a Christian Different?, 1989, Family of the King, Dynamics of Metaphor in the Gospel According to John, 1999, God's Message for Children, 1999; translator (New Testament into Modern Afrikaans) Die Boodskap, 1998; mem. editl. bd. Neotestamentica, 1995, Rev. for Biblical Lit., 1999. Named researcher Alexander von Humboldt sitftung, 1990—. Mem. South African Acad. Arts and Scis., New Testament Soc. South Africa (exec. sec. 1995), Studiorum Novi Testamenti Soc. (co-chair Johannine seminar 1998). Avocation: photography. Home: 404 Queen's Crescent, Lynwood Pretoria, South Africa 0081 Office: U Pretoria, Lynnwood Rd, Brooklyn Pretoria, South Africa 0002

VANDER WEIDE, VERNON JAY, lawyer; b. East Grand Rapids, Mich., Apr. 3, 1940; s. Henry Thomas and Della (Van Zoeren) V.W.; m. Gretchen Laurie Clemmons, Sept. 11, 1965; children: Jennifer, Stephanie, Vanessa. AA, Grand Rapids Jr. Coll., 1960; BA, U. Mich., 1962, LLB, 1965; LLM, George Washington U., 1971. Bar: D.C. 1970, Mich. 1970, Minn. 1977, U.S. Dist. Ct. Minn. 1977. Staff asst. House Rep. Conf., Washington, 1965-66; staff atty. ICC, Washington, 1969-70; br. chief atty. SEC, Arlington, Va., 1970-76; shareholder Wiese & Cox, Mpls., 1970-76; shareholder, bd. dirs. Head, Seifert & Vander Weide, Mpls., 1982—; lectr. Continuing Legal Edn. Corp. Orgn., 1981, 87, 98. Writer, analyst, columnist for neighborhood newspaper, Mpls., 1982-94. Mem. task force Supt.'s Blue Ribbon Commn., Mpls., 1982; bd. deacons Westminster Presbyn. Ch., Mpls., 1993-99, Minn. Futures Forum, 1998-99. Capt. U.S. Army, 1966-69. Mem. ABA, Minn. Bar Assn., Hennepin County Bar Assn. Avocations: sailing, investments, reading, teaching, family. Office: Head Seifert & Vander Weide 120 S 6th St Minneapolis MN 55402-1803

VAN DER WESTHUIZEN, JACOB, criminologist, retired research institute director; b. Heidelberg, South Africa, Sept. 15, 1929; s. Jacob and Gezina Christina Regina (Du Plessis) Van der W.; m. Debora Magrietha Van Heerden, July 10, 1954; children: Deborah, Jacob, Regina. BA with honors, U. South Africa, 1968, MA cum laude, 1970, PhD, 1977. Clk. Farmer's Coop., Nylstroom, South Africa, 1948-50; lab. asst., rschr. Indsl. Firm, Germiston, South Africa, 1951-53; tchr., divsn. head Edn. Dept., Gauteng, South Africa, 1954-70; lectr., sr. lectr. U. South Africa, Pretoria, 1970-75, sr. rsch. officer Inst. Criminology, 1976-79, prof. criminal justice, dir. rsch., 1980-89, rschr., cons., 1989—; rschr., cons. South African Police Svcs., Pretoria, 1991-94; cons. Univ. South Africa, Pretoria, 1989—. Author (handbook) Security Management, 1990; co-author (handbook) Security Forum, 1990; editor, co-author (handbook) Prediction of Parole Failure and Maladjustment, 1983; Portents of Violence (whorls and fingerprint patterns), 1983, Wheels of Misfortune: alcohol and drug abuse, 1988, Forensic Criminalistics, 1993; co-author: International Handbook of Contemporary Developments in Criminology, 1983, Protocol: Evaluating the Performance of Trained Police Dogs in Identifying Humans by Scent, 1997. Fellow Inst. Security (bd. dirs. 1985—), Internat. Biog. Assn.; mem. Internat. Assn. Chiefs of Police, Internat. Narcotic Enforcement Officers Assn. (Africa rep.), Planetary Soc., Nat. Geog. Soc. Achievements include research protocol for describing, explaining, predicting and controlling stress at the asset protection workplace, comprehensive computerization for the South African Policy Svc.-a systems approach. Avocations: reading, painting, writing, music, birdwatching. E-mail: jacobvw@mweb.co.za. Home: 37 Buffels Rd Rietondale, Pretoria 0084, South Africa

VAN DER WOUDE, ADAM SIMON, religious studies educator; b. Village Oosterlittens, Frisia, The Netherlands, Oct. 16, 1927; s. Dirk Van Der Woude and Feikje Stremler; m. Frederika Catharina Sanders, Apr. 3, 1954 (dec. Mar. 1998). BA in Theology cum laude, Groningen U., 1950, MA in Semitic Langs. and Lit. cum laude, 1955; ThD, U. Groningen, The Netherlands, 1957; DD, U. Munich, 1972, U. St. Andrews, Scotland, 1985. Min. Dutch Ref. Ch., 1957-60; prof. Old Testament U. Groningen, 1960-92; mem. bd. supervisory dirs. pub. house J.H. KOK, Kampen, 1983-98. Author: (book) The Job-targum from Cave 11 of Qumran, 1971, Commentaries on the Minor Prophets, 1974-84; editor: Jour. Study of Judaism, 1970-97. Named Companionship of the Order of the Dutch Lion, Dutch Govt., 1989. Fellow royal Dutch Acad. Scis. and Arts, Acad. Europea; mem. Brit. Soc. Old Testament Study (hon.). Mem. Dutch Ref. Ch. Avocation: gardening. Home: Domela Nieuwenhuislaan 57, 9722 LJ Groningen The Netherlands

VAN DER WOUDE, FOKKE JOHANNES, physician; b. Leeuwarden, The Netherlands, Sept. 30, 1953; m. H. Griesen, Jan. 14, 1978; children: Joanne, Diane. MD, State U. Groningen, 1977, PhD, 1984. Intern State Univ. Hosp. Groningen, 1975-77, resident, 1977-82; jr. staff mem. Renal Transplantation Unit, Groningen, 1982-85; postdoctoral fellow dept. pediatrics U. Minn., Mpls., 1985-87; head renal transplant unit, assoc. prof. medicine Univ. Hosp., Leiden, The Netherlands, 1987-95; prof., dir. V Med. Clinic U. Heidelberg, Germany, 1995—; full prof. U. Heidelberg; head V Med. Clin., Klinikum Mannheim, Germany; project leader European ANCA Study Group, EEC, Brussels, 1989-95. Contbr. articles to profl. jours. Postdoctoral fellow Dutch Kidney Found., 1985. Fellow Royal Soc. Medicine; mem. Dutch Soc. Nephrology, Dutch Soc. Immunology, Dutch. Soc. Transplantation, British Transplant Assn., Internat. Soc. for Nephrology, Am. Soc. Nephrology, Tranplantation Soc. Office: V Med Clinic Mannheim, Theodore Kutzer Uferi 3, 68135 Mannheim Germany

VAN DER WYCK, HERMAN CONSTANTYN, investment banker; b. The Hague, The Netherlands, Mar. 17, 1934; arrived in Eng., 1966; s. Hendrik Lodewyk and Berendina Johanna (Van Welderen Baroness Rengers) van der W.; m. Edina Nathalie, Patrick Henri Louis, Edzard Lorillard, Alexander Lodewyk. MA in Polit. Sci., U. Geneva, 1959; MBA, Rotterdam U., 1968, U. Mich., 1968. With S.G. Warburg & Co., Ltd., 1969-73, dir., 1973-87; vice chmn. S.G. Warburg Group plc, London, 1987-95; vice chmn., mng. dir. Warburg Dillon Read, 1995-99; chmn. UBS Warburg (Nederland) B.V., 1999—; dir. Compagnie Internat. Placements et DE Capitalizaion, Paris; dir. Wilken USA Select Fund, Atlanta. Capt. Dutch Cavalry, ret. Mem. Inst. Econ. Affairs. Avocations: swimming, skiing, music. Office: Warburg Dillon Read BV, Herengracht 564, 1017 CH Amsterdam EC2M 2PP, The Netherlands

VAN DE SANDE, CHRISTIAN C.G.A., chemist; b. Bad-Honnef, Germany, Jan. 25, 1949; s. Armand and Cécile (De Clercq) Van de S.; m. Beatrys Filliaert, Apr. 6, 1973; children: Tine, Sara. BSc in Chemistry, State U. Gent, Belgium, 1970, DSc in Chemistry, 1973, Diploma in Middle Mgmt., 1986. Postdoctoral rsch. assoc. Cornell U., Ithaca, N.Y., 1974; jr. rsch. assoc. Nat. Fonds voor Wetenschappelijk Onderzoek, Gent, 1970-73, rsch. assoc., 1975-78; rsch. scientist Agfa-Gevaert NV, Mortsel, Belgium, 1978-83, synthetic group mgr., 1983-86, dept. head chemistry, 1986-90, dept. head basic. photographic rsch., 1991-96, dir. photochem. R & D, 1996—; sr. v.p. R & D materials Agfa-Gevaert Group, Mortsel, 1999—. Contbr. more than 40 articles to internat. jours.; more than 50 patents and rsch. disclosures dealing with various aspects of photography. Recipient Stas medal Royal Acad. Scis., 1974, Otto Bayer medal Otto Bayer Stiftung, 1990. Mem. AAAS, Am. Chem. Soc., Koninklyke Vlaamse Chemische Vereniging, Kiwanis. Office: AGFA-Gevaert NV, Septestraat 27, B-2640 Mortsel Belgium

VAN DE VEN, WILLEM JAN MARIE, molecular genetics educator, researcher; b. Veghel, The Netherlands, May 22, 1947; arrived in Belgium, 1989; s. Martinus Antonius and Wilhelmina Maria (Van Der Cammen) Van De V.; m. Elisabeth Berdina Klaassen, July 4, 1973 (div. Sept. 1984); 1 child, Patrick Michiel. BS, U. Nijmegen, The Netherlands, 1970, MS, 1973, PhD, 1978. Rsch. fellow U. Nijmegen, 1973-78; postdoctoral Frederick Cancer Rsch. Ctr./Nat. Cancer Inst./NIH., Frederick, Md., 1978-80, vis. scientist, 1980-81; head rsch. Katholieke U., Nijmegen, Belgium, 1982-86; assoc. prof. Katholieke U., Nijmegen, 1986-89; prof. Katholieke U., Leuven, Belgium, 1989—; rsch. cons. K.U. Nijmegen, 1989—; rsch. cons. in biotech. K.U. Leuven, 1989—; chmn. Icarus Rsch. Found., Maastricht, The Netherlands, 1995—. Contbr. over 200 articles to profl. jours; patentee in field. Recipient Triennal Alexandre et Gaston Tytgat prize for cancer rsch., Belgium, 1995. Mem. Am. Assn. Cancer Rsch., Belgian Soc. Biochemistry, Belgian Soc. Cell Biology, Netherlands Soc. Biochemistry, Netherlands Soc. Genetics, Netherlands Soc. Microbiology, European Soc. Human Genetics, Human Genome Orgn., N.Y. Acad. Scis. Avocations: travel, opera. E-mail: wim.vandeven@med.kuleuven.ac.be. Office: Lab Molecular Oncology, Ctr Human Genetics, 3000 Leuven Belgium

VAN DEVENTER, JANNIE STEPHANUS JAKOB, engineering educator; b. Laingsburg, We. Cape, South Africa, May 18, 1955; arrived in Australia, 1995; s. Gert and Susanna (Odendaal) van D.; m. Winifred Snyman, Dec. 15, 1979; children: George, Ben. B. Engring. with honors, U. Stellenbosch, South Africa, 1978, B. Com. with honors, 1982, PhD in Engring., 1985, D. Com., 1991; D in Engring., U. Stellenbosch, 1999. Profl. engr. Sr. lectr. U. Stellenbosch, South Africa, 1981-86; assoc. prof. U. Stellenbosch, 1987-90, prof., head chem. engring. dept., 1990-95; prof. mineral and process engring. U. Melbourne (Australia), 1995—. Mem. editl. bd. Minerals Engring. Jour., 1993—. Decorated medal Brit. Assn., 1992; recipient P.E. Rousseau award for excellence, 1984, Pres.'s award Found. for Rsch. Devel. South Africa, named Category A researcher, 1994. Mem. South African Inst. Mining and Metallurgy (corr.). Avocations: wine collecting, jogging. Office: U Melbourne, Dept Chem Engring, Melbourne VIC 3010, Australia

VANDEVER, JUDITH ANN, county official; b. Hemstead, N.Y., Aug. 6, 1941; d. John Anthony Klym and Kathryn M. (Lane) Trexler; children: Garret, Kimberlee Vandever Johnson. Dep. recorder Clark County Recorder, Las Vegas, Nev., 1979-91, chief dep. recorder, 1991-93, asst. recorder, 1993-94, county recorder, 1995—. State chair. Nev. Young Woman of the Yr., 1991; mem. S.M.A.R.T. Team Clark County Sch. Dist., 1994-95, ctrl. com. State/County Dem. Ctrl. Com., 1988—; state dir. Women Officials Nat. Assn. Counties, 1997. Recipient Leadership Dedication award Amigos De HIP, 1996, Women Elected Ofcls. Spotlight award Women's Dem. Club, 1996. Mem. ASPA, Nat. Assn. County Recorders and Clks. (bd. dirs. 1999—), Nat. Assn. County Recorders, Election Ofcls. and Clks. (bd. dirs. 1999-02), Assn. of Profl. Mortage Women,Assn. of Recorders Mgrs. and Adminstrs., U. Nev.-Las Vegas Jean Nidetch Women's Ctr. (original founder), Leadership Las Vegas Alumni Assoc., Las Vegas C. of C. (bd. of trustees, cmty. coun. 1995-98). Office: Clark County Recorder 500 S Grand Central Pkwy Las Vegas NV 89106-4506

VANDEVER, WILLIAM DIRK, lawyer; b. Chgo., Aug. 1, 1949; s. Lester J. and Elizabeth J. V.; m. Kathi J. Zellmer, Aug. 26, 1983; children: Barton Dirk, Brooke Shelby. BS, U. Mo., Kansas City, 1971, JD with distinction, 1974. Bar: Mo. 1975, U.S. Dist. Ct. (we. dist.) Mo. 1975. Dir. Popham Law Firm, Kansas City, Mo., 1975—; lectr. in field, Kansas City Mo., 1979—. Issue editor U. Mo.-Kansas City Law Rev., 1974. Fellow Am. Bd. Trial Advs. (Best Lawyers in Am.-tort law); mem. ABA, ATLA, Mo. Assn. Trial Attys., Kansas City Met. Bar Assn. (treas., sec., pres., elected to 16th Jud. Commn. 1988-94), Kansas City Bar Found. (treas. 1992, sec. 1994, pres. 1996-98, pres. award domestic violence 1999), Interest on Lawyer Trust Accts. of Mo. (bd. govs.), Kansas City Mem. Svcs. (pres. 1988—, commr. 16th jud. cir. selection com.), U. Mo. Kansas City Found. (fin. com. 1998), Phi Delta Phi, Beta Theta Pi. Avocations: tennis, skiing, running, reading. Home: 11380 W 121st Ter Shawnee Mission KS 66213-1978 Office: Popham Law Firm 1300 Commerce Trust Bldg Kansas City MO 64106

VAN DE VOORDE, ANDRE, scientific officer; b. Lokeren, Flanders, Belgium, Dec. 8, 1943; s. Faldoni Van de Voorde and Celestine Baeke; m. Monique de Backer; 1 child, An. PhD, U. Ghent, Belgium, 1971. Asst. U. Ghent, 1967-73, staff scientist, 1973-87; lab. dir. Innogenetics N.V., Zwijnaarde, Belgium, 1987-96; chief sci. officer Innogenetics N.V., Zwijnaarde, 1996—; cons. IWT, Belgium, 1987-95, European Cmty., 1995—. Author: Research Advances in Alzheimer's Disease and Related Disorders, 1995. Mem. external adv. group Cell Factories of the European Commn. Sub lt. Belgian Med. Svc., 1968-69. Mem. Belgian Biochem. Soc., Belgian Immunol. Soc. Avocations: literature, music, arts. Office: Innogenetics NV, Industriepark Zwijnaarde 7, 9052 Zwijnaarde Belgium

VAN DE WAL, HENRY J.C.M., cardiopulmonary surgeon; b. Oss, The Netherlands, Sept. 8, 1951; s. Theo and Berny (Govers) van de W.; m. Carla Vermeulen, Apr. 14, 1976 (div. Feb. 2000); children: Sjoerd, Marloes, Rolf Babette. MD, Cath. U., Nymegen, The Netherlands, 1979, PhD, 1986. Resident Juliana Hosp., Apeldoorn, The Netherlands, 1979-81; resident St. Radboud U. Hosp., Nymegen, The Netherlands, 1981-85, cons. cardiopulmonary & vascular surgery, 1985-86, cons. cardiopulmonary surgery, 1986-91; head dept. cardiopulmonary surgery Wilhelmina Children's Hosp., Utrecht, The Netherlands, 1991-98; vis. cardiac surgeon Royal Liverpool Children's Hosp., Eng., 1986-87, Royal Hosp. Sick Children, Edinburgh, Scotland, 1987-88, Boston Children's Hosp., 1989; vis. prof. cardiac surgery Laennec Hosp., Paris, 1996-97, Inst. Cardiovasculaire Paris Sud, 1996-97. Rsch. fellow St. Radboud U. Hosp., 1978-79. Mem. Dutch Soc. Thoracic Surgery, European Assn. Cardio-Thoracic Surgery, European Assn. Pediatric Cardiologists. Avocations: painting. Home: Nieuwe Hesche weg 104, NL5342EE Oss The Netherlands Office: Univ Klinikum Essen, Hufeland strasse 55, D 45122 Essen Germany

VANDE WALLE, GASTON, retired economics educator, researcher; b. Ghent, E Flanders, Belgium, June 25, 1923; s. August Regina and Maria Magdalena (De Wulf) VW.; m. Jeanne Claes, Nov. 2, 1953; children: Annick, Peter. Cert. primary sch. tchr., Normal Sch., Ghent, Belgium, 1942, cert secondary sch. sci. tchr., 1944; lic. Comml. and Fin. Scis., U. Ghent, 1948, D in Econ. Scis., 1963. Tchr. primary sch. Mcpl. Ghent, Belgium, 1944-45; tchr. French Secondary Sch. Province E. Flanders, Ghent, 1945-48; tchr. comml. scis. Normal Sch., Ghent, 1946-48, Higher Tech. Schs., Ghent, Belgium, 1948-57; asst. prof. econs. U. Ghent, 1958-64; lectr. Higher Comml. Sch., Antwerp, Belgium, 1964-65; lectr. State U. Ctr., Antwerp, 1965-69, ordinary prof. econs., 1969-88; lectr. U. Ghent, 1969-88; mem. coll. of censors Nat. Bank Belgium, Brussels, 1967-92; vis. prof. Nat Inst. Devel. Adminstrn., Bangkok, Thailand, 1995-96. Author: (Books) The Conjunctural Evolution in Belgian Congo and Ruanda-Cerundi, 1966, History of Economic Thought, 1976, 3d rev. edit., 1990; co-author: General Economics, 1981, 3d rev. edit. 1993, Domestic and Foreign Trade, 1986, 3d rev. edit. 1992, Staff Management and Communication in Organizations, 1995. Pres. Tchrs. Trade Union, Ghent, 1952-58, Sec. Socialist Study Circle, Ghent, 1964-72, pres., 1972-79; pres. Higher Coun. non-Univ. Higher Edn., Brussels, 1977-82. Decorated Great Officer of Order of Leopold II, Belgium Ministry Fgn. Affairs, 1988. Mem. Flemish Socialist Party. Avocations: bridge, swimming, walking. Home: Aan de Bocht 10, 9000 Ghent E Flands, Belgium

VAN DE WINKEL, JAN, immunology educator; b. Venray, The Netherlands, Mar. 1, 1961; s. Matheus Wilhelmus and Maria Petronella Gerarda (Van Kempen) Van de W.; m. Helena Wilhelmina Van Maarseveen, Aug. 16, 1991; children: Lisa, Koen, Erik. MSc, U. Nymegen, The Netherlands, 1985, PhD, 1988. Postdoctoral rschr. Utrecht (The Netherlands) U., 1988-89; asst. prof. dept. immunology Utrecht (The Netherlands) U. Hosp., 1990-92, assoc. prof., 1992-96, prof., 1996—; sci. dir. Medarex Europe, Utrecht, 1996—; chief sci. officer Genmab, Copenhagen, 1999; mem. sci. adv. bd. IDM, Paris, 1994-97; mem. Sci. Coun., The Netherlands Cancer Found., 1998—; mem. bd. advisors The Thai Network for Biomed. Rsch., Thailand, 1997—. Editor: Human IgG Fc Receptors, 1996, The Immunoglobulin Receptors and Their Physiological and Pathological Roles in Immunity, 1998. Mem. Am. Assn. Immunologists, Brit. Soc. Immunology, Dutch Soc. Immunology. Fax: 31 0 30-2504305. Office: U Med Ctr Utrecht, Dept Immunology KC2-0852, 3584EA Utrecht The Netherlands

VAN DIEM, MIKE, film director, writer. Grad., Netherlands Film & TV Acad., 1989. Dir. (film) De Andere Kant, 1988, (TV series) Pleidooi, 1993; writer, dir. (films) Karakter, 1997, Alaska, 1997. Office: First Floor Features, Bolderweg 22, 1332 AV Almere The Netherlands*

VAN DIEST, PAUL JOANNES, pathologist, consultant; b. Rotterdam, The Netherlands, Apr. 29, 1963; s. Leo Van Diest and Maria Van Raay. MD, Free U. Amsterdam, The Netherlands, 1988, PhD, 1990, degree in Pathology, 1996. Bd. cert. pathologist. Rsch. fellow Free U. Amsterdam, 1988-90, postdoctoral worker, 1990-91, resident pathology, 1991-96, cons. pathology, 1996—, assoc. prof. pathology, 1999—; cons. Dianon Inc., Amsterdam, 1990-91; vis. prof. U. Ancona, Italy, 1994; chmn. breast cancer working group Free U. Hosp., Amsterdam, 1996-2000, dir. pathology program, 2000—. Author: Manual of Quantitative Pathology in Cancer Diagnosis and Prognosis, 1990; editor: Quantitative Cyto-and Histoprognosis, 1992; editor Diagnostic Quantitative Pathology Newsletter, 1992-96, Jour. Clin. Pathology, 1998—; mem. editl. bd. Jour. Clin. Pathology, 1996-97, Electronic Jour. Pathology, 1994—, Analytical Quantitative Cytology & Histology, 1995—, Molecular Pathology, 1998—. Grantee Dutch Cancer Found., 1995, Dutch Heart Found., 1995. Mem. Dutch Soc. Pathology Den Bosch, Internat. Soc. Diagnostic Quantitative Pathology (sec. 1994—), European Soc. Analytical Cellular Pathology (sec. 1999—). Avocations: running, tennis, windsurfing, music. Fax: 0756878171. Office: Free U Hosp Dept Pathology, PO Box 7057, 1007 MB Amsterdam The Netherlands

VAN DIJK, BOB ALFRED, blood transfusion specialist; b. Utrecht, The Netherlands, Jan. 4, 1950; s. Gerard and Sara Hendrika (Thijssen) van D.; m. Albertine Milatz, Jan. 11, 1975; children: Daan Reyer, Marianne Reyertje. MD, State U., Utrecht, The Netherlands, 1974; PhD, State U., Leyden, Holland, 1991. Asst. surgeon Cath. Hosp., Hilversum, Holland, 1976-78; asst. blood transfusion physician Blood Bank, Amsterdam, The Netherlands, 1978-80; head blood transfusion dept. U. Hosp., Groningen, The Netherlands, 1980-85, Nijmegen, The Netherlands, 1985-95; med. dir. SeroConsult, Groningen, The Netherlands, 1996—. Mem. ISBT, DMMA. Avocations: skiing, sailing, motorcycling. E-mail: serocons@dds.nl. Home and Office: Reitdiepskade 1001/AB, 9718 BP Groningen The Netherlands

VAN DIJK, ROBERT PETER ADRIAAN, aerospace company executive; b. Rotterdam, The Netherlands, Dec. 20, 1943; s. Christiaam Gerrit Van Dijk and Adriana Mathilda Van Boven; m. Magdalena Rijneke, Dec. 16, 1970; children: Roger, Tamara. BS, Tech. Coll., Haarlem, The Netherlands, 1967. Cert. aeronautical engr. Tech. officer Royal Netherlands Air Force, 1967-69; sales mgr. Hollinda, The Hague, 1969-73; sales engr. Fokker, Amsterdam, 1973-77, mktg. mgr., 1977-96; dir. bus. devel. Argo Systems, Inc., Sunnyvale, 1996-97, Boeing Info. and Comm. Sys. Divsn., 1997—. 1st lt. Royal Netherlands Air Force, 1967-69. Office: Vlietenburg 55, 2804 WR Gouda The Netherlands

VAN DIJL, JAN MAARTEN, molecular biologist, educator; b. Zwolle, Overijssel, The Netherlands, June 1, 1961; s. Jan and Annemarie Berta Zilla (Eichentopf) van D.; m. Henrica Maria Werink, June 28, 1991; children: Lotte, Mark. MSc cum laude, U. Groningen, Netherlands, 1985, PhD in Math. and Natural Scis., 1990. Postdoc. rschr. U. Groningen, 1990-94, rschr., lectr., 1996—; postdoc. rschr. Biozentrum, U. Basel, Switzerland, 1994-96; spkr. in field. Patentee in field; contbr. articles to profl. jours. Dutch Orgn. Fundamental Scientific Rsch. scholar, 1994; European Union fellow, 1994, European Molecular Biology Orgn. fellow, 1994. Avocations: sailing, horseback riding, literature. Office: Dept Pharm Biology U Gronin, A Deusinglaan 1, 9713 AV Groningen The Netherlands

VAN DILLEWIJN, JASPER CORNELIS, consultant; b. Sukanagara, Indonesia, Apr. 27, 1942; s. Jasper Jan and Derkje Johanna Van D.; m. Brenda Eunice Rada; children: Derkje, Gisela, Marolina, Jasper. PhD, Colo. State U., 1980. Tech. Botanical Garden, Caracas, Venezuela, 1963-68; instr. INCE, Caracas, Venezuela, 1968-78, internat. coord., 1978-87, CEO, 1987—; freelance cons. Caracas, Venezuela, 1987—; CEO AADEM, Caracas, Venezuela, 1987—; cons./trainer Vocat. Edn. Tchr. training, Supr. & Mgmt., Statis. Quality Control, "Green" Bus. Mem. Venezuelian Soc. Natural Sci., Planetary Soc., Andropological Devel. Found.(hon. mem.), Ecuatorias Soc. Quality and Productivity (hon. mem.), Nat. Geog. Soc., IAPA. Avocations: environmental protection, chess, aquariolgist, astronomy, speaks Spanish, Dutch, German, French.

VAN DINE, ALAN CHARLES, advertising agency executive, writer; b. Ford City, Pa., Jan. 12, 1933; s. Albert and Helen (Remaley) Van D.; m. Joan Anne Hodges, Jan. 29, 1955 (div. Jan. 1971); children: Lynn, Mark, Barbara, Michael; m. Holly Long Shefler, Apr. 23, 1977. BA, Duquesne U., 1955; postgrad., U. Pitts., 1968-71. Editor Mt. Lebanon News, Pa., 1956-58; editorial dir. Pitts. Suburban Newspapers, 1958-61; writer and assoc. creative dir. Batten, Barton, Durstine & Osborne, Pitts., 1961-70; pres., creative dir. Van Dine, Horton, McNamara, Manges, Inc., Pitts., 1970-89; chmn. Van Dine, Humphrey, Inc., Pitts., 1989-95; cons. in field, 1996—; mem. adv. coun. Internat. Poetry Forum, Pitts., 1969-80. Author: Can You Imagine?, 1967, Unconventional Builders, 1977, (humor) The Encyclopedia of Advertising, 1987, Clyde Hare's Pittsburgh, 1994; columnist Pitts. mag., 1977-78, Pa. Illustrated, 1979-81; contbr. articles, essays, short stories, and poems to mags. Bd. dirs. Allegheny Land Trust. 1st lt. USAR, 1956. Recipient numerous awards Art Dirs. Club N.Y., 1964—, Bus. and Profl. Advt. Assn., 1964—. Mem. Chartiers Country Club. Avocations: golf, tennis, darkroom photography, cartooning, computer programming.

VAN DINE, VANCE, investment banker; b. San Francisco, July 2, 1925; s. Melvin Everett and Grace Winifred (Harris) Van D.; m. Isabel Erskine Brewster, Sept. 8, 1956; 1 dau., Rose M. (dec.). BA, Yale U., 1949; LLB, NYU, 1955. Assoc. Morgan Stanley & Co., N.Y.C., 1953-59, 61-63; ptnr. Morgan Stanley & Co., 1963-75; mng. dir. Morgan Stanley & Co., Inc., N.Y.C., 1970-83; adv. dir. Morgan Stanley & Co., N.Y.C., 1983—; cons. Internat. Bank for Reconstn. and Devel., 1959-61; chmn. Doane Western Co. Author: The Role of the Investment Banker in International Transactions, 1970, The U.S. Market After Controls, 1974. Bd. dirs. Yale U. Alumni Fund, Combined Health Appeal of Greater N.Y., Rec. for Blind, Inc., N.Y.C., 1979-89; trustee Cancer Rsch. Inst., N.Y.C., Nassau County Art Mus., L.I. U., 1979-91; gov. dir. Fgn. Policy Assn., 1980-89. With USN, 1943-46. Recipient Yale Class of 1949 Disting. Service award, 1983. Mem. The Pilgrims of the U.S., Union Club, Piping Rock Club, N.Y. Yacht Club, Seawanhaka Corinthian Yacht Club, Church Club, Yale Club (N.Y.C.), Met. Opera Club. Republican. Episcopalian. Office: Morgan Stanley & Co Ste C2E 1221 Avenue Of The Americas New York NY 10020-1008

VANDIVER, FRANK EVERSON, institute administrator, former university president, author, educator; b. Austin, Tex., Dec. 9, 1925; s. Harry Shultz and Maude Folmsbee (Everson) V.; m. Carol Sue Smith, Apr. 19, 1952 (dec. 1979); children: Nita, Nancy, Frank Alexander; m. Renée Aubry, Mar. 21, 1980. Rockefeller fellow in humanities, U. Tex., 1946-47, Rockefeller fellow in Am. Studies, 1947-48, MA, 1949; PhD, Tulane U., 1951; MA (by decree), Oxford (Eng.) U., 1963; HHD (hon.), Austin Coll., 1977; DHL (hon.), Lincoln Coll., 1989, BA (hon.), 1994. Apptd. historian Army Service Forces Depot, Civil Service, San Antonio, 1944-45, Air U., 1951; prof. history La. State U., summers 1953-57; asst. prof. history Washington U., St. Louis, 1952-55; asst. prof. history Rice U., Houston, 1955-56, assoc. prof., 1956-58, prof., 1958-65, Harris Masterson Jr. prof. history, 1965-79, chmn. dept. history and polit. sci., 1962-63, dept. history, 1968-69, acting pres., 1969-70, provost, 1970-79, v.p., 1975-79; pres., chancellor N. Tex. State U., Denton and Tex. Coll. Osteo. Medicine, 1979-81; pres. Tex. A&M U., College Station, 1981-88, pres. emeritus, disting. U. prof., 1988—; founding pres. Acad. Marshall Plan, 1992; Sara and John Lindsey chair in humanities, 1988; Harmsworth prof. Am. history Oxford U., 1963-64; vis. prof. history U. Ariz., summer 1961; master Margarett Root Brown Coll., Rice U., 1964-66; Harmon lectr. Air Force Acad., 1963; Keese lectr. U. Chattanooga, 1967; Fortenbaugh lectr. Gettysburg Coll., 1974; Phi Beta Kappa assoc. lectr., 1970—; vis. prof. mil. history U.S. Mil. Acad., 1973-74; hon. pres. Occidental U., St. Louis, 1975-80; chmn. bd. Am. U. Cairo, 1992-97, acting pres., 1997-98. Editor: The Civil War Diary of General Josiah Gorgas, 1947, Confederate Blockade Running Through Bermuda, 1981-65: Letters and Cargo Manifests, 1947, Proceedings of First Confederate Congress, 4th Session, 1953, Proceedings of Second Confederate Congress, 1959, A Collection of Louisiana Confederate Letters; new edit., J.E. Johnston's Narrative of Military Operations; new edit., J.A. Early's Civil War Memoirs, The Idea of the South, 1964, Battlefields and Landmarks of the Civil War, 1996; author: Ploughshares Into Swords: Josiah Gorgas and Confederate Ordnance, 1952, Rebel Brass: the Confederate Command System, 1956, Mighty Stonewall, 1957, Fields of Glory, (with W.H. Nelson), 1960, Jubal's Raid, 1960, Basic

History of the Confederacy, 1962, Jefferson Davis and the Confederate State, 1964, Their Tattered Flags: The Epic of the Confederacy, 1970, The Southwest: South or West?, 1975, Black Jack: The Life and Times of John J. Pershing, 1977 (Nat. Book Award finalist 1978), (address) The Long Loom of Lincoln, 1986, Blood Brothers: A Short History of the Civil War, 1992, Shadows of Vietnam: Lyndon Johnson's Wars, 1997, 1001 Things Everyone Should Know About the Civil War, 1999; also hist. articles, mem. bd. editors: U.S. Grant Papers, 1973—. Mem. bd. trustees Am. U. in Cairo, 1988, chmn., 1992-97. Recipient Laureate Lincoln Acad., Ill., 1973, Carr P. Collins prize Tex. Inst. Letters, 1958, Harry S. Truman award Kansas City Civil War Round Table, Jefferson Davis award Confederate Meml. Lit. Soc., 1970, Fletcher Pratt award N.Y. Civil War Round Table, 1970, Outstanding Civilian Svc. medal Dept. Army, 1974, Nevins-Freeman award Chgo. Civil War Round Table, 1982, T. Harry Williams Meml. award, 1985, Pres. medal Am. U. in Cairo, 1999; named Hon. Knight San Jacinto, 1993, Hon. Mem. Sons of Republic of Tex., 1986; rsch. grantee Am. Philos. Soc., 1953, 54, 60, Huntington Libr. rsch. grantee, 1961; Guggenheim fellow, 1955-56. Fellow Tex. Hist. Assn.; mem. Am. Hist. Assn., So. Hist. Assn. (assoc. editor jour. 1959-62, pres. 1975-76), Tex. Inst. Letters (past pres.), Jefferson Davis Assn. (pres., chmn. adv. bd. editors of papers), Soc. Am. Historians (councillor), Tex. Philos. Soc. (pres. 1978), Civil War Round Table (Houston), Orgn. Am. Historians, Phi Beta Kappa, SAR of Tex. (hon., Knight San Jacinto 1993). Clubs: Cosmos, Army and Navy (Washington); Briarcrest Country (College Station). Achievements include originating idea of Coll. space grant program. Office: Tex A&M U Mosher Inst Internat Policy Studies College Station TX 77843-0001

VANDIVER, RENEE LILLIAN AUBRY, interior designer, architectural preservator; b. New Iberia, La., Nov. 7, 1929; d. Harold George and Josephine Fortier (Brown) Aubry; m. Arthur Roderick Carmody, Jr., Jan. 1952 (div. 1979); children: Helen Bragg Carmody Stroud, Renee Josephine Carmody Mathews, Arthur Roderick III, Patrick Gerard, Timothy H.A., Mary Joellyn, Virginia Caroline, Joseph Barry; m. Frank Everson Vandiver, Mar. 21, 1980. BFA, Sophie Newcomb Coll. Tulane U., 1951; postgrad., U. Paris, 1951-52, Centinary Coll., 1966-68, La. State U., Shreveport, 1978. Designer, supt. art New Iberia Parish Elementary Schs., 1951; archtl. drafter and designer Perry L. Brown, Inc., Baton Rouge, 1950-52; tchr. art St. Joseph's Elem. Sch., Shreveport, 1960-69; designer, illustrator, saleswoman Stierwalt Interiors, Shreveport, 1974-78; design cons. for president's homes and gardens North Tex. State U., Tex. A&M U., Denton, College Station, 1980-88; design cons., planner, saleswoman, pres. Renee Aubry Vandiver Interiors, College Station, Tex., 1980—; design cons. Am. U. in Cairo, 1997—; interior design and house constrn. cons. Heritage Antiques and Interiors, New Iberia, 1972—; interior design cons., Tenn., La., S.C., 1980—; invited student Middle Eastern master painter Sabri Raghab. Mem. NAFE, DAR, Constrn. Specifications Inst., Dallas Market Ctr., Houston Market Ctcr., Jr. League, Textile Mus., Mus. Women in Arts, Tex. A&M U. Women's Club (hon. pres. 1981—), Fedn. Tex. A&M U. Mother's Club. Avocations: painting, playing piano, gardening, travel, reading. Home: PO Box 10600 College Station TX 77842-0600

VAN DOESBRUG, BART, business consultant executive, consultant; b. Sassenheim, The Netherlands, Mar. 19, 1958. BA, Hogere Tech. Sch., Amsterdam, The Netherlands, 1980; MBA, Rotterdam Sch. Mgmt., The Netherlands, 1999. Programmer, project mgr. Hoogovens, Ymuidan, The Netherlands, 1984-91; info. sys. mgr. Castrol NL, Voorburg, The Netherlands, 1991-97, Amsterdam Uit Buro, Amsterdam, 1997-98; CEO, cons. Bizzo, Amsterdam, 1998—. Mem. Mgr. Netwerk Nederland. Office: Amer 14, 2105 ZA Heemstede The Netherlands

VAN DONGEN, HANS PHILEMON ANNA, research scientist, educator; b. Bergen op Zoom, The Netherlands, June 21, 1969; came to U.S., 1998; s. Marinus Elvire Johannes and Agnes Catharina Maria (Van Willegen) Van D.; m. Judith Catharina Van Peppen, Aug. 20, 1999. MSc in Astrophysics, Leiden U., The Netherlands, 1993, PhD in Chronobiology, 1998. Post doctoral fellow U. Pa., Phila., 1998-99, rsch. asst. prof. sleep and chronobiology, 1999—; mem. Sleep Ctr. Rsch. Com., U. Pa., 1999, Institutional Rev. Bd., U. Pa., 2000—; pres. rsch. group physiol. systems analysis Leiden U., 1994-98; invited lectr. in field, 1995—. Contbr. articles to profl. jours. Recipient Trainee Rsch. Merit award Associated Profl. Sleep Socs., 1999, Microsoft Corp. award, Internat. Soc. Chronobiology, Congress, 1999. Mem. Am. Psychol. Soc., Internat. Soc. Chronobiology, Soc. for Rsch. Biol. Rhythms, European Sleep Rsch. Soc., European Soc. Chronobiology, Sleep Rsch. Soc., Dutch Soc. for Sleep-Wake Rsch., David Mahoney Inst. Neurol. Scis. Avocations: tenor vocalist, sailing, open water diving. Office: U Pa Sch Medicine 423 Guardian Dr 1019 Blockley Hall Philadelphia PA 19104

VAN DOOREN, RENE, mechanics educator; b. Willebroek, Antwerp, Belgium, May 17, 1943; s. Camiel Van Dooren and Eugenie Cantraine; m. Denise Roelants, Dec. 23, 1967. DSc in Mech. Engring., Free U. Brussels, 1972. Asst. Free U. Brussels, 1965-72, 1st asst., 1972-78, asst. prof., 1978-86, prof., 1986—; guest rschr. CNRS, Marseille, France, 1973, U. Birmingham, U.K., 1971. Contbr. articles to profl. publs. Recipient 1st prize The Problemist, Brit. Chess Problem Soc., 1987, Hlas L'udu, 1993, 2d prize The Problemists, BCPS, 1984. mem. Belgian-Romanian Cultural Friendship Orgn., Belgian Assn. Problemists. Office: Free U Brussels Dept Mech E, Pleinlaan 2, 1050 Brussels Belgium

VAN DOVER, ROBERT BRUCE, physicist; b. Eatontown, N.J., Apr. 30, 1952. BS, Princeton U., 1974; MS, Stanford U., 1975, PhD, 1980. Disting. mem. tech. staff Bell Labs., Lucent Techs., Murray Hill, N.J., 1980—. Patentee in field. Fellow Am. Phys. Soc. (sec.-treas. topical group on magnetism and its applications); mem. IEEE (sr.), IEEE Magnetics Soc., AAAS, Materials Rsch. Soc. Office: Bell Labs, Lucent Techs 700 Mountain Ave Rm 1t-106 New Providence NJ 07974-1208

VAN DRIEL, WIM, astronomer; b. Rotterdam, The Netherlands, Sept. 28, 1956; s. Teunis and Anna Catharina (Van Alphen) Van D.; m. Lidia Maria Gesztelyi, May 27, 1988; 1 child, Luca. Doct. in Astronomy, Leiden U., 1981; PhD in Astronomy, Groningen U., 1987. Asst. prof. U. Paris VII, 1987-88, U. Amsterdam, The Netherlands, 1988-92; assoc. prof. U. Tokyo, 1992-94, U. Paris VII, 1994-95; astronomer Paris Obs., France, 1995—; dir. Nançay Radio Obs., France, 1994—; mem. Commn. on Radio Astronomy Frequencies of European Sci. Found., Sci. Commn. on Allocation of Frequencies for Radio Astronomy and Space Sci. of Internat. Coun. of Sci. of UNESCO. Contbr. articles to profl. jours. Mem. com. for dialogue with Europe, Region Centre, France, 1996-97. Mem. Internat. Astron. Union, Am. Astron. Soc., Internat. Union for Radio Sci. (corr.). Avocations: reading, music, martial arts. Office: USN Obs de Paris Meudon, 5 Place Jules Janssen, 92195 Meudon France

VAN DRIEL-GESZTELYI, LIDIA, astronomer, researcher; b. Satoraljaujhely, Hungary, May 28, 1951; d. Tibor and Magdolna (Forhencz) Gesztelyi; m. Wim van Driel, May 27, 1988; 1 child, Luca. MSc, Lorand Eotvos U., Budapest, Hungary, 1974; PhD in Astronomy, Charles U., Prague, Czech Republic, 1990. Sci. fellow Heliophys. Obs. Hungarian Acad. Scis., Debrecen, 1974-92; guest rschr. U. Utrecht (The Netherlands) Astron. Inst., 1988-92, Kiso (Japan) Obs., U. Tokyo, 1992-94, Obs. Paris, Meudon, France, 1994—. Contbr. articles to profl. jours. Recipient prize for best poster European Phys. Soc., Debrecen, 1990. Mem. Internat. Astron. Union (mem. organizing com. commn. 10 1997—), Internat. Astron. Soc., European Geophys. Soc., Com. on Space Rsch., Dutch Astronomer's Soc. Avocations: traveling, reading. E-mail: lidia.vandriel@obspm.fr. Fax: 33 1 45 07 79 59. Home: 2 allée Louis Chevrolet, F-92150 Suresnes France Office: Obs Paris, 5 place Jules Janssen, F-92195 Meudon Cedex, France

VAN DUSEN, BLANCHE BAKER, actress, sculptor; b. N.Y.C., Dec. 20, 1956; d. Jack and Carroll (Baker) Garfein; m. R. Bruce Vandusen; children: Zane, Dara, Wynn. Student, Wellesley Coll. Sculpture rep. by River Gallery, Irvington, N.Y., Sculpture Showcase, New Hope, Pa. Appeared in films The Handmaid's Tale, Shakedown, Raw Deal, Sixteen Candles, Cold Feet, The Seduction of Joe Tynan, TV program Holocaust (Emmy award for Best Supporting Actress); sculpture exhibited in shows at Nat. Arts Club, N.Y.C., Pen and Brush Club, N.Y.C., Salmagundi Club, N.Y.C., Cropsey-Newington Found., N.Y., Perry House Galleries, Alexandria, Va., Balch Inst., Phila., Alexandria Mus. Art, La., Coos Art Mus., Coos Bay, Oreg., Pound Ridge (N.Y.) Mus., Farmington Mus., N.Mex., Nat. Sculpture Soc., N.Y.C.; solo show Grants Pass Mus. Art, Eugene, Oreg., 2000. Named Anti-defamation League Woman of Achievement, 1979; recipient Philip Isenberg award Pen and Brush Club, 1995, Leonard Meiselman award Salmagundi Club, 1998, Agop Agopoff Meml. award Salmagundi Club, 1998, 2000, Leonard Meiselman award The Pen and Brush Club, 1999, Agop Agopoff Meml. award Newington Cropsey Found., 1998, H.A. Fahdli award Salmagundi Club, 1996, Pietro Montana award HVAA Newington Cropsey Found., 1997, 98, Helen Beling award Coos Art Mus., 1998; winner Manhattan Artists Showcase Manhattan Arts Internat., 1996-98; named Best in Show Pound Ridge Mus., 1998.

VAN DUSEN, GLENN T., controller, secretary, treasurer; b. Houston, Dec. 25, 1944; s. Glenn Thornton Van Dusen and Barbara L. (Folse) Hanna; m. Jeanette Bearden Nosky, Feb. 14, 1976; children: Cheryl C., Kimberly D. BBA in Acctg., U. Tex., 1972. Store controller Montgomery Ward, Brownsville, Tex., 1972-78; acctg. mgr. Norton Co., Brownsville, 1978-83; owner Photo Finish, Missouri City, Tex., 1984-85; corp. controller Basic Sys., Inc., Houston, 1985-87, Backlog Group, Houston, 1988-95, Staff Force, Inc., Houston, 1995—. Treas. PTA, Katy, Tex., 1987-89, Homeowner's Assn., Katy, 1994-96. With U.S. Army, 1967-71, Germany. Mem. Inst. Mgmt. Accts., Tex. Assn. Staffing. Republican. Avocations: golfing, geneaology, traveling, coins. Office: Staff Force Inc 15915 Katy Fwy Ste 160 Houston TX 77094-1707

VAN DUYSE, FRANCIS DONALD, publisher; b. Sturgeon Bay, Wis., May 2, 1926; s. Francis Lewis and Gertrude (Simon) Van D.; m. Dorothy Marie Walden, May 15, 1953 (div. Feb. 1978); children: Susan, Rebecca, Francis Roy, Sarah. BBA, Spencerian Coll., 1949. Baseball announcer Albany (Ga.) Cardinals, 1953-54, Waycross (Ga.) Bears, 1955, Valdosta (Ga.) Tigers, 1956; pub., editor Wis. All-Sports, Green Bay, 1958-68; sports dir. WLUK-TV, Channel 11, Green Bay, 1962-63; pub., editor Wis. Playground, Pro Football Exclusive, Green Bay, 1969-72; CEO, announcer Gemini Broadcasting Co., Appleton, Wis., 1980-82; pres., CEO MegaPrint Internat., Sturgeon Bay, Wis., 1986—. Author: History of the Green Bay Packers, 1965; editor, pub. (yearbooks) Salute to the Packers 1961-1968. With USN, 1944-46. Avocations: writing, fitness, marathons, chess. Home: 1811 Michigan St Apt 1E Sturgeon Bay WI 54235-3704 Office: MegaPrint Internat PO Box 88 Sturgeon Bay WI 54235-0088

VAN DYKE, GENE, oil company executive; b. Normal, Ill., Nov. 5, 1926; s. Harold and Ruby (Gibson) Van D.; children: Karen, Scott, Janice, Mary Katherine, Tor, Staffan. BS in Geol. Engring., U. Okla., 1950. Geologist Kerr-McGee, Oklahoma City, 1950; chief geologist S.D. Johnson Co., Wichita Falls, Tex., 1950-51; ind. geologist, oil operator, 1951-58; ptnr. Van Dyke and Mejlaender, Houston, 1958-62; owner, pres. Van Dyke Oil Co. (now Vanco Energy Co.), Houston, 1962—; also bd. dirs.; bd. dirs. Van Dyke Netherlands, Inc.; chmn. operating com. Vanco Gabon Group. Compiler index of geol. articles to South La. With AC U.S. Army, 1945. Mem. Am. Petroleum Inst., Ind. Petroleum Assn., Am. Assn. Petroleum Geologists, Houston, Houston Petroleum, Houstonian, Houston Petroleum, Houstonian, University. Republican. Episcopalian. Office: Vanco Energy Co One Greenway Pla Houston TX 77046

VAN DYKE, JOSEPH GARY OWEN, computer consulting executive; b. N.Y.C., Dec. 21, 1939; s. Donald Wood and Gladys Ann (Tague) Van D.; m. Lynne Diane Lammers; June 25, 1966; children: Alison Baird, Jeremy Wood, Matthew Kerr. BA, Rutgers U., 1961; postgrad., R.I. Sch. of Design, 1962, Am. U., 1964-67. Computer programmer System Devel. Corp., Paramus, N.J., 1962-64; sect. head computer tech. div. System Devel. Corp., Falls Church, Va., 1964-67; project mgr. Informatics Inc., Bethesda, Md., 1967-70; dept. dir. Informatics Inc., Rockville, Md., 1970-74, v.p., gen. mgr., 1974-78; owner, pres. J G Van Dyke and Assoc., Inc., Bethesda, 1978—; chmn. bd., chief exec. officer The Outreach Group, Inc., 1987—. Bd. dirs. Westbrook Sch., Bethesda, 1981-82, St. Columba's Ch., Washington, 1980-84; founder Computer Edn. Workshop, Bethesda, 1981; coach MSI soccer, Bethesda, 1979-89. Mem. Inst. Elec. Engring. Democrat. Episcopalian. Avocations: coaching soccer, sailing, graphic designing. Home: 5117 Dalecarlia Dr Bethesda MD 20816-1801 Office: JG Van Dyke & Assocs Inc 7900 Westpark Dr # T100 Mc Lean VA 22102-4242

VAN DYKE, LARRY DAVID, consultant; b. Healdsburg, Calif., Sept. 9, 1947; s. Lester Myers and Marjorie E. Van D.; m. Candise Maureen Ellwood, Dec. 19, 1970; children: David, Shawn, Todd. BA, U. Wash., 1978; MAR, Emmanuel Sch. Religion, 1982. Dir. pub. rels. Emmanuel Sch. Religion, Johnson City, Tenn., 1978-85, exec. dir. devel., 1985-88; pres. CMA Resource Devel., Inc., Johnson City, Tenn., 1988-96; sr. cons. Goettler Assocs., Columbus, Ohio, 1997—; instr. NSFRE, Alexandria, Va. With USN, 1969-73. Decorated Navy Achievement medal. Mem. Nat. Soc. Fund Raising Execs. (cert.). Republican. Avocations: fly fishing, canoeing, skiing, wood working. Home: 519 Laurels Rd Johnson City TN 37601-5213 Office: Goettler Assocs 580 High St Columbus OH 43215

VAN DYKEN, AMY, swimmer, Olympic athlete; b. Engelwood, Colo., Feb. 15, 1973; m. Alan McDaniel, Oct. 1995. Attending, Colo. State U. Swimmer U.S. Nat. Resident Team, Colorado Springs, Colo., 1994; swimmer U.S. Olympic Team, Atlanta, Ga., 1996, Sydney, Australia, 2000. Named Female NCAA Swimmer of the Year, 1994, Am. Record Holder 50 meter and 50 meter freestyle; recipient Bronze medal World Championships, 1994, Triple Gold medals Pan Am. Games, 1995, Silver medal Pan Am. Games, 1995, Gold medals: 50 meter freestyle, 100 meter butterfly, 4x100 meter freestyle relay, 4x100 meter medley relay Olympic Games, Atlanta, 1996., Gold Medal, 4 x 100m freestyle, Olympic Games, Sydney, 2000. Achievements include being the first Am. woman athlete to win 4 gold medals in any event during a single Olympic game. Office: US Swimming Inc 1 Olympic Plz Bldg 2A Colorado Springs CO 80909-5770

VANE, JOHN ROBERT, pharmacologist; b. Worcestershire, Eng., Mar. 29, 1927; s. Maurice and Frances Florence V.; m. Elizabeth Daphne Page, Apr. 4, 1948; children: Nicola, Miranda. BSc in Chemistry, U. Birmingham, 1946; MSc in Pharmacology, Oxford U., 1949, D Phil., 1953, DSc, 1970; MD (hon.), U. Cracow, Poland, 1977, Copernicus Acad. Medicine, Cracow; Hon. doctorate, Rene Descartes U., Paris, 1978; DSc (hon.), CUNY, 1980, Aberdeen U., 1983, N.Y. Med. Coll., Birmingham U., U. Surrey, 1984, Camerino U., Italy, 1984, Louvain, 1986, Buenos Aires, 1986; D honoris causa in Medicine and Surgery, U. Florence; DSc (hon.), U. London, 1995. Fellow Therapeutic Rsch. Coun., Oxford U., 1946-48; rsch. worker Sheffield U., 1948-49; rschr. worker Nuffield Inst. Med. Rsch., Oxford U., 1949-51; Stothert rsch. fellow Royal Soc., 1951-53; instr., then asst. prof. pharmacology Yale U. Med. Sch., 1953-55; mem. faculty Inst. Basic Med. Scis., Royal Coll. Surgeons Eng., 1955-73, prof. exptl. pharmacology, 1966-73; group R & D dir. Wellcome Found. Ltd., Beckenham, Kent, 1973-85; dir.-gen. William Harvey Rsch. Inst. St. Bartholomew's/Royal London Sch. of Medicine/Dentistry, Queen Mary/Westfield Coll., U. London, 1986-97, hon. life pres. William Harvey Rsch. Inst., 1997—; bd. dirs. De Code Genetics Inc., Iceland, Sparta Pharms. Inc., U.S. Co-editor: Adrenergic Mechanisms, 1960, Prostaglandin Synthetase Inhibitors, 1974, Metabolic Functions of the Lung, Vol. 4, 1977, Handbook of Experimental Pharmacology, 1978, Prostacyclin, 1979, Interactions Between Platelets and Vessel Walls, 1981, Endothelin I, 1989, II, 1991, III, 1993, IV, 1995, V, 1998, New Targets in Inflammation, 1996, Selective Cox-2 Inhibitors, 1998; contbr. numerous articles to profl. jours. Freeman City of Scranton (Pa.), 1988, Taipei (Taiwan), 1989, New Orleans, 1995. Decorated knight bachelor; recipient Baly medal Royal Coll. Physicians, Albert Lasker Basic Med. Rsch. award; Peter Debye prize, Nuffield Gold medal, Ciba Geigy Drew medal Soc. for Endocrinology, 1981, Nobel prize in physiology or medicine, 1982, Galen Medal Worshipful Soc. Apothecaries, 1983, Louis Pasteur Found. prize, Santa Monica, Calif., 1984, Nat. Headache Found. award, 1988, Hamburg Gold medal Royal Pharm. Soc. Great Britain, 1996. Fellow ACP (hon.), Inst. Biology, Royal Coll. of Surgeons of Eng. (hon.), Royal Soc. (Royal medal 1989), Brit. Pharm. Soc. (hon.), Royal Coll. Pathologists (hon.), Royal Nat. Acad. Medicine (hon.), Royal Coll. Physicians London (hon.); mem. NAS (fgn. assoc.), Polish Pharm. Soc. (hon.), Physiol. Soc. (hon.), Royal Acad. Medicine Belgium, Royal Netherlands Acad. Arts and Scis., Polish Acad. Scis. (fgn.), Am. Acad. Arts and Scis. (fgn. hon.), Soc. Drug Research, Alpha Omega Alpha (hon.). Office: William Harvey Rsch Inst St Bartholomew Royal London, U London Queen Mary Coll, London EC1M 6BQ, England

VANE, SYLVIA BRAKKE, anthropologist, publisher, cultural resource management company executive, writer; b. Fillmore County, Minn., Feb. 28, 1918; d. John T. and Hulda Christina (Marburger) B.; m. Arthur Bayard Vane, May 17, 1942; children: Ronald Arthur, Linda, Laura Vane Ames. AA, Rochester Jr. Coll., 1937; BS with distinction, U. Minn., 1939; postgrad,, Radcliffe Univ., 1944; MA, Calif. State Univ., Hayward, 1975. Med. technologist Dr. Frost and Hodapp, Willmar, MN, 1939-41; head labs. Corvallis Gen. Hosp., OR, 1941-42; dir. lab. Cambridge Gen. Hosp., OR, 1941-42, Cambridge, MA, 1942-43; staff Peninsula Clinic, Redwood City, CA, 1947-49; vice pres. Cultural Systems Rsch. Inc., Menlo Park, CA, 1978—; pres. Ballena Press, 1981—; cons. resource mgmt. So. Calif. Edison Co., Rosemead, 1978-81, San Diego Gas and Elec. Co., 1980-83, Pacific Gas and Elec. Co., San Francisco, 1982-83, Wender, Murase & White, Washington, 1983-87, Yosemite Indians, Mariposa, Calif., 1982-91, San Luis Rey Band of Mission Indians, Escondido, Calif., 1986-89, U.S. Ecology, Newport Beach, Calif., 1986-89, Riverside County Flood Control and Water Conservation Dist., 1985-95, Infotec, Inc., 1989-91, Alexander & Karshmer, Berkeley, Calif., 1989-92, Desert Water Agency, Palm Spgs., Calif., 1989-90, Metropolitan Water Dist., 1992—, Nat. Park Svc., 1992-2000, Applied Earthworks, Inc., 1997-99. Author: (with L.J. Bean), California Indians, Primary Resources, 1977, rev. edit., 1990, The Cahuilla and the Santa Rosa Mountains, 1981, The Cahuilla Landscape, 1991, Ethnology of the Alta California Indians, vol. I Pre Contact, vol. II POst Contact, 1992, Spanish Borderlands Sourcebooks, vols. 3, 4; contbr. chptrs. to several books. Mem. United Ch. of Christ. Mem. bd. dirs. Sequoia Area coun. Girl Scouts U.S., 1954-61; bd. dirs., vice pres., pres. LWV, S. San Mateo County, calif., 1960-65. Fell. Soc. Applied Anthropology, Am. Anthropology Assn.; mem. Southwestern Anthropology Assn. (prog. chmn. 1976-78, newsletter editor 1976-79), Soc. for Am. Archaeology, Soc. Calif. Archaeology (Martin A. Baumhoff Spl. Achievement awd. 1998). Office: Ballena Press 823 Valparaiso Ave Menlo Park CA 94025-4206

VANEČEK, JIŘI, physiologist, researcher; b. Prague, Czech republic, Sept. 26, 1951; s. Jiři and Nina (Ubiriová) V.; m. Ivana Valkounová, July 3, 1976; children: Kateřina, Tomáš. MD, Charles U., 1976; PhD, Czech Acad. Scis., Prague, 1982. Postdoctoral fellow Inst. Physiology, Prague, 1981-83, rsch. scientist, 1985-87, lab chief, 1992—; vis. fellow, vis. scientist NIH, Bethesda, Md., 1984, 90-92; rsch. scientist J. Gutenberg U., Mainz, Germany, 1988-89. Contbr. articles to profl. jours. Mem. European Pineal Soc., European Soc. for Chronobiology, Czech Physiol. Soc. Office: Inst of Physiology, Videňska 1083, 142 20 Prague 4, Czech Republic

VAN EECKHOUT, NICO JOHAN, pharmacist, researcher; b. Oudenaarde, Belgium, Dec. 22, 1972; s. Lucie Clara Creyf. Pharmacist, U. Ghent, Belgium, 1995, M.Pharm.Sci., 1996. Lic. pharmacist, Belgium. Rschr. Lab. of Phys. Pharmacy, Ghent, 1995-97; rschr. Lab. of Food Analysis, Ghent, 1997-99, asst., 1999—. Contbr. articles to profl. jours. Office: Lab of Food Analysis, Harelbekestraat 72, 9000 Ghent Belgium

VAN EEKELEN, WILLEM FREDERIK, senator; b. Utrecht, The Netherlands, Feb. 5, 1931; m. Johanna Wentink; 1 child. Student, Utrecht U., Princeton U., 1950-52; degree in law, Utrecht U., 1954, Ph.D. cum laude, 1964. Mem. Netherlands Diplomatic Service, 1957-77, Lower House of Parliament, 1977-78, 81-82; state sec. defense The Netherlands, 1978-81, state sec. fgn. affairs, 1982-86; minister of def. 2d Lubbers govt., The Netherlands, 1986-88; sec. gen. Western European Union, 1989-94; chmn. European Movement, 1995—. Office: Else Mauhslaan 187, 2597 HE The Hague The Netherlands

VANĚK, PŘEMYSL, chemist, researcher; b. Prague, Czech Republic, June 3, 1951; s. Přemysl and Květa Voldánová V.; m. Ljuba Marková, Apr. 12, 1979; children: Přemysl, Ljuba. Grad., Charles U., Prague, 1974, D in Chemistry, 1977; PhD in Physics, Inst. Physics, Prague, 1983. Rsch. fellow Inst. Physics, 1974-77, 82-83, rsch. worker, 1983-89, head tech. group, dept. dielectrics, 1989—; guest scientist U. des Saarlandes, Saarbrücken, Germany, 1987, 88. Contbr. numerous articles to internat. rsch. jours. Mil. duty, Czech Republic, 1977-78. Recipient rsch. grant, Grant Agy. of Czech Republic, 1996. Mem. Union Czech Mathematicians and Physicists, Czechoslovak Assn. for Crystal Growth. Avocation: hiking. Home: Nad Rokoskou 41, CZ-18200 Prague Czech Republic Office: Inst Physics AV CR, Na Slovance 2, CZ-18221 Prague Czech Republic

VAN ELTEREN, MELCHIOR CORNELIS MARIA, sociologist; b. Breda, The Netherlands, Apr. 14, 1947; s. Marinus Adrianus van Elteren and Maria de Laat; m. Nancy Ann Schaefer, Mar. 27, 1998. MA in Sociology, Tilburg (The Netherlands) U., 1973, MA in Psychology, 1985, PhD, 1987. Asst. prof. State U. Utrecht, The Netherlands, 1977-79, Erasmus U., Rotterdam, The Netherlands, 1979-91; assoc. prof. sociology Tilburg (The Netherlands) U., 1991—. Co-editor: American Culture in The Netherlands, 1996, Beat Culture and Beyond: American Counterculture in the 1950s, 1999. Avocations: American popular music, U.S. national parks. Office: Tilburg U, Warandalaan 2, 1000 LE Tilburg The Netherlands

VAN ENTER, AERNOUT COERT DANIEL, researcher in theoretical physics; b. Rotterdam, Netherlands, Oct. 4, 1951; s. Coert Herman Johan and Truus (Pit) van E.; m. Sonia Fanny Zirinsky, Feb. 20, 1987; children: Daniel Johan, Rebecca Leona, Benjamin Jasha. Grad., Rijksuniversiteit Groningen, Netherlands, 1972, Dr Nature Studies, 1976, PhD, 1981. With U. Heidelberg, Germany, 1981-86; Lady Davis rsch. fellow Technion, Haifa, Israel, 1986-88; vis. lectr. U. Tex., Austin, 1988-89; rsch. fellow Royal Dutch Acad. Arts and Scis., Netherlands, 1989-94; sr. rschr. Rijksuniversiteit Groningen, 1994—. Editor Jour. Statis. Physics, 1994-96, Nederlands Tijdschrift voor Natuurkunde, 1997—. Avocation: playing cello. E-mail: aenter@phys.rug.nl. Office: Inst Theoret Physics RUG, Nijenborgh 4, Groningen Netherlands 9747AG

VAN EVELGHEM, ERWIN MARIA LOUIS, business executive; b. Dendermonde, Flanders, Belgium, Mar. 12, 1970; s. Roger Van Evelghem and Ghislaine Philips. Student, Hemaco Coll., Dendermonde, 1988; MSc, U. Leuven, Belgium, 1993; postgrad., Belgische Kamer Van Rekenplichtigen, Antwerp, Belgium, 1996. Assoc. mgr. Gemeentekrediet, Antwerp, 1993-97; CEO Ivarex Roofmart, Antwerp, 1997—. Mem. Liberal Vlaams Studentenverbond, Brussels, 1989, Green Students, Leuven, 1990-92; vol. Vlaamse Kruis, Antwerp, 1995—, Red Cross, Dendermonde, 1993—. Mem. Alumni Lovanienses, Fin. Forum. Agnostic. Avocations: reading, culture, sports. Office: Ivarex Roofmart, Deurnebaan 46, 2170 Merksem-Antwerp Flanders, Belgium

VAN GEEL, MAURITS, artistic director. MA in Art History and Crafts, Rietveld Art Acad., Amsterdam, 1978. Tchr. arts and crafts, history art and folk dance Van Overbeeke Sch., Utrecht, The Netherlands, 1978-89; artistic asst. The Internat. Dance Theater, Amsterdam, The Netherlands, 1989-95, mem. artistic bd., 1995-97, artistic dir., 1997—; tchr. workshops, The Netherlands, Belgium, Germany, 1980—; guest tchr. Rotterdam Conservatory, 1985; dance cons. City of Amsterdam, 1987-90; bd. dirs. Folklore in Sch. Found., 1989—, De Nieuwe Kring elem. sch., 1998—; mem. adv. com. Doe-Dans Festival, 1982—. Office: Het Internat Danstheater, Postbus 16885, 1001 RJ Amsterdam The Netherlands

VAN GELDEREN, ELLY, linguistics educator, researcher; b. Geertruidenberg, The Netherlands, Sept. 20, 1958; d. Antonij Johannes and Elsje (Schuttevaar) van G.; m. Harry M. Bracken, June 19, 1985. BA, Utrecht U., The Netherlands, 1979, MA, 1981; PhD, McGill U., Montreal, Can., 1986. Assoc. prof. Ariz. State U., Tempe, 1995—; chair, Com. on Linguistics, 1998—. Author: The Rise of Functional Categories, 1993, Verbal Agreement, 1997, A History of English Reflexive Pronouns, 2000. Chair Amnesty Internat. Can., Ottawa, 1984-85. Mem. Soc. Germanic Linguistics (pres. 2000—). Office: Ariz State Univ PO Box 870302 Tempe AZ 85287-0302

VAN GENDEREN, MARC JACCO, chemist; b. Utrecht, The Netherlands, Aug. 29, 1968; s. Arie Cornelis Gysbert and Elisabeth Antonia (Van Der Hagen) Van G.; m. Margaretha Hendrina Linnenbank, Sept. 14, 1995; 1

child, Tim. D, U. Utrecht, 1991; PhD, Tu Delft, 1995. Rsch. asst. Tu Delft, The Netherlands, 1991-95; sr. rschr. Hoogovens R&D, Ymuiden, The Netherlands, 1995-99; mgr. quality dept. CM2 Corus Ljmuidew Hoogovens R&D, Ymuiden, 1999—. Contbr. articles to profl. jours. Mem. Bond v Materialenkennis. Avocations: reading, skiing, cycling. Home: Floraronde 290, 1991LG Velserbroek The Netherlands Office: Hoogovens R&D, PO Box 10000, 1970CA Ymuiden The Netherlands

VANGERVEN, PAUL MARIE, financial executive; b. Achel, Belgium, June 29, 1946; s. Petrus Vangerven and Francisca Kerkhofs; m. Anne-Marie Hugues, May 31, 1972; children: Lucie, Saskia, Alexandre, Isabelle. M of Bus., U. Leuven, Belgium, 1968. Asst. mgr. fin. and adminstrn. NCR Belgium, Brussels, 1970-78; mgr. fin. and adminstrn. NCR Belgium SA, Brussels, 1978-81; fin. dir. Maes Brewery SA, Waarloos, Belgium, 1981-83, gen. mgr., 1983-98; mng. dir. Alken Maesbrewery, Waarloos, 1988-93, Brepols SA, Turnhout, Belgium, 1994-98; dir. Epifine BV, Maarssen, The Netherlands, 1998—; chmn. of bd. Foresco NV, Turnhout; mng. dir. Belgian Media Holding, Brussels. Lt. Infantry, 1969-70. Fax: 00-31-30-2410882. E-mail: sales@epifine.nl. Home: Watertorenlaan 30, B-1930 Zaventem Belgium Office: Epifine BV, Postbox 6016, 3600 HA Maarssen The Netherlands

VAN GERWEN, LUCAS JOSEPH, foundation executive, psychologist; b. Amsterdam, The Netherlands, Feb. 23, 1952; s. Joop B. van Gerwen and Joke M. Van Gerwen-Resink; m. Maartje H. van Niedek; 1 child, Marieke L.B. Comml. pilot lic., Dan Aviation, Mo., 1977; psychologist, U. Utrecht, The Netherlands, 1985, psychotherapist, 1988. Cert. aviation psychologist, human factor specialist, clin. psychologist. Crisis mgr. Stichting Opvang Jongeren Apeldoora, Apeldoorn, The Netherlands, 1980-86; therapist First Lyn, Den Bosch, The Netherlands, 1986-88, Riagg Rotterdam Noordoost, Rotterdam, The Netherlands, 1988-90; dir. Valk Found., Leiden, The Netherlands, 1990—. Author: Vliegangst, 1988, Help I Have Got to Fly, 1996; contbr. articles to profl. jours. Mem. European Assn. Aviation Psychology, Vereniging Voor Gedrags Theradie, Nederlands Inst. Psychology. Avocations: skiing, running, reading, flying. Office: The Valk Found, PO Box 110, 2300 AC Leiden The Netherlands

VAN GEYT, HENRI LOUIS, architect; b. Brussels, Feb. 2, 1947; s. Jerome Charles and Marie Jose (Van Den Weghe) Van G.; m. Annie Claire Van Laere, Dec. 22, 1973; children: Celine, Adriaan. BArch, St. Lukes U., Brussels, 1972. Registered architect. Trainee Archiduk A & E, Leuven, Belgium, 1973-75, project architect, 1975-78, assoc., 1978-98; pvt. practice, 1999—; cons. ACT, Brussels, 1990—. Pres. Jaycees, Leuven, 1988; expert adviser Commn. European Communities, 1993—. Mem. Hospibel (bd. dirs., pres. 1990-93, 97-98, hon. pres. 1993—). Avocations: tennis, golf, classical music. Home: Kouter 15, 3060 Bertem Belgium

VAN GOETHEM, JOHAN WILLEM MATHILDE, neuroradiologist, researcher; b. Wilrijk, Belgium, Apr. 1, 1961; s. Jozef and Bernardina (Schouten) V.; m. Isabelle Biltjes; children: Alexia, Olivia, Félicia. MD, U. Antwerp, Belgium, 1986; Degree in Computer Sci., Vrije U., Brussels, 1987. Cert. neuroradiologist, Belgium. Resident U. Hosp., Antwerp, 1987-91; fellow VA Med. Ctr., San Diego, 1991; vice-departmental head dept. neuroradiology U. Hosp., Antwerp, 1991—; dir. MR MR St-Niklaas, 1993—; rschr. U. Antwerp, 1995—. Author: MR Imaging of the Postoperative Lumbar Spine, 1999. Lt. Belgian Army, 1991—. Recipient Assn. Students and Residents award, Antwerp, 1988. Mem. Am. Soc. Neuroradiology, Am. Soc. Spine Radiology, Am. Roentgen Ray Soc., European Soc. Neuroradiology. Avocation: gaviation. Office: Univ Hosp Antwerp, Wilrijkstraat 10, 2650 Edegem Belgium

VANHAECKE, ERWIN S. F., quality assurance and regulatory affairs manager; b. Brugge, Belgium, Oct. 10, 1960; s. Robert and Liliane (Boghmans) V.; m. Kathleen Van Den Haesevelde, Sept. 10, 1988; children: Laurens, Liselotte. Pharmacist, State U., Ghent, Belgium, 1983, indsl. pharmacist, 1985, PhD in Pharmacy, 1989; postgrad. bus. mgmt., Vlaemse Ekonomische Hoge Sch., Brussels, 1989. Rsch. asst. State U., Ghent, 1983-89, lectr., 1987-89; quality assurance mgr. Alcon-Couvreur, Puurs, Belgium, 1990-98, quality assurance and regulatory affairs mgr., 1999—. Contbr. numerous articles to profl. jours. Lt. Belgian M.C., 1985-86. Mem. Parenteral Drug Assn., Regulatory Affairs Profl. Soc., EyeCare Industries, Ophthalmic Spl. Interest Group (chmn. 1997-99). Avocations: marathon running, motorbiking. Home: Aalterveld 62, B-9880 Aalter Belgium Office: Alcon-Couvreur NV, Rijksweg 14, B-2870 Puurs Belgium

VANHANEN, JUHA PETTERI, management executive; b. Mikkeli, Finland, May 27, 1967; s. Matti Ilkka and Marja-Liisa (Ollinen) V.; m. Tiina Irmeli Rasanen, Sept. 5, 1992; 2 children, Vilma and Sanni. MS, Helsinki Univ. Tech., Finland, 1991, licentiate of tech., 1993, D in tech., 1996. Rsch. scientist Helsinki Univ. Tech., 1991-97; cons. Otaniemi Cons. Group, Helsinki, 1993-99; mng. dir. Gaia Group, Helsinki, 2000—. ontbr. articles to profl. jours. mem. of Internat. Assoc. for Hydrogen Energy and Internat. Solar Energy Soc. Avocations: golf, tennis. Home: Vallikuja 4A4, FIN-02600 Espoo Finland Office: Gaia Group, Lonnrotinkatu 19B, FIN-00120 Helsinki Finland

VANHANEN, TATU, political science educator; b. Vuoksenranta, Finland, Apr. 17, 1929; s. Taavi and Anna (Jantunen) V.; m. Anni Tiihonen, July 15, 1951; children: Rauno Juhani, Matti Taneli, Tuomo Tahvo. Candidate, Sch. Social Scis., Finland, 1958, licentiate, 1963; D Social Scis., U. Tampere, Finland, 1968. Editor Kyntäjä Rural Youth Union, Helsinki, Finland, 1959-61; chief article service Agrarian Party/Ctr. Party, Helsinki, 1962-69; acting assoc. prof. U. Jyväskylä, Finland, 1969-72; researcher Acad. Finland, Helsinki, 1972-74; assoc. prof. U. Tampere, Finland, 1974-92. Author: Power and the Means of Power, 1979, The Emergence of Democracy: A Comparative Study of 119 States, 1850-1979, 1984, The Process of Democratization: A Comparative Study of 147 States, 1980-88, 1990, Politics of Ethnic Nepotism: India as an Example, 1991, On the Evolutionary Roots of Politics, 1992, Strategies of Democratization, 1992, Prospects of Democracy: A Study of 172 Countries, 1997, Prospects for Democracy in Asia, 1998, Ethnic Conflicts Explained by Ethnic Nepotism, 1999. Grantee Acad. Finland, 1970, 72, 75-76, 79-80, 86, Scandinavian Inst. Asian Studies, 1976, 80, 84, 88, 97; Fulbright scholar, 1973-74. Mem. Assn. for Politics and Life Scis., Internat. Polit. Sci. Assn., Finnish Polit. Sci. Assn. (pres. 1986-88). Mem. Center Party. Lutheran. Avocation: sculpture. Home: Suopolku 4 D, 01800 Klaukkala Finland

VANHARTEN, PETER NICOLAAS, psychiatrist; b. Rotterdam, The Netherlands, Aug. 23, 1956. MD, U. Groningen, The Netherlands, 1981. Resident in psychiatry Acad. Hosp., Groningen, 1989; psychiatrist Psychiat. Inst. Capriles Clinic, Curaçao, 1990-95; dir. psychiat. residency, chmn. dept. psychiat. rsch. Welterhof Psychiat. Ctr., Heerlen, The Netherlands, 1995-98; dir. psychiat. residency Psychiat. Ctr., Amersfoort, The Netherlands, 1998—. Contbr. numerous articles to profl. jours. Office: Psychiat Ctr Zon & Schild, PO Box 3051, 3800 DB Amersfoort The Netherlands

VANHATALO, SAMPSA KULLERVO, physician; b. Tampere, Finland, June 18, 1971; m. Ulla Vanhatalo, 2000. MD, U. Helsinki, Finland, 1998, PhD, 1995. Rsch. assoc. U. Helsinki, 1993-99, asst. prof. in neurobiology, 1999—. Contbr. articles to profl. jours. Lt. Finnish Arty., 1990-91. Rsch. grantee Finnish Med. Found., 1994, 95, U. Helsinki, 1993-95, Finnish Cultural Found., 1996. Mem. Soc. for Neurosci., European Neurosci. Assn. Avocations: music, skiing, carpentry, hunting. Office: U Helsinki Inst Biomedicine, U Hosp Helsinki, PO Box 281, 00029 Helsinki Finland

VANHECKE, LIEVEN NOEL ADOLF, mathematics educator; b. Brugge, Belgium, May 26, 1939; s. Bruno Rene and Elza (Lagaeysse) V.; m. Magda Van Oyen, July 30, 1966; children: Bruno, Peter, Rebecca. Lic. in scis., Cath. U. Leuven, Belgium, 1963, cert. in edn., 1963, DSc, 1966. Rsch. asst. Nat. Fund for Scientific Rsch., Leuven, 1964-65; prof. Voorbereidend Inst. Cath. U. Leuven, 1965-66, docent faculty of scis., 1966-70, prof. math., 1970-72, ordinary prof. math., 1972—; prof. math. U. Antwerp, Belgium, 1972-85; vice dir. class of scis. Royal Acad. Belgium, 1984, dir., 1985, rep., 1985-95; pres. Nat. Com. math., Belgium, 1988—; hon. prof. U. Antwerp, 1985. Author: Analytic Geometry, 1973, 1989, part A, 1993, part B, 1994, manual, 1996, Isotropic and Pseudo-Isotropic Submanifolds of an n-dimensional Lorentz Manifold, 1976, Homogenous structures on Riemannian manifolds, 1983, Generalized Heisenberg Groups and Damek-Ricci Harmonic Spaces, 1995, Riemannian Manifolds of Conullity Two, 1996; editor: Differential Geometry and Mathematical Physics, 1982; contbr. articles to profl. jours. With Belgian Air Force, 1963-64. Decorated comdr. Order of Leopold, comdr. Order of Leopold II; recipient Triennial prize Vlaamse Leergangen Leuven, 1967; rsch. grantee NATO, CNR (Italy), Nat. Fund for Sci. Rsch., Belgium, Cath. U. Leuven. Mem. Royal Acad. Belgium, Am. Math. Soc., Math. Assn. Am., Tensor Soc., N.Y. Acad. Scis., Math. Soc. Palermo, Austrian Math. Soc., Belgian Math. Soc., Italian Math. Soc., Real Acad. Galega de Ciencias (corr.), Acad. Canaria de Ciencias (corr.), London Math. Soc., European Math. Soc., Balkan Soc. Geometers, Spanish Math. Soc. Roman Catholic. Home: Prinses Lydialaan 15, B-3001 Leuven Belgium Office: Cath Univ Leuven Dept Math, Celestijnenlaan 200B, B-3001 Leuven Belgium

VAN HECKE, LUC AIMÉ, zipper company executive; b. Sleidinge, Belgium, Sept. 6, 1951; s. Gerard and Angela (Criel) Van H.; m. Ingrid Boone, Aug. 25, 1976 (dec. Nov. 2000); 1 child, Tine. Ind. engr., H.R.I.T.H.O., 1974. Lay-out engr. Volvo Cars, Ghent, Belgium, 1974-76, group leader, 1976-81; mgr. B.N. Spoorwegmaterieel, Brugge, Belgium, 1981-84; mgr. N.V. H. Desseaux, Dendermonde, Belgium, 1984-87, tech. dir., 1987-91, exec. dir., 1991-95; exec. dir. N.V. Louis de Poortere, Mouscroen, Belgium, 1996; gen. mgr. N.V. Beaulieu Wielsbeke, Belgium, 1997-99, N.V. Eclair-Prym, Belgium and France, 1999-2000; mng. dir., CEO, bd. mem. Group Bonduel-Prm, Comines, Belgium, 2000—; bd. dirs. G.U.T., Aachen, Germany, M.I.D., Deventer, The Netherlands, Bergoss, Oss, The Netherlands. Trainer outward bound J.C.I., Kortrijk, Belgium, 1983, pres. local orgn., Meetjesland, Belgium, 1985, nat. trainer, Flanders, Belgium, 1985. Recipient Presdl. award Nat. Pres. J.C.I., Tongeren, Belgium, 1985. Fellow Rotary. Avocations: horses, running, windsurfing, skiing. E-mail: luc.vanhecke@online.be. Home: L Reychlerstraat 56, 9250 Waasmunster Belgium Office: NV Bonduel Prym, Ave de la Sideho 3/5, B-7780 Comines Belgium

VAN HEESCH, EGBERTUS J.M., researcher; b. Utrecht, The Netherlands, Feb. 15, 1951; m. M.C. Haagen; children: Bas, Stijn. PhD, U. Utrecht (The Netherlands), 1982. Rsch. asst. EUT, Eindhoven, The Netherlands, 1975; rschr. FOM, Nieuwegein, The Netherlands, 1975-84; rsch. asst. U. Sask., Saskatoon, Can., 1984-86; asst. prof. EUT, Eindhoven, 1986—. E-mail: e.j.m.v.heesch@tue.nl. Home: Eijerven 20, 5646 JL Eindhoven The Netherlands Office: Eindhoven U Tech, PO Box 513, 5600 MB Eindhoven The Netherlands

VAN HEMMEN, J. LEO, physicist, educator; b. Groningen, The Netherlands, May 9, 1947; s. Jan and Lina (Boersma) Van H.; m. Paulina N.D. Broek, June 28, 1972; children: Paul, Saskelina. PhD, U. Groningen, 1976; Habil., U. Heidelberg, Germany, 1983. Rsch. asst. U. Groningen, 1972-76; vis. mem. IHES, Bures-sur-Yevette, France, 1976-77; asst. prof. math. Duke U., Durham, N.C., 1977-78; rsch. assoc. U. Heidelberg, 1978-83, provatdozent, 1983-89; prof. physics Tech. U. Munich, 1989—. Editor/author: Models of Neural Networks, 1991—; contbr. articles to profl. jours. Netherlands Orgn. for Advancement of Pure Rsch. stipend, 1976. Fellow Am. Phys. Soc.; mem. Am. Math. Soc., European Phys. Soc. Avocation: photography. Office: Tech Univ Munich, Physics Dept, 85747 Garching Germany

VANHEMS, PHILIPPE MICHEL, physician, researcher; b. Mascara, Algeria, June 16, 1960; s. Michel and Nicole (Molinier) V.; m. Elyse Trudeau, May 30, 1998; 1 child, Mathilde. MS, Med. Sch. Nancy, France, 1991, MD, 1992; PhD in Epidemiology and Pub. Health, U. Montreal, Can., 1998. Registered with specialty in epidemiology and pub. health Lyon Bd. Physicians. Physician divsn. infectious diseases U. Hosp. Geneva, 1989-92; rschr. U. Montreal, 1992-97, U. Wash., Seattle, 1997—; assoc. prof. Sch. Medicine, Lyon, France, 1999; epidemiologist Inst. Internat. Health, Lyon, France, 1999—; acad. visitor Nat. Ctr. in HIV Epidemiology and Clin. Rsch., U. NSW, Sydney, Australia, 1995; dir. Master degree students Lyon U., 1997-99; cons. clin. rsch. Inst. Montreal. Contbr. articles to profl. jours. Recipient grants Swiss HIV Cohort Study, Geneva, 1995-98, Glaxo Welcome Inc., Montreal, 1997, Sidaction, Lyon, 1999. Mem. Internat. AIDS Soc., European Soc. Microbiology and Infectious Diseases, French Assn. Epidemiologists. Avocations: sailing, skiing, scuba diving. Home: 36 Rue de la Garde, 69005 Lyon France Office: Lab Epidemiology Pub Health, 8 Av Rockefeller, 69373 Lyon Cedex 08 France

VAN HOOF, VIVIANE ODILIA, pathologist, researcher; b. Lubumbashi, Congo, May 8, 1955; d. Jozef Lodewijk Van Hoof; m. Herman Lodewijk Vansweevelt, Oct. 29, 1976; children: Jef, Dirk. MD, U. Antwerp, Belgium, 1979, PhD, 1992. Clin. pathologist Unilab, Antwerp, 1983-86; resident clin. chemistry, clin. pathologist Univ. Hosp., Antwerp, 1986-90, sr. resident dept. clin. chemistry, clin. pathologist, 1990-97, head dept. clin. chemistry, clin. pathologist, 1997—; guest prof. U. Antwerp, 1995—, rschr., 1997—. Contbr. articles to profl. jours. Adminstr. Caisse de Prevoyance pour Medecins, Dentistes et Pharmaciens, Brussels, 1992—. Grantee Nat. Fund Sci. Rsch., 1993-96, 95-99. Mem. Am. Assn. Bone and Mineral Rsch., Am. Assn. Clin. Chemistry, Belgische Vereniging voor Klinische Biologie en Klin. Chemie, Med. Women's Assn. Belgium (co-founder, pres. 1991-93), algemeen Syndicaat der Gemeeskundigen U. Belgie. Avocations: silk painting, hiking, reading. Office: U Hosp Antwerp, Wilrijkstraat 10, B-2650 Edegem Antwerp Belgium

VAN HOUT, BAS, brain surgeon; b. Amsterdam, The Netherlands, May 22, 1959; s. Joop van Hut and Marja Terpstra; m. Hanja May Wegge, May 5, 1987; children: Jantje, Pietje, Klaasje. Diploma, Lagere, Amsterdam, 1979; M in Brain Surgery, U. Vinkeveen, The Netherlands, 1986. Gen. brain surgeon EVermaatziekenhuis, Hilversum, The Netherlands; surgeon gen. Den Haag (The Netherlands) Vandaag; dir. Koninklijk Huis, Soestdijk, The Netherlands, 1985-91, cons., Den Haag. Author: How to Operate on a Brain, 1986 (Med. award 1987), The First 5 Minutes After the Operation, 1987 (Med. award), Speedoperations on the Brain, 1991 (Med. award 1992). Chmn. Ctrl. Brainsurgeons Orgn., Monnickendam, CDA, Staphorst. Col. BVD, 1976-80. Roman Catholic. Avocations: medical affairs, politics, crime, Emerson Vermaat. Fax: 0031235730892. Home: Marnix van Sint Aldegondestraat 15, 2042 AN Zandvoort The Netherlands Office: PS Brain Transplant, m van st Andegondestr 15, 2042 AN Zandvoort The Netherlands

VANHOUTTE, PAUL MICHEL GEORGES, medical research executive, vascular biologist, pharmacologist, educator; b. Merelbeke, Oost-Vlaanderen, Belgium, Nov. 26, 1940; became Am. Citizen, 1992; s. Robert Edouard and Alice (Hubert) V.; m. Jacqueline A. Vandenberghe, Apr. 2, 1966; children: Valerie, Jacqueline, Paul-Robert, Alexis. BS magna cum laude, U. Gent, Belgium, 1961, MD magna cum laude, 1965, MS cum laude, 1970, PhD, U. Antwerp, Belgium, 1973. Rsch. asst. Lab. Normal and Pathol. Physiology, U. Gent, Belgium, 1965-68, first asst., 1969-71; rsch. asst. dept. physiology and biophysics Mayo Clinic, Rochester, Minn., 1968-69, rsch. assoc., 1972-73, cons. depts. physiology and biophysics, cardiovasc. medicine, 1981-89; head dept. internal medicine Lab. Pathophysiology U. Antwerp, Wilrijk, Belgium, 1973-75, head divsn. internal medicine Lab. Pharmacology, 1975-81; dir. dept. medicine Ctr. Exptl. Therapeutics Baylor Coll., Houston, 1989-92; v.p. rsch. Inst. de Recherches Internationales Servier, Courbevoie, France, 1992—; prof. medicine, physiology, pharmacology Inst. de Recherches Internationales Servier, Courbevoie; lectr. in pathophysiology Nat. U. of Rwanda, Butare, 1967; asst. prof. physiology Mayo Med. Sch. U. Minn., Rochester, 1972-73, vis. lectr., 1974-75, prof. physiology and pharmacology, 1981-89; asst. lectr. physiopathology U. Antwerp, Wilrijk, 1973, lectr. in physiology and pathophysiology, 1974, lectr. in physiology Premed. Sch., 1974-77, prof. pharmacology and physiology, 1975-81; vis. prof. Polish Acad. Scis., Warsaw, 1979; vis. faculty mem. Mayo Clinic and Mayo Found., Rochester, 1979-80; ad hoc mem. experimental cardiovascular scis. study sect. NIH, 1984, mem. program project rev. com. A Nat. Heart and Lung Inst., 1988-92, chair, 1991-92, mem. reviewers res., 1992—; prof. medicine, pharmacology and physiology Baylor U., Houston, 1989-95; Fouad A. Bashour vis. prof. U. Tex., Dallas, 1988; Philip Dow lectr. Med. Augusta, Ga., 1988; Lorenzini lectr., Padova, Italy, 1989; vis. prof. Brit. Heart Found., Royal Postgrad. Med. Sch., London, 1989, Royal Coll. Physicians and Surgeons Can., Winnipeg, 1989; Wellcome vis. prof. in basic med. scis. Tulane U., New Orleans, 1990; Louis B. Bishop lectr. Am. Coll. Cardiology, New Orleans, 1990; ICI/Manchester (Eng.) U. Prize lectr., 1991; Founders lectr. in basic sci. Assn. Acad. Surgery, 1991; Pfizer vis. prof. in cardiovasc. medicine N.Y. Med. Coll., 1992; chmn. nomenclature and drug classification com. on receptor Internat. Union Pharm. Scis., 1989-98, sec.-gen., 1998—; hon. prof. Pekin U. Med. Coll., Beijing. Author: (with J.T. Shepherd) Veins and Their Control, 1975, (with J.T. Shephard) The Human Cardiovascular System: Facts and Concepts, 1979, Japanese edit., 1983, (with T.F. Lüscher) The Endothelium: Modulator of Cardiovascular Function; co-editor: Mechanisms of Vasodilation, 1978, Vascular Neuroeffector Systems, 1980, Vasodilatation, 1981, 5-Hydroxytryptamine in Peripheral Reactions, 1982, Cardiovascular Pharmacology of the Prostaglandins, 1982, Vasodilator Mechanisms, 1984, Serotonin and the Cardiovascular System, 1985, Calcium Entry Blockers and Tissue Protection, 1985, Central and Peripheral Mechanisms of Cardiovascular Regulation, 1986, The Endothelium: Relaxing and Contracting Factors, 1988, Vasodilatation: Vascular Smooth Muscle, Peptides, Autonomic Nerves and Endothelium, 1988, Calcium Antagonists: Pharmacology and Clinical Research, 1988, Serotonin: From Cell Biology to Pharmacology and Therapeutics, 1990, Endothelium-derived Relaxing Factors, 1990, Endothelium-derived Contracting Factors, 1990, Cardiovascular System, Hypertension and Serotonin Antagonists, 1990, The Coronary Circulation in Physiological and Pathophysiological States, 1991, Mechanisms of Vasodilation, 1990, Fish Oil and Blood-Vessel Wall Interactions, 1991, Return Circulation and Norepinephrine, 1991, Serotonin From Cell Biology to Pharmacology and Therapeutics, 1993, Cardiovascular Pharmacology and Therapeutics, 1993, Endothelium-Derived Hyperpolarizing Factor, 1996; author chpts. to books; assoc. editor: Am. Jour. Physiology, Heart and Circulation Physiology, 1987-92, News in Physiol. Sci., 1987—, Jour. Vascular Medicine and Biology, 1989—, Jour. Neurol. Scis., 1986-92; editor-in-chief Jour. Cardiovascular Pharmacology, 1989—; mem. editl. bd. numerous med. jours.; contbr. over 450 rsch. papers and 400 revs. and articles to profl. jours. Internat. Postdoctoral fellow PHS, 1968-69; grantee Minn. Heart Assn. 1969, Belgian Nat. Founds. for Rsch. and Med. Rsch., 1975-80, Action grantee Belgian Govt., 1976-81; recipient Spl. prize U. Gent, 1965, 1st Place award Young Investigators Competition Am. Coll. Cardiology, 1973, Assubel prize, 1979, Outstanding Rsch. award Internat. Soc. Heart Rsch., 1984-85. Fellow Am. Coll. Angiology, Am. Coll. Cardiology, Am. Heart Assn. (mem. stroke coun., mem. coun. on high blood pressure rsch., med. adv. bd., mem. coun. circulation), Am. Physiol. Soc. (mem. cardiovascular sect., mem. com. liaison for industry 1987-91), Soc. Vascular Medicine and Biology; mem. Am. Soc. Clin. Investigation (emeritus), Am. Soc. Pharmacology and Exptl. Therapeutics, Assn. Am. Physicians, Assn. des Pharmacologistes (France), Belgian Soc. Physiology and Pharmacology, Biophys. Soc., Brit. Pharm. Soc., Internat. Soc. Hypertension, Internat. Soc. Endothelialization in Cardiovasc. Surgery (founding mem.), Acad. Europea, Brazilian Acad. Medicine (hon.), Koninklijke Acad. voor Geneeskunde van Belgie (corr.), Inter-Am. Soc. Hypertension, European Biomed. Rsch. Assn. (founding mem.), German Soc. Angiology (hon.), Panamerican Coll. Endothelium (hon.), Purine Club (rep. France), Serotonin Club (founder, past pres.), Sigma Xi. Avocation: classical music. Fax: 331 55 72 72 76. E-mail: vanhoutt@servier.fr. Office: Inst Recherches Internat Servier, 6 place des Pléiades, 92415 Courbevoie Cedex, France

VANHOVE, DOMINIQUE MICHEL, chemical engineering educator; b. Tourcoing, France, July 1, 1945; s. Henri Noel and Eugenie Philomene (Ghesquier) V.; m. Anne-Marie Regina Lancelot, July 17, 1971; children: Etienne, Florence, Guillaume. Lic. in phys. sci., U. Lille, France, 1966; DEA, 1967; PhD, U. Poitiers, France, 1973. Asst. U. Poitiers, 1968-74, maitre asst., 1974-81; postdoctoral U. Ghent, Belgium, 1973-74; prof. U. Claude Bernard, Lyon, France, 1981-91, Ecole Ctrl. de Lille, France, 1991—; head dept. process engring. Ecole Ctrl., Lille, 1991—; dir. rsch. lab., 1991—; cons. various orgns., Lyon and Lille, 1987—. Contbr. articles to profl. publs., conf. procs. Pres. Assn. LGCA-Roger Loison, Lille, 1991—. Home: Rue de la Cense à l'Eau, 59700 Marcq-en-Baroeul France Office: Ecole Ctrl Lille, Blvd P Langevin, 59651 Villeneuve d'Ascq France

VANHOVE, NORBERT, regional development director, economics educator; b. Torhout, West Flanders, Belgium, Sept. 24, 1935; s. Julien V. and Maria Doyen; m. Elisabeth Bleck, Sept. 30, 1960; children: Ann, Dries. M in Econ. Scis., State U. Ghent (Belgium), 1958; PhD in Econs., Erasmus U., Rotterdam, The Netherlands, 1961. Asst. U. Ghent (Belgium), 1958-62; mem. staff Westvlaams Economisch Studiebureau/Westvlaaamse Economische Raad, Brugge, Belgium, 1962-68; dep. dir. Westvlaams Economisch Studiebureau/Westvlaamse Economische Raad, Brugge, 1968-76; dep. dir. gen. Regional Devel. Authority West Flanders, Brugge, 1976-79, dir. gen., 1979-95, adminstr. gen., 1995—; dir. gen. Westvlaams Economisch Studiebureau, Brugge, 1979—; asst. prof. Coll. of Europe, Brugge, 1963-71, extra-ordinary prof., 1971—; extra-ordinary prof. U. Antwerp (Belgium), 1990—. Author: Regional Policy: A European Approach, 1980, 2d edit., 1999, Greek translation, 3rd edit. 1987, reports, 23 other books. Recipient Two Yrs. prize Assn. Economists, 1967, Pro Civitate prize Credit Communal Belgique, 1972; decorated officer Order of the Crown (Belgium), 1994. Mem. Orde Van de Prince, Tourist Rsch. Ctr. (sec. gen. 1965), Assn. Internat. du Tourisme (v.p. 1994—), Assn. Internat. d'Sci. du Tourisme. Avocations: gardening, cycling, tennis, writing. Home: Krakkestraat, 3 8200 Brugge Belgium Office: RDA West Flanders, Baron Ruzettelaan 33, 8310 Assebroek Brugge, Belgium

VAN HOVELL TOT WESTERFLIER, BARON ZWEDER OTTO HUBERT MARIE, banker; b. Bandung, Indonesia, June 18, 1942; m. Maria Pia Dreesmann, Aug. 31, 1968; 5 children. Student, U. Leiden, Netherlands, 1965. Several positions Hollandsche Bank Unie, 1966-70, Amsterdam Rotterdam Bank NV, Rotterdam, Netherlands, 1970-89; CEO, Staal Bankiers NV, The Hague, Netherlands, 1989-99; mem. exec. bd. Achmea Holding NV, Zeist, Netherlands, 1994—.

VAN HOVEN, JAY, retired school system administrator; b. Holland, Mich., Aug. 11, 1944; s. Leonard Jay and Mary Helene (Schaap) Van Hoven; m. Nancy L. Voight, June 27, 1975; children: Joshua, Janna, Lydia. B.A., Hope Coll., 1966; student, Wayne State U., 1966-68; M.A., No. Mich. U., 1971; postgrad., Mich. State U., 1973-75. Vol. Peace Corps, S.Am., 1968-69; tchr. St. Dunstans Sch., U.S. V.I., 1969-70; community sch. dir. Des Moines Schs., 1970-72; adminstr. Ctr. for Community Edn., Alma, Mich., 1973-75; asst. ombudsman Mich. State U., East Lansing, 1975; fin. mgr. Sch. Nursing U. N.C., Chapel Hill, 1976-78; desegregation specialist Ind. U., Indpls., 1979-82; ptnr. Westlake Profl. Services, Indpls., 1982-85; asst. supr. fin. Melvindale (Mich.) Schs., 1985-86; supt. Detour (Mich.) Schs., 1986-91, Mendon Schs., 1991-93, Mason Schs., 1993-97; ret., 1997; pres. Med. Specialty Disability Ins. Corp., Indpls., 1983-86. Rep., Interurban Coll. and Univ. Consortium, Des Moines, 1971-72; adminstr. Urban Cities, Flint, Mich., 1970; mem. Hispanic Edn., Des Moines, 1971-72; mem. Ind. Community Edn. Adv., Indpls., 1979—. Mott fellow, 1970-71, 73-75, 79-85. Mem. Mich. Assn. Sch. Adminstrs., Phi Delta Kappa. Lutheran.

VANHOYE, ALBERT FELIX, religious educator; b. Hazebrouck, France, July 24, 1923; s. Maurice Felix and Lucie Marie (Collewet) V. Lic. in Classics, Sorbonne, Paris, 1946; lic. in Philosophy, Vals, France, 1950; lic. in Theology, 1955; PhD in Scripture, Biblical Inst. Rome, 1961. Tchr. Greek S.J. Juniorate, Yzeure, France, 1946-47, 50-51; scripture lectr. S.J. Scholasticate, Chantilly, France, 1959-62; scripture prof. Biblical Inst. Rome, 1963-93; dean of faculty, 1969-75, rector, 1984-90, emeritus prof., 1993—; pres. Colloquium Biblicum, Leuven, Belgium, 1984, S.N.T.S., Internat., 1995-96. Author: Structure and Theology of the Accounts of the Passion, 1967, Old Testament Priests and the New Priest, 1986, Structure and Message of the Epistle to the Hebrews, 1989; contbr. articles to profl. jours. Recipient Chevalier de l'Ordre Nat. Merit, French Govt., 1990. Mem. Studiorum Novi Testamenti Societas, Assn. Catholique Francaise pour l'Etude de la Bible. Roman Catholic. Avocations: reading poetry, walking. Home: via della Pilotta 25, 00187 Rome Italy Office: Pontifical Biblical Inst, Piazza della Pilotta 35, 00187 Rome Italy

VANICEK, JIRI, computer science educator, government advisor; b. Prague, Czechoslovakia, Feb. 3, 1937; s. Vlastimil and Jirina (Zahourova) V.; m. Hana Svobodova, June 2, 1937; children: Tomas, Petr, Jan. MSc in Math., Charles U., Prague, 1960, PhD in Math., 1964; PhD in Computer

Sci., Czech Tech. U., Prague, 1986. Asst. prof. Charles U., 1960-65; sci. worker Rsch. Inst. for Computers, Prague, 1965-72, head software rsch., 1972-90; dir. gen. Inst. for Info. in Edn., Prague, 1990-95; prof. Czech Tech. U., 1995-97, Czech U. Agr., Prague, 1997—; pres. Czech Nat. Standardization Com. for Info. Tech.; govt. councillor Ministry of Economy, Czech Republic, 1995-96; govt. councillor-in-chief Govt. Office for State Info. Sys., Prague, 1996—. Contbr. articles to profl. jours. Mem. Armed Forces Comm. and Electronics Assn. (1st prize 1996). Office: Czech U for Agr PEF KI, Kamycka 129, CZ 16521 Prague 6, Czech Republic

VANIER, JERRE LYNN, art director; b. Phoenix, June 11, 1957; i. Jerry Dale Barber and Betty Jane (Brady) Barber Hughes; m. Kent Douglas Wick, May 4, 1979 (div. June 1994); 1 child, Jared Kent Wick; m. Jay David Vanier, June 6, 1994; 1 child, Jolie Jacqueline. BA in Art History magna cum laude, Ariz. State U., 1978, MA in Humanities. Chmn., vice chmn. Internat. Friends of Art, Scottsdale, Ariz., 1990-96; dir. 19th and 20th century art Joy Tash Gallery, Scottsdale, 1996-97; dir. estate art Vanier Fine Art, Ltd., Scottsdale, 1997-98, dir., 1998—; dir. Vanier Galleries on Marshall, Scottsdale, 1999—. Mem. pub. art collection adv. bd. Scottsdale Cultural Coun., 1990—, Phoenix Jr. League, Art Renaissance Initiative Faces of Ariz. Mem. DAR (Ariz. page continental congress 1993, Ariz. vice chmn. Jr. Am. Citizen com. 1998, 3d vice regent Camelback chpt. 1993), Colonial Dames Am., Daus. Republic of Tex. (non-resident), Nat. Soc. Arts and Letters (Valley of Sun chpt. bd. dirs. 1988-92, art chmn. 1988-90, membership chmn. 1990-92), Jr. League Phoenix, Alpha Delta Pi, Phi Kappa Phi. Republican. Avocations: genealogy, collecting contemporary art. Office: Vanier Galleries on Marshall 4142 N Marshall Way Scottsdale AZ 85251-3838

VAN JAARSVELDT, HENDRIK JACOBUS, industrial engineer; b. Louis Trichardt, Transvaal, South Africa, Aug. 17, 1957; s. Johannes Victor and Jacoba (Swart) Van J.; m. Maria Magdalena Van Burick, Dec. 6, 1975; children: Stephen, Eloise. BS, U. South Africa, Pretoria, 1983; BA with honors, U. Stellenbosch, South Africa, 1987, MBA, 1990; Executive Devel Prog Mgmt Technology, U Capetown. Prodn. supr. De Beers, Springs, South Africa, 1975-76, computer programmer, 1977-81; computer programmer De Beers, Shannon, Ireland, 1982; analyst/programmer De Beers, Springs, 1983-84, head dept. computers, 1985-88, prodn. mgr., 1988-90, tech. mgr., 1991—; computer programmer Scandiamant AB, Robertsfors, Sweden, 1982. Sgt. South African Army, 1976-77. Mem. Computer Soc. South Africa, South African Soc. for Quality (sr.), Production Mgmt. Inst. of South Africa. Dutch Ref. Ch. Achievements include research and development in synthetic diamond manufacture. Avocations: cricket, fly fishing, running. Home: PO Box 3427, Springs 1560, South Africa

VAN KAMPEN, MICHAEL, radiation oncologist, physician, educator; b. Bad Kreuznach, Germany, Mar. 5, 1963. MD, U. Erlangen, Germany, 1990. Cert. med. specialist in radiation oncology, 1995. Resident dept. radiation diagnostics U. Nurnberg, Germany, 1989-90, resident dept. radiotherapy, 1991-93; resident U. Heidelberg, Germany, 1993—, German Cancer Ctr., Heidelberg, 1994; sr. staff U. Heidelberg, 1996-2000; chief dept. radiation oncology U. Frankfurt, 2000—. Mem. European Soc. Therapeutic Radiation Oncology. Office: U Heidelberg, Dept Rad Oncol, KH Nordwest, Steinbacher Hohl 2-26, D-60488 Frankfurt Germany

VANKELECOM, HUGO, pharmacology educator; b. Halle, Belgium, Aug. 12, 1964. Pharmacist, U. Leuven, Belgium, 1987; PhD, U. Leuven, 1992. Postdoctoral fellow U. Oxford, U.K., 1993-94; postdoctoral fellow U. Leuven, Belgium, 1993-96, prof. pharmacology, 1997—. Recipient short-term fellowship European Sci. Foun., 1993, Royal Soc. fellowship, 1994, long-term fellowship European Molecular Biology Orgn., 1994, Wellcome Travelling Rsch. fellowship, Oxford, 1994. Office: U Leuven, Gasthuisberg Herestraat 49, Leuven B-3000, Belgium

VAN KEMENADE, ANS MARIA CORNELIA, linguistics educator; b. Eindhoven, The Netherlands, Sept. 4, 1954; d. Martinus Johannes Cornelius and Gertrude Johanna (van der Kruys) van Kemenade; m. Jos Antonius Eugène Heuer, Oct. 12, 1984 (divorced); children: Iris, Floris. Cand. Letters, U. Utrecht, 1976, Dr. Letters, 1979, PhD, 1987. Rschr. Nederlandse Organisatie voor Wetenshappelijk Onderzoek, Utrecht, 1982-85; lectr. U. Leiden, The Netherlands, 1985-86; lectr. linguistics Vrije U. Amsterdam, 1986-99; prof. English lang. U. Nymegen, 1999—. Author: Syntactic Case and Morphological Case in the History of English, 1987; editor Lingua, 1993, Parameters of Morpho Syntactic Change, 1997; contbr. articles to profl. jours. Nederlandse Organisatie voor Wetenshappelijk Rsch. grantee, 1982-85. Mem. Dutch Linguistics Soc. (bd. dirs. 1989-94, pres. 1994), Internat. Soc. Hist. Linguistics, European Soc. for Study of English, Generative Linguistics in the Old World. Home: Prof van Bemmelenlaan 32, 3571EM Utrecht The Netherlands Office: U Nymegen Dept English, PO Box 9103, 6500 Nymegen The Netherlands

VAN KERCKHOVE, GILBERT RACHEL, engineering executive; b. Gent, Belgium, Dec. 31, 1948; s. Gaston and Germaine (Van Den Berghen) V. K.; m. Danielle Brosse, 1971 (div. 1973); 1 child, Marianne; m. Bin Sun; 1 child, Valerie. MSEE, RUG, Gent, 1973. Reg. dir. China ACEC, Beijing, 1980-88; dir. Far East BARCO, Hong Kong, 1988-89; country mgr. Indochina, Burma Alcatel, Bangkok, Thailand, 1990-93; adv. to mng. dir. Alcatel Brazil, Sao Paulo, Brazil, 1993-94; sr. rep. Alcatel Spain, Beijing, China, 1994-95; dir. East China Alstom, Shanghai, China, 1995-99; pres., adviser for fgn. trade Belgium, China Strategy Ltd., Beijing, 2000—. Mem. Belgian Bus. Forum. Avocations: health club, diving, music, writing. Home and Office: Julong Garden, 5-3-201 Xinzhong Str 68, 100027 Beijing China

VAN KESTEREN, HENRICUS HUBERTUS, trade mark agent; b. Heemstede, The Netherlands, Dec. 22, 1944; s. Petrus Adrianus van Kesteren and Helena Petronella Hendriks; m. Woudina van Jaarsveld, Nov. 26, 1974; children: Ilse, Wouter. cert. trade mark agt. Haarlem Regional Ct. Tchr. Stichting Sch. & Wereld, Santpoort, The Netherlands, 1972-92; trade mark agt. Keesom & Hendriks N.V., The Hague, The Netherlands, 1995—; sec. gen. European Group Audiovisual Devel., Brussels, 1978-88. Writer documentary Migration and Starvation, 1979; prodr. documentaries; author: Heirs to a Paradise, 1982. Avocations: photography, making videos. Fax: 0031-703504963. E-mail: tmlaw@keesom.nl. Office: Keesom & Hendriks NV, Delistraat 45, 2585 VX The Hague The Netherlands

VAN KLINK, ED GERARDUS MARIA, veterinarian; b. Alphen Aandenrijn, The Netherlands, Nov. 19, 1956. DVM, Fac. Vet. Scis., Utrecht, The Netherlands, 1983; PhD in Agriculture, Wageningen (The Netherlands) U, 1994. Swine fever control rschr. Ministry Agriculture, The Netherlands, 1983; dist. vet. officer Ministry Agriculture, Zambia, Africa, 1985-87, vet. rsch. officer, 1987-90; policy officer Ministry Agriculture, The Netherlands, 1991-97, sr. policy expert, 1997—; rsch. asst. Fac. Vet. Medicine, Utrecht, The Netherlands, 1983-85; rsch. fellow U. Wageningen, The Netherlands, 1990-91; com. mem. Soc. Vet. Epidemiology and Preventative Medicine, England, 1998—; lectr. European U., 1999. Author: Aspects of Productivity of Traditionally Managed Barotse Cattle in the Western Province of Zambia, 1994; contbr. articles to profl. jours. Mem. Soc. for Vet. Epidemiology and Preventive Medicine, Dutch Vet. Soc. Avocations: speed skating, skeelering, running, drawing and painting, folk music and dance. Home: Vlietenburg 26, 2804WS Gouda The Netherlands Office: Nat Reference Ctr Agricult, PO Box 482, 6710 BL Ede The Netherlands

VANKOV, IVAN DANAILOV, nuclear engineer, educator; b. Sofia, Bulgaria, Jan. 12, 1936; s. Danail Lukov and Maria Ivanova (Andreicheva) V.; m. Maria Ilieva Dimitrova, Dec. 6, 1959; 1 child, Danail Ivanov. Diploma in electronic engring., Higher Mech. and Electrotech. Inst., Sofia, 1959; PhD, Inst. Physics, Sofia; DSc, Inst. Nuclear Rsch. and Nuclear Energy, Sofia. Rschr. Inst. Physics, Sofia, 1960-69, sr. rschr., 1969-73; prof. nuclear electronics Tech. Univ., Sofia, 1971—; head divsn. rsch. Inst. Nuclear Rsch. and Nuclear Energy, Sofia, 1973—, vice dir., 1984-88, prof., 1988—, dir., 1989-93, pres. sci. coun., 1993-95, v.p. sci. coun., 1995—. Co-author: Nuclear Electroics, 1978, CMOS Integrated Circuits, 1987, Pulse Circuits and Devices, 1989; contbr. articles to profl. jours.; patentee in field. Mem. Nat. Qualification Commn. Electrotechnics and Automation, European Nuclear Soc., Union Bulgarian Scientists. Avocations: tourism, skiing. Office: Inst Nuclear Rsch & Nuclear Energy, Tzarigradsko Shaussee 72, BG-1784 Sofia Bulgaria

VAN KRANENBURG, HERMA, material scientist, educator; b. Buren, Gelderland, The Netherlands, Sept. 12, 1964; d. Dick and Mini (Van Wyk) van K.; m. James Micola von Fürstenrecht, Dec. 19, 1989; children: Malou, Pauline. MSc, U. Twente, 1988, PhD, 1992. Rschr. U. Twente, Enschede, The Netherlands, 1992-93; asst. prof. MESA Rsch. Inst. U. Twente, Enschede, 1993—; rschr. Basic Rsch. Labs. NTT, Tokai, Japan, 1989. Author: Obliquely Co-evaporated Thin Films for Magnetic Recording, 1992; co-editor: Proc. 25th European Solid State Device Rsch. Conf., 1995; contbr. articles to profl. jours. Office: Univ Twente MESA Rsch Inst, Drienerlolaan 5, 7522 NB Enschede The Netherlands

VAN KUYK, JEF JOHANNES, psychologist; b. Nijmegen, The Netherlands, Mar. 31, 1941; s. Sjef Hendricus and Elisabeth Maria (Kersten) N.; m. Jacoba Maria Moonen, Dev. 15, 1965; children: Maaike, Maartje, Rogier. PhD, Tilburg Univ., 1985. Tchr. various, Nijmegen, 1964-71; tchr. secondary sch. Montessori Coll., Nijmegen, 1971-72; lectr. Univ. Tilburg, 1980-84; scientific project leader Cito Nat. Ednl. Testing Ctr., Arnhem, 1979—; adv. Min. of Edn. The Hague, 1990-94. Author, editor: How to Improve Primary Education, 1987, 91; contbr. articles to profl. jours. Chmn. Soc. of A House in France, 1980—; art adv. Internat. Art Gallery, Heeswijk, Den Bosch, 1989—. E-mail: jef.vankuyk@cito.nl. Fax: 0263521494. Home: Henri Dunantstraat 68, Nijmegen 6543KS, The Netherlands Office: Cito, Nieuwe Oeverstraat 50, Arnhem 6801MG, The Netherlands

VAN LAER, FRANK ANDREAS, nurse; b. Kasterlee, Antwerpen, Belgium, Mar. 2, 1957; s. Joannes Emilius Van Laer and Julia Regina Nuydens; m. Hilde Greta Marichal, Aug. 21, 1982; children: Jeroen, Tine, Pieter, Anneleen. RN, Hoger Rijksinstituut, Ghent, Belgium, 1978, postgrad., 1980; cert. tropical medicine, Prince Leopold Inst., Antwerpen, 1979; cert. infection control, U. Antwerp, Belgium, 1991. Male nurse Inst. Tropical Medicine, Antwerp, 1979-87; infection control male nurse U. Hosp. Antwerp, Edegem, Belgium, 1987—; tchr. infection control Karel de Grote-Hogeschool, Antwerp, 1999, Vormingscentrum Hoger Inst. voor Verpleegkunde Sint-Elisabeth, Turnhout, Belgium, 1999. Contbr. articles to profl. jours. Mem. Agalev. E-mail: frank.van.laer@uza.uia.ac.be. Fax: 32 3 825 42 81. Home: Pieter van den Bemdenlaan 124, B-2650 Edegem Antwerp, Belgium Office: Univ Ziekenhuis Antwerpen, Wilrijkstraat 10, B-2650 Edegem Antwerp, Belgium

VAN LEEUWEN, DIRK JACOB, hepatology educator; b. Emmen, The Netherlands, Nov. 9, 1951; s. Hendrik J. and Gerarda C. Creutzberg. MD, U. Amsterdam, 1979, PhD, 1988. Internist, gastroenterologist Dutch Splst. Registration Com. Med. dir. hepatobiliary unit Acad. Med. Ctr. U. Amsterdam, 1987-92; med. dir. hepatology and liver transplantation U. Ala., Birmingham, 1992-95, assoc. prof., medicine, pub. health, hepatologist, 1992—. Editor: Imaging in Hepatobiliary and Pancreatic Disease, 2000. Mem. Am. Assn. Study of Liver, Am. Gastroenterology Assn., Internat. Liver Pathology Study Group (Elves), European Assn. Study of Liver. Office: U Ala Liver Ctr 703 S 19th St Birmingham AL 35294-0001

VAN LEEUWEN, EDWIN HANS, research and development executive; b. Haarlem, The Netherlands, Oct. 4, 1950; arrived in Australia, 1951; s. Johannes Dirk and Matilda Van Leeuwen; m. Silvana Maria Puzsar, Dec. 4, 1982; children: Lara Michelle, Natasha Maria. BSc with honors, Australian Nat. U., Canberra, 1974, Monash U., Melbourne, Australia, 1976; PhD, Monash U., Melbourne, Australia, 1981. Sr. rsch. scientist dept. def. Def. Sci. and Tech. Orgn., Melbourne, 1981-85; prin. rsch. scientist BHP, Melbourne, 1985-87, mgr. advanced sys. engring., 1987-89; mgr. aerospace and electronics BHP, Sydney, Australia, 1989-90; mgr. external R & D BHP, Melbourne, 1990-94, mgr. tech. and bus. devel., 1994—; bd. dirs. Ctr. for Robost and Adaptive Sys., Canberra, Australia, IMS Internat., Toronto, Can., Australian Maritime Engring. Ctr., Launceston, Australia; chmn. Internat. Holonics Mfg. Sys., Toronto, 1995—; dep. chmn. IMSAC-Australia, Canberra, 1995—, head delegations IMS Australia, 1999—. Contbr. articles to profl. jours. Advisor Australian Space Industry Group Sub-com. to Australian Space Office, Canberra, 1988-91, Royal Melbourne U., 1996—; mem. Adv. Coun. for the Nat. Strategic Rev. of Math. in Australia, Sydney, 1994-95. Mem. Australian Math. Soc. Avocations: reading, skiing, bush walking, swimming, tennis. Office: BHP 245-273 Wellington Rd, Mulgrave VIC 3170, Australia

VANLERBERGHE, GUY, retired cosmetics executive; b. Bollezeele, France, July 14, 1932; s. Bernard and Clara (David) V.; m. Rose Schneider; children: Bruno, Thierry. BS, Coll. St. Jacques, 1950; degree in engring., ENSAT; lic. es scis., U. Toulouse, 1955; degree in engring., ESACG, 1956. Rschr. L'Oreal, Paris, 1959-67, dir. dept. rsch., 1967-97; lectr. ESACG, Paris, 1965-97, CPE, Lyon, France, 1997, U. Paris XII, 1993, U. Paris VI, 1997. Patentee in field; contbr. chpts. to books. Recipient Medaille Legrand Soc. Pour la Promotion de L'industrie, 1995. Mem. N.Y. Acad. Scis., AaAS, Assn. Pour L'etude des Corps Gras. Roman Catholic. Avocations: literature, philosophy, botany, foreign languages, working with wood and stone. Home: 40 Rue Charles de Gaulle, 77410 Villevaude France

VAN LOOSEN, JOHN, otorhinolaryngologist, head and neck surgeon; b. Vlissingen, The Netherlands, Feb. 7, 1957; s. Johan and Anna (Loerakker) Van L.; m. Arstrid Van Heusden; children: Hanna, Annette, Rian. M of Medicine, U. Rotterdam, The Netherlands, 1983; M of Dentistry, U. Amsterdam, The Netherlands, 1984; MD, U. Liverpool, Eng., 1997; PhD, Erasmus U., Rotterdam, 2000. Lic. otorhinolaryngologist and head and neck surgeon. Sr. rsch. assoc. U. Liverpool, 1987-97; jr. staff mem. ear, nose, and throat U. Rotterdam, 1989-90; sr. staff mem. ear, nose, and throat Royal Sophia Childrens Hosp., U. Rotterdam, 1990-93; sr. rsch. assoc. Erasmus U., Rotterdam, 1984—, Dalhousie U., Halifax, N.S., Can., 1995-98; head of ear, nose, and throat dept. Antonius Hosp., Sneek, The Netherlands, 1993—; dir. Fuse Ltd., 1989—. Col. Dutch Royal Navy, 1992—. Fellow Royal Coll. Medicine; mem. Internat. Coll. Surgeons, Royal Dutch Navy Club (hon.). Home: Elisabethstraat 1, 3063 BA Rotterdam The Netherlands Office: Antonius Hosp, PO Box 20 000, 8600 BA Sneek The Netherlands

VAN LOUCKS, MARK LOUIS, venture capitalist, business advisor; b. Tampa, Fla., June 19, 1946; s. Charles Perry and Lenn (Bragg) Van L.; m. Eva Marianne Forsell, June 10, 1986; children: Brandon, Charlie; m. Lee Ann Rose, Oct. 1, 1998. BA in Comm. and Pub. Policy, U. Calif., Berkeley, 1969. Sr. v.p. mktg., programming and corp. devel. United Cable TV Corp., Denver, Colo., 1970-81, advisor, 1983-89; sr. v.p., office of chmn. Rockefeller Ctr. TV Corp., N.Y.C., 1981-83; advisor United Artists Commun. Corp., Englewood, 1989-91; investor, business advisor in pvt. practice Englewood, 1983—; founder, prin. owner Glory Hole Saloon & Gaming Hall, Central City, Colo., 1990—, Harrah's Casino, Black Hawk, Colo., 1990—; chmn., CEO Bask Internat., Englewood, 1990—; bd. dirs. Wild West Devel. Corp., Denver; sr. v.p., bd. dirs. GSI Cable TV Assocs., Inc., San Francisco, 1984-90; guest lectr. on cable TV bus., 1985-91; cons. Telecommunications, Inc., Denver, 1989-93. Producer HBO spl. Green Chili Showdown, 1985; producer TV spl. 3 Days for Earth, 1987; producer, commd. artist nuclear war armament pieces; contbr. articles to profl. jours. Chmn. Cops in Crisis, Denver, 1990—; bd. dirs. The NOAH Found., Denver, 1976—; founding dir. Project for Responsible Advt., Denver, 1991-92; chmn. mayor's mktg. adv. bd., Central City, Colo. Named hon. capt. Denver Police Dept., 1991—, fin. advisor L. Rose Co., 1995—. Mem. Casino Owners Assn. (founding dir. 1989—), Colo. Gaming Assn. (dir. 1990—), recipient S'nnaeel Evol award, 1995), Glenmoor Country Club, The Village Club. Republican. Jewish. Avocations: music, woodworking, philanthropy, vintage autos. Office: MLVL Inc 333 W Hampden Ave Ste 1005 Englewood CO 80110-2340

VANMARCKE, ERIK HECTOR, civil engineering educator; b. Menen, Belgium, Aug. 6, 1941; came to U.S., 1965, naturalized, 1976; m. Louis Eugene and Rachel Louisa (van Hollebeke) V.; m. Margaret Maria Delesie, May 25, 1965; children: Lieven, Ann, Kristien. BS, U. Louvain, Belgium, 1965; MS, U. Del., 1967; PhD in Civil Engring, MIT, 1970. From instr. to prof. civil engring. MIT, Cambridge, 1969-85; Gilbert W. Winslow Career Devel. prof. MIT, 1974-77, dir. civil engring. systems group, 1976-80; prof. civil engring. and ops. rsch. Princeton U., 1985—, dir. grad. studies civil engring. and ops. rsch., 1990—; cons. Office Sci. and Tech. Policy, 1978-80; vis. scholar in engring. Harvard U., 1984-85; Shimizu Corp. vis. prof. Stanford U., 1991; cons. various govt. agys. and engring. firms; mem. exec. com. Princeton Materials Inst., 1991-93; mem. Princeton Environ. Inst., 1996—; affiliated faculty mem. Princeton U. Bendheim Ctr. Fin., 1998—; mem. com. on vulnerability of critical infrastructure Nat. Res. Coun., 1999—. Author: Random Fields: Analysis and Synthesis, 1983, Quantum Origins of Cosmic Structure, 1997; editor: Internat. Jour. Structural Safety, 1981-91. Recipient Sr. Scientist award for study in Japan, Japan Soc. for Promotion of Sci., 1991. Mem. ASCE (Raymond C. Reese rsch. award 1975, Walter L. Huber rsch. prize 1984, chair com. on risk assessment and mgmt. of the Geo-Inst. 1996—, chair com. on risk and vulnerability, Coun. Natural Disaster Reduction 1998—), Am. Geophys. Union, Seismol. Soc. Am., Internat. Soc. Soil Mechanics and Geotech. Engring. (chair com. TC32 on risk assessment and mgmt. 1998—), Royal Acad. Arts and Scis. of Belgium (fgn.). E-mail: evm@princeton.edu. Home: 578 Province Line Rd Hopewell NJ 08525-3104

VANMEER, MARY ANN, publisher, writer, researcher; b. Mt. Clemens, Mich., Nov. 22, 1947; d. Leo Harold and Rose Emma (Gulden) VanM. Student, Micha. State U., 1965-66, 67-68, U. Sorbonne, Paris, 1968; BA in Edn., U. Fla., 1970. Pres. VanMeer Tutoring and Translating, N.Y.C., 1970-72; freelance writer, 1973-79; pres. VanMeer Publs., Inc., Clearwater, Fla., 1980-88, VanMeer Media Advt., Inc., Clearwater, 1987-88; exec. dir., founder Nat. Ctrs. for Health and Med. Info., Inc., Palm Beach, Fla., 1990-93; pres., CEO The Thrifty Traveler, Inc. (formerly Traveling Free Pubs.), 1993—. Author: Traveling with Your Dog, U.S.A., 1976, How to Set Up a Home Typing Business, 1978, Freelance Photographer's Handbook, 1979, See America Free, 1981, Free Campgrounds, U.S.A., 1982, Free Attractions, U.S.A., 1982, VanMeer's Guide to Free Attractions U.S.A., 1984, VanMeer's Guide to Free Campgrounds, 1984, The How to Get Publicity for Your Business Handbook, 1987, Asthma: The Ultimate Treatment Guide, 1991, Allergies: The Ultimate Treatment Guide, 1993, Thrifty Traveling, 1995, 2d edit., 1996; pub. Nat. Health and Med. Trends Mag., 1986-88, The Thrifty Traveler Newsletter, 1993—, online edit., 2000, Over 50 Traveler Newsletter, 1997-98, Net News for the Thrifty Traveler Newsletter, 1997-98; webmaster ThriftyTraveler.com web sites, 1999—. Pub. info. chairperson, bd. dirs. Pinellas County chpt. Am. Cancer Soc., Clearwater, 1983-84, 86-88; mem. fin. devel. com. ARC, Palm Beach County, 1990-92. Mem. Am. Booksellers Assn., Soc. Am. Travel Writers. Office: ThriftyTraveler.com Inc PO Box 8168 Clearwater FL 33758-8168

VAN MEERWIJK, JOOST P.M., research scientist, educator; b. Leiderdorp, The Netherlands, Jan. 5, 1964; s. Frank van Meerwijk and Marijke (Peters) Lodder; m. Paola R. Romagnoli, Feb. 9, 1991; children: Nora, Giorgio. PhD, U. Utrecht, 1991. Postdoctoral fellow NIH, Bethesda, Md., 1991-93, Ludwig Inst., 1994-98; prof. immunology Paul Sabatier U., Toulouse, 1998—; rsch. group leader INSERM, Toulouse, 1998—. Contbr. articles to profl. jours. including Jour. Exptl. Medicine, Sci., Jour. Immunology, Internat. Immunology, Blood, EMBO Jour., others. Office: INSERM, CHU Purpan/BP 3028, 31024 Toulouse Cedex 3, France

VAN MEGEN, HAROLD JAN GEERT MARIA, psychiatrist; b. Nijmegen, The Netherlands, Jan. 8, 1960; s. Johannus Martinus and Bertha Hermina (Decates) van M.; m. Clarisse van Gorkom, Aug. 24, 1990; children: Sera Anna Isabel, Thomas Salamon Willem. MD, U. Amsterdam, 1986; PhD, U. Utrecht, The Netherlands, 1995. Assoc. prof. psychiatry U. Utrecht, The Netherlands, 1991—; med. dir. Anxiety Rsch. Ctr., The Netherlands, 2000—. Avocations: singing, biking. Office: U Hosp Utrecht, Heidelberglaan 100, 3584 CX Utrecht The Netherlands

VAN MIL, JAN WILLEM FOPPE, pharmacist, researcher; b. Waalwijk, The Netherlands, July 16, 1950; s. Harrie J. C. and Joop (Van Der Oord) Van M.; m. Roelf J. Bijleveld, Apr. 6, 1977. PharmD, U. Utrecht, The Netherlands, 1977; PhD in Sci., U. Groningen, 2000. Cert. pharmacist. Chief pharmacist Apotheek Lewenborg, Groningen, The Netherlands, 1977-79; chief pharmacist Zuidlaarder Apotheek, Zuidlaren, The Netherlands, 1979-81, owner, pharmacist, 1981—; rschr. U. Groningen; chmn. Pharm. Care Network Europe, Groningen, 1996-99; cons. in field. Editor: (book) Aids and Pharmacist, 1997; co-author: (books) The Drug, 1996, Slikwijzer, 1987; co-author, rschr.: (book) Dutch Drugs in Developing Countries, 1993; chief editor Pharmacy World and Sci. Recipient Innovation award Royal Dutch Assn. Advancement Pharmacy, 1993, Opwierda award, 1995. Mem. Internat. Soc. Pharmacoepidemiology, European Soc. for Clin. Pharmacy, Internat. Pharm. Fedn. Home: Margrietlaan 1, 9471 CT Zuidlaren The Netherlands

VAN MINGROOT, ERIK ALFONS, educator; b. Maldegem, Belgium, Sept. 1, 1937; s. Cornelius Van Mingroot and Marcella Naert; m. Monique De Facq, Dec. 30, 1961; children: Kathy, Marian, Hans, Gert. MPhil and Letters, Cath. U., Louvain, Belgium, 1959, PhD in History, 1969; diploma in archivist-palaeographer, Gen. State Archives, Brussels, 1962; diploma in mediaeval studies, Cath. U., Louvain, 1968. Aspirant Nat. Fund for Sci. Rsch., Belgium, 1961-64; asst. and sr. asst. Cath. U., Louvain, 1964-71, reader, 1971-74, lectr., 1974-77, prof. and full prof., 1977-99, emeritus prof., 1999—. Author: A Diplomatic and Comparative Study of the Bull of Foundation of the University of Louvain, December 9, 1425, 1994; co-author: Monasticon belge, Province de Flandre orientale, vol. IV, 1984, Limburg in kaart en prent, 1985 (gov. Roppe award 1987), Scandinavia in Old Maps and Prints, 1987. With Belgian Army, 1960-61. Recipient Officer in Order of Leopold, Kingdom Belgium, 1985. Roman Catholic. Home: Merellaan 18, 3210 Linden Belgium Office: Faculty Letters, Blijde-Inkomststraat 21, 3000 Leuven Belgium

VAN MONTAGU, MARC CHARLES ERNEST, chemist; b. Gent, Belgium, Oct. 11, 1933; s. Jearl Van Montagu and Irene Van Beveren; m. Nora Podgaetchi. BSc in Organic Chemistry, Rijksuniversiteit Gent, 1955, PhD in Organic Chemistry, Biochemistry, 1965. Prof., dir. U. Gent, 1965-99; prof. IPBO, 1999—; scientific dir. genetics dept. Flanders Interuniv. Inst. Biotech., 1965-99, Plant Genetic Sys. Inc., Belgium, 1982-96; adj. prof. Free U. Brussels, 1970-89; vis. prof. Fudan U., Shangai, China, U. Helsinki, Finland, U. Durham, Eng., U. Utah, Cold Spring Harbor Lab., N.Y., U. Iowa, others; organizer for numerous congresses. Mem. editl. bd. Plasmid, Genetical Rsch., Biofutur, Cell Biology, Mechanisms of Devel., Biotecnologia Aplicada, Biotech., Agro-Food-Industry High-Tech, Plant and Molecular Biotech. Series, FEBS Letters, Internat. Jour. Developmental Biology, Jour. Crop Prodn., Trends in Plant Scis., Biochimica et Biophysica Acta; contbr. over 700 articles to profl. jours. Named Francqui Chair Univ. Catholique de Louvain, Belgium, 1971-72, 94-95, U. Libre de Bruxelles, Belgium, 1986-87; recipient Stevens prize, Belgium, 1985, Rank prize for nutrition, London, 1987, IBM-Europe prize, 1988, Dr. Rudolf Maag prizes, 1990, Charles Léopold Mayer prize Acad. Scis., Paris, 1990, Gulden Spoor prize, Belgium, 1998, Theodor Bücher medal France, 1999. Mem. AAAS, NAC, Internat. Forum Biophilosophy (bd. dirs.), Belgische Vereniging voor Biochemie, Belgische Vereniging voor Celbiologie, Vlaamse Chemische Verenining, Am. Soc. Microbiology, Soc. Gen. Microbiology, Am. Soc. Plant Phys., Am. Phytopathological Soc., Agrl. Chem. Soc. Japan, European Molecular Biology Orgn. Fax: (32)(9)2648795. E-mail: marc.vanmontagu@rug.ac.be. Home: de Stassartstraat 120, 1050 Brussel Belgium Office: Lab voor Genetica Univ Gent, K L Ledeganckstraat 35, B-9000 Gent Belgium

VAN MOORSEL, JOANNES LUDOVICUS F., lawyer; b. Wassenaar, The Netherlands, Dec. 3, 1932; s. Adrianus Josephus M. Van Moorsel and Johanna Elisabeth Poelhekke; m. Hedwig Maria J. Van der Lande, Sept. 7, 1963; children: Lodewijk J.F., Robert C.M. LLM, L. Leiden, The Netherlands, 1959. Bar: Rotterdam 1966. Clk., asst. dist. atty. Rotterdam (The Netherlands) Ct., 1960-66; assoc. Van Velzen Law Firm, Schiedam, The Netherlands, 1966-70; ptnr. Trenité Van Doorne, Rotterdam, 1971-98; chmn. supervisory bd. Vanderlande Ind. BV, Veghel, The Netherlands, 1979; also other supervisory directorships. Chmn. Com. on Nat. Interests, Rotterdam, 1989-96; chmn. Erasmus Trust, Rotterdam, 1992—; hon. consul of Austria, Rotterdam, 1993—; sec. Opzoomerdag Trust, Rotterdam, 1993-94. Lt. col. The Netherlands Ct. Martial, 1954-88. Decorated officer Order Orange Nassau (The Netherlands) (v.p.). Mem. Netherlands Hon. Consular Assn. (v.p. 1996—), Broekpolder Golf Club (hon., pres. 1989-93). Mem. Conservative Party. Roman Catholic. Avocations: golf, skiing, reading. Home:

Zeestraat 77, 2518 AA The Hague The Netherlands Office: Trenité Van Doorne, Plaza Weena 666, 3012 CN Rotterdam The Netherlands

VAN MOORT, JAN CENT, geochemistry educator, consultant; b. Haren, Groningen, The Netherlands, Feb. 27, 1933; arrived in Australia, 1965; s. Jan Cent and Catharina Anna Maria (van't Veer) van M.; m. Johanna Gerardina Kapteijn, Dec. 31, 1964; children: Jan Cent Paul, Klaaske Godelieve, Catharina Anna Maria. Candidate in geology cum laude, Rijksuniversiteit, Utrecht, 1957, MSc in Petrology and Gen. Geology, 1961, DSc, 1965. Rsch. asst. Rijksuniversiteit Utrecht, 1959-61; rsch. fellow U. Tasmania, 1961-65, 69, lectr., 1965-72, sr. lectr., 1972—; prin. rschr. Australian Inst. of Nuclear Scis. and Engring., 1988—, Australian Rsch. Coun., 1995—; Humboldt Found. vis. prof. Mineral. Inst., Heidelberg, 1979, 90. contbr. articles to profl. jours. Fellow ZWO Dutch Orgn. for Sci. Rsch., 1965, Alexander von Humboldt Found., 1972; Dutch Govt. scholar, 1953-58; scholar Bourse d'Etat, Clermont-Ferrand, France, 1958. Mem. Internat. Assn. Exptl. Geochemistry, Geol. Soc. Australia, Internat. Electron Paramagnetic Resonance Soc., Australian New Zealand Assn. for Advancement of Sci. (treas.). Anglican. Avocations: swimming, horse riding, landscaping. E-mail: J.vanMoort@geol.utas.edu.au. Office: U Tasmania Dept Earth Scis, GPO Box 252-79, 7001 Hobart Tasmania, Australia

VAN NEERVEN, WILLY LODEWIJK, physicist, researcher; b. Weert, Limburg, The Netherlands, May 31, 1947; s. Antoon and Nelly Josepha (Goedhart) Van N. Grad., U. Nijmegen, The Netherlands, 1968, doctoral degree, 1970, PhD, 1975. Physics tchr. High Sch., Amsterdam, 1975, Delft, 1975-76; postdoctoral fellow U. Nijmegen, 1976-78, CERN, Geneva, 1979-80, Nikhef-H, Amsterdam, 1981-83, U. Dortmund, Germany, 1983-85; assoc. prof. U. Leiden, The Netherlands, 1985—. Mem. European Phys. Soc. Budapest. Avocation: history. Office: U Leiden, Niels Bohrweg 2, 2333 CA Leiden Holland, The Netherlands

VAN NESS, PATRICIA CATHELINE, composer, violinist; b. Seattle, June 25, 1951; d. C. Charles and Marjorie Mae (Dexter) Van N. Student, Wheaton (Ill.) Coll., 1969-70, Gordon Coll., 1972. Composer: ballet score for Beth Soll, 1985, 87, 94, for Monica Levy, 1988, for Boston Ballet, 1988, 90, for Charleston Ballet Theatre, 1994; text and music for voices and early instruments with text translated into Latin for Evensong, 1991, Five Meditations, 1993, Cor Mei Cordis, 1994, Arcanae, 1995, Ego sum Custos Angels, 1995, Tu Risa, 1996, The Nine Orders of the Angels, 1996; various scores, 1985-2000; rec. violinist A&M Records, Private Lightning, 1980, Telarc Internat. Arcanae and Ego sum Custos Angela, 1996, Telarc Internat. Michael and Thronorum, 1999, Telarc Internat. The Fourth River, 1999; composer-in-residence Coro Allegro, 1998, First Church in Cambridge (Mass.), Congregational, 1996—. Grantee Mass. Cultural Coun., 1993, 96, New Eng. Biolabs. Founds., 1989, Mass. Arts Lottery Coun., 1988, Meet the Composer, 1997, 98; recipient Spl. Recognition award Barlow Internat. Composition for Evensong, 1993, 1st prize His Majestie's Clerkes Choral Competition, 1997. Mem. ASCAP (Std. award 1996-2000), Chamber Music America, Am. Music Ctr., Alliance of Women in Music. Avocation: major league baseball.

VAN NESS, PETER, international studies educator; b. Paterson, N.J., Mar. 26, 1933; m. Anne A. Gunn; children: Stephen H., Thomas G., Harry A. BA in Polit. Sci., Williams Coll., 1955; B in Fgn. Trade, Am. Grad. Sch. Internat. Mgmt., 1959; MA in Polit. Sci., U. Calif., Berkeley, 1961, PhD in Polit. Sci. and Chinese Studies, 1967. Vis. lectr. Chinese U. Hong Kong, 1964-65; asst. prof. Grad. Sch. Internat. Studies, U. Denver, Colo., 1966-70; assoc. prof. Grad. Sch. Internat. Studies, U. Denver, 1970-98; fellow dept. internat. rels. Rsch. Sch. Pacific Studies, Australian Nat. U., Canberra, 1985-93, vis. fellow Contemporary China Ctr.,, 1998—; mem. rsch. pol. scientist Ctr. for Chinese Studies, U. Mich., Ann Arbor, 1968-69; bd. dirs. Human Rights in China, Nat. Com. on U.S.-China Rels., 1971-84; fellow Woodrow Wilson Internat. Ctr. for Scholars, Smithsonian Instn., Washington, 1973-74; Fulbright lectr. U. Tokyo, Keio U., Hitotsubashi U., Japan, 1978; lang. and rsch. fellow inter-univ. program for Chinese lang. studies Taipei, 1983; vis. prof. faculty of law Keio U., Tokyo, 1991. Author: Revolution and Chinese Foreign Policy: Peking's Support for Wars of National Liberation, 1970; editor, contbr.: Market Reforms in Socialist Societies: Comparing China and Hungary, 1989; co-author: (with Ian Russell and Chua Beng-Huat) Australia's Human Rights Diplomacy, 1993; editor: Debating Human Rights, 1999; corr. editor: Chinese Social Scis. Quar.; editorial adv. bd.: Jour. Contemporary China; editorial bd.: Bull. Concerned Asian Scholars; contbr. chpts. to books and articles to profl. jours. Named Nat. Def. Fgn. Lang. fellow, 1961-62, Inter-Univ. Program for Chinese Lang. Studies grantee, Taipei, Taiwan, 1963-64; Overseas fellow Ctr. for Chinese Studies, U. Calif., Berkeley, 1964-65; recipient Social Sci. Rsch. Coun. fellowship, 1973-74, Mellon Program in Chinese Studies fellowship Am. Coun. Learned Socs., 1982, Fulbright Rsch. grant, Tokyo, 1991. Mem. Internat. Studies Assn., Am. Polit. Sci. Assn., Assn. for Asian Studies. Office: Australian Nat U, Rsch Sch Pac-Asian Studies, Canberra ACT 0200, Australia

VAN NEVEL, GEORGE CHARLES, marketing manager; b. Beernem, Belgium, Jan. 29, 1953; s. Gaston and Paula (Lonneville) Van N.; m. Linda Brouckaert; children: Tine, Sarah, Willem. Lic. in econ. scis., U. Antwerp, Belgium, 1976; Lic. Mktg., Vlerick-Rug, Belgium, 1977. Acct. exec. BBDO, Belgium, 1980, Arte, Belgium, 1980; acct. dir. Vandekerckhove, 1985—; mng. ptnr. DVN; bd. dirs. Interdirect, U.K.; pres. congress St. Marketing, Belgium, 1991—. Contbr. articles to profl. jours. Recipient various creative awards. Avocation: soccer. Office: DVN, Kasteellaan 160, B-9000 Gent Belgium

VANNIASINGHAM, SAMUEL KANAGASABAPATHY, accountant; b. Singapore, Oct. 16, 1950; arrived in U.K., 1974; s. Nathan Kesagar and Mabel Gnanaratnam (Subramaniam) V.; m. Heather Christine Clark, August 5, 1981; children: Daniel James, David Joseph. Diploma in Acctg., Stamford Ctr., Singapore, 1972; degree Profl. Acctg., Chartered Assn. Cert. Accts., London, 1979. Articled clk. Peat, Marwick, Mitchell, Singapore, 1974-75; part-time tchr. Adult Edn. Bd., Singapore, 1972-75; mgmt. trainee E. Russell Ltd., London, 1977-79, accounts mgr., 1980-85; mgmt. acct. MAT Transport Internat. Ltd., London, 1985-86, group mgmt. acct., 1986-87, group acct., 1988; group fin. contr. and co. sec. C & S Group, 1989; mgr. fin. acct. Channel Four TV, London, 1989-92; pvt. practice Sam Vann & Co., Chartered Cert. Accts., 1992—; non-exec. dir. Trans Enterprise Computer Comm., Ltd., 1999—. Staff sgt. in nat. svc. Police dept., Singapore, 1968-75. Recipient Bravery commendation medal Police Force, Singapore, 1974. Fellow Chartered Assn. Cert. Acct., Mem. Brit. Inst. Mgmt., Singapore Cricket Assn. (test cricketer 1971-75), North London Enterprise Club (dir. 1994—), North London C. of C. (co-opted dir. 1999—). Methodist. Club: Hazelwood Squash (North London). Avocations: squash, cricket. Home: 17 Hyde Way, Edmonton, London N9 9RU, England Office: Sam Vann & Co, DPK House 186 Chase Side, London N14 5HN, England

VANNIER, ALAIN ROBERT, film company executive; b. Paris, May 3, 1935; s. Robert and Renée (Seligman) V.; m. Daniele Jeanne Machavoine; 1 child, Nicolas. Pres. Roissy Films, France, 1975-96; mng. dir. Orly Films, Paris, 1996—. Office: Orly Films, 10 Ave George 5, 75008 Paris France

VAN NOBELEN, ROBERT, electrical engineer, researcher; b. Haarlem, The Netherlands, Oct. 20, 1968; arrived in New Zealand, 1977; came to U.S., 1997; s. John and Trudy (van der Heyde) van N. BSEE with honors, U. Canterbury, New Zealand, 1990; MSEE, U. Canterbury, 1992, PhD, 1996. Rschr. AT&T Bell Labs, Florham Park, N.J., 1997—; bd. dirs. Niche Software Ltd., Christchurch, New Zealand. Contbr. articles to profl. jours.; patentee in field. Telecom Rsch. grant, 1993-94, Bus. Devel. grant Christchurch City Coun., 1995. Mem. IEEE. Avocations: software development. Office: AT&T Bell Labs 180 Park Ave Florham Park NJ 07932-1004

VAN NORMAN, GAIL A., aneshtesiologist; b. Bakersfield, Calif., May 9, 1955; d. Melvin F. Van Norman and Wilma J. Sibrel. BS in Microbiology with honors, U. Wash., 1977, MD, 1981, cert. health care ethics, 1993. Diplomate Am. Bd. Internal Medicine, Am. Bd. Anesthesiology. Internist Puget Sound Group Health Coop., Seattle, 1985-86; resident in anesthesiology U. Wash., Seattle, 1986-88, fellow in cardiothoracic anesthesiology, 1988-89, acting instr., 1994-95, acting asst. prof., 1995-97, asst. prof., 1997—; pvt. practice Swedish Hosp., N.W. Hosp., Seattle, 1989-94; consulting internist Spokane (Wash.) Urban Indian health Ctr., 1984-85; consulting anesthesiologist Med-Legal Malpractice Claims, Seattle, 1994—; co-chmn. ethics adv. com. U. Wash. Med. Ctr., Seattle, 1997—. Reviewer Anesthesia & Analgesia, 1997—; contbr. articles to profl. jours. Mem. Am. Soc. Anesthesiologists (mem. ethics com. 1992—), Soc. Carciovasc. Anesthesiologists, Wash. State Soc. Anesthesiologists (co-chair edn. 1992—). Avocations: hiking, biking, dog training. Office: U Wash Dept Anesthesiology PO Box 356540 Seattle WA 98195-6540

VAN NOTEN, FRANCIS, museum director; b. Mechelen, Belgium, Apr. 28, 1938; s. Karel and Maria (Van Der Veken) Van Noten; m. Eliane Possemiers; children: Filip, Berthie. MA in Archaeology, U. Ghent, Belgium, 1963, MA in African History, 1964, PhD in African History, 1967. Head prehistory archaeology Royal Mus. Ctrl. Africa, Tervuren, Belgium, 1965-88; head dept. archaeology Royal Mus. of Art and History, Brussels, 1987-88, dir., 1988—; prof. U. Leuven. Mem. Flemish Mus. Assn. (Belgian nat. com. 1998—), Internat. Coun. Ams., Internat. Coun. Museums. Office: Royal Mus Art and History, 10 parc du Cinquantenaire, 1000 Brussels Belgium

VAN NOY, TERRY WILLARD, health care executive; b. Alhambra, Calif., Aug. 31, 1947; s. Barney Willard and Cora Ellen (Simms) V.; m. Betsy Helen Pothen, Dec. 27, 1968; children: Bryan, Mark. BS in Bus. Mgmt., Calif. State Poly. U., 1970; MBA, Pepperdine U., 1991. CLU. Group sales rep. Mutual of Omaha, Atlanta, 1970-74, dist. mgr., 1974-77; regional mgr. Mutual of Omaha, Dallas, 1977-82; nat. sales mgr. Mutual of Omaha, Omaha, Neb., 1982-83; v.p. group mktg. Mutual of Omaha, Omaha, 1983-87; div. dir. Mutual of Omaha, Orange, Calif., 1987-95; pres., CEO, Amil Internat., Las Vegas, 1995-98; prin. Van Noy Consulting Group, Henderson, Nev., 1998—; bd. dirs. State Nev. Reinsurance Program. Presenter in field. Vice chmn. Morning Star Luth. Ch., Omaha, 1987; mem. adv. bd. Chapman U. Sch. Bus.; mem. exc. com. ABL Orgn.; trustee Desert Rsch. Inst.; mem. State of Nev. Reins. Bd. Mem. Am. Soc. CLU, Orange County Employee Benefit Coun., We. Pension and Benefits Conf., Las Vegas Valley Soaring Assn. (v.p.). Republican. Avocations: skiing, scuba diving, soaring. Home and Office: 2312 Prometheus Ct Henderson NV 89014-5324

VANNUKUL, VIRACHAI, management consultant; b. Bangkok, July 21, 1934; s. Oh Kyo Shiu and Vannukul Mansong. MBA, Pepperdine U., 1978; MA, Claremont Coll., 1983, Exec. MBA, 1985; MA, Nat. Def. Coll., Thailand, 1990. Mgmt. cons. U.S., Europe, Asia, Mid. East, 1977—; advisor to chmn. Bangkok Met. Bank, 1984, sr. exec. v.p., 1988-90; advisor to exec. chmn., CEO Bangkok Bank plc, 1994—; chmn. VG Cons. Group; prof. Internat. MBA Program Bangkok U., 1999—. E-mail: Virachai@VGConsultant.com. Office: VG Cons Group Riverside Twr, Rama 3 Rd Bangklo Dist, Bangkok 10120, Thailand

VAN NULAND, ERIC, physics engineer; b. Schijndel, Netherlands, Jan. 21, 1965; s. Jan and Anie (van Gerwen) van N.; m. Paula Soto, June 27, 1998. Ing., Hogeschool Eindhoven, Netherlands, 1990. Holographist Dutch Holographic Lab., Eindhoven, 1992-96, Hologramas de Mex., Mexico City, 1996-98; dir. DDD, Mexico City, 1997—, Cinco Stands, Mexico City, 1998—. Rschr. in development of office holoprinter. Sgt. Van Huist, 1991-92. Mem. Internat. Soc. for Optical Engring. Avocations: reading, movies, internet. E-mail: ericddd@npsnet.com.mx. Home and Office: Guty Cardenas 166-2, Col Guadalupe Inn, Mexico City 01020, Mexico

VAN OSDOL, DONOVAN HAROLD, mathematics educator; b. Plymouth, Ind., Sept. 27, 1942; s. Harold Isaac Van Osdol and Freida Marie (Culp) Mangus; m. Marie A. Gaudard, Jan. 2, 1983. AB, Earlham Coll., Richmond, Ind., 1964; AM, U. Ill., 1966, PhD, 1969. Asst. prof. Wilkes Coll., Wilkes-Barre, Pa., 1969-70; from asst. prof. to assoc. prof. U. N.H., Durham, 1970-79, prof., 1979—; rsch. assoc. U. Oslo, 1972-73; assoc. exec. dir. Am. Math. Soc., Providence, 1989-91; vol. assoc. sec. Math. Assn. Am., Washington, 1994-98. Contbr. rsch. articles to math. jours. Lance cpl. USMC, 1962-64. Mem. Am. Legion. Office: U NH Dept Math Durham NH 03824

VAN PATTEN, JAMES JEFFERS, education educator; b. North Rose, N.Y., Sept. 8, 1925; s. Earl F. and Dorothy (Jeffers) Van P.; married. BA, Syracuse U., 1949; ME, Tex. Western Coll., 1959; PhD, U. Tex., Austin, 1962. Asst. prof. philosophy and edn. Central Mo. State U., Warrensburg, 1962-64, assoc. prof., 1964-69; assoc. prof. fis. overseas U. Okla., Norman, 1969-71; prof. edn. U. Ark., Fayetteville, 1971-99, prof. emeritus, 1999—; visiting scholar, U. Mich., 1981, UCLA, 1987, U. Tex., Austin, 1987; vis. prof./scholar U. Fla., Gainesville, 1994; adj. Fla. Atlantic U., 2000. Editor: Conflict, Permanency and Change in Education, 1976, Philosophy, Social Science and Education, 1989, College Teaching and Higher Education Leadership, 1990, Social-Cultural Foundations of Educational Policy in the U.S., 1991; author: Academic Profiles in Higher Education, 1992, The Many Faces of the Culture of Higher Education, 1993, 2d edit. 2000, (with John Pulliam) History of Education in America, 7th edit., 1999, The Culture of Higher Education: A Case Study Approach, 1996, What's Really Happening in Education: A Case Study Approach, 1997, Individual and Collective Contributions to Humaneness In Our Time, 1997; editor: Watersheds in Higher Education, 1997, Challenges and Opportunities For a New Millennium, 1998, Challenges and Opportunities for Education in the 21st Century, 1999, Higher Education Culture, Case Studies For A New Century, 2000, A New Century In Retrospect and Prospect, 2000; contbr. articles to profl. jours.; founder Jour. of Thought. Served with inf. U.S. Army, 1944-45. Decorated Purple Heart. Mem. Am. Ednl. Studies Assn., Southern Future Soc., World Future Soc., Am. Philosophy Assn., Southwestern Philosophy of Edn. Soc. (pres. 1970), Am. Ednl. Rsch. Assn., Edn. Law Assn., Nat. Assn. Legal Assts., Kiwanis, Phi Delta Kappa (pres. chpt. U. Ark. 1976-77). Home: 434 W Hawthorn St Fayetteville AR 72701-1934

VAN POELJE, SARI JANNEKE, management consultant; b. Oranjestad, Aruba, Dutch Antillen, May 5, 1963; d. Willem and Epke (Van Steenbergen) Van P. PhD in Psychology, U. Leiden, The Netherlands, 1988. Cert. provisional tchg. and supervising transactional analyst. Trainer/cons. INTACT, internat. tng. and consultancy, Leiden, 1985-96; lectr. dept. human resources Cath. U., Brabant, The Netherlands, 1990-96; trainer/cons. KLM-Royal Dutch Airlines, Schiphol, 1996—; mgmt. cons. and coach, The Netherlands, 1985—. Author: Transactional Analysis in Organizations, 1996. Bd. dirs. Bailadores Found., 1988-89. Mem. European Assn. Transactional Analysis (v.p. 1993-96), Internat. Transactional Analysis Assn. (Eric Borne Fund for the Future award 1993), MUTA, MIP. Avocations: salsa dancing, tennis. Fax: 030-2760127. Home: A Bloemaertstr 16, 351U VP Utrecht The Netherlands

VAN PRAAG, HERMAN MEIR, psychiatrist, educator, researcher; b. Schiedam, The Netherlands, Oct. 17, 1929; s. Marinus Maurits and Charlotte Frederigue (Leverpoll) V.P.; m. Cornelia Eikens; children: Marinus, Gido, Charlotte, Bart. MD, Leiden U., The Netherlands, 1956; PhD in Neurobiology, U. Utrecht, The Netherlands, 1962. Chief of staff dept. psychiatry Dijkzigt Hosp., Rotterdam, The Netherlands, 1963-66; founder, head dept. biol. psychiatry Psychiat. Univ. Clinic State U., Groningen, The Netherlands, 1966-77; prof., head dept. psychiatry Acad. Hosp. State U., Utrecht, 1977-82, Albert Einstein Coll. Medicine, Bronx, N.Y., 1982-92; prof., chmn. dept. psychiatry and neuropsychology Acad. Hosp. U. Maastricht (The Netherlands), 1992-99, scientific advisor dept. psycholgy and neuropsychology, 1999—; emeritus prof. Albert Einstein Coll. Medicine, 1992—; psychiatrist-in-chief Montefiore Med. Ctr., Bronx, 1982-92; Lady Davis vis. prof. Hebrew U. Hadassah U. Hosp., Jerusalem, 1976-77; head WHO Nat. Ref. Ctr. for Study of Psychotropic Drugs, 1969; head WHO Collaborating Ctr. for Rsch. and Tng. in Biol. Psychiatry, 1974; guest lectr. numerous univs. around the world. Editor: Psychiatria Neurologia Neurochirurgia, 1968-70, Advances in Biological Psychiatry, 1978—; editor-in-chief Psychiatria Neurologia Neurochirurgia, 1971-74, Biology of Behavior, 1975-82, Handbook of Biological Psychiatry, 1975-81, Einstein Monograph Series in Experimental and Clinical Psychiatry, 1988—; European chief-editor Progress in Neuro-Psychopharmacology, 1993—; mem. editl. bd. numerous publs. in field; reviewer Am. Jour. Psychiatry, Archives of Gen. Psychiatry, Jour. Nervous and Mental Disease; mem. internat. scientific commn. Jour. Brazilian Psychiat. Assn. Decorated Knight in the Order of the Dutch Lion, Order Beatrix of The Netherlands, 1988; recipient numerous awards and honors. Fellow Am. Coll. Neuropsychopharmacology; mem. Royal Acad. of Scis. of The Netherlands, Soc. Biol. Psychiatry, Collegium Internationale Neuro-Psychopharmacologicum, Assn. for Advancement of Psychotherapy, Internat. Group for Study of Affective Disorders, Internat. Soc. Psychoneuroendocrinology, European Brain and Behavior Soc., Internat. Assn. for Suicide Prevention, Brit. Pharmacol. Soc., European Soc. for Clin. Investigation, Bataafsch Genootschap der Proefondervindelijke Wijsbegeerte, Am. Coll. Neuropharmacology, Deutsche Gesellschaft fur Psychiatrie und Nervenheilkunde, Israel Med. Assn., Psychiat. Rsch. Soc., N.Y. Acad. Medicine, Am. Psychopathol. Assn., Internat. Coll. Neurobiology, Biol. Psychiatry and Psychopharmacology, Serotonin Club, Internat. Soc. for Rsch. on Emotion, Internat. Soc. Psychoneuroendocrinology, Arbeitsgemeinschaft fur Neuropsychpharmakologie und Pharmakopsychiatrie. Office: Acad Hosp Maastricht, PO Box 5800, 6202 AZ Maastricht The Netherlands

VAN PUYVELDE, ERIC MICHEL, editor-in-chief, journalist; b. Brussels, Belgium, Sept. 26, 1945; s. Thierry and Ghislaine (Lassalle) Van P.; m. Martine Marie Allais, May 2, 1981. Lic. Sci. Econs., Cath. U., Louvain, Belgium, 1971. Collaborator RTBF, Brussels, Belgium, 1972-75; journalist Europe Info. Svcs., Brussels, 1975-85, editor-in-chief, 1985—; journalist European Report, Europolitique. Under lt. Belgian Air Force, 1971-72. Roman Catholic. Avocation: music. Home: Av Père Damien, 14, B-1150 Brussels Belgium Office: Europe Info Svc, Ave Adolphe Lacomblé 66, B-1030 Brussels Belgium

VAN RAALTE, JOHN A., research and engineering management executive; b. Copenhagen, Apr. 10, 1938; came to U.S., 1955; s. John A. and Laura W.M. (Louwerier) van R.; m. Andrée Valentine Greene, Dec. 28, 1963; children: Kirsten A., James E. BSEE, MIT, 1960, MSEE, 1960, elec. engrs. degree, 1962, PhD, 1964. Rsch. asst. MIT, Cambridge, 1960-64; mem. tech. staff RCA David Sarnoff Rsch. Ctr., Princeton, N.J., 1964-70, head display rsch., 1970-79, head videodisc record and playback, 1979-83, dir. videodisc systems rsch., 1983-84, dir. display systems rsch., 1984-87; dir. materials and process tech. lab. David Sarnoff Rsch. Ctr. subs. SRI Internat., Princeton, N.J., 1987-90; mgr. CRT engring. Thomson Consumer Electronics N.Am. Tube Div., Lancaster, Pa., 1990-92; gen. mgr. Electron Optics Lab., Thomson Tubes & Displays, Genlis, France, 1992-99; sr. tech. advisor Philips Components B.V., Sittard, Netherlands, 1999—; mem. steering com. Internat. Display Rsch. Conf., U.S., Europe, Japan, 1981-88. Author: (with others) Electronic Engineer's Reference Handbook, 4th and 5th edits. Chmn. ednl. coun. MIT, N.J., 1978-83. Fellow IEEE, Soc. for Info. Display (pres., v.p., treas., sec. 1981-88, chmn. and program chmn. Internat. Symposium 1973-78); mem. MIT Club of Princeton, Chevalier du Tastevin, Sigma Xi, Tau Beta Pi, Eta Kappa Nu (pres. Boston chpt. 1964). Home: Aylvalaan 9B-01, 6212 BA Maastricht The Netherlands Office: Philips Components BV, PO Box 7 Bldg D, 6130 AA Sittard The Netherlands

VAN RANST, ALFRED E., information technology security consultant. BS, Cornell U., 1974, MBA, 1976. CPA, Mass. Ptnr. KPMG LLP, Boston, 1975—. Office: KPMG LLP 99 High St Boston MA 02110-2320

VAN REENEN, JOHN MICHAEL, economist, educator; b. London, Dec. 26, 1965; s. Lionel and Ann (Williams) Van R. BA, Queens Coll., Cambridge, Eng., 1988; MSc, London Sch. Econs., 1990; PhD, Univ. Coll. London, 1993. Rsch. asst. London Sch. Econs., 1989-92; project mgr. Inst. for Fiscal Studies, 1993; lectr. Univ. Coll. London, 1994—. Mem. editl. bd. Jour. of Indsl. Econs., 1995, Rev. of Econ. Studies; contbr. articles to profl. jours. Avocations: music, reading, squash, travel. Office: Inst Fiscal Studies, 7 Ridgmount St, London WC1E 7AE, England

VAN REGENMORTEL, MARC HUBERT VICTOR, immunochemist; b. Brussels, Belgium, Dec. 6, 1934; s. Joseph and Catherine (Stinkens) van R.; m. Johanna Alida Boltman, Aug. 1958 (div. 1972); children: Sonia, Loubie; m. Petra Jeanne Schonborn, June 24, 1972. BSc, Stellenbosch, South Africa, 1957, MSc, 1959; PhD, Capetown (South Africa) U., 1961. Lectr. U. Stellenbosch, 1960-61, sr. lectr., 1961-65; rsch. fellow U. Calif., Berkeley, 1965-66; prof. U. Stellenbosch, 1967-70; vis. prof. U. Strasbourg, France, 1970-72; prof. U. Capetown, 1972-77; rsch. dir. Inst. of Molecular and Cellular Biology, Strasbourg, 1978—; bd. dirs. Biacore Corp., Sweden. Author: Serology and Immunochemistry of Plant Viruses, 1982, Synthetic Peptides as Antigens, 1999; editor: Synthetic Polypeptides as Antigens, 1988, Structures of Antigens, Vol. I, 1992, Vol. II, 1993, Vol. III, 1996, Immunochemistry of Viruses, Vol. I, 1985, Vol. II, 1990, Immunochemistry, 1994; editor Advances in Virus Rsch., 1985—, Archives of Virology, 1987—, Rsch. in Virology, 1987-97, Immunol. Investigations, 1987—, Jour. Molecular Recognition, 1988—, FEMS Immunology Medical Microbiology, 1988—, Seminars in Virology, 1990—, J. Immunological Methods, 1994—, Biologicals, Molecular Immunology Serodiagnosis and Immunotherapy in Infectious Diseases, 1993—, Analytical Biochemistry, 1995—. Mem. Internat. Union Microbiol. Scis. (vice chmn. virology divsn. 1984-87, chmn. 1987-90, sec.-gen. 1990, pres. internat. com. on taxonomy viruses 1996—). Office: Ctr Nat Rsch Sci, 15 rue Descartes, 67000 Strasbourg France

VAN REMSBURG, BOTHA JANSE, accountant, educator; b. Rustemburg, South Africa, July 13, 1940; s. Petrus Janse and Isabella Janse Van R.; m. Louisa Janse Meiring, Feb. 17, 1963; children: Petro, Pieter, Isabel, Louis. BCom, PU for CHE, South Africa, 1960; MCom, U. Pretoria, South Africa, 1966; DCompt, UNISA, South Africa, 1978. Chartered acct. Trainee acct. CAFIAM, South Africa, 1964-66; lectr. UMISA, South Africa, 1967-71, sr. lectr., 1972-77, assoc. prof., 1978, prof., 1979-87, head of dept., 1988—; mem. EDCO SAICA, South Africa, 1988—, PAAB, South Africa, 1993-96, Umisa Senate, South Africa, 1979—. Mem. SAICA. Avocations: cycling, woodworking, gardening, farming. Home: Zamia Palm St, Montana Park, Pretoria Gauteng, South Africa Office: UNISA, PO Box 392, Pretoria Gauteng, South Africa

VAN RENSSELAER, MILES, artist, sculptor; b. Morristown, N.J., Aug. 30, 1973; s. Robert Mickle Miles Van Rensselaer and Hilary Jenkins Prouty. BA, Kenyon Coll., 1996; cert. lang. study and art, Kegervan Inst., Indonesia, 1995. Studio mgr. Tobin Studios, Coopersburg, Pa., 1996—; Exhibited in group shows Heller Gallery, N.Y.C., 1999, Marta Hewitt Gallery, Cin., 1999, Rachael Collections, Aspen, Colo., 1999. Recipient Art award Boston Globe, 1991, Harlov-Davis award Phillips Hill Art Assn., 1998, Centerfold winner Art Calender Mag., 1999. Mem. Am. Craft Coun., Internat. Sculpture Ctr. Democrat. Avocations: photography, travel, S.E. Asia. E-mail: babirussa8@aol.com. Home: PO Box 272 Riegelsville PA 18077-0272

VAN RENTERGHEM, TONNY, writer; b. Amsterdam, The Netherlands, June 28, 1919; s. Antoine F.M. and Marguerite (Warnant) van R.; m. Susanne Severeid, Mar. 5, 1977. Officer Netherlands Army Cavalry, 1938-47; chief of staff Netherlands Resistance, Amsterdam-Z., 1943-45; officer on staff HRS Prince Bernhard, Netherlands Armed Forces, 1945-47; ptnr. Comatec Inc./Real Estate, L.A., 1949-57; dir. rsch., adv. George Stevens Sr. Prodns., 20th Century Fox, others, L.A., 1958-66; dir. product evaluation Growth Tech. Inc., L.A., 1967-69; pres. Malibu Inst., L.A., 1970-90; writer Zandvoort, The Netherlands, 1990—; cons., lectr. Author: Four Gospels Analysis, 1960, Jesus Speaks, 1961, When Santa Was a Shaman, 1995; dir., cinematographer (film documentary) The Last Hussars, 1987; corr. Hollywood Fgn. Press Assn., L.A., 1948-51. Bd. dirs. Liberal Internat., London, 1946-47; chmn. Cambridge U. Congress, 1947; adv. bd. Netherlands Hist. Cavalry Mus. Decorated War Cross, Resistance Cross Meml.; recipient Cert. of Honor Righteous Among Nations, Yad Vashem, 1988. Mem. CANDLES (dir. rsch. 1985—), Assn. Netherlands Cavalry Officers, Netherlands-Am. Soc. Avocations: bicycling, photography, historical research, languages. Office: c/o M Guggenheim 22 Paseo Margarita Camarillo CA 93012-8120

VAN RHENEN, DIRK JAN, health facility administrator, medical educator; b. De Bilt, Utrecht, The Netherlands, Oct. 13, 1948; s. Willem and Lena Hendrika (Van der Kuil) van R.; m. Hendrika Wilhelmina Holling, June 29, 1974; children: Anna, Kirstin, Elin. MD, Free U., Amsterdam, The Netherlands, 1974; PhD, Free U., 1982. Med. dir. Bloodbank Maastricht, The Netherlands, 1983-92; head lab. Univ. Hosp., Maastricht, 1983-92; med. dir. Bloodbank Rotterdam, The Netherlands, 1992—; mem. ISBT Working

Party Blood Group Serology, Bristol, Eng., 1993—; mem. Coun. Blood Transfusion, Amsterdam, 1994—; treas. ISH/EHA Congress Organizing Com., The Netherlands, 1999—; prof. transfusion medicine. Mem. Internat. Soc. Blood Transfusion (working party blood group serology 1993—), European Haematology Assn. (treas. congress organizing com. 1996-98), Internat. Soc. Haematology. Office: Bloodbank Rotterdam, Wytemaweg 10, 3001 KJ Rotterdam The Netherlands

VAN RHOON, GERARD CORNELIS, physicist; b. The Netherlands, Feb. 13, 1956; s. Jan and Geertrui (Harlaar) Van R.; m. Hubertina J.M. Schlösser, Oct. 5, 1984; children: Martyn, Marieke. BS, Polytechnical Sch. Dordrecht, 1977; PhD, Delft Tech. U., The Netherlands, 1994. Physics engr. Erasmus U., Rotterdam, 1977-83; rschr., scientist Daniel Den Hoed Cancer Ctr., Rotterdam, 1985-96; head hyperthermia and rschr. Acad. Hosp., Rotterdam, 1996—; cons. Dutch Health Coun., The Hague, 1995-97. Recipient Lund Sci. award ESHO, 1987. Office: Acad Hosp Rotterdam, Box 5201 3008 AE, Rotterdam The Netherlands

VAN RIENEN, URSULA HELGA, mathematician, educator; b. Düsseldorf, Germany, May 2, 1957; d. Josef August and Anna Margarete (Briesch) Götte; m. Gereon van Rienen, July 23, 1983; children: Jan Martin, Viola Christina. Diploma, Friedrich-Wilhelm U., Bonn, Germany, 1983; PhD, Tech. Hochschule, Darmstadt, Germany, 1989, Dr.habil., 1997. Math. diplomate. Rsch. asst. Deutsches Elektronen Synchrotron, Hamburg, Germany, 1983-89, postdoctoral, 1989-90; postdoctoral Prof. Dr. Thomas Weiland, TH Darmstadt, 1990-92; univ. asst. Tech. Hochschule, Darmstadt, 1992-97; prof. U. Rostock, Germany, 1997—; guest scientist Accelerator Divsn., Los Alamos (N.Mex.) Nat. Lab., 1986. Contbr. articles to profl. jours. Deutsche Forschungsgemeinschaft scholar, 1995. Mem. Assn. Angewandte Math. and Mechanik, Deutsche Math. Vereinigung, German Phys. Assn. Office: U Rostock, Albert-Einstein-Strabe 2, D18051 Rostock Germany

VAN ROERMUND, ARTHUR H.M., educator; b. Delft, The Netherlands, Nov. 25, 1951; m. Marianne Platell, June 25, 1976; children: Bram, Timo, Mark, Mieke. MS, Delft U. Tech., The Netherlands, 1975, PhD, 1987. Mem. sr. sci. staff Philips, Eindhoven, The Netherlands, 1975-92; prof., chmn. Delft U. Tech., The Netherlands, 1992-99; prof., chmn. mixed-signal microelectronics group Eindhoven U. Tech., 1999—; cons. in field. Mem. IEEE (sr., assoc. editor 1998-99). Roman Catholic. Avocations: hockey, church. Office: Eindhoven U Tech, Den Dolech 2, Eindhoven The Netherlands

VAN ROMPUY, PAUL FRANS, economics educator; b. St. Kat Waver, Antwerp, Belgium, Dec. 18, 1940; m. Karine Van Rompuy, Aug. 4, 1995; children: Joeri, Heiko, Elke. MS in Econs., U. Ill., Belgium, 1966; PhD in Econs., U. Louvain, Belgium, 1970. From asst. prof. to prof. econs. U. Louvain, 1970—, rsch. dir., 1970-75, chmn. dept. econs., 1982-85; mng. dir. Fed. Holding Co., 1995—. Advisor, Vice-Prime Minister, Brussels, 1988-89; chmn. fin. com. High coun. Pub. Fin. Govt., 1989. Fullbright fellow, 1962. Mem. Am. Econ. Assn., European Econ. Assn., Royal Acad. Scis. and Arts of Belgium, Belgian Inst. Pub. Fin. (chmn. 1999—). Home: Leeuwerikweg 37, B-3140 Keerbergen Belgium Office: Federal Holding Co FPM, Av Louise 54/1, B-1050 Brussels Belgium

VAN ROMPUY, VICTOR MAURICE, retired educator; b. Begijnendyk, Belgium, Feb. 27, 1923; m. Germaine Geens, Dec. 1, 1921; children: Herman, Eric, Anita, Christine. D of Econs., Cath. U. Leuven, Belgium, 1951. Assoc. prof. U. Antwerp, Belgium, 1951-65; prof. Cath. U. Leuven, 1965-88, prof. emeritus, 1988—; chmn. exec. com. Fed. Coun. for Fin., Brussels, 1991-99. Author: (with W. Moesen, textbook) Public Finance, 5th edit., 1996; co-author: (with R. Vertonghen, textbook) Cost-Benefit Analyses, 3d edit., 1995; editor: (textbook) Economics, 1975. Recipient Laureate award Ministry Edn., 1952; Belgian Fedn. Industries traveling scholar, 1962. Mem. Belgian Inst. for Pub. Fin. (chmn. 1986-96), Internat. Inst. for Pub. Fin. Mem. Christian Democrat Party. Home: Bevrydingslaan 40, 1932 Saint-Stevens-Wolume Belgium

VAN ROSENDAAL, JOHN, journalist; b. Steenbergen, The Netherlands, Nov. 18, 1962; s. Bas and Jo Van R.; m. Kyoko M. Shiotani, June 12, 1994; 1 child, Kai. MS, Columbia Sch. of Journalism, 1990; Dutch LLM, Utrecht U., 1989. Nat. copyreader Dow Jones & Co., N.Y.C., 1990-91; staff corr. Dow Jones & Co., Zurich, 1992-93; U.S. corrs. Elsevier, Het Financieele Dagblad, N.Y.C., 1993-98, Teleac/NOT, JvR Media, N.Y.C., 1997—; CEO PlanSponsor.com, Greenwich, Conn., 1999—. Fulbright grantee The Netherlands, 1989-90. Mem. Fgn. Press Assn. (asst. treas. 1997—). Avocations: travel, photography. E-mail: jvr@plansponsor.com. Office: PlanSponsor.com 125 Greenwich Ave Greenwich CT 06830-5527

VAN SAMBEEK, MARC R.H.M., surgeon; b. Veldhoven, Netherlands, Dec. 7, 1958; s. Walter and Joke (Van Heesch) Van S.; m. Marie-Suzanne Riphagen, Oct. 30, 1992. MD, U. Nijmegen, 1986; Surgeon, U. Rotterdam, 1995, PhD, 1998. Cons. vascular surgery U. Hosp. Rotterdam, 1996—. Contbr. author: (book) Indications in Vascular and Endovascular Surgery, 1998; contbr. articles to profl. jours. Mem. Endovascular Forum (sec.). Roman Catholic. Home: Essenlaan 82-B, 3062 NR Rotterdam Netherlands Office: U Hosp Rotterdam, Dr Molewaterplein 40, 3015 9D Rotterdam Netherlands

VAN SCHAIK, IVO NORBERTUS, neurologist, researcher; b. Monster, The Netherlands, June 3, 1962; s. Frits Fvans and Martina (Van Berkestyn) Van S. Grad. in Medicine, U. Amsterdam, The Netherlands, 1986, MD cum laude, 1989; PhD, U. Amsterdam, 1995. Resident in internal medicine Andreas Hosp., Amsterdam, 1989-90; resident in neurology Acad. Med. Ctr., Amsterdam, 1990-91, registrar in neurology, 1992-95; postdoctoral rsch. fellow dept. neurology U. Cambridge, Eng., 1996; sr. registrar in neurology Acad. Med. Ctr., 1997-99; hon. rsch. fellow dept. immunohematology Acad. Hosp. Leiden, The Netherlands, 1992—. Contbr. articles to profl. jours. Mem. European Neurol. Soc., Dutch Neurology Assn. Avocations: sailing, speed-skating, long-distance running, classical music/opera. Office: Acad Med Ctr U Amsterdam, PO Box 22700, 1100 DE Amsterdam The Netherlands

VAN SCHOONENBERG, ROBERT G., lawyer; b. Madison, Wis., Aug. 18, 1946; s. John W. and Ione (Henning) Schoonenberg. BA, Marquette U., 1968; MBA, U. Wis., 1972; JD, U. Mich., 1974. Bar: Calif. 1975, Fla. 1976. Atty. Gulf Oil Corp., Pitts., 1974-81; sr. v.p., gen. counsel, sec. Avery Dennison Corp., Pasadena, Calif., 1981—; judge pro tem Pasadena Mcpl. Ct., 1987-89. Dir., v.p. fin. adminstrn. Am. Cancer Soc., San Gabriel Vally Unit, 1987—; v.p., treas., dir., v.p. investments Pasadena Symphony Assn.; bd. dirs. Pasadena Recreation and Parks Found., 1983-84; mem. Pasadena Citizens Task Force on Crime Control, 1983-84; dir. Boy Scouts, San Gabriel Valley Coun., dir. public coun.; bd. dirs. Verugo Hills Hosp. Found.; trustee Southwestern U. Sch. Law. Mem. ABA, Am. Corp. Counsel Assn. (bd. dirs.), Am. Soc. Corp. Secs. (bd. dirs., pres. Southern Calif. chpt.), L.A. County Bar Assn. (past chair, corp. law dept. sect.), Corp. Counsel Inst. (bd. govs.), Jonathon Club, Flint Canyon Tennis Club, The Calif. Club, Pasadena Athletic Club, Wis. Union. Clubs: Athletic (Pasadena); Wis. Union. Office: Avery Dennison Corp 150 N Orange Grove Blvd Pasadena CA 91103-3534

VAN SCHOOTE, JEAN-PIERRE, university president, priest; b. Ghent, Belgium, June 10, 1923. Licentiate in Philosophy, Faculty of Soc. of Jesus, Louvain, Belgium, 1948, Licentiate in Theology, 1958; Licentiate in Romance Philology, Cath. U. Louvain, Belgium, 1953. Ordained priest, Soc. of Jesus, Roman Cath. Ch. Spiritual dir. student Lessius Univ. Coll., Leuven, 1960-66; spiritual dir. for seminarians L.Am. Coll., Leuven, 1966-70, course dir. of preparation for work in L.Am., 1974-88, pres., 1988-95; spiritual dir. for seminarians Pope John XXIII Sem., 1970-84; mem. L.Am. Episc. Coun. Author: Brandde ons hart niet in ons?, 1986; editor, Emmaüs, De Boodschap. Home and Office: Waversebaan 220, B-3001 Heverlee Belgium

VAN SCHYNDEL, ADRIANUS WILHELMUS, physicist, researcher; b. Sint-Oedenrode, The Netherlands, Dec. 4, 1964; s. Adrianus Johannes Van Schyndel and Wilhelmina Van Der Mee; m. Cornelia Maria Van Hoof. Bachelor's degree, Poly. U. Eindhoven, The Netherlands, 1988; Master's degree, U. of Tech. Eindhoven, 1990. Rsch. engr. U. of Tech. Eindhoven, 1991-98, lectr., 1998—. Contbr. articles to profl. jours. Sgt. Dutch Infantry, 1988-89. Avocations: volleyball, guitar.

VAN SON, JACQUES A., pediatric cardiac surgeon; b. Veldhoven, The Netherlands, Oct. 31, 1952; s. Marinus and Wilhelmina (Van den Meerendonk) Van S.; m. Christiane Berndt, May 9, 1984; children: Monique, Jean-Pierre, Maurice. MD, Catholic U., Nijmegen, The Netherlands, 1979, PhD, 1990. Clin. fellow Mayo Clinic, Rochester, Minn., 1991-93, Children's Hosp., Phila., 1993-94; clin. instr. U. Calif., San Francisco, 1994-95; cons. cardiac surgeon Herzzentrum, Leipzig, Germany, 1995-2000. Author: Coarctation Repair in Infancy, 1990, Histology of Internal Mammary Artery, 1993. Mem. European Assn. Cardiothoracic Surgery, Mayo Alumni Assn., Soc. Thoracic Surgeons. Avocations: long distance running, collecting authentic American music. Fax: 032-14-557105.

VANSTAN, STEPHEN THOMAS, business executive; b. Fremantle, Australia, Sept. 16, 1948; s. Roy Thomas and Patricia May (Donovan) V.; m. Lynette Joy Thorp, July 5, 1969 (div. 1982); 1 child, Nikola Joy; m. Lesley Kay Francis, July 30, 1983; 1 child Bradley William. BA in Bus., Curtin U., Perth, Australia, 1981. Engr. Alcoa, Perth, 1968-69, Kaiser Engrs., Perth, 1969-70, Bechtel, Melbourne, 1970-73; engr. mgr. Fluor Corp., Melbourne, 1974-83; dir., gen. mgr. Motherwell Systems, Perth, 1984-97; chief exec. Royal Soc. for Prevention of Cruelty to Animals, 1997—; mem. Dept. Tng. R&D Forum, 1994-96; dir. Control Systems Internat. Projects, Australia, 1986-96, CSI Engring. Cons., Australia, 1987-95. Contbr. numerous articles to profl. jours. Coun. City South Perth Coun., Australia, 1992-94; mem. Rotary, Australia, 1993-95. Recipient Design award Australian Design Coun., 1990, Export award Austrade, 1992, Engring. Excellence award Inst. Engrs. Australia, 1993. Fellow Australian Inst. Company Dirs., assoc. fellow Australian Inst. Mgmt. ; mem. Inst. Instrumentation & Control, Australian Grain Inst., CALM Animal Ethins Comm. Mem. Uniting Ch. in Australia. Avocations: golf, power boating, reading, gardening, Australian rules football. Office: RSCPA-WA Inc, PO Box 463 Cannington, 6987 Western Australia Australia

VANSTAPEL, MARYSE, French language educator; b. Boekhout, Belgium, Apr. 29, 1944; d. Herman Vanstapel and Maria Houbrechts; m. Theo Hendriks, July 20, 1972; 3 children. Grad., U. Grenoble, 1987. Tchr. French to young people Inst. Mater Dei, Overpelt, Belgium, 1964—.

VANSTONE, AMANDA, Australian government official; married. Cert. in mktg. studies, South Australian Inst. Tech., 1972, grad. diploma in legal practice, 1983; BA, U. Adelaide, Australia, 1981, LLB, 1983. Retailer, wholesaler; pvt. practice barrister and solicitor South Australia; mem. for South Australia Australian Senate, 1984—, shadow spl. min. of state, spokesperson on status of women; parliamentary sec. to dep. leader of the opposition; min. for employment, edn., tng. and youth affairs Australia, 1996-97, min. for justice, 1997-98, min. for justice and customs, 1998—. Mem. Liberal-Nat. Party Coalition. Office: Parliament House Ste MF48, Canberra ACT 2600, Australia

VAN SUSTEREN, GRETA CONWAY, news anchor, lawyer; b. Appleton, Wis., June 11, 1954; d. Urban Peter and Margery (Conway) Van S.; m. John Purcell Coale, Oct. 12, 1987. BA in Econs, U. Wis., 1976; JD, Georgetown U., 1979, LLM, 1982. Bar: D.C. 1979, U.S. Supreme Ct. 1982, Md. 1985, Wis. 1987, U.S. Ct. Appeals (D.C., 2d and 4th cirs.). Ptnr. Milliken, Van-Susteren & Canan, Washington, 1982—; with CNN, 1991—, co-host Burden of Proof, legal cons. The World Today; adj. prof. Georgetown Law Ctr., Washington, 1985—; lectr., panelist Jud. Conf., Washington, 1986. Bd. dirs. Stuart Stiller Found., Washington, 1982—. Stiller fellow Georgetown Law Ctr., 1980. Mem. ABA, Assn. Trial Lawyers Am. (lectr. conf. 1986—), D.C. Bar Assn. Office: CNN-Atlanta One CNN Center Atlanta GA 30303

VAN SWAAY, WILLIBRORDUS PETRUS M., chemist, educator; b. Nymegen, The Netherlands, Jan. 10, 1942; s. christiaan and Jacoba (Bosman) van S.; m. Johanna Jacoba van den Berk, June 4, 1966; children: Nieneke, Louise, Jos, Emmy, Claaitje. Jr. Chem. Engr., Tech. U. Eindhoven, The Netherlands, 1965, PhD, 1967; DES, U. Nancy, France, 1966, DSc (hon.), 1996. Rsch. scientist Shell Rsch./U. Nancy, 1965-67, Shell Rsch., Amsterdam, 1965-72; prof. Twente U., Enschede, The Netherlands, 1972—; cons. Shell, Amsterdam, 1984—, DSM, Duphar, Unilever, TNO, EPS, others; sci. dir. Nat. Dutch Grad. Sch. Process Tech., 1992—. Author: Chemical Reactor design and Operation, 1984; contbr. over 300 articles to profl. jours.; patentee in field. Sec. bd. Hosp. Enschede, 1974-84; mem. Energy Commn. of Provence of Overysel Zwolle, 1983-87. Recipient Dow Chem. Energy prize Dow/Royal Dutch Acad. Scis., 1985, Grand Prize du Genie des Procedes, Acad. Scis., Paris, 1996; named Knight of the Order of the Netherlands Lion, 1997. Mem. Dutch Acad. Engring. Scis., Royal Dutch Acad. Scis., Royal Instn. Engrs. (bd. dirs. divsn. petroleum tech. 1979-89, bd. dirs. divsn. chem. engrs. 1971-75). Avocations: sailing, surfing, bird watching, photography, history. Home: Sportlaan 60, 7581 BZ Losser The Netherlands Office: Twente Univ, PO Box 217, 7500 AE Enschede The Netherlands

VAN SWOL, CHRISTIAAN F., medical physicist; b. Breda, The Netherlands, May 12, 1966; s. Jan Pieter van Swol and Wilhelmina Cornelia de Bie; m. Dorota Jolanta Iskra, Aug. 29, 1991. MSc, Eindhoven U. Tech., The Netherlands, 1990; PhD, Utrecht U., The Netherlands, 1998. Cert. med. physicist Dutch Assn. Med. Physics. Rsch. scientist dept. urology U. Hosp. Utrecht, 1991-98; med. physicist U. Med. Ctr. Utrecht, 1999—; bd. dirs. Urolog Found., Bussum; conf. chair SPIE, Bellingham, Wash., 1997—. Author: (book) New Surgical Modalities for the Treatment of Benign Prostatic Hyperplasia, 1998. 1st lt. Dutch Infantry, 1990-91. Mem. Internat. soc. for Optical Engring., Internat. Orgn. Med. Physics, European Laser Assn., Dutch Assn. Urology, Dutch Med. Laser Assn. (treas. 1998—). Roman Catholic. Avocations: soccer, music, scuba diving. Fax: 31 30 2542002. E-mail: cswol@id.azu.nl. Office: U Med Ctr Utrecht, Heidelberglaan 100, 3584 CX Utrecht The Netherlands

VAN TETS, IAN GERARD, ecophysiologist; b. Canberra, Australia, Oct. 28, 1967; s. Gerard Frederick and Patricia Anne (Johnston) van T.; m. Christina Joy Scott-Branagan, Feb. 21, 1992. BSc with honors, Monash U., Melbourne, Australia, 1991; PhD, U. Wollongong, Australia, 1997. Fellow U. Cape Town, South Africa, 1997-99, Mitrani Ctr. for Desert Ecology, Midreshet Ben-Gurion, Israel, 1999—; vis. rschr. Limburg U., Diepenbeek, Belgium, 1999; cons. in field. Contbr. articles to profl. jours. Recipient Rsch. award Australian Rsch. Coun., 1992-95, Joyce W. Vickery award Linnaean Soc. N.S.W., 1994, Postdoctoral Bursary, Found. for R & D, South Africa, 1997-98. Mem. Zool. Soc. So. Africa, Ecol. Soc. Australia, Australian Mammal Soc., Zool. Soc. Israel, Nederlands Inst. Biology. Anglican. Avocations: shogi, chess, long-distance running, cricket. Office: Mitrani Ctr Desert Ecology, Jacob Blanstein Rsch Inst, 84990 Midreshet Ben-Gurion Israel

VAN THIEL, PIETER-PAUL A.M., internist, infectious diseases specialist; b. Eindhoven, The Netherlands, July 30, 1948; s. Paul P.G.M. and Joke P.M. (Slaats) van T.; m. Suze J.T.M. Schriks May 20, 1972; children: Machtelt, Hylke. MD, U. Leiden, The Netherlands, 1977; internist, U. Amsterdam, The Netherlands, 1991; infectious diseases specialist, IOEM, 1994. Sr. house officer, dept. ob-gyn. surgery Arnhem, The Netherlands, 1977-79; govt. med. officer Ministry of Health, Malawi, 1979-85; locum gen. practitioner The Netherlands, 1979, 85; sr. house officer, dept. neurology and urology Addenbrooke's Hosp., Cambridge, Eng., 1985; resident in internal medicine Acad. Med. Ctr., Univ. Hosp., Amsterdam, 1985-91, cons. internal medicine, 1991-95; cons. internal medicine, infectious diseases, tropical med. Acad. Med. Ctr. and Ministry of Def., Amsterdam, 1995—. Contbr. articles on infectious diseases to internat. med. jours. Res col. physician Royal Netherlands Army Med. Svc., missions, 1995—. Fellow and/or member of numerous nat. and internat. med. orgns., especially in the field of infectious diseases and tropical medicine; mem. Netherlands Assn. Internal Medicine. Avocation: oratorium choir. Home: Moerbeilaan 13, 1214 LT Hilversum The Netherlands Office: U Amsterdam Acad Med Ctr, Meibergdreef 9, 1105 AZ Amsterdam The Netherlands

VANT-HULL, LORIN L., physics educator, consultant; b. Matlack, Iowa, June 26, 1932; s. John Vant-Hull and Bessie A. Vissar, June 15, 1935; children: Julia, Barry, Brian. BS, U. Minn., 1955; MS, UCLA, 1957; PhD, Calif. Inst. Tech., 1967. Rsch. asst. Calif. Inst. Tech., Pasadena, 1959-67; staff scientist Ford Scientific Lab., Newport Beach, Calif., 1966-69; dir. solar thermal program Energy Lab., U. Houston, 1975-98, assoc. prof., 1969-78, prof. physics, 1978—. Author, editor: Solar Power Plants, 1991. Mem. Am. Solar Energy Soc. (bd. dirs. 1995—), Internat. Solar Energy Soc., Phi Beta Kappa, Sigma Xi, Phi Kappa Phi. Avocations: pottery, camping, hiking, water skiing. E-mail: vanthull@uh.edu. Home: 4145 Osby Dr Houston TX 77025-4637 Office: U Houston Dept Physics Houston TX 77004

VAN TIEL, DAGMAR HELGA, retired designer, educator; b. Liegnitz, Silesie, Poland, July 7, 1926; d. Gustav Adolf and Giesela Henriette (Hartmann) Wenz; m. Jan Van Tiel, May 14, 1959 (dec. Nov. 1989); children: Wouter, Astrid, Pieter. Ecole e'art, Burg Giebichenstein, Allemagne Halle, 1948. Designer Munchen Allemagne, designer, selling agt.; dir. design Van Tiel, Amsterdam, The Netherlands, 1959-75; designer Danbonne, France, 1975-89; editor Van Tiel, Monaco, 1995-98; ret., 1998. Author, editor, photographer: French Riviera Golf, 1996. Mem. Oxford Club (life), Club Allmand, France Etat Uni. Avocations: photography, golf, bridge. E-mail: dagmar@vantiel.com. Fax: 0033-493757595. Home: 28 Bd de Belgique, MC 98000 Monaco Monaco

VAN TIEL, FRANK HERMAN, medical microbiologist; b. Amsterdam, The Netherlands, May 4, 1953; s. Nicolaas and Guusta Marianna (Green) Van T.; m. Yvette Jacqueline Kraat; children: Robert, Brigitte. MD, State U. of Utrecht, The Netherlands, 1980, PhD, 1986. Cons. med. microbiologist lab. infectious diseases Mcpl. Health Svc., Amsterdam, 1986; postdoctoral fellow in infectious diseases Stanford (Calif.) U. Med. Sch., 1986-88; cons. med. microbiology Univ. Hosp. Maastricht, The Netherlands, 1988—; asst. prof. med. microbiology U. Maastricht, 1992—. Contbr. articles to profl. jours.; editor: Blueprint Pediatric Antimicrobial Therapy, 1995. Mem. AAAS, Am. Soc. Microbiology, European Soc. Clin. Microbiology and Infectious Disease, Dutch/Flemish Soc. Infectious Diseases. Avocations: modern literature, gardening, skiing.

VAN TINE, MATTHEW ERIC, lawyer; b. Tomahawk, Wis., June 21, 1958; s. Kenneth G. and Louise (Olson) Van T.; m. Rena Marie David, Apr. 30, 1988; 1 child, Kristen. AB cum laude, Harvard Coll., 1980; JD magna cum laude, Boston U., 1983. Bar: Ill. 1983, Mass. 1983, U.S. Dist. Ct. Mass. 1984, U.S. Dist. Ct. (no. dist.) Ill. 1986. Law clk. to Hon. Raymond J. Pettine U.S. Dist. Ct. R.I., Providence, 1983-84; assoc. Palmer & Dodge, Boston, 1984-85, Schiff, Hardin & Waite, Chgo., 1985-88; asst. corp. counsel City of Chgo., 1988-92; assoc. to ptnr. Saunders & Monroe, Chgo., 1993-99; of counsel Miller Faucher and Cafferty, Chgo., 2000—. Exec. editor: Boston University Law Rev., 1982-83. Mem. ABA, Chgo. Bar Assn., Inns of Ct. Office: Miller Faucher and Cafferty 30 N Lasalle St Ste 3200 Chicago IL 60602-2506

VANTINE, RENA MARIE, attorney; b. Bangalore, Karna-taka, India, Aug. 8, 1961; came to U.S., 1963; d. Murphy Samuel and Indra Mary David; m. Matthew Eric VanTine, Apr. 30, 1988; 1 child, Kristen Marie VanTine. JD, N.Y. Law Sch., 1986; B in gen. studies, Oakland U., Rochester Hills, Mich., 1982. Atty. assoc. Albert Speisman and Assocs., Chgo., 1986-87; atty. Cook County State's attys. office, Chgo., 1987-99, Ill. State Comptroller's office, Chgo., 1999—; chairperson Ill. State Comptroller's Ethics Commn., 1999—. co-treas. Indo Am. Democratic Orgn., Chgo., 1999-2000 (recipient cert. appreciation, 2000); dir. Asian Am. Democratic Orgn., Chgo., 2000; del. Democratic Nat. Convention, L.A., 2000. Recipient Cert. Appreciation Asian Am. Coalition, 2000. Mem. Asian Am. Bar Assn. (pres. 1999-2000), Women's Bar Assn Polit. Action Com. (chairperson 1999-2000), State's Attys. Asian Am. Counsel (chairperson 1999—), Alliance Bar Assns. for Judicial Screening (hearing chair 1998—). Democrat. Presbyterian. Avocations: triathlons, travel. E-mail: vantirm@mail.ioc.state.il.us. Home: 10643 N Loron Ave Chicago IL 60646 Office: Ill Office Comptroller 100 W Randolph St Ste 15-500 Chicago IL 60601-3282

VANTREASE, ALICE TWIGGS, marketing executive; b. Augusta, Ga., Aug. 29, 1943; d. Samuel Warren and Harriett Alice (Wright) Twiggs; m. John Mulford Marks, July 8, 1964 (div. Oct. 1972); children: John Mulford, Sarah Elizabeth; m. James David Vantrease, May 9, 1980 (div. Mar. 1988). Student, Winthrop Coll., 1961-62, Augusta Coll., 1962-64. Sales staff Chalker Publ. Co., Waynesboro, Ga., 1972-74; with Creative Displays, Inc., Tuscaloosa, Ala., 1974-78; sales mgr. GMC Broadcasting, Chattanooga, 1978-80; corp. sales, mktg. dir. Creative Displays Inc., Augusta, 1983-91, Beaufort, S.C., 1991-95; corp. sales, mktg. dir. Twiggs of Savannah, 1995—. Author: The Rabbit in the Moon, 1996; editor: The Met. Spirit Newspaper, 1989-91, Beaufort Mag., 1991-92. Bd. dirs. Bette Bus. Bur., 1987-89; pres. Good Luck Found., 1988-91. Named to Coop. Advt. Hall of Fame, 1989. Mem. Outdoor Advt. Suppliers Assn. (v.p. 1984-87, pres. 1987-88, editor newspaper 1985-88), Nat. Spkrs. Assn., Am. Assn. Coop. Advt. Profls., Outdoor Advt. Assn. Am. Instrs. Episcopalian. Avocations: painting, writing. Home and Office: 241 Abercorn St Savannah GA 31401-4018

VAN TUYL, OTTO ARIE, technical director, quality systems auditor; b. Gameren, The Netherlands, Apr. 9, 1950; s. Cornelis and Jakomyntje Van Tuyl; m. Geertje Hilda (Van Der Vinne) Dec. 24, 1970 (div. June 25, 1995); children: Margon, Korak; m. Helena Marta Catharina Brusselaars, Apr. 7, 1996. Grad. in Engring., Agrl. Coll., Drouten, The Netherlands, 1969; grad. in Poultry, Barnebeld (Netherlands) Coll., 1970; grad. in Labour Rels., Potchefstroom U., South Africa, 1986. Tech. mgr. Modern Farms Devel., Beirut, 1971-75, Mikzayoo Bros., Teheran, Iran, 1976-78; accouts mgr. Big Dutchman, Leezep, The Netherlands, 1978-80; tech. mgr. Mulders Hatchery, Voortheiiden, The Netherlands, 1981; asst. gen. mgr. N.P.B. Pty. Ltd., Meyerteen, South Africa, 1982-86; tech. svcs. mgr. Ross Breeders Ltd., Newbridge, Scotland, 1987-91; tech. dir. E.P.I. B.V., Roermond, The Netherlands, 1991—. Deacon Dutch Reformed Ch., South Africa, 1983-85; elder Reformed Ch., The Netherlands, 1993-95. Mem. WPSA. Mem. Reformed Polit. Fedn. Avocations: walking, swimming, reading (history theology), cooking. Home: Heesterbos 13, 4614 GV Bergen op Zoom The Netherlands

VAN'T VEER, ANNE, banking executive; b. Assendelft, The Netherlands, July 27, 1947; s. Gerrit and Geertje (Visser) V-V.; m. Marianne Wijthoff (div. Dec. 1995); children: Ernst Anne, Sophia Miriam; m. Johanna Wilhelmina Van Nieuwenhuyzen, June 12, 1998. Degree in econs., U. Amsterdam, 1974. Fin. analyst Ministry of Econ. Affairs, The Netherlands, 1974-76; econ. rschr. Min. Finance, The Netherlands, 1976-77; asst. IMF, Washington, 1977-80; dep. dir. Amro Bank, Amsterdam, 1980-85; mng. dir. NCM, Amsterdam, 1985-98; sec.-gen. Berne Union, London, 1998—. Office: Berne Union, 1-2 Castle Ln, London SW1E 6DR, England

VAN TYNE, ARTHUR MORRIS, geologist; b. Syracuse, N.Y., Aug. 12, 1925; s. Roy Hanford and Isabelle Marguerite (Hoag) Van T.; m. Patricia Wilson Boyd, July 13, 1946; children: Judith, Cynthia, Mark, Peter. AB, Syracuse U., 1951, MS, 1958. Cert. petroleum geologist; lic. geologist, Pa. Field asst. Syracuse U. Rsch. Inst., 1951-53; geologist Shell Oil Co., Rockies, Gulf Coast, 1953-57; sr. geologist-in-charge N.Y. State Geol. Survey-Oil and Gas Rsch. Office, Wellsville and Alfred, N.Y., 1958-81; geol. cons. Van Tyne Cons., Wellsville, N.Y.C., 1981—; gov. appointee mem. N.Y. State Oil, Gas, and Solution Mining Adv. Bd., 1996. Contbr. articles to profl. jours. Bd. dirs. Jones Meml. Hosp., Wellsville, 1974—, bd. chmn. 1986-95; bd. dirs. Wellsville United Way, 1968-80, pres. 1974-75; bd. dirs. Drake Well Found.; dep. mayor Village of Wellsville, 1992—; committeeman Rep. Party, 1962-77, 98-2000. Recipient Cert. of Appreciation Am. Petroleum Inst., 1975, 80, Award of Merit Internat. Oil Scouts Assn. and Appalachian Sect., 1961, 66, 88. Mem. N.Y. Acad. Scis., Am. Assn. Petroleum Geologists (nat. and Ea. sect. hon. mem., sec., dir. 1989-91, Disting. Svc. award Ea. sect. 1987, Nat. Disting. Svc. award 1994, John T. Galey Meml. award Ea. sect. 1997), Russian Assn. Oil and Gas Geologists, N.Y. State Oil Producers Assn. (dir., exec. com. 1980—, Svc. award 1981), Ind. Oil and Gas Assn. N.Y. (pres. 1985-88), No. Appalachian Geol. Soc. (pres. 1966-68), Geol. Soc. Am., Rotary (pres. Wellsville 1979-80, Paul Harris fellow 1994). Achievements include discovery of gas production from queenston formation in N.Y., discovered Bass Islands thrust structure, a major oil and gas producer in N.Y.

and Pa.; contributed for N.Y. State to Appalachian Gas Atlas. Home: 24 Oak St Wellsville NY 14895-1026 Office: Van Tyne Cons PO Box 326 159 1/2 N Main St Wellsville NY 14895-1149

VAÑURA, PETR, chemical technology educator; b. Brno, Czech Republic, June 1, 1946; s. Josef and Božena (Brázdilová) V.; m. Eva Dufková, July 7, 1977; 1 child, Eva. Engr., Inst. Chem. Tech., Prague, Czech Republic, 1968; postgrad., Nuclear Rsch. Inst., Řež, Czech Repubic, 1968-73; PhD, Czech Acad. Scis., Prague, 1980. Rschr. Nuclear Rsch. Inst., Řež, 1973-82, head rsch. group, 1982-87; rschr. Inst. Chem. Tech., Prague, 1987-91, tchr., rschr., 1991—. Contbr. articles to profl. jours., chpts. to books. Mem. Mensa Czech Republic, Czech Chem. Soc. Office: Prague Inst. Chem Tech, Technická 5, 16628 Prague 6 Czech Republic

VAN VELDHOVEN, PAUL PHILIP, biology educator; b. Wijnegem, Belgium, May 5, 1957. BS, Katholieke U. Leuven, 1979, MS, 1979, PhD, 1986. Post-doctoral rsch. fellow Duke U. Med. Ctr., Durham, N.C., 1986-88; assoc. prof. Katholieke U. Leuven, 1991-97, prof., 1997—. Rschr. in field. Recipient Kring der Alumni van de U. Stichting Biol. Scis. prize, 1988, Smith-Kline-Beecham prize, Koninklijke Academie der Geneeskunde, Brussels, 1992. Mem. Internat. Soc. for the Study of Fatty Acids and Lipids, Am. Soc. for Biochemistry and Molecular Biology, Soc. for the Study of Inborn Errors of Metabolism, Am. Oil Chemists Soc. Office: Katholieke U Leuven, Campus Gasthuisberg, Leuven B-3000, Belgium

VAN VELZEN, JOHANNES HENRICUS MATTEUS, library director; b. Alphen aan den Rijn, The Netherlands, July 7, 1952. Libr. City Libr. Haarlem, The Netherlands, 1975-78; dir. Pub. Libr. Spijkenisse, The Netherlands, 1978-88; mng. dir. Pub. Libr. Amsterdam, The Netherlands, 1988—; Bd. dirs. Dutch Libr. Svc. Mem. Dutch Libr. Assn. (bd. dirs.), North Holland Libr. Assn. (sec. bd. dirs.), Amsterdam Libr. Assn. (chmn. bd. dirs.), PICA/Ctr. for Libr. Automation. Office: Keizersgracht 440, 1016 GD Amsterdam The Netherlands

VAN VLIET, CAROLYNE MARINA, physicist, educator; b. Dordrecht, Netherlands, Dec. 27, 1929; emigrated to U.S., 1960, naturalized, 1967; d. Marinus and Jacoba (de Lange) Van V. BS, Free U. Amsterdam, Netherlands, 1949, MA, 1953, PhD in Physics, 1956. Rsch. fellow Free U. Amsterdam, 1950-54, rsch. assoc., 1954-56, asst. dir., 1958-60; fellow U. Minn., Mpls., 1956-57; faculty U. Minn., 1957-58, 60-70, prof. elec. engring. and physics, 1965-70; prof. theoretical physics U. Montreal, Que., Can., 1969-95; sr. rschr. math. rsch. ctr. U. Montreal, Que., 1969-2000; prof. emerita U. Montreal, 1998—; vis. prof. U. Fla., 1974, 78-88; prof. elec. and computer engring. Fla. Internat. U., 1992—. Contbg. author: Fluctuation Phenomena in Solids, 1965; contbr. articles to profl. jours. Rsch. grantee NSF, Air Force OSR, Nat. Sci. and Engring. Rsch. Coun., Ottawa. Fellow IEEE; mem. Am. Phys. Soc., N.Y. Acad. Scis., Associated Artists, Mid. Ea. Dance. Office: Ctr Engring & Appl Scis Fla Internat U 10555 W Flagler St Miami FL 33174-1630

VAN VLISSINGEN, P. FENTENER, gas, oil industry executive. CEO, chmn. bd. SHV Holdings NV, Utrecht, chmn. supervisory bd. *

VAN VOORHIS, REBECCA ANN, sociology educator; b. Walnut Creek, Calif.; d. John Daniel and Karen Judith (Wacker) Van V.; 1 child, George Nathaniel. BA, U. San Francisco, 1987, JD, 1990; PhD, U. Calif., Berkeley, 1999. Bar: Calif. 1990. Assoc. Gordon & Rees, San Francisco, 1990; asst. prof. dept. sociology and social svcs. Calif. State U., Hayward, 1999—. E-mail: rvanvoor@csuhayward.edu. Office: Calif State U Dept Sociology/Social Svcs Hayward CA 94542

VAN VOORST, ROBERT E., theology educator, minister; b. Holland, Mich., June 5, 1952; s. Robert Eugene and Donna Mae (Boeve) Van V.; m. Mary Lind Bos, June 15, 1974; children: Richard William, Nicholas John. BA, Hope Coll., 1974; MDiv, Western Sem., 1977; PhD, Union Sem., N.Y., 1988. Ordained to ministry Classis of Holland Reformed Ch. in Am., 1977. Pastor Rochester Reformed Ch., Accord, N.Y., 1977-89; prof. religion Lycoming Coll., Williamsport, Pa., 1989-99, dept. chair, 1997-99; prof. New Testament Western Theol. Sem., Holland, Mich., 1999—; adj. prof. Susquehanna U., Selinsgrove, Pa., 1991, Bucknell U., Lewisburg, Pa., 1993; vis. prof. Westminster Coll., Oxford, Eng., 1997; interim pastor Lycoming Presbyn. Ch., Williamsport, 1997-99. Author: Ascents of James, 1989, Building New Testament Vocabulary, 1990, 2nd edit., 1999, Anthology of World Scriptures, 1994, 3rd edit., 1999, Readings in Christianity, 1996, 2d edit., 2000, Jesus Outside the New Testament, 2000, Anthology of Asian Scriptures, 1999; co-author: Death of Jesus in Early Christianity, 1998; contbr. articles Eerdmans Dictionary of the Bible, 2000; contbr. numerous articles to profl. jours. Mem. Phi Beta Kappa, Phi Kappa Phi, Eta Sigma Phi, Phi Sigma Iota. Avocations: golf, cooking. Home: 1114 Post Ave Holland MI 49424-2550 Office: Western Theol Sem 101 E 13th St Holland MI 49423-3622

VAN VROONHOVEN, JOS CORNELIS WALTERUS, mechanical engineer; b. Eindhoven, The Netherlands, Apr. 21, 1963; s. Wil A.L. and Veronica T. (Dykmans) Van V.; m. Anna M.T.C. Van Den Berk, June 5, 1996; children: Thijs, Pim. MSc in Math., Tech. U. Eindhoven, 1988, PhD in Mech. Engring., 1996. Lectr. Tech. U., Eindhoven, 1988; rsch. scientist Physics and Electronics Lab., The Hague, 1988-89, Philips Rsch. Labs., Eindhoven, 1989-97; sr. designer Philips Display Components, Eindhoven, 1998—; sci. cons. Philips Ctr. for Mfg. Technologies, Eindhoven, 1992-98, Philips Display Components, Eindhoven, 1991-97; rsch. asst. Philips Semiconductors, Nymegen, 1989-90; gen. dir. Josephus Brewery, Nuenen, 1990—; damage control expert, Lausanne, Switzerland, 1994; numerical analysis expert Munich, 1995. Author: Dynamic Crack Propagation in Brittle Materials: Analyses Based on Fracture and Damage Mechanics, 1996; contbr. articles to profl. jours.; editor Pint-News Mag., Utrecht, 1993-98. Vice chmn. Parish of St. Paul, Eindhoven, 1995-98. 1st lt. royal Netherlands Army, 1988-89. Mem. Roerstok, PINT, ESIS. Roman Catholic. Avocations: gardening, brewing beer. E-mail: jos.van.vroonhoven@philips.com. Office: Philips Display Components, PO Box 218 Bldg RAF-1, 5600MD Eindhoven The Netherlands

VAN VUUREN, JAN H., education educator; b. Durban, South Africa, Feb. 2, 1969; s. Jan and Annalene W. (Greyvenstein) Van V. BSc, U. Stellenbosch, South Africa, 1989; BSc with honors, U. Stellenbosch, 1990, MSc, 1992; PhD, U. Oxford, Eng., 1995. Lectr. U. Stellenbosch, 1996, sr. lectr., 1997—. Contbr. articles to profl. jours. Mem. South Africa Ops. Rsch. Soc., South Africa Math. Soc. Avocation: music. Office: Stellenbosch U, PO Box XI Dept Appl Math, 7602 Stellenbosch South Africa

VAN WACHEM, LODEWIJK CHRISTIAAN, petroleum company executive; b. Pangkalan Brandan, Indonesia, July 31, 1931; m. Elisabeth G. Cristofoli, June 10, 1958; 3 children. Degree Mech. Engring., Delft U., Delft, The Netherlands., 1953. With Bataafsche Petroleum Maatschappij, The Hague, The Netherlands, 1953; pres. Royal Dutch Petroleum Co., The Hague, The Netherlands, 1982-92; chmn. com. mng. dir. Royal Dutch/Shell Group, The Hague, The Netherlands, 1985-92; chmn. supr. bd. Royal Dutch Petroleum Co., The Hague, The Netherlands, 1992—; chmn. bd. dirs. Shell Oil Co. USA, 1982-92, De Nederlandsche Bank N.V., 1987-92; non-exec. dir. IBM Corp., Armonk, 1992—, Credit Suisse Holding, Zurich, 1992-96, Atco Ltd., Calgary, 1993—, Zurich Fin. Svcs., 1993—, AAB Area Brown Boveri Ltd., Zurich, 1996-99; mem. supervisory bd. AKZO Nobel n.v., Arnhem, 1992—, Philips Electronics n.v., Eindhoven, 1993—, chmn. supervisory bd., 1999; mem. supervisory bd. BMW A.G., Munich, 1994—, Bayer A.G., Leverkusen, 1997—. Decorated C.B.E. (hon.), Knight Brit. Empire (hon.), Comdr. Order of Oranje Nassau, Knight Order Netherlands Lion, Pub. Svc. Star (Singapore). Office: Royal Dutch Petroleum Co, 30 Carel van Bylandtlaan, 2596 HR The Hague The Netherlands

VAN WALSUM, PETER, diplomat; b. Rotterdam, The Netherlands, June 25, 1934. Law Degree, U. Utrecht, The Netherlands. Legal officer Civil Def. Staff, Ministry Gen. Affairs, 1962-65; desk officer polit. sect. Directorate for Internat. Orgns., Ministry Fgn. Affairs, 1963-65; second sec. Permanent Mission to NATO, Brussels, 1965-67, Royal Netherlands Embassy, Rumania, 1967-70; first sec. Permanent Mission to the UN, N.Y., 1970-74, Royal Netherlands Embassy, India, 1974-75; counsellor Royal Netherlands Embassy, U.K., 1975-79, Permanent Representation to the European Cmty., Brussels, 1979-81; dir. Western Hemisphere Ministry Fgn. Affairs, 1981-85; amb. of the Netherlands Thailand, 1985-89; dir.-gen. polit. affairs Minstry Fgn. Affairs, 1989-93; amb. of the Netherlands Germany, 1993-98; permanent rep. of the Netherlands UN, 1998—. 1st lt. Field Artillery, 1960-62. *

VAN WAMELEN, JOOP, technical assessment consultant; b. Delft, The Netherlands, June 8, 1939; s. Bastiaan and Maria Hendrika van Wamelen; m. Andriesa Cornelia Brink, Oct. 6, 1962; children: Paul Bastiaan, Arend Andries, Riaan Joop. BSc in Math. and Applied Math., U. Pretoria, South Africa, 1960, BSc in Engring., 1966. Cert. profl. engr., South Africa. Various civil engring. positions South Africa, 1966-77; civil engr. Atomic Energy Commn. Licensing Br., Pretoria, 1977-80; sr. chief rsch. officer, head environ. engring. Nat. Bldg. Rsch. Inst., Pretoria, 1980-87; mgr. energy design CSIR Bldg. and Constrn. Tech., Pretoria, 1988, project leader infrastructure, 1989-93, mgr. energy efficiency in housing, 1998; mgr. Agrement South Africa, Pretoria, 1993-98, cons., 1999—; chmn. inaugural meeting World Fedn. Tech. Assessment Orgns., Pilanesberg, South Africa, 1995. Contbr. papers, articles, and reports to profl. jours. Treas. Rapportryers, Wonderboomfort, Pretoria, 1996-2000. Mem. So. African Soc. for Trenchless Tech. (bd. dirs., founder pres. 1992-93, v.p. 1992-2000, pres. 2000—), South African Instn. for Civil Engring. Avocations: recorded classical music, photography, do-it-yourself projects, reading. Fax: 27 12 841 2539. E-mail: jvwamele@csir.co.za. Office: Agrement South Africa, PO Box 395, 0001 Pretoria Gauteng, South Africa

VAN WANING, JACOB JAN-WILLEM, parliamantarian, retired; b. The Hague, The Netherlands, Feb. 12, 1938; s. Christiaan Jan-Willem and Francine Lucia (Van Maaren) Van W.; m. Petra Burger, Dec. 28, 1962; children: Anna Lucia, Anita Christine. B in Naval Scis., Royal Netherlands Naval Coll., 1959; MA, Georgetown U., 1982. Qualified submarine commanding officer, NATO, 1970. Commdg. officer HNLMS Zeehond, 1971-73; asst. naval attache Washington, 1979-83; strategic planner Netherlands Defense Staff, 1983-86; commdg. officer Den Helder Naval Base, 1986-89; bus. intelligence mgr. DAF Trucks N.V., Eindhoven, The Netherlands, 1989-91; sr. advisor Netherlands Inst. Internat. Rels., Clingendael, 1993-94; mem. Lower House of Parliament The Hague, 1994-98; exam. com. U. Brabant, 1991-96; dir., owner VWB Cons., Eindhoven, The Hague, 1991-94. Co-author: The Netherlands Submarine Service 1906-1966, 1966; co-author: Pergamon-Brassey's International Military and Defense Encyclopedia, 1988, Grote Winkler Prins, 1990; contbr. articles to profl. jours. Chmn. Democrats 66 study group on security and def., 1992-93, 98-2000.; Capt. Royal Netherlands Navy, 1984-89. Recipient legion of merit award U.S. Sec. Def., Washington, 1983; named hon. officer Order of Orange Nassau, 1989; recipient award Municipality of Den Helder, 1989. Mem. Internat. Inst. for Strategic Affairs, U.S. Naval Inst., Amnesty Internat. (mil. sect.), The Netherlands Soc. Internat. Affairs (vice chmn. 1992—), Royal Netherlands Maritime Soc. (mem. adv. bd. 1996—). Avocations: field hockey, cricket, tennis, yachting. Fax: 36 70 3247889. Home: Neuhuyskade 55, 2596 XJ The Hague The Netherlands

VAN WESTEN, FRANS, finance executive; b. Brussels, Mar. 6, 1956; arrived in The Netherlands, 1963; s. Pieter Johannes and Catherina Gesina (Koets) Van W.; m. Margriet Rijkmans; 3 children. BA, European Sch., Bergen, The Netherlands, 1974; M in Econs. cum laude, State U. Groningen, 1979; diploma in corp. fin. mgmt., Harvard U., 1991. Fin. analyst Esso Netherlands, 1981-83; asst. credit mgr. Esso Benelux, 1983-85, bus. planner, 1985-86, head fin. ops., 1986-88; treas. Royal Dutch Papermills, 1988-93; v.p. fin., treas. KNP-BT, Amsterdam, The Netherlands, 1993-98; exec. v.p., CFO Ahrend, Amsterdam, The Netherlands, 1998—. Contbr. articles to profl. jours. including Fin. Mgmt. & Orgn. and Treas. Handbook. 1st lt. The Netherlands Mil., 1980-81. Mem. Assn. Corp. Treasurers (Netherlands and U.K.). Home: Mauritslaan 3, 3818 GJ Amersfoort The Netherlands Office: Koninklijke Ahrend NV, Singel 130, 1015 AE Amsterdam The Netherlands

VAN WIJNGAARDEN, LEENDERT, fluid mechanics engineering educator; b. Delft, Mar. 16, 1932; s. Cornelis M. van Wijngaarden and Jeanne Severijn; m. Willy F. de Goede, 1962; 2 children. Grad., Gymnasium B, Delft, Tech. U. Delft. Head hydrodynamics dept. Netherlands Ship Model Basin, Wageningen, 1962-66; prof. fluid mechanics Twente U., Enschede, The Netherlands, 1966-97, prof. emeritus, 1997—. Contbr. 70 articles to profl. jours. Mem. Acad. Europaea, Royal Netherlands Acad. Sci., Internat. Union Theorectical and Applied Mechanics (pres. 1992-96, v.p. 1996-2000). Avocations: tennis, chess, literature, music. Home: Von Weberlaan 7, 7522 KB Enschede The Netherlands Office: Univ Twente, PO Box 217, 7500 AE Enschede The Netherlands

VAN WIMERSMA GREIDANUS, TJEERD BUWE, pharmacology educator; b. Utrecht, The Netherlands, July 17, 1936; s. Herman Theodorus and Catharina Esther (Jaeger) van W.; m. Jenny Koekkoek, Mar. 23, 1962 (div.) children: Buwe, Hajo Tjeerd, Ydke Hendrike; m. Anja Francisca Van Dam, July 22, 1983; 1 child, Daniel Cornelis. Degree Biology, Utrecht U., 1966; PhD, 1970, experimental pharmacologist, 1977. Asst. prof. dept. med. pharmacology U. Utrecht, 1972-76, assoc. prof., 1976-80, prof., 1980—, chmn. dept. med. pharmacology, 1985-99; chmn. Netherlands Soc. Olympic Participants, 1986-99; bd. dirs. Med. Faculty U. Utrecht, 1984-87, chmn. preclin. sect., 1975-78; chmn. Netherlands Ctr. Doping Affairs, Arnhem, 1989—; mem. coun. Utrecht U., 1995-99. Author and editor of over 250 scientific papers and chapters in neuroendocrinology, sports and doping. Mem. bd. Dutch Rowing Assn., Amsterdam, 1967-71; chef d'equipe Dutch Rowing Team European Champions, Olympic Games Mex., 1967-68; chef de Mission Netherlands Olympic Team, Sarajevo, L.A., 1984; bd. mem. Netherlands Olympic com., The Hague, 1985-89. Sgt. Royal Air Force, 1956-58. Recipient Medal of Honor Netherlands Olympic Com., 1985, Medal of Honor, Faculty Medicine Utrecht U., 1997; named Honorary mem. Utrecht Students Rowing Club Triton, 1965. Mem. Netherlands Soc. Olympic Participants (hon.). Home: Kameraarsweide 14, 3437 CB Nieuwegein The Netherlands Office: Rudolf Magnus Inst Neuroscis, Universiteitsweg 100, 3584 CG Utrecht The Netherlands

VAN WINKLE, WESLEY ANDREW, lawyer, educator; b. Kansas City, Mo., Sept. 22, 1952; s. Willard and Cleone Verlee (O'Dell) Van W.; m. Ruth Kay Shelby, Apr. 10, 1984. JD, San Francisco Law Sch., 1987. Bar: Calif. 1987, U.S. Dist. Ct. (no. dist.) Calif. 1987, U.S. Supreme Ct. 1994. Atty. Bagetelos & Fadem, San Francisco, 1987-91; pvt. practice Berkeley, Calif., 1991—; prof. law San Francisco Law Sch., 1990—; apptd. mem. Calif. Appellate Indigent Def. Oversight Adv. com., 1997-99. Editor (legal newspaper/rev.) Res Ipsa Loquitur, 1986. Mem. Calif. Attys. for Criminal Justice, Calif. Appellate Def. Counsel (pres. 1998-99), San Francisco Law Sch. Alumni Assn. (bd. dirs.), Delta Theta Phi. Democrat. Office: PO Box 5216 Berkeley CA 94705-0216

VAN WISSEN, GERARDUS WILHELMUS JOHANNES MARIA, consulting engineering company executive; b. Voorburg, The Netherlands, Aug. 2, 1941; s. Johannes J.G. and Wilhelmina (Houweling) van W.; divorced; children: Elise W.G., Wikke M., Annemarliese. Ir. Civil engr., Tech. U. Delft, The Netherlands, 1967. Asst. expert FAO, Rome, 1967-70; hydraulic engr. water master plan Rio Cai Agrar- und Hydrotechnik GmbH, Brazil, 1970-72; tech. dir. Ferrenafe irrigation scheme Agrar- und Hydrotechnik GmbH, Peru, 1972-74; team leader Tanga water master plan Agrar- und Hydrotechnik GmbH, Tanzania, 1974-76; regional dir. Africa dept. Essen, Fed. Republic Germany, 1976-78, sales mgr., 1978-82, mng. dir., 1982-94; pres. AHT Group GmbH, 1994-2000, AHT Group AG, Essen, 2000—. Mem. Pro Ruhrgebiet, Essen, 1984—. Mem. Royal Inst. Engrs., Verband unabhängig beratender Ingenieurfirmen (export com. 1982—), Industrie und Handelskammer (export com. 1983). Avocations: painting, fly fishing. Office: AHT Group AG, Huyssenallee 66-68, D-45128 Essen Germany

VAN WYMEERSCH, CHARLES PAUL, economics and business educator; b. Liege, Belgium, May 7, 1946; s. Paul H. and Nelly F. (Meulemans) Van W.; m. Genevieve X. Byvoet, June 30, 1972; 1 dau., Laurence. Elec. Engr., Cath. U. Louvain, 1969, B in Econs., 1972; MBA, Cornell U., 1973. Rsch. asst. Cath. U. Louvain, Belgium, 1971-72; attache Banque Bruxelles Lambert, 1973-76; prof. corp. fin. Namur U., Belgium, 1976—, chmn. dept. bus. adminstrn., 1980-98; exec. dir. Advanced Array Tech., 1998—; dir. C. of C., Namur; mem. adv. bd. Bank Brussels Lambert (ING Group), Namur. Author: Traite d'Analyse Financiere, 1996; editor: Traite pratique des comptes annuels, Guide des comptes annuels pour le Luxembourg. E-mail: charles.vanwymeersch@fundp.ac.bd. Office: U Namur, Dept Bus Adminstrn, 8 Rempart de la Vierge, B5000 Namur Belgium

VANYUSHIN, BORIS FEDOROVICH, biochemistry educator; b. Tula, USSR, Feb. 16, 1935; s. Fedor Georgievich and Tatyana Sergeevna (Kokoreva) V.; m. Valeria Ivanovna Ovchinnikova, Oct. 8, 1971. MS, Moscow State U., 1957; DSci., 1973; PhD, Biochem. Inst. Acad. Sci. USSR, 1961. Jr. rsch. scientist plant biochemistry dept. Moscow State U., 1957-64, sr. rsch. scientist lab. bioorganic chemistry, 1965-73, head dept. molecular bases of ontogenesis Belozersky Inst., 1973—; postdoct. rsch. fellow Virus Rsch. Unit ARC, Cambridge, Eng., 1964-65; Regent's lectr. dept. biochemistry U. Calif., Irvine, 1976; UNESCO expert in molecular biology Lucknow U., India, 1978; vis. prof. U. Catania (Italy), 1990; vis. rsch. fellow Nat. Ctr. Toxicol. Rsch., Jefferson, Ark., 1994-95; head Lab. Molecular Mechanisms of Hormonal Regulation of Plant Ontogenesis Inst. Agrl. Biotech., Moscow, 1985-96; mem., vice-chmn. The Biology Expert Coun. Highest Cert. Commn. Russia, 1974-95. Author: Molecular and Genetic Mechanisms of Aging, 1977; contbr. over 400 articles to profl. jours; mem. editl. bd. Biology Bull. Russian Acad. Scis., 1983—, Jour. Evolutionary Biochemistry and Physiology, 1977-97, Bilogicheskie Nauki Moscow, 1976-91, Biol. Sci. Bull., 1971-76. Grantee Russian Found. Fundamental Rsch., 1993-95, 96-98, 99—, Internat. Sci. Found., 1994-95. Avocations: swimming, computing. Home: Flat 576, Lomonosovsky prospect 14, 117296 Moscow Russia Office: Moscow State U, Belozersky Inst, 119899 Moscow Russia

VAN ZANDWIJK, JAN PETER, scientific researcher; b. Haarlem, The Netherlands, Nov. 10, 1968; s. Cornelis and Margaretha (Van Leuvensteijn) Van Z. MS in PHysics, Vrye U., Amsterdam, The Netherlands, 1993, PhD in Human Movement Scis., 1997. Contbr. articles to profl. jours. Avocation: chess.

VAN ZIJL, NELLY MARIA, physicist, researcher; b. Karlskrona, Blekinge, Sweden, Aug. 23, 1961; d. Johannes Benjamin and Britta Maria (Olen) van Z. BS, U. Lund, Sweden, 1981, PhD, 1987. Tchg. asst. theoretical physics U. Lund, 1983-87; post-doctoral staff theoretical physics U. Cape Town, South Africa, 1988; rschr. CelsiusTech Electronics, Jarfalla, Sweden, 1989-95; mgr. microwave devel. CelsiusTech Electronics, Jarfalla, 1996—; bd. dirs. High Frequency Electronics, Sweden. Contbr. articles to profl. jours. Avocations: photography, gardening, jewelry making. Home: Bravallagatan 3, S-113 36 Stockholm Sweden Office: CelsiusTech Electronics, Nettovagen 6, S-175 88 Jarfalla Sweden

VAN ZIJL, PIET-HEIN, finance company executive; b. The Netherlands, Dec. 15, 1965. BBA, Nigenrode, Breukelen, The Netherlands, 1987; MBA, IESE, Barcelona, 1991. Various positions in fin. Adam Opel A.G., Rüsselsheim, Germany, 1991-98, CFO, 1998—. Lt. Intendance The Netherlands, 1990-91. Office: Opel Nederland BV, Baanhoek 188, 3361 GN Sliedrecht The Netherlands

VAN ZUTPHEN, LAMBERTUS F. M. (BERT VAN ZUTPHEN), geneticist, educator; b. Gemert, The Netherlands, Oct. 27, 1941; s. Johannes and Petronella (Van den Berg) Van Z.; m. Anna Maria Rooymans; children: Yvonne, Esther. BS in Agrl. Engring., Agrl. Coll., Roermond, The Netherlands, 1961; M in Biology, U. Utrecht, The Netherlands, 1969, PhD, 1974. Biology tchr. Vitus Coll., Bussum, The Netherlands, 1968-69; asst. prof. U. Utrecht, 1969-76; prof., dept. head U. Utrecht, Bar Harbor, Maine, 1983—; assoc. prof. U. Utrecht, 1977-83; Fogerty fellow Jackson Lab., Bar Harbor, Maine, 1976-77; chmn. govt. com. Alternatives Animal Expts., 1986—; mem. Biotechnology, 1993; chmn. 2d World Congress on Alternatives and Animal Use in the Life Scis., Utrecht, The Netherlands, 1993-96. Editor: Animal Experimentation: Legislation and Education, 1989, Proefdieren en dierproeven, 1991, Principles of Laboratory Animal Science: A Contribution to the Humane Use and Care of Animals and to Experimental Results, 1993, Welfare Aspects of Transgenic Animals, 1997, Animal Alternatives, Welfare and Ethics, 1997; mem. editl. bd. jours. JEANS, ATLA, LAS; contbr. articles to profl. jours. Advisor HLO Coll., Utrecht, 1990-97; vice-chmn. Nat. Adv. Com. on Animal Experimentation, Den Haag, 1985—; chmn. NWO com. Animal Alternatives, 1996—. Fellow Fogarty NIH 1976-77. Mem. Com. European Sci. Found., Nat. Soc. Lab. Animal Sci. (pres. 1978-82), Netherlands Fedn. Lab. Animal Sci. Assn. (sec. 1984—), Animal Alternatives, Welfare Ethics. Avocations: badminton, walking, cycling. Home: Sanatoriumlaan 87, 3705 AN Zeist The Netherlands Office: U Utrecht, Yalelaan 2, Utrecht The Netherlands

VAN ZWIETEN, PETER A., clinical pharmacologist, medical educator, consultant; b. Heemstede, The Netherlands, May 20, 1937; s. Frans C. Van Zwieten and Dora Van Son. PhD, U. Amsterdam, The Netherlands, 1961; MD, U. Kiel, Germany, 1968; prof. hon. causa, Med. U., Beijing, 1995, Tongji Med. U., Wuhan, China, 1997. Bd. cert. clin. pharmacologist. Postdoctor U. Vienna, Austria, 1963-65; lectr. U. Kiel, Germany, 1965-68, assoc. prof., 1968-71; prof. faculty pharmacy Acad. Hosp., U. Amsterdam, 1971-85, prof. faculty medicine, 1985—; cons. clin. pharmacology, 1985—; dean faculty pharmacy U. Amsterdam, 1972-85. Author: (with others) Drug Therapy in Cardio-Thoracic Surgery, 1997, Antihypertensive Drugs, 1997; contbr. articles to profl. jours. With Royal Netherlands Army, 1961-63, reserve officer, 1963-99. Mem. German Acad. Scis., Academia Europea, Order of Netherlands' Lion (knight). Avocations: art, languages. Fax: 31.20.69 68 704. Office: Acad Med Ctr U Amsterdam, Meibergdreef 15, 1105 AZ Amsterdam The Netherlands

VAN ZYL, HERMIAS CORNELIUS, religous lecturer, clergyman; b. Rustenburg, South Africa, June 6, 1947; s. Petrus Lodewicus and Hester Sophia (Van der Walt) Van Z.; m. Cecilia Amanda Geldenhuys, July 4, 1970; children: Debbie, Wikus, Nico. BA, U. Pretoria, South Africa, 1969, BD, 1973, DD, 1987. Ordained to ministry Dutch Reformed Ch. Min. Dutch Reformed Ch., Benoni, South Africa, 1975-78; lectr. U. South Africa, Pretoria, 1979-84, U. Free State, Bloemfontein, South Africa, 1985—; lectr. Bible Sch., Bloemfontein, 1985—. Author: Stand Up and Live, 1996, Good News for the World, 1987; co-author: Biblelennium, 1999; co-editor: Afrikaans Reference Bible,; editor Neotestamentica, 1989-95. Mem. Soc. Bibl. Lit., N.T. Soc. South Africa (publ. sec. 1989-95). Avocation: jogging. E-mail: tlghc@rs.uovs.ac.za. Office: U Free State Dept New Test, PO Box 339, Bloemfontein 9300, South Africa

VARADHARAJAN, VIJAY, computer scientist, educator; b. New Delhi, July 2, 1960; s. Gopalakrishnan and Ramani (Sounderrajan) V.; m. Meera Srinivasan, June 7, 1987; children: Roopa, Preeltra. BSc with honors in Elec. Engring., U. Sussex, Eng., 1981; PhD, U. Plymouth and Exeter, Eng., 1984. Chartered engr., math. Rsch. asst. dept. comm. engring. Plymouth U., 1981-84; rsch. fellow, lectr. U. Plymouth, U. Reading, Eng., 1984-86; rsch. mgr. Brit. Telecom Rsch. and Tech. Applications Lab., Ipswich, Eng., 1987-88; project leader Hewlett-Packard Labs., Bristol, Eng., 1988-89, project mgr., 1989-92, sr. project mgr., 1992-94; prof. of Computing Found., dir. sys./network security rsch. U. Western Sydney, 1994—, head Sch. of Computing and Info. Tech., 1998—; cons. various European project activities, 1985-94, Cost-11, 534, 1985-87, Erkena, Race, 1987-88, mem. expert panel, 1987-88, mem. expert task force, 1992-93; sr. cons., architect various projects; mem. program com., chair session, program chair, gen. co-chair various confs. Co-author: Security Mechanisms for Computer Networks, numerous articles, conf. and tech. reports. Fellow Inst. Math. and Applications, Inst. Elec. Engrs., Brit Computer Soc., Australian Computer Soc. (tech. bd. dirs.), Australian Inst. Engrs.; mem. IEEE, Internat. Assn. Cryptologic Rsch., Acad. Scis. N.Y., Scientists Group Indian High Commn. Avocations: chess, travel. Office: U Western Sydney Dept Computing, Nepean PO Box 10, Kingswood NSW 2747, Australia

VARADI, JANOS, engineering educator; b. Budapest, Hungary, Apr. 12, 1920; s. Joseph and Jane (Wagner) V.; m. Sarah Csapo; 1 child, Catherina. MSc, Tech. U. Budapest, 1945; PhD (hon.), Agrl. U., Gödöllö, Hungary, 1990; Golden Diploma, Tech. U., Gödöllö, Hungary, 1995. Registered mech. engr., Hungary. Engr. State Material Testing Inst., Budapest, 1941-

46; draftsman Tungsram Ltd., Budapest, 1946-49; devel. engr. Ikarus Bus. Works, Budapest, 1950-51; assoc. prof. Agrl. U., Gödöllö, 1951-58, prof., 1959-90, prof. emeritus, 1990—, dean, 1952-63, pro-rector, 1963-64; dir. Ganz-Mávag Works, Budapest, 1964-65. Co-author: Tractors and Automobiles, 1958-77, Vehicle and Tractor Engines, 1978; contbr. articles to profl. jours. Recipient Order of Labor, Hungarian State, 1958, Medallion for Serving the Homeland, Min. of Def., 1970; named Outstanding Tchr. Min. of Edn., 1990. Mem. Soc. Agrl. Engring. Budapest (chmn. 1957-90, hon. chmn. 1990—). Avocations: technical history, cats, model railroading. Home: Tallér u 8, H-1145 Budapest Hungary Office: St Stephan Univ, Páter K u 1, H-2103 Gödöllö Hungary

VARADINOVA-GEORGIEVA, TATIANA LUKANOVA, biology educator; b. Sofia, Bulgaria, Sept. 17, 1947; d. Lukan Galabov and Nora Kirova (Petrova) Varadinova; m. Georgi Stefanov Georgiev, Jan. 9, 1982; children: Ognjian, Vjara. MS, U. Sofia, 1971, PhD, 1976. Asst. prof. Sofia U., 1977-86, prof., 1986—; head lab. Sofia U., 1989—. Author: Dictionary of Microbiology, 1993, Immunology, 1985, 88, Molecular Virology of Tumor Viruses; mem. editl. bd. Metal-Based Drugs, 1996; contbr. articles to profl. jours.; patentee in field. Mem. Edn. Com., Internat. Union Immunol. Socs., European Soc. Biomodulation and Chemotherapy, Internat. Soc. Antivirals. Avocations: skiing, swimming, collecting postcards. Home: z k Dianabad 15/20, 1172 Sofia Bulgaria Office: Sofia U Faculty of Biology, Dragan Tzankov Blvd 8, 1421 Sofia Bulgaria

VARADY, TIBOR, law educator; b. Zrenjanin, Yugoslavia, May 25, 1939. Degree in law, Belgrade (Yugoslavia) U., 1962, LLM, 1967; LLM, Harvard U., 1968, SJD, 1970. Assoc. Varady Law Firm, Yugoslavia, 1962-63; rom asst. prof. to prof. law Novi Sad U., 1963-92; minister of justice Govt. of Yugoslavia, 1992-93; prof. law, dept. legal studies Ctrl. European U., Budapest, Hungary, 1993—, also head dept. legal studies, 1993-97, pro-rector, 1994-97; vis. prof. U. Fla. Coll. Law, 1981, Emory U., Sch. Law, 1988, 90, 92, 94, 96, 98, U. Calif., Berkeley, 1991, Cornell U. Sch. Law, 1993, 95, 97; mem. Hague Permanent Ct. of Arbitration, 1989-93; chmn. panel of AsserColl., Europe, 1996—; mem. World Law Inst. Faculty, 1997—; internat. lectr. in field. Author: Great legal Handbook, 1972, 2d revised edition, 1977, International and Internal Conflict Rules, 1975, International Technology Transfer under Yugoslav Law, 1980, International Business Law-Selected topics, 1981, Private International Law, 1983, 3d revised edition, 1996; co-author: Settlement of Disputes by Arbitration, 1973, Joint Ventures, Long-Term Economic Cooperation with foreign firms, 1979, International Commercial Arbitration, 1999; contbr. articles to profl. jours.; editor in chief Letunk rev. for social sics., 1990—; corr. Netherlands Internat. Law Rev., 1985—. Mem. Serbian Acad. Scis. and Arts (corr.), Vojvodina Acad. Scis. and Arts, Hungarian Acad. Scis. (assoc.), Internat. Law Assn., Soc. de la Legislation Comparé, Assn. Alumni of Hague Acad. Internat. Law. Office: Ctrl European U Dept Legal, Nador Utca 9, 1051 Budapest Hungary

VÁRALLYAY, GYÖRGY, soil scientist, research educator; b. Debrecen, Hungary, July 17, 1935; s. György Várallyay and Erzsébet Pentelényi; m. Éva Skach, July 2, 1963; children: György, Éva. PhD, Agr. U., Gödöllö, Hungary, 1964, CSc, 1968, DSc, 1988. Soil surveyor Nat. Inst. Agrl. Quality Testing, Mosonmagyaróvár, Hungary, 1957-60; sci. assoc. Rsch. Inst. Soil Sci. & Agrl. Chemistry, Budapest, 1960-75, head soil sci. dept., 1976-96, inst. dir., 1981-96; prof. of soil sci. Gödöllö Agr. U., 1988—. Contbr. over 500 articles to profl. jours., book chpts. Decorated Order of Merit, Order of Work, comdrs. cross Prs. of State (Hungary); recipient Excellent Work for Water Mgmt. award Nat. Water Authority, Budapest, 1976, Michal Oczapowski medal Polish Acad. Sci., 1991. Mem. Internat. Union Soil Sci. (pres. commn. VI 1982-86), Hungarian Soil Sci. Soc. (pres. 1990-99), Hungarian Acad. Scis., Slovak Acad. Agrl. Sci. Home: Battai lépcsö 10, 1025 Budapest Hungary Office: RISSAC, Herman O 15, 1022 Budapest Hungary

VARANDAS, ANTONIO JOAQUIM DE CAMPOS, chemistry educator; b. Mata Curia, Anadia, Portugal, Sept. 19, 1947; s. Alfredo Cerveira and Lusitana Batista (de Campos) V.;m. Edite Maria Dias Carvalheira, Feb. 26, 1972; children: Antonio Miguel, Pedro Luis. Diploma in chem. engring., U. Oporto, Portugal, 1971; PhD in Theoretical Chemistry, U. Sussex, Eng., 1976. Aux. prof. U. Coimbra, Portugal, 1977-82, assoc. prof., 1982-88, prof., 1988—, head chemistry dept., 1989-92, chmn. chem. sci. coun., 1992-95; vis. rsch. scholar dept. chemistry Mpls. Supercomputer Inst., U. Minn., 1988; invited prof. Inst. Superior Ciencias y Tecnologia Nucleares, La Habana, 1998—. Co-author: Molecular Potential Energy Functions, 1984, Estrutura e Reactivadade Molecular, 1986, Introdução â Programação Fortran e Cálculo Cientifico, 1994; editor, reviewer Portuguese Jour. Chemistry, 1985-92; bd. editors Asian Jour. Spectroscopy, 1997—; mem. adv. editl. bd. Internat. Jour. Quantum Chemistry, 1999—; mem. adv. edtl. bd. Internat. Jour. Molecular Scis., 2000—; contbr. more than 180 articles to profl. jours. Lt. Portuguese Navy, 1978-79. NATO scholar, 1973-76, Brit. Coun. scholar, 1978; recipient Artur Malheiros prize for physics and chemistry Lisbon Acad. Scis., 1985. Mem. Am. Phys. Soc., European Phys. Soc. (bd. dirs. chem. physics sect. 1987-95), Royal Soc. Chemistry, N.Y. Acad. Scis., Portuguese Chem. Soc. (v.p. Lisbon chpt. 1985-89, Ferreira da Silva prize 1991), Portuguese Phys. Soc. Roman Catholic. Home: R Infanta D Maria 460 4E, 3030 Coimbra Portugal Office: U Coimbra, Dept de Quimica, 3049 Coimbra Portugal

VARATHARAJAN, JEBBAT KUMBANG WASSADE, chief executive officer; b. Kuala Lumpur, Malaysia, Sept. 11, 1960; s. Shanmugavelu and Kamala Devi (Mudaliar). BS with hons., 1983; M in Bus. Adminstrn., Asia Pacific U., New Zeland, 1996; D Medicine, Internat. U. Complementary Med, Sri Lanka, 1992; PhD, Bedfont Theol. Sem., U.K., 1985; D Sci., Internat. U. Complementary Med, Sri Lanka, 1993, PhD in Alternative Medicines, 1999. Chartered cons., U.K., accredited tng. cons., U.K., cert. bus. mgr., Germany, cert. profl. mgr., U.K., cert. tng. instr., U.S. Chief oper. officer Entreprenuers Cartel, Malaysia, 1988-90, Sys. Rsch. Agy., Malaysia, 1990-91; v.p. Sai Sadhana Satsang, Malaysia, 1990-95; vis. prof. Internat. U., Malaysia, 1995-97; pres. Whitefield Group Cos., Malaysia, 1997-98; chief exec. officer Hazrat Corp., Malaysia, 1999—. Office: Hazrat Cons Corp SDN BHD, GPO Box 13058, 50798 Kuala Lumpur Malaysia

VARDA, AGNES, screenwriter, director; b. Brussels, May 30, 1926; d. Eugène Jean and Christiane (Pasquet) V.; m. Jacques Demy, Jan. 8, 1962; children: Rosalie, Mathieu. Student, Coll. de Sète, U. Paris, Ecole du Louvre. Ofcl. photographer Théâtre Nat. Populaire, 1951-61; filmmaker, dir., 1954—. Films include: La Pointe Courte, 1954; Cléo de 5 a 7, 1961; Le Bonheur, 1964; Les Créatures, 1966; Lions Love, 1969; Nausicaa, 1970; Daguerréotypes, 1975; L'Une Chante l'Autre Pas, 1976; Mur Murs, 1980; Documenteur, 1981; Sans Toit ni Loi (Vagabond), 1985, Kung-Fu-Master, 1987, Jane B. par Agnès V., 1987, Jacquot de Nantes, 1990, Les demoiselles ont eu 25 ans, 1993, L'univers de Jacques Demy, 1993, Les Cent et une Nuits, 1994; short films include: O Saisons, O Chateaux, 1957; L'Opéra-Mouffe, 1958; Du Côté de la Côte, 1958; Salut les Cubains, 1963; Elsa la Rose, 1966; Uncle Yanco, 1967; Black Panthers, 1968; Réponse de Femmes, 1975; Plaisir d'Amour en Iran, 1976; Ulysse, 1982; Les Dites Cariatides, 1984, 7P. cuis., s. de b., 1985, T'as de beaux escaliers...tu sais, 1986. Decorated comdr. des Arts et des Lettres, comdr. de l;ordre du Mérite, officier de la Légion d'Honneur; recipient Prix Melies, 1962, Prix Louis Delluc, 1965, David Selznick award, 1965, Bronze Lion, Venice Festival, 1964, Golden Lion, 1985, Silver Bear, Berlin Festival, 1965, 1st prize Oberhausen, Popular Univs. Jury, 1970, Grand Prix Taormina, Sicily, 1977, Golden Plaque award, Chgo., 1993, French Cesar award, 1986.

VARDHAN, PEETA BOBBY, journalism educator; b. Nandiraju Thota, India, Aug. 25, 1958; s. Peeta Ankamma and Peeta Anasuya; m. Peeta Bobby, June 21, 1981; children: Chaitanya Deep, Sowjanya Roop. BCommerce, Arts Coll., Bapatla, India, 1981; MALitt., Nagarjuna U., Guntur, India, 1983; BJMC, Andhra U., Visakhapatnam, India, 1984; MJMC, Berhampur U., 1986. Lectr. Tutorial Coll., Bapatla, India, 1981-83; subeditor Andhra Bhoomi, Visakhapatnam, 1984-90; tchg. faculty Andhra U., Visakhapatnam, 1990-94, head & chmn., 1994—; dir. Info. & Pub. Rels., Visakhapatnam, 1995-96; cons. Indian Railways, 1995-97; performer All India Radio, 1995-96; investigator Ministry of Info. and Broadcasting, Ministry Human Resource Devel., Ministry Space, India. Editor: A.U. Srujana, 1990—; translator/author Dr. B.R. Ambedkar Works, 1995; editor: Farmabeat, 1996; author: World Chid, 1993. Mem. AMIC, CAE JAC, Pub. Rels. Soc. India (exec. 1991—). Avocations: literary crittcism, film appreciation, commn. councilling, writing for radio. Home: Pitapuram Beach Qrts, 530 003 Visakhapatnam India Office: Andhra U., Waltair, 530 003 Visakhapatnam Andhra, India

VARDHIREDDY, SUNKARA MANORAMA, physicist, researcher; b. Poona, India, May 21, 1963; d. Venkataveerareddy and Ashwarthamma (Narireddy) V.; m. Narendranadh Reddy Sunkara; children: Nishanth, Ashwitha. BSc, Fergusson Coll., Poona, 1983; MSc, Poona U., 1985, MPhil, 1987, PhD in Physics, 1990. Rsch. assoc. Indian Inst. Chem. Tech., Hyderabad, 1991-94, Quick Recruitment Scheme fellow, 1996-98, scientist C, 1998—; pool officer Coun. of Scientific and Inds. Rsch./Indian Inst. Chem. Tech., Hyderabad, 1994-96. Mem. MRSI (life). Hindu. Avocations: music, cooking, trekking. Home: TRU-3 IICT Quarters, Habshiguda, Hyderabad 500007, India Office: Indian Inst Chem Tech, Uppal Rd, Tarnaka, Hyderabad 500007, India

VARELA, MARTA B., city agency administrator, lawyer; b. Oakland, Calif., Sept. 9, 1953; d. Antonio Bouzas and Maria Josefa Varela Garcia; m. William Peter Barbeosch, Sept. 6, 1986. AB cum laude, Harvard U., 1977; JD, Fordham U., 1985, LLM in Internat. Trade, 1994. BBar: N.J. 1986, N.Y. 1989, D.C. 1990, U.S. Supreme Ct. 1996. Registered rep. E.F. Hutton & Co., N.Y.C., 1978-79; sales asst. Lehman Bros. Kuhn Loeb, N.Y.C., 1979-81; assoc. Seward & Kissel, N.Y.C., 1985-87, Carter, Ledyard & Milburn, N.Y.C., 1987-88; commn. chair N.Y.C. Commn. on Human Rights, 1994—; mem. Coun. on Fgn. Rels., N.Y.C., 1996—. Contbr. articles to profl. jours. Bd. dirs. Fountain House, N.Y.C., 1997—; mem. adv. bd. Ams. divsn. Human Rights Watch, N.Y.C., 1999-2000; mem. judicial screening com. First Dept., N.Y.C., 1998—. Office: Commn on Human Rights 40 Rector St Fl 10 New York NY 10006-1705

VARELAS, PANAYIOTIS, neurologist; b. Athens, Greece, Dec. 8, 1959; came to U.S., 1994; s. Nikolaos and Eleni Varela; m. Marianna Spanaki, Oct. 8, 1995. Med. diploma, U. Athens, 1983. Specialist in neurology Greek Ministry of Health. Neurology resident U. Athens Med. Sch., 1988-91; rsch. fellow Baylor Coll. Medicine, Houston, 1994; intern Meth. Hosp., Memphis, 1994-95; neurology resident Yale U. Sch. Medicine, New Haven, Conn., 1995-97, neurology chief resident, 1997-98, neurology instr., 1997-98; neurocritical care unit sr. fellow Johns Hopkins Hosp., Balt., 1998-00; internal medicine resident Athens Med. Sch., 1996, psychiatry resident, 1998; anesthesiology resident 251 Air Forces Hosp., Athens, 1994-95. Lt. Air Force of Greece, 1993-95. Hon. scholar U. Athens Med. Ctr., 1977-83, scholar NATO, 1994-95, Alexander Onassis Found., 1994-95. Mem. Am. Acad. Neurology (scholar for residents 1998), Am. Epilepsy Soc., Greek Neurol. Assn., Athens Med. Assn. Greek Orthodox. Avocation: chess. E-mail: pvarelas@mcw.edu.

VAREY, RICHARD JOHN, corporate communications consultant, educator; b. Beverley, Eng., Nov. 10, 1955. BSc in Scis., U. Newcastle-Upon-Tyne, U.K., 1980; MSc in Mgmt. Scis., Manchester (U.K.) Sch. Mgmt., 1990, PhD, 1996. With sales and mktg. dept. Thorn-EMI, 1980-86; freelance cons. Mktg. Mgmt. and Quality Mgmt., U.K., 1986-92; sr. lectr. mktg. Sheffield (Eng.) Bus. Sch., 1992-94; dir. BNFL Corp. Comm. unit/assoc. head rsch. The Grad. Sch. Mgmt., U. Salford, Eng., 1995—. Contbr. papers to profl. jours. Named Inst. Mgmt. Young Mgr. of Yr., 1991. Mem. Chartered Inst. Mktg. Avocations: reading, writing. Office: U Salford, The Mgmt Sch, Salford M5 4WT, England

VARGA, CSABA, biologist, educator; b. Debrecen, Hungary, May 21, 1959; s. József and Erszébet (Matkó) V.; m. Gabriella Ildikó Kövér, Aug. 2, 1980; children: Szabolcs, Orsolya Gyöngyi. BSc/MSc, L. Kossuth U., Debrecen, 1983, Dr.Universitatis, 1987, PhD in Biology, 1996; Candidate Sci. in Medicine, Hungarian Acad. Sci., Budapest, 1998; Dr.habil.med., U. Szegred, 2000. Microbiologist Biogal Pharm. Works, Debrecen, 1983-85, TRV Waterworks, Balmazujvaros, Hungary, 1985-90; asst. lectr. U. Med. Sch., Debrecen, 1990-96, asst. prof., 1996-99; assoc. prof. U. Med. Sch., Pécs, Hungary, 1999—; sec. Environ. Protection Com. Hajdu-Bihar County, Debrecen, 1992-96; part-time head tchr. Sch. Pub. Health, Debrecen, 1997-99. Pvt. first class Hungarian People's Army, 1977-78, 84. Recipient Pro Hygiene award Soc. Hungarian Hygienists', Budapest, 1998; Phare fellow European Union, Brescia, Italy, 1991, 93. Mem. European Environ. Mutagen Soc., Soc. Hungarian Human Geneticists, Hungarian Soc. Pub. Health. Avocations: classical music, traveling, literature, painting. Office: Dept Preventive Medicine, U Pécs, H-7643 Pécs Hungary

VARGA, DEBORAH TRIGG, music educator, entertainment company owner; b. Dayton, Ohio, Dec. 15, 1955; d. Ernest Cushman and Phyllis Ann (Martz) Trigg; m. Ali M. Abadi, Dec. 30, 1980 (div. July 1987); 1 child, Darren Vincent; m. Richard Charles Varga, June 25, 1994; 1 child, Kathryn Lenore. B of Music Edn. in Violin Performance, Converse Coll., Spartanburg, S.C., 1977. Music educator Seminole County Sch. Bd., Sanford, Fla., 1978-92, Howard County Pub. Schs., Ellicott City, Md., 1993—; co-founder, co-owner Gold Star Entertainement, Inc., Orlando, Fla., 1984-86, Ctr. Stage Entertainment, Inc., Maitland, Fla., 1986-92; owner Varga Music Entertainement, Highland, Md., 1993—. Composer children's songs, 1990—, Martin Luther King Tribute, Human Rights Commn., Howard County, 1997-00. Mem. Am. Fedn. Musicians, Music Educators Nat. Conf., Am. String. Tchrs. Assn., Nat. Orch. Assn. Avocations: waterskiing, whitewater rafting, tennis, golf, reading. Home: 13464 Allnutt Ln Highland MD 20777-9743

VARGA, JANOS MIKLOS, molecular immunologist, biochemist; b. Nagyoroszi, Hungary, June 19, 1935; arrived in Austria, 1988; s. Janos Varga and Maria Toth; m. Eva Pierrou (div. 1989); children: Paul, Elisabet. Diploma in chem. engring., U. Tech., Budapest, 1959; PhD, Eotvosl. U., Budapest, 1965. Cert. chem. engr. Rsch. assoc. Drug Rsch. Ctr., Budapest, 1960-67, Royal Inst. Tech., Stockholm, 1967-69; sect. head Pharmacia Co., Uppsala, Sweden, 1969-71; asst. prof. Yale U., New Haven, 1973-76, assoc. prof., sr. scientist, 1976-84; program dir. NIH-Nat. Cancer Inst., Bethesda, Md., 1984-87; prof. U. Innsbruck, Austria, 1988—; cons. Epipharm, Linz, Austria, 1988-95. Patentee in field. Recipient Career Devel. award NIH, 1976. E-mail: jmv@tci001.uibk.ac.at. Home: Loaweg 7, A-6091 Goetzens Austria Office: Dept Theoretical Chem, U Innsbruck, A-6020 Innsbruck Austria

VARGA, NICHOLAS, historian, archivist, retired educator; b. Elizabeth, N.J., Sept. 13, 1925; s. Joseph and Anna (Buchko) V.; m. Margaret Joan Skinner, Sept. 8, 1951; children: Deidre Kayne, Damian Guy, Colin Pierce. BS cum laude, Boston Coll., Chestnut Hill, Mass., 1951, MA, 1952; PhD with honors, Fordham U., 1960. Instr. history Loyola Coll., Balt., 1955-59, asst. prof., 1959-62, assoc. prof., 1962-66, prof., 1966-92, chmn. dept., 1964-68, prof. emeritus, 1992—, coll. archivist, 1976—. Author: Baltimore's Loyola, 1990. Advisor Jo Tydings Election Campaign, Balt., 1964, 70; bd. dirs. UN Assn. Md., Balt., 1966-70; pres. Woodbourne Sch. PTA, Balt., 1967-68; mem. Howard County Bicentennial Com., Ellicott City, Md., 1974-77. Publ. grantee Md. Hist. Soc., 1989. Mem. AAUP (founder, pres. Loyola Coll. chpt. 1966-69), Am. Hist. Assn. (interviewer Cate report 1966), Am. Cath. Hist. Assn. (nominating com. 1975-78), Soc. Am. Archivists, Mid-Atlantic Region Archivists Conf., Alpha Sigma Nu (hon.). Democrat. Byzantine Catholic. Office: Loyola Coll 4501 N Charles St Baltimore MD 21210-2601

VARGA, THOMAS, materials science educator; b. Szombathely, Hungary, Sept. 1, 1935; s. Emil and Carola (Klein) V.; m. Helga Caroline Kirnbauer, Sept. 8, 1962 (dec. Dec. 1984); m. Gerda Marie-Luise Hunold, July 30, 1986. Mech. engring. diploma, Tech. U., Vienna, Austria, 1960; D in Tech. Sci., Swiss Fed. Inst. Tech., Zürich, Switzerland, 1966. Group leader Sulzer Bros. Ltd., Winterthur, Switzerland, 1966-78; lectr. Swiss Fed. Inst. Tech., Zürich, 1972—; full prof. U. Tech., Vienna, 1979—; expert Swiss Fed. Nuclear Safety Inspectorate HSK, 1974-98; dep. head Inst. for Testing and Rsch. in Materials Tech., 1979—. Author: Eisenwerkstoffe, 1972; contbr. numerous tech. articles to profl. jours. Fellow Am. Soc. for Metals; mem. ASTM, Austrian Soc. for Materials Tech., German Welding Soc., German Soc. Materials Rsch. and Testing, Swiss Soc. Materials Tech., Hungarian Acad. Engring. (hon.). Lutheran. Avocations: literature, travelling, fossils. Office: U of Tech Vienna, Karlsplatz 13, Vienna Austria

VARGA, ZSOLT ANTAL, vascular surgeon; b. Budapest, Hungary, Mar. 8, 1955; s. István and Maria (Pászty) V. MD, Semmelweiss U. of Medicine, 1982; PhD, Hungarian Acad. Scis., 1995. Fellow in gen. surgery Postgrad. U. Medicine, Budapest, 1986, fellow in vascular surgery, 1989; asst. surgeon Robert Cmty. Hosp., Budapest, 1982-87; asst. vascular surgeon Ctrl. Mil. Hosp., Budapest, 1987-89; vascular surgeon dept. cardiovascular surgery Semmelweiss U. Medicine, Budapest, 1989-91; rsch. registrar, hon tutor dept. surgery U. Bristol, Eng., 1991-93; asst. lectr. dept. cardiovascular surgery Haynal U. for Health Scis., Budapest, 1993-94; dep. chmn., chief vascular surgeon Zala County Hosp., Hungary, 1994-97; lectr., cons. dept. surgery Pécs U., Hungary, 1999—. Author articles in vascular surgery and autotransfusion in surgery. Mem. European Soc. Vascular Surgery, Hungarian Soc. Surgeons, Hungarian Soc. Angiology, Hungarian Soc. Cardiac Surgeons, Surg. Rsch. Soc., Autransfusion Spl. Interest Group. Avocations: big game hunting, horse riding, wine tasting. Home: 6 Kacsoh P u, 7624 Pécs Hungary Office: II Dept Surgery Pécs U, Faculty Medicine 2 Rakoczi, 7623 Pécs Hungary

VARGAS, ANTONIO PINHO, composer, musician, educator; b. Porto, Portugal, Aug. 15, 1951; s. Antonio Alberto Pinho Vargas Silva and Isaura Cunha Faria; m. Ana Mafalda Castro; children: Ana Madalena Leite de Castro Pinho Vargas, João Antonio Leite de Castro Pinho Vargas. Grad. in history, U. Porto, 1983; grad. in piano, Porto Conservatory, 1986; grad. in composition, Rotterdam Conservatory, 1991. Tchr. Higher Mus. Sch., Lisbon, Portugal, 1992—; cons. Fundação Serralves, Porto, 1994. Composer various chamber music pieces and orch. works, 1983—, (film music) Tempos Difíceis, 1986 (Best Film Music award IPC 1989), Cinco Dias, Cinco Noites, 1996 (Best Film Music award Granado 1996), (operas) èdipo, 1996, Ôs Dias Levantados. Decorated comendator Order Infante D. Henrique. E-mail: aspirahovargas@mail.telepac.pt. Office: Av India 30-B, 1300 Lisbon Portugal

VARGAS, JORGE ANTONIO, mathematician, educator; b. Canals, Córdoba, Argentina, Sept. 20, 1949; s. Antonio Alfonso V. and Lucia Ines Sanchez; m. Pilar Elsa Ristorto, 1973; children: Irene, Lara. Licentiate in Math., U. Córdoba (Argentina), 1972; PhD, Columbia U., 1977. Postdoctoral fellow Inst. Advanced Study, Princeton, N.J., 1977-78; prof. titular plenario U. Córdoba (Argentina), 1978—; vice dean Faculty of Math., Astronomy and Physics, Córdoba, Argentina, 1992-94; guest Internat. Ctr. for Theoretical Physics, Trieste, Italy, 1991-92, U. Brasilia, Brazil, 1991; sec. Math. Union of Argentina, 1994-97. Contbr. articles to profl. jours. Mem. Jockey Club (treas. 1985-87, 89-91). Home: A Contte 507, 5016 Cordoba 1, Argentina Office: FAMAF, Ciudad Universitaria, 5000 Cordoba Argentina

VARGAS, JOSE ISRAEL, academic administrator; b. Paracatu, Minias Gerais, Jan. 9, 1928. BS in Chemistry, Fed. U. Minias Gerais, 1952; PhD, U. Cambridge, 1959. Dir. Inst. for Rsch. in Radioactivity, 1962; mem. Nat. Nuclear Energy Commn., 1964; lab. rschr. U. Grenoble, France, 1965-72; chmn. Tech. Ctr. of Minas Gerais, 1975-79; v.p. UN Adv. Com. on Tech. Devel., 1980-85; prof. Brazilian Ctr. for Rsch. in Physics, 1988-97; vis. prof. phys. chemistry Fed. U. Minas Gerais, 1965-67; rsch. leader Atomic Energy Commn., Paris, 1966-72; v.p. exec. coun. UNESCO, Paris, 1983-87. Contbr. articles to profl. jours. State sec. for sci. and tech., Minas Gerais, 1977-79, sec. for indsl. tech., ministry of industry and trade, 1979-84, min. of state for sci. and tech., 1992-94, min. of sci. and tech., 1994-98. Mem. Brazilian Acad. Scis. (v.p. 1984—), 3d World Acad. Scis. (v.p. 1988—, pres.). Office: Ministry Sci & Tech Third World Acad Scis, Via Beirut 6 PO Box 586, 34100 Trieste Italy*

VARGAS, VERA MARIA FERRÃO, biologist; b. Venâncio Aires, Brazil, Aug. 15, 1948; d. Antenor Silva and Petronilla (Marx) F.; m. Luiz Telmo Romor, Oct. 6, 1973; children: André, Cláudia. Diploma, Fed. U. Rio Grande Sul, Porto Alegre, 1973, MS in Genetics, 1978, PhD in Genetics with high praise, 1992. Elem. tchr. Padre Léo, Porto Alegre, Brazil, 1969-70; organic pollution rschr. State Found. for Environ. Protection, Porto Alegre, 1980-82, rschr. in environ. mutagens, 1983—, rsch. coord., 1984—, head rsch., 1992—; prof. in genetics Fed. U. Rio Grande Sul, 1992-93, prof. in genetics and molecular biol., 1998—; prof. zoology Pontifícia Catholic U. Rio Grande Sul, 1998—; sci. initiation staff Nat. Rsch. Coun. Porto Alegre, 1971-73, postgrad. fellow, 1975-78, 90-92, rsch. fellow, 1993—; assoc. rschr. Fed. U. Rio Grande Sul, 1983-92. Contbr. articles to profl. jours. Recipient 1st place award Sci. and Tech. Devel. Support Program-Fin. Co. for Studies and Projects, 1993, 97. Mem. Brazilian Mutagenic Soc. (treas. 1991-93, v.p. 1998-99, pres. 2000—), Genetic Soc., Rsch. Insts. Orgn. (v.p. 1999—). Roman Catholic. Avocations: reading, walking, music, swimming. Home: Palmeira Ave 644, 90470300 Porto Alegre Brazil Office: Fundação Estadual de Proteção Ambiental, Salvador França Ave 1707, 90690000 Porto Alegre RS, Brazil

VARGAS-ZAPATA, RUBEN ANTONIO, physics educator; b. Barranquilla, Colombia, May 28, 1940; s. Miguel Antonio and Olga (Zapata) Vargas; m. Rosa Navia, Nov. 25, 1965; children: Reinaldo, Olga Stella. BSc, U.P.T.C., Tunja, 1962; MSc in Physics, U. P.R., 1969, U. Ill., 1974; PhD in Physics, U. Ill., 1977. Physics tchr. Buenaventura (Colombia) High Sch., 1962-65; lectr. physics U. Valle, Cali, Colombia, 1965-67, 69-73, prof. physics, 1977—. Mem. Am. Phys. Soc., Am. Inst. Physics, Internat. Soc. for Solid State Ionics, Colombian Phys. Soc., Sigma Xi. Home: Carrera 60 No 11B-41, Cali Valle, Colombia Office: U Valle Physics Dept, Apartado Aereo 25360, Cali Valle, Colombia

VARGHA, ANDRÁS, psychology educator; b. Budapest, Hungary, Nov. 29, 1949; s. Domokos György and Domokosné (Stolte) V.; m. Anna Borbély, June 28, 1980; children: Flóra Zsuzsanna, György Domokos. MS in Math., Eötvös Loránd U., Budapest, 1974, MA in Psychology, 1976, PhD in Psychology, 1981, CSc, 1994. Asst. prof. psychology Eötvös Loránd U., 1975-82, assoc. prof., 1982-94, sr. lectr., 1994—; vis. prof. U. N.Mex., Albuquerque, 1996. Author: A Guide to Applied Psychological Statistics, Vol. 1, 1978, Vol. 2, 1981, Vol. 3, 1983, The Tables of the Hungarian Rorschach Standard, 1989, The Psychometry of the Szondi Test, 1994, The MiniStat Statistical Program Package Version 3.2, 1999, Mathematical Statistics with Applications in Psychology, Linguistics, and Biology, 2000; assoc. editor Hungarian Rev. Psychology, 1991-98; also articles. Named Excellent Educator, Hungarian Min. Culture, 1985; rsch. grantee Hungarian Acad. Scis., 1987, 91, 95, Fulbright grantee, Albuquerque, 1996, Rsch. Support Scheme of the Open Soc. Found., 1998. Mem. Hungarian Psychol. Assn. Calvanist. Avocations: music, excursions, travel. Office: Eötvös Lorand U, Izabella u 46, H-1064 Budapest Hungary

VARGHESE, GEORGE, physician, educator; b. India, Aug. 11, 1944; came to U.S., 1971; m. Molly Varghese; children: Smitha, Sapna, Martin. MD, St. John's Med. Coll., Bangalore, Ind., 1969. Diplomate Am. Bd. Phys. Medicine and Rehab., Am. Bd. Electrodiagnostic Medicine. Intern Nazareth Hosp., Phila., 1972; resident N.Y. Med. Coll., N.Y.C., 1973-75, rehab. med. instr., 1976-77; asst. prof. rehab. medicine U. Kans. Med. Ctr., Kansas City, 1977-81, assoc. prof. rehab. medicine, 1981-86, asst. dean for student affairs, 1999—, prof. rehab. medicine, 1986—; vis. prof. Med. Coll. Trivandru, India, 1980, Nat. Spinal Injury Ctr., Stoke Mandeville, London, Eng., 1985; invited examiner Am. Bd. Phys. Medicine and Rehab., 1982-98; presenter in field. Author: (with others) Rehabilitation of Burn Patients, 1984, Orthotics et cetera, 1983, Rehabilitation Management of Amputees, 1983, Traumatic Brain Injury, 1992; contbr. articles to profl. jours. including Jour. Kans. Med. Soc., Orthotics and Prosthetics, Strasibmus, Paraplegia. Recipient Appreciation award Kans. chpt. Nat. Head Injury Assn., 1984; named Miracle Worker Kansas City Mag., 1983; grantee Internat. Latex Corp., Kans. U., Knit-Rite Corp., Norwich-Eaton Labs. Mem. AMA, Am. Spinal Injury Assn., Am. Assn. Electrodiagnostic Medicine, Am. Acad. Phys. Medicine and Rehab., Assn. Acad. Physiatrists, Kans. Med. Soc., Wyandotte/Johnson County Med. Soc. Office: U Kans Med Ctr 3901 Rainbow Blvd Kansas City KS 66160-0001

VARGHESE, MARIAMMA, academic administrator; b. Kottayam, Kerala, India, Apr. 5, 1941; d. Ittiavira and Saramma (Punnen) Mathew; m. Abraham Cheeran Varghese, Jan. 11, 1970; children: Vivek Abraham,

Mathew Abraham. BSc, Lady Irwin Coll., India; MSc, M.S. U., India; PhD, Iowa State U. Lectr. M.S. U., 1968-69, reader, 1969-71; reader Jadaupa U., India, 1971-81; prof. S.N.D.T. Women's U., Mumbai, India, 1982-84, dir. postgrad. studies, rsch. in H-Sc, 1987-96, vice chancellor, 1996—; prin. S.V.T. Coll., India, 1984-87; dir. CFBD Consserve Tesly Lab, India, 1990—. Author: Women in Modern India, 1978, 3d edit., 1980, Women Administrators in Education, 1987, Resources Management, 1984. Recipient Best Tchr. award Maharashtra Govt., 1989, award Sahyoy Found., 1999; named Hon. Col., Def. Ministry, New Delhi, 1996. Mem. Homesan Assn. India (pres. 1994-99), Nat. Soc. Clean Air. Avocations: reading, music, swimming. Home: Gurukul, SNDT Annex 6th Fl, Mumbai 400 020, India Office: SNDT Women's U, 1 Nathibai Thackersey Rd, Churchgate Mumbai 400 020, India

VARGHESE, PARAMBETH GEORGE, production engineer, executive; b. Trichur, Kerala, India, Mar. 19, 1944; s. Parambeth Vareed George and Panikulam Kunjipalu Mariamma; m. Parmabeth Varghese Pulikan Thankamma, Jan. 9, 1972; 1 child, Sindhu. B in Engring., Regional Engring. Coll., Warangal, India, 1965. Lectr. Govt. Engring. Coll., Trivandrum, India, 1965-66; probationary engr. Hindusthan Aeronautics Ltd., Bangalore, 1966-68, prodn. engr., 1968-74, sr. mgr., 1974-86, chief mgr., 1986-96, dep. gen. mgr., 1996—; chief prodn. engr. advanced light helicopter Hindusthan Aeronautics Ltd., Bangalore, 1987-89. Pres. Cath. Assn., Bangalore, 1983-90. Mem. Aero. Soc. India (assoc.), Indian Inst. Material Mgmt. Roman Catholic. Avocations: music, sports, pets, reading. Home: 115 AECS, 1st Stage 15th Cross, Sanjay Nagar 560094, India Office: Hindusthan Aero Ltd, Helicopter Design Bur, Bangalore india

VARGHESE, ZAC, biochemist, immunologist; b. Kalayapuram, India, July 21, 1938; s. Gee Varghese Kanisseril and Aleyamma V.; m. Elizikutty Cherian, Nov. 25, 1963; 1 child, Sageh Zac-Varghese. BS, U. Kerala, India, 1959; B of Pharm., Andhra U., India, 1963; MS, U. Surrey, England, 1969, U. Brunel, England, 1972; PhD, U. London, 1979. Rsch. asst. CMC Vellore, India, 1962-63; biochemist Royal Free Hosp., London, 1964-83, cons. biochemist, 1983—, dir. tissue typing lab., 1968—, assoc. dir. rsch. unit, 1979—; dir. Internat. Inst. Scientific Acad. Collaboration, 1998—; vis. prof. SIUT, Karachi, Pakistan, 1996. Fellow Royal Coll. Pathologists. Avocations: writing, meditation. Office: Royal Free UCL Sch Medicine, Pond St, London NW3 2QG, England

VARGHESE, ZUBIN ABRAHAM, computer vision engineer, consultant; b. Alleppey, Kerala, India, Jan. 29, 1962; s. Abraham and Annie (Abraham) V.; m. Rachel George, June 24, 1994; children: Ratan Abraham, Nithin George. B Tech. with honors, Indian Inst. Tech., Kharagpur, 1986; MS, U. Mass., 1989; PhD, Pa. State U., 1991. Registered profl. engr., New Brunswick, Can. Dir. rsch. and devel. Lizotte Cons. Ltd., Green River, N.B., Can., 1992—; project leader rsch. and devel. Machine Vison Inspection of Seams of Food Cans, 1997, Computer Vision Inspection and Grading of Herring Roe, 1998. Mem. Soc. Mfg. Engrs., Am. Soc. Agrl. and Biol. Engrs., Internat. Soc. Optical Engring. Avocations: tennis, stock market, politics. Home: 37 Sormany, Edmunston, NB Canada E3V 1Y3 Office: Lizotte Cons Ltd, 4 Montreuil St, Green River, NB Canada E7C 2M6

VARI, SANDOR GEORGE, physician, research scientist; b. Turkeve, Hungary; came to the U.S., 1988; s. George Peter and Rozalia Roza (Balpataki) V.; m. Julianna Irma Gaal, Dec. 23, 1982; 1 child, Judith. MD, Semmelweis Med. U., Budapest, Hungary, 1978; Surgeon, Postgrad. Sch. Medicine, Budapest, Hungary, 1985. Resident Semmelweis Med. U., Budapest, Hungary, 1978-85, asst. prof. surgery, 1985-90; rsch. fellow Cedars-Sinai Med. Ctr., L.A., 1988-89, rsch. scientist, 1990—; vis. scientist Found. Rsch. Tech., Hellas, Heraklion, Greece, 1994, Laser-und Medizin Tech., Berlin, 1995, 96, 97, 98; spkr. USA Fulbright Assn., Washington, 1993-94; invited ind. expert European Commn., 1996. Contbr. articles to profl. jours. Founder Hungoptika Hungarian chpt. Internat. Soc. Optical Engring., 1989-90, Hungarian Fulbright Assn. Fulbright scholar Cedars-Sinai Med. Ctr., 1989-90; small bus. innovation rsch. grant NIH and Dept. of Def., 1991, 93-97; recipient numerous grants NIH, Dept Defense, European Union Cmty. R & D. Mem. Am. Fedn. Clin. Rsch., Am. Soc. Laser Medicine Surgery (chair conf. 1991-93), Internat. Soc. Optical Engring. (chair conf. 1989), Internat. Biomed. Optical Soc. (chair conf. 1989, 93, 96-99), Internat. Soc. Laser Surgery Med. (chair conf. 1991, 95), European Laser Assn. (chair conf. 1989), Hungarian Coll. Surgeons. Achievements include patent for fluorescence based biopsy needle, 1994, for biodistribution of fluorescence substances, 1995, for spectroscopy of blood perfusion, 1995, for fiber-optic endodontic apparatus, 1996, for spectroscopic burn injury evalutaion, 1997; research and applications of optics and photonics; research in spectral characterization of cervical cancer, multi dimensional spectroscopy in pathology, spectral topography microscope for histopathology evaluation; research and technology development in health telematics; development of optical imaging and integrated telematics applications for healthcare. E-mail: vari@cshs.org. Office: Cedars-Sinai Med Ctr Laser Rsch and Tech Devel Ctr 650 S San Vicente Blvd Los Angeles CA 90048-4620 Address: PO Box 17623 Encino CA 91416-7623

VARIAS, ANDREW GEORGE, research engineer, consultant; b. Vrodades, Chios, Greece, Nov. 12, 1962; s. George Andrew and Christina (Kasidoni) V.; m. Evangelia Kapetanaki, June 14, 1987; children: Christina, Chrysoula. Diploma, Nat. Tech. U. Athens, Greece, 1986; MSc, Brown U., 1988, PhD, 1991. Cert. engr. From rsch. asst. to rsch. assoc. Brown U., Providence, 1988-92; assoc. rsch. scientist Shell Rsch., Arnhem, The Netherlands, 1993-94, Amsterdam, The Netherlands, 1994-95; pvt. practice Athens, 1996—; instr. Hellenic Naval Acad., Piraeus, Greece, 1997-99; lectr. Malmö U., Sweden, 2000—. Contbr. articles to profl. jours. Student scholar Ioannis Pateras Found., Nat. Found. Scholarships, Athens, 1983, 84-85, Grad. Studies scholar Bodossaki Found., Athens, 1987-88, Brown U. fellow, Providence, 1987. Mem. European Structural Integrity Soc., Tech. Chamber Greece (Student award 1983-85), Greek Assn. Computational Mechanics, Sigma Xi. Avocations: attending/reading drama, fishing. E-mail: varias@hol.gr and andreas.varias@ts.mah.se. Home and Office: Makedonias 17, 141 21 Neon Iraklion Athens, Greece

VARIK, MATTI, sculptor; b. Leisi, Saaremaa, Estonia, Mar. 2, 1939; s. Hans and Magda Helene (Vaino) V.; m. Urve Salumaa, Oct. 1, 1966; children: Kerttu, Kattri, Martti. Degree, Tallinn (Estonia) Art Inst., 1964. Tchr. Tallinn Art U., 1964-66; sculptor Estonian Artists' Soc., Tallinn, 1966-83; tchr. art Estonian Art Acad., Tallinn, 1983-91, docent, 1991—; cons. Stone Sculpture Symposium, Berlin, 1984, Kankanpaa, Finland, 1995. Prin. works include Lullaby, 1966, Silence 1978, Message, 1980, Unicorn, 1986, Monument Gate of Freedom, Stockholm, 1994. Recipient award Latvian Artists' Union, 1980, 7th Internat. Small Sculpture Exhbn., Budapest, Hungary, 1987. Mem. Estonian Artists' Soc. Home: E Bornhöhe 34, 11911 Tallinn Estonia Office: Estonian Art Acad, Raja 11 A, EE 0026 Tallinn Estonia

VARILO, TEPPO TAPIO, geneticist, researcher; b. Helsinki, Finland, Nov. 17, 1961; s. Esko Tapio Varilo and iris-Lilja Lassila; m. Susanna Kati Teronen, July 1, 1988; children: Miro, Vilma., Reko. MD, U. Tampere, Finland, 1988; PhD, U. Helsinki, 1999. Rsch. scientist dept. human genetics Nat. Pub. Health Inst., Helsinki, 1994—. Contbr. articles to profl. jours. Grantee Finnish Cultural Found., 1997, Finnish Med. Found., 1997. Office: Nat Pub Health Inst Hum Mol, Genet Mannerheimintie 166, 00300 Helsinki Finland

VARIS, ANNA-LIISA, entomologist; b. Antrea, Finland, Aug. 25, 1925; d. Onni Ivar and Eeva Liisa (Kiesi) Tuomola; m. Eero Aulis Varis, Dec. 18, 1955; children: Liisa, Olli, Heikki. MS in Agriculture, U. Helsinki, 1953, DSc, 1972. Researcher Agrl. Rsch. Ctr., Vantaa, Finland, 1953-74; prof. U. Helsinki, 1974-90, prof. emeritus, docent, 1990—; mem. Nat. Rsch. Coun. for Agr. and Forestry, 1983-88. Chief editor: Annales Entomologici Fennici, Acta Entomologica Fennica, 1977-86; co-author: Diseases and Enemies of Honey Bees, 3d edit., 1993. Grantee Acad. Finland, U. Helsinki, Finnish Cultural Found. Fellow Royal Entomol. Soc. London; mem. Finnish Entomol. Soc. (Badge of merit 1997), Finnish Agrl. Soc., Nordic Agrl. Researchers (v.p. Finnish sect. 1985-87), Soc. Environ. Sci., Order White Rose Finland (knight first class 1973), Plant Protection Soc. Finland (Badge of merit 1985, v.p. 1984-86, pres. 1987-89, standing coms. European Congresses of Entomology 1997), European Sci. Journalists, N.Y. Acad. Scis. Home: Sointeentie 11, FIN-04310 Tuusula Finland Office: U Helsinki, U Helsinki Dept Applied Zoo, PO Box 27, FIN00014 Helsinki Finland

VARIS, P. TAPIO, media studies educator; b. Ruokolahti, Finland, June 17, 1946; s. Pekka Jeremias and Margareta (Hanninen) V.; m. Riitta Liisa Pellinen, Aug. 24, 1968; children: Sunnu Aulikki, Pekka Juhani. MA, U. Tampere, Finland, 1969, lic. in social scis., 1972, PhD, 1973. Instr., rschr. U. Tampere, 1969-72, lectr., 1973; lectr., rschr. Acad. Finland, Helsinki, 1974-78; dir. Peace Rsch. Isnt., Tampere, 1979-84; rector U. for Peace, San Jose, Costa Rica, 1986-89; dir. U. Indsl. Arts, Helsinki, 1990-92; prof., dir. faculty of arts U. Lapland, Rovaniemi, Finland, 1992-94; vis. prof. U. Salzbur, Austria, 1985; reader U. Tampere, 1973—, prof., chair, 1997—; reader U. Helsinki, 1977—; rsch. fellow Finnis Inst. Internat. Affairs, Helskinki, 1986; sr. rsch. fellow U. Art and Design, 1994—; cons. Wider/UNU Helsinki, 1993—; UNESCO chmn. Autonomous U. Barcelona, 1996—; mem. faculty European Peace Univ. Ctr.; acting pres. Global Univ. System, 1999—; expert European Parliament, 2000. Author: International Flow of TV Program, 1985; co-author: Television Traffic-A One Way Street, 1974, Transnational Communication, 1982; editor: Peace and Communication, 1986, The Media of the Knowledge Age, 1995; editor-in-chief Current Rsch. on Peace, 1977-84. Chmn. subcom. Finnis Unesco Commn., 1978-86; expert mem. disarmament com. Fgn. Min., 1981-87; speaker spl. session on disarmament UN Gen. Assembly, N.Y., 1982, 88; bd. dirs. Info. Ctr., Ch. of Finland, 1990—; mem. com. learning techs. Min. Edn., 1992—. Mem. Assn. Progressive Sci. in Finland (editorial bd. 1992—). Evangelical Lutheran. Avocations: accordian playing, mushrooms and forests, old documents, leaflets. Home: Immolantie 25 C, 00780 Helsinki Finland Office: U Tampere, PO Box 607, 33101 Tampere Finland

VARJU, DEZSOE, biologist, educator; b. Gasztony, Hungary, May 22, 1932; arrived in Germany, 1956; s. Johann and Anna (Hirschmann) V.; m. Heide Agner. Diploma Physics, U. Budapest, Hungary, 1956; PhD, U. Goettingen, Germany, 1958; univ. tchr., U. Tuebingen, Germany, 1967. Rsch. asst., rsch. assoc. Max Planck Inst., Tuebingen, 1958-59, 60-68; postdoctoral fellow Calif. Tech., Pasadena, 1959-60; prof. U. Tuebingen, 1968-97, prof. emeritus, 1997—. Author: Systems Theory, 1977, Mit den Ohren Sehen und den Beinen Hören, 1998; editor: Localisation and Orientation in Biology and Engineering, 1984; co-editor: Biological Cybernetics Jour., 1993; mem. adv. bd. Jour. Comp. Physiology. Avocations: gardening, skiing, tennis. Office: U Tuebingen, Auf der Morgenstelle 28, 72076 Tuebingen Germany

VARKEY, THATHOTHE ABRAHAM, laboratory director; b. Cochin, Kerala, India, Sept. 6, 1949; s. Thathothe Varkey Abraham and Thathothe Abraham Mariam; m. Sarada Varkey Unni, Oct. 21, 1980; children: Sujith, Sudheer. BSc with honors, All India Inst. Med. Scis., New Delhi, 1975. Lab. technician Chistian Med. Coll. and Hosp., Vellore, India, 1969-71, Govt. Health Svcs., Pondichery, India, 1971-72; tech. asst. U. Coll. Med. Scis., New Delhi, 1976-78; med. technologist Aramco, Dharan, Saudi Arabia, 1978-86; sr. med. technologist Aramco, Abqaiq, Saudi Arabia, 1986-90; dir. Medilab, Cochin, India, 1992—. Pres. Y's Mens Club, Ernakulam, India, 1995; sec. Cochin chpt. Alzheimer's and Related Disorders Soc. India, 1997—; treas. Environment Monitoring Forum, Cochin, 1998. Mem. Am. Assn. Clin. Chemistry, Kerala Pvt. Med. Technician's Assn. (pres. 1998—), Lions (treas. Ernakulam chpt. 1997), Lotus Club. Orthodox Syrian Christian. Avocations: swimming, cards, public speaking, reading. Home: 44/1889 Asoka Rd, Cochin 682017, India Office: Medilab, Doraiswamy Iyer Rd, Cochin 682035, India

VÁRKONYI-KÓCZY, ANNAMÁRIA RITA, electrical engineer, educator, researcher; b. Budapest, Hungary, Apr. 18, 1957; d. László Romulus and Zsuzsanna Ildikó (Nagy) Kóczy; m. Péter Ferenc Várkonyi, July 2, 1977; children: Péter László, Dániel Tamás, Teréz Anna. MSEE, Tech. U. Budapest, Hungary, 1981, MSMET, 1983, PhD, 1996. Rsch. fellow Rsch. Inst. Telecom., Budapest, 1981-87; rsch. assoc. dept. engring. mechanics Tech. U. Budapest, 1987-91, asst. prof. dept. measurement and instrument engring., 1991-96, sr. asst. prof. dept. measurement and instrument engring., 1996-98, assoc. prof. dept. measurement and info. sys., 1998—; corr. Math. and Phys. Jour. for Secondary Schs., Hungary, 1976-81; cons. Scripta Pub. Co., U.S., 1984-89; tchr. computer sci. Application Ctr. Computer Sci., Budapest, 1992—; head subdept. for univ. publs. Tech. U. Budapest, 1996-97, dep. dir. sci. and rsch. affairs, Tech. U. Budapest, 1998—. Co-author: Neural Networks and Its Applications (in Hungarian), 1995, Operating Systems--An Engineering Approach (in Hungarian), 2000; editor: Technical University of Budapest (in Hungarian), 1996; co-editor: (with K. Koudovosi) Operating Systems-An Engineering Approach (in Hungarian), 1999; contbr. articles to profl. jours. Founding mem. Márton Áron Soc., Hungary, 1987, Assn. Hungarian Nobility, 1994; oblata Ordonis Sancti Benedicti, Hungary, 1989. Mem. IEEE (sr.), EURASIP, N.Y. Acad. Scis., John von Neumann Hungarian Computer Soc., Measurement and Automation Soc., Hungarian Fuzzy Assn. (vice chair). Christian Democrat. Roman Catholic. Avocations: collecting books, oceanology, tennis, bridge, wind surfing. Home: Ady Endre 113, H-1221 Budapest Hungary Office: Budapest U Tech and Econs, Muegyetem rkp 9, H-1521 Budapest Hungary

VARMA, ANOOP RANJAN, neurologist, researcher; b. Chandausi, U.P., India, July 22, 1961; arrived in U.K., 1993; s. Paras Nath and Chhabishree (Bannerji) V. MBBS, SMS Med. Sch., Jaipur, India, 1984, MD, 1988; DM, Sree Chitra Med. Inst., Trivandrum, India, 1992. Jr. resident medicine SMS Med. Sch., Jaipur, 1985-88; sr. resident neurology Sree Chitra Med. Inst., Trivandrum, 1989-92; sr. registrar neurology Jaslok Hosp., Bombay, 1992-93; clin. rsch. fellow Nat. Hosp. Queen Sq., London, 1993-94; clin. fellow Manchester (Eng.) Royal Infirmary, 1994-95, rsch. fellow, 1995-2000; specialist registrar neurology dept. Royal Preston Hosp., Fulwood, Eng., 1995-2000; specialist registrar dept. neurology Hope Hosp., Salford, Eng., 2000—; rschr. in neuroimaging in dementias; cognitive and behavioral neurology. Contbr. articles to profl. jours. Recipient SMS Gold medal U. Rajasthan, India, 1984, Raghu Sinha Gold medal U. Rajasthan, 1988, Bhamasa award Mewar Found., Udaipur, India, 1984; Dr. P.N. Berry scholar High Commn. India, London, 1993. Mem. Royal Coll. Physicians, Manchester Med. Soc., Brit. Neuropsychiat. Assn., Internat. Brain Rsch. Orgn., Assn. Brit. Neurologists. Avocations: reading, hill walking. Home: Heaton Mersey, 28 Boddens Hill Rd, Stockport SK4 2DG, United Kingdom Office: Neurology Dept, Hope Hosp, Salford PR2 9HT, England

VARMA, ANUPAM, virologist; b. New Delhi, July 23, 1940; s. Satya Vrat and Kunti (Johri) V.; m. Prabhati Adaval, June 26, 1964; children: Mandira, Avijit. BSc, Allahabad (India) U., 1959, MSc, 1961; PhD, London U., 1967. Commonwealth fellow Rothamsted Exptl. Sta., Harpenden, U.K., 1964-67; sr. plant virologist Indian Agrl. Rsch. Inst., New Delhi, 1968-79, from prof. to head plant pathology divsn., 1982-95, dean, 1995-2000, nat. prof., 2000—; applied plant virologist Food & Agrl. Orgn. UN, Ibadan, Nigeria, 1979-81. Editor: Vistas of Plant Pathology, 1984; editor Indian Phytopathology, 1988-94, Internat. Jour. Tropical Plant Diseases, 1981—, Jour. Phytopathology, 1990—. Indian Nat. Sci. Acad. fellow, 1987, NAS fellow, 1988, Nat. Acad. Agrl. Scis., 1989; recipient Vasvik Found. award, 1989, Om Prakash Bhasin award, Bhasin Found., 1992. Mem. Nat. Acad. Agrl. Scis., Internat. Soc. Plant Pathology (sec. gen. 1993-98, v.p. 1999—). Avocations: social service, education, reading. Home: B-15 IARI, 110012 New Delhi India Office: Indian Agrl Rsch Inst, 110012 New Delhi India

VARMA, ARVIND, chemical engineering educator, researcher; b. Ferozabad, India, Oct. 13, 1947; s. Hans Raj and Vijay L. (Jhanjhee) V.; m. Karen K. Guse, Aug. 7, 1971; children: Anita, Sophia. BS ChemE, Panjab U., 1966; MS ChemE, U. N.B., Fredericton, Can., 1968; PhD ChemE, U. Minn., 1972. Asst. prof. U. Minn., Mpls., 1972-73; sr. research engr. Union Carbide Corp., Tarrytown, N.Y., 1973-75; asst. prof. chem. engring. U. Notre Dame, Ind., 1975-77, assoc. prof., 1977-80, prof., 1980-88, Arthur J. Schmitt prof., 1988—, chmn. dept., 1983-88; vis. prof. U. Wis., Madison, fall 1981; Chevron vis. prof. Calif. Inst. Tech., Pasadena, spring 1982; vis. prof. Ind. Inst. Tech.-Kanpur, spring 1989, U. Cagliari, Italy, summer, 1989, 92; vis. fellow Princeton U., spring 1996. Co-author: Mathematical Methods in Chemical Engineering, 1997, Parametric Sensitivity in Chemical Systems, 1999; editor: (with others) The Mathematical Understanding of Chemical Engineering Systems, 1980, Chemical Reaction and Reactor Engineering, 1987; series editor: Cambridge Series in Chemical Engineering, 1996—; contbr. numerous articles to profl. jours. Recipient Tchr. of Yr. award Coll. Engring. U. Notre Dame, 1991, Spl. Presdl. award 1992, R.H. Wilhelm award AIChE, 1993, Burns Grad. Sch. award 1997, E.W. Thiele award AIChE, 1998, Chemical Engring. Lectureship award, ASEE, 2000; Fulbright scholar; Indo-Am. fellow, 1988-89. Home: 52121 N Lakeshore Dr Granger IN 46530-7848 Office: Dept Chem Engring U Notre Dame Notre Dame IN 46556

VARMA, HARI KRISHNA, biomedical scientist, researcher; b. Chertala, Kerala, India, May 18, 1963; s. Rama Kalappattumadom and Nalini Rama Varma; m. Prabha Harikrishna Nilambur Kovilakom, Sept. 12, 1994; 1 child, Parvathi. BS, U. Kerala, India, 1983, PhD, 1993; MS, Vikram U., Ujjain, India, 1986. Cert. biomed. scientist. Jr. rsch. fellow Coun. Sci. and Indsl. Rsch., Trivandrum, India, 1987-89; sr. rsch. fellow Coun. Sci. and Indsl. Rsch., Trivandrum, 1989-93; scientist SCTIMST, Trivandrum, 1994—. Contbr. articles to profl. jours. Recipeint Merit Scholar award Indian Cryogenic Coun., 1990, Best Paper award Metallurgy Assn. India, 1990; Postdoctoral fellow Lady Davis Fellowship Trust, Technion, Haifa, Israel, 1993; vis. fellow Interdisciplinary Rsch. Ctr. in Biomed. Materials, Queen Mary and Westfield Coll., U. London, 1995, postdoctoral fellow Sci. and Tech. Agy., Japan, 1998. Mem. Indian Ceramic Soc., Indian Inst. Metals, Soc. fro Artifical Internal Organs. Achievements include patents pending for preparation and processing of hydroxy aapatite and B-Tricalcium phosphate bioceramic materials for bone substitution applications. Avocations: cricket, shuttle badminton, chess. Home: C-6 Faculty Apt Poojappura, Trivandrum Kerala, India Office: Biomed Tech Wing, SCTIMST Poojappura PO, Trivandrum 695012, India

VARMA, JAGMOHAN SINGH, surgeon; b. Nairobi, Kenya, Jan. 23, 1952; arrived in U.K., 1972; s. Ranjit Singh and Taravati (Puri) V.; m. Dawn Helen Sibbald, Aug. 22, 1986; children: Arlen, Jamie, Lewis. BSc with honors, U. Med. Sch., Edinburgh, Scotland, 1977; MD, U. Med. Sch., Edinburgh, 1988; FRCS, Royal Coll. of Surgeons, Edinburgh, Scotland, 1982; Diploma Higher Surg. Tng., Royal Coll. of Surgeons, 1990. Lectr. dept. pathology U. Edinburgh, 1978-80, Wellcome Trust surg. rsch. fellow, 1983-85; rotating registrar Basic Surg. Tng., Edinburgh, 1981-83; surg. sr. registrar Edinburgh Tchg. Hosp., 1988-91; cons. surgeon/sr. lectr. U. Newcastle-upon-Tyne and Royal Victoria Infirmary, 1993—; vis. lectr. Chinese U. Hong Kong, 1987-88; clin. audit officer dept. surgery Royal Victoria Infirmary, 1993-95. Contbr. articles to profl. jours. and publs. Mem. Surg. Rsch. Soc. U.K., Brit. Soc. Gastroenterology, Assn. Surgeons Gt. Britain, Internat. Continence Soc., others. Avocations: fishing, shooting, home improvement, gardening. Home: West Wing/Netherton Hall, Nedderton Village, Northumberland NE22 6AS, England Office: Univ Newcastle-Upon-Tyne, The Med Sch Dept Surgery, Newcastle-Upon-Tyne NE2 4HH, England

VARMA, PROMOD KR, information scientist; b. Faizabad, UP, India, Feb. 19, 1946; s. S.S. and B. Devi V.; m. S. Khurana, Nov. 26, 1972; children: Anuj, Abhinav. BA, Lucknow U., India, 1966; BLS, Kurukshetra U., Haryana, India, 1972; MA, Rajasthan U., Jaipur, India, 1985; M in Libr. Info. Scis., Madras U., India. Libr. asst. dept. pub. adminstrn. Lucknow U., 1965-68; profl. asst. Indian Inst. Tech., New Delhi, 1968-75; dy mgr., power sector - tech. svcs. Bharat Heavy Electricals Ltd., Noida, India, 1975-88, 89—; chief documentation officer rsch. and reference divsn. Ministry Info. and Broadcasting, Govt. India, New Delhi, 1988; tech. officer Dist. Rehab. Ctr. Ministry of Welfare, Govt. India, New Delhi, 1988-89. Mem. Indian Libr. Assn. (life), Soc. Info. Sci. (life), Computer Soc. India. Home: IVB-13 D-3 29 West Ave, Delhi New Delhi 110 016, India Office: Bharat Heavy Electricals, Fl 3 Kribhco Bhavan A 8-10, Sect 1 Noida 201301, India

VARMA, RAJENDER SINGH, organic chemist; b. New Delhi, India, July 26, 1951; came to U.S., 1983; s. Raj Mal and Roopvati V.; m. Manju Chandna, Dec. 18, 1977; children: Abhishek, Prashant. BS in Chemistry and Physics, Punjab (India) U., 1970; MS in Organic Chemistry, Kurukshetra (India) U., 1972; PhD in Organic Chemistry, Delhi (India) U., 1976; postgrad. diploma in pulp and paper, Norwegian Inst. Technology, Trondheim, Norway, 1978. Rsch. fellow Coun. Sci. & Indsl. Rsch., New Delhi, India, 1973-75; sr. rsch. fellow Ctr. Advanced Study in Chemistry, New Delhi, 1975-76; rsch. scientist Gwalior Rayon Silk Mfg. Co. Ltd., Calicut, Kerala, India, 1976-77; norad fellow Norwegian Inst. Technology, Trondheim, 1977-79; post-doctoral rsch. fellow The Robert Robinson Lab. The Univ. Liverpool, England, 1979-82; sr. rsch. assoc. U. Tenn., Knoxville, 1983-86; group leader Houston Biotechnology Inc., The Woodlands, Tex., 1986-90; asst. prof. Baylor Coll. Medicine, Ctr. for Biotechnology, The Woodlands, 1986-93; rsch. scientist Houston Advanced Rsch. Ctr., 1993—; rsch. prof. dept. chemistry Sam Houston State U., Huntsville, Tex., 1995-99; chemist U.S. Environ. Protection Agy., Cin., 1999—. Patentee in field; contbr. chpts. to books, encys. and over 160 rsch. articles to profl. jours. Norad fellow Govt. of Norway, 1977; grantee Am. Cancer Soc., 1988, 89-92, NIH, 1991—. Mem. Am. Chem. Soc. Avocations: reading, jogging. Home: 8294 Millview Dr Cincinnati OH 45249-2240

VARMA, RAJENDRA SINGH, chemistry educator, researcher, editor; b. Bangwan, India, June 25, 1941; s. Prasad Lakshman and Parvati Devi; m. Prem Lata, June 16, 1962; children: Meeta, Neeta, Rakesh. BSc, Lucknow (India) U., 1959, MSc, 1961, PhD, 1963, DSc, 1974. Scientist Regional Rsch. Lab., Hyderabad, India, 1963-65; rsch. assoc. U. Miss., 1965-67, Ga. State U., Atlanta, 1968; asst. prof. Lucknow U., 1969-85, assoc. prof., 1985-95, prof., 1995—; prin. investigator rsch. project Coun. Sci. and Indsl. Rsch., New Delhi, 1993-96, Indian Coun. Med. Rsch., New Delhi, 1992-95; coord. MSc Tech. Pharm. Chem. program Lucknow U., 1994—; convenor nat. seminar Kakatiya U., Warangal, India, 1995. Chief editor: Antifungal Drugs-Past and Future Prospects, 1998; editor-in-chief Indian Jour. Heterocyclic Chemistry, 1991; contbr. over 150 articles to profl. jours. Gen. sec. Anupam Pk. Citizen's Coun., Lucknow, 1994. Sr. fellow Alexander von Humboldt Found., Bonn, 1979; travel grantee Coun. Sci. and Indsl. Rsch., New Delhi, 1994, grantee Indian Nat. Sci. Acad., New Delhi, 1995. Fellow Indian Chem. Soc. (coun., v.p. 2000—, pres. Lucknow br. 1995-97); mem. Nat. Acad. Chemistry and Biology (life, gen. sec. 1991-97), Uttar Pradesh Assn. for Advancement of Sci. (life). Avocations: popularization of science, travel, cooking, current affairs. E-mail: profrsv@lw1.vsnl.net.in. Home: C-85 Sector-B Aliganj, Lucknow 226 024, India Office: Lucknow U, Dept Chemistry, Lucknow 226007, India

VARMA, VIKAS, advertising executive; b. Calcutta, India, Oct. 3, 1967; s. Shiva Prakash and Dolly (Bakshi) V.; m. Arshi Singh, Dec. 20, 1991. BA, St. Xavier's Coll., Calcutta, 1986; diploma in advt., U. Bombay, 1987. Fashion designer Futura Fashions, Bombay, 1986-88; client svc. exec. Frank Simoes Advt., Bombay, 1988-90; client svc. mgr. Madison DMBB Advt., Bombay, 1990-92; dir. Touché Comms., Bombay, 1992-94, pres., mng. dir., 1996—; mktg. cons. Golden Swan Group, Bombay, 1993—; design cons. Friday Club, N.Y., 1993-94, Ipcon Sys., Toronto, Can., 1994—; Indian rep. Dialogue Internat., Brussels, 1995—. Art dir. Indal-Windows, 1995 (Dialogue Creative award 1996). Recipient Udyon Ratna award Indian Econ. Soc., 1996, Excellence award Indian Econ. Soc., 1997. Mem. Am. Advt. Agys. Assn. (internat. mem.), Advt. Club Bombay, Golden Swan Country Club. Avocations: poetry, photography, scuba diving, cricket, hang gliding. Office: B-3-37/38 Green Fields, OPP Fantasy Land, Bombay India Office: Touche Comms Pvt Ltd, D-8-41 Greenfields, 400093 Bombay India

VARMUS, HAROLD ELIOT, health science administrator, educator, science researcher; b. Oceanside, N.Y., Dec. 18, 1939; s. Frank and Beatrice (Barasch) V.; m. Constance Louise Casey, Oct. 25, 1969; children: Jacob Carey, Christopher Isaac. AB, Amherst Coll., 1961, DSc (hon.), 1984; MA, Literature, Harvard U., 1962; MD, Columbia U. Med. Sch., 1966. Lic. physician, Calif. Intern, resident Presbyn. Hosp., N.Y.C., 1966-68; clin. assoc. NIH, Bethesda, Md., 1968-70; lectr. dept. microbiology U. Calif., San Francisco, 1970-72, asst. prof., depts. microbiology and immunology, biochemistry and biophysics, 1972-74, assoc. prof., 1974-79, prof., 1979-83, Am. Cancer Soc. research prof., 1984-93; dir. NIH, Bethesda, Md., 1993-99; pres., CEO Meml. Sloan-Kettering Cancer Ctr., N.Y.C., 2000—; chmn. bd. on biology NRC. Editor: Molecular Biology of Tumor Viruses, 1982, 85; Readings in Tumor Virology, 1983; assoc. editor Genes and Development Jour., Cell Jour.; mem. editorial bd. Cancer Surveys. Named Calif. Acad.

Sci. Scientist of Yr., 1982; co-recipient Lasker Found. award, 1982, Passano Found. award, 1983, Armand Hammer Cancer prize, 1984, GM Alfred Sloan award 1984, Shubitz Cancer prize, 1985, Nobel Prize in Physiology or Medicine, 1989. Mem. AAAS, NAS, Inst. Medicine of NAS, Am. Soc. Virology, Am. Soc. Microbiology, Am. Acad. Arts and Scis. Democrat. Achievements include research (with J. Michael Bishop) on the replication of retroviruses. Office: Meml Sloan-Kettering Cancer Ctr 1275 York Ave New York NY 10021-6094

VÁRNAGY, LÁSZLÓ ELEK, veterinarian; b. Eger, Heves, Hungary, Jan. 11, 1948; s. László and Klotild Klára (Szokoly) V.; m. Anikó Amália Ravasz, Sept. 26, 1971; children: Ákos, Katalin. Diploma in vet. medicine, U. Vet. Sci., Budapest, 1971; PhD, DSc. Pathologist Vet. Svc., Budapest, Hungary, 1971-73; instr. U. Veszprém, Hungary, 1973-76; asst. prof. Pannon Agrl. U., Keszthely, Hungary, 1976-83, assoc. prof., 1983-95, full prof., 1995—, head dept., 1983—, dean Georgikon Faculty, 1994-97; temp. expert WHO, Geneva, 1993; reporter Hungarian Vet. Jour., 1990—. Author: Professional Health and Hygiene, 1979, 2d edit., 1983, Teratological Effect of Pesticides, 1985, Methyl Parathion, 1993, Agrochemical Hygiene, 1995. Avocations: reading, travel, music. Office: U Veszprem Georgikon Fac Ag, Deák F u 16, H-8360 Keszthely Zala Hungary

VARNALS, SIMON PAUL, advertising executive; b. London, Sept. 18, 1954; s. Francis Arthur and Irene May (Stickland) V.; m. Nicola Jane Hall, Apr. 5, 1980; children: Benjamin, Camilla, Frederick. Cert., Inst. Practioners in Advt., Inst. Math. Mktg. exec. Ted Bates, London, 1976-78; account mgr. Broadbents & Priners, London, 1978-80; account dir. Cranfords, London, 1980-85, KHBB, London, 1985-95; group account dir. K-Advt., London, 1995-96; bd. account dir. Saatchi & Saatchi, London, 1996—. Com. exec. NRA, Northwood, 1998. Mem. Ch. of Eng. Avocation: rowing. Home: 9 Roy Rd, Northwood HA6 1EQ, England Office: Saatchi & Saatchi, 80 Charlotte St, London HA6 1AQ, England

VARNER, CHARLEEN LAVERNE MCCLANAHAN (MRS. ROBERT B. VARNER), nutritionist, educator, administrator, dietitian; b. Alba, Mo., Aug. 28, 1931; d. Roy Calvin and Lela Ruhama (Smith) McClanahan; student Joplin (Mo.) Jr. Coll., 1949-51; BS in Edn., Kans. State Coll. Pittsburg, 1953; MS, U. Ark., 1958; PhD, Tex. Woman's U. 1966; postgrad. Mich. State U., summer, 1955, U. Mo., summer 1962; m. Robert Bernard Varner, July 4, 1953. Apprentice county home agt. U. Mo., summer 1952; tchr. Ferry Pass Sch., Escambia County, Fla., 1953-54; tchr. biology, home econs. Joplin Sr. H.S., 1954-59; instr. home econs. Kans. State Coll., Pittsburg, 1959-63; lectr. foods, nutrition Coll. Household Arts and Scis., Tex. Woman's U., 1963-64, rsch. asst. NASA grant, 1964-66; assoc. prof. home econs. Central Mo. State U., Warrensburg, 1966-70, adviser to Colhecon, 1966-70, adviser to Alpha Sigma Alpha, 1967-70, 72, mem. bd. advisers Honors Group, 1967-70; prof., head dept. home econs. Kans. State Tchrs. Coll., Emporia, 1970-73; prof., chmn. dept. home econs. Benedictine Coll., Atchison, Kans., 1973-74; prof., chmn. dept. home econs. Baker U., Baldwin City, Kans., 1974-75; owner, operator Diet-Con Dietary Cons. Enterprises, cons. dietitian, 1973—, Home-Con Cons. Enterprises. Mem. Joplin Little Theater, 1956-60. Mem. NEA, Mo., Kans. state tchrs. assns., AAUW, Am., Mo., Kans. dietetics assns., Am., Mo., Kans. home econs. assns., Mo. Acad. Scis., AAUP, U. Ark. Alumni Assn., Alumni Assn. Kans. State Coll. of Pittsburg, Am. Vocat. Assn., Assn. Edn. Young Children, Sigma Xi, Beta Sigma Phi, Beta Beta Beta, Alpha Sigma Alpha, Delta Kappa Gamma, Kappa Kappa Iota, Phi Upsilon Omicron, Theta Alpha Pi, Kappa Phi. Methodist (organist). Home: PO Box 1009 Topeka KS 66601-1009

VARNER, HELEN, communications educator; b. Biddeford, Maine, Jan. 21, 1946; d. E. Harold Kemper and Darlene Ruth (Marcus) Meeks; m. Foy E. Varner, Jr., May 26, 1977; children: Dawn Hedgpeth, Jennifer Thompson, Foy E. III. B in Applied Arts and Scis., Stephen F. Austin State U., 1981, MA, 1983; EdD, Tex. A&M U., 1990. Reporter Galveston (Tex.) Daily News, 1964-65; acct. exec. John Gilbert Advt. Agy., Miami, Fla., 1965-67; chief Correspondence Sch., U.S. Army Edn. Ctr., Mannhiem, Germany, 1967-70; coord. pub. info. Galveston Coll., 1970-74; pub. rels., advt. dir. Sea-Arama Marineworld, Inc., Galveston, 1974-77; owner, chief exec. officer The Varner Pub. Rels. & Advt. Agy., Galveston, 1977-81; instr. Stephen F. Austin State U., Nacogdoches, Tex., 1981-88; assoc. prof. journalism N.E. La. U., Monroe, La., 1988-90, Chaminade U. of Honolulu, 1990-91; assoc. prof. comm. Hawaii Pacific U., Honolulu, 1991—, v.p. univ. rels. and dean of comm., 1998; pres. Galveston Conv. & Vis. Bur., Galveston, 1978-79. Pres. Galveston Press Club, 1977, ARC, Galveston Chpt., 1976, Nacogdoches Chpt., 1980; dir. Girl Scouts Am, Gulf Coast, Galveston, 1976. Named Outstanding Adviser Pub. Rels. Student Soc. Am., 1989, Outstanding Prof. Omicron Delta Kappa, 1989, Favorite Prof. Alpha Lambda Delta, 1988; recipient Mentor award Mortarboard Sr. Leadership Soc., 1990, Outstanding Adviser award Women In Communication, Inc., 1986-87, 85-86. Mem. Assn. for Edn. in Journalism and Mass Communication, Tex. Pub. Rels. Assn. (pres. 1987-88), Pub. Rels. Soc. Am., Pub. Rels. Assn. La. (sec. 1989), So. Pub. Rels. Fedn., Women In Communications (pres. Honolulu Profl. chpt. 1995-96), Orgn. of Women Leaders (Woman Leader of Yr. 1995-96), Pub. Rels. Found. Tex. Avocation: miniatures collection. Home: 46-082 Puulena St Apt 1224 Kaneohe HI 96744-3754 Office: Hawaii Pacific U 1132 Bishop St Ste 504 Honolulu HI 96813-2820

VARNES, JON EINAR, software company executive; b. Narvik, Trondheim, Norway, Nov. 12, 1948. MS, Tech. Univ. of Norway, Norway, 1971. Chief engr. KVO (Generator of Electric Energy), Norway, 1979-96; pres. Powel Data, Trondheim, 1996—. Mem. Lions. Office: Powel Data, Narvdovegen 4B, N-7034 Trondheim Norway

VARNEY, ROBERT NATHAN, retired physicist, researcher; b. San Francisco, Nov. 7, 1910; s. Frank Hastings Sr. and Emily Patricia (Rhine) V.; m. Astrid Margareta Riffolt, June 19, 1948; children: Nils Roberts, Natalie Rhine. AB with highest honors in Physics, U. Calif., Berkeley, 1931, MA, 1932, PhD, 1935; DSc (hon.), Leopold Franzens U., Innsbruck, Austria, 1983. Instr. NYU, 1936-38; asst. prof., assoc. prof., prof. Washington U., St. Louis, 1938-64; mem. rsch. lab. Bell Labs, Murray Hill, N.J., 1951-52; sr. mem. rsch. lab., sr. sci cons. Lockheed Missiles & Space Co., Palo Alto, Calif., 1964-75; guest prof. Leopold Franzens U., Innsbruck, 1977-78; mem. Mo. Gov.'s Sci. Adv. Com., St. Louis, 1960-64. Author: Engineering Physics, 1948; (with others) Methods of Experimental Physics, 1968, Introduction to ... Atmospheric Pollution, 1972, Brain Injury without Head Injury, 1999; contbg. author textbook; contbr. 82 articles to scholarly and profl. jours. Comdr. USNR, 1931-57. Fulbright fellow Leopold Franzens U., Innsbruck, 1971-72, 76-77, NSF sr. postdoctoral fellow Inst. Tech., Stockholm, 1958-59, NRC sr. postdoctoral fellow U.S. Army Ballistic Rsch. Lab., Aberdeen, Md., 1975-76; recipient Cross of Honor 1st Class Austrian Govt., 1981. Fellow Am. Phys. Soc.; mem. Am. Assn. Physics Tchrs., Phi Beta Kappa, Sigma Xi, Tau Beta Pi, Omicron Delta Kappa. Episcopalian. Achievements include research in electron swarms and atmospheric pollutants; studies of closed head brain injuries. Home: 4156 Maybell Way Palo Alto CA 94306-3820

VARNI, DAVID GRANT, SR., arborist; b. Hartford, Conn., Oct. 14, 1938; s. Louis Walter and Dorothy Grant Varni; children from previous marriage: David Jr., Cynthia, William; m. Marjorie Arline; 1 child, Deborah. Diploma, Glastonbury (Conn.) H.S. Lic. arborist, Conn. Mem. Conn. Tree Protective Assn., Nat. Arborist Assn., Internat. Arborists, Glastonbury C. of C., Elks. Avocation: private pilot. Home: 236 Forest Ln Glastonbury CT 06033-3920

VARNIENE, REGINA, bibliographer; b. Pasvalys, Lithuania, Apr. 18, 1950; two children. Diploma, Vilnius U., Lithuania, 1975, DSc, 1986. Rschr. and lectr. Vilnius U., 1976-88; rschr. Info. Inst., Vilnius, 1988-89; dir. of libr. Vilnius Tech. U., 1989-92; dir. Ctr. Bibliography and Book Sci. Nat. Libr., Lithuania, 1992—, dep. dir. Martynas MaUvydas, 1998—. Contbg. author Lithuanian Integrated Libr. Info. Sys., 1995; contbr. articles to profl. jours. Office: Nat Libr Lith Ctr Bibli, K. Sirvydo 4, 2600 Vilnius Lithuania

VARNISH, PETER, engineering executive; b. Leamington, Warwics, May 30, 1947; s. John and Ilma Hilary (Godfrey) V.; m. Shirley A. Bendelow; children: Jason, David. BSc with honors, U. Coll. North Wales, Wales, 1968; PhD, Sheffield U., Yorks. Head Admiralty Surface Weapons Establishment, Portsdown, 1978-82; supt. Def. Evaluation and Rsch. Agy., Funtington, 1982-89; dir. Def. Evaluation and Rsch. Agy., Hants, 1995—, Def. Rsch. Agy., Portsdown, 1989-91; dir. gen. Min. of Def., London, 1993-95; dir. DERA, Hants, 1995—; non sxec, dir. Weisstech, Herts, 1999, EMC Ltd., Camberlay; coun. ERA, Surrey, 1993-96; bd. U. Surrey, 1981-96; chmn. adv. com. U. Portsmouth, 1989-96. Contbg. editor Navy Stealth, 1994; contbr. articles to profl. jours.; patentee in field. Chmn. Rowlands Castle Assn., Hants, 1993. Active Falklands War. Named Officer Brit. Empire, Her Majesty the Queen, 1982. Fellow IEEE, Royal Acad. Engring., Royal Soc. Arts, Inst. Elect. Engrs. Avocations: rugby football, re-engineering, mountain walking, politics, IT applications. Home: 1 Greatfield Way, Rowlands Castle PO9 6AG, United Kingdom Office: Def Evaluation and Rsch Agy, Ively Rd, Farnborough GU14 0LX, United Kingdom

VARNUM, KEITH ADDISON, entrepreneur; b. Titusville, Pa., Apr. 15, 1948; s. Herbert Earle and Maryanne Varnum. BA in Comm., U. Mich., 1970. Lic. acupuncturist, Mass. Dir. East-West Ctr., L.A., 1970-72; v.p. mktg., bd. dirs. Erewhon Natural Foods, Boston, 1973-76; owner-chef Boca Loca Natural Foods Restaurants, Boston, 1977-79; dir. Touchstone Wellness Ctr., Cambridge, Mass., 1980-84; profl. acupuncturist Oriental Arts Ctr., Boston, 1984-88; facilitator Avatar course, Phoenix, 1989-94; founder, dir. The Dream Seminars, Phoenix, 1995—; Host radio talk show: Beyond Belief. Author: Living the Dream, 1997. Bd. dirs. Nat. Hypertension Inst., Phoenix, 1986-88. Avocations: hiking, travel, cooking, writing, reading. Home and Office: The Dream 11248 N 11th St Phoenix AZ 85020-5827

VARONOS, AGAMEMNON, mechanical engineer, researcher; b. Athens, Greece, Mar. 19, 1972; s. Apostolos and Ephemia (Metallinos) V. Diploma in mech. engring., Nat. Tech. U. Athens, 1994, PhD in Mech. Engring., 1999; diploma in fluid dynamics-turbomachinery, Vonkarman Inst. Fluid Dynamics, 1995. Tchg. and rsch. asst. Nat. Tech. U. Athens, 1995-99, rsch. assoc., 1999—. Contbr. articles to profl. jours. Scholar State Instn. Scholarships, Athens, 1990-94, scholar postgrad. studeis Von Karman Inst. for Fluid Dynamics, Brussels, 1994-95. Mem. Inst. Marine Engrs. U.K., Combustion Inst. (Greek sect.), Tech. Chamber Greece (3 prizes for excellence in mech. engring. studies 1991, 92, 94). Avocations: mountain skiing, tennis, flying small planes. Home: 10 Nymfeou St, 115-28 Athens Greece

VAROTSOS, CONSTANTINOS ANTONIOS, physicist, educator; b. Patras, Greece, Aug. 14, 1956; s. Antonios and Efrosini (Diamantopoulou) V.; m. Katerina Antipa, May 18, 1980; 4 children, Eleftheria, Panagiotis, Giorgos, Antonios. BhD, Nat. and Kapodistrian U., Athens, 1980; PhD, Aristotelean U., Thesaloniki, 1984. Rschr. dept. atmospheric physics Lab. Clarendon, Oxford (Eng.) U., 1984-85; rschr. dept. applied physics Lab. of Meteorology, U. Athens, 1986-88, asst. prof., 1988-99, assoc. prof., 1999—; sci. coord. various rsch. projecxts funded by EU, WMO, NATO. Co-author: The Physics of the Atmospheric Greenhouse Effect,, 1994, Remote Sensing and Global Climate Change, 1994, Environmental Physico-Chemistry, Vol. 1, Radiation, Greenhouse effect, Climate Change, 1996, Environmental Physico-Chemistry, Vol. 2, The Atmospheric Effects of Aircraft Emissions, Health Effects of Air Crew Members from Radiation, 2000, Atmospheric Ozone Variability, 2000; author more than 500 rsch. articles, congress presentations, reports. Fellow Brit. Meteorol. Soc.; mem. AAAS, Am. Geophys. Union, Remote Sensing Soc., Am. Acad. Scis. Office: Univ of Athens, U Athens Dept Appl Physics, Panepistimiololis, Bld Phys, Athens 157 84, Greece

VARRIALE, CHRISTINA MARIE, computer company executive; b. Valley Stream, N.Y., May 20, 1977. B in Mktg., U. N.C., 1999. Owner Internat. Ho. Pancakes, Little Neck, N.Y., 1996—; assoc. dir. sales/mktg. ecom, Jacksonville, N.C., 1998—. Mem. Young Reps. Recipient Platinum Sponser award March Dimes, 1999, 2000, Gold Sponser award United Way, 1999, 2000. Office: ecom 1650A Gum Branch Rd Jacksonville NC 28540-5201

VARRIALE, PHILIP, cardiologist; b. N.Y.C., July 30, 1934; s. John J. and Florence (Ferrara) V.; m. Eileen D. Rubencamp, Dec. 28, 1968; children: Donna, Philip, David. BA, NYU, 1955; MD, SUNY, 1959. Attending physician Dept. of Medicine, St. Vincent Hosp., 1963—; chief of cardiology Cabrini Med. Ctr. of N.Y., 1964—. Co-author: Textbook of Vectorcardiography, 1970; author: Cardiac Pacing, A Concise Guide to Clinical Practice, 1979. Lt. col. U.S. Army Med. Corps, 1968-70. Fellow ACP, Am. Coll. of Cardiology, Am. Coll. of Chest Physicians. Avocations: music, trumpet player. Home: 37 North Rd Bronxville NY 10708-1930 Office: 222 E 19th St New York NY 10003-2607

VARRÓ, VINCE, medical educator; b. Budapest, Hungary, Oct. 13, 1921; s. Bela Aladar and Berta (Glancz) V.; m. Magda Bonta, Dec. 16, 1950 (dec. Jan. 1987); children: Andrea, Andras. LLD, Pazmany U., Budapest, 1946; MD, Szeged (Hungary) U., 1949, PhD, 1957, DSc, 1965. Asst. Szeged U. Med. Sch., 1949-57, asst. prof. medicine, 1957-70, prof., dir. dept., 1970-91, prof. emeritus, 1991—. Author: Gastric Acid Deficiency, 1962, Gastorenterologia, 1964, 2d edit., 1997, Absorption and Malabsorption, 1984; contbr. over 500 articles to profl. jours., chpts. to books. Mem. Hungarian Soc. Gastroenterology (pres. 1972-82), Hungarian Soc. Internal Medicine (pres. 1986-94), European Assn. Gastroenterology (pres. 1976-80), World Assn. Gastroenterology (hon. pres.). Avocations: history, literature, swimming. Fax: 36-62-545-185. E-mail: vavi@inlst.szote.u-szeged.hu. Office: SZOTE 1st Dept Medicine, Koranyi fasor 8, H-6720 Szeged Hungary

VARSHAVER, NINA BORISSOVNA, geneticist; b. Moscow, Dec. 27, 1914; d. Boris Abramovich and Anna Lvovna (Bank) V. Diploma, Moscow State U., 1936, PhD, 1940. Rschr. Moscow State U., 1940-41, Inst. Epidemiology and Microbiology, Tashkent, Uzbekistan, 1941-43, Inst. Sci. and Tech. Info., Moscow, 1956-61, Inst. Viral Preparations, Moscow, 1961-64, Inst. Atomic Energy, Moscow, 1964-78, Inst. Molecular Genetics, Moscow, 1978—; opera singer Stanislavsky Opera and Drama Theatre, Moscow, 1944-47; chamber singer Uzbek State Philharm. Soc., Tashkent, 1947-56. Contbr. articles to profl. jours. Scholarship Russian Acad. Scis., 1997; Diploma for Discovery Patent cert. by USSR State Com. for Inventions and Discoveries, 1987; recipient Medal for Honored Labor, 1991, Order of Labor Red Flag Govt. award, 1990. Mem. V.I. Vavilow Soc. Geneticists and Breeders. Avocation: classical music. Home: Kuussinen St 17-55, 125252 Moscow Russia Office: Inst Molecular Genetics, Kurchatov Square, 123182 Moscow Russia

VARSHNEY, DINESH, physics educator, researcher; b. Bhopal, India, Dec. 3, 1965; s. Ramjilal and Padmavati Varshney; m. Meenu Varshney, Apr. 14, 1995; 1 child, Aditi Varshney. BSc, Barkatullah U., Bhopal, 1986, MSc, 1988, MPhil, 1989, PhD, 1993. Lectr. Barkatullah U., Bhopal, 1988-89, Vikram U., Narsingharh, India, 1989-93; lectr. Devi Ahilya U., Indore, India, 1993-94, sr. lectr., 1994—; rsch. fellow Abdus Salam Internat. Ctr. Theoretical Physics, Pisa, Italy, 1998-99. Recipient Young Scientist award Madhya Pradesh Coun. Sci. and Tech., Bhopal, 1994, Internat. Acad. Phys. Scis., 1997, Indian Sci. Congress Assn., 1998. Mem. Indian Physics Assn., Material Rsch. Soc. of India. Avocations: reading, writing, outdoor sports, camping, philately. Home: 387 Indrapun Colony, Indore 452001, India Office: Sch Physics Devi Ahilya U, Khandwa Rd, Indore 452001, India

VARTAK, ARVIND M., plastic surgeon, consultant; b. Alibag, Maharashtra, India, Aug. 29, 1942; s. Madhusudan and Malti Vartak; m. Hemalata Naik, May 31, 1972; children: Ninad, Nandan. MB BS, Grant Med. Coll., Mumbai, India, 1967, MS, 1974, MS in Plastic Surgery, 1978. Sr. resident J.J. Hosp., Mumbai, 1969-70, sr. registrar, 1970-72; resident in surgery Port Trust Hosp., Mumbai, 1972-83; plastic surgeon cons. Mumbai, 1983—; hon. plastic surgeon B.J. Wadia Hosp. for Children, Mumbai, 1985—, Masina Hosp., Mumbai, 1986—, S.L. Raheja Hosp., Mumbai, 1996—, M. Dalvi Hosp., Mumbai, 1996—; presenter numerous papers at confs., symposia. Contbr. articles to profl. jours. including Burns, Indian Jour. Occupl. Health. Recipient J.M. Shah scholarship U. Mumbai, 1962. Mem. Burns Assn. India, Indian Burns Rsch. Soc., Internat. Soc. for Burns Injuries, Assn. Plastic Surgeons India, Indian Soc. for Critical Care Medicine, Indian Soc. for Reconstructive Surgery Hand, Assn. Surgeons India, Indian Med. Assn., Assn. Med. Consultants, Loss Prevention Assn. Assn. India Ltd., Consumer Guidance Soc. India, Peoples Med. Relief Soc., Indian Edn. Soc., Assn. Brit. Coun. Scholars. Avocation: photography. Office: 17 A Partha, 4 Ganesh Peth, Off NC Kelkar Rd, Dadar Mumbai 400 028, India

VARTHALITIS, IOANNIS ISSIDOROS, oncologist; b. Piraeus, Attiki, Greece, Jan. 24, 1955; s. Sotirios and Anastasia (Gavala) V.; m. Ekaterini Palla, June 26, 1992; children: Nefeli, Fivos. Grad., U. Thessaloniki, Greece, 1980, U. Athens, Greece, 1987, Jules Bordet, Brussels, 1991, U. Libre de Bruxelles, Belgium, 1992. Lic. med. practitioner specialization internal medicine, med. oncology, infectiology. Intern medicine Air Force Gen. Hosp., Athens, 1980-82, Nat. Health Sys., Edipsos, Greece, 1983-84, Chase Farm Hosp., London, 1984, Gen. Hosp., Piraeus, Greece, 1984-87; med. oncologist Metaxas Cancer Hosp., Piraeus, 1987-97; infectious diseases physician Jules Bordet, Brussels, 1990-91; mem. staff dept. med. oncology and infections Evangelismos Hosp., Athens, 1997—; mem. ethical com. Metaxa Cancer Hosp, Piraeus, 1993-96, dir., 1995—. Contbr. articles to profl. jours. Treas. Balcan Sch. Oncology, 1995—; med. br. Amnesty Internat., Athens, 1985-87 Lt. Greek Air Force, 1980-82. Grantee European Sch. Oncology, Milan, 1989; scholar for infectious diseases in cancer patients Ministry Health, 1990-91. Mem. European Orgn. for Rsch. and Treatment (treas. Invasive Fungal Infectiopns Coop. Grp. 1991-95), Cancer Breast Cancer Coop. Group, Internat. Immunocompromised Host Soc., Balcan Union Oncology (treas. 1995—). Democrat. Christian Catholic. Avocations: photography, swimming, archeology. Home: Papadiamanti 6, 15126 Maroussi Athens, Greece Office: Evangelismos Hosp, Ipsilantou 45-47, 10676 Athens Greece

VARTIA, MATTI, plastics company executive; b. Hameenlinna, Finland, Aug. 5, 1937; s. Heikki Ilmari and Elna (Kivilahti) V.; m. Terhi Marjatta Karelahti, Apr. 11, 1939; children: Matti Juhani, Sari Elina. MS in Engring., Helsinki Inst. Tech., 1961; postgrad., Harvard U., 1986. Planning engr. Printal Oy, Helsinki, 1961-62, tech. dir., 1972-77; factory mgr. Oy Sako AB, Riihimäki, Finland, 1962-69; tech. dir. Bensow Oy-AB, Helsinki, 1970-72, Oy G.W. Sohlberg AB, Jyväskylä, Finland, 1978-86; dir. div. Oy G.W. Sohlberg AB, Helsinki, 1987-89; mng. dir. Perlos Oy, Nurmijärvi, Finland, 1990-97; also bd. dirs.; headmaster Sako Vocat. Sch., Riihmäki, 1966-69. Decorated 1st class Order of Suomen Leijona (Finland). Mem. Finnish Plastic Mfrs. Assn., Finnish Handball Assn. (chmn. 1990—), Rotary. Avocations: handball, tennis, literature, genealogy. hOME: Eino Leinonkatu 6 C 38, SF-00250 Helsinki Finland Office: Perlos Oy, Mahlamäentie 2, Nurmijärvi Finland

VARTIAINEN, AHTI TOIMI PAAVALI, military officer; b. Joensuu, Finland, Sept. 2, 1943; married; 1 child, Maria-Kristina. Tng. & engr. officer Finnish Mil., 1966-70, instr. Mil. Acad., 1971-74, student officer War Coll., 1974-77, dept. commdg. officer Engr. Depot, 1977-78, chief divsn. Air Force Hdqs., 1978-84, dept. commdg. officer, commdg. officer Engrs. Depot, 1984-88; commdg. officer Finnish Battalion UN Observer Force, Damascus, Syria, 1988-89; chief engrs. dept. Def. Staff Finland, 1990-91; inspector engrs. & nuc., biol. & chem. warfare def., 1991-94; force commdr. UN Peace Keeping Force, Cyprus, 1994-97; spl. advisor for chief of ops. in def. staff, 1997-98; comdr., brig. gen. Helsinki Mil. Province, 1998—. Commdr. Helsinki Mil. Province, 1998, Brigadier Gen. Decorated Commdr. Order of Lion Finland, Knight 1st Class, Comdr. Order of White Rose, Knight 1st Class; recipient Medal of Mil. Credits, UN, medals UN Disengagement and Observer Force, UN Force in Cyprus. Office: HQ Helsinki Mil Province, PO Box 169, Helsinki 00141, Finland

VARTIAINEN, ERKKI ARMAS, medical director, medical educator; b. Pieksämäki, Finland, Mar. 29, 1954; s. Kaarlo and Saara (Hänninen) V.; m. Anneli Rinkinen, July 16, 1977; children: Hannes, Ossi, Ville. MD, U. Kuopio, Finland, 1981, PhD, 1983. Rsch. asst. U. Kuopio, 1979; sr. rschr. Nat. Pub. Health Inst., Finland, 1981-88; head lab. Nat. Pub. Health Inst., 1990—, dep. dir. dept. epidemiology and health promotion, 1991—; temporary advisor WHO, 1982-96; assoc. prof. U. Kuopio, 1985—; vis. scientist Ctrs. for Disease Control, Atlanta, 1989-90; cons. World Bank, China and Hungary, 1990-96; nat. rep. European Union, Health Promotion Com., 1996—; investigator in field; dir. European Network on Young People and Tobacco, European Union, 1996—; vis. prof. U. Edinburgh, U.K., 2000—. Contbr. articles to profl. jours. Office: Nat Pub Health Inst, Mannerheimintie 166, 00300 Helsinki Finland

VARTIAINEN, HENRI JUHANA, economics educator; b. Sortavala, Finland, May 5, 1933; s. Pekka Juhana and Anna Viola (Böök) V.; m Liisa Pirkko Huuhtanen, Jan. 30, 1955; children: Juhana, Marianna, Petra, Lotta. MA in Econs., U. Helsinki, 1955, DSc in Econs., 1968. Head dept. Bank of Finland, Inst. for Econ. Rsch., Helsinki, 1960-73; head desk OECD, Paris, 1969-72; sr. rsch. assoc. Confedn. Finnish Industries, Helsinki, 1974-76; dir. Ctr. of Policy Rsch., Helsinki, 1976-79; sr. rsch. assoc. Conf. Br., Brussels, 1979-81; sr. lectr. Finnish Inst. of Mgmt., Helsinki, 1982-88; sr. rsch. assoc. various rsch. insts. and rsch. projects, Helsinki, 1982—; chmn. sci. bd. Kymi Rgional Assn., Kotka, finland, 1982-89; prof. U. Helsinki, U. Joensuu, U. Rovaniemi, Swedish Sch. Bus. Adminstrn., 1972-92; sec. Mgmt. Rsch. Group LIFIM, 1993—. Author: National Economy -- Our Joint Venture, 1979, Economic Relations Between Finland and South Africa, 1990, Apprenticeship Training in Selected European Countries, 1994; editor: Handbook on Monetary Economics, 1989; contbr. articles to profl. jours. Mem. Internat. Inst. Pub. Finance, Inst. of Fiscal Studies, Internat. Joseph A. Schumpeter Soc. (founding), Econ. Policy Soc. of Conservative Party (bd. dirs.), Rotary (gov. local dist. 1998-99). Avocations: history, cats. E-mail: henri.vartiainen@pp.inet.fi.

VARTIAINEN, OSMO OIVA, engineering company executive; b. Rovaniemi, Finland, May 29, 1926; s. Toimi Emil and Martta (Pasanen) V.; m. Anita Lindberg, June 21, 1953; children: Asmo, Kai, Pekka, Maria. MSc., U. Tech., Helsinki, Finland, 1952; Lic. Sc., U. Tech., 1972. Rsch. engr. Tech. Rsch. Centre Finland, Helsinki, 1951-54; sr. rsch. metallurgist Rhodesian Select. Trust Svc., Zambia, 1954-57; rsch. metallurgist Outokumpu Oy, Pori, Finland, 1957-60; supt. Outokumpu Oy, Kokkola Works, Kokkola, Finland, 1960-72; works mgr. Imatra (Finland) Steel Works, 1973-77; sr. v.p. Ekono Oy, Espoo, Finland, 1978-85; mng. dir. Osmo Vartiainen-Engring. Co., Helsinki, 1985—; pres., cons.Osmo Vartiainen-Engring. Co., Helsinki, 1985—. Contbr. articles to profl. jours.; inventor, patentee in field. Bd. dirs. Cen. C. of C., Helsinki, 1973-77, Engring. Soc. in Finland, Helsinki, 1972-75; supr. Union Bank Finland, Espoo, 1973—;. Paul Harris fellow Rotary Club, Espoo, 1966—. Mem. Finnish Assn. Cons. Engrs., Assn. Finnish Mining and Metallurgy, Inst. Mining and Metallurgy (United Kingdom), European Fedn. Chem. Engring. (England). Avocations: tennis, skiing, design. Office: OV Eng Oy, Telkkakuja 7 A1, 00200 Helsinki Finland

VARTIOVAARA, ILKKA JUHANI, publishing executive, medical writer; b. Helsinki, Finland, Feb. 14, 1946; s. Klaus Veikonpoika and Sirkka Marjatta (Lång) V.; m. Anne-Maria Tuulikki Kujala, Feb. 26, 1971; 1 child, Markus. B, Helsinki U., Finland, 1980; MD, Helsinki U., 1973. cert. medicine, psychiatry. Editor-in-chief The Medisiinari Mag., Helsinki, 1969-70; primary physician Commune of Imatra, Finland, 1974-75; psychiatrist U. Helsinki, 1975-78; editor-in-chief The Finnish Med. Jour., 1978-90, Terveys 2000, Helsinki, 1990-92; exec. chief Kipsimies Inc., Helsinki, 1986—; med. writer The Duodecim Jour., Helsinki, 1990—, Suomen Kuvalehti, 1982—; med. columnist, 1996-99; mem. Internat. Com. Med. Editors, 1981-90; mem. pub. bd. Duodecim, Helsinki, 1990—. Author over 20 med. books, 1969—, including Myocardial Infarct, Diabetes, Smoking and Lung Cancer, Allergy, Back Pain, Sexual Diseases, Burn-Out, The Dolphin's Song-New Data from Medicine, 1995, From Burnout to Recovery-A Time To Cry, A Time To Laugh, 1996, The Limits of Endurance, 2000; editor-in-chief: (CD-ROM) Family Doctor, 2000. Active mem. Com. of Ethical Problems in Medicine, 1979-90. Sub-lt. in res. Finnish Navy, 1964. Recipient Bronze Hon. medal Finnish Med. Jour., 1990. Mem. The Finnish Med. Assn. (Silver medal 1990, Bronze, 1997), Finnish Psych. Assn. Avocations: literature, music, photography, videography. Home and Office: Kaavintie 17 B, 01650 Vantaa Finland

VARUGHESE, KURUVILLA, agronomy educator, researcher; b. Neeratupuram, India, Dec. 14, 1952; s. Ampravil Varkey and Ampravil Mariamma (Mathew) V.; m. Anitha Elizabeth George, Aug. 25, 1983; children: Rohin George, Jithin Varughese. BSc in Agriculture with honors, Jawaharlal

Nehru U., Jabalpur, India, 1976, MSc in Agriculture Agronomy, 1978; PhD, Tamil Nadu Agrl. U., Coimbatore, India, 1991. Agrl. officer Min. Agriculture, Kerala, India, 1978; instr. Kerala Agrl. U., 1979-80, asst. prof., 1980-89, assoc. prof., 1989—. Contbr. rsch. articles to profl. jours. Indian Coun. Agriculture sr. fellow, New Delhi, 1988. Mem. Indian Soc. Agronomy (councillor 1994-96, editor 1999-2000), Indian Soc. Root Crops, N.Y. Acad. Scis. Christian Marthoma. Avocations: gardening, reading, basketball, music, swimming. Home: Ampravil House, Kavadithalakal, 695013 Kerala India Office: Kerala Agrl U, Vellayani, 695522 Kerala India

VARWIG, FREYR ROLAND, secondary educator; b. Bad Homburg, Germany, Mar. 28, 1944; s. Roland and Hildegard (Wallhäuser) V.; m. Mirjam Bettina de Boor, June 4, 1976; children: Marianne, Bettina, Cornelia. Degree, Johann Wolfgang-Goethe U., Frankfurt, Germany, 1969, PhD, 1973, Habilitation, 1992; degree, Humboldtschule, Bad Homburg, 1973. Jr. educator Humboldt-Gymnasium, Bad Homburg, 1971-73, master of sec. sch., 1975-77, headmaster, 1977-78; asst. master Gesamtschule-Freigericht, Germany, 1973-75; wiss. oberrat Johann Wolfgang-Goethe U., Frankfurt, 1978-92, univ. lectr., 1992—; asst. studiendirektor Studienseminar III, Frankfurt, 1974-78. Author: Der rhet. Naturbegriff bei Quintilian, 1976; editor: Sprechkultur im Medienzeitalter, 1986, Ainigma: Festschrift H. Rahn, 1987; contbr. articles to profl. jours. Bd. dirs. Dt. Gesellschaft für Sprechwineuschaft ur Sprecherticbung, Wiesbaden, 1984—, pres. 1996—; bd. dirs. Hölderlingesellschaft, Tübingen, 1992—; town-councillor Town Coun. of Bad Homburg, 1986-90; mcpl. coun. Mcpl. Coun. Bad Homburg, 1990-94. Mem. Evangelical Free Ch. Avocations: house music, piano, jazz band: Echoes of Harlem 1971-91, banjo/guitar. Home: Roemerstrasse 14, D-61352 Bad Homburg Germany Office: Joh Wolfg-Goethe Univ, Senckenberganlage 27, 60054 Frankfurt Germany

VARZEGAR, MINOO, English educator, reading specialist; b. Kerman, Iran; d. Abdolrahim and Amjad (Vali) V.; m. Saeid Khan Fatemi, May 8; children: Delaram, Arezou. BA in English, U. Tehran, 1966; MA in Tchg. English, U. Tchr. Edn., 1967; MA in Psychology, U. Tehran, 1969; MA in Tchg. English as a Second Lang., U. Ill., 1971, PhD in Tchg. English as a Second Lang., 1975, postgrad., 1994. Cert. tchr. English, cert. high acad. adminstrn. Asst. prof. U. Tehran, 1979-84, assoc. prof., 1984-94, prof. dept. English, 1984-97, head Dept. English of Evening Classes, 1975-83, dir. Lang. Lab., 1975-80, dir. lang. ctr., 1981-83, head dept. English, 1983-97; vis. prof. U. Ill., Champaign-Urbana, 1997-99, rsch. scholar, 1997-99; assoc. faculty Columbia U., N.Y.C., 1999—; lectr. Rutgers U., Newark, 1999—, William Paterson U., Wayne, N.J., 1999—; dir. Ctr. for testing and Psychometrics, Min. of Culture and Higher Edn., Tehran, 1975-77. Author: Children's English series, 1990-95, Reading Through Reading (Best Acad. Book), 1992, Testing and Measurement (Best Acad. Book), 1993, A Comprehensive Grammar of English, 1996, Testing TEFL, 1997; author/editor: Issues in Teaching English as a Second Language, 1990, English for the Students of Medicine, 1989; co-author: English for Medical Students, 1974; editor: English for the Students of Medicine (II), 1993, Novin English-Persian Dictionary, vols. I and II, 1993; co-editor: Yadvareh Persian-English Dictionary, vols. I, II, III, 1991, Yadvareh English-Persian Dictionary, vols. I and II, 1991, Yadvareh Unabridged English-Persian Dictionary, 1993, others; contbr. numerous articles to profl. jours. Mem. com. for Ctr. for Studying and Compiling Univ. Books in Humanities, Min. of Culture and Higher Edn., Tehran, 1984-97, com. for curriculum devel., 1984-97, com. for testing, 1977-79; mem. com. for lang. testing Tehran U. Lang. Ctr., 1979-81. Recipient Award for creating an Innovative Model of Reading Comprehension, U. Ill., 1975, Cert. of Appreciation for best adminstrn. U. Mich., 1998, award for extraordinary ability INS, 1998; U. Ill. grantee, 1975; Fulbright scholar, 1970-75; fellow in rsch. U. Ill., 1973-75. Mem. Tchrs. of English to the Speakers of Other Langs., U. Ill. Alumni Assn., Am. Assn. for Applied Linguistics, Nat. Coun. Tchrs. English. Avocations: computers, reading, painting, tennis, swimming. Home: 277 Prospect Ave Hackensack NJ 07601-2512 Office: Rutgers Univ 232 Smith Hall 101 Warren St Newark NJ 07102-1811

VASAIKAR, BABULAL FAKIRA, principal; b. Nandurbar, India, June 1, 1942; s. Fakira Dhondu and Bhagabai Fakira (Shewale) V.; m. Malatibai Babulal Baviskar, May 13, 1969; children: Nalini Babulal, Hemant Babulal, Devendra Babulal. BA, Poona U., India, 1967, MA, 1970, BEd, 1971. Tchr. P.A.J.B.S.U. Mandal, Bhiwandi, India, 1967-72, head master, 1972-75, lectr., 1975-93, vice-prin., 1994-95, prin., 1995—. Spl. exec. magistrate Gov. Maharashtra, India, 1984-86. Recipient Samat Gaurav Puraskar award. Avocations: reading biographies, philosophical books, studying Hindi philosophy, chess, Kabaddi, games. Home: Staff Quars BNN Coll, Vidyashram Bhiwandi, India Office: BNN Coll, College Rd, Vidyashram Bhiwandi, India

VASANTA RAM, VENKATESA IYENGAR, mechanical and aeronautical engineering scientist and educator; b. Bangalore, Karnataka, India, June 1, 1938; s. M.C. Seshadri and M. Indiramma (Seshadri) Iyengar. B of Engring., U. Mysore, Bangalore, India, 1957; M of Engring., Indian Inst. Sci., Bangalore, India, 1959; D of Engring., Tech. U., Braunschweig, Germany, 1966. Jr. sci. officer Gas Turbine Rsch. Ctr., Bangalore, India, 1959-61; mech. engr. Brown Boveri & Cige, Baden, Switzerland, 1967-68; asst. prof. Inst. Indian Tech., Kanpur, Uttar Pradesh, India, 1968-70; wissenschaft. mitarbeiter Ruhr U., Bochum, Germany, 1970-76, pvt. dozent, 1976-93, prof., 1993—. Avocations: classical music (western and Indian). Office: Ruhr U Bochum, Universitaetsstrasse 150, D-44801 Bochum Germany

VASARU, GHEORGHE, retired physicist; b. Manastireni, Romania, July 16, 1931; s. Teodor and Maria (Ghita) V.; m. Raveca Tarlea, June 12, 1967; children: Daniela, Dan. PhD, U. Cluj, Romania, 1954. Asst. faculty physics U. Cluj, Romania, 1954-58; sci. rschr. Inst. Atomic Physics, Cluj, 1958-68; sr. rsch. scientist Inst. Isotopic and Molecular Tech., Cluj, 1968-99; assoc. prof. faculty physics U. Cluj, 1992—; head sci. coun. Inst. Isotopic and Molecular Tech., 1993-99; vis. scientist JSPS Rsch. Program, Tokyo, 1981. Author: Methods of Separating Stable Isotopes, 1965, Thermal Diffusion in Isotopic Gaseous Mixtures, 1967, Thermal Diffusion, A Bibliography, 1968, Izotopii stabili, 1968, Thermal Diffusion Column. Theory and Practice with particular Emphasis on Isotope Separation, 1969, Les Isotopes Stables, 1970, Separation of Isotopes by Thermal Diffusion, 1975, Tritium Isotope Separation, 1993, Separarea tritiului, 1987, Deuterium and Heavy Water. A Selected Bibliography, 1975, Zirconium and his Implications in Nuclear Energetics, 1989, Thermal Diffusion Bibliography 1965-1995, 1996, Mic dictionar Ecologic, 1997, Geocronologie nucleara. 1998. Mem. Romanian Physics Soc. (v.p.), Romanian Sci. Assn., Romanian Scientists Acad., Nat. Geog. Soc. Avocations: travel, arts, music, numismatics. E-mail: infovision@mail.dntcj.ro. Home: Str Tarnita Nr 7 Apt 11, RO-3400 Cluj 15, Romania Office: INFOVISION, Str Tarnita 7 Apt 11, RO-3400 Cluj-Napoca 15, Romania

VASARY, TAMAS, concert pianist, conductor; b. Debrecen, Hungary, Aug. 11, 1933; m. Ildikó Kovacs, 1967. Educated, Franz Liszt U. Music, Budapest; pvt. studies with, Lajos Hernadi, Jozsef Gat, Zoltan Kodaly. First solo performance at age 8; tchr. theory Franz Liszt Acad.; recitalist Leningrad, Moscow, Warsaw; settled in Switzerland, 1958; London debut, 1961, N.Y.C., 1962; debut as condr. Menton Festival of Music, 1971; has since appeared in europe, South Africa, S.Am., U.S., Can., India, thailand, Hong Kong, Australia, Japan, Mex.; mus. dir. No. Sinfonia, Newcastle, 1979-82; prin. condr. Bournemouth Sinfonieta, 1989-98; music dir., prin. condr. Hungarian Radio and TV, Sinfonia, 1992—. Recs. for Deutsche Grammophone include: 3 records works of Franz Liszt, 8 of Chopin, 3 of Rachmaninoff, one of Debussy and Mozart. Recipient Liszt prizes, Queen Elizabeth of Belgium prize, Marguerite Longue prize, Paris, Chopin prizes Internat. Competition, Warsaw, Internat. Competition Brazil, Bach and Paderewski medals, London. Office: IMG (Europe), Lovell Ho 616 Chiswick High St, London 5RX UK, England*

VASCONCELLOS, CARLOS ALBERTO, agronomist, researcher; b. Rio de Janeiro, Brazil, Aug. 6, 1943; s. José Joaquim and Jandyra (Fernandez) V.; m. Vaneza Aparecida Figueiredo; children: Alesandra Figueiredo, Carlos Henrique, Christiane Figueiredo, Rafael Leandro. BS, U. F. Rural de Rio de Janeiro, Brazil, 1967; MS, Vicosa (Brazil) Fed. U., 1973; DS, Sao Paulo U., 1976. Rschr. DHPEA, Campo Grande, Brazil, 1968-75; rschr. EMBRAPA, Londrina, Brazil, 1975-77, Sete Lagoas, Brazil, 1978—. Mem. Brazilian Soil Sci. Soc. Avocations: gardening, reading, walking, theological study. Home: Rua Tarcilia dos Santos 285, 37 700 Sete Lagoas Brazil

VASCONCELOS, MARCIO MOACYR, pediatrics educator; b. Recife, Pernambuco, Brazil, July 9, 1960; s. Francisco Moacyr and Wanda (Saldanha) V. B Econs., U. State Rio de Janeiro, 1981; MD, U. Rio de Janeiro, 1987. Resident in pediat. Hosp. Servidores do Estado, Rio de Janeiro, 1989-91, resident in child neurology, 1992-93; fellow in child neurology Children's Hosp., Washington, 1993-96; head child neurology sect. Ctrl. Hosp. Inst. Assistencia do Servidoresdo Estado, Rio de Janeiro, 1997-98; adj. prof. pediat. Fed. U. Fluminense, Niteroi, Brazil, 1998—; adj. prof. pediat. and neurology George Washington U., Washington, 1996. Translator, editor: Nelson's Textbook of Pediatrics, 1996; contbr. articles to med. jours., including Pediatric Neurology, Arquivos de Neuropsiquiatria. 2d lt. Brazilian Army, 1988-89. Mem. Child Neurology Soc., Brazilian Soc. Pediat. (cert. in child neurology). Avocations: reading, listening to music, computers, fixing broken objects. Home: Apt 208, Rua das Laranjeiras 391, 22240002 Rio de Janeiro Brazil Office: U Fed Fluminense Hosp Pedro, Av Marquês de Parana 303, 24030210 Niterói RJ, Brazil

VASCONCELOS, VITOR MANUEL, biology educator; b. Guimaraes, Braga, Portugal, Feb. 22, 1963; s. Delfim Araujo and Maria Helena (Oliveira) V. BSc, U. Porto, Portugal, 1985, MSc, 1990, PhD, 1995. Rsch. asst. Porto U., 1985-95, asst. prof., 1995-99, assoc. prof., 1999—. Contbr. articles to profl. jours. including Toxicon, Natural Toxins, Water Rsch., and Aquatic Toxicology. Mem. Internat. Assn. Water Quality, Soc. Environ. Toxicology and Chemistry, Societas Internat. Limnologia. Avocations: scuba diving, gardening, photography. Office: Fac Sci, Praca Gomes Teixeira, 4050 Porto Portugal

VASELLA, DANIEL LUCIUS, pharmaceutical marketing executive; b. Fribourg, Switzerland, Aug. 15, 1953; came to U.S., 1988; s. Oskar Emil and Ursulina Isabella (Vieli) V.; m. Anne-Laurence Moret, May 12, 1978; children: Emilia Anna, Mauro Giovanni, Flavio Bernardo Placi. Swiss fed. physician diploma, U. Berne, Switzerland, 1979, MD, 1980; postgrad., Harvard U., 1989. Resident in pathology U. Berne, 1980-81, psychoanalyst, 1983-88; resident in internal medicine Inselspital, Berne, 1982-83, attending physician, 1984-88; resident in internal medicine Waid-Spital, Zurich, Switzerland, 1983-84; mgr. spl. projects Sandoz Pharms. Corp., East Hanover, N.J., 1988-90, product mgr., 1990-91, dir. mktg., 1991-92; asst. to COO Sandoz Pharms. AG, Basel, Switzerland, 1992-96; pres. Novartis Agy. (Sandoz Pharms. AG), Switzerland, 1996—; lectr. U. Fribourg, Berne and Fribourg, 1985-88. Author: (with others) Psychosomatische Medizin, 1986; contbr. articles to profl. jours. Speaker various orgns., U.S.A. and Switzerland, 1985-92. Recipient Patron award U. Mich., 1992. Mem. Am. Mgmt. Assn., Swiss Med. Assn. (bd. cert. for internal medicine 1985), Swiss Soc. for Geriatrics, Swiss Psychosomatic Assn., Swiss Psychoanalytical Assn. (candidate), Deutsches Kollegium fuer Psychosomatik. Avocation: art. Office: Sandoz Pharms Assn 59 State Route 10 East Hanover NJ 07936-1005 also: Lichstrasse 35, CH-4002 Basel Switzerland*

VASENKOV, ALEKSEY VIKTOROVICH, physicist, educator; b. Chirchik, Uzbekistan, June 21, 1969; s. Viktor Yakovlevich and Antonina Mikhailovna (Andrianova) V.; m. Irina Alexandrovna Ankilova, Aug. 8, 1997. MSc, Novosibirsk (Russia) State U., 1991, DSc, 1996. Part-time lectr. Novosibirsk State U., 1995—; rschr. Inst. Thermal Physics, Novosibirsk, 1996-98, sr. rschr., 1998—; chmn. young scientist coun. Inst. Thermal Physics, Novosibirsk, 1997—; vis. postdoctoral rschr., dept. chemistry, U. B.C., Vancouver. Contbr. articles to sci. jours. Scholar Soros Found., Russia, 1995-96, Russian State scholar, 1997. Fax: 7-3832-343480. E-mail: vasenkov@itp.nsc.ru. Office: U BC Dept Chemistry, 2036 Main Mall, Vancouver BC CAN V6T 1Z1

VASHI, RAJENDRA THAKORBHAI, chemistry educator; b. Navsari, Brahmin, India, Nov. 24, 1954; s. Thakorbhai Bhimbhai and Shardaben Thakorbhai V.; m. Bina Rajendra Desai, May 3, 1983; 1 child, Tanvay. BSc, South Gujarat U., Surat, 1975, MSc, 1977, LLB, 1979, PhD, 1982. Lectr. Mahila Coll., Navsari, India, 1982-83; lectr. Navyug Sci. Coll., Surat, 1983-98, prof. in charge post graduate ctr., 1998—; prin. investigator Univ. Grants Commn., New Delhi, Surat, 1989; coord. All Gujarat Fedn. Amateur Astronomers, Vadodra, India, 1998. Co-author: Science-Technology and Development, 1994, Inorganic Chemistry, 1996, Inorganic Chemistry (Paper III), 1997. Active Bhartiya Janta Party, Navsari, 1993. Univ. Grants Commn. fellow, New Delhi, Surat, 1979, Indian Coun. Med. Rsch. fellow, New Delhi, Surat, 1977-78, 82. Fellow Indian Chem. Soc.; mem. Indian Assn. Water Pollution Control, Indian Assn. Nuclear Chemists and Allied Scientists. Avocations: astronomy, corrosion research, pollution research. Office: Navyug Sci Coll, Rander Rd, Surat 395009, India

VASHISTH, PUNIT, research scientist; b. Meerut, India, Dec. 11, 1967; s. Jagdish Narain and Krishna (Sharma) V.; m. Rashmi Misra, Mar. 3, 1995; 1 child, Lavanya. BSc, Meerut (India) U., 1988, MSc, 1990, MPhil, 1993. Scientist-B Def. R & D Orgn., Manali, India, 1991-95; scientist-C Def. R & D Orgn., Manali, 1996-97, Dehradun, India, 1997—. Contbr. papers to internat. confs. Mem. Glaciological Soc. India, Optical Soc. India (life). Avocations: trekking, cricket.

VASHITZ, ODED, biochemical engineer; b. Israel, Nov. 12, 1938; s. Josef and Dina (Shalom) V.; m. Judith Altmann, Aug. 23, 1966; children: Yael, Geva, Oshrath, Ayeleth. BSc with distinction, Israel Inst. Tech., Haifa, 1966, DSc, 1988; MSc, Imperial Coll., London, 1967. From plant engr. to tech. dir. Zohar Detergent Factory, Kibbutz Dalia, Israel, 1968-84, chief process engr., 1989-99; R&D mgr. Bio Dalia-Becker, Kibbutz Dalia, Israel, 1991—, Zohar Dalia (Biotech.), Kibbutz Dalia, Israel, 1991—; cons. in field. Contbr. articles to profl. jours.; patentee in field. Sgt. maj. Israel Def. Force, 1956-59. Bnai Brith London Lodge grantee, 1967. Mem. Israel Inst. Chem. Engrs., Israel Mgmt. Ctr., Assn. Engrs. and Architects in Israel. Home: 19239 Kibbutz Dalia Israel Office: Zohar Dalia, 19239 Kibbutz, 19239 Kibbutz Dalia Israel

VASHKOVSKY, ANATOLY VASILIEVICH, physicist; b. Opochka, Pskov, Russia, Dec. 19, 1931; s. Vasily Fedorovich and Evgenia Nikitichna (Korsakova) V.; m. Marina Dmitrievna Gospodarskaya. Diploma in radioengineer, Moscow Power Engring. Inst., 1955; degree Cand Sci, Acad. Scis. USSR, Moscow, 1962; DSc, Acad. Scis. USSR, 1972. Prof. acad. sci. on radiophysics. Rschr. Inst. Radio Engring. and Electronics Acad. Sci., Moscow, 1955-63, sr. rschr., 1963-68, head lab., 1968—; invited prof. Moscow Power Engring. Inst., 1998-99; founder of USSR microwave spinwave conf., 1982-91. Co-author: Properties of Ferrite-Semiconductor Layered Structures, 1979, Magnetostatic Waves in Microwave Electronics, 1993; mem. editl. bd. Jour. Radiotehnika i Elektronika, 1982—. Laureate State prize USSR, 1988. Mem. Sci. Coun., Russian Acad. Scis. (coun. phys. electronics 1985—). Avocation: gardening. Office: Russian Acad Scis, Vvedensky 1, 141120 Fryazino Russia

VASHOLZ, LOTHAR ALFRED, retired insurance company executive; b. Milw., Feb. 20, 1930; s. Alfred and Charlotte Vasholz; m. Marji Cartwright, Dec. 26, 1954; children: Julie, Ann, Eric. BS, U. Colo., 1952; M (hon.), U. Rio Grande. ChFC. Sr. cons. Life Ins. Mktg. & Rsch., Hartford, Conn., 1966-70; v.p. N.Am. Life, Chgo., 1970-73; sr. v.p. Bankers Mut., Freeport, Ill., 1973-75; sales dir. Security Life of Denver, 1975-81; v.p. Union Cen. Life Ins. Co., Cin., 1981-85, sr. v.p., 1985-86; mgr. Union Cen. Life Ins. Co., Columbus, Ohio, 1986-87; sr. v.p., chief mktg. officer Union Cen. Life Ins. Co., Cin., 1987-91, exec. v.p., corp. mktg. officer, 1991-95; chmn. Carillon Investments, 1991-95; cons. on mktg. and sales to life ins. industry, 1995—; cons., owner Transitions Unltd., Cin., 1995—. Trustee U. Rio Grande, Ohio; elder Presbyn. Ch. Fellow Life Mgmt. Inst.; mem. Phi Delta Theta (past internat. pres.). Republican. Fax: (760) 771-9593.

VASIĆ, VOISLAV, natural history educator, researcher; b. Beograd, Yugoslavia, Mar. 9, 1945; s. Filip and Jelisaveta (Vukovic) V.; m. Zorana Nedic, Jan. 13, 1973 (div. 1981); children: Filip, Milica; m. Olga Rajacic, Mar. 6, 1983. Grad., U. Belgrade, Yugoslavia, 1967, PhD in Biology, 1984. Rsch. asst. Inst. Biol. Rsch., Belgrade, 1969-84, rsch., sci., 1985—, tchr. faculty of biology, 1991-2000; dir. Natural History Mus., Belgrade, 1984—; mem. exec. bd. Inst. for Protection of Nature, Belgrade, 1988-91, Sci. Mus., Belgrade, 1993—; expert Group for Ecol. Edn., Belgrade, 1992-97. Author: Catalogue of the Birds of Yugoslavia, 1973, Birds of Durmitor and Tara Canyon, 1990; editor: Biodiversity of Yugoslavia, 1995, editor Bull. Natural History Mus., 1984—; corr. Birds of the Western Palearctic, 1980-95. Mem. Union Yugoslav Soc. Biosystematics (sec. 1973-77), Union Yugoslav Biol. Soc. (sec. 1989-96), Union Yugoslav Ornithology Soc. (pres. 1987-91), Serbian Acad. Sci. (sec. com. of fauna 1984-97), Serbian Ecol. Soc. (pres. 1991-94), Matica Srpska. Avocations: painting, translating. E-mail: nhbeo@beotel.yu. Office: Natural History Mus, Njegoševa 51, Belgrade 11000, Yugoslavia

VASILE, NICOLAE, electrical engineer, educator; b. Ludesti, Romania, June 16, 1954; s. Stefan and Gheorghita V.; m. Floarea Matache, May 8, 1981; 1 child, Matei. BS, Poly. U. Bucharest, 1978, DSc, 1985. Engr. Cable Factory, Bucharest, 1978-79; from engr. to gen. mgr. Rsch. Inst. Elec. Engring., Bucharest, 1979—. Author: Topics in Boundary Element Research, 1990; contbr. articles to profl. jorus. Mem. Romanian Assn. Accreditation, Romanian Assn. Standardization, Romanian Tech. Acad. Office: Rsch Inst Elec Engring, 313 Splaiul Unirii, Bucharest Romania 74204

VASILE, RADU, Romanian politician, academic; b. Sibiu, Romania, Oct. 10, 1942; m. Mariuca Vasile; 3 children. Grad., U. Bucharest. Historian Village Mus., Bucharest, Romania, 1967-69; sci. rschr. History Inst. Nicolae Iorga Romanian Acad., 1969-72; asst. lectr. Acad. Econ. Studies, Bucharest, 1972, asst. prof., vice dean faculty trade, 1990; prof. Acad. Econ. Studies, 1993; v.p. Romanian Senate, 1996-98; head Romanian del. Parliament Assembly Coun. Europe, 1996-98, v.p., 1997-98; mem. Christian Dem. Nat. Peasant Party, 1990—, sec. gen., 1996-98; pres. Senate Parliament Group, 1996-98; prime minister Govt. of Romania, 1998—. Author: World Economy, Avenues and Stages of Modernization, 1987, Currency and Economy, 1994, Currency and Fiscal Policy, 1995, From the Iron Century to the Second World War, 1998. Avocations: poetry, satirical literature, chess, football. Fax: (1) 592018. Office: Office Prime Min, Piata Victoriei nr 1, 71201 Bucharest Romania*

VASILEV, VICTOR SERGEEVICH, scientific researcher; b. Moscow, July 31, 1958; s. Sergey Petrovich and Alexandra Alexeevna (Mitrohina) V. Process Engr., Mendeleev Moscow Chem. Tech., Inst., 1981. Probationer Kurnakov Inst. of Gen. and Inorganic Chemistry, Moscow, 1981-83, jr. rschr., 1983-96, rschr., 1996—. Author: (book) Fundamentalnye nauki - narodnomu hozyastvu, 1990; contbr. articles to profl. jours. Mem. of com. trade union Kurnakov Inst. of Gen. and Inorganic Chemistry, 1992-97. Fellow Mendeleev Chem. Soc. Avocations: theatre, music. Office: Kurnakov Inst Gen/Inorganic, Chemistry/Leninskii pr 31, 117907 GSP-1 Moscow Russia

VASILIEV, ALEKSEY NIKOLAYEVICH, chemist, researcher, educator; b. Kiev, Ukraine, Apr. 25, 1960; s. Nikolay Vasilievich Tudel and Rimma Vladimirovna Vasilieva; m. Larisa Pavlovna Savchenko, June 28, 1986; 1 child, Inna. MS, Kiev State U., 1982; PhD, Inst. Phys. Organic Chemistry Coal Chemistry, Kiev, 1991. Engr. Inst. Molecular Biology and Genetics, Kiev, 1982-83, Inst. Organic Chemistry, Kiev, 1983-86; jr. rschr. Inst. Phys. Organic Chemistry and Coal Chemistry, 1987-90; rschr. Inst. Bioorganic Chemistry and Petrochemistry, 1990-96; assoc. prof. U. Buenos Aires, 1997—, Nat. Technol. U., Cordoba, Argentina, 1997—; external cons. Tecnomyl s.r.l., Villetta, Paraguay, 1998—; rep. in Ukraine and Russia for MVTechnologies, Inc., Akron, Ohio, 1995—; external cons. Tecnomyl S.T.L., Paraguay, 1998—. Contbr. articles to profl. jours.; inventor in field. Mem. Green Party of Ukraine, Kiev, 1991-93. Recipient grant Internat. Sci. Foun., 1994. Mem. Internat. Soc. Heterocyclic Chemistry, N.Y. Acad. Scis. Avocations: skiing, trakking, tourism, ecology. Home: PO box 305, 01034 Kiev Ukraine Office: Nat Technol Univ, CC 17, 5016 Cordoba Argentina

VASILIEV, ALEXANDER BORISOVICH, physicist; b. Novogrodovka, Ukraine, May 24, 1954; m. N.V. Chistyakova; 1 child, Anna. Grad., Lomonosov Moscow State U., 1978, PhD, 1989. Assoc. prof. dept. physics Lomonosov Moscow State U., Moscow, 1997—, dep. dean dept. physics, 1997—. E-mail: abv@phys.msu.su. Office: Lomonosov Moscow State Univ, Vorobiobi gory, Moscow Russia

VASILIEV, GLEB ALEXANDROVICH, toxicologist, researcher; b. Petropavlovsk, Kazakhstan, Sept. 20, 1930; s. Alexandr Mikhailovich and Susanna Spiridonovna (Tuksuzova) V.; m. Tamara Andreevna Ermolaeva, Dec. 30, 1956; children: Andrew, Julia. MD, 2d Med. Inst., Leningrad, Russia, 1954; PhD, 1st Med. Inst., Leningrad, Russia, 1960; D of Med. Sci., Inst. Radiol. Medicine, Leningrad, Russia, 1967. Sr. rschr. 1st Med. Inst. Marine, Leningrad, 1955-72; head of lab. Rsch. Inst. Ship-Bldg., Leningrad, 1972-84, Rsch. Inst. Prometeus, St. Petersburg, 1984—; prof. toxicology, 1983. Author: Reference Book of Radioprotectors, 1962, 64, Endocrine System in Hypoxia, 1974, Combination Effect of Industrial Pollutants, 1975, Reference Book of Hygiene Polymers, 1984. Named Vet. of Labor, Soviet Ministers, Moscow, 1995. Mem. Spl. Sci. Bd. Prometeus. Avocations: reading fiction, table tennis, skiing, swimming. Home: Apt 70, Moskovskii Prospekt 194, 196070 St Petersburg Russia Office: RschInst Prometeus, 49 Shpalernaya Ulitsa, 193015 St Petersburg Russia

VASILIEVICI, ALEXANDRU PETRU, electrical engineer, educator; b. Timisoara, Timis, Romania, Mar. 8, 1940; s. Alexandru Milivoi and Barbara Maria (Martin) V.; m. Maria Bud; 1 child, Mihaela. MSc, U. Polytechnica Timisoara, Romania, 1961; PhD, U. Polytecnica Timigoara, Romania, 1969. Asst. U. Polytechnica Timisoara, 1961-68, lectr., 1968-76, reader, 1976-90, prof. elec. engring., 1990—, vice dean electrotech. faculty, 1976-84, dir. dept., 1984. Editor: Elements of Low Tension Device Technology, 1981, Electric Devices, 1986, Materiaux Dielectriques et Materiel Electrique, 1997, Equipements à logique programmé, 1998, Le transport de l'énergie en courant continuu, 1998; patentee in field. Capt. Romanian Mil. Recipient Prize of Min. of Edn., 1964, Golden Scroll of Excellence, IBC, Cambridge, Eng., 1998; named Man of the Yr., Am. Biog. Inst., 1997. Mem. IEEE, CTE, Lions. Avocation: symphonic music. Home: Intrarea Zenit 2, R-1900 Timisoara Timis, Romania Office: Univ Politechnica, B-dul V Parvan 2, R-1900 Timisoara Timis, Romania

VASILIKIOTIS, GEORGE, chemistry educator, researcher, consultant; b. Thessaloniki, Greece, Apr. 19, 1931; s. Stergios and Sophia (Vasilikioti) V.; m. Liolia Christides, July 31, 1960; children: Christos and Sophia. BSc in Chemistry, Aristotelian U., Greece, 1955; MSc in Pharm. Chemistry, Madison (Wis.) U., 1963; PhD in Chemistry, Aristotelian U., 1964, DSc in Chemistry, 1968. Cert. in analytical and environ. chemistry. Rsch. asst. U. Wis., Madison, 1960-63; lectr. Aristotelian U., 1964-68, asst. prof., 1968-69, assoc. prof., 1969-74, full prof., 1974—; dir. Lab. Analytical Chemistry, Thessaloniki, Greece, 1969-98, Lab. Environ. Pollution Control, and State Pollution Control Lab., 1976-82, Dept. Phys., Analytical and Environ. Chemistry, 1982-90, 94-96. Author: Analytical Chemistry: Qualitative Analysis, 1971, 2d edit., 1976, 3d edit., 1982, Quantitative Analysis, vol. I, 1974, 2d edit., 1977, 3d edit., 1981, vol. II, 1976, 2d edit., 1980, 3d edit., 1986, Environmental Chemistry, 1981, Environmental Pollution Control, 1986. Pres. Environ. Protection Coun., Ministry No. Greece, 1976-82; nat. rep. European Chemistry, 1986—; counselor Nat. Orgn. Tourism, Athens, 1990-93; v.p. Nat. Marine Rsch. Ctr., Athens, 1990-94, mem. sci. com., 1999—; mem. Com. Environ. Protection, 1994—. Lt. Ammunition, Greece, 1955-58. Fulbright scholar U. Wis., 1960-64. Mem. Greek Chemist Assn. (pres. 1994-97), Greek Sci. Soc. (pres. 1998—), Assn. No. Greece Chemists (treas. 1957-60), Mediterranean Sci. Assn. Environ. Protection (nat. rep. 1991—), Royal Chemistry Soc., Rotary (pres. Thessaloniki-East mem. 1978-79, gov. Greek dist. 1987-89), Balkan Environ . Assn. (v.p. 1998—). Greek Orthodox. Avocation: stamp collecting. Home: 13 Papakyriazi, Thessaloniki 54645, Greece Office: Aristotelian U, Lab Analytical Chemistry, Thessaloniki 54006, Greece

VASILIU, CRISTINA, obstetrician/gynecologist, educator; b. Bucharest, Romania, Dec. 28, 1957; d. Alexandru Cezar and Magdalena (Marculescu) Dumitriu; m. Constantin Ion Vasiliu, Nov. 23, 1990; 1 child, Alexandra. MD, U. of Medicine, Bucharest, 1982; PhD, U. of Medicine, 1998. Asst. prof. U. of Medicine, Bucharest, 1991-99, lectr., 1999—. Author: Hormonal Contraception, 1999; co-author: (with Vartej) Obstetrics-Normal

and Pathology, 1995. Mem. Romanian Soc. Ob-Gyn., Romanian Soc. Endocrinol. Gynecology, Balkanique Med. Union, N.Y. Acad. Scis. Eastern Orthodox. Avocations: universal literature, travel, psychology. Home: Str Batiste Nr 35 Apt 5 Parter, 70206 Bucharest Romania Office: Univ Hosp, Splaiul Independentei 169, Bucharest Romania

VASILIU-OPREA, CLEOPATRA TIMOFTE, science educator; b. Iasi, Romania, Nov. 25, 1934; d. Timofte and Varvara (Petrov) Vasiliu; m. Spiridon Oprea, June 23, 1962; children: Liviu, Dana. MSChemE, Poly. Inst., Iasi, 1957; PhD, Tech. U. Leuna, Merseburg, Germany, 1965. Asst. prof. Poly. Inst., 1957-62, lectr., 1966-70, assoc. prof., 1970-80; rsch. fellow Tech. U., 1962-65; prof. Gh. Asachi Tech. U., Iasi, 1980—; sci. counselor Macromolecular Chemistry Inst., Iasi, 1971—; vice rector Poly. Inst., 1984-90. Author: Mechanochemistry of Macromolecular Compounds, 1967, Russian edit., 1970; (with others) Polymerization Kinetics and Technology, 1973, Treatise of Macromolecular Compounds Chemistry, vol. 1, 1973, Polymers-Theory of Process Synthesis, 1986, Polymers-Structure and Properties, vol. II, 1986, Fracture of Polymers-Theory and Applications, 1992, Elastomer Technology Handbook, 1993; patentee in field; contbr. articles to profl. jours. Recipient Gheorghe Spacu prize Romanian Acad., 1980, Gold medal EUREKA, 1994, 95, 96, H. Coanda Gold medal Romanian Soc. Inventors, 1996; named Elite Inventor Patent Romanian Acad. and Romanian Soc. Inventors, 1992; grant DAAD, 1974, 92. Avocations: flowers, cats. Home: St Ralet No 7 Sc A Apt 3, 6600 Iasi Romania Office: Gh. Asachi Tech Univ, B dul Carol No 22, 6600 Iasi Romania

VASILIYEVA, ELENA FIODOROVNA, immunologist, researcher; b. Moscow, Russia, Dec. 13, 1946; d. Fiodor Petrovich and Nina Emeliyanovna (Sinyakova) Abramov; m. Viktor Nikolaevich Vasiliyev, June 19, 1973 (div. Aug. 1982); 1 child, Ann V. Kolosova. M, Moscow State U., 1973; PhD, Med. Biol. Problem Inst., Moscow, 1989. Specialist physiology man and animals, clin. lab. immunology; candidate biol. sci. Asst. Inst. Immunology, Moscow, 1973-77; jr. rschr. Inst. Medico-Biol. Problems, Moscow, 1977-89; chief clin. lab. Spl. Med. Clinic, Moscow, 1990-92; sr. rschr. Mental Health Rsch. Ctr., Moscow, 1992—. Editor: The New Jerusalem and Its Heavenly Doctrine, 1996. Mem. Soc. Immunology. Mem. Orthodox Ch. Avocations: pets, mountain skiing, theatre. Home: Valdayskiy proezd 7-22, 125445 Moscow Russia Office: Mental Health Rsch Ctr RAMS, Zagorodnoe schosse 2, 113152 Moscow Russia

VASILJEV, ALEXANDER VALERJOVICH, economist; b. Kuragata, Kazahstan, June 21, 1955; s. Valery Alexandrovich and Olga Vladimirovna Vasiljev; m. Marina Genadievna Tuzovskay, Dec. 31, 1985; children: Olga, Nataliya. Diplomate of engring., Metall. Inst., 1977; Candidate Scis., Inst. Engring., Moscow, 1982; postgrad., Inst. Sociology Acad. Scis., Moscow, 1992; PhD in Econs., Acad. Mgmt. Russia, Moscow, 1993. Jr., then sr. scis. employee Inst. Mariupol, Ukraine, 1980-84, mgr. rsch. lab. socioecon. problems., 1985-87; mgr. socially econ. lab. Inst. Labour of Ukraine, Mariupol, 1987-90; mgr. sect. social econ. problems of port's indsl. cities Inst. Econ.-Law Rsch., Nat. Acad. Scis. Ukraine, Mariupol, 1993-98, organizer Mariupol br., 1995-97; chmn. sci. coun. Inst. Econ. and Social/Cultural Rsch., Mariupol, 1989—; prof. PriAzov State Tech. U., Mariupol, 1993-98; v.p. Azov, Ukrainian Dept., Acad. Econ., Scis. and Entrepreneurship, Mariupol, 1999—. Author monographs in field. Pres. Fond Internat. Gerald Union, Volodarska, 1998; chmn. Civil Com. on Restortion Orthodox Ch. in Hist. Ctr. of Mariupol, 1990. Scholar Acad. Russia, 1991-92; recipient cert. Frederick P. Furth Found., 1990, medal "Met. Gotey & Cafa, St. Ignatia", 1999. Mem. N.Y. Acad. Scis., 1817 Heritage Soc. N.Y. Acad. Scis., Union Econ. Ukraine, Acad. Econ. Scis. and Entrepreneurship (hon.). Avocations: tennis, windsurfing, travel. E-mail: 481990@nyas.org. Home: Fl 41 Zelinsky 1 St, 87534 Mariupol Ukraine Office: Inst Econ/Social/Cult Rsch, Stroiteley 39 Ave Box N7, 87534 Mariupol Ukraine

VASILJEV, VALERY ALEXANDEROVICH, economist, metallurgical engineer; b. Novo-Ukrainka, Ukraine, July 10, 1929; s. Alexander Pavlovich and Olga (Andreyvna) V.; m. Olga Vladimirovna Vasilejeva; 1 child, Alexander. Diploma in engring., Tech. Inst. Odessa, USSR, 1952; degree in econs., Moscow Inst. Mgmt., 1978. Chief tech. office Igorsky Plant, St. Petersburg, Russia, 1952-54; main engr. Collective Farms, Kuragata, Dgambul, Kazakhstan, 1955-56; chief Br. metall. Plants of Ukraine, 1957-74; chief econ. dept. Ukrgipromez, Mariupol, Ukraine, 1975-84; chief rsch. sector Metall. Inst. Mariupol, 1985-86; sr. lectr. PriAzov, State Tech. Mariupol U., 1987—; mem. section sci. coun. Inst. Econ.-Law Rsch. NAS Ukraine, Mariupol, 1996-97; dir. Inst. Econ.-Social and Cultural Rsch., Mariupol, 1995—; pres.-chief Azov, Ukrainian Dept., Acad. Econ., Scis. and Entrepreneurship, 1999—. Recipient medal UFE, 1955, Labour-Vet. medal USSR, 1989, medal "Met. Gotey and Cafa, St. Ignatja", 1999, cert. Frederick P. Furth Found., 1990. Mem. Econ., Sci. and Entrepreneurship, Acad. Econ. Ukraine, N.Y. Acad. Scis. (cert.). Avocations: travel with family. Home: Fl 24, Nahimova, 122 St, 87534 Mariupol Donesk, Ukraine Office: Inst Econ Social Cultur Rsch, Stroiteley, 39 St, Box N7, 87534 Mariupol Donesk, Ukraine

VASILLIEV, LEONID NIKOLAEVICH, geophysicist; b. Moscow, Oct. 12, 1931; s. Nikolai Vasillievich and Glafira Nikolaevna Vailliev; m. Nina Nikolaevna Ish, July 12, 1955 (div. May 1981); 1 child, Alexander; m. Alvira Andreevna Sheveleva, June 24, 1981. Diploma in photogrametry, U. Geodesy, Moscow, 1954, PhD, 1959. Prof., dean U. Geodesy, Cartography and Air-Photography, Moscow, 1955-78; scientist Inst. Geography Russian Acad. Scis., Moscow, 1978—. Editor: Geographic Interpretation of Remote Sensing DATA, 1988 (Sci. award Russian Acad. Sci. 1989), Remote Sensing of Biosphere, 1990 (Sci. award Russian Acad. Sci. 1991). Travel grantee Internat. Sci. Found., 1996. Avocations: swimming, skiing, jogging. Home: 3-3-455, 26 Bakinskikh Komissarov, 117571 Moscow Russia Office: Inst Geography, Staromonetny 29, 109017 Moscow Russia

VASILYAK, LEONID MIKHAILOVICH, physician; b. Severouralsk, Sverdlovsk, Russia, Oct. 8, 1946; s. Mikhail Varnavovich and Nina Nickolaevna (Trenikhina) V.; m. Lyudmila Ivanovna Bibikhina, Feb. 15, 1986; m. Irina Eugenievna Glinko, Aug. 21, 1973; 1 child, Sergei. Magister, Moscow Inst. of Physics and Tech., 1971, Postgrad., 1971-74, PhD in Physics, 1975; DSc, Russian Acad. of Scis., 1996. Rsch. scientist Inst. for High Temperatures/USSR Acad. of Scis., 1974-85, sr. scientist, 1985-92, assoc. prof., 1992-98; prof. Inst. for High Temperatures/USSR Acad. Scis., 1999, head of lab. High Energy Density Rsch. Ctr., 1998—; mem. PhD exec. com. Inst. for High Temperatures, 1988—, Moscow Inst. of Physics and Tech., 1992—, mem. scientific coun., 1992-98, scientific coun. Joint Inst. for High Temperatures, 1999. Contbr. articles to profl. jours.; patentee in field. Grantee Soros Assoc. Prof., Internat. Soros Edn. Program, 1998, Russian Found. of Basic Rsch., Russian Govt. Edn. Dept., 1992-95. Mem. Am. Phys. Soc., N.Y. Acad. Scis. Avocation: art. Office: Russian Acad Scis Inst Thermophysics Extremal States, Izhorskay 13/19, 127412 Moscow Russia

VASKO, FEDOR T., physicist, researcher, educator; b. Kiev, Ukraine, June 6, 1946; s. Trofim A. and Polina E. (Kozachek) V.; m. Antonina I. Vasina, Dec. 25, 1969; 1 child, Natalia. MS in Physics, Kiev State U., 1969; PhD, Inst. Semiconductors, Kiev, 1976, DSc in Physics, 1986. Jr. rschr. Inst. Semiconductors, Kiev, 1968-69, rschr., 1971-76; sr. rschr. Inst. Semiconductors, 1976-86; head of group Inst. Semiconductor Physics, Kiev, 1986—; assoc. prof. physics, Kiev State U., 1984-86, prof., 1986-93. Author: Electronic States and Optical Transitions in Heterostructures, 1993, 98; contbr. articles to profl. jours. Lt., Soviet Army, 1969-71. Multiple rsch. grantee Fund of Fundamental Rschs., Ukraine, 1992—; rsch. grantee Internat. Sci. Found., 1995, 96. Mem. Am. Phys. Soc., High Certification Commn. Ukraine (expert). Home: 42 Listopadnaya, 252028 Kiev Ukraine Office: Inst Semiconductor Physics, pr. Nauki 45, 252650 Kiev Ukraine

VASKO, PETER THEODORE FREDERICK, priest; b. Bklyn., Nov. 28, 1943; s. Theodore Frederick and Catherine (Buday) V. BA in Philosophy, Cath. U. Am., 1966, BD in Theology, 1969; postgrad., Duke U., 1972-73, Franciscan Studium Biblicum, Jerusalem, 1985-86. Ordained priest Roman Cath. Ch., 1987. Pub. rels. asst. Holiday Inn/Oak Grove, Durham, N.C., 1972-74; dir. devel. NAA, Charlotte, N.C., 1974-76; dir. CETA, New Orleans, 1976-78; v.p. sales Peachtree Corners Corp. Travel, Atlanta, 1978-81; bd. dirs. Franciscan Custody, Jerusalem, 1992—; pres. The Holy Land Found., Jerusalem, 1994—. Editor photo essay See the Holy Land, 1993, The Holy Land and the Milennium, 2000; editor The Holy Land Mag., 1993-95; writer, narrator video On the Road of Christ, 1994; narrator video The Life of Jesus: Scriptural Journey, 1997; guest on Mother Angelica Live, 1996, 97, 98, Pat Robertson 700 Club, 1996, others; co-prodr. documentary Crisis in the Holy Land, 1994. Bd. dirs. St. Ives Soc., Jerusalem, 1992-94; guide White House Via U.S. Embassy, Jerusalem, 1992—; chaplain U.S. Marines/U.S. Consulate, Jerusalem, 1988—. Recipient Achievement in Pub. Rels. award Pub. Rels. Soc., Raleigh, 1975; named Jaycee of Yr., N.C. chpt., 1973; decorated mem. Equestrial Order of the Holy Sepulchre, 1992.

VASQUEZ, JOHN, political scientist; b. Hartford, Conn., Nov. 1, 1945; s. John C. and Helen J. Cristina V.; m. Marie T. Henehan, Sept. 23, 1952; 1 child, Elyse. AB, Boston U., 1967; MA, Syracuse U., 1972, PhD, 1974. Instr. Le Moyne Coll., Syracuse, 1973-74; asst. prof. Earlham Coll., Richmond, Ind., 1974-75; prof. of polit. sci. Rutgers U., New Brunswick, N.J., 1975-93, Vanderbilt U., Nashville, 1993—. Mem. editl. bd.: Internat. Studies Quarterly, 1995—; author: (book) The Power of Power Politics, 1998, The War Puzzle, 1993; co-author: (book) In Search of Theory, 1981; contbr. articles to profl. jours. Grantee NSF, 1999-2001, U.S. Inst. of Peace, 1989-90; Fulbright Rsch. Prof., 1985. Mem. Nature Conservancy, Peace Sci. Soc. (pres. 1998-99), Internat. Studies Assn. (v.p. 1993-94). Office: Vanderbilt U/Dept Polit Sci 21st Ave S-Calhoun Hall Nashville TN 37235

VASQUEZ BAUTISTA, FRANCISCO NEFTALI, cardiologist, military officer; b. Cotui, Dominican Republic, Dec. 11, 1946; s. Pedro Vasquez and Dominga Bautista; m. Juana Nuñez, Oct. 9, 1974; children: Carol, Natalia, Johanna. MD cum laude, U. Autonoma Santo Domingo, 1975. Physician Hosp. Inmaculada Concepcion, Cotui, 1975-76; commd. 1st lt. Ejercito Nat., 1976, advanced through grades to col., 1992; physician Hosp. Mil. Enrique W.L. Ceara E.N., Santo Domingo, 1976-78; cardiology resident Hosp. Mil. Ctrl. Gomez Ulla, Madrid, 1979-82; dir. critical care unit Hosp. Mil. Enrique W.L. Ceara E.N./Hosp. Ctrl. Fuerzas Armad, Santo Domingo, 1982-88; med. adminstrv. subdir. Hosp. Ctrl. de las FFAAYPN, Santo Domingo, 1988-89, dir. critical care unit, 1989-93, med. exec. subdir., 1993-94, dir. internal medicine dept., 1996-98, coord. internal medicine residence; Tchr. med. Ibero Americans U. Treas. Med. Mil. Soc., Santo Domingo, 1986; pres. Junta de Vecinos, Edificio, Proyecto Jose Contreras, 1993. Mem. Assn. Medica Dominicana, Soc. Dominicana Cardiologia, Assn. Mil. Ciencias Medicas, N.Y. Acad. Sci. Roman Catholic. Avocations: fishing, hunting, reading. E-mail: neftali.vasquez@codetel.net.do. Home: C/A Manzii Edif II, Proyecto Jose Contreras, Santo Domingo Dominican Republic Office: Centro Medico Ravely, Mella St, Santo Domingo Dominican Republic

VASQUEZ MARTINEZ, CLAUDIO RAFAEL, educator, university administrator, author; b. Marinilla, Antioquia, Colombia, May 22, 1957; came to Mexico, 1988, naturalized, 1997; BS in Indsl. Tech., U. San Buenaventura, Medellin, Colombia, 1981; postgrad., EAFIT U., Medellin, 1983, Linguaphone Inst., London, 1984, Internat. System Medellin, 1985; MS in Edn., U. Antioquia, Medellin, 1985; PhD in Edn., Autonomous U. Guadalajara, Mex., 1990; BS in Indsl. Engring., SEP, Mex., 1998. Assessor adminstrn., prodn., costs, market Polimeros and Viamacol, Bello, Antioquia, 1982-85; rschr. didactics dept. Autonomous U. Guadalajara, Mex., 1985—, prof. Sch. Indsl. and Elec. Mech. Engring., 1988-95, prof. thesis advising Sch. Indsl. & Electric Mech. Engring., 1988-98, prof. Dentistry Sch., 1988-95, prof. seminar sci. rsch. I, II, III, 1988-95, prof. Sch. Econ., 1988-95, prof. Sch. Computer Engring., 1988-89, prof. bio stats., 1989-90, prof. rsch. methods, 1988-98, prof. history, philosophy, edn., 1989, prof. stats., 1989-91, prof. Inst. Humanities, 1989-98, prof. Nursing Sch., 1989-90, prof. Sch. Teaching Tng., 1989-90, prof. comm. & leadership Master's degree adminstrn. program, 1990, prof. Sch. Acctg., 1990, prof. seminar for degree, 1990-98, rschr. DIRPLAC-UAG, 1991-93, rschr. Ctr. Ednl. Rsch. CIE-UAG, 1993-98, prof. Sch. Bus. Studies, 1993, prof. Sch. Comm., 1995-98, prof. Sch. Info. Scis., 1995-97, prof. Sch. Tourism, 1995-98; prof. honoris causa Die St. Lukas Akademie, Bamberg, Germany, 1998; prof., investigator, U. Tel Tolima, Colombia, 1998—; prof. ops. rsch. U. Colombia Popular del Risaralda, 1999—; cons. in field; rschr. Nat. Svc. Learning, Medellin, 1981, Higher Acad. & Indsl. Tech. Svcs., 1980-82, Modern Inst. Edn., 1982-85, Ctr. Ednl. Rsch. U. Antioquia, 1983-86, Sch. Edn. U. San Buenaventura, 1985-87; assessor adminstrn., prodn. costs, numismatics, re-engring., philately, specialists, lepidoptory, Rionegro, 1983-96; advisor epistemology, rhochrematics, Guadalajara, 1983-96; with UNESCO, 1985-98; advisor adminstrn., planning & devel. La Floresta Reforest Co., Rionegro, Antioquia, 1980-94, markets and adminstrn. DOMETAL, Medellin, 1986, prodn. & costs Casa de Reyes, Style Furniture & Decoration, 1980-81; asst. in prodn. Dimadera, Design & Decoration, Medellin, 1981-84; dean CREAD Pascual Bravo Tech. Inst., Rionegro, 1985-86, basic math. tutor Coll. Elec. & Mechanic Tech., 1985; adminstrv. advisor Modern Inst. Edn., Medellin, 1984-87; prof. rsch. techniques Coll. Pub. Adminstrn. ESAP, 1986, prof. gen. acctg., 1986; prof. ecology in civil engring. Antioquia Coll. Engring., 1987; prof. rsch. methods Coll. Indsl. Tech. Jaime Isaza Cadavid Colombian Polytechnic Inst., Rionegro, 1986-87, prof. indsl. practices, 1986-87, coord. indsl. practices, 1986-87, prof. rsch. methods Coll. Civilian Constrns., 1987; vis. prof. Beijing Normal U., 1997, Sao Paulo U., 1995, Sydney U., 1996, Waseda U., 1996, Tampere U., 1998, Cape Town U., 1998, Oxford U., 1997. Author: Quality and Social Impact, 1986, The Open Education, 1986, Methodology of Predictive Analysis of Mogers Space in the Arches of Subjects during Mixed Dentition, 1991, Computers in Education: Their Teaching, Research and Languages, 1992, Methodology of Incidence of Malocclusions in 3 to 5 year old Pre-school Children, 1994, Methodology of Incidence of Cavities Related to Bacterial Plaque in 3 to 5 year old Pre-school Children, 1994, Methodology of Detection of Oral Habits in 3 to 5 year old Pre-school Children and its Consequences in Primary Dentition, 1994, Methodology of the Baby Bottle Syndrome in 3 to 5 year old Pre-school Patients, 1994; contbr. articles to profl. jours; numerous internat. one-man shows, 1988—. Avocation: track and field. E-mail: rvasquez@uagunix.gdl.uag.mx. Home: Carrera 17 7-120 Torre 1-203, Pereira Risaralda Colombia

VASS, JOZSEF, software developer, researcher; b. Budapest, Hungary, Apr. 22, 1972; came to U.S., 1995; s. Gyozo and Kerlalin (Aulich) V.; children: Zachary, Jared; m. Sheila Ann Vass, Mar. 28, 1999. Diploma, Tech. U. Budapest, 1995; MS, U. Mo., 1996, PhD, 2000. Intern NASA Goddard Space Flight Ctr., Greenbelt, Md., summer 1996; rsch. assoc. U. Mo., Columbia, 1995-2000; sr. multimedia software developer Infranet Solutions, Vancouver, B.C., Can., 2000—. Contbr. articles to profl. jours.; patentee in field. Recipient award NSF, 1994, scholarship Soros Found., Hungary, 1995, rsch. award U. Mo., 1997, 98. Mem. IEEE (student mem.). E-mail: vass@cecs.missouri.edu.

VASSALLO, FRANCIS, bank executive. Gov. Ctrl. Bank of Malta; pres. Francis J. Vassallo & Assoc.; former Gov. for Malta Internat. Monetary Fund. Office: Ctrl Bank Malta, Castille Place, Valletta CMR 01, Malta*

VASSILACOS, DIMITRI GEORGE, bank advisor; b. Athens, Greece, Oct. 20, 1968; s. George and Helen (Sarlis) V. MSME, Nat. Tech. U. of Athens, 1994; MBA, Inst. Superieur des Affaires at HEC Group, Jouy-en-Josas, France, 1996; MA in Law and Diplomacy in Internat. Bus., Tufts U., 1997. Advisor to gov. Nat. Bank of Greece, Athens, 1996—. Avocations: jazz music, ethnic music, Greek folk art. Fax: 301-334-1075. E-mail: dgv@net.ethnodata.gr. Home: 23 Ioulianou St, 106 82 Athens Greece Office: Nat Bank Greece, 86 Eolou St, 10232 Athens Greece

VASSILAKOS, NICHOLAS, energy consultant; b. Athens, Jan. 1, 1954; s. Peter N. and Theodora G. (Sotiropoulou) V.; m. Erifili N. Kriari, May 9, 1987; children: Peter, Alexander. BSChE, Nat. Tech. U., 1976; MSChE, Calif. Inst. Tech., 1978, PhD, 1980. Registered chem. engr., Greece. Asst. prof. dept. chem. engring. U. Tex., Austin, 1981-84; assoc. prof. dept. chem. engring. U. Patras, Greece, 1985; sr. advisor Prime Min.'s Office Econ. Affairs, Athens, 1986-87; sect. gen. Ministry of Industry, Energy and Technology, Athens, 1988-89; mng. dir. Technion S.A. Energy and Environ. Systems, Athens, 1990-92; gen. dir. Network Cons. Group Ltd., Athens, 1993—; energy expert European Commn. Directorate Gen. for Transport and Energy, 1992—; mem. permanent energy commn. Tech. Chamber of Greece, Athens, 1991-98; mem. governing bd. Inst. for Continuing Edn. of Chem. Engrs., Athens, 1989-93. Author: Renewable Energy Sources in Greece, 1989, Energy Saving Technologies and Equipment for the Chemical Industry, 1994, Energy-Efficient Industrial Gas Equipment and Technologies, 1995, Economic Instruments for the Application of Environmental Policies in the Energy Sector, 1997; author, editor: Advances in Coal Chemistry, 1988. Recipient Cert. of Recognition NASA, 1982, 88. Mem. Am. Chem. Soc. (Bituminous Coal Rsch./R.A. Glenn award 1983), Hellenic Mgmt. Assn., Sigma Xi. Greek Orthodox. Avocations: poetry, art, art critique. Fax: 00301-9510800. Home: 20 Armatolon St Daphne, 17235 Athens Greece Office: Network Cons Group, 56 Arapaki Str, 17676 Kallithea Athens Greece

VASSILEV, GEORGE ALEKSANDROV, lawyer; b. Rudozem, Bulgaria, Dec. 25, 1957; s. Aleksander Georgiev and Violeta Yordanova (Dimitrova) V.; m. Antoaneta Liubenova Bozleva, Mar. 18, 1979; children: Aleksander, Elena. M of Laws, Sofia (Bulgaria) U., 1981. In house lawyer Wholesale, Russe, Bulgaria, 1982-84, Prodexim, Sofia, 1984-86; arbitrator Sofia City Arbitration Ct., 1986-92; judge Sofia City Ct., 1992-93; assoc. Legacom Antov & Ptnrs., Sofia, 1993—. Avocations: fishing, shooting, taking walks with pet dogs. Office: Legacom Antov and Ptnrs, 47 Burel St, 1408 Sofia Bulgaria

VASSILEV, HRISTO STOYNOV, engineer; b. Troyan, Lovech, Bulgaria, Mar. 21, 1969; s. Stoyno Vlkov and Victoria Todorova (Dimitrova) V.; 1 child: Christopher Hristov Vasilev. Engr. in Radioelectronics, HMSA "G. Benkovski", D. Mitropolya, Bulgaria, 1993. Flight navigator, lt. Bulgarian Air Force, Sofia, Bulgaria, 1993-94; engr. self-employed Troyan, Bulgaria, 1995; assoc. Advt. Agy., Troyan, Bulgaria, 1996. E-mail: hristo vassilev@yahoo.com. Home: HR Botev #9, 5600 Troyan Bulgaria

VASSILIKOS, VASSILIOS PERICLES, cardiologist, educator; b. Thessaloniki, Macedonia, Greece, Feb. 4, 1959; s. Pericles and Cathy (Prevedouraki) V.; m. Zoe Metaxa, Oct. 11, 1997; children: Catherine, Pericles. MD, Med. Sch. Thessaloniki, 1983, PhD, 1989. Med. diplomate. Registrar St. Bartholomew's Hosp., London, 1990-93; attending physician Onassis Cardiac Surgery Ctr., Athens, Greece, 1993-99; lectr. Aristotle U., Thessaloniki, 1999—. Author: Electrocardiography of Tachycardias, 1993; contbr. articles to profl. jours. Fellow European Soc. Cardiology; mem. N.Am. Soc. Pacing and Electrophysiology, Brit. Pacing and Electrophysiology Group. Greek Orthodox. Avocations: sailing, photography, mountaineering. Home: 45 Alex Svolou St, 54621 Thessaloniki Greece Office: Aristotelian U Thessaloniki, Med Sch, Thessaloniki Greece

VASSILIOU, GEORGE VASSOS, former president of Cyprus, consulting company executive; b. Famagusta, Cyprus, May 20, 1931; s. Vassos George and Sophia Othonos (Yavopoulou) V.; m. Androulla Georgiadou, Oct. 9, 1966; children: Sophia, Evelthon, Vassiliki. D of Econs., U. Geneva; postgrad., Budapest U., 1957; doctorate (hon.), Budapest U., Hungary, U. Athens, Greece. Market researcher Reed Paper Group, London, 1960-62; establisher MEMRB Internat., Nicosia, Cyprus, 1962—, chmn., 1962—; pres. Cyprus, 1988-93; leader United Dems. (formerly Free Dem. Movement), Cyprus, 1993—; Vis. prof. Cranfield Sch. Mgmt.; founder, prin. Middle East Ctr. for Mgmt. Studies, 1984; frequent speaker internat. confs. and seminars Middle East, 1972-82; head negotiating team for accession of Cyprus to EU. Author: Marketing in the Middle East, 1980; Marketing Handbook, 1986. Contbr. articles to various publs. Bd. dirs. Cyprus State Fair Authority, 1970-78; mem. Edn. Adv. Coun., econ. adv. coun. Ch. of Cyprus, 1980-88, internat. adv. com. Ctr. European Policy Rsch., Brussels; chmn. UN Univ./World Inst. Devel. Econs. Rsch.; mem. InterAction Coun., Tokyo, Trilateral Commn., Europe; bd. govs. Shimon Peres Inst. for Peace. Decorated Grand Cross of the Legion of Honour, France, Grand Cross of the Order of the Saviour, Greece, Grand Cross of the Holy Sepulchre, Greek Orthodox Patriarchate of Jerusalem; recipient distinctions, awards and decorations fgn. govts. including Standard (Flag) Order, Hungary. Office: MEMRB Internat, PO Box 22098, Nicosia Cyprus

VASSILOPOULOS, YERASSIMOS GEORGE, marketing and merchandising company executive; b. Athens, Greece, May 14, 1957; s. George and Natalia (Valsamakis) V. B in Bus., Higher Sch. Econs., Athens, 1980; MBA, Northwestern U., 1982. Merchandising mgr. V Giant Supermarket, Athens, 1984-87; gen. mgr. Bass & Bass Ltd., Athens, 1987—. Served with Greek Navy, 1982-84. Mem. Athens Coll. Alumni Assn., Athens C. of C. (export dept.). Avocations: sports, plants. Office: Bass & Bass Ltd, 3 Codrou, Filothei, 15237 Athens Greece

VASTA, EDWARD, humanities educator; b. Forest Park, Ill., Jan. 18, 1928; s. Joseph and Josephine (Mallimaci) V.; m. Geraldine Stocco, Nov. 28, 1953; children: John, Paula, Joseph, Catherine, Barbara, Salvatore. BA in English, U. Notre Dame, 1952; MA in English Lang. and Lit., U. Mich., 1954; PhD in English and Humanities, Stanford U., 1963. Tchg. intern, acting instr. Stanford U., Palo Alto, Calif., 1956-58; instr. U. Notre Dame, Ind., 1958-61, asst. prof., 1961-66, assoc. prof., 1966-69, prof., 1969-97; prof. emeritus U. Notre Dame, 1998—; fellow Medieval Inst. U. Notre Dame, Ind., 1993—. Author: The Spiritual Basis of Piers Plowman, 1965; editor: Middle English Survey, 1965, Interpretations of Piers Plowman, 1968; co-editor: Chaucerian Problems and Perspectives, 1979; co-translator: Dante Alighieri, Vita Nuova, 1995. With USN, 1946-48. Fulbright scholar, 1952-53; Grad. Honors fellow Stanford U., 1958, 59; Danforth grantee, 1961; Creative Writing fellow Nat. Endowment for Arts, 1979. Democrat. Roman Catholic. Home: 52140 Harvest Dr South Bend IN 46637-2923 Office: U Notre Dame 517 Flanner Notre Dame IN 46556-5644

VASTAGH, GEORGE FREDERICK, physician; b. Budapest, Jan. 11, 1936; s. Alajos Gusztaf and Ilona Kuthan Vastagh; m. Ann Beam Devos, Mar. 12, 1976 (div. Aug. 1987); children: Andrew, Victoria, Joseph, Vincent. MS, U. Budapest, 1954; MD, U. Graz, 1959; DSc (hon.), U. Budapest, 1963; JD (hon.), U. Minn., 1971. Prof. medicine U. Tex., Dallas, 1962-72; assoc. med. dir. Abbott Labs., North Chicago, Ill., 1972-82; med. dir. Schering-Plough Co., Memphis, 1982-87; pres. G.F. Vastagh, Memphis, 1987—; legal med. cons. Tenn. Bar Assn., Memphis, 1987-91. Author: Muscle Metabolism, 1971; patentee in field; contbr. articles to profl. jours. Maj. U.S. Army, 1960-62. Fellow Rockefeller Inst.; mem. Pilots Assn., Hungarian Univ. Students in Exile (pres. 1960). Roman Catholic. Avocations: woodworking, flight instructor, gourmet cooking. E-mail: Gvastagh@aol.com. Home and Office: 2427 Redbud Trail Dr Germantown TN 38139-6427

VASTI, THOMAS FRANCIS, III, lawyer; b. Poughkeepsie, N.Y., Sept. 22, 1966; s. Thomas F. Jr. and Faith Vasti; m. Suzanne Hammond, Aug. 17, 1991; children: Annelise Nicole, Matthew Thomas. BA, U. Notre Dame, 1988; JD, U. St. John's, 1991. Bar: N.Y. 1992, Conn. 1992, U.S. Dist. Ct. (ea. dist.) N.Y. 1995, U.S. Dist. Ct. (so. dist.) N.Y. 1995. Law clk. Vasti & Rutberg, Pleasant Valley, N.Y., 1988-91; assoc. Vasti & Sears, Pleasant Valley, 1991-96; v.p., sr. atty. Vasti & Sears, P.C., Pleasant Valley, 1996—; spkr. Landlord/Tenant Litigation Nat. Bus. Inst., 1995. Treas., head coach No. Dutchess Raiders Pop Warner, Millbrook, N.Y., 1991—. Mem. ABA, ATLA, N.Y. State Bar Assn., N.Y. State Trial Lawyers Assn., Dutchess County Bar Assn., Pleasant Valley C. of C. (v.p., trustee 1992—), KC, Notre Dame Alumni Club (sec. mid. Hudson Valley 1997, 98, v.p. 1999—). Republican. Roman Catholic. Avocations: youth sports coaching, golf, hunting, fishing, trombone playing. Office: Vasti & Sears PC 1733 Main St Rte 44 PO Box 656 Pleasant Valley NY 12569-0656

VASUDEV, KADABA SRINATH, histopathologist, cytopathologist, consultant; b. Mysore, India, May 5, 1943; s. Srinath Vedanta Kadaba and Lalitha (Krishna Iyengar) S.; m. Pratibha Narayan, June 29, 1972; children: Naveen, Chetan, Archana. MB BS, U. Bangalore, India, 1966. Lectr. in pathology Bangalore Med. Coll., 1968-69; sr. house officer Withington Hosp., Manchester, Eng., 1969-70, registrar in pathology, 1970-72; sr. registrar N.W. Regional Health Authority, Manchester, 1972-77; cons. in pathology Blackpool (Eng.) Victoria Hosp. NHS Trust, 1977—, clin. dir. directorate of pathology, 1993-96; postgrad. tutor U. Manchester, Blackpool, 1982-93, undergrad. tutor, 1982-93. Bd. govs. St. George's H.S., Blackpool; mem. standing adv. coun. on religious edn., Blackpool Borough Coun. Fellow Royal Coll. Pathologists (U.K.); mem. Internat. Acad. Pathology, Brit. Med. Assn. (sec. Blackpool divsn.), Overseas Doctors Assn. (pres. Blackpool divsn.), Life Edn. Ctr. Lancashire, Rotary Club of Blackpool Palatine (pres. 1995-96, drug awareness advisor Rotary Dist. 1190), Blackpool Ehtnic Minorities Liaison Group, trustee, Handicapped Aid Trust, Lytham. Hindu. Avocations: music, theatre, photography, coin collecting, cricket. Home: 10 Silverdale Rd, Saint Annes Lancs FY8 3RE, England

Office: Blackpool Victoria Hosp, Whinney Heys Rd, Blackpool Lancs FY3 8NR, England

VASUDEVAN, M. K., petroleum company executive; b. Rewa, India, Sept. 1, 1953; s. M. S. and K.R. (Padma) Krishnaswamy; m. Dhaya Rajanarayanan, Nov. 5, 1989; 1 child, Divya. B of Tech. in Chem. Engring., Indian Inst. Tech., Chennai, 1975; MS in Chem. Engring., Stanford U., 1977. Registered profl. engr., Calif., 1982. Process engr. Envirotech Corp., Belmont, Calif., 1977-79, Bechtel Corp., San Francisco, 1979-83, Advanced Micro Devices, Sunnyvale, Calif., 1984; sr. process engr. Madras Fertilizers, Chennai, India, 1988; dep. mgr. devel. Madras Refineries, Chennai, 1989-94, mgr. corp. planning, 1994—; engring. cons., Chennai, 1985-87. Vol. The Hunger Project Internat., San Francisco, 1978-83. Hindu. Avocations: professional journals, news, entertainment and sports shows, computers, travel, family. Home: 5D 5th Fl Front Blk, 57/2 B East Coast Rd, Thiruvanmiyur 600041, India Office: Madras Refineries Ltd, 552 Anna Salai Teynam Pet, Chennai 600018, India

VASUDEVAN, THIRUMALAI CHAKRAVARTHI, mathematician, educator; b. Kanchipuram, Madras, India, Sept. 19, 1946; s. Thirumalai Chakravarthi Ghanta Vijayaraghava Chariar and Thirumalai Chakravarthi Amirtha Amirthammal; m. Vasudevan Vanaja, Feb. 7, 1977; 1 child, T.C. Vijaya Raghavan. BSc, Pachaiappas Coll., Kanchipuram, 1967; MSc, Vivekananda Coll., Madras, 1969; PhD, Tata Inst Fundamental Rsch., Bombay, 1979. Grad. tchr. Govt. H.S., Madras, 1969-70; from lectr. to prof. Vivekanada Coll., Madras, 1970-86, prof., 1986—; vis. mem. Tata Inst. Fundamental Rsch., Bombay, 1973-77, Internat. Ctr. Pure and Applied Math., Nice, France, 1992, Max Planck Inst., Bonn, Germany, 1992, U. Münster, Germany, 1992. Reviewer Math. Reviews, 1989; patentee in field; contbr. articles to profl. jours. Recipient Dr. Radhakrishnan's award for best tchrs. Govt. Tamil Nadu. Mem. Am. Math. Soc., Ramanujan Math. Soc. (life), Assn. Math. Tchrs. India (joint acad. sec. 1990), Indian Math. Soc. Hindu-Brahmin. Avocations: Indian classical music, reading Sanskrit scriptures, travel, card games, book collecting. Home: 24 VSV Koil St, Mylapore 600004, India Office: Ramakrishna Mission, Vivekananda Coll Mylapore, Madras 600004, India

VASVARI, BELA, physics educator emeritus; b. Bekescsaba, Hungary, Feb. 2, 1932; s. Etelka (Hild) B.; m. Maria Szilagyi; children: Aniko, Bela. Diploma, U. Szeged, 1954. Tchr. U. Szeged, 1954-58, U. Debrecen, 1958-67; physics rschr. Cen. Rsch. Inst. for Physics, Budapest, 1967-84; prof. physics Tech. U. Budapest, 1984-98, emeritus prof., 1998—; scientific dir. Inst. Solid State Physics of the Cen. Rsch. Inst. for Physics, Budapest, 1971-79; dir. Inst. of Physics, Tech. U. Budapest, 1984-92. Co-author books in field, 1969, 84; contbr. articles to profl. jours. Office: Tech U Budapest, Budafoki ut 8/POB 112, Budapest H-1111, Hungary

VASYLYEV, OLEKSIY VSEVOLOD, information brokering company executive; b. Taganzog, Rostov, Russia, Apr. 12, 1959; s. Vsevolod Victor and Lilia Alexey (Simak) V.; m. Victoria Vladimir Tchetch, Apr. 28, 1994; children: Artur, Daria. Diploma Engr., Kiev (Ukraine) Poly. U., 1982; PhD, Nat. Acad. Sci., Kiev, 1991. Engr., rschr. Poly. U., Kiev, 1982-85; sci. rschr. Nat. Acad. Sci., Kiev, 1985-92; dep. dir. Vernadsky Ctrl. Sci. Libr., Kiev, 1992-93; dir. Internat. Info. Ctr./DZXXI, Kiev, 1993-95; dep. dir. FRACSIM-IMM Ltd., Kiev, 1995-96, Book Chamber of Ukraine, Kiev, 1996—. Mem. IEEE, Assn. for Computing Machinery, N.Y. Acad. Sci. Avocation: travel. Office: FRACCSIM-IMM Ltd, PO Box 110, 01010 Kyiv Ukraine

VATAKAS, LEANDROS CONSTANTINOS, ophthalmologist; b. Thessaloniki, Macedonia, Greece, June 29, 1942; s. Constantinos Leandros and Eve Nikolaos (Asimopoulou) V.; m. Victoria George Samaras, Dec. 14, 1968; children: Constantinos, Helen. MD, Aristotels U., Thessaloniki, Greece, 1968, diploma in ophthalmology, 1972. Asst. ophthalmology Hippokration Hosp., Thessaloniki, 1969-72, sr. registrar Eye Clinic, 1974-77; hon. registrar Moorfields Eye Hosp., London, 1972-73; rsch. fellow Inst. Ophthalmology, London, 1973-74; pvt. practice Thessaloniki, 1974—; cons. eye dept. Saratianos Gen. Clinic, Thessaloniki, 1977-90, eye dept. Galinos Gen. Clinic, Thessaloniki, 1990—; responsible for doctors Amnesty Internat., Thessaloniki, 1984-87; gen. sec. Pvt. Practice Doctors, Thessaloniki, 1985-87, Soc. Practising Ophthalmologists, Thessaloniki, 1980-83; responsible for Thessaloniki Experiment in Internat. Living, 1962-63; co-founder, joint-owner Irmos Art Galery, Thessaloniki, 1984—. Translator, editor: T.S. Eliot - Collected Poems, 1994, Theatrical Works, 1998; producer 16 sci. films, 1970-77; contbr. numerous articles to profl. jours. Elected mem. City Coun., Thessaloniki, 1982-86; pres. 1st Sch. Com. Thessaloniki, 1987-92; gen. sec. Assn. Thessalonikean Students Aristotel's U., 1960-63; bd. dirs. Mcpl. Theatre Orgn. Thessaloniki, 1985-88. Recipient Hon. Diploma, Mayor and City Coun. Thessaloniki, 1988, Hon. Diploma and Medal, Mayor and City Coun., 1992. Fellow Royal Coll. Ophthalmologists (U.K.); mem. Greek Ophthal. Soc., Greek Soc. Cataract and Refractive Surgeons, Ophthal. Soc. No. Greece, N.Y. Acad. Scis., European Soc. Cataract and Refractive Surgeons, Panhellenic Ophthal. Soc., Bridge Club Thessaloniki, Mensa Internat. (spkr.). Liberal Democrat. Mem. Christian Orthodox Ch. Avocations: art, poetry, bridge, classical music, reading. Home: Lida-Maria Danai 2, 57001 Thermi Thessaloniki, Greece Office: 36 Hermou Str, 54623 Thessaloniki Greece

VATANDOOST, NOSSI MALEK, art school administrator; b. Teheran, Iran, May 22, 1935; d. Abdullah Goodar and Mahtaban (Goodar) Malek; B.A., Western Ky. U., 1970; m. Ira Vatandoost, May 30, 1964; children: Debbie, Cyrus. Art tchr. Met.-Davidson County Sch. System, Nashville, 1970-71; dir., owner Nossi Coll. Art, Goodlettsville, Tenn., 1973—, dir. Tenn. Proprietary Bus. Sch. Assn., Inc., pres. Crimson Corp.; treas. Malek & Assos. Inc., 1976; dir. EXCEL Edn. Corp., 1980-86; vis. lectr., cons. EXCEL Bus. Inst., 1980-86. Active mem. Nat. Trust for Hist. Preservation. Mem. NAFE, Nat. Mus. Women in the Arts (charter), Nat. Assn. of Schs. of Art and Design, Hendersonville Art Council, Hendersonville Art Guild (com. chmn.), Career Coll. Assn., Art Inst. Nashville (founder, CEO), Internat. Coun. Design Schs. (pres. 1997-98). Club: Soroptimists (Upper Cumberland Valley, Tenn.). Home: 105 Country Club Dr Hendersonville TN 37075-4024 Office: 907 Two Mile Pky Goodlettsville TN 37072-2324

VATAVUK, WILLIAM MICHAEL, chemical engineer, author; b. Sharon, Pa., Jan. 30, 1947; s. William James and Amelia Agnes (Lenarcic) V.; m. Betsy Ann Chandler, Oct. 27, 1973; 1 child, William Chandler. B in Engring., Youngstown State U., Ohio, 1969. Registered profl. engr., N.C. Chem. engr. E.I. DuPont de Nemours, Richmond, Va., 1969-70; sr. chem. engr. U.S. EPA, Durham, N.C., 1970-99; pres. Vatavuk Engring., 1999—. Author: Dawn of Peace, 1989 (Pulitzer nomination 1990), Estimating Costs of Air Pollution Control, 1990, Marketing Yourself with Technical Writing, 1992; editor Environ. Progress jour.; inventor Vatavuk Air Pollution Control Cost Indexes; contbr. articles to profl. jours. Chmn. Bennett Pl. Hist. Site Adv. Com., Durham, 1992—; publicity chmn. Hist. Preservation Soc. Durham, 1989-90; bd. dirs. N.C. 4-H Devel. Fund, Raleigh, N.C., 1990-93; tchr., Sunday sch. CCD, 1993; mem. mgmt. com. Durham Youth Coordinating Bd., 1999—. Capt. USPHS, 1970-99. Mem. N.C. Farm Bur., N.C. Grange, USPHS Commd. Officers Assn. (pres. N.C. br. 1975-76, 84-85), Ret. Officers Assn. (life). Democrat. Roman Catholic. Avocations: reading, writing, jogging, gardening, solving puzzles. Office: 3512 Angus Rd Durham NC 27705-5404

VATCHER, JAMES GORDON, retired physician; b. Long Beach, Calif., June 14, 1925; s. Marshall James and Elise Ione (McElhinney) V.; m. Helen Stockwell (div.); children: Michael Gordon, Howard Peter, Donald Alan, Mary Helen, Kimberly Ann; m. Dorothy Caswell, June 1978. BA, Leland Stanford Jr. U., 1950; MD, Stanford U., 1954. Intern in surgery Stanford (Calif.) U. Hosp., 1953-54; resident Stanislaus County Hosp., Calif., 1954-56; physician surgeon Calif. Instn. for Women Dept. Corrections, Frontera, Calif., 1982-97; ret. Bsn Mate III USN CB, 1943-46. Democrat. Avocations: complementary medicine, nutrition, anti oxidant molecular/functional medicine, communication. Home: 872 S Cedarwood St Orange CA 92869-5301

VATER, HEINZ, linguist; b. Frankfort on the Oder, Germany, July 29, 1932. PhD, U. Hamburg, 1962, PhD habilitation, 1969. Asst. prof. U. Hamburg, 1963-69; assoc. prof. Ind. U., Bloomington, 1969-72; prof. U. Cologne, Fed. Republic Germany, 1972-97. Author: Das System der Artikelformen im gegenwärtigen, Deutsch, 1963, 2d edit., 1979, Dänische Subjekt - und Objektsätze, 1973, Strukturalismus und Transformationsgrammatik, 1982, Einführung in die Raumlinguistik, 1991, 3rd rev. edit., 1996, Einführung in die Zeitlinguistik, 1994, 3rd rev. edit., 1994, Einführung in die Textlinguistik, 1992, Einf in die Sprachwissenschaft, 1994, 3rd rev. edit., 1999; editor: (series) Linguistische Arbeiten, Deutsch-polnisches Jahrbuch, Fokus, KLAGE; several anthologies; contbr. numerous articles to profl. jours. Mem. German Linguistic Soc. (chmn. 1986-88), Linguistic Soc. Am., Soc. Linguistica Europaea, Germanistenverband. Office: Univ Cologne, Inst Deutsche Sprache u Lit, D 50923 Cologne Germany

VATNE, KAARE BIRGER, company executive; b. Torsken, Troms, Norway, Feb. 2, 1943; s. Ivar Paulsen and Laura (Karlsen) V.; m. Ingrid Linea Hermansson, July 28, 1984. Cert. engr., Gøteborg Tech. Inst., Sweden, 1962; BSc with honors, U. Strathclyde, Glasgow, Scotland, 1967. Devel. mgr. Procter & Gamble, Newcastle & London, 1968-71; devel. mgr. Elopak, Oslo, 1971-75, v.p., 1983-93, exec. v.p., 1993-98; mktg. mgr. Uddeholm, Skoghall, Sweden, 1975-78; devel. mgr. Allpak, London, 1978-83; pres. VATNE Consulting, Asker, Norway, 1998—; chmn. Unifill Internat. AG, Switzerland, 1995-98; mng. dir. Unifill Spa, Modena, Italy, 1997-98; bd. dirs. Catering Devel., Sweden, 1990-98; chmn. Norester S.A., France, 1995-98. Mem. Norwegian Soc. Chartered Engrs. Home and Office: Prinsessetien 17, 1391 Vollen Norway

VATTILANA, JOSEPH WILLIAM, retired chief state safety inspector; b. Wilmington, Del., Mar. 22, 1928; s. Andrew and Elizabeth (Castiglione) V.; (div. 1974); children: Joseph W., Joy Ann; m. Gladys Mary Spence, Nov. 18, 1978. Student, Del. Tech. Community Coll., 1966-70, 89—, Pa. State U., 1976-80. Cert. field instr., instr. for radiation control, work zone safety supr., dir. fleet maintenance, flagger instr. Heavy equipment mechanic Dept. Hwys. and Transp., Bear, Del., 1963-70; equipment supt. Dept. Hwys. and Transp., Bear, 1970-79, hwy. safety engr., 1979-84, chief safety inspector, 1984—; instr. Flagger-Nat. Safety Coun., 1997; safety cons. for pvt. engring. co., 1994—; speaker and instr. in field. Author: Safety Manual Pass the Word, 1987, Equipment Certification Manuel, 1987, Do Something-Traffic Controls for Emergency Personnel, 1999. Dep. chief, asst. chief-chief driver, bd. dirs., capt. of rescue, sec. Talleyville (Del.) Vol. Fire Co., 1946-98; instr. ARC Del. chpt., Wilmington, 1956—; hon. life mem. Wilmington Manor Vol. Fire Co., 1985—. Recipient disting. svc. award State of Del., 1986, Lammot duPont Jr. meml. award Del. chpt. ARC, 1989, nat. safety award Am. Traffic Safety Svcs., 1992, Outstanding Vol. of Yr. award Del. Safety Coun., 1996; named man of yr. 1994 Am. Soc. Hwy. Engrs., hon. staff officer Del. State Police, 1994; recipient spl. recognition safety award Federal Hwy. Adminstrn., 1994. Mem. Am. Soc. Hwy. Engrs. (exec. dir. 1st State chpt. 1997), New Castle County Fire Chiefs Assn. (pres. 1985-86), New Castle County Vol. Firemans Assn. (pres. 1986-87), Del. State Fire Chiefs Assn. (pres. 1993-94), Del. Hwy. Engrs. (1st and 2nd v.p. 1987-89), Soc. Hwy Engrs. (pres. 1st state chpt. 1988-90), Del. State Fire Police Assn. (hon. life), Del. Safety Engrs. (pres. 1986-87), Am. Legion (life), VFW (life). Roman Catholic. Avocations: woodworking, gardening, fishing. Home: 3333 Silverside Rd Wilmington DE 19810-4804

VAUCHEZ, ANDRÉ, school administrator, history educator; b. Thionville, Moselle, France, July 24, 1938; s. Antoine and Georgette (Rabbe) V.; m. Denise Mayeur, May 25, 1962; children: Etienne, Anne, Antoine. Grad., The Sorbonne, Paris, 1961, LittD, 1978. Cert. univ. tchr., rschr. Asst. prof. The Sorbonne, Paris, 1968-72; asst. dir. French Sch. at Rome, 1972-79; prof. medieval history Rouen (France) U., 1980-82, U. Paris X, Nanterre, 1983-95; dir. French Sch. at Rome, 1995—. Fellow Ecole Normale Supérieure, 1958-63, sr. fellow Inst. Univ. de France, 1991-95, 98—. Mem. Academie des Inscriptions et Belles-Lettres, Pontificio Comitato Di Scienze Storiche, Accademia Dei Lincei. Office: French Sch at Rome, Piazza Farnese 67, 00186 Rome Italy

VAUDREY, BARBARA, physician, surgeon; b. Walthamstow, Eng., Oct. 29, 1922; d. Reginald Guley and Katharine (Day) Lewis; m. Oliver Claude Vaudrey, July 10, 1954; children: Claude William, Joseph Henry, Caroline Ann. BS, BS, London U., 1953. House physician Barnet Gen. Hosp., Eng., 1953-54, hosue surgeon, 1954-55; gen. practice medicine London, 1955-57, Suffolk, Eng., 197-&; asst. police surgeon Suffolk County Constabulary, 1974-87. Contbr. articles to profl. jours. Mem. parish coun., Stoke Ash, 1972-88, chmn., 1981-84; mem. com. Women's Inst. Stoke Ash, 1970-84, chmn., 1971-72; mem. Royal Brit. Legion, 1983—, pres., 1985. Served with Aux. Territorial Svc., 1942-46. Mem. Royal Coll. Gen. Practitioners (faculty bd. 1975-88), Med. Women's Fedn., Brit. Med. ASsn. Anglican. Avocations: knitting, reading, church bell ringing, drawing, metal work.

VAUGEL, MARTINE OLGA, sculptor, educator; b. N.Y.C., Jan. 24, 1950; d. Ernest Peter and Simone Lee (Jehan) V.; m. Jim. Vaccanella, 1995; children: Taj, Collin. Student, Phila. Coll. Art, 1966, Rockland Community Coll., 1967, Beaux Art Paris, 1973. Sculptor, instr., 1966—; founder Vaugel Sculpture Studio, Vihiers, France, 1989, Venice Sculpture Studio; co-founder Venice Painting, Drawing and Sculpture Studio; sculpture dir. N.Y. Acad. Art, 1987-89. Prin. works in Japan's Hakone Open Air Mus., Martin Luther King Jr. Meml., Bank of Am. World Trade Ctr., L.A. Mus. Contemporary Art, Rockefeller Collection, collection's of Pres.'s Bush, Reagan and Carter, Corazon Aquino, Mikhail Gorbachev, Mayor Tom Bradley, Sir Richard Attenborough, Mother Teresa, City of L.A., on Manhatma Gandhi's ashes at the Self Realization Fellowship. Recipient Hakone Open Air Mus. award, 1992, Utsukushi-Ga-Hara Open Air Mus. award, 1990. Home: Les Cerqueux Sous Passavanc, Vihiers 49310, France

VAUGHAN, DINDY BELINDA, media company executive; b. Sydney, Kogarah, Australia, Dec. 26, 1938; d. Geoffrey Samuel and Honora Marie Julienne (Duggan) V. BA with honors, Sydney (Australia) U., 1967; MA, Flinders U., Adelaide, Australia, 1970. Lectr. Royal Melbourne Inst. of Tech., Melbourne, Australia, 1972-74; contract lectr. Footscray Inst. of Tech. (now Victoria U. of Tech.), Melbourne, 1974-83; acad. assessor Deakin U., Geelong, Australia, 1983-96; dir. Vaughan Willoughby Pub., Melbourne, 1987—, Gallery Without Walls, Melbourne, 1990—; founding tutor Footscray (Australia) Cmty. Arts Ctr., 1975-84; guest lectr. arts Interstate Univs., Adelaide, 1978; cmty. arts officer Nunawading City Coun., Melbourne, 1979-82; guest composer Utassy Ballet, Nachtmusique Chamber Group, Melbourne, 1984-96; rschr., writer Australia Coun., Sydney, 1985-87; bd. mem. Dandenong Ranges Cultural Ctr., Melbourne, 1997. Author: Multiculturalism and the Arts, 1985, Perspective on Visual Arts, 1987, Environmental Action Resource Catalogue, 1990; editor books on arts and the environment, 1984-98; columnist on arts, 1979-82, 94-96; composer, pub.: Out of Home Piano Music and Songs vols. 1 and 2, 1991, Wimmera Quartet Flute and Strings, 1992, Reconciliation Octet, 1996, Kununurre, 1998. Founding mem. Croydon Cmty. Svc. Group, Melbourne, 1974, Cmty. Arts Network, Melbourne, 1975-84; environ. cons. Environment Victoria, Koonung Mullum Forestway Assn., Candlebark Cmty. Nursery, Croydon City Coun., Melbourne, 1988-98. Recipient Alumni award for achievement in cmty. svc. U. Sydney, 1996. Mem. Australian Geog. Soc., Australian Conservation Found., U. Sydney Alumni Assn. (life). Avocations: bushwalking, planting and regenerating native bushland, recording oral history. Office: Gallery Without Walls, PO 668, Ringwood VIC 3134, Australia

VAUGHAN, EUGENE H., investment company executive; b. Brownsville, Tenn., Oct. 5, 1933; s. Eugene H. Sr. and Margaret (Musgrave) V.; m. Susan Bolinger Westbrook, May 11, 1963; children: Margaret Corbin, Richard Bolinger. BA, Vanderbilt U., 1955; MBA, Harvard U., 1961. CFA, 1967. Security analyst Putnam Mgmt. Co., Boston, 1961-64; dir., dir. rsch. Underwood, Neuhaus & Co., Inc., Houston, 1964-70; pres., chief exec. officer Vaughan, Nelson & Boston, Inc., Houston, 1970-77, Vaughan, Nelson, Scarborough & McCullough, L.P., Houston, 1970—; chmn. bd. dirs. Founders Asset Mgmt. Co., Denver, 1970—. Chair Fin. Analyst Fedn., N.Y.C., 1973-74, bd. dirs., 1969-76; pres. Houston Soc. Fin. Analysts, 1967-68; bd. dirs., chmn. investment com. Presbyn. Bd. Pensions (USA), Phila., 1988-95; trustee exec. com. Vanderbilt U., Nashville, 1972—, St. John's Sch., Houston, 1980-85, Goodwill Industries, Houston, 1978—, United Way of Tex. Gulf Coast, 1994—; elder First Presbyn. Ch., 1976—; founding chmn., trustee Presbyn. Sch., Houston, 1986-90. Lt. USN, 1955-58. Recipient Disting. Svc. award Fin. Analyst Fedn., 1978, Humanitarian award Am. Jewish Com., 1993, Disting. Svc. award Houston Soc. Fin. Analysts, 1993, Bus. Leader of Yr. award U. St. Thomas, 1996. Mem. Inst. Chartered Fin. Analysts (trustee 1986-93, chmn. 1989), Assn. for Investment Mgmt. and Rsch. (founding chmn. 1990-91, gov. 1990-93), Greater Houston Partnership (bd. dirs. 1990—, exec. com. 1993—, chair Ctr. Houston's Future 1999—), Houston Club (pres. 1983-84, bd. dirs. 1979-85, chair centennial celebration, 1992-94), Houston Country Club, Coronado Club (Houston), Houston Forum (pres. 1991-92, chmn. 1992-93), Harvard U. Bus. Sch. Club Houston (pres. 1968-69, bd. dirs. 1966-71, 86-90), Vanderbilt Club Houston (chmn. 1984—, pres. 1966-68, Disting. Svc. award 1994), Conferie des Chevaliers du Tastevin, Belle Meade Country Club (Nashville). Republican. Avocations: traveling, sailing. Home: 3465 Inwood Dr Houston TX 77019-3129 Office: Vaughan Nelson Scarborough & McCullough 6300 Chase Tower Houston TX 77002

VAUGHAN, GWEN MORRIS, poet; b. Mar. 17, 1937. Grad. h.s., Portsmouth, Va., 1955. Paraprofl. Portsmouth Sch. Bd., 1964-67, 88, 93.

VAUGHAN, HERBERT WILEY, retired lawyer; b. Brookline, Mass., June 1, 1920; s. David D. and Elzie G. (Wiley) V.; m. Ann Graustein, June 28, 1941. Student, U. Chgo., 1937-38; BS cum laude, Harvard U., 1941, LLB, 1948. Bar: Mass. 1948. Assoc. Hale and Dorr, Boston, 1948-54, jr. ptnr., 1954-56, sr. ptnr., 1956-89, co-mng. ptnr., 1976-80, of counsel, 1990-95, ptnr., 1996-2000; ret., 2000; mem. bd. dirs. and fin. com. Boston and Maine R.R., 1961-64. Mem. standing com. The Trustees of Reservations, 1986-98, chmn., 1988-92, sec., 1992-98, asst. sec., mem. adv. coun., 1998—; mem. bd. trustees Am. Friends New Coll. (Oxford U.); mem. adv. coun. James Madison Program in Am. Ideals and Instns., Princeton U. Fellow Am. Bar Found. (life); mem. ABA, Chesterton Soc. (internat. com.), Mass. Bar Assn., Boston Bar Assn., Am. Law Inst., Am. Coll. Real Estate Lawyers, Am. Coun. Trustees and Alumni (mem. alumni leadership coun.), Bay Club, Badminton and Tennis Club, Union Club (Boston), Boston Econ. Club, Longwood Cricket Club (Brookline). Office: Hale and Dorr LLP 60 State St Boston MA 02109-1816

VAUGHAN, OTHA H., JR., retired aerospace engineer, research scientist; b. Anderson, S.C., July 1, 1929; s. Otha H. and Ethel (Mayfield) V.; m. Betty Frances McCoy; children: Thera Virginia, Leslie, Frances. BS in Mech. Engring, Clemson U., 1951, MS in Mech. Engring., 1959; postgrad., U. Tenn. Space Inst., Tullahoma, 1975-81, U. Ala., Huntsville, 1974-75. Registered profl. engr., Ala. Commd. 2nd lt. USAF, 1951, advanced through grades to lt. col., 1972; mem. Von Braun R&D group Army Ballistic Missile Agy. (ABMA), Redstone Arsenal, Ala., 1956-60; retired USAF, 1979; rsch. engr., charter mem. NASA Marshall Space Flight Ctr., Huntsville, Ala., 1960-99, ret., 1999. Contbr. over 60 articles to profl. jours. Charter Mem. Aviation Hall of Fame, Dayton, Ohio. Fellow AIAA (assoc., Herman Oberth award Ala.-Miss. sect. 1999); mem. Air Force Assn. (past v.p. Huntsville chpt., life), Res. Officers Assn. (past pres. Huntsville, life), Minute Man Soc. Ala., Antique Aircraft Assn. (life), Exptl. Aircraft Assn., Soc. Interplanetary Free Floaters (zero-gravity flights in NASA KC-135 aircraft), 8th Air Force Hist. Soc. Blackbirds, Masons, Shriners, Nat. Space Club. Achievements include patent in Lunar Communications Receiver and Transmitter for Lunar Surface Missions; participation in design of rocket and space vehicle systems, research and development of Redstone, Jupiter, Jupiter C, Juno, Saturn I, Saturn IB, and Saturn V, Skylab and Apollo program, and the Space Shuttle launch vehicle systems; development of design criteria for lunar surface operations and mobility for Lunar Rover program; research in environmental design criteria for lunar and planetary exploration vehicles, zero-g atmospheric cloud physics, and atmosphere electricity research. Home: 10102 Westleigh Dr SE Huntsville AL 35803-1647

VAUGHAN, RODNEY GRANT, electrical engineer, communications scientist; b. Hamilton, New Zealand, Nov. 20, 1953; s. William and Lorna (Wason) V.; m. Helen Mary Smith, Apr. 16, 1977; children: Meta Louise, Elliot Graeme, Gregory Kendall. B in Engring., U. Canterbury, 1975, M in Engring., 1976; PhD, Aalborg U., 1985. Asst. prof. New Zealand Post Office, Wellington, 1976-77; from scientist to sr. rsch. engr., program leader Dept. Sci. and Indsl. Rsch., Lower Hutt, New Zealand, 1978-92; from team leader to programme leader New Zealand Inst. Indsl. Rsch., Lower Hutt, 1992—; cons. in field, 1989—. Contbr. articles to profl. jours. Mem. IEEE (sr.). Avocations: piano, classical guitar. Home: 12 Junction St Fairfield, Fairfield Lower Hutt 1, New Zealand Office: New Zealand Inst Indsl Rsch, Gracefield Rd PO Box 31310, Wellington New Zealand

VAUGHN, THOMAS JOSEPH, earth science educator, administrator; b. Lawrence, Mass., Dec. 23, 1944; s. Thomas Wilbur and Dorothy Agnes (Mallon) V.; m. Priscilla Margaret Bastian, June 30, 1973; children: Matthew Thomas, Judith Diane. BA in History/Geography, Mt. Carmel Coll., Niagara Falls, Ont., Can., 1968; AM in Geography, Boston U., 1972; MEd in Secondary Ednl. Adminstrn., U. Lowell, Mass., 1977; CAGS in Computers in Edn., Lesley Coll., Cambridge, Mass., 1985. Cert. tchr. earth sci., geography, history, cert. gen. supr., jr.-sr. h.s. prin., Mass. Tchr. earth sci. DeSales H.S., Louisville, 1968-69; tchg. fellow Boston U., 1969-71; liberal arts prof. Bryant-McIntosh Jr. Coll., Lawrence, 1971-72; asst. dir. project ESTEEM Harvard-Smithsonian, Cambridge, 1993; adult edn. instr. Arlington (Mass.) Pub. Schs., 1985-90; instr. earth sci. Northeastern U., Boston, 1997—; earth sci. tchr., lead sci. tchr. Arlington H.S., 1972—; telecomms. moderator Harvard U. Sci. Tchr. Network, Cambridge, 1986-89; chair study groups for sci. edn. reform Mass. Dept. Edn., Malden, 1995—, sci. tchr. leader, 1998. Co-author: Integrating Computers in Your Classroom: Middle and Secondary Science, 1994, Harvard Smithsonian Project IMAGE, 1997; presenter in field. Lector St. Theresa's Ch., Billerica, Mass., 1975—; trustee Billerica Pub. Libr., 1993—; mem. Billerica Friends of the Libr., 1995—. Recipient Pathfinder award in tech. Mass. Dept. Edn., 1991, Sci. Educator of Yr. award for Middlesex County, Mass. Assn. Sci. Tchrs., 1998, Presdl. award for excellence in tchg. math. and sci. NSF, 2000, Disting. Alumni award U. Mass., Lowell, 2000; Tandy Tech. scholar, 1996; inducted into Mass. Sci. Educators Hall of Fame, 1992. Mem. Nat. Assn. Geosci. Tchrs. (regional pres.), Nat. Sci. Tchrs. Assn., Nat. Geog. Soc., Mass. Assn. Scis. Tchrs. (award sect.), Gamma Theta Upsilon (local pres.). Democrat. Roman Catholic. Avocations: computers, telecommunications and Internet, reading journals and books, walking. Office: Arlington HS 869 Massachusetts Ave Arlington MA 02476-4701

VAURIO, JUSSI KALERVO, engineer and scientist; b. Lapua, Finland, Mar. 4, 1940; s. Juho and Rauha (Hietala) V.; m. Eija Hyotylainen, July 27, 1963; three children. Diploma in engring., U. Technology, Helsinki, Finland, 1967, DSc, 1971. Operating engr. Reactor Lab., Espoo, Finland, 1966-68; rschr. engr. Tech. Rsch. Ctr., Espoo, 1968-72; nuclear engr. Imatra Power Co., Helsinki, 1972-75, Argonne (Ill.) Nat. Lab., 1975-80; rsch. program mgr. ANL & DOE, Argonne, 1980-84; program mgr., head of tng. Imatra Power Co., Loviisa, Finland, 1984—; lectr. reliability and risk analysis Lappeenranta U. Tech., 1985—; reliability and risk analysis specialist. Contbr. 130 articles to sci. pubs. Mem. Am. Nuclear Soc., European Nuclear Soc., Soc. Risk Analysis. Achievements include comprehensive risk assessment and event data analysis system for nuclear power plant as well as methods and models in reliability and risk analysis, statistical analysis and stochastic processes. Office: Fortum Power and Heat, PO Box 23, 07901 Loviisa Finland

VAVILOV, GUENNADY ALEKSSEVICH, composer, music educator; b. Abdulino Orenburgskaia, Russia, May 7, 1932; s. Aleksey Sergeevich and Aleksandra Fedorovna (Pankeeva) V.; m. Natalia Ivanovna Romanenko, Mar. 17, 1971; 1 child. Ed., Conservatory, Leningrad, Russia, 1962-66, Conservatory, Moscow, 1973, 83, Univ., Petrozanodsk, Russia, 1978, Conservatory, Petrozanodsk, 1989, 99. Composer Union of Composers, Moscow, 1968—; tchr. theory of music and composition High Music Sch., Petrozavodsk, 1966-68; asst. prof. Conservatory, Petrozavodsk, 1968-99, prof., 1999—. Composer Cantata, 1958 (2d place Young Composers Competition), Peerileiki, 1978, Songs About War and Peace, 1971 (Komsomol prize 1978), My Music and Improvisation, 1996 (Platinum record for exceptional performance 1996). Mem. Culture Found. Bd., Karelia, 1986. Named Honoured Composer of Karelia, 1981, 95, Honoured Composer of Russia, 1987, Man of Yr., ABI, U.S., 1996, 97. Mem. Union of Composers of

Russia. Avocations: travel, chess. Home: Lenin str 13-3, 185000 Petrozavodsk Russia Office: Conservatory, Leningradskaia str 15, 18500 Petrozavodsk Russia

VAYDA, ANDREW P., human ecology and anthropology educator; b. Budapest, Hungary, Dec. 7, 1931; came to U.S., 1939; s. Sándor Vajda and Zelma Szentgyörgyi; m. Indah Setyawati, July 10, 1991 (div. July 1997). BA, Columbia U., 1952, PhD, 1956. From asst. prof. to assoc. prof. Columbia U., N.Y.C., 1960-68, prof., 1968-72; prof. Rutgers U., New Brunswick, N.J., 1972—; cons. World Wide Fund for Nature, Jakarta, Indonesia, 1992, 93, 98, Ford Found., Jakarta, 1981-84; disting. vis. scholar Ctr. for Internat. Forestry Rsch., Bogor, Indonesia, 1996. Author: (book) War in Ecological Perspective, 1976, (booklets) Bugis Settlers in East Kalimantan, 1996, Finding Causes of the 1997-98 Indonesian Forest Fires, 1998; editor-in-chief: (periodical) Human Ecology, 1971-77. Recipient Disting. Vis. Scholar award Ctr. for Internat. Forestry Rsch., 1996, Fulbright Lectr./Rsch. award USIA, 1989-90; vis. scholar grantee Ford Found., 1998; rsch. grantee NOAA, 2000. Fellow AAAS, Am. Anthropol. Assn., Borneo Rsch. Coun., Inst. Human Ecology. Avocations: food, traveling, playing squash. E-mail: vayda@aesop.rutgers.edu. Office: Rutgers U Dept Human Ecology New Brunswick NJ 08901

VAYENAS, CONSTANTINOS GEORGE, chemical engineering educator; b. Athens, Sept. 22, 1950; s. George Constantinos and Julia George (Kourousopoulou) V.; children: Julia, Vassia. Diploma, N.T. Univ., 1973; PhD, U. Rochester, 1977. Assoc. prof. MIT, Cambridge, 1981-83; dean of engring. U. Patras, Greece, 1983-86; vis. prof. Yale U., New Haven, 1991-92, EPFL, Lausanne, Switzerland, 1994; pres. Nat. Hellenic Rsch. Found., Athens, 1995-96; prof. U. Patras, Greece, 1981—, vice rector, 1998—; asst. prof. MIT, 1977-81, Yale U., 1976-77; v.p. Hellenic Bur. of Fgn. Acad. Degrees, Athens, 1988-89. Contbr. articles to profl. jours. Recipient Chemistry award Empirikion Found., Athens, 1994, Acad. of Athens, 1992, Wason medal Am. Concrete Inst., 1992, Alexander von Humboldt fellowship, 1990, H.F.C. Dreyfus award H.C. Dreyfus Found., 1981, Outstanding Achievement award of the High Temperature Materials Divsn. of the Electrochem. Soc., 1996. Mem. ACS, Hellenic Catalysis Soc. (pres. 1993-96), European Working Party on Catalysis and Reaction Engring. Home: Amerikis 7 St, Agios Vassilios Patras GR-26500, Greece Office: Univ Patras, Dept of Chem Engring, GR-26500 Patras Greece

VAYNER, BORIS VIKTOROVICH, physicist, researcher; b. Rostov on Don, Russia, May 31, 1949; came to U.S., 1992; s. Victor L. and Vera V. (Friedlander) V.; m. Olga M. Lysenko, Dec. 15, 1973; children: Yelena, Maria, Lev. MS in Theoretical Physics, Rostov State U., Rostov on Don, 1972; PhD in Astrophysics, Tartu Inst. Astrophysics, Estonia, 1978; ScD in Astrophysics and Radioastronomy, Moscow U., 1991. Rschr. dept. astrophysics Rostov U., Russia, 1972-79; assoc. prof. dept. astrophysics Rostov U., 1979-84, sr. rschr. dept. space rsch., 1984-92; NASA/Nat. Rsch. Coun. rsch. assoc. NASA/Lewis Rsch. Ctr., Cleve., 1994-97; physicist Lewis Rsch. Ctr. NASA, Cleve., 1997—; vis. rschr. dept. astronomy Case Western Res. U., Cleve., 1992-94. Contbr. papers to profl. jours. including Astronomy and Astrophysics, Astrophys. Space Sci., Astron. Jour., Jour. Spacecraft and Rockets. Recipient Silver medal Min. Edn., Russia, 1966; Nat. Rsch. Coun./NASA grantee, 1994. Mem. AIAA, Am. Astron. Soc. (high energy astrophysics 1992—), Am. Phys. Soc. Achievements include research in instability of low ionized plasma due to negative ions; the origin of gravitons in the Friedman Universe with the primordial perturbations; distortions of distribution function for collisionless particles by high-frequency gravitational waves (quasilinear theory); electromagnetic interference generated by arcing on the spacecraft surfaces, arcing on solar arrays. Office: NASA/Lewis Rsch Ctr MS 302-1 21000 Brookpark Rd Cleveland OH 44135-3191

VAZ, GASPAR GAITAN, geologist; b. Tuticorin, India, Oct. 17, 1951; s. T. Gaspar and G. Lourdes (Corera) V.; m. T. Crescentia Devotta, Jan. 31, 1981; children: G. Niranjan, G. Sudesh. BS, V.O.C. Coll., 1971; MS, Presidency Coll., Madras, India, 1976. Geol. asst. Gr. Water Dept., Madras, India, 1972-74; demonstrator Presidency Coll., Madras, 1976-77; jr. geologist Geol. Survey India, Visakhapatnam, 1977-92, sr. geologist, 1992—; divsnl. mgr. Tamilnadu Minerals Ltd., Madras, 1986-88. Contbr. articles to profl. jours. Roman Catholic. Avocations: outdoor games, music, fine arts, correspondence. Office: Marine Wing Geol Survey Ind, 41 Kirlampudi Layout, Visakhapatnam 530017, India

VAZQUEZ, TERESA CORONA, neurologist; b. Mexico City, Mex., Nov. 29, 1956; d. Rodolfo Corona Sotelo and Luz Maria (Vazquez) Araujo; m. Arturo Abundes Velasco, June 30, 1992; 1 child, Rodolfo. MD, Nat. U. Mex., 1980. Resident UNAM, Mex., 1980-85, clin. rschr., 1986; prof. medicine Nat. Inst. Social Security, Mex., 1987; staff specialist neurology Nat. Med. Ctr., Mex., 1988-92; mem. neurology divsn. Nat. Inst. Neurology, Mex., 1992—, chief multisclerosis clinic, 1992—, chief divsn. capacitation in human source, 1993-98; titular rschr. Natural Insts. Health, Mex., 1996—; chief direction teaching Nat. Inst. Neurology & Neurosurgery, Mex., 1998—. Contbr. articles to profl. jours. Fellow Am. Acad. Neurology; mem. Mexican Acad. Neurology (treas. 1992-94), Nat. Systems Rschrs, Mexican Soc. Neurology and Neuropsychiatry, Mexican Assn. Neurologists (founder, pres. 1991-93), Mexican Coun. Neurology, Mexican Acad. Scis., Nat. Acad. Medicine, Mexican Assn. Multiple Sclerosis, Spain Soc. Neurology, World Fedn. Multiple Sclerosis. Roman Catholic. Office: Nat Inst Neurology, Insurgentes Sur 3877, Mexico City DF 14269, Mexico

VÁZQUEZ-ABAD, FELISA JOSEFINA, operations research educator, electrical engineer; b. La Habana, Cuba, Mar. 14, 1960; arrived in Can., 1991; d. Jesús and Felisa J. (Abad) Vázquez. BS in Physics, Univ. Nat. Autonoma de Mex., 1984, MS in Stats. and Ops. Rsch., 1984; PhD in Applied Maths., Brown U., 1989. Tchg. asst. in physics Univ. Nat. Autonoma de Mex., 1982-83, rsch. asst., 1983-85; rsch. asst. divsn. applied math. Brown U., 1986-87; postdoctoral rschr. Nat. Inst. Sci. Rsch.-Telecom, U. Quebec, Can., 1990-91, rsch. asst., 1991-92; lectr. dept. computer sci. and ops. rsch. U. Montreal, Can., 1992-93, asst. prof. dept. computer sci. and ops. rsch., 1993-96; rsch. fellow dept. elec. and electronic engring. U. Melbourne, Australia, 1998-99; assoc. prof. dept. computer sci. and ops. rsch. U. Montreal, 1996—; vis. rsch. assoc. divsn. applied math. Brown U., 1989, vis. asst. prof., 1989-90; vis. rschr. dept. computer sci. and ops. rsch., U. Montreal, 1993; vis. rschr. dept. math. and stats. U. Melbourne, 1997-99; vis. prof. Nat. Inst. Sci. Rsch.-Telecom, U. Que., 1998—; lectr. in field. Web editor INFORMS Coll. Simulation, 1998—; assoc. editor Conf. Editl. Bd. IEEE Control Systems Soc.; reviewer numerous jours.; contbr. articles to profl. jours. Recipient numerous research grants, 1993—. Mem. IEEE Comm. Soc., INFORMS, Soc. Indsl. and Applied Math., Am. Math. Soc. Fax: 514-343-5834. Office: Univ Montreal, PO Box 6128 Downtown Sta, Montreal, PQ Canada H3C 3J7

VAZSONYI, BALINT, concert pianist, television producer, political philosopher; b. Budapest, Hungary, Mar. 7, 1936; came to U.S., 1959; s. Miklos and Hedvig (Felsner) V.; m. Barbara Whittington, Feb. 26, 1960; 1 child, Nicholas. Artist Diploma, Franz Liszt Acad., Budapest, 1956; MMus, Fla. State U., 1960; PhD, U. Budapest, 1982. Concert and recording career worldwide, 1948—; prof. music Ind. U., Bloomington, 1978-84; pres. Telemusic, Inc., Bloomington, 1983-98; sr. fellow The Potomac Found., McLean, Va., 1993—; dir. Ctr. of the Am. Founding, 1996—; tchr. master classes in piano Yale, Harvard, New Eng. Conservatory, Dartmouth Coll. Author: Erno Dohnanyi, 1971, The Battle for America's Soul, 1995, America's 30 Years War: Who Is Winning?, 1998; author, producer, presenter TV biographies Beethoven, 1983, Mozart, Schubert, 1986, Brahms, 1987; first chronological cycle of Beethoven Sonatas, N.Y., 1976. Hon. Cultural Counselor of the Republic of Hungary, 1993-95; decorated Officer's Cross of the Republic of Hungary, 1999; recipient Americanism award DAR, 2000, Hon. Citizen of Indpls., 2000, Key to City of Charleston, W.Va., 2000. Office: The Potomac Found 1311 Dolley Madison Blvd Mc Lean VA 22101-3925

VČEV, ALEKSANDAR IVAN, medical educator; b. Orahovica, Slavonia, Croatia, Dec. 27, 1960; s. Ivan Aleksandar and Rura Včev; m. Andrijana Nana Vegar, Jan. 18, 1992; 1 child, Ivan. MD, Med. Faculty, Zagreb, Croatia, 1985; MSc, Med. Faculty, Rijeka, Croatia, 1989, internist, 1993, PhD, 1994. Physician Med. Ctr. Osijek and Zadar, Croatia, 1985-86; asst. Med. Faculty, Zagreb, 1986-98; gastroenterologist Clin. Hosp., Osijek, 1989; asst. prof. Med. Faculty, Osijek, 1999. Author: (book) Alimentation and Ulcer Disease, 1997; contbr. articles to profl. jours. Mem. Croatian Soc. Gastroenterology, Croatian Med. Chamber, Croatian Physicians Trade Union. Avocations: basketball, swimming. Office: Clin Hosp Osijek, Huttlerova 4, 31 000 Osijek Slavonia, Croatia

VDOVENKOVA, TATIANA ANATOLIEVNA, physics researcher; b. Kiev, Ukraine, May 3, 1962; d. Anatoliy Andreevich Vdovenkov and Galyna Mikhaylovna Tropina; m. Aleksey Alekseevich Shmatov, Aug. 10, 1991; 1 child, Ann. MSc with honors, Shevchenko U., Kiev, 1984, PhD in Physics and Math., 1989. From jr. rschr. to rschr. dept. radio physics Shevchenko U., 1987-98, asst. prof., 1991-96, sr. rschr., 1998—; guest rschr. Ghent (Belgium) U., 1996; sci. cons. Analytic Ltd., Kiev, 1999—. Contbr. articles to sci. jours., including Thin Solid Films, Applied Surface Sci., others. Sci. grantee Ghent U., 1996, Internat. Sci. Edn. Program, Vdovenkova, 1998, INTAS, 1997-99. Mem. Ukranian Phys. Soc., N.Y. Acad. Scis. Avocations: Internet, music. Office: Shevchenko U Dept Radiophys, 64 Volodymyrska, 01033 Kiev Ukraine

VDOVIN, VLADIMIR IL'ICH, physicist, researcher; b. Balkhash, Kazakhstan, Russia, Feb. 6, 1952; s. Ilya Moiseevich and Nina Alexandrovna (Shahalova) V.; m. Irina Rostislavovna Kotlyarova, Mar. 9, 1974; 1 child, Ilya. MS, Moscow Steel and Alloys Inst., 1974; PhD, Inst. Semiconductors, Kiev, Ukraine, 1987. Engr. Inst. Rare Metals, Moscow, 1974-87, rsch. scientist, 1987-91, sr. rschr., 1991-96; sr. rschr. Inst. Chem. Problems of Microelectronics, Moscow, 1996—. Contbr. articles to profl. jours. Avocations: photography, wood carving. Fax: 095-953-8869. E-mail: icpm@mail.girmet.ru. Home: Alabyan St Bldg 10 Apt 62, 125080 Moscow Russia Office: Inst Chem Problems Microele, B Tolmachevsky per 5, 109017 Moscow Russia

VDOVIN, YURIY ALEKSANDROVICH, physicist, educator; b. Moscow, Dec. 3, 1928; s. Aleksander and Maria (Ganter) V.; m. Lyudmila Prokhorova, Oct. 6, 1956; two children. Diploma in engring., Moscow Engring. Phys. Inst., 1952, PhD, 1955, Dsc, 1969. From lectr. to prof. physics Moscow Engring. Physics Inst., 1952—. Co-author: Theoretical Physics, 1962, vol. 3, 1973; contbr. articles to profl. jours. Office: Moscow Engring Physics Inst, Kashirskoe Shosse 31, 115409 Moscow Russia

VEACH, ROBERT RAYMOND, JR., lawyer; b. Charleston, S.C., Nov. 28, 1950; s. Robert Raymond and Evelyn Ardell (Vegter) V.; m. Lori Sue Erickson, May 27, 1989. Student, St. Olaf Coll., 1968-70; BS in Acctg., Ariz. State U., 1972; JD, So. Meth. U., 1975. Bar: Tex. 1975, Nebr. 1975, U.S. Dist. Ct. Nebr. 1975, U.S. Dist. Ct. (no. dist.) Tex. 1975, Temporary Emergency Ct. Appeals 1975. Acctg. instr. Sch. Bus. So. Meth. U., Dallas, 1973-74; law clk. to Hon. Joe E. Estes U.S. Dist. Ct. No. Dist. Tex.-Temp. Emergency Ct. Appeals, Dallas, 1975-76; assoc. Locke Purnell Boren Laney & Neely, Dallas, 1976-80; v.p. The Lomas & Nettleton Co., Dallas, 1980-83, Rauscher Pierce Refsnes, Inc., Dallas, 1983-87; pres. RPR Mortgage Fin. Corp., Dallas, 1985-87; sr. shareholder Locke Purnell Rain Harrell, Dallas, 1987-97; exec. v.p. Precision Imaging Solutions, Inc., Dallas, 1998—; pvt. practice Dallas, 1998—; allied mem. N.Y. Stock Exch., 1985-87; lectr. securities and banking confs.; bd. dirs. pvt. corps.; trustee Correctional Properties Trust (NYSE-CPV), chmn. audit and finance com., 1998—. Author legal articles. Dir. North Tex. affiliate Am. Diabetes Assn., Dallas, 1978-81; mem. Gov.'s Task Force Wash. State Housing Commn., 1982-83. Mem. ABA, State Bar of Tex., Nebr. State Bar Assn., Fed. Bar Assn., Dallas Bar Assn. Republican. Methodist. Avocations: golf, antique Am. firearms. Home: 4223 Brookview Dr Dallas TX 75220-3801 Office: 2911 Turtle Creek Blvd Ste 1240 Dallas TX 75219-6277

VEATCH, ELIZABETH WILSON, educational administrator; b. Bloomington, Ind., July 26, 1946; d. Henry Babcock and Mary Jane (Wilson) V. BA, Ind. U., 1968; MS, Georgetown U., 1970. Researcher Inter-Am. Found., Arlington, Va., 1971-73, program officer, 1973-86; asst. dir. Office of Fellowships and Grants, Smithsonian Instn., Washington, 1986-96; dir. Nat. Security Edn. Fellowship Program, Acad. Ednl. Devel., Washington, 1996—; cons. Ford Found., N.Y.C., 1986-88, Inter-Am. Dialogue, Washington, 1990. Bd. dirs. Life Skills Ctr., Washington, 1988-96, Arlington County Community Found., 1991, fundraising com. Mem. Nat. Trust for Historic Preservation, Nat., Dem. Women's Club, Latin Am. Studies Assn. Democrat. Episcopalian. Office: NSEP/AED 1825 Connecticut Ave NW Washington DC 20009-5708

VECCHIO, ROBERT PETER, business management educator; b. Chgo., June 29, 1950; s. Dominick C. and Angeline V.; m. Betty Ann Vecchio; Aug. 21, 1974; children: Julie, Mark. BS summa cum laude, DePaul U., 1972; MA, U. Ill., 1974, PhD, 1976. Instr. U. Ill., Urbana, 1973-76; mem. faculty dept. mgmt. U. Notre Dame, 1976—, dept. chmn., 1983-90, Franklin D. Schurz Prof. Mgmt., 1986—. Editor Jour. of Mgmt., 1995-2000. Mem. Acad. Mtm., Am. Psychol. Assn., Am. Inst. Decision Scis., Midwest Acad. Mgmt., Midwest Psychol. Assn., Phi Kappa Phi, Delta Epsilon Sigma, Phi Eta Sigma, Psi Chi. Home: 16856 Hampton Dr Granger IN 46530-6907 Office: U Notre Dame Dept Mgmt Notre Dame IN 46556

VECCHIOTTI, JULIUS, philosophy educator; b. Rome, June 27, 1930; s. Umberto and Anna Maria Nicolina V. Diploma, U. Faculty of Lurizfrudence, Rome, 1950, U. Rome, 1955. Ordinary Internat. Insts., Italy, 1960-81; assoc. U. Urbino, 1981-90, first degree ordinary, 1990—; dir. Pacific Sch., U. Urbino, 1973-79, dir. of Inst., 1992-98. Author books in field. With Italian Army, 1943-44. Avocations: comparative linguistics, philology.

VECELLIO, LEO ARTHUR, JR., construction company executive; b. Beckley, W.Va., Oct. 26, 1946; s. Leo Arthur and Evelyn (Pais) V.; m. Kathryn Grace Cottrill, Nov. 29, 1975; children: Christopher Scott, Michael Andrew. BCE, Va. Poly. Inst. and State U., 1968; MCE, Ga. Inst. Tech., 1969; LLD, Northwood U., 1992. Sr. v.p. Vecellio & Grogan, Inc., Beckley, 1973-96, pres., CEO, chmn. bd. dirs., 1996—; mng. ptnr. Deerfield Property Assocs., 1988—, Vecellio Realty Co., 1990—; pres. Vecellio Realty Inc., 1997—; mng. ptnr. Orlando Property Assn. Ltd., 1997—, WRQ Property Assn. Ltd., 1997—; pres. Vecellio Contracting Corp. and subs. (Ranger Constrn. Industries, West Palm Beach, PAVEX Corp., Deerfield Beach, White Rock Quarries, Miami 1990—), Fla., 1982—; bd. dirs. Nations Bank Palm Beach County (formerly Barnett Bank); founder, past dir. Gulf Nat. Bank, Sophia, W.Va.; founder, past dir. Nat. Bankers Trust, Beckley. Chmn. bd. dirs. Econ. Coun. Palm Beach County, Fla., 1985—, chmn.-elect, 1987, chmn., 1989; gov. Northwood U., West Palm Beach, 1985—; organizer, trustee Beckley Area Found., 1985; v.p., trustee Vecellio Family Found., Beckley, 1972-96, pres., trustee, 1996—; active Mini-Grace Commn., Fla. Coun. 100, 1989—, vice-chmn., 1991—; commn. dir., v.p. Criminal Justice Commn.; chmn. Budget Rev. Task Force, Budget Oversight Task Force; bd. dirs. Palm Beach County Cultural Coun. and Art Sch. Task Force, Fla. Coun. 100, Floridians for Better Transp., exec. com.; corporator Schepens Eye Rsch. Inst., Harvard U., 1993—; mem. engring. coun. 100 Va. Tech. Capt USAF, 1969-73. Recipient Free Enterprise medal Palm Beach Atlantic Coll., 1988. Mem. Am. Rd. and Transp. Builders Assn. (dir. 2000), Flexible Pavements Assn. (found, bd. dirs. 1979—), Contractors Assn. W. (bd. dirs. 1975—). Republican. Roman Catholic. Clubs: Mayacoo Lakes Country (West Palm Beach), Adios Golf (Coconut Creek, Fla.), Jupiter Hills (Fla.), Lost Tree. Avocations: golf, boating, skiing. Home: 771 Village Rd North Palm Beach FL 33408-3331 Office: Vecellio Contracting Corp PO Box 15065 West Palm Beach FL 33416-5065

VECHT, CHARLES J., neurologist, neuro-oncologist, consultant; b. Zwolle, Netherlands, Jan. 21, 1947; s. Jacob M.Th. and Paulien (Droste) V.; m. Roselien van den Bergh; children: Nathan, Daniel. MD, U. Groningen, Netherlands, 1973, PhD, 1975. Resident in neurology U. Amsterdam, 1975-77; resident in psychiatry Ursula Clinic, Wassenaar, Netherlands, 1978; fellow in neuro-oncology Meml. Sloan Kettering Cancer Ctr., N.Y.C., 1979-80; staff neurologist Slotervaart Hosp., Amsterdam, 1981; neurologist Diaconessenhuis, Voorburg, Netherlands, 1982-86; staff neuro-oncologist Daniel den Hoed Cancer Ctr., Rotterdam, Netherlands, 1986—; neuro-oncologist U. Hosp., Rotterdam, Netherlands, 1986—, head dept. neuro-oncology, 1989-2000; cons. neuro-oncologist Comprehensive Cancer Ctr. West, Lyden, Netherlands, 1982—. Author: Haemostasis in acute neurological disorders, 1975; mem. editl. bd. several med. jours. Mem. Dutch Soc. Neurology, EORTC Brain Tumor Study Group (chmn.), Am. Acad. Neurology. Home: Wilhelminapark 16, 2342 AG Oegstgeest The Netherlands Office: MCH Westeinde Hosp, PO Box 432, 2501 CK The Hague The Netherlands

VÈCSEI, LASZLO IMRE, neurology educator; b. Kiskunleyegyhaza, Hungary, Sept. 10, 1954; s. Bela Jozset and Margit Neszte (Nagy) V.; m. Eszter Maria Karg, 1980; children: Bertalan, Dalma, Miklos. MD, Szent-Györgyi U., Szeged, Hungary, 1979; CSc, Hungarian Acad. Sci., 1986; PhD, Lund (Sweden) U., 1989; DSc, Hungarian Acad. Sci., 1992. Rsch. assoc. Szent-Györgyi U., 1980-84; asst. prof. Pecs (Hungary) U., 1984-87; rsch. fellow Lund U., 1987-89, Harvard U., Boston, 1989-90; assoc. prof. Pecs U., 1991-93; prof., head Szent-Györgyi U., 1993—; mem. exec. com. Danube Symposium Neurology, 1997—. Recipient Markusovsky Györgyi Semmelweis award Weekly Med. Jour., Hungary, 1997. Mem. European Fedn. Neurol. Soc. (sci. com. 1997—, program com. 1998—), Hungarian Pain Soc. (pres. 1999—). Office: Szent Györgyi Univ, Semmelucis str 6, 6725 Szeged Hungary

VEDESHWAR, AGNIKUMAR GANAPATI, physicist; b. Gokarn, India, July 21, 1959; s. Ganapati Mahabaleshwar and Shachidevi Ganapati V.; m. Rajeevi Agnikumar, May 20, 1990. BSc, Karnataka Sci. Coll., Dharwad, India, 1981; MSc, Karnatak U., Dharwad, India, 1983, PhD, 1988. Jr. rsch. fellow Karnatak U., Dharwad, 1983-88; rsch. assoc. Indian Inst. Tech., Kanpur, India, 1988-90, Indira Gandhi Ctr. for Atomic Rsch., Kalpakkam, India, 1990-93; lectr. dept. physics Delhi (India) U., 1993—. Contbr. articles to profl. jours. Active Indian Classical Music Concerts at Ednl. Inst., 1994—. Recipient Rsch. award Univ. Grants Commn., India, 1998-99. Mem. Indian Physics Assn., Indian Acad. Sci., Indian Vacuum Soc. Hindu. Avocations: Indian classical music, painting, fine arts, handicrafts, theater. Office: Univ Delhi, Dept Physics & Astrophysics, 110007 Delhi India

VEDOURAS, ANNA, federal lawyer; b. Cleveland, Ohio, Feb. 21, 1960; d. John and Emily (Peters) Vedouras. BA, U. Mich., 1981; JD, Cleve. State U., 1985. Bar: Ohio 1989. Atty. LIGHTNET, New Haven, Conn., 1985-86; contract adminstr. Constrn. Control Svcs., Inc., Boston, 1986-87; project mgr. Legal Support Svcs., Boston, 1987-89; sr. assoc. counsel Dept. of Defense, Cleveland, Ohio, 1989—. Pres. Young Friends Cleve. Mus. Art, 1993-95; trustee, v.p. Ctr. for Prevention of Domestic Violence, 1993-98; trustee Cleve. Play House, 1991-96; v.p. Cleve. Film Soc., 1993—, Cleve. Ctr. Contemporary Arts, 1996—, Spaces, 1999—; bd. dirs. Near West Theatre, 1996—. Recipient No. Ohio Live award of achievement, 1996, Disting. Fed. Svc. award, 1999; named one of 50 most interesting people Cleve. Mag., 1995; named Titan of Style, Sun Newspapers, 1995. Mem. Cleve. Bar Assn.

VEDRINE, HUBERT, French government official. Min. fgn. affairs Govt. of France, 1997—. Office: Ministry Fgn Affairs, 37 quai d'Orsay, 75700 Paris Cedex 07, France*

VEERAPANENI, SUNAINA, plant pathologist; b. Ambala, Haryana, India, Jan. 11, 1947; d. Inder Bal and Susheela (Chopra) Vohra; m. Kishore Veerapaneni, Dec. 7, 1970; children: V. Vandna, V. Vivek. BSc, Punjab U., Chandigarh, India, 1967; MSc 1st class hons., Punjab Agrl. U., Hissar, 1970; PhD 1st class hons., Meerut (India) U., 1993. Lectr. HAU, Hissar, 1970-72; scientist S Ctrl. Potato Rsch. Inst., Shimla, 1975-76, scientist S-1, 1976-82, sr. scientist, 1983—. Patentee in field. Mem. Indian Phytopathol. Soc. (life), Indian Potato Assn. (life). Avocations: reading, painting, cycling, declamation, fancy dress. Home: 35 B I Lines, Meerut 250001, India Office: Ctrl Potato Rsch Inst, Modipurm, Meerut 250110, India

VEERS, PAUL STEVEN, mechanical engineer; b. Marshfield, Wis., June 20, 1956; s. Charles George and Bertha Emma Anna (Hollatz) V.; m. Karen Ann Radtke, Sept. 5, 1987; children: Emma, Anna, Elisabeth, Margaret. BSEM, U. Wis., 1978, MSEM, 1980; PhD, Stanford U., 1987. Disting. mem. tech. staff Sandia Nat. Labs., Albuquerque, 1980—. Editor Wind Energy Symposium, 1991-92; assoc. editor Jour. of Solar Energy Engring., 1993-2000; contbr. more than 35 articles to various publs. Counsel mem. Shepherd Luth. Ch. and Sch., Albuquerque, 1988-97; sci. advisor Humphrey Elem. Sch., Albuquerque, 1990-96; mem. sch. bd. Shepherd Luth. Sch., 1998—. Recipient Sandia award for excellence Sandia Labs., 1993, 94, Tech. award Am. Wind Energy Assn., 1997. Mem. ASTM (com. fatigue and fracture 1987—), ASME (wind energy com. 1993—). Lutheran. Home: 9615 Admiral Dewey Ave NE Albuquerque NM 87111-1315 Office: Sandia Nat Labs Wind Energy Tech Dept Albuquerque NM 87185-0708

VEGA, ALFREDO, neurosurgeon, educator; b. Cuenca, Ecuador, Oct. 19, 1955; s. Rodrigo Borrero and Lucia (Vega) B.; m. Myriam Vallejo Ullauri, Apr. 4, 1990; children: Jose Alfredo, Daniel Juan David, Maria Juliana, Rodrigo Bordero. Grad., Univ. Cuenca, 1980, U. Mex., 1997. Cert. specialist neurosurgery, subspecialty spine surgery Mex. Bd. Neurosurgery. Neurosurgeon Iess, Cuenca, 1987-90, Met. Hosp., Quito, Ecuador, 1991—; chief neurosurg. dept. Inst. Cancer, 1993—; prof. San Francisco U., Quito, 1997—; prof., chief neurosurg. svc. Met. Hosp., 1997—, prof., chmn.; fellowship in Spine Ochner Clinic, New Orleans, La. Mem. Spine Ecuatonion Soc. (pres. 1999—). Avocations: running, music, history. E-mail: borrero@vio.statnet.net. Office: Med Ctr Hosp, Met Hosp, Quito 17088116, Ecuador

VEGA, RAYNETTE NORMA, hotel official; b. Kohala, Hawaii, Feb. 26, 1962; d. Antone Tony and Ramona Mona Vega. Student, Fayetteville (N.C.) Tech. Sch., 1980-81, Youth with a Mission, Sunland, Calif., 1982-83. Christian counselor Centrum of Hollywood, Calif., 1983-84; security officer Hawaii Protective Assn., Kamuela, 1984-87, Puakea Bay Ranch, Kapaau, Hawaii, 1987-93; concierge Hyatt Regency Waikoloa, Hawaii, 1988-89; youth Christian counselor New Covenant Ch., Waimea, Hawaii, 1985-86. Author: (poetry) Rainbows of Poems from Heaven Above, 1987, Heart Beat in Love, 1993. Recipient Golden Poet award World of Poetry, 1987-91, award Poetry Acad., 1993, Poet of Merit award Internat. Soc. Poets, 1993, Internat. Hall of Fame, 1996. Avocations: jogging, tennis, reading, writing poetry.

VEGA, STEVE, protective services official, poet; b. Manhattan, N.Y., Nov. 13, 1949; s. Exio Ocasio Vega; m. Veronica Gonzalez, Jan. 3, 1971; children: Katherine, James-Paul Christian (Eagle Scout Jan. 2000), Diamond Zhane. Cert. in bus. mgmt., Marion Bus. Coll., 1973; cert., John Marshall Law Sch., 1977; cert. in corrections and probations svcs., Chgo. Loop Coll., 1986; BA, Coll. of Commr. Sci., 1995, M of Commr. Svc., 1996, postgrad., 1997; PhD, Lord Baden-Powell Coll., Lake Geneva, Wisc., 1998; wilderness survival course, with APO wardogs, 1988; winter camping survival course, OKPIK, Woodstock, Ill., 1996; sea badge course, Great Lakes Navy Base, 1998. Adult probation officer Cook County, Ill., 1979-93; pub. safety officer, police-fireman aide Morton Grove (Ill.) emergency Svcs. and Disaster Agy., 1998—; union chief steward Cook County Adult Probation Dept., AFSCME, 1989-91; 1st v.p. AFSCME local 3486 APD officers, Chgo., 1991-92; cons. Chgo. Police Dept., FBI, U.S. Secret Svc. Contbr. poetry to over 20 anthologies worldwide, 1974—; appeared in over 18 major films incl. Only the Lonely, Music Box, Gladiator, Mo' Money, Hero, Hoffa, Natural Born Killers, others. Vol., mem. com. City of Chgo. Health Systems Agy., 1981-85; asst. coun. commn. Boy Scouts Am., Chgo. 1997. With USAF, 1970. Decorated USAF Commendation medal, 1969, knight comdr. European Order of Knighthood, 1982, (Italy); recipient Presdl. Commendations, Pres. Ronald Reagan, George Bush, 1987, 88, 90, Arrowhead awardBoy Scouts Am., 1994; named One of World's Great Living Poets, 1991 by The Dictionary of Intl. Biography 24th ed. IBC, England; recipient Man of the Year, Am. Biographical Inst., 1991, 92, Most Admired Man of the Decade, ABI, 1993, awarded title "His Excellency", ABI, 1993; collection of poetry encased in a Pegasus Time Capsule in Hall of Fame, withint World of Poetry Castle in Calif. Mem. ASCAP (composer, writer), Fraternal Order of Police (officer 1988, sgt.-at-arms), Sovereign, Military and Hospitaller Order of St. George in Karinthia (titular head), Internat. Biog. Ctr. (hon., mem. adv. coun.). Roman Catholic. Avocations: singing, composing, guitarist, motorcycle riding, chess, screen writing. Address: PO Box 221 Morton Grove IL 60053-0221

VEGA-CARRILLO, HECTOR RENE, nuclear engineer; b. Juchipila, Zacatecas, Mex., June 7, 1957; s. Pedro Vega-Banuelos and Evangelina Carrillo-Rodriguez; m. Maria Glafira Sandoval-Benavides, Dec. 22, 1981; 1 child, Maria G. Engr., U. Aut. de Zacatecas, Mex., 1980; MSc in Nuclear Engring., U. Aut. de Nvo. Leon, Monterrey, Mex., 1984; PhD in Nuclear Engring., U. Tex., 1995. Prof. nuclear engring. U. Aut. de Zacatecas, 1981-90, 95—, health physics head, 1982-90, 95-99; rsch. asst. U. Tex., Austin, 1991-95. Author: Introduccion al metodo cientifico experimental, 1987; co-author: Introduccion a las ciencias nucleares, 1985, Seguridad Radiologica, 1992; inventor in field. Recipient award for best tech. presentation Am. Nuclear Soc., 1991, Best paper award; rschr. Nat. Rschrs. Sys., Mex., 1996. Mem. Mex. Phys. Soc., Am. Assn. Physics Tchrs., Am. Phys. Soc., Health Physics Soc., Alpha Nu Sigma. Avocation: philately. Home: Britania 15 Fracc los Prados, Guadalupe Zacatecas, Mexico Office: Centro Regional Estud Nucl, C Cipres 10 Fracc la Penuela, 98068 Zacatecas Mexico

VÉGH, LUDEVÍT, civil engineering educator; b. Košice, Czechoslovakia, Aug. 26, 1921; s. Salamon and Olga (Braunstein) V.; m. Anna Doubková, 1950 (div.); children: Olga, Peter; m. Svetla Stryhalová, Sept. 1985. BS, U. Prague, 1949; PhD, Tech. U., Prague, DSc. From site engr. to chief engr. NHKG, Ostrava, Czechoslovakia, 1950-53; jr. asst. prof. Czech Tech. U., Prague, 1948-50, from asst. prof. to prof., 1953-88; from field expert to sr. expert UNESCO, India & Turkey, 1967-71; cons. pvt. practice, Prague, 1989-90, Fed. Ministry of Environ., 1991-92, STANGER Sci. & Environ., Prague, 1990-99; bd. dirs. Black & Veatch, Czech Republic; chmn. internat. confs. on concrete structures, 1978-88, on environ. impact assessment, 1991-2000; cons. in field, 1991—. Author, co-author over 15 books and textbooks; contbr. numerous articles to profl. and sci. pubs.; patentee in field. Com. mem. Czech Antifascist Orgn., Prague, 1953— (medal, 1973). Mem. Czech Union Civil Engrs., IASS (chmn. nat. com. 1995—, internat. adv. com.), Czech Assn. IUAPPA (hon. pres. 1993—), Czech Concrete Soc. (pres. 1991-93), Cement and Concrete Assn. Avocations: music, environment, philosophy, tennis. E-mail: vegh@mbox.vol.cr. Home and Office: Doubravčicka 10, 10000 Prague 10, Czech Republic

VEGH, MIHALY, ophthalmologist; b. Szeghalom, Hungary, Mar. 28, 1952; s. Mihaly and Gizella (Toth) V.; m. Andrea Boronkai, June 27, 1981; 1 child, Zsuzsa. MD, Med. U., Szeged, Hungary, 1976, Habilitation; Ophthalmologist, Med. Postgrad. U., Budapest, Hungary, 1980; PhD, Hungarian Acad. Scis., Budapest, 1994. Asst. lectr. Med. Univ., Szeged, 1980-94, sr. lectr., 1995—; dir. Contact Lens Lab., Dept. Ophthalmology, Med. U., Szeged, 1993—. Patentee in field. Recipient Javal Internat. Contactological award, 1997. Mem. Hungarian Contact Lens Soc. of Ophthalmologists and Optometrists (chmn. 1990—), European Soc. of Ophthalmic Plastic and Reconstructive Surgery (com. mem. 1991-95), European Contact Lens Soc. of Ophthalmologists (com. mem. 1990—), European Soc. of Dacryology (com. mem. 1995—), Hungarian Acad. of Scis. (prize 1987), Hungarian Soc. Ophthalmologists (prize 1985, 87), Alumni Assn. Med. U. (chmn. 1996—), Szent-Györgyi Meml. House Found. (chmn. 1999—). Avocations: computer technic, music. Office: U Szeged Dept Ophthalmology, Koranyi fasor 10-11, 6720 Szeged Hungary

VEHMAANPERA, JARI OLAVI, molecular biologist; b. Gothenburg, Sweden, Apr. 11, 1956; arrived in Finland, 1956; s. Erkki Olavi and Helina Johanna (Peltonen) V.; m. Johanna Petronella Ackermans, May 11, 1984; children: Edwin Olavi, Sonja Maria. MSc, U. Helsinki, Finland, 1981, PhD, 1990. From microbiologist to project mgr. Alko Rsch. Labs., Helsinki, 1981-94; project mgr. Primalco Biotec R & D, Rajamaki, Finland, 1995-97; R&D mgr. Rohm Enzyme Finland Oy, Rajamaki, Finland, 1997-98; sr. rsch. scientist VTT Biotech., Espoo, Finland, 1998—; vis. scientist U. Groningen, The Netherlands, 1991. Contbr. articles to profl. jours. Avocations: tennis, badminton. Office: VTT Biotech, PO Box 1500, FIN02004 Espoo Finland

VEHMAS, (ANTTI) TAPIO, radiologist; b. Helsinki, Finland, Apr. 5, 1959; s. Aatos Ensio and Kerttu Anna Liisa Vehmas; m. Tuija Kristiina Vehmas; children: Joanna, Tatu. Grad. high sch., Helsinki; MD, Helsinki U., 1984, PhD, 1991. Radiologist resident Helsinki U. Ctr. Hosp., 1987-91, radiologist, 1993-99; radiology lectr. Helsinki U., 1991-93; chief radiologist The Finnish Inst. Occupational Health, 1999—; sec. ethical com. Dept. of Radiology Helsinki U. Ctrl. Hosp., 1992-93; cons. radiologist The Patient Injury Bd., Helsinki, 1998—. Contbr. articles to profl. jours. Mem. The Finnish Radiol. Soc. (radiation protection com., bd. dirs., Prize fgn. sci. article 1992, Prize Finnish sci. article 1993), Finnish Med. Assn. Helsinki Duodecim. Office: Finnish Inst Occup Health, Topeliuksenkatu 41 a A, FIN00250 Helsinki Finland

VEIDERMA, MIHKEL, chemist, educator; b. Tallinn, Estonia, Dec. 27, 1929; s. Aleksander and Magdalena (Vihalem) V.; m. Silvia Poolak, Aug. 24, 1957; children: Anne, Liis, Riin. Degree in chem.-tech., Poly. Inst., Tallinn, 1953; Candidate Sci., Inst. Fertilizers, Moscow, 1965, DSc, 1972. Chief engr. Chem. Combine, Maardu, Estonia, 1956-60; docent Poly. Inst., Tallinn, 1960-73; prof. inorganic chemistry Tech. U. (formerly Poly. Inst.), Tallinn, 1973-97, dean chem. faculty, 1978-82; head dept., chair inorganic chemistry Tech. U., Tallinn, 1972-87, 94-97, prof. emeritus, 1997—; v.p. Estonian Acad. Scis., Tallinn, 1987-99, sec. gen., 1999—; supr. fertilizers tech. lab. Poly. Inst., 1965-92; dir. Office of Pres. of Estonian Republic, Tallinn, 1992-94; mem. Estonian Rsch. Fund Coun., Tallinn, 1994—; chmn. Estonian Acad. Scis. Energy Coun. Author: Technology of Important Chemical Products, 1970, Phosphorite Deposits, 1988; contbr. articles to profl. jours. Mem. Estonian Chem. Soc. (hon.), Finnish Chem. Soc. (corr. Helsinki), Estonian Acad. Scis., Finnish Acad. Tech. (fgn.), Estonian Naturalists' Soc. (hon.). Lutheran. Avocations: history of culture and science, gardening. Home: Jääraku 54, 12015 Tallinn Estonia Office: Estonian Acad Scis 6 KOHTU Str, 10130 Tallinn Estonia

VEIGA, CARLOS ALBERTO WAHNON DE CARVALHO, prime minister of Cape Verde; b. Mindelo, Sao Vincente, Oct. 21, 1949; s. Alfredo Carvalho and Augustus (Wahnon) V.; children: Augusto, Muxima, Victor, Ricardo, Carla. Degree in law, U. Clássica, Lisbon, Portugal, 1971; degree in polit. sci. (hon.), U. Bridgeport, 1993. Judge Ministry of Pub. Adminstrn., 1975-80; dir. gen. Internal Adminstrn.; atty. gen. Min. of Justice; pvt. practice law, legal cons. state cos. and bus. Praia; dep. v.p. Spl. Permanent Commn., 1975-90; pres., founder Movimento Para Democracia, 1990; prime minister of Cape Verde, 1991—. Avocations: soccer, swimming. Office: Office of Prime Minister, Palácio Do Governo Várzea CP 16, Praia Santiago, Cape Verde*

VEIGA, MANUEL M.M. ALTE DA, philosophy educator; b. Mogofores, Portugal, Jan. 4, 1941; s. Eugenio De Brito De Alte and Maria Isabel De Melo Alte Da (Sampayo) V.; m. Maria Filomena A.P.C. Alte Da Correia, July 27, 1974; children: Maria Manuela, Diogo Maria, Maria Luisa. Grad., Faculty Philosophy, Braga, Portugal, 1965; PhD, U. Aveiro, Portugal, 1985. Tchr. H.S. St. John Brito, Lisboa, Portugal, 1965-67; asst. prof. U. Aveiro, Portugal, 1976-86, prof., 1986-88; assoc. prof. U. Do Minho, Braga, Portugal, 1988—. Author: Philosophy of Education and Aporias of Religion, 1988, Life-Violence-School-Family, 1998; contbr. articles to profl. jours. Pres. Pastoral of Health, Braga, 1993—; deputy Coun. Aveiro, 1984-86; exec. mem. Tchrs. Syndicate, Porto, Portugal, 1991—. With Portuguese Army, 1969-71. Recipient Clin. Psychology award Cath. U., Louvain, Belgium, 1972-76. Mem. Philosophy Edn. Soc. Gt. Brit., Comparative and Internat. Edn. Soc., Soc. Portuguese Scis. Edn., Assn. Moral Edn. Roman Catholic. Avocations: model trains, walking, poetry. Home: Jaime Sottomayor 59-1-E, 4710-396 Braga Portugal Office: U Do Minho, Gualtar, 4710 Braga Portugal

VEIJALAINEN, HEIKKI SAKARI, forester; b. Kaukola, Finland, Apr. 1, 1941; d. Arvi and Helena (Hynninen) V.; m. Pirjo Marja-Leena Kiema, Sept. 1964; children: Kaisa, Marjukka. BSc, U. Helsinki, 1964. Rschr. Forestry Rsch. Inst., Helsinki, 1965—; mem. Nat. MAB Com., Helsinki, 1975, Com. for Forest Berries and Edible Fungi, Helsinki, 1979-80; sec. Forest 2000, Helsinki, 1979-80; sec., mem. working group for mktg. of forest berries and edible fungi, Helsinki, 1981-90. Mem. Internat. Peat Soc. Avocations: bird watching, horse races, volleyball, skiing, forestry. Office: Finnish Forest Rsch Inst, Box 18, 01301 Vantaa Finland

VEIL, SIMONE, government official; b. Nice, France, July 13, 1927; d. Jacob Andre and Yvonne (Jacob) Steinmetz; m. Antoine Veil, Oct. 26, 1946; children: Jean, Claude, Pierre-Francois. Student, Lycee in Nice; LLB, Inst. Polit. Studies, Paris. Apptd. to the Magistrature, 1956; apptd. titular attachee Ministry of Justice, France, 1957; various posts Ministry of Justice, 1957-69; mem. pvt. office of Mr. Pleven Lord Chancellor, 1969; appt. to High Coun. of Magistrature, 1970; mem. bd. dirs. French Radio and TV Authority, bd. dirs. Fondation de France, 1972; apptd. Min. of Health, 1974; also responsible for Social Security, 1977; apptd. chmn. Info. Bd. on Nuc. Power, 1977; Minister of Health and Family, 1978; mem. European Parliament, 1979-93, pres., 1979-82, chmn. legal affairs com., 1982, re-elected, 1984-93; min. des affairs sociales, de la Santéet de la Ville, 1993-95; chmn. Liberal and Democratic Group of European Parliament, 1984-93, state min. social affairs and urban health, 1993-95; mem. Conseil Constnl., 1998—. Author: (with Prof. Launay and Dr. Soule): Les donnees psycho-sociologiques de l'adoption. Decorated Medaille penitentiaire (medal for svcs. to prisons adminstrn.), Medaille de l'Edn. Surveillee, knight Nat. Order of Merit, France; Grand Cross 2d class Order of Merit, Fed. Republic Germany, grand officer of Merit of Republic of the Ivory Coast, grand officer Order of the Lion, Senegal, Grand Cross Order of Rio Branco, Brazil, grand officer Order Isabel La Catolica, Grand Cross of the Blue Cross of Social Security, Spain, Grand Cross of Senegal; comdr. Wissam al' Auwit, Morocco, Grand Cross Order of Merit, Luexembourg, Grand Cross Order of the Phoenix, Greece, Grand Cordon Order of the Liberator, Venezuela; recipient Athenès prize Found. Onassis, 1980, Jabolinsky prize, 1983, Charlemagne prize, 1985, Found. Klein philadelphie prize, 1991, other awards, honors, numerous hon. degrees fgn. univs. Office: 1 rue Bixio, 75007 Paris France*

VEINBERG, GRIGORY, chemist, researcher; b. Jaroslavl, Russia, July 17, 1941; arrived in Latvia, 1944; s. Adolf and Sophia (Scheinker) V.; m. Natalia Licht, Aug. 1, 1969; 1 child, Michael. PhD, Acad. Scis., Latvia, 1971; DS, Acad. Scis., Russia, 1987; D.Habil.Chem., Latvian Inst. Organic Synth, 1991. Jr. rsch. worker Latvian Inst. Organic Synthesis, 1970-74, sr. rsch. worker, 1975-83, leading rsch. worker, 1984—; vis. prof. Tech. U. Riga, Latvia, 1989—, State U. Riga, 1989—; expert commn. chemistry sci. Sci. coun. Latvia, 1993—. Recipient prize Presidium Acad. Scis. Latvia, 1985. Mem. Am. Chem. Soc. E-mail: veinberg@osi.lv. Home: 1/3 Terbatas St Apt 19 a, LV 1050 Riga Latvia Office: Latvian Inst Organic Synth, 21 Aizkraukles St, LV 1006 Riga Latvia

VEISBERGS, ANDREJS, linguistics educator, lexicographer, interpreter; b. Riga, Latvia, Feb. 22, 1960; s. Gunars and Olita (Gross) V.; m. Ruta Ola, July 29, 1984; 1 child, Kaspars. Higher Edn. Cert., U. Latvia, 1983, Dr. Habil. Philol., 1993; PhD, Acad. of Scis. of Latvia, 1986. Lectr. U. Latvia, Riga, 1983-89, asst. prof., 1989-94, prof., 1994—, head dept. linguistics, 1989—; mem. Latvian Habilitation Bd., Riga, 1995—; exec. sec. jour. Humanities and Social Scis., Latvia, 1992—; examiner Internat. Baccalaureate, Cardiff, Wales, 1994—; translator, interpreter. Author: False Friends: Latvian-English-Latvian, 1994; editor, author: The New Latvian-English Dictionary, 2000, (monograph) Latvian and English Word Formation, 1997, (monograph) Idioms in Latvian, 1999; gen. editor: Contrastive and Applied Linguistics, 1991—; editor Linguistica Lettica, 1998—; dep. editor Humanities and Social Scis., 1995. Recipient Tempus awards European Union, 1993, 95, 98; Brit. Coun. scholar, 1991. Mem. EURALEX (Verbatim awrd in lexicography 1993), Latvian Assn. Translators and Interpreters (chmn. 1998—), N.Y. Acad. Scis. Avocations: classical music, history, walking, mountaineering, swimming. Home: Maza Nometnu 55-3, LV-1002 Riga Latvia Office: Dept Contrastive Linguistic, U Latvia Visvalza 4A, LV-1050 Riga Latvia

VEIT, CLAIRICE GENE TIPTON, measurement psychologist; b. Monterey Park, Calif., Feb. 20, 1939; d. Albert Vern and Gene (Bunning) Tipton; children: Steven, Barbara, Laurette, Catherine. BA, UCLA, 1969, MA, 1970, PhD, 1974. Asst. prof. psychology Calif. State U., L.A., 1975-77, assoc. prof. psychology, 1977-80; rsch. psychologist The Rand Corp., Santa Monica, Calif., 1977—; rsch. cons. NATO Tech. Ctr., The Hague, The Netherlands, 1980-81; faculty Rand Grad Sch., Santa Monica, 1993—. Developer subjective transfer function (STF) method to complex sys. analysis and the mental health inventory. Mem. LWV, NOW, Soc. Med. Decision-Making, Soc. for Judgement and Decision-Making, L.A. Opera League. Avocations: mountain climbing, playing piano, travel, music, theatre. Office: The Rand Corp 1700 Main St Santa Monica CA 90401-3297

VEIT, IVAR EMILS, engineer, acoustician; b. Liepaja, Latvia, Apr. 21, 1936; s. Janis Nikolajs and Erna Elfriede (Galins) V.; m. Heidi Lore Klumpp, May 12, 1982; 1 child, Janis. Diploma engr., Tech. U., Ilmenau, Germany, 1960; D in Engring., Tech. U., Aachen, Germany, 1971. Engr. Vakutronik, Dresden, Germany, 1960-61; lab. head Siemens, Erlangen, Germany, 1961-75; dept. head Battelle-Inst., Frankfurt, Germany, 1975-78; dir. Acad. Hearing Aid Acoustics, Luebeck, Germany, 1978-81; dept. head Inst. Structural Acoustics, Stuttgart, Germany, 1981-84, Sennheiser Electronic, Wedemark, Germany, 1984-92, Tech. Inspection Soc., Eschborn, Germany, 1992-94; rschr. Continental Tire, Hannover, Germany, 1994—; assoc. lectr. U. Kiel, Germany, 1979-81. Author: Technical Acoustics, 1974, Hydroacoustics, 1979, Architectural Acoustics, 1997; co-author: Technical Acoustics, 1978. Chmn. Latvian Ctrl. Com. in Germany, Muenster, 1992—. Recipient award Hearing Aid Acousticians U.S.A., 1973, Assn. Spanish Audiologists, 1979. Mem. Acoustical Soc. Am., German Acoustical Soc., Electrotech. Soc. Germany. Avocations: foreign languages, politics, travel.

VEITCH, JAMES ALEXANDER, religious studies educator; b. Christchurch, New Zealand, Sept. 27, 1940; m. Janice Margaret Gregory; three children. BA, Otago U., 1963, BD, 1965, MTheol, 1967; PhD, U. Birmingham, 1969; ThD, Australian Coll. Theology, 1999. Lectr Asian religion Sekolah Tinggi Theologia, Sulawesi, Indonesia, 1969-75, Trinity Theol. Coll., Singapore, 1975-78; sr. lectr. religious studies Victoria U., Wellington, New Zealand, 1978-99; assoc. prof. Victoria U., Wellington, 1999—. Author: The New Testament in Modern Translation, 5 vols., 1993-95, Jesus of Galilee: Myth and Reality, 1994, The Birth of Jesus: History or Myth?, 1997, Jesus of Galilee: Discovering for the First Time Jesus of History; editor: Can Humanity Survive?, The World's Religions and the Environment, 1996; editor Fourth R, 1999—. Fellow Royal Asiatic Soc., Westar Inst. Presbyn. Avocations: classical music, tending to olive trees, small farming enterprise, Highland cattle adn stud sheep. Office: Victoria U, Religious Studies Dept, Wellington New Zealand

VEITH, MICHAEL, chemist; b. Görlitz, Germany, Nov. 9, 1944; s. Werner and Inge (Reichert) V.; m. Marie-Martine Hars, Oct. 1, 1971; children: Frederike, Sebastian, Charlotte, Emilie. Diploma in chemistry, U. Munich, Fed. Republic of Germany, 1969, PhD, in Natural Sci., 1971; Habilitation, U. Karlsruhe, Fed. Republic of Germany, 1977. Asst. U. Karlsruhe, 1971-77, lectr., 1977-79; prof. U. Braunschweig, Fed. Republic of Germany, 1979-84, U. Saarland, Saarbrücken, Fed. Republic of Germany, 1984—; Gignard/Wittig lectr., 1994. Contbr. articles to profl. jours. and chapts. to books. Recipient chemistry award Acad. Wissenschaften, Göttingen, Fed. Republic of Germany, 1982, Leibniz award German Sci. Found., Bonn, 1991; Winnacker scholar, Frankfort, Fed. Republic of Germany, 1978, Heisenberg scholar, German Sci. Found., 1978. Office: U of Saarlandes, Stadtwald, D-66041 Saarbrücken Saar, Germany

VEJBY-CHRISTENSEN, HANS, internist, cardiologist, consultant; b. Odder, Denmark, Feb. 29, 1944; m. Agnethe Nielsen; children: Lise, Jacob. MD, U. Aarhus, Denmark, 1970, PhD, 1976; SDH, Herning Sch. Mgmt. Sci., Denmark, 1992. Lectr. in physiology U. Aarhus, 1970-76, registrar in internal medicine, 1976-79, sr. registrar in cardiology, 1982-85; sr. registrar in internal medicine Randers, Denmark, 1979-81; cons. internal medicine Herning (Denmark) Ctrl. Hosp., 1985-91, chief exec. physician, 1991—. Home: Frijsenborgvej 35, DK-7400 Herning Denmark Office: Herning Ctrl Hosp, Gl Landevej 61, DK-7400 Herning Denmark

VEJRAŽKA, FRANTIŠEK, radio engineer, educator; b. Pardubice, Czech Republic, Apr. 6, 1942; s. František and Marta (Svobodová) V.; m. Zdeňka Skovajsová, July 6, 1968; children: Jan, (twins) Martin and Jiří. Grad., Tech. Coll., Pardubice, 1960; MS in Radio Engring., Czech Tech. U., 1965, PhD, 1972. Asst. prof. Czech Tech. U., Prague, 1969-80; head Computer Ctr. Czech Sci. Soc., Prague, 1973-88; assoc. prof. Czech Tech. U., 1981-95, dep. head dept. radio engring., 1990-93, head dept. radio engring., 1994—, prof., 1996—, vice-dean faculty elec. engring., 2000—; sec. dept. radio engring. Czech Tech. U., 1974-89, sci. coun., 1990-93. Author: Signals and Systems, 1983 (Czech Tech. U. award 1984), (in Czech) Digital Radio Communications, 1994, (in Czech) Satellite Navigation, 1996; mem. editl. bd. GPS World (USA), 1998—; contbr. articles to profl. jours. Recipient PECO grant European Communities, Brussels, 1993-95, grant Grant Agy. Czech Republic, 1993-95, 96-98, 98—. Mem. Internat. Navigation Assn., Royal Inst. Navigation London, Czech Inst. Navigation (pres. 1995-99), Inst. Navigation. Achievements include development of satellite navigation in Czech Republic; improvement of satellite navigation systems precision by geostationary overly; project of navigation equipment for Czech plane L610; precision improvement of Omega system receivers in Europe and in states of Berlin agreement. Office: Czech Tech Univ, Technická 2, 166 27 Prague Czech Republic

VÉKÁS, LADISLAU NICOLAE, physicist, researcher; b. Arad, Romania, Dec. 5, 1945; s. Emeric and Ilieana (Krieb) V.; m. Elena Magdalena Porfirean, Aug. 8, 1974; 1 child, Claudia. MS, U. Timisoara, Romania, 1968; D of Physics, U. Iasi, Romania, 1983. Physicist, sci. rschr. Rsch. Ctr. for Hydraulic Machines, Timisoara, 1971-74; sr. rschr. Poly. U., Timisoara, 1974-97, assoc. prof.; rschr. Romanian Acad. Scis., Timisoara, 1968-71, sr. rschr., 1997—, head Lab. Magnetic Fluids,, 1997—; v.p. adv. bd. Nat. Inst. Electrochemistry and Condensed Matter, Timisoara, 1997—. Contbr. articles to profl. jours. guest editor Proceedings of the 8th Internat. Conf. on Magnetic Fluids, Timisoara, Romania, 1998. Mem. European Acad. Scis. and Arts, Internat. Steering Com. on Magnetic Fluids. Roman Catholic. Avocations: symphonic music, opera, tennis, basketball. Office: Romanian Acad Timisoara Bd, Mihai Viteazul Nr 24, 1900 Timisoara Timis, Romania

VEKEMANS, MARCEL GEORGES J., obstetrician/gynecologist; b. Mechelen, Belgium, Feb. 8, 1944; s. Emiel Vekemans and Georgina De Prins; m. Claire Verougstraete; children: Marc, Johan. MD, U. Libre Brussels, 1969. Cert. in tropical medicine, in epidemiology, stats., pub. health. Asst. gynecology St.-Pierre Hosp., Brussels, 1969-80, adj. chief clin., 1980—; aspirant Fonds Nat. Rsch. Sci., Belgium, 1973-76; resident advisor Rwanda and Rabat John Snow Inc., 1993-95; charge de cours U. Libre Brussels, 1987—; cons. WHO, UN Fund for Population Activities, U.S. AID. Co-author: L'Avortement en Belgique et Dans Les Pays Voisins, 1992; editor, co-author: Planification Familiale Dans Les Pays en Voie de Developpement, 1993. Office: Intrah Sch Medicine U NC CB 1800 1700 Airport Rd Ste 300 Chapel Hill NC 27599-8100

VEKSHIN, NIKOLAI L., biophysicist, researcher; b. Vladivostok, USSR, Jan. 11, 1954; m. Olga M. Vekshina; children: Antonina, Evgeniya, Ekaterina, Vera, Nikita. Grad. in biophysics, Moscow Med. Inst., 1977; PhD, Inst. Chem. Physics, Moscow, 1987; D Biophysics, Inst. Biochem. Physics, Moscow, 1998. Jr. rschr. Inst. Biol. Physics, Pushchino, USSR, 1977-84, rschr., 1984-91; sr. rschr. Inst. Cell Biophysics, Pushchino, 1991-98; head rschr. Inst. Cell Biophysics, 1998—. Author: Photonics of Biological Structures, 1988, Transfer of Excitation in Macromolecules, 1989, Energy Transfer in Macromolecules, 1997, Photonics of Biopolymers (in English), 1999; contbr. over 50 articles to sci. jours., including Jour. Photochemistry and Photobiology B, Biochemistry Internat., Chem. Phys. Letters, European Jour. Biochemistry, Jour. Biochem. and Biophys. Methods; patentee in field. Grantee Nat. Ctr. Sci. Rsch., France, 1992, Netherlands Orgn. Scientific Rsch., 1999-01. Mem. Fedn. European Biochem. Soc. (grantee 1996), Internat. Soc. Optical Engring., Optical Soc. Am. Achievements include patents in field. Avocation: aphorisms. E-mail: vekshin@venus.iteb.serpukhov.su. Office: Russian Acad Scis, Inst Cell Biophysics, 142290 Pushchino Moscow, Russia

VELAGAPUDI, SATYANARAYANA VENKATA, electronics executive, consultant; b. Khammam, India, Sept. 10, 1967; s. Vankateswararao and Nagendramma (Katamaneni) V.; m. Neeta Vemulapalli, Apr. 26, 1993; children: Shivam, Ayush. B in Engring., Andhra U., Visakhapatnam, India, 1988. Prodn.-in-charge Kaivalli Electronics Pvt. Ltd., Hyderabad, India, 1988-89; tech. officer Marine & Comm. Electronics (India) Ltd., Visakhapatnam, 1989-94; dep. mgr. Phoenix Telecomm. Ltd., Hyderabad, 1989-2000; cons. Lucent Techs. Australia Ltd., Sydney, 2000—; bd. dirs. Laxmi Telecomm. Pvt. Ltd., Hyderabad. Mem. IEEE, Inst. Electronics and Telecom., Nat. Ctr. Quality Mgmt., Electromagnetic Compatibility Engrs. India. Avocations: chess, gardening, stamp collecting. Home: 1-8-88 Jubleepura, Khammam 507003, India

VELANO, EDSON ANTÔNIO, university official; b. Alfenas, Brazil, Sept. 26, 1943; s. José do Rosário and Alzira (Rodrigues) V.; m. Maria do Rosário Araujo, July 31, 1976; children: Larissa Araújo, Viviane Araújo. Law Degree, Faculdade de Direito Varginha, 1983. Tchr. State Jr. Sch., Alfenas, 1963-72; practice law, Alfenas, 1979-82; rector U. Alfenas, 1988—; mem. Edni. State Coun. Minas Gerais, Belo Horizonte, Brazil, 1992-99. Vice mayor City of Alfenas, 1983-85; proxy Alfenas Mcpl. Legislature, 1990-91. Mem. Found. Ensino e Tech. Alfenas (pres. 1966—). Office: U Alfenas, Rodovia MG 179 KM 0, 37130000 Alfenas MG, Brazil

VELARDO, JOSEPH THOMAS, molecular biology and endocrinology educator; b. Newark, Jan. 27, 1923; s. Michael Arthur and Antoinette (Iacullo) V.; m. Forresta M.-M. Power, Aug. 12, 1948 (dec. July 1976). AB, U. No. Colo., 1948; SM, Miami U., Oxford, Ohio, 1949; PhD, Harvard U., 1952. Rsch. fellow in biology and endocrinology Harvard U., Cambridge, Mass., 1952-53; rsch. assoc. in pathology, ob-gyn. and surgery Sch. Medicine Harvard U., Boston, 1953-55; asst. in surgery Peter Bent Brigham and Women's Hosp., Boston, 1954-55; asst. prof. anatomy and endocrinology Sch. Medicine, Yale U., New Haven, 1955-61; prof. anatomy, chmn. dept. N.Y. Med. Coll., N.Y.C., 1961-62; cons. N.Y. Fertility Inst., 1961-62; dir. Inst. for Study Human Reprodcn., Cleve., 1962-67; prof. biology John Carroll U., Cleve., 1962-67; mem. rsch. and edn. divs. St. Ann Ob-Gyn. Hosp., Cleve., 1962-67, head dept. rsch., 1964-67; prof. anatomy Stritch Sch. Medicine Loyola U., Chgo., 1967-88, chmn. dept. anatomy Stritch Sch. of Medicine, 1967-73; v.p. Universal Rsch. Systems, Warren, Ohio, 1975—; pres. University Rsch. Systems, Lombard, 1979—, Internat. Basic and Biol.-Biomed. Curricula, Lombard, Ill., 1979—; course moderator laparoscopy Brazil-Israel Congress on Fertility and Sterility, and Brazil Soc. of Human Reproduction, Rio de Janeiro, 1973; organizer, chmn. symposia in field. Author: (with others) Annual Reviews Physiology, Reproduction, 1961, Histochemistry of Enzymes in the Female Genital System, 1963, The Ovary, 1963, The Ureter, 1967, rev. edit., 1981; editor, contbr.: Endocrinology of Reproduction, 1958, The Essentials of Human Reproduction, 1958; cons. editor, co-author: The Uterus, 1959; contbr. Progestational Substances, 1958, Trophoblast and Its Tumors, 1959, The Vagina, 1959, Hormonal Steroids, Biochemistry, Pharmacology and Therapeutics, 1964, Human Reproduction, 1973; co-editor, contbr.: Biology of Reproduction, Basic and Clinical Studies, 1973; contbr. articles to profl. jours.; live broadcasts on major radio and TV networks on subjects of bioscis., biomed. careers and biomed. subjects; co-author, co-dir. med. movie on human reprodn. The Soft Anvil. Apptd. U.S. del. to Vatican, 1964; charter mem. U.S. Rep. Presdl. Task Force, 1988—; charter mem. U.S. Rep. Nat. Senatorial Com., 1988—; mem. Rep. Senate Adv. Coun., 1997—; rep. U.S. Senate Inner Circle, 1988—, U.S. Rep. Senatorial Commn., 1991—. With USAAF, World War II, 1943-45. Decorated Presdl. Unit citation, 2 Bronze Stars; recipient award Lederle Med. Faculty Awards Com., 1955-58, Cert. of Achievement U.S. Rep. Nat. Senatorial Com., 1999, Disting. Alumni award, The William R. Ross award in sci., U. No. Colo., 1999; named hon. citizen City of Sao Paulo, Brazil, 1972; U.S. del. to Vatican, 1964. Fellow AAAS, N.Y. Acad. Scis. (co-organizer, chmn., consulting editor internat. symposium The Uterus), Gerontol. Soc., Pacific Coast Fertility Soc. (hon.); mem. French Nat. Soc. for Study of Sterility and Fertility (exec. hon. pres. IVth World Congress on Fertility and Sterility 1962), Am. Assn. Anatomists, Am. Soc. Zoologists, Soc. for Integrative and Comparative Biology (organizer symposium The Uterus), Am. Physiol. Soc. (vis. prof. 1962), Endocrine Soc., Soc. Endocrinology (Gt. Britain), Soc. Exptl. Biology and Medicine, Am. Soc. Study Sterility (Rubin award 1954), Internat. Fertility Assn., Pan Am. Assn. Anatomy (co-organizer symposium Reproduction 1972), Midwestern Soc. Anatomists (pres. 1973-74), Mexican Soc. Anatomy (hon.), Harvard Club, Sigma Xi, Kappa Delta Pi, Phi Sigma, Gamma Alpha, Alpha Epsilon Delta. Roman Catholic. Achievements include extensive original research and publications on the physiology and development of decidual tissue (experimental

equivalent of the maternal portion of the placenta) in the rat; biological investigation of eighteen human adenohypophyses (anterior lobes of the human pituitary glands); induction of ovulation utilizing highly purified adenohypophyseal gonadotropic hormones in mammals; the pacemaker action of ovarian sex steroid hormones in reproductive processes; and the interaction of steroids in reproductive mechanisms. Office: 607 E Wilson Ave Lombard IL 60148-4062

VELASCO-MILLS, JOHN ANTHONY, music publishing company executive; b. Rugby, Eng., July 19, 1945; came to U.S., 1985; s. Robert Victor and Brenda Mona (Velasco) Mills; m. Fiona Davis, Aug. 16, 1984; children: Jack, Adam, Christian. Student photography, Sch. Art, Coventry, Eng., 1963. Dir. Canopy Music, London, 1965-68, Edwin H. Morris Ltd., London, 1968-71; mng. dir. United Artists Ltd., London, 1971-74, Pure Cream Entertainment Ltd., London, 1974-77, Interworld Ltd., London, 1977-80, Audio Visual Media Ltd., London, 1980-83, Cherry Lane Ltd., London, 1983-85; v.p. CBS Songs Inc., N.Y.C., 1985-87; pres. Music Pub. Internat. Inc., N.Y.C., 1987—, North Am. Entertainment Ltd., N.Y.C., 1988-89; mgr. Randy Edelman, L.A., 1983—, Joe Raposo, N.Y.C., 1986-89, Jimmy Webb, N.Y.C., 1988-94, Andy Street, L.A., 1996—; cons. Telecare, Direct Source (Can.), Those Characters from Cleveland, Phil Ramone, D.L. Toffner, V.I.P. Group, Foxwedge Inc.; exec. producer Sesame St. Record Series, 1988, audio series Batman, Superman, Spiderman, Capt. Am., Archie, 1990; producer Osibisa in India; bd. dirs. Am. Theatre Networks, N. Am. Entertainment Group, Inc. Prodr. Azendé video, 1997. Chmn. music adv. bd. Recording Artists, Actors and Athletes Against Drunk Driving; content provider how2.com.; pres. Hollywood On Air, Inc. Recipient achievement award Nat. Assn. Boys Clubs, London, 1983. Mem. Performing Rights Soc., Royal Automobile Club (London), Variety Club Internat., Nat. Acad. Popular Music, Nat. Acad. Recording Arts and Scis. Avocations: tennis, swimming, golf.

VELASQUEZ-COCK, ALVARO, industrial company executive, consultant; b. Medellin, Colombia, Oct. 16, 1939; s. Antonio Velasquez and Betty Cock; m. Elena de Bedout, May 31, 1972; 1 child, Juan Diego. Grad. in econs., U. Antioquia, Medellin, 1964; postgrad., London Sch. Econs., 1965-68. Lectr. econs. U. Antioquia, 1968-71, dean faculty econs., 1971-72; head Colombian Bur. Stats., Bogota, 1972-78; mgr. Corp. Financiera Nacional, Bogota, 1979-84; pres. Multicentros S.A., Bogota, 1984-89; gen. mgr. Apple Computers Distbn. Orgn., Bogota, 1989-91, Immobiliaria Progreso S.A., Bogota, 1991-93, Flores Acuarela y Prisma S.A., Bogota, 1993-94; advisor Group ETHUS, 1994—; lectr. econs. U. Antioquia, 1968-71; bd. dirs. Banco de Bogota (Panama), Panama City, Corp. Financiera Colombiana, Bogota; fin. cons. Mem. adv. coun. Compartir, Bogota, 1990—. Mem. AAAS, Internat. Statis. Inst., Inst. Math. Stats., N.Y. Acad. Scis. Mem. Liberal Party. Roman Catholic. Avocations: philately, sea fishing. Home: Carrera 5 81-50, Apt 906, Bogota Colombia

VELAZCO, JORGE, orchestra conductor, research musicologist; b. Mexico City, Jan. 12, 1942; s. Roberto Velazco and Columba Muñoz; m. Marcia Elizabeth Velazco, May 25, 1983; children: Diego, León, Sebastián. Licenciado en Derecho, Univ. Nat. Autonoma Mex., 1968; diploma in orchestral conducting, Acad. Chigiana, Siena, Italy, 1975; studied with, Herbert von Karajan, Berlin, 1976-77. Head music dept. Univ. Nat. Autonoma Mex., 1973-74, subdir. gen. difusión cultural, 1974-76; artistic dir. Univ. Nat. Autonoma Mex. Philharmonic, 1985-89; asst. Herbert von Karajan, Salzburg, Austria, 1977; artistic dir. Minería Symphony Orch., Mexico City, 1978-85, 96—; programming com. mem. Interamerican Music Festival, Washington, 1980-85, 88-91; prin. guest conductor Orch. Camera Fiorentina, Florence, Italy, 1990—, Sinfonietta RIAS, Berlin, 1983-85; music rschr. Inst. Investigaciones Estéticas, Mex., 1974—; artistic com. mem. Music Interpretation Internat. Sem., Ischia, Italy, 1988-92; dir. internat. studies Tex. Music Festival, Houston, 1991—; Wortham chair performing arts U. Houston, 1991; vis. prof. musicology Oviedo U., La Granda, Spain, 1994, U. Houston, 1997-98; mem. Robert Stevenson Prize jury, Washington, 1999. Author: La Música por Dentro, 1988, De Música y Músicos, 1981; conductor (CD) with Berlin Symphony Music by Antonio Gomezanda, Berlin, 1996, with Sinfonietta RIAS: Music by Boccherini & Danzi, Berlin, 1985, Music by Arriaga, Soler-Halffter & Sarrier, Berlin, 1989. John Simon Guggenheim Meml. Found. fellow, N.Y.C., 1987-88. Mem. Spanish Soc. Musicology, Internat. Musicology Soc., Royal Musical Assn., Italian Musicology Soc. Home: Cedros 18, San Miguel Ajusco, Tlalpan DF 14700, Mexico

VELAZQUEZ-SQUEGLIA, SHARON KATHLEEN, elementary education educator, language educator; b. Melrose, Mass.; d. Thomas Ashmore and Eleanor Marion (Smith) Samuels; div.; children: Sarah Squeglia, Oscar Velazquez, Martin Velazquez. BA in English Lit., U. Mass., 1971; MA in Intercultural Edn., U. Americas, Mex. City, 1975. Cert. elem. tchr., Mass. Tchr. English Inst. Politecnico Nacional, Mex. City, 1974-79; elem. tchr. Am. Sch., Veracruz, Mex., 1980-82; tchr. elem. bilingual Oakland Ave. Sch., Methuen, Mass., 1983-84; elem. tchr. Breen Sch., Lawrence, Mass., 1987-88; tchr. English Inst. Tecnologico Estudios Superiores Monterrey, Villas de Hda., Estado Mex, 1995-96. Avocations: reading, swimming, jogging, embroidery, cooking. Home: 33 Jordan St Apt 1 Lawrence MA 01841-4730

VELCIC-CANIVEZ, MIRNA, linguist, university scholar; b. Zagreb, Croatia, Oct. 30, 1952; arrived in France, 1991; d. Veseljko and Ivana (Vidas) V.; m. Patrice Canivez, Apr. 20, 1990. MA, Fac. Philosophy, Zagreb, 1979; PhD, Zagreb U., 1984. Lectr. Grenoble (France) U., 1976-78, U. Zagreb, 1979-87; Fulbright scholar Georgetown U. and Ind. U., Washington/Bloomington, 1987-88; rsch. fellow Inst. Anthropology, Zagreb, 1988-90; assoc. prof. U. Lille, France, 1992—; Mem. CNRS, Paris. Author: Uvod U Lingvistiku Teksta, 1987, Otisak Priče, 1991; contbr. articles to profl. jours. Mem. MLA. Avocations: skiing, hiking. Office: Univ Lille III, BP 149, 59653 Villeneuve d'Ascq Nord, France

VELDE, JOHN ERNEST, JR., investment company executive; b. Pekin, Ill., June 15, 1917; s. John Ernest and Alga (Anderson) V.; m. Shirley Margaret Walker, July 29, 1940 (dec. 1969); 1 dau., Drew; m. Gail Patrick, Sept. 28, 1974 (dec. July 1980); m. Gretchen Swanson Pullen, Nov. 7, 1981. A.B., U. Ill., 1938. Pres. Velde, Roelfs & Co., Pekin, 1955-60; dir. Herget Nat. Bank, 1948-75, Kroehler Mfg. Co., 1974-81; pres. Paisano Prodns., Inc., 1980-94, mng. ptnr., 1994—; mng. ptnr. The Gardner Partnership, 1994—. Trustee Pekin Pub. Library, 1948-69, Pekin Meml. Hosp., 1950-69, Everett McKinley Dirksen Rsch. Ctr., 1965-74, Am. Libr. Assn. Endowment, 1976-82, Joint Coun. Econ. Edn., 1977-83, Ctr. Am. Archeology, 1978-83, Western Heritage Mus., Omaha, 1994—; chmn. Am. Libr. Trustee Assn. Found., 1976; chmn. trustees, bd. dirs. Ctr. Ulcer Rsch. and Edn. Found., 1977-82; mem. bd. councilors Brain Rsch. Inst. UCLA, 1977-82; mem. Nat. Commn. on Libr. and Info. Sci., 1970-79; mem. adv. bd. on White House Conf. on Librs., 1976-80; bd. dirs. U. Ill. Found., 1977-83, Omaha Pub. Libr. Found., 1985-92, James Madison Coun. Libr. Congress, 1990—; vice chmn. U. Ill. Pres.' Coun., 1977-79, chmn., 1979-81, mem. fin. resources coun. steering com., 1976-78; mem. adv. coun. UCLA Grad. Sch. Libr. and Info. Sci., 1981-82; pres. Ill. Valley Library System, 1965-69; dir. Lakeview Ctr. for Arts and Scis., Peoria, Ill., 1962-73; mem. Nat. Book Com., 1969-74. Served as lt. (j.g.) USNR, World War II. Mem. Am. Libr. Trustee Assn. (regional v.p. 1970-72, chmn. internat. rels. com. 1973-76), Internat. Boy Scouts (Baden-Powell fellow 1987—), Kappa Sigma. Clubs: Chgo. Yacht, Internat. (Chgo.); California (Los Angeles); Outrigger Canoe (Honolulu); Thunderbird Country (Rancho Mirage, Calif.); Chaine des Rotisseurs, Chevaliers du Tastevin; Circumnavigators (N.Y.C.); Omaha, Omaha Country; Happy Hollow, Old Baldy (Saratoga, Wyo.), Eldorado Country (Indian Wells, Calif.). Home: 8405 Indian Hills Dr Omaha NE 68114-4099 also: 40-231 Club View Dr Rancho Mirage CA 92270-3527 also: 123 Arapahoe Dr Saratoga WY 82331

VELDEN, MANFRED H., psychology educator; b. Jülich, Rhineland, Germany, Nov. 17, 1939; s. Franz and Luise (Beissel) V. Diploma in psychology, U. Bonn, Germany, 1966; postgrad., U. Calif., Berkeley, 1967-68; Dr in Psychology, U. Mainz, Germany, 1972, Habilitation, 1978. Asst. U. Mainz, 1968-79, prof., 1979-80; prof. Tech. U. Berlin, 1980-81; prof. U. Osnabrück, Germany, 1981—, dir. dept. psychology, 1982-83, 99—. Author: Signalentdeckungstheorie, 1982, Psychophysiologie, 1994; contbr. articles to sci. jours. With German mil., 1960-61. Mem. APA, Internat. Orgn. Psychophysiology (assoc. editor 1989-2000). Home: Quellwiese 45, 49080 Osnabrück Germany Office: Univ Osnabrück, Dept Psychology, 49069 Osnabrück Germany

VELDHUIS, JOHANNES G. F. (JAN VELDHUIS), university president; b. Hengelo, Oct. 4, 1938; s. Bernardus J. and Berendina J. (Tijhuis) V.; married Monica M.H. Thier, 1968; children: Bernd-Pieter, Geert, Tiddo. Grad., U. Utrecht, U. Minn.; D in History and Polit. Sci., U. Fla. With Ministry of Fgn. Affairs, 1968-70; sec. univ. bd. U. Leiden, 1970-74; dep. sec.-gen. Ministry of Edn. and Sci., 1974-79, dir.-gen., inspector-gen. of edn. and sci., 1979-86; pres. Utrecht U., 1986—; sec. Bd. Med. Inst. Paramaribo, Suriname, 1972-74; chair Netherlands delegation OECD Edn. Com., 1984-86; chair bd. Netherlands-Am. Com. Ednl. Exch., Fulbright Commn., 1984—, Found. Decartes, Amsterdam, Netherlands Inst. for Art History, Florence, Netherlands Assn. Internat. Affairs, dist. Utrecht, 1995—; bd. dirs. State Inst. War Documentation, Netherlands History Inst., Rome, Nat. Mus. Catharijneconvent, Netherlands and Arab Archaeol. Inst., Cairo, Japan-Netherlands Inst., Tokyo, L. Bernstein Found., Amsterdam, Netherlands Insts. St. Petersburg & Athens. Author various pubs. in ednl. and pub. adminstrn. Bd. hosp. Med. Centrum Haaglanden. Fulbright grantee; decorated Chevalier Legion of Honor, France, officer, The Netherlands. Fellow Internat. Vis. Program. Avocations: lit., botany, tennis, skiing, bridge. Home: Roucooppark 12, 2251 AV Voorschoten The Netherlands Office: Utrecht U, Heidelberglaan 8 PO Box 80125, 3508 TC Utrecht The Netherlands

VELEZ, DIANA, historian, educator; b. N.Y.C., Mar. 11, 1949; d. Ismael Velez Rodriguez and Adoracion Pineiro Wiscovitch Velez. BA, CUNY, 1971; MA, PhD, Princeton U., 1977. Assoc. dir. Ctr. Latin Am. Studies U. Pitts., 1984-87; sr. program officer Tinker Found., N.Y.C., 1987-90; asst. dean arts & scis. U. Ctrl. Fla., Orlando, 1991-95, history faculty, 1995—. Doctoral fellowship Ford Found., 1971. Mem. Am. Hist. Assn., Soc. Spanish and Portuguese History, Conf. on Latin Am. History. E-mail: velez@pegasus.cc.ucf.edu. Office: U Ctrl Fla History Dept PO Box 161350 Orlando FL 32816-1350

VELICS, GABRIELLA, journalist, sociologist; b. Szombathely, Hungary, June 7, 1970; d. János and Jánosné Farkas Velics. Diploma, Berzsenyi Daniel Tchrs. Coll., 1992, U. Eötvös Loránd, 1995, 97. Freelance journalist Vas Népe, Szombathely, Hungary, 1986-95, Tér-Kép, Szombathely, Hungary, 1989-91; tchr. Indsl. Tech. Secondary Sch., Szombathely, 1992-93; editor of news Radio Szó-Köz, Szombathely, 1994—; editor Dzsungel, Szombathely, 1996; media cons., editor Nonprofit Info. Ctr., Szombathely, 1996—; asst., European studies coord. dept. sociology & polit. sci. Daniel Berzsenyi Coll., Szombathely, 1999-2000, asst. lectr. dept. Comm., 2000—; lectr. in field; owner, mgr. VG, Szombathely, 1996—. Mem. Kung-fu Sch., Szombathely, 1996. Mem. Austria Kung-fu Assn. Avocations: Yang Tai Chi Chuan, collecting cacti and succulents, formula 1 racing. Office: VG, Körmöc u 27, H-9700 Szombathely Hungary

VELISARIS, CHRIS NICHOLAS, financial analyst; b. Berwyn, Ill., June 2, 1961; s. Nicholas Chris and Panagiota Nicholas (Georgiou) V.; m. Mary Elizabeth Vlahos, July 23, 1994; children: Christopher Nicholas, Madalyn Penelope. BS, U. Ill., 1983; MS, U. Wash., 1985; MBA, Dartmouth Coll., 1990; postgrad., U. Naples, Italy, 1991-94. Rsch. engr. Amoco Chem. Co., Naperville, Ill., 1983, 85-94; cons. Orco Ltd., Athens, 1989; rsch. mgr. U. Wash., Seattle, 1990-94; sr. staff specialist corp. fin. United Airlines, Chgo., Ill., 1994-99; project mgr. corp. fin. GATX Corp., Chgo., Ill., 1999—; founder, prin. officer Velisaris Investment Cons. Svcs., Inc., Brookfield, Ill., 1994—; cons. in field. Author: Proc. 31st Ann. Nat. Sampe Symp., 1986, Polymer Engring. and Sci., 1986, 88, Proc. of the 5th European Conf. on Comp. Materials, 1992. Counselor Valleyview Correctional Ctr., Ill. Benedictine Coll., St. Charles, 1988; advisor Jr. Achievement of Chgo., Naperville, 1987-88. Mem. Tri-Orgn. of Amoco Corp. (bd. dirs. 1987-88). Greek Orthodox. Avocations: skiing, golf, tennis, chess, investing. Home: 59 Drexel Ave La Grange IL 60525-5845 Office: United Airlines WHQFT PO Box 66100 Chicago IL 60666-0100

VELLUCCI, SHERRY LYNN, library and information science educator; b. Paterson, N.J., Nov. 14, 1948; d. Peter and Eleanor M. Vellucci; m. Robin A. Leaver, June 10, 1988. AB, Rutgers U., 1972; MS in Libr. Sci., Drexel U., 1983; D in Libr. Sci., Columbia U., 1995. Catalog libr. Princeton (N.J.) U., 1977-78; choral libr. Westminster Choir Coll., Princeton, 1978-83, libr. dir., 1983-92; asst. prof. St. John's U., Jamaica, N.Y., 1992-98, assoc. prof., 1998—. Author: Bibliographic Relationships in Music Catalogs, 1997; co-author: Notes in the Catalog Record, 1989; mem. editl. bd. Cataloging and Classification Quar., 1998—; contbr. chpts. to books and articles to profl. jours. Mem. Internat. Assn. Music Librs. (bd. dirs. 1996-98, pres. 1999—), Music Libr. Assn. (treas. 1986-90, bd. dirs. 1991-93, Spl. Achievement award 1998), Music Libr. Assn., Am. Libr. Assn., Spl. Libr. Assn., Beta Phi Mu. E-mail: velluccs@stjohns.edu. Office: St Johns Univ DLIS 8000 Utopia Pkwy Jamaica NY 11439-0001

VELMAHOS, GEORGE, physician, surgeon; b. Athens, Mar. 23, 1962; came to U.S., 1994; s. Constantinos and Elpida (Valakis) V.; m. Irene Souter, June 20, 1993; 1 child, Elpida. MD, Athens Sch. Medicine, 1985, PhD, 1991. Resident in surgery Hippokration Hosp., Athens, 1986-91; surgeon in rural svc. Kalamata (Greece) Gen. Hosp., 1991-92; trauma fellow Baragwanath Hosp., Johannesburg, South Africa, 1991-94; asst. prof. in surgery L.A. County/U. So. Calif. Med. Ctr., L.A., 1994—. Contbr. articles to Am. and internat. jours. Fellow ACS, Royal Coll. Surgeons Edinburgh, Royal Coll. Surgeons Glasgow. Avocations: basketball, tennis. Office: Los Angeles Co-USC Med Ctr 1200 N State St Los Angeles CA 90033-1029

VELMANS, MAX LEOPOLD, psychologist, educator, philosopher, engineer; b. Amsterdam, Holland, May 27, 1942; arrived in Eng., 1967; s. Isaac and Anna (Cok) V.; children: Catherine, Emily, Benjamin, Samuel. BEE, U. Sydney, 1964; MPhil(Qual), U. London, 1967, PhD in Psychology, 1974. Chartered psychologist, Eng. Sys. analyst EMAIL, Sydney, 1965-66; lectr. City U., London, 1967-68; from psychology lectr. to reader in psychology U. London, 1969—; chmn. bd. trustees Inst. for the Study of Consciousness, London, 1994—; cons. Brit. Tech. Group, London, 1977-87. Author, editor: The Science of Consciousness, 1996, Understanding Consciousness, 2000; contbr. articles to profl. publs.; inventor hearing aid for the deaf. Grantee Brit. Tech. Group, 1977-82, Med. Rsch. Coun., 1985-87; Fulbright scholar, 1984. Fellow Brit. Psychol. Soc. (assoc., chmn. mind-body spl. interest group 1987-92, elected rep. sci. affairs bd. 1988-91); mem. Brit. Fulbright Scholar Assn., Russian Acad. Scis. (Moscow). Achievements includes inventor of a new frequency transposing hearing aid for the sensory-neural deaf and extensive theoretical devel. within the science of consciousness and related ares in philosophy of the mind. Office: U London, Goldsmiths, Lewisham Way, New Cross, London SE14 6NW, England

VELOSO, PAULO AUGUSTO SILVA, computer science educator, researcher; b. Porto Alegre, Brazil, Apr. 18, 1944; s. Paulo Dias and Lia (Silva) V.; m. Sheila Regina Murgel, Apr. 28, 1970; children: Paula Murgel, Flavia Murgel. BS in Electronic Engring., Tech. Inst. Aeronautics, São Jose Dos Campos, Brazil, 1968; MS in Elec. Engring., Fed. U., Rio de Janeiro, 1970; MA in Math., U. Calif., Berkeley, 1974, PhD in Elec. Engring. and Computer Sci., 1975. Rsch. asst. Nancy (France) U., 1968; instr. Fed. U., Rio de Janeiro, 1969-70, assoc. prof., 1975-77; assoc. prof. Cath. U., Rio de Janeiro, 1977-86, prof., 1986-96; prof. Fed. U., 1996—; vis. scientist U. Western Ont., London, 1977; vis. rschr. Paris U., 1980; chmn., Cath. U., 1981; sr. vis. fellow Imperial Coll., 1986, 90, 91, 92. Co-author: (chpt.) Application-Oriented Approaches, 1986, (chpt.) Fork Algebras, 1997; contbr. articles to profl. jours. Recipient Sr. Rsch. 1A grant Brazilian Nat. Rsch. Coun., 1992, Admiral Alvaro Alberto prize for sci. and tech. Brazilian Nat. Rsch. Coun., 1995, Sr. Rschr. 1A grant Brazilian Nat. Rsch. Coun., 1996.

VELTMAN, MARTINUS J., retired physics educator; b. Netherlands, 1931. PhD, U. Utrecht, Netherlands, 1963. John D. MacArthur prof. physics U. Mich., Ann Arbor, now prof. emeritus. Recipient High Energy and Particle Physics prize European Phys. Soc., 1993, P.A.M. Dirac Medal and Prize, Internat. Center for Theoretical Physics, 1996, Nobel Prize in Physics, 1999. Home: Schubertlaan 15, 3723 LM Bilthoven The Netherlands Office: U Mich Dept Physics 2477 Randall Lab 500 E University Ave Ann Arbor MI 48109-1120*

VELTRUP, CLEMENS GERHARD, psychologist, researcher; b. Haren, Germany, Nov. 22, 1960; s. Hermann and Thekla (Cloppenborg) V.; m. Barbara Dierse Veltrup, June 19, 1995; 1 child, Hannah. PhD, 1995. Psychological diplomate. Addiction rsch. Med. U., Luebeck, Germany, 1988-97; chief psychologist Dept. Addiction and Psychosomatics, Germany, 1997-99; mgr. clinic group Therapieverbund Ostsee, Luebeck, Germany, 1999—; cons. Lipha Pharma, Germany, 1995, TUEV Nord, Germany, 1995. Author: Abstinenzgefaehrdung und Abstinenzbeendigung bei entzugsbehandelten Alkoholabhaengigen, 1995, (with T. Wetterling) Diagnose und Therapie bei Alkoholproblemen, 1997. Pres. Cath. German Scouts, Osnabrueck, 1980-86. Mem. Deutsche fuer Gesellschaft Suchtforschung, Gesellschaft gegen Drogengefahren. Roman Catholic. Office: Therapieverbund Ostee, Weidenweg 9-15, D-23563 Luebeck Germany

VELU, PALANI T., materials processing engineer, researcher; b. Dindigul, India, May 20, 1964; came to U.S., 1992; s. Sundaram and Nallathai Thiraviyam; m. Annachelvi Paramasivam, May 27, 1996; 1 child, Preetha. BE, U. Madras, Coimbatore, India, 1985; MS, U. Nev., Reno, 1995; PhD, U. Ala., Tuscaloosa, 1997. Prodn. engr. S.S. Miranda Ltd., Ankleshwar, India, 1986-88; rsch. engr. Indian Space Rsch. Orgn., Trivandrum, 1988-92; process devel. engr. RF Monolithics, Inc., Dallas, 1997—. Mem. IEEE, ASM Internat., Electrochem. Soc., The Minerals, Metals, Materials Soc. Avocations: travel, photography. Office: RF Monolithics Inc 4347 Sigma Rd Dallas TX 75244-4598

VELZ, JOHN WILLIAM, literature educator; b. Englewood, N.J., Aug. 5, 1930; s. Clarence Joseph and Harriet Josephine (O'Brien) V.; m. Sarah Elizabeth Campbell, Oct. 18, 1967; children: Jody, Emily; 3 children from previous marriage. BA in English with high distinction and honors, U. Mich., 1953, MA in English and French, 1954; PhD in English and Classical Tradition, U. Minn., 1963. Instr. Coll. St. Thomas, St. Paul, 1958-60; asst. prof. English Rice U., Houston, 1963-69; prof. U. Tex., Austin, 1969-96, prof. emeritus, 1996—; vis. prof. U. Paul Valery, Montpelier, France, 1977-78, Julius Maximillians U., Wuerzburg, West Germany, 1981-82, 85-86; asst. dir., lit. adv. Odessa Shakespeare Festival, 1977; faculty mem. Oreg. Shakespeare Festival, 1979; lectr. tour Cen. and Ea. Europe univs., 1993; dir. acad. prodns. of Shakespeare and medieval drama; mem. Acad. Adv. Coun. Globe Theatre Ctr., 1981—; mem. U.S. Com. for Shakespeare's Globe, 1990—; presenter over 100 papers and lectures to learned socs.; reviewer over 100 books and theatrical prodns. Author: Shakespeare and the Classical Tradition, 1968, electronic edit., 2000 (ALA citation, Assn. Coll. and Rsch. Librs. citation); editor: Julius Caesar in MLA's New Variorum Shakespeare, 1966-95, (N.Am.) Cahiers Elisabethains, 1979-81; Shakespeare's English Histories: A Quest for Form and Genre, 1996; co-editor: Collected Papers of James G. McManaway, 1969, One Touch of Shakespeare: Letters of Joseph Crosby to Joseph Parker Norris 1875-1878, 1986, Pegasus Bibliography of Shakespeare's Roman Works, 2000; contbr. over 60 scholarly, interpretive articles, mainly on Shakespeare and on medieval drama, to profl. jours.; mem. editl. bd. Shakespeare Quar., 1975-98, Classical and Modern Lit., 1981-85, Tex. Studies in Lit. and Lang., 1969-92, Shakespeare and the Classroom, 1993—; mem. editl. adv. bd. Complete Works of Shakespeare, 3d edit., 1980, 4th edit., 1992, 5th edit., 1997; cons. editor South Ctrl. Rev., 1989-92; mem. cons. com. Internat. Studies in Shakespeare and His Contemporaries, 1990—. Recipient Fulbright award, 1977-78, 81-82; recipient Oreon E. Scott award U. Mich., 1953; NEH fellow, 1967-68; Folger Library fellow, 1968. Mem. MLA (life), Assn. Lit. Scholars and Critics, Internat. Shakespeare Assn. (charter), Shakespeare Assn. Am., Malone Soc., Renaissance English Text Soc., Medieval and Renaissance Drama Soc., Marlowe Soc. of Am., H.W. Fowler Soc. (charter), Internat. Soc. Classical Tradition, Phi Beta Kappa, Phi Kappa Phi, Phi Eta Sigma. Home: 809 W 32d St Austin TX 78705-2115

VENABLE, WILLIAM RALPH, III, marketing executive, banking executive; b. Kansas City, Mo., Mar. 18, 1959; s. William Ralph and Kathleen Loretta (Krivas) V. BS in Journalism, U. Kans., 1981; MBA in Mktg. and Fin., Rockhurst Coll., 1984; PhD, U. Mo., 2000. Film booker 20th Century Fox Film Corp., Kansas City, Mo., 1981-83; dir. alumni rels. Rockhurst Coll., Kansas City, Mo., 1983-86; fin. cons. Merrill Lynch, Kansas City, Mo., 1987-89; ops. mgr. AMC Entertainment, Kansas City, Mo., 1990-91; mktg. mgr. SecureAmerica, Omaha, 1991-92; event mgr. CCL-Hallmark Cards, Kansas City, 1993; dir. reseller rels. Ruf Strategic Solutions, Olathe, Kans., 1993-96; v.p., dir. database mktg. and strategies UMB Bank, N.A., Kansas City, Mo., 1997—; adv. bd. Barley's Ltd., 1995-97, LatAm Internat. Trading LLC; adv. dir. Marketsolutions LLC, 1995—, cons. River City Products, Inc., North Kansas City, 1986—. Author: (book) How to and Where of Kansas City Barbeque, 1989, Kansas City Barbeque Book, 1996; author, editor: (book) Absolute Barbeque, 1994. Founder O.E. Ellis Soc., Kansas City, 1984, Greater Omaha BBQ Soc., 1991, co-founder Students of the Social Sci. Consortium, Kansas City, 1996; co-chmn. Jazz Feast for Project ReStart, 1997-99, bd. dirs., 1999—; bd. dirs. Am. Cancer Soc., Kansas City, 1983-88; mem. exec. programs adv. com. U. Mo., 1997-2000; rsch. com. In itiative for Competitive Inner Cities, Kansas City, Mo., 1996-98. Recipient Arthur Mag PhD fellowship U. Mo., 1996-97, Marjorie Powell Allen Grad. fellowship U. Mo., 1995-96. Mem. SAR (Kans. state treas. 1988), Greater Kansas City C. of C. Centurions (retreat chair 1986-87, steering com. 1994-95, 97-2000, alumni pres.-elect 1997-98, alum ni steering com. 1992-95, pres. 1999-2000), Native Sons of Kansas City, Univ. Club Kansas City (mem. house com. 1996-97, bd. dirs. 1997-99), Phi Kappa Sigma, Alpha Kappa Psi, Gamma Omicron Beta, University Senate. Republican. Roman Catholic. Avocations: writer, chef, historic renovator. E-mail: wvenable@cctr.umkc.edu. Home: 8723 Aberdeen Dr Leawood KS 66206-1611 Office: UMB Bank PO Box 419226 Kansas City MO 64141-6226

VENABLE KING, GIOVAN, lawyer, minister; b. Winston-Salem, N.C., Dec. 10, 1956; d. Joel William and Jo Ann (Harbour) V. AB in Music magna cum laude, Dartmouth Coll., 1979; MDiv, Harvard U., 1983; JD, Stanford U., 1988. Bar: Calif. 1989, D.C. 1990, U.S. Supreme Ct. 1994; ordained minister Congregational Ch., 1984. Assoc. Wyman Bautzer Kuchel & Silbert, L.A., 1988-90; assoc. Gipson Hoffman & Pancione, L.A., 1990-92; pvt. practice L.A., 1992—. Contbr. articles to profl. jours.; editor Cal West Congregationalist, 1990—; mem. Stanford Law Rev., 1987-89. Mem. The Ebell L.A., Phi Beta Kappa. Achievements include being the first woman ordained at the oldest Protestant Ch. in Southern California and the first woman to head a Southern California Congregational Church in 1992. Avocations: piano, running, travel, tennis. Office: 419 N Larchmont Blvd Los Angeles CA 90004-3013

VENABLES, JOHN ANTHONY, physics educator; b. Leicester, Eng., May 19, 1936; s. Peter and Ethel (Howell) V.; m. Delia Poole, Oct. 21, 1961; children: Julian Paul, Gail Catherine. BA, Cambridge (Eng.) U., 1958, MA, PhD, 1961. Rsch. assoc. U. Ill., Urbana, 1961-64; lectr. U. Sussex, Brighton, Eng., 1964-71, reader, 1971-88, prof., 1988—; prof. associé U. Aix-Marseille (France), 1973-82; vis. scientist Max Planck Inst., Stuttgart, Fed. Republic Germany, 1969; prof. Ariz. State U., Tempe, 1985—. Fellow Inst. Physics, Electron Microscopy and Analysis Group (chair 1972-74); mem. Am. Inst. Physics, Electron Microscope Soc. Am. Office: U Sussex Sch CPES, U Sussex Sch CPES, Brighton BN1 9QJ, England Office: Ariz State U Dept Physics Ariz State U Dept Physics & Astronomy Tempe AZ 85287

VENATOR, MICHAEL, radiologist; b. Cologne, Germany, Aug. 21, 1953; s. Hans H. Rolf and Ursula (Landwehr) V.; m. Dorothea Kraus, June 27, 1979. Cert. gen. radiology. Intern St. Mary's Hosp., Bergisch-Gladbach, 1981-82, asst. dept. radiology, 1983-85, asst. dir., 1985-86; asst. dept. radiotherapy Essen, 1982-88; mem. staff MRI-Inst., Cologne, 1989-91; dir. MRI Dept., Pforzheim, 1992, Remscheid, 1992-95; mem. in charge of MRI Radiologic Group Practice, Lünen, 1995—. Founding mem. Movement for a Free an Dem. Rhineland, 1991. Mem. Radiologic Soc. of the Rhineland. Avocations: collecting art, related multiples-forgery. Office: Radiologische Gemein, Kurt-Schumacher Str 12, D-44534 Lünen West Germany

VENCES, MIGUEL, zoologist; b. Cologne, Germany, Apr. 24, 1969; s. Sergio and Ursula (Kilfitt) V. Diploma in biology, Rheinische Friedrich Wilhelm U., 1996, PhD, 2000. Zoologist Zoologisches Forschungsinst. and Mus. Koenig, Bonn, Germany, 1996—. Co-author: A Field Guide to

Amphibians and Reptiles of Madagascar, 1992, 2d edit., 1994; contbr. articles to profl. jours. Home: Zulpicher Str 79, 50937 Cologne NRW, Germany Office: Muséam Nat Historie Naturelle, Lab Reptiles and Amphibies, rue Cuvier 25 Paris 75005, France

VENDEL, STEFAN, psychologist; b. Breznica, Czechoslovakia, Jan. 20, 1951; s. Stefan and Anna (Mandulova) V.; m. Maria Dudasova, Apr. 23, 1977; children: Natalia, Ariadna, David. PhD, U. J.A. Komenskeho, Slovak Republic, 1982; habil., Mathias Bell U., Slovakia, 1999. Psychologist Nat. Com. Kosice City, Slovak Republic, 1974-77, Košice Psychol. Adv. Bd., Slovak Republic, 1977-90; asst. prof. Prešov U., Slovak Republic, 1990—. Author: (monograph) Čim budem; mem. editl. bd. Psychológia a patopsychológia dietata; contbr. articles to profl. jours. Mem. Slovak Psychol. Assn. Avocations: tennis, travel. E-mail: vendel@unipo.sk. Home: Turgenevova 3, 040 01 Kosice Slovakia Office: Filozofická fakulta PU, ul 17 novembra č 1, 080 78 Prešov Slovakia

VENDIK, IRINA BORISOVNA, electrotechnology educator; b. Fergana, USSR, May 15, 1936; d. Boris Sergeevich and Vera Grigorevna (Elkina) Abramov; m. Orest Genrikhovich Vendik, Mar. 13, 1957; children: Andrei, Olga. Diploma of Engring., Leningrad Elec. Engring. U., 1959, PhD, 1966; DrSc in Physics, A.F. Ioffe Phys.-Tech. Inst., Russia, 1990. Rschr. Leningrad Elec. Engring. Inst., 1959-64, asst. prof., 1964-67, assoc. prof., 1967-91; prof. St. Petersburg (Russia) Electrotech. U., 1991—; cons. Svetlana Electronics Co., Leningrad, 1970-85. Co-author: Microwave Switches and Phase Shifters, 1985, High Temperature Superconductor Devices for MIcrowave Signal Processing, 1997. Recipient award Ministry of Edn. of USSR, 1986, award Ministry of Electronics of USSR, 1986, Sign of Honor of Gov. of Russia, 1999; Soros Found. grantee, 1990. Mem. IEEE. Orthodox Christian. Avocations: music, swimming. Home: 42-1 Apt 456, Korablestroiteley Str, 199155 Saint Petersburg Russia Office: St Petersburg Electrotech U, 5 Prof Popov Str, 197376 Saint Petersburg Russia

VENDIK, OREST GENRIKHOVICH, electronics educator; b. Leningrad, Russia, Apr. 16, 1932; s. Genrikh Adamovich and Yelena Mikhailovna (Kalistratova) V.; m. Irina Borisovna Abramova, Mar. 13, 1957; children: Andrej, Olga. Diploma of Engr., Leningrad Elec. Engring. Inst., Russia, 1954, PhD, 1957, DSc, 1966. Asst. prof. Leningrad Elec. Engring. Inst., Russia, 1957-63, assoc. prof., 1963-67, prof., 1968-69, dept. head, 1969-89; prof. Electrotechnical U., St. Petersburg, Russia, 1989—; rschr. on leave Surrey U., London, 1967-68; presenter at profl. confs. Author: (book) Antennas with Non-Mechanical Scanning, 1965, High Temperature Superconductor Devices for Microwave Signal Processing, 1997; editor: Ferroelectrics at Microwaves, 1979, High-Tc Superconductors: Physical Principles of Microwave Applications, 1991; contbr. papers to profl. confs. Del. XIII Congress of Young Communist League of USSR, Moscow, 1958. Recipient State prize of USSR, Govt. of USSR, 1988, Soros Prof. grant Soros Found., 1994; named Man of Sci. Russian Fedn., Pres. Russian Fedn., 1999. Mem. IEEE, St. Petersburg Assn. of Scientists. Orthodox. Avocations: music, tourism, skiing, swimming. Home: Bldg 42-1 Flat 456, Korablestroiteley St, 199155 Saint Petersburg Russia Office: Electrotech U Bldg 5, Prof Popov St, 197376 Saint Petersburg Russia

VENDITTI, CLELIA ROSE See PALMER, CHRISTINE

VENDRIG, ALEXANDER ANTONIUS, clinical psychologist; b. Montfoort, The Netherlands, Oct. 16, 1969; s. Gerard Vendrig and Agaath Spruit. MS, U. Maastricht, 1993, U. Leiden, 1994; PhD, U. Nymegen, 1999. Clin. psychologist Rug Advies Centra Nederland, Zeist, 1994—. Avocations: automobile restoration, gliding. Office: Rug Advies Centra Nederland, Utrechtseweg 92, 3702 AD Zeist The Netherlands

VENET, CLAUDE HENRY, architect, acoustic engineer; b. Lyon, France, Aug. 10, 1946; came to U.S., 1981; s. René Joseph and Marcellé (Michel) V.; m. Valerie Picq, Sept. 22, 1997; 1 child, Elle Cassiopée Mariana. Dipl. electronic engr., ESTA, Rochefort, France, 1968; Lic. Physics, U. Paris, 1971; MArch, So. Calif. Inst. Architecture, 1986. U.K. mgr. Ling Dynamics/Altec, Royston, Eng., 1971-72; mng. dir. CVE Enterprises, London, 1972-75; sales dir. Macinnes/Amcron France, Paris, 1975-77; tech. dir. Audio Cons. Coordination, Rio de Janeiro, 1977-81; cons. Paramount (Sound) Films Corp., Glendale, Calif., 1981-82; pres. CV Acoustics, Arch. & Engring., Belleville, France, 1986-91, Archicoustics Inc., Miami and Rio de Janeiro, 1991—; lectr. U. Miami Sch. Architecture, 1995—. Vol. Architects Without Frontiers, Paris, 1990—. Named Most Outstanding Consulting Engr., Miami AIA. Mem. AIA, AAAS, Am. Inst. Physics, Acoustical Soc. Am., Nat. Coun. Acoustical Cons., Audio Engring. Soc., N.Y. Acad. of Sci., Order French Architects, Chamber French Cons. Engrs. Achievements include design of computer-driven, polymorphic, multi-use theatre with continous variable acoustics/geometry, variable-shape, multi-acoustics polymorphous concept in recording studio design; more than 1,000 consulting projects with international companies, including Citicorp, Club Med, Credit Lyonnais, Disney, Eurodisney, Jeressati (BZ), Universal, also numerous hotels. Office: Archicoustics Inc 630 NE 55th St Miami FL 33137-3008

VENETI, SMARAGDA, cytopathologist; b. Athens, Feb. 22, 1938; d. George and Olga (Hatjianagnostou) Zachariadou; m. Athanasios Venetis, Sept. 6, 1969; children: Anastasia, Olga. BA, Scripps Coll., Claremont, Calif., 1960; Medicine, U. Athens, 1967, Doctorate, 1975. MD. Asst. B Gen. Hosp., Chalkis, Greece, 1967-69, Evagelismos Hosp., Athens, 1969-75; cons. Social Security Orgn., Athens, 1975-78; asst. A Laiko Gen. Hosp., Athens, 1978-82; dir. MTS Gen. Hosp., Athens, 1982-86, Lito Hosp. for Women, Athens, 1986—; cons. in field, Athens, 1983—. Author/editor: Contribution of Cytology to CNS, 1974, Hormonal Receptors in Endometrial Neoplasia, 1987; contbg. author: Honorary Volume for Prof. Eleftheriou, 1978, Hon. Vol. for Prof. Chrysospathis, 1990, Pathology of Uterine Cervix - Colposcopy, 1991, Hon. Vol. for Prof. Papacharalambous, 1992, Hon. Vo. for Dr. Papaioannou, 1993, Modern Senology, 1996; contbr. articles to med. jours. Recipient Fulbright scholarship, 1957-60. Mem. Greek Soc. Cytology (founding mem., exec. coun. 1975—, v.p. 1996-98), Greek Soc. Senology (mem. exec. coun. 1996—), Greek Soc. Gen. Pathology and Pathol. Anatomy, Internat. Acad. Cytology, Brit. Soc. Clin. Cytology. Mem. Christian Greek Orthodox. Avocations: photography, travel, art. Office: Lito Hosp for Women, 7-13 Mousson St, 11524 Athens Greece

VENGATESAN, BALASUBRAMANIAN, materials scientist; b. Villupuram, India, June 4, 1962; s. Balasubramanian and Indra B.; m. Vengatesan Kusuma, May 26, 1991; children: Kowshik, Kaviya. BS, Madras U., 1982; MS, Annamalai U., 1984; PhD, Anna U., 1990. Rsch. fellow CSIR, India, 1984-89; lectr. Anna U., India, 1989-93; scientist Canare Elec. Co. Ltd., Japan, 1993—. Author: Proceedings of Crystal Growth, 1987; contbr. articles to profl. jours. Mem. Indian Assn. Crystal Growth, IEEE. Avocations: swimming, cycling, learning new technologies, watching TV, social service. Office: Canare Elec Co Ltd, 2888-1 Rikka Kumabari, Nagakute Aichi 480-1101, Japan

VENGROW, MICHAEL IAN, neurologist; b. Brookline, Mass., Apr. 10, 1949; s. Max and Mary V.; m. Lucy Lee Smith, Aug. 4, 1979; children: Robert David, Mary Elizabeth. BS in Chemistry magna cum laude, U. Mass., 1971; MD, U. Mass., Worcester, 1977. Diplomate Am. Bd. Psychiatry and Neurology, Am. Bd. Clin. Neurophysiology, Am. Bd. Electrodiagnostic Medicine, Am. Acad. Pain Mgmt., Nat. Bd. Med. Examiners. Rsch. chemist, asst. KFA-Julich, West Germany, 1970; rsch. chemist, asst. biomed. svcs. divsn. Damon Corp., Needham, Mass., 1971-72; rsch. chemist, head Shrine Burn Inst., Boston, 1972-73; intern Naval Regional Med. Ctr., San Diego, 1977-78; battalion med. officer Third Combat Engr. Battalion, Third Marine Divsn., Okinawa, Japan, 1978-79; resident, chief resident in neurology Nat. Naval Med. Ctr., Bethesda, Md., 1979-82; fellow in clin. neurophysiology Walter Reed Army Med. Ctr., Washington, 1982-83; neurologist, head divsn. diagnostic neurophysiology Naval Hosp. San Diego, 1983-85; neurologist Neurology Ctr. No. Ariz., Flagstaff, 1985-96, Neurology Cons. of Dallas, 1996-98; sr. reviewer Ariz. Long Term Care Sys., Phoenix, 1986-94; dir. Alzheimer's unit Kachina Point Health Ctr., Sedona, Ariz., 1986-93, dir. neurol. rehab. unit, 1989-93; dir. neurophysiology lab. Kingman Regional Med. Ctr., 1985-95, Flagstaff Med. Ctr., 1985-95, Chmty. Med. Edn. dir., 1988, chief medicine, 1989; mem. profl. adv. bd. Epilipsy Soc., Phoenix, 1987-96, Multiple Sclerosis Soc., Phoenix, 1989-96, Quantum Health Resources; cons. First Western Med. Group, Fresno, Calif., 1991-93, Long Term Care Program Ariz. Long Term Care System, 1987-95, Marcus J. Lawrence Hosp., Cottonwood, Ariz., Pub. Health Svcs. Hosp., Tuba City, Ariz.; ind. med. examiner, Ariz.; agreed med. examiner, qualified med. examiner, electromyographer BH Mgmt. Med. Group, Fresno, 1993—; instr. emergency medicine L.A. C.C. Overseas, Uniformed Svcs. U. Health Scis., Bethesda; clin. lectr. dept. neurology sch. health scis. U. Ariz., Tucson; clin. asst. prof. neurology U. Tex. Southwestern Med. Sch.; rschr. in field; presenter in field. Contbr. articles to profl. pubs. Bd. dirs. Flagstaff Symphony, 1991-94; sponsor Am. Youth Soccer Orgn., 1988-90. LCDR, USN, 1978-85, capt. M.C., USNR. Pub. Health scholar, 1975, State Bd. Higher Edn. Scholar, 1967-71, 75, Armed Forces Health Svcs. Profl. scholarship, 1975-77, Religious High Edn. scholar, 1965; recipient Navy commendation Operation Team Spirit, 1978, letter commendation Operation Desert Storm, 1991. Fellow Am. Acad. Neurology (govt. section), Am. EEG Soc. (practice com.), Am. Assn. Electrodiagnostic Medicine, Am. Electromyographic Soc.; mem. AMA, Ariz. Med. Assn., Tex. Med. Assn. (subcom. on accreditation, lectr. stroke project), Am. Mil. Surgeons U.S., Am. Epilepsy Soc., Uniformed Svcs. Neurology U.S., U.S. Navy Neurol. Soc., Am. Soc. Clin. Evoked Potentials, Am. Soc. Neuroimaging, Am. Med. EEG Assn., Naval Res. Assn, Am. Biographical Inst. Rsch. Assn., (life, dep. gov., bd. govs.), Am. Biographical Inst. (Man of Yr., 1992), Phi Eta Sigma, Phi Kappa Phi, Phi Beta Kappa. Avocations: scuba diving, rugby, bicycling, sailing, billiards. Home: 5977 Temple Dr Plano TX 75093-8707

VEN HORST, MARIE E., retired university dean; b. Pleasant Valley, Iowa; d. John R. and Helena (Venes) Ven H. BS, St. Ambrose/Marycrest Coll., Davenport, Iowa, 1942; MS, St Louis U., 1943; PhD, U. Iowa, 1952. Instr. chemistry and physics Marycrest Coll., Davenport, 1943-64, chair divsn. natural sci. and math., 1965-71, dir. establishment MA programs in edn., 1968-74, established admin./acad. computing sys., 1968, 72; lectr. mechanics Caterpillar Tractor Co., Mt. Joy, Iowa, 1977-81; prof. chemistry Marycrest Coll., Davenport, 1972-81, founder, dir. weekend coll., 1981-94; assoc. dean Marycrest Internat. U., Davenport, 1981-96, chief acad. officer, 1997-99; cons. Clarke Coll., Dubuque, Iowa, 1975; on-site evaluator U.S. Dept. Edn. Libr. Tech. Title 11-A, Washington, 1993. Contbr. more than 30 articles to profl. jours. Recipient Henderson medal for outstanding achievement Marycrest Alumnae, 1982, Leadership award Rock Island-Scott County Math. Tchrs. Assn., 1968; Damon Runyon rsch. grantee, 1955; grantee Am. Acad. Arts and Scis., 1956, AEC, 1961, 62, 63, NSF, 1956, 57, 63, 64, 65. Democrat. Roman Catholic. Home: 1361 W 12th St Davenport IA 52804-3755

VENIAMIS, THEODORE ELEFTHERIOS, ship owner, business executive; b. Vrontados, Greece, Nov. 17, 1950; s. Eleftherios Michael and Irene Eleftherios (Tsamoutalou) V.; m. Eleni George Gabriel; children: Eleftherios, Merini, Nikolas. BA, Athens (Greece) Sch. Econs., 1973. Pres., mng. dir. Golden Union Shipping Co. S.A., Panama, 1977—, Golden Union Enterprises S.A., Panama, 1979—, World Mgmt. Inc., Liberia, 1993—; pres. Sea Devel. S.A., Panam, 1996—; chmn., CEO Cape Investments Co., Cayman Islands, 1997—; mem. Greek com. Det Norske Veritas Classification A.S., Oslo, 1980—. Mem. Orthodox Hellenic-Russian Assn., Athens, 1991—, Panhellenic Club Friends of Mt. Athos, Athens, 1991—. Mem. London Steamship Owners' Mut. Ins. Assn. Ltd. (com. mem. 1983—), Yacht Club Greece. Avocations: hunting, underwater fishing, gardening. Office: Golden Union Shipping Co SA, 8 Aegaleo St, 185 45 Piraeus Greece

VENIARD, JOSE M., bank officer; b. Buenos Aires, Argentina, Feb. 11, 1935; came to U.S., 1970; s. Eduardo A. and Amalia (Bassi) V.; children: Maria, Sofia, Natalia, Clara. MS in Civil Engring., Buenos Aires U., 1962; MBA, Stanford U., 1972. Spl. asst. Minister of Pub. Works, Argentina, 1968-70; sr. ops. officer Stanford Rsch. Inst., Menlo Pk., Calif., 1971-73; sr. economist The World Bank, Washington, 1974-76, project mgr., 1976-81, 91—, asst. to v.p., 1981-85; ops. mgr. The World Bank, Beijing, 1985-91; cons. econ.-transp., 1963-68. Contbr. numerous articles, papers, to confs. and profl. publs. Fellow Econ. Devel. Inst. Home: 10005 Carter Rd Bethesda MD 20817-1416

VENITIS, BASIL, financial consultant; b. Korthi, Andros, Greece, May 9, 1945; came to U.S., 1968; s. Anthony and Maria (Stratis) V.; m. Carolyn Anketell, 1977 (div. Jan. 1987). PhD, Ohio U., 1973. Pres. Tradetix Co., N.Y.C., 1973-88, Chaos Trading Club, N.Y.C., 1988—. Contbr. articles to profl. jours. Mem. Chaos Trading Club (pres. 1990—, chief chaologist 1988). Republican. Avocations: ballroom dancing. E-mail: venitis@hotmail.com. Home: 68 Achilles, 175 62 Faliro Greece

VENIZELOS, LILY THERESE E., sea turtle conservationist; b. Athens, Greece, Apr. 10, 1933; d. John S. and Angela J. (Politis) Charamis; m. Elefterios K. Venizelos, Oct. 24, 1954; 1 child, Angela. Diploma in English, Cambridge U., Athens, Greece, 1949; secretarial degree, Winkfield Place, Weybridge, Eng., 1953. Pres., founder Mediterranean Assn. to Save the Sea Turtles, Medasset, U.K., 1998, Mediterranean Assn. to Save the Sea Turtles/Greece, Athens, 1993; internat. lectr. on sea turtle conservation and related Mediterranean problems, 1986—, including Royal Geog. Soc., London, 1987, European Youth Ctr., Strasbourg, France, 1987, Archeol. Soc. Greece, Athens, 1988, NHK/TV Symposium Okayama, Japan, 1992, others; coun. mem. Hellenic Soc. Protection of Nature (HSPN), Athens, 1986-95, Greek Animal Welfare Fund (GAWF), London, 1986—; regional rep. Global 500 Forum, Europe, 1992-94. Contbr. articles to profl. jours., bulls., publs., and the press. Mem. coun. Fund Edn. for Needy Wmen, Athens, 1952-58. Recipient Global 500 award UN Environ. Program, 1987, Athens Acad. award, 1988, Hellenic Red Cross, Gold Cross distinction, Athens, 1997, award Kay Gray Brit. Chelonia Group (BCG), U.K., 1999, Friends of the Red Cross high distinction, Athens, 2000. Mem. World Wide Fund for Nature, Greenpeace, Brit. Chelonia Group. Avocations: skin diving, music, collage painting, antiques, conversant in three langs. (Greek, English, French). E-mail: medasset@hol.gr. Office: MEDASSET, 1(c) Licavitou Str, 10672 Athens Greece

VENKAPPAYYA, DEVASHYA, chemistry educator; b. Karnataka, India, Dec. 2, 1942; s. Gowramma and Vasudeva (Mayya) V.; m. Devashya Amrutheshwari, Oct. 14, 1947; children: vandana V., Vinay V. BSc, Madras U., India, 1963; MSc, Indian Inst. Tech., Madras, India, 1965, PhD, 1969. Commonwealth scholar U. Strathclyde, Glasgow, Eng., 1970-72; pool officer Andhra Univ., Visakhappatnam, India, 1972-74; lectr. Regional Engring. Coll., Tiruchirapplli, India, 1974-75, asst. prof, 1975-80, prof., head chemistry, 1980-97, dean academics, 1997—. Mem. editl. bd. Samyak Jour. Chemistry, 1997—. Recipient Gold medal for Sanskrit, Madras U., 1963; named Commonwealth scholar Assn. Commonalwealth Univ., 1970. Mem. Chem. Soc., Indian Thermal Analysis Soc., Indian Soc. for Tech. Edn. Hindu. Avocations: gardening, walking in countryside. Home: No 5 5th ST, REC Staff Quarters, Tiruchirappalli 620015, India Office: Regional Engring Coll, Dean's Office, Tiruchirappalli 620015, India

VENKATA, RAMASASTRY, medical practitioner, editor; b. Manchili, India, Dec. 10, 1947; s. Sastry Venkata and Lakshmi Rajya Vedula. BSc, Andhra U., Waltair, India, 1967, MSc in Tech., 1970, Postgrad. Diploma in Applied Stats., 1970, PhD, 1975; MA, Windsor (Ont.) U., Can., 1976; postgrad. in hydrology, Padova (Italy) U., 1977; MD, DSc, Open Internat. U., Sri Lanka, Colombo, 2000. Diploma in Alloypathy, Homoeopathy, Ayurveda, and Registered Med. Practitioner. Rsch. asst. to assoc. Great Lakes Rsch. Project, Can., 1975-76; expert cons. Quanta Consulting Engrs., Tehran, Iran, 1976-77; sr. lectr. U. Benin, Benin City, Nigeria, 1977-86; chmn. Siveast Consultants, Inc., Dover, Del., 19886-90; editor-in-chief Worldwide Mil. and Police Scroll Awards, 1990-99; lectr., head acad. affairs Royal U., Ltd., Dublin, Ireland, 1995-99; v.p. Samuktha Med. Welfare Soc., Kovvur, India, 1997—; life mem. Medicina Alternativa, Open Internat. U., Colombo, Sri Lanka. Contbr. numerous articles to profl. jours. and conf. procs.; editor Western Strategies, Confident Christian, 1980-98. Mem. India Meteorol. Soc. (life mem. Visakhapatnam br., Andhra), Basic Med. Practitioners' Assn. (Rajahmundry, India), Andhra Med. Practitioners' Assn. Avocations: swimming, jogging, reading. Home: 23 Sanchez Ave Saint Augustine FL 32084-3285 Office: Royal U Ltd Europe, PO Box 8510, Kathmandu Nepal

VENKATARAMAN, MANGUDI SANKARAN, medical educator, surgeon; b. Chennai, Tamil Nadu, India, Apr. 15, 1931; s. Sankaran and Karpagam Sankaran; m. Jayalakshmi, Apr. 29, 1959; children: Lakshmi, Vani, Shankar Kumar. MBBS, Madras Med. Coll., Chennai, Tamil Nadu, 1955, MS in Gen. Surgery, 1960. Hon. asst. surgeon Govt. Gen. Hosp., Chennai, Tamil Nadu, 1960-77; hon. surgeon Govt. Gen. Hosp., Chennai, 1977-87; prof. surg. oncology Muthulakshmi Coll. Oncol. Scis., Cancer, Chennai, 1987-89; pvt. practice, 1989-99, ret., 2000—; hon. clin. prof. surgery Madras Med. Coll., Chennai, 1977-87; bd. mem. Trauma Care Consortium; cons. surgeon Cancer Inst., Adyar, Chennai, 1965-87. Author: The Gentle Tyrant, 1999; editor, contbr.: Kuraivattra Selvam, 1981, 2nd edit., 1990, Digestive System, 1999, Organ Transplantation, 1999. Fellow Royal Coll. Physicians and Surgeons Glasgow, Am. Coll. Surgeons; mem. Assn. Surgeons India, Indian Med. Scis. Acad. (treas. Tamil Nadu divsn. 1997), Madras Cricket Club, Lions Club Internat. Avocations: music, journalism, photography. Home: 26/2 Second Main Rd, CIT Colony Mylapore, Chennai Tamil Nadu 600 004, India Office: ENT Diagnostic Ctr, 26/1 2nd Main Rd CIT Colony, Mylapore Chennai, Tamil Nadu 600 004, India

VENKATARAMAN, NANGAVARAM SRINIVASA, federal official; b. Tiruchirapalli, Tamil Nadu, India, Dec. 20, 1940; s. Nangavaram Ranganatha Srinivasan and Srinivasan Venkalakshmi; m. Venkataraman Chellam, May 5, 1968; children: Venkat Srinivas, Sudha Nagaraj. D in Engring., Indian Inst. Sci., Bangalore, 1968. Chartered engr. Coun. Engring. Instns., U.K. Sr. aero. engr. Hindustan Aeronautics Ltd., Bangalore, 1966-70; asst. prof. aero. engring. Madras (India) Inst. Tech., 1970-78, prof. aero. engring., 1978—, head dept. aero. engring., 1980-90, dean faculty engring., 1989-93; dir. Madras Inst. Tech., Anna U., 1990-94; mission dir. TIFAC, DST, Govt., India, Delhi, 1994—; vis. prof. NSF, 1980; panel mem. Aeronautics R&D Bd. Ministry Def., Delhi, 1980—; adj. prof. Engring. Staff Coll. India, Hyderabad, 1995—. Recipient Nat. award for devel. and application of sci. and tech. Wisitex Found., India, 1990, Disting. Aeroalumnus award Indian Inst. Sci., Bangalore, 1992. Fellow Instn. Engrs. India (life), Aero. Soc. India (life, v.p. 1992-95, 98—, hon. sec. gen. 1995-98, Nat. award for excellence in aerospace edn. 1992); mem. Royal Aero. Soc., Soc. for Exptl. Stress Analysis, Indian Soc. for Tech. Edn. (life), Indian Soc. for Advancement of Materials and Process Engring. (life, dir.). Avocations: science for youth programs, counseling and career guidance for youth, numismatics, military training, taking composite materials to all walks of engineering. Office: MD TIFAC DST GOI, Technology Bhawan, New Delhi 110016, India

VENKATESH, BYRAPPA, molecular biologist, researcher; b. Bangalore, Karnataka, India, Apr. 16, 1953; arrived in Singapore, 1987; s. Gulapura Hanumanthappa Byrappa and Mariamma; m. Mangala Venkataramiah, Nov. 24, 1983; 1 child, Aparna. B in Fisheries Sci., Coll. Fisheries, Mangalore, India, 1974, M in Fisheries Sci., 1976; PhD, Nat. U. Singapore, 1991. Instr. Coll. Fisheries, Mangalore, 1976-77; scientist 1 Ctrl. Inland Fisheries Rsch. inst., Barrackpore, India, 1977-83; devel. officer Nat. Bank for Agrl. and Rural Devel., Bombay, 1983-87; jr. rsch. fellow Inst. Molecular and Cell Biology, Singapore, 1991-92, rsch. fellow, 1992-96, rsch. assoc., 1996-97, sr. scientist, 1998—. Contbr. articles to profl. jours. Recipient State award Govt. Karnataka, Bangalore, 1978. Mem. Human Genome Orgn. Office: Inst Molecular & Cell Biol, 30 Medical Dr, Singapore 117609, Singapore

VENKATESWARLU, PALADUGU, engineering educator; b. Moparru, India, Aug. 14, 1951; s. Paladugu Venkatramaiah and Paladugu Sitaramamma; m. Paladugu Vani, June 25, 1981; children: Rama Sita, Haritha. B in Chem. Engring., Andhra U., Visakhapatnam, India, 1973, M in Chem. Engring., 1976, PhD in Chem. Engring., 1988. Rschr. Andhra U., Visakhapatnam, 1976-79, lectr., 1979-91, assoc. prof., 1991—. Contbr. articles to profl. jours. Trustee Yoga Edn. Trust, Visakhapatnam, 1996—. Fellow Soc. Advancement Electrochem. Sci. Tech.; mem. Indian Inst. Chem. Engrs., Indian Soc. Tech. Edn. (life). Home: Moparru Guntur, Andhra Pradesh India Office: Dept Chem Engring, Coll Engring Andhra Univ, Visakhapatnam 530 003, India

VENKITESWARAN, S., lawyer; b. Kozhikode, Kerala, India, Jan. 22, 1941; s. Pazhayanur Subramanian and Subramanian Parvathi (Narayana Iyer) Pazhayanur; m. Venkiteswaran Lakshmi Krishnan, Nov. 13, 1967; children: Subramanian, Krishnan. BSc, Khalsa Coll., Bombay, 1960; LLB, Govt. Law Coll., Bombay, 1962. Enrolled advocate, 1962, sr. advocate, 1988. Mem. Nat. Shipping Bd. India, Com. for Drafting Admiralty Law of India, Mcht. Shipping Amednments, Ctrl. Shipping Legislation and Rev. Port Legislations. Mem. ABA, Supreme Ct. India Bar Assn., Internat. Bar Assn., Union Internat. Des Advocats. Hindu. Avocations: music, reading, literature. Home: 121 Nirvana, Mumbai 400022, India Office: 114-B Maker Chambers III, Mumbai 400021, India

VENKOV, PENCHO VASSILEV, molecular biology educator; b. Sofia, Bulgaria, Dec. 5, 1934; s. Vassil Penchev and Luba Ivanova (Boadjieva) V.; m. Liliana Vassileva Waltscheva, Aug. 17, 1964; 1 child, Ivo. MD, Sch. Medicine Sofia, 1959; PhD, Bulgarian Acad. Scis., Sofia, 1972. Head microbiology lab. City Hosp., Vidin, Bulgaria, 1960-62; vis. rschr. Inst. Genetics, Cologne, Germany, 1968-70, Washington U., St. Louis, 1971-72; rschr. Inst. Molecular Biology, Bulgarian Acad. Scis., 1963-68, head yeast lab., 1972-82, head dept. molecular genetics, 1983—, prof., 1985—; part-time prof. Sofia U., 1984—; mem. UNESCO Molecular Cell Biology Network, 1992. Author: (textbook) The Genetics of Bacteria, 1988; co-author: The Molecular Biology of Genes, 1980. Fellow Internat. Soc. for Yeasts; mem. Bulgarian Union Scientists (biochemistry and biophysics sect.). Home: St Naum St 49, 1126 Sofia Bulgaria Office: Bulgarian Acad Scis, Inst Molecular Biology, 1113 Sofia Bulgaria

VENN, GRAHAM ERSKINE, surgeon; b. Mar. 22, 1954; married. MD, U. London, 1977. House surgeon Middlesex Hosp., 1978, registrar, 1981-85; sr. registrar Harefield Hosp., 1985-86; Jules Thorne Neurol. rsch. fellow The Middlesex Hosp., 1986-87, sr. registrar, 1987-88; sr. registrar Hammersmith Hosp., 1988-89; staff surgeon Hosp. Broussais, Paris, 1989; cardiac and thoracic surgeon St. Thomas' Hosp., London, 1989—; clin. dir. cardiothoracic svcs. Guy's and St. Thomas' Hosp. Trust; hon. sr. lectr. cardiothoracic surgery Guy's and St. Thomas' Hosps., U. London; presenter in field. Contbr. articles to profl. jours. Named Hunterian prof. Royal Coll. of Surgeons of Eng., 1989; grantee DuPont (U.K.) Ltd., 1990, British Heart Found., 1991-92, Schiapparelli Searle, 1991-92, St. Thomas' Hosp. Rsch., 1991-92, The Jules Thorn Charitable Trust, 1991-92, Gensia (Europe) Ltd., 1991-92, Biomedica Foscama, 1993, Wellcome Trust Project, 1993-95, British Heart Found. PhD Studentship, 1993-96, European Soc. of Cardiology Rsch. Fellowship, 1994-95. Mem. Royal Soc. of Medicine (sect. cardiothoracic surgery, coun. mem. clin. sect.), Cardiac Surg. Rsch. Club, British Cardiac Soc., European Assn. for Cardiothoracic Surgery, European Cardiac Soc., Cardiovsascular Rsch. Soc., British Soc. for Cardiovascular Rsch., European Soc. for Cardiovascular Surgery, The Worshipful Soc. of Apothecaries of London. Avocations: sailing, skiing, golf. Office: London Bridge Hosp Emblem House, 27 Tooley St Ste 203, London SE1 2PR, England also: St Thomas Hosp Dept Cardiothoracic Surge, Lambeth Palace Rd, London SE1 7EH, England

VENN, WILLIAM FREDERICK, petroleum industry engineer/manager; b. Kirkuk, Iraq, May 14, 1956; s. Frederick John and Patricia Emily (Pinkney) V.; m. Isabelle Marie Madeleine Brodard, June 24, 1992; 1 child, Gwendoline. Grad. in Chem. Engring., U. London, 1977. Trainee prodn. engr. BP Petroleum, Aberdeen, U.K., 1977-78; prodn. engr. Sohio Petroleum Co., San Francisco, 1978-82; ops. engr. Sohio Alaska Petroleum Co., Anchorage, 1982-85; prodn. engr. BP Petroleum, London, 1985-89; supt. BP Petroleum, Shetland, U.K., 1989-93; devel. and environ. engr. Tyumen Task Force/World Bank, Brussels, 1993; cons. EQE Internat. Ltd., Aberdeen, U.K., 1994-96; consulting engr. Woodhill HSE and Engring. Cons., Woking, U.K., 1996-99; cons. Trident & Haden Freeman Risk Mgmt., 1999—; cons. Conoco U.K. Ltd., Aberdeen, 1997-98. Contbr. articles to profl. jours. Neighborhood engr. Engring. Coun., Nottingham, U.K., 1993. Recipient Assoc. award City and Guilds Inst., London, 1977. Mem. AIChE, European Engrs., Inst. Chem. Engrs. U.K., Soc. Petroleum Engrs. of AIME, Inst. Petroleum, Safety and Reliability Soc., Exploration Soc. U.K. Avocations: travel, outdoor sports, ancient history, computers, environment/ecological

issues. Home and Office: 76 Westgate Southwell, Nottinghamshire NG25 0JX, United Kingdom

VENSEL, VELLO, statistics educator; b. Keila, Harju, Estonia, Dec. 28, 1941; s. Voldemar Vensel and Salme (Niinemae) Ausing; m. Lia Seepold, Aug. 7, 1970; children: Keili Segerberg, Eneli Vensel. Diploma in econs., U. Tartu, 1965; Dr.sci., Estonian Acad. of Scis., 1983. Economist Ministry of Fin., Tallinn, Estonia, 1965-68; asst. Tallinn Tech. U., 1971-73, lectr., 1973-77, docent, 1977-83, prof., 1983—, head of dept., 1992-2000. Author: Correlation and Regression Analysis, 1978, Production Fuctions and Growth Functions, 1979, Adaptive Statistical Models, 1985; co-author: English-Estonian Dictionary in Economics, 1992, Basic Microeconomics, 1996, Basic Statistics, 1996. Recipient State award in Sci. Estonian Govt., 1987; rsch. grantee Internat. Rsch. and Exch. Bd., 1994, European Commn., The Phare Ace Program, 1994, 97. Mem. Am. Econ. Assn., Internat. Atlantic Econ. Soc., Internat. Lions Clubs. Lutheran. Avocations: farming, bridge, numismatics. Home: 10 Teaduse Poik Str, Keila 76609, Estonia Office: Dept Econs Tallinn Tech Univ, 101 Kopli Str, Tallinn 11712, Estonia

VENTEGODT, SOREN, research center administrator; b. Copenhagen, Mar. 26, 1961; s. Ole and Ina (Dybdahl) V.; m. Thorup Ventegodt (div.); 1 child, Alexander Thorup. MD, U. Copenhagen, 1992. Poet, writer Copenhagen, 1979-81, gardener, 1981-82, taxi driver, 1982-83; project leader Quality of Life Rsch. Ctr., Copenhagen, 1989-91, dir., 1994—; rsch. leader U. Hosp., Copenhagen, 1991-94; spkr., cons. Peoples' U. Copenhagen, 1987-91, 600 orgns. in Denmark, 1990-99; leader study groups, sci. groups, Copenhagen, 1991-99; organizer, sponsor sci. meetings, Niels Bohr Inst., Copenhagen, 1996. Author: Measuring the Quality of Life from Theory to Practice, 1996, Working-Life Quality, 1999. Recipient of Quality-of-Life award Mölnlycke, 1994. Mem. Danish Med. Assn. Avocations: flute, amateur art, philosophy of life,. writing. Home: Berggrensgade 8, DK-2100 Copenhagen Denmark Office: Quality of Life Rsch Ctr, St Kongensgade 70, DK-1264 Copenhagen Denmark

VENTURA, HECTOR OSVALDO, cardiologist; b. Buenos Aires, Mar. 21, 1951; came to U.S., 1981; s. Osvaldo Domingo and Nelida (Scocozza) V.; m. Laurie Anne Zeringue, Apr. 21, 1990; children: Austin Alejandro, Leighton Leandro, Kendra Mariel. BS, Nat. No. 10 Coll., Buenos Aires, 1968; MD, U. Buenos Aires, 1974. Diplomate Am. Bd. Internal Medicine with subspecialty in cardiovascular diseases. Resident in internal medicine Mil. Hosp., Argentina, 1975-78; rsch. fellow hypertension Ochsner Found., New Orleans, 1981-84; internal medicine resident Oschsner Found. Hosp., New Orleans, 1984-86, cardiology fellow, 1986-88; heart failure/heart transplant fellow Loyola U., Chgo., 1989; co-dir. heart failure heart transplant Oshsner Med. Inst., New Orleans, 1989-97, transplant adv. bd., 1992-97, mem. ethics com., 1995-97; assoc. prof. medicine La. State U. Sch. Medicine, New Orleans; co-dir. advanced heart failure/cardiac transplant Tulane U. Med. Ctr., New Orleans, 1998—; prof. medicine tulane U. Sch. Medicine, New Orleans; jour. manuscript reviewer. Editl. bd. Jour. Heart & Lung Transplantation, 1994; contbr. articles to profl. jours. 1st lt. Argentine Army, 1974-80. Ochsner Found. fellow, 1985, 86. Fellow Am. Coll. Cardiology; mem. Am. Soc. Transplant (organ thoracic com. 1993—), Am. Heart Assn. Roman Catholic. Avocations: tennis, aerobic exercise. Home: 3746 Rue Chardonnay Metairie LA 70002-1500 Office: Tulane Univ Med Ctr HC-19 1415 Tulane Ave New Orleans LA 70112-2605

VENTURA, MANUEL MATEUS, biochemist, educator; b. Fortaleza, Brazil, June 17, 1921; s. Antonio Rodrigues and Maria Raymunda (Lima) V.; m. Aglaeda Facó; children: Rita-Maria, Sandro, Manuel, Maria Monica. BSc, Agrl. Sch. Ceara, Fortaleza, 1943. Asst. prof. Agrl. Sch. Ceara, Fortaleza, 1945-48, prof., 1949-68; prof. Inst. of Chemistry of Fed. U. Ceara, Fortaleza, 1969-75; prof. biochemistry Inst. Biology, U. Brasilia, Brazil, 1975-91, prof. emeritus, 1992—; dir. Inst. Chemistry of Fed. U. Ceara, 1958-68. Contbr. articles to profl. jours. Recipient Anisio Teizeira prize Ministry of Edn., Brazil, 1981, Sci. Merit medal Fed. U. Ceara, 1988, Nat. Scientific Merit Order Ministry of Sci. and Tech., 1995. Mem. Brazilian Acad. Sci., N.Y. Acad. Sci., Protein Soc. Avocations: classical music, photography. Home: SQN 107 BL H Apto 504, 70743 Brasilia Brazil Office: U Brasilia Lab Biofisica-CEL-IB, Campus Universitario, 70910 Brasilia Brazil

VENTURI, PAOLO, corporate strategy professional; b. Reggio Emilia, Italy, Oct. 7, 1962; s. Lorenzo and Franca (Giordani) V. Diploma in Science, Liceum, Reggio, Italy, 1981; Degree in Aeronautical Engring., Univ., Pisa, Italy, 1988; MBA, SDA Bocconi, Milan, Italy, 1995. Chartered engr., 1988. Software engr. Trast, Pisa, Italy, 1988; project engr. Aermacchi, Varese, Italy, 1988-90; program mgr. Alenia, Gorizia, Italy, 1990-94; cons. BCG, Milan, Italy, 1995-96, 98—, Sydney, Australia, 1997-98. Author: (book) GPS Navigation Manual, 1997. Vol. Civil Protection, Italy, 1994—. Mem. Engrs. Assn. Avocations: adventure travels, sailing, playing piano and guitar, designing racing sailboats, off road driving instructor, organizing car races, Camel Trophy Italian team member, soccer. Home: Via Caduti Bettola 51, 42030 La Vecchia RE, Italy

VENUGOPAL, PANKAJALAKSHMI VELLORE, microbiologist; b. Bangalore, Karnataka, India, May 10, 1937; d. Balakrishna Vellore and Visalatchi (Meigandadevan) V. MBBS, Madras (India) Med. Coll., 1959, MD, 1967; postgrad., Emory U., 1981; PhD, Med. Alternativa Internat., Colombo, Sri Lanka, 1988. Tutor in physiology Kilpauk Med. Coll., Madras, India, 1962-64; tutor in bacteriology Madras Med. Coll., 1964-65, asst. prof. bacteriology, 1970, assoc. prof. microbiology, 1972-81, prof. microbiology, 1985-87; civil asst. surgeon King Inst. Preventive Medicine, Madras, 1966-70; reader bacteriology, head dept. Coimbatore (India) Med. Coll., 1970-71; prof., head dept. microbiology Thanjavur (India) Med. Coll., 1981-85, Stanley Med. Coll., 1987-88; mycologist Ministry of Health Hosps., Qatif, Dammam and Hofuf, Saudi Arabia, 1988-91; dir., prof. upgraded inst. microbiology Madurai (India) Med. Coll., 1991-95; cons. microbiologist Kumaran Hosp., Madras, 1995-96, Pallava Hosp., Madras, 1995-96; prof., head dep. Vinayaka Missions Med. Coll., Salem, India, 1996—; Colombo plan rsch. fellow in med. mycology, U.K., 1971-72; chief microbiologist Coimbatore Med. Coll. Hosp., 1970-71, Thanjavur Med. Coll. Hosp. and Rajah Mirasdar Hosp., 1981-85, Govt. Stanley Hosp., Madras, 1987-88; microbiologist Govt. Gen. Hosp., Madras, 1972-81; chief microbiologist, dir. Govt. Rajaji Hosp., Madurai, 1991-95; mem. bd. postgrad. studies Tamil Nad Dr. M.G.R. Med. U., Madras, 1994—; organizing sec., program dir. workshop on diagnosis and mgmt. of fungal infections Inst. Microbiology, Madurai Med. Coll., 1993, nat. workshop on fungal infections, 1994, 95; organizing sec. 3d Nat. Conf. SIHAM, 1st Internat. Symposium on Micuses in the New Millennium Ramachandra Med. Coll. and Rsch. Inst., Chennai, 2000. Contbr. articles to profl. publs., chpts. to books. Mem. Indian Assn. Med. Microbiologists (pres. Tamil Nadu and Pondicherry chpt. 1994-95, life), Indian Officers Assn. (life), Thuluva Vellala Assn. (life), Nat. Acad. Med. Scis., Internat. Found. Alt. Medicine, Homeo Found., N.Y. Acad. Scis., Internat. Soc. Human and Animal Mycology, Am. Soc. Microbiology, Internat. Leptospirosis Soc. (v.p.), Soc. for Indian Human and Animal Mycologists, Soc. for Health Edn. and Rsch. Avocations: films, music, gardening, Tamil literature, science fiction. Home: Malar Mangai, 2 1st Ave, Ashok Nagar Madras 600 083, India

VENUGOPAL, RAYASAM, educator; b. Harapanahalli, India, July 28, 1955; s. Rayasam Srinivasarao and Rayasam Sarada Rao; m. Rayasam Sudha, May 16, 1984; children: Sridevi Rayasam, Shilpa Rayasam, Srilekha Rayasam. BSc, Univ. Madras, Madras, India, 1976; MASC, Karnatak Univ., India, 1980; PhD in mineral engring., Indian Sch. Mines, Dhanbad, India, 1986. Jr. rsch. fellow Indian Sch. of Mines, Dhanbad, India, 1981-82; lectr. I.S.M., Dhanbad, India, 1982-87, asst. prof., 1987-93, prof., 1993—, head of dept., 1995-98, 2000—; mem. acad. coun. ISM, 1983—; mem. mgmt. bd. Ocean Sci. and Tech. Coll., Dept. Ocean Devel., govt. India, 1998—. Contbr. articles to profl. jours. Mem. expert group on beneficiation Min. of Mines Gov. India, 1996-97; adv. Union Public Svc. Commn. Gov. India, 1997. Recipient Nat. Mineral award Min. of Mines Gov. India, 1996. Mem. Indian Inst. Mineral Engrs. (life), Inst. of Engrs. (assoc.), Indian Inst. of Metals, Mining, Geological and Metallurical Inst. of India. Hindu. Avocations: cricket, Indian classical music and dance, writing feature articles, reading. E-mail: rvenu ism@hotmail.com. Home and Office: No V/12 Tchr's Colony, Indian School of Mines, 826004 Dhanbad India Office: Indian Sch Mines, Dept Fuel & Mineral Engring, 826004 Dhanbad India

VENUGOPAL, TARALAKSHMI VELLORE, pathologist, consultant; b. Trichy, Tamil Nadu, India, Mar. 11, 1944; d. Balakrishna Vellore and Visalatchi Vellore (Meiganda Devan) V.; m. Pandurangan Conjeevarum Nithyanandam, May 28, 1969; children: Gopal Pandurangan, Abirami Pandurangan, Meenakshi Pandurangan. MBBS, Madras (India) Med. Coll., 1966, MD in Pathology, 1972. Tutor in Pathology Stanley Med. Coll., Madras, 1967-69; tutor in Pathology Madras Med. Coll., 1969-72, from asst. prof. to dir., 1972-91, dir., 1991-93, addl. prof. Pathology, 1993—; prof., head dept. Pathology Madurai (India) Med. Coll., 1981-84; mem. bd. studies Madras U.; organizing sec. Symposium on Renal Pathology, Madras Med. Coll., 1999. Author: (with others) The New International Textbook of Medicine, 1981, 86, IADVL Textbook and Atlas of Dermatology, 1994; contbr. articles to profl. jours. Fellow Internat. Med. Scis. Acad., Madras Med. Coll.; mem. Nat. Acad. Med. Scis., Tamil Nadu Med. Svc. Assn., Indian Assn. Pathologists Microbiolists, Assn. Surgeons India. Avocations: barathanatyam, carnatic and film music, tamil lit. Home: Malar Mangai 2 1st Ave, Ashok Nagar, Madras Tamil Nadu 600 083, India Office: Madras Med Coll, Madras 600 003, India

VENZKE, ANDREAS WILLI, author, journalist, translator; b. Berlin, June 3, 1961; s. Gerhard and Adolphine (Schmidt) V. MA, Freie U. Berlin, 1986. Author: Der Entdecker Amerikas-Aufstieg und Fall des Christoph Kolumbus, 1991, Christoph Kolumbus, 1992, Johannes Gutenberg-Der Erfinder des Buchdrucks, 1993, Gasparan oder Die letzte Fahrt des Francis Drake, 1996, Veit und ein anderer Tag, 1996, Zwei Fluchten, 1997, Tarzan auf dem Mammut, 1998, Carlos kann doch Tore schiesen, 1999, Johannes Gutenberg und seine Zeit, 2000.

VEPSÂLÂINEN, JOUKO, chemist, educator; b. Varpaisjárvi, Finland, Nov. 13, 1960; s. Olavi and Aili (Martikainen) V.; m. Sirpa Peràniemi, Nov. 18, 1960. DSc, U. Joensuu, 1992. Rsch. chemist Leiras Oy, Tampere, Finland, 1985-91; from lab. supervisor to prof. U. Kuopio, Finland, 1991—. Avocation: fishing. Office: U Kuopio, PO Box 1627, Kuopio Finland 70211

VERA, PIERRE, nuclear medicine physician; b. Le Havre, France, Aug. 10, 1964; s. Roger and Sylvianne (Follain) V.; m. Isabelle Anne-Marie Busquet, Apr. 7, 1990; children: Antoine, Alexandre. MS in Biophysics, Paris, 1993, MS in Math., 1993; MD, U. Rouen, 1989; PhD, U. Paris, 1999. Resident in nuclear medicine Faculty of Medicine, Paris, 1989-93; sr. house physician Paris-Beaujon Hosp., Paris, 1993-96; lectr. in biophysics Faculty of Medicine, Rouen, 1996—, asst. prof., head dept. nuclear medicine, 1996—. Contbr. articles to profl. jours. Recipient Spl. award in Pediatric Imaging Soc. of Nuclear Medicine, 1996. Mem. European Soc. of Nuclear Medicine, French Soc. of Nuclear Medicine (Best Comm. Scientific paper 1996, 98). Avocations: tennis, jogging, golf. Home: 21 Rue de Lille, 76000 Rouen France Office: Nuclear Med Dept, 1 Rue D'Amiens, 76000 Rouen France

VERAS, MARCIA PEREIRA, educator; b. Porto Alegre, Brazil, July 13, 1937; d. Amaro Junqueira and Hilda (Marc) Pereira; m. Paulo Avila Veras, Sept. 5, 1959; children: Patricia Pereira Veras, Valeria Veras Burigo, Roberta Veras do Lago. BA in Libr., UFRGS, Brazil, 1969; MA in Polit. History, UFSC, Brazil, 1979. Prof. Fed. U. Amazonas, Brazil, 1971-72, Fed. U. Santa Catarina, Brazil, 1975-91; dir. Fed. Dist. Children'sLibr., Brasilia, Brazil, 1973-75; coord. Librarianship Ext. Project, Santarem, Brazil, 1982-90; head dept. Fed. U. Santa Catarina, 1989-91. Contbr. articles to profl. jours. Home: Rua Esteves Jr, No 428 Apt 1101, 88015530 Florianopolis Brazil

VERBERNE, ANTHONY JOHANNES, scientist; b. Zaandam, The Netherlands, July 9, 1957; s. Hendrikus Josephus and Mathilda Elizabeth Verberne; m. Johanna Louise Douglas, May 8, 1982; children: Michael Anthony, Thomas Walter. BSc with 1st class honors, U. Melbourne, Australia, 1978, PhD, 1982. Nat. Heart Found. Overseas Rsch. fellow U. Limburg, Maastricht, The Netherlands, 1989-90, U. Va., Charlottesville, 1990-91; Nat. Health and Med. Rsch. Coun. Australia Rsch. fellow U. Melbourne, 1993—. Contbr. articles to profl. jours. Avocations: amateur radio, electronics. E-mail: tonyv@austin.unimelb.edu.au. Fax: 61 3 9459 3510. Home: 49 Wilfred Rd, Ivanhoe East VIC 3079, Australia Office: Univ Melbourne, Austin & Repatriation Med, Heidelberg VIC 3084, Australia

VERBITSKAYA, L.A., academic administrator. Rector St. Petersburg State U., Russia. Office: St Petersburg State U, Universitetskaya nab 7/9, 199034 Saint Petersburg Russia*

VERBITSKII, VLADIMIR BORIS, ecologist, educator; b. Dnepropetrovsk, Ukraine, Apr. 24, 1952; s. Boris Iefim and Slava Boris (Lelgant) V.; m. Tamara Ivan Omelchuk, May 27, 1978; children: Victor, Ann. Postgrad., All Union Sci. Rsch. Inst., Dmitrov, Russia, 1981-84, PhD, 1985. Sci. rschr. State Sci. Rsch. Inst. Lake's Fisheries Economy, Gorky, USSR, 1978-80, Inst. Biology of Inland Waters-Russian Acad. Scis., Borok, USSR, 1984—. Contbr. articles to profl. jours.; inventor in field. Fouder sci. edn. ecological ctr., Borok, 1996—; leader Child Ecology Sch.-Camp, Borok, 1994—. Grantee Dept. Ecology Russia, Moscow, 1993-95, Russian Fund Fundamental Rschs., Moscow, 1995-96, 98-2000, Soros Found., Moscow, 1995, ISAR, Washington, 1996. Fellow Hydrobiology Soc. of Russian Acad. Scis.; mem. Assn. Ecology Edn. Avocations: poetry, video tape recordings. Office: Inst Biology Inland Waters, 152742 Borok YaroNeko, Russia

VERBOOM, GERRIT KLAAS, physicist, researcher; b. Waarder, Zuid, Holland, Sept. 16, 1941; s. Gerrit and Clara Wilhelmina (Hogendoorn) V.; m. Antje Elizabeth Goudriaan, Dec. 18, 1964; children: Peter Alexander, Robert Paul. MS in Physics, Tech. U. Delft, Holland, 1965; PhD in Physics, Math., U. Utrecht, Holland, 1971. Rschr. jr. Fundamental Rsch. on Matter, Utrecht, 1967-71; rschr. math. dept. Delft Hydraulics, 1971-74, head, 1974-80, math. specialist, 1980-83, project mgr. dept. estuaries and seas, 1983-87, sr. staff officer spl. duties R&D dept., 1987-92, mgr. bus. unit, 1992-98; product mgr. Delft 3D, 1998—. 1st lt. Spl. Svcs., 1965-67. Mem. IEEE, Dutch Phys. Soc., European Phys. Soc., Internat. Assn. Hydraulic Rsch., Assn. Computing Machinery. Avocations: gardening, wine making, reading. Home: 2 Stationsstraat 230, Zoetermeer 2718AC, Holland Office: Delft Hydraulics, PO Box 177, Delft 2600MH, Holland

VER BOVEN, JOS, marketing professional; b. Mimia, Congo; s. Joseph Ver Boven and Daisy ver Hassel; m. Micheline Nuytten, July 12, 1974. Diploma in engring., Inst. Industries Fermentation-Inst. Meurice Chinrie, Brussels, 1975; diploma in mktg., Inst. Carières Commls., Brussels, 1977. Quality control inspector Syntex, Louvain-la-Neuve, Belgium, 1976-77; sales rep. Abbott, Antwerp, Belgium, 1978-87; product mgr. Analis, Namur, Belgium, 1988-93; sales mgr. Innogenetics, Gent, Belgium, 1994-99; sales mgr. Benelux Ventana Med. Sys., Brussels, 1999—. Avocations: chess, ballroom dancing, hiking. Home: 48 Av Mésanges, B-1640 Rhode Saint Genese Belgium

VERBOVEN, PETER ERIC, engineering company executive; b. Mortsel, Antwerp, Belgium, Sept. 14, 1959; s. Jean Justin L. and Nelly Christiane R.V.H. (van Glabeke) V.; m. Krista Van Belle, Oct. 21, 1988 (div. 2000); children: Alex, Barbara. MSc, U. Ghent, Belgium, 1982, PhD, 1987. Sci. collaborator State U., Ghent, 1983-86; scientifically responsible engr. Siemens, Oostkamp, Belgium, 1987-90, Munich, Germany, 1987-90; tech. R&D mgr. LASAG, Thun, Switzerland, 1990-95; tech. dir. Seghers, Willebroek, Belgium, 1995-99; cons. OIP, Ghent, 1983-85, BARCO, Ghent, 1985-86, SMH, Biel, Switzerland, 1990; lector KVIV, Antwerp, 1990, 98, VDI Germany, 1995, 99. Contbr. articles to profl. jours. Cpl. Royal Mil. Acad., Brussels, 1982-83. Mem. Royal Assn. Flemish Engrs., Flemish Academicians, Royal Chess Club Mechelen. Avocation: chess. Home: Acaciastr 84, Mechelen Antwerp B-2800, Belgium

VERBRUGGEN, L. A. J., NATO official; m. Henny Palmen; 2 children. Grad., Royal Netherlands Naval Acad., 1963. Joined Royal Netherlands Navy, 1960, advanced through grades to capt., resigned, 1989; various capacities in early mil. career with Royal Netherlands Naval Air Arm; fixed wing and helicopter pilot, lt. comdr., adc. SACLANT, Norfolk, Va., 1977-79; frigate exec. officer; comdr. in charge of all helicopter matters Royal Netherlands Navy, comdr. HNLMS Callenburgh, 1984-86; assigned as mil. advisor to Netherlands Permanent Rep. to NATO, 1986-89; joined NATO as dir. coun. ops. and info. sys. NATO, 1989-93, exec. sec., 1993—. Office: NATO Hdqrs, Blvd Leopold III, 1110 Brussels Belgium

VERBURG, EDWIN ARNOLD, management consultant; b. Lakehurst, N.J., Oct. 6, 1945; s. Edwin Donald Verburg and Dorothy (Orrell) Hoodless; m. Joyce Elaine Majack, Sept. 14, 1968; children: Adelle Kristine, Wendi Elizabeth. BS, Calif. Polytech. U., 1968; M in City Planning, U. Calif., Berkeley, 1970; D in Pub. Adminstrn., George Washington U., 1975. Asst. planner City of Inglewood (Calif.), 1970-71; planner City of Glendale (Calif.), 1971-72; grad. assoc. U.S. Army Corps Engrs., Washington, 1974-75; mgr. fiscal analysis Met. Washington Council Govts., 1975-77; sr. program analyst U.S. Fish and Wildlife Service, Washington, 1977-79, asst. div. chief, 1979-80, div. chief, 1980-82, asst. dir. planning and budget, 1982-86, dep. asst. dir. policy budget and adminstrn., 1986-87; dir. office of fin. U.S. Dept. Treas., Washington, 1987-88, dir. fin. svcs. directorate, 1988-91, dir. fin. svcs. directorate, dep. CFO, 1991-95; assoc. adminstr. adminstrn. FAA, 1995-98; prin. ptnr. Avant Mgmt. Group, Inc., 1998-99; prin. fedn. govt. svcs. Kelly, Anderson & Assocs., 1999—. Author: Local State and Federal Fiscal Flows, 5 Vols., 1976; contbr. articles to fed. jours. Recipient Disting. Pub. Svc. award George Washington U., Sch. Bus. and Pub. Mgmt., 1994, Sec. of Treasury Disting Svc. award, 1995, Fin. Mgmt. Svc. Commrs. award, 1996. Mem. Am. Inst. Cert. Planners, Am. Planning Assn. (cert. govt. fin. mgr., Merit award Calif. chpt. 1973, First award Nat. Capital area chpt. 1980, Peer award for pub. svc. Dept. of Treasury 1990, sec. of treas. cert. appreciation 1991, Pres.'s Meritorious Svc. award 1991, Commr.'s Citation Fin. Mgmt. Svc. 1996, Pres.'s award Combined Fed. Campaign 1997), Arlington Kiwanis (bd. dirs. 1999-2000). Home: 538 N Oakland St Arlington VA 22203-2219

VERBURG, PETER, research scientist; b. Loenen, Utrecht, The Netherlands, May 18, 1972; s. Rinus Verburg and Josta Koeleman. MSc, Wageningen Agrl. U., The Netherlands, 1996. Jr. rschr. Wageningen U., 1996—. Fax: 31-317-482419.

VERCESI, HAYDÉE MARGARITA CHACHA, biomedical scientist; b. Bahia Blanca, Argentina, Sept. 24, 1959; came to U.S., 1988; d. Hector Vercesi and Elisa Martinez; m. Frederick Chanyapate Lahser, May 13, 1995; 1 child, Christopher Arthur Lahser-Vercesi. DVM, Nat. U. Ctr. Buenos Aires, 1983; MS, Tex. A&M U., 1994. Technician Tex. A&M U., College Station, 1988-90; rsch. technician Ctr. Behavioral Neurosci., SUNY, Stony Brook, 1995-97; rsch. coord. Mt. Sinai Med. Ctr., N.Y.C., 1997-99; assoc. scientist Schering Plough Rsch. Inst., Kenilworth, N.J., 1999—. Campaign coord. Amnesty Internat., Ronkon Koma, N.Y., 1998. Mem. Soc. Neurosci. Avocations: flag collecting, writing, music, reading. E-mail: haydee.vercesi@spcorp.com. Home: 467 Valley St Maplewood NJ 07040-1306

VERCRUYSSE, JEROOM AUGUST JOHAN GHISLEEN, retired education educator; b. Ukkel, Belgium, Feb. 10, 1936; s. Guillaume and Augustina (Borremans) V.; m. Jacqueline A.M. Vanderschrick, July 11, 1970; children: David, Nathalie. Lic. philosophy and lit., U. Libre, Brussels, 1959, D Philosophy and Lit., 1965. Tchr. French and morals various schs., Belgium, 1959-67; rsch. fellow Ctr. Nat. Rsch. Sci., Belgium, 1967-68; prof. Vrye U., Brussels, 1968-96; prof. emeritus Vrye U., 1996—; dir. studies on Enlightenment Vrye U., Brussels, 1972-84; bd. dirs. Nouvelles Annales Prince de Ligne, Oeuvres Completes Prince de Ligne. Contbr. articles to profl. jours. Sec. gen. Internat. Studies Eighteenth Century Soc., 1971-79, v.p., 1979-83; founder, past pres. Belgian-Dutch 18th Century Soc., Livres-Instns. Soc., Belgium. Served with Belgian Army, 1961-62. Avocations: travel, reading, philately, paleontology, printing techniques. Home: Olmenlaan 5, B1750 Saint M Lennik Belgium

VERDE, JUAN, accountant; b. Greci, Avellino, Italy, Feb. 19, 1924; arrived in Argentina, 1929; s. Rafael and Teresa (Clemente) V.; m. Elida Veros, Feb. 26, 1949; children: Hector Augusto, Juan Andres, Maria Alejandra. CPA, U. Del Litoral, Rosario, Prov. Santa Fe, 1949. CPA, Pergamino. Acct. Proper Studio, Pergamino, Argentina, 1949—; prof. Comm. Coll., Pergamino, 1949-51; counselor Consejo Profl. de Ciencias Economicas Provincia de Buenos Aires, La Plata, 1964; founder, pres. Caja De Créditos Pergamino (now Credicoop), Buenos Aires, 1959. Mcpl. acct. Mcpl. de Pergamino, 1958-60. Mewm. Masons (venerable master 1985). Avocations: poetry, little mosaics. Home: Santiago del Estero 1039, BA Pergamino 2700, Argentina

VERDE, RUI ALEXANDRE, educator; b. Lisbon, Portugal, July 25, 1966; s. Antonio Santos and Maria Helena (Dias) V.; m. Maria Isabel Magalhaes, July 20, 1990. Degree in law, Cath. U., Lisbon, Portugal, 1989; postgrad. in law, Automonous U., Lisbon, Portugal, 1992; PhD in Law, U. Newcastle, U.K., 1998. Chief staff, dean, dir. planning dept. U. Autonoma, Lisbon, 1989-91; dir. law affairs IPG Corp., Lisbon, 1992-93; dir. U. Independente, Lisbon, 1993—; prof. U. Autonoma, 1989-91, U. Independente, 1993—; vis. prof. U. Santa Cat, Brazil and F. Cath., Brazil. Mem. Legal Studies Ctr., Sto. Estavao Polo Club, Jesuits Alumni Assn., Remioliterario. Avocations: reading, travel, horseback riding, poetry, swimming. Home: Herdade Zambujeiro 25p, 2130 Benavente Portugal Office: U Independente, Av Marechal Gomes Costa 9, 1800 Lisbon Portugal

VERDE GONZALEZ, LUIS S., agronomy educator; b. Mercedes, Uruguay, June 30, 1930; arrived in Argentina, 1969; s. Daniel U. Verde and Maria Isabel Gonzalez; m. Sonia Chifflet, July 12, 1961; children: Gabriela, Luis Abel. Degree in agron. engring., U. Republica, Montevideo, Uruguay, 1960; MSc, Iowa State U., 1965. Prof. animal physiology Coll. Agrl. Scis., UNMP, Balcarce, Argentina, 1970-93, prof. animal nutrition, 1972-93; rschr. INTA Argentina, Balcarce, 1969-94; genetic resources coord. INTA Argentina, Buenos Aires, 1994; internat. coord. Procisur-IICA OEA, Montevideo, 1985-94; dir. basic scis. Coll. Agrl. Scis. UCA, Buenos Aires, 1994—; cons. in field; asst. dir. INTA-Argentina, 1992-95. Recipient Edmondo Gastal award Procisur IICA-OEA, 1991. Mem. AAPA (pres. 1979-81), AUPA (pres. 1996-98), N.Y. Acad. Scis. Home: Calle 32 No 938, 7620 Balcarce Argentina Office: Coll Agrl Scis UCA, Freire 183, 1426 Buenos Aires Argentina

VERDIER, DAVID D'OOGE, ophthalmologist, educator; b. Grand Rapids, Mich., Jan. 22, 1949; s. Leonard D'Ooge and Anita Beatrice (Carvalho) V.; m. Beverly Deane Johnson; children: Renée Leigh, Travis D'Ooge, Eric Leonard. BA in Polit. Sci., U. Mich., 1971; MD, U. Mich. Med. Sch., 1977. Resident in family practice Med. U. S.C., Charleston, 1977-80; resident in ophthalmology Pitts. Eye and Ear, U. Pitts., 1980-83; corneal and external eye fellowship U. Iowa, Iowa City, 1983-84; pvt. practice med. and surg. ophthalmology Verdier Eye Ctr. P.C., Grand Rapids, Mich., 1984—; assoc. clin. prof. Mich. State U. Coll. Medicine, East Lansing, 1986—; med. dir. Mich. Tissue Bank, Lansing, Mich., 1995-98, SEECOM, Mich., 1995—. Contbr. articles to profl. jours. and textbook chpts. Bd. dirs. East Grand Rapids (Mich.) Sch. Found., 1992-2000, Macatawa Bay Yacht Club, Holland, Mich., 1988-90, 94-95, Grand Rapids Art Mus., 1995—; bd. dirs. Macatawa Park Cottagers Assn., Holland, 1993-99, pres., 1993-98. Named to Galens Hon. Med. Soc., 1975-77. Mem. Mich. Ophthalmologic Soc (bd. dirs. 1994-2000), Mich. State Med. Soc. (del. 1993-2000). Home: 3043 Mary St SE Grand Rapids MI 49506-3150 Office: Verdier Eye Center PC 1000 E Paris Ave SE Ste 130 Grand Rapids MI 49546-3680

VERDONCK, PATRICK BERNARD, researcher, science educator; b. Elsene, Belgium, May 9, 1958; arrived in Brazil, 1988; s. Rudi Marinus V. and Julia Baeyens; m. Margareth Satiko Tatumi, Aug. 17, 1996; 1 child, Natalia Satie. Elec. Engr., Cath. U. Leuven, Belgium, 1981; PhD, UNICAMP, Campinas, Brazil. Researcher KUL, Leuven, Belgium, 1981-84; process engr. CTI, Campinas, Brazil, 1984-86; researcher IMEC, Leuven, Brazil, 1986-88; guest prof. U. São Paulo, 1988-90, researcher, 1990—; cons. Tech. H.S. of Technology, São Paulo, 1992; rschr. U. São Paulo, 1990-99; assoc. prof. 1998—. Contbr. articles to profl. jours., chpt. to book; editor proceedings 11th Brazilian Microelectronics Conf., 1996. Mem. Brazilian Microelectronics Soc. Avocations: sports. Home: Ed Santa Clara Apt 22, Av Candido Motta Felho 521, 05351001 São Paulo Brazil Office: LSI PEE EPUSP, Av Luciano Gualberto trav 03 158, 05508900 São Paulo SP, Brazil

VERDU, SERGIO, engineering educator; b. Barcelona, Spain, Aug. 15, 1958; came to U.S., 1980; s. Tomas Verdu and Visitacion Lucas; m. Mercedes Paratje, Jan. 19, 1982; 1 child, Ariana. Diploma telecomm. engr., Polytech. U. Barcelona, 1980; MS, U. Ill., 1982, PhD, 1984. Asst. prof. Princeton (N.J.) U., 1984-89, assoc. prof., 1989-92, prof., 1993—; prin.

investigator U.S. Office Naval Rsch., N.J. Dept. Higher Edn., U. S. Army Rsch. Office, N.J. Commn. Sci. and Tech., NSF, U.S.-Israel Binational Sci. Found.; vis. prof. U. Calif., Berkeley, 1998. Author: Multiuser Detection, 1998, Information Theory: Fifty Years of Discovery, 1999; mem. editl. bd. Transactions on Info. Theory, 1990-94; contbr. numerous articles to profl. jours, book chpts. Recipient Nat. U. prize Ministry Edn., Spain, 1982, Presdl. Young Invesitgator award NSF, 1988, Frederick E. Terman award Am. Soc. Engring. Edn., 2000. Fellow IEEE (Outstanding Paper award 1998, Millennium medal 2000); Info. Theory Soc. (v.p. 1995, pres. 1997, bd. govs. 1989—, Golden Jubilee Paper award 1998). Office: Princeton U Dept Elec Engring Princeton NJ 08544-0001

VERECZKEI, LAJOS, medical educator; b. Tokod, Hungary, Feb. 9, 1937; s. Lajos and Ida (Barna) V.; m. Hajna Losonczy, Aug. 19, 1941; 1 child, András. MD, U. Med. Sch. Pécs, Hungary, 1961; PhD, Eötvös Lóránd U., Budapest, Hungary, 1964. Resident Neurol. Clinic, Pécs, 1961-62; asst. prof. dept. philosophy Inst. Physiology, Pécs, 1962-86; prof. Inst. of Behavioral Scis., Pécs, 1986—. Author: The Conception of Consciousness in the Mirror of Learning, Reinforcement and Motivation Theories, 1975; editor: Philosophy - Man - Sciences, 1979; contbr. articles to profl. jours. Mem. Hungarian Acad. Scis. (regional com.), Scientists Club (pres.). Avocations: music, reading, travel. Office: U Pécs Faculty Medicine, Inst Behav Scis Szigeti ut 12, 7624 Pécs Hungary

VERECZKEY, GÁBOR, anesthesiologist, intensive therapist, cardiologist, consultant; b. Budapest, Nov. 25, 1958; s. György and Éva (Keleti) V.; m. Cosima Verebély, June 10, 1988; children: Döme Dávid Sonó, Luca Lili Maku. MD, Semmelweis Med. U., Budapest, 1984; Specialist in Anaesthesia and Intensive Care, Postgrad. Med. U., Budapest, 1989. Diplomate European Acad. Anaesthesiology; cert. cardiology specialist. Registrar Wexham Park Hosp., Slough, E. Berkshire, England, 1989-92; med. dir. Pfizer, Budapest, 1993-95; head of ICU HIETE Postgrad. Faculty Internal Med. and Cardiovascular Ctr. Heart and Vascular Surgery Clinic, Budapest, 1995—; cons. Hewlett-Packard Med., Budapest, 1992-94, Radiometer, Budapest, 1992—, Ask-Boeringer, Budapest, 1995—; med. dir. "Televisit"-Second Opinion Hungary, Telemedicine: Hungary-UCSF, 1997—. Author: Tissue Oxygenation in Critical Care The Radiometer Concept, 1996, What is Impedance Cardiography?, 1996; co-author Inodilator Therapy, 1996. Mem. European Acad. Anaesthesiology. Avocations: swimming, kayaking, bicycling, classical music, pop-rock. Home: 24 Országház Utca, H-1014 Budapest Hungary Office: HIETE Postgrad Faculty Internal & Cardivascular Ctr, 35 Szabolcs Utca, H-1135 Budapest Hungary

VERECZKEY, LASZLO FERENC, physician, researcher; b. Budapest, Hungary, June 16, 1942; s. Laszlo and Ilona (Sulkovszky) V.; m. Erzsebet Kalocsai, Dec. 30, 1968; children: Ildiko, Katalin. MD, Semmelweiss U., Budapest, Hungary, 1967; PhD, Hungarian Acad. Scis., 1983. Asst. prof. Semmelweis U., Budapest, 1967-71; head dept. Chem. Works of Gedeon Richter, Budapest, 1971-90; dep. dir. Inst. for Drug Rsch., Budapest, 1990-92; sci. dir. Biorex Ltd., Budapest, 1993; head dept. Chem. Rsch. Ctr. Hungarian Acad. Scis., Budapest, 1991—. Author: (with O. Gaal and G. Medgyesi) Electrophoresis in the Separation of Biological Micromolecules, 1980; contbr. articles to profl. jours. Mem. Internat. Soc. Study Xenobiotics (councillor 1991-94, 96-99). Avocations: swimming, Latin language. Office: Hung Acad Scis/Chem Rsch, Pusztaszeri 59-67, H-1025 Budapest Hungary

VEREEN, WILLIAM JEROME, uniform manufacturing company executive; b. Moultrie, Ga., Sept. 7, 1940; s. William Coachman and Mary Elizabeth V.; m. Lula Evelyn King, June 9, 1963; children: Elizabeth King, William Coachman. BS in Indsl. Mgmt, Ga. Inst. Tech., 1963. With Riverside Mfg. Co., Moultrie, 1967—; from v.p. to exec. v.p. Riverside Mfg. Co., 1970-77, pres., 1977-84, pres., treas., CEO, 1984—; v.p., dir. Moultrie Cotton Mills, 1969—; exec. v.p. Riverside Industries, Inc., Moultrie, 1973-77; pres. Riverside Industries, Inc., 1977-84, CEO, 1984—, also dir.; v.p. Riverside Uniform Rentals, Inc., Moultrie, 1971-80, pres., 1980-84, CEO, bd. dirs.; pres. Riverside Mfg. Co. (Ireland) Ltd., 1977—, Right Image Corp., Riverside Mfg. Co. GmbH, Germany, 1979—, also CEO, dir., 1984; pres., treas., CEO G.A. Rivers Corp., Riverside Mfg. Co. (U.K.) Ltd.; pres., treas. CEO, bd. dirs. Textile Clothing Tech. Corp.; chairholder Tyner eminent scholars, prof. coll. human scis. Fla. State U., 1993-94, mem. coll. human scis. devel. bd.; bd. dirs. Ga. Power Co., Gerber Sci., Inc., Blue Cross/Blue Shield Ga., Cerulean Cos., Inc., Trade and Tourism, Ga. Rsch. Alliance, Ga. Corp. Indsl. Devel.; mem. trilateral commn. apparel labeling NAFTA; so. regional dir. Nations Bank of Ga., N.A.; advisor textile and apparel tariffs and quotas U.S. Dept. State Bd.; mem. World Econ. Forum, Davos, Switzerland. Bd. dirs. Moultrie-Colquitt County (Ga.) Devel. Authority, 1973-77, Moultrie-Colquitt County United Givers, 1968-75, Moultrie YMCA, 1968-75, Colquitt County Cancer Soc., 1969-73; trustee Cmty. Welfare Assn. Moultrie, 1970—, Pineland Sch., Moultrie, 1971-75, Leadership Ga., 1972—, Ga. Coun. Econ. Edn.; trustee Am. Apparel Edn. Found.; adv. bd. Ga. Tech. sch. of textile and fiber engring.; elder 1st Presbyterian Ch. Capt. USMCR, 1963-67. Decorated Bronze Star with combat V, Purple Heart. Mem. Internat. Apparel Fedn. (2d v.p., 1st v.p., bd. dirs., exec. com., chmn. 1991-92), Am. Apparel Mfrs. Assn. (bd. dirs., exec. com., edn. found. com., 2d vice chmn., chmn. 1990-91), Nat. Assn. Uniform Mfrs. and Distbrs. (bd. dirs. 1988-91), Am. Apparel Edn. Found. (v.p., trustee), Capital City Club (Atlanta), Commerce Club (Atlanta), World Econ. Forum, Sunset Country Club, Ga. C. of C., Elks, Kiwanis, Sigma Alpha Epsilon. Home: 21 Dogwood Dr Moultrie GA 31768-6537 Office: PO Box 460 Moultrie GA 31776-0460

VERE HODGE, RICHARD ANTHONY, pharmaceutical executive, consultant; b. Burnham-on-Sea, Somerset, Eng., Dec. 27, 1943; s. Francis and Eleanore Mary V. H.; married; 3 children. BA, Trinity Coll., Dublin, 1966; DPhil, Worcester Coll., Oxford, Eng., 1969. With Beecham Pharms. (now SmithKline Beecham Pharms.), Eng., 1969-96, project mgr. human interferon project, 1974-76, chief biochemist antiviral chemotherapy project, 1981-92, with world-wide strategic product devel., 1992-93; assoc. dir., 1995-96; dir. Vere Hodge Antivirals Ltd., Reigate, Surrey, Eng., 1996—; cons. Pharmasset, Inc., Atlanta, 2000—. Contbr. articles to profl. jours., chpts. to books; patente for treatment of latent infection of herpesvirus, 1999. Founding mem. Ch. Roof Fund Com., Leigh, Reigate, Surrey, Eng., 1989-99. Mem. Royal Soc. Chemistry, Am. Soc. Microbiology, Internat. Soc. Antiviral Rsch., The Chromatography Soc. Avocations: bell-ringing, gardening, hill walking. Office: Vere Hodge Antivirals Ltd, Leigh, Reigate Surrey RH2 8RD, England

VERESEGYHÁZY, TAMÁS PÉTER, veterinarian, educator; b. Makó, Hungary, Dec. 5, 1947; s. László and Eszter (Csüllög) V.; m. Zsuzsanna Márta Szacsvay; Children: Éva, Andrea. Vet. diploma, U. Vet. Sci., Budapest, Hungary, 1971. Veterinarian Kiskun Coop., Kiskunlacháza, Hungary, 1971-74; asst. prof. U. Vet. Scis., Budapest, 1974-80, sr. lectr., 1980-95, assoc. prof., 1995—. Author (lab. manual) Biochemistry, (book) Comparative Biochemistry, 1995. Mem. Hungarian Biochem. Soc. Avocations: classical music, travel. Home: Ifjusag U 15/B, 2310 Szigetsze Hungary Office: U Vet Sci, István 2, H-1078 Budapest Hungary

VERESHCHAGIN, IGOR PETROVICH, electrical engineer, educator; b. Moscow, Russia, Oct. 25, 1931; s. Peter Nicolaevich Vereshchagin and Alexandra Alexeevna Legchilina; m. Lidia Dmitrievna Zhedilina, Oct. 15, 1960; children: Maria, Michael. Candidate in Sci., Moscow Power Engring. Inst., 1960, DSc, 1975. Diplomat Russian Min. Edn. Rschr. Moscow Power Engring. Inst., 1958-67, lectr., 1967-77, prof., 1977-88, head dept., 1988-97, pres. scientific ednl. ctr., 1994—, prof., 1997—; fellow expert bd. High Diploma Degree Commn. Russian Ministry Sci. and Tech., Moscow, 1975-98; fellow dr. degree bd. Moscow Power Engring. Inst., 1978—; chmn. cons. com. Ozone Generators and Ozone Application, 1985-99; chmn. sect. new electrophys. techs. Russian Acad. Scis., Moscow, 1990-98. Author: Corona Discharge in Electrotechnological Installations, 1985; co-author: Electrogasdynamic Grounds of Disperced Materials, 1974, Smoke Electrostatic Precipitators, 1980, Physical Grounds of Electrostatic Separation, 1983, Equipment and Technology for Coating in the Electric Field, 1990, Electro-physical Grounds of High Voltage Engineering, 1993; mem. editl. bd. Facta Universitatis. Grantee Russian Found. Fundamental Investigations, 1991-93. Mem. Internat. Soc. Electrostatic Precipitation (hon. mem., dir. bd. dirs., Outstanding Contbn. to Sci. award 1990), Russian Ozone Assn. (chmn. 1996-99), Internat. Ozone Assn., European Fedn. Chem. Engring. (working party 1991—). Home: Energeticheskaya St 22 100, 111116 Moscow Russia Office: Moscow Power Engring Inst, Krasnokazarmennaya 14, 111250 Moscow Russia

VERESHCHETIN, VLADLEN S., judge of international court of justice. Judge Internat. Ct. of Justice, The Hague. Office: Internat Ct Justice, Peace Palace Carnegieplein 2, 2517 KJ The Hague The Netherlands

VERESS, GYÖRGY, microbiologist, researcher; b. Debrecen, Hungary, June 15, 1966; s. György and Maria (Trefil) V.; m. Marianna Nagy, July 02, 1988; children: Balazs, Zsofia Borbala. MSc in biology, Kossuth U., Debrecen, Hungary, 1990; PhD in medicine, U. Med. Sch., Debrecen, Hungary, 1999. Jr. sci. fellow U. Med. Sch., Debrecen, Hungary, 1990-92, asst. lectr., 1993-99, asst. prof., 1999—. Contbr. articles to profl. jours. Mem. Hungarian Soc. Microbiology. Avocations: gardening, touring. E-mail: veregy@jaguar.dote.hu. Office: Dept Microbiol/Fac of Med, U Debrecen POB 17, Debrecen H-4012, Hungary

VERESS, TIBOR, forensic chemist; b. Debrecen, Hungary, May 22, 1956; s. József V. and Emma Pinczés; m. Tiborné Judit Kovács; 1 child, Viktória. BS in Chem. Engring., U. Veszprém, Hungary, 1980, MSc in Analytical Chemistry, 1986; EdD, Tech. U. Budapest, Hungary, 1993, PhD, 1997. Forensic chemist Inst. Forensic Scis., Budapest, 1980—. Contbr. articles to scientific jours. Mem. Hungarian Chem. Assn. Avocation: music. Office: Inst Forensic Sciences, PO Box 314/4, H-1903 Budapest Hungary

VEREVKIN, SERGEY PETROVICH, chemistry educator, research scientist; b. Kaunas, Lithuania, Mar. 31, 1956; arrived in Germany, 1992; s. Petr Dmitrievich and Tamara Stepanova (Smoliankina) V.; m. Elena Viktorovna Malenkova, Aug. 21, 1979; children: Daria, Nikita. MS in Chemistry and Chem. Engring., Kuibyshev (USSR) Poly. Inst., 1978; diploma in patent law, Kuibyshev Patent Inst., 1978; PhD in Phys. Chemistry, Byelorussian State U., Minsk, Russia, 1984. Cert. phys. chemistry and chem. engring. Jr. rsch. scientist Sci. Rsch. Ctr., Kuibyshev Poly. Inst., 1978-80, rsch. scientist, 1984-86, sr. rsch. scientist, 1986-92; rsch. scientist U. Freiburg (Germany) Inst. Organic Chemistry & Biochemistry, 1992-96; asst. prof. U. Rostock (Germany) Inst. Phys. Chemistry, 1996—; adj. prof. chemistry dept. Kuibyshev Constrn. Inst., 1984-92; exec. sec. of the com. Com. Project for Coordination Devel. Chemistry and Chem. Tech. in Volga-River Region of Russia, Samara, 1987-92; presenter in field. Contbr. articles to profl. jours. Fellow Fellowship of Found. Deutsche Akademische AustauschDienst, Bonn, Germany, 1988-89, Alexander von Humboldt Found., Bonn, 1992-93. Avocations: mountain climbing, music, journey. Fax: 0049-381-498-1854. Office: U Rostock Inst Physikalisce, Hermannstr 14, 18051 Rostock Germany

VERGADOS, JOHN (IOANNIS) DEMETRIOS, physics educator; b. Sparta, Laconia, Greece, Dec. 9, 1937; s. Demetrios Ioannis Vergados and Vasiliki (Dionysiou) Tournas; m. Deirdre Di Marco, Sept. 15, 1973; children: Vasiliki, Emilie, Demetrios, Niki-Rhea. BSc, U. Athens, Greece, 1963; MSc, U. Mich., 1965, PhD, 1968. Rsch. assoc. SUNY, Stony Brook, 1968-71; rsch. physicist Lawrence Berkeley (Calif.) Lab., 1971-73; asst. prof. U. Pa., Phila., 1973-77; prof. U. Ioannina, Greece, 1978—; chmn. physics dept. U. Ioannina, 1982-83, 84-89, pres., 1991-94. Author: topics in Mathematical Physics, 1985, Basic Physics, Vols. I & II, 1986, Mathematical Methods in Physics, Vols. I & II, 1988, Elementary Particles, 1990, Statistical Physics, 1990, Group Theory, 1991, Classical Electrodynamics, 1993, Vector Analysis, 1996; contbr. over 100 articles to profl. jours. Recipient Alexander von Humboldt rsch. award; Fulbright fellow. Mem. Am. Phys. Soc., European Phys. Soc., Greek Phys. Soc., Greek Soc. for Study of High Energy Physics. Home: Pedini, GR 45500 Ioannina Greece Office: U Ioannina, GR 45110 Ioannina Greece

VERGARA, PATROCINIO (PATRI VERGARA), physiology educator, researcher; b. Embid de Ariza, Aragon, Spain, July 11, 1955; d. Benito and Patrocinio (Esteras) V. DVM, Zaragoza U., 1978, PhD in Vet. Scis., 1983. Tchg. asst. Zaragoza U., 1979-83; physiology lectr. Autonomous U. Barcelona, Bellaterra, 1984—, vet. libr. coord., 1990-94, vice-dean vet. sch., 1995-98; postdoctoral fellow Inst. Animal Physiology, Cambridge, 1985; vis. rsch. fellow McMaster U., Hamilton, Ont., Can., 1991, Beth Israel Hosp., Boston, 1998. Contbr. articles to profl. jours. including Life Scis., Regulatory Peptides, Am. Jour. Physiology, Jour. Pharmacology and Exptl. Therapeutics, Annals N.Y. Acad. Scis., Neurogastroenterol. Grantee Centre d'Informació i Reserca d'Innovacions Tecnologiques, 1986, Autonomous U., 1989, Edn. Ministry, 1991, Dirección General de Investigación en Ciencia y Tecnologia, 1993, 96, 99, Commissionat Universitats i Recerca, 2000. Mem. Sociedad Espanola de Ciencias Fisiologicas, Sociedad Espanola para las Ciencias del Animal de Laboratorio (founder, gov. bd. dirs. 1990-97), Internat. Coun. for Lab. Animal Sci. (sci. rep. 1994, mem. gov. bd. 1995-99, treas. 1999—), European Gastrointestinal Motility Soc. Office: U Autonoma de Barcelona, Facultad Veterinaria U Fisiologia, 08193 Bellaterra Spain

VERGHESE, GEORGE THOMAS, editor; b. Madras, Tamil Nadu, India, Dec. 14, 1945; s. Thomas Kurien and Mary George; m. Meera John, Feb. 21, 1982; children: Vikram, Johann. BA, U. Madras, India, 1966, MA, 1968. Reporter Indian Express, Madras, India, 1967-68; journalist Econ. Times/Times of India, 1969-82; editor Indo British Rev.--A Jour. of History, 1982—. Editor:(books) C. Rajagopalachari - Gandhi's Southern Commander, 1986, Society, Religion and the State, 1996. Indian Orthodox Christian. Home and Office: Nelson Manickam Rd, 21 Rajaram Mehta Ave, T Nadu Madras 600 029, India

VERGHESE, JOE, neurologist; b. Cochin, Kerala, India, May 29, 1965; s. Joseph and Lucy Verghese; m. Ann Ambrose, 1992; children: Tanya, David. MBBS, St. Johns Med. Coll., Bangalore, India, 1989. Intern St. Johns Med. Coll., Bangalore, 1988-89; sr. house officer in medicine Princess Royal Hosp., Telford, Eng., 1991-94; registrar in neurology St. James U. Hosp., Leeds, Eng., 1994-95; resident in neurology Albert Einstein Coll. Medicine, Bronx, N.Y., 1995-98, fellow in neurology, 1998-99, asst. prof. neurology, 1999—; clin. rschr. Einstein Aging Study, Bronx, 1996—. Contbr. articles to profl. jours. Am. Acad. Neurology travel fellow, 1999. Mem. AMA, Royal Coll. Physicians (Ireland), Am. Acad. Neurology, Am. Geriatric Soc. Avocations: Scrabble, art, creative writing.

VERGILIS, JOSEPH SEMYON, mechanical engineering educator; b. Odessa, Ukraine, Aug. 14, 1934; came to U.S., 1988; s. Semyon E. and Zinaida I. (Gleizerman) V.; m. Zhanna S. Berenfeld, Apr. 30, 1963; children: Helen, Irene. BS in Mfg. Engring., Poly. Inst., Odessa, 1958; PhD in Mech. Engring., Exptl. R&D Inst. Machine Tools, Moscow, 1973. Mfg. engr. Factory of Machine Tools, Odessa, 1958-66; sr. scientist R&D Inst. ENIMS, Moscow, 1966-87; cons. Beltran Assn., Inc., Bklyn., 1988-90; prof. mech. engring. Murray (Ky.) State U., 1990-92; cons. Russtrad, Inc., Richmond, Mass., 1992-93; prof. mech. engring. U. Turabo, Gurabo, P.R., 1993-94, CCNY, 1994—. Author: Fine-Boring Heads, 1972, Spindle Heads for Precision Tools, 1975; contbr. articles to profl. jours. Mem. ASME, Soc. Mfg. Engrs. (sr. mem.), Am. Soc. Engring. Edn. Republican. Jewish. Achievements include patents for tool holders for machine tools. Home: 868 E 24th St Brooklyn NY 11210-2822 Office: CCNY Convent Ave at 135 St New York NY 10031

VERGOS, EVANGELOS-APOSTOLOS, agriculturist, educator; b. Thessaloniki, Greece, Mar. 24, 1957; s. Apostolos and Zohe (Vergou) V.; m. Georgia-Leonidas Tapouri, Sept. 19, 1959; children: Zohe Vergou, Parthenope Vergou, Apostolos-Leonidas. Grad., Aristotelian U., 1984; PhD, U. Coll. Dublin, 1991. Tech. dairy dept. Am. Farm Sch., Thessaloniki, 1977-80, translator, 1980-83; mgr. faculty Agr. Exptl. Farm, Thessaloniki, 1984-88; asst. prof. dept. animal prodn. U. Thessaly-Volos, 1991-92; prof. Tech. Ednl. Inst., 1992—; dean Dimitris Perrotis Coll. Agrl. Studies Am. Farm Sch., 1996—; rschr. dept. physiology of reproduction Aristotle U., Thessaloniki, 1991-92; mng. dir. Exptl. Farm Tech. Ednl. Inst. Thessaloniki, 1993—; scientific cons. Am. Farm Sch., 1993—, Greek Productivity Ctr., Thessaloniki, 1993—; dean Dimitris Perrotis Coll. of Agrl. Studies, 1996—. Author two books. With Greek Navy, 1985-86. Scholar Agrl. Bank Greece, 1973-76, Ministry of Agriculture, 1976-77, Nat. Scholarship Found., 1988-91. Mem. Am. Farm Sch. Alumni Soc., Greek Agrl. Soc., Hellenic Soc. Animal Prodn., Physiopathology of Reprodn. Soc., Internat. Embryo Transfer Assn., European Embryo Transfer Assn., Soc. for Study of Fertility, European Soc. Human Reprodn. New Democrat. Greek Orthodox. Avocations: fishing, jogging, basketball, diving, sailing. Home: Kanari 26, 56626 Sykies Thessaloniki Greece

VERHAEGEN, FRANS JOSEPHINA WILLEM, physicist, researcher; b. Willebroek, Antwerpen, Belgium, Sept. 9, 1965; s. Raoul Talboom and Marianne Eisner. Engr. in Physics, U. Ghent, Belgium, 1990, PhD in Physics, 1996. Rschr. Euratom, Geel, Belgium, 1990, U. Ghent, 1990-99, Inst. Cancer Rsch., Royal Marsden Hosp., 1999—. Contbr. some 30 articles to profl. jours. Recipient Young Investigator award European Cmty./12th Microdosimetry Conf., Oxford, 1996, Young Scientist award Assn. Radiation Rsch., Annual Meeting of the Assn. of Radiation Rsch. Oxford, 1997. Mem. European Soc. Radiation Biology, Am. Assn. Physicists in Medicine. Avocations: classical music, opera. Home: Vaderlandstraat 66, B-9000 Ghent Belgium Office: U Ghent, Proeftuinstraat 86, B-9000 Ghent Belgium

VERHASSELT, YOLA LOUISA GUSTAVE, geography educator; b. Antwerpen, Belgium, Aug. 14, 1937; s. Louis and Johanna (Cornelis) V. DSc, U. Libre, 1966. Asst. U. Libre, Brussels, 1959-61; rsch. fellow Nat. Fund for Sci. Rsch., Belgium, Belgium, 1961-65; rsch. asst. U. Antwerp, 1966-69, sr. asst., 1970-74; lectr. Vrije U., Brussels, 1968-74, prof., 1974—. Author, co-author 4 books; guest editor: Social Sci. and Medicine, Geojour., Geo-Eco-Trop, Bull. Soc. Neuchâteloise de Géographie, Revue Belge de Géographie; contbr. over 105 articles to profl. jours. Recipient Prix de Géographie Maurice Rahir Soc. Royale Belge de Géog, 1966; Lauréat d'Honneur Internat. Geog. Union, 1996. Mem. Academia Europaea, Eurasian Acad. Scis., Royal Acad of Overseas Scis. (permanent sec.), ICSU (treas.), Com. Nat. Geography (pres.). Avocations: theatre, poetry, music, tennis, swimming. Office: Vrije U Brussel, Geog Inst Pleinlaan 2, 1050 Brussels Belgium

VERHOFSTADT, EDWARD CORNELIUS, foreign language educator; b. Maldegem, E.Flanders, Belgium, Mar. 4, 1926; s. Aloysius Louis and Marguerite Marie Louise (Norro) V.; m. Leni Margaretha Denève, Aug. 17, 1963; children: Natasja, Marnix, Moira. D.Germanic Philology, U. Ghent, Belgium, 1961. Asst. and lectr. U. Ghent, 1957-69, full prof. German lit., 1969-91, prof. emeritus, 1991—, dean faculty of arts, 1988-90. Author: Daniel Casper von Lohenstein: Untergehende Wertwelt und ästhetischer Illusionismus, Fragestellung und dialektische Interpretationen, 1964; contbr. articles to profl. jours. Recipient Red Cross award Belgian Red Cross, 1984. Mem. Internat. Arbeitskreis für Barockliteratur, Hugo von Hofmannsthal-Gesellschaft. Home: Bergwegel 74, B-9820 Merelbeke Belgium Office: U Ghent, Blandijnberg 2, B-9000 Ghent Belgium

VERHULST, MICHEL JOSEPH JULIEN, naval officer; b. Brussels, May 19, 1942; s. Joseph and Georgette (Michel) V.; m. Geneviève Lefeure, Apr. 2, 1971; children: Veronique, Frédérique, Anne-Catherine, Nancy, Jean-Michel. Civil engr. degree, U. Degree, Brussels, 1966; grad., Naval Staff Coll., Greenwich, U.K., 1982, Royal Superior Inst. for Def., 1983. Cert. engr. Comdg. officer Frigate, Wielingen, 1984-85; plans and policy staff Joint and Naval Staff, 1985-88; comdr. Tng. Establishment, Belgium, 1989-92; comdr. in chief Belgian Fleet, 1992; chief ops. Joint Staff, Belgium, 1992-95; chief naval staff Belgian Navy, 1995—; nat. rep. Sci. Com. NATO Undersea Rsch. Ctr., La Spezia, Italy, 1988-95; equerry King of Belgians, 1972-82. Named comdr. de l'ordre de Leopold, Belgium, officer de laLégion d'honneur et de l'ordre nat. du Merite, France; recipient Grand Croix de l'ordre du 25Mai, Argentina. Mem. Belgian Royal Maritime Acad. Roman Catholic. Office: Quartier Reine Elisabeth, Rue D Evere Naval Staff, 1140 Brussels Belgium

VERIN, ALEXANDER D., biochemistry educator, researcher; b. Moscow, May 13, 1960; came to U.S., 1990; s. Dmitriy M. and Lilia A. Verin; m. Tatyana Yakusheva; 1 child, Alexander A. MS in Biology, Moscow State U., 198, PhD in Biology, 1990. Sr. technician Inst. Molecular Biology, USSR Acad. Scis., Moscow, 1981-82, fellow rschr. Inst. Organic Chemistry,, 1982-84; jr. sci. officer Moscow State U., 1984-90; postdoctoral fellow Ind. U., Indpls., 1990-97, asst. scientist and prof., 1997-98; asst. prof. medicine Johns Hopkins U., Balt., 1998—. Contbr. articles to sci. jours., including Am. Jour. Physiology, Biochem. Jour., Biochemistry. Grantee Am. Lung Assn., 1995-97. Mem. Am. Physiol. Soc., Am. Soc. for Cell Biology, Am. Heart Assn. (grantee 1996-99). Avocations: touring, fishing, mushroom hunting. E-mail: averin@welch.jhu.edu. Office: Johns Hopkins U 5501 Hopkins Bayview Cir Baltimore MD 21224-6821

VERISSIMO, RAMIRO FILIPE, medical educator, researcher, psychiatrist; b. Espinho, Portugal, Oct. 19, 1951; s. Manuel Ramiro and Margarida Pinto (Barbosa) V.; m. Maria Teresa Oliveira; children: Patricia, Luis Filipe, Leonor. MD, Porto (Portugal) Med. Sch., 1983, PhD in Medicine (Neuroscis.), 1998. Cert. gen. practitioner, psychiatrist. Gen. practitioner Hosp. S. Joao, Porto, 1984-87; lectr. Porto Med. Sch., 1986-87, probationary asst., 1987-89; resident in psychiatry Hosp. S. Joao, 1987-91, hosp. asst., psychiat. dept., 1991-97; asst. prof. Porto Med. Sch., 1987-91, prof. med. psychology, 1998—. Served as officer, arty. Portuguese MIl., 1973-75. Mem. AAAS, Am. Psychosomatic Soc., N.Y. Acad. Scis., Portuguese Soc. Psychosomatic Medicine. Avocations: photography, computing/informatics. Home: Rua Aurelia de Sousa 19-1, 4000 099 Porto Portugal Office: Porto Med Sch, Al Prof Hernani Monteiro, 4200 319 Porto Portugal

VERKHIVKER, GENNADY M., chemist; b. Odessa, Ukraine, May 29, 1954; s. Michael A. and Frima (Zukerman) V.; m. Victoria A. Bykova, Oct. 6, 1961; 1 child, Alex G. MS in Chemistry and Math., Odessa State U., 1976; PhD in Phys. Chemistry, Inst. of Phys. Chemistry/, Acad. of Scis., Moscow, 1986. Rsch. scientist Inst. of Phys. Chemistry, Odessa, Ukraine, 1979-86, sr. rsch. scientist, 1986-88, group leader, 1988-90; postdoctoral rsch. fellow dept. chemistry U. Ill., Chgo., 1990-91, rsch. scientist, 1991-92; rsch. scientist Agourow Pharms., Inc., San Diego, Calif., 1993-95, sr. scientist, 1995-98; sr. scientist II Agourow Pharms., Inc., San Diego, 1998-99. Home: 13217 Kingsfield Ct San Diego CA 92130-1507 Office: Agouzon Pharms Awazhrz- 3301 N Torrey Pines Ct La Jolla CA 92037-1022

VERKHODANOV, OLEG VASIL'EVICH, astrophysicist; b. Novgorod, Russia, Mar. 17, 1965; s. Vasilij Fyodorovich and Lyudmila Konstantinovna (Telitsyna) V.; m. Natalia Viktorovna Smirnova, Apr. 15, 1989; 1 child, Vasilisa. MSc, Leningrad (Russia) State U., 1987; PhD, Spl. Astrophys. Observatory, Karachaj-Cherkessia, Russia, 1993. Jr. scientist Spl. Astrophys. Observatory, 1987-93, scientific rschr., 1993-95, sr. scientist, 1995—; chief, Astron. Scs. and Olympiads, Spl. Astrophys. Observatory, 1994—; vis. scientist MIT, Cambridge, Mass., 1995; active Internat. Astron. Union, 1997. Contbr. articles to profl. jours. Office: Spl Astrophys Observatory, Nizhnij Arkhys, 357147 Karachaj Cherkessia Russia

VERKHOVODOV, PETRO OLEXANDROVYCH, physicist, researcher; b. Rostov-on-Don, Russia, Nov. 3, 1936; s. Olexander Jackovych and Olena Ivanivna (Kolesnyk) V.; m. Daredzhan Shalvovna Kipshidze, Oct. 31, 1960 (div. Dec. 1964); children: Oxana, Hanna; m. Lidija Tarasivna Nemezhykova, Jan. 8, 1965; 1 child, Maxim. Physicist, Rostov-on-Don U., 1960; Cand. Scis., Irkutsk U., 1969; PhD, Ukrainian Acad. Scis., 1992. Chief dept. Inst. Non-Ferrous Metallurgy, Krasnoyarsk, Russia, 1960-72; sr. rschr. Inst. Elec. Welding, Kyiv, 1972-75, Inst. Material Scis. Problems, Kyiv, 1975-95, Kyiv Cons. Group, 1995—. Author: X-Ray spectrometric Analysis: Problems of Theory and Modes Calibration, 1984, X-Ray Spectrometric Analysis: Separated corrections for Physical Processes, 1992; contbr. articles to profl. jours.; patentee in field. Mem. N.Y. Acad. Scis., Internat. Radiation Phys. Soc. Avocations: folk art, classical music. Office: Kyiv Consulting Group, Box 51/3, 03142 Kyiv Ukraine

VERKRUIJSSE, PIETER JOZIAS, classicist, educator; b. Groede, The Netherlands, Jan. 27, 1943; s. Jannis Abraham Verkruijsse and Maria Herrebout; m. Johanna H.T.J. de Feyter, Mar. 15, 1968 (div. 1985); 1 child, Elisabeth Maria. PhD, U. Amsterdam, 1983. Tchr. Dutch lit. U. Amsterdam, 1968—. Editor (periodical) Neder-L, 1996—. Avocations: bibliography, palaeography, archivist. Home: 6 Weissenbruchlaan, NL 2421

Nieuwkoop The Netherlands Office: U Amsterdam, 134 Spuistraat, NL-1012 Amsterdam The Netherlands

VERLEGER, ROLF, psychophysiologist, neuropsychologist; b. Ravensburg, Germany, Dec. 17, 1951; s. Ernst and Helga (Drexler) V.; m. Anne Bangert, Dec. 19, 1983; children: Simon, Katharina. Diploma in Psychology, U. Konstanz, Germany, 1976; D Social Sci. in Psychology, U. Tuebingen, Germany, 1986; Habilitation, Med. U., Luebeck, Germany, 1994. Rsch. asst. Ctrl. Inst. Mental Health, Mannheim, Germany, 1977-85; rsch. asst. dept. psychology U. Tuebingen, 1985-86; sr. rschr. dept. neurology Med. U. Luebeck, Germany, 1988—, prof., 1998—. Contbr. articles to profl. jours. Mem. German Soc. of Psychophysiology (pres. 2000—). Jewish. Avocations: jazz pianist. Office: Med U Dept Neurology, Ratzeburger Allee 160, 23538 Lübeck Germany

VERLINDE, CLAUDE, artist; b. Paris, June 24, 1927; s. Antoine and Leylavergne Yvonne V.; m. Marie-Therese Langard, Nov. 25, 1957; 1 child, Gilles. One-man shows include Galerie R. Duncan, Paris, 1948, Sigmund Rothschild Gallery, N.Y.C., 1966, Calerie Morantin, Paris, 1968, 70, French Inst., Stockholm, 1974, Gothenburg Mus., Sweden, 1974, Orebro Mus., Sweden, 1974, Musee Galliera, Paris, 1976, Musee Reims, France, 1979, Galerie d'Art Place Beauvau, Paris, 1980, 84, 89, Japon, 1985, Zoute Art, Belgium, 1991, Orangerie Charlottenburg, Berlin, Germany, 1992, Musee Tour Carree, Sainte-Maxime, France, 1993, Galerie Michelle Boulet, Paris, 1994, 98, 2000, many others. Home: 12 Beaumarchais, 75011 Paris France

VERLOOP, NICO, education educator; b. Dordrecht, The Netherlands, Apr. 22, 1949; s. Mattheüs and Lena (Van Driel) V. MEd cum laude, Utrecht U., The Netherlands, 1977; PhD cum laude, Leiden U., The Netherlands, 1989. Asst. prof. Nijmegen U., The Netherlands, 1977-80; sr. rschr. CITO, Nat. Inst. for Ednl. Measurement, The Netherlands, 1980-91; prof. edn. Leiden U., 1991—, dir. grad. sch. edn., 1992-95; dean Iclon Grad. Sch. Edn., 1995—; bd. dirs. Nat. Inst. for Ednl. Measurement, The Netherlands, 1994—; mem. steering com. European Network Life-Long Learning in Tchr. Edn., 1996—; mem. mgmt. team Inter-univ. Ctr. for Ednl. Rsch ICO, 1996—; mem. steering com. Thematic Network on Tchr. Edn. in Europe, 1996—. Author, editor: Educational Theory, 1995; author/editor Studies in Ednl. Evaluation jour., 1994; mem. editl. bd. Studies in Ednl. Evaluation, 1981—, Tchg. and Tchr. Edn., 1993—; contbr. articles to profl. jours. Mem. European Assn. for Rsch. and Learning and Instrn. (co-chair divsn. 1995—), Dutch Ednl. Rsch. Assn. (gen. bd. 1991—, pres. 1996—), Am. Ednl. Rsch. Assn., Pedagogische Studiën (editor 1995-99), European Ednl. Rsch. Assn. (exec. com. 1996—), Internat. Coun. on Edn. for Tchg. Home: Roland Holststraat 140, 3511 MN Utrecht The Netherlands Office: Leiden Univ ICLON Grad Sch Edn, PO Box 9555, 2300 RB Leiden The Netherlands

VERMA, BABU LAL, law educator; b. Bharatpur, India, Mar. 4, 1944; s. Bhagirath Singh and Sohan (Devi) V.; m. Uma Verma. BA, U. Rajasthan, India, 1964; LLB, U. Rajasthan, 1966, LLM, 1968, PhD, 1981. Asst. prof. U. Rajasthan, India, 1968-86, assoc. prof., 1986-87, prof., 1987—; mem. syndicate U. Rajasthan, 1992-99; chmn. B.O.S. in Law, 1987—; dir. Enviorn. Law Cell, U.O.R., 1991—; principal, Law Coll. U. Rajasthan, 1992-95. Author: (books) Muslim Vidhi, Rajasthan Balak Adhiniyam, Indian Legal System. Pres. B.S.V. Samiti, Jaipur, 1990—. Mem. Indian Law Inst., Gujrat Consumer Protection Cen. Home: Jawahar Nagar, 302004 Jaipur India Office: U Rajasthan, Bapu Nagar, 302004 Jaipur India

VERMA, BABU LAL, biostatistics professional; b. Barabanki, India, July 4, 1949; s. Vidya Prasad and Maina Devi Verma; m. Sushila Verma, July 1, 1964; children: Prachi, Pradyumna. PhD in Stats., Bundelkhand U., Jhansi, India, 1982. Statistician-cum-lectr. MLB Med. Coll. and Hosp., Jhansi, 1974-85, asst. prof. med. stats., 1986-88, assoc. prof. med. stats., 1988—, co-investigator and incharge, WHO rsch. project, 1980-86. Co-editor: (proc.) Principles and Practice of Statistics in Medicine, 1985, (ref. book) Biostatistics, 1995, Sexual Medicine, 1996; co-editor Jour. Indian Assn. for Communicable Diseases, 1981-85; book rev. editor ISMS Bull., 1991, 99. Joint sec. U.P. State Med. Coll. Tchrs. Assn., Lucknow, 1990-99. WHO fellow, Sri Lanka and Thailand, 1991. Mem. Nat. Acad. Med. Scis., Indian Soc. Med. Stats (sec. 1983-88), Internat. Epidemiol. Assn. (regional councillor 1999—), Indian Sci. Congress Assn. Hindu. Avocations: international travel, scientific speaking, creative work. Home: Flat #5, Med Coll Campus 284128, Jhansi India Office: MLB Medical Coll, Dept Social/Prev Med, Jhansi 284 128, India

VERMA, CHAMAN LAL, building materials research institute official; b. Ludhiana, Punjab, India, Oct. 22, 1944; s. Sohan Lal and Sheela Rani Verma; m. Raji Malhotra, Sept. 28, 1968; children: Neeraj, Neeti. B Tech. in Chem. Engring., Indian Inst. Tech., Kanpur, India, 1967; M Tech. in Chem. Engring., Indian Inst. Tech., Bombay, 1969; PhD, U. Roorkee, India, 1986. Tech. tchr. trainee Govt. of India, Bombay, 1967-70; lectr. chem. engring. U. Roorkee, 1970-73; scientist C Ctrl. Bldg. Rsch. Inst., Roorkee, 1973-81, scientist E-I, 1981-87, scientist E-II, 1987-93, scientist F, dep. dir., 1993—, rsch. project leader, 1973-81, R & D project leader, 1981-87, 93, chmn. coms. on deputation and study leave and safety, 1991-93; presenter at profl. seminars and confs., 1969—; mem. standing com. on pollution abatement for thrust area project on low cost and alt. bldg. materials and components Coun. for Sci. and Indsl. Rsch., 1987-92; mem. com. on pollution control from lime kilns H.P. State Pollution Control Bd., Shimla, India, 1988-92; mem. steering com. on formulatoin emission stds. for lime kilns Ctrl. Pollution Control Bd., Delhi, India, 1990-92; mem. sectional com. on lime and lime products Bur. Indian Stds., New Delhi, 1992-94, chmn., 1994—; mem. Nat. Com. on Pollution Abatement in Aluminum Industries, 1993-94. Contbr. articles to sci. jours., including Chem. Processing and Engring., Chem. Concepts, Indian Concrete Jour., Chem. Era, Jour. Instn. Engrs. India, Indian Planner and Builder, Chem. Engring. World, Jour. Indian Bldg. Congress, Jour. Sci. Indsl. Rsch. Recipient numerous awards. Fellow Instn. Engrs. (India); mem. Indian Inst. Chem. Engrs., Materials Rsch. Soc. India, Loss Prevention Assn. India (life), Indian Bldgs. Congress, Indian Concrete Inst., Indian Soc. for Constrn. Materials and Structures (life), Indian Assn. Environ. Mgmt. Hindu. Home: A-13 CBRI Colony, PO Shanti Nagar, Roorkee 247 667, India Office: Ctrl Bldg Rsch Inst, Roorkee 247 677, India

VERMA, LALIT, ophthalmologist, consultant; b. New Delhi, Delhi, India, July 1, 1959; s. Om Parkash and Shanta (Katira) V.; m. Neeta Malik, Feb. 19, 1987; children: Nitin, Neha. MBBS, All India Inst. Med. Sci., New Delhi, 1982, MD, 1985. Med. diplomate (eye surgery). Rsch. officer All India Inst. Med. Sci., New Delhi, 1986, sr. resident, 1986-89, asst. prof., 1989-95, assoc. prof., 1995—. Mem. Nat. Acad. Med. Scis., All India Ophthalmol. Soc. (joint sec. 1999—, mem. scientific com. 1999—), Delhi Ophtalmol. Soc. (treas. 1995-97, sec. 1997-99). Hindu. Avocations: travel, long drives, reading, writing. Home: E-78 Ansari Nagar AIIMS, 110029 New Delhi India Office: Dr R P Ctr AIIMS, Ansari Nagar, 110029 New Delhi India

VERMA, MAHESH, dentistry educator, consultant; b. Nangaldam, Punjab, India, Aug. 25, 1957; s. L.R. Verma and Satya Wati Jagota Verma; m. Meera Singh, Apr. 20, 1988; 1 child, Minaal. B in Dental Surgery, Dental Wing Med. Coll., Trivandrum, India, 1980; M in Dental Surgery, Dental Coll. Trivandrum, 1984. Resident H.P. Med. Coll. & Snowdon Hosp., Shimla, India, 1981-82; sci. pool officer Coun. of Scientific and Indsl. Rsch., India, 1985; asst. prof. Dental Wing Maulama Azad Med. Coll., New Delhi, 1985-91, assoc. prof., 1991-95, prof., head dental sch., 1995—; vis. fellow Sch. Dental Medicine SUNY, Buffalo, 2000; cons., head dept. of dental Lok Nayak Hosp., New Delhi, 1985-95, cons. and head of dental, 1995—. Joint editor Jour. Indian Dental Assn., Delhi Br., 1987-89, Jour. Indian Prosthodontic Soc., 1991-93. Recipient Disting. Svcs. award Lok Nayak Hosp., 1999. Fellow Am. Coll. Dentists, Internat. Coll. Dentists (joint editor jour. 1998—), Pierre Fauchard Acad., Acad. Dentistry Internat. Avocations: travel, meeting people. Home: D-129 Anand Vihar, New Delhi 110092, India Office: Dental Wing, Maulana Azad Med Coll, New Delhi 110092, India

VERMA, OM PRAKASH, translator; b. Apr. 17, 1956; s. Shri Gulab Chand and Smt. Sarraswati Devi. MA, U. Allahabad, 1976, LLB, 1979; B.J., Banaras Hindu U., 1981, Dip Yoga, 1983; Dip. Advance Mgmt., BPC, Baroda, India, 1987, EKS, Germany, 1987; Patrakarita Visharad, HSS, Allahabad, 1989, Shiksha Visharad, 1990; Dip EPMA, MIER, Jammu, 1990; D.D.E., IGNOU, 1991, DCE, 1993, DHRM, 1994, MADE, 1995, DCH, 1995, CIG, 1997, DRD, 1996, PGDHE, 1998, DNHE, 1999, CTE, 1999, CES, 2000; CFN, Nalanda OU, 1992; DEMT, Annamalai, 1994; DPM, NIPM, Calcutta, 1996; Dip. Translation Studies, U. Hydrabad, 1996; Dip. U.N. and Internatl. Understanding, Inst. of United Nations Studies, New Delhi, 1988; Dip. in Tng. and Devel., Indian Soc. for Tng. and Devel., New Delhi, 1986. Sr. translator NML, SCIR, Jamshedpur, India; guide NIHRD, Madras, NILEM, Madras, TASMAc, Pune, India. Hon. animal welfare officer Am. Welfare Bd. India, Madras; pres. Bihar br. Yowan; pres. Bihar branch NINC, Bombay. Recipient Spl. Svc. prize Bihar Dalit Acad., others; Nat. Merit scholar; Ambedkar fellow. Mem. Indian Soc. for Tng. and Devel. (life), Indian Inst. Pub. Adminstrn. (life), Mgmt. Studies Promotion Inst. (life), Inst. Constl. and Parliamentary Studies (life), Indian Adult Edn. Assn. (life), Indian Soc. Health Adminstrs. (life), Indian Sci. Congress Assn. (life), All India Assn. for Ednl Rsch. (life), Translators Assn. India (life), All India Nature Cure Fedn. (life), Indian Med. Acad. (life), Nat. Soc. for Prevention of Blindness (life), Common Cause (life), Consuemr Edn. and Rsch. Soc. (life), Vivekanand Kendra (life), Ved Sansthan (life), others. Office: E-4/ NML, CSIR, Jamshedpur India 831 007

VERMA, PRAMOD KUMAR, geologist; b. Chaibasa, Bihar, India, Jan. 7, 1961; s. Krishna Ballabh and Pan Devi (Lal) Prasad; m. Neelima Das, Apr. 30, 1987; children: Priyali, Pragya. BS with honors, Ranchi (India) U., 1982, MS, 1985; MPhil, Vikram (India) U., 1986, PhD, 1991. Lectr. Vikram U., 1986-95, reader, 1996—. Editor: Medicinal Plants of Malwa Region, 1997. German Acad. Exch. Svc. fellow, Bonn, Germany, 1993, Indian Nat. Sci. Acad. fellow, New Delhi, 1997; recipient Young Scientist award Govt. M.P., Bhopal, India, 1990. Fellow Geological Soc. India; mem. Am. Geophys. Union (life), Assn. Geoscientists for Internat. Devel. (life), Internat. Assn. Hydrological Scis. Avocations: travel, social service. Home: F-2/34 Vikram Univ Campus, 456010 Ujjain India Office: Vikram Univ, Sch Studies in Geology, 456010 Ujjain India

VERMA, RAKESH MOHAN, computer science educator; b. Meerut, India. BEE with honors, Inst. Tech., Varanasi, India, 1984; MS in Computer Sci., SUNY, Stony Brook, 1985, PhD in Computer Sci., 1989. Asst. prof. U. Houston, 1989-95; scientific cons. Ctr. for Devel. of Telematics, New Delhi, India, 1991; scientific cons., vis. prof. INRIA Lorraine, Nancy, France, 1995, 96-97; assoc. prof. computer sci. U. Houston, 1995—; vis. prof. SUNY, Stony Brook, 1999;. Contbr. articles to profl. jours. Mem. program com. Rewriting Techniques and Applications Confs., U.K., 2000. Recipient Gold medal Inst. of Technology, Varanasi, 1984, Catacosinos fellowship SUNY, Stony Brook, 1988, Inria fellow France, 1995, 96-97; rsch. grantee NSF, 1990-2001. Mem. Assn. for Computing Machinery. Avocations: reading, travel. Office: Univ Houston/Computer Sci 4800 Calhoun Rd Houston TX 77204-0001

VERMA, RAM VILAS, geography educator, researcher; b. Bhatauli, Unnao, India; s. Lakshamana Prasad Verma and Ram Pyari; m. Sushila Verma, May 13, 1964; children: Vivek Kumar, Vibha, Alok Kumar. BA, Vikramajit Singh Sanatan Dharm Coll., Kanpur, India, 1957, MA in Geography, 1959; PhD, Agra (India) U., 1968. Lectr. Vikramajit Singh Sanatan Dharam Coll., Kanpur, India, 1960-72, sr. lectr., 1972-86, reader, 1986-94; dir. Inst. Regional Devel. Studies, Kanpur, India, 1994—, dir. (hon.), 1984—; mem. dist. environ. com. Directorate of Environ. Govt. of Uttar Pradesh, Lucknow, India. Author: Evolution of Settlement Pattern in Oudh, 1971, Bharat Ka Bhaugolik Vivechan, 1977, Bharat Ka Sankshipt Bhaugolik Vivechan, 1979; editor: (internat. rsch. jour.) Regional Symbiosis, 1993—; contbg. editor: India: A Regional Geography, 1976. Sec. Azadnagar Assn., Kanpur, 1985-86. Vis. scholar Academic Exch. Programme Cairo U. Grants Commn. Govt. India, 1989. Mem. Indian Coun. Geographers (life), Uttar Bharat Boogal Parishad, Region Sci. Assn. (life), Nat. Assn. Geographers (life). Office: Inst Regional Devel Studies, 3A/37 Azad Nagar, 208002 Kanpur Uttar Pradesh, India

VERMA, RAMTEJ JAYRAM, zoology educator, researcher; b. Faizabad, Uttar Pradesh, India, Jan. 1, 1959; s. Jayram Ramdeo and Laungaben Jayram V.; m. Bina Ramtej Verma, Mar. 16, 1975; children: Kamlesh R. Verma, Ramesh R. Verma. MSc, U. Baroda, India, 1979, PhD, 1983. Lectr. Bhavnagar (India) U., 1985-90, sr. lectr., 1990-93; reader Gujarat U., Ahmedabad, India, 1993—. Author numerous rsch. papers; contbr. articles to sci. jours. including Pavo, Indian Jour. of Exptl. Biology, Indian Jour. Med. Rsch., Indian Phytopathology, others; rschr. in field. Mem. NAS (Indian chpt., life), Soc. Toxicology (Indian chpt., life), Gujarat Sci. Acad. (Assoc.). Avocations: reading, writing articles, teaching, listening to music, gardening. Home: Readers Row Houses, Gujarat Univ Campus, Ahmedabad Gujarat 380009, India Office: Gujarat Univ Dept Zoology, Univ Sch Scis, Ahmedabad Gujarat 380 009, India

VERMA, SURJIT KUMAR, retired school system administrator; b. India, May 17, 1940; arrived in Canada 1966; s. Sohara Lal and Gian Devi V.; m. Raj Verma; 1 child, Soania. MEd, St. Francis Xavier U., N.S., 1975; postgrad., Dalhousie U., N.S., U. Ottawa, Ont., Can, 1979. Cert. tchr. Nova Scotia. Sci. dept. head Halifax County Bedford Dist. Sch. Bd., N.S., Canada, 1968-88, curriculum supr., 1988-94; ret., 1995; served on C.T.F. Project Overseas Can. Teams, W.I., Nigeria, 1976, 77; mem. provincial sci. task force, biology rev. com., elem. sci.; mem. Internat. Sci. Symposium, 1979; mem. selection panel PromoSci. Program. Natural Scis. and Engring. Rsch. Coun. of Can.; mem. exec. coun. N.S. Inst. Sci.; worksop presenter numerous sci. workshops. Contbr. to profl. jours. Chmn. First Metro Halifax Dartmouth Reg Sci. Fair, 1975; co-chmn. Canada Wide Sci Fair, 1984. Recipient Sci. Tchg. Achievement Recognition award U.S. Nat. Sci. Tchrs. Assn. and Am. Gas Assn., 1993, Profl. Devel. award N.S. Tchrs. Union, Tchg. Excellence in Sci., Tech. and Math. award Prime Min. Can., 1993, 94, Sci. on Display award NASCO, 1993-94, Outstanding Achievement in Sci. Edn. award Halifax County Sch. Bd., 1993, Surjit Verma award for tchg. excellence created in his honor Halifax County Bedrod Dist. Sch. Bd., 1994, Michael Smith award Industry Can., 1996; U. Ottawa fellow, 1979, Dalhousie U. grad. fellow, 1980, Math. Sci. Tech. Edn. fellow Royal Bank Queen's U., 1994; Dalhousie U. Rsch. Devel. grantee, 1979; N.S. Tchrs. Union scholar, 1979; Can./N.S. Tech. Devel. grantee, 1995. Mem. Nova Scotia Inst. Sci. (coun. mem.), Natural Sci. and Engring. Rsch. Coun. (mem. selection panel promosci. project). Avocations: jogging, yoga. Home: 49 Rosewood Ave, Timberlea, NS Canada B3T 1C6

VERMAAT, JOHN ARTHUR EMERSON, reporter; b. Arnhem, The Netherlands, Oct. 22, 1947; s. Jan George and Carolina Geertruida (Van Welie) V.; m. Ilse Catharina Goudriaan, Oct. 31, 1970 (div. 1990). Grad. in law, State U., Leyden, The Netherlands, 1978. Asst. Dutch Parliament, The Hague, The Netherlands, 1969-73; TV, radio reporter EOTV/Radio, Hilversum, The Netherlands, 1973—. Author: World Council of Churches and Politics, 1989, Reporting in Situations of War and Crisis, 1995 (in Dutch), In the Name of Allah...Islamic Fundamentalism, 1997 (in Dutch), The Crime Web: The Globalization of Crime, 2000 (in Dutch); contbg. author: The New Image Makers, 1988. Mem. Dutch Assn. Journalists, Netherlands Assn. Internat. Affairs, Netherlands Internat. Law Fedn. Mem. Netherlands Reformed Ch. Avocations: skiing, reading, writing, traveling. Office: PO Box 1944, 1200 BX Hilversum The Netherlands

VERMANI, LEKH RAJ, mathematics educator; b. Udoana, India, May 5, 1940; s. Ladha Ram and Sita Devi (Bhutani) V.; m. Raj Dua, May 9, 1968; children: Vandana, Shalini. BA, Govt. Coll., Rohtak, India, 1960; MA in Math., Kurukshetra (India) U., 1964, PhD in Math., 1970. Tutor in math. Kurukshetra U., 1964-65, asst. lectr., 1965-67, lectr., 1967-76, reader, 1976-86, prof. math., 1986-2000, chmn. dept., 1989-92; vis. prof. Seth Jai Parkash Mukarid Lal Inst. tech., Raddaur, India; vis. scientist, prof. Panjab U., Chandigarh, 1986-87, 95, Steklov Inst. Math., Moscow, 1990, Aichi U. Edn., Igaya-Cho, Kariya-shi, Japan, 1994. Author: Lectures in Cohomology of Groups, 1994, Elements of Algebraic Coding Theory, 1996; contbr. articles to profl. jours. Recipient Commonwealth fellowship Commonwealth Scholarship Commn., U. Exeter, Eng., 1972-74, Visitorship U. Man., Winnipeg, Can., 1979. Fellow Nat. Acad. Scis. India; mem. Indian Math. Soc., Am. Math. Soc. Hindu. Avocations: reading, long walks.

VERMASVUORI, JUHA KALEVI, religious studies educator; b. Helsinki, Finland, July 19, 1936; s. Jalo Johannes and Anna Kyllikki (Henelius) V.; m. Maire Kaarina Permanto, July 19, 1967; children: Terhi, Juhana, Sirpa, Mikko. M of Theology, U. Helsinki, 1964, D of Theology, 1980, lectr. religious edn., 1992. Min. Alppila Parish, Evangelic-Luth. Ch. of Finland, 1964-67; asst. prof. Theology Libr., U. Helsinki, 1967-71, asst. prof. dept. practical theology, 1971-98, prof. ordinarius religious edn., 1998—. Co-author: (with Kari E. Nurmi) The Learning Results (Knowledge & Attitudes) in Confirmation Education 1-3 I, 1982, II, 1984, III, 1992; author: Religious Education Studies in Open University, 1997, Experiences and Results of Studying Religious Education as Multiform, 1997. Mem. bd. Union Univ. Assts. and Rschrs., 1984-91, vice chmn., 1990-94, chief shop steward, 1986-96. Avocations: choirsinging, volleyball. E-mail: juha.vermasvuori@helsinki.fi. Office: U Helsinki Dept Prac Theol, Aleksanterinkatu 7, 00100 Helsinki Finland

VERMEEND, WILLEM A. F. G., government official, state secretary finance; b. Zuilen, The Netherlands, Dec. 21, 1948. PhD. Mem. bd. dirs. PvdA, mem. second chamber, 1984—, pres. second chamber com. for pub. finance; former min. finance Govt. of The Netherlands, The Hague, state sec. for fin.; prof. European taxation U. Maastricht; mem. adv. coun. of Mars-concern, Veghel, Bus. Creation Results, Rotterdam, A.S.N. Bank, The Hague, Kluwer Fin. Edits. Author numerous books; contbr. articles to profl. jours. Home: Samuel van Houtenplein 18, 2314 EE Leiden The Netherlands Office: Ministry of Finance, PO Box 20201, 2500 EE The Hague The Netherlands*

VERMEER, CEES, biochemist, educator; b. Lisse, Holland, The Netherlands, Dec. 14, 1946; s. Cornelis and Johanna Maria (Moolenaar) V.; m. Helene Knulst, Jan. 15, 1970. BSc, State U., Leiden, The Netherlands, 1969, PhD, 1973. Cert. biochemistry. Rsch. fellow Red Cross, Amsterdam, The Netherlands, 1973-74; staff mem. U. Maaastricht, The Netherlands, 1975-76, sr. scientist, 1976-84, divsn. leader, 1984—, dept. head, 1987-90, faculty bd. faculty medicine, 1991-93; cons. Roche, Basel, Switzerland, 1995—. Editl. advisor Biochem. Jour., London, 1990-96; contbr. articles to profl. jours.; patentee in field. Temporary advisor WHO, Geneva, 1994. Lt. Dutch Land Forces, 1973-74. Mem. Internat. Soc. for Thrombosis and Hemostasis. Office: U Maastricht Dept Biochem, PO Box 616, 6200 MD Maastricht The Netherlands

VERMEER, MARTIN, engineering educator; b. Hardinxveld, The Netherlands, Jan. 27, 1953; s. Cornelis Arie Vermeer and Adriana van der Giessen; m. Eeva Liisa Hietala, June 24, 1982. Diploma in Geodetic Engr., Delft U. Tech., 1981; PhD, Helsinki U., 1985. Rschr. Finnish Geodetic Inst., Helsinki, 1981-88, dept. head, 1992-2000; rschr. Nat. Survey & Cadastre, Copenhagen, 1989-92; docent Helsinki U. Tech., 1994—, prof., 2000—; vis. prof. Delft U. Tech., 1993. Author: (software) MGM -- Mass Point Geopotential Modelling, 1988-97; mem. editl. bd. Jour. of Geodesy, 1994—; book rev. editor, 1994-99. Chmn. IAG Subcomm. for the Geoid in Europe, 1991-99, IAG Inst. Gravity and Geoid comm., 1999—. Mem. Geophys. Soc. Finland (chmn. 1999), Soc. for Surveying Scis. in Finland (chmn. 1999). Avocations: Linux use and advocacy, astronomy. Office: Helsinki U Tech, Dept Surveying, PO Box 1200, FIN02015 Hut Finland

VERMEER, PHILIPPUS JACOBUS, healthcare company executive; b. Utrecht, The Netherlands, Jan. 6, 1951; s. Gerrit and Cornelia Maria (Kok) V.; m. Didwi Gerise de Haan, Mar. 24, 1974 (div. Aug. 1988); m. Ah Ryung Sunu, July 27, 1991; children: Nathalie Françoise Zjihi, Fayette Juanita Zjuyung. Engr., Koninklyke Hogere Zeevaartsch, Utrech, 1970; Degree in Mktg., Praktyk Inst., Amsterdam, 1974; Mktg. A degree, Nima, The Hague, The Netherlands, 1975, Mktg. B degree, 1977. Group product mgr. Johnson & Johnson Benelux, Amersfoort, The Netherlands, 1975-77; product dir. Johnson & Johnson Can., Montreal, Que., 1977-79; gen. mktg. and sales mgr. Johnson & Johnson Benelux, Amersfoort, 1979-81; gen. mgr. Johnson & Johnson Ireland, Dublin, 1981-83; mktg. dir. Johnson & Johnson Malaysia, Kuala Lumpur, 1983-84, mng. dir., 1984-88; mktg. and sales dir. Johnson & Johnson Australia, Sydney, 1988-90; mng. dir. Johnson & Johnson Singapore and Malaysia, 1990-91, Johnson & Johnson Pacific, Sydney, Australia, 1991-94; internat. v.p. Johnson & Johnson Internat., Sydney, 1994—. Home: 48A Bay St, Mosman NSW 2088, Australia Office: Johnson & Johnson Internat, Stephen Rd, Botany NSW 2019, Australia

VERMES, GEZA, religious studies educator; b. June 22, 1924; arrived in Eng., 1957, naturalized, 1962; s. Ernö and Terezia (Riesz) V.; m. Pamela Hobson, May 12, 1958 (dec. 1993); m. Margaret Unarska, 1996. Lic. Oriental philology and history, Louvain U., 1952, ThD, 1953; MA, Oxford U., 1965, DLitt, 1988; DD (hon.), Edinburgh U., 1989, Durham U., 1990; DLitt, Sheffield U., 1994. Rschr. Ctr. Nat. Recherche Scientifique, Paris, 1954-57; lectr. religious studies U. Newcastle, Tyne, Eng., 1957-64; sr. lectr. U. Newcastle, Tyne, 1964-65; reader Jewish studies Oxford U., 1965-89, prof. Jewish studies, 1989-91, prof. emeritus, 1991—; gov. Ctr. for Hebrew Studies, 1972-92, dir. publs., 1987-91; dir. Oxford Forum for Qumran Rsch., 1991—. Author: Scripture and Tradition in Judaism, 1961, The Dead Sea Scrolls in English, 1962, 3d edit., 1987, Jesus the Jew, 1973, Jesus and the world of Judaism, 1983, The Religion of Jesus the Jew, 1993, The complete Dead Sea Scrolls, 1998, Providential Accidents: An Autobiography, 1998, Discoveries in the Judaean Desert XXVI, 1998, An Introduction to the complete Dead Sea Scrolls, 1999, The Dead Sea Scrolls, 2000, The Changing Faces of Jesus, 2000; editor: Jour. Jewish Studies, 1971. Fellow Brit. Acad.; mem. Soc. for Old Testament Study, European Assn. for Jewish Studies (pres. 1981-84), Brit. Assn. for Jewish Studies (pres. 1975-88). Mem. Liberal Party. Avocation: studying wildlife. Home: West Wood Cottage, Foxcombe Ln, Boars Hill Oxford OX1 5DH, England

VERMES, LASZLO PETER, agronomist; b. Budapest, Mar. 20, 1936; s. Laszlo Zoltan and Laszlone Margit (Brezovszky) V.; m. Laszlone Zsuzsanna Metz, Mar. 5, 1959; children: Judit, Csaba. MSc in Farm Irrigation, U. Agrl. Scis., 1962, PhD, 1970; CSc, Hungarian Acad. Scis., 1975, DSc, 1996. Cons. Land Reclamation and Improvement Co., Debrecen, Hungary, 1959-60; supr. Ministry of Agrl., Budapest, 1960-61, head of sect., 1991-93; scientific cons. Rsch. Ctr. for Water Rsch. Devel., Budapest, 1961-82; asst. prof. U. Agrl. Scis., Gödöllö, Hungary, 1983-90; univ. prof., head of dept. U. of Horticulture and Food Industry, Budapest, 1993-99; univ. prof. Szent Istvan U., Budapest, 2000—; subnetwork liaison officer FAO European Cooperative Network on Animal Waste Utilization, Budapest, 1977-80; vice chmn. ECE/ FAO Working Party on Rels., Geneva, 1991-93. Editor, co-author: Land Application of Sewages and Sewage Sludges, 1980; author: Waste Management, Waste Utilization, 1993; contbr. articles to profl. jours. Mem. Hungarian Hydrological Soc. (Pro Aqua 1977), Hungarian Acad. Scis. (commn. of agrl. water mgmt. 1977—, commn. of microelements 1980—, sec. 1996—, Pro Re Rustica Promovenda 1987), Farmers Tng. Soc. Janos Nagyvathy, Hungarian Soc. of Agrl. Scis. (chmn. of sect. on agrl. water mgmt. 1986—, chmn. sect. on soil contamination 1994—). Avocations: concerts, opera performances, playing piano, travelling abroad, swimming. Office: Szent Istvan U, Villanyi ut 35-43, H-1118 Budapest Hungary

VERMILLION, RICHARD DICKENS, investment securities company executive; b. Milw., Aug. 25, 1920; s. Gifford Tanner and Gertrude (Dickens) V.; m. Marcia Doherty; children: Nancy Elder, Louise Monroe, Richard Dickens Jr., James D. BS in Econs., U. Va., 1942. In sales Ketcham & Noncard, adro., 1946-50; v.p., regional mgr. Smith Barney & Co., Milw., 1950-76; registered rep. Dean Witter, Naples, Fla., 1977-87; 1st v.p. Robert W. Baird & Co., Naples, 1987—. Lt. USN, 1942-46. Mem. NASD (vice chmn. 1974-77, gov.), Naples Yacht Club, Hole-in-the Wall Golf Club (Naples). Republican. Episcopalian. Avocation: golf. Home: 718 Springline Dr Naples FL 34102-5063 Office: Robert W Baird & Co 5811 Pelican Bay Blvd Naples FL 34108-2752

VERMILYA, DALE NELSON, accountant; b. Columbus, Ohio, June 15, 1959; s. Ray Nelson and Linda Jo (Way) V.; m. Ellen Kathryn Von Hagen, Nov. 3, 1984; children: Christopher Dale, Samara Lyn, Jenna Renée, Joseph Ray. BBA, U. Akron, 1981. CPA, Ky., Ohio, Mich. Sr. auditor Ashland Oil Inc., Ky., 1981-84; advanced auditor Owens-Corning Fiberglas corp., Toledo, 1984-87; sr. fin. analyst Monroe (Mich.) Auto Equipment Co., 1987-88, sr. cost analyst, 1988-89, mgr. accounting, 1989-90; plant controller Hartwell (Ga.) Facility, 1990-94, dir. fin., 1994-95; dir. investor rels. and bus.

planning Hayes Lemmerz Internat. Inc., Romulus, Mich., 1995-97; corp. contr., chief acctg. officer Hayes Lemmerz Internat., Inc., Northville, Mich., 1997—. Mem. AICPA, Inst. Mgmt. Accts., Ohio Soc. CPAs, Nat. Investor Rels. Inst., Christian and Missionary Alliance, Beta Alpha Psi, Beta Gamma Sigma. Republican. Home: 2332 Eversham Ct Toledo OH 43617-2230 Office: Hayes Lemmerz Internat Inc 15300 Centennal Dr Northville MI 48167-9629

VERMILYE, PETER HOAGLAND, banker; b. N.Y.C., Jan. 17, 1920; s. Herbert Noble and Elise Tace (Hillyer) V.; m. Lucy Shaw Mitchell, Oct. 14, 1950; children: Peter H., Dana R., Andrew R., Mary S. AB, Princeton U., 1940. V.p. pension investments J.P. Morgan & Co. and Morgan Guaranty Trust, 1940-64; ptnr. State St. Research & Mgmt., Boston, 1965-69; pres. Alliance Capital Mgmt., N.Y.C., 1970-77; sr. v.p., chief investment officer Citibank, N.Y.C., 1977-84; chmn. Baring Am. Asset Mgmt., Boston, 1984-89; sr. advisor Baring Asset Mgmt., 1990-95, Harbor Capital Mgmt., Boston, 1996—; chmn. emeritus Huntington Theatre, 1989-96; bd. dirs. Engelhard Hanovia, Breadstreet Holdings Corp. Trustee Boston U., 1970—. Clubs: Brook, Somerset, Myopia. Home: 157 School St Manchester MA 01944-1236 also: 107 Chestnut St Boston MA 02108-1038 Office: Harbor Capital Mgmt 125 High St Fl 26 Boston MA 02110-2704

VERMILYEA, STANLEY GEORGE, prosthodontist, educator; b. Portland, Oreg., Jan. 29, 1946; s. Stanley Edmonds and Hattie Willamina (Bittner) V.; m. Barbara Jean Koester Ternus, June 23, 1967 (div. Dec. 1979); 1 child, Sheryl Eileen; m. Ileana Esther Villamarzo, July 3, 1980; 1 child, Michael Enrique. BS, Portland State Coll., 1970; DMD, U. Oreg., Portland, 1971; MS in Dental Materials, U. Mich., 1976; cert. in prosthodontics, Walter Reed Army Med. Ctr., Washington, 1985. Diplomate Am. Bd. Prosthodontics. Commd. 2d lt. U.S. Army, 1971, advanced through grades to col., 1985; dentist U.S. Army, various locations, 1971-76; rschr. dental materials U.S. Army Inst. Dental Rsch., Washington, 1976-80, chief dental materials rsch., 1980-83; prosthodontist U.S. Army, various locations, 1983-89; co-dir. residency in prosthodontics U.S. Army, Washington, 1989-92, ret., 1992; asst. prof. Coll. Dentistry Ohio State U., Columbus, 1992-95, chmn. primary care, 1996—. Contbr. chpt. to book and articles to profl. jours. Fellow Am. Coll. Prosthodontists, Acad. Gen. Dentistry; mem. Internat. Assn. Dental Rsch. Achievements include research on the corrosion characteristics of dental alloys as well as the compositions and microstructural features of dental materials. Office: Ohio State U Coll Dentistry 305 W 12th Ave Columbus OH 43210-1267

VERMUND, STEN HALVOR, infectious disease epidemiology educator; b. Mpls., Jan. 31, 1954; s. Halvor and Karen (Bergfjord) V.; m. Pilar Vargas, Apr. 8, 1978; children: Julian, Gabriel. BA, Stanford U., 1974; MD, Albert Einstein Coll. Medicine, 1977; MSc, London Sch. Hygiene and Tropical Medicine, 1981; PhD, Columbia U., 1990. Diplomate Am. Bd. Pediatrics, Am. Bd. Preventive Medicine. Intern Presbyn. Hosp., N.Y.C., 1977-78, resident in pediatrics, 1978-80; asst. prof. Columbia U., N.Y.C., 1982-85, Albert Einstein Coll. Medicine, Bronx, N.Y., 1985-88; chief epidemiology br. div. AIDS Nat. Inst. Allergy and Infectious Diseases, Bethesda, Md., 1988-92; chief vaccine trials and epidemiology br. div. AIDS Nat. Inst. Allergy and Infectious Diseases, Bethesda, 1992-94; prof. epidemiology, internat. health, medicine & pediatrics U. Ala., Birmingham, 1994—, chmn. dept. epidemiology, 1994-98, dir. divsn. geographic medicine, 1994—, sr. scientist Comprehensive Cancer Ctr., 1994—, assoc. dir. Ctr. for AIDS Rsch., 1994—, pres. Gorgas Meml. Inst., 1995—, dir. John J. Sparkman Ctr. for Internat. Pub. Health Edn., 1999—; cons. N.Y.C. Dept. Environ. Protection, 1986-88, Med. Bd. Nat. Coun. Chs., N.Y.C., 1984-85, Ctrs. for Disease Control, Atlanta, 1989—, FDA, Rockville, Md., 1991-94, NIH, 1994—; mem. Inst. Medicine Panel on Perinatal Transmission of HIV, 1997-98, mem. Inst. Medicine Panel on HIV Prevention, 1999—. Contbg. author: AIDS Epidemiology, 1993, Until the Cure: Caregiving for Women with HIV, 1993, Parasitic Protozoa, 2d edit., vol. 6, 1993, HIV in Women, 1995, AIDS, 4th edit., 1997; co-editor, contbg. author: Preventing HIV Infection in Developing Countries, 1999; contbr. articles to profl. jours. Mem. adv. bd. health rsch. tng. program N.Y.C. Dept. Health, 1986-88; mem. sci. adv. bd. World AIDS Found., 1994-95. Recipient Curnan award Babies Hosp., N.Y.C., 1980, Lalcaca medal U. London, 1981, Commrs. Spl. Svc. award N.Y.C. Dept. Health, 1988, Merit award USPHS, Bethesda, 1989, Cert. of Appreciation, U.S. Surgeon Gen., 1993, Superior Svc. award USPHS, 1994; med. rsch. grantee Ctrs. for Disease Control, Nat. Cancer Inst., Nat. Inst. Allergy Infectious Diseases, Nat. Inst. Child Health and Devel., others, 1986-88, 94—. Fellow Am. Acad. Pediatrics (sec., founding mem. regional com. on homeless children 1986-88), Am. Coll. Epidemiology, Soc. Adolescent Medicine, Royal Soc. Tropical Medicine and Hygiene, Infectious Disease Soc. Am.; mem. APHA, Internat. AIDS Soc., Internat. Epidemiologic Assn., Am. Soc. Tropical Medicine and Hygiene. Avocations: hiking, tennis, violin, table tennis. Office: U Ala Birmingham 845 19th St S # Bbrb203 Birmingham AL 35294-0001

VERNANT, JEAN-PIERRE, philosophy educator; b. Provins, France, Jan. 4, 1914; s. Jean and Anna (Heilbron) V.; m. Lida Nahimovitch, Nov. 30, 1939 (dec. 1991); 1 child, Claude. Tchg. cert. in Philosophy, Sorbonne, 1937; PhD (hon.), U. Chgo., 1979, U. Bristol, 1987, U. Brno, 1997, U. Naples, 1999, U. Oxford, 1999. Tchr. philosophy Lycée de Toulouse, France, 1940-44; instr. Lycée Jacques Decour, Paris, 1946-48, from rsch. attaché, chargé of rsch., 1948-58; dir. studies Sch. Higher Studies, Paris, 1958-74; prof. comparative study ancient religions Coll. de France, Paris, 1974-84, hon. prof., 1984—. Author: Les Origines de la pensée greque, 1962, Mythe et pensée chez les grecs, 1965, (with Pierre Vidal-Naquet) Mythe et tragédie en Grèce ancienne, 1972, Mythe et société en Grèce ancienne, 1974, (with Marcel Detienne) Les Ruses de l'intelligence: La Metis des grecsi Flammarion, 1974, La Cuisine du sacrifice en pays grec, 1979, Religion, histoires, raisons, 1979, (with Gherado Gnoli) La Mort, les morts dans les societes i anciennes, 1982, La Mort dans les yeux, 1986, (with Vidal-Naquet) Mythe et tragédie deux, 1986, (with Charles Malamoud) Corps des dieux, 1986, (with Vidal-Naquet) Oedipe et ses mythes, 1988, (with Vidal-Naquet) Travail et esclavage en Grèce ancienne, 1988, L'Individu, la mort, l'amour, 1989, Mythe et religion en Grèce ancienne, 1990, Figures, idoles, masques, 1990, Mortals and Immortals, 1991, Entre mythe et politique, 1996, Dans l'oeil du miroir, 1997; editor: Problèmes de guerre en Grèce ancienne, 1968; contbr. Divination et rationalité, 1974. Head dept. Armée Secrète, lt. col., 1942-45. Decorated Croix de Guerre, Croix de la Liberation, commdr. Legion of Honor (France); recipient Gold medal Recherche Scientifique, 1984, Premio di Storia, U. San Marino, 1991. Fellow Brit. Acad. (corr.); mem. Royal Acad. Belgium (assoc.), Am. Acad. Arts and Scis. (fgn. hon., Humanistic Studies award 1994). Home: 112 Grande Rue, 92310 Sèvres France Office: Coll de France Dept Ancient Religions, 11 Pl Marcelin Berthelot, 75005 Paris Cedex 05, France

VERNENGO, MARCELO JORGE, pharmaceutical educator; b. Buenos Aires, Argentina, June 11, 1930; s. Roberto Esteban Vernengo and Leiza Villa Monte; m. Margarita Caimari, Jan. 10, 1964; children: Martin, Matias. Diploma in Chemistry, U. Buenos Aires, Buenos Aires, 1953, ChD, 1955; PhD in Organic Chemistry, U. Cambridge (Eng.), 1961. Rsch. chemist Squibb Labs., Buenos Aires, 1954-58; assoc. prof. chemistry U. Buenos Aires, 1961-67; dir. Nat. Inst. Pharmacology, Buenos Aires, 1967-73; policies advisor Pan Am. Health Orgn., Sao Paulo, Rio de Janeiro, 1974-90; sci. advisor U.S. Pharm., Buenos Aires, 1990-99; prof. chemistry U. Buenos Aires, 1990-94; prof. U. Belgrano, Buenos Aires, 1994—, dean Sch. Scis., 1996—. Contbr. articles to profl. jours. NIH rsch. grantee, Washington, 1961-68. Fellow Am. Chem. Soc., Royal Soc. Chemistry, Argentine Chem. Assn. (pres. 1994-2000). Roman Catholic. Home: Rep Arabe Siria 2711 5to Piso, 1425 Buenos Aires Argentina

VERNET-MAURY, EVELYNE, neurophysiologist, researcher; b. Lyon, France, June 23, 1936; d. Treillefort Maury; m. Françoise Vernet; children: Emmanuel, Jean Luc. MS, U. Lyon I, 1960, DEA, 1962. Asst. U. Lyon I, 1960-68, maitre asst., 1968-85, maitre de conf., 1985-93, maitre de conf. hors classe, 1993—; mem. com. CNRS, Paris, 1983-86; mem. CCPPRB, Lyon, 1992-95. Contbr. articles to profl. jours., chpts. to books. Co-pres. biol. com. U. Lyon I, 1990-95. Decorated Palmes Académiques, 1996. Mem. Internat. Soc. Automatic Nervous Sys., European Chem. Rsch. Orgn., IBRO, Neurosci. Soc. Avocations: cinema, theatre, travel, walking. Home: 72 Rue des Aqueducs, F69005 Lyon France Office: Univ Lyon I/INSA Lyon, Batiment 401, F69621 Villeurbanne France

VERNETTI, FRANCISCO DE JESUS, international consultant; b. Pelotas, Brazil, Feb. 6, 1925; s. Francisco de Paula and Ondina (Torino) V.; m. Maria Helena Moreira Amarante, July 30, 1952; children: Cristina Helena, Francisco Jr., Lourdes Helena, Isabel Helena, Luiz Roberto. 1st and 2d degrees, Coll. Munic. Pelotense, Pelotas, 1945; agronomist engr., Fed. U. Pelotas, 1949; MS, Purdue U., 1963; PhD, U. São Paulo, Brazil, 1974. Cert. plant genetics and breeding agronomist. Rsch. agronomist Ministry of Agr. and Brazilian Enterprise Agrl. Rsch./Agr. Rshc, Ctr. for Temperate Climate, Pelotas, 1951-98; dir. crops rsch. divsn. Ministry of Agr., Brasilia, 1970-71; assoc. prof. Fed. U. Pelotas, 1973-79; dir. Brazilian Enterprise Agrl. Rsch./Soybean Nat. Rsch. Ctr., Londrina, Brazil, 1975; rsch. dir. Brazilian Enterprise Agrl. Rsch./Lowland Agrl. Rsch. Ctr., Pelotas, 1990-92; assessor to dean Fed. U. Pelotas, 1998-99; cons. Interam. Inst. Agrl. Cooperation, Paraguay, 1974, Uruguay, 1975, Protecno, Mozambique, 1978-84, UN Food and Agr. Orgn. and Interam. Inst. Agrl. Cooperation, Nicaragua, 1985-87, UN Food and Agr. Orgn. and World Bank, Bolivia, 1988, FAO, Cameroon and Ghana, 1990, UN Food and Agr. Orgn., Cuba, 1992-93, UN Food and Agr. Orgn., Inst. Nacional de Investigaciones Forrestales, Agricolas y Pecuarias, and Interam. Inst. Agrl. Cooperation, Mexico City, 1998—. Author, editor: (2-vol. book) Soja: Plt., Climate, Pests, Diseases, Weeds, vol. I, 1983, Soja: Genetics and Breeding, vol. II, 1983; author: A Cultura da Soja no Paraguay, 1974; contbr. articles to profl. publs. and procs. Named Agronomist of Yr., Assn. Engring. Agronomists of Pelotas, 1986, Soc. of Agronomy of R.G. do Sul state; recipient Mérito Rural, Assn. Rural, 1990, Sci. and Rsch. award Com. Orgn. R.P.S., 1997. Mem. Soc. Agron. do R.G. do Sul, Rotary Club Pelotas North. Avocations: music, soccer, traveling, movies, reading. Home and Office: Rua Andrade Neves 3129/201, 96020080 Pelotas Brazil

VERNICOS, GEORGE ALEXANDER, business executive, economist; b. Athens, Greece, Feb. 11, 1950; s. Alexander Nicolaos and Marina (Kanaki) V.; m. Dimitra Dimitrios Vezyrouli, Sept. 30, 1974 (div. April 1980); 1 child, Marina; m. Maria Aristovoulos Petzetaki, Dec. 1989. Grad., U. Athens, U. London. Chmn. Vernicos Yachts, Athens, 1976—; mng. dir. Hellenic Register of Shipping, Athens, 1992—; pres. Attica Enterprises SA, Athens, 1992-94. Contbr. articles to profl. publs. Sec. gen. Greek-European Movement of Youth, 1969-72, Hellenic Dem. Youth, 1975-77; leader Anti-Dictator Student Movement, 1971-74; city councillor City of Athens, 1982-87; pres. G. and A. Chatziconstas Orphanage Inst., 1986-89; v.p. Greenpeace, 1991—. Mem. Hellenic Profl. Yacht Owners Assn. (dir. 1990—), Assn. Greek Tourist Enterprises (dir. 1991—), Hellenic Tourist Orgn. (dir. 1996-99), Hellenic Chamber of Chipping (dir. 1984—). Avocations: travel, sailing, scuba diving, water skiing, mountain skiing. Office: Vernicos Yachts, 11 Poseidonos Ave, 17455 Alimos Athens, Greece

VERNIKOV, ARKADY, magnetics company executive, consultant, educator; b. Odessa, Ukraine, Feb. 27, 1948; arrived in The Netherlands, 1991; s. Jakov and Maria (Fishman) V.; m. Irina Passek, Aug. 23, 1974; 1 child, Alexei. MS in Engring. with honors, Tech. U. Odessa, 1970; MS in Internat. Trade, Tech. U. Moscow, 1986; postdoctorate, Tech. U. Odessa, 1988. Chief designer Inst. Magnetics, Odessa, 1975-80, tech. mgr., 1980-91; chief expert Ctrl. Patent Office, Moscow, 1985-91; prof. indsl. engring. Inst. Advanced Edn., Odessa, 1989-91; tech. mgr. Walker-Hagou, Bladel, The Netherlands, 1991—; cons. magnetics Med. U. Odessa, 1981-91, Agrl. U. Odessa, 1981-91. Author: Electromagnetic Plates, 1976, Magnetization and Demagnetization Systems, 1979, Magnetic and Electromagnetic Fixtures in Metal Working, 1984, Magnetic Equipment, 1986, Magnetic and Electromagnetic Equipment for Machinery, Basics on Magnets and Electromagnets: Application in Industry, 1993, Magnetic Equipment Marketing: A Winning Strategy, 1995; contbr. over 100 articles, stds. and reports to profl. jours. and publs.; inventor and patentee in field (50 inventions). Recipient Gold medal State Technol. Exhbn., Moscow, 1983, Silver medal, 1988. Mem. IEEE Magnetics Soc. Avocations: travel, popular science. Home: H Heyermanslaan 9, 5531 TB Bladel The Netherlands Office: Walker-Hagou BV, Industrieweg /9 POB 35, 5530 AA Bladel The Netherlands

VERNON, CLARE CHRISTINE, oncologist, consultant; b. Geelong, Melbourne, Australia, Oct. 23, 1951; arrived in Eng., 1961; d. Stephen and Mary (Dewhirst) V.; m. George Evans, July 17, 1976 (div. July 1990). MB, BChir, Cantab, Cambridge, 1976, MA, 1979. Sr. house officer Nat. Health Svcs., Whittington Hosp., London, 1977-78, Nat. Health Svcs., Sr. Barts Hosp., London, 1978-79; registrar Nat. Health Svcs., Royal Free Hosp., London, 1979-81, Nat. Health Svcs., Mt. Vernon Hosp., Middlesex, Eng., 1981-82; sr. registrar oncology Nat. Health Svcs., London, 1982-86, cons. oncology, 1992—; cons. MRC (med. rsch. counc.), London, 1986-92; dir. Teenage Cancer Unit, Hammersmith Hosp., 1994-97. Editor: Principles and Practice of Thermo Radiotherapy, 1996, Hyperthermic Clinical Practice, 1997; contbr. articles to profl. jours. Sec. 1951 Club, Eng., 1987-97. Fellow Royal Coll. Radiologists (bd. mem. 1994-97, coll. tutor 1994—, Varian scholar 1990), ESHO (mem. clin. com. 1990—, mem. edit. bd. 1991—, pres. 1993-96). Conservative. Roman Catholic. Home: 18 Brookfield Ave, Ealing London W5 1LA, England Office: Hammersmith Hosp Clin Oncol, Du Cane Rd, London W12 OHS, England

VERNON, DORIS SCHALLER, retired writer; b. Petoskey, Mich., Mar. 7, 1915; d. Harve and Edna (Covey) Frederickson; m. William Albert Schaller, Oct. 18, 1938; children: Kirk, Karen, Brent. Student, Cleary Coll., 1936-37, North Cen. Mich. Coll., 1960-61, 66-69. Sec. Mr. Beebe, Dean Freshman Coll., Petoskey, Mich., 1934-35, Dr. Dean C. Burns, Burns Clinic, Petoskey, 1937-38; with Probate and Juvenile Ct. Register, Petoskey, 1956-60; sec. bd. No. Mich. Rev., Inc., Mich., 1960-93; ret., 1996. Contbr. travel stories to profl. publs. Cub scout leader, Petoskey; treas. Camp Daggett Bd.; pres. Bus. and Profl. Women's Club, Petoskey, 1974-75; state bd. Don't Waste Mich., Riga and Lansing, 1989—, bd. dirs. No. bd., 1988—; civic gardening chair Petoskey Area Garden Club, sec., 1986; program chair Keenagers, First Christian Ch.; choir mem. First Christian Ch.; dir. Friendship Chorus for Care Ctrs. Singing Monthly Programs, Emmet County. Recipient cert. of commendation Guardian of the Earth, No. Mich., 1997. Avocations: square dancing, quilting. Home: 1028 Hoffman St Petoskey MI 49770-3213

VERNON, LAWRENCE GORDON, librarian; b. Belize City, Belize, May 19, 1937; s. Angus Vernon and Anna Drucilla (Elliott) Vernon Gabourel; m. Crystal Yvonne Gibson, July 18, 1959; children: Marlon, Dylan, Karen. Assoc., Brit. Library Assn. Corr. Course, London, 1959-63. Library asst. Nat. Library Svc., Belize, 1956-58, jr. asst. librarian, 1958-66, asst. librarian, 1966-76, sr. librarian, 1976-78, chief librarian, 1978-92; asst. librarian Univ. Coll. Belize, 1992, libr. dir., 1993-96, assoc. libr., 1996—. Co-author: Among my Souvenirs, 1966. Sec. bd. govs. Excelsior Community High Sch., Belize City, Belize, 1979; vice-chmn. Coun. of Vol. Social Svcs., 1986, rec. sec., 1989; chmn. Belize Scholarship Com., 1983. Mem. Belize Library Assn. (treas. 1978). Methodist.

VERNON, STEPHEN ANDREW, ophthalmologist; b. Manchester, Lancashire, Eng., Feb. 10, 1955; s. Alan and Phyllis Mary (Owen) V.; m. Alison Elizabeth Walton, Sept. 1, 1985; children: Olivia, Simon. M.B.Ch.B., U. Bristol, Eng., 1978; DM, U. Nottingham, Eng., 1994. House physician Profl. Med. Unit, Bristol, 1978-79; house surgeon Frenchay Hosp., Bristol, 1979; demonstrator in anatomy U. Bristol, 1979-80; resident in ophthalmology Bristol Eye Hosp., 1980-83; sr. registrar in ophthalmology Oxford (Eng.) Eye Hosp., 1983-86; cons. ophthalmologist Queen's Med. Ctr., Nottingham, 1986—. Author: Differential Diagnosis in Ophthalmology, 1999; lead author: National Guidelines Royal College Guidelines Ocular Hypertension and Glaucoma, 1997; co-editor: Key Advances in the Treatment of Glaucoma, 1999; contbr. articles to profl. jours. Recipient John William Clarke award Brit. Med. Assn., 1991; Glaucoma Soc. grantee, 1989. Fellow Royal Coll. Surgeons (Eng.), Royal Coll. Ophthalmologists (regional advisor 1994—, examiner 1991—), U.K. and Eire Eye Study Group, European Glaucoma Soc., U.K. and Eire Glaucoma Soc., Midland (Eng.) Ophthalmol. Soc. (pres. 2000—). Avocations: golf, music, opera. Office: University Hosp, Queen's Med Ctr, Nottingham NG7 2UM, England

VERNON, WESTON, III (WES VERNON), broadcaster, writer, actor; b. N.Y.C., Aug. 23, 1931; s. Weston, Jr. and Adelaide (Neilson) V.; m. Alida Steinvoort, Oct. 5, 1951; children: Rosanne, Weston IV, Diane, John Randall. Student, Utah State U., 1949-50, Brigham Young U., 1953-54. Early broadcasting career on staff of radio stas., in Utah and Wyo., 1950-54; news and announcer KBMY, Billings, Mont., 1954-63; news dir., polit. specialist KSL Radio-TV, Salt Lake City, Utah, 1963-68; bur. chief Bonneville Internat. Corp., Washington, 1968-72; corr. CBS Radio Stas. News Svc. CBS Radio, Washington, 1972-97; host CBS Crosstalk, 1975-97. Columnist The High Green, The Timetable; contbr. to Crossrail, NationalCorridors.org, CNSNews.com, NewsMax.com. Bd. dirs. Winding-Orchard Citizens Assn., Wheaton-Glenmont, Md., 1974-77, 86—, pres., 1975-76. Served with AUS, 1951-52. Recipient Journalism awards Mont. A.P. Press Stas., 1960, Journalism awards Utah Bar Assn., 1965, Journalism awards Utah Broadcasters Assn., 1965-66. Mem. SAG, AFTRA (exec. bd. Balt.-Wash. local 1997—), Am. Legion (comdr. Yellowstone Post 4 1962-63), Chesapeake Rlwy. Assn. (pres. 1992-94, bd. dirs.). Office: 1605 Billman Ln Silver Spring MD 20902-1417

VERÖ, JÓZSEF, geophysicist; b. Sopron, Hungary, July 23, 1933; s. József Sóndor and Erzsébet (Artner) V.; m. Mária Hetényi, Feb. 3, 1958; 1 child, Mária. Diploma in geophysics, Tech. U., 1956; Dr.techn., Miskolc U., 1964; DrSc, Hungary Acad. of Scis., 1974. Geophysicist Uranium Mines, Pécs, Hungary, 1956; rschr. Geophys. Rsch. Lab., Sopron, Hungary, 1957-63; sr. scientist Geodetic and Geophys. Rsch. Inst., Sopron, 1973-95, rsch. prof., 1996—, prof., 1991—. Editor-in-chief Acta Geodaelica et Geophysica Hung.; contbr. articles to profl. jours. Mem. Assn. of Tech. Socs. (v.p. 1985—), Rotary Club (pres. 1993-94), Hungarian Acad. Sci. (corr. mem.), Hungary Assn. Geophysics (scientific com. 1990—, Eötvös medal 1990), Hungarian Assn. Tech. Socs. (steering com. 1985-90, MTESz-prize 1990). Roman Catholic. Avocations: stamp collection. Home: Deák tér 21-23, H-9400 Sopron Hungary Office: Geodetic/Geophys Rsch Inst, POB 9, H-9401 Sopron Hungary

VEROLLA, STEVEN MICHAEL, French language educator; b. Flushing, N.Y., Dec. 21, 1957; s. Steve Charles Verolla and Anna Theresa DePietto. BA in French magna cum laude, Hofstra U., 1980; MA in French, Stony Brook U., 1984; MPhil, ABD, CUNY Grad. Ctr., 1998. Tchg. cert. Rassias Methods Workshop. Lectr. French Molloy Coll., Rockville Centere, N.Y., 1985-87; instr. French Nassau C.C., Garden City, N.Y., 1987-90; dean, acad. coord. Am. Hi-Tech. Bus. Sch., N.Y.C., 1988; dir. lang. lab., lectr. French John Jay Coll., N.Y.C., 1988-96; instr. French Hofstra U., Hempstead, N.Y., 1983-87, 96—; lectr. French Hunter Coll., N.Y.C., 1991—, City Coll., N.Y.C., 1998—; rep. exec. com. French Doctoral Program, N.Y.C., 1996-2000; moderator confs.; spkr. in field. Contbr. poetry to anthologies. Nice scholar Hofstra U., 1978. Mem. MLA, Assn. for Devel. of Fgn. Langs., Am. Assn. Tchrs. of French, Alliance Française Atelier, Camus Studies Assn. (sponsor), Phi Beta Kappa, Pi Delta Phi, Phi Sigma Iota. Avocations: singing, theater, tennis.

VERONA, ANTE FEDOR MARIA, management executive; b. Zagreb, Croatia, May 19, 1941; arrived in Italy, 1987; s. Albert and Mira Verona; m. Vesna Veselic; 1 child, Graziella Maria. Degree, U. Naval Engring./Ship Bldg., Zagreb; diploma in naval engring. Sales mgr. Schöller-Bleckmann, Vienna, 1972-75, V.E.W., Vienna, 1975-80, V.E.W. Branch Office of Africa, Nairobi, 1980-84; mng. dir. Boehler Steel Africa, Johannesburg, 1984-87, Boehler Acciai Italia, Milan, 1987-95; CEO, v.p. Böhler-Uddeholm Italia, Milan, 1995—. Companion Inst. of Sales and Mktg. Mgmt.; mem. Assn. Tech. Maritime et Aeronautique, Assn. Metall. Italiana, Muthaiga Country Club (Nairobi, Kenya), Johannesburg Country Club, Margara Golf Club (Alessadria, Italy). Avocations: golf, sailing, ancient lit. Office: Böhler-Uddeholm Italia, via Palizzi 90, 20157 Milan Italy

VERONELLI, JUAN CARLOS, physician, consultant; b. Buenos Aires, Aug. 16, 1933; s. Carlos Alberto and Alcira (Retamal Olmos) V.; m. Magali Correch, mar. 21, 1957; children: Magali, Maria Gracia, Paula Andrea, Carlos Alberto. MD, U. Buenos Aires, 1956, MPH, 1966; Cert. of Polit. Studies, Paris U., 1972; Hon. diploma, U. Chile, 1983. Chief health programming Ministry of Pub. Health, Buenos Aires, 1970-71; short term cons. Pan Am. Health Orgn.-WHO, Chile, Mex., 1974-84; regional advisor planning PAHO-WHO, Washington, 1984-85; sec. pub. and environ. health City of Buenos Aires, 1986-88; inter-country regional cons. PAHO/WHO, Bolivia, Honduras, Nicaragua, Peru, Uruguay, 1988-92; rep. PAHO/WHO, Montevideo, Uruguay, 1992—; prof. U. Buenos Aires, Mex., Chile, Veracruz, Lima, 1961-83; prof. ad honoreum UROU, U. del Salvador ARG. Author: Anatomy of the Nervous System and Hygiene, 1965, Medicine, Government and Society, 1975, Health in Latin America, 1983, The Health of the Uruguayans, 1994 (1st prize Nat. Lit. Award 1994). Advisor pub. health Radical Party Argentina, 1969-75. Recipient Eduardo Wilde award Sch. Medicine, Argentina, 1975. Mem. Mex. Acad. Surgery. Home: # 1709, Luis A de Herrera 1042, 11300 Montevideo Uruguay

VERPLAETSE, ALFONS REMI EMIEL, bank administrator; b. Zulte, Oost-Vlaanderen, Belgium, Feb. 19, 1930; s. Leon and Alida (Baert) V.; married, July 9, 1954; children: Patrick, Sibylle, Stefan, Bruno, Sabien. Licencié en sciences commerciales et consulaires, Université Catholique de Louvain, Belgium. With Nat. Bank of Belgium, 1953-81, dir., then dep. gov., 1988; gov. Nat. Bank of Belgium, Brussels, 1989-99; cabinet prime min., 1981-88; hon. gov., v.p. The Superior Fin. Coun./Bank for Internat. Settlements, Basle, Switzerland, 1999—, adminstr., 1999-03. Fax: 00 322 221 32.43. Home: Schaveyslaan 25, 1650 Beerse Brabant, Belgium

VERPLANCKE, JAN M. A., semiconductor company executive, nuclear physicist; b. Brugge, Belgium, Jan. 30, 1953; s. August and Ivonne (Declerq) V.; m. Annie A. V. Goossens, Oct. 11, 1980; children: Steven, Katrien. Lic. in physics, Cath. U. Louvain, Belgium, 1976, DSc, 1981. Rsch. asst. Cath. U. Louvain, 1976-81; mgr. applied sys. for Europe, Canberra Industries, U.S.A., 1991-95; mgr. R & D, Canberra Semicondr., Olen, Belgium, 1983-86, mgr. S & M., 1986-91, mng. dir., 1995—. Contbr. over 25 articles to sci. jours. With Belgian Army, 1981-82. Mem. Belgian Phys. Soc., French Phys. Soc., European Phys. Soc., Belgian Nuclear Soc. Office: Canberra Semicondr NV, Lammerdries 25, B-2250 Olen Belgium

VERRANDO, PATRICK, researcher in biochemistry; b. Nice, France, Dec. 19, 1953; s. Maurice and Angèle (Di Natale) V. DEUG, U. Nice, France, 1975, MSc, 1978, PhD in Biochemistry, 1981. Fellow L'Oreal Co., Sophia Antipolis, France, 1981-82, Faculty of Medicine, Nice, 1982-88; rschr. INSERM, Nice, 1988-93, Marseille, France, 1993—; cons. DIPTA, marseille, 1997—; fellow in dermatology Stanford (Calif.) U., 1990-91; cons. in cutaneous biology, 2000—. With French Army, 1975-76. Mem. Soc. for Rsch. in Dermatology (sec. 1994-98), European Soc. for Pigment Cell Rsch., N.Y. Acad. Sci., ESDR Europa. Avocations: hiking, bicycling, swimming. Office: LIMP, 46 Blvd de la Gaye, 13009 Marseille France

VERRILL, CHARLES OWEN, JR., lawyer; b. Biddeford, Maine, Sept. 30, 1937; s. Charles Owen and Elizabeth (Handy) V.; m. Mary Ann Blanchard, Aug. 13, 1960 (dec.); children: Martha Anne, Edward Blanchard, Ethan Christopher, Elizabeth Handy, Matthew Lawton, Peter Goldthwait; m. Diana Baber, Dec. 11, 1993. AB, Tufts U., 1959; LLB, Duke U., 1962. Bar: D.C. 1962. Assoc. Weaver & Glassie, 1962-64; assoc. Barco, Cook, Patton & Blow, 1964-66, ptnr., 1967; ptnr. Patton, Boggs & Blow, 1967-84, Wiley, Rein & Fielding, Washington, 1984—; adj. prof. internat. trade law Georgetown U. Law Ctr., Washington, 1978—, Charles Fahy Disting. adj. prof., 1993, Internat. Trade Law, Duke U. Law Sch., 1998—; conf. chmn. The Future of Internat. Steel Industry, Bellagio, Italy, 1984, U.S. Agenda for Uruguay Round, Airlie House, Warrenton, Va., 1986, Polish Joint Venture Law, Cracow, Poland, 1987, Internat. Steel Industry II, Bellagio, 1987, Bulgaria and the GATT, Washington, 1977; chair, spkr. Protection of Intellectual Property from Theft and Piracy Abroad Southwestern Legal Found. Fgn. Investment Symposium, 1995, chair, panel on NAFTA 2 1/2 Years Later, 1996. Local dir. Tufts U. Ann. Fund, 1965-69; mem. Duke Law Alumni Coun., 1972-75; trustee Internat. Law Inst., 1981—, chmn. bd. trustees, 1983-87; trustee Bulgarian Am. Friendship Soc., 1992—. Christ Ch., Dark Harbor, Maine; apptd. to roster of dispute settlement panelists World Trade Orgn., 1995, 97; chmn. adv. bd. Inst. for Attitudinal Studies, 1997—; mem. adv. com. rules U.S. Ct. Internat. Trade, 1998—; mem. adv. com. D.C. Cable Television, 1999—; mem. bd. visitors Duke U. Law Sch., 2000—; bd. visitors Duke U. Law Sch., 2000—. Mem. ABA, Internat. Bar Assn., D.C.

Bar Assn., Order of Coif, Theta Delta Chi, Phi Delta Phi, Met. Club (Washington), Chevy Chase Club (Md.), Tarratine Club (Dark Harbor, Maine). Home: 3000 Q St NW Washington DC 20007-3080 Office: 1776 K St NW Washington DC 20006-2304

VERRILL, JOHN HOWARD, museum director; b. Biddeford, Maine, June 17, 1947; s. Charles Owen and Elizabeth Martha (Handy) V.; m. Carol Christine Cory, Sept. 8, 1967; 1 child, Nathan Lawrence. BA, Campbell U., 1969. Tchr. St. Mary's County Schs., Leonardtown, Md., 1969-73; sales mgr. Kable News Co., N.Y.C., 1973-79; contract adminstr. Fischbach and Moore, L.K. Comstock, Lanham, Md., 1979-83; agrl. entrepreneur Jubilee Farm, Hebron, Md., 1983-87; mus. mgr. NASA, Wallops Island, Va., 1985; exec. dir. Purnell Mus., Snow Hill, Md., 1986-93, Ea Shore of Va. Hist. Soc., Onancock, Va., 1993—; faculty mem. Seminar for Hist. Adminstrn. at Colonial Williamsburg, 1999-2000. Editor: (book) Trustee, Board Member Handbook, 1995. Pres. Wicomico County Fair, Salisbury, Md., 1986, S.E. Shore Travel Coun., Salisbury, 1988, Lions Club, Hebron, Md., 1991; active Historical Adminstrn. 1999-00. Recipient Gov.'s citation, Maryland Gov. Schaeffer, 1994. Mem. Am. Assn. Mus., S. Ea. Mus. Conf. (mentor 1994)), Va. Assn. Mus. (mentor 1997), Am. Assn. State and Local History, Small Mus. Assn. (chmn. 1990, bd. dirs. 1997), Rotary Club Melfa, Va. (pres. 1995). Episcopalian. Avocations: home restoration, gardening, boating, travel. Office: Ea Shore Va Hist Soc PO Box 193 Onancock VA 23417-0193

VERSACE, DONATELLA, fashion designer; b. Reggio di Calabria, Italy, 1955; d. Antonio and Francesca V.; m. Paul Beck; children: Allegra, Daniel. Degree in lit., U. Florence, Italy. With Gianni Versace Group, 1978-97; creative dir. Gianni Versace Group, N.Y.C., 1997—. Office: care Keeble Cavaco and Duka Inc 450 W 15th St Ste 604 New York NY 10011-7082*

VERSCHOOR, JOHN, IV, physician assistant; b. Phoenix, Mar. 19, 1949; s. John Verschoor III and Dorothy (Killman) Hibbard; m. Nancy Lorel Welsh, Jan. 24, 1970; children: Bianca Dawn, Jared Moroni, Renee Ann, Benjamin Thayer. AS, Ariz. Western Coll., Yuma, 1972; Assoc. Med. Sci., Emory U., 1975; MD, Spartan Health Sci. U., St. Lucia, West Cast, 1985. Lic. nurse, Ariz., Ga., Tex., physician asst., Ariz. Orderly Yuma Regional Med. Ctr., 1967-68, emergency rm. nurse, 1970-72; commd. U.S. Army, 1972, advanced through grades to maj., 1990; physician asst. S.W. Med., Yuma, 1975-80; comdr. 12th Spl. Force Group, Albuquerque, 1980-85; exec. officer 996th Med. Co., Glendale, Ariz., 1985-88; bn. comdr. indsl. facility Fitzsimmons Army Hosp., 1988-92; physician asst. Deseret Diagnostic Ctr., Mesa, Ariz., 1990—; med. svc. officer CIA, Langley, Va., 1988—; exec. officer Tripler Army Med. Ctr., HI, 1992—; Lectr. U. Utah, Salt Lake City, 1990-94; bd. dirs. Lazerus Group, Inc., Las Vegas, 1989—. V.p. Clnica de Mormona, Guadalajara, Mexico, 1981. Mem. Wilderness Med. Soc., Am. Acad. Physician Assts. Republican. LDS Ch. Avocations: orienteering, primitive camping. Office: Deseret Diagnostic Ctr 215 S Power Rd Ste 106 Mesa AZ 85206-5236

VERSCHOORE, MICHÈLE RACHEL, medical products company executive, researcher; b. Tebessa, Algeria, May 16, 1953; d. Edouard David and Simone Bensakkoun; m. Verschoore, July 21, 1978 (dec. May 1984); 1 child, Oliver. MD, Nice (France) U., 1982, degree in dermatology, 1986, degree in clin. pharmacology, 1987. Clin. pharmacologist Internat. Ctr. Dermatol. Rsch., Sophia Antipolis, France, 1982-83, clin. rsch. mgr., 1983-85; rsch. and devel. coord. Galderma Rsch. and Devel., Paris, 1986-94, corp. mktg. mgr., 1994-99; internat. sci. rels. mgr. Rsch. Ctr. L'Oréal, Paris, 1999—; instr. Sch. Pharmacy, Marseille, France, 1985—. Avocations: golf, sailing, literature, music, theater. Home: 12 rue Chauveau, 92 200 Neuilly/ Seine France Office: L'Oreal DGRD Ctr C Zviak, 90 Av Roguet, 92583 Clichy France

VERSCHUEREN, KAREL, environmental engineer; b. Antwerp, Belgium, Feb. 21, 1944; s. Alphons and Germaine (Smets) V.; m. Renee-Marie Hansen, Feb. 24, 1968; children: Tim, Katia, Yves. Degree in chem. engring., Cath. U. Leuven, 1967. Environ. engr. Esso Refinery, Antwerp, Belgium, 1967-74; environ. coord. Fed. Chem. Ind. Belgium, Brussels, 1974-75, Concawe, The Hague, The Netherlands, 1975-81; sr. engr. Heidemy Advies Bur., Arnhem, The Netherlands, 1981-87; dir. IMd-Micon, 's-Hertogenbosch, The Netherlands, 1987-95, VEC Environ. Cons., 's-Hertogenbosch, The Netherlands, 1996—. Author: Air Pollution in cities, 1973, Handbook of Environmental Data on Organic Chemicals, 1977, 2d edit., 1983, 3d edit., 1995, 4th edit., 2000, Material Environmental Data Sheets, 1995. Achievements include patents on clean technology to degrade organic pollutants in soil, technology to clean steel drums using vacuum technology, a clean technology to cool fodder pellets using vacuum technology. Home: Oude Baan 36, 5244 JB Rosmalen The Netherlands

VERSCHUUR, HENDRIK PIETER, otolaryngologist; b. Eindhoven, The Netherlands, Mar. 16, 1961; s. Hendrik Pieter and Denyse Madeleine Jeanne (Basse) V.; m. Sandra Joan Van Loon Verschuur, Aug. 13, 1994; children: Eva Nadine, Charles Hendrik. MD, U. Groningen, The Netherlands, 1986; PhD, U. Utrecht, The Netherlands, 1994. Med. resident U. Paris XIII, 1986-89, U. Utrecht, The Netherlands, 1989-94; otolaryngologist Netherlands Cancer Inst., Amsterdam, 1994-95; head and neck fellow U. Toronto, 1995-96; otolaryngologist Westeinde Hosp., The Hague, 1996—, U. Hosp., Leiden, The Netherlands, 1997—; pres. ENT-Residents Soc., The Netherlands, 1990-93; v.p. LVAG, Utrecht, The Netherlands, 1991-93. Author: Protein Phosphorylation in Head and Neck Cancer, 1994; contbr. articles to profl. jours. Praeses Student Soc. Mutuafides, Groningen, The Netherlands, 1980-81; nestor De Griffe, Groningen, The Netherlands, 1982-97. Mem. Dutch ENT Soc., French ENT Soc. Office: Westeinde Hosp, Lynbaan 32, 2501 CK The Hague The Netherlands

VERSEPUT, JOHANNES PIET, retired oil company executive; b. Zonnemaire, The Netherlands, Aug. 2, 1924; s. Jacob Johannes and Maria Jansje (Geluk) V.; m. Maatje Willemina Stevense Verseput, June 28, 1930; children: Jacob Johannes, Jan Steven, Hubert Marines. MS, Tech. U., Delft, The Netherlands, 1951. Tech. mgr. Shell Curacao, 1952-63; head of refinery maintenance dept. Shell Internat., The Hague, The Netherlands, 1963-65; constrn. mgr. of refinery ext. Shell Singapore, 1965-67; head tech. dept. Shell Rsch., 1967-70; mfg. advisor for Far East, Shell Internat. Petroleum Co., 1970-82; owner, mng. dir. Deltabron Netherlands, Zonnemaire, 1982-93; ret., 1982; bd. mem., bd. pres. Van der Straaten B.V., Netherlands, 1976-94, 1985-94. Author of software progrms for medical profession, 1982-94; contbr. articles to profl. jours. Mem. AAAS, Royal Inst. Engrs. (v.p. The Hague 1976-82), Probus Club Schouwen Duiveland. Avocations: sailing, hunting, software. Home: Zuidweg 1, 4316AA Zonnemaire The Netherlands

VERSHBOW, ALEXANDER R., diplomat; m. Lisa Vershbow; two children. BA in Russian and East European Studies, Yale Coll., 1974; MS in Internat. Rels., Columbia U., 1976. Various fgn. svc. positions, 1977—; dir. Office of Soviet Union Affairs U.S. Dept. of State, 1988-91; prin. dep. asst. Sec. of State for European and Can. Affairs, 1993-94; spl. asst. to pres. and sr. dir. European Affairs Nat. Security Coun., 1995-97; U.S. amb. NATO and permanent rep. to North Atlantic Coun., 1998—; mem. Pres.'s delegation for NATO's 50th ann. Summit, Washington, 1999; involved in devel. of U.S. and NATO policy on Kosovo, others. Contbr. articles to profl. jours. Recipient Anatoly Sharansky Freedom award Union of Couns. of Soviet Jews, 1990, 1st ann. Joseph J. Kruzel award, Sec. of Def. William Cohen, 1997. Office: NATO Hdqtrs, Blvd Leopold 3, Brussels 1110, Belgium

VERSHININ, VLADIMIR LEONIDOVICH, ecologist, researcher; b. Sverdlovsk, Ural, USSR, July 15, 1957; s. Leonid Grigorievich and Larisa Alexandrovna (Ogibenina) V.; m. Irina Jurevna Ustinova, Dec. 10, 1982; 1 child, Vladimir Vladimirovich. Student, Ural State U., 1974-79; postgrad., Inst. Plant and Animal Ecology, Ekaterinburg, 1979-82. Biol. diplomate. Rschr. Inst. Plant and Animal Ecology, Ekaterinburg, USSR, 1982-86, head rsch. group, 1986-91; sr. rsch. assoc. Inst. Plant and Animal Ecology, Ekaterinburg, Russia, 1992-97, head Lab. Ecol. Monitoring, 1998—; declining amphibian populations task force World Conservation Union Species Survival Commn. Recipient Silver medal Exhbn. Achievements Commonwealth. Avocations: rock music, miniature sculpture. Home: A Valeka St 17-6, 620077 Ekaterinburg Ural, Russia Office: Inst Plant/Animal Ecology, 8 Marta St 202, 620144 Ekaterinburg Ural, Russia

VERSHUBSKY, GALINA GRIGORIEVNA, laboratory administrator, researcher; b. Moscow, Apr. 6, 1957; d. Grigory Vladimirovich and Inga Anatolievna Vershubsky; m. Andrei Igorevich Kozlov, Apr. 3, 1987. Degree in Engring., Moscow Inst. Oil Industry, 1979. Engr., rschr. State Rsch. Inst. Drilling Engring., Moscow, 1979-87; tchr. physics and computer sci. Sch., Tjumen, Russia, 1987-88; rschr. Tjumen Med. Inst., 1988-92; tech. dir. ArctAn-C Innovative Lab., Moscow, 1992—. Co-author: The Kola Saami: The Results of Medical-Anthropological Investigations, 1997, Medical Anthropology of the Native Inhabitants of the North of Russia, 1999. Mem. European Anthropol. Assn. E-mail: ggver@mail.ru. Home and Office: ArctAn-C Innovative Lab, Rajnis Blvd 7-27, 123363 Moscow Russia

VERSTAPPEN, HARRIE, photographer, audio-visual director; b. Curaçao, Netherlands Antilles, Dec. 12, 1940; m. Willy Hoekstra, 1970; 1 child, Natasha W. BS, Canisius Coll., Nymegen, The Netherlands, 1958; postgrad., U. Nymegen, 1958-61. Staff mem. Imag N.V., The Hague, The Netherlands, 1963-64, Cibaf N.V., The Hague, The Netherlands, 1964-66; dir. Vistafilm, The Hague, The Netherlands, 1964—, Fotomatiko N.V., Curaçao, Netherlands Antilles, 1987—. Still photographer (TV documentary) Eight Miles High, 1969; sound engr. Overal Zijn Indianen, 1970, Dennis Potter, Ileana Melita, 1970, Kaprisho Antiano, 1988, Rhythms and Caresses, 1989, You Can't Walk Home, 1989, Muhé Grandi, 1989, Cantiko Caribe, 1990; dir., prodr. Edgar Palm En Otrabanda, 1992, (feature film) Drop Out, 1969, Blue Movie, 1971, VD, 1972, Frank & Eva, 1972, Dakota, 1973, Alicia, 1973, My Nights, 1974, Mens Erger Je Niet, 1975, Pastorale 1943, 1977, Grijpstra & De Gier, 1979, Het Verboden Bacchanaal, 1982, Zwarte Ruiter, 1984; sound engr. (TV show) The Cats, 1971, The Shephards, 1971, (TV series) Poets, 1970; still photographer Historia Di Korsow, 1985; lights engr. Pentagram, 1986; sound engr. Antilliaans Verhaal, 1987; still photographer (film short) Kapsalon, 1971, Straf, 1973; cinematographer (documentary film) Ship-To-Ship, 1972, Antiyas, Triangulo Pa Futuro, 1980, Mosaiko Kultural, 1981, (filmograph) Cosmic Comics, 1973, (TV commercial) Anesco, 1981, Comwest, 1982, Curaçao Candle Co., 1982; prodr.: Del Curazao que se fué, 1996, (CD-ROM) The Werbata Maps-Curaçao, 1998, (CD-ROM) The Werbata Maps-II Dutch West Indies, 1999; contbr. photographs and articles to numerous publs. Curaçao del. Stichting ter bevordering van contacten met Zuid Amerika en het Caraïbisch gebied, The Netherlands, 1985; founding bd. mem. Corpus Mysticum, Curaçao, 1995. Sgt. Air Recon, 1961-63, The Netherlands and France. Recipient hon. mention Hollywood Erotic Film & Video Festival, 1984. Mem. Smithsonian Instn. (assoc.), Com. for Sci. Investigation of Claims of Paranormal (assoc.), Corpus Mysticum (sec. 1995-96). Home/Office: Plantage Bai Klaas, Curaçao Netherlands Antilles

VER STEEG, DONNA LORRAINE FRANK, nurse, sociologist, educator; b. Minot, N.D., Sept. 23, 1929; d. John Jonas and Pearl H. (Denlinger) Frank; m. Richard W. Ver Steeg, Nov. 22, 1950; children: Juliana, Anne, Richard B. BSN, Stanford, 1951; MSN, U. Calif., San Francisco, 1967; MA in Sociology, UCLA, 1969, PhD in Sociology, 1973. Clin. instr. U. N.D. Sch. Nursing, 1952-63; USPHS nurse rsch. fellow UCLA, 1969-72; spl. cons., adv. com. on physicians' assts. and nurse practitioner progs. Calif. State Bd. Med. Examiners, 1972-73; asst. prof. UCLA Sch. Nursing, 1973-79, assoc. prof., 1979-94, asst. dean, 1979-81, chmn. primary ambulatory care, 1976-87, assoc. dean, 1983-86, prof. emeritus, chair primary care, 1994-96, prof. emeritus, 1996—; co-prin. investigator PRIMEX Project, Family Nurse Practitioners, UCLA Ext., 1974-76; assoc. cons. Calif. Postsecondary Edn. Commn., 1975-76; spl. cons. Calif. Dept. Consumer Affairs, 1978; accredited visitor Western Assn. Schs. and Colls., 1985; mem. Calif. State Legis. Health Policy Forum, 1980-81; mem. nurse practitioner adv. com. Calif. Bd. RNs, 1995-97; mem. Edn. Industry Interface, Info. Devel. Mktg. Sub Coms., 1995-99; archivist Calif. Strategic Planning Com. Nursing/Colleagues in Caring Project, 1995—. Contbr. chpts. to profl. books and articles to profl. jours. Recipient Leadership award Calif. Area Health Edn. Ctr. Sys., 1989, Commendation award Calif. State Assembly, 1994; named Outstanding Faculty Mem., UCLA Sch. Nursing, 1982. Fellow Am. Acad. Nursing; mem. AAAS, AAUW, ANA (pres. elect Calif. 1977-79, pres. Calif. 1979-81), ANA C (interim chair Calif. 1995-96), Nat. League Nursing, Calif. League Nursing, N.Am. Nursing Diagnosis Assn., Am. Assn. History Nursing, Stanford Nurses Club, Sigma Theta Tau (Alpha Eta chpt. Leadership award Gamma Tau chpt. 1994), Sigma Xi. Home: 708 Swarthmore Ave Pacific Palisades CA 90272-4353 Office: UCLA Sch Nursing Box 956917 Los Angeles CA 90095-6917

VERSTEEGH, NANNO, chemical company executive; b. Batavia, Indonesia, June 22, 1940; s. Ferdinand and Wilhelmina (Berg) V.; m. Gerta Ooijevaar Versteegh, Dec. 29, 1966; children: Okke S., Kara H. HBS-B, Lyceum, Alkmaar, The Netherlands, 1960; degree chem. analytical engring., Coll. Analytical Chem., Arnhem, Netherlands, 1966; degree in propaedeuse econ., U. Rotterdam, Netherlands, 1968; MS in Mgmt., Boston U., Brussels, 1988. Chem. rsch. engr. AKZO-Nobel, Arnhem, Netherlands, 1962-67; mktg. specialist GE Plastics, Bergenopzoom, Netherlands, 1967-74; sales mgr. Harcros, Roermond, The Netherlands, 1974-80; mgr. sales and mktg. Morton Internat., Brussels, Belgium, 1980—. Contbr. articles to profl. jours. Chmn. Liberal Party VVD, Roerstreek, 1992-2000. Avocation: golf. E-mail: nverstee@morton.com. Home: Boterbloemdreef 6, NL6075DK Herkenbosch The Netherlands Office: Morton Internat Heiveldekens 7, Industriepark Blauwe Steen, B 2550 Kontich Belgium

VERSTRAETE, MARC, hematologist, educator; b. Brugge, Belgium, Apr. 1, 1925; s. Louis and Jeanne (Coppin) V.; m. Bernadette Moyersoen, July 12, 1955; children: Anneli, Benedicte, Luc, Frances, Beatrijs. MD with great honors, U. Leuven, Belgium, 1951, PhD, 1955; doctorate (hon.), U. Cordora, Argentina, 1983, U. Bologna, Italy, 1988, U. Bordeaux, France, 1989, U. Edinburgh, Scotland, U. London, 1996. Lectr. U. Leuven, 1957-61, asst. prof., 1961-63, assoc. prof., 1963-68, full prof., 1968—; rsch. fellow U. Oxford, U.K., 1955, Cornell U., N.Y.C., 1956. Author numerous books including Thrombosis, 1980, Bleeding Disorders, 1982, Cardiovascular Thrombotic disorders, 1992, 2d edit., 1998; contbr. articles to profl. jours. Col. Belgium Army res. Decorated enobled baron, 1996. Fellow ACP, Am. Coll. Cardiology (hon.), Royal Coll. Medicine Edinburgh and London (hon.); mem. Internat. Soc. on Thrombosis and Hemostosis (pres. 1986-88), Internat. Soc. Hematology, European Soc. Cardiology. Home: Minderbroedersstraat 29, B-3000 Leuven Belgium Office: U Leuven Ctr Molecular & Vascular Rsch, Herestraat 49, B-3000 Leuven Belgium

VERSTRINGHE, MARC EMILE SIDONIE, restauranteur, consultant; b. Bruges, Belgium, Dec. 18, 1934; came to Eng., 1957; s. Honore and Suzanne (Scherrens) V.; m. Carole Anita Finnimore, Nov. 4, 1967; children: Simon Marc, James Dominic. Diploma Ecole Moyenne, St. Bernardus Inst., Knokke, Belgium, 1951; Advanced Mgmt. Program, Swansea U., Wales, 1972. Apprentice Norfolk Hotel, Knokke, 1951-54; maitre d'hotel Lygon Arms, Broadway, Eng., 1957-59; mng. dir. Sutcliffe Catering Group, London, 1960-75; founder, chmn. Catering & Allied Svcs. Internat., London and Amsterdam, 1975-99; dir. Quality Catering Ptnrs., Zurich, Eurocater; chmn. Digby Trout; mem. adv. bd. Centre for Internat. Bus. and Mgmt.-The Judge Inst., Cambridge U. Chmn. trustees and mgmt. com. Advanced Mgmt. Programme Internat., Oxford, Eng. Decorated chevalier Confrerie des Chevaliers du Tastevin, France, 1978; recipient Catey award, 1989, Blue Riband award Cost Sector Catering, 1997; named commandeur of the Confreric, 1999. Fellow Royal Soc. Arts, Inst. Dirs. London, Hotel Catering and Instnl. Mgmt. Assn. (award for personal achievement 1999), European Catering Assn. (hon. pres., bd. dirs.); mem. Soc. for Foodservice Mgmt. USA, Foodservice Cons. Soc. Internat. (Spl. Distinction award 1992), Acad. Food and Wine (hon. fellow), Ampic Club. Office: Ctrl House, Balfour Rd, Hounslow TW3 1HY, England

VERTES, ALAIN ANDRE GUY, microbiologist; b. Saint-Maur-Les-Fosses, Val-De-Marne, France, May 22, 1963; s. Robert Emile and Germaine Louise (Galaret) V. BS in Engring., U Tech. of Compiegne, France, 1987; MS, U. Ill., 1989; PhD, U. Lille Flandres Artois, France, 1991. Rsch. and tchng. asst. U. Ill., Urbana-Champaign, 1987-89; rsch. engr. Inst. Pasteur, Paris, 1989-91; researcher Mitsubishi Chem. Co., Tsukuba, Japan, 1991-94; prin. rsch. scientist, leader procaryotic molecular biology group Battelle Meml. Inst., Columbus, Ohio, 1995-98; rsch. and bus. devel. advisor Eli Lilly and Co., Strasbourg, France, 1998—; rschr. sequencing by hybridization, Ministry of Internat. Trade and Industry, CO2 Fixation Project, Rsch. Inst. of Innovative Tech. for the Earth, Kyoto, Japan, 1993-94. Holder U.S. and Japanese patents; contbr. articles to profl. jours. Recipient Lavoisier fellowship, French Fgn. Office, Paris, 1988. Mem. N.Y. Acad. Scis., Am. Soc. Microbiology, Inst. of Food Technologists, The Biochem. Soc., Gamma Sigma Delta. Avocations: chess tournaments (mem. Internat. Corrs. Chess Fedn.). E-mail: avertes@freenet.columbus.oh.us or vertes alain@lilly.com. Home: 15 rue de l'Argonne, 67000 Strasbourg France Office: Lilly France BP 10, 2 Rue du Colonel Lilly, F-67642 Fegersheim Cedex France

VÉRTESY, GÁBOR, physicist, researcher; b. Budapest, Hungary, Mar. 25, 1951; s. Miklós and Ilona (Kocsis) V.; m. Zofia Potarska, July 24, 1976; children: Ágnes, Mónika. MS in Physics, Eotvos U., Budapest, Hungary, 1974; PhD in Physics, Hungarian Acad. Sci., Budapest, Hungary, 1995. Phys. Diploma. Rsch. fellow Hungarian Optical Works, Budapest, 1974-79, group leader, 1979-86; sr. scientist Ctrl. Rsch. Inst. Physics, Budapest, 1986-87, dep. head, 1987-92; lab. head Rsch. Inst. Materials Sci., Budapest, 1992—; Presenter in field. Contbr. over 50 articles to scientific jours. Avocations: tourism, swimming. Home: Szittya u 5, H-1118 Budapest Hungary Office: Rsch Inst Materials Sci, Konkoly Thege ut 29-33, H-1121 Budapest Hungary

VERTIY, ALEXEY, educator; b. Uman, Kiev, Ukraine, Oct. 11, 1947; s. Alexey Georgiy and Elena Tikhon (Bagbiy) V.; m. Vera Georgiy Sinitzina, June 15, 1974; 1 child. MS, Inst. Radioelec. Phys.-Tech., Kharkov, Ukraine, 1970, PhD, 1974; DSc, Kharkov State U., 1987. Rsch. Inst. Radiophysics and Electronics, Kharkov, 1970-77, sr. rschr., 1978-86, leading rschr., 1987-93, head dept., 1994—, head sci. coun., 1988-97, mem. editl. bd., 1996—; prof., dir. Turkish-Ukrainian Joint Rsch. Lab.; mem. coun. nondestructive testing Russian Acad. Sci., Moscow, 1988—; mem. editl. bd. Infrared and Millimeter Waves, N.Y., 1993—. Co-author: Polarization of Nuclear Targets by Millimeter Waves, Diffraction Radiation Generators; contbr. articles to profl. jours.; over 20 patents in field. Rep. Ministry Ukraine for Sci. and Intellectual Property, Kiev, 1999—. Mem. Nat. Acad. Scis. Turkey (Ukranian rep. 1999—). Christian Orthodox. Avocations: tennis, alpine skiing, music. Home: PO Box 21, Tubitak Lojman 25/5, 41470 Gebze Kocaeli, Turkey Office: Tobitak-MRC, PO Box 21, 41470 Gebze Kocaeli, Turkey

VERVARCKE, JAN MARIA, clinical psychiatrist; b. Brugge, Belgium, Dec. 15, 1938; s. Emiel and Godelieve (Chielens) V.; m. Anita Gerarda Piessen, Apr. 1, 1965; children: Diederik, Willem. MD, U. Leuven, Belgium, 1966. Clin. psychiatrist Onze Lieve Vrouw Psychiat. Hosp., Brugge, 1972-89, electro-encephalographist, 1972—, head Gerontopsychiat. Clin., 1990—; med. dir. SPS Mental Health Ctr., Brugge, 1975—; free lance drug investigator for pharm. cos. Mem. Belgian Coll. Neuro-psycho-pharmacology, Belgian Assn. Neurologists and Psychiatrists, Belgian Assn. Sleep Study, Similes Orgn. Fax: 32-50-38-49-17. E-mail: 100543.2336@compuserve.com. Office: Onze Lieve Vrouw Psych Hosp, Koning Albert Laan 8, Fld 8200 Brugge Belgium

VERWAAL, VICTOR JILBERT, surgeon; b. Annhem, The Netherlands, Nov. 20, 1963; s. Dick and Ina (Jansen) V. DS, U. Hosp. Nymegen, The Netherlands, 1988, MD, 1990. Surgeon Cath. Hosp., The Netherlands, 1991, 94-95, U. Hosp. Nymegen, The Netherlands, 1992-94, 97—, Elizabeth Hosp., Tilburg, The Netherlands, 1995-97. Mem. Nederlandre Vereniging voor Meetbunde, Nederlandre Vereniging voor Transatologie. Avocations: sailing, skiing. Home: De Schoren 17, 6581DK Malden The Netherlands

VERWEIJ, MARTIN DANIËL, electromagnetic theory educator, researcher; b. Alphen Aan Den Rijn, The Netherlands, May 9, 1961; s. Daniël and Dina Maria (Kooij) V. BSc, Mcpl. Poly. Sch., The Hague, The Netherlands, 1983; MSc cum laude, Delft U. Tech., The Netherlands, 1988, D, 1992. Asst. rschr. Delft U. Tech., 1988-92, asst. prof. electromagnetic theory, 1992-98, rsch. fellow, 1993-98; assoc. prof. electromagnetic theory, 1998—. Author: Transient Acoustic Waves in Continuously Layered Media, 1992. Sgt. Royal Dutch Army, 1983-84. Rsch. fellow Royal Netherlands Acad. Arts and Scis., Amsterdam, 1993-98. Mem. Acoustical Soc. Am. Mem. Reformed Ch. Office: Delft U Tech, Mekelweg 4, 2628 CD Delft ZH, The Netherlands

VERWER, CHRISTIAAN PIETER, lawyer; b. Breda, The Netherlands, Dec. 5, 1947; s. Jozef and Agnes (ten Braak) V.; m. Ineke Marjolein Harms, June 13, 1981; children: Juliette, Patricia, Jacqueline, Christiaan Jr. LLD, U. Amsterdam, 1976. Legal advisor Royal Air Force, The Netherlands, 1972-76, Ministry of Transp., The Hague, 1976-81; policy advisor Ministry of Econ. Affairs, The Hague, 1981-85; legal counsel State Supr. of Mines, Rijswijk, The Netherlands, 1985—; cons. B.M.B., Lagos, Nigeria, 1978. Author: Liability for Damage to Luggage, 1976, 2d edit. 1987; contbr. articles to profl. jours. Lt. Dutch Royal Air Force, 1972-76. Mem. Internat. Bar Assn. Roman Catholic. Office: State Supervisor of Mines, State Supervision of Mines, PO Box 90, 2280 AB Rijswijk The Netherlands

VERWOERD, WILHELM JOHANNES, geology educator; b. Cape Town, South Africa, Sept. 5, 1929; s. Hendrik Frensch and Elizabeth (Schoombee) V.; m. Anna Elizabeth Smit, Dec. 18, 1954; children: Hendrik, Dirk, Wilhelm, Gideon. BS, U. Stellenbosch, 1949, MS cum laude, 1953, DSc, 1963. Geologist Geol. Survey, South Africa, 1954-67; officer-in-charge Geol. Unit Atomic Energy Bd., South Africa, 1960-63; sr. lectr. Rand Afrikaans U., Johannesburg, South Africa, 1968-71; prof. U. Stellenbosch, South Africa, 1972-92, rsch. scientist, 1992—; vis. scientist Geophys. Lab. Carnegie Instn., Washington, 1977-78; geologist South African Geol. and Biol. Expedition to Marion and Prince Edward Islands, 1965; mem. Am. geol. expedition to Skaergaard in Greenland, 1974; mem. South African Com. for Stratigraphy, 1982—; nat. corr. Internat. Assn. Volcanology and Chemistry of Earth's Interior, 1972-90; mem. UNESCO-IGCP Project on Alkaline and Carbonatite Magmatism, 1990-95. Author: The Carbonatites of South Africa and South West Africa, 1967; editor: Mineralization in Metamorphic Terrains, 1978; assoc. editor: Volcanoes of the Antarctic Plate, 1990; contbr. articles to profl. jours. and chpts. to books. Recipient Jr. Capt. Scott medal Biol. Soc. South Africa, 1955. Mem. Geol. Soc. South Africa (hon., pres.), Suid-Afrikaanse Akademie vir Wetenskap en Kuns (Havenga prize 1987). Avocations: hiking, photography, philately. Office: U Stellenbosch, Dept Geology, Stellenbosch 7600, South Africa

VESA, KARRI ANTERO, public relations executive; b. Nokia, Finland, Nov. 14, 1960; s. Harri Antero and Aili Kyllikki (Lamminsivu) V.; m. Minna Marjatta Rasila, Aug. 13, 1988; children: Samu, Martta, Söpö. MSc, U. Tech., Tampere, Finland, 1986. Design engr. ABB, Helsinki, Finland, 1986-87; jr. cons. Hill & Knowlton, Helsinki, 1987-90, sr. cons., 1990-95; mng. dir. Harkonsalo & Vesa, Espoo, Finland, 1995—; lectr. in stratetic comm. and reputation mgmt., Estonia and Finland. Mem. Nat. Election Com., Espoo, 1992—. Sgt. Finnish armed forces, 1980. Mem. Finnish Orgn. Communicators. Avocations: coaching boys football, tennis, squash. Home: Sokinmåki 7A, 02760 Espoo Finland Office: Harkonsalo & Vesa, Niittykatu 8A, 02200 Espoo Finland

VESA, MIKKO JUHANI, retired editor-in-chief; b. Virrat, Finland, Feb. 3, 1937; s. Armas Johannes and Olga Maria (Äijälä) V.; m. Hilkka Marjatta Kotajärvi, 1963; children: Juha, Elina ja Olli, Ville. Diploma, Ilmajoen Yhteiskoulu, 1957; MSc in Agr., Helsingin yliopisto, 1965. Newspaper editor Maaseudun Tulevaisuus, Helsinki, Finland, 1965-69; mng. editor Maaseudun Tulevaisuus, Helsinki, 1969-84, editor-in-chief, 1984-2000; ret., 2000. Home: Huvilarinne 13A, 02730 Espoo Finland

VESELINOVIČ, DRAŠKO, stock exchange executive; b. Ljubljana, Slovenia, Feb. 26, 1959; s. Branko and Breda (Pokorn) V.; 1 child, Eva. M of Internat. Fin., U. Ljubljana, 1986, DSc in Econs., 1996. Fgn. exch. dealer Ljubljanska Bank, fgn. exch. and internat. treasury mgr.; prof. Faculty of Econs.; fin. adviser Slovene Govt.; CEO Ljubljana Stock Exch., gen. mgr., 1993—; mem. econ. chamber Slovene Parliament; founder The Yugoslav Stock Exch., 1989. Author: Foreign Exchange Trading, 1987, Stock Exchange Handbook, 1991, 95, Options and Other Derivative Financial Instruments, 1998; author over 100 articles. Avocations: tennis, music. Office: Ljubljana Stock Exchange Inc, Slovenska c 56, 1000 Ljubljana Slovenia

VESELKA, JOSEF, cardiologist; b. Prague, Czechoslovakia, Mar. 23, 1965; s. Jan and Milada Veselka; m. Helena Kubasova, 1992; children: Helena, Marketa. MD, Charles U., Prague, 1989; PhD, Charles U., 1998. Cert. medicine and cardiology Czech Republic. Resident, fellow 4th internal dept. Charles U., Prague, 1989-95, cons. 2nd internal dept. 3rd Med. Sch., 1995, cons., head cardiology unit 4th internal dept. 1st Med. Sch., 1996; head diagnostic unit, vice head divsn. cardiac surgery U. Hosp. Motol, Prague, 1997—. Author: (textbook) Valvular Heart Disease; contbr. articles to profl. jours. Avocation: sports. E-mail: veselka.josef@usa.net.

VESELOV, ALEXANDRE IVANOVICH, physicist; b. Khabarovsk, Russia, Apr. 14, 1946; s. Ivan Alexandrovich and Polina Arsent'evna (Shelestova) V.; m. Alla Leonidovna Samofalova, Sept. 24, 1968 (div. Nov. 1972); m. Galina Ivanovna Glazunova, June 4, 1976. BSc, Moscow Phys. Engring. Inst., 1969; BSc in Math., Moscow State U., 1973; PhD, Inst. Control Sys., Moscow, 1978. Jr. rschr. Inst. Nuc. Geophysics and Geochemistry, Moscow, 1969-70; engr. Inst. Control Sys., Moscow, 1971-79; sr. rschr. Advice on Cybernetics, Moscow, 1985-87, Inst. Theoretical and Exptl. Physics, Moscow, 1979-85, 87—. Russian Orthodox. Avocations: water travel, fishing. Home: Kutuzovskii pr 24-56, 121151 Moscow Russia Office: Inst Theor and Exptl Phys, B Cheremushkinskaja 25, 117259 Moscow Russia

VESELY, DAVID LYNN, medical educator, research scientist; b. Omaha, Mar. 6, 1943; s. Raymond James and Cecila Jane (O'Keefe) V.; m. Clo M. Farrell; children: Susanna, Catherine, Matthew, Brian, Jonathan. BS in biology, Creighton U., 1967; MD, U. Ariz., 1972, PhD, 1972. Asst. prof. medicine U. Miami Med. Sch., 1974-78; asst. prof., chief endocrinology U. Ark. Med. Sci., Little Rock, 1978-79, assoc. prof., 1979-83, prof., 1983-89; prof. medicine, physiology, biophysics Univ. S. Fla. Med. Sch., Tampa, 1989—; chief endocrinology and metabolism J.A. Haley Vets. Hosp., Tampa, 1993—; disting. vis. prof. Christchurch, New Zealand, 1995. Author: Atrial Natriuretic Hormones, 1992, 97; contbr. over 240 articles to profl. jours. Rsch. advisor Am. Heart Assn. Fla. Affiliate, 1993—; chmn. profl. com. Am. Diabetes Assn. Ark. chpt. 1982-85. Recipient Alumni Medal U. Ariz, 1992, Native Son award C. of C., Scribner, Nebr., 1990; grantee NIH, Dept. Vets. Affairs, Am. Heart Assn.; Sr. Fogarty Internat. fellow, Nice, France, 1984-85. Fellow ACP, Am. Coll. Endocrinology; mem. Endocrine Soc. (chmn. membership 1983-86), So. Soc. Clin. Investigation, N.Y. Acad. Sci. Achievements include discovery of three new peptide hormones, made by the heart, which lower blood pressure and increase sodium and water excretion, also useful in the treatment of congestive heart failure and renal failure. Office: Univ S Fla Health Scis Ctr 13000 Bruce B Downs Blvd Tampa FL 33612-4745

VESELY, VÍTĚZSLAV, mathematician, educator, researcher; b. Brno, Moravia, Czech Republic, Dec. 12, 1947; s. Josef and Emilie (Klukanová) V.; m. Marie Doupovcová, Nov. 11, 1978; 1 child, Eva. M in Natural Sci., Masaryk U., Brno, 1972, D in Natural Sci., 1974, PhD, 1990. Rsch. fellow Rsch. Inst. Gen. Engring. Works, Brno, 1973-81; rschr. Inst. Phys. Met., Czech Acad. Sci., Brno, 1982-90, rsch. scientist, 1990-91; project mgr. Tricolor Line, Ltd., Brno, 1992; sr. lectr. Masaryk U., 1993-94, assoc. prof., 1994—. Contbr. articles to profl. jours. Mem. Union Czech Mathematicians and Physicists, Am. Math. Soc., SIAM. Avocation: hiking. Office: Masaryk Univ Dept Math, Janáčkovo nám 2a, 66295 Brno Czech Republic

VESELY, VLADIMÍR, hematologist, consultant; b. JindØichv Hradec, Czech Republic, May 30, 1931; s. Vaclav and Anna (Jindrová) V.; m. Vendulka Pujmandová, May 12, 1958; children: Vendulka, Vladimír. MD, Charles U., Plzen-Prague, Czech Republic, 1957, Cert. in Internal Medicine, 1960, Cert. in Hematology/Blood Transfusion, 1963, PhD, 1975. Physician Univ. Hosp., Plzen, 1957-74; chief med. dept. Itegue Menen Hosp., Asmara, Ethiopia, 1964-67; chief blood transfusion ctr. Gen. Univ. Hosp., Prague, 1974—; chief blood bank St. John's Hosp., G'Mangia, Malta, 1981-83, 84-85; cons., adviser in blood transfusion Ctrl. Bohemia Country, Prague, 1974-92; external tchr. Postgrad. Inst., Brno, Czech Republic, Prague. Author: (manual) Blood Donor Recruitment, 1979, 3d edit., 1990, The Transfunding Medical Officer in Czech, 1998; editor jour. Transfuze Dnes, 1990-95. Expert Regional Ct., Plzen, 1975—; councilor Ministry of Health, Prague, 1975-97; mem. sci. com. ESTM, Milan, Italy, 1992—. Fellow ISBT (mem. com. 1992-96), DGTI, Czech Soc. for Transfusion Medicine (hon., pres. 1994-98). Avocation: flying gliders. Home: Háje 571, 149 00 Prague Czech Republic Office: Blood Transfusion Ctr, U Nemocnice 2, 128 08 Prague Czech Republic

VESETH, LEIF, physics educator; b. Vefsn, Nordland, Norway, July 19, 1942; s. Jorgen and Emma (Moeller) V.; m. Anne Haakanes, July 28, 1973; children: Siri, Tone, Ingvild. Candidatus realium, U. Oslo, 1967, PhD, 1971. Rsch. asst. U. Oslo, 1966-69, fellow, 1969-73, assoc. prof., 1973-93, prof., 1993—. Contbr. articles to profl. jours. Home: Veslefrikkveien 3, 0851 Oslo Norway Office: Dept Physics, Univ Oslo, 0316 Oslo Norway

VESHKURTSEV, JURIY MIKHAILOVICH, communications educator; b. Tumen region, Russia, Aug. 12, 1940; s. Mikhail Andrianovich and Varvara Polycarpovna (Pyrieva) V.; m. Alexandra Semenovna Shuhleeva, Oct. 18, 1961; 1 child, Dmitry Jurievich. Engr., Tomsk Polytechnic Inst., 1962, BS, 1970; DS, Moscow Energetic Inst., 1990. Engr. Rsch. Inst. Instrument Making, Omsk, Russia, 1962-70; instr., prof. Omsk Polytechnic Inst., 1970-91, chmn., 1992—; dean Rector Inst. Radioelecs. Svc. & Diagnosis, 1997—. Inventor in field; contbr. articles to profl. jours. Mem. Russian Soc. Non-Destructive Testing & Tech. (chmn.), Acad. Internat. Higher Edn. Acad. Scis. Office: OmSTY, Mira Ave 11, 644050 Omsk Russia

VESNA, VIKTOR ALEKSEEVICH, physicist, researcher; b. Uzlovaja, USSR, June 5, 1938; s. Aleksej Iosifovich Vesna and Galina Semenovna Efimova; m. Ekaterina Vladimirovna, Mar. 4, 1976; children: Antonina, Vera. Postgrad., Leningrad (USSR) Poly. Inst., 1958-64; PhD, Leningrad Nuclear Phys. Inst., 1978. Cert. in engring. physics. Locksmith VEF Factory, Riga, USSR, 1956-58; jr. sci. rschr. Leningrad Nuclear Physics Inst., Gatchina, 1964-78, sci. rschr., 1978-83, sr. sci. rschr., 1983-92; prof. Petersburg Nuclear Physics Inst., Gatchina, 1993—. Contbr. articles to profl. jours. E-mail: vesna@lnpi.spb.su. Office: Petersburg Nuclear Phys Ins, Orlova Roscha 1, Gatchina 188350, Russia

VESNAVER, GORAZD, chemist; b. Ljubljana, Slovenia, July 28, 1941; s. Ljuboslav and Carmen (Svetek) V.; m. Marija Pretnar, Mar. 19, 1966; children: Ales, Luka. BS in Chemistry, U. Ljubljana, 1965, MS, 1970, PhD, 1973. Grad. instr. U. Ljubljana, 1965-77, asst. prof., 1977-82, assoc. prof., 1982-88, prof., 1988—; postdoctoral fellow Rutgers U., New Brunswick, N.J., 1973-74, 79-80, vis. prof., 1987-88, 94-95; head phys. chemistry lab. U. Ljubljana, 1988-92; mem. D7 mgmt. com. COST, Brussels, 1993—; prin. investigator U.S.-Slovene Rsch. Project, Ljubljana, 1996—. Contbr. articles to profl. jours. Recipient Fund award B. Kidric Found., 1984, award for inventions, 1986. Avocations: skiing, tennis, mountain hiking. Home: Trubarjeva 29, 1000 Ljubljana Slovenia

VESNOVSKII, STANISLAV PETROVICH, radiochemist, environmental scientist; b. Nizhny Novgorod, USSR, Nov. 27, 1933; s. Petr Vasilievich and Nina Nikolaevna (Karpova) V.; children: Sergei Stanislavovich, Irina Stanislavovna. BS, Nizhny-Novgorod State U., USSR, 1956; PhD, All Russian Exptl. Physics Rsch. Inst., Arzamas-16, 1968. Engr. All Russian Exptl. Physics Rsch. Inst., Arzamas-16, USSR, 1956-60; sr. engr. All Russian Exptl. Physics Rsch. Inst., Arzamas-16, 1961-62, head rsch. group, 1963-70, sr. scientist, 1970-74, head lab., 1975-84, head radiochem. dept., mem. sci. and tech. coun., 1985-97, coord. internat. program in radiochem. isotopes/environ., 1997—; dep. dir. Inst. Nuclear and Radiation Physics. Contbr. chpts. to book, articles to mag.; inventor in field. Named Russian Fedn. Laureaut in Radiochemistry State Premium Russian Fedn. Govt., 1985. Mem. Russian Nuclear Soc., Internat. Nuclear Target Devel. Soc. Avocations: photography, tourism, swimming. Office: Russian Fed Nuclear Ctr, pr Mir 37, 607 190 Sarov Russia

VEST, CHARLES MARSTILLER, academic administrator; b. Morgantown, W.Va., Sept. 9, 1941; s. Marvin Lewis and Winifred Louise (Buzzard) V.; m. Rebecca Ann McCue, June 8, 1963; children: Ann Kemper, John Andrew. BSME, W.Va. U., 1963; MSME, U. Mich., 1964, PhD, 1967; DEng (hon.), Mich. Tech. U., 1992, W.Va. U., 1994, Ill. Inst. Tech., 1998, U. Notre Dame, 1998, Musashi Inst. Tech., 1999. Asst. prof., then assoc. prof. U. Mich., Ann Arbor, 1968-77, prof. mech. engring., 1977-90, assoc. dean acad. affairs Coll. Engring., 1981-86, dean Coll. Engring., 1986-89, provost, v.p. acad. affairs, 1989-90; pres. MIT, Cambridge, 1990—; bd. dirs. E.I. du Pont de Nemours and Co., IBM; vis. assoc. prof. Stanford (Calif.) U., 1974-75. Author: Holographic Interferometry, 1979; assoc. editor Jour. Optical Soc. Am., 1982-83; contbr. articles to profl. jours. Trustee Woods Hole Oceanographic Inst., New Eng. Aquarium; adv. trustee Environ. Rsch. Inst. Mich. Recipient Excellence in Rsch. award U. Mich., 1980, Disting. Svc. award, 1972, Disting. Visitor award U. La Plata, Argentina, 1979, Centennial medal Am Soc. Engring. Edn., 1993. Fellow AAAS, Am. Acad. Arts and Scis., Optical Soc. Am., ASME; mem. NAE, Sigma Xi, Tau Beta Pi, Pi Tau Sigma. Presbyterian. Office: MIT 77 Massachusetts Ave Cambridge MA 02139-4307

VEST, JAMES MURRAY, foreign language and literature educator; b. Roanoke, Va., Mar. 27, 1947; s. Eddie Lewis and Irene (Cannaday) V.; m. Nancy Foltz, June 6, 1970; 1 child, Cecelia. BA, Davidson (N.C.) Coll., 1969; MA, Duke U., 1971, PhD, 1973. From asst. to assoc. prof. Rhodes Coll., Memphis, 1973-91, chmn. French dept., 1983-98, prof., 1991—, head French program, 1984-98; adminstr. Rhodes in Paris Program, France, 1978-87; organizer faculty teaching seminars, 1988—. Author: The French Face of Ophelia, 1989, The Poetic Works of Maurice de Guérin, 1991; contbr. articles to profl. jours. Chmn. Urban Outreach Commn., Memphis, 1978-81; leader youth groups, 1983—. Capt. U.S. Army Res., 1973—. Recipient campus svc. award Sears-Roebuck, 1990, Outstanding Teaching award Clarence Day Found., Memphis, 1984, Am. Assn. Higher Edn., 1988; Woodrow Wilson fellow, 1971, NDEA Title IV fellow, 1969. Mem. MLA, So. Atlantic Modern Lang. Assn., Am. Assn. of Tchrs. of French, Am. Coun. Teaching Fgn. Lang. Avocations: cinema, hiking. Office: 2000 N Pkwy Rhodes C Memphis TN 38112

VEST, STEVEN LEE, gastroenterologist, hepatologist, internist; b. Mpls., July 30, 1948; s. Lee Herbert and Marian Mize (Rains) V.; m. Gayle Maureen Southworth, Nov. 27, 1971; 1 child, Matthew Steven. BA, U. Minn., 1970, MD, 1974. Diplomate Am. Bd. Internal Medicine, Am. Bd Gastroenterology. Intern internal medicine Milw. County Hosp., 1974-75; resident internal medicine So. Ill. U., Springfield, 1975-77; fellow in gastroenterology and hepatology Duke U. Med. Ctr., Durham, N.C., 1978-80; gastroenterology-hepatology and internal medicine cons. Lonesome Pine Hosp., Big Stone Gap, Va., 1980—; gastroenterology and internal medicine cons. St. Mary's Hosp., Norton, 1983—, Norton Community Hosp., Norton, Va., 1985—; chmn. med. care evaluation, Lonesome Pine Hosp., Big Stone Gap, 1984-88, chmn. pharmacy, therapeutics & transfusion com., 1992-94; chief of medicine Norton Cmty. Hosp., 1991-93, 97-99, exec. com., 1991-93, 97-99, also bd. dirs. 1993—, credentials com., 1995-97, bylaws com., 1996-97. Fellow ACP, Am. Coll. Gastroenterology; mem. Am. Gastroent. Assn., Am. Soc. Internal Medicine, Va. Med. Soc. (state del. 1992), Wise County Med. Soc. (treas. 1984-86, v.p. 1991-92, pres. 1992-93), Am. Assn. Christian Counselors, Wise County C. of C. Methodist. Avocations: kayaking, jogging, skiing, photography, karate. Fax: (540) 679-0245. Home: Powell Valley 1800 Egan Rd Big Stone Gap VA 24219-4224 Office: NCH Med Arts Bldg #2 98 15th St NW Ste 202 Norton VA 24273-1600

VESTAL, JUDITH CARSON, occupational therapist; b. Memphis, Dec. 22, 1939; d. Carl Thomas and Emma Winifred (Stewart) Carson; m. Tommy Vestal, June 22, 1974. BS in Elem. Edn., U. Tenn., 1961; BS in Occupl. Therapy, Washington U., St. Louis, 1964; MA in Guidance and Counseling, La. Tech. U., 1978; PhD, Tex. Woman's U., 1997. Cert. occupl. therapist, La. Occupl. therapist Sewall Rehab. Ctr., Denver, 1964-67, Whittington Hosp., London, 1967-70, The London Hosp., 1970-74, N.W. La. Rehab., Shreveport, 1975-77, Caddo Bossier Assn. for Retarded Children, Shreveport, 1977-81; occupl. therapist La. State U. Med. Ctr., Shreveport, 1981-87, asst. prof. occupl. therapy, 1986-92, assoc. prof. clin. occupl. therapy, 1992—. Editl. bd. Am. Jour. Occupl. Therapy, 1984-87; contbr. articles to profl. jours. Bd. dirs. Children's Learning Ctr., Shreveport, 1980-89; mem. Spl. Edn. Adv. Coun., Shreveport, 1985-91; mem., sec. vestry Ch. of Epiphany, Shreveport, 1992-96. Mem. Am. Occupl. Therapy Assn. (sec. com. on state assn. pres. 1989-92, Svc. award 1992), La. Occupl. Therapy Assn. (v.p. 1983-86, pres. 1986-90, Pres.'s award 1991, Award of Merit 1994), Soc. for Rsch. in Child Devel., Neurodevelopmental Treatment Assn., Internat. Soc. for Alternative and Augmentative Comm., Phi Kappa Phi. Reformed Episcopal Ch. Avocations: reading, travel, music. Home: 176 Preston Ave Shreveport LA 71105-3306 Office: Louisiana State Univ Health Scis Center Sch Allied Health Prof 1501 Kings Hwy Shreveport LA 71103-4228

VESTERGAARD, PETER, plant ecologist, researcher, educator; b. Nakskov, Denmark, Oct. 24, 1940; s. Hans Christian and Karen Ragnhild (Skafte) V.; married; 3 children. Grad., U. Copenhagen, 1969. Asst. prof. U. Copenhagen, 1969-73, assoc. prof., 1973—; mem. coun. European Union for Coastal Conservation, The Netherlands, 1991-95; mem. Nature Protection Coun., Denmark, 1992-96. Author: Vegetation Ecology, 1993, 2d edit., 1998, Salt Marsh monograph, 2000; author numerous sci. papers and monographs; editor: Opera Botanica, 1989; mem. editl. bd. Jour. Coastal Conservation, 1994—. Recipient Carl Rasch bot. award, 1979; San Cataldo Instn. grantee, 1991. Mem. Internat. Assn. for Vegetation Sci., Danish Bot. Soc. (pres. 1986-92), Danish Landscape Ecol. Soc. (bd. dirs. 1997—), Brit. Ecol. Soc., Swedish Phytogeographical Soc. Office: Botanical Inst, Øster Farimagsgade 2D, DK-1353 Copenhagen Denmark

VESZPRÉMI, TAMÁS, chemist, educator; b. Budapest, Hungary, Feb. 11, 1947; s. Tibor and Ibolya (Mandler) V.; m. Zsuzsánna Németh, Dec. 30, 1972; children: Nóra, Ágnes. MSc, Tech. U. Budapest, 1970, PhD, 1974; DSc, Acad. Scis., Budapest, 1993. Cert. chem. engr. Sr. lectr. Tech. U. Budapest, 1970-76, 1976-90, reader, 1990-93, prof. chemistry, 1993—; postdoctoral fellow Tokyo U., 1980-81; guest prof. Riken Inst., Japan, 1996. Contbr. more than 100 articles to profl. jours. Recipient Erdey prize Acad. Scis. Budapest, 1983, 96, Pruszt prize, 1997; Humboldt Found. fellow, 1986-87. Avocation: collecting minerals. Home: Kisvábhegyi u 4-6, 1122 Budapest Hungary Office: Technical University, Gellért tér 4, 1521 Budapest Hungary

VETÖ, FERENC DÉNES, biophysicist, researcher; b. Zalabesenyö, Hungary, 1932; s. Ferenc Vetö and Jolán Horváth; m. Judit Gross, 1955; children: Ferenc, Zoltán. MS, Eötvös L. Univ., Budapest, Hungary, 1955; PhD, Hungarian Acad. Scis., Budapest, Hungary, 1970. Rschr., lectr. Biophysical Inst. Med. U. Pécs, Hungary, 1956-93; lectr. Janus Pannonius U., Pécs, 1990-94; cons. German Acad. Austauschdienst, Jülich, Frankfort, Munich, Germany, 1981. Co-author: Biofizika, 1977, Biomembránok, 1989; contbr. articles to profl. jours. Mem. Hungarian Biophysical Soc. Budapest (founder), Hungarian Cell Membrane Club (founder). Home: Úrhajós u 13, H 7623 Pécs Hungary

VETRANO, FLAVIO BASIL, physicist; b. Genova, Ligury, Italy, Jan. 1, 1946; s. Vittorio and Candida (Puddu) V.; m. Lucia Calabria, Oct. 6, 1973; 1 child, Vittorio. Physics Degree, U. Genova, 1969. Rschr. CNR, Genova, Italy, 1972; asst. U. Urbino, Italy, 1972-82, prof., 1982—; dir. physics dept. U. Urbino, 1995—; rschr. INFN, Firenze, Italy, 1988—; external rsch. dir. ENEL, Urbino, 1993-94; cons. scientist Dist. Adminstrn., Ancona, Italy, 1996—; participant VIRGO Gravitational Antenna Project, 1998—. Contbr. articles to profl. jours. Officer Italian Artillery, 1970-72, Rome. Mem. Italian Phys. Soc. Office: Physics Dept/U Urbino, S Chiara 27, I-61029 Urbino Italy

VETRIN, VALERI ROMANOVICH, geologist, researcher; b. Pskov, Russia, Nov. 1, 1937; m. Margarita Alexandrovna Martinova, May 6, 1965; children: Elena, Leonid, Natalia. BSc, State U., Leningrad, Russia, 1960; PhD, Inst. Mineralogy Geochemistry Rare Elements, Moscow, 1968. Rsch. scientist State U., Leningrad, 1960-63; rsch. scientist Geol. Inst. Russian Acad. Sci., Apatity, Russia, 1965-76, sr. rsch. scientist, 1976-86, leading rsch. scientist, chief of dept., 1986—. Author: Granitoids of Murmansk Block, 1984; co-author: Reconstruction of the Process of Infracrustal and Crustal-Mantle Magmatism and Metasomatism, 1992, Archean Complex in the Section of the Kola Super-Deep Well, 1991, The Structure of Litosphere of the Baltic Shield, 1993, Endogenous Regimes and Evolution of the Magmatism on the Early Precambrian, 1991, Precambrian Granitoids of the Northeastern Baltic Shield, 1978, Precambrian Magmatic Formations of the Northeastern Baltic Shield, 1985, others; contbr. articles to profl. jours. Mem. trade union com. Geol. Inst. RAS, Apatity, 1970-90, chmn., 1978-80. Internat. Sci. Found. emergency grantee, N.Y., 1994; Russian Found. Fundamental Investigation grantee, Moscow, 1999—; INTAS grantee, 1995-98. Avocation: Alpine skiing. Office: Russian Acad Sci Geol Inst, 14 Fersman Str, 184200 Apatity Russia

VETRO, AGNES, child psychiatrist; b. Szeged, Hungary, July 21, 1947; d. Janos and Olga (Nogradi) V.; m. Istvan Gorzo, July 24, 1970; children: Laura, Dora. MD, Szent-Gyorgyi Albert Med. U., Szeged, 1971; splty. in pediatrics, Postgrad. Med. Sch., Budapest, 1975, splty. in child & adolescent psychiatry, 1978, splty. in child neurology, 1983, PhD in Med. Scis., 1987. Resident Clin. Child Psychiatry, Rheinhöhe, Germany, 1982-83, Wurzberg (Germany) U., 1990, Manchester (Eng.) U., 1993; resident dept. child and adolescent psychiatry Glasgow U., 1990-91, 93; lectr. dept. pediatrics Szent-Gyorgyi Albert Med. U., 1971-75, sr. lectr. psychiat. clinic, 1975-82, assoc. prof., 1982-83, assoc. prof. psychiat. clinic, 1983-93, assoc. prof. dept. pediatrics, 1993—, dept. head child and psychiat. dept., 1995—; dir. child and adolescent psychiatry Szent-Gyorgyi Albert Med. U., 1995—, dept. head psychiat. clinic CAP unit, 1984-93. Editor: Child and Adolescent Psychiatry, 1996; author: Mass Media and the Child, 1993; mem. adv. bd. European Jour. Child and Adolescent Psychiatry, 1993; mem. editl. bd. Psychiatrica Hungarica, 1991. Mem. Hungarian CAP Specialists (gen. sec. exec. coun. 1991-95), Hungarian Pediatrists (exec. coun. 1995—), Assn. of Empathy (pres. 1994-96), Found. for Mental Health of Children (pres. 1995—), German Assn. for Child and Adolescent Psychiatry (corr.), Hungarian Assn. for Child Neurology and Psychiatry (pres. 1990-94), Hungarian Psychiar. Assn. (exec. coun. 1989-94), European Assn. Child and Adolescent Psychiatry (v.p. 1995). Avocations: literature, painting, sports. Office: Szent-Gyorgyi Albert Med U, Semmelweis u 6, 6725 Szeged Hungary

VETTER, CLAUS JOHANNES, financial-real estate management company executive; b. Berlin, Aug. 5, 1941. Diploma in engring., Tech. U., Berlin, 1969; MBA, European Inst. Adminstrn., Fontainebleau, France, 1975. Rep. Wüstenrot, Berlin, 1964-70; pres. ABI Bldg. Corp., Berlin, 1970-74, INTORG GmbH, fin. and real estate mgmt., Berlin, 1979—; cons. Libyan Real Estate Bank, Tripoli, 1966, World Bank, Kinshasa, Zaire, 1976, govt. agy for real estate devel. Tunis, Tunisia, 1977-78, cons French investment group Berlin Area. Author handbooks on real estate investment and related tax shelter matters in Berlin and East Germany, 1980—. Avocation: sailing. Office: INTORG GmbH, Bonhoeffer Ufer 4, D-10589 Berlin Germany

VETTER, JÁNOS, biologist; b. Zirc, Hungary, Sept. 24, 1946; s. László and Koller (Éva) V.; m. Éva Majláth, Sept. 23, 1970; 1 child. PhD in Biology, U. Eötuös Loránd, Budapest, 1985, DSc, 1996. q. Asst. U. Scis. Eötvös L., Budapest, 1970-72; sci. worker U. Vet. Sci., Budapest, 1972-83, asst. prof., 1983-94, prof., head dept., 1995—. Co-author: Pilzanbau, 1991, Gombahatározó, 1991; editor: Gombahatározó/Key to Identification of Fungi, 1991. Mem. Mycol. Soc. (pres. 1983-91), Hungarian Mycol. Soc. (pres. 1992—), Mycol. Soc. Am. Avocation: history. E-mail: vetterj@univet.hu. Office: Rottenbiller 50, 1078 Budapest Hungary

VETTER, JORG, physicist; b. Meissen, Fed. Republic Germany, Aug. 12, 1954; s. Eberhard and Ilse Vetter; m. Catrin Vetter; children: Nora, Björn. Diploma of physics, U. Karl-Marx-Stadt, 1980, Dr of Exptl. Physics, 1984. Scientific asst. U. Karl-Marx-Stadt, 1983-90; head of PVD lab. Metaplas Lonon GmbH, Bergisch Gladbach, Fed. Republic of Germany, 1990—. Co-author, editor 2 books; contbr. over 85 articles to profl. jours.

VETTER, RALF-ACHIM HORST, physiologist; b. Duisburg, Germany, Aug. 3, 1962; s. Horst Paul and Renate Klara (Juwig) V.; m. Susanne Glang, May 13, 1994; children: Anna Louisa, Carolin Marie. Diploma in biology, Heinrich-Heine U., Düsseldorf, Germany, 1989; PhD in Biology summa cum laude, Christian-Albrechts-U., Kiel, Germany, 1992. Asst. sales mgr. Tobaccoland, Mülheim, Germany, 1982-83; sci. head eco-physiol. lab. Biologische Anstalt, Helgoland, Germany, 1993—; guest scientist Carleton U., Ottawa, 1996. Editor: Crustaceologen, 1997; contbr. articles to profl. jours. Vice head local com. Deutscher Bund f. Vogelschutz, Duisburg, 1978-81. Studienstiftung des Deutschen Volkes scholar, Bonn, Germany, 1986-89, 90-92. Mem. Deutsche Zoologische Gesellschaft, N.Y. Acad. Scis. Avocation: ballroom dancing. Home: Rablinghauser Landstr 53, 28195 Bremen Germany

VETTIVEL, SELVAKUMAR, anatomist, researcher; b. Palayamkottai, Tamilnadu, India; s. James and Lily Vettivel; m. Olive Duraisami, May 21, 1970; children: Samuel Nitishkumar, Solomon Satnishkumar, Ivan Prithishkumar. Reader in anatomy Christian Med. Coll., Vellore, 1973—. Contbr. articles to profl. jours. Mem. Am. Assn. Clin. Anatomists, Anat. Soc. India (life). Mem. Ch. South India. Home: Christian Med Coll Campus, Christian Med Coll Campus, 611B5 Brook Rd, Vellore 632 002, India Office: Christian Med Coll, Dept Anatomy, Vellore 632 002, India

VEVSTAD, VEGARD, retired textile company executive; b. Eidanger-Porsgrunn, Telemark, Norway, July 9, 1926; s. Jens and Elise (Tufte) V.; m. Reidunn Dahl; children: Snorre, Stine, Marte. Student, Skien Sch. Econs., 1949-50, Manchester Coll. Commerce, 1950-51, Norwegian Sch. Econs., 1953-56. Personal adminstrn. staff Norsk Hydro., Porsgrunn, Norway, 1952-53; dir. Th. Dahl Ltd., Skien, Norway, 1956-67; mng. dir. Th. Dahl Ltd., Skien, 1968-96; ret. Mem. Skien Rotary Club, Grenland Golf Club. Avocations: fishing, golfing. Home: Rising Terrasse 70, 3716 Skien Telemark, Norway

VEZVAEI, MAHBOBEH, mathematics educator; b. Tehran, Iran, Oct. 3, 1952; came to U.S., 1978; d. Hosain and Ehteram (Ghaderi) V.; m. Mosthea Rahmani, June 21, 1978; children: Rouhollah, Mona, Mariam, Haumed. MS, Informatic Inst., Tehran, 1978, Case Western Res. U., 1983; PhD, Case Western Res. U., 1987. Cert. healthcare nursing. H.S. tchr. Tehran, 1972-75; instr. Ertebatat U., Tehran, 1978; dir. divsn. statistics Bonyad Khayria, Tehran, 1975-78; cons. Case Western Res. U., Cleve., 1986; lectr. Kent State U., Kent, Ohio, 1983-99; asst. prof. Kent State U., 1999—. Rschr. in field. Recipient grad. assistantship Case Western Res. U., 1979-82. Mem. Am. Statis. Assn., Iranian Statis. Assn., Assn. of Women in Math. Avocations: reading, walking, cooking, being with family, sewing. E-mail: vezvaei@mcs.kent.edu. Office: Dept Math & Computer Sci Kent State U Kent OH 44242-0001

VIAL, JORGE, lawyer, educator; b. Santiago, Chile, Oct. 10, 1969; s. Jorge and Soledad (Alamos) V.; m. Magdalena Armanet, Sept. 30, 1995. LLM, U. Mich., 1997. Assoc. Claro y Cia. Law Firm, Santiago, Chile, 1991-96, Sidley & Austin, N.Y.C., 1998; ptnr. Simonetti y Cia. Law Firm, Santiago, Chile, 1998—; prof. law Cath. U. of Chile, Chile, 1995—. Recipient Fulbright scholarship Fulbright Commn., Santiago, 1996, Mideplan scholarship, Santiago, 1997. Mem. San Cristóbal Polo Club, Catholic U. Law Sch. Mem. Renovación Nat. Party. Roman Catholic. Avocations: golf, fishing, skiing. Office: Simonetti y Cia Law Firm, Office 1202 Alcantara 200, Santiago Chile

VIALLAT, ANNIE, physicist, researcher; b. Toulon, Var, France, Oct. 11, 1958; d. Pierre and Madeleine (Cointe) V.; life ptnr. Jean Pierre Cohen Addad; children: Vincent, Jade. Degree in engring., Ecole Poly., Paris, 1982, Genie Rural Eaux Forets, Paris, 1984; PhD, Grenoble (France) U., 1987. Rschr. in physics CNRS, France, 1988—; prof. U. Grenoble, 1989—; vis. scientist materials dept., U. Calif., 1988. Contbr. articles to profl. publs. Mem. Soc. Française Physique, European Phys. Soc. Avocations: skiing, hiking, reading. Home: 3 Rue Dr Bailly, 38000 Grenoble France Office: Lab Spectrometric Physique, BP 87, 38402 Saint-Martin d'Heres France

VIART, GUY, corporation executive; b. Arras, France, May 16, 1957; s. Micheline and Denis (Brasseur) V.; m. Lydie Delpouve, Dec. 30, 1995; children: Marc, Sophie, Celine. D in Engring., Enstimd, Douai, France, 1980; grad. in Bus. Mgmt., IAE Lille, France, 1986. R & D mgr. USINOR Wire Group, 1980-83, export mgr., 1983-85, project mgr. in prodn. restruc-

turation, 1985-86; tech. mgr., dir. bd. SOFAMOR, Paris, 1986-91; chmn., mng. dir. Interactif, Beaurains, France, 1991-94; mng. dir. Eurosurgical, Beaurains, 1994—; pres. Spine Network Group, Beaurains, 2000—, Spinet GmbH, Burscheid, Germany, 2000—; indsl. rep. mem. Argos Internat. Group of Spine Surgeons, 2000—; auditor internat. orgn. OIPEEC, 1981-85. roman Catholic. Home: 6 Rue de Vaulx-Vraucourt, 62128 Saint Leger Les Croisilles France Office: Eruosurgical, 18 Rue Robespierre, 62217 Beaurains France

VIBAR, BELEN MATIAS, librarian; b. Iriga, The Philippines, Dec. 14, 1935; d. Jose Bonafe and Adela (Matias) V. BS in Edn., U. St. Tomas, Manila, 1957, postgrad., 1974. High sch. libr. St. Paul Coll. Manila, Manila, 1961-67, Ateneo de Manila U., Quezon City, The Philippines, 1967-68; circulation libr. St. Paul Coll. Manila, Manila, 1968-69; libr. grad. sch. De La Salle U., Manila, 1969-75, libr. readers svcs., 1975-82; curriculum libr. Internat. Sch., Makati, The Philippines, 1982-84; head libr. Paref Woodrose Sch., Alabang, The Philippines, 1984-91; univ. libr. U. Asia & The Pacific, Pasig, The Philippines; bd. dirs. Libr. Integrated Svcs. Coop., Makati. Bd. dirs. Philippine Bd. on Books for Young People, 1995, auditor, 1996-98; mem. Nat. Commn. on Culture & Arts, Com. on Libr. and Info. Svc., 1995; chair Ortigas Ctr. Libr. Consortium, 1998. Mem. Assn. of Spl. Librs. of the Philippines (sec. 1978-79, treas. 1977, pres. 1987, v.p., pres-elect 1995, pres. 1996, exec. offcr., 1997, brd. advisors, 1998), Philippines Librs. Assn. Inc. (v.p., pres.-elect 1988-90, pres. 1995, trustee 1996, treas, 1997), Philippine Assn. of Acad. and Rsch. Librs. (bd. dirs. 1993, v.p. 1994, pres. 1995, ex-officio 1996), U. St. Thomas Libr. Sci. Alumni Assn. (pres. 1988-91). Roman Catholic. Avocations: stamp collecting, watching cultural shows, watching sports competition. Home: 201-D Kanlaon St SMH, Quezon City 1114, The Philippines Office: U Asia & The Pacific, Pearl Dr Ortigas Ctr, 1605 Pasig The Philippines

VIBE, KJELD, ambassador; b. Stavanger, Norway, Oct. 5, 1927; came to U.S., 1989; s. Christopher Andreas and Thordis (Amundsen) V., July 1, 1953; m. Beate Meyer; children: Annette, Margery, Johan Christopher, Ingeborg. LLD, U. Oslo, 1954; grad., Fgn. Svc. Sch., Oslo, 1955. Sec. of Norwegian Embassy, del. to NATO and OEEC Paris, 1956-59; prin. pvt. sec. to fgn. min. Norwegian Ministry of Fgn. Affairs, Oslo, 1962-65; counsellor Norwegian Embassy, Washington, 1965-69; dep. dir. gen. polit. affairs Ministry of Fgn. Affairs, Oslo, 1969-72, dir. gen. for polit. affairs, 1972-77, sec. gen., 1984-89; amb. to NATO Brussels, 1977-84; amb. to U.S. Washington, 1989-96; mem. Norwegian Govt. Commn. on the Freedom of Expression, 1996-99. Home: Holmenkollv 35, Oslo 0376, Norway

VIBHUTE, KHUSHAL IRWANTRAO, law educator, researcher; b. Khanapur, Maharashtra, India, Mar. 2, 1951; s. Irwantrao Hullappa and Geeta Irwantrao V.; m. Bharati Khushal Patil, May 2, 1980; children: Poonam, Prashant. BSc (gen.), Marathwada U., Aurangabad, India, 1973, LLB (gen.), 1975; LLB (new), Marathwada U., Aurangabad, India, 1976; LLM, Pune U., India, 1979; PhD, Pune (India) U., 1992. Advocate, India. Lectr. in law U. Pune, India, 1979-87; reader in law U. Pune, 1987-94, prof. law, 1994-95, prof. law, dept. head, 1997—; bd. dirs. Students' Welfare, U. Pune, 1990-92; mem. exec. coun., Pune U. Tchrs.' Forum, 1984-85, exec. com. Sch. Environ Scis, 1987—; mem. senate and acad. coun., U. Pune, 1990-92, PhD admission com. in law, 1992-94, 97—; head dept. law U. Pune, 1992, 97—; lectr. Law Coll., Nanded, 1979, vis. prof. U. Pune, environ. scis. dept., 1980—; vis. prof. law Bharati Vidyapeéth, Pune, 1985-87, U. Bremen, Germany, 1992, 94, 99, Mara Inst. Tech., Shah Alam, Malaysia, 1994-97; rsch. adv. com. rsch. unit for socio-legal studies U. Calgary, Can., 1998—; vis. fellow Max Planck Inst. for Comparative Pub. and Internat. Law, Heidelberg, Germany, 1999. Author: (books) Author: Enforcement of Foreign Commercial Arbitral Awards, 1994, International Commercial Trade and State Immunity, 1999; editor: (books) Principles of Legislation and Judicial Process, 1992, Dr. Ambedkar and Empowerment: Constitutional Vicissitudes, 1994. Recipient fellowship Univ. Grants Commn., 1977-79, fellowship from Hague Acad. Internat. Law, 1987, fellowship, Internat. Inst. Human Rights, Strasbourg, France, 1990, scholarship to Ctr. for Human Rights, Geneva, 1990. Mem. Indian Law Inst., New Delhi, Indian Soc. Internat. Law, New Delhi, Environ. Scientists Assn. India (joint sec. 1992—), Internat. Jurists Orgn. Asia. Fax: 91-20-5653899. E-mail: vibhute@unipune.ernet.in. Home: U Pune, Dept Law, Pune 411 007, India Office: U Pune Dept of Law, Pune 411 007, India

VIBRANS, GERWIG ERNST, retired material science educator; b. Braunschweig, Germany, Sept. 24, 1924; s. Walther and Marie (Scheele) V.; m. Edith Lindemann, Mar. 20, 1955; children: Heike, Gerhard, Elmar. Diploma in physics, Tech. U., Braunschweig, Germany, 1954, Dr. Engring., 1959. Engr. Telefunken Corp., Ulm, Germany, 1954-57; rsch. asst. Tech. U., Braunschweig, 1957-59, prof., 1964—; rsch. scientist USN Naval Weapons Lab., Dahlgren, Va., 1959-61; staff scientist MIT Lincoln Lab., Lexington, Mass., 1962-64. Author: Feinstrukturuntersuchungen in der Werkstoffkunde, 1974; editor: Lead and Lead Alloys, 1970; inventor electron tubes; contbr. numerous articles to profl. publs. Home: Schoeppenstedter Str 7, 38170 Berklingen Germany Office: Institut for Werkstoffe, Langer Kamp 8, 38106 Braunschweig Germany

VIBY-MOGENSEN, JØRGEN, medical educator; b. Ring, Jutland, Denmark, June 13, 1938; s. Antonius and Kathrine (Viby-Petersen) V.-M.; m. Grethe Funder, Mar. 17, 1962; children: Palle, Anders, Jens. MD, Århus (Denmark) U., 1966; Specialist in Anaesthesia, U. Copenhagen, 1974, MD, 1983. Resident Aalborg (Denmark) Hosp., 1966-70; sr. resident U. Copenhagen, Righospitalet, Copenhagen, 1970-75, prof. chmn., 1989—; assoc. prof. Gentofte (Denmark) Hosp., 1975-76, Herlev (Denmark) Hosp., 1976-89, King Khalid U. Hosp., Riaydh, Saudi Arabia, 1985. Fellow Coll. Anaesthetists; mem. Danish Soc. Anaesthesiologists (sci. contbn. prize 1989), Scandinavian Soc. Anaesthesiologists, Am. Soc. Anaesthesiologists, World Fedn. Socs. Anaesthesiologists (European regional sect.). Avocations: tennis. E-mail: viby@rh.dk. Home: Soemarksvej 3, DK 2900 Hellerup Denmark Office: Rigshospitalet, Dept Anaesthesia, Blegdamsvej 9, DK 2100 Copenhagen Denmark

VICARY, DOUGLAS REGINALD, priest, headmaster; b. London, Sept. 24, 1916; s. Reginald William and Nellie Mary (Fairman) V.; m. Hester Ruth Hickinbotham, Mar. 22, 1947; children: Teresa, Margaret, Joseph, Simon. BA, Trinity Coll., Oxford, Eng., 1938, BSc, 1939, MA, 1942; diploma in Theology, Oxford U., Eng., 1940. Ordained Deacon, 1940, priest, 1941 Ch. of Eng. Anglican. Chaplain St. Lawrence Coll., Ramsgate, Eng., 1940-44; tutor, chaplain Wycliffe Hall, Oxford, Eng., 1945-48; chaplain Hertford Coll., Oxford, Eng., 1945-48; dir. edn. Diocese of Rochester, Kent, Eng., 1948-57; canon residentiary Rochester Cathedral, Eng., 1952-57; headmaster The King's Sch., Rochester, Eng., 1957-75; canon residentiary, precentor Wells Cathedral, Somerset, Eng., 1975-88; chaplain to Her Majesty the Queen of Eng., 1976-86. Co-author: (with others) Canterbury Chapters, 1976; contbd. articles to profl. jours. Mem. Kent Edn. Com., Eng., 1948-57; chmn. Choir Schs. Assn., Eng., 1967. Avocations: music, reading, walking. Home: 8 Tor Street, Wells Somerset BA5 2US, England

VICE, ROY LEE, history educator; b. Lynchburg, Va., Oct. 12, 1950; s. Cline Lowell and Ruth Burchell (Newman) V. BA in History, BS in Physics, Carson-Newman Coll., 1972; MA in History, U. Chgo., 1976, PhD in History, 1984. Lectr. Continuing Edn. program U. Chgo., 1985-86, 87-88, rare books asst. univ. librs., 1986; asst. prof. Pacific Luth. U., Tacoma, 1986-87, Clemson (S.C.) U., 1988-90; asst. prof. Wright State U., Dayton, Ohio, 1990-95, assoc. prof., 1995—. Contbr. articles to profl. jours. Vol. tutor CYCLE Cabrini-Green Projects, Chgo., 1981-86; vol. lectr. LaSalle St. Ch., Chgo., summers 1989-98. With U.S. Army, 1972-74. Mem. Am. Hist. Assn., 16th Century Studies Conf. Democrat. Baptist. Home: 229 E 2nd St Dayton OH 45402-1719 Office: Wright State U Dept History 3640 Colonel Glenn Hwy Dayton OH 45435-0001

VICENTE, ANA, retired social scientist; b. Lisbon, Portugal, Feb. 8, 1943; d. Luis Oliveira and Susan Lowndes Marques; m. Antonio Pedro Vicente, July 18, 1970; children: Filipa, Antonio. Degree in religious culture, Higher Sch. Cath. Culture, Portugal, 1966; degree in pedagogy of English lang., U. Paris, 1973; degree in modern lang. and lit., U. Lisbon, 1987. Tchr., translator Lang. Inst., Portugal, 1966-74; officer Portuguese Commn. for Equality and Womens Rights, 1974-82; pvt. practice rschr. and cons. Spain, 1983-86; exec. sec. Nat. Drug Program, Portugal, 1988-91; pres. Ofcl. Commn. for Equality and Womens Rights, Portugal, 1992-96, cons., 1996-98; ret., 1998; cons. WHO, 1983—, UN Fund for Population Activities, 1984—, Coun. of Europe, 1997. Author: Mulheres em Discurso, 1987, Portugal visto por Espanha, 1992, As Mulheres em Portugal na Transição do Milénio, 1998, Os Poderes das Mulheres, os Poderes dos Homens, 1998, with Antonio Pedro Vicente, O Principe Real, Luiz Filipe de Bragança, 1998, Direitos das Mulheres, Direitos Humanos, 1999; contbr. articles to profl. jours., sects. to books. Bd. mem. New Future for Children, Portugal, 1996—, Assn. Women of So. Europe, Paris, 1996—; coord. We Are Ch. Internat. Movement, Portugal, 1997. Scholar Rotary Found., Paris, 1972-73. Mem. Assn. Women's Studies Portugal, Amnesty Internat. Roman Catholic. Avocations: looking at the sea, reading, listening to music. Home: Av João XX1 4-3 E, 1000-301 Lisbon Portugal

VICENTE, JEAN-CLAUDE, geologist, researcher, educator; b. Paris, May 22, 1941; s. Marius and Eliette (Roumaillac) V.; m. Véronique Garcia, Nov. 11, 1971; children: Chloé, Ghislaine. Degree in natural scis., U. Paris, 1965, DSc in Structural Geology, 1965. Assoc. prof. structural geology U. Paris, 1963-66; prof. geotectonics U. Chile, Santiago, 1966-76; prof. structural geology U. San Agustín, Arequipa, 1977-83; maître conf. geotectonics U. P. & M. Curie, Paris, 1983—; emeritus prof. U. San Augstín, Arequipa, 1983, dir. Geol. Rsch. Inst., 1977-83; expert tech. coop. French Fgn. Office, 1966-83; mem. internat. coms. Chilean Mantle and Geodynamics Projects, Andean magmatism, Circum-Pacific Rsch., Commn. on Jurassic and Cretaceous Rsch., Correlation of Jurassic Events in S.Am., Tectonic Evolution of the Pacific Gondwana Margin; mem. Commn. Specialistes, U. P. & M. Curie, 1993—, edn. coord., 1996—, campus rep., 1991—. Contbr. articles to profl. jours. Fellow Geol. Soc. Am., Argentine Geol. Assn. (hon.); mem. Geol. Soc. Chile (Premio Herbert Thomas 1991), Geol. Soc. France, Geol. Soc. Germany, Geol. Soc. Peru (Peruanist award 1997), Swiss Geol. Soc., Soc. for Sedimentary Geology. Avocation: saxophone, harmony orchestra. Home: 91 Bd Richard Lenoir, 75011 Paris France Office: U P&M Curie Dept Geotecton, 4 Place Jussieu, F 75252 Paris Cedex 05 France

VICENTIN, RICCARDO, project manager, consultant; b. Torino, Italy, June 25, 1969; s. Augusto and Natalia (Teppati) V. Elec. engr., Politech. of Torino, 1996. Project leader CRF, Torino, 1996; designer Eltrac, Torino, 1996-99; project leader IRISBUS, Torino, 1999—; cons. Montepaschi, Torino, 1995—. Mem. IEEE. Roman Catholic. Avocations: tennis, soccer. Home: Corso Francia 301, 10141 Torino Italy Office: IRISBUS, Viale Puglia Ingr 4, 10100 Torino Italy

VICENZI, ANGELA ELIZABETH, nursing researcher; b. N.Y.C., Aug. 19, 1938; d. Peter Christiaan and Angeline Elizabeth (Rudtke) Richard; m. Richard Emil Vicenzi, Nov. 11, 1961; children: Richard Martin, Paul Andrew, Stephen Mark, Douglas Emil. Diploma, St. Vincent's Hosp. Sch. Nursing, N.Y.C., 1959; BSN, Western Conn. State U., 1977; MEd in Cmty. Health Nursing, Columbia U., 1980, EdD in Health Edn., 1984. Pub. health nurse City of N.Y., 1960-61; pediat. staff nurse Norwalk (Conn.) Hosp., 1970-73; profl. nurse traineeship Columbia U. Tchrs. Coll., N.Y.C., 1978-80; clin. instr. Norwalk C.C., 1977-78; asst. prof. Sacred Heart U., Fairfield, Conn., 1980-83; from. asst. prof. to assoc. prof. So. Conn. State U., New Haven, 1985-95, prof., 1995-2000, prof. emeritus, 2000; cons. Corp. Health Cons., Norwalk, 1980-90; pres. faculty senate So. Conn. State U., 1991-94. Editor, pub. Complexity & Chaos in Nursing Jour., 1994—; contbr. articles to profl. jours. Mem. St. Jerome Parish Coun., Norwalk, 1995-97. Recipient Virginia A. Henderson award Conn. Nurses Assn., 1996; grantee Conn. State U., 1994-95, Profl. Nurse Traineeship grantee Health and Human Svcs., 1991-94. Mem. AAUP (treas. So. Conn. State U. chpt. 1995-97, pres. 1998-2000), Assn. Cmty. Health Nursing Educators (program chmn. 1995), Mu Beta, Sigma Theta Tau (pres. 1992-94).

VICHERKOVA, MIROSLAVA, plant physiologist; b. Holasovice, Czech Republic, Apr. 2, 1933; d. Jaroslav and Anna (Grimova) Bens; m. Jiri Vicherek, Oct. 19, 1957; children: Jana, Pavel. D, Masaryk U., Brno, Czech Republic, 1956; PhD, Masaryk U., Czech Republic, 1968. Asst. prof. dept. plant physiology Masaryk U., Czech Republic, 1956-90, assoc. prof., 1990-97, prof., 1997—. Contbr. articles to profl. jours. Grantee Grant Agy. Czech Republic, 1993-95, U. Devel. Fund, Praha, Czech Republic, 1993, 94, 96, 97. Mem. European Soc. Plant Physiology, Internat. Allelopathy Soc. Avocations: family, gardening, reading, music. Office: Masaryk U Faculty Sci, Kotlarska 2, 611 37 Brno Czech Republic

VICHIOLA, CHRISTOPHER MICHAEL, educator, writer; b. Bridgeport, Conn., Apr. 27, 1959; s. Michael Richard and Delores (Distaci) V.; m. Clementine Gant, Feb. 6, 1991 (div. July 1992); m. Tracey Vichiola, Nov. 12, 1997; children: Michael, Christopher. AS, Western Conn. State U., 1981, BA, 1983; grad., Colonel James "Bo" Gritz's Spec. Forces Green Beret On-Field Med. Surg. Sch. Cert. nursing asst. Martial arts tchr. Am. Bujinkan Dojo, Danbury, Conn., 1993—; owner Omega Ninpo Inst., Bethel, Conn., 1993—; tchr., distbr. Ctr. for Action, Kamiah, Idaho, 1997—; educator, cons. Primerica Fin. Svcs., Danbury, 1997—; educator Christic Inst. Law Firm, Washington, 1995—. Author: Above the Law - The Real Story's Files, 1995, Above the Law Part II, 1995, The Real Story of Christopher Vichiola and Colonel Gritz, 1997, The Real Story of Christopher Vichiola's and Colonel Gritz's Training, 1997. Educator Rev. Jesse L. Jackson's Rainbow Coalition, Washington, 1992—, Mayor Eugene Eriquez Dem. Party, Danbury, 1987—, Rep. Jack Brooks, 1991—, Gov. Michael Dukakis, 1989—. Black belt in Ninjutsu, 1997; recipient Eagle award Col. James "Bo" Gritz, 1997, Spike Navy Seal Scuba badge Col. James "Bo" Gritz, 1997. Avocations: camping, scuba diving, basketball, football, martial arts. Home: 48 Candlewood Lake Rd S Apt 3 New Milford CT 06776-4562 Address: PO Box 117 Bethel CT 06801-0117

VICK, FRANCES BRANNEN, publishing executive; b. Trinity, Tex., Aug. 14, 1935; d. Carl Andrew and Bess (courtney) B.; m. Ross William Vick Jr., June 23, 1956; children: Karen Lynn, Ross William III, Patrick Brannen. BA, U. Tex., 1958; MA, Stephen F. Austin State U., 1968. Teaching fellow Stephen F. Austin State U., Nacogdoches, Tex., 1966-68, lectr., 1968-69; lectr. Angelina Coll., Lufkin, Tex., 1969-71, Baylor U., Waco, Tex., 1974-75, 77-78; vice prin. Vanguard Sch., Waco, 1975-77; pres. E-Heart Press, Inc., Dallas, 1979—; co-dir. UNT Press U. North Tex., Denton, 1987-89, dir., 1989—. Publisher 170 books; editor 50 books. Leadership coun. Ann Richards Com., Austin, 1990-94; amb. Inst. Texan Cultures; mem. Tex. Commn. on Arts, Lit., 1991. Named to Tex. Inst. of Letters. Mem. AAUW, Book Pubs. Tex. (v.p. 1990-96, pres. 1996), Tex. Folklore Soc. (councillor 1991-93), Tex. Humanities Resource Ctr. (bd. dirs. 1990-91), Western Lit. Assn., Philos. Soc. Tex., Tex. Inst. of Letters, Pen Ctr. U.S.A. West, Tex. State Hist. Assn. (life), East Tex. Hist. Assn. (life), Soc. Scholarly Pub., Women in Scholarly Pub., Rocky Mountain Book Pubs. Assn., Leadership Tex., Leadership Am., Tex. Humanities Alliance, UNT League Profl. Women. Democrat. Episcopalian. Home: 3700 Mockingbird Ln Dallas TX 75205-2125 Office: U North Tex PO Box 311336 Denton TX 76203-1336

VICKERMAN, ROGER WILLIAM, economics educator; b. Blackpool, Lancashire, England, Aug. 31, 1947; s. William and G. Ethel (Passingham) V.; m. Christine Ann Wragg, July 28, 1973; children: Stephen, Jennifer, Karen, Thomas. BA, Cambridge U., Cambridge, England, 1968; PhD, Sussex, England, 1972. Lectr. U. Hull, Eng., 1972-76; lectr. econs. U. Kent, Canterbury, Eng., 1977-79, sr. lectr., 1979-87, reader, 1987-89, prof. regional and transport econs., 1989-98, Jean Monnet prof. European econs., 1998—; specialist adviser House of Commons, London, 1989; cons. expert Commn. European Communities, 1989; cons. Dept. Transport, U.K.; mem. standing adv. com. Trunkroad ASsessment, U.K., 1996-99. Author: Economics of Leisure and Recreation, 1975, Spatial Economic Behaviour, 1980, Urban Economies, 1984. Fellow Royal Soc. Arts, Chartered Inst. Transport, Inst. Logistics and Transport; mem. Regional Sci. Assn., Regional Studies Assn. Avocations: travel and transport, langs., music. Office: U Kent, Canterbury CT2 7NP, England

VICKERS, JOHN STUART, government official; b. Eastbourne, Eng., July 7, 1958; s. Aubrey and Kay V.; m. Maureen Freed, 1991; children: James, Zoe, Hannah. BA, Oxford U., 1979, MPhil, 1983, DPhil, 1985. Fellow All Souls Coll., Oxford, Eng., 1979-84, 91—, Nuffield Coll., Oxford, 1984-90; Drummond prof. pol. economy Oxford U., 1991—; exec. dir., chief economist Bank of England, London, 1998-2000; dir. gen. Office of Fair Trading, London, 2000—. Author (with G. Yarrow): Privatization: An Economic Analysis, 1988 (with M. Armstrong and S. Cowan) Regulatory Reform, 1994; contbr. articles to jours. Fellow British Acad., Econometric Soc. Fax: 020 7211 8920. Office: Office of Fair Trading, 2-6 Salisbury Sq, London EC4Y 8JX, England

VICKERY, HAROLD KIRBY, JR., lawyer; b. Worcester, Mass., July 4, 1941; arrived in Thailand, 1968; s. Harold Kirby and Mary Letitia (Miller) V. BA, Trinity Coll., Hartford, Conn., 1963; JD, U. Pa., 1966. Bar: Mass., 1967, U.S. Supreme Ct., 1970. Asst. dir. Houston Hall Student Union, U. Pa., Phila., 1966-67; judge advocate USAF, Minot AFB, N.D., 1967-68; judge advocate, fgn. claims commr. USAF, U-Tapao Airfield, Thailand, 1968-70; mil. judge Headquarters, 7/13th Air Force, Bangkok, Thailand, 1970-72; assoc. Price, Sanond & Assocs., Ltd., Bangkok, 1972-74; ptnr. Vickery & Worachai Ltd., Bangkok, 1975—; ret.lt. col. USAFR, 1989. Bd. dirs., v.p. Community Svcs. of Bangkok, 1988-93; chmn. com. Reps. Abroad Thailand, 1990-92; vice chmn. Asia-Pacific Coun. Am. C. of C., 1992-94; mem. bd. fellows Trinity Coll., 1994-2000. Decorated Bronze Star. Mem. ABA, Mass. Bar Assn., Worcester County Bar Assn., Am. C. of C. in Thailand (gov. 1981-84, 86-87, 89-92, 94-97, 99—, pres. 1984, Disting. Svc. award 1990), Am. Philatelic Soc., Army and Navy Club, Capitol Hill Club, Royal Bangkok Sports Club. Republican. Roman Catholic. Home: 31A Tower Pk, 52/144 Soi 3, (Nana Nua), Sukhumvit Rd, Bangkok 10110, Thailand Office: 16th Fl Diethelm Tower A, 93/1 Wireless Rd, Bangkok 10330, Thailand

VICKERY, JON LIVINGSTONE, neurologist; b. Freeport, Ill., May 30, 1955; s. Eugene Livingstone and Millie Margaret (Cox) V.; m. Diane Antoinetti; children: Daniel Scott, John Michael. BA, Northwestern U., 1976; MD, U. Ill., Chgo., 1980. Diplomate Nat. Bd. Med. Examiners. Resident in neurology U. Va., Charlottesville, 1980-84; staff neurologist Pinnacle Health Sys., Harrisburg, Pa., 1984—; ptnr. Pa. Neurol. Assocs., Lemoyne, Pa., 1984—; assoc. prof. of medicine Hershey Med. Ctr., Pa. State U., 1984-99; chief of medicine Holy Spirit Hosp., Camp Hill, Pa., 1992-95; asst. coach Dickinson Coll. Fencing Team. Mem. AMA, Am. Acad. Neurology, Dauphin County Med. soc. (del. 1985—), U.S. Fencing Coaches Assn., U.S. Fencing Assn., Am. Orchid Soc. (cert. judge, mem. conservation com, 1989-91), Beaufort Hunt Club, Masons, Shriners. Avocations: fencing, photography, raising orchids, theater. Office: Pa Neurol Assocs 108 Lowther St Lemoyne PA 17043-2012

VICTOR, ANDRAS, environmental educator; b. Tahi, Hungary, Aug. 23, 1943; s. Janos and Piroska (Bereczky) V.; m. Zsuzsanna Thoma. MS, Eotvos U., 1967, PhD, 1971. Tchr. Sanitary Vocat. Sch., Budapest, 1967-71; lectr. Nat. Pedagogical Inst., Budapest, 1971-77; sr. lectr. Eotvos U., Budapest, 1977—; vice prin. Eotvos U., 1986-92, head dept. chemistry, 1992-95. Author: Biology, 1972, Language and Thinking, 1977, The Man in the Time and Space, 1980; editor: Pedagogy of Chemistry, 1988. Mem. IUCN Com. on Edn. in Hungary (chair 1985—), Hungarian Biology Soc. (sec. didact sect. 1989—), Hungarian Soc. for Environ. Edn. (co-chair 1993—), Green Heart Youth Environ. Movement (chair 1999—). Avocations: playing piano and recorder, hiking, botanics, birdwatching. Home: Lajos 105, H-1036 Budapest Hungary Office: Eotvos U Tchr Tng Faculty, Marko 29, H-1055 Budapest Hungary

VICTOR, JEFFREY SPENCER, sociology educator; b. N.Y.C., Oct. 1, 1941; s. Bert Lawrence and May Victor; m. Michele Marie Honoré, July 17, 1965; 1 child, Mathieu. BS in Social Studies Edn., SUNY, Oneonta, 1963; postgrad., U. Md., 1963-65; MS in Sociology and Psychology, SUNY, Buffalo, 1969, PhD in Sociology, 1974. Prof. sociology Jamestown (N.Y.) C.C., 1965—; mem. adv. bd. False Memory Syndrome Found., Phila., 1992—. Author: Human Sexuality, 1980, Satanic Panic, 1993; also articles. Recipient Chancellor's award for teaching excellence SUNY, 1988, H.L. Mencken Book Awd., 1994. Mem. Internat. Soc. for Contemporary Legend Rsch. Unitarian. Home: 30 Hillcrest Ave Jamestown NY 14701-6118 Office: Jamestown CC 525 Falconer St Jamestown NY 14701-1920

VICTOR, TETZ VENIAMIM, microbiologist; b. Leningrad, Mar. 28, 1949; s. Tetz I. Veniamin and Lozinskaya G. Gilda; m. Achkinazi I. Rimma; 1 child, George. Diploma, Inst. Pavlov Med. Inst., Leningrad, 1972. Medical diplomate. Rschr. Influenza Inst., Leningrad, 1972-75; asst. prof. Inst. Pavlov Med. Inst., Leningrad, 1975-90, assoc. prof., 1990-91; prof. head of dept. State Pavlov Med. U., St. Petersburg, Russia, 1991—. Author: (books) Self-Regulation of Parasitogenic Systems, 1987, Manual of Clinical Microbiology, 1994; author, editor: (book) Molecular Biology of Bacteria; author/editor: (book) Cells Communities, 1998. Mem. Russian Acad. of Natural Scis., Russian Soc. Microbiology, Am. Soc. Microbiology, N.Y. Acad. Scis., Russian Soc. Clin. Microbiology (pres. St. Petersburg br.). Home: 27 Lensoveta str 95, 196066 Saint Petersburg Russia Office: St Petersburg State Pavlov, Med U/L Tolstoy str 6/8, 197089 Saint Petersburg Russia

VICTORINUS See KONG-HI YOUN

VIDAL, ALAIN JEAN BAPTISTE, agricultural and environmental engineer; b. Livry-Gargan, France, Oct. 6, 1961; s. Hervé Ernest Andre and Solange Marie Jeanne (Brunet) V.; m. Pascale Lydie Michele Ringenbach, July 1, 1983; children: Caroline, Alexandrine, Céline, Thomas, Jean-Nita. Degree in Agronomy Engring., Inst. Nat. Agronomique Paris-Grignon, Paris, 1984; Degree in Agri. & Environ. Engring., Ecole Nat. du Genie Rural des Eaux et des Forets, Paris, 1985; PhD in Water Scis., U. Montpellier (France) II, 1989; habilitation dir. rsch., U. Paul Sabatier, Toulouse, France, 1996. Engr. Cemagref, Toulouse, 1985-86; project mgr. Cemagref, Montpellier, 1988-91, rsch. leader, 1992-96, sr. scientist, 1996-98; tech. adviser Ormvag, Kenitra, Morocco, 1986-88; reg. theme mgr. Iptrid, Rome, Italy, 1998—; expert European Commn., Brussels, 1995-98, SPOT-IMAGE, Cairo, 1995. Author: Teledetection et Irrigation, 1990 (Vermeil medal French Acad. Agr. 1991); editor Thermal Remote Sensing, 1994, Use of Remote Sensing Techniques in Irrigation and Drainage, 1995, Télédétection et systémes d'information géographiques en irrigation et drainage, 1998, Remote Sensing and Geographic Information Systems in Irrigation and Drainage, 2000. Mem. Assn. Francaise pour l'Etude des Irrigations et du Drainage (vice chmn. 1996—). Roman Catholic. Avocations: music, choir conducting. Office: Iptrid, V d Terme di Caracalla, 00100 Rome Italy

VIDAL, CARLOS EUGÊNIO SOTO, veterinarian, immunologist, researcher; b. Pelotas, Brazil, July 31, 1963; s. Francisco Dias da Costa and Ana Elisa Soto (Peralta) V. Med.Vet., Fed. U. Pelotas, 1984; biotech. specialist diploma, Fed. U. Rio Grande do Sul, Porto Alegre, Brazil, 1988; animal toxicology specialist diploma, Pontifical Cath. U. Rio Grande Do Sul, Porto Alegre, 1987; MPhil, U. Edinburgh, Scotland, 1997. Rsch. trainee Fed. U. Pelotas, 1987-89; rsch. trainee Brazilian Agrl. Rsch. Agy., Sobral, 1985-87, jr. rschr., 1989-97; rschr. Brazilian Agrl. Rsch. Agy., Concórdia, 1997—. Contbr. articles to sci. jours., including Revista Microbiologia, Small Ruminant Rsch. Mem. Brazialian Assn. Veterinarians Specialized on Pigs. Office: Embrapa, Suinos e Aves, Caixa Postal 21, 89700000 Concórdia SC, Brazil

VIDAL, DAVID JONATHAN, insurance company executive, journalist; b. Bayamón, P.R., Oct. 11, 1946; s. Jesus Maria and Ercira Audacia (Mejia) V.; m. Watuza Leal, Jan. 25, 1975; 1 child, Katalyn. AB cum laude, Princeton U., 1968; student, Sch. Advanced Internat. Studies, Washington, 1982-83; MBA, Columbia U., 1991. Reporter The Caracas (Venezuela) Daily Jour., 1969-70; reporter, news editor AP, Caracas, N.Y., Sao Paulo, 1970-73; corr. AP, Brasilia, Brazil, 1973-75; reporter, bur. chief N.Y. Times, N.Y.C. and Rio de Janeiro, 1975-80; spl. asst., White House fellow Dept. State, Washington, 1980-81; cons. U.S. AID, Washington, 1981-82; dept. mgr. task force Pres.'s Pvt. Sector Survey on Cost Control, Washington, 1982-83; exec. dir. Nat. Commn. Secondary Schooling for Hispanics, Washington, 1983-84; dir. pub. affairs N.Y.C. Partnership, 1984-85; asst. v.p. Continental Ins., N.Y.C., 1985-95; v.p. Coun. on Fgn. Rels., N.Y.C., 1995-97; dir. rsch. global corp. citizenship The Conf. Bd., N.Y.C., 1997—; adj. prof. journalism Columbia U. Grad. Sch. Journalism, N.Y.C., 1985-86; bd. dirs. Pub. Affairs Coun., Washington, 1988-95; trustee Found. for Pub. Affairs, Washington, 1989-95; mem. Contbns. Adv. Group, 1988-95, chmn., 1994-95; mem. corp. adv.

group Schomburg Ctr. for Rsch. in Black Culture, 1988-95, Ad Hoc Com. on Charter Revision, 1988, Nat. Hispanic Agenda, 1988; mem. adv. group Latino Leadership Fund, 1991-95; vice-chmn. Nat. Civic League, 1999—. Author newspaper series N.Y. Times, 1980; contbr. articles and reports in field. Trustee N.Y. Theol. Sem., N.Y.C., 1990—; elder, trustee West End Presbyn. Ch., N.Y.C., 1986—; mem. Coun. of Fgn. Rels.; prin. Coun. for Excellence in Govt., Washington, 1992—; dir. Coun. on Internat. Ednl. Exchange, N.Y.C., 1997—. Recipient Hispanic Achievement award Wall Street chpt. IMAGE, N.Y.C., 1989; Fulbright scholar, Washington and Venezuela, 1968. Mem. N.Y. Regional Assn. Grantmakers (dir., sec. 1988-95), Nat. Inst. Industry Assn. (corp. adv. group 1990-95), Nat. Civic League, Internat. Platform Assn., Coun. on Fgn. Rels. Democrat. Office: The Conf Bd 845 3rd Ave New York NY 10022-6601

VIDAL, HECTOR MARCELO, foreign trade manager; b. Buenos Aires, Sept. 18, 1946; s. Roberto and Carmen (Vazquez) V. Grad., Sch. Comml., Buenos Aires. With cost-import-export dept. GTE-Sylvania Argentina S.A., Buenos Aires, 1963-72; chief of import-export dept. Lab. Roux Ocefa S.A., Buenos Aires, 1973-87; mgr. fgn. trade Microsules Argentina S.A., Buenos Aires, 1987-90; pruchase and fgn. trade dir. Microsules y Bernabo S.A., Buenos Aires, 1987—. Contbr. articles to trade jours. Mem. Chamber of Hosp. Equipment (bd. dirs. 1976-87), Chamber of Fine Chems. Prodrs. and Pharm. Raw Material (bd. dirs. 1982-90), Chamber of Importers and Exporters of Republica Argentina (pres., chmn. 1995-2000). Office: Av Pueyrredon 936 Piso 3 Dept 17, 1032 Buenos Aires Argentina

VIDAL, RAOUL FRANCOIS, ophthalmologist; b. Olargues, France, Nov. 27, 1943; s. Raoul Alexis and Genevieve (Grand) V.; m. Elisabeth Marie Brault, July 31, 1969; children: Francois, Anne-Claire. Degree, Nat. Ctr. Ophthalmology, Paris, 1973; advanced diploma in histo-cytology, U. Sci., Paris, 1977. Bd. cert. diplomate in ophthalmology. Corneal rsch. fellow U. Fla. Coll. Medicine, Gainesville, 1974-75; vis. rsch. assoc. prof. Sch. Pharmacy Hebrew U., Jerusalem, 1977-78; med. dir. Chibret Lab. Merck Sharp Dohme, Paris, 1979-80; asst. head dept. Inst. A. Vernes, Paris, 1980-92; ophthal. surgeon Am. Hosp. of Paris, 1992—. Editor Rev. Chibret du Glaucome, 1980-81. Gen. sec. French Eye Bank, Paris, 1975-78, Claude Bernard Assn., Paris, 1982-90. Mem. French Soc. Ophthalmology, European Soc. Cataract and Refractive Surgeons, Paris Soc Ophthalmology (bd. dirs.). Avocations: swimming, photography, numerised images. Office: 33 ave de Villiers, 75017 Paris France

VIDAL, RICARDO CARDINAL, archbishop of Cebu; b. Mogpog, Marinduque, Philippines, Feb. 6, 1931; s. Fructuoso and Natividad (Jamin) V. ordained priest Roman Cath. Ch., 1956. Consecrated bishop Titular Ch. Claterna, 1971; archbishop Lipa, Philippines, 1973-81, Cebu, Philippines, 1982—; proclaimed cardinal, 1985. Office: Chancery, PO Box 52, 6000 Cebu The Philippines*

VIDAL-MADJAR, ALFRED, astrophysicist; b. Cairo, Sept. 13, 1942; s. Edouard Papoulard and Hilda (Ruggiero) V.; m. Annie Lafferrerie, Nov. 23, 1963 (div. Dec. 1985); children: Boris, Maxime, Jeremie; m. Nicole Vittaut, Dec. 12, 1995. PhD, U. Paris, 1973. Maitre de recherche CNRS, Paris, 1977-84, dir. rsch. II, 1984-89, dir. rsch. I, 1989—; maitre de conf. Ecole Polytechnique, Palaiseau, France, 1977-91; cons. CNES, Paris, 1973-88, European Space Agy., Paris, 1976-88; mem. FUSE (Far Ultraviolet Spectroscopic Explorer) sci. team NASA, Balt., 1992—; bd. dirs. Can.-France-Hawaii Telescope, Waimea, Hawaii, 1990-96. Author: Atlas d'Astronomie (ency.), 1985, Il pleut des planetes, Hachette, 1999 ; editor: Circumstellar Dust Disks, 1995, Sommes nous seuls dans l'univers?, 2000. Lt. French Mil., 1963-65. Chevalier Ordre Nat. du Merite, France, 1989, CNRS Silver medalist, 1988. Mem. Internat. Astron. Union. Achievements include detection of deuterium in interstellar space; indentificatoin of the sun inside an interstellar cloud; discovery of comets falling on the star Beta Pictoris; possible historical first detection of an extrasolar planet around Beta Pictoris. Avocations: swimming, travel. Office: CNRS-IAP, 98 bis Blvd Arago, 75014 Paris France

VIDELL, JARED STEVEN, cardiologist; b. Phila., Apr. 9, 1947; s. Harry and Rose (Malken) V.; m. Cyla Trocki, Dec. 27, 1969; children: Haviv Elana, Mikhael Alon, Samara Pilar. BEd, U. Miami, 1969; DO, Phila. Coll. Osteo. Medicine, 1976. Resident and chief resident in internal medicine Atlantic City (N.J.) Med. Ctr., 1976-79; fellow in cardiovascular diseases Albert Einstein Med. Ctr., Phila., 1979-81; rsch. fellow in nuclear cardiology Deborah Heart and Lung Ctr., Browns Mills, N.J., 1981-82; dir. employee health svcs. Deborah Heart and Lung Ctr., Browns Mills, 1982-84; asst. dir. cardiology Pritikin Longevity Ctr., Downington, Pa., 1984-87; cardiologist, dir. clin. lab. Physician Care, P.C., Towanda, Pa., 1987-90; from co-chmn. intensive care to dir. cardiac stress lab. Meml. Hosp., Towanda, 1987-90; dir. house staff, intensive/cardiac care Lower Bucks Hosp., Bristol, Pa., 1992-94; dir. house staff ICU-CCU North Phila. Health Systems, 1994-97; med. dir. North Phila. Health Sys. Girard Med. Ctr., 1997—, chmn. clin. medicine, 1997—; med. dir. Am. Cancer Soc. chpt., 1989-90; state peer rev. KEPRO, 1989-90. Contbr. rsch. articles to profl. jours. Fellow Am. Coll. Angiology; mem. AMA, Am. Coll. Chest Physicians, Am. Soc. Internal Medicine, Internat. Soc. Internal Medicine, Internat. Soc. Endovascular Surgery, Am. Coll. Physician Execs., Internat. Platform Assn., Pa. Med. Soc., Phila. County Med. Soc., Alumni Assn. Phila. Coll. Osteo. Medicine, Nat. Assn. Managed Care Physicians (mem. medicine, law, and ethics). Jewish. Avocations: squash, cycling, cross country skiing, traveling, fishing. Home: 408 N Exeter Ave Margate City NJ 08402-1868

VIDIGAL, EULER COSTA, orthopedic surgeon, traumatologist, consultant; b. Caxias, Brazil, Oct. 10, 1933; s. Edesio and Alice Smith (Torreao da Costa) V.; m. Conceicao Lyra Pessoa, Dec. 20, 1960; children: Euler Costa Vidigal Jr., Erik Lyra Pessoa Vidigal. MD, U. Maranhao, Sao Luiz, Brazil, 1963. Resident Inst. of Orthopaedics, U. Sao Paulo, Brazil, 1964-65; staff orthopedic surgeon Fundacao Hospitalar, Brazilia, Brazil, 1966-96; fellow in orthopedic surgery Bristol (Eng.) Hosps., 1973-74; asst. prof. orthopedics U. Brasilia, 1967-70; chief in orthopedics Hosp. de Base, Brasilia, 1979-82. Co-author: Newborn Routine Manual, 3d edit., 1997; contbr. articles to profl. jours. Fellow Brazilian Coll. Surgeons, Brazilian Soc. Orthopedics and Traumatology, Brazilian Soc. Pediatric Orthopedics, Brazilian Soc. Foot Surgery (co-founder 1975), Brit. Orthopaedic Assn. (Overseas fellow); mem. N.Y. Acad. Scis. Avocations: Spanish guitar, jazz, Bossa Nova. Home: SHIS QL 12, Conjunto 04, Casa 13, 71630 Brasilia Brazil Office: SMHN-Quandra 2 Bloco A, Edificio das Clinicas/6o, 70710 Brasilia Brazil

VIDÓCZY, TAMÁS, chemist; b. Budapest, Hungary, Nov. 11, 1948; s. Tamás and Erzsébet (Simon) V.; m. Andrea Vendel, June 13, 1976; children: Katalin, Judit. MS in Chemistry, Eötvös U., 1972, MS in Math., 1976, PhD in Phys. Chemistry, 1976; degree, Hungarian Acad. Sci., 1986. Jr. rsch. assoc. Ctrl. Rsch. Inst. for Chemistry, Budapest, 1972-76, rsch. assoc., 1976-86, sr. rsch. assoc., 1986-93, head of group, 1993—. Editor: Combustion Efficiency and Air Quality, 1995; editor-in-chief Jour. Photochemistry and Photobiology B: Biology, 1999—; contbr. articles to profl. jours. Mem. European Soc. for Photobiology (newsletter editor 1996-99), European Photochemistry Assn. (sec. 1989-93). Avocations: hiking, photography. Office: Chem Rsch Ctr, Pusztaszeri ut 59-67, H-1025 Budapest Hungary

VIDOVIĆ, DAVORKO, social welfare administrator; b. Sisak, June 26, 1956; married; 2 children. Degree in sociology and physiology, U. Zagreb, 1980. H.s. tchr. sociology, philosophy, psychology Sisak; v.p. SDP, 1993, 96, min. labor and social welfare, 2000—. Res. maj. Croatian Army, 1991-92. Office: SDP, Sisak Croatia

VIDYASAGAR, PANDIT BHALCHANDRA, biophysicist, educator; b. Amalner, India, Sept. 1, 1953; s. Bhalchandra Hanumant and Pushpa Bhalchandra (Kulkarni) V.; m. Sandhya Vasant Mujumdar, Nov. 23, 1981; children: Ketan, Kunal. BSc, Ahmednagar (India) Coll., 1973; MSc in Physics, U. Pune (India), 1975; PhD, U. Pune, 1980. Lectr. Nat. Def. Acad., Pune, 1979; lectr. U. Pune, 1979-91, reader, 1991, dir. Sch. of Basic Med. Sci., 1994, dir. Bioinformatics Ctr., 1996, 99—, chmn. Bd. of Studies, 1997—; mem. Acad. Coun., chmn. Students' Welfare, U. Pune. Author: Medical Instrumentation, 1995; asst. editor Jour. Physics Edn.; contbr. articles to profl. jours. Found. for Med. Rsch. fellow, Bombay, 1976-79, fellow Maharastra Acad. Scis., 1997; assoc. Abdus Salam-Internat. Ctr. Theoretical Physics, Triest, Italy, 1998—. Mem. Inst. Physics (U.K.), Indian Physics Assn. (Hari Om Trust Presit 1991, M.W. Chiplonkar award 1996, sec. Pune chpt. 1982-84), Indian Biophys. Soc. (nat. exec. body 1992-96), Jidnyasa Sci. Club (pres. 1991). Avocation: scientific writing. E-mail: pbv@physics.unipune.einet.in. Home: B-9 Suyognagar, Pune 411016, India Office: Dept Physic U Pune, Ganeshkhind, 411 007 Pune India

VIE, GEORGE WILLIAM, III, lawyer; b. Tampa, Fla., Mar. 21, 1961; s. George William Jr. and Cheri Ann (Bass) V. BS magna cum laude, U. Houston, Clear Lake, Tex., 1985; JD, U. Tex., 1988. Bar: Tex. 1989, U.S. Dist. Ct. (so. dist.) Tex. 1990, U.S. Ct. Appeals (5th cir.) 1990, U.S. Mil. Ct. Appeals 1995, U.S. Supreme Ct. 1995; bd. cert. civil appellate law Tex. Bd. Legal Specialization. Legal asst. Bankston, Wright & Greenhill, Austin, Tex., 1985-89; atty. Bankston, Wright & Greenhill, Austin, 1989-90; ptnr. Mills, Shirley, Eckel & Bassett, Galveston, Tex., 1990—; spkr. in field. Contbr. articles to legal publs. Fellow Tex. Bar Found.; mem. FBA, State Bar Tex., Phi Kappa Phi, Sigma Phi Epsilon. Office: Mills Shirley Eckel & Bassett 2228 Mechanic St Ste 400 Galveston TX 77550-1591

VIÉ, JEAN CHRISTOPHE, veterinarian; b. Alger, Algeria, Feb. 9, 1962; s. Paul and Nicole (Duchene-Maullaz) V.; 1 child, Cyuelle. DVM, Maison Alfort, France, 1986; PhD in Ecology, Montpellier U., France, 1998. Veterinarian Ctr. Internat. Recherches Medicales, Franceville, Gabon, 1987-88; head psychology unit Institut Pasteur, Cayenne, French Guiana, 1990-91; wildlife veterinarian Wildlife Rsch. Ctr., Taif, Saudi Arabia, 1992; resident Calif. U., Davis, 1992-93; dir. wildlife rescue rsch. programme Petit Saut, Kovrov, French Guiana, 1993-98; pres. Assn. Kwata, Cayenne, French Guiana, 1995—; cons. Natural Reserves, French Guiana, 1994—, TerraAmazone, French Guiana and Brazil, 1999; expert VICN, 1993—, IUCN, 1999—. Contbr. articles to profl. jours. Founder NGO Kwata, French Guiana, 1994. Avocations: travel, sports, photography, plane piloting, nature. Office: Assn Kwata, 1 Pl Schoelcher BP672, 97335 Cayenne French Guiana

VIEDMA, ANTONIO, engineering educator; b. Torreperogil, Jaen, Spain, Oct. 18, 1960; s. Andres and Elena (Robles) V.; m. Rosario Guiard, Dec. 15, 1985; children: Elena, Maria del Valle, Andres. Aero. Engr., U. Politecnica, Madrid, 1983, D Aero. Engring., 1988. Cert. aero. engr. Rsch. asst. U. Politecnica, Madrid, 1984-85, asst. prof., 1985-90, assoc. prof., 1990-94, prof. engring., 1994—; sub-dir. Sch. Aero. Engring., Madrid, 1991-93, Sch. Indsl. Engring., Cartagena, Spain, 1996-97; v.p. U. Politecnica, Cartagena, 1998-99; dir. thermal and fluids enging. dept., Univ. Politecnica, Cartagena, 1999—. Lt. Spanish Air Force, 1983-85. Recipient Francisco Arranz 2, Aero. Engring. Assn., Spain, 1983, Premio Nat. Estudios U., Ministry Edn., Spain, 1984. Office: ETS Ingenieros Industriales, P Alfonso XIII 48, 30 203 Cartagena Murcia, Spain

VIEIRA, DAVID GUEIROS, retired history educator; b. Garanhuns, Brazil, Sept. 12, 1929; s. Aggeu Vieira da Silva and Noemi (Gueiros) Vieira; m. Anne Taylor Pettit, July 3, 1952 (div. 1967); children: David Jr., Taylor; m. Heloisa Guimaraes Domingues, Apr. 16, 1973; children: Daniel, Regina Maria. BA in U.S. History, King Coll., Va., Tenn., 1952; MA in U.S. History, U. Richmond, 1960; PhD in Latin Am. History, Am. U., 1973; diploma, Escola Superior de Guerra, Rio de Janeiro, 1979. Prof. history Longwood Coll., Farmville, Va., 1961-65; pres. Vieira Enterprises Inc., Caldwell, N.J., 1968-73; prof. history U. Brasilia, Brazil, from 1973; chairperson dept. history U. Brasilia, 1974-78; pres. U. Brasilia Press., 1978-79; cons., rep. Fed. U. Amapá, Brasilia, 1998, vice-rector, 1998; mem. Nat. Commn. for the Celebration of the 500th Yr. of the Discovery of Brazil, 1998—; pres. Found. for Devel. of Rsch. and Culture of Fed. U. Amapá, 1998. Author: Protestantismo, Maçonaria e a Questao Religiosa no Brasil, 1980, Uma Luz na Montanha: Colégio XV de Novembro, 1999; contbr. articles to profl. jours. Mem. Pi Sigma Alpha, Phi Alpha Theta. Presbyterian. Home: SQN 202 Bloco G Apt 506, 70832070 Brasilia DF, Brazil

VIEIRA, LUIZ CARLOS, microbiologist, consultant; b. Sao Paulo, Brazil, Apr. 28, 1951; s. Laius Fernandes and Zelia Gonzaga V.; m. Maria Aparecida Faria Gomes, April 9, 1985. BSc, U. Sao Paulo, 1978, MSc, 1999. Lab. analyst Bayer S.A., Sao Paulo, 1979-80; microbiology analyst Cyanamid Chem., Resende, Brazil, 1982, Stanley Home Ltd., Sao Paulo, 1983-88; biologist Bruch Labs., Sao Paulo, 1989-90, Trilab Diagnostics, Sao Paulo, 1990-95; master degree Inst. Biomed. Scis., Sao Paulo, 1996-99; Cons. Proteika Foods, Belo Horizonte, Brazil, 1982-83, Bruch Labs., Sao Paulo, 1989-90; quality control supr. Confrio Co., Sao Paulo, 1981. Contbr. articles to profl. jours. Mem. Cosmetics Brazilian Assn. Avocations: movies, sports, TV, internet, music. E-mail: lcvieira@yahoo.com.

VIEIRA DA SILVA, JORGE, agronomy researcher and consultant; b. Lisbon, Portugal, June 11, 1929; arrived in France, 1963; s. Antonio and Vitoria (Bravo) Vieira da S.; m. Teresa Valadas, Sept. 17, 1949; children: Isabel, Jorge. Degree in Agronomy, Higher Inst. Agronomy, Lisbon, 1953; PhD, U. Paris, 1970. Geneticist Cereals Inst., Angola, 1953-57; agronomist Mission for Agr., Angola, 1967-60; sec. for agr. Govt. of Angola, Luanda, 1961-62; rschr. Overseas Rsch. Corp., Ivory Coast, 1963-71; prof. U. Paris, 1971-97; cons. Paris, 1977—. Author: Cattle Management in Angola, 1960, Introduction to Ecological Theory, 1979; contbr. more than 120 articles to profl. jours. Recipient Gold medal Acad. of Agr., Paris, 1975. Mem. AAAS, N.Y. Acad. Sci. Avocations: gardening, painting. Office: Devel Cons, Les Belliards, 41320 Maray France

VIEL, ANTOINE, management consultant; b. France, 1963. Engr., 1986, MBA, 1986. Mng. dir. Mozartis, Neuilly/Seine, France, 1993—. Office: Mozartis, 6 bd Julien Potin, 92200 Neuilly/Seine France

VIENKEN, JOERG HANS, chemical engineer; b. Wittlich, Fed. Republic Germany, June 1, 1948; s. Walter and Ruth (Würtenberger) V.; m. Karin Bock; children: Hans, Peter, Claudia. Diploma Ing., Tech. U., Darmstadt, Fed. Republic Germany, 1975; D. Ing., Tech. U., Aachen, Fed. Republic Germany, 1980. Scientist Nuclear Rsch. Ctr. Jülich, Fed. Republic Germany, 1976-84, Inst. Biotechnology, Würzburg, Fed. Republic Germany, 1984-85, R&D Bus. Unit Membrana, Wuppertal, Fed. Republic Germany, 1985-88; head dept. Inst. Med. Membrane Application Akzo Wuppertal, 1988-95; rsch. dir., head dept. sci. svcs. Fresenius Med. Care, 1996-98, v.p. bus. unit sci. and product consulting, 1999—; prof. Internat. Faculty for Artificial Organs, 1996; guest prof. Danube U., Krems, Austria; hon. prof. Internal Med. Assn., Bulgaria. Contbr. chpts. to books. Fellow Bulgarian Soc. Nephrology (bd.; mem. European Soc. Artificial Organs, Internat. Soc. Artificial Organs. Home: Mozart Strasse 14, D-61250 Usingen Germany Office: Fresenius Med Care, Else Kroener Str 1, D-61352 Bad Homburg Germany

VIENONEN, MIKKO ANTERO, health care executive; b. Helsinki, Jan. 19, 1946; s. Erkki Tapio and Kaarina Helena (Lehtonen) V.; m. Sinikka Hellevi Olin, July 29, 1967; children: Ilkka Mikael, Venla Katriina, Aleksi Johannes. MD, U. Helsinki, 1971; specialist in gen. practice, Nat. Bd. Health, Helsinki, 1980; PhD, U. Kuopio, Finland, 1986. Cert. competency in health adminstrn. and mgmt. Nat. Bd. Health, Helsinki; spl. competency in internat. health Finnish Med. Assn., Helsinki. Intern Univ. Hosp. Helsinki, 1971; resident in general practice Ctrl. Hosp. Middle Finland, 1978-79; leading physician Health Ctr., Saarijarvi, Finland, 1973-82; chief med. officer Nat. Bd. Health, Helsinki, 1983-89; project dir. Health Devel. Cooperation Group, Helsinki, 1990-92; regional advisor WHO-EURO, Copenhagen, 1993-99; spl. rep. dir. gen. WHO, Moscow, Russia, 1999—. Author: Critical Challenges for Health Care Reform in Europe, 1998; co-author: Health and Disease in Developing Countries, 1994, European Health Care Reforms: Analysis of Current Strategies, 1997; editor: Citizens' Choice and Patients' Rights, 1996; mem. editl. bd. Laaketieteen Termit, 1991. Lt. Finnish Army, 1972-73. Mem. Finnish Med. Assn., Finnish Drs. Scientific Assn. Avocations: visual arts, culinary explorations, culture, human language. Home: Sysimiehenkuja 1, 00670 Helsinki Finland Office: WHO Regional Office Europe, UN House Ostozhenka St, 119034 Moscow Russian Fedn

VIERECK, WOLFGANG WILHELM, linguist; b. Berlin, Sept. 4, 1937; s. Wilhelm and Irmgard (Linck) V.; m. Karin Anna-Maria Ditschuneit, Sept. 21, 1973; 1 child, Nina. PhD summa cum laude, U. Hamburg, Germany, 1966; DLitt, U. Mainz, Germany, 1970; PhD honoris causa, Eötvös Loránd U., Budapest, Hungary, 1989, U. Uppsala, Sweden, 1996, U. Poznan, Poland, 1999. Rsch. asst. English dept. U. Hamburg, 1963-69; from asst. to assoc. prof. English dept. U. Mainz, 1969-73; prof., head English dept. U. Graz, Austria, 1973-78; prof. English linguistics and medieval English lit. U. Bamberg, Germany, 1978—; expert adviser German Rsch. Coun., Bonn, Germany, 1988-95; mem. Internat. Expert Com. on Modern Lang. and Lit., Amsterdam, The Netherlands, 1992-95; pres. Internat. Congress Dialectology, Bamberg, 1990. Author, editor 23 books, including: Studies on the Influence of the English Language on German, 1980, English in Contact with other Languages, 1986, The Computer Developed Linguistic Atlas of England, vol. 1, 1991, vol. 2, 1997; editor Dialectologia et Geolinguistica, 1993—, Univ. Bamberg Studies in English Linguistics, 1979—; mem. editl. bd. Atlas Linguarum Europae, 1992—; contbr. articles to profl. jours. Recipient Rector's medal U. Poznań, Poland, 1987, U. Helsinki, Finland, 1988, Basque Acad., Bilbao, Spain, 1990, Medal of Merit U. Poznań, 1992, Internat. Cultural awards Foyer, Rome, 1998, Catania, 1998; Rsch. fellow Japan Soc. for the Promotion Sci., 1992, Am. Coun. Learned Soc. fellow, N.Y., 1966-67. Mem. Internat. Soc. for Dialectology and Geolinguistics (v.p. 1989-97, pres. 1997—), Atlas Linguarum Europae (v.p. 1992-98, pres. 1998—), Internat. Assn. U. Profs. English (pres. 1998—), N.Y. Acad. Scis., Royal Humanistic Acad. Scis. (Uppsala, Sweden), Royal Gustavus Adolphus Acad. (Uppsala), Internat. Acad. Scis. Avocations: gardening, music. Home: Obere Dorotheenstr 5a, 96049 Bamberg Germany Office: Univ Bamberg, An der Universität 9, 96045 Bamberg Germany

VIERENDEELS, PAUL, chemist; b. Oberhausen, Germany, Sept. 11, 1952; m. Anne-Marie Soete; children: Lennert, Lei. MSc in Chemistry, Vrije Universiteit, Brussels, 1977. Area sales mgr. Kaneka Belgium, Belgium, 1979-84; with comml. devel. dept. Phillips Petroleum, Belgium, 1984; product mgr. Ethyl Corp., Belgium, 1987-90, bus. mgr., 1990-95; SAP project implementation leader Albemarle, France, 1996-97; bus. dir. Albemarle, Louvain-La-Neuve-Sud, Belgium, 1995-96, bus. dir. fine chemicals, 1997—. Office: Albemarle Europe SARL, 9 Rue du Bosquet, B 1348 Louvain La Neuve Sud Belgium

VIERHELLER, TODD, software engineering consultant; b. Winter Park, Fla., June 22, 1958; s. Irvin Theodore and Jeanne Marie (Zeller) V.; m. Susan Lindhe Watts, Dec. 22, 1984; children: Renate Jeanne, Clark, Lindhe Marie, Kent. BS in Computer Sci., U. Mo., Rolla, 1980; MA in Bibl. Studies, Multnomah Sch. Bible, Portland, Oreg., 1986. Tech. writer, software engr. Tektronix, Beaverton, Oreg., 1981-86; software engr., supr. Intel Corp, Hillsboro, Oreg., 1986-88; software engring. mgr. Summation, Hillsboro, Oreg., 1989-90, 1989-90; software cons. Quality First, Lynnwood, Wash., 1990—; software engr. mgr. Net Market Group, Inc., Bellevue, Wash., 1999; QA engr. PeerLogic Inc., Phoenix, 2000—; software engring. cons. Digital Equipment Corp., Bellevue, Wash., 1990-91, GTE, Bothell, Wash., 1990-91, Frank Russell Co., Tacoma, Wash., 1992-93, InterConnections, Inc., Bellevue, 1993, Novell, San Jose, Calif., 1993, Heartstream, Inc., 1996, N.Am. Morpho Sys., Inc., 1996, Air Touch Cellular, 1996-97; software engring. mgmt. cons. Weyerhauser, Federal Way, Wash., 1991-92, Frank Russell, Tacoma, Wash., 1994, ConnectSoft, Inc., Bellevue, 1994, Microsoft, Redmond, Wash., 1995-96, Nordstrom, Seattle, 1997-98, AT&T Wireless, Redmond, 1999, Ernst & Young, LLP, Seattle, 1998-99; tech. writer, cons. Air Touch Cellular, Bellevue, Wash., 1996-97. Mem. IEEE, NRA, Upsilon Pi Epsilon, Kappa Mu Epsilon. Mem. Republican Constn. Party. Mem. Evang. Christian Ch. Avocations: camping, bicycling, shooting sports, kung fu. Home: 460 E Cascada Rd Litchfield Park AZ 85340-4822

VIERO, GAETANO, marketing executive; b. Arzignano, Vicenza, Italy, Sept. 10; m. Giuseppina Baglieri; children: Andrea, Fabio. Diploma in Econs., Padua U., 1970. Tchr. Tech. H.S., Verona, Italy, 1960-62; tech. worker Lumingom, Verona, 1962-72; pres. Manens Intertecnica, Verona, 1971—. Avocation: mountaineering. Office: Manens Intertecnica Srl, Via Campofiore N 21, 37129 Verona Italy

VIERTL, REINHARD KARL WOLFGANG, statistician, educator, consultant; b. Hall i Tirol, Austria, Mar. 25, 1946; s. Johann Andreas and Hildegard (Waltl) V.; m. Dorothea Elisabeth Pittner, June 24, 1972; children; Nikolaus, Philipp. Dipl.Ing, U. Tech., Vienna, 1972, Dr.tech., 1974. Asst. U. Tech., Vienna, 1972-79, dozent, 1979-80, prof., 1982—; vis. lectr., U. Calif.-Berkeley, 1980-81; vis. dozent U. Klagenfurt, Austria, 1981-82; vis. prof. U. Innsbruck, Austria, 1991-93; dir. Rsch. Projects, Vienna, 1978-84; cons. gov. orgns., Vienna, 1983-84; organizer of confs. 1986, 90, 93, 2000. Author, co-author, editor books on reliability, math. and stats.; hon. theme editor for probability and statistics, UNESCO Encyclopedia of Life Support Systems; contbr. articles to profl. jours. Head Nat. Conf. Sci. Personal, Vienna, 1981-82; mem. Austrian Coun. Rsch., Vienna, 1981-82. With Basic Tng. Artillery, Austria, 1974. Rsch. fellow U. Calif., Berkeley, 1980-81, Max Kade Found. fellow, 1980. Fellow Royal Statis. Soc., Inst. Statisticians; mem. Austrian Math. Soc., Austrian Statis. Soc. (head 1987-95), Austrian Bayes Soc. (head, founder), Internat. Statis. Inst., German Statis. Soc., N.Y. Acad. Scis. Roman Catholic. Office: Vienna U Tech, Wiedner Hauptstr 8-10, 1040 Vienna Austria

VIETA, EDUARD, psychiatrist, educator; b. Barcelona, Spain, Jan. 16, 1963; s. Eduardo and Maria Dolores (Pascual) V.; m. Gloria Fernandez-Esparrach, June 26, 1994. MD, Autonomous U., Barcelona, 1987; PhD, U. Barcelona, Spain, 1994. Cert. psychiatrist. Resident Hosp. Clinic, Barcelona, 1988-91, rsch. fellow, 1992, staff psychiatrist, 1993-94; staff psychiatrist, liaison psychiatry unit, cons. Hosp. Clinic, 1994—, dir. bipolar disorders program, 1998; prof. U. Barcelona, Spain, 1993—; rsch. dir. clin. inst. psychiatry and psychology U. Barcelona, 2000; staff psychiatrist, liaison psychiatry unit, cons. Hosp. Clinic Barcelona, 1994—; sci. cons. Investigacion Medica Permanente, Barcelona, 1991-92; congress organizer European Assn. Psychiatry, Barcelona, 1992. Contbr. articles to profl. jours. in the field. Founder pres. Nat. Bipolar Assn., Barcelona, 1994. Grantee Clinic Found., Barcelona, 1992; named Best Young Investigator Soc. Española de Medicina Psicosomática, 1993. Mem. AAAS, Catalan Psychiat. Soc. (sec. 1997-99), Spanish Biol. Psychiatr. Soc. (Best Doctoral Theses Second award). Avocations: literature, music, soccer, chess, anthropology. Office: U Barcelona Hosp Clinic, Villarroel 170, 08036 Barcelona Spain

VIETOR, ILJA, molecular biologist, researcher; b. Bratislava, Slovakia, Sept. 3, 1964; s. Alexander and Nina (Zidovska) V. D in Natural Scis., Comenius U., Slovakia, 1987; PhD, Slovak Acad. Scis., Slovakia, 1993. Asst. Inst. Exptl. Endocrinology Slovak Acad. Scis., Bratislava, 1983-87, fellow, 1988-91, staff scientist, 1993-94; rsch. fellow in microbiology NYU Med. Ctr., 1991-92, postdoctoral fellow in microbiology, 1994-96; postdoctoral fellow in cell biology Rsch. Inst. Molecular Pathology, Vienna, 1996—. Contbr. articles to profl. jours. including Jour. Biol. Chemistry, Lymphokine and Cytokine Rsch., and European Jour. Pharmacology, Procedures Nat. Acad. Sci. U.S.A., Biochem. Biophys. Actc. Cpl. Dukla, Army Sports Unit Czechoslovak Army, 1987-88. Mem. N.Y. Acad. Scis. Russian Orthodox. Avocations: horseback riding, dressage. Home: Schönbrunnerstrasse 29B8, A-1050 Vienna Austria Office: Rsch Inst Molecular Pathol, Dr Bohr-gasse 7, A-1030 Vienna Austria

VIETOR-ENGLANDER, DEBORAH JUDITH, foreign languages educator, researcher; b. London, Sept. 23, 1946; d. Otokar Elieser and Doris May (Henley) Englander; m. Gustav Vietor; 1 child, Miriam Stella. BA with honors, U. London, 1968; PhD magna cum laude, U. Tübingen, Germany, 1986. Sr. lectr. U. Saarbrücken, Germany, 1972-92, Technische U., Darmstadt, 1992—. Editor: (series) Exil-Dokumente, Jüdische Bibliothek; contbr. articles to profl. jours. E-mail: englande@hrz1.hrz.tu-darmstadt.de. Home: Am Finther Weg 8, 55127 Mainz-Drais Germany Office: Sprachenzentrum Technische U Darmstadt, Hochschul str 1, 64289 Darmstadt Germany

VIGFUSSON, JOHANNES ORN, physicist, scientific officer; b. Akureyri, Iceland, Mar. 15, 1945; s. Vigfus Thorarinn Jonsson and Sigridur Huld Johannesdottir; m. Barbara Ruth Keller, Oct. 18, 1980; 1 child, Vanessa Stefania. Diploma in theoretical physics, U. Zurich, Switzerland, 1974, PhD, 1975; M in Piano, Conservatory Zurich, 1977. Asst. U. Zurich, 1974-75, rschr., 1975-83, 85-87; sci. officer Swiss Fed. Nuclear Safety Inspectorate, Würenlingen, 1987—; vis. asst. prof. CUNY, 1983-84; vis. fellow Princeton

(N.J.) U., 1984-85; tchr. Reisehochschule Zurich, 1968-87; concert pianist, 1977—. Contbr. articles to profl. jours. Pres. Friends of Iceland Soc., 1970-72, 73-78. Recipient Landolt prize Conservatory Zurich, 1975. Mem. Am. Phys. Soc., Swiss Phys. Soc., Icelandic Phys. Soc., N.Y. Acad. Scis., Iceland Soc. Switzerland (pres. 1998—), Planetary Soc., Icelandic Club Switzerland (counsellor 1989-90). Avocations: skiing, sailing, history of culture and civilization. Home: alte Ehrendingerstrasse 325, 5423 Freienwil Switzerland Office: HSK, 5232 Villigen-HSK Switzerland

VIGLIANCO, RICARDO ALBERTO, computer scientist, educator; b. Cordoba, Cor, Argentina, Feb. 19, 1960; s. Tito Mario and Teresa Aide (Pavon) V.; m. Graciela Patricia Rodriguez Garay, May 16, 1981; children: Nicolas Alberto, German Agustin, Victoria Andrea. B, Immaculada Inst., Cordoba, 1978; Sys. Analyst, Gral Urquiza, Rosario, Argentina, 1992. Cert. computer sys. analyst, sys. programmer. Tchg. asst. Gral Urquiza Sch., Rosario, 1991-92; tchr. Jorge Cura Sch., Rosario, 1992-93; tchg. asst. biochem. faculty U. Nat. de Rosario, Rosario, 1993—; technician Ifise-Conicet, Rosario, 1981-85, prin. technician, 1985—; tchr. Lola Mora Sch., Rosario, 1993—; asst. mgr. Kidlink Orgn., Noruega, 1995—; cons. Anesthesiology Soc., Rosario, 1995; cons. province program on AIDS, 1993-98, virtual libr. mgr., Biochem. Fac., 1999—; CEO RG & Assocs. Author: Develop of a Computer System for AIDS Research in Argentina, 1993, Epidemiology of AIDS Followups, 1986-98. Mem. Planetary Soc., Internet Soc. Avocations: fishing, internet, vans. E-mail: rviglian@citynet.net.ar. Office fax: 54 341 4 396664. Home: 2000, Caferatta 1652, 2000 Rosario Santa Fe, Argentina Office: Virtual Libr Biochem Fac, Suipacha 531, 2000 Rosario Santa Fe, Argentina

VIGMO, JOSEF, retired geriatrician; b. Reykjavik, Iceland, Nov. 12, 1922; arrived in Sweden, 1956; s. Olaf Johan Olsen-Vigmostad and Aline Josefine (Zachariassen) Hervik; m. Soffia Axelsdóttir, Jan. 24, 1953; children: Terje, Sylvi Aline. MD, U. Iceland, 1953; postgrad., U. Gothenburg, Sweden, 1960. Lic. in internal medicine, cardiology, geriatrics, Sweden. Asst. med. officer Sandträsks Tuberculosis Sanatorium, Sweden, 1953-54; resident in pulmonary diseases Sandträsks Tuberculosis Sanatorium, 1956-57; rotating intern White Meml. Hosp. and Clinic, Loma Linda U., L.A., 1954-55; resident in internal medicine Piteå County Hosp., Sweden, 1958-59, Kalix and Skene County Hosps., Norrköping Gen. Hosp., Sweden, 1961-65; sub-chief med. officer Hultafors Health Ctr., Sweden, 1960; sub-chief med. officer geriatric dept. Borås Gen. County Hosp., Sweden, 1966-77; chief med. officer geriatric dept. Borås Gen. County Hosp., 1977-87; ret., 1987; consulting cardiologist, Borås Gen. County Hosp., 1978—, lectr. Sch. Nursing, 1967—. Recipient Gold medal Älvsborg County Council, 1987. Mem. Swedish Med. Assn., Swedish Geriatrics Assn., Swedish Assn. Chief Med. Officers, South-Älvsborg County Assn. Chief Med. Officers. Lutheran. Avocations: linguistics, genealogy. Home: Båleröd, Sjövägen 1, S-452 97 Strömstad Sweden

VIGNA, CARLO, cardiologist, researcher; b. Cosenza, Italy, Mar. 8, 1957; s. Rocco and Giulia V.; m. Alessandra Trotta, Oct. 21, 1990; children: Edoardo and Beatrice (twins). MD, Cath. U., Rome, 1981, Cardiology Specialization, 1985, Internal Medicine Specialization, 1990. Med. diplomate. Cardiology fellow Cath. U., Rome, 1981-86; clin. cardiologist CSS-IRCCS Hosp., San Giovanni Rotondo, Italy, 1986—. Reviewer Am. Jour Cardiology, 1999; contbr. articles to profl. jours. Mem. A.N.M.C.O. Roman Catholic.

VIGNE, (JAMES) RANDOLPH, historian, researcher; b. Kimberley, South Africa, July 10, 1928; arrived in U.K., 1964; s. James Coplen Langford and Frances Mary Noël (Creswell) V.; m. Gillian Augusta Rea, May 8, 1953; children: Piers James Creswell, Lucy Vigne Camm. MA, U. Oxford, Eng., 1949. Fellow Huguenot Soc., London, 1966—, Soc. Antiquaries, London, 1986—; mem. Inst. Hist. Rsch., U. London, 1993—; hon. rsch. fellow U. Natal, Pietermaritzburg, South Africa, 1995-96; editor New African, Cape Town and London, 1962-70, Huguenot Soc. Publs., London, 1986—; assoc. editor So. African Rev. of Books, Cape Town, 1989—. Author: A Dwelling Place of Our Own, 1973; author, editor: A Gesture of Belonging, Letters from Bessie Head, Guillaume Chenu de Chalezac, The French Boy at the Cape of Good Hope, 1993, Liberals Against Apartheid, The History of the Liberal Party of South Africa, 1953-1968, 1997. Nat. dep. chmn. Liberal Party, South Africa, 1960-63; chmn. Namibia Support Com., Gt. Britain, 1969-90, Friends of Nambia Soc., 1997—. Anglican. Avocations: art collecting, genealogy, African travel. Office: Huguenot Soc Care Univ Coll, Gower St, London WCIE 6BT, England

VIGOUROUX, EMILE LÉON, retired animal physiology educator; b. Laguiole, France, Dec. 2, 1937; s. Jean Léon and Françoise (Remise) V.; m. Bernadette Louise Grosperrin, July 15, 1961; children: Marie-Ange, Sylvain, Elisabeth. Bachelor, U. Paris, 1958; DSc, U. Paris VI, 1964, state doctor, 1974. Asst. U. Scis. Faculty, Paris, 1961-64; conf. master U. P. et M. Curie, Paris, 1964-81; prof. U. Montpellier (France) II, 1981-98, dir. Comparative Physiology Lab., 1984-98; dir. Lab. Physiologic CompareII, UM2, 1984—. Contbr. articles to profl. jours. Mem. French Physiol. Assn., European Thyroid Assn., N.Y. Acad. Sci. Roman Catholic. Avocations: classical music, operas, lectures. E-mail: emile.vigouroux@diligo.fr.

VIHAK, VASYL, mechanics specialist, physicist, mathematician; b. Stryi, Lviv, Ukraine, May 5, 1936; s. Mykhailo and Anna (Boykiv) V.; m. Zvenyslava Soletska, July 7, 1966; children: Mykhailo, Natalya. Higher edn. diploma in mechanics-math., Franko State U., Lviv, 1958, Candidate in Physics and Math., 1973; DSc in Physics and Math., Russian Acad. Scis., Novosibirsk, Russia, 1990; prof. cert., Ukrainian Nat. Acad. Scis., 1993. Cert. in mechanics. Engr., sr. engr., team engr. Enterprise for Orgn. Thermal Electric Power Stas., Lviv, 1960-75; sr. sci. rschr., lab. chief Pidstryhach Inst. for Applied Problems Mechanics and Math., Lviv, 1975-90, head mechanics deformable solids dept., 1990—. Author: Optimal Control of Nonstationary Temperature Regimes, 1979, Control of Thermal Stresses and Displacements, 1988; contbr. articles to sci. jours., including Math. Methods and Physicomech. Fields. Mem. Sci. Soc. Taras Shevchenko, Nat. Com. Ukraine for Applied and Theoretical Mechanics. Fax: (380-322) 65-42-40. E-mail: dept11@iapmm.lviv.ua. Home: 6/118 Naukova St, 79053 Lviv Ukraine Office: Pidstryhach Inst App Prob, 3b Naukova St, 79601 Lviv Ukraine

VIHOL, JAYSINGH NATHUSINGH, paper company executive; b. Vadasan, Gujarat, India, May 1, 1951; s. Nathusingh Kalusingh and Maguben Nathusingh (Chawada) V.; m. Nayna Jaysingh Patel; children: Minesh J., Upasana J., Mihir J. Diploma in accountancy, Saraiya Inst., Ahmedabad, India, 1970; diploma in paper tech., H.M.P.I., Pune, India, 1972, City and Gills London, 1974; postgrad., Banares Hindu U., Varanasi, India, 1999. Prodn. mgr. Sardar Paper Mills, Bardoli, India, 1974-75, Prabhat Bord Mills, Karjat, India, 1975-77; propr. Apco Paper Industries, Ahmadabad, 1977-80; mng. dir. D.C.E. Pvt. Ltd., Ahmadabad, 1980—, J & J Timber Co. Ltd., Chana, 1988—, Janu Impex Pvt. Ltd., Ahmadabad, 1995—, Janvi Pharm. Ptd. Ltd., Utkarsh Housing Pvt. Ltd.; mng. dir., bd. dirs. Baskin Investments Ltd., London, 1995—; cons. Cambrige Paper Co., Planpur, India, 1980-82, African Gold Field Ltd., Ghana, 1988-90; coord. Banares Hindu U., 1999—; mem. Indian Textile Com., Indian Investment Ctr., India Engring. Export Promotion Coun., India Apparel Exprot Promotion Coun., India Cotton Textile Export Promotion Coun., Indian S.R.T.E.P.C. Hon. counsel and diplomat Govt. of Liberia, Ahmedabad, 1995. Comdt. Gujarat Home Guards, 1995-98. Mem. Indian Pulp and Paper Tech. Assn., Pulp and Paper World, Gujarat C. of C. Achievements include research on and development of hydrogen fuel. Home: DCE Pvt Ltd M-55 Yashkamal, Soc New Vikas Gruh Rd Paldi, Gujarat Ahmedabad 380 007, India

VIHROVS, IGORS, Olympic athlete. Winner Gold medal gymnastics floor exercise Sydney, 2000. Office: Latvian Gymnastics Fedn, Skanstes 13/15, LV-1013 Riga Latvia*

VIIK, TÕNU, astronomer; b. Harjumaa, Estonia, Dec. 12, 1939; s. Ferdinand-Leopold and Hilda-Maria (Velström) V.; m. Malle Unga, Sept. 14, 1968; children: Kalle, Heino, Maria. Grad., Tartu U., Estonia, 1963, Cand. of Physics and Math., 1970, ScD, 1991. Jr. rsch. assoc. Inst. of Physics and Astronomy, Tartu, Estonia, 1965-71, sci. sec., 1971-76; sr. rsch. assoc. Inst. of Astrophysics and Atmospheric Physics (name now Tartu Obs.), Tartu, 1976-85, dir., 1985-99; sr. rsch. assoc., 1999-2000, vice dir., 2000—. Mem. editl. bd. Jour. Quantitative Spectroscopy and Radiative Transfer. Sgt. Soviet Army, 1963-65. Decorated 3d class Order of the White Star (Estonia); recipient Estonian Acad. Scis. medal, 1998. Mem. Internat. Astron. Union, European Astron. Soc. Lutheran. Avocations: bird watching, hiking, wood carving, reading. Home: Observatooriumi 1-2, 61602 Toravere Tartumaa Estonia Office: Tartu Observatory, Toravere, 61602 Tartumaa Estonia

VIIKKI, OLLI JUKKA, electrical engineer; b. Helsinki, Finland, July 20, 1970; s. Erkki Antero and Iiris Helena Viikki; m. Merja Liisa Klaavu, Aug. 13, 1994. MSc in Engring., Tampere (Finland) U. Tech., 1995, lic. tech., 1997, PhD, 1999. Rsch. asst. Nokia Rsch. Ctr., Tampere, 1994-95, rsch. engr., 1995-98, rsch. project mgr., 1998—. Guest editor Speech Communication, 1999—. Grantee Tampere U. Tech., 1999. Mem. IEEE (pub. reviewer Signal Processing Soc. 1998), Internat. Speech Communication Assn. Fax: 358 3 2725888. Office: Nokia Rsch Ctr, PO Box 100, Visiokatu 1, 33721 Tampere Finland

VIJ, SATISH KUMAR, rail transportation company executive; b. New Delhi, Mar. 12, 1949; s. Chuni Lal and Rama (Pandoi) V.; m. Meeta Wadera, Apr. 21, 1978; 1 child, Shuchita. BSc in Civil Engring., Delhi Coll. Engring., New Delhi, 1969; MS in Civil Engring., Cornell U., Ithaca, N.Y., 1973; MA in Def. Studies, Nat. Def. Coll., New Delhi, 1989. Engr. Rwys., India, 1973-79; engr., cons. engr. Iraqi Rwys., 1979-82; sr. engr. Rwys., India, 1983-87, chief engr., 1989-97, divisional rwy. mgr., 1997-99; chief engr., track Indian Rwys., New Delhi, 1999. Named Min. Rwys., Ministry of Rwys., New Delhi, 1995, 99. Fellow Inst. Pkwy. Engrs. India, Instn. Engrs. India. Avocations: travel, photography, golf, table tennis, national security study. Home: XIV/11045 E Park Rd, New Delhi 110005, India Office: Indian Rwys, Rm 141 Rail Bhavan Rlwys, New Delhi 110001, India

VIJAYAKRISHNAN, KUMARALINGAM GOPALAKRISHNAN, linguistics educator; b. Chennai, Tamil Nadu, India, Feb. 10, 1952; s. Kumaralingam and Karpagavalli (Rajam) Gopalakrishnan; m. Rajalakshmi Gopalamurthy, May 10, 1979; 2 children. Bachelor's degree, Loyola Coll., Chennai, 1971; Master's degree, Madras Christian Coll., Chennai, 1973; PhD in English, Cen. Inst. English/Fgn. Lang., Hyderabad, India, 1983. From lectr. to reader Cen. Inst. for English and Fgn. Lang., Hyderabad, 1979-96, prof., 1996—; guest rschr. NWO, Leiden U., The Netherlands, 1999. Classical mus. performer All India Radio, 1973. Music tchr. Neighborhood Free Sch., Hyderabad, 1998—. Fulbright fellow, 1993. Hindu. Avocations: literature, cinema. Office: Cen Inst English/Fgn Lang, 500007 Hyderabad India

VIJAYA KUMAR, RAVICHANDRAN, cutting tool manufacturing executive; b. Palani, India, May 9, 1966; s. Vijaya Kumar and Sarojini Mummoorthy Kumarswamy; m. Somasundaram Saraswathi; 1 child, Aswathi. Diploma in mech. engring., Govt. Polytech., 1986; diploma in bus. and small industry, ITCOT, Chennai, 1991; diploma in Mgmt., IIIE, Mumbai. Jr. engr. Guindy M/C Tools Ltd., Chennai, 1986-88; planning asst. Usha Hydralics Ltd., Hosur, 1988-89; time study asst. Lakshmi Automatic Ltd., Hosur, 1989-93; indsl. engr. Indomatic System Ltd., Chengalpattu, 1993-96; asst. mgr. indsl. engring. Addison & Co., Chennai, 1996—. Literary assn. sec. LMS Boys H.S., Marthandam, 1981-83; rotract club treas. Govt. Polytech., 1983-86; covener Amnesty Internat., 1989-93. Mem. Nat. Inst. Quality and Reliability, Inst. Std. Engrs., Madras Mgmt. Assn. Hindu. Avocations: reading, philately, numismatic. E-mail: ravichandran-vmrt@yahoo.com. Home: H-14-G High Flats, Double Tank Colony, KK Nagar Chennai 600 078, India Office: Addison & Co Ltd, 4 Smith Rd, Chennai 600 002, India

VIJAYAKUMAR, T., research scientist; b. Varkala, Kerala, India, Apr. 9, 1947; s. P.N. Thankappan Pillai and K. Swarnamayi Amma; m. Gurija Devi Amma, May 28, 1973; children: Sindhu, Bindu. BSc, U. Kerala, Trivandrum, India, 1967, MSc, 1969; MSc, Osmania U., Hyderabad, India, 1976; PhD, U. Calicut, India, 1989. Jr. lectr. Govt. Coll., Trivandrum, India, 1969-70; jr. sci. asst. Export Inspection Coun., 1970-72; sci. asst. Med. Coll., Trivandrum, 1972-79, sr. rsch. officer, 1979-89, 98—; sci. officer Dept. Sci. and Tech., 1989-98; officer-in-charge Gas House, 1972-79, Clin. Biochemistry, 1972-79; guide for PHD, MD and MS students U. Kerala, 1989—; vis. faculty mem. Cochin U., 1993—. Author: Laboratory Technician; mem. editl. bd. Jour. Cancer, France, 1989-96, Biomed. jour., India, 1995—; contbr. over 160 articles to profl. jours., 14 chpts. to books. Recipient Cancer Rsch. award Indian Coun. Med. Rsch., 1989, Oration award Indian Dental Assn., 1992, Pres.' award Indian Med. Assn., 1995. Fellow Royal Soc. Chemistry London, Inst. Biology London, Internat. Med. Sci. Acad., Indian Chem. Soc. Avocations: cinema, reading, music, teaching. Home: Aiswarya, TC 13/2193 Mulavana, Trivandrum Kerala 695037, India Office: Med Coll, Ctrl Rsch Lab, Trivandrum 695011, India

VIJAYAKUMARAN, K.P. (KUTTAM POIL) (KUTTAM POIL VIJAYAKUMARAN), chartered psychologist, researcher; b. Mokkam Kozhikode, Kerala, India, June 15, 1958; s. K.P. Andikutty and K.P. (Perumpadappil) Savithri. MA in Psychology (1st rank, 1st class), U. Calicut, India, 1992. Chartered physchologist British Psychol. Soc. Contbr. articles to profl. jours. Recipient ODASS award ODA, London, 1994, Postgrad. bursery Conf. Cognitive Psychology-Brit. Psychol. Soc., Bristol, Eng., 1995; named Univ. Grants Commn. lectr., India, 1992. Mem. APA (assoc. mem.), Brit. Psychol. Soc. (chartered; divsn. tchrs. and rschrs. in psychology, affiliate divsn. clin. psychology, divsn. neuropsychology, divsn. health psychology), Can. Psychol. Assn. (assoc.), World Fedn. Mental Health, Indian Psychol. Assn. Avocations: collecting rare things, collecting books, reading, publishing articles, correspondence. Home: Cleveland Kapumala Estate, Mokkam PO Kozhikode, Kerala State 673 602, India

VIJAYAMOHANAN, KUNJUKRISHNAPILLAI, scientist, educator; b. Elamadu, Kerala, India, May 28, 1960; s. Padmanabhapillai Kunjukrishnapilla and Ambujakshi Amma Vijayalekshmi Amma; m. Leelabhai Manju Malu, Apr. 28, 1989; children: Harikrishnan, Jayakrishnan. BSc, Fatima Coll., Kerala, 1980; MSc, Univ. Coll., Trivandrum, Kerala, 1982; PhD, Indian Inst. Sci., Bangalore, Karnataka, 1989. Rsch. assoc. Indian Inst. Sci., Bangalore, 1989-91; scientist Nat. Chem. Lab., Pune, India, 1991—; cons. Barat Electronics, Pune, 1993-96, Ohm Solitronics, Pune, 1995-97. Recipient medal Materials Rsch. Soc. India, 1997. Mem. IUPAC (assoc.), Indian Physics Assn. (life), Soc. Advancement of Electrochem. Soc. (life). Socialist. Hindu. Avocations: chess, shuttle badminton, reading. Fax: 91-020-5893044. E-mail: viji@ems.ncl.res.in. Home: SA 82 NCL Colony Pashan Rd, Pune 411008, India Office: Nat Chem Lab, Pashan Rd, Pune 411008, India

VIJAYARATNAM, KANAPATHIPILLAI, chartered civil and environmental engineer, consultant, director; b. Analaitivu, Sri Lanka, May 10, 1948; arrived in Eng., 1979, naturalized, 1990; s. Kathirvelu Kanapathipillai and Parvathy Ponniah; m. Sakuntala Mylwaganam, Oct. 31, 1979. BSc in Engring. with honors, U. Ceylon, Peradeniya, 1971; M in Engring., Asian Inst. Tech., Bangkok, 1977; MSc in Pub. Health Engring., Imperial Coll. U. London, 1982; cert. sustainable bus. challenge, World Bus. Coun. Sustainable Devel., 1999. Chartered engr., U.K. Instr. civil engring. U. Ceylon, Peradeniya, 1972; civil engr. Mahaweli Devel. Bd., Colombo, Sri Lanka, 1972-75, Renardet Engring., Singapore, 1977-80; engr. Chanton Engring. Ltd., Middlesex, U.K., 1984-85, S.P. Collins Assocs., Cambridge, U.K., 1985-86; cons. civil engr. Coulsdon, U.K., 1986-88; sr. engr. Neilcot Constrn. Ltd., Kent, U.K., 1988-90; engr. clean water dept. Binnie & Ptnrs., Cons. Engrs., Redhill, U.K., 1990-94; sr. engr. grade 1 SMHBinnie Cons. Engrs., K.L., Malaysia, 1995-96; dep. project mgr., prin. engr. S.S.P. Consulting Engrs., Kuala Lumpur, Malaysia, 1996-97, engring. cons., 1998-99; dir. Rosebury Cons., Ltd., 1999—; engring. cons., Civil, Water & Environ. Engring. Projs., 1998-99, participant, presenter various internat. confs. and seminars, Am. (Pitts., MIT, Las Vegas), U.K. (London, Oxford, Newcastle), Europe (Netherlands, Sweden, Switzerland, Italy), Asia (Malaysia, Singapore, Thailand, Australia). Orig. contbr. to re-engring. of water ind. orgs., Broader Edu. of Civil Engs. in 21st Century, Cost and Performance Optimization of Water Treatment System (conceptual and mathematical), Sustainable Development of Infrastructure in Water and Environ. Engring., Environmentally Sound Dam and Water Power Devel., Emergence and Complexity in Urban Environmental Engring Mgmt. in 21st Century, 1999, Environ. Engring. Edn. in 21st Century, 1999, and Future Dir. Tech. Edn. in Asia, 1999, Project Mgmt. Water Supply and Treatment Projects in Asia, Future Direction Engrin. Edn. for a Sustainable World in the New Millenium; dir. Rosebury Cons. Ltd., 1999, Sustainable Waste Mgmt., 2000. Contbr. articles to profl. jours. U.K. Govt. scholar, 1976-77; NATO Advanced Inst. grantee, 1981, UNESCO/Colo. State U. grantee, 1981. Mem. ASCE, ASEE, Instn. Civil Engrs. London, Iternat Water Assn., Internat. Assn. Hydraulic Rsch. and Engring., Internat. Assns. and Water Resources, Water Power, Soc. of Risk Analysis, Internat. Coun. on Systems Engring. Avocations: golf, travel, reading, writing, fine arts. E-mail: vijay@vijayaratnam.com. Home: 1 Ashcroft Rise, Coulsdon Surrey CR5 2SS, England

VIJTIUK, NADA MIRYAM, immunologist, researcher; b. Zagreb, Croatia, Mar. 21, 1961; d. Antun Vouk and Zdravka Prgin; m. Vladimir Vijtiuk, July 28, 1984; 1 child, Juraj. BSc in Biology, U. Zagreb, 1983, MSc, 1990, PhD, 1994. Rsch. fellow U. Zagreb Faculty of Sci., 1983-84; clin. immunologist Clin. Hosp., Banja Luka, Bosnia and Herzegovina, 1984-90; rsch. asst. U. Zagreb Vet. Faculty, 1991-94; dir. VIN-TEH, Zagreb, 1994—; asst. prof. U. Zagreb, 1997—. Contbr. articles to profl. jours. Mem. AAAS, N.Y. Acad. Scis., Scandinavian Soc. for Immunology, Croatian Soc. for Immunology. Avocations: playing piano, aquarel painting, computer graphics, aquaristics. Home and Office: Jablanska 50, 10 000 Zagreb Croatia

VIKHAGEN, HÅVARD, artist; b. Hjørungavåg, Norway, June 8, 1952; s. Håkon and Margaret Nykrem Vikhagen. Student, Norwegian Acad. Fine Arts, 1975-82. Chmn. Norwegian Nat. Jury Fine Arts, 1992-93. Exhibited at Gallery K, Kunstnerforbundet, Gallery Christian Dam, Copenhagen, Hennie Onstad Art Ctr., 1987-98, prin. exhibitioner Bergen Internat. Festival, Norway, 1996. Mem. Norwegian Artist Assn. Fine Arts, Nordic Fine Arts Assn. (chmn. Norwegian sect. 1991-95). Home: Skøyen Terrasse 21, 0276 Oslo Norway

VILA, ANTONIO ALEJANDRO, travel agent; b. Buenos Aires, June 25, 1953; s. Antonio José Vila and Maria de Los Angeles Africa Fernandez; m. Claudia Norma Legari, Mar. 4, 1978; children: Gabriel Alejandro, Pablo Julian. BA, Coll. Guadalupe, Buenos Aires, 1970. Credit cons. Caja Nacional Ahorro y Seguro, Buenos Aires, 1973-75; dir., mgr. Bareco Argentina S.A.C. é I., Florida, Buenos Aires, Argentina, 1977-93, Shopping Tour EVT, Florida, Buenos Aires, 1991-93. With Argentine Army, 1974-75. Roman Catholic. Avocation: soccer. Office: Kensington Viajes EVT, Gral Roca 1572, 1602 Las Flores Buenos Aires, Argentina

VILA, GILBERT, psychiatrist; b. Toulouse, Haute-Gar, France, Aug. 20, 1959; s. Henri and Solange (Munier) V.; m. Catherine Bertrand, Sept. 17, 1994. Medicine, Rangueil Faculty, Toulouse, 1984; Resident, Xavier Bichat Faculty, Paris, 1989, MD, 1989. Medical diplomate in psychiatry. CCA Necker Hosp., Paris, 1989-92, P.H., 1992—; cons. Necker Hosp., 1989—; rsch. child psychiat. unit IFREM, Necker, 1995—. Author various books and articles in field. Aspirant mil. health dept. Larey Hosp., 1987-88, Toulouse. Fellow APFJ-SH/Paris. Office: Centre Hosp Necker, Enfants Malades/149 Rue Sev, 75015 Paris France

VILA, MARÍA CRISTINA, psychologist; b. Buenos Aires, Apr. 14, 1943; d. Fernando and Berta (GoniK) V.; m. Ignacio Gerlic, Oct. 14, 1965 (div. Oct. 1987); children: Sebastian, Valeria. Sci. degree in psychology, U. Buenos Aires, 1966. Psychologist supr. family violence area Consejo de la Majer, Buenos Aires, 1993-94; pvt. practice psychology, Buenos Aires; Argentine rep. L.Am. Seminar on Family Violence, World Coun. Chs., 1993, also coord. course on family violence for psychologists, program assistance and prevention of family violence; organizer in charge advising on family violence Argentine Union C(?), 1996—; supr. tel. assistance svc. Autonomous Govt. City of Buenos Aires, 1997; advisor on family violence psychiat. divsn. Hosp. Italiano, 1997—; adviser to govt. agys. and internat. orgns. on family violence and violence on job, including Permanent Assembly on Human Rights, Hosp. Pinero, Hosp. Clinicas, Hosp. Durand, Hosp. Alvear, U. Buenos Aires, Ministry Edn.; psychologist expert on violence befor criminal and civil cts.; coord., mem. faculty program of clin. dept. Christian Studies Ctr.; advisor Panam. Health Office. Author: Family Violence-Batered Women, Coercive Sexual Relations, Are We Living in a Violating Culture?; prodr. TV program Prevention of Family Violence. Mem. Argentine Soc. Victimhood (v.p.), Argentine Soc. Family Therapy (coord. dept. violence). Office: Beruti 3032, Buenos Aires Argentina

VILALLONGA DAVIDSON, ELIANA, lawyer; b. Buenos Aires; d. Federico A. Volallonga and Maria Forgas; m. William David Davidson, 1982. BA, U. Fla., 1975; JD, U. Va., 1992. Bar: Va. Rsch. analyst Nat. Econ. Rsch. Assocs., Washington, Boston, 1976-78; dir. rsch. Commonwealth Rsch. Group, Inc., Boston, 1978-82; exec. dir. Inst. Psychiatry & Fgn. Affairs, Washington, 1982-88; atty. U.S. Dept. State, Washington, 1992-95, from asst. dep. gen. counsel to dep. gen. counsel, 1995—. Office: YS Dept Def The Pentagon Rm 3e969 Washington DC 20310-0001

VILANOVA, MERCEDES, history educator; b. Barcelona, Catalonia, Spain, June 16, 1936; d. Xavier Vilanova and Mercedes Ribas; m. Juan Antonio Subirana, Oct. 1, 1960 (div. 1979); children: Miriam, Brian. Master's degree, Barcelona U., Spain, 1959; PhD, Valencia U., 1965. Vis. prof. Boston U., 1962-69; prof. contemporary history U. Barcelona, 1969—; assoc. Barnard W. Ctr., N.Y.C., 1987-88; rsch. assoc. Nat. Ctr. for Sci. Rsch., Paris, 1988; fellow Wilson Ctr., Washington, 1989-90; vis. scholar Harvard U., Cambridge, Mass., 1991-92, 98-99. Author: (books) Illiteracy in Spain between 1887 and 1981 (1st prize Spanish Rsch. 1990), The Invisible Majorities, 1996; contbr. articles to profl. jours. Mem. Internat. Oral History Assn. (pres. 1996-2000), Historia, Antropologia y Fuentes Orales (dir., founder 1989-97). Avocations: skin diving, sailing, skiing, reading, music. Home: Pelayo 44, 08001 Barcelona Spain Office: U Barcelona, Baldiri Reixach S/N, 08028 Barcelona Spain

VILAR, ANTÓNIO, lawyer, law educator; b. Porto, Portugal, Jan. 19, 1952; s. António Ribeiro and Herminia Ferreira V.; m. Marie Amélia Dias da Silva; 1 child, Joao António Vilhena Marques Vilar Ribeiro. Degree in Law, Coimbra (Portugal) U., 1976. Pres. A. Vilar Law Offices, Porto, 1977—; labor matters cons. Internat. Assn., Germany, 1976; consulting lawyer Oliveira Martins Found., Porto, 1977-79; lectr. labor law Porto U., 1979—. Contbr. articles to profl. jours. Chmn. Civic Assn. Devel. North, Oporto, Inst.-Euro-Atlântico; pres. Fundaçao Afro-Lusitana, Oporto; pres. north region Social Dem. Party, 1981-88; dep.: Portuguese Parlement, 1981-84. Named Chevalier, L'Ordre Des Palmes Académiques, France, 1991. Mem. Internat. Assn. Young Lawyers, Internat. Assn. Profl. Rels., Inst. Conciliation and Arbitration (v.p.), Forum Portucalense (hon., chmn.), Centro Juvenil De Canpanhã. Avocations: reading, writing. Office: A Vilar Law Offices, Rua De Ceuta 118-2, 4050 Porto Portugal also Office: Av Antonio Augusto Aguiar, 183, R/C Dto, 1050 Lisboa Portugal also Office: 10 Rue de Richelieu 6, 75001 Paris France

VILARDELL, FRANCISCO, gastroenterologist, educator; b. Barcelona, Spain, Apr. 1, 1926; s. Jacinto Vilardell and Mercedes Viñas; m. Leonor March; children: Mercedes, Carmen, Xavier. MD, U. Barcelona, 1949, DSc, 1961; DSc in Medicine, U. Pa., Phila., 1962; PhD (hon.), U. Toulouse, France, 1974, U. Zaragoza, Spain, 1990. Resident medicine Hosp. del Mar, Barcelona, 1949-52; fellow gastroenterology Hosp. de la Santa Cruz & San Pablo, 1952-55, chief gastroenterology svc., 1963—; fellow gastroenterology Grad. Hosp., Phila., 1959-62; prof., dir. Postgrad. Sch. Gastroenterology U. Barcelona, 1970—; hon. prof. U. Valparaiso, Chile, 1996; pres. European Assn. Study Liver, 1975-76, Coun. Internat. Orgns. Med. Scis. coms., 1987-91; sec.-gen. World Orgn. Gastroenterology, 1974-82, pres., 1982-90. Editor: Enfermedades Difusas del Estomago, 1962, others; assoc. editor Bockus Gastroenterology, 3rd edit., 1972, edtl. cons., 4th edit., 1986; contbr. articles to profl. jours. Asst. dir. gen. med. edn. Spanish Ministry Health, 1978-80, dir. gen. health planning, 1980-82, mem. med. rsch. coun., 1982-91. Fellow ACP, Royal Coll. Physicians, Royal Coll. Physicians Edinburgh, Am. Coll. Gastroenterology; mem. Catalan Soc. Bioethics (pres. 1994-96); hon. mem. French Gastroenterology Soc., Brit. Gastroenterology Soc., German Gastroenterology Soc., Japanese Gastroenterology Soc., Spanish Gastroenterology Soc., Polish Gastroenterology Soc., Hungarian Gastroenterology Soc., Portuguese Gastroenterology Soc., Argentinian Gastroenterology Soc., Colombian Gastroenterology Soc., Nat. Health Coun. Avocations: music,

philology, medical history. Home: Johann Sebastian Bach 11, 08021 Barcelona Spain Office: Hosp Santa Cruz & San Pablo, 08025 Barcelona Spain

VILCASSIM, MOHAMED NAWAZ JIFFRY, bank officer; b. Colombo, Sri Lanka, Singapore, Nov. 27, 1945; s. Jiffry Cader and Zareena Jiffry (Ismail) V.; m. Yasmin Muhseen, Dec. 26, 1975; children: Fathima Shahla, Nabeel Nawaz, Imran Hussein. LLB, U. Ceylon, 1967. Pvt. practice Ceylon, 1970-71; crown counsel Office of Atty. Gen. of Ceylon, 1971-73; sec. Rollei Group of Cos., Singapore, 1973-81; dep. co. sec., then co. sec. DBS Bank, Singapore, 1982-91, v.p., sr. v.p. Investor and Trusts Svcs., 1990-99, mng. dir. Investor and Trusts Svcs., 1999—; bd. dirs. DBS Asset Mgmt. Ltd., DBS Nominees Pte Ltd., DBS Trustee Ltd., DBS Securities Nominees Pte Ltd, Thai Danu-DBS Ltd., Thailand, Hwang DBS Custodian Svcs. Sdn Bhd, Malaysia; presenter in field of investing in Sri Lanka, also economist confs. and Singapore Trade Devel. Bd. Contbr. articles to profl. jours. Mem. Singapore-Sri Lanka Bus. Assn. (pres. 1995-98). Moslem. Avocations: collecting antiques, old currency and coins. Office: DBS Bank, 6 Shenton Way, Singapore Republic of Singapore

VILČEK, ŠTEFAN, molecular biologist, researcher; b. Vyšny Orlik, Slovakia, Dec. 1, 1950; s. Štefan and Maria (Kostova) V.; m. Sept. 10, 1978; children: Štefan, Martin. Ing., Czech Tech. H.S., Prague, 1974; PhD, Comenius U., Bratislava, Slovakia, 1981; DSc, U. P.F.J. Safarik, Kosice, Slovakia, 1999. Sci. worker U. P.F.J. Safarik, Kosice, Slovakia, 1974-81, U. Vet. Medicine, Kosice, 1981—; head dept. genetic engring. U. Vet. Medicine and Rsch. Inst. Vet. Medicine, Kosice, 1986—; tchr. U. P.F.J. Šafarik, 1990—, assoc. prof., 1994. Patentee in field; mem. editl. bd. Jour. Vesmir, 1989—. Wellcome Trust grantee, 1997—. Mem. Czechoslovak Microbiol. Soc. Avocations: hiking, shooting, photography, popularization of science. Office: Univ of Vet Medicine, Komenskeho 73, SK-04181 Kosice Slovakia

VILCHEZ, RICARDO S., library supervisor; b. Masaya, Nicaragua, Jan. 20, 1953; s. Adrian Zamora and Maria M. Vilchez; children: Ricardol E., Nidia E. BA, Fordham U., 1990; MBA, CES, Managua, Nicaragua, 1978; diploma, Inst. of Christian Econs., 1982; MLS, Pratt Inst., Bklyn., 1995. With Nat. Police Nicaragua, Managua, 1968-72; presdl. asst. Govt. Nicaragua, 1972-74; libr. asst. Ctrl. Bank Libr., Managua, 1974-75; asst. presdl. office Ctrl. Bank Managua, 1975-79; libr. supervisor Fordham U., N.Y.C., 1989—. Editor (CD) Los Motivos Del Lobo, 2000. V.p. Nicaraguan Children's Found., N.Y.C., 1999—; cultural dir. Nicaraguan Support Group, N.Y.C., 1999—; pres. Comision Hispana Pro Obra Rubén Dario N.Y., 1998—. Mem. Am. Libr. Assn., Am. Soc. Info. Sci., Libr. Congress. Republican. Roman Catholic. Avocations: cultural activities, travel, walking, rare books, community activities. Home: 13 Van Pelt Ave Staten Island NY 10303-2478 Office: Fordham U 113 W 60th St New York NY 10023-7484

VILENCHIK, MICHAEL MARC, biophysicist, physician, virologist, radiobiologist; b. Brjansk, Russia, May 30, 1938; s. Marc and Grunja G. (Smoljakova) V.; m. Valentina I. Vasilieva, Jan. 12, 1964 (div. 1967); 1 child, Joan; m. Julia N. Runova, Mar. 6, 1968 (div. 1971); 1 child, Vera. MD, 1st Med. Inst., St. Petersburg, Russia, 1961; PhD, Inst. Virology, Moscow, 1967. Postgrad. rsch. Inst. Virology, Moscow, 1963-66; rsch. scientist, sr. biophysicist, sr. resident Inst. Biophysics, Pushchino, Moscow, 1966-90; vis. scientist Med. Rsch. Coun., Didcot, England, 1990—; rschr. Inst. for Environ. Rsch., Tel Aviv, 1991; rsch. scholar SUNY Health Sci. Ctr., Syracuse, 1991-93, Cornell U., Ithaca, N.Y., 1993-94; rsch. scientist Longevity Achievement Found. and Sally Balin Med. Ctr., Media, Pa., 1994—. Author: Biological Fundamentals of Aging and Longevity, 1976, 87, 89, Radiobiological Effects and Environment, 1983, 91, Rules of Molecular-Genetic Action of Chemical Carcinogens, 1977, Dynamic DNA Instability and the Late Radiobiological Effects, 1987, Modification of Carcinogenic and Antitumor Actions of Ionizing Radiation; contbr. articles to profl. jours., also to Ency. Gerontology, Vol. 2, Acad. Press, 1996, others; monographs in fields of biophysics of aging and carcinogenesis; mechanisms of radiation effects and biophysics of the genome.

VILHJALMSSON, THOR, judge; b. Reykjavik, Iceland, June 9, 1930; s. Vilhjalmur T. and Inga Gislason; m. Ragnhildur Helgadottir, Sept. 9, 1950; children: Helgi, Inga, Kristin, Thorunn. Student, St. andrews U., Scotland, 1949-50; grad., U. Iceland, Reykjavik, 1957; also postgrad. studies. Asst. judge Reykjavik Civil and Maritime Ct., 1960-62, judge, 1962-67; prof. U. Iceland, 1967-76; judge Supreme Ct. of Iceland, 1976-93; judge European Ct. Human Rights, Strasbourg, France, 1971-98, v.p., 1998; judge EFTA Ct., Geneva, 1994-97; judge EFTA Ct., Luxembourg, 1996—, pres., 2000—. Author: Civil Procedures, Vols. 1-4, 1971. Office: EFTA Ct, 1 rue Fort Thungen, L-1499 Kirchberg Luxembourg

VILJANTO, JOUKO ALEKSI, pediatric surgeon, educator; b. Sortavala, Finland, Jan. 27, 1933; s. Mikko and Klaudia (Spiridonov) V.; m. Raili Mirja Torila, June 20, 1959; 1 child, Tanja. Legitimated physician, U. Turku, Finland, 1958, D.Med.Sci., 1964, Specialist in surgery, 1966, Specialist in pediatric surgery, 1970. Asst. in med. chemistry U. Turku, 1960-63, asst. in surgery, 1963-66, docent exptl. surgery, 1969-71, docent surgery, 1971-76, docent surgery and pediatric surgery, 1976-88, 90-98; specialist surgeon Turku U. Central Hosp., 1966-68, pediatric surgeon, 1968-76, assoc. chief pediatric surgery, 1976-88, assoc. prof. surgery, 1988-90, chief pediatric surgery, 1990-96. Contbr. articles on exptl. and clin. studies on wound healing, 1960—. Chmn. Turun Lääkärikeskus ja Laboratoriot Oy, 1977-88. Decorated Ordinis Leonis Finlandiae 1st class; WHO scholar, 1967; Research Council for Medicine grantee, 1974-79, 84-85. Mem. Finnish Surg. Assn., Scandinavian Assn. Pediatric Surgeons, Docent Assn. Turku U. (sec. 1976-78), Finnish Assn. Pediatric Surgeons (sec. 1978-80, chmn. 1991-94, hon. 1996), Scandinavian Surg. Assn., Estonian Soc. Pediatric Surgeons (hon.), Wound Healing Soc. Avocation: research in wound healing. Home: Terhokatu 18, SF-20720 Turku Finland

VILJOEN, KAREL STEPHANUS, geologist, research scientist; b. Worcester, South Africa, Nov. 29, 1960; s. Karel Stephanus and MAria (Bothma) V.; m. Marta Muscolino, Sept. 24, 1994. BSc with honors, U. Stellenbosch, South Africa, 1982; MSc, U. Capetown, South Africa, 1988; PhD, U. Witwatersrand, South Africa, 1994. Divisional geologist De Beers Consol. Mines (Pty) Ltd., Johannesburg, South Africa, 1983—. Contbr. articles to profl. jours. Mem. Geol. Soc. South Africa (assoc.). Office: De Beers Geosci Centre, PO Box 82232, Southdale 2135, South Africa

VILKKI, PANU ILMARI, retired pediatric surgeon, educator; b. Viitasaari, Finland, May 16, 1927; s. Joel Adiel and Suoma Eliisa (Kallo) V.; m. Liisa Fredriika Vestala, July 1, 1952; children: Jaana, Mikko (dec.), Juha, Vesa. MD, Turku U., 1951, PhD, 1956. Asst. chief surgery U. Hosp., Turku, Finland, 1963-67; chief pediat. surgery U. Hosp., Turku, 1967-90, lectr., 1967-90; ret.; pediat. surgeon Univ. Children's Clinic, Helsinki, 1963; rschr. Biochem. Inst., Helsinki, 1952-54, 60-61; vis. scientist NIH, Bethesda, Md., 1959-60, 78; chmn. coun. Lansetti Surg. Cons., Ltd., 1961-87; examiner pediat. surgery Nat. Bd. Finland, 1963-90. Contbr. articles to profl. jours. Chmn. Red Cross, Turku, 1966-67; fgn. sec. Med. Students Orgn., Turku, 1949-50, Child Accident Prevention Com., Finland, 1980—. Recipient NIH Centennial medal, 1987; NIH, USPHS grantee, 1961, Commonwealth Fund N.Y. grantee, 1967. Mem. Finnish Med. Assn., Assn. Pediat. Surgeons Finland (chmn. 1976-79), Brit. Assn. Pediat. Surgeons, German Assn. Pediat. Surgeons, Scandinavian Assn. Pediat. Surgeons, Scandinavian Assn. Pediat. Surgeons, Finnish Surg. Assn., Finnish Pediat. Assn., Finnish Orthopedic Assn., Fraternitas 68, Syrak. Lutheran. Avocations: sailing, beekeeping. E-mail: panvil@utu.fi.

VILLA, PAOLO, business advisor; b. Milan, Italy, Jan. 23, 1962; s. Claudio and Anna Maria (De Ambrogi) V. Degree in econs., U. Cattolica del Sacro Cuore, Milan, 1990. Ptnr. Studio Dr. Vincenzo de Biasi, Milan, 1990—; statutory auditor Yagi S.R.L., Milan, 1994—, Samsung Italia S.R.L., Milan, 1993—, Acheson Italiana S.R.L., Milan, 1992—, Plastica Italiana S.P.A., Milan, 1992—, cons. to numerous cos. Home: Via Marchesi de Taddei 4, 20145 Milan Italy Office: Studio Dr Vincenzo de Biasi, Piazza Belgiojoso 2, 20121 Milan Italy

VILLAMIZAR-C, ALVARO, civil engineer; b. Santafe de Bogota, Colombia, Mar. 14, 1935; s. Federico and Angela (Caicedo) V.; m. Rosalina Aurora Ruiz, Aug. 24, 1963; children: Alvaro Mauricio, Diana Angela, Daniel Javier, Joana Paola. Degree civil engring., U. Nacional, Bogotá, 1963, M in Hydraulic Resources, 1971; degree in irrigation engring., Instituto de Hidrologia, 1974. Resident engr. Salazar & Garcia Engrs., Bogotá, 1963-64; design engr. A. Olarte Engring. and Constrn., Bogotá, 1965-67; irrigation unit chief INCORA, Bogotá, 1967-76; design unit chief HIMAT, Bogotá, 1976-77; engring. dept. chief RIOPAILA Sugar Mill, LaPaila, Colombia, 1977-79; cons. engr. TAHAL Cons. Engr., Israel, 1975-83, Alvaro Villamizar, Bogotá, 1980-86; cons. irrigation engr. SNC Lavalin Internat., Montreal, Can., 1986-98; sec. Nat. Commn. on Irrigation, 1972-77. Author: Earth Dam Design, 1984; contbr. articles to profl. jours. Mem. ASCE (life), Colombian Soc. of Civil Engrs. Roman Catholic. Avocation: stamp and coin collecting. Home: Trnsversal 48 N 45-04, Santa Fe de Bogotá Colombia Office: Apartado Aereo 55635, Santa Fe de Bogotá Colombia

VILLANUEVA, LUCREZIA JACINTA GARCIA, librarian; b. Manila, The Philippines, July 3, 1940; d. Mauro and Pilar (Cruz) Garcia; m. Fidel Buenaventura Villanueva, Nov. 19, 1966; children: Leah Villanueva Ignacio, Loida Zita G. BS in Libr. Sci., U. The Philippines, 1961. Lic. librarian, The Philippines. Libr. Liberty Flour Mills, Inc., Mandaluyong City, The Philippines, 1961-62, Ramon Magsaysay Award Found. Asian Libr., The Philippines, 1962-66, Inst. Planning UP, The Philippines, 1967-70, Ctrl. Bank of Philippines, The Philippines, 1970-93; bank officer III Bangko Sentral ng Pilipinas Libr., 1993—; cons. libr. Philippine Columbian Assn. Libr., The Philippines, 1974—. Compiler: (book catalogues), Books in Libr. Philippine Columbian Assn., Aug. 31, 1974, Sept., 1987, Aug., 1995. Mem. Assn. Spl. Librs. Philippines, Philippine Libr. Assn., U. Philippines Libr. Sci. Alumni Assn. Avocations: reading, watching videos. Home: 7230 Marcelo Ave, Marcelo Green Village, Parañaque 1700, The Philippines Office: Bangko Sentral ng Pilipinas, A Mabini St Malate, Manila 2801, The Philippines

VILLAPALOS SALAS, GUSTAVO, law educator; b. Madrid, Spain, Oct. 15, 1949; s. Gustavo and Juana V-S. D (hon.), numerous instns. Prof. faculty of law U. Madrid, 1970-75; prof. law U. Complutense de Madrid, 1976—, dir. dept. history of law, 1980-84, dean faculty of law, 1984-87, former rector, from 1987; rsch. fellow Instituto de Estudios Jurídicos, 1972-74, Centro de Investigaciones Juridicas, Económicas y Sociales, 1975; vis. prof. U. Calif. at Berkeley, 1976, U. Freiburg, 1976-77. Author: Colección Diplomática del Archivo Municipal de Santander: Documentos Reales II (1525-1599), 1982, Los Regímenes Económicos Matrimoniales en la Historia del Derecho Español: Prelección, 1983, El Fuero de León: Comentarios, 1984, Cortes de Castilla en el siglo XV, 1986, La Baja Edad Media Vol. IV, Historia General de Cantabria, 1986, La Alta Edad Media, Vol. III, 1987. Recipient Gran Cruz de la Orden de Alfonso X el Sabio, Gran Cruz del Mérito Civil, Hon. C.B.E. Avocations: astronomy, cinema, classical music, reading. *

VILLAR, EUGENIO, electronic system design, educator, researcher; b. Valencia, Spain, May 1, 1957. BS, U. Cantabria, Santander, Spain, 1979, PhD, 1984. Asst. prof. electronics U. Cantabria, Santander, 1979-84, prof. electronics, 1984—. Contbr. articles to profl. jours., chpt. to book. Mem. IEEE. Office: U Cantabria ETSI Indsl Tele, Avda Los Castros S/N, 39005 Santander Spain

VILLAR, RICHARD NEVILLE, orthopaedic surgeon; b. Selsey, Sussex, Eng., Apr. 24, 1953; s. George Roger and Diana Mary (Thomas) V.; m. Barbara Louise Lobban, June 4, 1983; children: Ruairidh, Angus, Felicity. BSc with honors, London U., 1974; B in Medicine, B in Surgery, St. Thomas Hosp., London, 1977; MS, Southampton U., 1987. Cert. orthopedic surgery. Trainee orthopaedic surgeon NHS, Eng., 1977-88; cons. orthopaedic surgeon Addenbrooke's Hosp., Cambridge, Eng., 1988—. Author: Hip Replacement, 1995, Knee Problems, 1996, Revision Hip Arthroplasty, 1996. Maj. Royal Army M.C., 1978-84. Named Lord of Manor of Twineham Benfield. Fellow Brit. Orthopaedic Assn., Royal Coll. Surgeons; mem. European Hip Soc., European Soc. Sports Medicine and Surgery of Knee. Avocations: classical guitar, cross-country skiing.

VILLARREAL, CARLOS CASTANEDA, engineering executive; b. Brownsville, Tex., Nov. 9, 1924; s. Jesus Jose and Elisa L. (Castaneda) V.; m. Doris Ann Akers, Sept. 10, 1948; children: Timothy Hill, David Akers. BA, U.S. Naval Acad., 1948; MS, U.S. Navy Postgrad. Sch., 1950; LLD (hon.), St. Mary's U., 1972. Registered profl. engr. Commd. ensign U.S. Navy, 1948, advanced through grades to lt., 1956; comdg. officer U.S.S. Rhea, 1951, U.S.S. Osprey, 1952; comdr. Mine Div. 31, 1953; resigned, 1956; mgr. marine and indsl. operation Gen. Electric Co., 1956-66; v.p. mktg. and adminstrn. Marquardt Corp., 1966-69; head Urban Mass Transit Adminstrn., Dept. Transp., Washington, 1969-73; commr. Postal Rate Commn., 1973-79, vice chmn., 1975-79; v.p. Washington ops. Wilbur Smith and Assocs., 1979-84, sr. v.p., 1984-86, exec. v.p., 1987—, also bd. dirs.; lectr. in field; mem. industry sector adv. com. Dept. Commerce; mem. sect. 13 adv. com. Dept. Transp., 1983-86; tchr. U.S. Naval Acad., 1954-56. Contbr. to profl. jours. Mem. devel. com. Wolftrap Farm Park for the Performing Arts, 1973-78; mem. council St. Elizabeth Ch., 1982-86, chmn. fin. com.; mem. bd. edn. St. Elizabeth Sch.; bd. dirs. Assoc. Catholic Charities, 1983-86; mem. fin. com. Cath. Charities, U.S.A.; mem. John Carrol Soc. Decorated knight Sovereign Mil. Hospitaller Order St. John of Jerusalem of Rhodes and Malta, 1981, Knight Equestrian Order of the Holy Sepulchre of Jerusalem, 1995; recipient award outstanding achievement Dept. Transp. Fellow ASCE, Am. Cons. Engrs. Coun. (vice chmn. internat. com.); mem. IEEE, NSPE (pres. D.C. soc. 1986-87, bd. dirs. 1988-91), Am. Pub. Transit Assn., Soc. Naval Architects and Marine Engrs., Soc. Am. Mil. Engrs., Am. Rds. and Transp. Builders Assn. (chmn. pub. transp. adv. coun.), Transp. Rsch. Bd., Washington Soc. Engrs., Internat. Bridge, Tunnel and Turnpike Assn., Inst. Traffic Engrs., Intelligent Transp. Soc. Am. (chmn. fin. com., bd. dirs.), Univ. Club, Army-Navy Club (pres.). Republican. Roman Catholic. Office: Wilbur Smith Assocs 2921 Telestar Ct Falls Church VA 22042-1205

VILLAT, CLAUDE MAX CHARLES HENRI, retired banker; b. Aarau, Switzerland, June 10, 1946; s. Marcel Charles and Anne Marie (Gloor) V. Maj. Degree in Commerce, U. Aarau, 1965; Cert., Swiss Merc. Sch., London, 1967; DBA, Univ. Ams., Panama; D honoris causa, U Buenos Aires, 1996. Stock exch. dealer Swiss Bank Corp., Lausanne, Switzerland, 1965-67; investment advisor, v.p. Nordfinanz-Bank, Zurich, 1968-77; with comml. mktg., asst. v.p. Sogenal Zurich, 1977-79; dir., sr. v.p. fin. svcs. Bankers Trust A.G., Zurich, 1979-91; chmn. Pensionfund BTAG, Zurich, 1980-91; mem. Swiss Stock Exch., 1981-88; chmn. Roi Ford GmbH Munchen (formerly M.C.D. GmbH Munchen), Munich, 1980-88, Roico A.G., Kusnacht, 1988-92. Bd. dirs. CKM Found. Vaduz (F. Liechtenstein), 1986—. Mem. RREC Club. Address: Alte Landstrasse 1, CH-8802 Kilchberg Switzerland

VILLAVERDE, SANTIAGO, chemical engineer, educator; b. Madrid, Dec. 12, 1968; s. Severino Eusebio Villaverde and Maria Concepcion Gomez. B-SChemE, U. Valladolid, Spain, 1991, MSChemE, 1992, postgrad., 1994, PhD in Chem. Engring., 1994. Rschr. U. Valladolid, 1991-94, asst. prof., 1997-98, assoc. prof., 1998—; rsch. asst. Inst. Nat. Applied Scis., Toulouse, France, 1991-94; postdoctoral rschr. Ctr. for Biofilm Engring., Bozeman, Mont., 1994-96; tutor fgn. students Spanish Agy. for Internat. Coop., Valladolid, 1992-93; cons. New U. Lisbon, Portugal, 1998; referee Internat. Assn. Water Quality; sci. evaluator Nat. Agy. Evaluagion and Prospective, Madrid, 1999. Contbr. articles to profl. jours. Vol. Assn. Donors of Blood and Organs, Spain, 1989-99; mem. Action Aid, Spain, 1996-99. Rsch. grantee European Commn., 1997, Fulbright Found., 1999. Mem. AIChE, Internat. Assn. Water Quality, Spanish Soc. Biotech.

VILLELLA, EDWARD JOSEPH, ballet dancer, educator, choreographer, artistic director, performing arts administrator; b. L.I., N.Y., Oct. 1, 1936; s. Joseph and Mildred (DeGiovanni) V.; m. Janet Greschler (div. Nov. 1980); 1 child, Roddy; m. Linda Carbonetta, Apr. 1981; children: Christa Francesca, Lauren. BS in Marine Transp., N.Y. State Maritime Coll., 1957; LHD (hon.), Boston Conservatory, 1985, hon. degree; hon. degree, Union Coll., Schenectady, N.Y., 1991; DHL (hon.), St. Thomas U., Miami, Fla., 1994, U.S.C., 1997; DFA (hon.), SUNY Maritime Coll., Bronx, 1998. Mem. N.Y.C. Ballet, 1957, soloist, 1958-60, prin. soloist, 1960-83; artistic dir. Ballet Okla., Oklahoma City, 1983-86; founding artistic dir., CEO Miami (Fla.) City Ballet, 1985—; vis. artist U.S. Mil. Acad., West Point, 1981-82; vis. prof. dance U. Iowa, 1981; resident Heritage chair arts and cultural criticism George Mason U.; Dorothy F. Schmidt artist-in-residence Coll. of Arts & Letters. Performed dances in Symphony C, Scotch Symphony, Western Symphony, Donizetti Variations, Swan Lake, La Source, The Nutcracker, Agon, Stars and Stripes, The Prodigal Son; premiered in Balanchine works including The Figure in the Carpet, 1960, Electronics, 1961, A Midsummer Night's Dream, 1962, Bugaku, 1963, Tarantella, 1964, Harlequinade, 1965, The Brahms-Schoenberg Quartet, 1966, Jewels, 1967, Symphony in Three Movements, 1972, Schéhérazade, 1975; choreography includes Narkissas, 1966, Shostakovitch Ballet Suite, 1972, Shenandoah, 1972, Gayane Pas de Deux, 1972, Salute to Cole, 1973, Sea Chanties, 1974, Prelude, Riffs and Fugues, 1980; TV appearances include The Ed Sullivan Show, Bell Telephone Hour, Mike Douglas Show, (TV spl.) Harlequin, 1975 (Emmy award), summer theaters, festivals, U.S. and abroad, 1957—; co-author: (autobiography) Prodigal Son, 1991. Mem. Nat. Coun. of Arts, 1968-74; chmn. Commn. for Cultural Affairs City N.Y., 1978; bd. visitors N.C. Sch. for the Arts; mem. dance adv. panel Nat. Endowment for Arts; trustee Wolf Trap Found. for the Arts. Recipient Dance Mag. award, 1964, Lions of the Performing Arts award N.Y. Pub. Libr., 1987, Capezio Dance award, 1989, Gold medal Nat. Soc. Arts and Letters, 1990, William G. Anderson merit award AAHPERD, 1991, Nat. Medal of Arts award 1997, Kennedy Ctr. Honors, 1997, Cultural Svc. award Bklyn. Ctr. for Performing Arts at Bklyn. Coll., 1998; named Miamian of Yr., UNICO Nat., 1993; inductee Fla. Artists Hall of Fame, 1997, Dorothy F. Schmidt Artist-in-Residence Dorothy F. Schmidt Coll. Arts and Letters, 2000-2001.

VILLENEUVE, JACQUES, race car driver; b. St.-Jean-sur-Richelieu, Que., Can., Apr. 9, 1971. Student, Jim Russell Racing Drivers Sch, Mont Tremblant, Can., 1986, Spenard-David Racing Sch., Shannonville, Ont., 1987. Race car driver, 1988—. 3-time winner, 2d pl. in championship Japanese Formula 3, 1992, 5-time winner, 3d in championship, Rookie of Yr. Formula Atlantic Championship, 1993, 1-time winner, Rookie of Yr. IndyCar World Championship, 1994, 4-time winner, 1995, World Champion Formula 1, 1997; named Athlete of Yr., Can., 1995. Office: William Grand Prix, Grove Wantage Station Rd, Oxon OX12 0DQ, England*

VILLENEUVE, JACQUES GRANDBOIS DE, lawyer; b. Buc, France, Aug. 8, 1937; s. Pierre Grandbois de Villeneuve and Anne Marie Buret de Sainte-Anne; m. Claude Gautheron. D in Law, U. Paris, France, 1960, Diploma in Econs., 1961; LLM, McGill U., Montreal, Can., 1963. Bar: France, 1957. Prof. law U. Cameroons, Yaounde, 1963-64; ptnr. Gide, Loyrette, Nouel Law Firm, Paris, 1964—; mem. exec. coun. Indsl. Property, Paris, 1985-96. Author: Les Cooperatives Agricoles Dans le Marche Commn., 1970; editor: Dictionnaire Joly des Societes Commerciales, 1970-94. Named chevalier Chancelory Legion Honor, 1993. Mem. Racing Club of France, Golf de la Boulie. Home: 212 Rue de Rivoli, 75001 Paris France Office: Gide Loyrette Novel Advocats, 26 Cours Albert 1er, 75008 Paris France

VILLIGER, KASPAR, Swiss government official; b. Lucerne, Switzerland, Feb. 5, 1941; m. Marié Villiger; 2 children. Degree in mech. engring., Swiss Fed. Inst. of Tech., 1966. Co-owner Villiger Söhne AG, Pfeffikon; mem. Parliament of Lucerne, 1972-82; nat. councillor, mem. def. com. Nat. Coun., 1983-87; mem. ways and means com. and transport com. Coun. of States, 1987-89; fed. councillor, chief dept. mil. Swiss Confederation, Bern, 1989-94, pres., 1995, chief dept. fin., 1995—. Capt. Armed Forces. Mem. C. of C. of Cen. Switzerland (v.p.), Swiss Employers' Cen. Assn., Chamber of Industry and Commerce of Canton of Aargau (v.p.). Mem. Liberal Party of Switzerland. Office: Fed Dept Fin, Bernerhof Bundesgasse 3, CH-3003 Bern Switzerland*

VILLOCH, KELLY CARNEY, art director; b. Kyoto, Japan, July 22, 1950; d. William Riley and stepdaughter Hazel Fowler Carney; m. Joe D. Villoch, Aug. 9, 1969; children: Jonathan Christopher, Jennifer. A in Fine Arts, Dade C.C., Miami, Fla., 1971; student, Metro Fine Arts, 1973-74, Fla. Internat. U., 1985-88. Design asst. Lanvin, Miami, 1971—, Fieldcrest, Miami, 1974-77; art dir. Advercolor, Miami, 1977-78; art dir. copywriter ABC, Miami, 1978-89; writer Armed Forces Radio & TV Network; multimedia dir. ADVITEC, 1989-91; art dir. writer Miami Write, 1979—; owner Beach Point Prodns., 1992—; editor-in-chief L'Avenue Mag., 1998—; lectr. Miami Dade C.C., cons. Studio Masters, North Miami, 1979-89; writer Lucent techs., telephonetics, algorhythm, inter-tel, 1997—; editor-in-chief Miami Mag.com., Floridajourney.com, 1999. Prin. works include mixed media, 1974 (Best of Show 1974), pen and ink drawing, 1988 (Best Poster 1988); writer, dir., editor, prodr. (video film): Bif, 1988, Drink + Drive = Die, 1994; writer, dir., prodr. (pub. svc. announcement) Reading is the Real Adventure, 1990; film editor Talent Times Mag.; author: Winds of Freedom, 1994; art dir., exec. com. Miami Hispanic Media Conf., 1992, 93, 94; editor-in-chief, film editor: In Grove Miami Mag., 1994-96; webmaster, web content provider, website design cons., writer, graphic artist Guru Comms., 1996; editor-in-chief In Grove Miami Mag., 1994-96, L'Avenue Mag., Miami Mag., Fla. Journey and Miami Guide, 1998-99; web content provider WEBCOM; webmaster Guru Comm., 1996; web site designer, multimedia dir. State of Fla. grantee LimeLite Studios, Inc., 1990, William Douglas Pawley Found. grantee, Frances Wolfson scholar, Cultural Consortium grantee, 1993. Mem. Am. Film Inst., Phi Beta Kappa. Avocations: pen and ink drawing, printmaking, skin diving, boating, painting.

VIMONT, RICHARD ELGIN, lawyer; b. Lexington, Ky., Aug. 3, 1936; s. Richard Thompson and Christine Frazee (Anderson) V.; m. Louise Marie Salyer, Sept. 20, 1960; children: Richard Thompson II, Margaret Anderson; m. 2d, Martha Jane Murray, Nov. 13, 1982 (div.); m. Mary Ann Farley, May 31, 1997. BS, U. Ky., 1958, JD, 1960. Bar: Ky. 1960, U.S. Dist. Ct. (ea. dist.) Ky. 1964, U.S. Ct. Appeals (6th cir.) 1964, U.S. Supreme Ct. 1966, U.S. Ct. Appeals (2d cir.) 1998. Assoc. Brown, Sledd and McCann, 1960-64; ptnr. Core, Vimont and Combs, 1964-68, Breckenridge, Vimont and Amato, 1968-70, Anggelis, Vimont and Bunch, 1970-78; ptnr. Vimont and Wills PLLC, Lexington, 1978—, mng. mem., 1998—; asst. commonwealth atty., 1973-75; vis. prof. Transylvania U., 1978-80, Midway Coll., 1992; bd. dirs. Equitania Ins. Co.; mng. dir. Equitania Ins. Co., 1990-93, pres., CEO, 1993-95; gen. counsel Pavenstedt Pauli (U.S.A.), Inc., 1990-92; adj. prof. U. Kent. Coll. of Law, 1998. City commr., Lexington, 1971-72; chmn. Lexington Mounted Police Bd., chair, 1997—; bd. dirs. Ky. World Trade Ctr., 1990-97, Lexington Ballet Co., 1989-90; ch. parliamentarian Christian Ch. (Disciples of Christ). Fellow U. Ky., U. Kent. Mem. ABA, Am. Acad. Trial Attys., Ky. Bar Assn., Ky. Acad. Trial Attys., Fayette County Bar Assn., Lexington C. of C., Thoroughbred Club of Am., Lexington Polo Club, Spindletop Hall Club (bd. dirs. 1978-81, 86-90), Rotary (sec. Lexington endowment 1994-97, Paul Harris fellow). Democrat. E-mail: rvimont@vimwil.com. Office: 155 E Main St Fl 3 Lexington KY 40507-1300

VIMPANI, GRAHAM VERNON, pediatrician; b. Adelaide, Australia, Feb. 12, 1944; s. Horace and Phyllis Vimpani; m. Anne Strachan, Jan. 24, 1970; 2 children. MB, BS, U. Adelaide, Australia, 1967; PhD, U. Edinburgh, 1977. Intern, registrar Queen Elizabeth Hosp., 1967, 70; registrar RMO Royal Children's Hosp., Melbourne, 1968, Adelaide Children's Hosp., 1969-71; lectr. dept. pediats. U. Adelaide, 1972; rsch. fellow dept. child life and health U. Edinburgh, 1974-77; coord. maternal and child health svcs. SA Health Commn., 1977-81; dir. rsch. and evaluation Child Adolescent and Family Health Svcs., 1981-83, dir. cen. sector, 1983-85; staff pediatrician, sr. lectr. Flinders Med. Ctr./Flinders U. South Australia, 1985-89; nat. project dir. Nat. Injury Surveillance and Prevention Project, 1987-89; prof. cmty., child and family health U. Newcastle, 1990—, dir. child adolescent and family health svc., 1990—; prof. pediat. and child health, 2000—; cons. home visiting Nat. Child Protection Coun., 1995-96; mem. NSW Govt. Internat. Yr. of Family Adv. Com., 1994-95; bd. dirs. Family Action Ctr., U. Newcastle, Nat. Organizing and Sci. Program Com., Internat. Conf. on Injury Prevention and Control, 1992-96; mem. internat. working group on injury surveillance methodology WHO, 1990, Better Health Commn. Injury Task Force, 1985-86. Author: (with T. L. Parry) Community Child Health: An Australian Perspective, 1989. Mem. NSW Child Protection Coun., 1997-99, NSW Child Death Rev. Team, 1997-99, NSW Premier's Crime Prevention Coun., 2000—. WHO fellow, 1989, Nestle Traveling fellow Australian Pediat. Assn., 1973, Heinz fellow Brit. Pediat. Assn., 1973. Fellow Aus-

tralian Faculty Pub. Health Medicine, Royal Australasian Coll. Physicians (mem. bd. continuing edn. 1994—, chair specialist adv. com. cmty. child health 1999—, exec. faculty cmty. child health 1991—), Child Accident Prevention Found. Australia (hon. life, chmn. op. planning com. 1991-96), Exec. Nat. Investment for the Early Years (chmn. 1999—). Avocations: running, bushwalking, early music, reading, spirituality. E-mail: gvimpani@mail.newcastle.edu.au. Office: Child/Youth Health Network, Locked Bag 1014 Wallsend, Wallsend NSW 2287, Australia

VINCENS, LOUIS-FRANÇOIS, surgeon; b. Treignac, France, June 11, 1939; s. Robert and Marie-Françoise (Maurin) V.; m. Catherine Laire, Apr. 3, 1970; 1 child, Xavier. MD, U. Clermont-Ferrand, France, 1968, student urology, 1971. Hosp. extern Clermont-Ferrand, France, 1959-63; hosp. intern Clermont-Ferrand, 1965-68, asst. hosp. clin. chief, 1969-71, practice medicine specializing in surgery, 1971—; gen.-pres., dir. Clinique des Domes, Clermont-Ferrand, 1987; expert Arreal Tribunal, Riom, 1975. Mem. French Assn. Urology. Roman Catholic. Lodge: Rotary. Avocations: castle restoration. Home: Les Malieves, 63114 Montpeyroux France Office: 99 Avenue de la Republique, 63000 Clermont France

VINCENT, BRIAN, chemistry educator, industrial consultant; b. London, Apr. 25, 1943; s. William Ernest and Winifred (Porter) V.; m. Mary Barker, Jan. 2, 1965; children: Susanne, Katherine. BSc, U. Bristol, Eng., 1964, MSc, 1965, PhD, 1968, DSc, 1982. Royal Soc. rsch. fellow U. Wageningen, The Netherlands, 1968-69; rsch. scientist I.C.I. Paints plc, Slough, Eng., 1969-72; lectr. U. Bristol, 1972-84, reader, 1984-92, prof., 1992—, Leverhulme Prof. Phys. Chemistry, 1996; sr. vis. fellow U. Melbourne, Australia, 1980; plenary lectr. Russian Acad. Scientists, Moscow, 1990, Taniguchi Conf., Kobe, Japan, 1993. Co-author: Polymers at Interfaces, 1993; co-editor: Polymer Adsorption and Dispersion Stability, 1984. Mem. Am. Chem. Soc. (plenary lectr. 1995), Internat. Assn. Colloid & Interface Scientists, Internat. Union Pure Applied Chemistry Commn. I.6 (sec. 1985-97), Soc. Chemistry Industry Colloid & Surface Chemistry (chmn. 1990-93), Soc. Chem. Industry (exec. com. 1993-96). Liberal Democrat. Avocations: cricket, swimming, hill walking, theatre. Office: U Bristol Sch Chemistry, Cantock's Close, Bristol BS8 1TS, England

VINCENT, CARL G., JR., real estate portfolio manager; b. Milford, Del., June 30, 1964; s. Carl G. Sr. and Phylis F. (Cash) V.; m. Rhonda L. Ross, May 26, 1990. BS, Oral Roberts U., 1985, MBA, 1988; JD, U. Tulsa, 1991. Bar: Okla. 1991; real property adminstr., facility mgmt. adminstr. BOMI Inst.; cert. facility mgr. Internat. Facilities Mgmt. Assn. Real estate market analyst 1st Am. Realty, Tulsa, 1985-87; real estate fin. analyst Boston Mgmt. Co., Tulsa, 1987-91; real estate tax cons. Burke & Nickel, Tulsa, 1991-94; dir. Tulsa ops. Ruffin Properties, Tulsa, 1994—; bus. advisor Alzheimers Found., Tulsa, 1991—; adj. prof. mktg., internat. bus. and econs., 1992—. Contbr. articles to profl. publs. Recipient Chair award Order of Curule. Mem. Phi Delta Phi, Phi Alpha Phi. Office: Ruffin Properties 7130 S Lewis Ave Ste 950 Tulsa OK 74136-5427

VINCENT, CHARLES ANTHONY, psychologist; b. London, July 12, 1952; s. Anthony Peyton and Angela Mary (Tingay) V.; m. Angela Emma Phillips; 1 child, Rhianne. BA, Oxford U., 1975; MPhil, London U., 1978; PhD, U. Coll. London, 1987. Clin. psychologist British Nat. Health, London, 1979-84; rsch. psychologist U. Coll. London, 1985-88, lectr. psychology, 1988-94, sr. lectr., 1994—, reader in psychology, 1998, prof. psychology, 2000—; cons. World Health Orgn., 1995. Author: Complementary Medicine: A Research Perspective, 1997; editor: Clinical Risk Management, 1995, 2d edit., 2000; co-editor: Safety in Medicine, 1999, Medical Accidents, 1993; contbr. articles to profl. jours. Office: U Coll London Dept Psychology, Gower St, London WC1E 6BT, England

VINCENT, DAVID RIDGELY, management consulting executive; b. Detroit, Aug. 9, 1941; s. Charles Ridgely and Charlotte Jane (McCarroll) V.; m. Margaret Helen Anderson, Aug. 25, 1962 (div. 1973); children: Sandra Lee, Cheryl Ann; m. Judith Ann Gomez, July 2, 1978; 1 child, Amber; stepchildren: Michael Jr., Jesse Joseph Flores (dec.). BS, BA, Calif. State U., Sacramento, 1964; MBA, Calif. State U., Hayward, 1971; PhD, Somerset U., 1991. Cert. profl. cons. to mgmt., 1994. Sr. ops. analyst Aerojet Gen. Corp., Sacramento, 1960-66; contr. Hexcel Corp., Dublin, Calif., 1966-70; mng. dir. Memorex, Vienna, Austria, 1970-74; sales mgr. Ampex World Ops., Friebourg, Switzerland, 1974-76; dir. product mgmt. NCR, Sunnyvale, Calif., 1976-79; v.p. Boole & Babbage Inc., Sunnyvale, 1979-85; gen. mgr. Inst. Info. Mgmt., Sunnyvale Calif., Calif., 1979-85; pres., CEO The Info. Group, Inc., Santa Clara, Calif., 1985—. Author: Perspectives in Information Management, Information Economics, 1983, Handbook of Information Resource Management, 1987, The Information-Based Corporation: stakeholder economics and the technology investment, 1990, Reengineering Fundamentals: Business Processes and the Global Economy, 1994-96; contbr. monographs and papers to profl. jours. U.S. Soccer Fedn. soccer referee emeritus. Mem. Nat. Alliance Bus. Economists, Am. Electronics Assn., Soc. Competitive Intelligence Profls., World Future Soc., Inst. Mgmt. Cons., Product Devel. and Mgmt. Assn., Assn. Fin. Profls. Home: 2803 Kalliam Dr Santa Clara CA 95051-6838 Office: The Info Group Inc 4675 Stevens Creek Blvd Ste 100 Santa Clara CA 95051-6763

VINCENT, JAMES LOUIS, biotechnology company executive; b. Johnstown, Pa., Dec. 15, 1939; s. Robert Clyde and Marietta Lucille (Kennedy) V.; m. Elizabeth M. Matthews, Aug. 19, 1961 (div. 1998); children: Aimee Archelle, Christopher James. BSME, Duke U., 1961; MBA in Indsl. Mgmt., U. Pa., 1963; DBA (hon.), U. New Haven, 1998. Mgr. Far East div. Tex. Instruments, Inc., Tokyo, 1970-72; pres. Tex. Instrument Asia, Ltd., Tokyo, 1970-72; v.p. diagnostic ops., pres. diagnostics div. Abbott Labs., North Chgo., Ill., 1972-74, group v.p., bd. dirs., 1974-81, exec. v.p., COO, bd. dirs., 1979-81; corp. group v.p., pres. Allied Health and Sci. Products Co. Allied Corp., Morristown, N.J., 1982-85; CEO Biogen, Inc., Cambridge, Mass., 1985-97, chmn. bd., 1997-99, chmn. bd., CEO, 1999-2000, chmn. bd., 2000—; bd. dirs. PhRMA, Found. for Nat. Tech. Trustee Duke U., Com. for Econ. Devel.; bd. overseers Wharton Grad. Bus. Sch., U. Pa.; bd. dirs. Mass. chpt. Nat. Multiple Sclerosis Soc. Recipient Young Exec. Achievement Young Execs. Club, Chgo., 1976, Disting. Alumni award Duke U., 1988, Biotech. award Wall St. Transcript, 1997. Mem. Econ. Club Chgo., Mass. Bus. Roundtable, The Comml. Club Boston, Shoreacres Country Club, Algonquin Club Boston, Chgo. Club, The Links (N.Y.C.). Republican. Presbyterian. Office: Biogen Inc 14 Cambridge Ctr Cambridge MA 02142-1481

VINCENT, JEAN-LOUIS, critical care physician; b. Brussels, Belgium, May 20, 1949; s. Georges and Claudine (Bonaerts) V.; m. Cong-Huyen Ton Nu Bach Hac, Sept. 29, 1981; 1 child, Amelie. MD, U. Brussels, 1973, PhD, 1982. Resident U. Brussels, 1973-77; fellowship in critical care medicine U. So. Calif., Los Angeles, 1977-79; staff physician U. Brussels, 1979—; head dept. intensive care Erasme U. Hosp., Brussels. Fellow Soc. Critical Care Medicine, Am. Coll. Chest Physicians; mem. European Soc. Intensive Care Medicine (pres. 1991-93), U. Brussels Alumni Assn. (pres. 1990-93), European Shock Soc. (pres. 1996-99). Home: Rue Marianne, 26, 1180 Brussels Belgium Office: Erasme Univ Hosp, Route de Lennik 808, 1070 Brussels Belgium

VINCENT, JOSEF GUSTAV, cardiac surgeon; b. Brno, Czechoslovakia, Jan. 12, 1937; arrived in The Netherlands, 1968; s. Gustav and Helena (Lenz) Vincent; m. Michaela Milada Houdek, Jan. 25, 1964; children: Monika, Libor. MD, U. J.E. Purkyne, Brno, 1961; postgrad., Tech. U., Brno, 1965-68. Diplomate Bd. Gen. Surgery, Bd. Cardiopulmonary Surgery; lic. physician The Netherlands, Belgium, Germany, Switzerland, Czech Republic. Resident Dist. Hosp. N. Bor & C. Lipa, Czechoslovakia, 1961-64; registrar U. Hosp., Brno, 1964-68; chief registrar U. Hosp., Leiden, The Netherlands, 1968-71; sr. staff mem., chief clinic U. Hosp., Nijmegen, The Netherlands, 1971-92; cons. cardiac surgery Zentralklinik Bad Berka D, 1993-95; cons. cardiac surgeon Herz-Zentrum Bodensee, Kreuzlingen, 1995-97, Klinik Im Schachen, Aarau, Switzerland, 1997—; prof. cardiac surgery Masaryk U., Brno, 1992—; rschr. cardiac surgery; cons. cardiac surgery tech. Contbr. articles to profl. jours.; patentee in field; author sci. and med. ednl. films. Recipient award for tech. innovation in surgery Davies & Geck Cyanamid Corp., 1986. Fellow European Bd. Thoracic and Cardiovasc. Surgery. Avocations: skiing, horse riding, hiking. Home: Tannengut 5, CH-5000 Aarau Switzerland Office: Klinik Im Schachen, CH 5001 Aarau Switzerland

VINCENT, JULIE, Russian literature educator; b. Moscow, Mar. 14, 1922; naturalized Belgian citizen; d. Guenadi Gregoire and Fayna (Heifez) Chkolnikoff; m. Marc Vincent, Dec. 26, 1942; children: Anne, Irene. Lic. in Roman philology, U. Brussels, 1943; agregation in Roman philology, U. Louvain, Belgian Congo, 1960; PhD in French, U. Pitts., 1963. Prof. French, Athénée Royal Léopoldville, Belgian Congo, 1952-58, C. of. C. Brussels, 1974-87; lectr. French and Russian, Cath. U. Am., Washington, 1960-61; teaching fellow in French, U. Pitts., 1961-62; lectr. French, Am. Coll. in Paris, 1963-66; asst. prof. French, Chatham Coll., Pitts., 1967-68; asst. prof. Russian, Howard U., Washington, 1968-71; prof. Russian lit. Ctr. Féminin Edn. Permanent, Brussels, 1987—. Home: 5 ave de la Sauvagine, B-1170 Brussels Belgium

VINCENT HOUDEK, MICHAELA MILADA, rheumatologist; b. Brno, Czechoslovakia, Feb. 24, 1940; arrived in The Netherlands, 1968; d. Jaromir and Milada (Wagner) Houdek; m. Josef Gustav Vincent, Jan. 25, 1964; children: Monika,, Libor. MD, U. J.E. Purkyne, Brno, 1963. Cert. in pediatrics and rheumatology. Intern Provincial Hosp, Usti n/L, Czechoslovakia, 1963-65, Dist. Hosp., Breclav, Czechoslovakia, 1965-66; pvt. practice, Breclav, 1966-68; staff mem. Univ. Hosp., Leiden, The Netherlands, 1969-71; mem. staff, then cons. Rheumatology Hosp. St. Martens, Nijmegen, The Netherlands, 1972-80; rheumatologist, chief dept. infection control Univ. Hosp., Nijmegen, 1981-94; rheumatologist Health and Rehab. Ctr. Sennerüti, Degersheim, Switzerland, 1995—. Contbr. articles to med. jours. Home: 1 m Tanneugut 5, CH-5000 Aarau Switzerland Office: Health and Rehab Ctr Sennerüti, Degersheim St Galen, Switzerland

VINCIGUERRA, SERGIO, geologist, researcher; b. Chatenay-Malabry, France, Feb. 15, 1969; s. Domenico and Nadia (Foiadelli) V.; m. Erika Mirabella, Sept. 1, 1998. Degree in geol. scis., U. Catania, Italy, 1992, PhD, 1998. Rsch. fellow U. Catania, 1993-95; postdoctoral fellow Univ. Coll. London, 1998—; vis. rschr. Inst. Nat. Geophys., Rome, 1996-98, MIT, Boston, 1998. Mem. AGU. Home: 24 Orpington Rd, Winchmore Hill N21 3PG, England Office: Dept Geol Scis UCL, Gower St, London WC1E 6BT, England

VINCK, KAREL, steel industry executive; b. 1938. MBA, Cornell U. Past mng. dir. Eternit Group; past CEO NV Bekaert SA, Kortrijk, Belgium, past CEO, chmn. exec. com.; CEO Union Miniere SA, Brussels. Recipient Silver award Fin. World Mag., 1994. Office: Union Miniere SA, rue du Marais 31, B-1000 Brussels Belgium*

VINCKE, JOHN JOZEF, sociology educator; b. Beernem, Belgium, Jan. 29, 1956; s. Valère Vincke and Maria Vermandel. PhD, U. Gent, Belgium, 1989. Rsch. asst. U. Gent, 1990-92, sr. rsch. asst., 1992-95, prof. sociology, 1995—; vis. asst. prof., Pomona Coll., Claremont, Calif., 1989-90; invited expert Tech. Working Group on Bisexuality and AIDS, WHO, 1991. Author: Sociology. A classic but contemporary introduction, 1999; co-author (with R. Mak and R. Bolton): Men with Men. Well Being and Relationships, 1991; contbr. chpts. to books, articles to profl. jours. Pres. AIDS Team, Belgium, 1992-99. Mem. Am. Sociol. Soc., N.Y. Acad. Scis. Avocation: jogging. Office: U Gent Dept Sociology, Universiteitstraat 4-8, B-9000 Gent Belgium

VINCKEN, WALTER G., respiratory physiology and pulmonology educator; b. Brussels, Mar. 25, 1952; s. Julien Vincken and Hilda Van Hyfte; m. Anne-Marie De Coninck; children: Frederik, Jonathan, Stefanie. MD, Free U. Brussels, 1976, PhD, 1989. Specialist-in-tng. Brugmann Hosp., Brussels, 1976-79; rsch. fellow McGill U., Montreal, Que., Can., 1981-83; specialist-in-tng. in internal and respiratory medicine Free U. Brussels, 1979-81, resident in intensive care Acad. Hosp., 1983-91, head respiratory divsn., 1991—, prof. respiratory physiology and pulmonology, 1993—. Contbr. over 300 articles to nat. and internat. med. jours. Mem. Am. Thoracic Soc., Am. Coll. Chest Physicians, European Respiratory Soc. Avocation: music. Office: Free U Brussels Acad Hosp, Laarbeeklaan 101, 1090 Brussels Belgium

VINE, P. A. L., author; b. Teddington, Middlesex, Eng., Dec. 13, 1927; s. Laurence Arthur and Nellie Florence (Ashley) V.; m. Rosalind Bradley, Dec. 18, 1969; children: Deirdre, Ashley, Peter, Edwina; m. Kay Bowen, June 10, 1992. Degree, Lincoln Coll., Oxford, Eng., MA. Exec. asst. Brit. Ins. Assn., London, 1953-56; controller Auto. Assn., London, 1956-71; advisor Ethiopian Tourist Orgn., Addis Ababa, 1971-74; permanent sec. Tourism and Civil Aviation Govt. of Seychelles, 1976-77; advisor Barbados Bd. Tourism, Bridgetown, 1979-90, Jamaica Tourist Bd., Kingston, 1990-92; cons. UN Devel. Plan World Tourism Orgn., 1994-96; dir. Auto Assn. of Jamaica, 1990-92; cons. Brit. Exec. Svc. Overseas, 1993-2000. Author: London's Lost Route to the Sea, 1965, 5th edit. 1996, London's Lost Route to Basingstoke, 1968, 2d edit. 1994, The Royal Military Canal, 1972, Pleasure Boating in the Victorian Era, 1983, London's Lost Route to Midhurst, 1995, others. Lt. Brit. Army, 1946-49. Recipient Silver medal World Univ. Games, 1951, Bronze medal, 1953, Bain prize Chartered Ins. Inst., 1954; British 220 yard hurdles champion, Amateur Athletic Assn., 1955-56. Mem. Sussex Canal Trust (v.p. 1970-90), Wey & Arun Canal Trust (v.p. 1973—), Surrey & Hampshire Canal Soc. (v.p. 1968—), Achilles Club (mgmt. com. 1952-55). Ch. of England. Avocations: athletics, aquatics, bibliography, lawn tennis, jeu de paume. Home: Templemead Coach House, Pulborough Sussex, England RH202BH Office: 13 Lower St, Pulborough Sussex RH20 2BH, England

VINECOUR, ONEIDA AGNES, nurse; b. Port Arthur, Tex., Oct. 15, 1917; d. Ernest Eugene and Gertrude Mary (Wooldridge) Thorn; m. Seymour Vinecour, Jan. 14, 1943 (dec. 1976); children: Seymour Jacob, Rebecca Leah. Diploma, St. Mary's Hosp. Sch. Nursing, Port Arthur, 1939; postgrad., cert. Surg. Tech., Anesthesia, Cook County Hosp., 1939-40; postgrad. U. Chgo., 1939-40, Tex. Coll. Mines, 1943, U. Tex. Health Ctr. R.N., cert. occupational audiometric technician, occupl. spirometric technician. Operating room supr., instr. Schumpert Meml. Hosp., Shreveport, La., 1940-41; anesthetist St. Joseph Hosp., Albuquerque, 1941-42; operating room supr., instr. Lynn City Hosp. (Mass.), 1946-48; staff anesthetist St. Mary's Hosp., Port Arthur, Tex., 1951-53, in service dir., 1971-73; staff nurse Tyler County Hosp., Woodville, Tex., 1964-65; dept. head, supr. Park Pl. Hosp., Port Arthur, 1965-71; operating room supr. Mid-County Hosp., Nederland, Tex., 1973-81; staff nurse Baptist Meml. Hosp., Beaumont, Tex., 1973-81; part time staff Health Care Svcs., Port Arthur, 1983—; indsl. nurse Synpol Inc., 1984-86; staff nurse Texaco Chem. Plant, Port Arthur, 1986-92, Olsten Health Care Svcs., 1992—, staff nurse Huntsman Petro-Chem. Corp., 1996—. Served as officer U.S. Army Nurse Corps, 1942-46. Mem. Am. Nurses Assn., Mass. Nurses Assn., Tex. State Nurses Assn., Assn. Occupational Health Nurses. Republican. Methodist. Home: 2502 Glenwood Dr Port Arthur TX 77642-2639

VINGE, LOUISE, literature educator; b. Hovås, Sweden, Nov. 24, 1931; d. Karl Axel and Märta (Lagerlöf) V. BA, Lund (Sweden) U., 1954, MA, 1963, PhD, 1967. Tchr. h.s. Sollefteå, Sweden, 1955-57; editor CWK Gleerup Pubs., Lund, 1962-64, 69; maî de confs. associé U. de Bordeaux, France, 1968-69; asst. prof. U. Lund, 1970-80, prof. comparative lit., 1980-96, prof. emeritus, 1996—. Author: The Five Senses, 1975, Morgonrodnadens Stridsmän, 1978, The Narcissus Theme, 1967, Skånska Läsningar, 1999; co-author, editor: Skanes Litteraturhistoria, vols. 1-2, 1996-97; editor: Svenskt Litteraturlexikon, 1964, 2d edit., 1969. Bd. dirs. Clara Lachmann's Found., Göteborg, 1995—. Recipient Gleerup's prize New Soc. of Letters, Lund, 1967, 99, Schück's prize Swedish Acad., 1980, Festschrift, Lärdomens Trädgård, 1996. Mem. New Soc. of Letters (sec. 1973-77), Royal Soc. Humanities (pres. 1994-95), Swedish Rsch. Coun. of Humanities (bd. dirs. 1987-92), Royal Acad. Letters, History and Antiquities, Royal Physiographic Soc. in Lund. Home: Hantverksgatan 32, S-22736 Lund Sweden Office: Litteraturvetenskapliga Inst, Helgonabacken 12, S-22362 Lund Sweden

VINGRYS, ALGIS JONAS, optometrist, educator, vision scientist; b. Melbourne, Victoria, Australia, Feb. 21, 1951; s. Bronius and Jadvyga (Narunas) V.; m. Lynnette Margaret Tollis, May 25, 1973; children: Janis, Kristan, Nathan. BSc in Optometry, U. Melbourne, 1981, PhD, 1985. Cert. optometrist. Cadet pilot Qantas, Sydney, Australia, 1969-70; flight instr. Schutt Air, Melbourne, 1970-71; sr. pilot MacAir, Lae, New Guinea, 1971-72; first officer Ansett Airways, Melbourne, 1972-75; postdoctoral fellow Sch. Optometry, Columbus, Ohio, 1985-87; sr. lectr. Dept. Optometry U. Melbourne, 1987-98, assoc. prof., 1998; chmn. Nat. Optometric Continuing Edn. Com., Melbourne, 1992-95. Author: Pilots and Presbyopia, 1985; contbr. articles to profl. jours, papers and chpts. to books. Fellow Victorian Coll. Optometry, Am. Acad. Optometry. Avocations: snow skiing, fishing, bush walking, gardening. Achievements include research on colour vision, perimetry, electrodiagnosis, nutritional effects on vision, disease of the eye. Office: U Melbourne, Dept Optometry and Vision Sci, Parkville 3052, Australia

VINH MAU, ROBERT, physics educator; b. Hue, Vietnam, Dec. 2, 1931; s. Buu Vien and Nguyen Thi Nguyet. DSc, U. Paris, 1960. Researcher Cen. Nat. Rsch. Sci., Paris, 1957-61; prof. U. Bordeaux, France, 1961-65; prof. U. Paris, 1965—, dir. dept. theoretical physics, 1974-77; dir. theory div. Inst. Physique Nucleaire, Orsay, France, 1976-86. Contbr. articles to profl. jours. Alexander von Humboldt Found. awardee, 1986; laureate Acad. Scis. (France); decorated Ordre Nat. du Merite. Mem. Am. Phys. Soc., Europhys. Soc., Societa Italiana Fisica, Societe Francaise Physique. Home: 29, rue Guenegaud, 75006 Paris France Office: U Paris P et M Curie, 4 Place Jussieu, 75252 Paris France

VINIAR, IGOR VASILIEVICH, physicist, researcher; b. Soroki, Moldova, USSR, May 26, 1957; s. Vasilii Alexeevich Viniar and Galina Iosifovna Vaschenko; m. Irina Mikhailovna Moguilevich, Mar. 10, 1980; children: Alex, Anna. MSc, St. Petersburg Tech. U., Russia, 1981, PhD, 1986. Jr. rschr. St. Petersburg State Tech. U., 1986-87, rschr., 1987-89, sr. rschr., 1989-91, vice dir. applied physics, 1991-98; gen. dir. PELIN, Inc. (Can.), 1998—; sr. rschr. Russian Ministry Sci., Moscow, 1991; mgr., head R & D divsn. Liral Internat. Trading, Inc., Moscow, 1996-99; head lab. on pellet injection St. Petersburg Tech. U., Russia, 1999—; cons. Mitsubishi Heavy Industry, Ltd., Kobe, Japan, 1996—, Oak Ridge (Tenn.) Nat. Lab., 1997—. Contbr. articles on fusion sci. to sci. jours. Recipient state prize for young rschr. Soviet Union, Moscow, 1989; rsch. grantee Nat. Inst. for Fusion Sci., Japan, 1994. Avocations: travel, books, chess. Home: Apt 16, 18/7 Grazhdanskaya Str, 190031 Saint Petersburg Russia Office: State Tech U Physics Dept, 29 Polytekhnicheskaya St, 195251 Saint Petersburg Russia

VINK, JOS PIÈRRE MARIE, soil scientist, researcher; b. Moordrecht, Zuid-Holland, The Netherlands, Sept. 25, 1963; s. Piet Hubert Marie and Jèssy Maria Agnes Antonia (Pinckaers) V. MS, Agrl. U., Wageningen, Netherlands, 1990, Phys. degree, Dr., 1997. Soil scientist U. Minn., 1989-90, Ryksdienst, Ysselmeerpolders, The Netherlands, 1990-92; leader dept. soil quality Ministry Transport, Pub. Works and Water Mgmt., The Netherlands, 1990-96; rsch. leader chemistry and ecotoxicology Inst. Inland Water Mgmt. and Waste Water Treatment (RIZA), The Netherlands, 1996—; govt. advisor on environ. chemistry., on environ. behavior of pesticides, 1992—. Author: Pesticide biotransformation and fate in heterogeneous environments, 1997. Smart Student scholar Agrl. U. Wageningen, 1988. Mem. Dutch Soil Sci. Soc. (bd. dirs. 1994—); mem. jury Hissink rsch. award NBV, The Netherlands, 1997. Office: Inst Inland Water Mgmt RIZA, PO Box 17 Maerlant 16, 8200 AA Lelystad Flevoland, The Netherlands

VINK, ROBERT, neuroscientist, researcher; b. Mijnsheerenland, The Netherlands, Oct. 2, 1958; arrived in Australia, 1961; s. Johan and Lijntje (Van Der Steen) V.; m. Jane Maria Fedrick, May 15, 1982; children: Nathaniel Robert, Merinda Jane. BS, Griffith U., Brisbane, Australia, 1982, BS with honors, 1983, PhD, 1986; Cert. Edn., James Cook U., Townsville, Australia, 1994. Postdoctoral fellow U. Calif., San Francisco, 1985-86, asst. rsch. neurochemist, 1987-88; rsch. fellow James Cook U., 1988-91, from lectr. to assoc. prof., 1991-95, head dept. physiology and pharmacology, 1995-98; adj. prof. neurosci. Georgetown U., 1999—; cons. Allegheny Singer Rsch. Inst., Pitts., 1992-93, Spinal Cord Soc. Australia, 1994—. Contbg. author: Head Injury: Pathophysiology and Management of Severe Closed Injury, 1997; mem. editl. bd. Jour. Neurotrauma, 1988—; contbr. over 100 articles to profl. jours. Recipient Sandoz Neurosci. fellowship U. Calif., 1987, Queen Elizabeth II Rsch. award, Australia, 1988. Mem. Internat. Soc. Magnetic Resonance in Medicine, Neurotrauma Soc., Internat. Soc. Neurochemistry, Soc. Neurosci., Neural Injury Soc. Australia (founder, pres. 1997—). Avocation: basketball referee (Australian Nat. Basketball League cert.). Home: 40 Morstone St, Townsville QLD 4814, Australia Office: James Cook Univ, Dept Physiology, Townsville QLD 4811, Australia

VINKEN, PIERRE JACQUES, publishing executive, neurosurgeon; b. Nov. 25, 1927. MD, U. Utrecht, The Netherlands, 1955; postgrad. in psychiatry, neurology, and neurosurgery, U. Amsterdam, 1957-63; hon. Dr., U. Paris, 1981. Staff neurosurgeon Univ. Clinic, Amsterdam, 1964-69; pres., mng. dir., chief editor Excerpta Medica Found., Amsterdam and Princeton, N.J., 1962-88; mng. dir. Elsevier Pub. Co., Amsterdam, 1972-78, chmn. bd. dirs., 1979-95; chmn. bd. dirs. Reed Elsevier, London, 1993-95; chmn. supervising bd. Elsevier, Amsterdam, Halder Holdings, The Hague, Blue Horse Prodns., Rotterdam, Medialand, Amsterdam, Optas, Rotterdam, Trust Theater Co.; bd. dirs. Wereldhave Investment Co., The Hague, Logica, London, Rotterdam, Aalberts Industries, Driebergen, Revisor, Amsterdam, Nat. Acad. Arts, Amsterdam; prof. med. database informatics U. Leyden, 1975-93; mem. Nat. Sci. Policy Coun., The Hague, 1983-90; chmn. Netherlands del. Intergovtl. Unisist Conf., Paris, 1970; mem. Netherlands Unisist Commn., 1971-79. Founder, editor-in-chief: Handbook of Clinical Neurology, 77 vols.; editor sci. books; contbr. articles to profl. jours. Chmn. Netherlands Commn. Bibliography and Documentation, 1972-81; pres. Internat. Congress Patient Counselling, 1976-79; chmn. The Lancet, London, 1991-95; chmn. Hiscom, Leyden, 1987-98; bd. dirs. Pearson, London, 1988-91, The Economist, London, 1989-92; chmn. Mees Pierson Bank, Amsterdam, 1994-97; dep. chmn. European Pubs. Coun.; mem. soc. adv. coun. Tinbergen Inst., Rotterdam, 1996—. Recipient Royal Netherland Acad. Sci. award, 1997. Mem. European Info. Providers Assn. (pres. 1980-83), Neurol. Soc. India (hon.), French Neurol. Soc. (hon.), Amsterdam Neurol. Soc. (hon.), Peruvian Soc. Psychiat. Neurology and Neurosurgery (hon.), Netherlands Rep. Soc. (founder 1996), Order Hipolitó Unanue (Peru, commdr.), Order of Netherlands' Lion (Knight), Order of Orange Nassau (Netherlands, commdr.). Home: 142 Bentveldsweg, 2111 EE Aerdenhout The Netherlands

VINKLER, PÉTER, scientific secretary; b. Szeged, Hungary, Oct. 25, 1941; s. Péter Makláry and Mária (Vinkler) M.; m. Judit Lőrincz, Jan. 17, 1970; 1 child, Zsuzsanna. Master, U. A. József, 1966, PhD, 1974; CSc, Hungarian Acad. Sci., 1981. Rsch. scientist Ctrl. Rsch. I. Chem., Hungarian Acad. Sci., Budapest, 1966-82, sr. rschr., 1982-88, head of dept., 1987—; sci. sec. Chem. Rsch. Ctr., Hungarian Acad. Sci., Budapest, 1998—; com. for libr. Found. Basic Hungarian Rsch. Projects, 1998—; cons. Rsch. Eval. com., Hungarian Acad. Sci., Budapest, 1985-90, head rsch. anal. com. , 1996—, com. for Sci. Equipment Hungarian Acad. Sci., 1985-89. Author: Revolt on the Green Planet, 1989; contbr. articles to profl. jours.; patentee in field. Recipient Std. prize Hungarian Broadcasting Co., 1976. Mem. Scientometrics (editl. bd.), Am. Soc. for Info. Sci. Avocations: science fiction, garden work. Home: Szellő 10, 1035 Budapest Hungary

VINNICHENKO, SERGEY VICTOROVICH, mathematician, researcher; b. Darasun, Ukraine, Mar. 7, 1958; s. Victor Iosifovich Vinnichenko and Eugeniya Leonidovna Grischenko. Grad., U. Novosibirsk, Russia, 1978, Pedagogical Inst., Chita, Russia, 1983; Candidate Phys. and Math. Scis., U. St. Petersburg, Russia, 1993. Engr. Natural Resources Inst., Chita, 1985-86, sr. engr., 1987-89, sci. rschr., 1989-93, sr. sci. rschr., 1993—; engr. Poly. Inst., Chita, 1986-87; program executor Ostanovka, 1990, Morozko, 1991. Co-author: Stopping Moments and Controlled Random Walks, 1992. Mem. N.Y. Acad. Scis. E-mail: mat@cinr.chita.su. Fax: 302-2 21-25-82. Home: Kurnatovskogo 76-30, 672012 Chita Russia Office: Natural Resources Inst, Butina 26, 672090 Chita Russia

VINOD, MADHAVAN PADMANABHAN, chemist, researcher, educator; b. Varakala, India, May 31, 1969; m. INdu Sreedhar, Nov. 16, 1999. BSc, U. Kerala, India, 1989; MSc, M.G. U., Kerala, 1992; PhD, Nat. Chem. Lab., Pune, India, 1997. Jr rsch. fellow Nat. Chem. Lab., Pune, 1992-97; postdoctoral fellow Technion-Israel Inst. Tech., Haifa, 1997-98; Alexander

von Humboldt fellow Inst. for Solar ENergy, Hannover, Germany, 1998—; rschr. in field. Contbr. aticles to chemistry jours. Avocations: chess, Indian classical music, reading, country walking. E0mail: mpvinod@isfh.apc.de. Home: Vidyabhavan, Maithanam, Varkala, Trivandrum Dist, Kerala India 695141

VINOGRADOV, ALEXANDER EVGENIEVICH, biologist; b. St. Petersburg, Russia, July 3, 1953. MS, St. Petersburg U., 1975; PhD in Biology, Inst. Cytology, St. Petersburg, 1984. Sr. rschr. Inst. Cytology, 1992—; participant expdns. in Ctrl. Asia, Carpathians, Caucasus, Zone of Chernobyl accident, White Sea. Contbr. articles to profl. jours. Recipient award Soros Found., 1992-93; grantee Russian Found. Basic Rsch., 1996-98, 99—; recipient Russian State Scientific stipend, 1997-99, 2000—. Office: Inst Cytology, Tikhoretsky Ave, 4, 194064 St Petersburg Russia

VINOGRADOV, GUEORGUI KONSTANTIN, electronics company executive, consultant; b. Moscow, Nov. 2, 1949; arrived in Japan, 1992; s. Konstantin Gueorgui and Valentina Mikhail (Rumyantseva) V.; m. Elena Vitalii Kolesova, Nov. 11, 1971; 1 child, Konstantin Gueorgui. MS, Leningrad State U., 1973; PhD, Topchiev Inst. USSR Acad. Sci., Moscow, 1980. Researcher Topchiev Inst., USSR Acad. Scis., Moscow, 1973-85, group leader, 1985-92; prof. Nagoya (Japan) U., 1992-95; gen. mgr. R&D MC Electronics Co., KEM Inc., Yamanashi, Japan, 1995-99; dep. chmn. Moscow Coun. Young Scientists, 1977-80; chmn. group of plasma polymerization Coun. High Energy Chemistry, USSR Acad. Scis., 1981-89; mem. program and organizing com. 12th Internat. Symposium Plasma Chemistry, 1994-95; internat. cons. in field. Contbr. articles to profl. jours. Mem. Moscow Coun. Inventors, 1989-92. Sr. Scientific fellow USSR Acad. Scis., 1985. Mem. Am. Vacuum Soc., Am. Chem. Soc. Avocation: alpen skiing. Office: KEM Inc., 907-8 Shimoimasuwa, Nakakoma-gun 400-0212, Japan

VINOGRADOV, MIKHAIL EVGENIEVITCH, oceanologist, researcher; b. Moscow, May 30; s. Evgenia Nikolaevna Vinogradova; m. Mina Georgievna Kabardina, Apr. 5, 1950 (dec. Mar. 1997); children: Ekaterine, George. Grad., Moscow Energetic Inst., 1944-48, Moscow State U., 1948-52; PhD (hon.), Moscow, 1955, DSc (hon.), 1965. Jr. scientist Inst. Oceanology, Moscow, 1952-57, scientist, 1957-71, head lab., 1971—; prof. Moscow State U., 1978-92; dep. rschr. Inst. Oceanology, 1967-97; pres. Inter-Dept. Tektialogical Commn., Moscow, 1993—. Chief editor Jour. Oceanology, 1998; author: Vertical Distribution Zooplankton in the Ocean, 1968, Ecosystems of the Black Sea, 1992; author, editor over 20 sci. books. Mem. Polish Acad. Sci. Russian Orthodox. Avocation: collecting stamps and shells. Home: Kotelnicheskaja 1/15-B-24, 109240 Moscow Russia Office: PP Shizshor Inst Oceanology, Nakchimova 36, 1 Moscow Russia

VINSON, ROY DOUGLAS, engineer; b. Ky., Nov. 13, 1914; m. Julia; children: Julianne, Lisa. Lt. col. Army Fort Knox, 1931-55; working for Vinson Trading Co., N.Y.C., 1945-52; sr. project engr. Rockwell Internat., 1961-72; sr. project engr., asst. to head of program Apollo Moon program, 1962; pres. Vinson World Magnetrain Corp., Covina, Calif., 1973—; tank comdr., instr. WWII served under Gen. Patton Major 1944-45 (won several ribbons in 4 major battles), dep. mil. gov. Frankfurt, Germany apptd. by DD Eisenhower to rebuild the nation of Germany, 1945-47. Patentee in field. Fax: 801-730-9527. E-mail: vwmc98@aol.com. Home: 18988 La Guardia St Rowland Hghts CA 91748-3827 Office: Vinson World Magnetrain Corp PO Box 1810 Covina CA 91722-0810

VINTEN, GERALD, auditing and ethics educator; b. Rochester, Kent, Eng., Feb. 8, 1948; s. George Edward and Winifred Grace (Bishop) V.; m. Alice Mei Whei Lin, Nov. 12, 1990. BA, Leeds U., Yorkshire, Eng., 1970, MA, 1971; DEd, Oxford U., 1972; DPA, London U., 1980; MSc, City U., London, 1989, South Bank U., 1994. Lic. acct., tchr., internal auditor. Counselor Richmond (Va.) Sch. Bd., 1972; mgmt. acct. Martins Printing Group, Rochester, Kent, Eng., 1973; tchr. Rainham (Kent) Secondary Sch. for Boys, 1973-74; inspectorate taxes Inland Revenue, Chatham (Kent), 1974-76; fin. planner South East Thames Regional Health Authority, Croydon, Surrey, Eng., 1976-80; sr. mgmt. auditor London Borough of Southwark, 1980-82; audit mgr. London Borough of Camden, 1982-83; dir. MSc in internal audit and mgmt. City U. Bus. Sch., London, 1983-91; Whitbread prof. bus. policy, dir. rsch. U. Luton, Bedfordshire, Eng., 1991-97; dep. dean, prof. mgmt. Southampton Bus. Sch., 1997-2000; dir. Toynbee Hall, London, 1981-83; assessor Higher Edn. Funding Coun.; insp. Further Edn. Funding Coun. Author: Whistleblowing Auditors: A Contradiction in Terms, 1992, Whistleblowing-Subversion or Corporate Citizenship?, 1994; co-author: Internal Auditing, 1988; editor: Focus on Fraud, 1990, Business Ethics--Salvation or Sop?, 1990; editor Managerial Auditing Jour., Jour. Royal Soc. Health. Recipient Sam Evans award Mayor of Southwark, London, 1981, Outstanding Contbr. award Internal Auditor Jour., Fla., 1988, 92. Fellow Royal Geog. Soc., Royal Soc. Arts, Royal Soc. Health (dir. 1986—), Inst. Dirs. (life); mem. Chartered Inst. Pub. Fin. and Accountancy (mem. of coun.), Inst. Internal Auditors (past pres. 1994—), Royal Inst. Pub. Adminstrn., Royal Soc. for Promotion of Health (past chmn.). Mem. Ch. of Eng./Methodist. Avocations: walking, music, travel, writing. Home: 82 Speed House, London, Barbican EC2Y 8AU, England Office: U Luton, Park Sq, Luton LU1 3JU, England

VINUESA, JULIO HECTOR, biologist, researcher; b. Capital Federal, Argentina, Nov. 18, 1947; s. Isidoro and Eulogia (Agraz) V.; m. Mabel Lilian Labal, Apr. 9, 1975; children: Martin Patricio, Maria Paula. Mercantile expert, Bartolomé Mitre, Olivos, Argentina, 1965; grad. in biol. scis., U. Buenos Aires, 1975, PhD, 1982. Rsch. asst. CIBIMA-CONICET, Buenos Aires, 1972-74, researcher, 1974-83; initiation in rsch. CONICET, Buenos Aires, 1975-77, perfecting in rsch., 1977-79, asst. researcher, 1979-83; adj. researcher CONICET, Ushuaia, Argentina, 1983-90, ind. researcher, 1991—; dir. sci. tech. Govt. of Tierra del Fuego, 1993-97; vice dir. CIBIMA-CONICET, Buenos Aires, 1981-83; fishery cons. Govt. of Tierra del Fuego, Ushuaia, 1979-81; sci. coord. CADIC-CONICET, Ushuaia, 1984-86; del. U. Nacional de la Patagonia, Ushuaia, 1984-86, adj. prof., 1984-85. Contbr. rsch. articles to profl. jours. Vice pres. Grad. Coll. Biol. Scis., Buenos Aires, 1980-82. Grantee SECYT, Ushuaia, 1979, Govt. of Tierra del Fuego, Ushuaia, 1979, CONICET, 1984-91. Mem. Assn. Argentina de Ecologia, Crustacean Soc. Roman Catholic. Avocations: cross country skiing, reading. Office: Cen Austral Investicient, Av Malvinas Argentinas S/N, 9410 Ushuaia Tierra Del Fuego, Argentina

VIOLA, MARY JO, art history educator; b. Yonkers, N.Y., July 25, 1941; d. William F. and May (Cleary) O'Connor; m. Jerome Joseph Viola, June 21, 1967 (dec. Feb. 1990). BA in Fine Arts, Coll. of Mt. St. Vincent, 1963; MA in Art History, NYU, 1966; MPhil in Art History, CUNY, 1983, PhD in Art History, 1992. Art history tchr. Georgian Ct. Coll., N.J., 1965-66, Hollins Coll., Roanoke, Va., 1966-67, Marymount Coll., Tarrytown, N.Y., 1967-71, Baruch Coll., CUNY, N.Y.C., 1974-97, Bklyn. Coll., 1990-97, Parsons Sch. of Design, N.Y.C., 1991-93, Rutgers U., 1993-95, CUNY, 1997—; curator exhbns. Baruch Coll. Gallery, N.Y.C., 1987-88. Editor: A World View of Art History, 1985; art exhibited at Tribes Gallery, N.Y.C., 1996;. Rschr. for ethnic festivals, N.Y.C., 1993—. Fellow Nat. Trust for Hist. Preservation, 1964, Marymount Coll., 1970, Boston Mus. Fine Arts/CUNY, 1978, Luce Found., 1988. Mem. Coll. Art Assn., Historians of Am. Art, City Lore. Avocations: tai chi, Argentine tango, ballroom dance. Home and Office: 37 Roosevelt St Yonkers NY 10701-5823

VIOLANTE, JOSEPH ANTHONY, lawyer; b. Jersey City, June 15, 1950; s. Carmine Joseph and Rosa (Cardillo) V.; m. Linda Lee Munn, July 5, 1972; children: Joseph Anthony II, Christy Anne, Gina Lee. Student, St. Peter's Coll., Jersey City, 1972-74; BA, U. N.Mex., 1975; JD, U. La Verne (Calif.), 1980. Bar: Calif. 1981, U.S. Dist. Ct. (cen. dist.) Calif. 1982, (6th dist.) Ohio 1992, U.S. Ct. Appeals (fed. cir.) 1990, U.S. Ct. Appeals (D.C. cir.) 1991, U.S. Ct. Vets. Appeals 1990. Sole practice Thousand Oaks, Calif., 1981-85; atty., cons. Bd. Vet. Appeals, Washington, 1985-90; staff counsel DAV, Washington, 1990-92, legis. counsel, 1992-96, dep. nat. legis. dir., 1996-97, nat. legis. dir., 1997—; mem. adv. com. Bowie Cable T.V., 1989-91, bd. dirs., 1992-94. Co-host cable TV show Vets. Forum, 1991-94. Asst. coach Am. Youth Soccer Orgn., Thousand Oaks, 1981-84, Little League, Thousand Oaks, 1981-84; del. John Glenn Calif. Dem. Presdl. Primary, Thousand Oaks, 1984; active campaign Combined Fed., Washington, 1985; mem. presdl. del. Prisoners of War/Missing in Action, Southeast Asia, 1996. With USMC, 1969-72. Mem. ABA (vice chmn. vets. benefit com. 1991-98), DAV (life, comdr. 1990-91), VFW (life, comdr. 1984-85), KC, Calif. Bar Assn., Fed. Cir. Bar Assn. (chmn. vets appeal com. 1992-96, co-chmn. legis. com. 1996—, nominating com. 2000), FBA (at-large bd. mem., vets. com. 1991-92), D.C. Bar Assn., Italian-Am. Bar Assn., Nat. Italian-Am. Found., Coun. of 1,000, Nat. Italian Am. Found. (nat. mentors program), Am. Legion, Italian Am. War Vets., Marine Corps League, 3d Marine Divsn. Assn. (life), 2d Bn. 4th Marine Assn. Democrat. Roman Catholic. Avocations: collecting coins, soccer, softball, reading. Home: 2515 Ann Arbor Ln Bowie MD 20716-1562 Office: DAV Nat Svc & Legis Hdqrs 807 Maine Ave SW Washington DC 20024-2410

VIQUEZ, EDUARDO ANTONIO, historian, geographer; b. Heredia, Costa Rica, Feb. 23, 1942; s. Eduardo and Angela (Coronado) V.; m. Clara Betsabe Alvergue, Aug. 6, 1966; children: Ranny, Do Ryan, Nandy. Grad., Coll. San Mateo, Calif., 1969, San Francisco State U., 1971, U. Costa Rica, San Pedro, 1977, U. Costa Rica, San Pedro, 1980. Counsel gen. staff Costa Rica, 1966-71; tchr. U. Costa Rica, 1972-78; dir. Planetary Obs., Escazu, Costa Rica, 1991—; architect, designer DIPSA, San Jose, Costa Rica, 1977-81; art designer ASCONA, San Jose, 1980-82; dir. Investments Verbena, San Jose, 1982—, Geoff Marcy Plan & Astro. Obs. of Tropics, Escaru, Costa Rica, 1991—; advisor design cons. Sojourner Mars Craft, 1997. Mem. AAAS, Planetary Soc., N.Y. Acad. Scis., Nat. Geog. Soc. Avocations: dancing, singing, painting, writing verses of Greek culture. Office: Geoff Marcy Planetary Obs, PO Box 376-1000, San Jose Costa Rica

VIRA, SOMA, writer, publisher; b. Lucknow, India; came to U.S., 1957; d. Shyam Lal and Shanta Bugali Devi. BA in Journalism, U. Colo., 1958, MA, 1960; PhD in Philosophy, NYU, 1967. Assoc. editor children's page Nava Bharat Times, Bombay, 1956-57; staff artist All India Radio, Bombay, 1956-57; asst. editor The Colo. Daily, Boulder, 1958-59; assoc. editor The Observer, Internat. House, 1962-63; speaker UN, N.Y.C., 1964-67; owner, pres. Vira Ins. Protection Svc., 1974—; prin., owner Space Link Books, 1992—; bd. dirs. ABI Rsch.; adv. bd. Chinatown Planning Council, 1980-81. Author: the Planet Keepers, 1996, The Trap Series, 1996, The Angel Trails Series, 1998, Little Bit India, Little Bit USA, 1993; contbr. stories to mags. Founder, dir. Daya Dharma Soma Ednl. Charitable Trust, India, 1992; bd. dirs. Bharatiya Vidya Bhavan. Recipient Publication award Writer's Digest, 1995, Editor's Choice award Nat. Libr. Congress, 1998. Mem. Internat. Small Bus. Consortium, Nat. Writers Union, Science Fiction Fantasy Writers Am., Freelancers Assn., Am. Booksellers Assn. (N.Y., N.J. chpts.), Publishers Mktg. Assn., Asian Am. Advantage Assn., Assn. Indians in Am., Hearts and Handicapped Assn., Sisters in Crime, Small Press Ctr. Republican. Hindu. Avocations: travel, cultural activities, writing. E-mail: soma@earthlink.net. Home: 77 W 55th St Apt 12J New York NY 10019-4923 Office: Space Link Books Ste 9-J 77 W 55th St Apt 9J New York NY 10019-4922

VIRÁGH, SZABOLCS, pathologist, medical researcher; b. Berekböszörmény, Bihar, Hungary, May 31, 1930; s. József and Emilia (Kotilla) V.; m. Julia Kiss, May 16, 1959; 1 child, Szabolcs. MD, Med. U., Szeged, Hungary, 1955; PhD, Med. U., Budapest, Hungary, 1969; DSc, Hungarian Acad. Sci., Budapest, 1986. Tchg. asst. Med. U., Szeged, 1955-63; rsch. assoc. Med. U., Budapest, 1963-69; asst. prof. Postgrad. Med. U., 1970-74, sr. lectr., 1974-80, prof., 1980—, head Electron Microscopy Lab., 1969—, vice dean acad., 1980-86; chmn. com. of cell and developmental biology Hungarian Acad. Sci., Budapest, 1985-91. Author: Atlas for Self-Assessment and Practice in Ultrastructural Pathology and Diagnostic Electron Microscopy, 1996; co-editor: Ultrastructure of the Mammalian Heart, 1973; contbr. over 110 articles to internat. jours. Named Disting. Univ. Tchr., Ministry of Edn. Hungary, 1977; recipient Gould medal decoration for labor Coun. of Pres. of Hungary, 1985, Albert Szeut-Györgyi award Min. Edn. Hungary, 1998. Mem. Hungarian Soc. Pathology (bd. dirs. 1984—), Hungarian Soc. Microscopy (bd. dirs. 1980—), Hungarian Soc. for Electron Microscopy (pre. 1980-90, mem. com. 1982-84). Avocations: gardening, handicrafts. Office: Imre Haynal U Health Scis, Szabolcs u 33, 1135 Budapest Hungary

VIRAS, LOIZOS GIORGE, chemist, researcher; b. Cairo, Egypt, Apr. 1, 1950; s. Giorge and Eleni (Colla) V. BSc in Chemistry, U. Athens, Greece, 1972; MSc in Chemistry, U. Manchester, Eng., 1973; PhD in Chemistry, U. Athens, 1988. Chemist Ministry of Environment, Athens, 1974—, head air pollution control sect., 1991—. Author: Advances in Environmental Science and Technology, 1991; contbr. articles to profl. jours. Mem. Assn. Greek Chemists. Home: Ithakis 60, 11251 Athens Greece Office: Ministry of Environment, Patision 147, 11251 Athens Greece

VIRAVAU, PHILIPPE, engineering educator; b. Nanterre, Hts de Seine, France, May 9, 1968; s. Jean and Raymonde V.; m. Valerie Revel, July 3, 1993. Phys. Master, U. Jussieu, Paris, 1990; Engr. Master, Ecole Nat. Superieure des Techniques Avancees, Paris, 1992. Digital signal processing engr. for radio altimeters Thomson-CSF-CNI, Boulogne, France, 1992; digital signal processing expert in radiocomms. and spectrum Thomson-CSF Comsys, Gennevillier, France, 1992-99; tchr. radiocomms. and electronic warfare Thomson-CSF Cooperation, Buc, France, 1999—. Contbr. article to profl. jour.; inventor signal processing. Office: Thomson-CSF Coop, 283 rue de la Miniere BP105, 78531 Buc France

VIRBICKAS, JUOZAS, ecologist, researcher; b. Anykščiai, Lithuania, Oct. 10, 1939; s. Boleslovas and Zofija (Simaskaite) V.; m. Aldona Sinkevičiute, Feb. 6, 1960; childre: Daiva, Tomas. Magister in Sci., Vilnius (Lithuania) U., 1962, DSc., 1968; D. Habilitation, A.N. Severcov Inst., Moscow, 1988. Fish mgr. Inst. Ecology, Vilnius, 1960-63, sect. head, 1963-64, dept. head, 1964-90, deputy dir., 1977-90, sect. head, 1990—, dir., 1990—; pres. Fishery Union, 1998. Co-author: Obligate Symbiosis of the Organism and its Digestive Tract Microflora, 1989, Ecosystem of the Water-Cooling Reservoir of Ignalina Nuclear Power Station at the Initial Stage of its Operation, 1992, The Butinge Oil Terminal: Ecological State, 1997; contbr. articles to profl. jours. Pres. Lithuanian Ecol. Soc. 1995; coun. mem. Lithuanian Nature Soc. Vilnius, 1995l; head coun. Fishery Stocks Renovation Vilnius, 1997. Recipient P. Kapica medal Russian Acad. Sci., 1995, Lithuanian Nat. Sci. award, 1993; named Hon. Prof. Vilnius U., 1991. Mem. Internat. Acad. Nature Social Sci., N.Y. Acad. Sci., Lithuanian Acad. Sci.; editor profl. jours. Avocations: travel, literature. Home: Kalvariju Str 134-14, 2042 Vilnius Lithuania Office: Inst Ecology Akademijos 2, 2600 Vilnius Lithuania

VIRDEBRANT, CARL-ERIK, government administrator; b. Växjö, Kronoberg, Sweden, May 20, 1924; s. Erik and Blenda (Nilsson) V.; m. Iréne Margareta Pettersson, Dec. 20, 1950 (dec. Nov. 1985); 1 child, Gunilla. BA, U. Stockholm, 1950, M Polit. Sci., 1953. Adminstrv. officer Nat. Bd. Edn., Stockholm, 1951-58; 1st sec. Ministry of Edn., Stockholm, 1959-62, head sect., 1962-64, asst. under-sec., 1964-74, expert in cultural affairs, 1979-90; adminstrv. dir. Nat. Coun. for Cultural Affairs, Stockholm, 1974-83; mem. Nordic Cultural Commn., 1968-71; mem. Commn. Support to Regional Music, 1968-69; mem. Commn. Coun. of Europe to establish Youth Ctr. at Strasbourg, Sweden, 1968-73; chmn. Commn. Acad. Artistic Edn., 1973-76; chmn. commn. adminstrv. coop. between ctrl. nat. mus., 1982-84. Bd. dirs. Nordic Popular Acad., Kungaelv, Sweden, 1969-77, Nordic Sami Inst., Kautokeino, Sweden, 1982-90, Drottningholm Ct. Theatre, Theatre Mus., 1984-94. Named to Order of the North Star by the King of Sweden, 1968; recipient medal of merit Drottningholm Ct. Theatre, 1994.

VIRGA, NINO, packaging company executive; b. Castelvetrano, Italy, Apr. 1, 1964; arrived in Belgium, 1990; s. Francesco and Carmela V.; m. Cheryl Dooley, May 27, 1995; children (twins): Francesco, Alessandra. Degree in computer sci., Pisa (Italy) U., 1987; MBA, European U., Brussels, 1994. Computer analyst R&D Labs, Ivrea, Italy, 1987-88; computer analyst, project mgr. Olivetti, Luxemburg, 1988; acccount mgr. Olivetti, Brussels, 1989-91, internat. sales mgr., 1992-94; dir. sales Europe AT&T, Brussels, 1994-97; mng. dir. Europe Pak 2000, London, 1997—; bd. dirs. VIRNI sprl. Health Info. Mgmt. Mem. Inst. of Dirs. London. Avocations: various sports, travel, theater, reading. Home: 21 Lulworth Ave, Osterley TW5 0TY, England

VIRGILI, ANTONIO, educator, consultant; b. Naples, Italy, June 13, 1957; s. Fernando and Elisa (Terracciano) V. Laurea in Sociology cum laude, U. Naples, 1980, degree in psychotechnology, 1984, degree in social psychiatry, 1985; diploma in community scis. (hon.), Faculty Scienze Comunita, Naples, 1992; postgrad in comm. didactic and tech., U. Rome, 1995; postgrad. in informatic for didactic, U. Florence, 1996; postgrad. in ednl. techs., U. Rome, 2000. Rsch. collaborator Centro Nazionale Italiano Tecnologie Educative, Rome, 1981; rschr., sociologist Centro Ricerche, Naples, 1982-83; lectr. Inst. Superiore Sociologia, Naples, 1982-88, Faculty Scienze Comunita, Naples, 1989-91; tchr. Italian Ministry Edn., Naples, 1986—; collaborator U. Naples, 1987—; cons. Edil Inform Pub. Co., Naples, 1989-91, Press Agy. Europal, Genova, 1986—; dir. Inst. Superiore Sociologia, 1990—; pres. Istituto Studi Internazionali, Naples, 1992—; bd. dirs. Centro Ricerche Giuridiche ed Economiche. Author: La Modernizzazione, 1982, La Regione dell 'Øresund, 1994, Il Turismo in Campania, 1994, Progettazione Formativa E Tecnologie Didattiche, 1996, Economia E Territorio in Danimarca, 1996, Saggi di Geografia Economica, 1996, Itinerari di Scienze Sociali, 1998, Storia Dell Ordine Militare e Ospedaliere di San Giovanni d'Acri e San Tommaso, 1999, Popolazioni e Societa, 1999; editor Studi Internazionali mag., 1995; co-editor: Trasformazioni Urbane, 1983. Regional bd. dirs. Fondo Mondiale per Natura. Recipient essay spl. prize Istituto, Superiore Educazione Fisica and Acad., Parnaso, 1993, Essay Silver prize Internat. Pontzen Acad., 1994, Parthenope Aurea award for profl. activity Accademia Neapolis, 1994, Academical Great Collar, Internat. Pontzen Acad., 1995, prize for essays Naples En Monde, 1995, Maecenas of the Culture award Unione Artisti Operatori Culturali, 1995, Essay prize Accademia Parmenideli, 1996, Gold medal of Merit Acad. Micenie, 1997, Gold Medal award Acad. di San Marco, 1997, Great Prize for Visual Arts, 1997, Japan Trophy for Arts, 1998, European prize in Paris, 1999; named Knight, Sovereign Mil. Order of the Most Holy Saviour and of St. Bridget of Sweden, 1996, Sovereign Order of St. John of Jerusalem, 1997, Knight Grand Cross, Mil. and Hospitaller Order of St. John of Acre and St. Thomas, 1995, Mil. and Hospitaller Order of St. Mary of Bethlehem, 1995, Sovereign Order of St. John of Jerusalem, Denmark, 1998, Sovereign Mil. Order of Swabia, 1998, Marchese di Sestino, Conte di Colle Alto; tng. grantee Ancifap-Centro Nazionale Formazione Professionale, 1986. Mem. Soc. Geografica Italiana, N.Y. Acad. Scis., Assn. Italiana Formatori, Unione Artisti Operatori Culturali (hon. life), Soc. Europea per Immagine e Comunicazione (pres. 1992—), Union Europeenne Conseillers, Societa Studi Geografici, Internat. Soc. Assn., Associazione Professionale Italiana Consulenti di Direzione e Organizzazione, Acad. Tiberina, Soc. Dante Alighieri, Soc. Italiana per Progresso delle Sci. (Silver medal 1998), Soc. Italiana Econ. Demografia e Statistica, Soc. Italiana per Orgn. Internat., Inst. Italiano per L'Africa e L'Oriente. E-mail: sestino@freemail.it. Office: Corso Amedeo di Savoia 218, 80136 Naples Italy

VIRGO, JOHN MICHAEL, economist, researcher, educator; b. Prestbury Village, Eng., Mar. 11, 1943; s. John Joseph and Muriel Agnes (Franks) V.; m. Katherine Sue Ulmrich, Sept. 6, 1980; 1 child, Debra Marie Riekstins. BA, Calif. State U., Fullerton, 1967, MA, 1969; MA, Claremont Grad. U., 1971, PhD, 1972. Instr. econs. Whittier (Calif.) Coll., 1970-71, Calif. State U., Fullerton and Long Beach, 1971-72, Claremont (Calif.) Grad. Sch., 1971-72; asst. prof. econs. Va. Commonwealth U., Richmond, 1972-74; assoc. prof. mgmt. So. Ill. U., Edwardsville, 1975-83, prof., 1984—; bd. dirs., founder Internat. Health Econ. & Mgmt. Inst., Edwardsville, 1983-87. Author: Legal & Illegal California Farmworkers, 1974; author, editor: Health Care: An International Perspective, 1984, Exploring New Vistas in Health Care, 1985, Restructuring Health Policy, 1986; founder, editor-in-chief Internat. Advances in Econ. Rsch.; contbr. articles to profl. jours. Served with USN, 1965-68. Mem. AMA, Am. Econ. Assn., Am. Soc. Assn. Execs., Internat. Atlantic Econ. Soc. (founder, exec. v.p., mng. editor Atlantic Econ. jour. 1973—), European Econ. Assn., Allied Social Scis. Assn. (chmn. exec. confs. 1982-84), Western Econs. Assn., Western Econ. Assn., So. Econs. Assn., Media Club (St. Louis). Democrat. Roman Catholic. Avocations: tennis, skiing. Home: 5277 Lindell Blvd Saint Louis MO 63108-1223 Office: Internat Atlantic Econ Soc 2nd Fl 4949 W Pine Blvd Saint Louis MO 63108-1431

VIRGO, KATHERINE SUE, health services researcher; b. East Alton, Ill., Feb. 14, 1959; d. John William and Doris Ann (Spencer) Ulmrich; m. John Michael Virgo, Sept. 6, 1980. BSBA, So. Ill. U., 1981, MBA, 1983; PhD in Health Svcs. Rsch., St. Louis U., 1991. From asst. coord. to exec. adminstr. Atlantic Econ. Soc., Edwardsville, Ill., 1978-86; co-founder, exec. adminstr. Internat. Health Econs. and Mgmt. Inst., Edwardsville, Ill., 1983-87; health sci. specialist VA Med. Ctr., St. Louis, 1986-93, clin. rsch. coord., 1993—; asst. prof. St. Louis U., 1991-96, assoc. prof., 1996—; bd. dirs. Internat. Health Econs. and Mgmt. Inst., Edwardsville, 1983-87. Assoc. editor Atlantic Econ. Jour., 1994—; dep. editor Internat. Advances in Econ. Rsch., 1995—; co-editor Cancer Patient Follow-Up, 1997; ad hoc reviewer Jour. of the AMA, 1995-96, Med. Care, 1995—, Women's Health Issues, 2000—; contbr. numerous articles to profl. jours. Mem. St. Louis Cathedral Basilica Choir. VA grantee. Mem. Am. Pub. Health Assn., Acad. Mgmt., Assn. for Health Svcs. Rsch., Health Econs. Rsch. Orgn. Democrat. Roman Catholic. Avocations: singing, piano, reading, swimming, boating. Home: 5277 Lindell Blvd Saint Louis MO 63108-1223 Office: VA Med Ctr 112JC 915 N Grand Blvd Saint Louis MO 63106-1621

VIRGO, MURIEL AGNES, swimming school owner; b. Liverpool, Cheshire, Eng., Apr. 3, 1924; d. Harold Thornhill and Susan Ann (Duff) Franks; m. John Virgo, Aug. 13, 1942; children: John Michael, Angela Victoria, Barbara Ann, Collin Anthony, Donna Marie. Grad. parochial schs. Co-owner Virgo Swim Sch., Garden Grove, Calif., 1967—. Mem. Ancient Mystical Order Rosae Crucis, Traditional Martinist Order. Republican. Roman Catholic. Avocation: ballroom dancing. Home: 12751 Crestwood Cir Garden Grove CA 92841-5250 Office: Virgo Swim Sch 12851 Brookhurst Way Garden Grove CA 92841-5205

VIRGO, PHILIP ARTHURTON, information technology forecaster; b. London, Nov. 24, 1946; s. Ernest Stanley and Olive May (Arthurton) V.; m. Marjorie Jean Mary McAllister, Aug. 20, 1977. B.A., Peterhouse Cambridge, 1968, M.A., 1970; M.Sc., London Grad. Sch. Bus. Studies, 1973. Programmer/analyst Standard Telephones & Cables, 1968-69; project mgr. ICL (Internat. computers Ltd.), 1969-75, bus. devel. mgr., 1975-77; corp. planner Wellcome Found., 1977-82; I.T strategy mgr. Nat. Computing Centre, London, 1982-86; IT strategy cons. to Nat. Computing Centre; dir. IT Strategy Services, 1986—; dir. Fedn. Against Software Theft, 1984-85; sec. gen. EURIM, 1994—. Author: Cashing in on the Chips, 1979, The Big Steal, 1980, Learning for Change, 1981, No End of Jobs, 1984. Chmn. Conservative Computer Forum, 1978-84; convenor Parliamentary Computer Forum, 1979-81; external vice chmn. Parliamentary Info. Tech. Co., 1981-82, exec. fins., 1981—. Mem. Brit. Computer Soc. (council mem.), Brit. Inst. Mgmt.

VIRGÓS, EMILIO CANTALAPIEDRA, biologist, researcher; b. Madrid, Sept. 26, 1967; s. Emklio Pla Virgós and Carmen Cantalapiedra Rochas. Degree in biology, Complutense U., Madrid, 1993, PhD in Biology, 1999. Coord., founding mem. Terrestrial Carnivores Group, Madrid, 1991—; mem. dept. animal biology U. Compultense, Madrid, 1993—; mem. otter group Spanish Soc. Study and Conservation of Mammals, Madrid, 1991—; cons. in field. Author: Ecology and Evolution of Carnivores, 1996, Effect of Forest Fragmentation in Spanish Plateaus, 1998; contbr. articles to profl. jours. Grantee Inst. for Nature Conservation, Madrid, 1993, Edn. and Sci. Ministry, Madrid, 1994; recipient postdoctoral grant Inst. Investigacion en Recursos Cinegeticos, 2000. Mem. Spanish Mammal Soc. (founding mem., membership com. 1995—). Avocations: music, cinema. Home: Valdebernardo St 25 7B, 28030 Madrid Spain Office: U Complutense, Faculty Biol Sci, 28040 Madrid Spain

VIRK, GURDEV SINGH, power company executive; b. Faislabad, Punjab, India, Dec. 24, 1937; s. Nahar Singh and Balwant Kaur (Gill) V.; m. Harbans Kaur Garcha, Oct. 19, 1964; children: Navtej Singh, Preetinder Kaur. BA in Physics and Math., Govt. Coll., Ropar, India, 1957; B in Elec. Engring. with honors, Indian Inst. Tech., Kharagpur, 1961; MSc in Elec. Power Systems, Punjab Engring. Coll., Chandigarh, India, 1967. Asst. engr., asst. dir. Punjab State Electricity Bd., Patiala, 1961-70, dep. dir. thermal designs, 1970-84, dir. thermal designs, 1984-93, chief engr. thermal designs, 1993-95, chief engr. comml., 1995; exec. dir., bd. dirs. Punjab Thermal Power Ltd., Chandigarh, 1996—. Fellow India Inst. Engrs. (life); mem. Press Club (corp.), Chadigarh Club Ltd. Avocations: photography, gardening, walking, pet care, socializing. Home: 3439 Sector 38D, Chandigarh 160037, India

Office: Punjab Thermal Power Ltd, SCO 62-63 Sector 34-A, Chandigarh 160 022, India

VIRK, GURVINDER SINGH, control systems engineering educator, consultant; b. Jullander, Punjab, India, July 13, 1956; came to U.K., 1964; s. Rajinder Singh and Pritam Kaur (Ghuman) V.; m. Ann Marie Conlon, Apr. 13, 1985; children: Bernadette Ann, Terese Elizabeth, Ciaran Singh. BSc in Elec. Engring. with honors, U. Manchester, 1977; PhD in Control Theory, U. London, 1982; Diploma, Imperial Coll., London, 1982. Design engr. GEC Telecomms., Coventry, Eng., 1977-78; rsch. asst. U. Sheffield, 1981-83; lectr. Sheffield City Poly., 1983-84, U. Southampton, 1985-86, U. Sheffield, 1986-91; sr. lectr. U. Bradford, 1992-94; prof. U. Portsmouth, 1995—; cons. Brit. Aerospace plc, Brough, Humberside, Eng., 1987—; rsch. collaborator Trend Control Systems Ltd., Horsham, Eng., 1990—, Dimplex (UK) Ltd., Southampton, 1993—, Concord Temperature Controls Ltd., Stourbridge, Eng., 1993—. Author: Computer Control of Real-time Processes, 1990, Digital Computer Control Systems, 1991; contbr. numerous articles to profl. jours.; patentee measurement of woven mesh. Rsch. grantee U.K. Sci. and Engring. Rsch. Coun., 1989, Brit. Aero. plc., 1990, UK-SERC, 1993, others. Fellow Instn. Elec. Engrs. (com. mem.), Chartered Instn. Bldg. Svcs. Engrs.; mem. IEE So. Centre Com., Inst. Math. and Its Applications. Sikh religion. Avocation: running, squash. Office: U Portsmouth, Anglesea Rd, Portsmouth P01 3DJ, England

VIRK, HARDEV SINGH, physicist, researcher; b. Kamoke, India, Feb. 23, 1942; s. Avtar Singh and Tej Kaur (Bajwa) V.; m. Ranjit Kaur Virk, Sept. 28, 1966; children: T.S., S.S., A.S. BS, Mohindra Coll., Patiala, India, 1961; MS, Muslim U., Aligarh, India, 1963; PhD, Pierre & Marie Curie U., Paris, 1972; diploma in French, P.U. Patiala, India, 1968. Lectr. G.N. Engring. Coll., Ludhiana, India, 1963-65; reader Punjabi U., Patiala, India, 1965-79; prof. G.N.D. U., Amritsar, India, 1979—; boursier French Govt., Paris, 1970-72; dean G.N.D. U., Amritsar, India, 1991-93; dir. Earthquake Rsch. Ctr., 1995—. Author 15 books including: Story of Cosmic Rays, 1968, Atomic Physics, 1977, Heat and Thermodynamics, 1976; contbr. over 300 rsch. papers in profl. jours. V.p. Physics Tchr's. Assn., Kanpur, India, 1984-98; pres. Nuclear Track Soc. India, Mumbai, 1998-00; mem. Internat. Nuclear Track Soc., 1985-00. Recipient Siromani award Punjab State Lang. Dept. Patiala, 1993, sr. fellow ICTP Trieste, Italy, 1988-93. Avocations: reading, writing, music, meditation. E-mail: virkhs@yahoo.com. Home: A-4 GND University Campus, Amritsar 143005, India

VIRKKALA, RAIMO OLAVI, scientist, ecologist; b. Helsinki, Finland, June 11, 1959; s. Kalevi Onni and Eila Jenny (Simola) V.; m. Leena Mari Vahala, July 14, 1989; 1 child, Anna-Maria Ilona. MS, U. Helsinki, 1985, PhD, 1990, Docent in Zoology, 1993. Rsch. asst. U. Helsinki, 1985-91, rschr., 1992-93; rschr. Nat. Bd. Waters and Environment, Helsinki, 1993-94; sr. scientist Finnish Environment Inst., Helsinki, 1995—; expert WWF Finland, Helsinki, 1987—. Home: Steniuksentie 10A1, 00320 Helsinki Finland Office: Finnish Environment Inst, PO Box 140, 00251 Helsinki Finland

VIRKLER, MARK WILLIAM, religious educator; b. Lowville, N.Y., Mar. 25, 1952; s. Clayton Einbeck and Lillian Amelia V.; m. Patricia Claire, Dec. 16, 1972; children: Charity, Joshua. BA, Roberts Wesleyan Coll., 1974; ThM, Miami Christian U., 1985; PhD, Carolina Christian U., 1994. Youth pastor Avon (N.Y.) Wesleyan Ch., 1971-74; asst. prof. Yorkshire (N.Y.) Free Meth. Ch., 1975; assoc. pastor Curriers (N.Y.) Cmty. Ch., 1976; founding pastor Pioneer Christian Fellowship, Arcade, N.Y., 1976-82; asst. pastor Full Gospel Tabernacle, Orchard Park, N.Y., 1982-89; pres. Communion with God Ministries, Elma, N.Y., 1989—; pres. Christian Leadership U., Elma, 1994—, Covenant Enterprises, Elma, 1994—; dir. Christian Restoration Fellowship Internat., Elma, 1998—. Author: Communion With God, 1983, Dialogue With God, 1985, Counseled By God, 1989, Naturally Supernatural, 1990, Go Natural, 1994. Avocations: reading, writing, researching, family time. E-mail: mark@cluonline.com. Office: Communion with God Ministries 1431 Bullis Rd Elma NY 14059-9656

VIROLA, JUHANI SEPPO ANSSI PEKKA, bridge engineer; b. Espoo, Finland, Aug. 4, 1941; s. Aarno Paavo and Hilkka Mirjami (Pokkinen) V.; m. Leena Anneli Pirttilä, Aug. 13, 1967; 1 child, Mikko. BSCE, Tampere (Finland) Inst. Tech., 1967. Rsch. engr. Tech. Rsch. Inst., Espoo, Finland, 1967; bridge engr. Oy Kjessler & Mannerstråle Ab, Helsinki, Finland, 1968-74; materials engr. Oy Lohja Ab Rudus, Helsinki, 1975-76; rsch. engr. Oy Lautex Ab, Helsinki, 1976-79; quality control mgr. OMP Arabia Ltd., Jubail, Saudi Arabia, 1980-82; project engr. Bldg. Info. Inst., Helsinki, 1983-84; tech. dir. Finnish Particleboard Assn., Helsinki, 1984-86; mktg. engr. Datamex Oy, Helsinki, 1987-88, Teemuaho Group, Helsinki, 1988—. Contbr. to original Guinness Book of Records, also articles to profl. jours. Named European Engr. Fedn. Europe Assn. Nat. Engrs., Paris, 1988. Mem. Assn. Finnish Constrn. Engrs. and Architects, Concrete Assn. Finland. Lutheran. Home: Keinulaudantie 5 C 75, FIN-00940 Helsinki Finland Office: Teemuaho Group, Fredriksberginkatu 2, FIN-00240 Helsinki Finland

VIRREIRA-REYES, GONZALO, physician; b. Cochabamba, Bolivia, Sept. 20, 1928; s. Rodolfo Virreira-Flor and Margarita Reyes-Elias; m. Esperanza Querejazu-Alvarez de Virreira, Dec. 9, 1987; children: Gonzalo, Martha, Anna Maria. BS, Sagrado Corazon, Sucre, Bolivia, 1945; MD, U. San Francisco Xavier, Sucre, Bolivia, 1953. Med. diplomate. Asst. prof. pathology U. San Francisco Xavier, Sucre, Bolivia, 1949-51, chief clinic in ob/gyn, 1960-72, prof. ob/gyn, 1972-94; pres. Med. Coll. Bolivia, Sucre, 1971-73; dean. med. scis. faculty U. San Francisco Xavier, Sucre, Bolivia, 1992-93; pres. Inst. Medicine, Sucre, Bolivia, 1993—; med. chief roads nat. svc. Sucre, Bolivia, 1977-94; chief ob/gyn dept. Petroleum Enterprising of Bolivia, 1978-94. Contbr. articles to profl. jours. Hon. consul Venezuela, Sucre, Bolivia, 1996—. Recipient Profl. Merit medal Med. Coll. Bolivia, Sucre, 1991, Distinction of Bolivian Surgery Soc., 1993, emeritus mem. Bolivian Surgery Soc., 1997. Mem. Bolivian Med. Coll., Med. Inst., Internat. Fertility Assn. Avocations: golf, music, reading. Home: PO Box 123, Arenales St, Sucre Bolivia Office: Sucre Med Inst, San Alberto St N30, Sucre Bolivia

VIRSU, VEIJO VESA ELIAS, neuropsychology educator; b. Paavola, Finland, Apr. 9, 1941; s. Heikki Oskari and Lyydi Iines Irene Virsu; children: Pauliina, Anja, Milja. Candidate philosophy, U. Helsinki, Finland, 1965, lic. philosophy, 1968, PhD, 1968. Lic. psychologist. Lectr. psychology U. Mich., Ann Arbor, 1968-70; vis. scientist Stanford U., Palo Alto, Calif., 1969, U. of Cambridge (Eng.) and King's Coll., 1970-71, Max-Planck Inst. for Biophys. Chemistry, Göttingen, Fed. Republic Germany, 1975, 78, 81-82; scientist Acad. of Finland, Helsinki, 1972-78; prof. neuropsychology U. Helsinki, 1979—. Author 2 books on vision and neural basis of psychol. processes, also over 100 articles for profl. jours., newspapers. Alexander von Humboldt Found. fellow, 1978; Alexander von Humboldt Found. grantee, 1980, also numerous grants and awards in Finland. Mem. Brain Rsch. Assn. Finland (v.p. 1973-78), Pattern Recognition Soc. Finland, Acad. Scis. Finland, Academia Europaea. Avocations: photography, computer graphics, music. Office: U Helsinki Dept Psychology, PO Box 13 Meritullinkatu 1, 00014 Helsinki Finland

VIRTA, ERKKI ENSIO, psychologist; b. Helsinki, Finland, Mar. 7, 1949; arrived in Sweden, 1975; s. Sulo Leonard and Toini Irene (Salo) V.; m. Arja Anneli Jokinen, July 20, 1978 (div. Dec. 1994); 1 child, Henri Leonard. BA in Psychology, Helsinki U., 1972, MA in Psychology, 1974, PhD in Psychology, 1994. Lic. psychologist, Sweden. Rsch. asst. Ctr. Occupational Hygiene Helsinki U., 1972-75; rschr., psychologist Ctr. Occupational Health, Helsinki, 1975; rsch. scholar Stockholm U., 1975-76; freelance journalist Invandrartidningen mag., Stockholm, 1976-84; postgrad. rschr. Stockholm U., 1984-88, rsch. asst. dept. psychology, 1988-92, rschr. Ctr. for Rsch. Internat. Migration Ethnic Rels., 1993—; sci. cons., Sweden, 1983—. Contbr. articles to profl. jours. Grantee Acad. Finland, 1972-76, Stockholm U., 1984-88, Swedish Rsch. Coun., 1988—. Avocations: music, tennis, spending time with son. Office: CEIFO, Stockholm U, SE 10691 Stockholm Sweden

VIRTANEN, JORMA ILMARI, dentist, researcher; b. Rantasalmi, Finland, Mar. 17, 1955; s. Pentti Olavi Ilmari and Taimi Ingeborg (Oikarinen) V.; m. Nancy Eva-Stina Kronqvist, June 22, 1991; children: Hanna Kristina, Mirjam Aino, Marta Katarina, Paula Susanna, Elsa Magdalena. DDS, U. Oulu, Finland, 1983, PhD, 1997; dipl. PH, Nordic Sch. Pub. Health, Gothenburg, Sweden, 1996. Mcpl. dentist H.C., Jakobstad, Finland, 1984-85; mcpl. dentist H.C., Nykarleby, Finland, 1987-89, mcpl. chief dentist, 1989-90; pvt. practice Jakobstad/Oulu, 1986-91; clin. instr. U. Oulu, 1991-94, 98—, rsch. fellow, 1994-98; lectr. Inst. Health Care, Oulu, 1991-95, Nordic Sch. Pub. Health, Gothenburg, Sweden, 1996—. 2d sgt. Parachute troops, 1976-77. Clin. rsch. grantee Med. Rsch. Coun., Acad. Finland, 1993, rsch. edn. grantee Med. Rsch. Coun., 1994, 95. Mem. Finnish Dental Soc. (bd. cariology 1997—). Evangelical Lutheran. Avocations: theology, archipelago.

VIRTANEN, SIMO KASPER, microbiologist; b. Varkaus, Finland, Nov. 4, 1925; s. Yrjo and Kirsti (Hyvarinen) V.; m. Raili Inkeri Mikkonen, Apr. 7, 1925. B of Medicine, U. Helsinki, Finland, 1947; MD, U. Turku, Finland, 1951, D of Med. Sci., 1960. Asst. U. Turku, Finland, 1952-59, asst. prof., 1960-90; head dept. Nat. Pub. Health Inst., Finland, 1962-90, prof. emeritus, 1990—; acting prof. microbiology U. Oulu, Finland, 1963, of hygiene Turku U., 1970; mgr. Lab. Ductus, Turku, 1967-89;vis. scientist Nat. Inst. Health, Bethesda, Md., 1964-65; cons. microbiologist U. Hosp. Turku, 1977-83. Sgt. Finnish Field Artillery, 1943-45. Mem. Am. Pub. Health Assn., Soc. Gen. Microbiology, Internat. Soc. Human and Animal Mycology, Internat. Union Against Tuberculosis and Lung Disease. Avocations: painting, gardening, forestry. Home: Vaha-Hameenk 14 A 21, 20500 Turku Finland

VISAGGIO, GIUSEPPE, physicist, educator; b. Molfetta, Italy, Mar. 15, 1947; s. Corrado and Susanna Azzolini V.; m. Marta Gigante, Jan. 10, 1976; children: Aaron Cozzado, Gloria. Degree in physics, U. Bari, 1972. Prof. computer sci., software engring. U. Bari, Italy, 1973—; cons. Italian Nat. Pub. Adminstrn., 1996-97, regional govts. Italy. Author: Frontier Decision Support Business Process Reengineering, 1994; contbr. articles to profl. jours. Mem. IEEE, Assn. Computing Machinery. Office: U Bari Dept Informatics, Via E Orabona 4, 70126 Bari Italy

VISARIA, PRAVIN, economist, researcher; b. Koday, India, Apr. 23, 1937; s. Meghji Poonshi and Monghiben (Vira) V.; m. Leela Shah, Dec. 28, 1963; children: Sujata, Abhijit. BA, U. Bombay, 1956, MA in Econs., 1958; PhD, Princeton U., 1963. Reader in demography U. Bombay, 1963-71, prof. demography, 1971-73; economist World Bank, Washington, 1973-80; prof. Sardar Patel Inst. Econ. and Social Rsch., Ahmedabad, India, 1980-83; prof., dir. Gujarat Inst. Devel. Rsch., Ahmedabad, 1983-96; vis. prof. Inst. Econ. Growth, Delhi, India, 1996-97; dir. Inst. Econ. Growth, Delhi, 1997—; chmn. governing coun. Nat. Sample Survey Orgn., New Delhi, 1991—; bd. dirs. Dena Bank, India, 1995-2000; mem. panel economists Planning Commn. India. Author: The Sex Ratio of the Population of India, 1972; Women in the Indian Working Force: Trends and Differentials, 1996; co-author: Contraceptive Use and Fertility in India, 1995; Child labor in India: Resultsof a Methodological Survey of Surendranagar and Surat Districts of Gujurat State, 1995; co-editor: Infant Mortality in India, 1988, Non-Agricultural Employment in India, 1994 Urbanization in Large Developing Countries: Brazil, China, India and Indonesia, 1997; Social Change Through Voluntary Action, 1998. Recipient Dr. V.K.R.V. Rao prize for demography Indian Coun. of Social Sci. Rsch., New Delhi, 1981. Mem. Internat. Union for Sci. Study of Population (chmn. sci. com. 1978-82), Indian Assn. for Study of Population (mem. exec. com. 1971-73, pres. 1994-96), Indian Coun. Social Sci. Rsch. Home: 4 Abhinav Colony Drive-In R, Ahmedabad Gujarat 380052, India Office: Inst Econ Growth, Univ Enclave, Delhi 110007, India

VISCOMI, B. VINCENT, civil engineering educator; b. Phila., Sept. 21, 1933; s. Joseph and Rose (Sidoti) V.; m. Mary Hughes, Feb. 15, 1958; children—Vincent Andrew, Christopher Michael, Roseann Marie. BS in Mech. Engring., Drexel U., 1956; MS in Mech. Engring., Lehigh U., 1957; PhD in Civil Engring., U. Colo., 1968. Nuclear reactor engr. Phila. Electric Co., 1957-64; Simon Cameron Long prof. civil and environ. engring. Lafayette Coll., Easton, Pa., 1964—. mem. Commn. on Higher Edn., 1982—. Patentee in field. Pres. Easton Bd. Health, 1972-78. Served to 1st lt. U.S. Army, 1958-64. Recipient Jones Faculty award, 1969, Superior Teaching award Student Body Lafayette Coll., 1974, 78, award Charles and Mary Lindback Found. for Superior Teaching, 1976, Thomas and Laura Jones award for scholarship, 1997. Mem. ASCE (past pres.), Am. Soc. Engring. Edn., N.Y. Acad. Scis., Am. Nuclear Soc., Phi Beta Kappa, Sigma Xi, Phi Kappa Phi, Tau Beta Pi. Home: 127 High St Easton PA 18042-1609 Office: Dept Civil Engring Lafayette Coll Easton PA 18042

VISCOVICH, SIR ANDREW JOHN, educational management consultant; b. Oakland, Calif., Sept. 25, 1925; s. Peter Andrew and Lucy Pauline (Razovich) V.; m. Roen Shirley Mulvana, Apr. 19, 1952 (div. Feb. 1985); children: Randal Peter, Andra Clair; m. Elena Beth Wong, Apr. 28, 1991; 1 child, Alison Wong. BA, U. Calif., Berkeley, 1949; MA, San Francisco State U., 1960; EdD, U. Calif., Berkeley, 1973; cert. labor dispute resolution, Golden Gate U., 1976. Assoc. supt. Oakland Unified Sch. Dist., Calif., 1970-77; supt. Palm Springs (Calif.) Unified Sch. Dist., 1976-79, Garvey Sch. Dist., Rosemead, Calif., 1979-88, Berkeley (Calif.) Unified Sch. Dist., Stockton, Calif., 1988-90; pres. Ctr. for Ednl. Rsch. in Adminstrn., Stockton, Calif., 1990—; adj. prof. U. Calif., Berkeley, 1965-67, Calif. State U., Hayward, 1970-76, L.A., 1971-8; exec. dir. Marcus Foster Edn. Found., Oakland, 1975-76; cons. Spanish Ministry Edn., 1987—, Republic of China Ministry Edn., Taipei, Taiwan, 1986-89, Croatian Ministry Edn., Zagreb, 1993—, Marriott Sch. Svcs, 1992—, CSHQH, Idaho; pre-sch. dir. Oakland Unified Sch. Dist., 1974-76; asst. dir. Bay Area Bilingual Edn. League, 1971-75; dir. Bay Area Tchr. Ctr., 1974, asst. dir. Far West Ednl. Lab., 1974; adj. assoc. prof. Calif. State U. at L.A.and Hayward, U. South Fla., U. Oreg., Coll. of Holy Names; exec. dir. ANRO Cons., Inc., Calif., 1973-82; state adminstr. Coachella Unified Sch. Dist., Thermal, Calif., 1992; nat. dir. supt. consulting svcs. Sodexho Marriott Corp., 1992-99. Author: Language Programs for the Disadvantaged, 1965, R.E.S. Plus, 1978; contbr. The School Principal, 1978. Chair United Way, Pasadena, Calif., 1985; pres. Croatian Scholarship Found., San Ramon, Calif., 1993-94. Served to ens. USNR, 1959-64. Recipient award for innovations in alternative schools Behavioral Rsch. Lab., San Francisco, 1973; named Knight of Civil Order of Merit King Juan Carlos of Spain, 1990. Mem. Am. Mgmt. Assn., Am. Assn. Sch. Adminstrs., Assn. Calif. Sch. Adminstrs., Calif. City Sch. Supts., Calif. Tchrs. Assn. (John Swett award 1978), Tau Kappa Epsilon. Avocations: golf, reading, travel. ultralite flying. Home: 3754 Fort Donelson Dr Stockton CA 95219-3211

VISHWAKARMA, HARI RAM, information executive; s. Gauri Shankar and Poornima V.; m. Mamta Vishwakarma, June 22, 1983; chldren: Archana, Manisha, Anudeep. BE, Govt. Engring. Coll., Jabalpur, India, 1984; M Tech., Indian Inst. Tech., Bombay, 1986. Lectr. Govt. Poly., Jabalpur, India, 1984-85, Waidhan, India, 1987; apprentice asst. exec. engr. ITI Ltd., Bangalore, India, 1987-88, computer programmer, 1987-89, asst. exec. engr., 1988-90, info. sys. analysis, 1990-91, exec. engr., 1991-94, LAN mgr., software developer, 1992-94, sr. engr., project mgr., 1995-2000, deputy chief engr., 2000—. Contbr. articles to profl. jours. Merit scholar Govt. Madhya Pradesh (India), 1977, Nat. scholar Govt. India, 1979, Rsch. scholar, 1985. Mem. IEEE, Instn. Engrs., Computer Soc. India, All India Mgmt. Assn. Hindu. Avocations: reading and writing literature, mathematical puzzles. Home: Bala Niras I Cross Main Rd, Ramamathy Nagar, 560016 Bangalore India Office: ITI Ltd Switching R&D Divsn, Info Tech Dept, Dooravani Nagar Bangalore 560016, India

VISSER, JOHANNES, research scientist, biographer; b. Leeuwarden, The Netherlands, Nov. 27, 1936; s. Eeuwe and Marie (Van der Heul) V.; m. Johanna Catherina Elisabeth Van Kolmeschate; children: Katja, Derek. Degree in Chem. Engring., Technical U. Delft, The Netherlands, 1965; PhD, Coun. for Nat. Acad. Awards, London, 1973. Rsch. scientist Unilever Rsch., Vaardingen, The Netherlands, 1965-69, Port Sunlight, Eng., 1969-71, Vlaardingen, 1971-93; rsch. scientist Netherlands Inst. for Dairy Rsch., Ede, 1993-96; invited scientist U. Minho, Braga, Portugal, 1997—; 1st dir. found. European Hygienic Equipment Design Group, 1997-98; organizer Symposium Protein Interactions, 201st annual meeting ACS, Atlanta, 1991. Editor: Protein Interactions, 1992, Simon Vestdijk, 1987; inventor in field; contbr. articles to profl. jours. Bd. dirs. Unilever Mgrs. Union, Rotterdam, 1977-91, chmn. Vestdijkkring, The Netherlands, 1998—; 1st lt. Dutch Signal Corps 1963-65. Recipient Friesian Press award Union of Friesian Journalists, Leeuwarden, The Netherlands, 1984, Author's award Unilever Rsch. Vlaardingen, 1992. Mem. Royal Dutch Chem. Soc., Genootschap voor Melkkunde, Canadian Assn. for Advancement of Netherlandic Studies. Avocations: photography, cycling. E-mail: hvisser@kabelfoon.nl; visser@deb.uminho.pt (Portugal). Home: Lijsterlaan 122, 3145 Maassluis The Netherlands

VISSICCHIO, ANDREW JOHN, JR., linen service company executive; b. N.Y.C., Dec. 21, 1941; s. Andrew John and Ann (Renna) V.; m. Patricia Ann Hunken, Jan. 18, 1964; children: Andrew John III, Douglas David. BS in Bus., L.I. U., 1963; postgrad., A.T. Roth Grad. Sch. Bus., 1963-64, Harvard U., 1995, 98. Gen. mgr. Allied Coat & Apron, Bklyn., 1963-72; ops. officer N.Y. Ocean Sci. Lab., Montauk, N.Y., 1972-76; gen. mgr. Am. Svc. Corp., Miami, Fla., 1976-79; dist. mgr. Am. Svc. Corp., Miami, 1979-83, v.p. ops., 1983-87; gen. mgr. Nat. Linen Svc., West Palm Beach, Fla., 1987-88; dist. mgr. Nat. Linen Svc., Atlanta, 1988-90, v.p., gen. mgr. linen supply divsn., 1990-94, regional v.p., 1994-96; v.p. FDR Svcs. Group, Hempstead, N.Y., 1997-99; regional v.p. Video Save Inc., N.Y.C., 2000—. Author: A Book of Simple Poems; Pianist recital Carnegie Hall, 1956, 57. Mem. fin com. City of Boca Raton. Recipient Dedicated Svc. award Montauk Fire Dept., 1976, Milliken award New Prodn. Devel. in Textile Rental Industry, 1996; Meadowbrook Bank scholar L.I. U., 1962-63. Mem. Textile Rental Svc. Assn. (strategic com. 1984-86), S.Am. Explorers Club, Am. Orchid Soc., Boca Raton Orchid Soc. (fin. com.), Coalition for Species Orchid. Republican. Roman Catholic. Avocations: collecting and growing orchids, writing poetry, boating, fishing, classical music-opera. Home: 2350 NW 38th St Boca Raton FL 33431-5439

VISVANATHAN, KANNUSWAMY, mechanical engineer; b. Kumbakonam, Tamil Nadu, India, Dec. 7, 1942; s. Marudhar Kannuswamy and Chellapapu; m. Visvanathan Mohana, Sept. 12, 1974; 1 child, Vibha. B Mech. Engring., Annamalai U., India, 1966; MSc in Engring., Madras (India) U., 1968. Asst. prof. Birla Inst. Tech., Ranchi, India, 1969-71; project engr. Indian Space Rsch. Orgn., Trivandrum, 1972-73; engr. Static Test and Evaluation Complex, Indian Space Rsch. Orgn., Sriharikota, 1973-75, dep. project dir. Range Complex, Sriharikota Range,, 1986-91, gen. mgr. Static Test and Evaluation Complex, 1991-93, gen. mgr. Vehicle Assembly and Statis Testing Complex, Range and Testing Entity, 1994-97; dep. dir. Vehicle Assembly and Static Testing Entity, 1998—. Mem. Astronautical Soc. India (life), Indian Soc. for Non-destructive Testing (life). Avocations: playing bridge, reading PC magazines. Home: 366 PHC-1, AP Sriharikota 524124, India Office: Indian Space Rsch Orgn SHAR Ctr, Vehicle Assmbly-Static Test, AP Sriharikota 524124, India

VISWANADHA RAO, TAMVADA, academic administrator, English studies educator; b. Parvathipuram, India, Aug. 6, 1950; s. Sankara Tamvada and Ayyagari Visalakshi; m. Tamuada Rajyalakshmi, Feb. 3, 1983; children: (twins) Kakthik, Kalpana. BA, Andhra U., Waltair, India, 1971, MA, 1973, PhD, 1980. Lectr. in English Andhra U., Kakinada, 1977-86, reader, assoc. prof. English, 1986—, head English dept., 1985, 93-96, 1997-99, rsch. guidance, 1983—. Mem. Indian Assn. Commonwealth Studies. Home: 5/162 PO Thimmapuram, Kakinada, Andhra Pradesh 533005, India Office: Andhra U, Dept English, Kakinada Andhra Pradesh 533005, India

VISWANATHAN, ANANTHARAMAN, physicist, educator; b. Madras, Tamilnadu, India, Aug. 9, 1945; s. Anantharaman and Meenakshi; m. Jumbunathan Vasantha, Sept. 26, 1976; children: V. Sri Vidhya, Vijay. MSc, Jamal Mohammad Coll., Trichi, India, 1974; MPhil, Presidency Coll., Madras, India, 1979; PhD in Energy, U. Madras, 1995. Demonstrator in physics Voorhees Coll., Vellore, India, 1966-68, Madras Med. Coll., 1968-72, Govt. Arts Coll., Ponneri, India, 1974-77; prof. physics Presidency Coll., 1977-93; prof. physics Govt. Arts Coll., Madras, 1993-95, 97—, Cheyyar, India, 1995-97. Named Best Tchr., Rotary Internat., 1999. Mem. Soc. for Advancement of Electrochem. Sci. and Tech., Indian Solid State Ionic Soc., N.Y. Acad. Scis. Avocations: music, watching television. E-mail: vasanvis@md4.vsnl.net.in. Home: A/21 Rajaram Colony, Kodambakkam, Madras Tamilnadu 600 024, India Office: Govt Arts Coll, Nandanam, Chennai Tamilnadu 600 024, India

VISWANATHAN, NURNI NEELAKANTAN, research scientist, educator; b. Palghat, Kerala, India, May 15, 1968; s. Ramachandran Nurni and Muthulakshmi Neelakantan; m. Usha Sankaranarayanan, Dec. 11, 1998. BSc in Physics, Govt. Victoria Coll., Palghat, 1988; M in Engring., Indian Inst. Sci., Bangalore, India, 1992, PhD, 1997. Vis. rsch. scientist dept. metallurgy Royal Inst. Tech., Stockholm, 1998—. Contbr. articles to profl. jours. Mem. Indian Inst. Metals. Avocations: volleyball, trekking, Indian classical music, Eastern philosophy. E-mail: vnurni@hotmail.com and vichu@metallurgi.kth.se. Fax: 46 8 7900939. Office: Royal Inst Tech Dept Metall, Brinel Vagen 23, S-10044 Stockholm Sweden

VISWANATHAN, SRINIVASA, business executive; b. Allahabad, Pradesh, India, Oct. 17; s. Subramania and Nagalakshmi Srinivasan; m. Viswanathan Lalitha Mahadevan, Apr. 3, 1968; 2 children. BSc, U. Madras, India, 1960, MSc, 1962. Dir. Ordnance Factory Bd., Calcutta, India, 1982-84, contr. of safety, 1993-98, sr. gen. mgr., 1995-97, additional dir. gen., 1998—; gen. mgr. High Explosives Factory, Pune, India, 1987-90, Coridte Factory, Arwankadu, India, 1990-93. Mem. Royal Soc. of Chemistry, Inst. of Indsl. Engring. Avocations: photography, traveling. Office: Ordnance Factory Bd, 10A SK Bose Rd, 700001 Calcutta India

VIT, PATRICIA ANTONELLA, biologist, educator, researcher; b. Caracas, Venezuela, Aug. 20, 1958; d. Giovanni and Giovanna (Olivier) V. Lic. biology, U. Simón Bolívar, Caracas, 1981, MSc in Food Sci., 1984; PhD in Honey and Cataracts, U. Wales, Cardiff, 1997. Prof. asst. U. de Los Andes, Mérida, Venezuela, 1985-89; prof. agregado U. de Los Andes, Mérida, 1989-93, prof. asociado, 1993-98, prof. titular, 1998—; coord. Nat. Mus. Apiculture, Mérida, 1988—, Lab. Apitherapy and Environ. Vigilance, Mérida, 1998—, L.Am. Sect. Internat. Honey Commn., Mérida, 1999—. Author: Miel de Abejas, 1993, Cataratas y Mieles Terapéuticas, 1997; editor Revista del Munapih, 1993. Scholar Gran Mariscal de Ayacucho, Caracas, 1986, CONICIT-BID-ULA, Caracas and Mérida, 1993; rsch. grantee CONICIT/CONIPET, Caracas, 1999. Mem. APIMONDIA (harmonisation d'analyse), ARVO, ICPBR. Achievements include patent for kit to detect honey frauds. Avocations: diving, painting, reading and writing poetry, tai chi, swimming. Office: CVI-ADG-FA-04-97, Fac Farmacia ULA, Merida 5101, Venezuela

VITA-FINZI, CLAUDIO, university educator; b. Sydney, New South Wales, Australia, Nov. 21, 1936; s. Paolo and Nadia (Touchmalova) V.-F.; m. Penelope Jean Angus, May 1, 1969; 1 child, Leo. BA, Cambridge U., Eng., 1958, PhD, 1962; ScD, Cambridge U., England, 1988. Research fellow St. John's Coll., Cambridge U., 1961-64; lectr. Univ. Coll., London, 1964-74, reader, 1974-87, neotectonics prof., 1987—. Author: The Mediterranean Valleys, 1969, Recent Earth History, 1973, Archaeological Sites, 1978, Recent Earth Movements, 1986. Recipient G.K. Warren prize Nat. Acad. of Sciences, 1994. Fellow Royal Geog. Soc. (Back award 1971), Geol. Soc. London; mem. Am. Philos. Soc. Home: 22 S Hill Park, London NW3 2SB, England Office: Univ Coll London, Gower St, London WCIE 6BT, England

VITAL BRAZIL, OSWALDO, research scientist, physician; b. Sã Paulo, Mar. 2, 1912; s. Vital and Maria Da Conceição (Pereira de Magalhães) Brazil; m. Stella Telles, Dec. 4, 1935; children: Aurea, Rosa. Med. diploma, Nat. Faculty Medicine, Rio de Janeiro, 1939; MD, Faculty Medicine USP, Sao Paulo, 1963. Asst. Inst. Vital Brazil, Niteroi, Brazil, 1940, head dept., 1945-48, sci. dir., 1945-48; asst. dept. pharmacology Sao Paulo, 1950-63; head dept. pharmacology facilty med. sci. State U. Campinas, Brazil, 1964-82. Contbr. numerous articles to profl. jours. Recipient medal Butantan Inst., 1981, plaque Faculty Agrarian and Vet. Sci., 1983; symposium held in his honor Acad. Scis. of State of Sao Paulo; dedicated edit. of Jour. Natural Toxins, 1993. Mem. AAAS (internat. mem.), Internat. Soc. Toxicology (plaque Pan Am. sect. 1992), N.Y. Acad. Scis., Brazilian Soc. Pharmacology and Therapeutics (hon.), Brazilian Soc. Toxinology (hon., founder, 1st pres.). Office: Stata U Campinas, Dept Pharmacol PO Box 6111, Campinas Brazil

VITALIANO, PETER PAUL, medical educator, researcher; b. Hazleton, Pa.; s. Salvatore and Mary (Gaudio) V. BA, Queens Coll., 1969; MS,

Syracuse U., 1973, Ph, 1975; postdoct., Fla. State U., 1976, U. Wash., 1977. Rsch. assoc. U. Wash., Seattle, 1978, from asst. to prof., 1979-88, prof., 1988—. editor: Annals of Behavioral Medicine, 1997; mem. editl. bd.: Psychoneuroendocrinologym 1985—, Health Psychology, 1996—, Internat. Behavioral Medicine, 1999; contbr. 180 articles to profl. jours. Grantee Nat. Inst. Aging, 1986-89, 94-99, Nat. Inst. Mental Health, 1988-93, 98—. Fellow Am. Psychol. Assn., Soc. Beahvioral Medicine, Gerontol. Soc. Am.; mem. Acad. Behavioral Medicine Rsch. (coun.). Avocations: art, nature, music. Office: U Wash PO Box 356560 Seattle WA 98195-6560

VITEČEK, ANTONIN, engineering educator; b. Opava, Silesia, Czech Republic, June 9, 1942; s. Jan and Ludmila (Kralova) V.; m. Janina Wruck, Oct. 30, 1965 (div. Apr. 1987); children: Anna, Stanislav, Pavla, Michal; m. Miluse Wawrziczkova, Aug. 13, 1988; 1 child, Petr. MSc, Warsaw Tech. U., 1967, PhD, 1972. Rsch. worker Tech. U. Ostrava, 1972-74, sr. lectr., 1974-81, dep. head of dept., 1981-86, head of dept., 1986-96, dean of faculty, 1996—, chmn. sci. coun., 1996—. Author: (with others) Control Systems in Deep Mines, 1977, Optimization of Electric Drives, 1989 (Min. Edn. prize 1989), Mathematical Methods of Automatic Control, 1988 (Rector prize 1988), System Optimization, 1992; assoc. editor, mem. editl. bd. Tech. U. Kosice, 1997—. Grantee Grant Agy. Czech Republic, 1993, 95, Min. Edn., 1992. Avocations: judo, travel. Home: Manesova 20, 74601 Opava 1 Silesia, Czech Republic Office: Tech U Ostrava, 17 Listopadu 15, 70833 Ostrava-Poruba Moravia, Czech Republic

VÍTEK, JIŘÍ ALEŠ, cell biologist; b. Ostrava, Moravia, Czech Republic, June 29, 1949; s. Ferdinand Jan and Marie (Římánková) V.; m. Vlasta Koubková, June 18, 1981; 1 child, Vítek Milan. RNDr., U. Masaryk, Brno, Czech Republic, 1972; PhD, Charles U., Prague, Czech Republic, 1981. Rsch. scientist Pediat. Rsch. Inst., Brno, 1971-87; sr. rsch. scientist Rsch. Inst. Child Health, Brno, 1987—. Author: Killifish, 1988; contbr. articles to profl. jours. Grantee Agy. Ministry Health, Prague, 1992, 94, 95. mem. Czech Biol. Soc., European Cell Biol. Orgn., European Tissue Culture Soc. Avocations: embryology and biology of Killifish, breeding and rearing of beetles. Home: Rolnická 7, 625 00 Brno Moravia, Czech Republic Office: Rsch Inst Child Health, Černopolní 9, 662 62 Brno Moravia, Czech Republic

VITELLI, GUILLERMO LUIS, economist, researcher; b. Buenos Aires, June 29, 1944; s. Angel and Alicia Beatriz (Prendergast) V.; m. Irma Beatriz Balcon, June 19, 1970; children: Federico Augusto, Ana Paula. Licenciado en economia politica, U. Buenos Aires, 1968. Rschr. U. Sussex, Inst. Devel. Studies, Eng., 1979-80; prof. U. Buenos Aires, U. Lanus, Argentina, 1983-90; rschr. Consejo Nat. de Investigaciones Cientificas y Tecnicas, Buenos Aires, 1984—; economist Econ. Commn. for Latin Am., Buenos Aires, Mexico. Author: Competencia Oligopolio y Cambio Tecnologico En La Construccion, 1976, 40 Years of Inflation in Argentina, 1986, Las Logicas De La Economia Argentina, 1990, Los Dos Siglos de la Argentina, 1999. Home: Arz Espinosa 55 Piso 12, 1157 Buenos Aires Argentina Office: U Buenos Aires, Cordoba 2122, Buenos Aires Argentina

VITE-TORRES, JAIME, chemistry educator, researcher; b. Pachuca, Mex., June 21, 1953; s. Neftali Vite-Teran and Maria Concepcion Torres-Vite; m. Maria Guadalupe Solares-Rivera, Apr. 25, 1992; children: Jaime Vite-Solares, Rafael Vite-Solares. PhD in Chemistry cum laude, T.H. Merseburg, Germany, 1986. Project mgr. Nat. Inst. Nuc. Investigations, Mexico City, Mex., 1987—. Contbr. articles to sci. jours.; inventor in field. Mem. Nat. Rschrs. Sys., Nat. Electrochem. Soc., Mexican Nuc. Soc. Avocations: sports, classical music, poetry, painting, reading. Fax: 3297332. Home: Apt 203, Bartolome de las Casas, CP 42050 Pachuca Hidalgo, Mexico Office: Inst Nac Invest Nucleares, Km 36 5 Carretera Mex Toluc, 52045 Mexico City Salazar, Mexico

VITHOULKAS, GEORGE, homeopath; b. Athens, Greece, July 25, 1932; m. Zissoula Antoniadou (Zissoula) V. Diploma in Homeopathy, Indian Inst. Homeopathy, India, 1966. Tchr. classical homeopathic medicine Athens, 1967—; founder, dir. Ctr. Homeopathic Medicine, Athens, 1970—; dean Internat. Acad. Classical Homeopathy, Alonissos, Greece, 1995—; prof. Kiev Med. Acad., Ukraine, 2000—; v.p. for Greece, LIGA Medicorum Internat. Homeopatica; founder (with others) Internat. Found. Homeopathy, U.S., 1978—; cons. creation of Vithoulkas Expert System (VES), U. Namur, Belgium, 1987-91; lectr. in field. Author: Homeopathy-Medicine of the New Man, 1975, 2d edit., 1992, The Science of Homeopathy, 1980, Materia Medica Viva, A New Model for Health and Disease, Talks on Classical Homeopathy, Essence of Mateia Medica Le Essenze Rubate, 1988, Essenzen Homoopathischer, 1990, Homeopattisia Laakeainekuvia, 1992, Homeopathic Conference Esalen The Bern Seminar, 1980; creator Greek Homeopathic Jour., 1972—; creator, editor European Jour. Classical Homeopathy, 1995—. Recipient Alternative Nobel Prize for health, Sweden, 1996, Gold Medal of Hungarian Democracy Pres. of Republic of Hungary, 2000, Gold Medal Internat. Congress of the LIGA, 1989, honored Internat. Hemeopathic Med. Soc., 1974; named Homeopath of the Millinnium Min. of Health of the Ctrl. Govt. of India, 2000. Mem. AAAS, Internat. Found. Heomepathy (pres.), Hellenic Homeopathic Med. Soc. (hon. pres.), Greek Soc. Homeopathic Medicine (founder), N.Y. Acad. Scis., Hahnemann Soc. Eng. (hon. v.p.), Sci. and Med. Network, Soc. Authors. Avocations: ecology, gardening, politics. Office: Internat Acad Homeopathy, 370 05 Alonissos Greece

VITIELLO, GIUSEPPE, physicist; b. Torre Annunziata, Napoli, Italy, Mar. 25, 1946; s. Pasquale Vitiello and Giuseppina Cuccurullo; m. Marina Avitabile; children: Manuela, Chiara. Maturitá, Liceo Classico, Torre-A-Italy, 1964; Laurea, U. Di Napoli, 1970; PhD, U. Wis., Milw., 1974. Prof. incaricato U. di Salerno, Italy, 1975-80, assoc. prof., 1980—; ricercatore - Gruppo Nazionale Struttura Della Materia, 1975-80, Inst. Nazional Fisica Nucleare, Italy, 1980—. Co-author: (book) Quantum Mechanics, 1985; contbr. articles to profl. jours. Office: Dept Physics, Univ Salerno, 84100 Salerno Italy

VITINS, GIRTS, chemist; b. Riga, Latvia, July 13, 1969; s. Uldis and Ingrida (Kaleja) V. MSc, U. Latvia, 1993, D in Chemistry, 1999. Guest rschr. U. Stockholm, Sweden, 1994-95, Tech. U. Denmark, 1996-97; rsch. asst. Inst. Solid State Physics, Riga, 1996—; leading rschr. Faculty of Chemistry, U. Latvia, Riga, 2000—. Avocations: slalom skiing, orienteering, cycling. Office: U Latvia Inst Solid St Phys, 8 Kengaraga St, LV-1063 Riga Latvia

VITKINE, ALEXANDRE, computer sculptor; b. Berlin, Mar. 1, 1910; arrived in France, 1926; s. Chaim and Olga (Abramowsky) V.; m. Anne-Marie Löwensohn, Feb. 14, 1948; children: Robert, Marc. Student, Sch. Elec./Indsl. Mechanics, Paris, 1926-28. Various positions in industry France, 1928-66; freelance photographer, Boulogne, France, 1967-96; computer sculptor Boulogne, 1992—. With French and Brit. Army, 1940-46, MTO, ETO. Mem. ARS Mathematica (pres. 1992—). Home and Office: 66 Rue d'Aguesseau, 92100 Boulogne France

VITKOWSKY, VINCENT JOSEPH, lawyer; b. Newark, Oct. 3, 1955; s. Boniface and Rosemary (Ofack) V.; m. Mary Gunzburg, May 16, 1981 (div. 1997); children: Vincent Jr., Victoria; m. Pandora Strasler, Sept. 18, 1999. BA, Northwestern U., 1977; JD, Cornell U., 1980. Bar: N.Y. 1981. Assoc. Hart and Hume, N.Y.C., 1980-84, Kroll & Tract, N.Y.C., 1984-87; of counsel Nixon, Hargrave, Devans & Doyle, N.Y.C., 1988-89; ptnr. Buchalter, Nemer, Fields & Younger, N.Y.C., 1990-95, Edwards & Angell LLP, N.Y.C., 1996—; lectr. in field. Contbr. articles to profl. jours. Mem. ABA (com. chmn.), Am. Arbitration Assn. (inernat. panel arbitrators), Internat. Bar Assn. (com. officer), Internat. Law Assn., Assn. Bar City of N.Y., Cornell Club, Human Rights Watch, IBA Human Rights Inst., Lawyers Com. for Human Rights. Home: 1 Irving Pl New York NY 10003 Office: Edwards & Angell 750 Lexington Ave Fl 12 New York NY 10022-1253

VÍTOVEC, JIŘÍ, physician, medical educator, researcher; b. Brno, Czech Republic, Feb. 25, 1951; s. Jan and Jiřina (Klapková) V.; Eva Stěpánková, Oct. 30, 1976 (dec. Jan. 1986); children: Jiří, Lenka; m. Lenka Jakubová, June 23, 1989. MD, Masaryk U. Sch. Medicine, Brno, 1975, CSc, PhD, 1988, postgrad. degree in internal medicine. Jr. physician U. Hosp., Brno, 1975-79, sr. physician, 1979-81, cons., 1981-91; asst. prof. Sch. Medicine, Brno, 1991-96, assoc. prof., 1996—; vice-dean Sch. Medicine U. Masaryk, Brno, 1997—; cons. cardiology ICU, U. Hosp., 1981-91. Author: Cardiology for G.P., 1994, Intensive Care for Nurses, 1994, Hypertension, 1999, Cardiovascular Pharmacy Therapy, 2000; contbr. articles to profl. jours. Mem. Internat. Soc. Cardiovascular Pharmacoth. Avocations: photography, sports. Home: Jana Uhra 26, 602 00 Brno Czech Republic Office: 2d Dept Medicine, Pekarska 53, 656 91 Brno Czech Republic

VITRAC, EMMANUEL CHARLES, communications executive; b. Le Cannet, France, Jan. 22, 1967; s. Jean-Jacques and Roswitha (Kähling) V.; m. Béatrice le Grom de Maret, May 30, 1998. BA in Polit. Sci., Whittier Coll., 1988; grad. degree in internat. mktg. & mgmt., Paris Grad. Sch. Mgmt., 1990. Operational auditor Nestlé Foods, Paris, 1992-93; corp. comm. sr. mgr. for Europe, Middle East, Africa Seagate Tech., Paris, 1993—; com. co-dir. Assn. des Anciens de l'Ecole Superieure de Commerce de Paris, 1993-96. V.p. devel. Jr. Chamber Internat., Paris, 1993-95; vol. XII Journées Mondiales de la Jeunesse, Paris, 1997. Lt. French Army, Berlin, 1990-91. Recipient Nat. Journalism award U.S. Quill and Scroll award 1984; named Outstanding Coll. Students of Am., Pres. Ronald Reagan, U.S. Govt., 1986. Mem. Info. Presse et Comm. Roman Catholic. Avocations: ceramics, sailing, horse riding, gourmet entertaining, golf. Fax: 33 1 41 86 10 40. Home: 133 ave Charles de Gaulle, F-92200 Neuilly-sur-Seine France Office: Seagate Technology, 62 bis ave André Morizet, F-92643 Boulogne-Billancourt France

VITRAC, JEAN-JACQUES CHARLES, international business consultant; b. Paris, May 31, 1942; came to U.S., 1972; s. Jean Bernard Vitrac and Paulette Aimée (Buisson) Mannerheim; m. Roswitha Kahling, Sept. 11, 1965; children: Emmanuel, François, Catherine. Diploma, Faculty of Law, Aix, France, 1963; post grad. in mktg., Institut National Du Marketing, Paris, 1972; post grad. in econ. scis., Institut Superieur Sciences Economiques, Paris, 1979. Devel. officer Europe-Africa Internat. Jaycees, Geneva, 1968-70; dir. econ. affairs Internat. Jaycees, Coral Gables, Fla., 1970-72; mktg. cons. Bernard Krief Internat., Paris, 1973-79; strategy cons. Euro-PacRim Internat., Walnut Creek, Calif., 1980—; owner Domaine Becquet Winery, Valley Springs, Calif.; chair task force on multinat. strategies Ctrl. Bank of France, Paris, 1974-78; mktg. cons. Aérospatiale, Paris, 1978; bd. dirs. Capsule Française Inc., Napa, Calif.; asst. prof. mktg. Inst. Français de Gestion, Paris, 1973-79; U.S. chmn. L'Entreprise Demain, Brussels, 1982-98; no. Calif. chmn. World Tech. Execs. Network, 1987-90. Author: Discover Export, 1974; co-author: Doing Business in California, 1989; editor World Tech. Execs. Network Review, 1989-90. Bd. dirs. E. Bay Internat. Trade Coun., 1996-97; chair parish coun. St. Patrick's Ch., 1998, 99; trustee Mark Twain St. Joseph's Hosp. Found., 1999—, exec. bd. mem., pub. rels. com. co-chair, 2000—. Named knight Equestrian Order of Holy Sepulchre of Jerusalem. Mem. KC (dep. grand knight 1998, treas. 1999), Am. Assn. Polit. Cons., Art Ranaissance Found. (hon., chair Calif. chpt. 1994—), Classical Philharmonic (v.p. 1995-96), Cal-France Coun. (v.p. 1996-97), Kiwanis Internat (gov.'s cabinet, dir. com. svc. 1996-97), French War Vets. (No. Calif. chpt. pres. 1996-97), Napa Kiwanis Club (disting. pres. 1993, bd. dirs. Calif.-Nev.-Hawaii Found. 1996-98), Wine Inst., Calaveras Wine Assn. Republican. Roman Catholic. Home: Becket's Ranch PO Box 467 Valley Springs CA 95252 Office: Euro PacRim Int Corp 2173 Hwy 12 East PO Box 1418 Valley Springs CA 95252-1418

VITRUK, NIKOLAÏ VASILIEVICH, judge, lawyer, educator; b. Zharovka, Tomsk, Russia, Nov. 4, 1937; s. Vitruk Vasily Zinovievich and Vitruk Ksenia Leontievna Zharova V.; m. Nakonechnaya Vitruk, 1968 (div. 1988); 1 child, Elena Nikolaevna. Student, Tomsk State U., Russia, 1954-59; postgrad., Kiev State U., Ukraine, 1963-66. Mgr. Legal Advice Bur., Tomsk, Russia, 1959-60; asst. to chair of theory and history of state and law Tomsk U., Russia, 1960-63; asst. to chair of theory of state and law, sr. tchr., asst. prof. Kiev State U., Ukraine, 1966-71; sr. scientific researcherInst. State and Law USSR Acad. Scis., Moscow, Russia, 1971-81; prof. chair of theory of state and law and constitutional law Acad. of Ministry of Internal Affairs USSR, Moscow, Russia, 1981-84, chief chair of state and law discipline High CorrespondenceLaw Coll., 1984-91; dep. chmn. Constitutional Ct. Russian Fedn., Moscow, Russia, 1991-93, acting chmn., 1993-95, judge, 1995—. Contbr. more than 300 articles to profl. jours. and books. Rep. Russian Fedn. European Commn. for democracy through law, assoc. mem. Venice Commn., Strasbourg, France, 1992. Recipient Labour Veteran medal, Medal for Irreproachable Svc. Avocations: theatre, modern realistic painting, culture of Russia of the Silver Age. Home: Flat 56 3 bld, ul Dovatoza, 119121 Moscow Russia Office: Constitutional Court Russian Fedn, 21 Iljinka St, 103132 Moscow Russia

VITTAL, VIJAY, electrical engineer; b. Bangalore, India, Dec. 25, 1955; arrived in U.S., 1979; s. H.S. Padmanabha and K. Shakuntala V.; m. Sunanda Vittal, June 8, 1980; children: Eknath, Vinayak. B in engring., B.M.S. Coll. Engring., Bangalore, India, 1977; M in tech., Indian Inst. of Tech., Kanpur, India, 1979; PhD, Iowa State Univ., 1982. Asst. prof. Iowa State Univ., Ames, 1982-86, assoc. prof., 1986-90; program dir. Nat. Sci. Found., Washington, 1993-94; prof. Iowa State Univ., 1990—; cons. Siemens Energy Automation, Plymouth, Minn., 1992-93, G.E. Power Systems, Schenactady, N.Y., 1999. Author: Power System Analysis, 2000, Power System Transient Stability, 1992; contbr. articles to profl. jours. Recipient Presdl. Young Investigator award NSF, 1985. Fellow IEEE (chair power sys. dynamic performance com.). E-mail: vittal@ee.iastate.edu. Office: Iowa State Univ 1126 Coover Hl Ames IA 50011-0001

VITTAS, DIMITRIOS, orthopedic surgeon; b. Athens, Greece, Mar. 21, 1939; arrived in Denmark, 1967; s. Haralambos I. and Elli (Askitis) V.; m. Asta Elvira Frausing. Diploma, Athens Coll., 1958; cert., U. Mich., 1958; MD, Athens U., 1964, U. Copenhagen, 1970; PhD, U. Crete, Greece. Med. officer Greek Army, 1965-66; jr. registrar Sundby, Glostrup, Bispebjerg Hosps., Copenhagen, 1967-73; sr. registrar St. Elizabeth, Hvidovre, Gentofte Hosp., Copenhagen, 1973-83; chief surgeon Gentofte Hosp., Copenhagen, 1983-86, Herlev Hosp., Copenhagen, 1992—; clin. lectr. U. Copenhagen, 1978-90; guest lectr. U. Crete, 1990—. Contbr. articles to profl. jours. Scholar Deutscher Acad. Austauschdienst, 1967-68. Mem. Hellenic Med. Assn., Danish Med. Assn., Internat. Soc. Lymphology. Greek Orthodox. Avocations: diving, travel, music. Home: Bagsvaerdvej 139, 2800 Lyngby Denmark Office: Herlev Hosp U Copenhagen, Herlev Ringvej, 2730 Copenhagen Denmark

VITULLI, WILLIAM FRANCIS, psychology educator; b. Bklyn., July 17, 1936; s. William S. and Sadie Rosaria (Stallone) V.; m. Betty Jean Sheubrooks, June 15, 1961; children: Paige Vitulli Baggett, Quinn Anthony, Sherik Vitulli Butler. BA, U. Miami, 1961, MS, 1963, PhD, 1966. Lic. psychologist, Ala. Grad. asst. U. Miami, Coral Gables, Fla., 1961-65; asst. prof. psychology U. South Ala., Mobile, 1965-69, assoc. prof., 1969-75, prof., 1975—, chair sr. faculty caucus, 1999; v.p. Ala. Bd. Examiners in Psychology, Montgomery, 1982-84; rsch. cons. Drug Edn. Coun., Mobile, 1988-94. Mem. editl. bd. Jour. Sport Behavior, 1978—; contbr. articles to profl. jours. Mem. adv. bd. Contact Mobile, 1987-92. Named Prof. of Quar., Alpha Lambda Delta, Faculty Mem. of Yr., 1993-94; recipient Outstanding Prof. award Alumni Assn., 1994. Mem. APA, Southeastern Psychol. Assn., Ala. Psychol. Assn. (pres. 1975), Italian-Am. Cultural Soc. South Ala. (chair hist.-cultural com. 1982), Sigma Xi (pres.-elect U. South Ala. chpt. 1996-97), Psi Chi (faculty adviser U. South Ala. chpt. 1972-80, chair sr. faculty caucus U. South Ala. 1999-00). Roman Catholic. Avocations: jogging, athletics research and analysis, fishing. Home: 2025 Maryknoll Ct Mobile AL 36695-3829 Office: U South Ala 307 University Blvd N Mobile AL 36688-3053

VITVITSKY, JACK, physician assistant; b. White Plains, N.Y., Mar. 8, 1945; s. Alexander Jack and Helen Louise Virginia (Rider) V. BS, U. Rochester, 1968; AAS, Cuyahoga C.C., Cleve., Ohio, 1978; postgrad., SUNY, Plattsburgh, 1964-66, 73-74, Liberty U., 1994—. Cert. first aid and CPR instr. ARC; cert. EMT instr. N.Y.; cert. ground and flight instr., multi-engine instr., written test examiner FAA. Physician's asst. Planned Parenthood No. N.Y., 1979-84, Dr. David P. Gorman, Malone, N.Y., 1980-81, N.Y. State Dept. Corrections, Dannemora, N.Y., 1981-84, N.Y. State Office Mental Retardation and Devel. Disabilities, Tupper Lake, N.Y., 1984-85, N.Y. State Dept. Corrections, Raybrook, N.Y., 1985—; owner Adirondack Computer Testing Ctr., 1996—. Contbr. articles to profl. jours. Active Lake Placid Vol. Ambulance Svc., Inc., 1975—, Nat. Ski Patrol System, 1975—; mem. aviation explorer program Boy Scouts Am. With U.S.Army Res., 1981-84, N.Y. Army N.G., 1984—. Mem. Am. Acad. Physician Assts. (cons. minority affairs com. 1999—), N.Y. State Soc. Physician Assts., Soc. Army Physician Assts. (del. to Am. Acad. Physician Assts. Ho. of Dels.), Adirondack Soc. Physician Assts. (sec. 1996—), Mid-Hudson Assn. Physician Assts., Fellowship Christian Physician Assts. (sec. 1992-97), Exptl. Aviation Assn., Aircraft Owners and Pilots Assn., U.S. Army Flight Soc. of Flight Surgeons, NRA, Gun Owners Am. Republican. Avocations: snowshoeing, skiing, writing, woodworking, equine activities. Home: 1686 County Route 38 Norfolk NY 13667-3236 Office: US Army Nat Guard Computer Testing Ctr Olympic Finishers Hangar 61 Lake Ave Saratoga Springs NY 12866-2315

VITZTHUM, HANS GEORG, surgeon; b. Dresden, Saxonia, Germany, Mar. 1, 1967; s. Hans Ekkehart and Christine (Grossmann) V.; m. Kathleen Dietrich, Mar. 2, 1990; children: Maria Sophie, Hans Ferdinand. MD, U. Magdeburg, 1999. Resident ENT dept. U. Magdeburg, Germany, 1993-95, resident, 1995-99; specialist, leader med. dept. Praxis, Madgeburg, Germany, 1999—; specialist in tinnitus treatment. Mem. German Soc. ENT, Head and Neck Surgery, German Soc. Acupuncture and Neuraltherapy. Avocations: downhill skiing, water skiing, surfing, historic cars. Home: Schenkendorfstr 9, D-39108 Magdeburg Germany Office: Praxis, Sternstr 21, D-39104 Magdeburg Germany

VITZTHUM, HANS-EKKEHART, neurosurgeon, consultant, educator; b. Plauen, Germany, Feb. 22, 1940; s. Hans-Julius and Irmgard (Herold) V.; m. Christine Bärbel Grossmann, July 23, 1967; 1 child, Hans-Georg. MD, U. Leipzig, Germany, 1966; Habil., U. Magdeburg, Germany, 1981. Physician Hosp., Plauen, Germany, 1966-71, cons. gen. surgery, 1971-75, cons. traumatology, 1975-78; cons. neurosurgery U. Magdeburg, 1978-90; prof. U. Leipzig, 1990—. Contbr. 98 chpts. to books, 57 articles to profl. jours. Sgt. German Army, 1958-60. Mem. German Soc. Neurosurgery, German Soc. Spinal Rsch. Avocations: history of art, art, sport. Home: Viertelsweg 40, D-04157 Leipzig Germany Office: Univ Leipzig, Neurosurgery Clinic, Johannisallee 34, D-04103 Leipzig Germany

VITZTHUM, OTTO GEORG, organic chemist; b. Nuremberg, Germany, Sept. 27, 1934; s. Otto Michael and Marie B. (Link) V.; m. Doris H. Griesel, Apr. 1, 1965; children: Michael, Matthias, Anabel. Diploma in Chemistry, U. Erlangen, Germany, 1960, DrRerNat, 1964. Chemist Kaffee HAG AG, Bremen, 1964-70, head sci. dept., 1970-71; dir. HAG GF AG, Bremen, 1971-86; dept. mgr. Jacobs Suchard, Bremen, 1986-90; dir. coffee chemistry worldwide Kraft Jacobs Suchard, Bremen, 1990-96; hon. prof. Tech. U. Braunschweig, Germany, 1988. Author: Kaffee und Coffein; contbr. articles to profl. jours.; numerous patents in field. Recipient Philip Morris award, 1995. Mem. ASIC (sci. sec. 1980, award 1985), European Decaffeination Assn. (v.p. 1994-96). Achievements include research and patents in coffee science, coffee refining process, new instant coffee process, elucidation of coffee aroma chemistry; supercritical extraction of cocoa, spices, tea coffee, tobacco. Home: Upper Borg 170, 28357 Bremen Germany

VIVIANI, ANTONIO, aerospace engineer, educator; b. Salerno, Italy, Sept. 22, 1958; s. Domenico and Giovanna (Chinni) V. Degree in aeronautical engring., U. Naples, 1983, PhD, 1988. From asst. prof. to prof. U. Naples, Italy, 1984—. Mem. AAAS, N.Y. Acad. Sci., European Low Gravity Rsch. Assn. (v.p.). Avocation: volleyball. Office: U Naples Dept Aerospace Eng, Via Roma 29, 81031 Aversa Italy

VIVIANI, FRANCO GIOVANNI, anthropologist, educator; b. Padua, Italy, Nov. 25, 1948; s. Rino Aldo and Jole (Garon) V.. Biology degree, U. Padua, 1972. Tchr. H.S., Padova, Italy, 1974-93; rschr. Faculty of Psychology U. Padua, Padova, 1993, prof. neurosci. Faculty of Psychology, 1994-96, 98—; prof. anthropology Higher Inst. Phys. Edn., Bologna, Italy, 1980—; rschr. U. Padua, Guatuso, Costa Rica, 1977, Bissau, Guinea, 1988, Italian Speleol. Soc., 1985, 86. Editor: Female Genital Mutilation, 1995, Canidia, 1997, Physical Activity and Health, 1998; contbr. articles to profl. jours. Recipient Hon. Mention award Belgian Royal Acad. Overseas Sci., 1990. Mem. AAAS, Internat. Soc. Advancement of Kinanthropometry, Internat. Coun. Phys. Activity and Fitness Rsch. (bd. dirs. 1996—), European Anthropol. Assn., World Leisure and Recreation Assn., Italian Anthropol. Assn., N.Y. Acad. Scis., Internat. No Circumcision Network (rep. Italy 1996). Home: via Armistizio 88, I-35142 Padua Italy Office: U Padua Psychology Dept, via Venezia 8, I-35131 Padua Italy

VIZCAINO, HENRY P., mining engineer, consultant; b. Hurley, N.Mex., Aug. 28, 1918; s. Emilio D. and Petra (Perea) V.; m. Esther B. Lopez, Sept. 16, 1941; children: Maria Elena, Rick, Arthur, Carlos. BS in Engring., Nat. U., Mexico City, 1941; geology student, U. N.Mex., 1951-54. Registered profl. engr. With Financiera Minera S.A., Mexico City, 1942-47; gen. mgr. Minas Mexicanas S.A., Torreon, Mex., 1947-51; exploration engr. Kerr McGee Corp., Okla., 1955-69; cons. Albuquerque, 1969-75, 84—; regional geologist Bendix Field Engring., Austin, Tex., 1976-79; staff geo-scientist Bendix Field Engring., Grand Junction, Colo., 1979-81; sr. geologist Hunt Oil Co., Dallas, 1981-84. Contbr. articles to profl. publs. Mem. AIME, Internat. Platform Assn., Aircraft Owners and Pilots Assn., Rotary, Elks. Republican. Congregationalist. Address: 12332 Los Arboles Ave NE Albuquerque NM 87112-2079

VIZOSO, FRANCISCO JOSE, surgeon; b. Fene, La Coruna, Spain, Jan. 8, 1959; s. Angel and Maria Luisa (Piñeiro) V.; m. Concepcion Consuelo Alvarez, July 27, 1985; 1 child, Francisco Javier. Lic. Medicine, U. Santiago, Spain, 1982, Grad. in Medicine, 1983; PhD, Oviedo, Spain, 1990. Physician Hosp. de Marina, Ferrol, Spain, 1982-84; med. resident Hosp. Gen. de Asturias, Oviedo, 1985-89; med. cons. in surgery Hosp. de Jove, Gijon, 1989—. Contbr. articles to profl. jours. Mem. AAAS, N.Y. Acad. scis., Spanish Assn. Surgeons (Nat. Award of Surgery 1992). Avocations: literature, fishing. Home: Avda Marola #16, 33400 Salinas Asturias, Spain Office: Hospital de Jove, Avda Eduardo castro S/N, 33290 Gijon Asturias, Spain

VIZZINI, CAROL REDFIELD, symphony musician, music educator; b. San Diego, Jan. 3, 1946; d. Ernest Sylvester and Eleanor Diana (Soneson) Redfield; m. Edward Tracy Browning (div. 1981); children: Victor, Charlotte; m. Joseph Russell Vizzini, Apr. 12, 1997. MusB, Phila. Musical Acad., 1968. Prin. cellist Somerset Hills Symphony, Basking Ridge, N.J., 1971-81, New Philharm. of N.W. N.J., Morristown, 1978-87; asst. prin. cellist Princeton (N.J.) Chamber Symphony, 1985-95; prin. cellist Orch. St. Peter-by-the-Sea, Point Pleasant, N.J., 1987-92; instr. in cello Westminster Conservatory, Rider U., Princeton, 1987—, head string dept., 1992—; chamber music coach Vt. Music and Arts Ctr., Lyndonville, 1980-81; coach Greater Princeton Youth Orch., 1989-92; chamber music coach N.J. Youth Symphonies, Summit, 1989—; chamber music coord. Westminster Conservatory, 1991-98. Author: Cello Scales, Volume One (One and Two Octave Scales), 1997, Cello Scales, Volume Two (Three and Four Octave Scales), 2000. Mem. Am. String Tchrs. Assn., Am. Fedn. Musicians, Music Tchrs. Nat. Assn. (string coord. 1989-93). Avocations: gardening, fly fishing, travel. Office: Westminster Conservatory of Music Rider Univ 101 Walnut Ln Princeton NJ 08540-3819

VLACHOGIANNIS, GEORGE, cinema owner, administrator; b. Thessaloniki, Greece, Dec. 11, 1944; s. Thomas and Ifigenia (Kazinaris) V.; m. Gesthimani Hemmanouilidis, Sept. 20, 1975; children: Ifigenia, Thomas. Merchant Home Appliances, Veria, Greece, 1965—; cinema owner, adminstr. Cinema Star, Veria, Greece, 1974—. Editor (newspaper) Free Step, 1983—. Polit. v.p., Veria Imathias, 1985-90; pres. Imathias Prefecture owner's property, 1965-99. 2d lt., Hellenic Army, 1964-66. Mem. Athens Film-Makers (v.p. 1964—). New Democrat. Greek Orthodox. Avocations: computers, internet. Office: Cinema Star, 57 Metropoleos St, GR-59100 Veria Greece

VLACHOS, DIMITRIOS, physicist, researcher; b. Lefkas, Hellas, July 18, 1966; s. Spirantonis Vlachos and Paraskevi Vagena. Diploma in physics, U.

Ioannina, Greece, 1988; PhD in Physics, U. Ioannina, 1997. Meteorologist Hellenic Air Forces, Preveza, 1995-97; rschr. U. Ioannina, 1997; postdoctoral rsch. asst. physics & astronomy U. Glasgow, 1998—. Contbr. articles to profl. jours. Christian Orthodox. Avocations: sports, music, painting. Office: U Glasgow, Kelvin Bldg, Glasgow G12 8QQ, United Kingdom

VLACHY, VOJESLAV, chemistry educator; b. Ljubljana, Slovenia, May 29, 1946; s. Adam and Jelka (Strazar) V.; m. Metka Luzar, Jul. 14, 1973 (dec. Mar. 1996); children: Katja, Nina. BS, Univ. Ljubljana, 1970, MS in chemistry, 1973, PhD, 1978. Tchg. asst. Univ. Ljubljana, Ljubljana, Slovenia, 1972-80, asst. prof., 1980-86, assoc. prof., 1986-91, prof., 1991—; vis. asst. prof. Univ. Calif., Davis, 1984-85, vis. scientist/lectr. Univ. Calif., Berkeley, 1985-86, vis. assoc. prof. Univ. Utah, Salt Lake City, 1989, vis. scientist Univ. Calif., Berkeley, 1991-92. Contbr. articles to profl. jours. Recipient Fulbright fellowship, 1984, B. Kidrič Fund award Min. of Sci., 1984, The Slovenian award, 1996. Mem. Internat. Union of Pure & Applied Chemistry. Office: Univ Ljubljana, Chem & Chemical Tech, 1000 Ljubljana Slovenia

VLAD, ROMAN, composer; b. Cernauti, Romania, Dec. 29, 1919. Student, Cernauti Conservatory, Rome. Pianist, lectr., 1944—; artistic dir. Accademia Filarmonica, 1954-58, 66-69, pres., 1996—; artistic dir. Maggio Musicale Fiorentino, 1964, Teatro Comunale Florence, Italy, 1968-72, Teatro alla Scala, Milan, Italy, 1995-97; pres. Filarmonica Romana, Rome, Italy, 1995-97; tchr. Dartington Summer Sch., 1954-55; prof. composition Perugia Conservatory, 1968; supr. Turin Radio Symphony Orch., 1976-80; artistic adviser Turin Settembre Musica Festival, 1985—. Co-editor Ency. dello spettacolo, 1958-62; composer (ballets) La Strada sul Caffé, 1943, La Dama delle Camelie, 1945, Fantasie, 1948, Masques Ostendias, 1959, Die Wiederkehr, 1962, Il Gabbiano, 1968, (operas) Storia di una Mamma, 1951, Il Dottore di Vetro, 1960, La Fantarca, 1967, Il Sogno, 1973, (orchestral works) Sinfonietta, 1941, Suite, 1941, Sinfonia all'antica, 1948, Variazzioni concertiani su una serie di 12 note dal Don Giovanni di Mozart for piano and orch., 1955, Musica per archi, 1957, Musica Concertata for harp and orch., 1958, Ode super Chrysae Phorminx for guitar and orch., 1964, Divertimento sinfonico, 1968, L'Arte della Variazione, 1996, A se stesso (IV Cantata) for bariton, chorus and orch., 1997, La Musica arriva da lontano, for soprano and instruments, 1998, (vocal works) Lettura di Michelangelo, 1964, Immer wieder for soprano and instruments, 1965, Piccolo divertimento corale, 1968, Lettura di Lorenzo Magnifico for chorus, 1974, La Vespa di Toti for bois' voices and instruments, 1976, L'Arte dilla Variazione for 6 Soloists, Chorus and Orchestra, 2000, (instrumental works) Divertimento for 11 instruments, 1948, string quartet, serenata, Il Magico Flauto di Severino for flute and piano, Mutazioni for guitari solo, 1996, numerous works for piano, also music for more than 100 films; author: Collected Essays, 1955, Luigi Dallapiccola, 1957, Storia della dodecafonia, 1958, Stravinsky, 1958, 3d edit., 1979, Essays on Busoni, Schoenberg and Stravinsky. Mem. Soc. Italian Composers (pres. 1987-93), ISCM (pres. Italian sect. 1960-63). Home: XXIV Maggio 51, 00187 Rome Italy Office: Rome Philharm Acad, via Flaminia 118, I-00196 Rome Italy*

VLAD, STAN MELU, research and development manager; b. Gemenele, Romania, Mar. 5, 1955; s. Stan and Enuta (Bostan) V.; m. Florica Stefanescu, Apr. 17, 1980; children: Mihaela-Camelia, Anca-Felicia. Engr., Poly. U., Bucharest, 1980; sr. engr., Microprocessors, Bucharest, 1990. Engr. Electronics and Automation Factory, Bucharest, 1980-82, rsch. engr., 1981-89, head of lab. R&D, 1990-92, sr. project mgr., 1992-98, head R & D dept., 1998—; mgr. MV Electronics, Bucharest, 1994-98; project mgr. internat. nuc. rsch. program Electronics and Automation Factory, 1999; cons. ASTI Control, Bucharest, 1994-96. Contbr. articles to sci. publs. Observer League for Protecting Human Rights, 1990, 92. Mem. Air-Instrument Assn. Romania, Alpin Club Romania. Avocations: car club, collecting stamps, football. Home: Edu Odobesti 5 Bl Zl Sc 4 Ap 57, 74576 Bucharest Sector 3, Romania Office: Electrons & Automation Fact, 242 Cal Floreasca, Bucharest Sector 1, Romania

VLADA, MARIN, information educator; b. Movila Verde, Constantza, Romania, June 12, 1953; s. Constantin and Maria (Moromete) V.; m. Roxana (Rosca) V., Oct. 18, 1979; children: Iulia, George. Lic. in Math. and Computer Sci., U. Bucharest, Romania, 1978; MSc, U. Bucharest, 1979; MSc in Computer Graphics, Inst. Informatics, 1983, MSc in Artificial Intelligence, 1987. Program staff Computer Ctr. Municipality, Bucharest, 1979-84; rschr. Computer Ctr. U. Bucharest, 1984-92; assoc. prof. dept. applied math. and informatics U. Bucharest, 1992—. Author: (with A. Posea) Computer Graphics in Fortran, 1988, 90, (with A. Posea, I. Nistor, C. Constantinescu) Computer Graphics in Pascal and C Languages Implementation and Applications, 1992; contbr. articles to profl. jours. Mem. IEEE Computer Soc. E-mail: vlada@math.math.unibuc.ro. Office: U Bucharest Dept Math, 14 Academei St, 70109 Bucharest Romania

VLADAREANU, RADU, physician, consultant; b. Cimpulung, Arges, Romania, Dec. 1, 1962; s. Mircea and Sonia (Tamas) V.; m. Ana-Maria Gherasim, July 21, 1991. MD, U. Medicine, Bucharest, Romania, 1987, PhD, 1995. Med. resident ob-gyn. Bucharest, 1991-94, specialist ob-gyn., 1994-98, cons. in ob-gyn., 1998—; univ. asst. U. Medicine, Bucharest, 1991-97, prof. asst., 1997—. Author: Fetal Hipotrophy, 1996, Medical Complications During Pregnancy, 1999; translator: Obstetrics and Gynecology-NMS, 1998; contbr. articles to profl. jours. Recipient diploma for exceptional med. rsch. Min. Edn., 1987. Mem. Ob-gyn. Soc. (sec. 1998—), Lions Club (Bucharest), Clinmed 22 Found. (pres. 1999—). Avocations: tennis, skiing. Home: 41 Mozart st ap 2, 71458 Bucharest Romania Office: U Medicine, 15 Dionisie Lupu, Bucharest Romania Address: Faculty Medicine, Floreasca St 54, 71401 Bucharest Romania

VLADEM, PAUL JAY, investment advisor, broker; b. Chgo., Apr. 5, 1952; s. Arthur I. and Elaine A. (Ascher) V.; m. Sondra Joyce Berman, Dec. 27, 1981; children: Ashley Sherree, Evan David. BSBA with honors and high distinction, U. Ill., Chgo., 1974. Lic. brokerage securities, Fla., Ill., Ariz., Conn., Ga., Ind., N.C., Colo., Md., Nev., N.Y., Ohio, Calif., Utah; registered investment advisor; lic. ins. agt., Fla., Ill., Ind., Utah, Conn.; CPA, Fla., Ill.; lic. real estate agt., Fla. In charge acct. Peat Marwick, Fort Lauderdale, Fla., 1974-76; mgr. McGladrey & Pullen, CPA, Fort Lauderdale, 1976-85; sr. v.p. fin. Integrated Resources formerly Easter Kramer, Boca Raton, Fla., 1985-89; pres. Associated Investor Svcs., Fort Lauderdale, 1989—. Bd. dirs. Israel Bonds, Ft. Lauderdale, 1994, Jewish Family Svc., Ft. Lauderdale, 1993; chmn. CPA Com. on Israel Bonds, Ft. Lauderdale, 1994, mem. prof. adv. com., 1992—. Named One of Top Ten Brokers of Yr. Registered Rep. Mag., 1994. Mem. AICPA (personal planning divsn.), Fla. Inst. CPAs (mem. personal fin. planning com., 1985), Internat. Platform Assn. Democrat. Jewish. Avocations: tennis, basketball, attending sporting events. Home: 6508 NW 103rd Ln Parkland FL 33076-2934 Office: Associated Investor Svcs 2699 Stirling Rd Ste A200 Fort Lauderdale FL 33312-6583

VLADEM, STEVEN ALLEN, writer, motivational speaker; b. Chgo., July 24, 1949; s. Arthur and Elaine Edythe (Ascher) V. BA with honors and distinction, U. Ill., Chgo., 1970; MEd in Math., Northeastern Ill. U., Chgo., 1973; MA in Ednl. Adminstrn./Supervision, Roosevelt U., Chgo., 1975; PhD in Computer Edn., Internat. U., Los Altos, Calif., 1992; ScD, London Sch. Applied Rsch., 1993. Tchr. math. Chgo. Bd. Edn., 1971-81, statistician and evaluator dept. rsch. and evaluation, 1979; supr. program svcs. dept. Planning, Chgo. City Hall, 1981; coord. alt. sch. without walls program Chgo. M.H.S., 1982-87, coord. computer assisted instrn., 1987-91; developer ednl. software Chgo., 1987-92, freelance computer cons., 1987-92, writer/lectr., 1994—; lectr. in field; judge Emmy awards, 1999. Author: The Jigsaw People (poetry), 1997; artist soapstone sculpture The Wise Owl, Gallery of Art, Internat. Congress of Arts and Comm., Keble Coll., Oxford U., Eng. Dep. mem. Internat. Parliament for Safety and Peace, Palermo, Sicily, 1993-95, London Diplomatic Acad.; hon. amb. for laureates Jr. Achievement and Chgo. Assn. for Bus. and Industry, 1990; support group leader, outreach vol. Nat. Keratoconus Found., L.A., 1995—; Natl. Coalition for Hlth. Care Reform (bd. dirs.) 1998—; docent Tour of Old Town, Old Town C. of C., Chgo., 1993; patron various arts orgns.; judge Daniel Webster Acad. Poets Competition, 1998. Named John W. Rogers Educator of the Yr., Jr. Achievement, Chgo., 1990; recipient Congress Star of Distinction, Internat. Congress on Arts and Comm./St. John's Coll., Cambridge U., 1992, World Lifetime Achievement award, 1991, Cert. of World Leadership Internat. Biog. Ctr., 1991, Internat. Cultural Diploma of Honor, 1991, Medal of Merit, Republic of Peru, 1992, Albert Einstein medal Holland, 1994, finalist, U.S. Natl. Memory Championship, N.Y.C., 1997, Champion in Alzheimers Rsch. award Alzheimers Assn. of Am., 2000, Torch for Global Inspiration award 2000. Mem. NATAS, Internat. Platform Assn. (bd. govs. internet team, red carpet com., Gold Ribbon Most Popular Artist 1995), United Writers Assn. (life fellow), World Univ. Roundtable, Toastmasters Internat., Internat. Order of Merit (Cambridge, Eng.), Daniel Webster Acad. Poets (Cert. of Merit 1995), Chrysopoets, Order of Templars of Jerusalem (knight), Lofsensic Ursinius Order (knight comdr.), Order of San Ciriaco (count), Am. Legion (gold medal, sch. leadership award 1967), Lions Club. Avocations: cinema, musical theatre, backgammon, architecture, world travel. Home: 6237 N Hamlin Ave Chicago IL 60659-1019

VLADIKOVA, DARIA EUGENIEVA, chemist, researcher; b. Sofia, Bulgaria, Dec. 12, 1949; d. Eugene Ivanov and Todorka Gavrailova (Gandeva) V.; m. Lazar Christoforov Ilkov, June 1, 1978; 2 children. MS, KL Ohridski U., Sofia, 1972; PhD, Inst. Chem. Tech., Sofia, 1989. Rschr. Bulgarian Acad. Sci., Sofia, 1972-78; info. scientist Chem. Inst. Industry, Sofia, 1978-80; rschr. Inst. Chem. Tech., Sofia, 1980-89, rsch. assoc., 1989-95; rsch. assoc. Bulgarian Acad. Scis., Sofia, 1995-98, assoc. prof., 1998—; lectr. Inst. Chem. Tech., 1991-95. Co-author: The Chemistry—Knowledge and Practice, 1980. Bd. dirs. Nat. Club Democracy, Bulgaria, 1989, Bulgarian Women's Union, 1994; v.p. Bulgarian Women's Union, 1995-97. Mem. Acad. Women's Soc. (v.p. 1997), Bulgarian Electrochem. Soc., Internat. Soc. Electrochem. Democrat. Avocations: charity, travel, skiing. Home: 209 Rakovski St Entr B, 1000 Sofia Bulgaria Office: CLEPS Bulgarian Acad Sci, 10 Acad G Bonchev Str, 1113 Sofia Bulgaria

VLADIMIROV, ALEXANDER PETROVICH, physicist, educator; b. Narofominsk, Russia, Aug. 10, 1952; s. Peter Vladimirovich and Alexandra Vladimirov; m. Valentina Alexandrovna Korshunkova, Feb. 11, 1977; children: Daniil, Evgenij, Michail. Student, Chuvash State U., Cheboksary, Russia, 1970-75. Locksmith Plant Elec. Mechanisms, Cheboksary, 1969-70; engr. Inst. Polymer Materials, Perm, Russia, 1975-78; jr. scientist Inst. Metal Physics, Sverdlovsk, Russia, 1979-87; scientist Inst. Engring. Sci., Yekaterinburg, Russia, 1987—; invited lectr. Urals Tech. U., Sverdlovsk, 1989-98, lectr., Yekaterinburg, 1998—. Author: Holographic Methods of Measurement and Monitoring, 1996. Mem. Russian Phys. Soc. Avocations: philosophy, gardening. E-mail: vap@imach.uran.ru. Home: Lobkova St 34-65, 620057 Yekaterinburg Chuvash, Russia Office: Inst Engring Sci, K Libknekht St, 620219 Yekaterinburg Chuvash, Russia

VLADIMIROV, SERGUEI V., physicist, educator; b. Saint Petersburg, Russia, Oct. 1, 1961; s. V.N. and G.I. (Zubovich) V.; m. Galina, Aug. 23, 1986; children: Vladimir, Anna. MSc, Moscow Inst. Physics & Tech., 1984, PhD, 1988; DSc, Gen. Physics Inst., Russian Acad. Scis., Moscow, 1999. Rsch. fellow Gen. Physics Inst., Moscow, 1989-92; Humboldt rsch. fellow Ruhr.U., Bochum, Germany, 1992-93, JSPS rsch. fellow, 1994-95; rsch. fellow U. Sydney, Australia, 1995—. Author: Modulational Interactions in Plasmas, 1995; contbr. articles to profl. jours. Office: U Sydney, Sch Physics, Sydney NSW 2006, Australia

VLADIMIR SERGEY, PAKHOMOV, chemical engineering educator; b. Moscow, Feb. 14, 1937; s. Sergey Dmitry and Maria Ivanovna (Vinogradova) P.; m. Nina Homutskaya, June 20, 1959; 1 child. Diploma in engring., Moscow Inst. Chem. Engring., 1959, Candidate in Tech. Scis., 1971; D in Tech. Scis., Karpov Inst. Phys. Chemistry, 1989. Cert. chem. engring. Asst. corrosion and anticorrosion dept. Moscow Inst. Chem. Engring., 1959-73, lectr. chem. engring., 1973-90, prof. corrosion and anticorrosion dept., 1990—, vice-rector, 1978—; tchr. Inst. Apparatuses of Chem. Industry, Havana, Cuba, 1964-66; tech. cons. Krupp VDM GmbH, 1995—. Authro: Corrosion and Anticorrosion in Chemical Engineering, 1983; mem. editl. bd. Protection of Metals, 1983-97; sci. cons. for film Corrosion and Metal Protection, 1974. People's assessor People's Ct. Moscow, 1967-69. Fellow Russian Corrosion Soc.; mem. Soviet Union Corrosion Soc. (chmn. divsn. 1985-90), N.Y. Acad. Scis., Ctrl. Scientists Club. Avocations: photography, video-film making, traveling. Office: Moscow State U Ecol Engring, 21/4 Staraya Basmannaya St, 107884 Moscow Russia

VLADUT, EMANOIL, occupational health physician; b. Medias, Sibiu, Romania, Aug. 11, 1951; s. Emanoil and Aneta (Gherdia) V.; m. Tatiana Predtesoiv, Oct. 25, 1978. MD, U. Medicine, Timisoara, Romania, 1994. Village dispensary Musetesti, Romania, 1976-77; dispensary Bratei-Sibiu, Romania, 1977-83, Vitrometan Works, Medias, 1984-88; with clinic dept. occuption therapy Medias, 1989—; chief Polyclinic Medias, 1994-2000; chief med. svcs. House of Health Ins., 2000—. Contbr. articles to profl. jours. Capt. Res. Med. Svcs. Mem. European Soc. Chronobiology Clermond Ferand, N.Y. Acad. Scis., Coll. of Drs. Democrat. Avocations: tennis, reading, chess. Home: 13 Nicolae Iorga St, 3125 Medias Russia Office: House of Health Ins, 13 St L Roth St, 3125 Medias Romania Address: Mem Gerb 90A Polyclinic, 3125 Medias St Nicolae Iorg, Judsibiu Romania

VLAEV, STOYAN JELEV, physics researcher, educator; b. Provadia, Varna, Bulgaria, Sept. 7, 1952; s. Jelyu Stoyanov and Ivanka Yordanova; m. Margaritka Lakova Marinova, Aug. 3, 1975; children: Irina Stoyanova, Milen Stoyanov. BSc, U. Sofia, Bulgaria, 1975, MSc, 1977, PhD in Solid State Physics, 1990. Rsch. assoc. Inst. Gen. and Inorganic Chemistry, Bulgarian Acad. Scis., Sofia, 1978-82, rsch. fellow, 1982-89, rsch. scientist, 1989—; rsch. prof. Sch. of Physics U. Autonoma de Zacatecas, Mex., 1996—. Patentee in field; contbr. articles to profl. jours. With Bulgarian Army, 1970-72. Recipient Gold medal Ministry of Edn., 1970, Prize of Nat. Physics Olympiad, 1970, Gold medal Ministry of Sci. and Higher Edn., 1975. Mem. Bulgarian Phys. Soc., Mex. Soc. Physics. Avocations: skiing, touring, bard music. Home: Mladost 1A Bl 510 VH2 Ap 38, 1729 Sofia Bulgaria Office: U Autonoma Zacatecas, Sch Physics Apt Postal C580, 98068 Zacatecas Mexico

VLAJKOVIC, SRDJAN M., medical researcher; b. Belgrade, Serbia, Yugoslavia; s. Miodrag V. and Leposava S. V.; m. Gordana P. Prodanovic, July 9, 1984 (div. Aug. 18, 1986); 1 child, Darko; m. Rozalia A. Stancin, Oct. 9, 1988; 1 child, Tijana. MD, U. Belgrade, 1982, MSc Sch. of Pharmacy, 1984, PhD in Medicine, 1990. Rsch. assoc. Immunology Rsch. Ctr., Belgrade, 1985-90, rsch. fellow, 1990-91, dir., 1991-94; rsch. officer U. Auckland, New Zealand, 1994-96, rsch. fellow, 1996—. Contbr. chpt. to book, also articles to med. jours. Mem. Dem. Party, Belgrade, 1992-94. Postdoctoral rsch. fellow Emory U., Atlanta, 1991. Mem. Physiol. Soc. New Zealand, Internat. Soc. Neuroimmunomodulation, N.Y. Acad. Scis. Avocations: chess, reading, basketball, swimming. Fax: +649-3737499. E-mail: s.vlajkovic@auckland.ac.nz. Office: PB 92019, U Auckland Dept Physiology, Auckland 1001, New Zealand

VLAMOS, PANAYIOTIS, research mathematician, educator; b. Athens, Greece, Mar. 3, 1970; s. Michalis and Maria (Kalogeropoulou) V. BSc in Math., U. Athens, 1991; PhD in Math., Nat. Tech. U. Athens, 1997. Instr. math. Greek Open U., Athens, 2000. Author: Mathematical Analysis, 1998; co-author: Euclidean Geometry for the Lyceum, 1999, Mathematics for the First Class of the Second Cycle for the Technical High School, 1999; co-author (ednl. software) Mathematical Software for the Lyceum, 1999. Mem. Am. Math. Soc., Greek Math. Soc., Edinburgh Math. Soc. Greek Orthodox. Avocations: basketball, chess, reading. Home: 40 Riga Ferraiou St, GR-18344 Athens-Moshato Greece Office: 100 Makriyianni Str, GR-18345 Athens-Moshato Greece

VLASE, IOAN-OREST, electrical engineer; b. Brasov, Romania, Jan. 4, 1955; arrived in Germany, 1991; s. Ilarion and Aglaia (Ungureanu) V.; m. Stanca-Mihaela Jurescu, July 23, 1977; 1 child, Anca-Monica. Degree in elec. engring., Poly. Inst. Bucharest, Romania, 1980, PhD in Elec. Engring., 1991; MS in Math., U. Bucharest, 1989. Devel. engr. Nat. Inst. Automation, Bucharest, 1980-82; rsch. engr. Poly. Inst. Bucharest, 1982-83, sci. asst., 1983-90, lectr., 1990-91; rschr. Tech. U. Darmstadt, Germany, 1991-97, German Plastic Inst., Darmstadt, 1997-99, Tech. U. Darmstadt, 1999—; asst. prof. Poly. Inst. Bucharest, 1991—. Author: Numerical Methods in Electromagnetics, 1989, Electromagnetic Shielding in the Technical of Heavy Currents, 1990; contbr. articles to profl. jours. Sub-lt. Romanian armed forces, 1974-75. Mem. Internat. Compumag Soc., IEEE (mem. tech. com. on computer graphics, mem. Computer Soc., Electromagnetic Compatibility Soc., Power Engring. Soc.), N.Y. Acad. Scis., Assn. for Computing Machinery. Christian Orthodox. Achievements include development of SimDur computation program of high voltage insulators of epoxy resin; development of miniaturized high-voltage sources based on planar technologies; high frequency resonance analysis of high-voltage transformers; contribution to design of the high-speed d.c. circuit breakers for underground railway in Bucharest. Avocations: history, personal computers. Home: Grafenstrasse 33, D-64283 Darmstadt Germany Office: Tech U High Voltage Lab, Landgraf-Georg-Str 4, D-64283 Darmstadt Germany

VLASINOVA, HELENA, botanist; b. Lomnicenad Popelkou, Czech Republic, Oct. 7, 1953; d. Emil Chalupa and Helene (Herberova) Chalupova; m. Mojmir Vlasin; children: Svetlana, Ondrej. Diploma Agr. Engring., Mendel U. Agr. and Forest, Brno, Czech Republic, 1979. Lab. U. Botanical Garden, Brno, 1979-85; rschr. dept. botany and plant physiology Mendels U., Brno, 1985—. Avocations: permacultural gardening, goat keeping, drawing. Office: Mendels Agrl Univ, Zemedelska 1, CZ-61300 Brno Czech Republic

VLASOV, ANDREI DANILOVICH, physical chemist, philosophy historian; b. Moscow, Russia, May 3, 1932; s. Daniil Vasilievich and Tatiana Alexandrovna (Zelenetskaya) V.; m. Lidiya Ivanovna Ribakova, Apr. 30, 1955 (div. Sept. 30, 1966); children: Nadezhda, Vladimir; m. Lubov Timofeevna Kabanova, Nov. 4, 1966; children: Timofei, Danil. DSc, Moscow Steel Inst., 1957, Moscow Marxism-Leninism U., 1961; cand. Chem. Scis. (PhD), Gen. and Inorganic Chem Inst., Moscow, 1964; sr. rsch. fellow in Phys. Chemistry, All Union Rsch Inst Chem Tech, Moscow, 1966. Engr. Spl. Space Design Bur., Moscow, Russia, 1957-58; rsch. fellow All Union Rsch. Inst. Chem. Tech., Moscow, 1958-71; sr. rsch. fellow Inst. Chem. Physics, Moscow, 1971-74; rsch. group chief All-Union Rsch. Inst for Metrology Svc., Moscow, 1974-83; sr. rsch. fellow All-Union Rsch. Inst for Surface and Vacuum Properies, Moscow, 1983-90; leading rsch. fellow Moscow Aviation Inst., 1990—; cons. Moscow Aviation Inst., 1989-90. Author: (books) Adventure of Objective Reality, 1993, Dictionary of Hegel's Philosophy, vol. I Phenomenology of Spirit, 1997, vol. II Science of Logic, 2000; contbr. 50 articles to profl. jours; inventor Calcium-thermal zirconium prodn., 1970; co-inventor Spl. application, 1965. Grantee Internat. Sci. Found., 1994. Mem. N.Y. Acad. Scis. Avocations: photography, fruit-growing, bicycling, skiing. Home: Kashirskoye Shosse 48, Korp2, Kv 2 115409 Moscow Russia Office: Moscow Aviation Inst, Volokalamskoye shosse 4, 125871 Moscow Russia

VLASOV, GENNADII KONSTANTINOVICH, physicist, researcher; b. Karaganda, Kazakhstan, USSR, Apr. 3, 1939; s. Konstantin Artemovich and Lydia (Semenova) V.; m. Nina Ivanovna Kravchenko, Sept. 25, 1963; 1 child, Olga. Diploma, Frontier Guard's Mil. Sch., Moscow, 1959, State U., Kiev, Ukraine, 1966; PhD in theoretical and Math. Physics, Inst. Physics, Kiev, 1970. Chief radio-comms. Frontier Guard's Staff, Khorog, USSR, 1959-60; jr. sci. worker Inst. Physics, Kiev, 1970-73; sr. sci. worker in physics Ukraine Acad. Scis., Kiev, 1973-84; sr. sci. worker Space Rsch. Inst., Moscow, 1989-92; leading sci. worker Ctr. for Program Studies, Moscow, 1992—; head project Astrophysika, Moscow, 1991-97; lectr. Ukrainian Soc. Knowledge, Kiev, 1972-82. Capt. USSR Armed Forces. Patentee in field. Avocations: composing and singing, swimming, exercise, piano, jazz. Home: PO Box 75, ul M Tcvetaevoi 1-121, 249810 Tarusa Kaluzhskaya Russia Office: Ctr for Program Studies, ul Profsoyuznaya 84/32, 117810 Moscow Russia

VLASOV, IVAN VESELINOV, microelectronic engineer; b. Sofia, Bulgaria, Oct. 20, 1967; s. Veselin Ivanov and Dafinka Ivanova (Kostadinova) V. Degree in engring., Tech. U., Sofia, 1993. Constructor Optico-mech. Plant, Sofia, 1993-96, Videoprint Svc. for Lineprinter, Sofia, 1996—. Avocations: collecting stamps, light music. Home: bul Bukston bl 13 vch A ap5, 1618 Sofia Bulgaria Office: Videoprint Svc Lineprinter, Telerig 10 kv Bojana, Sofia Bulgaria

VLASSOV, VALERI VLADIMIROVICH, science researcher; b. Moscow, May 5, 1956; s. Vladimir Georgievich and Valentina Mihailovna (Bolshakova) V.; m. Olga Alexandrovna Zabenina, Aug. 9, 1977; 1 child, Anton. BA, Moscow Aviation Inst., 1977, MS, 1979, PhD, 1986. R&D engr. Moscow Aviation Inst., 1979-82, scientist, 1982-86, chief of group, 1986-93; chief of dept. BIOR, Moscow, 1993-94; rschr. INPE, S.J. Campos, Brazil, 1994—; asst. prof. MAI, 1990-93; cons. Internat. Ctr. COSMOS, Moscow, 1991-92; vice-dir. R&D dir. Thermal Ctr., Moscow, 1992-93; adj. prof. ITA/ME, S.J. Campos, Brazil, 1994-98; leader of thermal group, 1997—. Author: (software) Optimization of Thermal Systems, 1982-96, (tutorials) Design of Thermal Devices, 1986-92; contbr. articles to profl. jours. Mem. AIAA, ABME. Avocations: sports, painting. E-mail: vlassov@dem.inpe.br. Fax: 55-012-3456226. Office: INPE/DEM, Ave dos Astronautas 1758, 12227010 SJ Campos SP, Brazil

VLASSOV, VASILY VICTOROVICH, physician; b. Novosibirsk, Russia, June 15, 1953; s. Victor Vasilievich and Olga Ivanovna (Smirnova) V.; m. Irina Alexandrovna Shmaevskaya, Nov. 23, 1973; 1 child, Anna. MD, Mil. Med. Acad., Saint Petersburg, 1976, DSc, 1993. Air surgeon Air Forces, Gomel, Belarus, 1976-79; head dept. clin. physiology Air Force Hosp., Irkutsk, Russia, 1980-88; head dept. aerospace medicine Saratov (Russia) Mil. Med. Faculty, 1988-95; head dept. philosophy and social scis. Saratov State Med. U., 1995—; dir. Agaton, Saratov; mem. Russian Nat. Com. Bioethics, Moscow; chair Russian br. Cochrane Collaboration. Mem. Russian Med. Assn. Avocation: painting. Home: PO Box 1528, 410601 Saratov Russia Office: Med U, B Kazachia 112, 410600 Saratov Russia

VLASTOU, CATHERINE, plastic surgeon; b. Athens, Greece, Sept. 2, 1945; came to U.S., 1972; d. Constantin and Maria (Kostoglou) V. MD, U. Athens, 1969. Bd. cert. surgery, plastic surgery. Resident in gen. surgery Buffalo Gen. Hosp., 1972-73, Mt. Sinai Hosp., Cleve., 1973-76; resident in plastic surgery Case Western Res. U., Cleve., 1976-78, instr. plastic surgery, 1978-80, asst. prof. plastic surgery, 1980-95; pvt. practice Athens, 1990—. Fellow ACS; mem. Am. Soc. Plastic and Reconstructive Surgeons, Am. Soc. Surgery of the Hand, Am. Soc. Reconstructive Microsurgery, Internat. Microsurg. Soc., Hellenic Soc. for Reconstructive Microsurgery (pres. 1994), Hellenic Soc. Surgery of Hand (pres.-elect 1996, pres. 1997). Home: 6 V Ipirou St, 15237 Athens Filothei, Greece Office: 105 7 Vas Sofias Ave, 11521 Athens Greece

VLAVIANOS, HARIS, poet; b. Athens, June 18, 1957; s. Alexander Vlavianos and Aglae (Chartofilakos) Moncada; m. Yanna Zour, Sept. 9, 1987 (div. 1990); 1 child, Alexander; m. Katerina Schina, June 19, 1993; 1 child, Irene. BS, Bristol U., 1979; M in Philosophy, Oxford U., 1984, PhD, 1988. Tutor history Oxford U., 1984-88; prof. history Am. Coll. Greece, 1989-96; poetry editor Nefeli Pubs., Athens, 1991—. Author: The Angel of History, 1999, Adieu, 1996, Another Country, 1994, The Nostalgia of the Skies, 1991, Greece 1941-1949: From Resistance to Civil War, 1992, (Greek translations) Walt Whitman: Selected Poems, 1986, Ezra Pound: Hugh Selwyn Mauberley, 1987, Ezra Pound: Draft & Fragments, 1991, Wallace Stevens: Adagia, 1993, John Ashbery: Self Portrait in a Convex Mirror, 1995, William Blake: The Marriage of Heaven and Hell, 1997, Carlo Goldoni: The Venetian Twins, 1997; editor: Poetry, 1991—. Recipient Poetry award Hellenic Found., 1988; scholar Onassis Found., 1984-88, Brit. Coun., 1984-88; grantee Rockefeller Found., 1999. Mem. Greek Soc. Writers. Home: 136 Stratigou Dagli St, 11145 Athens Greece

VLEUGELS, MICHEL PETRONELLA, physician; b. Maastricht, Netherlands, Nov. 4, 1951; s. Hubertus and Maria Moes V.; m. Hendrica Verheul, July 15, 1978 (Jan. 1990); children: Renske, Ardi, Tessa; m. Helena van Sambeek, Dec. 2, 1993; children: Myrte, Romy. B of Medicine, Nymegen U., The Netherlands, 1973, MD, 1975, PhD, 1984; MD, Utrecht U., The Netherlands, 1977; postgrad., Royal Inst. of Amsterdam, The Netherlands, 1978. Resident tng. tropical medicine St. Johns Gasthuis, Hoorn, The Netherlands, 1977-78; med. officer-in-charge Turiani Hosp., Tanzania, 1979-82; tng. for gynecologist St. Joseph Hosp., Eindhoven, The Netherlands, 1983-87; tng. for gynecology U. Hosp., Utrecht, The Netherlands, 1987-88; dep. gynecology Partnership Gynaecologists Hilversum Streekziekenhuis,

Hilversum, The Netherlands, 1988-90, ptnr., 1990; jr. cons. St. Willibrordus Hosp., Deurne, The Netherlands; dir. Turiani Hosp., Tanzania, 1979-82; co-dir. Registrar Tng. Gynecology Canisius Wilhelmina Hosp., Nijmegen, 1998—; presenter workshops in field. Contbr. articles to profl. jours. Mem. Dutch Soc. Med. Specialists, Dutch Soc. Ob/Gyn, Dutch Soc. for Ultrasound, Dutch Soc. Gynecol. Endoscopy, European Soc. of Human Reprodn. and Embryology, European Soc. for Gynaecol. Endoscopy, Internat. Soc. Gynecol. Endoscopy, others. Roman Catholic. Avocations: sailing, piano, snow skiing. Office: Canisius Wilhelmina Hosp, Ob/Gyn Weg Door Jonkerbo100, 6500 GS Nijmegen The Netherlands

VLK, MILOSLAV, archbishop; b. Lišnice, Czechoslovakia, May 17, 1932. Student, Faculty of Philosophy, Charles U., Prague, Czechoslovakia, 1955-60, Faculty of Theology, Litoměřice, Czechoslovakia, 1964-68. Ordained priest Roman Cath. Ch., 1968. Archivist Trebon and Jindrichuv Hradec, 1960-61, Ceské Budejovice, 1961-64, Czechoslovak State Bank, Prague, 1986-88; sec. to Roman Cath. Bishop of Ceské Budejovice, 1968-71; priest Laziste and Rozmital pod Tremsinem, 1971-78; denied permission to work as priest, 1978; window cleaner Prague, 1978-86; parish priest Sumava Mtns., 1989-90; consecrated bishop of Ceske Budejovice, 1990-91, archbishop of Prague, 1991—; elevated to cardinal Roman Cath. Ch., 1994—; mem. Consilium Conferentiarum Episcopalium Europae, 1990, pres., 1993—, Pontificium Consilium pro Dialogo cum non Credentibus, 1991-93, Pontificium Consilium de Communicationibus Socialibus, 1994—, Congregatio pro Ecclesiis Orientalibus, 1994—. Contbr. articles to profl. jours. Office: Archibiskupství prazské, Hradcanské nam 16/56, 119 02 Prague 1, Czech Republic*

VLOKH, IRYNA JOSIPIVNA, medical university administrator; b. Lviv, Ukraine, Aug. 1, 1941; d. Josip and Sophia Stas; m. Orest Vlokh, Aug. 10, 1961; 1 child, Rostyslav Orestovich. Psychiatrist, Med. U., Lviv, 1964; PhD, Ukrainian Acad., Kiev, 1992; prof., Ministry of Higher Edn., Kiev, 1993; academician, High Acad. Edn., Kiev, 1993. Psychiatrist Mental Hosp., Lviv, 1965-78; asst. Chair of Psychiatry, Lviv, 1977-82, docent, 1983; head Course of Psychiatry, Lviv, 1989-91, Chair of Psychiatry and Med. Psychology, Lviv, 1991—; DMS Lviv Med. U., 1992; prof. academician Lviv Med. U. H.S. Edn., 1993; dir. Western med. region dept. Ukrainian H.S. Acad. Edn., 1993. Author: (sci. manual) Post-Graduate Specializing Course, 1987, (handbook) Psychopatologic Syndromes in the Clinics of Inner Diseases, 1997, Directory of Therapy in Psychic Diseases, 1998, Lectures on Psychology for Foreign Students, 1999; mem. editl. bd. Psychiatria Danubina, 1997, Dir. of Therapy in Psychic Diseases, 1998; contbr. articles to profl. jours. Mem. Trade-Union, Lviv Med. U., 1982; academician Ukrainian H.S. Edn., 1993. Recipient award of Yaroslav Mudriy Ukrainian Acad., 1997, silver medal and Diploma of IBC, Cambridge, 1998. Mem. Ukrainian Assn. Psychosocial Rehab. (dir. 1997), Administry of Psychiatrists of Ukraine, Danubian Psychiat. Assn. (adminstrv. bd. 1995), World Coun. of Psychotherapy, World Assn. Psychosocial Rehab., N.Y. Acad. Scis. (academician 1995), All-Ukrainian Assn. Psychosocial Rehabilitation (pres. 1998), German and Polish Assn. Psychiatrists, Assn. European Psychiatrists, World Phsychiat. Assn., Internatl. Counc. of Psych., 1998. Greek-Catholic. Avocations: music, art, literature, slalom. Home: 22A Yaroslavenska St Apt 17, 290026 Lviv Ukraine Office: Med U, 69 Pekarska, 290021 Lviv Ukraine

VLOKH, OREST-STEPAN GRYGOROVICH, physicist; b. Lviv-Vynnyky, Ukraine, July 2, 1934; s. Grygoriy Oleksiyovich and Olga Stepanivna (Kiyak) V.; m. Aug. 10, 1961; 1 child, Rostislav Orestovich. Physicist, Ivan Franko State U., Lviv, 1957, Cand. Phys.-Math. Scis., 1963; PhD, USSR Acad/Inst. Crystallograph, Moscow, 1979. Asst. prof. Ivan Franko State U., Lviv, 1963-65, docent, 1965-79, head dept. nonlinear optics, 1979-95; dir. Spl. Constructive Bur. Modulator, Lviv, 1982-85, Inst. Phys. Optics, Lviv, 1992—; dir. Western Sci. Ctr. of Ukrainian Acad. Scis. of Higher Edn., Lviv, 1997; creator Tng. of Engring./Rsch. Specialization Optoelectronic Implements and Sys., 1979, Tng. of Radiation Ecology Specialists, 1990, Sci. Sch. Crystal Optics and Structural Phase Transition; chief Spl. Rada of Doctors Dissertations Optics, Lazer Physics. Author: Phenomena of Space Dispersion in Parametric Crystal Optics; editor in chief Ukrainian Jour. Phys. Optics, 2000; contbr. articles to profl. jours. Dep. Ukrainian Parliament, Kyiyv, 1990-94; 1st chief Civic-Polit. West Ukrainian Region Orgn. "RUKH", Lviv, 1989; head Lviv Province Orgn. of Dem. Party of Ukraine, 1991. Recipient Gold medal, Moscow, 1980, Diploma for electrogyration discovery, Moscow, 1980, Honored Diploma for invention in sci., Kyiyv, 1981, Honored Rep. of Sci. and Tech. of Ukraine, 1991, Order Zazaslugy for merits III Degree, Pres. of Ukraine, 1997, silver medal and Diploma of IBC, Cambridge, 1998, awd. of St. Volodymyr/Ukrainian Higher Edn. Acad. of Scis., 1998. Mem. Phys. Soc., Shevchenko Sci. Soc., Internat. Union Crystallography, Internat. Soc. Optical Engring., N.Y. acad. Scis. Greek Catholic. Avocations: poetry, art, sport, yachta, slalom, Alpinism. Email: VlokhIFO@ifo.lviv.ua. Home: 22A Yaroslavenka St Apt 17, 790026 Lviv Ukraine Office: Inst of Phys Optics, 23 Dragomanov St, 790005 Lviv Ukraine

VOCELKA, KARL GERHARD, university educator; b. Vienna, Austria, May 23, 1947; s. Karl J. and Helene (Banar) V.; m. Sylvia E. Zeidler, Mar. 17, 1976 (div. 1986). PhD, U. Vienna, 1971. Univ. asst. U. Vienna, 1972-78, univ. prof., 1978—; vis. prof. Viennese dept. Stanford U., 1980-87, Midwest Consortium for Studies Abroad, Vienna, 1987—. Author: Rudolf II u seine Zeit, 1986, K.U.K. Karikaturen, 1986, Trümmerjahre Wien, 1985, Verfassung oder Konkordat, 1978, Die Lebenswelt der Habsburger: Kultur- und Mentalitatsgeschichte einer Familie, 1997, Die private Welt der Habsburger: Leben und Alltag einer Familie, 1998. Recipient Akademie der Wissensch Böhlau prize, Vienna, 1982, Sandoz prize, 1985, Förderungs prize, Vienna, 1988. Mem. Inst. Österreichische Geschichtsforschung. Mem. Green Party. Home: Ledergasse 33/12, A-1080 Vienna Austria Office: Inst Osterreichische Geschichsforschung, Dr Karl Luegerring 1, A-1010 Vienna Austria

VODOPYANOV, LEV KONSTANTINOVICH, physicist; b. Tomsk, Russia, Aug. 28, 1931; s. Konstantin Alexeevich and Felitsiana Ignat'evna (Vergunas) V.; m. Irina Vasil'ovna Lebedeva, Apr. 1952 (div. 1967); 1 child, Konstantin; m. Inna Cladimirovna Kucherenko, Sept. 17, 1968; children: Kinstantin, Tatiana. Grad., Moscow U., 1954; PhD, Lebedev Phys. Inst., Moscow, 1962, DS, 1975. Jr. rschr. Lebedev Phys. Inst., Moscow, 1955-58, rschr., 1962-63, leading rschr., prof., 1993—; vis. rschr. Faculty Scis. Paris, 1967, UCLA, 1973; vis. prof. Simon Fraser U., Vancouver, Can., 1992-93. Contbr. articles to profl. jours. Grantee Can. Govt. Fgn. Rels., 1992, Russian Found. Basic Rsch., Moscow, 1994, 97; vis. rsch. fellow London U., 1962-63. Mem. Russian Phys. Soc. Avocations: skiing, cross country skiing, hunting, fishing. Home: 50 Frunzenskaya naberejnaya, 119270 Moscow Russia Office: PN Lebedev Phys Inst, 53 Leninski Prospect, 117924 Moscow Russia

VOEGELS, RICHARD L., otolaryngologist, researcher; b. Sao Paulo, Brazil, Dec. 22, 1966; s. Dietrich E. and Ana M. (Silveira) V.; m. Daniela F. Farina, Feb. 17, 1995; 1 child, Julia Farina. MD, U. Sao Paulo, 1990, PhD, 1999. Asst. physician U. Sao Paulo Hosp. and Clinics, 1993-97, chief of otolarynlogy infirmary, 1997—; prof. U. Sao Paulo Med. Sch., 1999—. Contbr. articles to profl. jours. Mem. Am. Acad. Otolaryngology, European Rhinologic Soc., N.Y. Acad. Scis. Avocations: tennis, soccer. E-mail: voegels@attglobal.net. Home: Ap 61-B, Rua Iubatinga 145, 05716110 Sao Paulo Brazil Office: U Sao Paulo Med Sch, Rua Pedroso Alvareuja 1255, 04531021 Sao Paulo Brazil

VOELKER, HANS-ULLRICH, physician; b. Frankenberg, Sachsen, Germany, Jan. 28, 1972; s. Gunther and Andrea (Schneider) V. German med. qualify cert. Mem. workgroup "compartment syndrome" Mil. Hosp., Ulm, Germany, 1996—, asst. dr. dept. pathology, 1999—. 2nd lit. German Fed. Armed Forces, 1996—. Mem. German Soc. Wound Healing (leader working group "pressure sore" 1997—), German Assn. Mil. Medicine. Avocations: private aviation, reading, biking, medical investigation.

VOELKER, STEFAN HUGO, lawyer; b. Stuttgart, Baden, Germany, Nov. 17, 1960; s. Hugo and Anneliese (Brenner) V. D of Law, U. Tuebingen, Germany, 1989. Lectr. in law Eberhard-Karls U., Tuebingen, 1986-89; atty. Bruckhaus, Duesseldorf, Germany, 1989-91, Gleiss Lutz Hootz Hirsch, Stuttgart, Germany, 1991—; lectr. in law Export Acad., Reutlingen, Germany, 1994—. Author: Freedom to Receive Service Under European Community Law, 1990, Pricing Law. The Law of Price Indication and Price-Related Advertising, 1996; co-author: Advertising Law in Practice, 1999, Professional Handbook European Economic Area, 3rd edit., 1994; contbr. articles to profl. publs. Mem. German Soc. of Intellectual Property and Copyright, Internat. Bar Assn., Internat. Trademark Assn. Office: Gleiss Lutz Hootz Hirsch, Maybachstrasse 6, 70469 Stuttgart Baden, Germany

VOGEL, CHRISTOPH, management consultant; b. Bochum, Germany, July 20, 1968; s. Friedhelm and Antonie (Schmitz) V.; m. Carina Felicitas Koenig, Nov. 15, 1994; children: Simon Benedict, Helena Maria, Aaron Johannes. Diploma in bus. engring., U. Kaiserslautern, Germany, 1992, D in Bus. Adminstrn. and Econs., 1999. Rsch. asst. U. Kaiserlautern, Germany, 1992-97; mgmt. cons. Siemens AG, Munich, 1997—. Mem. Verband Deutscher Witschaftsingenieure e.V., Alumni Assn. of the Kaiserslauterer Wirtschaftsingenieure (pres. 1996—). Avocations: soccer, philosophy, politics, research and technology policy. Home: Johann Hackl Ring 28, 85630 Grasbrunn Bavaria, Germany Office: Siemens AG Mgmt Consulting, St Martin Str 76, 81541 Munich Bavaria, Germany

VOGEL, CLAUS, Indology educator; b. Saarbrücken, Germany, July 6, 1933; s. Ernst-August and Annelise (Lührs) V. PhD, U. Marburg, Germany, 1956; habil., U. Marburg, 1964. State examination in classics. Lectr. in Indian and Tibetan philology U. Marburg, 1964-69, prof., 1969-76; prof. Indology U. Bonn, Fed. Republic Germany, 1976-98; emeritus prof. U. Bonn, 1998; hon. prof. Tibetology, U. Göttingen, Fed. Republic Germany, 1989—. Author: Vagbhata's Astangahrdayasamhita, 1965, The Teachings of the Six Heretics, 1970, Indian Lexicography, 1979; editor: Th. Zachariae, Opera Minora, 1977; contbr. 60 articles to profl. jours. Fellow Royal Asiatic Soc.; mem. German Oriental Soc., Rheno-Westphalian Acad. Letters and Scis. Avocation: model railway. Home: Londoner Strasse 11, 53117 Bonn 1, Germany Office: U Bonn Indologisches Seminar, Regina-Pacis-Weg 7, 53113 Bonn Germany

VOGEL, GERHARD, HANS, pharmacologist, toxicologist; b. Bucarest, Roumania, Sept. 9, 1927; s. Eugen Georg and Emilie Katharina (Sturm) V.; m. Anna Theresia Zoller, Dec. 23, 1988. Pharmacist degree, U. Erlangen, 1951; physician degree, U. Tubingen, 1955; assoc. prof. degree, U. Marburg, 1967; honorary prof. degree, U. Frankfurt, 1979. Resident City Hosp., Heidenheim, Germany, 1956-57; senior scientist endocrinology lab. Dept. of Pharmacology, Hoechst AG, Frankfort, Germany, 1958-69, dir., 1967-78; dir. Pharma Rsch. Experimental Medicine, Hoechst AG, Frankfort, Germany, 1977-79, Pharma Preclinical Evaluation and Devel., Hoechst AG, Frankfort, Germany, 1980-88, Decision Bd. on Pharm. Devel., Hoechst AG, Frankfort, Germany, 1989-90; cons. Pharmaceutical and Medical Rsch. Devel., Ottobrunn, Germany, 1990—; mem. several scientific assns., Germany/USA, 1970—; cons. in drug evaluation and devel. Editor: Drug Discovery and Evaluation: Pharmacological Assays, 1997; contbr. over 100 articles on biomechanics to profl. jours. Home: Ulmenstr 2, D-85521 Ottobrunn Germany Office: Hoechst AG, Bruening Strasse, D-65926 Frankfurt am Main Germany

VÖGEL, HANS-JÖRG, technology researcher, educator; b. Oberstaufen, Germany, Feb. 1, 1968; s. Peter and Rita (Kennerknecht) V. Diploma in engring., Munich U. Tech., 1993. Rschr. Munich U. Tech., 1993-2000, The Fantastic Corp., Manno, Lugano, 2000—. Co-author: GSM-Vermittlung, Dienste & Protokolle in Digitalen Mobilfunknetzen, 1997, 2d edit., 1999, GSM-Global System for Mobile Communication, 1998. Recipient Best Paper award European Wireless Conf., 1999. Mem. IEEE, Corps Vitruvia (pres. 1997—). Avocations: sailing, travel. E-mail: hjv@hjvoegel.de. Office: The Fantastic Corp R&D SA, Via Cantonale, CH-6928 Manno Lugano

VOGEL, HOWARD STANLEY, lawyer; b. N.Y.C., Jan. 21, 1934; s. Moe and Sylvia (Miller) V.; m. Judith Anne Gelb, June 30, 1962; 1 son, Michael S. BA, Bklyn. Coll., 1954; JD, Columbia U., 1957; LLM in Corp. Law, NYU, 1969. Bar: N.Y. 1957, U.S. Supreme Ct. 1964. Assoc. Whitman & Ransom, N.Y.C., 1961-66; with Texaco Inc., 1966-99, gen. atty., 1970-73, assoc. gen. counsel, 1973-81, gen. counsel Tex. Philanthropic Found. Inc., 1979-82; gen. counsel Jefferson Chem. Co. Texaco Chems. Can. Inc., 1973-82; assoc. gen. tax counsel, gen. mgr. adminstr. Texaco Inc., White Plains, N.Y., 1981-99; counsel Allegaert Berger & Vogel LLP, N.Y.C., 1999—; gen. tax counsel Texaco Found. Inc., 1995-99; pres., dir. 169 E. 69th Corp., 1981—. Served to 1st lt. JAGC, U.S. Army, 1958-60. Mem. ABA, Aassn. Bar City N.Y., Fed. Bar Coun., Assn. Ex-Mems. of Squadron A., Princeton Club (N.Y.C.). Home: 169 E 69th St Apt 9D New York NY 10021-5163 Office: 18th Fl 111 Broadway Fl 18 New York NY 10006-1901

VOGEL, ROGER, pharmaceutical consultant, physician; b. Liverpool, Eng., Mar. 21, 1943; came to U.S., 1986; s. Arthur John and Joan Beatrice Mary Vogel; m. Patricia Janet Vogel, Feb. 20, 1969 (dec. Mar. 1991); children: Alexandra, William, Rosie; m. Ellen Ruth Strahlman, July 18, 1993. MB BChir, Univ. Coll. Hosp., London, 1966. Ptnr. Drs. Adams Potts Kirisy and Vogel, Redditch, Eng., 1968-78; sr. house officer Birmingham (Eng.) Midland Eye Hosp., 1978-79; clin. rsch. physician Merck Sharp & Dohme, Hoddeson, Eng., 1979-86; sr. dir. Merck & Co., Phila., 1986-95; pres. Clarity Consulting Group, Rochester, N.Y., 1995-97; v.p. Clinicor Inc., Austin, Tex., 1997—. Contbr. articles to sci. jours. Mem. parish coun. Barnham Parish Coun., Hertfordshire, Eng., 1984, Beoley Parish Coun., Worcestershire, Eng., 1973. Fellow Royal Coll. Physicians; mem. Royal Coll. Surgeons, Royal Coll. Ophthalmology, Am. Acad. Ophthalmology, Assn. for Rsch. in Vision and Ophthalmology. Avocations: violinist, painting, windsurfing. E-mail: rogervogel@aol.com. Office: Clinicor Inc 1717 W 6th St Austin TX 78703-4773

VOGEL, RONALD BRUCE, food products executive, real estate broker; b. Vancouver, Wash., Feb. 16, 1934; s. Joseph John and Thelma Mae (Karker) V.; m. Carol Vandecar, Mar. 16, 1958; children: Joseph S., Rhonda L., Theresa J., Denise R.; m. Donita Dawn Schneider, Aug. 8, 1970 (dec. June 1974); 1 child, Cynthia Dawn. BS in Chemistry, U. Wash., 1959. Glass maker Penberthy Instrument Co., Seattle, 1959-60; lab. technician Gt. Western Malting Co., Vancouver, 1960-62, chief chemist, 1962-67, mgr. corp. quality control, 1967-72, mgr. customer svcs., 1972-77, v.p. customer svcs., 1977-79, v.p. sales, 1979-84, gen. mgr., 1984-89, pres., CEO, 1989-95; ret.; gen. ptnr. Rou Vogel Family Partnership. Chmn. bd. dirs. Columbia Empire Jr. Achievement, Portland, Oreg., 1991-92. With U.S. Army, 1954-56. Recipient numerous awards. Mem. Master Brewers Assn. Am. (pres. 1996), Am. Malting Barley Assn. (chmn. 1984-86, 89-91), Vancouver C. of C. (chmn. 1991-93), Applied Phytologics, Inc. (bd. dirs.). Office: 54 317 NE 104th Ave Vancouver WA 98664

VOGEL, SILVIA ANGELIKA EMMA, mathematician, educator; b. Brotterode, Thuringia, Germany, Feb. 1, 1951; d. Karl and Marie (Baldauf) Rohmeiss; m. Jürgen Vogel, Mar. 22, 1975; children: Daniel, Andreas. Dr.rer.nat., Tech. U., Dresden, Germany, 1977; Dr.rer.nat. habilitation, Tech. U., Ilmenau, Germany, 1991. Asst. lectr. Tech. U. Dresden, 1976-77; asst. lectr. Tech. U. Ilmenau, Germany, 1977-92, prof. probability theory and math. stats., 1992—.

VOGEL, VICTOR GERALD, medical educator, researcher; b. Bethlehem, Pa., Mar. 14, 1952; s. Victor Gerald Jr. and Margaret Moser (Smith) V.; m. Saralyn Sue Schaffner, June 25, 1977; children: Heather Marie, Christiaan Keith. Diplomate Am. Bd. Internal Medicine, Am. Bd. Preventive Medicine, Nat. Bd. Med. Examiners. Resident in internal medicine Balt. City Hosps., 1978-81; fellow in med. oncology Johns Hopkins Oncology Ctr., Balt., 1983-86; Andrew W. Mellon fellow Johns Hopkins Sch. Hygiene Pub. Health, Balt., 1984-86; asst. prof. medicine and epidemiology U. Tex./M.D. Anderson Cancer Ctr., Houston, 1986-93, assoc. prof. clin. cancer prevention, 1993-95; asst. prof. epidemiology U. Tex. Sch. Pub. Health, Houston, 1987-95; prof. medicine and epidemiology U. Pitts. Cancer Inst./Magee-Women's Hosp., 1996—, dir. comprehensive breast cancer program, 1996—; epidemiologist Tex. breast screening project Am. Cancer Soc., 1986-93; mem. data and safety monitoring bd. Women's Health Initiative, NIH, 1994—; bd. dirs. Nat. Surg. Adjuvant Breast and Bowel Project Found., Inc., 1997—, AMC Cancer Ctr., Denver, 1996—. Contbr. articles to profl. jours. Founding mem. Nat. Surg. adjuvant Breast and Bowel Project Found., Inc. Served with USPHS, 1981-83. Named Med. Vol. of Yr., Am. Cancer Soc., 1983, award 1987, career devel. award, 1990-93; fellow Susan G. Komen Breast Cancer Found., 1990-93. Fellow Am. Coll. Preventive Medicine, ACP; mem. Am. Soc. Clin. Oncology, Am. Soc. Preventive Oncology, Christian Med. and Dental Soc., Am. Assn. Cancer Rsch. Republican. Presbyn. Avocation: flying. Office: University of Pittsburgh Cancer Inst Magee-Womens Hosp 300 Halket St Rm 3524 Pittsburgh PA 15213-3108

VOGEL, WILLIAM DICKERMAN, telecommunications executive; b. N.Y.C., Oct. 21, 1961; s. Ralph B. and Mabel (Harris) V.; m. Mary Anne Taylor. AB, Harvard Coll., 1984. CFA. Rsch. asst. George W. Ball, Princeton, N.J., 1986; corp. search cons. Korn/Ferry Internat., Hong Kong, 1987; equity rsch. analyst The Boston Co., Boston, 1988-93; telecom. analyst Nat. West Securities, N.Y.C., 1993-95; sr. v.p., head telecomm. equity rsch. Dillon, Read & Co., N.Y.C., 1996; mng. dir., head telecomm. equity rsch. NationsBanc Montgomery Securities, N.Y.C., 1997-98; sr. v.p. strategic planning Winstar Comm., N.Y.C., 1999-2000; chmn., CEO Ticket-Planet.com, 2000—. Author: Strategic Assessment, Regional Bell Telephone Cos., 1994. Trustee St. Paul's Sch., Concord, N.H. Mem. Assn. Investment Mgmt. and Rsch., Boston Security Analysts Soc., N.Y. Soc. Security Analysts, New Eng. Hist. and Geneal. Soc. Avocations: tennis, skiing, mountain biking, geneal. rsch.

VOGEL, ZVI, scientist; b. Gedera, Israel, Dec. 31, 1940; s. Shlomo and Kathe (Kramer) V.; m. Tikva Kivity, Mar. 30, 1996; children: Eyal, Orit, Noga. MSc, Hebrew U., Jerusalem, 1963; PhD, Weizmann Inst. Sci., Rehovot, Israel, 1970. Sr. scientist Weizmann Inst. Sci., 1973-75, assoc. prof., 1978-96, prof., 1996—; vis. assoc. NIH, Bethesda, Md., 1975-78, vis. scientist, 1981-82, 91-93. Editl. bd. Jour. Neurosci. Rsch., 1997. Mem. Internat. Soc. Neurochemistry, Soc. Neurosci. Office: Weizmann Inst Sci, Dept Neurobiology, 76100 Rehovot Israel

VOGELEY, CLYDE EICHER, JR., engineering educator, artist, consultant; b. Pitts., Oct. 19, 1917; s. Clyde Eicher and Eva May (Reynolds) V.; m. Blanche Wormington Peters, Dec. 15, 1947; children: Eva Anne, Susan Elizabeth Steele. BFA in Art Edn., Carnegie Mellon U., 1940; BS in Engring. Physics, U. Pitts., 1944, PhD in Math., 1949. Art supr. Pub. Sch. System, Spingdale, Pa., 1940-41; rsch. engr. Westinghouse Rsch. Labs., East Pitts., Pa., 1944-54; adj. prof. math. U. Pitts., 1954-64; sr. scientist Bettis Atomic Power Lab., West Mifflin, Pa., 1956-59; supr. tech. tng. Bettis Atomic Power Lab., West Mifflin, 1959-71; mgr. Bettis Reactor Engring. Sch., West Mifflin, 1971-77, dir., 1977-92; cons. U.S. Dept. Energy, Washington, 1992-95; cons. Bettis Atomic Power Lab., W. Mifflin, 1954-56; U.S. Navy Nuclear Power Schs., Mare Island, Calif., Bainbridge, Md., 1959-69. Author: (grad. sch. course) Non-linear Differential Equations, 1954; (rev. text) Ordinary Differential Equations, Rev. edit. 5, Shock and Vibration Problems, Rev. Edit. 6, 1991; rsch. report distributed to Brit., Can. and U.S. Govts. for use in design of airborne radar systems, 1944; oil painting represented in permanent Latrobe collection; acrylics, water colors and Christmas card designs in several pvt. collections; oil painting included in Barbara H. Nakle's A Unique Vision of Art, 1997, water color included in collection Superior Ct. of Pa. 1999. Pres., trustee Whitehall (Pa.) Pub. Libr., 1985. Recipient letter of commendation naval reactors br. USN, 1992. Mem. IEEE (life), Am. Phys. Soc., Assoc. Artists Pitts. (hon.), Pitts. Watercolor Soc., Sigma Xi, Sigma Pi Sigma, Sigma Tau. Presbyterian. Achievements include patents for Automatic Continuous Wave Radar Tracking System, Modulating Signals Passing Along Ridged Waveguides, Ridged Waveguide Matching Device, Method for Joining Several Ridged Waveguides, Antenna Feed Modulation Unit, others. Home: 185 Peach Dr Pittsburgh PA 15236-2145

VOGELGESANG, SANDRA LOUISE, business executive, writer; b. Canton, Ohio, July 27, 1942; d. Glenn Wesley and Louise (Forry) Vogelgesang; m. Geoffrey Ernest Wolfe, July 4, 1982. BA, Cornell U., 1964; MA, Tufts U., 1965, MA in Law and Diplomacy, 1966, PhD, 1971. With Dept. State, Washington, 1975-97, policy planner for sec. state and European Bur., 1975-80, dir. Econ Policy Office, Orgn. Econ. Coop. and Devel., 1981-82, econ. minister U.S. Embassy, Ottawa, Can., 1982-86, dep. asst. sec. Internat. Orgn. Affairs Bur., 1986-89; dep. asst. adminstr. Office Internat. Activities Environ. Protection Agy., Washington, 1989-92; with Dept. State, Washington, 1992; sr. policy advisor Agy. for Internat. Devel., 1993; U.S. amb. to Nepal Dept. State, Washington, 1994-97; pres. Everest Assocs. and Himalaya, 1997—; bd. dirs. Ctr. for Econ. Devel. and Population Activities; chair women and conservation com. World Wildlife Fund, 1997-98, nat. coun., 1998—, mem., 1999—; bd. advisors Am.'s Soc., N.Y.C., 1986-89; mem. Pres.'s Coun. of Cornell Women, Cornell U., 1998—; adv. com. Dept. of Treasury com. on Internat. Child Labor Enforcement, 1999—. Author: Long Dark Night of the Soul, The American Intellectual Left and the Vietnam War, 1974, American Dream-Global Nightmare: The Dilemma of U.S. Human Rights Policy, 1980. Bd. dirs. Crafts Ctr., 1999—. Recipient Meritorious Service awards, 1973, 74, 82, 83, 86, Disting. Honor award, 1976 Dept. State, Pres.' Disting. Service award, 1985. Mem. Council on Fgn. Relations. E-mail: everest.associates@erols.com. Office: 9009 Charred Oak Dr West Bethesda MD 20817-1923

VOGEL-SPROTT, MURIEL DORIS, psychology educator, researcher; b. Waterloo, Can., Aug. 20, 1934; d. Henry and Anne Ellen (Stroh) V.; m. David Arthur Sprott, Dec. 16, 1961; children: Anne Ellen, Jane Barry. BA, McMaster U., Can., 1955; MA, U. Toronto, 1957; PhD, 1960. Rsch. assoc. Addiction Rsch. Found., Toronto, Can., 1959-61; asst. prof. Psychology U. Waterloo, Can., 1961-65; assoc. prof., 1965-69, prof., 1969-96, rsch. prof., 1996-97, disting. prof. emerita, 1997—; Author: Alcohol Tolerance and Social Drinking, 1992; contbr. numerous chpts. and rsch. papers in profl. publs. in field. Recipient Rsch. award AA Found. for Traffic Safety, 1988; named Disting. Psychopharacologist, Can. Psychol. Assn., 1988, grantee Govt. and Pvt. agys. in Can. and USA. Fellow APA, Can. Psychol. Assn., Psychonomic Sci. Office: Dept Psychology, University of Waterloo, Waterloo, ON Canada

VOGELZANG, JEANNE MARIE, professional association executive, attorney; b. Hammond, Ind., Apr. 15, 1950; d. Richard and Laura Ann (Vanderaa) Jabaay; m. Nicholas John Vogelzang, May 17, 1971; children: Nick, Adam, Tim. BA, Trinity Christian Coll., Palos Heights, Ill., 1972; MBA, U. Minn., 1981; JD, U. Chgo., 1987. Bar: Ill. 1987; CPA, Ill. Tchr. Timothy Christian H.S., Elmhurst, Ill., 1972-74; tchg. assoc. in fin. U. Minn., Mpls., 1980-81; fin. analyst Quaker Oats Co., Chgo., 1982-84; assoc. Baker & McKenzie, Chgo., 1987-89, Jenner & Block, Chgo., 1989-91; pres., owner J.M. Vogelzang & Assocs., Western Springs, Ill., 1991-99; exec. dir. Structural Engrs. Assn. Ill., Chgo., 1992—, Nat. Coun. Structural Engrs. Assn., Chgo., 1996—; pub., editor Structure mag., 1996—. Mem. jud. code com. Christian Reformed Ch. N.Am., Grand Rapids, Mich., 1991-97; bd. dirs. Austin Christian Law Ctr., Chgo., 1989-92, Barnabas Found., Palos Heights, 1989-95; com. mem. Western Springs Planning Commn., 1991-95, village trustee, 1995-99, chmn. fin. com., chmn. gen. govt. com.; mem. adv. bd. Coll. DuPage Internat. Trade Ctr., Glen Ellyn, Ill., 1992-94; bd. dirs., mem. acad. affairs com., planning com., exec. com. sec. Trinity Christian Coll., 1992-98; mem. trustees' evaluation com. Christian Ref. Ch. N.Am., 1998; treas. The Tower Party of We. Springs, 1999—. Fellow Ill. Lincoln Excellence in Pub. Svc., 1999. Mem. ABA, Am. Soc. Assn. Execs., Ill. Bar Assn., Chgo. Bar Assn. Mem. Christian Reformed Ch. Office: 203 N Wabash Ave Ste 2010 Chicago IL 60601-2418

VOGES, UDO, systems engineer, researcher; b. Aurich, Niedersachsen, Germany, Aug. 3, 1946; s. Friederich and Katharina Voges; m. Barbara Zimmermann; children: Verena, Karsten. Diploma in Math., Ludwig-Maximilians U., Munich, 1971; Dr. Rer. Nat., U. Karlsruhe (Germany), 1989. Rsch. scientist Kernforschungszentrum, Karlsruhe, Germany, 1971-84, UCLA, 1984-85, Forschungszentrum, Karlsruhe, 1985—; cons. European Cmty., Brussels, 1988-95. Author: Software Diversity and Its Modelling, 1989; editor: Software Diversity in Computerized Control Systems, 1988; contbr. articles to profl. jours. Mem. IEEE, Assn. for Computing Machinery, Gesellschaft für Informatik. Avocations: gardening, photography. Office: FZK/IAI, HV Helmholtz-Platz 1, D-76344 Eggenstein Leopold, Germany

VOGES, WOLFGANG GUSTAV JULIUS, sociology, social policy researcher; b. Goslar, Germany, July 29, 1947; m. Gabriele Girnghuber-Voges, Apr. 4, 1986; 2 children. Diploma in ednl. scis., U. Munich, 1975, MSc, 1977; PhD, U. Tuebingen, Germany, 1981; Habilitation, U. Bremen, Germany, 1993. Lectr. dept. social work Sch. Applied Studies, 1978-82; lectr. dept. sociology U. Munich, 1981-83, sr. rschr. dept. sociology, 1983-84; lectr. Acad. for Social Professions, 1985-87; rsch. fellow dept. sociology Free U. Berlin, 1986-88; prof. Inst. Sociology and Ctr. Social Policy Rsch. U. Bremen, 1989—; vis. fellow Inst. for Rsch. on Poverty, U. Wis., Madison, spring 1991, Survey Rsch. Ctr., ISR, U. Mich., Ann Arbor, fall 1992, Ctr. for Urban Affairs and Policy Rsch., Northwestern U., Evanston, Ill., fall 1995, dept. econs. U. Göteborg, Sweden, 1996, Inst. for Sociology, U. Leipzig, 1998-99, CEPS/INSTEAD, Luxembourg, 1999. Editor: Dynamic Approaches to Comparative Social Research. E-mail: wvoges@zes.uni-bremen.de. Office: Univ Bremen Ctr Social Pol, Parkallee 39, 28209 Bremen Germany

VOGLINO, GIANFRANCO LUIGI, biologist; b. Avigliana, Turin, Italy, Nov. 15; s. Giovanni and Agnese Lodovina V.; m. Gallo Joan Cleland, Nov. 15, 1980; children: Simone, Emanuele, Alessandro. Diploma in Biology, U. Turin. Asst. CNR, Rome, 1968-70; maitre de rsch. CNRS, Paris; lab. dir. Sant'Anna Hosp., Turin, 1977—. Lt. Italian army, 1970-72. Avocation: flying hang-gliders. Office: Dept Clin Path/Lab Molecula, Path/Sant'Anna Hp/Corso 60, Turin 10128, Italy

VOGT, CARSTEN, computer scientist; b. Hannover, L Saxony, Germany, Feb. 24, 1961. Dipl., U. Bonn, 1986; Dr., U. Hamburg, 1990. Rschr. FFM/FGAN, Wachtberg, Germany, 1985-90; scientific advisor IBM, Heidelberg, Germany, 1991-93; prof. Fachhochschule U Applied Scis., Cologne, Germany, 1994—. Contbr. articles to profl. jours. Mem. Assn. Computing Machinery, Gesellschaft Info. Office: FH Cologne FB NT, Betzdorfer Str 2, 50679 Cologne NRW, Germany

VOGT, ERICH WOLFGANG, physicist, academic administrator; b. Steinbach, Man., Can., Nov. 12, 1929; s. Peter Andrew and Susanna (Reimer) V.; m. Barbara Mary Greenfield, Aug. 27, 1952; children: Edith Susan, Elizabeth Mary, David Eric, Jonathan Michael, Robert Jeremy. BS, U. Man., 1951, MS, 1952; PhD, Princeton U., 1955; DSc (hon.), U. Man., 1982, Queen's U., 1984; LLD (hon.), U. Regina, 1986; DSc (hon.), Carleton U., 1988, U. B.C., 1999; LLD (hon.), Simon Fraser U., 1996. Rsch. officer Chalk River (Ont.) Nuclear Labs., 1956-65; prof. physics U. B.C., Vancouver, 1965-95, prof. emeritus, 1995—, assoc. dir. TRIUMF Project, 1968-73, dir. TRIUMF Project, 1981-94, v.p. univ., 1975-81; chmn. Sci. Council B.C., 1978-80. Co-editor: Advances in Nuclear Physics, 1968—; Contbr. articles to profl. jours. Decorated officer Order of Can.; recipient Centennial medal of Can., 1967. Fellow Royal Soc. Can., Am. Phys. Soc.; mem. Can. Assn. Physicists (past pres., gold medal for achievement in physics 1988). Office: Triumf, 4004 Wesbrook Mall, Vancouver, BC Canada V6T 2A3

VOGT, EVON ZARTMAN, III (TERRY VOGT), merchant banker; b. Chgo., Aug. 29, 1946; s. Evon Zartman Jr. and Catherine C. (Hiller) V.; m. Mary Hewit Anschuetz, Sept. 26, 1970; 1 child, Elizabeth Christine. AB, Harvard U., 1968; MBA, U. Colo., 1976. Vol., then staff mem. U.S. Peace Corps., Brazil, 1968-72; v.p. Wells Fargo Bank, Sao Paulo, Brazil, 1977-81; mng. dir. Wells Fargo Internat. Ltd., Grand Cayman, 1982-84; mgr. global funding Wells Fargo Bank, San Francisco, 1984-86; pres. ARBI Transnational, Inc., San Francisco, 1986—; also bd. dirs. Arbi Transnational, Inc., San Francisco; bd. dirs. Magtech Ammunition Co., Inc., Las Vegas, 1990—. Bd. dirs. Internat. Diplomacy Coun., San Francisco, 1990-98, 2000—, pres. 1995-97; active No. Calif. C.A.R.E. Found., 1993-95, The Mex. Mus., 1994-96; bd. dirs. World Affairs Coun. of No. Calif., 1996—. Recipient Order of Rio Branco, Brazilian Govt., 1996. Mem. Brazil Soc. No. Calif. (pres. 1989-94), Pan Am. Soc. Calif. (bd. dirs., pres. 1991-94), World Affairs Coun. No. Calif. (bd. dirs.). Office: ARBI Transnational Inc 601 California St San Francisco CA 94108-2805

VOGT, HARTMUT, education educator; b. Berlin, Oct. 18, 1923; s. Alfred and Luise (Thiele) V.; m. Helga Hellebrand, July 16, 1952. State exam for tchr., U. Berlin, 1950, PhD, 1956. State tchr. Berlin, 1950-51; from lectr. to asst. prof. Univs. Berlin, Tübingen, Marburg, Fed. Republic Germany, 1951-70; full prof. U. Dortmund, Fed. Republic Germany, 1970-89, prof. emeritus, 1989—. Author several books in field; contbr. articles to profl. jours. 1st lt. German Air Force, 1941-45. Mem. Flying Club. Avocation: piloting. Home: Otterbach 80 H 18, D-53902 Bad Muenstereifel Germany Office: Univ Dortmund, Emil-Figge-Strasse 50, D-44221 Dortmund 50, Germany

VOGT, MARKUS WALTER, internist, educator; b. Buelach, Zurich, Switzerland, Feb. 14, 1951; s. Walter and Antonia (Frei) V.; m. Paula Christiina Stroemberg, May 22, 1977; children: Kaj-Phillip, Ina-Joanna. MS, Coll. Schwyz, 1971; MD, Med. Sch. Zurich, 1978. Bd. cert. internal medicine and infectious diseases. Intern U. Hosp. Zurich, 1978-79; resident Hosp. Ilanz, Switzerland, 1979-81, U. Hosp. Zurich, 1981-85; rsch. fellow Mass. Gen. Hosp., Boston, 1985-87; asst. prof. U. Zurich Hosp., 1987-92; prof. medicine Med. Clinic County Hosp., Zug, 1992—; cons. Schulthess Clinic, Zurich, 1987—. Contbr. chpts. in books and articles to profl. jours. Capt. Swiss Army Med. Br. Recipient Ludolph Brauer award Internal Medicine Germany, 1988. Mem. Rotary Internat. Roman Catholic. Avocation: fly fishing. Home: Unterleh 15, CH-6300 Zug Switzerland Office: Medical Clinic, Kantonsspital, CH-6300 Zug Switzerland

VOGT, PETER MARIA, surgeon, plastic surgeon; b. Braunschweig, Germany, Jan. 21, 1958; s. Herbert Arthur and Margret (Grobecker) V.; Susanne M. Vogt; children: Christopher, Maryam. MD, J.W. Goethe U., Frankfurt, 1983; PhD, Ruhr U., 1994. Resident in surgery Hannover (Germany) Med. Sch., 1985-91; rsch. fellow in plastic surgery Frankfurt U. Hosp., 1980-84; rsch. fellow in surgery Harvard Med. Sch., Boston, 1991-93; resident, asst. prof. surgery and plastic surgery BG-Kliniken Bergmannsheil, Ruhr U., Bochum, Germany, 1993—. Contbr. articles to profl. jours. Surgeon maj., 1984-85. Recipient Joseph E. Murray award New Eng. Soc. of Plastic and Reconstructive Surgeons, 1993. Mem. N.Y. Acad. Sci., Wound Healing Soc., German Surg. Soc. (Von Langenbeck award 1994), Plastic Surgery Rsch. Coun. (assoc.). Office: Dept Plastic Surgery BG Kliniken, Burkl-de-la-Camp Platz 1, 44789 Bochum Germany

VOGT, PHILIP PATRICK, attorney; b. N.Y.C., Sept. 29, 1955; s. Philip P. and Catherine N. V.; m. Donna Marrone, Nov. 17, 1979; children: Philip J., Erin E., Jennifer L. BA, CUNY, 1977; JD, Brooklyn Law Sch., 1980. Lawyer Alter & Vogt, N.Y.C., 1989—. Roman Catholic. E-mail: pvogt55@aol.com. Office: Altier & Vogt LLC 450 7th Ave New York NY 10123-0101

VOGT-SPIRA, GREGOR, classics educator; b. Freiburg, Germany, May 27, 1956; m. Bettina Rommel. MA, U. Freiburg, 1982, PhD, 1986, D in habilitation, 1993. Lectr. U. Trier, Germany, 1984; asst. prof. U. Konstanz, Germany, 1985-88, U. Freiburg, 1988-94; prof. U. Greifswald, Germany, 1994—; mem. Studienstiftung, Bonn, Germany, 1976-84, Rsch. Ctr. Orality-Literacy, Freiburg, 1988-94. Author: Dramaturgie des Zufalls, 1992; co-author: Plautus Barbarus, 1991; editor: Strukturem der Muendlichkeit, 1990, Rezeption und Identitaet, 1999, I.C. Scaliger Poetics, 5 vols., 1994-2000. Office: Inst for Altertumswissen, Univ Greifswald, D-17487 Greifswald Germany

VOHIDOV, ALISHER, diplomat. Rep. to UN Govt. of Uzbekistan, 1997—. Office: Permanent Mission Uzbekistan 866 U N Plz Rm 326 New York NY 10017-1822*

VOHRA, S. RAY, accountant; b. New Dehli, Dec. 8, 1972; s. Satish C. and Anju Vohra. BBA, Angelo State U., 1995; MPA, U. Tex., 1997. Sr. acct. Deloitte & Touche, LLP, N.Y.C., 1997—. Mem. Big Bros. & Big Sisters, N.Y., 1999. Carr Acad. scholar Carr Found., 1992. Mem. Alpha Chi, Beta Alpha Psi, Mu Delta Mu. Avocations: golf, tennis, painting, sketching, sailing. Fax: 212-436-5977. Office: Deloitte and Touche LLP 2 World Financial Ctr Fl 4 New York NY 10281-1400

VOHRA, SWASTI SHRIMALI, psychology educator; b. New Delhi, July 9, 1964; d. Parmanand and Vijay (Bhaskar) Sharma; m. Pankaj Vohra, Jan. 26, 1992; children: Madhav, Parth. BA in Psychology, U. Delhi, 1985, MA in Applied Psychology, 1987, PhD in Social Psychology, 1991. Asst. prof. dept. psychology Lady Shriram Coll., U. Delhi, 1987-88, asst. prof. dept. applied psychology Gargi Coll., 1989-90; assoc. prof. dept. psychology South Campus, U. Delhi, New Delhi, 1990—; vis. prof. U. Pa., 1988-89, Postgrad. Ctr. Mental Health, N.Y.C., 1993-95, Fordham U., N.Y.C., 1993, Ctr. for Creative Leadership, San Diego, 1993. Contbr. articles to profl. jours. Fellow Int. REBT, N.Y.C., summer 1993. Fellow APA; mem. Soc. Cross Cultural Rsch., Nat. Acad. Psychology India, Indian Acad. Applied Psychology, Delhi Assn. Clin. Psychologists, Internat. Assn. Cross Cultural Psychology. Avocations: writing poetry, acting in plays, music, arts and crafts, badminton. Home: 805 B Beverly Park I, DLF City, Gurgon Haryana 122002, India Office: U Delhi South Campus Psych, Benito Juarez Rd, New Delhi 110021, India

VOHRAH, LAL CHAND, judge, barrister; b. Melaka, Malaysia, June 3, 1934; s. Ralia Ram Vohrah and Yeo Ah Chee; m. Pauline May, 1960; children: R.C., A.R. LLB, U. Bristol, Eng., 1958, LLD, 1997; cert. of attendance, The Hague Acad. Internat. Law, 1967; LLM, U. Cambridge, Eng., 1968. Advocate, solicitor High Ct. of Malaysia. Magistrate, sr. asst. registrar High Ct. of Malaya, 1961-64; pres. Sessions Ct., Malaya, 1964-66; sr. fed. counsel Malaysia, 1968-77, dep. commr. for law revision, 1968-69; head internat. law divsn. Atty. Gen.'s Chambers, Malaysia, 1973, head internat. law and adv. divsn., 1976-77; chmn. Spl. Commrs. of Income Tax, Malaysia, 1977; justice High Ct. of Malaya, 1978-93; judge Internat. Criminal Tribunal for former Yugoslavia, 1993—. Mem. Malaysian del. UN Conf. on Law of Treaties, Vienna, 1969, Sessions of Asian-African Legal Consultative Com., 1970-76, UN Gen. Assembly 25th session, 1970, 3d UN Conf. on Law of the Sea, Caracas, Venezuela, 1974. Recipient Johan Setia Mahkota award Govt. of Malaysia, 1974, Darjah Cemerlang Seri Mahkota award State Govt. of Melaka, 1980, Panglima Setia Mahkota, Govt. Malaysia, 2000. Mem. Lake Club (Kuala Lumpur), Royal Selangor Club (Kuala Lumpur), Royal Selangor Golf Club (Kuala Lumpur), De Witte Club (The Hague), Palm Resort Golf and Country Club (Johore). Avocations: swimming, walking, reading. Office: Internat Criminal Tribunal, Churchillplein 1 PO Box 13888, 2501 EW The Hague The Netherlands

VOHS, JAMES ARTHUR, health care program executive; b. Idaho Falls, Idaho, Sept. 26, 1928; s. John Dale and Cliff Lucille (Packer) V.; m. Janice Hughes, Sept. 19, 1953 (dec. Oct. 1999); children: Lorraine, Carol, Nancy, Sharla. B.A., U. Calif., Berkeley, 1952; postgrad., Harvard Sch. Bus., 1966. Employed by various Kaiser affiliated orgns., 1952-92; chmn., pres., CEO Kaiser Found. Hosps. and Kaiser Found. Health Plan, INc., Oakland, Calif., 1975-92, chmn. emeritus; chmn. bd. dirs. Holy Names Coll., 1981-92; chmn. Marcus Foster Inst., 1981—; chmn. Fed. Res. Bank San Francisco, 1991-94; bd. dirs. The Clorox Co. Bd. dirs. Oakland-Alameda County Coliseum Complex, 1986-96, Bay Area Coun., 1985-94, chmn., 1991-92; mem. Oakland Bd. Port Commrs., 1993-96. With AUS, 1946-48. Mem. NAS, Inst. Medicine.

VOI, MALI, Samoa government official; b. Pelagai, Papua New Guinea, Aug. 28, 1946; s. Voikapi Olopu and Geno Varage Kiniwari; m. Ruth Bual, Aug. 30, 1969; children: JoAnna, Mali, Mathias, Angela, Hugh. MA, Macquarie U., 1983. Dir. secondary edn. Dept. of Edn., Papua New Guinea, 1973-76; dir. cultural affairs Nat. Cultural Coun., Papua New Guinea, 1977-79; dir. 3rd Festival of Pacific Arts, Papua New Guinea, 1979-80; 1st asst. sec. gen. edn. Dept. Edn., Papua New Guinea, 1983; sec. Dept. of Ctrl. Province, Pub. Svc., Papua New Guinea, 1983-87; registrar Papau New Guinea U. Tech., 1988-90; mng. dir. Tourism Devel. Corp., Papua New Guinea, 1991-93; cultural advisor UNESCO, Apia, Western Samoa, 1992—; chmn. Gerehu Sch. Bd., Papua New Guinea, 1974-80; mem. UNESCO's Adv. Com. on Oceanic Cultures, 1976-83; dept. chmn. Commn. for Higher Edn., 1984-92; chmn. Nat. Cultural Coun., 1984-90. Contbr. articles to profl. jours. Sec. Tertiary Students Fedn., Port Horesby, 1965-66, pres. SRC Port Horesby Tchr.'s Coll., 1966; chmn. Keakalo Devel. Assn., 1974-80. Recipient Instrs. Cert. Royal Australian Surf-Live Saving Assn., 1963, Most Excellent Order of British Empire Queen Elizabeth II, 1981; recipient Faithful and Disting. medal Papua New Guinea Govt., 1983. Mem. Pacific Circle Consortium, Nat. Geographic Soc., Samoa UN Assn. Avocations: reading, tennis, swimming, mix netball. Office: UNESCO, Matautu, Apia Western Samoa

VOICHAK, ANATOLY VLADIMIROVICH, economics educator, researcher; b. Kharkov, Ukraine, Oct. 24, 1950; s. Vladimir Mikhailovich and Lidiya Gerasimovna (Gubskaya) V.; m. Liliya Nikolayevna Khimich, June 29, 1975 (dec. Jan. 1992); m. Tatyana Mikhailovna Tsigankova; children: Dmitry, Nikolay. B in Econs., Inst. Nat. Economy, Kiev, Ukraine, 1976; PhD, Moscow Inst. Nat. Economy, 1980; M, Internat. Mgmt. Inst., Kiev, Ukraine, 1991; D of Econs., Higher Edn. Accreditation Com., Kiev, Ukraine, 1992. Asst. prof. Kiev Nat. Econ. U., 1976-80, assoc. prof., 1981-93, prof., 1994—; v.p. Internat. Christian U., Kiev, 1993—; prof. Internat. Mgmt. Inst., Kiev, 1991—; participant European Assn. for Internat. Edn., Amsterdam, The Netherlands, 1996—. Author: Inventory Techniques for Raw Materials, 1989, Industrial Raw Material Reference Book, 1991, Managerial and Economic Mechanism of Intermediating and Wholesaling, 1991, Marketing Management, 1997, Marketing, 1999, Marketing Management, 2000. Bd. dirs. Inst. Market Economy and Fin., Kiev, 1991-93. Served with Soviet Army, 1969-71. Recipient letter of honor Ministry of Edn. of Ukraine, 1997. Mem. Mktg. Assn. of Ukraine (v.p. 1997—). Avocations: hunting, fishing, driving, music, soccer. Office: Internat Christian U Kiev, Peremohy Ave 54/1, 252057 Kiev Ukraine

VOICU, VICTOR AURELIAN, physician; b. Bolovani, Romania, June 29, 1930; s. Aurelian Voicu and Elena Ion (Ilie) Cristescu; m. Marilena Jiquidi, Jan. 5, 1975; children: Theodor, Andreea. MD, U. Medicine, Bucharest, Romania, 1962, PhD, 1971; sr. physician, Ministry of Health, 1974. Asst. prof. U. Medicine, Bucharest, 1962-66, prof. pharmacology and toxicology, 1992—; sci. rschr. Mil. Med. Rsch. Ctr., Bucharest, 1964-67, head dept. pharmacology, 1968-88, comdr., 1988—; prof. pharmacology U. Craiova, Romania, 1972; invited scientist Ctr. Blood Rsch., Harvard U., Boston, 1992. Author: Enzyhmatic Mechanisms in Pharmacodynamics, 1977, Pharmacologic Mechanisms at Membranar Interfaces, 1994; co-editor: NBC Risks, 1999; contbr. over 250 articles to sci. jours.; 18 patents for drugs. Pres. Found. Carol Davila, Bucharest, 1992, Found. Hemorheology, Bucharest. Brig. Gen. Romanian armed forces, 1990—. Recipient Gold medal Eureka, 1992, Danielopolu prize Romanian Acad., 1994. Mem. AAAS, Romanian Acad. Med. Sci. (pres. sci. coun.), Romanian Agy. Medicines, Romanian Acad. (corr. mem.), Romanian Soc. Pharmacology (pres. 1997—), European Assn. Clin. Toxicology, European Assn. Clin. Pharmacology, N.Y. Acad. Scis. Christian Orthodox. Home: 70 Ion Neculce St, 78179 Bucharest Romania Office: Mil Med Rsch Ctr, 37 CA Rosetti St, Bucharest Romania

VOIGHT, JON, actor; b. Yonkers, N.Y., Dec. 29, 1938; s. Elmer and Barbara (Camp) V.; m. Lauri Peters, 1962 (div. 1967); m. Marcheline Bertrand, Dec. 12, 1971 (div.); children: James Haven, Angelina Jolie. BFA, Cath. U., 1960; studied with Sanford Meisner and Samantha Harper, N.Y.C. Stage appearances include O Oysters Revue, 1961, The Sound of Music, 1961, A View from the Bridge, 1965, Romeo and Juliet, 1966, The Tempest, 1966, Two Gentlemen of Verona, 1966, That Summer-That Fall, 1967 (Theatre World award 1967), A Streetcar Named Desire, 1973, The Hashish Club, 1975, Hamlet, 1976, The Seagull, 1992; TV appearances include Cimarron Strip, Gunsmoke; films include Fearless Frank, 1967, Hour of the Gun, 1967, Out of It, 1969, Midnight Cowboy, 1969 (Best Actor Acad. award nominee 1969, N.Y. Critics Circle award 1969, L.A. Film Critics Best Actor award 1969, Brit. Acad. Most Promising Newcomer to Leading Film Role award 1969), Catch-22, 1970, The Revolutionary, 1970, Deliverance, 1972, The All American Boy, 1973, Conrack, 1974, The Odessa File, 1974, End of the Game, 1976, Coming Home, 1978 (Best Actor Acad. award 1978, Golden Globe award 1978, Cannes Internat. Film festival award 1978, N.Y. Film Critics Best Actor award 1978, L.A. Film Critics Best Actor award 1978), The Champ, 1979 (Golden Globe award 1979), Runaway Train, 1985 (Acad. award nominee 1986, London Film Critics award nominee 1986), Desert Bloom, 1986, Eternity, 1990, Heat, 1995, Mission Impossible, 1996, Rosewood, 1997, Anaconda, 1997, Most Wanted, 1997, The Rainmaker, 1997, Boys Will Be Boys, 1997, U Turn, 1997, Varsity Blues, 1998, I Once Had a Life, 1998, Enemy of the State, 1998; TV films include Chernobyl: The Final Warning, 1991, The Last of His Tribe, 1992; actor, prodr., co-writer film Lookin' To Get Out, 1982, the Fixer, 1998; actor, prodr. film Table for Five, 1983, A Tribute to Dustin Hoffman, 1999, Noah's Ark, 1999 (tv miniseries), A Dog Flanders, 1999, Second String, 2000. Winner Best Actor awards for Midnight Cowboy and Coming Home, Cannes Internat. Film Festival, Golden Globe award for Best Actor, Coming Home and The Champ, Acad. award for Best Actor, Coming Home 1979, N.Y. Film Critics award, Los Angeles Film Critics award for Best Actor, Midnight Cowboy, Coming Home.

VOIGT, DAWN A., college program adminstrator, consultant; b. Caledonia, Minn., Jan. 26, 1960; d. Merlin Otto and Evangeline Martha Voigt. Student, U. London, 1980-81; BA in Psychology and Sociology, Winona (Minn.) State U., 1982; MA in Indsl. and Orgnl. Psychology, DePaul U., 1989, PhD in Indsl. and Orgn. Psychology, 1993. Rschr. Johnson O'Connor Rsch. Found., Chgo., 1989-92; rsch. coord. Jewish Vocat. Svc., Chgo., 1989-92; human resource assessor Stephen A. Laser and Assocs., Chgo., 1990-92; sr. test and measurement specialist Med. Coll. Wis., Milw., 1992-94; assessment and grants mgr. Family Svc. of Milw., 1995-97; adminstr., edn. coord. Walker's Point Ctr. for the Arts, Milw., 1997-98; program devel. and evaluation coord. Waukesha (Wis.) County Tech. Coll., 1998—; cons. Milw. Mental Health Consultants, 1997—. Project analyst Home Visitation Developmental Assessment Scale, 1996. Bd. dirs. Walker's Point Ctr. for the Arts, Milw., 1999—, chair edn. subcom., 1999—; vol. Jobs for Youth, Inc., Chgo., 1998-92. Mem. APA, Am. Assn. Women in Cmty. Colls. Avocations: origami and paper arts, gardening, sewing, outdoor activities. Home: 2672 N 67th St Wauwatosa WI 53213-1461 Office: Waukesha County Tech Coll 800 Main St Pewaukee WI 53072-4601

VOIGT, EHRHARD, geology and paleontology educator; b. Schoenebeck, Germany, July 28, 1905; s. Karl Adolf and Mira (Stadelmann) V.; m. Ellinor Margarete Adelheid Bucerius, May 22, 1947; children: Werner, Wolfgang, Irmgard. Dr.rer.nat., U. Halle, 1929; Dr.honoris causa, U. Bordeaux, France, 1961. Asst. Geol. Inst., U. Halle/S., Germany, 1929-36; docent Geol. Inst., U. Halle/S., 1936-39; extra ord. prof., dir. Geol. Staatsinstitut Hamburg, Federal Republic Germany, 1939-42; ord. prof. Geol. Staatsinstitut Hamburg, 1942-70, prof. emeritus of geology and paleontology, 1970—. Editor Palaeont. Zeitschrift jour., 1937-39; contbr. articles to profl. jours. Recipient Hans-Stille-Medaille, Deutsche Geologische Gesellschaft, Berlin, 1961, H.G.S. medaille, Hungarian Geol. Svc., Budapest, 1969, Joachim Jungius Medaille, 1989, others. Mem. Palaeontologische Gesellschaft (pres. 1963-64), Deutsche Geologische Gesellschaft (v.p. 1953-56), Geologische Vereinigung, Societe Geologique de France (assoc. mem.), Internat. Bryozoan Assn., Naturwiss Verein Hamburg Soc. Geograph. Lima Gesellschaft fur Geschiebekunde, Royal Acad. Scis. (Copenhagen). Avocations: walking, travel. Home: Parkallee 7, 20144 Hamburg Germany Office: Geol Palaontol Inst U Hambu, Bundesstrasse 55, 20146 Hamburg Germany

VOIGT, HANS-DIETER, oil company executive, researcher, educator; b. Jüterbog, Germany, Oct. 23, 1941; s. Gustav and Helene (Atlas) V.; m. Edeltraut Lorenz, May 12, 1967; children: Kristin, Astrid. MS, Mining Acad., Freiberg, Germany, 1968, PhD, 1977. Group leader Erdöl-Erdgas Stendal, Germany, 1968-72; sect. leader Erdöl-Erdgas Gommern, Germany, 1973-90, project mgr., 1991-96; project mgr. VEGO OEL GmbH, Germany, 1992—, Kazgermunai, Kazakhstan, 1997-98, EUROGAS Deutschland GmbH, Germany, 1999—; lectr. Mining Acad., 1979—; cons. Geothermie Neubrandenburg, Germany, 1987-90. Author: Geohydrodynamics, 1985, Heat and Mass Flow, 1992, Geothermics, 1991; also numerous articles; numerous patents in field. With German Army, 1962-63. Mem. German Sci. Soc. for Erdöl, Erdgas und Kohle, Soc. Petroleum Engrs. Avocations: reading, sports, travel. Home: B-Brecht-Strasse 14C, 39120 Magdeburg Germany Office: EUROGAS Deutschland GmbH, Friedrich Str 95, 10117 Berlin Germany

VOIGT, RUEDIGER BERG, administrative science educator; b. Flensburg, Fed. Republic Germany, Apr. 7, 1941; s. Kurt and Erika (Berg) Voigt; m. Konstanze Voigt, Apr. 6, 1968; children: Karsten Gerald, Marten Hendrik, Eike Jorren. PhD, U. Kiel, Fed. Republic Germany, 1973. Exam in legal sci., 1969. Asst. tchr. Sch. Law, U. Kiel, 1969-72; lectr. U. Siegen, Fed. Republic Germany, 1972-76; asst. prof. Free U., Faculty of Econs., Berlin, 1976-78; sr. lectr. in polit. sci. U. Siegen, Fed. Republic Germany, 1978-81, prof., 1981-90, sr. lectr. in polit. sci. dept. governance studies, 1995—; prof., chmn. adminstrv. sci. U. the Armed Forces, Munich, 1990—, dean fac. social scis., 1993-95; chmn. Convent the U. Siegen, 1980-81, Ctr. for Studies on Changing Norms and Mobility, Siegen, 1982-90; guest lectr. comparative jurisprudence U. Sydney Law Sch., Australia, 1991, 92, 94; guest lectr. in jurisprudence Faculty of Law U. Sydney. Editor, author: Der Leviathan, 2000, Globalisierung Des Rechts, 1999, Der Neue Nationalstaat, 1998, Des Staates Neue Kleider, 1996, Der Kooperative Staat, 1995, Gebietsreform in Laendlichen Raeumen, 1994, Abschied vom Staat-Rueckkehr zum Staat, 1993, 2d edit., 1998, Foederalismus in der Bewaehrungsprobe, 1991, 2d edit., 1994, Politik und Recht: Beitraege zur Rechtspolitologie, 1990, 3d edit., 1993, Symbole der Politik-Politik der Symbole, 1989, Limits of Legal Regulation, 1989, Law and Legal Science, 1986, 3d edit., 1991, Abschied vom Recht, 1983; co-author: Rechtspolitologie, 1985. Leader Social Dem. Party, Netphen, Fed. Republic of Germany, 1980-90. Recipient rsch. grant U. Siegen, 1987, 88. Mem. Internat. Assn. Philosophy of Law. Avocation: photography. Home: 90 Hilchenbacher Str, D-57250 Netphen Germany Office: U Armed Forces Munich Fac Social Sci, Dept Govtl Studies Head 1995-, D-85577 Neubiberg Germany

VOISIN, GUY-ANDRÉ, immunologist, researcher; b. Paris, Dec. 11, 1920; s. Maurice Roger and Marguerite Jeanne (Nommés) V.; m. Janine Edmée Terrassier, July 16, 1959; children: Jacques-André, Jean-Michel, Véronique. MS, U. Paris, Sorbonne, 1943; MD, U. Paris, 1945, DSc, 1958. Intern, resident Hosps. of Paris, 1947-51; fellow Johns Hopkins U., Balt., 1951-52; chief clinics Faculty Medicine Paris, 1953-54; dir. rsch. team CNRS, Paris, 1968-87; dir. rsch. Claude Bernard Assn. of Hosps. of Paris, 1964-90; sci. dir. INSERM Rsch. unit on immunopathology and exptl. immunology, 1970-88; dir. Ctr. Immunopathology Claude Bernard Assn. of Hosps. of Paris, 1971-90, dir. rsch. emeritus, 1991—; sci. advisor in immunology Clin-Midy/Sanofi, Montpellier, France, 1974-87; mem. several nat. sci. coms.; lectr. in field. Author, editor: Immunologie de la Reproduction, 1990; mem. edit. bd. several internat. jours.; patentee in field; contbr. numerous sci. articles to internat. jours. and books. Med. lt. French Army, 1944-46. Decorated Chevalier Légion d'Honneur, France, 1975; recipient Prix Prince Albert 1st de Monaco, Nat. Acad. Medicine, 1971. Mem. French Soc. Immunology (pres. 1974-78), Internat. Soc. Immunology Reprodn. (pres. 1986-89, pres. of honor), French League Against Multiple Sclerosis (pres. med. and sci. com. 1988-96, pres. of honor), Assn. Scientists Forever (pres. 1998—), European Soc. Reproductive and Devel. Immunology (founding pres. 1996-99). Avocations: history of arts and sciences, swimming, skiing. Home: 40 rue Condorcet, 75009 Paris France Office: Hosp Paul Brousse, Immuno-Pathology & Reprodn ICIG, 94800 Villejuif France

VOITENKO, VLADIMIR ANDREEVICH, physics educator; b. St. Petersburg, Russia, Jan. 17, 1956; s. Andrei Pavlovich Voitenko and Rema Mikhailovna Vlasova; m. Olga Ivanovna Sukhanova, Apr. 26, 1981; 1 child, Anna Vladimirovna. Degree in rsch. engring., M.I. Kalinin Poly. Inst., 1978, PhD, 1984. Researcher in exptl. physics M.I. Kalinin Polytech. Inst., 1979-82, asst. prof., 1984-93; researcher A.F. Ioffe Phys. Tech. Inst., 1977—; prof. State Tech. U.(formerly M.I. Kalinin Poly. Inst.), St. Petersburg. Contbr. articles to profl. jours. Home: Apt 122, 36 Nalichnaya St Block 6, 199-226 Saint Petersburg Russia Office: State Tech U, 29 Politechnicheskaya St, 195-251 Saint Petersburg Russia

VOITOVICH, NIKOLAI NIKOLAYEVICH, mathematician, researcher; b. Vitchivka, Rivne, Ukraine, Mar. 23, 1940; s. Nikolai Panasovich and Olena Demydivna (Parchuk) V.; m. Lyudmila Fedorivna Korchagina, Dec. 23, 1972; children: Oksana, Dmytro. MSc, Ivan Franko State U., Lviv, Ukraine, 1961; PhD, Radioengring. and Electronics, Moscow, 1968; DSc, State U., Kharkiv, Ukraine, 1982; D (hon.), Ivan Franko State U., 1991. Sr. rschr. Inst. Radioengring. and Electronics, Moscow, 1961-71; sr. rschr. Inst. Ap-

plied Problems Mechanics and Maths., Lviv, 1971-84, chair dept., 1984—; chair dept. Ivan Franko State U., Lviv, 1989—. Author: Table of Rieman Functions of Complex Arguments, 1970, Generalized Eigen Oscillation Method in Diffraction Theory, 1977, Electrodynamics of Antennas with Semitransparent Aperture, 1989, Synthesis of Antennas According to Amplitude Radiation Pattern, 1993, Generalized Method of Eigenoscillation in the Diffraction Theory, 1999. Recipient State award Ukraine in Area of Sci. and Tech., 1989. Mem. IEEE (chpt. chair 1994). Office: Inst Appl Probls Mech-Math, Naukova St 3 B, 79601 Lviv Ukraine

VOITSEKHOVSKAYA, OLGA KUZMINICHNA, physicist, researcher; b. Tomsk, USSR, Feb. 29, 1944; d. Kuzma Alekseevich Tsytsarev and Lidia Il'inichna Titova; m. Alexander Vasilievich Voitsekhovskii, Mar. 12, 1963; 1 child, Andrei. PhD, Tomsk State U., 1975; D in Phys.-Mathemat. Scis., Inst. Atmospheric Optics, Tomsk, 1989. Jr. scientist Siberina Phys.-Tech. Inst., Tomsk, 1966-69; sr. scientist Inst. Atmospheric Optics, Tomsk, 1969-94; prof. Tomsk State U., Russia, 1994—. Author: Information System on High Resolution Spectroscopy, 1988; contbr. article to profl. jour. Grantee Russian Found. Fundamental Rsch., 1995, 98, Univs. Russia Fundamental Rsch., 1998. Avocations: music, literature. Home: Kievskaya st 96-97, 634034 Tomsk Russia Office: Tomsk State U, 36 Lenin Ave, 634050 Tomsk Russia

VOJNITS, ANDRÁS MÁTYÁS, zoologist, educator, researcher; b. Budapest, Hungary, Jan. 2, 1941; s. Jenö and Gabriella (Rózsa) V.; m. Katalin Bonyhádi, May 15, 1963 (div. 1975); 1 child, Eszter; m. Éva Márta Herczeg, Deg. 24, 1976; 1 child, Kinga. Diploma in biology and geography, Eötvös Loránd U., Budapest, 1965, PhD, 1967. Rschr. Plant Protection Inst., Budapest, 1965-72; dep. dir. Hungarian Natural History Mus., Budapest, 1972-94; lead tchr. Mihály Táncsics Secondary Sch., Dabas, Hungary, 1995—. Recipient Comitat Pest award for sci., 1996, Frivaldszky award for ent. Teleki Samuel award for geography. Mem. Hungarian Geog. Soc. (chmn. expedition dept. 1998—), Hungarian Entomol. Soc. (sec. 1974-78), Hungarian Biol. Soc. (sec. 1980-83), Soc. Europaea Lepidopterologica (coun. 1982-86), Assn. Tropical Lepidoptera (adv. coun. 1994—), Assn. Palearctical Lepidoptera (adv. coun. 1994—), N.Y. Acad. Scis. Roman Catholic. Home: Haller utca 88, 1091 Budapest Hungary

VOJTA, PAUL ALAN, mathematics educator; b. Mpls., Sept. 30, 1957; s. Francis J. and Margaret L. V. B in Math., U. Minn., 1978; MA, Harvard U., 1980, PhD, 1983. Instr. Yale U., New Haven, 1983-86; postdoctoral fellow Math. Scis. Rsch. Inst., Berkeley, Calif., 1986-87; fellow Miller Inst. for Basic Rsch., Berkeley, 1987-89; assoc. prof. U. Calif., Berkeley, 1989-92, prof., 1992—; mem. Inst. for Advanced Study, Princeton, 1989-90, 96-97. Author: Diophantine Approximations and Value Distribution Theory, 1987. Recipient perfect score Internat. Math. Olympiad, 1975. Mem. Am. Math. Soc. (Frank Nelson Cole Number Theory prize 1992), Math. Assn. Am., Phi Beta Kappa, Tau Beta Pi. Avocations: computer, skiing. Office: Univ Calif Dept Math Berkeley CA 94720-0001

VOKAC, DAMIJAN D., cardiologist; b. Maribor, Slovenia, Apr. 23, 1957; s. Danilo J. and Zlata S. (Medic) V.; m. Nadja M. Kokalj, Dec. 27, 1986; children: Hana, Jakob. MD, U. Ljubljana, 1982. Intern Gen. Hosp. Maribor, 1982-84, resident, 1984-90, internist, 1990-92; clin. fellow in cardiology Montreal Hearth Inst., 1993-94; from attending to cons. cardiologist Gen. Hosp. Maribor, 1995—; asst. prof. U. Ljubjana, 1999. Mem. N.Am. Soc. Pacing and Electrophysiology, Slovenian Soc. Cardiology. Avocations: music, art, mathematics, golf. Home: Turnerjeva 25, 2000 Maribor Slovenia Office: Gen Hosp Maribor, Ljubljanska 5, 2000 Maribor Slovenia

VOKHNIK, OLGA MIKHAILOVNA, physicist; b. Moscow, June 6, 1949; d. Michail Danilovich and Nonna Georgievna (Orlova) V. Diploma in physics, M.V. Lomonosov Moscow State U., 1972, PhD in Physics and Math., 1979. Sci. rschr. Inst. Nuc. Physics M.V. Lomonosov Moscow State U., 1975-90, sr. scientist Faculty Physics, 1990—; cons. students and rsch. groups, supr. student practice Faculty Physics, M.V. Lomonosov Moscow State U., 1973—. Author: (text books) Solid-State Laser, 1980, Nonlinear Optical Effects, 1985, Phase Conjugation of Optical Radiation, 1992. Communist. Avocations: philately, arts. E-mail: omv@srdlan.npi.msu.su. Home: 12-4-597 Academ Anokhin Str, Moscow 117602, Russia Office: MV Lomonosov Moscow State U, Fac Physics, Vorob'evy Gory, Moscow 119899, Russia

VOKIN, ALEXANDER INNOKENT'EVICH, physical chemist, researcher; b. Novo-Nikolsk Village, Chita, USSR, Jan. 1, 1956; s. Innokentii Andriyanovich and Pelageya Alexandrovna (Polyntseva) V.; m. Tamara Leonidovna Stepanova, Feb. 22, 1979; children: Il'ya, Nataliya. Grad. in physics, Irkutsk (USSR) State U., 1978; postgrad., Irkutsk Inst. Organic Chemistry, 1978-80. Cert. in chemistry. Engr. Irkutsk Inst. Organic Chemistry, 1980-86, jr. rsch. worker, 1986-90, rsch. worker, 1990-92; sr. rsch. worker Irkutsk Inst. Chemistry, Siberian divsn. Russian Acad. Scis., 1992—. Author: Targets in Heterocyclic Systems, 1997; contbr. articles to profl. jours., including Russian Chem. Bull., Russian Jour. Gen. Chem., Bull. Acad. Scis. USSR. Avocation: music. E-mail: valtur@irioch.irk.ru. Home: 285 Lermontova St Apt 10, 664033 Irkutsk Russia Office: Irkutsk Inst Chem Russ AcSc, 1 Favorsky St, 664033 Irkutsk Russia

VOLAKIS, JOHN LEONIDAS, engineering educator; b. Chios, Greece, May 13, 1956; came to U.S., 1973; s. Leonidas I. and Maria L. (Makarigakis) V.; m. Maria I. Papouras, 1985; children: Leo, Alexandro. BE summa cum laude, Youngstown State U., 1978; MS, Ohio State U., 1979, PhD, 1982. Mem. tech. staff Rockwell Internat., Columbus, Ohio, Lakewood, Calif., 1982-84; asst. prof. elec. engring. and computer sci. U. Mich., Ann Arbor, 1984-89, assoc. prof., 1989-94, prof. computer sci., 1994—; prof. elec. engring., dir. radiation lab, 1998—; gen. chmn. IEEE Antennas and Propagation Internat. Symposium and Radio Sci. Meeting, 1993; mem. tech. coms. COMPUMAG Conf., 1994, 95, 98, Advanced Computational Electromagnetics Conf., 1995, 96; mem. Senate Assembly, U. Mich. rsch. policies and acad. affairs coms., 1994-97, elec. engring. dept. exec. com., 1997-99, grad. divsn. com., 1990—. Co-author: (books) Approximate Boundary Conditions in Electromagnetics, 1995, Finite Element Methods for Electromagnetics, 1998; contbr. chpts. or articles to 15 other books, 160 articles to refereed jours., 170 technical papers to sci. symposiums or confs.; assoc. editor IEEE Antennas and Propagation Transactions, 1989-93, IEEE Antennas and Propagation Mag., 1992—, Radio Sci., 1994-97, Jour. Electromagnetics Waves and Applications, 1995—; co-inventor slot spiral antenna with integrated balun and feed, patent pending. Fellow IEEE (numerous coms. including adminstrv. com. 1996-99, past chmn. antennas symposium); mem. Internat. Union of Radio Sci., Sigma Xi, Phi Kappa Phi, Tau Beta Pi. Office: U Mich 1301 Beal Ave Ann Arbor MI 48109-2122

VOLBERG, HERMAN WILLIAM, electronics engineer, consultant; b. Hilo, Hawaii, Apr. 6, 1925; s. Fred Joseph and Kathryn Thelma (Ludloff) V.; m. Louise Ethel Potter, Apr. 26, 1968; children: Michael, Lori. BSEE, U. Calif., Berkeley, 1949. Project engr. Naval Electronics Lab., San Diego, 1950-56; head solid state rsch. S.C. div. Gen. Dynamics, San Diego, 1956-60; founder Solidyne Solid State Instruments, La Jolla, Calif., 1958-60; founder, v.p. electronics divsn. Ametek/Straza, El Cajon, Calif., 1960-66; founder, cons. H.V. Cons., San Diego, 1966-69; sr. scientist Naval Ocean Systems Ctr., Oahu, Hawaii, 1970-77; chief scientist Integrated Scis. Corp., Santa Monica, Calif., 1978-80; founder, pres. Acoustic Sys. Inc., Goleta, Calif., 1980-84; founder, pres. Invotron, Inc., Lafayette, Calif., Murray, Utah, 1984—; sr. scientist Reson, Inc., Santa Barbara, Calif., 1992—; cons. Lockheed-Martin, 1985—, U. Utah Ctr. for Engring. Design, 1991; cons. on autonomous underwater vehicle sonar systems Mitsui/U. Tokyo, 1992; lectr. solid state course UCLA and IBM, 1956-62; instr. Applied Tech. Inst., Columbia, Md., 1988—; contbr. to undersea acoustical rsch. and devel. programs European Union, 1990—. Contbr. articles to IRE Bull., IEEE Ocean Electronics Symposium, IEEE/MTS Oceans, UDT Conf. Procs. Mem. adv. panels for advanced sonar systems and for high resolution sonars, USN, 1970-77. 1st lt. U.S. Army, 1944-47, ETO. Recipient award of merit Dept. Navy, 1973, 94. Mem. IEEE, AAAS, NRA, Acoustical Soc. Am., Mine Warfare Assn., N.Y. Acad. Scis., Marine Tech. Soc., U.S. Naval Inst., Planetary Assn., Libr. Congress Assocs. (charter), Old Crows, Masons, Elks. Achievements include patents for device for detecting and displaying the response of tissue to stimuli, high rate neutralizer (HIRAN), crane high-voltage sensing system. Home and Office: 41 W 6830 S Murray UT 84107-7124

VOLBORTH, ALEXIS VON, geochemistry and geological engineering educator; b. Viipuri, Finland, July 11, 1924; came to U.S. 1955, naturalized; m. Nadia Hasso, 1947; children: Tatyana, Swetlana, Maria, Gregory, Anna, Nicholaus H.W., Elisabeth. PhC, U. Helsinki, 1950, PhLic and PhD in Geology-Mineralogy, 1954. Mineralogist, rsch. assoc., assoc. prof., prof. U. Nev., Reno, 1956-68; Killam vis. prof. geology, Killam rsch. prof. Dalhhousie U., Can., 1968-72; vis. prof. NASA Lunar Sci. Inst., U. Houston, 1972-73; vis. rsch. chemist U. Calif., Irvine, 1973-76; prof. geology and chemistry N.D. State U., 1975-78; prof. geology, scientist Nucleaar Radiation Ctr., Wash. State U., Pullman, 1978-79; prof. geochemistry and chemistry Mont. Coll. Mineral Sci. and Tech., Butte, 1979-94, prof. geol. engring., 1987-92, dir. accelerator lab., 1983-86, sr. radiation safety officer, 1983-86; prof. emeritus Mont. Tech./U. Mont., Butte, 1995—; prin. investigator Stoichiometry Study Lunar Rocks, NASA, 1972-73; cons. AEC, 1961-63, NASA, 1965-73, Anaconda Co., 1968, Atomic Energy Orgn. Iran, 1975, King Abdul Aziz U., Jeddah, Saudi Arabia, 1975-76, Johns Manville Corp., Chevron, 1980-83, Pegasus Gold Inc., 1987, Placer Dome Inc., Echo Bay, Inc., 1990; U.S. rep., del. 2d Conf. on Natural Reactors, IAEC, Paris, 1977; U.S. rep. Internat. Geol. Correlation Program, 1990-96; interpreter, Russian translator in Soviet Siberia for U.S. and Can. mining cos., 1990-96. Contbr. articles to profl. jours. Traveling rsch. fellow Outokumpu Found., U. Vienna, U. Heidelberg, 1954-55, Hoover fellow Calif. Inst. Tech., 1955-56, sr. fellow Australian Acad. Sci., 1965, fellow Guggenheim Found., 1965-66; fossil Elkoceras Volborthi named in his honor. Fellow Mineral. Soc. Am., Am. Inst. Chemists; mem. Am. Chem. Soc., Am. Nuclear Soc., Soc. Econ. Geologists, Internat. Precious Metals Inst. Home and Office: PO Box 80 Dayton MT 59914-0080

VOLCHOK, IVAN PETROVICH, materials science educator; b. Pivaschy, Minsk, Belorussia, Feb. 7, 1935; arrived in Ukraine, 1962; s. Peter Nikitich and Elena Antonovna (Loyko) V.; m. Janna Grigorievna Oretschenko, Jan. 29, 1961. Degree in engring., Poly. U., Minsk, 1962; PhD, Machinebuilding Tech. INst., Zaporozhye, Ukraine, 1966, D of Tech. Sci., 1980. Chief of rsch. lab. Machinebuilding Inst., Zaporozhye, 1965-79, prof., 1979-80, chief of dept., 1980—; rector Tech. U., Zaporozhye, 1997. Author: Steel and Cast Iron Fracture Resistance, 1993, Technology of Structural Materials, 1995. Mem. Regional Coun., Zaporozhye, 1988-90. Served with Soviet mil., 1954-57. Recipient Badge of Honor, Soviet Govt., Moscow, 1986; named Meritorious Sci. Worker, Govt. of Ukraine, Kiev, 1992. Mem. Acad. of H.S. (Kiev, Ukraine), N.Y. Acad. Scis. Avocation: chess. Home: Lenin Ave 150 flat 44, 69095 Zaporozhye Ukraine Office: State Tech U, Zhukovskogo 64, 69063 Zaporozhye Ukraine

VOLCKER, PAUL A., economist; b. Cape May, N.J., Sept. 5, 1927; s. Paul A. and Alma Louise (Klippel) V.; m. Barbara Marie Bahnson, Sept. 11, 1954 (dec. June 1998); children: Janice, James. AB summa cum laude, Princeton U., 1949, LLD (hon.), 1982; MA, Harvard U., 1951, LLD (hon.), 1985. Economist Fed. Res. Bank N.Y., 1952-57, pres., 1975-79; economist Chase Manhattan Bank, N.Y.C., 1957-61, v.p., dir. planning, 1965-68; with Dept. Treasury, Washington, 1961-65, 69-74, dep. under sec. monetary affairs, 1963-65, under sec., 1969-74; chmn. bd. govs. Fed. Res. Bd., Washington, 1979-87; prof. emeritus internat. econ. policy Princeton U., 1988; chmn. Nat. Commn. on Pub. Svc., 1987-90, Trilateral Commn., Group of Thirty; bd. dirs. Prudential Ins. Corp; overseer TIAA-CREF. Active Internat. House Fin. Svcs. Vol. Corps. Sr. fellow Woodrow Wilson Sch. Pub. and Internat. Affairs, 1974-75. Mem. Am. Coun. Germany (dir.), Japan Soc. (dir.), Inst. Internat. Econs. (dir.).

VOLCZER, ARPAD, retired philosophy educator; b. Kolozsvar, Rumania, Oct. 31, 1928; arrived in Hungary, 1945; s. Arpad and Arpadne Maria (Dragan) V.; m. Arpadne Jolan Harmati, May 21, 1952. LLB, Eotvos Lorand Tudományegyetem, Budapest, 1951; Candidate's degree, Magyar Tudomanyos Akad., Budapest, 1976. Trainee Eotvos Lorand Tudomanyegyetem, Budapest, 1951-54, demonstrator, 1954-58, lectr., 1959-68, assoc. prof., 1968-89, retired, 1989—; vice-dean Eotvos Lorand Tudomanyegyetem, 1977-80. Co-author: (books) Historical Materialism, 1970, Selected Questions of Historical Materialism, 1975; co-editor: Philosophical Little Encyclopedia, 1976; contbr. articles to profl. jours. Mem. Hungarian Philos. Soc. Mem. Hungarian Socialist Party.

VOLETI, SHRIRAM MURTI, engineering educator; b. Amalapuram, India, June 8, 1943; s. Venkat Raju and Surya Ranganayakamma (Kuchiminchi) V.; m. Lalitha Duttaluru, May 25, 1967; children: Madhavi, Anand, Anurag. BSc in Engring., Agra (India) U., 1964; M in Engring., Osmania U., Hyderabad, India, 1976; PhD, Indian Inst. Tech., Madras, India, 1987. Assoc. lectr. Osmania U., Hyderabad, 1965-67, lectr., 1967-83, reader, 1983-91, prof., 1991—, faculty advisor mech. engring. dept., 1987—, chmn. bd. studies Coll. Engring., 1999—. Contbr. articles to profl. jours. Fellow Inst. Engrs.; mem. Indian Soc. Mech. Engrs. Avocation: life master in bridge. Home: 101 Prashanta Towers, Hyderabad 500076, India Office: Mech Engring Dept, Osmania Univ, Hyderabad 500007, India

VÖLGYES, TAMÁS, investment company executive, consultant; b. Budapest, Hungary, May 17, 1948; s. Miklós Weiss Völgyes and Marta Lax; m. Eva Romsics, Oct. 16, 1999; 1 child, Jennifer.; BSc, Budapest Econ. U., 1977, Mo Shi Minh, Budapest, 1978. Advisor, CEO Budapest Tech. Libr., 1970-80; dir. Stats. Publ. Dept., Budapest, 1980-82; media staff Hungarian Radio, Budapest, 1982-90; dir. sales Radio Budapest, 1990-92; pvt. practice network mktg. Budapest, 1992—; CEO Kódexpress Investments, Budapest, 1996—; dep. chmn. Kódexpress Ins., Budapest, 1998. Contbr. articles to profl. jours. Capt. Internat. Commn. Control and Supervision, 1973. Recipient ICCS award, 1975. Mem. Hungarian Mktg. Assn., Artist's and Journalists, Budapest Lions. Jewish. Avocations: driving, collecting watches. Office: Kódexpress, Marek 31, 1078 Budapest Hungary

VOLK, PATRICIA GAY, fiction writer, essayist; b. N.Y.C., July 16, 1943; d. Cecil Sussman and Audrey Elaine (Morgen) Volk; m. Andrew Blitzer, Dec. 21, 1969; children—Peter Morgen, Polly Volk. BFA cum laude, Syracuse U., 1964; student, Sch. Visual Arts, N.Y.C., 1968, New Sch., N.Y.C., 1975, Columbia U., 1977-88. Art dir. Appelbaum & Curtis, N.Y.C., 1964-65, Seventeen Mag., Triangle Publs., N.Y.C., 1966-68; copywriter Doyle, Dane, Bernbach, Inc., N.Y.C., 1969-88, also sr. v.p., creative mgr., 1969-87, sr. v.p.- assoc. creative dir., 1987-88; columnist N.Y. Newsday, 1995-96; fiction instr. Yeshiva Coll.; fiction instr. Playwrights Horizon Theater Sch., Marymount Coll. Author: The Yellow Banana, 1985 (Word Beat Press Fiction Book award 1984), White Light, 1987, All it Takes, 1990; contbr. articles to N.Y. Times mag., Redbook, Allure, Mirabella, Family Circle, The New Yorker, The Atlantic, Playboy, others; contbr. short stories to popular and small press publs. and anthologies. Recipient Stephen E. Kelly award, 1983, various Andy, Clio, Effie and One Show awards, 1970-88; Yaddo fellow, 1983, 99, MacDowell fellow, 1984. Mem. Author's Guild, PEN.

VOLK, WOLFGANG FRIEDRICH, mathematician; b. St.-Etienne, France, Feb. 15, 1950; s. Helmut Erich and Helene (Werner) V.; m. Ingeborg Hundt, May 17, 1996. Degree in Engring., Fachhochschule, Frankfurt, Germany, 1972; diploma, Freie Univ., Berlin, 1978, D in Natural Scis., 1982. Engr. ÖbVI Dr.-Ing. L. Keck, Offenbach, Germany, 1972-73; sci. collaborator Heinrich-Hertz-Inst., Berlin, 1978, Hahn-Meitner-Inst., Berlin, 1979-83; software engr. Sietec, Berlin, 1983-84, project mgr., 1984-90, workgroup mgr., 1990-96; software engr. SNI, Berlin, 1996-98, subproject mgr., 1998—; lectr. in field. Contbr. articles to profl. jours., chpts. to books. Mem. Deutsche Mathematiker Vereinigung, European Math. Soc., Berliner Mathematische Gesellschaft (adv. bd. 1992—). Avocation: mathematical research. Home: Nymphenburger Strasse 11, 10825 Berlin Germany Office: SICAD Geomatics, Rohrdamm 85, 13629 Berlin Germany

VOLKE, FRANK GERHARD, physicist, educator; b. Leipzig, Saxonia, Germany, Oct. 23, 1953; s. Gerhard Volke and Gisela (Giessner) Koepp; m. Teresa Schostok, Oct. 28, 1981. Physicist, U. Leipzig, 1977, PhD, 1981, Habil, 1987. Rschr., lectr. U. Leipzig, Germany, 1977-98; head magnetic resonance group Fraunhofer Inst. Biomed. Engring., Ingbert, Germany, 1998—; lectr. U. Saarland, 1999—. Patentee in field; contbr. articles to profl. jours. Mem. AAAS, Biophys. Soc. U.S., Deutscher Hochschulverband, Verband Deutscher Chemiker, Nuclear Magnetic Resonance. Office: Fraunhofer Inst Biomed Engring, Ensheimer St 48, D-66386 Saint Ingbert Germany

VOLKEN, PAUL, educator. Lic. law, Faculty Law Fribourg/Geneva, 1970, D of Law, 1977, privatdozent, 1986; diploma, Hague Acad. Internat. Law, 1973; LLM, Harvard U., 1976. Legal advisor Swiss Fed. Dept. Justice, 1972-73, sec. gen., 1973-78; vice-chmn. Spl. Commn. for Prep. New Swiss Pvt. Internat. Law Statute, 1978-82; head of sect. Swiss Fed. Dept. Justice, 1979-83, dep. head of divsn., 1984-88; prof. Faculty of Law U. Fribourg, 1988—; lectr. Faculties of Law, Zurich, 1980-81, Fribourg, 1981-87, Belgrade, 1987, Dubrovnik, 1985, 87, 89, 91, 96, 98, Hague Acad., 1990, Almae Matres, Sion, 1991-96, Case Western Res. U., Cleve., 1992, St. Gallen, 1993, Forum Internat., Peter Sanders, The Hague, 1993, Lucerne, 1994, 96, Coun. Europe, Prague, 1994, Swiss Inst. Permanent Formation, 1995-96, Study Ctr., Lugano, 1997-98, Faculty Humanities, U. Moscow, Lomonosov, 1999, Europa Inst., Zürich, 1999. Office: Faculty of Law, 11 av de Beauregard, CH-1700 Fribourg Switzerland

VOLKENANDT, MATTHIAS, dermatologist; b. Holtwick, Germany, Mar. 2, 1957; s. Otto and Ruth (Sohn) V. Student, Dormition Abbey, Jerusalem, 1978-79, U. Glasgow, Scotland, 1984-85; diploma in theology, MD, U. Bonn, Germany, 1986; med. degree, Ednl. Commn. Fgn. Med. Grads., 1988. Clin. fellow dept. oncology U. Münster, Germany, 1986-88; rsch. fellow dept. molecular pharmacology, devel. therapy and clin. investigation program Meml. Sloan-Kettering Cancer Ctr., N.Y.C., 1988-91; rsch. and clin. fellow dept. dermatology U. Munich, 1991—. Co-editor: Jour. Med. Ethics. With German Army, 1975-76. Mem. Acad. for Ethics in Medicine, Am. Soc. for Clin. Oncology, Am. Assn. for Cancer Rsch., Am. Soc. Hematology, Soc. for Investigative Dermatology, N.Y. Acad. Scis. Roman Catholic. Avocation: playing violin. Home: Landwehrstrasse 66, D-80336 Munich Germany Office: U Munich Dept Dermatology, Frauenlobstrasse 9, D-80337 Munich Germany

VOLKMANN, BODO, mathematician, researcher; b. Berlin, Apr. 16, 1929; s. Walter and Hedwig (Heyer) V.; m. Waltraut Rohrbach, Aug. 18, 1956; children: Angelika, Cordula, Evelina, Gesina. BSc, U. Göttingen, Fed. Republic Germany, 1948, MSc, 1950; PhD, U. Mainz, Fed. Republic Germany, 1951, Habilitation, 1955. Privatdozent U. Mainz, 1955-64; assoc. prof. math. U. Stuttgart, Fed. Republic Germany, 1964-66, prof. math., 1966-94, prof. emeritus, 1994—; vis. asst. prof. U. Utah, Salt Lake City, 1955-56, UCLA, 1956-57; vis. prof. U. Utah, 1962-63, U. Hawaii, Honolulu, 1966-67. Author books on Christian subjects, over 40 math. research articles. Chmn., Christian Democratic Union State Com. on Univs. and Colls., Baden-Württemberg, 1972-83. Mem. German Assn. U. Profs., Deutsche Mathematiker-Vereinigung, Am. Math. Soc, Österreichische Mathematische Gesellschaft. Home: PO Box 1108, D-71692 Möglingen Germany

VOLKOV, ANDREY YURIEVICH, physicist; b. Krivoj Rog, Ukraine, Jan. 5, 1962; s. Yuri Nikolaevich and Anna Fedorovna (Pokrovskaya) V.; m. Olga Nikolaevna Zhilina, Sept. 15, 1984; 1 child, Maxim. MS, Moscow Engring. Physics Inst., 1986; PhD, Obninsk Inst. of Nuclear Power Engring., 1998. Tech. asst. Moscow Engring. Physics Inst., Obninsk, 1980-85; engr. Obninsk Inst. Nuclear Power Engring., 1986-93, rschr., 1994-97, sr. rschr., 1998—; cons. Sci.-Industry Co. Technology, Obninsk, 1987-93; dep. dir. Dosimetr Control Dept., Chernobyl Nuclear Power Sta., Ukraine, 1986. Contbr. articles to profl. jours.; patentee in field. Leader Komsomol Orgn. of Obninsk Inst. of Nuclear Power Engring., 1985-90, Student Trade-Union of Nuclear Faculty, 1983-85. Recipient medal for work against Chernobyl Holocaust, Nuclear Ministry, Moscow, 1988; grantee Internat. Sci. Found., Washington, 1993, Russian Found. for Basic Rsch., Moscow, 1992, 93. Mem. Young Scientist's Club of Obninsk Inst. of Nuclear Power Engring., Obninsk Club of Scientists. Avocations: fishing, photography, water tourism. Home: 34 Gagarin St Apt 28, Obninsk/Kaluga 249034, Russia Office: Obninsk Inst Nuclear Power Engring, Studgorodok 1, Obninsk 249040, Russia

VOLKOV, VICTOR LVOVICH, chemist; b. Zvyagino, Russia, Nov. 13, 1938; s. Lev Sergeevich and Aleksandra Ivanovna (Sachazova) V.; m. Ludmila Nikolaevna Chetvirikova, Jan. 13, 1962 (div. May 1988); children: Michail Victorovich, Aleksey Victorovich; m. Galina Stepanovna Zacharova, June 2, 1988; 1 child, Aleksey Victorovich. Grad., Ural Poly. Inst., Sverdlovsk, Russia, 1965; post-grad., Inst. Chemistry, 1970; D of Chem. Scis., Inst. Solid State Chemistry, Ekaterinburg, Russia, 1992. Chemist Inst. of Chemistry, Sverdlovsk, 1957-58, Sverdlovsk-Ekaterinburg, 1959—; lab. asst. Inst. Solid State Chemistry, Sverdlovsk, 1957-65, scientific researcher, 1965-67, 70-72, head rsch. group, 1972—; head trade union com. Inst. of Chemistry, 1975-77; head All-Union Soc. Rationalizer and Inventor-The Inst. of Chemistry, 1978-85. Author: (with A.A. Fotiev and V.K. Kapustkin) Oxide Vanadium Bronzes, 1978; Phases of Inclusion Based on Vanadium Oxides, 1987; patentee iron-selective electrode; contbr. articles to profl. jours. Recipient Hon. diploma All-Union Soc. Chemistry, 1975, Bronze medal Exhibition of Nat. Econ. Achievements, 1982. Mem. Orthodox Ch. Avocations: horticulture, fishing. Home: Krasnolesey St 18-10, 620016 Ekaterinburg Russia Office: Inst Solid State Chemistry, Pervomaiskaya St 91, 620219 Ekaterinburg Russia

VOLKOV, VLADIMIR YAKOVLEVICH, biophysicist, researcher; b. Pronkino, USSR, Mar. 6, 1946; s. Yakov Ivanovich and Ekaterina Efimovna (Tarachteeva) V.; m. Lilia Alexandrovna Evgrafova, Nov. 4, 1970; children: Olga, Ekaterina. Diploma, U. Kazan, USSR, 1970, PhD, 1977; D in Chemistry, Microbiology Inst., USSR, 1992. Scientist U. Kazan, 1973-76; chief radiospectroscopy dept. State Rsch. Ctr. for Applied Microbiology, Obolensk, Russia, 1976-80, chief biophysics dept., 1980-89, dir. of postgrad. students, 1977—, deputy dir., 1989—; prof. State Rsch. Ctr. for Applied Microbiology, 1994—; hon. prof. Zhejiang Agrl. U., China, 1997—. Mem. editl. coun. Jour. Probl. Cryobiology, 1989—; contbr. over 140 articles to profl. jours. including Biophysics, Biotechnology, Microbiology, also others; 10 patents in field. Recipient USSR Govt. medal for labor in valor, 1981, Silver medal Exhbn. High Achievements in Econs., Moscow, 1984, Russian Pres.' medal in memory of 850th anniversary of Moscow, 1997, Order of Friendship Russian Govt., 1999. Fellow N.Y. Acad. Scis.; mem. Botechnological Soc. (USSR), Internat. Electron Paramagnetic Resonance Soc., Nat. Geographic Soc. Avocations: skiing, traveling, radioengineering, electronics. Office: State Rsch Ctr Applied Microbi, 142279 Obolensk Moscow, Russia

VOLKOVA, EKATHERINE ALEXANDER, physicist; b. Moscow, Feb. 5, 1958; d. Alexander B. and Galina I. (Eremeeva) Ishuroff; m. Alexander Michail Volkov, Mar. 24, 1981; children: Peter, Basil. Degree, Moscow State U., 1981, PhD in Physics and Math., 1985. Jr. scientist M.V. Lomonosov Sci. Rsch. Inst. Nuc. Physics Moscow State U., 1985-91, scientist, 1991-97, sr. scientist, 1997—. Author: Nonstationary Problems in Quantum Mechanics, 1997; contbr. articles to sci. publs. Grantee, Internat. Sci. Found., 1991, 92, Russian Fund for Basic Rsch., 1994, 96. Office: Inst Nuc Physics, Vorobjovi, Gory, 119899 Moscow Russia

VOLLER, RUDOLF LAMBERT, mathematician, researcher; b. Hilden, Germany, Apr. 6, 1952; s. Rudolf Heinrich and Else (Bousch) V.; m. Angelika Marianne Vogt, May 11, 1983; children: Benedikt, Jessica. Diploma in Math., Heinrich-Heine U., Düsseldorf, Germany, 1976, PhD, 1982, PhD, Habilitation, 1989. Sci. collegue Heinrich-Heine U., Düsseldorf, 1976-83, sci. asst., 1983-89, mem. sci. staff, 1989-91; cons. Orgalogic GmbH, Cologne, Germany, project mgr., 1991-98; prof. Niederrhein U. Applied Scis., 1998—. Co-author: Vieweg Mathematiklexikon, 1988 (2 awards 1993). Mem. Gesellschaft für Angewandte Mathematik und Mechanik, Deutsche Mathematiker Vereingung. Social Democrat. Roman Catholic. Home: Am Koppelshof 37, 40629 Düsseldorf Germany Office: FH Niederrhein FB07, Webschulstr 31, D-41065 Mouchengladbach Germany

VOLLES, ERWIN, neurologist, educator; b. Oberhausen, Germany, Apr. 18, 1935; s. Karl and Emilie (Weber) V.; m. Rezwandokht Payami, Apr. 29, 1963; children: Nina, Marco, Maja, Ingo. Final med. exam., U. Hamburg, Germany, 1962; MD, U. Göttingen, Germany, 1962. Mem. neurol. dept. U. Göttingen, 1964-74, neurologist, 1971-75, lectr. neurology, 1975-82, prof., 1982—; dir. neurol. dept. Asklepios Clinic Schildautal, Seesen, Germany,

1974—. Mem. German Soc. for Neurology (treas. 1985—). Fax: 0049-5381-741290. Office: Asklepios Clin Schildautal, Karl Herold Strasse 1, D-38723 Seesen Germany

VOLLHARDT, DIETER, physicist; b. Bad Godesberg, Fed. Republic Germany, Sept. 8, 1951; s. Adam and Elfriede (Hummel) V.; m. Jutta Muttenhammer, Aug. 22, 1986; 1 child, Matthias. B., United World Coll. of Atlantic, St. Donat's Castle, U.K., 1971; diploma in physics, U. Hamburg, Fed. Republic Germany, 1977, D. in Natural Scis., 1979, D. Habilitation, 1984. Rsch. fellow U. So. Calif., L.A., 1976-79; rsch. assoc. Max-Planck Inst. for Physics and Astrophysics, Munich, 1979-85, Heisenberg fellow of German Sci. Found., 1985-87; prof. physics, dir. Inst. Theoretical Physics Aachen (Fed. Republic Germany) Inst. Tech., 1987-96; chaired prof. Inst. Physics U. Augsburg, Germany. Author: (book) The Superfluid Phases of Helium 3, 1990. Mem. Am. Phys. Soc. (life), Deutsche Physikalische Gesellschaft. Office: U Augsburg, Theoretical Physics III, 86135 Augsburg Germany

VOLLMANN, JOCHEN, psychiatry and medical ethics educator; b. Dortmund, Germany, Sept. 1, 1963; s. Wolfgang and Christel (Kraft) V. MD, U. Giessen, Germany, 1991, PhD, 1996. Intern U. Giessen (Germany) Sch. Medicine, 1989-90, U. Munich, 1990; resident U. Freiburg, Germany, 1991-94; asst. prof. Free U. Berlin, 1995-96; prof. U. Applied Sci., Berlin, 1996—, mem. univ. senate and coun., 1997-99; vis. fellow Kennedy Inst. of Ethics, Georgetown U., Washington, 1994-95; chmn. rsch. ethics com. Ctr. Pub. Health, Tech. U. Berlin, 1997—; vis. prof. med. ethics Mt. Sinai Sch. Medicine, N.Y.C., 1999-2000, U. Calif. Sch. Medicine, San Francisco, 1999—. Contbr. numerous articles to profl. jours. Supporter, donor German com. Emergency Doctors, 1984—. Recipient award for brain rsch. in geriatrics U. Witten/Herdecke, 1999; grantee German Acad.Exch. Svc., Bonn, 1988, German Rsch. Coun., 1994; scholar German Nat. Scholarship Found., 1985. Mem. European Soc. Philosophy of Medicine and Healthcare, German Acad. Med. Ethics, The Hastings Ctr. (assoc.), others. Avocations: modern art and architecture, classical music, modern dance, sailing, mountain climbing. Office: Free U Berlin Inst History, Med Klingsor Strasse 119, D-12203 Berlin Germany

VOLLMER, JAMES E., high technology management executive; b. Phila., Apr. 19, 1924; s. Edward L. and Elizabeth (MacMichael) V.; m. Mary Campolieto, Nov. 16, 1946 (dec. July 1992); children: Jamie, Kurt, Kimarie; m. Avalon E. Kolar, Jan. 27, 1994. BS, Union Coll., Schenectady, 1945; MA, Temple U., Phila., 1951, PhD, 1956; grad., Advanced Mgmt. Program, Harvard U. Bus. Sch., 1971. Instr. physics Temple U., 1946-51; research supr. Honeywell Corp., Phila., 1952-59; with RCA, 1959—, dir. Advanced Tech. Labs., Camden, N.J., 1959-72; div. v.p., gen. mgr. Govt. Systems Group, RCA, Moorestown, N.J., 1972-79; corp. group v.p. Govt. Systems Div., Comml. Communications Div. and Picture Tube Div. RCA, Cherry Hill, N.J., 1979-83; corp. sr. v.p. RCA, Princeton, N.J., 1983-84; pres. James Vollmer Assocs. Inc., Jupiter Inlet Colony, Fla., 1984-89; disting. lectr. Am. Soc. Engring. Edn., 1972. Author; patentee in field. Vice pres. Palm Beach County (Fla.) United Way, 1974-75; exec. adv. council Fla. Atlantic U., Boca Raton, Fla., 1974-75; vice chmn. campaign Camden County (N.J.) United Way, 1980; bd. dirs. W. Jersey Hosp., Camden, 1980; bd. govs. Franklin Inst., Phila., 1980; chmn. bd. Bartol Rsch. Found., 1980-87. With USNR, 1943-45. Fellow IEEE, AAAS; mem. Am. Phys. Soc., Nat. Security Indsl. Assn. (nat. trustee, past pres. Phila. chpt.), World Affairs Coun. Phila. (bd. dirs. 1982-85), Navy League (life), S. Jersey C. of C. (dir. 1975-77), Tequesta Country Club, Phi Beta Kappa, Sigma Xi, Sigma Pi Sigma, Eta Kappa Nu. Home: 212 Turtle Creek Dr Tequesta FL 33469-1545

VOLLMER, MICHAEL, physicist, educator; b. Hambach/Pfalz, Germany, Mar. 20, 1957; s. Claus and Erika (Claudé) V. Diploma in physics, U. Heidelberg, Germany, 1983, PhD in Physics, 1986, habilitation physics, 1991. Scientist, rschr. Univ. Heidelberg, Germany, 1986-87, 88-91, U. Calif., Berkeley, 1987-88, U. Kassel, Germany, 1991-94; prof. physics Fachhochschule, Brandenburg, Germany, 1994—; Deutscher Akademischer Austausch Dienst vis. prof. U. Bangkok, Thailand, 1994. Author: Optical Properties of Metal Clusters, 1995. Elected mem. bd. (German Physical Soc. 1997). Avocations: dancing, volleyball, traveling.

VOLLMERS, HEINZ PETER, cell biologist; b. Stade, Niedersachsen, Germany, Feb. 19, 1952; s. Heinz and Ursula (Kalisch) V.; m. Annette Büchner, Sept. 29, 1979; children: Philipp, Christopher, Frederic, Sophie. Diploma Biology, U. Tübingen, Germany, 1978, PhD, 1981. Postdoctoral fellow Max Planck Soc., Tübingen, 1981-85; univ. asst. Inst. Pathology, Würzburg, Germany, 1986-91, asst. prof., 1991-98, prof., 1998—. Cpl. Germany Army, 1971-73. Mem. Am. Assn. Cancer Rsch., N.Y. Acad. Sci., Deutsche Krebs Gesellschaft, Deutsche Gesellschaft für Immunologie, Planetary Soc. Lutheran. Avocations: science fiction, cartoons, classic cars. Home: Budapesterstr 23, 97084 Würzburg Germany Office: Univ of Würzburg Inst Pathology, Josef Schneiderstr 2, 97080 Würzburg Germany

VOLLUM, ROBERT BOONE, management consultant; b. Abington, Pa., Sept. 13, 1933; s. Charles Milton and Marion (Yocum) V.; m. Gayle Lorraine Timmerman, July 8, 1956; children: Robert Boone III, Jeffrey Charles. BS in Engring. and Sci., U.S. Naval Acad., 1955. Sr. cons., group leader Stevenson, Jordan & Harrison, Inc., N.Y.C., 1959-65; asst. to pres., plant supt., sales engr. W.L. Gore & Assocs., Inc., Newark, Del., 1965-69; gen. mgr. Philmont Pressed Steel subs. Gulf & Western Industries, Inc., Bethayres, Pa., 1969-72, Air Shields div. Narco Sci. Industries, Inc., Hatboro, Pa., 1972-75; pres. Advanced Airflow Tech., Inc., Warminster, Pa., 1975-76, R.B. Vollum & Assocs., Huntingdon Valley, Pa., 1986—, RBV Mktg. Inc., Willow Grove, Pa., 1992—; chmn. bd. dirs., CEO SFM Technologies, Willow Grove, 1994—; prin. mfg. cons. Sperry Corp., Blue Bell, Pa., 1976-84; dir. cons. Creative Output, Inc., Milford, Conn., 1984-86; spkr. in field. Contbr. articles to profl. jours. Bd. dirs. Upper Moreland Little League, 1965-76. Served to lt. USN, 1955-59. Fellow Am. Prodn. and Inventory Control Soc. (chpt. pres. 1984-85); mem. soc. Mfg. Engrs (sr. mem.), Computer and Automated Systems Assn. (sr. mem.). Republican. Episcopalian. Home: 525 Overlook Ave Willow Grove PA 19090-2818 Office: PO Box 206 Huntingdon Valley PA 19006-0206

VOLMER, SUZANNE, artist; b. Montpelier, Vt., Nov. 25, 1956; d. William S. and Carolyn Lawton Volmer.; BFA with honors, Pratt Inst., 1979. writer, art critic Arts Mag., N.Y.C., 1982-84; instr. RISD, Providence, 1985-89; arts adv. bd. Warwick (R.I.) Mus., 1989-92; guest artist Mass. Coll. Art, Boston, 1995-96. One-woman shows include Hydrangea House Gallery, Newport, R.I., 1992, Newport Art Mus., 1996; group exhbns. include Twining Gallery, N.Y.C., 1987, RISD, Providence, 1988, 89, Die Skulptur Aus Ton, Galerie Schneider, Freiburg, Germany, 1988 (Elisabeth Schneider preis 1989), Galerie Ortillés-Fourcat, Paris, 1999. Recipient 1st prize juried sr. fine art show Pratt Inst., Bklyn., 1979. Home: 25 Livingston St Lincoln RI 02865-1920 Studio: 702 Great Rd Lincoln RI 02865-1421

VOLOBUEV, ANDREY NICOLAEVICH, biophysics educator; b. Moscow, July 3, 1947; s. Nocilay Alexandrovich and Irina Nicolaevna (Pleshenko) V.; m. Natalia Nicolaevna Tutova, Feb. 9, 1973; 2 children. Dr.habil.sc.ing., Traum. Inst., Riga, Latvia, 1993; Dr.tech.sc., Nostrification, Moscow, 1994. Sr. tchr. Med. State U., Samara, Russia, 1975-85; docent Med. State U., Samara, 1986-95, prof., 1995-96, head chair biophys., 1996—. Inventor in field. Mem. European Bioelec. Assn., N.Y. Acad. Scis., Soc. Neurosci., Samara Phys. Soc. (head 1998). Home: Box 1423, 443079 Samara Russia Office: Samara State Med U, St Chapaevskaja 89, 443099 Samara Russia

VOLODIN, VYACHESLAV VLADIMIROVICH, science administrator; b. Sverdlovsk, Ural, Russia, May 3, 1943; s. Vladimir Ivanovich and Ekaterina Petrovna Volodin; m. Tatjana Evgenjevna Susanina, July 8, 1970; 1 child, Svetlana. Engring. Degree, Moscow Aviation Inst., 1966, PhD, 1973. Chief rsch. lab. Moscow Aviation Inst., 1967-74; vis. prof. U. Ill., Urbana, 1975-76; head sci. group Rsch. Inst. Automatic Sys., Moscow, 1977-89, chief Info. and Rsch. Ctr., 1989—. Author: Features of VTOL Design, 1976, Computer Aided Design of Aircraft, 1991, Technical System Definition, 1992; editor: GosNIIAS History, 1996. Br. leader Communisty Party of the Soviet Union, 1985-90. Recipient three medals of the SU and Russian Govt. Mem. AIAA, Znanie Assn. Avocations: old coin collecting, gardening. Home: Zyuzinskaya St 4-4-31, 117418 Moscow Russia Office: GosNIIAS, Victorenko St 7, 125319 Moscow Russia

VOLODKO, ANTON G., physicist, researcher; b. Krasnojarsk, Russia, Jan. 2, 1938; s. Grigorii and Nina (Fufaeva) Volodko; m. Nelli Kotova, Sept. 13, 1965; 1 child, Irina. BSc, Gorky (Russia) U., 1960, postgrad., 1960; PhD, Joint Inst. for Nuclear Rsch., Dubna, Russia, 1972. Physicist Joint Inst. for Nuclear Rsch., Dubna, 1961-72, sr. physicist, 1972-85, leader of dept., 1985—. Author more than 100 publs. in nuclear physics, nuclear instruments and methods and physics letters. Mem. Dubna Chess Club. Avocation: fishing. Home: Sakharov St 15-12, 141 980 Dubna, Moscow Region Russia Office: Joint Inst Nuclear Rsch, Joliot-Curie St 6, 141 980 Dubna, Moscow Region Russia

VOLOSCHIN, LUIS MARÍA, medical researcher; b. Buenos Aires, July 18, 1935; s. Leon Voloschin and Raquel Bourd; m. Diana Beatriz Aisenson, Apr. 2, 1970; 1 child, Diego. MD, Buenos Aires U., 1960. Fellow Argentine Sci. and Tech. Rsch. Coun., Buenos Aires, 1962-65, rschr., 1968-99; fellow Neurophysiological Lab. Henri Roussel Hosp., Paris, 1967; fellow dept. anatomy U. Rochester, N.Y., 1967-68; mgr. Neurophysiology Lab. Neurobiology Inst., Buenos Aires, 1968-2000; dir. Neuroendocrinology Lab. C. Durand Hosp., Buenos Aires, 1988-2000; mem. adv. com. Argentine Sci. and Tech. Rsch. Coun., Buenos Aires, 1995-96, 2000, mem. physiology and pharmacology adv. com., 1996; mem. sci. com. Assn. Neuroendocrine Studies, Argentine Acad. Scis., Buenos Aires, 1987-89. Contbr. articles to profl. jours. Mem. Soc. Study Reproduction, N.Y. Acad. Scis. Avocations: art history, music, movies. Home: Avda Las Heras 1850 10 B, 1127 Buenos Aires Argentina Office: Inst Neurobiologia, Serrano 669, 1414 Buenos Aires Argentina

VOLOSHINOV, ALEXANDER VICTOROVICH, mathematics and philosophy educator; b. Saratov, Russia, Aug. 3, 1947; s. Victor Semyonovich and Lyudmilla Josephovna (Kasatik) V.; m. Elena Victoirovna Kotelkova, Mar. 22, 1975; children: Dmitry, Darya. B in Math., Saratov State U., 1970, M in Math., 1973, PhD in Math., 1974; DSc in Philosophy, Moscow State U., 1993. Assoc. prof. Saratov State Tech. U., 1974-76, 78-93, prof., 1993-94, head culturology dept., 1994—; assoc. prof. Annaba (Algeria) U., 1976-78; prof. Ministry High Edn., Moscow, 1994; academician Internat. Info. Acad., Moscow, 1997; mem. PhD-Degree Awarding Coun., Saratov, 1996—, DSc-Degree Awarding Coun., Saratov, 1996—. Author: Mathematics and Art, 1992, Pythagoras - Union of Truth, Kindness and Beauty, 1993, Trinity of Andrev Rublyov: Geometry and Philosophy, 1997; contbr. articles to profl. jours. Mem. All-Russian Soc. for Protection of Monuments of History and Culture, Moscow, 1985-94, Internat. Movement Educators for Peace and Mutual Understanding, Moscow, 1997. Grantee Soros Found., Moscow, 1993, Russian Found. for Basic Rsch., 1997. Mem. Internat. Assn. Empirical Aesthetics, Internat. Soc. for Group Theory in Cognitive Sci., Internat. Soc. for Math. Aesthetics. Mem. Orthodox Church. Avocations: alpinism, alpine skiing, classical music. Home: Apt 14, 6 Delovaya St, 410040 Saratov Russia Office: Saratov State Tech U, 77 Polytehnicseskaya St, 410054 Saratov Russia

VOLPE, ANDREW ARNOLD, securities company executive, mathematician; b. Moscow, Feb. 17, 1952; arrived in Latvia, 1966; s. Arnold Maxim and Olga Pavel (Nikitina) V.; m. Natalia Volpe, Aug. 11, 1983; children: Alexander A., Lydia A. MS in Technique, Riga Red Banner Civil Aviation Engring. Inst., Latvia, 1975, PhD in Technique, 1985; DSc Engring., Tech. U., Riga, 1993. Mathematician, programmer, sr. engr. Riga Red Banner Civil Aviation Engring. Inst., 1975-78, lectr., sr. tchr., 1978-88, asst. prof., 1988-92; vice chmn. bd. Slavu Bank, Riga, 1992-93; dir. computer tech. and info. sys. dept. Bonus Inc., Riga, 1993; sr. mgr. Bonus Trust Ltd., Riga., 1993-94; dir. Moscow's Rep. Kredo Bank, Riga, 1994-95; gen. mgr. Remora Ltd., Riga, 1995-96; pres. Joint-Stock Brokerage Co. Fincross Securities, Riga and San Francisco, 1996—; docent, asst. prof., chair software and computer sci. USSR Highest Attestation Com., Moscow, 1990. Contbr. articles to profl. jours. Mem. Latvian Assn. Profl. Participants Securities Market. Avocations: classic music, poetry, literature, tennis. E-mail: president@fincross.lv. Home: 11 Cesu St Apt 23, Riga LV-1012, Latvia Office: Fincross Securities, 33/35 Gertrudes St, Riga LV-1011, Latvia

VOLPE, RACHELE, pathologist; b. Civitavecchia, Rome, Mar. 22, 1951; d. Gennaro and Maria (Riccio Cobucci) V. MD, Naples (Italy) U., 1977; postgrad., Parma (Italy) U., 1980. Asst. pathologist Nat. Cancer Inst., Milan, Italy, 1977-78, Genoa, Italy, 1979-83; attending pathologist Nat. Cancer Inst., Aviano, Italy, 1984—. Contbr. numerous articles to profl. publs. Mem. Life Quality Assn. (pres. 1988). Avocations: reading, cooking, music. Home: Piazza del Popolo 56, 33077 Sacile Pordenone Italy Office: Centro Riferimento, Oncologico, 33081 Aviano Pordenone Italy

VOLPÉ, ROBERT, endocrinologist, researcher, educator; b. Toronto, Ont., Can., Mar. 6, 1926; s. Aaron G. and Esther (Shulman) V.; m. Ruth Vera Pullan, Sept. 5, 1949 (dec. Jan. 1997); children: Catherine, Elizabeth, Peter, Edward, Rose Ellen. MD, U. Toronto, 1950. Intern U. Toronto, 1950-51, resident in internal medicine, 1951-52, 53-55, fellow in endocrinology, 1952-53, NRC fellow, 1955-57, sr. rsch. fellow dept. medicine, 1957-62, McPhedran fellow, 1957-65, from asst. prof. to prof., 1962-92, prof. emeritus, 1992—, dir. divsn. endocrinology and metabolism, 1987-92, chmn. centennial com., 1987-88; attending staff St. Joseph's Hosp., Toronto, 1957-66; active staff Wellesley Hosp., Toronto, 1966—; dir. endocrinology rsch. lab. Wellesley Hosp., 1968-97, physician-in-chief, 1974-87; trans-Atlantic vis. prof. Caledonia Endocrine Soc., 1985; Hashimoto Meml. lectr. Kyushu U., Fukuoka, Japan, 1992; K.J.R. Wightman vis. prof. Royal Coll. Physicians, Can., 1994; celebratory lectr. commemorating 200th anniversary of birth of Robert Graves, Dublin, Ireland, 1996. Author: Systematic Endocrinology, 1973, 2nd edit., 1979, Thyrotoxicosis, 1978, Auto-immunity in the Endocrine System, 1981, Auto-immunity and Endocrine Disease, 1985, Thyroid Function and Disease, 1987, Autoimmune Diseases of the Endocrine System, 1990, The Autoimmune Endocrinopathies, 1999; past editl. bd. mem. Jour. Clin. Endocrinology and Metabolism, Clin. Medicine, Clin. Endocrinology, Annals Internal Medicine, Endocrine Pathology, American Journal of Physiology, Opinions in Endocrinolgy Metabolism, Thyroid; mem. editl. bd. Jour. Royal Soc. Medicine; contbr. over 320 articles to profl. jours. Served with Royal Can. Naval Vol. Res., 1943-45. Recipient Goldie medal for med. rsch. U. Toronto, 1971, Novo-Nordisk prize Irish Endocrine Soc., 1990; Med. Rsch. Coun. Can. grantee, 1960-97. Master ACP (gov. for Ont. 1978-83); fellow Royal Coll. Physicians Can. (coun. 1988-96, chmn. ann. meetings com. 1988-94, sci. program com. 1988-94, chmn. rsch. com. 1994-96, v.p. medicine 1994-96), Royal Coll. Physicians Edinburgh and London, Royal Soc. Medicine (editl. bd.); mem. AASS, Can. Soc. Endocrinology and Metabolism (past pres., Sandoz prize lectr. 1985, Disting. Svc. award 1990), Toronto Soc. Clin. Rsch. (Baxter prize lectr. 1984), Can. Soc. Clin. Investigation (Disting. Svc. award 1998), Am. Thyroid Assn. (pres. 1980-81, Disting. Scientist award 1991), Assn. Am. Physicians, Endocrine Soc., Am. Fedn. Clin. Rsch., Can. Soc. Nuclear Medicine (Jamieson prize lectr. 1980), Can. Inst. Acad. Medicine, N.Y. Acad. Sci., European Thyroid Assn. (corr.), L.Am. Thyroid Assn. (corr.), Soc. Endocrinology and Metabolism of Chile (hon.), Caledonia Soc. Endocrinology (hon.), Japan Endocrine Soc. (hon., gold medal 1986), Alpine Ski Club (bd. dirs. 1987-89), U. Toronto Faculty Club. Home: 3 Daleberry Pl, Don Mills, ON Canada M3B 2A5 Office: Wellesley Hosp, Toronto, ON Canada M4Y 1J3

VOLPERT, WALTER, psychologist, educator; b. Munich, Aug. 27, 1942. Dipl., U. Munich, 1966; D, Tech. U. Berlin, 1969. Prof. Pedagogical H.S., West Berlin, Germany, 1972-75, Tech. U. West Berlin, 1975—. Author: Wie Wir Handeln, 1992, Zauberlehrlinge, 1985; contbr. articles to profl. jours. Office: Tech Univ, Ernst Reuter Platz 7, D-10587 Berlin Germany

VOLSKI, GEORGE, economist; b. Tbilisi, Ga., Jan. 18, 1957; s. Zurab and Maggie (Machavariani) V.; m. Nino Sologashvilli, Nov. 13, 1978; children: Zura, Sandro, George Jr. BS, Tbilisi State Univ., 1978. Sr. economist Min. of Trade, Tbilisi, 1978-84; instr. of organizational dept. dist. com. Communist Ctrl. Com. of Ga., Tbilisi, 1984-86, instr. of dept. commerce city com., 1986-89; instr. Communist Cen. Com. of Ga., Tbilisi, 1989-90; deputy head of organizational dept. Trade Union Coun. of Ga., Tbilisi, 1990; head of organizational dept. Conf. of Ind. Trade Union of Ga., Tbilisi, 1990-91; deputy permanent rep. of Ga. Ga. in the Russian Fedn., Moscow, 1991-93; deputy permanent rep. Mission of Ga. to the United Nations, N.Y., 1993—. Avocations: tennis, music. E-mail:misgeorgia@aol.com Fax number: 212 759 1832. Home: 5807 Liebig Ave # 2 Bronx NY 10471-2111 : Office: Permanent Mission of Ga to United Nations One UN Plaza 26th Fl New York NY 10017 :

VOLTAN-ACAR, NILÜFER, psychology educator; b. Istanbul, Turkey, Jan. 1, 1952; d. Bekir and Nurhan (Sirmay) Voltan; m. Bülent Hayri Acar, Sept. 29, 1985; 1 child, Basak. Higher lic., Hacettepe U., Ankara, Turkey, 1974, M in Counseling, 1975, PhD, 1980; MSW, U. Utah, 1975-77. Rsch. asst. Hacettepe U., Ankara, 1977-85, asst. prof., 1985-87, assoc. prof., 1985-94, full prof., 1994—; cons. Ministry Edn., Ankara, 1995-97, Ministry Justice, Ankara, 1999—. Editor Turkish Psychol. Counseling and Guidance Jour., 1995—. Recipient award Fulbright, 1975-77, award Altrusa Internat., 1976. Mem. Internat. Sch. Psychology Assn., Internat. Coun. Psychology, Turkish Psychol. Counseling and Guidance Assn. (chairperson 1995—), Delta Kappa Gamma. Office: Hacettepe U, Dept Psychol Counseling, Beytepe Ankara 06532, Turkey

VOLTES, PEDRO, historian, economist, educator; b. Reus, Spain, July 1, 1926; s. Pedro and Ursicina (Bou) V.; m. Maria-Jose Buxo-Dulce Montesinos, Apr. 18, 1963; children: Joaquin, Maria-Jose, Milagro. DPHL, U. Madrid, 1952, MA in Polit. Sci., 1955; JD, U. Barcelona, 1957; MA in Econ. Sci., U. Valencia, Spain, 1970; MA in Info. Sci., U. Barcelona, 1981. Prof. history U. Barcelona, 1948-68, full prof. econ. history, 1968-91; lectr. in field; vis. prof. U. Bundeswehr, Hamburg, Germany, 1990. Author 80 books on history and social sci.; editor: La Vanguardia, 1948-75; contbr. articles to profl. jours. Dir. Mcpl. Inst. History, Barcelona, 1957-82. Recipient Palmes Academiques, France, Knight Comdr. Merit Republic of Italy, 1957, Knight Comdr. Order Isabella the Cath., 1980, Order Civil Merit, Mil. and Naval Merit, Medal to Merit in Labor, 1977, Cross of Honor in Sci. & Art of Austria, 1993. Mem. Assn. Journalists, Corp. Lawyers Barcelona, Royal Acad. History, Royal Acad. Econ. Scis., N.Y. Acad. Scis., Internat. Soc. Sys. Sci., Circulo Ecuestre Club. Home: Angli 2, 08017 Barcelona Spain

VOLTTI, HILKKA ANNIKKI, chemist; b. Mikkeli, Finland, Dec. 6, 1944; s. Heikki and Vera Maria (Pyhala) V. MS in Biochemistry, U. Oulu, Finland, 1970, PhD, 1974. Asst. dept. biochemistry U. Oulu, Finland, 1970-72; rsch. asst. Finnish Nat. Rsch. Coun., Oulu, 1972; reader, assoc. prof. frpy. med. biochemistry U. Oulu, 1973-79, lectr. biochemistry, 1980-81; chemist U. Hosp., Oulu, 1982-84; clin. chemist Ctrl. Hosp. Kymenlaakso, Kotka, Finland, 1985—. Contbr. articles to profl. jours. Mem. Soc. Clin. Chemistry, Soc. Biochemistry, Biophysics & Microbiology. Avocations: cycling, fitness, travel, nature. Office: Ctrl Hosp Kymenlaakso, 48210 Kotka Finland

VOLTZ, STERLING ERNEST, physical chemist, researcher; b. Phila., Apr. 17, 1921; s. Harry John and Gertrude Irene (Derr) V.; m. Betty Morgan, Nov. 6, 1943; children: Sandra Elizabeth, Karen Lee. BA, Temple U., 1943, MA, 1947, PhD, 1952. Rsch. chemist Houdry Process Corp., Linwood, Pa., 1951-58; group leader Sun Oil Co., Marcus Hook, Pa., 1958-60; supervising engr. GE, Phila., 1960-62; cons. liaison scientist GE, Valley Forge, Pa., 1962-68; rsch. assoc. Mobil Rsch. & Devel. Corp., Paulsboro, N.J., 1968-80, adminstrv., 1980-86; pvt. practice Media, Pa., 1986—. Contbr. articles to Jour. Phys. Chem., Jour. Am. Chem. Soc., Jour. Organic Chemistry, Analytical Chemistry, Jour. Soc. Automotive Engrs., Jour. Chem. and Engring. Data, Jour. Am. Inst. Chem. Engrs. and others. Lt. (j.g.) USN, 1943-46, ETO. Mem. AAAS, Am. Chem. Soc. (Phila. sect.), Catalysis Soc., Catalysis Club. Phila. (sec.-treas., chmn., dir. 1957-60), Am. Legion, Disabled Am. Vets., Sigma Xi. Achievements include 23 patents for Simulation of Catalytic Cracking Process, for Compatible Mixtures of Coal Liquids and Petroleum Based Fuels, for Reactivation of Automotive Exhaust Oxidation Catalyst, for Increasing Antiknock Value of Olefinic Gasoline, for Preparation of Aromatic Hydrocarbons, for Process for Dehydrocyclizing Heterocyclic Organic Compounds, for Alumina Stabilized by Thoria to Resist Alpha Alumina Formation, for Method of Treating Chromium Oxide, others; invention of plastic dry bag; co-development of commercial methanol-to-gasoline process, of fuel cell for space power applications, including first successful operation in space flight; development of catalysts and processes for petroleum and petrochemical conversions, of electronic apparatus to measure dielectric properties during oxidation reactions and establish reaction kinetics; establishment of relationship between catalytic properties, surface chemistry, and semiconductivity properties of metal oxide catalysts; research on catalytic systems for automotive emissions control including kinetic model of oxidation of carbon monoxide and hydrocarbons. Home: 6 E Glen Cir Media PA 19063-4712

VÖLTZKE, DIETER WOLFGANG, chemist, ceramist; b. Greifswald, Germany, Aug. 23, 1956; s. Herbert Johannes and Irmgard Minna (Hey) V. Diploma in chemistry, M.L. U. Halle-Wittenberg, Halle, Germany, 1983, PhD in Natural Scis., 1986. Rsch. student Martin Luther U. Halle-Wittenberg, 1982-85, rsch. fellow, 1985-00; rsch. engr. Max-Planck Inst. for Microstructure Physics, Halle, 2000—. Postdoctoral fellow Inst. New Materials, Saarbrücken, Germany, 1992-93. Avocation: photography. Office: Inst Anorg Chem ML Univ, Kurt Mothes Str 2, 06120 Halle SachAnhl, Germany

VOLYNETS, OLEG NAZAYOVICH, earth scientist; b. Irkutsk, Siberia, USSR, Feb. 25, 1937; s. Nazar Matveevich and Maria Yakovlevna (Pougachenko) V.; m. Janna Grigorievna; children: Genady, Artem, Anna. Student, Moscow U., 1959; Candidate of Geol.-Mineral. Scis., Inst. Petrology, Minerologyand Geochemistry, Moscow, 1967; D of Geol.-Mineral. Scis., Moscow State U., 1993. Older sci. engr. employee Kamchatkan Expdn. of AS of USSR, 1959-61; jr. sci. employee Inst. Volcan. Geology and Geochemistry, Petropavlovsk-Kamchatsky, USSR, 1961-71, sr. sci. employee, 1971-91, Ledind sci. employee, 1991—; cons. Geol. Office Kenchatke, Petropavlovsk-Kamchatsky, 1975-98. Author: (books) Plagioclases of Effusive and Subsurface Intrusions of Kamchatka, 1976, Geochemical Peculiarities of Quaternary Volcanic of Kamchatka, 1981. Grantee in field. Mem. Am. Geographic Soc., N.Y. Acad. Scis. Home: Piip Blvd 4 Fl 2, 683006 Petropavlovsk-kamchatsky Russia Office: Inst Volcan Geol and Geochm, Piip Blvd 9, 683006 Petropavlovsk-Kamchatsky Russia

VOLYNSKY, ANATOLY BORISOVICH, chemist, researcher; b. Moscow, Aug. 10, 1956; s. Boris Yakovlevich and Nadezhda Andreevna (Denisova) V.; m. Saule Abdykhanovna Arystanbekova, Feb. 9, 1980; 1 child, Viktor. MSc, Lomonosov Moscow State U., 1978; PhD, Vernadsky Inst. Geochemistry and Analytical Chemistry, Moscow, 1987. Rsch. asst. Vernadsky Inst., Moscow, 1978-80, jr. rsch. chemist, 1980-86, rsch. chemist, 1986-91, sr. rsch. chemist, 1996—; sr. rsch. chemist Lomonosov U., Moscow, 1991-93, sr. rsch. chemist, 1993-96; sr. rsch. chemist Zelinsky Inst. Organic Chemistry, Moscow, 1999—; guest rschr. Ulm (Germany) U., 1995-97. Contbr. articles to profl. jours.; sci. editor Russian Jour. Analytical Chemistry, 1986—. Scholar Alexander von Humboldt Found., Bonn, Germany, 1995-97, 2000. Avocations: literature, philosophy. Office: Vernadsky Inst Geochem Anal Chem, Anal Chem Kosygin Str 19, 117975 Moscow Russia

VOLZ, ARMIN, biochemist, researcher; b. Stuttgart, Germany, Feb. 14, 1959; s. Dietmar and Doris (Schwenkedel) V.; m. Barbara Schick Volz, May 5, 1989; children: Carolin Tabea, Manuel Hendrik. Diploma in Biochemistry, Eberhard-Karls U., Germany, 1988; PhD, Free U., Germany, 1994. Technician IBM-Germany, Stuttgart, 1981-82; scientist Free U., Berlin, 1990-95; tech. advisor Fa. Geiger Laborbedarf, Tuebingen, Germany, 1989—; scientist charité Humboldt U., Berlin, 1995—. Mem. bd., 1992, pres., 1993-99, Rock'n Roll Club, Starlights, Berlin. 1st Lt. ABC Defense, 1979-81. Avocations: Rock 'n roll dancing, production of videos, computers. Home: Archivstr 17, D-14195 Berlin Germany Office: Inst Immungenetik, Spandauer Damm 130, D-14050 Berlin Germany

VOLZ, HEINRICH JAKOB, chemistry educator; b. Frankfurt, Germany, July 25, 1928; s. Karl August and Katharina (Frasch) V.; m. Maria de Lecea Lumbreras, 1958; children: Margarita, Maria-Henriette. Diploma, U. Frankfurt, 1956, DPhil in Chemistry, 1957. Rsch. asst. J.W. Goethe U., Frankfurt, 1957-58; rsch. fellow Harvard U., Cambridge, Mass., 1958-59;

asst. Fridericiana U., Karlsruhe, Germany, 1960-65, lectr. chemistry, 1965-71, prof., 1971—; prof. European Sch. Higher Indsl. Chemistry Studies, Strasbourg, France, 1987—. Contbr. articles to sci. jours. Mem. German Chem. Soc., Am. Chem. Soc., Soc. for Biol. Chemistry, N.Y. Acad. Scis. Avocations: history, biology, woodworking. Home: Roland 52 A, 76135 Karlsruhe Germany Office: U Fridericiana, Kaiserstrasse, 76128 Karlsruhe Germany

VOM DAHL, STEPHAN, physician, researcher; b. Bielefeld, Westphalia, Germany, Sept. 19, 1962; s. Dieter and Rosel (Wiegleb) Vom D.; m. Christa Bertram, Aug. 3, 1990; children: Antonia, Ariane. MD, Med. Sch. Dusseldorf, Germany, 1989. Resident Freiburg, Germany, 1989-91; physician Freiburg, 1992-94, U. Hosp., Dusseldorf, 1995—. Contbr. over 60 articles in hepatology to profl. jours. Capt. German Army, 1991-92. Internat. Rotary Found. scholar, 1987-88; grantee Deutsche Forschunge Gemeinschaft, 1995—. Mem. German Assn. Intestinal and Metabolic Diseases, German Assn. Study Liver, German Soc. for Biochemistry and Molecular Biology. Avocations: music. Office: Gastroenterology, U Hosp Moorenstr 5, 40225 Düsseldorf Germany

VON ARNIM, HANS HERBERT, political science educator; b. Darmstadt, Germany, Nov. 16, 1939; s. Herbert and Katja Emmy (Leonhard) von A.; m. Ulrike Liebmann, Feb. 25, 1966; children: Felix, Vera, Eva. LLM, U. Heidelberg, Germany, 1962, M Econs., 1966, D Pub. and Canon Law, 1970; D Iuris Habilis, U. Regensburg, Germany, 1976. Dir. Karl Bräuer Inst., Wiesbaden, Germany, 1968-78; prof. U. Marburg, Germany, 1978-81; prof. pub. law and constl. theory German Postgrad. Sch. Adminstrv. Scis., Speyer, Germany, 1981—; rector Postgrad. Sch. Adminstrv. Scis., Speyer, Germany, 1993-95; mem. Commn. on Election Laws and Mcpl. Structure, Parliament of State of Rhineland-Palatinate, Mainz, Germany, 1988-90; mem. Fed. Presdl. Commn. on Party Financing, 1992-93; mem. Constl. Ct., State of Brandenburg, Potsdam, Germany, 1993-96. Author: The Common Good and Group Interests, 1977, State Theory of the Federal Republic of Germany, 1984, Power Makes Inventive, 1988, The State as Spoils, 1993, State without Servants, 1993, paperback edit., 1995, We Are the State, 1995, Parties, Members of Parliament and Money, 1996, The Glutton as Caterer, 1997, paperback edit., 1999, Servants of Many Masters, 1998, Principles of Economic Policy, 6th edit., 1998, The Bright Shine of Democracy, 2000. Office: Verwaltungswissenschaften, Freiherr-von-Stein-Str 2, Hochschule D-67324 Speyer Germany

VON ARX, DOLPH WILLIAM, food products executive; b. St. Louis, Aug. 30, 1934; s. Adolph William and Margaret Louise (Linderer) von A.; m. Sharon Joy Landolt, Dec. 21, 1957; children: Vanessa von Arx Gilvarg, Eric S., Valerie L. BSBA, Washington U., St. Louis, 1961; LHD, St. Augustine Coll., 1988. Account exec. Compton Advt., N.Y.C., 1961-64; v.p. mktg. Ralston Purina Co., St. Louis, 1964-69; exec. v.p. mktg. Gillette Personal Care Div., Chgo., 1969-72; exec. v.p. gen. mgmt. group T.J. Lipton Inc., Englewood Cliffs, N.J., 1973-87; pres., chief exec. officer R.J. Reynold Tobacco Co., Winston-Salem, N.C., 1987-88; chmn., chief exec. officer Planters LifeSavers Co., Winston-Salem, 1988-91; bd. dirs. Interat. Multi Food, Mpls., Ive Mackenzie, Toronto, Boca Raton, Fla., No. Trust Fla. Corp., Miami, Cree Rsch. Inc., Durham, N.C., Ruby Tuesday Inc., BMC Fund Inc., Isolux Corp., Naples, Fla.; chmn. Morrison's Restaurant Atlanta, 1996-98. Bd. visitors U. N.C., 1988-92; chmn. bd. trustees Wake Forest U. Grad. Sch. Mgmt., 1988-96; pres. bd. trustees N.C. Dance Theater, Winston-Salem, 1989-90; bd. dirs. Forsyth Meml. Hosp., 1988-92, Naples Conservancy, Naples Philharmonic Ctr. for Arts, Florida Arts Coun., Reynolds Mus. Am. Art, Naples Cmty. Hosp., chmn., 1994-99, bd. dirs. health care sys., chmn., 1995—. Mem. Belle Haven Club (Greenwich) (bd. dirs. 1983-87), Naples Yacht Club, Univ. Club (N.Y.C.), Linville Ridge Country Club (Linville, N.C.), Royal Poinciana Club (Naples, Fla.). Avocation: tennis. Home: Pent House 1 4351 Gulf Shore Blvd N Naples FL 34103-2697

VON BASSENHEIM, GUSTAVO MARCELO, veterinary surgeon, consultant; b. Buenos Aires, Nov. 16, 1957; s. Johann M. and Maria S. (Castex) von B.; m. Maria Cristina Gnecco, July 2, 1983; children: Agustín, Santiago, Josefina. MSc, U. Buenos Aires, 1985, Inst. Altos Estudios Empresariales U. Austral, Argentina, 1996. Dir. Cabaña Aricola Jorju, Buenos Aires, 1990—, Jorju SA, Buenos Aires, 1990—, Nutrovo SA, Buenos Aires, 1995—, Molinos Tressor SA, Buenos Aires, 1996—; pres. Labs. Gema SA, Buenos Aires, 1998—; pres. sci. com. Argentine Bd. of Poultry Industry, 1989—; bd. dirs. Poultry Work Force of Veterinarians, Argentina. Pres. Young Activist Dem. and Ctr. Politics, Hurlingham, Argentina, 1983-86. Mem. Marriage Encounter of Argentina (lectr. 1994—), Hurlingham Club. Roman Catholic. Avocations: fishing, outdoor activities, tennis, squash. Home: Gaboto 911, 1686 Hurlingham Buenos Aires Argentina Office: Cabaña Aricola Jorju SA, Uriarte 1635, 1414 Buenos Aires Argentina

VON BAUER, ERIC ERNST, venture capital and investment banking executive; b. LaHabra Heights, Calif., Apr. 12, 1942; s. Kurt Ernst and Margaret Ross (Porter) V.; children: Suzanne Lynn Vine, Katherine Jean. Student, Occidental Coll., L.A., 1960-63; MBA, U. Chgo., 1973; postgrad., U. Chgo. Law Sch., 1973. Registered rep. Piedmont Internat. Ltd. subs. Piedmont Capital Corp., Frankfurt, West Germany, 1968-71; fin. adv. trust dept. 1st Nat. Bank Chgo., 1971-72; sec.-treas., contr. Am. Med. Bldgs. Inc., Milw., 1973-75; sr. mng. cons. Mgmt. Analysis Ctr., Inc., Chgo., 1975-79; v.p., gen. mgr. corp. fin. adv. svcs. divsn. Continental Ill. Nat. Bank Trust Co., Chgo., 1979-82; pres., CEO The Capital Strategy Mgmt. Co., Chgo., 1982—; dir., pres. Chgo. chpt. N.Am. Soc. Corp. Planning, 1981-84; faculty mem. Keller Grad. Sch. Mgmt., Chgo., 1987—; guest lectr. U. Chgo. Grad Sch. Bus. Author: Knowing Your Product Line Profitability: Key to Greater Strategic Success, 1984, Meaningful Risk and Return Criticsm for Strategic Investment Decisions, 1982; co-author: Zero Base Planning, Budgeting, 1977; contbr. articles to profl. publs. Bd. dirs. Chgo. chpt. Reading is Fundamental, 1972-73; dist. adv. com. Fremont (Ill.) Unified Sch. Dist. 1st lt. C.E. U.S. Army, 1964-67. Decorated Army Commendation award. Mem. Assn. Corp. Growth, Midwest Planning Assn., Friends of Small Bus., Am. Mgmt. Assn. C. of C. (dir. Chgo. jr. chpt. 1971-73), Rotary (Chgo.), Chgo. Bar Assn. Presbyterian. Office: Mgmt Co 233 S Wacker Dr Chicago IL 60606-6306

VON BERNUTH, CARL W., rail transportation executive, lawyer; b. N.Y.C., Feb. 2, 1944. BA, Yale U., 1966, LLB, 1969. Bar: N.Y., Pa. Corp. atty. White and Case, N.Y.C., 1969-80; assoc. gen. counsel Union Pacific Corp., N.Y.C., 1980-83, dep. gen. counsel, 1983-88; v.p., gen. counsel Union Pacific Corp., Bethlehem, Pa., 1988-91; sr. v.p., gen. counsel, sec. Union Pacific Corp., Omaha, Nebr., 1997—; trustee Inst. Law and Econs. U. Pa., Phila. Mem. Am. Corp. Counsel Assn., Assn. Transp. Practitioners, Practicing Law Inst. Home: 5205 Burt St Omaha NE 68132-2223 Office: Union Pacific Corp 1416 Dodge St Rm 1230 Omaha NE 68179-0001

VON BOEHM, GERO, journalist, film director, producer; b. Hannover, Germany, Apr. 20, 1954; m. Christiane von Salmuth, 1975; children: Katharina, Julia, Felix. Freelancer DIE ZEIT, Germany, 1973-82; pres. Interscience Film GmbH, Heidelberg, Germany, 1978—. host Wortwechsel, 1980-89, SAT 1, 1990-91, over 100 documentaries on sci. and art, 1977—; author: Odyssey 3000, 1998, I.M. Pei: Light in the Key, 2000, Balthus: The Painter's House, 2000. Upjohn fellow, 1984; recipient TV award Hartmannbund, 1978, 94, Medicine and Media award, Culture award Eduard-Rhein Found., 1993, TV award Bavaria, 1994. Office: Intersci Film GmbH, Interscience Film GmbH, Am Buchsenackerhang 41, D-69118 Heidelberg Germany

VON BOETTICHER, CHRISTIAN ULRIK, member of European parliament; b. Hannover, Fed. Republic Germany, Dec. 24, 1970. Mem. European Parliament, Rellinger, Germany, 1999—; mem. Group of the European People's Party (Christian Democrats) and European Democrats; mem. com. on citizen's freedoms and rights, justice and home affairs, com. on petitions; substitute mem. com. on regional policy, transport and tourism; mem. delegation to the EU-Latvia Joint Parliamentary Com. •

VON BOSE, MICHAEL JOERG, physician, consultant, educator; b. Munich, Germany, Feb. 13, 1948; s. Hans-Juergen Karl and Margit (Niedermeier) Boettner; m. Janet Patricia Powell, Apr. 9, 1980 (div. Jan. 1985); m. Dorothee Marianne Scheid; children: Julia Teresa, Fiona Olga Louisa. Dr.med, Ludwig-Maximlian U., 1978; MD (FLEX-examm), Boston, 1982. Bd. cert. Neurology and Psychiatry, 1994 (Germany); diplomate Am. Bd. Emergency Medicine. Resident Dept. Surgery, U. Hosps., Munich, 1977-78; resident dept. anesthesiology Krecke Hosp., Munich, 1978-79; resident Dept. Surgery, Bklyn.-Cumberland Med. Ctr., N.Y.C., 1979-82, Dept. Surgery, Jersey City (N.J.) Med. Ctr., 1982-86, Dept. Neurology Stådt Krankenhaus Bogenhausen, Munich, 1987-90, 90-94; attending physician ICU Dept. Neurology Stådt Krankenhaus Bogenhausen, 1994—; Am. Heart Assn., ACLS instr., course dir. UMDNJ, Newark, 1984—; cons. for Internat. Emergency Systems, Munich, 1995—; mem. European Resuscitation Coun., U.K., 1993—; adj. asst. prof. dept. emergency medicine George Washington U., Washington, 1999. Co-author: manual on personality disorder examination, 1996; contbr. articles to profl. jours. Lt. German Navy, 1969-72. Recipient grant from The Laerdal Found., Norway, 1994, scholarship Max-Planck Soc., Munich, 1987-90. Fellow Am. Coll. Emergency Physicians, European Soc. for Intensive Care Medicine, Assn. for Resuscitation Tng. (chmn. 1994—), Soc. for Internat. Advancement of Emergency Med. Care. Avocations: cruise ship medicine, hyperbaric medicine, sailing, diving. Home: Aschafeldstr 10, 83250 Marquartstein Germany Office: Staedt Krankenhaus, Englschalkingerstr 77, 81925 Munich Germany

VON BRAUN, PETER CARL MOORE STEWART, finance company executive; b. Greenwich, Conn., June 24, 1940; s. Carl Conrad and Martha Irwin (Moore) von B.; m. Elisabeth Esser, July 1, 1967 (div. Dec. 1980); m. Denene Jensen, Sept. 26, 1987; children: Christina Stewart, Alexander Stewart. BA with high honors, Yale U., 1964; PhD summa cum laude, U. Cologne, 1966. Assoc. McKinsey & Co., Inc., N.Y.C., 1966-72, prin., 1972-77; chief internat. program devel. Order of St. John, London, 1977-80; exec. dir. Sight Programme, London and Sultanate of Oman, 1977-84; mng. ptnr. Leyton Assocs., Greenwich, 1980—; chmn., CEO Am. Microtrace Corp., Virginia Beach, Va., 1987-95, RusPetrol (USA), LLC, Greenwich, Conn., 1989-99; mng. dir. LabelADD, LLC, Greenwich, Conn., 1987—. Author: Die Verteidigung Indiens, 1968, How to Save a Life, 1977, How to Save An Eye, 1981; contbr. articles to profl. jours.; producer (film) How to Save a Life, 1977. Chmn. Battle Harbour Found., Greenwich, 1972—; vestryman Trinity Parish, N.Y.C., 1977-84; chmn. Anglican Svc. Tng. & Relief Orgn., London, 1986—; bd. dirs. Presiding Bishop's Fund, N.Y.C., 1977-81; mem. exec. bd. Greenwich Coun. Boy Scouts Am. With USN, 1956-58, U.S. Army, 1958-64. Decorated knight of grace and knight of justice Order of St. John, companion with star Order of Merit (Cyprus), other fgn. and U.S. decorations; Fulbright scholar, 1964-66. Republican. Episcopalian. Clubs: Cavalry, Guards Polo (London); N.Y. Yacht (N.Y.C.), Yale Club, Indian Harbor Yacht Field Club (Greenwich, Conn.), Battle Harbour Yacht (Newfoundland, Can.), Commodore. Avocations: sailing, military history, cooking. Home: 36 Zaccheus Mead Ln Greenwich CT 06831-3753

VON BREDOW, WILFRIED, political science educator; b. Heinrichsdorf, Fed. Republic Germany, Jan. 2, 1944; s. Christoph and Anja (von Oettingen) von B.; m. Monika Schlesier; 1 child, Fenimore. PhD, Bonn (Fed. Republic Germany) U., 1969. Asst. Seminar Fuer Politische Wissenschaft U. Bonn, 1969-72; prof. polit. sci. Philipps U., Marburg, Fed. Republic Germany, 1972—, v.p., 1975-77; vis. prof. U. Social Sci., Toulouse, 1981, Trinity Coll. U. Toronto (Ont., Can.), 1986-87. Author 14 books on polit. theory, internat. rels. and mil. security; contbr. numerous articles to profl. jours. Served to lt. inf. German Army, 1962-64. Recipient John S. Diefenbaker award, Can. Coun., Ottawa, 1994. Mem. Assn. Can. Studies in German Speaking Countries (pres. 1999—). E-mail: wvb@mailer.uni-marburg.de. Home: Altes SchulhausGoett, D-35094 Lahntal Germany Office: Philipps U, W-Roepke St 6, D-35032 Marburg Germany

VON BRENTANO, PETER, physicist, researcher; b. Zurich, Switzerland, May 22, 1935; s. Bernard and Margot (Gerlach) von B.; m. Tremezza Brigitte Künzel, July, 1966. PhD, U. Heidelberg, Germany, 1960-63; Habilitation, U. Heidelberg, 1969. Rsch. assoc. Max-Planck-Inst. Nuclear Physics, Heidelberg, 1963-66, group leader, 1968-71; vis. assoc. prof. physics U. Tex., Austin, 1966-67; sr. rsch. assoc. U. Washington, Seattle, 1967-68; prof. U. Cologne, Germany, 1971—, dir. nuclear physics lab.; mem. adv. bd. nuclear physics Fed. Min. Germany Edn. Rsch., Bonn, 1996-2000. Contbr. over 360 articles to profl. jours. Mem. German Rsch. Assn. (referee nuclear physics 1992-2000), German Physical Soc. (mem. nuclear physics bd. 1977-79), European Physical Soc. (chmn. nuclear physics bd. 1981-85), Euroball Coord. Com. E-mail: brentano@ikp.uni-koeln.de. Office: Inst Nuc Physics, Zülpicher St 77, 50937 Cologne Germany

VON BROSDA KUPFERBER, BARON ALEXANDER CHRISTIAN, investment banker; b. Huckeswagen, N. Rhine, Germany, Apr. 26, 1970; came to U.S., 1994; s. Christian-George and Emmi-Martina (Laugallies) B.; m. Katerina. Diploma, Humanistic-Classical and, Econ. Sch., Wuppertal, Germany, 1991. Investment banker various, Dusseldorf, Germany, 1991-92; exec. product mgr., sales trainer AWD, Hanover, Germany, 1992-93; chmn., CEO ABMK & Co. Internat. Ent., Inc., N.Y.C., 1994; v.p., mktg. dir. Lyon Mountain Spring Water, Inc., Stamford, N.Y., 1994—; shareholder, 1994; bd. dirs. The Maui Inst., Hawaii, 1994—; pres. A.B.A. Enterprises, Inc., Stamford, N.Y., 1995—, Stamford Inst. for Rsch., Consulting and Internat. Comm., 1995—; CEO and chmn. bd. Stamford Fin. Theatrical Fund, Inc., 1995—; exec. v.p., treas. European Mkt. Stamford Fin., Inc., N.Y., 1994-97; co-chmn. Taurus Internat. Investments, Inc., 1995. Chmn. ball com. Christmas Feeling Fund, Stamford, N.Y., vice chmn. of Fund. Recipient 20th Achievement award U.S. Libr. Congress, Degree of Merit for outstanding contribution to Finance and Industry, Melrose Press Ltd.; named Man of Yr., ABI, 1996, Hon. Dep. Gov., ABIRA, Hall of Fame of Internat. Bus. People. Mem. Club of Intellectuals, Cambridge, England, C. of C., Stamford, N.Y., Congressional Group, German-American C. of C., European-American C. of C., Rotary Internat., Police Benevolent Assn. (hon.), Comthur of Aragon Priory Order of St. John. Roman Catholic. Avocations: golf, reading, sailing, racing, diving. Office: Taurus Internat Investments Inc Braden Fin Ctr Ste 905 1401 Manatee Ave W Bradenton FL 34205-6770

VON CAMPE, HILMAR A., investment company executive, writer; b. Halle, Germany, Apr. 11, 1925; came to U.S., 1990; s. Alfred and Margarete von C.; m. Ubaldina Angelica Gamio, Dec. 1, 1972; children: Stefan, Sabrina. Diplom, Hamburg (Germany) U., 1950. Bd. mem. Moral Rearmament Germany, L.Am., 1958-69; asst. to pres. Adela Investment Co., Lima, Peru, 1971-72; regional mgr. Adela Investment Co., Kingston, Jamaica, 1973-76; mgr. Cotinco, S.A., Mexico City, 1977-79; exec. dir. Formamex S.A. de CV, Mexico City, 1980-92; owner 5 Continents, Inc., Colorado Springs, Colo., 1993—. Author: Feigheit und Anpassung, 1989, Moral Meltdown, 1996, Connecting with the Power of God, 1996, Deutschland im Globalen Bürgerkrieg, 2000. Bd. mem. Berlin Sculpture Fund, Inc. Decorated Iron Cross, Assault Medal. Mem. Am. Ret. Officers Assn., Order of St. John (knight). Lutheran. E-mail: voncampe@aol.com. Office: Five Continents PO Box 60326 Colorado Springs CO 80960-0326

VON CLARMANN, THOMAS, meteorologist, researcher; b. Munich, Sept. 15, 1959. Diploma, Ludwig-Maximilians U., 1986; Dr.rer.nat., U. Fridericiana, 1989. Scientist Forschungszentrum Karlsruhe, 1987—, group supr., 1995—. Contbr. articles to profl. jours.

VON COLLANI, GERNOT ULRICH, psychology educator, researcher; b. Swinemuende, Germany, Apr. 25, 1942; s. Hans-Joachim and Gertraude Karoline (Schmidt) von C.; m. Sonja Setiawaty Surya, July 7, 1980; children: Marcel Niklas, Patrice Dominic. B.A., Univ. Hamburg, 1966, M.A., 1969; Ph.D., Tech. Univ., Braunschweig, Fed. Republic Germany, 1973;Dr. rer. nat. habil., 1986. Research asst. dept. stats. Univ. Konstanz, Fed. Republic Germany, 1969-72; univ. asst. dept. psychology Univ. Braunschweig, 1972-81, asst. prof. dept. psychology, 1981-85, prof., 1992; prof. U. Leipzig, 1993. Author: Social Network Analysis, 1987; contbr. articles to profl. jours. Lutheran. Avocations: classical music, photography, letters. Office: Inst Psychology, Spielmannstrasse 19, D 38106 Braunschweig Germany

VONDERBANK, RALF SEBASTIAN, research engineer, energy executive; b. Bremen, Germany, Oct. 19, 1964; s. Sebastian and Renate (Weist) V.; m. Sabine Heltewig, Feb. 12, 1996; children: Katharina-Victoria, Helena. M in Engring., Tech. U., Darmstadt, Germany, 1990, D in Engring., 1993. Rsch. asst. Tech. U., Braunschweig, Germany, 1990-93; process engr. Steinmüller Gmbh, 1993-99, project mgr., 1997-99; vis. rschr. Pub. Power Corp. of Greece, 1991, State Electricity Commn., Australia, 1991, N.E. China Elec. Power, 1995; scholar Nat. Entity of Elec. Energy, Italy, 1995-96; rsch. engr. ENEL SpH, Italy, 1999-2000, Rolls-Royce Deutschland GmbH, 2000—. Inventor: slot burner for lignite combustion, 1994, process for combustion of lignite, 1995, patentee 1995, 97; also contbr. articles to profl. jours. Avocation: deep sea sailing. E-mail: vonderbank@gmx.net.

VON DER ESCH, HANS ULRIK, lawyer; b. Nurnberg, Germany, Jan. 27, 1928; s. Hans Joachim and Kerstin Marianne (Sandstedt) von der E.; m. Marianne Hedvig Margaretha Celsing, Aug. 23, 1975; children: Ulric, Fredrik; 1 child by previous marriage: Alexandra Louise. MBA, U. Gothenburg, 1951; LLB, U. Stockholm, 1954. Bar: Sweden 1966. With Dist. Ct. Svc., Nykoping and Stockholm, 1954-57; pres.'s asst. counsel Bonniergroup, Stockholm, Hamburg, Geneva, N.Y., 1957-63; atty. Bonniergroup, Stockholm, 1963-66, assoc., ptnr., sr. ptnr; with Advokatfirman Landahl, 1966-96; sr. ptnr. Landahl & Wistrand, Advokatbyrå, 1997-98; advokat HU von der Esch AB, 1999—; chmn., bd. dirs. Swedish and fgn. cos. With Swedish Army Calvary, 1946-48, maj. Res. Decorated Swedish Sign of Distinction, Finnish Golden Order of Merit, Norwegian Badge of Honor, Knight of the Order of St. John in Sweden. Mem. ABA, Swedish Lawyers Assn. (divsn. dir. 1974-79, del. 1979-88, mem. disciplinary bd. 1984-88, 92-98), Swedish Army and Air Force Res. Officers League (pres. 1975-78), Swedish Parachute Assn. (pres. 1966-68), Royal Swedish Aero Club (bd. dirs. 1966-78, gen. counsel 1967-78, v.p. 1983-88), Internat. Bar Assn., Internat. Fiscal Assn., Nya Saellskapet Club. Mem. Swedish Ch. Lic. pvt. pilot for airplane, helicopter and glider; holder 5 world class records piston engine: Class C-1-c, speed record over recognized course: Sal, Rep. of Cape Verde to Funchal, Madeira 224.06 km/hr, Class C-1-c light aircraft 1750-3000 kgs, Funchal, Madeira to Lisbon 256.131 km/hour, Class C-1-c Paris to Stockholm, 248.67 km/hour, Class C-1-b light aircraft 500-1000 kgs, Stockholm to Rovaniemi, Finland, 126.31 km/hour and Class C-1-b Rovaniemi, Finland to Murmansk, U.S.S.R., 150.59 km/hour. Home: 25 2nd Strandvägen, 11456 Stockholm Sweden Office: Strandvagen 25 1st, PO Box 5495, 11484 Stockholm Sweden

VON DER GABLENTZ, OTTO MARTIN, college rector; b. Berlin, Oct. 9, 1930; s. Otto Heinrich and Hilde (Zietlow) von der G.; m. Hetti Blanche-Koelensmid, Nov. 1999; children: Georg, Alexandra, Jessica, Johanna, Julia. Law degree, U. Freiburg, Germany, 1952; grad., Coll. Europe, Bruges, Belgium, 1953; BPhil, Oxford (Eng.) U., 1955; Doctor Honoris Causa, U. Amsterdam, The Netherlands, 1997. With Coll. of Europe, Bruges, 1955-56; asst. rschr. German Assn. Fgn. Affairs, 1958-59; with German Diplomatic Svc., 1959-95; amb. to The Netherlands The Hague, 1983-90; amb. to Israel Tel Aviv, 1990-93; amb. to Russia Moscow, 1993-95; rector Coll. of Europe, Bruges, 1996—; coord. German-Dutch Conf. Recipient A. de Tocqueville prize European Inst. Pub. Adminstrn., Maastricht, 1989; Harkness fellow Harvard U., 1956-57, hon. fellow Hebrew U., Jerusalem, 1993. Home: Hoornstraat 4, B-8000 Brugge Belgium Office: Coll of Europe, Dijver 11, B-8000 Brugge Belgium

VON DER LÜHE, OSKAR FRIEDRICH HARALD, astronomer; b. Celle, Fed. Republic Germany, Mar. 20, 1954; s. Harald Hans Erich and Miranda (Laubender) Von Der L.; m. Ruth Maria Fell, Oct. 11, 1984; children: Christina Pauline, Barbara Maria, Verena Carola. Diploma in Physics, U. Freiburg, Freiburg, Fed. Republic of Germany, 1979, Dr. rer. nat. in Physics, 1986. Researcher Kiepenheuer Inst., Freiburg, Fed. Republic Germany, 1979-86; astrophysicist Nat. Solar Obs., Sunspot, N.Mex., 1986-88; oberassistent ETH (Fed. Inst. Tech.), Zürich, Switzerland, 1988-90; astrophysicist European So. Obs., München, 1990-97; prof., dir. Kiepenheuer Inst., Freiburg, Germany, 1997—. Editor: (book) High Resolution Solar Observations, 1989. Recipient resident rsch. associateship Nat. Rsch. Coun., Air Force Geophysics Lab., Sunspot, N.Mex., 1986-87. Mem. Astronomische Ges., Deutsche Physikalische Ges., Optical Soc. Am., Soc. Photo-Optical Instrumentation Engrs., European Optical Soc. Office: Kiepenheuer Inst, Schoenechstr 6-7, D-79104 Freiburg Germany

VON DER MALSBURG, CHRISTOPH, biophysics and computer science educator; b. Kassel, Hesse, Germany, May 8, 1942; s. Raban and Gisela von der M.; m. Annegret Riedesel Freiin zu Eisenach, Aug. 16, 1975. Diploma in physics, Ruprecht-Karl U., Heidelberg, Germany, 1967, Dr. rer. nat. physics, 1970. Rsch. fellow Ctr. European pour la Recherche Nucleaire, Geneva, 1970-71; postdoctoral fellow Max-Planck-Inst. Biophys. Chemistry, Göttingen, Germany, 1971-74; mem. sci. staff Dept. Neurobiology, 1974-88; prof. computer sci. and neurobiology U. So. Calif., L.A., 1988—; prof. sys. biophysics Ruhr U., Bochum, Germany, 1990—. Recipient Pioneer award IEEE Coun. for Neural Networks, 1994. Mem. Internat. Neural Network Soc. (founding governing bd.), Academia Europaea. Office: Univ So Calif Univ Park Hedco Neurosci Los Angeles CA 90089-0001 Office: Inst fur Neuroinformatik, Systembiophysik-Ruhr Univ, 44780 Bochum Germany

VON DER MOSEL, HEIKO, mathematician, researcher; b. Wesel, Germany, Mar. 11, 1965; s. Hermann and Irmgard Maria (Fink) V. MS, U. Wis., Madison, 1990; Diplom, U. Bonn, Germany, 1993, PhD, 1996. Rsch. asst. SFB/U. Bonn, 1993-96, rschr. in math., 1996—; rsch. fellow Friedrich-Ebert Found., Bonn, 1988-93. Contbr. articles to profl. jours. Adminstr. Chor Modus Novus, Cologne, Germany, 1990-98; group leader Ch., Lingen, Germany, 1980-84; mem. Friedrich-Ebert-Stiftung, Bonn, 1988-93; singer Frankfurt a capella, 1995—; mem. North Atlantic Coun., 1989—. Lt. German Army, 1984-86. Recipient Friedrich Ebert fellow, 1988-93, U. Bonn stipend, 1989-90, Schloessmann award Max-Planck Soc., 2000. Avocations: singing, piano playing, marathon running, hiking. Home: Fahrenheitstrasse 41, 53125 Bonn Germany Office: Math Inst Univ Bonn, Beringstrasse 4, 53115 Bonn Germany

VON DER OSTEN-WOLDENBURG, HARALD HENNING RUEDIGER THEODOR, geophysicist; b. Munich, July 3, 1956. Degree in geophysics, Ludwig-Maximilian U., Munich, 1984, postgrad., 1986-91. Team mem. German Antarctic rsch. sta. Georg von Neumayer Alfred-Wegener Inst. Polar Rsch., Bremerhaven, Germany, 1984-86; chief geophysicist Landesdenkmalamt Baden-Wuerttemberg, Stuttgart, Germany, 1991—; geophysicist Dept. Antiquities, Stuttgart. Editor (procs.) Geophysikalische Prospektion, 1998. Violinist Sinfonie Orch., Zorneding, Munich, 1972-91. With German mil., 1977-78. Mem. Johanniter-Orden (Ehrenritterkreuz 1998). Avocations: astronomy, orchestra, sports, trekking. Office: Landesdenkmalamt, Silberburgstrasse 193, D-70178 Stuttgart Germany

VON DER SCHMIDT, EDWARD, III, neurosurgeon, veterinarian; b. Jan. 13, 1953. BS in Animal Sci., Rutgers U., 1975; DVM, Cornell U., 1979; MD, U. Medicine and Dentistry N.J., Newark, 1984. Diplomate Nat. Bd. Med. Examiners, Am. Bd. Neurol. Surgery. Veterinarian Secaucus (N.J.) Animal Hosp., 1979-82; pvt. practice vet. medicine N.J., 1980-85; gen. surg. intern Washington Hosp. Ctr., Washington, 1984-85; resident in neurosurgery George Washington U. Med. Ctr., Washington, 1985-90; pvt. practice neurosurgery Princeton (N.J.) Healthcare Ctr., 1990—; neurosurgeon Robert Wood Johnson U. Hosp., New Brunswick, N.J., St. Peter's Med. Ctr., New Brunswick, Somerset Med. Ctr., Somerville, N.J.; chief neurosurgery sect. The Med. Ctr. at Princeton; mem. search com. for chief divsn. neurosurgery U. Medicine and Dentistry N.J./Robert Wood Johnson Med. Sch. Mem. AMA, AAAS, Am. Assn. Neurol. Surgeons/Congress of Neurol. Surgeons (joint sect. on disorders of the spine and peripheral nerves, task force com. to create nat. guidelines in spinal cord injury trauma 1997—), Med. Soc. N.J. (physician advocacy program), Middlesex County Med. Soc., Middlesex Med. Soc. (trustee), N.Y. Acad. Sci., N.J. Neurosurg. Soc. (sec. treas. 1998—), Soc. Critical Care Medicine, Soc. Exec. Physicians, Am. Coll. Physician Execs., Am. Assn. Med. Transcription (bd. dirs. Ctrl. N.J. chpt.), Alpha Zeta (Best Freshman award). Home: 140 Hodge Rd Princeton NJ 08540-3014 Office: Princeton Healthcare Ctr 419 N Harrison St Ste 204 Princeton NJ 08540-3521

VON DEWITZ, VICTOR BOTHO JOBST, diesel engine manufacturing company executive; b. Gumbinnen, East Prussia, Germany, Jan. 16, 1942; arrived in Eng., 1974; s. Berndt and Albertine (von Grueber) von D.; m. Ingrid M. Larsson, July 8, 1967; children: Carina, Susanne, Michael. Arbitur, Walldorf Sch, Benefeld, Fed. Republic Germany, 1963. Salesman Jung VW, Hamburg, Fed. Republic Germany, 1967-69; buyer Deutz Svenska,

Stockholm, 1969-73, parts mgr., 1969-74; parts mgr. Deutz Engines Ltd KHD, London, 1974-83; mng. dir. Diesel Power Ltd., London, 1983—; bd. dirs. Factorprime Ltd., London. With German Army, 1965-66. Home: 18 Arlington Rd, Richmond, Surrey TW10 7BY, England Office: Diesel Power Ltd, Diesel Power Ltd, 12 Mitcham Indstrl Ests, Mitcham Surrey CR4 2AP, England

VON EFANS-TARAFDAR, QUENTIN (KNIGHT, COUNT VON VLORE, BARON DE NARES), diplomat, real estate developer; b. Hollywood, Calif., Feb. 10, 1947; s. Georg Herbert and Elizabeth Jeanne (Calfreath-Stephens) von Efans-T. BA in internat. econs., Am. Coll. Switzerland, 1972, BBA in internat. bus., 1972; MS in Internat Econs., U. Ilminster, 1989. Journalist UPI-Netherlands, Sub-saharic Africa, 1972-74; ptnr. Wiramex SL Holland Andorra, London, 1974-81; fgn. risk and pub. rels. cons. CLAS Inc., Houston, 1981-83; real estate salesperson Versailles Inc., Houston, 1983-84; real estate broker Houston, 1984-85; dir., developer of family-owner propr. Canary Islands, Spain, 1986—; vice counsel of the Order of Malta Ecumenical Rep. of Guinea-Bissau, 1986-99; consul gen., plenipotentiary Order of Malta Ecumenical Rep. of Equatorial Guinea, Malabo, 1993—; mem. Royal Cabinet of Albania, 1990—, The Internat. Policy Inst., Washington, 1989—, Assn. Commerce of Lauzarota, Canary Islands, 1987-99. Capt. U.S. Army Spl. Forces (Green Berets), 1966-70, Vietnam; maj. Legion of Frontiersmen U.K., 1997—. Decorated Knight Comdr. Grand Cross of Grace, Order of Malta Ecumenical, Cross of Gallantry Govt. of Vietnam, Bronze Stars (2), numerous medals. Mem. Spl. Forces Assn., Parachute Regiment Assn. U.K. Avocations: military parachuting, equestrian activities, scuba, classical ballet, music. Home: Villa Cuatro Vientos Africa, 17, 35510 Canary Islands Spain Office: PO Box 229, Puerto del Carmen Lazareto, 35510 Canary Islands Spain

VON ESCHEN, ROBERT LEROY, electrical engineer, consultant; b. Glasgow, Mont., Oct. 3, 1936; s. Leroy and Lillian Victoria (Eliason) Von E.; m. Carolyn Kay Frampton, Dec. 14, 1965 (dec. Feb. 1999); children: Eric Leroy, Marc Alfred. BSEE, Mont. State U., 1961; postgrad., U. Liberia, Lakeland C.C., Glendale C.C. Registered profl. engr., Pa. Hydro constrn. engr. U.S. Army Corps of Engrs., Mont. and S.D., 1961-62; hdqrs. chief engr. Eagle Constrn. Co., Colo., 1962; resident transp./distbn. elec. engr. Stanley Cons., Inc., West Africa, 1962-63; hydro cons., startup engr. Stanley Cons., Inc., Manila, West Africa, 1965-66; with Stanley Cons., 1962-68, Gilbert Assoc./United Energy Svc., 1968-92; performance based assessment program sect. engr., maintenance planning engr., condition assessment survey sec. mgr. Gilbert Assocs., Inc., Tex., 1992—; bd. dirs. Kidsworld Multimedia; cons. engr. fossil power plant, Ky., Colo., Mo., Korea; site project mgr., Ariz., Aruba; nuclear constrn. startup engr., Pa., Ala., Ohio; safety sys. functional inspector, Calif., Wis., Oreg.; performance based assessment program project mgr., Tex.; tech. cons. World Bank, Liberia; engring. cons. USN, Manila, 1967; founding dr. Madison Comptr. Soc., Ohio, 1983-85; v.p., dr. Boy Scouts Am., 1981-84. Founder, dir. Madison (Ohio) Computer Soc., 1983-85; v.p., bd. dirs. N.E. coun. Boy Scouts Am., Painesville, 1983-85. Recipient Silver Beaver award Boy Scouts Am., 19 other awards. Mem. IEEE, NRA, NPSE, NARP, Soc. Am. Mil. Engrs., Nat. Def. Indsl. Orgn., Profl. Engring. Soc. Ohio, Profl. Engring. Soc. Tex., Masons (life), Shriners. Avocations: target and skeet shooting, constrn. design, computers, electronics. Home: 3445 Gladstone Ln Amarillo TX 79121-1525 Office: Mason & Hanger Mason Corp PO Box 30020 Amarillo TX 79120-0020

VON EULER, CHRISTOPHER ULFSON, anesthesiologist, retired; b. Stockholm, Apr. 27, 1933; s. Ulf Svante and Jane Margareta (Sodenstierna) Von E.; m. Ulla Larsson Barnholdt, 1957 (div. 1964); children: Fredrik, Anne, Gabriel; m. Anne Charlotte Ryberg, 1970 (div. 1974); 1 child, Caroline. MD, Karolinska Inst., 1963. Resident Danderyd Hosp., Stockholm, 1963-71; registrar Serafimer Hosp., Stockholm, 1971-74, Huddinge U. Hosp., Stockholm, 1974-90; cons. St. Göran Hosp., Stockholm, 1990-98; retired, 1998; cons. StErik Eye Hosp., Stockholm, 1990—. Avocations: antiques, old cars.

VON EYBEN, FINN EDLER, physician, researcher; b. Copenhagen, Denmark; s. William Edler and Ragna von Eyben; m. Merete von Eyben (div. 1978); children: Thomas Edler, Rie. MD, U. Copenhagen, 1972; PhD, Lund (Sweden) U., 1983. Sr. rschr. Med. Rsch. Unit, Ringkoebing County, Denmark. Author, translator: Leave the Pack Behind, 1999. Grantee Danish Heart Assn., Danish Cancer Soc. Christian. E-mail: feesc@ringamt.dk. Office: Med Rsch Unit Amtsradhuset, Torvet Postbox 142, DK-6950 Ringkoebing Denmark

VON FETTWEIS, YVONNE CACHÉ, archivist, historian; b. L.A., Nov. 28, 1935; d. Boyd Eugene and Georgette Louisa (Tilmann) Adams; m. Maurice Lee Caché, Jan. 8, 1955 (div. 1962); children: Maurice C.B. II, Michele-Yvonne (Mrs. Vernon Young Sr.); m. Rolland Phillip von Fettweis, July 22, 1967. BA, Wagner Coll., 1954; postgrad, Am. U., 1973, Bentley Coll., 1981. Legal sec., asst. Judge, Davis, Stern, Orfinger & Tindall, Daytona Beach, Fla., 1961-66; head rec. sect., bd. dirs. 1st Ch. Christ Scientist, Boston, 1969-71, rsch. assoc., 1971-72, adminstrv. archivist, 1972-78, sr. assoc. archivist, 1979-84, records adminstr., 1984-91, div. mgr. records mgmt./orgnl. archives, 1991-92, divsn. mgr. ch. history, 1992—, divsn. mgr. ch. history and healing ministry, 1995; divsn. mgr. ch. history, 1995-96; ch. historian 1st Ch. Christ Scientist, Boston, 1996—; cons. Christian Sci. Bd. Dirs., 1999—; mem. Religious Pub. Rels. Coun. Co-author: Mary Baker Eddy: A Lifetime of Healing, 1996, Mary Baker Eddy: Christian Healer, 1997. Trustee Ch. Hist. Trust, 1995—; exec. sec. Volusia County Goldwater campaign, Daytona Beach, 1964; mem. Christian Sci. Bd. Lectureship, 1998. Mem. Soc. Am. Archivists (editor The Archival Spirit), Automated Records and Techniques Task Force, Am. Mgmt. Assn., Orgn. Am. Historians, Ctr. for Study Presidency, Religious Pub. Rels. Coun., New Eng. Archivists, Assn. Records Mgrs. and Adminstrs. (bd. dirs. 1983—), Assn. Coll. and Rsch. Librs., Bay State Hist. League, Order Ea. Star, Order Rainbow (bd. dirs. 1972-77). Republican. Christian Scientist. Home: 147 Bosarvey Dr Ormond Beach FL 32176-5237 Office: 1st Ch Christian Sci 175 Huntington Ave # A221 Boston MA 02115-3117

VON FRIEDERICHS-FITZWATER, MARLENE MARIE, health communication educator; b. Beatrice, Nebr., July 14, 1939; d. Paul M. and Velma B. (von Friederichs) Fitzwater; children: Richard Nielson, Kevin T. Young, James L. Nielson, Paul M. Nielson. BS, Westminster Coll., 1981; MA, U. Nebr., Omaha, 1981; PhD, U. Utah, 1987; cert. in death edn., Temple U., 1982. Various pub. rels., writing and editing positions, 1957-78; teaching fellow in comm. U. Nebr., Omaha, 1978-83, U. Utah, Salt Lake City, 1978-83; asst. prof. mass comm. U. So. Colo., Pueblo, 1983-85; prof. comm. studies Calif. State U., Sacramento, 1985—, chair comm. studies, 1996-2000; assoc. clin. prof. family practice Sch. Medicine U. Calif., Davis, 1987—; condr. workshops on communication skills for health care profls. Bergan Mercy Hosp., Omaha, 1980-81, Mercy Care Ctr., Omaha, 1980-81, Am. Cancer Soc., 1981-82, Hospice of Salt Lake, Utah, 1981-82; condr. seminars, workshops and courses on health communication, death and dying, patient edn. and compliance, other related topics, 1983—; presenter in health communication various profl. orgn. meetings and confs., 1981—; dir., cofounder The Health Communication Rsch. Inst., Sacramento, 1988—. Contbr. articles to profl. jours. Trainer United Way, Sacramento, project mgr., 1986—; pres. bd. dirs. Hospice Care Sacramento, Inc., 1986-87; instr. vol. tng. program Hospice Consortium Sacramento; hospice vol. 1980—. Recipient numerous state, regional and nat. awards for writing, editing, publ. design and photography. Fellow Am. Acad. on Physician & Patient; mem. Internat. Communication Assn. (health communication div., newsletter editor 1987-89, sec. 1989-91), AAUP, Assn. Behavioral Scis. and Med. Edn., Assn. Women in Sci., Pub. Rels. Soc. Am. (bd. dirs. Calif. Capital chpt. 1987-91), Soc. Tchrs. Family Medicine, Soc. Health Care Pub. Rels. and Mktg. No. Calif. Home: 5020 Hackberry Ln Sacramento CA 95841-4765 Office: Calif State U Communication Studies Dept 6000 J St Sacramento CA 95819-2605

VON FRIZBERG, HELMUT FRANZ MICHAEL, industrialist, historical writer; b. Graz, Austria, Oct. 8, 1910; s. Alois Julius Richard Michael and Pauline (Heresch) V.; m. Lore Wilhelmine Franziska Sekanina-Pawluszkiewicz, Feb. 9, 1943; children: Elisabeth, Bernahrd, Gilbert. Grad., Community U., Vienna, 1930; LLD, U. Graz, 1932, DJ Jubil. (50 yrs.) (hon.), 1983. Ct. practice, lawyers tng. Graz, 1933-34; govtl. councillor Styrian Adminstrn., 1935-39; mng. ptnr. Hereschwerke Frizberg KG, Wildon, 1946-96; mng. ptnr. other family cos.; mem. Austrian-Russian Commn. Natural Gas, 1971-75; gen. mgr. Steirische Ferngas-Ges, Graz, 1966-77; mgr. Osterreichische Erdgaswirtschaftses Vienna, 1968-77; pres. Austria Ferngas-Ges, Vienna, 1976-77, mgr., 1967-75. Bd. dirs. Hauptrerband d. Osterr. Sozialversicherung, Vienna, 1951-52, Pensionsversicherungs anstalt d. Arbeiter, Vienna, 1951-66, Societé d'Achat de Gas Algerien Pour l'Europe, Brussels, 1973-76. Served to lt., 1940-45; Russia, France. Recipient Grosses Ehrenzeichen der Republik Osterreich, Grosses Goldenes Ehrenzeichen des Land Steiermark, 1977; named Kommerzialrat Council of Commerce, 1971; Knight (of Grace and Devotion) of the Sovereign Mil. Order of Malta, 1964. Mem. vereinigung Osterr. Elektrizitaetswerke (pres. Graz 1950-80, hon. 1980), Verband d'Elektrizitaetswerke Osterreichs (v.p. Vienna 1953-80), Assn. Austrian Industrialists (chmn. 1963-83), Styrian C. of C. (counsillor Graz 1969-80). Österreichs Volkspartei. Roman Catholic. Home: Schloss Afram-Marienhof, A-8410 Wildon, Austria

VON HAARTMAN, HARRY ULF, international transportation consultant; b. Sundvall, Sweden, Mar. 19, 1942; s. Nils Erik and Ulla Margareta (Lavonius) von H.; m. Heidi Savolainen, Sept. 5, 1969; children: Harriet, Henri, Hans. MSc in Engring., Helsinki (Finland) U. Tech., 1967; BS in Econs., Helsinki U., 1971. Trainee Beton Monierbau, Braunschweig, Germany, 1965; researcher Oy Partek Ab, Parainen, 1966; engr. Erkki Juva oy, Helsinki, 1967; dep. mgr. Rakennustietosäätiö, Helsinki, 1967-70; sales mgr. Oy Lohja AB, Helsinki, 1970-72, R&D mgr., 1972-73, export mgr., 1974-77; dir. material adminstrn. Oy Lohja AB, Virkkala, Finland, 1977-82; pres. Oy Victor Ek ab, Helsinki, 1982-96; mem. bd. Finnish Forw Assn., Helsinki, 1984-96, Nordic F. Assn., 1992-94; mem. adminstrv. coun. Yrittäjäin Fennia, Helsinki, 1988-98; chmn. Travek Travel Bur., 1982-96; mem. bd. Cargo Express, Helsinki, 1987-89, Freeport of Finland Ltd., 1991-95; vice chmn. Employers Confedn., 1986-96. Chief author: Lightweight Concrete, 1975. Lt. Finnish inf., 1961-62. Named to Order of Lions in Finland, 1st Class. Mem. Helsinki C. of C. (adminstrv. coun. 1989-96). Liberal. Avocations: sports, bridge.

VON HAGEN, HEINRICH OTTO, retired zoologist; b. Cottbus, Germany, Feb. 15, 1933; m. Dorothee Anna Hueffmeier, Apr. 27, 1962; children: David, Babette, Ellen. D Natural Scis., 1962. Lectr. zoology U. Fridericiana, Karlsruhe, Germany, 1971-74; prof. Philipps U., Marburg, Germany, 1974-98; ret., 1998. Achievements include research in systematics and behavior of Crustacea and Mammalia. Home: Hoehenweg 39, 35041 Marburg Germany Office: Fachbereich Biologie, 35032 Marburg Germany

VON HAHN, BARON KARL, lawyer; b. Oldenburg, Germany, June 2, 1945; s. Hasso and Thekla (Schoen) von H.; married; children: Anna, Friedrich. Student, U. Heidelberg, Germany, 1964-65; JD, U. Hamburg, Germany, 1968, Dr jur, 1972; MBA, European Inst. Bus. Adminstrn., Fontainebleau, France, 1974. Bar: Hamburg 1972. Jr. lawyer State of Hamburg and C. of C. of Paris, 1966-72; ptnr. Seifert, Hahn, Recke, Hamburg, 1975-91, Huth Dietrich Hahn, Hamburg, 1992—; chmn. bd. Bau-Verein zu Hamburg AG, 1991-99, vice chair, 1998—; chmn. bd. Otto Kunststofftechnik GmbH, Neuruppin, Germany, 1992—; vice chmn. Wünsche AG, Hamburg, 1989—. Contbg. author: Financial Times Handbook, 1993. Chmn. econ. com. Liberal Party, Hamburg, 1982-86, chmn. bd., 1983-85. Scholar Brit. Law Soc., 1973. Mem. Hamburg Bar Assn., Transnat. Taxation Network (supervisory bd. 1992-96). Avocations: golf, skiing, shooting. Office: Huth Dietrich Hahn, Warburgstrasse 50, 20354 Hamburg Germany

VON HEIMBURG, DENNIS, plastic surgeon; b. Frankfurt, Germany, Sept. 11, 1967. MD, Frankfurt Med. Sch., 1993. Diplomate German Bd. Plastic Surgery, European Bd. Plastic Reconstructive Aesthetic Surgery. Plastic surgery resident St. Markus Hosp., Frankfurt, Germany, 1993-94, U. Hosp., Aachen, Germany, 1995—. Contbr. articles to profl. jours. Recipient Year award Assn. of German Plastic Surgeons, Leipzig, 1995, Seeon, 1999; winner European Conf. Scientists and Plastic Surgeons, Maastricht, 1999; grantee European Com. Rsch., 2000. Mem. Assn. German Plastic Surgeon, Interplast Germany. Office: U Technology Dept Plastic Surgery, Pauwelsstr 30, D-52057 Aachen Germany

VON HENTIG, HARTMUT, education educator; b. Poznan, Poland, Sept. 23, 1925; s. Werner Otto von Hentig and Natalie von Kügelgen. BA, Elizabethtown Coll., 1950, DLitt (hon.), 1991; MA, U. Chgo., 1951, PhD, 1953. Tchr. Greek and Latin Uhland Gymnasium, Tübingen, Germany, 1956-63; prof. edn. Göttingen (Germany) U., 1963-68; prof. edn. Bielefeld (Germany) U., 1968-87, prof. emeritus, 1987—; rsch. dir. Bielefeld Laborschule and Bielefeld Oberstufen-Kolleg, 1970-87; fellow Wissenschaftskolle zu Berlin, 1981-82; v.p. Deutsche Acad. für Sprache und Dichtung, Darmstadt, Germany, 1987-93. Author: Platonisches Lehren, 1966, Systemzwang und Selbstbestimmug, 1977, Die Menschen Stärken, Die Sachen Klären, 1985, Ergötzen, Belehren, Befreien, 1985, others; co-editor Neue Sammlung, 1993—. Active Präsidium des Deutschen Evangelischen Kirchetages, 1988-2000; founder, pres. Hope e.V. for Internat. Understanding, Berlin and Samara, Russia, 1989. Lt. German Wehrmacht, 1943-45. Recipient Schiller-Preis der Stadt Mannheim, 1969, Lessing-Preis der Stadt hamburg, 1986, Sigmund-Freud-Preis für Wissenschaftliche Prosa, 1986, Comenius prize Comenius-Stiftung, Germany, 1994, Ernst Christian Trapp prize Deutsche Gesellschaft für Erziehungswissenschaft, 1998. Home: Kurfürstendamm 214, D-10719 Berlin Germany

VON HERTZEN, LEENA CARITA, microbiologist, researcher; b. Helsinki, Finland, May 6, 1954; d. Kai Karl-Wilhelm and Ritta Elina (Joutsenlahti) Roos; m. Raimo Kari Von Hertzen, Jan. 6, 1994. MSc in microbiology, Helsinki Univ., 1979; M in public health, Nordic Sch. Pub. Health, Gothenburg, 1989; licentiate in health care, Helsinki Univ., 1991, PhD, 1996. Microbiologist Helsinki City Water-Works, Helsinki, 1979-82; rsch. asst. Vilhonkatu Health Ctr., Helsinki, 1982-83; product chief Medica Pharmaceuticals, Helsinki, 1983-85; rsch. coord., rschr. Leiras Pharmaceuticals, Helsinki, 1986-96; sr. researcher Nat. Pub. Health Inst., Helsinki, 1992-95; researcher The Finnish Lung Health Assn., Helsinki, 1996—, docent, 1999. Contbr. articles to profl. jours. Recipient The Finnish Anti-Tuberculosis Assn. award, 1992, 95, 97, The Yrjo Jahnsson Found. award, 1994. Mem. The Finnish Soc. Microbiologist, The Assn. of Infectious Diseases Rsch. Lutheran. Avocations: antiques, piano playing. Home: Hakolahdentie 3 C 37, 00200 Helsinki Finland Office: The Finnish Lung Health Assn, Sibeliuksenkatu 11A1, 00250 Helsinki Finland

VONK, GERRIT ROKUS, radio executive, consultant; b. Utrecht, Netherlands, Aug. 1, 1962; s. Pieter Gysbert and Jenny (Turkstra) V. BBA, Erasmus U., Rotterdam, Netherlands, 1984, MBA, 1988. Cons. Europe Transfer Cons., Rotterdam, 1988-89; mgr. Videonics Netherlands, Rotterdam, 1990-91; pres., gen. mgr. Holland FM Radio Chain, Rotterdam, 1991-95; owner, pres. Red Butler Real Estate Devel., Rotterdam, 1989-92; sr. cons. Europe Transfer Cons., Rotterdam, 1990-94; dir. Stads Radio Rotterdam, 1996-97; several logistical positions Medicins Sans Frontiers, Rwanda/Congo, 1998—; bd. mem. City FM Radio, Amsterdam, gen. mgr. Sun FM Radio, Rotterdam, Music of your Live Radio Network, N.Y. Author: Venture Capital Beyond Boundaries, 1988, A Natural Link; co-author (with others) Building European Ventures, 1990 (EFER 1990); contbr. articles to profl. jours. Avocations: field hockey, tennis, architecture. Home: Veldlaan 13, 3737 AM Groenekan The Netherlands Office: Emmalaan 33, 3581 HP Utrecht The Netherlands

VONKA, VLADIMIR, virologist; b. Prague, Czech Republic, July 31, 1930; s. Edvard and Vlasta (Bartunkova) V.; m. Jarmila Karasova, July 27, 1957; 1 child, Richard. MD, Charles U., Prague, 1955, PhD, 1963; DS, Czech Acad. Sci., Prague, 1981. Physician Regional Ctr. Health, Usti, Czech Republic, 1955-56; postdoctoral fellow Rsch. Inst. Immunology, Prague, 1957-60, head dept. virus biology, 1961-70; head dept. exptl. virology Inst. Sera and Vaccines, Prague, 1971-91, Inst. Hematol. and Blood Transfusion, Prague, 1991—; vis. prof. virology Baylor Coll., Houston, 1968-69; vis. scientist Pa. State U., Hershey, 1983-84; tchr. virology, med. molecular biology Charles U., Prague, 1972—, prof. microbiology, med. faculty, 1992—; expert WHO, Geneva, 1969-91' tchr. I.A.R.C. Internat. Sch. Oncology, Lyon, France, 1987. Contbr. more than 240 sci. articles to profl. jours. Vice chmn. sci. coun. Ministry of Health, Prague, 1990-92; chmn. sci. coun. Inst. Sera and Vaccines, Prague, 1989-91; mem. com. Granting Agy. Czech Republic, Prague, 1992-97. Recipient G. Mendel Silver medal Czech Acad. Sci., 1991; WHO grantee Baylor Coll., 1964-65. Fellow Am. Acad. Microbiology (chmn. Rogoza Morrison com. 1996-99), Czech Med. Soc., Learned Soc. Czech Republic, European Assn. Cancer Rsch. (mem. coun. 2000—), European Acad. Sci. & Arts, Sigma Xi. Avocations: history, philosophy of science, modern arts, literature. Office: Inst Hematology and Blood Transfusion, U Nemocnice 1, Prague 128 20, Czech Republic

VON KAISENBERG, CONSTANTIN, obstetrician-gynecologist; b. Heidenheim, Germany, Apr. 6, 1964; s. Ernst-Nikolaus and Kathrin (Bardt) von K. 1st Part State Exam, Ruprecht Karls U., Heidelberg, Germany, 1987, 2nd Part State Exam, 1989, 3rd Part State Exam, 1990; postgrad., Technische U., Munich, 1991-92; Diploma in Fetal Medicine, Kings Coll., London, 1999. Scientific asst., tutor anatomy U. Heidelberg (Germany), 1986, 1987, rsch. asst. dept. exptl. pharmacology, 1988; rsch. asst. Inst. Surgical Rsch. Ludwig Maximilian U., Munich, 1991; sr. house officer detp. ob-gyn. U. Tchg. Hosp. U. Hamburg, Eppendorf, Germany, 1993; rsch. fellow Harris Birthright Rsch. Ctr. Fetal Medicine King's Coll. Hosp., London, 1994-96, rsch. fellow dept. molecular medicine Rayne Inst., 1995-96; registrar, sr. registrar dept. ob-gyn. U. Tchg. Hosp. U. Kiel (Germany), 1997—; vis. rsch. fellow Anatomisches Inst. U. Freiburg, Germany, 1995-97; presenter, lectr. in field. Contbr. chpts. to books, numerous articles to med. jours. Grantee Deutsche Forschungsgemeinschaft, 1994-96. Home: Jungfernstieg 29A, 24116 Kiel Germany Office: U Hosp, Ob-Gyn, 24105 Kiel Germany

VON KALINOWSKI, JULIAN ONESIME, lawyer; b. St. Louis, May 19, 1916; s. Walter E. and Maybelle (Michaud) von K.; m. Penelope Jayne Dyer, June 29, 1980; children by previous marriage: Julian Onesime, Wendy Jean von Kalinowski. BA, Miss. Coll., 1937; JD with honors, U. Va., 1940. Bar: Va. 1940, Calif. 1946. Assoc. Gibson, Dunn and Crutcher, L.A., 1946-52, ptnr., 1953-85, mem. exec. com., 1962-82, adv. ptnr., 1985—; CEO, chmn. Litigation Scis., Inc., Culver City, Calif., 1991-94; chmn. emeritus Litigation Scis., Inc., Torrance, Calif., 1994-96, Dispute Dyamics, Inc., Torrance, Calif., 1996—; instr. Columbia Law Sch., Parker Sch. Fgn. and Cooperative Law, summer 1981; instr. antitrust law and litigation So. Meth. Sch. of Law, summer 1982-84, bd. visitors, 1982-85; v.p., bd. dirs., dir. W.M. Keck Found.; mem. faculty Practising Law Inst., 1971, 76, 78, 79, 80; instr. in spl. course on antitrust litigation Columbia U. Law Sch., N.Y.C., 1981; mem. lawyers dels. com. to 9th Cir. Jud. Conf., 1953-67; UN expert Mission to People's Republic China, 1982. Contbr. articles to legal jours.; author: Antitrust Laws and Trade Regulation, 1969, desk edit., 1981; gen. editor: World Law of Competition, 1978, Antitrust Counseling and Litigation Techniques, 1984; gen. editor emeritus Antitrust Report. With USN, 1941-46, capt. Res. ret. Fellow Am. Bar Found., Am. Coll. Trial Lawyers (chmn. complex litigation com. 1984-87); mem. ABA (ho. of dels. 1970, chmn. antitrust law sect. 1972-73), State Bar Calif., L.A. Bar Assn., U. Va. Law Sch. Alumni Assn., Calif. Club, L.A. Country Club, La Jolla Beach and Tennis Club, Phi Kappa Psi, Phi Alpha Delta. Republican. Episcopalian. Home: 12320 Ridge Cir Los Angeles CA 90049-1151

VON KLEIN, MICHAEL HANS ULLRICH, industrial designer; b. Paehl, Bavaria, Fed. Republic Germany, Aug. 23, 1944; s. Rolf Harald and Tilly (Wiedemann-Weirether) von K.; m. Monika Jungk, May 24, 1974; 1 child, Martina. Diploma in Indsl. Design, Fachhochschule fuer Gestautung Schwaebisch-Gmuend, Fed. Republic Germany. With Daimler-Benz AG, Sindelfingen, Fed. Republic Germany, 1969-91; field specialist Mercedes-Benz AG, Sindelfingen, 1985-91; ind. cons., 1992—; cons. Traffic Authorities, Leipzig, 1991—; lectr. design techniques Fachhochschule Fuer Gestaltung, Berufsakademie Stuttgart Schwaebisch-Gmuend, 1990—. Contbr. articles to profl. jours. Mem. Verband Deutscher Industrie-Designer (responsible for Baden-Wuertemberg region 1978-81). Achievements include numerous patents and inventions; design of exteriors and interiors of trucks, urban buses, coaches, VIP-helicopters and other special projects. Home: Hinderburgstr 18, 71149 Bondorf Germany

VON KOHORN, BARON RALPH STEVEN, retired investment banker, author; b. Chemnitz, Germany, Dec. 14, 1919; arrived in N.Z., 1963; s. Baron Oscar and Valerie (Wirth) von K.; m. Jillian Annette Bussell, Feb. 25, 1967; children by previous marriage: Karen Janne, Kirk Steven. Student, U. So. Calif., U. Mich. Dep. chmn. various world wide bus. orgns., 1945-62; ret.; settlor von Kohorn Family Trust Controlling Genrock Group of Cos., N.Z. and Australia. Author: Abstract Paintings by Forty New Zealand Artists, 1966; What You Always Wanted to Know about Single Sideband Radio and Never Dared to Ask, 1976, VHF/FM Marine Radio, 1977, Columbia Cruises South, 1977, Columbia Cruises North, 1978, Management of a General Ancillary Licence for Clubs, 1978, Your Guide to Marine Search and Rescue, 1980; co-author, cartographer: A Cruising Man's Guide to the Marlborough Sounds, 1979, A Cruising Guide-Cape Palliser to Marlborough Sounds and Tasman Bay, 1982, The Sounds Cruising Guide, including Cape Palliser to Farewell Spit, 1986, The Cohorn Clan, 1987, The Cohorn Clan 2, 1988, New Zealand Cruising Guide-Central Area, 1989, 2d edit., 1994, 3rd edit., 1999, The Cohorn Clan 3, 1996. Founding sr. v.p., dir. Am. C. of C., 1965-74; bd. dirs. Am. Edn. Found. (Fulbright), 1965-94, Kennedy Meml. Fellowship, 1972-94, East-West Ctr., Honolulu, 1972-78; selector Eisenhower Fellowships, 1966-68, 78, 81, 86; trustee Wellington Visual Arts Trust, 1968-72, Found. for Newborn Child, 1977-96, N.Z. Oral History Archives, 1981-94, Wellington Maritime Mus., 1989-96, founder, pres.; trustee, dir. N.Z. Sports Found., 1977-85, gov., 1986-94, hon. life mem.; nat. treas. N.Z. Water Safety Coun., 1979-87, Small Boat Safety Com., 1977-90; com. chmn. N.Z. Yachting Fedn., hon. life mem. Recipient Graham Hayter trophy, 1973-74, 78-79; Lane Bryant Internat. Vol. award, 1969, Water Safety award Minister of Internal Affairs, 1987, Merit award Minister of Transport, 1987, Outstanding Vol. Svc. award Wellington, N.Z., 1987, Tribute of Appreciation award U.S. Govt., 1987, N.Z. Yacht Cruising award. Fellow Inst. Dirs. (London), N.Z. Inst. Mgmt. (counselor); mem. Royal Yachting Assn. (London, life), Past Commodores Assn. N.Z. (pres.), Internat. Order Past Commodores (internat. v.p. 1982-93, v.p. emeritus 1993—, hon. life mem., patron 1996), N.Z. Am. Assn., Wellington Planetarium Soc. (life, vice-chmn. 1968-73), Inst. Advanced Motorists (life, vice-chmn. 1969-73), Mus. Wellington (life, boardroom named in his honor), Nat. Press Club, Wellesley Club (Wellington), Tattersalls Club (Sydney), U. Club, Royal N.Z. Yacht Club, Royal Port Nicholson Yacht Club (life), Mana Cruising Club (life, past commodore). Home: Herbert Gardens, 186 The Terrace, Wellington New Zealand Office: PO Box 2837, Wellington New Zealand

VON KROGH, GEO, dermatologist, venereologist; b. Bergen, Norway, Jan. 25, 1943; arrived in Sweden, 1970; s. Morten and Aslaug (Hegland) von K. MD, U. Bergen, 1967; PhD, Karolinska Inst., Stockholm, 1981. Intern Hosp. Drammen, Norway, 1967-68; resident in diving medicine Naval Hosp. Bergen, 1969-70; resident in dermatology and venereology So. Hosp., 1970-78; resident in psychiatry Hosp. Beckomberga, Stockholm, 1970; rsch. dermatologist U. Calif., San Francisco, 1979-82, asst. prof., 1983; assoc. prof., staff dermatologist Karolinska Hosp., 1988—. Author: (chpts.) Safety and Efficacy of Topical Drugs and Cosmetics, 1982, Dermatotoxicology, 2d edit., 1983, Occupational Skin Disease, 1983, Dermatology, 2d edit., Vol. 1, 1984, Infections in Reproductive Health, Vol. II, 1985, Dermatologic Immunology and Allergy, 1985, Treatment of Sexually Transmitted Diseases, 1986, Papillomaviruses, 1987, Genitoanal Papilloma Virus Infection: A Survey for the Clinician, 1989, Genital Papillomavirus Infections: Advances in Modern Diagnosis and Therapy, 1990, Papillomavirus in Human Pathology, 1990, Clinics in Dermatology, Vol. 3, 1991, Orticaria Angioedema, 1991, Dermatology & Perspectives, 1993, Papillomavirus in Human Pathology, 1995, Current Problems in Dermatology, Vol. 24, 1996; contbr., editor Human Papillomavirus Infections in Dermatovenereology, 1997; editor: Sexually Transmitted Diseases, 1990; co-editor: Genitoanal Papilloma Virus Infection, 1989, Diagnostic and Therapy in Primary Care, 1990, Papilloma Viruses, Part Two, 1997, Human Papilloma Virus Infection. A Clinical Atlas, 1997; contbr. articles to British Jour. Venereol Disease, Acta Dermatology Venereol, Sexually Transmitted Diseases, Archive Dermatology Rsch., Dermatologica, Contact Dermatitis, Jour. Swedish Med. Assn., Mykosen, Lancet II, Clin. Immunology Immunopathology, Scandinavian Jour. Infectious Diseases, Genitourinary Medicine, Jour. Am. Acad. Dermatology, Jour. Oral Pathology, Internat. Jour. STD and AIDS,

others. With Norwegian Navy, 1969-70. Mem. Swedish Acad. Dermatology, Scandinavian Soc. Genito-urinary Medicine, Internat. Soc. Study Vulvar Disease, Internat. Papillomavirus Workshop Group, Swedish Physicians Against AIDS, European Acad. Dermatology Venereology, Internat. AIDS Soc., Internat. Soc. STD Rsch., Med. Soc. Study Venereal Diseases, Am. Venereal Disease Assn., Swedish Soc. Dermatologic Surgery, European Human Papilloma Virus Associated Pathology (pres. 1993-96), Internat. Union Against Sexually Transmitted Infections (bd. sci. mem. 1996, European br., mem. editl. bd. Genital Infectious and Neoplasia Update 1998). E-mail: geo.von.krogh@ood.ki.se. Home: Bondegatan 1 C, 11623 Stockholm Sweden Office: Dept Dermatovenereology, Karolinska Hosp, 17176 Stockholm Sweden

VON KYAW, DIETRICH, diplomat; b. Stettin, Pommerania, Germany, June 9, 1934; arrived in Belgium, 1993; s. Jobst-Willrich von K. and Helga Ruth Matthias; m. Elisabeth Berner, 1964; children: Felicitas, Benita. Student Polit. Sci., Law, Chgo. U., 1954; LLD, U.Bonn, Germany, 1957; student Polit. Sci., Law, U. Liège, Belgium, 1958. 2nd state exam in law Düsseldorf Regional Ct., Germany, 1963. Vice-consul German Consulate, L.A., 1964-65; sec. German embassies Brazzaville, Congo and Bangui, Ctrl. African Republic, 1966-69; officer outer space policies econ. dept. Fgn. Office, Bonn, 1970-73; counsellor, German permanent rep. UN, N.Y.C., 1973-77, chmn. 3d com., 31st Gen. Assembly; head divsn. EC policies econ. dept. Fgn. Office, Bonn, 1977-83; min. econs. Embassy of Fed. Republic of Germany, Washington, 1984-88; head directorate East-West econ. rels., trade promotion, export controls econ. dept. Fgn. Office, Bonn, 1988-89, head directorate European cmty. affairs, dep. dir. gen. econ. dept., 1989-93; amb., permanent rep. of Germany to European Union, Brussels, 1993-99; ret., 1999; bd. dirs. Asta-Gevaert Co., Antwerpen, Belgium; commentator Fin. Times Deutchland; advisor European Union enlargement issues. Office: Miquelstrasse 45, D-14195 Berlin Germany

VON LAWZEWITSCH, IRENE, veterinary science educator; b. Kibarty, Kovno, Lithuania, May 30, 1924; arrived in Argentina, 1949; d. Luis Estanislao and Eugenia (Heidrich) von L. MD, Albertus U., Königsberg, Germany, 1944; Baccalaureate, Tomas Guido Sch., Buenos Aires, 1955; MD, U. Buenos Aires, 1960, PhD in Medicine, 1963. Chief lectr. histology, cytology and embryology U. Buenos Aires Sch. Medicine, 1968-74, asst. prof., 1975-90; assoc. prof. U. Buenos Aires Sch. Vet. Scis., 1975-78; full prof. U. Buenos Aires-Sch. Vet. Scis., 1978-89, vice dir. dept. physiology and basic scis., 1989-91, emeritus prof. histology and embryology, 1990—; rsch. asst. Inst. Biology and Exptl. Medicine, U. Buenos Aires, 1950-59, rschr., 1959-70; prin. rschr. Nat. Coun. for Sci. and Tech. Rsch., Buenos Aires, 1970—, dir. histological studies on endocrine glands program, 1980-2000; expert judge rsch. projects evaluation U. LaPlata, 1996. Co-author, editor: Aparato Genital de la Gallina, 1982, Lecciones Embriologia Veterinaria (6 vols.), 1985, Lecciones Histologia Veterinaria (9 vols.), 1985; contbr. over 125 articles to profl. jours. Recipient Maissa Found. prize, Argentine Acad. Medicine, 1970, Buenos Aires, 1970, José M. Mezzadra award with gold medal prize, Buenos Aires, 1970, Centennial prize, U. La Plata, Argentina, 1983. Mem. Zool. Soc. Japan, Soc. for Exptl. Biology and Medicine, World Soc. Vet. Anatomists, Am. Soc. Mammalogists. E-mail: ebmessi@overnet.com.ar. Office: Histología y Embriología, Chorroarín 280, C1427CWO Buenos Aires Argentina

VON LERSNER, HEINRICH FREIHERR, former German government official; b. Stuttgart, Germany, July 14, 1930; s. Albert Freiherr and Clotilde (von Groll) von L.; m. Uta von Weyhe, 1968; children: Ludwig, Marita, Brigitta, Charlotte. Dr. iur., U. Tubingen, Fed. Republic of Germany, 1955. Adminstr. of State of Baden-Wurttemberg, Fed. Republic Germany, 1959-61; with Ministry of Interior, Bonn, Fed. Republic of Germany, 1961-73, head of subdiv. 1970-73; pres. Fed. Environ. Agy., Berlin, 1973-95; prof. U. Cottbus, 1994—. Author, editor various books on environ. law. Home: Murtener Strasse 1, D-12205 Berlin Germany

VON LEYDEN, WOLFGANG MARIUS, retired philosophy educator, author; b. Berlin, Dec. 28, 1911; came to Eng., 1939; s. Victor Ernst and Luise Anna (Reichenheim) von L.; m. Iris Edith Sharwood Smith, July 11, 1953; children—Lucie Marion, Victor James. Student U. Berlin, 1931-32, U. Gottingen, 1932-33; Ph.D., U. Florence, 1936; D.Phil., U. Oxford, 1944. Lectr. philosophy U. Durham, Eng., 1946-56, sr. lectr., 1956-62, reader, 1962-77; vis. prof. SUNY, 1966-67; disting. vis. scholar, dept. govt. London Sch. Econs. and Polit. Sci., 1978-83. Editor: John Locke, Essays on the Law of Nature, 1954. Author: Remembering, 1961; Seventeenth Century Metaphysics, 1968; Hobbes and Locke, 1982; Aristotle on Equality & Justice, 1985. Rockefeller Found. grantee Oxford U., 1940-45. Avocations: travelling; reading; gardening. Home: 5 Pimlico, Durham DH1 4QW, England

VON LINSOWE, MARINA DOROTHY, information systems consultant; b. Indpls., July 21, 1952; d. Carl Victor and Dorothy Mae (Quinn) von Linsowe; m. Clayton Albert Wilson IV, Aug. 11, 1990; children: Kira von Linsowe Parker, Lara Carla von Linsowe-Wilson, Tami Cheri von Linsowe-Wilson. Student Am. River Coll., Portland State U. Cert. Prodn. and Inventory Mgmt. Verbal operator Credit Bur. Metro, San Jose, Calif. and Portland, Oreg., 1970-72; computer clk. Security Pacific Bank, San Jose, 1972-73; proof operator Crocker Bank, Seaside, Calif., 1973-74; proof supr. Great Western Bank, Portland, 1974-75; bookkeeper The Clothes Horse, Portland, 1976-78; computer operator Harsh Investment Co., Portland, 1978-79; data processing mgr. Portland Fish Co., 1979-81; data processing mgr. J & W Sci. Inc., Rancho Cordova, Calif., 1981-83; search and recruit specialist, data processing mgr. Re:Search Exec. Recruiters, Sacramento, Calif., 1983; sr. systems analyst Unisys Corp. (formerly Burroughs), 1983-91; sr. systems cons. FileNet Corp., Portland, Oreg., 1991-92; owner Optimal System Svcs., Portland, Oreg., 1992—; bus sys. analyst, software design and devel., mfg. specialist Portland. First violinist Am. River Orch. Recipient Bank of Am. Music award, 1970. Mem. NAFE, Am. Prodn. and Inventory Control Soc. (cert.), Am. Mgrs. Assn., MENSA, Data Processing Mgmt. Assn. Republican. Lutheran. Address: 3280 SW 170th Ave Apt 1780 Beaverton OR 97006-8612

VON LIPHART, GEORGE, mortgage company executive; b. N.Y.C., Aug. 9, 1946; s. George and Faina (Chesnokoff) von L.; m. Barbara Sawyer Sutton, Mar. 21, 1980; 1 child, Nicholas Sawyer. AB, Harvard U., 1967, MBA, 1969. Exec. v.p. The Stearns Co., San Francisco, 1980-86; ptnr. Bouret, von Liphart & Dunwoody, Atherton, 1987-88; mng. dir. Carriger Capital, Inc., San Francisco, 1988-92; prin. Hanford/Healy Cos., San Francisco, 1992-96; sr. v.p. GMAC Coml. Mortgage Corp., San Francisco, 1996—; mng. dir. GMAC Coml. Mortgage Japan, K.K., Tokyo, 1998—; asst. chair Japan coun. Urban Land Inst., Washington, 1998—. Trustee Chinese Am. Internat. Sch., San Francisco, 1983-98. Office: GMAC Coml Mortgage Japan KK, 3 12 Kioicho, Chiyoda-ku Tokyo 102 0094, Japan

VON LOEWENICH, VOLKER CLEMENS HELMUT, neonatologist, educator; b. Erlangen, Bavaria, Germany, Mar. 23, 1937; s. Walther Eugen and Elisabeth Maria (Thielicke) v.; m. Katharina Elisabeth Lagois, Dec. 28, 1965; children: Friederike, Clemens, Maria. MD, U. Erlangen, 1961. Resident Inst. Physiology, U. Erlangen, 1963-66; resident Univ. Children's Hosp., Frankfurt, Germany, 1966-72, dir. dept. neonatology, 1973—; prof. pediats. U. Frankfurt, 1973—. Contbr. articles to profl. jours.; co-author: Pediatric Intensive Care Medicine, 1974. Mem. Austrian Soc. Pediats. (corr.), German-Austrian Soc. for Neonatology and Pediat. Intensive Care Medicine (pres. 1981-85), German Soc. for Perinatal Medicine (pres. 1985-87, 89-91), Acad. Med. Ethics. Lutheran. Avocations: music (flute and violoncello), photography, wind-surfing. Home: Bruno Stuermer Str 27, D-60529 Frankfurt Germany Office: Univ Hosp, Dept Neonatology, D-60590 Frankfurt Germany

VON LÖHNEYSEN, HILBERT, physicist; b. Göttingen, Germany, Oct. 25, 1946; s. Hans-Wolfgang and Marianne (Zetsche) von L. Diploma in physics, U. Göttingen, 1970; PhD in Physics, U. Cologne, Germany, 1976; Habilitation, Tech. U. Aachen, Germany, 1981. Rsch. asst. U. Cologne, 1973-77; postdoctoral fellow Nat. Ctr. Sci. Rsch., Grenoble, France, 1977-78; rsch. asst. Tech. U. Aachen, 1978-81, docent, 1981-85, chair-interim, 1985-86; chair, full prof. U. Karlsruhe, Germany, 1986—, dean of faculty, 1992-94; mem. Senate Deutsche Forschungsgemeinschaft, 1995—. Recipient Maier-Leibnitz prize Ministry of Edn. and Sci., 1983. Office: U Karlsruhe, Physikalisches Inst, 76128 Karlsruhe Germany

VON MANDEL, MICHAEL JACQUES, lawyer; b. Yokohama, Japan, Oct. 20, 1941; came to the U.S., 1946; s. Michael Maximillan and Suzanne (Jacques) V.M.; m. Mary Denise Bienvenue, Dec. 22, 1984; 1 child, Michelle Denise. AB in Econs., Georgetown U., 1964; JD, Cath. U., 1968; LLM in Taxation, NYU, 1970. Bar: Washington 1969, Conn. 1969, Ill. 1976, U.S. Dist. Ct. (no. dist.) Ill. 1976, Fla. 1977, U.S. Ct. Appeals (7th cir.) 1976. Trial atty. FTC, Washington, 1968-69; trial atty. tax divsn. U.S. Dept. Justice, Washington, 1970-76; pvt. practice Chgo., 1976-93; ptnr. Von Mandel & Von Mandel, Chgo., 1994—; adj. prof. grad. tax program DePaul U., Chgo., 1980-83. Contbr. chpts. to books. Mem. ABA (tax and litigation sects. 1976—), Chgo. Bar Assn. (fed. tax com. 1976—), Fed. Bar Assn. (bd. dirs. 1981-93), Bar Assn. 7th Fed. Cir., Union League Club. Roman Catholic. Address: 79 W Monroe St Ste 708 Chicago IL 60603-4915

VON MARTENS, HANS JÜRGEN, electrical engineer, researcher; b. Bernburg, Germany, Nov. 17, 1939; s. Gerhard and Ingeborg (Rammelt) Spielmeyer; m. Edda Wolfermann, Mar. 22, 1974; children: Franziska, Tobias. MSEE, Tech. U. Dresden, Germany, 1964; PhD in Engring., Tech. U. Ilmenau, Germany, 1975. Registered profl. engr. Scientist Agy. for Standardization, Metrology and Commodity Testing, Berlin, 1964-70, head. lab., leader rsch. and devel. projects, 1970-90; head lab., leader rsch. and devel. projects Physikalisch-Technische Bundesanstalt, Berlin, 1991—; leader standardization projects Coun. Mutual Econ. Assistance, Moscow, 1970-90, Internat. Orgn. Legal Metrology, Paris, 1987—, Internat. Orgn. Standardization, Geneva, 1993—; lectr. in field. Contbr. numerous articles to profl. jours.; patentee in field. Recipient Nat. award Ministry of Sci. and Tech., 1987. Avocations: music, sports. Home: St 76 Q# 44, 12524 Berlin Germany Office: Physikalisch-Technische Bundesanstalt, Fürstenwalder Damm 388, 12587 Berlin Germany

VON MERING, OTTO OSWALD, anthropology educator; b. Berlin, Germany, Oct. 21, 1922; came to Switzerland, 1933, to U.S., 1939, naturalized, 1954; s. Otto O. and Henriette (Troeger) von M.; m. Shirley Ruth Brook, Sept. 11, 1954; children: Gretchen, Karin, Gregory, Hilary, Celia. Grad., Belmont Hill Sch., 1940; BA in History, Williams Coll., 1944; PhD in Social Anthropology, Harvard U., 1956. Instr. Belmont Hill Sch., Belmont, Mass., 1945-47, Boston U., 1947-48, Cambridge Jr. Coll., 1948-49; rsch. asst. lab. social rels. Harvard U., 1950-51, Boston Psychopathic Hosp., 1951-53; Russell Sage Found. fellow N.Y.C., 1953-55; asst. prof. social anthropology U. Pitts. Coll. Medicine, 1955-60, assoc. prof., 1960-65, prof. social anthropology, 1965-71; prof. child devel. and child care U. Pitts. Coll. Allied Health Professions, 1969-71; prof. anthropology and family medicine U. Fla., 1971-76, prof. anthropology in ob-gyn, 1979-84, prof. anthropology and gerontology, 1986-96, prof. anthropology and gerontology emeritus, 1998, joint prof. dept. medicine, coll. medicine, 1994-96; lectr. Sigmund Freud Inst., Frankfurt, Germany, 1962-64, Pitts. Psychoanalytical Inst., 1960-71, Interuniv. Forum, 1967-71; tech. adviser Maurice Falk Med. Fund, 1964-75; Fulbright vis. lectr., 1962-63; Richard-Merton guest prof. Heidelberg U., Germany, 1962-63; vis. prof. Dartmouth, 1970-71; vis. lectr. continuing edn. Med. Coll. of Pa., 1990-92, vis. lectr. U. Sheffield, Eng., Fall, 1995, U. Liverpool, 1995, U. Augsburg, 1997, U. Heidelberg, fall 1997; hon. vis. prof. U. Coll. London Med. Sch., fall 1997; bd. dirs. Tech. Assistance Resource Assocs., U. Fla., 1979-84; supr. grad. study program Ctr. Gerontologic Studies, U. Fla., 1983-85, assoc. dir. 1985-86, dir. 1986-96, prof. emeritus 1998; mem. coordinating com. Geriatric Edn. Ctr., Coll. of Medicine, U. Fla., 1986-96; mem. nat. tech. expert panel on long-term care Health Care Financing Adminstrn., Washington; chair, mem. adv. bd. Internat. Exchange Ctr. on Gerontology State U. System of Fla., 1987-92; adv. bd. Second Season Broadcasting Network, Palm Beach, Fla., 1989-92, Fla. Policy Exch. Ctr. on Aging, State U. System Fla., 1991-95, Assoc. Health Industries of Fla., Inc., Nat. Shared Housing Resource Ctr., Balt.; cons. mental hosps. Author: Remotivating the Mental Patient, 1957, A Grammar of Human Values, 1961, (with Mitscherlich and Brocher) Der Kranke in der Modernen Gesellschaft, 1967, (with Kasdan) Anthropology in the Behavioral and Health Sciences, 1970, (with Maria Alvarez) Aging, Demography and Well-Being in Latin America, 1989; (with R. Binstock and L. Cluff) The Future of Long Term Care, 1996; also articles; commentary editor: Human Organization, 1974-76; corr. editor Jour. Geriatric Psychiatry; mem. editl. bd. Med. Anthropology, 1976-84, Ednl. Gerontology, 1990—, Australasian Leisure for Pleasure Jour., 1995—, Jour. Cross-Cultural Gerontology, 1996—. Mem. nat. adv. bd. Nat. Shared Housing Resource Ctr., 1994-95; pres. Dedicated Alt. Resources for the Elderly, 1996-98; mem., bd. dirs. No. Ctrl. Fla. chpt. Alzheimer's Assn., 1996—; bd. dirs. Shepherd's Ctrs. Am., Gainesville, 1998-2000. Recipient Fulbright-Hayes Travel award, 1962-63; grantee Wenner-Gren Found., N.Y., 1962-63, Am. Philos. Soc., 1962-63, Maurice Falk Med. Fund, 1970-71, US-DHHS, 1979-83, Walter Reed Army Inst. Rsch., 1987-91. US-ADA/Fla. Dept. of Elder Affairs, 1993-94; spl. fellow NIMH, 1971-72. Fellow AAAS, Am. Anthrop. Assn. (mem. James Mooney award com. 1978-81, vis. lectr. 1961,-62, 71-74, 91-92), Am. Gerontol. Soc., Royal Soc. Health, Acad. Psychosomatic Medicine, Am. Ethnological Soc., Soc. Applied Anthropology, Royal Anthrop. Inst.; mem. Assn. Am. Med. Colls., Assn. Anthrop. Gerontol. (pres.-elect 1991-92, pres. 1992-93), Am. Fedn. Clin. Research, Am. Public Health Assn., Canadian Assn. Gerontology, British Soc. Gerontology, Med. Group Mgmt. Assn., World Fedn. Mental Health, Internat. Assn. Social Psychiatry (regional counselor 1973-81), Internat. Hosp. Fedn., Help Age Internat. (London). Home: 818 NW 21st St Gainesville FL 32603-1027 Office: U Fla Dept Anthropology Turlington Hall Gainesville FL 32611

VON MEYER, LUDWIG KURT, forensic toxicologist; b. Bad Elster, Germany, Nov. 27, 1942; s. Kurt Bruno and Irene (Ludwig) von M.; m. Renate Eleonore Kohmann; children: Alexander, Eckart. Staatsexamen in Pharmacy, U. Erlangen, Germany, 1968, Dr.rer.nat., 1975; MD, U. Munich, 1983. Sci. rschr. U. Munich, 1970-82, akademischer rat, 1982-85, akademischer oberrat, 1985-96, prof., 1990—, akademischer direktor, 1996—. Contbr. articles to profl. jours. and books. Mem. Internat. Assn. of Forensic Toxicologists, Assn. of Toxicologic and Forensic Chemistry, German Soc. of Legal Medicine. Avocation: photography. Home: Kerschensteinerstr 240, D-82110 Germing Germany Office: Inst Legal Medicine, Frauenlobstr 7a, D-80337 Munich Germany

VON MINCKWITZ, BERNHARD ALBERT ROMAN, publishing house executive; b. Göttingen, Germany, Aug. 11, 1944; s. Erasmus and Mary (von Lilienfeld) von M.; m. Cornelia Böhning; children: Alexis, Vanessa, Nicolas. Diploma Kaufmann, U. Berlin, 1971. Mem. bd. Bertelsmann Buch AG, Munich. Mem. Verband Bayerische Zeitschriftenverlage (bd. mem.). Office: Bertelsmann Fachinformation, Neumarkter Str 18, 81673 Munich Germany*

VON MOLTKE, GEBHARDT, diplomat; b. Wernersdorf, Silesia, Germany, June 28, 1938; married; 2 children. Student, U. Heidelberg, U. Grenoble, U. Berlin, U. Freiburg, 1958-63. Legal tng., 1963-67; with Fed. Fgn. Office, Bonn, 1968-71; with German Embassy, Moscow, 1971-75, Yaunde, 1975-77; with personnel adminstrn. office Fed. Fgn. Office, Bonn, 1977-82; with German Embassy, Washington, 1982-86; head U.S. dept., with Fed. Fgn. Office, Bonn, 1986-91; asst. sec.-gen. for polit. affairs NATO, 1991-97; amb. from Fed. Republic of Germany to Ct. of St. James London, 1997-99; per. rep. of Fed. Republic of Germany, North Atlantic Coun. NATO, Brussels, 1998—. Office: NATO Hdqrs, Blvd Leopold III, 1110 Brussels Belgium

VON MOLTKE, LISA L., pharmacologist, educator. BA, Wellesley Coll., 1981; MD, Mich. State U., 1987. Diplomate Am. Bd. Internal Medicine, Am. Clin. Pharmacology. Intern and resident internal medicine New Eng. Med. Ctr. Hosp., Boston, 1987-90; fellow clin. pharmacology Tufts U. Sch. Medicine, 1990-94; fellow clin. pharmacology dept. psychiatry and medicine New Eng. Med. Ctr. Hosp., 1990-94; rsch. asst. prof. dept. pharmacology & exptl. therapeutics Tufts U. Sch. Medicine, 1994—; assoc. medicine New Eng. Med. Ctr. Hosp., 1995—. Contbr. chpts. to books and articles to profl. jours. Grantee NIMH, 1995-2000. Mem. ACP, Internat. Soc. for the Study Xenobiotics, Am. Coll. Clin. Pharmacology, Mass. Med. Soc., Alpha Omega Alpha. Office: Tufts U Sch medicine New Eng Med Ctr Hosp Boston MA 02111

VON MÜHLENDAHL, KARL ERNST, pediatrician; b. Berlin, Jan. 14, 1939; s. Ernst and Esther (von Rennenkampff) von M.; m. Maja von Cube, Oct. 3, 1970; children: Alexander, Paul, Peter. MD, U. Munich, 1964. Med. diplomate; cert. pediatrician. Intern Med. U. Clinic, Düsseldorf, Germany, 1968; rsch. asst. Med. U. Clinic, Geneva, 1969-70; intern Pediatric U. Clinic, Heidelberg, 1971-72; intern in pediatrics Free U., Berlin, 1973-75, privatdozent, 1976, sr. registrar, 1976-78; asst. dir. Poison Control Ctr., Berlin, 1976-78; head clinic Children's Hosp., Osnabrück, Germany, 1979—; prof. U Münster, 1980—; head documentation and info. ctr. and commn. environ. questions German Acad. Pediatrics, 1991—. Author: Intoxications in Childhood, 2d edit., 1983, Pediatrics in Clinics, 1987, 6th edit., 1997, Pediatrician and Environment, 1994, III, 1996; editor: Intoxications in Childhood, 1979, 3d edit., 1995, Pediatric Emergencies, 1992, Pediatrician and Environment, 1992; contbg. editor European Jour. of Pediats.; co-editor Umweltmedizin in Forschung und Praxis; contbr. over 300 articles to profl. jours. Capt. German Army, 1966-67. Office: Kinderhospital, Iburger Str 187, D 49082 Osnabrück Germany

VONNEGUT, KURT, JR., writer; b. Indpls., Nov. 11, 1922; s. Kurt and Edith Sophia (Lieber) V.; m. Jane Marie Cox, Sept. 1, 1945 (div. 1979); children: Mark, Edith, Nanette; adopted nephews: James, Steven and Kurt Adams; m. Jill Krementz, 1979, 1 child, Lily. Student, Cornell U., 1940-42, U. Chgo., 1945-47; MA in Anthropology, U. Chgo., 1971. Reporter Chgo. City News Bur., 1946; pub. relations with Gen. Electric Co., 1947-50; freelance writer N.Y.C., 1950-65, 74—; lectr. writers workshop U. Iowa, Iowa City, 1965-67; lectr. in English Harvard U., Cambridge, Mass., 1970; disting. prof. CCNY, 1973-74. Author: (novels) Player Piano, 1951, Sirens of Titan, 1959, Mother Night, 1961, Cat's Cradle, 1963, God Bless You, Mr. Rosewater, 1964, Slaughterhouse-Five, 1969, Breakfast of Champions, 1973, Slapstick, or Lonesome No More, 1976, Jailbird, 1979, Deadeye Dick, 1982, Galápagos, 1985, Bluebeard, 1987, Hocus Pocus, 1990, Timequake, 1997, (collected stories) Welcome to the Monkey House, 1968; (play) Happy Birthday, Wanda June, 1970; (TV Script) Between Time and Timbuktu or Prometheus-5, 1972; (essays) Wampeters, Foma and Granfalloons, 1974; (Christmas Story with illustrations by Ivan Chermayeff) Sun Moon Star, 1980; (autobiographical collage) Palm Sunday, 1981, (collection of speeches and essays) Fates Worse Than Death, 1991, Timequake, 1997, (collection of short stories) Bagombo Snuff Box, 1999; also short stories, articles, revs. Served with inf. AUS, 1942-45. Guggenheim fellow, 1967-68. Mem. Nat. Inst. Arts and Letters (recipient Lit. award 1970). Fax: (212) 223-7561. Office: c/o Donald C Farber 6th Fl 750 Lexington Ave New York NY 10022-1906

VON NIESSEN, WOLFGANG, physicist, educator, chemist, educator; b. Wuppertal, Germany, Jan. 23, 1941; s. Alfred and Helma (Berg) Von N.; m. Karin Thelen, Mar. 21, 1969 (div. 1989); children: Yorck, Cornelia. MSc, Cornell U., 1966; Dr.rer.nat., Tech. U. Munich, 1970, Dr.rer.nat.habil., 1976. Postdoctoral fellow IBM Rsch. Lab., San Jose, 1969-70; sci. asst. Max-Planck-Inst. of Astrophysik, Munich, 1970-72, Tech. U. Munich, 1972-77; prof. Tech. U., Braunschweig, Germany, 1977—, dir. Inst. Physical and Theoretical Chemistry, 1984-88. Contbr. over 270 sci. articles to profl. jours. Mem. Am. Phys. Soc., German Phys. Soc., Bunsengesellschaft f. Physikalische Chemie. Avocations: music (piano), arts. Office: Tech Univ, Inst Phys and Theoret Chem, D-38106 Braunschweig Germany

VON OETINGER, BOLKO-ALEXANDER, consulting company executive; b. Berlin, Feb. 27, 1943; s. Gustav and Alexandra (von Hedemann) von O.; m. Marie-Luise Fürer von Haimendorf; children: Christina, Verena, Stephanie. D Social and Econ. Scis., Free U. Berlin, 1972, diploma Polit. Sci., 1968; MBA, Stanford U., 1974. Cons. The Boston Cons. Group, Menlo Park, Calif., 1974, Paris, 1974-75, Munich, Germany, 1975; v.p. The Boston Cons. Group, Munich, 1979-87, sr. v.p., 1987—; dir. The Boston Cons. Group Strategy Inst., Munich, 1999—; adv. bd. The Stanford Graduate Sch. Bus., 1999. Editor: Das Boston Consulting Group Strategie-Buch, 1993, (with Heinrich von Pierer) Wie kommt das Neue in die Welt?, 1997, Strategien für die neue Weltwirtschaft, 1998, (with John Seely Brown) Ergebnis Innovation, 1998. Bd. mem. Frauenstein Stiftung, Frankfurt, 1988. 2d lt. German Army, 1962-64. Mem. Münchner Herrenclub. Avocation: horseback riding. Office: The Boston Cons Group, Sendlingerstr 7, 80331 Munich Germany

VON PHILIPSBORN, WOLFGANG DIETRICH, chemist, educator; b. Anklam, Pomerania, Germany, Sept. 25, 1929; s. Maximilian Joseph and Lieselott Margarethe (von Welczeck) von P.; m. Heidi Wild, May 21, 1963; children: Andreas, Francisca. BSc in Chemistry, Free U., Berlin, 1952; PhD, U. Zürich, Switzerland, 1956. Fellow MIT, 1959-60; lectr. U. Zürich, 1963-66, asst. prof., 1966-69, assoc. prof., 1969-74, prof. chemistry, 1974-97; hon. prof. U. Zürich, 1997, dir. Inst. of Organic Chemistry, 1983-84; Swiss delegate Internat. Union of Pure and Applied Chemistry, 1985-97; vis. prof. Israel Inst. Tech., Haifa, 1972, U. Amsterdam, The Netherlands, 1975, U. Florence, Italy, 1988, U. Md., 1994, 97, U. Tel Aviv, 1995. European editor Magnetic Resonance in Chemistry, 1976—; adv. bd. internat. jours.; contbr. articles to profl. jours. Recipient Centennial medal Case Inst. of Tech., 1980. Mem. German Chem. Soc., Royal Soc. of Chemistry (London), N.Y. Acad. Sci., Am. Chem. Soc., Internat. Soc. of Magnetic Resonance, Swiss Chem. Soc. (hon. mem., 1996, pres. 1990-92, Alfred Werner prize 1963). Avocations: music, literature, arts, travel. Home: Mosacher 4, CH-8126 Zumikon Switzerland Office: Orgn Chem Inst U Zurich, Winterthurerstrasse 190, CH-8057 Zurich Switzerland

VON PIDOLL, ULRICH, explosion prevention executive, researcher; b. Cologne, Germany, Feb. 24, 1956; s. Heinrich and Angelika (Gambs) von P.; m. Christine Urban, June 14, 1991; 1 child, Viktoria. Diploma, U. Darmstadt, 1981, D in Engring., 1984. Rschr. U. Darmstadt, 1981-84; sci. referent Feldmuehle, 1985-90; rschr. Phys. Tech. Bundesanstalt, 1990—. Author: History of the Von Pidolls, 1981, VW-Beetle: A Car Writes History, 1994; patentee in field. Recipient prize Helmholtz Found., 1993. Avocation: historical cars. Office: Phys Tech Bundesanstalt, Bundesallee 100, D-38116 Braunschweig Germany

VON PIERER, HEINRICH, manufacturing executive; b. 1941. With legal dept. Siemens, Minich, 1969-77; dir. power plant divsn. KWU Power Sta. Unit, Siemens, 1977-88, comml. dir., 1988-89; mem. adminstrv. bd. Siemens AG, Munich, 1989-91, dep. chief exec., 1991-92, pres., chief exec., 1992—. Avocation: tennis. Office: Siemens AG, Wittelsbacherplatz 2, 80333 Munich Germany also: Siemens KWU Inc 1301 Avenue of Americas New York NY 10019-6022*

VON PROSCHWITZ, TED JÖRGEN, zoologist; b. Fröskog, Sweden, Oct. 10, 1957; s. Yngve and Mari-Ann (von Proschwitz) Johnsson. BS, U. Göteborg, Sweden, 1979, PhD, 1991. Mus. curator Mus. Natural History, Göteborg, 1985-89, head curator invertebrate zoology, 1989—. Author: Zoogeographical Studies on the Land Mollusca of the Province of Dalsland, 1994; tech. editor Checklist of European Continental Mollusca, 1997—; contbr. 80 articles to profl. jours. Mem. Deutsch Malakozoologische Gesellschaft. Home: Eklandagatan 29A, S-41282 Göteborg Sweden Office: Natural History Mus, PB 7283, S-40235 Göteborg Sweden

VON QUITZOW, CARL MICHAEL, law educator, consultant; b. Malmoe, Scania, Sweden, Nov. 26, 1962; m. Eva Kämmerling, Oct. 30, 1998; one child, Philip Christian Georg. LLM, Lund U., 1986, LLD, 1995. Trainee Arthur Andersen & Co., Malmoe, 1985-86; asst. prof. European Cmty. law Inst. European Mkt. Law, Copenhagen, 1987-89; expert advisor Ministry of Fgn. Affairs, Dept. Trade, Stockholm, 1989-91; assoc. Advokatfirman Landahl & Bauer, Stockholm, 1991-96; sr. lectr. U. Lund, 1995-96, assoc. prof. European Cmty. law, 1997, Jean Monnet prof. European Cmty. Law, 1997—; cons. in field. Author: Free Movement of Goods in the EC, 1995; co-author: EC Law, A New Legal Source in Sweden, 1992; contbr. articles to profl. jours. Recipient Award of King Oscar II for disting. doctoral dissertation Lund U., 1996. Mem. Danish Assn. of EC Law (bd. dirs. 1987-89), Coldinu Order (knight 1991—). Lutheran. Avocations: hunting, sailing, tennis. Office: Lund Univ Fac of Law, Box 207, S-221 00 Lund Sweden

VON RAFFLER-ENGEL, WALBURGA (WALBURGA ENGEL), linguist, cross-cultural communications specialist, lecturer, writer; b. Munich, Germany, Sept. 25, 1920; came to U.S., 1949, naturalized, 1955; d. Friedrich

J. and Gertrud E. (Kiefer) von R.; m. A. Ferdinand Engel, June 2, 1957; children: Lea Maxine, Eric Robert von Raffler. DLitt, U. Turin, Italy, 1947; MS, Columbia U., 1951; PhD, Ind. U., 1953. Free-lance journalist, 1949-58; mem. faculty Bennett Coll., Greensboro, N.C., 1953-55, U. Charleston (formerly Morris Harvey Coll.), W.Va., 1955-57, Adelphi U., CUNY, 1957-58, NYU, 1958-59, U. Florence, Italy, 1959-60, Inst. Postuniversitario Orgn. Aziendale, Turin, 1960-61, Bologna Center of Johns Hopkins U., 1964; assoc. prof. linguistics Vanderbilt U., Nashville, 1965-77, prof. linguistics, 1977-85, prof. emerita, sr. rsch. assoc. Inst. Pub. Policy Studies, 1985—; dir. linguistics program Vanderbilt U., 1978-86; chmn. com. on linguistics Nashville U. Ctr., 1974-79; Italian NSF prof. Psychol. Inst. U. Florence, Italy, 1986-87; prof. NATO Advanced Study Inst., Cortona, Italy, 1988; pres. Kinesics Internat., 1988—; vis. prof. linguistics Shanxi U., Peoples Republic China, 1985; vis. prof. U. Ottawa, Ont., Can., 1971-72, Lang. Scis. Inst., Internat. Christian U., Tokyo, 1976; grant evaluator NEH, NSF, Can. Coun.; manuscript reader Ind. U. Press, U. Ill. Press, Prentice-Hall; advisor Trinity U., Simon Frazer U.; lectr. in field; dir. internat. seminar Cross-Cultural Comm., 1986-87; mem. Ctr. for Global Media Studies, 1999; State Dept. Italy del. to Congress of the Hague. Author: Il prelinguaggio infantile, 1964, The Perception of Nonverbal Behavior in the Career Interview, 1983, The Perception of the Unborn Across the Cultures of the World, Japanese edit., 1993, English edit., 1994 (transl. into Chinese), A Traveler's Guide to Cross-Cultural Business Communications, 2000; co-author: Language Intervention Programs, 1960-75; editor, co-editor 12 books; author films and videotape; contbr. articles to profl. jours. Grantee Am. Coun. Learned Socs., NSF, Can. Coun., Ford Found., Kenan Venture Fund, Japanese Ministry Edn., NATO, UNESCO, Finnish Acad., Meharry Med. Coll., Internat. Sociol. Assn., Internat. Coun. Linguists, Tex. A&M U., Vanderbilt U., others. Mem. AAUP, Internat. Linguistic Assn., Linguistic Soc. Am. (chmn. Golden Anniversary film com. 1974, emerita 1985—), Linguistic Assn. Can. and the U.S., Internat. Assn. for Applied Linguistics (com. on discourse analyses, sessions chmn. 1978), Lang. Origins Soc. (exec. com. 1985-97, chmn. internat. congress, 1987), Internat. Sociol. Assn. (rsch. com. for sociolinguistics, session co-chmn. internat. conf. 1983, session chmn. profl. conf. 1983), Internat. Coun. Psychologists, Internat. Assn. for Intercultural Comms. Studies, Internat. Assn. for Study of Child Lang. (v.p. 1975-78, chmn. internat. conf. Tuscan Acad. Scis., Florence, Italy 1972), Inst. for Nonverbal Comm. Rsch. (workshop leader 1981), Southeastern Conf. on Linguistics, 1980— (hon. mem. 1985—), Semiotic Soc. Am. (organizing com. Internat. Semiotics Inst. 1981), Nat. Assn. Scholars, Tenn. Assn. Scholars (bd. dirs. 1998-99), Internat. Assn. for Intercultural Comms. Studies (panel organizer 1999), United Europe Movement (sect. chmn. 1944-45), Internat. Comm. Assn., Internat. Pragmatics Assn. Achievements include being instrumental in forcing Vanderbilt U. to enroll women on an equal basis with men. Home and Office: 116 Brighton Close Nashville TN 37205-2501

VON RANDOW, GERO, science writer, editor; b. Hamburg, Germany, Jan. 22, 1953; s. Thomas and Cornelie (Kleikamp) Von R.; m. Birgit Radow, June 6, 1975 (div. 1988); 1 child, Kathrin; m. Beate Ratter, June 2, 1995. Grad., Hamburg U. Freelance writer Bochum and Hamburg, Germany, 1984-92; editor Die Zeit, Hamburg, 1992—. Author: Das Ziegenproblem, 1992, Robuster Unsere Nächsten Verwandten, 1997; editor: Das Kritische Computerbuch, 1989; editor, author: Mein Paranormales Fahrrad, 1993, Der Fremdling im Glas, 1996. Recipient Robert-Mayer prize, 1997; named Reporter der Wissenschaft, Com. Reporter der Wissenschaft, 1992. Mem. Soc. for the History of Tech., History of Sci. Soc. Office: Die Zeit, Speersort Pressehaus, D-20079 Hamburg Germany

VON RETYI, ANDREAS, artist, writer; b. Munich, Germany, Oct. 10, 1963; s. Georg and Elisabeth (Filla) V.R. Freelance artist Carl-Zeiss Planetarium, Stuttgart, Germany, 1987-92. Author: Jupiter and Saturn, 1985, Halley, 1985, Danger from Outer Space, 1992, We are Not Alone!, 1994, Alien Empire, 1995, Meteorites, 1996, Century's Comet, 1997, The UFO-Connection, 1998, Secret Base Area 51, 1998, Stargate Conspiracy, 2000; editor: Star Observer. Mem. Planetary Soc., Internat. Assn. for Astron. Arts, Ancient Astronaut Soc. Avocations: meteorites, practical astronomy, music. Office: Langen Mueller Pubs, Kopp Publs, Graf-Wolfegg Str, 72108 Rottenburg Germany

VON ROSEN, RÜDIGER, stock exchange executive; b. Grocholin, June 21, 1943. Diploma, U. Frankfurt, 1970; PhD, 1973. With Deutsche Bundesbank, 1974-86; exec. vice-chmn. Fedn. German Stock Exchanges, 1986-93; speaker bd. mng. dirs. Frankfurter Wertpapierbörse AG, Frankfurt, 1990-92; mem. bd. mng. dirs. Deutsche Börse AG, Frankfurt, 1993-94, mng. dir., 1995—; mng. dir. Deutsche Aktieninstitut EV, Frankfurt; hon. prof. Frankfurt U., 1998. Office: Deutsches Aktieninstitut EV, Biebergasse 6-10, D-60313 Frankfurt Germany

VON ROTH, WALTER EMIL, civil engineer; b. Lauchringen, Germany, Aug. 10, 1940; s. Walter Armin and Ida (Maier) von R.; m. Maria de los Angeles Rechy, Feb. 9, 1940; children: Walter, Emil, Jose-Guadalupe. Engr., Tech. Coll., Karlsruhe, Germany, 1963, Diploma in Engring., 1968, D Engring., 1978. Tutor Tech. U., Karlsruhe, 1968-70; rschr. Fed. Res. Inst., Hamburg, Germany, 1970-89; lector U. Hamburg, 1970-87; prof. U. Monterrey, Mexico, 1989-93, U. Applied Sci., Neubrandenburg, Germany, 1994—; head Inst. Wood Tech., U. Monterrey, 1989-93; dean U. Applied Sci., Neubrandenburg, 1996-2000. Mem. Fed. Ministry Bldg., 1981-89. Recipient Gruen and Bilfinger prize, 1968. Mem. German Found. Studies. Roman Catholic. Office: Univ Applied Sci, Brodaer Strasse 2, D-17033 Neubrandenburg Germany

VON RYDINGSVARD, URSULA KAROLISZYN, sculptor; b. Deensen, Germany, July 26, 1942; cmae to U.S., 1950; d. Ignacy and Konegunda (Sternal) Karoliszyn; m. Pual Greengard. BA, MA, U. Miami, Coral Gables, Fla., 1965; postgrad., U. Calif., Berkeley, 1969-70; MFA, Columbia U., 1975; PhD (hon.), Md. Inst. Art, 1991. Instr. Sch. Visual Arts, N.Y.C., 1981-82; asst. prof. Pratt Inst., Bklyn., 1978-82, Fordham U., Bronx, N.Y., 1980-82; assoc. prof. Yale U., New Haven, 1982-86; prof. grad. divsn. Sch. Visual Arts, N.Y.C., 1986—. One-woman shows include Laumeier Sculpture Gallery, St. Louis, 1988, Capp St. Project San Francisco, 1990, Lorence-Monk Gallery, N.Y.C., 1990-91, Zamek Ujazdowski Contemporary Art Ctr., Warsaw, Poland, 1992, Storm King Art Ctr., Mountainville, N.Y., 1992-94, Galerie Lelong, N.Y.C., 1994, Weatherspoon Art Gallery, Grensboro, N.C., 1994, Univ. Gallery, Amherst, 1995, Mus. Art, Providence, 1996, Mus. Art R.I. Sch. Design, Providence, 1996, Yorkshire Sculpture Pk., Wakefield, England, 1997, Nelson-Atkins Mus., Kansas City, Mo., 1998, Madison (Wis.) Art Ctr., 1998, Chgo. Cultural Ctr., 1998, Indpls. Mus. Art, 1999, The Contemporaty Mus., Honolulu, 1999, Barbara Krahow Gallery, Boston, 1999; exhibited in group shows at Contemporary Arts Ctr., Cin., 1987, Damon Brandt Gallery, N.Y.C., 1989, Met. Mus. Art, N.Y.C., 1989-93, Whitney Mus. Contemporary Art, 1990, Cultural Ctr., Chgo., 1991, Ctrl. Bur. Art Exhbns., Warsaw and Krakow, Poland, 1991, The Cultural Space/Exit Art, N.Y.C., 1992, Galerie Lelong, N.Y.C., 1993, Denver Art Mus. and Columbus Art Mus., 1994—, others; outdoor exhbns include Pelham Bay Park, Bronx, N.Y., 1978, Neuberger Mus., Purchase, N.Y., 1979, Artpark, Lewiston, N.Y., 1979, Laumeier Sculpture Park, St. Louis, 1989-94, Walker Art Ctr., Mpls., 1990-93, Oliver Ranch, Geyserville, Calif., Storm King Art Ctr., Mountainville, N.Y., 1992-93; contbr. articles to profl. jours. Fulbright Hays travel grantee, 1975; grantee N.Y. State Coun. Arts, Am. the Beautiful Fund, Nat. Endowment for Arts, Creative Artists Program Svc.; Griswald traveling grantee Yale U., 1985; Guggenheim fellow, 1983-84; Nat. Endowment for Arts individual artists grantee, 1986-87; recipient Acad. award in Art, Am. Acad. Arts and Letters, 1994, Alfred Jurzykowski Found. Fine Arts award, 1996, Joan Mitchell award, N.Y., 1997. Studio: 429 S 5th St Brooklyn NY 11211-7425*

VON SAMSON-HIMMELSTJERNA, ARMIN, retired shipping executive; b. Dettendorf, Germany, Nov. 2, 1924; s. Alfred and Anna (Gräfin von Waldersee) von Samson-H.; m. Edda Maria Demal, June 27, 1967; children: Matthias, Silvia, Raynold, Thilo, Hubertus. Laborer U.S. Steel Co., Pitts., 1950-51; export clk. J.P. Sauer & Son A.G., Eckernförde, Germany, 1951-53; shipping mgr. Blumenfeld & Co., Hamburg, Germany, 1954-60; sec. gen. WDA, Geneva, 1960-67; shipping expert UNDP, N.Y., Taiwan, 1967-70; mng. dir. Ulrich Harms Salvage Co., Hamburg, 1971-84. Home: 274 Penyaparda Montgo, E 03730 Javea Alicante, Spain also: Montgo 274, E 03730 Javea/Alicante Spain

VON SEGESSER, LUDWIG KARL, cardiovascular surgeon, researcher, educator; b. Lucerne, Switzerland, Mar. 15, 1952; s. Ludwig and Mathilde (Glutz) von S.; m. Marie Dinh, June 27, 1979; children: Ludwig, Jeanne. MD, U. Basel, Switzerland, 1979, PD, 1989. Cert. Surg. Bd. Switzerland, 1985. Resident Kantonsspital Obwalden, Sarnen, Switzerland, 1979; resident Univ. Hosp., Geneva, 1980-83, mem. staff cardiovascular surgery, 1983-85; fellow cardiovascular surgery Tex. Heart Inst., Houston, 1986; staff surgeon Clinic for Cardiovascular Surgery Univ. Hosp., Zurich, Switzerland, 1987-96; acad. appointee Zurich (Switzerland) U., 1989-96; prof., chief dept. cardiovascular surgery Univ. Hosp. Lausanne, Vaud, Switzerland, 1996—; Mem. European Bd. of Cardiovascular Perfusion, chmn. 1993—; clin. prof., 1996—; head clinic cardiovascular surgery CHUV U. Hosp., Lausanne, Switzerland, 1996; gen. sec. Union Swiss Surg. Socs., 1996—. Author: Arterial Grafting for Myocardial Revascularization, 1990; asst. editor Perfusion, 1992—, European Jour. Cardio-Thoracic Surgery, 1994—; mem. adv. editl. bd. Thorac Cardiovasc. Surg., 1996—; corr. editor Cardiovascular Engring., 1997—; mem. editl. bd. Swiss Medical Weekly, Zeitschrift für Herz-, Thorax-und Gefässchiurgie, Jour. of Cirulatory Support, Heart, Swiss Surgery; contbr. over 400 articles to profl. jours. Recipient Goetz-Preis award U. Zurich, 1991, award Swiss Cardiology Found., 1991. Fellow ACS; mem. AAAS, Am. Assn. Thoracic Surgery, Swiss Soc. Thoracic and Cardiovascular Surgery (sec. 1989—), Swiss Soc. Vascular Surgery, Union Swiss Surg. Socs. (gen. sec. 1996—), Swiss Soc. Angiology, Swiss Soc. of Cardiology, German Soc. Surgery, German Soc. Thoracic and Cardiovascular Surgery, European Soc. Cardiology, European Assn. Pediat. Cardiology, European Assn. Cardio-Thoracic Surgery, European Soc. Cardiovascular Surgery, European Soc. Vascular Surgery, Am. Heart Assn., European Soc. Artificial Organs, Soc. Critical Care Medicine, Internat. Soc. Heart & Lung Transplantation, Internat. Soc. for Minimally Invasive Cardiac Surgery, Internat. Soc. Surgery, The Soc. Thoracic Surgeons, Soc. Laparoendoscopic Surgeons, Assn. Advancement Med. Instrn., Am. Soc. Artificial Internal Organs, Internat. Soc. Artificial Organs, Extracorpeal Life Support Orgn., Internat. Soc. Endovascular Surgery, Soc. Laparoendoscopic Surgeons. Achievements include research on improvement of blood exposed surfaces for cardio-pulmonary bypass and mechanical circulatory support. Office: Univ Hosp CHUV, Dept Cardiovascular Surgery, CH-1011 Lausanne Switzerland

VON SEIDLEIN, PETER C., architect; b. Munich, June 24, 1925; s. Peter and Mea (Kronenbitter) von S.; m. Karen Schoeningh, July 5, 1930; children: Maria Theresia, Lorenz, Rupert. D Engring., Tech. U. Munich, 1999; Reg. Baumeister, State Bavaria, 1953. Asst. prof. arch. Tech. U. Munich, 1955-59; pvt. practice architect Munich, 1958—; prof. architecture U. Stuttgart, 1974—, dir. Inst. for Bldg. Constrn., 1984—; bd. dirs. Suddeutscher Verlag, Munich, 1960—. Mem. City Bldg. Commn., Munic, 1976-86. Recipient German Archtl. prize, 1985. Mem. Bund Deutscher Arch. (chmn. Bavarian chpt. 1970-72, recipient prizes 1969, 85), Bavarian Chamber of Architects (del.), Acad. Arts Berlin. Roman Catholic. Avocations: gas ballooning, skiing. Home and Office: Fluggenstrasse 11, 80639 Munich 19, Federal Republic Germany

VONSOVICI, ADRIAN PETRU, physicist, researcher; b. Pitesti, Arges, Romania, Aug. 23, 1965; arrived in England, 1997; s. Victor and Veronica Vonsovici; m. Monica Lucia Ritco, Aug. 20, 1994; children: Mihai, Sergiu. MSc in Technol. Physics, U. Bucharest, Romania, 1989; MSc in Electronics, U. Paris, Orsay, 1993, PhD in Physics, 1996. Rschr. Inst. Physics, Bucharest, 1990-92; rsch. assoc. Inst. D'Electronique Fondamentale-U. Paris, Orsay, 1993-96; rsch. fellow U. Southampton, Eng., 1998, U. Surrey, Guildford, Eng., 1998-2000; devel. engr. Bookham Tech., Ltd., 2000—. Contbr. papers to profl. jours. Lt. Alpine Infantry, 1983-84. Grantee French Govt., 1992. Avocations: football, basketball, history, music.

VON STOCKAR, URS C., chemical engineering educator; b. Zurich, July 17, 1942; s. Walter and Georgine E. (Koch) von S.; m. Denise Y. Bridel, Aug. 28, 1971; children: Beryl, Sabine. Diploma engring. chemistry, Swiss Fed. Inst. Tech., 1967, PhD, 1973. Lectr. U. Calif., Berkeley, 1976; chemist Ciba-Giegy, Basel, Switzerland, 1977; assoc. prof. Swiss Fed. Inst. Tech., 1977-82, prof., 1982—; assoc. prof. U. Geneva, 1991-96. Contbr. articles to profl. jours., co-author 1 book. Capt. Swiss Artillery, 1973-96. Postdoctoral fellow U. Calif., 1973-76. Mem. Europ. Fed. Biotech. (exec. com. 1988—, chmn. 1996-97). Home: Ch de Cret-de-Plan 39, CH-1095 Lutry Switzerland Office: Swiss Fed Inst Tech, Ecole Polytech Fed Ecublens, CH-1015 Lausanne Switzerland

VON STREMPEL, ARCHIBALD HEINRICH, spine surgeon, consultant, researcher; b. Velbert, Germany, Apr. 28, 1950; s. Gustav-Adolf and Liselotte (Hoerder) von S.; m. Sabine Maria Franke; children: Maja, Alexandra-Charlotte. DEng., U. Berlin, 1984, MD, 1986. Med. asst. Prof. Ruecker, Berlin, 1982, Dr. Zielke, Bad Wildungen, 1983-85; asst. physician Dr. Pueschel and Dr. Eckhardt, Vogtareuth, 1985-87, Prof. Refior, Munich, 1987-89; orthopaedist Munich, 1989; asst. med. dir. Prof. Wirth, Hanover, 1989-94; med. dir. Annastift e.V., Hanover, 1995—; prof. orthop., 1999—. Author: In-vitro Untersuchungen an Menschlichen Wirbeksäken zur Stabilitaetsbestimmung von Bogenwurzelschrauben, 1992, Die Instabilitaet des Lumbosakralen Scharniers, 1992, Operative Behandlung der Spondylolisthesis durch distrahierende und transpedikulaere Stabilisierung ueber Sakralknieaufbau nach Zielke, 1986; inventor segmental spinal correction system. Mem. Deutsche Gesellschaft fuer Orthopaedie und Traumatologie, European Spine Soc., N.Am. Spine Soc. Office: Annastift eV Klinik III, Heimchenstrasse 1-7, 30625 Hannover Germany

VON SYDOW, AKE CHRISTIAN, marketing executive; b. Waxholm, Sweden, Sept. 5, 1926; s. Christian F.C.H. and Margit (Lowenborg) S.; m. Margit Lorvall, June 21, 1952; children: Carl, Martin, Daniel. MSc, Royal Inst. Tech., Stockholm, 1952; postgrad., MIT, 1952-53. Chartered engr., U.K. Pres. Stal-Laval (UK) Ltd., 1959-66; mktg. dir. Stal-Laval AB, Finspong, Sweden, 1967-80; sr. v.p. ASEA/ABB, Vasterås, Sweden, 1981-92; pres. Advance Mktg. AB, Vasterås, 1992—; condr. seminars in field. Contbr. numerous articles to profl. jours. Sr. advisor Swedish Trade Coun., 1992-99, Provincial Govt. Vasterås, 1995-99; vice chmn. Ctr. for Pacific Asia Studies, Stockholm U., 1986—. Maj. Swedish Army Res., 1972-96. Mem. Rotary (pres. 1974). Conservative. Lutheran. Avocations: music, church organs, house construction. Office: Advance Marketing AB, Aasgatan 19, 724 63 Vasterås Sweden

VON SYDOW, BJORN, federal official; b. Nov. 26, 1945; married; four children. BSc, Stockholm U.; PhD in Polit. Sci. Prof. polit. sci., sec. to former Prime Min. Tage Erlander, 1970-74; mcpl. councilor Solna, 1979—; mem. SDP Program Commn., 1987—; mem. Parliament, 1994—, min. trade, industry and commerce, 1996, min. def., 1997—; vis. prof. U.S.; rschr. in field. Mil. svc. Enkoping and Stockholm. Mem. Social Democratic Party. Office: Jakobsgatan 9, S-103 33 Stockholm Sweden*

VON TRIER, LARS, film director; b. Denmark, 1956. Dir. Nocturne, 1981, Images of a Relief, 1982, The Element of Crime, 1984, Epidemic, 1987, Medea, 1988, Europa, 1991 (Cannes Jury prize 1991), The Kingdom, 1994, Breaking the Waves, 1996 (Grand Prix Cannes Film Festival 1996), Idioterne, 1988, (TV mini-series) Riget II, 1997, D-dag, 2000, Dancer in the Dark, 2000 (Golden Palm, Cannes Film Festival 2000). Office: Zentropa Entertainments, Ryesgade 106, 4, DK-2100 Copenhagen Denmark Office: Zentropa Prodn, Avedore Tuaevej 10 Box 505, 2650 Huiodoure Denmark*

VON TURKOVICH, BRANIMIR FRANCIS, engineering educator, researcher; b. Zagreb, Croatia, Dec. 24, 1924; came to U.S., 1951; s. Francis von Turkovich and Ana (Vuchinich) Wolff; m. Maria Eulalia Forgas Del Rio, June 21, 1951; children: Edward, Francis, Richard, Karl, Ivan. MS in Naval Engring., U. Madrid, 1951; PhD in Mech. Engring. and Physics, U. Ill., 1961. Chartered naval engr., Spain. Prof. mech. and indsl. engring. U. Ill., Urbana, 1962-70; prof. mech. engring. U. Vt., Burlington, 1971—; vis. prof. mech. engring. Poly. U., Turin, Italy, 1966-67, U. Palermo, Italy, 1976, U. Pisa, Italy, 1987, U. Natal, South Africa, 1983; dir. divsn. NSF, Washington, 1988-91; cons. various cos., 1965—. Contbr. over 100 rsch. articles to sci. publs.; patentee in field. Fellow ASME (svc. medal 1987), Soc. Mfg. Engrs. (rsch. medal 1975); mem. Am. Phys. Soc., Materials Soc., Italian Soc. Mechanics (silver medal 1976), Internat. Instn. for Prodn. Engring. Rsch. (hon. mem., past pres.), Sigma Xi. Roman Catholic. Achievements include patents in field and research in materials processing. Avocations: hunting, skiing. Office: U Vt 201 Votey Bldg Burlington VT 05401

VON UNGERN-STERNBERG, SARA MARGARETA, information scientist; b. Vörå, Finland, June 25, 1940; d. Jarl Auno Elias and Aida Margareta (Simons) Ek; m. Rudolf Leo von Flittner, Aug. 26, 1961 (dec. 1988); children: Gabriella Maria, Michaela Anna Margarek, Joachim Einar Gottfried; m. Claes Erik von Ungern-Sternberg, Sept. 3, 1993. MS in Chemistry, Helsinki (Finland) U., 1967; PhD Libr. and Info. Scis., Åbo Acad. U., Finland, 1994. Rsch. asst. dept. physics Helsinki U., 1967-68; chemist Vet. U., Helsinki, 1968-70; info. specialist Turku (Finland) U., 1974-85; sr. lectr. Åbo Acad. U., Turku, 1985-95, prof., 1995-98, asst. prof., 1998—; docent Oulu U., 1998—. Author: Student and the Library, 1996, A Tool for Planning Information Provision in interdisciplinary Fields, 1994, Analysis of National Collections in the Sciences, 1989. Recipient Rsch. award Waldemar von Frenckells Found., 1990. Mem. Finnish Soc. for Info. Studies (bd. dirs. 1989—), Swedish Libr. Assn. Finland (edn. com. 1996—). Achievements include research on information and learning, informetrics. Home: Dragonvägen 4 B 11, FIN00330 Helsinki Finland Office: Åbo Acad U, Tavastgatan 13, FIN20500 Turku FInland

VON WARTBURG, WALTER P., chemical industry executive; b. Liestal, Switzerland, Aug. 26, 1939; m. Helen A. Imbach; children: Christian, Claudia, Phillip. Diploma, U. Paris Sorbonne, 1959; Lic. Optime, U. Basel, Switzerland, 1962, Doctorate magna cum laude, 1963; LLM, Harvard U., 1966. Bar: Basel. Sec. to dept. Ct. of Appeal, Basel; mem. legal staff Law Office of Dres. Goetschel et al, Basel; head Dept. Health Policy and Health Legislation, Basel, 1966-76; dir., mem. exec. com. Pharma divsn. Ciba-Geigy Ltd., Basel, 1977-89; head Ciba Comms., Basel, 1989—, 1990-97; head Novartis Comm., 1997-99; pvt. practice, 1999—; prof. in selected fields of pub. law, specially pub. health St. Gall Grad. Sch. Econs., Bus. and Pub. Adminstrn. Contbr. numerous articles to profl. jours. Founder, pres. Swiss Found. for Mentally Handicapped; chmn. bd. dirs. Basel Opera, Ballet and Theatre; mem. adv. coun. Bologna Ctr. of Paul H. Nitze Sch. Advanced Internat. Studies, Johns Hopkins U., Washington and Bologna, Italy. Recipient Eastman prize Am. Arbitration Assn., 1966.

VON WOGAU, KARL, member of European Parliament; b. Freiburg, Germany, July 18, 1941. Grad. in Law, Fed. Republic of Germany; diploma, Insead, Fontainebleau, France; Doctor degree, Fed. Republic of Germany. Mgr. Sandoz Ltd., Basel, Switzerland, 1971-84; ptnr. lawfirm Bappert, Witz, Selbherr, Freiburg, 1984—; mem. European Parliament, 1979—, chmn. com. on econ. and monetary affairs and indsl. policy, 1994—. Author: Der Milliardenjoker, 1988, Soziale Marktwirtschoft Modell für Europa, 1999. Mem. CDU (regional exec. com. Südbaden), Econ. and Ind. Bus. Assn. of the EEP (v.p.), Kangaroo Group (co-founder 1981, chmn.), Junge Union, Com. Econ and Monetary Affairs, Com. Constl. Affairs (substitute mem., spokesman), Delegation for Rels. with Mashreq countries and Gulf States. Mem. Christlich Demokratische Union. Roman Catholic. Fax: 49-761-2180871 or 322-284-9301. E-mail: wogau.freiburg@t-onlline.de, kwogau@europarl.eu.int. Office: Büro von Wogau, Kaiser-Joseph Str 284, D-79098 Freiburg Germany

VON WOLFERSDORF, LOTHAR, mathematics educator; b. Zeitz, Germany, June 13, 1934. Diploma, U. Halle, 1957, Dr., 1961; PhD, Tech. U. Bergakademie, Freiberg, 1966. Asst. Martin Luther U. Halle-Wittenberg, Halle, 1957-64; sci. worker Bergakademie Freiberg, Germany, 1965-67, assoc. prof., 1967-68, prof., 1968-99. Mem. Sächs Akad. Wissensch. Leipzig. Office: TU Bergakademie Freiberg, Akademie-Strasse 6, Freiberg Sachsen D-O9596, Germany

VON WRIGHT, GEORG HENRIK, philosopher, writer; b. Helsinki, Finland, June 14, 1916; s. Tor von Wright and Ragni Elisabeth Alfthan; m. Baroness Maria Elisabeth von Troil, 1941; 2 children. Educated, U. Helsinki, Cambridge U.; D honoris causa, Helsinki U., Liverpool U., Lund U., U. Turku, Tampere U., Buenos Aires U., Salta U., Bologna U., St. Olaf Coll., Abo Acad., Tromso U., Stockholm U., Leipzig U., Innsbruck U. Lectr. in philosophy U. Helsinki, 1943-46, prof. philosophy, 1946-61; prof. philosophy Cambridge U., 1948-51, Tarner lectr. Trinity Coll., 1969; hon. fellow Trinity Coll., Cambridge; vis. prof. Cornell U., 1954, 58, U. Calif., 1963, U. Pitts., 1966, U. Karlsruhe, 1975, U. Leipzig, 1994-95; Gifford lectr. U. St. Andrews, 1959-60; rsch. fellow Acad. Finland, 1961-86; Andrew D. White prof.-at-large Cornell U., 1965-77; chancellor at Abo Acad., 1968-77; Woodbridge lectr. Columbia U., 1972; Nellie Wallace lectr. U. Oxford, 1978. Author: The Logical Problem of Induction, 1941, A Treatise on Induction and Probability, 1951, An Essay in Modal Logic, 1951, Logical Studies, 1957, The Varieties of Goodness, 1963, Norm and Action, 1963, The Logic of Preference, 1963, An Essay in Deontic Logic, 1968, Explanation and Understanding, 1971, Causality and Determinism, 1974, Freedom and Determination, 1980, Wittgenstein, 1982, Philosophical Papers, I-III, 1983-84, Intellectual Autobiography, 1989, The Tree of Knowledge, 1993, Normen, Werte und Handlungen, 1994, Six Essays in Philosophical Logic, 1996, In the Shadow of Descartes, 1998. Recipient Wihuri Found. Internat. prize 1976, Alexander von Humboldt Found. rsch. award, 1986, Tage Danielsson Humanist award, 1998. Fellow Finnish Soc. Sci. (pres. 1966-67); mem. Philos. Soc. Finland (pres. 1962-73), Internat. Union History and Philosophy of Sci. (pres. 1963-65), Inst. Internat. de Philosophie Paris (pres. 1975-78), Royal Swedish Acad. Sci., Brit. Acad., Royal Danish Acad. Sci. Norwegian Acad. Sci. and Letters, European Acad. Arts, Scis. and Humanities, World Acad. Arts and Scis., Am. Acad. Arts and Scis. (hon. fgn. mem.). Address: 4 Skepparegatan, Helsinki Finland

VON ZUR MÜHLEN, ALEXANDER MEINHARD, physician, internal medicine educator; b. Riga, Latvia, May 13, 1936; arrived in Germany, 1939.; s. Alexander and Kira (Velitschkowski) von zur M.; m. Karen Berg, 1958 (div. 1977); children: Insa, Friederike, Patrick; m. Ulrike Warnecke, 1977; children: Constantin, Nicolas. Grad., Med. Sch. Freiburg, Fed. Republic Germany, 1963. Asst. Med. Sch. Göttingen, Fed. Republic Germany, 1965-74, sr. asst., 1974; prof. Internal Medicine Med. Sch. Hannover, Fed. Republic Germany, 1974—. Contbr. articles to profl. jours. Mem. German Soc. Endocrinology, German Soc. Internal Medicine. Office: Med Hochschule Hannover, Konstanty-Gutschow Str 8, D-30625 Hannover Germany

VOORHEES, KENT JAY, chemist; b. Provo, Utah, Sept. 7, 1943; s. Melrose and Beulah Madge (Hansen) V.; m. Tamara Lee Lasson, June 9, 1966; children: Christian Ward, Danielle Kay. BS, Utah State Univ., 1965, MS, 1968, PhD, 1970. Fellow Mich. State Univ., East Lansing, 1970-72; instr. Univ. Utah, Salt Lake City, 1971-73, asst. rsch. prof., 1973-76, assoc. rsch. prof., 1976-79; asst. prof. Colo. Sch. Mines, Golden, 1979-83, assoc. prof., 1983-86, prof., 1986—; cons. 1979—; scientific adv. bd. Colo. Health Care, Denver, 1997—; bd. dirs. Petrex, Golden, 1982-86; editorial bd. Analytical Pyrolysis, Amsterdam, The Netherlands, 1991—. Author: Analytical pyrolysis, 1982; contbr. articles to profl. jours. Recipient Rsch. award Am. Chem. Soc., 1995, ORISE Faculty fellowship Food and Drug Adminstrn., 1995. Mem. ACS (nominations and elections com. 1988-92, coun. policy com. 1999—), Colo. Am. Chem. Soc. (councilor 1981—), Am. Soc. Mass Spectrometry. Avocations: golf, fishing, boating. E-mail: kvoorhee@mines.edu.

VOORHEES, STEPHANIE ROBIN NEE FAUGHT, retired art educator; b. Indpls., Dec. 18, 1951; d. Edward Francis and Dorothy Marie (Teague) F.; m. James Osborn Voorhees, June 19, 1999. BFA, Montclair (N.J.) State U., 1973, postgrad., 1974-76. Substitute tchr. Woodbridge (N.J.) Twp. Bd. of Edn., 1971-73, elem. art tchr., 1973-84, 85-86; middle sch. art tchr. Colonia (N.J.) Middle Sch., 1984-85; high sch. art tchr. Woodridge High Sch., 1986-90; middle sch. art tchr. Avenel (N.J.) Middle Sch., 1990-94; art tchr. John F. Kennedy H.S., Iselin, N.J., 1994-98, ret., 1998; spkr. Woodbridge River Watch, 1991; pvt. art tchr., 1983-93; yearbook advisor Woodbridge H.S., 1989-90, Avenel Mid. Sch., 1991-94, John F. Kennedy H.S., 1995-98; play set designer, 1989, 94-97. Illustrator (book) Care of the Lower Back, 1975, Touching All the Bases, 1993. Campaign vol. Rep. Party, Woodbridge, 1992; sec. to the producer Fgn. Broadcast Svc. Dem./Rep. Nat. Convs., Miami, 1972. Recipient Gov.'s Tchr. Recognition award State Dept. of Edn., 1992, Excellence in Edn. award C of C., 1992. Mem. AAUW, Woodbridge Twp. Fedn. of Tchrs. (v.p. 1980-83, pres. 1983-95, Cert. of

Merit, 1982), Art Educators of N.J., Met. Mus. of Art, Ecology Club (advisor 1990-94), Am. Legion Post 24 Ladies Aux. (historian), Cabane 880 (historian), VFW Post 10141 Ladies Aux. (sec.). Baptist. Avocations: singing, playing piano, dancing, writing, cruise travel. Home: 29 River Isles Bradenton FL 34208-9003

VOORHES, MARY MARGARET, research center executive; b. Augusta, Ga., Aug. 20, 1955; married; 2 children. BA cum laude, Wesleyan U., Middletown, Conn., 1977; M of Internat. Policy, Johns Hopkins U., 1989. Exec. asst. Am. Com. U.S.-Soviet Rels., Washington, 1977-79; rsch. analyst Investor Responsibility Rsch. Ctr., Washington, 1980-82, sr. analyst, 1983-86, asst. dir. South Africa program, 1986-90, dir. So. Africa Svc., 1990-98, dir. social issues svc., 1997—. Author: The Modernization of Apartheid, 1982; co-author: Two Decades of Debate: The Controversy Over U.S. Companies in South Africa, 1983, Religion and Fair Employment in Northern Ireland, 1990, Private Sector Involvement in Southern Africa, 1996, How Sanctions Work, 1999; editor (quarterly jour.) South Africa Reporter, 1983-94, (monthly jour.) South Africa Investor, 1995-98, (monthly jour.) Corporate Social Issues Reporter, 1997—; co-editor The Sweatshop Quandary: Corporate Responsibility on the Global Frontier, 1999; spkr. in field. Mem. Women's Fgn. Policy Group, adv. coun. Greener Business Guide. Office: Investor Responsibility Rsch Ctr 1350 Connecticut Ave NW Washington DC 20036-1722

VOORHOEVE, JORIS, Dutch government official; b. The Hague, The Netherlands, Dec. 22, 1945; married; 4 children. Graduate, Coll. Higher Agrl. Edn., Ede, 1965; BSin Econs., Agrl. U., Wageningen, 1971; MA in Polit. Scis., Leiden U., 1972; PhD in Internat. Rels., Johns Hopkins U., 1983. With policy analysis dept. World Bank, Washington, 1973-77; chair internat. affairs working group adv. coun. on govt. policy, 1977-79; prof. internat. rels. Agrl. U., Wageningen, The Netherlands, 1979-86; dir. Clingendael Netherlands Inst. Internat. Rels., 1990-94; prof. internat. orgns. U. Leiden, The Netherlands, 1990-94; min. def., min. Netherlands Antilles and Aruban Affairs Govt. of Kingdom of Netherlands, 1994—; min. Netherlands Antilles and Aruban affairs; mem. adv. coun. peace and security, nat. adv. coun. devel. cooperation. dir. People's Party for Freedom and Democracy rsch. orgn., 1979-82, MP lower house, 1982-89; chmn. parliamentary People's Party for Freedom and Democracy, 1986—. Mem. Help the Afghans Assn. (chmn.), Politics of Peace Assn. (bd. dirs.), Netherlands Eurepean Movement. People's Party for Freedom and Democracy. Office: Min Netherlands Antillean, Herengracht 19 A, 2511 EG The Hague The Netherlands also: PO Box 20051, 2500 EB The Hague The Netherlands*

VOORSANGER, BARTHOLOMEW, architect; b. Detroit, Mar. 23, 1937; s. Jacob H. and Ethel A. (Arnstein) V.; m. Lisa Livingston, 1964; m. Catherine Hoover, Sept. 10, 1983; children—Roxanna Virginia (dec.), Matthew Ansley. AB cum laude, Princeton U., 1960; diplome, Fontainebleau, 1960; MArch, Harvard U., 1964. Assoc. Vincent Ponte, Montreal, Que., Can., 1964-67, I.M. Pei & Ptnrs., 1968-78; dir. I.M. Pei & Ptnrs., Iran, 1975-78; co-chmn. Voorsanger & Mills (Architects), N.Y.C., 1978-90; founder, prin. Voorsanger & Assocs., Architects, N.Y.C., 1990—; founder Taylor/Voorsanger Urban Designers, 1991; lectr. Bennington (Vt.) Coll., U. Pa., Columbia U., Harvard U.; guest critic, lectr. Yale U., Pratt Inst., CUNY, R.I. Sch. Design, U. Cin., Syracuse U., U. Tex., Arlington; mem. adv. bd. Parson Sch. Architecture; mem. archtl. rev. panel Port Authority of N.Y. & N.J.; advisor to Samsung Corp., Korea. Exhbns. include: NYU, Archtl. Assn., London, Harvard Grad. Sch. Design, Vacant Lots Housing Study, N.Y., Deutsches Architeckur Mus., Frankfurt, Mus. Finnish Architecture, Avery Lib.Centennial Exhbn. Columbia Univ., Helsinki, Bklyn. Mus.; major projects include: Le Cygne Restaurant, Neiman houseboat, NYU Midtown Ctr., NYU Bus. Sch. Library, La Grandeur housing, NYU dormitories, Hostos Community Coll., N.Y.; finalist Bklyn. Mus. masterplan internat. competition, expansion and master plan Pierpont Morgan Libr., Wethersfield Carriage Mus., Amenia, N.Y.; Montana and Wyoming Residences; Advanced Tng. Ctr., NYU, New York Apt., N.Y.C., Riverdale (N.Y.) Jewish Ctr.; fellow J. Pierpont Morgan Libr., N.Y., Asia Soc., NY, Brody Residence, VA, Daniels/Falks Residence, Ariz.; Port Authority N.Y./N.J. Air Traffic Control Towers, Bayly Art Mus., U. Va. Mem. vis. com. R.I. Sch. Design, U. Tex., Arlington; mem. N.Y. Hist. Soc., also mem. archtl. cir. steering com.; chmn. bd. advisors Temple Hoyne Buell Ctr., Study Am. Architecture, Columbia U., N.Y.C., 1989—; mem. adv. bd. Parsons Sch. Architecture; chair archtl. rev. panel Port Authority N.Y. and N.J.; bd. dirs. Worldesign Found.; mem. Regent's Panel N.Y. State U., N.Y. State Regents' Com. on Schs; chmn. N.Y. Found. for Architecture 2000-2001. 1st lt. U.S. Army, 1960-61. Recipient awards N.Y.C. chpt. AIA, AIA/Better Homes, Bard City Club, Interiors mag., Stone Inst., AIA/Libr., Lumen, Pratt Inst., NYU, N.Y.C. Art Commn. Fellow AIA (bd. dirs. N.Y.C. chpt. 1979-81, v.p. 1987, chmn. Brunner award com. 1978-80, Bard award pres.-elect N.Y.C. chpt. 1984, Nat. Honor award, N.Y. State award); mem. Archtl. League N.Y.C. (bd. dirs.), Sir John Soane Mus. Found., N.Y. Found. for Arch. (bd. dirs.), Worldesign Found., N.Y., Century Assn., Wadawanuck Club, Alumni Coun. Grad. Sch. Design Harvard. Office: 246 W 38th St Fl 14 New York NY 10018-5805

VORA, KIRIT H., environmental consultant; b. Bombay, India, Dec. 17, 1948; came to U.S., 1970; BS, U. Bombay, 1969; MA, U. Scranton, 1974. Dir. OHS Am. Can Co., Greenwich, Conn., 1976-82; dir. N.E. ops. Clayton Environ. Cons., Edison, N.J., 1983-92, v.p., 1987-97, sr. v.p., 1997—, dir. comml. progperty group, 1997—. E-mail: ksvora6060@aol.com. Home: 62 Overhill Rd East Brunswick NJ 08816-4212

VORA, MAYUR JAYKUMAR, food products executive; b. Mumbai, India, Jan. 9, 1958; s. Jaykumar Tulsidas and Lilavati Jaykumar (Sanghvi) V.; m. Rajvi Mayur Sheth, Oct. 17, 1981; children: Nikunj, Yutika, Kushala. BA in Econs., Fergusson Coll., Pune, India, 1978; MBA, Indian Inst. Mgmt., Bangalore, India, 1980; diploma Internat. Program Practicing, Mgmt., INSEAD. Fin. exec. Voltas Ltd., Bombay, 1979-80, transport mgr., fin. exec., 1981-82, fin. exec., 1981—; ptnr. Mahableswar Fruit Products, Panchgani, India, 1988-00; CEO Mapro Foods, Mahableswar, India, 1989-97; mng. dir. Mapro Foods Pvt. Ltd., Mahableswar, India, 2000—; mem. Internat. Program in Practicing Mgmt., INSEAD. Pres. Rotary Club Panchgani, 1989-90; trustee Vasantbhai Charitable Trust, trustee VM Kapol Boarding Sch., Mumbai. Mem. Rotary Internat. (zonal rep. 1995-96), Panchgani Gymkhana (sec. 1992-00). Avocations: traveling, reading, walking, philosophy. Home and Office: Kushal Kunj, Panchgani 412805, India Office: Mapro Foods, PO Box 64, Panchgani 412805, India

VOREMBERG, RHODERICK PETER GROSVENOR, solicitor; b. Trowbridge, Wiltshire, England, Nov. 19, 1954; s. Rudolf Peter and Rosella Mary Grosvenor (Bartelot) V.; m. Susan Mary Burnet, Mar. 15, 1980; children: Jessica, Rupert, Olivia. BA with honors, Magdalene Coll., Cambridge, Eng., 1977. Trainee Burges Salmon, Bristol, Eng., 1978-80, asst. solicitor, 1980-82; asst. solicitor Wilsons, Salisbury, Eng., 1982-84, ptnr., head pvt. client dept., 1985—. 2d lt. Royal Artillery, 1973, Hong Kong. Mem. Country Landowners' Assn. (tax com. 1987-92), English Eight Club (pres. 1993), English Match Rifle Eight (capt. 1993). Avocations: match rifle shooting, fly fishing, silversmithing. Office: Wilsons Solicitors, Steynings House Fisherton St, Salisbury SP2 7RJ, England

VORGIAS, GEORGE, obstetrician, gynecologist; b. Athens, Greece, Oct. 2, 1965; s. Constantine and Denise Vorgias. Student, PreMed. Coll., Athens U., 1983; MD, Patras U., 1990, PhD of Medicine, 1998. Resident Patras (Greece) U. Hosp., 1990-91, Leukas (Greece) Regional Hosp., 1992-93; chief resident Metaxa Meml. Cancer Hosp., Athens, 1993-95, Tzanio Gen. Hosp., Athens, 1995-97; cons. Iaso Maternity Hosp., Athens, 1997-99, St. Savas Cancer Inst., Athens, 1999-2000, Metaxa's Meml. Cancer Hosp., 2000—. Contbr. articles to profl. jours. Fellow European Coll. Oncology; mem. Hellenic Cancer Soc. (cons.), Greek Senologic Soc., Internat. Senologic Soc., N.Y. Acad. Scis. Avocation: mountain walking. Home: 22 Alon St, 16674 Glyfada Athens, Greece Office: 46B Metaxa Str, Glytada, 16674 Athens Greece

VORLAUFER, KARL HERMANN, geography educator; b. Bremen, Germany, Sept. 15, 1937; s. Karl Friedrich and Hildegard (Warnke) V.; m. Renate Görlich, May 4, 1984; children: Miriam, Tobias. PhD, Johann Wolf Goethe U., Frankfurt-a. Main, 1967. Prof. J. W. Goethe U., Frankfurt aus Main, 1972-87; prof. geography Heinrich Heine U., Düsseldorf, Germany, 1987—. Author: Physiognomie, Struktur u. Funktion Gross-Kampalas/Uganda, 1967, Dar Es Salaam, 1972, Ferntourismus und Dritte Welt, 1984, Kenya, 1990, Tourismus in Entwicklungsländern, Mäglichkeiten und Grenzen einer nachhaltigen Entwicklung durch Fremdenverkehr, 1996; editor-in-chief (jour.) Zeitschrift für Wirtschaftsgeographie, 1983—. Home: Heidenfeldstr 11, 65812 Bad Soden Germany Office: Heinrich Heine U, Geographisches Inst, Düsseldorf Germany

VORLÍČKOVÁ, MICHAELA, biophysicist, researcher; b. Jicin, Czech Republic, June 19, 1945; d. Oldrich and Miloslava (Mazankova) Fisera; 1 child, Hana. Prom.Biol., Purkinje U., Brno, Czech Republic, 1968, MD, 1971; PhD, Acad. Sci., Prague, 1976, DSc, 1992. Head of lab. Inst. Biophysics, Acad. Sci., Brno, Czech Republic, 1991—; mem. assembly Czech Acad. Sci., 1994-98. Contbr. articles to Nucleic Acids Rsch., Jour. Molecular Biology, Jour. Biomolecular Structure Dynamics, Biophys. Jour., others. Recipient Fogarty Internat. Rsch. Collaboration award Czech Acad. Sci., NIH. Mem. Biophys. Soc. Avocations: tennis, skiing, travel. Home: Ramesova 5, 61200 Brno Czech Republic Office: Inst Biophysics, Kralovopolska 135, 61265 Brno Czech Republic

VORMFELDE, STEFAN VIKTOR, clinical pharmacologist, medical educator; b. Köln, Germany, Oct. 22, 1965; s. Reinhold and Erika (Sautter) Löser; m. Saskia Vormfelde, Nov. 22, 1996. MD, U. Goettingen, Germany, 1992. Resident in gen. and clin. pharmacology U. Goettingen, 1992-97; asst. lectr. dept. gen. pharmacology U. Goettingen Med. Sch., 1992-94, asst. lectr. dept. clin. pharmacology, 1994, asst. prof. dept. clin. pharmacology, 1995—. Airman 1st class German Air Force, 1984-85. Mem. German Assn. Physicians in Clin. Pharmacology. Avocations: classical and Latin Am. dancing. Office: U Goettingen Dept Clin Phar, Robert Koch str 40, 37075 Goettingen Germany

VOROBIEV, IGOR ANDREJEVICH, finance company executive, science educator; b. Nizhny Novgorod, USSR, Sept. 23, 1937; s. Andrey Vasilievich and Evgenia Ivanovna (Nazarova) V.; m. Zinaida Pavlovna Popova, Nov. 7, 1937; children: Marina, Alexei. D Tech. Scis., Tech. U., Nizhny Novgorod, USSR, 1989. Dep. chief process engr. Normal Plant, Nizhny Novgorod, 1963-73; chief metallurg. engr., 1973-89, chief designer, 1989-93; chief engr. Joint Stock Co. Normal, Nizhny Novgorod, 1993-97; dep. gen. dir., 1997—; prof. Tech. U., Nizhny Novgorod, 1997—. Recipient prize USSR Coun. Miniatures, 1985. Mem. N.Y. Acad. Scis. Avocation: technical sciences. Office: Joint Stock Co Normal, 74 Litvinova St, 603600 Nizhny Novgorod Russia

VORONCOV, VLADIMIR, electronics engineer; b. Uzice, Serbia, Yugoslavia, Apr. 25, 1962; s. Nikola and Milka (Kravcov) V.; m. Tatjana Petrovic, Aug. 3, 1992. BEE with honors, U. Belgrade, 1988. Design engr. Mihailo Pupin Inst., Belgrade, Yugoslavia, 1988-92, Lochard Environ. Systems, Melbourne, Australia, 1993, Fujitsu Australia, Melbourne, 1993-95; sr. design engr. VDO Australia, Melbourne, 1995-97; dir., cons. Tesseract Solutions, Melbourne, 1993-97; sr. design engr. Telspec Australia P/L, 1997—. Avocations: alpine skiing, literature.

VORONENKO, BORIS IVANOVICH, physical metallurgist; b. Vereshchagino, Russia, Sept. 25, 1938; s. Ivan Ivanovich Purtov and Nadezhda Spiridonovna Voronenko; m. Galina Grigorievna Golubeva, June 28, 1975 (div. Apr. 1979); m. Albertina Israelevna Liogonkaia, May 19, 1979; children: Evelina, Julianna, Roman. Metall. Engr., Perm (Russia) State U., 1960; Candidate Tech. Sci., Gorki (Russia) Poly. Inst., 1965; cert. sr. rsch. worker, Gorki State U., 1978. Tech. engr. Aviation Elec. Generator Works, Sarapul, Udmurtia, Russia, 1960-62; rsch. worker, mgr. phys. metallurgy lab. Gorki Rsch. Physico-Tech. Inst., Gorki State U., 1965-85; sr. rsch. worker Nizhny-Novgorod Rsch. Inst. Engring. Materials "Prometei", Russia, 1985—; sci. reviewer All-Union Inst. Sci.-Tech. Info., Acad. Scis. USSR, Moscow, 1975—. Author: Investigation of the Phase Transformations, Structure and Properties in High Strength Stainless Steels, 1970, Acoustic Emission in Physical Metallurgy, 1980; contbr. articles to Russian jours. Mem. Russian Phys. Metallurgists Assn. (v.p. Nizhny-Novgorod dept. 1995—). Avocations: bellesletters, music. Office: Inst Engring Materials Prometei, ul Barrikad 1 GSP Sormovo, Nizhny Novgorod 603603, Russia

VORONIN, PAVEL YU, plant physiologist; b. Riga, Latvia, May 18, 1960; . Ioury and Eugenia V.; m. Olga Efimtsev, June 6, 1987; 1 child, Nikita. PhD, Inst. Plant Physiology, Russian Acad. Sci. Moscow, 1992. From exec. sec. to dep. editor-in-chief Russian Jour. Plant Physiology, Moscow, 1993—. Mem. Russian Soc. Plant Physiologists. Office: Inst Plant Physiology RAS, Botanicheskaya 35, Moscow Russia 127276

VORONKOV, MIKHAIL GRIGORIEVICH, research chemist; b. Orel, Russia, Dec. 6, 1921; s. Grigori Vasilievich and Raisa Mikhailovna Voronkov; m. Lilia Iliinichna Makhnina, Aug. 8, 1922; children: Viktor Mikhailovich, Valentina Mikhailovna. BS, Leningrad (Russia) U., 1942, PhD, 1947; DSc in Chemistry, Acad. Scis. USSR, Moscow, 1961; Dr. Honoris Causa, Gdansk (Poland) Poly. Inst., 1975. Sr. scientist Leningrad U., 1944-54; prof., head of lab. Inst. Silicate Chemistry Acad. Scis. USSR, Leningrad, 1954-61; prof., head of lab. Inst. Organic Synthesis Latvian Acad. Scis., Riga, 1961-70; academician, dir. Inst. Organic Chemistry Siberian divsn. Acad. Scis. USSR, Irkutsk, 1970-94, head of dept., sci. advisor Inst. Organic Chemistry, 1995—; sci. advisor Mongolian Acad. Scis., Ulan-Bator, 1975—, Industr. Corpor-n., Jilin, China, 1992—, Kiev (Ukraine) Poly. Inst., 1964—; co-dir. Inst. Applied Chemistry, St. Petersburg, 1995—. Contbr. more than 1000 rsch. articles to profl. jours. V.p. of presidium East Siberian Affiliation Siberian br. of USSR Acad. Sci., 1973-77. Lt. comdr. Leningrad Front, 1941-42. Mem. Braunschweig Chem. Soc. (corr.). Avocation: stamp collecting, chemical humour. Office: Irkutsk Inst Chemistry RAS, 1 Favorsky St, 664033 Irkutsk Russia

VORONOV, VICTOR IVANOVITCH, science educator; b. Moscow, Dec. 16, 1944; s. Ivan Matveevitch and Zinaida Victorovna (Korovtchinskaya) V.; m. Natal'ya Aleksandrovna Bizyaeva, Oct. 6, 1977; 1 child, Tat'yana. Degree in engring., State Tech. U., Kazan, Russia, 1968, PhD, 1974, DS, 1997. Lab. asst. State Tech. U., 1964-68, engr., 1968-71, postgrad. fellow, 1971-74, asst. lectr. sci., 1974-76, sr. lectr., 1976-82, assoc. prof., 1982-97, prof., 1998—; rschr. in laser optics and computer simulation. Contbr. articles to sci. jours. Avocations: travel, reading, photography, tennis, gymnastics. Home: Kul-Gali 5-113, 420141 Kazan Tatarstan Russia Office: State Tech U, Karl Marx 10, 420111 Kazan Tatarstan Russia

VORONTSOV, ALEXANDRE VALERYEVICH, research scientist; b. Novosibirsk, USSR, Oct. 11, 1971; s. Valery Alexandrovich Vorontsov and Eugenia Lasarevna Vorontsova. MSc, Novosibirsk (Russia) State U., 1994; PhD, Boreskov Inst. Catalysis, Novosibirsk, 1998. Rsch. asst. Boreskov Inst. Catalysis, Novosibirsk, 1994-99, rschr., 1999—; postdoctoral asst. U. Cin., 1999. Scholar Boreskov Inst. Catalysis, 1993, Internat. Soros Sci. Edn. Program, 1997, 98, Zamaraev Internat. Charitable Sci. Found., 1998. Avocations: mountain climbing, hiking. Office: Boreskov Inst Catalysis, Pr. Ak. Lavrentyeva 5, 630090 Novosibirsk Russia

VORONTSOV, YULIY MIKHAYLOVICH, ambassador; b. Leningrad, Russia, Oct. 7, 1929; m. Faina A. Vorontsova. Grad., Inst. Internat. Rels., Moscow, Russia, 1952. Various positions Ministry Fgn. Affairs, 1952-54; U.S.S.R. rep. UN, N.Y.C., 1954-58, 63-65; counsellor U.S.S.R. Embassy, Washington, 1966-70, counsellor-envoy, 1970-77; amb. to India Govt. of U.S.S.R., 1977-83; amb. to France Govt. of U.S.S.R., Paris, 1983-86; first dep. min. fgn. affairs Govt. of U.S.S.R., 1986-90, amb. to Afghanistan, 1988-90; amb. to UN Govt. of Russian Fedn., N.Y.C., 1990-92; advisor to pres. Govt. of Russian Fedn., Moscow, 1992-94; amb. to U.S. Govt. of Russian Fedn., Washington, 1994-98; under sec. gen. UN, 1998—. Office: Permanent Rep Russian Fedn 136 E 67th St New York NY 10021*

VORONTSOV-VELYAMINOV, PAVEL NIKOLAEVICH, physicist, educator; b. St. Petersburg, Russia, July 1, 1936; s. Nikolay Pavlovich and Sophia Nikolayevna (Poddubnaya) Vorontsov-V.; m. Elena Nikolaevna Ushakova, Oct. 11, 1937. Grad. Physics, U. St. Petersburg, 1961, Candidate Sci., Physics, Math., 1968, D Physics Math., 1981. Jr. scientist U. St. Petersburg, 1961-62, asst., 1962-75, docent, 1975-85, prof. physics, 1985—; mem. Collaborative Computational Project, Daresbury, Eng., 1993—; mem. sci. dissertation coun. in thermo-physics and molecular physics U. St. Petersburg, 1985—. Contbr. articles to profl. jours. Soros professorship grantee, 1997, Russian Found. Fundamental Rsch. grantee, 1996-97, 99—. Avocations: wind surfing, sea diving, books, languages, stamps, minerals. E-mail: voron.wgroups@pobox.spbu.ru. Home: 17-2 Apt 46, Gostilitskoye Shosse, 198504 Saint Petersburg Russia Office: St Petersburg U, Ulianouskaya 1, 198504 Saint Petersburg Russia

VÖRÖS, IMRE, educator; b. Budapest, Hungary, Oct. 20, 1944; s. Imre and Maria (Pisanov) V.; m. Krisztina Veress, Apr. 13, 1972; children: Krisztian, Szabolcs. JD, U. Scis. Budapest, 1968. Counsel Chemokomplex Fgn. Trade Co., Budapest, 1967-69; rschr. Inst. Legal Scis. Hungarian Acad. Scis., Budapest, 1969-90; prof. U. Miskolc, Hungary, 1983-98; judge Constl. Ct., Budapest, 1990-99; prof. U. Györ, Hungary, 1998—; assoc. prof. Ctrl. European U., Budapest, 1992-98, Donau U., Krems, Austria, 1991—. Author: Market Behaviour-Competition Law, 1981, International Co-operation Contracts, 1995, Handbook of European Competition Laws, 1996, Public Tenders, 1984; editor Conflict of Laws, 1997; editor-in-chief Law Sci. Rev., Budapest, 1972—. Rep. Bros. of the Christian Schs., 1990—; pres. Found. Count Széchenyi, Budapest, 1993—; comdr. Mil. and Hospitaller Order St. Lazarus, France, 1994—. Recipient Great Silver Medal of Honour Republic Austria, 1994, Medium Cross with the Star of the Medal of Honour of Republic of Hungary, 1999. Mem. Assn. Internat. de Droit Economique,Hungarian Assn. for Protection Intellectual Property, Hungarian Assn. Competition Law, German-Hungarian Lawyers Assn. Avocations: skiing, swimming. Home: Sasadi ut 146, H-1110 Budapest Hungary Office: Constl Ct Hungary, Donati u 35-45, 1015 Budapest Hungary

VÖRÖS, PÉTER PÁL, internist, nephrologist, diabetologist, researcher; b. Ujpest, Hungary, Jan. 19, 1949; s. Sándor and Jlona (Lichtneckert) V.; m. Isabella Jajzak, Dec. 2, 1974; children: P=248ter, Noémi. MD, Semmelweis U., Budapest, Hungary, 1973, PhD in Diabetology, 1998. Diplomate in internal medicine, nephrology, diabetology. Tng. in internal medicine Semmelweis U., 1973-78, tng. in nephrology, 1993; physician Hungarian Rkwy., Budapest, 1973-75; physician Szent István Hosp., Budapest, 1975-86, 1st asst., 1986-88, chief physician, 1988-98, dept. chief physician, 1998—; chief medicine FMC Dialysis Ctr., Budapest, 1998; guest lectr. Semmelweis U., 1999. Co-author: Peritonealis Dialysis, 1996; contbr. articles to med. jours., including Nephrology Dialysis Transplant, Geriatric Nephrology and Urology. Chamn. D-D Found., 1997. Recipient award Hungarian Min. Health, 1986. Mem. Hungarian Diabetes Assn., EDTA/ERA, Internat. Soc. Nephrology, EASD. Avocatins: skiing, tennis, fine arts. Office: Szent István Hosp, Nagyvarad ter 1, 1096 Budapest Hungary

VOROTINOV, ALEKSANDR MICHAILOVICH, physicist, researcher; b. Krasnoyarsk, Russia, Oct. 23, 1961; s. Michail Andreevich and Valentina Ivanovna (Fadeeva) V.; m. Olga (Fadeeva) Vorotinova, Sept. 24, 1983; 1 child, Eugenii. Grad., Krasnoyarsk (Russia) State U., 1984; PhD, Inst. Physics, Krasnoyarsk, 1998. Rschr. Inst. Physics, Krasnoyarsk, 1984—. Home: Akademgorodok 10-29, 660036 Krasnoyarsk Russia Office: Inst Physics, Akademgorodok, 660036 Krasnoyarsk Russia

VOROTNIKOV, VLADIMIR IL'ICH, mathematician, educator; b. Nizhuy Tagil, Sverdlov, Russia, June 8, 1954. PhD, Moscow State U., 1979, DSc, 1988. Cert. engr., Russia. Asst. prof. Ural State Tech. U., Nizhuy Tagil, 1976-79, assoc. prof., 1979-88, prof., head dept. math., 1989—, dep. dir. Nizhny Tagil Inst., 1992—. Author: Partial Stability, 1991, Partial Stability and Control, 1998; contbr. articles to profl. jours. Grantee Internat. Sci. Found. and Russian Found. for Basic Rsch., 1995, Russian Found. for Basic Rsch., 1995-97, 99—. Fellow Acad. Engring. Sci. Office: Ural State Tech U, ul Krasnogvardeyskaya 59, 622031 Nizhuy Tagil Russia

VORSTER, PIETER, botanist, researcher, educator; b. Pretoria, South Africa, Aug. 12, 1945; s. Lourens Marthinus D. and Rentia (De Wet) V.; m. Elsa Christina Brittz, Apr. 17, 1971; 1 child, Lourens. BS in Agr., U. Pretoria, 1967, BS (honours), 1968, MS in Agr., 1970, DS, 1978. Sr. prof. officer Bot. Rsch. Inst., Pretoria, 1967-78; sr. rsch. officer U. Stellenbosch, South Africa, 1979—. Co-author: Pelargoniums of Southern Africa, vol. 2, 1981, vol. 3., 1988. Recipient Augustin-Pyramus Decandolle prize Soc. Physique et D'Histoire Naturelle De Geneve, Switzerland, 1986. Avocations: botany, music, aviation. Office: Univ Stellenbosch, Botany Dept, Pvt Bag X1, 7602 Matieland South Africa

VORYS, ARTHUR ISAIAH, lawyer; b. Columbus, Ohio, June 16, 1923; s. Webb Isaiah and Adeline (Werner) V.; m. Lucia Rogers, July 16, 1949 (div. 1980); children: Caroline S., Adeline Vorys Cranson, Lucy Vorys Noll, Webb I.; m. Ann Harris, Dec. 13, 1980. BA, Williams Coll., 1945; LLB, JD, Ohio State U., 1949. Bar: Ohio 1949. From assoc. to ptnr. Vorys, Sater, Seymour & Pease LLP, Columbus, 1949-82, sr. ptnr., 1982-93, of counsel, 1993—; supt. ins. State of Ohio, 1957-59; bd. dirs Vorys Bros., Inc., others. Trustee, past pres. Children's Hosp., Greenlawn Cemetery Found.; trustee, former chmn. Ohio State U. Hosps.; regent Capital U.; del. Rep. Nat. Conv., 1968, 72. Lt. USMCR, World War II. Decorated Purple Heart. Fellow Ohio State Bar, Columbus Bar Assn.; mem. ABA, Am. Judicature Soc., Rocky Fork Headley Hunt Club, Rocky Fork Hunt and Country Club, Capital Club, Phi Delta Phi, Chi Psi. Home: 5826 Havens Corners Rd Columbus OH 43230-3142 Office: Vorys Sater Seymour & Pease LLP PO Box 1008 52 E Gay St Columbus OH 43216-1008

VOS, EDGAR J. (WATTY VOS), Aruban government official. Min. justice & pub. works Govt. of Aruba, Oranjestad. Office: Min Justice and Public Works, LG Smith Blvd 76, Oranjestad Aruba*

VOS, HENK, physicist, educational consultant; b. Huizen, N. Holland, The Netherlands, Oct. 10, 1943; s. Hermanus and Elbertje (Wouda) V.; m. Dineke Mastenbroek, June 27, 1968; children: Albert, Gerard, Herman, Maarten, Willem-Jan. M in Physics, Maths, Free U. Amsterdam, 1968, PhD in Physics, 1972. Tchg. lic. Free U. Amsterdam, 1972. Physics tchr. Tchr. Tng. Coll., Amsterdam, 1973-79; faculty trainer Gadja Mada U., Yogyakarta, Indonesia, 1979-83; physics tchr. Poly., Utrecht, The Netherlands, 1984; ednl. cons. elec. engring. U. Twente, The Netherlands, 1985—. Contbr. articles to profl. jours. Mem. Dutch Soc. Ednl. Rsch., Dutch Physics Soc., Dutch Assn. Edn. Sci., Am. Ednl. Rsch. Assn. Avocations: judo, aikido. Home: Dr Zamenhoflaan 216, 7522KW Enschede The Netherlands Office: U Twente Dept Elec Engring, PO Box 217, 7500 AE Enschede The Netherlands

VOS, JORIS MICHAEL, diplomat; b. Ede, Netherlands, Mar. 17, 1940; s. Willam Vos and Eva Louise Douwes Dekker; m. Yvonne Marguerite Rydemark, Oct. 1, 1966; children: Sebastiaan F.A., Annabelle M.C. JD, U. Utrecht, Netherlands, 1964. 3d sec. of embassy Netherlands Embassy, Prague, 1968-70; 2d sec. of embassy Netherlands Embassy, Accra, Ghana, 1970-72; polit. officer for Middle Easat Ministry of Fgn. Affairs, The Hague, 1972-74, prin. pvt. sec. to fgn. min., 1974-77, dir. for Atlantic coop. and security affairs, 1977-80; polit. counsellor Netherlands Embassy, The Hague, 1982-86; ambassador Netherlands Embassy, Canberra, Australia, 1986-90, Moscow, 1990-93, Washington, 1997—; under sec. for polit. affairs Ministry Fgn. Affairs, The Hague, 1993-97. Avocations: classical music, fine arts, literature, golf, skiing. Home: 2347 S St NW Washington DC 20008-4015 Office: Netherlands Embassy 4200 Linnean Ave NW Washington DC 20008-3896

VOŠAHLÍKOVÁ, PAVLA, historian, researcher; b. Prague, Czech Republic, Mar. 20, 1951; d. Otto and Lidie (Jersáková) V. PhD, Charles U., Prague, 1975; Candidate of Sci., Acad. Scis., 1980, DSc, 1998. Rschr. Inst. History, Acad. Sci. Czech Republic, Prague, 1974—; tchr. Czech Tech. U., Prague, 1982-88, Faculty Architecture, Prague, 1995-96. Author: Slovak Political Currents at the Turn of the 20th Century, 1979, The Czechoslovak Social Democracy and the National Front, 1985, Living in the Times of Emperor František Joseph I, 1996, The Golden Age of Czech Advertisement, 1999; editor: On the Journey-Published Memories, 1994, From The Official Power-Published Memories, 1998. Mem. Historians' Club (exec. com.

1996—). Avocation: kynology. Office: Inst History AS ČR, Prosecká 76, 190 00 Praha/Prague Czech Republic

VOSEVICH, KATHI ANN, writer, editor, scholar; b. St. Louis, Oct. 12, 1957; d. William and Catherine Mildred (Kalinowski) V.; m. James Hughes Meredith, Sept. 6, 1986. AB with honors, St. Louis U., 1980, MA, 1983; PhD, U. Denver, 1988. Tchg. fellow St. Louis U., 1980-83, acad. advising fellow, 1983-84; tchg. fellow U. Denver, 1985-87; prof. ESL, BNM Talensch., Uden, The Netherlands, 1988-91; instr. English, mentor U. Ga., Athens, 1992-94; vis. asst. prof. Colo. Coll., Colorado Springs, 1994; sr. tech. writer and editor Titan Client/Server Techs., Colorado Springs, 1994-96, head documentation, libr., 1996-97; documentation mgr. Beechwood, Colorado Springs, 1997-98, tech. mgr., 1998-99; tech. writer Microsoft, Redmond, Wash., 1999-2000; documentation and process mgr. Sprint, Denver, 2000—; forensic judge USAF Acad., Colo., 1987-88; edn. officer Volkel (The Netherlands) Air Base, 1988-91; instr. English European divsn. U. Md., The Netherlands and Belgium, 1989-91. Author: Customer Care User's Guide, 1996, Interview with Joseph Heller, 1999, Conversations with Joseph Heller in Understanding the Literature of World War II, 1999, Office Update, 1999-2000; editor: Subscription Services System Documentation, 1996, Titan Process Documentation, 1994-96; copy editor: Language, Ideas, and American Culture; War, Literature and the Arts; contbr. over 100 electronic texts and articles to profl. jours. Colo. scholar U. Denver, 1985-86, grad. dean scholar, 1988; NEH fellow U. Md., 1994. Mem. MLA, Phi Beta Kappa, Alpha Sigma Nu. Roman Catholic. Avocations: writing, drawing, raising Bernese mountain dogs. Office: SprintENS 7900 E Union Ave Ste 1100 Denver CO 80237-2746

VOSKA, KATHRYN CAPLES, consultant, facilitator; b. Berkeley, Cal., Dec. 26, 1942; d. Donald Buxton and Ellen Marion (Smith) Caples; m. David Karl Nehrling, Aug. 15, 1964 (div. Nov. 1980); children: Sandra E. Nehrling, Barbara M. Nehrling, Melissa A. Nehrling-Holmgren; m. James Edward Voska, Aug. 31, 1985. BS, Northwestern U., 1964; MS, Nat.-Louis U., 1989. Cert. teacher, Ill. Tchr. pub. schs., Northbrook and Evanston, Ill., 1964-65; acting phys. dir. YWCA, Evanston, Ill., 1975; quality control technician Baxter Travenol, Morton Grove, Ill., 1978-80; sr. quality assurance analyst Hollister Inc., Libertyville, Ill., 1980-85; info. ctr. trainer, tech. training mgr. Rand McNally, Skokie, Ill., 1985-92; cons., facilitator Capka & Assocs., Skokie and Kansas City, 1992—; dir. edn. Nat. Office Machine Dealers, 1992-94; career and mgmt. cons. Right Mgmt. Cons., Overland Park, Kans., 1994—; pvt. practice estate conservator; bd. dirs. Coro/Kansas City, 1996—. Telephone worker Contact Chgo. Crisis Hotline, 1989-90; CPR instr. trainer Amer. Heart Assn., Chgo., 1977-89; aquatic dir. YMCA, Evanston, Ill., 1969-80; rep. Alumnae Panhellenic Coun., Evanston, 1969-75; grad. Leadership Overland Park, 1996, mem. 15th anniv. special task force. Mem. ASTD (bd. dirs. Kansas City chpt. 1997-99), ASCD, Soc. Human Resource Mgmt., Midwest Soc. Profl. Cons., Assn. for Mgmt. Orgn. Design, Chgo. Orgn. Data Processing Educators, Chgo. Computer Soc., Info. Ctr. Exch. of Chgo., Assn. Quality and Participation, Am. Soc. for Quality (teller N.E. Ill. sect. 1982-84), Internat. Soc. for Performance Improvement, Internat. Assn. Career Mgmt. Profls. (interim pres. Kansas City chpt. 2000—), The Learning Resource Network. Presbyterian. Avocations: scuba diving, swimming, hiking, camping, traveling. Home: 1001 E 118th Ter Kansas City MO 64131-3828 Office: Right Mgmt Cons 7300 W 110th St Ste 800 Overland Park KS 66210-2387

VOSKRESENSKY, DMITRI NICKOLAEVICH, physicist, educator; b. Moscow, Jan. 27, 1951; s. Nickolai Semenovich and Lidiya Ivanovna (Tregubova) V.; m. Nina Ivanovna Chadaeva, July 19, 1975; children: Ivan, Mariya, Alexey. Diploma, Moscow Engring. Phys. Inst., 1974, PhD, 1977, ScD, 1991. Jr. sci. worker Moscow Engring. Phys. Inst., 1978-84, asst prof., 1985-87, assoc. prof., 1988-91, prof., 1992—; head in grantees Am. Phys. Soc., Soros Found., 1993, Russian Fund of Fundamental Rsch., 1993-95, Internat. Sci. Found., 1995, Internat. Sci. Found./Russian Govt., 1995; key participant in grantees Sci. Tech. Collaboration, 1997-99, German Rsch. Soc., 2000-2002. Sci. editor Yad. Fiz (Soviet Nuclear Physics), Moscow, 1977-94; contbr. articles to profl. jours. Home: P Korchagina 11/1 41, 129278 Moscow Russia Office: Moscow State Eng Phys Inst, Kashirskoe St 31, 115409 Moscow Russia

VOSS, GERHARD MARIA, monk, theologian; b. Recklinghausen, Germany, July 25, 1935; s. Franz Heinrich and Margarete Henriette (Riedel) V. D Theologiae, Univ. Wuerzburg, 1965. Ordained priest Roman Catholic Ch., 1961. Leader Ecumenical Inst., Niederaltaich, Germany, 1963—; editor Una Sancta, Meitingen, 1968—, Die Beiden Tuerme, Niederaltaich, 1995—. Author: Die Christologie der Lukanischen Schriften, 1965, Dich als Mutter zeige, 1992, Astrologie Christlich, 1980, Musik des Weltalls wiederentdecken, 1996. Pres. Coun. of Churches in Bavaria, 1987-97. Recipient Jiri Tranovsky medal Silesian Evangel. Ch. in the Czech Republic, 1992, Golden Charter of Peace and Humanism, Internat. League of Humanists, 1998. Home: Mauritiushof 1, D-94557 Niederaltaich Germany Office: Oekumenisches Inst, Tassilostrasse 6, D-94557 Niederaltaich Germany

VOSS, JÜRGEN, chemistry educator; b. Hamburg, Germany, Feb. 19, 1936; s. Adolph Bruno and Berta Frieda (Schüler) V.; m. Jutta Voss, Feb. 19, 1965; children: Eva Lotte, Sibylle Konstanze. D. in Natural Scis., U. Hamburg, 1965, Habilitation, 1972. Asst. U. Hamburg, 1964-73, lectr., 1973-77, prof., 1977—. Author: (with others) Houben-Weyl's Handbook, 1985, Comprehensive Organic Synthesis, 1991; contbr. 165 articles to sci. jours. Confidential agt. Friedrich-Ebert-Found., Bonn, Germany, 1980—. Mem. Gesellschaft Deutscher Chemiker. Lutheran. Home: Hochestieg 34A, 22391 Hamburg Germany Office: U Hamburg, Martin Luther King Platz 6, 20146 Hamburg Germany

VOSS, KATHERINE EVELYN, international management consultant; b. Cleve., Sept. 2, 1957; d. Wendell Grant and Ann Terry (Miller) Voss; m. James Everett Mathias, Oct. 6, 1984 (div. Dec. 1988). BS, Bowling Green State U., 1979, MBA, 1981. Sci. systems analyst Eli Lilly & Co., Indpls., 1981-83, systems tng. cons., 1983-84; customer liaison mgr. Ind. U., Bloomington, 1985; prodn. ops. mgr. Ind. U., Indpls., 1985-86; prin. systems cons. Wang Labs., Inc., Carmel, Ind., 1986-93; mgmt. cons. AMT-Sybex (I) Ltd., Dublin, 1994-99; sr. cons. mgr. AMT-Sybex, Ltd., U.K., Letchworth, 1999—; cons. Ind. Univ., Bloomington, 1984-85, Allied Irish Bank, Dublin, Ireland, 1990-91. Contbr. (book) Introduction to Business, 1980, Introduction to Accounting, 1981, Computers and Data Processing, 1981. Presidental advisor Jr. Achievement, Indpls., 1982-83; pres. PEO Chpt. AM, Indpls., 1987-89, Irish rep., 1995—. Mem. Assn. for Image and Info. Mgmt. (Master of Info. Tech. award 1997, Laureate Info. Tech. award 1999), Irish Computer Soc., Beta Beta Beta. Republican. Presbyterian. Avocations: scuba diving, photography, biking, crafts. Home: Glaed Hame Cottage, Pasture Rd, Letchworth SG6 3LW, England Office: AMT-Sybex Ltd, Spirella Bldg Bridge Rd, Letchworth SG6 3LW, England

VOSS, WERNER KONRAD KARL, architect, engineer; b. Muenster, Germany, Dec. 9, 1935; s. Reinhard and Maria (Ewers) V.; m. Sabine Gerda Franziska Glaser, Nov. 28, 1963; children: Katharina, Alexander, Franziska. Diploma in civil engring., U. Braunschweig, Braunschweig, Fed. Republic Germany, 1964, diploma in archtl. engring., 1968. Asst. U. Braunschweig, 1964-69, chief engr., 1969-79; prin. Werner Voss & Ptnrs., Ascheberg, 1969—. Fellow Chamber of Architects. Office: Werner Voss & Ptnrs, Davensberger Str 5, D-59387 Ascheberg Germany

VOSSEN, RAINER, linguistics educator; b. Duesseldorf, Northrine-Westphalia, Germany, Dec. 6, 1951; s. Hugo and Margot (Koerbes) V. MA, U. Cologne, Germany, 1977, PhD, 1982; Habilitation, U. Bayreuth, Germany, 1990. Acad. asst. U. Cologne, 1979-82; acad. asst. U. Bayreuth, 1984-90, asst. prof., 1990-92; assoc. prof. U. Munich, 1992-93; assoc. prof. U. Frankfurt upon Main, 1993-99, prof., 1999—; dir. Inst. African linguistics U. Frankfurt, Main, 1996—, dean faculty arts, 1997-99; organizer internat. and nat. confs., Cologne, Bayreuth, Munich, 1982-94. Author The Eastern Nilotes, 1982, The Complete Linguist, 1995; co-editor Sugia, 1979—; mem. editl. bd. Jour. African Langs. and Linguistics; contbr. more than 60 articles to profl. jours. Grad. German Acad. Exch. Svc., 1977, 79. Mem. German Rsch. Soc. (rsch. fellow 1982-94, project leader Bayreuth sect. 1986-94, Frankfurt sect. 1995—), Groupement de Recherche Europeen. Avocations: soccer, tennis, badminton, arts, reading. Office: U Frankfurt upon Main, Kettenhofweg 135, 60054 Frankfurt upon Main Hesse, Germany

VOTAW, JOHN FREDERICK, educational foundation executive, educator; b. Richmond, Va., May 9, 1939; s. Frederick Lee and Katherine (B.) V.; m. Joyce Marie Miller, June 8, 1961; children: Laura, Cynthia, Mary, John Jr. BS, U.S. Mil. Acad., 1961; MA in History, U. Calif., Davis, 1969; grad., U.S. Army Colls., 1970, 85; PhD in History, Temple U., 1991. Commd. 2d lt. U.S. Army, 1961, advanced through grades to lt. col., 1976; comdr. Company C 1st bn. 69th Armor U.S. Army, Hawaii, 1964-65; comdr. Troop A 1st Squadron 11th ACR U.S. Army, South Vietnam, 1966-67; comdr. C&C Squadron 11th ACR U.S. Army, Fulda, Germany, 1975-77; asst. prof. history U.S. Mil. Acad., West Point, N.Y., 1970-73, asst. dean for plans and programs, 1980-81, asst. prof., 1981-82; dep. dir. U.S. Army Mil. History Inst., Carlisle Barracks, Pa., 1983-86; ret. U.S. Army, 1986; dir. First Divsn. Mus., Wheaton, 1986—; exec. dir. Cantigny First Divsn. Found., Wheaton, 1991—; adj. asst. prof. history Dominican U. (formerly Rosary Coll.), River Forest, Ill., 1991-98, adj. assoc. prof. history, 1998—; dir. Col. Robt. R. McCormick Rsch. Ctr., Wheaton, 1991—; series editor Cantigny Mil. History Series. Contbg. author: The D-Day Ency., 1993, The Ency. of Am. Wars - The First World War, 1994, The European Powers in the First World War: An Ency., 1996, Encyc. of the Vietnam War, 3 vols., 1998, A Guide to the Study and Use of Military History, 1979; contbr. articles to profl. jours. Mem. adv. com. Ctr. for the Study of Force and Diplomacy, Temple U., 1996—. Decorated Legion of Merit, Bronze Star with "V" device, Purple Heart (3 awards) and others. Mem. Am. Hist. Assn., Orgn. Am. Historians, Soc. for Mil. History, Am. Assn. Mus., U.S. Naval Inst. (life), U.S. Army War Coll. Alumni Assn. (life), Ret. Officers Assn. (life), Assn. Grads. U.S. Mil. Acad., U. Calif. Davis Alumni Assn. (life), Am. Vets. (life), Am. Legion (life), Kiwanis (Wheaton club 1986—, pres. 1991-92), Phi Alpha Theta, Phi Kappa Phi (life). Avocations: reading, writing, classical music, golf. Office: First Divsn Mus at Cantigny 1 S 151 Winfield Rd Wheaton IL 60187-6097

VOTLOKHIN, YURIY ZINOVEVICH, engineer, physicist; b. Grozny, Russia, Jan. 11, 1933; came to the U.S., 1993; s. Zinoviy Abramovich and Maria Iosifovna Votlokhin; m. Alla Moiseevna Laventman, Jan. 26, 1963; children: Robert, Greta. BS, Russian Acad. Scis., Grozny, 1955, PhD, 1969. Chief Lab. Phys. Modelling of Reactionary Apparatus, Petroleum Rsch. Inst.-Russian Acad. Scis., Grozny, 1969-79, chief Lab. Elaboration of New Processes, 1980-93; sr. lectr. Petroleum Coll., Grozny, 1972-88. Contbr. articles to profl. jours.; patentee in field. Jewish. Achievements include numerous patents in technical fields. Home: 3260 Coney Island Ave Apt 15B Brooklyn NY 11235-6625

VOTRUBA, MARCELA, ophthalmic surgeon; b. Prague, Czech Republic, Sept. 26, 1962; d. Milan Frank Votruba and Alena Milue Rychecka; m. Paul Graham-Sheffield Cornes. BA in Physiol. Scis., Oxford U., Eng., 1984, MA in Physiol. Scis., 1987, BM, BChir, 1987; PhD, U. London, 2000. House surgeon, physician Oxford and High Wycombe, London, 1987-88; jr. neurosurgeon St. Bartholomew's Hosp., London, 1989; sr. house officer in ophthalmology S.W. London Hosps., 1990-92; registrar in ophthalmology Bristol, Eng., 1992-94; Welcome Trust Vision Rsch. fellow Inst. Ophthalmology, London, 1994-98; specialist registrar Moorfields Eye Hosp., London, 1998-2000, medical rehnor fellow, 2000—. Contbr. articles to profl. jours. Fellow Royal Coll. Ophthalmologists; mem. Royal Soc. Medicine (Ophthalmology prize 1996), The Assn. for Rsch. into Vision & Ophthalmology. Fax: 0171 608 6803. E-mail: mvotruba@hgmp.mrc.ac.uk. Office: Dept Molecular Genetics, Inst Ophthal 11-43 Bath St, London EC1V 9EL, England

VOUDOUKIS, IGNATIOS JOHN, internist, cardiologist; b. Skalohorion, Lesvos, Greece, July 8, 1927; came to U.S., 1955; s. John Ignatios and Christina (Hatzilias) V.; m. Penny Christakos, July 15, 1962; 1 child, Christine Antoinette. MD, Nat. U. Athens, 1954. Intern Meml. Hosp., Albany, N.Y., 1955-56; resident Episcopal Hosp., Phila., 1956-58, Hahnemann Med. Coll. and Hosp., Phila., 1958-59; fellow in cardiology Jackson Meml. Hosp. and U. of Miami, Fla., 1959-61, Jewish Gen. Hosp., Montreal, 1961-63; rsch. assoc. in cardiology Maine Med. Ctr., Portland, 1963-64; assoc. physician Henry Ford Hosp., Detroit, 1964-67; adj. instr. medicine Wayne State U., Detroit, 1969, clin. asst. prof. medicine, 1973, clin. assoc. prof. internal medicine, 1981—; pvt. practice Detroit, 1967—; active staff Harper Hosp., Detroit, Hutzel Hosp., Detroit. Mem. lab. facilities coun. Dept. Pub. Health, State of Mich., 1968-74; pres. Hypertension Coord. and Planning Coun. of Southeastern Mich., 1974. Recipient St. Paul Medallion, Greek Orthodox Diocese and Archdiocese of N. and S. Am., Detroit, 1986. Fellow ACP, Am. Coll. Angiology; mem. Am. Soc. Nephrology, Am. Soc. Hypertension (charter), Hellenic Univ. Club (pres. 1968-69), Detroit Athletic Club. Greek Orthodox. Office: Hutzel Hosp Profl Bldg 4727 Saint Antoine St Ste 402 Detroit MI 48201-1461

VOUGIOUKA, OLGA E., pediatrician; b. Agia Paraskevi, Greece, Dec. 21, 1953; d. Efstratios P. and Irini N. (Manolaki) V. MD, U. Athens, 1977; DSc, Univ. Sch. Medicine Athens, 1988. Gen. practitioner Med. Rural Svc., Mytilini, Greece, 1977-78; intern in pediatrics Tchg. Hosp. Athens, 1980-81, registrar, 1981-84, sr. registrar, 1985-89; hon. registrar CRC Northwick Park Hosp., London, 1989-90; cons. Tchg. Hosp. Athens, 1990—; cons. pediatric rheumatology Aglaia Kyriakou Children's Hosp., Athens, 1990—. Avocations: swimming, tennis, dancing. Home: 35 Pavlou Mela Str, 15125 Athens Greece Office: P & A Kyriakou Children's, Thivon & Levadias Str, 11527 Athens Greece

VOUGIOUKLIS, THOMAS NICHOLAOS, mathematics educator; b. Serres, Greece, Nov. 8, 1948; s. Nicholaos Thomas and Eleni Vougiouklis; m. Penelope Thomas Kambakis, June 14, 1981; children: Eleni, Suzannah. B in Math., Aristotles U., Thessaloniki, Greece, 1971; PhD in Algebra, Democritus U. Thrace, Xanthi, Greece, 1980. Lectr. math. Democritus U. Thrace, 1980-88, asst. prof., 1988-92, assoc. prof., 1992-95, prof., 1996-97, head dept. math., 1995-97, dean sch. edn., 1998—; vis. scholar MIT, Cambridge, 1981-82; vis. prof. U. Udine, Italy, 1988, U. Wales, Bangor, 1988-89; hon. prof. Inst. Base Rsch., Molise, Italy, 1994—. Author: Hyperstructures and Their Representations, 1994; editor: Algebraic Hyperstructures Applied, 1991, New Frontiers in Hyperstructures and Related Algebras, 1996. Chmn. Cultural Assn. Xanthi, 1977-78. Fellow Romanian Soc. Fuzzy Sys. (award). Avocations: gardening, swimming, nutrition. Home: Neapoli 14-6, 67100 Xanthi Greece Office: Democritus U Thrace, Dept Primary Edn, 68100 Alexandroupolis Greece

VOUNTESMERI, VALERI, science educator, researcher, inventor; b. Trostianets, Sumy, Ukraine, July 2, 1941; s. Semion and Anastasia (Gienco) V.; m. Gana Gilitskaja, Sept. 16, 1967; children: Olga, Julia. BSc, Radio-electronics Coll., Kiev, Ukraine, 1961; MS, Poly. Inst., Kiev, 1969, PhD, 1973; DSc in Tech. Sci., Coun. of Ministers, Soviet Union, 1988. Cert. in elec. engring. Fellow, rschr. Poly. Inst., Kiev, 1973-76, asst. prof., 1976-80, assoc. prof., 1981-90, prof., 1990-95, leader sci. program, 1976-95; expert State Com. for Sci. and Tech., Kiev, 1992-95; vis. scientist U. Oslo, Norway, 1980-81; vis. scientist Nat. U., Mexico City, 1995—, sci. coord., 1995—. Author: Radio Engineering. Encyclopedic Educational Reference-Book, 1999; patentee magnetoresistive electromagnetic field converter, others; contbr. some 85 articles to profl. jours. Recipient 2 medals Presisium of Supreme Coun. of the Soviet Union, 1982, 90; State Com. for Sci. and Tech. grantee, Moscow and Kiev, 1973-93, Nat Com. for Sci. and Tech. grantee, Mexico City, 1995. Mem. IEEE, Popov Soc., Nat. Investigation Sys. of Mex. Avocations: fishing, yoga, wind surfing. Office: Centro de Instrumentos UNAM, Apdo Postal 70-186/Univ, 04150 Mexico City DF, Mexico

VOUTSAS, EPAMINONDAS, chemical engineer; b. Athens, Greece, Mar. 11, 1968; s. COnstantinos and Asimo (Economou) V.; m. Alexandra Mikeli, Jul. 1, 1995. Diploma in chem. engr., Aristoteleon Univ., 1991; PhD, Nat. Tech. Unic., Athens, 1997. Fellow Nat. Tech. Univ., Athens, 1997—. With Supply and Transport Corps, 1991-93. Mem. Tech. Chamber of Greece. Home: 61 Odysseos St, GR 12461 Athens Greece Office: Nat Tech Univ, 9 Heroon Polytechniou St, GR 15780 Athens Greece

VOVES, JAN, electronics educator, researcher; b. Prague, Apr. 6, 1960; s. Jaromír and Hana (Dedková) V.; m. Rut Šilarová, July 20, 1984; children: Tomás, David, Lucie. MS, Charles U., Prague, 1984; PhD, Czech Tech. U., Prague, 1993. Researcher Czech Tech. U., Prague, Czech Republic, 1984-87; asst. prof. CTU Prague, Czech Republic, 1987-96, assoc. prof., 1996—; guest lectr. Katolicke Industriele Hogeshool West Vlandern, Oostend, Belgium, 1991-92, U. Hull, Eng., 1994, Leeds Met. U., Eng., 1996, Technics of Informatics and Microelectronics for Computer Architecture Multi-Project Circuits Lab., Grenoble, France, 1998. Author: (textbook) Quantum Electronic Structures, 1995, (textbook) TCAD for Electronics, 1995, Electronic Devices of a New Generation, 1995, Physics of Semiconductor Devices, 1997; contbr. article to profl. jour. Grantee Ministry of Edn., Czech Republic, 1994. Mem. IEEE, Electron Devices Soc., Union of Czech and Slovak Mathematicians and Physicists, N.Y. Acad. Scis., Inst. of Radioengring. Czech Acad. of Scis. (scientific coun.). Mem. Evangel. Ch. Avocations: tourism, music. Home: Nad Pomníkem 14, 152 00 Prague 5, Czech Republic Office: CTU Prague FEL, Technická 2, 166 27 Prague 6, Czech Republic

VOVK, IGOR VLADIMIROVICH, physicist, researcher; b. Dnepropetrovsk, Ukraine, Apr. 11, 1939; s. Vladimir Iakovlevich and Evgenia Stepanovna (Titkova) V.; m. Maya Ivanovna Kotenko, June 24, 1961; 1 child, Olga. Diploma in elec. engring., Poly. Inst., Kiev, Ukraine, 1961; diploma in phys.-math. scis., Inst. Hydrodevice, Kiev, Ukraine, 1975, Inst. Hydromechanic NAS, Kiev, Ukraine, 1987; habilitation, Inst. Hydromechanic NAS, Kiev, Ukraine, 1995. Engr., sr. engr. Rsch. Inst. Hydrodevice, Kiev, 1961-73, sr. rsch. scientist, 1973-81, chief lab., 1981-89; prin. rsch. scientist Inst. Hydromechanics Nat. Acad. Sci., Kiev, 1989-93, chief lab., 1993—, v.p. coun. awarding degrees of doctor, 1987—; chief postgrad. students Inst. Hydromechanic, 1980—. Author: Wave Problems of Scattering Sound on Elastic Shells, 1986; mem. editl. bd. Jour. Acoustic Bull, 1998—, Applied Hydromechanics, 1998—; contbr. articles to profl. jours. G. Soros grantee, 1994-95. Mem. Acoustical Soc. Am., East-European Acoustical Sci. Soc. Avocations: mountain skiing, swimming, photography, travel. E-mail: vovk@sabbo.net. Fax: 044 446-42-29. Home: Apt 70, 16 Institutskaya St, 01021 Kiev Ukraine Office: Inst Hydromechanic NAS, 8/4 Zhelyabov St, 03057 Kiev Ukraine

VOVK, SERGEI MIROSLAVOVITCH, physicist; b. M. Kheta, Krasnoyarsk, Russia, Oct. 23, 1953; s. Miroslav Ivanovitch and Maya Alexandrovna (Kovalekno) V.; m. GAlina Ivanovna Nakhnyova, Apr. 4, 1974; children: Kirill, Ivan. Engr. Rsch. and Devel. Inst. of Power Engring., Zarechny, Russia, 1976-79, head group, 1979-80, scientist, 1980-89, head lab., 1989-91, dir. dept., 1991-96, dir. br., 1996—. Author: Diagnosis of Mammal Gland Cancer, 1999; editor: Problems of Radioecology and Boundary Disciplines, 1998, 99; author 74 papers; 34 patents in field. Dep. chmn. adv. bd. Zarechny Technopolis, 1996-99; mem. Economy, Industry and Sci. Com. of Sverdlovsk Region, 1999; mem. Guardianship, Leader in Bus., 1999; chmn. state certifying commn. Ural State Tech. U., Ekaterinburg, 1998-99. Mem. Optic Soc. Avocation: chess. Home: 64 16 Leningradskaya str, 624501 Zarechny Russia Office: ENTEK, PO Box 96, 624051 Zarechny Russia

VOVNA, VITALY IVANOVICH, physicist; b. Vladivostok, Russia, Jan. 18, 1942; s. Ivan Ivanovich and Anastasia Petrovna Vovna; m. Irina Veniaminovna Reizer, July 3, 1965 (div. Dec. 1995); children: Dmitry, Maria; m. Svetlana Vasilyevna Plokhikh, Apr. 25, 1996. MS in Physics, Far Ea. State U., Vladivostok, 1969, PhD in Physics, 1974, D of Chemistry, 1989. Asst. Far Ea. State U., Vladivostok, 1969-75, sr. lectr., 1975-76, asst. prof. physics, 1975-86, head electron spectroscopy lab., 1986-90, head exptl. theoretical spectroscopy dept., 1990—, dir. Ctr. New Ednl. Techs., 1993—, dir. Pacific Inst. Distance Edn., 1999—; mem. dissertation couns. in chemistry Far East sect. Russian Acad. Scis., Vladivostok, 1990—, chmn., 1996—; mem. dissertation couns. in chemistry Far Ea. State U., 1993—. Contbr. articles to profl. jours. Recipient Soros Professorship Open Soc. Inst., N.Y.C., 1997, 98, 99. Mem. Far Ea. Sci. Assn., Primorski Prof.'s Club. Avocations: tennis, fishing. Office: Pacific Inst Distance Edn, Oktyabrskaia 27, 690600 Vladivostok Russia

VOVOS, NICHOLAS ANESTE, engineering educator; b. Salonica, Greece, Apr. 11, 1951; s. Aneste Nicholas and Ermione Demetrius (Vekopoulos) V.; m. Stamatia Panage Vassilatos, Aug. 25, 1974; children: Aneste, Panage. Diploma, Poly. U., Patras, Greece, 1974; PhD, Poly. U., Patras, 1978; MSc, U. Manchester Inst. Sci. Tech., Manchester, Eng., 1975. Rsch. asst. U. Patras, 1976-77, asst., 1977-79, tutor, 1979-82, lectr., 1982-83, asst. prof., 1983-90, reader, 1990-97, prof., 1997—. Author: Electrical Power Systems I, 1986, Electrical Power Systems II, 1988, Power System Protection, 1985, Electromechanical System Dynamics, 1985; contbr. numerous articles to jours. in field. Served with Greek mil., 1976. Mem. IEEE, Tech. Chamber of Greece, Internat. Conf. Grands Réseaux Elec. Avocations: fishing, ping pong. Home: 6 Acheloou Str, 26442 Patras Greece Office: U Patras, Dept Elec and Computer Engr, GR 26500 Patras Greece

VOWLES, RICHARD BECKMAN, literature educator; b. Fargo, N.D., Oct. 5, 1917; s. Guy Richard and Ella (Beckman) V.; m. Ellen Noah Hudson, Aug. 1, 1942 (div. 1969); children: Elizabeth Ellen, Richard Hudson. B.S., Davidson Coll., 1938; postgrad., U. N.C., 1938-39, U. Stockholm, 1939-40; M.A., Yale U., 1942, Ph.D., 1950. Engr. Hercules Powder Co., Wilmington, Chattanooga, 1941-43; chemist Rohm & Haas, Knoxville, Tenn., 1943-44; econ. cons. War Dept., 1944; Am. vice consul Gothenburg, Sweden, 1945-46; asst. prof. English Southwestern U., Memphis, 1948-50, Queens U., N.Y.C., 1950-51; asso. prof. English U. Fla., 1951-60; prof. Scandinavian and comparative lit. U. Wis., Madison, 1960-85; prof. emeritus U. Wis., 1985—, chmn. comparative lit., 1962-63, 64-67, 71-72, chmn. Scandinavian studies, 1977-80; Am. specialist in Scandinavia Dept. State, summer 1963; vis. prof. N.Y.U., summer 1964, U. Helsinki, Finland, spring 1968, Stockholm, 1969; lectr., Sydney, Australia, 1975, Paris, 1975; master ceremonies Santa Fe Scandinavian Film Festival, 1984. Editor: Eternal Smile, 1954, Dramatic Theory, 1956, Comparatists at Work, 1968; Adv. editor: Nordic Council Series, 1965-70, Herder Ency. of World Lit; contbr. articles to profl. jours. Am.-Scandinavian Found. fellow Stockholm, 1939-40, Lassen fellow Am. Scandinavian Found., 1986; Fulbright fellow Copenhagen, 1955-56; Strindberg fellow Stockholm, 1973; Swedish govt. research award, 1978; Norwegian Govt. fellow, summer 1978. Mem. Modern Lang. Assn., Soc. Advancement Scandinavian Study (mem. exec. com.), Internat. Comparative Lit. Assn., Am. Comparative Lit. Assn. (adv. bd.), Strindberg Soc., Phi Beta Kappa. Home: 1115 Oak Way Madison WI 53705-1420

VOYNET, DOMINIQUE, government official; b. Montbeliard, France, Nov. 4, 1958; married; 2 children. Degree in medicine, 1986. Environ. activist, 1976-86; co-founder Greens, 1984; Dole mcpl. councilor European Parliament, 1989-91; nat. spokesman Greens, 1991—; mem. Franche-Comte Regional Coun., 1992-94; presdl. candidate, 1995; nat. assembly deputy Dole-Arbois, 1997; min. Ministry Territorial Mgmt. & Environment, Paris, 1997—. Office: Ministry Territorial Mgmt, 20 ave de Segur, 75302 Paris France*

VOZNESENSKY, EUGENE ARNOLDOVICH, geology educator; b. Moscow, Jan. 13, 1960; s. Arnold Vikentievich Rotshtein and Tatiana Nikolaevna Voznesenskaya; m. Vera Vasilievna Ukhova, Feb. 10, 1979. MS, Moscow State U., 1982, PhD in Geology, 1985, DSc in Geology, 2000. Jr. rschr. Moscow State U., 1985-90, asst. prof. engring. geology, 1990-92, assoc. prof. engring. geology, 1992—; mem. bd. experts Fed. Found. Univs. of Russia Geology Br., 1992—; projects cons. Fed. Ctr. Geol. Systems, Moscow, 1995-97; vis. prof. U. B.C., Vancouver, 1993, N.T.N.U., Trondheim, 1995. Author: Quasi-thixotropic Alterations in Clay Soils, 1990, Encyclopedia for Children, Geology Vol., 1996, Soil Behavior under Dynamic Loads, 1997, Dynamic Instability of Soils, 1999; contbr. articles to profl. jours. (Young Scientists Coun. award 1988); patentee in field. Rsch. grantee Fed. Program Crystallogenesis, Moscow, 1997, Russian Found. for Basic Rsch., 1998, Fed. Program "Integratzia", 1998, Inst. Sustainable Cmtys., 1999; travel grantee Internat. Sci. Found., 1992, 95, 97, INTAS, 1998; recipient award for outstanding contbns. to world sci. and sci. edn., Internat. Sci. Found., U.S., 1997, II Shuvalov medal, 2000. Mem. N.Y. Acad. Scis., Internat. Assn. Engring. Geology, Nat. Geographic Soc. Avocations: ancient literature and history, poetry, pets, travel. Home: Apt 175, 9 Vorontsovskie prudy St, 117630 Moscow Russia Office: Moscow State U Dept Eng Geo, Vorobiovy Gory, 119899 Moscow Russia

VOZNICA, PETR, army officer; b. Karviná, Morava, Czech Republic, Nov. 7, 1954; s. Josef and Olga (Wienckowiczová) V.; m. Milada Vasicková, Apr. 16, 1977; 1 child, Radka. Diploma in Engring. of Chemistry, Mil. Coll., Vyškov, Czech Republic, 1977; MSc, Mil. Acad., Brno, Czech Republic, 1987. Comdg. and staff officer Czech Army, 1977-92; NBC def. chief Mil. Command Middle, Olomouc, Czech Republic, 1992-94; dep. comdr. 2nd Army Corps, Olomouc, Czech Republic, 1994-96; comdr. 2nd Army Corps, Olomouc, 1997, Territorial Def. Forces, Tábor, Czech Republic, 1997-99; chief dir. def. planning Ministry Def., Prague, Czech Republic, 1999—; advanced through grades to maj. gen. Czech Army, 1997; cons. Mil. Coll., Vyškov, Czech Republic, 1982-85; mem. bd. sci. Mil. Acad., Brno, 1999—. Decorated Cross of Merit, Medal for Merit. Avocations: classical music, squash, tourism. Home: Mikulaskovo Namesti 12, 62500 Brno Czech Republic Office: Ministry Def PO Box 15, Vitezne Namesti 5, Prague Czech Republic

VOZOFF, KEEVA, geophysicist consultant; b. Mpls., Jan. 26, 1928; s. Max and Ida (Abrams) V.; m. Elizabeth Philp, Oct. 12, 1957; children: Jennifer, Nancy, Stephen, Andrew. B in Physics, U. Minn., 1949; MSc, Penn State U., 1951; PhD, MIT, 1956. V.p., dir. Geoscience Inc., Cambridge, Mass., 1964-69; prof. Macquarie U., Sydney, Australia, 1972-94, IGM U. Cologne, Germany, 1993-95; dir., cons. HarbourDom P/L, Sydney, 1994-99. With USN, 1945-47. Recipient Humboldt prize von Humboldt Found., Germany, 1993. Fellow Australian Acad. Tech. Sci. & Engring.; hon. mem. Soc. Exploration Geophysicists, Australian Soc. Exploration Geophysicists. E-mail: kvozoff2@ozemail.com.au. Office: V & A Geoscience, PO Box 996, Spit Junction 2088, Australia

VRACHAS, CONSTANTINOS AGHISILAOU, aeronautical engineer; b. Jaffa, Palestine, Mar. 22, 1931; s. Aghisilaos Costas and Helen Nicola (Karatzas) V.; m. Maria Georghiou Papanastassiou, Dec. 31, 1955; children: Helen, Danae Cleopatra. Diploma in aero. engrin., Brit. Air U., 1954; BBA, Cyprus Coll., 1971. Chartered engr., Euro. engr., accredited aviation cons. Apprentice Cyprus Airways, Nicosia, 1949-51, aircraft engr., 1954-56; insp. Arab Airways, Amman, Jordan, 1956-58, Aden Airways, 1958-60; sr. chief engr. Cyprus Airways, 1960-89; chief airworthiness surveyor Dept. Civil Aviation, Ministry of Communications and Works, Nicosia, 1990-94; dir. Cyprair, 1993-2000; chief engr. CSM Aviation Ltd., 1996-99; engring. cons. Civil Aviation, Min. of Comm. and Works, 2000—. Contbr. articles to profl. jours. Fellow Royal Aero. Soc., British Inst. Mgmt., Chartered Inst. Transp., AIAA (fellow). Home: 28 Irinis St, Flat 4 Strovolos, Nicosia CY-2018, Cyprus

VRANES, JASMINA, microbiologist, researcher, educator; b. Gospic, Lika, Croatia, Feb. 20, 1961; d. Milan and Marija (Stilinovic) V. MD, Zagreb U., 1984, MSc, 1989, PhD, 1993. Intern U. Hosp. Osijek, 1984-86; staff assoc. Med. Sch. Zagreb U., 1986-89, rsch. asst., 1989-97, asst. prof., 1997—. Contbr. articles to profl. jours. including Jour. Chemotherapy, Chemotherapy, among others. Recipient Young Scientist award Internat. Soc. Chemotherapy, 1993, Hosp. Infection Soc., 1994, Fedn. European Microbiol. Socs., 1997. Mem. Croatian Soc. for Med. Microbiology, Internat. Soc. for Infectious Disease, European Soc. Clin. Microbiology and Infectious Disease (Young Scientist award 1997), N.Y. Acad. Scis. Office: Zagreb U Med Sch, Rockefeller Str 4, 10000 Zagreb Croatia

VRANICAR, MICHAEL GREGORY, lawyer; b. Hammond, Ind., Mar. 11, 1961; s. Melvin G. and Maryann R. (Szarek) V.; m. Marianna C. Livas, May 28, 1994. BSEE, U. Ill., 1983; JD, U. San Diego, 1987. Bar: Calif. 1987, Ill. 1988. Engr. Gen. Dynamics, San Diego, 1983-88; judge advocate USMC, Okinawa, Japan, 1988-91; assoc. Stellato & Schwartz, Chgo., 1992-94; ptnr. Plesha & Vranicar, Chgo., 1995—; arbitrator Cook County Arbitration Bd., Chgo., 1994—; judge regional competition Nat. Moot Ct., Chgo., 1992. Mem. Marine Corps Scholarship Found., Chgo. Ball Com. Maj. USMC Res., 1996—. Mem. Chgo. Bar Assn., Okinawa Bench and Bar Assn., Am. Legion. Republican. Roman Catholic. Office: 10540 S Western Ave Ste 103 Chicago IL 60643-2529

VRANITZKY, FRANZ, Austrian government official; b. Vienna, Austria, Oct. 4, 1937; s. Franz and Rosa V.; m. Christine Kristen. Grad., Vienna Acad. of Trade and Commerce. With Austrian Nat. Bank, Fed. Res. Bd., 1961-70; pres. Vienna Inst. for Devel. and Coop., 1990—; personal asst. to Minister for Finance, Austria, 1970-76; dep. chmn. mng. bd. Creditanstalt Bankverein, 1976-81; chmn. mng. bd. Laenderbank, 1981-84; fed. min. fin., Govt. of Austria, 1984-86, fed. chancellor, 1986-96. Mem. Socialist Party of Austria, chmn., 1988—; past mem. Austrian Nat. Basketball Team. Office: care SPÖ Office Fed Chancellor, Weyrgasse 5, A-1030 Vienna Austria*

VRAZAS, JOHN IOANNIS, radiologist; b. Melbourne, Victoria, Australia, July 25, 1963; s. Apostolos Ioannis and Eleni V.; m. Vickie Katsioulas, Jan. 19, 1985; children: Paul, Elisabeth. MB, BS, U. Melbourne, 1987. Diplomate Med. Practitioners Bd., Victoria. Intern med. officer St. Vincents Hosp., Melbourne, Victoria, 1988-89; pediat. resident med. officer Nonash Med. Ctr./Royal Children's Hosp., Melbourne, 1989-94; fellow in interventional radiology, clin. instr. Alexandria Hosp./George Washington U. Med. Ctr., Alexandria, Va., 1994-96; cons. interventional radiologist Royal Melbourne Hosp., 1996-97; dir. interventional radiology, non-invasive vascular lab. Western Hosp., Melbourne, 1997-99, dir. diagnostic and interventional radiology, 1999—; dir. diagnostic and interventional radiology St. Vincent's Hosp., dir. body interventional radiology; vis. interventional radiologist Royal Melbourne Hosp., 1996—; asst. sect. Australian Vascular Ultrasound Accreditation Bd., 1998—; sr. lectr., profl. assoc. dept. radiology U. Melbourne, 1996—. Contbr. articles to profl. jours. Fellow Royal Australian and New Zealand Coll. Radiologists; mem. Australasian Soc. Ultrasound in Medicine (mem. com., ednl. bd. 1998—), Interventional Radiology Soc. Australasia (examining coun. 1998—), Melbourne Vascular and Interventional Radiology Group (pres. 1998—). Avocations: powerlifting, golf, information technology. Fax: (613) 9830294. Home: 60 Highfield Rd, Canterbury VIC 3126, Australia Office: St Vincents Hosp/Dept Rad, Victoria Pde, Fitzroy VIC 3065, Australia

VRDOLJAK, SNJEŽANA, archaeologist, researcher; b. Zenica, Bosnia-Herzegovina, Jan. 12, 1966; d. Ilija and Kata (Andrijanić) V. Diploma in history and archaeology, U. Zagreb, Croatia, 1992, M in Archaeology, 1994. Sci. asst. dept. archaeology U. Zagreb, 1992—. Contbr. rsch. articles to profl. pubs. including Antiquity, Opuscula Archaeologica 16, 18. Mem. Croatian Archeol. Soc., Internat. Union Prehistoric and Protohistoric Scis. Roman Catholic. Avocations: mountain climbing, swimming, fitness, music. Office: U Zagreb Dept Archeol Philo, Ivana Lucica 3, 10 000 Zagreb Croatia

VREE, TOM B., chemist; b. Amsterdam, Dec. 25, 1942; s. P. H.J. and E.J. (Dissel) V.; m. Ursula M. Hoeben, Apr. 28, 1967; children: Jeroen B., Monika L., Veronika W.S., Daniel K.W. Diploma in Chemistry, U. Amsterdam, 1967; PhD cum laude, Med. Faculty Nymegen, 1973. Staff rschr. dept. clin. pharmacy to prof. anesthesiology Sint Radboud Hosp., U. Nijmegen, The Netherlands, 1974—; vis. rsch. fellow dept. anesthesiology, Stanford U., Palo Alto, Calif., 1973; mem. numerous scientific coms. including Nat. Epilepsy Rsch., Utrecht, 1992, DADA Cons., Nijmegen, 1990, Farma Rsch., Nijmegen, 1985, others; mem. Staff Nat. Inst. Doping and Drugs Rsch., U. Utrecht, 1995, Instnl. Rev. Bd. Farma Rsch., Nijmegen, 1997. Editl. bd. Archives Internat. de Pharmacodyamie et de therapie, 1985, Pharmaceutisch Weekblad, 1985, Tijdschrift voor Geneesmiddel, Onderzoek en Therapie, 1984, others; author/editor: (books) Pharmacokinetics of sulphonamides, 1985, Clinical Pharmacokinetics of Sulphonamides and their metabolites, 1987; contbr. articles to profl. jours. Office: Acad Hosp Nijmegen St Radbd, Geert Grooteplein Zuid 10, 6525 Nijmegen The Netherlands

VREELAND, VICTORIA LYNN, lawyer; b. Ravenna, Nebr., Nov. 7, 1948; d. Nelson Eugene Vreeland and Bernice Schmale Sadler; children: Ted Mansfield, Aleksander Ferguson, Cole. BA, Ea. Wash. U., 1972; JD, Gonzaga U., 1976. Bar: Wash. 1976. Jud. clk. Wash. State Ct. of Appeals, Spokane, 1976-78; asst. atty. gen. State of Wash., Seattle, 1978-83; ptnr. Gordon Thomas Honeywell, Seattle, 1983—; Contbr. articles to profl. jours. mem. Wash. State Bar Assn. (gov. 1999—), Wash. State Trial Lawyers Assn. (dir. 1994-98). Avocation: pianist. Office: Gordon Thomas Honeywell 2100 One Union Sq Seattle WA 98101

VREL-ALLEN, DOMINIQUE LAURENT, physicist; b. Bois-Colombes, France, Apr. 1, 1967; s. Christian Paul and Monique Gisele (De Meulder) Vrel; m. Jennifer Jacques Allen, Jan. 3, 1997; 1 child, Theodore. Engr., U. Paris XIII, Villetaneuse, 1990, Master, 1991, PhD, 1995. Cert. materials engr., chem. engr. Postdoctoral fellow U. Kumamoto, Japan, 1995-97; rschr. CNRS, Vlletaneuse, 1997—. Author: Technologie des Hautes pressions, 1997; contbr. articles to profl. jours. Mem. Am. Phys. Soc. Avocations: long-distance running, archery. E-Mail: vrel@limhp.univ.paris13.fr. Office: CNRS-LIMHP, Avenue J B Clément, 93430 Villetaneuse France

VREMAN, ANNA AURORA, artist, technical writer; b. Miami, Fla., July 8, 1956; d. Gerhard Jan Willem and Josina Hendrika (Schouten) V.; m. Lowell B. Symmes, Feb. 16, 1996. BS in Elec. Engring., U. Vt., Burlington, 1983. Electronics technician IBM Corp., Essex Junction, Vt., 1976-83, elec. engr., 1983-90; tech. writer United Engrs., Essex Junction, Vt., 1991-92; tech. writer, cons., owner Lamoille Valley Tech. Svcs., Milton, Vt., 1990—; artist Milton, 1999—. Mem. Soc. Tech. Comm. (employment mgr. 1996-98), No. Vt. Artists Assn., So. Vt. Art Ctr. (artist mem.). Office: Lamoille Valley Tech Svcs 623 W Milton Rd Milton VT 05468-3396

VRESTAL, JAN, chemist; b. Brno, Czech Republic, Feb. 16, 1939; s. Jan and Aneska (Kvasnickova) V.; m. Marie Tenkova, Aug. 15, 1965; children: Ludmila, Jan. D, Masaryk U., Brno, Czech Republic, 1967; PhD, Acad. Sci., Prague, Czech Republic, 1984, DS, 1996. Rschr. Inst. Phys. Metallurgy, Brno, Czech Republic, 1961—, dir. group thermodynamics, 1989-91; tchr. U. Trnava, Slovakia, 1989-92; dir. inst. phys. chemistry Masaryk U., Brno, 1993—; cons. in field. Author: Physical Chemistry for Material Engineers, 1989, Mass Spectrometry, 1998, 2d edit., 2000. Grantee Acad. Scis., Prague, 1992, 96, Ministry Edn., Prague, 1997, 99. Mem. Chem. Soc. Czech Republic, Phys. Soc. Czech Republic, Material Sci. Soc. Avocations: cross-country skiing, orienteering. Office: Masaryk U Inst Phys Chemistry, Kotlarska 2, 611 37 Brno Czech Republic

VRHUNEC, MIHA MARKO, ambassador; b. Ljubljana, Slovenia, May 31, 1946; s. Marko Vicenc and Nusa Ernestina (Juvancic) V.; m. Breda Krizman, July 9, 1949; children: Tina, Lenka. M in Econs., U. Ljubljana. Amb. Ministry of Fgn. Affairs, Kinshasa, Zaire, 1989-91; sec.-gen. Ministry of Fgn. Affairs, Ljubljana, 1992-94; amb. Ministry of Fgn. Affairs, Athens, 1994-98; counsellor internat. rels. Pres. Republic Slovenia, 1998—. Author 2 books, several articles.

VRIEND, WILLEM HENDRIK, retired rural surgeon; b. Haarlem, The Netherlands, Sept. 24, 1928; arrived in Australia, 1990; s. Cornelis and Engelina Maria Adriana (Van Kampen) V.; m. Engeltje Gijsbertha de Jong, Sept. 27, 1955; children: Evertje Engeline, Cornelis, Ingeborg Johanna, Adriaan, Simonjan. MD, U. Leiden, The Netherlands, 1955, postgrad., 1956; PhD, Vrije Universiteit, Amsterdam, 2000. Cert. health inspector for Indonesian govt.; med. expert Dutch Fgn. Office, pioneer/cmty. worker Highlands of Irian Jaya. Intern Deaconess Hosp., Leiden, 1955-56, resident in gen. surgery, ob-gyn. and urology, 1959-60, 64-65; resident in orthopedics and neurosurgery Deaconess Hosp., Utrecht, The Netherlands, 1975-76; intern in orthopedics and neurosurgery Deaconess Hosp., Leiden, 1975-76; resident in tubal surgery U. Leiden, 1981-82, intern in tubal surgery, 1981-82; mission doctor, tropical surgeon, health inspector Gereja Masehi Injili Timor Min. Health, Kupang, Indonesia, 1956-59; mission physician, tropical surgeon Gereja Kristen Injili, Angguruk, Irian Jaya, Indonesia, 1960-75; bilateral med. expert, tropical surgeon Gereja Kristen Injili Secretariat Cabinet Republic Indonesia, Wamena, Irian Jaya, 1976-86; mission doctor, tropical surgeon Gereja Keristen Injili-World Mission Australia, Wamena, 1987-93; pioneer Gereja Keristen Injili-Opening of the Yalimo area, 1961-65; cmty. developer Gereja Keristen Injili, Angguruk, 1965-75, rural surgeon, Angguruk and Wamena, 1961-93. Author: (film) SPT 100, 1970, (book trilogy) Smoky Fires, The Merits of Development Cooperation for Inculturation of Health Improvements, 2000. Grantee SIMAVI, The Netherlands, 1956-93, VEM, Barmen-Wuppertahl, 1965, Prof. Dr. P.H. van Thiel, The Netherlands, 1956-94. Mem. Netherlands Soc. Tropical Medicine, N.Y. Acad. Scis. Mem. Uniting Ch. of Australia. Avocations: appropriate missiology, tribal housing, computer programming. E-mail: wimvr@ozemail.com.au. Home and Office: 13 Cronin Dr, Wellington Pt Brisbane QLD 4160, Australia

VRIES, GERRIT DE, architect, consultant, educator; b. Groningen, The Netherlands, July 12, 1937; s. Gerrit and Geertje R. (van Blanken) de V.; m. Maja Horowitz (div. 1991); children: Marjan R., Bart I., Paul A.; m. Dorothea V. Oorthuys, May 9, 1995. Grad. in Engring., Tech. U. Delft, The Netherlands, 1963. Arch. Zanstra Ptnrs. Arch., Amsterdam, The Netherlands, 1966-71, Van Woerden Schneider Arch., Soest, The Netherlands, 1971-75; tchr. Tech. U. Delft, The Netherlands, 1971—; arch. Prof. Pennink Arch., Amsterdam, 1976-80, Gerrit de Vries Arch., Amersfoort, 1980—; chmn. Nederlands Normalisatie Inst. Com., Delft, 1985-89; chmn. regional dept. Bond Nederlandse Architecten, 1983-88. Author: Ontwerpen van utilitaire gebouwen, 1988, Utilitair Ontwerp, 1998; prin. works include civic and utilitarian bldgs., housing. Lt. Army, 1965-66. Office: Tech Univ Bouwkunde, Berlageweg 1, 2628 CR Delft The Netherlands

VRŠANSKY, PAVOL, pediatric surgeon; b. Bratislava, Slovakia, Apr. 6, 1949; s. H. Vladimir and Maria (Saturova) V.; m. Anna Lehocka; children: Pavol, Juraj. MD, PhD, Komensky U., Bratislava, Slovakia, 1973. Intern U. Children's Hosp., Bratislava, Slovakia, 1973-77; asst., sr. asst. & chief sect. Med. Faculty, Komensky U., Bratislava, 1977-90; chief medicine U. Children's Hosp., Bratislava, 1990-91; sr. specialist asst. Kinderchirurgische Abteilung, LKH, Salzburg, Austria, 1991; sr. asst. Med. Faculty Komensky U., 1991-93; chief clin. assoc. U. Hosp. St. Jacques, Besançon, France, 1993-94; med. specialist attache assoc. Hosp. Delafontaine, St. Denis, France, 1994—. Contbr. articles to profl. jours. Home: Líščie Udolie 198, 84102 Bratislava Slovakia Office: Hosp Delafontaine, 2 Rue Dr Delafontaine BP279, 93205 Saint Denis France

VSEVOLOZHSKAYA, TATIANA ALEXEEVNA, physicist, educator; b. Moscow, Feb. 29, 1936; d. Alexey Vsevolodovitch and Tatiana Vladimirovna (Shaposhnikova) V.; m. Gregory Ivanovitch Silvestrov, Oct. 17, 1959; children: Peter G., Ivan G. Grad., Moscow State U., 1960; postgrad., 1965-68. Sr. technician Kurchatov Inst., Moscow, 1960-62; sr. technician Budker Inst. Nuclear Physics, Novosibirsk, 1962-65, jr. rschr., 1968-77, sr. rschr., 1977—; physics educator State U. Novosibirsk, 1965-68, 79-82. Contbr. articles to profl. jours. Recipient State medal For Labour Distinction, 1971. Home: 4-21 Zhemchuzhnaya St, 630090 Novosibirsk Russia Office: Budker Inst Nuclear Physics, Pr Lawrentiev 11, 630090 Novosibirsk Russia

VU, KHOA, construction import/export company executive; b. Hatay, Vietnam, Sept. 27, 1936; s. Dinh Thuan Vu and Thi Dinh Do; m. Doan Thi Thien; children: Kieu Nga, Vu Quynh Nga. Engring. degree, Moscow Constrn. U., 1962; DSc, Polytech. U., Prague, Czechoslovakia, 1976. Officer Office State Planning Com., 1962-64, Office Prime Min. Vietnam, 1964-66; dept. chief State Constrn. Com. Vietnam, 1966-70; dept. chief, dep. dir. Gen. Inst. Constrn. Economy, 1976-79; dir. gen. Gen. Hydropower Stas. Constrn. Corp. & Union Constrn. Machinery, 1979-88; dir. gen., chmn. Vietnam Import-Export Constrn. Corp., 1988—; chmn. Vina-Leighton, Hanoi, Vietnam, 1994—; vice chmn. Vinata Corp., Hanoi, 1992—. Author: Mechanization of Stone Works, 1970, Economics of Construction Works, 1976, Construction Machinery, 1978. Mem. mgmt. com. Commerce & Industry Vietnam, 1992—. Recipient State Labour Excellent Job Performance medal Pres. Vietnam, 1990, Honor Builder medal Min. Constrn. Vietnam, 1992. Mem. Vietnamese Soc. Civil Engrs. (ctrl. mem. ctrl. com. 1976—), Nat. Club Bossess J/V Cos. Communist. Buddhist. Avocations: travel, music, photography, film. Home: 6 Hoa Ma, Hanoi Vietnam Office: Vietnam Import-Export Constrn Corp, Hanoi Vietnam

VU, THE BAO, engineering educator; b. Hiep Hoa, Vietnam, Oct. 1, 1935; arrived in Australia, 1956; s. Dinh Phan and Quynh Van Vu; m. Annemarie Luise Ruthenbeck, Jan. 22, 1966; children: Timothy Anh Tung, Natalie My Lan. Grad., U. Saigon, 1956; B of Engring., U. Adelaide, 1962, PhD in Elec. Engring., 1968. Rsch. scientist CSIRO, Sydney, Australia, 1966-68; lectr. U. NSW, Sydney, Australia, 1968-71, sr. lectr., 1971-77, assoc. prof., 1978—, head dept. communications, 1990-98; prof. City U. Hong Kong, Kowloon, 1999—. Contbr. over 160 technical articles to profl. jours. and internat. confs.; mem. internat. editorial bd. Jour. Electromagnetic Waves and Applications, Asia Pacific Engring. Jour. Fulbright sr. scholar, 1975. Fellow Inst. Engrs. Australia; mem. IEEE, N.Y. Acad. Scis., Electromagnetic Acad, Colombo Plan fellow, 1962-65, Fulbright senior scholar, 1975. Achievements include contribution to methods of accurately estimating effect of surface errors on radiotelescope performance; work on corrugated waveguide feed horns for radiotelescope and monopulse tracking applications; originator of null steering by amplitude-only control for electronic counter counter measure applications. Office: City U EE Dept, 83 Tat Chee Ave, Kowloon Tong Hong Kong China

VUCAK, MARIJAN, chemical engineer; b. Umag, Croatia, Mar. 21, 1967; s. Boze and Mira (Kegalj) V. BS, U. Split, Croatia, 1989; MS, U. Zagreb, Croatia, 1993; PhD, U. Split, 1996. Rsch. scientist faculty chem. tech. U. Split., Croatia, 1990-96; head R&D PCC Schaefer Kalk, Germany, 1996—; rsch. scientist CNRS, Nancy, France, 1994-95. Contbr. articles to profl. jours. Mem. Croatian Chem. Soc., Croatian Soc. Protection Water & Sea, Engrs. & Techs. Soc. Roman Catholic. Avocations: foreign languages, travel, jogging, hiking, skiing. E-Mail: marijan.vucak@schaeferkalk.de. Home: Mestrovicevo set 31, 21000 Split Croatia Office: Schaefer Kalk, Louise-Seher-Str 6, 65582 Diez Germany

VUCELIC, DUSAN, education educator; b. Belgrade, Yugoslavia; s. Rados and Vukosava (Tabakovic) V.; m. Vera Milakovic, Sept. 18, 1966; 1 child, Morana. BS, U. Belgrade, 1964, PhD in Phys. Chemistry, 1970. Scientific assoc. Begrade U., 1964-71, asst. prof., 1971-83, prof., 1983—; pres. bd. Holding Inst. Gen. and Phys. Chemistry, Belgrade, 1990—, ZEOLITE MIRA, Mira, Italy, 1997—; scientific assoc. Stanford U., Calif., 1980-81; pres. IUPAB Comm. on Radiation and Environ. Biophysics, 1984-94. Contbr. more than 100 articles to profl. jours. and publs. Recipient Steinkopff prize German Colloid. Soc., Germany, 1993. Mem. N.Y. Acad. Scis., Yugoslav Biophys. Soc. (pres. 1986-96). Avocations: books, farming, tennis, skiing. Home: Kralja Petra 46, 11000 Belgrade Yugoslavia Office: Zeolite MIRA S P A, Riviera Matteotti 12, 30034 Mira Venezia Italy

VUCKOVIC, GORDANA NENAD, chemist, educator; b. Grdelica, Yugoslavia, Sept. 1, 1953; d. Nenad and Jevrosima (Stamenkovic) Mihajlovic; m. Vojislav Vuckovic, Apr. 1, 1978; children: Dusan, Ksenija. BS, U. Belgrade, 1978, MS, 1981, PhD, 1987. From tchg. asst. to assoc. prof. chemistry U. Belgrade, Yugoslavia, 1978—. Fellow Japan Soc. Promotion of Sci., 1988-89. Mem. Serbian Chem. Soc. Avocations: music, cycling. Home: Majke Jevrosime 4, 11000 Belgrade Serbia, Yugoslavia Office: Studentski trg PO Box 158, 11004 Belgrade Serbia, Yugoslavia

VUČKOVIĆ-DEKIĆ, LJILJANA, researcher, immunology educator; b. Tekija, Serbia, Yugoslavia, Feb. 1, 1943; d. Nenad and Branislava (Stojićević) V.; m. Miodrag Dekić, July 9, 1967; children: Ivan, Vladimir. MD, U. Belgrade, Yugoslavia, 1967; MSc, U. Belgrade, 1975, PhD, 1980. Rsch. asst. Inst. Med. Rsch., Belgrade, 1969-75, asst. prof. rsch., 1975-88; assoc. prof. rsch. Inst. for Oncology and Radiology, Belgrade, 1988-94, prof. rsch., 1994—; asst. dept. immunology Med. Faculty, U. Belgrade, 1980-85, assoc. prof. immunology, oncology, biol. regulation, 1985-94, supr. postgrad. students, 1990—, prof. immunology, oncology, biol. regulation, 1994—, head exptl. oncology dept., 1999—. Contbr. articles to sci. jours., including Neoplasma, Jour. Exptl. Clin. Cancer Rsch., Archives Immunol. Therapy Expts., Panminerva Medica, Internat. Congress for Lung Cancer, Internat. Jour. Thymol, Bull. Hematology, Archives Oncology, Period Biology Oncology Reports, Biol. Medicine, Lung Cancer, Polish Jour. Immunology, Jour. BUOn. Mem. European Assn. for Cancer Rsch., Balkan Union Oncologists, N.Y. Acad. Scis. Avocation: theatre. Office: Inst for Oncology-Radiologyof Serbia, Pasterova 14, 11000 Belgrade Serbia, Yugoslavia

VU-DINH, TUONG, design engineer; b. Nam Dinh, Vietnam, Sept. 11, 1952; arrived in Australia, 1982; Diploma in Engring., Tech. U., Aachen, Germany, 1978; PhD in Elec. Engring., Wollongong (Australia) U., 1988. Part-time tutor math. Tech. U. Aachen, 1973-76; mem. acad. staff Duisburg U., Germany, 1979-82; design engr. Standard Telephones & Cables, Alexandria, NSW, Australia, 1986-88, Amalgamated Wireless Australasia, North Ryde, NSW, 1988-89; rsch. engr. Telecom Australia Rsch. Labs., Clayton, Victoria, 1989-93; design engr. ERG Ltd., Balcatta, Asutralia, 1993-94, Martin Comms. Pty. Ltd., Mulgrave, Victoria, 1994-99; sr. engr. RLM Sys. Pty. Ltd., Burwood East, Victoria, Australia, 1999-2000; sr. sys. engr. (Mobile comm. design divsn.) ACT Australia Pty.-Ltd., Melbourne, Australia, 2000—. Contbr. papers to internat. tech. jours. and confs. Mem. IEEE, Assn. for Computing Machinery. Avocation: astronomy.

VU HOAI, CHUONG, statistician, researcher; b. Hanoi, Vietnam, Aug. 6, 1945; s. Vu Boi Tan and Ngo Thi Ninh; m. Chu Thi Cam-Tu, May 20, 1985; children: Bao Linh, Hoan Khue. MEE, Budapest (Hungary) Tech. U., 1970, MSc in Math., 1973, D in Tech., 1983; PhD in Math., Hungarian Acad. Scis., 1978. Asst. lectr. Budapest Tech. U., 1971-73, postgrad. fellow, 1975-78; tchr. Vietnamese Hungarian Ministry Fgn. Affairs, Budapest, 1973; tchr. Hungarian Coll. Fgn. Langs., Hanoi, 1974; postgrad. fellow Budapest Tech. U., 1975-78; dep. head dept. statis. Inst. Info. Tech., Hanoi, 1979-85, head dept. statis., 1987—; sec. State Nat. Rsch. Project on Stats., Hanoi, 1980-85; mgr. Ministerial Rsch. Project on Numerical and Statis. Methods, Hanoi, 1997-98. Author: Hungarian-Vietnamese Scientific Vocabulary, 1967 (Spl. award Min. Edn. Vietnam 1968); editor-in-chief: Hungarian-Vietnamese Dictionary, 1974 (Spl. award Min. Culture and Edn. Hungary 1974, Spl. award Min. Edn. Vietnam 1975). Founding mem., mem. governing body Vietnamese-Hungarian Friedly Soc., Hanoi, 1990—. Recipient second prize nat. contest in math. Ministry Edn. Vietnam, Hanoi, 1963, first prize met. contest Chinese lang. Ministry Edn. Vietnam, Hanoi, 1963, silver badge of blood donor Min. Health France, Paris, 1986; CNRS scholar U. Paris Sud, Orsay, France, 1986-87. Mem. Internat. Assn. Hungarian Studies, Vietnamese Math. Soc., N.Y. Acad. Scis. Avocations: reading, television, music, onomastics. Home: 42A Ham Long, Q Hoan Kiem, Hanoi 10000, Vietnam Office: Inst Info Tech, Vien Congnghe Thongtin, Nghiado Hanoi 10608, Vietnam

VUILLEUMIER, PATRIK OLIVIER, neurologist, researcher; b. Geneva, Jan. 26, 1965; came to the U.S., 1997; s. Norbert Henri Vuilleumier and Irene Jenny Rapp; m. Sophie Isabelle Schwartz, Sept. 27, 1997. BS, Claparede Coll., Geneva, 1984; MD, U. Geneva, 1991. Neurology cert. Swiss Fedn. Physicians. Contbr. articles to profl. jours. mem. Swiss Soc. Behavioral Neurology, 1997, Swiss Soc. Neurology, 1997; rsch. fellow U. Calif., Davis, 1997-99, U. Coll. London, 1999. E-mail: pvuilleumier@ucl.acl.uk and patrick@ebire.org. Home: 458 Hudson St Oakland CA 94618-1137 Office: Inst Cognitive Neurosci, 12 Queen Sq, London WC1N, England

VUJANIC, GORDAN, pediatric pathologist; b. Banjaluka, Yugoslavia, Jan. 25, 1954; arrived in U.K., 1990; s. Milan and Melanija (Borozan) V.; m. Aleksandra Vojvodic, Apr. 25, 1991; children: Aleksandra, Ana, Milan. MD, Belgrade Sch. Medicine, 1978, DS in Pathology, 1984, PhD in Pathology, 1989. From registrar in pathology to head dept. pediat. pathology Mother & Child Health Inst., Belgrade, Yugoslavia, 1980-90; postdoctoral rsch. fellow Bristol Children's Hosp., England, 1990-91; cons. sr. lectr. pediat. pathology U. Wales Coll. Medicine, Cardiff, 1991—; renal tumors panelist UK Children's Cancer Study Group, 1992—, working party, 1992—. Fellow Royal Coll. Pathologists; mem. Internat. Soc. Pediat. Oncology (renal tumors panelist 1986—), Internat. Acad. Pathology, Pathol. Soc. Great Britain, Assn. Clin. Pathologists, Soc. Pediat. Pathology, Paediatric Pathology Soc. (hon. sec. 1996—). Mem. Christian Orthodox Ch. Avocations: history, opera. Office: U Wales Coll Medicine Dept Pathology, Heath Park, CF4 4XN Cardiff Wales

VUK, DAMIR, information technology specialist, consultant; b. Novoselec, Croatia, Nov. 24, 1955; s. Stjepan and Henrijeta (Schoenauer) V.; m. Srebrenka Ursic. BS in Physics, U. Zagreb, 1980. Reliability specialist Riz-Semiconductors, Zagreb, 1981-85, reliability mgr., 1985-88, quality control mgr., 1988-90; info. tech. cons., mgr. Systemcom/Sistemprojekt Group, Zagreb, 1990—; info. tech. cons. State Intellectual Propr. Office, Zagreb, 1993—, Meteorol. Hydrol. Svc. Croatia, Zagreb, 1995—. Contbr. articles to

profl. jours. Mem. N.Y. Acad. Sci. Achievements include rsch. in semiconductor failure analysis. Avocations: tennis, swimming, chess. Office: Systemcom Ltd, C Zuzoric 31, 10000 Zagreb Croatia

VUKASINOVIC, ZORAN STANISA, orthopaedic surgeon, educator; b. Valjevo, Serbia, Yugoslavia, July 12, 1959; s. Stanisa Milijan and Vukosava Sava (Urosevic) V.; m. Zorica Momcilo Zivkovic, Dec. 22, 1984; children: Ivan, Teodora. MD, H.S. Medicine, Belgrade, Yugoslavia, 1982, MSc, 1991, PhD, 1993. Resident Inst. Orthop. Surgery Banjica, Belgrade, 1982-89, chief ultrasound diagnostics, 1990-94, head paediat. orthopaedics dept., 1995—; asst. prof. Univ. H.S., Belgrade, 1989-96, prof., 1996—. Author: Sport Traumatology, 1993, Paediatric Hip, 1994, Paediatric Orthopaedics, 1999; editor Acta Orthopaedica Iugoslavica. Mem. Yugoslav Paediat. Orthopaedic Soc. (pres. 1994—), Yugoslav Orthopaedic Assn. (sec. gen. 1994—), World Orthopaedic Assn., European Paediat. Orthopaedics Soc. (nat. del. 1997—), European Fedn. Orthopaedic Surgeons and Traumatologists (nat. del. 1997—). Home: 9 Ivana Milutinovica, 11000 Belgrade Serbia, Yugoslavia Office: Inst Orth Surg Banjica, 28 Mihajla Avramovica, 11041 Belgrade Serbia Yugoslavia

VUKIĆ, ZORAN, lawyer, banking and corporate law consultant; b. Rijeka, Croatia, Apr. 3, 1962; s. Jure and Mila (Sjaus) V.; mem. Gina Kontić, Oct. 15, 1994; children: Luka, Iva, Ema. LLB, U. Rijeka, 1985. Assoc. Sprajc Law Office, Rijeka, 1985-88; ptnr. Sprajc and Vukić, Rijeka, 1989-95; sr. ptnr. Vukić, Jelušić & Šulina, Rijeka, 1996—. Contbr. articles to profl. jours. Mem. Croatian Bar Assn., Internat. Bar Assn., Croatian C. of C. (arbitar permanent arbitration ct. 1997—), Yacht Club Galeb (Kostrena) (sec. 1987). Avocations: sailing, basketball, collecting art. E-mail: vukiclaw@ri.tel.hr. Home: Tizianova 9, 51000 Rijeka Croatia Office: Vukić Jelusić Sulina, N Tesle 9, 51000 Rijeka Croatia

VUKMIR, MLADEN, lawyer; b. Zagreb, Croatia, Sept. 15, 1960; s. Branko and Stanka (Katičić) V.; m. Marina Sanguinetti, Sept. 11, 1999. Diploma in law, Zagreb Faculty of Law, 1985; M of Intellectual Property, Franklin Pierce Law Ctr., 1990. Atty. at law Croatian Bar Assn.; patent agt. Croatian Intellectual Property Office. Assoc. Hanzekovic and Radakovic, Zagreb, 1986-90; fgn. assoc. Fenwick & West, Palo Alto, Calif., 1990-91; fgn. counsel Pavia e Ansaldo, Milan, 1991-92; founding ptnr. Vukmir Law Offices, Zagreb, 1991—; hon. fellow Ctr. for Internat. Legal Studies, Salzburg, Austria, 1996; expert advisor UNIDO, Vienna, Austria, 1993-94, Croatian Patent Office, Zagreb, 1991-92; pres. Slow Food Croatia, Zagreb, 1996-98. Author: Copyright Act, 1995; co-author: The United Nations, 1996. Journalist START, MOL, POLET, Zagreb, 1978-85. Mem. Assn. Internat. pour la Protection de la Propriete Industrielle (sec. of Croatian group 1995-98), Internat. Trademark Assn., Internat. Bar Assn., Royal Danish Counsul Gen. (hon.), Computer Law Assn., Croation Copyright Soc. (mem. steering com.). Avocations: skiing, wine. Office: Vukmir Law Offices, Pantovcak 35, 10000 Zagreb Croatia

VUKSANOVIĆ, MIRO, library director, writer; b. Krnja Jela, Montenegro, May 4, 1944; s. Milutin and Koja (Grdinić) V.; m. Milana Dzuver; children: Danilo, Jelena. Grad., U. Belgrade, Yugoslavia, 1969. Secondary sch. tchr. Tech. Sch., Sombor, Yugoslavia, 1970-75; dir. City Libr. Karlo Bijelicki, Sombor, 1975-88, Biblioteka Matice srpske, Novi Sad, Yugoslavia, 1988—. Author: (novels) Kletva Peka Perkova, 1977, Gradista, 1989, Daleko bilo, 1995, Semolj gora, 2000; (short stories) Gorske oci, 1982, Nemusti jezik, 1984, Vucji tragovi, 1987; (poems) Tamooni, 1992, Moracnik, 1994; and other writings. Mem. Assn. of Writers (pres. 1985-86), Fedn. Socs. of Writers Belgrade (pres. 1984-86), Fedn. Socs. of Librs. Yugoslavia (pres. 1985-87), Fedn. Nat. Librs. (pres. 1988-92), Serbian Sci. and Cultural Soc. Matica srpska (collaborator 1988, mem. adminstrv. com. 1988). Office: Matice Srpske Libr, Matice Srpske 1, 21000 Novi Sad Yugoslavia

VULIC, NENAD, mechanical engineer; b. Split, Croatia, Aug. 26, 1960; s. Zdenko and Ida (Cotic) V.; m. Denis Mladinic, Aug. 16, 1986; 1 child, Marko. Dipl-Ing, U. Split, Croatia, 1983; MSc in Mech. Engring., U. Zagreb, Croatia, 1989, PhD, 1995. Lead assessor by exam. Brit. Standardisation Inst.; leading auditor quality systems. Engr. in shipyard Brodosplit Shipyard, Split, 1983-84, surveyor, 1984-88, sr. surveyor, 1988-92, prin. surveyor, 1992-94; head machinery and materials dept. Croatian Register of Shipping, Split, 1994—; faculty asst. Faculty of Elec. and Mech. Engring. and Naval Architecture, U. Split, 1992-98, asst. prof., 1998—. Contbr. articles to profl. jours. Mem. Croatian Soc. Mechanics, Croatian Soc. for Constrn., Croatian Soc. Mathematics, IACS/WP/Machinery. Roman Catholic. Avocations: swimming. Home: Sukoisanska 37, 21000 Split Croatia Office: Croatian Register Shipping, Marasoviceva 67, 21000 Split Croatia

VULLIAMY, (JOHN-NA'VRED) GRAHAM, education educator; b. Richmond, Eng., Apr. 12, 1946; s. Edmund Lewis and Rosamond Daphne (Farrell-Palliser) V.; m. Valerie Kilroy, Sept. 2, 1978 (div. 1985); m. Rosemary Ellen Webb, Nov. 22, 1996. BA in Econs., Cambridge (Eng.) U., 1968; postgrad. cert. in edn., U. London Inst. Edn., 1969; MA, Cambridge (Eng.) U., 1970; MSc, U. London Inst. Edn., 1972; DPhil, U. York, Heslington, Eng., 1985. Lectr. in sociology Cambridge U. Coll. Arts and Tech., 1969-72; sr. lectr. in edn. U. York, 1972—. Author or editor of 10 books, including: Teacher Research and Special Educational Needs, 1992 (Times Ednl. Supplement/Nat. Assn. Spl. Ednl. Needs Annual Book award 1993); contbr. over 80 articles to books and profl. jours.; exec. editor Brit. Jour. Sociology of Edn., 1982—, Internat. Jour. Ednl. Devel., 1982—; mem. editl. bd. Popular Music, 1980-91. Avocations: golf, tennis, windsurfing. Home: Hall Farm, High Catton, York YO41 EH, England Office: U York, Dept Educational Studies, Heslington YO10 5DD, England

VULSMA, THOMAS, pediatric endocrinologist, biochemist; b. Krommenie, The Netherlands, Feb. 20, 1948; s. Thomas and Cornelia (Ekkerman) V.; m. Elisabeth Heek, Dec. 23, 1969; children: Vincent, Thomas. MD, U. Amsterdam, The Netherlands, 1980, MSc in Biochemistry, PhD, 1991. Pediatrician subdivsn. pediat. endocrinology Emma Children's Hosp., Acad. Med. Ctr., Amsterdam, 1984-91, pediatric endocrinologist subdivsn. pediat. endocrinology, 1991—; rschr. U. Amsterdam, 1984—, tchr., 1980—. Contbr. articles to profl. jours. Mem. European Thyroid Assn. Avocations: wood carving, cycling, music, antique collecting. Home: Geerdinkhof 36, 1103 PP Amsterdam The Netherlands Office: Emma Children's Hosp-AMC, Meibergdreef 9, 1105 AZ Amsterdam The Netherlands

VUNJAK-NOVAKOVIC, GORDANA, chemical engineer, educator; b. Belgrade, Yugoslavia, Aug. 26, 1948; came to U.S., 1993; d. Vlajko and Mila (Simeunovic) Vunjak; m. Branko Novakovic, Oct. 27, 1974; 1 child, Stasha. BS, U. Belgrade, 1972, MS, 1975, PhD, 1980. From asst. prof. to prof. chem. engring. Belgrade U., 1981—; adj. prof. chem. engring. Tufts U., Boston, 1994—; from rsch. scientist to prin. rsch. scientist MIT, Cambridge, Mass., 1992—. Contbr. over 140 articles to sci. jours. and books. Fulbright Found. fellow, 1986-87. Fellow Am. Inst. Med. and Biomed. Engring.; mem. AAAS, AAUW, AIChE, Assn. Fulbright Scholars. Avocations: literature, classical music, film, travel. Office: MIT E25-342 77 Massachusetts Ave Cambridge MA 02139-4301

VUONG, LARRY VIET, chiropractor; b. Dalat, South Vietnam, Mar. 24, 1974; s. Anthony Phuoc and Diana (Duyen) V. Student, U. Alberta, Can., 1994; D of Chiropractic, Palmer Coll. Chiropractic West, 1997. Cert. chiropractor, Calif., Colo. Chiropractic and rehab. doctor, cons., office mgr. Fed. Med. Ctr., Denver, 1997—. Mem. Internat. Chiropractic Assn., World Chiropractic Alliance, Colo. Chiropractic Assn. Avocations: martial arts, ice hockey, tennis, hiking, skiing. Home: 229 Kenton Dr Santa Ana CA 92704-1430 Office: Fed Med Ctr 50 S Federal Blvd Denver CO 80219-2044

VUONG, PHAT NGOC, pathologist, cytologist, researcher; b. Hanoi, Vietnam, Feb. 2, 1945; s. Quynh Duy and Tan Thi (Nguyen) V.; m. Phuong Nguyen, 1969 (div. 1979); children: Tam Ngoc, Lan Ngoc; m. Sarra Houissa, Oct. 15, 1981; children: Anh Asma, Hien Hella. MD, U. Saigon, Vietnam, 1971, postgrad., 1973; postgrad., U. Paris, 1977, 78, 82, PhD in Sci., 1992; DSc, U. Rouen, 1997. Titular intern Saigon Hosp., 1969-72, asst. prof. faculty medicine, 1972-73; affiliated pathologist Hosps. of Paris, 1975-82; dep. dir. Ctrl. Lab. St. Michel Hosp., Paris, 1981-83, chief dept. A.C.P., 1984-88, head unit A.C.P., 1988—; co-dir. Lab. Anatomical and Cytol. Pathology, Bièvres, France, 1979—; ad hoc expert for legal testimony anatomical and cytol. pathology French Ministry for Justice Superior Ct., Versailles, Paris, 1986—; affiliated researcher Natural History Mus., Paris, 1985—, U. Rouen, 1997—. Contbr. articles, papers to profl. jours., books. Lt. MD South Vietnamese Army, 1973-74. Fellow Internat. Acad. Cytology; mem. AAAS, N.Y. Acad. Sics., European Soc. Pathology, Internat. Acad. Pathology, French Soc. Clin. Cytology, Anatomic Soc. Paris, French Soc. Lymphology, French Assn. Quality Assurance in Anatomic Pathology and Cytopathology., Coll. Med. Hosps. Paris. Office: Lab Anat Cytol Pathologiques, 20 Ave de la Gare, 91570 Bièvres France

VUORILEHTO, KAI, electrochemist, researcher; b. Imatra, Carelia, Finland, May 30, 1965; s. Simo Sakari V. and Liva Söderhjelm; 1 child, Helena. BSc in Vet. Medicine, Helsinki Coll. Vet. Medicine, Finland, 1988; MSc in Chem. Engring., Helsinki U. Tech., 1990, PhD in Chem. Engring., 1993. Scientist Helsinki U. Tech., 1990-93; free scientist Karl-Winnacker-Inst. der Dechema e.V., Frankfurt am Main, Germany, 1993-96; sr. scientist Vaisala Oyj, Vantaa, Finland, 1997—. Contbr. numerous articles to profl. jours.; inventor and patentee in field, 1994. Lt., Finnish Coast Arty., 1991, Helsinki. Recipient rsch. grants Imatran Voima Found., 1993, Deutscher Akademischer Austauschdienst, 1994, Helsinki U. Tech., 1995. Mem. Rotary. Avocations: ornithology, philately. Home: Otakuja 3C35, 02150 Espoo Finland Office: Vaisala Oyj, PO Box 26, 00421 Helsinki Finland

VUORINEN, MATTI KEIJO, mathematician; b. Turku, Finland, Nov. 6, 1948; s. Keijo Hugo and Aino (Kallio) V.; m. Sinikka Juusti, July 5, 1975; children: Ville, Elias (dec. 1995), Salla. MSc, U. Helsinki, 1973, PhD, 1977. Docent U. Helsinki, 1980; rsch. fellow Acad. Finland, Helsinki, 1979-85; vis. scholar Institut Mittag-Leffler, Djursholm, Sweden, 1977-78, 82, U. Mich., Ann Arbor, 1979-80, 91-92; sr. rsch. fellow Acad. Finland, 1994-99. Author: Conformal Geometry and Quasiregular Mappings, 1988, (with G.D. Anderson and M.K. Vamanamurthy) Conformed Invariants, Inequalities, and Quasiconformal Maps, 1997. Lt. Finland Arty., 1968-69. Alexander von Humboldt grantee Tech. U. Berlin, 1988-89; sr. scientist Acad. of Finland, 1990-95. Office: U Helsinki Math Dept, U Helsinki Math Dept, Yliopistonk 5, 00100 Helsinki Finland

VURAL, VOLKAN, Turkish representative to UN; b. Istanbul, Turkey, Dec. 29, 1941; married. Grad., Ankara U. With Turkish Ministry Fgn. Affairs, 1964—; internat. officer, polit. dept. NATO Hdqrs., 1976-82; head econ. dept., envoy, dep. dir. gen. bilateral econ. aff. Ministry Fgn. Affairs, 1982-87; Turkish amb. to Tehran, 1987-88, Moscow, 1988-93; dep. under-sec., amb., spokesman Ministry Fgn. Affairs, 1993, chief advisor to prime min., dep. under-sec., 1993-95; Turkish amb. Bonn, Germany, 1995-98; rep. from Turkey to UN, 1998—. Office: Permanent Del of Turkey/UN 821 U N Plz Fl 11 New York NY 10017-3520

VUURSTEEN, KAREL, beverage industry executive; b. Arnhem, The Netherlands, July 25, 1941; s. Cornelis Willem and Hendrika Eliza (Weddepohl) V.; m. Juliette H.J. Pronk, Apr. 4, 1964; 3 children. Cert. agrl. engr., Agrl. U. Wageningen, The Netherlands, 1968. With Philips, The Netherlands, 1968-79; consumer goods dir. Philips, Sweden, 1979-81; CEO Philips, Norway, 1982-83; consumer goods dir. Philips, Germany, 1984-87; CEO Philips, Austria, 1987-90; pres., CEO Philips Lighting Co., U.S.A., 1990-91; mem. exec. bd. Heineken N.V., Amsterdam, The Netherlands, 1991-92, dep. chmn. exec. bd., 1992-93, chmn. exec. bd., 1993—; bd. dirs. Whitbread PLC, London, Gucci Group N.V., The Netherlands, Nyenrode U., The Netherlands, AB Electrolux, Sweden; mem. adv. coun. ING Group N.V., The Netherlands; mem. adv. bd. CVC Capital Ptnrs., B.V., The Netherlands. Office: Heineken NV, Tweede Weteringplantsoen 21, 1017 ZD Amsterdam The Netherlands

V. WYSOCKI, KLAUS, accounting educator; b. Solingen, Fed. Republic Germany, Aug. 12, 1925; s. Josef and Paula (Lampe) v. W.; m. Ursula, Aug. 15, 1957. Dr.rer.pol., U. Muenster, Fed. Republic Germany, 1955, Habilitation, 1960. Prof. Univ. Mannheim, Fed. Republic Germany, 1961-62, 67-72, Freie Univ. Berlin, 1962-67, U. Munich, 1972—; dr. rer. pol. h.c. U. Mannheim, 1999; hon. prof. U. Wien, Austria. Author publs. in fields of acctg. and auditing. Mem. Rotary (pres. Munich club 1986-87). Roman Catholic. Home: Am Rupenhorn 6a, D-14055 Berlin Germany

VYHOVSKA, YAROSLAVA, hematology researcher, educator; b. Snyatyn, Ukraine, Aug. 12, 1930; s. Illya and Anna (Borys) Nykyforuk; m. Volodymyr Vyhovsky. Physician, Med. Inst., Lviv, Ukraine, 1953; PhD, Med. Inst. Lviv, 1961, MD, 1972. Rschr. Inst. of Haematology and Blood Transfusion, Lviv, 1953-65, sr. rschrs., 1965—, chief of haematology Lviv Affil. Br.; chief haematology Lviv Rsch. Inst. Blood Pathology and Transfusional Medicine, 1998—, prof., 1982. Author: Haematological Syndromes in Clinical Practice, 1981, Manual of Clinical Laboratory Diagnostics, 1992, Reference Book on Haematology, 1997. Mem. Animal Protection Soc. Mem. Ukrainian Med. Soc. of Haematologists and Transfusiologists, Taras Shevchenko Scientific Soc. Greek Catholic. Avocations: swimming, breeding Persian cats. Home: 32 Lychakivska St ap 4, 79010 Lviv Ukraine

VYMAZAL, JOSEF, physician, researcher; b. Prague, Aug. 5, 1962; s. Josef Vymazal and Marie (Zamrzlova) Vymazalova. MD summa cum laude, Charles U., Prague, 1986, PhD, 1990. Diplomate Bd. Neurology, Bd. Radiology. Intern, resident in neurology Med. Sch. Prague, 1986-91, intern, resident in radiology, 1996-99; physician Postgrad. Med. Sch., Prague, 1986-91; rsch. scientist NIH, Bethesda, Md., 1991-96; physician Hosp. na Homolce, Prague, 1996-99, chief MRI dept., 1999—. Contbr. articles to profl. jours.; reviewer: Magnetic Resonance in Medicine, 1999—, Jour. Radiosurgery, 1997—, Jour. Computer Assisted Topography, 1994—; mem. editl. bd. Jour. Radiosurgery, 1997—; lectr. in field. Active St. Matej Ch., Prague, organist, 1978—. Mem. Internat. Soc. Magnetic Resonance, Leksell Gamma Knife Soc., Czech Med. Soc., European Soc. for Magnetic Resonance in Medicine, (award 1996). Avocations: photography, foreign languages. Office: Hosp NA Homolce, Dept MRI, 15119 Prague Czech Republic

VYMĚTAL, JAN KAREL, information executive; b. Olomouc, Czechoslovakia, Feb. 13, 1941; s. Karel and Bohumila (Fák) V; m. Ružena Prachovsky, July 23, 1966; children: Petr, Dušan. M Engring., Inst. Chem. Tech., Prague, Czech Republic, 1969, PhD, 1972. Rschr. Urxovy Závody, Valašské Mezirici, Czechoslovakia, 1959-72, head rsch. group, 1972-90; head info. dept. DEZA Corp., Valašské Mezirici, Czech Republic, 1990—; tchr. asst. High Pedagogical Sch., Ostrava, Czechoslovakia, 1969-80, cons., 1980-89; cons. U. Palacky, Olomouc, Czechoslovakia, 1980-92; assoc. prof. U. Ostrava, 1994—. Author: Inform. Dep. In Firm Praxis, 1996, Chemical Literature and Information, 2000. Mem. IUPAC, N.Y. Acad. Scis., Czech Soc. Chemistry, Am. Chem. Soc. Avocations: symphonic and chamber music, travel. Home: Mírová 500, CZ 75701 Valasske Mezirici Czech Republic Office: DEZA Crp, Masarykova 753, CZ-75728 Valasske Mezirici Czech Republic

VYPLEL, ZDENĚK, language educator, translator; b. Kladno, Bohemia, Czechslovakia, Sept. 22, 1936; s. Ladislav and Marie (Holovska) V.; m. Jirina Brixova, Nov. 14, 1959; children: Vitezslav, Radka. PhD, Charles U., Prague, Czechoslovakia, 1978. Rsch. worker Acad. Scis., Czechoslovakia, 1970-78; head congress dept. Tech. & Sci. Soc., Czechoslovakia, 1978-86; lang. instr. Charles U., Prague, 1986-90, Czech Tech. U., Prague, 1990—; translator, 1970—. Translator: Prague: Eleven Centuries of Architecture, 1992, Baustilkunde, 1998. Major Czechoslovak Army, 1961-70. E-mail: vyplel@regionet.cz. Home: Uvoze, 27351 Braskov Czech Republic Office: Czech Tech U, Thakurova 7, 16629 Prague Czech Republic

VYSEKANTSEV, IGOR PAVLOVICH, research scientist, physician; b. Talalayevka, Ukraine, Jan. 1, 1950; s. Pavel Yemelyanovich and Nadezhda Mikhajlovna (Shabalina) V.; m. Nina Ivanovna Kireyeva, Mar. 9, 1973; 1 child, Kozak Olga Igorievna. MS, Med. Inst. Kharkov, Ukraine, 1973; PhD, Inst. Crybiology, Kharkov, 1983; postgrad., Acad. Postdiploma Edn., Kharkov, 1996. Head dept. Sanitary Epidemiology Sta., Kharkov, 1974-75; jr. rschr. Inst. Immunology, Kharkov, 1974-76; leading rschr. Inst. Cryobiology, Kharkov, 1976—; asst. prof. Nat. U., Kharkov, 1995—. Co-author: Cryobiology and Biotechnology, 1987, Cold Stress and Biosystems, 1991; patentee in field. Avocation: hunting. Home: 6 Elizarova St, 610098 Kharkov Ukraine Office: Inst Problems Cryobiology, 23 Pereyaslaskaya St, 610015 Kharkov Ukraine

VYSOTSKY, VITALY SERGEEVICH, physicist; b. Moscow, Aug. 22, 1948; s. Serguei S. and Valentina B. (Kuprina) V.; m. Valentina V. Muzaleva, Nov. 3, 1972; 1 child, Anna. MS summa cum laude, Moscow State U., 1972; PhD, Russian Acad. Sci., 1986. Rschr. Lebedev Phys. Inst., Moscow, 1972-93; vis. scientist MIT, Cambridge, Mass., 1993-96; assoc. prof. Kyushu U., Fukuoka, Japan, 1996—; cons. Mitsubishi Electric Co., Amagasaki, Japan, 1993, 98, Intermagnetic Gen. Corp., Latham, N.Y., 1995, Kyushu Electric Power Co., Fukuoka, Japan, 1996-98. Contbr. articles to profl. jours. Mem. IEEE, Moscow Phys. Soc., Moscow House of Scientists. Avocations: fishing, outdoor, skiing. Office: Kyushu U Fac Engring, 6-10-1 Hakozaki Higashi-ku, Fukuoka 812-8581, Japan

WAAG, KARL LUDWIG, pediatric surgeon, educator; b. Linz, Donau, Austria, July 31, 1942; s. Karl Friedrich and Margarethe (Klein) W.; m. Dorothea Weber, July 4, 1969 (div. 1984); children: Miriam, Gregor, Frederik; m. Susan Juliette von Stenglin, Oct. 9, 1986; children: Bastian-Ludwig, Nikolas-Jürgen. Student, U. Vienna, Austria, 1961-67; MD, U. Heidelberg, Germany, 1968. Cert. specialist in gen. surgery and pediat. surgery. Sr. house officer U. Liverpool, Eng., 1970-71; asst. U. Munich, 1971-73; cons. U. Heidelberg, Germany, 1973-79, U. Frankfurt, Germany, 1979-89; prof. U. Düsseldorf, Germany, 1989-91; prof., chief pediat. surgery dept. U. Mannheim and U. Heidelberg, 1991—; del. Body Sci. Med. Specialist Orgn., Germany, 1984—, World Fedn. Pediat. Surg. Assn., 1986—, Union European Medicines Specialists, Brussels, 1990—; mem. adv. coun. Assn. Pediat. Surgery, Germany, 1990—. Author: Pediatrics, 1986; co-author: Therapy of Diseases in Childhood and Youth, 1996, Pediatric Pneumatology; editl. cons. Pediat. Surgery Internat., Zentralblatt Kinderchirurgie. Mem. Assn. Pediat. Surgeons (com. mem.), Assn. Surgery (com. 1992-95), Assn. Pediat. Avocations: guitar, classics. Office: Heidelberg Univ Hosp, Klinikum GmbH, 68167 Mannheim Germany

WAAGE, JAN, retired engineering executive, researcher; b. Bergen, Norway, Aug. 14, 1931; s. Ragnar and Edith (Kaaresen) W.; m. Kirsten Laache Waage, Sept. 17, 1960; children: Jan Andreas, Margrethe. ME, Bergen (Norway) Tech. Coll.; BSME, S.D. Sch. Mines & Tech., Rapid City, 1958. Profl. engr. Design engr. Western Gear Corp., Indsl. Machinery, Seattle, 1958-62; mgr. devel. Horten (Norway) Ship Yards, Indsl. Divsn., 1962-74, Kongsberg (Norway) Def. Ltd. Adminstrn. Electronics, 1974-97. Contbr. rsch. in field. Bd. mem., 1976, pres., 1976-77, Kongsberg Profl. Engr. Charter. Mem. Norske Sivilingeniors Forening. Sgt. Airforce, 1953-55, Norway. Avocations: genealogy, photography, travel, swimming. E-mail: jawaage@online.no. Home: Halvdan Svartesgate 80, 3186 Horten Norway

WAALER, BJARNE ARENTZ, physician, educator; b. Bergen, Norway, Apr. 18, 1925; s. Rolf and Gudrun Waaler; m. Gudrun Arentz, Dec. 19, 1950; children: Hans Michael Arentz, Finn, Astrid. MD, U. Oslo, 1950, DM, 1959. Various positions Norwegian hosps., 1950-56; rsch. fellow physiology lab. physiology Oxford (Eng.) U., 1958-61; prof. physiology U. Oslo Med. Faculty, 1962-92, dean med. faculty, 1974-77, rector, 1977-85; ret., 1992. Contbr. articles to profl. jours. Decorated comdr. Royal Order St. Olav; recipient medal Order of Grand Duke Gediminas, Lithuania. Mem. Norwegian Acad. Sci. and Letters (pres. 1990-97), Physiol. Soc. Engring. Office: U Oslo Dept Physiology, Postbox 1103 Blindern, 0317 Oslo 3, Norway

WABNIG, HARALD WERNER, systems analyst, researcher; b. Lustenau, Austria, Sept. 19, 1968; s. Werner and Marlies (Drexel) W.; m. Eveline Sauerczopf, Sept. 14, 1996. Diploma in computer sci., Tech. U. Vienna, 1990. Rschr. Inst. Angewandte Info. U. Vienna, 1991-95; system analyst Software Data Svc., Vienna, 1995—. Contbr. articles to profl. jours. Recipient Civil Svc. honors Ministry of the Interior, Vienna, 1995. Avocations: tennis, soccer. E-mail: Harald.WABNIG@SDS.-WIEN.RAIF-FEISEN.ada.at. Fax: 43-1-21156-3590. Office: Software Daten Svc, Millennium Tower, A-1200 Vienna Handelskal 94-96, Austria

WACHEWSKI, ROBERT THOMAS, health facility administrator; b. Bklyn., May 29, 1952; s. Henry and Sophie (Kaptur) W. BBA, Baruch Coll., 1975; MPA, NYU, 1981. Mgr. fed. funding City of N.Y. Dept. Mental Health, N.Y.C., 1976-80; assoc. dir. fin. Bronx-Lebanon Hosp. Ctr.-Crotona Park Cmty. Mental Health, 1980-82; dir. fin. Maimonides Cmty. Mental Health Ctr., Bklyn., 1982-86; assoc. adminstr. dept. psychiatry Maimonides Med. Ctr., Bklyn., 1986-90, asst. dir. fin., 1990-92, asst. v.p., 1992—; bd. dirs., treas. The Heights Players, Inc., Bklyn., 1992—. Co-prodr. various plays and musicals, 1992—. Mem. Healthcare Fin. Mgmt. Assn. Democrat. Home: 66 Orange St Apt 4A Brooklyn NY 11201-1738 Office: Maimonides Med Ctr 4802 10th Ave Brooklyn NY 11219-2844

WACHINGER, BURGHART, German literature educator; b. Munich, June 10, 1932; s. Walther and Liselotte (Langewiesche) W.; m. Marie-Helene Gravert, July 25, 1966; children: Eva, Lorenz. PhD, U. Munich, Germany, 1958. Asst. U. Munich, Germany, 1958-59, 61-69; lectr. Bryn Mawr (Pa.) Coll., 1959-60, Harvard U., Cambridge, Mass., 1960-61; prof. U. Tübingen, Germany, 1969-98. Author: Studien zum Nibelungenlied, 1960, Sängerkrieg, 1973, Der Mönch von Salzburg, 1989; editor in field; contbr. articles to profl. jours. Recipient Leibniz-Preis, Deutsche Forschungsgemeinschaft, 1988. Office: Univ Tübingen, Wilhelmstrasse 50, D-72074 Tübingen Germany

WACHMAN, MARVIN, former university chancellor; b. Milw., Mar. 24, 1917; s. Alex and Ida (Epstein) W.; m. Adeline Lillian Schpok, Apr. 12, 1942; children: Kathleen M., Lynn A. B.S., Northwestern U., 1939, M.A., 1940; Ph.D., U. Ill., 1942; LLD (hon.), U. Pa., 1964, Lincoln (Pa.) U., 1970, Del. Valley Coll. Sci. and Agr., 1973, Med. Coll. Pa., 1982, Bloomfield Coll., 1987, Albright Coll., 1991; DHL (hon.), Gratz Coll., 1973; LittD (hon.), Jewish Theol. Sem. Am., 1973, Drexel U., 1980; LHD (hon.), Colgate U., 1975, Widener U., 1976; DSc (hon.), Thomas Jefferson U., 1980; LHD, U. New Eng., 1997; DHL, Phila. Coll. Textiles and Sci., 1999. Asst. in history U. Ill., 1940-42; instr. Biarritz Am. U., Biarritz, France, 1945-46; vis. asst. prof. San Diego State Coll., summer 1948, U. Minn., 1950; assoc. prof. history U. Md. in Europe, 1952-53; from instr. to prof. Colgate U., 1946-61, dir. upper class core program, 1956-61; pres. Lincoln (Pa.) U., 1961-70; v.p. acad. affairs Temple U., 1970-73, pres., 1973-82, chancellor, 1982-2000, Dir. Salzburg Seminar in Am. Studies, 1958-60, pres. Fgn. Policy Rsch. Inst., 1983-89; acting exec. dir. Pa. Higher Edn. Assistance Agy., 1989; acting pres. Phila. Coll. Textiles and Sci., 1991; pres. Albright Coll., 1991-92; past chmn. Nat. Ctr. for Higher Edn. Mgmt. Sys.; specialist in Africa for State Dept., 1965, 68; mem. adv. coun. World Learning, Inc.; mem. Colgate Nat. Coun.; dir., chair COLLEGIS, Inc.; dir. emeritus Germantown Ins. Co. Author: History of Social-Democratic Party of Milwaukee, 1897-1910, 1945; contbr. articles to profl. jours. and newspapers, also chpts. in books. Mem. bd. overseers Coll. V.I.; hon. trustee Albright Coll.; hon. life trustee Temple U.; vice chair Fgn. Policy Rsch. Inst.; trustee emeritus Balch Inst. Ethnic Studies; mem. adv. coun. Greater Phila. Urban Affairs Coalition, World Affairs Coun.; mem. bd. mgrs. Phila. Found.; hon. dir. Phila. Contributionship; alumni regent Phila. area Northwestern U. With AUS, 1942-46. Mem. NAACP, Am. Studies Assn. (past mem. exec. com.), AAUP (past pres. Colgate U. chpt.), Am. Hist. Assn., ACLU, Pa. Assn. Colls. and Univs. (past chmn., pres. 1993), Phi Beta Kappa. Office: Temple U Philadelphia PA 19122-6096

WACHMANN, ERIC JAMES, music educator, symphony musician; b. Pa., May 26, 1964; s. Constantin and Brenda (Michael) W.; m. Maria Paula Survilla, July 18, 1987; 1 child, Anton. MusB, U. Ottawa, Ont., Can., 1987; MusM, U. Mich., 1990; MusD, UNC, Greensboro. Asst. prof. music Wartburg Coll., Waverly, Iowa, 1994—; clarinet player Waterloo (Iowa) and Cedar Falls Symphony Orch.; artist Yamaha Music, Grand Rapids, Mich. Avocations: sailing, hiking, skiing, camping. Fax: 319-532-8501. E-mail: Wachmann@wartburg.edu. Office: Wartburg Coll 222 9th St NW Waverly IA 50677-2215

WACHSMAN, HARVEY FREDERICK, lawyer, neurosurgeon; b. Bklyn., June 13, 1936; s. Ben and Mollie (Kugel) W.; m. Kathryn M. D'Agostino, Jan. 31, 1976; children: Dara Nicole, David Winston, Jacqueline Victoria, Lauren Elizabeth, Derek Charles, Ashley Max, Marea Lane, Melissa Roseanne. B.A., Tulane U., 1958; M.D., Chgo. Med. Sch., 1962; J.D., Bklyn. Law Sch., 1976. Bar: Conn. 1976, N.Y. 1977, Fla. 1977, D.C. 1978, U.S. Supreme Ct. 1980, Pa. 1984, Md. 1986, Tex. 1987. Diplomate Nat. Bd. Med. Examiners; cert. Am. Bd. Legal Medicine, Am. Bd. Profl. Liability Attys. (pres.); cert. civil trial advocate Nat. Bd. Trial Advocacy (trustee). Intern surgery Kings County Hosp. Ctr., Bklyn., 1962-63; resident in surgery Kingsbrook Med. Ctr., Bklyn., 1964-65; resident in neurol. surgery Emory U. Hosp., Atlanta, 1965-69; practice medicine specializing in neurosurgery Bridgeport, Conn., 1972-74; ptnr. Pegalis & Wachsman, Great Neck, N.Y., 1977—; trustee SUNY, chmn. health sci. and hosp. com.; pres., CEO Found. Excellence & Ethics in Medicine. Author: American Law of Medical Malpractice, Vol. I, 1980, 2d edit., 1992, American Law of Medical Malpractice, Vol. II, 1981, 2d edit., 1993, American Law of Medical Malpractice, Vol. III, 1982, 2d edit., 1994, Cumulative Supplement to American Law of Medical Malpractice, 1981, 82, 83, 84, 85, American Law of Medical Malpractice, 2d edit., Vols. I, II and II, Lethal Medicine, 1993; mem. editl. bd. Legal Aspects of Med. Practice, 1978-82. Trustee SUNY, chmn. health sci. and hosp. com. Fellow Am. Coll. Legal Medicine (mem. bd. govs. 1986, chmn. edn. com. 1983—, chmn. 1985 nat. meeting, New Orleans, chmn. 1988 nat. meeting, Va., bd. dirs. ACLM Found.), Am. Acad. Forensic Scis., Royal Soc. Medicine, Royal Soc. Arts (London), Royal Soc. Medicine (London), Roscoe Pound Found. of Assn. Trial Lawyers Am.; mem. ABA, Am. Soc. Law and Medicine, Congress Neurol. Surgeons, Assn. Trial Lawyers Am., Soc. Med. Jurisprudence (trustee), N.Y. Bar Assn., Conn. Bar Assn., Fla. Bar Assn., D.C. Bar Assn., N.Y. Acad. Scis., Assn. Trial Lawyers Am. (bd. govs.), N.Y. Trial Lawyers Assn., Conn. Trial Lawyers Assn., Fla. Acad. Trial Lawyers, Md. Trial Lawyers Assn., Tex. Trial Lawyers Assn., Pa. Trial Lawyers Assn., Nat. Bar Assn. (mem. com. on South Africa), Nassau County Bar Assn., Fairfield County Med. Soc., Nassau-Suffolk Trial Lawyers Assn. Club: Cosmos (Washington). Office: 175 E Shore Rd Great Neck NY 11023-2430

WACHSTEIN, JOAN MARTHA, dental hygienist; b. Phila., Nov. 12, 1941; d. Milton and Mabel Louise (Friedman) Hertzfeld; m. Mortimer Berwyn Wachstein, July 14, 1962 (dec. 1989); 1 child, Esther Lynn. RDH, Temple U., Phila., 1961. Registered dental hygienist; cert. gerontology referral Union Am. Hebrew Congregations and Hebrew Union Coll. Jewish Inst. Religion. Dental hygienist Dr. M.B. Wachstein, Newark, Del., 1970-89; campaign mgr. Milton and Hattie Kutz Home for Capital Campaign, 1995. Mem. allocations panel and planning coms. United Way, Wilmington, Del., 1986-92, bd. dirs., 1994-99, chair allocations panel, 1994-98, mem. strategic planning com., ethics com., 1994-95, chair spl. gifts divsn. United Way campaign, 1996; bd. dirs. Jewish Family Svcs., del., 1983-99, rec. sec., 1984-86, 88-91, pres., 1992-94, treas. 1989-91; bd. dirs. Milton and Hattie Kutz Home, Inc., 1987-99, v.p., 1988-96, treas., 1994-96, pres., 1997-99, chair nominating com., 2000—; bd. dirs. Assoc. Jewish Family and Childrens Agys., 1995-99; bd. dirs. Jewish Fedn. Del., 1983-89, 91-92, 94-97, 99, mem. exec. com., 1992-93, mem. Jewish Cmty. endowment com., 1993-99, Mid-Atlantic coun. Union Am. Hebrew Congregations, 1981—, vice chair biennial program com., 1990-92, chair 1992-94, bd. dirs., 1994—, v.p. 1992-98, pres., 1998—; trustee Union of Am. Hebrew Congregations, 1994—, mem. com. on Jewish family, 1997—, mem. commn. on religious living, mem. outreach commn. exec. com., chair com. on older adults, 1996—, com. on small congregations UAHC, 2000, biennial program com., 2000, budget com., 2000; mem. Women of Reform Judaism, Fedn. Temple Sisterhoods, 1975-97, v.p. 1987-89, 89-91, 91-93, mem. at-large bd. dirs., 1993-97; pres. Beth Emeth Sisterhood, 1968-70; mem. jr. bd. Christiana Care Del., Inc.; apptd. commn adult entertainment establishments, State of Del., 1993—; mem. N.Am. bd. World Union Progressive Judaism; mem. exec. com. ARZA/World Union N.Am., 1999—; chair Women for Carper com. for Gov. State of Del., 1993-96; vol. ombudsman State of Del. Divsn. Svcs. for Aging Adults and Adults with Phys. Disabilities, 2000. Recipient Community Builder award NCCJ, 1985, Keva cert. Ctrl. Conf. Am. Rabbis and Nat. Assn. Temple Educators. Mem. Nat. Coun. Jewish Women, Orgn. for Ednl. Resources and Tech. Tng., Temple U. Dental Hygiene Alumni Assn., B'nai B'rith, Hadassah. Jewish. Home: 3331 Silverside Rd Wilmington DE 19810-4804

WACHTEL, HANS WILHELM, multimedia company executive; b. Geldern, Germany, July 10, 1954; m. Ellen Kugler, Jan. 30, 1978; children: Jan, Lena, Timo. Diplom informatiker, RWTH, Aachen, Germany, 1980. Sys. programmer Nixdorf Computer, Paderborn, Germany, 1980-82; asst. to bd. mem. Gruner & Jahr, Hamburg, 1983-84, head dept. info. sys., 1984-86; exec. mem. G&J Electronic Media Svc. GMBH, Hamburg, 1986—; divsn. mgr. G&J Press, 1004—. Avocations: tennis, family activities. Office: G&J Electron Media Svc GMBH, 20444 Hamburg Germany

WACHTEL, JOSEPH H., sculptor; b. Gura-Putila, Ukraine, Apr. 12, 1914; came to U.S., 1962; s. Israel and Shendel W.; m. S. Pouse (dec. 1991); 1 child, Peter L. Grad. H.S., Gura-Putila, 1936; student, Palm Beach (Fla.) C.C., 1983, 1999. Mech. technician Ukraine, 1939-41; pres. Salisbury Fashion, N.Y.C., 1968-78; quality control Space Legs, N.Y.C., 1979-88. Author: (book) Escape from the Hounds of Hell, 1993. Sculptures on permanent display at Temple Beth Tikvah, Lake Worth, Fla., Yad Vashem, Jerusalem, Nat. Holocaust Mus., Washington, Mus. of Tolerance, L.A. Mem. B'nai B'rith, Holocaust Survivors Orgn. Democrat. Jewish. Avocations: fishing, walking, reading. Home: 313 Knotty Pine Cir Apt A-2 Lake Worth FL 33463-9053

WACHTEL, THOMAS LEE, surgeon; b. Mansfield, Ohio, July 25, 1938; s. Earl J. and Lorena Fredona (Lehman) W.; m. Carolyn Coleman, May 15, 1965; children: John Matthew, David Earl-Martin, Julianne Maria. AB, Western Res. U., Cleve., 1960; MD, St. Louis U., 1964; cert. naval flight surgeon, Naval Flight Sch., Pensacola, Fla., 1970; MMM, Tulane U., 1998. Diplomate Am. Bd. Surgery, Am. Bd. Med. Mgmt.; cert. added qualification in surg. critical care. Intern in surgery U. Ky., Lexington, 1964-65, resident in surgery, 1965-66; resident in surgery St. John's Mercy Hosp., St. Louis, 1966-69; pvt. practice Hamilton & Wachtel, Corbin, Ky., 1973-74; mem. surg. faculty U. N.Mex., Albuquerque, 1974-77; mem. surg. faculty U. Calif., San Diego, 1978-84, 91-96, burn dir., 1980-84, head trauma divsn., 1982-84; med. dir. trauma Samaritan Regional Med. Ctr., Phoenix, 1984-90; program dir. Phoenix Integrated Surg. Residency, 1986-90; med. dir. trauma Sharp Meml. Hosp., San Diego, 1990-96; chmn. bioengrng. faculty Ariz. State U., 1984-90; dir. trauma Centura Health St. Anthony Hosp. Ctrl., Denver, 1996—; mem. surg. faculty F. Edward Hebert Sch. Medicine USPHS, Bethesda, 1988—; mem. surg. faculty U. Ariz., Tucson, 1993—; mem. nat. faculty Advanced Burn Life Support, Omaha, 1988—; mem. surg. faculty U. Colo., Denver, 1996—. Author: Medical Exploring, 2 edits., 1973, 76, Current Topics in Burn Care, 1983, Burns of the Head and Neck, 1984; editor: A Symposium on Burns, 1985. Mem. Nat. Commn. on Exploring Boy Scouts Am., Arlington, Tex., 1972-85; mem. Flynn Found. on Commn. on Med. Manpower, Phoenix, 1987-88. With USNR, 1961-98, capt. Res. Recipient Family Practice Teaching award Am. Acad. Family Practice, Phoenix, 1985; rsch. grantee U.S. Army, NIH, HSA-HEW. Fellow ACS (gov. 1995—), Am. Assn. Surgery of Trauma, Am. Coll. Critical Care Medicine; mem. Am. Burn Assn. (pres. 1989-90), Phi Gamma Delta, Phi Chi (pres. Phi Rho chpt. 1963-64), Omicron Delta Kappa, Sigma Delta Psi. Roman Catholic. Avocations: travel, hiking, woodworking, fishing, skiing. Office: Centura Health St Anthony Hosp Ctrl Trauma Dept 4231 W 16th Ave Denver CO 80204-1335

WACHTELL, ESTHER, non-profit management executive, consultant; b. June 30; m. Thomas Wachtell, Jan. 27; children: Roger Bruce, Wendy Anne, Peter James. BA in Phil., Conn. Coll., 1956; MA in Literature, Cornell U., 1957. Pres. Music Ctr. of Los Angeles County; founder, pres. The Wachtell Group, TWG, Inc.; lectr. UCLA Grad. Sch. of Mgmt. Bd. dirs. Town Hall of Calif.; bd. visitors George L. Graziadio Sch. of Bus. Pepperdine U., The Ventura County Mus. of History and Art; chair non-profit rsch. ctr. Sch. of Pub. Policy and Devel. U. of Southern Calif.; bd. regents Children's Hosp. L.A. Mem. Regency Club. Fax: 805-649-3303.

WÄCHTERSHÄUSER, GÜNTER, patent lawyer, researcher; b. Giessen, Hesse, Germany, Aug. 30, 1938; s. Wilhelm and Lina (Kieper) W.; m. Dorothy Laura Gray, May 23, 1970. Diploma in chemistry, U. Marburg, 1963, D in Natural Scis., 1965. Registered German patent atty. 1970; rep. European Patent Office, 1978. Pvt. practice Munich, 1970—; second Sol Spiegelman lecture, 1998. Contbr. articles to profl. jours. Recipient Ann. award Bavarian Acad. Sci., 1993, Bonn Chemistry award U. Bonn, 1999; named hon. prof. U. Regensburg, 1994. Mem. Gesellschaft Deutscher Chemiker, Deutsche Patentanwaltskammer, Internat. Fedn. Indsl. Property Attys., Internat. Soc. for Study of Origin of Life. E-mail: info@patent.de. Office: TAL 29, D-80331 Munich Germany

WACHTMEISTER, THOMAS AXEL WILHELM, manufacturing company executive; b. Stockholm, Oct. 23, 1931; s. Shering and Adrienne (de Geer) W.; m. Aurore von Essen, 1956; children: Alexandra, Carl-Frederik, Philip. Grad., Stockholm Sch. Econs., 1956. Various positions in shipping and banking U.S., 1956-59; asst. to mng. dir. Atlas Copco AB, Stockholm, 1959-73, group pres., 1975-91, vice chmn., 1991-98; lord chamberlain to King of Sweden, 1973-75; chmn. Sweden-China Trade Coun., Optima Batteries; bd. dirs. Brit.-Swedish C. of C., Investment AB, Norsk Hydro, Norway, North Atlantic Nat. Resources, Swedish-Am. C. of C., N.Y.; chmn. Inkina. Mem. Gen. Export Assn. Sweden (vice chmn.). Fax: 46 0 8 662 3115. Office: Tom wacco AB, Box 5501, S-114 85 Stockholm Sweden

WACHUTKA, GERHARD KARL MAXIMILIAN, electrotechnological physics educator, researcher; b. Cham, Oberpfalz, Germany; s. Kurt and Anna (Zierl) W.; m. Renate Adelheid Haberer, June 7, 1985; children: Leonhard, Korbinian. MS, Ludwig-Maximilian U., Munich, 1973, DSc., 1985. Rsch. asst. U. Munich, 1978-85; modeling engr. Siemens Cen. R&D, 1985-88; sr. scientist Fritz Haber Inst. of Max Planck Soc., Berlin, 1989-90; sr. rschr. Swiss Fed. Inst. Tech., Zurich, Switzerland, 1990-94; prof. tech. U. Munich, Germany, 1994—; cons. Siemens Rsch. Lab., Munich, 1989—. Contbr. numerous articles to profl. jours. Squad leader Civil Svc., Munich, 1972-85. Recipient Best Paper award Eurosensors, San Sebastian, Spain, 1992. Mem. IEEE, Am. Electrochem. Soc., German Phys. Soc. Roman Catholic. Avocations: mountaineering, sailing, folk dancing. Home: Schwanenweg 28, D-81827 Munich Germany Office: Tech U Physics Electrotech, Arcisstrasse 21, D-80290 Munich Germany

WACKER, ELISABETH, sociologist, educator; b. Hohenstadt, Bavaria, Germany, Dec. 23, 1954; d. Erich Walter and Maria Theresia (Hesse) W.; m. Friedrich August Bootz, May 21, 1987; children: Philip Friedrich, Robert Jakob. BSc in Theology, U. Tübingen, Germany, 1980, D in Sociology, 1989. Lectr. sociology Tech. Coll., Stuttgart, Germany, 1980-81; rschr. U. Tübingen, 1982-86, dir. rsch. inst. on lives of handicapped persons, 1982-96; lectr. Coll. Edn., Reutling, Germany, 1995-96; prof. U. Dortmund, Germany, 1996—, dean faculty rehab., 1998—. Mem. German Sociol. Assn., Internat. Erich Fromm Assn., Inst. for Rehab. Sci. (mem. mng. com. 1994—). Avocations: tennis, skiing. Home: Domänenstr 52, D-44225 Dortmund Germany Office: Univ Dortmund Dept Sociol, Faculty 13 Figge St 50, D-44221 Dortmund Germany

WACKER, SUSAN REGINA, cosmetic design director; b. Red Bank, N.J., Apr. 29, 1954; d. Durward Richard and Margaret Rose (Williams) W. BFA, Pratt Inst., 1978. Asst. art dir. Lesley-Hille Inc., N.Y.C., 1975-79; art dir. Kasica, Lefton, Brown, Inc., N.Y.C., 1979-80, Marinelli & Hnath Assocs., Inc., N.Y.C., 1980-82; sr. design dir. Elizabeth Arden Co., N.Y.C., 1982-99; art dir. Cosmair/L'Oreal Retail Divsn., N.Y.C., 2000—. Exhibited at The Nature of Diamonds, Mus. Natural History, N.Y.C., 1997-98; patentee in field. Fellow Mus. Modern Art; supporting mem. Cooper Hewitt Mus.; friend mem. Whitney Mus.; active Met. Mus. Art. Recipient (4) DESI awards, 1980, ANDY award, 1980, Fragrance Found. award, 1988, 91, 92, Silver award N.J. Packaging Execs. Club, 1990, ADDY Excellence citation, 1991, Edison Best New Products Gold Medal award, 1991, (2) Gold awards Nat. Paperbox & Packaging Assn., 1992, (2) Gold awards, 1994, Silver award Paperboard Packaging Coun., 1993, Excellence award, 1993, Silver Excellence award Nat. Paperbox & Packaging Assn., 1993, (10) Silver Excellence awards, 1994, Mobius 1st Place Statuette award, 1995, Gold award Nat. Paperboard Coun., 1995, Prix Francois 1st de L'Emballage de Luxe, 1995, OMA Gold award, 1995, Oscar de L'Emballage Prestige à Lyon, 1995, Mobius award First Place Statuette for Elizabeth Taylor's Black Pearls perfume product line/package design, 1996, OMA Gold award for Elizabeth Arden's 5th Avenue tester display, 1996, OMA Bronze award for Elizabeth Taylor's Black Pearls tester display, 1996, Lagerfeld, Jako Mchdsg., 1998, CPC "Package of the Month" (October), Elizabeth Arden's 5th Avenue fragrance line, 1996, Natl. Paperboard Packaging Conc. award, 1996, OMA Bronze award Lagerfeld JAKO Merchandising Program, 1998. Mem. Internat. Perfume Bottle Assn., Cosmetic Exec. Women Found., Fashion Group Internat. Avocations: skiing, tennis, horseback riding, photography. Office: Cosmair/L'Oreal Retail Divsn 575 Fifth Ave New York NY 10017

WACKERMANN, GABRIEL, education educator; b. Woerth, Alsace, France, Mar. 18, 1928; s. George and Marie (Zimmermann) W.; m. Arlette Martin; children: Marie Francoise, Jean Brice, Marie Emmanuelle. LLB, Lycee de Haguenau, France, 1946; M in Geography, U. Strasbourg, France, 1951, D in Geography, 1973; Prof Agrege, Paris, 1975. Prof Lycee Couffignal of Strasbourg, 1952-72; Prof. agrege U. Strasbourg III, 1975-79; prof. U. Haute-Alsace, 1979-90, U. Sorbonne, Paris, 1990—; dir. Inst. Promotion Superieure du Travail, U. Strasbourg, 1972-76, dept. Langs. Etrangeres Appliquees, U. Haute-Alsace, 1978-80, dean of faculty of lettres and human scis., 1980-86, dir. Internat. Inst. Transp.; dir. Doctorate Sch. in Transp., U. Sorbonne, 1990—. Author 40 books, including Tourisme et transport, 1994, Loisir et tourisme-une internationalisation, Géopolitique de l'espace Mondial, 1997, La nouvelle Europe Centrale, 1997, La civilisation des services, 1997, Façades Maritimes en mutation, 1998, La Géographie humaine—Une approche socio-politique, 2000; contbr. more than 400 articles to profl. jours./publs. Chmn. econ. and social group, Alsace FEC, Strasbourg, 1980—; chmn. European Congress of Recreation, Strasbourg, 1961-83; pres. FEC/Strasbourg; adviser Geopolitics of Ency. U. Paris, 1987—. Hon. dir. Inst. de Promotion Supérieure du Travail of Louis-Pasteur of Strasbourg U., 1979. Mem. Acad. Planning of Germany (corr. mem.), Acad. Messina/Italy, French Assn. Sci. Experts of Tourism (vice-chmn. 1980-94), Nat. Com. of Geography/France (treas., vice chmn. 1988-96), French Assn. Geographers (mem. com. 1986—), U. Pluridisciplinaire Paris, Cannes-Univ. Home: 180 Rte d'Oberhausbergen, F-67200 Strasbourg France Office: Inst Geographie U Paris-Sorbonne, 191 Rue Saint-Jacques, F-75005 Paris France

WACKERMANN, JIRI, research scientist; b. Roudnice, Czechoslovakia, Mar. 14, 1955; s. Vaclav and Helena (Hrdlickova) W.; m. Ladislava Svandova, Sept. 20, 1976 (div. 1980); 1 child, Margareta; m. Anna Neradova, Dec. 6, 1985; children: Marie, Katerina. Diploma in psychology, Charles U., Prague, Czechoslovakia, 1981, DPhil, 1985. Rsch. worker Inst. Physiol. Regulations, Czech Acad. Scis., Prague, 1983-88; asst. lectr. Inst. Postgrad. Med. Studies, Prague, 1989-90; rsch. worker Psychiat. Rsch. Inst., Prague, 1990-92; gen. mgr. Neurosci. Tech. Rsch., Prague, 1993-97; head of psychophysiology dept. Inst. fur Grenzgebiette der Psychologie, Freiburg, Germany, 1998—; organised symposium "Cognition and Volition under Anomalous Conditions", 10th IOP Congress, Sydney, 2000, symposium "Frontiers of Psychology I, II", Prague, 1999, 2000. Postdoctoral rsch. fellow U. Hosp. Dept. Neurology, Zurich, 1991, 92-93. Mem. AAAS, Czech Med. Assn., N.Y. Acad. Scis., Soc. for Scientific Exploration, Parapsychol. Assn. Avocations: history of science and philosophy, astronomy.

WADA, MASAOMI, pediatrician; b. Himeji, Hyogo, Japan, Mar. 12, 1964; s. Hiroshi and Taeko (Watanabe) W.; m. Yumiko Yoshino, July 7, 1995; children: Hiiro, Kanon. PhD, Oita (Japan) Med. U., 1995. Med. chief Fujimoto Childrens Hosp., Oita, 1995—, Oita Med. U. Hosp., Oita, 1997—. Mem. Japan Pediat. Soc., Japanese Soc. Child Neurology. Office: Oita Med Univ, Dept Pediat, 879-5593 Oita Japan

WADA, TAKAO, physics educator; b. Kawasaki, Kanagawa, Japan, July 23, 1930; s. Akira and Yoshimi Suzuki; m. Tomoko Wada, Mar. 23, 1960; children: Noriko, Takanobu, Mototake. BEE, Ehime U., Matsuyama, Japan, 1954; postgrad., Osaka (Japan) U., 1959; PhD in Engring., Nagoya (Japan) U., 1965. Researcher Kobe (Japan) Kogyo Corp., 1954-59; rsch. asst. Nagoya U., 1959-65, lectr., 1965-66, assoc. prof., 1966-70; prof. Mie U., Tsu, Japan, 1970-84; prof. Nagoya Kogyo U., Nagoya Inst. Tech., 1984-94, life prof. emeritus, 1994—; prof. Daido Inst. Tech., Nagoya, 1994—; vis. scholar Northwestern U., Evanston, Ill., 1974-75. Contbr. over 190 articles to profl. jours. Grantee Ministry Edn., 1985-87, Casio Sci. Found., 1984, Murata Sci. Found., 1985, NEC Corp., 1985-92. Mem. Japan Soc. Applied Physics (councillor 1982-89), Phys. Soc. Japan, Inst. Electronics, Info. and Comm. Engrs. (councillor 1984-89), Electrochem. Soc., N.Y. Acad. Scis. Achievements include patents on methods of impurity doping. Avocation: painting. Home: 293-7 Torii-cho, Tsu 514, Japan Office: Daido Inst Tech, Daido-cho, Minami-ku, Nagoya 457, Japan

WADA, YUTAKA, patent information executive; b. Sapporo, Hokkaido, Japan, Feb. 2, 1932; s. Hiroshi and Toki (Hirano) W.; m. Makiko Hirate, Apr. 15, 1940; children: Takeshi, Kaori. BA, Tokyo U., 1953; Grad., London Sch. Economics, 1963. Cert. Nat. Civil Svc. With Ministry of Internat. Trade and Industry, Tokyo, 1953-64; first sec. Japanese Embassy to United Arab Rep., 1964-68; dir. policy review and assessment sec. Small and Medium Enterprise Agy. MITI, Tokyo, 1968-69; counselor Japanese permanent delegation Internat. Orgn., Geneva, 1972-75; dir. gen. multilateral trade dept. MITI, Tokyo, 1975-76; dir. gen. first examination dept. Patent Office, Tokyo, 1978-79, dir. gen., gen. adminstrn. dept., 1979-80; dir. gen. Bur. of Equipment, Defense Agency, Tokyo, 1980-82; exec. dir., bd. dir. The Overseas Economic Cooperation Fund, Tokyo, 1982-84; with Sharp Corp., Osaka, 1984—, exec. dir., bd. dir., 1985—, group gen. mgr. internat. bus. group, 1986-89, sr. exec., dir., mem. of exec. com., 1989-91, sr. exec., v.p. for internat. bus., mem. exec. com., 1991-95, sr. exec. v.p., then corp. sr. exec. v.p. external rels., mem. exec. com., 1995—; interviewed by CNN Worldwide, 1994. Bimonthly articles contbr. (under Yasuhiko Hiromi) Keizai-kai Bus. Jour., 1980-82; contbr. articles Nippon Keizai Shinbun, 1994, The Nikkei Weekly, 1994, The Asian Wall Street Journal, 1994. Mem. Kansai Economic Fedn. (spl. com. on internat. bus. mgmt., 1993-94), The Osaka Indsl. Assn. (internat. community rels. com. 1993—), Osaka Fgn. Trade Assn. (dir. 1994—), Japan-China Investment Promotion Orgn. (dir. 1993—). Avocations: golf, swimming, skiing, go, reading. Office: Japan Patent Info Orgn, 1-7 Toyo 4 chome Koto-ku, Tokyo 135-0016, Japan

WADDINGTON, DAVID JAMES, chemistry educator; b. Edgware, Middlesex, U.K., May 27, 1932; s. Eric James and Marjorie Edith (Harding) W.; m. Isobel Hesketh, Aug. 17, 1957; children: Matthew James, Rupert John, Jessica Katharine. BSc, Imperial Coll., London, 1953, PhD, 1956. Head of sci. dept. Wellington Coll., Berkshire, 1960-64; sr. lectr. U. York, U.K., 1965-78, prof., 1978—. Co-author: Organic Chemistry Through Experiment, 4th edit., 1985, Modern Organic Chemistry, 4th edit., 1985, Chemistry: The Salters' Approach, 1990, Chemical Storylines, Salters Advanced Chemistry, 1994, Chemical Ideas, Salters Advanced Chemistry, 1994; editor: Chemical Education in the Seventies, 2d edit., 1982, Teaching School Chemistry, 1985, Education, Industry and Technology, 1987, Bringing Chemistry to Life, 1992, Science for Understanding Tomorrow's World: Global Change, 1994, Global Environmental Change Science: Education and Training, 1995, Partners in Chemical Education, 1996, Salters Higher Chemistry, 1999, The Essential Chemical Industry, 1999. Recipient Nyholm medal Royal Soc. of Chemistry, 1985, Brasted award Am. Chem. Soc., 1988, Brazilian Nat. Order Scientific Merit, 1997; hon. prof. Mendeleev U. of Chem. Tech., Moscow, 1998. Mem. Internat. Coun. Sci. Unions (chmn. com. tchg. sci. 1989-93). Office: U York, York YO 10 5DD, England

WADDINGTON, GORDON STUART, physiotherapist, researcher; b. Sydney, NSW, Australia, June 26, 1959; s. Russel Stuart and Nancye Kinman (Gordon) W.; m. Catherine Margaret Pearson, Mar. 30, 1985; children: Anna, Freya, Ainsley, Ross. BS, U. Sydney, 1981; B in Applied Sci. Physiotherapy, Cumberland U., Sydney, 1986, diploma in applied sci., 1989; M in Applied Sci. Exercise, U. Sydney, 1994, M in Applied Sci. Sports Physiotherapy, 1995. Physiotherapist Wyo. Physiotherapy, Gosford, 1986-88, North Gosford Hosp., 1988-91; chief physiotherapist Berkeley Vale Hosp., 1991-93, Wyo. Physiotherapy, Gosford, 1993-97, Brindabella Physiotherapy, Canberra, 1997—; dir. Brindabella Phys. Rehab. Rsch. Ctr., Canberra, 1997—. Co-author: Clinical Workbook Sports Physiotherapy, 1995; contbr. articles to profl. jours. including Phys. Therapy Revs., Australian Jour. Physiotherapy. Fellow Sports Medicine Australia; mem. Australian Physiotherapy Assn. (specialization com. 1998—, acad. stds. com. 1996—), Internat. Triathlon Union (sec. med. com. 1996-98), Am. Coll. Sports Medicine, Internat. Fedn. Sports Medicine. Avocations: running, cycling. Office: Brindabella Physiotherapy, 14/5 Dann Close, Garran ACT 2605, Australia

WADDINGTON, JOHN PAUL, social sciences researcher, educator, consultant; b. Bradford, Yorks, Eng., Aug. 31, 1937; s. Walter and Ada Beatrice (Hobden) W.; m. Sheila Kathryn Ingham; children: Clare Elizabeth, Hugh James, Katherine Emma, Anna Bridget, Megan Jean. BA with honors, U. Durham, 1958; postgrad. diploma in town planning, Coll. of Arts, Birmingham, Eng., 1964. Chartered town planner. Various planning positions Staffordshire, Coventry & Notts, Derbies Local Authorities & John Madin Design Group, 1961-69; cmty. worker Coventry Nottinham CVS, 1969-70; lectr. in urban and social planning Coventry Polytechnic, 1971-73; rsch. fellow U. York, 1973-76; sr., prin. lectr. U. Ctrl. Eng., Birmingham, 1976-83, head of dept., asst. dean, 1983-93, emeritus prof. applied social studies; profl. rsch. fellow, cons., rschr. Shropshire Social Svcs. Dept., Shrewsbury, 1992—, Sandwell Health Authority and Social Svcs. Dept., West Bromwich, 1992-96, Warwickshire Health Authority, Social Svcs. Dept., and Arley G.P. Practice, 1995-97, Neptune Health Park Project, 1996-98, Beyond the Surgery Walls Project, Coventry Health Authority, 1998-99, Ladywood Primary Care Group, Birmingham, 1999—. Author: (with N. Moor) From Rags to Ruins, 1980; contbr. more than 50 articles to profl. publs. Mem. coun. Royal Town Planning Inst., London, 1964-66; chair Digbeth Trust, Birmingham, 1990, Charities Evaluation Svcs., London, 1993. Lt. Royal Engrs. Army, 1959-61. Rockefeller grantee U. Durham, 1958. Mem. Lunar Soc. Roman Catholic. Avocations: family, walking, reading, writing, gardening. Office: U Ctrl Eng Fac Health & Social Scis, Perry Barr, Birmingham B42 Z5U, England

WADDLES, LORI BOBBITT, lawyer; b. Detroit, May 2, 1963; d. Darwin and Alice Belden; m. Robert Terry Bobbit, Jr., July 15, 1989 (div. Oct. 30, 1994); 1 child, Erin Elyse Bobbitt; m. Alvin Bernard Waddles, June 22, 1996; 1 child, Dominic Christopher Darwin. BA, Western Mich. U., 1985; JD, Detroit Coll. Law, 1988. Law clk. Mich. Supreme Ct., Detroit, 1988-90; assoc. atty. Howard & Howard, Bloomfield Hills, Mich., 1990-95; asst. corp. counsel City of Detroit, 1995-96; asst. gen. counsel Blue Cross & Blue Shield Mich., Detroit, 1996-99; chief investigator Office of Investigator/Detroit Police, 1999—. Trustee Western Mich. U., Kalamazoo, 1993—. Avocation: singing. Office: Office of Chief Investigator 2111 Woodward Ave Fl 8 Detroit MI 48201-3421

WADE, CLAIRE MARGARET, animal scientist, educator; b. Bankstown, N.S.W., Australia, Jan. 25, 1964; d. Keith austin and Adele Margaret (Stork) W. BSc with honors, U N.S.W., 1986, PhD, 1990; Grad. Cert. in Edn., U. Queensland, 1997. Quantitative geneticist Victorian Inst. of Animal Sci., Melbourne, 1990-91; lectr. animal breeding and genetics U. Queensland, Brisbane, 1992—. Contbr. articles to profl. jours. Mem. Assn. for advancement of Animal Breeding and Genetics. Avocations: reading, sailboarding, horseback riding. Office: Univ of Queensland, Sch of Vet Sci, Brisbane 4072 QLD, Australia

WADE, DAVID, biochemist; s. George H. and Agnes Wade. BS, Del. Valley Coll.; MS, Fairleigh Dickinson U.; PhD, U. Medicine and Dentistry N.J. Rsch. assoc. Rockefeller U., N.Y.C., 1988-91; postdoctoral fellow P.E.N.C.E., U. Alberta, Can., 1992-93; vis. scientist Karolinska Inst., Stockholm, 1994, 96-98, Haartman Inst., Helsinki (Finland) U., 1998, 99; asst. prof. Kuwait U. Faculty of Medicine, 1998—. Contbr. articles to profl. jours. Recipient Alumni award in Sci., Del. Valley Coll., 1991. Mem. AAAS, Am. Peptide Soc., European Peptide Soc. Office: Kuwait U Faculty Medicine, Dept Biochem PO Box 24923, 13110 Safat Kuwait

WADE, HENRY WILLIAM RAWSON, legal scholar, author; b. London, Jan. 16, 1918; s. Henry Oswald and Eileen Lucy (Rawson-Ackroyd) W.; m. Marie Osland-Hill, Oct. 15, 1943 (dec. 1980); children: John Michael Ackroyd, Edward Henry Rawson; m. Marjorie Grace Hope Browne, Oct.

15, 1982. BA, U. Cambridge, Eng., 1939; DLitt (hon.), U. Cambridge, 1998. With His Majesty's Treasury, 1940-46; lectr. U. Cambridge, 1947-59, reader, 1959-61, master Gonville and Caius Coll., 1976-88, Rouse Ball prof. English law, 1978-82; prof. English law U. Oxford, Eng., 1961-76. Author: (with B. Schwartz) Towards Administrative Justice, 1963, Legal Control of Government, 1972, Constitutional Fundamentals, 1980, (with Sir R. Megarry) The Law of Real Property, 2000, (with C.F. Forsyth) Administrative Law, 2000; contbr. articles to profl. jours. Named to Queen's Counsel, 1968, Knight Bachelor The Queen, 1985. Fellow Brit. Acad. (v.p. 1981-83); mem. Alpine Club, London. Avocations: mountaineering, gardening, music. Home: The Green 1A Ludlow Ln, Cambridge CB1 5BL, England Office: Gonville and Caius Coll, Cambridge CB2 1TA, England

WADE, NICHOLAS JAMES, psychologist, educator; b. Retford, Eng., Mar. 27, 1942; s. William John and Sarah Ellen (Ostick) W.; m. Christine Whetton; children: Rebecca Jane, Helena Kate. BSc, U. Edinburgh, 1965; PhD, Monash U., 1968. Lectr., reader U. Dundee, U.K., 1970-91; prof. U. Dundee, 1991—. Author: Psychologists in Word and Image, 1995, Visual Perception: An Introduction, 1991, Visual Allusions, 1990, Brewster and Wheatstone on Vision, 1983, A Natural History of Vision, 1998. Fellow Royal Soc. Edinburgh. Office: Dept Psychology, Univ Dundee, Dundee DD1 4HN, Scotland

WADE, ROBERT ALAN, lawyer; b. Coronado, Calif., July 10, 1955; s. John William and Betty Lou (Schrader) W.; m. Barbara Louise Waters, June 18, 1977 (div.); children: John Robert, Matthew Waters; m. Eileen L. Guest, Sept. 24, 1990; stepchildren: Nathaniel Craig, Adrian Louise. BA, Coll. William and Mary, 1977; JD magna cum laude, Harvard U., 1980. Bar: Pa. 1980, U.S. Dist. Ct. (ea. dist.) Pa. 1980. Assoc. Schnader, Harrison, Segal & Lewis, Phila., 1980-85, Kalogredis Law Assocs., Ltd., Wayne, Pa., 1985; ptnr. Kalogredis & Wade Law Assocs., Wayne, 1986-89, Beck & Anders Law Assocs., Plymouth Meeting, Pa., 1989-93, Wade, Goldstein, Landau & Abruzzo, PC, Berwyn, Pa., 1993—; lectr., cons. and spkr. in field. Contbr. articles to profl. jours. Spkr. to various civic, local, and nat. groups. Mem. ABA, Pa. Bar Assn. (com. on profl. responsibility and legal ethics 1987-96), Phila. Bar Assn. (mem. sect. on probate trust law, office practices com. 1981-86). Democrat. Presbyterian. Home: 4020 Prospect Hill Ln Pottstown PA 19464-2245 Office: Wade Goldstein Landau & Abruzzo PC 61 Cassatt Ave Berwyn PA 19312-1325

WADE, ROYCE ALLEN, financial services representative; b. Medford, Wis., Apr. 30, 1932; s. Charles L. and Mildred H. (Clarin) W.; m. Corinne Mae Weber, June 30, 1956; children: Suzanne Mae, Debra Ann. BS (acad. scholar), U. Wis., Stevens Point, 1954; MDiv, Garrett Theol. Sem., Evanston, Ill., 1960; MS in Adult Edn., U. Wis., Milw., 1968; postgrad., U. Wis., Madison, 1970-75; grad., Realtors Inst. Ordained to ministry Meth. Ch., 1960; cert. pastoral counseling and interpersonal relations. Pastor Richmond (Wis.) Meth. Ch., 1956-58, Asbury United Meth. Ch., Janesville, Wis., 1958-61; tchr., guidance counselor Edgerton (Wis.) H.S., 1961-62; assoc. pastor Community United Meth. Ch., Whitefish Bay, Wis., 1962-66; pastor Simpson and Gardner United Meth. Chs., Milw., 1966-68; assoc. pastor St. Luke United Meth. Ch., Sheboygan, Wis., 1968-69; pastor Poynette and Inch United Meth. Chs., 1969-74; dir. Adult Study Ctr., Portage, Wis., 1974-75; dir. growth and devel. Profl. Products & Svcs., Inc., Sauk City, Wis., 1976-83; realtor Dick Marquardt Agy., Poynette, 1983-86, Don Lee Realty, Inc., Portage, 1986-87, Noble Properties, Poynette, 1987, Anchor Real Estate Svcs., Madison, 1988-93; personal fin. analyst Primerica Fin. Svcs., Madison, 1992-2000; HRD cons., 1983-96; curriculum cons. U. Wis. Sch. Nursing, 1974-76, instr. small group seminar, 1974-76, supr. behavioral disabilities student tchrs., 1974-76; adult edn. instr. Wis. Conf. United Meth. Ch., 1964-69. Village trustee Poynette, 1977-81; mem. Police Aux., Whitefish Bay; bd. dirs. North Shore Coun. Human Relations, Milw., Inter Faith Coun., Milw., Poynette Area Cmty. Devel. Orgn., 1983-87. Served with C.I.C., U.S. Army, 1954-56. Mem. ASTD, Adult Edn. Assn., Nat. Assn. Realtors, Wis. Realtors Assn., Optimists, Phi Delta Kappa. Achievements include research on participation in adult instructional groups using Eriksonian ego-stage theory. Home: PO Box 115 Poynette WI 53955-0115

WADHER, BHARAT JIVRAJ, microbiology educator; b. Nagpur, Maharastra, India, July 6, 1952; s. Jivraj Chhotalal and Bhagwati Jivraj (Patriwala) W.; m. Rekha Bharat Chowhan, May 2, 1982; children: Paras, Dimple. BSc in Biology, Nagpur U., 1975, MSc in Microbiology, 1977, PhD in Microbiology, 1985. Lectr. Nagpur U., 1977-85, sr. lectr., 1986-90, reader, 1991—, mem. bd. studies, 1995-99, mem. faculty sci., 1995-99, mem. bd. exam., 1995-99, mem. PhD referee com., 1995-99; postdoctoral fellow King's Coll., London, 1987-89. Author: Textbook of Diagnostic Microbiology, 1995; co-author: Citric Acid as a Antimicrobial Agent, 1998. Recipient jr. rsch. fellowship Univ. Grant Commn. New Delhi, 1978, postdoctoral fellowship Govt. India, New Delhi, 1987. Mem. Assn. Microbiologists of India (life), Hosp. Infection Soc. (life), Assn. U. Tchrs. (exec. mem. 1998—). Avocations: reading, writing, yoga, educational tours, management of annual social gathering. Home: Pannase Layout, Jaitala Rd, Nagpur 440016, India Office: Nagpur U LIT Premises, Microbiology Dept, Nagpur 440010, India

WADSTRÖM, LARS BERNHARD, urologist, medical administrator; b. Saltsjöbaden, Stockholm, Mar. 10, 1925; s. Carl Bernhard and Gunild Maria (Österberg) W.; m. Anita Maria Wehtje, Dec. 18, 1949; children: Carl, Jonas, Anna, Malin, Tomas. MD, Karolinska Inst., Stockholm, 1950, PhD, 1962; Dipl. R&D, CEI, Geneva, Switzerland, 1970. Med. diplomate in gen. surgery and urology. Postgrad. med. tng. Univ. Hosps., Stockholm, 1950-59; asst. prof. Karolinska Inst., Stockholm, 1962-70; med. dir. Univ. Clinics, Basel, Switzerland, 1970-76; chmn. dept. urology Malmö Gen. Hosp. U. Lund, Sweden, 1976-90; cons. WHO, Geneva, 1991-93; pvt. practice Falsterbo, Sweden, 1990—; chmn. State Coun. Urology Edn., Stockholm, 1986-92; pres. Regional Oncologic Bd., Lund, 1986-92, Found. for Urology Rsch., Malmö, Sweden, 1976—. Contbr. articles to profl. jours. Vice pres. Sch. Authority, Djursholm/Stockholm, 1960-70. Comdr. Royal Swedish Navy, 1956-66. Fellow Internat. Urol. Soc.; mem. Swedish Urol. Soc. (hon., pres. 1982-88), Swedish Med. Assn. (ednl. com. 1985-91), Swiss Urol. Soc. (corr.), Rotary (bd. dirs. 1985-91). Avocations: farming, travel, hunting, skiing, yachting. Home and Office: S Fågelsträcket 20, S-23940 Falsterbo Sweden

WADSWORTH, BILL, producer; b. Chickasha, Okla., Mar. 12, 1941; s. Evard W. and Ann Wadsworth; children: Pamela Goode, Amanda Ogden. BBA, U. Okla., 1964; MA, U. So. Calif., 1970. Dir. Omega Prodns., Milw., 1970-71; prodr., dir. Univ. Wis. Media Ctr., Milw., 1971-76; faculty Univ. Tex., Austin, 1977; prodr., dir. Bill Wadsworth Prodns., Austin, 1978—. Dir., writer: Tailypo: An Appalachan Tale, 1990 (Booklist Editor's Choice 1990), Another Half, 1985 (Booklist Editor's Choice 1986), First Things First, 1983 (Golden Eagle award Coun. Internat. Non-theatrical Events 1983); dir. Porfirio Salinas: Boy Born to Paint, 1995 (Silver Star award Houst Internat. Film Fest award 1995). Capt. U.S. Army, 1964-67. Recipient Gold plague award Chgo. Internat. Film Fest, 1990, 4 Golden Eagle awards Coun. Internat. Nontheatrical Events, 1973-90. Mem. Film Arts Found. Democrat. Office: Bill Wadsworth Prodns 3660 Church St Occidental CA 95465

WAERN, RASMUS LENNART, editor, architect; b. Gothenburg, Sweden, Dec. 14, 1961; s. Lennart Fredrik and Kerstin Edit (Bäckman) W.; m. Karin Maria Åberg, Sept. 2, 1989; children: Mauritz, Tom, Felix. MArch, Chalmers U., Gothenburg, Sweden, 1988, PhD, 1996. Author: The Time of the Competitions, 1996, Guide to the Architecture of Stockholm, 1998; editor Bibliotekstjänst AB, 1986—, Arkitektur, 1996—, Bra Böckers Lexikon 2000 (all architecture and town planning), 1996-99; contbr. articles to profl. jours. Vice pres. Swedish Mus. Architecture, 2000—; curator Architecture of the 20th Century: Sweden exhbn. German Arch. Mus., 1998. Melchior Wernstedt Found. grantee, 1989; recipient Olle Engkvist prize Stockholm Bldg. Soc., 1991. Mem. Nat. Assn. Swedish Architects, Assn. Internat. Critiques d'Art. Avocations: skating, sailing. Home: Daggstigen 3, S-16355 Spånga Sweden Office: Arkitektur, PO Box 1742, S-11187 Stockholm Sweden

WAESCHE, R(ICHARD) H(ENLEY) WOODWARD, combustion research scientist; b. Balt., Dec. 20, 1930; s. J(oseph) Edward and Margaret Steuart (Woodward) W.; m. Lucy Spotswood White, June 29, 1957; children: Charles Russell, Ann Spotswood. BA, Williams Coll., 1952; postgrad. U. Ala., 1956-58; MA, Princeton U., 1962, PhD, 1965. Rsch. scientist Rohm & Haas Redstone div., Huntsville, Ala., 1954-59; rsch. asst. Princeton U., 1961-64; sr. rsch. scientist Rohm & Haas, Huntsville, 1964-66; sr. rsch. engr. United Tech. Rsch. Ctr., East Hartford, Conn., 1966-81; prin. scientist Atlantic Rsch. Corp., Gainesville, Va., 1981-93, Sci. Applications Internat. Corp., 1993—; cons. Goodyear Corp., 1959-60, Princeton U., 1965, NRC, 1985-86, NASA, 1987—, Def. Adv. Rsch. Project Agy., 1988—, Directed Techs, 1989—, Atlantic Rsch. Corp., 1992—, Battelle Meml. Inst., 1992—, Calif. Inst. Tech., 1995—. Assoc. editor Jour. Spacecraft and Rockets, 1975-80, editor-in-chief, 1980-86, Jour. Propulsion and Power, 1986—; contbr. numerous articles to profl. jours.; mem. exec. bd. Dictionary of Modern Science and Technology; mem. exec. adv. bd. Encyclopedia of Physical Science and Technology. Chmn. Fine Arts Commn., Glastonbury, Conn., 1975-77. Served to cpl. U.S. Army, 1952-54. Recipient JANNAF Recognition award, 1988; Guggenheim fellow, 1959-61. Fellow AIAA (chmn. propellants and combustion tech. com. 1975-77, propulsion tech. group coord. 1979-81, tech. activities com. 1979—, publs. com. 1980—, inst. devel. com. 1988-93, fin. com. 1988—, dir. propulsion & energy 1992-95, bd. dirs. 1992-95, Best Paper in Solid Rockets 1989); mem. Am. Phys. Soc., Combustion Inst., Nat. Def. Indsl. Assn., Internat. Pyrotechnics Soc., Sigma Xi. Episcopalian. Home: 4319 Banbury Dr Gainesville VA 20155-1122 Office: Sci Applications Internat Corp 1410 Spring Hill Rd Mc Lean VA 22102-3008

WAFULA, RICHARD MAKHANU, literary critic, researcher; b. Bungoma, Kenya, Jan. 1, 1960; came to U.S., 1998; s. Makhanu Nicholas and Naliaka Rezpah (Makhanu) W.; m. Margaret N. Situluku, Apr. 18, 1989; children: Gideon, Eddah, Jael, William. BEd in ARts, Nairobi U., Kenya, 1984, MA in Lit., 1992. Tchr. Tchrs. Svc. Commn., Kenya, 1984-87; lectr. Kenyatta U., 1989-92, 92-98, Nairobi U., 1992; lit. critic, rschr., 1998—. Editor: (collection of short stories) Pendo La Heba na Hadithi Nyingine, 1997; author: (criticism-drama) Uhakiki Wa Tamthilia, 1999. Educator, Ford-Kenya Civic Edn., Kenya, 1992. Mem. Writers Assn. Kenya (asst. sec. 1993-94). Quaker. E-mail: rwafula@indiana.edu. Home: Box 204, Tongaren, Bungoma Kenya Office: Comparative LIt Dept Ballan 914 Bloomington IN 47405

WAGA, MATEUSZ TOMASZ, engineer; b. Wroclaw, Poland, Nov. 1, 1972; s. Zbigniew Tomasz and Maria (Kryszakowicz) W. MSc, Tech. U. of Wroclaw, 1998. Specialist Inst. of Telecomm., Wroclaw, 1997—. Mem. AIKIKAI. Avocations: aikido, mountain cycling, philosophy.

WÄGELE, JOHANN WOLFGANG, zoologist; b. Neuwied, Germany, Oct. 21, 1953; s. Gerhard and Christa (Banse) W.; m. Heike Stanjek, July 30, 1982; children: Leonard, Richard. Biologist, U. Kiel, 1977, PhD, 1980. Rsch. asst. U. Oldenburg, Germany, 1981-91; head dept. zoology U. Bielefeld, Germany, 1991-96, U. Bochum, Germany, 1996—. Office: Faculty Biology, Ruhr Univ Bochum, 44780 Bochum Germany

WAGELMANS, ALBERT PETER MARIE, economics educator; b. Rotterdam, Netherlands, Nov. 19, 1960; s. Pieter Frederik and Augustine Elise (Vredeveld) W.; m. Kerry Marie Malone, Apr. 25, 1996; children: Rory Pieter Joseph Malone, Kyran Timothy Robert. MSc in Econometrics, Erasmus U., Rotterdam, 1985, PhD, 1990. Asst. prof. ops. rsch. Erasmus U., Rotterdam, 1986-2000; assoc. prof. ops. rsch., 2000—; assoc. dir. Erasmus Rsch. Inst. Mgmt. Erasmus U., Rotterdam, 1999—; dir. Rotterdam Inst. for Bus. Econ. Studies, 1999—; vis. scientist Ctr. for Econometrics and Ops. Rsch., Louvain-la-Neuve, Belgium, 1989, MIT, 1990-91. Referee sci. jours, 1986—; contbr. articles to profl. jours. Active Amnesty Internat., Rotterdam, 1988-98. Rsch. grant Erasmus Trust Fund, 1990; Netherlands Orgn. for Sci. Rsch. fellow, 1990. Mem. Inst. for Ops. Rsch. and the Mgmt. Scis., Oper. Rsch. Soc., Netherlands Soc. for Ops. Rsch. Avocations: biking, running, music, cooking. E-mail: wagelmans@few.eur.nl. Office: Erasmus U Rotterdam, PO Box 1738, Rotterdam 3000DR, Netherlands

WAGEMAKER, ALLARD J., military officer; b. Renkum, The Netherlands, June 23, 1962; s. Gerard and Wilma (Welling) W.; m. Linda C. de Wyn, May 27, 1992; children: Lana, Puck. BC in Internat. Rels., Royal Naval Acad., Den Helder, The Netherlands, 1988; MA in Land Warfare, Am. Mil. U., 1996. Exch. officer, ops. officer Group Operational Units Marine Corps, Doorn, The Netherlands, 1992-95; liaison officer Hdqrs. UN Protection Force, Sarajevo, Bosnia, 1995; ops. officer Hdqrs. Royal Navy, The Hague, The Netherlands, 1996; co. 2IC Group Operational United Marine Corps, Doorn, 1996-97, co. comdr., 1997-99; pers. mgr. Hdqrs. Royal Netherlands Marine Corps, Rotterdam, The Netherlands, 1999—. Mem. editl. bd. Marineblad, 1995—, QuaPatet Orbis, 1999—; contbr. articles to profl. jours. Avocations: military history, politics, parachuting, long distance running. Home: Neptunus 43, 3962KX Wyk by Duurstede The Netherlands Office: HQ RNLMC, Noordsingel 250, 3032 BN Rotterdam The Netherlands

WAGENER, KLAUS PAUL, physics educator; b. Halle/Saale, Ger., July 27, 1930; s. Ewald and Margarete (Ladendorf) W.; Ph.D., U. Goettingen, 1959, dipl. in physics, 1956; docent phys. chemistry Tech. U. Berlin, 1964; m. Gisela Jander, Aug. 31, 1957; children: Jens, Dirk, Silke, Ulf, Bjoern, Birte, Karen; m. Angela de Luca Rebello, June 12, 1987. Asst., U. Goettingen (Ger.), 1958; rsch. assoc. U. Zurich, 1959-61; dept. head Hahn-Meitner Inst. Nuclear Rsch., Berlin, 1964-67; assoc. prof. U. Calif., La Jolla, 1966-67; prof. biophysics Tech. U. Aachen, Fed. Republic Germany, 1969—; dir. Just. Phys. Chemistry Nuc. Rsch. Ctr., Julich, Germany; dir. Just. prof. dept. chem. Pontificia U. Catolica, Rio de Janeiro, 1983-99; vis. prof. U. N.C., 1976; expert solar energy Sci. Commn. of European Cmty., 1977-84; prin. investigator Mariculture on Land, 1983-85; dir. Inst. Phys. Chemistry, Nuc. Rsch. Ctr., Jülich, Ger., 1968-78; active in sci. devel., Brazil, 1969, in implementation of biotech. in 3d world countries. Co-editor: Biomass Handbook, 1990; mem. editl. bd. Environ. Biophysics, 1974-78. Mem. N.Y. Acad. Scis. Home: Rua Dos Oitis 44, 22 451-050 Rio de Janeiro Brazil

WAGER, WALTER HERMAN, author, communications director; b. N.Y.C., Sept. 4, 1924; s. Max Louis and Jessie (Smith) W.; m. Sylvia Liebowitz Leonard, May 6, 1951 (div. May 1975); 1 child, Lisa Wendy; m. Winifred McIvor, June 4, 1975. BA, Columbia U., 1943; LLB, Harvard U., 1946; LLM, Northwestern U., 1949. Bar: N.Y. 1946. Spl. asst. to Israel dir. Civil Aviation, 1951-52; freelance writer N.Y.C., 1952-54; editor UN, N.Y.C., 1954-56; freelance TV and mag. writer N.Y.C., 1956-63; editor-in-chief Playbill mag., N.Y.C., 1963-66; editor Show mag., N.Y.C., 1965; cons. pub. rels. and editorial dept. ASCAP, N.Y.C., 1966-72, dir. pub. relations, 1972-78; cons. pub. relations Nat. Music Pub. Assn., N.Y.C., 1978-84; dir. communications Juilliard Sch., N.Y.C., 1985-86; counsel pub. relations Mann Music Ctr., Phila., 1986-87, Eugene O'Neill Theater Ctr., N.Y.C., 1987-89; dir. pub. info. U. Bridgeport, 1991-93; tchr. Northwestern U., 1949, Columbia U., 1955-56; spl. asst. to atty. gen. N.Y. State investigation hate lit. in elections, 1962; bd. dirs. Jazz Hall of Fame, 1975-77. Author: Death Hits the Jackpot, 1954, Operation Intrigue, 1956, I Spy, 1965, Masterstroke, 1966, Superkill, 1966, Wipeout, 1967, Countertrap, 1967, Death Twist, 1968, The Girl Who Split, 1969, Sledgehammer, 1970, Viper Three, 1971 (filmed as Twilights's Last Gleaming 1977), Swap, 1972, Telefon, 1975 (filmed in 1977), My Side-By King Kong, 1976, Time of Reckoning, 1977, Blue Leader, 1979, Blue Moon, 1980, Blue Murder, 1981, Designated Hitter, 1982, Otto's Boy, 1984, 58 Minutes, 1987 (filmed as Die Hard 2, 1990), The Spirit Team, 1996, Tunnel, 2000; (non-fiction) Camp Century, 1962, Playwrights Speak, 1967, (with Mel Tillis) Stutterin' Boy, 1984. Pres. Columbia Coll., class 1944. Fulbright fellow Sorbonne, Paris, 1949-50, Northwestern U. Law Sch. fellow, 1948-49. Mem. Writers Guild Am., Mystery Writers Am. (bd. dirs. 1988-94, 97-2000, now sec.). Democrat. Jewish. Avocation: traveling. Home and Office: 200 W 79th St New York NY 10024-6212

WAGIH, MOHAMED-RASHEAD ELSAYED, biotechnology researcher, research manager; b. Alexandria, Egypt, Feb. 6, 1954; s. Elsayed Mohamed-Elsayed Wagih and Ferdous Abdel-Razik Ibrahim Desokey; m. Nagat Abdel-Kader Mohamed Mousa, Feb. 6, 1986; children: Ramy, Omar, Manar. BS with honors, U. Alexandria, 1978, MS, 1983; MS, U. Queensland, Brisbane, Australia, 1984, PhD, 1990. Tutor, genetics U. Alexandria, 1978-82, lectr., genetics, 1989-91; sr. lectr., biotechnology U. Technology, Lae, Papua New Guinea, 1992-98, exec. dir., 1998—; assoc. prof. biotech. Internat. Devel. Program Australian Univs. and Colls., 1999; cons. agrl. biotechnology; negotiating mem. APEC Biotechnology Experts, 1997—; vis. prof. Mubarak City for Scientific Rsch., Alexandria, 1999, U. Menoufia, Egypt, 1999, U. Louis Pasteur, Strasbourg, France, 1998, U. Hasanuddin, Indonesia, 1996, 97; cons., sr. advisor The Sugar and Integrated Industries Co., Cairo, 1997-98; sr. advisor U. Alexandria, 1996—; mem. Commonwealth Sci. Coun. Biotech. Experts, 1999. Co-author: (book) Non-Seed Carbohydrate Producing Plants, 1996, Vol. 9; editor: African Crop Science Jour., 1993—, Sci. in New Guniea Jour., 1996—; Harvest Jour., 1999. Advisor Farmers Assn., Cocoa and Coconut Rsch. Inst., Coffee Rsch. Inst., Papua New Guinea, 1993—; chmn. adv. coun. for village devel., Papua New Guinea, 1993—. Soldier Egyptian Air Def., 1979-80. Recipient scholarships AusAID, Australia, 1982, 86, Faculty of Agr., Alexandria, 1978. Mem. Internat. Assn. Plant Tissue Culture and Biotech., Soc. Advancement Breeding Rschs. Asia and Oceania, Rotary (internat. dist. 9600 1993-94). Muslim. Avocations: Greek, Roman and free wrestling, reading, travel. Office: Univ Technology, PMB LAE, Morobe Province Papua, New Guinea

WAGNER, ARTHUR WARD, JR., lawyer; b. Birmingham, Ala., Aug. 13, 1930; s. Arthur Ward and Lucille (Lockheart) W.; m. Ruth Shingler, May 11, 1957; children: Celia Wagner Minter, Julia Wagner Dolce, Helen Wagner McAfee. BSBA, U. Fla., 1954, JD, 1957. Bar: Fla. 1957, U.S. Dist. Ct. (so. dist.) Fla. 1957, U.S. Dist. Ct. (mid. dist.) Fla. 1975. Ptnr. Wagner, Johnson, & McAfee, P.A., West Palm Beach, Fla., 1959—; lectr. in field. Author: Art of Advocacy: Jury Selection, 1981; co-author: Anatomy of Personal Injury Lawsuit I & II, 1968 and 1981. Mem. 15th Jud. Nominating Com., Palm Beach City, 1979-82, 4th Dist. Nominating Commn., Palm Beach City, 1982-86; mem. pres.'s coun. U. Fla.; vestry, chancellor Holy Trinity Parish; bd. dirs. U. Fla. Found., 1996-2000. Fellow Internat. Acad. Trial Lawyers, Am. Coll. Trial Lawyers, Internat. Soc. Barristers, Am. Bd. Trial Advs.; mem. Assn. Trial Lawyers Am. (pres. 1975-76, hon. life trustee Roscoe Pound Found.), So. Trial Lawyers Assn. (pres. 1991), U. Fla. Law Coll. Alumni (mem. bd. govs.). Democrat. Episcopalian. Office: Wagner Johnson & McAfee PA 1818 S Australian Ave West Palm Beach FL 33409-6452

WAGNER, CARRUTH JOHN, physician; b. Omaha, Sept. 4, 1916; s. Emil Conrad and Mabel May (Knapp) W. A.B., Omaha U., 1938; B.Sc., U. Nebr., 1938, M.D., 1941, D.Sc., 1966. Diplomate: Am. Bd. Sugery, Am. Bd. Orthopaedic Surgery. Intern U.S. Marine Hosp., Seattle, 1941-42; resident gen. surgery and orthopaedic surgery USPHS hosps., Shriners Hosp., Phila., 1943-46; med. dir. USPHS, 1952-62; chief orthopaedic service USPHS Hosp., San Francisco, 1946-51, S.I., N.Y., 1951-55; health mblzn. USPHS Hosp., 1959-62; asst. surgeon gen. dep. chief div. hosps. UPHS, 1957-59; chief div. USPHS, 1962-65, USPHS (Indian Health), 1962-65; dir. Bur. Health Services, 1965-68; Washington rep. AMA, 1968-72; health services cons., 1972-79; dept. health services State of Calif., 1979—. Contbr. articles to med. jours. Served with USCGR, World War II. Recipient Pfizer award, 1962; Meritorious award Am. Acad. Gen. Practice, 1965; Disting. Svc. medal, 1968, Calif. Dept. Health Svcs. Pub. Health Recognition award, 1995. Fellow A.C.S. (bd. govs.), Am. Soc. Surgery Hand, Am. Assn. Surgery Trauma, Am. Geriatrics Soc., Am. Acad. Orthopaedic Surgeons; mem. Nat. Assn. Sanitarians, Am. Pub. Health Assn. Sanitarians, Am. Pub. Health Assn., Washington Orthopaedic Club, Am. Legion, Alpha Omega Alpha. Lutheran. Club: Mason (Shriner). Home: 6234 Silverton Way Carmichael CA 95608-0757 Office: PO Box 638 Carmichael CA 95609-0638

WAGNER, CHARLENE BROOK, publishing consultant; b. L.A.; d. Edward J. and Eva (Anderson) Brook; children: Gordon, Brook, John. BS, Tex. Christian U., 1952; MEd, Sam Houston U., 1973; postgrad., U. Tex., Austin, 1975, Tex. A&M U., 1977. Sci. educator Spring Branch Ind. Sch. Dist., Houston, 1970-98; ret., 1998; dir. CompuKidZ, Houston, 1998—; cons. Scott Foresman, Addison Wesley, Ginn, Houston; cons. Scott Foresman Pub. Co., Houston; owner Sci. Instrnl. Sys. Co., 1988—; dir. Compukidz. Mem. Houston Symphony League, 1992, Mus. Fine Arts, Mus. of Art of Am. West, Houston, 1989, Mus. Natural Scis., Women's Christian Home, Houston, 1991; mem. Houston Grand Opera Guild, mem. exec. bd. 1999-2000, rec./corr. sec.; social chmn. Encore, 1988; mem. Magic Circle Rep. Women's Club. Mem. NEA, NAFE, AAUW, Tex. State Tchrs. Assn., Spring Branch Edn. Assn., Internat. Platform Assn., Wellington Soc. for Arts (Houston chpt.), Shepherd Soc., Watercolor Arts Soc., Art League Houston, Clan Anderson Soc., Heather and Thistle Soc., Houston Highland Games Assn., Space City Ski Club. Episcopalian. Avocations: painting, watercolor media. Home: B54 2670 Marilee Ln Apt B54 Houston TX 77057-4264 Office: 2301 Fountain View Dr Apt 85 Houston TX 77057-4620

WAGNER, DONALD B(LACKMORE), historian; b. Sudbury, Ont., Can., June 22, 1943; s. William James and Edith Winifred Wagner; m. Annie Winther, June 4, 1981. SB in Math., MIT, 1965; Cand.mag. in Chinese, PhD, U. Copenhagen, 1976, DPhil, 1993. Computer sys. programmer Project MAC MIT, Cambridge, 1965-67; computer sys. programmer A/S Regnecentralen, Copenhagen, 1968-72; rsch. fellow Scandinavian Inst. Asian Studies, Copenhagen, 1976-80, Danish Rsch. Coun. for Humanities, Copenhagen, 1982-85, U. Copenhagen, 1986-90, Needham Rsch. inst., Cambridge, Eng., 1990-91, 94-96; assoc. prof. U. Copenhagen, 1998—; vis. prof. Tech. U. Berlin, 1993-94, 97-98. Author: Iron and Steel in Ancient China, 1993, The Traditional Chinese Iron Industry and Its Modern Fate, 1997, A Classical Chinese Reader: The Han Shu Biography of Huo Guang, 1998, The State and the Iron Industry in Han China, 2000. Avocation: research. E-mail: dbwagner@hum.ku.dk. Home: Reverdilsgade 3 1 th, DK-1701 Copenhagen V, Denmark Office: U Copenhagen Dept Asian Stu, Leifsgade 33, DK-2300 Copenhagen Denmark

WAGNER, DONALD EDWARD, minister; b. Medina, N.Y., Sept. 3, 1942; s. Donald E. and Thelma C. (Nelson) W.; children: Jay Douglas, Matthew, Anna. BA, Westminster Coll., 1964; MA, Princeton Sem., 1967; ThM, Princeton Theol. Sem., 1969; DMin, McCormick Sem., 1984. Ordained to ministry Presbyn. Ch., 1968. Asst. to dean Princeton (N.J.) Sem., 1965-67; assoc. minister Elmwood Presbyn. Ch., East Orange, N.J., 1967-69, West Side Presbyn. Ch., Ridgewood, N.J., 1970-73, 1st Presbyn. Ch., Evanston, Ill., 1973-80; nat. dir. Palestine Human Rights Campaign, Chgo., 1980-90; dir. Middle East program Mercy Corps Internat., Chgo., 1990-94; assoc. prof. religion North Park U., Chgo., 1994-00; nat. dir. Evangelicals for Middle East Understanding, 1991-00' dir. Middle East Studies Ctr., North Park U., 1995-00. Author: All in the Name of the Bible, 1987, Anxious for Armageddon, 1994; co-author: Peace in Ammageddon, 1993; editor: Israeli Settler Violence, 1986, Dying in the Land of Promise, 2000. Recipient Arab Am. U. Grads. award 1982, Disting. Svc. award Arab community Ctr., Chgo., 1993, Ann. Martin Luther King Disting. Clergy award Morehouse Coll., 1992, Human Rights award Am. Arab Anti-Discriminat Com., 1993. Avocations: travel, running, writing. Office: North Park Univ 3225 W Foster Ave Chicago IL 60625-4823

WAGNER, ERIC ARMIN, sociology educator; b. Cleve., May 31, 1941; s. Armin Erich and Florence (Edwards) W. AB, Ohio State U., 1964; MA, U. Fla., 1968, PhD, 1973. Instr. sociology Ohio U., Athens, 1968-73, asst. prof., 1973-75, assoc. prof., 1975-83, prof., 1983-87, chmn. sociology & anthropology, 1974-78, 86-91, 94-97, vice chmn. faculty senate, 1982-84, prof. emeritus, 1997. Contbr. articles on internat. sports and soc. to books and profl. jours. Dir. Planned Parenthood of Southeast Ohio, 1990-96, pres. 1992-94. Mem. Internat. Sociol. Assn., Midwest Assn. Latin Am. Studies (pres. 1979-80), U.S. Orienteering Fedn. (dir. 1976-82, sec.-treas. 1976-79, v.p. 1979-80, sec. 1980-82), Delta Sigma Phi. Presbyn. Home: 2615 NW 82d St Gainesville FL 32606-8623

WAGNER, EWALD, orient language educator; b. Hamburg, Germany, Aug. 8, 1927; s. Karl and Leni (Ewald) W.; m. Ida S. Patilla, Sept. 20, 1974; children: Georg, Elisabeth, Angelica. Dr. phil., U. Hamburg, 1951. Scholar German Rsch. Found., Mainz, Fed. Republic Germany, 1951-52, Akademie der Wissenschaften und der Literatur, Mainz, 1952-53; libr. U. Mainz, 1955-64; prof. orient lang. studies U. Giessen, 1964-93. Contbr. articles to profl. jours. Mem. German Oriental Soc. (2d sec. 1972-91). Home: Eichendorffring 2, D-35394 Giessen Germany Office: Univ of Giessen, Otto-Behaghel-Str 10, D-35394 Giessen Germany

WAGNER, FRANK, literature educator; b. Ueckermunde, Germany, May 1, 1927; s. Johannes and Ella (Schneider) W.; m. Edith Schönmeier, Aug. 15,

1953; children: Christiane, Bettina. PhD, Humboldt U., 1957. Lectr. U. Poznan, Poland, 1957-59; adviser Min. Higher Edn., 1959-65; rsch. scientist Akad. der Wissenschaften, Berlin, 1965-74; asst. prof. U. Lublin, Poland, 1974-78; prof. Humboldt U., Berlin, 1978-90; prof. Peking U., China, 1983-85. Author: Literatur auf Kriegskurs, 1961,...der Kurs auf die Realitat, Anna Seghers 1935-43, 1975, Auf den Spuren Jüdischer Mifbürger in Uekermünde, 1998; co-author: Geschichte der deutschen Literatur, 1917-1945, 1973; co-editor: Anna Seghers-Eine Biographie in Bildern, 1994. Avocation: philately. Home: Theobaldstrasse 5, 13053 Berlin Germany

WAGNER, GERHARD ADAM, sociologist; b. Donzdorf, Germany, Nov. 27, 1958; s. Georg and Genofeva (Feth) W.; m. Marina Sabine Roth, Sept. 28, 1983; 1 child, Ruben. MA, U. Heidelberg, Germany, 1987; Dr.rer.soc., U. Bielefeld, Germany, 1992, habilitation, 1998. Lectr. U. Heidelberg, 1987-90, U. Bielefeld, 1990—. Author: Validity and Normative Coercion, 1987, Social Theory as Political Theology?, 1993, The Challenge of Diversity, 1999; editor: Max Weber's Philosophy of Science, 1994, Responsibility, Action and Social Order, 1998, The End of the Book, 1998, The Logic of Social Systems, 2000, Sociology and Anti-Sociology, 2000; editor Simmel newsletter, 1991—. Mem. German Sociol. Assn. Avocation: creative writing. Home: Feldbergstrasse 58, D-68163 Mannheim Germany Office: U Bielefeld, Universitätsstrasse 25, D-33615 Bielefeld Germany

WAGNER, GUSTAV ALFRED, retired medical educator; b. Hannover, Germany, Jan. 10, 1918; s. Gustav and Anna Wagner; m. Inge Winiarz, Dec. 6, 1941; 1 child, Klaus-Dieter. MD, U. Berlin, 1944. Resident physician Mcpl. Dermatol. Hosp., Hannover, 1946-51; asst. prof. U. Dermatol. Hosp., Kiel, Fed. Republic of Germany, 1951-64; prof. medicine, dir. German Cancer Research Ctr., Heidelberg, Fed. Republic of Germany, 1964-86; ret. German Cancer Research Ctr., Heidelberg, 1986. Author/editor over 70 books and 300 jours. articles. Recipient Ernst von Bergmann medal Chamber German Physicians, 1980. Mem. German Soc. of Med. Informatics (hon.), European Fed. of Med. Informatics (hon.), Internat. Working Group of Bone Tumours (hon.), Assn. German Medical Press. (hon.). Avocation: philately. Home: Bluetenweg 64, 69198 Schriesheim Baden Wurtt Germany

WAGNER, HEINZ GEORG, physical chemistry educator; b. Hof Bavaria, Federal Republic of Germany, Sept. 20, 1928; s. Georg and Friedl Wilhelmine (Spiess) W.; m. Renate Charlotte Heuer, July 24, 1974. Diploma in Phys. Chemistry, Technische Hochschule Darmstadt, Fed. Republic of Germany, 1953, Doctor rer. nat., 1956; Dr. h.c. Bochum U., 1989. Dozent U. Gö ttingen, Fed. Republic Germany, 1960-64, prof. phys. chemistry, 1971-97; prof. U. Bochum, Fed. Republic Germany, 1965-70; dir. Max-Planck-Institut fur Stromungsforschung, Gottingen, 1971-97. Contbr. articles on combustion, reaction kinetics, thermodynamics of liquid mixtures to profl. publs. Recipient Achema-Plakette, 1982, Numa Manson medal, 1987, Bundesverdienstkreuz, 1987, Dionizy Smolenski medal, 1991, Dechema medal, 1997, Grosses Bundesverdienstkreuz, 1999. Mem. Deutsche Bunsen-Gesellschaft (hon., pres. 1983-84, Fritz Haber prize 1963, Walther-Nernst-Denkmünze 1993), Combustion Inst. (internat. sec. 1982-92, Bernard Lewis Gold medal 1972), Am. Phys. Soc., Royal Soc. Chemistry (v.p. Farady div. 1978-82), Acad. Sci. Göttingen (sec.), Internat. Acad. Astronautics, Acad. Sci. Heidelberg, Deutsche Akad. Naturforscher Leopoldina, Academia Europaea: Fng. mem. of the Russian Acad. of Sci., Moscow, Deutsche Forschungsgemeinschaft (v.p. 1983-89). Office: Institut fur Physikalische Chemie, U Göttingen, Tammannstrasse 6,. 37077 Göttingen Germany

WAGNER, HELMUT MICHAEL, economics professor; b. Schwandorf, Germany, Aug. 24, 1951; s. Alfons and Marianne (Ries) W.; m. Mechthild Schweers, Dec. 18, 1981. Diploma in Econs., U. Regensburg, Germany, 1974; diploma in Sociology, U. Regensburg, 1975, PhD in Econs., 1976; Habilitation, U. of Aachen, 1981. Lectr. U. Regensburg, Regensburg, 1977; asst. prof. U. Aachen, Aachen, 1978-82; prof. (chair) U. Hamburg, Hamburg, Germany, 1982-95; prof., chair U. Hagen, Fern U., Hagen, Germany, 1995—; vis. prof. U. Calif., Riverside, Berkeley, 1982-83; vis. scholar MIT, Cambridge, Mass., 1987; vis. rsch. prof. Bank of Japan, Tokyo, 1988; vis. fellow Princeton (N.J.) U., 1991-92; vis. scholar AICGS (Johns Hopkins U.), 1997, IMF, Washington, 1997. Mem. Royal Econ. Assn., Am. Econ. Assn., European Econ. Assn., Verein fur Socialpolitik, Arbeitskreis Politische Okonomie. Home: IM Eichenwald 2, 58093 Hagen Germany Office: Fern Univ Hagen, Feithstr 140, 58084 Hagen Germany

WAGNER, JÉRÔME, media/communications company executive; b. Oran, Algeria, Jan. 4, 1962; arrived in France, 1962; s. Jacques and Claudine (Fabre) W.; m. Emmanuelle Perrier; twins: Julien and Mathieu. Bachelor, Lycée Daudet, Nimes, France, 1979; grad. in Mktg., Hautes Etudes Commerciales, Paris, 1985. Sales exec. Robert & Ptnrs., Paris, 1987; mktg. comm. dir. Hachette Distbn./Relaish, Lagardere Group, Paris, 1987-93; worldwide sales mktg. dir. Symah Vision, Lagardere Group, Paris, 1993—; tchr. mktg. Inst. Supérieur Commerce Bus. Sch., Paris, 1993-94; mktg. cons. Claude Aburbé & Assoc. Cabinet, Paris, 1995. Author: Eau Fraiche, 1988; contbr. articles to profl. jours. With French Marines, 1985-87. Mem. Hautes Etudes Commerciales Info. Media Group, HEC Advt. Group. Avocations: literature (poetry), cinema, tennis. Home: 48 rue de Laborde, 75008 Paris France Office: Symah Vision, 27 rue Jean Bleuzen BP 47, 92174 Vanves France

WAGNER, MARTIN G., chemical engineer, researcher; b. Bklyn., Mar. 19, 1942; s. Joseph Bernard and Anne Bleifer Wagner; m. Aylene Parker, Apr. 15, 1965; children: Gaylia, Aaron. B in Chem. Engring., The Cooper Union, 1962; MS in Chem. Engring., Northwestern U., 1964, PhD in Chem. Engring., 1967. Sr. tech. assoc. DuPont Co. Ctrl. Sci. and Engring., Wilmington, Del., 1966—. Dir. Welcome House Adoption Agy., Doylestown, Pa., 1983-88. Mem. AIChE, Soc. Rheology, Sigma Xi. Achievements include 7 patents in field. Avocations: sailing, reading, woodworking. E-mail: martin.g.wagner@usa.dupont.com. Home: 1013 Overbrook Rd Wilmington DE 19807-2235 Office: DuPont Ctrl Sci & Engring PO Box 80323 Wilmington DE 19880-0323

WAGNER, MARY ANN, human resources executive; b. St. Louis, May 24, 1947; d. John Gerard and Carmela Lucy (Cozza) Blethroad; 1 child, John Patrick. BA, Webster U., St. Louis, 1979, MA, 1982. Tchr. Our Lady of Fatima, St. Louis, Wetterau, St. Louis; personnel mgr. Venture, St. Louis, 1979-81; customer svc. coord. Venture, O'Fallon, Mo., 1981-84, personnel mgr., 1984-86; regional personnel mgr., 1986-88, dir. tng. and devel., 1988-92; divsn. v.p. dir. of assoc. rels. May Merchandising, St. Louis, 1995-98; sr. v.p. human resources Meier & Frank, Portland, Oreg., 1998—; adj. prof. Webster U., 1990-95, divisional v.p. tng. and devel., 1992—. Chmn. United Way, O'Fallon, 1985, bd. dirs. Mem. AAIM Mgmt. Assn., Am. Soc. Tng. and Devel., Am. Mgmt. Assn. Roman Catholic. Avocations: antiques, music, sports. Home: 325 Perceval Dr Saint Charles MO 63304-5708

WAGNER, MICHAEL DUANE, lawyer; b. Shiner, Tex., July 4, 1948; s. Martin Matthew and Mary Margaret (Prasek) W.; m. Patricia Ann Miller, July 1, 1972; children: Matthew Miller, Michael Patrick. BA, Tex. Christian U., 1970; JD, St. Mary's Sch. Law, San Antonio, 1973. Bar: Tex. 1973, U.S. Supreme Ct. 1977. Assoc. counsel United Svcs. Automobile Assn., San Antonio, 1973-78, asst. v.p., counsel, 1978-80; v.p., counsel United Svcs. Automobile Assn., San Antonio, 1980-98, sr. v.p., gen. counsel, 1999—; counsel investment mgmt. co. United Services Automobile Assn., San Antonio, 1980—, pres., chmn. bd. dirs. fed. credit union, 1981-84. Counsel United San Antonio Found., 1982; rep. Target 90/Goals for San Antonio, 1985; chmn. bd. advisors Daus. Charity Svcs. San Antonio; trustee Boysville, 1988; bd. dirs. De Paul Family Ctr., San Antonio, 1985, Cancer Therapy and Rsch. Ctr., Friends of McNay, ARC, San Francisco, Archdiocese of San Antonio. Named one of Outstanding Young Men in Am., U.S. Jr. C. of C., 1984. Mem. ABA, Fed. Bar Assn., State Bar of Tex. (ethics and grievance com.) San Antonio Bar Assn., Phi Delta Theta, Phi Alpha Delta. Roman Catholic. Avocations: running, home renovation.

WAGNER, PATER BENEDIKT FRANZ, archivist, librarian; b. Sonntagberg, Austria, Mar. 17, 1929; s. Anton and Maria (Ertlthaler) W. Theologian, Salzburg Sch. Cath. Theology, Austria, 1957; MPh, U. Vienna, 1968, PhD, 1969. Joined Benedictine Order, 1955, ordained priest Roman Cath. Ch. 1957. Tchr. Greek and Latin langs. Seitenstetten (Austria) Secondary Sch., 1965-94; archivist Stiftsarchiv, Seitenstetten, 1969—; libr. Stiftsbibliothek, Seitenstetten, 1976—; headmaster Stiftsgymnasium, Seitenstetten, 1983-94. Author: (book) Stift Seitenstetten und seine Kunstschätze, 1988; editor (book) Seitenstetten - Udalschalks Erbe im Wandel der Zeit, 1980; editor (periodical), Bote aus Seitenstetten, 1958-62; editor (exposition catalog) Julius Raab -Aussaat und Ernte, 1992. Recipient Ehrenring for outstanding promotion Pres. of Austria, 1969, Ehrenkreuz für Wissenschaft und Kunst, Pres. of Austrian Republic, 1994. Office: Benediktinerstift, Am Klosterberg 1, A-3353 Seitenstetten Lwr Aus, Austria

WAGNER, PAUL ANTHONY, JR., education educator; b. Pitts., Aug. 28, 1947; s. Paul A. and Mary K. Wagner; children: Nicole S., Eric P., Jason G. BS, N.E. Mo. State U., 1969; MEd, U. Mo., 1972; MA in Philosophy, 1976, PhD in Philosophy of Edn., 1978. Internal expeditor electromotive div. GM, La Grange, Ill., 1970-71; instr. Moberly (Mo.) Jr. Coll., 1972-73; instr. U. Mo., Columbia, 1973-78, acting dir. instl. rsch. and planning, 1990-92, dir. univ. self study, 1991-92; instr. Mo. Mil. Acad., 1978-79; prof. edn. and philosophy U. Houston-Clear Lake, Atrium Cir. Disting. Rsch. Prof., 1980, Chancellor's Disting. Svc. Prof., 1985; dir. Inst. Logical and Cognitive Studies, 1980—; dir. Project in Profl. Ethics; chmn. dept. edn. U. Houston-Clear Lake, 1989-92; adj. prof. bus. mgmt. U. Houston-Victoria; judge Sears Intercollegiate Ethics Bowl, Dallas, 1998; pres. Wagner & Assocs. Ednl. Consulting, 1988-93; dir. Tex. Ctr. for Study Profl. Ethics in Tchg., 1988-95; rsch. assoc. Ctr. for Moral Devel., Harvard U., 1985-86; vis. scholar Stanford U., Palo Alto, Calif., 1981; cons. to various sch. dists., 1979—; cons. in total quality mgmt. Golden Gate U., 1992-93, M.D. Anderson Cancer Ctr. and Hosp., 1992-93, U. Houston-Victoria, 1993; cons. on strategic planning Houston ChronicleNewspaper, 1997; chair So. Accreditation of Colls. and Schs. steering com. U. Houston-Clear Lake, 1990-93; mem. bd. dirs., chair planning and budgeting com. Houston Tenneco Marathon, 1992-94; bd. dirs. Houston Meth. Healthcare Sys. Marathon, 1994-2000; mem. steering com. Trilateral Conf. and Supershow Greater Human Partnership, 1994-95; cons. and ethics trainer Am. Leadership Forum, 1995-98; mem. planning com. Tex. Ethics in Govt. Ann. Conf., 1995-98; pres. faculty senate U. Houston-Clear Lake, 1999—. Author: (with F. Kierstead) The Ethical Legal and Multicultural Founds. of Teaching, 1992, Understanding Professional Ethics, 1996; contbr. articles on sci. edn., mgmt. theory and philosophy of edn. to profl. jours. Mem. editl. bd. Jour. of Thought, 19815, Focus on Learning, 1982-85; editorial cons. Instrnl. Scis., 1981-83; editorial assoc. Brain and Behavioral Scis., 19865. Mem. Human Rights Commn., Columbia, Mo., 1976-79, vice chmn., 1978-79; Sunday sch. tchr. Mary Queen Cath. Ch., Friendswood, Tex., 1979-85; founding bd. mem. Bay Area Symphony Soc., 1983-85; capital campaign com. Soc. Prevention Cruelty to Animals, 1989-91; publicity com. Am. Cancer Soc., Houston chpt., 1989-92; cons. in strategic planning to M.D. Anderson Cancer Ctr. vol. divsn.; mem. steering com. City of Houston Emerging Bus. Conf., 1994-95, Trilateral Conf., Greater Houston Partnership, 1994-95; active Houston Bus. Promise; chair strategic planning com. Leadership Houston, 1996-98; bd. dirs. Houston Vol. Ctr., 19985; bd. dirs. Leanna Saprianno Dance Co., 20005; mem. Linda Lorelle Scholarship Com., 19995; coun. mem. Project Grad Coordinating Coun., 19995; emcee, expert commentator for pub. TV, Channel 8 in Houston, 19905. Sgt. Mo. NG, 1970-76. Recipient Cert. of Appreciation, City of Columbia, 1978; K.E. Graessle scholar, 1968, Mo. Peace Studies Inst. grantee, 1971. Mem. AAUP, Assn. Applied and Profl. Ethics, Am. Assn. Pub. Adminstrs. (ethics com.), Am. Philos. Assn., Assn. Philosophers in Edn. (exec. bd., v.p.), Philosophy of Edn. Soc. (exec. sec.-treas., hospitality chair 1995-96), Am. Ednl. Studies Assn., Philosophy Sci. Assn., S.W. Philosophy Edn. Soc., Tex. Network for Tchr. Tng. in Philosophy for Children (bd. dirs. 1983-90), Tex. Ctr. for Ethics in Edn. (bd. dirs. 19885), Tex. Ednl. Found. Soc. (pres. 19865), Tex. Assn. Coll. Tchrs., So. Assn. Colls. Coord., Houston Bar Assn. (mem. steering com. NAFTA Conf. 1993-94), Informal Logic Assn., Leadership Houston, Friends Hermann Pk., Clearlake Cir. (chair 1979-85), Phi Delta Kappa, Kappa Delta Pi. Roman Catholic. Avocations: running, racquetball, reading, opera, ballet. Address: RR 4 Box 217 Navasota TX 77868-9413 Office: U Houston 2700 Bay Area Blvd Rm 338 Houston TX 77058-1002

WAGNER, PETER HANS, educator; b. St. Ingbert, Saarland, Germany, Jan. 18, 1949; s. Theodor Josef and Maria (Spaniol) W.; m. Odile Allain, Aug. 4, 1973; children: Anne-Claude, Marie-Laure, Roland. PhD, U. Saarland, 1978, Sorbonne, Paris, 1986; Habil., Sorbonne, Paris, 1987. Lectr. Coll. of William and Mary, 1973-75, U. Bath, Eng., 1978-80, U. Aston, Eng., 1980-81; asst. prof. U. Eichstätt, Germany, 1981-93; prof. U. Landau, Germany, 1993—. Author: Puritan Attitudes Toward Recreatioin in 17th C New England, 1980, (rev. 1990), Reading Leonatext, 1995; editor: Erotica and the Englighenment, 1991, Icon,Texts Leonotexts, 1996; contbr. 55 articles to profl. jours., 60 revs. Mem. Anglistenverband, Am. Soc. 8th C Studies, Canadian Soc. 8th C Studies. Avocations: sailing, boules, cycling, lepre chauning. Office: Univ of Landau, Im Fort 7, D-76829 Landau Germany

WAGNER, PHIL, publisher, writer; b. Port Chester, N.Y., July 7, 1951; s. Philip Frank and Jean Mary (Miles) W.; m. Mary Ann Sherry, Oct. 1, 1977; 1 child, Samuel. Pres. Wagner Labs and Enterprises, Mohegan Lake, N.Y., 1982—; pub., editor Iconoclast Mag., Mohegan Lake, N.Y., 1992—; free-lance writer various orgns. and locations, 1975—. Author: Marlowe in the South Seas, 2000. Mem. Coun. Literary Mags. Presses. Avocations: book collecting, reading, investing, hiking, music. Office: Wagner Labs and Enterprises 1675 Amazon Rd Mohegan Lake NY 10547-1804

WAGNER, SAMUEL ALBIN MAR, records management executive, educator; b. Brighton, Colo., Feb. 23, 1942; s. Jacob Doer and Leota Garnet (Wilson) W.; m. Donna Dee Person, Mar. 20, 1987; children: Kurt, Andrea, Autumn, Jan, Arthur. BA in History, U. Colo., 1964, MA in History, 1965; STB (MTS) in History of World Religions, Harvard U., 1968; cert. in archival adminstrn., U. Denver, 1978. cert. records mgr.; cert. archivist. Archival asst. Harvard U. & Harvard Bus. Sch., 1965-68; asst. curator we. hist. collections U. Colo., 1968-70; sr. asst. archivist Cornell U., Ithaca, N.Y., 1971-73; editor Brighton Blade, Ft. Lupton Press, Colo., 1973-77; city archivist City of Providence, 1978-80; state records analyst Wyo. State Archives, Cheyenne, 1979-83; pres. Records Mgmt. Cons. Internat., 1983—; records mgr. Ft. Collins (Colo.) Police Dept., 1984-87; pub. records adminstr. State R.I., Providence, 1987-90; asst. prof. master archival studies program U. B.C., Vancouver, Can., 1990-93; editor Mo. State Archives, Jefferson City, 1994-96; prodr. community access Sta. JCTV, Jefferson City, 1994-96; chief N.J. Bur. Records Mgmt., Trenton, 1996—; pres. Historic Rsch. Svcs., Jefferson City, Trenton, 1994—; instr. Chapman, U., 1981-87, Colo. State U., 1985-87, Lincoln U., 1995-96, U. B.C., 1990-93; speaker in field. Author: Brighton Reflections, 1976, Adams County: Crossroads of the West, 1977, Directory of Automated Records Management Systems, 1985-91, Crossroads of the West: A History of Brighton and the Platte Valley, 1987; editor The Fort Lupton Story, 1987; contbr. articles to profl. jours. Officer, bd. dirs. Adams County Hist. Soc., 1973-77; county historian Adams County, Brighton, 1976-77; mem. Brighton Human Rels. Commn., 1977-78; bd. dirs. Brighton Bicentennial Com., 1975-76, Ft. Lupton Bicentennial Com., 1975-76, R.I. RSVP, 1978-80, R.I. Pub. Records Adv. Coun., 1987-90, R.I. Hist. Records Adv. Bd., 1987-90; chmn. info. profls. legis. task force Freedom of Info. and Privacy Assn., 1991-93; chmn. oral history project Cole County Hist. Soc., 1996. Recipient Hist. Preservation award Adams County Hist. Soc., 1978, award Freedom of Info. and Privacy Assn., 1993; grantee Ethnic Heritage Project Colo. Humanities Coun., 1977, Humanities and Social Scis. U. B.C., 1993, Nat. Historic Pub. & Records, 1988-92; Ford Found. fellow, 1964-65. Mem. Assn. Records Mgrs. and Adminstrs. (pres. No. Colo. chpt. 1984-85, v.p. Ocean State chpt. 1987-90, bd. dirs., editor Vancouver chpt. 1991, bd. dirs. Ctrl. N.J. chpt. 2000—, mem. records mgmt. standards and glossary task forces, Mem. Yr. 1985, microcomputer/PC industry action com., chmn. 1984-86, editor Software Dir. 1985-91, co-chmn. tech. applications com. 1989-90, chmn. Archives ISG 1997-99, ISG mid-year seminar program com. 1998—, mgr. edn. sector 1999—), Inst. Cert. Records Mgrs. (regional coord., exam proctor, grader 1982—, cert. records mgr. 1983), Soc. Am. Archivists (com. automated records and techniques 1990-94, select com. task force on automated records and techniques 1994—, chmn. MicroMARC users group 1994-96, rep. joint SAA-ARMA Com. 1995-97), Nat. Assn. Govt. Archivists an Records Adminstrs., Archives Assn. B.C. (freedom of info. and privacy legis. com. 1990-93), Assn. Can. Archivists (electronic records select com. 1991-93, Acad. Cert. Archivists (outreach com. 1996-98, mem. commn. on future of archival enterprise 1999—), Am. Hist. Soc. of Germans from Russia (charter mem.), Mid-Atlantic Archives Conf. (program com. 1999-2000. Democrat. Unitarian. Avocations: local history, art, photography, film and TV production, hiking. Home: 231 Hobbs Ave Cheyenne WY 82009-4720

WAGNER, SIEGFRIED, gastroenterologist, researcher; b. Roetz, Germany, Sept. 28, 1957; s. Siegfried and Emma (Nothas) W. MD, Tech. U., Munich, 1983; PhD, Ludwig-Maximillian U., Munich, 1984. Rsch. scientist dept. physiology Free U. Berlin, 1985-86; resident, fellow in gastroenterology and hepatology Med. Hochschule, Hannover, Germany, 1986-93, cons. gastroenterology and hepatology, 1993-95, asst. prof. gastroenterology and hepatology, 1995-99, assoc. prof. medicine, 1999—. Co-editor sci. books; contbr. over 150 articles to books and profl. jours. Capt. German Med. Corps, 1984. Recipient Sci. grants Deutsche Forschungs Gemeinschaft, 1991, 93, 96, 99. Mem. German Soc. Gastroenterology, German Assn. Study of Liver, German Soc. Ultrasound in Medicine, Am. Gastroenterol. Assn. Avocations: tennis, skiing, theater. Office: Med Hochschule Hannover, Gastroenterology/Hepatology, D-30623 Hannover Germany

WAGNER, TERRANCE, consultant; b. Olympia, Wash., July 24, 1947; s. John Philip Wagner and Elsie Dora Lewis; m. Evelyn Adela Ruiz, Aug. 17, 1973; children: Marco, Kellie, Christopher, Lisa. BS in Bus. Adminstrn., U. Phoenix, 1981; MBA, Golden Gate U., 1983. Retail mgr. Army and Air Force Exch. Svc., Great Falls, Mont., 1977-79; chief inventory mgmt. Army and Air Force Exch. Svc., Oakland, Calif., 1979-85; asst. chief Pacific field office Army and Air Force Exch. Svc., Tokyo, 1985-92; divisional merchandise mgr. Army and Air Force Exch. Svc., Dallas, 1992-95, v.p. consumables divsn., 1995-98, v.p. main store hardlines, 1998-99; proprietor TdblU Consulting, DeSoto, Tex., 1999—. Avocations: genealogy, aviation, motorcycling, reading. E-mail: tdblu@worldnet.att.net. Office: TdblU Consulting 705 Bent Creek Dr Desoto TX 75115-3655

WAGNER, WILFRIED, educator; b. Tarutung, Indonesia, Sept. 10, 1935; s. Heinrich Hermann Peter and Erna (Michel) W.; m. Sigrun Fischer, July 5, 1968. Abitur, C.W. Schule, 1957; PhD, U. Frankfurt, 1968. Asst. prof. U. Frankfurt (Germany), 1968-71; reader U. Dortmund (Germany), 1971-74; prof. U. Bremen (Germany), 1974—; dean Faculty Social Scis., Bremen, 1980-81. Social worker Luth. Ch., Dortmund, 1971-74. Mem. Ostasiatischer Verein Bremen, Internat. Assn. historians Asia. Avocations: walking, gardening, restoring old furniture. Office: U Bremen Dept History, PO Box 330440, D-28334 Bremen Germany

WAGNER, WILLIAM MICHAEL, investment company executive; b. Saratoga Springs, N.Y., May 6, 1949; s. Harold Wilbur and Alice Frieda (Stauffacher) W.; m. Barbara Lee Galarneault, Jan. 25, 1980; 1 child, Harold Galarneault Wagner. BA, Bradley U., 1971; MA, U. Tex., 1973. Tchr. Happy Grove High Sch., Hector's River, Jamaica, 1974-75; specialist software systems U. Tex., Austin, 1977-88, asst. dir., 1988-93; 2nd v.p. TIAA-CREF, N.Y.C., 1993-98, v.p. technol. integration, 1998—. Contbr. articles to profl. jours. Mem. Software AG User Group Internat. (ADABAS product rep. 1986-87, v.p. 1987-88, pres. 1989-91, adv. bd. 1990-93), Computer Measurement Group, Littlefield Soc., Chancellor's Coun., Tex. Leadership Soc., Mensa, Phi Eta Sigma, Phi Kappa Phi, Omicron Delta Kappa, Sigma Pi Sigma, Kappa Delta Rho. Republican. Avocations: cycling, skiing, physics and cosmology, naval history, railroads. Office: TIAA-CREF 730 3d Ave New York NY 10017-3206

WAGNER, WOLFGANG, pharmaceutical industry executive; b. Hohenpeissenberg, Germany, June 29, 1950; s. Josef and Irmgard (König) W.; m. Karin Schuett, Dec. 23, 1997. MD & PhD, U. Munich, 1975; DiplPharmMed, FAPI, 1997. Med. dir. Duphar Pharma (Solvay Group), Hannover, Germany, 1984-91; internat. clin. dir. Solvay Pharms., Marietta, Ga., 1991-93; corp. med. dir. Solvay Human Health Divsn., Hannover, 1993-94; v.p. global drug safety and surveillance worldwide Solvay Pharmaceuticals, Hannover, 1995—; lectr. in med. ethics and clin. pharmacology. Contbr. to books and articles to profl. jours. Decorated Internat. Order of Merit. Fellow Faculty of Pharm. Medicine, Royal Colls. Physicians of U.K.; mem. Acad. Ethics in Medicine, Kennedy Inst. Ethics at Georgetown U. Avocations: moral philosophy, music, organ works by J.S. Bach. Home: Adolf-Ey-Str 3, D-30519 Hannover Germany Office: Solvay Pharmaceuticals, Hans-Böckler-Allee 20, D-30173 Hannover Germany

WAGNER, WOLFGANG HERIBERT, patent lawyer; b. Wels, Austria, May 5, 1951; s. Hans and Karla (Lughofer) W. MSc in Physics, Eidgenossische Technische Hochschule, Zurich, 1975; PhD in Physics, U. Zurich, 1980. Asst. U. Zurich, 1975-80; trainee in patent law BBC Brown Boveri, Baden, Switzerland, 1982-84; software engr. Polydynamics Ltd., Zurich, 1984-86, Oerlikon Bührle, Zurich, 1986-88; trainee in patent law R.A. Egli & Co., Zurich, 1988-91, patent atty., 1991-93, head patent dept., 1993-95; ptnr. Zimmerli, Wagner & Ptnr. AG, Zurich, 1995—; profl. rep. European Patent Office, 1991. Contbr. articles to profl publs. Mem. Verband der beim europaischen Patentamt eingetragenen freiberuflichen schweizerischen Patentanwälte, Assn. internat. pour la protection de la propriete intellectuelle, Inst. fur gewerblichen Rechtsschutz. Office: Zimmerli Wagner & Ptnr AG, Löwenstrasse 19, CH-8001 Zurich Switzerland

WAGNER-DÖBLER, ROLAND, scholar, consultant, educator; b. Essen, Germany, Jan. 12, 1954; m. Smiljana Primorac, June 17, 1994; 2 children. Diploma, Libr. Sch. Frankfurt, Hochschule für Politik, Munich; PhD, U. Augsburg, Germany, 1989, habilitation, 1997. Scientist Tech. U. Munich, 1990-92, U. Munich, 1992-93; lectr. U. Augsburg, Germany, 1997—; ind. info. broker, 1987-96, cons., 1997—. Author: (in German) Growth Cycles of Technological and Scientific Creativity, 1997; co-author (with Jan Berg): Mathematische Logik von 1847 bis zur Gegenwart, 1993; contbr. articles to profl. jours. Mem. Rsch. Assn. Sci. Comm. and Info. (founding), Gesellschaft für Wissenschaftsforschung Berlin, Internat. Soc. Scientometrics and Informetrics. Avocations: chess, mountaineering. Home: Gewürzmühlstr 10, D-80538 Munich Germany

WAGO, MILDRED HOGAN, municipal official; b. N.Y.C., Aug. 16, 1918; d. Andrew James and Gunhild (Olsen) Hogan; m. Charles Leonard Wago, Nov. 24, 1949 (dec.); children: Linda G., Charlene C. Grad. bus. sch., White Plains, N.Y. Clk. Met. Life Ins. Co., N.Y.C., 1938-50; publican Town of North Castle, Armonk, N.Y., 1960—. Mem. N.Y. State Assn. Receivers and Collectors (v.p. 1983—), Westchester County Assn. Receivers and Collectors (v.p., pres. 1987—), Nat. Assn. Exec. Females. Republican. Home: 3 Wago Ave Armonk NY 10504-1447

WAGONER, G. RICHARD, JR., automotive company executive; b. Wilmington, Del., Feb. 9, 1953. BS in Econs., Duke U., 1975; MBA, Harvard U., 1977. Analyst in treas.'s office, mgr. Latin Am. financing, dir. Can. and overseas borrowing, dir. capital analysis and investment GM, N.Y., 1977-81; treas. GM, Sao Paulo, Brazil, 1981-84, exec. dir. fin., 1984-87; v.p., fin. mgr. GM, Can., 1987-88, group dir. strategic bus. planning, 1988-89; v.p. fin. GM, Zurich, Switzerland, 1989-91; pres. GM, Brazil, 1992-93; head Worldwide Purchasing Group GM, 1993-94, exec. v.p., pres. North Am. ops., 1994-98, pres., COO, mem. bd. dirs., 1998—, CEO, 2000—. Chmn. bd. visitors Fuqua Sch. Bus. Duke U.; trustee Detroit County Day Sch. Mem. Soc. Automotive Engrs. (mem. VISION 2000 exec. com.). Office: GM Corp 300 Renaissance Ctr Detroit MI 48265-0001

WAHAB, HAJI MUHAMMAD ABDUL, company executive; b. Dhaka, Bangladesh, Mar. 3, 1956; s. Haji Abdul Halim and Shamsun (Nahar) Begum; m. Amina Wahab, Jan. 30, 1987; children: Enamul Hasan, Erfanul Hasan. B.Com.(hons.) for Bus. Mgmt./Adminstrn., Dhaka U., 1976. Owner, operator M/S Abdul Wahab, Dhaka, 1976-89; dir. Haji Abdul Halim and Sons, Dhaka, 1978-81, Abdus Salam and Co., Dhaka, 1981-85; owner Halim Plastic and Rubber Industry, Dhaka, 1985—; mng. dir. Nahar Industries. Mem. Bangladesh Footwear Mfrs. Assn. (exec. mem. 1985—), Dhaka C. of C. and Industry, Bangladesh Hardware and Machinery Merchant's Assn. (exec. mem. and Comml. Important Person). Muslim. Avocations: travel, reading. Home: 34/36 Nanda Kumar Dutta Rd, Dhaka 1211, Bangladesh Office: Halim Plastic and Rubber, Halim Plastic & Rubber Ind, 36 Nanda Kumar Dutta Rd, Dhaka 1211, Bangladesh

WAHASS, SAEED HADI, psychologist, educator; b. Al-Freain, Saudi Arabia, Dec. 19, 1960; s. Hadi Mohyee Wahass and Mohrah Aiyed Qohtani; m. Sheikhah Awad; children: Atheer, Abdulhadi, Zeyad, Tarqe, Alla. BS, U. Saudi Arabia, 1986, MA, 1991; PhD, 1997. Asst. lectr. Jao Coll., Saudi Arabia, 1986-91; lectr., clin. psychologist King Faisal U., Saudi Arabia, 1991-97, asst. prof., 1997—, cons. clin. psychologist. Mem. APA, Br. Psychol. Soc., Br. Assn. Behavioural and Cognitive Psychotherapy, Advancement Assn. Behavioral Therapy, Soc. Behavior Med. Fax: 3-857-2327. E-mail: swahass@dammam.kfu.edu.sa. Office: King Fahd Tchg Hosp, Dept Psych Box 40185, 31952 Al-Khobar Saudi Arabia

WAHID, ABDURRAHMAN, president of Indonesia; b. East Java, Indonesia, Aug. 4, 1940; married; 4 daughters. Student, Al Azhar U., Egypt, Islamic U. of Baghdad. Leader Nat. Awakening Party Republic of Indonesia, 1999—, elected nat. pres., 1999—. Avocation: classical music. Office: Office of Pres, Istana Merdeka, Jakarta 10110, Republic of Indonesia*

WAHID, MOHAMMAD REZWANUL, pediatrician, educator; b. Mymensingh, Bangladesh, Sept. 6, 1962; s. Mohammad Abdul Wahid and Samsun (Nahar) W.; m. Rokeya Tasneen, Feb. 5, 1988; children: Tasmia Rezwan, Mayumi Rezwan. MD, Dhaka (Bangladesh) Med. Coll., 1987; PhD, Kagoshima (Japan) U., 1996. Lic. physician. Intern Dhaka Med. Coll. Hosp, Dhaka, 1987-88; rsch. and tchg. assoc. Kagoshima U., 1996—; gen. physician Dhaka, 1988-91; rsch. and tchg. assoc. Kagoshima U., 1996-97; pediatrician Dhaka Shishu Hosp., 1998-99. Recipient Monbusho scholarship Ministry Edn., Japan, 1992-96; fellowship, Japanese Soc. Promotion Sci., 1999—. Mem. Bangladesh Med. Assn., Kagoshina U. Fgn. Students Assn. (pres. 1995-96). Avocations: books, music, movies. E-mail: mitan@citechco.net. Home: House No 103, Rd No 7, Sector 4 Uttara, Dhaka 1230, Bangladesh

WAHIDI, BADER A., insurance executive; b. Kuwait, Aug. 28, 1949; s. Ahmed A. Wahidi and Qad A. Zaman; m. Patrice Wahidi, Jan. 15, 1973. Student, Carnegie Mellon U.; MA in Econometrics, U. Calif., Santa Barbara; postgrad., U. Colo. Gen. mgr. Arab Ins. Group; dir., bd. mem. Bahrain Internat. Bank, KMMC, Kuwait, Allied Insurance Investors, Egypt, Arab Jordanian Insurance Group, Jordan; chmn. Arig Health & Gen. Insurance, Bahrain; bd. dirs., Arab Lebanese Ins. Group, Arab Tunisian Ins. Group, Gulf Arab Investment Corp., Egypt; exec. bd. dirs. CNIA, Morocco. Office: ARIG, PO Box 26992, Manama Bahrain

WAHL, BERNT RAINER, mathematician, writer, software engineer; b. Santa Monica, Calif., June 24, 1960; s. Bruno W. and Ursula (Nunn) W. BA in Math., U. Calif., Santa Cruz, 1984, BS in Physics, 1986; MBA, U. Calif., Davis, 1999; cert. mgmt. tech., U. Calif., Berkeley, 2000. Founding mem. Berkeley (Calif.) Macintosh User Group, Berkeley, 1984—; CEO Dynamic Software, Berkeley, Calif., 1986—; mem. Bootstrap Inst., Fremont, Calif., 1996—; chief creative officer Yellow Giant, Inc., Oakland, Calif.; tech. advisor Reliacom, Reston, Va., Quantal, Berkeley, Calif., Jhane Barnes, Inc., N.Y., 1995—; lectr. U. Calif., Berkeley, U. Calif., Davis, U. Calif., Santa Cruz, 1995-96; adj. prof. bus. Golden Gate U., San Francisco; bd. dirs. Sportabella, Inc. Author: Chaos, 1988, Exploring Fractals, 1995; co-author: Virtual Playhouse, 1994; host (video series) Fractals, 1995, Info. Tech., 1996; film dir./prodr.: Swing City, 1999. Mem. AAAS, Nation Ednl. Film and Video Festival (jury chair), Assn. Computing Machinery. Avocations: Olympic photography, America Cup Heart of Am. E-mail: bernt@wahl.org. Office: Dynamic Software PO Box 13991 Berkeley CA 94712-4991 also: Quantal 1936 University Ave Ste 355 Berkeley CA 94704-1071

WAHL, MARTIN, marine biologist, researcher; b. Wiesbaden, Germany, Apr. 15, 1955. Masters, U. Montpellier, France, 1979, U. Kiel, Germany, 1982; PhD, U. Kiel, Germany, 1987, Habilitation, 1996. Rschr. Lab. Arago U. Paris, France, 1983-87; asst. prof. Kiel, 1987-91; postdoctoral Scripps Instn. of Oceanography, San Diego, 1991-92; postdoctoral Inst. Marine Scis. U. N.C., Morehead City, 1992-93; asst. prof. Kiel U., 1993-97, assoc. prof., 1997-99; sr. lectr. U. Namibia, Windhoek, 1999—. E-mail: mwahl@unam.de.

WAHL, MICHAEL GUENTER, educator; b. Hamm, Germany, Oct. 10, 1953; s. Albert W. and Gertrud (Struchhold) W. Dipl. ing., U. Siegen, 1982, Dr.ing., 1988. Researcher U. Siegen (Germany), 1982-89; cons. MW Consulting, Siegen, 1989-93; prof. U. Siegen, 1993-99, SWT, San Marcos, 1999—; project mgr. ECE, Siegen, 1989-93. Author: Testmustererzeugung fuer Digitale Schaltungen, 1988. Recipient Outstanding Contbn. award USA EDIF User's Group, 1991, Significant Contbn. Reward, 1993. Mem. IEEE. Avocations: biking, dancing. Home: Friedrich Wilhelm Str 215, D 57074 Siegen Germany Office: U Siegen, Hoelderlinstrasse 3, 57068 Siegen Germany

WAHL, ROBERT ARNULF, surgeon; b. Stuttgart, Germany, June 25, 1943; s. August Robert and Hermine Anna (Lederle) W.; m. Heidemarie Van Hoffs, Jan. 10, 1974; children: Julia Katharina, Mathias Franz. MD, U. Munich, 1969. Resident in surgery U. Heidelberg, 1970-76, registrar in surgery, 1977-79; asst. prof. U. Marburg, 1980-84; assoc. prof. U. Frankfurt, 1985—; head of surgery Bürger Hosp., Frankfurt, 1985—; cons. German Thyroid Patients Orgn., 1995—; lectr. in field. Contbr. over 400 articles to profl. jours. Mem. German Assn. Endocrine Surgeons (sec. 1982-88), German Surg. Assn., Internat. Assn. Endocrine Surgery, Internat. Soc. Surgery, N.Y. Acad. Scis., Collegium Internationale Chirurgie Digestive. Roman Catholic. Avocations: contemporary literature and music, skiing, canoeing. Fax: 0049(0)69/1500-0-401. Office: Bürgerhospital, Nibelungenallee 37-41, D-60318 Frankfurt Germany

WAHLERS, THORSTEN, thoracic and cardiovascular surgeon; b. Germany, Feb. 8, 1958; married; 2 children. Grad. in Basic Med. Sci., U. Dusseldorf, Germany, 1979; grad. in Clin. Medicine, U. Cologne, Germany, 1983. Diplomate German Bd. Surgery. Resident thoracic and cardiovascular surgery Hannover (Germany) Med. Sch., 1983-84, practice in traumatology, 1985-86, practice in gen. surgery, 1987-89, cardiothoracic surgeon, 1989-98; staff surgeon div. thoracic and cardiovascular surgery U. Hosp. Jena, Germany, 1999; chief dept. cardiac, toracic and vascular surgery Friedrich Schiller U., Jena, 1999—. Recipient fellowship Harefield Hosp., 1986-87. Mem. German Soc. for Thoracic and Cardiovascular Surgery (Ethicon prize 1992, Franz Köhler prize 1993), German Surg. Soc., Internat. Soc. for Heart and Lung Transplantation (Pres.'s award 1989), European Soc. for Heart and Lung Transplantation, German Soc. Transplant Ctrs. Office: Friedrich Schillar U, Dept Cardiac Thoracic and Vascular Surge, 07740 Jena Germany

WAHLESTEDT, APRIL P., communications executive; b. Cheverly, Md., Apr. 9, 1968; d. James Anthony Pazienza and Beth Lewisa Catherwood; m. Claes R. Wahlestedt, June 15, 1991 (div. July 1996). BS in Fgn. Svc., Georgetown U., 1989; M Internat. Affairs, Columbia U., 1999. Program asst. Spanish Inst., N.Y.C., 1990-92; spl. asst. Oscar de la Renta, Ltd., N.Y.C., 1992-94, 95-96; rschr. Bank Credit Analyst, Montreal, Que., Can., 1994-95; dir. comms. Coun. on Fgn. Rels., N.Y.C., 1996—. Republican. Roman Catholic. E-mail: awahlestedt@cfr.org.

WAHLGREN, MIKAEL ULF LENNART, legal counsel; b. Helsingborg, Skane, Sweden, May 4, 1965; m. Jeanna Louise Linton, Nov. 14, 1992; children: Karolina Märta Wilhelmine, Douglas Knut Magnus. M of Law, U. Lund, Sweden, 1991. Paralegal Swedish Internat. Devel. Authority, Stockholm, 1988, 89; clk. Jönköping (Sweden) Dist. Ct., 1991-92; legal counsel Skanska Internat. Civil Engring. AB, Stockholm, 1992-94, 95-97; legal mgr. Uri Civil Contractor AB, New Delhi, 1994-95; legal counsel ABB Bus. Svcs., Baden, Switzerland, 1997-2000; sr. legal counsel Rolls-Royce Power Ventures Ltd., London, 2000—; dir. Skanska Internat. Equipment Svcs. Ltd., Colombo, Sri Lanka, 1995-97, Quaraka Indsl. Park Ltd., Nairobi, Kenya, 1995-96; co. sec. Skanska Dredging AB, Göteborg, Sweden, 1996-97, Skanska Raise Borring AB, Stockholm, 1996-97. Author: (book) What a Swedish Party Has to Consider When He Intends to Make a Contract in Kenya, 1991. Chmn. Moderate Party, Helsingkrona, 1981-82, Helsingborg Student Fraternity, Lund, 1988-89. 2d lt. 3d Anti-Aircraft Regiment, 1984-85. Fellow Roundtable # 31; mem. Swedish In-House Lawyers' Assn. Avocations: cultural events, shooting, golf, riding, skiing. Office: Allington House, 150 Victoria St, London SW1E 5LB, England

WAHLIN, ÅKE LENNART THOMAS, neuropsychologist, psychology researcher; b. Halstahammar, Sweden, June 19, 1956; s. Lennart Edward and Brita Josefina (Svenningsson) W.; m. Tarja-Brita Hannele Robins, Mar. 26, 1989; children: Emma, Iida, Emil. Psychologist, Stockholm U., 1990; PhD, Karolinska Inst., Stockholm, 1996. Rsch. asst. Stockholm Gerontology Rsch. Ctr., 1990-91; neuropsychologist Huddinge Hosp., Stockholm, 1992-93; postdoctoral rschr. Karolinska Inst., 1997—; vice asst. dir. psychology sect. Stockholm Gerontology Rsch. Ctr., 1997—. Contbr. chpt. to book, articles to profl. jours. Sgt., Swedish Army Arty., 1975-76, Jönköping. Rsch. grantee Forskningsradsnamnden, Swedish Coun. for Rsch. in Humanities and Social Scis., Sweden, 1997. Mem. APA, European Brain & Behavior Soc., Gerontological Soc. Am. Office: Stockholm Gerontology Rsch, Olivecronasväg 4, S-11382 Stockholm Sweden

WÅHLIN, VAGN, history educator; b. Copenhagen, Jan. 16, 1935; s. Frederik M. Andersen and Erna M. (Kretzschmer) W.; m. Birgitte M. Nielsen, June 19, 1964 (div. 1981); children: Sidsel, Rane; m. Barbara E. Dunn, Dec., 1984 (div. 1991); stepchildren: Sara D., Simon D.; m. Kaisu K. Salmia, 1995. Degree, U. Copenhagen, 1968. Amanuensis U. Aarhus, Denmark, 1968-73, mem. study bd. Hist. Inst., 1973-93, 95—, lectr., docent, 1989—; dir. Ctr. North Atlantic Studies, Denmark, 1990-94, bd. dirs., 1995—: Denmark, USA, Nordic Cultural History, The Faroe Islands, commentator in Danish and English in the press, radio and tv. Author: Historien i kulturhistorien, 1988, Trosliv og skolevirke, 1991, Mellem Faerøsk og Dansk Politik, 1917-1920, 1994, more than 50 rsch. articles in Danish and internat. jours., 1964—, editor of North Atlantic Studies, 1989—, other rsch. jours. Rsch. fellow Univ. Coll., London, 1973-74. Mem. North Atlantic Fishery History Assn., Hejredalsparken Bldg. Soc. (vice chmn. 1991—). Social Democrat. Lutheran. Avocation: music. Office fax: 45-86256589. Home: Emmasvej 18, DK 8220 Brabrand Aarhus Denmark Office: Historisk Inst, Aarhus U, DK 8000 Århus Denmark

WAHLSTRÖM, BO ANDERS, government agency administrator; b. Göteborg, Sweden, July 11, 1942; s. Arne L. A. and Maj-Brita S. (Lindberg) W.; m. Agneta E. Pallinder, Oct. 28, 1962 (div. Oct. 1971); children: Katarina, Susanna; m. Anita L. Moberg, Aug. 1, 1981; children: Robert, Daniel, Magnus. BS, Göteborg U., 1965, MS, 1969, PhD, 1971; toxicology diploma, Karolinska Inst., Stockholm, 1980. From univ. tchr. to assoc. prof. Göteborg U., 1965-76; rschr. Nat. Food Adminstrn., Uppsala, Sweden, 1976-80; rsch. asst. Geneva (Switzerland) U., 1974-76; head pesticide divsn. Products Control Bd., Solna, Sweden, 1980-95; head dept. sci. tech. Nat. Chems. Inspectorate, Solna, 1986-90, dir. internat. affairs, 1991-98; sr. scientific adv. UNEP Chems., Geneva, Switzerland, 1998—; sec. Swedish Govt. Chems. Policy Com., 1996-97; postdoctoral fellow Royal Soc. London, 1971-72; chmn. OECD Chems. Group, Paris, 1996-98. Sgt. Coast Artillery, 1960-61. Mem. Swedish Soc. Toxicology (pres. 1991-92). Avocations: sports, mountain hiking. Office: UNEP Chemicals, 11-13 Chemin des Anémones, CH-1219 Châtelaine Geneva Switzerland

WAHLSTROM, LENNART STIG, chemical engineer, scientist; b. Fagersta, Sweden, Mar. 11, 1952; s. Lindor Victor and Märta Cecilia (Holmquist) W.; m. Ann-Marie Inga Jonsson; children: Jeanette, Peter, Michael. Chmn. engr., Zimmermansm Skolan, 1972; chemistry/biochemistry, Uppsala U., 1979; psychology, Örebro Hogskola, 1991. Chem. engr. Pharmacia, Uppsala, Sweden, 1972-74; rsch. engr. Pharmacia Instrument Devel., Uppsala, 1974-80; sect. head mgr. Pharmacia Biotech., Uppsala, 1980-86; sr. scientist Biacore AB, Uppsala, 1990—; dept. head Bionsensor AB, 1986-89; cons. Gems Pet, Uppsala, 1991-93. Author numerous posters. Mem. Internat. Food Tech., Am. Assn. Analytical Chemists, Sci. Assn. Dedicated to Analytical Excellence, Leatherhead Food RA. Avocations: reading books, fishing, psychology, wood working. Office: Biacore AB, Rapsgatan 7, S-75450 Uppsala Sweden

WAHSNER, RENATE MERKEL, philosopher, researcher; b. Lausen, Leipzig, Germany, Mar. 25, 1938; d. Albert and Irmgard (Kirchhof) Merkel; children: Nikos, Sirko. Diploma in Philosophy, Humboldt U., Berlin, 1961, PhD, 1966; D Sci. Philosophy, Acad. Scis. Germany, Berlin, 1978. Sci. asst. Coll. Econs., Berlin, 1961-63; sci. sr. asst. Humboldt U. Inst. Philosophy, Berlin, 1966-70; v.p. natural scis. Urania Soc. Circulation Sci. Knowledge, Berlin, 1970-74; mem. sci. staff Inst. Astrophysics Acad. Sci. Germany, Potsdam, 1974-82, mem. sci. staff Einstein Lab., 1982-91; mem. sci. staff Centre History and Philosophy of Sci., Berlin, 1992-95; mem. sci. staff, sr. scientist Max Planck Inst. History of Sci., Berlin, 1995—; lectr. Free U. Inst. Philosophy, Berlin, 1990-96, U. Potsdam Inst. Philosophy, 1995. Author: Mensch und Kosmos-die copernicanische Wende, 1978, Das Aktive und das Passive. Zur erkenntnistheoretischen Begründung der Physik durch den Atomismus-dargestellt an Newton und Kant, 1981, Prämissen physikalischer Erfahrung. Zur Helmholtzschen Kritik des Raum-Apriorismus und zur Newton-Marxschen Kritik des antiken Atomismus, 1992, Zur Kritik der Hegelschen Naturphilosophie. Über ihren Sinn im Lichte der heutigen Naturerkenntnis, 1995, Naturwissenschaft, 1998; co-author: Newton und Voltaire. Zur Begründung und Interpretation der klassischen Mechanik, 1980, Physikalischer Dualismus und dialektischer Widerspruch. Studien zum physikalischen Bewegungsbegriff, 1989, Die Wirklichkeit der Physik. Sudien zu Idealität und Realität in einer messenden Wissenschaft, 1992; co-editor: Ernst Mach, Die Mechanik in ihrer Entwicklung. Historisch-kritisch dargestellt, 1988, Voltaire, Elemente der Philosophie Newtons. Verteidgung des Newtonianismus. Die Metaphysik des Neuton, 1997; editor: Gravitation und Kosmos. Beiträge zu Problemen der Allgemeinen Relativitätstheorie, 1988; co-author, co-editor: Messung als Begründung oder Vermittlung? Ein Briefwechsel mit Paul Lorenzen Über Protophysik und ein paar andere Dinge, 1995. Recipient postgrad. scholarship Humboldt U., Inst. Philosophy, Berlin, 1963-66. Mem. German Phys. Soc., Soc. Analytic Philosophy, Kant Soc., Internat. Hegel Soc., Internat. Hegel Union, Internat. Feuerbach Soc., Austrian Soc. Hist. Scis. Office: Max Planck Inst History Sci, Wilhelmstr 44, D-10117 Berlin Germany

WAI, PING-KONG ALEXANDER, engineering educator; b. Hong Kong, Jan. 22, 1960; s. Yung Tong Wai and Shiu Ngan Chan; m. Sheila Tang, Nov. 20, 1995. BS, U. Hong Kong, 1981; MS, U. Md., 1985, PhD, 1988. Rsch. physicist Sci. Applications Internat. Corp., McLean, Va., 1988-90; rsch. assoc. dept. elec. engring. U. Md., Balt., 1990-96; asst. prof. dept. electronic engring. Hong Kong Poly. U., Hung Hom, 1996-97, assoc. prof. dept. electronic and info. engring., 1997—; chief tech. cons. Vast Team Unltd., Hong Kong, World Tone Internat. Ltd. Contbr. articles to profl. jours. Mem. IEEE (sr.), Optical Soc. Am. Avocations: martial arts, golf, roller-blading, reading. Fax: (852) 2362-8439. E-mail: enwai@polyy.edu.hk. Office: Hong Kong Poly U, Dept Elec & Info Engring, Hung Hom Hong Kong China

WAID, JOHN SAVILLE, ecologist; b. Alverstoke, England, Nov. 16, 1927; s. Saville Charles and Edith Alice (Venelle) W.; m. Sally Cecilia Taylor, May 29, 1953; children: Caroline, Giselle, Saville, Natasha, Arabella. BS with honors, London U., 1951; MS, Oxford U., England, 1953, DPhil, 1959. Rsch. scientist Grassland Rsch. Inst., England, 1953-55, Nature Conservancy, England, 1955-58, Fisons Fertilisers, England, 1958-62; sr. lectr. U. New England, Australia, 1962-64; rsch. assoc. Cornell U., 1964-65; lectr. U. Reading, England, 1965-69; reader microbiology Canterbury U., New Zealand, 1969-74; found. prof. microbiology La Trobe U., 1974-92, dean sch. biol. scis., 1977-79, 83-85, prof. microbiol. emeritus, 1993—; adh. prof. microbiology U. Sunshine Coast, 1997—; adj. prof. Univ. Sunshine Coast, 1997—; team leader Colombo Plan, Faculty Sci., Khon Kaen, Thailand, 1974, Australian Program Assistance Agrl. U., Bogor, Indonesia, 1986; dir. Victoria Biotech. Cons., 1986-95; cons. in field. Editor: PCBs and the Environment, 1986; co-editor: (with D. Parkinson) Ecology of Soil Fungi, 1960; editor-in-chief Soil Biology & Biochem., 1969—; contbr. articles to profl. jours. Erskine Travel fellow Canterbury U., 1973, Hector and Andrew Stewart Meml. fellow U. Western Australia, 1990. Fellow Australian Inst. Biology; mem. Australian Soc. Microbiology, Internat. Soc. Soil Sci. E-mail: jswaid@optusnet.com.au. or sallywaid@bigpond.com.au. Address: 10 Royal Dr, Buderim 4556, Australia

WAIDELICH, RAPHAELA MARIA, urologist, researcher; b. Munich, Bavaria, Germany, Sept. 14, 1958; d. Georg and Elisabeth (Kollmannsberger) Fuersich; m. Wilhelm Rudolf Waidelich, June 19, 1984; 1 child, Daniel. MD, U. Munich, 1984. Lic. urologist. Resident in surgery Hosp. Martha Maria, Munich, 1990-91; resident in urology Univ. Hosp., Munich, 1991-96, asst. prof. urology, 1996—. Editor: (books) Laser in Medicine, 1987, 89, 91, 93, 95, 97. Mem. Internat. Soc. Laser Surgery and Medicine (bd. dirs. 1997—), Cen. European Assn. Urology (founding mem.), German Soc. Urology, German Soc. Laser Medicine. Avocations: tennis, swimming, cycling. Home: Becker-Gundahlstr 32, D-81479 Munich Bavaria, Germany Office: U Hosp Munich, Dept Urology, D-81366 Munich Bavaria, Germany

WAIDLER, BEVERLY MAE, music teacher; b. Eau Claire, Wis., Jan. 14, 1941; d. George Hiram and Myrtle Julianna (Gunderson) Gilbertson; m. Brian Edmund Waidler Sr., Aug. 12, 1961; children: Brian Edmund jr., Sonvy Kristina, Heidi Julianna. BS in Elem. Edn., U. Md., 1962, MEd in Music and Piano/Voice, 1976. Cert. elem. and music tchr. Tchr. 5th grade Pub. Schs. Prince George's County, Bladensburg, Md., 1962; GS 5 mortgage notes accts. clk. Fed. Housing Authority, Washington, 1963-64; 4th grade substitute tchr. Amidon Sch., Washington, 1966; music tchr. vocal and gen. Parkland Jr. H.S. Montgomery County Pub. Schs., Rockville, Md., 1966-67; pvt. piano tchr. Rockville, 1966-80; salesperson, then office worker Sears Montomery Mall, Bethesda, 1989-91; substitute tchr. Pub. Schs. D.C. and Montgomery County, Rockville, Gaithersburg, Washington, 1991-95; pvt. piano and voice instr. Rockville, 1995—. Singing recitals include Weisbaden, Germany, 1982, Kaiserslautern, Germany, 1982, Pirmasens, Germany, 1983. Election office worker Dem. gubinatorial race, Wheaton, 1992; unit pres. Ch. Women United, 1976-78, mem. 1997—; lobby participant Internat. Women's Year, 1975. Mem. AAUW, Phi Theta Delta, Friday Morning Music Club. Democrat. Baptist. Avocations: art appreciation, reading biographies, walking, yoga. Home: 7036 Wick Ln Rockville MD 20855-1963

WAILLY, ALAIN JAMYL DE, biologist; b. Fez, Morocco, Jan. 5, 1938; s. Louis and Lamia Sophie (Abourizk) de W.; m. Mireille Sarran, July 16, 1960; children: Georges, Hélène. MS, Mohammed V U., Rabat, Morocco, 1963. Head dept. Promagri, Casablanca, Morocco, 1965-67, Sasma, Casablanca, 1968-79; dir.'s asst. INRA, Bordeaux, France, 1979-81; head dept. King's Secretariat, Casablanca, 1981-86; cons. Pessac, France, 1986—. Patentee med. apparatus; contbr. articles to Bull. Archeol. Morocco and Acta Biotheor. Mem. Biol. Theory French Soc., Mensa. Home: 11 Ave du Poujeau, 33600 Pessac France

WAIN, GEOFFREY THOMAS, academic administrator, mathematics educator; b. London, May 5, 1933; s. Arthur Henry and Esther Annie Dorothy (Smith) W.; m. Victoria Elizabeth Cooledge, Aug. 12, 1967 (div. 1974); children: Alexis, Rupert; m. Zakiah Mohamed Noor, July 20, 1975; children: Johann, Noreena, Daniel. Grad., King's Coll., London, 1954; Diploma in Edn., Bradford U., 1970. Tchr., house master Gordonstoun Sch., Elgin, Scotland, 1958-61; prin. lectr. Balls Park Coll., Hertford, Eng., 1961-70; sr. lectr. U. Leeds, Eng., 1970-94; prof. U. Malaysia, Sarawak, 1994-96; acad. mgr. No. Consortium/U. Manchester Inst. Sci. and Tech., Manchester, Eng., 1997-98; sec. Joint Math. Coun. U.K., 1981-86; cons. ODA/Brit. Coun., South Africa, 1978-94, 98; cons. ODA, Sierra Leone, 1985. Author, editor: Issues in Mathematical Education, 1994, Mathematics Teacher Education Project, 2 vols., 1980; (with S. Flower) Mathematics Homework on a Microcomputer, 1989; editor, author: Mathematics Education, 1978. Lt. comdr. Royal Navy, 1955-58, Res., 1958-72. Grantee European Cmty., Czech Republic and Slovenia, 1992-94, Univ. Grants Com., 1987, U. Leeds, 1992. Avocations: boating, military history, reading, stamp collecting, music. Home and Office: 39 Jackson Ave, LS8 1NP Leeds England

WAINE, COLIN, director health programs; b. Bishop Auckland, Durham, Eng., Mar. 12, 1936; s. Anderson and Annie (Bowron) W.; m. Gwendoline Jameson; children: Jennifer, Anna. MB BS with honors, U. Durham, 1959; MRCGP with distinction, Royal Coll., U.K., 1975. House officer Bishop Auckland (Eng.) Gen. Hosp., 1959-60, Maternity Hosp., Newcastle upon Tyne, Eng., 1960-61; pvt. practice Bishop Auckland, 1961-93; hosp. practitioner pediatrics Gen. Hosp., Bishop Auckland, 1963-89; part-time unit mgr. Cmty. Unit, Bishop Auckland, 1983-89; dir. Health Authority, Sunderland, Eng., 1993—; cons. U.K. del. European Health Com., Strasbourg, France, 1983-85; chmn. Royal Coll. of Gen. Practitioners, London, 1990-93; mem. Health Edn. Authority, London, 1988-90, No. Regional Health Authority, Newcastle, 1984-88. Editor 21 books; contbr. articles to profl. jours. Fellow Royal Coll. of Gen. Practitioners, Royal Coll. of Pathologists, Royal Soc. of Arts; mem. British Med. Assn. Avocations: reading, gardening, cricket, family. Home: 42 Etherley Ln, Bishop Auckland DL14 7QZ, England Office: Sunderland Health Authority, Durham Rd, Sunderland SR3 4AF, England

WAINSZTEIN, NESTOR ADRIAN, physician; b. Buenos Aires, Dec. 4, 1956; s. Jaime and Fanny (Kesselman) W.; m. Edith Susana Paternò, Aug. 27, 1983; children: Vanina, Agustina. MD, U. Buenos Aires, 1980. Resident Guenes Pvt. Hosp., Buenos Aires, 1981-83, chief resident, 1984-85, chief critical care unit, 1985-93, 93—, chief dept. critical care & emergency, 1991-93, head internal medicine, 1993; prof. internal medicine Favaloro U., 1996—; chief critical care unit Inst. Cardiology and Cardiovascular Surgery Favaloro Found., 1992—; head dept. critical care Inst. of Neurologic Investigations Raul Carrea Fleni, 1994—; head dept. of edn. Favaloro Found. Editor-in-chief Intensive Medicine Argentina, 1987—; contbr. articles to profl. jours. Fellow Am. Coll. of Chest Physicians, Am. Coll. Critical Care Medicine, Internat. Coll. Physicians & Surgeons; mem. Soc. Critical Care Medicine, Soc. Argentina de Terapia Intensiva (dir. pubs. 1987).

WAINWRIGHT, CHERRY LINDSEY, science educator, researcher; b. Blackpool, Eng., Feb. 11, 1960; d. Frederick Henry and Doreen (Slinger) W.; m. Peter James Marks, July 24, 1992; children: Bethany Wainwright Marks, Chloe Davies Marks. BSc, Aberdeen U., Scotland, 1981; PhD, Strathclyde U., Glasgow, Scotland, 1984. Postdoctoral rsch. fellow Strathclyde U., 1984-88, Janssen Found. rsch. lectr., 1988-93, lectr., 1993-94, sr. lectr., 1994—. Editor: Myocardial Preconditioning, 1996-99; editor Brit. Jour. Pharmacology, 1996—; assoc. editor Pharmacology and Therapeutics, 1994—; contbr. articles to profl. jours. Fellow European Soc. Cardiology; mem. Internat. Soc. for Heart Rsch., Am. Heart Assn., Internat. Soc. Cardiovascular Pharmacotherapy, Brit. Soc. Cardiovascular Rsch. (hon. treas. 1996-98), Brit. Pharmacol. Soc., Clydesdale Amateur Rowing Club (com. mem. 1990-93). Church England. Avocations: rowing, wine tasting, interior decorating, music. Office: U Strathclyde, U Strathclyde/Dept Phys/Phm, 51BS 27 Taylor St, Glasgow 94 ONR, Scotland

WAINWRIGHT, ELAINE MARY, religious studies educator; b. Toowoomba, Queensland, Australia, Aug. 25, 1948; d. Norman Thomas and Kathleen Veronica (O'Connell) W. BA with honors, U. Queensland, Brisbane, Australia, 1981; MA in Theology, Cath. Theol. U., Chgo., 1985; Élève diplomé, École Biblique, Jerusalem, 1986; PhD, U. Queensland, Brisbane, 1991. Secondary tchr. All Hollow's Sch., Brisbane, 1973-74; lectr. Pius XII Seminary, Brisbane, 1981-83; lectr. bibl. studies Brisbane Coll. Theology, 1987—; founder, exec. mem. Women Scholar Religion and Theology, 1992-98; mem. editl. com. New Testament, Concilium, Nijmegen, The Netherlands, 1993—, mem. editl. com. feminist studies, 1993—; adj. fellow Griffith U. Sch. Theology, Brisbane, 1998—. Author: Towards a Feminist Critical Reading of the Gospel According to Matthew, 1991, Shall We Look for Another: A Feminist Rereading of the Matthean Jesus, 1998; mem. editl. bd. Jour. for the Study of the New Testament, 1997—; contbr. articles to profl. jours. Mem. mgmt. com. Project Esther, Brisbane, 1994-98. Mem. Soc. Bibl. Lit., Cath. Bibl. Assn. Australia (pres. 1991-92), Nat. Found. Australian Women. Home: 7/37 Marathon St, Aspley QLD 4034, Australia Office: Brisbane Coll Theology, Approach Rd, Banyo QLD 4014, Australia

WAISANEN, CHRISTINE M., lawyer, writer; b. Hancock, Mich., May 27, 1949; d. Frederick B. and Helen M. (Hill) W.; m. Robert John Katzenstein, Apr. 21, 1979; children: Jeffrey Hunt, Erick Hill. BA with honors, U. Mich., 1971; JD, U. Denver, 1975. Bar: Colo. 1975, D.C. 1978. Labor rels. atty. U.S. C. of C., Washington, 1976-79; govt. rels. specialist ICI Americas, Inc., Wilmington, Del., 1979-87; dir. cultural affairs City of Wilmington, 1987; founder, chief writer Hill, Katzenstein & Waisanen, 1988—. Chmn. Delaware State Coastal Zone Indsl. Control Bd., 1993—. Mem. Fed. Bar Assn., Jr. League of Wilmington (v.p. 1985-86), Women's Rep. Club of

Wilmington (bd. dirs. 1988-93), U. Mich. Club of Del. (pres. 1999—). Republican. Presbyterian. Home: 1609 Mt Salem Ln Wilmington DE 19806-1134

WAISBEIN, HÉCTOR, hospital administrator; b. Buenos Aires, Aug. 10, 1935; s. Saúl and Berta (Wainer) W.; m. Amanda Teresa Martinez, Nov. 24, 1966; children: Claudia Amanda, Saúl Daniel y Pablo Eduardo. MD, Buenos Aires, 1962. Physician imaging dept. Hosp. Alvear, Buenos Aires, 1963-79; chief of imaging dept. Hosp. Oncológico, Buenos Aires, 1980-81, Hosp. Tornú, Buenos Aires, 1979-80, Hosp. Piñero, Buenos Aires, 1981—; assoc. prof. Buenos Aires U., 1991. Contbr. articles to profl. jours. Jewish. Home: Av Juan B Justo 4353, 1416 Buenos Aires Argentina Office: Hosp P Piñero, Varela 1301, 1406 Buenos Aires Argentina

WAISER, JOHANNES ERHARD, nephrologist; b. Nuremberg, Germany, Aug. 29, 1963; s. Max Erhard and Herta Magdalena (Horner) W.; m. Silvia Wurm; 2 children. Physician, Friedrich-Alexander U., 1990, MD, 1992; internist, Humboldt U., 1998. Resident Friedrich-Alexander U., Erlangen, Germany, 1991-94; transplant coord. Deutsche Stiftung Organ Transplantation, Nuremberg, Germany, 1994-95; chief resident Humboldt U., Berlin, 1995—. Author: (with others) Blutreinigungsverfahren, 1997; contbr. articles to profl. jours. Lance cpl. Telecommunications, 1982-83. Mem. Internat. Soc. of Nephrology. Roman Catholic. Avocations: hockey, skiing, tennis, jogging, piano. Office: Humboldt U Dept Nephrology U Hosp Charite, Schumannstrasse 20/21, 10117 Berlin Germany

WAISMAN, DAN ISRAEL, neonatologist, researcher; b. Buenos Aires, Sept. 4, 1958; arrived in Israel, 1984; s. David Ber and Elena (Kemper) W.; m. Neta Strelski, Aug. 23, 1990; children: Gal, Amit. Grad. high sch., Reconquista, Buenos Aires, 1976. Resident in pediat. Carmel Med. Ctr., Haifa, Israel, 1985-92; fellow in neonatology B.C. Children's Hosp., Vancouver, 1992-95; rsch. fellow Pulmonary Rsch. Lab. St. Paul's Hosp., Vancouver, 1993-95; attending neonatologist Bnai-zion Med. Ctr., Haifa, 1997—, Carmel Med. Ctr., Haifa, 1997—; rsch. assoc. Shock Rsch. Lab. Carmel Med. Ctr., 1997—. Mem. Israeli Med. Assn., Israeli Neonatal Soc., Israel Soc. for Hyperbaric and Diving Medicine and Physiology. E-mail: dwaisman@netvision.net.il. Office: Carmel Hosp Dept Neonatol, 7 Michal St, 34362 Haifa Israel

WAISMAN, MARC, orthopaedic surgeon; b. Resistencia, Argentina, Nov. 4, 1943; s. David Ber and Elena (Kemper) W.; m. Ana Brisanof, Sept. 9, 1969 (div. 1989); children: Gabriel, Michal, Danit, Keren, Guy, Ofer. MD, U. Medicine, Buenos Aires, 1968; orthopaedic surgeon, Rambam Med. Sch., Israel, 1977. Resident in orthopaedic surgery Rambam Hosp., 1969-75, 76-77; sr. cons. and rschr. Carmel Hosp., Haifa, Israel, 1977-86; guest fellow in spine surgery St. Mary Hosp., Mpls., 1986, Long Beach (Calif.) Meml. Hosp., Jackson Meml. Hosp., Miami, Fla., 1986; chief dept. orthopaedics Zvulun Med. Ctr., Israel, 1982; chief spine surgery unit Carmel Med. Ctr., Haifa, Israel, 1987—. Contbr. articles to profl. jours. Capt. Israel Def. Forces, 1975-95. Mem. Israel Med. Assn., Israel Orthopaedic Assn., Asociacion Argentina Ortopedia y Traumatologia (hon.). Office: PO Box 5153, Kyriat Bialik 27000, Israel

WAISMAN, WARNER, pharmacist; b. N.Y.C., Apr. 22, 1931; s. Abraham Herbert and Pearl (Brand) W. BS in biochemistry, BS in sociology, Queens Coll., 1955; BS in pharmacy, Bklyn. Coll. Pharmacy, 1958. Registered pharmacist, N.Y., La. Pharmacist Schreir Pharmacy, N.Y.C., 1962-63; pharmacist Dew Drug, N.Y.C., 1963-66, Raysol Pharmacy, N.Y.C., 1966-70, 72-75, Bellevue Hosp., N.Y.C., 1970-72, Bronx State Hosp., N.Y.C., 1975-78, Coler Hosp., N.Y.C., 1978-95. Mem. N.Y. State Health-Sys. Pharmacists. Democrat. Jewish. Home: 13215 Rico Pl Jamaica NY 11417-2017

WAISSER, KAREL, chemist, educator; b. Hradec Králové, Czech Republic, Feb. 14, 1936; s. Karel and Marie (Voborniková) W.; m. Marie Krámová, July 6, 1967; children: Karel, Petr. MSc, Charles U., Prague, Czech Republic, 1961, PhD, 1966, DSc, 1992. Postdoctoral fellow U. New Brunswick, Fredericton, Can., 1967-68; rsch. assoc. Laval U., Que., Can., 1968-69, Charles U., 1969-72; asst. prof. chemistry Charles U., Hradec Králové, 1972-88, assoc. prof. chemistry, 1988-93, head dept. chemistry, 1990—, prof. chemistry, 1993—, sub-dean for sci., 1994-97. Author: Structure and Nomenklature of Organic Compounds, part 1, 1993, Struktura a nomenklatura organickych sloučenin, 1996, Reaktivita organickych sloučenin, 1996, Bioorganická chemie, 1998, Organická chemie, vol. I, 1999; contbr. numerous articles to profl. jours. Czech Republic grantee, 1993, 96, 99, 2000, Min. of Edn. grantee, 1994, 96, 98, 99, 2000. Mem. Czech Chem. Soc. (hon.; vice-chmn. organic chem. group), Czech Chem. Soc. (hon. mem.), Slovak Pharm. Soc. (hon.). Achievements include patents on varied antituberculous drugs and on antimycotic drugs. Office: Faculty of Pharmacy, Charles U Heyrovsky St 1203, CZ500 05 Hradec Králové Czech Republic

WAIT, CHARLES VALENTINE, banker; b. Albany, N.Y., May 28, 1951; s. Newman Edward Jr. and Jane Caroline (Adams) W.; m. Candace Ellin Hollar, May 27, 1978; children: Charles Valentine Jr., Christopher David, Alexandra Dallas Wait. BA, Cornell U., 1973; cert. in banking, Rutgers U., 1981. Asst. v.p. The Adirondack Trust Co., Saratoga Springs, N.Y., 1974, treas., 1978-81, sec., treas., 1981-84, pres., 1984—, also bd. dirs.; bd. trustees N.Y. Bus. Devel., 1997; mem., Saratoga County Indsl. Development Agency, 1998—, nom. com. Fed. Reserve Bank N.Y.; mem. Yaddo Corp., Saratoga Springs, 1996—, corp. sec. and asst. treas., 1997—, asst. treas., 1998—; bd. dirs. N.Y. Bus. Devel. Corp. Trustee Skidmore Coll., Saratoga Springs, 1984—, Nat. Mus. Dance, Saratoga Springs, 1987—, N.Y. Racing Assn., Nat. Mus. Racing, 1988-91, v.p., 1989-91; trustee Charles R. Wood Found., 1991-98; chmn. Saratoga Springs City Ctr. Authority, 1983-89; treas. Saratoga Performing Arts Ctr., 1987, chmn., 1989-97, chmn. Saratoga Care, Inc., Face of the Future Capital Campaign. Named Outstanding New Yorker, N.Y. State Jaycees, 1984; recipient Pvt. Sector Initiative award Pres. Ronald Reagan, Commitment to Community award, N.Y. State Bus. Coun., 1983, Liberty Bell award Saratoga County Bar Assn. for cmty. svc., Good Scout award Twin Rivers Coun., 1997, Exec. of Yr. award Capital Dist. Bus. Rev., 1999; Paul Harris fellow Dist. 7190, 1997, Sam Walton Bus. Leader Awd., 1997. Mem. Ind. Bankers Assn. of N.Y. State (bd. dirs., sec. 1986-87), N.Y. Bankers Assn. (bd. dirs. 1987, treas. 1995—, chmn. 1997-99), N.Y. State Bankers Retirement System (trustee 1987-95, vice chmn., chmn. 1992-94), Am. Inst. Banking (Counsel of Yr. 1976), Greater Saratoga C. of C., Pillar Soc. Republican. Home: 658 N Broadway Saratoga Springs NY 12866-1624 Office: The Adirondack Trust Co 473 Broadway Saratoga Springs NY 12866-2262

WAITE, ANDREW JONATHAN, lawyer; b. Salisbury, Wiltshire, England, Feb. 25, 1950; s. Eric Peter and Beryl Margaret (Gunn) W.; m. Cheryl Anita Russell, Aug. 25, 1979; children: Rachel, Benjamin. BA in Law, Oxford (Eng.) U., 1973, MA, 1977. Bar: solicitor, Eng. Solicitor Clintons, London, 1975-76, Lambeth Comty. Law Ctr., London, 1976-80; lectr. U. Southampton, Eng., 1980-88; acting dir. environ. law ctr. U. Southampton, 1984-87; head environment dept. Masons, London, 1988-90; coord. environ. group Linklaters & Paines, London, 1990-93; ptnr., coord. environ. group Berwin Leighton, London, 1993—; vis. prof. environ. law U. Ga. Law Sch., Athens, 1987; mem. editl. bd. Environ. Law and Mgmt., Eng., 1989—, Nat. Resources, Energy and Environ. Law, ABA, U.S., 1993—; mem. Internat. Coun. Environ. Law, Bonn, Germany, 1992—, Internat. Ct. of Environ. Arbitration and Conciliation, Mex., 1994—, Internat. Union for the Conservation Nature Commn. on Environ. Law, 1999—. Co-author: Environmental Law in Property Transactions, 1997; editor: (book) Butterworth's Environmental Law Handbook, 1994, 2nd edit., 1997; prin. contbr. Internat. Encyclopedia Environ. Law: United Kingdom, 1992; adv. editor Encyclopedia of Forms and Precedents: Public Health and Environ. Law, 1992; contbr. articles to environ. publs., 1988—. drafter forestry legislation Sierra Leone, FAO, 1989; advised UK govt. on environ. legislation, Brownlands Group, London, 1993—, Ukranian Govt. Coun. Europe, 1995. Mem. UK Environ. Law Assn. (co-founder, mem. coun. 1986-97, sec. 1986-90), European Environ. Law Assn. (bd. dirs., v.p. 1992-99, pres. 1999—), Internat. Ctr. Comparative Environ. Law (v.p. 1994—), Confedn. Brit. Industry (chmn. ad hoc subcom. on environ. liability 2000—). Anglican. Avocations: history, archeology, countryside, films, theatre. Office: Berwin Leighton Solicitors, Adelaide House London Brdg, London EC4R 9HA, England

WAITE, DONALD EUGENE, medical educator, consultant; b. Columbus, Ohio, Aug. 25, 1925; s. Sidney B. and Louise Alice (Lipsey) W.; children: David L., Larry R., James A., Steve C., Debra J., Julie A., Craig D., Tracy E., Christopher R. DO in Osteopathic Medicine, U. Osteo. Medicine and Health Scis., 1955; MPH, U. Calif., Berkeley, 1989. Intern Doctors Hosp., Columbus, Ohio, 1955-56; pvt. practice Columbus, 1956-72; prof. family medicine Mich. State U., East Lansing, 1972-90, prof. emeritus, 1990—; cons. Environ. Health Conss., Columbus, East Lansing, 1990—; mem. occupl. health del. to Poland, Hungary and Czechoslovakia, 1992; mem. Aerospace Med. Assn. del. to People's Republic of China, 1993. Author: Your Environment, Your Health and You, 1991, Environmental Health Hazards, 1994. Med. examiner FAA, East Lansing, 1964-90; asst. scoutmaster Boy Scouts Am., East Lansing, 1980-83. With USN, 1943-45. Mem. Am. Osteo. Assn., Am. Coll. Occupl. Medicine, Aerospace Med. Assn., Ohio Osteo. Assn., Mich. Assn. Osteo. Physicians. Avocations: skiing, fishing, hunting. Home: 117 Agate Way Williamston MI 48895-9434 Office: Mich State U Dept Family Medicine East Lansing MI 48824

WAITE, RONALD SCOTT, educator, tennis instructor; b. Toledo, Ohio, Nov. 20, 1950; s. Ralph Edward and Virginia (Scott) W.; m. Suzanne Marie D. Stefano, Dec. 23, 1973 (div. 1987); 1 child, Sean Eamonn. BA, Fairfield U., 1972, MA, 1976. Prof. Manchester (Conn.) C.C., 1975-78, Albertus Magnus Coll., New Haven, 1975—; owner Photosportacular, New Haven, 1998—; cons. Conn. Reps., Hartford, 1998—. Justice of peace State Conn., New Haven, 1996—. Mem. AAUP, Soc. Am. Magicians, U.S. Profl. Tennis Registry, U.S. Tennis Writers Assn. Roman Catholic. Avocations: guitar, chess, computers. Home: 578 Whitney Ave New Haven CT 06511-2247 Office: Albertus Magnus Coll 700 Prospect St New Haven CT 06511-1224

WAITHE, MARY REBECCA, personnel director, dance instructor; b. N.Y.C., Oct. 10, 1934; arrived in Barbados, 1982; d. Edward A. and Beryl Margaret (Roberts) Waithe. BSc in Bus. and Pub. Adminstrn., NYU, 1973, MBA, 1975. Adj. asst. prof. Bronx (N.Y.) Community Coll., 1970-76; adminstr., chief personnel officer NYU Sch. Law, N.Y.C., 1977-81; purchasing agt., office mgr. South Bronx Devel. Orgn. Inc., N.Y.C., 1982-86; human resource mgr. Intel Barbados Ltd., 1982-86; personnel officer Barbados Mut. Life Assurance Soc., St. Michael, 1987-91; dir. human resources Cunard Paradise Village Beach Club, 1991-92; human resource mgr. Barbados Hilton Hotel Internat., 1993-99, Cobblers Cove Hutch, 1999—; personnel cons. Bonhus Ltd., Barbados, 1989—; tutor Barbados C.C. Hospitality Sch., pers. mgmt., supervisory mgmt., 1997, 98; part-time tutor Ctr. Mgmt. Devel. U. West Indies exec. diploma mgmt., 1999. Choreographer: Black Franchise Dance, 1989 (cert 1989), Flight of the Bird, 1989 (Gold Cup 1989). Mem. Phi Chi Theta, Mau Gamma Tau. Avocations: modern-Afro-Caribbean dance instructing, community activities, travel. Home: 22 10th Ave, Newton Terr, Christ Church Barbados

WAIZUMI, KENJI, chemistry educator; b. Niitzu, Niigata, Japan, Apr. 19, 1962; s. Michio and Sumiko (Satoh) W.; m. Chie Oda, Mar. 11, 1989; children: Hiroki, Tatsuyuki. BS, Tohoku U., Sendai, Japan, 1986, MS, 1988; D Engring., Nagoya (Japan) Inst. Tech., 1994. Tech. assoc. Inst. Molecular Sci., Okazaki, 1991-93; lectr. Yamaguchi (Japan) U., 1993-96, assoc. prof., 1996—. Mem. Chem. Soc. Japan, Japanese Assn. Crystal Growth. Home: Sento-Cho 9-5, Yamaguchi 753-0076, Japan Office: Yamaguchi U Faculty Edn, Yoshida 1677, Yamaguchi 753-8513, Japan

WAJAND, JAN ALEKSANDER, engineering educator, designer; b. Katowice, Poland, Oct. 17, 1929; s. Jan Teodor Wajand and Gertrud Lucy (Siwiec) Gavel; m. Donata Teresa Wieczorek, Apr. 29, 1927; 1 child, Jan Tomasz. MSc, Technical U. Lodz, Poland, 1951, DSc, 1959; DSc, Technical U. Lodz, Poland, 1964. Head Heat Piston Engine chair Technical U. Lodz, 1966-70, 93—, vice-dean Mechanical Engring. Dept., 1966-73, dir. Inst. Technology and Automotive Engring., 1973-93, dean Machine Bldg. Dept., 1987-93; designer Sulzer AG Winterthur, Switzerland, 1982-83. Author: (books) Automobile Compression Ignition Engines, 1958, Piston Engines Supercharging, 1962, Automotive Compression Ignition Engines, 1966, 73, 80, 88, Damages of Automotive Internal Combustion Engines, 1969, Measurements of Fast Varying Pressures in Engines, 1974; co-author: Low and Medium Speed Engines, 1971, 76, 83, Microcomputer Calculations of IC Engines, 1990, Piston IC Engines, 1993, 2d edit., 1997, Research Piston Engines, 1998; contbr. more than 140 articles to profl. jours. Mem. Polish Orgn. Automobile Experts (pres. 1982-95, hon. pres. 1995—), Fedn. Internationale des Experts en Automobiles (pres. 1992-95, hon. pres. 1995—). Avocations: photography, hiking, music. Home: Al Armii Krajowej 165, PL43309 Bielsko-Biala Poland Office: Technical U Lodz-Branch in Bielsko-Biala, ul Willowa 2, PL 43309 Bielsko-Biala Poland

WAJED, SHEIKH HASINA, prime minister; b. Tungipara, Gopalgang, Sept. 28, 1947; parents Bangabandhu Sheikh Mujibur Rahman; m. M.A. Wazed Miah; 2 children. Grad., U. Dhaka, 1973. Pres. Awami League, 1981; leader Opposition in Parliament; prime min. People's Republic of Bangladesh, 1996—. *

WAKABAYASHI, HAJIMU, materials engineer, research center manager; b. Kyoto, Japan, Nov. 9, 1940; s. Tsuezo and Kinue (Yamanaka) W.; m. Tomoko Hayashi, Nov. 8, 1969; children Yutaka, Makoto. BSc. in Engring., Nagoya (Japan) Inst. Tech., 1965; D in Engring., Kyoto (Japan) U., 1986. Chief sr. rschr., mgr. Osaka Nat. Rsch. Inst., Ikeda, Osaka, Japan, 1965-94; sr. mgr. New Glass Rsch. Ctr. Nihon Yamamura Glass Co., Ltd., Nishinomiya, Hyogo, Japan, 1994—; mem. com. Small Bus. Promotion Corp., Tokyo, Japan, 1993—. Contbr. articles to profl. jours. Fellow New Glass Forum, Tokyo; mem. The Ceramic Soc. Japan (Acad. award 1990), Magnetics Soc. Japan. Buddhist. Avocations: mountaineering, tennis, skiing, travel, gardening. E-mail: wakaba@po.iijnet.or.jp and Wak@iris.dti.ne.jp. Home: 3-3-6 Kamo, Kawaniski, Hyogo 666-0025, Japan Office: Nihon Yamamura Glass Co Ltd, Rsch Ctr 2-1-18 Naruohama, Nishinomiya Hyogo 663-8142, Japan

WAKAMATSU, TAKASHI, political science educator; b. Nakano, Tokyo, Japan, Aug. 16, 1946; s. Eitaro and Kiyo Wakamatsu; 1 child, Eiko. LLB, U. Tokyo, Japan, 1971. Instr. comparative politics Chuo U., Tokyo, 1972-77, asst. prof. comparative politics, 1977-85, prof. comparative politics, 1985—. Author: Road to a Civil War: Studies in the Spanish Second Republic, 1986, Contemporary History of Spain, 1992; editor: The Spanish Civil War and International Politics, 1990; co-editor: Concise History of Spain, 1987. Rsch. scholar Sakuradakai, Tokyo, 1989, 99. Mem. Japanese Polit. Sci. Assn. Home: Hirayama 3-12-8, Hino 191-0043, Japan Office: Chuo Univ, Higashinakano 742-1, Hachioji 192-0393, Japan

WAKAMATU, NOBUYUKI, environmental engineer; b. Tokyo, Feb. 22, 1949; parents; Kouhei and Yasuko (Tukasa) W. Grad., Kwanto-Gakuin U., Yokohama, Japan, 1971. Lic. Architect. Engr. Yasui Architect and Engrs., Osaka, Japan, 1971-79, chief engr., 1979—. Mem. Soc. Heating, Air Conditioning and Sanitary Engrs. of Japan. Home: Midoriga-oka Kitamachi 13-8, Kawachi-nagano Osaka 586, Japan Office: Yasui Architect and Engrs, Shimamachi 2-7, Higashi-ku, Osaka 540, Japan

WAKATSUKI, TOSHIKAZU, surgeon; b. Tokyo, June 26, 1910; s. Kosaku and Mochizuki (Aki) W.; m. Tsugie Takahashi, May 1936; children: Kenichi, Toshiko. MD, U. Tokyo, 1936, PhD, 1947. Surgeon Hosp. Imperial U. Tokyo, 1936-45; chief surgeon, dir. surgery, supt. Saku Ctrl. Hosp., Usada, Japan, 1945—. Author: Combating Ailments in Rural Communities, 1971, Health Hazards by Environmental Pollution, 1973, Toshikazu Wakatsuki's Selected Works, 1986, Along with Local Farmers in 50 Years, 1994. Mem. Japanese Assn. Rural Medicine, Internat. Assn. Agrl. Medicine & Rural Health, Asian Assn. Agrl. Medicine & Rural Health, Nat. Rsch. Fedn. Japan. Avocations: oil painting, poet, essayist. Home: 2211-2 Usada, 384-03 Nagano Japan Office: Saku Ctrl Hosp, Saku Ctrl Hosp, 197 Usuda, 384-0301 Usuda Japan

WAKEFIELD, EDWARD HUMPHREY TYRRELL, business executive; b. London, July 11, 1936; s. Edward Birkbeck and Constance Lalage (Perronet-Thompson) W.; m. Elisabeth Sophia Sidney, Feb. 11, 1966 (div. 1972); 1 child, Maximilian Eward Vereker; m. Katharine Alice Baring; children: Mary, John Baring. BA, Cambridge U., 1960, MA, 1966. Furniture expert Christie's Auction Ltd., London, 1960-62; furniture expert Mallet Antiques, London, 1962-66, dir., 1975-78; exec. v.p. Mallet Antiques, N.Y.C., 1969-75; furniture expert, architect Lough Cutra Castle, Ireland, 1966-69; owner Chillingham Castle, Eng., 1981—; writer, lectr. in field; attended expdns. to Everest, Antarctic, North Pole; advisor U.S. Russian, European crafters and factories on detailing of replica of works of art and antiques. Prin. works as arch. include Lough Cutra Castle, Chillingham Castle, Merion Sq.; contbr. articles to profl. jours. Campaign coord. Conservative party, active Red Cross, London, 1978-81; pres. Avison Trust, Avison Ensemble; patron Medicine for Chernobyl; pres. Northumberland Fell & Mountain Rescue; chmn. Wilderness Trust; fellow Pierpont Morgan Libr. Capt. Brit. Mil. Fellow Royal Geog. Soc.; mem. Scott Polar Inst. (life), Guards and Chivalry Club, Harlequin Rugby Football Club, Turf Club. Mem. Ch. of England. Avocations: horse riding, shooting, music, mountaineering, travel. Home: Chillingham Castle, Chillingham NE66 5NJ, England

WAKEFIELD, THOMAS WILLIAM, vascular surgeon, educator; b. Toledo, Jan. 28, 1954; s. William Henry and Doris Alice (Antolini) W.; m. Mary Margaret Reas, June 17, 1977; children: Andrew Thomas, Victor Walter. BA, U. Toledo, 1975; MD, Med. Coll. of Ohio at Toledo, Toledo, 1978. Lic. gen. surgeon, Mich.; lic. vascular surgeon, Mich.; lic. surg. critical care, Mich. Instr. surgery Med. Ctr. U. Mich., Ann Arbor, 1984-86, asst. prof., 1986-92; assoc. prof. U. Mich., Ann Arbor, 1992-98, prof., 1998—. Author: (with others) Textbook of Surgery: Scientific Principles, 1996 and Practice, 3rd edit., 2000, Current Therapy in Vascular Surgery, 4th edit., 2000, Vascular Surgery, 5th edit., 2000, others; contbr. numerous articles to profl. jours. Recipient Gov.'s award Am. Coll. Cardiology, 1972, 3d Pl. award for Rsch. in Venous Disease, Am. Venous Forum, 1991, 1st Pl. award sponsor for Rsch. in Venous Disease, 1998; NIH grantee. Fellow ACS; mem. Soc. Univ. Surgeons, European Soc. Vascular Surgery, Ctrl. Surg. Assn., Frederick A. Coller Surg. Soc. (Conrad Jobst award for vascular surgery rsch. 1982), Assn. Acad. Surgery, Midwest Vascular Surg. Soc. (sponsor Guthrie award 1996), Internat. Soc. for Cardiovascular Surgery (N.Am. chpt.), Western Surg. Assn., Am. Venous Forum (sec.), Soc. Vascular Surgery, Phi Kappa Phi (grad. scholar 1975). Roman Catholic. Avocations: running, basketball. Office: U Mich Med Ctr 1500 E Medical Center Dr Ann Arbor MI 48109-0005

WAKEHAM, LORD JOHN, former parliamentarian; b. Eng., June 22, 1932; s. Walter John and Eva Rose (Webb) W.; m. Anne Roberta Bailey, 1965 (dec. Oct. 1984); children: Jonathan, Benedict; m. Alison Bridget Ward, July 19, 1985; 1 child, David. Charterhouse, Surrey. Asst. govt. whip London, 1979-81, Lord Commr. of the Treasury, 1981, parliamentary Undersec. of State for industry, 1981-82, Minister of State, Treasury, 1982-83, govt. chief whip, 1983-87; Lord Privy Seal, House of Commons, London, 1987-88, Leader, 1987-89, Lord Pres. of the council, 1988-89, sec. of state for energy, 1989-92; Lord Privy Seal, Leader, House of Lords, London, 1992-94; chmn. Press Complaints Commn., London, 1995—; non exec. dir. Bristol & West, plc. 1997—, Enron Corp., 1994—, N.M. Rothschild & Sons, Ltd., 1995—; pres. Michael Page Group plc, 1997—; chancellor Brunel U., 1998—; chmn. Royal Commn. Reform Ho. Lords, 1999. Conservative. Clubs: Carlton (chmn. 1992-98), St. Stephen's Constitutional, Garrick, Buck's, Royal Yacht Squadron. Avocations: farming, sailing, racing, reading. Office: House of Lords, London SW1A OPW, England*

WAKELEY, CHARLES JOHN, consulting radiologist; b. London, May 3, 1959; s. John Cecil and June (Leney) W.; m. Rachel Morag Penrose, Sept. 1, 1984; children: Rupert William, Arthur Charles. BSc, U. London, 1980, MB BS, 1983. House surgeon U. London, 1983-84; house physician Chester, 1984; sr. house officer, 1984-85, sr. house officer orthopedics, 1985-86, sr. house officer surgery, 1986, registrar in radiology, 1988-91, sr. registrar in radiology, 1991-95; cons. radiologist musculoskeletal and oncol. imaging United Bristol Healthcare NHS Trust, Eng., 1995—. Fellow Royal Coll. Surgeons, Royal Coll. Radiologists. Avocations: woodcarving, waterskiing, fishing. Office: Clin Rad Bristol Royal Inf, Marlborough St, Bristol B52 8HW, England

WAKELEY, JOHN CECIL NICHOLSON, retired surgeon; b. London, Aug. 27, 1926; s. Cecil and Elizabeth Muriel (Nicholson-Smith) W.; married Apr. 10, 1954; children: Nicholas, Charles, Amanda. MBBS, U. London, 1950. Cons. surgeon Chester Hosps., 1961-88; ret., 1988. With RAF, 1953-54. Comdr. Order of St. John of Jerusalem, 1960, Baronet, Eng., 1982. Fellow ACS, Royal Coll. Surgeons (lic., councillor 1971-83). Avocations: photography, model trains, music. Home: Mickle Lodge, Mickle Trafford, Chester CH2 4EB, England

WAKEMAN, RICHARD JOHN, chemical engineering educator; b. Cuckfield, England, Apr. 15, 1948; s. Ronald and Kathleen (Smith) W.; m. Patricia Joan Morris, July 24, 1971; children: Simon Richard, Mark Andrew. BS, UMIST, 1970, MS, 1971, PhD, 1973. Rsch. asst. UMIST, Manchester, England, 1972-73; lectr. U. Exeter (England), 1973-86, reader, 1986-90, prof., 1990-95; prof. U. Loughborough, England, 1995—; cons. in field. Author: Filtration Post-Treatment Processes, 1975; contbr. scientific papers to profl. publs. Com. mem. Sci. & Engring. Rsch. coun., England, 1984—; chmn. Incofilt, 1995—; panel mem. British Stds. Inst., London, 1992-94. Fellow Inst. Chem. Engrs., Royal Acad. Engring. Home: 1 Cornmill Close, Elvaston Meadows, Elvaston, Derbyshire DE72 3UA, England Office: U Tech, Dept Chem Engring, Loughborough LE11 3TU, England

WAKHLU, ASHISH, pediatric surgeon; b. Lucknow, India, Jan. 24, 1965; s. Autar Kishen and Indu (Gupta) W.; m. Geeta Agarwal, June 24, 1988; children: Anvita, Akshay. MBBS, King George's Med. Coll., Lucknow, 1988, MS in Gen. Surgery, 1991; MCh in Pediatric Surgery, U. Rajasthan, Jaipur, India, 1994. Specialist qualification in pediatric surgery. Rotating intern Gandhi Meml. and Associated Hosps., Lucknow, 1987-88; resident gen. surgery King's George's Med. Coll., Lucknow, 1988-91; sr. resident pediatric surgery Sawai Man Singh Med. Coll., Jaipur, 1992-94; asst. prof. dept. pediatric surgery King George's Med. Coll., Lucknow, 1994—; presenter nat. and internat. confs. Contbr. articles to profl. jours. Mem. Indian Med. Assn., Indian Acad. Pediatrics, Indian Assn. Pediatric Surgeons (mem. exec. com. 1995-97). Hindu. Avocation: photography. Home: 1/147 Vivek Khand, Gomti Nagar, Lucknow India Office: King Georges Med Coll, Lucknow 226003, India

WAKID, SHUKRI ABU, information technology director; b. Kfarshima, Lebanon, Dec. 20, 1945; came to U.S., 1967; s. Edward Bou and Renee Bou Wakid; m. Jane Abraham, May 29, 1978; children: Edward, Jacob. BS, Am. U. Beirut, 1967; postgrad., U. Pitts., 1967; PhD, La. State U., 1971. Chmn. dept. physics, math, CS Haigazian Coll., Beirut, 1972-76; postdoctoral fellow La. State U., 1976-77; asst. prof. computer sci. U. Pitts., Johnstown, 1977-78; sr. rsch. assoc. NASA/Goddard Space Flight Ctr., Greenbelt, Md., 1978-79; sr. mem. tech. staff Computer Scis. Corp., Seabrook, Md., 1980; mem. tech. staff Bell Labs., Holmdel, N.J., 1981-84; group mgr. then chief adv. sys. divsn. Nat. Inst. Stds. and Tech., Gaithersburg, Md., 1988-95, dir. info. tech. lab., 1995-99, CIO, 1999—; adj. prof. Lebanese U., Beirut, 1973-76. Founder: The North American Integrated Svcs. Digital Network Forum (Top 25 Comm. Leaders 1989, Newsmaker 1988); contbr. articles to profl. jours. Recipient Fed. 100 award Fed. Computer Week, 1991, Silver medal U.S. Dept. Commerce, 1992, Presdl. Rank award for meritorous exec. U.S. Govt., 1993; Fulbright-Hays exch. fellow U.S. Govt., 1967. Mem. IEEE (sr., vice-chair tech. adv. bd. Computer Soc. 1997—), Instnrl. Mgmt. Sys. Bd. Achievements include standardization of Intergrated Svcs. Digital Network technology, measurement techniques for high speed networks; theoretical prediction of positronium formation in hydrogen at low energy positron-hydrogen collisions; inelastic resonances in helium and lithium. Home: 12526 Hialeah Way Gaithersburg MD 20878-3784 Office: NIST MS 3207 100 Bureau Dr Bldg 222 Gaithersburg MD 20899-0003

WAKIM, ALAIN, pediatric surgeon, researcher; b. Dakar, Senegal, Aug. 1950; s. Khalil and Georgette (Chebeh) W.; m. Mitsa Breidi, June 22, 1979; children: Sebastien, Pascale. Bacalureat serie C, Assez-Bien Notre Dame, Beirut, Lebanon; MD, Diplome D'Etat Francais, Beirut, Lebanon. Diplo-

mate European Bd. Paediatric Surgery. Physician in gen. surgery Paris, 1988—, physician in paediatric surgery, 1990, assoc. prof. paediatric surgery, 1996. Contbr. articles to profl. jours. Mem. Soc. Francaise de Chirurgie Pedatrique, European Soc. Paediatric Urology, internat. Children's Continence Soc. Home: 122 Rue Lauriston, 75116 Paris France Office: 40 Boulevard de Courcelles, 750017 Paris France

WAKISAKA, MASAMI, urologist; b. Nakasuge, Tottori, Japan, June 6, 1947; parents Urao and Kikue (Shinohara) W. MD, Chiba (Japan) U., 1981. Lectr. Chiba (Japan) U., 1976-81, asst. prof., 1981-88; dir. sect. Funabashi (Japan) Chu-oh Hosp., 1988—. Contbr. articles to profl. jours. Mem. AAAS, Japanese Urol. Assn., Japanese Cancer Assn., Japan Soc. Cancer Therapy, N.Y. Acad. Scis., The Planetary Soc. Avocations: tennis, swimming, going to the theater. Office: Social Ins Funabashi Chu-oh Hosp, 6-13-10 Kaijin, Funabashi 273, Japan

WAKITA, HIROSHI, environmental sciences and geochemistry educator; b. Nishinomiya, Hyogo, Japan, Sept. 29, 1936; s. Masataka and Yasuko (Terawaki) W.; m. Kikuko Nishikawa, May 5, 1964; children: Ken, Reiko. BSc, Gakushuin U., Tokyo, 1962, MSc, 1964, PhD, 1968. Rschr. Japan Atomic Energy Rsch. Inst., Tokyo, 1964-68; rsch. assoc. Oreg. State U., Corvallis, 1968-71; lectr. U. Tokyo, 1971-77, assoc. prof., 1978-86, prof., 1986-97, prof. emeritus, 1997; prof. Gakushuin Women's Coll., Tokyo, 1998—; dir. Lab. Earthquake Chemistry, Faculty Sci., U. Tokyo, 1988-97, Fgn. Student Ctr., Gakushuin Women's Coll., Tokyo, 1998—. Author: Earthquake Prediction Techniques, 1982; assoc. editor Applied Geochemistry, 1992-96. Lectr. Bunkyo-City, Tokyo, 1990—. Mem. Geochem. Soc. Japan (pres. 1992-93), Geochemistry Rsch. Assn. (v.p. 1996, Miyake prize 1989). Avocations: tennis, mountain climbing. Home: 2-18-8 Yayoi, Bunkyo-ku Tokyo 113-0032, Japan Office: Gakushuin Womens Coll, 3-20-1 Toyama, Shinjuku-ku Tokyo 162-8650, Japan

WAKO, AMOS, Kenyan government official, lawyer; b. 1946. LLB, U. East Africa; BS, LLM, U. London. Chmn. Law Soc. Kenya and Pub. Law Inst., 1979-81; sec. gen. Inter-African Union of Lawyers; atty. gen. Govt. of Kenya, Nairobi, 1993—; bd. trustees UN Voluntary Fund, 1982; spl. rapporteur UN Commn. on Human Rights, 1982. Office: Atty Gen State Law Office, Harambee Ave 4th Fl Rm 402 BOX 40112, Nairobi Kenya*

WAKS, NATHAN, music director; b. Sydney, NSW, Australia, Jan. 23, 1951; s. Leo and Anna (Jakubowicz) W.; m. Candice Williams; children: Sam, Mina. Student, Sydney Conservatorium, Paris Conservatoire. Mem. BBC Symphony Orch., 1969; prin. cello Sydney Symphony Orch., 1970, Fidelio String Quartet, 1971-75, Elizabethan Theatre Trust Orch. (opera and ballet), 1971-75; dir. music Australian Broadcasting Corp., Sydney, 1993-97; mng. dir. Symphony Australia, 1997-99; chair music fund Australia Coun., 1998—; bd. dirs. Australian Chamber Orch., Australian Music Ctr.; artist-in-residence Sydney Conservatorium, 1975-85, Hong Kong Acad. Performing Arts, 1985-87, artistic advisor Australia Chamber Orch., 1989; musical advisor Melbourne Internat. Festival, 1992; advisor Australia Coun. Music. Bd. Prodr. recordings Sony Classical Internat., 1991—; dir. Musica Viva Easter Festival, 1993; writer film scores My Brilliant Career, 1978, For Love Alone, 1985, Kangaroo, 1986, Hunger, 1986. Avocations: photography, bridge, wine, cooking. Office: Australia Coun, 372 Elizabeth St, Surry Hills 2010 NSW, Australia

WAKUMOTO, YOSHIHIKO, electronics company executive, grants executive; b. Bunkyo-Ku, Tokyo, June 4, 1931; s. Yoshitaro and Fumie (Oka) W.; m. Reiko Tanaka, Mar. 28, 1959; children: Yoshiaki, Yoshiyuki. BA, Tokyo U., 1955; postgrad., Columbia U., 1960-61. Dep. mgr. license negotiation Toshiba Corp., Tokyo, 1964-67, mgr. overseas mfg. ops., 1967-72, mgr. fin. divsn., 1972-74, gen. mgr. internat. fin. divsn., 1974-81, gen. mgr. internat. affairs divsn., 1981-88, v.p., dep. group exec.-internat. staff group, 1988-91, exec. v.p. for corp. planning, info. sys. and group cos., 1991-95, exec. v.p. for internat. rels., 1995-96, bd. dirs., advisor, 1996—; exec. dir. Japan Found. Ctr. for Global Partnership, Tokyo, 1996—; bd. dirs. Schlumberger Ltd.; mem. Japan nat. com. United World Colls. Co-author: Foreign Exchange Risk and International Financial Strategy, 1973, The Run-up of 21st Century, 1991; translator: Management By Exception, 1968. Mem. Internat. House of Japan, Am.-Japan Soc., Fgn. Corr. Club Japan (assoc.), Bus. Rsch. Inst., Inc. (trustee). Home: 3-43-18 Hongo Bunkyo-ku, Tokyo 113-0033, Japan Office: Toshiba Corp, 1-1-1 Shibaura Minato-Ku, Tokyo 105-8001, Japan

WAKURI, YUTARO, mechanical engineering educator; b. Fukuoka, Kyushu, Japan, July 7, 1928; m. Masako Yasumura, Mar. 28, 1958; children: Seiich, Satoko, Watanabe Yoshiko. B of Engring., Kyushu U., Fukuoka, 1952, D of Engring., 1962. Rsch. fellow lab. Mitsubishi Ship Bldg. and Engring. Co. Ltd., Nagasaki, Japan, 1952-63; assoc. prof. Kyushu U., Fukuoka, 1963-70, prof., 1970-92; prof. Fukuoka U., 1992-99, ret., 1999; jury mem. Japan Soc. for Promotion of Sci., Tokyo, 1990-97, Nat. Instn. for Acad. Degrees, Yokohama, Japan, 1991-99; mem. Sci. Coun. of Japan, Tokyo, 1985-94. Contbr. articles to profl. jours. Recipient award for contbn. to engine sys. field Japan Soc. Mech. Engrs. Mem. Soc. Automotive Engrs. Japan (bd. dirs. 1976-92, award for contbn. to sci. rsch. 1993), Japan Soc. Mech. Engrs. (bd. dirs. 1982-84, v.p. 1988-89), Marine Engring. Soc. Japan (v.p. 1991-93, Doko prize 1989), Engring. Acad. Japan. Avocations: model engineering, photography, Igo. Home: 1-6-45 Torikai Chu-ō-ku, 810-0053 Fukuoka Japan Office: Fukuoka U Faculty Engring, 8-19-1 Nanakuma Jonan-ku, 814-0180 Fukuoka Japan

WALBESSER, HENRY HERMAN, computer science educator; b. Buffalo, May 9, 1935; s. Henry Herman and Florence (Schoenl) W.; m. Diane L. Walker, Aug. 16, 1958; children: Henry, Kathleen, James. BS, SUNY, Buffalo, 1958; MA, U. Md., 1960, PhD, 1965; DSc, U. of the Republic, Uruguay, 1976. Asst. prof. U. Tex., Austin, 1961-63; assoc. dir. AAAS, Washington, 1963-68; assoc. prof. U. Md., College Park, 1968-76, assoc. dean/assoc. provost, 1971-76; prof., chair U. Md., Catonsville, 1976-92, prof. emeritus, 1992—; prof. Baylor U., Waco, Tex., 1992—, dean, 1992-96. Author: Evaluation Model, 1965; co-author: Descriptive Data Analysis, 1991, Inferential Data Analysis, 1994; contbr. articles to jour. Rsch. in Math. Edn., 1972. Active adv. bd. Gov.'s Econ. Devel. Office, Annapolis, Md., 1988-91, Strecker Mus., Waco, 1992—, Lyric Opera of Waco, 1997—; worker Habitat for Humanity, Waco, 1996—. Fulbright-Hays fellow, 1967, 68, SEAMEO fellow, 1981, 82, OECD fellow, 1988. Fellow AAAS; mem. Nat. Hist. Soc. Democrat. Baptist. Avocations: bioinformatics, history of university presidents, gardening. E-mail: henry walbesser@baylor.edu. Home: 400 Shadow Mt Waco TX 76712 Office: Baylor U PO Box 97356 Waco TX 76798-7356

WALCH, WILLIAM JEFFREY (HUTCH WALCH), corporate consultant; b. San Diego, Sept. 20, 1955; s. Warren Joseph Walch and Vernette June Melanese; m. Marie Ann, Aug. 16, 1980; children: Aubry Marie, Kale Jeffrey. Degree in Theology, Azusa (Calif.) Pacific Coll., 1978. TV/radio mgmt. CBS KUAM TV8/FM/AM, Guam, 1979-82; radio broadcasting co-host Guam Cable/KOKU FM, 1982-88; radio broadcaster KGUM FM, Guam, 1988-92; prin., owner Sound Factory Music Stores, Guam, 1992-94; nat. sales mgr. Trillium Tech., Roseville, Minn., 1995-97; prin., owner Bennett Russell & Walch, Minnetonka, Minn., 1997-98; mng. ptnr. Working Relationships, Inc., Eden Prairie, Minn., 1998—; bd. dirs. Bloomington City Coun. co-prodr., star three TV spls., Hutch & Jeffrin Hollywood, 1980, 81, 82 (Press Club award 1980, 81, 82). bd. mem. Kiwanis Internat., Guam, 1980-83. Recipient Ancient Order of Chamori award Guam Govt. Legislature, 1994, Legis. Resolution award Guam Govt. Legislature, 1994. Mem. Twin West Chamber, MIMA Internet Mktg. Assn. Protestant. Fax: 612-941-4334. E-mail: hwalch@workingrelationships.com. Office: Working Relationships Inc 6468 City West Pkwy Eden Prairie MN 55344-3245

WALCKIERS, ROLAND ALAIN, obstetrician-gynecologist; b. Brussels, Brabant, Belgium, Apr. 14, 1944; s. Alfons Petrus Walckiers and Julienne Therese Vander Elst; m. Martine Alberte Buyze, Mar. 8, 1969; children: Stephen, Stephanie. BChir, U. Catholique Louvain, Belgium, 1967; specialist ob-gyn., Katholieke U. Leuven, Belgium, 1972. Cert. Bd. Ob-gyn. Flanders, Belgium. Head dept. ob-gyn. City Hosp., Sint-Niklaas, Belgium, 1983—; tchr. for trainees Katholiche Univ. Leuven, 1989—. Capt. Colt Mil., 1972-90. Mem. Coll. Physician Using Ultrasound Machine (bd. dirs. Coll. Ob-Gyn.). Avocations: international contacts, languages. Home fax: 3237768876/office fax: 323 7806686. Home: Rietvelde 20, B9100 Sint-Niklaas Belgium Office: City Hosp, 10 Azalealaan, B9100 Sint-Niklaas Belgium

WALCOTT, DEREK ALTON, poet, playwright; b. Castries, St. Lucia, Jan. 23, 1930; s. Warwick and Alix W.; m. Fay Moston, 1954 (div. 1959); 1 son; m. Margaret Ruth Maillard, 1962 (div.); 2 daus.; m. Norline Metivier (div.). BA, U. West Indies, Kingston, Jamaica, 1953, DLitt, 1972. Former tchr. St. Lucia, Grenada, Jamaica; poet-in-residence Hollins Coll., Roanoke, VA, 1980; prof. English Boston U.; founding dir. Trinidad Theatre Workshop, 1959—; lectr. Rutgers U., Yale U.; vis. prof. Columbia U., 1981, Harvard U., 1982, Boston U., 1985. Author: (poetry) Twenty-Five Poems, 1948, Epitath for the Young: A Poem in XII Cantos, 1949, Poems, 1953, In A Green Night: Poems, 1948-1960, 1962, Selected Poems, 1964, The Castaway and Other Poems, 1965 (Heinemann award Royal Soc. Lit. 1966), The Gulf and Other Poems, 1969 (Cholmondeley award 1969), Another Life, 1973 (Jock Campbell/New Statesman prize 1974), Sea Grapes, 1976, Selected Verse, 1976, The Star-Apple Kingdom, 1979, The Fortunate Traveller, 1981 (Heinemann award Royal Soc. Lit. 1983), Selected Poetry, 1981, Midsummer, 1984, Collected Poems, 1948-1984, 1986 (L.A. Times Book Rev. prize 1986), The Arkansas Testament, 1987, Omeros, 1990 (W.H. Smith Literary award 1991), Selected Poetry, 1993, Antiles: Fragments of Epic Memory, 1993; (plays) Henry Christophe: A Chronicle in Seven Scenes, 1950, Henry Dernier, 1951, Wine of the Country, 1953, The Sea at Dauphin: A Play in One Act, 1953, Ione: A Play with Music, 1957, Drums and Colours: An Epic Drama, 1958 (Jamaica Drama Festival prize 1958), Ti-Jean and His Brothers, 1958, Malcochon; or, Six in the Rain, 1959, Dream on Monkey Mountain, 1967 (Obie award 1971), In a Fine Castle, 1970, The Joker of Seville, 1974, The Charlatan, 1974, O Babylon!, 1976, Remembrance, 1977, Pantomine, 1978, The Isle Is Full of Noises, 1982, The Last Carnival, 1986, Beef, No Chicken, 1986, A Branch of the Blue Nile, 1986, The Odyssey, 1992. Recipient Guinness award, 1961, Nat. Writer's Coun. prize Welsh Arts Coun., 1979, Queen Elizabeth II Gold Medal for poetry, 1988, Nobel Prize for Lit., 1992; Rockefeller Found. fellow, 1957, 58; Eugene O'Neill Found.-Wesleyan U. fellow, 1969; MacArthur Found. grantee, 1981; decorated Order of the Hummingbird, Trinidad and Tobago, 1969. Achievements include being the founder of Trinidad Theater workshop. Home: 71 Saint Marys St Boston MA 02215 Office: 165 Duke of Edinburgh Ave, Diego Martin Trinidad and Tobago also: care Farrar Straus & Giroux 19 Union Sq W New York NY 10003-3304

WALCZAK, BEATA, chemist, educator; b. Lublin, Poland, Mar. 31, 1955; d. Ireneusz and Wanda (Pardela) W. MS in Chemistry, Silesian U., 1979, PhD of Chemistry, 1984; DSc in chemistry, Jagiellonian U., Cracow, Poland, 1997. Lectr. Silesian U., Katowice, Poland, 1984-99, prof. analytical chemistry, 1999—. Contbr. chpts. in books and articles to profl. jours. Mem. Polish Chem. Soc. Office: VUB FABI, Laarbeeklaan 103, B-1090 Brussels Belgium Office: Silesian U Inst Chemistry, 9 Szkolna St, 40 006 Katowice Poland

WALCZAK, JOANNE CAROL, accountant; b. Buffalo, Feb. 8, 1959; d. Joseph Charles and Carol Dolores (Nicklas) Moorhouse; m. John T. Walczak, Aug. 2, 1980; 1 child, Bryan. BS in Acctg., SUNY, Geneseo, 1986; MBA in Fin. and Corp. Acctg., U. Rochester, 1991. CPA, N.Y. Staff acct. Genesee C.C., Batavia, N.Y., 1986-87; sr. acct. Strong Meml. Hosp., Rochester, N.Y., 1987-88; ptnr. J&L Assocs., Batavia, 1988-93, Landers & Walczak, Batavia, 1993—; adj. faculty Genesee C.C., 1988—. Bd. dirs. YWCA Genesee County, Inc., Batavia, 1989-90; mem. bus. devel. com. Genesee County C. of C., 1992—; v.p. Zonta Club of Batavia-Genesee, 1994-95, pres. 1996-97. Mem. N.Y. State Soc. CPAs. Roman Catholic. Avocations: golf, tennis, bowling, reading, crafts. Home: 16 Linwood Ave Batavia NY 14020-3714 Office: Landers & Walczak 12 Center St Batavia NY 14020-3204

WALCZAK, ZBIGNIEW KAZIMIERZ, polymer science and engineering researcher; b. Gostyn, Poland, Mar. 27, 1932; came to U.S. 1964.; s. Ignacy P. and Stanislawa (Zychlewicz) W.; m. M. Krystyna Szymusik-Zygmuntowicz; 1 child, Agatha C. Engr. master, Poly. of Lodz, Poland, 1956. Tech. mgr. Coop. Chem. Industries, Lodz, 1956-59; chief chemist Persöner Concernen AB, Ystad, Sweden, 1960-62; rsch. chemist A.B. Casco, Stockholm, 1962-63, Shawinigan (Que.) Chems. Ltd., 1963-64, E.I. DuPont De Nemours Inc., Old Hickory, Tenn., 1964-67; sr. project leader Phillips Petroleum Co., Bartlesville, Okla., 1967-70, M & T Chems., Inc., Rahway, N.J., 1970-73; rsch. assoc. Inmont Corp., Clifton, N.J., 1973-82; rsch. fellow Kimberly-Clark Corp., Roswell, Ga., 1982-95; ind. rschr., cons., 1995—; contract prof. polymer sci., Xavier U., Cin., 1980-81. Author: Formation of Synthetic Fibers, 1977, Thermal Bonding of Fibers, 1992, novel organic compounds; patentee synthetic fibers. Active Underground Boy Scouts as part of Polish Resistance Movement of Armia Krajowa, 1943-45. Address: 56.5.4, Passeig De Sant Gervasi, 08022 Barcelona Spain

WALDECK, JOHN WALTER, JR., lawyer; b. Cleve., May 3, 1949; s. John Walter Sr. and Marjorie Ruth (Palenschat) W.; m. Cheryl Gene Cutter, Sept. 10, 1977; children: John III, Matthew, Rebecca. BS, John Carroll U., 1973; JD, Cleve. State U., 1977. Bar: Ohio 1977. Product applications chemist Synthetic Products Co., Cleve., 1969-76; assoc. Arter & Hadden, Cleve., 1977-85, ptnr., 1986-88; ptnr. Porter, Wright, Morris and Arthur, Cleve., 1988-90, ptnr. in charge, 1990-96; ptnr. Walter & Haverfield, Cleve., 1996—; bd. advisors Litigation Mgmt., Inc., 2000—. Chmn. Bainbridge Twp. Bd. Zoning Appeals, Chagrin Falls, Ohio, 1984-94; trustee Greater Cleve. chpt. Lupus Found. Am., 1978-91, sec., 1979-86; trustee LeBlond Housing Corp., Cleve., 1990-96, sec., 1996, Univ. Circle, Inc., 1993-97, Fairmount Ctr. for Performing and Fine Arts, Novelty, Ohio, 1993-96, sect., 1994-95; bd. dirs. Geauga County Mental Health Alcohol and Drug Addiction Svc. Bd., Chardon, Ohio, 1988-97, treas., 1991-93, vice-chmn., 1993-95, chmn., 1995-97; mem. bd. advisors Palliative Care Svcs., Cleve. Clinic Cancer Ctr., 1989-91, Litigation Mgmt. Inc., 2000. Mem. Ohio State Bar Assn. (real property sect. bd. govs. 1992), Greater Cleve. Bar Assn. (real property, corp. banking sect, co-chair real estate law inst. 1990, 95, 96). Roman Catholic. Avocations: beekeeping, gardening, jogging. Home: 18814 Rivers Edge Dr W Chagrin Falls OH 44023-4968 Office: Walter & Haverfield 50 Public Square 1300 Terminal Tower Cleveland OH 44113

WALDEGRAVE, LORD OF NORTH HILL, financial services company executive; b. Aug. 15, 1946; s. Earl Waldegrave; m. Caroline Burrows, 1977; 4 children. Grad., Corpus Christi Coll., U. Oxford, Eng. Fellow All Souls Coll., U. Oxford, Eng., 1971-86; mem. ctrl. policy rev. staff Cabinet Office, 1971-73; mem. polit. staff Office of Prime Min., London, 1973-74; head Office Leader of Opposition, London, 1974-75; justice of peace Inner London Juvenile Ct., 1975-79; M.P. for Bristol West Ho. of Commons, London, 1979-97; parliamentary under sec. state Brit. Dept. Edn. and Sci., 1981-83; parliamentary under sec. state Brit. Dept. Environ., 1983-85, min. state for environ. and countryside, 1985-87, min. state for planning, 1986-88, min. state for housing, 1987-88; min. state Fgn. and Commonwealth Office, 1988-90; sec. state for health, 1990-92; chancellor Duchy of Lancaster, 1992-94; min. agr., fisheries and food London, 1994-95, chief sec. to treasury, 1995-97; exec. dir. Dresdner Kleinwort Benson, London, 1998—; dir. Birstol & West, p.l.c., RMLIT plc, Waldegrave Farms Ltd. Author: The Binding of Leviathan, 1977. Kennedy fellow Harvard U. Mem. Beefsteak Club, Pratt's Club, Clifton Club (Bristol). Office: Dresdner Kleinwort Benson, 20 Fenchurch St, London EC3 P3DB, England

WALDEKRANZ, RUNE, film educator emeritus; b. Södertälje, Sweden, Sept. 14, 1911; s. Einar August Valdemar and Olga Waldekranz; m. Brita Klein, Nov. 27, 1947; children: Cecilia Waldekranz Piselli, Jan. MA, Uppsala U., Sweden, 1937. Critic literature and film Svenska Dagbladet, 1939-42; film prodr. Sandrew Film, Sweden, 1942-64; head film sch. Swedish Film Inst., 1965-70, also bd. dirs.; prof. film research Stockholm U., 1970-78; pres. Swedish Film Acad., 1977-80. Author: The Growth of Film, 1941, The Birth of Film Drama, 1976, Film History, The First Hundred Years I-III, 1985-95, others. Recipient Prize for Hist. Rsch., Royal Swedish Acad., 1989, Golden Plaque of Svenska Vitterhets, Historie & Antikvitets Acad., King Carl XVI Gustaf, 1996. Address: Lovisinsgatan 5, 151 73 Södertälje Sweden

WALDEMAR, GUNHILD, neurologist; b. Give, Denmark, July 18, 1957; d. Tage Søndervang Waldemar and Linda Kirstine Poulsen; m. Henrik Heerdegen Jakobsen, May 30, 1987; children: Victor, Elisabeth. MD, Copenhagen U., 1985. Intern, resident various hosps., Copenhagen, 1985-87, 91-95; rsch. fellow dept. neurology Copenhagen U. Hosp., Rigs Hosp., 1987-91, dir. Memory Clinic, 1995—. Bd. dirs. No Rage, 1991—. Recipient Heide Nielsen award The Heide Nielsen Found., 1995. Mem. Danish Alzheimer Soc. (bd. dirs. 1991—), European Fedn. Neurol. Socs. (chmn. task force working group). Home: 10 Raagevej, DK-2900 Hellerup Denmark Office: Rigs Hosp Dept Neurology, Univ Hosp 9 Blegdamsvej, 2100 Copenhagen Danmark

WALDEN, CHRISTOPHER CHARLES, chemical company executive, consultant; b. London, Oct. 4, 1971; arrived in South Africa, 1992; s. Geoffrey Gordon and Georgina (Shennan) W. BA in German, Goethe Inst., London, 1991. Dir. Blendwell Cape C.C., Cape Town, South Africa; dir. Capeability Chems., Cape Town, Cleaning Chem. Warehouse, Paarl, Walden Properties, Cape Town, Fresh From Africa, Johannasburg, Anchorprop Pty. Ltd., Cape Town. Mem. Ch. of Eng. Avocations: skiing, walking, theatre, antiques, art. E-mail: blendwel@iafrica.com. Office: Blendwell Cape CC, PO Box 214, Eppindust, Cape Town 7475, South Africa

WALDEN, DAVID MICHAEL, historian, consultant; b. Omaha, Nov. 6, 1947; s. Blake Chester and Charlotte Walden. BS, Iowa State U., 1969; MA, U. Guam, Mangilao, 1979, Brigham Young U., 1989. Cert. tchr., Utah. Tchr. biology and history pvt. and pub. schs., Guam, 1974-79; historian, writer, 1982—; adj. instr. U.S. history Salt Lake C.C., Salt Lake City, 1993—; bd. editors Assn. for History of Chiropractic, 1989-93; mem. history com. Utah Med. Assn., Salt Lake city, 1989-91; rschr. KUTV documentary A Century of Smog, 1991. Author (60 hist. profiles) International Directory of Company Histories, 1991-2000, Protestant and Catholic Churches of Provo, 1986, A Guide to Utah Medical History, 2000; co-author: Miles Goodyear and His Historic Cabin, 1995; (50 co. profiles) Centennial Utah, 1995, St. Mark's Hospital, 1872-1997, 1999; editor: As a Rose, 1982, Out of Obscurity, 1985; contbr. articles to profl. publs. Sec. West Liberty Neighborhood Assn., Salt Lake City, 1996-99; voting dist. chair, county and state del. Utah Rep. Party, Provo and Salt Lake City, 1984—. Grantee Charles Redd Ctr. for Western Studies, 1987, Brigham Young U. Ctr. for Family and Cmty. History, 1988; Folklore scholar Utah Arts Coun., 1983. Mem. League Utah Writers, Utah State Hist. Soc., History of Medicine in Utah, Inc. (founder, sec.), Oral History Assn., Beehive Intermountain Naval Acad. (sec. alumni chpt. 1994-96), Chi Omicron Gamma. Mem. LDS Ch. Avocations: chess, photography, collecting shells, swimming, collecting jokes. Home and Office: 4981 S 1645 E Salt Lake City UT 84117-5972

WALDEN, HENRY RUSSELL, architect, educator; b. Timaru, Canterbury, New Zealand; s. Rolan Moore and Alice Wilson (Rennie) W.; m. Helen Elizabeth Green, Aug. 25, 1962; children: Nicolas Rolan, Alison Margaret, Andrew Russell. BArch, U. New Zealand, 1962; MArch with honors, U. Auckland, 1965; PhD, U. Birmingham, Eng., 1978. Arch. Auckland, 1960-64, City Archs., Birmingham, 1969-71; sr. lectr. Ctrl. U. Eng., 1972-78; reader Victoria U. of Wellington, 1978-93, assoc. prof., 1994—; postgrad. rschr. Found. Le Corbusier, Paris, 1973-78. Author: Voices of Silence, New Zealand's Chapel of Futuna, 1987, Finnish Harvest: Kaija and Heikki Sirens Chapel of Otaniemi, 1998; editor: The Open Hand: Essays on Le Corbusier, 1978. Fellow New Zealand Inst. Archs. (Nat. Arch. award 1993). Avocations: trout fishing, golf, photography, travel. E-mail: russell.Walden@vuw.ac.nz. Home: 24 Napier St, Wellington 3, New Zealand Office: Victoria U of Wellington, Sch Arch and Design, Box 600 Wellington New Zealand

WALDEN, JOHAN, mathematician; b. Stockholm, Sweden, May 24, 1969; s. Lars Johan and Jennifer Mary (Rawlins) W.; m. Petronella Carlberg. BA in History, Uppsala U., 1992, MS in Engring. Physics, 1992, MS in Econs., 1996, PhD in Numerical Analysis, 1996. Asst. prof. dept. sci. computing Uppsala U., Sweden, 1996-97; postdoctoral rsch. assoc. dept. math. Yale U., New Haven, 1997-99; cons. McKinsey & Co., Stockholm, 1999—. Avocations: volleyball, friends.

WALDEN, JOSEPH LAWRENCE, career officer; b. Paducah, Ky., Oct. 2, 1956; s. Thomas Lorenzo and Betty Jo (Miller) W.; m. Julia Kay Johnson, Oct. 9, 1982; children: Amber Marie, Bobbi Michelle. BS in Rural Sociology, N.C. State U., 1978; MBA, Fla. Inst. Tech., Melbourne, 1988; MS in Sys. Mgmt., Fla. Inst. Tech., 1989; grad., USAF Command and Staff Coll., 1990, U.S. Army/Command Gen. Staff, 1992, U.S. Army War Coll., 1994, U.S. Air War Coll., 1997, U.S. Army Sch., Advanced Mil. Studies, 2000. Commd. U.S. Army, 1978, advanced through grades col., to date; supply platoon leader 25th Inf. divsn. U.S. Army, Schofield Barracks, Hawaii, 1979-81; supply control officer U.S. Army, 1981-82; installation supply officer Signal Sch. U.S. Army, Ft. Gordon, Ga., 1983; brigade logistics officer 2d Signal Brigade U.S. Army, Ft. Gordon, 1983-84; co. comdr. Co. B, 3rd Batallion, 2d Signal Brigade, Ft. Gordon, 1984-86; logistics plans officer Combat Devel., Quartermaster Sch., Ft. Lee, Va., 1988-89; chief gen. support U.S. Army Quartermaster Sch., Ft. Lee, Va., 1989-91; assigned to U.S. Army Command and Gen. Staff Coll., Ft. Leavenworth, Kans., 1991-92; exec. officer 19th Corps Materiel Mgmt. Ctr., Wiesbaden, Germany, 1992-94; chief supply mgmt. 3D Corps Support Command, Wiesbaden, 1994-95; comdr. Materiel Mgmt. Ctr., Ft. Irwin, Calif., 1995-97; program mgr. Logistics Reengring., Ft. Lee, Va., 1997-99; sr. fellow adv. operational art Ft. Leavenworth, Kans., 1999-2000; mem. faculty U.S. Army Sch. Advanced Mil. Studies, 2000—; mem. adj. faculty St. Leo Coll., Ft. Lee, 1988-91; mem. faculty City Coll. of Chgo., 1994-95; pres. Walden Fitness Systems, Ft. Leavenworth, 1984-92. Contbr. articles to profl. jours. Mem. Bldg. Code Appeals Bd., City of Hopewell, 1988-91. Armed Forces Powerlifting Champion, 1983, Va. State Powerlifting Champion, 1990, Kans. State Powerlifting Champion, 1992, Nat. Powerlifting Champion, 1992, European Armed Forces Powerlifting Champion, 1993, 94. Mem. APICS, Internat. Soc. of Logistics, Warehousing Edn. and Rsch. Coun. (mem. edn. com.), Va. Assn. of U.S. Powerlifting Fedn. (pres. 1989-91), U.S. Golf Assn., Am. Sunbathing Assn., Fellowship Christian Athletes, Fla. Sheriffs Assn., San Diego Zool. Soc., Assn. Quartermasters, Mus. Tolerance, Las Vegas Sun Club, Save the Manatee Club. Republican. Methodist. Avocations: powerlifting (1992 Nat. Champion), naturist, golfing.

WALDENFELS, HANS, theologian; b. Essen, Germany, Oct. 20, 1931; s. Bernhard and Therese (Schröder) W. LicPhil, Berchmanskolleg, Munich, Germany, 1956; LicTheol, Sophia U., Tokyo, 1964; DrTheol, Gregorian U., Rome, 1968; DrTheolHabil, U. Würzburg, Germany, 1976; DrTheol (hon.), U. Warsaw, 1993. Joined Soc. of Jesus, 1951; ordained priest Roman Catholic Ch., 1963. Prof. fundamental theology, theol. non-Christian religions, U. Bonn., Germany, 1977-97, prof. philosophy of religion, 1977-97, dean, 1979-80, 88-90. Author: Offenbarung, 1969, Absolute Nothingness, 3d edit., 1980, Japanese, Korean and English edits., Faszination des Buddhismus, 1982, Kontextuelle Fundamentaltheologie, 3d edit., 2000, also Italian, French, Polish, Spanish and Croatish Tschech. edits., An der Grenze des Denkbaren, Meditation-Ost und West, 1988, Begegnung der Religionen, Theologische Versuche I, 1990, Phänomen Christentum, 1994, Polish, Italian ed. GOTT, 2d edit., 1997, Polish, Spanish, Italian ed. Gottes Wort in des Fremide. Thelogische Versuche II, 1997; editor: FS Glazik.Willeke, 1978, FS Dolch, 1982, FS Dumoulin, 1985, Lexikon der Religionen, 2d edit., 1988, pocket-book 4th edit., 1999, Italian Tschech, Polish, Bras./Post edit. Mem. Internat. Assn. Mission Studies, Internat. Inst. Studies of Missions (chmn. 1978-98), German Soc. Theol. Missiology, European Acad. for Arts and Scis., Assn. History Religion, Rotary. Home: Grenzweg 2, D-4000 Düsseldorf 31, Germany

WALDER, DENNIS JEAN, literature educator, author; b. Cape Town, Republic South Africa, Feb. 7, 1943; came to Eng., 1965; s. Jean Walder and Ruth (Von Liebenstein) Lodge; m. Frances Moodie Powell, Feb. 13 1968 (div. Oct. 1974); m. Mary MacLeod, Mar. 26, 1979; children: Anna Ruth, Rohan James. BA Comm., U. Cape Town, 1964; MA with honors, U. Edinburgh (Scotland), 1967; M.Litt., 1969, PhD, 1979. Asst. lectr. English U. Edinburgh, 1969-73, Workers Edn. Authority, 1970-71; staff tutor arts Open U., Edinburgh, 1974-81; lectr. lit. Open U., Milton Keynes, Eng., 1981-88; sr. lectr. lit., 1989-99, prof., head dept., 1999—; presenter ednl. radio adn TV programs BBC; speaker in field; external examiner, 1981—.

Author: Dickens and Religion, 1981; Athol Fugard, 1984, Ted Hughes, 1987, Literature in the Modern World, 1990, Post-Colonial Literatures in English, 1999; contbr. articles to ednl. jours. Aytoun fellow U. Edinburgh, 1970-73. Avocations: travel, films, theatre. Office: Faculty Arts Open U, Walton Hall, Milton Keynes MK7 6AA, England

WALDHÄUSL, WERNER KLAUS, physician; b. Leipzig, Germany, Sept. 27, 1937; s. Friedrich Wilhelm and Therese Auguste (Falke) W.; m. Marianne Hann-Kirchberger, 1965; children: Martin, Bernhard, Christoph. MD, U. Vienna, 1962. Instr. dept. exptl. pathology U. Vienna (Austria) Med. Sch., 1963-65, instr. dept. internal medicine, 1965-68; rsch. assoc. div. endocrinology and metabolism U. Mich. Med. Sch., Ann Arbor, 1968-70; with dept. internal medicine U. Vienna Med. Sch., 1970—; head div. clin. endocrinology and diabetes, mellitus, 1975, assoc. prof. internal medicine, 1978—, vice chmn. dept. internal medicine, 1985, chmn., 1987, head endocrinology and metabolism, 1992, chmn. dept. medicine III, 1992, prof. medicine; E.F.F. Copp lectr., Los Angeles, 1983; Claüde Bernard lectr., EASD Rome, 1986. Editor-in-chief Diabetologia, 1998—; contbr. articles on internal medicine, endocrinology and metabolism to med. jours. Recipient Stosius prize, 1970, 72, Sandoz prize, 1975, F. von Brücke prize, 1976, Paul Langerhans medal, Leipzig, 1998. Mem. European Soc. Clin. Investigation, Am. Diabetes Assn., Endocrine Soc., European Assn. Study Diabetes (v.p. 1982-84), Internat. Diabetes Fedn. (sci. sec. 10th congress). Office: Univ Hosp/AKH Dept Internal Med, Währinger Gurtel 18-20, A 1090 Vienna Austria

WALDMAN, ALAN I. (ALAWANA), songwriter, composer, lyricist, computer programmer, emergency medicine provider; b. Elkins Park, Pa., Jan. 20, 1955; s. Harry and Anna Waldman; m. Deborah Anne Fulkerson, Dec. 9, 1998; 1 child, Penelope Anne. Student, U. Okla., 1973-76, U. Oreg., 1978, 79; BS in Econs., U. Wis., 1979; MS in Stats., U. Iowa, 1985. Performing songwriter, composer, lyricist Deerfield Beach, Fla., 1986—; ind. computer programmer; cons. Internet and World Wide Web; cardiopulmonary resuscitation and emergency cardiovascular care provider. Author: Poetic Universe Collection, How to Form Your Own Publishing Entity and Operating it Thereafter; lyricist, composer (song collections) Hit The Market, Down to Home, Sphere of Influence, Next Galaxy, Quality Rainbow, Predicaments of Life, Great Guidelines for Living, Collection of Alawana, Vol. I, 1993, The Artist Dimension Song Collection, Vols. II, III, Artsist Dimension Collection. Charter mem. Rep. Presdl. Task Force, Washington, 1984-92. Mem. U. Iowa Alumni Assn. Republican. Avocations: music clubs, book clubs, audio book clubs, computer books training and improvement. Home: 1830 NE 48th St Apt 317 Pompano Beach FL 33064-6532

WALDMAN, JAY CARL, judge; b. Pitts., Nov. 16, 1944; s. Milton and Dorothy (Florence) W.; m. Roberta Tex Landy, Aug. 28, 1969. B.S., U. Wis., 1966; J.D., U. Pa., 1969. Bar: Pa. 1970, D.C. 1976, U.S. Supreme Ct. 1976. Assoc., Rose, Schmidt, Dixon & Hasley, Pitts., 1970-71; asst. U.S. atty. western dist. Pa., Pitts., 1971-75; dep. asst. U.S. Atty. Gen., Washington, 1975-77; counsel Gov. of Pa., Harrisburg, 1978-86; sr. ptnr., Dilworth, Paxson, Kalish & Kauffman, Phila., 1986-88; judge U.S. Dist. Ct. (ea. dist.) Pa., 1988—. Dir. Thornburgh for Gov. campaign., Pa., 1977-78; commr. Pa. Convention Ctr. Authority, 1986-88. Fellow Am. Bar Found.; mem. ABA, Fed. Bar Assn., Union League Phila. Republican. Office: US Dist Ct Pa 9613 US Courthouse 601 Market St Philadelphia PA 19106-1713

WALDMANN, HELMUT, psychiatrist, educator; b. Karlsruhe, Germany, Nov. 6, 1933; s. Hubert and Inge (Otto) W.; m. Silvia Knickenberg, Sept. 23, 1961; children: Sabine, Georg, Ruth. MD, U. Munich, 1961; psychiatrist, neurologist, Bonn (Germany) U., 1967, psychoanalyst, 1968. Scientific asst. U. Bonn, 1964-72; vice dir. Max-Planck-Inst., Munich, 1972-75; dir. Clinic Uhlandstrasse, Munich, 1975-97, Clinic Bischofsried, Diessen, Germany, 1997—; hon. lectr. U. Munich, 1975-82. Author: Phantastika im Untergrund, 1970; editor: Therapie der Drogenabhängigkeit, 1975, Medikamentenabhängigkeit, 1985; contbr. numerous chpts. to books, articles to profl. jours. Recipient Bundesverdienstkrenz, 1988, Oberbayerische Verdienstmedaille, 1997. Mem. Deutsche Gesellschaft fü Suchtforschung und Suchttherapie (v.p. 1985-89), Bayerische Landesstelle Gegen Suchtgefahren (pres. 1989-96), Diessen Sailing Club Weiss-Blau (pres. 1998—). Mem. Social Democrat. Home: Brentanostr 21, D-80807 Munich Germany Office: TZB Red Cross, Bischofsried 3, D-86911 Diessen Germany

WALDNER, VERYL CULVER, artist; b. Elk City, Okla., Feb. 23, 1913; d. Luther Coma and Lura Hapgood (Archer) Kirksey; m. Joseph Carl Culver Nov. 23, 1930 (dec. 1986); children: Irene, Lura; m. Glenn Waldner (dec. 1991). Student, Coll. of the Redwoods, 1960-90. pres., treas. Old Town Art Gallery, Eureka, Calif., 1960—. Artist Book on Encaustic Painting, 1990. Mem. Redwood Art Assn. (various offices 1960—, numerous awards), South Humboldt Art Assn. Avocations: church activities, women's clubs, walking, travel. Home: 2575 Christensen Way Eureka CA 95501-3329

WALDOCK, WILLIAM DAVID, aeronautical science and aviation safety educator; b. Ft. Worth, Tex., Aug. 4, 1952; s. Wallace Gordon and Annabelle (Wolfe) W.; m. Barbara A. Wisler, Sept. 14, 1974; children: Andrew, Kathleen. BA in History, U. Fla., 1975; student, Miami-Dade Coll., Miami, Fla., 1977-78; M of Aero. Sci. with honors, Embry-Riddle Aero. U., 1982; postgrad., Kennedy-Western U. Prof. aero. sci. Embry-Riddle Aero. U., Prescott, Ariz., 1982—, chief investigator aircraft accidents, 1991-96, assoc. dir. Ctr. Aerospace Safety Edn., 1986—, dir. Robertson Aviation Safety Ctr., 1995—; pres., chief cons. Sys. Safety, Inc., Prescott, 1990—; cons. Am. West Airlines, Phoenix, 1996-99; presenter numerous safety confs. Contbr. articles to profl. publs.; guest various T.V. shows. Lt. commdr. USCG, 1975-96, ret. Mem. SAFE Assn. (Gen. Spruance award for Outstanding Contbns. to Safety Through Edn. 1990), Aircraft Owners and Pilots Assn., Aircraft Rescue and Firefighting Working Group, Am. Soc. Safety Engrs., World Safety Orgn. (cert.), Internat. Soc. Air Safety Investigators (pres. Ariz. chpt. 1987—). Achievements include over 75 field investigations; research in accident history. Avocations: flying, hiking, boating, history. Office: Embry-Riddle Aero U Bldg 29 3200 Willow Creek Rd Prescott AZ 86301-3721

WALDREN, WILLIAM HENRE, historian, museum administrator; b. N.Y.C., May 2, 1924; s. William Harry and Alice Huetter Schminke Waldren; m. Yvette Mignaro, 1954 (div. 1958); m. Jacqueline Dee Brown, Jan. 23, 1960; children: CC, Talis, Deia, Tana, Mya. DPhil, U. Oxford, Eng., 1982, MA (hon.), 1991; art diploma, Art Student's League, N.Y.C. Cert. in prehistory-prehist. archaeology. Founder, dir. Deia Archaeol. Mus. Rsch. Ctr., Mallorca, Spain, 1962—; rsch. assoc. Baden Powell Quaternary Rsch. Ctr. Pitt Rivers Mus., U. Oxford, 1982—; sub-faculty archaeology Oxford U., 1989—; dir., prin. investigator Earth Watch Inst., Boston, 1972—. Editor: Damarc Archaeological Series, 1962—; editor, chmn. Internat. Confs. of Prehistory; editor Brit. Archael. Reports, 1998—. Tech. sgt. U.S. Army, 1943-46. Christensen Rsch. fellow St. Catherine Coll., Oxford U., 1987-88. Mem. Linacre Coll., U. Oxford (life), Churchill Coll., U. Cambridge (life, Winston Churchill Rsch. fellow 1990-92), Oxford/Cambridge Club (life). Avocations: fine art, computer science, music, reading. Office: Baden Powell Quaternary Ctr, 60 Banbury Rd, Oxford OX2 6PN, England

WALDREP, ALVIS KENT, JR., non-profit foundation administrator; b. Austin, Tex., Mar. 2, 1954; s. Alvis Kent and Denise Carol (Wolfe) W.; m. Lynn Burgland, Dec. 6, 1980; children: Trey, Charles. BBA, Tex. Christian U. and Kennedy Western U., 1992. Exec. Nat. Paralysis Found., Dallas, 1985—; chmn. Turbo Resins Internat., Dallas, 1991—, Dallas Rehab. Inst., 1981-93; bd. dirs. Tex. Rehab. Commn., Austin, 1989—. Member Job Accomodations Network, Washington, 1986-89, Internat. Alliance on Disability, Washington, 1986—; chmn. Tex. Gov.'s Com. for Disabled Persons, Austin, 1987-90; founder Am. Paralysis Assn., 1979—. Recipient Spirit of Tex. award ABC-TV Affiliate, 1984, Spl. award Tex. Sports Hall of Fame, 1975, Family of the Yr. award Dallas YWCA, 1998; named one of Ten Outstanding Young Ams., U.S. Jaycees, 1985. Mem. Nat. Soc. Fund Raising Execs. (bd. dirs. 1983-84), Nat. Coun. on Disability (vice chair 1983-94), Nat. Rehab. Assn., Neurotrauma Soc., Tex. Jaycees. Republican. Methodist. Avocations: bridge, swimming, public speaking. Office: Nat Paralysis Found 16415 Addison Rd Ste 550 Addison TX 75001-3234

WALDRON, ARTHUR NELSON, international relations educator; b. Boston, Dec. 13, 1948; s. William Augustus and Gertrude Lill (Nelson) W.; m. Xiaowei Yu, June 25, 1988; children: Charles William, Theodore Nelson. AB, Harvard U., 1971, PhD, 1981. Asst. prof. history and East Asian studies Princeton (N.J.) U., 1985-91; prof. strategy and policy U.S. Naval War Coll., Newport, R.I., 1991-97; Lauder prof. internat. rels. U. Pa., Phila., 1998—; dir. Asian Studies Am. Enterprise Inst., Washington, 1997—; sr. fellow Fgn. Policy Rsch. Inst., Phila., 1997—; cons. Freedom House, N.Y., 1985—, Dept. Def., Washington, 1991—. Author: The Great Wall of China, 1990, From War to Nationalism, 1995; editor: How the Peace Was Lost, 1992. Mem. Coun. on Fgn. Rels., The Hist. Soc., Nat. Assn. Scholars, Am. Hist. Assn., Assn. for Asian Studies, Soc. Harvard Club (N.Y.C. and Boston), Navy League, U.S. Naval War Coll., Somerset Club (Boston). Republican. Episcopalian. Avocation: travel. Home: 906 Coopertown Rd Bryn Mawr PA 19010-3722 Office: U Pa Dept History 3401 Walnut St Philadelphia PA 19104-6228

WALDRUP, KENNETH ARLEN, veterinarian, researcher; b. Waco, Tex., May 8, 1954; s. James Arlen and Ann Pendleton (Ellen) W.; m. Darcy Lynn Tammen, Aug. 9, 1975 (div. Aug. 1987); m. Carol Smith, June 6, 1998; 1 child, Matthew Ryan Ponder-Waldrup; 1 stepchild, Ashley Nicole Bradford. BS, Okla. State U., 1976, MS, 1980, DVM, 1983; PhD, Tex. A&M U., 1991. Lic. vet. Okla., Tex., Ark. Vet. Animal Care Ctr., Poplar Bluff, Mo., 1983-85; vet. scientist AgResearch Invermay, Mosgiel, New Zealand, 1991-95; vis. prof. Okla. State U., Stillwater, 1995-96; support epidemiologist Tex. Animal Health Commn., Austin, 1997—. Author: (with others) Zoo & Wild Animal Medicine III, 1993, Infectious Diseases of Wild Mammals, 2000. Recipient Performance award Ministry of Agr. & Fisheries, Mosgiel, 1992. Mem. AVMA, Wildlife Disease Assn., Am. Assn. Small Ruminant Practitioners (com. co-chmn. 1997—), Am. Assn. Wildlife Vets. Avocations: fishing, hunting, photography, music, camping. E-mail: kenw@tahc.state.tx.us. Office: Tex Animal Health Commn PO Box 3041 Cleburne TX 76033-3041

WALDSCHMIDT, JÜRGEN WILHELM ROLF, pediatrician; b. Brüel, Germany, Oct. 20, 1935; s. Rudolf Waldschmidt and Hildegard Ilgmann; m. Astrid Benda, May 17, 1974; children: Ulrike, Stefan, Johannes, Matthias. Student, Free U., 1962, med. asst., 1964. Wiss asst. Free Univ., Berlin, 1964-72, head pediatric surgery, 1972—. Author: Akutes Abdomen in Kindesalter, 1990, Akutes Skrotum, 1990, Maldescensls testis, 1990, Cholestasis in Neonates, 1988. Recipient Bundesverdienstkreuz am Bande, 1984, Ehrenmitglied Panhellenic Assoc. Pediatric Sugery, 1978. Mem. German Assn. Laser Medicine (pres.). Evangelist. Home: Kreutzer Weg 21, 12203 Berlin Germany Office: Free Univ Ben Franklin Hosp, Hindenburgdamm 30, 12200 Berlin Germany

WALDVOGEL, SIEGFRIED R., chemistry educator, researcher; b. Konstanz, Bodensee, Germany, June 9, 1969; s. Siegfried W. and Martha (Vogel) W. Diploma in Chemistry, U. Konstanz, 1994; PhD, U. Bochum, Germany, 1996. Rschr. MPI-Mueiheim, Germany, 1994-97; postdoctoral fellow TSRI, LaJolla, Calif., 1997-98; asst. prof. U. Muenster, Germany, 1998—. Recipient Jugend Forscht, Germany, 1989, Otto-Hahn medal, Germany, 1996. Mem. GdCH, ACS. Home: Gescherweg 21, D-48161 Muenster Germany Office: U Muenster Org Chem Inst, Correnssstr 40, D-48149 Muenster Germany

WALENDY, UDO BRUNO, publisher; b. Berlin, Germany, Jan. 21, 1927; s. Bruno and Paula (Brandts) W.; m. Margarete Schneider, Aug. 22, 1931; 1 child, Ute Marita. Cert., German Jounalsim Aachen, 1949; Diploma, German Hochschule Politik, Berlin, 1956. Dir. Volkshochschule, Herford, 1960, Gildenhaus e.V., Bielefeld, Germany, 1961-62; polit. docent Bildungsarbeit Büro Bonner Berichte and Arbeitsgemein, Kreise, Germany, 1960-65; docent Staatsrecht, 1960-66; pub. Verlag für Volkstum, Vlotho, Germany. Author, pub.: Wahrheit fur Deutschland-Die Schuldfrage des Sweiten Weltrieges, 2d edit., 1965, Europa in Flammen 1939-1945, 1967, Bild'dokumente' fur die Geschichtsschreibung?, 1973, Historische Tatsachen, 1975-99, No. 1-77, Die Weltanschauung des Wissens, 5 vols., 1969, 88, Auschwitz im IG-Farben Prozess, 1981. Mem. Nat. German Dem. Party, 1965-72. With German Army, 1944-45. Home: Postfach 1643, D 32590 Vlotho Germany Office: Verlag fur Volkstum, Postfach 1643 Winterberg St, D 32602 Vlotho Weser, Germany

WALENTA, KURT, retired mineralogy educator; b. Prague, Czech Republic, Dec. 1, 1927; s. Eduard and Maria (Rott) W.; m. Marianne Bleicken, Apr. 3, 1956; children: Susanne, Wolfgang. Diploma in geology, U. Stuttgart, Germany, 1953, PhD, 1956, habilitation, 1962, prof., 1967. Scientific asst. Inst. Mineralogy and Crystallography, U. Stuttgart, 1956-63, lectr., 1963-67, prof. mineralogy, 1967—, dir., 1972-94; ret., 1994. Author: The Minerals of the Black Forest, 1992; contbr. over 170 articles to internat. profl. jours. Mem. German Mineral. Soc., Oberrheinischer Geologischer Verein, Vereinigung der Freunde der Mineralogie und Geologie, Verein der Freunde von Mineralien und Bergbau Oberwolfach. Home: Kremmlerstr 43, D-70597 Stuttgart Germany Office: Inst Mineralogy U Stuttgart, Pfaffenwaldring 55, D-70569 Stuttgart Germany

WALES, JEREMY KENNETH HARVARD, pediatric endocrinologist; b. Scarborough, Yorkshire, England, July 28, 1954; s. Kenneth Collinson and Marjorie (Mallard) W.; m. Clare Draper July 19, 1980 (div. 1988); children: Harry Johnathan, Mark Nicholas; m. Gillian Kirsten Sankey, July 10, 1989; children: Oscar Jeremy, Montgomery Kenneth Sankey. BM, BCh, U. Oxford, Eng., 1976, MA, 1980, DM, 1990. Accreditation UK, Europe in pediatric endocrinology,. Sr. lectr. U. Sheffield, Eng., 1990—; head med. directorate Sheffield Children's Hosp., 1994-95, Nat. Health Svc. Trust, Eng., 1994-2000. Fellow Royal Coll. Physicians, Royal Coll. Pediatrics and Child Health (registered advisor 1997—); mem. Brit. Soc. Pediatric Endocrinology (chmn. 1998—), European Soc. Pediatric Endocrinology, Internat. Soc. for Pediat. and Adolescent Diabetes. Avocations: cosmology, cycling. Office: Sheffield Childrens Hosp, Dept Pediatrics, Sheffield S10 2TH, England

WALES, RAYMOND GEORGE, retired physiology educator; b. Melbourne, Victoria, Australia, Aug. 24, 1931; s. John and Eileen Veronica (Mulkearns) W.; m. Margaret Anne Mitchell, Aug. 15, 1959 (dec. Aug. 1996); children: Amanda Jane, Peter John, Katherine Anne. B of Vet. Sci., Sydney (Australia) U., 1955, PhD, 1960, D of Vet. Sci., 1972. Vet. officer Agr. Dept., Victoria, 1955; lectr. Sydney U., 1960-64, sr. lectr., 1965-71, assoc. prof., 1972-74; prof. Murdoch U., Perth, Australia, 1975-96; vis. scientist Med. Rsch. Coun., London, 1984; vis. prof. U. York, Eng., 1993; mem. senate Murdoch U., 1978-84, 86-90. Contbr. articles to profl. jours. Mem. nat. exec. Fedn. Australian U. Staff Assns., 1980-83. Population Coun. fellow U. Pa., 1966, Sr. Hays Fulbright fellow Washington U., St. Louis, 1973. Mem. Nat. Terr. Edn. Union (life), Australian Soc. for Reproductive Biology (found. treas. 1969-72), Rotary club Applecross (pres. 1999-2000). Avocations: art acquisition and practice, gardening. Home: 19 Strome Rd, Applecross 6153, Australia

WALESA, LECH, former president of Poland, foundation administrator; b. Popowo, Poland, Sept. 29, 1943; s. Boleslaw and Feliksa W.; m. Miroslawa Danuta, 1969; children: Bogdan, Slawomir, Przemyslaw, Jaroslaw, Magdalena, Anna, Maria-Victoria Brygida. Student, Tech. State Vocat. Sch., Lipno, Poland; PhD (hon.), Alliance Coll., Pa., 1981, U. of Columbia, 1981, Cath. U., Louvain, 1981, MacMurray Coll., Ill., 1982, U. Notre Dame, 1982, Providence Coll., 1981, St. Denis U., Paris, 1982, Seton Hall U., 1982, U. Paris, 1983, Harvard U., 1983, Fordham U., 1984, Dundee U., Great Britain, 1984, McMaster U., Hamilton, Can., 1989, Simon Fraser U., Can., 1989, Gdańsk U., 1990, Copernicus U., Toruń, Poland, 1990. Electrician Lenin Shipyard, Gdansk, 1966-76, 80—, chmn. strike com., 1970, 80; co-founder, chmn. Nat. Coordinating Com. of Independent Trade Union Solidarity, 1980; held in detention, 1981-82; chmn. nat. exec. com. NSZZ Solidarnosc, 1981-90; pres. of Poland, 1990-95; v.p. Lech Walesa Inst. Found., Warsaw, Poland, 1995—. Author: A Way of Hope, 1987, The Struggle and the Triumph, 1991. Named Man of the Yr., Time mag., 1981, The Fin. Times, 1980, The Observer, 1980, Polish Radio and TV, 1989, Saudi Gazette, Saudi Arabia, 1989; recipient Free World prize Norway, 1982, Le Point, 1981, Le Soir, 1981, l'Express, 1981, Freedom medal, Phila., 1981, Die Zeit, 1981, Die Welt, 1980, Peace prize of Arbetet, 1981, Love Internat. award, 1981, Medal of Merit Polish Am. Congress, 1981, Internat. Democracy award, 1982, Social Justice award, 1983, Am. Friendship medal, 1983, Nobel prize for Peace, 1983, Social Justice award, 1983, Am. Friendship medal, 1983, Humanitarian Pub. Svc. medal, 1984, Pro Fide et Patria medal, Poland, 1985, Internat. Integrity award, 1986, Phila. Liberty medal, 1989, Coun. of Europe Human Rights prize, 1989, U.S. Medal of Freedom, 1989, George Meany Human Rights award, 1989; decorated Order of Francisco de Miranda, 1989, knight of the Grand Cross of the Order of the Bath, 1991, Grand Cross of Legion of Honour, 1991, Grand Order of Merit, Republic of Italy, 1991, Ordine Piano I classe Cavalliere di Collare, 1991, Grand Sash of Order of Leopold, 1991, Grande Colar da Ordem da Liberdade, 1993, Grand Cross of White Rose with Chains, Finland, 1993, Royal Order of Seraphim, Sweden, 1993, Order of the Elephant, Denmark, 1993, Grand Cross of Order of Merit, Republic of Hungary, 1994, knight of Order of Rebirth of Poland, knight of Order of White Eagle, Poland, Path to Peace award Apostolic Nuncis to UN, 1996. Home: ul Polanki 54, 80-308 Gdańsk Poland Office: Lech Walesa Institute, Al Jerozolimskie 11/19, 00-508 Warsaw Poland*

WALFORD, GEOFFREY, education policy educator; b. London, Apr. 30, 1949. PhD in Physics, U. Kent, 1975; MPhil in Sociology, U. Oxford, 1978; MA in Ednl. Adminstrn., U. London, 1986; MBA, Open U., 1996. Tchr. Stowe Sch., Buckingham, 1976; rsch. fellow U. Kent, 1976; SSRC conversion fellow St. John's Coll., Oxford, 1976-78; lectr. sociology of edn. dept. ednl. enquiry Aston U., 1979-83, lectr. in edn. policy and mgmt., Aston Bus. Sch., 1983-90; lectr. in ednl. studies, fellow Green Coll. U. Oxford, 1995-97, reader in edn. policy, fellow of Green Coll., 1997-99; dir. rsch. project on technology for religious minorities Spencer Found., Eng., 1999-2001; prof. edn. policy Sreen Coll., 1999—. Author: Life in Public Schools, 1986, Restructuring Universities: Politics and Power in the Management of Change, 1987, Choice and Equity in Education, 1994, Educational Politics: Pressure Groups and Faith-Based Schools, 1995, (with Henry Miller) City Technology Coll., 1991, others; editor: British Public Schools: Policy and Practice, 1984, Schooling in Turmoil, 1985, Doing Sociology of Education, 1987, Doing Education Research, 1991; co-editor: Affirming the Comprehensive Ideal, 1997; joint editor Brit. Jour. Ednl. Studies; series editor Studies in Ednl. Ethnography. Office: Dept Ednl Studies U Oxford, 15 Norham Gardens, Oxford OX2 6PY, England

WALI, ANIL, petrochemical company executive; b. Srinagar, India, May 13, 1959; s. Brij Krishen and Lata (Dhar) W.; m. Rashmi Raina, Oct. 23, 1992; children: Shivashish, Ridhima. BS, Jammu U., India, 1980, MS in Chemistry, 1982; PhD in Chemistry, Indian Inst. Tech., Delhi, 1987. Sr. scientific officer Atic Industries, Valsad, India, 1987-88; rsch. officer Indian Petrochem. Corp. Ltd., Vadodara, India, 1988-92, sr. rsch. officer, 1992-98; dep. mgr. I.P.C.L., Vadodara, 1999—. Contbr. articles to profl. jours.; inventor in field. Rsch. scholar Indian Inst. Tech., Delhi, 1982-87; Rsch. fellow C.S.I.R., Delhi. Fellow Indian Soc. Analytical Scientists, Indian Chem. Soc.; mem. Am. Chem. Soc., Catalysis Soc. India (life). Hindu. Avocations: recreational activities. Home: 79/5 Trikuta Nagar, Jammu Tawi India Office: Indian Petrochem Corp Ltd, Rsch Ctr, 391 346 Vadodara India

WALI, MAHMOUD ANWAR, surgeon, educator; b. Zagazig, Sharkia, Egypt, Aug. 27, 1955; s. Anwar Soliman Wali and Fat'hia Mahmoud El-Shahed; m. Taha Deyanah, Mar. 3, 1989; children: Tasneem, Ahmad, Salsabeil, Kawthar, Omar. MBBCh, Kasr El-Ainy, Cairo, 1979, MSc in Gen. Surgery, 1986. Registrar in vascular surgery St. James Hosp., Dublin, Ireland, 1991, sr. registrar in vascular surgery, 1992-94, sr. registrar in gen. surgery, 1994-95; specialist in gen. surgery Ministry of Health, Cairo, 1992; cons. vascular surgeon Ministry of Health, Madina Munawara, Saudi Arabia, 1995-96; asst. prof. King Khalid U., Abha, Saudi Arabia, 1996—; cons. vascular surgeon Asiv Ctrl. Hosp., Abha, Saudi Arabia, 1996—; instr. ACS, 1997—. Contbr. articles to profl. jours. 2nd lt. Egyptian Army, 1981-83. Fellow Royal Coll. Surgeons Ireland; mem. Internat. Soc. Cardiovasc. Surgery, Assn. Study Med. Edn., N.Y. Acad. Scis. Avocations: swimming, golf, tennis. Home: 24 Honeysuckle Crescent, Ancaster, ON Canada Office: King Khalid U, Coll Medicine, PO Box 641, Abha Saudi Arabia

WALIA, BRIJ NANDAN SINGH, pediatrician, hospital administrator; b. Hoshiarpur, India, June 23, 1933; s. Rajendra Singh and Gursharan K.; m. Harkanwal Walia, Dec. 7, 1959; 1 child, Ramnik. MBBS, Agra, 1954; MD, 1957; cert. in Health Planning, Johns Hopkins Sch. Pub. Health, Balt., 1975. Asst. prof. Pediatrics All India Inst. Med. Scis., New Delhi, 1961-65; assoc. prof. Post Grad. Inst. Med. Edn. and Rsch., Chandigarh, 1965-71, prof., 1971-91; emeritus prof. Punjab Hlth. and Peds., 1983; dir. Post Grad. Inst. Med. Edn. and Rsch., Chandigarh, 1991-95; dean faculty medicine Baba Farid U. Health Scis., Faridkot, 1999-2000; chmn. Punjab Health Sys. Corp., 1996. Contbr. articles to med. jours. and chpts. to several books. Chmn. Blood Bank Soc., Haryana Soc. Welfare Hearing Impaired. Recipient Honorary fellowship Indian Acad. Pediatrics, Nat. Acad. Med. Scis.; founder fellow Royal Coll. Pediatrics and Child Health, Eng.; worker as mem. WHO Ccom. on treatment of respiratory infection and several WHO (SEARO) coms. on pediatric edn.; examiner vis. prof. to several univs. in India, abroad. Fellow Royal Coll Peds. & Child Hlth.; mem. Indian Acad. Pediatrics (pres. 1983). Home: 1004 Sector 11-C, Chandigarh 160011, India

WALJI, JABIR MOHAMED, management consultant, commercial analyst; b. Kampala, Uganda, Mar. 2, 1959; s. Razahusein Virji and Kubra (Mauji) W.; m. Ahlam Jaffer Ali, Nov. 8, 1989. BS with honors, John Moores U. Liverpool, Eng., 1982; DMS, U. North London, 1986; MBA, Manchester Bus. Sch., Eng., 1996. Mktg. officer Tara Arts Group, Eng., 1985-86; internal cons. Indus Textile Mills Ltd., Pakistan, 1987-94; dir. Indus Marines, Pakistan, 1988-92; cons. Shell Oils, Eng., 1996-98, svc. team, 1998—. Mem. Royal Soc. Arts, Chartered Inst. Mktg., Inst. Mgmt. Consultants, Strategy and Planning Soc., Dubai Soc., Inst. Leisure and Amenity Mgmt., Assn. MBA, Tourism Soc. Avocations: jet skiing, squash, cinema, cuisine. Home fax: 020 8958-7593; office fax: 020 7346-0746. Home and Office: 6 Penshurst Ct, Penshurst Gardens, Edgware Middlesex HA8 9TL, England

WALKER, ALICE MALSENIOR, author; b. Eatonton, Ga., Feb. 9, 1944; d. Willie Lee and Minnie (Grant) W.; m. Melvyn R. Leventhal, Mar. 17, 1967 (div. 1976); 1 dau., Rebecca Walker Leventhal. BA, Sarah Lawrence Coll., 1966; PhD (hon.), Russell Sage U., 1972; DHL (hon.), U. Mass., 1983. Co-founder, pub. Wild Trees Pr., Navarro, Calif., 1984-88; writer in residence, tchr. black studies Jackson State Coll., 1968-69, Tougaloo Coll., 1970-71; lectr. literature Wellesley Coll., 1972-73, U. Mass., Boston, 1972-73; disting. writer Afro-American studies dept. U. Calif., Berkeley, 1982; Fannie Hurst Prof. of Literature Brandeis U., Waltham, Mass., 1982; cons. Friends of the Children of Miss., 1967. Author: Once, 1968, The Third Life of Grange Copeland, 1970, Five Poems, 1972, Revolutionary Petunias and Other Poems, 1973 (Nat. Book award nomination 1973, Lillian Smith award So. Regional Coun. 1973), In Love and Trouble, 1973 (Richard and Hinda Rosenthal Found. award Am. Acad. and Inst. of Arts and Letters 1974) Langston Hughes: American Poet, 1973, Meridian, 1976, Goodnight, Willie Lee, I'll See You in the Morning, 1979, You Can't Keep a Good Woman Down, 1981, The Color Purple, 1982 (Nat. Book Critics Circle award nomination 1982, Pulitzer Prize for fiction 1983, Am. Book award 1983), In Search of Our Mothers' Gardens, 1983, Horses Make a Landscape Look More Beautiful, 1984, To Hell With Dying, 1988, Living By the Word: Selected Writings, 1973-1987, 1988, The Temple of My Familiar, 1989, Her Blue Body Everything We Know: Earthling Poems, 1965-1990, 1991, Finding the Green Stone, 1991, Possessing the Secret of Joy, 1992, (with Pratibha Parmar) Warrior Marks, 1993, (with others) Double Stitch: Black Women Write About Mothers & Daughters, 1993, Everyday Use, 1994, Alice Walker Banned: The Banned Works, 1996, Everything We Love Can Be Saved: A Writer's Activism: Essays, Speeches, Statements and Letters, 1997, The Same River Twice, 1997; editor: I Love Myself When I'm Laughing... And Then Again When I'm Looking Mean and Impressive, 1979, By The Light of My Father's Smile, 1998. Recipient first prize Am. Scholar essay contest, 1967, O. Henry award for "Kindred Spirits", 1986, Nora Astorga Leadership award, 1989, Fred Cody award for lifetime achievement Bay Area Book Reviewers Assn., 1990, Freedom to Write award PEN Ctr. USA West, 1990; Bread Loaf Writer's Conf. scholar, 1966; Merrill writing fellowship, 1967; McDowell Colony fellowship, 1967, 77-78; National Endowment for the Arts grantee, 1969, 77; Radcliffe Inst. fellowship, 1971-73; Guggenheim fellow, 1977-78. Address: care Joan Mira 1563 Solano Ave Berkeley CA 94707-2116

WALKER, ANDREW MORRIS, retired statistics educator; b. Glasgow, Scotland, U.K., Dec. 21, 1921; s. Andrew and Elizabeth (Morris) W.; m. Monica Anne Creasy, July 9, 1959; children: Ruth Helen, Gordon Peter. BA in Math., Cambridge U., Eng., 1943. Sci. officer U.K. Civil Svc., London, 1946-49; rsch. asst. U. Manchester, 1949-55; grad. asst. U. Oxford, 1955-58; lectr. math. U. Cambridge, 1958-68; sr. lectr. U. Sheffield, 1968-70, reader dept. probability and statistics, 1970-72, prof., 1972-82; ret.; vis. prof. Stanford U., 1968; vis. fellow Australian Nat. U., 1963-64. Contbr. about 30 articles to profl. jours. Fellow Royal Statis. Soc.; mem. Inst. Math. Stats. Ch. of England. Avocations: piano playing, singing, hill walking. Home: 12 Clumber Rd, Sheffield England S10 3LE

WALKER, ANNE KATHLEEN, state official; b. Toledo, Ohio, Oct. 20, 1944; d. Charles LeRoy and Nina Eloise (Weber) Shrock; m. Danny James Walker, Nov. 28, 1963; 1 child, James Allen. Acctg. asst. Tropicana Products, Bradenton, Fla., 1977-78; exec. sec. Colo. Refractories Corp., Canon City, 1978-79; asst. sec. Naples (Fla.) Fed. Savs. & Loan, 1979-81; acctg. technician II Dept. Corrections, Canon City, 1981-83, adminstrv. officer II, 1983-86; sr. policy budget analyst Dept. Corrections, Colorado Springs, Colo., 1986-89, prin. policy budget analyst, 1989-93, dir. fin. and budget, 1993—. Republican. Lutheran. Avocations: exercising, boating, fishing. E-Mail: kathy.walker@state.co.us. Office: Dept Corrections 2561 N Circle Dr Ste 400 Colorado Springs CO 80909-1167

WALKER, ANNETTE, counseling administrator; b. Birmingham, Ala., Sept. 20, 1953; d. Jesse and Luegene (Wright) W. BS in Edn., Huntingdon Coll., 1976; MS in Adminstrn. and Supervision, Troy State U., 1977, 78, MS in Sch. Counseling, 1990, AA in Sch. Adminstrn., 1992; diploma, World Travel Sch., 1990; diploma in Cosmetology, John Patterson Coll., 1992; MEd in higher Edn. Adminstrn., Auburn (Ala.) U., 1995. Cert. tchr., adminstr., Ala.; lic. cosmetologist, Ala. Tchr. Montgomery (Ala.) Pub. Sch. System, 1976-89, sch. counselor, 1989—; lit. tchr. Federal Bureau of Justice, 1997—; tchr. Fed. Govt., 1997—, U.S. Bur. Justice, 1997—; gymnastics tchr. Cleveland Ave. YMCA, 1971-76; girls coach Montgomery Parks and Recreation, 1973-76; summer sch. sci. tchr. grades 7-9, 1977-88; chmn. dept. sci. Bellingrath Sch., 1987-90, courtesy com., 1987-88, sch. discipline com., 1977-84; recreation asst. Gunter AFB, Ala., 1981-83; calligraphy tchr. Gunter Youth Ctr., 1982; program dir. Maxwell AFB, Ala., 1983-89, vol. tchr. Internat. Officer Sch., 1985—, Adult Laubach Reading Prog., Ala. Goodwill Amb., 1985—, day camp dir., 1987, calligraphy tchr., 1988; trainer internat. law for sec. students, Ala., 1995—; leader of workshops in field; evening computer tchr. high sch. diploma program, 1995—; sales rep. Ala. World Travel, 1990—; behavior aid Brantwood Children's Home, 1996—; computer tchr. h.s. diploma program Montgomery County Sch., 1995—; behavior aide Brantwood Children's Home, 1995—; hotel auditor, 1995—; Am. del. to China, People to People Internat., 1998. Mem. CAP; tchr. Sunday sch. Beulah Bapt. Ch., Montgomery; vol. zoo activities Tech. Scholarship Program for Ala. Tchrs. Computer Courses, Montgomery, Ala.; bd. dirs. Cleveland Ave. YMCA, 1976-80; sponsor Bell-Howe chpt. Young Astronauts, 1986-90, Pate Howe chpt. Young Astronauts, 1991-92; judge Montgomery County Children Festival Elem. Sci. Fair, 1988-90; bd. dirs. Troy State U. Drug Free Schs., 1992—; chmn. Maxwell AFB Red Cross Youth, 1986-88; goodwill amb. sponsor to various families (award 1989, 95); State of Ala. rep. P.A.T.C.H.-Internat. Law Inst., 1995; bd. dirs. People to People Internat., 2000. Recipient Outstanding high Sch. Sci./Math. Tchr. award Sigma Xi, 1989, Most Outstanding Youth Coun. Leader award Maxwell AFB youth Ctr., 1987, Outstanding Ala. Goodwill Amb. award, 1989, 95; named Tchr. of the Week, WCOV-TV, 1992, Ala. Tchr. in Space Program, summer 1989, Local Coodr. Young Astronaut Program, 1988, Tchr. of Yr. award Paterson Sch., 1990, Career Infusion Award (Most Appreciated Tchr. award 1987), Montgomery Pub. Sch., 1982, 84, Earthwatch Ednl. award, Israel, 1997; Fulbright scholar, Japan, 1999; selected Citizen Amb. to China, People to People Internat., 1999, 20 Class award Maxwell AFB Internat. Fgn. Officer Program. Mem. NEA, Internat. Platform Assn., People to People Internat. (founder, bd. trustees, organizer, pres. Ala. chpt. 1998), Nat. Sci. Tchrs. Assn., Ala. Sch. Counselors, Montgomery Sch. Counselors Assn., Montgomery County Ednl. Assn., Space Camp Amb., Huntingdon Alumni Assn. (sec.-treas.), Ala. Goodwill Amb., Montgomery Capital City Club, Young Astronauts, Ea. Star, Japan Friends of Fulbright Meml. Fund Tchr. Prog., Water Watch, Montgomery, AL, Zeta Phi Beta, Chi Delta Phi, Kappa Pi. Avocations: international travel, calligraphy, international food, cruising. E-mail: awalke123@aol.com. Home: 3504 Oak Ave SW Birmingham AL 35221-1436 Office: MacMillan Internat Sch 25 Covington St Montgomery AL 36104-3015

WALKER, ANTHONY DAVID MORTIMER, physicist; b. Port Shepstone, South Africa, Dec. 7, 1937; s. Frank Arthur Mortimer and Joan Margaret (Bland) W.; m. Caroline Rae Glencross, Apr. 14, 1967; children: Andrew, Kenneth, Harriet. BS, Rhodes U., South Africa, 1958, BS with honors, 1959, MS, 1962; PhD, Cambridge U., England, 1966. Lectr. Rhodes U., South Africa, 1966-69, sr. lectr., 1969-72; prof. U. Natal, South Africa, 1972—, dean faculty sci., 1991-95; sr. visitor Cambridge U., 1969-70; cons. Johns Hopkins U. Applied Physics, Laurel, Md., 1981, 84-85, 91; vis. scientist Max Planck Inst. Aeronomie, Lindau, Germany, 1977-78; chmn. Star Working Group SCAR, Cambridge, 1994—, v.p., 1998—. Author: Plasma Waves in the Magnetosphere, 1993; contbr. numerous scientific papers to profl. pubs. Chmn. bd. trustees U. Natal Retirement Fund, South Africa, 1995—. Recipient de Beers gold medal South African Inst. Physics, 1998; Alexander von Humboldt Found. fellow, Germany, 1977-78. Fellow Royal Soc. South Africa; mem. Nat. Acad. Sci. South Africa (founder), Am. Geophys. Union. Avocations: watercolor painting, gardening. Home: 12 Chase Pl, Westville 3630, South Africa Office: U Natal, Sch Pure & Applied Physics, 4041 Durban South Africa

WALKER, BETTY STEVENS, lawyer; b. N.Y.C., Feb. 3, 1943; d. Randolph Blakney and Anne (Stevens) Wood; m. Paul Thomas Walker, Aug. 27, 1942; children: Camarf, Tarik, Kumi. BA in Polit. Sci. and History, Spelman Coll., 1964; JD, Harvard U., 1967. Bar: U.S. Dist. Ct. (DC) 1981, U.S. Ct. Appeals (DC cir.) 1977, U.S. Supreme Ct. 1996. Coord. southern schs. Legal Def. and Ednl. Fund, N.Y.C., 1964; asst. prof. polit. sci. Shaw U., Raleigh, N.C., 1968-69; faculty fellow Shaw U., Raleigh, 1969-70; corp. atty. Southern Railway Co., Washington, 1974-77; exec. asst. to adminstr. Farmers Home Adminstrn. USDA, Washington, 1977-81; assoc. Walker & Walker Assoc., P.C., Washington, 1981—. Democrat. Mem. African Meth. Ch. Office: Walker & Walker Assoc PC 2807 18th St NW Washington DC 20009-2205

WALKER, BRIAN WILSON, former field science foundation director; b. Chipping Norton, Oxon, Eng., Oct. 31, 1930; s. Arthur Harrison and Eleanor Mary (Wilson) W.; m. Nancy Margaret Gawith, Mar. 4, 1954; children: Peter, Clare, Dorcas, Grainne, Siobhan, Sarah. MA, Oxford U., 1983. Mgmt. scholarship Pye Radio, Kendal, 1952-56; personnel mgr. Pye Radio, Northern Ireland, 1957-61; personnel mgr. Nat. Dist. and Chem. Corp., Northern Ireland, 1961-68, gen. mgr. R&D, 1968-70, gen. mgr. mfg., 1970-74; dir. gen. Oxfam, Oxford, 1974-83; dir. ICIHI, Geneva, 1983-85; pres. IIED, London, 1985-89; exec. dir. Earthwatch Europe, Oxford, 1989-95; founder, chmn. New Ulster Movement, 1969-74; mem. standing commn. Human Rights/No. Ireland, 1974-77; mem. European NGO Liaison Com., Belgium, 1976-83; chmn. Cambodia NGO Liaison Com., Belgium, 1976-83; chmn. Cambodia NGO Consortium, Oxford, 1979-83; chmn. Bandaid/Live Aid, London, 1985-91; U.K. mem. Internat. Com. on Food and Peace, Indian, 1989-94; chmn. Govs. Dallam Sch. Cumbria, 1996; Oxford U. meml. lectr. on environ. and devel., 1996. Editor: Report on African Emergency of 1984-86; co-author: World Guide to Environmental Issues, 1990, Britain's Overseas Aid, 1979, others. Founder, chmn. New Ulster Movement, Northern Ireland, 1969-73; chmn. SOS Sahel, London, 1989-93; trustee Cambodia Trust, London, 1989-95, Artizan Trust, London, 1992-95, Nginnkaret Found. for Cambodia, 1993-2000. Mem. Athenaeum Club. Quaker. Avocations: gardening, walking, reading. Home: Biskets Church Hill, Arnside Cumbria LA5 ODW, England

WALKER, BRIGITTE MARIA, translator, linguistic consultant; b. Stolp, Germany, Sept. 20, 1934; came to U.S., 1957; d. Joseph Karl and Ursula Maria Margot Ehrler; m. John V. Kelley (div.); 1 child, John V. Jr.; m. Edward D. Walker, July 3, 1977. Grad., Erlangen Translator's Sch., Germany, 1956; grad. fgn. corres., Berlitz Sch., Germany, 1956. Bilingual sec., translator Spencer Patent Law Office, Washington, 1959-62; office mgr., translator I. William Millen, Millen and White, Patent Law, Washington, 1962-67; prin. Tech. Translating Bur., Washington, 1967-68, St. Petersburg Beach, Fla., 1968—; cons. for patent law offices, Washington, 1962—; ofcl. expert for ct. Paul M. Craig, Patent Atty., Rockford, Ill., 1981; cons. to sci. editor Merriam-Webster, Inc., Springfield, Mass., 1987—. Author: German-English/English-German Last-Resort Dictionary for Technical Translators, 1991, (poetry) The Other Side of the Mirror, 1992 (Poetry award Nat. League Am. Pen Women 1994); co-translator: The Many Faces of Research, 1980; holder of trademark in field. Evaluator fgn. textbooks Pinellas County Sch. Bd., St. Petersburg, 1987, German judge, 1988. Recipient Recoginition award Pinellas County Sch. Bd., 1988, Meritorious Pub. Svc. award City of St. Petersburg Beach, 1987, poetry award Nat. League Am. Pen Women, 1994, 99, 2000, essay award, 1996, short story award, 1997, Grand prize for poem DDDD Publs., 1998. Mem. Mensa (Winner Nat. award Best Fiction 1996). Democrat. Lutheran. Avocations: swimming, aerobics, piano, painting. Home and Office: 7150 Sunset Way Apt 1007 Saint Petersburg FL 33706-3650

WALKER, CAROLYN SMITH, college services administrator, counselor; b. Atlanta, May 9, 1946; d. George Taft and Lonnie Bell (Bates) Smith; 1 child from previous marriage, Gary Sherard Walker II. BA in Psychology, Clark Coll., Atlanta, 1970; MS in Counseling & Guidance, U. Nebr., Omaha, 1975. Lic. and cert. profl. counselor, Ga. Adult basic edn. instr. Atlanta Pub. Schs., 1970-71, adult basic edn. site coord., 1971; adult basic edn. instr. Omaha-Nebr. Tech. C.C., Omaha, 1971-74, dir. adult basic edn., 1974; guidance counselor Omaha Pub. Schs., 1974-76; recruitment counselor Minority Women Employment Program, Atlanta, 1976-77; career planning and employment preparation instr. Discovery Learning Inc., Job Tng. and Pntrship Act, Atlanta, 1985-86; dir. counseling and testing svcs. Atlanta Met. Coll., 1977—, assoc. v.p. for student affairs, 1998—; test supr. Ednl. Testing Svc., Princeton, N.J., 1980—, Psychology Corp., San Antonio, 1991—, Law Sch. Admissions Test, Newtown, Pa., 1991—; cons. Commn. on Colls., So. Assn. Colls. and Schs., Atlanta, 1978—; jr. c.c. rep. Placement & Coop. Edn., Atlanta, 1987-90. Editor newsletters Romar On-Line, 1997, The Brief, 1984, 85, Guided Studies News, 1974; contbg. author: (manual) AJC Self-Study, 1981, 2000; author: (manual) Policies and Procedures for Coordinated Counseling, 1981, 3d edit., 1999, Policies and Procedures for Learning Disability Services, 1997, 2d edit., 1999, Women's Coalition for Habitat for Humanity in Atlanta, 1993-95, 97. Pres. Atlanta Barristers Wives Inc., 1984, 85; mem. steering com. Atlanta Mayor's Masked Ball, 1987; mem. memberships sales com. Atlanta Arts Festival, 1986, Neighborhood Arts Ctr., 1986; state host Dem. Nat. Conv., Atlanta, 1988; mem. Heritage Valley Cmty. Neighborhood Assn., 1982—. Recipient Outstanding Svc. award Nat. Orientation Dirs. Assn., 1985, 86, Literacy Action, Inc., 1978, Atlanta Met. Coll., 1987, others. Mem. Ga. Coll. Personnel Assn., Ga. Mental Health Counselors Assn., Nat. Coun. Student Devel., Univ. System Counseling Dirs., 100 Women Internat. Inc. (charter mem.), Am. Assn. Community and Jr. Colls., The Links Inc., Ga. Assn. Women Deans, Counselors and Adminstrs., Ga. Coll. Conselors Assn. Democrat. Methodist. Avocations: tennis, travel, horticulture. Home: 3511 Toll House Ln SW Atlanta GA 30331-2330 Office: Atlanta Metro Coll 1630 Metropolitan Pkwy SW Atlanta GA 30310-4448

WALKER, CHARLES DODSLEY, conductor, organist; b. N.Y.C., Mar. 16, 1920; s. Marshall Starr and Maude Graham (Marriott) W.; m. Janet Elizabeth Hayes, May 30, 1949 (dec. Feb. 1997); children: Peter Hayes, Susan Starr. BS, Trinity Coll., 1940; AM, Harvard U., 1947. Organist, choirmaster Am. Cathedral, Paris, 1948-50, Ch. of the Heavenly Rest, N.Y.C., 1951-88; music dir. Blue Hill Troupe, Ltd., N.Y.C., 1955-90, The Chapin Sch., N.Y.C., 1961-85; mem. organ faculty Union Theol. Sem., N.Y.C., 1962-73, NYU, 1968-80; dean, music dir. Berkshire Choral Inst., Sheffield, Mass., 1982-91; organist, choirmaster Trinity Episcopal Ch., Southport, Conn., 1988—. Contbr. articles to profl. jours. Lt. comdr. USNR, 1942-46. Recipient Disting. Alumnus award Cathedral Choir Sch., 1988. Fellow Am. Guild of Organists (nat. pres. 1971-75); mem. Am. Fedn. of Musicians, Canterbury Choral Soc. (founder, conductor 1952—), Saint Wilfrid Club, The Bohemians. Avocations: travel, photography. Home: 160 W 96th St Apt 15N New York NY 10025-9212 Office: Trinity Episcopal Ch 651 Pequot Ave Southport CT 06490-1416

WALKER, CLARENCE EUGENE, psychology educator; b. Monongahela, Pa., Jan. 8, 1939; s. Lewis G. Walker and Olga T. Brioli; divorced; children: Chad Eugene, Kyle Lewis, Cass Emanuel. BS in Psychology summa cum laude, Geneva Coll., 1960; MS in Clin. Psychology, Purdue U., 1963, PhD in Clin. Psychology, 1965. Lic. psychologist, Okla. Asst. prof. Westmont Coll., 1964-68; pvt. practice clin. psychology Santa Barbara, Calif., 1965-68; from asst. prof. to assoc. prof. Baylor U., 1968-74; pvt. practice clin. psychology Waco, Tex., 1970-74; assoc. prof. med. sch. U. Okla., Oklahoma City, 1974-80; chief pediatric psychology svc. Okla. Children's Meml. Hosp., 1974-80, dir. out-patient pediatric psychology clinic, 1974-80; prof. med. sch., dir. pediatric psychology tng. program U. Okla., Oklahoma City, 1980-95, prof. emeritus, 1995; assoc. chief mental health svcs. Children's Hosp. Okla., 1980-95; intern in clin. psychology Riley Children's Hosp., West 10th St. VA Hosp., Indpls., 1963-64; psychology trainee West 10th St. VA Hosp., Indpls., 1962-63; pres. Psychol. Cons., Inc., 1998—; cons. Head Start Program, Waco, 1968-70, VA Hosp, Waco, 1969-74, VA Ctr., Temple, Tex., 1969-74, Region XII Ednl. Svc. Ctr., Waco, 1971-74, Rusk (Tex.) State Hosp., 1972-74, Bapt. Children's Home, Oklahoma City, 1975-79; rsch. cons. Los Alamos (N.Mex.) Pub. Schs., 1975-79; chmn. div. edn. and psychology Westmont Coll., 1966-68; consulting psychologist, 1995—. Author: Learn to Relax, 1975, 2nd edit., 1991, (with P. Clement, A. Hedberg and L. Wright) Clinical Procedures for Behavior Therapy, 1981, (with B.L. Bonner and K. Kaufman) The Physically and Sexually Abused Child, 1988, others; editor: The History of Clinical Psychology in Autobiography, Vol. I, 1992, Vol. II, 1993, (with M.C. Roberts) Handbook of Clinical Child Psychology, 1992; contbr. articles to profl. jours. Fellow APA; mem. AAAS, Southwestern Psychol. Assn. (pres. 1977), Okla. Psychol. Assn. (pres. 1983), Soc. Pediat. Psychology (pres. 1986), Ctrl. Tex. Psychol. Assn. (pres. 1973), Sigma Xi. Avocations: reading, wine tasting, travel.

WALKER, CLIVE THOMAS, nuclear fuel technologist, microbeam analyst; b. Coalville, Eng., Nov. 22, 1947; s. Wilfred Wallace and Vera May (Brown) W.; m. Janet Patricia Vernon, Sept. 11, 1970. Diploma, U. Surrey, Guildford, Eng., 1971, PhD, 1974. Head EPMA lab. Inst. Transuranium Elements, Karlsruhe, Germany, 1978—, dep. head tech. physics, 1998—; vis. scientist Risoe Nat. Lab., Roskilde, Denmark, 1992; mem. exec. bd. European Microbeam Soc., Antwerp, Belgium, 1993—; advisor ISO (TC 202), Geneva, Switzerland, 1997—, Internat. Congress on X-ray Optics and Microanalysis, 1998—, European Conf. on Applied Surface and Interface Analysis, 1999—. Contbr. articles to profl. jours., including Nature, Jour. Electrochem. Soc., Nuclear Tech., Jour. Nuclear Materials, others; patentee in field. Mem. 94th Livery Co., City of London, 1998—. Recipient Freeman award, City of London, 1998. Fellow Inst. Materials (London), Inst. Physics (London), Royal Microscopical Soc. (Oxford), Internat. Union of Microbeam Analysis Socs. (treas./sec. 2000—). Christian Democrat. Baptist. Avocations: books, bicycling, gardening, golf, oenology. E-mail: Clive.Walker@itu.fzk.de. Fax: 49 7247 951 590. Home: Hegenbergstr 8, D-76327 Woeschbach Germany Office: Inst Transuranium Elements, PO Box 2340, D-76125 Karlsruhe Germany

WALKER, DALE MAXWELL, city official; b. Big Rapids, Mich., Dec. 18, 1947; s. Lewis M. and Hilma I. (Windquist) W.; m. Joanne Kay Richmond, June 22, 1968; children: Christina Elizabeth, Heather Marie. BS, Ferris State Coll., 1970; MBA, Ctrl. Mich. U., 1981. Dir. fin. City of Owosso, Mich., 1970-74; corp. treas. Mich. Bapt. Homes, Detroit, 1976-77; dir. fin. City of Cadillac, Mich., 1977—; pres. Gospel Bookstore, Inc., Cadillac, 1983-98. Bd. dirs. Wexford County United Way, 1980-82, Shiawassee County United Way, 1971-72; sec.-treas. Cadillac Police and Fire Retirement System, 1977-87, bd. dirs. 1987—; chmn. Mcpl. Employees Retirement System, Mich., 1997—. Fellow Govtl. Fin. Officers Assn. U.S. and Can. (Profl. Achievement award 1984-2000); mem. Mich. Mcpl. Fin. Officers Assn. (bd. dirs. 1983-85), Internat. City Mgrs. Assn., Mich. Mcpl. Treas. Assn., Mcpl. Treas. Assn. U.S. and Can. (bd. dirs. 1982-84), McGuires Golf Club. Republican. Baptist. Avocations: golf, swimming, reading. Home: 901 Lincoln St Cadillac MI 49601-2035 Office: 200 N Lake St Cadillac MI 49601-1829

WALKER, DEWARD EDGAR, JR., anthropologist, educator; b. Johnson City, Tenn., Aug. 3, 1935; s. Deward Edgar and Matilda Jane (Clark) W.; m. Candace J. Arroyo; children: Alice, Deward Edgar III, Mary Jane, Sarah, Daniel, Joseph Benjamin. Student, Ea. Oreg. Coll., 1953-54, 56-58, Mexico City Coll., 1958; BA in Anthropology with honors, U. Oreg., 1960-61, PhD in Anthropology, 1964; postgrad., Wash. State U., 1962. Asst. prof. anthropology George Washington U., Washington, 1964-65; asst. prof. anthropology Wash. State U., Pullman, 1965-67, research collaborator, 1967-69; assoc. prof., chmn. dept. Sociology/Anthropology, lab. dir. U. Idaho, Moscow, 1967-69; prof. U. Colo., Boulder, 1969—, research assoc. in population processes program of inst. behavioral sci., 1969-73, assoc. dean Grad. Sch., 1973-76; founder, v.p. Walker Rsch. Group, Ltd., Boulder, Colo. Founder, co-editor Northwest Anthropol. Rsch. Notes, 1966—; editor, Plateau Vol.: Handbook of North American Indians, 1971-98; author, co-author 150 books, reports, articles and papers. Mem. tech. steering panel Hanford Environ. Dose Reconstrn. Project, 1988-95, Basalt Waste Isolation Project, Hanford, 1986-88; advisor on Native Am. affairs. With U.S. Army, 1954-62. Fellow NSF, 1961, NDEA, 1961-64. Fellow Am. Anthropol. Assn. (assoc. editor Am. Anthropologist 1973-74), Soc. Applied Anthropology (hon. life, exec. com. 1970-79, treas. 1976-79, chmn. 1980-95, cons., expert witness tribes of N.W., editor Human Orgn. 1970-76, rschr. over 65 projects with 150 monographs, articles, reports, and papers, editor High Plains Applied Anthropologist); mem. AAAS, Am. Acad. Polit. and Social Scis., N.W. Anthropol. Conf. Avocations: geology, mining. Home: PO Box 4147 Boulder CO 80306-4147 Office: U Colo PO Box 233 Boulder CO 80309-0233

WALKER, DIANE RUTH, communications executive; b. Kansas City, Mo.; m. R. Wayne Walker; children: Molly, Joshua. BA, U. Mo., 1978. Cert. bus. communicator. Reporter, asst. city editor Kansas City (Kans.) Kansan, 1978-84; asst. mgr. comm. Greater Kansas City C. of C., Kansas City, 1984-87; pub. rels. dir. Penn Valley C.C., Kansas City, 1987; comm. specialist Peoples Natural Gas, Omaha, 1988-90; comm. adminstr. Mo. Pub. Svc., Raytown, 1991-97; corp. comm. UtiliCorp United, Kansas City, 1997—. Asst. coach softball and soccer Liberty Parks and Recreation, Liberty, Mo., 1996-1999; vol. Youth Friends, Kansas City, Mo., 1996—; mentor William Jewell Coll., Liberty, 2000—; pres. PTA Lewis & Clark Elem. Sch., Liberty, 1999—; mem. key messages com. Liberty Sch. Bond Election, 2000. Mem. Internat. Assn. Bus. Comm. (co-chmn. conf. materials com. regional conf., 1997, Bronze Quill award 1994, 1998). Fax: 816-467-9686. E-mail: dwalker@utilicorp.com. Office: UtiliCorp United 20 W 9th St # 2133 Kansas City MO 64105-1704

WALKER, DONALD J., automotive executive; b. London, Ont., Can., Aug. 29, 1956; s. Cyril Reginald and Margaret Marilyn (Wallace) W. BSc, U. Waterloo, Ont., 1980. Sr. engr., supt. GM; asst. to chair Magna Internat. Inc., Markham, Ont., 1987-88, dir. corp. mtkg. and strategic planning, 1988-89, v.p. product devel., 1989-90, exec. v.p., COO, 1990-92, pres., CEO, 1992—. Bd. dirs. Hunter Coll. Found. Mem. Automotive Parts Mfrs. Assn. (bd. dirs. 1993—), Assn. Profl. Engrs. Ont. Office: Magna Internat Inc, 337 Magna Dr, Aurora, ON Canada L4G 7K1

WALKER, DORIS I., writer, historian, educator; b. Cleve.; d. Alphonse Charles and Rose Emma (Gibbons) Isaak; children: Brent Evan Walker, Blair Dana Walker. AB, Case Western Reserve U.; postgrad., Northwestern U., U. Calif., Irvine. Publs. editor Brunswick Corp., Chgo.; pub. rels. mgr. Dana Point (Calif.) Harbor, 1970-84; field rsch. writer Kessler Exch., L.A., Calif., 1984-89; instr. Calif. history South Orange County C.C. Dist.; lectr. schs., colls., civic venues. Author: Sections of Orange, Dana Point Harbor/Capistrano Bay: Home Port for Romance, Mission Viejo: The Ageless Land, Coastal Reflections, Tallships and Spanish Spice on the Citrus Coast, Orange County Adventures With Children, The Whales of Capistrano Bay, The Heritage of San Clemente, A Guide Book of Numismatic-Philatelic Covers; contbr., editor, photographer newspapers, mags. Commr. Orange County Hist. Commn., 1994—; founder, coord. Dana Point Festival of Whales, 1975-84. Recipient over 100 awards including Am. History award DAR, Clarion award, Unique Coverage award Women in Comm., Woman of Distinction award Capistrano Bay Area, Soroptimist Internat., Crisis Comm. Award Internat. Coun. Indsl. Editors, cert. of recognition Calif. State Senate; named Orange County Woman of Achievement in Comm., YWCA. Mem. AAUW (pres. San Clemente-Capistrano Bay br.), Nat. Fedn. Press Women (Nat. first place book award history), Calif. Media Profls., Calif. Press Women (pres. Orange County dist., state sec.), Dana Point Hist. Soc. (hon. life, founder, dir.), San Juan Capistrano Hist. Soc. (dir.), Orange County Hist. Soc. (dir.). Avocations: travel, photography, granddaughter. Office: PO Box 546 Dana Point CA 92629-0546

WALKER, EDWARD FAHEY, lawyer, honorary consul; b. Laredo, Tex., Oct. 17, 1946; s. John Fahey Walker and Betty Ann Crockett; m. Sirkka Walker, Nov. 9, 1973; children: Caroline Helene, Mark Crockett. AB in Econs., Coll. of William and Mary, 1969; JD, U. Tex., 1976; LLM in Tax, So. Meth. U., 1981. Bar: Tex. 1976, U.S. Dist. Ct. (no. and so. dists.) Tex. 1977, U.S. Tax Ct. 1980, U.S. Supreme Ct. 1980; cert. mediator. Assoc. Wood & Burney, Corpus Christi, Tex., 1976-79; assoc. Jenkens & Gilchrist, Dallas, 1980-83, ptnr., shareholder, 1984—; spkr. in field. Contbr. articles to profl. jours. Hon. consul of Finland, 1991—; dean Dallas-Ft. Worth Consular Corps, 2000—. Lt. (j.g.) USNR, 1969-73. Mem. ABA, State Bar Tex. (real property sect.), Dallas Bar Assn. Avocations: travel, reading, golf, horses, dogs. Office: Jenkens & Gilchrist 1445 Ross Ave Ste 3200 Dallas TX 75202-2785

WALKER, EDWARD JOSEPH, marketing executive, marketing consultant, editor; b. Chiswick, London, Eng., Jan. 5, 1958; s. Edward Joseph and Lorna Ruth (Benfell) W.; m. Sheila Mary Rooney; children: Rosa, Clara. BSc in Econs., London Sch. Econs., 1980; MSc, Brighton (Eng.) U., 1985. Copywriter Howard Design, Eindhoven, Tbe Netherlands, 1985-87, Bus. Address Ltd., London, 1987-89; mktg. comm. cons., London, 1989-94; mktg. comm. mgr. SAS Inst., Heidelberg, Germany, 1995—; vis. lectr. U. Westminster, London, 1994-95, U. North London, 1992-94. Editor, Inform, 1995—; European editor SAS Comm., 1995—, Exec Solutions, 1996-98. Mem. Chartered Inst. Mktg., Nat. Union of Journalists, Cosmopolitan Cricket Club (Hassloch). Avocations: hill walking, motorcycling, sports. Home: Eisenbahnstrasse 11, 68535 Edingen-Neckarhausen Germany Office: SAS Inst, Neuenheimer Landstr 28-30, 61920 Heidelberg Germany

WALKER, ELJANA M. DU VALL, civic worker; b. France, Jan. 18, 1924; came to U.S., 1948; naturalized, 1954; m. John S. Walker, Jr., Dec. 31, 1947; children: John, Peter, Barbara. Pres. Loyola Sch. PTA, 1959-59; bd. dirs. Santa Claus Shop, 1959-73; treas. Archdiocese Denver Catholic Women, 1962-64; rep. Cath. Parent-Tchr. League, 1962-65; pres. Aux. Denver Gen. Hosp., 1966-69; precinct committeewoman Arapahoe County Women's Com., 1973-74; mem. re-election com. Arapahoe County Rep. Party, 1973-78, Reagan election com., 1980; block worker Arapahoe County March of Dimes, Heart Assn., Hemophilia Drive, Muscular Dystrophy and Multiple Sclerosis Drive, 1979-81, cen. city asst. Guild Debutante Charities, Inc. Recipient Dist. Svc. award Am.-by-choice, 1966; nmaed to Honor Roll, ARC, 1971. Mem. Cherry Hills Symphony, Lyric Opera Guild, Alliance Franciase (life mem.), ARC, Civic Ballet Guild (life mem.), Needlework Guild Am. (v.p. 1980-82), Kidney Found. (life), Denver Art Mus., U. Denver Art and Conservation Assns. (chmn. 1980-82), U. Denver Women's Lib. Assn., Chancellors Soc., Passage Inc., Friends of the Fine Arts Found. (life), Children's Diabetes Found. (life), Littleton Pub. Sch. Pioneers, Union (Chgo.), Denver Athletic, 26 (Denver), Welcome to Colo. Internat. Roman Catholic. Address: 2301 Green Oaks Dr Greenwood Vlg CO 80121-1562

WALKER, GEORGE KONTZ, law educator; b. Tuscaloosa, Ala., July 8, 1938; s. Joseph Henry and Catherine Louise (Indorf) W.; m. Phyllis Ann Sherman, July 30, 1966; children: Charles Edward, Mary Neel. BA, U. Ala., 1959; LLB, Vanderbilt U., 1966; AM, Duke U., 1968; LLM, U. Va., 1972; postgrad. (Sterling fellow), Law Sch. Yale U., 1975-76. Bar: Va. 1967, N.C. 1976. Law clk. U.S. Dist. Ct., Richmond, Va., 1966-67; assoc. Hunton, Williams, Gay, Powell & Gibson, Richmond, 1967-70; pvt. practice Charlottesville, Va., 1970-71; asst. prof. Law Sch. Wake Forest U., Winston-Salem, N.C., 1972-73, assoc. prof. Law Sch., 1974-77, prof. Law Sch., 1977—; mem. bd. advisors Divinity Sch. Wake Forest U., 1991-94; Charles H. Stockton prof. internat. law U.S. Naval War Coll., 1992-93; vis. prof. Marshall-Wythe

Sch. Law, Coll. William and Mary, Williamsburg, Va., 1979-80, U. Ala. Law Sch., 1985; cons. Naval War Coll., 1976—, Nat. Def. Exec. Res., 1991—, Naval War Coll., Operational Law Adv. Bd., 1993—. Co-author: Moore's Federal Practice, 3rd edit., 1997; contbr. articles to profl. jours. With USN, 1959-62, capt. USNR, ret. Woodrow Wilson fellow, 1962-63; recipient Joseph Branch Alumni Svc. award, Wake Forest, 1988; named Hon. Atty. Gen. N.C., 1986. Mem. ABA, Va. Bar Assn., N.C. Bar Assn. (v.p. 1997-98), Am. Soc. Internat. Law (exec. coun. 1988-91), Internat. Law Assn., Am. Judicature Soc., Am. Law Inst., Maritime Law Assn., Order of Barristers, Order of the Coif (hon.), Piedmont Club, Phi Beta Kappa, Sigma Alpha Epsilon, Phi Delta Phi. Democrat. Episcopalian. Home: 3321 Pennington Ln Winston Salem NC 27106-5439 Office: Wake Forest U Sch Law PO Box 7206 Winston Salem NC 27109-7206

WALKER, IAIN ALEXANDER, psychology educator; b. Kilwinning, Scotland, Apr. 24, 1960; arrived in Australia, 1968; s. William McConnochie and Annette (Hanlon) W.; m. Jane Mary Keogh, June 2, 1989; children: Alex, Joel, Patrick. BA, U. Adelaide (Australia), 1980; BA with honors, Flinders U., Adelaide, 1981; MSc, U. Calif., Santa Cruz, 1984, PhD, 1987. Lectr. Murdoch U., Perth, Australia, 1986-94, sr. lectr., 1994-99, assoc. prof., 2000—; dir. Inst. Social Issues Biotech. and Health, Perth, 1994—. Co-author: Social Cognition: An Integrated Introduction, 1995; contbr. articles to profl. jours. Grantee Australian Rsch. Coun., 1993-95, 96, Med. Rsch. Fund Western Australia, 1996-97. Mem. APA (fgn. affiliate), Soc. Australasian Social Psychologists (founding mem.). Office: Dept Psychology, Murdoch U, Murdoch 6150, Australia

WALKER, JENNIE LOUISE, fundraising director; b. Ft. Hood, Tex., Nov. 27, 1962; d. Homer Lee and Jennie Louise (Smith) Walker; m. Philip Jerome King, Apr. 23, 1994 (div. Mar. 1999). BA in Speech Comms., Columbus State U., 1984; postgrad., Mercer U., 1987-90. Intern Senator Mack Mattingly, Washington, 1984, Congressman Richard Ray, Washington, 1984; rsch. asst. The Robinson Humphrey Co., Inc., Atlanta, 1985-89; mktg. asst. Norrell Corp., Atlanta, 1989-90; dir. rsch. The Carter Ctr., Inc., Atlanta, 1990-94, Boys & Girls Clubs Am., Atlanta, 1994-2000; dir. philanthropic initiatives The WEBMD Found., Inc., Atlanta, 2000—; mem. adv. bd. The Found. Ctr. - Atlanta, 1997—. Vol. Richard Ray for Congress Campaign Com., 1984, The Atlanta Project, 1992, Sta. WPBA-TV, Channel 30; mem. adv. bd. Ga. Addiction Pregnancy and Parenting Family Enrichment Ctr., 1994-96. Mem. NARAS (assoc.), Nat. Soc. Fundraising Execs., Ga. Music Industry Assn. Inc. (v.p. 1992-93, 95-98, pres. 1998—, bd. dirs. 1991-93, 95—, publicity chair, 1991-93, fundraising chair 1995—, Pres. award for vol. svc. 1997), Broadcast Music Inc., Nat. Acad. Songwriters, Am. Prospect Rsch. Assn. (pres. Ga. chpt. 1993-94, 96-97), Soc. Competitive Intelligence Profls., Spl. Librs. Assn., Columbus State U. Alumni Assn. Methodist. Avocations: songwriting, singing. Office: The WEBMD Found Inc 400 The Lenox Bldg 3399 Peachtree Rd NE Atlanta GA 30326-1120

WALKER, JEWETT LYNIUS, clergyman, church official; b. Beaumont, Tex., Apr. 7, 1930; s. Elijah Harvey and Ella Jane (Wilson) W.; m. Dorothy Mae Croom, Apr. 11, 1965; children: Cassandra Lynn, Jewett L., Kevin, Michael, Ella, Betty Renne, Kent, Elijah H. BA, Calif. Western U., 1957; MA, Kingdom Bible Inst., 1960; BRE, St. Stephens Coll., 1966, DD, 1968; LLD, Union Bapt. Sem., 1971; grad., St. Paul Sch. Theology, 1979, Nat. Planned Giving Inst., 1981, Philanthropy Tax Inst., 1982; DD, Clinton Jr. Coll., 1992. Ordained to ministry A.M.E. Zion Ch., 1957. Pastor Shiloh A.M.E. Zion Ch., Monrovia, Calif., 1961-64, Martin Temple A.M.E. Zion Ch., L.A., 1964-65, 1st A.M.E. Zion Ch., Compton, Calif., 1965-66, Met. A.M.E. Zion Ch., L.A., 1966-73, Logan Temple A.M.E. Zion Ch., San Diego, 1973-74, Rock Hill A.M.E. Zion Ch., Indian Trail, N.C., 1974-79, Bennettsville A.M.E. Zion Ch., Norwood, N.C., 1979-86, Price Meml. A.M.E. Zion Ch., Concord, N.C., 1986-89, Mt. Zion A.M.E. Zion Ch., Hickory Grove, S.C., 1989-91, New Hope A.M.E. Zion Ch., Lancaster, S.C., 1993—; sec.-treas. dept. home missions, brotherhood pensions and relief A.M.E. Zion Ch., Charlotte, N.C., 1974-92; mem. exec. bd. Prophetic Justice Unit Com. Nat. Coun. Chs., co-chairperson pers. com.; mem. World Meth. Coun., del. 14th World Conf. Author: Is There a Man in the House, 1975, Lets Get Serious about Missions, 1991, The Denominational Dollar, 1992, also articles. Chmn. Minority Affairs Adv. Com., Mecklenburg County; trustee Clinton Coll., dir. planned giving, 1992; trustee Rock Hill, Lomax-Hannon Coll., Greenville, Ala., Union Bapt. Theol. Sem., Birmingham, Ala.; bd. mgrs. McCrorey br. YMCA; pres. Am. Ch. Fin. Svc. Corp., Carolina Home Health Svc. Inc., Meth. Life Ins. Soc. Inc., bd. trustees State N.C. Coll. Found., Inc., 1987, del. Presbyn. Ptnrs. in Ecumenism Nat. Coun. Chs. Christ, 1986, pres., 1988—; pres. Walker Funeral Home Inc. (formerly The House of Irma Funeral Home), Concord, Am. Ch. Econ. Devel. Corp.; del. Presbyn. Ch. U.S. Gen. Assembly, 1985; mem. citizens parole accountability com. Mecklenburg County, Charlotte, 1993; mem. planned giving adv. bd. Livingston Coll., Salisbury, N.C.; pres. Jewett L. Walker & Assocs.; chmn. minority affairs adv. com. Mecklenburg County; com. mem. Charlotte Mecklenburg Citizen Parole Accountability Com., 1994, vice chmn., 1998; pres. Pardue St. Apts. Inc., Lancaster, S.C., 1997—, Am. Ch. Econ. Devel. Corp., 1999. Fellow Nat. Assn. Ch. Bus. Adminstrs., Ch. Bus. Adminstrn., Presbyn. Ch. Bus. Adminstrn. Assn.; mem. NAACP (life), Nat. Soc. Fund Raising Execs., Am. Bible Soc. (state dir. vols., N.C. and S.C. dir. vol.), Nat. Spkrs. Bur., Christian Ministries Mgmt. Assn., Am. Soc. Assn. Execs., Funeral and Cremation Soc. South, Inc. (founder 1998), Shriners, Masons (33 deg.), Prince Hall Affiliation. Republican. Home: 910 Bridlepath Ln Charlotte NC 28211-2022 Office: 4501 Walker Rd Charlotte NC 28211-2047

WALKER, JOHN, molecular biologist; b. Chesterfield, Eng., June 28, 1965; s. Alan Joseph and Sheila Valerie (Weakford) W.; m. Jane Harris, July 12, 1996. BSc in Biology with honors, U. Derby, 1986; PhD in Biochemistry, U. Aberystwyth, 1990. Rsch. fellow in biochemistry U. Aberystwyth, 1990-93; sr. rsch. fellow U. Glasgow, 1993-96, 1996-97; biology educator Fundacion Colegio de Inglaterra, Bogotá, Colombia, 1997-2000; head biochemistry dept. Corp. Centro Internacional de Entrenamiento e Investigaciones Medicas, Cali, Colombia, 2000—; vis. sr. rsch. fellow Ctrl. Vet. Inst., Lelystad, The Netherlands, 1995. Contbr. articles to profl. jours. Mem. British Soc. for Parasitology, Biochem. Soc. Avocations: scuba diving, football, angling, natural history, skiing. Office: CIDEIM, Avenida 1 Norte 3-03, Cali Colombia

WALKER, JOHN ERNEST, molecular biologist; b. Halifax, Eng., Jan. 7, 1941; s. Thomas Ernest and Elsie (Lawton) W.; m. Christina Jane Westcott, 1963; 2 children. BA, St. Catherine's Coll., Oxford, Eng.; MA, Oxford (Eng.) U., DPhil, 1969; DSc (hon.), U. Bradford, U. Haddersfield, U. Leeds, 1999, UMIST, Buenos Aires, 1999, Gröningen U., 1999, Oxford (Eng.) U., 1999. Vis. rsch. fellow U. Wis., 1969-71; NATO rsch. fellow CNRS, Gif-sur-Yvette, France, 1971-72; EMBO rsch. fellow Pasteur Inst., Paris, 1972-74; sr. scientist lab. molecular biology Med. Rsch. Coun., Cambridge, Eng., 1982-98, dir. Dunn Human Nutrition Unit,, 1998—. Contbr. articles to profl. jours. Recipient Johnson Found. prize U. Pa., 1994, Ciba medal and prize Biochem. Soc., 1996; named Nobel Laureate in Chemistry, 1997. Fellow Royal Soc.; mem. European Molecular Biology Orgn. (Knight Bachelor 1999). Avocations: cricket, opera music, walking. Fax: 44 (0) 1223 413763. Office: Dunn Human Nutrition Unit, Med Rsch Coun, Cambridge CB2 2XY, England

WALKER, JOHN SUMPTER, JR., lawyer; b. Richmond, Ark., Oct. 13, 1921; s. John Sumpter, Martha (Wilson) W.; m. Eljana M. duVall, Dec. 31, 1947; children: John Stephen, Barbara Monika Ann, Peter Mark Gregory. BA, Tulane U., 1942; MS, U. Denver, 1952, JD, 1960; diploma Nat. Def. U., 1981. Bar: Colo. 1960, U.S. Dist. Ct. Colo. 1960, U.S. Supreme Ct., 1968, U.S. Ct. Appeals (10th cir.) 1960, U.S. Tax. Ct., 1981. With Denver & Rio Grande Western R.R. Co., 1951-61, gen. solicitor, 1961-89; pres. Denver Union Terminal Ry. Co. Apptd. gen. counsel Moffat Tunnel Commn., 1991; life mem. Children's Diabetes Fund. With U.S. Army, 1942-46. Decorated Bronze Star. Mem. Colo. Bar Assn., Arapahoe County Bar Assn., Alliance Francaise (life), Order of St. Ives, U. Denver Chancellors' Soc., Cath. Lawyers Guild, Denver Athletic Club. Republican. Roman Catholic.

WALKER, LANNON, foreign service officer; b. Los Angeles, Jan. 17, 1936; s. James Orville and Esther W.; m. Arlette Daguet, July 16, 1954; children: Rachelle, Anne. B.S., Georgetown U., 1961. Fgn. service officer Dept. State, 71961; polit. officer Dept. State, Rabat, Morocco, 1962-64; prin. officer Dept. State, Constantine, Algeria, 1964-66; assigned Exec. Secretariat Dept. State, 1966-69; econ. counselor Dept. State, Tripoli, Libya, 1969-70; dep. chief mission Dept. State, Yaounde, Cameroon, 1971-73; adminstrv. counselor Dept. State, Saigon, Viet Nam, 1973-74; dep. chief mission Dept. State, Kinshasa, Zaire, 1974-77; dep. asst. sec. African Affairs Dept. State, Washington, 1977-82; spl. adviser African affairs Dept. State, 1983-84, dep. insp. gen., 1984-85, ambassador to Senegal, 1985-88, amb. to Nigeria, 1989-92; mem. Policy Planning Coun. Dept. of State, Washington, 1993-95; ambassador to Cote d'Ivoire Abidjan, 1995-98; employed in pvt. sector, 1982-83; sr. assoc. Carnegie Endowment, 1988-89; pres. Africa Strategy Corp., Bethesda, Md. Served with USAF, 1953-58. Mem. Am. Fgn. Service Assn. (chmn. 1966-69). Roman Catholic.

WALKER, LARRY KENNETH ROBERT, professional baseball player; b. Maple Ridge, B.C., Dec. 1, 1966. Grad. high sch., B.C., Can. With Montreal Expos, 1989-94; outfielder Colo. Rockies, 1995—. Named "The Sporting News" Nat. League All-Star Team, 1992, "The Sporting News" NAt. League Silver Slugger Team, 1992; recipient Gold Glove as outfielder, 1992-93. Office: Colo Rockies Coors Field 2001 Blake St Denver CO 80205-2008

WALKER, LEE E., lawyer; b. Mesquite, Nev., Sept. 22, 1925; s. Ernest A. and Julia (Reber) W.; m. Evaline Peterson, Dec. 27, 1945 (div. Dec. 1995); m. Kathleen Seeley, July 30, 1996; children: Kathren, Merrilee, Michele, Marc, Lizbeth, Brooke, Darrel. BS, Brigham Young U., 1958; MS, George Washington U., 1962, JD, 1964. Bar: Nev., 1964. Lawyer Nev. State Bar, Las Vegas, 1964—; mem. senate Nev. Legislature, 1972-80. mem. No. Las Vegas Planning Commn., Nev., 1980-88. With U.S. Army, 1941-43. Decorated Purple Heart, Silver Star. Democrat. Home and Office: 1729 Arrowhead St North Las Vegas NV 89030-7242

WALKER, LUCY DORIS, secondary school educator, writer; b. Ridgeway, N.C., May 6, 1951; d. Edgerton Verl and Mary Ellen (Williams) Plummer; m. William A. Walker Jr., June 21, 1969 (div. Aug. 1974); 1 child, Lucretia Marie. BA in English Edn., Fairleigh Dickinson U., 1975; MA in Theater Arts, Montclair State U., 1977. Cert. English and theater arts tchr., N.J. Tchr., dir., actor, writer Ctr. Modern Dance Edn., Hackensack, N.J., 1978; writer, dir. Am. Theater Actors, N.Y.C., 1978-79; tchr. multicultural hub Ctr. Internat. Studies, Cultural Events, Teaneck (N.J.) H.S., 1979—; artistic dir. Teaneck H.S. dance ensemble, 1989—; program coord. African & African-Am. Studies Resource Ctr., 1990—. Writer and choreographer various plays, 1979-95. Recipient Acad. Achievement award Fairleigh Dickinson U. Opportunities Program, 1974, Black Heritage award Nat. Assn. Negro Bus. & Profl. Women's Clubs, 1991. Mem. NEA, N.J. Edn. Assn. Democrat. Baptist. Avocations: sewing, gardening, hiking, painting, music. Home: 363 Washington Pl Englewood NJ 07631-3232 Office: Teaneck HS 100 Elizabeth Ave Teaneck NJ 07666-4713

WALKER, MALCOLM CONRAD, food products company executive; b. Feb. 11, 1946; s. Willie and Ethel Mary M.; m. Nest Rhianydd, 1969; three children. Mgr. trainee F.W. Woolworth & Co., 1964-71; founder Iceland Frozen Foods plc, 1971-73; chmn., CEO Iceland Group (formerly Iceland Frozen Foods plc), 1973—; bd. dirs. DFS Furniture Co., plc, 1993—. Avocations: skiing, shooting, gardening. Office: Iceland Group plc, 2d Ave Deeside Indsl Park, Deeside Flintshire CH5 2NW, Wales*

WALKER, MARGARET SMITH, real estate company executive; b. Lancashire, Eng., Oct. 14, 1943; came to U.S., 1964; d. Arthur Edward and Doris Audrey (Dawson) Smith; m. James E. Walker, Feb. 6, 1992. Lic. real estate agt., Hawaii. Broker Lawson-Worrall Inc. (now Mary Worrall/Sotheby), Honolulu, 1974-81; pres. Maggie Parkes & Assocs., Inc., Honolulu, 1981—. Bd. dirs. Hawaii Combined Tng. Assn., Honolulu, 1985-97; com. chmn. Hawaii Opera Theatre, 1997, chmn. Opera Ball, 1997. Mem. Am. Horse Shows Assn., Hawaii Horse Shows Assn., Outrigger Canoe Club. Episcopalian. Avocations: dressage riding, horse show management. Office: PO Box 25083 Honolulu HI 96825-0083

WALKER, MILES RAWSTRON, Isle of Man government member; b. Colby, Isle of Man, Nov. 13, 1940; s. George Denis and Alice (Whittaker) W.; m. Mary Lilian Cowell, Oct. 11, 1966; children: Mark, Claire. Degree in agr., Shropshire Coll. Agr., 1960; LLD (honoris causa), Liverpool U., 1994. Mem., chmn. Arbory Parish Commn., 1970-76; mem. Ho. of Keys Isle of Man Govt., 1976—, chief min., 1986-96. Decorated comdr. Order Brit. Empire; named Knight Bachelor. Anglican. Office: Isle of Man Govt, Bucks Rd, Douglas Isle of Man

WALKER, MOIRA KAYE, sales executive; b. Riverside, Calif., Aug. 2, 1940; d. Frank Leroy and Arline Rufina (Roach) Porter; m. Timothy P. Walker, Aug. 30, 1958 (div. 1964); children: Brian A., Benjamin D., Blair K., Beth E. Student, Riverside City Coll., 1973. With Bank of Am., Riverside, 1965-68, Abitibi Corp., Cucamonga, Calif., 1968-70; with Lily div. Owens-Illinois, Riverside, 1970-73; salesperson Lily div. Owens-Illinois, Houston, 1973-77; salesperson Kent H. Landsberg div. Sunclipse, Montebello, Calif., 1977-83, sales mgr., 1983-85; v.p., sales mgr. Kent H. Landsberg div. Sunclipse, Riverside, 1985—. Mem. NAFE, Women in Paper (treas. 1978-84), Kent H. Landsberg President's Club (1st female to make club, 1994, 95, 96). Lutheran. Office: Kent H Landsberg Div Sunclipse 1180 W Spring St Riverside CA 92507-1327

WALKER, NATHAN BELT, trade association administrator; b. Macon, Mo., Apr. 18, 1952; s. Wendell K. and Azalea B. (Belt) W.; children: Madison, Samuel. BS in Agrl. Journalism, U. Mo., 1974, MS in Cmty. Devel., 1995. Owner, pub., editor La Plata (Mo.) Home Press, 1978-82; state rep. dist. 12 State of Mo., Anabel, 1981-85; dir. Mo. Divsn. Hwy. Safety, Jefferson City, 1985-91; dir. adminstrn. Mo. Office Atty. Gen., Jefferson City, 1991-93; exec. dir. Mo. Head Injury Assn., Jefferson City, 1993-94; dir. econ. devel. City of Boonville, Mo., 1994-96; dir. devel. Kemper Mil. Sch. and Coll., Boonville, 1996-98; dir. ops. Mo. Automobile Dealers Assn., Jefferson City, 1998—. Republican. Fax: 573-636-5834. Home: 3709B Struemph Ct Jefferson City MO 65109-4992 Office: Mo Automobile Dealers Assn 3322 American Ave Jefferson City MO 65109-1079

WALKER, PAUL CRAWFORD, medical practitioner, health systems consultant; b. Nuneaton, Eng., Dec. 9, 1940; s. Joseph Viccars and Mary Tilley (Crawford) W.; m. Barbara Georgina Bliss, Mar. 16, 1963; children: Mary Kate, Victoria Barbara Louise, Caroline Penelope. MA, Cambridge U., 1962, MB BChir, 1965. Pub. Health Diplomate. Regional med. officer N.E. Thames Regional Health Authority, London, 1978-85; dist. gen. mgr. Frenchay Health Authority, Bristol, Eng., 1985-89; dir. pub. health Norwich Health Authority, Norfolk, Eng., 1989-93; sr. lectr. U. Wales Coll. Medicine, 1993-94; sr. ptnr. Independent Pub. Health, Bristol, 1994—. Author: Healthy Norfolk People, 1990; editor: Helping People With Disabilities in East Anglia, 1991. Trustee Frenchay Cmty. Care Trust, Bristol, 1993-97, Norwich and Norfolk Care Trust, Norfolk, 1991-93; justice of peace, Epping and Ongar, Eng., 1980-85; councillor Bristol City, 1995-99. Mem. The Athenaeum, Brit. Med. Assn. Rehab. Medicine. Mem. Labour Party. Avocations: music, railway history. E-mail: paul@crawfordwalker.freeserve.co.uk. Home: 8 Church Avenue, Bristol BS9 1LD, England Office: Ind Pub Health, PO Box 48, Westbury on Trym Bristol BS9 1HT, England

WALKER, PETER JOHN, research scientist; b. Brisbane, Queensland, Australia, Mar. 31, 1953; s. John Stanley and Florence May (Barter) W.; m. Jantana Maiyanij, July 3, 1999; children: James, Andrew. BSc, U. Queensland, Brisbane, 1975, PhD, 1981. Rsch. officer Queensland Inst. Med. Rsch., Brisbane, 1981-83; scientist Queensland Dept. Primary Industries, Brisbane, 1984-87; sr. rsch. scientist Csiro Tropical Animal Prodn., Brisbane, 1987-93; prin. rsch. scientist Csiro Tropical Agr., Brisbane, 1993—; program leader Aquaculture CRC Ltd., Sydney, Australia, 1998—; adj. assoc. prof. Griffith U., Brisbane, 1995—, U. Queensland, Brisbane, 2000—; assoc. editor Virus Genes, London, 1995—; expert cons. in fish health Food and Agr. Orgn., Rome, 1999—. Contbr. articles to profl. jours., chpts. to books. Rsch. grantee Australian Dairy Rsch. Corp., 1988-91, Australian Ctr. for Internat. Agrl. Rsch., 1989—, Coop. Rsch. Ctr. for Vaccine Tech., 1992-96. Mem. Soc. for Gen. Microbiology, World Aquaculture Soc., Australian Marine Sci. Assn. Avocations: music, squash, Thai history.

WALKER, RANDALL WAYNE, lawyer; b. Pampa, Tex., Mar. 13, 1956; s. Jimmy Wayne and Dorothy Evelyn (Mercer) W.; m. Patricia Gale Vernon Walker, Dec. 12, 1992; children: Alissa Gail Walker, Angie Marie Walker Grimsey, Cory Wayne, Nicholas Russell Rattan. AA, Clarendon (Tex.) Coll., 1980; BS, West Tex. State U., Canyon, 1984; JD, Tex. Tech. U., Lubbock, 1986. Bar: Tex., 1987. Pvt. practice Clarendon, Tex., 1987-91; asst. atty. gen. Tex. Atty. Gen. Office, Wichita Falls, Tex., 1991—; mng. atty. Tex. Atty. Gen. Office, Wichita Falls, 1992—. Cubmaster Boy Scouts Am., Clarendon, 1988-89. Mem. State Bar Tex., Wichita County Bar Assn., Lions (v.p. Clarendon 1989). Avocations: fishing, camping, woodworking. Office: Attorney General Office 813 8th St Wichita Falls TX 76301-3305

WALKER, RICHARD BRIAN, chemistry educator; b. Quincy, Mass., May 14, 1948; s. George Edgar and Eva Mary (Taylor) W. BS in Biochemistry, U. So. Calif., 1970; PhD in Pharm. Chemistry, U. Calif., San Francisco, 1975. Rsch. assoc. Oreg. State U., Corvallis, 1975-76, U. Wash., Seattle, 1976-78; lectr. U.S. Internat. U., San Diego, 1978-81, Hamdard Sch. Pharmacy, New Delhi, India, 1981-82; rsch. scientist Biophysica Found., San Diego, 1982-83; assoc. prof. chemistry U. Ozarks, Clarksville, Ark., 1983-84; asst. to assoc. prof. chemistry U. Ark., Pine Bluff, 1984-96, prof. chemistry, 1996—; prin. investigator minority biomed. rsch. support program NIH, Bethesda, Md., 1986—; project dir. Ark. Systemic Sci. Initiative. Contbr. articles to profl. jours. Coord. home Bible fellowship The Way Internat., Pine Bluff, 1984-99; judge Ctrl. Ark. Sci. Fair, Little Rock, 1986—. NIH rsch. grantee, 1986, 89, 93. Mem. Am. Chem. Soc., Ark. Acad. Scis., Am. Assn. Pharm. Scientists, Sigma Xi. Avocations: fishing, golf, skiing. Office: U Ark Dept Chemistry 1200 University Dr Pine Bluff AR 71601-2799

WALKER, RODERICK BRYAN, pharmaceutical scientist; b. Johannesburg, South Africa, Oct. 3, 1961; s. William James and Florence (Wood) W.; m. Rosemary Ann Starkey, Dec. 10, 1988. B in Pharmacy, Rhodes U., 1983, PhD, 1995. RPh, South Africa. Grad. asst. Rhodes U., Grahamstown, South Africa, 1985, 86, 89, teaching asst., 1987, 88, 91, jr. lectr., 1990, 92, lectr., 1993-97, sr. lectr., 1998—; dep. dean faculty pharmacy Rhodes U., Grahamstown, 1998—; clin. trial and analytical monitor biopharmaceutics rsch. inst. Rhodes U., 1993-95, cons., 1996, 97, 98; quality assurance officer Pharmaceutics, 1999; nat. examiner South African Pharmacy Coun., 1996; mem. expert com. Medicines Control Coun., 2000. Contbr. articles to profl. jours. H.G. Bradlow scholar, 1985; Adcock Ingram travel grantee, 1992; named "Y" Rated Scientist Nat. Rsch. Found., 2000, Disting. Tchr. of Yr. South African Acad. of Pharm. Scis., 2000. Mem. South African Pharmacy Coun., Acad. Pharm. Scis., Pharm. Soc. South Africa, Royal Soc. South Africa, Am. Assn. Pharm. Scientists, Controlled Release Soc., Grahamstown Golf Club (exec. com. 1996-97). Presbyterian. Office: Rhodes U Sch Pharm Scis, Grahamstown 6140, South Africa

WALKER, RONALD R., writer, editor, educator; b. Newport News, Va., Sept. 2, 1934; s. William R. and Jean Marie (King) W.; m. O. Diane Mawson, Apr. 16, 1961; children: Mark Jonathan, Steven Christopher. BS, Pa. State U., 1956; postgrad., Harvard U., 1970-71. Reporter, news editor, sr. editor, editorial page editor, mng. editor San Juan Star (P.R.), 1962-73, Washington columnist, 1982-84, city editor, 1984-87; instr. journalism Pa. State U., State College, 1973-74; asst. prof. Columbia U. Grad. Sch. Journalism, N.Y.C., 1974-76; editor The Daily News, V.I., 1976-77; press sec. Gov. V.I., 1978-79; spl. asst., chief of staff Rep. James H. Scheuer, U.S. Congress, 1980-82, Resident Commr. Jaime B. Fuster, U.S. Congress, 1987-92; spl. asst., press sec. Resident Commr. Antonio J. Colorado, 1992-93; ind. profl. writer, weekly columnist editl. page San Juan Star, 1993—; regular columnist St. John Times, 1997—. Contbr. articles to nat. mags. and jours. including The Nation, The N.Y. Times, The Washington Post, and others. Served with U.S. Army, 1957-59. Nieman fellow in journalism Harvard U., 1970-71. Mem. Soc. Nieman Fellows, Leica Hist. Soc. Am. Address: PO Box 1358 Saint John VI 00831-1358

WALKER, SAVANNAH T., executive assistant, legislative assistant; b. Lubbock, Tex., Nov. 23, 1930; d. John Hansford and Lenore Belle (Muecke) Tunnell; m. Julius Waring Walker, Jr., July 29, 1956; children: Savannah Waring, Lucile Lenore, George Julius Stewart. BA, Tex. Tech. U., 1951; student, Radcliffe Coll., 1951. Cert. secondary sch. tchr., Tex. Tchr., English and journalism Phillips (Tex.) Ind. Sch. Dist., 1951-52; asst. to congressman Mahon U.S. Congress, Washington, 1952-54, admisntrv., exec. asst., 1954-58, 63-66; legis. asst. to chmn. House Appropriations U.S. Ho. of Reps., Washington, 1973-78; exec. asst. to v.p. Nat. Assn. Mfrs., Washington, 1985-89; exec. asst. to pres. Ogilvy Pub. Rels. Worldwide, Washington, 1990-99; sr. mgr. Pres. of the Americas, Ogilvy Pub. Rels. Worldwide, 2000—. Vol., fundraiser for charitable orgns., Chad and Eng., 1966-73; pres. Am. Women in London, 1971-72, Am. Women in Liberia, Monrovia, 1979-80. Mem. AAUW, PEO, Am. Women in the Arts Mus., DAR, Internat. Women's Club (founder pres.) (Ouagadougou, Burkina Faso), Delta Delta Delta. Avocations: church work, bridge, reading, needlework, writing. Home: 3801 Jenifer St NW Washington DC 20015-1917 Office: Ogilvy Public Relations Worldwide 1901 L St NW Ste 300 Washington DC 20036-3506

WALKER, STUART CARTER, educator; b. Boston, Jan. 6, 1944; s. Robert Stringfellow and Ruby (Shelledy) W.; m. Keiko Shingai, Mar. 27, 1993. BA, Harvard U., 1967; JD, Stanford U., 1973. Bar: Calif. Tchr. Aiglon Coll., Chesieres, Switzerland, 1967-69; atty. McCutchen, Doyle, Brown & Enersen, San Francisco, 1973-77, Bank of Am., San Francisco, 1977-78; prof. Tribhuvan U. Law Sch., Kathmandu, Nepal, 1979-80; tchr. French Lincoln Sch., Kathmandu, 1980-85; dir. Edn. Systems Lang. Svcs., Tokyo, 1986-87; dir. Studies Key West Club, Sapporo, Japan, 1987-91; prof. Seishu Jr. Coll., Sapporo, Japan, 1991-93, Sapporo Internat. U., 1993—. Contbr. articles to profl. jours. Mem. Japan Assn. Lang. Tchrs.-Hokkaido (pres. 1991-92, rec. sec. 1990, membership chmn. 1989). Home: Kiyota 5-1-5-24, Sapporo Hokkaido 004-0845, Japan Office: Sapporo Internat U, 4-1 Kiyota 4-jo 1-chome, Sapporo, Hokkaido 004-8602, Japan

WALKER, WILL EARL, educator; b. Nov. 17, 1961. PhD, Princeton U., 1998. Asst. prof. U. Vt., Burlington, 1997-98.

WALKER, WILLIAM D., physicist, educator, researcher; b. Nov. 23, 1923; s. William D. and Mildred Ramsey Walker; m. Suzanne Porter, Dec. 23, 1946 (div. Oct. 1975); m. Constance Kalbach, Oct. 16, 1975; children: Nancy Walker Davis, Elizabeth Walker Schenkel, Samuel. BA, Rice U., 1944; PhD in Physics, Cornell U., 1949. Asst. prof. Rice U., Houston, 1949-51; lectr. U. Calif., Berkeley, 1951-52; asst. prof. U. Rochester, N.Y., 1952-54; from asst. prof. to prof. U. Wis., Madison, 1954-71; prof. physics Duke U., Durham, N.C., 1971-98; chmn. dept. physics U. Wis., Madison, 1964-66, Max Mason disting. prof., 1969-71; J.B. Duke disting. prof. Duke U., Durham, N.C., 1990-94, chmn. dept. physics, 1975-81, prof. emeritus, 1993—; chmn. users com. Argonne Nat. Lab., Lemont, Ill., 1960-63, Fermi Nat. Accelerator Lab., Aurora, Ill., 1971-74; mem. physics adv. bd. NSF, Washington, 1962-65. Discovered several elementary particles. Deacon Episc. Ch., 1964-71; elder Presbyn. Ch., 1993—. Fellow Am. Phys. Soc. Avocation: tennis. Home: 907 Green St Durham NC 27701-1507 Office: Duke U Physics Dept Durham NC 27708

WALKER, WILLIE MARK, electronics engineering executive; b. Bessemer, Ala., Aug. 18, 1929; s. Johnnie and Annie Maimie (Thompson) W.; m. Mae Ruth Fulton, Apr. 28, 1952; children: Patricia Ann, Mark William, Karen Marie. BEE, Marquette U., 1958; MSEE, U. Wis., 1965. Registered profl. engr., Wis. Devel. technician AC Spark Plug, Milw., 1953-56, project engr., 1956-60, engring. supr., 1960-65; sr. devel. engr. AC Electronics, Milw., 1965-71; sr. prodn. engr. Delco Electronics, Oak Creek, Wis., 1871-94; owner, prin. Walker Engring., 1994—. Author various proprietary reports. Pres. Potawatomi Area coun. Boy Scouts Am., Waukesha, Wis., 1982-84, chief camp insp. area 1, east ctrl. region, 1987, 99, v.p. program area 1, 1988-93, v.p. area 3 ctrl. region, 1993-96, mem. ctrl. region bd., 1994—, commr. east ctrl. region Scout Jamboree, 1989, internat. commr. ctrl. region Scout Jamboree, 1993; loaned exec. United Way Greater Milw., 1983; uhser, min. communion St. Mary Cath. Ch., Menomonee Falls, Wis., 1967—. With USAF, 1949-53. Elected to Black Achievers in Bus. and Industry, Milw.

Met. YMCA, 1984; recipient Civic Svc. award Rotary Club, 1983, GM award for Excellence, 1980, St. George award Milw. Archdiocese, 1974; Silver Beaver award Boy Scouts Am., 1973, Silver Antelope award, 1987. Mem. IEEE (computer soc., sr. mem.), Computer Automated Sys. Assn., Soc. Mfg. Engrs., Wis. Soc. Profl. Engrs., Inst. Indsl. Engrs. (sr. mem., cert. sys. integrator), BRA (life), N.Am. Hunting Club (life), Lions (chpt. pres. 1979-80, sec. 1974-75), KC (recorder 1966-67, advocate 1975-76).

WALKER, WOODROW WILSON, lawyer, cattle and timber farmer; b. Greenville, Mich., Feb. 19, 1919; s. Craig Walker and Mildred Chase; m. Janet K. Keiter, Oct. 7, 1950; children: Jonathan Woodrow, William Craig, Elaine Virginia. BA, U. Mich., 1943; LLB, Cath. U., 1950. Bar: D.C. 1950, U.S. Supreme Ct. 1958, Va. 1959. Operator family farm, 1937-39; dir. Libr. of Congress Fed. Credit Union, 1957-60; atty. Am. law div. legis. reference Libr. Congress, Washington, 1951-60; pvt. practice, Arlington, Va., 1960—; counsel Calvary Found., Arlington, 1970-85, first pres., 1972; judge moot ct. George Mason Law Sch., 1986; owner-operator Walker Farm Front Royal, Va., 1972—. Co-author rsch. publs. for U.S. Govt.; featured in Washington Post. V.p. Jefferson Civic Assn., Arlington, 1955-61; pres. Nellie Custis PTA, Arlington, 1960-61; sec. Arlington County Bd. Equalization Real Estate Assessment, 1962, chmn. 1963; com. chmn. Arlington Troop 108 Boy Scouts Am., 1964-69; mem. Arlington County Pub. Utilities Commn., 1964-66, vice chmn., 1965-66; pres. Betschler Class Adult Sunday Sch., Calvary United Meth. Ch., Arlington, 1965. Served with U.S. Army, 1943-45, PTO. Cited for notable deed in conduct of his legal duties Washington Post, 1996. Mem. ABA, Arlington County Bar Assn., Va. Farm Bur., Va. Cattleman's Assn. Methodist. Democrat. Home: 2822 Ft Scott Dr Arlington VA 22202-2307 Office: 2055 N 15th St Ste 203 Arlington VA 22201-2613

WALKER-BROWN, ANDREW BELSHAM, science tertiary educator; b. Birmingham, Eng., Feb. 17, 1956; s. Thomas Charles and Helga (Steinhardt) Brown; m. Julie Patricia Walker, Mar. 31, 1985; children: Rosemary, Edward. BSc with honors in Biol. Scis., U. Plymouth, Eng., 1977; MSc in Microbiology, Birbeck London, 1980. Chartered biologist Inst. Biology; cert. edn. Sr. technician scis. Oaklands Coll., St. Albans, Eng., 1977-80; sect. leader scis. South Devon Coll., Torquay Devon, Eng., 1980—; examiner So. Examing Group, Guildford, 1986-88, No. Exam Bd., Manchester, 1988-92; external verifier EDEXCEL, London, 1994—. Mem. Nat. Assn. Tchrs. in Further and Higher Edn. Avocations: environmental interests, outdoor recreation, family interest. Office: South Devon Coll, Newton Rd Torquay, Torquay TQ2 5BY, England

WALKOW, TONY, ophthalmologist; b. Riesa, Elbe, Germany, Sept. 15, 1968; s. Jordan T. and Uta J. Walkow. MD, Humboldt U., Berlin, 1994. Ophthalmology intern U. Zurich, Switzerland, 1993; ophthalmology resident Free U. Berlin, 1994-96; ophthalmology fellow Humboldt U., Berlin, 1996-99; retina cons., 2000—. Contbr. sci. papers to profl. jours. Recipient 2d award 1st European Students Conf., 1990; 1st Award scholar Humboldt U., 1991. Mem. Am. Acad. Ophthalmology, Deutsche Ophthalmologische Gesellschaft, Assn. for Rsch. in Vision and Ophthalmology, Deutsche Gesellschaft fuer Intraokularlinsenimplantation. Avocations: tennis, theater, volleyball, windsurfing. Home: Lindenstr 15a, D-12527 Berlin Germany Office: AOK St Polten Augenklinik, Propst-Fuhrer-Str 4, A-3100 Saint Polten Austria

WALL, BRIAN RAYMOND, forest economist, business consultant, researcher; b. Jan. 26, 1940; s. Raymond Perry and Mildred Beryl (Pickert) W.; m. Joan Marie Nero, Sept. 1, 1962 (div. Aug. 1990); children: Torden Erik, Kirsten Noel. BS, U. Wash., 1962; MF, Yale U., 1964. Forestry asst. Weyerhaeuser Timber Co., Klamath Falls, Oreg., 1960; inventory forester West Tacoma Newsprint, Klamath Falls, Oreg., 1961-62; timber sale compliance forester Dept. Nat. Resources, Kelso, Wash., 1963; rsch. forest economist Pacific N.W. Rsch. Sta., USDA Forest Svc., Portland, Oreg., 1964-88; cons., 1989—; co-founder, bd. dirs. Cordero Youth Care Ctr., 1970-81; owner Brian R. Wall Images and Communications; owner Nikken ind.; distbr. Sage Mentor Lifestyles; owner Sage Mentors Bus. Consultancy; cons. to govt. agys., Congress univs., industry, small bus.; freelance photographer. Co-author: An Analysis of the Timber Situation in the United States, 1982; contbr. articles, reports to profl. publs., newspapers. Interviewed and cited by nat. and regional news media. Recipient Cert. of Merit U.S. Dept. Agr. Forest Svc., 1982. Mem. ACLU, Soc. Am. Foresters (chmn. Portland chpt. 1973, Forester of Yr. 1975), Conf. of Western Forest Economists Inc. (founder, bd. dirs. 1988-91, treas. 1982-87), Portland Photographic Forum, Common Cause, Oregon Economists Assn., Nat. Audubon Soc., Amnesty Internat., Zeta Psi. E-mail: b.r.wall@worldnet.att.net. Home: 12360 SW Walnut St Tigard OR 97223 Office: Sage Mentors Consultancy PMB 1162 10117 SE Sunnyside Rd Ste F Clackamas OR 97015-7708

WALL, CHARLES TERENCE CLEGG, mathematics educator, researcher; b. Bristol, Eng., Dec. 14, 1936; s. Charles and Ruth (Clegg) W.; m. Alexandra Joy Hearnshaw, Aug. 22, 1959; children: Nicholas, Catherine, Lucy, Alexander. BA, Cambridge U., 1957, PhD, 1960. Lectr. Cambridge U., 1961-64; reader Oxford U., 1964-65; prof. math. U. Liverpool, 1965-99, prof. emeritus, 1999—; vis. prof. CIEA, Mex., 1967. Author: Surgery On Compact Manifolds, 1970; mem. editl. bd. Compositio Math., 1967-92; contbr. articles to profl. jours. Sr. fellow Sci. and Engring. Rsch. Coun., 1983-88. Fellow Cambridge Philos. Soc., Royal Soc. (coun. mem. 1974-76, Sylvester medal 1988); mem. London Math. Soc. (pres. 1978-80, Whitehead prize 1976, editor procs. 1992-98), Royal Danish Acad. Democrat. Avocations: gardening, walking. Home: 5 Kirby Park, Wirral West Kirby CH48 2HA, England Office: U Liverpool, Liverpool L69 3BX, England

WALL, DIANE EVE, political science educator; b. Detroit, Nov. 17, 1944; d. Albert George and Jean Carol Bradley. BA in History and Edn., Mich. State U., 1966, MA in History, 1969, MA in Polit. Sci., 1979, PhD in Polit. Sci., 1983. Cert. permanent secondary tchr., Mich. Secondary tchr. Corunna (Mich.) Pub. Schs., 1966-67, N.W. Pub. Schs., Rives Junction, Mich., 1967-73; lectr. Tidewater C.C., Chesapeake, Va., 1974-77; instr. Wayne State U., Detroit, fall 1980, Lansing (Mich.) C.C., 1981-83; prof. dept. polit. sci. Miss. State U., 1983—, undergrad. coord., 1993—; instr. Ctrl. Mich. U., Mt. Pleasant, spring 1982; pre-law advisor Miss. State U., 1990-93, chair, 1993—. Co-editor spl. issue Southea. Polit. Rev.; contbr. articles, revs. to profl. jours., chpt. to book. Evaluator Citizen's Task Force, Chesapeake, Va., 1977; panelist flag burning program Ednl. TV, Mississippi State, 1990, prayer in pub. sch., Starkville Cmty. TV, 1995. Recipient Paideia award Miss. State U. Coll. Arts and Scis., 1988, Miss. State U. Outstanding Woman Tchg. Faculty award Pres.'s Commn. on Status of Women, 1994, Acad. Advising award Miss. State U., 1994, Outstanding Advisor award Nat. Acad. Advising Assn. and ACT, 1995, Miss. State U. Upper Level Undergrad. Tchg. award Miss. State U. Alumni Assn., 2000; Grad. Office fellow Mich. State U., 1980; Miss. State U. rsch. grantee, 1984. Mem. ASPA (exec. bd. Sect. for Women 1987-90, Miss. chpt. pres. 1992-93), LWV (Chesapeake charter pres. 1976-77), Miss. Polit. Sci. Assn. (exec. dir. 1991-93), Miss. State U. Soc. Scholars (pres. 1992-93), Miss. State U. Faculty Women's Assn. (v.p. 1985-86, pres. 1986-88, scholar 1987-89), Phi Kappa Phi (v.p. 1985-86, pres. 1986-88), Pi Sigma Alpha (Ann. Chpt. Activities award 1991). Democrat. Methodist. Avocations: dog obedience training, Corvette activities, gardening. Office: Miss State U PO Drawer PC Mississippi State MS 39762

WALL, JACQUELINE REMONDET, industrial and clinical psychologist, rehabilitation counselor; b. Paris, Dec. 25, 1958; came to U.S., 1959; d. Jack Whitney and Hazel Aline (Riley) Hargett; m. David Gordon Wall, Jan. 27, 1990; 1 child, Jeanette Renee. BA, Southeastern La. U., 1978; MA, U. Tulsa, 1982, PhD, 1989; postgrad., Ill. Inst. Tech., 1995. Lic. psychologist, Ind. Program coord. Hillcrest Med. Ctr., Tulsa, 1982-88; coord. psychol. svcs. Rebound Inc.-Cane Creek Hosp., Martin, Tenn., 1989-90; psychologist Sea Pines Rehab. Hosp., Melbourne, Fla., 1990; indsl. psychology intern Morris & Assocs., Jackson, Miss., 1990-91; ind. cons. indsl. psychology, 1991-92; clinic coord. Ill. Inst. Tech., Chgo., 1992-94, postdoctoral fellow clin. respecialization program, 1992-94; intern psychology dept. U. Miss. Med. Ctr., Jackson, 1994-95; postdoctoral fellow Rehab. Inst. Mich., Detroit, 1995-97; asst. prof., dir. psychol. svcs. U. Indpls., 1997—; instr. Tulsa Jr. Coll., 1989; rsch. asst. U. Tulsa, 1981-82, 84-86, La. State U., Baton Rouge, 1980, Med. Sch., Tulane U., New Orleans, 1979-80; instr. Wayne State U., 1991, IIT, 1994; presenter in field. Contbr. book chpts. and articles to profl. jours. Recipient rsch. grant U. Tulsa, 1982; NIH postdoctoral fellow, 1996-97. Mem. APA, Nat. Acad. Neuropsychology, Soc. for Indsl.-Orgnl. Psychology, Southeastern La. U. Thirteen Club, Sigma Xi, Psi Chi, Phi Kappa Phi, Phi Lambda Pi. E-mail: jwall@uindy.edu. Office: U Indpls Dept Psychology 1400 E Hanna Ave Indianapolis IN 46227-3630

WALL, LEONARD J., bishop; b. Windsor, Ont., Can., Sept. 27, 1924; Ordained Roman Catholic priest, June 11, 1949; ordained titular bishop of Leptiminus and aux. bishop of Toronto, 1979-92; archbishop of Winnipeg Archdiocese of Winnipeg, 1992—. Office: Archdiocese of Winnipeg, 1495 Pembina Hwy, Winnipeg, MB Canada R3T 2C6

WALL, PATRICK DAVID, educator, scientist; b. Nottingham, Eng., Apr. 5, 1925. MA, U. Oxford, Eng., 1947; B.M., B.Ch., Middlesex Hosp. Med. Sch., London, 1948; D.M., U. Oxford, 1959; MD (hon.), U. Siena, 1987, F.R.S., 1989. Instr. in physiology Yale U., New Haven, 1948-50; asst. prof. anatomy U. Chgo., 1950-53; instr. physiology Harvard U., 1953-55; assoc. prof. biology MIT, Cambridge, Mass., 1957-59, prof. physiology, 1959-67; prof. anatomy U. London, 1967—; vis. prof. Hebrew U., Jerusalem, 1972—; editor Pain-Internat. Assn. for the Study of Pain, 1975—. Contbr. articles to profl. jours. Recipient Gunn award, 1987, Bonica medal Internat. Assn. Study Pain. Fellow Royal Coll. of Physicians (Sherrington medal 1987, Wakeman award 1988, Bristol-Myers award 1988). Mem. Labour Party. Office: St Thomas Hosp, Ctr for Neurosci Rsch, Hodgkin Bldg/King's Coll, London SE1 1UL, England

WALLA, PETER, biologist; b. Feldkirch, Austria, July 26, 1967; s. Helmuth and Edith (Ess) W. Mag.rer.nat., U. Vienna, 1993, Dr.rer.nat., 1998. Investigator Sch. Neuropsychology, St. Andrews, Scotland, 1996, Inst. Zoology, Yokohama, Japan, 1992; investigator U. Clinic Neurology, Vienna, 1996-98, prin. investigator, 1999—. Recipient Theodor Koerner Found. award, Vienna, 1998. Mem. Austrian Neurosci. Assn. Avocations: running, video filming, painting, travel, friends. Office: U Clinic Neurology, Waehringer Guertel 18-20, 1090 Vienna Austria

WALLAART, (JOHN)JOHANNES CHRISTIAAN, occupational health educator, chemist; b. Bandoeing, Indonesia, Dec. 31, 1948; arrived in New Zealand; s. John and Liz (Veltmeyer) W.; m. Jane Eleanor Hurrell. Diploma in chemistry, New Zealand, 1971; diploma in mgmt., NZ Inst. Mgmt., Sydney, Australia, 1978; diploma in internat. mgmt., Massey U., Sydney, 1976, diploma in occupl. health & safety mgmt., 1995, MBA, 1998. Chemist Dumedin Electroplaters, 1965-73, New Zealand Aluminum Smelting, 1972-82; orgnl. devel. New Zealand Aluminum, 1982-85, occupl. health officer, 1985-95; cons., 1995—; presentor in field; referee New Zealand Found. Rsch., Sci. and Tech. Contbr. articles to profl. jours. Advisor New Zealand Fire Svce. Hazardous Substances. Fellow New Zealand Inst. Chemistry (past com. mem.); mem. New Zealand Occupl. Hygiene Soc. (past. com. mem.), New Zealand Soc. Scientists, New Zealand Mgmt. (assoc. fellow), Internat. Soc. Respiratory Protection (bd. dirs. 1995). Avocations: commercial pilot. Home: 117 Nikau Paum Rd, Nikau Valley Paraparaumu, Wellington New Zealand

WALLACE, ARTHUR WILLIAM, cardiac anesthesiologist, researcher; b. Oakland, Calif., Nov. 2, 1959; children: Alfred, Andrew. BS in Engring. and Applied Sci., Yale U., 1981; MD, PhD in Biomed. Engring., Johns Hopkins U., 1988. Diplomat Am. Bd. Anesthesiology. Lectr. U. Calif., San Francisco, 1993, asst. prof., 1994—; attending anesthesiologist Vets. Affairs Med. Ctr., San Francisco, 1994—. Recipient Young Scientist award Am. Heart Assn., 1996-97. Mem. Found. Anesthesia Edn. Rsch. (Young Investigator award 1992-93), Multicentered Stuy Perioperative Ischemia. Office: Vet Affairs Med Ctr 4150 Clement St San Francisco CA 94121-1545

WALLACE, EDWIN RUTHVEN, IV, psychiatrist, neuropsychiatrist psychotherapist; b. Portsmouth, Va., Mar. 10, 1950; s. Edwin Ruthven III and Laura Essie (Catron) W.; m. Laura Martin Elmore, May 13, 1972; children: Laura Martin, Edwin Ruthven V. BS cum laude, U. S.C., 1970, BA magna cum laude, 1976; MD, Med. U. S.C., 1973; MA summa cum laude, Johns Hopkins U., 1978. Diplomate Am. Bd. Psychiatry and Neurology. Intern in neurology Richland Meml. Hosp., Columbia, S.C.; resident in psychiatry and neurology William S. Hall Psychiat. Inst., Columbia, S.C., 1973-75; chief resident William S. Hall Psychiat. Inst., Columbia, 1975-76; postdoctoral fellow in neuropsychiatry and hosp. psychiatry Yale U. Sch. Medicine, New Haven, 1977; postdoctoral fellow in history of science and medicine Sch. Medicine Johns Hopkins U., Balt., 1978; asst. prof. neuropsychiatry Sch. Medicine U. S.C., Columbia, 1978-80; asst. prof. psychiatry Yale U. Sch. Medicine, New Haven, 1980-82; assoc. prof., vice chmn. dept. psychiatry & health behavior Med. Coll. Ga., Augusta, 1982-87, prof. psychiatry and health behavior, 1987-95, acting chmn. Dept. Psychiatry, 1987-90; prof. social work U. Ga. Grad. Sch., Athens, 1988—; clin. prof. psychiatry and health behavior Med. Coll. Ga., 1995—; rsch. prof. bioethics and med. humanities U. S.C., 1995—, adj. prof. history, philosophy & religious studies, 1996—; instr. in neuropsychiatry U. S.C. Sch. Medicine, 1975-76; cons. Army Health Svc. Command, U.S. Army Med. Corps, 1986-94, VA Hosps. Augusta, 1988-94; mem. history and libr. com., Am. Psychiat. Assn., Washington, 1986-89; vis. scholar Com. on Conceptual Foundations of Sci., U. Chgo., 1990. Author: Dynamic Psychiatry in Theory and Practice, 1983, Spanish edit., 1991, Freud and Anthropology: a History and Reappraisal, 1983 Japanese edit., 1993, Historiography and Causation in Psychoanalysis, 1985, Italian edit., 1991, 140 articles and chpts. in scholarly and profl. jours. and edited books and encyclopedias; sr. editor: Essays in the History of Psychiatry, 1980; mem. editl. bd. Bull. of History of Medicine, Balt., 1980-88, Second Opinion: Jour. Health, Faith and Ethics, Chgo., 1987-95, Rev. of Psychoanalytic Books, 1995-97; sr. edit. bd. Philosophy, Psychiatry and Psychology, 1993—. Trustee J.B. White Nat. Charitable Found., Augusta, 1988-98; co-capt. Inner City Soup Kitchens, Augusta, 1984-87. Recipient NEH fellowship, 1990. Mem. AAAS, AMA, Am. Hist. Assn., Am. Assn. for the History of Medicine, Am. Coll. Psychiatrists, Assn. for Advancement of Philosphy and Psychiatry (co-founder, exec. com.), Group for the Advancement of Psychiatry, Phi Beta Kappa, Alpha Epsilon Delta. Episcopalian. Fax: 803-777-4575. Home: 1829 Senate St Apt 3E Columbia SC 29201-3837

WALLACE, EUAN MORRISON, obstetrician; b. Dumfries, Scotland, May 26, 1963; s. John and Elizabeth Anne (Morrison) W.; m. Karen Jane Gordon, Oct. 24, 1987; children: Duncan, Ailsa. MBChB, U. Edinburgh, 1986, MD, 1997. WHO rsch. fellow Med. Rsch. Coun., Edinburgh, Scotland, 1987-90; registrar Lothian Health Bd., Edinburgh, 1990-92; lectr. U. Edinburgh, 1993-96; fellow Monash U., Melbourne, Australia, 1996-97, sr. lectr., 1997-99, assoc. prof., 2000—. Contbr. articles to profl. jours.; patentee Inhibin-A in Down's Syndrome, 1994. Rsch. grantee Birth Defects Found., 1995, U. Edinburgh, 1994-95, Monash U., 1997-98, Viertl Found., 1997. Fellow Edinburgh Obstetric Soc. (coun. 1987), Soc. for Endocrinology, Endocrine Soc., Royal Aust. Coll. Gynaecology; mem. Royal Coll. Gynaecology. Avocations: skiing, art, oenology. Office: Monash Med Ctr Dept Obstetr, 246 Clayton Rd, Clayton 3168, Australia

WALLACE, FRANKLIN SHERWOOD, lawyer; b. Bklyn., Nov. 24, 1927; s. Abraham Charles and Jennie (Etkin) Wolowitz; m. Eleanor Ruth Pope, Aug. 23, 1953; children: Julia Diane, Charles Andrew. Student, U. Wis., 1943-45; BS cum laude, U.S. Mcht. Marine Acad., 1950; LLB, JD, U. Mich., 1953. Bar: Ill. 1954. Practice law Rock Island, Ill.; ptnr. Winstein, Kavensky & Wallace; asst. state's atty. Rock Island County, 1967-68; local counsel UAW at John Deere-J.I. Case Plants. Former bd. dirs. Tri City Jewish Ctr.; former trustee United Jewish Charities of Quad Cities; former bd. dirs. Blackhawk Coll. Found. Mem. ABA, Ill. Bar Assn. (chmn. jud. adv. polls com. 1979-84), Rock Island County Bar Assn., Am. Trial Lawyers Assn., Ill. Trial Lawyers Assn., Nat. Assn. Criminal Def. Lawyers, Ill. Appellate Lawyers Assn., Am. Judicature Soc., Blackhawk Coll. Found. Democrat. Jewish. Home: 3405 20th Street Ct Rock Island IL 61201-6201 Office: Rock Island Bank Bldg Rock Island IL 61201

WALLACE, IAN NORMAN DUNCAN, barrister; b. Smyrna, Turkey, Apr. 21, 1922; s. Duncan Gardner and Eileen Agnes (Wilkin) W.; m. Valerie Mary Hollman, Mar. 28, 1961 (div. 1965). MA, Oriel Coll., Oxford U., Eng., 1947. Barrister-at-law, U.K. Pvt. practice London, 1948—, Queen's counsel, 1973—; vis. prof. King's coll. London Centre of Constrn. Law, 1988—; vis. scholar Boalt Hall Sch. Law, U. Calif., Berkeley, 1978—. Author: Hudson on Building and Engineering Contracts, 8th edit., 1959, 9th edit., 1965, 10th edit., 1970, 11th edit., 1994, Construction Contracts, Principles and Policies, 1986, Vol. II, 1996, The International Civil Engineering Contract, 1974, 2d edit., 1980, The Ice Conditions of Contract, 1976, Building and Civil Engineering Standard Forms, 1969, 2d edit., 1973. Lt. Royal Navy Vol. Res., 1940-46. Mem. Landsdowne Club, Hurlingham Club. Avocations: shooting, art, wine. Home: 53 Holland Park, London W11 3RS, England Office: Atkin Chambers, 1 Atkin Bldg, Grays Inn, London WC1 5AT, England

WALLACE, JANE HOUSE, retired geologist; b. Ft. Worth, Aug. 12, 1926; d. Fred Leroy and Helen Gould (Kixmiller) Wallace; A.B., Smith Coll., 1947, M.A., 1949; postgrad. Bryn Mawr Coll., 1949-52. Geologist, U.S. Geol. Survey, 1952-97, chief Pub. Inquiries Offices, Washington, 1964-72, spl. asst. to dir., 1974-97, dep. bur. ethics counselor, 1975-97, Washington liaison Office of Dir., 1978-97; ret., 1997. Recipient Meritorious Service award Dept. Interior, 1971, Disting. Svc. award, 1976, Sec.'s Commendation, 1988, Smith Coll. medal, 1992. Fellow Geol. Socs. Am., Washington (treas. 1963-67); mem. Sigma Xi (asso.).

WALLACE, JESSE WYATT, pharmaceutical scientist; b. Canton, Ga., Jan. 24, 1925; s. Jesse Washington and Lula (Wyatt) W.; m. Myra Brown, Jan. 2, 1949; children: Karin, Kimberly, Stephen, David. BBA magna cum laude, U. Ga., 1954; MS, Ga. Inst. Tech., 1960. Chmn. svc. groups Ga. Tech, Atlanta, 1953-57; adminstrv. mgr. Am. Viscose Corp., Marcus Hook, Pa., 1957-61; various exec. positions FMC Corp., Phila., 1961-85; pres., dir. Wallco Internat. Corp., Wilmington, Del., 1985-89, 96—; v.p., sec. Pharm. Svc. and Tech., Inc., Woodbury, N.J., 1989-95; bd. dirs. Artist Alive, Inc.; adv. bd. Pharm. Tech. Conf., 1986—. Editor: Controlled Release Systems, 1988; contbr. Encyclopedia, 1989; contbr. articles to profl. jours; author (manual) Problem Solver, 1980. Vice chmn. Ch. Deacons, Wilmington; v.p., pres. Wilmington Gideons, 1969-71; v.p., bd. dirs. ACA Acad., 1971-73; vice chmn. Del. Family Found., 1990—. Lt. USN, 1943-46, 50-53. Recipient Publ. award Pharm. Technology, 1989. Fellow Acad. Pharm. Scis., Am. Asnsn. of Pharm. Scientists; mem. Internat. Platform Assn., La. Fedn. Internat. Pharm., Am. Assn. Pharm. Scientists, Mensa, Delta Sigma Pi (life), Delta Mu Delta. Republican. Baptist. Avocations: family, reading, golf, racquet ball, travel. Office: Wallco Internat Corp 1106 Grinnell Rd Wilmington DE 19803-5126

WALLACE, KEITH, lawyer; b. London, June 5, 1945; s. William and Sheila Agnes (Hopper) W.; m. Christine Wallace, Mar. 17, 1973; children: Jasper, William, Dougal. Postgrad. cert., Kings Coll., London. Solicitor Supreme Ct., London; ptnr. Richards, Butler law firm, London, 1984—; chmn. Maldon Unit Trust Mgrs., Eng., Ind. Pension Trustee, Eng.; dir. Beaufort Trust Corp., Eng. Editor Pension Lawyer periodical, 1984-99; editor/commentator Pension TV Network, 1992—. Recipient award Assn. Pension Lawyers, 1999. Office: 15 Saint Botolph St, London EC3A 7AA, England

WALLACE, MATTHEW WALKER, retired entrepreneur; b. Salt Lake City, Jan. 7, 1924; s. John McChrystal and Glenn (Walker) W.; m. Constance Cone, June 22, 1954 (dec. May 1980); children: Matthew, Anne; m. Susan Struggles, July 11, 1981. BA, Stanford U., 1947; MCP, MIT, 1950. Prin. planner Boston City Planning Bd., 1950-53; v.p. Nat. Planning and Rsch., Inc., Boston, 1953-55; pres. Wallace-McConaughy Corp., Salt Lake City, 1955-69, Ariz. Ranch & Metals Co., Scottsdale, 1969-84, Idaho TV Corp., Channel 6, ABC, Boise, 1976-78; chmn. Wallace Assocs., Inc., Salt Lake City, 1969-98; dir. 1st Interstate Bank, Salt Lake City, 1956-90, dir. Arnold Machinery Co., 1988—, dir. Roosevelt Hot Springs Corp., 1978—; mem. adv. bd. Mountain Bell Telephone Co., Salt Lake City, 1975-85. Pres. Downtown Planning Assn., Salt Lake City, 1970; chmn. Utah State Arts Coun., Salt Lake City, 1977; chmn. hon. bd. Planned Parenthood; mem. Humanities and Scis. Coun., Stanford U., also mem. athletics bd., mem. alumni assn. exec. bd., bd. vis. sch. law; mem. nat. adv. bd. Coll. Bus., U. Utah; lifetime dir. Utah Symphony Orch.; chmn. arts, adv. coun. and Capital Campaign Westminster Coll. Lt. (j.g.) USN, 1944-46, PTO. Recipient Contbn. award Downtown Planning Assn., 1977, Gov.'s award in the Arts, 1991, Utah Nat. Guard Minuteman award, 1994. Mem. Am. Inst. Cert. Planners (charter), Am. Arts Alliance (bd. dirs. 1991), Alta Club (dir.), Cottonwood Club (pres. 1959-63), Salt Lake Country Club (dir.), Desert Island Golf and Country Club (Rancho Mirage, Calif.), Flat Rock Club (Island Park, Idaho pres. 1994-98), Phi Kappa Phi (hon., life). Home: 2510 Walker Ln Salt Lake City UT 84117-7729

WALLACE, PETTER, television producer, director; b. Stavanger, Norway, Aug. 13, 1957; s. Haakon Waldemar and Sigrid (Wallace) Andersen.; m. Hege WØlstad-Knudsen, Aug. 14, 1987; children: Benedikte, Karoline. BS summa cum laude, Ohio U., Athens, Ohio, 1981; postgrad., San Diego State U., 1982. Comty. access supr. Athens Comty. TV, 1981; founder, dir. Program Prodns. Scandinavia, Oslo, Norway, 1983-86; producer Firma Petter Wallace, Oslo, 1988-89; commissioning controller TV3 Broadcasting Group Ltd., West Drayton, Eng., 1989-92; mng. dir. Missing Link Ltd., Twickenham, Eng., 1992-93, Rubicon TV AS, Oslo, 1993-97; co-mng. dir. Dragonfire Ent. Ltd., London, 2000—; bd. dirs. Norwegian Film & TV Prodns. Assn., 1994—. Co-author: Brevomber, 1985; exec. producer Way North--Roald Dahl, 1985, Syv Søstre, 1996; prodr., dir. Fort Boyard (Norway and Denmark), 1993, Hjemme Hos Paus, 1994; prodr. Bak Din Rygg, 1995, Snow Children, 1999-2000; dir. Hotel Ceasar, 1998-99. Avocations: family, writing, the arts. Office: PO Box 163, N 1321 Stabekk Norway

WALLACE, ROANNE, hosiery company executive; b. Greenwood, Miss., Dec. 18, 1949; d. Robert Carter and Lois Anne (Vick) W. BM, U. Tenn., 1971; MA, U. N.C., 1976; MBA, Wake Forest U., 1982. Exec. dir. Am. Bd. Clin. Chemistry, Winston-Salem, N.C., 1977-78; administrv. officer Winston-Salem/Forsyth County Office Emergency Mgmt., 1978-79, sr. asst. dir., 1979-82; with Sara Lee, Winston-Salem, 1982—; mktg. dir. Sara Lee Hosiery/Just My Size, Winston-Salem, 1988—; product mgr. L'eggs Products, Inc., Winston-Salem, 1986-88. Mem. adv. coun. Winston-Salem/Forsyth County Office Emergency Mgmt.; v.p. audience devel., bd. dirs. Opera Theatre, Inc. Miss U. Tenn., 1970. Home: 803 Devon Ct Winston Salem NC 27104-1263 Office: Sara Lee Hosiery 5650 University Pkwy Winston Salem NC 27105-1312

WALLACE, ROBERT BRUCE, environmental company executive; b. Ithaca, N.Y., Oct. 25, 1942; s. Maury and Ida (Musto) W.; m. Donna Hoyt, Dec. 25, 1964 (div. 1972); children: Christopher, Matthew. MET, SUNY, Binghamton, 1967. Cert. environ. specialist. Millwright, foreman Wallace Steel, Inc., Ithaca, 1967-70; engr., mgr. Ingersoll-Rand Co., Painted Post, N.Y., 1970-74, J.I. Case Co., Racine, Wis., 1974-77; gen. mgr. engring. L.O Smith/Wis. Foundry Products, Milw., 1977-81; pres., gen. mgr. Corning (N.Y.) Materials, Inc., 1981-83; dir. ops. N.Y. Office Mental Health, Albany, 1983-88; dir. quality assurance Splty. Systems, Inc., Indpls., 1988-90; v.p. Alliance Environ., Inc., 1990-91; pres., CEO Alliance Environ., Indpls., 1991—; chief instr. N.Y. State Govs. Office, Albany, 1985-88. Petentee scrap reduction and environ. remediation process; contbr. articles to profl. publs. Scoutmaster Boy Scouts Am., 1969-78, vol., 1959—; regional dir. ToughLove, Corning, 1982-85; recycling dir. Southerntier Recycling Ctr., Elmira, N.Y., 1983-85. With U.S. Army, 1961-64, Laos. Eagle Scout, 1955. Mem. Am. Foundrymen's Soc. (chpt. pres. 1983-85), Nat. Asbestos Coun., Internat. Maintenance Inst. (chpt. pres. 1975-77), Am. Inst. Plant Engrs. (chpt. pres. 1978-79), Am. Soc. Safety Engrs., Spl. Forces Assn., 82d Airborne Assn. Republican. Episcopalian. Avocations: tour biking, canoeing, water sports, skiing. Home: 5707 Blue Spruce Dr Indianapolis IN 46237-2712 Office: Alliance Environ Inc 1433 Sadlier Circle Indianapolis IN 46237-3015

WALLACE, ROGER JAMES, educator, researcher; b. Swan Hill, Australia, Aug. 29, 1950; s. Dugald and Patricia (Ashton) W.; life partner Cheryl Lynn Evans; 1 child, Lachlan John. B in Applied Sci., Royal Melbourne Inst. Tech., Australia, 1973; BSc (Hons.), Monash U., 1975; Dip Ed, U. Melbourne, 1981; PhD, La Trobe U., 1988. Lectr. mgmt. info. sys. Deakin U., Melbourne, 1985—; exch. prof. Winthrop U., Rock Hill, S.C., 1992, statis. cons. Pacific Plants, Vancouver, Can., 1992-96, Deakin Australia, Melbourne, Australia, 1997, Nelson Publishers, Melbourne, 1999, Cicada Bay Software, Melbourne, 1999; spkr. in field. Co-author: Time Series

Analysis, 1988, co-designer FECRT field test, 1992—; contbr. articles to profl. jours. Grantee Bowater Industries, 1987, 91, Siddons Industries, 1983, Deakin U., 2000, Deakin U. Sch. Mgmt. Info. Systems, 2000. Mem. Carlton Football Club. Anglican. Avocations: Native American history, parenting, golf, jogging, chess. Office: Deakin U Sch Mgmt Info Sys, Burwood Hwy, Burwood Victoria 3125, Australia

WALLACE, WILLIAM JOHN, history educator; b. Leicester, Eng., Mar. 12, 1941; s. William Edward and Mary Agnes (Tricks) W.; m. Helen Sarah Rushworth, Aug. 24, 1968; children: Harriet, Edward. BA in History, Cambridge U., 1962; PhD in Govt., Cornell U., 1968; PhD h.c., Free U. Brussels, 1992. Lectr. govt. Manchester (Eng.) U., 1967-77; dir. studies Royal Inst. of Internat. Affairs, London, 1978-90; Walter F. Hallstein fellow St. Antony's Coll., Oxford, Eng., 1990-95; reader internat. rels. London Sch. Econs., 1995—; vis. prof. internat. studies Ctrl. European U., 1994—. Author: The Transformation of Western Europe, 1990, Regional Integration: The West European Experience, 1994; editor: The Dynamics of European Integration, 1990, Policy-making in the European Union, 1996. Vice chmn. policy com. Liberal Party of Britain, 1976-88; mem. House of Lords, 1995—. Office: London Sch Econs, Dept Internat Rels, London WC2A 2AE, England

WALLACE-CRABBE, CHRISTOPHER KEITH, poet, English language educator; b. Melbourne, Victoria, Australia, May 6, 1934; s. Kenneth Eyre d'Inverell and Phyllis Vera May (Cock) W.; m. Helen Margaret Wiltshire, June 16, 1958 (div. 1978); children—Ben, Georgia; m. Marianne Sophie Feil, Nov. 25, 1978; children—Toby, Joshua Leo. BA, U. Melbourne, Australia, 1956, MA, 1964. Jr. tech. officer Royal Mint, Melbourne, 1950-52; tchr. Haileybury Coll., Hampton, Victoria, 1957-58; Lockie fellow U. Melbourne, Parkville, 1961-63, lectr., 1964-76, reader in English, 1977-86, personal chair, 1987—; prof. Australian studies Harvard U., 1987-88, prof. emeritus, 1998—. Author: The Music of Division, 1959, Eight Metropolitan Poems, 1962, In Light and Darkness, 1963, The Rebel General, 1967, Where the Wind Came, 1971, Selected Poems, 1973, Chris-Wallace Crabbe Reads from His Own Verse, 1973, The Foundations of Joy, 1976, The Emotions are not Skilled Workers, 1979, Melbourne or the Bush: Essays on Australian Literature and Society, 1974, Splinters, 1981, Toil and Spin: Two Directions in Modern Poetry, Three Absences in Australian Literature, 1983, The Amorous Cannibal, 1985, I'm Deadly Serious, 1988, For Crying Out Loud, 1990, Falling into Language, 1990, Rungs of Time, 1992, Selected Poems, 1995, Whirling, 1998; editor: Six Voices: Contemporary Australian Poets, 1963, The Australian Nationalists: Modern Critical Essays, 1971, Australian Poetry 1971, 1971, The Golden Apples of the Sun: Twentieth Century Australian Poetry, 1980, (with P. Pierce) Clubbing of the Gunfire: 101 Australian War Poems, 1984, (with K. Flattley) From the Republic of Conscience, 1992, Author, Author!, 1998. Served to cpl. RAAF, 1952-53. Harkness fellow Yale U., 1965-67. Mem. Australian Acad. Humanities. Avocations: tennis, cricket, drawing, body surfing. Home: 102 Davies St, Brunswick 3056, Australia

WALLACH, HOWARD FREDERIC, psychiatrist; b. Chgo., Sept. 4, 1923; s. Leo and Mildred (Ebert) W.; m. Laurie Rochelle Gettleman, Sept. 15, 1945 (div. July 1968); children: Joan, John, Richard; m. Gloria Bunny Jackman, July 14, 1968; children: Rand, Steve, Beth. MD, U. Ill., Chgo., 1946; M.Social Psychiatry, UCLA, 1969. Diplomate Am. Bd. Psychiatry and Neurology. Intern Cook County Hosp., Chgo., 1946-47, resident internal medicine, 1947-49; pres. Mount Sinai Hosp. Med. Rsch. Found., 1952-64; asst. clin. prof. psychiatry UCLA, 1968-80, assoc. clin. prof., 1980—; chief allied mental health Brentwood VA Hosp., L.A., 1970-72; chief psychiatry Sepulveda VA Hosp., L.A., 1972-74; pvt. practice L.A.; resident internal medicine Cook County Hosp., Chgo., 1947-49; bd. govs. Cedars-Sinai Med. Ctr., L.A., 1985—, mem. exec. com., 2000—; cons. VA Med. Ctr., L.A., 1982-90; developer maj. high rise apts., Chgo., 1951-64. Contbr. articles to profl. jours. Sec. Am. Psychiat. Found., Washington, 1990-99; bd. dirs. Nat. Mus. Health and Medicine, Washington, 1989-99; v.p. Jewish Family Svc. of L.A., 1997-98; bd. dirs., pres. Young Men's Jewish Charities, Chgo., 1951-62; mem. Cook County Blue Ribbon Commn., 1959-63. 1st lt. U.S. Army, 1943-46. Recipient Bronze award Boys Clubs of Am., 1962, Pres.'s Spl. Achievement award So. Calif. Psychiat. Soc., 1991. Fellow Am. Coll. Psychoanalysts, Am. Psychiat. Assn. (exec. com. 1982-88), Am. Acad. Psychoanalysis; mem. Calif. Psychiat. Assn. (pres. 1986-88), So. Calif. Psychiat. Soc. (pres. 1979-80, mem. coun. 1975-83), Alpha Omega Alpha. Avocations: photography, computers, golf, walking, presidential manuscript collecting. Office: 2080 Century Park E Los Angeles CA 90067-2001

WALLAERT, BENOIT, chest physician, medical educator; b. Lille, France, Mar. 17, 1952; s. Raymond Wallaert and Antoinette Wallaert-Hache; m. Monique Tillie; children: Virginie, Jimmy, William, Marine, Elliot. MD, U. Lille, France, 1982. Cert. in pulmonology, allergology, cancerology U. Lille II. Intern, resident Ctr. Hosp. Regional et Univ., Lille; rschr. Pasteur Inst., Lille, 1986—; prof. medicine, asst. chief svc. dept. pulmonology U. Lille II Faculty Medicine, Lille, 1989—. Mem. editl. bd. European Respiratory Jour.; contbr. articles to med. jours. Mem. Am. Thoracic Soc., European Respiratory Soc. (Cournand lectr. 1996). Office: BLD Leclercq-Hosp Calmette, Dept Pneumology, 59037 Lille France

WALLAND, JAKOB, master mariner; b. Haugesund, Rogaland, Norway, Dec. 1, 1954; s. Kristian and Astrid (Kvilhaug) W. Student, Haugesund Navigation Sch., Norway, 1975; Master Mariner, Haugesund Maritime Tech. Sch., Norway, 1991. Master mariner class I. Chief officer Balder Mgmt., Oslo, Norway, 1981-84; marine supr. Primary Fuels, Houston, 1984-87; master mariner Leiren Group, Bergen, Norway, 1988-90, Klaveness Group, Oslo, Norway, 1991—; shipping cons. Ellefsen Marine, N.Y., 1987-93. Mem. Norwegian Sea Officers Orgn., Subic Yacht and Country Club. Conservative. Lutheran. Avocations: boating, yacht clubs, travel, trekking. Home and Office: Medhaugsv 11, 4270 Akrehamn Norway

WALLANDER, JAN RICKARD, banker; b. Stockholm, Sweden, June 8, 1920; s. Sven and Elna (von Zweigbergk) W.; m. Ann-Charlotte Westergren, Aug. 26, 1941 (div. 1982); children: Anna Rogberg, Malin Wallander-Olsson, Fanny Borgstrom; m. Birgitta Celsing, Sept. 7, 1983. With Indsl. Inst. for Econs. and Social Research, 1945-48, pres., 1953-61; research mgr. Indsl. Council for Social and Econ. Studies, 1950-51, pres., 1951-53; pres. Sundsvallsbanken, 1961-70; pres. Svenska Handelsbanken, Stockholm, 1971-78, chmn., 1978-91, hon. chmn., 1991—. Contbr. articles to profl. publs. Chmn. bd. Jan Wallander and Tom Hedelius Found., Ab JC Architect, Wenner-Gren Found. for Sci. Rsch.; Tore Browaldh Found.; bd. dirs. Peter and Birgitta Celsing Found.; past mem. Nat. Bd. Univ. and Coll.; past chmn. bd. Swedish State Railways, AB IRO, 1978-84, Swedish Securities Register Ctr., 1971-84, Tidnings AB Marieberg, 1978-88, Bahco. Decorated Knight Comdr.'s cross Royal Order of Vasa; recipient Kings medal of the 12th Dimension with the Ribbon of the Seraphims. Home: Klockberga, S-178 02 Drottningholm Sweden Office: Svenska Handelsbanken, Kundstradgardsgatan 2, S-106 70 Stockholm Sweden

WALLAS, ARMIN ALEXANDER, German literature researcher; b. Villach, Austria, Apr. 21, 1962; s. Johann and Emilie (Reichmann) Wa. Mag. phil., U. Klagenfurt, Austria, 1985, PhD, 1989. Rsch. scientist dept German lit. U. Klagenfurt, 1990—. Editor: Texte des Expressionismus, 1988, Simon Kronberg: Werke, vol. 2, 1993; (with Klaus Amann) Expressionismus in Österreich, 1994; Max Zweig: Zuedische Dramen, 1999, Eugen Hoeflich: Tagebuecher 1915-1927, 1999, (with Andrea Lauritsch) Mnemosyne, 1987—; (with Primus-Heinz Kucher) Edition Mnemosyne, 1993—; author: Albert Ehrenstein, 1994, Zeitschriften und Anthologien des Expressionismus in Österreich, vol. 2, 1995; contbr. articles to profl. jours. Fellow Verband Deutschsprachiger Schriftsteller in Israel; mem. Mnemosyne-Gesellschaft für Erinnerung (chmn. 1992—). Home: Rennsteiner Str 118, A-9500 Villach Austria Office: Univ Klagenfurt Dept German Lit, Universitätsstr 65-67, A-9020 Klagenfurt Austria

WALLBERG, BÖRJE CARL-GUSTAF, retired Swedish army officer, philately consultant; b. Södertälje, Sweden, Feb. 28, 1923; s. John A. and Eugenia M. (Palm) W.; m. Annie-Marie Kvarforth, 1951 (div. 1973); m. Evabritta G. Personne, Feb. 10, 1973; children: Matilda, Magnus Ph. Student, Mil. Staff Coll., Stockholm, 1954-56, Mil. Def. Coll., Stockholm, 1970, 78. Commd. officer Swedish Army, 1946, advanced through grades to brig. gen., 1974, insp. logistics, supply, transp. and med. svcs.; ret., 1983; owner, mgr. Wallberg Cons. HB, Enebyberg, Sweden, 1987—; sec.-gen. World Philatelic Exhbn. Stockholmia, 1986; internat. judge 25 world stamp exhbns., 1976—; cons. to Swedish Post Office, 1987-97; expert to Swedish Govtl. Humanitarian Law Commn., 1978-84; mem. Swedish Govtl. Internat. Humanitarian Law Del., 1984-88. Author: The Albatross Mail 1914-1918, 1972; contbr. numerous articles on philately and internat. security questions to profl. publs. Pres., chmn. ctrl. bd. Swedish Red Cross Soc., 1981-87; v.p. Swedish Vol. Truck Drivers Fedn., 1979-81, 87-89, pres., 1989-93; pres. FIP Commn. for Trad Phil., 1996-2000. Decorated comdr. Royal Order of Sword (Sweden); recipient King Carl XVI Gustaf personal medal for vol. svcs. and philatelic activities, 1991. Fellow Royal Philadelic Soc. London; mem. Swedish Philatelic Fedn. (sec. 1967-84, v.p. 1985-87), Acad. Philatelic (Paris corr.), Roll of Disting. Philatelists of World (Signator 1994, bd. election 1998—). Avocations: philately, Red Cross work. Home and Office: Örskärsvägen 6, SE182 49 Enebyberg Sweden

WALLBERG, MARILYN, personnel recruiting company executive; b. N.Y.C., Dec. 18, 1942; d. Walter and Frances (Steinfeld) Sitomer; divorced; children: Ruth Dyan, Allison Jo. BA, U. Vt., 1964; MA, Columbia U., 1968. Legal recruiter Stephen M. Haas Legal Placement, Inc., N.Y.C., 1983—. Mem. Nat. Assn. Legal Search Cons. Avocations: cooking. Office: Stephen M Haas Legal Placement 60 E 42nd St New York NY 10165-0006

WALLDAL, SIGURD, investment company executive; b. Göteborg, Sweden, Jan. 18, 1939; s. Carl O. and Daga C.S. (Berggren) W.; m. Elvi L. Andersson, May 18, 1966; children: Charlotte, Sverker, Louise. MSc in Engring., Chalmers Inst. of Tech., 1961; grad. in bus. adminstrn., Göteborg Bus. Sch., 1964. With orgn. dept. AB Turitz & Co., Sweden, 1964-67; mgr., dir. planning dept. NK/Turitz Group, Sweden, 1967-72; dir. fin. and adminstn. EKA AB, Sweden, 1972-85; sr. v.p. EKA Nobel AB, Sweden, 1986-91; group chief exec. AB Geveko, Sweden, 1991—; chmn. tech. physics sect. Assn. of Alumni Chalmers Inst. of Tech., Göteborg, 1998—. Radar engr. Coast Artillery of Sweden, 1964-86. Mem. IVA Väst, Chalmerska Ingenjörs Föreningen. Avocations: bridge, golf, sailing, wine, family. Home: Skårsgatan 36, S-41269 Göteborg Sweden Office: AB Geveko, PO Box 2137, S-40313 Göteborg Sweden

WALLEN, CARL JOSEPH, JR., education educator; b. Glendale, Calif., Dec. 12, 1931; s. Carl Joseph and Winifred (Batten) W.; m. LaDonna Leigh Stanley, Nov. 29, 1959; children: Erik Stanley, Todd Alan, Michael Carl. BA, U. Calif., Santa Barbara, 1956; MA, San Francisco State U., 1960; EdD, Stanford U., 1962. Tchr. 5th grade Mt. Eden Sch. Dist., Hayward, Calif., 1956-58; tchr. 3d and 6th grades Pacifica (Calif.) Sch. Dist., 1958-60; grad. asst. Stanford U., Palo Alto, Calif., 1960-62; asst. prof. Oreg. State U., Corvallis, 1962-65; assoc. prof. tchg. rsch. Oreg. Sys. Higher Edn., Monmouth, 1965-67; assoc. prof. U. Oreg., Eugene, 1967-73; dir. of U.S. Office of Edn. fellowship program U. Oreg., 1972-73; prof., chmn. dept. elem. edn. Ariz. State U., Tempe, 1973-78, prof., 1978-97, prof. emeritus, 1997—; cons. to schs., dists. and state depts. edn. in Oreg. and Ariz., 1962—. Author: Competency in Teaching Reading, 1973, 82, Cognition and Effective Instruction, 1993, 94, 95, 96; co-author: Effective Classroom Management, 1978, Fraud Recognition: Claims Adjustors, 1993; also monographs and jour. articles. Mem. com. Am. Friends Svc. Com., Oreg. and Ariz., 1963—; co-founder, pres. Ariz. Ctr. to Reverse Arms Race, Phoenix, 1978-82; rep. Ariz. Ecumenical Coun., 1978—, pres., 1990-93, prison visitation and support, 1997—. With U.S. Army, 1952-54. U.S. OfficeEdn. fellow, 1972-73. Mem. Am. Ednl. Rsch. Assn., Phi Delta Kappa. Democrat. Quaker. Avocations: woodworking, stained glass making, gardening. Home: 525 E Alameda Dr Tempe AZ 85282-3822

WALLENBERG, PETER, banker, investor; b. Stockholm, May 29, 1926; s. Marcus Wallenberg and Dorothy Mackay; divorced; 3 children. LLM, U. Stockholm; hon. degree, Stockholm Sch. Econs., Augustana Coll., Sioux Falls, S.D., Upsala Coll., Stockholm, 1984, Georgetown U. Various positions Atlas Copco Group, 1953-67; dep. mng. dir. Atlas Copco AB, 1970-74, chmn., 1974; first vice chmn. Skandiaviska Enskilda Banken, 1984-96, hon. chmn. bd. dirs.; investor AB, Wallenberg Found.; hon. pres. ICC. Avocations: hunting, tennis, sailing. Office: Investor AB, 10332 Stockholm Sweden Address: Arsenalsgatan 8c, S-10332 Stockholm Sweden*

WALLENIUS, CLAES, psychologist; b. Malmo, Sweden, Oct. 29, 1958; s. James and Gunnel (Skog) W. Clin. psychologist Sweden, 1987-88; rsch. psychologist Nat. Def., Sweden, 1988—. Office: Nat Def Coll, Jarnvagsgatan 6, SE 65225 Karlstad Sweden

WALLENIUS, ILKKA JYRKI, management educator; b. Kuusankoski, Finland, Oct. 11, 1949; s. Jukka Ilmari and Valvikki Vilhelmiina Wallenius; m. Hannele Elina Heinonen, Aug. 25, 1973; 1 child, Johanna Kristiina. MS in Econs., Helsinki (Finland) Sch. Econs., 1971, PhD in Managerial Econs., 1975. Assoc. prof. U. Jyväskylä, Finland, 1979-88; prof. Helsinki Sch. of Econs., 1990—, dir. Basic Rsch. Inst., 1993-95, founding dir. Ctr. Innovative Edn., 1996-98, dir. internat. ctr., 1998—, vice rector, 1999—; vis. prof. Purdue U., West Lafayette, Ind., 1979-80, Ariz. State U., Tempe, 1984-86, Tex. A&M U., College Station, 1991-92. Author: (periodicals) Management Science, 1975, 76, 78, 83, 84, 92, 99; contbr. articles to profl. jours.; editor European Jour. Operational Rsch., 1999—. 2d lt. Finnish Army, 1977-78. Recipient Pareto-Edgeworth award Int. Soc. Multiple Criteria Decision Making, 1994. Avocations: tennis, skiing. Office: Helsinki Sch Econs, Runeberginkatu 14-16, 00100 Helsinki Finland

WALLER, ALAN GEORGE, management consultant, educator; b. Wolverhampton, Eng., Dec. 20, 1944; s. Joseph Herbert and Elsie Victoria (Clarke) W.; m. Patricia Rosemund Jones, Aug. 17, 1968; children: Benjamin, Timothy, Sarah, Katherine, Victoria. MA in Math., Oxford (Eng.) U., 1967; diploma in mgmt. studies, Leicester (Eng.) Poly., 1970; MSc in Operation Rsch., Cranfield Sch. Mgmt., 1971. Grad. trainee Brit. Steel, Eng., 1967-68, asst. plant mgr., 1968-70, control engr., 1970-72; lectr. Leicester (Eng.) Sch. Mgmt., 1972-74; cons. Coopers & Lybrand, Eng., 1974-76; lectr. Warwick (Eng.) U. Bus. Sch., 1976-78; sr. lectr. Cranfield Sch. Mgmt., Eng., 1978-86; ptnr. Coopers & Lybrand, Eng., 1986—; dir. Cranford Ctr. Logistics and Transp. Cranfield Sch. Mgmt., Eng., 1997—; chmn. Faculty of Freight, Eng.; pres. Cranfield Logistics Soc.; chmn. European Coun. on Supply Chain & Logistics, 1997—. Contbr. articles to profl. jours. Chmn. Oringbury Parish Coun., End., 1985-88, chmn. Home Farm Trust Friends, Northants, Eng., 1986—; ch. warden Orlinebury Parochial Ch. Coun., Eng., 1990-97. Fellow Chartered Inst. Transport (dir. 1991—), Inst. Mgmt., Inst. Mgmt. Cons., Inst. Mgmt. Svc., Fellowship for Operational Rsch.; mem. Wellingborough (Eng.) Rotary Club. Anglican. Avocations: family activities, golf, music, art. Home: Garden House, Rectory Ln, Orlingbury NN14 1JH, England Office: Price Waterhouse Coopers, 1 Embankment Pl, London WC2N 6NN, England

WALLER, EPHRAIM EVERETT, retired professional association executive; b. Sioux City, Iowa, Aug. 10, 1928; s. Everett and Ruth Emma (Little) W.; m. Virginia Louise Harper, Oct. 3, 1959. BA, U. Iowa, 1951, MA, 1959; grad., Strategic Intelligence Sch., 1955, Army Security Agy. Sch., 1962, Nat. Cryptologic Sch., 1966, Comd. and Gen. Staff Coll., 1966; grad. with honors, State Dept. Fgn. Svc. Inst., 1967, Turkish Lang. Sch., 1968; grad., Indsl. Coll. Armed Forces, 1972; EdD with honors, U. S.D., 1981. Cert. fgn. area specialist, cryptologist. Commd. 2d lt. U.S. Army, 1951, advanced through grades to lt. col., 1967, retired, 1979; exec. dir. Midwest Agrl. Chems. Assn., Sioux City, Iowa, 1981-95; cons., 1996—; mem. sci. and regulatory oversight coun. Am. Crop Protection Assn., Washington, 1990-95; mem. interregional coord. coun. Joint Body U.S. Regional Agrl. Assns., Dawson, Ga., 1991-95. Contbr. numerous articles to profl. jours. Mem. coms. 1st Congrl. Ch., Sioux City, 1937—. Decorated Bronze Star, Cross of Gallantry with Silver Star, Legion of Merit with oak leaf cluster, Chinese and Vietnamese Honor medals, Meritorious Svc. medal with oak leaf cluster, Joint Svc. Commendation medal with oak leaf cluster, Army Commendation medal with oak leaf cluster, Army Gen. Staff badge, Vietnamese Combat Merit medal. Mem. Retired Officers Assn., Siouxland C. of C. (com. mem. 1981-95), Interprofessional Inst., Scottish Rite, Masons, Eastern Star, Phi Delta Kappa, Delta Sigma Rho. Avocations: swimming, hiking, travel, stamp collecting, writing. Home: 2847 Valley Dr Sioux City IA 51104-4071

WALLER, GEOFFREY NICHOLAS HUGH, biologist, zoologist; b. Tunbridge Wells, Kent, Eng., July 25, 1955; s. John Richard and Ruth Mary (Roder) W. BSc in Marine Zoology, U. Wales, Bangor, 1976; PhD in Toothed Whale Biology, U. Cambridge, Eng., 1980. Monbusho scholar U. Tokyo, 1980-82; rsch. asst. Univ. Coll. London, 1983-88; rsch. fellow H. Steinitz Marine Biology Lab., Israel, 1989-91; rsch. asst. Natural History Mus., London, 1991-97. Author, editor: Sealife: A Complete Guide to the Marine Environment, 1996; editor: Eyewitness Shark, 1992 (U.K. Bestseller); contbr. articles to profl. jours. Spl. Trustees grantee U. London, 1995-97; recipient Rsch. award Med. Rsch. Coun., U. London, 1982-84, Rsch. award Engring. and Physical Sci. Rsch. Coun., 1994-96. Mem. European Assn. Aquatic Mammals. Office: c/o Marine Biol Assn, The Laboratory, Plymouth PL1 2PB, England

WALLER, JOHN LOUIS, anesthesiology educator; b. Loma Linda, Calif., Dec. 1, 1944; s. Louis Clinton and Sue (Bruce) W.; m. Jo Lynn Marie Haas, Aug. 4, 1968; children: Kristina, Karla, David. BA, So. Coll., Collegedale, Tenn., 1967; MD, Loma Linda U., 1971. Diplomate Am. Bd. Anesthesiology. Intern Hartford (Conn.) Hosp., 1971-72; resident in anesthesiology Harvard U. Med. Sch.-Mass. Gen. Hosp., Boston, 1972-74, fellow, 1974-75; asst. prof. anesthesiology Emory U. Sch. Medicine, Atlanta, 1977-80, assoc. prof., 1980-86, prof., chmn. dept., 1986—; chief anesthesiology Emory U. Hosp., Atlanta, 1986-94, med. dir., 1993-95; assoc. v.p. info. svcs. Woodruff Health Scis. Ctr., 1995-97; chief info. officer Emory U. System Healthcare, Atlanta, 1995-97; cons. Arrow Internat., Inc., Reading, Pa., 1988—; bd. dirs. Clifton Casualty Co., Bermuda; mem. adv. com. on anesthetic and life support drugs FDA, Washington, 1986-92; numerous vis. professorships and lectures. Contbr. articles to med. jours. Maj. M.C., USAF, 1975-77. Recipient cert. of appreciation Office Sec. Def., 1983. Fellow Am. Coll. Anesthesiologists, Am. Coll. Chest Physicians; mem. AMA, Am. Soc. Anesthesiologists, Soc. Cardiovascular Anesthesiologists (pres. 1991-93), Internat. Anesthesia Rsch. Soc. (trustee 1984—, sec. 1996-98, chair 1998-2000), Assn. Univ. Anesthesiologists, Soc. Acad. Anesthesia Chairmen (councillor 1989—), Assn. Cardiac Anesthesiologists. Avocations: tennis, sailing, swimming. Office: Emory U Hosp Dept Anes 1364 Clifton Rd NE Atlanta GA 30322-1061

WALLER, PETER WILLIAM, public affairs executive; b. Kewanee, Ill., Oct. 1, 1926; s. Ellis Julian and Barodel (Gould) W.; m. Anne-Marie Appelius van Hoboken, Nov. 10, 1950; children: Catherine, Hans. BA with hons., Princeton U., 1949; MA with hons., San Jose State U., 1978. Bur. chief Fairchild Publs., San Francisco, 1953-55; freelance writer Mountain View, Calif., 1956-57; pub. relations coord. Lockheed Missiles and Space, Sunnyvale, Calif., 1957-64; info. mgr. for 1st missions to Jupiter, Saturn, Venus NASA Ames Rsch. Ctr., Mountain View, 1964-83, mgr. pub. info., 1983-95; cons. NASA-Ames Galileo, Lunar Prospector, 1996-97; prodr. space films PacPAW Assoc., 1998—; speechwriter for pres. Lockheed Missiles and Space, 1960-64. Producer (documentary) Jupiter Odyssey, 1974 (Golden Eagle, 1974); producer, writer NASA Aero. program, 1984; contbr. articles to profl. jours, encyclopedias. Cons. on preservation of Lake Tahoe, Calif. Resources Agy., Sacramento, 1984. Mem. No. Calif. Sci. Writers Assn., Sierra Club. Democrat. Congregationalist. Avocations: skiing, travel, architecture, construction, hiking. Home: 3655 La Calle Ct Palo Alto CA 94306-2619

WALLER, PHILIP JOHN, history educator; b. Rochdale, Lancashire, Eng., Jan. 31, 1946; s. Eric and Marjorie (Atkinson) W.; m. Jane Christine O'Rafferty, Aug. 14, 1971; children—Matthew James, Amy Alexandra, Joseph Lawrence. B.A., Oxford U. Wadham Coll., 1967. Fellow by examination Magdalen Coll. Oxford U., 1968-71, fellow and tutor in modern history Merton Coll., 1971—; vis. prof. U. S.C., Columbia, 1979, Colo. Coll., Colorado Springs, 1985. Author: Democracy and Sectarianism, 1981; Town, City and Nation, 1983; editor: Politics and Social Change in Modern Britain, 1987, The English Urban Landscape, 2000; joint editor: Chronology of the Modern World, 1763-1992, 1994, Chronology of the 20th Century, 1995, rev. 1996. Office: Merton Coll, Oxford OX1 4JD, England

WALLER, WILHELMINE KIRBY (MRS. THOMAS MERCER WALLER), civic worker, organization official; b. N.Y.C., Jan. 19, 1914; d. Gustavus Town and Wilhelmine (Claflin) Kirby; m. Thomas Mercer Waller, Apr. 7, 1942. Ed., Chapin Sch., N.Y.C. Conservation chmn. Garden Club Am., 1959-61, pres., 1965-68, chmn. nat. affairs, 1968-74, dir., 1969-71; mem. adv. com. N.Y. State Conservation Commn., 1959-70; mem. Nat. Adv. Com. Hwy. Beautification, 1965-68; trustee Mianus River Gorge Conservation Com. of Nature Conservancy, 1955—, Arthur W. Butler Meml. Sanctuary, 1955-79; dir. Westchester County Soil and Water Conservation Dist., 1967-74; adviser N.Y. Gov.'s Study Commn. Future of Adirondacks, 1968-70; adv. com. N.Y. State Parks and Recreation Commn., 1971-72; adv. com. to sec. state UN Conf. Human Environment, 1971-72; mem. Pres.'s Citizens Adv. Com. on Environ. Quality, 1974-78. Mem. planning bd., Bedford, 1953-57; mem. Conservation adv. coun., Bedford, N.Y., 1968-70, Westchester County Planning Bd., 1970-88; bd. govs. Nature Conservancy, 1970-78; Mem. Lyndhurst council Nat. Trust for Historic Preservation, 1965-74; bd. dirs. Scenic Hudson, Inc., 1985-88. Recipient Frances K. Hutchinson medal Garden Club Am., 1971, Holiday mag. award for beautiful Am., 1971, Conservation award Am. Motors Corp., 1975, Oak Leaf award Nature Conservancy, 1988. Mem. Nat. Soc. Colonial Dames, Huguenot Soc. Am., Daus. of Cincinnati. Address: Tanrackin Farm Bedford Hills NY 10507

WALLER, WILMA RUTH, retired secondary school educator and librarian; b. Jacksonville, Tex., Nov. 15, 1921; d. William Wesley and Myrtle (Nesbitt) W. BA with honors, Tex. Woman's U., 1954, MA with honors, 1963, MLS with honors, 1976. Tchr. English Dell (Ark.) High Sch., 1953-54, Jefferson (Tex.) Ind. Schs., 1954-56, Tyler (Tex.) Ind. Schs., 1956-68; librarian Wise County Schs., Decatur, Tex., 1969-71, Thomas K. Gorman High Sch., Tyler, 1971-74, Sweetwater (Tex.) Ind. Sch. Dist., 1974-86; ret.; lectr., book reviewer for various clubs. Active in past as vol. for ARC, U. Tex. Health Ctr. Ford Found. fellow, 1959; recipient Delta Kappa Gamma Achievement award, 1992. Mem. UDC, Smith County Ret. Sch. Pers., Bible Study Group, Delta Kappa Gamma. Republican. Baptist. Avocations: reading, gourmet cooking, piano, writing letters. Home: 1117 N Azalea Dr Tyler TX 75701-5206

WALLERSTEIN, JUDITH SARETSKY, marriage and divorce researcher; b. N.Y.C., Dec. 27, 1921; d. Samuel Saretsky and Augusta (Tucker) Weinberger; m. Robert S. Wallerstein, Jan. 27, 1949; children: Michael, Nina, Amy. BA, CUNY, 1943; MS, Columbia U., 1946; PhD in Psychology, Lund (Sweden) U., 1978. Sr. lectr. U. Calif., Berkeley, 1966-91, sr. lectr. emeritus, 1991—; dir. Calif. Children of Divorce Project, Marin County, Calif., 1971—; founder, former exec. dir. Judith Wallerstein Ctr. Family in Transition, Corte Madera, Calif., 1980-93. Author 4 books; contbr. over 100 articles to profl. jours. Mem. adv. com. on family law Calif. Senate Subcom. on Adminstrn. of Justice, 1977-79; mem. task force on family equity Calif. State Senate, 1986. Recipient Koshland award in social welfare San Francisco Found., 1975, Renè Spitz award Denver Psychoanalytic Soc., 1991, Geri Taylor Meml. award No. Calif. Psychiat. Soc., 1993, Presdl. citation APA Divsn. Family Psychology, 1995, Dale Richmond award Am. Acad. Pediat., 1996, others; fellow Ctr. Advanced Study in the Behavioral Scis., Stanford, Calif., 1979-80, Rockefeller Found. Study Ctr., Bellagio, Italy, 1992. Mem. NASW, Am. Psychoanalytic Assn. (hon.), N.Y. Freudian Soc. (hon.), San Francisco Psychoanalytic Soc. (interdisciplinary mem.), Am. Orthopsychiat. Assn., Assn. Child Psychoanalysis (mem. exec. coun. 1977-80), Assn. Family Conciliation Cts., Phi Beta Kappa. Achievements include principle investigator follow-up study effects of divorce on children and their parents, study of good marriages.

WALLERSTEIN, ROBERT SOLOMON, psychiatrist; b. Berlin, Jan. 28, 1921; s. Lazar and Sarah (Guensberg) W.; m. Judith Hannah Saretsky, Jan. 26, 1947; children: Michael Jonathan, Nina Beth, Amy Lisa. BA, Columbia U., 1941, MD, 1944; postgrad., Topeka Inst. Psychoanalysis, 1951-58. Assoc. dir., then dir. rsch. Menninger Found., Topeka, 1954-66; chief psychiatry Mt. Zion Hosp., San Francisco, 1966-78; tng. and supervising analyst San Francisco Psychoanalytic Inst., 1966—; clin. prof. U. Calif. Sch. Medicine, Langley-Porter Neuropsychiat. Inst., 1967-75, prof., chmn. dept. psychiatry, also dir. inst., 1975-85, prof. dept. psychiatry, 1985-91, prof.

emeritus, 1991—; vis. prof. psychiatry La. State U. Sch. Medicine, also New Orleans Psychoanalytic Inst., 1972-73, Pahlavi U., Shiraz, Iran, 1977, Fed. U. Rio Grande do Sul, Porto Alegre, Brasil, 1980; mem., chmn. rsch. scientist career devel. com. NIMH, 1966-70; fellow Ctr. Advanced Study Behavioral Scis., Stanford, Calif., 1964-65, 81-82, Rockefeller Found. Study Ctr., Bellagio, Italy, 1992. Author 18 books and monographs; mem. editl. bd. numerous profl. jours.; contbr. over 275 articles to profl. jours. With AUS, 1946-48. Recipient Heinz Hartmann award N.Y. Psychoanalytic Inst., 1968, Disting. Alumnus award Menninger Sch. Psychiatry, 1972, J. Elliott Royer award U. Calif., San Francisco, 1973, Outstanding Achievement award No. Calif. Psychiat. Soc., 1987, Mt. Airy gold medal, 1990, Mary Singleton Sigourney award, 1991, Outstanding Contbn. to Psychoanalytic Edn. award Internat. Fedn. Psychoanalytic Edn., 1999. Fellow ACP, Am. Coll. Psychoanalysts, Am. Psychiat. Assn., Am. Orthopsychiat. Assn.; mem. Am. Psychoanlytic Assn. (pres. 1971-72), Internat. Psychoanalytic Assn. (v.p. 1977-85, pres. 1985-89, hon. v.p. 1999—), Group for Advancement Psychiatry, Mexican Psychoanalytic Assn. (hon.), Brit. Psycho-Analytical Soc. (hon.), Phi Beta Kappa, Alpha Omega Alpha. Home: 290 Beach Rd Belvedere CA 94920-2472

WALLGREN, CARITA CHRISTINA HELENA, lawyer; b. Ekenäs, Finland, Oct. 2, 1953; d. Åke Oskar Viking and Helena (Pitkänen) Lindholm; m. Georg Johan Wilhelm Wallgren, Aug. 7, 1976; children: Johanna Helena Antoinette, Sofia Karin Marie, Christina Wilhelmina Isabel. Student, W. Ga. Coll., 1974; Diploma English Philology, Polit. Sci., U. Helsinki, Finland, 1977, Diploma Roman Philology, French, 1977, LLM, 1979. Bar: Finland, 1983; trained at the bench, 1983. Rschr. U. Helsinki, Finland, 1979-81; trainee Surrey & Morse, Paris, 1979; assoc. lawyer S.G. Archibald, Paris, 1981-82; assoc. lawyer Roschier-Holmberg & Waselius, Attorneys Ltd., Helsinki, Finland, 1984-89, ptnr., 1989—; mem. legis. com. for Contracts Act Finnish Ministry of Justice, 1987-90; bd. dirs. The Spanish-Finnish Trade Assn., 1993-96. Author: Letters of Intent (Swedish), 1983. Mem. Internat. Bar Assn., Assn. Internat. des Jeunes Avocats, Juridiska Föreningen i Finland, Ctrl. C. of C. Finland (bd. dirs., bd. arbitration 1996—), Finnish Arbitration Assn. (bd. dirs. 1996—), Lex Mundi (bd. dirs 1996—). Lutheran. Achievements include languages spoken Finnish, Swedish, English, French. Avocations: traveling, literature, country life, tennis, skiing. Home: Armas Lindgrens väg 15 H, 00570 Helsinki Finland Office: Roschier-Holmberg & Waselius, Attorneys Ltd Keskuskatu 7A, 00100 Helsinki Finland

WALLGREN, GEORG RABBE, retired surgeon; b. Helsinki, Finland, Nov. 28, 1920; s. Georg-Wilhelm and Rea (Strahle) W.; m. Karin Synnove Molander, Apr. 1, 1950; children: Georg-Wilhelm, Jean-Peter, Jeanette, Christoffer. MD, U. Helsinki, 1948. Resident in surgery Kotka (Finland) Gen. Hosp., 1949-53; surgeon Univ. Children's Hosp., Helsinki, 1953-56; asst. chief surgeon Aurora Hosp., Helsinki, 1956-79, chief surgeon, 1979-83; surgeon Eira Hosp., Helsinki, 1964-85; prin. med. officer Fennia Ins. Co., Helsinki, 1964-85, Svensk-Finland Ins. Co., Helsinki, 1968-90. Contbr. articles to profl. jours. Decorated several war medals for disting. service; recipient ASLA-Fulbright scholarship Colo. Gen. Hosp., Denver, 1957; named Medicinalråd Pres. Koivisto of Finland, 1984. Mem. Brit. Assn. Pediatric Surgeons, German Pediatric Surgery Assn., Scandinavian Assn. Pediatric Surgeons (gen. sec. 1964-80, pres. 1980-86, hon. 1986), Sulamaa Soc. (chmn. 1980-82, hon. 1986). Lutheran. Club: Nylandska Jakt. Lodges: Masons, Rotary. Home: Parkgatan 11-A-13, 00140 Helsinki Finland

WALLGREN-PETTERSSON, CARINA, physician; b. Helsinki, Uusimaa, Finland, July 26, 1956; d. Henrik Wallgren and Carin Forsius-Wallgren; m. Tom E. Pettersson, 1980; children: Tobias, Katarina. MD, U. Helsinki, 1982, PhD, 1990, Specialist in Med. Genetics, 1994. Lic. physician, 1982. House officer in paediatrics Helsinki, 1982-84; researcher Children's Hosp./Univ. Helsinki, 1984-90; sr. registrar dept. med. genetics Väestöliitto, Helsinki, 1990-91; rsch. fellow Inst. Med. Genetics/Univ. Wales, Cardiff, U.K., 1991-92; sr. registrar Dep. Clin. Genetics Univ. Helsinki, 1992-94, researcher, 1994—; head of genetics The Folkhälsan Dept., 1995Ö; coord. ENMC Internat. Consortium on Myotubular Myopathy, 1993-99, ENMC Internat. Consortium on Nemaline Myopathy, 1996—. Contbr. articles to profl. jours. Mem. European Soc. Human Genetics, Clin. Genetics Soc. Office: Univ Helsinki Dept Med Genetics, PO Box 211, FIN00251 Helsinki Finland

WALLING, ARTHUR KNIGHT, orthopedist; b. Oskaloosa, Iowa, Apr. 25, 1950; m. Rebecca Lynn; children: Christopher Albert, Eleanor Eckhoff. BS, Iowa State U., 1972; MD, Creighton U., 1976. Diplomate Nat. Bd. Med. Examiners, Am. Bd. Orthopedic Surgeons. Resident in surgery Creighton Univ. Affiliated Hosps., Omaha, 1976-77; resident in orthopedic surgery U. South Fla. Affiliated Hosps., Tampa, 1977-80; fellow in musculoskeletal pathology U. Fla., 1980-81; clin. instr. U. Fla., Gainesville, 1981-82; acting chief orthopedic surgery James A. Haley VA Hosp., Tampa, 1982-85; chief orthopedic surgery H. Lee Moffitt Cancer Ctr., Tampa, 1985-89, 96—; clin. assoc. prof. U. South Fla., Tampa, 1989—; vis. asst. prof. U. So. Fla., 1982-85; dir. Tampa Orthopedic Program, 1991—; bd. dirs. Fla. Orthopedic Inst., 1989—; chief orthopedics H. Lee Moffitt Cancer Ctr., 1996—. Fellow Am. Acad. Orthopedic Surgeons; mem. AMA, Am. Orthopedic Assn., Am. Bone and Joint Surgeons, Am. Orthopedic Foot and Ankle Soc., Internat. Soc. Limb Salvage, So. Med. Assn., Southeast Oncology Group, So. Orthopedic Group, Assn. Bone & Joint Surgeons, Pediat. Oncology Group, Fla. Orthopedic Soc., Bay Area Orthopedic Soc., Pediat. Oncology Group, Hillsborough County Med. Soc., U. Fla. Orthopedic Assn., U. South Fla. Orthopedic Alumni Assn. Office: Fla Orthopedic Inst 4175 E Fowler Ave Tampa FL 33617-2011

WALLINGER, JOHN D(AVID) A(RNOLD), investment banker; b. Buenos Aires, May 1, 1940; (parents Brit. citizens); s. Sir Geoffrey Arnold Wallinger and Diana (Peel-Nelson) Clarabut; m. Rosamund Elizabeth Clifford-Wolff, Feb. 22, 1966; 1 child, Mark Robert Arnold. BA in French, German and History, Cambridge (Eng.) U., 1962. Various positions to gen. ptnr. Panmure Gordon, London, 1963-75; gen. ptnr. Rowe and Pitman, London, 1975-87; dir. S.G. Warburg Securities, London, 1987-93; vice chmn. S.G. Warburg Internat., London, 1993-96; exec. dir. SBC Warburg, London, 1996-99; cons. UBS A.G., 1999—; chmn. Gen. and Oriental Ltd., 1999—. Mem. Inst. Investment Mgmt. and Rsch. Anglican. Avocations: golf, fishing. Office: UBS AG, 1 Curzon St, London W1Y 7FN, England

WALLIS, BEN ALTON, JR., lawyer; b. Llano County, Tex., Apr. 27, 1936; s. Ben A. and Jessie Ella (Longbotham) W.; children from previous marriage: Ben a. III, M. Jessica; m. Joan Mery, 1987. BBA, U. Tex., 1961, JD, 1971; postgrad., Law Sch. So. Meth. U. Bar: Tex. 1966, U.S. Dist. Ct. (no. dist.) Tex. 1971, U.S. Ct. Appeals D.C. 1974, U.S. Dist. Ct. D.C. 1975, U.S. Dist. Ct. (we. dist.) Tex. 1975, U.S. Dist. Ct. (no. dist.) Calif. 1983, U.S. Ct. Appeals (5th cir.) 1975, U.S. Ct. Appeals (8th cir.) 1980, U.S. Ct. Appeals (11th cir.) 1981, U.S. Dist. Ct. (ea. dist.) Wis. 1983, U.S. Supreme Ct. 1974. Pvt. practice Llano, 1966-67, Dallas, 1971-73; investigator, prosecutor State Securities Bd. Tex., 1967-71; v.p. of devel. Club Corp. Am., Dallas, 1973; assoc. counsel impeachment task force U.S. Ho. of Reps. Com. on Judiciary, Washington, 1974; prin. Law Offices of Ben Wallis, P.C., San Antonio, 1974—. Chmn. Nat. Land Use Conf., 1979-81; mem. Gov.'s Areawide Planning Adv. Com., 1975-78; pres. Inst. Human Rights Rsch., 1979-2000. Mem. ATLA, FBA, Coll. of State Bar of Tex., State Bar Tex. (former chmn. agr. tax com.), D.C. Bar Assn., San Antonio Bar Assn., Delta Theta Phi, Delta Sigma Pi. Republican. Baptist. Office: GPM South Tower 800 NW Loop 410 Ste 350 San Antonio TX 78216-5619

WALLIS, KENNETH FRANK, econometrics educator; b. Mexborough, Yorkshire, Eng., Mar. 26, 1938; s. Leslie and Vera Daisy (Stone) W.; m. Margaret Sheila Campbell, July 26, 1963. BSc, Manchester (Eng.) U., 1959, MScTech, 1961; PhD, Stanford U., 1966; D (hon.), Groningen (Germany) U., 1999. Rsch. staff economist Yale U., New Haven, 1965-66; lectr./reader London Sch. Econs., 1966-77; prof. econometrics U. Warwick, Coventry, Eng., 1977—; chmn. H.M. Treasury Acad. Panel, London, 1987-91. Co-editor Econometrica, 1977-83; contbr. sci. articles to profl. jours.; author various textbooks. Coun. mem. Royal Statis. Soc., 1972-76. Fellow Econometric Soc., 1975. Fellow Brit. Acad.; mem. Royal Econ. Soc. (coun. mem. 1989-94). Home: 4 Walkers Orchard, Stoneleigh, Coventry CV8 3JG, England Office: U Warwick, Dept of Econs, Coventry CV4 7AL, England

WALLISER, OTTO HEINRICH, paleontology educator; b. Krettenbach, Germany, Mar. 3, 1928; s. Wilhelm and Martha (Fahr) W.; m. Edith H. Grill, Aug. 24, 1954; children: Thomas W., Matthias O. Diploma in geology, U. Tübingen, Germany, 1954, D Natural Scis., 1954; D Habilitation, U. Marburg, Germany, 196l. Asst. prof. U. Marburg, 1954-65; prof. paleontology U. Göttingen, Germany, 1965—, head dept. geology and paleontology, 1965-93; leader project 216, Internat. Geol. Correlation Program, 1984-91. Author, editor numerous books on paleontology and geology, Devonian, Variscides and evolution; contbr. numerous articles to profl. jours. Mem. Paläontologische Gesellschaft (pres. 1974-76), Internat. Paleontol. Soc. (sec. gen. 1976-84), Acad. Scis. Göttingen, Russia, Krakow and Warsaw, Poland. Office: Inst Geol Paleontology, Goldschmidt Strasse 3, D-37077 Göttingen Federal Republic of Germany

WALLMAN, CHARLES JAMES, historian; b. Kiel, Wis., Feb. 19, 1924; s. Charles A. and Mary Ann (Loftus) W.; m. Charline Marie Moore, June 14, 1952; children: Stephen, Jeffrey, Susan, Patricia, Andrew. Student, Marquette U., 1942-43, Tex. Coll. Mines, 1943-44; BBA, U. Wis., 1949. Sales promotion mgr. Brandt, Inc., Watertown, Wis., 1949-65, v.p., 1960-70, exec. v.p., 1970-80, v.p. corp. devel., 1980-83; guest spkr. dept. German, U. Wis., Madison, 1987, Watertown H.S., 1986-99; former dir., former sec. The Friends of the Max Kade Inst. for German Am. studies U. Wis., Madison. Author: Edward J. Brandt, Inventor, 1984, Pioneer Memoirs of Early Watertown, 1986, The Joe Davies Scholars, 1988, The German-Speaking Forty-Eighters: Builders of Watertown, Wisconsin, 1990, Built on Irish Faith, 150 Years at St. Bernard's, 1994, Combat. . .and More, 1996, (with others) The Prisoners of War of the 12th Armored Division, 1988. Former mem. exec. bd. Potawatomi coun. Boy Scouts Am., also former v.p. coun.; former bd. dirs., former pres. Earl and Eugenia Quirk Found., Inc.; trustee, mem. Joe Davies Scholarship Found.; writer history Watertown Country Club 75th Anniversary Program, 1997; former bd. dirs., former mem. exec. com. Watertown Meml. Hosp., now dir. emeritus. Served with armored inf. AUS, 1943-45; ETO. Decorated Bronze Star; recipient Local History award of Merit State Hist. Soc. Wis., 1994. Mem. Am. Legion (life), East Ctrl. Golf Assn. (past pres.), Wis. Alumni Assn. (local pres. 1950-52, 89-91, bd. dirs. nat. orgn. 1989-91), 12th Armored Divsn. Assn. (life), Watertown Hist. Soc. (life; past bd. dirs.), Am. Ex-Prisoners of War Inc. (life), Watertown Country Club (past bd. dir.), Rotary (past pres., former bd. dirs., Paul Harris fellow), Elks (life; past officer), Phi Delta Theta (mem. Golden Legion). Home: 604 Votech Dr Watertown WI 53098-1124

WALLMANN, JEFFREY MINER, author; b. Seattle, Dec. 5, 1941; s. George Rudolph and Elizabeth (Biggs) W. BS, Portland State U., 1962; PhD, U. Nev., 1998. Pvt. investigator Dale Sys., N.Y.C., 1962-63; asst. buyer, mgr., pub. money bidder Dohrmann Co., San Francisco, 1966-69; dir. pub. rels. London Films, Cinelux-Universal, Trans-European Publs., 1970-75; editor-in-chief Riviera Life mag., 1975-77; instr. U. Nev., Reno, 1990—, Las Vegas, 1998—; cons. Mktg. Svcs. Internat., 1978—. Author: The Spiral Web, 1969, Judas Cross, 1974, Clean Sweep, 1976, Jamaica, 1977, Deathtrek, 1980, Blood and Passion, 1980, Brand of the Damned, 1981, The Manipulator, 1982, Return to Conta Lupe, 1983, The Celluloid Kid, 1984, Business Basic for Bunglers, 1984, Guide to Applications Basic, 1984, The Western: Parables of the American Dream, 1999, (under pseudonym Leon DaSilva) Green Hell, 1976, Breakout in Angola, 1977, (under pseudonym Nick Carger) Hour of the Wolf, 1973, Ice Trap Terror, 1974, (under pseudonym Margaret Maitland) The Trial, 1974, Come Slowly, Eden, 1974, How Deep My Cup, 1975, (under pseudonym Amanda Hart Douglass) First Rapture, 1972, Jamaica!, 1978, (under pseudonym Grant Roberts) The Reluctant Couple, 1969, Wayward Wives, 1970, (under pseudonym Gregory St. Germain) Resistance # 1: Night and Fog, 1982, Resistance #2: Magyar Massacre, 1983, (pseudonym Wesley Ellis) Lonestar on the Treachery Trail, 1982, numerous others, (pseudonym Tabor Evans) Longarm and the Lonestar Showdown, 1986, (pseudonym Jon Sharpe) Trailsman 58: Slaughter Express, 1986, numerous others in Trailsman series, also others under pseudonyms; co-author, under pseudonym William Jeffrey) Duel at Gold Buttes, 1980, Border Fever, 1982, Day of the Moon, 1983, The Western: Parables of the American Dream, 1999; contbr. articles and short stories to Argosy, Ellery Queen's Mystery Mag., Alfred Hitchcock's Mystery Mag., Zane Grey Western, Venture, Oui, TV Guide. Mem. Mystery Writers Am., Sci. fiction Writers Am., We. Writers Am., Nat. Coun. tchrs. English, Crime Writers Am., Nev. state Coun. Tchrs. English, Esperanto League N.Am., We. Lit. Assn., Internacia Soc. Amikeco Kaj Bonvolo, Sci. Fiction Rsch. Assn., Internat. Assn. Fantastic in the Arts, We. Lit. Assn. Office: care of Barry Malzberg PO Box 61 Teaneck NJ 07666-0061

WALLNER, FRANZ, engineer; b. Berlin, Mar. 24, 1937; s. Franz and Kundry (Siewert) Wallner-Basté. Diploma in engring., Tech. U. Berlin, 1964, DEng, 1970. Rsch. fellow Tech. U. Berlin, 1964-69, prof. automobile engring., 1974—; rsch. fellow Westend Surg. Clinic, Westend Surg. Clinic, Free U. Berlin, 1969-75; pres. BMT Messtechnik GmbH, Berlin, 1976—. Contbr. numerous articles on automobile and artificial heart rsch. and bioengring. to profl. jours. Mem. Soc. Automotive Engrs., Verein Deutscher Ingenieure, Verein Deutscher Elektrotechniker, Internat. Ozone Assn., Reitclub Grunewald, Brandenburger Hunting Club. Home and Office: Argentinische Allee 32a, D-14163 Berlin Zehlendorf, Germany

WALLNER, FRIEDRICH, philosopher, educator; b. Weiten, Austria, July 21, 1945; s. Alois Pehm and Theresia W.; m. Rosemarie Micka, Apr. 12, 1973; children: Christian, Monika. MA, U. Vienna, Austria, 1969, PhD, 1972, Habilitation, 1981. Secondary tchr. Bundesoberstufenrealgymnasium, Wiener Neustadt, Austria, 1969-87; asst. prof. philosophy U. Vienna, 1981-87, prof., 1987—; speaker Wittgenstein Conf., Kirchberg, Austria, 1977-86; lectr. sci confs. Europe and N.Am., 1981—; organizer Popper Conf., Vienna, 1983; speaker advanced tng. for tchrs. Austrian Ministry Edn., 1983—; founder Inst. Constructive Realism, 2000. Author: Philosophical Problems of Physics, 1980, 2d edit., 1982, Boundaries of Language and Knowledge, 1983, The Philosophical Life-Work of Wittsenstein as Unity, 1983, Philosophy and Science, 1985 (book series) Philosophica, 1985—. Recipient Innitzerpreis Roman Cath. Ch., Vienna, 1984, Körnerpreis Pres. of Austria, 1985, sci. stipend City of Vienna, 1986. Mem. Kant Soc., Hegel Soc., Soc. German Philosophers, Soc. Austrian Philosophers. Roman Catholic. Avocations: bicycling, swimming, jogging. Home: Renngasse 10, A 2604 Theresienfeld Austria Office: U Vienna Inst Wissenschaftstheorie, Sensengasse 8 und Wissenschaftsforschung, A-1090 Vienna Austria

WALLNOFER, HEINRICH, physician; b. Klagenfurt, Austria, June 27, 1920; s. Franz and Auguste (Scherrl) W.; m. Lorenza Pichler Mandorf, 1943; children: Peter, Anton, Maria Donata Bayer. MD, U. Vienna, 1948. Diplomate in psychotherapy, psychosomatic. Dir. Margareten and Urania Adult Colls., Vienna, 1945-48; with Inst. of Hygiene U. Vienna, 1948-49; with Heart Disease Clin., Vienna, 1949-60; asst. phys. Cardiol. Hosp., Vienna, 1948-60; dir. dept. psychosomatic medicine HFI/U. Innsbruck, 1966-88; dir. Internat. Coll. for Autogenic Tng., Austria, 1969-75; pvt. practice psychotherapy Vienna, 1948—; lectr. U. Vienna, U. Innsbruck, U. Fribour; guest rschr. Komazawa U., Tokyo; physician, Nolan D.C. Lewis vis. prof. Carrier Found., Belle Mead, N.J. Co-author: Golden Treasury of Chinese Medicine, 30 other books; contbr. numerous articles to profl. jours. and publs.; patentee for re-animation apparatus. Leader Austrian Legitimist Resistance, Carinthia, WWII. Lt. comdr. Austrian Res. Air Force. Recipient High Off., Order of St. George of Carinthia. Mem. Austrian Soc. for Med. Hypnosis and Autogenic Tng. (founder, first pres., hon. pres.), German Soc. for Med. Hypnosis and Autogenic Tng., Internat. Comm. for Coord. Clin. Application and Tgn. of Autogenic Therapy, Japanese Soc. Autogenic Tng. (hon.). Avocations: sailing, Chinese philosophy, music. E-mail: h.wallnoefer@abacus.at. Office: U Tokyo, Pyrkergasse 23, 1190 Wien Austria

WALLNY, HANS JOACHIM, biochemist, science administrator; b. Esslinger/Neckar, Germany, May 15, 1962; s. Franz Josef W. and Helga Meta (Wittig) W.-Strohm; m. Mechthild Schlipf, June 8, 1990; children: David Benedikt, Simon Julian. Diplom Biochemist, U. Tübingen (Germany), 1990, PhD, 1992. Scientist Basel (Switzerland) Inst. Immunology, 1992-95; lab. mgr. Biotest Pharma GmbH, Dreieich, Germany, 1995-97, Novartis Pharma AG, Basel, 1997—. Contbr. chpts. to books, articles to profl. jours. Recipient Award for Students Hoechst AG, 1991. Mem. Soc. for Biochemistry and Molecular Biology. Avocations: volleyball, biking. Office: Novartis Pharma AG, WKL-681 3 46, CH4002 Basel Switzerland

WALLOT, GEORGE PAUL, electronics engineer; b. Mt. Vernon, Ohio, Nov. 15, 1941; s. George Armond and Madeleine Elizabeth (Lambillotte) W.; m. Ellen Maxine Jones, Feb. 9, 1963 (div. Mar. 1990); 1 child, Paula. BEE, Ohio Northern U., 1969. Sr. devel. engr. Gen. Electric Co., Fort Wayne, Ind., 1969-81; project mgr. Zenith Electronics Corp., Glenview, Ill., 1981-92; v.p. mfg. EOS Corp., Camarillo, Calif., 1992-95; dir. mfg. engring. Condor Inc., Oxnard, Calif., 1995-97; mgr. engring. Invensys, San Diego, 1997—. Patentee in field. With U.S. Army 1962-64. Mem. Tau Beta Pi (engring. hon. soc.), Phi Kappa Phi (acad. hon. soc.). Avocation: computing. E-mail: gwallot@hotmail.com. Home: 2042 N Nutmeg St Escondido CA 92026-3316 Office: Invensys 2727 Kurtz St San Diego CA 92110-3109

WALLOT, JEAN-PIERRE, archivist, historian; b. Valleyfield, Que., Can., May 22, 1935; s. Albert and Adrienne (Thibodeau) W.; m. Denyse Caron; children: Normand, Robert, Sylvie. BA, Coll. Valleyfield, 1954; lic. es lettres, U. Montreal, 1957, MA in History, 1957, PhD in History, 1965; D (hon.), U. Rennes, France, 1987, U. Ottawa, Can., 1996. Reporter Le Progres de Valleyfield, 1954-61; from lectr. to prof. dept. history U. Montreal, 1961-85, dept. chmn., 1973-75, vice-dean studies faculty arts and scis., 1975-78, vice-dean research Faculty Arts and Scis, 1979-82, academic v.p., 1982-85; nat. archivist, Can., 1985-97; historian Nat. Mus. Man, Ottawa, Ont., 1966-69, assoc. prof. U. Toronto, 1969-71; prof. Concordia U., Montreal, Que., 1971-73; vis. prof. U. Ottawa, 1997—, dir. Ctr. de Rsch. en Civilisation Canadienne-Francaise, 2000—; dir. Etude Assn. Ecole Pratique des Hautes Etudes en Scis. Sociales, Paris, 1975, 79, 81, 83, 85, 87, 89, 94. Author: Intrigues françaises et americaines au Canada, 1965, (with John Hare) Les Imprimés dans le Bas-Canada, 1967, Confrontations, 1971, (with G. Paquet) Patronage et Pouvoir dans le Bas-Canada, 1973; Un Quebec qui bougeait, 1973; Editor: (with R. Girard) Memoires de J.E. McComber, bourgeois de Montréal, 1981; (with J. Goy) Evolution et eclatement du monde rural, 1986. Pres. internat. adv. com. on memory of the world, UNESCO, 1993-98. Decorated officer Order Arts et Lettres (France); officer Order of Can.; recipient Marie Tremaine medal, 1973, Tyrrell medal, 1982, Royal Soc. Centenary medal, 1994, Jacques Ducharme prize, 1997. Fellow Royal Soc. Can. (sect. pres. 1985-87, pres. 1997-99); mem. Am. Antiquarian Soc., Acad. des Lettres du Quebec, Inst. d'Histoire l'Amerique Francaise (pres. 1973-77), Can. Hist. Assn. (pres. 1982), Assn. Can.-Francaise l'Avancement Scis. (pres. 1981-83, emeritus mem.), Assn. Archivists Que., Assn. Can. Archivists, Internat. Coun. on Archives (v.p. 1988-92, pres. 1992-96, pres. emeritus). Roman Catholic. Office: U Ottawa Inst Can Studies, PO Box 450 Sta A, Ottawa, ON Canada K1N 6N5

WALLS, CARMAGE LEE, JR., newspaper publisher/executive, consultant; b. Cleveland, Tenn., May 4, 1962; s. Carmage Lee Walls Sr. and Sarah (Smith) Bailey; m. Jeanne Marie Waller, June 4, 1989; children: Courtney Marie, Kathryn Jessica. BA in Journalism and English, U. Ala., Birmingham, 1988. Writer Birmingham News, 1987; exec. v.p. Cleveland Newspapers Inc., Birmingham, 1989—; pres., creative dir. Walls New Media, Inc., 1997—. Republican. United Methodist.

WALLS, JAMES DOUGLAS, minister; b. Washington, Aug. 1, 1931; s. George Washington and Emma (Benson) W.; m. Donna Marie Payne, June 16, 1962; children: Quentin Douglas, Janice Marie. Student, Washington Bible Inst., 1957-61; DD, Faith Evangelistic Christian Coll., Detroit, 1990, So. Calif. Sch. Ministry, Inglewood, 1991; HHD (hon.), Faith Evang. Christian Schs., Detroit, 1991. Ordained to ministry Ch. of God, 1960. Pastor Ch. of God, Xenia, Ohio, 1968—; mem. program and planning com., nominating com. Nat. Assn. Ch. of God, West Middlesex, Pa., 1983-89, coord. nat. preachers clinic, 1984—, mem. mass comm. bd., 1988-92, mem. ch. rels. bd., 1989-93; chair. bd. dirs. Women's Abuse of Substance Intervention Tactics, 1990-94. Editor Words of Truth, 1972-84, Xenia Herald, 1988—. Mem. Cumberland Ridge Civic Assn., Columbus, Ohio, 1971—. With U.S. Army, 1952-54. Mem. Urban Christian Leadership Assn., Xenia Area Assn. Chs., African Am. Ministerial Alliance, Ohio State Ch. of God Missionary Bd. Home: 3032 Pine Valley Rd Columbus OH 43219-1643

WALLS, MARTHA ANN WILLIAMS (MRS. B. CARMAGE WALLS), newspaper executive; b. Gadsden, Ala., Apr. 21, 1927; d. Aubrey Joseph and Inez (Cooper) Williams; m. B. Carmage Walls, Jan. 2, 1954; children: Byrd Cooper, Lissa Walls Vahldiek. Student pub. schs., Gadsden. Pres., dir. Walls Newspapers, Inc., 1969-70; sec., treas., dir. Summer Camps, Inc., Guntersville, Ala., 1954-69; CEO, pres., dir. So. Newspapers, Inc., Houston, 1970—; pres., dir. So. Newspapers of Ala., Inc., Scottsboro; v.p., dir. Ft. Payne (Ala.) Newspapers, Inc. Bay City (Tex.) Newspapers, Inc., Galveston Newspapers, Inc.; dir. Monroe (Ga.) Newspapers, Inc.; sec., dir. Mil. Publs., Inc., Portales, N.Mex.; bd. dirs. Jefferson Pilot Corp., Greensboro, N.C., 1990-98, Jefferson-Pilot Life Ins. Co., 1990-98, Jefferson Pilot Comm., 1990-98. Bd. dirs. Montgomery Acad., 1970-74. Mem. Soc. Profl. Journalists, The Houstonian. Episcopalian. Office: So Newspapers Inc 1050 Wilcrest Dr Houston TX 77042-1608

WALLY, YOUSSEF AMIN, Egyptian government official; b. Cairo, Apr. 2, 1931. BSc in Agr., Cairo U., 1951, MSc in Horticulture, 1955, PhD in Horticulture, 1958. Prof. horticulture dept. Ain Shams U., until 1982; min. of state for agr. and food security Govt. of Egypt, Cairo, 1982-87, dep. prime min., 1985—, min. agr. and land reclamation, 1987—; cons. on agr. to the Libyan Govt., 1962; pres. Mediterranean Group of Plant Physiology, World Food Coun., 1989-92. Editor Egyptian Jour. of Horticulture, 1973—, Agr. Annals, 1982—; author books on horticulture; contbr. articles to profl. jours. Gen. sec. Nat. Dem. Party; cons. Ministry of Sci. Rsch. and Ministry of Agr. and Land Reclamation, 1969-82. Mem. AAAS, Am. Soc. for Hort. Sci., Scandinavian Soc. for Plant Physiology, Egyptian Horticulture Soc. (chmn. bd.). Office: Min of Agr, Sharia Nisaret al-Ziraa, Dokki 702677, Egypt*

WALMSLEY, JULIAN KENNETH, economist, consultant, software developer; b. Bangor, Northern Ireland, Nov. 21, 1948; s. Kenneth M. and Kathleen M. (Patterson) W.; m. Danena J. Wrightson-Hunt, Aug. 8, 1976. BA in Econs., Cambridge (Eng.) U., 1970. CFA. Economist Barclays Bank, London, 1970-77, econ. advisor, 1977-81; v.p. Barclays Bank, N.Y.C., 1981-86; dir. Panmure Gordon Bankers, London, 1986-88; sr. investment officer Oil Ins., Hamilton, Bermuda, 1988-90; chief investment officer Mitsubishi Fin., London, 1990-91; mng. dir. Askeaton Assocs., Ltd., London, 1991—; hon. fellow Isma Ctr., U. Reading, Eng., 1992—. Author: Dictionary of International Finance, 1979, Foreign Exchange and Money Markets Handbook, 1983, 3d edit., 2000, Global Investing, 1990, New Financial Instruments, 1986, 2d edit., 1998, The Repo Market in Euro: Making it Work, 1997, New Frontiers in Clearing and Settlement, 1999; editor newsletter The Euro Zone, 1997—. Mem. Assn. for Investment Mgmt. and Rsch., Chartered Inst. Bankers U.K. Avocations: theatre, art galleries. Home: Duncliffe Church St, West Stour, Dorset SP8 5RL, England

WALOTSKY, RON, illustrator; b. Bklyn., Aug. 21, 1943; s. Joe and Rebecca (Cohen) W., divorced; 1 child, Lennon. Student, Sch. of Visual Arts, 1962-66. Illustrator Fantasy and Sci. Fiction Mag., Cornwall, Conn., 1967—, St. Martins Press, N.Y.C., 1989—, Avon Books, N.Y.C., 1970—, Doubleday Book and Music Club, N.Y.C., 1980—, TOR Books, N.Y.C., 1980—; tchr. Sullivan County C.C., Hurleyville, N.Y., 1981-82, Daytona C.C., 2000—. One-man shows include Herst Gallery, Long Island, N.Y., 1967, Spectrum Gallery, N.Y.C., 1969, West Beth, N.Y.C., 1972, John O'Rourke Gallery, N.Y.C., 1977, Martin Mulinary Gallery, N.Y.C., 1987, The Pike St. Arts Ctr., Port Jervis, N.Y., 1990; exhibited in group shows at The Pendragon Gallery, L.A. and Annapolis, Md., 1986, Bryce Gallery, Phila., 1988, York Atrium, N.Y.C., 1989-90, Works of Wonder Gallery, Washington, 1992-99, Canton (Ohio) Art Inst., 1996, Ormond Beach Art Mus., 1997-98, Butterfield Garage Gallery, 2000; author: Inner Visions The Art of Ron Walotsky, 2000. Recipient Frank R. Paul award, Kublacon, Nashville, Tenn., 1987, first prize Boscon, Boston, 1986; first prize I.S.D.C., 1988, first prize Lunacon, N.Y., 1988, 1st prize in painting Oasis, 1994; named guest artist U.S. Cultural Ctr., U.S. Embassy, Paris, France, 1979; given Key to City, New Orleans, 1994; Hugo Award nominee, 1996. Mem.

Graphic Artist Guild, Assn. Sci. Fiction Artists. E-mail: walotsky@arpent.com. Home: 3634 S Central Ave Flagler Beach FL 32136-4117

WALPEN, LAURENT, chief of police, lawyer; b. Sion, Switzerland, Apr. 14, 1950; s. Albert and Cecile (Besse) W.; m. Monique Jocelyne Clivaz, Jan. 14, 1952; three children. LLB, U. Lausanne, 1975; LLD (hon.), U. Western Ill., 1995. Police commr. Police of Geneva, Switzerland, 1978-85; police chief Police of Valais, Switzerland, 1985-89, Police of Geneva, 1989—; dir. of investigations UN Internat. Criminal Tribunal for Rwanda, Kigali. Mem. Internat. Police Assn., Swiss Criminal Law Soc., Internat. Assn. Chiefs of Police, Rotary. Roman Catholic. Avocations: precious stones, jazz, fly fishing, hiking, golf. Office: UN ICTR, Box 749, Kigali Rawanda

WALRAVENS, JAN, foreign language educator; b. Duffel, Belgium, June 28, 1957; s. Frans and Angela (Steylaerts) W.; m. Christel Idon, Dec. 12, 1981; children: Nils, Nina. MA, U. Iowa, 1982; DPhil, U. Brussels, 1991. Teaching asst. U. Brussels, 1985-91; prof. Haute Ecole F. Ferrer, Brussels, 1991—; adj. prof. Vesalius Coll, Belgium, 1988—. Co-author: Uit Jezelf, 1987; co-editor: Literaire Escapades, 1996; translator: (plays) A Streetcar Named Desire, 1989, Solo, 1997. Mem. Belgian Luxemburg Am. Studies Assn., Assn. des Neerlandistes de Belgique francophone. Avocations: theater, film. Office: Haute Ecole F Ferrer, Pl Anneessens 11, 1000 Brussels Belgium

WALROND, ERROL RICARDO, surgeon; b. Mar. 19, 1936; m. Beverley Walrond; children: Maurice, Maya. BS in Anatomy with honors, London U., 1958; Degree, Conjoint Coll. Royal Coll. Physicians and Surgeons Eng., 1960; MB, BS, London U., 1961; FRCS, Royal Coll. Surgeons Eng., 1964. House physician Guy's Hosp., London, 1960-61, ENT house surgeon, 1961; house surgeon Putney Hosp., London, 1961-62, casualty officer, 1962-63; surg. registrar Alton (Eng.) and Lord Mayor Treloars Hosp., 1963-65; sr. surg. registrar Queen Elizabeth Hosp., Barbados, 1965-66, U. Hosp., Jamaica, 1966-67; commonwealth fellow thoracic surg. dept. Guy's Hops., London, 1967-68; lectr. dept. surgery U. W.I., Mona, Jamaica, 1968—, sr. lectr. dept. surgery, 1971-76, prof. surgery, 1976-96; vice-dean faculty of medicine U. W.I., Barbados, 1977-86, dean faculty med. scis., 1986-92, 96—; sci. sec. of Commonwealth Caribbean Med. Rsch. coun., 1973-99; appt. mem. expert adv. panel health manpower WHO, 1980-92; mem. coun. Caribbean Rsch. and Epidemiology Ctr., 1979-99; chmn. Med. Coun., Barbados, 1985-87, 92-96. Editor: BAMP Bulletin, 1983-85; contbr. numerous articles to profl. jours. Fellow ACS; mem. Assn. Surgeons Jamaica (sec. 1964-73), Barbados Assn. Med. Practitioners (v.p., chmn. ethical com. 1975-76, pres. 1976-82, v.p. 1982-87, chmn. task force on AIDS, nat. adv. com. on AIDS 1987-94, Companion of Honor Barbados 1990). Home: 34 Sandy Ln, Saint James Barbados Office: U WI, Faculty Med Scis, Bridgetown Barbados

WALSA, ROBERT EDMUND, neurologist; b. Budapest, Aug. 11, 1923; s. Elmer and Ann (Czakler) W.; m. Martha Maria Szikszai, Oct. 21, 1950 (div. 1968); 1 child, Martha; m. Melinda Barbara Gaspar, Apr. 25, 1981. MD, U. Scis., Budapest, 1948; neurologist, Semmelweis U., 1953, psychiatrist, 1961; candidate of medicine, Acad. Scis., 1969; electroencephalography EEG specialist, Hungary Postgrad. U., 1979. Chief med. officer, EEG cons. Ctrl. Army Hosp., Budapest, 1954-83; EEG cons. Hungarian Transport Svcs. and Budapest Traffic Svc., 1954-83. Contbr. Hungarian Med. Jour., 1971; editor Hungarian Jour., 1991—; contbr. numerous articles to profl. jours. Recipient Markusovszky prize Hungarian Med. Jour. Editl. Bd., 1964, 68, 87, 93, Lissak medal Bd. of the Hungarian EEG Soc., 1987. Home: Pasaréti ut 79, 1026 Budapest Hungary Office: Orvosi Hetilap, Muzeum u 9, 1088 Budapest Hungary

WALSER, MARTIN, writer; b. Wasserburg-Bodensee, Mar. 24, 1927; s. Martin and Augusta (Schmid) W.; m. Kathie Jehle, 1950; 4 daughters. Ed. Theologische-Philosophische, U. Tubngen. Writer, 1951—. Publs. include: (short stories) Ein Flugzeug uber dem Haus, 1955, Lugengeschichten, 1964; (novels) Ehen in Philippsburg, 1957, Halbzeit, 1960, Das Einhorn, 1966, Fiction, 1970, Die Gallistl'sche Krankheit, 1972, Der Sturz, 1973, Jenseits der Liebe, 1976, Ein filehendes Pferd, 1978, Seelenarbeit, 1979, Das Schwanenhaus, 1980, Brief an Lord Liszt, 1981, Brandung, 1985, Dorle und Wolf, 1987, Jagd, 1988, Die Verteidigung der Kinheit, 1991, Ohne Einander, 1994, Finks Krieg, 1996, Ein Springender Brunnen, 1998; (plays) Der Abstecher, 1961, Eiche und Angora, 1962, Uberlebensgross Herr Krott, 1963; Der schwarze Schwan, 1964, Die Zimmerschlacht, 1967, Ein Kinderspiel, 1970, Das Sauspiel, 1975, In Goethes Hand, 1982, Die Ohrfeige, 1986, Das Sofa, 1993, Kaschmir in Parching, 1997; (essays) Beschreibung einer Form, Versuch uber Franz Kafka, 1961, Erfahrungen und Leseerfahrungen, 1965, Heimatkunde, 1968, Wie und wovon handelt Literatur, 1973, Wer ist ein Schriftsteller, 1978; (poems) Der Grund zur Freude, 1978; (essay) Uber Ironie, 1981, Liebeserklaerungen, 1983, Gestaendnis auf Raten, 1986, Vormittag eines Schriftstellers, 1994, Ich vertraue.Querfeldein, 2000. Decorated Orden pur le Mérite; recipient Group 47 prize, 1955, Hermann-Hesse prize, 1957, Schiller prize, 1980, G. Buechner prize, 1981, Hoelderlin prize, 1996, Peace prize German Booksellers, 1998. Address: Zum Hecht 36, Nussdorf Überlingen 88662, Germany

WALSER, PETER, mining engineer; b. Linz, Upper Austria, Austria, May 22, 1943; s. Andreas and Elisabeth (Hagleitner) W.; m. Nora Lohmann, Oct. 13, 1970 (dec. 1990); children: Ingrid, Gudrun, Gerfried; m. Maria Hörbiger, Nov. 26, 1999. BS, Mining U., Leoben, Austria, 1968, PhD, 1970. Site mgr. Bauxit Parnasse, Greece, 1969; exploration asst. Mining U., Leoben, 1970; exploration mgr. Sabina Mines Ltd., Can., 1971-72; mine mgr. GKB Fohnsdorf, Austria, 1972-76, Gold Mine Minerven, Venezuela, 1977-78; site mgr. Arge Bosruck Tunnel, Austria, 1979-80; mine mgr. WBH Tungsten Mine Mittersill, Austria, 1980-87, gen. mgr., 1987—. Mem. Sport Club Mittersill (pres. 1982-90), Freunde der Montan U., Bergmann Verein Osterreich. Roman Catholic. Club: VDST (Leoben). Avocations: skiing, tennis, mountaineering, golfing. Office: Wolfram Bergbau, A5730 Mittersill Austria

WALSH, ARTHUR CAMPBELL, psychiatrist; b. Vancouver, B.C., Can., Dec. 21, 1919; came to U.S., 1964; s. William Charles and Kathleen (Patterson) W.; m. Bernice Martha Hessom, Dec. 26, 1944; children: Kathleen, David, Thomas. MD, U. Alta., Edmonton, 1943. Intern Vancouver Gen. Hosp., B.C., 1943; pvt. practice Vancouver, B.C., 1964-67; resident psychiatry U. Pitts., 1967-99, clin. asst. prof. psychiatry, 1967-99; semi-ret., 1999; pvt. practice Pitts., 1969-2000; pres. Ctr. Senility Studies Alzheimer Treatment Rsch. Ctr., Pitts., 1969-98; psychiat. cons. VA, Pitts., 1969-89, Woodville State Hosp., Pitts., 1969-86. Author: Conquering Senility; co-author: Mental Capacity: Legal and Medical Aspects of Assessment and Treatment, 2nd edit., 1999; contbr. med. articles to profl. jours. With Royal Can. Army Med. Corps, 1943-45. Mem. AMA, Am. Psychiat. Assn., Pa. Med. Soc. Home and Office: 279 Norman Dr Cranberry Township PA 16066-4235

WALSH, CRAIG WILKINSON, food products company executive; b. Honolulu, May 11, 1949; s. John Joseph and Shirley Rae (Wilkinson) W.; m. Marcia Ellen Chapman, Mar. 12, 1971 (div. Jan. 1986); 1 child, Chase Wilkinson; m. Marjorie Janet Wilson, Apr. 26, 1986. BSc, Rensselaer Poly. Inst., 1970. Security analyst Security Pacific Nat. Bank, L.A., 1970-71; underwriter Prudential Ins. Co., Newark, 1971-74; from credit analyst to asst. v.p. corp. banking Bank of Hawaii, Honolulu, 1975-84; v.p. comml. loans Aloha Nat. Bank, Kihei, Hawaii, 1984-85; dir. Transax plc, Birmingham, Eng., 1986-96; pres. The Poi Co., Honolulu, 1997—; bd. dirs. Transax (Ireland) Ltd., Dublin, Transax Australia PLC, Adelaide, Retail Credit Mgmt. Ltd., Birmingham, Transax Ltd., Auckland, New Zealand. Republican. Office: The Poi Co Inc 749 Kopke St Honolulu HI 96819-3316

WALSH, DAVID JAMES, lawyer; b. Dubuque, Iowa, Aug. 10, 1949; s. James and Helen Walsh; m. Alice Chebba; children: Elizabeth, James. BA, Loras Coll., 1971; JD, U. Wis., 1974; MBA, Alaska Pacific U., 1990; postgrad. in Internat. Bus., City U. London, 1991. Bar: Wis. 1974, Alaska 1975. Asst. dist. atty. State of Alaska, Anchorage, 1975-78; pvt. practice Anchorage, 1974-75, 78-90; co-founder, chmn. exec. com. Internat. Assn. Ins. Suprs., 1992-95; dir. ins. State of Alaska, 1990-95; gen. counsel Domestic Brokerage Group Am. Internat. Group, N.Y.C., 1995-98; pres. Nat. Assn. Ins. Commrs., 1994; exec. v.p., corp. counsel Swiss Re Life & Health, Stamford, CT; mem. Gov.'s Transition Team, 1982-83; mem. U.S./Alaska R.R. Transfer Team, 1982-84; vice chmn. State Rolyalty Oil and Gas Adv. Bd., 1985-87. Chmn. Anchorage Mcpl. Assembly, 1976-86; bd. dirs. Alaska Mcpl. League, 1976-86, pres., 1980; mem. exec. bd. Greater N.Y. coun. Boy Scouts Am., 1997—. Mem. Assn. Internationale de Droit des Assurances (presdl. coun. 1995—). Office: Swiss Re Life & Health 969 High Ridge Rd Stamford CT 06905-1608

WALSH, DOLORES ANN GONCZO (LORRY WALSH), special education educator; b. Detroit, Sept. 3, 1933; d. Joseph John and Dolores (Carey) Gonczo; m. Bernard Waldrup, Aug. 23, 1958 (div. 1980, dec. 2000); children: Elizabeth, Carey, Leslie, Bernard III; m. Deleon Walsh, Sept. 3, 1982 (dec. 1990). Student, Barat Coll., 1951-52; PhB, U. Detroit, 1955; MPS, Manhattanville Coll., 1978. Tchr. 2d grade East Detroit (Mich.) Pub. Schs., 1955-58; tchr. 4th grade Birmingham (Ala.) Schs., 1958-59, St. Francis Xavier Sch., Birmingham, 1959-62; homebound tchr. Greenburg Cen. #7, Hartsdale, N.Y., 1969-73; tchr. spl. edn. Greenburg Cen. 7, Hartsdale, N.Y., 1973-91; ret., 1998; tchr. English, China, summer 1998. Dist. leader Dem. Party Greenburgh, 1981-89; sec. Greenburgh Health Cen. Bd., Greenburgh, N.Y., 1986-89; leader Girl Scouts U.S., 1968-69; CCD tchr. Convent of Sacred Heart, Greenwich, Conn.; vol. West Valley Art Mus., 1992—. Mem. Epsilon Phi chpt. Delta Zeta.

WALSH, ELIZABETH JAMESON, musician; b. Panhandle, Tex., Oct. 23, 1913; d. Edwin Reece and Lela (Blackshear) Jameson; m. Thomas Norris Walsh, Nov. 1, 1951 (dec. May 5, 1990); children: Thomas Edwin, Richard Malcolm, Lela Elizabeth. MusB, U. North Tex., 1941, MusM, 1942. Cert. tchr. music. Piano tchr. U. North Tex., Denton, 1940-42; music tchr. Perryton (Tex.) H.S., 1942-43, Plainview (Tex.) H.S., 1943-45; choir dir. Presbyn. and Disciples Ch., Plainview, 1943-45; music tchr. Dallas Pub. Schs., 1945-53; organist, choir dir. Midway Hills Ch., Dallas, 1954-60; piano tchr. Hockaday Pvt. Sch., Dallas, 1960-70; music tchr. Dallas Pub. Schs., 1970-82; organist, choir dir. Greenville Ave. Christian Ch., Dallas, 1975-82, Grace Meth. Ch., Dallas, 1982-91, St. Andrews Episcopal Ch., Farmers Branch, Tex., 1991—. Composer (operetta) Day in Mexico, 1971, various titles for choir, 1996—; author: The Echo Tower, 1987, The House on the Hill, 1989; appeared as Cleopatra as Caesar and Cleopatra, Dallas Little Theatre, 1933, Jane in Jane Eyre, Amarillo Little Theatre, 1935, Anna in Anna and the King of Siam, Northway Ch. Players, 1971. Mem. Dallas Civic Chorus, 1960-65, Dallas Symphony Chorus, 1970-75, Farmer's Br. Women's Club, 1995—. Recipient 2nd prize in Nat. Recording Contest, Nat. Piano Guild, 1973. Mem. Dallas Music Tchrs. Assn., Dallas chpt. Am. Guild Organists, Musical Arts Club, Daus. of Republic of Tex. (chaplain 1993-95, pres. James Butler Bonham chpt. 1997—, Mamie Wynne Cox award 1995, sec. 1995-97), Pro Musica (pres. 1976-77, 85-86, treas. 1980-81, 96-97), Pi Beta Phi, Mu Phi Epsilon. Avocations: reading, travel. Home: 14339 Tanglewood Dr Farmers Branch TX 75234-3855

WALSH, FRANCIS R., law educator; b. Newark; s. Francis Richard and Loretta Marie Walsh; m. Ethel A Nerney, Mar. 12, 1944; 1 child, Jeffrey R. BSBA, Seton Hall U., 1944; JD, Georgetown U., 1948. Bar: Calif. 1949, U.S. Supreme Ct. 1957. Law clk. to Judge Healy U.S. Ct. Appeals (9th cir.), 1948-49; prof. law Georgetown U., 1949-51, U. San Francisco, 1951-54; pvt. practice, San Francisco, 1954-57; prof. law U. San Francisco, 1957-74, dean, 1957-70; chief Broadcast Bur., FCC, Washington, 1970-71; prof. law U. Calif. Hastings Coll. Law, San Francisco, 1974—. Lt. USNR, 1943-46, PTO. Mem. Meadow Club. Roman Catholic. Avocations: golf, travel. Home: 28 Spring Rd Kentfield CA 94904-2625 Office: U Calif Hastings Coll Law 200 Mcallister St San Francisco CA 94102-4707

WALSH, JAMES JOSEPH, lawyer; b. New Orleans, June 21, 1948; s. Francis Michael and Violet (Young) W.; m. Priscilla Robson Ferris, Oct. 12, 1972; children: Caitlin Marian, Alison Robson. BA, La. State U., 1970, JD, 1975. Bar: La. 1975, Mich. 1977, U.S. Ct. Appeals (6th cir.) 1981, U.S. Supreme Ct. 1991. Law clk. Mich. Ct. Appeals, Detroit, 1975-77; assoc. Bodman, Longley & Dahling, Detroit, 1977-84, ptnr., 1984—, head litigation practice group; counsel Outdoor Advt. Assn. Mich. Editor: La. Law Rev., 1975. Named to Hall of Fame, La. State U. Law Sch., 1988. Mem. ABA, State Bar Mich., Washtenaw County Bar Assn., Ann Arbor Club, Detroit Athletic Club. Avocations: fishing, gardening, carpentry. Home: 8025 Mast Rd Dexter MI 48130-9301 Office: Bodman Longley & Dahling 110 Miller Ave Ste 300 Ann Arbor MI 48104-1339

WALSH, JAMES WILLIAM, mental health professional; b. Pottsville, Pa., Aug. 15, 1948; s. William John and Anna Mae (Carl) W.; m. Celia Marie Ruggiero, Sept. 14, 1974; children: Tara Marie, Christine Ann, James William, Jr. Student, Wilmington Coll., 1971-72, Pa. State U., 1972-74; BA, Bapt. Christian Coll., 1985; MA, La. Bapt. U., 1991, PhD, 1998. With Residential Pilot Program for Developmentally Disabled United Cerebral Palsy, Pottsville, Pa., 1974; with Direct Care with Developmentally Disabled Regional Devel. Corp., Pottsville, 1982-83; vocat. program specialist Habilitation Inc., Pottsville, 1992-96; mental health profl. Kids Peace, Temple, 1996-98; mental health profl., chair autism coun. Family Svc. Agy., Pottsville, 1997—; mem. steering com. Habilitation, Inc., Pottsville, 1993-94; mem. behavior intervention com. Schuylkill County, Pottsville, 1995; mem. behavior intervention com. United Cerebral Palsy, Pottsville, 1995; mem. middle Atlantic states accreditation presentation com. Kids Peace, 1996. Author: Don't Take Any Wooden Nickels, 1994. Autism coun. chair Family Svcs. Agy., 1997. With USCG, 1966-70. Democrat. Methodist. Avocations: bicycling, reading, writing. Home: 238 W Bacon St Pottsville PA 17901-3913

WALSH, JOE, government official; b. Ballineen, Ireland, 1943; married; 5 children. Student, St. Finbarr's Coll., Cork, Ireland, U. Coll., Cork, Ireland. Mem. Cork County Coun., Ireland, 1974-91, mem. com. agrl., 1974-88, chmn. com., 1976-77, 85-86, mem. Dail, 1977—, mem. vocat. ednl. com., 1979-91, sen., 1981-82; min. State Dept. Agrl. & Food, Ireland, 1987-92, Ministry Agrl. Food & Forestry, Ireland, 1992-97, 97—. Home: 5 Emmet Sq, Clonakilty Co Cork Ireland Office: Dept Agrl Food & Forestry, Kildare St, Dublin 2, Ireland

WALSH, JOHN BREFFNI, aerospace consultant; b. Bklyn., Aug. 20, 1927; s. George and Margaret Mary (Rigney) W.; m. Marie Louise Leclerc, June 18, 1955; children: George Breffni, John Leclerc, Darina Louise. BEE, Manhattan Coll., 1948; MS, Columbia U., 1950; postgrad., NYU, 1954-62. Asst., instr. Columbia U., N.Y.C., 1948-51, asst. prof., asst. dir. Electronics Rsch. Labs., 1953-66; various positions through tech. dir. Intelligence and Reconnaissance Div., Rome Air Devel. Center, N.Y., 1951-53; dep. for rsch. to asst. sec. Air Force, 1966-71; sr. staff mem. Nat. Security Council, 1971-72, asst. to Pres.'s sci. advisor, 1971-72; dep. dir. Def. Research and Engring., 1972-77; asst. sec. gen. for def. support NATO, 1977-80; holder chair in systems acquisition mgmt., dean exec. inst. Def. Systems Mgmt. Coll., Ft. Belvoir, Va., 1981-82; prof. emeritus Def. Systems Mgmt. Coll., Ft. Belvoir, 1982—; v.p., chief scientist Boeing Mil. Airplane Co., Wichita, Kans., 1982-89; v.p. rsch. and engring. programs Boeing Aerospace and Electronics div., Seattle, 1990-92; v.p. strategic analysis Boeing Defense and Space Group, Seattle, 1992-93; prin. John B. Walsh Assocs., 1993—; mem. aeros. adv. com. NASA; mem. Congl. Adv. Com. on Aeros., 1984-85; assoc. Def. Sci. Bd.; mem. indsl. adv. bd. Wichita State U. Coll. Engring., adj. prof. elec. engring., 1989-90; chmn. tech. working group Def. Trade Adv. Group Dept. State, 1992-95; chmn. com. on adv. group on aeronautics R & D, NATO, 1981-82. Author: Electromagnetic Theory and Engineering Applications, 1960, (with K.S. Miller) Introductory Electric Circuits, 1960, Elementary and Advanced Trigonometry, 1977; contbr. tech. papers to publs.; patentee in field. Mem. planning bd., Cresskill, N.J., 1964-66; commr. Kans. Advanced Tech. Commn., 1985-86; bd. dirs. Kans. Inc., 1986-90; mem. math. scis. edn. bd. NRC, 1989-92. Served with U.S. Army, 1946-47, USAR, 1947-52. Recipient Air Force Exceptional Civilian Service award, 1969; recipient Dept. Def. Meritorious Civilian Service award, 1971, Disting. Civilian Service award, 1977, Air Force Assn. citation of honor as outstanding Air Force civilian employee of year, 1971, Theodore von Karman award Air Force Assn., 1977. Fellow IEEE (life), AIAA (v.p. tech. 1987-89); mem. Internat. Inst. for Strategic Studies, N.Y. Acad. Scis., GPS Internat. Assn., Electromagnetics Acad., Sigma Xi, Eta Kappa Nu. Roman Catholic. Office: 8800 Prestwould Pl Mc Lean VA 22102-2231

WALSH, J(OHN) B(RONSON), lawyer; b. Buffalo, Feb. 20, 1927; s. John A. and Alice (Condon) W.; m. Barbara Ashford, May 20, 1966; 1 child, Martha. AB, Canisius Coll., 1950; JD, Georgetown U., 1952. Bar: N.Y. 1953, U.S. Supreme Ct. 1958, U.S. Ct. Internat. Trade 1969, U.S. Ct. Customs and Patent Appeals 1973. Trial atty. Garvey & Conway, N.Y.C., 1953-54; vol. atty. Nativity Mission, N.Y.C., 1953-54; ptnr. Jaeckle, Fleischmann, Kelly, Swart & Augspurger, Buffalo, 1955-60; pvt. practice Buffalo, 1961-75; ptnr. Jaeckle, Fleischmann & Mugel, Buffalo, 1976-80; with Walsh & Cleary, P.C., Buffalo, 1980-84; pvt. practice, 1984—; spl. counsel Ecology and Environment, Inc., Lancaster, N.Y., 1989—; trial counsel antitrust div. Dept. Justice, Washington, 1960-61; spl. counsel on disciplinary procedures N.Y. Supreme Ct., 1960-76; appointee legal disciplinary coordinating com. State of N.Y., 1971; legis. counsel, spl. counsel to mayor Buffalo, 1995—; counsel to sheriff Erie County, 1969-72; legis counsel Niagara Frontier Transp. Authority; cons. Norfolk So. R.R., Ecology and Environment on Govtl. Affairs; guest lectr. univs. and profl. groups. Author: (TV series) The Law and You (Freedom Found. award, ABA award, Internat. Police Assn. award). Past pres. Ashford Hollow Found. Visual and Performing Arts; past trustee Dollar Bills, Inc.; past co-producer Grand Island Playhouse and Players. With U.S. Army, 1945-46. Recipient Gold Key Buffalo Jr. C. of C., 1962, award Freedom Found., 1966. Fellow Am. Bar Found.; mem. ABA (del. internat. conf. Brussels 1963, Mexico City 1964, Lausanne, Switzerland 1964, Award of Merit com. 1961-70, sec., vice chair, chmn. sect. bar activities 1965-69, mem. ho. of dels. 1969-70, mem. crime prevention and control com. 1968-70, vice chair sr. lawyers divsn., com. legislation and adminstrn. regulations 1992—, vice chair sr. lawyers divsn. membership com. 1993-94), N.Y. Trial Lawyers Assn., Am. Immigration Lawyers Assn., Am. Judicature Soc., N.Y. State Bar Assn. (past exec. sec.), Erie County Bar Assn., Buffalo Bar Assn., Nat. Pub. Employer Labor Relations Assn., Capital Hill Club of Buffalo, Am. Assn. Airport Execs., N.Y. State Bus. Coun. (environ. law subcom., chmn. subcom.), Buffalo Irish Club (bd. dirs.), Buffalo Athletic Club (past bd. dirs., past v.p.), Buffalo Canoe Club, Buffalo Club, Ft. Orange of Albany Club, KC, Knights of Equity, Leoknights, Phi Delta Phi, Delta Gamma. Roman Catholic. Home: 95 North Dr Eggertsville NY 14226-4158 Office: 368 Pleasant View Dr Lancaster NY 14086-1316 also: 210 Ellicott Sq Bldg Buffalo NY 14203-2402

WALSH, KENNETH JOSEPH, design and engineering executive, consultant; b. Chorley, Lancashire, Eng., Apr. 10, 1965; s. Kenneth Bernard and Delia Anne (Ogden) W.; m. Pamela May Berry, Aug. 5, 1989; children: Damian David, Thomas Ian. Grad. mech. and prodn. engring., Bolton Inst. Higher Edn., 1989. Chartered engr. Technician apprentice Bae, Bolton, 1981-86, prodn. engr., 1986-91, sr. prodn. engr., 1991-92; mfg. mgr. Global Pumping Systems Ltd., Hailsham, Eng., 1992-93; gen. mgr. Global Pumping Systems Ltd., Manchester, Eng., 1993-95; tech. dir. Verder Ltd., Leeds, Eng., 1995—. Mem. Inst. Elec. Engrs. Avocations: reading, cycling, karate.

WALSH, MARIE LECLERC, nurse; b. Providence, Sept. 11, 1928; d. Walter Normand and Anna Mary (Ryan) Leclerc; m. John Breffni Walsh, June 18, 1955; children: George Breffni, John Leclerc, Darina Louise. Grad., Waterbury Hosp. Sch. Nursing, Conn., 1951; BS, Columbia U., 1954, MA, 1955. Team leader Hartford (Conn.) Hosp., 1951-53; pvt. duty nurse St. Luke's Hosp., N.Y.C., 1953-57; sch. nurse tchr. Agnes Russel Ctr., Tchrs. Coll. Columbia U., N.Y.C., 1955-56; clin. nursing instr. St. Luke's Hosp., N.Y.C., 1957-58; chmn. disaster nursing ARC Fairfax County, Va., 1975; course coord. occupational health nursing U. Va. Sch. Continuing Edn., Falls Church, 1975-77; mem. disaster steering com. No. Va. C.C., Annandale, 1976; adj. faculty U. Va. Sch. Continuing Edn., Falls Church, 1981; disaster svcs. nurse ARC, Wichita, Kans., 1985-90; disaster svcs. nurse Seattle-King County chpt. ARC, Seattle, 1990-96; ret.; rsch. and statis. analyst U. Va. Sch. Continuing Edn. Nursing, Falls Church, 1975; rsch. libr. Olive Garvey Ctr. for Improvement Human Functioning, Inc., Wichita, 1985. Sec. Dem. party, Cresskill, N.J., 1964-66; county committeewoman, Bergen County, N.J., 1965-66; pres., v.p., Internat. Staff Wives, NATO, Brussels, Belgium, 1978-80; election officer, supr. Election Bd., Wichita, 1987, 88; v.p. McLean Newcomers, 1997-99, pres., 1999-2000. Mem. AAAS, AAUW, N.Y. Acad. Sci., Pi Lambda Theta, Sigma Theta Tau. Avocation: travel, gardening. Home: 8800 Prestwould Pl Mc Lean VA 22102-2231

WALSH, MARY NOELLE, publishing executive; b. Birmingham, Warwicksh., Eng., Dec. 26, 1954; d. Thomas and Marrie (Ferguson) W.; m. David Howard Heslam, Oct. 15, 1988; children: Ciara, Calum. BA with honors in European History and German, U. East Anglia, Norwich, Eng., 1976. News editor Cosmopolitan, London, 1979-85; editor London Week, 1985-86; dep. editor Good Housekeeping Mag., London, 1986-86, editor, 1987-91; editor You & Your Family, Daily Telegraph, London, 1991-92; co-dir. Value for Money Co., London, 1991—. Author: Hot Lips: The Ultimate Kiss and Tell Guide, 1985, The Good Deal Directory, 1994, 7th edit. 2000, Baby on a Budget, 1995; co-author: The Home Shopping Handbook, 1995, Wonderful Wedding that Won't Cost a Fortune, 1996, The Factory Shopping and Sightseeing Guide to the UK, 1996, The Mail Order Guide, 1996. Fellow Royal Soc. Arts. Home and Office: PO Box 4, Lechlade Gloucestershire GL7 3YB, England

WALSH, PETER JOSEPH, multimedia marketing professional; b. Newport, R.I., Jan. 22, 1948; s. Alexander Ronald and Mary (O'Connell) W.; m. Virginia Diana Santore, May 11, 1978 (div. May 1992); children: Bridget, Peter, Lara, Elizabeth, Vanessa. BA, Santa Clara U., 1970; MA, Johns Hopkins U., 1978. V.p. Noblemet Internat., N.Y.C., 1978-80; mktg. dir. Multi-Arc Scientific Coatings, St. Paul, Minn., 1980-88; sr. v.p. Projects Devel., Inc., N.Y.C., 1988-91; pres. Kiser Rsch., Inc., Washington, 1990-93; sr. v.p. multi-media Sonalysts Studios, Waterford, Conn., 1993—; mem. tech. adv. com. U. R.I., 1997—. Bd. dirsl Portsmouth Abbey Sch. Alumni, Portsmouth, R.I., 1996—. Roman Catholic. Avocations: tennis, golf, running. Home: 96 Mary St Newport RI 02840-3150 Office: Sonalysts Inc 215 Parkway N Waterford CT 06385-1209

WALSH, RAOUL ANTHONY, behavioural medicine consultant; b. Sydney, N.S.W., Australia, June 8, 1951; s. Desmond William and Joan May (Bullock) W.; m. Janet Elizabeth Greenhalgh, June 2, 1979; children: Aidan, Dorian, Magnus, Fergus, Stirling. BA Dip. Edn., Macquarie U., Sydney, 1972; PhD, Newcastle U., N.S.W., 1995. Health educator Mental Health Program, Sydney, 1974-75, Hunter Drug Adv. Svc., Newcastle, Australia, 1975-79; team leader Hunter Drug Adv. Svc., Sydney, 1980-85; dir. drug and alcohol svcs. Hunter Area, N.S.W., 1986-88; lectr. U. Newcastle, 1989-94; cons. Hunter Ctr. for Health Advancement, 1995-2000; cons. WHO, Geneva, 1996—, Nat. Breast Cancer Ctr., 1997-98; sr. rsch. academic NSW Cancer Coun., 1999—. Mem. editl. bd. Drug and Alcohol Rev.; contbr. articles to profl. jours. Sec. Newcastle Addiction Treatment Orgn., 1976-79; cons. N.S.W. Cancer Coun., Sydney, 1989-99; mem. Hunter Area Rsch. Ethics Com., 1992-94, U. Newcastle Rsch. Ethics Com., 1994; chmn. Hunter Family Life Movement, Newcastle, 1979-89. Rsch. grantee Commonwealth AIDS Rsch., 1990-92, Dept. Health, Housing and Cmty. Svcs., 1993-95, Nat. Health and Med. Rsch. Coun., 1994-96. Mem. Australian Soc. Health Educators (v.p. 1980-82), Australian Profl. Soc. on Alcohol and Other Drugs, N.S.W. Cmty. Health Assn., Australian Coun. of Alcohol and Other Drugs Assn. Avocations: gardening, cricket, tennis, reading, music. Home: Dawson's Hill, Singleton 2330 NSW, Australia Office: NSWCC Cancer Edn Rsch Prog, Locked Bag 10, Wallsend 2287 NSW, Australia

WALSH, THOMAS FRANCIS, JR., producer, writer, director; b. N.Y.C., Aug. 15, 1956; s. Thomas Francis and Catherine Alice (May) W.; m. Adriana Mia Stastny, Oct. 19, 1996. BFA, NYU, 1977. Pres. Tom Walsh Prodns. Inc., N.Y.C. and Del., 1977-89; chmn., CEO I.D.L. Inc., N.Y.C. and Calif., 1989-91, Wonderland Dream Factory Inc., Calif. and Del., 1991-93, Enteraktion Inc. and Enteraktion.Net, Pompano Beach, Fla., 1993—. Prodr.: (feature film) Denial, 1991; (CD-ROM) The Arrival, 1996; exec. prodr.: (TV) We Dare You!, 1982, House to House, 1982, Mismatch, 1979; prodr., dir.: The Whole Truth, 1977. Scholar Helena Rubenstein Co., N.Y.C., 1976-77; recipient 1st prize for best TV show Conn. Assn. Profl. Communicators, 1974, Bronze and Silver awards Nat. Forensic League, 1977, Kate Garland award NYU/Columbia Pictures, 1976. Mem. Psi Upsilon (Delta chpt.), Alpha Epsilon Rho. Avocations: boating, diving, trains, water skiing. Office: Enteraktion Inc 2401 E Atlantic Blvd Ste 410 Pompano Beach FL 33062-5243

WALSH, THOMAS J., JR., lawyer; b. Newark, Jan. 23, 1961; s. Thomas J. and Ellen M. Walsh; m. Catherine M. Twomey, Nov. 19, 1988; children:

Christopher, Claire. JD, U. Conn., Hartford, 1983; BA, U. Conn., 1986. Ptnr. Marsh, Day & Calhoun, Southport, Conn., 1986-98; town atty. Town Fairfield, Conn., 1993-97; prin. Brody, Wilkinson and Ober, P.C., Southport, 1999—; mem. bd. dirs. Bridgeport C. of C., 1990—; mem. bd. mgrs. YMCA, Fairfield, 1999—; dir. Bridgeport Neighborhood Fund, 1999—. Mem. ABA, Conn. Bar Assn., Bridgeport Bar Assn. Avocations: tennis, politics. Office: Brody Wilkinson and Ober PC 2507 Post Rd Southport CT 06490-1259

WALSH, THOMAS JOHN, infectious disease physician, oncologist, researcher, educator; b. Hartford, Conn., May 5, 1952; s. John Thomas and Frances (Zeneski) W.; m. Sherril Ross, Apr. 8, 1989; 1 child, Laura. BA in Biology/Chemistry, Assumption Coll., Worcester, Mass., 1974; MD, The Johns Hopkins U., 1978. Diplomate Am. Bd. Internal Medicine, Am. Bd. Infectious Diseases, Am. Bd. Med. Oncology. Resident in medicine Michael Reese Hosp., U. Chgo., 1978-82; fellow pathology Johns Hopkins Hosp. and Univ., Balt., 1979-80; fellow infectious diseases U. Md., Balt., 1982-85, fellow med. oncology, 1985-86; fellow med. oncology Nat. Cancer Inst., Bethesda, Md., 1986-87, sr. staff fellow, 1987-88, med. officer, 1988-93, sr. investigator, 1993—, head mycology unit, 1993—, chief immunocompromised host sect., 1996—; assoc. prof. U. Md. Sch. Medicine, Balt., 1992-98, prof., 1998—; lectr. The Johns Hopkins U. Sch. Medicine, Balt., 1985—. Contbr. chpts. to Management of Infections in Patients with Cancer, 1985, Critical Problems in Trauma Care, Vol. II Medical Management, Current Therapy in Hematology/Oncology, 1987, Tenth Congress of the International Society for Human and Animal Mycology-ISHAM Proceedings, 1988, Diagnosis and Therapy of Systemic Mycoses, 1989, Respiratory Diseases in the Immunosuppressed Host, 1990, Hematology: Basic Principles and Practice, 3d edit., 1999, Medical Microbiology, 3d edit., 1991, Pediatric AIDS, 1990, Current Therapy in Critical Care Medicine, 1990, Emerging Targets in Antibacterial and Antifungal Chemotherapy, 1991, The Principles and Practice of Medical Intensive Care, 1993, Aspergillus: The Biology and Industrial Applications, 1991, New Strategies in Fungal Disease, 1992, Oral Fungal Infections in Immunocompromised Patients, 1991, Current Therapy in Pediatric Infectious Diseases, 3d edit., 1993, Hematopoietic Growth Factors and Mononuclear Phagocytes, 1993, Fungal Diseases of the Lung, 2d edit., 1993, Manual of Clinical Microbiology, 7th edit., 1994, Infectious Diseases, 1994, Infectious Complications of Cancer, 1995, Principles and Practice of Pediatric Oncology, 2d edit., 1996, Current Therapy in Adult Medicine, 4th edit., 1997, Cutaneous Infection and Therapy, 1997, Manual of Bone Marrow Transplantation, 1997, Adrenomedullin, 1998, Transplant Infections, 1998, Hunter's Tropical Medicine, 1999, others; contbr. more than 200 publications to profl. jours. and 146 rsch. abstracts. Comdr. USPHS, 1991—, NIH. Recipient Med. Mycology Fellow award Nat. Found. for Infectious Diseases, 1984, Young Investigator award ICAAC and Am. Soc. Microbiology, USPHS Commendation medal, 1993. Fellow ACP, Am. Acad. Microbiology, Infectious Diseases Soc. Am., Am. Coll. Chest Physicians. Achievements include development of exptl. and clin. found. for new approaches to diagnosis, treatment and prevention of invasive candidiasis and aspergillosis in immunocompromised patients; devel. of new understanding of pathogenesis, diagnosis, and treatment of emerging mycoses; devel. new approaches to augmentation of host defenses in neutropenic hosts against invasive mycoses. Office: NIH 9000 Rockville Pike Bethesda MD 20892-0003

WALSH, THOMAS JOSEPH, neuro-ophthalmologist; b. N.Y.C., Sept. 18, 1931; s. Thomas Joseph and Virginia (Hughes) W.; m. Sally Ann Maust, June 21, 1958; children—Thomas Raymond, Sara Ann, Mary Kelly, Kathleen Meghan. BA, Coll. Fordham, 1954; MD, Bowman Gray Med. Sch., 1958. Intern St. Vincent's Hosp., N.Y.C., 1958-59; resident ophthalmology Bowman Gray Med. Sch., Winston-Salem, N.C., 1961-64; fellow neuro-ophthalmology Bascom Palmer Eye Inst., Miami, Fla., 1964-65; practice medicine specializing in neuro-ophthalmology Stamford, Conn., 1965—; dir. neuro-ophthalmology service, asst. prof. ophthalmology and neurology Yale Sch. Medicine, New Haven, 1965-74; assoc. prof. Yale Sch. Medicine, 1974-79, prof., 1979—, also bd. permanent officers; dir. ophthalmology Stamford Hosp., 1978-83; mem. staff St. Joseph Hosp., Yale New Haven Hosp.; fellow Yale Sch. Mgmt., 1999; cons. to surgeon gen. army in neuro-ophthalmology Walter Reed Hosp., Washington, 1966—, VA Hosp., West Haven, 1965—, Silver Hill Found., New Canaan, Conn., 1974—; adj. prof. Dartmouth Med. Sch.; frequent lectr. various univs. Contbr. articles to various publs. Mem. adv. bd. Stamford Salvation Army, 1972-92; mem. med. bd. Darien Nurses Assn., Conn., 1972—; surgeon Darien Fire Dept., 1969—. With AUS, 1959-61. Decorated Knight of Malta, 1983; Centennial fellow Johns Hopkins, 1976. Mem. AMA, Conn., Fairfield County med. socs., Acad. Ophthalmology, Oxford Ophthal. Congress, Acad. Neurology, Am. Assn. Neurol. Surgeons, Internat. Neuro-Ophthalmology Soc., Soc. Med. Cons. to Armed Forces, Cosmos Club (Washington), Darien County Club, Yale Club (N.Y.C), Lions, Army-Navy Club. Office: 1250 Summer St Ste 205 Stamford CT 06905-5318

WALSH, WILLIAM DESMOND, investor; b. N.Y.C., Aug. 4, 1930; s. William J. and Catherine Grace (Desmond) W.; m. Mary Jane Gordon, Apr. 5, 1951; children: Deborah, Caroline, Michael, Suzanne, Tara Jane, Peter. BA, Fordham U., 1951; JD, Harvard U., 1955. Bar: N.Y. State bar 1955. Asst. U.S. atty. So. dist. N.Y., N.Y.C., 1955-58; counsel N.Y. Commn. Investigation, N.Y.C., 1958-61; mgmt. cons. McKinsey & Co., N.Y.C., 1961-67; sr. v.p. Arcata Corp., Menlo Park, Calif., 1967-82; gen. ptnr. Sequoia Assocs., 1982—; pres., chief exec. officer Atacra Liquidating Trust, 1982-88; chmn. bd. dirs. Consol. Freightways Corp., Menlo Park, Calif., Clayton Group, Inc., Tampa, Fla., Newell Mfg. Corp., Lowell, Mich., Newell Indsl. Corp., Roanoke, Va., Neuroscis. Inst./Scripps; bd. dirs. URS Corp., San Francisco, Basic Vegetable Products, San Francisco, UNOVA, Woodland Hills, Calif., Crown Vantage, Cin., Ohio, Ameriscape, Inc., North Salem, N.Y., Bemiss Jason Corp., Newark, Calif. Mem. Harvard Law Sch., co-chair dean's adv. bd.; trustee Fordham; mem. bd. overseers Hoover Inst.; adv. bd. Agincourt, Annapolis, Md. Mem. N.Y. State Bar Assn., Harvard Club (N.Y.C. and San Francisco), Fordham Club No. Calif., Knights of Malta. Home: 279 Park Ln Atherton CA 94027-5448 Office: Bldg 2 3000 Sand Hill Rd Ste 140 Menlo Park CA 94025-7113

WALSH, WILLIAM JOSEPH, business educator, labor arbitrator; b. Passaic, N.J., May 26, 1944; s. David Michael and Catherine Elizabeth Walsh; m. Paula Ruth Walsh, June 5, 1968; children: Brent W., Shannon C. (deceased). BS, USAF Acad., 1968; MA, Ind. U., 1974, PhD, 1986. Profl. cert. pilot. Commd. 2d lt. USAF, 1968, advanced through grades to lt. col., 1985, ret., 1990; assoc. prof. USAF Acad., Colo., 1984-86; dir. ops., tng. Tech. Tng. Group, Rantoul, Ill., 1986-87; inspector gen. Chanute Tech. Tng. Ctr., Rantoul, Ill., 1987-90; assoc. prof. bus. Ill. Wesleyan U., Bloomington, 1990—; cons. McLean County Hist. Soc., Bloomington, 1991-96; mem. adv. bd. W.M. Putnam Co., Bloomington, 1994-97. Co-author: Collective-Bargaining & Impasse Resolution, 1988. Vice chmn., treas. OSF/St. Joseph's Med. Ctr. Found., Bloomington, 1995—;. Recipient Disting. Paper award Midwest Acad. Legal Studies, 1997. Mem. Midwest Soc. for Human Resources/Indsl. Rels. (pres. 1999-2000, Disting. Paper awrad 1998), Rotary (pres. Paxton chpt. 1985-86). Roman Catholic. Avocations: flying, acting. Office: Ill Wesleyan U PO Box 2900 Bloomington IL 61702-2900

WALSHAM, BRUCE TAYLOR, mining company executive; b. Grimsby, England, Feb. 28, 1936; s. Arthur and Phyllis Elsie (Stokes) W.; m. Denise Cox, 1961; m. Ann Barry; children: Alexandra, Nicola; m. Carole Moore, Jan. 3, 1998. BS in Geology with honors, Birmingham (Eng.) U., 1958. Profl. soccer player, 1958-65; provincial and rep. Cricketer, 1955-70; geologist Union Corp. Ltd., Johannesburg, Republic of South Africa, 1958-62; geologist in charge Union Corp. Ltd., London, 1964-71; geologist MacKay and Schnellmann Ltd., London, 1962-64; dir. MacKay and Schnellmann P.L., Brisbane, Queensland, Australia, 1971-72; exploration mgr. Bond Corp., Perth, West Australia, 1971; v.p. Freeport of Australia Inc., Melbourne, Victoria, Australia, 1972-76, pres., 1979-89; v.p. Freeport Explorn Co., Reno, Tucson, Nev., Ariz, 1976-79, Freeport Minerals Co., New Orleans, 1986-89; pres. Pittston Mineral Ventures Internat. Ltd., Melbourne, 1989-93; exec. chmn. Panorama Resources Australia, 1993-98; chmn., pres., CEO Diamond Works Ltd, Vancouver, 1997—; dir. Aurora Gold Ltd, Perth, 1994-98, Tonganyika Gold, Perth, 1998—. Contbr. articles to profl. jours. Fellow Inst. Mining and Metallurgy, Australasian Inst. Mining and Metallurgy; mem. Am. Inst. Mining Engrs., Soc. Econ. Geologists, Soc. for Geology Applied to Mineral Deposits (v.p. 1986-90), Geol. Soc. South Africa, Australian Club, Carlton Club. Avocations: philately, photography, various sports, theatre, films.

WALSH-MCGEHEE, MARTHA BOSSE, conservationist; d. Leon and Lenore (Carter) Bosse; m. Leo S. Walsh, Sept. 30, 1972 (div. Oct. 1982); m. Donald B. McGehee, Aug. 6, 1992. Student, U. Mo., 1966, Baker U., 1966-67, Marymount-Manhattan, 1980-82. Flight attendant TWA, N.Y.C., 1967-78; pres. Island Conservation Effort, 1988—; chmn. bd. dirs. The Tortoise Preserve; trustee Rare Ctr. for Tropical Bird Conservation, Phila., 1987-91; rsch. assoc. N.C. Mus. Natural Sci. Ptnr. in conservation World Wildlife Fund, Washington, 1986—; assoc. World Resources Inst., Washington, 1987—; mem. St. Croix Environ. Assn., 1987—; mem. Saba Conservation Found. Nature Conservancy. Mem. Caribbean Conservation Assn., St. Lucia Naturalists Soc., Cedam Internat., Soc. Caribbean Ornithology (exec. coun. mem., bd. dirs.), Friends of Abaco Parrot, Assn. Parrot Conservation, Tropical Audubon, Ctr. for Marine Conservation. Republican. Avocations: reading, bird watching, horseback riding, scuba diving. Home: 90 Edgewater Dr Apt 901 Coral Gables FL 33133-6918 also: Windwardside, Saba Netherlands Antilles

WALSS-RODRIGUEZ, RODOLFO J., obstetrician-gynecologist; b. Monclova, Coahuila, Mexico, June 13, 1945; came to the U.S., 1992; s. Rodolfo Walss-Polendo and Consuelo Rodriguez Walss; m. Maria Eugenia Aurioles; children: Maria Eugenia, Consuelo, Rodolfo, Patricia, Leonardo. MD, U. Coahuila, Torreon, Mexico, 1970; Degree in Ob-gyn., U. W.Va., 1977. Diplomate Am. Bd. Ob-gyn. Prof. faculty medicine Autonomous U. Coahuila, Torreon, 1978-92; prof. faculty medicine Mexican Inst. Social Security, Torreon, 1986-92, chief svc., 1986-90, chief divsn., 1990-92; attending Columbia Valley Regional Med. Ctr., Brownsville, Tex., 1992—; chief of svc. Columbia Valley Regional Med. Ctr., Brownsville, 1994-96; chief tchg. and rsch. Inst. Social Svcs. for State Workers, Torreon, 1981-86. Contbr. articles to profl. jours. Pres. Alumni Soc., Torreon, 1964-65, Nat. Orgn. Med. Students, Mexico, 1965-67, Obstetrical Soc. La Laguna, Torreon, 1986-88. Fellow ACOG, ACS; mem. Am. Soc. Clin. Hypnosis. Roman Catholic. Avocation: painting.

WALSTON, RODERICK EUGENE, state government official; b. Gooding, Idaho, Dec. 15, 1935; s. Loren R. and Iva M. (Boyer) W.; m. Margaret D. Grandey; children: Gregory Scott W., Valerie Lynne W. A.A., Boise Jr. Coll., 1956; B.A. cum laude, Columbia Coll., 1958; LL.B. scholar, Stanford U., 1961. Bar: Calif. 1961, U.S. Supreme Ct. 1973. Law clk to judge U.S. Ct. Appeals 9th Cir., 1961-62; dep. atty. gen State of Calif., San Francisco, 1963-91, head natural resources sect, 1969-91, chief asst. atty. gen. pub. rights div., 1991-99; spl. dep counsel Kings County, Calif., 1975-76; gen. counsel Metropolitan Water Dist. So. Calif., 2000—; mem. environ. and natural resources adv. coun. Stanford (Calif.) Law Sch. Contbr. articles to profl. jours.; bd. editors: Stanford Law Rev., 1959-61, Western Natural Resources Litigation Digest, Calif. Water Law and Policy Reporter; spl. editor Jour. of the West. Co-chmn. Idaho campaign against Right-to-Work initiative, 1958; Calif. rep. Western States Water Coun., 1986—; environ. and natural resources adv. coun., Stanford Law Sch. Nat. Essay Contest winner Nat. Assn. Internat. Rels. Clubs, 1956, Stanford Law Rev. prize, 1961; recipient Best Brief award Nat. Assn. Attys. Gen., 1997; Astor Found. scholar, 1956-58. Mem. ABA (chmn. water resources com. 1988-90, vice chmn. and conf. chmn. 1985-88, 90—), Contra Costa County Bar Assn., U.S. Supreme Ct., Hist. Soc., Federalist Soc., World Affairs Coun. No. Calif. Office: Calif Atty Gen's Office 455 Golden Gate Ave Ste 11000 San Francisco CA 94102-3660

WALTER, BERNHARD, bank executive. Chmn. bd. mng. dirs. Vreschner Bank AG, Frankfurt, Germany, 1998—. Avocations: golf, joggong, music. Office: Dreschner Bank AG, Juergen Ponto Platz 1, 60301 Frankfurt Germany*

WALTER, GEORGE ANTHONY, elementary education educator; b. Cin., July 16, 1948; s. George Winton and Yvonne Iola (Rivard) W. AA, Brevard C.C., 1968; BA in Edn., U. Fla., 1970; MEd, Stetson U., 1978. Tchr. Brevard County Sch. Sys., Vierra, Fla., 1971—. V.p. Rockledge Little League, 1991—; v.p. bd. dirs. Fla. Miss Softball, 1988; pres. bd. dirs. Rockledge Miss Softball, 1988-89; mem. Rep. Nat. Party. With U.S. Army, 1970-76, USAR. Recipient Newspapers in Edn. cert. Fla. Today, 1997. Mem. Brevard Fedn. Tchrs., Am. Legion. Republican. Avocations: photography, softball. Home: 155 Becora Ave Merritt Island FL 32953-3141

WALTER, HORST, musicologist; b. Hannover, Lower Saxony, Germany, Mar. 5, 1931; s. Julius and Gertrud W.; m. Liesel Roth, Aug. 31, 1959; two children. PhD, U. Cologne, 1962. Editor Joseph Haydn Inst., Cologne, 1962-96, dir., 1992-96. Editor: Haydn Studies, Collected Haydn Edit.; contbr. articles to profl. jours./publs. in field.

WALTER, HUGO GÜNTHER, humanities educator; b. Phila., Mar. 12, 1959; s. Paul and Elli R. Walter. BA, Princeton U., 1981; PhD in Lit., Yale U., 1985; MA in Humanities, Old Dominion U., 1989; PhD in Interdisciplinary Humanities, Drew U., 1996. Adj. instr. Yale U., New Haven, 1981-85, Old Dominion U., Norfolk, Va., 1988-89; asst. prof. Washington and Jefferson Coll., Washington, Pa., 1989-92, Fairleigh Dickinson U., Madison, N.J., 1992-96, Kettering U., Flint, Mich., 1996-99, Berkeley Coll., White Plains, N.Y., 1999—; vis. asst. prof. Rhodes Coll., Memphis, 1986-87, U. Mo., Columbia, 1987-88. Author: (poetry) The Fragile Edge, 1988, Velvet Rhythms, 1989, Amber Blossoms and Evening Shadows, 1990, Golden Thorns of Light and Sterling Silhouettes, 1991, Waiting for Babel Prophesies of Sunflower Dreams, 1992, Along the Maroon-Prismed Threshold of Bronze-Pealing Eternity, 1992, The Light of the Dance Is the Music of Eternity, 1993, Dusk-Gloaming Mirrors and Castle-Winding Dreams, 1994, Amaranth-Sage Epiphanies of Dusk-Weaving Paradise, 1995, 2d edit., 1996, (monographs) The Apostrophic Moment in 19th and 20th Century Lyric Poetry, 1988, Space and Time on the Magic Mountain: Studies in the 19th and 20th Century European Literature, 1999. Mem. Acad. Am. Poets, Internat. Soc. Poets. Avocations: music, painting. Home: 157 Loomis Ct Princeton NJ 08540-3438

WALTER, JEREMY CANNING, lawyer; b. Esher, U.K., Aug. 22, 1948; s. Richard and Beryl (Pugh) W.; m. Judith Jane Rowlands, Aug. 24, 1973 (div. 1983); children: Emma Canning, Alison Canning; m. Dawna Beth Rosenberg, Oct. 17, 1992. MA with 1st class honors, Cambridge (Eng.) U., 1969, LLB with 1st class honors, 1970. Trainee solicitor Ellis Piers & Co., London, 1971-73; asst. solicitor Simmons & Simmons, London, 1973-77, ptnr., 1977—, dep. mng. ptnr. corp. dept., 1994-96, head corp. dept., 1996—; mem. ICC Fin. Svcs. Commn., 1992—. Cons. editor Jour. Soc. Advanced Legal Studies, 1998—. Mem. East-West Forum of bus. law sect. IBA; vice chair IBA Arab Regional Forum Coun., 2000; com. mem. City of London Law Soc., 1999—. Mem. ABA, Internat. Bar Assn., Securities Inst., Law Soc. (London ins. law com. 1991-99), Brit. Polish Legal Assn. (exec. com.). Office: Simmons & Simmons, 21 Wilson St, London EC2M 2TX, England

WALTER, JOHN FREDERICK, historical researcher, genealogist; b. Bklyn., Sept. 27, 1939; s. William O. and Madeline (Dittrich) W.; m. Margaret Killeen, Feb. 9, 1963; children: Mark, Michael, Robin, Brian. Student, St. John's U., 1955-61. Records mgr. Ladenburg Thalmann & Co., N.Y.C., 1961-76, W.R. Family Assocs., N.Y.C., 1976-94; dir., owner Inst. for Civil War Rsch., Middle Village, N.Y., 1994—. Merit badge counselor Boy Scouts Am., Middle Village, 1990—. Sgt. U.S. Army Res., 1961-65. Mem. Nat. Geneal. Soc., Co. Mil. Historians, Assn. Profl. Genealogists, Cartophilic Soc. Great Britain. Roman Catholic. Avocations: walking, volleyball, racquetball, cigarette card collecting. E-mail: ICWRJOHN@AOL.COM. Home and office: 79-13 67 Dr Middle Village NY 11379

WALTER, KENNETH GAINES, library director; b. Atlanta, Mar. 14, 1932; s. Gaines Winningham and Freddie Lou (Thigpen) W.; m. Eva Lou McClelland, June 10, 1965; children: Regina Eileen, Kevin Michael. BA, Emory U., 1954, MS, 1958; postgrad., U. Vienna, Austria, 1962; MSLS, U. N.C., Chapel Hill, 1966; EdD, U. Ga., 1995. Asst. cataloging libr. Ohio U., Athens, 1961-65, head cataloging libr., 1965-68; faculty rep. Bapt. Student Union Ohio U., New Haven, 1965-68; asst. dir. librs. U. S.C., Columbia, 1968-75; dir. librs. Ga. So. U., Statesboro, 1975-84; dir. libr. svcs. So. Conn. State U., New Haven, 1985-97, dir. libr. svcs. emeritus, 1997—; cons. libr. strategic planning, budgeting, evaluation of book collections; faculty advisor Delta Tau Delta, Statesboro, 1976-83; book reviewer Libr. Jour., 1970-78. Contbr. articles to profl. jours. Mem. Conn. State U. Sys. Lib. Autom. RFP com., 1991-93, lib. dirs. com., 1985-97, Conn. Coun. Acad. Lib. Dirs., 1989-97 (emeritus mem. 1997—), Interagy. Libr. Planning Com., Hartford, Conn., 1986-89; mem. com. in-state svc. Conn. Acad. Libr. Dirs., 1985-89; mem. cataloging bd. New Haven Colony Hist. Soc., 1987-89; mem. Statesboro-Ga. So. Community Chorus, 1980-84; chmn. bd. suprs. CORE Credit Union, Statesboro, 1978-81. Staff sgt. U.S. Army, 1956-57. Recipient scholarship Emory U., 1950-53; Fulbright scholar, 1961-62; grantee Austrian Govt., 1961-62. Mem. ALA (life), Acad. Libr. Dirs. (mem. Ga. regents com. 1975-83), Assn. Coll. and Rsch. Librs., Libr. Adminstrn. and Mgmt. Assn., Reference and User Svcs. Assn., Southeastern Libr. Assn., Ga. Libr. Assn., Conn. Libr. Assn., Cen. Ga. Assoc. Librs (pres. 1980-82), East. Ga. Libr. Triangle (pres. 1976-83), Ga. Acad. Sci., Ga. Assn. Coll. and Rsch. Librs. (pres. 1983), Rotary (New Haven), Sigma Gamma Epsilon, Beta Phi Mu, Phi Delta Kappa, Delta Tau Delta. Baptist. Avocations: camping, rock collecting, philately, woodworking. Home: 512 Wallingford Rd Cheshire CT 06410-2844

WALTER, MICHAEL CHARLES, lawyer; b. Oklahoma City, Nov. 25, 1956; s. Donald Wayne and Viola Helen (Heffelfinger) W. BA in Polit. Sci., BJ, U. Wash., 1980; JD, Univ. Puget Sound, 1983. Bar: Wash. 1985, U.S. Dist. Ct. (9th cir. 1985). Ptnr. Keating, Bucklin & McCormack, Seattle, 1985—; instr. Bellevue (Wash.) C.C., 1983—. FAX: 206-223-9423. Mem. ABA, Wash. State Bar Assn., Seattle-King County Bar Assn., Wash. Assn. Def. Counsel, Seattle Claims Adjustors Assn., Wash. Assn. Mcpl. Attys., Def. Rsch. Inst., Am. Planning Assn., Def. Rsch. Inst. Avocations: running, swimming, hiking, coin collecting, photography. Fax: (206) 223-9423. Home: 11920 27th Pl SW Burien WA 98146-2438 Office: Keating Bucklin & McCormack Inc PS 4141 SeaFirst 5th Ave Pla Seattle WA 98104

WALTER, NIKOLAUS, religious studies educator; b. Wolfen, Germany, Mar. 11, 1932; s. Robert and Caritas (Flügel) W.; m. Katharina Wossidlo, Jan. 2, 1967; children: Hanna, Bettina. D of Theology, Martin Luther U., Halle, Germany, 1961. Wissenschaftlicher asst. Inst. Deutsche Acad., Berlin, 1955-64; lectr. Kirchliche Hochschule, Naumburg, Germany, 1964-86; prof. U. Jena (Germany), 1986-97; retired, 1997. Author: Der Thora-Ausleger Aristobulos, 1964, Fragmente Hellenistisch-jüdischer Historiker, 1976, Praeparatio Evangelica, 1997. Fellow Deutsche Acad. Wissenschaften Berlin, Halle, 1955-64. Mem. Soc. New Testament Studies, Acad. gemeinnütz/Wissenschaften Erfurt. Home: Wilhelm-Wagner-Str 7, D-06618 Naumburg Germany

WALTER, ROLF WILHELM, mathematician, educator; b. Karlsruhe, Germany, Feb. 1, 1937; s. Willi Gottlob and Hedwig Lydia (Siebler) W. Dipl-Math, Technische U., Karlsruhe, 1960; DrRerNat, U. Freiburg, Fed. Republic Germany, 1963. Mem. faculty Technische U., Karlsruhe, 1960-62, U. Freiburg, 1962-72; ordinary prof. math. U. Dortmund, Fed. Republic Germany, 1972—, chmn. dept. math., 1984-87. Author: Differentialgeometrie, 1978, rev. edit., 1989, Einführung in die lineare Algebra, 1982, Lineare Algebra und analytische Geometrie, 1985; author more than 20 rsch. articles on differencial geometry. Mem. Am. Math. Soc., Deutsche Mathematiker-Vereinigung, Hochschulverband. Office: U Dortmund, Faculty Math, 44221 Dortmund Germany

WALTER, WILLIAM PAUL, retired bioengineer; b. Youngstown, Ohio, Sept. 14, 1925; s. John William and Susan Irene (Herald) W.; m. Rita Elizabeth Lang, Aug. 24, 1986. BS, Mt. St. Mary's, Emmitsburg, Md., 1948; bioengrng., U. Md., 1953; MD, Loyola Coll., 1954; postgrad., U. Wis., 1963. Registered microbiologist. From microbiologist to lab chief Pilot Plant Div. Lab., Ft. Detrick, Md., 1951-63; project engr., prin. investigator Bioengrng. Div., Ft. Detrick, 1963-74; prin. investigator, bioengr. chief Biol. Defense Group, Edgewood Arsenal, Md., 1971-74; retired, 1974; cons. Pitman and Moore, Indpls., 1974-75, Johnson and Johnson, Washington, 1974-76, Merck Pharm., Rahway, N.J., 1976-77, Peebles Hosp., Brit. Virgin Islands, 1977-78, NASA, Washington, 1966. Contbr. articles to profl. jours. Supr. Monocacy Fed. Credit Union, Frederick, Md., 1969. With USN, 1944-46. Mem. Am. Soc. Microbiology, Am. Acad. Microbiology (Nat. Registry of Microbiologist), Sigma Xi (Achievement award 1965, 67, chmn. publicity com. 1966, social com. 1970). Republican. Roman Catholic. Avocations: boating, fishing, bowling, basketball referee, snorkeling. Home and Office: 101 Dreamtime Ave Lake Placid FL 33852-6290

WALTER, WOLFGANG LUDWIG, mathematics educator; b. Schwab Gmünd, Germany, May 12, 1927; s. Eugen and Hildegard (Reich) W.; m. Irmgard Scheu, Feb. 21, 1957; children: Wolfgang, Susanne, Katrin. Student, U. Tubingen, 1947-52, PhD, 1956. Asst. math. U. Karlsruhe, Germany, 1957-59, dozent, 1959-63, prof. math., 1963—; vis. prof. U. Md., 1958-59, Notre Dame U., 1965-66, U. Wis., 1969-70, Colo. State U., 1973-74, U. Tenn., 1977, UCLA, 1978, U. Fla., Gainesville, 1982, Ga. Inst. Tech., Atlanta, 1983, U. Conn., 1987, Utah State U., 1988, UNICAMP Campinas, Brazil, 1994. Author: Gewöhnliche Differentialgleichungen, 7th edit., 2000, Differential and Integral Inequalities, 1970, Analysis I and II, 5th edit., 1999, Distributionentheorie, 3d edit., 1994, Ordinary Differential Equations, 1998; mem. editl. bd. Applicable Analysis, 1971—, Nonlinear Analysis: Theory, Methods and Applications, 1976—, Dynamical Systems and Applications, 1992—, Jour. Inequalities and Applications, 1996—; contbr. articles to profl. jours. Mem. Deutsche Mathematiker Vereinigung, Assn. for Angew. Math. and Mechanik (pres. 1986-89), Am. Math. Soc., Math. Assn. Am., Soc. Indsl. and Applied Math. Avocation: music. Home: Breslauer St 66 G, D-76139 Karlsruhe Germany Office: U Karlsruhe Math Inst I, D-76128 Karlsruhe Germany

WALTERS, SIR ALAN ARTHUR, economist, educator; b. Leicester, Eng., 1926. BSc in Econs., U. London, 1951; MA, Oxford U., 1981; DLit (hon.), U. Leicester, 1981; D in Social Sci. (hon.), U. Birmingham, 1984; PhD, Francisco Marroquin, Guatemala. Lectr. dept. econometrics and stats. U. Birmingham (Eng.), 1952-60, prof., 1961-68, head dept., 1961-68; Sir Ernest Cassel prof. econs. U. London, London Sch. Econs., 1968-75; prof. econs. Johns Hopkins U., Balt., 1975-91; resident scholar Am. Enterprise Inst., Washington, 1983-84; vis. prof. Northwestern U., 1959-60, U. Va., 1966-67, MIT, 1967-68, Monash U. (Australia), 1971; past cons. various ctrl. banks; mem. Commn. on London's Third Airport (Roskill), 1968-70; econ. adviser World Bank, 1976-80; chief econ adviser to Prime Minister, U.K., 1981-83, 89; dir. Am. Internat. Trading Group, Washington, 1991. Author: (with R.W. Clower, G. Dalton and M. Harwitz) Growth Without Development, 1966; Integration in Freight Transport, 1968; The Economics of Road User Charges, 1968; An Introduction to Econometrics, 1968, 2d edit., 1969, Money in Bloom and Slump, 3d edit., 1971, Noise and Prices, 1975, (with P.R.G. Layard and McGraw Hill) Microeconomic Theory, 1978, (with E. Bennathan) Port Pricing and Investment in Developing Countries, 1979, Britqain's Economic Renaissance, 1986, Sterling in Danger, 1990, The Economics and Politics of Money, 1998; editor: Money and Banking, 1970; contbr. articles to profl. publs. Decorated knight; recipient Francis Boyer Lecture award Am. Enterprise Inst., 1983. Fellow Econometric Soc. Office: AIG Trading Group, 9 Thomas More Square, London E1 9WZ, England

WALTERS, BARBARA, television journalist; b. Sept. 25, 1931; d. Lou and Dena (Selett) W.; 1 child, Jacqueline. Grad., Sarah Lawrence Coll., 1953; LHD (hon.), Ohio State U., Marymount Coll., Tarrytown, N.Y., 1975, Wheaton Coll., 1983. Former writer-producer WNBC-TV; then with Stas. WPIX and CBS-TV; joined Today Show, 1961, regular panel mem., 1964-74, co-host, 1974-76; moderator syndicated program Not For Women Only, 1974-76; newscaster ABC Evening News (now ABC World News Tonight), 1976-78; host The Barbara Walters Spls., 1976—; co-host ABC TV news show 20/20, 1979—; co-exec. prodr., co-owner, co-host The View, ABC, N.Y.C., 1997—. Contbr. to ABC programs Issues and Answers. Author: How To Talk With Practically Anybody About Practically Anything, 1970; contbr. to Reader's Digest, Good Housekeeping, Family Weekly. Recipient award of yr. Nat. Assn. TV Program Execs., 1975, Emmy award Nat. Acad. TV Arts and Scis., 1975, Mass Media award Am. Jewish Com. Inst. Human Relations, 1975, Hubert H. Humphrey Freedom prize Anti-Defamation League-B'nai B'rith, 1978, Matrix award N.Y. Women in Communications, 1977, Barbara Walters' Coll. Scholarship in Broadcast Journalism established in her honor Ill. Broadcasters Assn., 1975, Pres.'s award Overseas Press Club, 1988, Lowell Thomas award Marist Coll., 1990, Lifetime Achievement award Internat. Women's Media Found., 1992, Lifetime Achievement award

Daytime Emmy Awards, 2000; named to 100 Women Accomplishment Harper's Bazaar, 1967, 71, One of Am.'s 75 Most Important Women Ladies' Home Jour., 1970, One of 10 Women of Decade Ladies' Home Jour., 1979, One of Am.'s 100 Most Important Women Ladies' Home Jour., 1983, Woman of Year in Communications, 1974, Woman of Year Theta Sigma Phi, Broadcaster of Yr. Internat. Radio and TV Soc., 1975, One of 200 Leaders of Future Time Mag., 1974, One of Most Important Women of 1979 Roper Report, One of Women Most Admired by Am. People Gallup Poll, 1982, 84, to Hall of Fame Acad. TV Arts and Scis., 1990. Office: 20/20 147 Columbus Ave Fl 10 New York NY 10023-5900*

WALTERS, DAVID MCLEAN, lawyer; b. Cleve., Apr. 4, 1917; s. William L. and Marguerite (McLean) W.; m. Betty J. Latimer, Mar. 25, 1939 (dec. 1983); 1 child, Susan Patricia (Mrs. James Edward Smith); m. Rebecca Brewer, Feb. 14, 1991. BA, Baldwin-Wallace Coll., 1938, LHD (hon.); LLB, Cleve. Sch. Law, 1943; JD, U. Miami, 1950; LHD (hon.), St. Thomas of Villanova U. Bar: D.C. 1950, Fla. 1950, Fed. 1950. Judge adminstrv. practices U.S. Dept. Justice, Washington, 1940-50; sr. law ptnr. firm Walters & Costanzo, Miami, Fla., 1950-80; of counsel firm Walters, Costanzo, Russell, Zyne, 1980-85; amb. to Vatican, 1976-78; fellow internat. medicine, bd. advisors Med. Sch., Boston U., 1985. Chmn. Fla. Harbor Pilot Commn., 1952-54, City of Miami Seaport Commn., 1953-54, Nat. Leukemia Soc., 1965-66, Archbishops Charities Dr., 1975-76; spl. bond counsel Dade County, 1957-58; gen. counsel Dade County Port Authority, 1957-58; vice-chmn. Nat. Dem. Fin. Coun., 1960-77; mem. Gov.'s Adv. Bd. on Health and Rehabilitative Svc., 1976-77; sec.-treas. Inter-Am. Ctr. Authority, 1960-74; bd. advisor St. Thomas Law Sch., 1985-88; personal rep. Pres. Reagan F.D.R. Meml. Commn., 1985; bd. dirs. Barry U.; chmn. bd. trustees Variety Children's Hosp.; pres. Miami Children's Hosp. Found., 1980—; trustee Gregorian Inst. Found., Rome. Served with Counter Intelligence Corps., U.S. Army, 1943-46. Decorated Bronze Star medal., Knight of the Grand-cross, Order St. Gregory the Great; recipient Silver medallion NCCJ, Resolution of Commendation award for civic contbn. Fla. Legislature, 1988. Mem. Am., Fla., Fed., D.C., Interam. bar assns., Am. Assn. Knights of Malta (v.p.), Serra Club, Sovereign Mil. Order Malta (master knight 1975—, exec. com. papal visit to U.S. 1987), Omicron Delta Kappa, Lambda Chi Alpha. Democrat. Roman Catholic. Home: 9202 SW 78th Pl Miami FL 33156-7590 Home (summer): 5 St Helens, Marine Parade Sandycove, Dublin Ireland Office: 3000 SW 62nd Ave Miami FL 33155-3065

WALTERS, JEFFERSON BROOKS, musician, retired real estate broker; b. Dayton, Ohio, Jan. 20, 1922; s. Jefferson Brooks and Mildred Frances (Smith) W.; m. Mary Elizabeth Espey, Apr. 6, 1963 (dec. July 22, 1983); children: Dinah Christine Basson, Jefferson Brooks; m. Carol Elaine Clayton Gillette, Feb. 19, 1984. Student, U. Dayton, 1947. Composer, cornetist Dayton, 1934—, real estate broker, 1948-88; ret., 1988. Condr., composer choral, solo voice settings of psalms and poetry Alfred Lord Tennyson; composer Crossing the Bar (meml. performances U.S. Navy band), 1961; composer The Yorktown Grand March (Good Citizenship medal SAR, 1988). Founder Am. Psalm Choir, 1965; apptd. deferred giving officer Kettering (Ohio) Med. Ctr., 1982-85. Served with USCGR, 1942-45, PTO, ETO. Mem. SAR (life), Greater Dayton Antique Study Club (past pres.), Dayton Art Inst., Montgomery County Hist. Soc., Masons (32d deg.). Brethren Ch. Home: 4113 Roman Dr Dayton OH 45415-2423

WALTERS, JERRY WILLARD, retired federal intelligence officer; b. Paducah, Ky., Aug. 26, 1936; s. Rex Willard and Dorothy Maureen (Smith) W.; m. Rita Ann Middledorf, Oct. 10, 1960; children: Rex Robert, Wade Alan, Stacy Lee. BA, U. Md., 1959. Fingerprint specialist FBI, Washington, 1955-57; commd. ensign USN, 1960; served as intelligence officer U.S. Naval Security Group, Alaska, and the Philippines, 1960-70; intelligence analyst Nat. Security Agy., Washington, 1966-69; human intelligence case officer U.S. Naval Intelligence, Japan, 1973-77; intelligence ops. officer Bur. Alcohol, Tobacco & Firearms, Washington, 1978-82; mgr. customs intelligence officer U.S. Customs Svc., Washington, 1982-93. Mem. Internat. Assn. Law Enforcement Intelligence Analysts (charter, bd. dirs. 1980-90, pres. 1986-89). Republican. Avocations: guitarist, video photography, oriental languages. Home: 10510 Cobbler Valley Ln Delaplane VA 20144-2018

WALTERS, JULIAN ROGER FORD, gastroenterologist, researcher; b. Weston-Super-Mare, England, Aug. 3, 1951; s. Roger and Dorothy (Ford) W.; m. Ann Frances Williams; children: Thomas, Anna, Owen, Huw. BA, U. Cambridge, England, 1972, MB BChir, 1976. Diplomate Am. Bd. Internal Medicine, Am. Bd. Gastroenterology. House physician Kings Coll. Hosp., London, 1976; resident physician Dudley Road Hosp., Birmingham, England, 1977-80; rsch. fellow Gen. Hosp., Birmingham, 1980-81; NIH tng. fellow SUNY at Buffalo, 1981-82, asst. prof., 1983-88; lectr. UMDS Guys Hosp., London, 1988-89; sr. lectr. RMPS Hammersmith Hosp., London, 1989-97, Reader Imperial Coll. Sch. Medicine, 1997—. Recipient numerous Research grants. Fellow Royal Coll. Physicians; mem. Am. Gastroenterological Assn., British Soc. Gastroenterology. Avocations: music, photography, industrial archaeology, virtual travel. Office: Gastroenterology Unit, Hammersmith Hosp, W12 0NN London England

WALTERS, KEITH FREDERICK ARTHUR, applied insect ecologist, researcher; b. Southampton, U.K., Oct. 23, 1956; s. Frederick William and Ailsa Edith (Mount) W.; m. Susan Margaret Jones, Sept. 8, 1979; children: Fawn Susan, Steffan Keith. BSc with honors, London U., 1978; PhD, U. East Anglia, Norwich, U.K., 1982. Rschr. U. East Anglia and Rothamsted Exptl. Sta., Norwich/Harpenden, Eng., 1978-82; sr. rsch. assoc. U. East Anglia, Norwich, 1982-83; entomologist Dept. Agr. and Fisheries for Scotland, Edinburgh, Scotland, 1983-88; entomologist Ctrl. Sci. Lab., York, Eng., 1988-92, head pest biology, modelling and mgmt., 1992—; sec. pests and diseases tech. subcom. Brit. Crop Protection Coun., London, 1992-98, chair pests and diseases expert working group, 1999; mem. organizing com. Brighton (U.K.) Crop Protection Conf., 1994, 96, 98, 2000; coordinated action group European Union, Brussels, 1992-2000. Author: The Ecology of Insect Overwintering, 1993; editor: Individuals, Populations and Patterns in Ecology, 1994, Populations and Patterns in Biology, 1996; sr. editor The Jour. Agrl. and Forest Entomology, 1999—; contbr. articles to profl. jours. Recipient numerous rsch. grants, 1984—. Fellow Royal Entomol. Soc. (coord. aphid spl. interest group 1991-99, v.p. 1994-95); mem. Royal Coll. Sci. (assoc.), Inst. Biology, Assn. Applied Biology. Mem. United Reformed Ch. Achievements include research in overwintering, biology of quarantine pests, cabbage stem flea beetle on oilseed rape; cabbage seed weevil on oilseed rape; pollen beetle on oilseed rape; cereal aphids on winter wheat; pea aphids on combining peas. Avocations: collector of Roman coins, long distance running. Office: Ctrl Sci Lab, Sand Hutton, York Y041 1LZ, England

WALTERS, KENN DAVID, computer scientist, computer company executive; b. Birmingham, Eng., July 1, 1957; s. Kenneth Walters; m. Barbara Grabert, Aug. 9, 1985; children: Natascha Ruth, Vanessa Marjorie. BSc in Computer Sci., Highbury Tech. Sch., Portsmouth, Eng., 1973; MSc in Computer and Info. Systems, Pacific Western U., Calif., 1989; PhD in Computer Info. Sytems, Pacific Western U., 1991. Programmer Arinco, London, 1973-75; project leader I.C.L., London, 1976-78; exec. cons. Globus Consulting (ITT Corp.), Eng., 1978-82; cons., project leader I.T.T., Fed. Republic Germany and U.S., 1982-86; div. mgr. Nixdorf Computers A.G., Munich, 1987-89; chief exec. officer Capricorn Systems Assocs., Munich, 1989-91, ESP Informatik GMbH, Munich, 1991-93; CEO Globus Cons., Munich and London, 1993—. Author: Programming Practices and Guidelines, 1985. Fellow Inst. Analysts and Programmers; mem. Data Processing Inst., Inst. for Data Processing Mgmt., N.Y. Acad. Scis. Avocations: shooting, reading, classic cars.

WALTERS, KENNETH C., retired educator; b. Constantine, Mich., Apr. 2, 1913; s. Roy Irvin and Pearl Valentine (Ashbaugh) W. Student, Western Mich. U., 1931-35; MA in Math., MA in Edn., U. Mich., 1948; PhD in Math., U. Fla., 1952. Tchr. coll. level, 1936-52. One man shows, Thousand Oaks, Calif.; author: (novels) Gone with the Winter, 1980, I, the President, 1980, (comedy, play) Irene, The Nurse's Aide, 1980, (instrnl.) Beginners Play Piano in 60 Minutes, 1996, over 100 poems; copyright 8,400 songs; standup comedian; composer songs for commls., Broadway musicals. Advisor to Bill Clinton. 4-yr. scholar Western Mich. U., 1931-35. Mem. Burbank Catalina Art Assn. (pres.), San Fernando Art Club. Home: 2233 N Catalina St Burbank CA 91504-3246

WALTERS, PETER INGRAM, petroleum company executive; b. Birmingham, Eng., Mar. 11, 1931; s. Stephen and Edna F. (Redgate) W.; m. Patricia Anne Tulloch, 1960 (dissolved 1991); 3 children; m. Meryl Marshall, 1992. Student, King Edward's Sch., Birmingham, Eng.; B.Com., U. Birmingham; D in Social Sci. (hon.), 1986. Chmn. Midland Bank, 1991—; chmn. Blue Circle Industries PLC, 1990—, dir., 1989—, dep. chmn., 1990—; with British Petroleum Co., 1954-90, mng. dir., 1973-90, chmn., 1981-90; v.p. BP N.Am., 1965-67; chmn. BP Chems., 1976-81; chmn. BP Chems. Internat., 1981, dir., 1981-89, dep. chmn., 1988-89; dir. Smithkline Beecham plc, 1989-90, dep. chmn., 1990-94, chmn., 1994—. Mem. Ind. Soc. Coun., 1975-90, Post Office Bd., 1978-79, adv. bd. Coal Industry, 1981-85, gen. com. Lloyds Register of Shipping, 1976-90, pres.'s com. CBI, 1982-90, Inst. Manpower Studies, 1986-88, v.p., 1977-80, pres., 1980-86; pres. Soc. Chem. Industry, 1978-80, gen. coun. British Shipping, 1977-78, Inst. Dirs., 1986—; chmn. govs. London Bus. Sch., 1987-91, gov., 1981-91; gov. Nat. Inst. Econ. and Social Affairs, 1981-90, mem. found. bd., 1982-83, chmn., 1984-86; trustee Nat. Maritime Mus., 1983-90, E. Mailing Res. Sta., 1983—. Created Knight, 1984; decorated comdr. Order of Leopold (Belgium), 1984. Avocations: gardening, sailing. Office: SmithKline Beecham, 22 Hill St, London W1X 7FU, England also: Midland Bank PLC/City London Corp Office, 27-32 Poultry, London EC2P 2BX, England also: SmithKline Beecham Plc, New Horizons Ct, Brentford England*

WALTERS, ROBERT ANCIL, physicist, mathematician; b. Russell Springs, Ky., Mar. 12, 1915; s. Robert Edmund Lee and Talitha Margaret (Wilson) W.; m. Etha Jane McKinley, Feb. 2, 1943; 1 child, Robert Ancil II; m. Sandra Faye Roy, June 29, 1969; 1 child, Forrest Wayne. BS, Western Ky. U., 1941; postgrad., George Washington U., 1943-45, Agrl. Grad. Sch., 1947-48, Am. U., 1951-52. H.S. asst. prin. Russell County Bd. Edn., 1941-42; physicist, head exterior ballistics U.S. Naval Weapons Lab., Dahlgren, Va., 1942-59; pres. Walters Ins. and Investment Counselor, Dahlgren, 1948-80; engr., head systems planning U.S. Naval Space Surveillance, Dahlgren, Va., 1959-69; R&D specialist, physicist interdisplinary math. cons. U.S. Naval Warfare Lab., Dahlgren, 1969-75; pres. Navel Weapons Lab. Fed. Credit Union, Dahlgren, 1968-74; bd. examiners Potomac River Naval Gom., Washington, 1953-56; biology lab. instr. Western Ky. U., Bowling Green, 1935-36. Chmn. Old Dominion Eye Bank, Richmond, Va., 1975-76; co-chair Dem. Party, 1937-42; pres. Nat. Fedn. Fed. Employees, Washington, 1963-69. Recipient Nat. Quality award Nat. Assn. Life Underwriters, 1976; named Ky. Col., gov. of Ky., 1976, Outstanding Citizen of Yr., VFW, 1981, Guest of Honor King George County Fall Festival, 1994. Mem. Lions Internat. (dep. dist. gov. 1976-77, Disting. Svc. award 1975). Baptist. Home: 5460 Potomac Dr PO Box 877 Dahlgren VA 22448-0877

WALTERS, ROBERT FREDERICK, illustrator, museum consultant; b. Phila., Mar. 24, 1949; s. Frederick and Cora Maxwell (Strother) W. Cert. in comml. graphics, Del. Valley Graphic Arts Assn., 1972; BFA in Graphics, Pa. Acad. of Fine Art, 1973. Pvt. illustration studio, 1978—; chief exhibits illustrator Acad. Nat. Scis., Phila., 1985-86, 97-98; exec. art dir., curator Dinofest Acad. Nat. Scis., 1998; muralist, illustrator Creative Discovery Mus., Chattanooga, 1994-95; guest curator dinosaur exhibit Bruce Mus., Yale Peabody Mus., Conn., 1997-98; guest lectr. Princeton U., N.J., Nat. Mus. History, Smithsonian Inst., Washington, Boston Mus. Sci., Longwood Gardens, Kennett Sq., Pa., Art. Inst. Phila.; instr. dinosaur reconstrn. course Acad. Nat. Scis. Illustrator The Age of Dinosaurs, The Encyclopedia of Dinosaurs, National Geographic World, The Complete T-Rex, Pterosaurs, Dinosaurs: Unearthing the Secrets of Ancient Beasts, Bigger Than T-Rex, 1997, The Great Hunters, 1997, others; illustrator, art dir. The Complete Dinosaur, 1998; illustrator, art editor The Ceratopsians: A Natural History, 1997; contbr. illustrations, artwork to Jurassic Park theme ride pre-show video, (CD-Rom) Dinosaur Discovery, Dinosaur Video Disk, Acad. Nat. Scis. and Boston Mus. Sci., (video disk) Coelophysis Excavation, Smithsonian, (TV series) The Dinosaurs, PBS, (TV show) Paleoworld, The Learning Channel, (ednl. video) Where Did They Go? A Dinosaur Update (silver medal Internat. Film and Video Festival, Sci. Edn.), others; advt. campaign Am. Mus. Nat. History; dinosaur calendar, 1994; cons., contbg. artist Dinosaur Poster Book; works exhibited at Cranbrook Inst. Sci., Ohio, Acad. Natural Scis., Longwood Gardens, Kennett Square, Pa., Nat. Aquarium, Balt., Saguaro Gallery, Park City, Utah; numerous traveling exhibits; permanent displays Nat. Mus. Natural History, Creative Discovery Mus., Chattanooga. Recipient Chesley award Assn. Sci. Fiction Artists, 1984, 85, 86, 91. Mem. Soc. Vertebrate Paleontology. Avocations: drumming, percussion. E-mail: bobtess@dinoart.com. Office: Walters & Kissinger 2634 Parrish St Philadelphia PA 19130-1829

WALTERS, SHERWOOD G., professor, consulant; b. Detroit, May 9, 1926; s. George Henry and Helen (Parker) W.; m. Alexandra (Sielcken) Walters, Sept. 4, 1952; children: Margaret Taylor Clifford, Karen Chapin, George Alexander, Virginai Sherwood McFee. BA cum laude, W. Maryland Coll., 1949; MS, Columbia U., 1950; MBA with distinction, Columbia U., Grad. Sch. Bus., 1953; PhD hons. scholar, N.Y. U., 1960. Assoc. prof., Econ. Sociology Coll. Bus. Econ., Lehigh U., Bethlehem, Pa., 1950-60; exec. v.p., dir. ctrs., retail planning mgr. Mobil Oil, N.Y.C., 1960-65; exec. officer, mktg. dir. Gen. Tire & Rubber Internat. Plastics Co., Chem. Plastics Divsn., Akron, Ohio, 1965-70; prof. Rutgers U., Newark, N.J., 1970-93; prof. emeritus mgmt. studies Rutgers U., Newark, 1993—, founding dir. interfunctional mgmt. program, 1970-88; evaluator/emissary U.S. NSF, 1980—, cons. in field. Co-author: Marketing Management Viewpoints, 2nd ed. 1970, Mandatory Housing Finance Programs, 1975, Managing the Industry University Cooperative Research Centers: A Guide for Directors and Other Stakeholders, 1998. Chmn. N.J. gov. public utility commission task force, 1973-75, U./Indsl. Partnerships, John Von Neumann Ctr., Princeton, N.J., 1986. 1st Lt. Infantry/Quartermaster, Corps, 1944-47. Mem. Newcomen Soc. Presbyterian. Avocations: deep sea fishing. Home: 110 Topsail Watch Ln Hampstead NC 28443-2728

WALTERS, WILLIAM ALLEN WILLCOX, obstetrician, gynecologist, medical educator; b. Adelaide, Australia, May 27, 1933; s. Lance Strother and Jeanie May (Willcox) W. MB, BS, U. Adelaide, 1956; PhD, U. London, 1964. House physician, house surgeon Royal Adelaide Hosp., South Australia, 1956-57; obstetric house surgeon and registrar Queen Victoria Maternity Hosp., Adelaide, 1957-58; sr. house officer gynecology Jessop Hosp. Women, Sheffield, U.K., 1958-59; Med. Rsch. Coun. Rsch. fellow and tutor Hammersmith Hosp., London, 1960-63; lectr. in ob-gyn. U. Aberdeen, Scotland, 1963-65; sr. lectr. ob-gyn. Monash U., Melbourne, Australia, 1965-70, assoc. prof., 1970-85; prof. reproductive medicine U. Newcastle, Australia, 1985—, dep. dean faculty medicine and health scis., 1993-96; chmn. div. ob-gyn. John Hunter Hosp., Newcastle, 1991—; chair maternal and perinatal com. N.S.W. Health Dept., Sydney, 1995—, mem. maternity svcs. adv. com., 1998—; mem. Hunter Area Health Svc. Bd., 1994-98. Editor: Human Reproduction: Current and Future Ethical Issues, Baillière's Clinical Obstetrics and Gynaecology, 1991; contbr. articles to profl. jours. Fellow Royal Soc. Medicine, Royal Coll. Obstetricians and Gynecologists, Royal Australian Coll. Obstetricians and Gynecologists, Australian Coll. Sexual Health Physicians; mem. N.Y. Acad. Scis., Australian Perinatal Soc., Australian Soc. Reproductive Biology, Australian Assn. Clin. Profs., Australian Bioethics Assn., Australian and N.Z. Perinatal Soc., Australian Soc. for Study of Hypertension in Pregnancy, Med. Protection Soc., Newcastle Ob-Gyn Soc., North of Eng. Ob-Gyn Soc., Obstetric Med. Group Australia, Asian Fedn. Ob-Gyn., Asia Oceania Fedn. Perinatal Socs., Internat. Fedn. World Placental Assns., Hunter Postgrad. Med. Inst., MacDonald Club. Avocations: Egyptology, English literature, classical music. Home: 49 Tyrrell St, Newcastle 2300 NSW, Australia Office: John Hunter Hospital, Lookout Rd, New Lambton 2305 NSW, Australia

WALTHER, GERD ERWIN, mathematics educator; b. Amberg, Bavaria, Germany, Aug. 3, 1945; s. Erwin Ernst and Maud (Schunk) W.; m. Maria Lisa Mueller, June 14, 1974; children—Sabine, Thomas-Eike. Diploma Math., Universitaet Erlangen, Germany, 1970; Dr. Paed., Paed. Hochschule, Dortmund, Germany, 1974, Privatdozent, 1979. Asst. prof. Paed. Hochschule, Dortmund, 1971-76, Akad. Rat, 1976-81, prof. math., Kiel, Germany, 1981—. Translator; contbr. articles to profl. jours., chpts. in books. Mem. Gesellschaft fuer Didaktik der Mathematik. Office: Paedagogische Hochschule, Olshausenstr 75, 24118 Kiel Germany

WALTHER, HELMUT G(ERHARD), medieval history educator; b. Bayreuth, Germany, July 4, 1944; m. Gisela Maassen, Feb. 21, 1975. PhD, U. Konstanz, 1970, Habilitation, 1978. Scholar U. Konstanz, 1970-78; prof. medieval history Christian-Albrechts U., Kiel, Germany, 1979-93, U. Göttingen, Germany, 1985-86, U. Hannover, Germany, 1990, U. Münster, Germany, 1991, Free U. Berlin, 1991-92, U. Rostock, Germany, 1992, Friedrich Schiller U., Jena, Germany, 1993—; vis. prof. medieval history German Hist. Inst., Rome, 1988-89. Author: Imperiales Konigtum, 1976, Hus in Konstanz, 1978, Aufbrueche 450 Jehre Hoche Schule Jena, 1998; editor: Buendnissysteme u. Aussenpolitik im Spateren Mittelalter, 1988. Office: Friedrich Schiller U, Humboldtstr 11, D-07743 Jena Germany

WALTHER, JOHANNES PETER, banker, financial consultant; b. Eindhoven, North Brabant, Holland, July 22, 1933; came to Argentina, 1961.; s. George Johannes Peter and Jantje Alida (Van Randwijk) W.; m. Anna de Boer; 1 child, Ingrid Christina. Grad. high sch., Holland. Chief dept. ABN Bank, Buenos Aires, 1961-72; mgr. subs. bank Continental Illinois NBT Co., Holland, 1972-75, Boston Bank, Buenos Aires, 1976-83; gen. mgr. NMB Bank, Uraguay, 1983-85; treas. Welfare Soc., Buenos Aires, 1986; fin. advisor Tucuman, Buenos Aires, 1986—. Home and Office: Roque Saenz Pena 692, Roque Saenz Pena 692, San Isidro 1642, Buenos Aires Argentina Office: Tucumán540, Floor 27, Buenos Aires Argentina

WALTHER, MANFRED ODO, philosopher, educator; b. Berlin, May 24, 1938; s. Odo and Ilse (Petersdorff) W.; m. Gudrun Spennes, July 21, 1978; 1 child, Rebecca. PhD, U. Frankfurt, 1968. Asst. theologian U. Munster, Fed. Republic of Germany, 1964-66; projectionist HIS GmbH, Hannover, Fed. Republic of Germany, 1969-71; dozent U. Hamburg, Fed. Republic of Germany, 1971-74, prof. in didactics of Jurisprudence, 1975—; prof. in Philosophy U. Hannover, Fed. Republic of Germany, 1985—; pres. Spinoza-Gesellschaft, 1988—. Author: Metaphysik als Antitheologie, 1971, Das Leben Spinozas—Eine Bibliographie, 1996; co-editor: (series) Studia Spinozana, 1985—, Fundamenta Juridica: Beiträge z. rechtswiss. Grundlagenforschung, 1985—, Schriften der Spinoza-Gesellschaft, 1991—. Home: Eisvogelring 42, 30196 Isernhagen Germany Office: U Hannover Fachbereich, Königsworther Platz 1, D-30167 Hannover Germany

WALTON, ANTHONY JOHN (TONY WALTON), theater and film designer, book illustrator; b. Walton on Thames, Eng., Oct. 24, 1934; s. Lancelot Henry Frederick and Hilda Betty (Drew) W.; m. Julie Andrews, May 10, 1959 (div. 1968); 1 child, Emma Kate; m. Genevieve LeRoy, Sept. 12, 1991; 1 stepchild, Bridget. Student, Oxford Sch. Tech. Art and Commerce, 1949-52, Slade Sch. Fine Art, London, 1954-55. Designer settings, costumes for theater prodns., London, off-Broadway, 1957-60, Broadway, 1961—; Broadway prodns. include Pippin, 1972 (Tony award 1972-73, Drama Desk award 1972-73), Shelter, 1973 (Drama Desk award 1972-73), Chicago, 1975, Sophisticated Ladies, 1981, The Real Thing, 1984, Hurlyburly, 1984, I'm Not Rappaport, 1985, House of Blue Leaves, 1986 (Tony award 1985-86), Drama Desk award 1985-86), Front Page, 1986, Social Security, 1986 (Drama Desk award 1985-86), Anything Goes, 1987, Grand Hotel, 1989, Six Degrees of Separation, 1990, The Will Rogers Follies, 1991, Death and the Maiden, 1992, Conversations with My Father, 1992, Four Baboons Adoring the Sun, 1992, Guys and Dolls, 1992 (Tony award 1991-92, Drama Desk award 1991-92), Tommy Tune Tonight, 1992, She Loves Me, 1993, A Grand Night for Singing, 1993, Laughter on the 23rd Floor, 1993, Picnic, 1994, A Christmas Carol, N.Y.C., 1994, Company, 1995, Moonlight, 1995, A Fair Country, 1996, A Funny Thing Happened on the Way to the Forum, 1996, The Shawl, 1996, Taller Than a Dwarf, 2000, Uncle Vanya, 2000, The Man Who Came To Dinner, 2000; dir., designer The Importance of Being Earnest, 1996, Major Barbara, 1997; dir. Noel Coward in Two Keys Bay St. Theatre Festival, 1996, Make Someone Happy, Bay St. Theater Festival, 1997, Not Waving, 1997, Steel Pier, 1997, King David, 1997, 1776, 1997; The Cripple of Inishman, 1998; Noel & Gertie, 1998; House, 1998; Ashes to Ashes, 1999; Annie Get Your Gun, 1999; On Raftery's Hill, 2000 (Dublin and London); dir. Missing Footage, 1999, If Love Were All, 1999; dir., co-writer, costume designer Oops! The Big Apple Circus Stage Show, 1999; ballets, principally San Francisco Ballet Co., Am. Ballet Theatre; films include Mary Poppins, A Funny Thing Happened on the Way to the Forum, Murder on the Orient Express, The Wiz, All That Jazz (Acad. award with Philip Rosenberg 1980), Prince of the City, Star 80, The Glass Menagerie, 1987, Regarding Henry, 1991; operas in London, 1963-68, Spoleto, Italy, 1965, Santa Fe, 1975, San Francisco, 1992, Chgo., 1993; author: Adelie Penguin in Wonders, 1981; illustrator Wonders, 1981, The Importance of Being Earnest, 1973, Lady Windemere's Fan, 1973, Popcorn, 1972, God Is a Good friend, 1969, Witches Holiday, 1971, others. Served with RAF, 1952-54. Recipient Emmy award Death of a Salesman, 1986; named to Theatre Hall of Fame, 1991; elected to Interior Design Hall of Fame, 1993. Mem. United Scenic Artists, Costume Designers Guild Calif., Acad. Motion Picture Arts and Scis. Office: care Martino ICM 40 W 57th St New York NY 10019-4001

WALTON, ANTHONY MICHAEL, lawyer; b. London, May 4, 1925; s. Henry Herbert and Martha Clara (Dobrantz) W.; m. Jean Frederica Hey, July 30, 1955; 1 child, Martin. MA, Oxford U., 1950, BCL, 1950. Queen's Counsel, 1970. pres. Oxford Union Trinity Term, 1945. Author: Ency. of Brit. and European Patent Law; editor: Russell on Arbitration. Bencher Mid. Temple, 1978, Master Reader Autumn, 1996. Home: 62 Kingsmead Rd, Tulse Hill London SW2 3JG, England

WALTON, BRENT, chemical company executive; b. Rochdale, Lancashire, Eng., Oct. 31, 1959; s. Frank and Phyllis (Chadwick) W. BSc in Applied Chemistry, Manchester (Eng.) Met. U., 1986; MSc in Chemistry, U. Salford, Eng., 1996. Rsch. technician Manchester Royal Infirmary, 1978-80; quality control analyst Ashe Labs., Rochdale, Eng., 1980-83; mass spectroscopist ICI Pharms., Alderley Edge, Eng., 1983-87; sr. analyst Manro Performance Chems. Ltd., Stalybridge, Eng., 1987—. Avocations: reading, astronomy, sports, science discoveries, cinema. Home: Croxton Ave, Rochdale OL16 2YR, England Office: Manro Performance Chems Ltd, Bridge St, Stalybridge SK15 1PH, England

WALTON, CLIFFORD WAYNE, chemical engineer, researcher; b. Phila., May 14, 1954; s. John Robert and Elizabeth Baird (Hamilton) W. BSChemE, Drexel U., 1976; MSChemE, Tex. A&M U., 1977, PhD, 1987. Registered profl. engr., Nebr.; cert. electroplater-finisher. Instr. U. Coll. div. U. Md., Stuttgart, Germany, 1978-79, Tex. A&M U., College Station, 1982-84; rsch. engr. Dow Chem. Co., Freeport, Tex., 1985; asst. prof. U. Nebr., Lincoln, Nebr., 1987-91; assoc. prof. U. Nebr., Lincoln, 1991-92; cons. Walton & Assocs., Lincoln, 1987-94; rsch. assoc. FMC Corp., Princeton, N.J., 1994-97, project leader, sr. rsch. assoc., 1997-00, project leader, assoc. fellow, 2000—; cons. Lincoln Plating Co., 1987-94, Mitsui Engring. and Shipbuilding Co., Ltd., Tokyo, 1989-93, Nat. Ctr. for Mfrs. Scis., Ann Arbor, 1990-94, J.P. Industries, Ann Arbor, 1990-94. Editl. bd. Plating and Surface Finishing, 1989-95; internat. editl. bd. Jour. of Clearner Prodn., 1990—; contbr. articles to profl. jours. Treas. Nebr. Wrestling Booster Club, Lincoln, 1990-92. 1st lt. U.S. Army, 1977-80. Named Outstanding Young Man in Am., U.S. Jaycees, 1982; recipient Ralph R. Teetor award Soc. Automotive Engrs., 1990. Mem. AIChE (sec.-treas. Nebr. br. 1989-91), ASTM (tech. com. 1989-96), Am. Electroplaters and Surface Finishers Soc. (br. pres. 1988-91, publs. bd. 1989-95, scholarship com. 1989-92, chair scholarship com. 1992-94, 95-96), Electrochem. Soc. Inc. (sec. IEEE divsn. 1996-98, symposium organizer 1989, 90, 92, 96, 97, 99, 2000, procs. vol. editor 1990, 97, 99, vice chair IEEE divsn. 1998-00, chair IEEE divsn. 2000-02, contbg. mem. com. 1999—). Avocation: physical fitness, amateur wrestling, boxing, church choir, church youth groups. Office: FMC Corp Chem Rsch & Devel Ctr PO Box 8 Princeton NJ 08543-0008

WALTON, CONRAD GORDON, SR., architect; b. Houston, June 18, 1928; s. John Edward and Evelyn Lucile (Gordon) W.; m. Rilda Ellen Akin, Dec. 10, 1954; children: Conrad Gordon, Evelyn Coleman, Rogerta Agnes. BS (Walsh scholar), Rice U., 1951; postgrad., U. Houston, 1955. Registered architect, Tex., NCARB. Pres. DCW Architects, Inc. Home: 9014 Springview Ln Houston TX 77080-1755 Office: 2425 Fountain View Dr Ste 225 Houston TX 77057-4834

WALTON, (DELVY) CRAIG, philosopher, educator; b. L.A., Dec. 6, 1934; s. Delvy Thomas and Florence (Higgins) W.; m. Nancy Young, June 6, 1965 (div. May 1977); children: Richard, Kerry; m. Vera Allerton, Aug. 30, 1980; children: Matthew, Ruth, Peter, Benjamin. BA, Pomona Coll., 1961; PhD, Claremont Grad. Sch., 1965. Asst. prof. U. So. Calif., L.A., 1964-68; asst. prof. No. Ill. U., DeKalb, 1968-71, assoc. prof., 1971-72; assoc. prof. U. Nev., Las Vegas, 1972-76, prof., 1976—, chmn. dept. philosophy, 1986-89, dir. Inst. for Ethics and Policy Studies, 1986—; presenter workshops in field. Author: De la recherche du Bien, 1972, Philosophy & the Civilizing Arts, 1975, Hobbes's Science of Natural Justice, 1987; translator: (intro.) Treatise on Ethics (Malebranche), 1992; bd. dirs. Jour. History of Philosophy, 1978—; contbr. articles to profl. jours. V.p. Nev. Faculty Alliance, 1984-86, pres. 95-97; mem. Clark County Sch. Dist. Task Force on Ethics in schs., 1987, 96-97. 1st lt. USAF, 1956-59. Recipient NDEA Title IV fellowship Claremont Grad. Sch., 1961-64, rsch. sabbaticals U. Nev., 1978, 85, 92; named Barrick Disting. scholar U. Nev., 1988. Mem. AAUP (pres. Nev. chpt. 1983-84), Internat. Hume Soc. (exec. com. 1979-81), Am. Philos. Assn., Soc. for Study History of Philosophy (founder and mem. exec. com. 1974-91), Internat. Hobbes Soc., Phi Beta Kappa. Democrat. Avocations: backpacking, hiking, snow-shoeing, salad-making, dog tng. Fax: (702) 645-3157. E-mail: cwalton@nevada.edu. Home: 6140 Eisner Dr Las Vegas NV 89131-2303 Office: U Nev Inst Ethics Policy Studies 4505 S Maryland Pkwy Las Vegas NV 89154-9900

WALTON, DAN GIBSON, lawyer; b. Houston, Mar. 26, 1950; s. Dan Edward and Lucy Frances (Gibson) W.; m. Martha Sandlin, June 24, 1972; children: Cole Gibson, Emily Wyatt. BA with honors, U. Va., 1972; JD with honors, U. Tex., 1975. Bar: Tex. 1975, U.S. Dist. Ct. (so. dist.) Tex. 1977, U.S. Ct. Appeals (D.C. cir.) 1975, U.S. Ct. Appeals (5th cir.) 1981; bd. cert. in civil trial law and personal injury. Law clk. to hon. Malcolm R. Wilkey D.C. Ct. Appeals (D.C. cir.), 1975-76; assoc. Vinson & Elkins, Houston, 1976-82, ptnr., 1982—; bd. dirs. The Meth. Health Care Sys., Houston. Bd. dirs. Meml. Pk. Conservancy, Houston, 2000—, Tex. Equal Access to Justice Found., 2000—, State Bar of Tex., 1999—, South Tex. Coll. Law, Houston, 1994—, Covenant House Tex., Houston, 1993—, Briarwood Sch./Brookwood Cmty., Houston, 1991—; trustee St. John's Sch., Houston, 1997—, Good Samaritan Found., 1998—; co-chancellor Tex. Ann. Conf., United Meth. Ch., Houston, 1996—. Fellow Am. Bar Found., Tex. Bar Found., Houston Bar Found. (chair 1994), Houston Bar Assn. (pres. 1998-99), Garland Walker Am. Inn of Ct. (master), Am. Bd. Trial Advocates (assoc.), Internat. Assn. Def. Counsel, Tex. Assn. Def. Counsel. Avocations: golf, skiing. Home: 3203 Ella Lee Ln Houston TX 77019-5923 Office: Vinson & Elkins LLP 2300 First City Tower 1001 Fannin St Ste 3201 Houston TX 77002-6706

WALTON, DEWITT TALMAGE, JR., dentist; b. Macon, Ga., May 25, 1937; s. DeWitt T. Sr. and Jimmie (Braswell) W.; m. Joan Robinson, June 11, 1960; children: Jimmie Walton Paschall, Gwen N., Gayle N., Joy A. BS, Howard U., 1960, DDS, 1961. Pvt. practice Macon, 1963—; Chmn. dental adv. com. Ga. Dept. Med. Assistance; dental svcs. adv. com. Dept. Physical Health, Ga. Dept. Human Resources; adv. bd. dirs. Wachovia Bank, Macon-Warner Robins area; bd. dirs. The Ga. Dept. Cmty. Affairs. Fin. chmn. Boy Scouts Am., Piedmont/Creek Dist., 1978-80, exec. bd., 1978-82, v.p. exec. com., 1983-84; apptd. Bibb County Bd. Edn., 1969-73; vice chmn. Macon-Bibb County Transit Authority, 1981-87; dir. exec. com. Devel. Corp. Mid. Ga., 1984-91; sec.-treas. Urban Devel. Authority, Macon-Bibb County, 1984-87; trustee Macon Heritage Found., 1983-87; bd. dirs. Ctrl. Ga. Speech and Hearing Ctr., 1984-87, Boys' Club Macon, Inc., 1986, 87, 88, The Grand Opera House, 1988, 89, 90, Booker T. Washington Ctr., 1993, Pub. Edn. Found., 1995—, Douglass Theater, 1995—; mem. oversight com. Minority Bus. Assistance Program, 1984-91; active Bibb County Commn. on Excellence in Edn., 1984; trustee United Way Macon-Bibb County, 1985, 86, 87; deacon, elder, treas. Washington Ave. Presbyn. Ch.; active Downtown Coun., Coalition for Polit. Awareness, So. Poverty Law Ctr., NAACP; mem. "Cmty. Hero"-torchbearer Olympic Torch Relay for 1996 Olympic games, Atlanta; advisory bd. Wachovia Bank, Macon, Warner-Robins; apptd. bd. dirs. Ga. Dept. Cmty. Affairs. With U.S. Army, 1961-63. Recipient Cert. of Appreciation State Bar of Ga., Citizenship award Bibb County Voter's Registration League, Inc., 1977, Community Svc. award NAACP, 1982, Community Svc. award Alpha Kappa Alpha Sorority, 1982, Meritorious Svc. award United Negro Co. Fund, 1983, Comml. Bldg. of Yr. award Macon Heritage Found., 1983, Faithful Svc. award Bibb County Dept. Family and Children's Svcs., 1983-90, citation Macon-Bibb County Beautification Clean Community Comm., 1983-84, Cert. appreciation Macon-Bibb County Econ. Opportunity Coun., 1984, Outstanding Svc. award So. Poverty Law Ctr., 1984, Proclamation Mayor George Israel Svc. on Macon-Bibb County Transit Authority, 1984, Outstanding Alumni award Coll. Dentistry Howard U., 1985, award for Outstanding Svc. Macon-Bibb County Urban Devel. Authority, 1987, award for Outstanding Svc. Macon-Bibb County Transit Authority, 1987, cert. Appreciation Close-Up Found., 1988, cert. Appreciation Ga. Dental Edn. Found., 1988, Community Svc. award United Way Macon-Bibb County, 1988, cert. Disting. Svc. Devel. Corp. Middle Ga., 1990, Continuous Corp. Support award Entrepreneurship and Black Youth Program U. Ga., 1990, cert. Recognition Outstanding Svc. So. Poverty Law Ctr., 1990, cert. Appreciation Keep Macon-Bibb Beautiful Commn. and Cherry Blossom Festival, 1990, James E. Carter award Ga. Dental Soc., 1993; named Olympic Torchbearer, 1996. Fellow Acad. Gen. Dentistry (Membership award 1983-85), Acad. Dentistry Internat., Am. Coll. Dentists, Ga. Dental Assn. (hon.), Internat. Coll. Dentists, Pierre Fauchard Acad.; mem. AAAS, ADA (alt. del. Ga. 1986-91, life mem.), Am. Analgesic Soc., Am. Endodontic Soc., Am. Fund Dental Health, Am. Sch. Health Assn., Am. Soc. Dentistry for Children, Nat. Dental Assn., Nat. Rehab. Assn., Ga. Dental Soc. (pres., 1978, Citizenship award 1979-80, Humanitarian award 1981-82, James E. Carter Jr. award 1993), North Ga. Dental Soc. (pres. 1978-79), Cen. Dist. Dental Soc. (peer rev. com., legis. com., alt. del. to Ga. Dental Assn. 1982, 83, 84, del. 1984, 85, 86, 87), Bibb County Dental Soc. (charter), Acad. Continuing Edn., Fed. Dentaire Internat. (life), Pres' Club Howard U. (life), Am. Running and Fitness Assn. (life), Greater Macon C. of C. (bd. dirs. 1995-97), Macon Tracks, Sigma Pi Phi, Omega Psi Phi (life). Presbyterian. Avocations: walking, jogging, aerobics, coin collecting, real estate. Home: 2988 Malibu Dr Macon GA 31211-2609 Office: DeWitt T Walton Jr DDS 591 Cotton Ave Macon GA 31201-7504

WALTON, JAMES STEPHEN, research scientist; b. Kingston-upon-Thames, Eng., Nov. 27, 1946; came to U.S., 1968, permanent resident, 1975, citizen, 1996; s. Ronald Walter and Jean Edna (Hudson) W.; m. Dorcas Ann Graham, July 20, 1974; children: Kirstyn Amy, Lars Timothy. Diploma in Phys. Edn., Leeds U., 1968; MA in Exercise Physiology, Mich. State U., 1970; MS in Applied Mechanics, Stanford U., 1976; PhD in Biomechanics, Pa. State U., 1981. Cert. tchr., Eng. Research asst. Stanford (Calif.) U., 1974-76; tchr. Gaynesford High Sch., Carshalton, Eng., 1969-70; dir. engring. Computerized Biomech. Analysis Inc., Amherst, Mass., 1978-79; sr. biomed. research scientist Gen. Motors Research Labs., Warren, Mich., 1979-85; applications engring. and product planning mgr. Motion Analysis Corp., Santa Rosa, Calif., 1985-87, v.p. applications engring., 1987-88; pres. 4D Video, Sebastopol, Calif., 1988—; cons. Sci. mag., 1982, 83, Mich. State U., 1984-85; trampoline coach several gymnastics clubs and univ. teams, 1968—; mem. organizing com. 22d Internat. Congress on High-Speed Photography and Photonics, 1996; mil. contractor; vis. prof. dept. anatomy U. P.R., San Juan, 1998; cons. in field. Contbr. articles to profl jours. Mem. Nat. Boy's Club Gt. Britain, London, 1964—; organizer summer workshop West Sonoma County Union H.S. Dist., Sebastopol, Calif., 1999, mem. dist. adv. com., 1996-97, cmty. rep. dist. tech. com., 1995—; mem. site coun. El Molino H.S., 1998—; mem. El Molino H.S. Bus. Roundtable, Forestville, Calif., 1995—. Recipient Research award Nat. Collegiate Gymnastics Assn., 1968-69; recipient Bd. Trustee's award West Sonoma County Union H.S. Dist., 1998. Fellow Brit. Assn. Phys. Tng. (hon.); mem. AAAS, Internat. Soc. Biomechanics, Internat. Soc. Biomechanics in Sports, Am. Acad. Forensic Scis., Am. Coll. Sports Medicine, Am. Soc. Biomechanics, Am. Soc. Photogrammetry and Remote Sensing (cert. photogrammetrist), Human Factors Soc., N.Y. Acad. Scis., Soc. Photo-Optical Instrumentation Engrs. (chmn. working group on high-speed photography, viedography and photonics 1994-96, 99-01), Digital Equipment Computer Users' Soc., Sun Users' Group, Mensa, U.S. Gymnastics Fedn., Brit. Trampoline Fedn., Stanford Alumni Club, Sigma Xi. Avocations: gymnastics, photography. Home: 3136 Pauline Dr Sebastopol CA 95472-9741 Office: 4D Video 825 Gravenstein Hwy N Ste 4 Sebastopol CA 95472-2844

WALTON, JOHN MICHAEL, drama educator; b. Newcastle-On-Tyne, England, May 10, 1939; s. Henry John and Ada Griffith (Young) W.; m. Susan Kathleen Hodge, July 29, 1967; children: Alice Louisa, Benjamin Toby, Mark Edwin. MA, St. Andrews U., 1962; PhD, Hull U., 1989. Trainee dir. theatre ABC TV, York, Eng., 1963-64; actor, dir. Profl. Theatre, Eng., 1964-65; asst. lectr. U. Hull, Eng., 1965-68, lectr., 1968-81, sr. lectr., 1981-87, reader, 1987-93, personal chair, 1992—, head dept. drama, 1990-91, 92-96, established chair, 1994—; vis. prof. U. Denver, 1972-73; vis. lectr. La. State U., Baton Rouge, 1991, UCLA, U. Calif. Riverside, 1994, San Diego, 1998-99, Univ. Coll. Dublin, 1999, Trinity Coll. Dublin, 1999; cons. Getty, Malibu, 1994; Plenary lectr. Northwestern, 1996, Thessaloniki, 1997, Getty, 2000; founder dir. The Performance Translation Ctr., 1997—; author, dir. Medea Complex, Delphi, 2000. Author: Greek Theatre Practice, 1980, 2d edit. 1991, Craig on Theatre, 1983, 3d edit., 1999, The Greek Sense of Theatre, 1984, 2d edit., 1996, Living Greek Theatre, 1987; (with Peter D. Arnott) Menander and the Making of Comedy, 1996; editor: Methuen Classical Greek Dramatists, 1987—; translator: Sophocles, Euripides, Menander, Terence. Gov. Rose Bruford Coll., Kent, U.K., 1984-90, Scarborough Coll., Yorks, U.K., 1994-2000; bd. mgrs. DESMI, Athens, 2000—; judge Onassis Internat. Th Co., 2000—. Mem. British Actors Equity, Dirs. Guild Great Britain (mem. tng. com. 1986-88), Soc. Theatre Rsch., The Primary Club, Assn. Univ. Tchrs. Avocations: cricket, classical music, walking. E-mail: michael.walton@drama.hull.ac.uk. Home: 103 Park Ave, Hull HU5 3EP, England Office: U Hull Dept Drama, Cottingham Rd, Hull HU6 7RX, England

WALTON, LEE, medical physicist; b. Grimsby, Eng., May 13, 1955; s. Kenneth Walton and Marjorie May Cant; m. Joan Mary King, June 18, 1977; 1 child, Rachel Elizabeth. BSc with honors in Applied Physics, Lanchester Poly., Coventry, Eng., 1977. Rsch. fellow J&P Engring., Reading, Eng., 1977-80; med. physicist Hallamshire Hosp., Sheffield, Eng., 1980-83, sr. med. physicist, 1983-90, prin. med. physicist, 1990—; vis. prof. U. Va., Charlottesville, 1991. Contbr. articles to profl. jours. Mem. Inst. of Physics, Inst. of Phys. Scis. in Medicine. Mem. Ch. of Jesus Christ LDS. Home: 66 Swinston Hill Rd, Dinnington S25 2SA, England Office: Weston Park Hosp, Royal Hallamshire Hosp, Glossop Rd, Sheffield S10 2JF, England

WALTON, RALPH GERALD, psychiatrist, educator; b. Darlington, Eng., Aug. 18, 1942; came to U.S., 1950; s. Kenneth and Paula (Weissman) W.; m. Ellen Paula Liebling, Feb. 15, 1970 (div. 1980); children: Deborah, Rachel; m. Mary Elaine Hultburg, Sept. 27, 1981; children: Lisa, Jonathan. AB, U. Rochester, 1963; MD, SUNY, Syracuse, 1967. Diplomate Am. Bd. Psychiatry and Neurology. Intern Strong Meml. Hosp., Rochester, N.Y., 1967-68, resident in psychiatry, 1968-71; asst. prof. psychiatry Sch. Medicine U. Rochester, N.Y., 1973-76; chief psychiatry Jamestown (N.Y.) Gen. Hosp., 1976-88; commr. mental health Chautauqua County, Jamestown, 1985-88; chmn. dept. psychiatry Western Res. Care System, Youngstown, Ohio, 1988-98; prof., chmn. dept. psychiatry N.E. Ohio Univs. Coll. of Medicine, Rootstown, Ohio, 1998—; med. dir. Profl. Recovery Plus Alcoholic Clinic, Youngstown, 1992—. Contbr. chpt. to: Dietary Phenylalanine and Brain Function, 1988; contbr. foreword to: Katherine It's Time, 1989; contbr. articles to profl. jours., 1972—. Maj. U.S. Army, 1971-73, Panama. Fellow Am. Psychiat. Assn. Jewish. Office: 725 Boardman Canfield Rd Youngstown OH 44512-4380

WALTON, REGGIE BARNETT, judge; b. Feb. 8, 1949; m. Debra Walton; 1 child, Danon. BA, W.Va. State Coll., 1971; JD, Am. U., 1974. Staff atty. Defender Assn. Phila., 1974-76; asst. U.S. atty. Office of U.S. Atty., Washington, 1976-80, chief career criminal unit, 1979-80, exec. asst. U.S. atty., 1980-81; assoc. judge Superior Ct. D.C., 1981-89, 91—, dep. presiding judge criminal divsn., 1986-89; assoc. dir. Office Nat. Drug Control Policy, Exec. Office of Pres., Washington, 1989-91; sr. White House advisor for crime, 1991; mem. U.S. Dept. Justice and ABA Ctrl. and East European Law Initiative Reform Project, Irkutsk, Russia, 1996. Active Big Brothers. Recipient Dean's award Washington Coll. Law, 1989, Disting. Svc. award Young Lawyers sect. Bar Assn. D.C., 1989, H. Carl Moultrie award D.C. br. NAACP, 1989, Sec.'s award Dept. Vets. Affairs, 1990, James R. Waddy Meritorious Svc. award W.Va. State Coll. Nat. Alumni Assn., 1990, County Spotlight award Nat. Assn. Counties, 1990, William H. Hastie award Jud. coun. Nat. Bar Assn., 1993, Honorable Robert A. Shuker Meml. award Asst. U.S. Attys. Assn., 1997, Friendship award Best Friends Found., 1998, Disting. Alumni award Am. U., 1999. Republican. Office: Superior Ct H Carl Moultrie Courthouse 500 Indiana Ave NW Washington DC 20001-2131

WALTON, S. ROBSON, discount department store chain executive; b. 1945; s. Sam Moore W.; married. Grad., Columbia U., 1969. Formerly with Conner, Winters, Ballaine, Barry & McGowen; with Wal-Mart Stores Inc., Bentonville, Ark., 1969—, sr. v.p., 1978-82, also bd. dirs., vice chmn. bd., 1982-92, chmn., 1992—. Office: Wal-Mart Stores Inc 702 SW 8th St Bentonville AR 72716-6299

WALTON, SUZY NICOLA, military psychologist, government administrator; b. Nottingham, England, Dec. 8, 1963; d. Michael and Greta Helen (Lowe) Brett; children: Benjamin Philip Charles, Elliot Michael. James. BSc, MSc, U. Hertfordshire, England, 1994; PhD in Suicide, Cranfield U. Coll. Aeronautics, England, 1997. Reporter, prodr. travel show London Broadcasting Co., 1984-88; news prodr., presenter BSky B Television, London, 1989-90; intern Betty Ford Clinic, Calif., 1992-93; rsch. psychologist Defense Rsch. Agy., England, 1995-96; sr. psychologist Ministry of Def., London, 1994—; lay mem. gen. coun. of Bar's Profl. Conduct and Complaints Com. Contbr. articles to profl. jours.; actress Children of a Lesser God, London, 1981-84. Fellow Royal Soc. for Encouragement of Arts, Royal Soc. of Medicine, Manufacture and Commerce, Brit. Psychol. Soc. (charter, assoc. fellow), Brit. Actors Equity Assn. Avocations: theatre, swimming.

WALTON OF DETCHANT, LORD JOHN NICHOLAS, neurologist; b. Rowlands Gill, Durham, Eng., Sept. 16, 1922; s. Herbert Walton and Eleanor (Watson) Ward; m. Mary Elizabeth Harrison, Aug. 31, 1946; children: Elisabeth Ann, Judith Mary, Christopher John. MB, BS with 1st class honors, U. Durham, Eng., 1945, MD, 1950; DSc, U. Newcastle, Eng., 1972; Dr. de L'Univ. (hon.), Aix Marseilles, France, 1976; DSc (hon.), U. Leeds, 1978, U. Leicester, 1979, U. Hull, 1982; Oxford Brookes U., 1994; MD (hon.), U. Sheffield, 1982; DCL (hon.), U. Newcastle, 1988; Laurea Hon Causa, Genoa, Italy, 1992; MD (hon.), Mahidol, Thailand, 1998. Prof. neurology U. Newcastle-upon-Tyne, Newcastle, 1968-83, dean of medicine, 1971-81; warden Green Coll., Oxford, Eng., 1983-89; pres. World Fedn. Neurology, 1989-97. Author: Essentials of Neurology, 6th edit., 1989, Brain's Diseases Nervous System, 10th edit., 1993, (autobiography) The Spice of Life, 1993; editor: Oxford Companion to Medicine, 1986, Oxford Medical Companion, 1994. From capt. to col. Brit. Army, 1947-49, 50-66. Named Knight Bachelor, U.K., 1979; named to Life Peerage and House of Lords as Baron Walton of Detchant, U.K., 1989. Fellow Royal Coll. Physicians (London), Acad. Med. Sci. (London), Royal Coll. Physicians Edinburgh (hon.), Royal Coll. Physicians Can. (hon.), Royal Coll. Pathologists (hon.), Royal Coll. Psychiatrists (hon.), Royal Soc. Medicine (hon., pres. 1984-86), Inst. Edn. U. London (hon.), Russian Acad. Medicine (hon.), Venezuelan Acad. Medicine (hon.), Brazilian Acad. Medicine (hon.); mem. Brit. Med. Assn. (pres. 1980-82), Gen. Med. Coun. (pres. 1982-89), Athenaeum Club, United Oxford and Cambridge Univ. Club. Methodist. Avocations: reading, music, cricket, golf. Home: North View Tanners Ln, Burford OX18 4NB, England Office: World Fedn Neurology, 13 Norham Gardens, Oxford OX2 6PS, England

WALTRICH, JOSEPH BEST, electronics engineer; b. Phila., Jan. 16, 1934; s. Joseph Jacob and Helen Anna (Best) W.; m. Mary Frances Rennick, Aug. 20, 1960; children: Mary Patricia, Mary Lisa. BA in Physics, La Salle U., 1957; MS in Physics, U. Notre Dame, 1960. With engring. lab. Leeds & Northrup, Phila., 1960-62; rsch. engr. SKF Industries, King of Prussia, Pa., 1962-69; corp. staff engr. Ametek, Paoli, Pa., 1969-70; dir. engring. Dynasciences, Blue Bell, Pa., 1970-78; test systems engr. Honeywell, Ft. Washington, Pa., 1978-85; mgr. digital spl. projects Motorola Broadband Comms. Sector, Horsham, Pa., 1985—; mem. advanced TV sys. FCC adv. com. on advanced TV, Washington, 1987—; sci. bd. assoc. Motorola. Contbr. numerous articles to profl. jours. Mem. IEEE, SMPTE, Soc. Cable TV Engrs. Republican. Roman Catholic. Avocations: licensed dog show judge, private pilot. Home: 228 Sylvania Ave Glenside PA 19038-4113

WALTZ, JOSEPH MCKENDREE, neurosurgeon, educator; b. Detroit, July 23, 1931; s. Ralph McKinley and Bertha (Seelye) W.; m. Janet Maureen Journey, June 26, 1954; children: Jeffrey McKinley, Mary Elaine, David Seelye, Stephen McKendree; m. Marilyn Liska, June 5, 1967; 1 child, Tristana McKendree. Student, U. Mich., 1950; B.S., U. Oreg., 1954, M.D., 1956. Diplomate Am. Bd. Neurol. Surgery. Surg. intern U. Mich. Hosp., 1956-57, gen. surg. resident, 1957-58, clin. instr. neurosurgery, 1960-63; neurosurg. assoc. St. Barnabas Hosp., N.Y.C., 1963—; assoc. dir. Inst. Neurosci., 1974—, dir. dept. neurol. surgery, 1977—; assoc. cons. in neurosurgery Englewood (N.J.) Hosp., 1964—; assoc. prof. neurosurgery NYU Med. Str., 1974—; asst. prof. dept. surgery (neurosurgery) N.Y. Coll. Osteo. Medicine, 1989—; bd. dirs. Neurol. Surgery Rsch. Found., 1978; mem. alumni bd. U. Mich. Med. Ctr., 1995. Author: (chpt.) Cryogenic Surgery, Neurology, 1982, Advances in Neurology, 1983, Textbook of Stereotactic and Functional Neurosurgery, 1997; contbr. articles to profl. jours.; patentee in field. Mem. sci. adv. bd. Dystonia Med. Research Found., 1980—; trustee St. Barnabas Hosp., 1980—. Served to capt. M.C. AUS, 1958-60. Recipient Bronze award Am. Congress Rehab. Medicine, 1967, World Cmty. Svc. award Rotary, Disting. Trustee award United Hosp. Fund, 1995. Mem. AMA, Am. Paralysis Assn., World Soc. Stereotactic and Functional Neurosurgery, Congress Neurol. Surgeons, Math. Assn. Am., Internat. Neural Network Soc., Soc. for Cryobiology, N.Y. State Med. Soc., Bronx County Med. Soc., N.Y. State Neurosurg Soc., Nat. Ski Patrol, Phi Beta Pi. Achievements include spl. rsch. on neurophysiology and treatment of epilepsy, basal ganglia disorders, abnormal movement disorders, cerebral palsy, also neurosurg. application stereotactic thalamic surgery and spinal cord stimulation. Home: Four B Island South 720 Milton Rd Rye NY 10580-3258 Office: St Barnabas Hosp Dept Neurosurgery Bronx NY 10457

WALTZ, SUSAN, international relations educator. Former chmn. Amnesty Internat., London; prof. internat. rels. Fla. Internat. U., Miami. Office: Fla Internat U Dept Internat Rels DM 498A Miami FL 33199*

WAMALA, EMMANUEL CARDINAL, archbishop; b. Kammagwa, Uganda, Dec. 15, 1926. Ordained priest Roman Cath. Ch., bishop, cardinal. Archbishop Kampala, Uganda, 1990—; created Cardinal Sacred Coll. Cardinals, 1994—. Office: Archbishop's House, PO Box 14125, Mengo, Kampala Uganda*

WAMBUZI, SAMSON WILLIAM WAKO, chief justice Uganda; b. Uganda, Jan. 23, 1931; s. Erukana and Miriam (Naigaga) Kakungulu Wako; m. Gladys Bulyaba Nsibirwa, Jan. 7, 1956; children: Phillip William Wako, Samson Enoka Wambuzi, Veronica Gladys Naigaga Hansa, Miriam Sarah Musekwa. LLB, U. London, 1958; barrister at law, Lincoln's Inn, London, 1959; LLB (hon.), U. Hull, Eng., 1960. With dept. of pub. prosecutions Govt. of Uganda, 1960-61, crown prosecutor, 1961-62, crown counsel, 1962-63, sr. parliamentary counsel, 1963-64, 1st parliamentary counsel, 1964-69; judge High Ct. Uganda, 1969-72, acting chief justice, 1972-73, chief justice, 1973-75, 79-80, 86—; pres. Ct. Appeal for East Africa; judge of appeal Ct. of Appeal, Kenya, 1977-79; pres. Ct. of Appeal Uganda, 1986; legal cons. Sebalu & Lule, Kampala, Uganda, 1981-86; sec. De Lestang Commn., 1966; chmn. Uganda Armed Forces Pensions & Gratuities Appeals Bd., 1968-69, Uganda Armed Forces Pensions Assessment Bd., 1970—, Law Council, 1972; external examiner criminal procedure, civil procedure and evidence Makerere U., Kampala, 1971-75, 80—; mem. Common Market Tribunal, East African Community, 1972. Mem. bd. govs. Busoga Coll., Mwiri, Uganda; patron Busoga Coll. Mwiri Old Boys Assn., 1986. Address: PO Box 801, Kampala Uganda Office: High Ct Uganda, PO Box 7085, Kampala Uganda*

WAMSTEKER, KEES, gynecologist, researcher; b. Haarlem, The Netherlands, May 29, 1946; s. Hendrik and Christine Albertine (Zaaijer) W.; m. Yvonne Marianne L. Bijlsma, Feb. 7, 1970; children: Sacha Marianne C., Simone Nathalie, Verena Marguérite. MD, State U. Leiden, The Netherlands, 1971, PhD, 1977. Bd. cert. ob-gyn. Resident in ob-gyn. State U. Leiden, 1971-76; cons. dept. ob-gyn. Mariastichting, Haarlem, 1977-89, Spaarne Hosp., Haarlem, 1989—; bd. dirs. Hysteroscopy Tng. Ctr., Spaarne Hosp., Haarlem; cons. Olympus Winter & Ibe, Hamburg, Germany; pres. European Soc. Hysteroscopy, 1988-90; mem. internat. adv. com. World Congress Gynaecol. Endoscopy, Bombay, 1993, Jerusalem, 1995; dir. Instn. Internat. Sch. Hysteroscopy, Chgo.-Haarlem-Paris, 1997—. Author: Hysteroscopie, 1977, Wamsteker e.a.: Imaging and Visual Documentation in Medicine, 1987, Diagnostic Imaging and Endoscopy in Gynecology: A Practical Guide, 1997; co-author: Lasers in Gynecology, 1992, Endoscopic Surgery for Gynecologists, 1993, Endometrial Ablation, 1993, The Fallopian Tube: Clinical and Surgical Aspects, 1994, Office Hysteroscopy, 1996; mem. exec. editl. bd. Gynaecological Endoscopy; referee Obstetrics and Gynecology, Gynaecological Endoscopy, European Jour. Ob-Gyn. and Reproductive Biology; mem. rev. com. Jour. Am. Assn. Gynecologic Laparoscopists; contbr. articles to profl. jours. Recipient Annual Internat. Soc. for Photoscopy Audiovisual award Internat. Soc. for Photoscopy, Fort Lauderdale, Fla., 1984. Mem. Internat. Soc. for Gynecologic Endoscopy (European chmn. sci. com. 3rd biennial meeting 1991, sec. 1994—, mem. exec. bd.), European Soc. Hysteroscopy (pres. 1988-90, mem. exec. bd.), European Soc. Gynaecological Endoscopy, Dutch Ob.-gyn. Soc. (bd. mem. 1993-95). Democrat. Avocations: playing saxophone and piano, tennis. Home: Noord Schalkwykerweg 167, 2034 JB Haarlem The Netherlands Office: Spaarne Hosp, van Heythuijzenweg 1, 2012 CE Haarlem The Netherlands

WAMUTOMBO, DIKEMBE MUTOMBO MPOLONDO MUKAMBA JEAN JACQUE See MUTOMBO, DIKEMBE

WAN, GUANGHUA, development consultant; b. Jiangdu, Jiangsu, China, Oct. 16, 1961; s. Yongrong and Guifang (Qiu) W.; m. Lingye Kong, Feb. 2, 1982; children: Rose, Roland. B of Agrl. Econs., Nanjing Agrl. U., 1982; MEc, U. New England, Armidale, Australia, 1985, PhD, 1990. Lectr. U. Sydney, Australia, 1990-96, sr. lectr., 1996—; cons. UN, N.Y.C., 1995, Winrock Internat., 1996; hon. prof. Chinese Acad. Agrl. Scis., Beijing, 1996; vis. prof. Ford Found., Beijing, 1998. Author: Chinese Economy Towards the 21st Century, 1999, also jour. articles. Unity Party candidate for Lower House, Sydney, NSW, 1999. Mem. Assn. for Chinese Econ. Studies (pres.), Australian Soc. Agrl. and Resource Economists. E-mail: g.wan@agec.usyd.edu.au. Office: U Sydney, Dept Agrl Econs, Sydney NSW, Australia 2006

WAN, JULIA CHANG, science educator; b. Hong Kong, Hong Kong, Oct. 13, 1937; d. Charles S.Y. and Lucy (Wong) Chang; m. Frederic Y.M. Wan, Sept 10, 1960. BA, Wellesley Coll., 1960, MA, 1970; EdD, Boston Coll., 1978. Mem. staff Bio Rsch. Inst., Cambridge, Mass., 1960-64; physics tchr. Watertown (Mass.) H.S., 1970-73; sci. dir. Watertown Pub. Schs., 1973-79; curriculum dir. Fed. Way Sch. Dist., Fed. Way, Wash., 1979-83; asst. supt. Bainbridge Island (Wash.) Sch. Dist., 1983-93; program dir. NSF, Washington, 1993-95; dir. Ctr. for Excellence in Sci. and Math. Edn.c Calif. State U., Fullerton, 1995—; mem. accreditation com. N.W. Assn. Schs. and Colls., Boise, Idaho, 1981-95; mem. edn. opportunity coun. AAAS, Washington, 1995-99; bd. dirs. Challenger Ctr., Alexandria, Va., 1997-2000. Author: Designing School Health Education Curricula, 1992, 2d edit. 1995; contbr. articles and revs. to sci. mags. Bd. dirs. NOW, 1985-88; mem. Commn. on Asian-Am. Affairs, Olympia, Wash., 1990-93; bd. trustees Girls, Inc., Orange County, Calif., 1995—. Recipient award profl. excellence We. Wash. U., Bellingham, 1988, exemplary program award Met. Life Found., N.Y.C., 1989; grantee: NSF (numerous), Arlington, Va., 1989—, Beckman Found., Irvine, Calif., 1998-2003. Mem. ASCD, Am. Ednl. Rsch. Assn., Nat. Sci. Tchrs. Assn., Phi Delta Kappa. E-mail: Jwan@fullerton.edu. Office: Calif State U Fullerton PO Box 6850 Fullerton CA 92834-6850

WAN, YUNG-LIANG, radiologist; b. Kalimpong, India, Oct. 18, 1953; arrived in Taiwan, 1967; s. Fu-Kuei and Chun-Hsia (Chao) W.; m. Tchun-Ching Lee, Oct. 22, 1982; children: Peter Li-Hau, Dinah, Nina. MD, Nat. Taiwan U., Taipei, 1980. Diplomate Taiwan Bd. Cert. Diagnostic Radiologists. Resident Chang Gung Meml. Hosp., Lin-Kou, Taiwan, 1980-84, staff radiologist, 1984-85, dept. dir., 1993—; staff radiologist Chang Gung Meml.

Hosp., Kao-Hsiung, Taiwan, 1985-93; assoc. prof. Chang Gung U. Coll. of Medicine, Lin-Kou, 1994-99, prof., 1999—; vis. fellow Mt. Sinai Med. Ctr., N.Y., 1985. Mem. editl. bd. Chang Gung Med. Jour., 1994—, Jour. Med. Ultrasound, 1994—, Internat. Med. Image Registry, 1995-96, Chinese Radiol. Jour., 1995. Recipient Rsch. award Nat. Sci. Coun., 1995, 96, 97, 98. Mem. Taiwan Soc. Ultrasound in Medicine and Biology (bd. dirs. 1994—), Radiol. Soc. Republic of China (bd. dirs. 1995—, Best Paper award 1987, 98, Good Sci. Exhibit award 1991, 2d Film Panel Interpretation award 1993). Avocations: tennis, bowling, golf. Office: Chang Gung Med Ctr/ Diag Rad, 5 Fu-Hsing Rd, Lin-Kou Taoyuan Taiwan

WAN ABAS, WAN ABU BAKAR, mechanical engineer, biomedical engineer, educator; b. Segamat, Malaysia, May 11, 1951; s. Wan Abas and Amah (Mohd Tahar) Wan M.; m. Hasimah Harun, Apr. 24, 1980; seven children. BSc, U. Strathclyde, 1974, PhD, 1978. From lectr. to prof., dean engrng. U. Malaya, Malaysia, 1978—. Author: Engineering Mechanics—Statics, 1989, Engineering Mechanics—Dynamics, 1993, Dictionary of Applied Mechanics, 1991. Mem. Instn. Engrs. Malaysia.

WAN ABDULLAH, WAN AHMAD TAJUDDIN, physicist, educator; b. Kuala Terengganu, Malaysia, June 8, 1960; s. Abdullah and Hamidah (Abdullah) Wan A.; m. Nur Azian Azizi; five children. BSc, Imperial Coll., London, 1982, PhD, 1985. From lectr. to assoc. prof. to prof. U. Malaya, Kuala Lumpur, Malaysia, 1985—. Author: Lawatan Lain, 1995, also chpts. in books and numerous papers in field. Recipient Nat. Young Scientist award, 1995; European Commn. fellow, 1991. Fellow Malaysian Inst. Physics; mem. Internat. Neural Network Soc., Artificial Intelligence Soc. Islam. Office: U Malaya, Jabatan Fizik, 50603 Kuala Lumpur Malaysia

WAN CHAT KWONG, TAYE WAH MICHEL, diplomat. Rep. to UN Govt. of Mauritius, 1996—. Office: Permanent Mission Mauritius UN 211 E 43rd St Fl 15 New York NY 10017-4707*

WANDEL, SHARON LEE, sculptor; b. Bemidji, Minn., Mar. 19, 1940; d. Roy J. and Bonnie (Englund) Opsahl; m. Thaddeus Ludwik Wandel, Oct. 17, 1970; children: Holly, Erika. BA, Gustavus Adolphus Coll., 1962; MSW, Columbia U., 1965; Cert. in Arts Mgmt., SUNY, Purchase, 1993. Caseworker Manhattan State Hosp., N.Y.C., 1963-64; caseworker/rschr. Cmty. Svc. Soc., N.Y.C., 1965-67; teaching asst. dept. medicine NYU Med. Ctr., N.Y.C., 1967-70; mem. adv. bd. Lamia, Inc., N.Y.C., 1999, 2000. One-person shows at Silvermine Guild of Artists, New Canaan, Conn., 1993, 97, Pen and Brush, N.Y.C., 1994, Clark Whitney Gallery, Lenox, Mass., 1994, James Cox Gallery, Woodstock, N.Y., 1994, 96, Cortland Jessup Gallery, Provincetown, Mass., 1998, Gallery Marya, Osako, Japan, 1999, Laura Barton Gallery, Westport, Conn., 2000, Firehouse Gallery, Damaviscotta, Maine, 2000; group shows include Nat. Acad. Design, N.Y.C., 1988, 90, 92, 94, 95, 97, 98, 99, 2000, Nat. Sculpture Soc., N.Y.C., 1989, 91, 93, 94, Palazzo Mediceo in Seravezza, Italy, 1994, Knickerbocker Artists, N.Y.C., 1989, 90, 92, Art of N.E. U.S.A., New Canaan, Conn., 1989, 92, Mus. of Hudson Highlands, Cornwall, N.Y., 1990, James Cox Gallery, 1992, 93, 95, 96, N.Y. Soc. Women Artists, Cork Gallery at Lincoln Ctr., 1991, Broome St. Gallery, N.Y.C., 1991, 92, Warner Comm., 1989, Lever House, N.Y.C., 1993, 94, 96, 98, Kohn Pederson Fox Gallery, N.Y.C., 1996, Patio Azul Gallery, Sedona, Ariz., 1995, Williamsville Sculpture Garden, 1995-2000, Kimberly Greer Gall., Northport, NY, 1999, 2000, Grounds for Sculpture (Hamilton), NJ, 1999, The Firehouse Gall., Damariscotta, Maine, 1999, 2000, Gall. Between The Muse, Rockland, ME, 1999, Cavalier Gallery, Nantucket, Mass., 2000, Elaine Benson Gallery, Bridgehampton, 1996, Chapel St. Art Gallery, New Haven, 1996, 97, U. Conn., 1996, Mirage Gallery, Albuquerque, 1997, Dora House, London, 1997-98, Lever House, N.Y.C., 1998, Sakai City (Japan) Mus., 1998, Cortland Jessup Gallery, Provincetown and N.Y.C., 1998-2000, Berkshires Bot. Garden, Mass., 1998, Sundance Gallery, Bridgehampton, N.Y., 1997, 98, Castle Gallery, Coll. of New Rochelle, 1998, Gallery Brocken, Tokyo, 1999, Canyon Ranch, Lenox, Mass. 1999, 2000, Internat. Sculpture Biennale, Toyamura, Japan, 1999, HBO, N.Y.C., 1999, Chesterwood, Lenox, Mass., 2000; works in permanent collections at Art Students League, 1989, Westinghouse Corp. Collection, Pitts., 1990, Nat. Acad. Design, 1994, Housatonic Mus., CT, 1998, C. of C., Toyamura, Japan, 1999; commns. include two 8' bronze figures for Ihilani Resort, Kapolei, Hawaii, 1993, 2 5" figures Silvermine Galleries, 1993. Mem. rsch. com. Arthritis Found., N.Y.C., 1968-69; mem. adv. bd. Lamia Ink. Recipient N.Am. Sculpture Exhbn. 2d place, 1991, Three River Arts Festival (Carnegie Inst.) Purchase award, 1990, Hakone Open Air Mus. (Japan) 3d and 4th Rodin Grand Prize Exhbn. Excellent Maquettes, 1990, 92, Matrix Gallery 1st prize for sculpture, 1990, Ariel Gallery Internat. Competition Group Show award, 1989, Salmagundi Club McReynolds award, 1989, Barret Coleco award, 1988, 1st place nat. competition Sundance Gallery, Bridgehampton, N.Y., 1997; Vt. Studio Ctr. fellow, 2000. Mem. Silvermine Guild of Artists (Solo Show award 1992), N.Y. Soc. Woman Artists (pres.), Knickerbocker Artists USA, The Pen and Brush (Meisner award 1990, Solo Show award 1993), Nat. Acad. Design (nat. academician 1994, Cleo Hartwig award 1990), Nat. Sculpture Soc. (Meisner award 1994, Hexter award 1993, Spring award 1991, Meiselman award 1990), Audubon Artists (Chaim Gross Found. award 1993), Sculptures Guild (bd. dirs.), Royal Soc. Brit. Sculptors (internat.). Avocations: travel, cooking, reading. Studio: PO Box 314 Croton On Hudson NY 10520-0314

WANDERMAN, MIRIAM, library studies educator; b. Bklyn.; m. Jay S. Wanderman, 1973; children: Adam, Joshua, Daniel. BA, Herbert Lehman Coll., 1970; MLS, Pratt Inst., Bklyn., 1972; MA, Herbert Lehman Coll., 1975. Adj. asst. prof. Libr. Svcs. Medgar Evers Coll., Bklyn., 1972-88; adj. asst. prof. Libr. Svcs. Adelphi U., Garden City, N.Y., 1988-95, Hofstra U., Hempstead, N.Y., 1995—. Pres. Lakeside Elem. Sch. PTA, Merrick, N.Y., 1995-97, Merrick Ave. Mid. Sch. PTA, Merrick, 1998-99, John F. Kennedy H.S. PTA, Bellmore, N.Y., 2000—; historian Nassau Dist. PTA, 1997-2000. Recipient N.Y. State PTA Hon. Life Membership award, 1990, N.Y. State PTA Disting. Svc. award, 1997, Merrick Union Free Sch. Dist. Disting. Svc. award, 1997, Nat. PTA Hon. Life Membership award, 1999, Golden Cir. of Leadership award N.Y. State PTA, 1998, 99. Mem. ALA, Nassau County Libr. Assn., Assn. of Coll. and Rsch. Librs./N.Y., N.Y. Libr. Assn. Home: 3039 Whaleneck Dr Merrick NY 11566-5324

WANDRASZ, JANUSZ WLADYSLAW, science educator, research scientist; b. Sosnowiec, Poland, Feb. 26, 1941; s. Jan and Lucyna (Wolska) W.; m. Kazimiera Hodorowska, Mar. 19, 1967; children: Andrzej Jan, Krzysztof Michál. MSc in Engrng., Silesian Tech. U., Gliwice, Poland, 1963, PhD, 1973, PhD, DSc, 1976. Prof. Silesian Tech. U., Gliwice, 1963-64, older asst., 1964-73, sr. asst., 1973-76, docent, 1976-86, extraordinary prof., 1986-96, ordinary prof., 1996—, dean Faculty Mechanics and Energetics, 1985-90; head Chair of Technologies and Installations for Waste Mgmt., Gliwice, 1987—; expert in field. Contbr. articles to profl. jours.; inventor in field. Recipient II reward Ministry of Height Edn. and Technic, 1984, 1st reward Ministry Environ. Protection, Natural Resources and Forestry, 1988, 91. Mem. N.Y. Acad. Scis., Solid Waste Assn., Polish Acad. Sci. (waste mgmt. com.), Russian Acad. Sci. Avocations: hunting, sculpture. Home: Kaszubska 14/1, 44-100 Gliwice Poland Office: Silesian Tech Univ, Konarskiego, 44-100 Gliwice Poland

WANDSCHNEIDER, DIETER FRITZ ERICH, philosopher, educator; b. Bremerhaven, Germany, Nov. 3, 1938; m. Anne Kerzmann. Diploma in Physics, Hamburg, 1965; PhD, Tübingen, 1970, postdoctoral habilitation, 1978. Prof. U. Tübingen, Germany, 1983-87, Tech. U., Aachen, Germany, 1988—. Author: Formale Sprache und Erfahrung. Carnap als Modellfall, (Formal Language and Experience. Carnap as a Model Case) 1975, Raum, Zeit, Relativität. Grundbestimmungen der Physik in der Perspektive der Hegelschen Naturphilosophie, (Space, Time, Relativity. Fundamental Categories of Physics from the Angle of Hegel's Philosophy of Nature) 1982, Basic Theory of Dialectics, Reconstruction and Revision of the Dialectical Development of Categories in Hegel's Science of Logic, 1995. Home: Am Chorusberg 57b, D-52076 Aachen Germany Office: Univ Aachen, Philosophical Inst, D-52056 Aachen Germany

WANDT, BIRGER NILS, cardiologist; b. Almhult, Sweden, Feb. 2, 1951; s. Hans Kristian and Elsa Karin (Nilsson) W.; m. Anne-Torin Nygaard, June 28, 1978 (div. 1994); children: Marcus, Thorstein. MD, U. Hosp., Linkoping, Sweden, 1979; PhD, Linköping U., 1998. Intern Mora (Sweden) Hosp., 1979-80; resident in internal medicine and cardiology Örebro, Sweden, 1981-85; resident in clin. physiology Gothenburg, Sweden, 1986-88; asst. physician Mora (Sweden) Hosp., 1979-81; asst. physician Regional Hosp., Orebro, Sweden, 1981-85, sr. physician, 1985-86; asst. physician Sahlgrenska Hosp., Gothenburg, 1986-88; dept. head Ctrl. Hosp., Karlstad, Sweden, 1989-99, Örebro (Sweden) Med. Ctr. Hosp., 1999—. Mem. Swedish Soc. Clin. Physiology (bd. dirs. 1994-96), Karlstad Soc. Medicine (chmn. 1994-95), Swedish Soc. Cardiology. Avocations: hunting, boating, reading, philosophy. Home: Skolgatan 16A, S-703 62 Örebro Sweden Office: Örebro Med Ctr Hosp, S-70185 Örebro Sweden

WANEK, WOLFGANG, plant physiologist, researcher; b. Vienna, Austria, Aug. 7, 1967; s. Alfred and Dietlinde (Kranzmayer) W. MSc, U. Vienna, 1993, PhD, 1996. Cert. first aid asst., stable isotope lab. mgr., radiation protection profl. Contract employee Inst. Ecology & Conservation Biology U. Vienna, 1992, project asst., 1993-95, postdoctoral rschr., 1996-97, univ. asst., 1997—; rschr. Biol. Sta. La Gamba, Costa Rica, 1998. With M.C., Austrian Army, 1995-96. Mem. Fedn. European Socs. Plant Physiologists, Austrian Soc. Plant Physiologists. Avocations: collecting minerals, carambol billiards, jogging. Home: Hormayrgasse 27/12, A-1170 Vienna Austria Office: U Vienna Inst Ecol & Conserv Biol, Althanstrasse 14, A-1091 Vienna Austria

WANG, AIHE, educator; b. July 14, 1954. MA, Chinese Acad. of Soc. Scis., Beijing, China, 1986, Harvard, Cambridge, MA, 1989; PhD, Harvard, Cambridge, MA, 1995. Artist, factory worker Beijing, China, 1971-83; asst. prof. Purdue Univ., W. Lafayette, IN, 1995-2000, U. Hong Kong, 2000—. Office: U Hong Kong, Dept Chinese, Pokfulam Hong Kong

WANG, ALBERT HUAI-EN, lawyer; b. Tainan, Taiwan, Feb. 21, 1967; s. Tien-Yu Wang and Shiu-Yin Chen. BA, UCLA, 1990, MA, 1990; JD, Cornell U., 1994. Bar: N.Y. 1995. Tax specialist KPMG Peat Marwick, L.A., 1990-91; assoc. Willkie Farr & Gallagher, N.Y.C., 1994-99, Schulte Roth & Zabel LLP, N.Y.C., 1999—; legal counsel, mem. adv. coun. Asian Am. Bus. Devel. Ctr., N.Y.C., 1999—. Legal counsel Asian Am. Bus. Dept. Ctr.; dir. Chinese Am. Voters Assn. of Queens, Orgn. of Chinese Ams. (N.Y. chpt.). Alumni scholar UCLA, 1986, Departmental scholar, 1989. Mem. ABA, N.Y. State Bar Assn., Chinese Fin. Soc., Phi Beta Kappa, Phi Delta Phi, Omicron Delta Epsilon. Democrat. Fax: (212) 593-5955. E-mail: albert.wang@srz.com. Home: 138-10 Franklin Ave Apt 5N Flushing NY 11355-3305 Office: Schulte Roth & Zabel LLP 900 3d Ave New York NY 10022

WANG, ALEXANDER TZE-CHE, physician; b. Changhwa, Taiwan, Mar. 28, 1939; s. Chieh Ching Wang and Yin Gee Tsai; m. Margaret M. Tsai, June 1, 1967; children: Jane, John, Gabrielle. MD, Nat. Taiwan U., 1965. Diplomate Am. Bd. Internal Medicine, Am. Bd. Cardiology. Rotating intern Nat. Taiwan U. Hosp., 1964-65, med. resident, 1966-69, chief med. resident, 1969-70; nephrology fellow U. Chgo. Hosp., 1970-74; attending cardiologist LaGrange (Ill.) Meml. Hosp., 1974-77; chmn. medicine Cathay Gen. Hosp., Taipei, 1977-79; chmn. medicine Taipei Med. Coll. Hosp., 1981-83, v.p. med. staff, 1991-92, dir. Ctr. for Med. Humanities, 1995-99; chmn. geriatrics Taipei Med. Coll. and Hosp., 1987—; cons. cardiologist Nat. Taiwan U. Hosp., Taipei, 1977—; organizer Symposium on Med. Ethics, 1997; columnist various newspapers. Lt. Res. Med. Officer, 1965-66. Fellow ACP, Am. Coll. of Cardiology; mem. Taipei West Rotary Club. Buddhist. Avocations: opera, golf, speech. Office: Taipei Med Coll Hosp, 252 Wu-Shing St, Taipei 105, Taiwan

WANG, ALLAN XU HUI, physician; b. Xindeng, Zhejiang, China, May 14, 1955; s. Hui Fu Wang and Ruo Nan Shi; m. Hui Huang, May 31, 1985; 1 child, Shubai. CMD, Shanghai U. Chinese Medicine, 1977, Post CMD, 1985. Physician Shanghai Yueyang Hosp./Coll. TCM, China, 1977-84; prof. Shanghai U. Chinese Medicine, 1985-93; pres. Inst. Traumatology and Orthopedics/Shanghai Acad. TCM, China, 1985-93; v.p. Internat. Med. Rsch., China, 1993-99, Internat. Med. Rsch. (Botanic Lab), Brea, Calif., 1999—; commr. Task Force on Cancer Pain of IASP, 1993—. Patentee in field; contbr. articles to profl. jours. Spl. subsidy expert China State Coun., 1992—, China scientist and inventist, 1995; recipient cert. for world-famous med. experts and qualified personnel World Pharm. Rsch. Ctr., 1997. Mem. All China Soc. Rheumatism (commr. 1988—), All China Com. Preventing and Treating Rheumatism (vice-chmn. 1994—). Avocations: art, music, sports, reading. Home: 11624 McDonald Tustin CA 92782-3345 Office: Bonanic Lab 2900B Saturn St Brea CA 92821-6203

WANG, ANHUA, solar energy educator; b. Changzi, China, Sept. 24, 1935; s. Wen Guang and Dong Ying (Zhau) W.; m. Bao Yin Gao, Jan. 1, 1958; children: Jun, Yui, Wei, Ling. Degree, Xian Tao Tong U., China, 1958, Colo. State U., 1983. Group head Hunan Inst. for Design Light and Chem. Industry, Chang Sha, China, 1958-65; div. head Gansu Xian Guo Xia Chem. Factory, Lanzhou, China, 1966-78; vice-dir., dir. Gansu Nature Energy Rsch. Inst., Lanzhou, 1978-92; pres. Gansu GNERI PV Co., Lanzhou, 1992—. Contbr. articles to profl. jours. Mem. Internat. Solar Energy Soc., Chinese Solar Energy Soc. (bd. dirs.), Chinese Renewable Energy Assn. (bd. dirs.), China Rual Energy Assn. (bd. dirs.). Invented new way of making antifreezing solar collector; set up Chinese Solar Building Technology; patents about solar collector, PV; founded Tianshui Wetern Solar Co. and Gansu GNERI PV Co.

WANG, AN-MING, composer; b. Shanghai, China, Nov. 7, 1926; Came to U.S., 1948; d. Cheng Hsu and Eling (Tong) W.; children: Elise, Darrell. BE, Central China U., 1947; MusB, Wesleyan Conservatory, Macon, Ga., 1950; MA in Music Edn., Columbia U., 1951. Freelance composer, 1951—. Composer: Songs for All Seasons, 1982, Requiem for chorus and orch. and organ, 1982, The Song of Endless Sorrow, 1985, Piano Concerto, 1990, Gloria for Chorus and Orch., 1991, The Christmas Gift for Chorus and Keyboard/Orch., 1993, Lan Ying (opera in 3 acts), 1995, East Wind for Flute and Piano, 1997. Mem. ASCAP, Internat. Alliance for Women in Music, Southeastern Composers League, Soc. of Composers, League Am. Pen Women, Nat. Fedn. Music Clubs, Am. Music Ctr., Friday Morning Music Club (Washington). Republican. Episcopalian. Home and Office: 11920 Canfield Rd Potomac MD 20854-2816

WANG, BAO-NING, chemist, researcher; b. Kunming, Yunnan, China, May 30, 1933; s. He-rong and Yu-zhen (Zhong) W.; m. Gui-na Tang, July 4, 1969; children: Xiao-feng, Xiao-jia. BSc, Yunnan U., Kunming, 1960. Cert., Chinese Acad. Scis. Asst. Changchun Inst. Applied Chemistry, Chinese Acad. Scis., 1960-78, asst. prof., 1978-85, assoc. prof., 1986-89; vis. prof. Kumamoto (Japan) U. Tech., 1987-88; dep. editor-in-chief Chinese Jour. Analytical Chemistry, Changchun, 1988-97, prof., 1990—. Author monograph; contbr. more than 50 articles to profl. jours. Recipient 2d grade prize for excellent periodicl publ. Chinese Acad. Scis., 1990, 96, 97, 2nd prize for Nat. Appraisal Excellent Sci-Tech Jours. of China, 1997. Mem. Chem. Soc. China (analytical chemistry com. 1988—). Office: Changchun Inst Appl Chem, 159 Renming St, Changchun China 130022

WANG, BAOSHAN, electronic engineer; b. Shanghai, Feb. 11, 1933; s. Xiaohou Wang and Fengnian Guo; m. Huijun Liu, Mar. 22, 1969; 1 child, Fred. BA, Zhe Jiang U., Hangzhou, China, 1953. Technician NRIET, Nanjing, China, 1953-63, engr., 1963-80, sr. engr., 1980-87, rsch. sr. engr., 1987—, chief engr. microelectronic divsn., 1990-94; sr. tech. cons. Nanjing Lopu Corp., 1993—; rschr. in field. Author: Electronic Packaging Technologies, 1997. Recipient 2d Class award Ministry of Electronic Industry, Beijing, 1986, 89, 1st Class award, 1994. Mem. IEEE (sr.) Chinese Inst. Electronics (sr.). Avocation: bridge. Office: Nanjing Lopu Corp, PO Box 3210-16, 210061 Nanjing Jiangsu, China

WANG, BU-XUAN, engineering educator; b. Jiangsu, China, Feb. 5, 1922; s. Shao-Ting and Yang-Qing (Rui) W.; m. Bao-Ci Gu, July 4, 1948; children: Ru-Qi Wang, Ru-Ji Wang, Ru-Jun Wang. BS, Tsinghua U., 1943; MS in Mech. Engrng., Purdue U., 1949. Assoc. prof. Peking U., 1950-52; assoc. prof. Tsinghua U., Beijing, 1952-61; prof. Tsinghua U., 1961—; chmn. power engrng. dept., Tsinghua U., 1961-84; dir. Rsch. Inst. for Thermal Sci. and Engrng., Tsinghua U., 1984—. Editor, mem. editl. bd. Internat. Jour. Heat and Mass Transfer, 1982—, Internat. Jour. Thermophysics, 1984—, Internat. Jour. Heat and Fluid Flow, 1995-98; contbr. more than 360 articles to profl. jours. Mem. China Acad. Scis. (academician), Chinese Soc. Engring. Thermophysics (pres.), Chinese Solar Energy Soc. (founding), N.Y. Acad. Sci. E-mail: bxwang@mail.tsinghua.edu. Home: Tsinhue U., Rm 13, Apt Bldg 11, Beijing 100084, China Office: Inst Thermal Sci and Engring, Tsinghua U, Beijing 100084, China

WANG, CHANGJIE, engineer; b. Lanzhou, Gansu, China, Nov. 2, 1959; came to U.S., 1995; s. Ansun Wang and Tinglan Zhao; m. Hong Yang; children: Wenqi, David W. BS, Lanzhou U., 1982; MS, U. N. Tex., 1997, postgrad., 1998—. Assoc. prof. S.W. Petroleum Inst., Nanchong, China, 1994-95; tchg. asst. U. N. Tex., Denton, 1996, rsch. asst., 1996-99; engr. Ball Semiconductor Inc., Allen, Tex., 1999-2000, STMicroelectronics Inc., Carrollton, Tex., 2000—; cons. Changqing Petroleum Inc., Gansu, China. Contbr. articles to profl. jours.; patentee engineered surface pattern of polymer gels. Mem. AAAS, Am. Physics Soc. (outstanding presentation 1996, 97), Sigma Xi. Avocations: chess, swimming, aesthetics, history. Home: 1607 W Oak St Apt 221 Denton TX 76201-8913

WANG, CHARLES PING, engineering executive; b. Shanghai, Republic of China, Apr. 25, 1937; came to U.S., 1962; s. Kuan-Ying and Ping-Lu (Ming) W.; m. Lily L. Lee, June 29, 1963. BS, Taiwan U., Republic of China, 1959; MS, Tsinghua U., Singchu, Republic of China, 1961; PhD, Calif. Inst. Tech., 1967. Mem. tech. staff Bellcomm, Washington, 1967-69; research engr. U. San Diego, 1969-74; sr. scientist Aerspace Corp., Los Angeles, 1976-86; pres. Optodyne, Inc., Compton, Calif., 1986—; adj. prof. U. Calif., San Diego, 1979-90; pres. Chinese-Am. Engr. and Scientists Assn. So. Calif., Los Angeles, 1979-81; program chmn. Internation Conf. of Lasers, Shanghai, 1979-80; organizer and session chmn. Lasers Conf., Los Angeles, 1981-84, program chmn., Las Vegas, 1985. Editor in chief Series in Laser Tech., 1983-91; contbr. articles to profl. jours.; inventor discharge excimer laser. Calif. Inst. Tech. scholar, 1965. Fellow Am. Optical Soc., AIAA (assoc., jour. editor 1981-83). Office: Optodyne Inc 1180 W Mahalo Pl Compton CA 90220-5443

WANG, CHARLESTON CHENG-KUNG, lawyer, engineer; b. Tainan, Republic of China, Oct. 17, 1956; came to U.S., 1972; s. Shan-Cheng and I-Tsen (Cheng) W.; m. Shirley Liao, Mar. 14, 1981; children: Vivian, Arthur Rex. BS in Econs. and Chem. Engring., U. Del., 1977; MBA in Internat. Bus., Xavier U., 1979; JD, No. Ky. U., 1982; postgrad., U. Cin., 1989, No. Territory U. Darwin, Australia, 1999. Bar: Ohio 1982, U.S. Dist. Ct. (so. dist.) Ohio 1983, U.S. Dist. Ct. (ea. dist.) Ky. 1983, U.S. Ct. Appeals (6th cir.) 1983; diplomate Am. Bd. Indsl. Hygiene; cert. indsl. hygienist. Chem. engr. Procter & Gamble, Cin., 1979-81, NIOSH, Cin., 1981-84; mng. ptnr. Groeber & Wang, Cin., 1982-85; compliance officer U.S. Dept. Labor, Cin., 1985-88; v.p., gen. counsel Environ. Enterprises, Inc., Cin., 1988—; adj. prof. No. Ky. U., 1983—, U. Cin., 1985—. Author: How to Manage Workplace Derived Hazards and Avoid Liability, 1987, OSHA Compliance & Management Handbook, 1991; assoc. editor No. Ky. Law Rev., 1980-82; contbr. articles to profl. jours. Mem. Am. Acad. Indsl. Hygiene, Am. Inst. Chem. Engrs., Am. Conf. Govt. Indsl. Hygienists, Chinese Am. Assn. Cin. (pres. 1987-88). Avocation: swimming. Home: 11321 Terwilligers Valley Ln Cincinnati OH 45249-2744 Office: Wanglaw Bldg 6924 Plainfield Rd Cincinnati OH 45236-3789

WANG, CHEN, radiologist; b. Shenyang, Liaoning, China, Mar. 5, 1959; s. Diankui and Chaiyun (Zhang) W.; m. Li Lu, Aug. 4, 1985; 1 child, Yanlu. MD, China Med. U., 1982, M of Med. Sci., 1988; D of Med. Sci., Uppsala U., 1998. Med. intern 2d Clin. Hosp., China Med. U., Shenyang, China, 1982-84, asst. physician, 1984-86, physician, 1986-90, chief physician, 1990-93; rsch. scholar Uppsala U. Hosp., Sweden, 1993-98; physician Uppsala U. Hosp., 1998—; asst. lectr. China Med. U., 1984-90, lectr., 1990-93. Contbr. articles to profl. jours. Avocations: philately, photography. Home: Djäknegatan 81, S-75425 Uppsala Sweden Office: Uppsala Univ Hosp, Dept Diagnostic Radiology, S-75185 Uppsala Sweden

WANG, CHEN CHI, electronics company, real estate, finance company, investment services, and international trade executive; b. Taipei, Taiwan, Aug. 10, 1932; came to U.S., 1959, naturalized, 1970; s. Chin-Ting and Chen-Kim Wang; m. Victoria Rebisoff, Mar. 5, 1965; children: Katherine Kim, Gregory Chen, John Christopher, Michael Edward. BA in Econs., Nat. Taiwan U., 1955; BSEE, San Jose State U., 1965; MBA, U. Calif., Berkeley, 1961. With IBM Corp., San Jose, Calif., 1965-72; founder, CEO Electronics Internat. Co., Santa Clara, Calif., 1968-72; owner, gen. mgr. Electronics Internat. Co., Santa Clara, 1972-81; reorganized as EIC Group, 1981; now chmn. bd., CEO EIC Investment Corp., 1982—; dir. Systek Electronics Corp., Santa Clara, 1970-73; founder, sr. ptnr. Wang Enterprises (name changed to Chen Kim Enterprises 1982), Santa Clara, 1974-75, Hanson & Wang Devel. Co., Woodside, Calif., 1977-85; chmn. bd. Golden Alpha Enterprises, San Mateo, Calif., 1979—; mng. ptnr. Woodside Acres-Las Pulgas Estate, Woodside, 1980-85; founder, sr. ptnr. DeVine & Wang, Oakland, Calif., 1977-83, Van Heal & Wang, West Village, Calif., 1981-82; founder, chmn. bd. EIC Fin. Corp. (now EIC Investment Corp.), Redwood City, Calif., 1985-90; chmn. bd. Maritek Corp., Corpus Christi, Tex., 1988-89; chmn. EIC Internat. Trade Corp., Lancaster, Calif., 1989-90, EIC Capital Corp., Redwood City, 1990-91; mng. mem. Sixtieth West, LLC, 1997—, Land Investment Co. Calif., LLC, 1998—, Aceh Capital, LLC, 1998—. Author: Monetary and Banking System of Taiwan, 1955, The Small Car Market in the U.S., 1961. Served to 2d lt., Nationalist Chinese Army, 1955-56. Mem. Internat. Platform Assn., Tau Beta Pi. Mem. Christian Ch. Home: 195 Brookwood Rd Woodside CA 94062-2302 Office: EIC Group Head Office Bldg 2055-2075 Woodside Rd Redwood City CA 94061-3355

WANG, CHENG, economics educator; b. Dan Yang, Jiang Su, China, Dec. 25, 1963; came to U.S., 1992; s. Li Chang Jing and Xiao Yu Wang; m. Ge Gao. BS, Fu Dan U., Shanghai, 1984, MA, 1987; PhD in econs., U. Western Ont., Can., 1994. Asst. prof. Carnegie Mellon U., Pitts., 1994—. Office: Carnegie Mellon U Grad Sch Indsl Orgn Pittsburgh PA 15213

WANG, CHENG XU, education educator; b. Jiangyin, Jiangsu, China, June 15, 1912; s. Jiefu and Yuyin (Chen) W.; m. Duanying Zhao, Aug. 8, 1939; children: Zhongwei, Zhongming. BEd, Zhejiang U., Hangzhou, China, 1936; MA, London (Eng.) U., 1941. Prof. edn., head dept. edn. Zhejiang U., Hangzhou, 1947-52; prof. edn., head dept. edn., dean Zhejiang Tchrs. Coll., Hangzhou, 1952-57; prof. edn., head Ctr. for Comparative Edn. Inst. Higher Edn. Hangzhou (China) U., 1958-98; prof. edn., head ctr. comparative edn. Zhejiang U. XIXI Campus, 1998—; vis. scholar Luce Found., U. So. Calif., 1985; hon. fellow Inst. Edn., London U., 1993. Editor: (textbooks) Readings in the Western Educational Classics, 1964, 80, 85, Comparative Education, 1982 (State Edn. Commn. award 1988), (book series) Western Higher Education, 1987, 88, 89, (book) Post-War English Education, 1992, London University, 1995, History of Comparative Education, 1998 (Ministry of Edn. award 1999), Short History of Comparative Studies of Chinese & Foreign Education, 1997 (State award 1999); translator: Burton Clark's Higher Education System, 1994, Clark Kerr's Higher Education Cannot Escape History, 2000. Mem. adv. com. regional coop. in edn. Asia and Pacific UNESCO, 1980-92; vice chmn. Chinese People's Polit. Consultative Conf., Zhejiang prov. com., 1985-92. Mem. China Comparative Edn. Soc. (advisor 1990—), China History of Edn. Soc. (coun. mem. 1979—), Zhejiang Higher Edn. Soc. (chmn. 1987—). Avocations: Chinese taiji and qigong. Home: 12-22 Hangda Xincun, Hangzhou Zhejiang 310007, China Office: Zhejiang Univ XIXI Campus, Dept Edn, Hangzhou Hangzhou Zhejiang 310028, China

WANG, CHENG-I, parasitologist, researcher in tropical medicine; b. Da Wu, China, June 2, 1910; s. Yi Wu and D.J. (Chen) W.; m. Qi Ho Zhang, Aug. 15, 1935 (dec. 1970); children: Wang Wanzhong, Wang Louan; m. Ping He Zhang, May 19, 1973. Student, U. Nanking, China, 1930-34; MD, Peiping Union Med. Coll., 1939; DTM, Calcutta Sch. Trop. Medicine, 1943; DrPH, U. Mich., 1948. Asst. Peiping (China) Union Med. Coll., 1939; resident, then vis. physician Szechwan Provincial Infectious Diseases Hosp., Cheng-du, China, 1940-44; postdoctoral fellow Tulane U. Med. Ctr., New Orleans, 1945-46; rsch. fellow U. Mich., Ann Arbor, 1946-48; prof. parasitology Chongqing (China) U. Med. Coll., 1949-51; prof. parasitology and microbiology West China U. Med. Scis., Cheng-du, 1952-67, chief dept. parasitology, 1970-75; prof., rschr., dep. dir., dir. Beijing (China) Tropical Medicine Rsch. Inst., 1979-85, 85-87, dep. dir., 1979-85, dir., 1985-87; mem.

com. on med. scis. Ministry of Health of People's Republic of China, Beijing, 1963-90; invited advisor to editl. bd. China Internat. Interchange Press. Author: Handbook on the Control of Hookwork Infections; adviser editorial bd. Jour. Practical Parasitic Disease, 1993—; contbr. numerous over 150 articles to profl. jours. Recipient various awards. Mem. Chinese Soc. Parasitologists (adviser), China Assn. Preventive Medicine (sr.). Avocations: Beijing opera, bridge. Home: Bdlg 20 Gate 2 Apt 501, Chong Wen Men East St, 100062 Beijing China Office: 94 Yong An Rd, Beijing 100050, China

WANG, CHIA PING, physicist, educator; came to U.S., 1963, naturalized; (parents Chinese citizens).; s. Guan Can and Tah (Lin) W. BS, U. London, 1950; MS, U. Malaya (now U. Singapore), 1951; PhD in Physics, U. Malaya (now U. Singapore) and U. Cambridge, 1953; DSc in Physics, U. Singapore, 1972. Asst. lectr. U. Malaya, 1951-53; mem. faculty Nankai U., Tientsin, 1954-58, prof. physics, 1956-58, head electron physics divsn., 1955-58; head electron physics Lanchow Atomic Project, 1958; faculty Hong Kong U.; faculty Chinese U., Hong Kong, 1958, prof. physics, 1959-63, acting head physics, math. depts., 1959; rsch. assoc. lab. nuclear studies Cornell U., Ithaca, N.Y., 1963-64; assoc. prof. space sci. and applied physics Cath. U. Am., Washington, 1964-68; assoc. prof. physics Case Inst. Tech. Case Western Res. U., Cleve., 1966-70; vis. scientist, vis. prof. Cavendish Lab. U. Cambridge (Eng.), Inst. Theoretical Physics, U. Leuven (Belgium), Cosmic Ray Lab., U.S. Naval Rsch. Labs., U. Md., MIT, 1970-75; rsch. physicist radiation lab. U.S. Army Natick (Mass.) R & D Command, 1975—; steering com. sci. and tech. directorate U.S. Army Natick R & D Command, 1993—; steering com. nuclear physics divsn. Nankai U., Tientsin, 1956-58; vis. scientist, vis. prof. U. Cambridge (Eng.), U. Leuven, Belgium, U.S. Naval Rsch. Labs., U. Md., MIT, 1970-75. Co-author: Atomic Structure and Interactions of Ionizing Radiations with Matter in Preservation of Food by Ionizing Radiation, 1982; contbr. more than 80 articles to profl. jours. and reports. Recipient Outstanding Performance award Dept. Army, 1980, Quality Increase award, 1980. Mem. AAAS, Am. Nuclear Soc., Am. Phys. Soc., Inst. Physics London, N.Y. Acad. Scis., Sigma Xi. Achievements include pioneering research in nuclear sub-structure (now often referred to as parton), nucleor sub-unit structure, multiparticle production, cosmic radiation, picosecond time to pulse-height conversion, thermal physics, laser steel melting, microwaves absorption and scattering, initiating cosmic-ray extensive air shower research in China. Office: US Army Natick 28 Hallett Hill Rd Weston MA 02493-1753

WANG, CHIEN-MING, structural engineer, educator, researcher; b. Alor Star, Kedah, Malaysia, Sept. 3, 1957; arrived in Singapore, 1982; s. Chang-Wai and Kim-Hoon (Kung) W.; m. Poh-Hong Aung, Feb. 2, 1980; children: Timothy Shing-Lern, Christopher Shing-Wen, Andrew Shing-Zhi, Stephanie Huifen. B of Engring. with 1st class honors, Monash U., Melbourne, Australia, 1979, M of Engring. Sci., 1980, PhD, 1982. Chartered engr., U.K. Lectr. Nat. U. Singapore, 1982-88, sr. lectr., 1988-97, assoc. prof., 1997—, assoc. dir. Ctr. for Devel. of Tchg. and Learning, 1999—; mem. internat. adv. com. Internat. Conf. on Optimization, Chengdu, China, 1995, Perth, Australia, 1998, Internat. Conf. on Structural Stability and Design, Sydney, Australia, 1995, Asian Pacific Conf. Computational Mechanics, Seoul, Korea, 1996, Internat. Conf. Computing Civil & Bldg. Engring., Seoul, 1997. Editor: Optimization Techniques and Applications, 1992, Computational Mechanics for the Next Millennium, 1999; co-author: Vibration of Mindlin Plates, 1998, Elsevier, Shear Deformable Beams and Plates: Relationships with Classical Solutions, 2000; co-editor-in-chief Internat. Jour. Structural Stability; mem. editl. bd. Computational Structural Engring.; contbr. articles to internat. jours. including Jour. Structural Mechanics, Jour. Engring. Mechanics, Jour. Structural Engring., Internat. Jour. Mech. Scis., Internat. Jour. Solids Structures, Jour. Sound and Vibration. Rsch. grantee Nat. U. Singapore, 1991, 92, 95, 99; recipient Engring. Faculty Innovative Tchg. award, 1997, Tchg. Excellence award, 1998. Mem. ASCE, Instn. Structural Engrs., Internat. Soc. for Structural and Multidisciplinary Optimization, Instn. Engrs. Singapore (pub. com. 1990—, best structural paper award 1994), Singapore Structural Steel Soc., Asian Pacific Assn. Computational Mechanics (mem. gen. coun.). Achievements include research in automating Rayleigh-Ritz method for structural analysis, relationships between solutions of higher-order and classical beam/plate theories; research in structural optimization. Avocations: chess, reading, traveling. Office: Nat U Singapore Dept Civil Engring, Kent Ridge, Singapore 119260, Singapore

WANG, CHI-LUEN, fiber optics engineer; b. Tainan, Taiwan, Nov. 27, 1960; came to U.S., 1985; s. Yu-Chung and Shoou-Hwa W.; m. Cecilia Huang, Sept. 20, 1996. BS in Physics, Nat. Tsing Hua U., Hsinchu, Taiwan, 1982; MSEE, Syracuse U., 1989, PhDEE, 1992. Rsch. asst. Dept. of ECE, Syracuse (N.Y.) U., 1986-92; asst. prof. Inst. Tech., SUNY, Utica, N.Y., 1992-93; assoc. rschr. Telecom. Labs. Ministry of Transp. and Comm., Taoyuan, Taiwan, 1994-96; rschr. Telecom. Labs. Chunghwa Telecom., Taoyuan, Taiwan, 1996; system group leader E-Tek Dynamics, San Jose, Calif., 1996-97, staff engr., 1998-99, mgr., 1998-99; v.p. R&D Fiver Labs, Fremont, Calif., 1999-2000, SDO Comms. Corp., Fremont, 2000—. Contbr. articles to profl. jours. and confs. Recipient grad. assistantship Syracuse U., 1986-92. Mem. IEEE, Internat. Soc. Optical Engring., Sigma Xi. E-mail: aclwang@yahoo.com. Home: 2849 Red Pine Ct Pleasanton CA 94588-9695 Office: SDO 42986 Osgood Rd Fremont CA 94539-5627

WANG, CHUNG-CHENG, neurosurgeon; b. Yan-tai, Shandong, China, Dec. 20, 1925; s. Xiang-shan and Shung-shi Wang; m. Yi-fang Han; children: Xin, Rui, Jin. MD, Beijing Med. U., China, 1950. Resident Tianjin (China) Gen. Hosp., 1950-55; attending physician Beijing Tongren Hosp., 1955-58; attending physician Beijing Xuanwu Hosp., 1958-78, prof., 1978—; researcher Beijing Neurosurg. Inst., 1977—, dep. dir., 1960-78, dir., 1978—; pres. Beijing Xuanwu Hosp., 1978-82, Beijing Tiantan Hosp., 1982-92; mem. WHO expert adv. panel on neurosci., 1982—. 1st author: Cerebral Angiography, 1965 (nat. award 1978), Neurosurgery I-III, 1974-84; author: Microneurosurgery, 1985; contbr. articles to profl. jours.; chief editor Chinese Jour. Neurosurgery, 1985—; vice chief editor Chinese Jour. Mental Diseases, 1977—. Recipient Nat. award Nat. Com. Sci. and Tech., Beijing, Ministry award Ministry Pub. Health, Beijing, Mcpl. award Beijing Com. Sci. & Tech., Bur. award Beijing Bur. Pub. Health. Mem. Am. Assn. Neurol. Surgs. (hon.), Japan Neurosurg. Soc. (hon.), Chinese Soc. Neurosurgery (pres. 1985—), Chinese Acad. Engring. Avocations: swimming, cool bathing, long running, table tennis. Home and Office: Beijing Neurosurgical Inst, Tiantan Xili, Beijing 100050, China

WANG, COLLEEN IONA, medical association administrator, writer; b. Mpls., Oct. 23, 1953; d. Dillard Wayne and Nova Bardeen (Vaught) Greenwood; m. Hansen Stephen Wang, Aug. 22, 1976; children: Hansen Jeremiah, Nathaniel Stephen. AS in Nursing, Loma Linda U., 1974. Registered nurse, Calif. Staff nurse cardio-thoracic ICU Loma Linda (Calif.) U. Med. Ctr., 1975-77, staff nurse pediats. ICU, 1978-80; staff nurse med.-surg. cardio-thoracic ICU St. Bernardine's Hosp., San Bernardino, Calif., 1977-78; nurse medically fragile, high risk infants, foster care San Bernardino County, Alta Loma, Calif., 1980-87; coord. support group So. Calif. chpt. San Bernardino-Riverside County Tourette Syndrome Assn., Loma Linda, 1987-97; med. liaison So. Calif. chpt. Tourette Syndrome Assn., Redlands, 1991-99, nursing educator, 1993—; bd. dirs. med. liaison Tourette Syndrome Assn., Encino, 1993-99; chmn. western regional med. conf. Tourette Syndrome Assn., Pasadena, 1994; bd. dirs., pres. Tourette Syndrome Assn., Encino, 1996; host chmn. with Tourette Syndrome Assn. N.Y. Tourette Syndrome Assn., Burbank, 1996; chmn. educators conf. Tourette Syndrome Assn., San Diego, 1998; chair western regional med. conf. Tourette Spectrum Disorder Assn., Ontario, Calif., 1999, med. v.p., bd. dirs., 1999—. Co-author, editor: Tourette Syndrome: A Continuing Education Program for Nurses, 1993, updated, 1996 (Outstanding Chpt. Achievement award Nat. Tourette Syndrome Assn. Inc. 1994); co-author: National Curriculum on Educating & Managing of Children with Neurobiological Disorders; contbr. articles to profl. jours. Founding officer, sec. Challenging Kids, Inc., Atlanta; vol. instr. gifted and talented math Mariposa Elem. Redlands (Calif.) Sch. Dist., 1990-91; mem. PTA Mariposa Elem., Redlands, Calif., 1992-95, vol. instr. first aid Flash Class, 1990-92; presenter-in-svc. edn. Multiple Schs. San Bernardino County, Riverside County, L.A. County, 1992—; mem. PTA Moore Middle Sch., Redlands, 1995-97, Redlands H.S., 1994—. Mem. Ams. for Nonsmoker's Rights, Tourette Spectrum Disorder Assn., Tourette Syndrome Assn. (nat. membership Bayside, N.Y. emm. com. underserved area conf. 1986-97). Avocations: computers, snorkeling, travel. Office: Tourette Syndrome Assn So Calif 30733 E Sunset Dr S Redlands CA 92373-7350

WANG, DAKAI, physics educator; b. Nanjing, China, Aug. 15, 1936; m. Yongping He; children: Lipo, Hongbing. Grad., 3d Sch. Wuhan (China) City, 1955, Northwestern U., Xian, China, 1959. Asst. Northwestern U., 1959-64, lectr., 1964-81, assoc. prof., 1983-86, prof., 1986—, head physics dept., 1984-89, head elec. dept., 1992-96, researcher of inst. of analytical sci., 1997—; vis. scholar U. Glasgow, Scotland, 1981-83; vis. rschr. Tech. U. Delft, The Netherlands, 1991-92; dir. Coun. for Teaching Elec. and Info. Sci., 1991—. Author: Methods and Applications of Modern Spectral Estimation, 1991; editor WULI, physics jour., 1983. Grantee Dutch Tech. Found., 1991. Fellow Chinese Phys. Soc., Chinese Elec. Soc., Am. Math. Soc. Office: Northwestern U, Da Xue Dong Lu, Xian 710069, China

WANG, DEHUA, chemist; b. Shaoxing, China, Sept. 27, 1937; m. Xiaolong Xu, Nov. 7, 1967; children: Kathy Yu, Wendy Lu. PhD, Syracuse U., 1985. Spectroscopist Atlanta U., 1985-86; prof. Wuhan Inst. Physics, China, 1986-89; vis. prof. Coll. Staten Island, N.Y., 1989-90; NMR rsch. scientist Kimberly-Clark Corp., Roswell, Ga., 1990—. Office: Kimberly-Clark Corp 1400 Holcomb Br Rd Roswell GA 30076

WANG, DE-JUNG (DEJUAN WANG), telecommunications educator; b. Fuzhou, Fujian, China, Feb. 15, 1927; s. Xin Ru and Qiong Ying (Lin) W.; m. Xin Hua Wang; children: Lijun, Min, Wei Wang. E, Shanghai Jiaotong U., 1951. Tchr. Tech. Sch. Posts & Telecomm., Nanging, China, 1952-55; lectr. U. Posts & Telecomm., Beijing, China, 1955-77; assoc. prof. Beijing U. Posts & Telecomm., 1978-86, prof., 1986—; concurrent prof. Grad. Sch. Academia Sinica, Beijing, 1982-93. Co-author: Theory of Network Synthesis, 1962; gen. dir., designer MH04 60 Ch. Transmultiplexer, 1985-89; gen. dir. Digital Multifrequency Sys, 1985-90; patentee in field; assoc. chief editor Jour. Beijing U. Posts & Telecomm., 1978, chief editor, 1982-90. Named Splendid Tchr. Beijing Govt., 1991, Model Worker of Nat. Edn. Sys., Chinese Nat. Edn. Com. and Pers. Ministry, 1991, Specialist with Outstanding Contbn. Chinese Govt., China, 1991. Fellow Chinese Inst. Electronics, Chinese Inst. Comm.; mem. IEEE (sr., chpt. chair SP 1993-96). Avocations: Beijing opera, appreciation of football game. Office: Beijing U, Posts & Telecomm, Beijing 100088, China

WANG, DONNA HUI, investigative medicine director; b. Guangdong, China, Aug. 20, 1961; d. Xuanwu and Huijuan (Ouyang) W.; m. Eugene J. Yu, June 8, 1985; 1 child, Eunice Yu. MD, Sun Yat-Sen Med. U., Guangzhou, China, 1984; postdoc. fellow, Eastern Va. Med. Sch., Norfolk, 1990. Resident Sun Yat-Sen Ophthalmic Ctr., Sun Yat-Sen Med. U., Guangzhou, China, 1984-85; vis. scholar dept. surgery and physiology Bowman Gray Sch. Medicine, Winston-Salem, N.C., 1985-87; rsch. assoc. dept. physiology Eastern Va. Med. Sch., Norfolk, 1987-90, asst. prof. dept. physiology, 1990-93; asst. prof. dept. internal medicine U. Tex. Med. Branch, Galveston, Tex., 1993-97, assoc. prof. dept. internal medicine, 1997-99; scientist, dir. histochemical core Sealy Ctr. for Molecular Cardiology, U. Tex. Med. Sch., Galveston, 1994-99; prof. dept. medicine Michigan State U., East Lansing, 1999—; dir. Investigative medicine, Dept. Medicine, Mich. State U., East Lansing, 1999—; mem. Pub. Com. Am. Heart Assn. Coun. for High Blood Pressure, Dallas, 1999-02. Editor: Angiotensin Protocol, Methods in Molecular Medicine, 2000; contbr. articles to profl. jours. Chair The Session of Physiology and Genetics of Angiotensin I and II Receptors, The 68th Scientific Sessions of Am. Heart Assn., Anaham, Calif., 1995, The Session of Hypertension, Am. Physiol. Soc., San Francisco, 1998; peer reviewer Am. Heart Assn-Western State Affiliates Peer Review, San Francisco, 1998-99; mem. prof. com. The Microcirculatory Soc. Inc., San Diego, 1997-01. Recipient First Ind. Rsch. Support Transition award, Nat. Inst. Health, 1993, 98, 1997 Outstanding Young Investigator Travel award, The Microcirculatory Soc., Inc., Hoechst Marion Roussel 1998 Young Scholar award, The Am. Soc. Hypertension, 1998, Established Investigator award Am. Heart Assn., 1999-03. Fellow Am. Heart Assn. Coun. for High Blood Pressure Rsxh. Pub. com. mem., 1995—, Cardiovascular sect., Am. Physiol. Soc. Woman in Physiology com. mem., 1999—; mem. The Microcirculatory Soc. Inc. E-mail: donna.wang@ht.msu.edu. Fax: 517-432-1326. Office: Dept Medicine B316 Clinical Center East Lansing MI 48824

WANG, ENGE, physics educator; b. Shenyang, Liaoning, China, Jan. 24, 1957; s. Zhaogai Wang and Qixiu Deng; m. Xiaoping Zhang, July 1984; 1 child, Yiren. BS, Liaoning U., Shenyang, China, 1982, MS, 1985; PhD, Peking U., Beijing, 1990. Postdoctoral rschr. Inst. Physics, Chinese Acad. Scis., Beijing, 1990-91, prof. physics, 1995—; rschr. Inst. Superieur d'Electronique du Nord, Lille, France, 1992; rschr. U. Houston, 1992-93, rsch. assoc., 1993-95; vis. prof. U. Oxford, Eng., 1996; dep. chmn. Degrees Appraising Coun. of Inst. Physics, Beijing, 1996—; dir. State Key Lab. for Surface Physics, Beijing, 1997—; mem. 100 talent program Chinese Acad. Scis., 1994. Contbr. articles to profl. jours.; patentee in field. Named Nat. Outstanding Young Rschr., Chinese Natural Sci. Found., 1995, Outstanding Young scholar Hong Kong "Qui Shi" Natural Sci. Found., 1996; recipient 1st Young Scientist award Chinese Acad. Sci., 1997. Mem. Internat. Ctr. for Materials Physics, Chinese Phys. Soc. (dir. surface sect. 1999—), Inst. Physics (dir. 1999—). Avocations: climbing, camping, basketball, reading, music. Office: Inst Physics CAS, PO Box 603 Nanshan 3rd St, Beijing 100080, China

WANG, EN-SI, organic chemist, administrator; b. Jilin, China, Nov. 15, 1955; s. Hang-Chuan and Su-Lan (Bi) W.; m. Xiao-Ping Zhang, Aug. 7, 1980; 1 child, Xi. BSc, Jilin U., Changchun, China, 1978, MSc, 1988; PhD, Chinese U. Hong Kong, 1994. Tchg. asst. Jilin U., 1978-85, lectr., 1985-92, assoc. prof. organic chemistry, 1992-99, prof., 2000—; mgr. Mailing biol. Co. Ltd., Changchun, 1995-96; vice gen. mgr. GeneSci. Pharms. Co. Lt., Changchun, 1997—. Contbr. articles to profl. jours. Recipient 2d award Jilin Edn. Commn., 1992, 1st award China Edn. Commn., 1995. Home: 1 Tianhe St, Changchun China Office: Jilin U Coll of Life Sci, 123 Jiefang Rd, Changchun China

WANG, ERQI, instrumentation engineering educator; b. Yong Chun, Fujian, China, Jan. 28, 1938; s. Jinji Wang and Peilan Chen; m. Dehui Song, Sept. 30, 1965; children: Youtong, Dahui. Diploma, Zhejiang U., Hangzhou, China, 1960. Gen. designer Xian (China) Inst. Applied Optics, 1960-85; dir. Inst. Tech. Xiamen (China) U., 1986-90, prof. dept. sci. instrumentation, 1990—. Contbr. articles to profl. jours. including Chinese Jour. Sci. Instrumentation; designer laser range finder, telescopic laser range finder, ophthalmic YAG laser disruptors, ruby laser range finder. Mem. China Instrument Soc. (bd. dirs.), China Optics Soc. (bd. dirs.), Xiamen Automation Soc. (standing bd. dirs.). Home: PO Box 8-502, Xia-da Bei-Cun, Fujian Xiamen 361005, China Office: Xiamen U, Dept Sci Instrumentation, Fujian Xiamen 361005, China

WANG, FRANCIS WEI-YU, biomedical materials scientist, researcher; b. Pei-Kang, Yun-Lin, Taiwan, July 21, 1936; came to U.S., 1956; s. Yin-Kwei and Tsai-Wei Wang; m. Susan Shu-Huei Liao, June 18, 1966; children: Anthony, Andrea, Edwin. BSChemE, Calif. Inst. Tech., 1961, MSChemE, 1962; PhD in Chemistry, U. Calif., San Diego, 1971. Chemist Pacific Soap Co., San Diego, 1962-66; rsch. asst. U. Calif.-San Diego, La Jolla, 1966-71; USPHS postdoctoral fellow Polytechnic U., Bklyn., 1971-72; group leader biomaterials Nat. Inst. Stds. and Tech., Gaithersburg, Md., 1972—; rep. Dept. Commerce Accredited Stds. Comm. MD156, Dental Materials, Instruments, and Equipment, Chgo., 1997—. Contbr. numerous articles to profl. jours. Recipient W.P. Slichter award Dept. Commerce, 1997, Bronze medal, 1985. Mem. Internat. Assn. for Dental Rsch., Soc. for Biomaterials, Am. Chem. Soc., Am. Phys. Soc. Achievements include patents on non-destructive method for fluorescence monitoring of polymerization and solidification of thermoplastic polymer, fluorescence monitoring of polymer injection molding, and fluorescence monitoring of polymer viscosity and orientation. Office: Nat Inst Stds and Tech 100 Bureau Dr Stop 8545 Gaithersburg MD 20899-8545

WANG, FU-ZHANG, medical researcher; b. Dali, Shaanxi, China, Mar. 23, 1964; p. Zeng-Suo Wang and Jun-Fang Yang; m. Jing Hou, Aug. 15, 1996. MB, Xian (China) Med. U., 1985; M in Medicine, Beijing Med. U., 1988, Karolinska Inst., Stockholm, 1995; PhD in Med. Scis., Karolinska Inst., Stockholm, 1999. Clin. physician Beijing Med. U., 1988-89, rsch. assoc., 1990-92; vis. scientist Karolinska Inst., Stockholm, 1992-93; rsch. assoc. Swedish Inst. for Infectious Disease Control, Stockholm, 1995-99; rsch. fellow U. Kans. Med. Ctr., Kansas City, 2000—. Contbr. articles to profl. jours. Mem. European Soc. for Clin. Virology, Swedish Soc. for Med. Microbiology. Avocations: swimming, tennis. E-mail: Fu-Zhang.Wang@smi.ki.se. Fax: 46-8-272231. Home: 3900 Booth St Apt 9 Kansas City KS 66103-2840 Office: Dept Microbiol/Molec Gen 3901 Rainbow Blvd Kansas City KS 66160-0001

WANG, GANG, neurologist, physiologist, researcher; b. Changsha, Hunan, China, Aug. 27, 1963; arrived in Japan, 1987; s. Xiangpu Wang and Yingshi Han; m. Shan Ding, Mar. 4, 1991; 1 child, Ridey Hsiao. BS, Huazhong U. Sci. Tech., Wuhan, China, 1984; MS, Kagoshima (Japan) U., 1990, PhD, 1993. Asst. prof. Hunan Med. U., Changsha, 1984-86; rschr. Kagoshima U., 1987-88, asst. prof., 1995-98, assoc. prof., 1999—; rschr. RIKEN Inst., Wako, Japan, 1993-95. Contbr. articles to profl. jours. Mem. Soc. Neurosci., Physiol. Soc. Japan, Japan Neurosci. Soc. Avocations: swimming, travel, hiking. Office: Kagoshima U Dept Bioengring, 1-21-40 Korimoto, Kagoshima 890-0065, Japan

WANG, GUANGMIAO, business executive, consultant; b. Ninghai, China, Jan. 19, 1947; came to U.S., 1992; s. Yuegnan and Hehua (Zhou) W.; m. Guiyan Xu, May 1, 1973; children: Haixiang, Haijia. BA, Hangzhou Coll. Fgn. Lang., China, 1969; grad., Shanghai Jiaotong U., China, 1985, U. N.D., 1993; postgrad., Heriot-Watt U., Edinburgh, U.K., 1997—. Supr. Heiman Ship Co., China, 1971-74; lectr. Zhejiang U. Tech., Hangzhou, 1974-91; exec. Kin Lin Corp., Kansas City, Mo., 1997—, Jia Xiang Inc., Springfield, Mo., 1997—; cons. Heimen Bus. Assn., 1972-74. Contbr. articles to profl. jours. U. N.D. grantee, 1992. Mem. Zhejiang Lang. Assn. (advisor 1980-91), N.Am. Chinese Restaurant Assn. (dir. 1997—), Phi Beta Delta. Avocations: golf, boating, photography, collecting stamps and coins. Home: 314 W Whiteside St Springfield MO 65807-2844 Office: 2118 S Campbell Ave Springfield MO 65807-2853

WANG, GUANGQIU, aerospace engineer; b. Beijing, Sept. 11, 1954; arrived in Germany, 1983; s. Zeying Wang and Defeng Liu; m. Mingming Yang, Dec. 9, 1998. Rschr. Inst. Aerospace Tech. U., Berlin, 1986-91; lectr. dept. math. Tech. U., Delft, The Netherlands, 1991-92; engr. BMW Rolls-Royce Aeroengines, Dahlewitz, Germany, 1992-94; mgr. rsch. tech. BMW Rolls-Royce, Dahlewitz, 1995—; cons. Aviation Industries China, Beijing, 1997—; lectr. Beijing U. Aeronautics/Astronautics, 1997—. Author: Visoelastic Rolling Contact of Two Rollers, 1988; book contbr. Three-dimentional Viscoelastic Rolling Contact, 1993; contbr. articles to profl. jours. Bd. dirs. China Spring mag., N.Y.C., 1993-94. Fellow Modern China; mem. German Aerospace Union. Avocations: football, basketball, golf, politics. Home: Hohenfriedbergstr 9, 10829 Berlin Germany Office: BMW Rolls-Royce AeroEngines, Eschenweg 11, 15827 Dahlewitz Germany

WANG, GUO ZHI, optician, educator; b. Yu Lin, Shaanxi, China, Sept. 15, 1936; s. ZiAn and Shi (Ling) W.; m. Li Juan Li, Feb. 1, 1962; children: Yu, Xin. B, ShaanXi Normal U., 1958. Asst. prof. Phys. Dept. ShaanXi Normal U., XiAn, China, 1958-77; asst. prof. Inst. Optic and Precision Mechanics Acad. Sinica China, XiAn, 1977-96, prof., 1996—. Inventor in field. Mem. Chinese Optics Soc., Chinese Physics Soc. Office: Acad Sinica Inst Optic & Precision Mechanics, 234 Friend W Rd, Xian 710068, China

WANG, HAIMING, research scientist; b. Linhai, Zhejiang, China, Feb. 15, 1958; s. Bingrong and Xiaochun (Du) W.; m. Shanlin Mi, May 15, 1984; 1 child, Katherine Y. B Engring. in Optical Engring., Zhejiang U., Hangzhou, China, 1982; MSc, Chinese Acad. Scis., Changchun, 1985, PhD, 1990. Tchg. asst. dept. precision machinery U. Sci. and Tech. China, Hefei, 1985-86; vis. scholar Siemens Ctrl. Rsch. Lab., Munich, Germany, 1988-89; postdoctoral scholar U. Kaiserslautern, Germany, 1990-92; rsch. engr. Centro Investigaciones en Optica, Leon, Mexico, 1992-97, KLA-Tencor Corp., San Jose, Calif., 1997—. Contbr. articles to profl. jours. Mem. Mexican Acad. Scis., Optical Soc. Am. Avocations: reading, Chinese Kungfu, go, drawing. Office: KLA-Tencor Corp 160 Rio Robles San Jose CA 95134-1809

WANG, HOAU-YAN, pharmacologist, educator; b. Kaoshiung, Taiwan, June 23, 1957; s. Yen-San and Hui-Ying Wang; m. Kim Eberle, Nov. 26, 1988; children: Ethan, Jordan. BS in Pharmacy, China Med. Coll., Taiwan, 1981; MS in Pharmacology, St. John's U., N.Y.C., 1985; PhD in Pharmacology, Med. Coll. Pa., 1988. Tchg. fellow St. John's U., 1984-86; instr. Med. Coll. Pa., Phila., 1990-92, asst. prof., 1992-94; asst. prof. Allegheny U. Health Scis., Phila., 1994-97; sr. scientist R.W. Johnson Pharm. Rsch. Inst., Spring House, Pa., 1998—; internat. referee N.Z. Neurol. Found., Newton/Auckland, 1995—. Author: the Role of Adenosine in the Regulation of Cardiac Function: The Effect of Age, 1998, Cocaine: Effects on the Developing Brain, 1998, Methods in Aging Research, 1999. Rsch. grantee Alzheimer's Disease and Related Disorders Assn., Inc., 1988, Nat. Inst. Aging, 1997, Southeastern Pa. affiliate Am. Heart Assn., 1995, March of Dimes Birth Defects Found., 1997. Mem. Am. Soc. Pharmacology and Exptl. Therapeutics, Soc. Neurosci., N.Y. Acad. Scis., Mid-Atlantic Pharmacology Soc. Avocations: classical music, painting. Fax: (215) 628-3297. E-mail: hwang2@prius.jnj.com. Office: RW Johnson Pharm Rsch Inst McKean and Welsh Rds Spring House PA 19477

WANG, HUIMIN, science educator; b. Baofeng, Henan, China, Dec. 5, 1956; arrived in Singapore, 1999; s. Baoqing Wang and Zhi Wei; m. Weirong Liang, Apr. 25, 1985; children: Ruifan, Sizhe. B of Engring., Northwestern Poly. U., China, 1983, M of Engring., 1988; PhD, Zhejiong U., China, 1993. From lectr. to assoc. prof. Zhejiang U., 1988-96; vis. scientist Tech. U. Berlin, 1995-96; prof. Shandong U., China, 1996-00; rsch. scientist Inst. Materials, Singapore, 1997-99; rsch. fellow (A) A.G. Internat., Singapore, 1999—; cons. Com. Composite Materials Devel., China, 1994—. Mem. editl. bd. FRP/Composites, 1994—, Thermo Setting Resin, 1988—; contbr. articles to profl. jours. Recipient LCP in-situ Composites award Nat. Advanced Materials Com. China, 1991, Nano-Polymer of Film award Nat. Nature Fund China, 1997, Multi Phase Polymer Sys. award Edn. Ministry of China, 1997. Avocations: photography, Tai Ji, badminton.

WANG, HUINING, engineer; b. Changchun, Jilin, China, Aug. 8, 1963; arrived in Finland, 1995; parents Wang Zhaoke and Suqin Weng; m. Xiumei Xu, Sept. 28, 1989; 1 child, Yiming. BS, Beijing Inst. Tech., 1985; Licentiate in Tech., Helsinki (Finland) U. Tech., 1997, postgrad., 1998—. Cert. sr. engr. China Aerospace Industry Corp. Sr. engr. China Aerospace Industry Corp., Beijing, 1985-94; design engr. Nokia Mobile Phones, Tampere, Finland, 1999—. Contbr. papers to profl. jours. Mem. IEEE (assoc.). Avocations: badminton, football. Fax: 358 10 505 6888. E-mail: huining.wang@nokia.com. Home: Insinoorinkatu 84 C 43, FIN33720 Tampere Finland Office: Nokia Mobile Phones Tampere, PO Box 83, FIN33721 Tampere Finland

WANG, JI ZU, finance educator, economics researcher; b. Xingta, Hebei, China, Oct. 24, 1924; s. Zhe and Yu Mei (Li) W.; m. Xi Ru Guo, 1958; children: Yan, Yang. BA in Econs., Nat. Polit. U., Chongqing, China, 1946; MA in Econs., U. Mo., 1951; PhD in Econs., U. Ill., 1954. Rsch. assoc. Inst. Internat. Rels., Chinese Acad. Sci., Beijing, 1957-61; rsch. assoc. Inst. Econs., Nankai U., Tianjin, People's Republic China, 1962-81, prof. fin., 1981—, chmn. dept., 1985-92, tutor PhD candidates, 1986—; econ. advisor Tianjin Mcpl. Govt., 1986—. Co-author: On Inflation, 1979, Outline of World Economics, 1984; translator: Interregional Trade and International Trade (B. Ohlin), 1986; also articles. Mem. Internat. Fin. Assn. North and N.W. China (vice chmn. 1990-96), Tianjin Fin. Assn. (vice chmn. 1986-96), Fgn. Trade Assn. (vice chmn. 1983—). Fax: 86-22-2350 4853. E-mail: wangjz@public.tpt.tj.cn. Office: Nankai U Fin Dept, Tiunjin 300071, China

WANG, JIAN GUO, economist; b. Wangchen, Hunan, People's Republic of China, Nov. 19, 1953; s. Zai Hua and Ai Zhen (Li) W.; m. Zhuo Wei Xiong, Jan. 2, 1991. BA, Wuhan Univ., 1982; MBA, Leuven U., 1985; PhD, Monash Univ., 1994. Math. tchr. No. 2 H.S., Changsha, People's Republic of China, 1971-78; sr. mgr. China Resources Co. Ltd., Hong Kong, 1985-87, China Venturetech Corp., Beijing, 1987; rschr. Hongkong Univ., 1988; lectr. U. N.S.W., Sydney, 1993—; prof. Nat. U. Singapore, 1996—, dir. Ctr. for Study of Transitional Economy, 1998—; prof. Peking U., 2000—; session organizer Am. Econ. Assn. Boston Meeting, 1994; chmn. Monash Internat. Conf., Melbourne, Australia, 1992; cons., lectr. in field. Contbr. articles and referee reports to profl. jours. Recipient Spl. Rsch. grantee U. N.S.W., 1994,

Project Rsch. grant The Ctr. for Modern China, 1991. Mem. Chinese Econ. Studies Assn. (pres. 1991, 92), Chinese Econ. Reform Assn. (standing mem. 1987-89), Australia-China C. of C. and Industry N.S.W. (standing mem. 1993-95), Australian Chinese Writers Assn., Am. Econ. Assn. Avocations: poetry writing, debating, walking, swimming, travelling. Office: Nat U Singapore Dept Econs and Stats, 10 Kent Ridge Crescent, Singapore 119260, Singapore

WANG, JIANGZHOU, engineering educator; b. Hubei, China, Nov. 15, 1961; s. Linqi and Jumei (Hu) W.; m. Leiping Xu; children: Belgie, California, Larry. BS, Xidian (China) U., 1983, MSc, 1985; PhD, U. Ghent, Belgium, 1990. Postdoctoral fellow U. Calif., 1990-92; sr. sys. engr. Rockwell USA, 1992-95; assoc. prof. dept. elec. engrng. U. Hong Kong, 1995—. Editor IEEE Transactions on Comm., 1998—; guest editor IEEE Jour., 1999; contbr. articles to profl. jours. Mem. IEEE (sr.). Avocations: running, tennis, swimming. Office: Univ of Hong Kong, Dept of EEE, Hong Kong Hong Kong

WANG, JIANSHE, optics and fine mechanics educator, researcher; b. Hou Ma, Shanxi, China, Dec. 2, 1958; s. Qinlu and Chunying (Liu) W.; m. Xiuying Zhang, Sept. 20, 1985; 1 child, Juntian. Bachelor, Taiyuan Inst. Heavy Machinery, China, 1983; Master, Changchun Inst. Optics and Fin, China, 1989, PhD, 1996. Asst. prof. Changchun Inst. Optics and Fine Mechanics, 1990-95, assoc. prof., 1995—; vis. scholar U. Wales, Swansea, U.K., 1997-98. Contbr. articles to profl. jours. Recipient scholarship Chinese Acad. Scis., 1996. Avocation: precision mechanical engineering. Office: Changchun Inst Optics, 140 People St, Changchun 130022, China

WANG, JIAN-SHENG, materials scientist; b. Taihe, Jiangxi, China, July 7, 1941; came to U.S., 1980; s. Shuo-Ru and Feng-Zi (Liu) W.; m. Hui-Jian Liu, Aug. 17, 1963; children: Yi-Bin, Yi-Min. MS, Northwestern Poly. U., China, 1963; PhD, Stanford U., 1985. Rsch. engr. Iron and Steel Rsch. Inst., Beijing, 1963-80; rsch. asst. Stanford (Calif.) U., 1982-85; sr. rsch. assoc. Harvard U., Cambridge, Mass., 1985-98; sr. rsch. sci. Northwestern U., Evanston, Ill., 1998-2000; sr. tech. staff Am. Superconductor, Westborough, Mass., 2000—; vis. scholar Stanford U., 1980-82; vis. scientist Max-Planck Inst. fü Eisenforschung, Düsseldorf, Germany, 1989-90; hon. prof. Northwestern Poly. U. China, 1994. Contbr. articles to profl. jours., proceedings and treatises; keynote speaker nat. and internat. confs. Recipient Nat. Prize sci. and technol. innovation China Nat. Com. Sci. and Tech., Beijing, 1981, various awards All China Sci. Cong., Beijing, 1978. Mem. Materials Rsch. Soc., Am. Soc. Metals, Am. Physics Soc., Am. Ceramic Soc. Achievements include patents for heat-resistant steels; notable findings in micromechanics and chemistry of interfacial fracture and brittle versus ductile transition; mechanisms of creep and creep rupture; the alloying principle and phase transformation in low-alloying steels and mechanical behaviors of coatings and thin films; contributed to linkage between materials science and solid mechanics. Home: 41 Briarwood Ln Apt 1 Marlborough MA 01752-2519 Office: 2 Technology Dr Westborough MA 01581-1727

WANG, JIE, research scientist, science administrator; b. Linhai, Zhejiang, China, May 3, 1956; came to U.S., 1992; s. Youyuan and Xianglian (Xu) W.; m. Wei Li, Jan. 25, 1984; children: Jing, Lisa. BS, Zhejiang U., Hangzhou, 1982, MS, 1984; PhD, SUNY, Syracuse, 1996. Tchr. Linhai County 2nd Mid. Sch., 1974-78; instr., then asst. prof. China Textile U., Shanghai, 1984-88; asst. prof. Shanghai Inst. Elec. Power, 1988-92; postdoctoral rschr. Iowa State U., Ames, 1996-98; sr. scientist, exec. PolymTech, Inc., Ames, 1999-2000; sr. scientist R&D Graphic Scis., Inc., Portland, 2000—; rsch. asst. Coll. Environ. Sci. and Forestry, SUNY, Syracuse, 1992-96; postdoctoral fellow Ames lab. U.S. Dept. Energy, 1997. Contbr. articles to sci. publs. Recipient Young Prof. award China Dept. Energy, Shanghai, 1991. Mem. Am. Chem. Soc., China Chem. and Engrng. Soc. Achievements include patents for 3-(p-substituted benzoyl)-2, 5-dichlorothiophenes; for 3 novel soluble organic electrooptical polythiophene derivatives possessing high molecular weight and high thermal stability; research in mechanical breaking theory and mechanism of polymeric materials and high-performance inks and coatings. Avocations: fishing, swimming, reading, travel. Home: 1403 Maxwell Ave Ames IA 50010-5658 Office: Graphic Scis Inc Ste L 7515 NE Ambassador Pl Portland OR 97220

WANG, JIEDONG, cell biologist, reproductive biologist; b. Qingdao, Shandong, China, July 24, 1950; s. Shengrong and Suqin (Bao) W.; m. Qijie Zhao, Aug. 30, 1980; 1 child, Simo. MD, Capital Med. U., Beijing, China, 1978; MS, Peking Union Med. Coll., Beijing, 1983. Jr. rschr. Beijing Med. Coll., 1983-84; vis. scholar U. Chgo., 1986-87; rsch. asst. Nat. Rsch. inst. for Family Planning, Beijing, 1984-86; rsch. assoc. Nat. Rsch. Inst. for Family Planning, Beijing, 1987-92, assoc. prof., 1992-96, prof., 1996—, dir. cell biology, 1992—; prin. investigator WHO, Geneva, 1990—, invited expert, 1996—, task force scientist, 1992—, mem. steering com. of task force Spl, Programme of Rsch., Devel. and Rsch. Tng. in Human Reprodn., 1997—. Contbr. articles to profl. jours. Recipient Wu Jieping-Paul Janssen Med. award Ministry of Health, 1995, Advance ofSci. and Tech. award State Family Planning Commn., 1995, Disting. Svcs. award State Coun., China, 1996. Mem. Soc. for Study of Reprodn., Reproductive Biology Soc. Avocations: travel, photography, music. Fax: 0086-10-62179119. E-mail: jdwnrifp@public3.bta.net.cn. Home and Office: Nat Rsch Inst Fam Planning, 12 Da Hui Si, 100081 Beijing China

WANG, JINGXIU, astronomer, educator; b. Fusun, Liaoning, China, May 21, 1944; s. Taizhi and Yulan Wang; m. Quifen Meng, July 1, 1972; children: Peng, Pai. BS, Beijing U., 1969; MS, Grad. Sch. Chinese Acad., Beijing, 1982; PhD in Astrophys., Beijing Astron. Obs., 1987. Tchr. Dagujia Mid. Sch., Qinyuan County, China, 1970-73; weather forecaster Qinyuan Meteor. Sta., Qinyuan County, 1973-78; rsch. assoc. Beijing Astron. Obs., Chinese Acad. Scis., 1982-89, assoc. prof., 1989-92, prof., 1992—; vis. assoc. Calif. Inst. Tech., 1983-84; vis. prof. Inst. Space and Astronautical Sci., Japan, 1996; chmn. astronomy com. Chinese Acad. Scis., 1997—; dep. dir. Nat. Astronomical Observatories, Chinese Acad. Scis. Editl. bd. mem. Astrophysics Reports publ. of Beijing Astron. Obs., 1991—, Progress in Astronomy, 1991—, Basic Rsch., 1993—, Acta Astrophysica Sinica, 1987—, Solar Physics, 1999—. Mem. Internat. Astron. Union (mem. commn. 10, commn. 12), Chinese Astron. Soc. (mem. coun. 1993—). Office: Beijing Astron Obs Chinese, Acad Scis A20 Datun Rd, Beijing 100012, China

WANG, JIN-LING, chemistry educator; b. Nanjin, Jiang Su, China, June 12, 1943; s. Enzhi and Baohua (Wu) W.; m. Songqi, Jan. 9, 1970; children: Wei, Pei. BS, Tianjin Industl Coll., China, 1960-64; Chemistry Reagent, Tianjin, 1964-80; MS in Chemistry, Nankai U., Tianjin, 1980-83. Engr. Inst. Chem. Reagent, Tianjin, China, 1964-80; assoc. prof. Tianjin Normal U., 1987-92, prof., 1992—; assoc. rschr. chem. dept. Okla. U., 1987-88; advisor Hong Kong Internat. Edn. Exch. Ctr. contbr articles and profl jours. mem. Am. Soc Advancenment of Scis., Inst. of Crystallography Chemistry. Chinese Chemical Soc., 1993—. mem. Chinese Chem. Soc., 1987—. Office: Tianjin Normal U, Insts. of Crystallography Chem, Tianjin 300074, China

WANG, JUNG-HUA, electrical engineering educator; b. Keelung, Taiwan, Sept. 15, 1959; s. Won-Shen and Pao-Yu (Chang) W.; m. Miao-Hwa Hung, Dec. 19, 1989; children: Christine, Ting-Yuan. BS, Nat. Cheng Kung U., Tainan, Taiwan, 1983; MSEE, Tex. Tech U., 1988, PhD, 1991. Engr. Tex. Instruments, Taipei County, Taiwan, 1983, Chung Shan Inst. Sci. and Tech., 1984; assoc. rschr. Indsl. Tech. Rsch. Inst., 1990; prof. Nat. Taiwan Ocean U., Keelung, 1991—; cons. Fastech Corp., Taipei, 1990—, Nat. Bur. Stds., 1998—. Contbr. articles to profl. jours. Rep. Ming-Hu Elem. Sch., Taipei, 1997, Nan-Hu Elem. Sch., Taipei, 1998. Recipient Best Tchr. award Minister of Edn., Taipei, 1994, Paper Contest award Chinese Inst. Elec. Engrng., 1996. Mem. IEEE, N.Am. Fuzzy Info. Processing Soc., Sigma Xi. Avocations: swimming, basketball, movies, computers. Office: Nat Taiwan Ocean U, 2 Peining Rd, Keelung Taiwan

WANG, JUNQIANG, software developer and programmer; b. Beijing, People's Republic of China, Aug. 31, 1955; s. Jian Wang and Aizhi Xia; m. Dazhen Wang; 1 child, Zhiyu. BSc in Physics, Hunan Tchrs. U., Changsha, China, 1981; MSc in Physics, Shanxi U., Taiyuan, China, 1988; PhD, U. of Tech., Sydney, Australia, 2000. Assoc. lectr. Taiyuan (People's Republic of China) Tchrs. Coll., 1982-85; lectr. of physics Shanxi Edn. Coll., Taiyuan, 1988-92; vis. scholar U. of Tech., Sydney, Australia, 1992-94, rsch. asst., 1994-96, lab demonstrator in physics, 1996-97; website developer May Murray Neighborhood Ctr., Sydney, 1998-99; software cons. Argus Techs., Sydney, 1999-2000; internet developer, web database programmer Microset, Sydney, 2000—. Mem. Internat. Soc. Optical Engrng., China Physics Soc., Shanxi Physics Soc. (coun. mem.).

WANG, KAI, wood industry executive, consultant; b. Xiangtan, Hunan, China, Nov. 14, 1917; s. Fengwu Wang and Shujin Tan; m. Chuanfu Luo, Nov. 14, 1941; children: Yu, Shen, Qin, Yan, Shou. BS, North West Agr. Coll., Yanlin, China, 1940; MS in Engrng., U. Mich., 1945. Technician Nat. Indsl. Rsch. Inst., Shanghai, China, 1946-49; chief engr. Kwan-Hwa Wood Complex, Beijing, China, 1950-79; v.p. Chinese Acad. Forestry, Beijing, China, 1980-86; ret., 1988; concurrent prof., Beijing and Nanjing Forestry U., China, 1985—; cons. Beijing Mcpl. Govt., 1990—; pres. Chinese Soc. Wood Industry, 1980—. Editor-in-chief: Forest Industry sect. China Ency., 1980, Forest Industry vol., China Agrl. Ency., 192; co-editor-in-chief Scientia Silvae Sinica, 1979—; editor-in-chief China's Wood Industry, 1986—. Recipient Nat. Sci. and Tech. 1st prize, Nat. Sci. and Tech. com., Beijing, 1988; recipient Emeritus Staff award, Ministry of Forestry, Beijing, 1988; recipient Prof. Liu award Prof. Lieu Award Found., Beijing, 1996. Mem. Chinese Soc. Forestry (hon.; v.p. 1978-93), Chinese Nat. Poplar Commn. (hon.), Sigma Xi. Avocations: music, travel. Office: Chinese Soc Wood Industry, Wan Shoushan, Beijing 100091, China

WANG, KEGANG, physicist, researcher; b. Lianhua, Jiangxi, People's Republic of China, Mar. 23, 1963; s. Jinqian and Sanmei (Li) W.; m. Li Song, Jan. 28, 1992; 1 child, David Shuo. BS, Jiang Xi Ednl. Coll., Nanchung, 1984; MS, Sichuan U., Chengdu, People's Republic of China, 1988; PhD, Chinese Acad. of Scis., Shenyang, People's Republic of China, 1992. Postdoctoral rschr. Bejing U. of Sci. and Tech., 1992-94, assoc. prof., 1997—; postdoctoral fellow U. Barcelona, Spain, 1994-95; postdoctoral assoc. U. Minn., 1995-96; vis. scientist Tohwa U., Japan, 1998-99; vis. scholar Rensselaer Polytech. Inst., 1999—. Contbr. articles to profl. publs. Postdoctoral fellowship Ministry Edn. and Sci. of Spain, 1994. Mem. Minerals, Metals and Materials Soc. Avocation: swimming. Office: Rensselaer Polytech Inst 110 8th St Troy NY 12180-3522

WANG, KESHENG, engineering educator, researcher; b. Shanghai, China, Mar. 12, 1945; arrived in Norway, 1985; s. Shaohua and Shuneng (Cheng) W.; m. Junxia Liu, May 1, 1976. BS, Shanghai (China) U. Tech., 1968, MS, 1981; PhD, Norwegian Inst. Tech., Trondheim, Norway, 1988. Engr. SEUIF, Shanghai, China, 1968-79; lectr. SUT, Shanghai, China, 1981-85; assoc. prof. NTH, Trondheim, Norway, 1989-92; prof. NTNU, Trondheim, Norway, 1993—; cons. SINTEF, Trondheim, Norway, 1989—, FEM Engring, AS, Trondheim, Norway, 1997. Author: Artificial Intelligence Applications to Mechanical Engineering, 1991, The Principles and Technology of Layer Manufacturing, 1997; editor: Applications of AI to Production engineering, 1997, Intelligent Production Systems, 1997. Mem. IFIP, NAIA, N.Y. Acad. Sci. Home: Tidemannsgate 20, N-7016 Trondheim Norway Office: Norweigian U Sci and Tech, Richard Birkelandsv 2B, N-7034 Trondheim Norway

WANG, LIAN TANG, pathologist, educator, consultant; b. Nanyang, Henan, China, Apr. 24, 1954; s. Bing Xin Wang and Shu Hua Zhang; m. Hui Li, Dec. 28, 1982; 1 child, Wei. MB, Zhongshan Med. Coll., Guangzhou, China, 1978; MD, Sun Yat-Sen U. Med. Sci., Guangzhou, China, 1982, PhD, 1996. Asst. Zhongshan Med. Coll., 1982-87; lectr. Sun-Yat-Sen U. Med. Sci., Guangzhou, 1988-92, prof., pathologist, cons., 1993—, supr. master students, 1993—. Author: Surgical Pathology, 1997; contbr. articles to profl. jours. Recipient Prize II, Guangdong Province, 1994; Nat. Health and Medicine Rsch. Com. fellow, Australia, 1995-96; Nat. Nature and Sci. Found. China grantee, 1997—. Mem. Chinese Medicine Assn., Chinese Path. Assn. Avocations: running, music, swimming, football. E-mail: pathol@gzsums.edu.cn. Office: Sun Yat Sen U Med Scis, Guangzhou 510089, China

WANG, LI-JUN, chemist, researcher; b. Zhu-Ji, Zhe-Jiang, China, May 11, 1971; parents Xin-Kang and Ju-Luo Wang; m. Yin-Bin Li, Feb. 2, 1998. B of Engrng., Dalian U. Tech., Liao-Ning, China, 1992; M of Engrng., Kangwon Nat. U., Chunchon, South Korea, 1998, postgrad., 2000—. Cert. in engrng. Engr. Shanghai Rsch. Inst. Chem. Industry, 1992-95; rsch. engr. Shanghai Hetex Chem. Co. Ltd., 1995-96. Mem. TAPPI, Pulp and Paper Tech. Assn. Can. (reviewer 1997—). Avocation: classical guitar. Fax: 82-361-257-9023. E-mail: li junwa@lycos.co.kr. Office: Kangwon Nat U, Hyoja 2-Dong 192-1 Chunchon, 200-701 Kangwon South Korea

WANG, LIN-FA, molecular biologist; b. Shanghai, May 31, 1960; arrived in Australia, 1989; s. Yun-Sheng Wang and Yun-Bao Wu; m. Meng Yu, Aug. 4, 1984; children: Scarlett, Nelson. BSc, East China Normal U., Shanghai, 1982; PhD, U. Calif., Davis, 1986. Postdoctoral rschr. U. Calif., Davis, 1986-89; sr. tutor Monash U., Melbourne, Australia, 1989-90, sr. rsch. officer, 1990; rsch. scientist Animal Health Lab. CSIRO, Geelong, Australia, 1990-92, sr. rsch. scientist, 1992-96, project leader, 1994—, prin. rsch. scientist, 1996—; adj. prof. molecular biology East China Normal U., 1989—; mem. editorial bd. Asia Pacific Jour. Molecular Biology and Biotechnology, 1996—, Immunology Lab Manuals, 1996—. Author: Methods in Molecular Biology: Epitope Mapping Protocols, 1996; patentee in field. Michael Swackhamer fellow U. Calif., Davis, 1986; recipient Young Scientist rsch. award NSF, 1990. Mem. Australian Soc. Microbiology, Australian Soc. Biochemistry and Molecular Biology. Avocations: tennis, gardening, reading. Office: CSIRO Australian Animal Health Lab, Pvt Mail Bag 24, Geelong VIC 3220, Australia

WANG, LIPO, educator, researcher; b. Wuhan, Hubei, China, 1963. BS, Nat. U. of Def. Technology, Changsha, China, 1983; PhD, La. State U., 1988. Postdoctoral fellow Stanford U., Calif., 1989, 90; Fogarty assoc. NIH, Bethesda, Md., 1991-94; lectr. Deakin U., Clayton, Victoria, Australia, 1995-98; assoc. prof. Nanyang Technol. U., Singapore, 1998—. Assoc. editor: Knowledge and Info. Systems jour.; co-author/editor: (book) Artificial Neural Networks: Oscillations, Chaos, and Sequence Processing, 1993; co-editor Procs. of the Second World Multi-Conference on Systemics, Cybernetics and Informatics, 1998; contbr. numerous articles to profl. jours. and publs. Mem. IEEE (sr.). Avocations: movies, reading. Office: Sch of EEE NTU, Block S2 Nanyang Ave, Singapore 639798, Singapore

WANG, LIQIAN, environmental science and technology researcher; b. Nanjing, Jiangsu, China, Jan. 23, 1933; parents Guangqing Wang and Lingmei Bian; m. Bentao Zhang, Jan. 28, 1965; 1 child, Yanzhe. BS, Nanjing (China) U., 1952. Cert. prof. Ministry Water Resources and Electric Power. Technician Shenyang Rsch. and Design Inst. Aluminum and Magnesium, China, 1952-56; engr. Shenyang Rsch. and Design Inst. Aluminum and Magnesium, 1956-80, profl. chief in engrng., 1980-82; dir. rsch. dept. Nanjing Environ. Protection Rsch. Inst. Ministry of Energy, China, 1983-85, vice dir. Nanjing Environ. Protection Rsch. Inst., 1986-92; chmn. China Electrostatic Precipitation Com., 1993—; guest prof. South-East U., China, 1999—; researcher in field. Author: Fluidization Engineering, 1962; chief editor: Electrostatic Precipitation and Gas Cleaning quar., 1995—; editor procs. Internat. Conf. Environ. Protection of Electric Power, 1996; inventor in field. Dept. Nat. People's Congr. China, Beijing, 1993-97; vice chmn. Chinese People's Polit. Consultative Conf. Nanjing Mcpl. Commn., 1993—. Nat. spl. contributions allowance China State Coun., 1992. Mem. China Soc. Physics (vice chmn. electorstatics commn. 1991-95), China Soc. Electric Engrng. (vice chmn. environ. protection commn. 1984—), Internat. Soc. Electrostatic Precipitation (bd. dirs. 1996—). Avocations: photography, swimming. Office: Nanjig Elec Power Environ, Nat Elec 10 Pudong Rd, 210031 Nanjing Jiangsu, China

WANG, LONG HUEI, microbiologist; b. Taichung, Taiwan, Sept. 5, 1940; s. Duey and Chao (Lin) W.; m. Chio-Huei Kan, Jan. 15, 1968; children: Hsien-Yih, Yih-Chuen. BS, Nat. Taiwan U., 1964, MS, 1967; PhD, Iowa State U., 1975. Mem. research staff Taiwan Sugar Research Inst., Tainan, 1967—, head dept. by-products utilization, 1982—, assoc. dir., 1995—, dir., 1989—. Recipient Outstanding Service award Taiwan Sugar Corp., 1980. Mem. Am. Soc. Microbiology, Soc. Indsl. Microbiology, Inst. Food Technologists, Chinese Agrl. Chemistry Soc., Biomass Energy Soc. of China, Chinese Biochem. Soc., Sigma Xi. Editor reports. Office: 54 Sheng-Chan Rd, Tainan 70123, Republic of China

WANG, MING CHANG, laser scientist, optical engineer; b. Chang Chun, Ji Lin, Peoples Republic of China, July 14, 1940; s. Xin Chuan Wang and Shu Hui Liu; m. Xiu Fen, Jan. 1, 1966; children: Xiao Zhuo, Ning. BS, U. Optics and Fine Mechanics, Chang Chun, 1963. Research asst. Inst. Optics and Fine Mechanics, Shanghai, Peoples Republic of China, 1963-78, research assoc., 1978-84, assoc. prof. optical engr., 1987-93, prof., 1993—, leader lab. free electron laser, 1988—, supr. PhD, 1997—; vis. prof. Seoul Nat. U. Korea, 1986-87. Author: Laser Physics, 1975; prin. researcher for devel. waveguide laser, 1979, optical klystrom, Beijing FEL and Bragg Cavity, 92, 95, Compact New Beam Source, 1999; editor Chinese Jour. Lasers. Recipient Research and Devel. award Academia Sinica, 1979, 92, 95, 98. Mem. Chinese Soc. Optics, Shanghai Soc. Laser. Office: Shanghai Inst Optics & Fine Mechanics, PO Box 8211, Shanghai 201800, China

WANG, MING DE, engineer; b. Yibin, Sichuan, Peoples Republic of China, July 4; came to U.S., 1994; d. Xisheng and Shoumai (Wu) W.; m. Guoxian Zhang, Oct. 4, 1970; 1 child, Ying. BSc in Chemistry, Nankai U., Tianjin, China, 1978, MSc in Organic Chemistry, 1981; PhD in Chemistry, U. Ottawa, Ont., Can., 1993. Rsch. asst. Nankai U., Tianjin, 1978-81, lectr., 1981-87; rsch. asst. in chemistry U. Ottawa, Can., 1987-89, rsch. asst., 1989-93; postdoctoral fellow in chemistry SUNY, Albany, 1994-95, U. Ottawa, 1995-96; process engr. Hadco Santa Clara, Calif., 1996-98, Carolina Circuits, C-MAC of Am., Inc., Greenville, S.C., 1998—. Co-author 3 chpts. to books; contbr. 16 articles to profl. jours. Cert. instr. CPR, ARC, SUNY, Albany, 1994—. Recipient scholarship Ont. Min. Edn. and Tng., 1992, Sci. and Tech. award Nat. Edn. Com. Peoples Republic of China, 1990. Mem. Am. Chem. Soc., Chem. Inst. Can., China Chem. Soc. Avocations: gospel music, classic movies, travel. Home: 107 Raleigh Ct Simpsonville SC 29681-1981 Office: Carolina Circuits C-MAC of Am Inc 200 Fairforest Way Greenville SC 29607-4609

WANG, MINGQI, physics researcher, engineer; b. Shanghai, China, Oct. 1, 1963; d. Wenbin Wang and Hongmei Huang. B in Engrng., Shanghai Inst. Mech. Engrng., 1985; lic., Uppsala (Sweden) U., 1995, PhD, 1997. Avocations: music, reading, traveling. Home: 805/6/303, Shanghai Zhong Shan Bei Rd, 200070 Shanghai China Office: Uppsala U, Box 530, S-75121 Uppsala Sweden

WANG, NINA, real estate executive. Chairwoman Chinachem Group, Kowloon, Hong Kong. Fax: 852-2311-3080. Office: Chinachem Golden Plz Top Fl, 77 Mody Rd Tsimshatsui East, Kowloon Hong Kong*

WANG, NINGSHENG, anthropologist, educator; b. Nanjing, China, May 8, 1930; s. Shouling Wang and Yu Ying Xu; m. Wang Yunhui; children: Wang Ge, Wang Jing. BA in Archaeology, Beijing U., 1959. Asst. prof. Cen. Nationalities Inst., Beijing, 1959-64; vice dir. Yunnan Nationalities Rsch. Inst., Kunming, China, 1980-83; sr. fellow dept. anthropology U. Pa., Phila., 1983-84; guest prof. Inst. Orient Art History Heidelberg U., Germany, 1984-85; prof., chmn. dept. history Yunnan Nationalities Inst., Kunming, 1987-91; vis. prof. dept. Oriental studies U. Oslo, Norway, 1991-92; vis. scientist dept. anthropology U. Wash., Seattle, 1992; vis. prof. Inst. Human Rights U. Oslo, 2000. Author: The Archaeology of Yunnan, 1980, 2d edit., 1992, The Rock Paintings in Yunnan, 1985 (1st prize of social sci. 1989), The Ethnohistory in Southwest China, 1989, Essays of Ethnoarchaeology, 1989, The Methodology of Cultural Anthropological Field Work, 1996, Academic Tour in SW China for 35 Years, 1998. Luce scholar Henry Luce Found., N.Y., 1983; scholar Norwegian Rsch. Coun. for Sci. and Humanities, Oslo, 1992. Sr. fellow Inst. for Study of Human Issues (hon.); mem. Archaeol. Soc. of China (bd. dirs. 1989-98), Anthropology Soc. of China (bd. dirs. 1980-98), Soc. of Ethnology in China (bd. dirs. 1979-98), Internat. Com. on Rock Art. Office: Yunnan Nationalities Inst, Beijiao Lianhuachi, 650011 Kunming Yunnan China

WANG, NORMAN JIN-SHYR, psychologist, consultant; b. Ping-Tung, Taiwan, Jan. 11, 1962; s. Pei Chich Wang and Ming-Feng Tu; Christina T.C. Wang-Chu; children: Wang, Ishi. BA in Psychology, Queen's U., Kingston, Canada, 1983, BS in Life Science, 1984; Masters in Theological Studies, Ontario Theol. Sem., Toronto, Canada, 1988; PhD in Psychology, Newport U., Calif., 1994. Triage worker Englewood Health Ctr., Chicago, 1988-90; crisis worker Loretto Hosp., Chicago, 1988-91; mental health worker III Alexian Brother Med. Ctr., Elk Grove, Ill., 1988-91; lctr., prof. Christian Discipleship Coll., Taiwan, 1992-93; founder, clin. psychologist Agape Counseling Ctr., Taiwan, 1992—; bd. dirs. Garden of Hope Found., Taiwan, 1995—, dir. ctr. sexual abused children, 1998-99; supr./ advisor Ministry of Edn., Taiwan, 1997—; lctr. Junio Chamber Internat. 1998-99 (excellence in lctrship., 1999); trainer, workshop leader. Author: Self-Development Mannual, Counseling Children of Attention Deficit Disorder, Counseling Depressive Children, The Touching Moments in Counseling, As Sun Rises-11 Cases of Psychotherapy, The Toddler's Years, Emotional Quotient Diary, Problems and Myths of Reincarnational Psychotherapy. Youth dir. Kwo-Ming-Tung party, Taipei City, 1999. Recipient The Ten Outstanding Young Person award Ministry of Edn., Ministry of Youth, Tawain, 1998, Asian-Pacific Trans-Century Customer Saisfactory Products Rim award, Coun. Promotion of Internat. Trade, 1999. Mem. APA. Mem. Kwa-Ming-Tung Party. Mem. Christian Ling-Liung Ch. Avocations: travel, painting, rock collecting, swimming, body building. Office: Agape Counseling Ctr, Ho-Ping Rd East Section 3, Taipei City Taiwan

WANG, PAO-KUAN, meteorologist, educator; b. Tainan, Taiwan, Dec. 1, 1949; came to U.S., 1973; s. Shou and Luan-Chao (Chiu) W.; m. Li-Bi Tseng, Aug. 28, 1926; children: Lawrence, Victor. BS in Atmospheric Scis., Nat. Taiwan U., Taipei, 1971; MS, UCLA, 1975, PhD, 1978. Rsch. meteorologist UCLA, 1978-80, adj. asst. prof., 1980; from asst. to assoc. prof. U. Wis., Madison, 1980-88; prof. U. Wis., 1988—, chmn. Atmospheric and Oceanic Sci., 1994-97; cons. Nelson Industries, Stoughton, Wis., 1985—; vis. prof. Nat. Taiwan U., 1993, U. Mainz, Germany, 1993, Mass. Inst. Tech., Cambridge, 1997. Author: Heaven and Earth, 1996 (10 Best Books), Cloud Physics, 1997. Recipient Humboldt award Alexander V. Humboldt Found., Mainz, 1993; S.C. JohnsonDisting. fellow Johnson Wax Co., Racine, Wis., 1993. Mem. Am. Meteorol. Soc. (chmn. Cloud Physics Com. 1990-93). Office: U Wis Dept Atmospheric Oceanic Sci 1225 W Dayton St Madison WI 53706-1612

WANG, PEIGUANG, mathematics educator, researcher; b. Harbin, China, Feb. 5, 1963; m. Zhihui Fan, Sept. 29, 1989; 1 child, Kainan. BS, Hebei U., Baoding, China, 1984, MS, 1987; PhD, Beijing Inst. Tech., 2000. Asst. Hebei U., 1987-91, lectr., 1991-96, assoc. prof., 1996-99, prof. math., 1999—, vice dean dept. math., 1994—; Contbr. articles to profl. jours. Recipient award for remarkable young tchrs. Edn. Com. of Peoples Republic of China, 1998, award for sci. and tech. progress Edn. Com. of Hebei Province, 1998, award for tchg. achievements Edn. Com. of Hebei Province, 1997. Avocations: table tennis, volleyball. Office: Hebei U Dept Math, 1 Hezue Rd, 071002 Baoding, Hebei China

WANG, PETER TSING-SHIH, fund management company executive; b. Singapore, Apr. 9, 1952; s. En Pao and Chwee Keng (Wong) W.; m. Grace Maria-Jovita Rivera, Dec. 7, 1985; 1 child, Clarence A. B Mgmt., Birmingham (Eng.) Poly., 1976; postgrad., Hotel Catring Inst. Mgmt., Eng., 1977; B Econs., U. London, 1979. Exec. Singapore Airlines, 1977-81, mgr., 1981-84; dir. Hyatt Internat., 1984-89, area dir., 1988-91; v.p. Wahchang Internat., 1991-95; exec. dir. Bayan Tree Gallery, 1991-95; gen. mgr. Thaiwan, 1991-95; pres. Tsing-Shi, Alexander & Assocs. (Asia), 1995—; chmn. IHT Ventures (Asia) Pvt. Ltd., 1999; pres. C2C Remittances, 1998-99. Designer layout pub. area Hyatt Internat. Bd. dirs. Mission for Asia, CBN (Asia) Philippines, 1998—, CBN (Asia) Singapore, 2000—. Officer Singapore Army, 1971-73. Recipient award for Best Design for Restaurant/Cafe, Design for Multi-Usage, 1985, The Philippines. Mem. Chaine des Rotisseur. Avocations: painting, antiques, art, creative writing. E-mail: peterwang@vasia.com. Home: 48 Ming Teck Park, Singapore Republic of Singapore

WANG, PETER ZHENMING, physicist; b. Quanzhou, Fujian, People's Republic of China, Nov. 30, 1940; came to U.S., 1983; s. Guohua and Shunhua (Chen) W.; m. Grace Ruhui Xu, Mar. 14, 1967; children: Yili, Yile. MS, Qinghua U., Peking, People's Republic of China, 1964; postgrad., U. Tex., Dallas, 1983-84. Sr. engr. Particle Accelerator Inst., Shanghai, 1964-83; electronic engr. Benchmark Media Systems, Inc., Syracuse, N.Y., 1984-87; project engr. McGaw Inc., Carrollton, Tex., 1988—; physicist High Energy Physics Inst., Peking, 1978-79. Co-author: (book) Vacuum World, 1984. Tchr. Bible study, Plano, Tex., 1990. Baptist. Achievements include research and design of a variety of proton and electron accelerators for low energy nuclear physics experiments, industries and hospitals; design of 50 GEV proton synchrotron, design of audio distribution amplifiers and consoles for BBC, ABC, and other TV and radio stations; development and design of air bubble detector, pressure transducer and noise reduction solution for the microprocessor based infusion therapy instrument used in hospitals. Home: 1510 Chesterfield Dr Carrollton TX 75007-2847 Office: McGaw Inc 1601 Wallace Dr Carrollton TX 75006-6666

WANG, PINCHAO, mathematics educator; b. Shanxian, People's Republic of China, May 4, 1942; s. Bang-jie and Liu Wang; m. Wu Fengyun, July 8, 1962; 1 child, Xuegong. Grad., Shandong Tchrs. Coll., Jinan, China, 1964. Prof. dept. math. Qufu (People's Republic of China) Normal U., 1964—. Editor: New Methods of Advanced Algebra, 1989; contbr. articles to profl. jours. Named Excellent Tchr. of Shandong Province, 1985. Mem. Chinese Math. Soc., Am. Math. Soc. Office: Qufu Normal U, Dept Math, Qufu Shandong 273165, China

WANG, PING, biomedical investigator; b. Qingzhou, China, Feb. 5, 1959; came to U.S., 1987, naturalized, 1998; s. Tangbang Wang and Xiuzheng Quan; m. Mian Zhou, May 14, 1986; children: Stephanie M., Christie M. MD, Changwei Med. Coll., Weifong, China, 1982; MS, 3d Med. U., Chongqing, China, 1985; MA, Brown U., 1998. Rsch. assoc. U. Wash., Seattle, 1987-88; rsch. assoc. Mich. State U., East Lansing, 1988-92, asst. prof. surgery, 1992-96; asst. prof. surgery Brown U. Sch. Medicine, Providence, 1996-97, assoc. prof. surgery, 1997-2000; prof. depts. surgery, physiology and pathology U. Ala. Sch. Medicine, Birmingham, 2000—. Recipient NIH Individual Rsch. Project award, 1998—, Ind. Scientist award NIH, 1996—, 1st Ind. Rsch. Support and Transition award NIH, 1995—, Grant-in-Aid award Am. Heart Assn., Dallas, 1994-98. Mem. AAAS, Am. Physiol. Soc., Shock Soc., Surg. Infection Soc., Assn. for Acad. Surgery, Soc. Critical Care Medicine, Am. Heart Assn. (cardiopulmonary and critical care coun.), N.Y. Acad. Scis. Fax: 205-975-9715. E-mail: ping.wang@ccc.uab.edu. Office: U Ala at Birmingham Dept Surgery 1670 University Blvd Dept S Birmingham AL 35294-0001

WANG, QI, process engineer, materials scientist; b. Nanchang, Jiangxi, China, Jan. 24, 1963; came to U.S., 1992; s. Zhifu Wang and Shunlin Qian; m. Fan Xu, Aug. 20, 1988; children: Xueyou, Jonah. BS, Nanchang U., China, 1984; MS, Inst. Metal Rsch., Shenyang, China, 1987; PhD, U. Minn., 1997. Rsch. scientist Inst. Metal Rsch., Shenyang, China, 1987-91; vis. lectr. Inst. Material Rsch. Tohoku U., Sendai, Japan, 1991-92; rsch. asst. U. Minn., Mpls., 1992-96; sr. prcess engr. Mitsubishi Silicon Am., Salem, Oreg., 1996—. Contbr. articles to profl. jours. Recipient 3rd Rank prize for natural sci. work Chinese Acad. Sci., 1990, Outstanding Paper award Acta Metallurgica, 1992. Mem. ACS, Am. Vacuum soc., Materials Rsch. Soc. Achievements include patents for superflat epitaxial wafer process, ultraclean epitaxial wafer process, and advances resistivity measurement method for n-type silicon wafers. Avocations: basketball, reading. Office: Mitsubishi Silicon Am PO Box 7748 3990 Fairview Indsl Dr SE Salem OR 97302

WANG, QING, mechanical engineer, educator; b. Shijiazhuang, China, Mar. 16, 1966; s. Weiping Wang and Guiying Zou; m. Xifang Sun, Aug. 6, 1991; 1 child, Kejing. MS, Beijing U., 1986, Shandong U. Tech., Jinan, 1991; PhD, Tongji (China) U., 1996. Assoc. prof. mech. engring. Shandong U. Tech., 1996-98, prof. mech. engring., 1999—; vis. prof. mech. engring. Kyushu Inst. Tech., Kitakyushu, Japan, 1999. Mem. Chinese Soc. Composites, Chinese Soc. Mechanics. Office: Shandong U Tech, Materials Engring Dept, Jinan 250061, China

WANG, QUAN, university educator; b. Shenyang, Liaoning, China, Feb. 8, 1967; s. Qiwen W. and Dexian Li; m. Chunhui (Maggie) Liu. MS, Peking U., 1991, PhD, 1994. Rsch. fellow Hong Kong U., 1994-95, Nanyang Tech. U., Singapore, 1995-97; rsch. asst. U. S.C., 1997-98, Purdue U., West Lafayette, Ind., 1998-99; asst. prof. Nat. U. Singapore, 1999—. Recipient Baogang award China Govt., 1993. Mem. ASME, ASCE. Office: Nat U Singapore Dept CE, Kent Ridge Crescent, Singapore 119260, Singapore

WANG, REN, mechanical engineering educator; b. Wuxing, Zhejiang, China, Jan. 2, 1921; s. C.S. and S.Y. (Chou) W.; m. Chong Jing Zhang, July 21, 1956; children: Mingyan, Mingzhen. BS in Aero. Engring., Nat. S.W. Associated U., Kunming, China, 1943; MS in Aero. Engring., U. Wash., 1950; PhD in Applied Math., Brown U., 1953. Design engr. 1st Aircraft Mfr., Kweiyang, China, 1944-45, 3d Aircraft Mfr., Taichong, China, 1946-48; rsch. assoc. Brown U., Providence, 1952-54; asst. prof. mech. engring. Ill. Inst. Tech., Chgo., 1954-55; from assoc. prof. to prof. mech. Peking U., Beijing, 1955—; mem. editorial bd. Internat. Jour. Mech. Sci., 1980-90; editor Jour. Pure Applied Geophysics, 1982-87, 95-98, Internat. Jour. Mechanical Engring. Edn., 1981—, Tectonophysics, 1981-92, Acta Mech. Sinica, 1985—, Acta Mech. Solida Sinica, 1988—, Acta Seismologica Sinica, 1988—; vice-dir. Nat. Natural Sci. Found. China, 1986-91; vis. prof. mech. engring. Yale U., New Haven, Conn., 1987. Author: Foundation of Plasticity, 1982, Foundation of Solid Mechanics, 1982; editor: Constitutive Relation for Finite Deformation, 1992, Mechanics Problems in Geodynamics I, 1995, II, 1996, Rheology of Bodies with Defects, 1998. Rockefeller Found. fellow, 1950-52. Mem. Chinese Soc. Theoretical Applied Mechanics (pres. 1990-94), Am. Geophysics Union, Internat. Union Theooretical Applied Mechanics bur. Achievements include work on the dynamic plastic buckling of shell 2d critical velocity, numerical inversion of stress field, simulation of earthquake sequence. Office: Dept Mechanics Engring Sci, Peking U, Beijing 100871, China

WANG, RONG, chemical engineer, educator; b. Nanchang, Peoples Republic China, Jan. 24, 1963; d. Binshen and Yuefen (Wan) W.; m. Weilie Ding, Jan. 25, 1989; 1 child, Yue. B, Zhejiang Univ, Hangzhou, China, 1984; PhD, Chemical Acad. Scis., Beijing, China, 1992. Asst. engr. Chima Gen. Mech. Engring. Co., Beijing, 1984-86; asst. prof. Chinese Acad. of Scis. Inst. of Chem. Metallurgy, Beijing, 1992-95, assoc. prof., 1996-99; indsl. rsch. scientist Environ. Tech. Inst., Nanyang Technol. U., Singapore, 1999—; deputy dir. rsch. dept. Chinese Acad. of Sci. Inst. of Chem. Metallurgy, 1995—. Contbr. articles to profl. jours. Recipient Excellence prize of Dir. Grad. Scholarship Chinese Acad. of Scis.,1 992, First Prize of Dir. Grad. Scholarship, 1992. E-mail: rwang@eti.org.sg. Office: Environ Tech Inst NTU, Innovation Ctr Unit 237, Singapore 639798, Singapore

WANG, RONG-MING, aeronautical engineer, researcher; b. Tai-Xing, Jiang-Su, China, June 25, 1969; s. Hong-Quan Wang and Cai-Zhen Meng; m. Xu Ning, Jan. 13, 1997. B, Peking U., Beijing, 1991, M, 1994; D, Beijing Inst. Aeronaut. Materials, 1997. Engr. Beijing Inst. Aeronautical Materials, 1997-98, sr. engr., 1999—, dri. Metal Physics Lab., 1998—. Contbr. articles to profl. jours. Recipient Nat. Mathemat. Olympia award Chinese Mathemat. Soc., 1986, Sci. and Tech. Advancement award Chinese Aviation Industries, 1998. Mem. Chinese Aeronaut. Material Engring. Soc., Assn. Young Scientists and Engrs. Beijing Inst. Aeronautical Materials. Avocations: Chinese chess, bridge, table tennis, badminton. Office: Beijing Inst Aeronaut Mater, PO Box 81-4, 100095 Beijing China

WANG, SANWU, physicist, educator; b. Tongcheng, Anhui, China, May 15, 1963; s. Zhoujie and Yuyan (Zhou) W.; m. Mei Wu. BSc, Anhui Laodong U., Hefei, China, 1982; postgrad. diploma, N.W. U., Xi'an, China, 1986; PhD, U. Newcastle, Australia, 1999. Assoc. lectr. physics Anhui Inst. Edn., Hefei, 1982-87, lectr. in physics, 1987-94, assoc. prof., 1994-95; physics rschr. U. Newcastle, 1995-99; rsch. assoc. Vanderbilt U., Nashville, 1999-2000, Fla. State U., Tallahassee, 2000—. Contbr. articles to profl. jours. Mem. Australian Inst. Physics, Am. Phys. Soc., Overseas Chinese Physics Assn., Minerals Metals & Materials Soc., Sigma Xi. Office: Fla State U CSIT Tallahassee FL 32306

WANG, SENHAO, Chinese government official; b. 1932. Grad., Beijing Inst. Mining, 1956. Mem. 6th, 7th, Nat. People's Congress for Shanxi; gov. Shanxi Province, 1983-93; dep. sec. Shanxi Province CCP, 1983-93; mem. CCP 12th, 13th Cen. Com., 1985—; engr.-in-chief, min. of coal industry Ministry of Coal Industry, 1993—. Office: Min of Coal Industry, 211 Hepinggli Beijie, Beijing China*

WANG, SHENG-DE, engineering educator; b. Taichung, Taiwan, Nov. 5, 1957; s. King-Don and Su-chin (Liaw) W.; m. Yu-Yu Cheng, Sept. 3, 1984; children: Jin-Han, Schen. BS, Nat. Tsing-Hua U., 1980; MS, Nat. Taiwan U., 1982, PhD, 1986. Assoc. prof. Nat. Taiwan U., Taipei, 1986-91, prof., 1991—; computer mgmt. dir. Computer Ctr., Nat. Taiwan U., Taipei, 1995—. Contbr. articles to profl. jours. Mem. IEEE, Assn. for Computing Machinery. Office: Dept of Electrical Engring, Nat Taiwan Univ, Taipei 106, Taiwan

WANG, SHIH-JEN, nuclear scientist; b. Kaohsiung, Taiwan, Feb. 26, 1950; s. Lin and I-Chu (Chen) W.; m. Min Chian, Nov. 12, 1978; children: Hao, Hsiung. BS, Chung-Cheng Inst. Tech., 1972; MS, Tsing-Hua U., 1976; PhD, U. Tenn., Knoxville, 1983. Cert. in nuclear engring. Tchg. asst. Chung-Cheng Inst. Tech., Tai-Chi, Republic of China, 1972-73; assoc. prof. Chung-Cheng Inst. Tech., Tai-Chi, 1976-77; rsch. asst. Inst. Nuclear Energy Rsch., Lung-Tan, Republic of China, 1973-74, asst. scientist, 1976-79, assoc. scientist, 1983—. Editor Nuclear Sci. Jour., 1993. Rsch. awardee Nat. Sci. Coun., Republic of China, 1991, 93. Mem. Chung-Hua Nuclear Soc. Achievements include contribution to modeling and simulation of nuclear power plants and Taiwan research reactor; development of boiling water reactor plant analyzer for the nuclear power plants in Taiwan; application of the simplex search method to nuclear power plants and Taiwan research reactor in identification of important plant parameters, control system design, and optimization of the plant performance; severe accident analysis of nuclear power plant. Avocations: bridge, stamp collecting, travel, reading. Office: Inst Nuclear Energy Rsch, PO Box 3-3, 32500 Lungtan Taiwan

WANG, SHOU CHUN, economics educator; b. Jiangyin, Jiangsu, Jiangsu, Peoples Republic of China, Dec. 26, 1930; s. Guo Guang and Ju Fen (Yao) W.; m. Juan Fen Guo, Aug. 1, 1959; children: Wang Pei, Wang Yi. MA, UIBE, 1955. Prof. U. Internat. Bus. and Econs., Peoples Republic of China; cons. Ministry of Fgn. Trade and Econ. Cooperation; rschr. Rsch. Inst. State Coun.'s Office of Hong Kong and Macao Affairs, Beijing, 1986-88. Author: New Development of China's Foreign Economic Relations and Trade, 1986, China's Foreign Economic Relations, 1988, Theory and Policy of China's Foreign Trade, 1992, China's Foreign Trade, 1994, Encyclopedia of China's Foreign Economic Relations and Trade System Reform, 1995, China's Foreign Trade Economics, 1994, Directory of Opening up World Market, 1997, 50 Years of China's Foreign Trade and Economic Cooperation, 1999. Mem. Assn. of Gen. Agreement on Tariffs and Trade (dir.), China Assn. of Internat. Trade (coun. mem. 1988-96). Avocations: literature, music, photography, film, TV. Home: Primary Sch Residential Apt, 2-401 Er li Gou, Beijing 100044, China Office: U Internat Bus and Econs, Hepingjie Beikou, Beijing 100029, China

WANG, SHUMAO, psychologist, consultant; b. Harbin, People's Republic of China, Feb. 24, 1938; s. Zhongru and Huizhen (Yang) W.; m. Xin Wang, Sept. 30, 1964; children: Peiqian, Peishi. B degree, Beijing U., 1963, MS, 1966. Worker Shenyang Liming Engring. Soc., 1968-70; vice dir. theory edn. dept. Liaoning Provincial Govt., Shenyang, 1970-79; rschr. Liaoning Provincial Acad. Social Sci., Shenyang, 1979-87; pres. Shenyang Edn. Coll., 1987-94; dir. Shenyang Inst. Psychology, 1994—; prof. Chinese Mayor Tng. Ctr., Beijing, 1985-97; mem. cons. com. policy decision making Liaoning Provincial Govt., Shenyang, 1995-97. Author: Psychology of Political Ideology, 1986 (3d Session China's Excellent Books competition prize 1989), The Mentality of Young People, 1984 (Nat. Excellence Books competition prize 1985), An Interesting Episode in Psychology, 1982 (Philos. and Social Sci. of Liaoning Province prize 1984). Mem. Shenyang Polit. Consultation Conf., 1993, Rsch. Group of the Comparison between the East Asian and North European Polit. Culture, Copenhagen, 1996. Recipient Nat. Excellence Ednl. Worker award Ednl. Com. and Pers. Dept. Com., Nat. Com. Ednl. Trade Union, People's Rep. of China, 1989, Spl. Subsidy of the Chinese Govt., State Coun. People's Rep. of China, 1992, Disting. scholar award Appalachian State U., 1984. Mem. APA, Shenyang Assn. Psychology (gen. dir. 1985-97), Psychology Assn. China (coun. mem., dir. popular sci. com. 1985-99), Internat. Soc. Polit. Psychology, World Fedn. Mental Health. Avocations: music, dance, travel, fishing, badminton. Office: Shenyang Inst Psychology, No 55 Wencui Rd Qingnian St, Shenyang Liaoning 110015, People's Republic of China

WANG, SHUMIN, physicist, researcher; b. Shanghai, Nov. 2, 1963; arrived in Sweden, 1989; s. Gang Wang and Zhuqing Cai; m. Hong Yang, May 20, 1994; 2 children. BS, Fudan U., Shanghai, 1985, MS, 1988; lic. in philosophy, Chalmers U. Tech., Göteborg, Sweden, 1992, PhD, 1994. Rsch. assoc. Chalmers U. Tech., 1994-97, dir. molecular beam epitaxy lab. dept. microelectronics, 1998—, assoc. prof., 1999—. Contbr. articles to internat. sci. jours., including Applied Physics Letters, Phys. Rev. B. Achievements include research in epitaxial growth of novel semiconductor heterostructures for high speed electronic and photonic devices. Avocations: philately, photography. Office: Chalmers U Tech, Dept Microelectronics, S-41296 Göteborg Sweden

WANG, SHU-RONG, neuroscientist, biophysicist; b. Henan, China, Dec. 20, 1939; s. Zhen-De and Jiao Wang; m. Yan Chen, Dec. 17, 1969; 1 child, Wang Qi. Diploma in biophysics, China U. Sci. and Tech., Beijing, 1964. Vis. scientist Brain Rsch. Inst., Zürich, Switzerland, 1977-78; rsch. assoc. Inst. Biophysics Academia Sinica, Beijing, 1964-76, asst. prof. Inst. Biophysics, 1979-83, assoc. prof., vice dir. Inst. Biophysics, 1983-86, prof., dir., 1986-90, 91-98; vice chmn. bioscientist com. Academia Sinica, Beijing, 1988-91, vice chmn. neuroscientist com., 1988-92. Author: Inspiration from the Nature, 1974 (Nat. award 1981, 97), Mysteries of Amphibians & Reptiles, 1984, (Academia Sinica award 1986); contbr. articles to profl. jours.; mem. of editors Acta Biophysica Sinica, 1986-90, Acta Biochimica et Biophysica Sinica, 1988-91, Visual Neurosci., 1987-89. Mem. Biophys. Soc. China (pres. 1986-90), Chinese Soc. Physiol. Scis., Chinese Soc. Popular Sci. Writers (Outstanding award 1990), Internat. Brain Rsch. Orgn. Avocations: collecting stamps, writing popular science papers, tourism. Office: Acad Sinica Inst Biophysics, 15 Datun Rd, Beijing 100101, China

WANG, SHUSEN, chemistry educator, researcher; b. Tianjin, China, Aug. 4, 1937; s. Guanjun and Shoumei (Yao) W.; m. Meiyun Zeng, Oct. 27, 1967; children: Xiaorong, Ju. BS, Tsinghua U., Beijing, 1964; MS, SUNY, Buffalo, 1982. Asst. Beijing Poly. U., 1964-71, asst. prof., 1972-79, assoc. prof., 1983-90, prof., 1991—; vis. scholar SUNY, Buffalo, 1980-82, Hong Kong U., 1989, Hong Kong Bapt. Coll., 1990-91, Hong Kong U. Sci. and Tech., 1992-93. Contbr. articles to profl. jours. Recipient Cert. award Nat. Sci. Meeting China, 1976, Cert. award City Govt. Beijing, 1979. Mem. Membrane Learned Soc. Beijing (dir. 1992—). Office: Beijing Poly Univ, 100 Ping Le Yuan, 100022 Beijing China

WANG, SHYH-YAU, engineering researcher; b. Taipei, Taiwan, Sept. 9, 1965; s. Chun-Ing and Tsai-Chi Chen Wang; m. Wen-Hwa Chen, Feb. 14, 1995; 1 child, Kevin. BS, Nat. Chun-Hsing U., Tauchubg, Taiwan, 1987; MS, U. Houston, 1993, PhD, 1998. Rsch. assoc. ITRI, Hsing-Chu, Taiwan, 1989-90, U. Houston, 1990—; conf. coord. CIGMAT conf., 1999, 2000. 2d lt. Chinese Army, 1987-89, Taiwan. Rsch. grantee Tex. Dept. Transp., Houston, GCHSRC, Tex. Mem. Am. Chem. Soc., Taiwan Profl. Environ. Engrs., Tex. Buddhist Assn. (exec.). Avocations: badminton, meditation, sports. Home: 2750 Holly Hall St Apt 310 Houston TX 77054-4148 Office: U Houston Dept Civil & Environ Engrng Houston TX 77204-0001

WANG, SING-WU, retired librarian; b. China, Dec. 24, 1920; s. Zhi-tang and Zhang Shi. B.A., U. Zhejiang, China, 1944; M.A., Australian Nat. U., 1969; m. May, Nov. 20, 1947; children: Angela, Ruth, Kristina. Chief cataloguer of Chinese books, Nat. Cen. Libr., Nanking, China, 1945-49; chief libr. Yang Ming Shan Inst. Libr., Taipei, Taiwan, 1949-55; dir. Taiwan Provincial Libr., Taipei, 1955-64; sr. specialist libr. Orientalia Sect., Nat. Libr. Australia, Canberra, 1964-73, chief libr., 1973-85; exchange libr. Cleve. Pub. Libr., 1959-60; examination passed Sch. Libr. Sci., Western Res. U., Cleve., 1959-60; assoc. prof., prof. libr. sci., dept. social edn. Taiwan Normal U., Taipei, 1957-65; lectr. modern Chinese history, Coll. Chinese Culture, Yang Ming Shan, Taiwan, 1963-64; lectr. Chinese classics, dept. of Chinese, Australian Nat. U., Canberra, 1966; vis. lectr. libr. sci. Beijing Normal U., 1985; exec. dir., bd. dirs. Libr. Assn. of China, 1953-64, dir. libr. tng. sch., Taipei, 1956-58. Fellow, The China Acad., Yang Ming Shan, 1968—; recipient fgn. libr. program award, U.S. Dept. State, 1959-60, medal of the Order of Australia, 1986. Mem. ALA, Libr. Assn. Australia, Assn. for Asian Studies, Asian Studies Assn. Australia, E. Asian Librs. Group of Australia (newsletter editor, 1980-82; chmn. 1982-85, vice chmn. 1985-86). Baptist. Author: Introduction to the Classification of Books (in Chinese), 1955, On Library Services in Taiwan (in Chinese), 1963, The Organization of Chinese Emigration, 1848-1888, 1978, Chinese translator: Lincoln (Nathaniel Wright Stephenson), 1958, contbr. articles to publs. in English and Chinese, papers to confs. Australia, China, South Korea, Japan and Taiwan (in English and Chinese).*Sing-wu Wang had the responsibility for escorting the National Central Library's first shipment of rare books to Taiwan in 1948, during a time of fear of the civil war. Through an agent in Hong Kong, he organized the purchase of important Mainland Chinese publications for use by the Yang-Ming-Shan Institute in Taipei. He successfully approached the Taiwan Provincial Government to grant land and finance to the Provincial Library to erect a new library building. He was instrumental in building up the largest and most comprehensive East Asian language collection in Australia in the National Library of Australia. He established exchange relations with libraries in China, Taiwan, Japan, South Korea, and North Korea* Home: 123 Namatjira Dr, Fisher ACT 2611, Australia

WANG, SONGLIN, dentist; b. Xiangxiang, China, Nov. 2, 1962; s. Xianju and Hexiu (Ding) W.; m. Yanying Xu, Jan. 19, 1988; 1 child, Yuxi. DDS, Beijing Med. U., 1984, PhD, 1989. Teaching asst. Beijing Med. U., 1984-89; lectr. Capital U. Med. Scis., Beijing, 1989-92, assoc. prof., 1992-98, prof., 1998—; cons. global cons. on oral health scis. edn. WHO, 1994—; vis. scientist NIH, 1996-98. Mem. AAAS. Office: Beijing Hosp Stomatology, Tian Tan Xi Li No 4, Beijing 100050, China

WANG, SUSHENG, economics educator; b. Suzhou City, Jiangsu, China, July 13, 1957; s. Xijie Wang and Lufeng Lin; m. Wei Yang, July 13, 1984; children: Tao Wang, Xiao Yang. BS in Math., Nankai (China) U., 1982, MS in Math., 1985; PhD in Econs., U. Toronto, Can., 1991. Lectr. Nankai U., 1985; asst. prof. Concordia U., Can., 1991-93, Hong Kong U. Sci. & Tech., 1993—. Contbr. articles to profl. jours. Grantee Social Scis. and Humanities Rsch. Coun. of Can., 1993, Rsch. Grants Coun. of Hong Kong, 1996. Mem. Am. Math. Soc. (reviewer 1986—), Econometric Soc., Am. Econ. Assn. Avocations: basketball, computers. Home: Sr Staff Quarter, Apt 24 HKUST, Hong Kong China Office: Hong Kong U Sci & Tech, Dept Econs, Clear Water Bay Hong Kong China

WANG, TAHUI, electronic engineering educator; b. Tao-Yuan, Taiwan, May 3, 1958; s. Kung-Kuo and Chi-Chen (Wu) W.; m. Ya-Tze Hu, May 30, 1992; children: Eric, Melody. BS, Nat. Taiwan U., 1980; MS, Northwestern U., 1981; PhD, U. Ill., 1986. Mem. tech. staff Hewlett-Packard Lab., Calif., 1985-87; assoc. prof. Nat. Chiao-Tung U., Hsin-Chu, Taiwan, 1987-91, prof., 1991—; sci. cons. U.S. Army Lab., N.J., 1985; tech. com. mem., session chair Internat. Electron Devices Mtg., 1999—; tech. com. mem. Internat. Reliability Physics Symposium, 1996; cons. Electronics Rsch. Svc. Orgn./ITRI, Taiwan, 1998, Macronix Internat. Co., Taiwan, 2000. Contbr. over 70 articles to profl. jours. Recipient Best Tchg. award Min. of Edn., Taiwan, 1991, IBM predoctoral fellow, 1984. Mem. IEEE (sr.). Avocations: hiking, mountain climbing. Office: Nat Chiao-Tung Univ, Dept Electronics Engring, Hsin-Chu Taiwan

WANG, TAO, ophthalmologist, researcher; b. Huairen, Shanxi, China, July 25, 1968; came to U.S., 1999; d. Yulan Zhao and Zilu Wang; m. Yun Zhang, Oct. 10, 1996. MD, Capital U. Med. Scis., Beijing, 1991, PhD, 1999. Resident Beijing Tongren Hosp., 1991-96, chief resident, 1996-97, physician in charge, 1996-99; postdoctoral rschr. Inst. Ocular Pharmacology, Tex. A&M U., College Station, 1999-2000; ophthalmologist, rschr. Inst. Ocular Pharmacology, Tex. A&M Univ., College Station, 2000—. Contbr. articles to profl. jours. Mem. Chinese Med. Assn. Avocation: table tennis. Office: Texas A&M U Dept Pharm & Toxic Inst of Ocular Pharmacology 304 Reynolds Medical Bldg College Station TX 77843-0001 also: Beijing Tong Ren Hosp, Capital Univ of Med Sci, Beijing People's Republic of China

WANG, TIANJI, physicist; b. Bayan, China, May 27, 1938; s. Yanfu and Xiangxian (Zhou) W.; m. Peiyun Li, Aug. 18, 1971; 1 child, Nanfei. BSc, Northeast U., 1963. Researcher Acad. Scis., Guangzhou, China, 1963-80; vis. scholar Stuttgart U., Germany, 1981-83; from rsch. assoc. to prof. Acad. Scis., 1984—. Author: Photonic Spip, 1980. Avocation: calligraphy. E-mail: gztjwang@public.guangzhou.gd.cn. Home: Rm 903 Bldg 5 81 Xianle Rd, 510070 Guangzhou China Office: Inst Elec Tech, 100 Xianlie Zhong Rd, 510070 Guangzhou China

WANG, TIEGUAN, petroleum engineer, educator; b. Shanghai, China, Dec. 4, 1937; s. Yuanbo and Xiumin (Wu) W.; m. Zhizhen Ren, Jan. 3, 1967; children: Jing, Lei. Student, Beijing Petroleum Geology Sch., 1956, Beijing Petroleum Inst., 1961-65. Lectr. Beijing Petroleum Geology Sch., 1956-61, Jianghan Petroleum Geology Sch., Hubei, 1965-78; lectr. Jianghan Petroleum Inst., Jingzhou, 1978-83, assoc. prof./prof., 1986-94; rsch. scholar U. Del., Newark, 1983-84; rsch. assoc. Oreg. State U., Corvallis, 1984-86; prof. U. Petroleum, Beijing, 1994—; courtesy prof. Jianghan Petroleum Inst., 1996—, Beijing Grad. Sch., China U. of Mining and Tech., Beijing, 1996—. Co-author: Formation and Mechanism of Oil from Coal, 1995 (China Natural Sci. award 2d class 1997); author: Genetic Mechanism and Occurance of Immature Hydrocarbons, 1995 (China Sci. and Tech. award 3d class 1997), Approach to Biomarker Geochemistry, 1990 (2d class Sci. and Tech. award of CNPC 1991); mem. editl. bd. Marine Origin Petroleum Geology, 1995—. Mem. China Soc. Geology (coun. mem. 1997), European Assn. Organic Geochemistry, Chinese Petroleum Soc. Avocation: philately. Home: Linyedaxuebei, 2-401 #5 Bldg #9 Yard-5, Beijing 100083, People's Republic of China Office: Univ of Petroleum/Geosci De, Shiku Rd Changping, Beijing 102200, People's Republic of China

WANG, TSUEY TANG, science educator, venture capitalist; b. Tainan, Taiwan, Nov. 12, 1932; came to U.S., 1958; s. Shih-Neng (dec.) and Tsun (Chen) W.; m. Margaret Mei-Tieh Lin, June 12, 1965; children: David, Marjorie, Vanessa. BS, Cheng Kung U., Tainan, 1955; PhD, Brown U., 1965. Asst. prof. Poly. U. N.Y., Bklyn., 1965-67; disting. mem. tech. staff AT&T Bell Labs., Murray Hill, N.J., 1967-88; vis. prof. Rutgers U., New Brunswick, N.J., 1988—; pres., chmn. bd. dirs. Transpac Capital Corp., Springfield, N.J., 1988—; vis. prof. Tokyo U. Agr. and Tech., 1984; mem. indsl. adv. bd. Nat. Ctr. Composite Materials, U. Del., 1986-89; bd. dirs. Internat. Power Devices, Inc., Boston, 1989-99; spl. invited vis. prof. Japan Ministry Edn., Tokyo, 1992; bd. dirs. Nat. Assn. Investment Cos., Washington, 1990-94. Author: (chpt.) Polymer Blends, 1978, (chpt.) Optical Telecommunications, 1979; editor: The Applications of Ferroelectric Polymers, 1988; patentee in field. Recipient Borden Corina Keen fellow Brown U., 1961. Fellow Am. Phys. Soc.; mem. ASME, Soc. Advancement Material and Process Engring., Materials Rsch. Soc., N.Y. Acad. Scis. Achievements include research in spinodal decomposition in polymer blends; melting point depression in compatible polymer blends. Office: Rutgers Univ Chem and Biochem Engring New Brunswick NJ 08854

WANG, WAYNE, film director. Dir.: Chan is Missing, 1982, Dim Sum: A Little Bit of Heart, 1985, Slamdance, 1987, Eat a Bowl of Tea, 1989, Life is Cheap...But Toilet Paper is Expensive, 1989, The Joy Luck Club, 1993, Smoke, 1995; co-dir. A Man, A Woman, and A Killer, 1975, The Stranger, 1992, Blue in the Face, 1995, Chinese Box, 1997, Anywhere But Here, 1999. Office: CIM Prodns 665 Bush St San Francisco CA 94108-3510 also: ICM c/o Bob Walker 40 W 57th St Fl 16 New York NY 10019-4001

WANG, WEI, lecturer; b. Shanghai, China, Feb. 23, 1958; m. Xueyun Qian, Aug. 28, 1983; children: Rong, Fei. BEd, East China Normal U., Shanghai, 1982; PhD, U. Wollongong, Australia, 1991. Tchg. asst. East China Normal U., 1982-83; tchg. fellow U. Wollogong, 1986-91; assoc. lectr. U. Sydney, Australia, 1991-95; lectr. Ctrl. Queensland U., Rockhampton, Australia, 1995—. Contbr. articles to profl. jours. Mem. Australian Psychol. Soc.,

Australasian Human Devel. Assn., Asian Assn. Social Psychology. Office: Ctrl Queensland U, Bruce hwy, Rockhampton Australia 4702

WANG, WEN CHUAN, chemical engineering educator; b. Sichuan, China, Aug. 26, 1941; s. Zhanxin and Zhongxiu (Fu) W.; m. Xiu Yu, Sept. 1, 1972; 1 child, Ruohan. BSChemE, Tianjin (China) U., 1962, MSChemE, 1965. Rsch. engr. Rsch. Inst. of Chem. Machinery, Lanzhou, China, 1967-85; assoc. prof. dept. chem. engring. Beijing U. of Chemical Technology, 1985-88, prof. dept. chem. engring., 1988—; vis. scholar dept. chem. engring. Purdue U., West Lafayette, Ind., 1981-83; vis. prof. Tech. U. Denmark, Lingby, 1990-91; sec. gen. Inst. Chem. Engring., China, 1997—; mem. econ. and tech. com. Ministry Chem. Industry, China, 1995—; chmn. organizing com. 2d Beijing Internat. Symposium on Thermodynamics in Chem. Engring. and Industry, 1994; co-chmn. programming com. 2d China-U.S. Joint Chem. Engring. Conf., Beijing, 1997. Assoc. editor: Chinese Jour. Chem. Engring., 2000—; contbr. over 110 articles to profl. jours. Recipient Giauque award 46th Calorimetry Conf., 1991, 2d prize for sci. and tech. Ministry of Chem. Industry, Beijing, 1995; postdoctoral fellow Purdue U., 1983. Mem. AIChE, Chem. Industry and Engring. Soc. China (vice dir. Japan com. 1994—), Internat. Union Pure and Applied Chemistry (nat. rep. solubility data commn. 1994—). Office: Beijing U Chem Tech Dept Chem Engring, PO Box 100, 100029 Beijing China

WANG, WEN QING, chemist, educator; b. Zhenhai, Zhejiang, China, Oct. 25, 1932; d. Yin Ting and Mei Yun (Yu) W.; m. Ji Lan Wu, Jan. 22, 1955; 1 child, Wu Yue Dong. Diploma in chemistry, Fudan U., Shanghai, 1953. Asst. Fudan U., Shanghai, 1953-54, Zhejiang U., Hangzhou, 1954-56; lectr. Beijing U., 1956-79, assoc. prof., 1979-85, prof., 1985—, PhD advisor, 1986—; vis. scholar U. Md., 1982-83, 89-90, Fla. State U., Tallahassee, 1983, Liege (Belgium) U., 1989. Author: The Problems of Physical Chemistry, 1981, 2d edit. 1999, The Principles of Extraction Chemistry, 1984, The Chemical Evolution of Life, 1994, Life Science, 1998, Cosmos-Earth-Life, 1999, Mind and Brain, 1999; contbr. over 200 articles to sci. jours. Recipient State Coun. Cert. Outstanding Contbn. in Divsn. of Higher Edn., China, 1989, 1st class prize sci. technique Progress of State Edn. Commn., Beijing, 1995. Mem. AAAS, N.Y. Acad. Scis., Internat. Soc. Study of Origin of Life. Home and Office: Beijing U, Dept Tech Physics, Beijing 100871, China

WANG, WEN-XIONG, science educator; b. Fujian, China, July 31, 1965; parents Yan-Fa Wang and Ya-Yun Chen; m. Zi-Jun Zhang, June 8, 1993; children: Elaine, Grace. BSc, Xiamen U., Fujian, 1984, MSc, 1987; PhD, SUNY, Stony Brook, 1996. Rsch. scholar SUNY, Stony Brook, 1991-96, rsch. assoc., 1996-97; asst. prof. dept. biology Hing Kong U. Sci. & Tech., Kowloon, Hong Kong; vis. scholar Plymouth (Eng.) Marine Lab., 1989-91; cons. applied math. SUNY, Stony Brook, 1996-97; grant reviewer Sea Grant, Tex., 1996. Contbr. sci. articles to profl. publs. Scholar NOAA Sea Grant, N.Y., 1991-96, Nat. Edn. Com., China, 1989, Natural Environ. Rsch. Coun., U.K., 1990; rsch. grantee Rsch. Grant Coun., Hong Kong, 1999. Mem. Am. Soc. Limnology and Oceanography, Soc. Environ. Toxicology and Chemistry, Ecol. Soc. Am., Am. Geophys. Union. Avocations: reading, swimming. Fax: 852 2358 1559. E-mail: wwang@ust.hk. Office: Hong Kong U Sci & Tech, Dept Biology, Kowloon Hong Kong

WANG, WENYI, music educator; b. Taipei, Taiwan, Oct. 30, 1964; came to U.S., 1986; d. Shih-Ming and Hsieh-Chu Wang. MusM, Ohio U., 1988; MusD, U. Mo., 1995; D in Music Edn., Ind. U., 2000. Prof., adminstr. Sch. Music Tainan (Taiwan) Coll., 1989-92; prof. Nat. Taiwan Acad. Arts, 1989-92, Nat Sun Yat-Sen U., Kaohsiung, Taiwan, 1990-92; mem. vis. faculty Sch. Music Ind. U., Bloomington, 1999—; mem. faculty dept. music George Mason U. Soloist-in-residence Nat. Chiang Kai Shek Cultural Ctr., Taipei, 1991-94; flutist Asian Composers League, Taipei, 1990-92; asst. prin. flutist Taiwan Symphony Orch., Taichung, 1984-86; contbr. articles to profl. publs. Nat. Art and Sci. Coun. scholar, Taiwan, 1989-92; Nat. rsch. grantee Ministry of Edn., Taiwan, 1989-92; named New Performing Star of Yr. Nat. Theatre and Concert Hall Planning and Mgmt. Coun., Taiwan, 1991. Mem. Coll. Music Soc., Music Edn. Nat. Conf., Soc. for Rsch. in Music Edn., Nat. Flute Assn. (life), European Recorder Tchrs. Assn., Internat. Soc. for Music Edn. (Eng.).

WANG, XIAN HUI, researcher; b. Jiangxi, China, Jan. 8, 1964; parents Shi Long Wang and Sai Yu Xiao; m. Moping Wang, July 1, 1987; 1 child, Zijing. BS, Wuhan U., Hubei, China, 1986, MSc, 1989; MSc, Nat. U. Singapore, 1999. Tchg. asst. Hubei Coll. Pharmacy and Clin. Lab. Scis., Wuhan, 1989-92, lectr., 1992-97; rsch. asst. Nat. U. Singapore, 1999—. Avocations: singing, swimming. Fax: 0065-7792486. E-mail: dbswxh@nus.edu.sg. Office: Nat U Singapore Biol Scis, Lower Kent Ridge Rd, Singapore 117600, Singapore

WANG, XIAODU, engineering educator; b. Beijing, Oct. 3, 1954; came to U.S. 1991; p. Yu Miao and Fang He; m. Yuhong Li, May 1, 1984; 1 child, Grace. BS, Beijing Inst. Aeronautics and Astronautics, 1982, MS, 1985; D in Engring., Yokohama (Japan) Nat. U., 1990. Asst. lectr. Beijing Inst. Aeronautics and Astronautics, 1985-86; rsch. engr. NKK Corp., Kawasaki, Japan, 1990-91; postdoctoral rsch. asst. U. Tex. Health Sci. Ctr., San Antonio, 1992-94, asst. instr., 1995-97, asst. prof., 1997-99; asst. prof. U. Tex., San Antonio, 1999—; faculty advisor Chinese Student and Scholars Assn., San Antonio, 1996-99. Contbr. chpt. to book and articles to profl. jours. Recipient Fgn. Rsch. Studentship, Ministry Edn. Japan, Yokohama, 1986-90, Biomed. Rsch. award The Whitaker Found., 1998; Japan Overseas Tech. Tng. scholar Japan Overseas Tech. Exch. Assn., Kawasaki, 1991; rsch. grantee NIH, 1999. Mem. ASME, Orthopaedic Rsch. Soc., Soc. for Biomaterials, Biomed. Engring. Soc. Avocations: reading, traveling, ancient history. E-mail: xwang@utsa.edu. Fax: 210-458-5589. Home: 7810 Parsley San Antonio TX 78240-2275 Office: Univ Tex 6900 N Loop 1604 W San Antonio TX 78249-1130

WANG, XIAOHUI, research physicist; b. Benbu, China, Feb. 13, 1965; s. Lianzhong and Fengying Wang; m. Hongwu Tong, Jan. 22, 1990. BSc, Nanjing (China) U., 1986, MSc, 1989; PhD, Frieburg (Germany) U., 1996. Postdoctoral rschr. Frieburg U., 1996; postdoctoral rschr. Lund (Sweden) U., 1997-98, asst. prof. physics, 1999—. Contbr. articles to profl. jours. Rsch. grantee Swedish Naturvetenskapliga Forskningsradet, Lund, 1997, 98. Mem. Am. Phys. Soc. Home: Vildandsvägen 14 L106, S-22734 Lund Sweden Office: Lund U Dept Theoretical Phy, Solvegatan 14A, S-22362 Lund Sweden

WANG, XUEBING, banker. With Peoples' Bank China, 1976-93; pres., chmn. bd. Bank of China, Beijing, 1993—; vice gen. mgr. Everbright Group, 1993; CEO China Constrn. Bank, Beijing. Office: China Constrn Bank, 4 Men No 28 West Dajie, Xuanwumen Beijing 100053, China*

WANG, XUEMING, English educator, translator; b. Fujian Province, China, Feb. 21, 1933; s. Gongxiu and Xiuhua (Li) W.; m. Xianlu Chang, Oct. 15, 1960; children: Wang Xiaowen, Wang Xiaodong. Student, Beijing Fgn. Studies U., 1951-55, 55-57. Head fgn. lang. teaching and rsch. sect. Kunming (China) U. Sci. and Tech., 1960-80, chmn. fgn. lang. dept., 1981—; mem. Nat. Commn. on Fgn. Lang. Textbook Evaluation and Syllabus Designing, Beijing, 1985-93; vice chmn. Translator's Promotion Com. under China Nat. Nonferrous Metals Industry Co., 1985-90. Editorial bd. Jour. of Kunming Inst. Tech., 1980—; author: English-Chinese Translation Course, 1991; translator: Abraham Lincoln, 1987; translator articles. Recipient Award for Outstanding Contbn., State Coun. China, 1992, Award for Excellent Textbooks, Chongqing U., 1991, Award for Excellent Textbooks, Nat. Edn. Commn., 1993. Mem. Yunnan Translators Assn. (dep. pres. 1987-93). Avocations: reading, music, table tennis. Office: Kunming U Sci & Tech, Lian Hua Chi, Kunming China

WANG, XUNGAI, engineering educator; b. Jianli, China, Jan. 21, 1966; p. Zhi Xiang Wang and Huang Gui Zhou; m. Zhu Hui Zhang, Dec. 8, 1990; 1 child, Senney. B in Engring., N.W. Inst. Textile Sci. & Tech., Xi'an, China, 1986; PhD, U. NSW, Sydney, Australia, 1992, diploma HEd, 1996. Lectr. U. NSW, Sydney, 1993-97, sr. lectr., 1997-98; assoc. prof. Deakin U., Geelong, Australia, 1998—. Mem. Textile Inst. Office: Deakin U Sch Engring & Tech, Pigdons Rd, Geelong 3217, Australia

WANG, YANQI, materials scientist, researcher; b. Junan, Shandong, China, Dec. 24, 1965; s. Zuoshan Wang and Shangzhen Li; m. Jing Wei, Dec. 19, 1993; 1 child, Tianlu. BS in Physics, Shandong Tchrs. Coll., Jinan, 1989; MS in Materials Sci. and Engring., Zhejiang U., Hangzhou, China, 1992, PhD in Materials Sci. and Engring., 1998. Asst. prof. Zheijiang U., 1992-94, rsch. assoc., 1994-98; rsch. asst. Space Vacuum Epitaxy Ctr., U. Houston, 1998—. Mem. AAAS, Am. Physics Soc., Sigma Xi. Avocations: table tennis, music. Fax: 713-747-7724. E-mail: ywang11@bayou.uh.edu. Home: 5415 Scott St Apt 7 Houston TX 77021-1539 Office: U Houston Space VAcuum Epitaxy Ctr 4800 Calhoun Rd Spc Vacuum Houston TX 77004-2610

WANG, YEONG-HER, electrical engineer, educator; b. Tainan, Taiwan, Dec. 2, 1956; s. Jin-Inn and Jin-Shan (Yang) W.; m. An-Chi Liu; children: Sze-Wen, Li-Wen. BS, Nat. Cheng-Kung U., Tainan, 1978; MS, Nat. Cheng-Kung U., 1980, PhD, 1985. Lectr. dept. elec. engring. Nat. Cheng-Kung U., Tainan, 1982-85, assoc. prof., 1985-92, prof., 1992—, assoc. dir. dept. elec. engring., 1993-96, dir. elec. labs., 1995-96, chmn. elec. engring., 1996—; mem. tech. staff AT&T Bell Labs., Murray Hill, N.J., 1989-91. Contbr. articles to profl. jours.; patentee in field. Young Scientist award Chinese Inst. Engring., 1995. Mem. IEEE, Chinese Inst. Engrs. (bd. dirs. 1997—). Avocations: stamp collecting, fishing. Home: 45-1 sec 1 Pei-mann Rd, Tainan 700, Taiwan Office: Dept Elec Engring, 1 University Rd, Tainan 701, Taiwan

WANG, YING-LUO, college dean, educator; b. Jin, Anhui, China, May 21, 1930; s. Shi-Qing and Qi-Zen (Cheng) W.; m. Xian-Ru Zhang, July 19, 1956; children: Shi-Hua, Shi Qi. BS, Shanghai Jiao-tong U., People's Republic China, 1952; MS, Harbin Tech. U., People's Republic China, 1955. Lectr. Shanghai Jiao-tong U., 1955-58; lectr., assoc. prof. Xi'an (People's Republic China) Jiao-tong U., 1959-78, prof., vice chmn. mech. dept., Inst. Systmes Engring., 1979—, prof., dean Sch. Mgmt., 1979—, v.p., 1984-88; cons. Shaanxi Province Govt., 1988, Xi'an City Govt., 1985. Fellow Am. Biographical Inst. (mem. rsch. bd. advisors 1989); mem. Systems Engring. Soc. China (v.p. 1986—), Internat. Fedn. Automatic Control (mem. systems engring. com. 1985—). Avocations: music. Office: Xian Jiao-tong U, Mgmt Sch, Xian 710049, China

WANG, YIXING, engineering educator; b. Shanghai, Sept. 20, 1937; s. Guochu and Quanyun (Song) W.; m. Meiqiu Zha, Feb. 10, 1966; children: Zhaohui, Shuangying, Zhaoyang. BS, No. Jiaotong U., Beijing, 1960. Asst. Jilin U. Tech., Changchun, People's Republic of China, 1960-77, lectr., 1977-83, assoc. prof., 1983-91, prof., 1991—, dep. dir. Chain Transmission Inst., 1979-94, chmn. acad. com. Chain Transmission Inst., 1994-97; dep. dir. Jilin Mech. Transmission Inst., Changchun, 1985—; mem. standing coun. Mech. Transmission Inst. of China Mech. Engring. Soc., Zhengzhou, People's Reppublic of China, 1987—; chmn. Nat. Tech. Com. for Standardization of Chain Transmission, 1995—; chmn. chain transmission Inst. Mech. Transmission Inst., 1996—; rsch. worker in field. Author: Chain Transmission, 1983 (Nat. award 1988), Match Theory in Chain Drive, 1989 (Ministry of the S.D. award 1991), CAD of Chain Products, 1991 (Ministry of the S.D. award 1994), GB/T 1243-1997 (Ministry of the S.D. award 1999). Recipient Outstanding Pers. award Jilin Province Govt., 1985, Ministry of Machine Bldg. Industry of People's Republic of China, 1991, Advanced Worker award China Mech. Engring. Soc., 1990, 96. Mem. ASME, Internat. Fedn. Theory of Machine and Mechanism (com. China, governing com. 1998—). Avocations: reading, travel, talking with young people. E-mail: wyx@jut.edu.cn. Home: Gong Da Apt # 10-20, Nan Lin St, Changchun 130022, China

WANG, YONG GANG, fuel chemistry researcher; b. Tongjiang, China, Oct. 18, 1960; s. Ji Wu Wang and Shu Min Fu; m. Ya Juan Liang; 1 child, Xiang Yu. BS, Anshan (China) Iron & Steel U., 1982; MS, Taiyuan (China) U., 1988; PhD, Kyushu U., Kasuga, Japan, 1999. Assoc. prof. Taiyuan U., 1992-94; vis. scientist Kyushu U., 1994—. Contbr. articles to profl. publs.

WANG, YONGJI, computer engineer; b. Gaizhou, Liaoning, China, Dec. 8, 1962; s. Xuesheng Wang and Shuzhen Zhao; m. Lu Jiang, Nov. 11, 1962; 1 child, Y. Daniel. BS in Aeronautics and Astronautics, Beijing U., 1984, MS in Aeronautics and Astronautics, 1987; PhD, Edinburgh U., 1995. Lectr. Tianjin (China) U., 1987-92; rsch. assoc. Edinburgh (Scotland) U., 1995-96; rsch. fellow Heriot Watt U., Edinburgh, 1996-98; sr. rsch. fellow Ctr. Sys. & Control Glasgow U., Scotland, 1998—. Contbr. articles to profl. jours. Recipient Excellent Young Rschr. award K.C. Wong Edn. Found., 1992-95. Mem. Chinese Automation Soc. Avocations: bridge, music, swimming, badminton, GO (Weiqi). Home: 1F1 86 Leamington Terr, Edinburgh EH10 4JU, Scotland Office: Ctr Sys & Control, Glasgow U, Dept Mech Engr, Glasgow G12 8QQ, Scotland

WANG, YOUXIN, marketing professional; b. Hangzhou, Zhejiang, China, Oct. 22, 1963; s. Xuanshou and Ruoying (Yao) W.; m. Lai Sun; children: Nancy, Jason. BS, Zhejiang U., Hangzhou, China, 1985; diploma in Mktg., Fachhochschue, Munich, 1998; M Mktg., Thunderbird, Glendale, Ariz., 1995. Bus. devel. mgr. Sulzer, Winterthur, Switzerland, 1996-97; mktg. mgr. Rieter Automotive Mgmt. AG, Winterthur, 1997—. Auditor English Connection, Switzerland, 1999, 2000. Avocations: skiing, swimming.

WANG, YU, telecommunication engineer; b. Dalian, Liaoning, China, Nov. 28, 1956; arrived in Switzerland, 1988; naturalized French citizen, 1994; d. Zhongtuo Wang and Wenzhu Deng; m. Ronan Boulic; children: Shuran Xixi, Tunvez. BSc in Applied Physics, Dalian U. Tech., China, 1982; PhD in Elec. and Electronics Engring., Tech. U. Vienna, Austria, 1987. Mem. faculty Beijing U. Post and Telecomms., 1982-83; rsch. asst. Ecole Poly. Federale Lausanne, Switzerland, 1987; rsch. scientist Ascom Tech Ltd., Berne, Switzerland, 1988-98; tech. expert Swisscom Ltd., Berne, Switzerland, 1998—. Contbr. articles to profl. publs.; patentee in field. Austrian Govt. grantee, 1983-85. Mem. IEEE Communication Soc., IEEE Lasers and Electo-optics Soc., Dalian U. Tech. Alumni Assn. Overseas (v.p. 1997). Avocations: world economics, Chinese calligraphy, Chinese cooking, Chinese medicine. Home: Engerain 26, CH 3004 Bern Switzerland Office: Swisscom Ltd, NWS-ENG, CH-3050 Berne Switzerland

WANG, YU LIANG, journal editor; b. Chongqing City, Pengshui, China, Nov. 3, 1933; s. Zhi Jun and Chen Shi Wang; m. Cai Xia Wu, Oct. 1, 1961; children: Xue-Ping, Dong-Ping, Xiao-Bo. BA, Beijing Tchrs. U., 1956, MA, 1958. Tchr. Yulin County No. 1 Middle Sch., Shaanxi, China, 1958-73; chief editor Jour. Yulin Edn., Shaanxi, 1973-80; editor Jour. Humanities, Xi'an, 1981-86, chief editor, 1986—; assoc. prof. philosophy Shaanxi Acad. Social Scis., Xi'an, 1987-90, prof., 1990—; prof. Enterprise Culture Inst., Beijing U., 1997—. Author: The Value Philosophy, 1989 (2d award Shaanxi Province Govt. 1993), A New Research of Value Philosophy, 1993, The Value Outlook of Deng Xiaoping, 1995 (Five First Engring. award Shaanxi Province Govt. 1996), Seek Value-Reread John Dewey, 1997, The New Theory of Value Philosophy in China and Japan, 1994 (1st award Shaanxi Philosophy Learned Soc. 1995). Recipient Shaanxi Province Govt. Outstanding Achievements Expert award, 1991, Govt. Specific Allowance, the State Coun., Beijing, 1992, Shaanxi Province Model Laborer award, 1997. Mem. Shaanxi Learned Soc. on Value Philosophy (chmn. 1996—), Chinese Anthropology Learned Soc. (dir. 1996—), Shaanxi Philosphy Learned Soc. (routine dir. 1991—). Mem. Communist Party of China. Avocations: watching TV, sports. Office: Shaanxi Acad Soc Scis, #7 South Sect Hanguang Rd, Xi'an 710065, China

WANG, YUHAI, magazine editor-in-chief; b. Lanxi County, China, Apr. 9, 1941; s. Xixian Wang and Jiayun Liu; m. Guimei Zhou; children: Ying yun, Xin yun. Student, Harbin (China) Tchr. Tng. Coll, China, 1967. Chinese lang. tchr. Heilongjiang Zhaodong 1st Mid. Sch., Zhaodong, China, 1960-65, Heilongjiang Zhaodong 2d Mid. Sch., Zhaodong, China, 1965-73; playwright Heilongjiang Zhaodong Theatre of Cultural Ctr., Zhaodong, China, 1973-77; Chinese lang. and lit. tchg. rsch. fellow Zhaodong Edn. Bur., 1978-82; v.p. Sch. for Tchrs.' Advanced Studies Daqing Municipality Ranghulu Region, 1982-87, vice leader Edn. Bur., 1982-87; editor-in-chief Ways to a Successful Composition (mag.), Daqing, 1987—; publ. lectr. in field of lang. and lit. edn. reform, and participant in various seminars and confs., 1982—. First vice editor-in-chief Education Art (bimonthly), Beijing; publisher 22 books and monographs (prize China Writing Assn.); contbr. over 150 articles to jours. and newspapers.;. Named in various ref. books on Chinese educators, editors, reporters, and people of outstanding ability; recipient Excellent Editor prize Heilongjiang Provincial Higher Edn. Jour. Assn., Heilongjiang Provincial Sci. Com., Pub. Bur. Press, and other orgns. Mem. Chinese Edn. Art Inst. (permanent coun. mem., vice sec.-gen. 1990—, rsch. and study awards), Chinese Edn. Artist Assn., Chinese Lang. and Lit. Press Assn. (permanent coun. mem., vice sec.-gen. 1990—, Excellent Editor prize), Chinese Teenagers Writing Inst. (permanent coun. mem., vice head learning sci. com. 1990—). Avocation: visiting places of historic interest and beauty. Office: Zuowen Chenggong Zhi Lu, 4-34 Dongfengxincun, Daqing 163311, China

WANG, YUWEN, chemist, researcher; b. Yangyuan, Hebei, China, Aug. 28, 1954; came to U.S., 1987; s. Ji Wang and Guiying Ma; m. Zengjuan Li, Jan. 6, 1981; children: Lei, Julie. B, Hebei U., 1977; PhD, Va. Poly. and U., 1997. Asst. rsch. fellow Hebei Acad. Scis., Shijiazhuang, China, 1978-81; assoc. dir. Hebei Acad. Scis., Shijiazhuang, 1982-86, assoc. rsch. fellow, 1989-91; rsch. assoc. Iowa State U., Ames, 1987-88; rsch. scientist Va. Poly. and State U., Blacksburg, 1992-2000; sr. scientist Boehringer Ingelheim Pharms. Inc., Ridgefield, Conn., 2000—; cons. Cultor Inc., Groton, Conn., 1995, Pfizer Inc., Groton, 1996. Contbr. articles to profl. jours.; mem. editl. bd. Internat. Jour. Information, 1999—. Recipient Chinese Nat. Sci. Progress award Nat. Sci. Com., 1985, Hebei Sci. Progress award Hebei Sci. Com., 1979, 83, 91. Mem. AAAS, Am. Chem. Soc., Assn. Students in Va. Tech. (v.p.), Phi Lambda Upsilon, Sigma Xi. Achievements include research on gas chromatography mass spectrometry, liquid chromatography capillary zone electrophoresis and atomic absorption spectroscopy, development of explosive stimulants, invention of electrogenerated chemiluminescence detector for HPLC, development of parts per trillion levels of cancerogenic compound detection methods. Avocations: tennis, racquet ball, jogging, singing. Home: 40 Lake Ave Apt 2 Danbury CT 06810-6345 Office: Boehringer Ingeheim Pharms Inc PO Box 368 900 Ridgebury Rd Ridgefield CT 06877-1058

WANG, ZHAO YIN, hydraulic engineer, educator; b. Jinan, Shandong, China, Oct. 25, 1951; s. Zhuyun Wang and Jinghua Guo; m. Xiuhua Chong, July 29, 1981; 1 child, Ruiyu. Bachelor, Ctrl.-South U. Tech., Changsha, China, 1979; Master, China Inst. Water Resources, Beijing, 1983, Doctor, 1985. Technician Yellow River Farm and Shandong No. 3 Geol. Team, 1969-76; sr. engr. China Inst. Water Resources and Hydro-Power Rsch., 1985-91; rsch. fellow Alexander von Humboldt Found., Germany, 1991-92; guest scientist U. Karlsruhe, Germany, 1993-94; prof. hydraulic engring. Internat. Rsch. and Tng. Ctr. on Erosion and Sedimentation, Beijing, 1995—; prof., chair Tsinghua U., 1999—; sec. gen steering com. for Three Gorges Project, Beijing, 1985-86; sr. expert UNDP Project, Beijing, 1995-97; initiator, organizer Sino-German Sediment Rsch. activities, Karlsruhe and Beijing, 1994—. Author: Hyperconcentrated Flow, 1994; contbr. articles to profl. jours. including Acta Geographica Sinica (1st prize of Sci. and Tech. Progress, 1991), Acta Mechanica Sinica (1st Prize of Sci. and Tech. Progress, 1990, 96), others; editor, chief editor Internat. Jour. Sediment Rsch. Mem. Nat. Com. of Acad. Degree, Beijing, 1996—, selection com. of the Prize of Outstanding Young Scientists of China, 1996—; vice-sec. gen. Chinese Assn. of Alexander von Humboldt fellows, Beijing, 1995—. Named Doctor of Great Contributions for China, Nat. Com. Acad. Degree, 1991, Excellent Scientist Who Made Great Contributions to the Three Gorges Project, Ministry of Water Resources of China, 1995, First Ning Chien prize, 1989, Outstanding Young Scientist of China, State Coun. of China, 1995. Mem. ASCE (mem. task force com. orr debris flow 1991-97), Internat. Commn. Large Dams (mem. sedimentation com. 1991-97), Internat. Assn. Hydraulic Rsch., N.Y. Acad. Scis. Achievements include research in laminated load motion, instability theory of non-Newtonian flow, time distortion of sediment model, drag reduction of hyperconcentrated flow, inertia of river bed, turbulence of bed load, buoyancy force of suspension, scale effects of wind tunnel modelling, mechanism of debris flow and unsteady sediment transport theory. Home: 20 Che-Gong-Zhuang Rd, Beijing 100044, China Office: IRTCES PO Box 366, 20 West Che-Gong-Zhuang Rd, Beijing 100044, China

WANG, ZHAO ZHONG, physics researcher; b. Shanghai, China, Jan. 23, 1946; s. Zhu-Kang and Shu-zhen (Chen) W.; m. Ya-Xin Yu, Sept. 17, 1971; children: Zhi-Yuan, Bin-Yuan. BA, U. Sci. & Tech. of China, Beijing, 1968; MA, U. Grenoble, France, 1981, PhD, 1985. Cert. solid state physicist. Worker Baotou Steel & Iron Co., Neimongou, People's Republic of China, 1968-74, technician, 1974-78; lectr. U. Sci. & Tech. of China, Hefai, People's Republic China, 1978-79; maitre de conf. U. Grenoble, 1984-85; rsch. assoc. Princeton (N.J.) U., 1985-88, rsch. staff mem., 1988-90; dir. rsch. Lab. Microstructures and Microelectronics Centre National de la Recherche Scientifique, Paris, 1990; part-time prof. Univ. Sci. and Tech. of China, 1993; pres. Association Scientifiques et Ingineurs chihoise en France, 1998; overseas assessor Chinese Acad. Scis., 1999. Mem. Assn. Sci. and Engrs. of China in France, Am. Phys. Soc., Assn. Chinese Scientists and Engrs. in France (pres.), N.Y. Acad. Scis. Home: 40 Rue des Aulnes, 92330 Sceaux France Office: L2M/CNRS, 196 Ave H Ravera, 92220 Bagneux France

WANG, ZHENG, computer scientist, researcher; b. Hangzhou, Zheijiang, China, Apr. 25, 1964; s. Yu Wang and Yafen Kong; m. Wei Dong, Feb. 26, 1991; children: Dylan, Netta. B Engring. in Electronics, Zhejiang U., Hangzhou, 1985; PhD in Computer Sci., U. London, 1992. Rsch. assoc. Cambridge (Eng.) U., 1990-92; rsch. fellow U. London, 1992-97; rsch. scientist Bell Labs. Lucent Tech., Holmdel, N.J., 1997—. Editor spl. edit. IEEE Network Internet Traffic Engring., 2000. Avocations: Do It Yourself, investing. Fax: 732-203-2268. E-mail: zhwang@ieee.org. Office: Bell Labs Lucent Tech 101 Crawfords Corner Rd Holmdel NJ 07733-1985

WANG, ZHENG MING, science educator; b. Wujin, Jiangsu, China, Aug. 16, 1943; s. You Zhi Wang and Xin Rong Yu; m. Chen Ji, Jan. 23, 1972; children: Zixun Wang, Ziyi Wang. BS, Tsinghua U., Beijing, 1967; MS, Chinese Acad. Scis., Beijing, 1981. Asst. engr. Haerbin Works of Steam Turbine, 1968-78; rsch. assoc. Chinese Acad. Scis., Beijing, 1982-86, assoc. rsch. prof., 1986-94, pprof., 1994—. Contbr. articles to profl. jours. Mem. Chinese Soc. Engring. Thermophysics, Chinese Soc. Aeronautics. Avocation: calligraphy in Chinese. Office: Chinese Acad of Scis, B12 Zhongguancun Rd, 100080 Beijing China

WANG, ZHENG PING, educator; b. Harbin, China, Sept. 21, 1949; s. Shu Yuan and Xing Cun (Dang) W.; m. Chun Yan Yin; 1 child, Zhen Fei. BS, Harbin Engring. U., China, 1982, M of Engring., 1989. Teaching asst. Harbin Engring. U., China, 1982-88, lectr., 1988-93, assoc. prof., 1993-98, prof., 1998—. Contbr. articles to profl. jours. Mem. AAAS, Optical Soc. Am., N.Y. Acad. Scis. Office: Harbin Engring U, 2 Yiman St, Harbin 150001, China

WANG, ZHI, economist, researcher; b. Beijing, Nov. 15, 1950; came to U.S., 1987; s. Wen Long and Xian Wen (Tian) W.; m. Zhong Hua Yan, Jan. 31, 1982; 1 child, Qian. MS, Chinese Acad. Agrl. Scis., Beijing, 1984, Ohio State U., 1990; PhD, U. Minn., 1994. Rsch. fellow Chinese Acad. Agrl. Scis., Beijing, 1985-87; cons. The World Bank, Washington, 1994-95; rsch. assoc. U. Minn., Mpls., 1995-97; economist Purdue U., Lafayette, Ind., 1997-98; agrl. economist USDA, Washinton, 1999—. Co-author: (book) Global Economics; contbr. articles to profl. jours. Bd. dirs. Hope Chinese Sch., Washington, 1995-98. Mem. Am. Economist Assn., Chinese Economist Soc. (bd. dirs. 1992-93), Am. Agrl. Economics Assn. E-mail: Zwang@usda.ers.gov. Home: 118 Apple Blossom Way Gaithersburg MD 20878-1165 Office: USDA Agrl Econs Rsch Svcs 1800 M St NW Washington DC 20036-5802

WANG, ZHIJIAN, optics scientist, educator; b. Le Ting, Tang Shan, China, May 27, 1941; s. Jingrong Wang and Zhenying Yan; m. Shulan Zhou, Apr. 28, 1967; 1 child, Peng. Bachelor Degree, Harbin (China) Inst. Tech., 1965. Engr. Huabei Optical Instrument Factory, Beijing, 1965-69, Taihang Mechanic Factor, Shijiazhuang, China, 1969-72; prof. Changchun (China) Inst. Optics and Fine Mechanics, 1972—; bd. dirs. Larte Laser Co., Dalian. Contbr. articles to profl. jours. Recipient China Sci. and Tech. Session prize State Coun. Peoples Republic China, Beijing, 1978, Secondary prize China Nat. Def. Industry Office, Beijing, 1981, Excellent Paper award China Mil. Assoc., Beijing, 1991. Mem. Internat. Soc. for Optical Engring., China

Optics Assn., China Optics Measurement and Test Com. Communist. Avocations: football, reading. E-mail: wangpeng@public.cc.jl.cn. Office: Changchun Inst Optics, 7 Weixing Rd PO Box 1003, Changchun 130022, China

WANG, ZHONG GAO, surgeon; b. Hangzhou, Zhejian, China, Sept. 3, 1937; s. Te Jian and Ei Zhen Jian W.; m. Yan Ping Zhao, Jan. 13, 1965; children: Dajie, Xiujie. MD, Shanghai Med. U., China, 1961. Resident to assoc. prof. Peking Union Med. Coll., Beijing, China, 1961-86; prof., chief dept. vascular surgery An Zhen Hosp., Beijing, China, 1986-92; prof., dir. Vascular Inst. Gen. Post & Telecom Hosp., Beijing, China, 1992—; vis. scholar Duke U. Med. Ctr., Durham, N.C., 1979-81. Author: Current Problems in Surgery, 1996; chief editor: Vascular Surgery, Vol. I, 1992, Vol. II, 1998, Chin J. Vascular Surgery, 2000. Recipient Rsch. Achievement award Internat. Coll. Angiology, 1996, 2d Award of Technology Advancement in China, Chinese Govt., Beijing, 1998, Life Achievement award ABI, 1998. Hon. mem. Soc. Vascular Surgery, Am. Coll. Angiology, Am. Coll. Phlebotomy, Cardiothoracic Vascular Soc. India, Chinese Vascular Soc. (pres. 1992—), Asian Vascular Soc. (pres. 1996-98), Internat. Union Angiology (v.p. 1999—). Home: Nan Wei Rd # 2 6-1-6-8, 100050 Beijing China Office: Gen Post & Telecom Hosp, Vascular Inst Long Rd, 100032 Beijing China

WANG, ZHONG-HAN, history educator; b. Dong-an, Hunan, China, Aug. 2, 1913; s. Xian-Lian and Gui-Xiang (Tang) W.; m. Yin-Sung Tu, Sept. 14, 1949; children: Xiang-Yun, Ying-Yun, Chu-Yun. BA, Yenching U., Beijing, 1938, MA, 1940; D in History, Harvard U., 1995. Instr. history Yenching U., 1940-41, lectr., 1943-46; lectr. Harvard U. Grad. Sch., 1946-48; assoc. prof. Yenching U., 1948-52; acting vice editor-in-chief Sinological Series, Harvard-Yenching Inst., Beijing, 1948-51; prof. Rsch. Ctr., Cen. U. Nationalities, Beijing, 1952-56, prof. history, 1956—, nat. life-time prof., 1986—. Author: Miscellanea on the History of Qing, 1957, New Studies on the History of Qing, 1990 (award 1991); editor: A Brief History of the Manchu People, 1979 (award 1984), Notes on Biographies of Qing, 1987, Continued Studies on the History of Qing, 1993, A History of Chinese Nationalities, 1994 (Nat. award 1995, Beijing Re-award 1996). Mem. Soc. History of Nationalities (cons. 1978—), Soc. Chinese History, Soc. Beijing History (cons. 1990—). Home: Cen Univ Nationalities, 5 Unit 34 Faculty Apts, Beijing 100081, China Office: Cen Univ Nationalities, Dept History, Beijing 100081, China

WANG, ZHONGYU, Chinese government official; b. Changchu City, Jillin, People's Republic of China, 1933. Mem. standing com. Jilin Province CCP, 1983—, dep. sec., 1985—; alt. mem. Chinese CCP 13th Cen. Com., 1987—; vice-gov. Jilin Province, 1988, gov., 1989-96; minister in charge State Econ. and Trade Commn., People's Republic of China; sec. State Coun. Secretariat. Mem. The Communist Party. Office: 8 Shan Li He Dong Lu, West Dist, Beijing 100820, China*

WANG, ZIDONG, electrical engineering and mathematics educator; b. Gaoyou City, Jiangsu, China, Feb. 21, 1966; arrived in Germany, 1997; s. Youpei Wang and Shunzhu Zhang; m. Naiwen Dou, Oct. 10, 1991; 1 child, Yuanchen. BSc, Suzhou (China) U., 1986; MSc, China Textile U., Shanghai, 1988; D in Engring., U. Sci. & Tech., Nanjing, China, 1994. Cert. elec. engr. Asst. prof. applied math. E. China Inst. Tech., Nanjing, 1988-90; lectr. Nanjing (China) U. Sci and Tech., 1990-94, assoc. prof., 1994-97; guest prof. Ruhr U. Bochum, Germany, 1997-98; sr. lectr. U. Kaiserslautern, Germany, 1999—. Contbr. 80 articles to profl. jours. Recipient Ann. Best Sci. Paper awards, Nanjing U. of Sci. and Tech., 1994, 95, 96; Nat. Sci. Investigator award Nat. Natural Sci. Found. of China, 1995, Outstanding Sci. and Tech. Devel. award Nat. Edn.l Com. China, Beijing, 1996, Alexander von Humboldt fellowship, Bonn, Germany, 1997. Mem. IEEE (with automatic control divsn. 1997—), Chinese Assn. Automation (automatic control 1994—), Chinese Assn. Math. (Stochastic Process), Chinese Soc. Stats (stochastic stats), Command and Control Soc. of Jiangsu Province, China (gen. sec. 1992—). Office: Dept Math, Univ Kaiserslautern, D-67663 Kaiserslautern Germany

WANG, ZONGLI, pathologist, educator, researcher; b. Shanghai, China, Apr. 4, 1937; s. Zheng Zhang and Xiuzhen; m. Chengsu Xu, Feb. 12, 1963; 1 child, Lezhi. MD, Shanghai Med. U., 1960. Asst. dept. pathology Peking Union Med. Coll., Beijing, 1960-77; lectr. dept. pathology Peking Union Med. Coll., 1978-85, assoc. prof. dept. pathology, 1985-86, prof., chmn. dept. pathology, 1987—; vis. rsch. fellow Melbourne (Australia) U., 1982-84. Author: Pathophysiology of Body Fluid Factors and Blood Circulation, 1989; standing editor editl. bd. Chinese Jour. Atherosclerosis, 1990—. Sci. rsch. grantee Nat. Com. for Sci. and Tech., Beijing, 1996, Chinese Natural Sci. Found., Beijing, 1997, 98, Ministry of Health, Beijing, 1998. Mem. Soc. Pathology Chinese Med. Soc. (bd. mem., com. mem.), Soc. Atherosclerosis (bd. mem., com. mem.). Achievements include pharmaceutical patent. Avocations: Chinese traditional medicine, Chinese musical instruments, swimming, singing. E-mail: yongyong-li@21cn.com. Fax: 011-8610-67635802. Office: Peking Union Med Coll, 5 Dong Dan San Tiao, Beijing 100005, China

WANG, ZUOBIN, engineering educator; b. Harbin, China, Jan. 21, 1960; parents Shiyuan Wang and Xiufang Gao; m. He Liu, June 24, 1985; 1 child, Wen Xiao. BSc in Opto-electronic Engring., Changchun Inst. Optics/ Mechs., 1982, MSc in Opto-electronic Engring., 1985; PhD in Optical Engring., U. Warwick, Coventry, Eng., 1998. Lectr. Changchun Inst. Optics & Fine Mechanics, 1985-93; assoc. prof. Changchun Inst. Optics & Fine Mechanis, 1993—; rsch. assoc. Cardiff (Wales) U., 1997—; dir. elec. and electronic engring. lab. Changchun Inst. Optics & Fine Mechanics, advisor sci. and tech. Contbr. articles to profl. jours. Recipient 3d prize for interpolation methods of moire fringe Sci. & Tech. Com. Jilin Province, 1991, 2d prize for laser scanning measurement sys. Ministry Machine Bldg., 1991. Mem. Internat. Soc. Optical Engring. Avocations: reading, writing, traveling. Fax: 44(0) 1222 874003. E-mail: wangz@cardiff.ac.uk. Office: Cardiff U Sys Engring Div, Queen's Bldg, Cardiff CF24 3TE, Wales

WANGCHINDORJ, LANGTAI BALJINNIAM, periodical editor; b. Khamar Dawa, Kubsukul, Mongolia, June 19, 1924; s. Shirab Baljinniam and Langtai Baldon; m. Rinchndo Baigal (div. 1979). Student, Nat. U., Ulan Bator, 1949-56, Internat. Rels. Inst., Moscow, 1956-57. Internat. econ. affairs officer Ministry External Rels., Ulan Bator, Mongolia, 1956-57; second sec. Mongolian Embassy, New Delhi, 1957-61; dep. head dept. Ministry External Rels., Ulan Bator, 1961-73; econ. affairs officer Econ. & Social Commn. Asia & Pacific, UN, Bangkok, 1973-76; sec. gen. Mongolian Nat. Commn., UNESCO, Ulan Bator, 1976-84; polit. observer Mongolian News Agy., Ulan Bator, 1984-86; chief editor Dharmaduta Jour., Internat. Asian Buddhist Orgn., Ulan Bator, 1986—. Contbr. numerous articles and essays to profl. pubs. Active supporter, spkr., writer for human rights and ednl. opportunities. With Mongolian Army, 1941-48. Mem. Lions. Avocations: photography, cooking, community activism. Home: PO Box 49/156, Ulan Balor 49, Mongolia

WANGCHUCK, HIS MAJESTY JIGME SINGYE, King of Bhutan; b. Thimphu, Bhutan, Nov. 11, 1955; s. Druk Gyalpo Jigme Dorji Wangchuk and Queen Ashi Kesang; married; 8 children. Student, North Point, Darjeeling, Wangchuk Acad., Paro, Bhutan, 1970-72; also in Eng. Crown prince, 1972, succeeded to throne, 1972, coronated King of Bhutan, head of state, 1974—; chmn. Planning Commn. Bhutan, 1972—, Coun. of Ministers, 1972—; also comdr.-in-chief armed forces. Address: The Royal Secretariat, Tashichhodzong, Thimphu Bhutan*

WANGLEE, THAMNOON, airline executive; married; 2 children. Grad., U. North Tex. Founder Alphatec Electronics, 1988—; pres. Thai Airways; sec. Thai Airways, Bangkok; senator Thailand. Dir. fundraising Thai Red Cross Soc. Fax: 662-513-5532. Office: Thai Airways, 89 Vibhavadi Rangsit Rd, Bangkok 10900, Thailand*

WANI, GHULAM MOHY-UD-DIN, education director; b. Koelmukam, Kashmir, India, Mar. 9, 1949; s. Sona-Ullah and Sara Wani; children: Paras, Gazanfer. B in Vet. Sci. and Animal Husbandry, Agrl. U., Rajasthan, India, 1972; M in Vet. Sci., GB Pant U., India, 1976; DVM, Vet. Sch., Hannover, Germany, 1984; PhD, IVRI, Izatnagar, India, 1985. Vet. asst. surgeon, 1972-74; rsch. assoc. GBPUA&T, Pantanagar, 1974-75; jr. scientist ICAR, IVRI/CIRG, 1976-81; sr. scientsit ICAR, CIRG, 1982-85; prof., head chief scientist S.K. U. Agrl. Scis., 1986-90, assoc. dean, dir. rsch., 1991-92, dean vet., 1992-95, dir. ext. edn., 1995—; vis. scientist U. Hohenheim, Germany, 1991, 94. Author: Pregnancy Diagnosis in Farm Animals, Advanced Techniques in Animal Reproduction, Embryo Biotechnology in Sheep and Goats; contbr. articles to profl. jours. Recipient Dr. Z.A. Hashmi award on animal rsch. and edn. U. Faisalabad, 1996, Merit of Honor, Ministry Info., Govt. India, 1997; named Internat. Acad. Ptnr., European Union, 1995; DAAD fellow U. Hohenhimi, 1980, Disting. fellow German Rsch. Found., 1991. Mem. J&K Acad. Scis. Avocations: poetry, social work, architecture, drawing, palmotry. Fax: 091-0194-461317. Home: Bismillah Ho Parraypora, Bhagat-e-Barzullah Box 461, Srinagar Kashmir 190 001, India Office: Sher-e-Kashmir U Agrl Sci, PO Box 461, Shalimar Srinagar Kashmir 190001, India

WANKE, KLAUS, physician, psychiatry educator; b. Kiel, Fed. Republic Germany, Nov. 18, 1933; s. Claus Henning Werner Konrad and Ella Lina Berta (Heuer) W.; m. Susanne Wanke, Sept. 18, 1998; 1 child, Miriam. Student, U. Heidelberg, 1954-56; D of Medicine, U. Hamburg, Heidelberg/Hamburg, Fed. Republic Germany, 1959. Intern Internal U. Clinic, Hamburg, 1960; staff psychiatrist Psychiat. U. Clinic, Hamburg, 1961-67; asst. med. dir. Psychiat. U. Clinic, Frankfurt, Fed. Republic Germany, 1967-72; lectr. Psychiat. U. Clinic, Frankfurt, 1972; prof., head Psychiat. U. Clinic II, Frankfurt, 1973-78; supt. Psychiat. U. Clinic, Homburg, Fed. Republic Germany, 1978—; professorial chair psychiatry U. Saarland, Homburg, 1978—, dean faculty of medicine, 1990-92. Author books on psychiat. subjects; contbr. articles to profl. publs. Mem. German Soc. Psychiatry, German Soc. Neurology. Avocation: collecting tin figurines. Office: Univ Kliniken, Dept Psy and Psychotherapy, D-66421 Homburg Germany

WANKMUELLER, JOHN ROBERT, finance company executive; b. N.Y.C., Sept. 6, 1949; s. Robert and Mary Wankmueller; married; children: Donna, David. BA in Math., Fordham U., 1971; MA in Math. Edn., NYU, 1974. Tchr. math. N.Y.C. Schs., 1972-80; systems analyst AT&T, White Plains, N.Y., 1980-91; dir. software engring. MasterCard Internat., Purchase, N.Y., 1991-93; dir. tech. assessment MasterCard Internat., Purchase, 1993-94, sr. dir. electronic commerce, 1994-96, prin. electronic commerce, 1996-98, v.p. electronic commerce, 1998—. Inventor in field. Cpl. USMCR, 1971-74. Recipient Best Banking Application award OnLine Banking Assn., San Francisco, 1997. Avocations: tennis, swimming, basketball. Fax: 914-249-4229. E-mail: john.wankmueller@mastercard.com.

WANLESS, DEREK, bank executive; b. Newcastle, U.K., Sept. 29, 1947; s. Norman Hall and Edna (Charlton) W.; m. Vera West, 1971; 5 children. BA in Math. with honors, MA, King's Coll., Cambridge, Eng.; student, Harvard U.; ScD (hon.), City Univ. With Nat. Westminster Bank, London, 1970—, mktg. mgr. domestic banking divsn., 1980-82, area dir. north-east area, 1982-85, dir. West Yorks area, 1985-86, dir. personal banking svcs., 1986-88, gen. mgr. U.K. br. bus., 1989-90, chief exec. U.K. fin. svcs., 1990-92, dep. group chief exec., group head NatWest Mkts., 1992, dir., 1991—, CEO, 1992-99; mem. bd. dirs Northern Rock plc, Newcastle Upon Tyne, 2000S; dir. NatWest Life, Ulster Bank, Isle of Man Bank, Nat. Westminster Home Loans, Nat. Westminster Ins. Svcs., Lombard North Ctrl., NatWest Mkts.; chmn. MasterCard and Eurocard Mems. (UK and Republic of Ireland) Forum Ltd., 1989. exec. com. The Institut Internat. D'Etudes Bancaires; chmn. Nat. Adv. Coun. for Edn. and Tng. targets; dir. UK-Japan 2000 Group. Chair Adv. Com. Bus. and the Environment, 1993-95, Nat. Forum Mgmt. Edn. and Devel., 1996—; mem. Investors in People U.K. Bd.; freeman City of London; dep. chmn. Bus. in the Cmty.; chmn. Bus. Edn. Leadership Team; chmn. Adv. Com. on Bus. and Environment II, 1991-93, chmn. fin. sector working party, 1992-93. Fellow Inst. of bankers; mem. Fin. Sector Working Group (chmn. 1991-93), Bus. in Environment, EC Consultative Forum on Environment, World Bus. Coun. Sustainable Devel., Inst. Statisticians, Brit.-Am. C. of C. (adv. bd.), Reform Club. Avocations: sports, chess, music, walking, gardening. Office: Northern Rock plc, Northern Rock House, Newcastle Upon Tyne NE3 4PL, England*

WANTZ, GEORGE EDWARD, surgeon; b. Charlevoix, Mich., Apr. 14, 1923; s. George Edward and Dorothy Alice (Armstrong) W.; m. Mary Jane Dyble, 1947 (dec. 1961); m. Diana Dilworth, Sept. 30, 1965; children: David DeWeese Hoguet, Diana Logan Hoguet. MD, U. Mich., 1946. Diplomate Am. Bd. Surgery. Intern Wesley Meml. Hosp., Chgo., 1947, Presbyn. Hosp., Chgo., 1948; asst. resident Presbyn. Hosp., 1949; intern in surgery The N.Y. Hosp., N.Y.C., 1949-50, asst. resident, 1950-52, 1954-55, resident, 1955-56, attending physician, 1956—; assoc. prof. Cornell U., N.Y.C., 1956-90, prof., 1990—. Author: Atlas of Hernia Surgery, 1991, Hernia Healers, An Illustrated History, 1998; editor: Problems in Surgery, 1961. Served to capt. USMC, 1952-54. Fellow ACS; mem. Am. Geriatric Soc., N.Y. Acad. of Medicine, Am. Surg. Assn., Academie de Chirurgie, Soc. Surgery of the Alimentary Tract, Century Assn. Republican. Home: 950 Park Ave New York NY 10028-0320

WAPLER, VINCENT, legal auctioneer; b. Linares, Spain, Dec. 3, 1947; s. Jean Jacques and Helene (Huffmann de Cock) W. M. History of Art, Lille; M.Law and Bus., Paris. Self-employed legal auctioneer Paris. Author: Jane Poupelet, Sculptor, 1969. Avocations: karate, golf, stag hunting, alpinism, contemporary art collecting. Office: 16 Place Des Vosges, 75004 Paris France

WAPNER, ALAN DEAN, security professional, mayor pro tem; b. Newark, May 26, 1956; s. Gerald Harold and Sandra Linda Wapner; m. Karen Dian Vaughn, Aug. 14, 1977 (div. May 1986); children: Robyn, Jennifer, Bryan, Amber; m. Judith Ann Vasquez, Aug. 29, 1993; 1 child, Sarah. BA in Polit. Sci./Pub. Rels., U. So. Calif., 1978; JD, Whittier Coll., 1981. Police sgt. City of Ontario, Calif., 1982-98, city councilman, 1994-98, mayor pro tem, 1998—; v.p. Ontario-Montclair Elem. Sch. Dist., 1991-94; prin. Alan D. Wapner & Assocs., Ontario, 1994—. Trustee Temple Sholom Ontario, 1994—; vice chmn. bd. dirs. City of Ontario Redevelopment Agy., 1994—, City of Ontario Housing Authority, 1994—; bd dirs. Inland Empire Econ. Partnership, San Bernardino, Calif., 1998—; mem. Calif.-Nev. Super Speed Train Commn., Las Vegas, 1998—. Mem. Pi Kappa Phi (housing corp. pres. 1996—). Republican. Jewish. Avocations: youth sports, baseball, travel. Fax: 909-988-8807. Home: 2733 S Monterey Pl Ontario CA 91761-8703 Office: City of Ontario 303 E B St Ontario CA 91764-4196

WARAKOMSKI, ALPHONSE WALTER JOSEPH, JR., sales and marketing executive; b. N.Y.C., Apr. 1, 1943; s. Alphonse Walter and Mary (Dupnock) W. BS in Chemistry, St. Bonaventure, Allegheny, N.Y., 1968; MBA in Mktg., Keller Grad. Sch., Chgo., 1981. Chemist, lab. mgr. Purification Scis., Geneva, N.Y., 1968-73; applications engr. Pollution Control Industries, Stamford, Conn., 1973; sales mgr. Kopper's Environ. Elements, Balt., 1974; mktg. specialist, regional mgr. Union Carbide Linde, Chgo., 1975-79; sales engr. Dorr Oliver, Chgo., 1980-81; dir. mktg. and sales Linde AG Lotepro, Valhalla, N.Y., 1981—; Contbr. articles to profl. jours. Contbr. articles to profl. jours. Mem. Am. Chem. Soc., Am. Inst. Chem. Engrs., Internat. Ozone Assn. (dir. internat. bd.), Pan Am. Group (group sec.), WEF, AWWA. Home: 15 Brevoort Dr Apt 1C Pomona NY 10970-3077 Office: Linde AG Lotepro 115 E Stevens Ave Valhalla NY 10595-1252

WARBERG, WILLETTA, concert pianist, writer, piano educator; b. Twin Falls, Idaho, June 2, 1932; d. George William Warberg and Ethel Margaret (Sargent) Warberg-Chandler; m. David Jacob Bar-Illan, Sept. 3, 1954 (div.); children: Daniela, Jeremy Oscar. Student, Colo. Women's Coll., 1950-51, Aspen Music Camp, 1951; studied with, Rudolph Firkusny, 1951-53; BS, Mannes Coll. Music, N.Y.C., 1954. Assoc. food editor Look mag., N.Y.C., 1956-61; food editor Status mag., N.Y.C., 1961-62, Ladie's Home Jour., N.Y.C., 1964-66; photog. stylist Gourmet mag., N.Y.C., 1961-64, freelance writer, photog. stylist, 1965-75; pres., owner Willettta Enterprises, advt. agy., Twin Falls, 1976-84; food columinst, music and arts critic Times News, 1978-87; duo-piano ptnr. with Robert Starer, N.Y.C., Woodstock, N.Y., 1991—; pvt. piano tchr., Saugerties, N.Y., 1991—; made feasibility study of restaurant situation in Israel, U.S. Dept. State ICA Point 4 Program, Washington and Israel, 1960; artist-in-residence Holy Cross Concert Series, Kingston, N.Y., 1994—. Concert pianist, Idaho, Oreg., Utah, Wash., Colo., N.Y.C., N.Y. State, 1940—; author: Cooking from Scratch, 1976, Space Age Cookery, 1977; syndicated food columnist Willetta Says, 1978-87; contbr. food and sci. articles to Cosmopolitan, Modern Maturity, Esquire, Sun Valley, Sci. Diegest, also other mags. Bd. dirs. N.W. Opera Assn., 1984-87; pres. bd. dirs. Woodstock Lyric Theatre, 1994—; v.p. bd. dirs. Woodstock Chamber Orch., 1993—; chmn. Friends of the Maverick Concerts Inc., Woodstock, N.Y., 1999—. Winner Rocky Mountain talent search contest Salt Lake Tribune and Salt Lake Telegram, 1949. Mem. Nat. Fedn. Music Clubs, Music Tchrs. Nat. Assn. (cert.), Kingston Music Soc.. Avocations: designing and sewing clothes, painting still lifes, swimming, developing recipes, writing science fiction book.

WARBURG, RICHARD JEREMY, patent lawyer; b. Eng., Apr. 12, 1957; came to U.S., 1981; s. Jeremy and Tessa (Lorant) W.; m. Ruth Passow, Apr. 1, 1984; children: Jeremy, Zachary, Jordan. BSc, Birmingham U., Eng., PhD, 1981; JD, Suffolk U., 1990. Postdoctoral fellow Brandeis U., Waltham, Mass., 1981-83, rsch. assoc., 1984-85; adj. asst. prof. Wellesley (Mass.) Coll., 1982; assoc. Brobeck Phleger & Horrison, San Diego; cons. Air Products and Chems. Corp., Allentown, Pa., 1983-84, U. Mass., Worcester, 1984-86, Nowegian Food Rsch. Inst., Norway, 1984-86. Author various publications. Mem. Mass. Bar Assn., Boston Bar Assn., Am. Soc. Microbiology, Boston Patent Law Assn. Achievements include patent for Microcentrifuge Tube Opener. Office: Brobeck Phleger & Horrison 12390 El Camino Rd San Diego CA 92130

WARBURTON, MINNIE, writer, art educator; b. Beverly, Mass., July 12, 1949; d. Barclay Harding and Margaret McKean (Vernon) W.; 1 child, Samantha. BA, Univ. of the South, 1994, MA in theology, 1994. Writer Procter & Gamble, Cin., 1980-81, ABC, L.A., 1991-82; owner Sargent Gallery, Sewanee, Tenn., 1996-99; owner/tchr. Pink Flamingo Studio, Sewanee, Tenn., 1999—. Author: Mykonos, 1979; author poetry. Fund raising vol. Sewanee Ele. Sch., 1997, vol. Hospitalty Shop, 1999. Mem. Writers Guild Am. E-mail: minsam@edge.net. Office: Pink Flamingo Studios 201 Kentucky Ave Sewanee TN 37375-2101

WARBURTON, PHILIP JOHN, management executive; b. Burnley, Eng., Jan. 29, 1957; s. Vincent and Joan Warburton; m. Teresa Neale, Apr. 12, 1982; children: Emma, Christopher, Rebecca. BS, U. Manchester, Eng., 1978; Postgrad. Diploma Mgmt. Studies, Manchester Poly., 1983. Mgmt. svcs. coord. Kellogg Co. (G.B.) Ltd., Manchester, 1979-97; head mgmt. svcs. Transport Devel. Group, Manchester, 1987-89; mgmt. cons. Coopers & Lybrand, Manchester, 1989-93, Melbourne, Australia, 1993-95; head ops. and logisticvs Coca-Cola Amatil, Sydney, Australia, 1995-98, gen. mgr. ops., 1998—. Mem. Australian Inst. Mgmt. Roman Catholic. Avocations: bushwalking, swimming, computing. E-mail: Phil.Warburton@ANZ.C-CAMATIL.com. Office: Coca-Cola Amatil, 71 MacQuarie St, Sydney NSW, Australia 2229

WARBURTON, RALPH JOSEPH, architect, engineer, planner, educator; b. Kansas City, Mo., Sept. 5, 1935; s. Ralph Gray and Emma Frieda (Niemann) W.; m. Carol Ruth Hychka, June 14, 1958; children: John Geoffrey, Joy Frances W. Tracey. B.Arch., MIT, 1958; M.Arch., Yale U., 1959, M.C.P., 1960. Registered architect, Colo., Conn., Fla., Ill., La., Md., N.J., N.Y., Va., D.C.; registered profl. engr., Conn., Fla., N.J., N.Y.; registered cmty. planner, Mich., N.J.; lic. interior designer, Fla. With various archtl. planning and engring. firms Kansas City, Mo., 1952-55, Boston, 1956-58, N.Y.C., 1959-62, Chgo., 1962-64; chief planning Skidmore, Owings & Merrill, Chgo., 1964-66; spl. asst. for urban design HUD, Washington, 1966-72, cons., 1972-77; prof. architecture, archtl. engring. and planning U. Miami, Coral Gables, Fla., 1972-2000, chmn. dept. architecture, archtl. engring. and planning, 1972-75, assoc. dean engring. and environ. design, 1973-74, dir. grad. urban and regional planning program, 1973-75, 81, 87-93, prof. emeritus, 2000—; advisor govt. Iran, 1970; advisor govt. France, 1973, govt. Ecuador, 1974, govt. Saudi Arabia, 1985; cons. in field, 1972—, lectr., critic design juror in field, 1965—; mem./chmn. Coral Gables Bd. Archs., 1980-82. Assoc. author: Man-Made America: Chaos or Control, 1963; editor: New Concepts in Urban Transportation, 1968, Housing Systems Proposals for Operation Breakthrough, 1970, Focus on Furniture, 1971, National Community Art Competition, 1971, Defining Critical Environmental Areas, 1974; contbg. editor: Progressive Architecture, 1974-84; editl. adv. bd.: Jour. Am. Planning Assn., 1983-88, Planning for Higher Edn., 1986-94, Urban Design and Preservation Quar., 1987-94; contbr. over 130 articles to profl. jours.; mem. adv. panel Industrialization Forum Quar., 1969-79, archtl. portfolio jury Am. Sch. and Univ., 1993. Mem. Met. Housing and Planning Coun., Chgo., 1965-67; mem. exec. com. Yale U. Arts Assn., 1965-70; pres. Yale U. Planning Alumni Assn., 1983—; mem. ednl. adv. com. Fla. Bd. Architecture, 1975; mem. grievance com. The Fla. Bar, 1996-99. Recipient W.E. Parsons medal Yale U., 1960; recipient Spl. Achievement award HUD, 1972, commendation Fla. Bd. Architecture, 1974, Fla. Trust Historic Preservation award, 1983, Group Achievement award NASA, 1976; Skidmore, Owings & Merrill traveling fellow MIT, 1958; vis. fellow Inst. Architecture and Urban Studies, N.Y.C., 1972-74; NSF grantee, 1980-82. Fellow AIA (nat. housing com. 1968-72, nat. regional devel. and natural resources com. 1974-75, nat. sys. devel. com. 1972-73, nat. urban design com. 1968-73, bd. dirs. Fla. S. chpt. 1974-75), ASCE, Fla. Engring. Soc., Nat. Acad. Forensic Engrs.; mem. NSPE, Am. Inst. Cert. Planners (exec. com. dept. environ. planning 1973-74), Am. Soc. Engring. Edn. (chmn. archtl. engring. divsn. 1975-76), Nat. Sculpture Soc. (allied profl.), Nat. Soc. Arch. Engrs. (founding), Nat. Trust Hist. Preservation (principles and guidelines com. 1967), Am. Soc. Landscape Architects (hon., chmn. design awards jury 1971, 72), Am. Planning Assn. (Fla. chpt. award excellence 1983), Am. Soc. Interior Designers (hon.), Am. Arbitration Assn., Omicron Delta Kappa, Sigma Xi, Tau Beta Pi. Home: 6600 SW 54th Ln South Miami FL 33155-6413 Office: 420 S Dixie Hwy Coral Gables FL 33146-2222 also: U Miami Sch Architecture Coral Gables FL 33124-5010

WARD, ALISTER CURTIS, molecular biologist, researcher; b. Ballarat, Victoria, Australia, Mar. 28, 1968; s. William James and Beverly Thelma (Robinson) W.; m. Tania Frances De Koning, Oct. 8, 1994. BSc with honors, U. Melbourne, Australia, 1989, PhD, 1994. Rsch. scholar Biomolecular Rsch. Inst., Melbourne, 1990-93; rsch. officer U. Melbourne, 1994-96; rsch. fellow Erasmus U., Rotterdam, Netherlands, 1997-99; sr. rsch. fellow Ludwig Inst. for Cancer Rsch., Melbourne, 2000—; demonstrator U. Melbourne, 1989-93; tutor Queen's Coll., Melbourne, 1992-93. Contbr. articles to profl. jours. Scholar Ormond Coll., 1986-87; postgrad. rsch. grantee Australian Govt., 1990-93; European Molecular Biology Orgn. fellow, 1997, 98; Viertel sr. med. rsch. fellow, 2000. Mem. Australian Soc. for Med. Rsch. (mem. schs. com.), Australian Soc. for Biochemistry and Molecular Biology (fellowship 1996). Avocations: hiking, duathlons, European history, cuisine, education. Office: Ludwig Inst Cancer Rsch, PO Box 2008, Royal Melbourne Hosp Parkville 3050, Australia

WARD, ANTHONY JOHN, lawyer; b. L.A., Sept. 25, 1931; s. John P. and Helen C. (Harris) W.; m. Marianne Edle von Graeve, Feb. 20, 1920 (div. 1977); 1 son, Mark Joachim; m. Julia Norby Credell, Nov. 4, 1978 (div. 1999). BA, U. So. Calif., 1953; LLB, U. Calif., Berkeley, 1956. Bar: Calif. 1957. Assoc. Ives, Kirwan & Dibble, L.A., 1958-61; ptnr. Marapese and Ward, Hawthorne, Calif., 1961-69; pvt. practice Torrance, Calif., 1969-76; ptnr. Ward, Gaunt & Credell, Torrance, 1976—. Served to 1st lt. USAF, 1956-58. Mem. ABA, Blue Key, Calif. Trial Lawyers Assn., Lambda Chi Alpha. Office: Pavilion A 21525 Hawthorne Blvd Torrance CA 90503-6600

WARD, BRIAN ERNEST, historian, educator, writer; b. Nolton, Lincolnshire, Eng., Apr. 24, 1961; s. Gerald Thomas and Edith Mary (Adshead) W. BA in Am. Studies with honors, U. East Anglia, Norwich, Eng., 1984; PhD in History, Cambridge (Eng.) U., 1995. Temp. lectr. in Am. history U. Durham, Eng., 1990-91; lectr. in Am. history U. Newcastle upon Tyne, Eng., 1991-98, reader in Am. history, 1998—; assoc. prof. U. Fla., 2000—; dir. Martin Luther King Jr. Meml. confs., Newcastle-upon-Tyne, 1993, 98. Author: Just My Soul Responding: Rhythm & Blues, Black Consciousness and Race Relations, 1998 (Am. Book award 1999, James A. Rawley prize 1999); co-editor: The Making of Martin Luther King and the Civil Rights Movement, 1996. Recipient Archie K. Davis fellow North Carolinana Soc., 1995; Carter G. Woodson Inst. postdoctoral fellow U. Va., 1995-96, Arts and Humanities Rsch. Bd. fellow, London, 1999—. Mem. Brit. Assn. for

Am. Studies, Orgn. Am. Historians, So. Hist. Assn. Office: U Fla Dept History 4131 Turlington Hall Gainesville FL 32611-7320 Home: 1714 NW 11th Rd Gainesville FL 32605-5322

WARD, COLLEEN ANN, psychologist, educator; b. New Orleans, Aug. 19, 1952; d. William Raymond Ward and Margaret Anna Lebrun; m. David Patrick Verrinder. BS summa cum laude, Spring Hill Coll., 1974; PhD in Psychology, U. Durham, Eng., 1977. Postdoctoral fellow U. of the W.I., Trinidad, 1978-79; sci. lectr. U. Malaysia, Penang, 1979-82; lectr. Nat. U. of Singapore, 1982-86, assoc. prof., 1993-2000; sr. lectr. U. Canterbury, Christchurch, New Zealand, 1986-92; prof. Victoria U. Wellington, New Zealand, 2000—; trainer Singapore Police, 1992-97, New Zealand Ministry of External Rels. and Trade, 1991, SOS, Singapore, 1985-86; cons., trainer Assn. of Women for Action and Rsch., 1992—. Author: (with A. Furnham and S. Bochner) Psychology of Culture Shock, 2000, Attitudes Toward Rape: Feminist and Social Psychological Perspectives, 1995; editor: Altered States of Consciousness and Mental Health: A Cross Cultural Perspective, 1989; co-editor (with T. Sugiman, M. Karasawa, J. Liu) Progress in Asian Social Psychology, 1999. Rsch. grant Asia 2000, 1998, Nat. U. of Singapore, 1992—, Social Sci. Rsch. Fund, 1989-92. Mem. Internat. Assn. for Cross-Cultural Psychology (sec. gen. 1992-94), Acad. of Intercultural Rsch., Asian Assn. of Social Psychology. Avocations: travel, tennis. Home: 80 Volga St Island Bay, Wellington New Zealand Office: Victoria U Wellington, PO Box 600, Wellington New Zealand

WARD, CURTIS WILLIAM, process engineer; b. Rochester, N.Y., Aug. 14, 1972; s. Joseph Wells and Jo Ann Ward. BS, Rensselaer Poly. Inst., 1993; MS, Cornell U., 1996, PhD, 1998. Rsch. asst. Clarkson U., Potsdam, N.Y., 1988-89; physicist Xerox Corp., Webster, N.Y., 1992-93; rsch. asst. Rensselaer Poly. Inst., Troy, N.Y., 1992-93, Cornell U., Ithaca, N.Y., 1993-98; sr. process engr. Intel Corp., Hillsboro, Oreg., 1998—. Contbr. articles to profl. jours. Rsch. fellow NSF, 1993. Mem. Am. Inst. Physics/Soc. Physics Students, Soc. Automotive Engrs., Sports Car Club Am. Avocations: auto racing, electronics. Fax: (503-613-8963. E-mail: Curtis.W.Ward@intel.com. Home: 309 NE Edison St Hillsboro OR 97124-3133 Office: Intel Corp 5200 NE Elam Young Pkwy Hillsboro OR 97124-6497

WARD, DOUGLAS ANDREW, Spanish and special education educator; b. Elgin, Ill., Mar. 24, 1958; s. Joseph James Ward and Agnes Jane Krecioch. BA, Rockford Coll., 1994, MAT, 1997. Cert. Spanish educator, Ill. Cook, bartender, asst. mgr. Nordic Steak Ho., W. Dundee, Ill., 1976-80; tel. operator Ill. Bell, Elgin, 1980-82; long distance tel. operator AT&T, Rockford, Ill., 1987-94; distn. clk. U.S. Post Office, Rockford, 1994-99; bilingual LD resource tchr. Barbour Two-Way Lang., Rockford, 1999, Nashold Sch., Rockford, 1999—. With USN, 1982-86. Mem. Phi Sigma Iota. Democrat. Roman Catholic. Avocations: singing, gardening, reading, soccer, piano. Home: 316 Dawn Ave Rockford IL 61107-5009 Office: Nashold Sch 3303 20th St Rockford IL 61109-2398

WARD, ELIZABETH DESPARD, medical association administrator; b. London, Oct. 10, 1926; d. Deny Ashley Ferion and Joyce (Fleming) Rynd; m. Nigel Yeoward Peirce, May 3, 1950; children: Susie, Timothy, Rebecca. Student, Cheltenham Ladies' Coll., Eng. Sales dir. N.Y.P. Ward & Co., Bordon, Hanis, Eng., 1956-66; pres. Brit. Kidney Patient Assn., Bordon, Eng., 1975—. Author: Timbo: A Struggle for Survival, 1986. Named Officer Order Brit. Empire, 1992. Avocations: opera, walking, music. Home: Oakhanger Pl, Bordon England Office: Brit Kidney Patient Assn, Bordon GU35 9JZ, England

WARD, GEORGE FRANK, JR., ambassador; b. Jamaica, N.Y., Apr. 9, 1945; s. George Frank and Hildegard Louisa (Evans) W.; m. Peggy Elizabeth Coote, June 12, 1965; 1 child, Pamela Ward Priester. BA, U. Rochester, 1965; MPA, Harvard U., 1980. U.S. vice consul Am. Consulate, Hamburg, Germany, 1970-72; ops. officer Office Sec. State, Washington, 1972-74; U.S. consul Am. Consulate Gen., Genoa, Italy, 1974-76; polit. officer Am. Embassy, Rome, 1976-77, exec. asst., 1977-79; polit. officer Am. Embassy, Bonn, Germany, 1984-85, dep. chief mission, 1989-92; polit.-mil. officer U.S. Dept. State, Washington, 1980-84, dep. dir. European Security and Polit. Affairs, 1985-88, prin. dep. asst. sec. Bur. Internat. Orgns., 1992-96; U.S. ambassador to Namibia U.S. Dept. State, 1996-99; dir. tng. program U.S. Inst. Peace, Washington, 1999—. Capt. USMC, 1965-69. Decorated Vietnamese Cross Gallantry (Vietnam); Naval Commendaton medal; recipient Presdl. Meritorious Svc. awards, 1992, 94, Disting. Honor award U.S. State Dept., 1992. Mem. Am. Fgn. Svc. Assn., Phi Beta Kappa. Episcopalian. Avocations: classical music, running, skiing, tennis. Home: 3404 Walnut Hill Ct Falls Church VA 22042-3546

WARD, HAROLD WILLIAM COWPER, oncologist, educator; b. Southend-On-Sea, Essex, Eng., Nov. 24, 1925; came to U.S., 1976; s. William Samuel and Winifred (Marjorie) W.; m. Barbara Mary Sanderson, Oct. 6, 1962; children: Belinda Mary Jane Morris, Rosemary Sylvia, Timothy Harold. MB BS, U. London, 1953; diploma in med. radiation therapy, Royal Coll. Physicians London, 1957. Cert. therapeutic radiology Am. Bd. Radiology, cert. basic cardiopulmonary resuscitation Am. Heart Assn. Intern Charing Cross Hosp., London, 1953, resident in radiotherapy, 1955-56; intern Royal Postgrad. Med. Sch., London, 1954-55; intern in surgery The Bolinbroke Hosp., London, 1954; sr. resident in radiotherapy Edinburgh (Scotland) Royal Infirmary, 1958-59; rsch. fellow in radiotherapy St. Bartholomew's Hosp., London, 1959-65; cons. radiotherapist Queen Elizabeth Hosp., Birmingham, Eng., 1965-75; clin. lectr. U. Birmingham, 1965-75; dir. radiation oncology Parkland Meml. Hosp., Dallas, 1976-78; prof. radiology U. Tex. Southwestern Med. Sch., Dallas, 1976-78; clin. prof. radiology divsn. radiation oncology U. Cin., 1978-82, assoc. prof. medicine divsn. hematology, 1980-82; dir. radiation oncology Meml. Med. Ctr., Corpus Christi, Tex., 1982-95; clin. assoc. prof. radiation oncology U. Tex. Med. Br., Galveston, 1984-90; mem. Oncology Assocs., Inc., Cin., 1978-82; travelling fellow in radiotherapy Meml. Hosp. for Cancer and Allied Diseases, N.Y.C., M.D. Anderson Hosp., Houston, U. Calif. Med. Sch., San Francisco, 1965; mem. U.K. Med. Rsch. Coun. Working Party for study of embryonal tumors of childhood, 1967-75; mem. steering com. U.K. Nat. Ovarian Cancer Clin. Survey, 1967-75; site vis. team NCI, 1984-87; physician advisor Tex. Med. Found. Peer Rev. Orgn., 1985—; mem. regional quality rev. com., 1989—. Bd. dirs. Symphony Orch., Corpus Christi, 1992-95. Fellow Royal Coll. Radiology; mem. AMA, Internat. Soc. for Pediatric Oncology, Royal Coll. Surgeons Eng., Royal Coll. Physicians, Soc. Apthecaries, Am. Soc. Therapeutic Radiologists, Am. Soc. Clin. Oncology, Am. Coll. Radiology, Am. Cancer Soc. (Nueces County br. 1984-88), Brit. Inst. Radiology, Brit. Med. Assn., Brit. Assn. for Cancer Rsch., Tex. Med. Assn., Southwestern Oncology Group, Nueces County Med. Soc. (pub. rels., environ. pollution control, Cancer adv. com. 1984-98, consultative fee rev. com. 1988-98). Episcopalian. Avocations: music, gardening. Home: 131 Naples St Corpus Christi TX 78404-1828

WARD, HARRY MERRILL, history educator; b. West Lafayette, Ind., July 30, 1929; s. Hiley L. and Agnes W. Student, U. Ill., 1947-49; BA, William Jewell Coll., 1951; MA, Columbia U., 1954, PhD, 1960. Social investigator N.Y.C. Dept. Welfare, 1958-59; asst. prof. Georgetown (Ky.) Coll., 1959-61; from asst. to assoc. prof. Morehead (Ky.) State U., 1961-65; vis. assoc. prof. So. Ill. U., 1967-68; assoc. prof. history U. Richmond, Va., 1965-77, prof. history, 1977—, William Binford Vest prof. history, 1993-99, William Binford Vest prof. history emeritus, 1999—; cons. in field. Author: The United Colonies of New England, 1643-1690, 1961, Department of War, 1781-95, 1962, 81, Unite or Die: Intercolony Relations, 1690-1763, 1971, Statism in Plymouth Colony, 1973, Duty, Honor or Country: General George Weedon and the American Revolution, 1979, Richmond: An Illustrated History, 1985, 88, Charles Scott and the Spirit of '76, 1988, Major General Adam Stephen and the Cause of American Liberty, 1989, Colonial America, 1607-1763, 1990, American Revolution: Nationhood Achieved, 1763-1788, 1994, General William Maxwell and the New Jersey Continentals, 1997, The War for Independence and the Transformation of American Society, 1999; co-author: Richmond During the Revolution, 1775-1783, 1977; contbr. articles to profl. publs. With USMC, 1951-53. Recipient Fraunces Tavern Mus. Book award, 1990; Scholar award in history Va. Social Sci. Assn., 1992. Fellow Pilgrim Soc.; mem. Am. Hist. Assn., Orgn. Am. Historians, So. Hist. Assn. Office: U Richmond Dept History Richmond VA 23173-0180

WARD, HILEY HENRY, journalist, educator; b. Lafayette, Ind., July 30, 1929; s. Hiley Lemen and Agnes (Fuller) W.; m. Charlotte Burns, May 28, 1951 (div. 1971); children: Dianne, Carolee, Marceline, Laurel; m. Joan Bastel, Aug. 20, 1977. BA, William Jewell Coll., 1951; MA, Berkeley Bapt. Div. Sch., 1953; MDiv, McCormick Theol. Sem., Chgo., 1955; student, Northwestern U., 1948, 54, 56-57; PhD, U. Minn., 1977. News asst. Christian Advocate, 1953-55; editor jr. publs. David C. Cook Pub. Co., 1956-59; editor Record, Buchanan, Mich., 1960; religion editor Detroit Free Press, 1960-73; asst. prof. journalism Mankato (Minn.) State U., 1974-76; assoc. prof. journalism Wichita (Kans.) State U., 1976; prof. journalism Temple U., Phila., 1977-96, prof. emeritus, 1997—, dir. news-editorial sequence, journalism dept., 1977-80, chmn. dept., 1978-80; instr. journalism Oakland U., Rochester, Mich., evenings 1963-66. Author: Creative Giving, 1958, Space-age Sunday, 1960, Documents of Dialogue, 1966, God and Marx Today, 1968, Ecumania, 1968, Rock 2000, 1969, Prophet of the Black Nation, 1969, The Far-out Saints of the Jesus Communes, 1972, Religion 2101 A.D., 1975, Feeling Good About Myself, 1983, Professional Newswriting, 1985, My Friend's Beliefs: A Young Reader's Guide to World Religions, 1988, Reporting in Depth, 1991, Magazine and Feature Writing, 1993, Mainstreams of American Media History, 1997; editor: Media History Digest, 1979-94; exec. editor: Kidbits, 1981-82; book editor: Editor and Publisher, 1989-98; contbr. articles to profl. jours., feature articles to newspapers and mags.; also short stories and poems. Religious Pub. Rels. Coun. fellow, 1970; recipient citation Religious Heritage Am., 1962, Leidt award Epsic. Ch., 1969, citation U.S. Am. Revolution Bicentennial Adminstrn., 1976, Text and Acad. Authors citation, 1997. Mem. Religion Newswriters Assn. (pres. 1970-72), Am. Soc. Journalists and Authors, Am. Journalism Historians Assn. (bd. dirs. 1994-96, Kobre lifetime achievement award 1999), Overseas Press Club. Home: PO Box 399 1263 Folly Rd Warrington PA 18976-1422

WARD, JOE HENRY, JR., retired lawyer; b. Childress, Tex., Apr. 18, 1930; s. Joe Henry and Helen Ida (Chastain) W.; m. Carlotta Agnes Abreu, Feb. 7, 1959; children: James, Robert, William, John. BS in Acctg., Tex. Christian U., 1952; JD, So. Meth. U., 1964. Bar: Tex. 1964, Va. 1972, D.C. 1974; CPA, Tex. Mgr. Alexander Grant & Co. CPA's, Dallas, 1956-64; atty. U.S. Treasury, 1965-68; tax counsel U.S. Senate Fin. Com., 1968-72; pvt. practice Washington, 1972-83; asst. gen. counsel, tax mgr. Epic Holdings, Ltd. and Crysopt Corp., 1983-87; pvt. practice Washington and Va., 1987-95; ret., 1995. Lt. USNR, 1952-56. Mem. ABA, AICPA, Am. Assn. Atty.-CPA's, Univ. Club. Home: 2639 Mann Ct Falls Church VA 22046-2721

WARD, ARCHBISHOP JOHN ALOYSIUS, archbishop; b. Jan. 24, 1929; s. Eugene and Hannah (Cheetham) W. Ed., Prior Park Coll., Bath, Eng. Received Capuchin Franciscan Friar, 1945; solemn profession, 1950, ordained priest, 1953; with Diocesan Travelling Mission, Menevia, 1954-60; guardian and parish priest Peckham, London, 1960-66; provincial definitor, 1963-69, provincial dir. of vocations, 1963-69, min. provincial, 1969-70; gen. definitor Rome, 1970-80; bishop coadjutor Menevia, 1980, bishop, 1981-83; archbishop Cardiff, Wales, 1983—. Office: Archbishop's House, 41-43 Cathedral Rd, Cardiff CF1 9HD, Wales*

WARD, JON DAVID, insurance company executive; b. Marshalltown, Iowa, Nov. 30, 1944; s. Wiley Granger and Maxine Lucille (Culbertson) W.; children: Wendy, Stacey, Christine. BS in Acctg., U. No. Iowa, 1969; MBA, Ill. State U., 1973. Cert. internal auditor; CLU. Audit dir. State Farm Ins. Cos., Bloomington, Ill., 1969—. Contbr. articles to profl. jours. and chpts. to books. Ct.-apptd. spl. advocate Child Protection Network and Children's Advocacy Ctr., Bloomington, 1997—; sec. Bloomington-Normal Sister Cities Commn., 1989-95. Fellow Life Mgmt. Inst.; mem. Inst. Internal Auditors (bd. dirs. 1984-97). Methodist. Avocations: racquetball, running, skiing, travel, reading. Home: 19325 Great Crane Rd Bloomington IL 61704-5231 Office: State Farm Ins Cos 1 State Farm Plz # B-2 Bloomington IL 61710-0001

WARD, KATHERINE NORA, medical virologist, educator; b. Brighton, Sussex, Eng., Mar. 14, 1948; d. Wilfred and Nancy Ward. BSc with honors, U. London, 1969, PhD, 1973; MB BChir, U. Cambridge, Eng., 1983, MA, 1990. Registered med. practitioner. Fellow Kennedy Rheumatology Inst., London, 1972-74; rsch. assoc. pathology dept. U. Cambridge, 1974-79; house officer Gen. and Addenbrooke's Hosps., Newmarket and Cambridge, 1984-85; registrar Pub. Health Lab., Manchester, Eng., 1985-87; clin. lectr. U. Cambridge, 1987-91; hon. sr. registrar Addenbrooke's Hosp., Cambridge, 1987-91; fellow, dir. studies Christ's Coll., Cambridge, 1987-91; sr. lectr., hon. cons. Royal Postgrad. Med. Sch./Hammersmith Hosp., London, 1991-98; cons. virologist, hon. sr. lectr. U. Coll. London Hosp. Trust, 1998—; mem. nat. standing sci. com. on virology Pub. Health Lab. Svc., 1996-98; mem. Pub. Health Lab. Svc. forum on diagnosis and mgmt. of immunocompromised patients, 2000, HIV Lab Diagnostic Network, 1999—; mem. med. res. coun. subgroup on Inflammatory Bowel Disorders and Autism, 1999-2000, antiviral working party Brit. Soc. Antimicrobial Chemotherapy, 1997—. Contbr. sci. papers to internat. jours. Rsch. grantee U.K. Med. Rsch. Coun., U.K. Action Rsch., Leukemia Rsch. Fund, The Wellcome Trust. Fellow Royal Coll. Pathologists; mem. Brit. Soc. for Immunology, Soc. for Gen. Microbiology, British Soc. Antimicrobial Chemotherapy, London Virus Group. Office: U Coll London Med Sch, Windeyer Bldg 46 Cleveland, London W1P 6DB, England

WARD, KEITH ALBERT, electronics engineer; b. Worcester, Eng., July 28, 1955; s. Harold Thomas and Irma Lisalotta (Hamphelt) W.; 1 child, Stephanie Alice. Degree in electronics, Tech. Coll., 1986. TV engr. Express TV, Malvern, England, 1972-80; svc. mgr. R. Hales Ltd., Cheltenham, England, 1980-85; sr. R&D engr. Insight Vision Systems, Malvern, 1985—; trainer overseas agts. Insight Vision, 1985-93. Mem. IEEE. Conservative. Mem. Church of England. Avocations: golf, reading, television, cinema. Home: 22 Matravers Rd, Malvern England

WARD, KEITH DOUGLAS, engineering research director; b. Birmingham, Eng., Feb. 25, 1955; s. Thomas Derek and Doreen Margaret (Johnson) W.; m. Hilary Janet Stubbs, Jan. 28, 1978. BA with honors, MA, Cambridge (Eng.) U., 1977; PhD, U. Birmingham, 1988. Rsch. scientist Def. Rsch. Agy., Eng., 1977-95; dir. TW Rsch. Ltd., Malvern, Eng., 1995—; chmn. tech. corp. panel internat. panel of experts on radar signal processing, Eng., 1988-95. Contbr. articles to profl. jours. Recipient Mountbatten prize, 1990. Fellow Inst. Elec. Engrs. (profl. group hon. editor), Royal Acad. Engrng.; mem. IEEE. Avocations: travel, walking, photography, music, gardening. Home and Office: Harcourt Barn, Harcourt Rd, Malvern WR14 4DW, England

WARD, KENNETH G., agricultural products executive; b. Bath, N.Y., Mar. 30, 1946; s. Kenneth Duel and Katherine E. (Gray) W.; m. Sharon Fowler, Apr. 22, 1966; chcildren: Scott Manley, Wendy Jo, Erica. AAS in Bus. Agrl., Alfred State Coll., 1966; BSA in Agrl. Econ., U. Ga., 1968. V.p. M.J. Ward & Son Inc., Bath, 1966-76, pres., 1976—. Chmn. bd. Village of Bath, 1978—; commr. Bath Electric Gas & Water, 1994—; pres. Bath Ctrl. Sch., 1986-96. Mem. Cooperative Feed Dealers (bd. dirs. 1976—, pres. 1991-99), Elks (exauted ruler). Republican. Protestant. Avocations: hunting, fishing. Office: MJ Ward & Son Inc PO Box 747 Bath NY 14810-0747

WARD, LESLIE, physicist; b. Sheffield, England, May 4, 1925; s. John Walter and Annie (Higgins) W.; m. Freda Annis Marper, July 24, 1954; children: Catherine, Richard. BSc, Sheffield U., 1945, MSc, 1949; PhD, London U., 1955. Rsch. physicist William Jessop & Sons, Sheffield, 1945-47; lectr. Univ. Coll. Gold Coast, Ghana, 1949-56, U. Aston, Birmingham, England, 1957-60; sr. lectr. Rutherford Coll. Tech., Newcastle, England, 1960-62; head dept. Coventry U., England, 1962-82, hon. rsch. fellow, 1982—; cons. Warwickshire Police, England, 1980-93. Author: Optical Constants of Bulk Materials and Films, 1988, 2d edit., 1994; co-author: High Vacuum Technology, 1967; contbr. articles to profl. jours. Fellow Inst. Physics. Avocations: music, art, archaeology. E-mail: lward42862@aol.com. Home: 43 Sunningdale Ave, CV8 2BY Kenilworth Warwickshire, England Office: Coventry U, Priory St, CV1 5FB Coventry England

WARD, LILLIAN HAZEL, music educator; b. Hastings, Colo., Sept. 19, 1920; d. Frank Joseph and Jane (Shields) Baker; m. Peter Joseph Ward, Sept. 12, 1942; children: Mary Jane Eickhoff, Michael George. Student, Western State Coll., 1938-42. Piano tchr. San Francisco, 1951-54, Los Altos, Calif., 1955—. Author: (composition for piano) Girl Scout Song Book, 1957. Leader brownies Girl Scouts USA, San Francisco, 1952-54, Los Altos, Calif., 1955-59; guardian coun. Jobs Daus., Los Altos, 1959-68; tchr., dir. United Meth. Ch., Los Altos, 1955-73. Mem. Nat. Music Tchrs. Assn., Calif. Assn. Profl. Music Tchrs. Avocations: gardening, reading, working with the blind, spending time with grandchildren, watercolor and oil painting. Home: 246 Alicia Way Los Altos CA 94022-2346

WARD, LLEWELLYN ORCUTT, III, oil company executive; b. Oklahoma City, July 24, 1930; s. Llewellyn Orcutt II and Addie (Reisdorph) W.; m. Myra Beth Gungoll, Oct. 29, 1955: children: Casidy Ann, William Carlton. Student, Okla. Mil. Acad. Jr. Coll., 1948-50; BS, Okla. U., 1953; postgrad. Harvard U., 1986. Registered profl. engr., Okla. Dist. engr. Delhi-Taylor Oil Corp., Tulsa, 1955-56; ptnr. Ward-Gungoll Oil Investments, Enid, Okla., 1956—; owner L.O. Ward Oil Ops., Enid, 1963—; mem. Okla. Gov.'s Adv. Coun. on Energy; rep. to Interstate Oil Compact Commn.; bd. dirs. Community Bank and Trust Co. Enid. Chmn. Indsl. Devel. Commn., Enid, 1968—; active YMCA; mem. bd. visitors Coll. Engrng., U. Okla.; mem. adv. coun. Sch. Bus., trustee Phillips U., Enid, Univ. Bd., Pepperdine, Calif.; Okla. chmn. U.S. Olympic Com., 1986—; chmn. bd. Okla. Polit. Action Com., 1974—, Bass Hosp.; Rep. chmn. Garfield County, 1967-69; Rep. nat. committeeman from Okla.; bd. dirs. Enid Indsl. Devel. Found. Served with C.E., U.S. Army, 1953-55. Mem. Ind. Petroleum Assn. Am. (chmn. 1996-98), Okla. Ind. Petroleum Assn. (pres., bd. dirs.), Nat. Petroleum Council, Enid C. of C. (v.p., then pres.), Alpha Tau Omega. Methodist. Clubs: Toastmasters (pres. Enid chpt. 1966), Am. Bus. (pres. 1964). Lodges: Masons, Shriners, Rotary (pres. Enid 1990-91). Home: 900 Brookside Dr Enid OK 73703-6941 Office: 502 S Fillmore St Enid OK 73703-5703

WARD, M. NEIL, research scientist; b. Leeds, Eng., Feb. 18, 1963; s. Michael Stanley and Kay Marion (Wilson) W.; m. Claire Margaret Halls, Mar. 29, 1986 (div. June 1994). BA with honors, U. Oxford, 1985, MA, 1986; PhD in Meteorology, U. Reading, 1994. Sr. sci. officer Hadley Ctr. for Climate Prediction and Rsch., Bracknell, Eng., 1985-95; from rsch. scientist to rsch. assoc. prof. IMGA-CNR/Univ. Okla., Modena, Italy, 1995-98, rsch. assoc. prof., 1998-2000; head forecast devel. Internat. Rsch. Inst. Climate Prediction, LDEO Columbia U., Palisades, N.Y., 2000—; vis. sci. advisor, cons. African climate diagnosis-prediction African Ctr. for Meteorol. Applications to Devel., Niamey, Niger, 1994—; task force mem. climate svcs. World Meteorol. Orgn., Geneva, 1994, internat. programs African climates, 1998—, marine ecosys. variability, 1997—. Co-author: IPCC Scientific Assessment, Climate Change, 1990, 92, 95, Prediction of Interannual Climate, 1993, Analysis of Climate Variability, 1995, Beyond El Niño-Decodal Variability in the Climate System, 1999; contbr. articles to profl. jours. Recipient rsch. prize Norbert Gerbier World Meteorological Orgn., 1996. Fellow Royal Meteorol. Soc. Avocations: jazz and classical music, playing guitar, cricket, football, table tennis coaching. Fax: (845) 680-4864. E-mail: nward@iri.columbia.edu. Office: Columbia U Internat Rsch Inst Clumate Prediction, Lamont-Doherty Earth Observ, 61 Rt 9W Monell Bldg, Palisades Italy

WARD, MARK GORDON, university dean, language educator; b. Hemel Hempstead, Eng., Feb. 4, 1951; s. Alan Gordon and Cicely Jean (Chapman) W.; m. Janet Helen Turner, Aug. 25, 1973; children: Christopher Gordon, Martyn William. BA, King's Coll., London, 1973. Tutorial rsch. scholar Bedford Coll., London, 1974-75; lectr. German Glasgow (Scotland) U., 1975-90, sr. lectr., 1990-97, prof., 1997—, vice dean Faculty of Arts,, 1992-95, dean Faculty of Arts,, 1995-99; dir. studies Crichton Coll., U. Glasgow, 1999—; prin. examiner German, Scottish Exam Bd., Dalkeith, 1987—. Author: Storm: Der Schimmelreiter, 1988, Laughter, Comedy and Aesthetics. Kleist's der Zerbrochne Krug, 1989; editor: From Vormärz to Fin de Siecle, 1986, Perspectives on German Realist Writing, 1995, Romantic Dreams, 1998, Theodor Storm--Narrative Strategies and Patriarchy, 1999. Recipient Willoughby prize English Goethe Soc., London, 1982. Avocations: music, gardening, sport. Home: 8 Crawford Crescent, Lnrkshr Glasgow G71 7DP, Scotland Office: U Glasgow Dept German, University Gardens, Lnrkshr Glasgow G12 8QQ, Scotland

WARD, MICHAEL PATRICK, business executive; b. Bad Kreuznach, Fed. Republic Germany, Jan. 1, 1964; naturalized citizen; s. Glenn Lee and Waldtraut (Lass) W.; divorced; 1 child, Shawn Michael. Cert. motorcycle repair tech., Motorcycle Mechanics Inst., Phoenix, 1994. With Site Mgmt. Inc., La Porte, Tex. Sgt. U.S. Army, 1982-92. Home: 1802 Jane Dr Pasadena CA 77502 Office: Site Mgmt Svcs Inc 400 E Main St La Porte TX 77571-5574

WARD, NINA GILLSON, jewelry store executive; b. Boston, Dec. 19, 1950; d. Rev. John Robert and Patricia (Gillson) Baker; m. Jorge Alberto Lievanos, June 6, 1981 (div.); children: Jeremy John Baker, Wendy Mara Baker, Raoul Salvador Baker-Lievanos; m. David Ward, July 24, 1998; stepchildren: Johnna Ward, Tavi Sterling. Student, Mills Coll., 1969-70; grad. course in diamond grading, Gemology Inst. Am., 1983; student in diamondtology designation, Diamond Coun. Am., 1986—. Cert. store mgr., Jewelers Cert. Coun., Jewelers Am. Artist, tchr. Claremont, Calif., 1973-78; escrow officer Bank of Am., Claremont, 1978-81; retail salesman William Pitt Jewelers, Puente Hills, Montclair, Calif., 1981-83, asst. mgr., 1983; mgr. William Pitt Jewelers, Puente Hills, Santa Maria, Calif., 1983-91, corp. sales trainer, 1988-89; sales and design specialist Merksamer Jewelers, Santa Maria, 1991; mgr. Merksamer Jewelers, San Luis Obispo, Calif., 1991-92, Santa Maria, Calif., 1992-94; diamond specialist cons. Merksamer Jewelers, Santa Maria, 1994-96; pres., ops. mgr. Dancer House Designs, Santa Maria, Calif., 1996; co-owner, pres. primary jewelry designer Dancer House Design Fine Jewelry, Inc., Kennebunk, Maine, 1997—. Artist tapestry hanging Laguna Beach Mus. Art, 1974; exhibited in Nat. Jeweler's Design Competition, 1999. Mem. Cen. Coast Pla. Adv. Bd., 1992. Recipient Cert. Merit Art Bank Am., 1968, 1st pl. Best of show award for jewelry design Maine Jeweler's Assn., 1998. Mem. NAFE, Internat. Platform Assn., Maine Jewelers Assn. (bd. dirs. 1999—), Speaker's Bur., Santa Maria C. of C., Compassion Internat. Republican. Avocations: tapestry weaving, creative writing. Office: Dancer House Design Fine Jewelry 6 York St Kennebunk ME 04043-7154

WARD, RICHARD HURLEY, university dean, writer; b. N.Y.C., Sept. 2, 1939; s. Hurley and Anna C. (Mittasch) W.; children from a previous marriage: Jeanne M., Jonathan B.; m. Michelle Pierczynski, June 15, 1987. BS, John Jay Coll., CUNY, 1968; M in Criminology, U. Calif., Berkeley, 1969, D in Criminology, 1971. Detective N.Y.C. Police Dept., 1962-70; coord. student activities John Jay Coll., N.Y.C., 1970-71, dean students, 1971-75, v.p., 1975-77, vice chancelor, 1977-93; assoc. chancellor and prof. internat. criminology U. Ill., Chgo., 1993-98; exec. dir. Office Internat. Criminal Justice, 1985-99; exec. v.p. MBF Edn. Group, Malaysia, 1996-97; dean Coll. Criminal Justice, Sam Houston State U., Huntsville, Tex., 1999—; vis. prof. Zagazig U., Egypt, Egyptian Police Acad., 1986, East China Inst. Politics and Law, Shanghai, 1990-91; lectr., various confs. in China, Egypt, Russia, Italy, Eng., Peru, Germany, Vietnam and U.S., 1983—. Author: (with others) Police Robbery Control Manual, 1975; Introduction to Criminal Investigation, 1975, An Anti-Corruption Manual for Administrators in Law Enforcement; (with Robert McCormack) Quest for Quality, 1984; gen. editor Foundations of Criminal Justice, 46 vols., 1972-75; editor: (with Austin Fowler) Police and Law Enforcement, Vol. I, 1972; Police and Law Enforcement, Vol. II, 1975; (with Harold Smith) International Terrorism: The Domestic Response, 1982, International Terrorism: Operational Issues, 1988; co-author: (with James Osterburg) Criminal Investigation: A Method for Reconstructing the Past, 1992, 3d edit., 1999. Mem. Near West Side Cmty. Conservation Coun., 1982-96, Mayor of Chgo.'s Blue Ribbon Pannel on Police Promotion; varsity baseball coach U. Ill., Chgo., 1980-82, John Jay Coll. Criminal Justice, N.U.C., 1971-72; chief investigator Mayor's Commn. Police Integrity, 1998. Cpl. USMC, 1957-61. Recipient Leonard Reisman award John Jay Coll. Criminal Justice, 1968, Alumni Achievement award, 1978, Richard McGee award U. Calif., Berkeley Sch. Criminology, 1971, Friendship medal Peoples Republic of China, 1994, Hans Mattick award Ill. Acad. Criminology, 1999; Justice Dept. fellow U. Calif., Berkeley, 1971. Mem. ASPA, Acad. Criminal Justice Scis. (pres. 1977-78, Founder's award

1985), Internat. Assn. Chiefs of Police (chmn. edn. and tng. sect. 1974-75), Am. Assn. for Higher Edn., Am. Acad. for Profl. Law Enforcement (nat. bd. dirs. 1978-85), Sigma Delta Chi. Office: Sam Houston State U Coll Criminal Justice Huntsville TX 77341

WARD, ROBERT RICHARD, lawyer; b. Spencer, Iowa, Nov. 7, 1948. BA, U. Calif., Berkeley, 1971; MBA, Calif. State U., Hayward, 1974; JD, Pepperdine U., 1978. Bar: Calif. 1978; U.S. Dist. Ct. (cen. dist.) 1979; U.S. Supreme Ct. 1978. Sr. ptnr. Mainstreet Law Offices, Inc., Yorba Linda, Calif., 1981—; real estate broker Award Properties, Yorba Linda, Calif., 1990—; bd. dirs. Colorbrite, Inc., Huntington Beach, Calif., 1990-96, Nat. Recreational Corp., San Jose, 1983-96, Ednl. Found., Yorba Linda, 1992-94, Sino Am., Dalian, China, 1992-96. Co-author: Alaska Pipeline Legislation, 1977. Pres. Placentia (Calif.) C. of C.; chmn. Planning Commn., Placentia; bd. dirs. Yorba Linda C. of C. Mem. Orange County Bar Assn., ATLA, Rotary Club, Exchange Club. Avocations: hunting, fly fishing, scuba diving. Office: Main St Law Offices Inc 4895 Main St Yorba Linda CA 92886-3413

WARD, WILLIAM EDWARD, museum exhibition designer; b. Apr. 4, 1922; s. Edward and Lura Dell (Eckelberry) W.; m. Evelyn Svec, Nov. 12, 1952; 1 child, Pamela. BS, Western Res. U., 1947, MA, 1948; diploma, Cleve. Inst. Art, 1947; postgrad., Columbia U., 1950. Mem. staff edn. Oriental depts. Cleve. Mus. Art, 1947—, designer, 1957—, ret. chief designer; prof. calligraphy and watercolor Cleve. Inst. Art, 1960—; prof., cons. graphic and installation exhbn., design cons. Egyptian Mus., Cairo, 1995—. Exhibited in numerous exhbns. including (with Evelyn Svec Ward) Oaxacan Inspirations: An Exhibition of Collage and Watercolor, 1986, Valley of Oaxaca: Exhibition of Watercolors and Photographs, Folk Art Gallery, Cleve., 1992, Cleve. Playhouse Gallery, 1984; designer George Gund Collection of Western Art Mus., 1972, Firemen's Meml., Cleve., sculpture design, 1968; designer ofcl. seals Case Western Res. U., also Sch. Medicine, 1969; curator Culcon exhbn. Masterpieces of World Art from Am. Museums, Tokyo and Kyoto, Japan, 1976; co-author (catalogue, exhbn.) Folk Art of Oaxaca: The Ward Colection, Cleve Inst. Art, 1987; textile designs in Cleve. Artists Found. collection; represented in permanent collections of Cleve. Mus. of Art, Akron Art Mus., Art Assn. of Cleve. Inst. of Art. Mem. Internat. Design Conf., Aspen, 1959—; mem. Tridecca Soc. (trustee 1995-98); mem. Fine Arts Adv. Com. City Cleve., 1966-90; mem. mayor's com. for selection of ofcl. seal City of Cleve., 1973, mem. design rev. com., 1991-92. Served with Terrain Intelligence, AUS, 1942-45, S.E. Asia Command. Recipient commn. award City Canvas competition Cleve. Area Arts Coun., 1975, No. Ohio LIVE Achievement award Cleve. Mus. Art, 1987, Hall of Fame award West Tech. Alumni Assn., 1995. Mem. Cleve. Soc. Contemporary Art, Artists Archives of the Western Reserve, Print Club Cleve., Cleve. Artist Found. (exhibiting mem. Beck Ctr. Gallery, Cleve. 1999), Rowfant Club, Women's City Club Cleve. (Arts Prize Spl. citation 1988). Home: 27045 Solon Rd Solon OH 44139-3452 Office: Cleve Mus Art 11150 East Blvd Cleveland OH 44106-1711

WARD, WILLIAM REGINALD, modern history educator; b. Chesterfield, Derbyshire, Eng., Mar. 23, 1925; s. William Gilmour and Clarice (Bowmer) W.; m. Barbara Elizabeth Uridge, Oct. 9, 1949; children: Faith, William Aidan, James Neil. BA, Oxford U., 1946, MA, 1951, DPhil, 1951. Resident tutor Ruskin Coll., Oxford, Eng., 1946-49; successively asst. lectr., lectr., sr. lectr. history U. Manchester, Oxford, Eng., 1949-65; warden Needham Hall, Manchester, Eng., 1959-65; prof. modern history U. Durham, Oxford, Eng., 1965-86; emeritus prof. U. Durham, Eng., 1986—. Author: The English Land Tax in the 18th Century, 1953, Georgian Oxford, 1958, Victorian Oxford, 1965, Religion & Society in England 1790-1850, 1972, Early Corr. of Jabez Bunting, 1972, Early Victorian Methodism, 1976, Theology, Sociology and Politics, 1979, Palatinate Studies, 1992, The Protest Evangelical Awakening, 1992, Faith & Faction, 1993, Parson and Parish in 18th Century Surrey, 1994, Parson and Parish in 18th Century Hampshire, 1995, Christianity Under the Ancién Régime, 1999, Kirchengeschichte Grossbritanniens, 2000. Leverhulme Trust grantee Oxford U., 1958-59; Sir James Knott fellow U. Durham, 1983-84; Peterson fellow Am. Antiquarian Soc., Worcester, Mass., 1987. Fellow Royal Hist. Soc. (coun. 1982-90, v.p. 1986-90); mem. Chetham Soc. (sec. 1964-84, pres. 1984-95), Eccles. History Soc. (pres. 1970-71), Surtees Soc. (council 1966-87). Methodist. Avocation: mountain walking, music. Home and Office: 21 Grenehurst Way, Petersfield, Hants GU31 4A2, England

WARDEN, JAMES BRYCE, bank executive; b. Pitts., June 28, 1937; s. James Benjamin and Emily (Bryce) W.; m. Sallie Eleanor McKee, Oct. 28, 1961; children: James McKee, Andrew Bryce. BA, Yale U., 1959. Trainee Phila. Nat. Bank, 1961, with credit dept., 1961-64, with internat. div., 1964-67, internat. banking officer, 1967-68, v.p., 1968-69; European rep. Phila. Nat. Bank, London, 1969; v.p. London, 1969-72, mgr. European area, 1972-77; mgr. internat. trading and funding, 1977-87, sr. v.p., 1987—; mng. dir. CoreStates Investment Banking, 1988-93; sr. rep. CoreStates Bank, London, 1994-98, ret., 1998. Served with USAR, 1960-66. Republican. Episcopalian. Clubs: Phila., Phila. Cricket; Pike Run Country (Jones Mills, Pa.); Yale (N.Y.C.); Caledonian (London), Overseas Bankers (London). Home: 2 Tennyson Mansions, Lordship Pl, London SW3 5HT, England

WARDEN, JOHN L., lawyer; b. Evansville, Ind., Sept. 22, 1941; s. Walter Wilson and Juanita (Veatch) W.; m. Phillis Ann Rodgers, Oct. 27, 1960; children: Anne W. Clark, John L., W. Carson. AB, Harvard U., 1962; LLB, U. Va., 1965. Bar: N.Y. 1966, U.S. Ct. Appeals (2d cir.) 1966, U.S. Dist. Ct. (so. and ea. dists.) N.Y. 1967, U.S. Ct. Appeals (10th cir.) 1971, U.S. Supreme Ct. 1972, U.S. Ct. Appeals (D.C. cir.) 1980. Assoc. Sullivan & Cromwell, N.Y.C., 1965-73, ptnr., 1973—. Pres. U. Va. Law Sch. Found.; trustee Am. Ballet Theatre. Fellow Am. Coll. Trial Lawyers; mem. ABA, Am. Law Inst., N.Y. State Bar Assn., Assn. Bar City N.Y., N.Y. County Lawyers Assn., Knickerbocker Club, Down Town Assn. Club, Doubles Club, Bedford Golf and Tennis Club, Lyford Cay Club. Republican. Episcopalian. Editor-in-chief Va. Law Rev., 1964-65. Office: Sullivan & Cromwell 125 Broad St Fl 28 New York NY 10004-2489

WARDE-NORBURY, WILLIAM GEORGE ANTONY, financial executive; b. Doncaster, Eng., Mar. 13, 1936; s. Harold George Warde-Norbury and Mary Betty Warde-Aldam; m. Philippa Marjorie Davies-Cooke, Oct. 15, 1938; children: Mark William Antony, Alastair George. Capt. Coldstream Guards, 1956-63; with Allied-Domec (then Allied-Lyons), 1964-66, dir. subs. companies, 1966-76; dir. Allied Breweries, 1976-82; main bd. dirs. Allied-Lyons and other cos., London, 1982-86; non-exec. chmn. Skol Internat. & Oldham Claudgen, Ind Coope African Invests., 1986-94; non-exec. dir. Provident Fin. plc, Bradford, 1988-97, chmn., 1995-96; non-exec. dir. Gallup Orgn., Weybridge, 1986-98; exec. chmn. Pvt. Farming Co., Doncaster, 1986—; chmn. Yorkshire Regional Coun. Prince's Trust; trustee Hardman Trust. Dep. lt., South Yorkshire, 1990—, high sheriff, 1996. Avocations: field sports, travelling, music. Home: Hooton Pagnell Hall, Doncaster DN5 7BW, England

WARD-HOWLETT, RONALD PETER HENRY, financial investment executive, consultant; b. London, May 5, 1932; s. Ronald Desmond and Hilda May (Stopforth-Rimmer) W. Student, Ealing (Eng.) Coll., 1947-49. Bank ofcl., mgr. Nat. Provincial Bank, London, 1950, 52-68; sr. exec. Joseph Sebag, London, 1968-73; mgr. Blankstone Sington & Co., London, 1973-84, Northcote & Co., Liverpool, 1973-84; fin. investment contr. Ernst & Young Internat., London and Liverpool, 1984-93; fin. investment exec./cons. Southport, Eng., 1993—; dir., co. sec. Brandon Ct. Properties, Ltd., Southport, 1972-84. Auditor Chamber of Trade and Commerce, Chalfont St. Peter, Eng., 1962-68; sch. gov. Ainsdale H.S., Merseyside, Eng., 1988-92; founder, trustee The Howlett Mabrouk Shanekoe Found., 1994—. With Royal Air Force, 1950-52. Fellow Zool. Soc. London, Linnean Soc., Inst. Fin. Accts. (Eng.); mem. Inst. Mgrs. (Eng.), Brit. Herpetol. Soc. (life), Victory Svcs. Club (life), Royal Overseas Club. Ch. of England. Avocations: herpetology, numismatics, antiques, reading, travel. Home and Office: 13 Brandon Pk Ct Argyle Rd, Southport PR9 9LX, England

WARD JOUVE, NICOLE ANNE, English educator; b. Marseille, Provence, France, July 6, 1938; arrived in England, 1962; d. Andre Julien and Marcelle (Bricard) Jouve; m. Anthony Ward, Sept. 5, 1962; children: Gilles, Cathy, Fabrice. Licence, Sorbonne, Paris, 1960, Agrégation, 1962; ancienne eleve, Ecole Normale Supérieure Jeures Fills, Paris, Sevres, France, 1962. Asst., tutor Cambridge U., Eng., 1962-63; asst. lectr. York U., Eng., 1963-69, lectr., 1970-79, sr. lectr., 1979-84; maitre-asst. Paris III Sorbonne-Nouvelle, 1975-76; reader York U., Eng., 1985-88, prof. English and related lit., 1988—; vis. lectr. U. Alberta, Can., 1969-70; participant French radio and TV work; participant radio and TV work BBC, Eng. Author: (short stories) Shades of Grey, 1977-82; author: Baudelaire, 1980, The Streetcleaner, 1982-86, Colette, 1987, White Woman Speaks With Forked Tongue: Criticism as Autobiography, 1991, Female Genesis: Creativity, Self and Gender, 1998; reviewer THES, City Limits, Women's Rev., PS Femmes, New Statesman, 1982-90. Mem. Amnesty Internat., London, 1984-2000. Disting. Vis. fellow Inst. for Advanced Study in the Humanities, U. Mass., Amherst, 1990. Mem. Comparative Lit. Assn., Network, Soc. des Etudes Romantiques. Roman Catholic. Office: York U, Heslington, York Y01 5DD, England

WARE, BENNIE, university administrator; b. Ponca City, Okla., Sept. 21, 1946; s. Clyde Elmer and Lois Aliene (Smith) W.; m. Sheridan Lee Welch, May 28, 1967 (div. 1976); 1 child, Winston Arthur; m. Claudia Borman, Dec. 21, 1979 (div. 1998); children: Jeffrey Bright, Amelia Marie; m. Eleanor Gallagher, Mar. 7, 1998. BS in Chemistry, Okla. State U., 1968; PhD in Biophys. Chemistry, U. Ill., 1972. Asst. prof. chemistry Harvard U., Cambridge, Mass., 1972-75, assoc. prof., 1975-79; prof., chmn. dept. chemistry Syracuse U., 1979-84, Kenan prof. sci., 1984-91, v.p. rsch., 1989-92, v.p. rsch., computing, 1992—. Contbr. articles to profl. jours. Grantee NIH, 1972, 74, 77, 80, 83, 86, 89, NIH, 1972, 74, 76, 77, 79, 81, 84, 86; Alfred P. Sloan fellow, 1976-80. Fellow AAAS; mem. Phi Beta Kappa, Phi Kappa Phi. Achievements include invention of electrophoretic light scattering; first to combine laser light scattering and fluorescence photobleaching recovery to distinguish mutual and tracer diffusion; first to apply laser Doppler velocimetry to protoplasmic streaming. Home: 333 Berkeley Dr Syracuse NY 13210-3041 Office: Syracuse Univ 3-014D Ctr Sci And Tech Syracuse NY 13244-0001

WARENIK-SZYMANKIEWIZ, ALINA, medical educator, endocrinologist, gynecologist; b. Bisk-Byteń, Poland, July 3, 1937; d. Józef and Julia Grynczyk Warenik; children: Jarosław, Ewa. MD, U. Med. Scis., Poznań, Poland, 1961, PhD, 1966. Assoc. prof. U. Med. Scis., 1982-92, prof., 1992—, chmn. divsn. gynecological endocrinology, 1993—, vice-dir. Inst. Gynecology and Obstetrics,, 1992-97. Contbr. articles to med. jours. and pubs. Mem. Polish Soc. Endocrinology (chmn. 1981-84), European Assn. Ob-Gyns, Polish Soc. Menopause adn Andropause (v.p. 1994—), Internat. Menopause Soc. Office: U Med Scis Divsn Gyn Endo, Polna 33, 60 535 Poznan Poland

WARFIELD, JOHN NELSON, retired engineering educator, consultant; b. Sullivan, Mo., Nov. 21, 1925; s. John Daniel and Flora Alice (Land) W.; m. Rosamond Arline Howe, Feb. 2, 1948; children: Daniel, Nancy, Thomas. BA, U. Mo., 1948, BSEE, 1948, MSEE, 1949; PhD, Purdue U., 1952. Assoc. prof. Pa. State U., University Park, 1949-55, U. Ill.-Urbana, 1955-57, Purdue U., West Lafayette, Ind., 1957-58; prof. elec. engring U. Kans., Lawrence, 1958-66; sr. research leader Battelle Meml. Inst., Columbus, Ohio, 1966-74; prof. elec. engring U. Va., Charlottesville, 1974-83; sr. mgr. Burroughs Corp., 1983-84; dir. Inst. for Info. Tech. George Mason U., Fairfax, Va., 1984-87, dir. Inst. for Advanced Study in Integrative Scis., 1987-98; prof. emeritus, 2000—; cons. IBM, Armonk, N.Y., 1979-82, Saudi Arabian Nat. Ctr. Sci. and Tech., Riyadh, 1978-82, Ghana Coun. for Sci. and Indsl. Rsch., Accra, 1989—, Niagara-Mohawk Power Co., 89, Ford Motor Co., 1990—, Defense Systems Mgmt. Coll., 1990—. Author: Societal Systems, 1976, A Science of Generic Design, 1990, A Handbook of Interactive Management, 1994; inventor interpretive structural modeling, 1973; editor: IEEE Transactions on Systems, Man, and Cybernetics, 1968-73, Systems Research, 1981-90. Recipient Excellence in Instrn. award Western Electric Co., 1966, Peace Pipe award Ams. for Indian Opportunity, 1987, Best Paper award European Conf. Cybernetics and Systems, 1988, Mayour's cert. City of Austin, 1993, Plaque of Recognition, Mex. Ministry of Social Devel., 1994, Spl. Recognition award Internat. Soc. Design and Process Sci., 1995. Fellow IEEE (life, outstanding contbn. award 1977, Centennial medal 1984, Third Millennium medal 2000), Soc. for Design and Process Sci. (fellow award, 1996); mem. Internat. Soc. Panetics, Assn. for Integrative Studies. Home: 2673 Westcott Cir Palm Harbor FL 34684-1746

WARGNIER, REGIS, film director. Dir.: La Femme de ma vie, 1986, Terres jaunes, 1989, I'm the King of the Castle, 1989, Une femme francaise; co-dir. Le Lumiere et Compagnie, 1997; asst. dir. Le Grand Pardon, 1981, Le Grand Frere, 1982, Le Bon Plaisir, 1984; writer Indochine, 1992 (Best Fgn. Lang. Film Acad. Awd, 1992). Recipient Lumiere et Campagnie, 1995, Uhe Femme Francaise, 1995, Est-Ovest, 1999. Office: Voyez Mon Agent, 20 Avenue Rapp, 75007 Paris France*

WARING, ANTHONY JOHN, chemistry educator; b. Stockport, Cheshire, England, Feb. 13, 1938; s. John and Phyllis Maud (Potter) W.; m. Rosemary Hope Goodson, June 27, 1963 (div. 1987); children: Mark Richard, Emma Jane Louise. BA, U. Cambridge, England, 1959, PhD, 1962, MA, 1963; DSc, U. Birmingham, England, 1985. Chartered chemist. Rsch. fellow U. Cambridge, 1962-63; Fulbright fellow Mich. State U., East Lansing, 1963-64; NATO fellow U. Southampton, England, 1964-65; lectr. in chemistry U. Birmingham, 1965—. Contbr. articles to profl. jours. Fellow Royal Soc. Chemistry (hon. treas. 1988-92, coun. mem. 1991-94, sect. chmn. 1994-97). Mem. Ch. of England. Avocations: classical music, church architecture. Office: Univ Birmingham, Sch Chemistry, Birmingham B15 2TT, England

WARING, MICHAEL JOHN, chemotherapy educator; b. Lancaster, Eng., Nov. 8, 1939; s. Frederick and Kathleen (Hadley) W.; m. Ann Josephine Milner, July 28, 1973 (div. 1978). BA, U. Cambridge, Eng., 1961, PhD, 1964, MA, 1965, ScD, 1975. Fellow Carnegie Inst., Washington, 1964-65; demonstrator biochemistry U. Cambridge, 1965-67, lectr. pharmacology, 1967-90, reader chemotherapy, 1990-99, prof. chemotherapy, 1999—; fellow, dir. studies Jesus Coll., Cambridge, 1965; hon. cons. Cancer Rsch. Lab., Auckland, New Zealand, 1975; vis. prof. U. Copenhagen, 1983, U. Montreal, Can., 1985, U. Paris, 1991, Calif. Inst. Tech., 1992, 99, U. Tex., Austin, 1998; mem. Stoke Mandeville Burns rsch. Trust Com., 1991; organizer internat. rsch. confs., London, 1980. Fontevraud, 1986, Padova, 1987, Cambridge, 1989, Roscoff, 1991, Copenhagen, 1993, Aussois, 1994, Ascoha, 1996, Bressanone/Brixen, 1999. Author: The Molecular Basis of Antibiotic Action, 1972, 2d edit., 1981; editor: Molecular Aspects of Anti-Cancer Drug Action, 1983, Biology of Carcinogenesis, 1987, The Science of Cancer Treatment, 1990, The Search for New Anti-Cancer Drugs, 1992, Molecular Aspects of Anti-Cancer Drug DNA Interactions, 1994, The Genetics of Cancer, 1995; editor jour. Molecular Recognition, 1991-94. Corr. mem. Mus. Nat. d'Histoire Naturelle, Paris, 1995—. Mem. Synod Ch. of Eng. Home: Jesus Coll, Cambridge CB5 8BL, England Office: U Cambridge Dept Pharmacology, Tennis Ct Rd, Cambridge CB2 1QJ, England

WARIS, MICHAEL, JR., lawyer; b. Phila., July 3, 1921; s. Michael and Esther (March) W.; m. Mary Luschyk, June 2, 1956. B.S. in Econs., U. Pa., 1942, J.D. cum laude, 1944. Bar: Pa., D.C. Law clk. to judge U.S. Tax Ct., Washington, 1946-48; trial counsel IRS, Washington, 1948-52; legis. atty. Legislation and Regulations div. IRS Washington, 1952-55; assoc. tax legis. counsel U.S. Treasury Dept., Washington, 1955-62; ptnr. Baker & McKenzie, Washington, 1962-88, of counsel, 1988—; adj. prof. Georgetown U. Law Sch., Washington, 1963-73. Bd. dirs. United Service Orgn. Nat. Capital Area, 1978-79; mem. adv. group to U.S. Commr. of IRS, Washington, 1979-80. Named Master of the Bench, J. Edgar Murdock Am. Inn of Ct., 1988. Fellow ABA; mem. Fed. Bar Assn., Bar Assn. D.C., Ukrainian-Am. Bar Assn. (past chmn. bd. govs.), Cosmos Club, Met. Club, Beta Gamma Sigma. Ukrainian Catholic. Home: 6707 Tusculum Rd Bethesda MD 20817-1521 Office: Baker & McKenzie 815 Connecticut Ave NW Washington DC 20006-4004

WARLIMONT, HANS, physical metallurgist; b. Osnabrueck, Germany, Sept. 4, 1931; s. Clemens and Liselotte (Hofmann) W.; m. Barbara Meier, June 4, 1966; children: Cora, Guido, Petra. Diploma in metallurgical engring., Bergakademie Clausthal, Germany, 1956; PhD, Max-Planck-Inst. Metals Rsch., Stuttgart, Germany, 1959. Rschr. U.S. Steel Corp., Monroeville, pa., 1959-62; head rsch. group Max-Planck-Inst. for Metals Rsch., 1962-74; head rsch. divsn. Swiss Aluminium Ltd., Neuhausen, 1974-77; dir. rsch. Vacuumschmelze GmbH, Hanau, Germany, 1977-91; authorized rep. for R&D of exec. bd. Metallgesellschaft AG, Frankfurt am Main, Germany, 1991-92; sci. dir. Inst. fuer Festkoerper-und Werkstofforschung Dresden, Germany, 1992-98; adj. prof. Inst. for Phys. Metallurgy U. Stuttgart, Inst. for Solid State Physics, Inst. Tech., Technische Hochschule Darmstadt, 1968-92; prof. materials sci. Technische U. Dresden, 1992—; 39th Hatfield Meml. lectr. Royal Soc., Inst. Metals U. Sheffield, Eng., 1991; mem. adv. coms. for several German rsch. ctrs. Author: (with E. Hornbogen) Metallkunde, 1972, 4th rev. edit., 2000, (with L. Delaey) Martensitic Transformations in Copper, Silver and Gold Based Alloys; contbr. numerous articles to profl. publs. Recipient Heyn-Medal for outstanding achievements Deutsche Gesellschaft für Materialkunde, 1989. Mem. German Magnetics Soc. (chmn. 1987-92), others. Office: Inst fuer Festkoerper and Werkstoffosschung Dresden, Helmholtzstr 20, D-01069 Dresden Germany

WARME, PIERRE MARIE, military officer engineer; b. Beaumont, France, July 28, 1938; s. Maurice and Genevieve (Latouche) W.; m. Daniele Marie Renard, Dec. 30, 1963; children: Catherine, Philippe. Lycee St. Louis, Paris, 1958; Engr., Ecole De L'Air, Salon de Provence, France, 1960; Brevet de Pilote Militaire, Tours, France, 1961; Engr., Inst. Econs., Strasbourg, France, 1966. Air base comdr. French Air Force, Nancy, France, 1982-84; chief gen. planning office French Air Force, Paris, 1984-86, dep. chief of staff for planning and procurement, 1986, 91; head of edn. and tng. French Air Force, Tours, 1991-94; chmn. advisor Dassault Aviation, Vaucresson, France, 1994-99. Author: (book) Infra-Red Line by Line, 1971. Served to gen. French Air Force. Decorated Medaille de L'Aeronautique, Legion d'Honneur, Merite Nat. Mem. AIAA. Avocations: golf, music, theatre, walking. Office: Dassault Aviation, 27 Rue Pauchet, 92420 Vaucresson France

WARMERDAM, LAURENCE VAN, physician, pharmacologist, researcher; b. Heemskerk, The Netherlands, Oct. 10, 1969; s. Jan Van and Riet Van (Stam) W. MD, Vrije U., Amsterdam, The Netherlands, 1990; PhD, U. Utrecht, The Netherlands, 1995. Clin. pharmacologist Slotervaart Hosp., Amsterdam, 1992-97; clin. rschr. Netherlands Cancer Inst., Amsterdam, 1992-97; phys. Antonius Hosp., 1998—. Author: Pharmacokinetics and Pharmacodynamics of Anticancer Agents, 1995. Recipient Antoni van Leeuwenhoek award, 1996. Avocation: music composition. Office: Apotheek Neth Cancer Inst, Louwesweg 6, 1066 EC Amsterdam The Netherlands

WARNAKULASURIYA, SAMAN, medical educator, scientist; b. Galle, Sri Lanka, Oct. 5, 1946; arrived in Eng., 1990; s. Ariyadasa and Lily Grace (Jayatillake) W.; m. Ranjini Fernando, Oct. 1971; 1 child, Samantha Roshini. BDS, U. Ceylon, 1969; PhD, U. Glasgow, Scotland, 1976. From acad. staff to prof. U. Peradeniya, Sri Lanka, 1976-89; sr. lectr. Royal Coll. Surgeons, King Coll., London, 1990-98; reader Kings Coll., London, 1999—; cons. in field. Mem. editl. bd., dep. editor Oral Diseases, 1995—; contbr. over 100 articles to profl. jours. Sr. Rsch. fellow WHO, 1996—, Travel awards, 1978, 82-83, Colombo Plan fellow British Coun., London, 1971-76; recipient Johnson & Johnson Internat. award in dentistry Internat. Dental Fedn., 1990. Fellow Royal Coll. Surgeons England, Royal Coll. Surgeons Edinburgh; mem. Internat. Assn. for Dental Rsch., British Soc. for Oral Medicine. Buddhist. Avocations: study of complimentary medicine and acupuncture, Buddhist civilization. E-mail: s.warne@kcl.ac.uk. Home: 5 Hillside Rd Cheam, Sutton SM26ET, England Office: Kings Coll Hosp, Caldecot Rd Denmark Hill, London SE59RW, England

WARNATZ, JÜRGEN, physics educator; b. Chemnitz, Sachsen, Germany, May 31, 1944; s. Hans-Heinrich and Brigitte (Schumann) W.; m. Christel Schröder, Aug. 23, 1973; children: Hans-Jörg, Melanie. Diploma in Physics, Göttingen (Germany) U., 1969, D of Natural Scis., 1971; Dr. rer. nat. habil., Darmstadt Tech. U., Germany; Dr.tech.h.c., Troudheim U., 1997. Asst. prof. Darmstadt (Germany) Tech. U., 1971-82; dep. prof., assoc. prof. Heidelberg (Germany) U., 1982-88; full prof. Stuttgart (Germany) U., 1989-94, Heidelberg (Germany) U., 1994—. Recipient Winnacker-Stipendium, Hoechst AG, 1981, Combustion Silver medal, 1982, Philip-Morris Rsch. award Philip-Morris Found., 1991, Leibniz award Deutsche Forschungs-Gemeinschaft, 1993, Gerhard-Damköhler medal Deutsche Vereinigung für Chemie-und Verfahrenstechnik, 1995. Mem. Internat. Combustion Inst., Bunsengesellschaft, Verein Deutscher Ingenieure, Gesellschaft Deutscher Chemiker, Deutsche Gesellschaft fur Chemisches Apparatewesen und Biotechnologie. Office: IWR Heidelberg U, Im Neuenheimer Feld 368, 69120 Heidelberg Germany

WÄRNE, ANDERS GUSTAV BERTIL, geriatrician, researcher; b. Lund, Sweden, May 5, 1949; s. Lars Bertil and Inga Anna-Stina (Lilienberg) W.; m. Greta Wärne-Nyman Klarin, Jan. 17, 1978 (div. Feb. 1987); children: Cecilia, Katrin. Degree Med., Goteborg U., 1977. Med. diplomate, 1979, geriatrics specialist, 1985, internal medicine spceialist, 1985. Intern Gallivaire Hosp., Norrbotnia, Sweden, 1977-79; with Boden Ctrl. Hosp., Norrbotnia, Sweden, 1980-85, sr. physician, 1985-87; asst. sr. phys. ward Vasa Hosp., Goteborg, 1987-94; tutor Inst. Geriatrics Goteborg U.; cons. Sahlgrens U. Hosp., 1997—; med. cons. Found. Alderdomshemmet, Göteborg, 1989-92. Avocations: medical acupuncture, philosophy, skiing. Home: DrLinds Gata 4, 41325 Göteborg Sweden Office: Sahlgrenska Moludal Sjukhus, Divsn Geriatrics, 43180 Mölndal Sweden

WARNECKE, HANS-JÜRGEN, engineering educator; b. Braunschweig, Germany, Apr. 2, 1934; s. Hans and Ella (Grobe) W. Diploma engring., Tech. U. Braunschweig, 1959, DEng, 1963; D honoris causa, U. Ljubljana, Yugoslavia, 1989; DEng (hon.), Tech. U. Magdeburg, Germany, 1989; D honoris cause, Tech. U. Timisoara, Romania, 1995, U. Žilina, Slovakia, 1998. Rschr. Inst. Machine Tools, Braunschweig, 1959-65; dir. Rollei-Werke, Braunschweig, 1965-70; prof. U. Stuttgart, Germany, 1970-93; mng. dir. Fraunhofer Inst. IPA, Stuttgart, 1971-93; pres. Fraunhofer-Gesellschaft, Munich, 1993—; bd. dirs. Mahle GmbH, Stuttgart, Bros Fahrzeugteile, Coburg, Deutz, Köln, Man Roland, Offenburg, J. Wagner Found., Friedrichshafen, KSB-Stiftung, Frankenthal, Anton-Klara Roser Stiftung, Stuttgart. Author: Der Produktionsbetrieb, Fertigunstechnik, 1985, The Fractal Co., 1993; editor Werkstattstechnik, 1980—. Decorated officer's cross Order of Merit (Fed. Republic Germany). Decorated officer's cross Order of Merit (Germany), officer's cross Order of Merit State Lower Saxony and State Baden-Württenberg. Mem. Verein Deutscher Ingenieure Assn. Prodn. Techniques (pres. 1995-97, adv. bd.), Assn. for Rationalization German Economy, Regional Soc. Engrs., Internat. Assn. for Prodn. Rsch., Nat. Acad. Engring., Acad. Scis. Croatia. Avocations: sailing, crafting. Office: Fraunhofer-Gesellschaft, Leonrodstr 54, 80636 Munich Germany

WARNER, ANTHONY ROWLAND, linguistics educator, researcher; b. Bishop's Stortford, Hertfordshire, Eng., Jan. 27, 1945; s. Roy Henry and Amy Eleanor (Le Page) W.; m. Patricia Anne Thornton, Mar. 27, 1976; children: Kate, David, Philip. BA with honors, U. Oxford, Eng., 1967; PhD, U. Edinburgh, Scotland, 1978. Lectr. U. Liverpool, Eng., 1971-75; lectr. U. York, Eng., 1975-94, head dept. lang. & linguistic sci., 1992-96, sr. lectr., 1994-97, prof., 1997—. Author: Complementation in Middle English and the Methodology of Historical Syntax, 1978, The Structuring of English Auxiliaries, 1985, English Auxiliaries: Structure and History, 1993; editor: (jour.) York Papers in Linguistics, 1979-97. Recipient rsch. readership Brit. Acad., 1997-99. Mem. Linguistics Assn. of Great Britain (sec. 1977-80), Philol. Soc. (coun. 1998—). Office: Univ York Heslington, Dept Lang & Linguistic Sci, York YO10 5DD, England

WARNER, DAVID SAMUEL, anesthesiologist; b. Evanston, Ill., July 20, 1953; s. James Daniel and Marcella Anne Warner; m. Rosanne T. Warner, June 14, 1980; children: Lindsay, Seth. BA, U. Wis., 1976, MD, 1980. Diplomate Am. Bd. Anesthesiology. Resident U. Iowa, Iowa City, 1980-84; rsch. assoc. U. Lund, Sweden, 1984-85; asst. prof. U. Iowa, Iowa City, 1985-89, assoc. prof., 1989-94; prof. anesthesiology Duke U., Durham, N.C., 1994—. Editl. bd. Jour. Neurosurg. Anesthesia, 1989—, Anesthesia and Analgesia, 1995—; contbr. over 120 articles to profl. jours. NIH grantee, 1987—. Mem. Soc. for Neurosurg. Anesthesia and Critical Care (pres. 1994-95), Soc. for Neurosci., Am. Soc. Anesthesiologists, Internat. Anesthesia Rsch. Soc. Episcopalian. Home: 1006 Camden Ln Chapel Hill NC 27516-7756 Office: Duke Univ Med Ctr Dept Anesthesiology PO Box 3094 Durham NC 27710-0001

WARNER, DOUGLAS ALEXANDER, III, banker; b. Cin., June 9, 1946; s. Douglas Alexander Jr. and Eleanor (Wright) W.; m. Patricia Grant, May 13, 1977; children: Alexander, Katherine, Michael. BA, Yale U., 1968. Officer's asst. J.P. Morgan & Co. Inc., N.Y.C., 1968-70; asst. treas. J.P. Morgan & Co., Inc., N.Y.C., 1970-72, asst. v.p., 1972-75; v.p. Morgan Guaranty Trust Co., N.Y.C., 1975-85; sr. v.p. J.P. Morgan & Co. Inc., N.Y.C., 1983-87, exec. v.p., 1987-89; mng. dir. Morgan Guaranty Trust Co., N.Y.C., 1989-90, pres., 1990-95, chmn., pres., CEO, 1995—, also bd. dirs.; bd. counselors Bechtel Group, Inc.; bd. dirs. GE Co., Anheuser-Busch Cos., Ind.; chmn. bd. of overseers and mgrs. Meml. Sloan-Kettering Cancer Ctr.; mem. The Bus. Coun. Trustee Pierpont Morgan Libr. Mem. Links Club, River Club, Meadowbrook Club (L.I.). Avocations: golf, skiing, shooting. Home: PO Box 914 New York NY 10268-0914 Office: J P Morgan & Co Inc 60 Wall St New York NY 10005-2888*

WARNER, FRANK SHRAKE, lawyer; b. Ogden, Utah, Dec. 14, 1940; s. Frank D. and Emma (Sorensen) W.; 1 child, Sheri; m. Sherry Lynn Clary. JD, U. Utah, 1964. Bar: Utah 1964. Assoc. Young, Thatcher, Glasmann & Warner, and predecessor, Ogden, 1964-67, ptnr., 1967-72; chmn. Pub. Svc. Comn. Utah, Salt Lake City, 1972-76; ptnr. Warner & Wikstrom, Ogden, 1976-79, Warner, Marquardt & Hasenyager, Ogden, 1979-82; pvt. practice Ogden, 1982-89, Warner & Phillips, 1989-96, Warner Law Firm, 1996—; mem. Utah Gov.'s Com. on Exec. Reorgn., 1978-80. Mem. Utah Bar Assn. (ethics and discipline com. 1981-90), Am. Inns of Ct, Am. Trial Lawyers Assn., Ogden Gun Club (past pres.). Office: 868 25th St Ogden UT 84401-2611

WARNER, FREDERICK EDWARD, chemical engineer, educator; b. London, Mar. 31, 1910; s. Frederick and Anne Elizabeth (Wooley) W.; m. Margaret Anderson McCrea; children: Robert Anderson, Elizabeth Jean, Peter Anderson, Judith Alexandrea; m. Barbara Ivy Reynolds. 2d class hons. in Chemistry, U. London, Eng., 1932, diploma in Chem. Engring., 1933; DSc. (hon.), Us. Aston, Bradford, Cranfield, Eng., 1968-85, Us. Heriot-Watt, Newcastle and, Open U., Essex, Eng., 1968-85. Sr. ptnr. Cremer and Warner, Eng., 1956-80; vis. prof. Imperial Coll., London, 1970-76, Univ. Coll., London, 1970-83, Univ. Essex, Eng., 1983—, Imperial Coll., London, 1993—; pres. Inst. Chem. Engrs., Eng., 1966-67; chmn. Coun. Sci. and Tech. Insts., 1987-90; pres. Fedn. des Assns. Nat. d' Ingenieurs, Europe, 1968-71, Inst. Quality Assurance, UK, 1987-90, Brit. Standards Inst., Eng., 1980-88. Author: Introduction in Risk: Analysis, Perception and Management, 1992, Extrapolation of Dose Response Data for Risk Assessment, 1995; co-author: The Treatment and Handling of Wastes, 1992, Radioecology after Chernobyl-Biogeochem Pathways of Artificial Radionuclides, 1993, Nuclear Test Explosions, 1999. Recipient Gold medal Czecho-Slovak Soc. for Internat. Rels, 1969, preis fur Umweltschutz Technische Ubersichungs Verein Rheinland, 1982, Gerard Piel award Sci. Am., 1991, Gold medal, World Fedn. of Engring. Orgns., 1993; named Knight-Bachelor, Her Majesty the Queen, 1968. Fellow Royal Soc., Royal Acad. Engring.; mem. Royal Soc. Chemistry (hon. fellow), Instn. Civil Engrs., Instn. Chemical Engrs., Sci. Com. on Problems Environ., otherws. Episcopalian. Avocations: archaeology, ceramics, gardens.

WARNER, JULIAN CHARLES, information science educator; b. London, Mar. 4, 1955; s. Victor and Norma (Rebuck) W. BA, U. Newcastle, England, 1977, MA, 1979; DPhil, Oxford (Eng.) U., 1984; MLS, Sheffield (Eng.) U., 1985. Rsch. asst. United Glass Rsch. & Devel., St. Alban, Eng., 1973-74; libr. trainee U. York, Eng., 1982-83; lectr. Queen's U., Belfast, Northern Ireland, 1984-96, asst. dir. rsch. Sch. Mgmt., 1996-99. Author: From Writing to Computers, 1994, Information, Knowledge, Text, 2000; contbr. articles to profl. publs. Mem. Inst. for Info. Scientists, Libr. Assn., Assn. Info. Mgmt., Am. Soc. for Info. Sci. Avocations: reading, cycling. Office: Queens U, Sch of Mgmt and Econs, Belfast BT7 1NN, Northern Ireland

WARNER, MALCOLM, educator, author, social scientist; b. Manchester, Eng., May 10, 1937; s. Simon and Gertrude W.; m. Jacqueline Ramseyer, Apr. 5, 1966; children: Raphael, Natasha. BA, Cambridge U., 1959, PhD, 1966. Postdoctoral researcher Columbia U., N.Y.C., 1966; sr. rsch. fellow London Bus. Sch., 1969-73; prof. Brunel U. and Henley Mgmt. Coll., Henley-on-Thames, Eng., 1973-87; vis. fellow Wolfson Coll., Cambridge, Eng., 1987-89; fellow Wolfson Coll., 1989—; judge Inst. Mgmt. Studies, Cambridge U. Co-author: Microelectronic Product Applications in Great Britain and West Germany, 1989, New Technology, Skills and Management, 1992; editor: Sociology of Workplace, 1973, Organizational Experiments, 1984, Management Reforms in China, 1987, New Technology and Manufacturing Management, 1990, How Chinese Managers Learn, 1992, The Management of Human Resources in Chinese Industry, 1995, International Encyclopaedia of Business and Management, 6 vols., 1996, (with S.H. Ng) China's Trade Unions and Management, 1998, Handbook of Management Thinking, 1998, Changing Workplace Relations in the Chinese Economy, 2000, others. Home: 10 Chalcot Crescent, London NW1 8YD, England

WARNER, MARTIN MICHAEL, philosophy educator; b. Epsom, Surrey, U.K., Sept. 27, 1940; s. Hugh Compton and Nancy le Plastrier (Owen) W.; m. Veronica Smith, July 28, 1972. MA, Oxford U., 1962, BPhil, 1965. Lectr. philosophy U. Coll., North Wales, Bangor, 1965-69; lectr. philosophy U. Warwick, Coventry, U.K., 1969-90, sr. lectr., 1990—; program dir. Ctr. for Rsch. in Philosophy and Literature, 1985-87. Author: Philosophical Finesse, 1989, A Philosophical Study of T.S. Eliot's, 1999; co-editor: Terrorism, Protest and Power, 1990, Addressing Frank Kenmode, 1991, The Language of the Cave; gen. editor: Transcending Boundaries in Philosophy and Theology, 1999—; editor: The Bible As Rhetoric, 1990, Religion and Philosophy, 1992; mem. editl. adv. bd. Philosophy and Lit., 1982-96; contbr. articles, critical notices and revs. to profl. lit. jours. and collections. Mem. Royal Inst. Philosophy (mem. coun. 1981—, exec. com. 1982—), Soc. for Applied Philosophy (exec. com. 1983-91), Aristotelian Soc., Mind Soc. Office: U Warwick, Dept Philosophy, Coventry CV4 7AL, England

WARNER, PATRICIA ANN, secondary school educator; b. Wooster, Ohio, Dec. 21, 1949; d. Kent Branson and Irene Mae (Graves) W. BA in English, Coll. of Wooster, 1972, MAT in English, 1973. Instr. in English Orrville (Ohio) H.S., 1974—, Wayne Col., Orrville, Ohio, 1988-91. Named Orrville (Ohio) City Schs. Tchr. of Yr., 1987-88, Jennings Scholar Jennings Found., 1994-95. Mem. NEA, NCTE, Ohio Council of Tchrs. of English and Language Arts. Office: Orrville HS 841 N Ella St Orrville OH 44667-1154

WARNER, RAY ALLEN, research scientist; b. Davis, Calif., May 5, 1938; s. William Lorenzo and Fern Edna (Squires) W.; m. Judith Rita Sauve, July 30, 1965. BS in Engring. Physics, U. Calif., Berkeley, 1961; PhD in Physics, U. Calif., Davis, 1969. Rsch. asst. U. Calif., Davis, 1964-69; rsch. assoc. Mich. State U., East Lansing, 1969-72, asst. prof., 1972-77; sr. rsch. scientist Battelle N.W., Richland, Wash., 1977—; advisor to U.S. delegation negotiating the Comprehensive Nuclear-Test-Ban Treaty, 1995—. Author articles in field of nuclear physics. Served to 2d lt. U.S. Army, 1961-62. Mem. AAAS, Am. Phys. Soc., Sigma Xi, Tau Beta Pi. Home: 62407 N 68 PR NW Benton City WA 99320-9672 Office: Pacific NW Nat Lab Battelle Blvd Richland WA 99352

WARNER, ROBERTA ARLENE, accountant, financial services executive; b. Binghamton, N.Y., Dec. 31, 1938; d. Murrilan Earl and Ethel Margaret (Bell) W. BA, SUNY, Binghamton, 1960; MBA, Ind. U., 1962, MHA with highest distinction, 1973. C.P.A., N.Y. State; lic. nursing home adminstr., N.Y. State. Sr. acct. Arthur Young & Co., C.P.A.s, Buffalo, 1962-66; acctg. supr. Children's Hosp., Buffalo, 1966-68; controller King Manor Nursing Homes-Ave. Bldg. Corp., Buffalo, 1968-71; asst. dir. health fin. Hosp. Assn. N.Y. State, Albany, 1973-80, dir. health fin., 1980-93; dir. health fin. Healthcare Assn. N.Y. State, Albany, 1994-97, dir. data analysis and standards, 1997-98; pres. Roberta A. Warner Co., 1999—. Author articles in field. Trustee Ednl. Found. of Am. Women's Soc. C.P.A.s/Am. Soc. Women Accts., 1985-87. Fellow Healthcare Fin. Mgmt. Assn.; mem. Am. Inst. C.P.A.s, Am. Acctg. Assn., Am. Soc. Women Accts. (pres. Buffalo chpt. 1967-68), Am. Women's Soc. CPAs, N.Y. State Soc. C.P.A.s, Ind. U. Alumni Assn. (life), SUNY Binghamton Alumni Assn. (life), Grange. Methodist. Home and Office: 569 NY Rte 79 Windsor NY 13865-2714

WARNER, SCOTT DENNIS, investment banker; b. York, Pa., July 13, 1963; s. Earl Dennis and Sandra Glee (Barnhart) W. SB in Elec. Engring., MIT, 1986, SB in Computer Sci. and Engring., 1986, SM in Elec. Engring. and Computer Sci., 1986; MBA in Fin., U. Chgo., 1990. Rschr., teaching asst. MIT Lab. for Computer Sci., Cambridge, Mass., 1982-86; intern IBM Corp., Yorktown Heights, N.Y., 1983-86; fin. analyst Merrill Lynch & Co., N.Y.C., 1986-88, assoc., 1990-94, v.p., 1994-95; summer assoc. Goldman, Sachs & Co., N.Y.C., 1989; v.p. Lipper & Co., L.P., N.Y.C., 1995-98, Gerard Klauer Mattison & Co., Inc., N.Y.C., 1998—. Nat. Merit scholar, 1981, ROTC scholar, 1981, teaching asst. scholar MIT, 1985, 86; Leon C. Marshall scholar U. Chgo., 1988. Mem. Nat. Eagle Scout Assn., Delta Upsilon Frat. Republican. Presbyterian. Home: 235 E 95th St Apt 34J New York NY 10128-4025 Office: Gerard Klauer Mattison & Co Inc 529 5th Ave New York NY 10017-4608

WARNER, SUSAN, federal agency administrator; b. Rochester, N.Y., July 20, 1956; d. Harold J. and Jeannette (Nichols) Warner; divorced; children: Jennifer Lynn, Kathryn Alice. BA, Miami U., Oxford, Ohio, 1978; postgrad., Xavier U. Loan specialist HUD, Columbus, Ohio, 1978-79, Cin., 1979-83; fin. planner IDS Fin. Services, Inc., Cin., 1983-86, Manufacturer's Hanover Mortgage Corp., 1986, Shawmut Mortgage Corp., 1986-87, U.S. Dept. HUD, St. Louis, 1987—; housing cons., Cin., 1985—. Author: Community Land Coop. Residents' Handbook, 1986. Adv. Cin. Tech. Coll., 1984—; mem. fin. com. Community Land Coop., Cin., 1985—; exhibits chair Conf. Cin. Women, 1985, corp. patrons chair, 1986, conf. coordinator, 1987—; vol. Am. Cancer soc., 1981-84, March of Dimes, 1996-99; leader Girl Scouts. Recipient profl. awards; Mercury awards IDS, Cin., 1984, award for superior performance U.S. Inspector Gen. HUD, 1990. Republican. Roman Catholic. Avocations: reading, costume designing, making teddy bears, softball, theater. Home: 771 Seven Hills Ln Saint Charles MO 63304-1436 Office: US Dept HUD 1222 Spruce St Saint Louis MO 63103-2818

WÄRNERSSON, INGEGERD, Swedish government official. Minister of schs. and adult edn. Ministry Edn. and Sci., Govt. of Sweden, Stockholm. Mem. Social Democratic Party. Office: Ministry Edn and Sci, S-103 33 Stockholm Sweden

WÄRNERYD, KARL-ERIK, economic psychology educator; b. Sweden, Dec. 20, 1927; s. Werner Hjalmar and Nanny Hildegard (Andersson) W.; m. Eila Anna Marita Nystrom, Aug. 9, 1957; children: Karl Mikael, Jan Erik. MBA, Stockholm Sch. Econs., 1950; PhD, U. Chgo., 1955; D in Econs. honoris causa, Helsinki Swedish Sch. Bus., 1989. Rsch. asst. Stockholm Sch. Econs., 1950-52, asst. prof., 1955-63, prof. econ. psychology, 1963-92; ret., 1992; rsch. asst. Psychometric Lab., U. Chgo., 1953-55; dep. chmn., chmn. Sci. Adv. Group, Commn. for Switching to Right-Hand Driving, Stockholm, 1964-67; expert Commn. on Advt., Stockholm, 1967-74; rsch. fellow Ctr. for Econ. Rsch., Tilburg U., The Netherlands. Co-editor: Handbook of Economic Psychology, 1988, Ethics and Economic Affairs, 1994, The Psychology of Saving, 1999. Mem. Internat. Assn. Rsch. in Econ. Psychology (bd. mem. 1981-92), Internat. Ass Applied Psychology (pres. div. econ. psychology 1984-90), Swedish Psychol. Assn. Home: Wollmar Yxkullsgatan 14, S-11850 Stockholm Sweden Office: Stockholm Sch Econs, Sveavägen 65, S-11383 Stockholm Sweden

WARNKE, MARTIN, art history educator; b. Ijui, Brasil, Oct. 12, 1937; s. Kurt Anton Friedrich and Hilka (Schomerus) W.; m. Freya Grolle; children: Philine, Vincenz, Jessica. PhD, Free U. Berlin, 1964; Habilitation, U. Münster, Fed. Republic Germany, 1970. Vol. Stiftung Preuss. Kulturbesitz Mus., Berlin, 1964-65; fellow Art History Inst., Florence, Italy, 1965-67; sci. asst. Westfälische Wilhelms U., Münster, 1967-70; prof., sci. asst. Philipps U., Marburg, Fed. Republic Germany, 1971-78; prof. art history U. Hamburg (Fed. Republic Germany), 1978—; com. mem. Alexander von Humboldt-Stiftung, Bonn, Germany, 1987—; bd. dirs. Kulturwissenschaftliche Inst., Essen, Germany, 1989, U. Hamburg, Germany, 1991. Author: Kommentare zu Rubens, 1965, Bau und Überbau, 1976, Hofkünstler, 1985; editor: Das Kunstwerk zwischen Wissenschaft und Weltanschauung, 1970. Wissenschaftskolleg grantee 1983-84, Getty Ctr. 1987, Leibniz-Preis 1990, Collegium Budapest, 1998-99. Office: U Hamburg Art History Sem, Edmund-Siemers-Allee 1, D-20146 Hamburg Federal Republic of Germany

WARNKE, UWE, writer, publisher; b. Wittenberge, Germany, Aug. 21, 1956; s. Vollrath and Ingeborg (Thoms) W.; 1 child, Max Böthig. Diploma in engring., Tech. U., Dresden, Germany, 1981. Founder, dir. Entwerter/Oder, Berlin, 1982—; founder, owner, dir. Uwe Warnke Verlag, Berlin, 1990—. Author: Uwe Warnke serielle texte, 1989, Numeralien, 1991, Das Fall, 1992, Übung vierhändig, 1996, Wortgang, 1996, text, 1998, Parodien, 1999. Recipient V.O. Stomps award The Town of Mainz, Germany, 1991. E-mail: warnke@snafu.de. Office: Uwe Warnke Verlag, Sonntag str 22, 10245 Berlin Germany

WARNOCK, WILLIAM REID, lawyer; b. Detroit, Mich., July 25, 1939; s. William G. and Margery E. (Ford) W.; m. Sandra L. Klarich, Dec. 27, 1961; children: Cheryl Lynn, Laura Ellen. BBA, U. Mich., 1961, JD with distinction, 1964. Bar: Ill. 1964, U.S. Dist. Ct. (no. dist.) Ill. 1965, U.S. Supreme Ct. 1972, Mich. 1995. With Ross & Hardies, Chgo., 1964-70; regional counsel U.S. Dept. HUD, Chgo., 1970-73; ptnr. Roan & Grossman, Chgo., 1973-82; sole practice Chgo., 1982-85; ptnr. Siegel & Warnock, Chgo., 1985-91; of counsel Donovan & Olsen, Chgo., 1991; pres. William R. Warnock P.C., LaGrange, Ill., 1992—; cons. Ill. Dept. Bus. and Econ. Devel., Chgo., 1977-78, Ill. Housing Devel. Authority, Chgo., 1973-78, Council State Housing Financing Agys., Washington, 1975-78; past pres., chmn. Atty.'s Title Guaranty Fund, Inc., Chgo., 1986-88, also bd. dirs., 1976—. Author: (legal references) Land Use and Zoning, 1974-88, Ward on Title Examination, 1975, Illinois Real Property Service: Real Estate Exchanges, 1988, Environmental Law and the Real Estate Lawyer, 1989-90. Mem. Ill. State Bar Assn., Am. Coll. Real Estate Lawyers, DuPage Club. Republican. Methodist. Avocations: boating, woodworking. Fax: 708-482-0977. Home: 13556 Pleasant View Rd Three Rivers MI 49093-8406

WARR, WENDY ANNE, information management specialist, researcher; b. Stoke-On-Trent, Eng., Mar. 7, 1945; d. Charles Stuart and Florrie (Allman) Dobson; m. Hilary Eric Warr, Aug. 5, 1967; children: Alastair Charles, Adrian Hedley. BA, U. Oxford, Eng., 1967, MA, DPhil, 1970. Rsch. asst. U. Oxford, 1968-70; rsch. chemist Robinson Bros. Ltd., West Bromwich, Eng., 1970-72; various positions systems dept. ICI Pharms., Cheshire, Eng., 1972-86, rsch. info. mgr., 1984-86, mgr. info. svcs., 1986-90, corp. external rels. exec., 1990-92; pvt. practice Wendy Warr & Assocs., 1992—. Author book and book chpts.; editor 9 books, Jour. Chem. Info. and Computer Scis., 1989—; contbr. articles to profl. jours. Fellow Inst. Info. Scientists, Royal Soc. Chemistry; mem. Am. Chem. Soc., Am. Soc. Info. Sci., Chem. Structure Assn. Methodist. Avocations: swimming, cycling, reading, singing, music. Home: 6 Berwick Ct, Holmes Chapel CW4 7HZ, England

WARRELL, ERNEST HERBERT, organist, choir master, educator; b. London, June 23, 1915; s. Herbert Henry and Edith (Peacock) W.; m. Jean Denton, May 24, 1952; children: Christopher John, Nicholas Leslie, Angela Mary. Grad. secondary sch., London. Organist, lectr. music Kings Coll., London, 1953-91; organist, choir master St. Mary's Primrose Hill, London, 1954-57; lectr. plainsong Royal Sch. Ch. Music, Croydon, 1954-59; orgainst, choir master St. John the Divine, Kennington, London, 1961-68; organist, dir. music Southwark Cathedral, London, 1968-76; musical dir. Gregorian Assn., London, 1969-82; chief examiner Internat. Baccalaureate, Geneva, 1983-88; chmn. acad. bd. Guild of Ch. Musicians, 1991-96. Author: Accompaniments to the Psalm Tones, 1942, Plainsong and the Anglican Organist, 1943; editor: (with others) An English Kyriale, 1988, (with Anne Kennedy) Seriously Silly Hymns, 1999. Capt. Brit. Army, 1940-46. Decorated Mem. Order Brit. Empire; fellow King's Coll., U. London, 1979, Trinity Coll., London. Fellow Guild Ch. Musicians (hon.); mem. Spl. Forces Club, Little Ship Club. Mem. Ch. Eng. Avocation: sailing. Home and Office: 41 Beechhill Rd, Eltham London SE9 1HJ, England

WARREN, ALBERT, publishing executive; b. Warren, Ohio, May 18, 1920; s. David and Clara W.; m. Margaret Virginia Yeomans, Jan. 9, 1947; children: Ellen, Paul, Claire, Daniel, Thomas, Joan. BA in Journalism, Ohio State U., 1942. Assoc. editor TV Digest, Washington, 1945-50, sr. editor, 1950-58, chief Washington Bur., 1958-61; chmn., editor, pub. Warren Comm. News, Inc., Washington, 1961—; lectr. Columbia Grad. Sch. Journalism, N.Y.C., 1962-75; mem. alumni adv. coun. Ohio State U., Columbus, 1982-88. Contbr. articles to profl. jours. Mem. adv. coun. sch. of journalism Ohio State U., 1982—. With USNR, 1942-45, PTO. Recipient Disting. Alumnus award Ohio State U. Sch. Journalism, 1995. Mem. Ind. Newsletter Assn. (co-founder 1963, pres. 1965-66), Newsletter Pubs. Assn. (Hall of Fame 1985), Broadcast Pioneers (Annual Recognition award 1982, Hall of Fame 1995), Cable TV Pioneers, Internat. Radio and TV Soc. Pubs., White House Corr. Assn., U.S. Congress Periodical Gallery, Soc. Profl. Journalists (Hall of Fame 1991), Cosmos Club. Home: 26 W Kirke St Chevy Chase MD 20815-4261 Office: Comm News Inc 2115 Ward Ct NW Washington DC 20037-1209

WARREN, ANDREW, geomorphologist, educator; b. Kalimpong, India, Oct. 27, 1937; arrived in England, 1947; s. Thomas and Janet Simpson (MacPhail) W.; m. Inga Marian Kerridge, Aug. 14, 1967; children: Ben, Anna. BS, Aberdeen U., 1959; PhD, Cambridge U., 1967. Soil surveyor Hunting Tech. Svcs. Ltd., Borehamwood, England, 1960-64; lectr. U. Coll. London, 1964-73, sr. lectr., 1973-95, prof., 1995—; cons. UNEP, Nairobi, Kenya, 1976-77, UNSO, N.Y.C., 1991. Co-author: Geomorphology in Deserts, 1974, Desert Geomorphology, 1991; co-editor: Conservation in Practice, 1973, Conservation in Perspective, 1984. Fellow Am. Coun. Learned Socs., 1967-68; recipient Back award Royal Geog. Soc., 1977. Home: Flat 5 44 Saffron Hill, London ECIN 8FH, England Office: U Coll London, 26 Bedford Way, London WC1H OAP, England

WARREN, BACIL BENJAMIN, writer, publisher; b. Leupp, Ariz., Oct. 21, 1915; s. Bacil Augustine and Margaret Adell (Norman) W.; m. Annelle Griffin, May 26, 1938 (dec. Apr. 1990); children: Jannelle Jedd, Bacil Christopher. BA, U. Ariz., 1938. Pub. info. officer U. Ariz., Tucson, 1937-38, Ariz. Dept. Social Security, Phoenix, 1938-42; supr. of continuity Ariz. Broadcasting Sys., Tucson, 1942-45; investigations supr. U.S. Civil Svc. Commn., Tucson, 1945-64; dir. pubs. U.S. Civil Svc. Commn., Washington, 1964-76; pub. Aileen Griffin Press, Tucson, 1976—. Supervising writer: Biography of an Ideal, 1974; author: Young at Any Age, 1978, Ernie, the Fast Horse (children's book), 1979, A History of Errors, 1984, On the Anacoluthe, 1994, Think Left, Look Right, 1996; prodr., dir. (documentary videos): Alamos, 1996, Land of the Long White Cloud, 1997, St. Mark's Jubilee, 1998, Spanish Missions of Santa Cruz, 1999, Copper Canyon Adventure, 1999, Kiwis Wild, Kiwis Tame, 2000; contbr. articles to profl. jours. Mem. Oral History Assn., Western History Assn., Ariz. Hist. Soc., Internat. Air Passenger's Assn., Royal Oak Soc., Nat. Press Club (founding mem. Found.), Phi Beta Kappa. Democrat. Presbyterian. Avocations: photography, videography, video editing. Office: Aileen Griffin Press 3737 E Pima St Tucson AZ 85716-3322

WARREN, GRAHAM BARRY, cell biology educator; b. London, Feb. 25, 1948; s. Charles Graham and Joyce Thelma (Roberts) W.; m. Philippa Mary Temple-Cole, June 18, 1966; children: Joanna, Eleanor, Katya, Alexandra. MA, Cambridge U., 1969, PhD, 1972. Group leader EMBL, Heidelberg, Germany, 1977-85; prof., chair dept. biochemistry U. Dundee, Scotland, 1985-88; prin. scientist ICRF, London, 1988-99; prof. cell biology Yale U. Med. Sch., New Haven, 1999—. Mem. editl. bd. Jour. Cell Biology, 1985-88, 95—. Fellow Royal Soc. (London); mem. Biochem. Soc., Am. Soc. Cell Biology, Academia Europaea, European Molecular Biology Orgn. Office: Yale U Med Sch 333 Cedar St New Haven CT 06510-3289

WARREN, JANET L., psychiatric medicine educator, psychotherapist; b. Winnipeg, Man., Can., Mar. 8, 1951; came to U.S., 1973; d. Clarence Robinson and Irene Margarite (Morrison) W.; m. David Dalley, June 14, 1974 (div. Aug. 1980); 1 child, Miran Anur Warren; m. Robert Scott Leventhal, June 18, 1995. BSW, U. Man., Winnipeg, 1973, MSW, 1975; D Social Work with distinction, U. Calif., Berkeley, 1982; postgrad., N.Y. Freudian Soc. Lic. clin. social worker, Va. Tchg. asst. U. Calif., 1977-78; instr. sociology dept. Piedmont C.C., Charlottesville, Va., 1980; instr. dept. behavioral medicine and psychiatry U. Va., Charlottesville, 1981-85; asst. prof. U. Va. Gen. Med. Faculty, Charlottesville, 1985-92, clin. assoc. prof. psychiat. medicine, 1992—, instr. divsn. med. ctr. social work, 1981-85, asst. prof., 1981=85; co-dir. Va. Inst. Justice Info. Sys. U. Va., 1992—; with Inst. Law, Psychiatry and Pub. Policy, Blue Ridge Hosp., Charlottesville; liaison behavioral scis. unit FBI Acad., Quantico, Va., 1997—; criminal and civil forensic cons. in U.S. and internationally, 1990—; pvt. practice psychoanalysis and psychoanalytic psychotherpay, Charlottesville; presenter state, nat. and internat. meetings and confs., also on TV and radio; jour. reviewer Hosp. and Cmty. Psychiatry, Jour. Interpersonal Violence, Jour. Family Violence, Violence Against Women, Aggression and Violent Behavior: A Rev. Jour. Mem. editl. bd. Threat Assessment; contbr. numerous articles to profl. jours., including Forensic Scis. Internat., Jour. Forensic Scis., Jour. Occupl. and Environ. Medicine, Jour. Quantitative Criminology, Internat. Jour. Law and Psychiatry, FBI Law Enforcement Bull., Jour. Interpersonal Violence, Bull. Am. Acad. Psychiatry and Law, Hosp. and Cmty. Psychiatry, Australian Jour. Medicine, Jour. Cons. and Clin. Psychology, Law and Human Behavior, Jour. Criminal Justice and Behavior. Gertrude Child scholar, 1973, Coun. Jewish Women scholar, 1973; Donald Vernon Snider Meml. fellow, 1974-75, grad. fellow U. Man., fellow AAUW, 1976, Can. Coun., 1976, 77; Guggenheim grantee, 1992-93, gtantee Forensic Info. Mgmt. Sys., 1987-999, Nat. Inst. Justice, 1992-94, 98-00, Va. Dept. Criminal Justice Svcs., 1995-99, Office Juvenile Justice and Delinquency Prevention, 1997-99. Mem. NASW, Nat. Orgn. Forensic Social Work (treas. 1985-86, pres.-elect 1986, pres. 1987-88, treas. Blue Ridge chpt. 1988-89), Nat. Fedn. Clin. Social Work (co-chmn. forensic subcom. 1992-96). Avocation: psychoanalysis. E-mail: jlw@virginia.edu. Office: Inst Law Psychiat-Pub Policy PO Box 100 Charlottesville VA 22902-0100

WARREN, JOHN COOLIDGE, private school dean, history educator; b. Boston, May 16, 1956; s. William Bradford and Mary-Elizabeth (Coolidge) W.; m. Laura Parker Appell, June 18, 1983; children: Ethan Reynolds Appell, Amanda Pfaltzgraff Appell. BA, Stanford U., 1978, MA, 1980; MEd, Harvard U., 1991, EdD, 1994. Tchr. history Robert Louis Stevenson Sch., Pebble Beach, Calif., 1979-81; tchr. history Milton (Mass.) Acad., 1981—, chmn. dept. history, 1992-95, acad. dean, 1995—; faculty cons. Ednl. Testing Svc., Princeton, 1990—, William Joiner Ctr., Boston, 1992—; editl. cons. Longman Inc., White Plains, N.Y., 1991—. Editor: America's Intervention in Vietnam, 1987. NEH fellow, 1985, advanced doctoral fellow, Harvard U., 1993. Mem. Am. Hist. Assn., Orgn. Am. Historians, Assn. Asian Studies, World History Assn., Boston Athaneum, Colonial Soc. Mass., Mass. Hist. Soc., Phi Beta Kappa. Avocations: canoeing, fishing. Home and Office: Milton Acad 170 Centre St Milton MA 02186-3338

WARREN, JOYCE WILLIAMS, English language educator, writer; b. Springfield, Mass.; d. Robert Frederic and Violet Victoria (Hill) W.; m. Frank A. Warren; children: Victoria, Catherine, Charlotte, Frank. BA, Brown U., MA; PhD, Columbia U., 1981. From lectr. to asst. prof. Queens Coll., Flushing, N.Y., 1981-94, assoc. prof., 1994—; dir. women's studies Queens Coll., 1993-94. Author: The American Narcissus, 1984, Fanny Fern: An Independent Woman, 1992, (children's book) A Mouse To Be Free, 1973; editor: Ruth Hall and Other Writings, 1986, The (Other) American Traditions, 1993, Challenging Boundaries, 2000. NEH grantee, 1987. Mem. Am. Lit. Assn., Modern Lang. Assn., Am. Studies Assn., Northeast Modern Lang. Assn. Office: Queens Coll Dept English Flushing NY 11367

WARREN, KENNETH, geography educator; b. Lincoln, Eng., Sept. 16, 1931; s. Arthur Robert and Doris May (Blow) W.; m. Jean Elizabeth Elcock, June 6, 1957; children: Peter, John, David. BA, U. Cambridge, Eng., 1954, PhD, 1960. From asst. lectr. to lectr. U. Leicester, Eng., 1956-66; lectr. U. Newcastle upon Tyne, Eng., 1966-70; lectr. and fellow U. Oxford, Eng., 1970-91; emeritus fellow Jesus Coll. U. Oxford, 1991—. Author: The American Steel Industry, 1973, Chemical Foundations, 1980, Mineral Resources, 1973, Armstrongs of Elswick, 1990, Triumphant Capitalism: Henry Clay Frick and the Industrial Transformation of America, 1996, Steel, Ships and Men: Cammell Laird, 1824-1993, 1998. Methodist. Avocations: gardening, walking. Home: Little Garth Leazes Ln, Hexham Northumberland NE46 3AQ, England Office: Jesus Coll, Oxford OX1 3DW, England

WARREN, PAUL ROBERT, dentist; b. Bromley, Kent, Eng., May 3, 1947; s. Charles Walter and Eva Marion (Powell) W.; m. Sally Elizabeth Draper, Sept. 24, 1970; children: Marcus Simon, Hannah Ruth, Robert James. Lic. Dental Surgeon, U. Sheffield, Eng., 1970. Registered dental surgeon, U.K. Lectr. U. Sheffield, 1970-75; pvt. practice gen. dentistry U.K., 1975-86; dental advisor ICI Pharms., U.K., 1986-93; dir. clin. rsch. Braun GmbH, Kronberg, Germany, 1993-2000; v.p. clin. rsch. and dental affairs Oral-B Labs., Kronberg, Germany, 2000—; hon. clin. rsch. asst. U. Wales, 1988-93; hon. clin. rsch. lectr. U. Manchester, 1986-90; examiner Royal Soc. Health, London, 1983-90. Contbr.: Practical Dental Health Education I and II, 1981, 83; contbr. articlesto profl. jours. Treas. Round Table, Riverdale, Eng., 1985-86; chmn. Club Beyond/Young Life, Frankfurt, Germany, 1995-96. Mem. ADA, Internat. Assn. Dental Rsch., Brit. Dental Assn. Office: Braun GmbH, Frankfurter Str 145, 61476 Kronberg Taunus, Germany

WARREN, PETER MICHAEL, archaeologist, educator; b. Crewe, Cheshire, Eng., June 23, 1938; s. Arthur George and Alison Joan (White) W.; m. Elizabeth Margaret Halliday, June 18, 1966; children: Diktynna Alison, Damian Arthur Charles. BA, U. Wales, 1960, U. Cambridge, 1962; MA, U. Cambridge, 1966, PhD, 1966. Rsch. fellow Corpus Christi Coll., Cambridge, 1965-68; rsch. fellow in arts U. Durham, 1968-70; asst. dir. Brit. Sch. at Athens, 1970-72; lectr., sr. lectr., reader in Aegean archaeology U. Birmingham, 1972-76; prof. ancient history and classical archaeology U. Bristol, 1977—; dir. excavations Myrtos, Crete, Greece, 1967-68, Knossos, Crete, 1971-73, 78-82, 97; chmn. mng. com. Brit. Sch. at Athens, 1979-83; vis. prof. U. Minn., Mpls., 1981; Geddes-Harrower prof. Greek art and archeol. U. Aberdeen, 1986-87; Neuberg lectr. and prize U. Göthenburg, 1986. Author: Minoan Stone Vases, 1969, Myrtos, An Early Bronze Age Settlement in Crete, 1972, The Aegean Civilizations, 1975, 2nd edit., 1989, Aegean Bronze Age, 1989; contbr. articles to profl. jours. Fellow Brit. Acad., Soc. Antiquaries of London (hon.), Archeol. Soc. Athens; mem. Austrian Acad. Scis. (corr.), Bristol and Gloucestershire Archaeol. Soc. (chmn. coun. 1981-84, trustee 1985, pres. 2000—), Soc. for Promotion of Hellenic Studies (mem. coun. 1978-81). Anglican. Avocations: Greek and Balkan history and society, botany and use of plants. Office: U Bristol, Dept Archaeology 43 Woodland Rd, Bristol BS8 1UU, England

WARREN, RAYMOND H.C., music educator, composer; b. Weston Super Mare, Eng., Nov. 7, 1928; s. Arthur H. and Gwendoline C. (Hallett) W.; m. Roberta L.A. Smith, Apr. 9, 1953; children: Timothy, Christopher, Benedict, Clare. Student, Cambridge (Eng.) U., 1949-52, MA, 1957, DMus, 1969. Lectr. Queen's U., Belfast, No. Ireland, 1955-67, prof. music, 1967-72; prof. music U. Bristol, U.K., 1972-94; ret., 1994. Author: Opera Workshop, 1995; composer oratorios, symphonies, opera songs, cantatas, church music. Mem. Brit. Acad. Composers and Songwriters. Avocation: walking. Home: 9 Cabot Rise, Portishead Bristol BS20 6NX, England

WARREN, RICHARD M., experimental psychologist, educator; b. N.Y.C., Apr. 8, 1925; s. Morris and Rae (Greenberg) W.; m. Roslyn Pauker, Mar. 31, 1950. BS in Chemistry, CCNY, 1946; PhD in Organic Chemistry, NYU, 1951. Flavor chemist Gen. Foods Co., Hoboken, N.J., 1951-53; rsch. assoc. psychology Brown U., Providence, 1954-56; Carnegie sr. rsch. fellow NYU Coll. Medicine, 1956-57; Carnegie sr. rsch. fellow Cambridge (Eng.) U., 1957-58, rsch. psychologist applied psychology rsch. unit, 1958-59; rsch. psychologist NIMH, Bethesda, Md., 1959-61; chmn. psychology Shimer Coll., Mt. Carroll, Ill., 1961-64; assoc. prof. psychology U. Wis., Milw., 1964-66, prof., 1966-73, rsch. prof., 1973-75, disting. prof., 1975-95, adj. disting. prof., 1995—; vis. scientist Inst. Exptl. Psychology, Oxford (Eng.) U., 1969-70, 77-78. Author: (with Roslyn Warren) Helmholtz on Perception: Its Physiology and Development, 1968, Auditory Perception: A New Analysis and Synthesis, 1999; contbr. articles to profl. jours. Fellow APA, Am. Psychol. Soc., Acoustical Soc. Am.; mem. AAAS, Am. Chem. Soc., Am. Speech and Hearing Assn., Sigma Xi. Office: U Wis Dept Psychology Milwaukee WI 53201

WARREN, RUSSELL JAMES, investment banking executive, consultant; b. Cleve., July 28, 1938; s. Harold Fulton and Agnes Elmina (Hawkswell) W.; m. Doris Helen Kenyeres, June 6, 1964. BS, Case Western Res. U., 1960; MBA, Harvard U., 1962. CPA, Ohio. With Ernst & Whinney, Cleve., 1962-87, ptnr. in charger merger and acquisition svcs., 1987—. Co-author: Implementing Mergers and Acquisitions in the Fin. and Svc. Industry, 1985; assoc. editor Jour. Corp. Growth, 1986-87, mem. editl. bd., 1988; contbg. editor Jour. Buyouts and Acquisitions, 1984-86; contbg. author venture capital financing study conducted in five countries for Asian Devel. Bank, Malaysia, Indonesia, Pakistan, Sri Lanka, Thailand, 1986. Trustee Case Western Res. U., 1980—, chmn. audit com., 1991—; trustee Cleve. Bot. Garden, 1995—, Western Res. Hist. Soc., 1996—, Cmty. Improvement Corp Summit, Medina and Portage Counties, 1992—, Cascade CDC, 1992—; trustee Fairmont Presbyn. Ch., 1987-93, elder, 1991-93; dir. Univ. Tech., inc., 1986-88; adv. bd. Shaker Investments, 1992—; v.p. M & A Internat., Inc., 1990-91, pres., 1992; bd. zoning appeals City of Lyndhurst, 1978—, chmn., 1980-82, 91-93, 2000—; mem. vis. com. Case Sch. Engring., Weatherhead Sch. Mgmt., 1998—. Mem. AICPA, Ohio Soc. CPA's, Assn. for Corp. Growth (bd. dirs. internat. orgn. 1988, v.p. Cleve. chpt. 1983-86, pres. 1986-87), Cleve. Com. on Fgn. Rels., Cleve. World Trade Assn., Union Club, Mayfield Country Club, Catawba Island Club, Harvard Club N.Y.C., Jesters. Office: The TransAction Group 500 Hanna Bldg Cleveland OH 44115

WARREN, WARREN SLOAN, chemist; b. Detroit, Aug. 16, 1955; s. Arthur Stanley and Pauline (Sloan) W.; m. Kathleen Elizabeth Horsch, Aug. 17, 1978; children: Julie Kathleen, Michael Sloan. AB, Harvard U., 1977; MS, U. Calif. Berkeley, 1979, PhD, 1980. Prof. chemistry Princeton U., N.J., 1982—, dir. Ctr. Ultrafast Laser Applications, 1997—; assoc. dir. Princeton Ctr. Photonics/Optoelectronic Materials, N.J., 1992—; editor: (jour.) Advances in Magnetic and Optical Resonance, Academic Press, 1988—. Author: (book) The Physical Basis of Chemistry, 1993, 2000; contbr. articles to profl. jours. Recipient McKnight Innovation award in neurosci., McKnight Found., Minneapolis, 1999. Fellow Am. Physical Soc.; mem. Am. Chem. Soc. (chmn. princeton section). Fax: 609-258-6746. E-mail: wwarren@princeton.edu. Office: Dept Chem Princeton U Princeton NJ 08544-0001

WARRLICH, ANNE CAROLINA, veterinarian, journalist; b. Frankfurt, Germany, June 28, 1961; d. Peter Gerisch and Ruth Bydekarken; children: Laura, Siri. D, Justus-Liebig U., Germany, 1985, DVM, 1988. Pvt. practice veterinarian Besigheim, Germany, 1986—; freelance journalist Besigheim, 1995—. Author: Meine Zwergkaninchen, 1999, 1. Hilfe für meinen Hund, 2000; contbr. numerous articles to profl. jours. Mem. Bundesverband Prakt. Tierärzte, Deutsche Teckelklub e.v. Avocation: American quarter horses. Office: Finkenweg 1, 74354 Besigheim Germany

WARSELIUS, LENNART ROLF, cardiologist, consultant; b. Stockholm, Oct. 7, 1954; s. Rolf Olov and Kerstin Elisabeth (Burö) W.; m. Anna-Karin Maria Lindkvist, Nov. 26, 1988; children: Pauline, Georg, Karl. MD, Karolinska Inst., Stockholm, 1981. Qualified internal medicine and cardiology specialist, Sweden. Intern St. Eriks Hosp., Stockholm, 1983-85, resident in internal medicine, 1985-86; resident Huddinge U. Hosp., Stockholm, 1986, attending cardiologist, 1991; resident Södersjukhuset, Stockholm, 1987-88, fellow in cardiology, 1988-91; cons. cardiologist Stockholm Heart Ctr., 1991-97, Sophiahemmet, Stockholm, 1997—. Lt. Swedish Army, 1988. Mem. Swedish Med. Assn., Swedish Soc. Cardiology, Swedish-Brit. Soc., lOrdre Amaranter, lOrdre l'Innocence. Mem. Conservative Party. Avocations: sailing, skiing, golf, hunting. E-Mail: lw@pi.se. Home: Falkvägen 37A, S-18350 Täby Sweden Office: Sophiahemmet, Box 5605, Hjärt-Kärlgr LM 5 Mott 2, S-11486 Stockholm Sweden

WARSHAWSKY, ISIDORE, physicist, consultant; b. N.Y.C., May 27, 1911; s. Morris and Esther (Sherman) W. BS cum laude, CCNY, 1930. Physicist Nat. Adv. Com. Aeronautics, Langley Field, Va., 1930-42; chief instrumentation sect. Nat. Adv. Com. Aeronautics, Cleve., 1942-50; chief instrument rsch. br. Nat. Adv. Com. Aeronautics/ NASA, Cleve., 1950-72; instrumentation cons. NASA, Cleve., 1972-90, ret., 1990, disting. rsch. cons. (unsalaried), 1990-95. Author: (textbook) Foundations of Measurement and Instrumentation, 1990; author 10 NACA/NASA tech. reports; contbr. 20 articles to sci. jours. and books. Fellow Instrument Soc. Am.; mem. Am. Phys. Soc., Combustion Inst., Am. Vacuum Soc, Phi Beta Kappa.

WARTENBERG, MARTIN B., physician, educator; b. Cali, Columbia, Apr. 14, 1944; s. Bertram and Haydee (Villegas) W.; m. Virginia Correa, Dec. 20, 1975; children: Federico, Juan Sebastian, Alejandro. MD, U. del Valle, 1969. Diplomate Am. Bd. Internal Medicine, Am. Bd. Cardiovascular Disease. Intern Princeton (N.J.) Hosp., 1971; resident in internal medicine Tulane U., New Orleans, 1974-76, fellow in cardiology, 1976; assoc. prof. medicine U. del Valle, Cali, Columbia, 1976—; exec. dir. Fundacion Valle del Lilli, Cali, 1983-85, med. dir., 1985—; dir. ICU Hosp. Univ. Valle, Cali, 1977-80; exec. sec. X Congreso Colombia Cardiology, Cali, 1983. Assoc. editor Revista Colombiana Cardiology, Bogota, Columbia, 1984—. Fellow Am. Coll. Cardiology; mem. Musser-Burch Soc., Soc. Colombian Medic-Interna, Soc. Colombiana de Cardiology, N.Y. Acad. Scis. Liberal. Roman Catholic. Clubs: Campestre (Cali) (bd. dirs. 1980-83), Colombia. Avocations: golf, history of medicine. Home: Carrera 2 B Oeste # 7-40, Cali Colombia Office: Fundaction Valle del Lili, Carrera 98 18-49, Cali Colombia

WARTEWIG, SIEGFRIED HERMANN, physicist, educator; b. Langensalza, Thueringen, Germany, May 11, 1938; s. Otto Alwin and Gertrud (Cohn) W.; m. Antje Lina Kofeld, May 22, 1963; children: Peter, Anne-Kristin. Diploma, U. Leipzig, Germany, 1961, Dr.rer.nat., 1968, Dr.habil., 1979. Asst. dept. physics U. Leipzig, 1961-70, asst. prof., 1970-79; prof. Tech. U., Merseburg, Germany, 1979-93, U. Halle-Wittenberg, Halle, Germany, 1993-95; prof. physics Inst. Applied Dermatopharmacy, Halle, 1995—; dir. dept. physics Tech. U., Merseburg, 1987-91, dir. Inst. Exptl. Physics, 1991-93. Mem. German Phys. Soc. Avocations: skiing, sailing. Office: Inst Applied Dermatopharm, Wolfgang-Langenbeck Str 4, D-06120 Halle Sachsen-Anhalt, Germany

WARTHMAN, LESLIE, administrative assistant, writer; b. Marquette, Ohio, June 21, 1960; d. Max Schultz and Ilona Doris Habermann; m. Randall Lee, June 26, 1976; children: Taran, Alaxandra. BA, Ohio State U., 1982. Intern WCMH-TV, Columbus, Ohio, 1980-81; reporter WMNI-AM/FM Radio, Columbus, Ohio, 1980-82; afternoon drive news dir. WSNY-FM Radio, Upper Arlington, Ohio, 1982-83; adv. copywriter Angeletti Ad Agy., Westerville, Ohio, 1983-85; spl. assignment copy writer, reporter This Week News, Worthington, Ohio, 1985-97; adminstrv. asst. Orange Twp., Lewis Ctr., Ohio, 1997—; freelance writer Bus. First, Columbus, 1985-97. Editor O.T. Newsletter, 1999; newsletter writer various orgs. including Family Weight Loss Ctrs., 1998. E-mail: imrightus@aol.com. Home: 7610 Park Bend Ct Westerville OH 43082-9796 Office: Orange Twp 7307 S Old State Rd Lewis Center OH 43035-9228

WARTIOVAARA, JORMA JUHANI, educator; b. Helsinki, Finland, July 25, 1938; s. Otso Uolevi and Maine Helmi Kaarina (Alanen) W.; m. Kirsti Anna Tuulikki Hyvarinen, 1964 (div. 1988); children: Katarina, Kirmo, Anna; m. Satu Kyllikki Koskimies, 1992. MD, Med. Sch. U. Helsinki, 1964, PhD, 1966. Jr. researcher Nat. Acad. Med. Sci. Finland, 1964-67; pathology assoc. U. Helsinki, 1970-74; sr. researcher Nat. Acad. Med. Sci. Finland, 1975-77; assoc. prof. biology U. Helsinki, 1978-87, prof., dir. dept. electron microscopy, 1988-95, rsch. dir. Inst. Biotechnology, 1996—. Co-editor: Medical Developmental Biology, 1976. Sect. chmn. cell & devel. biology Finnish-Soviet Commn. Coop. in Sci. adn Tech., Helsinki, 1981-92. Grantee Nat. Acad. Med. Sci., Finland, 1970-89, Sigrid Juselius Found., Finland, 1970-87, U. Helsinki, 1989. Mem. Scandanavian Soc. Electron Microsci. Soc. (pres. 1980-82), Internat. Soc. Devel. Biologists (sec.-treas. 1973-82), European Devel. Biology Orgn. (v.p. 1982-89). Avocation: graphic arts. Office: U Helsinki Inst Biotech, Viikinkaari 9 PO Box 56, 00014 Helsinki Finland

WARWICK-SMITH, MYLES HUMPHREY, hygiene and sanitation company executive; b. Dec. 26, 1929; s. Reginald Sidney and Eileen (Maclean) W.-S.; m. Diana Mary Freeman, Jan. 16, 1952; children: Penny, Nella, Robert, Peter. Student, Nautical Coll., Worcester, 1944-47, Eaton Hall Officer Cadet Sch., Chester, 1950. Mgmt. trainee Bick Internat. Ltd., London, 1953-59; sales mgr. Eucryl Group Ltd., Southampton, Eng., 1959-65; mng. dir. Fogarty Ltd., Boston, 1965-67, Solignum Ltd., London, 1967-70, LRC Indsl. Holding, London, 1970-81, Elsan Ltd., Sussex, 1981—; dir. LRC Internat., PLC, London, 1970-81. Author: Toiletries and Cosmetics in Europe, 1980. Com. mem. Brit. Wood Preserving Assn., 1968. Served to capt. Brit. Army, 1950-56, Royal warrant, 1969. Fellow Inst. Dirs., Brit. Inst. Mgmt.; mem. Internat. Sales and Mktg., Inst. Export, Am. Wood Preserving Assn., Brit. Productivity Assn., Pharm. Assn. Gt. Britain, Dirs. Club London, Pub. Sch. Club, East India Club (London). Conservative. Mem. Ch. Eng. Fax: 44 0 1825 761212. Office: Elsan Ltd, Buxted, Sussex,, Elms Barn Isfield Uckfield, Sussex TN22 5XG, England

WASACZ, EMIL, federal official; b. Zabratowka, Aug. 1, 1945; married; 3 children. Gradn., Lodz U. Tech., 1969; postgrad., Warsaw Sch. Econs., 1994. With Apator, Torun, 1969-71, R&D Ctr. Propulsion Control instruments, 1971-94, Huta Katowice Steel Mill, 1976-94; mng. dir. Huta Katowice SA, 1991-94, chmn. bd. dirs., 1991-97; dep. chmn. supervisory bd. progress Nat. Investment Fund, 1995-96; chmn. bd. dirs. Huta Szczecins S.A., 1995-97; min. Treasury, Warsaw, 1997—. Solidarity Election Action. Office: Min Treasury, ul Krucza 36/Wsp Ólna 6, 00-522 Warsaw Poland*

WASEEM, MOHAMMAD, engineer; b. Jhang, Punjab, Pakistan, Mar. 21, 1951; s. Mohammad Amjad Hussain and Naseema (Ul-Nisa) Amjad; m. Nighat Siddiqui, Feb. 24, 1989; children: Mohammad Arsalan Waseem, Madeeha Waseem, Zaiya Waseem. SSC, Lahore Bd., 1966; FS, Sargodha Bd., 1968; BS in Mech. Engring., U. Engring. and Tech., Lahore, 1973. Cert. fin. acct., cost acct., mgr. IBA. Apprentice engr. Brit. India Engring., Karachi, 1974; apprentice engr. Pak-Am. Fertilizers Mianwali, 1974-75, asst. deputy mgr., 1975-80; mech. engr. Nat. Refinery Ltd., Karachi, 1980-91, sr. project engr., 1992-95; mgr., sr. mgr. Nat. Refinery Ltd., 1995—. Pres. N.R. Officers Assn., Karachi, 1991, 92. Mem. Instn. Engrs., ASME Internat., Pakistan Engring. Coun. Avocations: Bridge, tennis, table tennis. Office: Nat Refinery Ltd, Karachi 75530, Pakistan

WASHBURN, KATHRYN HAZEL, government agency executive; b. L.A., May 22, 1944; d. S. Edward and Hazel Irene Lafler; m. Wilcomb Edward Washburn, Jan. 2, 1985 (Feb. 1997); m. William A. Niskanen, Apr. 23, 2000. BA, UCLA, 1966; MA, George Washington U., 1974. Planner Orange County, Santa Ana, Calif., 1966-70; urban planner So. Calif. Assn. Govt., L.A., 1970-71; planner U.S. Dept. Transp., Washington, 1971, U.S. EPA, Washington, 1972, Hwy. Users Fedn., Washington, 1972-73; regional mgr. North Atlantic NOAA, U.S. Dept. Commerce, Washington, 1974-89; dir. internat. affairs U.S. Dept. Interior, Washington, 1989—. Bd. dirs. Am. Inst. Cert. Planners, Washington, 1977-79, Preservation Md., Balt., 1997—, Salisbury State U. Found., 1997—; bd. dirs. Rsch. Ctr. Delmarva History and Culture, Salisbury (Md.) U., 1996—; mem. Chesapeake Bay Found. Mem. Nat. Audubon Soc., Wildlife Conservation Soc., Nature Conservancy, Sierra Club. Home: 648 E Capitol St NE Washington DC 20003-1233 Office: US Dept Interior Dept Internat Affairs 1849 C St NW # Ms4426 Washington DC 20240-0001

WASHINGTON, ANTHONY NATHANIEL, mechanical engineer; b. L.A., Jan. 19, 1969; s. Ralph Anthony and Naomi (Jemison) W. BSME, A&M U. Prairie View, 1992; postgrad., U. Phoenix, 1999—. Engr. Detroit Edison Co., 1992-95, GMC, Dayton, Ohio, 1995-96; area supr. Chrysler Corp., Detroit, 1997-99; product engr. Daimler Chrysler Corp., Detroit, 1999—. Mem. Nat. Black MBA Assn., Nat. Soc. Black Engrs., Metro Detroit Optimist Club, Kappa Alpha Psi Fraternity Inc., Pi Tau Sigma. Avocations: sports, music, travel, reading. Home: 26678 E Carnegie Park Dr Southfield MI 48034-6151

WASHINGTON, CHARLES HENDERSON, laser systems designer, consultant; b. Little Rock, Ark., Apr. 8, 1953; s. John David and Antoinette LaVerne (Henderson) W. BA in Comm., U. Ill., 1979; PhD in Comm., Columbia State U. Lineman apprentice IBEW, Springfield, Ill., 1976-80; data comms. specialist State of Ill., Springfield, Ill., 1980-85; v.p. engring. NATAC, Springfield, Ill., 1983—; cons. North Am. Tec-Hec, Springfield, Ill., 1991-93. Author: Datacom Systems Operation Manual, 1984, Datacom Systems Configuration Manual, 1985. Mem. A. Philip Randolph Inst., Springfield, 1994. With U.S. Navy, 1970-75. Named to Outstanding Young Men of Am., 1984. Mem. AAAS, Internat. Soc. Photo-Optical Engrs., N.Y. Acad. Sci., Omega Psi Phi, Phi Theta Kappa. Methodist.

WASHINGTON, DOLORES, art association administrator; b. Trenton, N.J., Jan. 28, 1936; d. Rachel William and Carrie W.; m. Percell Moody, Apr. 7, 1956 (div. Jan. 1978); children: Sherri, Lawrence, Tyhem, Terron. BA in Liberal Arts, Coll. New Rochelle, 1999. Real estate salesperson Century 21-Willenger Real Estate, N.Y., 1990-93; technician X-Ray darkroom No. Westchester Hosp. Ctr., Mt. Kisco, N.Y., 1990-95; mktg. asst. Westchester Arts Coun., White Plains, N.Y., 1995—; office mgr. GHR Mktg. Network, N.Y.C., 1996—; print model Ford Modelling Agy., N.Y.C.; actress Herbert Mark Newman Theatre, N.Y.C.; founder Designs from Shekinah, 1997—. Film appearances include It Could Happen to Your, 1995, Asylumn of the Soul, 1998. Vol. ESL-Manhattanville Coll., 1998, Sr. Outreach to Sr., White Plains, 1996-98. Nat. Exch. Club-Preventive Child Abuse Parent Aide, White Plains, 1996-97, SHARE Program, White Plains, 1996-98. Recipient Woman of Essence award Zeta Phi Beta, 1997. Avocations: tap dancing, horseback riding, ice skating, singing. Home: PO Box 8622 Tarrytown NY 10591-8622 Office: Westchester Arts Coun 31 Mamaroneck Ave White Plains NY 10601-3300

WASHINGTON, PATRICK JOHN, underwater services company executive; b. Melbourne, Victoria, Australia, Aug. 25, 1943; s. Francis Patrick and Margaret Isobel (Gardner) W.; m. Joan Patricia Massey, July 4, 1969; children: Daniel Geoffrey, David Patrick. Diploma, St. Augustine's Christian Brothers Coll., Yarraville, Australia, 1959. Cert diver/diving supr. Assn. Offshore Diving Contractors (Eng.); cert. fin. mgmt. Sales rep. Ducon Condensers, Melbourne, 1960-64; sales mgr. Plessey Elect, Melbourne, 1965-68; diving supt. Internat. Divers/Australia/U.K. S.E.A., 1968-70; mng. dir. Subsea Svcs., Bairndale, Austrlaia, 1970-73; ops. mgr. Oceaneering Australia, Sale, Perth, 1977-80, gen.mgr., 1980—, mng. dir., 1987—; chmn. bd. dirs. Australian Nat. Underwater Tng. Ctr., beauty Point, Tasmania, 1992-94; diving industry rep. Stds. Assn., Sydney, 1985—; dep. chmn. Nat. Occupl. Diver Tng. Com., Melbourne, 1991—. Chmn. bd. dirs. Victorian Recreational Fishing Body, 1996—, Melbourne, 1994-99; pres. East Gippsland Football League, Bairnsdale, 1985-86, Bairnsdale Fly Fishers, 1994—. Recipient Order of Australia medal Royal Assent, Melbourne, 1994. Mem. Australian Diving Contrs. Assn. (pres. 1987—). Mem. Liberal Party. Roman Catholic. Avocations: fly fishing, fly tying, golf. Office: Oceaneering Australia p/L, 141 Patten St, Sale VIC 3850, Australia

WASHINGTON, REGINALD LOUIS, pediatric cardiologist; b. Colorado Springs, Colo., Dec. 31, 1949; s. Lucius Louis and Brenette Y. (Wheeler) W.; m. Billye Faye Ned, Aug. 18, 1973; children: Danielle Larae, Reginald Quinn. BS in Zoology, Colo. State U., 1971; MD, U. Colo., 1975. Diplomate Nat. Bd. Med. Examiners, Am. Bd. Pediatrics, Pediatric Cardiology. Intern in pediatrics U. Colo. Med. Ctr., Denver, 1975-76, resident in pediatrics, 1976-78, chief resident, instr., 1978-79, fellow in pediatric cardiology, 1979-81, asst. prof. pediatrics, 1982-1988, assoc. prof. pediatrics, 1988-90, assoc. clin. prof. pediatrics, 1990—; staff cardiologist Children's Hosp., Denver, 1981-90; v.p. Rocky Mountain Pediatric Cardiology, Denver, 1990—; chief of staff Presbyn./St. Lukes Med. Ctr., 1999—; mem. admissions com. U. Colo. Sch. Medicine, Denver, 1985-89; chmn., bd. dirs. Coop. Health Care Agreements, 1994-98; chmn. dept. pediatrics Presbyn./St. Lukes Med. Ctr. Denver, 1996-99, pres.-elect med. staff, 1997-99; adv. coun. Nat. Heart Lung Blood Inst., NIH, 1996-98. Cons. editor Your Patient and Fitness, 1989-92. Chmn. Coop. Health Care Agreements Bd., State of Colo., 1994-98; adv. bd. dirs. Equitable Bank of Littleton, Colo., 1984-86; bd. dirs. Ctrl. City Opera, 1989-95, Cleo Parker Robinson Dance Co., 1992-94, Rocky Mountain Heart Fund for Children, 1984-89, Rainbo Ironkids, 1989-95; nat. bd. dirs. Am. Heart Assn., 1992-96; bd. dirs. Nat. Coun. Patient Info. and Edn., 1992-98, Children's Heart Alliance, 1993-94, Colo. State U. Devel. Coun., 1994—, Caring for Colo. Found., 1999—; trustee Denver Ctr. Performing Arts, 1994—, Regis U., 1994-99; mem. Gov.'s Coun. Phys. Fitness, 1990-91; mem. Colo. State Bd. Agr., 1996—, adv. coun. of Nat. Heart Lung Blood Inst. NIH, 1995-98. Named Salute Vol. of Yr. Big Sisters of Colo., 1990; honoree NCCJ, 1994, Physician of Yr., Nat. Am. Heart Assn., 1995. Fellow Am. Acad. Pediatrics (cardiology subsect., chmn. sports medicine and fitness com. 2000—), Am. Coll. Cardiology, Am. Heart Assn. (coun. on cardiovascular disease in the young, exec. com. 1988-91, nat. devel. program com. 1990-94, vol. of yr. 1989, pres. Colo. chpt. 1989-90, Torch of Hope 1987, Gold Heart award Colo. chpt. 1990, bd. dirs. Colo. chpt., exec. com. Colo. chpt. 1987—, grantee Colo. chpt. 1983-84, mem. editorial bd. Pediatric Exercise Scis. 1988—), Soc. Critical Care Medicine; mem. Am. Acad. Pediatrics/Perinatology, , Am. Acad. Pediatrics/Pediatric Cardiology (exec. com. 1996—), N.Am. Soc. Pediatric Exercise Medicine (pres. 1986-87), Colo. Med. Soc. (chmn. sports medicine coun. 1993-94), Leadership Denver 1990, Denver Athletic Club, Met. Club, Glenmoor Golf Club. Democrat. Roman Catholic. Avocations: golf, fishing. Office: Rocky Mountain Pediatric Cardiology 1601 E 19th Ave Ste 5600 Denver CO 80218-1255

WASHINGTON, VALORA, non-profit administrator; b. Columbus, Ohio, Dec. 16, 1953; d. Timothy Washington and Elizabeth (Jackson) Barbour; children: Omari, Kamilah. BA in Social Sci. with honors, Mich. State U., 1974; PhD, Ind. U., 1978; PhD (hon.), Bennett Coll., 1992. Assoc. instr. sch. edn. Ind. U., Bloomington, 1975-77; dir., cons. Urban League Ind., Indpls., 1977-78; substitute tchr. Indpl. Pub. Schs., 1978; dir. U. N.C., Chapel Hill, 1980-82; congrl. sci. fellow Soc. for Rsch. in Child Devel., Washington, 1981-82; prof. edn. U. N.C., Chapel Hill, 1978-83; asst. dean, assoc. prof. Howard U., Washington, 1983-86, Am. U., Washington, 1986-87; prof., v.p. Antioch Coll., Yellow Springs, Ohio, 1987-90; v.p. Kellogg Found., Battle Creek, Mich., 1990-99; exec. dir. Unitarian Universalist Svc. Com., 1999—; cons. Ford Found., N.Y.C., 1990; project evaluator Carnegie Corp., N.Y.C., 1989-90, Ohio Bd. Regents, Columbus, 1990—. Author: (with others) Creating New Linkages for the Adoption of Black Children, 1984, Project Head Start: Past, Present and Future Trends in the Context of Family Needs, 1987, Black Children and American Institutions: An Ecological Review and Resource Guide, 1988, Affirmative Rhetoric, Negative Action: The Status of Black and Hispanic Faculty in Higher Education, 1989; contbr. articles to profl. jours; contbr. chapters to numerous books. Recipient Capital U. award, 1990, award Springfield Alliance Black Educators, 1989; named one of Ten Outstanding Young Women Am., 1980, Outstanding Young Woman N.C., 1980, one of 100 Young Women of Promise Good Housekeeping Mag., 1985, one of 25 Most Influential Working Mothers, Working Mothers Mag., 1997. Mem. Nat. Coun. Negro Women (chmn. 1982-83), Am. Assn. for Higher Edn. (sec. black caucus 1989), Soc. for Rsch. in Child Devel. (pres. black caucus 1987-89), Nat. Assn. for the Edn. of Young Children (sec. of bd. dir. 1990—), Phi Delta Kappa, Delta Kappa Gamma.

WASHINGTON-KNIGHT, BARBARA J., career officer, nurse; b. Chgo., July 13, 1948; d. Lewis and Carrie Mae (Randolph) Washington; m. William S. Knight, Aug. 23, 1986 (separated); children: Carlton, Carrie. Diploma, St. Elizabeth's Hosp., Chgo., 1971; B in Health Scis., Chapman Coll., 1979, postgrad. CCRN. Commd. lt. USAF, 1972, advanced through grades to lt. col.; asst. head nurse med. unit USAF, Fairfield, Calif., 1976-78, asst. head nurse orthopedic unit, 1978-79; asst. head nurse spl. care unit USAF, Montgomery, Ala., 1979-80, head nurse spl. care unit, 1980-82; head nurse spl. care unit USAF, Riverside, Calif., 1982-85; head nurse surg. ICU USAF, San Antonio, 1985-87, clin. supr. dept. of critical care, 1987-88; head nurse spl. care unit USAF, Riverside, Calif., 1988-91, coord. quality improvement, 1990-92; asst. chief nurse, clin. nurse specialist inpatient svcs. USAF, Tinker AFB, Oklahoma City, 1992-93; clin. nurse post critical care unit Moreno Valley (Calif.) Cmty. Hosp., 1993—. Recipient Nurseweek's Mag. Clin. Excellence award, 2000. Mem. Soc. Ret. Air Force Nurses, Am. Assn. Critical Care Nurses (pres. Inland Empire chpt.), Am. Assn. Legal Nurse Cons. (cert.), Air Force Assn., Air War Coll. Assn., Women's Meml. Found., Nat. Coun. Negro Women, Ret. Officers Assn., Citizen Amb.

WASHIYAMA, JUNICHIRO, chemical engineer; b. Sapporo, Hokkaido, Japan, Aug. 25, 1958; s. Fumoto and Reiko (Machida) W.; m. Makiko Kinoshita, May 19, 1985; 1 child, Yuya. BEng, Tokyo Inst. Tech., 1981, MEng, 1983, PhD in Polymer Engring., 1994. Rschr. Showa Denko K.K., Kawasaki, Japan, 1983-90, chief rschr., 1990-95; chief rschr. Japan Poly-

olefins, Kawasaki, 1995-99; group leader, chief rschr. Montell-SDK-Sunrise Ltd., Kawasaki, 1999—; vis. scientist Cornell U., Ithaca, N.Y., 1990-92. Inventor in field; patents pending. Mem. Am. Chem. Soc., Soc. Polymer Sci. Japan. Mem. Liberal Dem. Party. Avocation: billiards.

WĄSIK, ZDZISŁAW, linguistics educator; b. Kłopotów, Poland, May 3, 1947; s. Jan and Anna (Podedworna) W.; m. Lidia Maria Rucka, Apr. 17, 1971 (div. 1993); 1 child, Hanna; m. Elżbieta Magdalena Lizis, Dec. 30, 1993; 1 child, Adam. MA in German, U. Wroclaw, Poland, 1971, PhD in Indo-European, 1977; DLitt in Gen. Linguistics, U. Poznan, Poland, 1986. Instr. gen. linguistics dept. and Cultural Studies Inst. Wroclaw (Poland) U., 1972-77, asst. prof. linguistics dept. and Cultural Studies Inst., 1977-88; assoc. prof. gen. linguistics dept. and English Lang. Inst. Opole U., 1988-92, prof. extraordinarius gen. linguistics dept, 1992-99, prof. extraordinarius, 1994-2000; prof. ordinarius Sch. English Adam Mickiewicz U., 1996-2000, Poznan, 2000—; prof., head linguistics dept. Fgn. Langs. Inst., State Higher Edn. Vocat. Sch., Walbrzych, Poland, 2000—; vis. prof. So. Ill. U., Carbondale, 1980, U. Fed. de St. Cat., Florianopolis, Brazil, 1987, U. Trondheim, Dragvoll, Norway, 1990, Rijksuniversiteit Groningen, Netherlands, 1990; dir. Gen. Linguistic Dept., Wroclaw, 1984-99; chief editor Studia Linguistica, Wroclaw, 1985-99; pres. Lang. Commn., Wroclaw, 1993—; expert in linguistics Polish-U.S. Fulbright Commn., Warsaw, 1993—; sr. lectr. Tchr. Tng. Coll., 1993-97. Author: A Structural Typology of Interrogative Utterances, 1979 (Min.'s award 1979), Semiotic Paradigm of Linguistics, 1988 (Min.'s award 1988), Systemic and Ecological Properties of Language in Interdisciplinary Investigative Approaches, 1997, An Outline for Lectures on the Epistemology of Semiotics, 1998; co-author, editor: From the Problems of the Ecology of Language, 1993, Heteronomies of Language, 1996; mem. editl. bd. Treatises of the Lang. Commn.; contbr. articles to profl. jours. Named Prof. Titular, Pres. of Republic of Poland, 1997; Fulbright rsch. grantee, 1982-84, JREX rsch. grantee, 1991. Mem. Polish Acad. Scis., Philol. Scis. Commn., European Cultures Commn., Polish Linguistic Soc., Soc. Linguistica Europaea, Polish Semiotic Soc., Wroclaw Sci. Soc., Internat. Assn. Semiotic Studies, Polish Fulbright Alumni Assn. Avocations: horse riding, choir singing. E-mail: wasik@ifa.amu.edu.pl. Office: Adam Mickiewicz U Poznan, Al Niepodlegtosci 4/Sch English, 61-874 Poznan Poland

WASILEWSKA, MARIOLA, chemist, educator; b. Kędzierzyn-Kozle, Poland, Dec. 18, 1966; d. Ryszard and Anna (Antul) Walawender; m. Grzegorz Wasilewski, Apr. 25, 1987; 1 child. MSc, Silesian U., Katowice, Poland, 1990; PhD, Poznan (Poland) Tech. U., 1997. Chemist Inst. Heavy Organic Synthesis, Kędzierzyn-Kozle, 1990-92, specialist, 1992-93, asst., 1993-97, lectr., 1997—; head of lab. Inst. Heavy Organic Synthesis, 1992—. Contbr. articles to profl. jours. NATO grantee, 1998. Mem. Polish Acad. Sci., Polish Standardizing Com. Roman Catholic. Avocations: music, dancing, traveling, literature. Home: B Krzywoustego 12F/10, 47-220 Kędzierzyn-Kozle Poland Office: Inst Heavy Organic, Synthesis Ul Energetykow 9, 47220 Kędzierzyn Kozle Poland

WASKO, STEVEN E., lawyer; b. Chgo., May 10, 1954; s. Theodore J. and Beverly W.; m. Elaine L. Enger, Oct. 3, 1981 (div. Aug. 1996); 1 child, Christine. B in Spl. Studies cum laude, Cornell Coll., 1976; JD cum laude, Kent U., 1979. Bar: Ill. 1979, U.S. Dist. Ct. (no. dist.) Ill. 1979. Assoc. atty. Blanshan & Summerfield, Park Ridge, Ill., 1979-81; ptnr. Summerfield & Wasko, Park Ridge, 1981-86; sole practitioner Steven Wasko and Assocs., Park Ridge, 1986-90, mng. ptnr., 1992-95; ptnr. Wasko & Michaels, Park Ridge, 1990-91, Steponate & Wasko Ltd., Park Ridge and Chgo., 1995—; dir. Kolan Corp., Park Ridge, 1988—. Great Books leader Field Sch. Dist., Park Ridge, 1997—. Avocations: jogging, watercolors and fine art. Office: 1580 N Northwest Hwy Park Ridge IL 60068-1444

WASKOW, MARK STUART, financial planner; b. Bklyn., Apr. 15, 1957; s. Bernard and Irene Lillian (Gorin) W.; m. Kathryn Lynn Ansell, June, 1980 (div.); children: Alexander James, Destiny Rose. BS, Cornell U., 1978. CLU, ChFC, fellow Life Underwriting Tng. Coun. Contbr. articles to profl. jours. Bd. dirs. Montpelier Rotary, 1988-91; bd. dirs., trustee The T.W. Wood Art Gallery, Montpelier, Vt., 1987-92; bd. dirs. Spl. Friends of Washington County, Barre, Vt., 1987-88; vol. Shelburne Mus., 1987-88; cons. Vt. Health Ins. Plan Bd., 1987. Mem. Vt. Assn. Life Underwriters (exec. bd., past pres.), Health Care Reform Task Force Vt. Assn. Life Underwriters (past chmn.), Nat. Assn. Life Underwriters, Nat. Assn. Health Underwriters, Cen. Vt. Assn. Life Underwriters (pres. 1985-86), Assn. Health Ins. Agts. (chmn. nat. mem. svcs. and comms. 1995-96). Avocations: antiques, wine tasting, Tae Kwon Do, reading, traveling. Office: The Waskow Group 95 Saint Paul St # 440 Burlington VT 05401-4428

WASMUHT, ULRIKE CONCETTA, sociologist, political scientist; b. Bamberg, Germany, June 17, 1957; d. Klaus and Christa (Michel) W. BA, Regensburg U., Germany, 1979; MA in Sociology, U. Colo., Boulder, 1981; PhD, Hamburg (Germany) U., 1986; Habilitation, Free U. Berlin, 1996. Head resident German Dept. Colo. Coll., Colorado Springs, 1979-80; teaching asst., instr. Dept. Sociology U. Colo., Boulder, 1980-83; rsch. asst. Inst. Peace Rsch. and Security Policy, Hamburg, Germany, 1983-85; pub. reader Fed. Ctr. of Polit. Edn., Bonn., Germany, 1985-87; cons., free lance writer Bonn., Germany, 1987-89; rsch. and teaching assoc., instr. Dept. Polit. Sci. Free U. of Berlin, Germany, 1989-95; rsch. assoc. German Armed Forces Inst. for Social Scis., Strausberg, 1996—. Author: Peace Movements of the 80's, 1987, History of Peace Research in Germany, 1998; editor, author: Alternatives to Old Politics, 1989, Peace Research, 1991, Conflict Administration, 1992, Is Knowledge Power?, 1992, Courage for Utopias, 1994. Named Dean's list Colo. Coll., Colorado Springs, 1980; Stipend grantee Friedrich-Ebert-Stiftung, Bonn, Germany, 1984-85, Deutsche Forschungsgemeinschaft, Bonn, Germany, 1994-95. Mem. German Assoc. Peace and Conflict Rsch., Assn. Military and Social Scis., European Peace Rsch. Assn. Avocations: sports, travel, photography, reading Arab literature, history, culture, belletristic, Latin Am. belletristic literature. Office: FU Berlin Fachbereich Politische Wissenschaft, Ihnestrasse 22, D-10717 Berlin Germany also: German Armed Forces Inst Social Scis, Proetzeler Chaussee, D-15344 Strausberg Germany

WASMUTH, CARL ERWIN, physician, lawyer; b. Pitts., Feb. 16, 1916; s. Edwin Hugo and Mary Blanche (Love) W.; m. Martha Conn., Aug. 25, 1939; children: Carl Erwin; m. Gertrude White Ruth, June 19, 1984; m. Wilhelmina Waterman Devine, May 12, 1990. BS, U. Pitts., 1935, MD, 1939; LLB, Cleve.-Marshall Law Sch., 1959. Diplomate Am. Bd. Anesthesiology. Bar: Ohio 1959. Intern Western Pa. Hosp., Pitts., 1939-40; fellow anesthesiology Cleve. Clinic Found., 1949-51, mem. emeritus staff, 1976—; pvt. practice medicine Dry Run, Pa., 1942-45, Scottdale, Pa., 1945-49; mem. dep. anesthesia Cleve. Clinic, 1951—, head dept., 1967-69; asso. prof. law Cleve.-Marshall Law Sch., 1959-66; adj. prof. Cleve. Marshall Law Sch., 1966-73. Author: Anesthesia and the Law, 1961, Law for the Physician, 1966, Law and the Surgical Team, 1968; Editor: Legal Problems in the Practice of Anesthesiology, 1973; contbg. editor: Hale's Anesthesiology; editorial bd.: Med. World News; Contbr. articles to profl. jours. Trustee Cleve.- Marshall Law Sch., chmn., 1969-71; bd. dirs. Scottdale Hosp. Found; chmn. bd. govs. Cleve. Clinic, 1969-77; trustee Cleve. Clinic Found., 1969-76, v.p., 1973-76; trustee Cleve. Clinic Ednl. Found., 1969-76, v.p., 1973-76; chmn. bd. trustees, pres. Cleve. Marshall Ednl. Found., 1972-81; bd. overseers Coll. Law, Cleve. State U., 1972-76; vis. com. Coll. Law, Case-Western Res. U., 1973-76; trustee United Torch Svcs.; hon. trustee Tucson Symphony Soc., 1983-84, 88; trustee Santa Cruz Med. Found., 1977, pres., 1978; bd. govs. Ohio World Trade Center; trustee Cancer Center Cleve., Ohio Coll. Podiatric Medicine, 1976, Am. Coll. Legal Medicine Research Found., 1984—; mem. U. Ariz. Found., 1978, World Congress Med. Law, 1967—, Keynoter 3d World Congress, 1971; sec. Commn. Med. Malpractice, HEW, 1972-73; vestryman St. Francis-in-the-Valley Episcopal Ch., Green Valley, 1990-93. Named Distinguished Eagle Scout Nat. Council Boy Scouts Am., 1977; named Outstanding Citizen Eagle Cuyahoga council, 1976; Citizen of Year Cleve. Area Bd. Realtors, 1976. Fellow Am. Coll. Anesthesiologists, Am. Coll. Legal Medicine (pres. bd. govs. 1966-69), A.C.P., Am. Coll. Chest Physicians, Law Sci. Acad.; mem. Am. Soc. Anesthesiologists (dir., pres. 1968, speaker ho. of dels.), Ohio Soc. Anesthesiologists (dir. 1960-69), Cleve. Soc. Anesthesiologists (pres. 1963), Internat. Anesthesia Research Soc., World Fedn. Soc. Anesthesiologists (vice chmn. Am. delegation 1967), Acad. Anesthesiology (chmn. program com. 1967), Am., Ohio med. assns., N.Y. Acad. Scis., Nat. Acad. Sci., NRC, Com. Cadaver Utilization, Cleve. Acad. Medicine, AAAS, Transplantation Soc. (charter), Am., Ohio, Cuyahoga County, Cleve. bar assns., Phi Rho Sigma, Delta Theta Phi, Masons, Lions (past pres. local clubs), Old Pueblo Club, Tucson Club, Country of Green Valley Club, Pleasant Valley Country Club, Mt. Kenya Safari Club, Nanyuki, Kenya, Ariz. Sr. Acad., The Lakes Club. Home: Apt C121 14515 W Granite Valley Dr Sun City West AZ 85375-6036

WASS, HANNELORE LINA, educational psychology educator; b. Heidelberg, Germany, Sept. 12, 1926; came to U.S., 1957, naturalized, 1963; d. Hermann and Mina (Lasch) Kraft; m. Irvin R. Wass, Nov. 24, 1959 (dec.); 1 child, Brian C.; m. Harry H. Sisler, Apr. 13, 1978. B.A., Tchrs. Coll., Heidelberg, 1951; M.A., U. Mich., 1960, Ph.D., 1968. Tchr. W. Ger. Univ. Lab. Schs., 1958-60; mem. faculty U. Mich., Ann Arbor, 1958-60, U. Chgo. Lab. Sch., 1960-61, U. Mich., 1963-64, Eastern Mich. U., 1965-69; prof. ednl. psychology U. Fla., Gainesville, 1969-92; prof. emeritus, 1992—; faculty assoc. Ctr. for Gerontol. Studies U. Fla., Gainesville; cons., lectr. in thanatology. Author: The Professional Education of Teachers, 1974, Dying-Facing the Facts, 1979, 2d edit., 1988, 3d edit., 1995, Death Education: An Annotated Resource Guide, 1980, vol. 2, 1985, Helping Children Cope With Death, 1982, 2d edit., 1984, Childhood and Death, 1984; founding editor (jour.) Death Studies, 1977-92; cons. editor: Ednl. Gerontology, 1977-92, (book series) Death Education, Aging and Health Care, 1980-96; contbr. approximately 200 articles to profl. jours. and chpts. in books. Mem. Am. Psychol. Assn., Gerontol. Soc., Internat. Work Group Dying, Death and Bereavement (bd. dirs.), Assn. Death Edn. and Counseling. Home: 6014 NW 54th Way Gainesville FL 32653-3265 Office: U Fla 346 Norman Hall Gainesville FL 32611-2053

WASSEF, RAAFAT KAMEL, physics educator; b. Cairo, Egypt, June 10, 1926; s. Kamel Salama Wassef and Kokab (Anton) Nagib; m. Kamilia Nagib Botros, July 20, 1952; children: Wafaa, Osama, Maged. BSc, Cairo U., 1946, MSc, 1950, PhD, 1954, DSc, 1968. Demonstrator in physics Cairo U., 1946-50, asst. lectr., 1950-54, lectr., 1954-60, asst. prof., 1960-68, chair prof., 1968—; vis. prof. Riyadh U., Saudi Arabia, 1970-73, Lorand Eotvös U., Budapest, Hungary, 1967-68; mem. Internat. Union of Pure and Applied Physics, UNESCO, 1981-86, 90-96. Author 8 books (in Arabic) including Physics, 1995, Solid-State Physics, 1996, Physics for Non-Majors, 1996, (in English) Physics for Life, 1996; contbr. more than 140 articles to profl. jours. Mem., chmn. physics commn. Sci. Syndicate, Cairo, 1984. Recipient Sci. State prize Egyptian Acad. Scis., 1963, 2 Sci. State medals in physics Egyptian Govt., 1963, 86. Christian. Avocations: music, painting in oil, psychology studies, gardening. Home: 7 Cairo University St, Giza Cairo Egypt Office: Cairo U, Dept Physics, Giza Cairo Egypt

WASSELIUS, JOHAN ANDERS, ophthalmology researcher, consultant; b. Boras, Sweden, Jan. 17, 1973; s. Anders Ragnar Andersson and Ulla Kerstin Marianne (Hallgren) A. MBA, U. Boras, 1996; BMed, Lund (Sweden) U., 1999, MSc in Biomed Sci., 1999. Cert. optician. Optician Glasgoncity AB, Boras, 1987-96; rschr. dept. ophthalmology Lund U., 1996—; rschr. Harvard U., Boston, 1998, Mass. Gen. Hosp./HHMI/Harvard Med. Sch., Boston, 1999. Actor, Vargladspexet, 1998—. Mem. City Parliament, Boras, 1994-96. Sgt., Swedish Army, 1992-93. Recipient Hennerlow award, Stockholm, 1998; Wallenberg Found. scholar, 1998, 99. Mem. Assn. Rsch. in Vision and Ophthalmology, Svenska Lakaresallskapet. Mem. Conservative Party. Avocations: working out, sailing, music, theater. Home: Sodra Esplanaden 16A, S-22352 Lund Sweden Office: Lund U Hosp, Dept Ophthalmology, S-22185 Lund Sweden

WASSELL, RICHARD CHARLES, educational consultant; b. Birmingham, Eng., Feb. 25, 1949; s. Bert and Dora Winifred (Didlock) W. BA with honors, King's Coll., London, 1970. Mktg. officer Victory Reinsurance, London, 1977-87; dir. Brit. Assn. Conf. Towns, Tunbridge Wells, 1988-89; overseas mktg. officer NRG Victory Reinsurance, London, 1989-91; dir., co. sec. TRi Electronics Plc, London, 1991-93; sec.-gen. Ctr. for Europe, London, 1993-97; European edn. and networking cons. Ctr. for Europe, Ctr. Européene d'Aide, others, 1997—; co-founder Ctr. for Europe, 1984, chmn. 1985-93; coun. mem. Fedn. Internat. des Maisons de l'Europe, Sarbrücken, 1991-98, Ctr. Européene d'Aide à la Vie Associative, Lille, 1997—; sec. Confederation Européene des Anciens Combattants, London, 1993—, Monte Cassino Fedn. for Remembrance and Reconciliation, London, 1993-98; internat. officer Veterans in Europe, London, 1998—. Hon. treas. European Movement Brs. Assn., London, 1991-98; vice-chmn. Cen. London Europe Group, 1977—, hon. treas., 1991—; dep. chmn. Westminster North Conservative Assn., London, 1986-89, European Dem. Forum, London, 1979-84; hon. sec. Charter Movement, London, 1995—, hon. treas., 1990-95; bd. dirs. European Movement, London, 1983-84, 85-86; founder Brussels Britain in Europe Group, 1974, hon. sec., 1974-75. Mem. Chartered Inst. Mktg., Chartered Ins. Inst. (assoc.). Avocation: languages. E-mail: rcw@accuk.co.uk. Home: 10A Tubs Hill Parade, TN13 1DH Seven Oaks Kent, England

WASSELL, STEPHEN ROBERT, mathematics educator, researcher; b. Santa Monica, Calif., Jan. 17, 1963; s. Desmond Anthony and Catherine Ann (Stephens) W. BS in Arch., U. Va., Charlottesville, 1984, PhD in Math., 1990, M in Computer Sci., 1999. Programmer, analyst UNISYS, McLean, Va., 1984-85, graphics artist, 1986; tutor summer transition program U. Va., Charlottesville, 1987-88, tchg. asst., 1986-90; asst. prof. math. Sweet Briar (Va.) Coll., 1990-96, assoc. prof. math., 1996—, dept. chmn., 1996-97, 99—; prof. of record Ctr. for the Liberal Arts, U. Va., 1991; vis. asst. prof. math., U. Va., Charlottesville, 1992, vis. assoc. prof. computer sci., 1998-99; doctoral cons., Charlottesville, 1989-90. Author: (with L.E. Thomas) Schrödinger Operators, 1992; author: Nexus 2: Architecture and Mathematics, 1998, Nexus 3: Architecture and Mathematics, 2000; contbr. chpt. to book. Recipient Grad. assistantship award U. Va., 1986-90; Gordon T. Whyburn fellow, 1985-86. Mem. AAUP (Sweet Briar chpt. sec.-treas. 1993-99), Am. Math. Soc., Math. Assn. Am., Am. Solar Energy Soc., Sigma Nu (Beta chpt. treas. 1985-86). Achievements include patents for solar powered lawnmower, for solar shed, for ear muffs. Home: 4500 Monacan Trail Rd North Garden VA 22959-2215 Office: Sweet Briar Coll Dept Math Scis Sweet Briar VA 24595

WASSERMAN, DANUTA ELISABETH, medical educator; b. Warsaw, Poland, Mar. 19, 1945; arrived in Sweden, 1968; d. Nikolai Stefan and Stephanie Maria (Smolarek) Wolk; m. Janusz Josef Szklarzewicz, Mar. 15, 1969 (div. Mar. 1973); children: Janek, Susanne; m. Jerzy Wasserman, June 16, 1979; 1 child, Camilla. Degree, Med. Faculty, Uppsala, Sweden, 1972; MD, PhD, Karolinska Inst., Stockholm, 1986. Cert. psychoanalyst. Med. and psychiat. resident Uppsala and Stockholm, 1972-92; rschr. Med. Rsch. Coun., Stockholm, 1989-92; assoc. prof. Karolinska Inst., Stockholm, 1990-95, head Nat. Ctr. Suicide Rsch. & Prevention Mental Ill Health,, 1995—; prof. psychiatry and suicidology Nat. Inst. Psychosocial Medicine/Karolinska Inst., Stockholm, 1995—; task force for suicide prevention Swedish Med. and Swedish Psychiat. Assn., 1994; sec. Planning Group of the Med. Rsch. Coun. for Suicide Rsch. in Sweden, Stockholm, 1990—; hon. pres. Estonian-Swedish Suicidological Inst., Tallinn, Estonia, 1993—. Author and co-author of 9 books; mem. editl. bd. Crisis, Archives Suicide Rsch., Italian Jour. Suicidology; dir. editl. bd. Epidemiol. Surveillance of Suicidal Behaviours; contbr. articles to profl. jours. Mem. Bd. of Health and Welfare's Nat. Coun. Suicide Prevention in Sweden, 1993—; mem. Club of 13, Karolinska Inst., Stockholm. Mem. Internat. Assn. Suicide Prevention and Crisis Intervention (v.p. 1995-97, dir. task force for identification of rsch. priorities in suicidology 1993—, Erwin Stengel Rsch. award 1993), Swedish Med. Assn. (rsch. award 1993), N.Y. Acad. Scis. Avocations: reading, history, travel, piano playing, gardening. Office: Nat Ctr Suicide Rsch/Prevention, Karolinska Inst Box 230, 171 77 Stockholm Sweden

WASSERMAN, IRENE, research scientist, educator; b. Uman, Ukraine, Russia, June 1, 1965; arrived in Israel, 1990; d. Avram and Ludmila (Khazin) W. MSc, Inst. Chem. and Chem. Engring., Dnjepropetrovsk, Russia, 1987; DSc, Technion, Haifa, Israel, 1994. R&D engr. Perlite Industries Ltd., Moshav Habonim, Israel, 1990-91; rschr. Golan Devel. Co., Katzrin, Israel, 1992-94; head concrete dept. Galilee Lab., Kiryat Shmonah, Israel, 1994-95; scientist Inst. for Bldg. Materials TU Munchen, Munich, Germany, 1996-97; lectr. Tel-Hi Coll., Israel, 1994-95, 97—; rsch. scientist Nat. Bldg. Rsch. Inst. Technion, Haifa, Israel, 1997—; cons. Nat. Bldg. Rsch. Inst., Haifa, 1995-96, coord. implementation dept., 1998—. Contbr. articles to profl. jours. Recipient Minerva fellow, 1996-97, fellow Hebrew Immigrant Aid Soc., 1991. Avocations: reading, art. Office: Nat Bldg Rsch Inst, Kiryat Technion, 32000 Haifa Israel

WASSERMAN, KAREN BOLING, clinical psychologist, nursing consultant; b. Olney, Ill., July 29, 1944; d. Kenneth G. and Betty Jean (Varner) Boling; m. James M. Wasserman, Apr. 14, 1965; children: Nicole C., Michael B. RN, Barnes Hosp. Sch. Nursing, St. Louis, 1965; BA, Antioch Coll., 1977; Dr. of Psychology, Wright State U., 1986. Lic. psychologist, Miss., Ohio, Ind.; RN, Miss., Mo., Ohio. Staff nurse various med. facilities, 1965-76; instr. practical nurse program Ind. Vocat. Tech. Coll., Richmond, 1976-77; staff, float nurse Good Samaritan Hosp., Dayton, Ohio, 1977-78; pub. health nurse coord. Bur. Alcoholism Svcs., Dayton, 1978-79; alcoholism counselor IV Bur. Alcoholism Svcs., Dayton, Ohio, 1979-82; practicum student Wright State U. Sch. Profl. Psychology, Dayton, 1983-85; psychology intern Balt. VAMC Consortium, 1985-86; clin. psychologist Dayton VAMC, 1987-89; founder, ptnr. dir. clin. svcs. Fairhaven Clinic, P.A., Biloxi, Miss., 1989-98; clin. psychologist Gulf Oaks Hosp., Biloxi, 1989-98; clin. psychologist Sand Hill Hosp., Gulfport, Miss., 1993-98, chief psychol. svcs., 1998; cons. pschologist Sr. Life Cons., Dublin, Ohio, 2000—; psychiat. nursing cons. Mercy Hosp., Omaha, Council Bluffs, Iowa, 1987; instr. William Carey Coll. on the Coast, 1993; owner/propr. Angel Garden, Ocean Springs, 1996-98; founder, co-owner Ebenzer's Antiques, Springfield, Ohio, 1999—. Chmn. cmty. svcs. Altrusa Internat., Biloxi, 1990-94, treas., 1993-94; mem. Evangelism com. First United Meth. Ch., Gulfport, Miss., 1991-93, coun. on ministries, 1994-95; Friend of the Rainbow Warrior, Greenpeace, 1986-93; mem. adminstrv. bd. Gulf Coast Ctr. for Nonviolence, 1996-98; mem. libr. com., ch. and soc. com. Worthington (Ohio) United Meth. Ch., 1999—. Recipient Alumnae award in Acads., Barnes Hosp. Sch. Nursing, 1965, Career Woman of Yr. award, Lighthouse of Biloxi chpt., Bus. and Profl. Women, 1994. Fellow Am. Acad. Psychologists Treating Addiction; mem. APA, Ohio Psychol. Assn. (legis. com.), Miss. Psychol. Assn. (region IV rep. exec. coun., continuing edn. com. 1990-95, chair 1994-95, chair membership com. 1997-98). Avocations: architecture, gardening, travel, movies. Office: Sr Life Consultants 6465 Reflections Dr Ste 110 Dublin OH 43017-2353

WASSERMAN, STANLEY, statistician, educator; b. Louisville, Aug. 29, 1951; s. Irvin Levitch and Jeanne (Plattus) W.; m. Sarah Wilson, Feb. 3, 1974; children: Andrew Joseph, Eliot Miles. BS in Econs., U. Pa., 1973; PhD in Stats., Harvard U., 1977. Asst. prof. U. Minn., Mpls., 1977-82; assoc. prof. U. Ill., Urbana, 1982-88, prof. psychology, stats., sociology, 1988—; prof. Beckman Inst., 1993—; vis. rschr. Columbia Univ., N.Y.C., 1978; cons., expert witness EEOC, Cleve., 1979-81; cons. V.A. Med. Ctr., Mpls., 1980-82, AT&T Communications, Basking Ridge, N.J., 1988-90. Author: Social Network Analysis, 1994; assoc. editor: Sociological Methodology, 1978-81, Jour. Am. Statis. Assn., 1987—, Psychometrika, 1988-2000, Am. Statistician, 1993-96, Structural Analysis, 1997-2000; guest editor: Sociol. Methods and Rsch., 1992; book review editor: Chance, 1993—; consulting editor Am. Jour. Sociology, 2000—. Treas. Montessori Sch. of Champaign-Urbana, Savoy, Ill., 1990-92. Grantee NSF, Washington, 1979-81, 84-89, 93—, NIH, 1995-98; postdoctoral fellow Social Sci. Rsch. Coun., N.Y.C., 1978. Fellow AAAS, Am. Statis. Assn.; mem. Psychometric Soc., Royal Statis. Soc., Classification Soc. N.Am. (sec., treas. 1993-95, bd. dirs. 1996-98. 99-2000), Internat. Network for Social Network Analysis (bd. dirs. 1997). Achievements include reseach in applied statistics, categorical data analysis, social network analysis. Home: 2066 County Road 125 E Mahomet IL 61853-8907 Office: U Ill 603 E Daniel St Champaign IL 61820-6232

WASSERMAN, STEPHEN ALAN, lawyer; b. Cleve., Apr. 7, 1948; s. Myron Earl and Eve Ruth (Milstein) W.; m. Sandra Shulamith Moltz, Oct. 20, 1978. BA, U. Wis., 1970; JD, Northeastern U., Boston, 1978. Bar: Mass. 1978, U.S. Dist. Ct. Mass. 1978. Housing atty. Neighborhood Legal Svcs., Lynn, Mass., 1978-83; ptnr. Barmack, Boggs and Wasserman, Lynn, 1983-91; pvt. practice Salem, Mass., 1991-97, 98—, Boston, 1997-98. Bd. dirs. North Shore Cmty. Action Program, Peabody, Mass., 1995—. Avocations: reading, baseball, jogging. Office: 32 Church St Salem MA 01970-3737

WASSERMAN, STEPHEN MILES, communications director; b. Chgo., Apr. 26, 1945; s. Samuel Isreal and Rayna (Krassner) W.; m. Faye Rita Samuelson, Oct. 17, 1971; children: Rayna, Alyssa. BA in Journalism, Bradley U., 1968. Mgr. corp. comm. Underwriters Labs., Inc., Northbrook, Ill., 1991-98, corp. mgr. global comm. svcs., 1997-98, dir. global comm. svcs., 1998—; mem. pub. rels. and fundraising com. Ill. Math. and Sci. Acad., Aurora, 1992-96; comms. chair Nat. Electric Safety Found., Washington, 1994-96. campaign chmn. United Way, Buffalo Grove, Ill., 1991-93, pres., 1994-95. Mem. Nat. Press Club. Office: Underwriters Labs Inc 333 Pfingsten Rd Northbrook IL 60062-2002

WASSERMAN, STEVE, editor; b. Vancouver, Wash., Aug. 3, 1952; s. Abraham and Ann (Dragoon) W.; m. Michelle Krisel, Mar. 7, 1982; children: Claire, Paul, Isaac. AB in Criminology, U. Calif., Berkeley, 1974. Asst. editor City Mag. of San Francisco, 1975-76; dep. editor opinion sect. Los Angeles Times, 1977-83; editor in chief New Republic Books The New Republic, N.Y.C., 1984-87; pub. Hill and Wang div. Farrar, Straus and Giroux Inc., N.Y.C., 1987-90, The Noonday Press div. Farrar, Straus and Giroux Inc., N.Y.C., 1987-90; editorial dir. Times Books divsn. Random House, N.Y.C., 1990-96; editor L.A. Times Book Rev., 1996—; founder L.A. Inst. Humanities, 1998—; cons. editor The Threepenny Rev., Berkeley, Calif., 1980-86, Tikkun, Oakland, Calif., 1986-90; founder, co-dir. L.A. Inst. for the Humanities, 1998—. Contbr. articles and revs. to mags. and newspapers. Mem. PEN. Office: LA Times 202 W 1st St Los Angeles CA 90012-4105

WASSMAN, E. ROBERT, JR., geneticist, medical educator, management consultant; b. New Rochelle, N.Y., Oct. 2, 1951; s. Edward Robert and Eleanor Elizabeth (Humphrey) W.; m. Susan Louise Woody; children: Edward Robert III, Anna Cecelia. BS in Biology cum laude, Yale U., 1973; MD, Albany (N.Y.) Med. Coll., 1977. Med. lic. N.Y. and Calif.; COQ cert. N.Y. State Lab Dir. ResidentN.Y. Hosp. Cornell U. Med. Ctr., N.Y.C., 1977-79; fellow med. genetics Harbor-UCLA Med. Ctr., Torrance, 1979-83; clin. asst. prof. pediatrics, 1983—; med. dir., rsch. dir. Alfigen, The Genetics Inst., Pasadena, Calif., 1983-89; v.p. corp. devel. Genetrix, Inc., Scottsdale, Ariz., 1990-94; chief So. Calif. Regional Offices Dept. Health Svcs., Childrens Med. Svcs., L.A., 1995-96; pres., CEO Perinatal Alliance Med. Group, Inc.; pres. and CEO ACCME, Internat., Seal Beach, Calif., 1990—; cons. AMX, Internat., Washington, 1994—; internat. assoc. Baker Internat. Assocs., Palm Beach, Fla., 1992—; trustee Billy Barty Found. Burbank, Calif., 1983—; v.p. corp. devel. and strategic alliances perinatal practice holdings Alfigen, Inc.; dir. bus. devel./genetics specialty labs., Santa Monica, Calif., 1996-97. Contbr. chpt. to Obstetrics and Gynecology Clinics of North America, 1993; contbr. articles to profl. jours.; presenter in field. Bd. dirs. med. adv. So. Calif. March of Dimes, L.A., 1987-90, Long Beach March of Dimes, chmn., 1984-89; mem. alumni schs. com. Yale U. Alumni Assn., Orange County, Calif., 1987—. Recipient Humanitarian award Found. for Children's Health Care, Long Beach, 1986; Giannini Found. fellow Bank of America, L.A., 1981-83; recipient Unsung Heroes award Harbor UCLA Med. Ctr., 1997. Fellow Am. Coll. of Med. Genetics founding, Am. Acad. of Pediat.; mem. AMA, NIH Alumni Assn. (life), Am. Soc. of Human Genetics, N.Y. Acad. Sci. Achievements include findings on causes of morbidity and mortality in short statured persons and inactivation of human X-chromosome, methods for growth of fetal cells in maternal bloodstream, Co-developer of first private genetic testing firm; developer of strategies for technology rationalization and deployment in managed care enviornments. Avocations: skiing, surfing, ice hockey, golf, tai chi. Home: 107 Ocean Ave Seal Beach CA 90740 Office: 31 W Del Mar Pasadena CA 91105

WASSMER, THEODORE MILTON, artist; b. Salt Lake City, Feb. 23, 1910; s. Theodore James and Hester Sadie (Hall) W.; m. Julia Farnsworth Lund, Dec. 8, 1945 (dec. May 1996). Student, Art Students League, N.Y.C., 1947-51; student under Raphael Soyer, Am. Art Sch., N.Y.C., 1949-51. Employed by engraving and wholesale hardware cos. Salt Lake City, 1925-42; artist N.Y.C., 1946-52, Woodstock, N.Y., 1952-85, Salt Lake City,

1985—; apprentice to Florence E. Ware painting murals for the WPA, 1934-39. More than 2,000 works are in museums, colls., schs. and pvt. collections in U.S., Europe and Japan; with wife donated more than 900 works to Springville Mus. of Art, Snow Coll., Brigham City Mus.-Gallery, Fairview Mus. of History and Art and Nora Eccles Harrison Mus. Art, Utah; solo show at Albany (N.Y.) Inst. History and Art, 1974; other solo shows in Alaska, Ariz., Tex., Utah, Fla., N.Y. and Calif.; in Art Access Gallery traveling show (Utah), exhibited with 4 other artists over 80, 1994; solo show of 50 recent works at Myra Powell Gallery, Ogden, Utah, 1997; works reproduced in various publs. Sgt. U.S. Army Air Force, 1942-45. Springville Mus. Art honored his 80th yr. with reception and 60-yr. retrospective show, 1930-90, showing 100 of his works and issuing a 24-page catalog. Avocation: collecting art. Home: 130 S 1300 E Apt 501 Salt Lake City UT 84102-1779

WASSON, JAMES WALTER, aircraft electronics manufacturing company executive; b. Pitts., Dec. 9, 1951; s. George Fredrick and Dolores Helen (Weurl) W.; m. Evelyn Fay Gonzales, Dec. 28, 1974; children: Robert, Brian. AST, Pitts. Inst. Aeronautics, 1972; BSET, Northrop U., Inglewood, Calif., 1981; MBA, U. Phoenix, 1988, govt. contracts mgmt. cert., 1989. Avionics technician various cos., 1972-74; electronics prodn. mgr. Ostgaard Industries, Gardena, Calif., 1974-75; sr. avionics design engr. Allied Signal Garrett Airesearch Aviation Co., L.A., 1975-81; v.p. engring., co-founder Avionics Engring. Svcs., Inc., Tucson, 1980-81; sr. tech. specialist Northrop Aircraft Div., Hawthorne, Calif., 1981-84; prog. mgr. McDonnell Douglas Helicopter Co., Mesa, Ariz., 1984-86; R&D projects mgr. McDonnell Douglas Helicopter Co., 1986-93; exec. v.p., co-founder Leading Edge Technologies, Inc., Mesa, 1991-95; mgr. bus. devel. McDonnell Douglas Helicopter Sys., Mesa, 1993-95; dir. tech. mktg. Smiths Industries, Aerospace & Def. Sys., Grand Rapids, Mich., 1995—; adj. prof. ops. mgmt. contract mgmt., program mgmt., proposal devel., strategic mgmt., mktg., tech. mgmt., rsch. projects U. Phoenix, 1990—; cons. in field. Author: Avionics Systems Operation and Maintenance, 1993, Business Opportunities in Artificial Intelligence, 1988; contbr. articles to profl. jours. Inventor in field. Com. chmn. industry adv. bd. Northrop U., 1981; chmn. bd. dirs., pres. Alta Mesa Community Assn., 1989; organizer Boy Scouts Am., Mesa, 1988. Named Engr. of Yr., Northrop U., 1980; recipient Disting. Alumnus award Pitts. Inst. Aeronautics, 1981, U. Phoenix, 1996; named to Hall of Fame, Career Colls. Assn., 1991. Mem. IEEE, NSPE, Assn. Avionics Educators, Soc. Automotive Engrs., Army Aviation Assn. (chpt. sr. v.p. 1988-91, treas. 1993-95), Nat. Def. Indsl. Assn., Assn. U.S. Army, Am. Helicopter Soc. (chmn. avionics com. 1990), Assn. Avionics Educators, Rotorcraft Industry Tech. Assn. (bd. dirs. 1998-99), Crystal Springs Country Club (fin. com. 2000—). Republican. Roman Catholic. Avocations: flying, scuba diving, hiking, golf, camping.

WASTBERG, OLLE M., diplomat; b. Stockholm, May 6, 1945; s. Erik and Greta (Hirsch) W.; m. Inger Claesson, Feb. 21, 1968; children: David, Elias. BA, U. Stockholm, 1972. Tchr. polit. sci. U. Stockholm, 1967-68; journalist polit. dept. Expressen, 1968-71; editor-in-chief, 1994-95; rsch. fellow Bus. and Soc. Rsch. Ctr., 1971-76; pres. Aktieframjandet, 1976-82; mem. Parliament, 1976-82; pres. Swedish Newspaper Promotion Assn., 1983-91; undersec. of state for fin. affairs Ministry of Fin., Stockholm, 1991-93; pres. bd. Nordic Investment Bank, 1992-94, Swedish Broadcasting Corp., 1996-99; consul gen. for Sweden in N.Y., 1999—; dir. Stockholm Stock Exchange, 1977-82, 88-92;group of 10 deputies IMF, 1991-93; Swedish del. meeting of ministries of fin., 1992; mem. govt. coms. on S. Africa consumer politics and stock market; pres. Bertil Ohlin Inst., 1996-2000. Author books on African problems, immigration politics and econ. topics; contbr. articles to profl. jours. Polit. sec. Liberal Youth Sweden, 1966, v.p., 1996-71; bd. Liberal Party, 1972-93, 97-2000, pres. exec. com., 1982-83; bd. dirs. Friends of Hebrew U. of Jerusalem. Recipient Gold medal Swedish Mktg. Group, 1982. Home: 600 Park Ave New York NY 10021-7010

WASZKEWITZ, BERNHARD CHRISTIAN HANS, psychologist, consultant; b. Schleswig, Germany, May 27, 1926; s. Ferdinand August and Annemarie Katharine (Speck) W.; m. Ingeborg Martens, April 14, 1955; children: Birgit, Peter. PhD, U. Kiel, Germany, 1952. Licensed psychologist. Cons. Inst. Psychology, München, Germany, 1956-67; personal mgr. Brücknerwerke, Leonberg, Germany, 1967-68; cons. Sr. Suchan UB, Weinheim, Germany, 1968-71; tchr. Acad. Oeconomy, Friedrichshafen, Germany, 1971-76; prof. Fachhochschule, Fulda, Germany, 1976-91. Author: Fundamente der Persönlichkeitspsychologie, 1960, Persönlichkeit und Verhalten, 1998, Wissenschaftliche Graphologie, 1998, Steuerungs-und Verhaltenssysteme, 1999, Mitarbeiterführung, 2000, Krankheit u. Normalität, 2000. Grenadier Deutsche Wehrmacht, 1945. Home: Weimarer StraBe 6A, D 36093 Künzell Germany

WATABE, TOMIJI, retired engineering educator, volunteer consultant; b. Tokyo, Oct. 26, 1927; s. Shoege and Mon (Ono) W.; m. Akiko Aoki, May 26, 1953; children: Hajime, Junko. DEng, Tokyo U., 1970. Machine designer Hitachi Co. Ltd., Tokyo, 1950-72, rschr., 1972-77; lectr. Tokyo Electric U., 1971-77; prof. mech. engring. Muroran (Japan) Inst. Tech., 1978-93; cons. vol., 1993—; cons. Muroran Inst. Tech., Narasaki Machine Mfg. Co., Ltd., Hitachi Co., Ltd., Hokkaido Devel. Bur., Ocean Engring. Inst. Teanjin, China, Haiyou Machine Mfg. Co., China. Inventor automatic machinery, ocean wave power device. Recipient Invention prize Japan Soc. Invention, Superior Paper award Found. for Promotion of Hydraulics and Pneumatics Tech., 1990. Achievements include research in automatic winders for coal and ore mine transportation, automatic winders for cable car transportation, coal cutter-loader governed by maximum power control, automatic power transmission for diesel powered vehicles, non-magnetic hydrostatic power transmission, constant loading rate controller for rotary bucket conveyer, large friction clutch for clash aster control, and ocean wave power converter pendulor; patent for anti-shock braking system, automatic power transmission, ocean wave power converter. Avocation: violin. Home and Office: T-Wave Consulting Volunteer, 5-23-3 Misono, Noboribetsu 059-0036, Japan

WATANA, YOD S., manufacturing company executive; b. Bangkok, Mar. 12, 1957; s. Arun S. and Konkaew (Pong-Kasem) W.; m. Suree S. Rojanavilaivut, Mar. 16, 1986; children: Yosawat, Yosawin. BA, Ramkhamhaeng U., Bangkok, 1982. Clk.-typist S. Watana Ltd., Bangkok, 1975-83, asst. mgr., 1983—; internat. mgr. Camping Equipment Ltd., Bangkok, 1983-91, mng. dir., 1992—; owner, editor Yan - Yong Motoring Mag., Bangkok, 1987—. Mem. editing staff Hi-Performance Motoring, 1981. Sec. The Consumer's Assn., Bangkok, 1975, Thai Traffic Safety Assn., Bangkok, 1981, also pres. Home: Patanakarn Rd, 209/7 Muangthong 2/2, Bangkok 10250, Thailand Office: Camping Equipment Ltd, 2140/38/2140/39, Ramkhamhaeng 34, Bangkok 10240, Thailand

WATANABE, HAJIME, lawyer; b. Tokyo, July 28, 1959; s. Takashi and Noriko (Nakagawa) W.; m. Mansumi Hanaya, Apr. 19, 1987; children: Rei, Kei. Diploma, U. Tokyo, 1981, LLB, 1985; diploma, Legal Tng. and Rsch. Inst., 1987; LLM, U. Ill., 1993. Bar: Japan, N.Y. Japan legal cons. Jenner & Block, Chgo., 1993-95; legal cons. The Fed. Trade Commn. of the U.S., Washington, 1995; ptnr. Mori Sogo Law Offices, Tokyo, 1997—. Author: Insider Trading Regulations, 1988, Defense Tactics in M&A, 1990, Internet Law, 1997. Mem. ABA, Japan Fedn. of Bar Assn., N.Y. State Bar Assn. Home: 5-9-14-402 Shibuya-ku, Tokyo 150-0014, Japan Office: NKK Bldg 1-1-2 Marunouchi, Chiyoda-ku, Tokyo 100-0005, Japan

WATANABE, HITOSHI, information technology educator, researcher; b. Taisha, Shimane, Japan, Dec. 26, 1930; s. Ryozo and Shimako (Fukuhara) W.; m. Reiko Yoshida, Jan. 22, 1958; children: Yuri Sato, Yosinori Watanabe. BE, Kyoto U., Japan, 1953, DEng, 1961. Registered profl. engr. Mgr. NEC Corp., Japan, 1965-71, gen. mgr., 1971-80, v.p., 1980-91; prof. Soka U., Hachioji, Japan, 1991—. Author: Transmission Network: Theory and Design, 1968 (Best Book award Inst. Electronics, Info. and Comm. Engrs. 1969); contbr. articles to profl. jours. Recipient sci. & tech. achievement award Gov. Tokyo, 1990, best paper awards, fellow Inst. Electronics Info. and Comm. Engrs. Jour., 1960, 67, 68. Fellow IEEE (life, IEEE Circuits and Sys. Soc. award 1991, centennial medal 1984, 2000, 3d millennium medal, Circuits and Sys. Golden Jubilee medal), Inst. of Electronicjs, Info. and Comm. Engrs., Info. Processing Soc. Japan (hon.). Avocations: tea ceremony, mixed chorus, muscle tng. Office: Soka Univ Faculty Engring, 1-236 Tangi-cho, Hachioji 192-8577, Japan

WATANABE, IWAO, chemist, educator; b. Osaka, Japan, Mar. 10, 1944. DSc, Osaka U., Toyonaka, Japan, 1973. Asst. dept. chemistry faculty of sci. Osaka U., 1971-86, assoc. prof. chemistry, 1987—. Home: Izumicho 4-21-6, Suita 564-0041, Japan Office: Dept Chemistry Grad Sch Sci, Osaka U Machikaneyama 1-1, Toyonaka 560-0043, Japan

WATANABE, KISHICHI, retired business educator; b. Omi-machi, Japan, Oct. 25, 1927; s. Asanosuke and Shin Watanabe; m. Kazuko Sudo, Apr. 11, 1965. MS, Meiji (Japan) U., 1960, PhD, 1963. Lectr. Kyoto (Japan) Sangyo U., 1968-71, assoc. prof. bus., 1971-80, prof. bus., 1980-98, prof. emeritus, 1998—. Contbr. numerous articles to profl. jours. Avocations: reading, walking. Home: 104 3 Bldg 6-6, Umezu-Onawaba-cho, Kyoto 615-0925, Japan

WATANABE, KOJI, epidemiologist; b. Otaru, Hokkaido, Japan, Dec. 10, 1959; s. Shoji and Eiko Watanabe; m. Yumiko Mayama, June 8, 1990. MD, Teikyo U., Tokyo, 1989; PhD, Hokkaido U., 1994. Nat. med. lic. Resident dr. Hokkaido U. Hosp., Sapporo, Japan, 1989-90, Naganuma Hosp., Sapporo, 1990-91, Inazumi-Park Hosp., Sapporo, 1991-94, Sapporo Tokushukai Hosp., 1994-95; staff dr. Hakodate (Japan) Bayside Hosp., 1995-96; staff dr. Hokkaido Indsl. Health Mgmt. Assn., 1996-98, chief dr., 1999—. Contbr. articles to med. reports. Mem. Japanese Soc. Gastroenterol. Mass Survey, Japanese Soc. Internal Medicine. Avocation: vacuum tube amplifier collector.

WATANABE, MAMORU, music historian; b. Tokyo, Oct. 9, 1915; m. Ilse Wetzel (dec. 1945). Student, Imperial U. Tokyo, Japan, 1939, U. Vienna, Austria, 1941-43. Prof. Philos. Faculty, U. Tokyo, 1965-76; dir. Japanese Cultural Inst., Cologne, Germany, 1976-82; min. Japanese Diplomatic Mission to Fed. Republic Germany, 1976-82; prof. Osaka Music Acad., 1982-94. Author: The Works of Richard Wagner, 1965, The Life of Richard Wagner, 1967, The Structure of Music, 1969, The Cultural History of Vienna Music, 1989, The Habsburg Din. and Music, 1997, The History of German Songs, 1997. Recipient Mainichi Book prize Mainichi Press, 1962, Gold Badge of Merit, State of Salzburg, Austria, 1978, Das Grosse Verdienstkreuz of German Fed. Republic, 1982, Kyoto Music prize City of Kyoto, Japan, 1989. Home: 9 Victoria Rd, Oxford OX2 7QF, England

WATANABE, NAOHARU, bio-organic chemistry educator; b. Hamamatsu, Shizuoka, Japan, July 30, 1950; s. Shuichiro Kajimura and Masako Watanabe; m. Mari Arai, Nov. 21, 1980; children: Yu, Ai. PhD, U. Tokyo, 1980. Rsch. scientist Taisho-Pharm. Co. Ltd., Ohmiya, Japan, 1980-89; assoc. prof. Shizuoka (Japan) U., 1989-98, prof. dept. applied biol. chemistry, 1998—. Author: Hana no Kaori wa Dokokara?, 1999. Recipient Ito-Kagaku Zaidan Kenkyu Shorei Sho, 1998. Avocation: drawing pictures. Home: 1036-68 Kusanagi, Shizuoka 424-0886, Japan Office: Shizuoka U, 836 Ohya, Shizuoka 422-8529, Japan

WATANABE, SEIICHI, electronics engineer; b. Nagoya, Japan, May 26, 1941; s. Fumio and Toshiko W.; m. Keiko Tsumura, Mar. 21, 1968; children: Ayako, Hirotake, Yuriko. BS, U. Tokyo, 1965, MS, 1967, DSc, 1989. From gen. mgr. Discrete Device to pres. Rsch. Ctr. SONY, Tokyo, 1985—. Author: High Frequency Devices for Electronic Tuners; contbr. articles to profl. publs. Mem. IEEE, Japan Soc. Applied Physics (trustee 1990—), Semicondr. Industry Rsch. Inst. Japan (trustee 1994-98). Avocations: golf, history, Japanese chess, Go. Home: 3-2-10 Tsukushino Machida, Tokyo 194-0001, Japan Office: 2-1-1 Shinsakuragaoka, Yokohama 240-0036, Japan

WATANABE, SHAW, pathologist, epidemiologist, nutritionist; b. Jan. 18, 1941; s. Tatsu and Shizu Watanabe; m. Hiroko Mutsui, Nov. 5, 1964; children: Daizo, Yuh, Tomo. MD, Keio U., Tokyo, 1970. Intern Keio U. Hosp., Tokyo, 1865-66, resident, 1966-70; asst. prof. Keio U., 1970-75; vis. scientist Nat. Cancer Inst., NIH, Bethesda, Md., 1975-76; chief pathology sect. Nat. Cancer Ctr., Tokyo, 1977-85, chief epidiology divsn., 1985-96; prof. dept. nutritional sci. & epidemiol. Tokyo U. Agr., 1996—. Editor: Jour. Epidemiology, 1993—, Japanese Jour. Clin. Oncology, 1993—, Acta Haematology Japan, 1985-90. Recipient Who Toh medal, 1993. Mem. Japan Med. Assn. (Med. award 1995), Japan Cancer Soc., Internat. Soc. Epidemiologists, Am. Assn. Cancer Rsch. Home: 1-14 Nishi, Kunitachi, Tokyo Japan Office: Tokyo Univ Agr, Sakuragaoka 1-1-1, Tokyo Setagaya ku 156-8502, Japan

WATANABE, TERUO, geologist, educator; b. Tokyo, Japan, Feb. 9, 1944; s. Mitsugu and Tsusoko (Okada) W.; m. Kinue Watanabe. DSc, Hokkaido U., Sapporo, Japan, 1975. Prof. geology Hokkaido U., 1994—. Office: Hokkaido Univ, Divsn Earth Planetary Scis, Sapporo 060, Japan

WATANABE, TOSHIHARU, ecologist, educator; b. Kyoto, Japan, June 6, 1924; s. Seizo and Fusa Watanabe; m. Sumiko Isebo, Nov. 3, 1952; children: Ikuko, Naoki. DSc, Kyoto U., 1961. Prof. Nat. Kanazawa (Japan) U., 1972-75, Nat. Nara (Japan) Women's U., 1975-88; prof. fgn. studies Kansai U., Hirakata/Osaka, Japan, 1988—; owner Diamond Resort Hawaii Owner's Club, 1989—; pres. Inst. Sci. Rsch. to Hydrospherical Ecology, 1990-95, adviser, 1995-2000. Author: Encyclopedia of Environmental Control Technology, 1990; editor: Japanese Jour. Diatomology, 1985-97, Japanese Jour. Water Treatment Biology, 1971—. Profl. mem. Ministry of Constrn., Kinki dist., 1980-96; vice-chmn. Com. on environ. pollution, Nara Prefecture and City, 1982-96, chmn., 1997—, com. mem. Wakayama, 1980—; pres. Environ. Coun., Nara Prefecture, 1996—, Nara City, 1997—. Recipient Blue Ribbon Order of the Navy, 1961. Avocations: Indian ink drawing, music. Home: Higashigawa-cho 518, Shinkyogoku St Nakagyo-ku, Kyoto 604 8046, Japan Office: Kansai U Fgn Studies, Kitakatahoko-cho 16-1, Hirakata Osaka 573, Japan

WATANABE, TSUNEO, newspaper executive; b. Tokyo, May 30, 1926; s. Heikichi and Hanako (Yanai) W.; m. Astuko Nabeshima, May 25, 1954; 1 child, Mutsumi. BA, U. Tokyo, 1949. With Yomiuri Shimbun, Tokyo, 1952—; chief Washington news bur. Yomiuri Shimbun, 1968-72; assoc. mng. editor, polit. editor Yomiuri Shimbun, Tokyo, 1975-77, dep. mng. editor, 1977-79, exec. editor, 1979-80, chmn. editl. bd., 1979-87, sr. exec. dir., 1980-87, pres., editor-in-chief; vis. rsch. scholar Ctr. for Strategic and Internat. Studies, Washington, 1995. Author: A Study of Political Party Factions, 1958, Inside the White House, 1971, Watergate: Background and Foreground, 1973, Practical Wisdom of Politics, 1976. Pvt. Japanese Army. Mem. Japan Nat. Press Club (dir. 1984—, editor-in-chief 1985—, sr. v.p. 1987). Office: Yomiuri Shimbun, 1-7-1 Ohtemachi, Chiyoda-ku Tokyo 100-8055, Japan Office: CSIS Office Japan Chair 1800 K St NW Washington DC 20006

WATANABE, YOSHIHISA, materials scientist, educator; b. Sakai, Osaka, Japan, June 2, 1952; s. Shigetaka and Setuko (Yamauchi) W.; m. Narumi Fujiwara; children: Koh, Mizuho. B in Engring., Kyoto (Japan) U., 1975, M in Engring., 1977; PhD, Tohoku U., Sendai, Japan, 1982. Rsch. assoc. Nat. Def. Acad., Yokosuka, Japan, 1979-84; lectr. Nat. Def. Acad., Yokosuka, 1984-87, assoc. prof., 1987-94, prof., 1994—, head advanced materials lab., 1996—, dept. chair, 1997—; vis. scholar U. Wash., Seattle, 1990-91; lectr. in field. Contbr. articles to profl. jours. Recipient 2nd place ceramographic awards Ceramic Soc. Japan, Tokyo, 1993, 96, Excellent Paper award Soc. for Hybrid Microelectronics, Tokyo, 1995, Yamasaki award Nat. Defense Acad., 1999. Mem. Am. Ceramic Soc., Japan Soc. Applied Physics, Materials Rsch. Soc. (prin. editor 1995—). Office: Nat Def Acad Dept Mat Sci, 1-10-20 Hashirimizu, Yokosuka Kanagawa 239-8686, Japan

WATANABE, YOSHIHITO, chemistry educator; b. Morioka, Iwate, Japan, May 30, 1953; s. Keiji and Teruko (Anetai) W.; m. Yumiko Iwabuch, Jan. 7, 1982; children: Haruka, Takuma. BS, Tohoku U., 1976; PhD, U. Tsukuba, 1982. Postdoctoral fellow U. Mich., Ann Arbor, 1982-84, asst. rsch. scientist, 1984-85; rsch. staff mem. Princeton U., Princeton, N.J., 1985-87; asst. prof. Keio U., Tokyo, 1987-89; sr. researcher Nat. Chem. Lab. for Industry, Tsukuba, Japan, 1989-90; assoc. prof. chemistry Kyoto U., 1990-94; prof. Inst. Molecular Sci., Okazaki, Japan, 1994—. Author: Macintosh for Scientific Presentation, 1990; contbr. articles to profl. jours. Mem. AAAS, Chem. Soc. Japan, Am. Chem. Soc., N.Y. Acad. Sci. Avocations: tennis, skiing, baseball. Office: Inst Molecular Sci, Okazaki 444, Japan

WATANABE, YOSHIO, cardiologist; b. Tokyo, Nov. 8, 1925; s. Yoshisada and Setsuko (Shiga) W.; m. Keiko Ohta, Nov. 18, 1958; children: Mari, Yuri. MD, Keio Gijuku U., 1951, DMS, 1960. Asst. instr. medicine Keio U. Hosp., Tokyo, 1952-60; assoc. prof. medicine, physiology and biophysics Hehnemann Med. Coll., Phila., 1961-72; prof. medicine, dir. cardiovascular inst. Fujita Health U., Toyoake, Japan, 1972-95; hosp. dir. Toyota (Japan) Regional Med. Ctr., 1995-99; cons. cardiologist Chiba Tokushukai Hosp., Funabashi, Japan, 1999—; scientific chmn. 5th Internat. Symposium Cardiac Pacing, Tokyo, 1976. Author: Cardiac Arrhythmias, Electrophysiologic Basis for Clinical Interpretation, 1977; co-author: International Textbook of Cardiology, 1986, Cardiac Electrophysiology, From Cell to Bedside, 1990; editor: Cardiac Pacing, 1977, Heart and Vessels, 1985-99. Recipient Kato Meml. prize Physiology and Medicine Kato Meml. Found., Tokyo, 1981. Fellow Am. Coll. Cardiology (co-dir. annual program on cardiac arrhythmias 1965-99); mem. Japanese Soc. Electrocardiology (hon., pres. 1989-90), British Cardiac Soc. (corr. mem.), Portuguese Soc. Cardiology (hon. mem.), Japanese Circulation Soc. (extraordinary mem.), Japanese Cardiac Pacing Soc. (hon. mem.), Coun. on Clin. Cardiology, Am. Heart Assn. (internat. fellow and rep. for Japan, Korea and Taiwan), N.Am. Soc. Pacing and Electrophysiology (mem. health policy com. 1997—). Buddhist. Avocations: cello, astronomy, hiking. Home: 2-6-3 Kugenuma-Fujigaya, Fujisawa 251, Japan Office: Chiba Tokushukai Hosp, 1-27-1 Narashinodai, Funabashi 274, Japan

WATANABE, YUMIKO MAYAMA, epidemiologist, geritrician; b. Kamaishi, Iwate, Japan, Apr. 2, 1963; d. Iwao and Yukiko (Miura) M. Mayama; m. Koji Watanabe, June 8, 1990. MD, Teikyo U., Tokyo, 1989; PhD, Hokkaido U., Sapporo, Japan, 1996. Resident Hokkaido U. Hosp., 1989-90, Aizen Hosp., Sapporo, 1990-96; staff physician Koshin Hosp., Sapporo, 1996-97; chief physician Facilty of Healthcare Svcs. for Elderly, Sapporo, 1997-99; vice dir. Sapporo Minami Seishu Hosp., 1999-2000; staff physician Shin-ei Hosp., Sapporo, 2000—. Contbr. articles to med. jours., including Hokkaido Jour. Med. Sci., Modern Medicine, others. Mem. Japanese Soc. Geriatric Medicine, Soc. Neurologica Japonica, Japanese Soc. Pub. Health. Avocations: gourmet cooking, poetry, piano. Office: Shin-ei 331, Kiyota-ku, Sapporo Hokkaido 004-0839, Japan

WATANACHAI, KASEM, health services administrator, consultant; b. Ratchaburi, Thailand, Apr. 28, 1941; s. Prapas and Porn W.; m. Ratchaneewan Siampakdee. MD summa cum laude, Chiang Mai (Thailand) U., 1967; DEd, Mahidol U., Bangkok, 1995. Diplomate Am. Bd. Internal Medicine, Am. Bd. Subspecialty in Cardiovascular Diseases. Head, sect. cardiology Faculty of Medicine Chiang Mai (Thailand) U., 1977-84, vice dean student affairs Faculty of Medicine, 1978-82, v.p. student affairs, 1985-87, v.p. academic affairs, 1987-89, pres., 1989-92, prof. emeritus, 1993; dep. perm. sec. Ministry U. Affairs, Bangkok, 1992-94, perm. sec., 1994-96; pres. Huachiew Chalermprakiet U., Bangplee Samutprakran, Thailand, 1997—. Senator Office of the Senate, Bangkok, 1996-2000. Recipient Gold Medal award Disting. Svc. in Medicine World Orgn. Alternative Medicine, Spain, 1992. Mem. Heart Assn. Thailand, Royal Coll. Physicians Thailand (founding mem.), Med. Assn. Thailand. Home: 1131/79 Therddumri Rd, 10300 Bangkok Thailand Office: Huachiew Chalermprakiet U, 18/18 Bangna-Trad Rd (18 km), Bangplee Samut Prakan Thailand

WATARI, AKIRA, trading company executive; b. Japan, Jan. 7, 1932; m. Yoko Watari; 1 child. Grad., Osaka (Japan) City U., 1954. With Nichimen Corp., 1954—, sr. gen. mgr. foodstuffs divsn., 1983-84, dir., 1984-87, mng. dir., 1987-89, sr. mng. dir., 1989-90; pres. Nichimen Am. Inc., 1990-91, Nichimen Can. Inc., 1991-93; exec. v.p. Nichimen Corp., Osaka, 1993-94; pres. Nichimen Corp., Tokyo, 1994—. Decorated Order Ranju Housho (Blue Ribbon) Japanese Govt., 1998. Avocations: reading, golf, bash writing. Office: 1-23 Shiba 4-chome, Minato-ku Tokyo 108-8405, Japan*

WATARU, WESTON YASUO, civil engineer; b. Honolulu, Mar. 30, 1957; s. Ralph Mitsuo and Anna Setsuko (Ogami) W.; m. Celine Jacqueline Teasdale, Nov. 1, 1986; children: Maile, Hope, Amber, Adam. BS, U. Hawaii, 1980. Registered profl. engr., Hawaii. Asst. engr. Dames and Moore, Honolulu, 1980-82; civil engr. I City and County of Honolulu Dept. Pub. Works, 1982-84, civil engr. IV, 1985-87, civil engr. V, 1987-89, svc. engr., civil engr. VI, 1989-98; civil engr. VI City and County of Honolulu Dept. Planning and Permitting, 1998—; mem. utilities coord. com. City and County of Honolulu, 1989—, mem. permit streamlining task force, 1995—. Mem. ASCE, NSPE, Am. Pub. Works Assn., Hawaii Govt. Employees Assn. Avocations: family, sporting events, basketball, reading. Office: City and County of Honolulu Dept Planning and Permitting 650 S King St Dept And Honolulu HI 96813-3078

WATERFALL, ROGER CLIVE, engineering lecturer; b. Sheffield, Yorkshire, Eng., Oct. 24, 1944; s. Harold and Vera (Crookes) W.; m. Nancy Lucas, July 15, 1987; children: Benjamin Diamuid, Daniel Kit. BSc, Birmingham U., 1965; MSc, Manchester U., 1972, PhD, 1981. Tech. asst. Ministry of Posts and Telecomm., Mauritius, 1965-66; grad. apprentice Yorks Elec. Bd., 1966-67; design engr. Ferranti Ltd., 1967-71; lectr. electronics engring. U. Manchester Inst. Sci. and Tech., 1971-96, reader, 1996—; hon. scientist North Staffs Health Authority, Stoke-on-Trent, 1984—; examiner Council Engring. Inst., London, 1984—. Contbr. articles to profl. jours. Mem. IEE (SEM sect. chmn. 1982-83). Anglican. Avocations: gardening, cycling. Office: UMIST Sackville St, Dept Elec Engring and Electronics, Manchester M6O 1QD, England

WATERHOUSE, JAMES MARIS, physiologist educator; b. Shoeburyness, Essex, England, Aug. 2, 1944; s. Charles Stanley and Emmeline Mary (Coe) W.; m. Maureen Elizabeth Dent, Sept. 6, 1969; children: Richard John, Philippa Jane. BA in Physiology, U. Oxford, Eng., 1966, DPhil, 1969. Lectr. U. Manchester, Eng., 1969-80, sr. lectr., 1981-89, reader, 1990-94, sr. rsch. fellow, 1995—; lectr. U. Liverpool, Eng., 1995—; cons. Cheshire Police Force, Chester, Eng., 1984-85; advisor Health and Safety Exec., Boothe, Eng., 1989-96. Co-author: Circadian Rhythms and the Human, 1981, Physiology and the Scientific Method, 1986, Circadian Rhythms and Performance, 1996; editor: Circadian Rhythms in Clinical Practice, 1988. Grant for Circadian Rhythms, Shiftwork, Med. Rsch. Coun., 1982-85, Irregular Sleep Schedules, Ministry of Defense, 1982-89, Shiftwork and Rhythms, Med. Rsch. Coun., 1985-95. Mem. European Soc. of Chronobiology (past pres. 1991-95), Internat. Soc. Chronobiology (pres. 1997—). Avocations: music, walking, photography. Home: 1 Blackthorn Ave Burnage, Manchester M19 1FT, England Office: Liverpool John Moores U Rsch Inst, Sport Exer Scis True Bldg Webs St, Liverpool L3 2ET, England

WATERMAN, DAVID MOORE, lawyer; b. San Francisco, July 23, 1947; s. Joseph and Muriel Yvette (Moore) W.; children: Kymberley Anne, Kevin David. BA, U. Ariz., 1970, JD, 1973; postgrad., U. Wash., 1978-80. Bar: Ariz. 1973, U.S. Dist. Ct. Ariz. 1973, U.S. Ct. Appeals (9th cir.) 1973; A-rated hearing officer 8J of Supreme Ct. Ariz. Assoc. Law Offices of William Berlat, Tucson, 1973-74, Law Offices of David K. Wolfe, Tucson, 1976-78, Rabinovitz, Dix & Rehling, Tucson, 1981-84; ptnr. Dix, Rehling & Waterman, Tucson, 1984-86, Dix & Waterman, Tucson, 1986-91; propr. Law Offices of David M. Waterman, 1991-95; mng. ptnr. Taylor & Assocs., Tucson, 1996-98; pvt. practice Tucson, 1998—; adj. prof. bus. law U. Puget Sound, Tacoma, Wash., 1978-80; instr. Highline C.C., Midway, Wash., 1978-79, U. Phoenix, 1992-93; staff assoc. Office of Atty. Gen., Seattle, 1978. Mem. ABA, ATLA, Ariz. Assn. Lawyers for Injured Workers, So. Ariz. Workers' Compensation Applicant's Assn. (pres. 1986-88), State Bar Ariz. Worker's Compensation (co-chair sect. 1985), Am. Soc. Law and Medicine. Office: 3900 E Broadway Blvd # 208 Tucson AZ 85711-3453

WATERS, TERRANCE J, architect; b. El Centro, Calif., Nov. 6, 1920; s. John and Grace May (Cox) W.; m. Beatrice Ecker, Sept. 15, 1944; 1 child, Michael Terrance. Student, L.A. City Coll., 1940, U. So. Calif., 1941, UCLA, 1948. Registered arch., Calif. Apprentice draftsman John Lautner Arch., L.A., 1949-51; prin. Arch. Terrance Waters, Malibu, Calif., 1956—; spkr. Internat. Conf. Low Cost Housing for Devel. Countries, Roorkee, India, 1985; presenter in field. Author: The Tungsten Conspiracy, 1968. Chmn., exec. sec. Malibu Citizens for Conservation, 1963-67. With USAAF,

1941-45, ETO. Recipient Svc. medal with 4 bronze stars. Mem. Am. Astonautical Soc. (sr.), Nat. Space Soc., Planetary Soc., Earthquake Engring. Rsch. Soc., Space Frontier Found. Achievements include patents for hyperboloid buildings, hyperboloidal deployable antennas and spacecraft.

WATERS, WILLIAM CARTER, III, internist, educator; b. Atlanta, Dec. 12, 1929; s. William Carter and Nannie Ellen (Starr) W.; m. Sarah Ann Bankston; children: William Carter IV, Sarah Walker Waters McEntire. AB, Emory U., 1950, MD, 1958. Diplomate in internal medicine and nephrology Am. Bd. Internal Medicine. Resident in internal medicine Grady Meml. Hosp./Emory U., Atlanta, 1958-60, 61-62; fellow in nephrology New Eng. Med. Ctr., 1960-61; practice medicine specializing in internal medicine and nephrology, Atlanta, 1962—; from instr. to assoc. prof. Emory U. Sch. Medicine, 1962-70, clin. assoc. prof., 1970-85, clin. prof., 1985—; chief staff internal medicine Piedmont Hosp., Atlanta, chmn. bd., 1991-94; 1st chmn. bd Promina Health Sys., Atlanta, 1994-96. Contbr. articles to med. jours. Served with USAF, 1951-52. Fellow ACP (master: gov. for Ga.); mem. AMA, Med. Assn. Ga., Med. Assn. Met. Atlanta, Am. Soc. Nephrology, S.E. Clin. Club, Atlanta Country Club, Piedmont Driving Club, Big Canoe Club. Methodist. Office: 35 Collier Rd NW Ste 150 Atlanta GA 30309-1604

WATERS, WILLIAM ESTLIN, medical educator; b. Toronto, Ont., Can., Nov. 6, 1934; came to U.K., 1947; s. Edward Thomas and Cicely (Weatherall) W.; m. Judith Isabel Lloyd, Mar. 14, 1964; children—Robert, David. M.B., B.S., U. London, 1958. Intern, Hither Green Hosp., London, 1959; resident Llandough Hosp., 1960, Sully Hosp., 1963-64; Leverhulm fellow, 1964-65; mem. sci. staff Med. Research Council, Cardiff, Wales, 1965-70; sr. lectr. U. Southampton, Eng., 1970-75, reader, 1975, prof. community medicine, 1976-90 . Hon. specialist in community medicine Wessex Regional Health Authority, Winchester, 1974-94, profl. fellow, 1990-94, emeritus prof., 1994— . Author, editor: The Elderly in Eleven Countries, 1983; (with others) Community Medicine: A Textbook for Nurses and Health Visitors, 1983; Headache, 1986. Served to capt. Brit. Army, 1960-62. Fellow Faculty of Community Medicine of the Royal Coll. Physicians; mem. Internat. Epidemiol. Assn. (past sec.), Brit. Ornithologists Union, Brit. Trust for Ornithology. Home: Orchards, Broxmore Park, Sherfield English, Romsey S051 6FT England Office: Community Medicine South Acad Block, Southampton Gen Hosp, Southampton Hampshire, England S09 4XY

WATERSON, IMOGEN MARGARET, pediatrician, consultant; b. London, Aug. 2, 1948; d. Donald Hibbert and Peronelle Imogen (Armitage-Smith) R.; m. John Merlin Waterson, June 19, 1971; children: Helen Natasha, Alexis Julian, Hugh Benedict. MA, Cambridge (Eng.) U., 1970, MBBCh, 1973. Cert. Higher Med. Tng. From house officer to sr. house officer medicine and surgery Salop AHA, Shrewsbury, Eng., 1973-78, registrar in pediats., medicine, 1978-81; from clin. med. officer to sr. clin. med. officer Norwich H.A., 1982-92; cons. pediatrician N.W.A. Healthcare Trust, Kings Lynn, Eng., 1992—. Author, editor (booklet) Preschool Surveillance, 1994. Fellow Royal Coll. Paediatrics and Child Health, Royal Coll. Physicians; mem. Royal Coll. Ob-Gyn (D Obstetrics), Assn. Rsch. Infant and Child Devel. Anglican. Avocations: hiking, choral singing, sailing. Office: NW Anglia Healthcare Trust, St James Extons Rd, Norfolk Kings Lynn PE30 5NU, England

WATERSON, MICHAEL JOHN, economics educator; b. Meriden, Eng., July 29, 1950; s. Geoffrey and Christine M. (Whitlock) W.; m. Sally Ann Davis, Dec. 16, 1974; children: Thomas Philip, Alice Jane. BA with 1st class honours, Warwick U., Coventry, Eng., 1971, PhD in econs., 1977; MSc in Econs., London Sch. Econs., 1972. Lectr. econs. U. Newcastle-upon-Tyne, Eng., 1974-86, reader, 1986-88; prof. Reading (Eng.) U., 1988-91, Warwick U., 1991—; vis. lectre. Sydney (Australia) U., 1987-88. Author: Economic Theory of the Industry, 1984, Regulation of the Firm and Natural Monopoly, 1988; assoc. editor Internat. Jour. Indsl. Orgns., 1985-93; mem. editorial bd. Jour. Indsl. Econs., 1986-2000en. editor, 1994-99. Mem. Indsl. Strategy Group, London, 1988-93; mem. good behavior adv. body Oftgem, 2000—. Fellow Royal Soc. Arts, Mfg. and Commerce; mem. European Assn. Rsch. Indsl. Econs. (pres. 1999—). Avocations: walking, playing musical instruments. Home: 60 Broadway Earlsdon, Coventry CV5 7NU, England

WATFORD, PAUL STEPHEN, finance analyst; b. Bklyn., Mar. 26, 1959; s. Paul and Evelyn J. Watford; m. Brenda A. Darrell, Oct. 16, 1993; 1 child, Everett A. BA in History, U. Rochester, 1980; BS in Mech. Engring., Howard U., 1982; MM in Fin., Northwestern U., 1989. Sr. prin. engr. Commonwealth Edison, Chgo., 1982-91; bus. analyst FMC Corp., Chgo., 1991-92; strategic planner United Airlines, Elk Grove Township, Ill., 1992-95; dir. fin. WTTW Ch. 11, Chgo., 1995-99; dir. fin. planning and analysis Sears Roebuck & Co., Hoffman Estates, Ill., 1999—. Trustee St. Mark's Sch., Southborough, Mass., 1993—; young leader Chgo. Cmty. Trust, 1995—. Mem. Nat. Black MBA Assn. (pres. Chgo. chpt. 1999-2000). Home: 4254 N Hermitage Ave Chicago IL 60613-1104

WATHELET, MELCHIOR, Belgian government official; b. Mar. 6, 1949. Student, U. Liege; LLM, Harvard U., 1976. Researcher U. Liege, 1973-77; sec. of state for regional economy and for housing, 1980-81, minister of new tech., planning and forestry, 1981-85, min., chmn. French Regional Exec. responsible for New Tech., Fgn. Affairs, Gen. Affairs and Pers., 1985-88, vice prime min., min. justice and econ. affairs, 1988-91, 1992-95, vice prime min., min. defense; judge European Ct. Justice, Luxembourg, 1995-. Office: Court Justice European Comm, Blvd Konrad Adenauer Kirchb, L-2925 Luxembourg Luxembourg*

WATHEN, CHRISTOPHER G., physician; b. Bebington, Cheshire, Eng., Aug. 11, 1955; s. John R. and Cicely W. BSc with honors, Edinburgh (Scotland) U., 1976, MBChB with honors, 1979, MD, 1980. Intern Hammersmith Hosp., London, 1981-82; lectr. in medicine Royal Infirmary, Edinburgh, 1982-89; sr. registrar City Hosp., No. Gen. Hosp., Royal Infirmary, Edinburgh, 1989-91; Lectr. in medicine Royal Infirmary, Edinburgh, Scotland, 1990-91; cons. physician Wycombe Hosp., High Wycombe, Eng., 1991—, Stoke Mandeville (Eng.) Hosp., 2000—; mem. edn. com. Nat. Asthma Campaign, London, 1992—. Contbr. numerous articles to profl. jours. Fellow Royal Coll. Physicians Edinburgh, Royal Coll. Physicians London; mem. Brit. Thoracic Soc., Am. Thoracic Soc. Office: S Buckinghamshire NHS Trust, Queen Alexandra Rd, High Wycombe HP11 2TT, England

WATKIN, BRUCE WYKEHAM, writer; b. London, Apr. 17, 1917; s. Frank Arthur and Eve Lewis (Reid) Bailey; m. Brigitte Paneth, Sept. 2, 1941 (div. 1967); children: Brian, Keir M.; m. Joan Adèle Haldane, Sept. 26, 1994. MA, Oxford (Eng.) U., 1939; BA, Open U., Milton Keynes, U.K., 1970; diploma in town planning and housing, Leeds (Eng.) Poly., 1948; diploma in town planning, Poly. Cen. London, 1953. Rsch. engr. Ricardo & Co., London, 1941-46; rsch. officer Ministry Town & Country Planning, Leeds, 1946-48; planning officer Staffordshire (Eng.) County Coun., 1948-49, London County Coun., 1949-51; field advisor Nat. Parks Commn., London, 1951-60; sec. Royal Fine Art Commn., London, 1961-81. Author: Shell Guide to Surrey, 1977, Shell Guide to Buckinghamshire, 1981, History of Wiltshire, 1989, Medieval Wellington, 1999; co-author: (with John Somerfield) The Pub and the People, 1943. Sec. Somerset Archaeol. and Natural History Soc., 1989-94, Surrey Amenity Coun., 1950-70, Green Belt Coun., London, 1965-75, Age Concern Wellington, 1997-2000; chmn. Warminster Civic Trust, Warminster, 1984-87, Taunton Civic Soc., 1989-91; active Somerset County Coun. Libr. Com., Taunton, 1991-95. Avocations: photography, glass engraving. Home: 55 Beech Hill, TA21 8ER Wellington England

WATKIN, JOHN RAYMOND, ecologist, writer; b. Kasanna, Zambia, July 31, 1968; s. Arthur Raymond Myles and Patrica Barbara (Marriot) W. BS in Applied Biology with honors, Nottingham Trent U., Eng., 1990; MS in Advanced Ecology, U. Durham, 1991. Cons. Mpala Rsch. Ctr., Laikipia, Kenya, 1995-96; film asst. BBC, Wamba, Zaire, 1996; mgr. Gallman Meml. Found, Laikipia, 1996-97; cons. African Butterfly Rsch. Inst., Nairobi, Kenya, 1997; program coord. African Conservation Ctr., Nairobi, 1997—; mentor to students; lectr., East Africa, 1992—. Contbr. articles to mags. Grantee various orgns. Avocations: birdwatching, reading, sports. Office: African Conservation Ctr, PO Box 62844, Nairobi 62844, England

WATKIN, VIRGINIA RUTH, financial professional; b. Pomona, Calif., Sept. 25, 1955; d. Charles Robertson Williams and Effie Ruth (Jones) Kettmann; m. Thomas Peter Watkin, Sept. 10, 1977; children: Shannon Ruth, Dana Erin. AA, Mt. San Antonio Coll., 1975; postgrad., Calif. State U., Fullerton, U. Guadalajara, Riverside (Calif.) City Coll. Mgmt. trainee Local Loan Co., La Puente, Calif., 1977, Morris Plan of Calif., Corona, 1977-78; cons. loan processor Glendale Fed., Riverside, 1978-81; cons. loan officer Glendale Fed., Riverside and Downey, Calif., 1981-84; sr. cons. loan officer Glendale Fed., Glendale, 1984-86; asst. v.p., consumer loan mgr. Hemet (Calif.) Fed. Savs. and Loan, 1986-91; underwriter Wells Fargo Bank, Santa Ana, Calif., 1992-93; sr. underwriter 1st Interstate Bank, Pasadena, Calif., 1993-96; reimbursements officer Dept. Veterans Affairs State of Calif., Barstow, 1996—; instr. Inst. Fin. Edn. Hemet/San Jacinto (Calif.) chpt. Consumer Fin. Rep. Calif. Community and Jr. Coll. Assn., Walnut, 1975. Mem. Nat. Assn. Female Execs., Calif. Savs. and Loan League (consumer loan com.), Hemet C. of C. Republican. Roman Catholic. Avocations: reading, water skiing, fishing, camping, gourmet cooking. Home: 17754 Siskiyou Rd Apple Valley CA 92307-1224 Office: Dept Veterans Affairs 100 Veterans Pkwy Barstow CA 92311-7003

WATKINS, ALAN KEITH, engineering executive; b. Oct. 9, 1938; s. Wilfred Victor and Dorothy Hilda W.; m. Diana Edith Wynne, 1963; 2 children. BS with honors, U. Birmingham, PhD. With Lucas Rsch. Ctr., 1962-69, Lucas Batteries, 1969-75; divsn. dir. Lucas Aerospace, 1975-87; mng. dir. Aerospace Lucas Industries, 1987-89; mng. dir., CEO, Hawker Siddeley Group, 1989-91; dep. chmn., chief exec. London Transport, 1992-94; dep. chmn. Sr. Engring. Group (now Senior plc), 1995-96, chmn., 1996—, also bd. dirs.; chmn. High Duty Alloys Ltd., 1997—. Fellow IEE, Inst. Materials, Inst. Mfg. Engrs. (v.p. 1991). Office: Senior Plc, Senior House, 59/61 High St, Rckmnwrt Hertfordshire WD3 1RH, England

WATKINS, JOEL SMITH, geophysicist, educator; b. Poteau, Okla., May 27, 1932; s. Joel Smith and Eva (Byers) W.; m. Carolyn Elizabeth Shoup, May 12, 1956 (div. Jan. 1971); children: Catherine DeHaven Watkins McKenna, Victoria Byers; m. Billie K. Dore, Mar. 27, 1971. AB, U. N.C., 1953; PhD, U. Tex., 1961. Geophysicist U.S. Geol. Survey, Washington, 1961-64; supr. geophysicist U.S. Geol. Survey, Flagstaff, Ariz., 1964-66; rsch. assoc. MIT, Cambridge, 1966-67; assoc. to full prof. U. N.C., Chapel Hill, 1967-72; prof. Med. Br. U. Tex., Galveston, 1973-74; prof. Marine Sci. Inst. U. Tex., Austin, 1975-77; dir., mgr., v.p. exptl. rsch. Gulf Oil, Houston, 1977-85; E.F. Cook prof. Tex. A&M U., College Station, 1985—, head dept. geophysics, 1988-93. Author: (textbook) Our Geological Environment, 1975; assoc. editor Am. Assn. Petroleum Geologists; contbr. articles to profl. jours. Lt. USMC, 1953-56. Home: RR 2 Box 165C Hearne TX 77859-9510 Office: Tex A&M U Dept Geology and Geophysics Halbouty Bldg College Station TX 77843-0001

WATKINS, LAURENCE DALE, neurosurgeon; b. Newport, UK, May 21, 1959; s. Barrie and Doreen W. MB, Cambridge U., 1984, BChir, 1984, MA, 1984. Sr. house officer, registrar Westminster Hosp., London, 1987-89; registrar Atkinson Morley's Hosp., London, 1989-90, Nat. Hosp., London, 1990-95; sr. registrar Newcastle Gen. Hosp., UK, 1995-99; sr. lectr. Inst. Neurology, London, 1999—. Author: Maxillofacial Surgery, 1998; contbr. articles to profl. jours. Fellow Royal Coll. Surgeons.

WATKINS, LOIS IRENE, English educator; b. Sterling, Nebr., Mar. 12, 1926; d. August Ralph and Magdalena Anna (Foss) Bargman; m. Morris Grant Watkins, Dec. 28, 1947 (dec. May 1996); children: Sharon Thomas, Stephen, Mark, Paul, Debra Walters, Joanna Hutchinson, David. Student, Concordia Tchrs. Coll., 1945-47; BA in Applied Linguistics, Calif. State U., Fullerton, 1976, MA in Applied Linguistics, 1978. 2d grade tchr. Canoga Park (Calif.) Luth. Sch., 1961-62; asst. prof. William Carey U., Pasadena, Calif., 1978-80; asst. to pres. All Nations Lit., Calif., Ind., Wash., 1972-92; dir. literature and literacy All Nations Lit., Colorado Springs, Colo., 1992-94, pres., bd. dirs., 1994-96; ESL curriculum specialist Internat. Bible Soc., Colorado Springs, Colo., 1996—; missionary wife Luth. Ch.-Mo. Synod, Uyo, Nigeria, 1950-52, Ogojo, Nigeria, 1959-63. Author, sr. instr. manual and video series Bridge of Love, 1994; co-editor: All Nations English Dictionary, 1990. Mem. Rep. Nat. Com., Washington. Mem. Luth. Soc. for Missiology (bd. dirs. 1994—). Avocations: reading, writing, gardening, computer graphics. Home: 5475 Jennifer Ln Colorado Springs CO 80917-1420

WATKINS, NICHOLAS WYNN, physicist; b. Poole, Dorset, Eng., May 8, 1962; s. Anthony Wynn and Christine Margaret (Blight) W. BSc, U. Coll., London, 1985; PhD, Sussex (Eng.) U., 1989; diploma in space studies, Internat. Space U., Toulouse, France, 1991. Rsch. fellow Space Sci. Ctr. Sussex U., Brighton, 1989-95; rsch. fellow space and astrophysics group U. of Warwick, Coventry, England, 1995-97; physicist Brit. Antarctic Survey, Cambridge, England, 1997—; stagiare Obs. of Paris, Meudon, France, 1996-97. Contbr. articles to profl. jours. Recipient scholarship Sci. Engring. Rsch. Coun./Space Edn. Trust, 1991; grantee USAF, 1993. Mem. Planetary Soc., Am. Geophys. Union. Office: Brit Antarctic Survey, Cambridge CB3 0ET, England

WATKINS, PAUL LINDSAY, company executive; b. Coventry, Eng., Oct. 16, 1947; s. Francis Harry and Betty Doreen (Lewis) W.; m. Maureen Ellen Sheehan, Nov. 16, 1968; children: Laura, Eleanor, Gareth. Surveyor Thomas Bates, Kenilworth, Eng., 1965-69, Turriff Corp., Warwick, 1969-70; exec. Miller Buckley, Rugby, 1970-75, Godiva Co., Coventry, 1975-78, Wilcon Group, Coventry, 1978-89, E.C. Harris & Ptnrs., West Midlands, Eng., 1989-91; pvt. practice, 1991—. Contbr. articles to profl. jours. Fellow Royal Soc. Arts and Sci., mem. Coventry C. of C. (chmn. bldg. 1977), Chartered Inst. Bldgs., Assn. Project Mgrs. (coun. mem.). Avocations: motor sports, flying. Home: 87 Rugby Rd Cubbington, Leamington Spa, Warwickshire CV327JH, England Office: 2 Hearsall Lane, Coventry CV5 6QR, England

WATKINS, RICHARD VALENTINE, investment banker; b. London, Sept. 23, 1950; s. Anthony and Audrey (Smith) W.; m. Charlotte Rosemary De Laszlo, June 1, 1978; children: Alexis, Clarissa, Nicholas. BSc, U. Loughborough, Eng., 1972. Rep. Kleinwort Benson, Venezuela, 1978-81; mgr. Kleinwort Benson, Australia, 1982-83; mng. dir. Phillips & Drew, N.Y.C., 1983-85; pres. Hoare Govett, N.Y.C., 1985-88; chief exec. Shroder Securities, London, 1988-92; founder, chief exec. BBV LatInvest, London, 1992-98, Liability Solutions, 1999—; chmn. bd. dirs. Deutsche Latin Am. Cos. Trust. Mem. Securities Inst. Avocation: skiing. Office: Liability Solutions Ltd, 17C Curzon St, London W1J 5HS, England

WATKINS, RUSSELL L., banker; b. Dermott, Ark., Dec. 9, 1960; s. Bruce L. and Barbara J. Watkins. Student, U. Miss., Oxford, 1993; BBA in Fin., Delta State U., Cleveland, Miss., 1995; postgrad., U. Memphis, 1999. Asst. v.p lending Union Planters Bank, Greenville, Miss., 1981-94; v.p., bank mgr. The Valley Bank, Greenville, 1994-96; v.p. lending Heartland Cmty. Bank, Monticello, Ark., 1996—. Bd. dirs. Drew County United Way, 2000—, Drew County Am. Cancer Soc., 2000—, March of Dimes, Miss. chpt., 1981-96, mem. exec. bd., 1997-2000; county del. Ark. Promise, 1997. Mem. Delta Mu Delta, Phi Kappa Phi. Democrat. Roman Catholic. Avocations: travel, art, writing, southern culture, blues and jazz. Home: 1020 Village Dr Apt 23 Arkadelphia AR 71923-2962 Office: Heartland Community Bank 473 Hwy Y25 N Monticello AR 71655

WATKINS, SHERRY LYNNE, elementary school educator; b. Bloomington, Ind., Oct. 13, 1944; d. Quentin Odell and Velma Ruth W. BSEd, Ind. U., 1966, MSEd, 1968. Tchr. 4th grade North Grove Elem. Sch., Ctr. Grove Sch. Dist., Greenwood, Ind., 1966-68; tchr. 4th and 6th grades John Strange Sch., Met. Dist. of Wash. Twp., Indpls., 1968-91; tchr. 4th grade Allisonville Sch. Met. Sch. Dist. of Wash. Twp., Indpls., 1991—; bd. dirs. ISTA Ins. Trust and Fin. Svcs. Mem. People for Ethical Treatment of Animals. Mem. NEA (nat. del. 1978—), ACLU, AAUW, Ind. Tchrs. Assn. (state del. 1966—), Washington Twp. Edn. Assn. (pres. 1986-89), World Confedn. Orgn. of Tchg. Profls. (del. Costa Rica 1990), Delta Kappa Gamma (chpt. pres. 1992-94, chmn. coord. coun. Indpls. area 1994-96, state legislature chair, 1997-99), Alpha Omicron Pi. Avocations: traveling, cultural activities. Office: Allisonville Sch 4920 E 79th St Indianapolis IN 46250-1615

WATKINS, TED ROSS, social work educator; b. Terrell, Tex., Dec. 2, 1938; s. Daniel Webster and Iva Lucy (Lowrie) W.; m. Betty Diane Dobbs, May 30, 1959; children: Evan Scott, Brett Dobbs, James David. BA in Psychology, U. North Tex., 1961; MSW, La. State U., 1963; D of Social Work, U. Pa., 1976. Staff social worker Mercer County Mental Health Ctr., Sharon, Pa., 1963-65; chief social worker, assoc. exec. Talbot Hall Treatment Ctr., Jonestown, Pa., 1965-70; chief social worker Harrisburg (Pa.) Mental Health Ctr., 1970-71; asst. prof. social work U. Tex., Arlington, 1971-76; dir. counseling svcs. Family Svcs., Inc., Ft. Worth, 1976-79; assoc. prof. social work U. Tex., 1979-85, dir. criminal justice, 1985-87, chair dept. sociology, 1987-91, assoc. prof., grad. advisor social work, 1991-99; assoc. prof., dir. Bachelor of Social Work program S.W. Tex. State U., San Marcos, 1999—; cons. in field. Author: (with James Callicutt) Mental Health Policy and Practice Today. Tex. del. to Pres.'s Commn. in Mental Health, Austin, 1978. Recipient Golladay Teaching award Coll. Liberal Arts, Arlington, 1990; named Outstanding Profl. Human Svcs., 1972. Mem. NASW (state bd. dirs. 1976-78, 80-82, unit chair, vol. lobbyist 1982), Acad. Cert. Social Workers (lic. master social worker, advanced clin. practitioner), World Assn. for Psychosocial Rehab., Alliance for the Mentally Ill, Nat. Assn. for Rural Mental Health, Nat. Social Sci. Assn. Democrat. Methodist. Avocations: music, painting, camping. Office: SW Tex State U Dept Social Work 601 University Dr San Marcos TX 78666-4685

WATKINS, WINIFRED MAY, biochemist, researcher; b. London, Aug. 6, 1924; d. Albert Edward and Annie (Delia) W. BSc, London U., 1947, PhD, 1950, DSc, 1963; DSc (hon.), Utrecht (The Netherlands) U., 1990. Head biochem. dept. Lister Inst., London, 1968-75; head divsn. immunochem. genetics Med. Rsch. Coun. Clin. Rsch. Ctr., Harrow, U.K., 1976-89; hon. sr. rsch. fellow Royal Postgrad. Med. Sch., Hammersmith Hosp., London, 1990—. Contbr. articles to profl. jours. Recipient Landsteiner award Am. Soc. Blood Banks, N.Y., 1967, Paul Ehrlich medal and prize Ehrlich Found., Frankfurt, Germany, 1969, Franz Oehlecker Gold medal German Soc. Transfusion Medicine, 1989, Philip Levine award Am. Soc. Clin. Pathologists, 1990. Fellow Royal Coll. Pathology, Royal Soc. (coun. 1984-86, Royal medal 1988), Royal Coll. Physicians (hon.); mem. British Biochem. Soc. (hon.), Genetical Soc. U.K., Immunol. Soc. U.K., Brit. Blood Transfusion Soc. (hon.), Polish Acad. Scis. (fgn.), Japanese Biochem. Soc. (hon.), Internat. Blood Transfusion Soc. (hon.), Royal Swedish Acad. Scis. (fgn.). Avocations: reading about art and architecture, travel. E-mail: w.watkins@ic.ac.uk. Office: Imp Coll Hammersmith Hosp, Dept Hematology Du Cane Rd, London W12 0NN, England

WATKINSON, CAROL, home economics educator, textile researcher; b. Graaff Reinet, Cape, South Africa, Sept. 26, 1947; d. Eric Thomas W. Higher diploma in Edn., Natal U., South Africa, 1979; Nat. diploma in Home Econs., Technikon Natal, Durban, South Africa, 1967. Tchr Home Econs. Estcourt H.S., South Africa, 1968, Salisbury Girls Sch., Zimbabwe, 1969; sr. lectr. Teknikon Natal, 1971-92; workshop presenter, (textiles and fabric recognition), Home Econs. Assn. South Africa Bi-Ann. Conf., 1995, Textile Inst. World Conf., 1996, Home Econs. Africa Assn., 1997, Internat. Fedn. Home Econs., 2000. Com. mem. Home Econs. Assn. South Africa, 1989-91. Recipient Plum award Fashion Dept. Technikon Natal, South Africa, 1993. Mem. Textile Inst. (com. mem. 1995-97), Internat. Textile and Apparel Assn., Home Econs. Assn. Africa, Internat. Fedn. Home Econs. Avocations: photography, writing. Office: Technikon Natal, PO Box 953, Durban 4000, Kwa Zulu Natal, South Africa

WATKINSON, JOHN RONALD, communications consultant; b. Hull, England, Mar. 29, 1950; s. George Ronald and Agnes (Smith) W.; m. Annette Friend, July 1974 (div. 1988); children: Howard, Matthew; m. Chrissie (Lewis) Wyle, May, 1995. BS with honors, Southampton U., 1971, MS, 1972. Rsch. officer Southampton U., Hampshire, United Kingdom, 1973-76; lectr. Digital Equipment Corp., Reading, United Kingdom, 1976-82, Sony Broadcast, Basingstoke, United Kingdom, 1982-84; tng. mgr. Ampex Great Britain, Reading, 1986-88; dir. Runlength Ltd., Reading, 1988—, Celtic Audio Ltd., 1997—; cons. United Kingdom Nat. Sound Archive, London, 1991—. Author: The Art of Digital Audio, 1988, 2d edit., 1994, The Art of Digital Video, 1990, 2d edit., 1994, The D-2 Digital Video Recorder, 1990, Coding for Digital Recording, 1990, R-DAT Digital Audio Tape, 1991, The D-3 Digital Video Recorder, 1992, Introduction to Digital Audio, 1994, Introduction to Digital Video, 1994, The Digital Video Recorder, 1994, The Art of Data Recording, 1994, The Art of Sound Reproduction, 1998, MPEG-2, 1999. Audio Engring. Soc. fellow, 1991; recipient Nat. Tng. award United Kingdom Dept. Trade and Industry, 1990. Mem. British Computer Soc. Avocations: helicopters, music, clocks. Home and Office: 2 Hillside, Burghfield Common, Berkshire RG7 3BQ, England

WATKIS, NICHOLAS CLIVE, marketing professional, management consultant; b. Kempston, Bedfordshire, Eng., Apr. 25, 1952; s. Jack Reginauld and Jeanne Kathleen (Shepherd) W.; m. Mary Jane Thornhill, Jan. 5, 1985; children: Andrew, Katherine. Postgrad. Diploma in Mktg., Chartered Inst. Mktg., 1976; Postgrad. Diploma in Indsl. Mktg., Inst. Mgmt. Consultancy, 1979. Cert. mgmt. cons. Territorial Army, 1972; salesperson Wellcome Found., Cheshire, 1971-73, Brit. Steel, Gwent, Eng., 1973-76; mktg. Tucker Products, Glamorgan, Eng., 1976-78; head mktg. Powell Duffryn Engring., Glamorgan, 1978-81; chief exec. Contract Mktg. Svcs., Pontypool, Eng., 1981-96, Virtual Office UK, Gloucester, Eng., 1996—; mng. dir. Money-for-Business.com Ltd., 2000. Author: The Western Front from the Air, 1999. With intelligence corps Territorial Army Svc., 1972-84, Royal Air Force Vol. Res., 1984-97, Royal Aux. Air Force, 1997—. Recipient Air Efficiency award Royal Air Force, 1984, Air Efficiency award CLASP, 1994. Mem. Brit. Longbow Soc., Chartered Inst. Mgmt., Inst. Mgmt. Consultancy (cert. mgmt. cons.), Cotswold Aero Club. Avocations: flying, military history, gardening, swimming, reading. Office: Virtual Office UK, "Thackers" Upton Ln, Gloucester GL4 5UY, England

WATLING, MICHAEL LEE, sculptor; b. Kansas City, Mo., Sept. 8, 1946; s. George Edward and Patricia June Watling; m. Reneé Lentz, Sept. 1, 1969 (div. Jan. 1974); m. Ruth Ann Watling, Oct. 10, 1981; 1 child, Benjamin Patrick. Life tchng. credential, Calif. C.C. Owner/operator Landscape Design-Build Firm, San Diego, 1974-77; prof. horticulture Coll. of the Desert, Palm Desert, Calif., 1977—; founding dir. Coll. of the Desert Arboretum, Palm Desert, 1988—; ptnr., cons. The Watling Co., Pinyon, Calif., 1990—. Sculptor large scale artwork, earthworks and pub. monuments. Rep., Pinyon Cmty. Coun., 1993-97. Home: 69-030 Pinesmoke Rd #51 Mountain Center CA 92561 Office: College of the Deser 43-500 Monterey Ave Palm Desert CA 92260

WATMORE, LESLIE JOHN, retired solicitor; b. London, May 8, 1929; s. Arthur and Edith Alice Watmore; m. Iris Daphne Enever, Dec. 19, 1953 (dec. June 1992); children: Stephen Charles, David Anthony; m. Wendy Joan Gunn, Apr. 1, 1998. MA, Oxford U., 1953. Ptnr. L. Bingham & Co. (Solicitors), London, 1959-76; sr. ptnr. L. Watmore & Co. (Solicitors), London, 1976-94; chmn. Legal Aid Area Com., London, 1982-85. Mem. Royal Automobile Club, City Livery Club, West Kent Golf Club (pres.). Avocations: golf, hill walking. Home and Office: Tudor Cottage, 10 Downs Hill Beckenham, Kent BR3 2HB, England

WATMOUGH, DAVID JOHN, medical products company executive; b. Oct. 18, 1938. BSc, St. Andrews U., Eng., 1961, PhD, 1965. Sr. lectr., head ultrasonic lab. U. Aberdeen, Eng., 1978-92; chief exec. Kings Coll. Aurora Instruments Ltd., Old Aberdeen, Eng., 1977; assoc. prof., chmn. physics dept. King Faisal U., Dammam, Saudi Arabia, 1992-96; chmn. dept. radiology Kuwait U., prof. physics; founding dir. Highland Innovation Ctr. Ltd., Inverness, Eng., 1998—; grant applications referee, Eng. Contbr. numerous articles to profl. jours. Fellow Inst. Acoustics; mem. IEE, European Soc. Hyperthermic Oncology, Brit. Inst. Radiology. Home: 16 Blackpark Terr, Scorguie IV3 8NE, England

WATNE, ALVIN L., surgeon, educator; b. Shabbona, Ill., Jan. 13, 1927; m. Diana Folio, Dec. 3, 1966; children: Carrie, Matthew, Andrew, Valer-

ie. B.S., U. Ill.-Chgo. Coll. Medicine, 1950, M.D., 1952, M.S., 1956. Diplomate: Am. Bd. Surgery. Intern Indpls. Gen. Hosp., 1952-53; resident U. Ill. Research and Edn. Hosps., Chgo., 1954-58; assoc. cancer surgeon Cancer Research, Roswell Park, Buffalo, N.Y., 1958, assoc. chief cancer research, 1959; assoc. prof. surgery W.Va. U., 1962-67, prof., 1967-72, acting chmn. dept. surgery, 1973-75, prof., chmn. dept. surgery, 1975-86; prof., chmn. dept. surgery U. Ill., Peoria, 1986-91; dir. Cancer Ctr. of Ga., 1991-94; assoc. dir. dept. surgery Ga. Bapt. Med. Ctr., 1994-97; cons. surgery VA, Clarksburg, W.Va., 1963—. Author: Gardner's Syndrome, 1977, (2d edit.), 1979, Melanoma of Head and Neck, 1981, Polyposis Coli, 1982. Pres. W. Va. div. Am. Cancer Soc., 1967-68, 80—, v.p., 1981. Recipient Hektoen Gold medal AMA, 1958; recipient Hektoen Silver medal AMA, 1960. Mem. ACS (pres. W.Va. chpt. 1972-73, chmn. local com. 1978—, gov. 1985—), Southeastern Surg. Congress (councilor 1980—), Soc. Surg. Oncology (exec. council 1980), Soc. Head and Neck Surgeons (pres. 1982), Am. Cancer Soc. (dir.-at-large 1985—). Office: 105 E Navaho Ave Shabbona IL 60550-9779

WATNE, DONALD ARTHUR, accountant, educator; b. Gt. Falls, Mont., Jan. 18, 1939; s. Arthur Leonard and Anne (Salo) W.; m. Patricia Elaine Schick, Aug. 12, 1961; children: Elizabeth Anne, Michael Arthur. BA with high honors, U. Mont., 1960, MA, 1961; PhD, U. Calif., Berkeley, 1977. CPA, Oreg. Acct. Piquet & Minihan, Eugene, Oreg., 1961-65; mgr. capital investment analysis Weyerhaeuser Co., Tacoma, 1965-68; mktg. rep. IBM Corp., Portland, Oreg., 1968-70; dir. EDP Ctr. in Concejo Mcpl., Barquisimeto, Venezuela, 1971-72; prof. acctg. Portland State U., 1976—; vis. prof. Xiamen (Fujian, People's Rep. China), 1985-86, U. Otago, Dunedin, New Zealand, 1985-86, U. Newcastle, Australia, 1985-86; cons. in field; acctg. qualifications com. Oregon State Bd. Acctg., 1989-98, CPE com., 1998—. Author: (with Peter B.B. Turney) Auditing EDP Systems, 2d edit. 1990; contbr. chpts. to books, articles to profl. jours. Del. to Soviet Union citizen amb. program People to People Internat., 1990; active Tng. the Trainers Program, Vilnius, Lithuania, 1993. Mem. AICPA, Am. Acctg. Assn., Oreg. Soc. CPAs, Mazamas Mountain Climbing Club, Mensa. Home: 2826 NE 26th Ave Portland OR 97212-3503 Office: Portland State U Sch Bus Adminstrn PO Box 751 Portland OR 97207-0751

WATNEY, LYNNE MOUNTFORD, interior designer; b. Capetown, South Africa, Nov. 20, 1953; d. Claude Mountford and Monica Nelson (Girdlestone) W.; m. Brian David Klass, July 27, 1983. With Watney Girls Restaurant, Cape Town, 1978-79; dir. Lakes Holiday Resort (Pty) Ltd., Wilderness, 1976-90; chief exec. officer Contract Interiors CC, Johannesburg, South Africa, 1979—; dir. Contract Installations, Johannesburg, 1980—, Stara Internat.; CEO Workplace Design Internat.; dir. Corp. Interplan Cons., Kessler Corp. Property, Steelcase South Africa. Contbr. articles to profl. jours. Avocations: reading, water skiing, squash. Home: 55289 Northlands, 2116 Johannesburg South Africa Office: Contract Interiors CC, Beau Arts Pl Willowbrook Close Melrose N, Johannesburg South Africa

WATSON, ALAN GORDON, software engineer, consultant, statistician; b. Bulawayo, Zimbabwe, Dec. 19, 1964; arrived in South Africa, 1978; s. Dennis Roy and Valerie Eleanor (Irons) W. BS, U. Witwatersrand, Johannesburg, 1985, BS with honors, 1986, MS, 1988; PhD, U. Minn., Mpls., 1990. Systems programmer Softserve Scientific, Johannesburg, 1985-86; software cons. Johannesburg, 1986; dir. Alan Watson Computer Consultancy C.C., Johannesburg; rsch. asst. U. Minn., Mpls., 1988-90; project leader Coun. for Sci. and Indsl. Rsch., Pretoria, South Africa, 1991-97; proprietor Corp. Techs., 1997—. Contbr. scientific papers to profl. jours. Recipient Nat. Postgrad. scholarship FRD, 1989, Outstanding Svcs. award South African Airways, 1996. Mem. Internat. Assn. for Math. Geology, Assn. Computing Machinery. Avocations: hiking, rock climbing, outdoor photography, writing. Home: 16 2d Ave, Edenvale 1610, South Africa

WATSON, ALEJANDRO, hotel executive; b. Mexico City, June 3, 1957; s. Eduardo Watson and Angelina Rincon; m. Claudia Bringas, Mar. 10, 1989; children: Andrea, Rodrigo, Paola. Degree in hotel mgmt., Ctr. Higher Edn. San Angel, Mexico City, 1981. Gen. dir. sales Posadas de Mex., Mexico City, 1991-92, v.p. Mex. sales force, 1993-94; corp. comml. dir. Wuss-Carrasco, Mexico City, 1994-95; comml. dir. met. divsn. svcs. Bancomer, Mexico City, 1995; assoc. dir. sales Ritz-Carlton, Cancun, Mex., 1996-97; dir. mktg. Camino Real Mex., Mexico City, 1997—; cons. Ctr. Higher Edn. Angel, 1995-99. Mem. Meeting Planners Incentive. Avocations: swimming, aerobics, music, reading, public relations. Home: Sierra Madre 380-B, 11000 Mexico City Mexico Office: Camino Real Mex Col Anzures, Mariano Escobedo 700, 11590 Mexico City Mexico

WATSON, BRADLEY CHARLES STEPHEN, political science educator, lawyer, writer; b. Toronto, Can., Jan. 7, 1961; s. Charles William and Winifred Nelsie Watson; m. Barbara Jean Morton, Aug. 27, 1988; children: Victoria Jean, Charles Morton. BA, U. B.C., 1983; LLB, Queen's U., Kingston, Ont., 1986; MA, Claremont (Calif.) Grad. Sch., 1992, PhD, 1996; MPhil, Cath. U. of Louvain, Belgium, 1995. Bar: B.C. 1987. Articled student Campney & Murphy, Vancouver, B.C., Can., 1986-87; assoc. Palkowski & Co., Vancouver, B.C., 1987-89; asst. prof. Norwich U., Northfield, Vt., 1996-99, St. Vincent Coll., Latrobe, Pa., 1999—; adj. faculty U. Redlands, Calif., 1994-96; vis. asst. prof. Claremont McKenna Coll., Claremont, 1995-96; adj. prof. Norwich U. Mil. Grad Program, 1997—; adj. fellow Claremont Inst. Study Statesmanship and Polit. Philosophy, 1998—, John M. Ashbrook Ctr. for Pub. Affairs, Ashland U., 1999—; fellow in politics and policy Ctr. for Econ. and Policy Edn., St. Vincent Coll., 1999—; dir. St. Vincent Coll. Govt. and Polit. Edn. Lecture Series, Culture and Policy Conf., Duquesne Club lecture series, Civitas Forum, George Washington Fellowship Program, 1999—. Author: Civil Rights and the Paradox of Liberal Democracy, 1999; contbr. Rethinking the Constitution, 1996, Microsoft Encarta Ency., 1997, 98, 99, 2000; editor: Liberalism in the New Millennium, 2000; contbr. articles to profl. jours. and other publs. Faculty fellow John M. Olin Found., 1997-98, postdoctoral fellow Social Scis. and Humanities Rsch. Coun. of Can., 1996, faculty fellowship Gould Ctr. for Humanistic Studies, Claremont McKenna Coll., 1996, Salvatori fellow Heritage Found., 1995. Mem. Am. Polit. Sci. Assn., Can. Polit. Sci. Assn., Nat. Assn. of Scholars. Anglican. Avocations: foreign travel, astronomy, skiing, photography. Office: St Vincent Coll Ctr for Econ and Policy Edn Latrobe PA 15650-2690

WATSON, BRENDA BENNETT, insurance company executive; b. Decatur, Ga., Aug. 26, 1940; d. Robert Joseph and Clarissa Mae (Weekes) Bennett; m. James H. Pair Jr., Apr. 4, 1969 (div. Aug. 1993); children: Richard S. Pair, Randall J. Pair, Ronald G. Pair; m. James Leigh Watson, Sept. 9, 1995. Student, DeKalb Coll., 1971. Lic. property and casualty agt., Fla., Ga., Okla., Tenn., Tex. Underwriter W. K. Stringer Co., Atlanta, 1961-65, Tharpe & Assocs., Atlanta, 1965-68; sr. v.p. Alexander - Howden, Atlanta, 1968-82; exec. v.p., ptnr. Pair Underwriting Mgrs. Inc., Atlanta, 1982-86; pres. Walkingstick-LaGere-Pair Underwriting Mgrs., Inc., Chandler, Okla., 1986-88; exec. v.p., dir. LaGere-Walkingstick Ins. Agy., Chandler, Okla., 1988—; exec. v.p. Nat. Am. Ins. Co., Chandler, Okla., 1987—, Austin, Tex., 1999—; exec. v.p., bd. dirs. Chandler Ins. Ltd., Cayman Islands, 1985—. Dir., past pres. Gateway to Prevention and Recovery, 1994-98. Mem. Nat. Assn. Ins. Women (pres. Atlanta chpt. 1978-79, Woman of Yr. 1979-80). Republican. Episcopalian. Home: 10002 Shinnecock Hills Dr Austin TX 78747-1315 Office: Wells Fargo Bank Bldg 2028 Ben White Blvd Ste 200 Austin TX 78741

WATSON, BRIAN COLBATH See COLBATH, BRIAN

WATSON, DONALD CHARLES, cardiothoracic surgeon, educator; b. Fairfield, Ohio, Mar. 15, 1945; s. Donald Charles and Pricilla H. Watson; m. Susan Robertson Prince, June 23, 1973; children: Kea Huntington, Katherine Anne, Kirsten Prince. BA in Applied Sci., Lehigh U., 1968, BSME, 1968; MSME, Stanford U., 1969; MD, Duke U., 1972. Diplomate Am. Bd. Thoracic Surgery, Am. Bd. Surgery. Intern in surgery Stanford U. Med. Ctr., Calif., 1972-73, resident in cardiovasc. surgery, 1973-74, resident in surgery, 1976-78, chief resident in heart transplant, 1978-79, chief resident in cardiovasc. and gen. surgery, 1978-80; clin. assoc. surgery br. Nat. Heart and Lung Inst., 1974-76, acting sr. surgeon, 1976; assoc. cardiovasc. surgeon dept. child health and devel. George Washington U., Washington, 1980-84, asst. prof. surgery, asst. prof. child health and devel., 1980-84, attending cardiovasc. surgeon dept. child health and devel., 1984-89, assoc. prof. surgery, 1984-89; assoc. prof. pediats. U. Tenn.-Memphis, 1984-90, prof. surgery, prof. pediats., 1990—, chmn. cardiothoracic surgery, 1984-99, assoc. chief med. officer, 1999—; mem. staff Le Bonheur Children's Med. Ctr., Memphis, chmn. cardiothoracic surgery, 1984—; mem. staff William F. Bowld Med. Ctr., Memphis, Regional Med. Ctr. at Memphis, Bapt. Meml. Med. Ctr., Memphis; cons. in field; instr. advanced trauma life support; profl. cons., program reviewer HHS. Contbr. chpts., numerous articles, revs. to profl. publs. Bd. dirs. Internat. Children's Heart Found., Child Health Alliance of the Mid-South. Served to lt. comdr. USPHS, 1974-76. Smith Kline & French fellow Lehigh U., 1967; NSF fellow Lehigh U., 1968; univ. interdepartmental scholar and univ. scholar Lehigh U., 1968. Fellow Am. Coll. Cardiology, Am. Coll. Chest Physicians (forum cardiovasc. surgery, coun. critical care), Southeastern Surg. Congress, Am. Acad. Pediats. (surgery sect.), ACS; mem. Assn. Surg. Edn., Am. Assn. Thoracic Surgery, Soc. Thoracic Surgeons, So. Thoracic Surg. Assn., Am. Thoracic Soc., Assn. Acad. Surgery, Internat. Soc. Heart Transplantation, Am. Fedn. Clin. Rsch., Found. Advanced Edn. in Scis., Andrew G. Morrow Soc., Norman E. Shumway Soc. (multiple bd. dirs.), Coun. on Cardiovasc. Surgery Am. Heart Assn., Soc. Internat. di Chirig., AAAS, N.Y. Acad. Sci., AMA, NIH Alumni Assn., Stanford U. Med. Alumni Assn., Stanford U. Alumni Assn., Lehigh U. Alumni Assn., Smithsonian Assocs., Sierra Club, U. Tenn. Pres.'s Club, LeBonheur Pres's Club, U.S. Yacht Racing Assn., Pilots Internat. Assn., Nat. Assn. Flight Instrs., Aircraft Owners and Pilots Assn., Order Ky. Cols., Crescent Club, Phi Beta Kappa, Tau Beta Pi, Pi Tau Sigma, Phi Gamma Delta. Republican. Presbyterian. Avocations: sailing, racquet sports, flying, computers. Office: Office of the CMO 66 N Panhine Ste 334 Memphis TN 38105-5123

WATSON, FRANK H., government official; b. Gordon's Long Island, Bahamas, Mar. 24, 1940. Diploma Pub. Adminstrn., U. West Indies; postgrad., U. London, 1962. Customs officer and businessman; employee various posts, then asst. comptroller, sr. dep. Bahamas Customs Dept., 1959-77; pres. Bahama Divers Water Sports and Tours Co., 1977—; owner Flora Creations; mem. for Carmichael Ho. of Assembly, Nassau, 1982—, chmn. Com. to Revise Retail Price Index, opposition whip, parliament and shadow min. for youth, min. pub. works and local govt., 1992-95, dep. prime min. and min. tourism, from 1995; now dep. prime min., min. nat. security Cabinet, Govt. of Bahamas, Nassau. Mem. Free Nat. Movement. Office: Ministry Nat Security, PO Box N 3217, Nassau Bahamas

WATSON, GEORGE WILLIAM, lawyer, legal consultant; b. Eaton Rapids, Mich., Mar. 1, 1926; s. George W. and Agnes R. (Nissen) W.; m. Ruth Carpenter Murphy, Oct. 1, 1949; children: G. William (dec.), Linda R.W. Macari, Daniel, Thomas, Rose Mary. AB, U. Mich., 1947, JD, 1950. Bar: Mich. 1951, U.S. Dist. Ct. (ea. and we. dists.) Mich. 1951, U.S. Ct. Military Appeals, 1991. Pvt. practice law Charlotte, Mich., 1951-53; dir. Kalamazoo Legal Aid Bur., 1953-54; asst. pros. atty. Kalamazoo County, 1955-56; gen. atty. Office Civil and Def. Mobilization, Battle Creek, Mich., 1956-62, Def. Civil Preparedness Agy., Washington, 1962-80; assoc. gen. counsel Fed. Emergency Mgmt. Agy., Washington, 1980=88, gen. counsel, 1988-91; cons. on adminstrn. law and govtl. affairs pvt. practice, Alexandria, Va., 1991—. Pres. Mt. Vernon/Lee Enterprises, Alexandria, Va., 1988-94; commordor Nat. Yacht Club, Washington, 1981; chmn. bd. dirs. Way Home Program, Georgetown, Del., 1999—. With USN, 1944-46, PTO. Mem. State Bar of Mich. Episcopalian. Avocations: community svc., sailboat racing. Home: 508 Candlelight Ln Bethany Beach DE 19930-9688 Office: 2610 Culpeper Rd Alexandria VA 22308-2135

WATSON, GEORGIANNA, librarian; b. Lock Haven, Pa., Feb. 18, 1949; d. George and Anna (Eisenhower) Rhine; children: Sharga Nicolle, George Winfield-Martin. BS in Edn., Lock Haven State U., 1971; MLS, Brigham Young U., 1978; M in Pub. Adminstrn., John Jay Coll. Criminal Justice, N.Y.C., 1986. Tchr. Mifflin County Sch. Dist., Lewistown, Pa., 1971-72; librarian Shiprock Boarding Sch. Bur. Indian Affairs, Shiprock, N.Mex., 1972-79, Ft. Sill Indian Sch. Bur. Indian Affairs, Lawton, Okla., 1979-80; librarian U.S. Mil. Acad., West Point, N.Y., 1980-83, head pub. services, library, 1983—. Mem. Southeastern N.Y. Library Resource Council (mem. continuing edn. com., chairperson govt. documents interest group), Southeastern N.Y. Reference Library Interest Group, Am. Quarter Horse Assn., Internat. Arabian Horse Assn., Pi Alpha Alpha. Republican. Home: 8 St Michaels Ln Walden NY 12586-2466 Office: US Mil Acad Dept Army West Point NY 10996-1799

WATSON, GRAHAM MICHAEL, urologist; b. London, Oct. 28, 1950; s. David Anthony and Elizabeth Rosemary (Bowen) W.; m. Caroline Anne Hausner, Feb. 14, 1980; children: Kathryn, Jessica, Phoebe. MB, BChir, Cambridge (Eng.) U., 1975, MD, 1988. Sr. lectr. St. Peter's Hosp., London, 1989-94; cons. urologist Eastborne, Eng., 1994—. Inventor in field. Chmn. Wannock Place Stables, 1996. Fellow Royal Coll. Surgeons England. Office: Esperance Pvt Hosp, Hartington Pl, Eastbourne BN21 3BG, England

WATSON, GUY EDWARDS, mechanical engineer, consultant; b. Los Angeles, Nov. 1, 1923; s. Russell Allen and Sacca Mauree (Hardesty) W.; m. Margie Anne Ruffin, July 10, 1948; one child, Kimberly Anne. BS, U. Calif., Berkeley, 1950; MSME, Santa Clara (Calif.) U., 1967; Engr. in Mech. Engring., Stanford U., 1972. Registered profl. engr., Calif., Kans. Sr. svc. rep. Fed.-Mogul Corp., Detroit, 1950-54; design and research engr. Coleman Co. Inc., Wichita, Kans., 1954-60; pres. Midwest Plastics Corp., Wichita, 1960-63; technical cons. Lockheed Missiles & Space Co., Sunnyvale, Calif., 1963-87; pres. Watson Mark Corp., Cupertino, Calif., 1987-94; gen. mgr. propeller divsn. Wings of History Air Mus., San Martin, Calif., 1994—; cons. Fahlin Propellers, Cupertino, Calif., 1980-91. Patentee in field. Served to capt. USAAF, 1942-46, PTO. Mem. AIAA (sr.), Quiet Birdmen. Home: 7723 Kilmarnok Dr San Jose CA 95135-2140

WATSON, HELEN RICHTER, educator, ceramic artist; b. Laredo, Tex., May 10, 1926; d. Horace Edward and Helen Mary (Richter) Watson. B.A., Scripps Coll., 1947; M.F.A., Claremont Grad. Sch. and U. Ctr., 1949; postgrad. Alfred U., 1966; Swedish Govt. fellow Konstfackskolan, Stockholm, 1952-53. Mem. faculty Chaffey Coll., Ontario, Calif., 1950-52; chmn. ceramics Mt. San Antonio Coll., Walnut, Calif., 1955-57; prof., chmn. ceramics dept. Otis Art Inst., Los Angeles, 1958-81; mem. faculty Otis-Parsons Sch. Design, 1983-88, ret. 1988; studio ceramic artist, Claremont, Calif. and Laredo, Tex., 1949—; design cons. Interpace, Glendale, Calif., 1963-64; artist-in-residence Clarement Men's Coll., 1977. Claremont Grad. Sch. fellow, 1948-49; Swedish Govt. grantee, 1952-53; recipient First Ann. Scripps Coll. Disting. Alumna award, Claremont, 1978. Mem. Artists Equity, Nat. Ceramic Soc., Am. Craftsmen's Council, Los Angeles County Mus. Art, Mus. Contemporary Art Los Angeles. Republican. Episcopalian. Address: 1906 Houston St Laredo TX 78040-7709

WATSON, HUGH ROBERT, clinical researcher; b. Cheltenham, U.K., Jan. 12, 1959; s. Charles Borthwick and Irene Isobel (Norrie) W. BS, U. Bath., U.K., 1982. Clin. rschr. Schering Health Care, Ltd., Burgess Hill, U.K., 1982-86; clin. project leader Schering Health Care, Ltd., Burgess Hill, 1987-92, Schering AG, Berlin, 1993-97; project dir. Searle European Clin. R&D, Paris, 1997—. Contbr. articles to profl. jours. Mem. European Soc. Vascular Surgery, Soc. Pharm. Medicine. Avocations: swimming, cycling, cinema, art. Office: Searle European Clin R&D, Immemble Elysees La Def/7Pl, 92056 Paris La Defense, France

WATSON, JAMES DEWEY, molecular biologist, educator; b. Chgo., Apr. 6, 1928; s. James Dewey and Jean (Mitchell) W.; m. Elizabeth Lewis, 1968; children: Rufus Robert, Duncan James. BS, U. Chgo., 1947, DSc (hon.), 1961; PhD in Zoology, Ind. U., 1950, DSc (hon.), 1963; LLD (hon.), U. Notre Dame, 1965; DSc (hon.), L.I. U., 1970, Adelphi U., 1972, Brandeis U., 1973, Albert Einstein Coll. Medicine, 1974, Hofstra U., 1976, Harvard U., 1978, Rockefeller U., 1980, Clarkson Coll., 1981, SUNY, 1983; MD (hon.), U. Buenos Aires, Argentina, 1986; DSc (hon.), Rutgers U., 1988, Bard Coll., 1991, U. Cambridge, 1993, Fairfield U., 1993, U. Stellenbosch, 1993, U. Oxford; MD, Charles Univ., Prague, 1998. Rsch. fellow NRC, U. Copenhagen, 1950-51; Nat. Found. Infantile Paralysis fellow Cavendish Lab., Cambridge U., 1951-52, 55-56; sr. rsch. fellow biology Calif. Inst. Tech., 1953-55; asst. prof. biology Harvard U., 1955-58, assoc. prof., 1958-61, prof., 1961-76; dir. Cold Spring Harbor Lab., N.Y., 1968-93, pres., 1994—; assoc. dir. Nat. Ctr. for Human Genome Rsch., NIH, 1988-89, dir. Nat. Ctr. for Human Genome Rsch.,, 1989-92; Newton-Abraham vis. prof. Oxford U., 1994. Author: Molceular Biology of the Gene, 1965, 4th edit., 1986, The Double Helix, 1968, (with John Tooze) The DNA Story, 1981, (with others) The Molecular Biology of the Cell, 1983, 2d edit., 1989, 3d edit. 1994, (with John Tooze and David Kurtz) Recombinant DNA, A Short Course, 1983, 2d edit., 1992. Named Hopn. fellow Clare Coll., Cambridge U.; recipient (with F.H.C. Crick) John Collins Warren prize Mass. Gen. Hosp., 1959, Eli Lilly award in biochemistry Am. Chem. Soc., 1959, Albert Lasker prize Am. Pub. Health Assn., 1960, (with F.H.C. Crick) Rsch. Corp. prize, 1962, (with F.H.C. Crick and M.H.F. Wilkins) Nobel prize in medicine, 1962, Presdl. Medal of Freedom, 1977, Kaul Found. award for excellence, 1993, Nat. Biotech. Venture award, 1993, Copley Medal, 1993, Charles A. Dana award, 1994, Lomonosov medal Russian Acad. Sci., 1995, Nat. medal of Sci., 1997. Mem. NAS (Carty medal 1971), Am. Philos. Soc., Am. Assn. Cancer Rsch., Am. Acad. Arts and Scis., Am. Soc. Biol. Chemistry, Royal Soc. (London), Acad. Scis. Russia, Danish Acad. Arts and Scis; Mendel Medal, Brno, 1998. Achievements include co-discovery of Double-Helix DNA. Office: Cold Spring Harbor Lab PO Box 100 Cold Spring Harbor NY 11724-0100

WATSON, JERRY CARROLL, advertising executive; b. Greenville, Ala., Aug. 22, 1943; s. William J. and Georgia Katherine (Mixon) W.; m. Judith Zeigler Brooks, Sept. 16, 1988; 2 child, Theodore William, Hunter Brooks. BS, U. Ala., Tuscaloosa, 1967; MS, U. Va., 1995. Staff writer Phillips, Eindhoven, The Netherlands, 1967-68; mgr. mktg. Fuller & Dees Mktg., Montgomery, Ala., 1968-70; v.p. Univ. Programs, Washington, 1970-73; pres. Coll. & Univ. Press, Washington, 1973-80; ptnr. Direct Response Consulting Svcs., McLean, Va., 1981-96; bd. dirs. Foxhall Corp., The Art Co. Founding mem. Am. Inst. Cancer Rsch. Mem. Direct Mktg. Assn., Non-Profit Mailer Fedn., Promotional Mktg. Assn., Nature Conservancy, Sierra Club, Falls Church (Va.) C. of C. (bd. dirs.). Avocation: gardening, astronomy. Home: Apt 402 850 Dolley Madison Blvd Mc Lean VA 22101-1821 Office: Direct Response Cons Svcs 6849 Old Dominion Dr Ste 300 Mc Lean VA 22101-3791

WATSON, JOANN FORD, theology educator; b. Ashland, Ohio, Apr. 11, 1956; d. Laurence Wesley and Edna Lucille (Garber) F.; m Duane Frederick Watson, June 2, 1984; 1 child, Christina Lucille. BA, DePauw U., 1978; MDiv, Princeton Theol. Sem., 1981; PhD, Northwestern U., 1984. Ordained to ministry, Presbyn. Ch. Asst. prof. hist. theology Ashland Theol. Sem., 1984-86, assoc. prof. theology, chair dept. ch. history and theology, 1989-95, H.R. Gill Prof. of theology, 1996—; chaplain Grady Meml. Hosp., Atlanta, 1986-87; co-pastor Tri-Ch. Parish United Meth. Chs. Northwestern, N.Y., 1987-89; pastor Camroden Presbyn. Ch., Rome, N.Y., 1987-89; clergy commr. del. Gen. Assembly of Presbyn. Ch., 1995. Author: Manna for Sisters in Christ, 1989, Mutuality in Christ, 1991, Meditations on Suffering, 1993, Study of Karl Barth's Doctrine of Man and Woman, 1995, Sister to Sister, 1998. Missionary vol. Mother Teresa's Missionaries of Charity, Calcutta, 1988; mem. Hospice Ashland County chpt., 1989-93; assoc. mem. Women's Symphony League, Ashland Symphony Orch., 1989-94. Doctoral fellowship Northwestern U., 1982-84. Mem. Internat. Assn. of Women Mins. (exec. bd., trustee 1990-95), Presbyn. Women in Leadership, Nat. Assn. of Presbyn. Clergywomen, Soc. of Biblical Lit., Am. Acad. of Religion, Alpha Lambda Delta, Phi Beta Kappa. Republican. Avocations: travel, music, water sports. Office: Ashland Theolog Sem 910 Center St Ashland OH 44805-4007

WATSON, JOHN RICHARD, English educator; b. Ipswich, Suffolk, Eng., June 15, 1934; s. Reginald Joseph Watson and Alice Mabel Tennant; m. Pauline Elizabeth Roberts, July 21, 1962; children: David James, Elizabeth Emma, Rachel Clare. BA, Oxford (Eng.) U., 1958, MA, 1961; PhD, U. Glasgow, Scotland, 1966. Lectr. U. Glasgow, 1962-66; lectr., then sr. lectr. U. Leicester, Eng., 1966-78; prof. English U. Durham, Eng., 1978-99, pub. orator, 1989-99. Author: The Poetry of Gerard Manley Hopkins, 1985, English Poetry of the Romantic Period, 1985, 2d edit., 1992, The English Hymn, 1997; editor: Everyman's Book of Victorian Verse, 1982. 2d lt. Royal Arty., 1953-55. Mem. Modern Humanities Rsch. Assn. (chmn. 1990-99), Internat. Assn. Univ. Profs. English (pres. 1995-98), Charles Wesley Soc. (v.p. 1994-98). Avocations: playing cello, bookbinding, cycling, walking. Home: Stoneyhurst, 27 Albert St, Durham DH1 4RL, England

WATSON, MARK BROWNLEE, psychology educator, researcher; b. Port Elizabeth, Ea. Cape, South Africa, Oct. 17, 1949; s. John Brownlee and Jean Campbell (Kay) W.; m. Lynnley Christine Anne Moys, July 28, 1979; children: Leanne, Neil. BA, U. Port Elizabeth, 1970, BA with honors, 1971, MA cum laude, 1973, PhD, 1985; nat. higher edn. diploma, Rhodes U., South Africa, 1974. Tchr., counselor Victoria Park H.S., Port Elizabeth, 1975-80; lectr. U. Port Elizabeth, 1980-85, sr. lectr., 1985-93, assoc. prof., 1993-97, prof., 1997—; mem. nat. exec. Ednl. Psychology, South Africa, 1996, 98; bd. advisors Career Success Program, South Africa, 1996. Author, editor: Career Psychology in the South African Context, 1999; author: (with others) Contextual Transformation and the Development of Black South African Youth, 2000; contbr. articles to profl. jours. Rsch. grant Human Scis. Rsch. Coun., 1989, 90, Overseas grantee Ctr. for Scientic Devel., 1991, 93, 95, 97, Rsch. and Overseas grant U. Port Elizabeth, 1989-99. Mem. Psychol. Soc. of South Africa (nat. exec. divsns. 1996-98), Profl. Bd. of Psychology. Presbyterian. Avocations: reading, gardening, collecting China. Office: U Port Elizabeth Dept Psych, PO Box 1600, Port Elizabeth 6000, Republic of South Africa

WATSON, MAVIS PAULINE, retired nurse; b. Bradford, Yorkshire, Eng., Aug. 8, 1939; d. Frank and Phyliss (Bradley) Robinson; m. Albert Edward Watson, July 9, 1964 (div. Aug. 1989); children: Jonathan David, Mark Edward. RN. Staff nurse Bradford Royal Infirmary, 1960-61; dist. nurse Bradford Cmty., 1962-67, dist. nurse, tchr., 1975-78; night sister Sirtitus Salts Hosp., Bradford, 1968-73, jr. sister, 1974, sr. sister, dep. matron, 1974-75; nursing officer pvt. patient oncology stomacare Royal Infirmary, Bradford, 1978-83, sr. clin. nurse, mgr. stomacare, 1984—. Decorated Order of Brit. Empire, 1999. Mem. Word Coun. Enterostomal Therapists (internat. del. 1985-88, v.p. 1988-92, pres. 1992-96), Japanese Nursing Assn. (hon.). Avocations: traveling, reading, swimming, knitting, walking.

WATSON, NEVILLE ROBERT, electrical engineering educator; b. Dunedin, Otago, N.Z., July 3, 1961; s. Donald Keen and Anne Helen (Mitchell) W.; m. Soesianawati Watson, Dec. 17, 1988; children: Jeremy, Stephen. BE with honors, U. Canterbury, Christchurch, N.Z., 1984, PhD, 1988. Temp. lectr. U. Canterbury, 1987-88, lectr., 1988-95, sr. lectr. elec. engring., 1996—. Co-author: Power System Harmonic Analysis, 1997, Power System Quality Assessment, 2000; contbr. articles to profl. jours., chpts. to books. Mem. IEEE (sr.), IPENZ. Office: Univ of Canterbury, Pvt Bag 4800, Christchurch New Zealand

WATSON, OLIVER LEE, III, aerospace engineering manager; b. Lubbock, Tex., Sept. 18, 1938; m. Judith Valeria Horvath, June 13, 1964; 1 child, Clarke Stanford. BSEE, U. Tex., 1961; MSEE, Stanford U., 1963; MBA, Calif. State U., Fullerton, 1972; cert., U. So. Calif., 1980. Cert. comm. & networks U. Calif., Irvine, 1999. Mgr. ballistic analysis Rockwell Internat. Autonetics Div., Anaheim, Calif., 1973-78, mgr. minuteman systems, 1978-83, mgr. preliminary engring., 1983-84; mgr. analysis group autonetics divsn. Rockwell Internat., Anaheim, Calif., 1984-85, mgr. aircraft sys. autonetics dept., 1985-93, dep. dir. integrated product devel. N.Am. aircraft aircraft modification divsn., 1993-94, dep. dir. engring. N.Am. aircraft modification divsn., 1994-96; dep. dir. engring. comm. and combat sys. divsn. Boeing N.Am., Anaheim, 1996-98; skills, process and metrics mgr. Comm. and Battle Mgmt., Anaheim, 1998-99; process, metrics and tools dir. Anaheim Site Engring., Space and Comm. Group, Anaheim, Calif., 1999—; lectr. engring. Calif. State U., Fullerton, 1981-90, mem. indsl. adv. bd., 1994—, vice chmn., 1995-97; spkr. welcome address Engring. & Computer Sci. Commencement, 1997, mem. ABET adv. com., 2000. Co-author Digital Computing Using Fortran IV, 1982; Fortran 77, A Complete Primer, 1986. Bd. dirs. Olive Little League, Orange, 1980; vol. Stanford U. Engring. Fund, Orange County, Calif., 1983, regional chmn. 1984-86, So. Calif. chmn. 1986-91; mem. Stanford Assocs., 1988—. Recipient Stanford Assocs. Centennial Medallion award, 1991; fellow N.Am. Aviation Sci.-Engring., L.A., 1962, 63, Inst. Advancement Engring., L.A., 1976. Mem. IEEE (sr., sec. v.p. 1974-75, sect. chmn. 1975-76), Jaycees (v.p. Orange chpt. 1973-74), Rockwell-Calif. State Univ. Alumni Club (v.p. 1993, pres. 1993-94), Lido Sailing Club.

Republican. Avocations: sailing, swimming, humor writing, scriptwriting, reading. Office: Boeing NAm 031-DA62 3370 E Miraloma Ave Anaheim CA 92806-1911

WATSON, REBECCA ELAINE, human resources software consultant; b. Dallas, Nov. 11, 1960; d. John Cephas and Mary Magdeline (Rhea) Bishop; m. Billy Don Wilkinson, July 31, 1982 (div.); children: Eric Tyler, Kristen Rhea; m. David John Watson, June 12, 1999. BEd, U. Dallas, 1982, MBA, 1995. Adminstrv. asst. IBM, Irving, Tex., 1982-85; equal opportunity coord. IBM, Irving, 1985-90; human resources data analyst IBM, Roanoke, Tex., 1990-94; sr. human resources/payroll application specialist Westinghouse Security Sys., Irving, 1994-97, team leader fin. and adminstrv. sys., 1996-97; sr. cons. Cambridge Tech. Ptnrs., 1997-98; sr. assoc. dir. Comp-U-Temp, USA, Tex., 1998-2000; v.p. WW Cons., 2000—; v.p. WW Cons., 2000—. Mem. NAFE, NOW, Greenpeace, Sigma Iota Epsilon. Democrat. Episcopalian. Avocations: needlework, rollerblading, reading, golfing, bowling.

WATSON, ROBERT FRANCIS, lawyer; b. Houston, Jan. 9, 1936; s. Louis Leon and Lora Elizabeth (Hodges) W.; m. Marietta Kiser, Nov. 24, 1961; children: Julia, Melissa, Rebecca. BA, Vanderbilt U., 1957; JD, U. Denver, 1959. Bar: Colo. 1959, U.S. Dist. Ct. (no. dist.) Tex. 1967, U.S. Supreme Ct. 1968, Tex. 1973, U.S. Ct. Appeals (5th cir.) 1973, U.S. Dist. Ct. (so. dist.) Tex. 1980, U.S. Ct. Appeals (11th cir.) 1981. Law clk. U.S. Dist. Ct. Colo., 1960-61; trial atty. SEC, Denver, 1961-67; asst. regional adminstr. SEC, Ft. Worth, 1967-72, regional adminstr., 1972-75; ptnr. Law, Snakard & Gambill, P.C., Ft. Worth, 1975-98, of counsel, 1998—; gen. counsel USPA&IRA, Ft. Worth, 1998—; counsel City of Ft. Worth Police Investigation Commn., 1975; spl. counsel Office Atty. Gen. State Ariz., 1977-78. Contbr. articles to profl. jours. Mem. Ft. Worth Crime Commn., 1987-93; former pres. bd. trustees Trinity Valley Sch., Ft. Worth; adv. dir., former pres. Lena Pope Home for Dependent and Neglected Children, Ft. Worth. Honoree 27th Ann. Rocky Mountain State-Fed.-Provincial Securities Conf. Mem. ABA, FBA, State Bar Tex., Colo. Bar Assn. (life fellow), Tex. Bar Found., Tex. Bus. Law Found. (bd. dirs. 1988-93), Tarrant County Bar Assn., Tarrant County Bar Found., U. Denver Law Sch. Alumni Coun., Coll. of State Bar Tex., Ft. Worth Club, Shady Oaks Country Club (Ft. Worth), Phi Delta Phi. Republican. Presbyterian. Office: USPA&IRA 4100 S Hulen St Fort Worth TX 76109-4953 also: Law Snakard & Gambill PC 500 Throckmorton St Ste 3200 Fort Worth TX 76102-3819

WATSON, S. MICHELE, home health nurse; b. Selma, Ala., Apr. 21, 1965; d. Kenneth and Linda (Bishop) Wilds; m. H. Alan Watson, May 30, 1987. AAS, Cleveland State Community Coll, Tenn., 1987, AS, 1985. RN, Tenn. Emergency room staff nurse Cleveland Community Hosp.; staff nurse ICU Meml. Hosp., Chattanooga; team leader Bradley Meml. Home Health, Cleveland. Home: 146 Hicks Rd NE Cleveland TN 37312-5853

WATSON, SEOSAMH, linguist, educator; b. Belfast, No. Ireland, Apr. 25, 1943; s. Joseph and Elizabeth (Allen) W.; m. Vivien Hick, Jan. 22, 1966; children: Rhonwen, Iarfhlaith, Somhairle, Darach, Rhiannon, Meirwen. MA, Cambridge U., Eng., 1965; MLitt, Edinburgh U., Scotland, 1968; PhD, Nat. U. Ireland, Dublin, 1978. Rsch. scholar Dublin Inst. Advanced Studies, 1965-67; adminstrv. officer revenue commrs. Irish Civil Svc., Dublin, 1968-70; mem. faculty U. Coll., Dublin, 1970—, prof., Found. Chair modern Irish lang. and literature, 1998—, dean faculty Celtic studies, 1996—; founder, dir. Oideas Gael, Donegal, Ireland, 1984—; mem. Irish nat. com. European Bur. Lesser Used Langs., Dublin, 1996-99; disting. vis. prof. D'Arcy-McGee Chair Irish Studies St. Mary's U., Halifax, N.S., Can., 1991; Canadian Commonwealth univs. rsch. fellow Ottawa (Ont.) U., 1983. Editor: Mac Na Míchomhairle, 1979; mem. editl. bd. : Atlas Linguarum Europae, 1990—, joint editor, 1998—; mem. editl. com. Dictionary Modern Irish, 1996—. Chmn. Bahá'í Nat. Assembly, Dublin, 1976-96. Scholar King's Coll., Cambridge, Eng., 1962-64, rsch. scholar UNESCO Nat. Com., Dublin, 1983. Mem. Internat. Soc. Dialectology and Linguistics (mem. internat. nominating com. 1993—), Eighteenth Century Ireland Soc. (mem. exec. com. 1988-91), Folklore Ireland Soc. (mem. exec. com. 1993—). Mem. Bahá'í. Avocation: walking. Home: 2 Harlech Downs, Goatstown, Dublin 14 Ireland Office: Dept Modern Irish/Univ Coll, JH Newman Bldg, Belfield Dublin 4, Ireland

WATSON, THOMAS STURGES, professional golfer; b. Kansas City, Mo., Sept. 4, 1949; s. Raymond Etheridge and Sarah Elizabeth (Ridge) W.; m. Linda Tova Rubin, July 8, 1973 (div.); children: Margaret Elizabeth, Michael Barrett. BS, Stanford U., 1971. Profl. golfer, 1971—. Winner Western Open, 1974, 1977, 1984; winner Byron Nelson Tournament, 1975, 78, 79, 80; winner Brit. Open, 1975, 77, 80, 82, 83; winner, U.S. Open, 1982; winner World Series, 1975, 80; winner Andy Williams San Diego Open, 1977, 80; winner El Prat, 1977; winner Masters, 1977, 81; winner Bing Crosby Nat. Pro-Am Golf Tournament, 1977, 78; winner Tucson Open, 1978, 84; winner Colgate Hall of Fame Classic, 1978, 79; winner Anheuser Busch Golf Classic, 1978; winner Meml. Tournament, 1979; winner Heritage Classic, 1979, 83; winner Tournament of Champions, 1979, 80, 84; Los Angeles Open, 1980, 82; Greater New Orleans Open, 1980, 81; Dunlop Phoenix, 1980, Atlantic Classic, 1981; Nabisco Championship, 1987, Hong Kong Open, 1992; Recipient Vardon Trophy, 1977, 78, 79, Byron Nelson award, 1977-78, 79-80; named to Ryder Cup Team, 1977, 81, 83, 89 (elected capt. 1992—); named Player of Year Profl. Golf Assn., 1977, 78, 79, 80, 82, 84; elected to PGA World Golf Hall of Fame, 1988, Kans. Golf Hall of Fame, 1991, William H. Richardson award 1990. Mem. U.S. Golf Assn., Profl. Golfers Assn., Golf Course Supts. Assn. of Am. (Old Tom Morris award 1992), Butler Nat. Golf Club, Shadow Glen Club, Preston Trails Golf Club, Oakwood Country Club, Par Club, Blue Hills Country Club, Kansas City Country Club, Royal and Ancient Golf Club St. Andrews. Achievements include being the leading money winner PGA, 1977-80, 84. Address: PGA PO Box 109601 100 Ave of Champions Palm Beach Gardens FL 33418-3665*

WATT, HELEN PATRICIA, bioethicist, researcher; b. Saskatoon, Sask., Can., July 17, 1962; d. Edward David and Janet Patricia (Hubble) W. BA with honors, U. Western Australia, 1983; PhD, Edinburgh (Scotland) U., 1993. Enquiries officer Commonwealth Dept. Edn., Perth, Australia, 1984-87; rsch. fellow Linacre Ctr. for Healthcare Ethics, London, 1992—; sr. rsch. assoc. Peterhouse, Cambridge, Eng., 1993-96. Author: Life and Death in Healthcare Ethics, 2000; Contbr. articles to profl. jours. Roman Catholic. Avocations: reading, walking, cinema.

WATT, KENNETH EDMUND FERGUSON, zoology educator; b. Toronto, July 13, 1929; s. William Black Ferguson Watt and Irene Eleanor (Hubbard) Dodd; m. Genevieve Bernice Bendig, Oct. 28, 1955; children: Tanis Jocelyn, Tara Alexis. BA with honor, U. Toronto, 1951; PhD in Zoology, U. Chgo., 1954; LLD, Simon Fraser U., 1970. Biometrician Rsch. div. Dept. Lands and Forests, Ont., Canada, 1954-57; sr. biometrician Can. Dept. Agr., Ottawa, Ont., 1957-60; head, statis. rsch. and svcs. Canadian Dept. Forestry, Ottawa, 1960-63; from assoc. prof. to prof. Dept. Zoology, U. Calif., Davis, 1963-93. Author: Ecology and Resource Management, 1968, Principles of Environmental Sciences, 1973, Understanding the Environment, 1982, Taming the Future, 1991; editor-in-chief: Human Ecology, The Encyclopedia Legacy of H.G. Wells, 2000. Recipient Gold medal Entomol. Soc., 1969. Achievements include development of new approach to forecasting future based on exhaustive statistic testing of non-linear math. equations to long runs of historical data; discovery that change through time in real world systems violates Markov principles. Home: 2916 Quail St Davis CA 95616-5711 Office: U Calif Dept Evolution & Ecology Davis CA 95616

WATTEAU, JOHN FRANCOIS, academic administrator; b. Paris, May 1, 1930; s. Charles Frederic and Suzanne Marie (Barbot-Ducau) W.; m. Aurore deFeuilhade de Chauvin, June 20, 1968 (div. Mar. 1974); children: Laetitia, Quentin; m. Marie Christine Amiot, June 18, 1977; 1 child, Jean-Felix. High Finance diploma, Statis. Inst., 1974; PhD cum laude, Sorbonne U., 1967. Dept. head Aerospatiale, Paris, 1960-69; sales mgr. EDP-Rolls Royce, Brussels, 1969-71; dir. R&D ITT, Paris, 1971-74; chmn. bd. Technitron, Paris, 1974-77; asst. CEO Amiot Group, Paris, 1977-82; prof., lab. dir. UCLA, 1982-88; pres. Air Acad. Assn., Paris, 1988—. Patentee in field. Advisor Presdl. Platform, Paris, 1994—. Lt. col. French Air Force, 1950-65. Recipient Cross with Gold Star Mil. Valour, Algeria, 1958; named Officer of Legion of Honor, Paris, 1989. Mem. Golf de Saint Cloud, Assn. High Fin. Inst. Alumni, Cercle-de-L'Union-Interalliée, Assn. Hereditary Hons. Roman Catholic. Avocations: golf, high sea fishing. Mailing: 90 Ave Henri Martin, 75116 Paris France

WATTERICH, ANDREA, physicist, researcher; b. Budapest, Hungary, Mar. 25, 1942; d. Ödön and Ödönné (Bauer) W. BS in Physis, Eötvös Roland U., Budapest, 1966; candidate, Hungarian Acad. Scis., Budapest, 1979, DSc, 1994. Rschr. Med. Univ., Budapest, 1966-75; rschr. Rsch. Lab. for Crystal Physics, Budapest, 1976-97, scientific advisor, 1994—; scientific advisor Rsch. Inst. Solid State Physics and Optics, Budapest, 1998—. Contbr. articles to scientific jours., including Phys. Rev., Jour. Phys. Chem. Solids, Solid State Comm., and Jour. Physics Condensed Matter. Mem. Eötvös Roland Phys. Soc. Office: Rsch Inst Solid State Physics & Optics, Konkoly-Thege M ut 29-33, 1121 Budapest Hungary

WATTERS, CORA TULA, musician; b. Portsmouth, Ohio; d. James Arthur and Nelle (Barber) W.; children: Gina Marie, Michael Earnest III, Lisa Michelle Iezzi, Patrice Annette England, Lora Diane Okwesa, James Vincent Yezzi (dec.). B in Gen. Studies cum laude, Ohio U., 1979; student, Miami U., Oxford, Ohio, LaSalle U., Rio Grande Grad. Sch., 1996. Mem. USMC Band, Quantico, Va., 1952-55; tchr. Musician Performer, 1950—; tchr. Spl. Edn. MRDD Sch., West Union, Ohio, 1983-88; dir. Shawnee Hills Sch. Fine and Performing Arts, 1983-88; tchr. Spl. Edn. West Union (Ohio) Elem. Sch., 1989-91; adjunct faculty music Southern State, Hillsboro, Ohio, 1989-92; tchr. Art West Union (Ohio) Jr. H.S., 1991-92; tchr. Music Seaman (Ohio) Elem. Sch., 1992-94; adjunct faculty Native Am. Studies Antioch Coll., Yellow Springs, Ohio, 1993—; tchr. Acad. Tutor Ohio Valley Vocat. Sch., West Union, 1994-97; tchr. Ohio Valley Schs., 1999-00; bldg. rep., state union rep., union rep., Ohio Valley Sch. Edn. Assn., 1992-96; owner Shawnee Hills Pub., 1996—; singer, dancer, profl. storyteller. Co-author: Brain Tanning-Indian Style, 1980; composer: Red, White and Blues, 1989, Watters and Daughter-At Last!, 1990, (CD) Red, White and Blues, 2000; music dir., screenwriter White Buffalo Media, Inc., 2000; author: Tales of 10 Moons, 1993, Jimmie's Place, 1996, Ohio Indians-Prehistoric to Present, 1997, Progressive Revelations of God, 1997, Progressive Revelation (Children's Workbook), 1997, Woodland Indians Children's Workbook, 1997, Digging Up Your Indian Roots, 1996, Meals from Tula's Lodge, 1997, Caproni's History and Cookbook, 1998; From the Rocking Chair, 1999; contbr. to Encyclopedia of Appalachia, 1999-2000; profl. storyteller of Appalachian & American Indian tales. Chair Humane Soc., Adams County, Ohio, 1980-83; bd. mem. Adams Brown Alcohol Coun., West Union, Ohio, Adams Co. Arts Coun., 1981-83; prin. chief Shawnee Nation-Ohio Blue Creek Band; minority rep., mem. exec. com. Adams County to Ohio Valley Regional Devel. Devel. Com. Cpl. USMC, 1952-55. Named Outstanding Tchr. Spl. Edn. Consortium, 1987, 95, Ashland Oil Outstanding Tchr. Nominee, 1992, 95, One of 1000 Outstanding Women (Native Am.) in OYOHO, 1982, 83; recipient Holloway Human Rights award State Ohio Edn. Assn., 1993, Ohio State Commendation award for outstanding tchg., 1993, found. & chair 4 yrs. of OMEA- Music Comp. for those with spec. needs (Ohio), 5 Gold medals regional winner music/drama Veterans Administration Creative Arts Competition, 2000. Mem. Am. Indian Inter-Tribal Alliance (leader), Ohio Shawnees Blue Creek Band (prin. chief), Am. Cancer Soc. (prin. chief), So. Ohio Nat. Am. Substance Abuse, Native Am. Coun. of Ohio, Ohio Mental Health and Ohio Arts Coun., N.Am. Alliance Ohio, Families and Children First. Baha'i Faith. Avocations: family, religion, my tribe. Home: 696 Blacks Run Rd Lynx OH 45650-9702

WATTERS, DAVID ALLAN KILPATRICK, surgeon, educator; b. Durban, Natal, South Africa, May 8, 1952; arrived in the U.K., 1952; s. Archibald Norman and Ann Margaret (Douglas) W.; m. Anne Sinclair (div. 1995); children: Douglas, Jennifer; m. Helga Koestenbauer. BSc with honors, Edinburgh (Scotland) U., 1974, MB, BChir, 1977, ChM, 1983. European cert. of specialist tng. in gen. surgery. Sr. house officer Victoria Hosp., Kirkcaldy, Scotland, 1978-79; registrar Lothian Health Bd., Edinburgh, 1979-81; rsch. fellow Wolfson G.I. Univ., Edinburg, 1981-82; sr. registrar King Edward VIII Hosp., Durban, South Africa, 1982-83; specialist surgeon McCord Zulu Hosp., 1983-84; sr. lectr. U. Zambia, Lusaka, 1985-90; lectr. Chinese U. Hong Kong, 1991; prof. U. Papua New Guinea, Port Moresby, 1992-2000; prof. surgery, Geelong Hosp. U. Melbourne, Victoria, Australia, 2000—. Author, editor: Care of the Critically Ill in the Tropics, 1991, Gastroenterology in the Tropics, 1995, Neurosurgery in the Tropics, 2000; author: Put Christ Back into Christmas, 1982; editor: Surgery in the Tropics, 1988; contbr. numerous articles to profl. jours., chpts. to books, numerous papers. Elder Ch. of Scotland, Kirkcaldy, Scotland, 1980-82; deacon Bapt. Ch., Durban, 1983; chief Caledonian Soc., Lusaka, Zambia, 1990; med. rep. Cancer Soc., Papua New Guinea, 1993-2000. Fellow Royal Coll. Surgeons Edinburgh, Assn. Surgeons East Africa (Zambia rep. 1989-90), Royal Australasian Coll. Surgeons, Hong Kong Coll. Surgeons; mem. Assn. Surgeons Papua New Guinea (mem. coun.), Asian Surg. Soc., Gen. Surgeons of Australia. Avocations: soccer, tennis, running, music. Home: 29 Challambra Cres, Highton VIC 3216, Australia Office: Dept Surgery Geelong Hosp, PO Box 281, Victoria Geelong 3220, Australia

WATTS, CAROLYN SUE, nurse; b. Baxter, Tenn., Mar. 18, 1950; d. John D. and Bettye F. (Montgomery) McDaniel; m. Roy L. Watts, Oct. 27, 1973 (div. Sept. 1984); children: Eric, Allison. BS, Olivet Nazarene U., Kankakee, Ill., 1971; MS in Nursing, U. Tenn., 1978. RN, Tenn.; cert. wound care nurse. Head nurse Martin Place Hosp., Madison Heights, Mich., 1971-75; nursing supr. Livingston Community Hosp., Tenn., 1975-78; dir. nursing Livingston Community Hosp., 1978-81; asst. dir. nursing DePaul Hosp., New Orleans, 1981-82; staff nurse Touro Infirmary Hosp., New Orleans, 1982-83; clin. nurse specialist, case mgr. Vanderbilt U. Med. Ctr., Nashville, 1983-2000; clin. edn. specialist Hollister, Inc., 2000—; cons. dept. nursing edn. Sch. Nursing, Vanderbilt U., 1983-2000, mem. adj. faculty, 1984-2000, assoc. in surgery Sch. Medicine, 1986-2000; frequent spkr. at profl. seminars. Assoc. editor Jour. Urol. Nursing, 1985-91; contbr. articles to profl. jours. Mem. ANA, Tenn. Nurses Assn., Southeastern Surg. Nurses Assn. (counsellor 1983-91), AACN, Wound Ostomy Continence Nurses Soc., Assn. Advancement Wound Care, Sigma Theta Tau. Avocations: reading, cooking, walking. Office: Hollister Inc 2000 Hollister Dr Libertyville IL 60048-3781

WATTS, CEDRIC THOMAS, English literature educator, author; b. Cheltenham, Eng., Feb. 19, 1937; s. Thomas Henry and Mary Adelaide (Cheshire) W.; m. Judith Edna Mary Hill, Jan. 3, 1983; children: Linda, William, Sarah. BA, Cambridge U., 1961, MA, 1963, PhD, 1965. Lectr. U. Sussex, Brighton, Eng., 1965-79; reader U. Sussex, Brighton, 1979-83, prof. English lit., 1983—. Author: Conrad's Heart of Darkness, 1977, A Preface to Conrad, 1982, rev. edit., 1993, R.B. Cunninghame Graham, 1983, The Deceptive Text, 1984, A Preface to Keats, 1985, William Shakespeare, Measure for Measure, 1986, Hamlet, 1988, Joseph Conrad, a Literary Life, 1989, Literature and Money, 1990, Joseph Conrad, Nostromo, 1990, Romeo and Juliet, 1991, Thomas Hardy: Jude the Obscure, 1992, Joseph Conrad, 1994, A Preface to Greene, 1997; co-author: Cunninghame Graham: A Critical Biography, 1979; editor: Joseph Conrad's Letters to R.B. Cunninghame Graham, 1969, The English Novel, 1976, Selected Writings of Cunninghame Graham, 1981, Conrad: Typhoon and Other Tales, 1986, Conrad: The Nigger of the Narcissus, 1988, Conrad: Heart of Darkness and Other Tales, 1990, Hardy: Jude the Obscure, 1999, Conrad: Victory, 1994, Conrad: the Heart of Darkness, 1995, Shakespeare: Romeo and Juliet, 1995, Conrad: Nostromo, 1995, Conrad: An Outcast of the Islands, 1996, Conrad: The Secret Agent, 1997, Shakespeare: Romeo and Juliet, 2000, Shakespeare: Macbeth, 2000, Shakespeare: Henry V, 2000; co-editor: Conrad: Lord Jim, 1986. Served with Brit. Navy, 1956-58. Office: U Sussex Arts Bldg, BN1 9QN Brighton BN1 9QN, England

WATTS, HELENA ROSELLE, military analyst; b. East Lynne, Mo., May 29, 1921; d. Elmer Wayne and Nellie Irene (Barrington) Long; m. Henry Millard Watts, June 14, 1940; children: Helena Roselle Watts Scott, Patricia Marie Watts Foble. BA, Johns Hopkins U., 1952, postgrad., 1952-53. Assoc. engr. Westinghouse Corp., Balt., 1965-67; sr. analyst Merck, Sharp & Dohme, Westpoint, Pa., 1967-69; sr. engr. Bendix Radio divsn. Bendix Corp., Balt., 1970-72; sr. scientist Sci. Applications Internat. Corp., McLean, Va., 1975-84; mem. tech. staff The MITRE Corp., McLean, 1985-94; ret., 1994; adj. prof. Def. Intelligence Coll., Washington, 1984-85. Contbr. articles to profl. jours. Mem. IEEE, AAAS, AIAA, Nat. Mil. Intelligence Assn., U.S. Naval Inst., Navy League U.S., Air Force Assn., Assn. Former Intelligence Officers, Assn. Old Crows, Mensa, N.Y. Acad. Sci. Republican. Roman Catholic. Avocations: photography, reading. Home: 4302 Roberts Ave Annandale VA 22003-3508

WATTS, MARVIN LEE, minerals company executive, chemist, educator; b. Portales, N.Mex., Apr. 6, 1932; s. William Ellis and Jewel Reata (Holder) W.; m. Mary Myrtle Kiber, July 25, 1952; children: Marvin Lee, Mark Dwight, Wesley Lyle. BS in Chemistry and Math., Ea. N.Mex. U., 1959, MS in Chemistry, 1960; postgrad., U. Okla., 1966, U. Kans., 1967. Analytical chemistr Dow Chem. Co., Midland, Mich., 1960-62; instr. chemistry N.Mex. Mil. Inst., Roswell, 1962-65, asst. prof., 1965-67; chief chemist AMAX Chem. Corp., Carlsbad, N.Mex., 1967-78, gen. surface supt., 1978-84; pres. N.Mex. Salt and Minerals Corp., 1984—; chem. cons. Western Woils Lab., Roswell, 1962-67; instr. chemistry N.Mex. State U., Carlsbad, 1967—; owner, operator cattle ranch, Carlsbad and Loving, N.Mex., 1969—; bd. dirs. Mountain States Mut. Casualty Co., 1981; gen. mgr. Eddy Potash, Inc., 1987—, v.p., gen. mgr., 1987-95; cons. Potash Industry, 1995—. Pres. Carlsbad Dept. Devel., 1996. N.Mex. BLM Resoource Adv. Coun., 1994; chmn. Eddy County Land USF Commn., Eddy County Labor Rels. Bd.; dir. Soil Conservation Svc.; mem. Roswell dist. adv. bd. Bur. Land Mgmt.; bd. dirs. Southeastern N.Mex. Regional Sci. Fair, 1996; mem. adv. bd. Roswell dist. Bur. Land Mgmt.; mem. Eddy County Fair Bd., 1976—, chmn., 1978, 82; mem. pub. sch. reform com.; chmn. higher edn. reform com.; mem. sponsor of N.Mex. pub. Sch. Reform Act; bd. dirs. Carlsbad Found., 1979-82; adv. bd. N.Mex. State U. at Carlsbad, 1976-80; vice chmn. bd. Guadalupe Med. Ctr.; bd. dirs. N.Mex. Legis, 1984-89; mem. Rep. State Exec. com., 1972—; Rep. chmn. Eddy County (N.MEx.), 1970-74, 78-82, dirs. Conquistador coun. Boy Scouts Am., Regional Environ. Ednl. Rsch. and Improvement Orgn. With Mil. Police Corps, AUS, 1953-55, Germany. Recipient Albert K. Mitchell award as outstanding Rep. in N.Mex., 1976; hon. state farmer N.Mex. Future Farmers Am.; hon. mem. 4-H. Fellow N.Mex. Acad. Sci.; mem. Am. Chem. Soc. (chmn. subsect.), Western States Pub. Lands Coalition, Carlsbad C. of C. (dir. 1979-83), N.Mex. Mining Assn. (dir.), AIME (chmn. Carlsbad potash sect. 1975), Carlsbad Mental Health Assn. (pres. 1994—), N.Mex. Inst. Mining and Tech. (adv. bd. mining dept.), Am. Angus Assn., Am. Quarter Horse Assn., N.Mex. Cattle Growers Assn. (bd. dirs. 1989—), Carlsbad Farm and Ranch Assn., Nat. Cattlemen's Assn., Kiwanis (Disting. lt. gov.). Baptist. Home: PO Box 56 Carlsbad NM 88221-0056 Office: PO Box 101 Carlsbad NM 88221-5603

WATTS, PAUL GRAHAM, oral and maxillofacial surgeon, consultant; b. Hull, Yorkshire, Eng., Jan. 17, 1949. B Dental Surgery, U. Dundee, Scotland, 1972. House officer Dundee Dental Hosp., 1972-73; sr. house officer Doncaster Royal Infirmary, Eng., 1973-77; registrar Addenbrookes Hosp., Cambridge, Eng., 1977-79; sr. registrar Kings Coll. Hosp., London, 1979-81, John Radcliffe Hosp., Oxford, Eng., 1981-87; cons. Kings Mill Centre, Sutton-in-Ashfield, Eng., 1988—; hon. clin. tutor U. Sheffield, Eng., 1991—; examiner Part II FDS Royal Coll. Surgeons, Edinburgh, 1989—; chmn. hosp. med. com. Kings Mill Centre, Sutton-in-Ashfield, 1995-97, vice chmn. theatre users com., 1993-97, chmn. theatre users com., 1997—; mems. rep. on coun. Brit. Assn. Oral and Maxillofacial Surgeons, London, 1986-88. Contbr. articles to profl. jours. Fellow Brit. Assn. Oral and Maxillofacial Surgeons, Royal Coll. Surgeons Edinburgh (fellow in dental surgery 1978, Ethicon Found. Fund award 1984), Royal Soc. Medicine; mem. Hosp. Cons. and Specialists Assn. Avocations: rugby football, cricket, reading, fine wines. Office: Kings Mill Centre, Mansfield Rd, Sutton-in-Ashfield NG17 4JL, England

WATTS, RICHARD ARTHUR, rheumatologist, consultant; b. London, Dec. 18, 1956; s. Richard We and Joan Em Watts; m. Lesley Diana King, Apr. 23, 1983; children: Oliver, Isobel. BA, Oxford (Eng.) U., 1978, MA, MB BChir, 1982, MD, 1992. Rsch. fellow Middlesex Hosp., London, 1985-90; sr. registrar Adderbrooke Hosp., Cambridge, Eng., 1990-92, Norwich (Eng.) Hosp., 1992-94; pvt. practice Ipswich, Eng., 1994—. Contbr. papers to profl. publs. Fellow Am. Coll. Rheumatology; mem. Brit. Soc. for Rheumatology, Brit. Med. Assn., Royal Coll. Physicians. Home: Bury Hill House Woodbridge, Suffolk IP1L 1JD, England

WATTS, ROSS LESLIE, accounting educator, consultant; b. Hamilton, Australia, Nov. 10, 1942; came to U.S., 1966; s. Leslie R. and Elsie B. (Horadam) W. m. Helen Clare Firkin, Jan. 15, 1966; children: Andrew David, James Michael. B Commerce with honors (Commonwealth Govt. scholar 1960-65), U. Newcastle (Australia), 1966; MBA (Ford Found. fellow 1967-68), U. Chgo., 1968, PhD, 1971. Audit clk. Forsythe & Co., Newcastle, Australia, 1960-64, acct., 1964-66; instr. Grad. Sch. Bus., U. Chgo., 1969-70; asst. prof. Simon Sch. Mgmt., U. Rochester (N.Y.), 1971-78, assoc. prof., 1978-84, prof., 1984-86; endowed chair Rochester Telephone Corp., 1986-98; William H. Meckling prof. U. Rochester (N.Y.), 1998—; prof. commerce U. Newcastle, 1974-76; hon. prof. City U. Hong Kong, 1996—; cons. to bus. firms, 1972—; disting. lectr. Hong Kong Univ. Sci. and Tech., 1994; hon. prof. Xiamen U., China, 1999—. Contbr. articles on acctg. rsch. to profl. jours.; assoc. editor Jour. Acctg. Rsch., 1972-78, Jour. Fin. Econs., 1974-89, Australian Jour. Mgmt., 1976-81; co-editor Jour. Acctg. and Econs., 1979—; editor Jour. Acctg. Abstracts, 1995-97; dir., editor Acctg. Rsch. Network, 1997—; mem. adv. bd. Midland Corp. Fin. Jour., 1983-88, Continental Bank Jour. of Applied Corp. Fin., 1988-94, Bank Am. Jour. Applied Corp. Fin., 1994—; mem. editorial bd. Contemporary Acctg. Rsch., 1983-85; cons. editor Asia Pacific Jour. Acctg. Econs., 1998—. Recipient Notable Contbn. award AICPA, 1979, 80, award Alpha Kappa Psi Found., 1985. Mem. Am. Acctg. Assn. (Outstanding Educator award 2000), Am. Fin. Assn., Inst. Chartered Accts. in Australia. Home: 17 Burncoat Way Pittsford NY 14534-2215 Office: U Rochester Simon Sch Mgmt Wilson Blvd Rochester NY 14627-2241

WATTS, ROSS WAKEFIELD, retired school principal, mayor; b. Harrisburg, Pa., Dec. 14, 1926; s. Ralph Ray Sr. and Laura Mae (Wakefield) W.; m. Mildred E. Urich, Jan. 29, 1949; children: Gordon W., Lori L. BS, Pa. State U., 1949, MEd, 1954. Cert. vocat. agr. and gen. sci. tchr., secondary sch. prin., supt. Tchr. vocat. agr. Jersey Shore (Pa.) Area H.S., 1949-59; asst. jr. H.S. prin. Spring Ford Jr. H.S., Royersford, Pa., 1959-60; prin. Palmyra (Pa.) Area H.S., 1960-89, ret., 1989. Contbr. articles to profl. jours. Planning commn. Palmyra Borough, 1965-73, borough councilman, 1974-76, recreation commn., 1975-76, mayor, 1990—. With U.S. Army, 1945-46. Mem. Mid. States Assn. (evaluator, chmn. 1959—), Pa. Assn. Secondary Prins. (pres. 1981-82), Mayors Assn. (pres. 1995-97), VFW, Am. Legion, Brownstone Masonic Lodge, Zembo Shrine, Hershey Shrine Club (pres. 1996, Plaque 1996). Republican. Methodist. Avocations: camping, photography, hiking, golf. E-mail: Rwatts@ezonline.com. Home: 701 S Duke St Palmyra PA 17078-2720

WATTS, VICTOR BRIAN, circuit judge; b. London, Jan. 7, 1927; s. Percy William and Doris Millicent (Peat) W.; m. Patricia Eileen Steer, July 31, 1965; children: Julia Mary, Martin William. MA, U. Coll., Oxford, Eng., 1948; B in Common Law, U. Coll. Oxford, 1949. Barrister: Mid. Temple 1950, Western Cir. 1953. Recorder Crown Ct., London, 1972-80; cir. judge London, 1980-99. Author: Cases on the Law of Contract, 1955, Landlord and Tenant Act, 1954; contbr. articles to profl. jours. Officer Royal Air Force, 1950-52. Mem. Hurlingham Club, London Rowing Club. Conservative. Roman Catholic. Avocations: arts, horse-back riding, tennis, traveling. Home: 28 Abinger Rd, Bedford Park, London W4 1EL, England

WATTS, VICTOR ERNEST, university administrator, educator; b. Bristol, Eng., Apr. 18, 1938; s. Fred Challenger and Bessie May (Oaten) W.; m. Mary Margaret Curtis, Apr. 4, 1964; children: Alison, Ann, John; m. Elaine Munroe, 1998. MA, Oxford U., 1964. Lectr. Durham U., 1962-74, sr. lectr., 1974-84; sr. tutor Grey Coll., Durham, 1984-89, master, 1989—, dean of arts, 1987-89, dean of colls., 1999—; hon. dir. English Place-name, Survey, 1993—. Translator: The Consolation of Philosophy, 1989; editor: De Proprietatibus Rerum, 1975; editor: The Cambridge Dictionary of English Place Names; contbr. articles to profl. jours. Chmn. Durham County Social Dem. party, 1979-81. Fellow Soc. of Antiquaries of London, Inst. Continuing Profl. Devel.; mem. Archtl. and Archaeol. Soc. of Durham and Northumberland (past pres.), Durham County Cricket Club. Avocations: onomastics, music, theatre, art, countryside. Home: High Close, Hollingside

Ln, Durham DH1 3TN, England Office: Grey Coll, South Rd, Durham DH1 3LG, England

WATTS, VINCENT CHALLACOMBE, educational administrator; b. Bristol, Eng., Aug. 11, 1940; s. Geoffrey Hilton and Lilian Florence (Pye) W.; m. Rachel Mary Rosser, June 15, 1967 (dec. 1998); children: Ben, Hannah. MA, U. Cambridge, Eng., 1963; MSc, U. Birmingham, Eng., 1967. Trainee acct. Arthur Andersen & Co., Eng., 1963-66; mgmt. cons. Andersen Cons. U.K., 1967-76, ptnr., 1976-97; vice chancellor U. East Anglia, Eng., 1997—; chmn. East of Eng. Devel. Agy., 1998—. Fellow Inst. Chartered Accts. Eng. and Wales (mem. coun. 1987-90), Inst. Mgmt. Cons.; mem. Ops. Rsch. Soc. (mem. coun. 1980-83), Com. Vice Chancellors and Prins. Office: U East Anglia, Norwich NR4 7TJ, England

WATZ, MARTIN CHARLES, brewery consultant; b. St. Louis, Oct. 31, 1938; s. George Michael and Caroline Theresa (Doggendorf) W.; m. Deborah Perkowski; children: Pamela, Kathlene, Karen. BS in Chemistry and Microbiology, SE Mo. State U., 1961; MBA, Washington U., 1966-67. Safety engr. McDonnell-Douglas, 1962-64; sr. brewing chemist Anheuser-Busch, Inc., St. Louis, 1965-68; asst. brewmaster Anheuser-Busch, Inc., Columbus, Ohio, 1968-79; sr. asst. brewmaster Anheuser-Busch, Inc., St. Louis, 1979-82; resident brewmaster Anheuser-Busch, Inc., Baldwinsville, N.Y., 1982-84, Williamsburg, Va., 1984-87; v.p. bakers yeast divsn. Anheuser-Busch Indsl. Products Corp., St. Louis, 1987-88, dir. brewing ops., 1988-89; sr. brewmaster Anheuser-Busch, Ft. Collins, Colo., 1989-99; brewing cons., 1999—. Patentee in field. With USAF, 1962-65. Mem. Master Brewers Assn. Am. (pres., nat. bd. govs.), Am. Soc. Brewing Chemists, Internat. Food Tech. Assocs., Aircraft Owners and Pilots Assn., U.S. Pilots Assn. Avocation: flying. Home and Office: 1417 N County Rd # 3 Fort Collins CO 80524-9312

WAUGH, MICHAEL BRIAN, filmmaker, film editor; b. Johannesburg, Transvaal, South Africa, Oct. 26, 1967; s. William Hardesty and Gaynor (Lawrence) W. Nat. diploma, Pretoria Technikon Film Sch., 1992. Set runner Brigadiers, Johannesburg, South Africa, 1991; site foreman Midwest Engring., Johannesburg, 1992; site mgr. Midwest Engring., Bulawayo, Zimbabwe, 1992-93; asst. editor Eklips Leisureco, Johannesburg, 1993-94, EyeLevel, Johannesburg, 1994-95; first asst. editor Duncan McNeilie Prodns., Johannesburg, 1995, Xencat/Chanel Four (U.K.), London and Johannesburg, 1996; editor Catalyst Films, Johannesburg, 1997, Xencat Pictures, Channel Four, Johannesburg, 1997; editor, cameraman The African Bush Telegraph Corp., Johannesburg, 1997—; prodr., tech. dir., mem. The Hurricane Factory, Johannesburg, 1997-98; editor Endemol Entertainment, Johannesburg, 1998-99, Soul City, Johannesburg, 1999; freelance editor The Refinery, Johannesburg, 1999—. With M.C. South African Def. Force, 1987-88. Recipient South African Guild of Editors award for best editing in a TV drama, 1999. Avocations: pottery, gym, movies, reading, socializing.

WAWRA, EDGAR, biochemistry educator; b. Vienna, Austria, Nov. 15, 1947; s. Edgar and Herta Wawra; m. Gabriele Kadanka, June 30, 1990; 1 child, Arian Maximilian. M in Natural Scis., U. Vienna, 1976, D in Natural Scis., 1981. Technician Osterreichische Studiengesellschaft für Atom-Energie, Seibersdorf, Austria, 1965-76, sci. employee, 1976-78; univ. asst. Inst. Molecular Biology, Vienna, 1978-89, assoc. prof. biochemistry, 1989—. Author: Biochemische Übungen für Mediziner, 1993, Chemische Übungen für Mediziner, 1993. Mem. Austrian Biochem. Soc. (sec. 1989-91), Austrian Soc. for Genetics and Gen-Tenique (treas. 1992-95). Avocations: sailing, skiing, home renovation, writing, cooking. Office: Inst for Molecular Biology Vienna Bioctr, Dr Bohrgasse 9, A-1030 Vienna Austria

WAWSZCZAK, WLODZIMIERZ STANISLAW, mechanical engineering educator; b. Lodz, Poland, May 8, 1940; children: Agata, Rafal. BS in Engring., Tech. U. of Lodz, 1962, MS in Engring., 1963, PhD in Engring., 1972, DSc in Tech. of Machine Bldg., 1995. Designer and sr. designer Tech. U. of Lodz, 1963-68, lectr. and sr. lectr., 1968-72, head of heat and mass transfer group, 1995-00; adj. lectr., Lodz, 1972-00; vis. Inst. of Compressors, Tech. U. of Leningrad, 1973-74, Inst. of Heat and Mass Transfer, Byelo Russian Acad. of Scis., Minsk, 1981; vis. prof. U. Calgary, Alberta, 1981-82, 83-84. Author: General and Uniform Investigation Method of One-Dimensional Models of Flow, 1990, Gas Flows in Channels, 1993; contbr. articles to profl. jours. and publs.; patentee in field. Mem. Ind. Trade Union Solidarity, 1980, adviser of farmers at Zelow Community in Solidarity, 1992; candidate to mem. parliament, 1993. Grantee R&D of High Rotating Heat Exchangers from the State Com. for Scientific Rsch. in Poland. Mem. Polish Mech. Engrs. Assn., Polish Theory and Appyied Mech. Assn., Polish Cons. Soc., Polish Acad. Scis. (thermodynamics sect. of thermodynamics and combustion com. com. 1999). Roman Catholic. Avocations: swimming, sailing, history of philosophy, Holy Scripture. Office: Tech Univ of Lodz, Stefanowski 1/15, 90-924 Lodz Poland

WAX, ARNOLD, physician; b. Bklyn., Mar. 11, 1949; s. Emanuel and Eleanor (Greenfield) W.; m. Francine Wax; children: Erin, Rachael, Adam, Benjamin. BS in Pharm. Scis., Columbia U., 1971; MD, SUNY, Buffalo, 1976. Diplomate Nat. Bd. Med. Examiners, Am. Bd. Internal Medicine, Am. Bd. Quality Assurance and Utilization Rev. Physicians, Am. Acad. Pain Mgmt.; lic. physician, Fla., Calif., N.D., Minn., N.Y., Nev., Ariz. Intern, resident Millard Fillmore Hosp., Buffalo, 1976-79; clin. asst. instr. SUNY, 1977-79; instr. medicine U. Rochester, N.Y., 1979-81; dir. internal medicine U. N.D., Grand Forks, 1982-83, clin. asst. prof., 1982-85; pvt. practice Las Vegas, Nev., 1987—; mem. staff Sunrise Hosp., Las Vegas, Desert Springs Hosp., Las Vegas, Nathan Adelson Hospice, Las Vegas. Contbr. articles to profl. jours. Grantee So. Nev. Cancer Rsch. Found., Ea. Coop. Oncology Group, Gynecol. Oncology Group, North Ctrl. Cancer Treatment Group, S.W. Oncology Group. Fellow Am. Coll. Physicians; mem. AMA, Am. Cancer Soc. (fellow 1979), Am. Soc. Clin. Oncology, Am. Coll. Physicians (gov. State of Nev.), Nev. Oncology So. (v.p.), Nev. Med. Soc., Clark County Med. Soc. (trustee, peer rev. com., treas.), Nev. Peer Rev. Orgn., U. Nev. Las Vegas Found., Nev. Dance Theater, Nev. Opera Theater, Las Vegas Symphony, Nev. Inst. Contemporary Art, Lied Mus., Allied Arts Coun., James Platt White Soc., U. Buffalo Found., Rho Chi (Bronze medal 1971). Home: 2224 Chatsworth Ct Henderson NV 89014-5309 Office: 3730 S Eastern Ave Ste 202 Las Vegas NV 89109-3321

WAX, NAOMI, science educator and researcher; b. Haifa, Israel, Feb. 12, 1939; d. Asher and Rachel (Shwartz) Berlinger; m. Ben-Zion Wax, 1958; children: Hagay, Omer, Ayelet. BSc in Biology, Hebrew U., Jerusalem, Israel, 1964, MSc in Biology, 1966; MA in Edn., Tel-Aviv U., 1978, PhD in Sci. Edn., 1994. Cert. h.s. tchr. Tchr. biology Zeitlin H.S., Tel Aviv, 1964-75; lectr. Levinsky Coll., Tel Aviv, 1981-84; sci. curriculum developer and rschr. Tel Aviv U., 1975-98, lectr., 1990—; head sci. tchg. project for elem. sch. Tel-Hay (Israel) Coll., 1995—; cons. Ctr. for In-Svc. Tchr. Tng., Tel Aviv U., 1984-98, Israel Ednl. TV, Tel Aviv, 1988-97; acad. coord. project in sci. edn. between Tel-Aviv U. and Al-Quos U., 2000—. Author learning units in books; editor newsletter Sci. Tchg. in Elem. Sch., 1979-83; contbr. articles to Human Devel., Cognitive Devel., Israel Exploration Jour., others. Mem. Sci. and Tech. Ednl. Ctr. Israel, Israeli Soc. Botany, European Assn. for Rsch. on Learning and Instrn. Avocations: poetry, music, swimming, travel. Home: 5 Habanim St, 45930 Ramot Hashavim Israel Office: Tel Aviv U Sch Edn, Ramat Aviv, 69978 Tel Aviv Israel

WAXENBERGER, GABRIELE MARIA, historical linguist; b. Muehldorf, Bavaria, Fed. Republic Germany, June 12, 1956; d. Ludwig Nikolaus and Suse Hermine (Tamler) W. MA, U. Munich, 1984, PhD, 1991. Interim tchr. English and German König-Karlmann-Gymnasium, Altoetting, Bavaria, Fed. Republic Germany, 1980; tchr. English Volkshochschule Waldkraiburg and Muehldorf, Waldkraiburg, Muehldorf, Bavaria, 1985—; asst. to prof. hist. linguistics Cath. U. Eichstätt, Bavaria, 1986-87; lang. asst. German Westfield Coll., U. London, 1987-88; coord. for program, head, lang. dept. English Volkshochschule Waldraiburg, 1989—; asst. to prof. methodology Cath. Univ. of Eichstätt, Germany, 1991-94; developer new tchg. concept for ESL, Success Line-Successful in English and Bus., 1996—. Mem. MLA, Am. Dialect Soc. Avocations: computer, langs., gardening, traveling, skiing, Old English and Old Frisian Runes. Home: 62 Stadtplatz, 826 Muehldorf Bavaria, 8260 Muehldorf Bavaria, Germany

WAYLAND-SMITH, ROBERT DEAN, retired banker; b. Oneida, N.Y., July 2, 1943; s. Robert and Prudence Cragin (Skinner) W.-S.; m. Kathleen Anne Schultz, Aug. 24, 1968 (dec. 1999); children: Kristin, Debra. BA in Econs., U. Rochester, 1965. Mgr. equipment svc. Strong Meml. Hosp., Rochester, N.Y., 1965-67; mgmt. trainee Chase Lincoln First Bank, N.A., Rochester, 1967-68, mgr. mcpl. securities, 1968-81, mgr. portfolio mgmt. depart., 1981-84, mgr. fin. and investment svc. dept., 1984-87, mgr. trust and fin. svc. dept., 1987-88; pres. and CEO Rochester region Chase Manhattan Bank, N.A., 1988-93, upstate trust and investment divsn. exec., 1993-98; ret., 1998; mem. adv. bd. Roberts Wesleyan Coll., Rochester, 1989-99; mem. adv. coun. J.W. Jones Sch. Bus. SUNY, Geneseo, 1990-99. Trustee Ctr. for Govtl. Rsch., 1985—, Rochester Visitors Assn., 1990-93, Rochester Downtown Devel. Corp., 1991-93; dir. United Neighborhood Ctrs., Greater Rochester Found., 1992—; mem. fin. execs. adv. bd. Coll. Bus. Rochester Inst. Tech., 1994—; mem. adv. bd. Help Our World Found., 1990—; bd. dirs. Oneida Cmty. Mansion House, 1988—, United Way Greater Rochester Corp., 1998—, Via Health, 1999—; bd. dirs. The Genesee Hosp., 1992—, bd. govs.; coll. coun. SUNY Coll. Geneseo, 1999—. Fellow Assn. for Investment Mgmt. and Rsch.; mem. Internat. Assn. Fin. Planners, Rochester Soc. Security Analysts, Greater Rochester Met. C. of C. (dir. 1992-95), Genesee Valley Club, Oak Hill Country Club. Avocations: golf, gardening, reading. Office: Chase Manhattan Bank One Chase Sq Rochester NY 14643

WAYNE, DONALD, editor; b. N.Y.C., May 13, 1913; s. Benjamin and Rose (Frank) W.; m. Elaine Pailthorpe, Nov. 23, 1938 (dec. July 1972); children—Arthur, Christina, Victoria, Alistair; m. Helena Paula Malinowska Burke, June 29, 1974. B.A., Cornell U., 1934. Editor Victory, Photo Review (overseas br. OWI), 1942-45; asst. mng. editor Parade mag., 1956-58, mag. editor, 1958-65; mng. dir. Roto Publs., Ltd., London, Eng.; editor-pub. Friday mag.; pub. Southeast Living mag.; editor The Am.; mng. dir. Am. Weekly Newspapers, Ltd.; pub. Historic London for Ams. Stage mgr. Broadway theatricals Ethan Frome, St. Helena, 1934-37; novelist, radio writer Broadway theatricals, 1937-40; screen writer, Selznick Studios, Hollywood, 1945-46, free lance writer nat. mags., 1945-56; Author: Fine Flowers in the Valley, 1937; screen Adaptation Thomas Wolfe's Look Homeward, Angel; film script: Arthur Kaestler's Scum of the Earth, 1983. Home: Russet Cottage Mill Ln, Burwell, Cambridge England CB5 0HJ

WAYNE, JEANETTE MARIE, auditor; b. Mt. Clemens, Mich., Apr. 17, 1965; d. Robert Thomas W. and Sharon Elaine (Mominee) Nole; m. Ronald Edward Klicki, Sept. 14, 1985 (div. Oct. 1989). Asst. mgr. Little Caesars, Mt. Clemens, Mich., 1981-83, Cheese & Co., Birmingham, Mich., 1984; courier Chevrolet, Detroit, 1984; libr. EDS Chevrolet, Detroit, 1985-86, migration specialist, 1987; software support EDS Saturn, Troy, 1988-89, ops. tech., 1990-93; ops. tech. cons. EDS Tech. Architecture, Plano, Tex., 1993-2000; sr. auditor EDS Corp. Audit, Plano, Tex., 1997-2000, program mgr., 2000—; leader bus. process reengineering. Republican. Office: EDS Corp Audit 5400 Legacy Dr Plano TX 75024-3199

WAYNE, JESSE, actor/stuntman, film production manager; b. L.A., Sept. 14, 1941; s. Frank Anthony and Edith Florence (Manning) W. appt. by L.A. mayor to facilitate TV and motion picture filming in city, 1971-72. Appeared in feature films, including Prey, Cincinnati Kid, Love Bug Rides Again, Hopscotch, Birds of Prey, The Messenger, Bless the Beasts and the Children, Pete's Dragon, Testament; TV shows include F-Troop, Cheers, Batman, Big Valley, Star Trek, The Steve Allen Show, Mickey Rooney Show, Beverly Hillbillies, Jack Cassidy's TV Special, Medical Center, Combat, The Faceless Man; prodn. mgr. films, including Music City Blues, Ticket to Heaven; asst. dir. films, including Solo, The Ghost Team, Blindside, Reflections, Every Girl Should Have One. Mem. Sons of Confederate Vets. (adj. 1980—), Stuntmen's Assn. (publicity dir., sec.-treas. 1961-84), NRA, So. Calif. Antique Radio Soc., Nashville Amateur Radio Club. Rep. Avocations: photography, electronic kits, fire arms collection, ham radio. Home: PO Box 8057 Universal City CA 91618

WAYNE, VICTOR SAMUEL, cardiologist; b. Melbourne, Australia, Jan. 7, 1953; s. Mark Isaac and Anita (Selzer) W.; m. Karen Susan Eisinger; children: Fairlie, Stephanie. MB, BS with honors, Monash U., 1976. Diplomate Australian Soc. Ultrasound in Medicine. Intern, resident med. officer, registrar Alfred Hosp., Melbourne, 1976-79, cardiology registrar, 1980-81; advanced cardiology fellow St. Vincent Hosp., Worcester, Mass., 1982-83; instr. medicine U. Mass., Worcester, 1982-83; sr. cardiologist, chmn. Divsn. Cardiology St. Francis Xavier Cabrini Hosp., Melbourne, 1983—; vis. physician, cardiologist Alfred Hosp., Monash U., Melbourne, 1983—; lecturer in field. Contbr. articles to profl. jours; co-author books. Grantee Nat. Heart Found., Alfred Hosp., 1982. Fellow Royal Australasian Coll. Physicians, Am. Coll. Chest Physicians, Internat. Acad. Chest Physicians and Surgeons, N.Y. Acad. Scis., Am. Coll. Cardiology, Internat. Coll. Angiology, European Soc. Cardiology; mem. Cardiac Soc. Australia and New Zealand, Australian Soc. Echocardiography, Internat. Soc. and Fedn. Cardiology. Jewish. Club: Nat. Golf of Australia. Avocations: reading, traveling, theater, property investment, piano. Home: 8 Carmyle Ave, Toorak Victoria 3142, Australia Office: Cabrini Med Ctr, 183 Wattletree Rd, Melbourne Victoria 3144, Australia

WAZEER, MOHAMED ISMAIL, chemistry educator; b. Galagedara, Sri Lanka, Apr. 5, 1947; s. Hadjilebbe Mohamed Ismail and Ummul (Noormohamed) Majida; m. Sithy Walidah Izadeen, Aug. 9, 1975; children: Azmath, Mona, Azim. BSc with honors, U. Ceylon, Sri Lanka, 1969; MSc, U. East Anglia, U.K., 1972, PhD, 1974. Lectr. U. Ceylon, Sri Lanka, 1974-79; sr. lectr. U. Peradeniya, Sri Lanka, 1980-81; asst. prof. U. Petroleum & Minerals, Saudi Arabia, 1981-83; assoc. prof. King Fahd U. Petroleum & Minerals, Dhahran, Saudi Arabia, 1983-95, prof., 1996—; vis. scientist Indian Inst. Sci., 1981; vis. scholar Harvard U., 1992-93. Contbr. articles to profl. jours. chmn. mosque mgmt. com. Peradeniya U., 1981. Commonwealth scholar U.K. Govt., 1971-74. Fellow Inst. Chemistry Ceylon; mem. Am. Chem. Soc. Home: King Fahd U Petroleum, Minerals Box 2038, Dhahran 31261, Saudi Arabia Office: King Faud U Petroleum &, Minerals Dept Chemistry, Dhahran 31261, Saudi Arabia

WAZZAN, OSAMA AHMED, communications systems engineering executive; b. Makkah, Saudi Arabia, Mar. 21, 1962; s. Ahmed Hasan and Khariyah Abdul-Rahman (Kamal) W.; m. Shereen Adel Abdul-Aziz, Feb. 1, 1990; children: Hasan, Addanah, Leena. BS in Indsl. and Sys. Engring., U. So. Calif., 1986. Cert. profl. engr. in indsl. engring. Sys. engr. Samarec, Jiddah, Saudi Arabia, 1986-90, asst. gen. mgr., 1990-92, project mgr., 1992-94; comm. sys. maintenance specialist Saudi Aramco, Jiddah, 1994—; gen. mgr. Hasan Wazzan Est., Jiddah, 1994—; cons. Saudia Airlines, Jiddah, 1989-92. Mem. Am. Inst. Indsl. Engrs., Jiddah Yacht Club (Yachtsman of Yr. 1994, 96). Avocations: flying, diving, swimming, sailing, reading. Office: Saudi Aramco, PO Box 5250 MC 437, Jeddah 21422, Saudi Arabia

WDOWIAK, LESZEK HIERONIM, public health physician, educator; b. Lublin, Poland, Sept. 30, 1948; s. Stanisław and Apolonia Wdowiak; m. Helena Turek, Nov. 15, 1969; 1 child, Artur. Physician, Med. Acad., Lublin, 1972; M in Social Medicine and Pub. Health, Med. Acad., Moscow, 1976; MD, Med. Acad., Łódz, Poland, 1977; PhD, Med. Acad. Lublin, 1985. Mgr. Basic Health Ctr., Puławy, Poland, 1972-74; lectr. dept. social medicine and pub. health Med. Acad. Lublin, 1977-78, head of dept. social medicine and pub. health, 1978—, head Inst. Social Medicine, 1991-93; from asst. prof. to prof. Med. Acad., Lublin, 1986-94; cons. Pres. of Main Bd. of Social Ins. Instn., Warsaw, Poland, 1988-98; regional specialist Govt. Specialistic Wnrol in Orgn. of Health Protection, Poland, 1983-98. Author: (books) The Outline of Organization of Medical Health Care in Poland, 1987, The Lexicon of Expert Medical Opinion, 1990; editor: (jour.) Problems of Social Medicine, 1992—; contbr. papers to profl. jours. Vice-chmn. State Coun. of Fedn. of Trade Union of Health Protection Employees, 1985-89; chmn. Trade Union of Employees of Med. Acad. Lublin, 1988—. Recipient Award of Min. of Health and Social Care, 1989. Fellow Polish Hosp. Soc.; mem. Polish Soc. of Social Medicine and Pub. Health (pres. 1996—). Democrat. Avocations: traveling, gardening, art history. Home: Wojciecha Zywnego, 20-854 Lublin Poland Office: Med Acad Lublin, Al Racławickie 1, 20-059 Lublin Poland

WEADON, DONALD ALFORD, JR., lawyer; b. Brisbane, Australia, Sept. 15, 1945; came to U.S., 1946; s. Donald Alford and Ellen Martha (Salisbury) W.; m. Suzanne Hayden Cameron, Sept. 9, 1995. BA, Cornell U., 1967; JD, U. Calif., 1975; MBA, Harvard U., Iran Ctr. Mgmt. Studies, Tehran, 1976. Bar: Calif. 1976, D.C. 1988. Assoc. Hancock, Rothert & Bunshoft, San Francisco, 1977-80; jr. ptnr. Bryan, Cave, McPheeters & McRoberts, Washington, 1980-83; ptnr., head internat. dept. Anderson Baker Kill & Olick, Washington, 1983-84; sr. ptnr. Weadon, Dibble & Rehm, Washington, 1984-88, Weadon, Rehm & Assocs., Washington, 1988-89, Weadon, Rehm, Thomsen & Scott, Washington, 1989-90, Weadon & Assocs., Washington, 1991—; speaker, cons. U.S. Dept. Commerce, 1980-83; cons. Internat. Mktg. Assn., 1980—; Scientific Apparatus Mfg. Assn., 1983—, Valve Mfrs. Assn., 1983—; internat. counsel Am. Electronics Assn., 1986—; adj. prof. internat. law Golden Gate U., San Francisco, 1979-82, George Mason U., Arlington, Va., 1989—. Contbr. articles to profl. jours. Trustee coun. Cornell U., 2000—. Lt. comdr. USNR, 1968-72. Mem. ABA (chmn. China trade law com. 1982-84, chmn. software and tech. data com. 1983-85), Olympic Club, Savage Club, Harvard Club, Press Club, Sovereign Mil. Order Temple Jerusalem (Grand Cross, Order of Merit), Delta Kappa Epislon (alumni pres. 1997—, nat. bd. dirs. 1998—). Episcopalian. Office: Weadon & Assocs Ste 550 1819 Pennsylvania Ave NW Washington DC 20006-3611

WEAH, GEORGE, professional soccer player. Soccer player Yaound, Munich, 1988-92, Paris Saint-Germain, AC Milan, Manchester City, U.K., 2000. Founder George Weah Found. Named World Player of Yr. FIFA, 1995, European Footballer of Yr., African Football Player of Yr., African Golden Ball, 1989, 94; championships include: Cameroon Champions, 1988, French Champions, 1994, French Cup Winners, 1993, 95, French League Cup Winners, 1995, European Cup Winners' Cup Finalists, 1992, AC Milan Champions, 1996. Office: Manchester City, Maine Rd Moss Side, Manchester M14 7WN, United Kingdom*

WEAKLAND, REMBERT G., archbishop; b. Patton, Pa., Apr. 2, 1927; s. Basil and Mary (Kane) W. AB, St. Vincent Coll., Latrobe, Pa., 1948, DD (hon.), 1963, LHD (hon.), 1987; MS in Piano, Juilliard Sch. Music, 1954; grad. studies sch. music, Columbia U., 1954-56, PhD in Musicology, 2000; LHD (hon.), Duquesne U., 1964, Belmont Coll., 1964, Cath. U. Am., 1975, Xavier U., Cin., 1988, DePaul U., 1989, Loyola U., New Orleans, 1991, Villanova U., 1992, Dayton U., 1993, Marian Coll., Fond du Lac, Wis., 1995, St. Anselm Coll., Manchester, N.H., 1996, St. Norbert Coll., De Pere, Wis., 1996, U. San Francisco, 1997, Scholastica Coll., 1998; HHD (hon.), St. Ambrose U., Davenport, 1990, Aquinas Inst. Theology, St. Louis, 1991, St Mary's Coll., Notre Dame, Ind., 1994; LLD (hon.), Cardinal Stritch Coll., Milw., 1978, Marquette U., 1981, Loyola U., Chgo., 1986, U. Notre Dame, 1987, Mt. Mary Coll., Milw., 1989, John Carroll U., Cleve., 1992, Fairfield U., 1994; D of Sacred Music (hon.), St. Joseph's Coll., Rensselaer, Ind., 1979; DST (hon.), Jesuit Sch. Theology, Berkeley, Calif., 1989, St. John's U., Collegeville, Minn., 1991, Santa Clara U., 1991, Yale U., 1993; DD (hon.), Lakeland Coll., Sheboygan, 1991, Ill. Benedictine Coll., Lisle, Ill., 1992, Regis Coll., Toronto, 1993, Trinity Coll., Hartford, 1996, Trinity Lutheran Sem., Columbus, Ohio, 1998; D of Ministry (hon.), Catholic Theol. Union, Chgo., 1999. Joined Benedictines, Roman Cath. Ch., 1945, ordained priest, 1951. Mem. faculty music dept. St. Vincent Coll., 1957-63, chmn., 1961-63, chancellor chmn. of bd. of Coll., 1963-67; elected co-adjutor archabbot, 1963; abbot primate Benedictine Confederation, 1967-77; archbishop of Milw., 1977—. Mem. Ch. Music Assn. Am. (pres. 1964-66), Am. Guild Organists. Office: PO Box 070912 Milwaukee WI 53207-0912

WEAKLEY, CLARE GEORGE, JR., insurance executive, theologian, entrepreneur; b. Dallas, Apr. 14, 1928; s. Clare George and Louise (Cunningham) W.; children: Clare George III, Carol J., Charles E.; m. Jean C. Burrow, July 20, 1962. BBA, So. Meth. U., 1948, ThM, 1967. Ordained min. Christian Cmty., 1967. With Employers Ins., Dallas, 1948-52; owner Weakley & Co., Dallas, 1952—; founder, pres. Am. Svc. Found., Inc., 1967—, Small Bus. Assn., Inc., 1988—; vis. prof. western bus. theory and Christian ethics Internat. Mgmt. Inst. (formerly Leningrad Internat. Mgmt. Inst.), St. Petersburg, Russia, 1990—; founder, leader The Christian Cmty., internat. ch. on World Wide Web. Author: In God We Trust, 1997, God 101, 1998; author, editor: The Wesley Library Series for Today's Reader, The Nature of the Kingdom, 1996, The Nature of Spiritual Growth, 1977, The Nature of Revival, 1987, The Nature of Salvation, 1988, The Nature of Holiness, 1988. Republican. Home: 13731 Goldmark Dr Apt 1207 Dallas TX 75240-4220 Office: Weakley & Co PO Box 516065 Dallas TX 75251-6065

WEATHERHEAD, BERNARD ANTHONY, hotelier; b. St. James, Barbados, Aug. 13, 1946; s. Keith and Hilda E. (Chandler) W.; m. Flor Marilda Sarria, Oct. 14, 1967; children: Alfredo, Rod. Student, Harrisons Coll., Barbados, Barbados Acad. Cert. pilot; justice of the peace. Chmn. Bernmar Investments Inc., Barbados, Sandridge Beach Hotel, Barbados. Mem. Barbados Hotel Assn. (pres. 1976-78, 84-86), Barbados Light Aero Club (chmn. 1983-91). Anglican. Avocation: flying. Home: #127 Sandy Ln, Saint James Barbados Office: Sandridge Beach Hotel, St Peter Barbados

WEATHERUP, ROY GARFIELD, lawyer; b. Annapolis, Md., Apr. 20, 1947; s. Robert Alexander and Kathryn Crites (Hesser) W.; m. Wendy Gaines, Sept. 10, 1977; children: Jennifer, Christine. AB in Polit. Sci., Stanford U., 1968, JD, 1972. Bar: Calif. 1972, U.S. Dist. Ct. 1973, U.S. Ct. Appeals (9th cir.) 1975, U.S. Supreme Ct. 1980. Assoc. Haight, Brown & Bonesteel, Santa Monica, Santa Ana, L.A., 1972-78, ptnr., 1979—; judge Moot Ct. UCLA, Loyola U., Pepperdine U.; arbitrator Am. Arbitration Assn.; mem. com. Book Approved Jury Instrns. L.A. Superior Ct. Mem. ABA, Calif. Acad. Appellate Lawyers, Los Angeles County Bar Assn., Town Hall Calif. Republican. Methodist. Home: 17260 Rayen St Northridge CA 91325-2919 Office: Haight Brown & Bonesteel PO Box 680 1620 26th St Ste 4000 Santa Monica CA 90404-4060

WEAVER, DONNA RAE, company executive; b. Chgo., Oct. 15, 1945; d. Albert Louis and Gloria Elaine (Graffis) Florence; m. Clifford L. Weaver, Aug. 20, 1966; 1 child, Megan Rae. BS in Edn., No. Ill. U., 1966, EdD, 1977; MEd, De Paul U., 1974. Tchr. H.L. Richards High Sch., Oak Lawn, Ill., 1966-71, Sawyer Coll. Bus., Evanston, Ill., 1971-72; asst. prof. Oakton Community Coll., Morton Grove, Ill., 1972-75; vis. prof. U. Ill., Chgo., 1977-78; dir. devel. Mallinckrodt Coll., Wilmette, Ill., 1978-80, dean, 1980-83; campus dir. Nat.-Louis U., Chgo., 1983-90, dean div. applied behavioral scis., 1985-89; dean Coll. Mgmt. and Bus., 1989-90; pres. The Oliver Group, Inc., Kenilworth, Ill., 1993-97; mng. ptnr. Le Miccine, Gaiole-in-Chianti, Tuscany, Italy, 1996—; cons. Nancy Lovely and Assocs., Wilmette, 1981-84, North Ctrl. Assn., Chgo., 1982-90. Contbr. articles to Am. Vocat. Jour., Ill. Bus. Edn. Assn. Monograph, Nat. Coll. Edn.'s ABS Rev., Nat. View. Mem. Ill. Quality of Work Life Coun., 1987-90, New Trier Twp. Health and Human Svcs. Adv. Bd., Winnetka, Ill., 1985-88; bd. dirs. Open Lands Project, 1985-87, Kenilworth (Ill.) Village House, 1986-87. Recipient Achievement award Women in Mgmt., 1981; Am. Bd. Master Educators charter disting. fellow, 1986. Mem. Nat. Bus. Edn. Assn., Delta Pi Epsilon (past pres.). Avocations: reading, traveling, decorating. Office: 505 N Lake Shore Dr Apt 4010 Chicago IL 60611-3619

WEAVER, E(LVIN) PAUL, minister; b. Everett, Pa., Oct. 13, 1912; s. Mahlon J. and Fanny S. (Ritchey) W.; m. Zalma Faw, Aug. 6, 1936 (dec. 1966); children: Nelda Weaver Sollenberger, Bruce H.; m. Eleanor Snare Carter, June 21, 1968. AB, Elizabethtown (Pa.) Coll., 1937; BD, BA, Bethany Theol. Sem., Chgo., 1945; postgrad., Kennedy Sch. Missions, Hartford, Conn., 1939. Ordained to ministry, Ch. of the Brethren, 1933. Missionary Ch. of the Brethren, Nigeria, 1940-44; pastor Ch. of the Brethren, Huntington County, Ind., 1945-51, Mexico (Ind.) Ch., 1951-59; dist. exec. Mid Dist. of Ind., North Manchester, Ind., 1959-71, Nappanee, Ind., 1971-80; pastor SS Valley & Cherry Ln., Everett, Pa., 1981-88; ret.; pres. Ind. State Pastor Conf., Indpls., 1955; bd. dirs. legis. counsel Ind. Coun. Chs., Indpls., 1948-78; del. Nat. Coun. Chs., Detroit, Dallas; accredited visitor World Coun. Chs. Assemblies II, VI, VII, VIII; Ind. Christian Endeavor, 1948-78; rep. Ch. of Brethren at UN SSD III, 1988. Author: Journey Into Faith, 1994. Mem. Pa. advocacy and action team Pa. Coun. of Chs., 1987—; founder Do Something for Peace program, Nigeria, 1999. Recipient Ecumenical award Ind. Coun. Chs., 1975, Pa. Coun. Chs., 1988. Home: 1672 Lower Snake Spring Rd Everett PA 15537-6651

WEAVER, JACQUELYN KUNKEL IVEY, artist, educator; b. Richmond, Ky., Mar. 14, 1931; d. Marion David and Margaret Tabitha (Brandenburg) Kunkel; m. George Thomas IveySr., 1951 (dec. 1989); children: George Thomas Ivey Jr., David Richard Ivey; m. Harrell Fuller Weaver, 1991. BFA, Wesleyan Coll., 1987. Owner J. K. Ivey Art, Macon, Ga., 1974-91, J.K. Ivey Bookkeeping and Tax Svc., Macon, Ga., 1976-84, Ivey-Weaver Art Studio, Macon, 1991—. Exhibited works in galleries including Mid. Ga. Art Assn. Gallery, Macon, 1980—, Mus. Arts and Scis., Macon, 1987, 91, 94, 96, 98, Attaway Cottage, Macon, 1990—, AAPL Salmungundi Club, N.Y.C., 1992, Frames and Art Gallery, Macon, 1995—, CLWAC Nat. Arts Club, N.Y.C., 1996, Stofko-Dixon Fine Arts, Bolingbroke, Ga., 1996—, Hilton Head Island Art League, Self Family Art Ctr., Hilton Head Island, 1997, Christopher Gallery, Cohasset, Mass., 1997, 98, Parthenon (Tenn. Art League) Centennial Park, Nashville, 1998, Lowndes/Valdosta Cult. Arts Ctr., Valdosta, Ga., 1992, 94, 95, 96, 97, 98, Thomasville (Ga.) Cultural Ctr., 1999, Martin Hall, Univ. of Mobile, Mobile, AL, 2000. Bd. dirs., treas. Mid. Ga. Art Assn., Macon, 1981-84, 92, publicity chmn., 1988-89, chmn. nominating com., 1997, mem. fin. com., 1998-99, audit com., 1998. Mem. Nat. Mus. Women in Arts (charter mem.), Wesleyan Coll. Alumnae Assn., Mus. Arts and Scis., Catherine Lorillard Wolf Art Club, Middle Ga. Art Assn., Portrait Painters Am., Inc. Presbyterian. Avocations: ballroom dancing, reading, walking, music. Office: Ivey-Weaver Art Studio 6183 Hwy 87 Macon GA 31210

WEAVER, JUDITH ANN, lawyer; b. South Bend, Ind., June 5, 1948; d. Raymond Joseph and Norma Jean DeVliegher; m. Edward Thomas Weaver, Sept. 3, 1983. BA, St. Mary's Coll., Notre Dame, Ind., 1970, JD, 1991; LLM, U. Mo., Kansas City, 1992. Bar: Mo. 1993, Kans. 1993, Colo. 2000. Social worker, dir. vol. svcs. S.C. Dept. Social Svcs., Charleston, 1970-73, adult day care licensure, 1973-75, title XX coord., 1975-78, asst. to commr., 1978-81, medicaid divsn. dir., 1981-83; mgmt. cons. Electronic Data Sys., Bethesda, Md., 1983-85; cons., adminstr. Booz Allen Hamilton, N.Y.C., 1985-89; pvt. practice Kansas City, Mo., 1992-93; assoc. Blackwood, Langworthy & Schmelzer, P.C., Kansas City, Mo., 1993-96; of counsel Lathrop & Gage, L.C., Kansas City, Mo., 1996—. Author: Health Law Handbook, 1995, 96; columnist Radiology Bus. Mgmt. Assocs. Jour., 1996-98. Bd. dirs. Samuel U. Rogers Cmty. Health Ctr., 1992-95, Mo. Family Health Coun., 1994-96, Katy's Place, 1996-99, Met. Orgn. to Combat Sexual Assault, 1998; trustee Swope Ridge Found., 1995-99; mem. Mo. Health Facilities Rev. Com., 1993-96, chair, 1995-96; Gubernatorial appointee Joint Legis. Com. to Study Health Planning Legislation, 1995; founder Fund for Gender Equity, Kansas City, 1998—; bd. mem. Bristlecone Hosp., Summit, Colo., 1999—; trustee Nat. Repertory Orch., Denver, 1999—. Gage fellow U. Mo., Kansas City, 1991-92. Mem. ABA, Am. Health Lawyers, Am. Assn. Homes for the Aging (Mo. gen. counsel), Mo. Bar, Kans. Bar, Colo. Bar. E-mail: ejweaver@earthlink.net. Home: PO Box 2146 Breckenridge CO 80424-2146 Office: Lathrop & Gage LC Ste 295 Grand Blvd Kansas City MO 64108

WEAVER, KITTY DUNLAP, author; b. Frankfort, Ky., Sept. 24, 1910; d. Arch Robertson and Rebecca (Johnson) Dunlap; m. Henry Byrne Weaver, June 29, 1933. Student, Sorbonne, Paris, summer 1930; AB, William and Mary Coll., 1932; MA, George Washington U., 1933; BS, U. Md., 1947; postgrad., Georgetown U., U. Pa., George Washington U., 1964-67, Moscow U., 1983; studied with Alfred Adler, Vienna, 1932. Jr. H.S. tchr., 1931-32, poultry farmer, 1947-55, author, 1970—. Author: Lenin's Grandchildren, 1971, Russia's Future, 1981, Bushels of Rubles, 1992. Mem. Sulgrave (Washington) Club, Aldie Hort. Soc., Chevy Chase (Md.) Club, Met. Club (Washington), Garden Club Am., Fauquier Loudoun Garden Club. Home: 40820 John Mosby Hwy Aldie VA 20105-2820 also: 603 Pennsylvania Ave NW Apt 504 Washington DC 20004-2602

WEAVER, PEGGY (MARGUERITE MCKINNIE WEAVER), plantation owner; b. Jackson, Tenn., June 7, 1925; d. Franklin Allen and Mary Alice (Caradine) McKinnie; children: Elizabeth Lynn, Thomas Jackson III, Franklin A. McKinnie. Student, U. Colo., 1943-45, Am. Acad. Dramatic Arts, 1945-46, S. Meisner's Profl. Classes, 1949, Oxford U., 1990, 91. Actress, 1946-52; mem. staff Mus. Modern Art, N.Y.C., 1949-50; woman's editor radio sta. WTJS-AM-FM, Jackson, Tenn., 1952-55; editor, radio/TV Jackson Sun Newspaper, 1952-55; columnist Bolivar (Tenn.) Bulletin-Times, 1986—; chmn. Ho. of Reps. of Old Line Dist., Hardeman County, Tenn., 1985-91, 94-97. Founder Paris-Henry County (Tenn.) Arts Coun., 1965; pres. Assn. Preservation of Tenn. Antiquities, Hardeman County chpt., 1991-95; charter mem. adv. bd. Tenn. Arts Commn., Nashville, 1967-74, Tenn. Performing Arts Ctr., Nashville, 1972—; chmn. Tenn. Libr. Assn., Nashville, 1973-74; regional chmn. Opera Memphis, 1979-91; mem. nat. coun. Met. Opera, N.Y.C., 1980-92, Tenn. Bicentennial Com., Hardeman County, 1993-96; sec. Mempis Brooks Mus. League, 1998-99. Mem. DAR, Nat. Soc. Colonial Dames Am. (treas. Memphis chpt. 1996-98, pub. rels. chmn. 1998-2000, v.p. 2000—), Oxford Alumni Assn. N.Y., English Speaking Union (London chpt.), Summit (Memphis), Dilettantes (Memphis) (treas. 1997-98). Methodist. Avocations: horseback riding, travel, theatre. Office: 402 Heritage Plantation Hickory Valley TN 38042

WEAVER, PHILIP PETER EDMUND, geologist; b. Chester, U.K., Dec. 4, 1952; s. Donald Victor and Dora (Corfield) W.; m. Marian Wren, Sept. 13, 1975; children: Oliver, James, Benjamin. BSc, Leicester (U.K.) U., 1974, DSc, 2000; PhD, Coun. Nat. Acad. Awards, Plymouth, U.K., 1978. Rschr. Plymouth Poly., 1977-80; scientist Inst. Oceanographic Scis., Wormley, U.K., 1980-95, Southampton (Eng.) Oceanography Ctr., 1995—; head seafloor processes divsn. Southampton Oceanography Ctr., 1997—; coord. EC project Sediment Transport on European Atlantic Margins, 1994-97. Contbr. articles to profl. jours. Fellow Geological Soc. London. Avocations: tennis, gardening. Office: Southampton Oceanography, Empress Dock, SO14 3ZH Southampton England

WEAVER, WILLIAM CLAIR, JR. (MIKE WEAVER), human resources development executive; b. Indiana, Pa., Apr. 11, 1936; s. William Clair and Zaida (Bley) W.; m. Janet Marcelle Boyd, Sept. 18, 1963 (div. 1978); 1 child, William Michael; m. Donna June Hubbuch, Feb. 10, 1984. B Aero Engring., Rensselaer Poly. Inst., 1958; MBA, Washington U., St. Louis, 1971; postgrad., Rutgers U.; grad., Armed Forces Indsl. Coll. Registered profl. engr. Engr. aerodynamics N.Am. Aviation, Los Angeles, 1959-60; engr. flight test ops. Boeing/Vertol, Phila., 1963-66; engr. flight test project Lockhead Electronics, Plainfield, N.J., 1966-69; project engr. advanced systems, sr. staff engr. Emerson Electric Co., St. Louis, 1969-72; pres. Achievement Assocs., Inc., St. Louis, 1972—; founder, charter mem. Catalyst, 1978—; speaker in field. Author: Winning Selling, 1983, Winning Manager, 1997; contbr. articles to profl. jours. Mem. adv. com. Boy Scouts Am., Bridgeton, Mo., 1974. Served to capt. USAF, 1960-63, USAFR. Mem. AIAA, NSPE, ASTD, Am. Soc. Bus. and Mgmt. Cons., Am. Ordnance Soc., Assn. MBA Execs., Air Force Assn., Am. Helicopter Soc., Acacia Frat., St. Louis C. of C., Mensa, Beta Gamma Sigma. Republican. Lutheran. Avocations: photography, music, sports. Home and Office: 13018 Ray Trog Ct Saint Louis MO 63146-1802

WEB, SHAW-BING, engineering educator; b. Hsinchu, Taiwan, Apr. 15; m. Luan-Hu Lo, Mar. 15, 1996. BS, Nat. Cheng-Kung U., Tainan, Taiwan, 1993, MS, 1995, PhD, 1997. Registered mining engr., Taiwan. Mining engr. Nat. Assistance Commn. for Retired Svc., Taipei, Taiwan, 1979, cons., 1979-80; lectr. Nat. Cheng-Kung U., 1980-87, assoc. prof., 1987-89, prof., 1998—, head dept., 1997—. Contbr. articles to profl. publs.; patentee in field. Lt. Taiwan Army, 1975-79. Mem. Chinese Inst. Mining and Metall. Engring. (bd. dirs. 1997—, Outstanding Dissertation award 1984, 95, 97)), Found. Mining and Metallurgy (bd. dirs. 1997). Avocation: fishing. Office: Nat Cheng-Kung U, Dept Resources engring, Tainan 70101, Taiwan

WEBB, ANN RUTH, scientific researcher; b. Leeds, Yorkshire, Eng., Nov. 20, 1960; d. Norman William and Winifred (Ayling) W.; m. Glenn Rich, Jan. 4, 1989; children: Caitlin Dawn, Adam. BS in Physics and Meteorology, Reading (Eng.) U., 1982; PhD in Environ. Physics, Nottingham (Eng.) U., 1985. Postdoctoral fellow Tufts U., Boston, 1985-87, Boston U., 1987-88; lectr. Reading U., 1988-93, sr. rsch. fellow, 1993-95; lectr. U. Manchester (Eng.) Inst. Sci. and Tech., 1995-99, sr. lectr., 1999—; cons. Chaim Sheba Med. Ctr., Israel, 1992, Emtech, U.K., 1992-93, Bausch and Lomb, N.Y.C., 1993, Calif. Suncare Inc., L.A., 1994—. Author: UV Instrumentation and Applications, 1998; contbr. book chpt.: Annual Review of Nutrition, vol. 8, 1988, Environmental UV Photobiology, 1993; contbr. more than 40 articles to profl. jours. Recipient various rsch. grants European Union, NERC, Agr. and Food Rsch. Coun.; Earth Obs. fellow Natural Environment Rsch. Coun., 1994-97. Mem. Inst. Physics (assoc., travel grantee 1985), Am. Soc. Photobiology, Royal Meteorol. Soc., N.Y. Acad. Sci. Anglican. Avocations: hot air balloon pilot, Karate (black belt), baritone horn player, yoga, sailing. Office: U Manchester Inst Sci and Tech, PO Box 88 Sackville St, Manchester M6O 1QD, England

WEBB, ANTHONY JOHN, surgeon, consultant, researcher; b. Bristol, Eng., Dec. 29, 1929; s. Charles Reginald and Gwendoline (Moon) W.; m. Audrie Ruth Bowen, Mar. 5, 1955; children: Maryl Idris Humfrys, Dominique Louise, Charlotte Ann, Jason Crispin John. MB, ChB, U. Bristol, Eng., 1953, ChM, 1974. House officer Bristol (Eng.) Royal Infirmary, 1953-55; registrar Frencbay Hosp., Bristol, 1957-59, Queen Elizabeth Hosp., Birmingham, Eng., 1960-62; sr. registrar Birmingham Hosps., Eng., 1962-67; cons. surgeon Bristol Royal Infirmary, 1967-94; sr. rsch. fellow dept. surgery U. Bristol, 1995—. Capt. Royal Army Med. Corps., 1955-57. Recipient Silver medal Bristol Royal Infirmary, 1953, McEwan medal Royal Coll. Surgeons Glasgow, Scotland, 1957, Erica Wachtel medal and named Erica Wachtel lectr. Brit. Soc. for Clin. Cytology, 1993; named Hunterian prof. Royal Coll. Surgeons Eng., 1975. Mem. Brit. Assn. Endocrine Surgeons (pres. 1992-94), Bristol Medico Chirurgical Soc. (pres. 1985), Surgical Club S.W. Eng. Conservative. Anglican Ch. mem. Avocations: choral singing, clin. cytology, history 1914-18, gardening. Home: 10 Grange Park, Bris Cty Bristol BS9 4BP, England Office: Cavendish Lodge, 7 Percival Rd, Clifton Bristol BS8 3CE, England

WEBB, COLIN, chemical engineering educator, consultant; b. Hereford, Eng., Oct. 11, 1954; s. Sidney Joseph and Stella Taylor (Botten) W.; m. Ann Elizabeth Kelly, Apr. 14, 1984; children: Richard Hereford, Kate Elizabeth. BSc with honors, U. Aston, Birmingham, Eng., 1976, PhD, 1980. Postdoctoral fellow U. Manchester (Eng.) Inst. Sci. and Tech., 1979-83, lectr., 1983-90, sr. lectr., 1991-94, Satake prof. grain process engring., 1994—; examiner 10B, 1997. Editor: Process Engineering Aspects of Immobilized Cell Systems, 1986, Plant and Animal Cells: Process Possibilities, 1987, Biochem. Engring. Jour., 1998. Fellow Instn. Chem. Engrs. Avocation: cyclist. Address: Holly Bank, Talbot Rd, Glossop Derbyshire SK13 7DP, England Office: U Manchester, Inst Sci & Tech, Dept Chem Engring PO Box 88, Manchester M60 1QD, England

WEBB, COLIN EDWARD, laser physics educator; b. Erith, Kent, Eng., Dec. 9, 1937; s. Alfred Edward and Doris (Collins) W.; m. Pamela M.C. White, June 6, 1964 (dec. Jan. 1992); children: Susan Patricia, Julie Diane. BSc in Physics with 1st class honors, U. Nottingham, Eng., 1960; PhD in Physics, U. Oxford, Eng., 1964. Mem. tech. staff Bell Labs., Murray Hill, N.J., 1964-68; AEI rsch. fellow dept. physics U. Oxford, Eng., 1968-71, lectr. in physics, 1971-90, reader in physics, 1990-92, prof. laser physics, 1992—, fellow Jesus Coll., 1973—; chmn. Oxford Lasers Ltd., Abingdon, 1977—; mem. adv. com. on opto electronics Rank Prize Funds, 1990—; pres. UK Consortium for Photonics & Optics, 1998—; vis. prof. Cranfield U., Eng., 1999—. Contbr. articles to profl. jours. Recipient award for export Her Majesty the Queen of Eng., 1987, awards for tech. Her Majesty the Queen of Eng., 1989, 91; named mem. Order of the British Empire, 2000. Fellow Optical Soc. Am. (dir. at large 1991-94), Inst. Physics (Duddell medal 1985, Glazebrook medal and prize 2001), Royal Soc. (Clifford Paterson lectr. and prize 1998). Achievements include patents in laser technology. Avocations: reading, traveling, music, photography. Office: Univ Oxford Clarendon Lab, U Oxford Clarendon Lab, Parks Rd, Oxford OX1 3PU, England

WEBB, DAVID JOHN, pharmacology educator, medical researcher, consultant; b. Greenwich, London, Sept. 1, 1953; s. Alfred William Owen and Edna May (Parish) W.; m. Margaret Jane Cullen, June 23, 1984; children: David Matthew, Matthew Owen Cullen, Mark Ewen. MB, BS, U. London, 1977, MD, 1990. Clin. rsch. fellow Med. Rsch. Coun. Blood Pressure Unit, Glasgow, Scotland, 1982-85; lectr. in pharmacology St. George's Hosp. and Med. Sch. U. London, 1985-89; sr. lectr. dept. medicine U. Edinburgh, Scotland, 1990-95, Christison prof. therapeutics and clin. pharmacology, 1995—; hon. cons. physician Lothian U. Hosps., NHS Trust, Edinburgh, 1990—, head dept. medicine, 1997; dir. clin rsch. ctr. U. Edinburgh, 1990-95; mem. physiol. medicine grants com. Med. Rsch. Coun., 1996; leader Wellcome Trust Cardiovasc. Initiative, 1997—; mem. MRC Adv. Bd., 1997, Wellcome Trust Physiology and Pharmacology Panel, 1997; chmn. Lothian Area Drug and Therapeutics Com., 1998—; head Ctr. for Cardiovascular Sci., 2000. Author: (with others) The Endothelium in Hypertension, 1997; contbr. articles to profl. jours. Hon. Trustee and Rsch. Dir for the High Blood Pressure Found., Edinburgh, 1991—. Fellow Royal Coll. Physicians Edinburgh, Royal Coll. Physicians (UK), Royal Coll. Physicians London, Faculty of Pharm. Med., Acad. Med. Sci. (U.K.); mem. Med. Rsch. Soc., Scottish Soc. for Exptl. Medicine (coun. 1994), Brit. Hypertension Soc. (exec. com. 1991-94), European Soc. Hypertension, Internat. Soc. Hypertension, Brit. Pharmacological Soc. (exec. com. clin sect. 1994-99, sec. 1995, Hon. sec., dir., trustee 1996-99), Scottish Cardiac Soc., Rsch. Defence Soc., Am. Heart Assn. (Hypertension and Cardiology), European Network of Therapeutics Tchrs., Assn. Physicians of Great Brit. and Ireland, Scottish Soc. Physicians, Assn. Clin. Profs. Medicine, Soc. for Medicines Rsch. Avocations: mountaineering, opera, bridge, chess. Fax: 0131-537-2003. E-mail: d.j.webb@ed.ac.uk. Home: 26 Inverleith Gardens, Edinburgh EH3 5PS, Scotland Office: Clin Pharm & Rsch Ctr, Western Gen Hosp Crewe Rd, Edinburgh EH4 2XU, Scotland

WEBB, DONNA LOUISE, academic director, educator; b. Yakima, Wash., Aug. 12, 1929; d. Manuel Lawrence and Rena May (Sewell) Matson; (div.); children: Marlene Park, Ed Webb III. AA in Vocat. Edn., Portland (Oreg.) Community Coll., 1976; BA in Psychology, Warner Pacific Coll., 1980; MEd in Career and Vocat. Edn., Oreg. State U., Corvallis, 1980, EdD in Career and Vocat. Edn., 1983. Dir. placement Andrews U., Mich., 1969-74; dir. career edn. and coop. work experience Portland, 1976-78; coord. youth program Fed. Experiment/Chronically Unemployed Youth, Vancouver, Wash., 1979; dir. career counseling Clark Coll., Vancouver, 1979; tchr. coop. edn. project Multnomah County ESD, Portland, 1981; pvt. practice counselor Portland, 1982-84; dir. career devel. & coop. edn. Walla Walla (Wash.) Coll., 1984-87; assoc. dir. Ctr. for Lifelong Learning Loma Linda (Calif.) U., 1987-91; corp. trainer Pacific Inst., Seattle, 1991-94, account mgr. consulting and rsch., 1994—; home decorator Frederick & Nelson; payroll and computerized bookkeeper Hilo Care Ctr.; with pers. office Flour-Utah Mining; employment counselor Snelling & Snelling Employment Agy.; tchr. bus. edn. Portland Adventist Acad. Contbr. articles to profl. jours. Mem. ASTD, Assn. Pers. Adminstrs. (columnist San Bernardino Sun newspaper), Coun. for Adult and Exptl. Learning, Calif. Assn. for Counseling and Devel., Coop. Edn. Assn., Nat. Commn. for Coop. Edn., Phi Delta Kappa. Office: 4501 W Powell Blvd Apt 72 Gresham OR 97030-5070

WEBB, EMILY, retired plant morphologist; b. Charleston, S.C., Apr. 10, 1924; d. Malcolm Syfan and Emily Kirk (Moore) W.; m. John James Rosemond, Apr. 23, 1942 (div. 1953); 1 child, John Kirk; m. Julius Goldberg, Sept. 9, 1954; children: Michael, Judith. AB in Liberal Arts and Sci. with honors, U. Ill., Chgo., 1968, MS in Biol. Scis., 1972, PhD in Biol. Scis., 1985. Undergrad. fellow in bacteriology Med. Coll. S.C., Charleston, 1952-54; teaching asst. U. Ill., Chgo., 1969-72, 77-84, rsch. asst., 1977; teaching fellow W.Va. U., Morgantown, 1974, instr., 1974-75; rsch. in N.Am. bot. needlework art, 1986—. Author: Studies in Several North American Species of Ophioglossum, 1986; translator Nat. Transl. Ctr., Chgo., 1976; contbr. articles to profl. jours. James scholar U. Ill., 1968-69. Mem. DAR. Democrat. Episcopalian. Avocations: garden design, writing, money management. Home and Office: 1356 Mandel Ave Westchester IL 60154-3433

WEBB, GEOFFREY IAN, computer scientist, educator; b. Melbourne, Victoria, Australia, Oct. 6, 1960; s. James Bawtree and Leslie Merele (Hayes) W.; m. Janine Carol McGuinness; 1 child, Daniel. BA, LaTrobe U., Melbourne, 1982, PhD, 1987. Lectr. Griffith U., Brisbane, Australia, 1986-88, Deakin U., Geelong, Australia, 1988-90; sr. lectr. Deakin U., Geelong, 1990-94, reader, 1995-98, prof., 1998—; cons. MMI Ins. Group, Sydney, Australia, 1997-98, Coles Myer Ltd., Melbourne, 1999—; bd. dirs. GI Webb & Assoc. Pty. Ltd. Contbr. articles to profl. jours. Commonwealth Postgrad. Rsch. scholar, Australia, 1982. Office: Sch Computing and Math, Deakin Univ, Geelong 3217, Australia

WEBB, JAMES R., finance educator, consultant; b. Granite City, Ill., Apr. 5, 1947; s. Gene and Lucille (Arney) W.; m. Anais Harding Brown, 1978; children: Clinton, Stuart, Carissa. BS in Mgmt., N. Ill. U., 1972, MBA in Fin., 1974; PhD in Fin., U. Ill., 1982. Asst. prof. fin. Kent (Ohio) State U., 1979-82; assoc. prof. U. Akron (Ohio), 1982-89; prof. fin. Cleve. State Coll. Bus., 1989—; vis. prof. U. Tex., Austin, 1987-88, U. Hong Kong, 1993, 95, 96, 98, U. We. Australia, Sydney, 1993, 97; dir. real estate U. Rsch. Ctr. Cleve. State U., 1992-99. Contbr. over 100 articles to profl. jours. Exec. dir., past pres. Am. Real Estate Soc., 1987—. Fellow Am. Real Estate Soc. Found., 1988—. Avocations: Japanese cloisonne, ornamental horticulture. Office: Cleve State U Dept Fin Cleveland OH 44114

WEBB, KARRIE, professional golfer; b. Ayr, Queensland, Australia, Dec. 21, 1974. Profl. golfer LPGA, 1995—. Won Weetabix Women's Brit. Open, 1995, 97, Healthsouth Inaugural, 1996, Sprint Titleholders Championship, 1996, SAFECO Classic, 1996, 97, ITT LPGA Tour Championship, 1996, Susan G. Koman Internat., 1997, Australian Ladies Masters, 1998, City of Hope: Myrtle Beach Classic, 1998, Wegman's Rochester Internat., 1999, Mercury Title-holders Championships, 1999, Standard Register PING, 1999, Australian Ladies Masters, 1999, 2000, The Office Depot, 1999, 2000, ier Classic, 1999, Nabisco Championship, 2000, Take Fuji Classic, 2000; recipient Vare Trophy LPGA, 1997; named Rolex Rookie of Yr., LPGA, 1996. Office: care LPGA 100 International Golf Dr Daytona Beach FL 32124-1082*

WEBB, KEITH, political science educator; b. London, May 25, 1943; m. Wanda Marie Cekalo, July 11, 1970; children: Laura F.G., Adam K.G. B.A. with honors, U. Keele, Eng., 1970; M.Sc. in Politics, U. Strathclyde, Scotland, 1972; PhD in Internat. Rels., U. Kent, Eng., 1994. Lectr. U. Iceland, Reykjavik, 1972-74, U. Strathclyde, Glasgow, 1974-75; research fellow City Univ., London, 1976-82; lectr. U. Kent, Canterbury, Eng., 1982—. Author: Growth of Nationalism in Scotland, 1978. Co-editor: New Approaches to International Mediation, 1987, Theory and Practice in Foreign Policymaking, 1994; contbr. articles to profl. jours. Mem. Conflict Research Soc. (sec.), Ctr. for Analysis Conflict, European Conflict Research Group (Coordinator 1980-85). Avocations: sailing, research. Home: 42 Somner Close, Canterbury England Office: U Kent Rutherford Coll, Canterbury CT2 7NZ, England

WEBB, LAMAR THAXTER, architect; b. Hapeville, Ga., Sept. 13, 1928; s. Eugene Garnette and Sara Ethel (Moore) W.; m. Bettye Jayne Jackson, Dec. 6, 1957; children: Mark Maynard, Robin Lynn. BBA in Fin., U. Ga., 1950; BS, Ga. Inst. Tech., 1959, BArch, 1960. Registered architect, Ga., Fla. Intern architect Abreu and Robeson, Inc., Brunswick, Ga., 1960-66; architect, pres. Webb & Baldwin, Inc., St. Simons Island, Ga., 1966-72; pres., owner Lamar Webb, Arch., Inc., St. Simons Island, 1972—. 1st lt. USAF, 1953-55. Mem. AIA (State bd. dirs. 1985—, v.p. Golden Isles chpt. 1988-89, pres. 1989-90), Am. Soc. Interior Designers, Am. Soc. Landscape Architects (assoc.), Audubon Soc., Nat. Hort. Soc., Humane Soc. (local bd. dirs. 1985-87), Smithsonian Assocs., Coastal Alliance for Arts, Nat. Trust for Hist. Preservation, Ga. Trust for Hist. Preservation, Coastal Ga. Hist. Assn., Met. Mus. Art, Golden Isles Gourmet Club (bd. dirs.) Chien de Rotessieurs, G.I. Chap. Avocations: cooking, drawing, painting, travel. Home: Marsh Oaks Saint Simons GA 31522 Office: 13 Retreat Pl Saint Simons Is GA 31522-2401

WEBB, MARK, professional society administrator; b. Ravenna, Ohio, July 22, 1956; s. James Cecil Webb and Edna Jeanette Santee; m. Christina Lauren Hamlett, Mar. 9, 1998. BA, U. Ariz., 1978, JD, 1981. Dep. county atty. Santa Cruz County Atty., Nogales, Ariz., 1982; assoc. Munger & Munger, Tucson, 1983-87; dep. dir. Ariz. Dept. Ins., Phoenix, 1987-88; counsel Am. Ins. Assn., Sacramento, 1988-93, asst. v.p., 1997-98, v.p., 1998—; prin. Richard Robinson & Assocs. Inc., Sacramento, 1993-97. pres. Associated Students, U. Ariz., Tucson, 1978; active Ariz. Opera Co., Tucson, 1985; mem. governing bd. Pima C.C. Bd. Govs., Tucson, 1986-88; del. McCain for Pres., Burlingame, Calif., 2000. Recipient Joseph S. Jenckes award ATLA, Tucson, 1981, Cert. Recognition, Am. Soc. Safety Engrs.-Orange Coast chpt., Calif., 1999. Mem. NRA (life), Am. Assn. Polit. Cons. (assoc.), Clan Keith Soc. Republican. E-mail: mewebb@earthlink.net and mwebb@we.aiadc.org. Home: 8827 Salmon Falls Dr Apt E Sacramento CA 95826-1953 Office: Am Ins Assn #2060 980 9th St Ste 2060 Sacramento CA 95814-2740

WEBB, O(RVILLE) LYNN, physician, pharmacologist, educator; b. Tulsa, Aug. 29, 1931; s. Rufus Aclen and Berla Ophelia (Caudle) W.; m. Joan Liebenheim, June 1, 1954 Idiv. Jan. 1980); children: Kathryn, Gilbert, Benjamin; m. Jeanne P. Heath, aug. 24, 1991. BS, Okla. State U., 1953; MS, U. Okla., 1961; PhD in Pharmacology, U. Mo., 1968. Diplomate Nat. Bd. Med. Examiners, Am. Bd. Family Practice; cert. medical examiner, 1999. Rsch. assoc. in pharmacology U. Okla., 1959-61; rsch. fellow NIH, 1962-66; instr. pharmacology U. Mo., Columbia, 1966-68, asst. prof., 1968-69; family practice New Castle, Ind., 1969-89; med. dir. VA Clinic, Lawton, Va., 1989-94, Comanche County Hosp., 1994-98; pvt. practice medicine, 1998—; med. dir. Southwestern Hosp., Lawton, Okla., 2000—; clin. assoc. prof. family medicine U. Okla. Coll. Medicine, 1989—; adj. assoc. prof. pharmacology U. Okla. Coll. Medicine, 1989—; mem. U. Okla. Medicine Admissions Bd., 1995-98; mem. staff Henry County Meml. Hosp., New Castle, 1969-89; guest prof. pharmacy and pharmacology Butler U. Coll. Pharmacy, Indpls., 1970-75; owner, dir. Carthage Clinic, 1975-89; clin. assoc. prof. family medicine Ind. U. Coll. Medicine, 1986-89; county physician, jail med. dir. Henry County, Ind., 1976-89. Author: (with Blissitt and Stanaszek, Lea and Febiger) Clinical Pharmacy Practice, 1972; contbr. numerous articles to profl. jours. Bd. dirs. Lawton Philharm., 1990-95. Recipient Cert. of merit in Pharmacol. and Clin. Med. Rsch., 1970, Med. Student Rsch. Essay award Am. Acad. Neurology, 1968. Fellow Am. Acad. Family Physicians, Am. Coll. Physician Execs.; mem. AMA (ann. award recognition 1975—), Ind. State Med. Assn., Am. Coll. Sports Medicine, Am. Coll. Occupational and Evnironmental Medicine, AAAS, N.Y. Acad. Scis., Am. Soc. Contemporary Medicine and Surgery, Festival Chamber Music Soc. (bd. dirs. Indpls. 1981-87), Nat. Fraternity Eagle Scouts, Mensa, Columbia Club, Skyline Club, Country Club, Kiwanis, Elks, Sigma Xi, Phi Sigma. Home: 30 Quail Creek Dr Lawton OK 73501-9026

WEBB, PAULINE MARY, broadcaster, writer; b. Wembley, Middlesex, U.K., June 28, 1927; d. Leonard Frederick and Daisy Winifred (Barnes) W. BA, King's Coll., London, 1948; diploma in tchg., Inst. Edn., London, 1949; STM, United Theol. Sem., 1966; ThD (hon.), Brussels U., 1985; LittD (hon.), Victoria U., Toronto, Ont., Can., 1986; LHD (hon.), Mt. St. Vincent U., Halifax, N.S., Can., 1987; DD (hon.), Birmingham U., U.K., 1997. Tchr. Thames Valley Grammar Sch., Twickenham, U.K., 1949-52; editor Meth. Missionary Soc., London, U.K., 1952-67; dir. lay tng. Meth. Ch., U.K., 1967-73, sec. Caribbean area overseas divsn., 1973-79; organizer religious broadcasting BBC World Svc., London, U.K., 1979-87; freelance broadcaster BBC, U.K., 1987-98; dir. First Conf. Estate, U.K., 1975—; bd. dirs. Ethical Investment Rsch. Svc., U.K.; adviser on ethical investment Credit Suisse, U.K., 1990—. Author: Salvation Today, 1974, Candles for Advent, 1989, She Flies Beyond, 1994; editor: Celebrating Friendship, 1989, A Long Struggle, 1994; co-editor Dictionary of the Ecumenical Movement, All Loves Excelling, 1997, Worship in Every Event, 1998. Vice moderator World Coun. Chs., Geneva, 1968-75; v.p. Meth. Conf., London, 1965-66; pres. Feed the Minds, 1998—. Fellow King's Coll., 1991. Mem. Christian Evidence Soc. (trustee 1989-99, v.p.), BBC Club. Mem. Labour Party. Home: 14 Paddocks Green, 99 Salmon St, London NW9 8NH, England

WEBB, ROBERT MILES, civil engineer; b. St. Brelades, U.K., Aug. 8, 1940; s. Arthur and Minnie (Stray) W.; m. Thérèse Alexandra Ord, Feb. 7, 1970 (dec. Nov. 1996); children: Louise Mary, Angela Lucy, James Arthur, Elizabeth Jane(dec. Sept. 1999), Rosemary Sarah. Diploma in civil engring., Brighton Tech. Coll., U.K., 1963; M in Engring., U. Liverpool, 1971. Asst. resident engr. Lewis & Duvivier, Chichester, U.K., 1963-64; asst. engr., engring. mgr. Sir William Halcrow & Ptnrs., Dubai, Philippines and, London, 1964-74; sr. engr. Livesy & Henderson, U.K. and Peru, 1974; engr.,

mgr. ocean engring. British Petroleum, London and Worldwide, 1974-88; mng. dir. Robin Webb Cons. Ltd., Colchester, U.K., 1989-94, 96—; assoc. dir. Billington Osborne Moss Engring. Ltd., U.K. and Malaysia, 1994-95; chmn. SUT Group on Environ. Forces, London, 1993-94, UKOOA Structural Working Group, London, 1975-78, UKOOA North West Approaches Group, London, 1985-88; mem. SUT Publs. Com., London, 1990-97. Translator/editor: Practical Guide: Environmental Loading on Offshore Platforms, 1996; contbr. articles to profl. jours. Neighborhood engr. Engring. Coun., Colchester, U.K., 1992-94. Indsl. fellowship SRC Halcrows, 1971; grantee Royal Acad. Engring., 1992, 93. Mem. ASCE, Soc. for Underwater Tech. (chmn. 1993), Instn. of Civil Engrs., Internat. Soc. for Offshore and Polar Engring. (session chmn. 1991-94). Achievements include patent for carbon fibre composite tethers; developed early computer model of litural drift. Home: 121 Maldon Rd, Colchester CO3 3AX, England Office: RWCL 3 West Stockwell St, Colchester, Essex CO11HQ, England

WEBB, STEVE, physicist, educator; b. Swindon, Wiltshire, United Kingdom, Nov. 26, 1948; s. Arthur Stanley and Adelaide Brenda (Revell) W.; m. Linda Margaret Badham, July 29, 1972; children: Thomas Llewelyn, David Samuel. BSc, U. London, 1970, PhD, 1973; DSc, Inst. Cancer Rsch., 1994. Lectr. Imperial Coll., U. London, 1973-74; lectr. Inst. Cancer Rsch., 1974-89, sr. lectr., 1989-93, reader, 1993-96, prof., 1996—; coun. mem. Inst. Cancer Rsch., 1996-99. Editor: The Physics of Medical Imaging, 1988; author: From the Watching of Shadows-The Origins of Radiological Tomography, 1990, The Physics of Three Dimensional Radiation Therapy, 1993, The Physics of Conformal Radiotherapy, 1997; contbr. articles to profl. jours. Fellow Inst. Physics, Inst. Physics and Engring. Medicine, Royal Soc. Arts. Avocations: Renaissance stringed instrument making, Italian language, railway history and models. Office: Inst Cancer Rsch, Joint Dept Physics Downs Rd, Sutton Surrey SM2 5PT, United Kingdom

WEBB, THOMAS IRWIN, JR., lawyer; b. Toledo, Sept. 16, 1948; s. Thomas Irwin and Marcia Davis (Winters) W.; m. Polly S. DeWitt, Oct. 11, 1986; 1 child, Elisabeth Hurst. BA, Williams Coll., 1970; postgrad., Boston U., 1970-71; JD, Case Western Res. U., 1973. Bar: Ohio. Assoc. Shumaker, Loop & Kendrick, Toledo, 1973-79, ptnr., 1979—, chmn. corp. law dept., 1992-94, mgmt. com., 1994-99; dir. Calphalon Corp., 1990-98, Yark Oldsmobile, Inc. Coun. mem. Village of Ottawa Hills, Ohio, 1979-85, Ohio divsn. Securities, 1979-85, commr. of taxation, 1999—; trustee Kiwanis Youth Found. of Toledo, 1982—; dir. Toledo Area Regional Transit Authority, 1989-91; trustee Arts Commn. Greater Toledo, 1993—, exec. com., 1994-99, v.p., 1994-96, pres., 1996-97; trustee Jr. Achievement of Northwestern Ohio, Inc., 1992—, Lourdes Coll. Found., 1995—, Toledo Orch. Assn., 1999—. Mem. ABA, Ohio Bar Assn. (corp. law com. 1989—), Toledo Bar Assn., Northwestern Ohio Alumni Assn. of Williams Coll. (pres. 1974-83), Toledo-Rowing Found. (trustee 1985—), Toledo Area C. of C. (trustee 1991-98, exec. com. 1993-98, fin. com. 1993—), Order of Coif, Crystal Downs Country Club, Toledo Country Club, The Toledo Club (trustee 1984-90, pres. 1987-90), Williams Club N.Y., Crystal Lake Yacht Club. Republican. Episcopalian. Office: Shumaker Loop & Kendrick 1000 Jackson St Toledo OH 43624-1573

WEBB, VERONICA, fashion model, journalist; b. Detroit, Feb. 25, 1965; d. Leonard Douglas and Marion (Stewart) W. Student, New Sch. Social Rsch., 1983; signed with, Ford Models, Inc., N.Y.C., 1992—. Contbg. editor, columnist Paper Mag., 1989—; contbg. editor features column Interview Mag., 1990—; spokesmodel Revlon, 1992-96. First featured on cover of Vogue, 1988; appearances incluce (films) Jungle Fever, 1991, Malcolm X, 1992, For Love or Money, 1993, Catwalk, 1995, 54, 1998, Holy Man, 1998, In Too Deep, 1999, The Big Tease, 1999. First African-Am. to receive exclusive cosmetics contract. Mem. Lifebeat (bd. dirs. 1994—). Office: United Talent Agy 9560 Wilshire Blvd Ste 500 Beverly Hills CA 90212*

WEBBER, PEGGY, actress, producer, director, writer; b. Laredo, Tex., Sept. 15, 1925; d. Mathew Edward and Margaret Ann (Pierce) Weber; m. Robert Sinskey, Aug. 8, 1951 (div. 1968); children: Teresa Dickinson, Patricia Wynn, Robert Marshall Jr.; m. Sean McClory, Mar. 17, 1983. Student, U. So. Calif., L.A., 1942-44; AA, CUESTA, 1973; student, Calif. Poly. U. Founder Calif. Artists Repertory and Radio Theatre, 1972—. Actress, writer, dir., prodr.: (TV drama series) Treasures of Literature (Outstanding Prodn. award Acad. TV Arts and Scis., 1948-49); writer, dir., prodr. Calif. Artists Radio Theatre Series, NPR series Mysteries in the Air; actress over 8,000 network radio broadcasts, and 300 nat. TV telecasts; actress: (films) Orson Welles' Macbeth, Hitchcock's The Wrong Man, Farrow's Submarine Command, others; exec. dir. 7 theatres; prodr., writer, dir. over 90 drama, lit., music prodns. for nat. pub. radio. Recipient Ray Bradbury Creativity award Woodbury U., L.A., 1998, Double Gold award Corp. for Pub. Broadcasting, 1992, 26 nat. and internat. awards. Mem. AFTRA, SAG, Actors Equity Assn., Pacific Pioneer Broadcasters (bd. dirs.). Avocations: walking, history, genealogy, archaeology. Office: Calif Artists Repertory and Radio Theatre 6612 Whitley Ter Los Angeles CA 90068-3221

WEBB-JENKINS, JOHN ESMOND, manufacturing executive; b. West Wickham, Kent, Eng., May 20, 1939; s. David John and Winnifred Rose (Webb) Jenkins; m. Clare Florence Cockshutt, Aug. 15, 1964; children: Timothy, Christian, Matthew, Lucy. BSc in Chemistry with honors, Bristol (Eng.) U., 1960. Shift chemist Distillers Co., Barry, 1960-61; comml. asst. ICI Plastics, Welwyn Garden City, 1961-65; tech. mgr. Stanley Smith, Isleworth, 1965-72; dir. mktg. Nestpack (Solvay G.P.), Watford, 1972-78; mng. dir. Stanley Smith, Isleworth, 1978-95; bus. devel. dir. Barlo plc, Isleworth, 1995-96; export sales dir. Stanley Smith, 1996-97; mng. dir. Kirkstone Plastics Ltd., Weybridge, Eng., 1997-98; CEO The Inst. Packaging, 1998—; chmn. Assn. Calendered UPVC Suppliers, London, 1985-98, Pkg. and Indsl. Films Assn., Nottingham, 1996-98, dir., 1992-2000; spkr. in field. Patentee in field. Chmn. Addlestone Playgroup, 1966-70. 2nd lt. Royal Signals Corp., 1962-65. Named Freeman of the City of London, Liveryman of the Worshipful Company of Light Mongers. Conservative. Roman Catholic. Avocations: golf, bridge, jazz. E-mail: info@iop.co.uk. Home: 8 High Pine Close, Weybridge Surrey KT13 9EA, England Office: Inst Packaging Sysonby Ldg, Nottingham Rd, Leicshr Melton Mowbray LE13 0NU, England

WEBER, ADOLF OTTO ALBERT, retired agricultural economics educator; b. Bucha, Saxony, Germany, July 17, 1922; s. Alfred and Gertrud (Hille) W.; m. Gisela Steiling, Oct. 28, 1949; children: Reglindis, Ruthild. Diploma in agr., U. Göttingen, Fed. Republic Germany, 1957, DSc in Agr., 1960. Farm adminstr. Saxony, 1937-41, 45-53; rsch. asst. U. Göttingen, 1953-65, lectr., 1965-68; prof. agrl. econs. U. Kiel (Fed. Republic Germany), 1968—, now prof. emeritus, 1989—; vis. prof. U. Minn., Mpls., 1970-71, 86; prof. U. Nairobi (Kenya), 1974-76, 80-82. Author: Meat Consumption in the E.E.C., 1961, Agricultural Advertising, 1965; co-editor Internat. Agr.; contbr. over 165 articles on world food problems to profl. jours. With German Air Force, 1941-45. Mem. Am. Agrl. Econs. Assn., European Assn. Agrl. Economists, Internat. Assn. Agrl. Economists. Lutheran. Home: Koppenhagener Allee 4, D-24109 Kiel Germany Office: U Kiel, U Kiel, Olshausenstrasse 40, D-24118 Kiel Germany

WEBER, ARNOLD I., lawyer; b. Little Cedar, Iowa, Oct. 4, 1926; divorced; children: Katherine Weber Hickle, Thomas, Margaret Weber Robertson. PhB magna cum laude, Marquette U., 1949; MA, Harvard U., 1950; JD, George Washington U., 1954, LLM, 1956. Bar: D.C. 1954, Md. 1961, Calif. 1962, U.S. Dist Ct. D.C. 1954, (no. dist.) Calif. 1962, (cen. dist.) Calif. 1992, U.S. Ct. Claims 1960, U.S. Tax Ct. 1965, U.S. Ct. Appeals (D.C. cir.) 1954, (9th cir.) 1962, (fed. cir.) 1991, U.S. Supreme Ct. 1959. Lawyer Housing and Home Fin., Washington, 1954; pvt. practice Washington, 1954-55; lawyer Tariff Commn., Washington, 1954-55, FCC, Washington, 1955-56, IRS, Washington, 1956-61; assoc. Brobeck, Phleger & Harrison, San Francisco, 1961-64; sr. gen. atty. So. Pacific Transp., San Francisco, 1964-84; western tax counsel Santa Fe Pacific Corp., San Francisco, 1985-88; pvt. practice San Francisco, 1988—. With USNR, 1944-54, PTO. Mem. ABA, Olympic Club, Bar Assn. San Francisco, State Bar of Calif. Office: 57 Post St Ste 502 San Francisco CA 94104-5020

WEBER, ARNOLD ROBERT, academic administrator; b. N.Y.C., Sept. 20, 1929; s. Jack and Lena (Smith) W.; m. Edna M. Files, Feb. 7, 1954; children: David, Paul, Robert. B.A., U. Ill., 1951; M.A., MIT, 1958, Ph.D. in Econs., 1958. Instr., then asst. prof. econs. MIT, 1955-58; faculty U. Chgo. Grad. Sch. Bus., 1958-69, prof. indsl. relations, 1963-69; asst. sec. for manpower Dept. Labor, 1969-70; exec. dir. Cost of Living Council; also spl. asst. to Pres. Nixon, 1971; Gladys C. and Isidore Brown prof. urban and labor econs. U. Chgo., 1971-73; former provost Carnegie-Mellon U.; dean Carnegie-Mellon U. (Grad. Sch. Indsl. Adminstrn.), prof. labor econs. and pub. policy, 1973-80; pres. U. Colo., Boulder, 1980-85; pres. Northwestern U., Evanston, Ill., 1985-95, chancellor, 1995-98, pres. emeritus, 1998—; bd. dirs. Diamond Tech. Ptnrs.; cons. union, mgmt. and govt. agys., 1960—, Dept. Labor, 1965; mem. Pres.'s Adv. Com. Labor Mgmt. Policy, 1964, Orgn. Econ. Coop. and Devel., 1987; vice chmn. Sec. Labor Task Force Improving Employment Svcs., 1965; chmn. rsch. adv. com. U.S. Employment Svc., 1966; assoc. dir. OMB, Exec. Office of Pres., 1970-71; chmn. Presdl. R.R. Emergency Bd., 1982; trustee Com. for Econ. Devel.; bd. dirs. Aon Corp., Burlington No./Santa Fe, Inc., Tribune Corp., Deere & Co.; asst. sec. manpower U.S. Dept. Labor, 1969-70. Contbr. articles to profl. jours. Trustee com. econ. devel., U. Notre Dame; trustee Aspen Inst. Lt. (j.g.) USCGR, 1952-54. Laureate, Lincoln Acad. Ill.; Ford Found. Faculty Rsch. fellow, 1964-65. Mem. Am. Acad. Arts and Scis., Indsl. Rels. Rsch. Assn., Nat. Acad. Pub. Adminstrn., Comml. Club Chgo. (pres., civic com.), Econ. Club Chgo. (pres. 1995-97), Phi Beta Kappa. Jewish. Office: Northwestern U Office of Pres Emeritus 555 Clark St 209 Evanston IL 60208-0805

WEBER, CHRISTIAN KARL GEORG, software development executive; b. Hamburg, Germany, Sept. 22, 1950; s. Dieter and Hanna (Dziekan) W.; m. Barbara Pietschke, Oct. 29, 1977; children: Johannes, Anke, Andreas. BS, U. Liverpool, Eng., 1973; diplome, U. Stuttgart, Germany, 1975, PhD, 1977. Programmer Computer Gesellschaft Konstanz, Germany, 1977-80, group head, 1980-85; head main group Siemens AG (now Fujitsu Siemens), München, Germany, 1985-95, dept. sys. strategy and arch., 1995—; standardization ECMA, Geneva, 1979-81, Internt. Standards Orgn., 1985-93. Author articles on math. and computer sci. Mem. Assn. for Computing Machinery, Gesellschaft für Informatik. Roman Catholic. Avocations: skiing, hiking, chess, science fiction. Home: Lindacherstr 3a, Poing Bayern 85586, Germany Office: Fujitsu Siemens, Otto-Hahn-Ring 6, München 81739, Germany

WEBER, CORNELIA SOFIE, clinical pharmacologist; b. Furth im Wald, Germany, Jan. 10, 1960; arrived in Switzerland, 1989; d. Helmut and Martha (Kolbeck) W. MSc, U. Regensburg, Germany, 1983, PhD, 1987. Rsch. asst. U. Regensburg, 1984-87; rsch. assoc. SUNY, Buffalo, 1988; clin. pharmacokineticist Hoffmann-La Roche Ltd., Basel, Switzerland, 1989-93; sr. clin. rsch. scientist Hofflann-LaRoche, Basel, Switzerland, 1993-96, clin. pharmacologist, 1996—. Contbr. articles to sci. publs. Mem. Cath. Youth Cmty., Furth im Wald, 1974-76. Mem. Am. Assn. Pharmacol. Sci., Drug Info. Assn. Avocations: gardening, photography, travel, squash, reading. Office: Hoffmann-LaRoche, Grenzacherstr, CH-4070 Basel Switzerland

WEBER, DAVID ALEXANDER, medical physicist; b. Lockport, N.Y., Mar. 6, 1939; s. Fred Leonard John and C. Gladys (Woodcock) W.; m. Sandra Jean Watson, Aug. 26, 1961; children: Sarah D. Beisheim, David A. Jr. BS, St. Lawrence U., 1956; PhD, U. Rochester, 1971. Rsch. asst. Sloan Kettering Cancer Inst., N.Y.C., 1961-68; fellow, asst., assoc. prof. U. Rochester, N.Y., 1970-87; sr. scientist, head nuclear medicine rsch. group Brookhaven Nat. Lab., Upton, N.Y., 1987-94; prof. radiology SUNY, Stony Brook, 1988-94; prof. radiology, vice chair rsch. radiology U. Calif. Davis, Sacramento, 1994-2000; dep. chief officer Office of Rsch. Compliance and Assurance Veterans Adminstrn., Washington, 2000—; mem. Nat. Coun. on Radiation Protection and Measurements, 1993—. Contbr. articles to profl. jours. Fellow Sr. Fogarty, 1978-79. Fellow Am. Coll. Nuclear Physicians; mem. Am. Assn. Physicists in Medicine (assoc. editor 1979-82, 88-97), Health Physics Soc. (chpt. pres. 1973-75), Soc. Nuclear Medicine (pres. computer coun. 1977-78, pres. instrumentation coun. 1986-87, chmn. Med. Internal Radiation Dose com. 1988-94), European Assn. of Nuclear Medicine, Assn. of Univ. Radiologists, Sigma Xi. Office: ORCA Dept Veteran Affairs 811 Vermont Ave NW Washington DC 20006

WEBER, ÉDITH, music educator, critic, researcher; b. Strasbourg, France, Oct. 31, 1925; d. Jean and Marthe (Antoni) W. BA in English and Musicology, Strasbourg U., D in Humane Letters, 1971. Asst. U. of Paris, The Sorbonne, 1958-62, maître asst., 1962-70, maître de confs., 1971, prof. sans chaire, 1972, prof. titulaire, 1972-94, prof. emeritus, 1994—; prof. music and English, Coll. Lucie Berger, Strasbourg, 1952-58; dir. Inst. of Musicology, founder, dir. Doctorate Sch., 1994; invited prof. Inst. Gregoriano, Lisboa, Portugal, Inst. Catholique, Paris, U. Inter-Ages, Paris; mem. com. Nat. Ctr. for Sci. Rsch.; cons. com. to univs. Author: La Musique Mesurées A l'Antique en Allemagne, 1974, Le Théâtre humaniste et scolaire dans Les Pays Rhénans, 1979, La musique protestante de langue Française, 1979, La musique protestante en langue allemande, 1980, La recherche musicologique, 1980, Le Concile de Trente et la musique, 1982, Histoire de la Musique Française 1500-1650, 1996; contbr. articles to scholarly and profl. jours. Named to Officier des Palmes Académiques; recipient prix de thése, Adrerus, 1972, prix Pays Protestants, Paris. Mem. Soc. of French Protestant History (com.), French Soc. Musicology, Internat. Soc. Musicology, Internat. Arbeitsgemeinschaft für Liturgik und Hymnologie (corr.), Hymn Soc. U.S. and Can., Internat. Heinrich Schültz Gesellschaft (founder French sect.), Soc. for Study of 16th Century. Avocations: music, hymnology, history, theology. Home: 10-16 rue Thibaud, F-75014 Paris France Office: U Paris IV Sorbonne, 1 rue Victor Cousin, F75230 Paris, Cedex 05 France

WEBER, EDWIN HANS-GEORG, organic chemistry educator; b. Mönchröden, Bavaria, Germany, Aug. 2, 1946; s. Arno and Grete (Rebhan) W. Diploma in chemistry, Jul.-Max. U., Würzburg, Germany, 1973, D Natural Scis., 1976; venia legendi in Organic Chemistry, Friedrich Wilhelm U., Bonn, Germany, 1984. Sci. asst. Friedrich Wilhelm U., 1976-80, 81-84, lectr., 1985-86, prof. organic chemistry, 1986-92; NATO grantee U. Wis., Madison, 1980-81; prof. Christian Albr. U., Kiel, Germany, 1991-92, Tech. U. Bergakademie, Freiberg, Sachsen, Germany, 1993—. Editor 13 books on current chemistry, 1984-98; contbr. over 200 articles to sci. jours.; patentee on complexants and bleaching activators. Home: Johann Sebastian Bach Str 1, D-09599 Freiberg Germany Office: Tech U Bergakademie, Leipziger Str 29, D-09596 Freiberg Germany

WEBER, EICKE RICHARD, physicist; b. Muennerstadt, Germany, Oct. 28, 1949; s. Martin and Irene (Kistner) W.; m. Monika Rähse, Aug. 28, 1999. BS, U. Cologne, Fed. Republic of Germany, 1970, MS, 1973, PhD, 1976, Dr.Habil., 1983. Sci. asst. U. Koeln, 1976-82; rsch. asst. U. Lund, Sweden, 1982-83; asst. prof. Dept. Material Sci. U. Calif., Berkeley, 1983-87, assoc. prof., 1987-91, prof. materials sci., 1991—; prin. investigator Lawrence Berkeley Lab., 1984—; vis. prof. Tohoku U., Sendai, Japan, 1990, Kyoto (Japan) U., 2000; cons. in field; internat. fellow Inst. for Study of Defects in Solids, SUNY, Albany, 1978-79; chmn. numerous confs.; mem. founding com. CAESAR Found., Bonn, 1995-97, mem. scientific coun. 1999—; lectr. in field. Editor: Defect Recognition and Image Processing in III-V Compounds, 1987, Imperfections in III-V Compounds, 1993; co-editor: Chemistry and Defects in Semiconductor Structures, 1989, others; series co-editor: Semiconductors and Semimetals, 1991—; contbr. over 380 articles to profl. jours. V.p. Alexander von Humboldt Assn. Am., 1999—. Recipient IBM Faculty award, 1984, Humboldt U.S. Sr. Scientist award, 1994; rsch. grantee Dept. of Energy, 1984—, Office Naval Rsch., 1985—, Air Force Office Sci. Rsch., 1988—, NASA, 1988-90, Nat. Renewable Energy Lab., 1992—. Mem. IEEE (sr.), Am. Phys. Soc., Materials Rsch. Soc. Achievements include first identification of point defects formed by dislocation motion in silicon; determination of the energy levels of antisite defects in GaAs, of 3d transition metal solubility and lattice site in silicon, of mechanism of internal gettering in silicon; research in defects formed in III/V thin films and interfaces; on lattice mismatched heteroepitaxial growth; in structure and electronic properties of metal GaAs heterostructures; in nature and electronic properties of defects in GaAs, GaN, and related compounds; in MBE growth of GaN and related compounds; in low-temperature MBE growth of As-rich GaAs; in transition metal gettering in silicon; polysilicon for photovoltaic applications; scanning tunneling microscopy of semiconductor thin films and interfaces; on electron paramagnetic resonance of defects in semiconductors. E-mail: weber@socrates.berkeley.edu. Office: U Calif Dept Materials Sci 475 Evans Hall Berkeley CA 94720-1767

WEBER, GEORG, sociologist, educator; b. Zendersch, Romania, Oct. 22, 1931; arrived in Germany, 1944; s. Georg and Sara (Bürger) W.; m. Renate Schlenther, Apr. 6, 1962; children: Cornelius, Markus, Ricarda. MTh, Wittenberg U., Springfield, Ohio, 1958; DrTheol, U. Münster, Germany, 1965, Habil in Sociology and Paedagogics, 1971; DrPhil honoris causa, U. Cluj, Romania, 1992. Ordained to ministry Lutheran Ch. Tchr. high sch., Münster, 1963-64, 68-69; rschr. U. Dortmund, Germany, 1961-62, Comenius Inst., Münster, 1965-68; asst. prof. Tchrs. Coll., Münster, 1970-72, assoc. prof., 1972-73; univ. prof., dir. inst. U. Münster, 1973—; cons. U. Cluj, 1976—; cons. Inst. de Cercetări Socio-Umane, Sibiu, Romania, 1990—; bd. dirs. AKSL, Heidelberg, Germany, 1980—. Author: Beharrung und Einfügung, 1968, Anspruch und Wirklichkeit, 1972; co-author: Altersbilder in der professionellen Altenpflege, 1997, Die Deportation von Siebenbürger Sachsen in die Sowjetunion 1945-1949, 3d vol., 1995, Soziale Hilfe-ein Teilsystem der Gesellschaft?, 1999; editor: Zugänge zur Gemeinde, Soziologische, historische und sprachwissenschaftliche Beiträge, 2000; co-author, editor other books; editor Archiv für Siebenbürgische Landeskunde, Studia Transilvanica, Schriften zur Siebenbürgischen Landeskunde, Studien zur interdisziplinären Thanatologie; co-editor other jours. Bd. dirs. Com. for Refugees, München, 1958-78. Mem. Deutsche Gesellschaft für Soziologie, Deutsche Gesellschaft für Erziehungswissenschaften. Avocations: history, literature, sports.

WEBER, GEORGE, former international social welfare administrator; b. Montreal, Que., Can., Apr. 18, 1946; s. Harry and Johanna (Alexopoulos) W.; m. Mary Ellen Morris, May 8, 1976. BEd, McGill U., 1970, MA, 1974; postgrad., Harvard U., 1989. Vol. instr., examiner, mem. staff Canadian Red Cross, 1963-73; field del. with Indochina operational group Canadian Red Cross, Vietnam, 1973-74; nat. dir. internat. affairs Canadian Red Cross, 1976-81, nat. dir. programs, 1981-83, sec. gen., CEO, 1983-93, hon. v.p., 1993—; field del. with Indochina Operational Group Internat. Red Cross, Vietnam, 1973-74; chief del., disaster relief officer League of Red Cross Socs., Geneva, 1974-76; founder, chmn., CEO Nat. Charity Coun., 1990-92; sec. gen., CEO Internat. Fedn. Red Cross and Red Crescent Socs., Geneva, 1993-2000. Contbr. articles to sci. jours. Bd. dirs. Nat. Capital Harvard Bus. Sch. Alumni Club, Amundsen Found. Recipient Vanier award, 1984, Internat. Comm. and Leadership award Toastmasters, 1985, Friendship medal Turkish Red Crescent Soc., 1988, Exceptional Humanitarian Svc. award Portuguese Red Cross, 1989, hon. medal of merit Venezuelan Red Cross Soc., 1991. Mem. Am. Coll. Sports Medicine, Canadian Inst. Internat. Affairs, Canadian Soc. Assn. Execs. (mem. bd. dirs.), Canadian Comprehensive Auditing Found., Nat. Health Agy's. CEO Orgn., Canadian Cross Soc. (hon. v.p.), Internat. Devel. Execs. Assn. (founder), Rideau Club, Harvard Club, Five Lakes Club. Avocations: diving, tennis, squash, skiing. Office: PO Box 372, CH-1211 Geneva 19, Switzerland*

WEBER, HARALD WOLFGANG, educator; b. Vienna, Austria, Oct. 25, 1944; s. Herbert F.J. Weber and Editha Wlaschutz; m. Felicity Ann Wallis, Feb. 14, 1986; children: Cornelia, Christoph, Alexander. PhD, U. Vienna, 1969; U. Docent, Tech. U. Vienna, 1975; D (hon.), Latvian U., Riga, Latvia, 1993. Univ. asst. Tech. U., Vienna, 1968-81, prof., 1981—. Author: Supraleitung, 1979; editor four books; contbr. articles to profl. jours. Mem. Am. Phys. Soc., AAAS, Austrian Phys. Soc., Rotary. Avocations: skiing, swimming, reading, classical music. Home: Hauptstrasse 76/2, Giesshubl A-2372, Austria Office: Atominstitut, Stadionallee 2, Wien A-1020, Austria

WEBER, HORST HANS EDWARD, musicologist, educator; b. Koblenz, Germany, Apr. 1, 1944; s. Max and Else (Koster) W.; m. Rita Oelsner, May 15, 1976. PhD, U. Vienna, Austria, 1968; Habilitation, Tech. U., Berlin, 1992. Asst. prof. U. Goettingen, Germany, 1970-72; fellow Bonn, Germany, 1972-74; asst. prof. U. Bonn, 1975-78; prof. Folkwang Hochschule, Essen, Germany, 1978—; dir. rsch. project Mus. Migration of Musicians to U.S., Bonn, 1994—. Author: Studies in Mozart's Musical Theatre, 1968, Alexander Zemlinsky, 1977; editor Metzler-Komponistenlexikon, 1992, Musik in der Emigration, 1994, Alexander Zemlinsky: Correspondence with Arnold Schoenberg, 1995. Office: Folkwang Hochschule, Klemensborn 39, 45239 Essen Germany

WEBER, JEAN JACQUES, English educator; b. Luxembourg, Aug. 31, 1952; s. Georges Weber and Yvette Morheng; divorced; children: Anne, Stephanie, Thomas. BA, Lancaster (Eng.) U., 1975; PhD, Louvain (Belgium) U., 1991. Cert. tchr., Luxembourg. Tchr. English Ministry Nat. Edn., Luxembourg, 1975-88; lectr. in English U. Ctr., Luxembourg, 1988-93, prof. English, 1993—; co-dir. Linguistics Rsch. Ctr., U. Ctr. Luxembourg, 1992—. Author: Critical Analysis of Fiction, 1992; co-author: The Literature Workbook, 1998; editor: The Stylistics Reader, 1996; co-editor: Twentieth-Century Fiction, 1995. recipient Fgn. and Commonwealth Office scholarship U. London, 1989. Mem. European Soc. Study of English (bd. mem. 1991-96), Poetics and Linguistics Assn. (bibliography compiler 1987-91), Belgian Luxembourg Am. Studies Assn. (v.p. 1999—), Assn. English Tchrs. in Higher Edn. Luxembourg (pres. 1993-96). Home: 4 Av Guillaume, L-1650 Luxembourg Luxembourg Office: Univ Ctr Luxembourg, 162A Av de la Faiencerie, L-1511 Luxembourg Luxembourg

WEBER, JEFFREY RANDOLPH, record producer; b. L.A., Feb. 3, 1952; s. Jerome and Doris (Robbin) W.; m. Denise Esola, Mar. 31, 1979 (div.); children: Jason Ryan, Jayme Nicole, Jordan Caitlin. BA, UCLA, 1973; JD, Southwestern Law Sch., 1976. Pres. Weberworks Inc., Beverly Hills, Calif., 1979—; specialist in high tech. rec. (digital, live 2 track); voice-over talent for comml., animation and films. Producer over 130 albums (6 Grammy nominations, 2 Grammy awards). Mem. NARAS (bd. govs. 1986-98, v.p. 1990-91, 95-96, trustee 1991-95). Avocations: films, collecting signed first edition mysteries, rare and exotic wood. Office: Weberworks PO Box 1451 Beverly Hills CA 90213-1451

WEBER, JOHN BERTRAM, architect; b. Evanston, Ill., Oct. 15, 1930; s. Bertram Anton and Dorothea W.; m. Sally Ann French; children: Suzanne French Roulston, Jane Marie McCarthy, Patricia Ann Blodgett, Nancy B. AB in Architecture, Princeton U., 1953; postgrad., Ill. Inst. Tech., 1959. Lic. arch.; registered interior designer. Field engr. United Constrn. Co., Riverdale, N.D., 1952; draftsman Bertram A. Weber Arch., Chgo., 1947, 53, architect, 1958-1973; field engr. Atkinson United Constrn. Co., Greenup and Ashland, Ky., 1956-58; ptnr., proprietor Weber & Weber Arch., Winnetka, Ill., 1973—; Mem. Ill. Architecture Act Revision task force, 1982-89. Prin. works include Prestwick Country Club, the 3175 Commercial Ave. Bldg., Northbrook, med. office bldg. and additions to Bi-county hospital, Warren, Mich., additions and alterations to Detroit Osteopathic Hosp., addition to Duraclean Internat. Bldg., Deerfield, additions to The Admiral (a retirement home in Chgo.), Villa Stresov, Borovets, Bulgaria, and numerous pvt. residences, churches, comml., ednl., and recreational bldgs. Active Winnetka Cmty. Caucus, 1965, 74; mem. Mayor's adv. com. on bldg. codes, Chgo., 1975-80; chmn. bldg. com. Winnetka Cmty. House, 1977-81; mem. Winnetka Zoning Bd. Appeals, 1983-88, chmn., 1987-88; mem. Winnetka Ad Hoc Zoning Com., 1995-96; deacon, elder Winnetka Presbyn. Ch. With USN, 1953-56. Fellow Ill. Soc. Arch. (bd. dirs. 1969-84, 91-99, pres. 1976-78), Assn. Lic. Arch.; mem. AIA (health com. 1969-76), Ill. Arch.-Engr. Coun. (chmn. 1981-82, del. 1976-87, 92-99), Northbrook C. of C., Architects Club Chgo. (pres. 1981, bd. dirs. 1976-86, 94), Assn. Energy Engrs., Constrn. Specifications Inst., Builders Club Chgo. (bd. dirs. 1966—, pres. 1973-74), Am. Legion, Old Willow Club (pres. 1983), Dairymen's Country Club. Office: Weber & Weber Architects 415 Berkeley Ave Winnetka IL 60093-2109

WEBER, JUERGEN, airline executive; b. Lahr, Germany, Oct. 17, 1941. Degree in aerospace engring., U. Stuttgart, Germany, 1965; postgrad., MIT, 1980. With engring. divsn. Lufthansa, Hamburg, Germany, 1967-74; sr. dept. head maintenance at home and abroad Lufthansa, Frankfurt, Germany, 1974-78; head main dept. flight equipment Lufthansa, Hamburg, 1978-87; fully-authorized gen. mgr. for tech. Lufthansa, 1987-89, dir. tech., dep. bd. dirs., 1989-90, dep. chmn., 1990; chmn. bd. Deutsche Lufthansa AG, Cologne, 1991—; now chmn. exec. bd. Deutsche Lufthansa AG; bd. dirs. Hapag-Lloyd AG. Office: Deutsche Lufthansa AG, Von-Gablenz Strasse 2-6, 50679 Cologne 21, Germany*

WÉBER, KATI, computing company executive; b. Ujpest, Hungary, Sept. 14, 1948; d. Mâtyás and Kati (Wirth) W. Dipl. Libr., Libr. Sch., Budapest, Hungary, 1972; BA, HoShiMinh Coll., Budapest, Hungary, 1979; MA, Kossuth U., Debrecen, Hungary, 1993. Libr., organizer arch. Rsch. Inst. for Econs., Budapest, 1972-73; sys. organizer Nat. Tech. Info. Ctr., Budapest, 1973-80; libr. Med. Rehab. Inst., Budapest, 1980-81; head libr. Indls. Rsch. Inst. of Acad., Budapest, 1981-86; advisor Szåmalk, Budapest, 1986-87; head of dept. Hungarian Telecom. Ltd., Budapest, 1987-98; chief cons. ICON Ltd., 1999—. Author: Thesaurus of Foreign Trade Terms, 1976; co-author: Thesaurus of Information Terms, 1972; contbr. articles to profl. jours. Mem. Hungarian Union of Database Suppliers, Infoclub. Avocations: classical music, skiing, weaving. Home: Zsigard u 13, H-1141 Budapest Hungary

WEBER, MICHAEL, computer science educator; b. Ramstein, Germany, Nov. 27, 1959; s. Albert and Elisabeth (Bachtler) W.; m. Karin Schmidt, Aug. 14, 1992; children: Daphne, Felicitas. PhD in Computer Sci., U. Kaiserslautern, Germany, 1990. Rsch. asst. U. Kaiserslautern, 1985-90; R & D engr. Litef, Freiburg, Germany, 1991-92; rschr. German Rsch. Ctr. for AI, Saarbrücken, Germany, 1992-94; prof. distributed systems U. Ulm, Germany, 1994-2000, prof. multimedia computing, 2000—. Mem. IEEE, Assn. Computing Machinery, Gesellschaft für Informatik.

WEBER, NICO, linguist, researcher, educator; b. Pétange, Luxembourg, May 28, 1957; arrived in Germany, 1977; s. Joseph Weber and Suzanne-Valentine Esch; m. Astrid Steiner. MA, U. Bonn, Germany, 1982, PhD, 1988, habilitation, 1997. Rsch. asst. U. Bonn, Inst. Comms., Rsch. and Phonetics, Germany, 1982-84; systems analyst Startext GmbH, Bonn, 1985-91; rsch. fellow U. Bonn Inst. Comm. Rsch. and Phonetics, 1991-95; prof. U. Applied Sci., Cologne, Germany, 1995—; rsch. fellow Coll. France, Paris, 1991. Author: Maschinelle Lexikographie und Wortbidungsstrukturen, 1990, Die Semantik von Bedeutungsexplikationen, 1999; editor Semantik, Lexikographie und Computeranwendungen, 1996, Machine Translation: Theory, Applications, and Evaluation, 1998; sci. and tech. suppr. Lëtzebuergesch dictionary project, Order Min. Culture, Luxembourg, 1999—; contbr. articles to profl. jours. Rsch. fellow Coll. France, Paris, 1991. Mem. Assn. for Linguistische Datenverarbeitung, Assn. pour le Traitement Automatique des Langues, Inst. Grand-Ducal Luxembourg (corr., linguistic sect.), Conseil Permanent de la Langue Luxembourgeoise. E-mail: nico.weber@fh-koeln.de. Office: Univ Applied Sci, Mainzer Strasse 5, 50678 Cologne Germany

WEBER, NORMAN JOSEPH, Seychelles government official, banker; b. Colombo, Sri Lanka, June 16, 1956; arrived in Seychelles, 1960; s. Francis Archibald and Sophia Nossta (Samsoodin) W.; m. Nadia Marise Delpech, June 14, 1981 (div. June 1991); 1 child, Martin Sean; m. Josette Priscilla Larue, Apr. 1997; children: Alexander Mervyn, Liam Louis Joseph, Rachel Regina. MSc, London Sch. Econs., 1982. Acct. treasury div. Seychelles Ministry Fin., Victoria, 1980, acct. gen., 1981-83, fiscal specialist fin. planning div., 1983-85, dir. gen. policy div., 1986-89, prin. sec., 1989-98; sec. of state Vice Pres.'s Office, Victoria, 1998—; chmn. Seychelles Petroleum Co., 1995—, Air Seychelles Ltd., 1996—; gov. Ctrl. Bank Seychelles; chmn. Land Marine Ltd. Fellow Chartered Assn. Cert. Accts. Avocations: diving, fishing. Office: Central Bank Bldg, PO Box 313, Victoria Mahé, Seychelles Also: Ministry of Finance, Independence Ave, Victoria Mahé, Seychelles*

WEBER, PAMELA ANN, ophthalmologist; b. Buffalo, Mar. 30, 1958; d. Carl Freden Weber and Lois Jean Germann; m. Michael Scott Levine, June 18, 1989; children: Randall Carl Weber-Levine, Carly Michaela Weber-Levine. BS, McGill U., Montreal, Que., Can., 1980; MD, Columbia U., 1984. Lic. physician, N.Y. Attending physician Univ. Hosp., Stony Brook, N.Y., 1990—, VA Hosp., Northport, N.Y., 1995—, St. Charles Hosp., Pt. Jefferson, N.Y., 1997—, John T. Mather Hosp., Pt. Jefferson, 1997—; asst. prof. Stony Brook U., 1990—; prin. investigator NIH Grant STOP-ROP, Stony Brook, 1995—; cons. Collaborative Connections Inc., East Setauket, N.Y., 1999—. Reviewer: Ophthalmology, 1990—; contbr. articles to med. jours. Med. dir. Gift of Sight-Rotary, Stony Brook, 1994—. Recipient Award for Vocat. Svc., 1993-94, Vol. award Rotary Internat., 1995, Cert. of Appreciation, Winthrop Hosp., 1991. Mem. AMA, Am. Acad. Ophthalmology. Assn. for Rsch. in Vision and Ophthalmology, Vitrebus Soc., Schepen's Internat. Retina Soc., N.Y. State Ophthalmology. Presbyterian. Avocations: inline skating, hockey, power boating, skiing, ice-skating. Office: Ea L I Retina Assocs 1500 William Floyd Pkwy Shirley NY 11967-1800

WEBER, RABBE JOHAN, small business owner, consultant; b. Dragsfjärd, Finland, May 28, 1956; s. Sven-Erik Alexander and Inga Birgitta (Lönnberg) W. Student, kandidat i Humanistiska vetenshaper, U. Helsingfors, Finland, 1977; student, HUK, Sch. Econs., Finland, 1977. Chief editor student mag., Helsingfors, 1984; mng. dir. Oy Weber Ab, Helsingfors, 1985—. Editor: (book) Studenter 1985, 1985-86; (serial mag.) Womppu, 1987-88; chief editor (newspaper) Studentbladet, 1984. Avocations: travel, photography, music, art. Home: Tölögatian 34 A15, 00260 Helsingfors Finland

WEBER, RAINER KARL, otorhinolaryngologist; b. Fulda, Hessen, Germany, May 18, 1961; s. Aloys and Agnes Elisabeth (Gutberlet) W.; m. Barbara Sieglinde Epple, June 19, 1987; children: Tobias, Maria. MD, Giessen (Germany) U., 1987. Resident ENT dept. State Clinic, Fulda, 1988-92, asst. med. dir., 1993—; prof. Univ. Dept. of Otorhinolaryngology, Magdeburg, Germany, 1999—. Author, (book) Minimally Invasive Endonasal Sinus Surgery, 1999, (CD-Rom) Endonasal Sinus Surgery, Postoperative care, 1999, Co-author (CD-ROM) Die Endonasale Pansinusoperation, 1994, Die Interdisziplinäre Chirurgie der Tränenwege, 1997, 10 others; contbr. over 120 to profl. jours. and books. Recipient Poster award German Soc. Skull Base Surgery, 1997. Mem. German Soc. ENT Head and Neck Surgery, Profl. Assn. of ENT, Paul Ehrlich Soc., German Soc. Acupuncture. Office: Otto-von-Guericke U Dept ENT, Leipziger Str 44, 39120 Magdeburg Germany

WEBER, RALPH EDWARD, history educator; b. St. Cloud, Minn., Apr. 19, 1926; s. Andrew A. and Kathryn (Desmond) W.; m. Rosemarie Hoyt; children: Mary, Elizabeth, Ralph A., Anne, Catherine, Neil, Therese, Thomas, Andrew. AB, St. John's U., Collegeville, Minn., 1948; MS in Edn., U. Notre Dame, 1950, PhD, 1956. Instr. U. Notre Dame, South Bend, Ind., 1953-54; asst. to dean Marquette U., Milw., 1954-57, registrar, dir. admissions, 1958-61, assoc. prof. history, 1961-69, prof. history, 1969—, chmn. history dept., 1993-96, bd. dirs. Marquette U. Press, 1994—; scholar-in-residence CIA, Washington, 1987-88, Nat. Security Agy., Ft. Meade, Md., 1991-92; bd. visitors Les Aspin Ctr., Washington, 1994—. Author: Notre Dame's John Zahm, 1961, U.S. Diplomatic Codes and Ciphers, 1979 (Best Scholarly Intelligence Book award Nat. Intelligence Study Ctr. 1980), Masked Dispatches, 1993, Spymasters: Ten CIA Officers, 1999; co-author: Admission to College, 1963; editor: From the Foreign Press, 2 vols., 1980, The Final Memoranda, 1988; co-editor: Voices of Revolution, 1972. With USN, 1944-46. Grantee Am. Philos. Soc., 1974, rsch. grantee Bradley Ctr., Milw., 1995, 98. Mem. Soc. for Historians Am. Fgn. Rels. (membership chmn. 1976-94), Am. Cath. Historians Assn. (exec. coun. 1972-75), Assn. Former Intelligence Officers (bd. dirs. 1994—), Am. Legion. Avocations: fishing, skiing, hunting, forestry, farming. E-mail: weberr@csd.mu.edu. Office: Marquette U History Dept Milwaukee WI 53233

WEBER, RICHARD DEAN, primary care physician, researcher; b. Downey, Calif., Aug. 26, 1938; s. Leslie Ward and Ethel Lucille (Kalangvin) W.; m. Fratie Gevedia Jackson, Aug. 30, 1958; children: Debra Lynn Weber Reilly, Shelley Annette, Weber Krahn. D Naturapathic Medicine magna cum laude, Am. U. Natural Therapeutics, Mesa, Ariz., 1980; MD Homeopathic, Western U., Phoenix, 1982; PhD in Psychol. Counseling, Golden State U., L.A., 1984; D of Oriental Medicine and Acupuncture, Calif. Acupuncture Coll., San Diego, 1986. Diplomate in preventive medicine Fla. Inst. Tech. Engr. Kern County Fire Dept., 1966-71, capt., 1971-76; chief paramedic, CEO Flynn Ambulance Co., Bakersfield, Calif., 1974-76; primary care assoc. physician in medicine North Kern Hosp., Wasco, Calif., 1976-78; naturopathic physician, dir. rsch. Southwestern U.S. Rsch. Ctr., Monett, Mo., 1978-80; homeopathic physician Bakers Holistic Health Ctr., Lake Geneva, Fla., 1980-81, Hollywood (Fla.) Treatment Ctr., 1981-83; naturopathic physician, dir. rsch. Soouthwestern U.S. Rsch. Ctr., Prescott, Ariz., 1983-87; Oriental medicine physician, acupuncturist, dir. rsch. Bio-Systems and Pain Ctr., Escondido, Calif., 1987—; qualified med. evaluator, acupuncturist State of Calif. Workmen's Compensation, Sacramento, 1992—; rsch. physician Rsch. Ctr., Prescott, 1978-87; v.p. bd. dirs. Calif. Acupuncture Coll., San Diego, 1985-86. Author (paper) Silver Amalgam, 1981. Sec. Nevada Naturopathic Med. Assn., Las Vegas, 1982-95,. Grantee primary care assoc. Stanford U., 1978. Mem. Calif. Soc. Indsl. Medicine and Surgery, Calif. Soc. Oriental Medicine and Acupuncture, Am. Assn. Acupuncture and Oriental Medicine. Republican. Mormon. Avocations: golf, astronomy, amateur radio, computer technology. Office: Bio-Sys & Pain Ctr 301 E Washington Ave Ste B Escondido CA 92025-2855

WEBER, ROLF ROLAND, oceanography educator; b. Sao Paulo, Brazil, Apr. 12, 1948; s. Rudolf Weber and Irngarth Ida Laux; m. Eliane Oliveira Sagulla, Nov. 1977 (div. 1979); m. Maria Angela Falsi Violani, Mar. 1987; 1 child, Lourenco Afonso Violani Weber. BChem, U. Sao Paulo, 1972, MS Organic Chemistry, 1975, PhD Analytical Chemistry, 1981; Postgrad. Diploma Marine Pollution, U. Liverpool, 1978. FAPESP scholarship U. Sao Paulo, 1973-75, rsch. chemist Oceanographic Inst., 1976-80, asst. prof. Oceanographic Inst., 1981-88, assoc. prof., 1988-90; prof., 1990—; head phys. oceanography dept. U. Sao Paulo, 1992-93, dir. Oceanographic Inst., 1997—; fellow Brit. Coun., Liverpool, U.K., 1977-78; rsch. chemist Oxiteno S.Am., Sao Paulo, 1980-81; postdoctorate Inst. Marine Sci. Kiel Univ., Germany, 1988-89; vis. scientist Monaco Lab. IAEA/ILMR, Monte Carlo, 1989. Co-author: (book) Principles of Catalysis, 1981, Chemical Oceanography, 1994. 2nd lt. Artillery Army, 1967-68, Sao Paulo. Recipient medal First Brazilian Antartic Expedition, Brazilian Navy, Brazil, 1983; rsch. fellow Brasilian Nat. Res. Coun., 1989-99. Mem. Internat. Mussel Watch Commn.; Brazilian Nat. Commn. on Oceans, Brazilian Soc. for Advancement of Sci., Brazilian Chemistry Soc. Lutheran. Avocations: scuba diving, swimming, sailing. Office: Oceanograph Inst U Sao Paulo, Praca do Oceanografico 191, 05508900 Sao Paulo Brazil

WEBER, THOMAS WALDEMAR, neurologist, researcher; b. Bonn, Germany, Oct. 21, 1954; s. Albrecht and Angela (Jaeger) W.; m. Karin Fischer, Dec. 30, 1986; children: Rchard, Robert. MD, U. Tech., Munich, 1981; privatdozent Dr. Med. habilitation, U. Göttingen, 1994. Stabsarzt Schiffahrtsmed Inst. Kiel, Germany, 1980-81; assistenzarzt Inst. für Neuropathologie, Düsseldorf, Germany, 1981-83, Neurologische Klinik Univ., Göttingen, 1983-85, 88, Psychiatrische Klinik U. Göttingen, 1990-91; assistenzarzt Neurolosische Klinik U. Göttingen, 1991-92, oberarzt, 1992, head rsch. group on prion diseases, 1993-95; assistenzart Niedersächsisches Landeskrakenhaus-Abteilung Psychiatrie, Moringen, 1989; privatdozent MD habilitation Neurologische Klinik U. Göttingen, 1994-95; chief dept. neurology Marienkrankenhaus, Hamburg, Germany, 1995—; vis. scientist Dept. Neurology, U. Tex., Houston, 1986; rsch. assoc. Dept. Virology and Epidemiology, Baylor Coll. Medicine, Houston, 1987. Author: (with others) Clinical Haemotology, Epidemiology of Haematological Disease, 1992, Neurology in Clinical Practice, 1995; mem. editl. bd. Jour. of Neurovirology, 1995. Lt. German Navy, 1980-81. Mem. Deutsche Gesellschaft für Neurologie, European Group for Rapid Viral Diagnosis, Am. Acad. Neurology. Fax: 49 40 2546-2600. E-mail: 100634.276@compuserve.com. Home: Denksteinweg 43, D-22043 Hamburg Germany Office: Neurol Klinik Marienkrankenhaus Hamburg, Alfred Str 9, D-22087 Hamburg Germany

WEBER, WILFORD ALEXANDER, education educator; b. Allentown, Pa., Apr. 29, 1939; s. Alexander F. and Kathryn A. (Campbell) W.; children from previous marriage: Kendra L., Brad A.; m. Cheryl Angelo. BA, Muhlenberg Coll., 1963; EdD, Temple U., 1967. Tchr., counselor New Life Boys Ranch, Harleysville, Pa., 1963-65; rsch. asst. Temple U., Phila., 1965-67; asst. prof. Syracuse (N.Y.) U., 1967-71; prof. U. Houston, 1971—, chair dept. curriculum & instrn. Author approximately 165 books, monographs, papers and articles. Grantee, Syracuse U., U. Houston. Mem. Am. Ednl. Rsch. Assn., Assn. Tchr. Educators. Avocation: sports. Home: 2015 Swift Blvd Houston TX 77030-1213

WEBER, WOLFGANG HANS, computer engineering educator; b. Berlin, Dec. 20, 1937; s. Hans Georg and Luise (Heckmann) W.; m. Elisabeth Maria Aumüller, Jan.27, 1961; children: Ralf Guido, Dirk Alexander, Lars Matthias. MS in Engring., U. Darmstadt, Germany, 1961; PhD i Engring., U. Karlsruhe, 1966, D Habilitation, 1969; DPhil (hon.), Marquis G. Scicluna U., 1985, U. Nis, Yugoslavia, 1991. Devel. engr. AEG-Telefunken, Germany, 1958-62, rsch. and devel. sr. fellow engr., 1961-66; asst. prof. U. Karlsruhe, 1966-69; prof. elec. engring. U. Kaiserslautern, Germany, 1970-73; prof. elec. engring. U. Bochum, Germany, 1973—, dean of faculty, 1975-77, v.p., 1977-79; founder Hagen Open U., 1976—; bd. dirs. numerous German cos. Contbr. articles to sci. and profl. jours. Mem. IEEE, Internat. Acad. Info. (pres. 1994—), N.Y. Acad. Sci., Russian Acad. Sci., Masons (pres. 1984-94). Avocations: history, philosophy, anthropology, human rights. Office: U Bochum Inst Computer Sci, Universitatstr 150, D44780 Bochum Germany

WEBER-SÁNCHEZ, ALEJANDRO, surgeon; b. Mexico City, July 24, 1956; s. Federico Weber-Tejeda and Virginia Sánchez-Aguilar; m. Asunción Alvarez-Del Campo, Dec. 12, 1986; children: Pablo, Alejandro. BS summa cum laude, Inst. Juventud, Mexico City, 1974; MD with honors, U. LaSalle, Mexico City, 1980; gen. degree, U. Nat. Autonoma Mex., Mexico City, 1985. Diplomate Mex. Bd. Gen. Surgery, Bd. Gastroenterology Surg. Intern Hosp. ABC, Mexico City, 1978-79; resident in gen. surgery Hosp. Gen. Mex., Mexico City, 1981-85; prof. surg. techniques U. LaSalle, 1986, prof. clinic, 1987-88; dir. Diplomate in Advanced Laparoscopic Surgery, Mexico City, 1994—; prof. laparoscopic surgery Inst. Nat. Perinatologia, Mexico City, 1995-96; bd. dirs. Mex. Bd. Gen. Surgery, Mexico City, 1994; cons. in laparoscopic surgery Hosp. Gen. Mexico, 1995—; vis. prof. U. Peruvian Cayetano Heredia, 1998—. Author: Laparoscopic Surgery, 1994, 2d edit., 1997, Manual de Colecistectomia Laparoscópica, 1994; co-author: Endoscopia Quirúrgica Ginelocologica, 1994, Cuidados Quirurgica Postoperatorios En Cirugia Laparoscopica de Urgencias, 1996, Urologic Laparoscopic Surgery, 1996, Interventional Radiology, 1997, Cirugia Laparoscópica Avanzada, 1997, others. Pres. Fed. Electoral Inst., Mexico City, 1997. Recipient Acknowledgement award Mex. Ministry of Health, 1993, Salvadorian Social Security Inst., 1996, Ecuadorian Soc. Surgery. Fellow Internat. Coll. Surgeons; mem. Mex. Assn. Gen. Surgery (bd. dirs. 1988-96), Mex. Assn. Laparoscopic Surgery (pres. 1994-95, cons. bd. 1995—, Pioneer of Laparoscopic Surgery award 1997), L.Am. Assn. Endoscopic Surgery, Salvadoran Laparoscopic Soc. (hon.), Peruvian Laparoscopic Soc. (hon.), Paraguayan Laparoscopic Soc. (hon.), Hidalguense Laparoscopic Soc. (hon.), Cuban Gastroenterologic Soc. (hon.), Soc. Am. Gastroenterologist and Endoscopic Surgeons. Roman Catholic. Avocations: crafts, swimming. Home: Fuente de la Palma # 13, 52788 Edo Mex Mexico Office: Grupo Med del Valle, Gabriel Mancera # 341, 03100 Mexico City Mexico also: Vialidad Barranca, CP 52763 Edo Mexico

WEBLEY, SIMON, research administrator; b. Bristol, Eng., Aug. 10, 1932; s. Charles Ewart and Kathleen Violet Alice (Forse) W.; m. Helen Edith Kelso Coulter, Sept. 27, 1958; children: Jonathan, Peter, Elizabeth. BA, Trinity Coll., Dublin, 1955, MA with honours, 1961. Rsch. economist Reed Internat. Found. for Bus. Responsibilities, London, 1958-65, dep. dir., 1965-69; dir. Brit.-N.Am. Rsch Assn., London, 1969-98, Brit-N.Am. Com., 1969-98; trustee Kennedy Meml. Trust, 1979-98; bd. dirs. Tear Fund, 1976-89, chmn., 1981-89; chmn. bd. govs. St. Lawrence Coll., Ramsgate, 1989—; rsch. dir. Inst. Bus. Ethics, 1998—; trustee Kirby Laing Found., 1990—, Ch. Pastoral Aid Soc. Patronage Trusts, 1989—. Author: Technology Transfer to Developing Countries, 1979, What Shall It Profit, 1981, The Law of the Sea Treaty, 1982, Multinational Corporations and Codes of Conduct, 1984, Stiffening the Sinews of the Nations, 1986, Company Philosophies and Codes of Business Ethics, 1989, Codes of Ethics and International Business, 1997, Company Use of Codes of Business Conduct, 1998. Ch. warden, mem. Ditton Parish Coun., Kent, Eng. Served with RAF, 1955-57. Mem. Reform Club. Anglican. Avocations: travel, Tudor houses. Office: Inst Bus Ethics, 24 Greencoat Pl, London SW1P 1BE, England

WEBSTER, CHRISTOPHER WHITE, foreign service officer; b. Boston, Oct. 30, 1953; s. Henry deForest and Marion (Havas) W. BA cum laude, Amherst Coll., 1975; MA, Johns Hopkins U., 1977. Asst. comml. attache Am. Embassy, Buenos Aires, 1977-79; econ. comml. officer Georgetown, Guyana, 1979-81; desk officer for Jamaica and Guyana Washington, 1982-84; econ. officer Office of Energy, Washington, 1984-86; fin. and devel. officer Lisbon, Portugal, 1986-89; econ. sect. chief Algiers, Algeria, 1989-92; dept. dir. Office of Pakistan, Afghanistan and Bangladesh Affairs, Washington, 1992-95; dep. chief of mission Khartoum, Sudan and Addis Ababa, Ethiopia, 1995-96; chief developer Country Trade Divsn., Washington, 1996-98; dep. dir. Office of Ctrl. Am. and Panamanian Affairs, Washington, 1998-00; dep. chief mission Dept. of State, Dhaka, Bangladesh, 2000—. Recipient Superior Honor award Dept. State, 1983, 91, 98-2000. Office: Dept of State 6120 Dhaka Pl Washington DC 20521-6120

WEBSTER, GEORGE ARNOLD, mechanical engineer, consultant; b. Wortley, Yorkshire, U.K., May 12, 1937; s. George and Bessie W.; m. Sheila Mary Hobday, Jan. 13, 1962; children: Andrea, Neil, Sharon. BS, Imperial Coll., London, 1958, PhD, 1962; DSc, London U., 1987. Engr. Eng. Electric Co. Ltd., Whetstone, 1962-63; rsch. assoc. Pratt & Whitney Aircraft, North Haven, Conn., 1963-65, sr. rsch., 1965-66; lectr. Imperial Coll., London, 1966-73, sr. lectr., 1973-82, reader, 1982-89, prof., 1989—. Fellow Inst. Materials, Inst. Mech. Engrs., City of Guild of London Inst. Avocations: walking, golf, theatre. Office: Mech Engring Dept, Imperial Coll, SW7 2BX London England

WEBSTER, HENRY DEFOREST, neuroscientist; b. N.Y.C., Apr. 22, 1927; s. Leslie Tillotson and Emily (deForest) W.; m. Marion Havas, June 12, 1951; children: Christopher, Henry, Sally, David, Steven. AB cum laude, Amherst Coll., 1948; MD, Harvard U., 1952. Intern Boston City Hosp., 1952-53, resident, 1953-54; resident in neurology Mass. Gen. Hosp., 1954-56, research fellow in neuropathology, 1956-59; prin. investigator NIH research grants for electron microscopic studies of peripheral neuropathy, 1959-69; mem. staffs Mass. Gen., Newton-Wellesley hosps.; instr. neurology Harvard Med. Sch., 1959-63, assoc. in neurology, 1963-66, asst. prof. neuropathology, 1966; assoc. prof. neurology U. Miami Sch. Medicine, 1966-69, prof., 1969; head sect. cellular neuropathology Nat. Inst. Neurol. Diseases and Stroke, Bethesda, Md., 1969-97; chief Lab. Exptl. Neuropathology, 1984-97; scientist emeritus Nat. Insts. Health, 1997—; disting. scientist, lectr. dept. anatomy Tulane U. Sch. Medicine, 1973; Royal Coll. lectr. Can. Assn. Neuropathologists, 1982; Saul Korey lectr. Am. Assn. Neuropathologists, 1992; chmn. Winter Conf. on Brain Rsch., 1985, 86; head neuropathology delegation to visit China in 1990, Citizen Amb. Program, People to People Internat.; mem. exec. com. rsch. group on neuromuscular disease World Fedn. Neurology, 1986-93. Author: (with A. Peters and S.L. Palay) The Fine Structure of the Nervous System, 1970, 76, 91; contbr. articles to sci. jours. Recipient Superior Svc. award USPHS, 1977, A. von Humboldt award Fed. Republic Germany, 1985, Sci. award Peripheral Neuropathy Assn., 1994; named hon. prof. Norman Bethune U. of Med. Scis., Chanchun, China, 1991. Mem. Am. Assn. Neuropathologists (v.p. 1976-77, pres. 1978-79, Weil award 1960), Internat. Soc. Neuropathology (councillor 1976-80, v.p. 1980-84, exec. com. 1980-84, 86-94, pres. 1986-90, hon. mem. 1999—), Internat. Congress Neuropathology (sec. gen. VIII 1978), Peripheral Nerve Study Group (exec. com. 1975-93, chmn. 1977 meeting), Japanese Soc. Neuropathology (hon.), Am. Neurol. Assn., Am. Acad. Neurology, Royal Soc. Medicine, Am. Soc. Cell Biologists, Soc. Neurosci., Rotary Internat., Ausable Club. Office: NIH Rm 4A 29 Bldg 36 Bethesda MD 20892-0001

WEBSTER, JEFFREY LEON, graphic designer; b. Idaho Falls, Idaho, Nov. 23, 1941; s. Leon A. and Marjory M. (McAllister) W.; student Sch. Associated Arts, St. Paul, 1962; m. Judith Kess, Apr. 17, 1965; children: Eric J., Marjorie P. Sci. illustrator Mayo Clinic, Rochester, Minn., 1963-66; layout artist Brown & Bigelow, St. Paul, 1966; graphic designer U. Minn., Mpls., 1966-67, U. Calgary (Alta., Can.), 1967-68; sr. artist Control Data Corp., St. Paul, 1968-70; mem. Idaho State U. Meml. Lectureship Com.; graphic designer Idaho State U., 1970-78; owner, operator studio, Harmony, Minn.; mktg. and advt. cons. to 45 regional and nat. firms, 1978—. Mem. Idaho Civic Symphony Bd. Chairperson rub. rels. Unitarian Ch. Rochester, 1991—; bd. dirs. Gift of Life Transplant House, Rochester, Minn. 1996, Rochester Orch. and Chorale, 1996. Recipient Profl. citation Libr. Congress, 1976; 1st Pl. Best Trucking ad, Overdrive Mag., 1990. Artist pub. ednl. exhibits. Home and Office: RR 1 Harmony MN 55939-9801

WEBSTER, JILL ROSEMARY, historian, educator; b. London, Sept. 29, 1931; arrived in Can., 1965; d. Harold James and Dora Elena (Andreini) W. BA in Hispanic Studies with honors, U. Liverpool, Eng., 1962, postgrad. cert. in edn., 1965; PhD in Spanish, U. Toronto, Can., 1969; MA in Spanish, U. Nottingham, Eng., 1964; BA in History with honors, U. London, Eng., 1978. Prof. U. Toronto, 1968-95, assoc. dean, 1978-81, dir. Ctr. for Medieval Studies, 1979-94, grad. chair dept. Spanish and Portuguese, 1993-94; prof. emeritus, 1995—. Author: Els Menorets: The Franciscans in the Realms of Aragon from St. Francis to the Black Death (1348), 1993, Per Déu o per diners - els mendicants i el clergat al pais valencià, 1998, Carmel in Medieval Catalonia, 1999, Els Franciaseans Catalans a l'Edat Mitjana, 2000. Recipient Creu de Sant Jordi award, Generalitat de Catalunya, 1999. Fellow Royal Soc. Can.; mem. Am. Cath. Hist. Assn., Am. Acad. Rsch. Historians of Medieval Spain (pres. 1990-95), Secció Històrico-Arqueològica Inst./d'Estudis Catalans (mem. corr.). Office: U Toronto St Michaels Coll, 81 St Mary St, Toronto, ON Canada M5S 1J4

WEBSTER, JOHN KINGSLEY OHL, II, health administrator, rehabilitation manager; b. L.A., July 27, 1950; s. John Kingsley Ohl and Inez (Gilbert) W.; children: David Lilly, Jason Kingsley McKnight. AA, Pasadena (Calif.) City Coll., 1973; BS, San Jose (Calif.) State U., 1975; MS, Calif. State U., L.A., 1989. Registered occupational therapist, Calif. Supervising occupational therapy cons. San Gabriel Valley Regional Ctr., 1976-79; supr. II occupational therapy cons. San Diego Regional Ctr., 1979-83; sr. occupational therapist Mesa Vista Hosp., 1983-84; pvt. practice Vista, Calif., 1983-85; occupational therapy cons. Calif. Children Svcs., State Dept. Health Svcs., L.A., 1985-86, regional adminstrv. cons., 1986-90; dir. occupational therapy Eureka Gen. Hosp., 1990; dir. ops. and mktg. Life Dimensions Inc., Newport Beach, Calif., 1990; occupational therapy cons., licensing and cert. Calif. Dept. Health Svcs., 1990-93; program dir. rehab. svcs. Scripps Meml. Hosp., Encinitas, Calif., 1993-94; dir. rehab. Vista (Calif.) Knoll, 1994; clin. dir. occupational therapy Sundance Rehab., San Diego, 1994-95; regional dir. ops. Quest Rehab, L.A., 1995-96; area mgr. Am. Therapy Svc., 1996; western divsn. dir. of ops. Accelerated Care Plus, L.A., 1996-97; clin. svcs. mgr. Tustin Rehab. Hosp., 1998-99; supr. therapist Calif. Childrens Svcs., 1999; regional dir. ops., pres. Health Point & Ergonomix, Vista, Calif., 2000—; cons. Hopi and Navajo Tribes, Winslow, Ariz., 1978; dir. Imperial County SPRANS grant, El Centro, Calif., 1986-88; pres., owner Ergonomix & Regs., San Diego, 1988—. Artist (sculpture) Free Form (3d pl. award 1973), (oil painting) Jamaican Woman (3d pl. award 1979). Recipient Esquire title Lady Elliott of STOBS, Edinburough, Scotland, 1973, spl. dept. recognition Calif. State U., 1989. Mem. Am. Occupational Therapy Assn., Inst. Profl. Health Svc. Adminstrs., Student Assn. of Am. Coll. Health Care Execs. Avocations: oil painting, sculpting, producing films, woodworking, tennis.

WEBSTER, LINDA JANE, clinical social worker, consultant; b. Whitinsville, Mass., Mar. 23, 1948; d. David and Erva Viola (Chesley) Longmuir; m. Barry Ward Webster, Dec. 16, 1988; 1 child, Jeffrey. BS magna cum laude, Springfield (Mass.) Coll., 1969; MEd, U. Hartford, 1971; M. in Social Work, U. Utah, 1981, PhD, 1997. Lic. clin. social worker Utah; diplomate Am. Bd. Examiners and Nat. Assn. Social Workers. Sch. psychologist Bd. Edn., New Britain, Conn., 1969-77; dir. Project React Capital Region Edn. Coun., Bloomfield, Conn., 1977-79; coord. acute and intensive treatment Valley West Mental Health Ctr., Salt Lake City, Utah, 1981-86; program dir. Western Inst. NeuroPsychiatry, Salt Lake City, 1986-88; social worker pvt. practice Murray, Utah, 1988—; cons. Episcopal Social and Pastoral Ministries, Salt Lake City, 1986-88; adj. faculty U. Utah, Grad. Sch. Social Work, Salt Lake City, 1986-93. Vol. Episcopalian Ch., Salt Lake City, 1980—; mentor Murray (Utah) H.S., 1997. Mem. Nat. Assn. Social Workers (sec. Utah chpt. 1986-88), Alumni Assn. U. Utah Grad Sch. Social Workers, (pres. 1986-89), Phi Kappa Phi. Avocations: skiing, tennis, basketball, teddy bears, crafts. Office: PhD LCSW 111 E 5600 S Ste 314 Murray UT 84107-8167

WEBSTER, MURRAY ALEXANDER, JR., sociologist, educator; b. Manila, Philippines, Dec. 10, 1941; s. M.A. and Patricia (Morse) W. AB, Stanford U., 1963, MA, 1966, PhD, 1968. Asst. prof. social rels. Johns Hopkins U., Balt., 1968-74, assoc. prof., 1974-76; prof. sociology, adj. prof.

psychology U. S.C., Columbia, 1976-86; vis. prof. sociology Stanford U., 1981-82, 85, 88-89; sr. lectr. San Jose State U., 1987-89; dir. sociology program NSF, 1989-91,99-2000; prof. sociology U. N.C., Charlotte, 1993—. Author: (with Barbara Sobieszek) Sources of Self-Evaluation, 1974, Actions and Actors, 1975, (with Martha Foschi) Status Generalization: New Theory and Research, 1988; mem. editl. bd. Am. Jour. Sociology, 1976-79, Social Psychology Quar., 1977-80, 84-87, 93—, Social Sci. Rsch., 1975—. NIH fellow, 1966-68; grantee NSF, Nat. Inst. Edn. Mem. AAAS, Am. Sociol. Assn., So. Sociol. Soc., Am. Psychol. Assn., Am. Psychol. Soc., N.Y. Acad. Scis. Presbyterian. Office: Univ NC Dept Sociology Charlotte NC 28223

WEBSTER, NIGEL ROBERT, anesthesia educator, consultant; b. Walsall, Eng., June 14, 1953; s. Derek Stanley and Sheila Margaret (Squire) W.; m. Diana C.S. Hutchinson, July 2, 1977; children: Lorna, Oliver, Lucy. BSc in Pharmacology, U. Leeds, Eng., 1974; MB, BChir, U. Leeds, 1977, PhD, 1984. Mem. sci. staff Med. Rsch. Coun., London, 1986-88; cons. St. James U. Hosp., Leeds, 1988-94; prof. U. Aberdeen, Scotland, 1994—; cons. Aberdeen Royal Infirmary, 1994—. Editor: Clinical Research in Anesthesia, 1988, Intensive Care: Developments and Controversies, 1992, Clinical Scenarios in Intensive Care, 1998. Fellow Royal Coll. Anesthetists, Royal Coll. Physicians. Avocations: flying, travel, photography. Office: Inst Med Scis, Foresterhill, Aberdeen AB25 2ZD, Scotland

WEBSTER, PETER DAVID, judge; b. Framingham, Mass., Feb. 12, 1949; s. Waldo John and Helen Anne (Borovek) W.; m. Michele Page Hernandez, Jan. 13, 1989; 1 stepchild, Alana Perryman. BS, Georgetown U., 1971; JD, Duke U., 1974; LLM, U. Va., 1995. Bar: Fla. 1974, U.S. Dist. Ct. (mid. dist.) Fla. 1975, U.S. Ct. Appeals (5th cir.) 1975, U.S. Dist. Ct. (so. dist.) Fla. 1977, U.S. Dist. Ct. (no. dist.) Fla. 1978, U.S. Supreme Ct. 1978, U.S. Ct. Appeals (11th cir.) 1981. Law clk. U.S. Dist. Judge, Jacksonville, Fla., 1974-75; assoc. Bedell, Bedell, Dittmar, Smith & Zehmer, Jacksonville, 1975-78; ptnr. Bedell, Bedell, Dittmar & Zehmer, Jacksonville, 1978-85; cir. judge State Fla., Jacksonville, 1986-91; judge Dist. Ct. of Appeal, First Dist., State of Fla., Tallahassee, 1991—; master of bench Chester Bedell Am. Inn of Ct., 1988-91, Tallahassee Am. Inn of Ct., 1992—; chmn. com. on standard jury instrns. in civil cases, chmn. court reporter cert. planning com.; mem. com. on trial ct. info. sys.; com. on confidentiality of records of jud. br. Fla. Supreme Ct. Contbg. author: Sanctions: Rule 11 and Other Powers, 1986, Florida Criminal Rules and Practice Manual, 1990. Bd. dirs. Jacksonville Area Legal Aid, Inc., 1978-82, River Region Human Svcs., Inc., Jacksonville, 1986-88; mem. adv. bd. P.A.C.E. Ctr. for Girls, Inc., Jacksonville, 1986-91; com. mem. Shawnee dist. North Fla. coun. Boy Scouts Am., 1974-78; mem. delinquency task force Mayor's Commn. on Children and Youth, City of Jacksonville, 1988-91; officer, mem. exec. bd. Suwanee River Area coun. Boy Scouts, 1991-96. Mem. Fla. Conf. Appellate Judges, Jacksonville Bar Assn., Tallahassee Bar Assn., Phi Beta Kappa, Phi Alpha Theta, Phi Eta Sigma. Office: 1st Dist Ct Appeal 301 Martin Luther King Blvd Tallahassee FL 32399-1850

WEBSTER, RICHARD, editor-in-chief; b. Derby, England, May 6, 1933; s. Alan Francis and Kathleen (Allen) W.; m. Mary Primrose Buxton, July 14, 1956; children: Daphne, Christopher, Rachel. BS, Sheffield U., England, 1954; DPhil, Oxford U., England, 1966; DS, Sheffield U., 1983; D (hon.), Louvain, Belgium, 1995. Soil chemist Govt. No. Rhodesia, 1957-61; rsch. officer Oxford U., England, 1961-68; sr., prin. scientific officer Rothamsted Exptl. Sta., HArpenden, 1968-73, sr. prin. scientific officer, 1974-90; sr. rsch. scientist CSIRO, Australia, 1973-74; rschr. Ecole des Mines Paris, 1990; dir. rsch. INRA, Montpellier, France, 1990-91; prof. Fed. Inst. Tech., Zurich & Lausanne, Switzerland, 1992-94, WSL, Zurich, 1994-95; editor-in-chief British Soc. Soil Sci., England, 1995—; vis. prof. Reading U., England, 1997—. Author: Quantitative Methods in Soil Classification and Survey, 1977, Statistical Methods in Soil and Land Resource Survey; contbr. articles to profl. jours. Fellow Royal Soc. Arts; mem. British Soc. Soil Sci. Methodist. Avocations: music, mountain walking, carpentry. Home: 29 Battlefield Rd, St Albans AL1 4DB, England Office: Rothamsted Exptl Sta, Harpenden AL5 2JQ, England

WEBSTER, RICHARD EDWARD, author, consultant, hypnotherapist; b. Auckland, New Zealand, Dec. 9, 1946; s. Frederick Edward and Margaret Helena Meredith (Mace) W.; m. Margaret Joan Shaw, July 24, 1971; children: Nigel Edward, Charlotte Leigh, Philip James. Cert. Nat. Guild Hypnotists (U.S.), Assn. Profl. Hypnotherapists and Parapsychologists (U.K.), New Zealand Hypnotherapy Assn., Profl. Hypnotherapy inst. N.Z., Internat. Registry Profl. Hypnotherapists. Trainee William Collins, New Zealand, 1964-67, 67-69, ednl. mgr., 1969-70; pres. Brookings Bookshop, New Zealand, 1971-72, Brookings Agys., New Zealand, 1973-80, Brookfield Press, New Zealand, 1981-86; writer, 1987—; dir. Action Hypnosis Ctrs., Auckland, New Zealand, 1981—; bd. dirs. Brookfield Press, Auckland. Author: Freedom to Read, 1972, Sun Sign success, 1982, The Stars and Your Destiny 1982, How to Read Tea Leaves, 1982, Discovering Numerology, 1983, How to Read Minds, 1984, Secrets of Ghost Writing, 1987, How to Develop Psychic Power, 1988, Revealing Hands, 1994, Dowsing for Beginners, 1996, Seven Secrets to Success, 1997, Aura Reading for Beginners, 1998, Astral Travel for Beginners, 1998, Chinese Numerology, 1998, 101 Feng Shui Tips for the Home, 1998, Feng Shui for Wealth and Happiness, 1999, Palm Reading for Beginners, 2000, Energy Within, 2000, others; writer series of monographs for magicians and mentalists. Recipient Benny award Variety Artists Club New Zealand, 1997, Scroll of Honour, 1995; named Mentalist of Yr., Psychic Entertainment Assn., 1990. Mem. New Zealand Radiesthesia Soc., Salespeople with a Purpose (v.p. 1996), Kiwanis Club of St. Heliers (v.p. 1989). Avocations: book collecting, classical music, mentalism, map collecting, antiques. Home and Office: 22 Marriott Rd, Pakuranga Auckland 6, New Zealand

WEBSTER, RONALD D., communications company executive; b. Richwood, W.Va., Aug. 9, 1949; s. Ralph D. and Victoria M. (Cisek) W.; m. Donna M. Falkenthal, Aug. 9, 1975; 1 child, Kathryn E. BSBA with high distinction, U. Ill., Chgo., 1971; MBA, U. Chgo., 1980. CPA, Ill. Sr. auditor Arthur Andersen & Co., Chgo., 1970-75; dir. corp. reporting Trans Union Corp., Lincolnshire, Ill., 1975-77; asst. group contr. Union Tank Car Co. (subs. of Trans Union Corp.), Chgo., 1977-83; treas. Telephone and Data Systems, Inc., Chgo., 1983-87, 88-97, v.p., 1992-97; v.p., chief fin. officer Ideal Sch. Supply Corp., Oak Lawn, Ill., 1987-88; sr. v.p., CFO, 21st Century Telecom. Group, Inc., Chgo., 1997—. Bd. dirs., v.p. fin. Ivy Glen Homeowners Assn., Aurora, Ill., 1972-73. Staff sgt. USNG, 1970-76. Mem. Fin. Execs. Inst., Am. Soc. CPAs (Elijah Watt Sells nat. honorable mention 1973), Ill. CPA Soc., Beta Gamma Sigma. Home: 7637 Ridgewood Ln Burr Ridge IL 60525-5132 Office: 21st Century Telecom Group Inc 350 N Orleans St Ste 600 Chicago IL 60654-1596

WECHSLER, ANDREW STEPHEN, surgery educator; b. N.Y.C., July 19, 1939; s. James Erwin and Nina (Wander) W.; m. Donna Clare Ramstein, Sept. 12, 1965; children: Jennifer Lynn, Hollis Ann. AB, Brandeis U., 1960; MD summa cum laude, SUNY-Downstate Med. Ctr., 1964. Diplomate Am. Bd. Thoracic Surgery (bd. dirs. 1986—). Resident in surgery Duke U. Med. Ctr.; asst. prof. surgery Duke U. Med. Ctr., Durham, N.C., 1974-77, assoc. prof., 1977-80, prof., 1980-88; chmn. dept. surgery Med. Coll. Va., Richmond, 1988—; chmn. surgery and bioengring. study sect. NIH, 1989—. Mem. editorial bd. Annals Thoracic Surgery, 1980-88, Circulation, 1985—, Jour. Cardiac Surgery, 1985—, Jour. Cardiac Anesthesiology, 1985—; contbr. numerous articles to profl. jours. Comdr. USPHS, 1966-68. Fellow ACS, Am. Coll. Cardiology. Address: 114 Pine St Philadelphia PA 19106-4312 Office: Med Coll Va PO Box 645 Richmond VA 23218-0645 also: Med Coll Va Hosp 401 N 12th St Richmond VA 23298-5035

WECHSLER, ARNOLD, osteopathic obstetrician, gynecologist; b. N.Y.C., June 10, 1923; s. David and Eva (Kirsch) W.; m. Marlene Esta Jurnovoy, Sept. 11, 1955 (div. Sept. 1986); children: Diane, Paul, Stewart. Grad., Rutgers U.; DO, Phila. Coll. Osteo. Medicine, 1952. Diplomate Am. Bd. Osteo. Obstetricians and Gynecologists; lic. physician, Pa., N.Y., Fla. Intern Hosps. of Phila. Coll. Osteo. Medicine, 1952-53, resident in ob-gyn. and gen. surgery, 1953-56; lectr. in ob-gyn. Nursing Sch. Phila. Coll. Osteo. Medicine; founder, mem. staff Tri County Hosp., Delaware County, Pa., from 1960, chief staff, 1960-62, chief dept. ob-gyn. surgery, 1960-77, dir. med. edn., 1968-71; attending and cons. in ob-gyn. surgery Met. Hosp., Phila., 1956-60, 71-75; chief dept. ob-gyn. Humana Hosp.-South Broward, Hollywood, Fla., 1980-84; cons. and attending in gynecol. surgery Drs. Hosp. of Hollywood, 1982-86; insp. for intern and resident tng. programs Bur. Hosps. of Am. Osteo. Assn., 1965-66; founder, med. dir. Women's Med. Svcs., 1973-77, Nutrients Inc., Phila., 1977-79, Supplements Inc., Phila., 1979-80, Alternative Lifestyle Ctr., Fla., 1983-86; founder, dir. A.W. Profl. Consultants, Inc.; cons. Practice Mgmt. Group, Med Temps Plus, Plantation, Fla.; provider ambulatory gyn. surgery for multiple gyn ctrs. in Dade, Broward and Palm Beach Counties, Fla. Author: Dr. Wechsler's New You Diet, 1978. Staff Sgt. Signal Corps, USAF, 1942-46, PTO, Japan. Fellow Am. Coll. Osteo. Obstetricians and Gynecologists, Internat. Coll. Applied Nutrition; mem. Am. Osteo. Assn., Pa. Osteo. Med. Assn., Philadelphia County Osteo. Soc., Fla. Osteo. Med. Assn., Broward County Osteo. Med. Assn., Am. Soc. Bariatric Physicians, Assn. Maternal and Child Welfare, Internat. Acad. Preventive Medicine, Inst. Food Technologists, Coun. for Responsible Nutrition, Internat. Coll. Gynecologic Laparoscopists, Assn. Reproductive Health Profls. Avocations: photography, sculpture, woodworking.

WECHSLER, BRADLEY J., film company executive; m. Patricia Newburger; children: Samantha, Kate, Robert James, David Eliot. BA, Brandeis U.; JD, Columbia U. Various oper. and fin. positions entertainment cos., including Home Box Office, Inc., Columbia Pictures; ptnr., media and entertainment group Drexel Burnham Lambert; chmn., CEO Imax Corp., 1994—, co-chief exec. officer, 1996—; chmn., CEO Entertainment Fin. Svcs. Inc.; gen. ptnr. Cinema Plus, L.P. Bd. dirs. Am. Mus. of the Moving Image, NYU Kids, NYU-Tisch Hosp., Kernochan Ctr. Law Media and Arts. Office: 110 E 59th St Fl 21 New York NY 10022-1304

WECHSLER, GIL, lighting designer; b. N.Y.C., Feb. 5, 1942; s. Arnold J. and Miriam (Steinberg) W. Student, Rensselaer Poly. Inst., 1958-61; BS, NYU, 1964; MFA, Yale U., 1967. Lighting designer Harkness Ballet, N.Y.C., 1967-69, Pa. Ballet, Phila., 1969-70, Stratford Shakespeare Festival, Ont., Can., 1969-78, 97, Guthrie Theatre, Mpls., 1971, Lyric Opera, Chgo., 1972-76, Met. Opera, N.Y.C., 1976-96, Equus, Stratford Sheakespeare Festival, 1997; tchr. NYU, Rensselaer Poly. Inst., 1998; guest lectr. Teatro Colon, Buenos Aires, Argentina, 1985, Yale U., New Haven, Conn., 1980, Broadway Lighting Designers, 1994-98; guest lighting designer Am. Ballet Theatre, N.Y.C., 1980, Paris Opera, 1983, Chatelet Theatre, Paris, 1991; dean's adv. bd. Sch. Rensselaer Poly. Inst., Troy, N.Y. Cons. editor Opera Quar., 1983-90. Recipient Emmy award nominations, Illuminating Engring. Soc., United Scenic Artists. Avocations: collecting ocean liner memorabilia, gardening, kayaking. Home: 1 Lincoln Plz New York NY 10023-7129

WECHSLER, SERGIO, automotive executive, consultant; b. Rio de Janeiro, Aug. 10, 1944; came to U.S., 1965; s. Michael and Gertrud (Putziger) W.; m. Suzana Brauer, June 26, 1969; children: Mark, Andrew. Student, Mackenzie U., 1962, Gen. Motors Inst. Engring., 1967; MBA in Internat. Bus., NYU, 1974; PhD in Internat. Bus., Kennedy-Western U., 1996. Quality supr. GM do Brasil, Sao Paulo, 1963-65, quality control supt., 1967-70; quality control mgr. Gillette Corp., Berlin, 1970-71; project mgr. GM, N.Y.C., 1971-76; plant mgr. GM de Portugal, Lisbon, 1976-79; project mgr. Adam Opel AG, Russelheim, Fed. Republic of Germany, 1979-81; quality dir. GM, Linden, N.J., 1981-85; dir. ops. and quality control GM, Warren, Mich., 1985-93, mgr. internat. programs, 1985-95; program mgr. Cadillac Luxury Car divsn. GM, Flint, Mich., 1995-96; pres. Marswex Global Enterprises, St. Petersburg, Fla., 1982—, Hudson (Fla.) Pla., 1984-99; chmn. Auto Exchange Club, Clearwater, Fla., 1997, MSX Internat., Detroit, 1997-99, v.p. German ops., 1999—. V.P. Temple Beth Jacob, Pontiac, Mich., 1986, pres., 1987-89. Mem. Am. Soc. Quality Control (cert. quality engr. 1992), Radio Club. Republican. Avocations: ham radio, travel, automobile restoration.

WECHTER, CLARI ANN, paint manufacturing company executive; b. Chgo., June 1, 1953; d. Norman Robert and Harriet Beverly (Golub) W.; m. Gordon Jay Siegel, Feb. 10, 1980; 1 child, Alix Jessica. BA, U. Ariz., 1975; BE, Loyola U., Chgo., 1977. Cert. tchr., Ill. Saleswoman, v.p. sales Federated Paint Mfg. Co., Chgo., 1979—. Republican. Jewish. Avocation: travel. Home: 25 E Cedar St Chicago IL 60611-1109 Office: Federated Paint Mfg Co 1882 S Normal Ave Chicago IL 60616-1013

WECHTER, IRA MARTIN, tax specialist, financial planner; b. Bkyn., June 26, 1947; s. Nathan Harris and Mollie (Bauer) W.; m. Myrna Ellen Rosenbaum, Dec. 22, 1968; 1 child, Megan Jill. BA, CCNY, 1969; MPA, Bernard Baruch Coll., 1973. CFP; cert. practitioner of taxation; accredited tax advisor; registered investment advisor; lic. gen. securities prin.; enrolled to practice before IRS; lic. gen. securities prin., life, health and disability ins., N.J., N.Y. Dir. adminstrv. svcs. N.Y.C. Dept. City Planning, 1971-77; dep. asst. budget dir. N.Y., N.Y.C. Office Mgmt. and Budget, 1977-81; dep. commr. N.Y.C. Dept. Environ. Protection, 1981-84; pres. Wechter Fin. Svcs., Inc., Parsippany, N.J., 1984—. Mem. Community Bd. No. 1 S.I., 1973-76, 1st v.p., 1976-77; treas. S.I. Coun. on Arts, 1974-75. Recipient Outstanding Citizenship award Borough Pres. of S.I., 1977. Mem. Nat. Assn. Enrolled Agts., Inst. Cert. Fin. Planners, Nat. Assn. Tax Practitioners, Nat. Soc. Tax Preparers, Nat. Soc. Pub. Accts. Republican. Jewish. Avocations: U.S. mint stamp collecting, organist. Office: Wechter Fin Svcs Inc 1719 State Rt 10 Ste 310 Parsippany NJ 07054-4507 also: 1719 Route 10 Ste 118 Parsippany NJ 07054-4507

WECK, GERHARD, computer scientist; b. Trier, Ger., Dec. 13, 1947; s. Hanns and Marianne (Philipp) W.; m. Christa Speicher, Apr. 2, 1974; children—Thomas, Martin. Diploma Physics, U. Saarlandes, 1971, Dr.rer.nat., 1975. Asst. tchr. U. Saarlandes, Saarbruecken, W.Ger., 1971-75, TH Darmstadt, 1975-76; asst. prof. Unicamp, Campinas, Brazil, 1976-77; asst. tchr. U. Saarlandes, 1977-80; sr. security cons. Infodas GmbH, Koeln, W.Ger., 1980—; surveyor Gesellschaft fur Mathematik und Datenverarbeitung, Bonn, 1973-74; expert DIN, Berlin, 1981—. Author: Prinzipien und Realisierung von Betriebssystemen, 1982, Datensicherheit, 1984, (with Volker Schmidt) Digitalelektronisches Praktikum, 1973. Mem. Assn. Computing Machinery, Computer Security Inst., Gesellschaft fuer Informatik. Roman Catholic. Office: Infodas GmbH, Rhonestr 2, 50765 Koeln Germany

WECKESSER, ELDEN CHRISTIAN, surgery educator; b. Marshallville, Ohio, Mar. 31, 1910; s. Christian and Ella Elizabeth (Long) W.; m. Kathryn Alice Tuttle, Mar. 17, 1937 (dec., 1998); children: Jane, Elizabeth, Nancy, Mary. Student, Duke U., 1928-29; AB, Western Reserve U., 1933, MD, 1936. Diplomate Am. Bd. Surgery. Intern Cin. Gen. Hosp., 1936-37; sr. intern surgery Univ. Hosps., Cleve., 1937-38, asst. resident gen. surgery, 1938-39, resident, 1939-40; from demonstrator in surgery to clin. prof. surgery Case Western Res. U., Cleve., 1940-74, prof. surgery, 1974-81, prof. emeritus surgery, 1981—; asst. surgeon Lakeside Hosp., Cleve., 1940-61, assoc. surgeon, 1961—; assoc. surgeon Highland View Hosp., St. Lukes Hosp., Cleve., 1961—; cons. surgeon VA Hosp., 1961—. Author: (books) Treatment of Hand Injuries, 1974, The Department of Surgery, Case Western Reserve University, 1843-1986, His Name Was Mudd, 1991, Fifty-Five Years of My Era of the Twentieth Century, 1999; co-author: Flynn's Hand Surgery, 1966, rev. edits., 1975, 82, 91; co-author: (chpts.) Medicine in Cleveland and Cuyahoga County 1810-1976, 1977; contbr. numerous articles to profl. jours. Lt. col. vol. M.C. AUS, 1942-46, Australia, New Guinea. Named Disting. Alumnus, Case Western Res. U., 1981. Mem. AMA, ACS (mem. trauma com.), Am. Bd. Surgery, Acad. Medicine Cleve. (v.p. 1965-66, pres. 1966-67), Ohio State Med. Assn., Cleve. Surg. Soc. (pres. 1964-65), Am. Assn. Surgery Trauma, Am. Soc. Surgery of Hand, Cen. Surg. Assn., Internat. Soc. Surgery, Cleve. Med. Libr. Assn. (v.p. 1973-74, pres. 1974-75), Western Res. Med. Alumni Assn. (pres. 1965-66), Alpha Omega Alpha. Republican. Presbyterian. Avocations: author. Home and Office: The Commons 1928 Campden Way Fairview PA 16415-1976

WEDBERG, WALTER CATO, science consultant; b. Bergen, Norway, Nov. 29, 1940; s. Ottar Cato and Gerda (Lohne) Olsen; m. Lena Birgitta Wedberg, Oct. 17, 1964; children: Torolf, Kristian. BA in Physics, U. Colo., 1966, MA in Physics, 1968. Assoc. physicist IBM Corp., N.Y.C., 1968-70; rsch. scientist Christian Michelsen Inst., Bergen, Norway, 1970-81, sr. scientist, 1981-88; sr. scientist U. Bergen/UNIFOB, 1988-90; sci. cons. pvt. practice, Bergen, 1990—; mgr. microanalysis lab. U. Bergen, 1975-88, mgr. indoor environ. project, 1991—; del. European Work Party Static Electricity, 1985-90, Norwegian Stds. Com. on Air Filtration, 1993—. Contbr. articles to profl. jours. With Norwegian Navy, 1959-60. Norwegian Rsch. Coun. grantee, 1985, 88, 92, 94. Mem. Norwegian Assn. Chartered Engrs. Avocations: mountaineering, skiing, music. Home: O Fredlundveg 15A, N-5073 Bergen Norway Office: U Bergen, Dept Physics, N-5007 Bergen Norway

WEDDERBURN, DOROTHY ENID COLE, educational administrator; b. London, Sept. 18, 1925; d. Frederick C. and Ethel C. Barnard. BA, Cambridge U., 1946, MA, 1950; DLitt (hon.), Warwick U., 1984, Loughborough (Eng.) U., 1989, Brunel U., 1990; LLd (hon.), Cambridge U., 1991; DSc (hon.), City U., 1991; D Social Sci. (hon.), Southampton U., 1999. Research officer dept. applied econs. Cambridge U., 1950-65; lectr., prof. indsl. sociology Imperial Coll. Sci. and Tech., London, 1965-81; sr. research fellow, 1981, hon. fellow, 1986; prin. Bedford Coll., London, 1981-85, Royal Holloway and Bedford New Coll., Egham, Surrey, Eng., 1985-90; pro vice chancellor U. London, 1986-89; hon. fellow Ealing (Eng.) Coll. Higher Edn., 1985. Author: White Collar Redundancy, 1964, Redundancy and the Railwayman, 1964, Enterprise Planning for Change, 1968, Old Age in Three Industrial Societies, 1968; co-author: The Aged in the Welfare State, 1965. Mem. Ct. of London U., 1981-90. Mem. Fawcett Soc. (hon. pres. 1986—). Home: 65 Ladbroke Grove Flat 5, London W11 2PD, England

WEDDERBURN OF CHARLTON, LORD KENNETH WILLIAM, law educator; b. London, Apr. 13, 1927; s. Herbert John and Mabel Ethel (Holland) W.; m. Nina Salaman, 1951 (div. 1960); children: Sarah Louise, David Roland, Lucy Rachel; m. Dorothy Cole, 1962 (div. 1969); m. Frances Ann Knight, Aug. 22, 1969; 1 child, Jonathan Michael. MA, Cambridge U., 1948, LLB, 1949; Hon. Dott. Giur., Pavia, 1987; Hon. Dott. Econs., Siena, 1991; LLD (hon.) Stockholm, 1995. Barrister, Middle Temple, Queen's Counsel, 1991. Fellow, tutor in law Clare Coll., Cambridge U., 1952-64, hon. fellow, 1997; lectr. in law U. Cambridge, 1953-64, prof. comml. law London Sch. Econs., U. London, 1964-92, prof. emeritus, 1992—. Author: The Worker and the Law, 3d edit. 1986, Employment Rights in Britain and Europe, 1991, Labour Law and Freedom, 1995; co-author: (with B. Aaron and others) Industrial Conflict, 1972; (with P. Davies) Employment Grievances on Disputes and Procedures, 1969; (with R. Lewis and J. Clark) Labour Law and Industrial Relations, 1983; The Social Charter-European Company and Employment Rights, 1989, I Diritti Del Lavoro, 1997; gen. editor Modern Law Rev., 1970-88. Chmn. ind. rev. com. Trades Union Congress, 1976—; pres. Inst. Employment Rights, 1989-95; asst. editor Clerk and Lindsell on Torts, 1989-95, I Diritti del Lonoro, 1997. Fellow Brit. Acad. Created life peer, baron, 1977. Mem. Labour Party. Office: U London Sch Econs, Houghton St, London WC2A 2AE, England*

WEDEL, MILLIE REDMOND, secondary school educator; b. Harrisburg, Pa., Aug. 18, 1939; d. Clair L. and Florence (Heiges) Aungst; m. T.S. Redmond, 1956 (div. 1967); children: T.S. Redmond II; m. Frederick L. Wedel, Jr., 1974 (div. 1986). BA, Alaska Meth. U., 1966; MEd, U. Alaska, Anchorage, 1972; postgrad. in comm., Stanford U., 1975-76. Lic. third class broadcasting, FCC. Profl. actress Charming Models & Models Guild of Phila., 1954-61; asst. dir. devel. in charge pub. rels. Alaska Meth. U., Anchorage, 1966, part-time lectr., 1966, 73; comm. tchr. Anchorage Sch. Dist., 1967-96; owner Wedel Prodns., Anchorage, 1976-86; cons. comms., media and edn.; pub. rels. staff Alaska Purchase Centennial Exhibit, U.S. Dept. Commerce, 1967; writer gubernatorial campaign, 1971; part-time instr. Chapman Coll., 1990-93; adj. instr. U. Alaska, Anchorage, 1972, 77-79, 89—; cons. Cook Inlet Native Assn., 1978, No. Inst., 1979; judge Ark. Press Women's Writing Contest, 1990-91; sec. exec. bd. Alaska Dept. Edn. Profl. Tchg. Practices Commn., 1993-94, mem. 1993-96. Bd. dirs. Sta. KAKM, Alaska Pub. TV, membership chmn., 1978-80, nat. lay rep. to Pub. Broadcasting Svc. and Nat. Assn. Pub. TV Stas., 1979; bd. dirs. Ednl. Telecom. Consortium for Alaska, 1979, Mid-Hillside Cmty. Coun., Municipality of Anchorage, 1979-80, 83-88, Hillside East Cmty. Coun., 1984-88, pres., 1984-85; rsch. writer, legal asst. Vinson & Elkins, Houston, 1981; v.p., bd. dirs. Inlet View ASD Cmty. Sch., 1994-95, pres., 1995-97; mem. Valley Forge Freedoms Found., Murdoch Scholarships, Valley Forge; bd. dirs. Rev. Richard Gay Trust, Alaska and Pa., 1992—; active Anchorage Opera Guild, Anchorage Concert Assn. Recipient awards for newspapers, lit. mags.; award Nat. Scholastic Press Assn., 1981, 82, 83, 84; Alaska Coun. Econs., 1982, Merits award Alaska Dept. Edn., 1982-93, Legis. commendation State of Alaska, Nat. Blue Ribbon Outstanding Sch. award, 1993. Mem. NEA (AEA bldg. rep., state del. 70s, 80s, 94-95), Assn. Pub. Broadcasting (charter mem., nat. lay del. 1980), Indsl. TV Assn. (San Francisco and Houston 1975-81), Alaska Press Club (chmn. high sch. journalism workshops, 1968, 69, 73, awards for sch. newspapers 1972, 74, 77), Alaska Fedn. Press Women (dir. 1978-86, 94-95, pres. 1995-96, h.s. journalism competition youth projects dir., award for brochures 1978, chair youth writing contest 1994-95), Internat. Platform Assn., World Affairs Coun., Chugach Electric (chair 1990, nomination com. for bd. dirs. 1988-90), Stanford U. Alumni Club (Alaska pres. 1982-84, 90-92, 99-2000, v.p. 1998-99), Petroleum Club of Anchorage, Anchorage East Rotary, Club at Pelican Bay (Fla.) Singles and Women's Club, Naples (Fla.) Philharm. League, Naples Players Theatre Guild, PB Singles and Women's League, Delta Kappa Gamma. Presbyterian. Office: PO Box 111489 Anchorage AK 99511-1489 also: PO Box 770662 Naples FL 34107-0662

WEDENIG, HARALD DIETER, consulting plastics engineer; b. Klagenfurt, Carinthia, Austria, Oct. 4, 1961; s. Karl Josef and Helga Anna (Salzmann) W. Diploma in plastics engring., U. Mining and Metallurgy, Leoben, Austria, 1989. Asst. U. Mining and Metallurgy, 1989-90, lectr., 1990-92, mem. exam. bd. for polymer tech., 1991—; with numerical analysis dept. Supercomputing, Salzburg, Austria, 1990; pvt. practice engring., Leoben, 1991; mgr. Bratsch & Wedenig, cons. engrs., Salzburg, 1992—; cons. Geoconsult, Salzburg, 1991-93, Steiner, Ried, Austria, Singapore, 1995—. Patentee for method of manufacturing hollow monolithic bodies from FRP materials, method of camouflaging radar antennas, crash barriers for car racing, motocycle racing, push nut, ski racing, QA cons. Mem. Verein Deutsches Ingenieure, Verbund Leobner Kunststofftechniker, Chamber Trade and Commerce Vienna. Roman Catholic. Home and Office: Schubeststrasse 10, A-8641 Saint Marein Austria

WEDENIWSKI, SEBASTIAN, software engineer; b. Aiud, Alba, Romania, Oct. 17, 1971; s. Horst Josef and Aurelia Wedeniwski; m. Esther Dahlstrom, July 4, 1997. Diploma in computer sci. and math., U. Tübingen, Germany, 1997. Self-employed software developer, Tübingen, 1993-97; software developer, IBM, Böblingen, Germany, 1998—. Contbr. articles to profl. jours.; patentee in field. Vol. in workshop for mentally and physically handicapped Anstalt Stetten, Waiblingen, Germany, 1992-93. Winner 12th nat. contest for computer sci. Gesellschaft für Informatik e.V., 1993; grantee Studienstiftung Deutschen Volkes, 1993. Avocation: decathlons. E-mail: wedeniws@de.ibm.com. Home: Beim Herbstenhof 39, 72076 Tübingen Germany Office: IBM Deutschland Entwicklung, Postfach 1380, 71003 Böblingen Germany

WEDER, HANS, theology educator; b. Diepoldsau, Switzerland, Dec. 27, 1946; s. Johann and Katharina Weder; m. Veronika Altherr; children: Christine, Katharine. PhB, U. St. Andrews, 1973; PhD, U. Zurich, Switzerland, 1977. Asst. U. Zurich, 1974-80, prof. theology, 1980—, dean faculty theology, 1986-88; editor Zurcher Bibelkommentare, Zurich, 1988—, Neues Testament Deutsch, Göttingen, 1989-2000; co-editor Zeitschrift für Theologie und Kirche, Tübingen, 1993—; dir. Inst. Hermeneutik, Zurich, 1994-98; editor: Theologische Literaturzeitung, Leipzig, 1995-2000; pres. U. Zurich, 2000—. Author: Die Gleichnisse Jesu als Metaphern, 1978, 90, Die "Rede der Reden", 1985, 94, Neutestamentliche Hermeneutik, 1986, 89, Einblicke ins Evangelium, 1992. Mem. Soc. N.T. Studies, Acad. Scis. Home: Zürichberstr 102, CH-8044 Zurich Switzerland Office: Rektorat, Kunstlergasse 15, CH-8001 Zurich Switzerland

WEDER, JUERGEN KURT, food chemistry educator; b. Berlin, Sept. 26, 1936; s. Kurt Paul and Elisabeth (Bellack) W.; m. Adelheid Trauzettel, Aug. 29, 1963. Diploma in engring., Tech. U. Berlin, 1962, DEng, 1965. Asst. Tech. U., Berlin, 1962-66; chief asst. Tech. U., Munich, 1966-77, acad. dir., 1977—, prof. food chemistry, 1981—. Contbr. articles to profl. jours. Mem. Gesellschaft Deutscher Chemiker, Gesellschaft Deutscher Naturforscher und Aerzte, Lebensmittelchemische Gesellschaft, European Assn. for Grain Legume Rsch. Office: Tech U Muenchen, Lichtenbergstrasse 4, D-85748 Garching Germany

WEDGEWORTH, ROBERT, former dean, university librarian, former association executive; b. Ennis, Tex., July 31, 1937; s. Robert and Jimmie (Johnson) W.; m. Chung Kyun, July 28, 1972; 1 child, Cicely Veronica. AB, Wabash Coll., 1959, DHL (hon.), 1980; MS, U. Ill., 1961; LittD, Park Coll., 1973; LLD, Atlanta U., 1982; DHL, Western Ill. U., 1983, Coll. William & Mary, 1988. Cataloguer Kansas City Pub. Library, 1961-62; asst. librarian, then acting librarian Park Coll., Parkville, Mo., 1962-64; librarian Meramec Community Coll., Kirkwood, Mo., 1964-66; acquisitions librarian Brown U. Library, Providence, 1966-69; asst. prof. Rutgers U., New Brunswick, N.J., 1971-72; exec. dir. ALA, Chgo., 1972-85; dean Sch. Library Service Columbia U., N.Y.C., 1985-92; univ. libr., prof. libr. adminstrn. U. Ill., Urbana, 1992-99; mem. Nat. Commn. on New Technol. Uses of Copyrighted Works, 1975-78, biomed. library rev. com. Nat. Library Medicine, 1975-78, chmn., 1978-79; mem. network adv. com. Library of Congress, 1977-78; nat. adv. bd., exec. com., council Ctr. for the Book, Library of Congress, 1978-82; bd. dirs. Newberry Library, Chgo., 1979—, Pub. Service Satellite Consortium, 1975-85; bd. visitors U. Miami Libraries, Air U.; mem. exec. bd. Internat. Fedn. Library Assns. and Instns., The Hague, 1985-91, pres. 1991-97; trustee Am. Library in Paris, 1986-92; trustee Wabash Coll., 1988—; alumni bd. Wabash Coll., pres. 1987-89; vis. prof. Sch. Library Sci. U. N.C., Chapel Hill, 1985; mem. adv. coun. Princeton U. Libraries, 1977-78, Stanford U. Librs., 1989-92, Harvard Coll. Libr. Vis. Com., 1994-97; mem. nat. adv. com. Gannett Ctr. for Media Services; mem. Accrediting Council on Edn. in Journalism and Mass Communication, 1989-97. Editor: Library Resources and Tech. Services, 1971-73; editor-in-chief: ALA Yearbook, 1976-85, World Encyclopedia of Library and Information Services, 3d edit., 1993. Chmn. U.S. Nat. Com. for UNESCO/PGI, 1976-81. Council on Library Resources fellow, 1969; recipient Medal of Honor Internat. Coun. Archives, 1996. Mem. ALA (life), NAACP (life), Am. Soc. Info. Sci., Grolier Club, Am. Antiquarian Soc. Home: 2008 Bentbrook Dr Champaign IL 61822-9204 Office: Univ of Illinois 230 Library 1408 W Gregory Dr MC-522 Urbana IL 61801-3607*

WEDGWOOD, IAN DUNCAN, power company executive; b. Manchester, Eng., Mar. 27, 1968; s. Carl and Susan Christine (Bardsley) W.; m. Veronica Alicia Martinez, Aug. 28, 1999. BSc with honors, U. St. Andrews, Scotland, 1990, PhD, 1994. Chartered mathematician. Computer programmer U. St. Andrews, 1989-90, math. tutor, 1990-93; rsch. officer U. Bath, Eng., 1993-94; rsch. mgr. BTR Tech. Svcs. Ltd., Burton, Eng., 1995-96, artificial intelligence specialist, 1996—; finite capacity scheduling and product configuration cons. BTR Tech. Svcs. Ltd., Burton, 1996; tech. mgr. BTR Tech. Svcs. Ltd., 1997; cons. BTR Change & Tech. Group, 1997-99; program mgr. INVENSYS Power Sys. Divsn., 1999—; dir. Wedgwood Packing, Manchester, Eng., 1993—, Governor, Oldfields Hall Sch., Uttoxeter, 1998-99. Contbr. articles to profl. jours. Mem. Inst. Math. and Applications, Am. Math. Soc., Computer Soc., IEEE. Avocations: golf, swimming, sketching, reading fiction, travelling. Office: Invensys Power Systems 2727 Kurtz St San Diego CA 92110-3109

WEE, ANDREW THYE SHEN, physics educator; b. Singapore, Oct. 28, 1962; m. Brenda Saw Al Yeoh. BA with honors, U. Cambridge, Eng., 1984, MA, 1984; PGCE, U. London, 1985; DPhil, U. Oxford, Eng., 1990. Lectr. dept. physics Nat. U. Singapore, 1990-94, sr. lectr., 1994-98, assoc. prof., 1998—, dir. Surface Sci. Lab., 1999—; asst. dir. Ministry Edn., Singapore, 1997. Contbr. numerous articles to profl. jours. Capt. arty. Singapore armed forces, 1995—. Rhodes scholar, 1987; Commonwealth Trust fellow, 1997. Mem. Materials Rsch. Soc., Inst. Physics Singapore (hon. sec. 1999—). Avocation: swimming. Office: Nat U Singapore Dept Physic, Lower Kent Ridge Rd, Singapore S119260, Republic of Singapore

WEE, IN-SUK, mathematics educator; b. Pusan, Korea, June 16, 1952; d. Kye-Saeng and So-Eui (Kim) W.; m. Joon Yong, Aug. 19, 1976; 1 child, Clara Haeseung. BS, Seoul Nat. U., 1975; PhD, U Minn., 1982. Tchg. asst. U. Minn., Mpls., 1975-82; asst. prof. La. State U., Baton Rouge, 1982-83; asst. prof. Korea U., Seoul, 1983-85, assoc. prof., 1985-89, prof., 1989—, chmn. dept. math., 1988-90, 93-95; vis. prof. U. Minn., Mpls., 1991-92; referee Korea Sci. and Engring. Found., Bull. and Jour. Korean Math. Soc. Contbr. more than 20 articles to profl. jours. including Jour. Korean Math., Jour. Korean Statis. Soc., Jour. Sci. and Engring. Korea U., among others. Grantee U. Minn., 1978, Korea Sci. and Engring. Found., 1983-88, 91-93, 96, 97-99, Math. Soc. Japan, 1990, Dawoo Found., 1993-94, Korea Rsch. Found., 1993-94, Ministry Edn. Korea, 1994-99. Mem. Korean Math. Soc. (chief editor 1997—, com. probabilty theory), Inst. Math. Statistics, Bernoulli Soc., Am. Math. Soc. Office: Korea U Dept Math, 1 Anam-dong, Sungbuk-ku, Seoul 136-701, Korea

WEE, MICHAEL YOONG KAN, anesthesiologist, consultant; b. Malacca, Malaysia; arrived in Eng., 1970; s. Robert Wee and Swee Kim Ong; children: Michelle, Camilla, Niels, Jasmine, Janine. BSc first class honors, Dundee (Scotland) U., 1978, MB, B of Surgery, 1982. Sr. registrar Dundee Tchg. Hosps., 1986-87, Hvidovre and Gentofte Hosps., Denmark, 1987-89, S.W. RHA, Eng., 1989-92; cons. anesthetist Poole (Eng.) Hosp. NHS Trust, 1992—; chmn. Obstetric Anesthetists Statutory Tng. Com., Eng., 1996—. Contbr. articles to profl. jours. Recipient R.D. Campbell Meml. prize, 1982. Fellow Royal Coll. Anaesthetists; mem. Wessex Obstetric Anaesthetists (chmn. 1995—), Obstetric Anaesthetists Assn. (com. 1996, sec.-elect 1999), Assn. Anaesthetists Gt. Britain and Ireland. Avocations: aerobics, gardening, fishing, cooking. Office: Poole Hosp NHS Trust, Longfleet Rd Anaesthesia, Poole BH15 2JB, England

WEED, MELVIN L., retired railroad conductor, small business owner; b. Detroit, Jan. 25, 1947; s. Merrill L. and Flora McMillan Galbraith (Thornton) W.; m. Malinda D. Ward-Corey, Jan. 29, 1966 (div. Feb. 1982). Railroad condr. Pennsylvania Railroad, Melvindale, Mich., 1966-68, Pen Cen. Railroad, Detroit, 1968-76, ConRail, Detroit, 1976-86, Amtrack, Detroit, 1986-88; proprietor Mel's Snow Removal, Madison Heights, Mich., 1978-84, Mel's Bldg. and Landscape Supply, Madison Heights, 1979-84; local chmn., union steward United Transp. Union, Detroit, 1967-69, local v.p., 1970-76. Author: (books) Do You Feel Like Me?, 1991; contbg. poet: (anthology) Reflections of Light, 1995; singer/songwriter/composer: Cloud Nine With an Angel, 1993, (album) Faces of Love, 1996. Guardianship/foster parent State of Mich., Oakland County, 1985. Recipient citation for citizen arrest, City of Madison Heights, 1987. Avocations: writing, singing, composing music. Office: Earnest Stone Publs PO Box 1288 Sterling Heights MI 48311-1288

WEED, ROGER OREN, rehabilitation services professional, educator; b. Bend, Oreg., Feb. 2, 1944; s. Chester Elbert and Ruth Marie (Urie) W.; m. Paula J. Keller; children: Nicholette, Andrew. BS in Sociology, U. Oreg., 1967, MS in Rehab. Counseling, 1969; PhD in Rehab. Counseling, U. Ga., 1986. Cert. rehab. counselor; cert. disability mgmt. specialist; lic. profl. counselor; cert. case mgr., cert. life care planner. Vocat. rehab. counselor State of Alaska, Anchorage, 1969-71; instr. U. Alaska, Anchorage, 1970-76; counselor Langdon Psychiat. Clinic, Anchorage, 1971-74; from asst. dir. to exec. dir. Hope Cottages, Anchorage, 1974-79; owner Profl. Resources Group, Anchorage, 1978-80; mng. ptnr. Collins, Weed & Assocs., 1980-84; assoc. dir. Ctr. for Rehab. Tech. Ga. Tech. U., Atlanta, 1986-87; catastrophic injury rehab. Weed & Assocs., Atlanta, 1984—; from asst. prof. to prof. Ga. State U., Atlanta, 1987—; adj. faculty Ga. Inst. Tech.; courtesy faculty U. Fla., 1996—; chmn. Ga. Composite Bd. for Licensing Profl. Counselors. Co-author: Vocational Expert Handbook, 1986, Transferable Work Skills, 1988, Life Care Planning: Spinal Cord Injured, 1989, 94, Life Care Planning: Head Injured, 1994, Life Care Planning for the Amputee, 1992, Rehab Consultant Handbook, 1994; editor: Life Care Planning and Case Management Handbook, 1999; mem. editl. bd. Jour. of Pvt. Sector Rehab., Athens, Ga., 1986—; mem. Disting. Editl. Bd. Vanguard Series in Rehab., Athens, 1988—; contbr. articles to profl. pubis. Chair Ga. Composite Bd. for Lic. Profl. Counselors, 2000—. Recipient Gov.'s award Gov.'s Com. on Employment, Alaska, 1982, Goldpan Svc. award Gov.'s Com. on Employment, Alaska, 1978, Profl. Svcs. award Am. Rehab. Counselors Assn., 1993. Fellow Nat. Rehab. Assn. (chair legis. com., bd. dirs. met. Atlanta chpt. 1988—, pres. Pacific region 1983-85, pres.'s award Pacific region 1986), Nat. Assn. Rehab. Profls. in Pvt. Sector (chair resh. and tng. com. 1988-93, pres. 1994-95, Educator of the Yr. award 1991, 97), Nat. Brain Injury Assn., Pvt. Rehab. Suppliers Ga., Rehab. Engring. Soc. N.Am., Anchorage Amateur Radio Club. Republican. Methodist. Avocations: sailing, skiing, bicycling, flying, computers. Office: Ga State U Coll of Edn Dept Counseling/Psychol Svc 9th Fl Atlanta GA 30303

WEEDE, ERICH HARTMUT, sociology educator; b. Hildesheim, Germany, Jan. 4, 1942; s. Erich and Käthe (Günther) W.; m. Hildegard Joeris, Feb. 19, 1971. Diploma in psychology, U. Hamburg, 1966; PhD in polit. sci., U. Mannheim, 1971, venia legend, 1975. Assoc. prof. sociology U. Cologne, 1978-97; prof. sociology U. Bonn, 1997—; Johns Hopkins U. vis. prof. internat. rels. Bologna Ctr., Italy, 1986-87; editl. bds. Jour. Conflict Resolution, 1997—, Internat. Interactions, 1988—, Pacific Focus, 1986—. Author: Asien und der Westen, 2000, Economic Development, Social Order and World Politics, 1996, Mensch und Gesellschaft, 1992, Wirtschaft Staat und Gesellschaft, 1990, Weltpolitik und Kriegsursachen im 20 Jahrhundert, 1975. Mem. Am. Polit. Sci. Assn., Am. Sociol. Assn., Internat. Studies Assn. (v.p. 1985-86), Peace Sci. Soc. Internat. (pres. 1982-83). Office: Seminar für Soziologie, Adenauerallee 98a, 53113 Bonn Germany

WEEDON, MARK JOHN HAYLEY, search consultant; b. Singapore, Oct. 28, 1940; m. Julie C.J. McLeod, May 22, 1971; children: James, Anna, Georgina. MA in Law, Cambridge (Eng.) U., 1963; MBA with distinction, Harvard U., 1969. Various mktg. positions Shell Co. of Australia, Sydney, Melbourne, 1964-72; sr. assoc. McKinsey and Co., London, 1972-77; mng. ptnr. Egon Zehnder Internat., London, 1977-88; founder Corp. Community Cons., London, 1988-92; ptnr. Merton Assocs., London, 1992-95; mng. ptnr. Alexander Hughes Ltd., London, 1995-98; chmn., founder Board Search, London, 1999-2000; dir. Norman Broadlent Internat., 2000—. Avocations: gardening, tennis, skiing, opera. Home: Parkview House, Highclere, Hampshire RG20 9RG, England Office: Norman Broadlent, 20 Lower Regent St, London SW14, England

WEEKES, JOHN, international organization executive; b. Toronto, Can., 1943; m. Arlene Harris; 2 children. BA in Polit. Sci. and Econs., U. Toronto, 1966. With Dept. of External Affairs, 1966; mem. Can. Embassy in Belgrade; amb. GATT, Ottawa, 1979-87; chmn. Uruguay Round Negotiating Group, GATT Coun., 1988-89, GATT Contracting Parties, 1989-90; amb. Gen. Agreement on Tariffs and Trade, Geneva; asst. dep. min. for trade policy, Cans. chief negotiator for N.Am. Free Trade Negotiations, 1991-94; coord. NAFTA Dept. of Fgn. Affairs and Internat. Trade; sr. asst. dep. min., 1993-95, chmn. WTO com. on regional trade agreements; chmn. Working Party on the Acession of Saudi Arabia to the WTO, APCO Worldwide's Global Trade Practice, Geneva; mem. Can. Delegation to Conf. on Security and Cooperation in Europe. Office: Hdqrs Global Trade Practice, 17 Chemin Louis-Dunant, 1202 Geneva Switzerland*

WEEKLEY, LESLIE BRUCE, veterinarian, pharmacologist; b. Palatka, Fla., Sept. 9, 1953; s. Leslie B. and Shirley (Roberts) W. BS, MS, Va. Commonwealth U., 1978; MS, Med. Coll. of Va., 1981; PhD, U. Wyo., 1985; DVM, Colo. State U., 1989. Toxicologist Va. Dept. Health, Richmond, 1989-90; rsch. scientist Va.-Md. Regional Coll. Vet. Medicine, Blacksburg, 1990-93; clin. veterinarian U. Tex. S.W. Med. Ctr., Dallas, 1993-96; sr. veterinarian Toxicology Rsch. Labs., Eli Lilly and Co., Greenfield, Ind., 1996-99; sr. rsch. veterinarian Merck Rsch. Labs., Merck and Co., Inc., West Point, Pa., 1999—; toxicology cons. George Washington U., 1987-90; lectr. Va. Commonwealth U., Richmond, 1990-91; mem. expert com. on vet. drugs U.S. Pharmacopeia, 2000—; mem. Annapolis Ctr. Workshop (to educate pub. and legislators on toxicology studies). Mem. bd. sci. reviewers Am. Jour. Vet. Rsch.; contbr. articles to profl. jours. including Biochem. Pharmacology, Cardiovasc. Rsch., Compendium on Continuing Edn., 1995, 98. Mem. AVMA, Am. Coll. Clin. Pharmacology, Am. Assn. Lab. Animal Sci., Am. Coll. Lab. Animal Medicine (diplomate, publ. com.), N.Y. Acad. Scis., Sigma Xi. Achievements include research on laboratory animal science and veterinary medicine to improve the welfare of animals and the scientific values of animal studies in toxicology and pharmacology. Home: 114 State St Lansdale PA 19446-5229 Office: Merck Research Labs Merck and Co Inc Dept Comparative Med WP 44-201 West Point PA 19486

WEEKS, CHRISTOPHER HENRY CLARK, writer, historian; b. Schenectady, N.Y., May 4, 1950; s. Maurice Harold and June King (Clark) W. BA, U. Va., 1972, MA, 1976. Cons. The Nat. Trust, Gloucestershire, U.K., 1973-74; writer, editor Md. Hist. Trust, Annapolis, Md., 1976-85; adj. lectr. U. Md., College Pk., 1978—; curator, cons. Centro Internazionale A. Palladio, Vicenza, Italy, 1976-80; lectr. Goucher Coll., Towson, Md., 1979; trustee Balt. Mus. of Art, 1985-90, Friends of the Am. Wing, 1999—, Ladew Topiary Gardens, Monkton, 2000; dir., v.p. Ctr. for Palladian Studies, Richmond, Va., 1980—; speakers' com. Md. Hist. Soc., Balt., 1978-84. Author: Architectural History of Westminster, 1978, Where Land and Water Intertwine, 1985, Between the Nanticoke and Choptank, 1985, AIA Guide to Washington, D.C., 1994, Alexander Smith Cochran, Modernist Pioneer in Traditional Baltimore, 1995, An Architectural History of Harford County, Maryland, 1996, Perfectly Delightful: The Life and Gardens of Harvey Ladew; co-author: W.L. Bottomley in Richmond, 1986, Clues to American Gardens, 1988; contbr. numerous articles to profl. jours. Trustee Ladew Topiary Gardens, 1999—. Named Knight of St. John., Episcopal Ch., 1989. Mem. Hist. Soc. of Harford County (dir. 1988—), Liriodendron Found. (dir. 1979—). Democrat. Episcopalian. Avocations: swimming, gardening, bridge. Home and Office: 230 Stony Run Ln Apt 4G Baltimore MD 21210-3023

WEEKS, CLIFFORD MYERS, musician, educational administrator; b. N.Y.C., Apr. 15, 1938; s. Vernal C. and Adeline (Campbell) W.; m. Ethel Lynn Fleming, Oct. 26, 1963 (dec. 1982); children: Clifford M. Jr., Michele Lynn. Diploma in Arranging and Composition, Berklee Coll. Music, 1962; MusB magna cum laude, Boston Conservatory Music, 1963, MusM, 1975; cert. in edn. adminstrn., Boston State Coll., 1977. Cert. secondary sch. adminstr. and tchr. music, Mass. Tchr. music Boston Pub. Schs., 1964-74, condr. All-City Stage Band, 1972-79, adminstrv. asst. to asst. supt., 1974-75, coordinator instrumental music, 1975-79, asst. prin., 1979, adminstrv. asst. to asst. supt., 1979-96, acting community supt., 1983, cluster coord., 1996—; arranger, composer, trombonist, 1963—; condr. Boston Coll. Jazz and Stage Band, Chestnut Hill, Mass., 1976-78. Composer Tryptych for tuba and piano, 1971, (oratorio) The King-Life and Teachings of Dr. Martin Luther King Jr., 1976; composer, arranger various jazz compositions, 1975. Mem. Medford (Mass.) Jaycees, 1975-76; adv. bd. Roxbury (Mass.) Boys and Girls Club, 1970—, Berklee Coll. Music, Boston, 1972. Named fellow Boston U., 1989. Mem. Boston Assn. Sch. Adminstrs. and Suprs. (adminstrs. union 1997—), Boston Tchrs. Union, Black Educators Alliance Mass. (treas. 1972-76, award 1976), ASCAP, Adminstrv. Assts. Assn. (chmn. local chpt. 1982—), Assn. for Supervision and Curriculum Devel., Omega Psi Phi. Methodist. Office: Boston Pub Schs Cluster Office # 4 40 Smith St Roxbury MA 02120-2702

WEEKS, JASON MARK, ecotoxicologist; b. Eastbourne, Sussex, Eng., May 10, 1966; s. Harold Derick and Joan Margaret (Pollard) W.; m. Sharon Denise Wellington, Sept. 12, 1987; children: Devon, Lorna. BSc with honors, U. London, 1987, PhD, 1990. Royal Soc. fellow U. Odense, Denmark, 1990-91, lectr., 1991-93; higher sci. officer NERC, Eng., 1993-94, sr. sci. officer, 1994-96, prin. sci. officer, 1997-2000; prin. scientist Nat. Ctr. for Environ. Toxicology, Marlow, Eng., 2000—. Editor: (book series) Ecological and Environmental Toxicology; mem. editl. bd. Biomarkers. Fellow Linnaeus Soc.; mem. Inst. Biology, Soc. Chartered Biologist. Avocations: fine wines, gardening, cooking. Office: NCET WRC-NSF, Henley Rd Medmenham, Huntingdon Marlow Buckinghamshr SL7 2HD, England

WEEKS, JEFFREY, sociologist, social historian; b. Rhondda, Wales, Nov. 1, 1945; s. Raymond Hugh and Eiddwen (Evans) W. BA with honors, U. Coll., London, 1967; M in Philosophy, U. Coll., 1973; PhD, U. Kent, Canterbury, U.K., 1983. History tchr. Sidcup Grammar Sch., London, 1969-70; rsch. officer London (Eng.) Sch. Econs., 1970-77; rsch. fellow Essex U., Colchester, Eng., 1978-79; lectr. in sociology U. Kent, Canterbury, 1980-83; rsch. fellow U. Southampton, Southampton, Eng., 1983-85; asst. registrar Coun. for Nat. Academic Awards, London, 1986-90; prof. social rels. U. West of Eng., Eng., 1990-94; prof. sociology South Bank U., 1994—, dean humanities and social sci., 1998—. Author: Coming Out, 1977, Sex, Politics and Society, 1981, Sexuality and It's Discontents, 1985 (socialist rev. book award, 1986), Sexuality, 1986, Against Nature, 1991, (with K. Porter) Between the Acts, 1990, 98, Invented Moralities, 1995, (with J. Holland) Sexual Cultures, 1996, Making Sexual History, 2000. Recipient Simon Sr. fellowship U. Manchester (U.K.), 1989-90. Mem. British Sociol. Assn., Writers Guild of Great Britain. Home: 26 Dresden Rd, London N19 3BD, England

WEEKS, ROBERT LEE, electronic engineer, program manager; b. Woonsocket, R.I., Mar. 8, 1957; s. Joseph Bernard and Claire Lorraine (Jolicoeur) W.; m. Christine Ann Bentley; children: Barbara Ann, Christopher Lee. BSEE, U. Ariz., 1985, postgrad., 1987; MBA, U. Phoenix, 1996. Laborer ASARCO Mine Inc., Sahuarita, Ariz., 1979-82; test engr. EMI and TEMPEST br. U.S. Army Electronic Proving Ground, Ft. Huachuca, Ariz., 1985-88, chief EMI and TEMPEST br., 1988-95; chief electromagnetics br. U.S. Army Electronic Proving Ground, Ft. Huachuca, 1995-96, mgr. R&D program, 1996—; mem. MIL-STD-461 Joint Working Group, 1989-94; mem. DOD and industry E3 standards com. Dept. Def., 1994—. Bd. dirs. Bristol Park Neighborhood Assn., Tucson, 1994—; vol. YMCA, 1994—. With USMC, 1975-79. Mem. IEEE (named Engr. of Yr. local chpt. 1994), Electromagnetic Compatibility Soc. of IEEE, Nat. Assn. Radio and Telecomms. Engrs. (cert. electromagnetic compatibility engr.). Democrat. Roman Catholic. Avocations: basketball, bowling, hiking. Office: US Army Electronic Proving Ground STEWS-EPG-TE Fort Huachuca AZ 85613

WEEKS, STANLEY BYRON, foreign and defense policy consultant; b. Oakland, Calif., Dec. 11, 1948; s. Charles Roy and Evelyn Maxcy Weeks; m. Kathleen Case, Mar. 17, 1973; children: Christine, Elizabeth, Brian, Anne. BS in Fgn. Affairs, U.S. Naval Acad., 1970; MA in Internat. Studies, Am. Univ., 1974, PhD in Internat. Studies, 1977. Commd. ensign USN, 1970, advanced through grades to comdr., 1985, ret., 1990; sr. scientist Sci. Applications Internat. Corp., McLean, Va., 1990—; adj. prof. Naval War Coll., Newport, R.I., 1994—; mil. cons. CBS News, N.Y.C., 1990—. Author: The Armed Forces of the USA in the Asia Pacific Region, 1999. Def. and fgn. policy advisor Dole Presdl. Campaign, Washington, 1995-96. Mem. Arms Control Assn., Navy League, U.S. Naval Inst., Internat. Inst. of Strategic Studies (London), Royal Inst. of Internat. Affairs (London), U.S. Coun. for Security Coop. in Asia-Pacific (bd. dirs. 1994—). Roman Catholic. Avocations: reading, skiing, travel. Home: 6221 Rockhurst Rd Bethesda MD 20817-1755 Office: Science Applications Internat Corp MS1-6-1 1710 SAIC Dr Mc Lean VA 22102-3799

WEEKS, TRESI LEA, lawyer; b. Brownwood, Tex., Dec. 3, 1961; d. Dean Moore and Patsy Ruth (Evans) Adams; m. Kevin Weeks, Oct. 26, 1998. BA in Fgn. Svc., BA in French, Baylor U., 1984, JD, 1987. Bar: Tex. 1987, U.S. Dist. Ct. (no. dist.) Tex. 1988, U.S. Ct. Appeals (5th cir.) 1989. Atty. Richard Jackson & Assocs., Dallas, 1987-91, Amis, Bell & Moore, Arlington, Tex., 1992-98. Vol. Legal Svcs. of North Tex., Dallas, 1988-97, Dallas Com. for Fgn. Visitors, 1989-92; bd. dirs. Plano Internat. Presch., 1995-96. Recipient Pro Bono Svc. award Legal Svcs. of North Tex., 1989, 90, 91. Mem. AAUW (pub. policy dir. Plano, Tex. br. 1992, 93-94, v.p. 1994-95), State Bar Tex. (mem. mentor program for lawyers com. 1994-98, mem. local bar svcs. com. 1994-96), Dallas Bar Assn., Dallas Women Lawyers Assn. (bd. dirs. 1989-90, v.p. 1992, pres. 1993). Avocations: scuba diving, reading, bicycling, hiking, growing herbs.

WEEKS, WILLIAM RAWLE, JR., oil company executive; b. Denver, Oct. 23, 1920; s. William Rawle Sr. and Besse Elizabeth (Griffith) W.; m. June Suzanne Stephens, Jan. 22, 1944 (div. 1980); children: Stephen R., Tacy A. Weeks Hahn. BA, Stanford U., 1943. With book prodn. divsn. Stanford U. Press, 1948-49; advt. exec. Palo Alto, Calif., 1949-50; with CIA, 1951—; gen. ptnr. Weeks, Brewer & Assocs., 1971; CEO Fort Collins Consol. Royalties, Inc., Cheyenne, Wyo., 1983—. Author: Knock and Wait Awhile, 1957 (Edgar Allan Poe award 1958, Commonwealth award 1958). Nat. press and media advance man Muskie Vice Presdl. Campaign, 1968. 2nd lt. U.S. Army, 1943-46. Mem. Nat. Press Club, Denver Petroleum Club, Heather Ridge Country Club. Avocations: flying, skiing, golfing, hiking. Home: 1201 Williams St Apt 11C Denver CO 80218-2678 Office: Fort Collins Consol Royalties Inc 1508 Stillwater Ave Cheyenne WY 82009-7349

WEERASINGHE, S. G. M. ARJUNA, surgeon, cardiothoracic researcher; b. Colombo, Sri Lanka, Apr. 25, 1963; arrived in Eng., 1994; s. Samaratunga G.M. and Amarawathie Indrani Weerasinghe. MB, BS with honours in surgery, U. W.I., Barbados, 1992. House officer Queen Elizabeth Hosp., Barbados, 1992, sr. house officer, 1993; sr. house officer Nat. Health Svc., Eng., 1994-97; cardiothoracic fellow U. London, 1997—, tutor in cardiology and cardiothoracic surgery, 1998—. Contbr. articles to med. jours., including Circulation, Annals Thoracic Surgery. Fellow Royal Coll. Surgeons (Eng.); mem. AAAS, Royal Coll. Physicians (U.K.), Soc. Cardiothoracic Surgeons Gt. Britain and Ireland, Brit. Assn. for Advancement of Sci. Avocations: light aviation, scuba diving. Office: Hammersmith Hosp Dept Cardiothoracic Surgery, Ducane Rd, London W12 0HS, England

WEETMAN, ANTHONY PETER, medical educator; b. Durham, Eng., Apr. 29, 1953; s. Kenneth and Evelyn (Healer) W.; m. Sheila Lois Thompson, Feb. 20, 1982; children: James, Chloe. B of Med. Scis., U. Newcastle-upon-Tyne, Eng., 1974, MB, BS, 1977, MD, 1983, DSc, 1993. Med. Rsch. Coun. tng. fellow U. Wales Med. Sch., Cardiff, 1980-84; Med. Rsch. Coun. travelling fellow NIH, Bethesda, Md., 1984-85; Wellcome sr. rsch. fellow Royal Postgrad. Med. Sch., London, 1985-88; lectr. U. Cambridge, Eng., 1988-90; prof. medicine, dean med. sch. U. Sheffield, Eng., 1991—; Haines lectr. Mayo Clinic, Rochester, Minn., 1992. Author: Autoimmune Endocrine Disease, 1991; contbr. papers to sci. jours. Fellow Royal Coll. Physicians of London (Goulstonian lectr. 1991), Am. Thyroid Assn., The Endocrine Soc., European Thyroid Assn., Assn. of Physicians (sec. 1992—), Am. Assn. Immunologists. Avocations: mountaineering, squash, ornithology. Office: Clin Scis Ctr, No Gen Hosp, Sheffield S57 AU, England

WEFERS, KLAUS PETER, dentist; b. Bottrop, Germany, Oct. 10, 1955; s. Heinrich Johann and Maria Theodora (Hilgert) W.; m. Sabine Kovermann, Aug. 22, 1986. DDS, Giessen U., 1986. From dental asst. to head subdept. gerodontology Giessen U., Germany, 1983-97; head Blend-a-med Rsch., Germany, 1997—; cons. Cen-Tec, Brussels, 1986-87, Stiftung Warentest, Berlin, 1996—, Deutsches Inst. für Normung, Berlin, 1998—; legal expert in prosthodontics, Hesse and Bavaria, Germany, 1988—. Mem. Arbeitskreis Gerostomatologie (pres. 1990-97), European Coll. Gerodontology (councillor 1993-98). Avocation: model railways. Home: Steinfurthstrasse 18, D-35444 Biebertal Germany Office: Procter & Gamble GmbH, Sulzbacher Strasse 40, D-65823 Schwalbach Germany

WEFERS, SABINE HILDEGARD, librarian, historian; b. Essen, Germany, Apr. 17, 1957; d. Ernst and Renate (Ferse) Kovermann; m. Klaus P. Wefers, Aug. 22, 1986. Grad., U. Giessen, Germany, 1982, PhD, 1987. Lectr. U. Giessen, Germany, 1981-84, scientific employee, 1984-86; scientific employee U. Libr., Frankfort, Germany, 1987-95, dir. catalogue dept., 1995-99; head univ. and state libr. Jena, Germany, 1999—; pres. Bd. Libr. Dirs., Thuringia, Germany, 1999—. Author: The Political System Emperor Sigismunds, 1989; editor Deutscher Bibliothekartag, 1995-98, Verein Deutscher Bibliothekare. Mem. VDB (councilor 1993-95). Avocations: dancing, literature, gardening. Office: Thulb, Postfach, D-07740 Jena Germany

WEFFORT, FRANCISCO CORREA, Brazilian government official; b. San Pablo, Brazil, May 17, 1937. Founder Worker's Party, sec. gen., 1984-86; min. culture Brazil, 1994—; sociologist; past asst. to Pres. Cardoso. Author. Office: Esplanda Mins, Bloco B-3, Andar 70068-900, Brazil*

WEGENER, BERND A., social scientist, educator; b. Swinemuende, Germany, Nov. 2, 1944; s. Edward and Hildburg (Sachsse) W.; m. Gabriele Molitor V. Muehlfeld, May 18, 1998; 1 child, Bernd Moritz. PhD, U. Hamburg, 1975; habilitation, U. Mannheim, Germany, 1986. Lectr. psych. dept. U. Hamburg, 1972-74; study dir. Ctr. for Surveys and Rsch., Mannheim, 1975-78, program dir., 1978-86; prof. Max Planck Inst. Devel. and Edn., Berlin, 1986-87; prof. sociology U. Heidelberg, Germany, 1987-93, U. Potsdam, Germany, 1993, Humboldt U., Berlin, 1993—; dir. Inst. Social Scis. Humboldt U., Berlin, 1997-99; vis. prof. dept. sociology Harvard U., Cambridge, Mass., 1984-85. Author: Kritik des Prestiges, 1988; editor: Social Attitudes and Psychophysical Measurement, 1982, Social Justice and

Political Change, 1995. Lt. German Navy, , 1964-66. Recipient Fritz Thyssen Found. award, 1985. Mem. Internat. Soc. Social Justice Rsch. (bd. dirs.). Office: Inst Social Scis, Humboldt U, D-10099 Berlin Germany

WEGENER, HEIDE, linguist, educator; b. Bitterfeld, Germany, Dec. 13, 1940; d. Werner and Meta (Woeste) W. Exam, Free U., Berlin, 1968; PhD, Tech. U., Berlin, 1984; habilitation, U. Augsburg, Germany, 1993. Asst. Free U., 1971-75; lectr. U. Sorbonne, Paris, 1976-82; docent U. Augsburg, 1982-93, Waseda U., Tokyo, 1988; prof. U. Heidelberg, Germany, 1993-94; prof. German and Linguistics U. Potsdam, Germany, 1994—. Author: Der Dativ im heutigen Deutsch, 1985, Die Nominalflexion des Deutschen, 1995; contbr. articles to profl. jours of German linguistics. Mem. Deutsche Gesellschaft fur Sprachwiss, Internat. Cognitive Linguistics Assn. Office: U Potsdam, PO Box 60 15 53, 14415 Potsdam Brandbrg, Germany

WEGENER, INGO, computer science educator; b. Bremen, Fed. Republic Germany, Dec. 4, 1950; s. Werner and Gisa (Luebsin) W.; m. Christa Muerbe, May 16, 1975. Diploma, U. Bielefeld, Fed. Republic Germany, 1976, PhD in Math., 1978, Habilitation in Math., 1981. Asst. U. Bielefeld, 1976-80; prof. computer sci. Johann Wolfgang Goethe U., Frankfurt am Main, Fed. Republic Germany, 1980-87; prof. computer science U. Dortmund, Fed. Republic Germany, 1987—; juror Jugend Forscht, Hamburg, Fed. Republic Germany, 1989-98; scientific leader German Computer Sci. competition, 1995—. Author: Search Problems, 1979 (transl. into Russian, 1982, English 1982), Efficient Algorithms for Fundamental Functions, 1989, The Complexity of Boolean Functions, 1987, Theoretical Computer Science, 1993, Theoretical Computer Science a Compendium, 1996, Computer Science-A Start-up, 1998, Highlights of Computer Science, 1996, Branching Program and Binary Decision Diagrams, Theory and Applications, 2000. Mem. Soc. for Info. (speaker theoretical computer sci. group 1989-91), Deutsche Forschungsgemeinschaft DFG (main referee 1992-2000). Avocations: soccer, tennis. Home: Lessingstrasse 58A, 33604 Bielefeld Germany Office: U Dortmund, FB Info LS II, 44221 Dortmund Germany

WEGENER, KLAUS, ophthalmologist; b. Wernigerode, Germany, Apr. 22, 1940; s. Franz and Eva (Schmidt) W.; m. Lissy Rehn, Sept. 20, 1968 (div. Apr. 1988); children: Sebastian, Andreas, Alexandra. Physikum, U. Kiel, Fed. Republic Germany, 1963; Staatsexamen, U. Freiburg, Fed. Republic Germany, 1966. Wiss. asst. U. Kiel, 1969, U. Heidelberg, Fed. Republic Germany, 1970; asst. arzt Katharinenhosp., Stuttgart, Fed. Republic Germany, 1970-73; ophthalmologist Krankenhaus/Travemünde, Lübeck, Fed. Republic Germany, 1974-81, Krankenhaus/Augsburg, Fed. Republic Germany, 1986; pvt. practice ophthalmology Kiel, 1986—. Kirchenvorstand, Protestantische Kirche, Niendorf, Ostsee, 1978-82. Mem. Christlich Democratic Party. Avocations: harpsichord, aviation. Office: Kirchhoffallee 35, 2300 Kiel Germany

WEGERT, ELIAS, mathematics educator; b. Nossen, Saxony, Germany, Mar. 20, 1955; s. Frieder Wegert and Waltraud (Möbius) Ssuschke; m. Petra Franck, May 5, 1978; children: Jenny, Henry. Diploma, Chemnitz (Germany) TH, 1980; PhD, Chemnitz Tech. U., 1984; habilitation, Bergakademie, Freiberg, Germany, 1988. Asst. Chemnitz (Germany) TH, 1980-84, Bergakademie TU, Freiberg, Germany, 1984-88; assoc. prof. Bergakademie TU, Freiberg, 1989-92, prof. math., 1992—. Author: (book) Nonlinear Boundary Value Problems for Holomorphic Functions and Singular Integral Equations, 1992; contbr. over 35 articles to profl. jours. Mem. Am. Math. Soc., Gesellschaft Angewandte Math. Mech., Deutsche Math. Ver. Avocation: climbing. Home: Dantestr 19, D-09127 Chemnitz Saxony, Germany Office: Freiberg Tech U Math Dept, Akademiestr 6, D-09596 Freiberg Germany

WEGMANN, RUDOLF, mathematician; b. Obergünzburg, Germany, Sept. 21, 1940; s. Magnus and Kreszentia (Grandi) W. D Natural Scis, U. Munich, 1968. Mem. staff Max-Planck Inst. for Astrophysics, Munich, 1968—. Contbr. articles to profl. jours. Home: Mühlfeldweg 56, 85748 Garching Germany Office: Max Planck Inst Astrophysik, Karl Schwarzschildstrasse 1, 85748 Garching Germany

WEGMARSHAUS, GERT RUEDIGER, political scientist, researcher; b. Berlin, Germany, June 12, 1954; s. Fredo Hilmar and Lieselotte Erika (Schubert) W.; m. Tatyana Vsevolodovna Shapayeva, Nov. 18, 1977; children: Katya, Ulrike. Grad., Arbeiter und Bauern-Fakultat, Halle, 1973; diploma, St. Petersburg U., 1978; PhD, Berlin Acad. Scis., 1987; Habilitation, Europa U. Viadrina, 1999. Rschr. Acad. Berlin, 1978-89; mng. dir. Inst. Sci. Theory, 1990-91; rschr. U. Calif., Irvine, 1992, KAlev, Berlin, 1992-93; lectr. Europe U., Frankfurt, 1993-96, rschr., 1997—. Author numerous books; contbr. articles to profl. jours. Fellow German Marshall Fund, 1992; grantee Deutsche Forschungs-Gemeinschaft, 1993-95, Hochschul-Sonder Programm-III, 1997-2000. Mem. Internat. Sociol. Assn., Am. Polit. Sci. Assn., Am. Assn. Advancement Slavic Studios. Home: Flemmingstrasse 23, D-12555 Berlin Germany Office: Europa U Viadrina, Grosse Scharrnstrasse 59, D-15230 Frankfurt Germany

WEGNER, AHARON, ophthalmologist; b. Munich, Nov. 1, 1957; s. Henryk Wegner and Ida Goldfarb-Wegner. MD, Sakler Sch. of Medicine, Tel Aviv, 1981; Acupuncturist, Ludwig Boltzmann Acupuncture, Inst., Vienna, Austria, 1993. Intern Tchilov Hosp., Tel Aviv, 1981-82; resident dept. ophthalmology Tech. U. Munich, 1989-93, dir. of glaucoma outpatient dept., 1993—. Capt. Israelia mil., 1982-87. Mem. Am. Soc. Laser Medicine and Surgery, European Glaucoma Soc., Internat. Perimetric Soc., Austrian Soc. Acupuncture and Auriculotherapy, N.Y. Acad. Scis. Home: 13 Geibel St, 81679 Munich Germany Office: Dept Ophthalmology Tech Univ, 22 Ismaninger St, Munich 81657, Germany

WEGNER, GUENTER PETER, prehistorian, history educator; b. Kleinostheim, Bavaria, Germany, Mar. 31, 1937; s. Engelbert and Berta (Hofmann) W.; m. Christine Elisabeth Jung, Dec. 23, 1970; 1 child, Patrick. D Cath. Theology, Wurzburg (Germany) U., 1968, PhD, 1975. Curator Staatliches Mus., Oldenburg, Germany, 1978-87; head dept. prehistory Landesmuseum, Hannover, Germany, 1987—; hon. prof. U. Göttingen, Germany, 1997—; chmn. Niedersaechsischer Landesverein Urgeschichte, Archaeologische Kommission Niedersachsen. Author: Die vorgeschichtlichen Flussfunde aus dem Main und aus dem Rhein bei Mainz, 1976; editor: Bronzezeit in Niedersachsen, 1996, Die Kunde jour., 1987-98. Roman Catholic. Office: Niedersaechsisches Landesmu, Willy-Brandt Allee 5, D-30169 Hannover Germany

WĘGRZYN, GRZEGORZ, biologist, researcher, educator; b. Gdańsk, Poland, June 27, 1963; s. Jan and Genowefa (Małek) W.; m. Alicja Beata Pawłowicz, June 5, 1993; 1 child, Aleksandra. MS, U. Gdańsk (Poland), 1987, PhD, 1991, DSc (Habilitation), 1995. Rsch. asst. U. Gdańsk (Poland), 1987-91, lectr., 1992-96, vice dean faculty, 1993-96, from asst. prof. assoc. prof., 1996-98, head dept., 1996—, prof., 1998—; rsch. fellow U. Nottingham (Eng.), 1991; postdoctoral rsch. fellow U. Calif., San Diego, 1992. Contbr. articles to profl. jours. Recipient award Young Polish Scientist Found. Polish Sci., 1993, award sci. work Min. Nat. Edn., 1995, award sci. work Prime Minister, 1997, award prof. Found. Polish Sci., 2000; grantee Polish State Com. Sci. Rsch., 1995; U.S.-Poland Marie Sklodowska-Curie Fund II, Volkswagen Found., European Union. Mem. Polish Biochem. Soc., Polich Genetical Soc. (pres. Gdańsk branch 1995). Home: Jednorozca 59/6, 80-299 Gdańsk Poland Office: U Gdańsk, Kładki 24, 80-822 Gdańsk Poland

WEGSCHEIDER, WOLFHARD, chemistry educator; b. Graz, Austria, Feb. 21, 1950; m. Susanne Rath, July 9, 1974; children: Stefan Ulrich, Beate Julia, Eva Clara. D of Tech. Sci., U. Tech. Graz, 1976. Cert. engr. tech. chemistry; prof. gen. and analytical chemistry. Rsch. assoc. U. Tech., Graz, 1974-75, univ. asst., 1975-77; rsch. assoc. U. Denver, 1977-78; univ. asst. U. Tech., Graz, 1978-80, asst. prof., 1989-93; prof. U. Leoben, Austria, 1994—. Home: Flurweg 11, A-8055 Graz Austria Office: U Leoben Inst Gen and Analytical Chemistry, Franz-Josef-Str 18, A-8700 Leoben Austria

WEGULO, STEPHEN NGAKHALA, plant pathologist, researcher; b. Kakamega, Kenya, Sept. 27, 1961; came to U.S., 1988; s. Gabriel and Florence Ngakhala; m. Consolatrix Akinyi, Aug. 4, 1989; children: Gibb, Maury, Marianne. BS, Davidson Coll., 1991; MS, Iowa State U., 1994, PhD, 1997. Tchr. Shikokho Secondary Sch., Kakakamega, 1985-88, dep. head master, 1985-86, headmaster, 1986-88; head math. dept. Vihiga (Kenya) H.S., 1991-92; rsch. asst. Iowa State U., Ames, 1992-97, rsch. assoc., 1997-99, asst. scientist, 1999—. Contbr. articles to profl. jours. Mem. AAAS, Am. Phytopathological Soc., Iowa Acad. Sci., Sigma Xi, Phi Kappa Phi, Gamma Sigma Delta. Avocations: classical music, soccer. Office: Iowa State U Dept Plant Pathology 351 Bessey Hl Ames IA 50011-0001

WEH, ALLEN EDWARD, airline executive; b. Salem, Oreg., Nov. 17, 1942; s. Edward and Harriet Ann (Hicklin) W.; m. Rebecca Ann Roberton, July 5, 1968; children: Deborah Susan, Ashley Elizabeth, Brian Roberton. BS, U. N.Mex., 1966, MA, 1973. Asst. to chief adminstrv. officer Bank N.Mex., Albuquerque, 1973; pres. N.Mex. Airways, Inc., Albuquerque, 1974; dep. dir. N.Mex. Indochina Refugee Program, Santa Fe, 1975-76; dir. pub. affairs UNC Mining & Milling Co., Albuquerque, 1977-79; pres., CEO, CSI Aviation Svcs., Inc., Albuquerque, 1979—. Mem. steering com. Colin McMillan for lt. gov., Albuquerque, 1982; bd. dirs. N.Mex. Symphony Orgh., Albuquerque Conv. and Visitors Bur., 1982; mem. Albuquerque Police Adv. Bd., 1977-78; event chmn. fin. com. Rep. Heather Wilson (Rep.-N.Mex.) Re-Election Campaign, 1999—; mem. state fin. com. G.W. Bush for Pres.; co-chmn. N.Mex. Victory, 2000; elected del. GOP Nat. Conv., 2000. Capt. USMC, 1966-71, Vietnam; col. USMCR, 1971-97, Col. USMC, 1990-91, Persian Gulf, 1992-93, Somalia. Decorated Silver Star, Legion of Merit, Bronze Star with V device, Purple Heart with two gold stars, Meritorious Svc. medal with gold star, Air medal. Mem. Marine Corps Res. Officers Assn. (life, bd. dirs. 1973, 86), Res. Officers Assn. U.S. (life), SCV (life), Mil. Order Stars and Bars (life), SAR, N.Mex. Retail Assn. (chmn. 1999-2000). Republican. Episcopalian. Home: 6722 Rio Grande Blvd NW Albuquerque NM 87107-6330 Office: CSI Aviation Svcs Inc 3700 Rio Grande Blvd NW Albuquerque NM 87107-2876

WEHBE, MIKHAIL, diplomat. Amb. permanent rep. Syrian Arab Republic U.N., N.Y.C. Office: Permanent Mission Syrian Arab Republic to UN 820 2nd Ave Fl 15 New York NY 10017-4504

WEHDORN, MANFRED, architect, educator; b. Vienna, Austria, Jan. 23, 1942; s. Franz and Gabriela (Nösterer) W.; m. Margaretha Dworak, July 2, 1970; children: Armine, Jessica. Diploma in engring., Tech. U. Vienna, 1966, D Technology, 1969. Lic. architect, Vienna. Univ. asst. Tech. U. Vienna, 1966-79, lectr., 1979-81, prof., 1981; pvt. practice Vienna, 1973—; mem. working group for situation of tech. and indsl. heritage in Europe, Coun. of Europe, Strasbourg, France, 1985-89. Author: Baudenkmäler, 1st edit., 1969, 2d. edit., 1972, Wiener Ringstrasse, 1979, Baudenkmäler der Technik, 4th vol., 1984, rev. edit., 1991, Phoenix, 1999, 101 Restaurierungen in Wien, 2000; contbr. to sci. publs. Recipient Osteseichisches Elvenkreuz fur Wissenschaft und Kunst, 1995, Goldenes Ehrenzeichen für Verdieuste um das Land Wien, 1999. Mem. Denkmalbeirat Osterr (pres. 1986-92), Fachbeirat (pres. 1991-99). Roman Catholic. Office: Tech U Vienna, Karlsplatz 13, A 1040 Vienna Austria

WEHNER, HENRY OTTO, III, pharmacist, consultant; b. Birmingham, Ala., Mar. 3, 1942; s. Henry O. Jr. and Carolyn (Kirkland) W.; m. Sammye Ruth Murphy, June 8, 1974 (div. July 1989); m. Sharron Marie Culp, Mar. 5, 1998. AA, Daytona Beach Community Coll., 1967; BS in Biology, North Ga. Coll., Dahlonega, 1971; BS in Pharmacy, U. Ga., 1978. Registered pharmacist, Fla., Ga.; cert. sci. tchr. grades 7-12, Ga. Tchr. biology Irwin County High Sch., Ocilla, Ga., 1971-75; extern Eckerd Drugs, Athens, Ga., 1977; intern/extern St. Mary's Hosp., Athens, 1977; pharmacy intern Button Gwinnett Hosp., Lawrenceville, Ga., 1978; co-owner, mgr. Hiawassee (Ga.) Pharmacy, 1978-79; staff pharmacist Dyal's Pharmacy, Daytona Beach, Fla., 1979, Little Drug Co., New Smyrna Beach, Fla., 1979-80; staff pharmacist, mgr. Super X Drugs, New Smyrna Beach, 1980-81; staff pharmacist Fish Meml. Hosp., New Smyrna Beach, 1981-92, Halifax Med. Ctr., Daytona Beach, Fla., 1992—; oncology pharmacist Regional Oncology Ctr. Halifax Med. Ctr., 2000—. With USAF, 1961-65. Mem. Am. Pharm. Assn., Fla. Soc. Hosp. Pharmacists, Volusia County Pharm. Assn., Ea. Shores Soc. Hosp. Pharmacists (charter, pres. 1995-96), Eastern Shores Fla. Soc. Hosp. Pharmacists, Phi Lambda Sigma, Phi Theta Kappa. Methodist. Avocations: painting, cycling, tennis. Office: Halifax Med Ctr PO Box 1350 303 N Clyde Morris Blvd Daytona Beach FL 32114-2709

WEHNER, KAY Y., poet; b. Brill, Wis., July 26, 1922; d. Burritt C. and Olivia P. Leonard; children: Kurt Thomas, Todd Craig. BA, U. Wis., 1945; postgrad., U. Calif., Berkeley, 1958-59. Author: (poetry) Granite and Kettle Moraine, 1980, Far Falcons, 1980, Incantations from Heron Lake, 1988, Spirit of Tallinn, 1991, Under the Rain, 1995, Torn Horizons, 2000. Home: 650 Hilldale Ave Berkeley CA 94708-1316

WEHNERT, MANFRED SIEGFRIED, human molecular geneticist, educator; b. Stralsund, Germany, Feb. 7, 1951; s. Siegfried and Erika (Stripp) W.; m. Susanne Christine Kittner, Oct. 6, 1989; children: Hendrikje, Sabine Susanne. Diploma in Biology, U. Greifswald, Germany, 1973, PhD, 1980, Habilitation, 1991. Cert. human geneticist. Faculty U. Greifswald, 1978-91; postdoctoral Baylor Coll., Houston, 1991-94; sr. faculty U. Greifswald, 1994—, prof. human molecular genetics, 1999—. Recipient award Johann-Lukas-Schoenlein Soc., Germany, 1990, award Fed. Min. Sci. and Tech., Germany, 1991. Fellow AAAS, Am. Soc. Human Genetics, European Soc. Human Genetics, Human Genome Orgn., World Muscle Soc. Achievements include research in post-and prenatal biochemical diagnosis of inborn; errors of metabolism; introduction of molecular genetics diagnosis of clotting disorders and muscle diseases; identification and characterization of human genes; codiscovery of the gene for Miller-Dieckér-Lisencephaly. Avocation: sailing. Office: Inst Human Genetics, Fleischmannstr 42/44, D-17487 Greifswald Germany

WEHR, JAMES PAUL, musician; b. Celina, Ohio, Feb. 19, 1960; s. Paul and Sally Wehr; m. Elisabeth Dawn Wehr, Sept. 1, 1964; 1 child, Alexander Clarence. BA, U. Ctrl. Fla., 1982; MusM, U. Cin., 1984; postgrad., Ind. U., 1985-87. Sch. sales rep. Allegro Music Ctr., Casselberry, Fla., 1983-87; bass trombonist Teatr Wielke Orch., Warsaw, Poland, 1988, Airforce Band New England, Hanscom AFB, Mass., 1989-92; classical buyer Virgin Megastore, Lake Buena Vista, Fla., 1998-99; dir. bands Pine Castle (Fla.) Christian Acad., 2000—; pub. over 200 compositions Wehr's Music Ho., 1991-99; founder Prima Poni-Orlando Trombone Choir, Orlando, Fla., 1994—, Cuarteto de la Asensión, 1997—. Composer 6 works for chamber ensemble, 1993-99; contbr. articles to jour. Internat. Trombone Assn. With USAF, 1989-92. Yamaha scholar Ind. U., 1980; recipient Van Wey Hill award Brevard (N.C.) Music Ctr., 1982, Quello award, Outstanding Musician award U. Ctrl. Fla., 1982. Mem. Pi Mu Alpha (pres. Sinfonia Mu Eta chpt. 1981-82). Republican. Lutheran. Avocations: model rockets, sports, outdoor activities. E-mail: wehrestate@aol.com. Home and Office: 3533 Baxter Dr Winter Park FL 32792-1704

WEHRHAHN, RICARDO AMÉZAGA, strategy consultant; b. La Paz, Bolivia, Feb. 16, 1963; arrived in Germany, 1998; s. Rudolfo and Mercedes (Amézaga) W.; m. Tatiana Dubravcic, 1993. Bachelor, German Sch., Bolivia, 1979; diploma informatiker, U. Hamburg, 1988. Head devel. dept. NONAS, S.A., Spain, 1987-89; head ESP and devel. Corso Computer and S.W. GmbH, Germany, 1989-91; dir. EDP and orng. distbn. Quelle S.A., Spain, 1991-96; freelance info. tech. cons. Madrid, 1996-97; sr. assoc. Booz-Allen & Hamilton, Munich, 1998—; founder Golf 4 You S.L., Madrid, 1993. Author photography exhbn. Mem. IEEE Computer Soc., U.S. Avocation: golf. Home: Erikaweg 3, 85375 Neufahrn Germany Office: Booz Allen & Hamilton, Lenbachplatz 3, D-80333 Munich Germany

WEHRMEYER, WALTER CLAUS HEINRICH, ecological management educator; b. Krefeld, Germany, May 23, 1962; arrived in the U.K., 1988; s. Wolfgang and Margaret (Segelken) W.; m. Susanne Lin Nelson, July 17, 1993. Zwischenexamen in Bus. Adminstrn., U. Marburg, Germany, 1985; diploma in devel. studies, U. Kent, Canterbury, U.K., 1988, MA in Mgmt., 1989, PhD in Environ. Mgmt., 1993. Rsch. asst. Canterbury Bus. Sch., 1990-91; rsch. fellow U. Kent, 1991-93, lectr. A, 1993-95, lectr. B, 1995-97; BG Surrey scholar in contaminated land Ctr. for Environ. Strategy, U. Surrey, 1998—; dir. Bus. in the Environment Program, U. Kent, 1994-97; sr. tutor external programme Wye Coll., U. Coll. London; cons. in field. Author: Environmental References in Business, 1994, Measuring Environmental Performance, 1995; author, editor: Greening People, 1996; co-editor: Growing Pains, 1999; guest editor Greener Mgmt. Internat. Jour., 1996, 97; editor Greener Mgmt. Internat.; mem. editl. bd. Jour. Indsl. Ecology, Environment, Devel. and Sustainability; contbr. chpts. to books and articles to profl. jours. Judge Industry in Kent Enviroment Award, 1994—. Fellow Royal Soc. Arts; mem. Inst. Environmental Mgmt. and Assessment. Avocation: sailing. E-mail: W.Wehrmeyer@surrey.ac.uk. Office: Ctr for Environ Strategy, Univ Surrey, Guildford Surrey GU2 5XH, United Kingdom

WEI, CHENG LIAN, physicist; b. Countryside, China, June 2, 1938; s. Lai An and Tian Tai (Li) W.; m. Min Hua Zhang, Nov. 12, 1969; 1 child, Dong. BS, Shanghai Univ. Sci. & Tech., Shanghai, China, 1963. Rsch. mem. Shanghai Univ. Sci & Tech., Shanghai, 1963—. Contbr. articles to profl. jours. Fellow Inst. of High Energy Physics; mem. Chinese Nuclear Physics Soc., High Energy Physics Soc. China, Chinese PHysics Soc. (synchrotron radiation com.), Am. Assn. Advancement Sci. Avocations: watching football matches, music, walking. Office: Inst of High Energy Physics Academia Sinica, PO Box 2732, 100080 Peijing China

WEI, FONG, nephrologist; b. Shanghai, May 2, 1941; came to U.S., 1941; s. Tseh Heen and Waling (Chung) W.; m. Theodora Mary Zopko, July 16, 1966; children: Christopher, Alexander. BA, Yale U., 1963; MD, Tufts U., 1967. Diplomate Am. Bd. Internal Medicine, Am. Bd. Nephrology. Intern Boston City Hosp., 1967-68, resident, 1968-69; resident Bronx (N.Y.) Mcpl., 1969-70; fellow in nephrology U. N.C., Chapel Hill, 1970-72; pvt. practice Princeton, N.J., 1974—; clin. assoc. prof. Robert Wood Johnson Med. Sch., New Brunswick, N.J., 1975—; pres. med. staff Med. Ctr. Princeton, 1981-82; prin. investigator Bristol Myers Squibb, Princeton, 1984—, Merck and Co., Princeton, 1988—; cons. Princeton U., 1990—; pres. Princeton Med. Group, 1982—. Med. advisor Princeton Regional Homemakers Assn., 1975—. Fellow ACP; mem. Am. Soc. Nephrology, Internat. Soc. Nephrology, Am. Soc. Hypertension. Office: Princeton Med Group 419 N Harrison St Princeton NJ 08540-3521

WEI, GAOYUAN, chemistry educator; b. Chenxi, Hunan, China, June 26, 1961; s. Xiangfu and Fuhua (Tian) W.; m. Weiwei Luan, 1993; 1 child, Kaihuan. B in Polymer Engring., South China Inst. Tech., Guangzhou, People's Rep. of China, 1982; MSc in Chem. Engring., Cornell U., 1985; PhD in Chemistry, U. Wash., 1990. Rsch. assoc. chemistry dept. U. Wash., Seattle, 1990; rsch. assoc. Cavendish Lab. U. Cambridge, Eng., 1990-92; lectr. chemistry dept. Coll. Chemistry and Molecular Engring., Peking U., Beijing, 1992-93, assoc. prof., 1993-99, prof., 1999—. Contbr. articles to sci. jours. Mem. Am. Chem. Soc., Am. Phys. Soc., Internat. Union Pure and Applied Chemistry, Inst. of Physics, N.Y. Acad. Scis., Chinese Chem. Soc. Avocations: writing, reading, jogging, hiking, badminton. Home: Yandongyuan Peking U, 606 Bldg 7A, Beijing 100871, China Office: Peking U, Dept Chemistry, Beijing 100871, China

WEI, GUANGHUA, mechanical engineer; b. Sanming, China, Nov. 18, 1969; parents Juyang Wei and Guijin Ni; m. Bifang Su, Nov. 5, 1993. BS, Shanghai Jiao Tong U., 1992; MS, Tex. A&M U., 1997. Engr. Yong-an Thermal Power Plant, China, 1992-94; rsch. asst. Tex. A&M U., College Station, 1994-97, rsch. assoc., 1997-99, sr. rsch. assoc., 1999—. Mem. ASME, ASHRAE, Sigma Xi. Avocations: classical music, travel, soccer, gardening. Home: 2800 Longmire Dr Apt 10 College Station TX 77845-5804 Office: Tex A&M U Energy Sys Lab Werc 068 College Station TX 77843-0001

WEI, GUANG-PU, science educator; b. Zhuji, Zhejiang, China, Jan. 9, 1939; s. Shao Yuan Wei and Ai Zhao He; m. Fei-Wen Sun; children: Ang, Hong. Degree, Nanjing (China) U., 1961; PhD, Osaka (Japan) U., 1996. Asst. prof. Shanghai U., 1961-65, lectr., 1965-84, assoc. prof., 1986-92, prof., 1992—; vis. rschr. Osaka U., 1984-86; vis. prof. Kobe (Japan) U., 1995-96; rschr. in field; bd. dirs. Shanghai U. Libr., 1996-99. Patentee amorphous silicon x-ray sensor, amorphous silicon devices, measurement equipments for solar cell. Bd. dirs. Shanghai Overseas Returned Student Assn., 1990. Recipient award of sci. and technique Ministry of Edn. of China, 1992, Shanghai City Govt., 1992, 99. Mem. Shanghai Phys. Soc. (bd. dirs. 1986-99), Shanghai Solar Energy Soc. (bd. dirs. 1987-99), N.Y. Acad. Sci. Avocation: music. Office: Shanghai U Inst Material Sc, No 20 Cheng Zhong Rd, Jaiding Shanghai 201800, China

WEI, GUO-QING, computer scientist; b. Jing-Tan, Jiangsu, China, Oct. 1, 1962; came to U.S., 1998; s. Lian-Gen and Xiao-Min (Dong) W.; m. Xiao-Wen Yin, Sept. 16, 1963; children: Catherine, Lucia. BSc, Nanjing (China) Inst. Tech., 1983, MSc, 1986; PhD, Southeastern U., Nanjing, 1989. Asst. prof. Chinese Acad. Scis., Beijing, 1989-91; sr. rsch. scientist German Aerospace Rsch. Establishment, Munich, 1991-98; mem. tech. staff Sienens Corp. Rsch., Inc., Princeton, N.J., 1998—. Contbr. numerous articles to profl. jours. Recipient Best Paper award Chinese Acad. Scis., 1991, Best Paper award German Assn. pattern Recognion and Austrian Assn. pattern Recognition, 1994, Olympus European Found. prize, 1997. Mem. IEEE (sr.). Avocations: walking, swimming, table-tennis. Office: Siemens Corp Rsch Inc 755 College Rd E Princeton NJ 08540-6632

WEI, LU-XIN, radiation health researcher; b. Tianjin, China, Sept. 21, 1922; s. Shao-Geng and Shu-Ying (Li) W.; m. Zhu-Kui Quan, Jan. 14, 1951; children: Gang, Ming, Qing, Quan-Xin. Diploma, Med. Coll. U., Beijing, 1950. From asst. to lectr. Sch. Hygiene Peking Univ. Med. Coll., Beijing, 1950-57; from lectr. to assoc. prof. Beijing Inst. Radiation Medicine, 1957-72; from assoc. prof. to prof. lab. indsl. hygiene Min. Pub. Health, Beijing, 1972—; expert com. Nat. Bur. Environ. Protection, Beijing, 1985—, Nat. Nuclear Safety Adminstrn., Beijing, 1986—; rep. UN Scientific Com., Vienna, 1987-89; expert adv. panelist Min. Health, Beijing, 1994—. Mem. Soc. Radiol. Medicine & Protection. Office: Lab Indsl Hygiene, 2 Xinkang St, Beijing 100088, China

WEI, MING, epidemiology researcher; b. Nanning, China, May 5, 1958; came to U.S., 1989; s. Shi-Phan Wei and Wan-Yan Liu; m. Kun Wang, July 14, 1987; children: Murlin K., Glyn K. MD, Guang Xi Med. Coll., Nanning, China, 1983, MS, 1986; MPH, U. S.C., 1992. Physician Guang Med. Coll. Hosp., Nanning, China, 1986-89; med. assoc. Iwate Med. U., Marioca, Japan, 1989; path. assoc. U. Pitts., 1989-91; rsch. asst. prof. U. S.C., Columbia, 1993-94; fellow U. Tex. Health Sci. Ctr., San Antonio, 1994—. Contbr. articles to profl. jours. Mem. AAAS, Am. Diabetes Assn., Soc. Epidemiol. Rsch., Chinese Med. Assn. Avocations: chess, fishing, travel, basketball, golf. Home: 6749 Spanish Moss Dr Plano TX 75024-5446 Office: U Tex Health Sci Ctr Dept Medicine/Clin Epidem 7703 Floyd Curl Dr San Antonio TX 78284-6200

WEI, SERH SHERNG, nephrologist; b. Singapore, Apr. 26, 1956; s. Chau and Song (Heng) Tan Wei; m. Mui Hua, Apr. 26, 1980; children: Lydia, James. MBBS, U. Singapore, 1980; MD, Nat. U. Singapore, 1988. Intern Min. Health, Singapore, 1980-81; med. officer Min. Def., Singapore, 1981-82; med. officer, registrar Min. Health, Singapore, 1983-90; vis. specialist Nat. Kidney Found., Singapore, 1990-91; sr. registrar, cons. Min. Health, 1990—. Author: Understanding Dialysis: An Illustrated Guide on Haemodialysis, 1994; contbr. articles to profl. jours. Mem. Singapore Med. Assn., Singapore Soc. Nephrology, Asian-Pacific Soc. Nephrology, Endocrine and Metabolic Soc. Singapore, Am. Soc. Artificial Internal Organs, Internat. Soc. Nephrology, Singapore Soc. Hypertension, Serangoon Country Club, Raffles Town Club. Methodist. Avocations: fishing, reading, table tennis, swimming, preaching.

WEI, SHYUE-WIN, electrical engineering educator; b. Peido, Changhua, Republic of China, June 9, 1958; s. Ching-hsi and Hsu chai-hsia (Hsu) W.; m. Yueh-hua Lin, Mar. 1, 1984; children: Shih-Ping, Yu-Ting. BS, Cen. Police Coll., Taoyuan, Taiwan, 1980; MS, Nat. Chiao-Tung U., Hsinchu/Taiwan, 1986, PhD, 1990. Cert. nat. police spl. examiner. Assoc. technician Inst. Police Telecomms., Taipei, Taiwan, 1980-82, technician, 1982-84; assoc. rschr. Telecom. Labs., Chungli, 1990-92; prof. elec. engring. Chung-Hua U., Hsinchu, 1992-2000, Chi-Nan U., Poli, Nan-Tou, Taiwan, 2000—; cons. Tailyn Comm. Co., Taoyuan, 1994-96, Data Secom Co., Taipei, 1994-95, Nat. Police Adminstr., Taipei, 1994, ITE Co., Santa Clara, Calif., 1996-98. Author: Principle of Data Communications, 1992; patentee in field. 2d lt.

mil. police, Taiwan, 1980. Recipient rsch. award Nat. Sci. Coun., Teipei, 1994. Mem. IEEE (sr.). Buddhist. Avocations: knights-errant novel, Judo. Home: No 5 Ln 67 Yuan-Ho St 3d Fl, 300 Hsinchu Taiwan Office: Chi-Nan U Dept Elec Engr, 1 University Rd, 545 Poli Nan-Tou, Taiwan

WEI, TIE-QUAN, biochemist; b. Feshan, Canton, China, Sept. 3, 1956; came to U.S., 1988; s. Yuan-Pu Wei and Shu-Gui Wang; m. Yun Yue, Nov. 20, 1986; children: Le, Jason. BS, Nankai U., Tianjing, China, 1982; MS, Chinese Acad. Scis., Beijing, 1986; PhD in Biochemistry, U. Ill., Chgo., 1993. Rsch. assoc. China-Japan Friendship Hosp., Beijing, 1986-88; postdoctoral fellow Loyola Med. Ctr., Chgo., 1993-95; devel. biochemist DuPont Med. Products, Newark, Del., 1995-96; sr. biochemist Dade Behring Inc., Newark, 1996—. Contbr. articles to profl. jours. Recipient Sci. Advancement award Chinese Acad. Scis., 1987, Travel award GenBio, Inc., 1995. Fellow Nat. Acad. Clin. Biochemistry, mem. Am. Assn. Clin. Chemistry (diplomate). Achievements include discovery and purification of Casein Kinase II from human erythrocyte membrane. Home: 115 George Ct Bear DE 19701-1882 Office: Dade Behring Inc Glasgow Site 707 PO Box 6101 Newark DE 19714-6101

WEI, YANG, olympic athlete; b. Hubei, China, Feb. 8, 1980. Mem. men's gymnastics team China; winner all-around silver medal Asian Games, 1998; winner team gold World Championship, 1999, winner bronze medal in high bar, 1999; winner team all-around Olympics, Sydney, Australia, 2000. Office: Chinese Gymnastics Assn, 9 Tiyuguan Rd, 100 763 Beijing China*

WEI, YAU-HUEI, biomedical research scientist; b. Taichung, Taiwan, Republic of China, May 29, 1952; s. Yuing-Kwei and Jen (Wu) W.; m. Yeh-Jen Lin, Aug. 11, 1978; children: Li-Sing, Tien-Sing, Mu-Sing, Teng-Sing. BS, Nat. Taiwan U., Taipei, Republic of China, 1974; PhD in Biochemistry, SUNY, Albany, 1980. Assoc. prof. biochemistry Nat. Yang-Ming Med. Coll., Taipei, 1981-85, prof., chair dept. biochemistry, 1985-91, dean student affairs, 1989-91; investigator Clin Rsch. Ctr. Taipei Vets Gen. Hosp., 1984—; cons. Taichung Vets Gen. Hosp. 1991-97; dir. Instrumentation Ctr., Nat. Yang Ming Med. Coll., Taipei, 1985-88; dir. Ctr. for Cellular and Molecular Biology, Nat. Yang-Ming U., 1993—; prof. biochemistry Sch. Life Sci., 1994—; coord. med. biochemistry and molecular biology study sect. Nat. Sci. Coun., Taiwan, 1997-99; nat. del. Gen. Assembly Internat. Union Biochemistry and Molecular Biology, 2000—. Author: New Experimental Biochemistry, 1986, Recent Advances in Molecular and Biochemical Research on Proteins, 1993; editor: Molecular Mechanism of Alcohol, 1989, Advances in Biotechnology and Molecular Biology, 1990; exec. editor Sci. Monthly, Taipei, 1989—, Chinese Biochem. Soc., Taipei, 1991—, Chinese Med. Jour., Taipei, 1994—; editor Jour. Biochemistry, Molecular Biology and Biophysics, 1996—. Recipient Biomed. Rsch. award Ching-Ling Med. Found., Taipei, 1983, 93, Disting. Rsch. award Republic of China Nat. Sci. Coun., Taipei, 1987-98, Disting. Teaching award Min. Edn., Taipei, 1989-90, Excellent Rschr. award Global Hope Med. Found., Taipei, 1998; William Evans fellow U. Otago, Dunedin, New Zealand, 1996; postdoctoral fellow SUNY, Albany, 1980. Mem. AAAS, Fedn. Asian and Oceanian Biochemists and Molecular Biologists (coun. 1991-93), Chinese Biochem. Soc. (bd. editors jour. 1986—, pres. 1991-93), Soc. for Chinese Bioscientists in Am., Chinese Physiol. Soc., Chinese Clin. Biochemistry Soc., N.Y. Acad. Scis., Biophys. Soc. of Republic of China (mem. coun. 1995—, chmn. membership com.), Chinese Soc. Cell and Molecular Biology (coun. 1994—). Baptist. Avocations: ping-pong, basketball, travel, stamp and coin collecting. E-Mail: joeman@ym.edu.tw. Home: 155 Li-Long St Sec 2, Fac Drm 23, Shih-Pai, Taipei 112, Taiwan Office: Nat Yang-Ming U Sch Lif Sci, 155 Li Long St, Sec 2, Shih-Pai Taipei 112, Taiwan

WEI, YI, physicist; b. Gaozhou, Guangdong, China, Oct. 9, 1965; came to U.S., 1989; s. Yisheng Wei and Xuefang Deng; m. Cynthia Xingshan He, July 12, 1992; 1 child, Jodie R. BS, Peking U., Beijing, 1987; PhD, Ariz. State U., 1995. Instr. Jinan U., Guangzhou, China, 1987-89; rsch. assoc. Ariz. State U., Tempe, 1989-95; rsch. scientist Tex. Instruments, INc., Dallas, 1995-97; staff engr., sect. mgr. Motorola, Inc., Tempe, 1997—. Contbr. articles to profl. jours. Mem. Am. Phys. Soc., Am. Vacuum Soc., Soc. Info. Display. Achievements include U.S., European and Japanese patents. Avocations: reading, hiking, cooking. E-mail: yi.wei@motorola.com. Fax: 480-755-5115. Home: 41 S Forest Dr Chandler AZ 85226-8616 Office: Motorola Flat Panel Display Divsn 7700 S River Pkwy Tempe AZ 85284-1808

WEI, YUCHUAN, mathematician, electrical engineer, physicist, researcher; b. Jiaozuo, Henan, China, Sept. 1, 1966; s. Bangfu and Cuilan (Liu) W. BS, Lanzhou U., 1988; MS, Chinese Acad. Sci., Beijing, 1994; PhD, Beijing U of Sci. and Tech., 1998. Asst. prof. Gansu Univ. of Industry, Lanzhou, 1988-91; lectr. dept. physics Beijing Univ. Sci. and Tech., 1994—; postdoctoral fellow dept. elec. engring. Beijing U. Aeronautics and Astronautics, 1999—; internat. advisor for Internat. Conf. on Math. Modelling of Nonlinear Systems, India Inst. Tech., Khakagpur. Office: Beijing U Sci & Tech, Dept Physics, Beijing 100083, China

WEI, ZIQING, geodesy researcher; b. Sui County, Henan, China, Apr. 15, 1937; s. Xiaowen Wei and Shaolan Zhou; m. Weide Luan, Apr. 29, 1969; children: Tong, Fang. Diploma, Beijing Inst. Surveying, 1960. Asst. engr. Beijing Rsch. Inst. Surveying and Mapping, Beijing, China, 1960-62; asst. engr. Xian Rsch. Inst. Surveying and Mapping, 1963-69, asst. prof., 1978-81, assoc. prof., 1981-83, prof., 1987—; vis. prof. Wuhan (China) Rsch. Inst. Surveying and Mapping, 1970-78; vis. scholar Ohio State U., Columbus, 1984-86; guest prof. Zhengzhou (China) Inst. Surveying and Mapping, 1995—, Xian Inst. Engring., 1995—; rschr. in field. Contbr. rsch. articles, reports to profl. publs., books; mem. editl. bd. Acta Geodaetica et Cartographica Sinica, 1997—. Recipient State Sci. Assembly award, 1978, 2d award of nat. sci. and tech. advance prize, 1990, 96; Chinese Govt. grantee, 1992—. Mem. Shaanxi Soc. Geodesy, Photogrammetry and Cartography (mem. geodetic commn. 1995—), Chinese Astron. Assn., Internat. Assn. Geodesy (assoc.), Chinese Acad. Engring., Internat. Union of Geodesy and Geophysics (Chinese com. 1998—). Office: Xian Rsch Inst Surveying, 1 Yanta Mid-Rd, 710054 Xian Shaanxi, China

WEIBLE, DIANE LYNN, minister; b. St Louis, Jan. 16, 1966; d. Donald Lawrence and Marlene Jo (Glanz) Dempsey; m. Timothy Scott Weible, Sept. 8, 1990; children: Rebecca Marie, Sarah Elizabeth, Joshua Michael. BA in Comms., Drury Coll., 1987; MDiv, Eden Theol. Seminary, St. Louis, 1991. Ordained minister United Ch. of Christ. Reporter, photographer Suburban Newspapers, Columbia, Ill., 1987-88; missionary United Ch. Bd. for World Ministries, Tono, Japan, 1991—. Avocations: reading, quilting, crafts, painting.

WEICHSELBERGER, KURT FRANZ, statistics educator; b. Vienna, Austria, Apr. 13, 1929; s. Franz X. and Paula (Grabner) W.; m. Ingeborg Bischoff, Aug. 23, 1955; children: Annette, Andreas, Eugen, Charlotte, Bettina. PhD, U. Vienna, 1953. Rsch. asst. Sozialforschungsstelle, Dortmund, Germany, 1953-60; teaching asst. U. Cologne, Germany, 1960-62, dozent, 1962-63; prof. Tech. U., Berlin, 1963-69, rector, 1967-68; prof. stats. U. Munich, 1969-97, prof. emeritus, 1997—. Author: Elementary Foundations of a More General Theory of Probability, vol. I, 2000 (in German); co-author: Price Index Numbers of Non-Commercial R and D for the Federal Republic of Germany 1968-77, 1978, A Methodology for Uncertainty in Knowledge-Based Systems, 1990. Mem. Internat. Statis. Inst., German Statis. Assn. (chmn. ednl. com. 1969-81, chmn. com. econ. and social faculties 1979-81). Home: Neû-Dichaû 5, D-85567 Grafing Germany Office: U Munich Rsch Group, Lüdwigstrasse 33, D-80539 Munich Germany

WEICHSLGARTNER, ALOIS JOSEPH, writer; b. Kelheim, Bavaria, Germany, Sept. 13, 1931; s. Alois and Maria (Hoetschl) W.; m. Sieglinde Anna Katharina Mair, Aug. 17, 1955; children: Petra, Norbert, Thomas, Gunther. Diploma, Gymnasium, Kelheim, Germany, 1951. Jr. editor Tagesanzeiger, Regensburg, Germany, 1955-58; editor Press Agy. "nld" Munich, 1958-62, freelance journalist and writer, 1962-69; editor Stadtanzeiger/Suddeutsche Zeitung, Munich, 1969-71; chief editor Altbayerische Heimatpost, Trostberg, Germany, 1972-94; freelance journalist and writer, 1995—. Editor: (poetry book) Bayerischer Psalter, 1975, 90; author: (poetry book) Wie Wolkenflug, 1991, (essays), Vom Nordgau zum Chiemgau, 1985, Bayer Originale: Ernst und Heiter, 1998, (book) Bayerisches Lesebuch, 1981. Recipient awards Herwig-Weber-Preis, Internat. Press Club of Munich, 1973, Bayerischer Poetentaler, Munchner Turmschreiber, Munich, 1982, Bundesverdienstkreuz am Bande, Germany, 1991. Mem. Internat. Press Club of Munich, Munchner Turmschreiber. Home: Lerchenstrasse 18, D-83308 Trostberg Germany

WEICKER, HELMUT GEORG, sports medicine administrator; b. Mainz, Germany, Mar. 6, 1920; s. Heinrich and Christine (Vollrath) W.; m. Irmgard Laule, Aug. 3, 1947; children: Ulrike, Karin. MD, Med. Sch., Frankfurt, 1946; doctor habil., Med. Sch., Heidelberg, 1957. Asst. Internal Med. County Hosp., Darmstadt, Germany, 1946-51; chief asst. Med. Policlinic, Heidelberg, Germany, 1952-58; rsch. fellow Tufts Med. Sch., Boston, 1959-61; head of dept. metabolic rsch. U. Heidelberg, 1970-72, chmn. dept. sportsmedicine, 1974-90, ret., 1990; rsch. assoc. Harvard Med. Sch., Boston, 1967-69; cons. scientific com. DSB, Frankfurt, 1975-85, Scientific Com. Bundesinstitut, Cologne, Germany, 1976-88. Author: Sportsmedicine: Physiological and Biochemical Basic Research and Practical Application, 1994; editor: Internat. Jour. Sports Medicine, 1980-90; patent for proteinelectrophoresis; contbr. articles for to profl. jours. Grantee Deutsche Forschungsgemeinschaft, 1970-90, Bundesinstitut Sportwissenschaft, 1970-90; recipient Bundesverdienstkreuz Govt., Bonn, 1988. Mem. Scientific Com. of Sportsmedicine (scientific publs., 1970-85), Soc. of Sportsmedicine (sect. of tchg. and rsch. 1975-88), Am. Coll. of Sportsmedicine. Avocations: sailing, windsurfing, skiing, tennis, track and field. Home: Remlerstr 1a, 69120 Heidelberg Germany Office: Dept Sportsmedicine, Hospitalstr 3, 69115 Heidelberg Germany

WEICKER, JACK EDWARD, educational administrator; b. Woodburn, Ind., June 23, 1924; s. Monald Henry and Helen Mae (Miller) W.; m. Janet Kathryn Thompson, May 29, 1946; children: John H., Kathryn Ann, Jane Elizabeth, Emily Jo. AB, Ind. U., 1947, MA, 1950. James Albert Woodburn fellow, All Univ. fellow; tchr. history and English Harrison Hill Sch., Ft. Wayne, Ind., 1947-48; tchr. history and English South Side H.S., Ft. Wayne, 1951-61, counselor, asst. prin., 1961-63, prin., 1963-90; mem. Ind. State Scholarship Commn., 1969-77; mem. exec. com. Midwest regional assembly Coll. Entrance Exam. Bd., 1974-77, chmn. nominating com., 1976-77, mem. nat. nominating com., 1979; mem. Midwest Regional Coll. Access Svcs. Com., 1982-84. Author: (with others) Indiana: The Hoosier State, 1959, 63; (monographs) Due Process and Student Rights/Responsibilities: Two Points of View, 1975, Back to Basics: Language Arts, 1976, College Entrance Exams--Friend or Foe?, 1981, How the Effective Principal Communicates, 1983, Readin', Writin', and Other Stuff, 1984, The Last 25 Years in Education: One Educator's Perspective, 1988, The Power of Poetry: A Muse for All Seasons, 1988, American Political Humor: Mark Twain to Mark Russell, 1992. Chmn. Easter Seal Telethon, Allen County Soc. Crippled Children and Adults, 1982, 83; moderator bd. trustees Disciples of Christ Ch., 1975-79. Recipient award for meritorious svc. Ball State U., 1980; Outstanding Prin. of Yr. award Ind. Secondary Sch. Adminstrs. Assn., 1981, Ind. Prin. of Yr., Ind. Assn. Ednl. Secs., 1986, Disting. Svc. award Midwestern Regional Assembly of Coll. Entrance Exam. Bd., 1987, Sagamore of the Wabash award Ind. Gov. Evan Bayh, 1989, South Side H.S. Disting. alumni award (hon.), 1997; Rotary Paul Harris fellow, 1985; South Side H.S. Prin. Emeritus, 1996. Mem. Ft. Wayne Prins. Assn., Nat. Assn. Secondary Sch. Prins. (conf. speaker New Orleans, 1985, 89), Ind. Secondary Sch. Adminstrs., PTA (life), Phi Beta Kappa, Phi Delta Kappa, Phi Alpha Theta, Ft. Wayne Rotary (dir. 1973-76, 79-82, pres.-elect 1981-82, pres. 1982-83), Quest (dir. 1979-81, v.p. 1988-89, pres. 1989-90), Fortnightly Club (v.p. 1984-85, pres. 1985-86, 91-92). Mem. Christian Ch. (Disciples of Christ). Home: 5200 N Washington Rd Fort Wayne IN 46804-1844

WEICKMANN, DIRK UDO, toxinologist, arachnologist; b. Weissenburg, Bavaria, Germany, Mar. 12, 1967; s. Peter Zwörner and Anita Weickmann. Toxinology cert., Hosp. Chemists, Weissenburg, 1988; student, Nat. Sci. & Tech. Acad., 1988, Chem. Inst. Stuttgart, 1997. Pharmacist Einhorn Chemists, Weissenburg, Germany, 1988; lab. chief Hosp. Chemists, Weissenburg, 1988-89, Cell Biology Lab., Munich, 1991-92; technician Inst. Anthropology of Ludwig Maximilian U., Munich, 1992-97; leader cytology researching group Inst. Cell Biology and Immunology Dr. Klehr, Munich, 1998-2000; leader, chief sci. rsch. group Angelwandte BioTechnologie, 2000—; leader biotech. co. ABiTec, 1999—; spider taxonomist Inst. Zoology, Alma-Ata/Kasachstan, 1991—; venomous plants taxonomist Ludwig Maximilian U., Munich, 1998—; organizer venomous animals and parasites exhbns., 1997—; chief Venomous Spiders and Latrodectus Working Group, Germany, 1993—. Editor Latrodecta, 1991—, Lotus News, 1997—, organizer Latrodectus and Venomous Spiders symposia, 1993, 95-98, chief, 1993-98, organizer scorpion symposia, 1996, 98, venomous animals and parasites exhbns., 1997—. Advisor Air Transport and Air Landing Schs., 1988-90. Recipient Bavarian Red Cross, 1993-99. Mem. Brit. Tarantula Soc., German Electrophoresis Soc., Am. Tarantula Soc., German Arachnological Soc. (spider and scorpion taxonomist 1998—), McFarlane Toys Collectors Club, Spawn Club, Top Cow Fan Club, German Carnivorous Plant Soc., Asian Game Fowl Soc., Club Deutscher Ur-und Kampfhuhnzüchter von 1977, Club Deutscher Zwerg-Kämpferzüchter, Sonderverein für Malaien, Sonderverein für Madras. Avocations: keeping venomous plants and animals, sports, fantasy stories, collecting scientific books, comics and action toys. Office: LATRODECTA, Ligsalzstr 36, 80339 Munich Bavaria, Germany

WEIDA, LEWIS DIXON, marketing analyst, consultant; b. Moran, Ind., Apr. 23, 1924; s. Charles Ray and Luella Mildred (Dixon) W.; student Kenyon Coll., 1943, Purdue U., 1946; B.S., Ind. U., 1948; M.S., Columbia U., 1950. Mgr. statis. analysis unit Gen. Motors Acceptance Corp., N.Y.C., 1949-55; asst. to exec. v.p. Am. Express Co., 1955-82. Served with USAAF, 1943-46; PTO. Mem. Internat. Platform Assn. Democrat. Club: Masons. Home: 25 Tudor City Pl New York NY 10017-6819

WEIDAW, KENNETH ROE, musician, educator, consultant; b. Toledo, Apr. 7, 1920; s. Fred Andrew and Ola Mae (Harris) W.; m. Margaret Ruth Lazear, Dec. 14, 1940;children: Patricia Ruth, Pamela Mae, Kenneth Roe Jr., Karen Louise. B in Music Edn., Vandercook Coll., 1942; MusB, Roosevelt U., 1942; MusM, U. So. Calif., 1953. Freelance musician, 1940—; several adminstrv. positions various music schs., colls. and vets. adminstrns., Chgo. and Los Angeles, 1940-54; tchr., coord. music Arcadia (Calif.) Unified Schs., 1952-81; musician Glendale (Calif.) Symphony, 1961-83, L.A. Rams Band, 1965-69, 74-80; regional coord. Am. Scandinavian Student Exch., Laguna Beach, Calif., 1980-84, student group escort, 1987—; area coord. Fgn. Study League and E.F. Inst. for Cultural Exch., L.A., 1975-79; musician L.A. City Concert Band, 1958-81; condr. San Gabriel (Calif.) Valley Junior Symphony, 1962-66; adjudicator, clinician, 1940—; hon. life mem. So. Calif. Sch. Band and Orch. Assn., pres., 1975-77; adj. prof. Calif. State U., L.A., 1984—; investment exec., Temple City, Calif., 1971—. Musician for (films) Paint Your Wagon and Heaven Can Wait; contbr. articles to profl. jours. Mem. Sun City (Ariz.) Concert and Renaissance Brass Band, 1998—. With USN, 1942-45. Recipient Am. Bicentennial medal, 1976; named Tchr. of Year, Santa Anita Industry-Edn. Council, 1972, Outstanding Music Educator, Los Angeles County Bd. Edn., 1983; Ann. Ken Weidaw Outstanding Music Student award named in his honor Arcadia Music Club, 1982. Mem. Am. Fedn. Musicians (life), Fin. Planning Assn., Plan Consultants Specializing in Investment/Retirement Planning (CEO 1985—), Music Educators Nat. Conf., Calif. Music Educators Assn. (pres. 1980-83), Am. Sch. Band Dirs. Assn., Assn. Calif. Sch. Adminstrs., Pi Kappa Lambda, Phi Mu Sigma. Avocations: golf, travel. Office: Plan Cons PO Box 493 Temple City CA 91780-0493

WEIDEKAMM, ERHARD, pharmacokineticist, pharmaceutical researcher; b. Willenberg, Germany, July 5, 1941; s. Ewald Otto and Christel Gertrud (Walpuski) W.; m. Christa Gisela Henningsen, Dec. 23, 1968; children: Julia, Claudia. Diploma, U. Freiburg, Germany, 1968, PhD summa cum laude, 1971; lectr. venia legendi, U. Konstanz, Germany, 1978. Instr. Tufts U., Boston, Mass., 1971-73; lectr. U. Konstanz, 1978—; group leader Hoffmann-LaRoche Ltd., Basel, Switzerland, 1982—. Author: Biological Systems, 1984, Advances in Veterinary Science and Comparative Medicine, 1986; contbr. articles to profl. jours. Lt. Bundeswehr, Germany, 1960-62. Recipient grant Max Planck Soc., U. Freiburg, 1968-73, Tufts-NEMCH, Boston, 1971-73. Avocations: piano, oil painting, swimming, skiing. Office: F Hoffmann-LaRoche Ltd, Grenzacherstrasse 124, CH-4002 Basel Switzerland

WEIDELE, HORST KARL, physicist; b. Radolfzell, Germany, May 15, 1961; s. Karl August and Rosa Waldburga (Seeberger) W.; m. Rebecca Ann Stevens, Oct. 10, 1986. Degree in physics, U. Konstanz, Germany, 1990, PhD, 1995. Scientific employee U. Konstanz, Germany, 1990-95; elec. developer MTU Friedrichshafen, Germany, 1999—. Contbr. articles to profl. jours. Postdoctoral fellow Belgian Nat. Found. Sci. Rsch., 1996, European Cmty., Belgium, 1997-98. Mem. German Phys. Soc., Marie Curie Fellow Assn.

WEIDEMANN, CELIA JEAN, social scientist, international business and financial development consultant; b. Denver, Dec. 6, 1942; d. John Clement and Hazel (Van Tuyl) Kirlin; m. Wesley Clark Weidemann, July 1, 1972; 1 child, Stephanie Jean. BS, Iowa State U., 1964; MS, U. Wis., Madison, 1970, PhD, 1973; postgrad., U. So. Calif., 1983. Advisor UN Food & Agr. Orgn., Ibadan, Nigeria, 1973-77; ind. rschr. Asia and Near East, 1977-78; program coord., asst. prof., rsch. assoc. U. Wis., Madison, 1979-81; chief institutional and human resources U.S. Agy. for Internat. Devel., Washington, 1982-85; team leader, cons. Sumatra, Indonesia, 1984; dir. fed. econs. program Midwest Rsch. Inst., Washington, 1985-86; pres., founder, pres. emeritus Weidemann Assocs., Arlington, Va., 1986-2000; pres. Weidemann Found., 2000—; cons. U.S. Congress, Aspen Inst., Ford Found., World Bank, Egypt, Nigeria, Gambia, Pakistan, Indonesia, AID, Thailand, Jamaica, Panama, Philippines, Sierra Leone, Kenya, Jordon, Poland, India, Egypt, Russia, Finnish Internat. Devel. Agy., Namibia, pvt. client Estonia, Lativa, Russia, Japan, Internat. Ctr. Rsch. on Women, Zaire, UN Food and Agriculture Orgn., Ghana, Internat. Statis. Inst., The Netherlands, Global Exch., 1986-87, Asian Devel. Bank, Mongolia, Nepal, Vietnam, Bangladesh, Indonesia, Philippines. Author: Planning Home Economics Curriculum for Social and Economic Development, Agricultural Extension for Women Farmers in Africa, 1990, Financial Services for Women, 1992, Egyptian Women and Microenterprise: The Invisible Entrepreneurs, 1992, Small Enterprise Development in Poland: Does Gender Matter?, 1994, Microenterprise and Gender in India, 1995; contbr. chpts. to books and articles to profl. jours. Fellow Am. Home Econs. Assn., 1969-73; grantee Ford Found., 1987-89. Mem. Nat. Rsch. Coun., Nat. Acad. Sci. (peer reviewer), Soc. Internat. Devel., Am. Sociol. Assn., U.S. Dirs. of Internat. Agrl. Programs Assn. for Women in Devel. (pres. 1989, founder, bd. dirs.), Coalition for Women's Econ. Devel. and Global Equality (co-chair), Internat. Devel. Conf. (bd. dirs., exec. com.), Am. Home Econs. Assn. (Wis. internat., chmn. 1980-81), Internat. Platform Assn., Pi Lambda Theta, Omicron Nu. Avocations: mountain trekking, piano/pipe organ, canoeing, photography, poetry. Office: Weidemann Assocs Inc 933 N Kenmore St Ste 401A Arlington VA 22201-2236

WEIDEMANN, VOLKER WULF JÜRGEN, astrophysicist, educator; b. Kiel, Germany, Oct. 3, 1924; s. Carl August Heinrich and Carla Ina Marie (Clausen) W.; m. Helga Kindt, June 4, 1954; children: Karen, Martin. Diploma math., U. Kiel, 1952, Dr.rer.nat., 1954. Ober reg.rat Phys. Tech. Bundesanstalt, Braunschweig, 1954-65; univ. prof. U. Kiel, 1965-93, prof., 1993—; rsch. fellow Calif. Inst. Tech., Pasadena, 1957-58, sr. rsch. fellow, 1961-62, rsch. assoc., 1971-72, 81-82. Editor: Phys. Berichte, 1958-77. Lt. Navy, 1941-46. Mem. Leopoldina, Deutsche Physikalische Gesellschaft, Astron. Ges., Astron Soc. Pacific. Lutheran. Home: Poeler Weg 3, 24107 Kiel Germany Office: Inst Astron Astrophys U, 24098 Kiel Germany

WEIDENFELD, WERNER, political science educator; b. Cochem, Germany, July 2, 1947; m. Gabriele Kokott-Weidenfeld. PhD, U. Bonn, Germany, 1971; Habilitation, U. Mainz, Germany, 1975; PhD (hon.), Middlebury Coll., 1994. Prof. polit. sci. U. Mainz, 1975-95; prof. associé Sorbonne, Paris, 1985-87; prof. polit. sci. U. Munich, 1995—; coord. German Govt. for German Am. Cooperation, 1987-99; mem. bd. Bertelsmann Found., Gütersloh, Germany. Editor Internat. Politk mag., Yearbook on European Integration, 1980—. Office: Univ Munich GSI, Oettingenstr 67, 80538 Munich Germany

WEIDLE, ULRICH HEINZ, biochemist; b. Ittelsburg, Bavaria, Germany, Jan. 12, 1949; s. Ulrich and Anneliese (Geymann) W. Diploma in Biochemistry, U. Tübingen, 1974, PhD in Natural Scis., 1978; postgrad., U. Zürich, Switzerland, 1979-82; D in Med. Habilitation, U. Würzburg, 1991. Group leader Boehringer Mannheim, Penzberg, Germany, 1982-89, sci. dir., head Oncology Dept, 1982—; lectr. U. Stuttgart, Germany, 1989—. Contbr. numerous articles to profl. jours; patentee in field. Co-recipient Landsteiner medal Austrian Soc. for Immunology, 1995. Mem. Am. Soc. for Microbiology. Avocations: football, car racing, parachuting. Office: Boehringer Mannheim, Im Nonnenwald 2, D 82372 Penzberg Bavaria, Germany

WEIDLICH, WOLFGANG, physics educator, researcher, author; b. Dresden, Germany, Apr. 14, 1931; s. Walther and Margarethe (Otto) W.; m. Evelyn Sievers, May 28, 1958 (dec. 1996); children: Sophia, Irene; m. Ursula Ronsch, Apr. 6, 1999. Diploma in physics and math., Free U. Berlin, 1955, D Natural Scis., 1957, Habilitation, 1963; D honoris causa, U. Umeå, Sweden, 1985. Asst. prof. U. Erlangen (Germany) and U. Berlin, 1957-63; assoc. prof. physics U. Stuttart, Germany, 1963-66, prof., 1966—, v.p., 1978-80. Author: Thermodynamics and Statistical Mechanics, 1977, Quantitative Sociology, 1983; editor: Interregional Migration, 1988, Physics and Social Science-The Approach of Synergetics, 1991, Sociodynamics-A Systematic Approach to MathematicalModelling in the Social Sciences, 2000; contbr. articles to profl. jours. Lutheran. Avocations: philosophy, theology, music. Office: U Stuttgart, Pfaffenwaldring 57, D-70550 Stuttgart Germany

WEIDNER, STANISŁAW MARIAN, biochemist, plant physiologist, educator; b. Wrzesnia, Poznan, Poland, Mar. 22, 1947; s. Jozef and Ludwika (Rominska) W.; m. Maria Magdalena Minakowska, Aug. 12, 1976; children: Magdalena, Janusz. Master, Olsztyn (Poland) U. Agrl. Tech., 1971, Doctor, 1980. Asst. Olsztyn U. Agr. and Tech., 1971-80, adj., 1980-89, asst. prof., 1989-92, prof., 1992-98; prof. U. Warmia and Mazury, Olsztyn, 1999—; vis. prof. Okayama U., 1998-99; mem. COST project European Coop., 1996—. Editor: (with Wacław Minakowski) Biochemistry of Vertebrates, 1998 (Minister's prize 1999). Recipient Silver Cross for achievements in sci. and edn. fields Pres. of Poland, 1994; Internat. Rsch. and Exch. Bd. fellow, 1990; State Com. for Sci. Rsch. grantee, 1993-96, 97—; Kosciuszko Found. fellow, 1997. Mem. Fedn. European Biochem. Socs., Fedn. European Socs. Plant Physiology. Roman Catholic. Achievements include research in possible involvement of cytoskeleton in regulation of cereal caryopses dormancy and germination. Home: Heweliusza St 24/24, PL-10718 Olsztyn Poland Office: U Warmia and Mazury, Kortowo Pl Lodzki 3, PL-10957 Olsztyn Poland

WEIER, ANDREAS, chemist; b. Frankfurt, Germany, Dec. 30, 1960; s. Carlos Adalberto Fluch Y Noebel and Ursula Weier; m. Anke Schumacher, July 22, 1988; 1 child, Patrick Andreas. BS in Chemistry, Hamburg (Germany) U., 1982, MS in Chemistry, 1985, PhD in Chemistry, 1988; postdoctorate, U. Calif., Irvine, 1988-89. Rsch. chemist Th. Goldschmidt AG, Essen, Germany, 1989Ô. Patentee in field. With German Army, 1979-80. Rsch. grantee, 1985, 88. Mem. German Chem. Soc., Am. Chem. Soc. Office: Th Goldschmidt AG, Goldschmidtstrasse 100, 45127 Essen Germany

WEIER, WINFRIED, educator; b. Fulda, Germany, Apr. 26, 1934; s. Ferdinand and Eva (Kind) W.; m. Ingrid Meier, Aug. 15, 1971; children: Ursula, Michael. Dr.phil, U. Mainz, 1959; Habilitation, U. Salzburg, 1966. Dozent Padagogischen Hochschule Wurzburg, 1962-72; dozent U. Wurzburg, 1972-74, prof., 1974-78, full prof., 1978—; prof. U. Salzburg, 1980. Author: Die Stellung des J. Clauberg in der Phlosophie, 1960, Sinn und Teilhabe. Das Grundthema der abendland. Geistesentwicklung, 1970, Strukturen menschlicher Existenz. Grenzen heutigen Philosophierens, 1977, Nihilismus. Geschichte, System, Kritik, 1980, Geistesgeschichte im Systemvergleich. Zur Problematik des historischen Denkens, 1984, Phänomene und Bilder des Menschseins. Grundlegung einer Dimensionalen Anthropologie, 1986, Die Grundlegung der Neuzeit. Typologie der Philosophiegeschichte, 1988, Brennpunkte der Gegenwartsphilosophie, Zentralthemen und Tendenzen im Zeitalter der Nihilismus, 1991, Religion als Selbstfindung, Grundlegung einer Existenzanalytischen Religionsphilosophie, 1991, Das Phänomen Geist. Auseinandersetzung mit Psychoanalyse, Logistik, Verhaltensforschung, 1995,

Sinnerfahrung menschlicher Existenz Neue Wege der Gotteserkenntnis, 1999; contbr. 54 articles to profl. jours. Home: Unterer Weinberg 66, 97234 Reichenberg Germany Office: Univ Wurzburg Theol Faculty, Sanderring 2, 97070 Wurzburg Germany 8700

WEIGAND, DANIEL ARTHUR, psychologist, educator; b. Portland, Oreg., Apr. 18, 1957; arrived in Eng., 1994; s. George Turner and Doris Betty (Spoon) W.; m. Judy Rae McIntosh, Sept. 11, 1983. BS with honors, Portland State U., 1986; MS, U. North Tex., 1993, PhD, 1994. Cert. sport psychology cons. Tchg. fellow U. North Tex., Denton, 1990-93; sr./prin. lectr., dir. mental skills tng. De Montfort U., Bedford, 1994—; assoc. editor Jour. of Sport Behavior, 1995—; mem. editl. bd. Jour. Sport Medicine & Physical Fitness, 1995—; editl. asst. APA Style Jour. Applied Sport Psychology, 1998—; sport psychology cons. to nat. and internat. athletes. Contbr. articles to profl. jours. Mem. APA (mem. presdl. com. 1996—), AAASP, BASES (psychology accreditation com. 1998-2000), ISSP. Avocations: golf, tennis, basketball, reading, travel. Office: De Montfort U, 37 Lansdowne Rd, Bedford MK40 2BZ, England

WEIGAND, ECKEHARD FRIEDRICH, chemist; b. Kaiserslautern, Germany, Apr. 2, 1949; s. Otto and Margarete W.; m. Huguette, Dec. 3, 1974; children: Holger, Bjoern. MS, U. Saarlandes, Saarbrueken, Germany, 1976, Dr.rer.nat., 1978. Product mgr. Bayer, Leverkusen, Germany, 1980-85; sect. mgr. application rsch. Sumitomo Bayer Urethanes Co., Amagasaki, Japan, 1985-88; sect. mgr. Bayer, 1989—. Contbr. articles to profl. jours. NIH Rsch. grantee, 1979. Mem. European Isocyanate Producers Assn. (chmn. task forces 1989—, chmn. coms. 1996—). Avocations: photography, ballroom dancing, research. Office: Bayer AG, PU-S/UP Bldg B211, D-51368 Leverkusen Germany

WEIGEL, RICHARD GEORGE, psychologist, educator; b. St. Louis, Feb. 23, 1937; s. George D. and Irene K. (Bretz) W.; children: Paul K., Laura K. BA, DePauw U., 1959; MA, U. Mo., Columbia, 1962, PhD in Psychology, 1968. Diplomate in clin. psychology Am. bd. Profl. Psychology; lic. psychologist Colo., Ill., Utah. Counselor/asst. prof. psychology Oreg. State U., Corvallis, 1964-67, acting dir. Counseling Ctr., 1967; asst. prof. to prof. and chmn. counseling psychology program Colo. State U., Ft. Collins, 1967-78; sr. cons. psychologist Rohrer, Hibler & Replogle, Inc., Denver, 1978-90, mgr., 1981-86; dir. and adj. prof. psychology Student Counseling Ctr., Ill. State U., Normal, 1990-92; dir. Counseling Ctr. U. Utah, Salt Lake City, 1992—, clin. prof. psychology, ednl. psychology and psychiatry, 1992—, asst. v.p. student devel., 1996-97, interim v.p. for student affairs, 1997-99; pvt. practice psychology, Ft. Collins, 1970-78; adj. prof. Denver U. Sch. Profl. Psychology, 1977-78, Counseling Psychology Program, Ctr. for Spl. and Advanced Programs of U. No. Colo., Greeley, 1975-78, vis. assoc. prof. counseling psychology program, summer 1975; lectr. continuing edn. for nurses Poudre Valley Meml. Hosp., Ft. Collins, 1975; selection psychologist Peace Corps, 1973-74; asst. prof. psychology divsn. continuing edn. Oreg. State Sys. Higher Edn., Salem, 1965; ind. practice marriage counseling, Corvallis, Oreg., 1965-67; clin. psychologist Mo. Tng. Sch. for Boys, summer 1964; instr. psychology U. Mo., Columbia, 1963-64; counselor Counseling Svc., Stephens Coll., Columbia, 1963-64, Univ. Testing and Counseling Svc., U. Mo., Columbia, 1961-62; instr. psychology, resident advisor George Williams Coll., Lake Geneva, Wis., summer 1961; tchg./rsch. asst. psychology U. Mo., 1960-61; rsch. asst. Purdue U., West Lafayette, Ind., 1960; VA clin. psychology trainee Indpls., 1959-60; vis. scientist/lectr. APA, Drury Coll., 1974; lectr. in field; condr. workshops in field; v.p. Bd. Psychologist Examiners State of Colo., 1973-76. Assoc. editor Cons. Psychology Jour.: Practice and rsch., 1991-93, editl. bd., 1990—; editl. bd. Jour. Coll. Student Devel., 1970-73, 92—, Profl. Psychology: Rsch. and Practice, 1990-92; reviewer Jour. Counseling Psychology, 1976, 94-96, Counseling Psychologist, 1994-98, Jour. Cons. and Clin. Psychology, 1977; editl. cons. Wadsworth-Brooks/Cole Pub. Co., 1974-78, Univ. Park Press, 1976; contbr. numerous articles to profl. jours.; co-author: Innovative Psychological Therapies, 1975, Innovative Medical-Psychiatric Therapies, 1976. Bd. dirs. Mental Health Assn., Benton County, Oreg., 1966-67; mem. Soc. Indiana Pioneers, 1990; mem. profl. adv. bd. Denver U. Sch. Profl. Psychology, 1976-78. NIMH grantee, 1977-82, Colo. State U. grantee, 1976-77, Oreg. State U. grantee, 1965-66, 66-67; Paul Harris fellow Rotary, 1981-86. Fellow APA (task force on revision of accreditation criteria 1977-78, vis. scientist 1974, divsn. cons. psychology pres.-elect 1995-96, pres. 1996-97, past pres. 1997-98, sec. 1993-95, exec. com. 1990-98, com. fellows 1989-93, chair 1991-93, program com. 1990, counseling psychology divsn. awards com. 1993-95, 98, edn. and tng. com. 1975-78, 91-93, coll. counseling interest group 1991 , clin. psychology divsn., group psychology and group psychotherapy divsn. com. on fellows 1991-93, 95 , chair 1992-93), Am. Psychol. Soc.; mem. AAUP, Assn. Univ. and Coll. Counseling Ctr. Dirs. (governing bd. 1993-95), Rocky Mountain Psychol. Assn. (pres. 1973-74, treas. 1971-72, Disting. Svc. award 1987), Rsch. Consortium of Counseling and Psychol. Svcs. in Higher Edn. (bd. dirs. 1993-95), Internat. Assn. Counseling Svcs. (site visitor 1991-95), Am. Coll. Pers. Assn., Utah Psychol. Assn., Colo. State Bd. Psychologist Examiners (vice chmn. 1974-76, del. to Am. Assn. State Psychology Bds. 1976), Coun. of Counseling Psychology Tng. Programs (bd. dirs. 1974-79, liaison to Am. Assn. State Psychology Bds. 1979), Newcomen Soc. U.S., Sigma Xi, Psi Chi, Phi Gamma Delta, Phi Mu Alpha, Phi Kappa Phi (hon., Golden Key). Avocation: history. Office: University of Utah 208 Park Building Salt Lake City UT 84112-1201

WEIGL, MICHAEL, religious studies educator; b. Vienna, Austria, Jan. 29, 1963; s. Oskar and Ilse (Hemmelmayr) W. ThM, U. Vienna, 1986, ThD, 1991; MA, U. Toronto, Ont., Can., 1993. Assoc. prof. O.T. studies U. Vienna, 1999—. Author: Zefanja und das "Israel der Armen," 1994 (Austrian Rsch. Coun. award 1994), Mein Neffe Achikar (Tob 1:11): Die aramäischen Achikar-Sprüche und das Alte Testament, 1999; contbr. articles to profl. jours., including Biblica, Bibel und Kirche. Mem. Soc. Bibl. Lit., Royal Can. Soc. for Mesopotamian Studies, Am. Soc. Oriental Rsch. Roman Catholic. Avocations: travel, classical music. Office: U Vienna Dept OT Studies, Schottenring 21, A-1010 Vienna Austria

WEIGLEIN, ANDREAS HEINRICH, anatomist; b. Graz, Styria, Austria, June 29, 1961; s. Heinrich Robert and Heidelinde Gertrude (Schwarz) W.; m. Marion Eva Ferk, May 4, 1962; children: Michaela Anna, Martin Andreas. MD, Med. Sch., Graz, Austria, 1988. Study asst. Anatomical Inst., Graz, 1982-88, univ. asst., 1988—, asst. prof., 1995—, assoc. prof., 1996—, vice chmn., 2000—; sec. S.E. European Sch. Minimally Invasive Surgery and Stapling. Mem. Anatomische Gesellschaft, Internat. Soc. Plastination (sec. 1994-96, pres. 1996—), Brit. Assn. Clin. Anatomy, European Assn. Clin. Anatomy, AAAS, N.Y. Acad. Scis., Am. Assn. Clin. Anatomy, Am. Assn. Anatomists, European Congress Radiology, Austrian Ent Soc. Roman Catholic. Avocations: skiing, travel, cooking, painting, theater. Office: Styria Anatomical Inst U Graz, Harrachgasse 21, Graz A-8010, Austria

WEIGLEY, RUSSELL FRANK, history educator; b. Reading, Pa., July 2, 1930; s. Frank Francis and Meta Beulah (Rohrbach) W.; m. Emma Eleanor Seifrit, July 27, 1963; children: Jared Francis Guldin, Catherine Emma Rohrbach. BA, Albright Coll., 1952; MA, U. Pa., 1953, PhD, 1956; HLD (hon.), Albright Coll., 1978. Instr. history U. Pa., Phila., 1956-58; asst. prof. Drexel Inst. Tech., Phila., 1958-60, assoc. prof., 1960-62; assoc. prof. Temple U., Phila., 1962-64, prof. history, 1964-85, Disting. Univ. prof., 1985-98, prof. emeritus, 1998—; vis. prof. Dartmouth Coll., Hanover, N.H., 1967-68; U.S. Army vis. prof. mil. history rsch. U.S. Army War Coll., U.S. Army Mil. History Rsch. Collection, Carlisle Barrakcs, Pa., 1973-74; pres. Am. Mil. Inst., Washington, 1975-76. Author: Quartermaster General of the Union Army: A Biography of M.C. Meigs, 1959, Towards an American Army: Military Thought from Washington to Marshall, 1962, History of the United States Army, 1967, 84, The Partisan War: The South Carolina Campaign of 1780-82, 1970, The American Way of War, 1973, Eisenhower's Lieutenants, 1981 (Athenaem of Phila. Spl. award for Nonfiction by a Phila. Author, 1983), The Age of Battles: The Quest for Decisive Warfare from Breitenfeld to Waterloo, 1991, A Great Civil War: A Military and Political History, 1862-1865, 2000; editor: The American Military: Readings in the History of the Military in American Society, 1969, New Dimensions in Military History, 1976, Philadelphia: A 300-Year History, 1982. Mem. hist. adv. commn. Dept. of Army, Washington, 1976-79, 88—, Pa. Hist. Records Adv. Com., Harrisburg, 1977-79; bd. dirs. Masonic Libr., Mus. of Pa., The Grand Lodge of Masons of Pa., Phila., 1990-95, 97—; Supreme Coun., Scottish Rite, No. Masonic Jurisdiction, 1999. Penrose Fund grantee Am. Philos. Soc., 1958; fellow John Simon Guggenheim Meml. Found., 1969-70; recipient Samuel Eliot Morison prize Am. Mil. Inst., 1989. Mem. Hist. Soc. Pa. (vice chmn. 1989-93, councilor 1983-89, 92-98, emeritus 1998—), Pa. Hist. Assn. (pres. 1975-78, v.p. 1967-75, coun. 1967—, editor jour. 1962-67), Am. Hist. Assn., Orgn. Am. Historians, Soc. Mil. Hist. (Disting. Book award 1992), So. Hist. Assn., Soc. Am. Historians Inc., Interuniv. Seminar on Armed Forces and Soc., Am. Philos. Soc., Masons (33d degree, Scottish rite supreme coun. northern Masonic jurisdiction 1999). Democrat. Unitarian. Home: 327 S Smedley St Philadelphia PA 19103-6717 Office: Temple U Dept History Philadelphia PA 19122

WEIGOLD, ADAM MARK, laser company executive, researcher; b. Washington, Jan. 18, 1966; s. Erich and Jocelyn Clare (Stebbins) W.; m. Jacqueline Bastow, Jan. 14, 1995; 1 child, Zachary Paul. BSc, Adelaide U., 1987; BSc with honors, Flinders U., Adelaide, 1988; PhD, Macquarie U., Sydney, Australia, 1993. Rsch. scientist Flinders U., Adelaide, 1987, Def. Sci. Tech. Organ., Adelaide, 1993-94; mng. dir. Photon Engring., Adelaide, 1994—; cons. Light Solutions Corp., Mountain View, 1994-95, CSIRO, Adelaide, 1998—; project leader Macquarie U., 1997-99; vis. rschr. Australian Nat. U., Canberra, 1991-92. Contbr. articles to profl. jours. including Optics Letters, Jour. Optical Soc. Am., Jour. Phys. B., Australian Jour. Physics. Recipient scholarship Macquarie U., 1988. Mem. Optical Soc. Am., Australian Optical Soc. Avocations: downhill skiing, golf, wine tasting, Australian rules football. Office: Photon Engring, PO Box 10269, Gouger St, Adelaide SA 5000, Australia

WEIHRAUCH, THOMAS ROBERT, internist, gastroenterologist, educator; b. Munich, Nov. 23, 1942; s. Hans Robert and Elna Sophie (Birch) W.; m. Birgit Ursula Kaethe Eggers, Mar. 7, 1969; children: Martin Robert, Julia Christine. MD, PhD, U. Munich, 1970; Habilitation in Internal Medicine, U. Mainz, Germany, 1979. Diplomate German Bd. Internal Medicine, German Bd. Gastroenterology. Intern U. Kiel (Germany) Clinics, 1969-70, Maricopa County Hosp., Phoenix, 1970-71; resident in internal medicine Univ. Clinic Medicine I, Mainz, 1971-79, chief resident, 1979-82; assoc. in exptl. pharmacology U. Mainz, 1971-75, lectr. clin. medicine, pathophysiology and clin. pharmacology, 1971-89; life prof. internal medicine and gastroenterology Free U. Berlin Klinikum Steglitz, 1981; head dept. clin. pathophysiology and clin. rsch. I Bayer AG Pharm. Rsch. Ctr., Wuppertal, Germany, 1982-85, head dept. medicine and devel., 1985-95, sr. v.p. global med. strategy and rels., 2000—; prof., lectr. clin. medicine and pathophysiology U. Düsseldorf, Germany, 1989—; head med. affairs internat. U. Düsseldorf, Wuppertal, Germany, 1995-2000; sr. v.p. global med. strategy and rels. Bayer AG, Wuppertal, Germany, 2000—; prof., lectr. clin. medicine and pathophysiology U. Düsseldorf, Germany, 1989—; med. examiner for clin. pharmacology; mem. bd. bus. group for self-medication Bayer AG, Leverkusen, Germany, 1984-87, mem. bd. bus. group pharma, 1991-93; bd. spokesman Paul-Martini-Found., Bonn, Germany, 1992-95; vice chmn. Ctr. Medicine Rsch. Internat., Carshalton, Eng., 1993-95, chmn. R&D bd., 1996—; mem. bd. Faculty Pharm. Medicine, U.K.; reviewer German and internal jours., pub. houses, sci. founds. and award coms. Author: (monograph) Esophageal Manometry, 1981; editor Therapy in Internal Medicine, 12 edits., 1975-98; contbr. numerous articles on gastroenterology and clin. pharmacology to med. jours. and ency. With German Army, 1962-63. Fellow Royal Soc. Medicine (London), Royal Coll. Physicians Faculty Pharm. Medicine U.K. (with distinction); mem. German Soc. Internal Medicine (spokesman for corp. mems. 1994—), numerous other German and internat. socs. Avocations: jogging, skiing, archaeology. Office: Bayer AG Pharm Rsch Ctr, Aprather Weg, D-42096 Wuppertal Germany

WEIL, CASS SARGENT, lawyer; b. N.Y.C., Nov. 6, 1946; s. Theodore and Ruth Frances (Sargent) W. BA, SUNY, Stonybrook, 1968; JD cum laude, William Mitchell Coll. of Law, 1980. Bar: Minn. 1980, U.S. Dist. Ct. Minn. 1980, U.S. Ct. Appeals (8th cir.) 1980, Wis. 1984, U.S. Ct. Appeals (7th cir.) 1984; cert. bankruptcy law specialist, consumer and bus. Am. Bd. Certification. Assoc. J.R. Kotts & Assoc., Mpls., 1980-81, Wagner, Rutchick & Trojack, St. Paul, 1981-83; ptnr. Zohlmann & Weil, Wilmar, Minn., 1983, Peterson, Franke & Riach, P.A., St. Paul, 1983-91, O'Connor & Hannan, Mpls., 1991-94, Moss & Barnett, P.A., Mpls., 1994—. Editor: Minn. Legal Forms, Bankruptcy, 1983, 87, 91, 92, 93. Recepient Leading Am. Atty. award Am. Rsch. Corp., 1994, 96, 98, Minn. Top Lawyers Mpls. St. Paul Mag., 1998. Mem. Minn. Bar Assn. (vice chmn. bankruptcy sect. 1984-88, chairperson 1988-89), Wis. Bar Assn., Am. Bankruptcy Inst., Comml. Law League Am., Order of Barristers. Democrat. Jewish. Office: Moss & Barnett PA 4800 Norwest Ctr Minneapolis MN 55402

WEIL, JACK BAUM, clothing manufacturing company executive; b. Denver, Nov. 13, 1928; s. Jack Arnold and Beatrice (Baum) W.; m. Elizabeth Fried, 1956 (div. 1969); children: Steven Eugene, Judith B. Weil Oksner; m. Candace Helene Taylor, 1973 (div. 1983). BA, Tulane U., 1952. V.p. Rockmount Ranch Wear Mfg. Co., Denver, 1954—, designer, sales mgr., 1957—; designer western apparel. Head planning group Humboldt Island Hist. Dist., Denver; planning com. City of Denver Chessman Park, 1996—; chmn. Commty. Coll. Denver Found. bd. dirs.; committeeman Denver Rep. Party, 1974—; del. Rep. county, dist. and state convs., 1974—; sec. Rep. Party Com., 1st Congl. Dist. Colo., 1993-94, chmn. 1995-99; sec. Colo. Rep. State Ctrl. Com., 1999—; mem. Colo. State Rep. Exec. Com., 1996—; bd. dirs. 1st Universalist Ch., Denver; mem. admissions com. Tulane U., 1994—; del. Rep. Nat. Conv., 1992, 96, nat. credentials com. 1st lt. U.S. Army, 1952-54. Mem. West Coast Western Mktg. Assn., Midwest Western Wear and Equipment Assn. (bd. dirs.), N.W. Western Wear & Equipment Travelers Assn. (pres. Mpls.), S.E. Western, English and Equine Assn. (bd. dirs. Altanta), Denver Western Wear and Equipment Assn., Hat Inst. Am. (del. 1974—), Denver Athletic Club, Town Club, Lincoln Club (bd. dirs. 1997—), Rump Club, Kappa Delta Phi. Avocations: painting, politics, physical fitness, travel. Home: 1025 Humboldt St Denver CO 80218-3121 Office: Rockmount Ranch Wear Mfg Co 1626 Wazee St Denver CO 80202-1314

WEIL, MARVIN LEE, pediatric neurologist; b. Gainesville, Fla., Sept. 28, 1924; s. Joseph and Ann (Abrams) W.; m. Joyce Sari Zimmerman, May 2, 1954; children: Daniel Ivan, Clifford Felix, Meredith. BS with high hons., U. Fla., 1943; MD, Johns Hopkins Sch. Medicine, 1946. Diplomate Am. Bd. Pediatrics, Am. Bd. Neurology with spl. competence in child neurology. Intern in pediatrics Duke U., Durham, N.C., 1946-47, resident in pediatrics, 1947-48; asst. chief neurotropic virus sect., div. virus and rickettsial diseases Army Med. Dept. Rsch. and Grad. Sch., Washington, 1948-50; resident in pediatrics Cin. Children's Hosp., 1950-52; clin. instr. in pediatrics U. Cin., 1952-53; clin. asst., prof. pediatrics U. Miami Sch. Medicine, 1954-65; asst. prof. pediatrics and neurology UCLA Sch. of Medicine, 1968-72, assoc. prof. pediatrics and neurology, 1972-78, prof. pediatrics and neurology, 1978-89, prof. emeritus, 1989—; acad. vis. dept. biochemistry U. Oxford, U.K., 1989—; cons. Torrance (Calif.) Sch. Dist., 1983-89; acting dir. Harbor Regional Ctr. for Developmentally Disabled, L.A., 1973-74; physician specialist chief, div. pediatric neurology, Harbor-UCLA Med. Ctr., Torrance, 1968-89. Contbg. author books in field; contbr. articles to profl. jours. Capt. AUS, 1948-50. Spl. fellow Nat. Inst. Neurol. Diseases and Blindness, Johns Hopkins U., UCLA, 1965-66, 66-68; sr. internat. fellow Fogarty Internat. Ctr./NIH, Karolinska Inst., Stockholm, Sweden, 1976-77. Fellow AAAS, Am. Acad. Pediatrics, Am. Acad. Neurology; mem. Am. Pediatric Soc., Child Neurology Soc. (bd. dirs. 1980-82), Am. Assn. Immunologists, Am. Assn. Mental Deficiency (exec. bd. region II 1971-76, chmn. region II 1973-74), Internat. Child Neurology Soc., L.A. Soc. Neurology and Psychiatry (sec./treas. 1978-80, pres. elect 1980, pres. 1981, bd. dirs. 1982-84), Western Soc. Pediatric Rsch., Calif. Child Neurology Soc., Dade County Med. Assn., N.Y. Acad. Sci. Democrat. Fax: 44-0-1865-794617. E-mail: mjweil@compuserve.com. Home: 82 Thames St, Oxford OX1 1SU, England Office: Dept Biochemistry/U Oxford, South Parks Rd, Oxford OX1 3QU, England

WEIL, RICHARD, III, surgeon, medical educator; b. N.Y.C., Feb. 22, 1936; s. Richard Jr. and Allene (Hall) W.; m. Polly Edgar, Aug. 22, 1959; children: Wendy, Richard. AB, Princeton U., 1957; MD, Columbia U. Coll. Physicians and Surgeons, 1961. Diplomate Am. Bd. Surgery, Nat. Bd. Med. Examiners. Intern in surgery Presbyn. Hosp., 1961-62, asst. resident in surgery, 1962-63, 65-67, chief resident in gen. surgery, 1968; chief resident in pediat. surgery Babies Hosp., 1969, chief resident in vasc. surgery, 1969, asst. attending surgeon, chmn. surg. house staff com., 1970-74, dir. kidney transplantation, 1973-74; asst. in surgery Columbia U. Coll. Physicians and Surgeons, 1967-68, instr. surgery, 1969, asst. prof. surgery, 1970-74; fellow in transplantation surgery U. Minn., 1970; assoc. prof. surgery U. Colo., 1974-79, prof. surgery, 1979-87, dir. transplantation, 1980-87; prof. surgery, dir. transplantation NYU, 1987-93; assoc. dean medicine, prof. surgery Brown U., Providence, 1993-98; cons. surgeon Manhattan VA Hosp., 1989-92, Denver VA Hosp., 1980-87, Denver Gen. Hosp., 1980-87, St. Anthony-Ctrl. Hosp. Denver, 1980-87; attending surgeon Bellevue Hosp. Ctr., 1989-93. Contbr. more than 130 articles to profl. jours. including Surg. Forum, Am. Jour. Surgery, Transplantation, Surgery, Jour. Pediat. Surgery, Surgery, Gynecology & Obstets., among others. Capt. U.S. Army Med. Corps, 1963-65, Germany. Mem. Am. Assn. Tissue Banks, ACS, Am. Fedn. Clin. Rsch., Am. Soc. Transplant Surgeons, Am. Soc. for Artificial Internal Organs, Am. Surg. Assn., Assn. for Acad. Surgery, Allen O. Whipple Surg. Soc. (recorder 1976-78), Ctrl. Surg. Assn., Clin. Immunology Soc., Denver Acad. Surgery, Harvey Soc., Intermountain End-Stage Renal Disease Network (exec. com. 1975-79), Internat. Cardiovasc. Soc., N.Y. Ctr. for Liver Transplantation, N.Y. Clin. Soc., N.Y. Regional Transplant Program (pres. 1991-92), N.Y. Surg. Soc., Rocky Mountain Vasc. Surg. Soc., Soc. Internat. de Chirurgie, soc. Univ. Surgeons, Transplantation Soc., Western Assn. Transplant Surgeons, United Network for Organ Sharing (councilor for Colo., Wyo., Nebr., Kans., Iowa, Mo. 1986-87).

WEIL, WITOLD ANDREW, energy company executive; b. Lodz, Poland, May 15, 1947; s. Jan and Wanda Halina (Tomaszewska) W.; m. Margaret Helcel, June 15, 1970 (div. 1979); m. Margaret Sawaryn, Dec. 20, 1980; children: Hubert, Olga. MSc, U. Mining and Metallurgy, Cracow, Poland, 1970, PhD in Engring., 1977. Exploration geologist Polish Oil and Gas Co., Wołomin, Poland, 1970-77; head dept. hdqrs. Polish Oil and Gas Co., Warsaw, Poland, 1977-80, head dept. geonafta divsn., 1985-90; v.p., COO Polish Oil and Gas Co., Warsaw, 1990-99; head dept. Petrobaltic, Gdansk, Poland, 1980-85; advisor Energy Market Agy., Warsaw, 1999—; cons. in field. Inventor peak-shaving power plant at underground gas storages; editor jour. Oil and Gas News from Poland, 1992-98; co-editor jour. chpt. in field. Recipient Gold medal for Polish geology Ministry of Environ., 1994, Silver medal Mining Live Saving Sta., 1995. Mem. Geol. Soc. Geos (medal 1996), Polish Soc. Petroleum Engring. (v.p. 1996—, medal 1997), Am. Assn. Petroleum Geologists. Avocations: classical music, theater, books, winter sports, basketball. Home: 3 Guderski Str Flat 43, 03-982 Warsaw Poland Office: Energy Market Agy, Mokotowska 43, 00551 Warsaw Poland

WEILENMANN DE TAU, MARIA ELISABET, agricultural engineer, researcher; b. La Plata, Argentina, Oct. 24, 1955; d. German Santiago and Lia Graciela (Poggi) Weilenmann; m. José Luis Tau, Aug. 29, 1980; children: Federico, Laura. B, Normal no 1, La Plata, 1973; Agrl. Engring. degree, Faculty Agriculture, La Plata, 1980; DSc in Agronomics, Faculte des scis. agronomics, Gembloux, Belgium, 1988. Rschr. Conicet, Salta, Argentina, 1981-84, Marcos Juarez, Argentina, 1988-92, Balcarce, Argentina, 1993—. Contbr. articles to profl. jours., chpts. to books. Avocations: reading, gardening, traveling, cinema, yoga. Home: 147 y 32, 7620 Balcarce Argentina Office: Conicet, 7620 Balcarce Argentina Address: Dept Agron INTA EEA, CC 276, 7620 Balcarce Argentina

WEILER, DOROTHY ESSER, librarian; b. Hartford, Wis., Feb. 21, 1914; d. Henry Hugo and Agatha Christina (Dopp) Esser; A.B. in Fgn. Langs., Wash. State U., 1935; B.A.L., Grad. Library Sch., U. Wash., 1936; postgrad. U. Ariz., 1956-57, Ariz. State U., 1957-58, Grad. Sch. Librarianship, U. Denver, 1971; m. Henry C. Weiler, Aug. 30, 1937; children—Robert William, Kurt Walter. Tchr.-librarian Roosevelt Elem. Schs., Dist. #66, Phoenix, 1956-59; extension librarian Ariz. Dept. Library and Archives, Phoenix, 1959-67; library dir. City of Tempe (Ariz.), 1967-79; assoc. prof., dept. library sci. Ariz. State U., 1968; vis. faculty Mesa Community Coll., 1980-84. Mem. public relations com. United Fund; treas. Desert Samaritan Med. Ctr. Aux., 1981, v.p. community relations Hosp., 1982, vol. asst. chaplain, 1988—, pastoral care vol. Named Ariz. Librarian of Yr., 1971; recipient Silver Book award Library Binding Inst., 1963. Mem. Tempe Hist. Soc., Ariz. Pioneers Hist. Soc., Am. Radio Relay League, Am. Bus. Women's Assn., ALA, Southwestern Library Assn., Ariz. State Libr. Assn. (pres. 1973-74), Ariz. Libr. Pioneer. Roman Catholic. Clubs: Our Lady of Mt. Carmel Ladies' Sodality, Soroptimist Internat. Founder, editor Roadrunner, Tumbling Tumbleweed; contbr. articles to mags. Home: 1605 E Southern Ave Tempe AZ 85282-5610

WEILL, MICHAEL, architect; b. Paris, Aug. 31, 1914; s. Edouard and Edmee (Hirschmann) W. Diplome d'architecte, Ecole des Beaux Arts, 1942. With Lagneau, Weill, Architects, Paris, 1947-55; cons. architect S.E.T.A.P., Paris, Neuilly, 1955-82, pres., Meudon, 1982—. Decorated chevalier Legion d'Honneur, Croix de Guerre (France); comdr. Alphonso le Sage (Spain). Fellow AIA (hon.); mem. Ordre des Architects, Academie d'Architecture, Union Internationale des Architectes (sec.-gen. 1970-78). Address: 1 rue des Pins, 92-100 Boulogne France

WEILL, SANFORD I., bank executive; b. N.Y.C., Mar. 16, 1933; s. Max and Etta (Kalika) W.; m. Joan Mosher, June 20, 1955; children: Marc P., Jessica M. B.A., Cornell U., 1955, student Grad. Sch. Bus. and Pub. Adminstrn., 1954-55. Chmn. bd., chief exec. officer Carter, Berlind & Weill (name changed to CBWL-Hayden, Stone, Inc. 1970, to Hayden Stone, Inc. 1972, to Shearson Hayden Stone 1974, to Shearson Loeb Rh, N.Y.C., 1960-84; dir., chmn. exec. com. Carter, Berlind & Weill (name changed to CBWL-Hayden, Stone, Inc. 1970, to Hayden Stone, Inc. 1972, to Shearson Hayden Stone 1974, to Shearson Loeb Rh, 1981-83, pres., 1983-85; chmn. Fireman's Fund, 1984-85; past pres., chmn. exec. com., mem. fin. com. Am. Express Co., until 1989; chmn., chief exec. officer Primerica Corp., N.Y.C., 1989—, pres., until 1992; chmn. Primerica Holdings Inc., N.Y.C.; chmn., pres., chief exec. officer Comml. Credit Co., Balt., 1986—; chmn., CEO Travelers Group, N.Y.C., 1996—, Citigroup, New York; dir. IDS Mutual Funds Group; vice chmn. adv. council The Johnson Grad. Sch. of Mgmt.; founder Acad. of Fin. Mem. bd. overseers Cornell Med. Coll.; chmn. Carnegie Hall, N.Y.C.; mem. bus. com. Mus. of Modern Art, N.Y.C. Mem. N.Y. Soc. Security Analysts. Clubs: Cornell (N.Y.C.), Century Country (Purchase, N.Y.), Harmonie (N.Y.C.). Office: Travelers Group 388 Greenwich St New York NY 10013-2375 Office: City Group 153 E 53rd St New York NY 10043-0001

WEILOVÁ, EVA SMOLKOVÁ-KEULEMANSOVÁ, chemistry educator; b. Prague, Czech Republic, Apr. 27, 1927; d. Oskar and Alice (Kaufmanova') W.; m. Aloysius Ignatius Maria Keulemans (dec. 1977); children: Eva, Petr. D of Natural Scis., Charles U., Prague, 1952, PhD, 1956, DSc, 1982. Asst. dept. analytical chemistry Charles U., 1956-66, assoc. prof., 1966-86, prof., 1986—; supr. PhD works, cons., organizer postgrad. courses in modern analytical separation methods. Author: Analysis of Substances in Gaseous Phase, 1991; co-author: Cyclodextrins and Their Analytical Uses, 1987, Instrumentation in Analytical Chemistry, 1991, Trends in Cyclodextrins and Derivatives, 1991, Comprehensive Supramolecular Chemistry, vol. 3, 1996; hon. mem. editl. bd. Chromatographia jour.; mem. editl. bd. STP Pharma Scis.; contbr. over 100 articles to profl. jours. Recipient Tswet medal Russian Acad., 1978, Hanus medal Czech Chem. Soc., 1996. Mem. Czech Chem. Soc. (com. chromatography and electrophoresis group 1949—), Chromatogr Soc. U.K. Avocations: music, sculpture, art, books, theatre. Office: Charles U Dept Analyt Chem, Albertov 2030, 12840 Prague 2, Czech Republic

WEIMANN, ROBERT KARL, cultural historian, critic, educator; b. Magdeburg, Germany, Nov. 18, 1928; s. Robert and Elsa (Weihe) W.; m. Maja H. Eisentraut, Nov. 12, 1991; children: Gundi, Meulein, Robbie, Charlotte. Tchr. diploma, Halle U., 1951; PhD, Humboldt U., Berlin, Germany, 1955, PhD habilitation, 1962; Doctorate (hon.), Potsdam U., 1988. Assoc. prof. Potsdam U., 1962-64; full prof. Humboldt U., Berlin, 1965-68; fellow, prof. Acad. Scis., Berlin, 1968-91; chair Forschungsschwerpunkt Literaturwissenschaft, Berlin and Munich, 1992-94; prof. U. Calif., Irvine, 1993—; vis. prof. Toronto U., 1982, Harvard, 1984, 89, U. Calif., Berkeley, 1986; cons. to Shakespeare prodns. Deutsches Theater, 1972, Volksbühne, 1977, Berliner Ensemble, 1986; v.p. Akademie Der Künste, Berlin, 1979-90, mem., 1990—; mem. PEN Internat., German Ctr., Berlin, 1982—; pres. Deutsche Shakespeare Soc., 1985-93; mem. exec. com. Internat. Shakespeare

Assn., 1986-96. Author: New Criticism, 1962, Shakespeare and the Popular Tradition in the Theatre, 1967, English edit., 1978, 87, Literaturgeschichte and Mythologie, 1971, Suhrkamp edit., 1977, Structure and Society in Literary History, 1984, Shakespeare und die Macht der Mimesis, 1988, Authority and Representation in Early Modern Discourse, 1996, Playing and Writing in Shakespeare's Theatre, 2000. Recipient Lessing prize, Kamenz, 1984. Mem. MLA (hon.), N.Y. Acad. Scis. Avocations: sailing, gardening. Home: Muhlenbecker Str 22, 16352 Basdorf Germany Office: Drama Dept Univ Calif Irvine CA 92697-0001

WEIN, HANNS-ULRICH HERBERT, editor, publisher; b. Crossen, Germany, Sept. 19, 1920; s. Karl August and Frieda (Kühnelt) W.; m. Siglinde Auguste Bartels, Sept. 13, 1953; children: Verena, Andrea, Wulf, Vivian. Final exam., Realgymnasium, Crossen, 1938. Newspaper editor Lüneburg, 1946-52, Kassel, 1952-56; officer German Army, 1956-76; editor, ind. pub. H-U Wein, Soltau, Germany, 1976—. Editor, pub.: (periodicals) Crossener Heimatgrüsse, 1969-95, Die neue Oder-Zeitung, 1981-95, (books) An der Grenze Schlesiens und der Mark, 1982, 89, Jahrbücher Wanderungen durch Südostbrandenburg, 1996-97, 97-98; pub. Heimat zwischen Bober und Lubst, 1978, 92. Mem. Dist. Coun., Soltau, 1949-52; mem. City Coun., Munster, 1970-76. Lt.-col. German Army, 1970-76. Mem. Social Democratic Party Germany. Lutheran. Avocations: history, traveling. Home and Office: August-Wöhler-Str 4, D-29614 Soltau Germany

WEIN, PETER, obstetrician, gynecologist, educator; b. Melbourne, Australia, Sept. 6, 1960; s. Reuben and Ruth Betty (Melzer) W.; m. Jennifer Ann Richtman, June 3, 1990; children: Daniel Moshe, Jeremy Avigdor. MBBS, U. Melbourne, 1983. Intern Royal Melbourne Hosp., Melbourne, 1984, jr. resident, 1985; resident med. officer Royal Women's Hosp., Melbourne, 1986, sr. resident, 1987, registrar, 1988, sr. registrar, 1989; registrar Leicester (Eng.) Royal Infirmary, 1990-91, Peterborough (Eng.) Gen. Hosp., 1991; sr. lectr. dept. ob-gyn. U. Melbourne Mercy Hosp. for Women, Melbourne, 1992-99; ob-gyn. Univ. Dept. Royal Women's Hosp., Melbourne, 2000—. Sub-editor Australian and New Zealand Jour. of Ob-gyn., 1994—; contbr. numerous articles to profl. jours. Fellow Royal Australian Coll. Ob-gyn.; mem. Australian Perinatal Soc., Jewish Med. Ethics Soc. of Victoria. Mem. Australian Labour Party. Jewish. Avocations: science fiction, watching cricket. Home: 12 Lempriere Ave, East St Kilda, Melbourne 3183, Australia Office: Mercy Hosp Women Ob-gyn, Royal Women's Hosp, 96 Grattan St Ste 3, Carlton 3053, Australia

WEINBERG, DANIEL H., federal agency administrator, economist; b. Bklyn., Dec. 17, 1949; s. Jack and Rachel (Levy) W.; m. Susan Spoeri, Sept. 6, 1986; children: Robert McGuckin, Catherine McGuckin, Garrett, Henry, George. SB, MIT, 1971; PhD, Yale U., 1975. Lectr. Yale U., New Haven, Conn., 1975-76; sr. economist Abt Assocs., Cambridge, Mass., 1976-80; divsn. dir., sr. economist U.S. HHS, Washington, 1980-89; divsn. chief U.S. Census Bur., Suitland, Md., 1989-00; chair Std. Occupl. Classification Revision Policy Com., Washington, 1996-99. Author: Economics of Housing Vouchers, 1982; editor: Fighting Poverty, 1986, Confronting Poverty, 1994. Recipient Presdl. commendation U.S. Pres., 1989, Bronze medal U.S. Dept. Commerce, 1996, V.P. Innovation award U.S. V.P., 1998, 99. Fellow Am. Statis. Assn. (sect. chair 1996-97); mem. Assn. Pub. Policy Analysis and Mgmt., Am. Econ. Assn., Soc. Govt. Economists. Office: US Census Bur Housing/Household Econ Stat Washington DC 20233-8500

WEINBERG, FÉLIX, historian, educator; b. Buenos Aires, Jan. 16, 1927; s. León Weinberg and Sara Malimovka; m. María Beatriz Fontanella, July 15, 1968; 1 child, Gabriel Félix. Prof. in History, Inst. Nac. Sup. del Profesorado, Buenos Aires, 1950. Asst. prof. U. Buenos Aires, 1957-66; prof. history sect. Inst. Nac. Superior del Profesorado, Buenos Aires, 1975-76; assoc. prof. U. Nac. del Sur, Bahía Blanca, Argentina, 1966-77, prof., 1977-92, extraordinary prof., 1992—, dir. Ctr. Regional Studies, 1981—; dir. history archives U. Nac. del Sur, Bahia Blanca, Argentina, 1992—. Author: El Salón Literario de 1837, 1958, 2d edit., 1977, Juan G. Godoy: Literatura y Política, 1970 (award 1972), Dos Utopías Argentinas de Principios de Siglo, 1976, 2d edit., 1986, Las Ideas Sociales de Sarmiento, 1988, Poblamiento, Inmigración y Cambio Social, 1991; contbr. more than 100 articles to profl. jours. Active Nat. Acad. History. Recipient 1st Nat. Regional Prodn. award Ministry Culture and Edn., 1972, 97; Guggenheim fellow, 1977-78. Home: Pasaje Delfino 352, 8000 Bahia Blanca Argentina Office: U Nac del Sur, 12 de Octubre y San Juan, 8000 Bahia Blanca Argentina

WEINBERG, FELIX JIRI, physics professor; b. Usti, Czechoslovakia, Apr. 2, 1928; came to England, 1945; s. Victor and Nelly Altschul W.; m. Jill Nesta Piggot, July 26, 1954; children: John Felix, Peter David, Michael Johnathan. BSc, London U., Eng., 1950; BSc in Special Physics, London U., 1951; DIC in Chem. Engring., Imperial Coll., 1953; PhD, London U., 1954, DSc in Applied Physics, 1960; DSc (hon.), Israel Inst. Tech., 1990. Chartered engr., physicist. Rsch. asst. Imperial Coll., London, 1951-54; asst. lectr. Imperial Coll., 1954-56, lect., 1956-60, sr. lectr., 1960-64, reader, 1964-67, prof., 1967—; vis. prof., lectr. various universities including U. Calif., 1960—; cons. industries, govt. agys., insts., 1960—. Author: Optics of Flames, 1963, Electrical Aspects of Combustion, 1969; editor, co-author: Advanced Combustion Methods, 1986; editor: Combustion Inst. European Symposium; contbr. articles to profl. jours. Recipient Silver Combustion medal The Combustion Inst., 1972, Bernard Lewis Gold medal, 1980, Rumford medal The Royal Soc., 1988, Italgas Prize for Rsch. and Innovation in Energy, Turin Acad. of Sci., 1991, Smolenski medal Polish Acad. Sci., 1999. Fellow Inst. of Physics, Inst. of Energy, The Royal Soc.; mem. The Combustion Inst., The Royal Instn. Avocations: eastern philosophies, travel, archery. Home: 59 Vicarage Rd, London SW14 8RY, England Office: Dept Chem Engring Imperial Coll, Prince Consort Rd, London SW 2BY, England

WEINBERG, ROBIN SUE, lawyer; b. Plainview, N.Y., June 22, 1969; d. Gary and Eileen M. Weinberg; m. Todd Pines, Sept. 13, 1997. BA, U. Pa., 1991; JD, NYU, 1996. Bar: N.Y. 1997, U.S. Dist. Ct. (so. and ea. dists.) N.Y. 1997, U.S. Dist. Ct. (we. dist.) N.Y. 1998, U.S. Dist. Ct. (no. dist.) N.Y. 1999, Conn. 1996. Assoc. Kelley Drye &Warren LLP, N.Y.C., 1996—. Pro bono counsel Lawyers Com. for Human Rights, N.Y.C., 1998—. Mem. ABA, N.Y. State Bar Assn., Penn Club N.Y. Avocations: photography, tennis. E-mail: rweinberg@kelleydrye.com. Home: 7 Gramercy Park W Apt 5C New York NY 10003-1759 Office: Kelley Drye & Warren LLP 101 Park Ave New York NY 10178-0002

WEINBERG, STEVEN, physics educator; b. N.Y.C., NY, May 3, 1933; s. Fred and Eva (Israel) W.; m. Louise Goldwasser, July 6, 1954; 1 child, Elizabeth. BA, Cornell U., 1954; postgrad., Copenhagen Inst. Theoretical Physics, 1954-55; PhD, Princeton U., 1957; AM (hon.), Harvard U., 1973; ScD (hon.), Knox Coll., 1978, U. Chgo., 1978, U. Rochester, 1979, Yale U., 1979, CUNY, 1980, Clark U., 1982, Dartmouth Coll., 1984, Columbia U., 1990, U. Salamanca, 1992, U. Padua, 1992; U. Barcelona, 1996, U. Barcelona, 1996; PhD (hon.), Weizmann Inst., 1985; DLitt (hon.), Washington Coll., 1985. Rsch. assoc., instr. Columbia U., 1957-59; rsch. physicist Lawrence Radiation Lab., Berkeley, Calif., 1959-60; mem. faculty U. Calif., Berkeley, 1960-69, prof. physics, 1964-69; vis. prof. MIT, 1967-69, prof. physics, 1969-73; Higgins prof. physics Harvard U., 1973-83; sr. scientist Smithsonian Astrophys. Lab., 1973-83; Josey prof. sci. U. Tex., Austin, 1982—; sr. cons. Smithsonian Astrophys. Obs., 1983—; cons. Inst. Def. Analyses, Washington, 1960-73, ACDA, 1973; Sloan fellow, 1961-65; chair in physics Coll. de France, 1971; mem. Pres.'s Com. on Nat. Medal of Sci., 1979-82, Coun. of Scholars, Libr. of Congress, 1983-85; sr. adv. La Jolla Inst.; mem. Com. on Internat. Security and Arms Control, NRC, 1981, Bd. on Physics & Astronomy, 1989-90; dir. Jerusalem Winter Sch. Theoretical Physics, 1983-94; mem. adv. coun. Tex. Superconducting Supercollider High Energy Rsch. Facility, 1987; Loeb lectr. in physics Harvard U., 1966-67, Morris Loeb vis. prof. physics, 1983—; Richtmeyer lectr., 1974; Scott lectr. Cavendish Lab., 1975; Silliman lectr. Yale U., 1977; Lauritsen Meml. lectr. Calif. Inst. Tech., 1979; Bethe lectr. Cornell U., 1979; de Shalit lectr. Weizman Inst., 1979; Cherwell-Simon lectr. Oxford U., 1983; Bampton lectr. Columbia U., 1983; Einstein lectr. Israel Acad. Arts and Scis., 1984; Hilldale lectr. U. Wis., 1985; Clark lectr. U. Tex., Dallas, 1986; Dirac lectr. U. Cambridge, 1986; Klein lectr. U. Stockholm, 1989; Brittin lectr. U. Colo., 1994; Sackler lectr. U. Copenhagen, 1994; Gibbs lectr. Am. Math. Soc., 1996, Bochner lectr. Rice U., 1997; Sanchez lectr. Tex. A&M Internat. U., 1998; Sloan fellow, 1961-65; mem. Supercollider Sci. Policy Com., 1989-93. Author: Gravitation and Cosmology: Principles and Application of the General Theory of Relativity, 1972, The First Three Minutes: A Modern View of the Origin of the Universe, 1977, The Discovery of Subatomic Particles, 1982; co-author (with R. Feynman) Elementary Particles and the Laws of Physics, 1987, Dreams of a Final Theory, 1992, The Quantum Theory of Fields - Vol. I: Foundations, 1995, Modern Applications, Vol. II, 1996, Supersymmetry, Vol. III, 2000; rsch. and publs. on elementary particles, quantum field theory, cosmology; co-editor monographs on math. physics Cambridge U. Press ; mem. adv. bd. Issues in Sci. and Tech., 1984-87; mem. sci. book com. Sloan Found., 1985-91; mem. editl. bd. Jour. Math. Physics, 1986-88; mem. bd. editors Daedalus, 1990—, Jour. Math. Physics, 1998—; mem. bd. assoc. editors Nuclear Physics B. Bd. advisors Santa Barbara Inst. Theoretical Physics, 1983-86; bd. overseers SSC Accelerator, 1984-86; bd. dirs. Headliners Found., 1993—. Recipient J. Robert Oppenheimer Meml. prize, 1973, Dannie Heineman prize in math. physics, 1977, Am. Inst. Physics-U.S. Steel Found. sci. writing award, 1977, Nobel prize in physics, 1979, Elliott Cresson medal Franklin Inst., 1979, Madison medal Princeton U., 1991, Nat. Medal of Sci. NSF, 1991, Andrew Gemant prize Am. Inst. Physics, 1997, Piazzi prize Govts. Sicily and Palermo, 1998, Lewis Thomas prize Rockefeller U., 1999. Mem. NAS (supercollider site evaluation com. 1987-88), Am. Acad. Arts and Scis. (past councilor), Am. Phys. Soc. (past councilor at large, panel on faculty positions com. on status of women in physics), Einstein Archivess (adv. bd. 1988—), Internat. Astron. Union, Coun. Fgn. Rels., Am. Philos. Soc., Royal Soc. London (fgn. mem.), Am. Medieval Acad., History of Sci. Soc., Philos. Soc. Tex. (pres. 1994), Tex. Inst. of Letters, Phi Beta Kappa. Clubs: Saturday (Boston); Headliners, Tuesday (Austin); Cambridge Sci. Soc.

WEINBERGER, CASPAR WILLARD, publishing executive, former secretary of defense; b. San Francisco, Aug. 18, 1917; s. Herman and Cerise Carpenter (Hampson) W.; m. Jane Dalton, Aug. 16, 1942; children: Arlin Cerise, Caspar Willard. AB magna cum laude, Harvard U., 1938, LLB, 1941; LLD (hon.), U. Leeds, Eng., 1989; LittD (hon.), U. Buckingham, 1995, Rennselear Poly., U. San Francisco. Bar: Calif., 1941, U.S. Ct. Appeals (D.C. cir.) 1990. Law clk. U.S. Judge William E. Orr, 1945-47; with firm Heller, Ehrman, White & McAuliffe, 1947-69, ptnr., 1959-69; mem. Calif. Legislature from 21st Dist., 1952-58; vice chmn. Calif. Rep. Ctrl. Com., 1960-62, chmn., 1962-64; chmn. Com. Calif. Govt. Orgn. and Econs., 1967-68; dir. fin. Calif., 1968-69; chmn. FTC, 1970; dep. dir. Office Mgmt. and Budget, 1970-72, dir., 1972-73; counsellor to the Pres., 1973; sec. HEW, 1973-75; gen. counsel, v.p., dir. Bechtel Power Corp., San Francisco, 1975-80, Bechtel, Inc., 1975-80, Bechtel Corp., 1975-80; sec. U.S. Dept. Def., Washington, 1981-87; counsel Law Firm of Rogers & Wells, Washington and N.Y.C., 1988-94; chmn. Forbes Magazine, New York, 1989—; formerly staff book reviewer San Francisco Chronicle; moderator weekly TV program Profile, Bay Area, sta. KQED, San Francisco, 1959-68; Frank Nelson Doubleday lectr., 1974; co-host World Bus. Review, 1996-99. writer column on Calif. govt., 1959-68; author: Fighting for Peace: Seven Critic al Years in the Pentagon, 1990, The Next War, 1996; co-author: Peter Schweizer.9. Chmn. Pres.'s Com. on Mental Retardation, 1973-75; former mem. Trilateral Commn.; former mem. adv. coun. Am. Ditchley Found.; former bd. dirs. Yosemite Inst.; former trustee St. Luke's Hosp., San Francisco, Mechanics Inst.; former chmn. nat. bd. trustees Nat. Symphony, Washington; former bd. govs. San Francisco Symphony; chmn. bd. USA-ROC Econ. Coun., 1991-94; co-chmn. Winston Churchill Travelling Fellowships Found., 1989-99; trustee Winston Churchill Meml. Trust, 1994—; bd. dirs. Chatham House Found., Inc., 1996—; mem. coun. on fgn. rels. Capt., inf. AUS, 1941-45; PTO. Decorated Bronze Star, Grand Cordon of Order of the Rising Sun (Japan), Hon. Knight Grand Cross Civil Div. Order of Brit. Empire, Order of Brillians Star with Grand Cordon, Taiwan; recipient Presdl. medal Freedom with distinction, 1987, Merite First Class, Mex., 1987, George Catlet Marshall medal, 1988, Civil award Hilal-i-Pakistan, 1989. Mem. ABA, State Bar Calif., D.C. Ct. Appeals, Century Club (N.Y.), Bohemian Club (San Francisco), Pacific Union Club (San Francisco), Harvard Club (Washington). Episcopalian (former treas. Diocese of Calif.). Office: Forbes Mag Office of Chmn 1101 17th St NW Ste 406 Washington DC 20036-4720

WEINBERGER, PETER, chemist; b. Vienna, Austria, Apr. 14, 1967; s. Franz and Helga (Wowk) W. MSc, Vienna U. Tech., 1993, PhD, 1998. Cert. computer networking. Asst. Inst. Inorganic Chemistry, Vienna U. Tech., 1993-94, rschr., 1994-97, univ. asst., 1998—. Contbr. article to profl. jours. Environ. activist Youth of the Austrian Peoples Party, Vienna, 1987-89. Recipient 9th Austrian Chemistry Olympiad 3rd prize Ministry Edn., Vienna, 1983, scholarships Inst. for Isotope Rsch. Hungarian Acad. Scis., Budapest, 1992, dept. chemistry Dundee (Scotland) U., 1993. Mem. Yacht Club Austria, Austrian Cruising Club. Avocations: downhill skiing, windsurfing, yachting, backbag travel. Fax: 43-1-58801-15399. E-mail: weinberg@mail.zserv.tuwien.ac.at. Office: Vienna U Tech, Getreidemarkt 9/153, A-1060 Vienna Austria

WEINER, EDWARD, civil engineer, federal agency administrator; b. Bklyn., Mar. 31, 1941; s. Abe C. and Elsie (Botwinick) W.; m. Joanne Jessen, Sept. 9, 1967 (div. Mar. 1988); children: Jennifer Lynn, Michael Andrew; m. Janis Lynn Wolford, Oct. 7, 1995. BA, NYU, 1963, BCE, 1963; MS in Civil Engring., Purdue U., 1964; M. in Pub. Adminstrn., U. So. Calif., 1978. Registered profl. engr. Hwy. research engr. Bur. of Pub. Rds., then Fed. Hwy. Adminstrn., Washington, 1964-70; mgr. urban analysis program Office Sec. of Transp., Washington, 1970-77, sr. policy analyst, 1978—; sec. Task Force on Pub. Transp., Transp. Research Bd., 1971-72, mem. Com. on Travel Behavior and Values, Oct. 1973—; mem. com. Econ. Devel. of Land and Transp. Systems, 1983-86; mem. group 1 council, transp. systems planning and adminstrn., 1984-90; mem. com. Intergovernmental Relations and Policy Process, Telecomm. and Travel Behavior; guest lectr. George Washington U., U. Va., Portland State U., U. Wis. Co-editor: Emerging Transportation Planning Methods, 1978; author, co-author: Urban Transportation Planning in the U.S., 1987, revised edit., 1999, National Transportation System Initiative, 1999; (monographs) Role of Taxicabs in Urban Transportation, 1974, Glossary of Urban Public Transportation Terms, 1978, Modal Split, 1966; co-editor Internat. Assn. for Travel Behavior newsletter, 1985-88; contbr. over 70 articles to profl. jours.; mem. editorial adv. bd. Transp., 1978-80, 92-2000. Asst. troop leader Girl Scouts Am., Silver Spring, Md., 1981-82; v.p. Unitarian Universalist Ch. of Silver Spring, 1984, pres., 1985-86, v.p., 1998-99. Edn. for Public Mgmt. fellow U.S. Dept. Transp., 1978; recipient Bronze medal Dept. Transp., 1981, Spl. Achievement award, 1990, 95, 98, 99, 2000. Mem. ASCE, Transp. Research Bd. Home: 16615 Harbour Town Dr Silver Spring MD 20905-4082 Office: US Dept Transp P-30 400 7th St SW Washington DC 20590-0001

WEINER, HOWARD MARC, physician; b. Feb. 25, 1946. BSc, Marietta Coll., 1967; MD, U. Cin., 1971; MPH, Med. Coll. Wis., 1994. Diplomate Am. Bd. Forensic Examiners, Diplomate Am. Bd. Internal Medicine, Am. Bd. Allergy, Asthma & Immunology, Am. Bd. Preventive Medicine/Occupl. Medicine; cert. ind. med. examiner. Intern in medicine Temple U. Hosp., Phila., 1971-72, resident in internal medicine, 1972-74; fellow in allergy and clin. immunology Hosp. of U. Pa., Phila., 1974-76; pres., physician Allergy & Asthma Assocs. West Boca, Boca Raton, Fla., 1988—; pres., med. dir. Med. Assessment Inst. Inc., Boca Raton, Fla., 1997—; chmn. ethics com. Palm Beach County Med. Soc., West Palm Beach, Fla., 1994-97; bd. dirs. Primus Physicians Svcs., Inc., So. Fla. Mem. Omicron Delta Kappa Soc., Pi Kappa Epsilon. Office: 9980 Central Park Blvd N Boca Raton FL 33428-1762

WEINER, KENNETH BRIAN, lawyer; b. N.Y.C., Oct. 13, 1954; s. Irwin I. and Elayne B. (Biffer) W.; m. Sandra Hong, Apr. 30, 2000. BSCE, Case Western Res. U., 1976; JD summa cum laude, N.Y. Law Sch., 1986. Bar: N.Y. 1986, Washington 1997; registered profl. engr., N.J. Quality control engr. Cosmic Constrn. Co., Newport News, Va., 1976-77; project engr., geotech. engr. Mueser Rutledge Cons. Engrs., N.Y.C., 1977-86; assoc. Olwine, Connelly, Chase, O'Donnel & Weyner, N.Y.C., 1986-91, Ballard Spahr Andrews & Ingersoll LLP, Washington, 1992; assoc. Reid & Priest LLP, Washington, 1992-95, ptnr., 1996-98; ptnr. Thelen Reid & Priest LLP, Washington, 1998—. Contbr. articles to profl. jours. Mem. Aircraft Owners and Pilots Assn., Mooney Aircraft Pilots Assn. Avocations: flying, skiing. Office: Thelen Reid & Priest LLP 701 Pennsylvania Ave NW Washington DC 20004-2608

WEINER, LAWRENCE, lawyer; b. Phila., Aug. 20, 1942; s. Robert A. and Goldie Weiner; m. Jane M. Coulthard, Feb. 28, 1976; 1 child, Kimberly. BS in Econs., U. Pa., 1964, JD, 1967. Bar: Pa. 1967, U.S. Dist. Ct. (ea. dist.) Pa. 1967, Fla. 1970, U.S. Dist. Ct. (so. dist.) Fla. 1976, U.S. Ct. Appeals (5th cir.) 1976, U.S. Tax Ct. 1984. Assoc., ptnr. Blank, Rome, Klaus & Comisky, Phila., 1967-71, 1975-77; ptnr. Weiner & Weisenfeld, P.A., Miami Beach, Fla., 1971-73, Pettigrew & Bailey, Miami, Fla., 1973-75; pres. Lawrence Weiner, P.A., Miami, 1977-83; ptnr. Spieler, Weiner & Spieler, P.A., Miami, 1983-89, Weiner & Cummings, P.A., Miami, 1989-94, Weiner, Cummings & Vittoria, Miami, 1994—; lectr. Wharton Sch. U. Pa., Phila., 1968-70; instr. bus. law and acctg. Community Coll. Phila., 1967-70; lectr. estate planning various non-lawyer groups, Miami, 1972—. Mem. Fla. Bar (liaison non-lawyers groups 1980-87), Pa. Bar Assn., Phila. Bar Assn., Dade County Bar Assn. (chmn. ins. com. 1977-78, probate law com. 1992—). Democrat. Jewish. Office: Weiner Cummings & Vittoria 1428 Brickell Ave Ste 400 Miami FL 33131-3436

WEINER, RICHARD MAX, physicist; b. Czernowitz, Romania, Feb. 6, 1930; s. Max and Pepi (Haber) W.; m. Nina Culic, Dec. 19, 1969; 1 child, Diana Free. MS, U. Bucharest, 1953, PhD, 1958. Rsch. fellow Physics Inst. Acad. Scis., Bucharest, 1951-69, U. Bucharest, 1968-69, European Nuclear Rsch., CERN, Geneva, 1969-70; vis. prof. Ind. U., 1970-72; sr. fellow Imperial Coll., London, 1972-73; prof. theoretical physics U. Marburg, Germany, 1974—; vis. scientist Los Alamos (N.Mex.) Nat. Lab., 1976-77, cons., 1978—; rschr. lab. physique theorique hautes energies Orsay U., Paris, 1995—. Co-editor: Local Equilibrium in Strong Interaction Physics, 1985, Correlations and Multiparticle Production, 1991; editor: Bose-Einstein Correlations in Particle and Nuclear Physics, 1997; author: Introduction to Bose-Einstein Correlations and Subatomic Interferometry, 1999; contbr. over 180 sci. papers to profl. jours. and books. Achievements include research on atomic, nuclear and elem. particle physics; prediction of nuclear isomeric shift and other physical effects in nuclear and particle physics. Office: U Marburg, Wieselacker 8, 35041 Marburg Germany

WEINER, ROBERT STEPHEN, federal agency administrator; b. Paterson, N.J., Apr. 3, 1947; s. Jess Joseph Weiner and Dorothea Violet (Slavin) Tabor. BA, Oberlin Coll., 1969; MA, U. Mass., 1974. Student coord. Hampshire County, dir. telephone bank Kennedy for U.S. Senate, Amherst, Mass., 1970; dir. nat. voter registration Young Dems. Am., Washington, 1971-72; dir. voter registration, media dir. get out the vote Dem. Nat. Com., Washington, 1972; legis. asst. Congressman Edward Koch, Washington, 1974-75; staff dir. subcom. health and long-term care U.S. Ho. of Reps., Washington, 1975-76, staff dir. com. aging, 1976-80; sr. assoc. Mgmt. Recruiters Internat., Springfield, Mass., 1981-83; dir. Robert Weiner Assocs., Amherst, 1983-86; media dir., press sec. com. narcotics U.S. Ho. of Reps., Washington, 1987-90, press sec./comms. dir. com. on govt. ops., 1990-95; sr. assoc. Mgmt. Recruiters Internat., Springfield, Mass., 1981-83; dir. Robert Weiner Assocs., Amherst, 1983-86; dir. comm. Ho. Judiciary com. Minority and Cong. John Conyers Jr., 1995; dir. pub. affairs White House Drug Policy Office, Washington, 1995—; dir. gen. press rm. Dem. Nat. Convention, Atlanta, 1988, N.Y.C, 1992, Chgo., 1996; cons. Carter-Mondale Transition, Washington, 1976-77, Congressman Claude Pepper, Washington, 1975-89. Represented in permanent exhbns. Nat. Mus. Am. History, Smithsonian Instn., Washington; contbr. numerous articles to profl. jours. Dem. nominee for U.S. Congress, Mass., 1986; chmn. Road Runners Am. Nat. 10 Mile Championship, Amherst, 1984; vice chmn. Dem. Town Com., Amherst, 1984-87; legis. chmn. Pioneer Valley Gray Panthers, Amherst, 1981-87; nat campaign aide Kennedy for Pres., Washington, 1980. Named Communicator of Yr., Washington Crime News Svcs., 1988, 89, 90; 2d place U.S. Nat. Masters Track Championship, 1994, 97. Mem. Assn. House Dem. Press Assts., Congl. Staff Club, Nat. Dem. Club, Sugarloaf Mountain Athletic Club (pres. 1984-86), White House Athletic Ctr. (exec. bd. 1995—), Potomac Valley Track Club, Capitol Hill Runners (pres. 1991—). Avocations: running, attending performing arts. Home: 1104 Sanford Ln Accokeek MD 20607-2324 Office: Exec Office of Pres Office Nat Drug Control Pol Washington DC 20500

WEINER, WALTER HERMAN, banker, lawyer; b. Bklyn., Aug. 29, 1930; s. Harry and Sylvia (Freifeld) W.; m. Nina Ester Avidar, Oct. 11, 1966; children: Thomas Field, Jon Michael. BA, U. Mich., 1952, JD, 1953. Bar: N.Y. 1953. Sr. ptnr. Kronish, Lieb, Weiner & Hellman, N.Y.C., 1965-79; chmn. exec. com., chief exec. officer Republic N.Y. Corp., 1980-81, pres., chief exec. officer, 1981-83, chmn. bd., chief exec. officer, 1983—; chmn. exec. com., chief exec. officer Republic Nat. Bank of N.Y., 1980-82, pres., chief exec. officer, 1981-86, chmn. bd., chief exec. officer, 1986—, also bd. dirs.; pres. WHW Mgmt. Corp., N.Y.C.; bd. dirs. Republic N.Y. Corp., Republic Nat. Bank of N.Y. Assoc. editor U. Mich. Law Rev. Bd. dirs., treas. Bryant Park Restoration Corp., Internat. Sephardic Edn. Found.; trustee Guild Hall, East Hampton, N.Y.; mem. N.Y. Holocaust Meml. Commn.; bd. visitors U. Mich. Law Sch. Recipient Humanitarian award NAACP, 1987, Human Rels. award Accts., Bankers, Factors and Fin. divsn. Am. Jewish Com., 1988, Man of Yr. award Bklyn. Sch. for Spl. Children, 1988, Good Scout award Greater N.Y. Couns./Boy Scouts Am., 1994, Jewish Theol. Sem.'s Louis Marshall award, 1994, numerous others. Mem. ABA, N.Y. State Bar Assn., Assn. of Bar of City of N.Y., Am. Bankers Assn., N.Y. Clearing House Assn., Bankers Roundtable. Office: WHW Mgmt Corp 425 Park Ave 26th Fl New York NY 10022-3506

WEINERT, HENRY M., biomedical company executive; b. Nordhausen, Kassel, Fed. Republic Germany, May 31, 1940; s. Heinrich V. Nennenstiehl and Martha H. Weinert; m. Helen Koopmans, Feb. 14, 1966 (div. June 1982); children: Jason C., Brian T.; m. Kerri V. Keaton, Sept. 25, 1989. BA in Sci., Columbia Coll., 1962; MBA, Harvard Grad. Sch. Bus., 1970. Med. rsch. assoc. Columbia Univ., N.Y.C., 1964-65; exec. v.p., founder Clin. Diagnostic Lab., New Haven, Conn., 1966-68; dir. planning, bus. devel. Lederle Labs./Am. Cyan., Pearl River, N.Y., 1970-73, mktg. dir., 1973-74; bus. devel. mgr. Corning (N.Y.) Glass Works, 1974-77; pres., founder Boston Biomed. Cons., Waltham, Mass., 1977—; spl. ltd. ptnr. MedVenture Assocs., San Francisco, 1965—, Interwest Ptnrs., San Francisco, 1989; presenter, lectr. in field. Patentee laser fabrication of microsuture needles; contbr. articles to profl. jours. Pres. Svc. Soc., Columbia Coll., 1959; chmn. Student Union Com., Columbia Coll., 1961; treas. Class 1962, Columbia Coll., 1962-64; others. Recipient Alumni Achievement award Columbia Coll., 1962; grantee NIH, 1964-66. Mem. Biomed. Mktg. Assn. (bd. dirs. 1978-86, Recognition award 1986), Am. Assn. Clin. Chemistry, Van Slyke Soc. (bd. mem. 1991—). Lutheran. Avocations: reading sci. fiction and mystery novels, sailing, cars, landscaping. Home: 86 Myles Standish Rd Weston MA 02493-2124 Office: Boston Biomed Cons 1000 Winter St Ste 1600 Waltham MA 02451-1469

WEINGARTZ, HANS, editor, educator; b. Bonn, Germany, Feb. 7, 1949; s. Hans and Irene (Gülden) W.; m. Dorothee Pass, Sept. 17, 1951; children: Tim, Jan, Pia. States exam., U. Bonn, 1973. Founder Kid-Verlag, Bonn, 1990—. Editor: Brd und Die Un-Kinderkonvention, 1991, Kinderrechte und Verfassung, 1992; editor (quar.) Kinderinformations Dienst, 1990, www.KidWeb.de. E-mail: hanswein@t-online.de. Office: Kid Verlag, Samansstr 4, 53227 Bonn Germany

WEINGAST, MARVIN, laboratory executive; b. Bklyn., Jan. 1, 1943; s. Abe and Rose (Altein) W. BS, L.I. U., 1967, MS, 1971; postgrad., Poly. Inst., 1967-68. Analytic and pollution chemist Amerada Hess Corp., Pt. Reading, N.J., 1969-73; asst. lab. dir. Chem. Constrn., North Brunswick, N.J., 1973-74; dir. Indsl. Hygiene Lab. Nat. Starch and Chemical, Bridgewater, N.J., 1974—; grant com. mem. Ctr. for Hazardous and Toxic Substance Mgmt., Newark, 1988—; mem. Sourland Regional Citizens Planning Coun., Neshanic, N.J., 1989—. Contbr. to book: Small Business Programs, 1980; contbr. articles to profl. jours. Recipient Chemistry Dept. award L.I. U., 1967, Teaching fellowship Poly. Inst., 1967, L.I. U., 1968. Mem. MENSA, Am. Chem. Soc., Am. Conf. Chem. Labeling, Soc. Toxicology. Achievements include development of improved system for identification of hazardous chemicals; organization of first global monitoring of indsl. workers to hazardous workplace chemicals. Office: Nat Starch & Chem Co 10 Finderne Ave Bridgewater NJ 08807-3355

WEINMANN, CHRISTOPH DAVID, economic advisor; b. Berlin, Germany, Nov. 26, 1963. MS in Econs., Free U. Berlin, 1992; cert. in devel.

studies, German Devel. Inst., 1993. Seaman Merchant Marine, Germany, 1982-86; cons. Treuhandanstalt, Berlin, 1993; asst. to the dir. Luso Consult GmbH, Hamburg, Germany, 1994-96; acting mgr. econ. policy analysis and adv. svcs. Luso Cons. GmbH, Hamburg, 1997-2000; program coord., advisor on reform and devel. Sml./Medium-Scale Enterprises (via State Econ./Trade Commn.), Beijing, 2000—. Textilien in Mosambik: Industrialisierung "von unten", 1993; contbr. articles to profl. jours. Mem. Kinderhilfe Hyvong e.V., Support Group of the Ecumenical Devel. Coop. Soc. Fax: 86-10-85275185. Office: GTZ Office Beijing Sunflower Towers Rm 1100, 37 Maizidian St Chaoyang Dist, 100026 Beijing China

WEINMANN, ERIC, retired lawyer; b. Teplice, Czech Republic, July 29, 1913; came to U.S., 1942; s. Ing Edmund and Josefine (Taussig) W.; m. Camilla Behn, May 4, 1946 (div. 1953); children: Edward Marvin, Gail Greenwood; m. Mary Ethel Carothers, Dec. 21, 1974. Diploma, Handelshochschule, Berlin, 1935; MA, Columbia U., 1943, JD, 1957; LLM, Georgetown U., 1963. Bar: N.Y. 1957, D.C. 1958, U.S. Supreme Ct. 1963. Assoc. counsel Legal & Monetary Subcom., Ho. of Reps., Washington, 1957-60; atty. SEC, Washington, 1960-63; counsel SBA, Washington, 1963-89. Contbr. articles to profl. jours. Trustee emeritus Folger Shakespeare Libr., Washington, 1985. Mem. Met. Club City of Washington, City Tavern Assn., N.Y. Athletic Club. Avocations: skin diving, mountain climbing, dressage riding. Home: 3244 Nebraska Ave NW Washington DC 20016-2704

WEINMEISTER, HANNS-WOLFGANG, forest engineer, educator; b. Linz, Austria, Feb. 9, 1939; s. Bruno and Gertrude (Weihs) W.; m. Elfriede Schernhammer; children: Gertrud, Siegmund, Hanna, Bruno. Diploma, U. Agrl. Scis., Vienna, Austria, 1963; PhD, U. Salzburg (Austria), 1984. Mountain risk engring. Engr. Forest Tech. Svc., Salzburg, 1963-66, sr. engr., 1968-78; engr. Fed. Forests, Golling, Austria, 1966-67; nature protection commr. Govt., Salzburg, 1979-90; u. prof. U. Agrl. Sci., Vienna, 1991—; expert cons. of ct., Salzburg, 1980—. Mem. scientific bd. Alpen Forum, Bern, Switzerland, 1995, Wilturland Foundry, Vienna, 1995-98; mem. scientific bd. Naturscheigbeiral, Salzburg, 1973-89, mem., 1975-90. Mem. S.A.B.O. (Japan), W.L.V., Avalance Assn. Avocations: music, walking, skiing.

WEINREB, MICHAEL PHILIP, physicist; b. Lakewood, N.J., Feb. 2, 1939; s. Sol and Lillian (Bolotsky) W.; m. Alice Kogan, Aug. 28, 1966; children: Jenya, Elizabeth. BA, U. Pa., 1960; MA, Brandeis U., 1963, PhD, 1966. Physicist NASA, Cambridge, Mass., 1965-70, U.S. Dept. Transp., Cambridge, 1970, Nat. Oceanic and Atmospheric Adminstrn., Washington, 1970—; adj. prof. math. Am. U., Washington, 1984-85. Contbr. articles to profl. jours. Recipient Gold medal U.S. Dept. of Commerce, 1998, Bronze medal, 1994. Mem. Optical Soc. Am., Am. Meteorol. Soc., Am. Geophys. Union, Phi Beta Kappa. Avocation: music. Office: NOAA NESDIS 5200 Auth Rd Camp Springs MD 20746-4304

WEINREICH, DAN, federal official; b. Feb. 16, 1946; s. Elieyou and Malka W.; m. Dalea Weinrich, Sept. 23, 1981; children: Ishay, Ron. BA in Polit. Sci. and Labour Studies, Tel Aviv U. Advisor, instr. World Zionist Orgn., summer 1970, part time social instr., 1968-71; coord. Student Home Tel Aviv Secondary Schs., 1966-72; tchr. BILU Sch., Tel Aviv, 1967-71; asst. spokesman Min. Def., State of Israel, 1976-77; spokesman pub. rels. Jewish Agy., World Zionist Orgn., 1972-75; spokesman Min. Def., State of Israel, 1977—. Mem., instr. Bnei Akiva Youth Movement, 1954-64. Served with Israeli Army, 1964-66. Mem. Israeli Assn. Polit. Sci., Israeli Assn. Pub. Rels. Avocations: music, sports, theater, cinema, reading. Office: Israel Ministry of Def, Hakirya, Tel Aviv 61909, Israel

WEINREICH, GABRIEL, physicist, minister, educator; b. Vilnius, Lithuania, Feb. 12, 1928; came to U.S., 1941, naturalized, 1949; s. Max and Regina (Szabad) W.; m. Alisa Lourié, Apr. 19, 1951 (dec. 1970); m. Gerane Siemering Benamou, Oct. 23, 1971; children: Catherine, Marc, Daniel, Rebecca, Natalie. AB, Columbia U., 1948, MA, 1949, PhD, 1954. Ordained priest Episcopal Ch., 1986. Mem. staff Bell Telephone Labs., Murray Hill, N.J., 1953-60; mem. faculty U. Mich., Ann Arbor, 1960—; prof. physics U. Mich., 1964-95; prof. emeritus, 1995—; Collegiate prof. U. Mich., 1974-76; adj. min. St. Clare's Episcopal ch., Ann Arbor, 1986-90; rector St. Stephen's Episcopal Ch., Hamburg, Mich., 1993-96. Author: Solids: Elementary Theory for Advanced Students, 1965, Fundamental Thermodynamics, 1968, Notes for General Physics, 1972, Geometrical Vectors, 1998; editor: Mechanics of Musical Instruments, 1995. Recipient Disting. Teaching award U. Mich., 1968, Klopsteg award Am. Assn. Physics Tchrs., 1992, Internat. medal French Acoustical Soc., 1992. Fellow Acoustical Soc. Am. (assoc. editor Jour. 1987-89). Home: 754 Greenhills Dr Ann Arbor MI 48105-2718 Office: Randall Lab U Mich Ann Arbor MI 48109-1120

WEINSCHELBAUM, EMILIO, lawyer; b. Rosario, Argentina, Oct. 25, 1935; s. Marcos Leib and Elka (Werbin) W.; m. Marina Lucila Scornik, Dec. 20, 1962; children: Fernando, Violeta. Student, Columbia U., 1952-53; Atty. at Law, Universidad Nacional, Buenos Aires, 1957, sociologist, 1975; postgrad., U. Sorbonne, Paris, 1978. Pvt. practice Buenos Aires, 1957—; personal del. from Pres. Alfonsin to Europe-Latin Am. Congress, Strasbourg, France, 1988; organizer Congreso Internacional sobre Reforma Constitucional, Buenos Aires, 1988. Editor, legal advisor Primera Plana newsmag., 1962-64; editor Plural newsmag., 1984—, El Ciudadano newsmag., 1988-89; editor: (TV program) Los Argentinos, 1987 (Martin Fierro award 1987). Pres. Fundacion Plural para la Participacion Democratica, Buenos Aires, 1984—; mem. Coun. for Consolidation of Democracy, Buenos Aires, 1985-89, Nat. Com. Politics and Strategies of Democracy, 1997—. Mem. Colegio Publico de Abogados de Buenos Aires, Fundacion Compromiso Ciudadano, Club del Progreso (v.p. 1999—), Fundacion del Alvear (pres. 1999—). Office: Av Santa Fe 900 piso 6, 1059 Buenos Aires Argentina

WEINSCHELBAUM, ERNESTO EDUARDO, surgeon, educator; b. Rosario, Santa Fe, Argentina, Apr. 24, 1942; s. Noe and Delia (Rotman) W.; m. Susnaa Ines Bucsdorff; children: Guillermo Jose, Greta Veronica. Degree in Surgery, Rosario Nat. U., 1955; Degree in Cardiovascular Surgery, Inst. Cardiol/Thoracic Surgery, Buenos Aires, Argentina, 1972. Chief of the surgery residence Inst. Cardiology/Thoracic/Cardiovsc., Hosp. Luis Guemes, Buenos Aires, 1974-93, chief of the surgery, 1974-93, chief cardiovascular surgery dept., 1993—; assoc. prof. cardiology and thoracic and cardiovascular surgery Salvador U., Buenos Aires, 1978-91; prof. cardiac surgery Inst. Biomed. Scis., Favaloro Found., Buenos Aires, 1993—. Contbr. articles to profl. jours. Recipient Rafael Bullrich award Nat. Med. Acad., 1975. Mem. Argentine Soc. Cardiology (dir. coun. 1985, Best Sci. Work award 1989), Argentine Coll. Cardiovascular Surgeons (pres. 1988, pres. honor ct. 1991-93), Rosario Soc. Cardiology (hon.), Peruvian Soc. Cardiology (hon.), Soc. Cardiovascular and Thoracic Surgery of Mendoza (hon.). Avocation: golf.

WEINSTEIN, ALAN EDWARD, lawyer; b. Bklyn., Apr. 20, 1945; s. John and Matilda W.; m. Patti Kantor, Dec. 18, 1965; children: Steven R., David A. AA, U. Fla., 1964; BBA, U. Miami (Fla.), 1965, JD cum laude, 1968. Bar: Fla. 1968, U.S. Dist. Ct. (so. dist.) Fla. 1968, U.S. Ct. Appeals (5th cir.) 1969, U.S. Supreme Ct. 1973, U.S. Ct. Appeals (4th & 11th cirs.) 1981. Assoc. Cohen & Hogan, Miami Beach, Fla., 1968-71; pvt. practice Miami Beach, 1972-81; sr. ptnr. Weinstein & Preira, Miami Beach, 1981-92; prin. Law Offices of Alan E. Weinstein, Miami, 1992—; lectr. continuing legal edn. programs. Mem. ABA (criminal and family law sect. 1968—, white collar crime commn. 1986—), Nat. Assn. Criminal Def. Lawyers, 1st Family Law Am. Inn of Court, Fla. Bar Assn. (criminal and family law sect. 1968—, ethics com. 1987-88, bench/bar com. 1988-89, grievance com. 1999—), Fla. Criminal Def. Attys. Assn. (pres. 1978-79), Fla. Assn. Criminal Def. Lawyers (treas. 1989-90), Miami Beach Bar Assn., Soc. Wig and Robe, Phi Kappa Phi. Avocations: marlin fishing, reading, travel. Office: 1801 West Ave Miami FL 33139-1431

WEINSTEIN, GEORGE, management consultant; b. N.Y.C., Mar. 20, 1924; s. Morris J. and Sara (Broder) W.; m. Shirley Beatrice Greenberg, Sept. 1, 1945; children: Stanley Howard, Jerrald, Sara Belle. BS, U. Ill., 1944, postgrad. Law Sch., 1944-55; MBA, NYU, 1947. Joined Morris J. Weinstein, Groothuis & Co., N.Y.C., 1944, ptnr., 1945-72; ptnr. Weinstein Assocs., Miami and Israel, 1973—; chmn. Weinstein Assocs. Ltd.; pres. dir. REIT Property Mgrs. Ltd., Milw.; pres. Hudson Valley Corp., WAL Ltd.; bd. dirs. Regency Investors, John Stewart, Axminster U.S.A., Ice Co. of Wis., Med. Mgmt. Am., Fla. Glass, Inc., chmn.; bd. mem. Israviation Ltd. Active United Jewish Appeal, Fedn. Jewish Philanthropies; bd. dirs., founder North Shore Hebrew Acad.; founder, past pres. Gt. Neck (N.Y.) Synagogue; founder, chmn. Lake Park Synagogue; bd. dirs. Milw. Jewish Home, Jewish Nat. Fund, Milw. Hillel Acad. Mem. Am. Inst. Accts., N.Y. Soc. CPAs, Hebrew Immigrant Soc., President's of U. Ill. Club, Westmoreland Club, Ambassadors Club of Yeshiva U., Milw. Athletic Club, Wisconsin of Milw. Club, Citrus Club, Masons (past master), Tau Delta Phi (nat. treas.), Delta Sigma Phi. Address: 5 Yismach Melech, Davids Village Jerusalem 94105, Israel

WEINSTEIN, HAREL, physiologist, biophysicist, educator; b. Romania, June 5, 1945; came to U.S., 1973; s. Adolf and Klara W.; m. Barbara Manski, June 9, 1967; 1 child, Elhav. BS, Technion-Israel Inst. Tech., Haifa, 1966, MS, 1968, DSc, 1971. Lectr. Technion-Israel Inst. Tech., 1971-73; rsch. assoc. chemistry Johns Hopkins U., Balt., 1973-74; asst. prof. pharmacology Mount Sinai Sch. Medicine, N.Y.C., 1974-76, assoc. prof., 1976-79, prof., 1979—, chmn., prof. physiology and biophysics, 1985—, dir. Inst. Computational Biomedicine, 1998—, dir. Inst. for Computational Biomedicine; cons. Merck, Sharp & Dohme, Rahway, N.J., 1979-81; mem. study sect. Nat. Inst. Drug Abuse, Bethesda, Md., 1979-83, 90—, chmn., 1997-98; mem. health & environ. rsch. adv. com. U.S. Dept. Energy, Washington, 1986-94; mem. scientific adv. bd. Terrapin Technology Inc., 1994—, Telik; cons. CytoMed, UCB, 1997—; mem. sci. adv. bd. N.Y. Acad. Medicine; mem. coun. Biophysics Soc., 1998—. Editor: Quantum Chemistry in Biomedical Sciences, Computational Approaches to Enzyme Structure and Function; contbr. over 190 articles to profl. jours. Recipient Irma T. Hirschl Career Scientist award, 1978-82, Alcohol, Drug Abuse & Mental Health Assn. Rsch. Scientist Devel. award, 1979-89, Outstanding Contbns. award Internat. Soc. Quantum Biology, 1988, Rsch. Scientist award Nat. Inst. Drug Abuse, 1990—; named Parke-Davies Disting. lectr. U. Mich., 1988. Mem. Assn. Chmn. Depts. Physiology (councillor 1989-91, pres.-elect 1991-92, pres. 1992-93); Internat. Soc. Quantum Biology and Pharmacology (pres. 1989), N.Y. Acad. Scis. (chair. biophysics sect. 1992). Office: Mt Sinai Sch Medicine 1 Gustave L Levy Pl New York NY 10029-6500

WEINSTEIN, HARRIS, lawyer; b. Providence, May 10, 1935; s. Joseph and Gertrude (Rusitzky) W.; m. Rosa Grunberg, June 3, 1956; children: Teme Ring, Joshua, Jacob. BS in Math., MIT, 1956, MS in Math., 1958; LLB, Columbia U., 1961. Bar: D.C. 1962. Law clk. to judge William H. Hastie U.S. Ct. Appeals (3d cir.), Phila., 1961-62; with Covington & Burling, Washington, 1962-67, 69-90, 1993—; chief counsel Office of Thrift Supervision U.S. Dept. of Treasury, Washington, 1990-92; asst. to solicitor gen. U.S. Dept. Justice, 1967-69; pub. mem. Adminstrv. Conf. of U.S., 1982-90; lectr. U. Va. Law Sch., 1996; mgmt. com. Undiscovered Mgrs., LLC, 1998—. V.p. Jewish Social Svc. Agy., 1995-98; mem. MIT Corp., 1989-95. Mem. Nat. Press Club. Home: 7717 Georgetown Pike Mc Lean VA 22102-1411 Office: Covington & Burling PO Box 7566 1201 Pennsylvania Ave NW Washington DC 20004-2401

WEINSTEIN, ILYA ALEXANDROVICH, engineer; b. Sverdlovsk, Russia, July 20, 1968; s. Alexandr Abramovich and Capitolina Pavlovna (Kutepova) W.; m. Nalalia Alexandrovna Savina, July 18, 1992 (dec. July 1998); 1 child, Veniamin. PhD, Ural State Tech. U., Ekaterinburg, Russia, 1997. Rschr. Ural State Tech U., Ekaterinburg, 1996-97, sr. rschr., 1997—. Mem. editl. bd. Red Burds, 1992—; contbr. articles to profl. jours. Lt. Soviet Army, 1985-87, 93-00. Avocation: tennis. Office: Ural State Tech Univ, Mira Str 19 Dept Phys & Tec, 620002 Ekaterinburg Russia

WEINSTEIN, LARRY B., business educator; b. N.Y.C., Mar. 9, 1953; s. Bernard and Gussie (Schultz) W.; m. Robin E. Weinstein, May 25, 1985. BS, U. Cin., 1985; MS, GMI Inst., Flint, Mich., 1989; PhD, U. Ky., 1996. Cert. Quality Auditor, Cert. Quality Engr.; cert. in Prodn. and Inventory Mgmt. Carillonneur Carillon Hist. Park, Dayton, Ohio; vis. asst. prof. Ea. Ky. U., Richmond, 1989-92, Ball State U., Muncie, Ind., 1992-93; asst. prof. Wright State U., Dayton, 1993—; v.p. Midwest Decision Sci. Inst.; sr. examiner Ohio Award for Excellence, Dayton Quality Award. Recipient Prix d'Excellence Nederlandse Beiaard Sch., Amersfort, the Netherlands, 1977, 1st prize Internat. Carillon Performance Competition, 1977, Dutch Carillon Soc. Competition, 1973, 74. Mem. Decision Sci. Inst., Dayton Am. Prodn. and Inventory Control Soc. (bd. dirs.). Office: Wright State Univ Col Glenn Hwy Dayton OH 45435

WEINSTEIN, RHONDA KRUGER, elementary mathematics educator, administrator; b. Boston, May 18, 1948; d. David Solomon and Henrietta Reina (Slocum) Kruger; m. Milton Charles Weinstein, June 14, 1970; children: Jeffrey William, Daniel Jay. AB, Mt. Holyoke Coll., 1970; MA, Suffolk U., 1973. Cert. supr./dir.; math. 7-12; elem. K-8; elem. prin.; supt., Mass. Tchr. grade 3 Brookline (Mass.) Pub. Schs., 1974-78, math. resource tchr. K-6, 1980-81, math. resource tchr. K-8, 1981-82, elem. curriculum coord. for math., 1982—; program evaluator Newton (Mass.) Pub. Schs., 1992-93; part-time instr. Suffolk U., Boston, 1976, 79; mem. math. adv. bd. Ency. Britannica, Chgo., 1993-95; cons. Mass. sch. sys. including Northborough/ Southborough, 1987-88, Sudbury, 1987, North Andover, 1993; spkr. profl. meetings Assn. Tchrs. Math. in New Eng., 1990, 94, 95, ASCD, Boston, 1988. Co-author: Calculator Activities, 1987; reviewer 2 books Arithmetic Teacher, 1991. Alumnae fund vol. Mt. Holyoke Coll., South Hadley, Mass., 1985-90; vol. Am. Heart Assn., Brookline, 1982-93; mem. PTO, Baker Sch., Brookline, 1983-95. Sarah Williston scholar Mt. Holyoke Coll., 1967; grantee Brookline Found., 1994, Tchrs. and Adminstrs. Tng. Fund, 1992, 96. Mem. Nat. Coun. Tchrs. Math. (nat. conv. com. chair 1995, speaker profl. meeting 1993), Nat. Coun. Suprs. of Math. (spkr. profl. meeting 2000), Assn. Tchrs. of Math. in Mass., Boston Area Math. Specialists, Phi Beta Kappa. Avocations: cross-country skiing, gourmet cooking, walking, swimming, playing piano. Home: 50 Princeton Rd Chestnut Hill MA 02467-3061 Office: Brookline Pub Schs 88 Harvard St Brookline MA 02445-7949

WEINSTEIN-BACAL, STUART ALLEN, lawyer, educator; b. Stuttgart, Germany, May 23, 1948; s. Marvin Stuart and Mae (Beal) W.; m. Holly Laurette Thompson, Aug. 7, 1982; children: Rachel Lee, Maximillian II, Sarah Nicole. BA, U. Va., 1970, MEd, 1973; JD cum laude, U. Miami, 1979. Bar: D.C. 1979, Va. 1981, V.I. 1985, P.R. 1988. Tchr., pvt. tutor various schs., Conn., Fla., Costa Rica, 1973-76; mem. prof. staff Merchant Marine and Fisheries Com. U.S. Ho. of Reps., Washington, 1978; assoc. Cameron, Hornbostel & Adelman, Washington, 1979-80, Burch, Kerns & Klimek, P.C., Washington, 1980, 81; staff atty. C.A.C.I., Washington, 1982, 83; sr. assoc. Dudley, Dudley & Topper, St. Thomas, U.S. Virgin Islands, 1984, 85; v.p., gen. counsel Redondo Construction Corp., San Juan, P.R., 1985-89; pvt. practice law San Juan, 1989-2000; sr. ptnr. Weinstein-Bacal and Assocs., P.S.C., Old San Juan, 2000—; owner Weinstein-Bocal & Assocs., P.S.C., 2000—; early neutral evaluator U.S. Dist. Ct. P.R. Contbr. articles to profl. jours. Capt. USAR, 1970-85. Mem. ABA, Am. Arbitration Assn. (pres., Caribbean region adv. coun. 1988—, arbitrator 1989—), Res. Officers Assn., Colegio de Abogados de P.R., U. Va. Alumni Assn., Nature Conservancy, Sovereign Order of the Oak (knight comdr.), Rotary Club of San Juan (bd. dirs. 1991-95), The Langley Club, Bankers Club P.R., Phi Alpha Delta. Avocations: sailing, golf, tennis, gourmet cooking, traveling. Home: Villas Del Mar E # 7D Carolina PR 00979 also: Mallory Chase Farm 35919 Turkey Roost Rd Middleburg VA 20117-3401 Office: Gonzalez Padin Bldg-Penthouse 154 Rafael Cordero St Plz Armas Old San Juan PR 00901

WEINSTOCK, LORD ARNOLD, electronics company executive; b. London, July 29, 1924; m. Netta Sobell, Oct. 23, 1949; children: Simon Andrew (dec.), Susan Gina. BSc in Econs., U. London, 1945; DSc (hon.), Salford, 1975, Aston, 1976, Bath, 1978, Reading, 1978, U. Ulster, 1987; LLD (hon.), U. Leeds, 1978, U. Wales, 1985, Keele U., 1997; DTech (hon.), Loughborough U., 1981; D(hon.), Anglia Polytechic U., 1994; D Econ Sci, London U., 1997. Jr. adminstrv. officer Admiralty, 1944-47; financier, property developer, 1947-54; with Radio & Allied (Holdings), Ltd., 1954-61; dir. GE Co., Plc., of Eng., London, 1961-63, mng. dir., 1963-96, chmn. emeritus, 1996—. Trustee Brit. Mus., 1985-95, Royal Philharm. Soc. Found. Fund. Created knight, 1970; life peer, 1980; hon. fellow Peterhouse, Cambridge U., London Sch. Econs.; hon. bencher Gray's Inn; officer Legion d'Honneur (France), 1991, commendatore Order of Merit (Italy), 1991. Fellow Royal Statis. Soc., Royal Coll. Radiologists (hon.). Avocations: racing, breeding horses, classical music. Home: 7 Grosvenor Sq, London W1, England Office: GE PLC, 1 Bruton St, London W1X 8AQ, England

WEINSTOCK, ROBERT, physics educator; b. Phila., Feb. 2, 1919; s. Morris and Lillian (Hirsch) W.; m. Elizabeth Winch Brownell, Apr. 22, 1950; children: Frank Morse, Robert B. Weinstock-Collins. AB, U. Pa., 1940; PhD, Stanford U., 1943. Instr. physics Stanford U., Calif., 1943-44, instr. math., 1946-50, acting asst. prof. math., 1950-54; research assoc. in radar countermeasures Radio Rsch. Lab. Harvard U., Cambridge, Mass., 1944-45; asst. prof. U. Notre Dame, Ind., 1954-58, assoc. prof. math., 1958-59; vis. assoc. prof. math. Oberlin Coll., Ohio, 1959-60, assoc. prof., 1960-66, prof. physics, 1966-83, emeritus prof., 1983—. Author: Calculus of Variations, 1952; contbr. numerous tech. articles to profl. jours. Fellow AAAS, Ohio Acad. Sci.; mem. ACLU, Am. Assn. Physics Tchrs., Am. Phys. Soc., History of Sci. Soc., British Soc. for the History of Sci., Sigma Xi. Avocations: concert going, reading, walking, traveling, letter writing. Home: 37 Kendal Dr Oberlin OH 44074-1902 Office: Oberlin Coll Dept Physics Oberlin OH 44074

WEINZIERL, KLAUS, utilities company executive; b. Danzig, Germany, July 29, 1942; s. Simon and Elsbeth (Skwarra) W.; m. Ute Schneider, May 20, 1988. Diploma, Tech. U. Karlsruhe, Germany, 1969; D of Engring., Tech. U. Hamburg, Germany, 1987. Tech. asst. U. Karlsruhe, 1969-70; from tech. mgr. to dir. plant design and constrn. VEW Energie AG, Dortmund, Germany, 1970-97, bd. dirs., 1997—; bd. dirs. Mitteldeutsche Energieversorgung AG. Editor: Optimization of Combined Cycles with Integrated Coal Gasification, 1987. Mem. Orgn. German Engrs. Avocations: mountain trekking, golf. Home: Milanweg 18, 44229 Dortmund Germany

WEINZWEIG, DANIEL, producer; b. Toronto, Ont., Can., July 23, 1947; s. John Jacob and Helen (Tenenbaum) W.; children: Noah, Joshua. Film & TV producer, distbr., head booker Internat. Film. Dist., 1964-67; sales mgr. Astral Films Ltd., 1968-69; pres. Danton Films Ltd., 1969-80; chief buyer, booker Cineplex Corp., 1980-83, sr. v.p., 1983; pres. Norstar Releasing, Inc., 1984-86; [res. Selluloid Screen Svc., Inc. & Ind. Prodn., 1986-88; producer advisor Cdn. Ctr. Advanced Film Study, 1989-90; chmn. Cinephile Ltd., 1989-93; chief exec. Mayfair Entertainment Internat., London, 1995-99; mng. dir. Korn Ferry Internat., Toronto, Can., 2000—; apptd. industry task force Fed. Min. Comm., 1986. Author: Making It - The Business of Film and Television in Canada. Co-chair Trade Forum, Fest of Fests, 1987. Mem. Motion Picture Inst. Can. (founding, sec.), Assn. Ind. & Can. Owned Motion Picture Distbrs. (founding, pres.), Brit. Acad. Film & Television Arts, Soho House Cannons Club. Avocations: running, swimming, movies. Office: Korn Ferry Intenrat, 40 Kinst St W Ste 4714, Toronto, Canada M5M 3Y2

WEIPPL, GERALD THEODOR, pediatrician, educator; b. Vienna, Austria, Aug. 4, 1927; s. Theodor and Ludmilla (Wagner) W.; m. Selma Völkl, Aug. 15, 1970; 1 child, Edgar. MD, U. Vienna, 1952. Intern, then resident in pediatrics Pediatric Univ. Clinic, Vienna, 1952-73; head premature unit Univ. Clinic, Vienna, 1962-73; head infectious disease dept. Wilheminen Hosp., Vienna, 1973-94; lectr. hematology U. Vienna, 1965-71, lectr. infectious disease, 1971—, prof. pediatrics, 1973—. Author: Iron Deficiency Anemias, 1975; editor Pädiatrie u Pädologie, 1965—; contbr. over 170 articles on pediatrics to med. jours. Recipient award for article U. Vienna Med. Faculty, 1965, 72. Mem. Austrian Pediatric Soc., European Pediatric Rsch. Soc., German Pediatric Soc., Austrian Hematologic Soc. Home: Trauttmansdorffgasse 50, A-1130 Vienna Austria

WEIR, DAVID JOHN, orthopaedic surgeon; b. Irvine, Scotland, Jan. 27, 1962; s. David and Helen (Jolly) W.; m. Alison Ann Wardle, July 12, 1991; 1 child, Rebecca Jane. MB ChB, U. Dundee, 1985. Anatomy demonstrator U. Dundee, Scotland, 1986-87; surg. registrar No. Region Health Authority, Eng., 1988-91; orthopaedic registrar South Tyneside NHS Trust, Eng., 1991-94, orthopedic sr. registrar, 1994-96; Knee fellow Freeman Hosp., Eng., 1996, cons. orthopedic surgeon, 1996—; medico-legal reporting, Britain, 1996—. Fellow Royal Coll. of Surgeons. Office: Freeman Hosp, Freeman Rd, Newcastle Upon Tyne NE7 7DN, England

WEIR, DAME GILLIAN CONSTANCE, concert organist, harpsichordist; b. Martinborough, New Zealand, Jan. 17, 1941; d. Cecil Alexander and Clarice M. Foy (Bignell) W. Grad., Royal Coll. Music, London, 1965; DMus (hon.), U. Victoria of Wellington, New Zealand, 1983; DLitt (hon.), Huddersfield U., 1997; DMus (hon.), Hull U., 1999. artist in residence numerous univs. including Wash. U., St. Louis, U. Western Australia, others; vis. lectr. Royal No. Coll. Music, Manchester, Eng., 1974-89; vis. prof. organ Royal Acad. Music, London, 1997-98; Prince Consort prof. Royal Coll. of Music, London, 1999—; spkr. BBC programs on music and performance. Concert appearances with leading Brit. Orchs. and Boston Orch., Seattle Orch., Australian ABC Orch., Wurttemberg Chamber and other fgn. orchs.; appeared in major internat. festivals including Edinburgh, Flanders, Aldeburgh, Bath, Proms, Europalia; appeared at concert halls including Royal Festival Hall, Royal Albert Hall, Lincoln Ctr., N.Y., Sydney Opera House; numerous radio and TV appearances in Brit. and world-wide including Royal Festival Hall Jubilee; organ cons.; adjudicator internat. competitions; contbr. The Messiaen Companion, 1995; contbr. articles to profl. jours.; recs. include complete organ works of Olivier Messiaen, others; TV documentary film on career, 1982, BBC TV programs The King of Instruments, 1989. Recipient Turnovsky award 1985, Evening Std. award for outstanding solo performance, 1998-99, Evening Std. award for individual performance, 1998; decorated Comdr. of Order of Brit. Empire, Dame Comdr., 1996. Fellow Royal Coll. Organists (hon., mem. coun. 1977—, mem. exec. 1981-85, pres. 1994-96, 1st Woman pres.), Royal Can. Coll. Organists (hon.); mem. Royal Acad. Music (hon.), Inc. Soc. Musicians (pres. 1992-93), Albert Schweitzer Assn. (Silver medal 1998), Soloists' Ensemble (pres. 1997). Office: care Karen McFarlane Artists 12429 Cedar Rd # 29 Cleveland OH 44106-3199

WEIR, HUGH WILLIAM LINDSAY, publishing executive, writer; b. Ireland, Aug. 29, 1934; arrive in Ireland; s. Terence John Collison Weir and Rosamund Suzanne (Gibson) Eekhout; m. Grania Rachel O'Brien, July 17, 1973. DLitt in History, Trinity Coll., Delaware, 1994. Ad writer Harmsworth Press, London, 1955-57; tchr. Cork Grammar Sch., 1958-59, Aravon Sch., Bray, 1960-61, St. Stephens Sch., Dublin, Ireland, 1961-63, Brook House Sch., Dublin, 1963-65; exec. Dr. Barnardos, Dublin, 1965-67; mng. dir. Weir Machinery Ltd., Whitegate and Limerick, Ireland, 1970-80; cons. Shannon (Ireland) Devel., 1982—; owner Bell'acards; mng. dir. Ballinakella Press, Whitegate; Irish heritage historian, 1980—. Author: Hall Craig-Words on an Irish House, 1983, O'Brien People and Places, 1984, Houses of Clare, 1986, O'Connor People and Places, 1994, C.Y.E.: A Social, Educational and Environmental Excercise, 1998; editor: Ireland-A Thousand Kings, 1988; contbr. publs. including Clare Champion (weekly), Ch. of Ireland Gazette (weekly), The Other Clare (ann.). Patron, past chmn. East Clare Clean Environ. Group, 1988—; v.p. Clare Hist. Soc.; pres. Clare Young Environmentalists; onetime Episcopal nominator, lay preacher Ch. of Ireland, mem. rep. body and standing com. Gen. Synod, 1980-89; selector Bishop's Clerical Selection Conf., Dublin, 1980, 89; mem. nat. coun. C.A.R.E., 1974-90; mem. pub. monuments adv. com. Clare County Coun., 1996—; dir. Christian Tng. Inst., 1999—; dir. The Hunt Mus. Trust, 2000—. Recipient Oidhreacht award for Journalism and Environ. Promotion, Iarnród Eireann, 1990. Fellow Royal Geog. Soc.; mem. Assn. for Tchrs. of Fgn. Students in Ireland (co-founder). Avocations: drawing, travel, youth work, angling, writing. Home: Ballinakella Lodge, Whitegate Co Clare, Ireland

WEIR, MICHAEL ECKFORD LIND, educational professional executive; b. Edinburgh, Lothian, Scotland, May 5, 1938; s. Norman James Lind and Gladys Eckford (Howden) W.; m. Hazel Dobson Cunningham, June 12, 1963; children: Andrew, Euan, Roger. MA, Edinburgh U., 1958, LLB, 1960. Apprentice Menzies & White, WS, Edinburgh, 1957-60; asst. West Anderson & Co. Solicitors, Glasgow, Scotland, 1960-61; prin. ptnr. Weir & Co., WS, Edinburgh, 1961-88; cons. in pvt. practice Edinburgh, 1988-93; exec. chief, legal advisor Scottish Export Assn., Edinburgh, 1993—; mem. Scottish Nat. Broadcasting Com., 1967-70; dir. Scottish Coun. Internat. Arbitration, Edinburgh, 1988-91; part-time mem. "Vat & Duties" Tribunal, Edinburgh, 1991-97. Author: The Law of Arbitration in Scotland, 1980,

revised edit., 2001. Pres. Edinburgh Jr. C. of C., 1966-67; senator, life mem. Jr. Chamber Internat. Avocations: photography, walking, Scottish history, improving French and German. Home and Office: Scottish Export Assn, 34 Swanston Ter, Edinburgh EH10 7DN, Scotland

WEIR, MORTON WEBSTER, retired academic administrator, educator; b. Canton, Ill., July 18, 1934; s. James and Frances Mary (Johnson) W.; m. Cecelia Ann Rumler, June 23, 1956; children: Deborah, Kevin, Mark. AB, Knox Coll., 1955; MA, U. Tex., 1958, PhD, 1959. Rsch. assoc., asst. prof. child devel. U. Minn., Mpls., 1959; asst. prof. child devel. U. Ill., Urbana, 1960-64, assoc. prof., 1964-68, prof., 1968-93, prof. emeritus, 1993—, head dept. psychology, 1969-71, vice chancellor acad. affairs, 1971-79, v.p. acad. affairs, 1982-88, chancellor, 1988-93, chancellor emeritus, 1993—, sr. found. rep., 1993-99; dir. Boys Town Center Study Youth Development, 1979-80. Contbr. numerous articles to profl. jours. Trustee Knox Coll., 1984—, chmn., 1995-99; trustee Menninger Found., 1993—; dir. RHR Internat. Co., 1986—. With AUS, 1960. NSF Predoctoral fellow, 1957-59. Fellow AAAS; mem. Soc. Rsch. in Child Devel. (chmn. bd. publs. 1971, chmn. fin. com. 1993-95), Sigma Xi, Phi Beta Kappa, Phi Kappa Phi.

WEIR, PETER LINDSAY, film director; b. Sydney, Australia, Aug. 21, 1944; s. Lindsay Weir and Peggy Barnsley; m. Wendy Stites, 1966; 2 children. Educated, Scots Coll., Sydney, Vaucluse Boys H.S., Sydney U. Worked in real estate until 1965; worked as stagehand in TV, Sydney, 1967; dir. film sequences in variety show, 1968; dir. amateur univ. revs., 1967-69; dir. for Film Australia, 1969-73; made own short films, 1969-73, ind. feature film producer, dir. and writer, 1973—. Films include: Cars That Ate Paris, 1973, Picnic at Hanging Rock, 1975, The Last Wave, 1977, The Plumber (TV), 1978, Gallipoli, 1980, The Year of Living Dangerously, 1982, Witness, 1985, The Mosquito Coast, 1986, Dead Poets Society, 1989, Green Card, 1990, Fearless, 1993, The Truman Show, 1997. Recipient various film awards. Mem. Australia A.M. Office: CAA care John Ptak 9830 Wilshire Blvd Beverly Hills CA 90212-1804

WEIR, SONJA ANN, artist; b. Hazleton, Pa., Oct. 12, 1934; d. Stephen and Anna (Prehatny) Tatusko; m. Richard Clayton Weir, Jan. 14, 1956; children: Robert, Carl, Donna, Lisa, Nancy. Studied with Mary Ellen Silkotch, 1963-83; student, Art Students League, N.Y.C., 1985-87. Artist Knickerbocker Toy Co., Middlesex, N.J., 1980; represented by Agora Gallery, Soho, N.Y., 1999; guest speaker career day Bridgewater H.S., 1993-94. One-woman shows include Johnson & Johnson, Piscataway, N.J., 1992, Somerset County Libr., Bridgewater, N.J., 1992-94, Manville (N.J.) Pub. Libr., 1994-99; exhibited in group shows at Raritan Valley Art Assn., 1982-83, 95, 98 (Best in Show award 1983, 2d prize 1995, 1st place for oil 1998), Ariel Gallery, N.Y.C., 1991, Am. Artists Profl. League, 1991, 94, Barren Art Ctr., Woodbridge, N.J., 1993, Agora Gallery, Soho, N.Y., 1995-99, Somerset County Libr., 1998-99, Am. Artists Profl. League, 1999; featured in Artis Apectrum mag., vol. 11/6, 1999, Star Ledger, 2000; represented in permanent collections N.W.B. Bank of South Bound Brook, N.J., Summit Bank. Featured in Artis Spectrum mag., 1999. Fellow Am. Artists Profl. League (nat. exec. bd. 1998-2000, editor newsletter 1992- 99, 99, v.p. N.J. chpt. 1988-91, pres. N.J. chpt. 1992-95, show chmn. 1989-91, publicity com. 1988-91); mem. Nat. Mus. of Women in the Arts, Raritan Valley Arts Assn. (pres. 1982-84), Nat. Miniature Assn. (assoc.), Miniature Art Soc. Fla. Home and Studio: 25 Madison St South Bound Brook NJ 08880-1244

WEIS, EBERHARD, modern history educator; b. Schmalkalden, Germany, Oct. 31, 1925; s. Julius and Elisabeth (Weidinger) W.; m. Ingeborg Weis-Koeniger, Apr. 16, 1953; children: Wolfgang, Reinhold. PhD, U. Munich, 1952, Dr. Phil. Habilitation, 1969. Archivist Bavarian State Archives, Munich, 1953-69; prof. modern history Free U. Berlin, West Berlin, 1969-70, U. Münster, Fed. Republic Germany, 1970-74, U. Munich, 1974—; pres. historische commn. Bayerischen Acad. Wissenschaften, 1987-97; chmn. adv. bd. German Hist. Inst. Paris, 1983-93; mem. adv. bd. German Hist. Inst. Rome. Author: Propyläen Geschichte Europas, vol. 4, 1978, (with K. Bosl) Die Gesellschaft in Deutschland bis 1848, 1976; editor: Reformen im Rheinbündischen Deutschland, 1984, Montgelas I, 1988, many other publs.; mem. editorial bd. Historische Zeitschrift. Mem. Bayerische Acad. Wissenschaften, Historisches Coll. Munich, Assn. for Italian-German Hist. Rsch. Home: Ammerseestr 102, D 82131 Gauting Germany Office: U Munich, Geschwister-Scholl Platz 1, D 80539 Munich Germany

WEIS, EDMUND BERNARD, JR., retired orthopaedist, educator, engineer, lawyer; b. Bismarck, N.D., Aug. 4, 1931; s. Edmund Bernard and Margaret Catherine (Rickert) W.; m. Annette Mary Fernandes, Nov. 19, 1972; children: John Paul, Giselle Anne, Susan Ellen, Melanie Elizabeth, Edmund Bernard III, Bronwyn Kristen. Attended, U. Utah, 1949-52; grad., U. Notre Dame, 1953; MD, U. Colo., 1957; MS in Bioengring., Drexel Inst. Tech., 1962; doctoral candidate in engring. mechanics, Ohio State U., 1968-71; JD, Newport U., 1994. Diplomate Am. Bd. Orthopaedic Surgery; Bar: Calif. 1994. Intern Good Samaritan Hosp., Phoenix, 1957-58; chief vibration and impact br. mercury astronaut crew selection Aerospace Med. Rsch. Labs., Wright-Patterson AFB, Ohio, 1958-66; resident in orthopaedics Ohio State U., Columbus, 1968-71; amputations tng. Dept. Vet. Affairs, Grossinger, N.Y., 1985; pedicle screw fixation tng. Cleve. Rsch. Inst., 1987; thermography tng. Acad. Neuromuscular Thermography, L.A., 1989; surg. lasers tng. Loma Linda (Calif.) U., 1992; rsch. med. officer USAF, Wright-Patterson AFB, Ohio, 1966-68; mem. staff Ohio Vets. Oupatient Ctr., Columbus, 1974-76, N.D. Vets. Hosp., Fargo, 1976-79; mem. staff VA Hosp., Omaha, 1979-85, acting chief rehab., 1983-85; mem. staff, chief orthopaedics VA Hosp., Loma Linda, 1985-99; mem. staff Loma Linda Cmty. Hosp., 1985-99, chief orthopaedics, 1989-90; mem. staff Loma Linda U. Med. Ctr., 1985-99, Redlands (Calif.) Cmty. Hosp., 1986-94, San Bernardino (Calif.) Cmty. Hosp., 1990-99, Moreno Valley (Calif.) Hosp., 1992-94, San Gorgonio Meml. Hosp., Banning, Calif., 1993-94; instr. to asst. prof. orthopaedics Ohio State U., 1971-76; assoc. prof. U. N.D., Grand Forks, 1976-79, asst. dean, 1977-79; prof. Creighton U., Omaha, 1979-85; clin. prof. Loma Linda U., 1985-99; bioengring. cons. Cox Coronary Heart Inst., Dayton, Ohio, 1962-66, Battelle Meml. Inst., Columbus, 1970-76; orthopaedics cons. Grand Forks AFB Hosp., 1976-79, Ehrling-Berquist AFB Hosp., Omaha, 1979-84, Jour. Bone and Joint Surgery, Waltham, Mass., 1980—; com. mem. Am. Acad. Orthopaedics Emergency Svcs. Contbr. numerous articles to profl. jours.; inventor sonic surg. tool; patentee method and sys. for control of a powered prosthesis. Maj. USAF, Wright-Patterson AFB, 1957-66. Recipient R & D award USAF, 1966, Rsch. award Dept. Vet. Affairs, 1988, U.S. Svc. award; rsch. fellow NIH, 1969-71, traveling fellow Am. Orthopaedics Assn., 1971. Fellow Am. Acad. Orthopaedic Surgeons (Rsch. and Edn. Found. award 1969), Am. Coll. Legal Medicine; mem. AMA, Orthopaedic Rsch. Soc., San Bernardino County Med. Soc., Calif. Med. Soc., Nat. Assn. Vet. Physicians, N.Am. Spine Soc., Phi Rho Sigma. Avocations: restoring old Fords. Home: 30555 7th Ave Redlands CA 92374-7619

WEISBERG, ADAM JON, lawyer; b. Cocoa Beach, Fla., June 5, 1963; s. Melvin H. Weisberg and Joan Julie (Carney) Vargo; m. Cheryl Lynn Scupp, June 25, 1994. BS in Bus. Econs., Rider Coll., 1985; JD, N.Y. Law Sch., 1988. Bar: N.Y. 1989, N.J. 1989, U.S. Dist. Ct. 1989, Fla. 1991. Law clk., asst. prosecutor Middlesex County Prosecutors Office, New Brunswick, N.J., 1988-90; workers' compensation atty. Levinson Axelrod Wheaton, Edison, N.J., 1990-91; trial atty. workers compensation Richard J. Simon, Esq., New Brunswick, 1991-92; pvt. practice lawyer New Brunswick, 1992—; pres. Asbury Music Co., Belmar, N.J. Mem. ABA, N.J. Bar Assn., Middlesex County Bar Assn., Monmouth County Bar Assn., Assn. Criminal Def. Lawyers. Avocations: fishing, surfing. Office: Monmouth Exec Plz II 1300 Highway 35 Ste 201 Ocean NJ 07712-3531 also: 46 Bayard St New Brunswick NJ 08901-2152

WEISBERG, DAVID CHARLES, lawyer; b. N.Y.C., June 25, 1938; s. Leonard Joseph and Rae M. (Kimberg) W.; m. Linda Gail Kerman, Aug. 27, 1975; children: Leonard Jay, Risa Beth. AB, U. Mich., 1958; LLB, Harvard U., 1961. Bar: N.Y. 1962, U.S. Dist. Ct. (so. and ea. dists.) N.Y. 1965, U.S. Supreme Ct. 1970. Assoc. firm Dreyer & Traub, Bklyn., 1962, Lee Franklin, Mineola, N.Y., 1962-65; pvt. practice Patchogue, N.Y., 1965-67, 77-80; ptnr. Bass & Weisberg, Patchogue, 1967-77, Davidow, Davidow, Russo & Weisberg, Patchogue, 1981-82, Davidow, Davidow, Weisberg & Wismann, Patchogue, 1982-87, Davidow, Davidow & Wismann, Patchogue, 1988-92, Weisberg & Wismann, Patchogue, 1992—; assoc. justice and justice Village of Patchogue, 1968-70, village atty., 1970-85; spl. asst. dist. atty. Suffolk County, Patchogue, 1970-85; assoc. estate tax atty., appraiser N.Y. State Dept. Taxation and Fin., Hauppauge, N.Y., 1975-85; lectr. estate tax Suffolk County Acad. Law, 1976-84, negligence law, 1994. Law chmn. Suffolk County Dem. Com., N.Y., 1975-85; bd. dirs. Temple Beth El of Patchogue. With USAR, 1961-62. Mem. ATLA, N.Y. State Bar Assn., Suffolk County Bar Assn., Nassau-Suffolk Trial Lawyers Sect., Lions (pres. Medford 1978-79, 2d v.p. 1984-85). Avocations: bicycling, skiing, backpacking.

WEISBIN, CHARLES RICHARD, nuclear engineer; b. Bklyn., Jan. 4, 1944; s. Alma (Schwartz) Lovitt; m. Alison Norma Weisbin, June 20, 1964; children: Daniel Mark, Amy Gayle. MS in Nuclear Engring., Columbia U., 1965, DSc in Nuclear Engring., 1969. Group leader Oak Ridge (Tenn.) Nat. Lab., 1977-80, section head, 1980-89, dir. Ctr. for Engring. Systems Advanced Rsch., 1982-89, dir. robotics and intelligence systems, 1986-89; mgr. telerobotics tech. Jet Propulsion Lab., Pasadena, Calif., 1991-92, mgr. robotic systems and advanced computer tech. sect., 1989-93, mgr. rover and telerobotic tech., 1993-95, Mars program technologist, 1994-96, mgr. robotics and Mars exploration tech., 1995-98; dep. mgr. Cross Enterprise Tech. Devel. Program, NASA, 1999—, thrust mgr. Surface Systems,, 1999—; mem. joint tech. panel on robotics DOD Joint Dirs. Labs., 1986-89; assoc. prof. computer sci. U. Tenn., Knoxville, 1984-89; program chmn. 2nd Internat. Conf. on Artificial Intelligence, IEEE Computer Soc., 1985; co-chmn. U.S. NASA Telerobotics Working Group, 1990-98, robotics and telepresence Space Tech. Interagency Group, 1992-96. Author: Sensitivity and Uncertainty Analysis of Reactor Performance Parameters, 1982; mem. editorial bd. Applied Intelligence, 1990-95; contbr. articles to profl. jours. Recipient NASA Exceptional Svc. medal, 1993, 99, Nova award, 1998, Thomas O. Paine award for advancement of human exploration to Mars, 1998. Mem. IEEE (Cert. Appreciation 1987), Am. Nuclear Soc. (program chmn. 1977-79), Robotics and Automation Soc., Sigma Chi, Tau Beta Pi. Republican. Jewish. Achievements include initiation of robotics and intelligent systems at Oak Ridge; rsch. on sensitivity analysis, non-destructive assay of spent nuclear fuel, supervised inspection, and emergency response robotics. Home: 775 Starlight Heights Dr La Canada Flintridge CA 91011-1854 Office: Jet Propulsion Lab 4800 Oak Grove Dr Pasadena CA 91109-8001

WEISBROD, NEIL L., film and television director; b. Bklyn., July 25, 1946; arrived in Israel, 1978; s. George B. and Marion Y. W.; m. Gilla Treibich, Aug. 31, 1976; children: Ariel, Moriah. BA, SUNY, Binghamton, 1968. From asst. dir. to dir. WGBH-TV, Boston, 1972-78; dir. sr. staff Israel TV (IBA), Jerusalem, 1978-2000, head drama and arts dept., 2000—; cons., filmmaker Smithsonian Instn./Nat. Mus. of Am. History, Washington, 1981—; instr. Boston U., 1973-78, Hadassah Coll., Jerusalem, 1993—. Dir. film: Musical Masterpiece at Masada, 1988, The Trek-Story of Exodus of Ethiopian Jews to Israel, 1993, Aulcie, 1994; dir. short films on permanent display in The Smithsonian Instn., 1983; dir. TV show: Weekend, 1997; dir. film project Israel's First Astronaut, 1999. Jewish. Home: 7 Hanassi St, Jerusalem 92188, Israel Office: Israel TV (IBA), Rommema, Jerusalem Israel

WEISBROT, MARVIN MYRON, retired healthcare administrator, consultant; b. Phila., Oct. 20, 1928; s. Lewis Harold Weisbrot and Rose (Horn) Weisbrot/Abel; m. Jan Levin, Feb. 14, 1954; 1 child, Michele Ann. BA, U. Pa., 1950; BS, Phila. Coll. Pharmacy, 1959; MBA, Temple U., 1973. Registered pharmacist, N.J. Pres. Drug Ctrs., Inc., Burlington, N.J., 1956-71; adminstrv. officer VA Med. Ctr., Tampa, Fla., 1973-74; adminstrv. officer, clin. studies coord. Drug Dependence Treatment Ctr. VA Med. Ctr., Phila., 1974-80; lectr. psychiatry Sch. Medicine U. Pa., Phila., 1974-93; adminstrv. officer, co-investigator, coord. Psychiatry Svc. VA Med. Ctr., Phila., 1980-90, clin. rsch. Med. Rsch. Svc., 1990-93; cons. on addictive disease Roxane Labs., Columbus, Ohio, 1995-97; bd. dirs. Drenk Mental Health Ctr., Mt. Holly, N.J., chair program com.; trustee Meml. Health Alliance, Mt. Holly, 1988-98; cons. addictive disease Bio Devel. Corp., McLean, Va., 1993-95; cons. health edn. Evesham (N.J.) sch. dists., 1995; cons. to Ministry of Health, Portugal, 1993-96, France, 1993. Author: Comparison of Modalities of Treatment for Narcotic Addiction, 1973;; contbr. papers and monographs to profl. jours. Mem., cons. Mcpl. Alliance for Drug and Alcohol Awareness and Edn. (DARE), Mt. Laurel, N.J., 1993—; mem. Legion of Honor, Chapel of Four Chaplains, Phila., 1977. 1st lt. U.S. Army, 1951-54. Named Outstanding Young Man of Yr., Jaycees, 1962, 64. Fellow Am. Coll. Apothecaries. Jewish. Avocations: photography, travel, golf. Home: 327 Carleton Ln Mount Laurel NJ 08054-3113

WEISE, OTFRIED REINHARD, physical geography educator; b. Waldenburg, Silesia, Germany, May 7, 1943; s. Richard Robert and Anna Elisabeth (Schwanitz) W.; m. Uta Dorothea Schollmeyer, Aug. 2, 1968 (div. Apr. 1977). DSc, U. Würzburg, Germany, 1967, habilitation, 1973; MSE, U. of the 7 Rays, N.J., 1994. Asst. lectr. U. Würzburg, 1967-73, sr. lectr., 1974-78; prof. phys. geography U. Giessen, Germany, 1978-83; pvt. cons. for soil erosion Giessen, 1984-85; pvt. cons. nutrition and health Munich, Vienna, 1985—; prof. esoteric scis. U. of the 7 Rays, 1997—; lectr. Tabula Smaragdina, Munich, Vienna, 1995—. Author: Harmonische Erhährung, 1990, Melone zum Frühstück, 1991, Zur Eigenen Kraft Finden, 1995, Entschlackung, Entsäuerung, Entgiftung, 2000, Die 7 Kosmischen Strahlen, 2000; co-author: Die 5 Tibeter Feinschmeckerküche, 1993. Avocations: eastern and western philosophy, psychology, meditation. Home and Office: Tabula Smaragdina, Anton-Langer-Gasse 46/2/5, A-1130 Vienna Austria

WEISER, FRANK ALAN, lawyer; b. L.A., Dec. 12, 1953; s. Carl and Rose (Klein) W.; m. Susan Koenig, Aug. 12, 1983. BA, UCLA, 1976; JD, Southwestern U., L.A., 1979; LLM in Taxation, U. San Diego, 1986. Bar: Calif. 1979, U.S. Dist. Ct. (cen. dist.) Calif. 1981, U.S. Tax Ct. 1982, U.S. Ct. Appeals (9th cir.) 1982, U.S. Supreme Ct. 1987, U.S. Ct. Claims 1987, U.S. Ct. Mil. Appeals 1988, U.S. Ct. Appeals (fed. cir.) 1989, U.S. Ct. Internat. Trade 1989, U.S. Ct. Appeals Temporary Emergency Ct., 1989, U.S. Ct. Vets. Appeals 1990, U.S. Dist. Ct. (no. and so. dists.) Calif. 1993. Tax cons., advanced underwriter Transam. Occidental Life Ins. Co., L.A., 1979-80; assoc. Law Offices Herman English, 1980-81; atty., owner Frank A. Weiser-A Law Corp., L.A., 1981—; judge pro tem L.A. County Mcpl. Ct., 1987—. Editor So. Calif. mag., 1987—; contbr. articles to profl. jours. Bd. suprs. Michael Antonovich Election Com., 1988; mem. World Affairs Coun., L.A.; mem. U.S. Ct. of Vets. Appeals, 1990; assoc. mem. Calif. Rep. Cen. Com. Recipient official resolutions from Calif. State Legislature, 1989, joint rules com. resolution for state assembly and sate senate, 1990, Calif. State Assembly and Senate, 1989, L.A. County Bd. of Suprs., 1989, City Coun. of L.A., 1987, Congressional Cert. of Appreciation; tribute to him placed into official Congl. record, 1989; Nat. Merit scholar, 1971. Mem. ABA (internat. labor com., arts control and disarmament com., internat. employment practices com., editorial advisor internat. law and practive sect. publs. com., internat. property, estate and trust com., fgn. investment in U.S. com.), Fed. Bar Assn. (internat. law com.), Inter-Am. Bar Assn., Am. Judicature Soc., Assn. Trial Lawyers Am., Calif. Trial Lawyers Assn., L.A. Trial Lawyers Assn., Internat. Bar Assn., World Affairs Coun. L.A., World Inst. Achievement, L.A. Athletic Club. Office: 3460 Wilshire Blvd Ste 903 Los Angeles CA 90010-2230

WEISER, JAROSLAV, entomologist, researcher, consultant; b. Prague, Czechoslovakia, Jan. 13, 1920; s. Martin and Anna (Beková) W.; m. Jaroslava Janáčková, 1947 (dec. Feb. 1998); children: Jaroslav, Helena. RNDr Nat. Hist., Charles U., Prague, 1947; DSc in Biology, Acad. Scis., Prague, 1960. Asst. prof. parasitology Charles U., Prague, 1947-51; vis. prof. med. faculty U. Sarajevo, 1949-50; chief dept. parasitology Acad. Scis., Prague, 1951-54; cons. Inst. Entomology Acad. Scis., Budejovice, 1989—; head dept. insect pathology Prague, 1954-88; vis. prof. pestology Simon Fraser U., Burnaby, B.C., Can., 1969-70; mem. steering com. WHO Biocontrol Vectors, Geneva, 1969-82, head Col. Ctr. Vector Pathology, Prague, 1969-84; chmn. COMECON perm. com. Biocontrol, Moscow, 1968-89; cons. SIAPA Pest Control, Rome, 1972-76. Author: Diseases of Insects, 1966, An Atlas of Insect Diseases, 1969, 2nd edit. 1977; co-author: Modern Insecticides, 1951, Medical Entomology, 1952. Recipient Czechoslakia State award, 1964. Mem. Soc. Invertebrae Pathology (pres. 1978-80), Czech Soc. Parasitology, Parasitology Soc. Germany (hon., R. Leuckart medal 1982). Home: Herálecká str 964, 140 00 Prague 4, Czech Republic Office: Inst Entomology Acad Sci, Branisovská 31, 370 05 Ceské Budejovice Czech Republic also: Parasitology Dept Univ, Vinicná 7, 128 44 Prague Czech Republic

WEISER, SHERWOOD M., hotel and corporate executive; b. Cleve., Mar. 9, 1931; s. Aaron A. and Helen W. (Scheiner) W.; m. Judith A. Zirkin; children: Douglas J., Warren P., Bradley A. BS, Ohio State U., 1952; LLB, Case Western Res. U., 1955. Bar: Ohio 1955. Ptnr. Weiser & Weiser, Cleve., 1955-65, Weiser & Lefton, Cleve., 1965-69; chmn., exec. officer Carnival Resort, CRC, Miami, Fla., 1970—; bd. dirs. Mellon United Nat. Bank, Miami, Carnival Corp., Miami, U. Miami, New World Symphony; trustee Fla. Internat. U., Miami, 1984-94. Trustee, chmn. bd. Ransom Everglades Sch., Miami, 1974-84; co-chair, bd. adv. Coconut Grove Playhouse, Miami, 1986—; trustee U. Miami, 1988—; chmn. Performing Arts Ctr. Found., Miami, 1995—. Recipient Silver medallion Nat. Conf. Christians and Jews, 1998. Mem. Riviera Country Club. Jewish. Office: CRC Holdings Inc 3250 Mary St Miami FL 33133-5232

WEISER, STANLEY, screenwriter; b. N.Y.C., Mar. 15, 1949. BFA in Film, NYU, 1973. Ind. film writer various studios, Calif., 1980—. Screenwriter (films) Coast to Coast, 1980, Project X, 1987, (with Oliver Stone) Wall Street, 1987, (TV movie) Murder in Mississippi, 1990 (Emmy nomination, DGA award), Fatherland, 1994, Witness to the Mob, 1998, (with Phil Alden Robinson) Freedom Song, 2000. Mem. TV Acad. of Sci. and Arts, Writers Guild Am. West, Acad. Motion Picture Arts and Scis. Office: care Writers Guild Am West 7000 W 3d St Los Angeles CA 90048-2420 also: care ICM 8899 Beverly Blvd Los Angeles CA 90048-2412 also: William Morris Agy 151 S El Camino Dr Beverly Hills CA 90212-2704

WEISERT, KENT ALBERT FREDERICK, lawyer; b. Passaic, N.J., Sept. 9, 1949; s. Frederick William and Waleska Anna Sophia (Bischoff) W.; m. Deborah Jean Searing, Mar. 12, 1983; 1 child, Christianna Lillian. BA magna cum laude, Rutgers U., 1971, JD, 1974. Bar: N.J. 1974, U.S. Dist. Ct. N.J. 1974, U.S. Tax Ct. 1975, U.S. Ct. Appeals (3d cir.) 1978, U.S. Supreme Ct. 1987. Adminstrv. asst. trust dept. Howard Savs. Bank, Newark, 1973-74; ptnr. Schwartz, Tobia & Stanziale, Montclair, N.J., 1975—; arbitrator U.S. Dist. Ct., Newark, 1985—. Contbr. chpt. to book New Jersey Transaction Guide, 1987. Pres. ch. coun. Holy Trinity Luth. Ch., Nutley, N.J., 1982-83; mem. Greater N.J. Estate Planning Coun.; trustee Oakside Bloomfield Cultural Ctr. Mem. N.J. State Bar Assn., Essex County Bar Assn., Rutgers Law Sch. Alumni Assn., Nat. Trust Hist. Preservation, N.J. Hist. Soc., Phi Beta Kappa, Phi Alpha Theta, Pi Delta Epsilon. Republican. Lutheran. Avocations: classical music, antiques, mil. and gen. history, hist. presevation, tennis. Home: 51 Fairway Bloomfield NJ 07003-5515 Office: Schwartz Tobia & Stanziale 22 Crestmont Rd Montclair NJ 07042-2902

WEISGALL, JONATHAN MICHAEL, lawyer; b. Balt., Mar. 17, 1949; s. Hugo David and Nathalie (Shulman) W.; m. Ruth Macdonald, June 3, 1979; children: Alison, Andrew, Benjamin. BA, Columbia Coll., 1970; JD, Stanford U., 1973. Bar: D.C. 1974, N.Y. 1974, U.S. Supreme Ct. 1982, Marshall Islands 1983. Law clk. to judge U.S. Ct. Appeals (9th cir.), San Francisco, 1973-74; assoc. Covington & Burling, Washington, 1974-79; from assoc. to ptnr. Ginsburg, Feldman, Weil & Bress, Washington, 1980-83; sole practice Washington, 1983-99; v.p. Legis. and Regulatory Affairs MidAmerican Energy Holdings Co., 1995—; adj. prof. law Georgetown U. Law Ctr. Author: Operation Crossroads: The Atomic Tests at Bikini Atoll, 1994; exec. prodr. documentary film Radio Bikini. Chmn. bd. dirs. Ctr. for Energy Efficiency and Renewable Techs.; trustee Arena Stage, Washington; bd. dirs. Meet the Composer. Mem. Geothermal Energy Assn. (past v.p., bd. dirs., pres.), Phi Beta Kappa. Jewish. E-mail: jweisgall@aol.com. Home: 5309 Edgemoor Ln Bethesda MD 20814-1323 Office: Ste 300 1200 New Hampshire Ave NW Washington DC 20036-6812

WEISINGER, RONALD JAY, government housing and economic development consultant; b. Youngstown, Ohio, Feb. 13, 1946; s. David S. and Sterna (Woolf) W.; m. Donna H. Kristaponis; children: Morgan, Megan. BS, Carroll Coll., 1968; MBA, U. Palm Beach, 1970. Dir. cash dept. Nat. United Jewish Appeal, 1975-78; exec. dir. Jewish Fedn. Pinellas County, Inc., Fla., 1978-80; prin. VIP Mortgage Trust Co., VIP Mgmt. and Realty, Inc., West Palm Beach, 1984-91; developer, econ. developer affordable housing, exec. search, 1991—; econ. devel. in Eastern Europe, former countries of Soviet Union and Mid. East. Jewish.

WEISKOPF, KIM ROBERT, television producer, writer; b. N.Y.C., Apr. 10, 1947; s. Robert Jerome and Eileen May (Ito) W.; m. Jo Ellen Erwin Legendre, May 17, 1980; 1 child, Kathleen. BA in English Lit., San Francisco State U., 1969. Story editor, writer TV show Good Times, Hollywood, Calif., 1977; exec. script cons., writer TV show Three's Company, L.A., 1979-80; prodr., writer TV show 9 to 5, L.A., 1981; exec. prodr., writer TV show What's Happening Now, Burbank, Calif., 1985-87; prodr., writer TV show Full House, Culver City, Calif., 1988-91; supervising prodr., writer TV show Rachel Gunn, R.N., Hollywood, 1992-93; supervising/co-exec. prodr., writer TV show Married...With Children, Columbia TV, Culver City and Hollywood, 1994-96; exec. prodr., writer TV show Malcolm & Eddie, Tri-Star TV, Culver City, 1996—; co-exec. prodr., writer TV show Sister, Sister Paramount, Hollywood, Calif., 1997; writer TV show Baywatch, 1998; writer TV show Pigs Next Door Saban, 1999; writer TV show Los Beltran Telemundo/Tristar TV, 1999.

WEISKRANTZ, LAWRENCE, neuropsychologist, educator; b. Phila., Mar. 28, 1926; s. Benjamin and Rose (Rifkin) W.; m. Barbara Edna Collins, Feb. 20, 1954; children: Conrad, Julia. BA, Swarthmore Coll., 1949; MSc, U. Oxford, Eng., 1950; PhD, Harvard U., 1953. Rschr. Inst. Living, Hartford, Conn., 1952-55; postdoctoral fellow U.S. Acad. Sci., Oxford, 1955-56; asst. dir. rsch. Cambridge (Eng.) U., 1956-66, reader physiol. psychology, 1966-67; prof. psychology U. Oxford, 1967-93, emeritus prof., 1993—. Editor: Analysis of Behavioral Change, 1968, Thought Without Language, 1988; author: Blindsight, 1986, Consciousness Lost and Found, 1997. Chmn. adv. com. Brit. False Memory Soc. Sgt. USAAF, 1944-46. Recipient Kenneth Craik award Cambridge U., St. John's Coll., 1976, Ferrier prize lecture Royal Soc., London, 1989, Hughlings Jackson lectr./medallist Royal Soc. Medicine, London, 1990; fellow Magdalen Coll., Oxford, 1967-93; William James fellow Am. Psychol. Soc., 1992. Fellow Royal Soc. (mem. coun. 1988-89); mem. U.S. Nat. Acad. Scis. Washington. Avocations: music, walking. Office: Dept Exptl Psychology, South Parks Rd, OX1 3UD Oxford England

WEISL, EDWIN LOUIS, JR., foundation executive, lawyer; b. N.Y.C., Oct. 17, 1929; s. Edwin L. and Alice (Todriff) W.; m. Barbara Butler, June 12, 1974; 1 child, by previous marriage, Angela Jane. A.B., Yale, 1951; LL.B., Columbia, 1956. Bar: N.Y. 1956, D.C. 1968. Assoc. Simpson Thacher & Bartlett, N.Y.C., 1956-64; mem. firm Simpson Thacher & Bartlett, 1964-65, 69-73; adminstr. parks, recreation and cultural affairs, commr. parks City of N.Y., 1973-75; asst. atty. gen. of U.S. in charge of land and natural resources division, 1965-67, asst. atty. gen. in charge civil div., 1967-69; asst. spl. counsel, preparedness investigating com. U.S. Senate, 1957-58; former pres. Internat. Found. for Art Research. Dir. N.Y. State Dem. campaign, 1964; mem. The 1001, World Wildlife Fund; mem. vis. com. dept. European paintings Met. Mus. Art; bd. dirs. Robert Lehman Found.; mem. corp. Presbyn. Hosp., N.Y.C.; bd. dirs. Old Master Exhbn. Soc. N.Y.; mem. Villa I Tatti Coun, Harvard Ctr. for Renaissance Studies. Lt. (j.g.) U.S. Navy, 1951-53. Mem. Explorers Club, Warrenton Hunt Club, Century Assn. Office: 50 E 77th St New York NY 10021-1842

WEISMAN, DAVID S., military officer; b. Poughkeepsie, N.Y.; m. Barbara Miller; 2 children: Michael, Brian. Bachelor, U. Tampa; M in Vocat./Ednl. Guidance, St. Bonaventure U.; M in Nat. Security and Strategy, Naval War Coll.; grad., Command and Staff Coll., British High Command and Staff. Commd. 2d lt. U.S. Army; advanced through grades to lt. gen.; various assignments U.S. and overseas; dep. dir. strategic plans and policy Office Dep. Chief of Staff for Ops., Washington; dep. dir. politico-mil. affairs (Europe and Africa) Strategic Plans and Policy Dir., Jt. Staff, Washington; vice dir. strategic plans and policy Jt. Staff, Army Hdqrs., Washington; U.S. mil. rep. NATO Mil. Com. Decorated Def. D.S.M., Def. Superior Svc. medal, Legion of Merit with 2 oak leaf clusters, Bronze Star with 1 oak leaf cluster, Meritorious Svc. medal. with 2 oak leaf clusters, Air medal.

WEISMAN, IRVING, social worker, educator; b. N.Y.C., May 6, 1918; s. Max and Sadie (Berkewitz) W.; m. Cyrille Gold, May 1, 1941; children: Seth, Adam. B.S., CCNY, 1939; M.S., U. Buffalo, 1942; Ed.D., Columbia U., 1962. Cert. social worker N.Y. State. Caseworker Nat. Refugee Service, N.Y.C., 1941; warden's asst. Fed. Detention Hdqrs., Bur. Prisons, Dept. Justice, N.Y.C., 1942-43; psychiat. social worker to chief social worker VA, Camden and Union City, N.J., 1946-49; case supr. Altro Health and Rehab. Service, N.Y., 1949-50; field instr., lectr. Columbia U. Sch. Social Work, 1950-57, assoc. prof., 1957-62, prof., 1962-84, prof. emeritus, 1984, adj. prof., 1984, acting dean, 1964-65; assoc. dean Hunter Coll. Sch. Social Work, 1967-69; exec. officer doctoral program social work Grad. Ctr. CUNY, 1975-78; clin. practice William Alanson White Inst., 1976-79; vis. prof. Sch. Social Work, Barry U., 1984-85; adj. prof. Sch. Social Work, San Diego State U., 1988—; UN adv. on social welfare to Ceylon Sri Lanka, 1963-64; sr. Simon research fellow U. Manchester (Eng.), 1970-71; cons. U.S. Office Juvenile Delinquency and Youth Devel., U.S. Children's Bur., NIMH, NIDA, HEW, N.Y.C. Dept. Personnel, Westchester County (N.Y.) Dept. Mental Health, Community Service Soc., Council Social Work Edn., Moblzn. for Youth, N.Y.C., Universidad Católica Madre y Maestra, Santo Domingo, Dominican Republic, 1983-84, United Jewish Appeal-Fedn. Jewish Philanthropies of N.Y.C., 1986-87, U. Puertorriqueña de los Antillas Aguadilla, P.R., 1993; condr. continuing edn. workshops, various univs. Contbr. articles to profl. jours., also monographs. With U.S. Army Air Corps., 1943-46. HEW and HHS grantee, 1961-62, 64-76, 77-81. Mem. Inst. Continued Learning, U.C. San Diego. Home: 4612 Monongahela St San Diego CA 92117-2415

WEISS, ANDREW RICHARD, lawyer, mediator, educator, optician; b. Hartford, Conn., Jan. 11, 1945; s. Irving and Clara E. (Miller) W.; m. Sara N. Brookwood, Apr. 3, 1981 (dec. June 1982); m. Avril M. Bell, Oct. 14, 1989. BA, Dartmouth Coll., 1967; MA, U. Wis., 1968; postgrad., Boston U., 1970; JD, Boston Coll., 1977. Bar: Mass. 1977, U.S. Dist. Ct. Mass. 1978, U.S. Supreme Ct. 1992; lic., cert. optician Am. Bd. Opticians. Tchr. English, Saddle River (N.J.) Country Day Sch., 1968-69; rsch. and writing asst. Soun-View Throg's Neck Cmty. Mental Health Ctr., Bronx, 1969-70; retail dispensing optician, 1972-97; legal adv. Mass. Advocacy Ctr., Boston, 1975-77; pvt. practice, Boston, 1978-89; atty. Resolution, Wellesley, Mass., 1989—; instr. New Eng. Sch. Whole Health Edn., 1995—, dean faculty, 1997—; dispensary mgr. North Shore Eye Splsts., Danvers, Mass., 1998-99, Wesson & Niro Eye Care, Acton, Mass., 1999—; instr. meditation Cambridge Ctr. Adult Edn., 1994 . Trustee Thacher Montessori Sch., Milton, Mass., 1981 , Newbury Insight Meditation Ctr., 1995 ; pres. Zaltho Found., Inc., Concord, Mass., 1994 . Fellow Nat. Acad. Opticians, Opticians Assn. Am.; mem. Mass. Bar Assn., Soc. Profls. Dispute Resolution, Internat. Alliance Holistic Lawyers, Order Interbeing Internat. (exec. coun. 1992). Avocations: music, motorcycles, hiking, pets. Home and Office: 20 Elm St Maynard MA 01754-2630

WEISS, ARMAND BERL, economist, association management executive; b. Richmond, Va., Apr. 2, 1931; s. Maurice Herbert and Henrietta (Shapiro) W.; m. Judith Bernstein, May 18, 1957; children: Jo Ann Michele, Rhett Louis. BS in Econs., Wharton Sch. Fin., U. Pa., 1953, MBA, 1954; DBA, George Washington U., 1971. Cert. assn. exec. Officer USN, 1954-65; spl. asst. to auditor gen. Dept. Navy, 1964-65; sr. economist Ctr. for Naval Analyses, Arlington, Va., 1965-68; project dir. Logistics Mgmt. Inst., Washington, 1968-74; dir. systems integration FEA, Washington, 1974-76; sr. economist Nat. Commn. Supplies and Shortages, 1976-77; tech. asst. to v.p. Sys. Planning Corp., 1977-78; chmn. bd., pres., CEO Assns. Internat. Inc., 1978—; chmn. bd. dirs., CFO Rail Digital Corp., 1988-91; v.p., treas. Tech. Frontiers, Inc., 1978-80; sr. v.p. Weiss Pub. Co., Inc., Richmond, Va., 1960—; v.p. Condo News Internat., Inc., 1981; v.p., bd. dirs. Leaders Digest Inc., 1987-88; sec., bd. dirs. Mgmt. Svcs. Internat. Inc., 1988-91; adj. prof. Am. U., 1979-80, 89-90; vis. lectr. George Washington U., 1971; assoc. prof. George Mason U., 1984; treas. Fairfax County (Va.) Dem. Com., 1992-94, assisted Pres. Clinton, v.p. Gore transition at White House, 1993; pres. Washington Mgmt. and Bus. Assn., 1993—; chmn. U.S. del., session chmn. NATO Symposium on Cost-Benefit Analysis, The Hague, Netherlands, 1969, NATO Conf. on Operational Rsch. in Indsl. Systems, St. Louis, France, 1970; pres. Nat. Coun. Assns. Policy Scis., 1971-77; chmn. adv. group Def. Econ. Adv. Coun. Dept. Def., 1970-74; resident assoc. Smithsonian Instn., 1973—; expert cons. Dept. State, GAO; undercover agt. FBI, 3 yrs. Co-editor: Systems Analysis for Social Problems, 1970, The Relevance of Economic Analysis to Decision Making in the Department of Defense, 1972, Toward More Effective Public Programs: The Role of Analysis and Evaluation, 1975; editor: Cost-Effectiveness Newsletter, 1966-70, Operations Rsch./Systems Analysis Today, 1971-73, Operation Rsch./Mgmt. Sci. Today, 1974-87, Feedback, 1969-93, Condo World, 1981, The Democrat, 1997-2000; assoc. editor Ops. Rsch., 1971-75; pub. IEEE Scanner, 1983-89, Spl. and Individual Needs Tech. (SAINT) Newsletter, 1987-88, Jour. Parametrics, 1984-88. Del. Pres.'s Mid-Century White House Conf. on Children and Youth, 1950; scoutmaster Japan, U.S.; leader World Jamborees, France, Can., U.S., 1945-61; Eagle scout, 1947; U.S. del. Internat. Conf. on Ops. Rsch., Dublin, Ireland, 1972; organizing com. Internat. Cost-Effectiveness Symposium, Washington, 1970; spkr. Internat. Conf. Inst. Mgmt. Scis., Tel Aviv, 1973, del., Mexico City, 1967; mem. bus. com. Nat. Symphony Orch., 1968-70, Washington Performing Arts Soc., 1974-88; bus. mgr. Nat. Lyric Opera Co., 1983—, Internat. Assn. Med. Sci. Educators, 1997-98, Data Adminstrv. Mgmt. Assn. Nat. Capital, 1992—, Potomac Pedalers Touring Club, 1990—, Am. Friends of London Region Sch. Econs., 1988-97; mem. mktg. com. Fairfax Symphony Orch., 1984-91; bd. dirs. McLean (Va.) Orch., 1992-94; exec. com. Mid Atlantic coun. Union Am. Hebrew Congregations, 1970-79, treas., 1974-79, mem. nat. MUM com., 1974-79; mem. dist. com. Boy Scouts Am., 1972-75; bd. dirs. Nat. Coun. Career Women, 1975-79, Va. Acad. Scis., 1991—; pres. Jewish Temple, 1970-72; adminstr. Daniel Heumann Fund for Spinal Cord Rsch., 1999—. Recipient Silver medal 50-yard free style and half mile swimming meet. No. Va. Sr. Olympics, 1990. Fellow AAAS, Washington Acad. Scis. (gov. 1981-92, v.p. 1987-88, pres.-elect 1989-90, pres. 1990-91, past pres. 1991-92), Ops. Rsch. Soc. Am. (chmn. meetings com. 1969-71, chmn. cost-effectiveness sect. 1969-70, Moving Spirit award 1994), Washington Ops. Rsch./Mgmt.. Sci. Coun. (editor newsletter 1969-93, sec. 1971-72, pres. 1973-74, trustee 1975-77, bus. mgr. 1976-93), Internat. Inst. Strategic Studies (London), Am. Soc. Assn. Execs. (membership com. 1981-82, assn. mgmt. co. sect. coun. 1995-98, cert.), Inst. Ops. Rsch. and the Mgmt. Scis., Am. Econ. Assn., Wharton Grad. Sch. Alumni Assn. (exec. com. 1970-73), Nat. Eagle Scout Assn., VFW, Am. Legion, Navy League of U.S., Greater Wash. Soc. Assn. Execs. (new ventures com. 1995-97), Alumni Assn. George Washington U. (governing bd. 1974-82, chmn. univ. publs. com. 1976-78, Alumni Svc. award 1980), Alumni Assn. George Washington U. Sch. Govt. and Bus. Adminstrn. (exec. v.p. 1977-78, pres. 1978-79), George Washington U. Doctoral Assn. (sr. v.p. 1968-69), Nat. Assn. Acad. Sci. (del. 1991-93), Wharton Sch. Washington (sec. 1967-69, pres. 1969-70, exec. dir. 1987—, Joseph Wharton award 1991). Home: 6516 Truman Ln Falls Church VA 22043-1821

WEISS, ARNOLD HANS, lawyer, consultant; b. Nurnberg, Germany, July 25, 1924; m. Artemis Lychos, May 5, 1956; children: Daniel L., Andrew A. B.A., U. Wis., 1951, J.D., 1952. Bar: Wis. 1953, D.C. 1958. Atty. advisor Office Gen. Counsel U.S. Treasury, 1953-60; atty. Inter Am. Devel. Bank, 1960-61, dep. gen. counsel, 1961-70, gen. counsel, 1970-77; ptnr. Arent, Fox, Kintner, Plotkin & Kahn, Washington, 1977-90; cons. Chevy Chase, Md., 1991; sec., gen. counsel Emerging Markets Corp., Washington, 1992—. With U.S. Army, 1942-47; served to lt. col. JAGC USAR, 1948-62. Decorated Bronze Star. Mem. ABA, Am. Soc. Internat. Law, Inter-Am. Bar Assn., Internat. Bar Assn., D.C. Bar Assn., Univ. Club of D.C., Univ. Club of Mexico City, Army and Navy Club (Washington). Office: Emerging Markets Corp 2001 Pennsylvania Ave NW # 1100 Washington DC 20006-1850

WEISS, CARL OTTO, nonlinear optics researcher; b. Rostock, Fed. Republic Germany, Dec. 14, 1941; s. Gottfried and Alida (Crasemann) W. Dr. Rer. Nat., U. Hannover, Germany, 1972. Physicist Physikalisch Technische Bundesanstalt, Braunschweig, Fed. Republic of Germany, 1972-75, researcher, 1975-88, dir., 1989-91; sect. head, prof. physics, 1991—; cons. rsch. funding orgns., Europe, N.Am., China, Japan; vis. prof. U. Copenhagen, Tokyo Inst. Tech.; sr. lectr. U. Queensland. Author: Dynamics of Lasers, 1991; contbr. articles to profl. jours. Avocation: classical music. Home: Saarbr Str 158, 38116 Braunschweig Germany Office: Phys Tech Bundesanstalt, Bundesallee 100, D-3300 Braunschweig Germany

WEISS, CHRISTOPH JOHANNES, physiologist, educator; b. Uelzen, Hannover, Germany, Apr. 24, 1926; s. Hermann Rudolf and Theodora Olga (Schleuning) W.; m. Ilse Wiebke Fuchs, July 6, 1955; children: Michael Gregor, Christiane. Diploma in medicine, U. Freiburg, Germany, 1952; MD, U. Hamburg, Germany, 1954; Dr.med.habil, U. Hamburg, 1960; PhD, U. London, 1960. Asst. Inst. Physiology U. Hamburg, 1953-55, 60-62, privat dozent Inst. Physiology, 1962-65, assoc. prof. Inst. Physiology, 1965-69; lectr., sr. lectr. dept. physiology U. Khartoum, Sudan, 1955-60; prof., dir. Inst. Physiology U. Kiel, Fed. Republic Germany, 1970-79, U. Lübeck, Germany, 1979-95; mem. Wissenschaftsrat, German Fed. Govt., 1975-78, head med. commn., 1978-80. Contbr. over 100 articles to profl. publs. Mem. Dentsche Physiologische Gesellschaft. Home: Bavernsee 3, 23627 Gross Sarau Germany Office: Inst Physiologie Med Univ, Ratzeburger Allee 160, 23538 Lübeck Germany

WEISS, DANIEL EDWIN, clergyman, educator; b. Kenosha, Wis., June 9, 1937; s. Edwin and Ruth J. (Stromquist) W.; m. Rachel A. Johnson, Aug. 9, 1958; children: Daniel E. Jr., Kristen R. BA, Wheaton Coll., 1959, MA, 1962; MDiv, Gordon Conwell Theol. Sem., South Hamilton, Mass., 1962; PhD, Mich. State U., 1964; DD (hon.), Judson Coll., 1976, Franklin Coll., 1990; DHL (hon.), Ottawa (Kans.) U., 1997; STD (hon.), Linfield Coll., 2000. Ordained to ministry Am. Bapt. Chs., 1962. Prof. ministry Gordon Div. Sch., Wenham, Mass., 1964-69; v.p. Gordon Coll., Wenham, 1969-73; pres. Eastern Coll., St. Davids, Pa., 1973-81, Eastern Bapt. Theol. Sem., Phila., 1973-81; exec. v.p. Pace U., N.Y.C., 1981-83; exec. dir. Am. Bapt. Bd. Edn. and Publ., Valley Forge, Pa., 1983-88; gen. sec. Am. Bapt. Chs. U.S.A., Valley Forge, 1988-2000; mem. ctrl. com. World Coun. Chs., Geneva, 1989-98; mem. gen. bd. Nat. Coun. Chs., N.Y.C., 1989-2000; mem. gen. coun. Bapt. World Alliance, Washington, 1985-2000.

WEISS, DIETER KARL, physics educator; b. Günzburg, Bavaria, Germany, Feb. 17, 1955; s. Karl Arkadius and Elfriede (Endhardt) W.; m. Susanne Bessling, Apr. 6, 1990; children: Lorenz, Verena. Diplom, U. Munich, Germany, 1982; PhD, Tech. U. Munich, 1987; Habil., U. Stuttgart, Germany, 1993. With Tech. U. Munich, 1982-85, Max-Planck-Inst., Stuttgart, 1985-95; prof. physics U. Regensburg, Germany, 1995—; cons. Bellcore, Red Bank, N.J., 1990-91. Contbr. articles to profl. jours. Recipient Otto-Klung Preis, Berlin, 1993. Mem. Deutsche Physikalische Gesellschaft, Am. Phys. Soc. Office: U Regensburg/Exp und Ang Ph, Universitatsstr 31, 93040 Regensburg Germany

WEISS, DIETER WALDEMAR, economics educator, consultant; b. Berlin, Dec. 2, 1935; s. Waldemar Weiss and Elsa Radke. Diploma in engring., Tech. U., Berlin, 1960, PhD, 1962. With policy planning sect. Fed. Ministry Econ. Cooperation, Bonn, Germany, 1962-65; chief Mid. East dept. German Devel. Inst., Berlin, 1965-80; prof. Freie U., Berlin, 1980—; John Foster Dulles vis. prof. Princeton U., 1994; mem. German econ. adv. mission to Pres. Anwar Sadat, Egypt, 1977. Author, co-author 10 books; contbr. over 120 articles to profl. jours. Named to Order of the Arab Republic of Egypt, Govt. Egypt, Cairo, 1977. Office: Freie U Berlin, Boltzmannstr 20, 14195 Berlin Germany

WEISS, EARLE BURTON, physician; b. Waltham, Mass., Nov. 23, 1932; s. Murray E. and Ruth R. (Pill) W.; m. Ruth Lithwick, Dec. 1, 1963; children—Ilana, Joshua. BS with honors, Northeastern U., 1955; MS, M.I.T., 1957; MD, Albert Einstein Coll. Medicine, 1961. Intern King's County Hosp., Bklyn., 1961-62; resident Boston City Hosp., 1962-64, Nat. Heart Inst. fellow, 1964-66; assoc. chief of medicine Tufts Med. Svc., 1969-71; founder/first dir. respiratory ICU, physician pulmonary svc. Boston City Hosp., 1964-71; dir. div. respiratory diseases St. Vincent Hosp., Worcester, Mass., 1971-89; also acting med. dir. St. Vincent Hosp., 1985-87; prof. medicine U. Mass. Med. Sch., 1977—; sr. pulmonary rsch. scientist, dept. anesthesia Rsch. Labs. Brigham and Womens Hosp., Boston, 1989—; cons. FDA, 1975-77; lectr. in medicine Tufts Med. Sch.; assoc. prof. life scis. Worcester (Mass.) Poly. Inst.; vis. prof. Faculty of Medicine, dept. of anesthesia Harvard Med. Sch., 1990—, vis. prof. U. Guadalajara, Mexico, 1973, 77; med. dir. Found. Rsch. in Bronchial Asthma and Related Diseases; Tb cons. Commonwealth of Mass., 1972-89; dir. regional inpatient Tv, Worcester County; vis. prof. U. Guadalajara, Mex., 1973, 77; prof. extraordinario faculty of medicine U. Guadalajara Med. Sch., 1977, 82. Author: Bronchial Asthma, 2d edit., 1976, 3d edit., 1993, Status Asthmaticus, 1978; contbr. (with artist Frank H. Netter) Ciba Collection: The Respiratory System and Clinical Symposia; contbr. numerous articles to profl. jours., abstracts, audio tapes and book chpts. Served to capt. USAF, 1965-70. Recipient 1st Dr. J. McKeever Meml. award for outstanding med. educator, 1970, Chadwick medal for meritorious contbn. to thoracic diseases Mass. Thoracic Soc., 1990, The Acad. Honor Soc. Fellow ACP, Am. Coll. Chest Physicians, Royal Coll. Physicians (assoc.); mem. AAAS, AMA, Mass. Thoracic Soc. (pres. 1976-78, Chadwick medal for meritorious contbn. 1990), Mass. Med. Soc., Am. Thoracic Soc. (co-founder clin. assembly, rep. councilor 1979-82, chmn. med. devices com. 1972-79), Am. Assn. Clin. Scientists, Am. Soc. Internal Medicine, Soc. Free Radical Rsch., N.Y. Acad. Scis., Interasthma, Sigma Xi. Achievements include pioneer use of mech. ventilation in respiratory failur of chronic lung disease, arterial blood gas profiles in status asthma, the role of calcium and oxygen toxic products in asthma and airways reactivity, and the training of numerous pulmonary physicians. Avocations: oil painting, cello, family. Home: 57 South St Natick MA 01760-5526 Office: Brigham and Womens Hosp Dept Anesthesia Rsch L Boston MA 02115

WEISS, EUGEN FRANZ JOSEF, veterinary pathology educator; b. Gmund, Bavaria, Fed. Republic Germany, Feb. 24, 1930. Student, U. Munich, 1954, DVM, 1955, Habilitation, 1960, DVM (hon.), 1990; DVM (hon.), U. Budapest, 2000. Vet. medicine diplomate. Asst. U. Munich, 1955-60, lectr., 1960-67; asst. prof. Wash. State U., 1962-63; prof., head dept. vet. pathology U. Giessen, Fed. Republic Germany, 1968-98. Author: Spezielle Pathologie, 5th edit., 1998; editor, author: Allgemeine Pathologie, 8th edit., 1990. Mem. Deutsche Akademie der Naturforscher Leopoldina. Home: Dietrich Bonhoeffer Str 9, D 35398 Giessen Germany Office: Frankfurter Str 96 Inst fur, Veterinarpathologie, D 35392 Giessen Germany

WEISS, JONATHAN ARTHUR, lawyer; b. May 1, 1939. BA, Yale U., 1960, LLB, 1963. Bar: D.C. 1994, N.Y. 1967, U.S. Supreme Ct. 1967. Mng. atty. Neighborhood Legal Svcs., Washington, 1964-66, Mobilization for Youth Legal Svcs., N.Y.C., 1969-71; with Ctr. on Welfare Law, Columbia U. Law Sch., N.Y.C., 1967-69; dir. Legal Svcs. for Elderly, N.Y.C., 1971—; lectr. Hebrew U., Jerusalem, 1966; vis. prof. Tex. So. U. Law Sch., Houston, 1971; adj. prof. Yeshiva U. Cardozo Law Sch., N.Y.C., falls 1983-85. Co-author, editor: The Law and the Elderly, 1976; co-author: Right and Wrong a Philosophical Dialogue and Between Father and Son, 1968; contbr. numerous articles and revs. to law and philos. jours. and newspapers, French and Russian transls. Bd. dirs. N.Y. Civil Liberties Union, Disability Legal Def. Fund. Recipient Disting. Scholar medal Hofstra U., 1972; Fulbright scholar, 1966. Mem. ABA (mem. Adv. Coun. ethics 2000 com.), Native Am. Bar Assn. Democrat. Office: Legal Svcs for Elderly 130 W 42d St New York NY 10036

WEISS, JONATHAN DAVID, obstetrician-gynecologist; b. N.Y.C., Oct. 18, 1954; s. Meyer Harry and Gloria Rea (Dymond) W.; m. Kiyo M. Watkins. AB, Brandeis U., Waltham, Mass., 1976; MD, Tufts U., Boston, 1980. Diplomate Am. Bd. Ob-Gyn. Intern Tufts U. Affiliated Hosp., Boston, 1980-81, resident, 1981-84, fellow maternal-fetal medicine, 1984-86; asst. prof. ob-gyn. Tufts U., Boston, 1984-86; perinatologist dept. maternal-fetal medicine Alta Bates Med. Ctr., Berkeley, Calif., 1986-95; perinatologist John Muir Med. Ctr., Walnut Creek, Calif., 1987—, Summit Med. Ctr., Oakland, Calif., 1995—. Fellow Am. Coll. Obstetricians and Gynecologists; mem. Soc. Perinatal Obstetricians, San Francisco Gynecol. Soc. Avocations: flying, alpine skiing. Office: 350 30th St Ste 230 Oakland CA 94609-3424 also: 9260 Alcosta Blvd Ste 17A San Ramon CA 94583 also: 2021 Ygnacio Valley Rd Walnut Creek CA 94598-3391

WEISS, JOSEF JOHANN, engineering educator, researcher; b. Weidling, Austria, June 5, 1937; s. Josef and Luise (Brandner) W.; m. Birgit Agnes Bartosch, 1967; children: Agnes, Julia. Diploma in Engring., U. Agr., Vienna, Austria, 1963, Doctor, 1970, Inauguration, 1980. Rschr. Fed. Coll. and Rsch. Inst. for Viticulture and Pomology, Klosterneuburg, Austria, 1963-67, head divsn., 1967-88, prof., 1988-99; prof. U. Agr., Vienna, 1987—. Recipient Franz Schwackhofer prize Assn. Austrian Food and Biotechnologists, 1974. Mem. Magyar Elelmezesipari Tudomanyos Egyesület (hon.).

WEISS, MANFRED ERWIN, anesthesiologist, educator; b. Wolfratshausen, Germany, Mar. 2, 1958; s. Erwin and Stefanie (Roemer) W. MD, Ruhr U. Bochum, Germany, 1983. Resident in anesthesiology U. Düsseldorf, Germany, 1984-86, 88-95; resident in internal medicine U. Aachen, Germany, 1986-88; staff anesthesiologist U. Ulm, Germany, 1995—, assoc. prof., 1997—. Author: Yearbook of Intensive Care and Emergency Medicine, 1996; contbr. articles to med. jours., including Blood, Cytokine, Jour. Pharm. Exptl. Toxicology. Mem. Soc. Critical Care Medicine, European Soc. Intensive Care Medicine, N.Y. Acad. Scis. Office: U Ulm Dept Anesthesiology, Steinhoevelstrasse 9, 89075 Ulm Germany

WEISS, PAUL, philosopher, educator; b. N.Y.C., May 19, 1901; s. Samuel and Emma (Rothschild) W.; m. Victoria Brodkin, Oct. 27, 1928 (dec. Dec. 31, 1953); children: Judith, Jonathan. BSS, CCNY, 1927; MA, Harvard U., 1928, PhD (Sears Travelling fellow), 1929; hon. degrees, Grinnell Coll., 1960, Pace Coll., 1969, Bellarmine Coll., 1973, Haverford Coll., 1974, Boston U., 1989. Instr., tutor philosophy Harvard U., also instr. Radcliffe Coll., 1930-31; assoc. in philosophy Bryn Mawr (Pa.) Coll., 1931-33, assoc. prof., 1933-40, prof., 1940-46, chmn. dept., 1944-46; Guggenheim fellow, 1938; vis. prof. Yale U., 1945-46, prof. philosophy, 1946-62, Sterling prof. philosophy, 1962-69, Sterling prof. emeritus, 1969—; fellow Ezra Stiles Coll.; vis. prof. philosophy Hebrew U., Jerusalem, 1951; Luce-Rabinowitz grantee for study, Israel and India, 1954; lectr. Aspen Inst., 1952, Chancellor's Forum, U. Denver, 1952; Orde Wingate lectr., 1954; Powell lectr. U. Ind., 1958; Gates lectr. Grinnell Coll., 1960; Matchette lectr. Purdue U., 1961, Wesleyan Coll., 1963; Aquinas lectr. Marquette U., 1963; Townsend Harris medalist, 1963; Rhoades lectr. Haverford Coll., 1964; Phi Beta Kappa lectr., 1968-69; resident scholar State U. N.Y., 1969, 70; vis. prof. U. Denver, spring 1969; Eliot lectr. Marquette U., 1970; William De Vane medalist Yale, 1971; Aquinas lectr. St. Mary's, 1971; medalist City Coll., 1973, Hofstra U., 1973; B. Means lectr. Trinity Coll.; lectr., Japan, 1981; Ann. McDermott Lectr. U. Dallas, 1983; vis. Heffer prof. Philosophy Cath. U. Am., 1969-91, 93-94. Author: Reality, 1938, Nature and Man, 1947, Man's Freedom, 1950 (Portugese transl., 1960), Modes of Being, 1958, Our Public Life, 1959, World of Art, 1961 (Hebrew transl., 1970), Nine Basic Arts, 1961, History: Written and Lived, 1962, Religion and Art, 1963, The God We Seek, 1964, Philosophy in Process, 12 vols., 1955-88, The Making of Men, 1967, Sport: A Philosophic Inquiry, 1969 (Japanese transl., 1985, Korean transl., 1993), Beyond All Appearances, 1974, Cinematics, 1975, First Considerations, 1977, You, I and The Others, 1980, Privacy, 1983, Toward a Perfected State, 1986, Creative Ventures, 1991, Being and Other Realities, 1995, Emphatics, 2000; co-author: Right and Wrong: A Philosophical Dialogue Between Father and Son, 1967, 71 (Hebrew transl., 1971), Approaches to World Peace, 1944, Perspectives on a Troubled Decade, 1950, Moral Principles of Action, 1952, Personal Moments of Discovery, 1953, Perspectives on Peirce, 1965, Dimensions of Job, 1969, Mid-Century American Philosophy, 1974, Philosophy of Baruch Spinoza, 1980, Existence and Actuality, 1984, When the Worst That Can Happen Already Has, 1992, The Philosophy of Paul Weiss: Autobiography, Replies to Critics, Drawings, and Bibliography, 1995; co-editor: Collected Papers of Charles S. Peirce, 6 vols.; founder, editor Rev. Metaphysics, 1947-63; mem. editl. bd. Judaism, Jour. Speculative Philosophy; contbr. articles to profl. jours. Mem. Assn. for Symbolic Logic (councillor 1936), Am. Philos. Assn. (co-pres. 1966), Conf. on Sci., Philosophy and Religion (founding), C.S. Peirce Soc. (founding, pres.), Metaphys. Soc. Am. (founder, pres. 1951-52, councillor 1953-58), Philos. Soc. for Study of Sport (co-founder, pres. 1973), Am. Friends Hebrew U., Philos. Edn. Soc. (founder), Washington Philosophic Club (C.S. Peirce award), European Soc. Culture, Internat. Acad. Philosophy of Art, Am. Assn. Mid. East Studies, Aurelian Club, Elizabethan Club, Phi Beta Kappa. Address: 2000 N St NW Washington DC 20036-2336

WEISS, ROBERT ALAN, surgeon; b. Chgo., Mar. 8, 1956; s. Harold Richard and Nancy (Rogoff) W.; m. Tina Haberer. MD, Chgo. Med. Sch., North Chicago, Ill., 1982. Diplomate Nat. Bd. Med. Examiners, Am. Bd. Ophthalmology, Am. Soc. Oculoplastic and Reconstructive Surgery. Flexible intern Cook County Hosp., Chgo., 1982-83; resident ophthalmology house staff Cornell U., N.Y. Hosp. & Meml. Sloan Kettering Cancer Ctr., N.Y.C., 1983-86, fellow ophthalmic oncology and orbital disease, 1986-87; fellow oculoplastic and reconstructive surgery Emory U. Med. Ctr., Atlanta, 1987-88; asst. clin. prof. ophthalmology Cornell U. Med. Ctr., N.Y.C., 1988-90; clin. assoc. prof. ophthalmology and neurosurgery U. Ill., Chgo. Med. Ctr., 1991—; attending oculoplastic surgeon Chgo. Eye Inst., 1991—; asst. dir. Cornell Med. Ctr. Robert Ellsworth-Ophthalmic Oncology Ctr., N.Y.C., 1988-90; credentialled specialist U. Ill. Divsn. Svcs. Cripped Children, Chgo., 1991—; co-dir. U. Ill. Retinoblastoma Bd., Chgo., 1992—; vis. prof. Lions Club, Bolivian Am. Med. Soc., S.Am. Med. Soc., Israel, Bolivia, Columbia, Equador, Philippines, Egypt, 1991, 93, 94, 98, 99, 2000, Egypt, 1991, 93, 94, 98, 99, 2000. Editor: Principles and Practice of Ophthalmic Plastic and Reconstructive Surgery, 1996. Recipient Golden Apple Tchg. award U. Ill., Chgo., 1994; named tchr. of yr. Chgo. Curriculum in Ophthalmology, 2000. Fellow Am. Soc. Oculoplastic and Reconstructive Surgery, Am. Acad. Ophthalmology, Alpha Omega Alpha. Avocations: gardening, photography, painting. Office: Chgo Eye Inst 3982 N Milwaukee Ave Chicago IL 60641-2703

WEISS, ROBERT MICHAEL, dentist; b. Bklyn., June 5, 1940; s. Henry and Rena (Bluth) W.; m. Irene Marilyn Sternick, June 30, 1962; children: Lori Ann, Julie Lynn, Karen Michelle. Trustees scholar, L.I. U., 1958-61; DDS, NYU, 1965; postdoctoral cert., LD Pankey Inst. for Advanced Dental Edn., 1979. Pvt. practice dentistry Avon, Conn., 1967—; pres. Avon Dental Group, P.C., 1972—; clin. prof. Coll. Dentistry U. Conn., 2000—; nat. cons. Conn. Gen. Ins. Co. for ins. coverage for Gen. Electric Co., 1980—; advisor dental assisting program Briarwood Coll.; cons. CNA Ins. Co., 1988—; bd. dirs. Sentinel Bank. Chmn. Children's Dental Health Week, Hartford County, Conn., 1971; chmn. Jewish Adult Edn., West Hartford, Conn., 1986-87; trustee Temple Beth Israel, 1983—. Served to capt. USAF, 1965-67. Fellow Acad. Gen. Dentistry, Am. Acad. Gen. Dentistry, Pierre Fauchand Acad. (hon.); mem. ADA, Am. Soc. Preventive Dentistry (pres. Conn. chpt.), Acad. Osseointegration, Internat. Congress Oral Implantologists, Hartford Dental Soc. (exec. com. 1993—, chmn. centennial yr., chmn. 100th anniversary 1996-97), Conn. State Dental Assn. (ho. of dels. 1992—), Chronic Fatigue Immune Dysfunction Syndrome (Conn. bd. dirs. 1992—), So. New Eng. Assn. Practice Adminstrn., Starnard Beach Assn. (pres. 1984-86), Avon Jr. C. of C. (pres. 1971-72), Masons, Alpha Omega, Sigma Alpha Mu. Home: 13 Alpine Meadow Ln Avon CT 06001-3935 Office: Avon Dental Group 20 W Avon Rd Ste 2 Avon CT 06001-3540

WEISS, RONALD PHILLIP, lawyer; b. Springfield, Mass., Apr. 28, 1947; s. Kermit Paul and Fay Roslyn (Robinovitz) W.; m. Janet Faye Landon, June 15, 1969; children: Emily, Katherine. BA, Dartmouth Coll., 1968; JD, U. Pa., 1972. Bar: Mass. 1972, U.S. Dist. Ct. Mass. 1975, U.S. Tax Ct. 1979, U.S. Ct. Appeals 2000. Assoc. Bulkley, Richardson and Gelinas, Springfield, Mass., 1972-78; ptnr. Bulkley, Richardson & Gelinas, LLP, Springfield, 1978—; pres. Estate Planning Coun. Hampden County, 1979-81; trustee Mass. Continuing Legal Edn. Inc., 1978-81. Author: (with others) Drafting Wills and Trusts in Massachusetts, 1990, 92, 94; editor: (with others) Massachusetts Corporate Tax Manual, 1986. Trustee Springfield Symphony Orch., 1986—, v.p. 1988-89, pres. 1989-91, chmn. 1991-94, clk., gen. counsel 1994—; mem. bd. advisors U. Mass. Family Bus. Ctr., 1992—; counsel Cmty. Found. of Western Mass.; trustee Jewish Fedn. Greater Springfield, 1986-90; mem. appropriations com. Town of Longmeadow, Mass., 1990-96, chmn. 1991-92, 95-96. Mem. ABA, Mass. Bar Assn. (chmn. taxation sect. 1978-81, bd. dels. 1979-81), Mass. Bar Found., Hampden County Bar Assn., Rotary. Office: Bulkley Richardson & Gelinas LLP 1500 Main St Ste 2700 Springfield MA 01115-0001

WEISS, SHOSHANA, alcoholism and drug researcher; b. Haifa, Israel, Jan. 3, 1952; d. Itzhak and Tova (Zikert) Rabinowitz; m. Avraham Weiss, June 27, 1974; children: Tali, Nirit. BSc, Technion, Haifa, 1974, instrn. cert.,

1974; DSc, Israel Inst. of Tech., Haifa, 1984; MA, Haifa U., 1979. H.S. tchr. Haifa, 1975; lectr. Sch. Edn. Haifa U., 1985-97; dir. alcohol abuse prevention and rsch. Israel Soc. for Prevention of Alcoholism, Ramat-Gan, 1984—. Author: (in Hebrew) Hashis and Marijuana, 1979, 4th edit., 1990, Alcohol and Drunkenness, 1984, 4th edit., 1988; author prevention kits on alcohol drinking in Russian, Amharic, Arabic and Hebrew, 1993-94 (1st place Internat. Markie awards 1995); editor ISPA Bull., 1993—; mem. editl. bd. Efshar-Jour., 1993—, Alcohol in Israel jour., 2000—; contbr. over 200 articles to profl. jours. in Hebrew and English. Officer Israel Def. Force, 1970-72. Sr. Scientist's fellow Govt. of Norway, 1993, Govt. of Finland, 1997; grantee Can. Govt., 1991; Prudential scholar, 1985; candidate UNESCO and Helena Rubenstein prize for women in sci., 1997. Mem. Kettil Bruun Soc. for Social and Epidemiol. Rsch. on Alcohol, European Soc. for Biomed. Rsch. on Alcoholism, Soc. for Med. Anthropology (alcohol and drug study group), Israel Assn. Canadian Studies, Israel Assn. Medicine and Law, Israel Soc. Addiction Medicine. Jewish. Home: 41A Ramim St, Karmiel 21861, Israel Office: Israel Soc Prevention Alcoholism, 4 Nordau St, Ramat-Gan 52464, Israel

WEISS, STEPHEN STEWART, electric insulation company executive; b. Birmingham, Eng., Mar. 18, 1945; s. Eric and Greta (Kobaltsky) W.; m. Liliane Lijn; children: Mischa, Sheba. BA, Pomona Coll., 1968. Trader mineral ore Naylor Benzon Ltd., London, 1968-70; founder, chief exec. Co-optic Ltd., London, 1970-76; mng. dir. Ericsten Investment Ltd., London, 1976—, Elmelin Plc, 1979—. Editor creative photography, 1973-76; editor, pub. Young British Photographers, Real Britain Postcards, 1973-76; exhibited in various one-man photgraphy shows. Arts Council Great Britain grantee, 1974. Mem. Engring. Employers Fedn. Home: 28 Camden Sq, London NW1 9XA, England Office: Elmelin Plc, 1 Betts Mews Ringwood Rd, London E17 8PP, England

WEISS, WILLIAM, retired pulmonary medicine and epidemiology educator; b. Phila., July 30, 1919; s. William and Anna (Grossman) W.; m. Esther E. Sabul, June 22, 1941; children: Winifred A., Seth S., Deborah E. BA, U. Pa., 1940, MD, 1944. Clin. dir. pulmonary disease svc. Phila. Gen. Hosp., 1950-74; chest cons. Norristown (Pa.) State Hosp., 1951-60; dir. Pulmonary Neoplasm Rsch. Project, Phila., 1957-67; faculty U. Pa. Grad. Sch. Medicine, Phila., 1952-66, Med. Coll. Pa., Phila., 1952-86; from assoc. prof. to prof. medicine Med. Coll. Pa., Hahnemann U., Phila., 1966-84, prof. emeritus, 1984—; cons. to various indsl. cos., Pa., N.J., 1962—. Editor Phila. Medicine, 1976-99; mem. editl. bd. Arch. Environ. Health, 1968-86; contbr. over 229 articles and 125 editls. to profl. jours., 18 chpts. to books. Bd. dirs. Am. Cancer Soc., Phila., 1980-86; cons. on asbestos Bd. Edn., Phila., 1983; mem. EPA Sci. Review Panel for Health Rsch., Washington, 1980-81, Toxics/Health Effects adv. com. Pa. Dept. Health, 1985-87. Capt. USAF, 1953-55. Recipient Ann. Sci. award Phila. divsn. Am. Cancer Soc., 1979, Cristol award Phila. County Med. Soc., 1989; picture on cover Cancer Rsch., Mar. 1, 1990 for lung cancer rsch. Fellow ACP, Coll. Physicians Phila., Am. Coll. Occupl. and Environ. Medicine (merit in authorship award 1974, 85); mem. AMA, Laennec Soc. Phila. (pres. 1970), Phila. Occupl. Med. Assn. (pres. 1980-81), Am. Thoracic Soc., Pa. Med. Soc., Phila. County Med. Soc. (Strittmatter award 1991, Gold medal). Avocation: classical music. Home: 3912 Netherfield Rd Philadelphia PA 19129-1014

WEISS, WOLFGANG, English language educator; b. Munich, Feb. 20, 1932; s. Josef and Caecilia (Stork) W.; m. Birgit Huber, March 23, 1957; children: Stephan, Alexander, Esther. PhD, U. Munich, 1964. Lektor U. Glasgow, Scotland, 1960-62; asst. lectr. U. Munich, 1962-68, konservator, 1968-70, full prof., 1974-2000; full prof. U. Cologne, Germany, 1970-74. Author: Die Elisabethanische Lyrik, 1976, Das Studium der Englischen Literatur, 1979, Das Drama der Shakespeare zeit, 1979, Der Anglo Amerikanische Universitatsroman, 1988, Swift und die Satire des 18 Jahrhunderts, 1992. Fellow Internat. Assn. Univ. Profs. English, Deutsche Shakespeare Gesellschaft, Internat. Shakespeare Assn. Roman Catholic. Home: Haid 7, D-94474 Vilshofen Bavaria, Germany

WEISSBARD, SAMUEL HELD, lawyer; b. N.Y.C., Mar. 3, 1947; children: Andrew Joshua, David S. BA, Case Western Res. U., 1967; JD with highest honors, George Washington U., 1970. Bar: D.C. 1970, U.S. Supreme Ct. 1974, Calif. 1998. Assoc. Fried, Frank, Harris, Shriver & Kampelman, 1970-73, Arent, Fox, Kintner, Plotkin & Kahn, 1973-78; prin. Weissbard & Fields, P.C., 1978-83; shareholder, v.p. Wilkes, Artis, Hedrick & Lane, Washington, 1983-86; ptnr. Foley & Lardner, Washington, 1986-97, L.A., 1997-98; co-chair creditors' rights workout and bankruptcy group Foley & Lardner, Washington, 1992-95; sr. counsel Cox, Castle & Nicholson, L.L.P., Newport Beach, Calif., 1998—. Editor in chief George Washington U. Law Rev., 1969-70. Bd. dirs. Luther Rice Soc., George Washington U., 1985-87, Atlanta Coll. Art, 1993, Nat. Learning Ctr., 1993-96, Georgetown Arts Commn. and gen. counsel 1995-96; Chmn. steering com. of Lawyer's Alliance for Nat. Learning Ctr. and Capital Children's Mus., 1989-90; mem. steering com. DC/NLC Don't Drop Out Campaign, 1992,93, bd. dirs., 1994-96; devel. com. Shelter for the Homeless, 1998—. Recipient John Bell Larner medal, 1970. Mem. ABA, D.C. Bar, Georgetown Bus. and Profl. Assn. (bd. dirs. 1993-96, sec., gen. counsel 1993-97), Orange County Bus. Assn. (legis. com. 1998—), Order of Coif. Office: Cox Castle Nicholson LLP Ste 600 19800 MacArthur Blvd Irvine CA 92612-2435*

WEISSBEIN, THOMAS JERALD, public health physician; b. Agrefeuille, France, Nov. 14, 1960; s. Arthur Sigmund Weissbein and Marie Martone; m. Anna Maria Bijak, Sept. 1, 1985; children: Maria Bijak-Weissbein, Jan Bijak-Weissbein. BA, U. Calif., Berkeley, 1982; MD, U. Vt., 1987. Diplomate Am. Bd. Internal Medicine, Polish Bd. Internal Medicine. Intern, resident John Hopkins Health Sys., Baltimore, 1987-90; physician at various clinics, 1990-92; physician Health Ctr., Md., 1990-92; rsch. scientist Inst. Neurology, Poland, 1992-94; physician Health Ctr., Hagerstown, Md., 1994-97, Health Svc., Poland, 1997—. Contbr. articles to profl. jours. Baha'i. Avocations: chess, walking, gardening, home improvement. Home: ul Barbackiego 93, 33-300 Nowy Sacz Poland

WEISSBUCH, ISABELLE, chemistry research scientist; b. Dorohoi, Suceava, Romania, Dec. 23, 1946; arrived in Israel, 1979; d. Gershon and Gizela (Moskovitch) Schächter; m. Leon Weissbuch, Nov. 4, 1936; children: Jeannine, Yulian. MSc in Chem. Engring., Polytech. Inst., Iassy, Romania, 1969; PhD in Chemistry, Weizmann Inst. Sci., 1985. Cert. profl. chemist, chem. engr. Asst. prof. Polytech. Inst., Iassy, Romania, 1969-78; assoc. staff scientist Weizmann Inst. Sci., Rehovot, Israel, 1987-1998, sr. staff scientist, 1999—. Author: (book chapters) 100 Years of Lock-and-Key Principle, 1994, Crystallization Technology Handbook, 1995, Comprehensive Supramolecular Chemistry, 1996, Advances in Chemical Physics, 1997, Molecular Modeling Applications in Crystallization, 1999; contbr. articles to profl. jours.; patentee in field. Recipient prize Gerhard M.J. Schmidt Meml. Fund, Israel, 1987. Mem. Israel Chem. Soc., Israel Assn. Crystal Growth, N.Y. Acad. Scis. Office: Dept Materials & Interfaces, Weizmann Inst Sci, 76100 Rehovot Israel

WEISSER, URSULA BRIGITTE, medicine historian; b. Schwaeb Hall, Germany, Jan. 12, 1948; d. Eberhard and Hannelore (Huebner) W. Dr.phil.nat., U. Frankfurt, Germany, 1974; Dr.med.habil, U. Erlangen, Germany, 1981. Docent Inst. History of Medicine, U. Erlangen, 1981-84, Inst. History of Medicine, U. Mainz, Germany, 1984-87; univ. prof. Inst. History of Medicine U. Hamburg, Hamburg, Germany, 1987-2000; ret., 2000. Co-editor Medizinhistorisches Jour., 1988. Home: Grandweg 3, Hamburg D-22529, Germany

WEISSMAN, ROBERT EVAN, information services company executive; b. New Haven, May 22, 1940; s. Samuel and Lillian (Warren) W.; m. Janet Johl, Aug. 27, 1960; children: Gregory, Christopher, Michael. BSBA, Babson Coll., Wellesley, Mass., 1964. Exec. v.p. Rediffusion Inc., Saugus, Mass, 1972-73; dir. corp. devel. Nat. CSS, Wilton, Conn., 1973-74, chmn., 1975-81; exec. v.p. Dun & Bradstreet Corp., N.Y.C., 1981-84, pres., 1985-93, chmn., CEO, 1994-96; chmn., CEO Cognizant Corp., Westport, Conn., 1996-98; CEO IMS Health, Westport, Conn., 1998-99, chmn., 1999—; bd. dirs. State St. Boston Corp., Gartner Group, Nielsen Media Rsch.; mem. adv. bd. N.Y. Stock Exch. Liste Co.; mem. bus. roundtable com. econ. devel. U.S.-Japan Bus. Coun. Vice chmn. bd. trustees Babson Coll. Mem. IEEE, Info. Tech. Assn. Am., Inst. Mgmt. Accts., Soc. Mfg. Engrs. (sr.). Office: IMS Health 200 Nyala Farms Rd Westport CT 06880-6267

WEISSMAN, SHARON BETH, physician; b. Washington, Mar. 24, 1963; d. Sherman Morton and Myrna Milgram W.; 1 child, Rachel. BS, Mass. Inst. Tech., 1985; MD, Columbia, 1991. Diplomate Am. Bd. Internal Medicine, Infectious Disease. Resident Beth Israel Hosp., Boston, 1991-94; fellow infectious disease Harvard Longwood Program, Boston, 1994-96; asst. prof. Case Western Res. Univ., Cleveland, 1996—; staff physician Vet. Affairs Medical Ctr., Cleve., 1996—, medical dir., 1997—, dir. medicine core clerkship, 1998; chmn. AIDS task force Vet. Affairs MEdical Ctr., Cleve., 1996—, internal medicine residency selection com. Univ. Hosp. Cleve., 1997., investigation review bd. Vet. Affairs Medical Ctr., 1998. Contbr. articles to profl. jours. Recipient numerous rsch. grants. Mem. Soc. Gen. Internal Medicine, Infectious Disease Soc. Am., Am. Coll. Physicians, Alpha Omega Alpha. Office: Cleveland Vet Affairs Medical Ctr 10701 East Blvd Cleveland OH 44106-1702

WEISSMAN-BERMAN, DEBORAH, composites engineer, researcher; b. N.Y.C., June 9, 1938; d. Raphael H. and Sarah S. (Schreiber) Weissman; m. Lewis H. Berman, Aug. 1, 1958 (div. Apr. 1966); 1 child, Michelle B. Marchildon. BFA, Columbia U., 1967; M of Engring. in Ocean Engring., Stevens Inst. Tech., Hoboken, N.J., 1980; profl. degree Civil Engr., Columbia U., 1985; ScD, Eurotech. Rsch. U., Hilo, Hawaii, 1989. Asst. prof. naval architecture U.S. Merchant Marine Acad., Kings Point, N.Y., 1980-81; asst. prof. engring. SUNY Maritime Coll., Ft. Schuyler, N.Y., 1981-82; sr. naval architect M. Rosenblatt & Son, N.Y.C., 1982-83; composites cons. Weissman-Berman & Co., Inc., Conn., N.Y., Fla., 1983-92; assoc./rsch. prof. engring. Webb Inst. Naval Architecture, Glen Cove, N.Y., 1986-89; assoc./courtesy scientist U. Fla., Gainesville, 1990—; rsch. scientist Nova Southeastern U., Dania, Fla., 1996—; creator composites software, COREDES PLATES, S.e.a. Software Corp., enFt. Lauderdale, Fla., 1992—; co-chair 2d Internat. Conf. Sandwich Composites, Gainsville, 1992. Author: Research Guidelines for Aluminum, 1993; contbr. sci. papers to Trans. SNAME, Procs. 2d Internat. Conf. Sandwich Composites; contbr. chpt. to SAMPE Internat. Ency. Composites, 1990; assoc. editor SAMPE Jour., 1992-95. Recipient grad. scholarship SNAME, Jersey City, N.Y., 1979. Mem. ASME (v.p. rsch. com. 1990-96), Soc. Naval Architects and Marine Engrs., Soc. Advanced Materials and Process Engring., Am. Soc. Composites. Democratic. Jewish. Achievements include derivation of sandwich beam and plate equations with core as elastic foundation, derivation of sandwich composites yield equations, derivation of the mechanics modulus of residual stiffness (alpha), definition of bi-geometrical structure of sandwich beams. Office: Nova Southeastern U Oceanographic Ctr 8000 N Ocean Dr Dania FL 33004-3033

WEISSMANN, CHARLES, molecular biologist; b. 1931. MD, PhD, U. Zurich, Switzerland; D honoris causa, U. Verona, Italy, 1992, U. Ghent, Belgium, 1994, Swiss Fed. Inst. Tech., Zurich, 1998, U. Zurich, 2000, U. St. Andrews, 2000. Dir. Molecular Biology Inst., 1967-99; pres. Swiss Soc. for Cell ane Molecular Biology; chmn. sci. bd. Biogen, 1984-86; pres. Ernst Hadorn-Stiftung, Zurich, 1986—; bd. dirs. F. Hoffmann-LaRoche Ltd., Basel; mem. sci. adv. bd. ZMB, Heidelberg, 1988-90, Roche Inst. Molecular Biology, Nutley, N.J., 1993-95, Osaka (Japan) Biosci. Inst., 1994—, Roche Molecular Sys., Alameda, Calif., 1994—, Swiss Inst. for Cancer Rsch., Lausanne, 1994-98; mem. sci. coun. Swiss Nat. Fund, 1989-94, Internat. Human Frontiers Rsch. Program, 1994-98; mem. internat. sci. adv. bd. The Netherlands Cancer Inst., Amsterdam; bd. govs. Tel Aviv U., 1997—; chmn. European Com. Group on Bovine Spongiform Encephalopathy, 1996; Samuel Rudin disting. vis. prof. Columbia U., N.Y.C., 1999. Assc. editor Molecular Medicine, 1994—. Decorated fgn. mem. Order for Merit for Sci. and Art (Germany); recipient Ruzicka prize in chemistry, 1996, Otto Warburg prize, 1980, H.P. Heineken prize, 1982, Sir. H. Krebs medal, 1974, Mercel Benoist prize, Bern, 1970, Scheele medal, Uppsala, 1982, Krebspreis Schweizerische Krebsliga, 1987, Jung prize for medicine, Hamburg, 1988, Gabor medal Royal Soc., London, 1993, Robert Koch medal, Bonn, 1995, Datta lectureship award FEBS, 1998, Charles Leopold Mayer prize French Acad. Sci., 1996, Royal Soc. Glaxo Wellcome prize, 1996, August Wilhelm von Hofmann Denkmünze, 1997, Klaus Joachim Zülch prize, 1997, Max Delbrück medal, Berlin, 1997, Wilhelm Exner medal, Vienna, 1997, Disting. Svc. award, Miami, 1998, Mendel medal Genetical Soc., London, 1998. Fellow Am. Acad. Microbiology, Mem. NAS, European Molecular Biology Orgn., Am. Acad. Arts and Scis., Swiss Acad. Med. Sic., Deutsche Akademie Naturforscher Leopoldina, Royal Soc. (fgn.), Weizmann Inst. Sci. (bd. govs. 1985—), Academia Europaea, Human Genome Orgn., Nordheim-Westfälischen Acad. Sci. (corr.), Berlin-Brandenburgischen Acad. Sci. (extraordinary). Office: Imperial Coll Sch Medicine, Norfolk Pl, London W2 1PG, England

WEISSMANN, HEIDI SEITELBLUM, radiologist, educator; b. N.Y.C., Feb. 4, 1951; d. Louis and June (Joseph) Seitel Bloom; m. Murray H. Weissmann, June 16, 1973; 1 dau., Lauren Erica. BS in Chemistry magna cum laude, Bklyn. Coll., CUNY, 1970; MD, Mt. Sinai Sch. Medicine, N.Y.C., 1974. Diplomate Nat. Bd. Med. Examiners. Intern Montefiore Med. Ctr. Bronx, N.Y., 1974-75, resident in diagnostic radiology, 1975-78; fellow in computerized transaxial tomography and ultrasonography N.Y. Hosp.-Cornell U. Med. Ctr., N.Y.C., N.Y., 1978-79; instr. in radiology and nuclear medicine Albert Einstein Coll. Medicine, Montefiore Med. Ctr., Bronx, N.Y., 1979-80; asst. prof. radiology and nuclear medicine Albert Einstein Coll. Medicine and Montefiore Med. Ctr., Bronx, N.Y., 1980-84, assoc. prof. nuclear medicine, 1984-94, assoc. prof. radiology, 1986-94; dir. Ctr. for Women, Medicine and Healthcare, Washington, 1994—; adj. attending physician Montefiore Med. Ctr., 1979-87; chmn. Nuclear Medicine Grand Rounds: Greater N.Y., 1980-87; physician coord. Nuclear Medicine Technologist In-Service Tng. Program, 1982-86; cons. NIH, 1984-86, NIH Diagnostic Radiology, 1985-86. Assoc. editor Nuclear Medicine Ann., 5 vols., 1979-84, editor, 5 vols., 1985—; contbr. chpts. to books, articles to jours.; editor Jour. Sci. and Engring. Ethics, 1994—; reviewer Jour. of Radiology, 1981—, mem. editl. adv. bd., 1985-86, assoc. editor, 1986—; reviewer. Jour. of Nuclear Medicine, 1981—, Am. Jour. of Roentgenology, 1986—, Gastroenterology, 1986—, Western Jour. of Medicine, 1985—; contbr. audiovisual programs and films. Recipient Saul Horowitz, Jr., Meml. award (Disting. Alumnus award), Mt. Sinai Sch. Medicine, 1980, Pres.' award, Am. Roentgen Ray Soc., 1979, Berta Rubinstein, M.D., Resident award, 1978, Cavallo award for moral courage, 1993, others. Mem. Radiol. Soc. N.Am. (mem. subcom. for nuclear medicine of program com., 1981, 82, 83, chmn. 1984, 85, 86), Soc. Nuclear Medicine (trustee 1983-87, 88—, sec.-treas. Correlative Imaging Council 1979-82, exec. bd. 1982-84, pres. 1984-86, exec. bd. 1986—, mem. acad. council 1980—, task force on interrelationship between nuclear medicine and nuclear magnetic resonance 1983-85 , gov. Greater N.Y. chpt. 1983-85, treas., 1985-86, 86-87, 2d ann. Tetalman award of Edn. and Research Found. 1982, mem., vice chmn. coms. and subcoms.), Soc. Gastrointestinal Radiologists, Am. Inst. Ultrasound in Medicine, N.Y. Acad. Scis., Assoc. Alumni Mt. Sinai Med. Ctr., Nuclear Radiology Club (chmn. 1983—). Phi Beta Kappa.

WEISZ, FERENC, mathematician; b. Mohács, Hungary, Jan. 25, 1964; s. Ferenc and Anna (Wagner) W.; m. Márta Ladányi, Oct. 22, 1988; children: Ágoston, Gellért, Ambrus. MA, Eötvös Loránd U., Budapest, Hungary, 1988; PhD, Hungarian Acad. Scis., Budapest, Hungary, 1991. Rsch. fellow Hungarian Acad. Scis., Budapest, 1988-91; asst. prof. Eötvös Loránd U., Budapest, 1991-94, assoc. prof., 1995—. Author: Martingale Hardy Spaces and Their Applications in Fourier Analysis, 1994; contbr. articles to profl. jours. Rsch. fellow Ludwig-Maximilians U., Munich, 1992-93, Johannes Kepler U., Linz, Austria, 1993-94, Humboldt-U. zu Berlin, 1998-99; recipient Pro Scientia medal Min. Edn., Hungary, 1989. Office: Eötvös Loránd U, Eötvös Loránd U, Pazmeny P Setany 1/D Numer, H-1177 Budapest Hungary

WEISZ, HERBERT, retired analytical chemistry educator; b. Wieselburg, Hungary, Apr. 25, 1922; s. Wilhelm and Paula (Ludwig) W.; m. Eva Swoboda, Jan. 15, 1949. Diplng, Tech. U. Brno, Czechoslovakia, 1944; DrTechn, Tech. U., Vienna, 1947. Asst. prof. Tech. U. Vienna, 1949-60; chair analytical chemistry U. Freiburg, Germany, 1960-84; univ. rsch. fellow U. Birmingham, Eng., 1955-56; guest prof. La. State U., 1959-60. Author: Microanalysis by the Ring-Oven Technique, 1961, 2d edit., 1970; contbr. more than 180 articles to profl. jours. Recipient Fritz Pregl prize Acad. of Scis., Vienna, 1967, others. Mem. Royal Soc. Chemistry, Gesellschaft Deutscher Chemiker, Gesellschaft Osterr. Chemiker. Home: Heuweilerweg 34, D 79194 Gundelfingen Germany Office: U Freiburg Chem Lab, Albertstr 21, D 79104 Freiburg Germany

WEITKAMP, CLAUS CARL HEINRICH, physicist; b. Wuppertal, Germany, June 30, 1935; s. Heinrich Friedrich and Emmi (Woyt) W.; m. Marga Christl Mors, Apr. 4, 1961; 1 child, Timm. Student, U. Tubingen, Fed. Republic of Germany, 1955-56; BS in Physics, U. Paris, Sorbonne, 1959; MS in Physics, U. Karlsruhe, Fed. Republic of Germany, 1958, PhD, 1962. With Lab. des Hautes Pressions Centre Nat. de la Recherche Sci., Bellevue, France, 1958-59; guest scientist physics divsn. Oak Ridge Nat. Lab., 1968-69; sr. scientist, leader nondestructive assay group Inst. for Applied Nuclear Physics, Karlsruhe, 1962-74; sr. scientist, head optics divsn. Inst. of Physics, Geesthacht, Germany, 1975-94; dir.-in-charge Inst. Phys. and Chem. Analytics, Geesthacht, Germany, 1995, head laser spectroscopy divsn., 1995-2000; cons. GKSS Forschungszentrum, Geesthadil, Germany, 2000—. Contbr. articles to profl. jours.; patentee in field. French Govt. rsch. fellow, 1958-59; named hon. citizen Gov. of Tenn., 1968. Mem. Optical Soc. Am. Home: Bergedorfer Weg 25, D-21465 Wentorf Germany Office: GKSS-Forschungszentrum, Postfach 1160, D-21494 Geesthacht Germany

WEITLAUFF, MANFRED, ecclesiastical history educator; b. Augsburg, Bavaria, Fed Republic Germany, July 31, 1936; s. Heinrich and Elisabeth (Maiss) W. Abitur, Realgymnasium, Augsburg, 1957; diplome of catholic theology, U. Munich, 1962, ThD, 1970, habilitation, 1977. Scientific asst. U. Munich, 1967-77, extraordinary prof., 1977-80, prof., 1980; ordinary prof. Faculty for Catholic Theology, Lucerne, Switzerland, 1981-86, U. Munich, 1986—; instr. philosophy and history Warse der Baycrischen Akademie der Wissenschaften, 2000. Author: Das Bistum Freising im Zeitalter des Barocks, 1989; editor: Joseph Bernhart Erinnerungen 1891-1930, 1992, Bischof Ulrich von Augsburg, 1993. Home: Ainmillerstrasse 29a, D 80801 Munich Germany Office: Faculty for Cath Theology, Geschw Scholl Platz 1, D 80539 Munich Germany

WEITZ, JEANNE STEWART, artist, educator; b. Warren, Ohio, Apr. 30, 1920; d. William McKinley and Ruth (Stewart) Kohlmorgan; m. Loyal Wilbur Weitz, Aug. 1, 1940 (dec. 1986); children: Gail, Judith, John, Marc. BS in Art and English, Youngstown U., 1944; MEd in Art, U. Tex., El Paso, 1964; postgrad., Tex. Tech U., 1976. Indsl. engr. Republic Iron & Steel, Youngstown, Ohio, 1942-43; art tchr. pub. schs., Bessemer, Pa., 1943-44; art tchr. El Paso (Tex.) Independent Sch. Dist., 1944-50, 54-78, art. cons., 1978-87; art tchr. Hermosa Beach (Calif.) Independent Sch. Dist., 1950-53, El Paso Mus. Art, 1960-65; lectr. in art U. Tex., El Paso, 1963-66; instr. El Paso Community Coll., 1970-78; free-lance artist, lectr. El Paso, 1987-91; supr. student tchr. U. Tex., El Paso, 1989-91; mgr. Sunland Art Gallery, 1994-95. Represented in group exhibitions at Sun CarnivalExhbn., 1961, El Paso Mus. Art, 1962; author highsch. curriculum guide; exhibited at LVAA Shows, 1990 (5 First Places), Westside Art Guild, 1992, LVAA, 1992 (1st in Watercolor). Coordinator art edn. El Paso Civic Planning Coun., 1985-86; chmn. art edn., art resources dept. City of El Paso, 1982-83. Recipient Purchase award El Paso Art Assn. Spring Show, 1995, 1st pl. award KCOS (PBS), 1996, 1st pl. award Westside Art Guild, 1996, 2d pl. El Paso Art Assoc., 1998, 1st pl. award West Side Art Guild, 1998, 99, H.M. El Paso Pastel Soc. Show, 1998. Mem. Tex. Art Edn. Assn. (conf. planner, local orgn. 1981, Hon. Mention award 1972), Nat. Soc. Arts and Letters (sec. El Paso chpt. 1988—), El Paso Mus. Art Guild, Lower Valley Art Assn. (Hon. Mention award 1988), Nat. Art Edn. Assn. (sec. 1988-93, two 1st Place award LVAA shows 1989), Westside Art Guild (pres. 1993-95), Nat. Soc. Am. Pen Women, Rio Bravo Watercolorists (sec. 1998), Pastel Soc. of El Paso (v.p. 1999-2000). Republican. Presbyterian. Avocations: printmaking, travel. Home and Studio: 1407 Camino Amparo NW Albuquerque NM 87107-2607

WEITZ, MARTIN, physicist; b. Mannheim, Germany, Oct. 26, 1964; s. Hans-Martin and Brigitte (Hofmann) W.; m. Susanne Weitz, Oct. 14, 1994; children: Carolina, Julia. PhD, U. Munich, Germany, 1992. Acting asst. prof. Stanford (Calif.) U., 1994; scientist Max-Planck Inst., Garching, Germany, 1994—. Contbr. articles to profl. jours. Mem. German Phys. Soc. Office: Max-Planck Inst, Hans-Kopfermann Str 1, 85748 Garching Germany

WEIZMAN, EZER, president of Israel, air force officer; b. Tel Aviv, June 15, 1924; married; 2 children. Student, Royal Air Force Staff Coll. Commd. Israel Air Force, 1948, advanced through grades to maj.-gen., officer, 1948-66, chief gen. staff br., 1966-69; min. transport Govt. of Israel, 1969-70, min. of def., 1977-80, min. comm., 1984-88, min. of sci., 1988-92, pres., 1993—; mem. Likud front, 1973-80. Author: On Eagles Wings, 1978, The Battle for Peace, 1981. Head Yahad Party in Nat. Unity Govt., 1984-89. Office: Pres Residence, Beit Hanassi, Jerusalem 92188, Israel Office: 2 Hadekel St, Caesarea Israel*

WEIZSACKER, RICHARD VON, former president of Federal Republic of Germany; b. Stuttgart, Germany, Apr. 15, 1920; m. Marianne von Kretschmann, Oct. 10, 1953; children: Robert, Andreas, Marianne, Fritz. Ed., Oxford U., DCL (hon.), 1988; ed., Dr. jur.; Dr. jur. (hon.), D. Weizman Inst. Tel Aviv, Grenoble, Loewen, Belgium, Istanbul, Sucre, Bolivia, Göttingen, Harvard U., Coimbra, Portugal, Oxford. Mem. CDU, 1954—, chmn. commn. on basic policy issues, chmn. regional group Berlin, 1981-83, fed. dep. chmn., 1983-84; mem. German Bundestag, 1969-81, v.p., 1979-81; dep. chmn. Christian Dem. Union/Christian Social Union Parliamentary Py, 1973-79; mem. Ho. of Reps., Berlin, 1979, 81-84; governing mayor City of Berlin, 1981-84; pres. Federal Republic of Germany, 1984-94; guest prof. Heinrich Heine U., Düsseldorf, Germany, 1996—. Recipient Theodor Heuss prize, 1983, Romano Guardini prize, 1987, Heinrich-Heine-Preis, 1991. Office: Office Former Pres, Am Kupfergraben 7, 10117 Berlin Germany

WEKHOF, ALEXANDER, physicist; b. Moscow, Oct. 19, 1943; came to U.S., 1979; naturalized, 1989; s. Alexis A. Wekhof and Lydia Gaber-Agapov; m. Sabine Christel Schradin, Mar. 15, 1989; 1 child, Tobias Eugene. Ed., Power Engring. Coll., Moscow, 1962; MS in Exptl. Physics with honors, Engring. Physics Inst., Moscow, 1969; PhD in Plasma Physics, Lebedev Physics Inst., Moscow, 1975. Staff scientist Lebedev Physics Inst., Moscow, 1969-75, Space Rsch. Inst., Moscow, 1975-78; staff scientist space sci. lab. U. Calif., Berkeley, 1979-80; staff scientist Lawrence Berkeley Lab., U. Calif., 1980-82; sr. engr. Intel Corp., Livermore, Calif., 1982-84; group leader Nat. Semiconductor Corp., Santa Clara, Calif., 1984-85; pres. Ultraviolet Energy Generators Inc., Oakland, Calif., 1988-93, Wekhof GmbH, 1993-96, Wek-Tec, 1996—; cons. joint projects Maxwell Labs., San Diego, Calif., 1986-87; coop work with Livermore Nat. Lab, 1991, chem. waste mgr., 1991;. Contbr. articles to profl. jours.; inventor, patentee in field. Mem. Am. Physics Soc. Avocations: skiing, swimming, visiting art galleries, theaters. Office: WEK-TEC Filter und UV Technik, Frankfurter Str 85 C, D-74072 Heilbronn Baden-Wurtenberg, Germany

WELBORNE, JOHN HOWARD, railway company executive, lawyer; b. July 24, 1947; s. William Elmo and Pauline Cornwell (Schoder) W.; m. Mary Martha Lampkin, Oct. 8, 1994. AB, U. Calif.-Berkeley, 1969; MPA, UCLA, 1974; JD, U. Calif.-Davis, 1977. Bar: Calif. 1977, D.C. 1980. Congl. intern Congressman John V. Tunney, Washington, 1969; assoc. firm Adams, Duque & Hazeltine, L.A., 1979-84, of counsel, 1984-96; gen. counsel Magnum Software Corp., Chatsworth, Calif., 1989-98; mgmt. cons., 1971—; dir. Pueblo Viejo Devel. Corp., 1979-88, Union Hardware & Metal Co., 1981—; pres. Angels Flight Railway Co., L.A., 1995—; COO Calif. Sesquicentennial Found., 1996-97; dir. Childrens Hosp. L.A. Centennial Celebration, 1998—. Contbr. articles to profl. jours. Mem. cen. bus. dist. project adv. com., downtown strategic plan adv. com., chmn. open space task force, mem. South Park task force City of L.A. Cmty. Redevel. Agy.; mem. L.A. Philharm. Men's Com., 1978-89; pres. L.A. County Host Com. for Olympic Games, 1984; mem. exec. com. Citizens's Task Force for Cen. Libr. Devel., L.A., 1981-83; bd. dirs. Angels Flight Railway Found., L.A., 1995—, chpt. ARC, 1986-89, Children's Bur. L.A., 1982-88, El Pueblo Park Assn., 1983-89, Friends of the USC Librs., 1999—, Inner City Law Ctr., 1992-95, Los Amigos del Pueblo, L.A. Libr. Assn., 1983-89, 92—, Windsor Sq. Assn.,

1980-87, 1999—, L.A. Beautiful, 1982-85, Pershing Sq. Restoration Campaign, 1986-87, Children's Bur. Found., 1997—; bd. dirs. In the Wings divsn. Performing Arts Ctr., Los Angeles County, 1982-86, pres. 1984-85; bd. dirs., officer L.A. 200 Com., 1978-91; bd. councilors U. So. Calif. Sch. Pub. Adminstrn., 1983-89; mem. adv. bd. The L.A. Conservancy, 1986—; trustee Windsor Sq-Hancock Park Hist. Soc., 1983-86, Nat. Trust Hist. Preservation, 1997—; fellow Amundsen Inst. U.S.-Mex. Studies, 1987. Capt. Adj. Gen.'s Corps., U.S. Army, 1970-71, USAR, 1972-79. Decorated Army Commendation medal with oak leaf cluster; Cross of Merit 1st class (Fed. Republic Germany). Mem. ABA, D.C. Bar Assn., State Bar Calif., Ordre des Coteaux de Champagne, Confrerie Saint-Etienne d'Alsace, Calif. Vintage Wine Soc. Episcopalian. Office: Angels Flight Railway PO Box 712345 Los Angeles CA 90071-7345

WELCH, CHARLES EDGAR, JR., retired English language educator, writer; b. Phila., July 20, 1918; s. Charles Edgar and Eva Dudley (Morris) W.; widower. BS in Edn., West Chester U., 1947; MA in Early Am. History, U. Pa., 1948, PhD in Folklore, 1970; cert. in 20th Century poetry, Oxford (Eng.) U., 1948. Cert. tchr., Pa. Lectr. English, Phila. Coll. Pharmacy and Sci., 1947-50, asst. prof., 1951-60, assoc. prof., 1960-69, prof., 1969-77, emeritus prof., 1977—, chmn. dept. langs. and social scis., 1950-77; adj. prof. ESL, Temple U., Phila., 1977-96; part-owner Trevose Summer Theater, 1950-52; contbr., cons. Ledger Syndicate, 1950-70; actor, asst. stage mgr. New Angola (Pa.) Summer Theater, 1955; program dir. Folk Fair, Nationalities Svc. Ctr., Phila., 1955-75; contbr. to humanities program Thomas Jefferson U.; writer Milestones, Phila.; a host You and Your Health, Sta. WFIL-TV, 1958-70; folklorist for documentary on Phila. Mummers Parade Look Who's Having Fun, 1986. Author: Oh! Dem Golden Slippers: A History of the Philadelphia Mummers Parade, 1970, revised, 1993, (with A. Osol): A Sesquicentennial of Service 1821-1971 of the Philadelphia College of Pharmacy and Science; contbr. articles and book revs. to profl. jours., newspapers and mags. Stage mgr. fund raising program, fund raiser Erlanger Theater, Phila., Internat. House, Phila. Mem. Acad. Natural Scis., Pa. Hist. Soc., Pa. Acad. Arts, Nat. Mus. Women in Arts (charter). Republican. Avocation: writing. Home: 2423 Pine St Philadelphia PA 19103-6416

WELCH, DAVID WILLIAM, lawyer; b. St. Louis, Feb. 26, 1941; s. Claude LeRoy Welch and Mary Eleanor (Peggs) Penney; m. Candace Lee Capages, June 5, 1971; children: Joseph Peggs, Heather Elizabeth, Katherine Laura. BSBA, Washington U., St. Louis, 1963; JD, U. Tulsa, 1971. Bar: Okla. 1972, Mo. 1973, U.S. Dist. Ct. (we. dist.) Mo. 1973, U.S. Dist. Ct. (ea. dist.) Mo. 1974, U.S. Ct. Appeals (8th cir.) 1977, U.S. Ct. Appeals (7th cir.) 1991. Contract adminstr. McDonnell Aircraft Corp., St. Louis, 1965-66; bus. analyst Dun & Bradstreet Inc., Los Angeles, 1967-68; atty. U.S. Dept. Labor, Washington, 1972-73; ptnr. Moller Talent, Kuelthau & Welch, St. Louis, 1973-88, Lashly & Baer, St. Louis, 1988-96, Armstrong Teasdale LLP, St. Louis, 1996—. Author: (handbook) Missouri Employment Law, 1988; contbr. book chpts. Missouri Bar Employer-Employee Law, 1985, 87, 89, 92, 94, Missouri Discrimination Law, 1999; co-editor: Occupational Safety and Health Law, 1996. Mem. City of Creve Coeur Ethics Commn., 1987-88, Planning and Zoning Commn., 1988-96; bd. dirs. Camp Wyman, Eureka, Mo., 1982—, sec., 1987-88, 2nd v.p. 1988-89, 1st v.p. 1990-92, pres., 1992-94. Mem. ABA, Fed. Bar Assn., Mo. Bar Assn., Okla. Bar Assn., St. Louis Bar Assn., Kiwanis (bd. dirs. St. Louis 1979—, sec. 1982-83, 93-94, v.p. 1983-84, 88-90, 92-93, Man of Yr. award 1985). Democrat. Mem. Christian Ch. (Disciples of Christ). Avocations: travel, landscaping, music. Home: 536 N Mosley Rd Saint Louis MO 63141-7633 Office: Armstrong Teasdale 1 Metropolitan Sq Ste 2600 Saint Louis MO 63102-2740

WELCH, JERRY, oil company executive; b. Marion, Ohio, Mar. 13, 1963; s. Arthur Leroy and Donna R. (Ellwood) W.; m. Sharon Carol Lee, 1995; children: Joseph Peterson, Shellie Peterson, James Peterson. BA, U. Colo., 1984. Exec. Amoco Oil, Houston, 1984—; CEO Brit. Inc., Paris. Mem. Internat. Platform Assn. Republican. Avocations: auto racing, tennis, sailing, swimming. Home: 31650 Hwy 44 E Eustis FL 31650 also: PO Box 470512 Lake Monroe FL 32747-0512

WELCH, J(OAN) KATHLEEN, entrepreneur; b. Pensacola, Fla., Jan. 28, 1950; d. Leslie Peter and Frances Louise (Hughes) Morales. Salesperson Arthur Murray Dance Studio, Colo., Fla., Pa. and N.J., 1970-81; sales rep. Warner-Lambert Co., Morris Plains, N.J., 1981-83; supr., mgr. Dance Club Internat., Chatham, N.J., 1983-90; dist. rep. Nat. Fedn. Ind. Bus., 1990-95; pres. I Am Consulting, 1993—; radio sales rep. Fress Media, 1995-96; acct. exec. Atlantic Lucent Techs., 1997; computer programmer Mailcraft, Inc., 1997-98; developed sales program Dance Club Internat.; judge Nat. Dance Coun. Am., 1977-90; dance coach, 1975-90; coached winners U.S. Ballroom Championships Hustle divsn., 1978, choreographer, 1971-90, competitor, 1972-81; condr. New Age lectrs., seminars and workshops, 1994—, Kofutu Touch Healing, 1994—, Reiki practitioner, 1995—, Kinesiology, 1995—, Regenesis Practitioner, 1996—; tchr. meditation, yoga, Tai Chi, Chee Gung (Qigong), 1995—; advanced clinical hypnotist, 1997, massage therapist, 1998. Co-prodr., promoter, talent scout for TV program: Astrology Today (formerly It's in the Stars), 1989-94; performed on nat. TV with leading personalities including George Raft, Donald O'Connor, and Mike Douglas. Recipient awards Arthur Murray Studio, 1971-81, 1st place counselor award Arthur Murray All Star Tournament, 1977, 1st place Supr. award Dance Club Internat., 1st place Registrar award Dance Club Internat. in the Tournament of Champions, 1984; ranked No. 1 rep. in Profls. Corner, N.Y. div. Nat. Fedn. Ind. Bus., 1991, ranked No. 2 rep., 1992; named Internat. Woman of Yr., 1993. Mem. Imperial Soc. Tchrs. of Dancing (assoc. Ballroom br., Latin-Am. br.), Am. Dance Tchrs. Assn. Mem. Unity Ch. Avocations: travel, yoga, astrology, theater, metaphysics and new age studies. Home and Office: 2000 W 92d Ave #443 Denver CO 80260

WELCH, JOHN FRANCIS, JR. (JACK WELCH), electrical manufacturing company executive; b. Peabody, Mass., Nov. 19, 1935; s. John Francis and Grace (Andrews) W.; m. Carolyn B. Osburn, Nov. 1959 (div. 1987); children: Katherine, John, Anne, Mark; m. Jane Beasley, Apr. 1989. B.S. in Chem. Engring. U. Mass., 1957; M.S., U. Ill., 1958, Ph.D., 1960. With Gen. Electric Co., Fairfield, Conn., 1960—, v.p., 1972, v.p., group exec. components and materials group, 1973-77, sr. v.p., sector exec., consumer products and services sector, 1977-79, vice chmn., exec. officer, 1979-81, chmn., chief exec. officer, 1981—; also dir. Gen. Electric Capital Services; chm National Broadcasting Corporation. Patentee in field. Mem. NAE, The Bus. Coun. (former chmn.), Bus. Roundtable. Office: Gen Electric Co 3135 Easton Tpke Fairfield CT 06431-0001

WELCH, JOSEPH DANIEL, lawyer; b. University City, Mo., Feb. 1, 1952; s. Robert Joseph and Mary Virginia (Church) W.; m. Sharon Susan Filipek, Mar. 16, 1973; children: Eric Ryan, Christopher Joseph, Colin Andrew, Maria Nicole, Theresa Katherine. BA cum laude, St. Louis U., 1974, JD, 1977. Bar: Mo. 1977, U.S. Dist. Ct. (ea. and we. dists.) Mo. 1977, U.S. Ct. Appeals (8th cir.) 1984, U.S. Supreme Ct. 1994. Assoc. Ely & Cary, Hannibal, Mo., 1977-79; ptnr. Ely, Cary & Welch, Hannibal, Mo., 1979-82, Ely, Cary, Welch & Hickman, Hannibal, Mo., 1982-99, Cary, Welch & Hickman, L.L.P., Hannibal, Mo., 1999—; mem. Mississippi River Pky. Commn., St. Paul, 1988-95, head Mo. del., 1988; prof. bus. law Hannibal-LaGrange Coll., 1993-98; mem. Nat. Heritage Corridor Commn., Washington, 1990-96; speaker various orgns. Editor: Year in Review-Bankruptcy, 1991-94, coauthor, 1988-90; speaker various profl. orgns.; contbr. articles to profl. jours. Bd. dirs. Mark Twain Area Physician's Recruitment Assn., Hannibal, 1984-85, Hannibal Free Pub. Libr., 1980-82, Hannibal C. of C., 1978-80; pres. Hannibal Ctrl. Bus. Devel., Inc., 1982-85; mem. Mo. Right-to-Life, 1977—; community adv. bd. St. Elizabeth Hosp., 1985-86; Birthright of Hannibal, Inc., 1980—, Holy Family Sch. Bd., 1990-95. Recipient acad. scholarship St. Louis U., 1970-74, recognition for Significant Contribution to Bush Administrn., Dept. Interior, 1993. Mem. ATLA, Mo. Assn. Trial Lawyers., Mark Twain Astron. Soc. (co-founder). Roman Catholic. Avocations: parenting, basketball, tennis, boating, creative writing. Home: 601 Country Club Dr Hannibal MO 63401-3033 Office: Cary Welch and Hickman LLP 1000 Center St Hannibal MO 63401-3449

WELCH, LINDA LUREE, physician; b. Lansing, Mich., Sept. 18, 1952; d. Richard Dale and Muriel Ruth (Frye) Welch; children: Sarah, Gabriel, Harry, Abigail. BS, Mich. State U., 1974, DO, 1978. Diplomate Am. Bd. Osteo. Family Practioners; cert. Am. Acad. Pain Mgmt. Intern Grand Rapids (Mich.) Osteo. Hosp., 1978-79; asst. prof. dept. family medicine Mich. State U. Coll. Osteo. Medicine, East Lansing, 1979-82, fellow in primary medicine edn., 1981; pvt. practice San Antonio, 1982—; chair dept. family medicine Bapt. Med. Ctr., 1998-99; children's counselor supr. South Tex. Billy Graham Crusade, 1997. Missionary physician to Romania, Travis Park United Meth. Ch., San Antonio, 1991; clin. preceptor for missionary trip to Mexico Christian Med. & Dental Soc., 1994. Recipient cert. of recognition Cristo Rey Clinic, Lansing, 1982, El Buen Pastor Meth. Ch., San Antonio, 1988, 89; named Sunday's Woman, San Antonio Light, 1989. Fellow Am. Acad. Disability Evaluating Physicians; mem. Am. Osteo. Assn., Am. Oseo. Coll. Family Practitioners, Am. Osteo. Coll. Pain Mgmt. & Sclerotherapy (bd. dirs. 1995-98), Tex. Osteo. Med. Assn., Tex. Coll. Family Practitioners, Mich. Assn. Osteo. Physicians, Mich. Assn. Osteo. Family Practitioners, Am. Acad. Med. Ethics, Am. Assn. Orthopedic Medicine. Avocations: swimming, metalsmithing, fishing, cooking, skiing. Office: 11312 Perrin Beitel Rd San Antonio TX 78217-2534

WELCH, NANCY L., urban planner; b. Rhinelander, Wis., Dec. 5, 1956; d. Leonard Chase and Nora Brokke Welch; m. Peter S. Glick, July 11, 1982 (div. Oct. 1989); 1 child, Nathaniel Welch Glick; m. David Hawthorne Plank, June 25, 1994; 1 child, Kelsey Thora Plank. BA, Oberlin Coll., 1979; MArch, U. Wis., Milw., 1991. Cert. planner Am. Inst. Cert. Planners. Asst. to registrar Mpls. Coll. Art and Design, 1979-84; archivist Wis. Archtl. Archive, Milw., 1989-93; planner City of Des Moines, 1993-99, City of West Allis, Wis., 1999—. Avocations: hiking, sailing, landscaping, historical research. E-mail: plankwel@execpc.com and nwelch@ci.west-allis.wi.us. FAX: 414-302-8401. Home: 6108 Washington Cir Wauwatosa WI 53213-2452 Office: City of West Allis 7525 W Greenfield Ave West Allis WI 53214-4648

WELCH, RICHARD LEROY, personal improvement company executive; b. Lincoln, Nebr., Oct. 15, 1939; s. Raymond Nathanial and Helen Lila (Ludwig) W.; m. Donna Lee Gysegem, Nov. 3, 1991; children: Terri L. Flowerday, Julie A. Kuhl; 1 stepchild, Shannon Panzo. Student, U. Nebr., 1958-59. Agt. Gurantee Mut. Life, Lincoln, Nebr., 1960-61; agt., mgr. Mut. of Omaha, 1962-68; gen. agt. Loyal Protective Life, Omaha, 1969-70; mgr. Mut. Benefit Life, Dallas, 1971-73; br. mgr. Great West Life, San Jose, Calif., 1973-74; pres. Internat. Speedreading Inst., Phoenix, 1975-80; founder, pres. Educom, Inc./Subliminal Dynamics, Aurora, Colo., 1980—; mem. adv. bd. Great West Life, San Jose, 1973; pres. bd. dirs. Internat. Speedreading Inst., Phoenix, 1975-80, Subliminal Dynamics, Inc., San Jose, 1980-93, Educom, Inc., Aurora, 1993—; scientist, spkr., author, educator in field. Author: Brain Management, 1996. Mem. Shriners, Masons (32d degree). Democrat. Avocations: sports, music, travel. E-mail: subdyn@subdyn.com Fax: (303) 627-2870. Office: Educom Inc DBA Subliminal Dynamics 19744 E Union Dr Aurora CO 80015-3486

WELCH, RICHARD LON See ABELL, RICHARD BENDER

WELD, JONATHAN MINOT, lawyer; b. Greenwich, Conn., Feb. 25, 1941; s. Alfred White and Sally (Duggan) W.; m. Jane Paige, June 19, 1965; children: Elizabeth, Eric. A.B. in History cum laude, Harvard U., 1963; J.D., Cornell U., 1967. Bar: N.Y. 1967, U.S. Ct. Appeals (2d cir.) 1969, U.S. Dist. Ct. (ea. and so. dist.) N.Y. 1970. Assoc. Shearman & Sterling, N.Y.C., 1967-75, ptnr., 1976—; ptnr. Shearman & Sterling, London, 1982-85; bd. dirs. Bank of N.S. Internat., The Evergreens. Bd. dirs. Bklyn. Hosp., St. Ann's Sch., Bklyn. Botanic Garden; former bd. dirs. Bklyn. Home for Children, Harvard Coll. Fund, Winant and Clayton Vols. Mem. ABA, N.Y. State Bar Assn. Office: 599 Lexington Ave Fl C2 New York NY 10022-6030

WELD, ROGER BOWEN, clergyman; b. Greenfield, Mass., Dec. 1, 1953; s. Wayland Mauney and Luvycie (Bowen) W.; m. Patricia Ann Kaminski, June 7, 1978 (div. 1979); m. Cynthia Lou Lang, Apr. 15, 1995. Grad., Sacred Acad. Jamilian U. of the Ordained, Reno, 1976-77, Seminary, 1978-82; student, U. Nev., 1983-85; postgrad., Sacred Coll. Jamilian Theology, 1988-90. Ordained to ministry, Internat. Comty. of Christ Ch. of Second Advent, 1977; appointed Rabban priest Internat. Comty. of Christ, 1993. Adminstrv. staff Internat. Community of Christ Ch. of Second Advent, Reno, 1977—, exec. officer dept. canon law, 1985—, exec. officer advocates for religious rights and freedoms, 1985—, exec. officer speakers bur., 1985—, exec. officer office pub. info., 1986—, mgr. Jamilian Univ. Press, 1987—, dir. advt. prodns., 1988—; founder, pres. Crown Rsch. Found., 1992—; mem. Chamber of Concerned Christians for Separation of Ch. and State. Author: Twelve Generations of the Family of Weld: Edmund to Wayland Mauney, 1986, A Steamboat in the Desert--A History of Steamboat Springs, Nevada, 1998; dir. photography, supervising editor: (video documentary) Gene Savoy's Royal Roads to Discovery, 1993, The Gran Vilaya Expeditions, Reclaiming a Legendary Lost City From the High Jungles of Peru, 1996. Staff sgt. USAF, 1971-75. Named Life Mem., Sacred Oversee, 1991. Mem. Nev. Clergyman's Assn., Andean Explorers Found. (Explorer's medal 1990), Ocean Sailing Club (exec. sec. 1988-94, v.p. 1994—, Participant's Silver Medallion 1989). Avocations: photography, cinematography, videography, print media. Office: Internat Cmty Christ Ch Second Advent of 2d Advent 643 Ralston St Reno NV 89503-4436

WELDEN, ALICIA GALAZ-VIVAR, foreign language educator; b. Valparaiso, Chile, Dec. 4, 1937; came to U.S., 1976; d. Pedro and Juanita (Vivar) Galaz; m. Oliver Welden, May 2, 1973; children: Arnold, Jacqueline, Cinthya, Jonathan. Grad., U. Chile, Santiago, 1955; PhD, U. Ala., Tuscaloosa, 1980. Prof. U. Chile, 1966-76; lectr. Appalachian State U., N.C., 1982-89; assoc. prof. U. Tenn., Martin, 1989—; dept. chair U. Chile, Antofagasta, 1966-68; founder, editor Tebaida Lit. Rev., Chile, 1968-70. Author: Antologia de Gongora, 1962, Jaula Gruesa, 1972, Oficio de Mudanza, 1987, Alta Marea, 1989, Senas Distantes, 1990. Regional pres. Pablo Neruda's Presidential Candidacy, Chile, 1969-70. Mem. MLA, Am. Coun. Tchrs. Fgn. Langs., Tenn. Philol. Assn., Soc. Chilean Writers, Ctr. Poetical Hispanic Studies, Phi Kappa Phi. Roman Catholic. Office: Univ Tenn Modern Fgn Langs Martin TN 38238-0001

WELDON, FAY, author; b. Alvechurch, Worcestershire, Eng., Sept. 22, 1931; d. Frank Thornton and Margaret (Jepson) Birkinshaw; m. Ronald Weldon, 1960; children: Nicholas, Daniel, Thomas, Samuel; m. Nicolas Fox, 1994. MA, U. St. Andrews, 1952, DLitt, 1990. Former propaganda writer Brit. Fgn. Office; former market rschr. Daily Mirror, Londom; advt. copywriter various firms; former mem. lit. panel Art Coun. Gt. Britain; chairperson judges' panel Booker McConnell Prize, 1983. Writings include: (novels) The Fat Woman's Joke, 1967, Down Among the Women, 1971, Female Friends, 1974, Remember Me, 1976, Words of Advice, 1977, Praxis, 1978, Puffball, 1979, The President's Child, 1982, The Life and Loves of a She-Devil, 1983, Shrapnel Academy, 1986, The Heart of the Country, 1987, Rules of Life, 1988, Leader of the Band, 1988, The Hearts and Lives of Men, 1988, Cloning of Joanna May, 1989, Darcy's Utopia, 1990, Life Force, 1992, Growing Rich, 1ž992, Trouble, 1993, Affliction, 1993, Splitting, 1995, Worst Fears, 1996, Big Women, 1998; (children's books) Wolf the Mechanical Dog, 1989, Party Puddle, 1989; (short story collections) Watching Me, Watching You, 1981, Polaris and Other Stories, 1984, Moon Over Minneapolis, 1991, Wicken Women, 1995, A Hard Time to be a Father, 1998; (non-fiction) Letters to Alice on First Reading Jane Austen, 1984; (essay collection) Godless in Eden, 1999; (libretto) A Small Green Space, 1989; (plays) Permanence, 1969, Time Hurries On, 1972, Words of Advice, 1974, Friends, 1975, Moving House, 1976, Mr. Director, 1978, Action Replay, 1979, I Love My Love, 1981, Wordworm, 1981, (adaptations) A Dolls House, 1990, Tess of the D'Urbervilles, 1991, Jane Eyre, 1994; (teleplays) The Fat Woman's Tale, 1966, Wife in a Bond Wig, 1966, Office Party, 1970, On Trial, 1971 (Soc. Film and TV Arts award 1971), Hands, 1972, Poor Baby, 1975, The Terrible Tale of Timothy Bagshott, 1975, Aunt Tatty, 1975, Married Love, 1977, Watching Me, Watching You, 1980, Life for Christine, 1980, Little Miss Perkins, 1982, Loving Women, 1983, The Wife's Revenge, 1983, Heart of the Country, 1989, Pride and Prejudice, 1985, Growing Rich, 1991, Big Women, 1998; (radio plays) Spider, 1972 (Best Radio Play award Writer's Guild 1978), Housebreaker, 1973, Mr. Fox and Mr. First, 1974, The Doctor's Wife, 1975, Polaris, 1978 (Giles Cooper Best Radio Play award 1978), Weekend, 19979, All the Bells of Paradise, 1979, Hole in the Top of the World, 1991, A Hard Time to be a Father, 1995, Hearts and Lives of Men, 1996; editor: New Stories 4: An Arts Coun. Anthology, 1979. Office: care Giles Gordon, 3 Ann St. Edinburgh E84 1PJ, Scotland also: Casarotto Co Ltd, National House 62-66 Wardour St. London W1V 3HP, England

WELDON, THEODORE TEFFT, JR., retail company executive; b. Evanston, Ill., July 19, 1932; s. Theodore Tefft and Dorothe Galbraith (Stover) W.; m. Barbara Ann Eskilson, Aug. 17, 1957; children: Lisa Courtney Weldon LeFevre, Theodore Tefft III, Margaret Helen. BA, Dartmouth Coll., 1954. Retail store salesman Sears Roebuck & Co., Gary, Ind., 1954-58; retail store mgr. Sears Roebuck & Co., Kankakee, Ill., 1958-62; sales mgr. Craftsman Sears Roebuck & Co., Chgo., 1962-69, advt. mgr. Craftsman, 1969-70, mktg. mgr. tires, 1970-81, sr. buyer sporting goods, 1981-82, nat. gen. catalog mgr., 1982-86; dir. home TV shopping Sears/QVC, Chgo., 1986-92; cons. Drake, Beam, Morin, Inc., Chgo., 1992-94, Focus Media, Inc., L.A., 1993-96, Std. Mktg. Corp., Naperville, Ill., 1993-98, King World Direct, L.A., 1993-97, Guthy-Renker, Las Vegas, 1997-98, Sears Roebuck and Co., 1997-2000, Ovation Group, 1997—, Home Depot, 1997-98, Kmart, 1997-98, Walmart, 1997-98, Pearle Vision, 1998, 3M, 1998, Tyee, 1998-2000, Target Stores, 1998, Panasonic 1997-2000; v.p. Link Tools Internat., USA, 1998—. Mem. Jr. Achievemnt, Chgo., 1966-68; rep. Winnetka (Ill.) Village Caucus, 1972-74; advisor Children's Theatre of Winnetka, 1972—; pres. Sunset Improvement Assn., Winnetka, 1975—. Avocations: internat. travel, theatre, swimming, biking, golf. Home and Office: 426 Sunset Rd Winnetka IL 60093-4232

WELFE, WLADYSLAW KAZIMIERZ, economics educator, consultant; b. Kolbuszowa, Rzeszow, Poland, May 20, 1927; s. Mieczyslaw and Zofia (Kielbinska) W.; m. Walentyna Kosidlo, Sept. 9, 1951; 1 child, Aleksander. MA in Econs., U. Lodz, Poland, 1949; PhD in Econs., Sch. Planning and Stats., Warsaw, Poland, 1961, Habilitation, 1964; D (hon.), U. Uppsala, Sweden, 1978, Acad. Econs., Cracow, Poland, 1995, U. Lyon 2, Lumiere, France, 1997. Sr. asst. Sch. Econs., Lodz, 1949-50, adj. asst. prof., 1950-64; adj. asst. prof. Sch. Planning and Stats., 1950-54; lectr. econs. U. Lodz, 1964-69, assoc. prof., 1969-74, prof., 1974—, dean Sch. Econs. and Sociology, 1966-70, vice rector, 1971-78, dir. Inst. Econometrics and Stats., 1980-97; chmn. subcom. Com. for Sci., Warsaw, 1994-2000; cons. in econ. forecasting; chmn. senate S. Sch. of Entrepreneurship and Mgmt., Lodz, 1996—; chmn. Senate Acad. of Bus. Lodz. Author: Indices of Production, 1966, Econometric Models of the Polish Economy, 1992, Applied Econometrics, 1996; co-author, editor: Econometric Models of Markets Vol. I, 1977, Vol. II, 1978, Vol. III, 1982, Quarterly Model of the Polish Economy, 1995, Economies in Transition. A System of Models and Forecasts for Germany and Poland, 1993, Medium-Term Econometric Model of the Polish Economy Under Transition, 1996, Economies in Transition and the World Economy. Models, Forecasts and Scenarios, 1997, Central and Eastern Europe on its Way to European Union, Simulation Studies Based on Macromodels, 1999, Principles of Macroeconometric Modeling, 1999; editor: Studies in Law and Economics; contbr. articles to sci. jours. Chmn. adv. coun. to pres. Town of Lodz, 1977-90; chmn. econs. sect. Adv. Coun. for Higher Edn., Warsaw, 1994-97. Recipient sci. award Lodz Volvodship, 1977; Copernicus and ACE grantee European Cmty., Brussels, 1992-96. Mem. Econometric Soc., European Econ. Assn. Assn. Applied Econometrics, Assn. for Forecasting Economies in Transition (pres. 1995-97), Lodz Sci. Assn. (chmn. sect. social scis. 1978-90, award 1993), Polish Acad. Sci. (corr. 1998—), Acad. Sci. of Ukraine (fgn. mem.). Avocations: travel, gardening, classical music. Home: Jaracza 65 m 9, 90-251 Lodz Poland Office: U Lodz Inst Econometrics/ Stats, Rewolucji 1905r 41, 90-214 Lodz Poland

WELISCH, EVA, physician, consultant; b. Steinmauern, Baden, Germany, May 23, 1961; m. Stefan Welisch, Sept. 21, 1987; 3 children. MD, Free U. Berlin, 1987. Asst. dr. in pediat. practice Minden, Germany, 1989-91; jr. house officer Otago Med. Sch., Wellington, New Zealand, 1951-52; resident U. Md. Med. Sys., Balt., 1952-94; fellow divsn. pediat. cardiology Heartctr., Bad Oeynhausen, Germany, 1994—. Fellow AAP/UVA; mem. Ruth-Tichauer Soc. (chair 1988—), Med. Bd. Westfalen-Lippe (cert. gen. pediats., pediat. cardiology). Office: Clinic Pediat Cardiology, Georgvstr 11, 32545 Bad Oeynhausen Nordhein-Westfalen, Germany

WELKE, ELTON GRINNELL, JR., publisher, writer; b. Berkeley, Calif., June 15, 1941; s. Elton Grinnell and Elsie Maud (Shattuck) W.; m. Anna Lange, July 28, 1963 (div. 1980); children: Allison Espy, Erik Grinnell; m. Bonnie Jean Lum, Jan. 24, 1981; 1 child, Erin Irene. BA in Zoology, U. Calif., Berkeley, 1962. Staff writer Sunset mag., Menlo Pk., Calif., 1962-65, assoc. editor, 1965-69, sr. editor, 1978-80; travel editor Better Homes & Gardens, Des Moines, 1969-71; mng. editor Apt. Life mag., Des Moines, 1971-72; exec. editor Sunset Spl. Interest mags., Menlo Pk., 1972-78; freelance editorial cons. San Francisco and Seattle, 1981-84; v.p., dir. Livingston & Co., Seattle, 1984-89; publisher Microsoft Press, 1989-98; chmn. North Wave Comms., Inc., Alaska, 1996—, Elton-Wolf Pub. Co., Seattle, 1999—; bd. dirs. Advance Online, Inc., Seattle; cons. Holland Am. Line, Seattle, 1983-84, Livingston & Co. Advt., Seattle, 1983-84. Author: How to Survive Being Alive, 1977, Place's to go With Children Around Puget Sound, 1987. Bd. dirs. Olympic Nat. Pk. Assocs., Washington, 1965-69, March of Dimes, Western Washington, 1987-92, chmn. campaign com., 1989-92. Recipient 1st Pl. award Washington Press Assn., 1985, 86, 88, WPA award, 1987. Mem. Soc. A. Travel Writers, PRSA, Internat. Assn. Bus. Communicators (Golden Quill award 1985), Washington Athletic Club, Safari Club, Alpha Delta Phi. Republican. Avocations: gardening, plant collecting, fly fishing, cattle ranching, Asian art. Home and Office: 11329 NE 103d St Kirkland WA 98033-5178

WELKER, BERNHARD GEORG, gynecologist, researcher; b. Herzogenaurach, Bavaria, Germany, Dec. 4, 1952; s. Rudolf and Pauline Welker; m. Claudia Christine Orben, Sept. 2, 1993. Approbation, U. Erlangen, Germany, 1980, MD, 1981; grad., U. Bonn, Germany, 1989. Lic. gynecologist and obstetrician, reproductive endocrinologist, prenatal ultrasonography specialist. Physician dept. surgery U. Bonn, 1980-81, physician dept. ob-gyn., 1986-89; physician dept. ob-gyn. U. Cologne, Germany, 1982-84; rsch. fellow U. So. Calif., 1984-85; gynecologist, obstetrician Outpatient Clinic, Bonn, 1990—; cons. Ministery of Pub. Health, Bonn, 1992—. Contbr. articles, papers and presentations to profl. jours. and procs. Rsch. fellow Deutsche Forschungsgemeinschaft, 1984-85. Mem. Wissenschaftliches Inst. Ärzte Deutschlands, European Soc. Human Reprodn. and Embryology, German Soc. for the Study of Fertility and Sterility, Deutsche Gesellschaft für Gynäkologie und Geburtshilfe, Am. Inst. for Ultrasound in Medicine, Am. Soc. Reproductive Medicine, Bundesverband Freier Berufe, N.Y. Acad. Scis. (life mem.), Deutsche Gesellschaft für Ultraschall in der Medizin. Roman Catholic. Avocations: music, painting. Home: Koenigstrasse 29, 53115 Bonn Germany

WELLEN, DANA THOMAS, engineering administrator; b. Warwick, R.I., Dec. 20, 1957; s. Robert G. and Thomasina (Morris) W.; m. Debra Ann Ciccarelli, July 18, 1987. AS, R.I. Jr. Coll., 1979. Electronic engring. technologist Cherry Semicondr. Corp., East Greenwich, R.I., 1979-88, adminstr. computer sys., computer programmer, 1987—, assoc. elec. engr., 1988—. Mem. Sun Users Group. Avocations: fishing, golf, bowling, photography. Home: 87 Helen Ave Coventry RI 02816-6347

WELLENS, DONALD LODEWIJK, pharmacologist; b. Koningshooikt, Antwerp, Belgium, May 11, 1936; s. Antoon Lodewijk and Margareta Maria (Voet) W.; m. Winifrieda Maria De Geeter, Aug. 1, 1961; children: Annemie, Inge, Geert. MSc in Biology, U. Leuven, Belgium, 1957; PhD, Nat. U. Belgium, 1964. Cert. sci. comm. officer. Lectr., demonstrator Sci. Palace World Expo, Brussels, 1958; prof. biology Cath. Flemish People U., Antwerp, 1959; lab. head UCB, Brussels, 1961-70, Janssen Rsch. Found., Beerse, Belgium, 1971-75; sci. comm. officer Janssen Pharmaceutica, Beerse, 1975—; lectr. Postgrad. Med. Courses, Belgium, 1976-90; lectr. Janssen Rsch. Found., 1975-95; session pres. Ann. Congress Angiology, Spain, 1978, Austria, 1980, France, 1986, host, organizer, Belgium, 1982. Author, editor: Calcium Entry Blockers in Cardiovascular and Cerebral Dysfunctions, 1984; assoc. editor Angiology, 1980-95; contbr. articles to profl. jours. Lectr. Citizen Amb. Program, China, 1985; head redaction Jour. Environ. Edn. Mens, 1991-96; organizer, jury mem. Thesis Awards, Belgium, 1992-96. Sgt. Med. Svcs., 1959-60. Recipient Popularisation of Sci. award Larousse Ency., U. Diepenbeek, 1983. Mem. Flemish Biologists Assn. (founder 1975). Avocations: environment and biology, dioxines, chess. Home: Stoktsebaan

23, 2350 Vosselaar Antwerp, Belgium Office: Janssen Pharmaceutica, Turnhoutseweg 30, 2340 Beerse Antwerp, Belgium

WELLER, CHERYL K., Internet service provider executive, educator; b. Rochester, Pa., Apr. 2, 1959; d. Glenn Stanley and Annabelle Lee (English) W. BA in English, Coll. Wooster, 1981; MA in English, Slippery Rock U., 1987; postgrad., Duquesne U. Instr. English Slippery Rock (Pa.) U., 1988-90; author centennial history Greek Cath. Union, 1990-92; instr. comms. Robert Morris Coll., 1992-96; owner, web-site developer Get-A-Site Internet Archs, Tucson, 1996—; instr. tech. writing C.C. Beaver County, 1997-98; tchr. St. Gregory Coll. Prep., 1998—. Editor: 20th Century History of Beaver County, 1989 (Best New Titles Pa. Mus. Commn. 1990); author: A Steadfast Commitment, 1993. Recipient Honorable Mention Sparrowgrass Poetry Forum, 1994; named Poet of Merit Am. Poetry Assn., 1989. Mem. NCTE, AAUW, N. Am. Soc. Study of Romanticism, Coll. English Assn. Avocations: antiques, cycling, tennis, racketball. Office: St Gregory Coll Prep English Dep 3231 N Craycroft Rd Tucson AZ 85712-5207

WELLER, DEBRA ANNE, elementary educator; b. New Orleans, Feb. 4, 1954; d. James Garretson and Elizabeth Gene (Blakely) Hyatt; m. Bruce Weller, June 15, 1974; children: Jenny, Todd. AA in Art, St. Petersburg Jr. Coll., 1974; BA in Art Edn., Glassboro State Coll., 1983; MS in Curriculum and Instrn., Nat. U., 1991. Cert. tchr. Profl. storyteller Mission Viejo, Calif., 1980—; tchr. Capistrano Unified Sch. Dist., San Juan Capistrano, Calif., 1989—; elem. tchg. asst. prin., stds. curriculum specialist Bathgate Elem., 1998—, stds. curriculum specialist; edn. dir. South Coast Storytellers Guild, Costa Mesa, Calif., 1990—; workshop presenter Orange County Dept. Edn., Costa Mesa, 1991—, Imagination Celebration, Irvine, Calif., 1993—; bd. mem. Calif. Kindergarten Assn. Author: (pamphlet) Image-U-Telling Clubs, 1995, also articles. Sec. Mission Viejo Cultural Com., 1995—. Cultural Arts grantee Dana Point (Calif.) Cultural Commn., 1993. Mem. NEA, Nat. Storytelling Network (Pacific region liaison), Calif. Tchrs. Assn., Calif. Kindergarten Assn. (bd. dirs.). Mormon. Avocations: calligraphy, composing, playing banjo, dulcimer and guitar.

WELLER, DOUGLAS LAFONTAINE, patent lawyer; b. Balt., Dec. 20, 1956; s. Weston Douglas and Jeanne Marie Weller; m. Frances Elizabeth Farrow, Sept. 7, 1991; 1 child, Weston John. BSEE, U. Calif., Davis, 1979; JD, U. Calif., Berkeley, 1983; MDiv, Western Sem., Portland, Oreg., 1990. Bar: Calif., 1983. Atty. Hewlett-Packard Co., Palo Alto, Calif., 1983-87; pvt. practice Santa Clara, Calif., 1987—. Prodr. TV show Search for Truth, San Jose, Calif., 2000—. Chmn., elder Valley Ch., 1999—. E-mail: patentcnsl@aol.com. Office: 431 Magnolia Ln Santa Clara CA 95051-5637

WELLER, KEITH A., lawyer, corporate officer; b. Camden, N.J.. AB, St. Joseph's U., 1984; JD, NYU, 1987. Bar: Pa. 1987, D.C. 1989, N.Y. 1991. Atty. Drinker Biddle & Reath, Phila., 1987-91, Brown & Wood LLP, N.Y.C., 1991-95; 1st v.p., assoc. gen. counsel Mitchell Hutchins Asset Mgmt. Inc., N.Y.C., 1995—; officer numerous investment cos. Articles editor NYU Jour. of Internat. Law and Politics, 1985-87. Mem. Union League of Phila.

WELLER, RAINER, language educator, writer; b. Schwaebisch, Gmuend, Germany, Aug. 16, 1938; s. Wilhelm and Anne (Froehlich) W.; m. Christel Hermanutz, Aug. 20, 1961; 1 child, Dirk. Student, U. Tuebingen, Germany, 1957-63. Cert. educator German and English lang. and lit. Tchr. U. Vienna, Austria, 1957-63; tchr. German and Eng. lang. Biberach, Germany, 1965; head dept. modern langs. Pestalozzi Gymnasium, Biberach, 1973—; collaborator, co-owner Weller House. Author: Sprachspiele, 1973, Luegen, Lauter Luegen, 1976, Spielend Texten, 1987, Von der Serie zum Gesamtkunstwerk, 1993, Kreative Spiele, 1999; contbg. author: (anthology) European Masters, Domestic Interiors, 1991. Home: Gartenstrasse 24, 88400 Biberach Germany Office: Pestalozzi Gymnasium, 88400 Biberach Germany

WELLER, ROBERT PAUL, anthropologist, consultant; b. Phila., Dec. 8, 1953; s. Sol. W. and Miriam D. W.; m. Alice E. Ingerson, Nov. 5, 1979; children: Ezra, Hannah. BA, Yale U., 1974; PhD, the Johns Hopkins U., 1980. Asst. prof. Duke U., Durham, N.C., 1980-86, asst. dean, 1986-90; rsch. assoc., assoc. prof. Boston U., 1990-96, prof., 1999—; cons. World Bank, Washington, 1994—, U.S. Dept. State, Washington, 1999, 00; adv. bd. Chinese Sociology and Anthropology, Canberra, Australia, 1992-95. Author: Unities and Diversities in Chinese Religion, 1987, Resistance, Chaos and Control in China, 1994, Alternate Civilities: Chinese Culture and the Prospects for Democracy, 1999; co-editor: Unruly Gods: Divinity and Society in China, 1996. Grantee NSF, Washington, 1977, Himalaya Found., Taiwan, 1998. Mem. Am. Anthropological Assn., Assn. Asian Studies (coun. mem. 1999-01). E-mail: rpweller@bu.edu. Office: ISEC Boston Univ 10 Lenox St Brookline MA 02446-4042

WELLER, THOMAS HUCKLE, physician, former educator; b. Ann Arbor, Mich., June 15, 1915; s. Carl V. and Elsie A. (Huckle) W.; m. Kathleen R. Fahey, Aug. 18, 1945; children: Peter Fahey, Nancy Kathleen, Robert Andrew, Janet Louise. A.B., U. Mich., 1936; M.S., 1937, LL.D. (hon.), 1956; M.D., Harvard, 1940; Sc.D., Gustavus Adolphus U., 1975, U. Mass., 1985; L.H.D., Lowell U., 1977. Diplomate Am. Bd. Pediatrics. Teaching fellow bacteriology Harvard Med. Sch., 1940-41, research fellow tropical medicine, pediatrics, 1947-48, instr. comparative pathology, tropical medicine, 1948-49, asst. prof. tropical pub. health Sch. Pub. Health, 1949-50, assoc. prof., 1950-54, Richard Pearson Strong prof. tropical pub. health, 1954-85, prof. emeritus, 1985—, head dept., 1954-81; intern bacteriology and pathology Children's Hosp., Boston, 1941; intern medicine Children's Hosp., 1942, asst. resident medicine, 1946, asst. dir. research div. infectious diseases, 1949-55; mem. commn. parasitic diseases Armed Forces Epidemiol. Bd., 1953-72, dir., 1953-59. Author sci. papers. Served to maj. M.C. AUS, 1942-46. Recipient E. Mead Johnson award for devel. tissue culture procedures in study virus diseases Am. Acad. Pediatrics, 1953, Kimble Methodology award, 1954, Nobel prize in physiology and medicine, 1954, George Ledlie prize, 1963, Weinstein Cerebral Palsy award, 1973, Stern Symposium honoree, 1972, Bristol award Infectious Diseases Soc. Am., 1980, Gold medal and diploma of honor U. Costa Rica, 1984, First Sci. Achievement award VZV Rsch. Found., 1993, Walter Reed medal Am. Soc. Tropical Medicine, 1996. Fellow Am. Acad. Arts and Scis., Royal Soc. Tropical Medicine & Hygiene (hon.); mem. AMA, NAS, Harvey Soc., Am. Epidemiological Soc., Am. Pediatric Soc., Assn. Am. Physicians, Soc. Exptl. Biology and Medicine, Am. Assn. Immunologists., Soc. Pediatric Research, Am. Soc. Tropical Medicine and Hygiene, Phi Beta Kappa, Sigma Xi, Alpha Omega Alpha. Home and Office: 56 Winding River Rd Needham MA 02492-1025

WELLING, HELEN GEERTRUIDA, architecture educator; b. Jersey City, Feb. 3, 1947; d. Hendrik Philippus Kelder and Johanna Catharina Dekker; m. Ib Welling, Jan. 13, 1969 (div. 1973); children: Casper, Jesper. BArch, Tech. U., Delft, The Netherlands, 1967; MARch, Royal Acad. Fine Arts, Copenhagen, 1972, PhD, 1987. Assoc. prof., chmn. arch. dept. Royal Acad. Fine Arts, 1975—, vis. asst. prof. Sch. Sculpture, 1978-79; assoc. prof. environ. design U. Calif., Berkeley, 1989; assoc. prof. Coll. Arch. and Urban Planning U. Mich., Ann Arbor, 1990-91; assoc. prof. Danish Internat. Studies U. Copenhagen, 1993; cons., rschr. Min. of Environ., Nat. Agy. for Protection of Monuments and Sites, Copenhagen, 1995—. Author: Modernism's Architecture--Fundamental Concepts and Perspectives on Preservation, 1999; contbr. articles to profl. publs. Bd. dirs. Danish Docomomo Working Party, 1996—. Mem. Danish Assn. Architects. Avocations: drawing, travel, gardening. Home: Dalmosevej 23, 2400 NV Copenhagen Denmark Office: Royal Acad Fine Arts, Philip de Langes Allé 10, 1435-K Copenhagen Denmark

WELLING, MICHAEL THEO, biologist; b. Osnabrueck, Germany, May 19, 1958; s. Theo and Hildegard W.; 1 child, Nefertari. Diploma (Biology), U. Mainz (Germany), 1984, PhD, 1990. Rsch. scientist Fed. Biol. Ctr. Agr. and Forestry, Darmstadt, Germany, 1985-93; head project "biol. locust control" Fed. Biol. Ctr. Agr. and Forestry, Darmstadt, 1993-95; exec. Senate Fed. Rsch. Ctrs., Braunschweig, Germany, 1995—. Author: Auswirkungen von Ackerschonstreifen, 1988; co-author: Regualtionsmoeglichkeiten von Schad-und Nutzarthropoden, 1991; editor-in-chief ForschungsReport, 1996—. Mem. Deutsche Phytomedizinische Gesellschaft, Deutsche Gesellschaft Allgemeine und Angewandte Entomologie. Office: Senate Fed Rsch Ctrs, Messeweg 11/12, D-38104 Braunschweig Germany

WELLINGS, VICTOR GORDON, retired judge; b. London, Eng., July 19, 1919; s. Gordon Arthur and Alice Adelaide (Scarrott) W.; m. Helen Margaret Jill Lovell, May 1, 1948; children: John Victor, Peter Henry, Christopher David. BA, Oxford (Eng.) U., 1940, MA, 1945; barrister at law, Gray's Inn, London, 1949. Pvt. practice barrister Oxford Circuit and London, 1949-73; mem. lands tribunal Eng., 1973-88, pres. lands tribunal, 1989-92, dep. high ct. judge, 1975-92. Editor: Woodfall on the Law of Landlord and Tenant, 1954-90; author books in field. Served with Indian Army, 1940-46. Named Queen's Counsel, 1973, hon. mem. Royal Instn. Chartered Surveyors, London, 1993. Mem. United Oxford and Cambridge Univ. Club. Mem. Ch. of Eng. Home: Cherry Tree Cottage, Whitchurch Hill, Near Reading RG8 7PT, England

WELLINGTON, KARL EVERARD, animal geneticist, researcher, agriculturist; b. Hopewell, Jamaica, Nov. 2, 1936; s. Phillip Nathaniel and Iris Viola (Scott) W.; m. Cecily Veronica Roye Wellington, Dec. 31, 1960 (widowed Feb. 6, 1989); children: Ruth, Delf, Heather, Max, Bryan; m. Bloom Stephanie Bourne Wellington, Aug. 15, 1992. BS, U. West Indies, St. Augustine, Trinidad, 1965, PhD, 1968. Agr. asst. Min. Agr., Kingston, Jamaica, 1957-65, agr. officer, 1965-79, dir. rsch. and devel., 1979-82; agr. dir. ALCAN, Mandeville, Jamaica, 1982-96; agriculturist pvt. practice, Jamaica, 1996—; cons. FAO/IICA, Trinidad, Brazil, 1980; part time lectr. and examiner U. West Indies, Trinidad, 1970—; dir. Jamaica Livestock Assn., Jamaica, 1991—, Agr. Devel. Corp., Jamaica, 1985—. Co-author: Fertilizer For Pastures, 1991; author, co-author: (rsch. station bulletins) Development of Jamaica Hope, Red Poll, and Brahman, 1972-83; contbr. rsch. papers to profl. jours. Patron Golden Eagle Marching Band, Mandeville, 1990-97; mem. West Indians Assn. Australia, Sydney, 1992—, Vet. Tribunal Jamaica, 1993-95; bd. mem. Regional Health Auth., Southern Jamaica, 1997—. Recipient Grace Kennedy award for sci. and tech. in Agr., Jamaica Soc. for Sci. and Tech., 1991, Silver Musgrave medal Inst. Jamaica, 1993, Order of Distinction, Jamaica Govt., 1993. Mem. Jamaican Soc. for Agr. Sci., British Soc. of Animal Sci., N.Y. Acad. Sci. Baptist. Avocations: farming, fishing, cricket, indoor games. Home: Knockpatrick PO, Daley's Grove, Mandeville Jamaica

WELLINK, NOUT, bank executive. Pres. Ctrl. Bank of the Netherlands, Amsterdam, 1997—. Office: De Nederlandsche Bank nv, Westeinde 1 POB 98, 1000 AB Amsterdam The Netherlands

WELLISCH, DIETMAR FRANZ, public finance, taxation educator, tax consultant; b. Sigmaringen, Germany, Dec. 26, 1960. Diploma in econs., U. Tübingen, Germany, 1988, PhD in Econs., 1991; habilitation econs., U. Dortmund, Germany, 1994. Rsch. asst. U. Tübingen, 1988-92, U. Dortmund, 1992-94; prof. pub. fin. and taxation U. Dresden, Germany, 1994-2000; prof. bus. taxation U. Magdeburg, Germany, 2000—; vis. asst. prof. Ind. U., Bloomington, 1992. Author: Intertemporale und internationale Aspekte staatlicher Budgetdefizite, 1991, Dezentrale Finanzpolitik bei hoher Moblilität, 1995, Theory of Public Finance in a Federal State, 2000, Public Economics I: Market Failures, 2000, Public Economics II: Theory of Taxation, 2000, Public Economics III: Public Debt, 2000. Mem. Verein für Socialpolitik. E-mail: Astrid.Bentlage@ww.uni-magdeburg.de, Dietmar.Wellisch@ww.uni-magdeburg.de. Office: Otto von Guerick Univ, Magdeburg PF 4120, 39016 Magdeburg Germany

WELLMAN, MICHAEL ALLEN, SR., executive search executive, consultant; b. Newton, Mass., May 29, 1953; s. John Garland and Charlottie Abbott Wellman; m. Dorothy Eleanor Trefts (div.); m. Lynn Grube Wellman, Nov. 12, 1983; children: Michael Allen Jr., Benjamin Robert, Zachary John. BS in Commerce, U. Va., 1975, MBA, 1979. Assoc. Chem. Bank, N.Y.C., 1975-76; cons. Bain & Co., Boston, 1979-81; pres., COO Lakewood Plantation Co., Columbia, S.C., 1981-84; prin. Johnson, Smith & Knisely, N.Y.C., 1984-89; dir. Spencer Stuart, Atlanta, 1989-91; cons. BM&W, Stamford, Conn., 1991; pres. Jefferson Ptnrs., Darien, Conn., 1991-92; v.p. Korn/Ferry Internat., N.Y.C., 1992-95, mng. dir. N.Y., 1996-98, mng. dir. N.E. region, 1998-99, pres. global specialties, 1999—, also bd. dirs. Mem. County Club of Darien, DeBordieu Club, The Sky Club, Assn. of Exec. Search Cons. Republican. Presbyterian. Avocations: golf, travel. Office: Korn/Ferry Internat 200 Park Ave Fl 37 New York NY 10166-3702

WELLS, ADRIAN, psychologist, researcher; b. Doncaster, England, Feb. 2, 1962; s. Kenneth Arthur and Marion (Johnson) W. BS with honors, Aston U., Birmingham, 1984, PhD, 1987; MS, Leeds U., 1989; Diploma, U. Pa., Phila., 1990. Chartered clin. psychologist. Rsch. fellow U. Pa., Phila., 1989-90; sr. rsch. clin. psychologist U. Oxford, 1990-95; sr. lectr., cons. U. Manchester, 1995—; BABCP rep. U.K. Coun. Psychotherapy, London, 1992-93; mem. steering group U. Oxford, 1992-95; assoc. editor Behav. Cognitive Psychotherapy, 1994—. Author: (books) Attention & Emotion: A Clinical Perspective, 1994, (with G. Matthews) Cognitive Therapy of Anxiety Disorders, 1997, Emotional Disorders and Metacognition: Innovative Cognitive Therapy, 2000, Bulimia Nervosa: A Self-Help Cognitive Therapy Programme, 2000; contbr. numerous articles to profl. jours. Mem. British Psychological Soc. (assoc. fellow), British Assn. Behav. & Cognitive Psychotherapy. Avocations: watercolour painting, music, woodworking, classic cars. Office: U Manchester-Dept Clin Psychology-Manchester Royal Infirmary, Oxford Rd, M13 9WL Manchester England

WELLS, BENJAMIN GLADNEY, lawyer; b. St. Louis, Nov. 13, 1943; s. Benjamin Harris and Katherine Emma (Gladney) W.; m. Nancy Kathryn Harpster, June 7, 1967; children: Barbara Gladney, Benjamin Harpster. BA magna cum laude, Amherst (Mass.) Coll., 1965; JD cum laude, Harvard U., 1968. Bar: Ill. 1968, Tex. 1973, U.S. Tax Ct. 1973, U.S. Ct. Claims 1975, U.S. Ct. Appeals (5th cir.) 1981, U.S. Dist. Ct. (so. dist.) Tex. 1985, U.S. Dist. Ct. (we. dist.) Tex. 1993. Assoc. Kirkland & Ellis, Chgo., 1968-69; assoc. to ptnr. Baker Botts, L.L.P. (formerly Baker & Botts, L.L.P.), Houston, 1973—. Contbr. articles to profl. jours. Mem. planned giving com. St. John's Sch., Houston (chmn. 1987-98); Harvard Legal Aid Bureau, 1966-68. Capt. U.S. Army, 1969-72. Fellow Am. Coll. Tax Counsel; mem. ABA (vice chair corp. tax com. sect. on taxation 1999—), Houston Tax Roundtable (pres. 1994-95), The Forest Club, The Houston Club, Phi Beta Kappa. Presbyterian. Office: Baker Botts LLP One Shell Plaza 910 Louisiana St Ste 3330 Houston TX 77002-4916

WELLS, CLAUDIA MAE ELLIS, nutritionist, educator; b. Reform, Ala., Apr. 25, 1911; d. Leven Handy and Mary (Sibley) Ellis; m. John Walter Wells, Sept. 10, 1935; 1 child, John Walter. BS in Home Econs., U. Ala., 1931, MS, 1933. Registered dietitian. Dietitian U. Ala., 1931-33; tchr. home econs., sci. Ala. high schs., 1942-50; sci. tchr. Marietta (Ga.) High Sch., 1950-53, head sci. dept., 1953-56; instr. biology U. Ga. Ctr., Marietta, 1953-56; asst. prof. nutrition and food sci. U. Ky., 1956-76; organizer Ga. Sci. Fairs, 1954-56, Lafayette (Ky.) High Sch. Band Club, Ctrl. Ky. Youth Orch. Assn., 1956-58; presenter papers in field. Author: History of Aiken Garden Club, 1990, Laborers Together, 1995, History of Pickens County Alabama and Families, 5 biographies, 1998; contbr. articles to profl. jours. Active ARC, YWCA, PTA, Ala., Ga., Ky.; sponsor Bapt. Student Union U. Ky., 1964; assoc. Young People's Dir., mem. Bapt. Tng. Union, Cmty. Missions divsn. Woman's Missionary Union, chmn., 1963-64, Elkhorn (Ky.) Assn.; tchr. ladies' Sunday Sch. class Aiken (S.C.) 1st Bapt. Ch., 1976-98, pres. ch. tng. group, 1978, 80, chm. nominating com., 1978-79; pres. Aiken Garden Club, 1978-80; active Aiken Garden Coun., 1978-80, parliamentarian, 1979-84; vol. Multiple Sclerosis Soc., 1980; pres. Sunshine Club, 1988-90, mem. sr. adult choir, 1990—; active Nat. Arbor Day Found., 1995—. Named Honorable Order of Ky. Col., 1976; honoree 50th Anniversary of Coll. Home Econs., U. Ala., 1981; named to Faculty Hall of Fame, U. Ky. Mem. NEA, Am. Ednl. Assn., Ga. Edn. Assn., Biology Tchrs. Am., Inst. Technologists, Inst. Food Technologists (historian Bluegrass sect. 1965-71), Am. Home Econs. Assn., Ky. Home Econs. Assn., Am. Dietetic Assn., Ky. Dietetic Assn. (pub. rels. chmn. 1968-71, co-editor bull. 1971-75), Bluegrass Dietetic Assn. (v.p. 1963-64, pres. 1964-65), Sigma Xi. Avocations: flower and vegetable gardening. Home: 121 Wexford Dr Apt 104 Anderson SC 29621-1799

WELLS, DAMON, JR., investment company executive; b. Houston, May 20, 1937; s. Damon and Margaret Corinne (Howze) W. BA magna cum laude, Yale U., 1958; BA, Oxford U., 1964, MA, 1968; PhD, Rice U., 1968. Owner, CEO Damon Wells Interests, Houston, 1958—; pres. Damon Wells Found., Houston, 1993—. Author: Stephen Douglas: The Last Years, 1857-61, 1971 (Tex. Writer's Roundup prize 1971), paperback edit., 1990. Bd. dirs. Child Guidance Ctr. of Houston, 1970-73; trustee Christ Ch. Cathedral Endowment Fund, 1970-73, 84-88, chmn., 1987-88, Kinkaid Sch., 1972-86, Kinkaid Sch. Endowment Fund, 1981-86; hon. friend of Somerville Coll., Oxford U., 1988—; mem. Sr. Common Room, Pembroke Coll., Oxford U., 1972—; trustee Camp Allen retreat of Episc. Diocese of Tex., 1976-78; founding bd. dirs. Brit. Inst. U.S., 1979-80; mem. pres.'s coun. Tex. A&M U., 1983-89. Named Hon. Comdr. Most Excellent Order of Brit. Empire by Her Majesty Queen Elizabeth II, 1991, Outstanding Alumnus Yr. by Kinkaid Sch., 1994; fellow Jonathan Edwards Coll. (assoc.), Yale U., 1982—, Sterling fellow Yale U., 2000—, hon. fellow Pembroke Coll., Oxford U., 1984—. Mem. English-Speaking Union (nat. dir. 1970-72, v.p. Houston br. 1966-73), Coun. Fgn. Rels., Houston Country Club, Houston Club, Yale Club (N.Y.C.), United Oxford and Cambridge U. Club (London), Cosmos Club (Washington), Buck's Club (London), Coronado Club (Houston), Little Ship Club (London). Episcopalian. Fax: 713-528-4832. Home: 5555 Del Monte Dr Houston TX 77056-4100 Office: 2001 Kirby Dr Ste 806 Houston TX 77019-6088

WELLS, DAVID ARTHUR, German language educator; b. Ware, Eng., Apr. 26, 1941; s. Arthur William and Rosina Elizabeth (Jones) W. BA, Cambridge (Eng.) U., 1963, MA, PhD, 1967. Asst. lectr. in German U. Southampton, Eng., 1966-67; lectr. in German U. Southampton, 1967-69, Bedford Coll., U. London, 1969-74; prof. German Queen's U., Belfast, 1974-87; prof. German Birkbeck Coll., U. London, 1987—, head Ctr. for Lang. and Lit., 1993—. Author numerous books, monographs and articles on medieval European lit. Mem. Modern Humanities Rsch. Assn. (hon. sec. 1969—), Internat. Fedn. for Modern Langs. and Lits. (sec.-gen. 1981—). Home: 128 Belgrave Rd, London SW1V 2BL, England Office: Birkbeck Coll Dept German, Malet St, London WC1E 7HX, England*

WELLS, DAVID MERLIN, lawyer; b. Decatur, Ill., Jan. 30, 1943; s. Arthur Merlin and Louise (Keller) W.; children: Melanie Adair, David Weston, Todd Ashley. BA, Northwestern U., 1965; JD, Georgetown U., 1971. Assoc. Pillsbury, Madison & Sutro, San Francisco, 1971-75; ptnr. Graham & James, San Francisco, 1975-76, Erickson, Zerfas & Adams, L.A., Jeddah, Saudi Arabia, 1976-78, Morrison & Foerster, San Francisco & Jeddah, 1978-81, Law Offices Dr. Mujahid M. Al-Sawwaf, Jeddah, 1981—; speaker on middle east law to profl. seminars, confs. Contbr. articles to profl. jours. Mem. ABA, Calif. Bar Assn., Internat. Bar Assn., Southwestern Legal Inst. (Adv. Coun. 1988-92). Home and Office: Law Offices Dr M Al-Sawwwaf, PO Box 5840, Jeddah 21432, Saudi Arabia

WELLS, FAY GILLIS, writer, lecturer, broadcaster, aviation historian; b. Mpls., Oct. 15, 1908; d. Julius Howells and Minnie Irene (Shafer) Gillis; student Mich. State Coll., 1925-28; m. Linton Wells, Apr. 1, 1935 (dec. 1976); 1 son, Linton Wells, II. Free-lance corr. in USSR for N.Y. Herald Tribune and AP, 1930-34, aviation mags., 1930-36; fgn. corr. Italy-Ethiopian War, N.Y. Herald Tribune, 1935-36, spl. Hollywood corr., 1937-38; contbr. book revs. Saturday Review, 1939-42; dep. chief of mission for U.S. Comml. Co., Portuguese W. Africa, 1942-46, syndicated boating columnist, 1960-62; White House corr. Storer Broadcasting Co., 1964-77; aircraft pilot, 1929; designer yacht interiors Alta Grant Samuels, 1958-62; now co-chmn. Internat. Forest of Friendship; hon. co-chmn. Nat. Air Heritage Council; mem. com. to select 1st journalist in space, 1985—; judge of trophy winners Nat. Air Space Mus., 1988—. Recipient Sherman Fairchild Internat. Air Safety Writing award, 1965, Amelia Earhart medal, 1967, Golden Age of Flight award Nat. Air and Space Mus.-Dept. Transp., 1984, Elder Statesman of Aviation, 1984, award Internat. Conf. Women Engrs. and Scientists, 1984, 99s Spirit of Inspiration award 1996, Lifetime Achievement award Women in Aerospace Scis., 1996, Disting. Achievements award San Diego Aerospace Mus., 1997, Disting. Alumni award Elizabeth N.J. Edn. Coun., 1997, Pres.'s Personal award of excellence, 1997, Inspiration award Internat. Orgn. Women Pilots, 1997, Ester Tufty Meml. award Am. Women in Radio and TV, 1998; named to Hall of Fame Women In Aviation Pioneers, 1992; Honors award Women in Aviation, 1990; asteroid # 4820 named in her honor, 1995. Mem. Aviation/Space Writers Assn., Am. Women in Radio and TV (pres. Washington chpt. 1968-69, CBS Charlotte Friel award 1972), Radio-TV Corrs. Assn., White House Corrs. Assn. (hon. life), Aircraft Owners and Pilots Assn., The Ninety-Nines (charter mem.; Most Valuable Pilot, Washington chpt. 1975), OX5 Aviation Pioneers (Outstanding Woman of Year award 1972), Internat. Soc. Woman Geographers, Broadcast Pioneers, Zonta Internat. (life hon.), DAR, Nat. Aero. Assn. (named elder statesman 1984). Clubs: Overseas Press (founding mem. 1939), Nat. Assn. Female Execs., Nat. Press, Internat. Forest Friendship (co-gen. chmn. 1976—, Fay Gillis Wells Gazebo dedicated 1991). Home: 4211 Duvawn St Alexandria VA 22310-2024

WELLS, FRANCIS CHARLES, cardiothoracic surgeon consultant, lecturer; b. Pontesbury, Shropshire, U.K., Feb. 20, 1950; s. Frank and Violet Mary (Mold) W.; m. Helen Marjorie Stubbs Wells; children: Joanna Claire, Nicholas Charles. BSc with honors, U. London, 1972; MB, BS, Charing Cross Hosp. Med. Sch., 1975; M in Surgery, U. London, 1985; MA, Cambridge U., 1996. House surgeon Charing Cross Hosp., London, 1976-77, lectr. in Anatomy, 1977; casualty officer Kings Coll. Hosp., London, 1977; resident surgical officer Brompton Hosp., London, 1978; registrar in surgery Addenbrookes Hosp., Cambridge, 1979; sr. registrar Cardiac Surgery Brompton Hosp., London, 1982-83; sr. rsch. fellow U. Ala., Birmingham, 1984; cons. Cardiac and Thoracic Surgeon Papworth Hosp., Cambridge, 1985—; assoc. lectr. U. Cambridge, U.K., 1985—; chmn. Thoracic Mgmt. Group, Papworth Hosp., 1991—. Author: Thoracic Surgical Techniques, 1990, Mitral Valve Disease, 1995; contbr. articles to profl. jours. and to design of surgical devices. Smith and Nephew Surgical Rsch. fellow, 1984; Hunterian Prof. Surgery, Royal Coll. Surgeon, London, 1985. Fellow Royal Coll. Surgeons; mem. Royal Soc. Medicine. Avocations: painting, pencil sketching, playing piano, armchair motor racing. Home: 40 West St, Great Gransden SG193AU, England Office: Papworth Everard, Papworth Hosp Dept CD Surg, CB3 8RE Cambridge England

WELLS, FRANCIS OWEN, physician; b. London, Mar. 7, 1936; s. Raymond Owen and Dorothy May (Waldron) W.; m. Janet Edith Tufton, May 14, 1960; children: Catherine Jane, Henrietta Claire. MBBS, London Hosp., 1960. FRCP, FRCPE, FFPM, London. Med. registrar West Suffolk Hosp., St. Edmunds, U.K., 1960-62; prin. ptnr. Ipswich, U.K., 1962-79; under-sec. Brit. Med. Assn., U.K., 1979-86; med. dir. Assn. of the Brit. Pharm. Industry, London, 1986-96; cons. Medico-Legal Investigations, 1996—, Howard Found. Rsch., Cambridge, 1996—. Editor: (books) Fraud and Misconduct in Medical Research, 1994, 2d edit. 1996, The Textbook of Pharmaceutical Medicine, 1993, 2d edit. 1995; contbr. articles to profl. jours. Councillor Tuddenham Parish Coun., Ipswich, 1996. Travel fellowship Geigy Pharm., Japan, 1978; hon. lectureship U. Surrey, 1994—. Fellow Royal Soc. Medicine, Brit. Med. Assn.; mem. Soc. Pharm. Medicine (chmn. 1995—), Assn. Rsch. Ethics Coms. (treas. 1999—). Mem. Ch. of England. Avocations: indsl. archaeology, classical music, art galleries.

WELLS, HUGH ALBERT, retired judge; b. Shelby, N.C., June 8, 1922; s. Charles Hudson and Tonce Walker Wells; m. Virginia DiaFabilo, Feb. 3, 1945 (div. Aug. 1958); children: Kathleen Mary, Hugh A. Jr.; m. Anne Hubner, June 30, 1962; 1 child, Joseph Walker; stepchildren: Rawell C. Cloninger Jr., Debi Cloninger McDaniel, Stephanie Cloninger Stadler, Michael Charles, Beth Cloninger Mayo. LLB, U. N.C., 1952. Bar: N.C. 1952. Gen. law practice Shelby, N.C., 1952-60, Atlanta, 1960-63, Raleigh, N.C., 1963-70; appt. N.C. Utilities Commn., 1969, 73-75; v.p. gen. coun. N.C. Elec. Inc., 1975-76; spl. counsel to joint utilities rev. com. N.C. Gen. Assembly, 1976-77; exec. dir. Pub. Staff N.C. Utilities Commn., 1977-79; judge N.C. Ct. Appeals, 1979-92; ret.; chmn. N.C. Utilities Commn., 1992-96; ret., 1996. Democrat. Methodist. Avocations: reading, music. Home: 310 Lamar Ave Shelby NC 28150-5468

WELLS, JAMES T., development and brokerage executive, consultant; b. Salt Lake City, Mar. 24, 1939; s. Calvin Young and Arvilla (Thomas) W.; m.

Luana P., July 7, 1967; children: Rebecca Ann, Elizabeth Marie, Rachel Diane, Jamie Danielle, Eden Michelle, Don Carlos, Natalie Rose. BA in Econs. and Bus. Law, U. Utah, 1964, MBA in Fin. and Acctg., 1966. Cert. real estate broker, Calif. Corp. staff fin. analyst Radio Corp. Am., N.Y.C., 1966-67; divsn. overhead budget adminstrn. Radio Corp. Am., Van Nuys, Calif., 1967-68; cons. KMPG Peat Marvick LLP (CPA), L.A., 1968-69; mgr. 3d party leasing and fin. Xerox Data Sys., Inc., El Segundo, Calif., 1970-72; v.p. fin. Holstein Industries, Inc., Costa Mesa, Calif., 1972-76; CEO, pres. Svc. Sta. and Mini Mart Sales, Inc., Costa Mesa, Calif., 1976-2000; pres. Mesa Verde Cmty., Inc., Calif., 1991-94. Author: Recent Real Estate Trends, 1966. Mem. Nat. Assn. Realtors, Calif. Assn. Realtors. Republican. Mem. LDS Ch. Avocation: church ministry. Office: Svc Sta and Mini Mart Sales Inc PO Box 3491 Costa Mesa CA 92628-3491

WELLS, JOHNNY ALLEN, electronics engineer; b. Poplar Bluff, Mo., Aug. 6, 1962; s. John Derrell Wells and Joy Marie hilterbrand; m. Gina K. Faries, Dec. 25, 1980 (div. jan. 1991); children: Kristen Kaye, Julie Anne; m. Michele Lee Brown, 2000. Logistics engr. Emerson Electric, St. Louis, 1987-90; sr. field svc. engr. Electronics and Space Corp., St. Louis, 1990-97; sr. engr. specialist Sys. and Electronics Inc., St. Louis, 1997—. With USN, 1980-86. Mem. Engrs. Club of Emerson Electric, Engrs. Club of Electronics & Space Corp. (sec. 1995-96). Avocations: reading, computers, radio, guitar and music, camping. Home: 5121 Hunning Rd High Ridge MO 63049-3009 Office: Systems and Electronics Inc 201 Evans Ln Saint Louis MO 63121-1126

WELLS, JONATHAN CHARLES KINGDON, nutritionist, educator; b. Winchester, Hampshire, U.K., May 14, 1968; s. Francis Roland and Elizabeth Peternel (McCall) W. BA in Social Anthropology, U. Cambridge, Eng., 1990; MPhil in Biol. Anthropology, U. Cambridge, 1991, PhD in Biol. Anthropology, 1994. Rsch. fellow Dunn Nutrition Unit, Cambridge, 1994-97; rsch. fellow Inst. Child Health, London, 1997-98, lectr., 1998—. Contbr. articles to profl. jours. Avocations: music, art, literature, hill walking, various sports. Office: Childhood Nutrition Rsch Ctr, 30 Guilford St, London WC1N 1EH, England

WELLS, KEIKO, humanities educator, folksong researcher. BA, Tsuda Coll, Tokyo, 1981, MA, 1983. Instr. Shugitsu H.S., Okayama, Japan, 1983-84; asst. prof. Ehime U., Matsuyama, Japan, 1987-92; assoc. prof. Ritsumeikan U., Kyoto, Japan, 1992—; v.p. Wells English-Math. Acad., Okayama, 1984-87. Contbr. articles to profl. jours., chpt. to book. Grantee Japan Edn. Min., Tokyo, 1993, 94, 97, 98, 99, Japan Railroad Co. Found., Tokyo, 1993, Ritsumeikan U., 1995. Mem. Japan English Lit. Soc., Am. Folklore Soc., Am. Studies Soc. Office: Ritsumeikan U, 56-1 Tojinkita, Kita-ku Kyoto 603-8577, Japan

WELLS, LIONELLE DUDLEY, psychiatrist, educator; b. Winnsboro, S.C., Nov. 22, 1921; s. Lionelle Dudley and Mary Wells; m. Mildred Wohltman, June 28, 1945 (dec. 1986); children: Lucia, Lionelle, John, Diane; m. Eilene Bromfield, Sept. 23, 1989. BS, U. S.C., 1943; MD, Med. U. S.C., 1945; grad., Boston Psychoanalytic Inst., 1960. Diplomate Am. Bd. Psychiatry and Neurology; lic. physician, S.C., Mass.; cert. in psychoanalysis. Intern Met. Hosp., N.Y.C., 1945-46; psychiatry resident VA Hosp., North Little Rock, Ark., 1948-50; asst. resident in Psychiatry Graylyn, Bowman-Gray Sch. Medicine, Winston-Salem, 1950-51; instr. psychiatry U. Ark., 1949-51, Mass. Gen. Hosp./Harvard Med. Sch., Boston, 1955-69; clin. instr. psychiatry Harvard Med. Sch., Boston, 1969-78; lectr. psychiatry Boston U. Sch. Medicine, 1977-98; asst. clin. prof. psychiatry Harvard Med. Sch., 1978-93; lectr. psychiatry Tufts U. Med. Sch., Boston, Mass., 1981—; cons. staff Newton-Wellesley Hosp., Newton, Mass., 1983-95, hon. staff, 1995—; assoc psychiatrist Mass. Gen. Hosp., Boston, 1975-82, psychiatrist, 1982-96, sr. psychiatrist, 1996—; courtesy staff Waltham Deaconess Hosp. and Med. Ctr., 1977-99; cons. Edith Nourse Rogers Meml. VA Med. Ctr., Bedford, Mass., 1966—; cons. in psychiatry VA Outpatient Clinic, Boston, 1959—, others in past; chmn. bd., chief exec. officer Bay State Health Care, 1984-91; nominating com. Am. Managed Care and Rev. Assn., 1988-89, others. Contbr. articles to profl. jours. Recipient Robert Wilson award, Med. U. S.C., 1943, 44. Fellow Am. Coll. Physician Execs., Am. Psychiat. Assn. (life); mem. AMA, Am. Psychoanalytic Assn., Am. Assn. Geriatric Psychiatry, Internat. Gero-Psychiatry Assn., Mass. Psychiat. Soc., Mass. Med. Soc., Boston Psychoanalytic Soc. and Inst., Boston Soc. for Gerontologic Psychiatry (mem. chmn. and dir. 1974-76). Home and Office: 73 Rolling Ln Weston MA 02493-2474

WELLS, MARTIN JOHN, zoology educator; b. London, Aug. 24, 1928; s. Frank Richard and Dora Margaret (Gibbons) W.; m. Joyce Finlay, Sept. 8 1953; children: Dominic John, Simon Finlay. BA, U. Cambridge, England, 1952, DS, 1966. Asst. Stazione Zoologica, Naples, 1953-56; demonstrator zoo dept. U. Cambridge, 1959-64; tutor Churchill Coll., Cambridge, 1962-75, dir. studies, 1962-85; lectr. U. Cambridge, 1964-76; reader zoology zoo dept. U. Cambridge, 1976—; fellow emeritus Churchill Coll., 1995—. Author: Brain and Behavior in Cephalopods, 1962, You, Me, and the Animal World, 1964, Lower Animals, 1968, Octopus: Physiology and Behavior of an Advanced Invertebrate, 1978, Civilization and the Limpet, 1998; contbr. over 130 articles to sci. jours. With Royal Air Force, 1947-49. Trinity Coll. fellow, Cambridge, 1956-59; recipient Silver medal Zool. Soc. London, 1968. Fellow Cambridge Philos. Soc.; mem. Royal Highland Yacht Club, Royal Yachting Assn., Cambridge Drawing Soc. Avocations: painting, yachting, carpentry, fishing. Home: The Bury Home End Fulbourn, Cambridge CB1 BS, England Office: U Cambridge, Zoo Dept, Downing St, Cambridge England

WELLS, PATRICIA TRENT, auditor; b. N.Y.C., June 29, 1943; d. Ralph Harold and Lorraine Mary (Parker) Trent; m. Peter Scoville Wells, Dec. 8, 1973. BA in History, Marymount Manhattan Coll., N.Y.C., 1992; MA in Folk Art Studies, NYU, 1999. Ops. mgr. customer svc. Bell Atlantic, N.Y.C., 1970-84, mktg. mgr., 1984-90, assoc. dir. internal auditing, 1990—, supervising sr. auditor, 1990—. Mem. Marymount Manhattan Coll. Adv. Bd. Mem. Sovereign Mil. Order of Temple of Jerusalem, N.Y. Jr. League, Inst. of Internal Auditors. Home: 449 E 78th St New York NY 10021-1649 Office: Bell Atlantic Corp 1095 Ave Americas New York NY 10036

WELLS, RAYMOND O'NEIL, JR., mathematics educator, researcher; b. Dallas, June 12, 1940; s. Raymond O. and Hazel (Rand) W.; m. Rena Schwarze, Aug. 1, 1963; children: Richard Andrew, René Michael. BA, Rice U., 1962; MS, NYU, 1964, PhD, 1965. Asst. prof. math. Rice U., Houston, 1965-69, assoc. prof., 1969-74, prof. math., 1974-2000, prof. edn., 1993-2000; chmn. dept. math., 1976-79; chmn. dept. edn. Rice U., Houston, 1994-98, dir. sch. math. project, 1987-2000, dir. computational math. lab., 1990-2000, prof. math emeritus, 2000—; vis. asst. prof. Brandeis U., Waltham, Mass., 1967-68; vis. prof. U. Göttingen, Germany, 1974-75, U. Colo., Boulder, 1983-84, U. Bremen, Germany, 1995-96, Internat. Univ. Bremen, 1998—; adj. prof. cmty. medicine Baylor Coll. Medicine, 1994—; active Inst. for Advanced Study, Princeton, N.J., 1970-71, 79-80; exch. visitor NAS, Sofia, Bulgaria, 1984; planning com. Internat. U., Bremen, 1997-99. Author: Differential Analysis on Complex Manifolds, 1973, Mathematics in Civilization, 1973, Twister Geometry and Field Theory, 1990, Wavelet Analysis: The Scaleable Structure of Information, 1998; editor: Mathematical Heritage of Herman Weyl, 1989, (book series) Expositions in Mathematics, 1988—; contbr. numerous articles to sci. jours. Pres. Stages Repertory Theater, Houston, 1989-90. Recipient Alexander von Humboldt Sr. U.S. Scientist award U. Göttingen, 1974-75; Fulbright fellow, 1968, Guggenheim fellow, 1974. Fellow AAAS (coun. 1989—); mem. Am. Math. Soc. (coun., editor 1978-88), Cosmos Club Washington. Home: Wilmannsberg 50, 28757 Bremen Germany Office: Internat Univ Bremen, PO Box 750561, 28725 Bremen Germany

WELLS, ROBERT HARTLEY, chemistry professional; b. Springfield, Mass., Mar. 23, 1926; s. Cecil and Anna (Coates) W.; m. Mary G. Frinzi, May 30 1952 (wid. May 1969); children: Michael J., Brian H., Donald L.; m. Alice G. Asplund, June 20, 1970. BS in Chemistry, U. Maine, 1948, MS in Chemistry, 1950. Instr. in chemistry Lafayette Coll., Easton, Pa., 1950-51; rsch. chemist Celanese Corp., Summit, N.J., 1952-56, S.D. Warren, Westbrook, Maine, 1956-58; epoxy rsch. engr. CIBA Corp., Toms River, N.J., 1958-66; sect. head Foundry Products Borden Cem., Bainbridge, N.Y., 1966-70; sr. rsch. engr. Amoco Chem., Naperville, Ill., 1970-73; product mgr. epoxies Wilmington (Del.) Chem., 1973-76; product mgr. epoxy resins AZS Corp., Lakeland, Fla., 1976-83; cons. chemist Lakeland, 1983—. Patentee in field; contbr. articles to profl. jours.; photographer exhibits in field. Mem. Toms River Sch. Bd., 1962-66, Garden State Symphony, Toms River, 1963-66; pres. Toms River Jaycees, 1962; photographer SPCA, Lakeland, 1993—; vol. photographer Fla. Presbyn. Homes, 1997—. Sgt. U.S. Army, 1944-46. Mem. AAAS, Am. Chem. Soc., Photographic Soc. (mem. chmn. 1993-95, Merit Svc. award 1994), Photographic Soc. Am., Am. Contract Bridge League, Bartow Camera Club (pres. 1988-91), Sigma Xi, Kappa Phi Kappa. Republican. Methodist.

WELLS, ROGER STANLEY, software engineer; b. Seattle, Apr. 13, 1949; s. Stanley A. and Margaret W. BA, Whitman Coll., 1971; postgrad., U. Tex., Austin, 1973-74; BS, Oreg. State U., 1977. Software evaluation engr. Tektronix, Beaverton, Oreg., 1979-83; computer engr. Aramco, Dhahran, Saudi Arabia, 1983-84; software engr. Conrac Corp., Clackamas, Oreg., 1984-85, Duarte, Calif., 1985; software analyst Lundy Fin. Systems, San Dimas, Calif., 1986-89; contract software analyst for various orgns. Seattle, 1989-92; sr. project engr. Illuminet, Olympia, Wash., 1993-2000, mem. Exec. Yr. 2000 com., 1998-99; configuration mgr. New Edge Networks, Vancouver, Wash., 2000—; bd. dirs. The Lydia Whitney Found., Collinsville, Conn. Bd. dirs. The Sci. Fiction Mus., Salem, Oreg., 1993—; co-founder, bd. dirs., pres. Oreg. Sci. Fiction Conv., 1979-81. Mem. IEEE, Nat. Speakers Assn., Am. Philatelic Soc., Nat. Assn. Parliamentarians, Am. Inst. Parliamentarians (chpt. v.p. 1996-97, pres. 1997-98), Fantasy Amateur Press Assn., Portland Sci. Fiction Soc., N.W. Sci. Fiction Soc., Internat. Platform Assn. (2d place Monologue contest 1997, conv. com. 1998-99, bd. govs. 1999—), Mensa, Assn. Computing Machinery, L.A. Sci. Fantasy Soc., Melbourne (Australia) Sci. Fiction Club, Toastmasters Internat. (pres. 1980, v.p. edn. 1994-95, area gov. 1994-95, dist. 32 parliamentarian 1996-99). Achievements include designing software program to transfer billing records for regional telephone companies. Avocations: traveling, public speaking, science fiction, stamp collecting. Home: 1701 Broadway St # 104 Vancouver WA 98663-3436

WELLS, RONALD HENRY CECIL, health sciences consultant; b. Saffron Walden, Essex, Eng., Feb. 6, 1926; arrived in Australia, 1962; s. Sidney Robin and Evelyn (Woods) W.; m. Betty Craggs, Dec. 1, 1948. BSc, St. Thomas Hosp., London, 1946, B Medicine B Surgery, 1950, MD, 1962. Specialist physician Singapore, 1952-61; specialist physician No. Terr, gen. supt. Darwin Hosp., Australia, 1962—; chmn. Canberra Hosps. Bd., Australia, 1970-73; dep. dir. gen. Commonwealth Dept. Health, Australia, 1973-74; chmn. Capital Terr. Health Commn., Australia, 1974-76, Nat. Hosps. and Health Svcs. Commn., 1976-77; pvt. cons. health svcs., Australia, 1987-95; cons. health stats. WHO, 1970-90. Author: Human Sex Determination, 1989, The Sexual Odds, 1989, Medieval Ancestries, 1996, 2nd edit., 1997, Varaha, 1996, Ancient Ancestors with Modern Descendants, 1998, 99. Fellow Royal Australian Coll. Physicians, Royal Australian Coll. Med. Adminstrs., Acad. Medicine Singapore, Royal Inst. Health; mem. Order Australia, Royal Coll. Physicians London, Univ. of Third Age (pres.). Avocations: farming, medieval history, golf. Home: 1/130 Shackleton Pk, Mawson ACT 2607, Australia

WELLS, RONALD JOHN, JR., clergyman; b. St. Paul, Jan. 25, 1953; s. Ronald John and Pearl Flowers (Halversen) W.; m. Brenda B. Burandt, May 28, 1977; children: Roland John III, Timothy Earl. BA in Pre-Theology, U. Minn., 1975; MDiv, Luther Theol. Sem., St. Paul, 1979. Ordained to ministry Am. Luth/ Ch., 1979. Youth dir. Advent Luth. Ch., Roseville, Minn., 1973-79; pastor Our Savior's and St. Paul's Luth. Chs., Cleveland, Minn., 1979-85; sr. pastor Hosanna Luth. Ch., Forest Lake, Minn., 1985-87, St. Paul's Evang. Luth. Ch., Mpls., 1988—; founder, dir. CitySpirit Ministries, Mpls., 1990—; founder, pres. Sch. Urban Ministry, Mpls., 1995—; mem. adj. faculty Am. Luth. Theol. Sem., St. Laul, 1997—; v.p. Great Commn. Network, Mpls., 1990-2000; bd. dirs. Luther Dell Luth. Bible Camp, Rerner, Minn., 1980-87. Author: (musicals) Spirit Walk, 1977, The Disciple-ship, 1984. Bd. dirs. Le Sueur County Devel. Activity Ctr., Waterville, Minn., 1982-85, Internat. Luth. Conf. on Holy Spirit, Roseville, 1989-99; asst. cubmaster, scoutmaster groop 401 Boy Scouts Am., Roseville, 1989—; mem. Hope Urban Devel., Mpls., 1999-2000. Recipient commendation Eddie Eagle Gun Safety Program, 1998. Mem. NRA (life). Avocations: hunting, custom rifle building. Office: St Paul's Evang Luth Ch 1901 Portland Ave Minneapolis MN 55404-2713

WELLS, SIMON JOHN, global investment management executive; b. Oxford, Eng., Sept. 11, 1955; s. Ronald and Joan Wells; m. Mirella Vivienne Vellucci, May 24, 1985; 1 child, Frederick. Fund mgr. Crown Agts., London, 1978-87; dir. Smith Barney Global Capital Mgmt., London, 1987-95, Smith Barney Shearson, Cayman Islands, 1993—; CEO PRICOA Asset Mgmt. Ltd., 1995—. Office: PRICOA Asset Mgmt, 100 Piccadilly, London W1V 9FN, England

WELLS, STEVEN WAYNE, lawyer; b. Ft. Walton Beach, Fla., Sept. 8, 1960; s. H. Wayne and Shirley A. W.; m. Lisa Stieler, May 20, 1983; Robert, James, Jessica. BA in Comm., Mich. State U., 1982; JD with distinction, Detroit Coll. of Law, 1985. Bar: Mich. Asst. prosecutor Oakland County, Pontiac, Mich., 1985-88; mng. ptnr. Schnelz, Bondy & Wells, P.C., Troy, Mich., 1988-93; shareholder, mng. ptnr. Cross Wrock, P.C., Detroit, 1993-99; prin. shareholder Schnelz, Wells, Monaghan & Wells PC, Birmingham, Mich., 1999—. Contbr. articles to State Bar Jour.; lectr. and presenter to legal forums. Pres. Bloomfield Village Bd. Fellow Mich. Bar Assn.; ABA, ATLA, Detroit Bar Assn., Mich. Trial Lawyers Assn., Nat. Dist. Attys. Assn. Avocations: golf, tennis, coaching youth baseball, soccer. Address: 255 S Old Woodward Ave Ste 200 Birmingham MI 48009-6184

WELLS, TENNYSON R., government official; b. Deadman's Cay, L.I., Bahamas, Dec. 30, 1947; married; 3 children. Degree in Econs. and Polit. Sci., St. Mary's U., Can.; Law Degree, London U. Admitted to Bahamas bar. Entered law practice, 1973; ptnr. Wells, Campbell & Co.; mem. for Bamboottown Ho. of Assembly, Nassau, Bahamas, 1987-92, min. agr. and fisheries, 1992-95, min. transport, 1995-97; min. justice, atty. gen. Cabinet, Govt. of the Bahamas, Nassau, 1997—. Mem. Free Nat. Movement. Office: Min Justice/Atty Gen, PO Box N-3007, Nassau Bahamas*

WELLS, ZELLA FAYE, assistant school superintendent, consultant; b. Prestonsburg, Ky., Oct. 15, 1948; d. Robert Jackson and Nancy Jane (Stephens) Wallace; m. Frank Allen Wells Jr., Aug. 11, 1972 (div. Dec. 1992). AS, Prestonsburg C.C., 1968; BA, U. Ky., 1970, MA, 1973, Ed.D, 1999. Tchr. Floyd County Schs., Prestonsburg, 1970-72; tchr., instrnl. supr., asst. prin., asst. supt. Johnson County Schs., Paintsville, Ky., 1972-95, 96—; disting. educator Ky. Dept. Edn., Frankfort, 1995-96; adj. instr. Prestonsburg C.C., 1983-91. Mem. Ky. Edn. Profl. Stds. Bd., Frankfort, 1996—, Morehead State U. Big Sandy Adv. Bd., Prestonsburg, 1996—, Ky. Testing and Internship Adv. Bd., Frankfort, 1993-98, Ky. Edn. Assn. Pub. Edn. Task Force, Frankfort, 1996-98. Named Disting. Educator, Ky. Dept. Edn., Frankfort, 1993; recipient Disting. Svc. award Ky. Coun. Tchrs. of Math., 1993, Outstanding Math. Edn. Achievement award Ea. Ky. Coun. Tchrs. of Math., 1993. Mem. ASCD, Am. Ednl. Rsch. Assn., Nat. Coun. Tchrs. of Math., Am. Guild Organists, Mid-South Ednl. Rsch. Assn., Ky. Assn. Tchr. Educators, Ky. Assn. Sch. Adminstrs., Ky. Assn. Sch. Supts., Kiwanis, U. Ky. Alumni Assn., Sierra Club, Phi Delta Kappa. Avocations: canoeing, running, birding. Home: PO Box 1024 Paintsville KY 41240-5024 Office: Johnson County Bd Edn 253 N Mayo Trl Paintsville KY 41240-1803

WELLSTEAD, PETER ERIC, engineering educator; b. St. Albans, Eng., June 27, 1944; s. John Edwin and Sarah (Foreman) W.; m. Jane Elizabeth Raply; children: Stephen Edwin, Sarah Jane. BSc, Hatfield (Eng.) Coll., 1967; MSc, Warwick (Eng.) U., 1968, PhD, 1970, DSc, 1988. Chartered engr. Lectr. UMIST, Manchester, 1972-80, sr. lectr., 1980-83, reader in control engring., 1983-92, prof. control engring., 1992—; Lucas prof. control engring. Lucas Industries, Birmingham, Eng., 1992-98; cons. GEC plc, London, 1999—, 3M Corp., St. Paul, 1998-00, TecQuipment, Nottingham, Eng., 1978—. Author: (books) Introduction to Physical System Modelling, 1979, Self Tuning Systems, 1997; editor: (book series) Control Systems Centre Book Series, 1991—, (jour.) IEE Procs., 1998—. Recipient Harold Hartley medal Inst. M.C., London, 1999, Honeywell Internat. medal, 1994. Fellow Inst. Elec. Engrs. (Blumein Browne Williams premium 1988). Avocations: walking, climbing, skiing. Office: Control Sys Ctr Unit, Sackville St PO Box 88, Manchester M60 1QD, England

WELMAN, JO MARK POLE, banker; b. London, Jan. 2, 1958; s. Eric Michael and Susanna (Solomon) W.; m. Alex Susan Burrell, Mar. 5, 1988; children: Ted, Rebecca. Degree in econs., Exeter U., 1979. With Baring Bros. & Co., London, 1979-89; mng. dir., investment mgr., dir. Rea Bros. Ltd., London, 1989-98; bd. dirs. Finsbury Income & Growth Investment Trust, Harlequin Ins., Varga Holdings Ltd., Dan Dare Corp.; chmn. Bayswater Growth, BRIT Ins. Holdings Plc, Close FTSE 100 Investment Trust Plc. Avocations: shooting, golf, rugby. Office: BRIT Ins Holdings Plc, 55 Bishopgate, London EL2N 3AS, England

WELSBY, JOHN KAY, rail transportation executive; b. May 26, 1938; s. Samuel and Sarah Ellen Welsby; m. Jill Carole Richards, 1964; 2 children. BA, U. Exeter; MSc, U. London. With Govt. Econ. Svc., 1966-81; dir. provincial svcs. British Railways Bd., 1982-84, mng. dir. procurement, 1985-87, bd. dirs., 1987-99, CEO, 1990-95, CEO, chmn., 1995-98, chmn., 1998-99; chmn. Inst. Transport, Eng., 1998-99; pres. Inst. Logistics and Transport, London, 1999—; freeman City of London, 1992; liveryman Carmen's Co., 1992; chmn. bd. dirs. Brit. Rwys.; bd. dirs. London & Continental Rys. Contbr. econs. articles to profl. jours. Decorated comdr. Brit. Empire. Mem. Inst. of Mgmt. (companion 1991). Avocations: walking, music, swimming. Office: 80 Portland Pl, London W1N 4DP, England

WELSCH, GLENN ALBERT, accounting educator; b. Woodward, Okla., Apr. 1, 1915; s. George Franklin and Minnie Melissa (Bowers) W.; m. Irma Richards, Apr. 5, 1942; children: Glenn Andrew, Linden Richards, Mary Ann Welsch Williamson. B.S., Northwestern State Coll., Alva, Okla., 1935; grad., Army Staff and Command Sch., 1943; M.S., Okla. State U., 1949; Ph.D., U. Tex., 1952. CPA, Okla., Tex. Comml. tchr. pub. high sch. Alva, Okla., 1937-40; mem. faculty Coll. Bus. Adminstrn., U. Tex., 1952-85, prof. acctg., 1956-85, chmn. dept., 1959-62, assoc. dean grad. studies, 1962-67, John Arch White prof. acctg., 1968-78, Peat, Marwick, Mitchell prof. acctg., 1978-83, Bayless chair in free enterprise, 1984-85, Bayless chair emeritus, 1985—; instr. Exec. Devel. Program, 1956-72; vis. prof. Carman G. Blough Disting. vis. prof. U. Va., 1970-71; Prickett Disting. vis. prof. Ind. U., 1975; cons. various companies on fin. acctg. and profit planning and control; expert witness. Author: (with Ronald W. Hilton and Paul Gordon) Budgeting: Profit Planning and Control, 5th edit., 1988, (with B.H. Sord) Business Budgeting: A Survey of Management Planning and Control Practices, 1958, (with C.T. Zlatkovich) Intermediate Accounting, 8th edit., 1989, (with C.H. Griffin and T.H. Williams) Advanced Accounting, 1966, (with Daniel G. Short) Fundamentals of Financial Accounting, 6th edit., 1987, (with R.N. Anthony) Fundamentals of Management Accounting, 4th edit., 1984. Served to maj. AUS, 1940-46. Recipient numerous awards for teaching excellence and service to acctg. profession, including Outstanding Educators award Amn. Acctg. Assn., 1985, Austin Area Tex. Execs. Outstanding Edn. Educator award, 1999; named to Hall of Fame, Coll. and Grad. Coll. of Bus. Adminstrn., U. Tex., 1988. Mem. Tex. Soc. CPA's (v.p. 1959-60), Am. Acctg. Assn. (pres. 1963), Am. Inst. CPA's (council 1968-73, acctg. prins. bd. 1970-73), Nat. Assn. Accts., Fin. Execs. Inst., Planning Execs. Inst., Beta Alpha Psi, Beta Gamma Sigma. Home: 3405 Taylors Dr Austin TX 78703-1047

WELSH, SIR ALFRED JOHN, lawyer, consultant; b. Louisville, May 10, 1947; s. Elvin Alfred and Carol (Kleymeyer) W.; m. Lee Mitchell, Aug. 1, 1970; children: Charles Kleymeyer, Kathryn Thomas. BA, Centre Coll., 1969; JD, U. Ky., 1972; LLM in Internat. Law cum laude, U. Brussels, 1973. Bar: Ky. 1972, U.S. Dist. Ct. (we. and ea. dists.) Ky. 1972, U.S. Ct. Appeals (6th cir.) 1972. Atty. Ky. Atty. Gen. Office, Frankfort, 1973-74; legis. counsel to congressman Ho. of Reps., Washington, 1974-77; mng. ptnr. Nicolas Welsh Brooks & Hayward, Louisville, 1977—, Boone Welsh Brooks and Hayward Internat. Law; hon. counsel of Belgium, 1983—; econ. devel. advisor Kimgdom of Belgium; mem. Ky. Econ. Adv. Coun.; pres. Transcontinental Trading Cons., Ltd.; participant in North African Mideast Econ. Summit Conf., Morocco, 1994; bd. dirs. Intervention Resources, Inc. Bd. dirs. Greater Louisville Swim Found., 1983-94, exec. com., 1994—; bd. dirs. Louisville com. Coun. Fgn. Rels., 1993—, also pres.; bd. dirs. Jefferson County Alcohol and Drug Abuse Found., Louisville, 1986—, Intervention Resource, Inc., Louisville, 1998—, Internet. Resolve; mem. econ. task force of Ky. Legis. Agts. Decorated knight Order of the Crown (Belgium). Mem. ABA (internat. law sect., commn. on impairment), ATLA, Ky. Bar Assn. (bd. dirs. 1981-82, pres. young lawyers divsn. 1981-82), Am. Judicature Soc., Louisville C. of C. Democrat. Presbyterian. Avocations: swimming, water polo, soccer. Office: Barristers Hall 1009 S 4th St Louisville KY 40203-3207

WELSH, CHARLES EDWIN, mathematician, educator, EMT; b. Lancaster, Pa., June 24, 1973; s. Charles Edwin and Barbara Ann W. BS, Calif. U. Pa., 1995. Tchr. Queen Anne's County Bd. Edn., Centreville, Md., 1995—; emergency med. tech. Queen Anne's County Emergency Svcs., Centreville, 1999—. Mem. Nat. Coun. Tchrs. Maths., Lions, Phi Sigma Pi. Democrat. Mem. Evangelical Congregational Church. Avocations: collecting farm toys, playing piano, collecting Cal Ripkin memorabilia. Office: Kent Island HS 900 Love Point Rd Stevensville MD 21666-2120

WELSH, DORIS MCNEIL, early childhood education specialist; b. Kansas City, Mo.; d. Zelbert Melbourne and Anna May (Main) McNeil; children: J. Randall, Valerie M. BA, U. Calif., Berkeley, 1950, MA, 1952; postgrad., U. San Francisco, 1980-82. Cert. tchr., counselor, supr., Calif. Asst. dir. Bing Sch., Stanford, Calif., 1966-76; family devel. specialist Children's Hosp., Stanford, 1976-78; rsch. cons. Stanford U. Med. Ctr., 1970-87; dir. One Fifty Parker Sch., San Francisco, 1978-99; assoc. Lawrence Hall of Sci., U. Calif., Berkeley, 1996—; citizen amb. del. edn. and childcare People to People Internat., St. Petersburg, Russia, Vilnius, Lithuania, Budapest, Hungary, 1993; pres. bd. dirs. Support for Parents of Spl. Children, San Francisco, 1986-87; bd. dirs. Family Svc. Assn. Mid-Peninsula, Palo Alto, Calif., 1970-80; leader Summer Camp for Pre-Schoolers, East Palo Alto, 1970-73; leader parenthood discussion groups U. Chgo., 1963-64; lectr. in field. Vol. Irving Mental Hosp., Chgo., 1963. Mem. Nat. Assn. Edn. Young Children, Assn. Childhood Edn. Internat., World Affairs Coun., Audubon Soc., Sierra Club. Avocations: natural sciences, hiking, horseback riding, gardening. Office: One Fifty Parker Sch 150 Parker Ave San Francisco CA 94118-2608

WELSH, JOHN FRANCIS, retired advertising executive; b. New Haven, May 19, 1916; s. Pierce Jerome and Irene (Kennedy) W.; m. Margaret Burke, Sept. 18, 1947; children: Peter Burke, Diana Margaret. B.A., Yale U., 1937. With Warwick & Legler, Inc., N.Y.C, 1946-81; exec. v.p., mgmt. supr., mem. mgmt. com.; vice chmn. Warwick, Welsh & Miller, Inc., 1973-81. Served with AUS, 1941-45. Decorated Bronze Star, Croix de Guerre France). Club: Tokeneke (Darien). Home: 98 Ridge Acres Rd Darien CT 06820-2616

WELSH, WILLIAM DANIEL, family practitioner; b. Balt., May 18, 1950; s. Joseph Leo and Bessie Mary (Tangires) W.; m. Loraine Lynn Barkhaus, July 11, 1985; children: Sean William, Ryan Daniel. Student, Johns Hopkins U., 1971; BS in Biology cum laude, Fairleigh Dickinson U., 1972; DO, Coll. Osteo. Medicine-Surgery, Des Moines, 1975. Diplomate Nat. Bd. Osteo. Physicians; cert. ATLS; approved supr. physician assts. Osteopathic Med. Bd. Calif.; radiography and fluoroscopy x-ray supr., operator Calif. Intern Martin Place Hosp., Madison Heights, Mich., 1975-76, resident in internal medicine, 1976-77; pvt. practice Detroit, 1977-79; pvt. practice, Whittier, Calif., 1979—; instr. ACLS, L.A., 1980-92; bd. dirs. Whittier Hosp. Med. Ctr., 1981, vice chief staff, 1982-84, med. dir. family asthma forum, 1979-88, med. dir. Summit Place alcohol treatment program, 1983-88; med. dir. Mirada Hills Rehab. Hosp., La Mirada, Calif., 1980-88; former clin. preceptor Coll. Osteo. Med. Pacific, Pomona, Calif., clin. assoc. prof. internal medicine; mem. dept. family practice, physician rev. com. Friendly Hills Regional Med. Ctr., La Habra, Calif., 1994-97; mem. staff Presbyn. Intercmty. Hosp., Whittier; med. dir. Berryman Health Convalescent Hosp., 1999. Participant Calif. Beach Clean Up Day, 1996. Recipient Physician Recognition award AMA, 1991, 95, 96, Commn. of Merit Rep. Nat. Com., 1995. Mem. Am. Osteo. Assn., Am. Coll. Osteo. Family Physicians, Osteo. Physicians and Surgeons Calif., Am. Coll. Osteopathic Family Practitioners (bd. cert. 1991, geriatrics 2000), L.A. Osteopathic County Med. Assn. Avocations: boating, skiing, reading, tennis. Home: 16871 Marina Bay Dr Huntington Beach CA 92649-2913

WELT, PHILIP STANLEY, lawyer, consultant; b. Freeport, N.Y., July 5, 1959; s. Morris and Rose (Offenberg) W.; m. Karen Teresa Gault, May 22, 1994. BBA summa cum laude, Hofstra U., 1983; MBA, Columbia U., 1988; JD cum laude, NYU, 1995. Bar: N.J. 1995, N.Y. 1995; U.S. Dist. Ct. N.J. 1995, U.S. Dist. Ct. (so. and ea. dists.) N.Y. 1996, U.S. Ct. Appeals (2d cir.), 1997, U.S. Ct. Appeals Armed Forces, 2000, U.S. Supreme Ct. 1999; CPA, N.Y. Sr. mgr. Deloitte & Touche, N.Y.C., 1983-92; assoc. Reboul MacMurray Hewitt Maynard & Kristol, N.Y.C., 1993, Davis Polk & Wardwell, N.Y.C., 1994, 96—; jud. clk. U.S. Dist. Ct. N.J., Newark, 1995-96; special asst. dist. atty. Kings Co., N.Y., 1999—; bd. dirs., treas. Pub. Interest Law Found., N.Y.C., 1993-94; guest spkr. Boy Scouts Am., Nassau County, 1984-91, Nat. Assn. Accts., N.Y./N.J., 1988-92, others. Sr. editor Columbia Jour. World Bus., 1986-88; sr. exec. editor Ann. Survey Am. Law, 1993-95; contbr. articles to profl. jours. Vol. income tax asst. Dept. Treasury, IRS, N.Y.C., 1981-87; vol. Variety-The Children's Charity, N.Y.C., 1985-87; advisor Friends of Jon Kaiman, Nassau County, 1995. Provost's scholar Hofstra U., 1981-83, Deloitt & Touche fellow Columbia U., 1986-88; recipient Appreciation cert. Dept. Treasury, IRS, 1981-87, Variety, 1985-87, Bovenaan Outstanding Cmty. Svc. award Hofstra U., 1983, Orison S. Marden Moot Ct. Advocacy award NYU Sch. Law, 1993, Seymore A. Levy meml. award, 1995. Mem. ABA, AICPA, N.Y. State Bar Assn., N.Y. State Soc. CPAs, Beta Alpha Psi, Beta Gamma Sigma. Avocations: golf, rock climbing, photography, philately, amateur radio. Home: 157 Mountain Wood Rd Stamford CT 06903-2107 Office: Davis Polk and Wardwell 450 Lexington Ave Fl 31 New York NY 10017-3982

WELTE, A. THEODORE, chamber of commerce executive; b. Mankato, Minn., Feb. 11, 1944; s. Arthur William and Bernice (Town) M.; m. Kathleen P. Browne, May 3, 1969; 1 child, Jason N. BA in Sociology, Psychology, Mankato State U., 1966, MA in Econs., 1972; cert., U. Notre Dame, 1987; cert. mgmt., Stonehill Coll., 1990. Cert. chamber exec. Program officer, br. officer Peace Corp, Washington, 1968-69; rsch. dir. Tech. Found., W.Va. Tech., Montgomery, 1969-70; project dir. Self-Help, Inc., Brockton, Mass., 1972-73; regional planner, planning supr. Old Colony Planning Coun., Brockton, 1974-81; pres., CEO Metro South C. of C., Brockton, 1981-90, MetroWest C. of C., Framingham, Mass., 1990—; trustee Brockton Regional Econ. Devel. Corp., 1982-90; treas. Brockton Area Pvt. Industry Coun., 1987-89. Cubmaster pack 68 Boy Scouts Am., Easton, Mass., 1989-90, com. chair troop 86, 1991-94, bd. dirs. Algonquin/Knox Trail coun., 1991—, v.p. exploring, 1996-99. Mem. New Eng. Assn. C. of C. Execs. (sec. 1990-91, 2d v.p. 1991-92, 1st v.p. 1992-93, pres. 1993-94), Mass. Assn. C. of C. Execs. (pres. 1988-89), Rotary (sec. Brockton 1988-90, v.p. Framingham 1990-92, pres. 1993-94). Presbyterian. E-mail: ted@metrowest.org. Office: MetroWest C of C 1671 Worcester Rd Ste 201 Framingham MA 01701-5400

WELTE, DIETRICH HUGO, geochemist; b. Würzburg, Germany, Jan. 22, 1935; s. Adolf T. and Charlotte (Wittmann) W.; m. Hildegunde HuBlein, Aug. 20, 1959. Diploma in geology, U. Würzburg, 1957, Dr. rer. nat., 1960. Rsch. geochemist Shell Internat. Oil Co., Den Haag, Netherlands, 1960-63; scientific asst., lectr. geochemistry U. Würzburg, 1963-67; sr. rsch. geochemist, rsch. coord. Chevron Oil Field Rsch. Co., La Habra, U.S., 1967-70; prof. geochemistry U. Göttingen, Germany, 1970-72; prof. geology, geochemistry and oil and coal deposits Rheinisch-Westfälische Technische Hochschule Aachen, Germany, 1972—; dir. inst. for petroleum and organic geochemistry Forschungszentrum Jülich, Germany, 1979—; mem. Geokommission, Bonn, Conseil Scientifique, Rueil-Malmaison, France, Scientific Program Com. WPC, London, 1992—; chmn. sci.-tech. coun. Forschungszentrum Jülich, Germany. Author: Petroleum Formation and Occurrence, 1978, '84; editor Advances in Petroleum Geochemistry; contbr. articles to profl. jours. Advisor Ministry Sci. and Tech., Germany. Recipient Alfred Treibs award Geochem. Soc. U.S.A., 1983, Carl Engler medal Deutsche Gesellschaft fur Mineralolwissenschaft und Kohl chemie, 1986. Mem. Am. Assn. Petroleum Geologists (Pres. award 1966), Deutsche Wissenschaftliche Gesellschaft fur Erdol, Erdgas und Kohle e.V., Geologische Vereinigung (Gustav Steinman award 1989), Deutsche Geologische Gesellschaft, European Assn. Organic Geochemists, Rhein.-Westf. Akademie d. Wissenschaften, Academia Europaea. Office: IES GmbH, Bastion St 11-19, 5248 Jülich Germany

WELTERMANN, BIRGITTA M., health care administrator; b. Munich, Germany, May 16, 1961; d. K. U. and M. P. W. MD, RWTH Aachen Med. Sch., Germany, 1987; MPH, U. Conn., 1993; postgrad., U. Dusseldorf, Germany, 2000—. Program dir. Med. Ethics U., 1988-89; clinician, scientist U. Conn., 1990-93, U. Cologne, 1994-97; clinician, scientist U. Munster, 1997-99, rschr., scientist, 1999—; health care mgr. TK Hamburg, Germany, 1999—; asst. clin. prof. dept. medicine & health care U. Conn., 2000—; vis. prof. U. Conn., 1999. Mem. Soc. Social Medicine Germany, German Neurol. Assn. Avocations: outdoors, sports. Office: Techiner Krankenkasse, 20233 Hamburg Germany

WELTNER, KLAUS VOLKER, physicist, educator; b. Rinteln, Germany, Jan. 8, 1927; s. Ernst and Elfriede Paula (Bülow) W.; m. Almuth Weltner, May 25, 1955; children: Bettina, Konstanze, Juliane, Martin. Diplom Physiker, U. Hannover, Germany, 1953, DrRerNat, 1956; DrHabil, U. Linz, Austria, 1970. Lectr. Adolf Reichwein Hochschule, Osnabrück, Germany, 1956-61, prof., 1961-69; prof. Pedagogical U., Berlin, 1969-70, U. Frankfurt, Germany, 1970-93; vis. prof. U. Salvador, Brazil, 1993—; dir. Inst. für Didaktic d. Physic, U. Frankfurt, 1972-75, 78-80, 86-88, dekan, dept. physics, 1991-92. Author: Measurement of Verbal Information in Psychology and Education, 1973, Autonomes Lernen, 1978, (CD-ROM) Mathematik für Naturwissenschaftler, 1998; author, editor: (books and study guides) Mathematics for Engineers and Scientists, 1986. Home: Schumannstr 57, 60325 Frankfurt Germany

WELTON, CHARLES EPHRAIM, lawyer; b. Cloquet, Minn., June 23, 1947; s. Eugene Frances and Evelyn Esther (Koski) W.; children: Spencer Sanda, Marshall Eugene. BA, Macalester Coll., 1969; postgrad., U. Minn., 1969-70; JD, U. Denver, 1974. Bar: Colo. 1974, U.S. Dist. Ct. Colo. 1974, U.S. Supreme Ct. 1979, U.S. Ct. Appeals (10th cir.) 1980. Assoc. Davidovich & Wanifuchi, Denver, 1974-77, Charles Welton and Assocs. and successor firms, Denver, 1978-86; ptnr. OSM Properties, Denver, 1982-97; prin. Brock House, LLC, Denver, 1997—; prin. Charles Welton, P.C., 1986—; adj. prof. Inst. Advanced Legal Studies U. Denver, 1991-98; polit. and social commentator; lectr. in field; instr. Nat. Inst. Trial Advocacy, 1998—. Author instrnl. materials; editor profl. publications; contbr. articles to profl. jours. Sch. pres. PTSA, Denver, 1983-84; coach Colo. Jr. Soccer League, 1980-85; coach Odessey of Mind (formerly Olympics of Mind), 1986-88; bd. dirs. Virginia Vale Swim Club, officer, 1989-91, Pioneer Jr. Hockey Assn., 1990-92. Served alt. mil. duty Denver Gen. Hosp., 1970-72. Mem. ATLA, Denver Bar Assn. (facilitator bench/bar retreat 1995, 96, legal fee arbitration com.), Colo. Bar Assn. (interprofl. com.), Colo. Trial Lawyers Assn. (bd. dirs. 1985-90, chmn. seminar com. 1986-88, exec. com. 1987-88, legis. com. 1988-94, case assistance com. 1995—, keyperson 1997—), Am. Bldg. a Lasting Earth (founder), Exec. Ventures Group of Am. Leadership Forum (founding adv. bd. 1987-90). Democrat. E-mail: welton@charles-welton.com. Home: 680 Vista Ln Lakewood CO 80215-6037 Office: The Brock House 1800 Gaylord St Denver CO 80206-1211

WELTON, JESSICA WHEAT, advertising executive; b. Richmond, Va., Sept. 25, 1953; d. Francis Conway and Catherine May (Murphy) W.; m. Steven Jake Ellerbroek, Mar. 17, 1973 (div. 1979); m. Patrick Siddall, July 6, 1985; children: Justin, Jeremy, Peyton, Jenny. BFA, Va. Commonwealth U., 1977. Finished artist The Martin Agy., Richmond, 1977-78; art dir. Morgan & Assocs., Richmond, 1978-79; art dir. Siddall, Matus & Coughter, Richmond, 1979-88, v.p., assoc. creative dir., 1988—. Active Goochland County Gifted Adv. Coun., Goochland County Commn. Future in Edn. Recipient over 100 nat. and internat. awards London Internat., 1990, One Show, CA, Print, Art Dirs., Athenas, Addies, MIRMS, Clios, Andys. Mem. Richmond Advt. Club (bd. dirs.), Va. Mus., Va. Hist. Soc., Peyton Soc. Va., Va. Mus. Friends of Art, Goochland County Hist. Soc. (bd. dirs.), Deep Run Hunt Pony Club (bd. dirs.). Episcopalian. Avocation: fox hunting. Home: Readers Br Farm 1737 Manakin Rd Manakin Sabot VA 23103-2650 Office: Siddall Matus & Coughter 830 E Main St Richmond VA 23219-2725

WELTON, MICHAEL PETER, dentist; b. Milw., Apr. 19, 1957; s. Lloyd Peter and Allegra (Nimmer) W.; m. Etsuko Suehiro, Nov. 21, 1986 (div. Nov. 1993); m. Lucia Aldon, Jan. 29, 1994. BS in Biology cum laude, Carroll Coll., 1979; DDS, U. Minn., 1983. Commd. lt. USN, 1983; resident Naval Hosp. Camp Pendleton, Oceanside, Calif., 1983-84; with periodontics dept. Naval Dental Clinic, Yokosuka, Japan, 1984-85; clinic dir. Negishi Dental Annex, Yokohama, Japan, 1985-87; gen. dentistry Br. Dental Clinic Mare Island Naval Sta., Vallejo, Calif., 1987-90; pvt. practice gen. dentistry Vacaville, Calif., 1990—; legis. extern Am. Student Dental Assn., Washington, 1982; student rep. Minn. Dental Assn., Mpls., 1980. Fellow Acad. Dentistry Internat.; mem. ADA, Calif. Dental Assn. (ho. of dels. 1996-98, com. rules and order 1998), Napa-Solano Dental Soc. (exec. com. 1995-98, bd. dirs. 1990-95, pres. 1997), Art Deco Soc. Calif., No. Calif. Golf Assn., Vacaville C. of C., Tilden Park Golf Club, Delta Sigma Delta (treas. Mpls. chpt. 1982-83, Outstanding Mem. award 1982-83), Vacaville Sunrise Rotary Club (dir. 1997-99, sec. 1999—), Ducks Unlimited (dinner com. 1997—). Avocations: golf, skiing, tennis, reading, gardening, hunting. Home: 480 Evelyn Cir Vallejo CA 94589-3259 Office: 3000 Alamo Dr Ste 103 Vacaville CA 95687-6345

WELTY, EUDORA, author; b. Jackson, Miss.; d. Christian Webb and Chestina (Andrews) W. Student, Miss. State Coll. for Women; B.A., U. Wis., 1929; postgrad., Columbia Sch. Advt., 1930-31. Author: A Curtain of Green, 1941, The Robber Bridegroom, 1942, The Wide Net, 1943, Delta Wedding, 1946, Music From Spain, 1948, Short Stories, 1949, The Golden Apples, 1949, The Ponder Heart, 1954 (William Dean Howells medal Am. Acad. Arts and Letters 1955), The Bride of the Innisfallen, 1955, Place in Fiction, 1957, The Shoe Bird, 1964, Thirteen Stories, 1965, A Sweet Devouring, 1969, Losing Battles, 1970 (Nat. Book award nomination 1971), One Time, One Place, 1971 (Christopher Book award 1972), The Optimist's Daughter, 1972 (Pulitzer prize in fiction 1973), The Eye of the Story, 1978, The Collected Stories of Eudora Welty, 1980 (Notable Book award ALA 1980, Am. Book award 1981), One Writer's Beginnings, 1985 (Am. Book award 1984, Nat. Book Critics Circle award nomination 1984), Eudora Welty Photographs, 1989, A Writer's Eye: Collected Book Reviews, 1994, Monuments to Interruption: Collected Book Reviews, 1994, The Shoe Bird, 1993, The First Story, 1999; editor: (with Ronald A. Sharp) The Norton Book of Friendship, 1991; contbr.: New Yorker. Recipient O. Henry award, 1942, 43, 68, Creative Arts medal for fiction Brandeis U., 1966, Nat. Inst. Arts and Letters Gold Medal, 1972, Nat. Medal for Lit., 1980, Presdl. Medal of Freedom, 1980, Commonwealth medal MLA, 1984, Nat. Medal of Arts, 1987; Lit. grantee Nat. Inst. Arts and Letters, 1944; Guggenheim fellow, 1942; Chevalier de l'Ordre des Arts et Lettres (France), 1987; National Women's Hall of Fame, 2000. Mem. Am. Acad. Arts and Letters. Home: 1119 Pinehurst Pl Jackson MS 39202-1812 Address: care U Press Miss 3825 Ridgewood Rd Jackson MS 39211-6497

WELZ, CHRISTIAN, law educator; b. Cuxaven, Germany, Nov. 26, 1958; s. Karl and Erika (Simon) W. M. U. Aix-en-Provence, France, 1983; DEA, U. Strasbourg, France, 1985. Lectr. U. Freiburg (Germany), 1986-90; rschr. Inst. Europaeische Politik, Bonn, Germany, 1990-92; dep. dir. Euro-Inst., Kehl, Germany, 1992-96; prof. law Fachhochschule Kehl, 1996-99; rsch. mgr. European Found., Dublin, Ireland, 2000—. Author: Europarecht, 3d edit., 1999; editor: Umweltrecht in Deutschland und Frankreich, 1996. Mem. Tönissteiner Kreis, Stifterverband Deutsche Wissenschaft. Avocations: hiking, travel. E-mail: christian.welz@eurofound.ie. Home: Blackrock, 34 Stradbrook Lawn, Dublin Ireland Office: European Found, Wyattville Rd Loughlinstown, Dublin Ireland

WEMELSFELDER, FRANCOISE, behavioral scientist, researcher; b. Utrecht, The Netherlands, Mar. 8, 1958; arrived in Scotland, 1993; d. Frans and Dineke (Nolst-Trenité) W. BSc, U. Groningen, 1981, MSc with honors, 1985; PhD (hon.), U. Leiden, 1993. Rsch. scientist Scottish Agrl. Coll., 1993—. Author: (2 chpts.) Stereotypic Animal Behavior, 1993, Animal Consciousness and Animal Ethics, 1997, Encyclopedia of Animal Rights and Animal Welfare, 1998, (1 chpt. with L.I.A. Birke) Animal Welfare, 1997, (chpt.) Attitudes to Animals;mem. editl. bd. Soc. and Animals, 1993—, Jour. Applied Animal Welfare Science, 1994—; contbr. articles to profl. jours. including Applied Animal Behavior Sci. Grantee Schweisfurth-Stiftung, 1991. Mem. Netherlands Soc. for Theoretical Biology (sec. 1987-90), Internat. Soc. for Applied Ethology, Assn. for Study of Animal Behavior. Avocations: hill-walking, windsurfing, playing the piano, dancing. Office: Scottish Agrl Coll, Divsn Animal Biol Bush Est, Penicuik Midlothian EH26 0PO, Scotland

WEN, CARSON, lawyer, politician; b. Hong Kong, Apr. 16, 1953; s. Sir Yung and Tsi Fung (Chu) W.; m. Julia Yuet Shan Fung, Jan. 30, 1983; 1 child, Ho. BA, Columbia U., 1975, Oxford (Eng.) U., 1977; MA, Oxford (Eng.) U., 1980. Solicitor Supreme Ct. Hong Kong and Eng. and Wales; attesting officer, China. Assoc. D.W. Ling & Co., Hong Kong, 1977-81; fgn. law cons. Masuda & Ejiri, Tokyo, 1981; ptnr. Siao, Wen and Leung, 1982—; bd. dirs. Delta Asia Bank (Banco Delta Asia SARL), Macau, Pearl Oriental Holdings Ltd.; lectr. on Hong Kong Law. Contbr. chpt. to book. Adviser on Hong Kong affairs Govt. of China, 1993—; vice chmn. Hong Kong Progressive Alliance, 1994—; mem. selection com. First Govt. of Hong Kong Spl. Adminstrv. Region, 1996; hon. pres. Hong Kong Indsl. Areas Industry and Trade Fedn., 1994—; dep. Nat. People's Congress, China, 1998—. Mem. Law Soc. Hong Kong, Law Soc. Eng., United Oxford and Cambridge Univs. Club (London). Avocations: reading, golf. Office: Hang Seng Bldg 15th Fl, 77 Des Voeux Rd Ctrl, Hong Kong China

WEN, CHUAN-DONG, medical physicist; b. Shou Guang, Shandong, China, May 4, 1960; s. Shangshu Wen and Xiu-Fang Wang; m. Ann Yan Liu, May 19, 1998. BSc, Shandong Tchrs. U., Jinan, China, 1982; MSc, James Cook U., Townsville, Australia, 1993. Asst. prof. Shandong Tchrs. U., 1982-84, lectr., 1984-87; med. physicist Townsville Gen. Hosp., Australia, 1993-95; sr. med. physicist Launceston Gen. Hosp., Australia, 1996-97; RTP specialist ADAC Labs., 1998—. Recipient Vis. scholarship World Bank, 1988, Overseas Rsch. Student scholarship Australia Govt., 1990-93. Mem. Am. Assn. Physicists in Medicine, Australasian Coll. Phys., Scientists and Engrs. in Medicine (assoc.), Australian and New Zealand Soc. Nuclear Medicine. Avocations: photography, table tennis, swimming, music, movies. Office: PO Box 4183, Mulgrave Business Centre, 3170 Mulgrave Victoria, Australia

WEN, FU-QIANG, pulmonologist, cellular biologist; b. Sichuan, China, Sept. 23, 1961; s. Bing Wen and Fang-xiu Sun; m. Ping Yan, May 1, 1987; 1 child, Xi. MD, 3rd Mil. Med. U., Chongqiang, China, 1983, MS, 1986; PhD, Fukuoka (Japan) U., 1997. Resident Chengdu (China) Gen. Hosp., 1987-88, attending physician, 1989-93, assoc. prof., 1994-99; rsch. assoc. U. Nebr., Omaha, 1999—; rsch. fellow Fukuoka U., 1994—. Contbr. articles to profl. jours. Recipient Grant-in-aid Ministry Culture, Edn. and Sci., Japan, 1995, 97; Internat. Cooperation fellow Kyushu U., Japan, 1997. Mem. European Respiratory Soc., Asian Pacific Soc. Respirology (chairperson 1988, plenary lectr. 1990). Office: U Nebr Med Ctr Omaha NE 68198-0001

WEN, GEYI, applied physics educator; b. Pingjiang, Hunan, China, Dec. 28, 1962; s. Zhiwu and Meiran (Li) W.; m. Jun Yuan, Jan. 22, 1988; 1 child, Nan. BS, Xidian U., Xian, China, 1982, MS, 1984, PhD, 1987. Lectr. S.E. U., Nanjing, China, 1988-90; assoc. prof. U. Electronic Sci. and Tech. China, Chengdu, 1990-92, prof., 1993—; vis. rschr. U. Calif., Berkeley, 1992-93; 97, chmn., 1997—; vis. prof. U. Waterloo, Can., 1998. Author: Modern Methods for Electromagnetic Computation, 1996, Advances in Electormagnetic Theory, 1999; contbr. articles to profl. jours. Recipient Talent through Century award Sichuan Province, Chengdu, China, 1994, Sci. and Tech. Progress award China Soc. Sci. and Tech., 1996, Talent through Century award Nat. Edn. Com., Beijing, 1996. Mem. IEEE (editl. bd. IEEE Transactions on Microwave Theory & Techniques 1992—), China Soc. Computational Physics (mem. couns. 1992—), China Inst. Electronics (editl. bd. Jour. Electromagnetic Waves 1997—). Avocations: table tennis, Chinese chess. Office: U Electronic Sci and Tech, Inst Applied Physics, 610054 Chengdu Sichuan, China Address: Rsch in Motion, 295 Phillip St, Waterloo, ON Canada N2L 3W8

WEN, HUNG TZU, neurosurgeon, educator; b. Tainan, Taiwan, Dec. 15, 1963; s. Sau Pei Wen and Yu Chieh Teng; m. Cecilia Emi Tsukamoto, Oct. 23, 1993. MD, U. São Paulo, 1987. Resident in neurol. surgery Hosp. Clinicas, Coll. Medicine U. São Paulo, 1988-93, chief resident divsn. neurosurgery, 1992-93; clin. fellow in vascular microneurosurgery Neurol. Inst. São Paulo, 1993, clin. assoc., 1998—; rsch. fellow in microneurosurgery dept. neurol. surgery U. Fla., Gainesville, 1993-96, clin. asst. prof. dept. neurol. surgery, 1999—; clin. attending in epilepsy and vascular diseases Hosp. das Clinicas U. São Paulo, 1996—; clin. assoc. Inst. Neurol. Scis., São Paulo, 1998—; lectr. in field; organizer, instr. courses on microneurosurgery. Contbr. articles to profl. jours., chpts. to books. Mem. Brazilian Soc. Neurosurgery, Brazilian Acad. Neurosurgery. Fax: 55-11-251-1766. E-mail: cicawen@uol.com.br. Office: Inst Neurol Scis, Praca Amadeu Amaral 27 5a, 01327010 São Paulo Brazil

WEN, HUNGTAO JOSEPH, management educator; b. July 20, 1958. PhD, Va. Commonwealth U., 1993. Asst. prof. N.J. Inst. Tech., Newark, 1994-98; assoc. prof. N.J. Inst. Tech., 1999—. Office: N J Inst Tech Sch Mgmt 211 Stewart Ave Newark NJ 07102-1982

WEN, JINGSONG (CHING-SUNG), aerosol and hydrosol scientist, atmospheric physicist; b. Beijing, China, Feb. 4, 1933; s. Gongyi and Jiaxin (Xiao) W.;m. Zhenhua Zhu; children: Hongxing, Hongyu, Hongqing, Hongsheng. Grad., Peking U., Beijing, 1957. Asst. prof. Inst. Atmospheric Physics Chinese Acad. Scis., Beijing, 1957-71; assoc. prof. Anhui Inst. Optics and Fine Machine Chinese Acad. Scis., Hefei, 1971-84; prof. physics Nankai U., Tianjin, 1984—. Author: An Introduction to Micro-Atmospheric Physics, 1989, Probability and Micro-Atmospheric Physics, 1995, The Fundamentals of Aerosol Dynamics, 1996; contbr. articles to profl. jours. including Scientia Sinica, Jour. Fluid Mechanics, Jour. Colloid and Interface Sci., among others. Recipient award Chinese Acad. Scis., 1978, Nat. Edn. Com., 1988, 96, 97, Nat. Natural Sci. Prize, 1999. Fellow Royal Soc. Meteorology; mem. Meteorol. Soc. Tianjin (dir. 1985), Chinese Inst. Aerosols (dir. 1990), Chinese Soc. Particuology (dir. 1996), Am. Assn. for Aerosol Rsch., N.Y. Acad. Scis., Am. Biograph. Inst. Avocations: reading, classical music, walking, watching television. E-mail: cswen@nankai.edu.cn. Home: Nankai U, No 103 Bldg 21 N Village, 300071 Tianjin China Office: Nankai U Dept Physics, No 94 Weijin Rd, 300071 Tianjin China

WEN, RUILIN, editor; b. Beijing, Apr. 30, 1939; d. Zongnong Wen and Tianjue Zhang; m. Jinling Du, Apr. 29, 1966; children: Du, Tong, Du, Jing. BS, Beijing U. Aeronautics, Beijing, 1963. Documentationalist China Aero-Info. Ctr., Beijing, 1963-87, chief editor Chinese Aerospace Abstracts, 1988-95, chief editor Fgn. Aeronautics Abstracts, 1990-94, hon. chief editor, 1996-97; vice dir. China Aero. Documentation and Info. Ctr., Beijing, 1990-94, ret., 1995; mem. 6th subcom. China Nat. Documentation Standardization Com., Beijing, 1993-96. Author: User Manual: Descriptive Cataloging Format for Scientific and Technological Documents, 1990; chief editor: Indexing Manual for Aeronautics Documents, 1992; co-translator: Vocabulary Control for Information Retrieval, 1982. Mem. China Periodical Soc. (exec. coun. 1992-96). Avocations: exercise, collecting coins and stamps. Home: Jia 4-2-501 Hepingli 5 qu, Dongcheng Dist, Beijing 100013, China Office: 14 Xiaoguan Dongli Anwai, Beijing 100029, China

WEN, SIHAI, materials scientist, mechanical engineer; b. Wuhu, Anhui, China, Oct. 26, 1970; s. Shizhong and Meizhu (Hu) W.; m. Xianping Li, Oct. 25, 1995. BS, Nanchang Inst. Aero-Tech., Jianxi, China, 1992; MS, South China U. Tech., Guangzhou, Guangdong, China, 1995. Rsch. asst. South China U. Tech., Guangzhou, 1992-95; materials scientist Guangzhou U., 1995-98; scholar, rsch. asst. SUNY, Buffalo, 1998—. Excellent Student scholar Nanchang Inst. Aero-Tech., 1988-92; grad. scholar South China U. Tech., 1992-95. Mem. Soc. for Advanced Materials. E-mail: sihaiwen@acsu.buffalo.edu. Home: 9 Kenville Rd Apt A Buffalo NY 14215-2958 Office: SUNY 321 Jarvis Hall Buffalo NY 14260-4400

WEN, WEIJIA, physicist, researcher; b. Chongqing, China, May 5, 1956; m. Gu Xu; 1 child, Wen He. BS, Chongqing U., 1982, MS, 1988; PhD, Chinese Acad. Sci., Beijing, 1995. Asst. prof. Chongqing U., 1982-88, lectr., 1988-92; rsch. fellow Hong Kong U. Sci. and Tech., 1995-97; postdoctoral fellow UCLA, 1999—; asst. prof. Hong Kong U. Sci. and Tech., 1999—. Contbr. articles to profl. jours. Mem. Materials Rsch. Soc., Chinese Physics Soc, Am. Physics Soc. Fax: 852-23581652. E-mail: phwen@ust.hk. Office: Hong Kong U Sci & Tech, Dept Physics, Hong Kong China

WEN, XIAOQING, engineer, educator; b. Beijing, China, Apr. 23, 1964; came to U.S., 1998; s. Tingzhe Wen and Yanxiu Qu; m. Kanako Hayashido. B in Engring., Tsinghua U., Beijing, 1986; M in Engring., Hiroshima (Japan) U., 1990; PhD, Osaka (Japan) U., 1993. Sys. engr. IC Instruments Co., Osaka, 1993; asst. prof. engring. Akita (Japan) U., 1993-97; rsch. fellow U. Wis., Madison, 1995-96; R&D project mgr. SynTest Technologies, Inc., Sunnyvale, Calif., 1998—; cons. Internat. Langs. Engring. Co. Ltd., Boulder, Colo., 1995-97, Excel Co. Ltd., Osaka, 1995-97, Sharp Co. Ltd., Nara, Japan, 1996-97. Contbr. articles to profl. jours. Recipient Rsch. Encouragement award Inst. Elec., Info. and Comm. Engrs., Japan, 1994. Mem. IEEE, Info. Processing Soc. Japan (Rsch. Encouragement award 1994). Avocations: movies, swimming, jogging, reading, walking. Office: 505 S Pastoria Ave Ste 101 Sunnyvale CA 94086-7583

WENDEBORN, RICHARD DONALD, retired manufacturing company executive; b. Winnipeg, Man., Can.; came to U.S., 1976; naturalized, 1988; s. Curtis and Rose (Lysecki) W.; m. Dorothy Ann Munn, Aug. 24, 1957; children: Margaret Gayle, Beverley Jane, Stephen Richard, Peter Donald, Ann Elizabeth. Diploma, Colo. Sch. Mines, 1952; grad. advanced mgmt. program, Harvard U., 1974. With Can. Ingersoll-Rand Co., Montreal, 1952—, gen. mgr., v.p., dir., 1968, pres., 1969-74, chmn. bd., 1976—; exec. v.p. Ingersoll-Rand Co., Woodcliff Lake, N.J., 1976-89; ret., 1989; mem. Can Govt. Oil and Gas Tech. Exch. Program with former USSR, 1972—, Minerals and Metals Mission to China, 1972—. Mem. Resource Fund Colo. Sch. Mines; past pres., dir. Town and River Civic Assn. Mem. Machinery and Equipment Mfrs. Assn. Can. (bd. dirs. 1974—, past chmn.), Royal Palm Yacht Club (commodore 1994), Internat. Order of Blue Gavel (past Commodore's Club, past pres. Royal Palm br. dist. 8), Useppa Island Club, Tau Beta Pi. E-mail: Dickandda@aol.com. Home: 9990 Cypress Lake Dr Fort Myers FL 33919-6020

WENDELBERGER, GUSTAV, ecology educator; b. Vienna, Austria, Mar. 29, 1915; s. Gustav and Maria (Schulz) W.; m. Elfrune Zelinka, July 13, 1950; 1 child, Rudiger. D. in Natural Scis., U. Vienna, 1941. Asst. prof. U. Vienna, 1950-72; sec. gen. Inst. for Nature Protection, Vienna, 1950-69; prof., chair for vegetation sci. U. Vienna, 1972-85. Author: Zur Soziologie der kontinentalen Halophytenvegetation Mitteleuropas, 1950 (Ac. Sciences Vienna award), Die Steichen Heterophyllae der Gattung Artemisia, 1960 (Bibliotheca Botanica Stuttgart). Lt. German Air Force, 1943-45. Home: Schlossgasse 30, A 2500 Baden Austria Office: U Vienna, Althanstrasse 14, A 1090 Vienna Austria

WENDELBURG, NORMA RUTH, composer, pianist, educator; b. Stafford, Kans.; d. Henry and Anna Louise (Moeckel) W.;. MusB, Bethany Coll., 1943; MusM, U. Mich., 1947, Eastman Sch. Music, 1951; postgrad., Eastman Sch. Music, 1964-65, 66-67, PhD in Composition, 1969; postgrad., Mozarteum, 1953-54, Vienna Acad. Music, 1955. Tchr. music edn., piano Wayne (Nebr.) State Coll., 1947-50; asst. prof. Bethany Coll., Lindsborg, Kans., 1952-53, U. Iowa, 1956-58; asst. prof. composition, theory, piano Hardin-Simmons U., Abilene, Tex., 1958-66, chmn. grad. com. Sch. Music, 1960-66, founder, chmn. ann. univ. festival contemporary music, 1959—; assoc. prof. music Dallas Bapt. Coll., 1973-75; rsch. asst. to dir. grad. studies Eastman Sch. Music, 1966-67; assoc. prof., chmn. dept. theory and composition S.W. Tex. State U., 1969-72; mem. faculty Friends Bible Coll., Haviland, Kans., 1977-83; guest composer several colls. including U. Ottawa, 1984; performed in Eng. and in Prague; performed Am. Conservatory Mus., Charles Ives Ctr. for Am. Music, 1990—; various solo recitals and festivals. Composer numerous works including Symphony, 1967, Suite for Violin and Piano, 1965, Song Cycle for Soprano, flutes, Piano, 1974, Music for Two Pianos, 1985, Affirmation, 1982, Interlacings (organ), 1983, (recorded) Suite No. 2 for Violin and Piano, 1989, Fantasy for Trumpet and Piano, 1990, Sonata for Clarinet and Piano, Sinfonietta, 1994, Concerto for Clarinet and

Orch.; performed Mosaic, Smetana Hall, Prague, 1999, Symphony Orch. of Prague, Smetana Hall, Prague, 1999, Symphony Hall, Boston, 1998, Concertino for Oboe and String Orch. Alice Tully Hall Lincoln Ctr., N.Y.C., 1999, Warsaw Rhapsody, Warsaw Philharm. Orch., Lutoslawski Hall, 1999; performed and recorded Warsaw Rhapsody, Warsaw, 1999. Recipient Meet the Composer award N.Y. State Coun. Arts, 1979; named Kans. Composer of Yr., Kans. Fed. Music Clubs, 2000; Composition scholar Composers' Conf. Middlebury (Vt.), 1950, Berkshire Ctr., 1953; Fulbright awardee, 1953-55; Resident fellow Huntington Hartford Found., 1955-56, 58, 61; MacDowell Colony fellow, 1958, 60, 70; Nat. Festival Performing Arts fellow, 1989. Mem. ASCAP (Composition awards 1988-90, 91-98), Music Tchrs. Nat. Conf., Am. Soc. Univ. Composers, Minn. Composers Forum, Am. Women Composers, Music Club (Hutchinson), Sigma Alpha Iota. Republican. Avocations: travel, photography, gardening. Address: 2206 N Van Buren St Hutchinson KS 67502-3738

WENDER, IRA TENSARD, lawyer; b. Pitts., Jan. 5, 1927; s. Louis and Luba (Kibrick) W.; m. Phyllis M.Bellows, June 24, 1966; children: Justin B., Sarah T; children by previous marriage: Theodore M., Abigail A., John B. Swarthmore Coll., 1942-45; JD, U. Chgo., 1948; LLM, NYU, 1951. Atty. Lord, Day and Lord, N.Y.C., 1950-52, 54-59; asst. dir. internat. program in tax. Harvard U. Law Sch., 1952-54; lectr. N.Y. U. Sch. Law, N.Y.C., 1954-59; ptnr. Baker and McKenzie, Chgo., 1959-61; founding ptnr. N.Y.C. office, 1961-71; sr. ptnr. Wender, Murase & White, 1971-82; of counsel, 1982-86; chmn. C. Brewer and Co., Ltd., Honolulu, 1969-75; pres., CEO A. G. Becker Paribas Inc., 1978-82; chmn., CEO Sussex Securities Inc., 1983-85; of counsel Patterson, Belknap, Webb & Tyler, N.Y.C., 1986-87, ptnr., 1988-93; of counsel, 1994—; chmn. Perry Ellis Internat., Inc., N.Y.C., 1994; bd. dirs. REFAC Tech. Devel. Corp., N.Y.C., Dime Bancorp, N.Y.C.; Deotexis Inc., Bermuda; bd. mgrs. Swarthmore Coll, 1978-89; pres., bd. mgrs. PARC Vendome Condominium, 1990-94; trustee Putnet (Vt.) Sch., 1985-92, 93—, vice chmn., 1998—; trustee Brearley Sch., N.Y.C., 1980-85. Author: (with E.R. Barlow) Foreign Investment and Taxation, 1995. Dir., treas. Fountain House, Inc., N.Y., 1998—; dir. Am. Near East Refuge Aid, Washington; mem. Coun. on Fgn. Rels. Mem. ABA, N.Y. State Bar Assn., Assn. of Bar of City of N.Y. Home: 115 E 67th St New York NY 10021-5951 Office: Patterson Belknap Webb & Tyler LLP Ste 2300 1133 Avenue Of The Americas Fl 22 New York NY 10036-6731

WENDERS, WIM, film director; b. Dusseldorf, Germany, Aug. 14, 1945. Dir. films including Summer in the City, 1970, The Goalie's Anxiety at the Penalty Kick, 1972, The Scarlet Letter, 1974, Alice in the Cities, 1974, The Wrong Move, 1975, Kings of the Road, 1976, The American Friend, 1977, Lightning Over Water (Nick's Movie, with Nicholas Ray), 1980, The State of Things, 1982, Hammett, 1982, Paris, Texas, 1984 (Palme d'Or, Cannes Internat. Film Festival), Tokyo-Ga, 1985, Wings of Desire, 1987 (Best Dir., Cannes Internat. Film Festival), Aufzeichnungen zu Kleiderund Stadten, 1989, Until the End of the World, 1991, Far Away, So Close, 1993 (Cannes Internat. Film Festival Grand Prize), The End of Violence, 1997; co-dir. Par Dela' Les Nuages, 1995, Lumiere et Compagnie, 1995, A Trick of the Light, 1996; writer, dir. Beyond the Clouds, 1995, The End of Violence, 1997; author: Emotion Pictures, 1986, Written in the West, 1987, Die Logik de Bilder, 1988, The Act of Seeing, 1992, Million Dollar Hotel, 1999, Buena Vista Social Club, 1999. Office: Road Movies Filmproduktion Gmbh, Potsdamer Strasse 199, 1000 Berlin 30, Germany*

WENDLINGER, ROBERT MATTHEW, communications and memory consultant; b. N.Y.C.; s. Harry and Rose (Pollock) W.; m. Dalis Peralta, 1955 (div. 1973); children: David, Marcella, Marta; m. Joan Hays Cole, June 23, 1984. Student U. Calif., Berkeley, 1942-43, Columbia U., 1947-52. Script editor Radio Free Europe, N.Y.C., 1950-52; assoc. editor Ind. Film Jour., N.Y.C., 1953-57; gen. mgr. Kermit Rolland and Assos., Princeton, N.J., 1957-59; exec. asst. in charge editorial services United Hosp. Fund of N.Y., N.Y.C., 1959-60; mgr. info. sect. Com. for Air and Water Conservation, Am. Petroleum Inst., N.Y.C., 1966-67; with Bank of Am. NT & SA, San Francisco, 1967-78, asst. v.p. communications, 1972-78; pres. Communications Cons. and Services, Berkeley, Calif., 1978-82; pres. Proust Press, Oakland, Calif., 1994—; mem. grad. faculty St. Mary's Coll., Moraga, Calif., 1975-78; mem. Astron Corp. Fellow Am. Bus. Communication Assn.; mem. Indsl. Communication Council (past pres.). Author: (with James M. Reid, Jr.) Effective Letters: A Program in Self-Instruction, 1964, 3d edit., 1978, Japanese edit., 1996, The Memory Triggering Book: Using Your Memories to Enhance Your Life and Your Relationships, 1995; contbr.; Everybody Wins; TA Applied to Organizations, 1973; Affirmative Action for Women, 1973; McGraw-Hill Ency. Professional Management, 1978. Office: 20 Treasure Hl Oakland CA 94618-2331

WENDT, ALEXANDER EDWARD, educator; b. Mainz, Germany, June 12, 1958; s. Hans Werner and Martha Ann W. BA, Macalester Coll., St. Paul, Minn., 1982; PhD, U. Minn., 1989. Asst. prof. Yale U., New Haven, Conn., 1989-97; assoc. prof. Dartmouth Coll., Hanover, N.H., 1997-99, U. Chgo., 1999—. Author: Social Theory of International Politics, 1999. E-mail: awendt@uchicago.edu. Office: Univ Chicago Dept Political Sci Chicago IL 60637

WENDT, DIRK, psychologist, educator; b. Harburg-Wilhelmsburg, Germany, Mar. 18, 1935; s. Heinrich and Aenne (Meyer) W.; m. Chrilla Gerlach, Dec. 23, 1961 (div. 1990); children: Katharina, Johannes. Diploma in psychology, U. Hamburg, 1959, PhD, 1966. Rsch. asst. U. Hamburg, 1959-60, tchg. asst., 1960-71, assoc. prof. psychology, 1971-73; prof. psychology U. Kiel, Germany, 1974—. Co-author: Quantitative Methoden der Psychologie, 1966, 74; author: Allgemeine Psychologie, 1989, Entwicklungspsychologie, 1997. Office: Inst Psychology, Olshausenstrasse 40, D-24098 Kiel Germany

WENDT, HANS W., life scientist; b. Berlin, July 25, 1923; s. Hans O. and Alice (Creutzburg) W.; m. Martha A. Linger, Dec. 23, 1956 (div.); children: Alexander, Christopher, Sandra; m. Judith A. Hammer, June 25, 1988. MSc, U. Hamburg, Germany, 1949; PhD in Psychopharmacology, U. Marburg, Germany, 1953. Diplomate in psychology. Rsch. asst. U. Marburg, 1949-53; rsch. assoc. Wesleyan U. and Office Naval Rsch., Middletown, Conn., 1952-53; asst. prof., field dir. internat. project U. Mainz, Germany, 1955-59; engring. psychologist to prin. human factors scientist Link Aviation, Apollo Simulator Systems, Binghamton, N.Y., 1959-61; assoc. to prof. psychology Valparaiso (Ind.) U., 1961-68; prof. psychology Macalester Coll., St. Paul, 1968-93; sr. rsch. fellow Chronobiology Labs. U. Minn., 1980—; prin. investigator A.v. Humboldt Geomedicine Collaboration (astrobiology), 1994—; cons. and reviewer, 1961—; hon. prof. sci. U. Marburg, Germany, 1971—; vis. prof. U. Victoria, B.C., Can., U. Marburg, U. Bochum, U. Bielefeld, U. Goettingen, all Germany, 1966-89. Contbr. articles to profl. jours., chpts. to books. Recipient Disting. Sr. Scientist award, Alexander von Humboldt Found., 1976. Home: 2180 Lower Saint Dennis Rd Saint Paul MN 55116-2831

WENDT, KAROL JEAN, marriage and family therapist, consultant, trainer; b. Prairie du Chien, Wis., Aug. 19, 1952; d. Lloyd Jule and Audrie Pearl (Knoble) Wood; m. James J. Wendt, Jr., Aug. 16, 1980; children: Jason Curt, Laura Jean. BS, U. Wis., Platteville, 1974; MSW, U. Wis., Milw., 1976. Cert. alcohol and drug counselor, Wis.; cert. ind. clin. social worker, Wis.; cert. marriage and family therapist, Wis. Family therapist Elmbrook Hosp., Brookfield, Wis., 1976-79, Family Svc. of Milw., 1979-87, Cedarspring Resource Ctr., 1987-90; pres. Systemic Perspectives, Inc., 1990—; mem. faculty Family Tng. Inst., Milw., 1986—; ind. trainer Children's Rsch. Ctr., Madison, Wis., 1998—. Resource person Compassionate Friends, Milw., 1978—; vol. Greendale (Wis.) Sch. Dist., 1993—; active Adoration Luth. Ch., Greenfield, Wis., 1986—. Named among Best Mental Health Profls. in Milw., Milw. Mag., 1994. Mem. NASW, Wis. Family Based Svc. Assn. (bd. dirs. 1992-94, pres. 1994, Crucible award 1994), Am. Assn. Marriage and Family Therapy (approved supr.). Democrat. Avocations: hiking, gardening, reading, music. Office: Systemic Perspectives Inc 2300 N Mayfair Rd Ste 505 Milwaukee WI 53226-1508

WENDT, MICHAEL, anesthesiologist, researcher; b. Bielefeld, Germany, Mar. 1, 1948; s. Georg-Gerhard and Ingeborg (Nickel) W.; m. Gertrud Breuer; 1 child, Sandra. MD, J. W. Goethe U., Frankfurt, Germany, 1972. MD. Resident Aug.Krankenhaus Altona, Hamburg, Germany, 1975-76; resident dept. anesthesia U. Münster, Germany, 1976-80, staff, 1980-92; head dept. anesthesia U. Greifswald, Germany, 1992—, med. dir., 1994-97. Med. officer Bundeswehr, 1972-74, Stade, Germany. Office: Klinik Anes-Intensive Med, Loefflerstrasse 23b, D-17489 Greifswald Germany

WENDT, ROBIN GLOVER, retired public official; b. Preston, England, Jan. 7, 1941; s. William Romilly and Doris May (Glover) W.; m. Prudence Ann Dalby, Sept. 11, 1965; children: Julia Margaret, Catherine Susan. BA, Oxford U., 1962, MA, 1992. Civil servant Dept. Health and Social Security, London, 1962-75; dep. sec. Cheshire (United Kingdom) County Coun., 1975-79, chief exec., 1979-89; sec. Assn. County Couns., London, 1989-97; CEO Nat. Assn. Local Couns., 1997-99; ret., 1999. Dep. lt. County of Cheshire, 1990—. Methodist. Avocations: music, travel, swimming, gardening, sports. Home: 28 Church Ln Upton, Chester CH2 1DJ, England

WENDT, VERNON EARL, internist, cardiologist; b. Cleve., Mar. 26, 1931; s. Raymond C. and Esther L. (Naujoks) W.; m. Hildegarde Caroline Moeller, Aug. 14, 1953; children: David, Frederick, Kathryn, Elizabeth, Doralyn, James, Vernon Earl, Jr. BS in Chemistry cum laude, Baldwin-Wallace Coll., 1952; MD, Columbia U., 1956. Intern Detroit Receiving Hosp., 1956-57, resident, 1959-62; USPHS postdoctoral fellow in cardiology Wayne State U. Sch. of Medicine, Detroit, 1962-65, from instr. to asst. prof. medicine, 1961-65; dir. rsch. Blodgett Meml. Med. Ctr., Grand Rapids, Mich., 1965-67; pvt. practice internal medicine and cardiology, Grand Rapids, 1967—. Capt. med. corps. USAF, 1957-59. Fellow Am. Coll. Cardiology, Am. Coll. Angiology; mem. ACP, Am. Heart Assn. of Mich. (pres. 1987-88, trustee 1973-93), Am. Lung Assn. of Mich. (pres. 1978-80), Mich. Soc. Internal Medicine (pres. 1991-92), Kent County Med. Soc., Coun. on Geriatric Cardiology, Am. Acad. Anti-Aging Medicine. Lutheran. Avocations: golf, gardening, walking. Home: 1620 Andover Rd SE Grand Rapids MI 49506-4710 Office: 1000 E Paris Ave SE Ste 208 Grand Rapids MI 49546-3680

WENEGRAT, SAUL S., arts administrator, art educator, consultant; b. Jersey City, Mar. 28, 1933; s. John and Tillie (Freeman) W. BA, Rutgers U., 1960; MPA, Harvard U., 1962; cert., London U., 1975. Dir. art program Port Authority of N.Y. & N.J., N.Y.C., 1962-95; prof. grad. divsn. Fashion Inst. Tech., N.Y.C., 1987-95; v.p. Forums Internat., 1995—; pub. art panelist N.J. State Com. Arts, Trenton, 1985-95, Conn. State Com. Arts, Hartford, 1988, N.Y.C. Cultural Affairs, 1980-88, Met. Transit Authority, N.Y.C., 1994-95. Editor: Art for the Public, 1985. Capt. USAF, 1953-57. Recipient Doris Freedman award Mayor of N.Y.C., 1984, Merit cert. Mcpl. Art Soc., 1980, 85; Carnegie fellow, 1960, Fels fellow, 1960. Mem. Nat. Assn. Corp. Art Adminstrn. (chmn. bd. 1985-95), Harvard Club. Avocations: bridge, walking, museums. Home: 2 Beekman Pl New York NY 10022-8058

WENG, CHENG-CHIANG, civil engineering educator, structural engineer; b. Taichung, Taiwan, Feb. 24, 1959. BS, Nat. Taipei Inst. of Tech., 1979; MS, Cornell U., 1984, PhD, 1987. Rsch. asst. civil engring. dept. Cornell U., Ithaca, N.Y., 1983-86; assoc. prof. civil engring. dept. Nat. Chiao Tung U., Hsinchu, Taiwan, 1986-92, prof. civil engring. dept., 1992—; vis. scholar U. Wash., Seattle, 1992-93. Contbr. articles to profl. jours. including Jour. of Structural Engring., Jour. of Materials in Civil Engring., Strain. Dir. Chinese Youth Goodwill Mission, Taipei, 1990, Taipei Folk Dance Group, 1991. Recipient Award of Excellence in Rsch. Nat. Sci. Coun., 1993, Outstanding Award in Tchg. Ministry of Edn., 1993, 94. Mem. ASCE, Chinese Soc. of Structural Engrs. (mem. exec. com. 1993—), Chinese Inst. of Steel Constrn., Chinese Soc. of Earthquake Engring. (mem. exec. com. 2000—), Chinese Soc. of Civil Engrs. (vice chmn. steel structures com. 1989-90). Avocations: tennis, golf, classic music, travel, folk arts. Home: 4th Fl No 6 Alley 1003, Ta Hsueh Rd, Hsinchu Taiwan Office: Nat Chiao Tung Univ/Civil Engring, 1001 Ta Hsueh Rd, Hsinchu Taiwan

WENG, CHENG-I, engineering educator; b. Tainan, Taiwan, Apr. 9, 1944; s. Ho-Fa and Fang-Chu (Liang) W.; m. Pi-Yuen Chen, Dec. 30, 1967; two children. BS, Nat. Cheng Kung U., Tainan, 1966; MS, U. Rochester, 1970, PhD, 1973. Rsch. assoc. dept. mech. engring. U. Rochester, 1972-73; assoc. prof. dept. mech. engring. Nat. Cheng Kung U., Tainan, 1973-77; prof., chmn. dept. mech. engring. Nat. Chiao Tung U., Hsinchu, Taiwan, 1977-80; prof., chmn. dept. mech. engring. Nat. Cheng Kung U., Tainan, 1980-86, prof., dir. Tjing Ling Mfg. Ctr., 1986-88, acad. dean, 1989-94; pres. Nat. Cheng Kung U., Nat. Sci. Coun.; cons. Machinery Industry Rsch. Lab., Hsin Chu, Taiwan, 1984-89; chmn. Taiwan Machinery Mfg., Kao Hsiung, Taiwan, 1988-89; dir. Automobile Testing R&D Ctr., Taipei, 1990-92; standing dir. Metal Industry R&D Ctr., Kao Hsuing, 1991-94. Contbr. articles to profl. jours. 2d lt. Air Force, 1966-67, Taiwan. Recipient Disting. Rsch. award Nat. Sci. Coun., Taiwan, 1988, 90, 92, 94, Acad. Publ. award Chung-San Acad. Found., Taiwan, 1990, Acad. award Ministry of Edn., Taiwan, 1991. Mem. Chinese Soc. Mech. Engring. (pres. Kao Hsuing br. 1995—), Chinese Soc. Theoretical and Applied Mechanics. Avocations: sports, music, mountaineering. Office: Nat Cheng Kung Univ, 1 Ta-Huseh Rd, Tainan Taiwan Also: Nat Sci Coun, 106 Ho-ping East Rd Sect 2, Taipei Taiwan*

WENG, JOHN JUYANG, computer science educator, researcher; b. Shanghai, Apr. 15, 1957; came to U.S., 1983; m. Min Guo, 1985; children: Colin S., Rodney D. BS in Computer Sci., Fudan U., Shanghai, 1982; MS in Computer Sci., U. Ill., 1985, PhD in Computer Sci., 1989. Rsch. asst. U. Ill., Urbana, 1984-88; rschr. Computer Rsch. Inst. Montreal, Can., 1989-90; vis. asst. prof. U. Ill., 1990-92; asst. prof. Mich. State U., East Lansing, 1992-98, assoc. prof., 1998—. Author: (chpt.) Early Visual Learning, 1996; co-author: (chpt.) Handbook of Pattern Recognition and Computer Vision, 1993, Motion and Structures from Image Sequences, 1993, Visual Navigation, 1997. Mem. IEEE (Computer Soc., assoc. editor IEEE Transactions on Image Processing 1994-97), Am. Soc. Engring. Edn., Sigma Xi, Phi Beta Delta. Achievements include contributions to understanding and computation of estimation of motion and structure from image sequences; co-inventor of Cresceptron, an experimental system for recognizing and segmenting objects from natural images; introducer of the concept of comprehensive visual learning for intelligent sensor-based machines; inventor of SHOSLIF, a general framework for visual learning by computers; an originator of the developmental approach to artificial intelligence -- patent pending "Developmental Learning Machine and Method." Office: Mich State Univ 3115 Engring Bldg East Lansing MI 48824

WENG, WEN-KAI, physician, medical researcher; b. Taipei, China, Dec. 11, 1962; arrived in U.S., 1990; s. Hua-Min and Lee (Chu) W. MD, Chung-Shan Med. & Dental Coll., Taichung, China, 1988; PhD, U. Minn., 1996. Rsch. asst. U. Minn., Mpls., 1990-96; resident in internal medicine U. Tex./Houston Med. Sch., 1996-99; fellow in oncology Stanford U., Calif., 1999—. Ad hoc reviewer Blood-Jour. Am. Soc. Hematology, 1996. Dir. acad. com. Minn. Chinese Soc. Biomed. Sci., Mpls., 1993-96; cons. Minn. Chinese Student Assn., Mpls., 1993-96. With Rep. of China Army, 1988-90. Recipient fellowship U. Minn. Grad. Sch., 1995-96, Nat. Rsch. Svc. award NIH, 1994-95. Mem. Chinese Med. Assn., Sigma Xi (Charles and Dorothy Andrew Bird award 1996). Avocations: wildlife photography, birding, rock climbing, computers. Office: Stanford U Divsn Oncology Medicine 1000 Welch Rd Ste 202 Palo Alto CA 94304-1808

WENG, XINZHI, physician, researcher, educator; b. Ningpo, Zhejiang, China, May 10, 1919; s. Van-lan and Van-zhen (Chen) W.; m. Heping Du; children: Weiren, Weili, Weixin. BS, Peiping Yenching U., Beijing, 1941; MD, West China Union U., Chendu, 1945. Asst. instr. Med. Sch. Peking (China) U., 1946-49; vis. physician, asst. prof. Ctrl. People's Hosp., Beijing, 1949-57; dir. med. dept. Beijing Sino-Soviet Friendship Hosp., 1957-65; dep. dir. hosp. Beijing Chaoyang Hosp., 1957-97; prof. Capital U. Med. Scis., 1979-97; head WHO Collaborating Ctr. for Tobacco or Health China, 1986—. Chief editor: Chronic Obstructive Pulmonary Disease and Chronic Cor Pulmonale, 1997, Chinese Jour. Internal Medicine, 1986-92, Chinese edit. Brit. Med. Jour., 1998—; editor: Dictionary of Internal Medicine, 1992, Collection of Academic Papers of Weng Xinzhi, 1995. People's del. 7th and 8th Beijing People's Congresses, 1977-86; mem. 7th Nat. People's Polit. Consultative com., 1987-92. Recipient WHO Tobacco or Health cert. and medal, Geneva, 1989, Progress of Sci. and Tech. award Ministry of Health, Beijing, 1992, 2d grade Progress of Sci. and Tech. award Beijing People's Govt., 1986, 91. Mem. N.Y. Acad. Scis., Chinese Acad. Engring., Chinese Med. Assn. (sr., standing bd. dirs. 1990-94), Chinese Med. Found., Beijing Med. Assn. (v.p. 1984-92). Avocations: music, stamp collecting, photography, movies. Fax: (8610) 6500 5359. Home: 9-5-1 Ti Yu Chang Dong Lu, Beijing 100020, China Office: Beijing Red Cross Chaoyang, Hosp, 8 Bai Jia Zhuang, Chaoyang Beijing 100020, China

WENGE, RALPH, newscaster; b. Phila.. BBA, Temple U. Anchor, co-producer KGW-TV News, 1973-83; anchor, producer, writer WTNH-TV, New Haven, Conn., 1970-73; exec. prodr. CNN, Atlanta, 1983—. Office: CNN PO Box 105366 1 CNN Ctr NW Atlanta GA 30348-5366

WENGER, LOWELL E., physics educator; b. Middlebury, Ind., Nov. 17, 1948; s. Theodore E. and Lavina A. W.; m. Andrea J. Goral, Dec. 26, 1976; children: Joel, Erin. BS, Purdue U., 1971, MS, 1973, PhD, 1975. From asst. prof. to prof. dept. physics Wayne State U., Detroit, 1976-98, prof., chair dept. physics, 1998—. Alfred Sloan fellow Sloan Found., 1978-79, Fulbright Rsch. fellow The Netherlands, 1982-83. Mem. Am. Physical Soc., Materials Rsch. Soc., Sigma Xi (pres. local chpt. 1996—). E-mail: wenger@physics.wayne.edu. Office: Wayne State Univ Dept Physics Detroit MI 48201

WENIGER-PHELPS, NANCY ANN, media specialist, photographer; b. Kingman, Kans., Sept. 4, 1948; d. Watson and Reva Jo (Schlup) W. BA in Phys. Edn., Ottawa (Kans.) U., 1970; MA in LS, U. Denver, 1980. Cert. K-12 media specialist, secondary phys. edn. tchr., Ariz. Phys. edn. tchr. Grand Junction (Colo.) Sch. Dist., 1970-73; dist. mgr. World Book Ency., 1973-74; personal sec. Younger Bail Bond Svc., Grand Junction, 1974-76; media specialist K-12, phys. edn. tchr. Kingman (Kans.) Unified Sch. Dist., 1976-78, Ovid (Colo.) Sch. Dist., 1980-82, Sargeant Sch. Dist., Monte Vista, Colo., 1982-84, Antonito Sch. Dist., Ovid, Colo., 1984-85; photographer's asst. Bill Westenberg Photography, Alamosa, Colo., 1985-86; sch. media specialist Window Rick (Ariz.) Unified Sch. Dist., 1986-96; profl. photographer; trainer adult and student storytellers; head dist. lib. computer program. Author: Photographic Uses in the Library; exhibited in group shows Gallup (N.Mex.) Gallery, 1989, Window Rock Elem. Sch., 1989, Sunflower Shop, Wichita, Kans. 1989-90, 96-98, also Alamosa, Colo., 1985-87, 1st Nat. Bank, Kingman (Kans.), Fernley (Nev.) Phys. Therapy, 1993. Mem. Washoe County Friends of Libr., Reno, Nev., vol. book sorter, vol. book sale. Mem. AAHPERD, ALA, Am. Fedn. Tchrs., Internat. Platform Assn., Ariz. Fedn. Tchrs., Window Rock Fedn. Tchrs., Ariz. Edn. Media Assn., Assoc. Photographers Internat. Ariz. Edn. Assn., Alpha Delta Kappa. Home: 3305 Farm District Rd Fernley NV 89408-8608

WENKANG, ZHANG, Chinese government official. Min. pub. health Govt. of China, Beijing. Mem. Communist Party. Address: Ministry Pub Health, 44 Hou Hai Bei Yan/West Dis, Beijing 100725, China*

WENNAR, AMÍ AYNE, foreign service officer program intern; b. Pittsfield, Mass., Oct. 30, 1972; d. Martin Howard and Elizabeth Wennar. BA, U.V.M., 1998; grad., Georgetown U., 2000, MS in Fgn. Sci., 2000. Tchg. asst. Dept. of Humanities U. Vt., Burlington, 1997; rsch. asst. Dept. Polit. Sci. U. Vt., 1997, rsch. asst. Dept. History, 1997; rsch. intern Washington Inst. for Near East Policy, 1997, 98; intern Seeds of Peace, Washington, 1999—; Marava Seminar participant Israeli Def. Forces, Haifa, Israel, 1995; rsch. cons. Leadership PhD Program, 1999; ednl. program participant Project Oren, Eilat, Israel, 1995. Cmty. Bd. Sch. Fgn. Svc., Georgetown U., 1999-2000, Debate Soc., Sch. Fgn. Svc. Avocations: languages (Arabic, Hebrew, French, Russian), photography, cooking, martial arts, travel. E-mail: awennar@hotmail.com.

WENNBERG, TERESA, artist; b. Stockholm, Dec. 30, 1944; d. Fredrik and Helen (Ankarcrona) W.; m. Pierre D. Lobstein, 1983; 1 child, Alexia. Student, U. Stockholm, 1968. Exhbns. include Fondation C. Gulbenkian, Lisbon, 1982, Hara Mus. Contemporary Art, Tokyo, 1987, Norrtälje Konsthall, Sweden, 1995, Royal Inst. Tech., Stockholm, 1998.

WENNER, CHARLES RODERICK, lawyer; b. New Haven, Jan. 10, 1947; s. Charles Bellew and Joan Rhoda (Morrison) W.; m. Jovita C. Vergara, June 11, 1999. BS, Coll. Charleston, 1969; JD, U. Conn., 1973. Bar: Conn. 1974, D.C. 1977. Law clk. Conn. Superior Ct., Hartford, 1973-74; staff atty. SEC, Washington, 1974-76, spl. counsel to chmn., 1976-77; assoc. Fulbright & Jaworski, Washington, 1977-81, ptnr., 1981—; lectr. law Sch. Law U. Conn., 1973-74. Trustee Calvary United Meth. Ch., Arlington, Va., 1993-95, 97-98; counselor Gospel Mission of Washington, 1991—; bd. dirs. Operation Friendship Internat., Inc., Washington, 1993—. Recipient Am. Hist. award DAR, Charleston, 1969. Mem. ABA, D.C. Bar Assn. Methodist. Avocations: running. Home: Apt 105 1101 S Arlington Ridge Rd Arlington VA 22202-1922 Office: Fulbright & Jaworski 801 Pennsylvania Ave NW Fl 3-5 Washington DC 20004-2623

WENNERÅS, CHRISTINE, physician, educator; b. Trondheim, Norway, Feb. 13, 1963; arrived in Sweden, 1963; d. Svein and Kari (Tøndell) W. PhD, Göteborg (Sweden) U., 1993, MD, 1995; postgrad., Pasteur Inst., 1996-97. Med. diplomate. Med. intern Sahlgren's Hosp., Göteborg, 1993-95; asst. prof. dept. med. microbiology Göteborg U., 1998—; med. resident Bacteriol. Lab. Sahlgren's Hosp., 1998—. Swedish rep. European Tech. Assessment Network, European Union, Brussels, 1998, 99. home: Klostergången 3, 41318 Göteborg Sweden Office: Dept Med Microbiology, Guldhedsgatan 10, 413 46 Göteborg Sweden

WENSELEERS, TOM HILAIRE, biologist, researcher; b. Antwerp, Brabant, Belgium, Nov. 2, 1973; s. Luc Wenseleers and Diane Sebrechts. MSc in Biology with 1st class honors, U. Leuven, Belgium, 1995. Univ. asst. Entomology Lab., U. Leuven, 1995—. Contbr. papers to sci. jours., including Internat. Jour. Insect Morphology and Embryology. Office: U Leuven Entomology Lab, Naamsestraat 59, B-3000 Leuven Brabant, Belgium

WENSKUS, OTTA HELENE, philologist; b. Marburg, Hessen, Germany, May 29, 1955; d. Reinhard Rudolf and Hella Elisabeth Wenskus; 1 child, Roland. PhD, U. Göttingen, Germany, 1982, Habil., 1988. Prof. of classics U Innsbruck, Austria, 1994—. Author: Ringkomposition im Hippokratischen Corpus, 1982, Astronomische Zeitangaben von Homer bis Theophrast, 1990, Emblematischer Code-Wechsel, Innsbruck, 1998; contbr. articles to profl. jours. Grantee Studienstiftung, 1975-82, Deutsche Forschungsgemeinschaft, 1985, 86-87, Heisenberg Found., 1990-94. Avocations: astronomy, botanics, modern languages, travel. Office: Univ of Innsbruck, Innrain 52, A-6020 Innsbruck Tirol, Austria

WENSLEY, PENELOPE, diplomat. Australian rep. to UN N.Y.C., 1997—. Office: Permanent Mission Australia 150 E 42nd St 33rd Fl New York NY 10017-5612*

WENTE, VAN ARTHUR, consultant, retired government official; b. Johnston City, Ill., Jan. 11, 1925; s. Edward H. and Pauline Lucille (Barham) W.; m. Jane Van Derveer Updike, Sept. 22, 1962; children: Gretchen Jane, Robert Edward. BSChemE, Washington U., St. Louis, 1945; grad., Nat. Def. U., 1977. Chem. engr. Firestone Tire & Rubber Co., Pottstown, Pa., 1945-50, USN Research Lab., Washington, 1950-56; info. officer U.S. Atomic Energy Agy., Germantown, Md., 1956-59, sci. advisor, 1959-61; documentation head NASA, Washington, 1961-64, systems head, 1965-80, sci. and tech. info. dir., 1981-89, sr. exec. svc., 1983-89; mem. adv. group on aerospace R & D info. NATO, 1983-89. Contbr. articles to profl. jours., chpts. to books. Chairperson adminstrv. coun. Concord-St. Andrews United Meth. Ch., 2000—. Recipient Presdl. award Mgmt. Improvement, 1970. Fellow Nat. Fedn. Abstracting and Info. Svcs. (hon., bd. dirs. 1986-88); mem. AIChE, Am. Soc. for Info. Scis., Chem. Engrs. Washington (treas. 1957-58, sec. 1958-59), Kenwood Golf and Country Club (bd. govs. 1995—), Mil. Officers Club, Omicron Delta Kappa, Sigma Xi. Avocations: tennis, music, photography. Home and Office: 5919 Gloster Rd Bethesda MD 20816-1144

WENTWORTH, DIANA VON WELANETZ, author; b. L.A., Mar. 4, 1941; d. Eugene and Marguerite (Rufi) Webb; m. Frederic Paul von Welanetz, Nov. 2, 1963 (dec. Mar. 19, 1989); 1 child, Lisa Frances von We-

lanetz; m. Theodore S. Wentworth, Dec. 9, 1989; stepchildren: Christina Linn, Kathryn Allison. Student, UCLA, 1958-60. Ptnr. von Welanetz Cooking Workshop, L.A., 1968-85; host New Way Gourmet, 1983-86; founder Inside Edge Found. Edn., Calif., 1985-93; spkr. in field. Author: The Pleasure of Your Company, 1976 (Cookbook of Yr.), With Love from Your Kitchen, 1976, The Art of Buffet Entertaining, 1978, The Von Welanetz Guide to Ethnic Ingredients, 1983, L.A. Cuisine, 1985, Celebrations, 1985, Chicken Soup for the Soul Cookbook, 1995. Treas. Louise L. Hay Found., Carson, Calif., 1988—; advisor Women of Vision, Calif., 1995—. Mem. Internat. Food, Wine & Travel Writers Assn., Internat. Assn. Cooking Profls., Angels of Arts/Orange County Performing Arts Ctr., Ctr. Club. Avocations: painting, fine art, travel writing, design. Office: 4631 Teller Ave Ste 100 Newport Beach CA 92660-8105

WENTWORTH, LARRY MARSHALL, lawyer; b. Knoxville, Tenn., June 16, 1951; s. Robert Benning and Lillian (Hicock) W. BA in Polit. Sci., Antioch Coll., 1974; JD summa cum laude, New Eng. Sch. Law, Boston, 1991. Bar: Mass., Conn., Federated States of Micronesia. Staff. atty., law clk. Supreme Ct. of Federated States of Micronesia, Chuuk, 1992—. Editor New Eng. Law Rev., 1989-91; contbr. articles to profl. jours. Avocations: vexillology, philately. Office: Federated States Micronesia, Supreme Ct PO Box 601, Chuuk Federated States of Micronesia

WENTWORTH, THEODORE SUMNER, lawyer; b. Bklyn., July 18, 1938; s. Theodore Sumner and Alice Ruth (Wortmann) W.; m. Sharon Linelle Arkush, 1965 (dec. 1987); children: Christina Linn, Kathrun Allison; m. Diana Webb von Welanetz, 1989; 1 stepchild, Lexi von Welanetz. AA, Am. River Coll., 1958; JD, U. Calif., Hastings, 1962. Bar: Calif. 1963, U.S. Dist. Ct. (no. and ctrl. dists.) Calif., U.S. Ct. Appeals (9th cir.), U.S. Supreme Ct.; cert. trial specialist; diplomate Nat. Bd. Trial Advocacy; assoc. Am. Bd. Trial Advocates. Assoc. Adams, Hunt & Martin, Santa Ana, Calif., 1963-66; ptnr. Hunt, Liljestrom & Wentworth, Santa Ana, Calif., 1967-77; pres. Solabs Corp.; chmn. bd., exec. v.p. Plant Warehouse, Inc., Hawaii, 1974-82; prin. Law Offices of Wentworth, Paoli & Purdy, Newport Beach & Temecula, Calif.; judge pro tem Superior Ct. Attys. Panel Harbor Mcpl. Ct.; owner Eagles Ridge Ranch, Temecula, 1977—. Pres., bd. dirs. Santa Ana-Tustin Cmty. Chest, 1972; v.p., trustee South Orange County United Way, 1973-75; pres. Orange County Fedn. Funds, 1972-73; bd. dirs. Orange County Mental Health Assn. Mem. ABA, Am. Bd. Trial Advocates (assoc.), State Bar Calif., Orange County Bar Assn. (dir. 1972-76), Am. Trial Lawyers Assn., Calif. Trial Lawyers Assn. (bd. govs. 1968-70), Orange County Trial Lawyers Assn. (pres. 1967-68), Lawyer-Pilots Bar Assn., Aircraft Owners and Pilots Assn., Bahia Corinthian Yacht Club, Pacific Club, Newport. Achievements include research in vedic prins., natural law, quantum physics and mechanics. Office: 4631 Teller Ave Ste 100 Newport Beach CA 92660-8105 also: 41530 Enterprise Cir S Temecula CA 92590-4816

WENTWORTH, WILLIAM EDGAR, journalist; b. Newton, N.H., Nov. 4, 1931; s. Charles Bertrand and Mildred Frances (Ingalls) W. BA in Journalism, U. Tenn., Knoxville, 1958. Reporter Rochester (N.H.) Courier, 1959; reporter, copy editor Foster's Daily Democrat, Dover, N.H., 1959-68; copy editor Florida Today, Melbourne, Fla., 1968-93, ret., 1993. Author: (book) Vital Records, 1790-1829, 1995, Journals of Enoch Hayes Place, 1998; editor: (periodical) Genealogical Record, 1995—. Data entry-online Dover Pub. Libr., N.H., 1993—. Sgt. USAF, 1950-54. Mem. Strafford County Genealogical Soc., Citizens Against Government Waste, Srs. Coalition, N.H. Hist. Soc., N.H. Soc. Genealogists, Maine Soc. Genealogists, New Eng. Hist. Genealogical Soc. Republican. Baptist. Avocation, genealogy research. Home: 13 Olde Madbury Ln Dover NH 03820-5439

WENZ, GERHARD KARL, macromolecular chemistry educator; b. Mainz, Germany, July 27, 1953; s. Werner and Marianne Wenz; m. Brigitte Klaus, June 2, 1986; children: Andreas, Katharina. Vordiplom, J. Gutenberg-Univ., Mainz, 1975; diplom, A. Ludwigs-Univ., Freiburg, Germany, 1979, D of Chemistry, 1984; Habilitation, J. Gutenberg-Univ., 1993. Rsch. asst. Staudinger Inst., Freiburg, 1984-85; postdoctoral fellow UCLA, 1985-86; rsch. asst. Max-Planck Inst. für Polymerforschung, 1986-93; prof. Polymer-Inst. U. Karlsruhe, 1993—. Patentee in field; contbr. articles to sci. jours. Mem. Gesellschaft Deutscher Chemiker, Am. Chem. Soc., Deutscher Hochschullehrer Verband. Office: Polymer-Inst Univ Karlsruhe, Hertzstr 16, 76187 Karlsruhe Germany

WENZEL, ANN, dentist, researcher; b. Aarhus, Denmark, Dec. 4, 1952; d. Ib Christian Wenzel and Ellen Margrete (Nielsen) Christensen; m. Jakob Kragstrup, June 27, 1951; children: Jon, Tue. Dentistry degree, Copenhagen Dental Sch., 1977; PhD, Royal Dental Coll., Aarhus, 1982, D of Odontology, 1991. Specialist in oral radiology; tchg. diplomate. Dental surgeon Danish Ch. Aid, Moshi, Tanzani, 1977-78; dentist in pedodontics Comty. Dental Health Care, Silkeborg, Denmark, 1979-81; rsch. fellow Inst. Orthodontics Royal Dental Coll., Aarhus, 1978-81, from asst. prof. to assoc. prof. dept. oral radiology, 1981-96, prof. dept. oral radiology, 1996—. Mem. editl. bd. Jour. Dentomaxillofacial Radiology, 1992—, Oral Surgery, Oral Medicine, Oral Pathology, Oral Radiology Endodontics, 1992—, Clin. Oral Implant Rsch., 1994—, Jour. Dental Rsch., 1999—. Bd. dirs. Children's Internat. Summer Villages, UNESCO, Aarhus, 1993-97; bd. dirs. Open U., Aarhus, 1987-89. Grantee Danisco Found., 1993, Dannin Sci. Rsch. Found., 1995, Aarhus U. Rsch. Found., 1996. Mem. Internat. Assn. Dental Rsch. (bd. dirs. Scandinavian divsn. 1988-97, pres. Scandinavian divsn. 1991-93, pres. diagnostic sys. group 1996-97). Office: Royal Dental Coll Dept Oral Radiology, Vennelyst Blvd, DK-8000 Århus Denmark

WENZEL, KLARA, company executive, educator; b. Budapest, Hungary, Jan. 22, 1939; d. Karoly Gerőfy and Margit Böckl; m. Gottfried Wenzel, Aug. 11, 1962; 1 child, Andras. Grad., Tech. U. Budapest, 1962, DR, 1976, PhD, 1992, D Engring., 1996. Engr. Metallurgy Works, Ózd, Denmark, 1962-63; tchr. secondary sch., Ózd, 1963-69; asst. prof. Tech. U. Budapest, 1969-76, assoc. prof., 1976-92, prof., 1992-98; devel. dir. Coloryte Inc., 1998—. Patentee for correction color deficiency, 1994, measuring color vision defects, 1996. Hungarian leader Divsn. A of CIE, 1996. Named to Order of Cabour Internat. Com. Vega, 1987. Mem. ICVS, ISCC. Avocations: reading, music, swimming. Office: Coloryte Inc, Kőzúzó ur 8, H-2000 Szentendre Hungary

WENZEL, LOREN ALVIN, accounting educator; b. Dec. 12, 1945; s. Alvin Karl Gustav and Lois LaVonne (Kuechenmeister) W.; children: Lisa Anne (Wenzel) Szumilas, Karl Louis, Sara Kirsten Wenzel; m. Nylah Onalee. DBA, U. Memphis, 1990. Asst. prof. acctg. Wichita (Kans.) State U., 1987-88; prof. acctg. Mankato (Minn.) State U., 1988-98, U. Md. European Divsn., Heidelberg, Germany, 1996-97, Buena Vista U., Storm Lake, Iowa, 1998-99, Austin Peay State U., Clarksville, Tenn., 1999-2000, Marshall U., Ona, W.Va., 2000—. Contbr. articles to profl. publs.

WENZEL, LYNN, writer, editor; b. San Francisco, Mar. 22, 1944; d. Ralph Everett and Roberta (Hansen) Shallenberger; m. Jeffrey Bruce Wenzel, June 28, 1964; children: Jennifer Ann, Michael Charles. BA magna cum laude, William Paterson U., 1976. Editor Womanspace, Hackensack, N.J., 1980-85; asst. editor New Directions for Women, Englewood, N.J., 1988-89, mng. editor, 1989-94; writer feature stories for nat. antique mag. Handed Down, Berkeley, Calif., 1996—; writers features, mags., newspapers, Newsweek, N.Y. Times, Newsday, On the Issues, among others, N.J., 1979—; editor lit. and visual arts Bergen County N.J. Sch., Hackensack, 1992, Maywood, N.J., 1974-93; graphic artist New Directions for Women, Englewood, 1974-93, Marine Field Trip Manual, N.Y.C., 1989-93. Author: I Hear America Singing, 1989, Past & Promise, 1992; poetry for photo-greeting cards Foto-Feelings, 1993. Apptd. constnl. bicentennial com. on women and the constn. Teaneck Mayor's Office, Teaneck, N.J., 1987. Recipient The World is Moving award Bd. Freeholders, 1993. Mem. NOW, No. N.J. Nat. Orgn. for Women (co-pres. 1985-87, chairwoman media task force 1987-89, 12th Annual Feminist Achievement award 1992), Bergen County Alliance for Women (chairwoman publicity/media 1986-88), Nat. Writers Union, Internat. Women's Writing Guild. Unitarian-Universalist. Avocations: antiques, reading, genealogy, photography, interior design.

WENZEL, PETER, English literature educator; b. Essen, Germany, Apr. 23, 1953; s. Karl and Marianne (Koenen) W. PhD, Ruhr U., Bochum, Germany, 1979, PD, 1986. Asst. Ruhr U., 1979-94, asst. prof., 1994-96; prof. English lit. RWTH, Aachen, Germany, 1996—, vice dean faculty of philosophy, 1998—. Author: Lear-Criticism in the 20th Century, 1979, Surprise Endings in Jokes and Short Stories, 1989. Roman Catholic. Office: Inst fuer Anglistik I, Karmanstr 17-19, 52056 Aachen Germany

WENZEL, VERA STEPANOWNA, mathematician; b. Novosibirsk, Russia, Dec. 1, 1943; d. Stepan Markowic and Klaudia Andreewna (Ishukowa) W.; Polewzew; m. Volker Wenzel, Jan. 15, 1970; children: Jost, Julia. Diploma with distinction, U. Moscow, 1966; PhD, Tech. U., Magdeburg, Germany, 1979. Rsch. asst. Poly. U., Tula, Russia, 1970-71; rsch. scientist Acad. Sci., Berlin, 1971-86, rsch. scholar, 1987-93; rsch. scholar Free U., Berlin, 1994—. Co-author: Faszination Licht, 1996; contbr. articles to profl. jours. Mem. European Assn. for Study of Sci. and Tech., Gesellschaft für Wissenschafts- und Technikforschung. Avocation: painting. Home: Schmidtstr 11, 12621 Berlin Germany Office: Free U, Malteserstr 74-100, 12249 Berlin Germany

WENZLER, EDWARD WILLIAM, architect; b. Milw., Feb. 17, 1954; s. William Paul and Dolores Ann (Rahn) W.; m. Georgine Marie Eggert, Apr. 3, 1976; children: Christopher E., Michael E. BArch, U. Milw., 1978. Registered architect Wis., 1981, Minn., 1996. Architect Gordon Sibeck, Dallas, 1978-79; assoc. Wenzler and Assocs., Milw., 1979-84, ptnr., 1984-91, pres., 1991—. Prin. works include Oak Hill Terr, Waukesha, Wis., The Student Ctr. Addition at U. Wis.-Whitewater, Laurel Oaks Retirement Cmty, Glendale, Wis., Ctr. for the Arts at U. Wis.-Whitewater, Seven Oaks Skilled Care Facility, Glendale, Weidner Ctr. Addition at U. Wis.-Greenbay. Mem. AIA, Nat. Coun. Archtl. Registration Bds., Constrn. Specification Inst. Home: 19600 Gebhardt Rd Brookfield WI 53045-4823

WERBITT, WARREN, gastroenterologist, educator; b. Phila., Jan. 29, 1939; s. Saull Boris and Pearl (Weiner) W.; m. Drue Natalie Engman Werbitt, Aug. 30, 1964; children: Julie Michele, Jeffrey Brian. BS in Pharmacy, Temple U., 1960; D in Osteopathy, U. Osteo. Med. and Health Sci., Des Moines, 1966; MD, Allegheny U. Hosps. Med. Coll., Pa., 1973. Diplomate Am. Osteo. Bd. Internal Medicine, also sub-splty. bd. Gastroenterology; diplomate Am. Bd. Internal Medicine, also sub-splty. bd. Gastroenterology. Intern Doctor's Hosp., Columbus, Ohio, 1966-67; resident in internal medicine Doctor's Hosp., Columbus, 1967-68, Kennedy Meml. Hosps., Cherry Hill, N.J., 1968-69, Mercy Cath. Med. Ctr., Phila., 1969-70; resident in internal medicine Allegheny U. Hosps.- Med. Coll. Pa. divsn., Phila., 1971-72, fellow in gastroenterology, 1970-71, 72-74, instr., 1973—, attending physician and cons. in gastroenterology, 1977-94; instr. Phila. Coll. Osteo. Medicine, Phila., 1973-75; chmn. divsn. gastroenterology Phila. Coll. Osteo. Medicine, 1975-77; clin. assoc. prof. medicine U. Medicine and Dentistry, N.J., 1977—; attending physician and cons. in gastroenterology Vet. Adminstrn. Hosp., Phila., 1972-75; chmn. Div. Gastroenterology, Dept. Medicine Phila. Coll. Osteopathic Medicine, 1975-77; chmn. Dept. Medicine Kennedy Meml. Hosp. U. Med. Ctr., Cherry Hill, 1979-81, chmn. subsect. Gastroenterology, 1979-87. Contbg. editor The N.J. Jour. for Ostepathic Physicians and Surgeons, 1980—; mem. scientific adv. com. Phila. chpt. Nat. Found. Ileitis & Colitis, Inc., 1982—; contbr. articles to profl. jours. Recipient Profl. Svc. award Med. Soc. N.J., 1991. Fellow Am. Coll. Physicians, Am. Coll. Gastroenterology, Acad. Med. N.J.; mem. AMA, Am. Soc. Gastrointestinal Endoscopy, Am. Gastroenterology Assn., Am. Soc. Parenteral and Enteric Nutrition, Am. Inst. Ultrasound in Medicine, Am. Assn. Gynecologic Laparoscopists, Phila. Gastrointestinal Rsch. Forum, State Med. Soc. N.J., Camden County Med. Soc., N.J. Endoscopic Soc., Del. Valley Soc. for Gastrointestinal Endoscopy, South Jersey Gastroenterological Soc., Am. Osteopathic Assn., N.J. Soc. Osteopathic Physicians and Surgeons, Am. Coll. Osteopathic Internists, Camden County Osteopathic Assn., Am. Cancer Soc. (bd. dirs. N.J. chpt.), Crohn's and Colitis Found. Am. Inc. (Phila. and Del.), Pres.'s Circle Am. U., N.Y. Acad. Scis., John Sherman Myers Soc., Med. Club Phila., Lambda Omicron Gamma. Avocations: golf, running, music, reading, American History. Office: Profl Gastroenterology Assn 1939 Route 70 E Ste 250 Cherry Hill NJ 08003-4507

WERESH, THELMA FAYE, sculptor, artist; b. Baca County, Colo., Mar. 15, 1919; d. William Lee Cotton and Myrtle Mae (Quiet) Cotton-Winston; m. Andrew Anthony Weresh, Jan. 28, 1939; children: Charlotte Maria, Catherine Ann. BA, Coll. St. Mary, 1967. Art tchr. Ralston (Nebr.) Pub. Schs., 1967-73, Father Flanagan's Boys Home, Boys Town, Nebr., 1973-75; bd. dirs. Alliance of Arts Coun., Lincoln, Nebr., 1975; chmn. Visual Arts Commn., Loveland, Colo., 1990-91. One person exhibn. includes Ariel Gallery, N.Y., 1991; featured in Artist's Profile KRMA TV, 1995. Recipient SOHO Internat. 1st Place, 1990, 1st Place United Coun., 1990, 2nd Place, 1991, 1st Place George Lewis, 1991, 1st Place Southwest Art, 1992, 1st Place Women Artists, 1992, Spl. award Mus. N.W., 1992, First Annual Hall of Fame award Revue mag., 1996. Mem. Allied Artists Am., Loveland (Colo.) Sculpture Group. Home: 2009 Lakewood Dr Loveland CO 80538-3423

WERMUTH, MANFRED JAKOB, urban engineering educator; b. Munich, Bavaria, Fed. Republic Germany, Feb. 1, 1941; s. Jakob and Gertraud (Lechner) W.; m. Rosemarie F. Papak, May 31, 1974; children: Tobias, Sebastian. Diploma in Math., Tech. U., Munich, 1967, D in Engring., 1978. Rsch. asst. Tech. U, Munich, 1967-81; prof. urban and regional planning Tech. U, Braunschweig, 1981-89, chief inst. urban engring., 1987—; mng. dir. Transp. Rsch. and Infrastructural Planning, Braunschweig, 1989—. Author: VPS3-An Analytical Transport Demand Model, 1973, Determinants of Transport Demand, 1978; co-author: HUETTE-The Fundamentals of Engineering Sciences, 2000. Chmn. Feuchtinger/Wehner-Found., 1998—. Recipient August-Loesch award, 1975, Feuchtinger-Wehner award, 1980. Mem. Regional Sci. Assn., German Transport Sci. Soc., Assn. Urban, Regional and State Planners, Rsch. Soc. for Road and Traffic Engring., Rotary. Roman Catholic. Home: Am Papenholz 8, 38104 Braunschweig Germany Office: Tech U Inst fuer Verketir Stadtbauwesen, Pockelsstr 4, 38106 Braunschweig Germany

WERNER, ERHARD ERICH, electronics executive; b. Breslau, Germany, Apr. 19, 1938; married, 1966; children: Lutz, Lars. Diploma in engring., Tech. U., Hannover, Germany, 1964, D Engring., 1971. Asst. prof. Tech. U., 1964-71; head electronic design Sennheiser, Germany, 1971-81, head product design, 1981-85, head rsch., 1985-94. Co-author: Microphone Engineering Handbook, 1994; contbr. articles to profl. publs. Mem. Acoustical Soc. Am., Acoustical Engring. Soc., Verband deutsche Electrotech., Deutsche Gesellschaft für Akustik, Internat. Electrotech. Commn., European Telecom. Standards Inst., Commn. Europeene des normes Electrotechnique, Deutsche Kommission für Elektrotechnik im VDE. E-mail: erhard.werner@t-online.de.

WERNER, GLORIA S., librarian; b. Seattle, Dec. 12, 1940; d. Irving L. and Eva H. Stolzoff; m. Newton Davis Werner, June 30, 1963; 1 son, Adam Davis. BA, Oberlin Coll., 1961; ML, U. Wash., 1962; postgrad. UCLA, 1962-63. Reference librarian UCLA Biomed Library, 1963-64, asst. head pub. services dept., 1964-66, head pub. services dept., head reference div., 1966-72, asst. biomed. librarian public services, 1972-77, asso. biomed. librarian, 1977-78, biomed. librarian, assoc. univ. librarian, dir. Pacific S.W. regional Med. Library Service, 1979-83; asst. dean library services UCLA Sch. Medicine, 1980-83; assoc. univ. librarian for tech. services, 1983-89, dir. libraries, acting univ. librarian, 1989-90, univ. librarian, 1990—; adj. lectr. UCLA Grad. Sch. Library and Info. Sci., 1977-83. Editor, Bull. Med. Library Assn., 1979-82, asso. editor, 1974-79; mem. editorial bd. Ann. Stats. Med. Sch. Libraries U.S. and Can., 1980-83; mem. accrediting commn. Western Assn. Schs. and Colls., N.W. Assn. Schs. and Colls. Mem. ALA, Assn. Rsch. Librs. (bd. dirs. 1993-98, v.p./pres.-elect 1995-96, pres. 1996-97, past pres. 1997-98). Office: UCLA Rsch Libr Adminstrv Office 405 Hilgard Ave Los Angeles CA 90095-9000

WERNER, GOTTFRIED, biochemist, researcher; b. Oberpreschkau, CZ, Aug. 26, 1919; s. Josef and Elfriede (Kleinpeter) W.; m. Helga Borchers, Aug. 12, 1963; children: Björn-Marko, Jens-Ingo. Diploma in chemistry, U. Würzburg, Germany, 1948, Dr.rer.nat., 1950; Dr.h.c., U. Unisinos, Sao Leopoldo, Brazil. Lectr. U. Marburg, Germany, 1960-84; prof. U. Frankfurt, Main, Germany, 1963-84; dir. sect. neurochemistry Max-Planck-Inst. Brain Rsch., Frankfurt, 1963-84. Author: Autoradiography. Home: Stettinerstr 105, 63150 Heusenstamm Hessen, Germany Office: Max Planck Inst Brain Rsch, Deutschordenstr 46, D 60528 Frankfurt Hessen, Germany

WERNER, PETER JOHANN, mathematics educator; b. Berlin, Oct. 15, 1932; s. Friedrich and Käthe (Rütters) W.; m. Heide Hertzberg, Dec. 23, 1975. Diploma in math., U. Bonn, Fed. Republic Germany, 1956; PhD in Math., Tech. U., Aachen, Fed. Republic Germany, 1959. Asst. prof. Tech. U. Aachen, 1957-62; asst. prof. U. Karlsruhe, Fed. Republic Germany, 1962-63, docent, 1963-66; prof. math. U. Stuttgart, Fed. Republic Germany, 1966—; rsch. assoc. U. Wis., Madison, 1961-62, 65-66, 68-69. Contbr. over 40 articles to profl. publs. Mem. Am. Math. Soc., Deutsche Math. Vereinigung, Gesellschaft Angewandte Math. and Mech. Home: im Asemwald 32/8, 70599 Stuttgart Germany Office: U Stuttgart Math Inst A, Pfaffenwaldring 57, 70569 Stuttgart Germany

WERNER, SAMUEL ALFRED, physics and astronomy educator; b. Elgin, Ill., Jan. 5, 1937; s. Charles August and Frances Agnes (Tasch) W.; m. Laura Louise Reed, Sept. 1, 1961; 1 dau., Catherine Louise. A.B., Dartmouth Coll., 1959, M.S., 1961; Ph.D., U. Mich., 1965. Staff scientist physics dept. Ford Motor Co., Dearborn, Mich., 1964-75; adj. prof. nuclear engring. U. Mich., Ann Arbor, 1968-75; prof. physics U. Mo., Columbia, 1975—, chmn. physics dept., 1981-83, Millsop Disting. prof., 1986—, Curator's prof., 1992—; vis. scientist A.B. Atomenergi, Studsvik, Sweden, 1970, Institut Laue-Langevin, Grenoble, France, 1977, Argonne Nat. Lab., Oak Ridge Nat. Lab., Brookhaven Nat. Lab.; cons. Argonne Nat. Lab., 1968—, mem. solid scis. div. rev. com., 1972-77, chmn. spl. com. Intense Pulsed Neutron Source, 1978-82; cons. Nat. Acad. Scis., 1977, 83; vis. scientist Nat. Bur. Stds, 1983-84; vis. scientist Nat. Inst. Stds. and Tech., 1996—, chmn. com. on assessment of physics lab., 1992-95. Contbr. numerous articles to profl. jours. Grantee NSF; fellow Swedish Research Council; recipient outstanding alumni award U. Mich., 1980, Chancellor's award for Outstanding Research U. Mo., 1980, Presdl. Research award U. Mo., 1983. Fellow Am. Phys. Soc.; mem. Sigma Xi. E-mail: werners@missouri.edu. Home: 7620 Augustine Way Gaithersburg MD 20879-4587 Office: U Mo Physics Dept Columbia MO 65211-0001

WERNER, STUART LLOYD, computer services company executive; b. N.Y.C., June 2, 1932; s. Leroy Louis and Frances Werner; m. Davideen Price, Jan. 6, 1990; children by previous marriage: Joan Leslie, Susan Lyn, Richard Wayne. BArch, Rensselaer Poly. Inst., 1954. Ptnr. in charge architecture Werner-Dyer & Assocs., Washington, 1959-68; v.p. REntex Corp., Phila., 1968-70; pres. Werner & Assocs., Inc., Washington, 1970-81; v.p. spl. projects ARA Svcs., Inc.; v.p. ARA, 1981-83; chmn. STN, Inc., Falls Church, Va., 1982-83; pres. Werner & Monk, Inc., 1983-90, STN, Inc., 1981-99; chmn. STN, Inc., Falls Church, Va., 2000—; nat. instr. filePro database programming. Author: FilePro Developer's Reference, 3d edit., 1999; contbr. articles to tech. jours. Bd. dirs. Watergate South, 1984-90, Washington Opera Soc., Friends of the Corcoran Gallery, Washington. With AUS, 1955-57. Mem. AIA, Am. Inst. Indsl. Engrs., Marinette Yacht Club, Masons, Tau Beta Pi. Republican. Home: 20281 E County Club Dr Apt 1502 Aventura FL 33180 Office: STN Inc 5113 Leesburg Pike Falls Church VA 22041-3204

WERNER, THOMAS BERND, environmental scientist; b. Muehldorf, Bavaria, Germany, July 5, 1955; m. Ruth Pia Brack; 1 child, Dominick. MS, U. Munich, 1981, PhD, 1986. Postdoctoral fellow GSF, Munich, 1986-88, scientist, 1988—; sci. advisor MIPS Martinsried, Germany, 1993-96. Edilt. bd. mem. Jour. In Silico Biology, 1997—; contbr. articles to profl. jours. Mem. AAAS. Office: GSF Nat Rsch Ctr Environ, Ingolstaedter Landstr 1, D-85764 Neuherberg Bavaria, Germany

WERNER, YEHUDAH LEOPOLD, zoologist, educator; b. Munich, June 16, 1931; arrived in Israel, 1935; s. Alfred Moshe and Anna Hanna (Gutmann) W.; m. Nurit B. Meyerstein, Jan. 3, 1964; children: Uri, Sharon, Wered. MSc, Hebrew U., Jerusalem, 1956, PhD, 1961. Asst., instr., lectr. Hebrew U., 1953-68, sr. lectr., 1968-73, assoc. prof. zoology, 1973-78, prof. zoology, 1978-99; mem. com. Zool. Terminology in Hebrew, Israel, 1963—; rsch. assoc. Princeton (N.J.) U., 1967-68; vis. assoc. prof. U. Chgo., 1977-78; vis. prof. U. Pa., Phila., 1994; curator amphibians and reptiles Hebrew U., Jerusalem, 1973-99, dir. life scis. collections, 1990-93; mem. sci. adv. com. Nature Reserves Authority, Israel, 1992-97. Author, photographer: A Guide to the Reptiles and Amphibians of Israel, 1995; editor Israel Jour. Zoology, 1973-89; contbr. over 280 articles to profl. jours. Staff sgt. Israel Def. Force, 1948-50. Mem. World Congress of Herpetology (exec. com. 1989-97), Asian Herpetol. Congress (organizing com. 1992—), Internat. Soc. Vertebrate Morphologists (exec. com. 1995—). Jewish. Avocations: photography, traffic safety. Office: Hebrew U., Dept Evolution Sys Ecol, 91904 Jerusalem Israel

WERNICK, EDWARD RAYMOND, company executive, computer consultant; b. Irvington, N.J., Mar. 11, 1955; s. Edward Joseph and Ann (Czech) W.; m. Ione Sharon Greenbaum, Nov. 2, 1984; 1 child, Elissa Ann. BS in Computer Sci., Kean Coll., 1977. Computer analyst N.Y. Life Ins., N.Y.C., 1978-81; computer cons. Horizons, N.Y.C., 1981-84; data base adminstr. oracle Standard & Poors, N.Y.C., 1984-88; tchr. sybase Sybase, N.Y.C., 1988-89; data base adminstr. sybase Merrill Lynch, N.Y.C., 1989-91, Paramount Comms., Old Tappan, N.J., 1991-95; v.p. Crossmar, Parsippany, N.J., 1995-98; pres., CEO Femasque Inc., 1998—; computer, fin. cons., pvt. practice, Oradell, N.J., 1981—; pres. FEMASQUE, Inc., 1998—. Designer stage lighting for more than 80 plays, 1978-84; writer relational scripts for Australian govt., 1994; exhibited sculpture in India, 1991, Brazil, 1992, Oslo, Norway, 1994. Mem. Rep. Nat. Com.; sec. Stockton (N.J.) Rifle Club, 1974; pres. Irvington (N.J.) Masquers, 1978. Named Outstanding Young Rep. Union, N.J., Rep. Com., 1976; Best of Show sculpture Art Assoc., Irvington, N.J., 1979; 100 yd. standing rifle champion Stockton (N.J.) Rifle Club, 1974. Mem. Assn. for Computing Machinery, Sybase Internat. Users Group, Relational Database Users Group, Oradell Arts Com., Internet Users Group. Roman Catholic. Avocations: lighting design, theater, logic. Home: 920 Oradell Ave Oradell NJ 07649-1925 Office: Crossmar 111 Sylvan Ave Englewd Clfs NJ 07632-1514

WERNICK, JUSTIN, podiatrist, educator; b. N.Y.C., Feb. 26, 1936; s. Charles and Ethel (Crown) W.; m. Susan Schoenfeld, Oct. 16, 1960 (div.); children: Elissa, Peter; m. Charlotte Kinsman, Mar. 5, 2000. Diplomate Am. Bd. Podiatric Orthopedics. Pvt. practice Seaford, N.Y., 1960-78; co-founder, exec. v.p. Langer Biomechanics Group, Inc., Deer Park, N.Y., 1969—; prof. orthopedics N.Y. Coll. Podiatric Medicine, 1969—, 1969—; med. dir. Eneslow Pediatric Inst.; mem. adv. bd. Rockport Shoe Co., Marlboro, Mass., 1988-92; clin. prof. N.Y. Coll. Podiat. Medicine, 1990—; chmn. dept. orthopedic scis., N.Y.C. Podiat. U, 1998—. Co-author: A Practical Manual for a Basic Approach to Biomechanics, 1972; guest editor Jour. Current Podiatric Medicine, 1989; editorial adv. Podiatry Tracts; contbr. Clin. Biomedics of the Lower Extremity, 1995. Fellow Am. Coll. Foot Orthopedics, Am. Acad. Podiatric Sports Medicine; mem. Am. Podiatric Med. Assn., N.Y. State Podiatric Med. Assn. (Podiatrist of Yr. award 1976), Nat. Acad. Practice in Podiatry (Disting. Practitioner award 1985). Republican. Jewish. Avocations: photography, skiing, traveling, golf. E-mail: justinlbg@aol.com. Home: 96 5th Ave Apt 6J New York NY 10011-7612 Office: NY Coll Podiatric Medicine 1800 Park Ave New York NY 10035-1940

WERNIG, ANTON, neurophysiology, educator; b. Klagenfurt, Austria, Oct. 14, 1944; s. Anton and Anna Wernig; m. Brigitte Wernig, June 21, 1975; children: Markus, Marius, Antonia-Dusa. MD, U. Innsbruck, Vienna, Austria, 1968. Asst. U. Innsbruck, 1968-73; Max Kade fellow, lectr. U. Denver, 1970-72; asst. Max Planck Inst. Psychiatry, Munich, 1973-80; prof. U. Bonn, Germany, 1980—; rsch. cons. D.T. Stiftung Querschnittlähmung, Germany, 1991. Author: Motorneuronal Connections, 1991; contbr. articles to profl. jours. Office: U Bonn, Physiol Inst, Wilhelmstr 31, 53111 Bonn Germany

WERRES, KARL JOSEF, university educator, academic administrator, lawyer; b. Mönchengladbach, Northrhine Westfalia, Germany, June 17, 1947; s. Franz Josef and Katharina (Misgeld) W.; m. Erika Baldus, Sept. 8, 1976 (div. 1983); 1 child, Thomas A.; m. Melanie Grabowski, Dec. 24, 1996. MA in Edn., Newport (Calif.) U., 1979, PhD in Edn., 1980; PhD (hon.), Clayton (Mo.) U., 1984; diploma in pedagogy, U. Koblenz-Landau, Germany, 1985; PhD in Behavioral Sci., U. Calif., La Jolla, 1988; postgrad. diploma in psychology, Postgrad. Med. U. Hungary, 1989; LLM in

European Law, U. St. Ivan Rilski, Sofia, Bulgaria, 1994; D honoris causa, Cath. U., La Paz, Bolivia, 1987, State U. Tarija, Bolivia, 1990, U. Oradea, Romania, 1998; Magister Jur, State U., Plovdiv, Bulgaria, 1996. Sch. counselling credential, Germany. Tchr., head dept. Dr. Jungbecker Sch., Düsseldorf, Germany, 1973-77; expert State Bd. Dist. Edn., Cologne, Germany, 1977-79; chief commr. edn. European Fedn. Schs., Solothurn, Switzerland, 1980-82; prof., dean European programs Newport U., 1982-83; prin., dir. West German Acad., Düsseldorf, 1983-89; prof., exec. dean State Univ. Coll., Magdeburg, Germany, 1990-92; prof., dean European faculty U. Mining and Geology, Sofia, 1993-97; bd. dirs. Acad. for European Law, Düsseldorf, 1995—, sec. gen., 1995—; project devel. dir. AER Cyberversity, 1997—; acad. v.p. Internat. Inst. Postgrad. Studies U. Oradea, Romania, 1999—, CEO Internat. Consortium Cybertechnological Us., Inc., 2000—; assoc. prof. Univ. Coll., Kempten, Germany, 1983-84; titular prof. U. Miskolc, Hungary, 1991-92; chmn. bd. Unicorp Rsch. Inc., Sofia, 1996-98; mem. supervisory bd. Novoplan AG, Düsseldorf, 1997-98. Author: (booklet) Le Comportement Humaine Face au Bilinguisme, 1985, (books) Creativita delle Scienze ed Educazione, 1989, The European Union, 1996; author, editor: Betriebswirtschaftliche Kompendien, 18 vols., 1989. With Germany Army, 1964-68. Decorated Laureat Van de Arbeid 1st class (The Netherlands); recipient spl. citation West Los Angeles Coll., 1977, nat. sci. award Republic of San Marino, 1985, European Cross Merit CEAC, Paris, 1998. Fellow Coll. Preceptors (U.K.); mem. Internat. Bar Assn., Interstate Bar Assn. (hon.), German Free Experts Assn. (trustee 1993—). Roman Catholic. Avocations: travel, languages, creative writing. E-mail: RaD@ctu.ie. Home: PO Box 27 01 29, 40549 Düsseldorf Germany Office: U Oradea, Str Armatei Romane Nr 5, 3700 Oradea Romania

WERRIES, E. DEAN, food distribution company executive; b. Tescott, Kans., May 8, 1929; s. John William and Sophie E. Werries; m. Marjean Sparling, May 18, 1962. B.S., U. Kans., 1952. With Fleming Foods Co., Topeka, 1955-89, exec. v.p., 1973-76; exec. v.p. Eastern ops. Fleming Foods Co., Phila., 1976-78; pres. Fleming Foods Co., Oklahoma City, 1978-81; pres., chief operating officer Fleming Cos., Inc., Oklahoma City, 1981-88, also dir.; pres., chief exec. officer Fleming Cos., Inc., 1988-89, chmn., CEO, 1989-93; chmn. bd. Sonic Corp., 1995-99. Sec. of Commerce State of Okla., 1995. With U.S. Army, 1952-54, Korea. Mem. Nat. Am. Wholesale Grocers Assn. (bd. dirs. 1979-93), Food Mktg. Inst. (bd. dirs. 1984—, chmn. 1989-91), Ind. Grocers Alliance (bd. dirs. 1984-94). Republican. Presbyterian. Office: Fleming Cos Inc 6307 Waterford Blvd Ste 230 Oklahoma City OK 73118-1125

WERRING, HENRI TUXEN, management educator; b. Kristiansund, Norway, Aug. 6, 1926; s. Sigurd and Germaine Amelie (Aubert) W.; m. Turid Andresen, Sept. 17, 1962. PhD in Philology, U. Oslo, Norway, 1954, practical pedagogics, 1954; mgmt. courses, 1972. Journalist Møre Dagblad/Morgenbladet, 1945-51; headmaster KA-Skolen, Oslo, 1959-65; pers. dir. Christiania Bank, Oslo, 1965-82; mng. dir. Norwegian Coll. Banking, Oslo, 1982-89, Norwegian Coll. Info. Tech., 1989-94; ednl. dir. Norwegian IT-Akademy, 1999—; dir. Inst. Polit. Knowledge, 1999—; chmn. Orgn. for Tchrs. within Industry, Norwegian Inst. Pers. Adminstrn., Students of Mgmt., Com. for Pers. Mgmt. in Norwegian Banks; bd. dirs. Earth Charter Norway. Author: (books) Active Personnel Work, 1979, The Power of Talking Together, 1988, Personnel, The Scandinavian Way, 1996, Organization and Management, 1999; editor: (book) Ethics for Managers, 1987; contbr. numerous articles to newspapers and profl. mags. Chmn., polit. leader Liberal Party; mem. City Com., Oslo. Maj. Norwegian Air Force, 1955-59. Mem. Norwegian Assn. Writers, Ethics and Soc., Rotary (pres.). Liberal. Roman Catholic. Avocations: literature, football. Home and Office: Rosendalsun 38, 1166 Oslo Norway

WERRY, JOHN SCOTT, physician, educator; b. Christchurch, New Zealand, Jan. 30, 1931; s. Chace Chenoweth and Edith Kathleen (Scott) W.; m. Jocelyn Margaret Loughnan, Dec. 1, 1956 (div. 1975); children: Edward, Timothy, Robert, Francine, William; m. Dianne Moya Moffitt, Nov. 11, 1978. B of Med. Sci., U. New Zealand, 1952, MB, BChir, 1955; diploma in Psychiatry, McGill U., Montreal, Can., 1963; MD, Otago U., Dunedin, New Zealand, 1975. Diplomate Am. Bd. Psychiatry. Asst. prof. McGill U., 1964-65; asst. prof. U. Ill., 1965-66, assoc. prof., 1966-70; prof. U. Auckland, New Zealand, 1970-92, emeritus prof., 1992—; psychiatrist Montreal Children's Hosp., 1962-64, Auckland Hosp., 1970-97; dir. Inst. Juvenile Rsch., Chgo., 1969-70. Contbr. over 150 articles to profl. jours. Fellow Royal Coll. Physicians Can., Royal Coll. Psychiatrists New Zealand, Am. Psychiat. Assn. (corr.), Am. Acad. Child and Adolescent Psychiatry (life, corr.). E-mail: j.werry@auckland.ac.nz. Home: 19 Edenvale Crescent, Mount Eden, Auckland 1003, New Zealand

WERSHOFEN, HERBERT ANTON, chemist, environmentalist; b. Mayen, Germany, Apr. 15, 1955; s. Karl and Maria (Maurer) W.; m. Ulrike Weyers, Dec. 20, 1990; children: Andreas, Dominik. Diploma in chemistry, Rhinelandic Frederick William, Bonn, Germany, 1983, Dr.rer.nat., 1988. Cert. nuclear chemist and environmentalist. Asst. U. Bonn, 1983-89; environmentalist Nat. Meterol. Inst. Germany, Braunschweig, 1989—. Mem. Internat. Radiol. Protection Assn. Office: Physik-Tech Bundesantalt, Bundesallee 100, D-38116 Braunschweig Germany

WERTHEIM, JOHN DAVID, investment and manufacturing executive; b. Leeds, Yorkshire, Eng., Mar. 12, 1945; came to U.S., 1971; s. Paul and Edith (Gale) W.; married. BA in Biochemistry, U. Cambridge, 1966, MA, 1970; MBA in Fin., Wharton Sch., U. Pa., 1973; MA in Econs., U. Pa., 1977. With Pfizer Ltd., London and Sandwich, Eng., 1966-69, United Molasses Co., London, 1969-71, Sandoz Group, U.S. and Europe, 1974-82, Allied-Signal, Inc., Morristown, 1982-86; pres., chmn. Commonwealth Investment Co., Inc., Madison, N.J., 1986—; dir. Penrice Ltd., Adelaide, South Australia, 1989-96, dep. chmn., 1991-96; dep. chmn. Brunner Mond Group plc, Northwich, Cheshire, Eng., 1991-95, chief exec., 1995—, chmn., 1998—; dir. Prospect St. Internat. Fund PCC Ltd., Guernsey, 1999—. Mem. N.W. Bus. Leadership Team, Eng., 1995—. Open scholar Gonville and Caius Coll., Cambridge, 1963; Thouron fellow U. Pa., 1971. Office: Brunner Mond Group plc, PO Box 4 Mond House, Northwich CW8 4DT, England also: Commonwealth Investment Co Inc PO Box 340 Madison NJ 07940-0340

WERTZ, JOHN ALAN, secondary school educator; b. Mpls., May 28, 1945; s. John Edward and Florence (Carlson) W.; m. Margaret M. Schlangen, 1993. BS, Hamline U., 1967; MS, St. Cloud State Coll., 1973; postgrad., George Washington U., 1985. Tchr. social sci. St. Cloud (Minn.) Community Schs., 1967—; trainer and field rep. New Games Found., San Francisco, 1980-83; tchr.-coach Apollo H.S. Mock Trial team, 1987—. Mem. com. social action Minn. Synod, Luth. Ch. Am., 1971-74; chair social action com. Salem Luth. Ch. Coun., St. Cloud, 1974-76; mem. affirmative action com. St Cloud Cmty. Schs., 1975-78, co-chair student assistance com., 1982-83, mem. site coun. Apollo H.S., 1994-96, co-chair site coun. Apollo H.S., 1995-96; chair St. Cloud Human Rights Commn., 1979-83; adv. Ctrl. Minn. Sexual Assault Ctr., 1981-83; bd. dirs. St. Cloud Area Tenants' Assn., 1975-77, St. Cloud Area Spl. Olympics, 1982-83, United Way St. Cloud Area, 1996—, Minn. Edn. Assn., 1996-99, Great River Roundtable, 1997—, sec., 1997-98; mem. Edn. Minn. Transition Bd., 1998-99, Edn. Minn. Governing Bd., 1999—. Recipient Merit award St. Cloud Area Coun. for Handicapped, 1976; grad. St. Cloud Area Leadership Program, 1995. Mem. ASCD, NEA, Am. Fedn. Tchrs., Edn. Minn., St. Cloud Edn. Assn. (chair govtl. rels. coun. 1978-83, 88-96), Am. Hist. Soc. Germans from Russia, St. Cloud Area C. of C. (edn. divsn. 1992-97, vice-chmn. PreK-12 com. 1993-94, chair edn. recognition com. 1994-96, Thayer Youth Leadership steering com. 1995-97). Avocations: theatre arts, travel, computing. Home: 816 Rilla Rd Saint Cloud MN 56303-1037 Office: Apollo High Sch 1000 44th Ave N Saint Cloud MN 56303-2036

WESBERRY, JAMES PICKETT, JR., financial management consultant, auditor, international organization executive; b. Columbia, S.C., Sept. 22, 1934; s. James P. and Ruby L. (Perry) W.; m. Lea Esdras Casteneda, June 13, 1975; children: Jonathan Jesse, Perry Latimer, Ruby Lee Nilda; children by previous marriage: James Pickett III, Elisa Marie, Lillian Sue, Paul Armand. BBA, Ga. State U., 1955; LLD (hon.), Atlanta Law Sch., 1967; MPA, Am. U., 1983. CPA, Ga.; cert. internal auditor, fraud examiner, govt. fin. mgr., fin. svcs. auditor. Page U.S. Ho. Reps., 1949-51; acct., mgmt. cons. Atlanta, 1956-67; v.p. fin. and adminstrn. Computer Tech. South, Atlanta, 1969-70; sr. cons. Inst. Pub. Adminstrn., N.Y.C., 1967-69, 70-76; cons. to comptr. gen. Peru, 1970-74, Ecuador, 1974-78; adv., prof. Latin Am. Inst. Auditing Scis. Peruvian and Ecuadorean Sch. Govtl. Auditing, 1971-78; dir. sys., stds. and procedures Days of Inns Am., Inc., 1979-80; chief auditor OAS, Washington, 1980-82; cons. World Bank, 1982-83; prin. advisor acctg. and auditing pub. sector Latin Am. and Caribean Region, 1994-97; dir. America's accountability/anti-corruption project Casals & Assocs., Arlington, Va., 1997—; founder, pres. Accountability 21, 1998—; advisor to pres. of Latin Am. Orgn. of Supreme Audit Instn., 1993-2000; sr. adv. to comptr. gen. U.S., 1983-85; dir. internat. ops. Price Waterhouse, 1985-88; sr. fin. advisor AID, 1988-93; pres., CEO Inst. Pub. Adminstrn., 1993-94, trustee; dir. N.Y. Bur. Mcpl. Rsch., 1993-94; mem. panel of experts in acctg. and auditing UN, 1972-82; adj. prof. Am. U., Washington, 1981-85; founding dir. Internat. Consortium Govtl. Fin. Mgmt., 1977-88, 94-97, pres., 1984-87; cons., tchr. all Spanish-speaking We. Hemisphere nations, Brazil, Haiti, Jamaica, The Netherlands Antilles, Guyana, Peoples Republic China, The Philippines, Can., U.S. Co-author: UN Handbook on Government Auditing for Developing Countries; editor: Latin American Manual of Professional Auditing in the Public Sector, Spanish Lang. newsletter Pistas de Auditoria, 1985-92; mem. editl. bd. Pub. Budgeting and Fin. Mgmt., 1982-92, The Govt. Accts. Jour.; contbr. articles to profl. jours. Mem. Ga. Senate, 1962-67, Fulton County Dem. Exec. Com., 1962-66. Decorated Order of Merit (Peru), 1972, Comptr. Gen. Venezuela, 1998; recipient Outstanding Career Achievement award USAID, 1993. Mem. AICPA (hon. life, chmn. interam. com. 1988-95), Interam. Acctg. Assn. (cert. assoc., bd. dirs. 1989-95, chmn. pub. sector com. 1989-91, 2000-2001, exec. com. 1994-95, Vet. Acct. Am. award 1987, lifetime acct. of Am. 1995), Am. Acctg. Assn., Assn. Govt. Accts. (Authors award 1981-82, 89-90, chmn. internat. affairs com. 1981-82, 89-91), Inst. Internal Auditors (v.p. Latin Am. 1978-79, internat. rels. com. 1977-82, 84-88, regional dir. Latin Am. 1986-88, chpt. bd. govs. 1981-87, v.p. 1982-84, pres. 1984-85, vice chmn. internat. membership com. 1989-90, chpt. Disting. Svc. award 1987, Bradford Cadmus Meml. award internat. orgn. 1989, Outstanding Author's award 1990), Honduras CPA Soc. (Hon. award 1990), Jr. Chamber Internat. (life senator), Quito (Ecuador) Inst. Internal Auditors (life bd. dirs.), Lina Coll. Pub. Accts. (hon.), Lima Jr. C. of C. (hon.), Pinchicha Coll. Pub. Accts. (hon.), Ecuador Fedn. Pub. Accts. (hon.). Baptist. E-mail: jimwes@casals.com. Home: 4004 Franconia Rd Alexandria VA 22310-2136 Office: Casals & Assocs 1199 N Fairfax St Alexandria VA 22314-1437

WESEL, UWE, law educator; b. Hamburg, Germany, Feb. 2, 1933; s. Alfons and Rotraut (Garbsch) W.; m. Natascha Wittbrodt; 1 child, Thomas. First Law Exam, U. Munich, Germany, 1961; LittD, U. Saarbrücken, Germany, 1965; Second Law Exam, State of Bavaria, Germany, 1966; habil., U. Munich, Germany, 1968. Univ. asst. U. Munich, Germany, 1961-68; prof. law Free U., Berlin, Germany, 1968—; v.p. Free U., Berlin, 1969-73. Author: Der Mythos vom Matriarchat, 1980, Früformen Des Rechts, 1985, Fast Alles Wa REcht Ist, 1992, Der Honecker Prozess, 1994, Geschichte des Rechts, 1997. Mem. Jury of Third Internat. Russell Tribunal, Frankfurt, Germany, 1978. Mem. P.E.N. Club. Home: Koenigs allee 41, 14193 Berlin Germany Office: Free U, Boltzmanstrasse 3, 14195 Berlin Germany

WESKAMP, KELLEY S., loan account manager, real estate company executive; b. Boulder City, Nev., Jan. 9, 1964; d. Dale P. and Phyllis J. (Cooper) W. BA in English Lang. Lit. with distinction, Loretto Heights Coll., 1985. Cons. Ely Leadership Mgmt., Lakewood, Colo., 1985-88; budget asst. Bureau Reclamation, Denver, 1988-90; real estate owned technician FDIC, Denver, 1990-93; real estate specialist Westfall and Co., Westminster, 1993-95; account mgr. Westfall and Co., 1995-97, Castle Advisors subs. Chgo. Title, 1998-99; sr. account mgr. Litton Loan Servicing, Houston, 1999—; participant Bench Mark Study, Pete Marwick Assocs., 1997. Contbr. article to mag. Democrat. Catholic. Avocations: weaving, reading, travel, cooking. Home: 12080 W Mexico Ave Lakewood CO 80228-3909

WESKER, ARNOLD, playwright, director; b. London, May 24, 1932; s. Joseph and Leah (Perlmutter) W.; m. Doreen Cecile Bicker, 1958; 4 children. BLitt (hon.), U. East Anglia, 1989; hon. degree, Denison U., London U. Worked as furniture maker's apprentice, carpenter's mate RAF, 1950-52; plumber's mate, farm labourer, seed sorter, kitchen porter; chmn. Brit. ctr. of Internat. Theater Inst., 1978-82; pres. Internat. Com. of Playwrights, 1979-83. Author, dir. (plays): The Four Seasons, Cuba, 1968, The Friends, Stadsteatern, Stockholm, 1970, London, 1970, The Old Ones, Munich, Their Very Own and Golden City, Aarhus, 1974, Love Letters on Boue Paper, Nat. Theatre, London, 1978, Oslo, 1980, Annie Wobbler, Birmingham, 1983, London, 1984; dir. The Entertainer (Osborne), Theatre Clwyd, 1983, Yardsale RSC Actor's festival, 1985, Whatever Happened to Betty Lemon and Yardsale, London, 1987, The Merry Wives Windsor (Shakespeare), Oslo, 1989; (workshop prodn.) Shylock, London, 1989; dir. (play) The Kitchen, U. Wis.-Madison, 1990, The Mistress, Rome, 1991, The Wedding Feast, Denison U., Granville, Ohio, 1995; author plays: The Kitchen, 1957, The Wesker Trilogy--Chicken Soup with Barley, 1958, Roots, 1959, I'm Talking About Jerusalem, 1960, Chips with Everything, 1962; (TV) Menace, 1963, Their Very Own and Golden City (Marzotto prize), 1964, The Four Seasons, 1965, The Friends, 1970, The Old Ones, 1972, The Journalists, 1972, The Wedding Feast, 1974, Shylock, 1975, Love Letters on Blue Paper, 1976, One More Ride on the Merry-Go-Round, 1978, Caritas, 1981, Sullied Hand, 1981; (collected essays and lectures): Fear of Fragmentation, 1971, Distinctions, 1985, Words as Definitions of Experience, 1976, Journey into Journalism, 1977; (stories) Six Sundays in January, 1971, Love Letters on Blue Paper, 1974, Say Goodbye You May Never See Them Again, 1974, Said the Old Man to the Young Man, 1978, Fatlips (children's book), 1978, The Journalists triptych, 1979, Collected Plays and Stories, 5 vols., 1979, 7 vols., 1989-94; (cycle of one woman plays) Annie Wobbler, 1983, Four Portraits, 1984, Yardsale, 1985, Whatever Happened to Betty Lemon, 1986, The Mistress, 1988, Letter To A Daughter, 1990, 98; (filmscript) The Wesker Trilogy, 1979, Lady O, 1983, Homage to Catalonia, 1990-91; (TV) play) Breakfast, 1983, Cinders, 1983, (play for radio) Bluey, 1984; 4 90-minute plays adapted for TV from Arthur Koestler's novel Thieves in the Night, 1985; When God wanted a Son, 1986, Badenheim 1939 (from a novel by Aharon Appelfeld), 1987, Lady Othello (from original film script), 1987; (one act plays for young people) Little Old Lady and Shoeshine, 1987; (community play celebrating 40th birthday of the Town of Basilden) Beorhtel's Hill, 1988; (4 60 minute plays adapted for TV from Doris Lessing's novel) Diary of a Good Neighbor, 1989, Three Women Talking, 1990, Blood Libel, 1991, Wild Spring, 1992, (autobiography) As Much As I Dare, 1994, (film script from the Lessing TV adaptation) Maudie, 1995, Circles of Perception, 1996, Denial, 1997, Break, My Heart, 1997, The Birth of Shylock and The Death of Zero Mostel, 1997, The King's Daughters, 1998; (TV play) Barabbas, 2000. Dir. Ctr. Forty two, 1961-70. Recipient bursary Brit. Arts Coun., 1959, Ency. Britanica award U.K., 1959, 61, Goldie award N.Y., 1987, Spectator and Critic's Gold medal, Madrid, 1961, 73, Evening Std. Drama award, London, 1959, Marzotto prize, Italy, 1966, Last Frontier Lifetime Achievement award Valdez, Alaska, 1999. Address: Hay on Wye, Hereford HR3 5RJ, England

WESLEY, JAMES PAUL, theoretical physicist, lecturer, consultant; b. St. Louis, July 28, 1921; s. Edgar Bruce and Nanny Fay (Medford) W.; m. Margaret Ellen Martin, June 1943 (div. 1952); 1 child, Martin Medford; m. Dorothy Ree Casey, Aug. 1952 (div. 1963); children: William Casey, David Douglas, Gina Teresa; m. Michele Dudek, June 1963 (div. 1967); 1 child, Sherry Allison; m. Gabriele Beate Modest, July 30, 1975; children: Carl-Eric, Julia Ann, Benjamin Fredrik. BA, U. Minn., 1943, MA, UCLA, 1949, PhD, 1952; postdoctoral, Scripps Inst. Oceanography, La Jolla, Calif., 1951-52. Various positions, 1943-50; prof. physics U. Idaho, Moscow, 1953-56; rsch. geophysicist Newmont Exploration, Ltd., Jerome, Ariz., 1955-56; rsch. physicist Lawrence Radiation Lab. U. Calif., 1956-61; NIH rsch. fellow, fellow Ctr. Advanced Study Behavioral Sci., Stanford, Calif., 1961-62; rsch. physicist U. Denver, 1962-63, Melpar, Inc., Falls Church, Va., 1963, Roland F. Beers, Inc., Alexandria, Va., 1964; assoc. prof. physics U. Mo., Rolla, 1964-74; lectr., cons. on quantum theory, space-time physics, others Berlin and Blumberg, Germany, 1974—. Author: Ecophysics, 1974, Causal Quantum Theory, 1983, Advanced Fundamental Physics, 1991, Classical Quantum Theory, 1996, To Appreciate Physics, 2000; co-editor: Proc. Internat. conf. on Space-Time Absoluteness, 1982, Proc. Conf. on Foundations of Mathematics and Physics, 1991, Physics as a Science, 1998; editor: Progress in Space-Time Physics, 1987; contbr. over 100 articles primarily on fundamental physics to profl. jours. Nat. Bur. Standards rsch. fellow, 1950. Mem. Am. Phys. Soc., AAAS. Unitarian. Avocations: oil painting, hiking. Home and Office: Weiherdammstrasse 24, 78176 Blumberg Germany

WESSEL, HORST A., manufacturing executive; b. Bonn, Germany, Apr. 12, 1943; s. Kaspar and Margarete (Kaulen) W.; m. Margareta Jocksch, Nov. 30, 1972; children: Christian, Martin. PhD, U. Bonn, 1979, U. Dusseldorf, Germany, 1995. Asst. prof. U. Bonn, 1973-76; mgr. German Soc. for Bus. History, Cologne, Germany, 1976-83; head dept. Mannesmann AG, Dusseldorf, 1983—, authorized clk., 1994—; v.p. Commn. History of Elec. Engring., Frankfurt, Germany, 1982—. Co-editor: (book) Historic Shares - Testimonies of Financial, Economic, Technical and Art History, 1981; author: The Development of Telecommunication in Germany and the Industry in Rhineland, From the Beginning to 1914, 1983, Continuity in Change, 100 Years of Mannesmann 1890-1990, 1990; editor: Thyssen & Co., Mulheim a.d. Ruhr. History of a family and its enterprise, 1991, The History of the Whell—An Important Part of Kronprinz, 1997. Pres. of the commn. of local, Cath. ch., Hilden, Germany, 1985-93; lectr. U. Dusseldorf, 1986—, U. Nuremberg, 1985—, Bochum, 1998—. Roman Catholic. Home: North Rhine Westphalia, Marie-Colinet-Str 5, D-40721 Hilden Germany Office: Mannesmann AG, Mannesmannufer 2 North Rhine Westphalia, D-40213 Dusseldorf Germany

WESSEL, INGRID, history educator; b. Bobersberg, Germany (now Poland), Jan. 11, 1942. MA, Lomonossov U., Moscow, 1967; PhD, Humboldt U., Berlin, 1972, Habilitation, 1982. Asst. Humboldt U., 1967-82, asst. prof. Indonesian history, 1982-88, univ. prof., 1988—. Author: (with H.D. Kubitscheck) Indonesian History, 1981; co-author: Social Process and Classes in Developing Countries, 1981; editor, co-author: Nationalism and Ethnicity in Southeast Asia, 2 vols., 1994, Indonesia at the End of the 20th Century, 1996. Mem. Euroseas. Office: Humboldt U, Unter Den Linden 6, D-10099 Berlin Germany

WESSEL, KARL FRIEDRICH MARIA, neurologist; b. Eslohe, Germany, Aug. 28, 1954; s. Johannes R.S. and Irmgard B. (Polzin) W.; m. Edeltraud J. Walter, Nov. 17, 1983; children: Maximilian, Sara, Jacob. MD, U. Freiburg, 1981. Bd. cert. neurologist. Intern U. Freiburg, Germany, 1980-81; registrar U. Cologne and Munich, 1981-83, U. Tübingen, 1983-87; cons. neurologist U. Lübeck, 1987-97; rsch. fellow NIH/NINDS, Bethesda, Md., 1992-93; head dept. neurology Städt. Klinikum Braunschweig, 1997—; head behavioral neurology inst. Tech. U. Braunschweig, 2000—. Contbr. articles to profl. jours. Lt. comdr. German Navy. Fellow Am. Acad. Neurology (corr.); mem. The Movement Disorder Soc., German Soc. Neurology. Avocations: sailing, golf, family, reading. Office: Städt Klinikum Braunschweig, Salzdahlumer Str 90, 38126 Braunschweig Germany

WESSEL, PETER LORENTZ, telecommunication systems engineer; b. Oslo, Nov. 22, 1938; s. Jan and Liv (Christiansen) W.; m. Karen Marie Bjornstad, Jan. 15, 1977; children: Ruth Charlotte, Jan Christopher. SB in EE, MIT, 1966; grad., Norwegian Sch. Mgmt., Oslo, 1973; diploma, North European Mgmt. Inst., Oslo, 1974. Project mgr. Radionette A/S, Oslo, 1966-72, Tanbergs Radiofabrikk A/S, Olso, 1972-79; sys. engr. A/S Elektrisk Bur., Asker, Norway, 1979-87; mgr. electronics dept. Control Comms. Ericsson Bus. Comms. AS, Asker, 1987-95; responsible for intellectual property rights Ericsson AS, Norway, 1995—; mem. coun. Electronics Rsch. Lab., Norwegian Inst. Tech., Trondheim, 1966-72; chmn. bd. SEAS A/S, Moss, Norway, 1980. Contbr. articles in field to profl. jours.; patentee in field. With Norwegian Air Force, 1957-62. Mem. IEEE, Norwegian Soc. Chartered Engrs., Sigma Xi, Tau Beta Pi, Eta Kappa Nu. Conservative. Home: Johs Hartmannsvei 12, 1395 Hvalstad Norway Office: Ericsson AS, Olav Brunborgsvei 6, 1396 Billingstad Norway

WESSELS, WOLFGANG THEODOR, political science educator; b. Cologne, Germany, Jan. 19, 1948; s. Theodor and Emma Wessels; m. Aysin Gurkan; children: Yasmin, Melanie. Diploma in econs., U. Cologne, Germany, 1973, PhD, 1979; habilitation, U. Bonn, Germany, 1990. Dir. Inst. Europäische Politik, Bonn, 1973-93, mem. exec. bd., 1993—; dir. dept. adminstrv. and polit. studies Coll. of Europe, Brussels, 1980-96; prof. U. Cologne, 1993—; Jean-Monnet chair European Commn., 1994—. Author: Europa von A-Z, 7th edit., 1995; editor: Jahrbuch der Europäischen Integration, 20th vol., 2000. Mem. Trans-European Polit. Studies Assn. (chmn. bd. dirs. 1995—). E-mail: wessels@uni-koeln.de. Office: Forschunginst Polit Sci, Gottfried-Keller Str 6, 50931 Cologne Germany

WESSING, ARMIN RICHARD EVERHARD, biologist; b. Essen, Germany, Oct. 10, 1924; s. Franz-Josef and Caroline (Van Ham) W.; m. Ingeborg Luebbert, Jan. 11, 1934; children: Roland, Gundo. Dr. Rer. Nat., U. Bonn, 1952. Asst. U. Bonn, 1952-63, asst. prof., 1963-67; prof. U. Giessen, 1968-94; dir. Zool. Inst. U. Giessen, Germany, 1967-94. Roman Catholic. Office: Zoological Inst, Heinrich-Buff-Ring 29, Hessen Giessen 35392, Germany

WESSJOHANN, LUDGER, chemistry educator, consultant; b. Melle, Germany, May 19, 1961. Diploma, U. Hamburg, Germany, 1987, PhD, 1990. Rsch. fellow U. Oslo, Norway, 1987-88; postdoctoral fellow Stanford (Calif.) U., 1990-91; guest prof. U. Federal de Santa Maria, Brazil, 1990, 93, 95; asst. prof. U. Munich, 1992-98; prof. bioorganic chemistry Free U., Amsterdam, The Netherlands, 1998-2000, Martin Luther U., Halle, Germany, 2000; head dept. natural product chemistry U. Halle Leibniz Inst. Plant Biochemistry, 2000—; cons. in field. Contbr. articles to profl. jours. Recipient Talented Student scholarship Studienstiftung Dt. Volk, 1984-87, Promotions stipend, 1988; named Royal Norwegian Postdoctoral fellow, 1987, Feodor Lynen fellow, 1990-91. Fellow Am. Chem. Soc., Gesellschaft Deutscher Chemiker, Am. Orchid Soc., Deutsche Orchideen Gesellschaft, Gesellschaft für Biochemie und Molekularbiologie, Royal Dutch Chem. Soc. Office: U Halle Leibniz Inst Plant, Pathology, Weinberg 3, D-06120 Halle (Saale) Germany

WESSNER, DEBORAH MARIE, telecommunications executive, computer consultant; b. St. Louis, Aug. 15, 1950; d. John George and Mary Jane (Beetz) Eyerman; m. Brian Paul Wessner, Sept. 15, 1972; children: Krystin, David. BA in Math. and Chemistry, St. Louis U., 1972; M Computer Info. Sci., U. New Haven, 1980. Statistian Armstrong Rubber Co., New Haven, 1972-74; programmer analyst Sikorsky div. United Techs., Stratford, Conn., 1974-77; project engr. GE, Bridgeport, Conn., 1977-79; software mgr. GE, Arlington, Va., 1979-81; mgr. software ops. Satellite Bus. Systems, McLean, Va., 1981-83; v.p. ops. DAMA Telecommunications, Rockville, Md., 1983-87; dir. network ops. and adminstrn. Data Gen. Network Svcs., Rockville, 1987-91; dir. bus. ops. Sprint Internat., Reston, Va., 1991-92; v.p. network adminstrn. Citicorp, Washington, 1992-93; v.p. telecomm. product mgmt. Citicorp, Reston, Va., 1994-95, v.p. product mgmt., 1996-97, v.p., dir. Yr. 2000 program, 1997—; assoc., cons. KDB Assocs., Columbia, Md., 1986—. Mem. exec. bd. Howard County PTA. Mem. Am. Bus. Women's Assn., NAFE. Avocations: sailing, windsurfing, tennis. Office: 1900 Campus Commons Dr Reston VA 20191-1535

WEST, DANA RENEE, secondary education educator; b. Williston, N.D., July 21, 1957; d. Walter Clifton and Ardyce Mildred Jones; m. Mark Terrance West, July 10, 1982; children: Cammie Jo and Kelsey Lee (twins). BS in Secondary Edn., U. Mont., 1979. Cert. Counselor, Mont. Tchr. Cut Bank (Mont.) Jr. H.S., 1980-82, Scobey (Mont.) H.S., 1982-84, Melstone (Mont.) H.S., 1984-88; tchr. history Havre (Mont.) H.S., 1988—; adj. instr. Mont. State U.-No., Havre, 1990-97; in-svc. cons., classroom presenter various confs., 1995-98. Vocalist, cantor St. Jude's Ch., Havre, 1992—; mem. Havre City Coun., 1995-96. Recipient Outstanding Young Educator award Scobey Jaycees, 1984. Mem. Mont. Coun. for Social studies, Havre Edn. Assn. (v.p. 1997-99). Democrat. Roman Catholic. Avocations: gardening, reading, skiing, travel. Home: 1016 20th St Havre MT 59501-5523 Office: Havre HS 900 18th St Havre MT 59501-5416

WEST, DANIEL CHARLES, lay worker, dentist; b. Trenton, N.J., July 23, 1955; s. Harry E. and Alma R. (Washburn) W.; m. Deborah L. Scott, May 28, 1977; children: Lauren Elizabeth, Colin Jeffrey. BS, Ea. Nazarene Coll., 1977; DMD, U. Pitts., 1982. Min. youth/music South Hills Ch. of the

Nazarene, Bethel Park, Pa., 1977-82; pvt. practice specializing in family dentistry Terre Hill, Pa., 1982-95; pvt. practice specializing in cosmetic, implant and reconstructive dentistry New Holland, Pa., 1995—; mem. Internat. Gen. Bd., Ch. of the Nazarene, Kansas City, Mo., 1989—, lay mem. dist. adv. bd. Phila. dist., Frazer, Pa., 1985—, coord. work and witness program, 1988-90, bd. dirs. compassionate ministries, 1990—; bd. dirs. Mission Am., 1997—; dir. Phila. dist. IMPACT, 1982-89; trustee Ea. Nazarene Coll., Wollaston, Mass., 1984—, mem. exec. com., chmn. dept. fin.; mem. clin. faculty U. Pa. Sch. Dental Medicine, Med. U. Ukraine, Kiev, Pediat. Med. U. Russia, Moscow; mem. Mission Am. Bd., 1997—. Contbr. articles to jours. Bd. dirs. Garden Spot Village Retirement Comty., 1996-97. Lt. USPHS, 1982-85. Recipient Alumni Achievement award Eastern Nazarene Coll., 1996. Fellow Am. Acad. Gen. Dentistry; mem. ADA (Cert. Recognition for Internat. Svc. in a Fgn. County 1996), Am. Acad. Cosmetic Dentistry, Pa. Dental Assn., Lancaster County Dental Soc. Republican. Home: 1442 Hay Field Dr East Earl PA 17519-9685 Office: 650 E Main St New Holland PA 17557-1410

WEST, JAMES REYENARD, dance educator; b. Jersey City, Nov. 28, 1960; s. James Albert and Juanita (Shorter) W.; life ptnr. Miguel Angel Negron. BA in Health Edn. summa cum laude, U. Palmers Green, London, 1983, MA in Social Work summa cum laude, 1985. Attendant U.S. Army Europe Terrace Officers Club, Frankfurt, Germany, 1984-85; mgr. King Creole's Restaurant, Frankfurt, 1985-86; asst. mgr. Dance Ctr. Frankfurt/Arthur Murray Dance Studio, 1986-97; coord. peer edn. AIDS Project R.I., Providence, 1997—, cons. youth programs, 1999—; instr. Burlington (Mass.) Sch. Dance, 1999—; cons. Dept. Human Svcs., Pitts., 1999. Founding mem., mem. adv. com. Gay Men of African Descent-N.E. Regional Capacity Bldg. Assistance Program, N.Y.C., 1999—; chmn. pub. rels. Enforcers, R.I., Providence, 1999; incorporator, exec. dir. Orgn. for Men of Ethnicity Geared to Advancement, 2000—. With USAF, 1981-83. Mem. World Profl. Dance Tchrs. Assn. (dual bachelor instr.). Democrat. Muslim. Avocations: weight training, travel, reading, movies, theatre. E-mail: rahjah@hotmail.com. Home: 1691 Broad St Apt 4 Cranston RI 02905-2731 Office: Burlington Sch Dance 171 Cambridge St Rm 3 Burlington MA 01803-2922

WEST, JOHN CARL, lawyer, former ambassador, former governor; b. Camden, S.C., Aug. 27, 1922; s. Shelton J. and Mattie (Ratterree) W.; m. Lois Rhame, Aug. 29, 1942; children: John Carl Jr., Douglas Allen, Shelton West Bosley. BA, The Citadel, 1942; LB magna cum laude, U. S.C., 1948; D (hon.), The Citadel, U. S.C., Davidson Coll., Presbyn. Coll., Francis Marion Coll., Wofford Coll., Coll. Charleston. Bar: S.C. 1947. Ptnr. West, Holland, Furman & Cooper, Camden, S.C., 1947-70; state senator Kershaw County State of S.C., 1954-66; lt. gov. State of S.C., 1966-70, gov., 1971-75; ptnr. West, Cooper, Bowen, Beard & Smoot, Camden, S.C., 1975-77; amb. to Saudi Arabia, 1977-81; sr. ptnr. West & West, P.A., Hilton Head Island, 1981-88; disting. prof. Middle East Studies U. S.C., 1981—; of counsel McNair Law Firm, Hilton Head Island, S.C., 1988-92, Bethea, Jordan & Griffin, P.A., Hilton Head Island, S.C., 1993—; bd. dirs. Donaldson, Lufkin & Jenrette, Inc. Maj. AUS, 1942-46. Decorated Army commendation medal; comdr. Order of Merit (West Germany); recipient Freedom award S.C. C. of C. Mem. Phi Beta Kappa. Democrat. Presbyterian. Address: PO Box 13 Hilton Head Island SC 29938-0013

WEST, LINDEN REGINALD, education educator, researcher; b. Stoke-on-Trent, Eng., Nov. 11, 1946; s. Alfred Reginald and Phyllis Annie (Barker) W.; m. Margaret Hughes, Feb. 16, 1973 (div. Mar. 1986); children: Keith, Louise, Lindsey, Charlotte; m. Helen Grace Reynolds, Dec. 7, 1990; 1 child, Hannah Lucy. BA with honors, Keele U., U.K., 1969; MPhil, Open U., U.K., 1985; postgrad. cert. psychotherapy, U. Kent, 1997, PhD in Edn., 1998. Further edn. tutor Cmty. Coll., Cumbria, U.K., 1973-81; head Adult Basic Edn. Unit, Edinburgh, Scotland, 1981-83; dist. sec. Workers Ednl. Assn., Oxford, Eng., 1983-90; lectr. theory and practice of continuing edn. U. Kent, U.K., 1990-96; sr. lectr. Kent Inst. Medicine and Health scis./U. Kent, U.K., 1997—; chair Our Right to Learn Campaign, Scotland, 1981-82; access cons. Oxon County Coun., U.K., 1988-90; external examiner, advisor U. Sussex, U.K., 1994—; advisor Brit. Postgrad. Med. Fedn., 1995-98; sr. vis. rsch. fellow U. East London, Canterbury, Christ Church U., 1999—. Author: Beyond Fragments: Adults, Motivation and Higher Education, 1996, Doctors on the Edge, 2000, (chpt.) Life Histories, Adult Learning and Identity, 1995. Parliamentary candidate Labour Party, Carlisle, U.K., 1979; city councillor Carlive City Coun., 1970-81; exec. dir. Stoke Arts Festival, U.K., 1971-72. Recipient Rsch. grant Dept. Edn. and Sci., U.K., 1985, Rsch. grant Higher Edn. Funding Coun., U.K., 1992, Rsch. grant Thames Postgrad. Med. and Dental Edn., U.K., 1996. Fellow Royal Soc. Arts, Mfrs. and Commerce. Mem. Ch. of Eng. Avocations: trainee psychotherapist, music, walking, gardening. Home: 5 Shepherdsgate Roper Rd, Kent Canterbury CT2 7RU, United Kingdom Office: Kent Inst Medicine Health, Keynes Coll Univ Kent, Kent Canterbury CT2 7NX, United Kingdom

WEST, MARTIN LITCHFIELD, classical scholar, educator; b. Eltham, London, U.K., Sept. 23, 1937; s. Maurice Charles and Catherine Baker (Stainthorpe) W.; m. Stephanie Roberta Pickard, Dec. 31, 1960; children: Rachel Ann, Robert Charles. MA, Oxford U., 1962, PhD, 1963, DLitt, 1994. Jr. rsch. fellow St. John's Coll., Oxford, U.K., 1960-63; fellow, praelector Univ. Coll., Oxford, 1963-74; prof. Greek U. London, 1974-91; sr. rsch. fellow All Souls Coll., Oxford, 1991—; vis. lectr. Harvard U., 1967-68; vis. prof. UCLA, 1986. Author: The Orphic Poems, 1983, Studies in Aeschylus, 1990, Ancient Greek Music, 1992, The East Face of Helicon, 1997, Runciman award 1998. Fellow Brit. Acad; mem. Hungarian Soc. Classical Studies (hon.), Akademie der Wissenschaften zu Göttingen (corr.), Academia Europaea. Avocation: music. Office: All Souls College, Oxford OX1 4AL, England

WEST, PAUL GAVIN, educator, administrator; b. Port Elizabeth, South Africa, Mar. 27, 1958. ND Man, Technikon, Port Elizabeth, 1985, NHD Man Prac, 1987; MBA, Northland Open U., Can., 1989. Mgr. Kodak/CPL, Port Elizabeth, 1987-89; sr. lectr. Technikon SA, Johannesburg, 1989-92; dir. Ctr. for Lifelong Learning Technikon SA, Joannesburg, 1993—. Mem. Inst. of Dirs., Inst. of Adminstrn. and Commerce, Johannesburg C. of C. Fax: 27-11-471-2603. E-mail: pgwest@pgw.org. Home: PO Box 276, 1710 Florida Gauteng, Republic of South Africa Office: Technikon SA, Pvt Bag X24, 1710 Florida Gauteng, Republic of South Africa

WEST, RICHARD GILBERT, botany educator; b. Hendon, Middlesex, Eng., May 31, 1926; s. Arthur G.D. and Daisy E.L. (Hutchinson) W. ScD, U. Cambridge, Eng., 1974. Prof. palaeoecology U. Cambridge, 1975-77, prof. botany, 1977-91; fellow Clare Coll, Cambridge, 1954—. Author: Preglacial Pleistocene, 1980, Pleistocene Palaeoecology, 1991, Pleistocene Geology and Biology, 1977, Plant Life of the Quarternary Cold Stages, 2000. Fellow Geol. Soc. London (Bigsby medal 1969, Lyell medal 1988), Royal Soc. London, Inst. Biology, Soc. Antiquaries London; mem. Royal Irish Acad. (hon.). Office: U Cambridge Botany Sch, Downing St, Cambridge CB2 3EA, England

WEST, ROBERT LEE, JR., marketing professional; b. Wilmington, N.C., Oct. 5, 1958; s. Robert L. Sr. and Elsie S. (Skipper) W.; m. Shari H., Aug. 1, 1998. BSBA, U. N.C., Pembroke, 1981; postgrad., U. Pa., 1988-90, 99. Divsn. controller Royster Co., Norfolk, Va., 1982-84; regional fin. mgr. Rohm & Haas Co., Memphis, 1984-86; head Asian ops. Franklin Mint, Hone Kong, 1986-88; head corp. cost improvement Franklin Mint, Phila., 1988-89; head European ops. Franklin Mint, London, 1989-90; v.p. fin. & ops. Paradise Galleries, Inc., San Diego, 1990-91; v.p., chief fin. officer Georgetown Collection, Inc., Portland, Maine, 1992-95; v.p. worldwide ops. Nat. Media Corp., Phoenix, 1995-97; pres., founder DCA Internat., Phoenix, 1990—; CEO, pres. Georgetown Collection, Inc., Portland, Maine, 1997-98; chief oper. officer LL Knickerbocker, Lake Forest, Calif., 1998-99; v.p., gen. mgr. Chevrolet Catalog, San Diego, 1999—; cons. to CEO J Crew, N.Y.C., 1990-91. V.p. Maxton (N.C.) Conservative Response, 1980-82. Mem. Am. Mgmt. Assn., Am. Fin. Assn., Inst. Mgmt. Accts., World Affairs Coun. Republican. Avocations: biking, flying, model railroading, tennis, long distance running. Home: 56 Monserrat Pl Foothill Rnch CA 92610-1903 Office: DCA Dynamic Cons Assocs 3646 E Ray Rd Ste B16-60 Phoenix AZ 85044-7116

WEST, TIMOTHY, actor, stage director; b. Oct. 20, 1934; s. Harry Lockwood and Olive (Carleton-Crowe) West; m. Jacqueline Boyer, 1956 (div.); m. Prunella Scales, 1963. Student, John Lyon Sch., Eng., Regent Street Poly., Eng. Dir. Old Vic Theatre Co., 1980-81; dir. in residence U. W. Australia, 1982. Appeared in (stage prodns.) Summertime, 1956, Caught Napping, 1959, The Life of Galileo, 1960, The Merry Wives of Windsor, 1964, Love's Labour's Lost, The Merchant of Venice, The Comedy of Errors, 1965, The Investigation, 1965, The Constant Couple, A Room with a View, 1967, Richard II, Edward II, 1969, Much Ado About Nothing, Abelard and Heloise, Exiles, 1970, Trelawny, Henry IV, 1971, King Lear 1972, Major Barbara 1973, Macbeth, 1974, Hedda Gabbler, 1975, Trelawny of the Wells, 1980, others; TV appearances include Edward VII, Horatio Bottomley, Hard Times, Crime and Punnishment, Churchill and the Generals, Brass, The Last Bastion, The Monocled Mutineer, A Very Peculiar Practice, The Good Doctor Bodkin Adams, What the Butler Saw, Harry's Kingdom, The Sealed Train, When We Are Married, Breakthrough at Reykjavik, Strife, A Shadow on the Sun, The Contractor, Blore, M.P., Beecham, Survival of the Fittest, Why Lockerbie?, Framed, Hiroshima, Eleven Men Against Eleven, Cuts; appeared in films, Twisted Nerve, Nicholas and Alexandra, The Day of the Jackal, Oliver Twist, Hedda, Joseph Andrews, The Devil's Advocate, Agatha, Masada, The Thirty Nine Steps, Rough Cut, Cry Freedom, Ever After, Joan of Arc. Recipient CBE by Queen Elizabeth, 1984. Avocations: traveling, music, exploring old railways, tennis.

WEST, WALLACE MARION, cultural organization administrator; b. N.Y.C., Aug. 30, 1921; s. Florian and Mary (Wziatek) Wesolowski. BSBA, L.I. U., 1966; cert. mus. mgmt., Columbia U. Estimating engr. Sperry Rand Corp., Lake Success, N.Y., 1957-65; sys. analyst Grumman Aerospace, Bethpage, N.Y., 1965-71; exec. dir. Queens Coun. on Arts, Jamaica, N.Y., 1971-76, Hall of Sci. of City of N.Y., Flushing, 1976-79; pres. Am. Inst. Polish Culture, Pinellas Park, Fla., 1982—; cons. arts mgmt. N.Y. State Coun. on Arts, 1968-71. Author: Handbook for Directors of Non-Profit Corporations, 1974; editor: Sharing Our Heritage, 1996; editor Polish Heritage Quarterly, 1985-99; contbr. articles to profl. jours. Recipient Order of Merit Republic of Poland, 1992; named Notable Am. of Bicentennial Era Am. Biog. Inst., 1976. Mem. Am. Inst. Polish Culture (pres., Polonian of Yr. 1985, Spl. Achievement award 2000), Am. Coun. Polish Culture (bd. dirs., Founders award 1992, Spl. Achievement award 2000, editor 1985-99), Polish Am. Soc., Polish Inst. Arts/Scis. in Am., Polish Am. Pulaski Assn., Kosciuszko Found., Pilsudski Inst. Am. Republican. Roman Catholic. Avocations: photography, crafts, electronics, swimming. Home: 6507 107th Ter Pinellas Park FL 33782-2432 Office: Am Inst Polish Culture 9190 49th St Pinellas Park FL 33782-5228

WEST, WILLIAM BRENT, judge; b. Salt Lake City, May 17, 1951; s. Richard William West and Beverly Jean (Woodhead) Monson; m. Judy Ann Hill, Mar. 18, 1971; children: Jennifer Lee, Jason William. BS, U. Utah, 1973; JD, Southern Meth. U., 1975. Bar: Utah, 1976. Pvt. practice Ogden, Utah, 1976-79; asst. corp. counsel City of Ogden, 1979-81, chief prosecutor, 1981-84; circuit court judge State of Utah, Ogden, 1996, dist. ct. judge, 1996—; presiding judge 3d Cir. Ct. Bd. Judges, 1985-88, 2d Cir. Ct. Bd. Judges, 1988-90; mem. Cir. Ct. Bd. Judges, 1986, 88-91, Utah Jud. Coun., 1991-94. Bd. dirs. Children's Aid Soc., treas. 1978-80, v.p. 1987-89, Ogden City Schs. Vols. Assn., pres. 1980-86, Moweda, 1985-87; active Common Ct. Boundaries Com., 1987, Utah Task Force on Gender and Justice 1986-89, Weber, Morgan Counties Child Abuse Co-ordination Coun., 1988-90; vice-chmn. Warrants Task Force, 1987; chmn. Uniform Bail Schedule Com., 1987-91; group leader Parents United, 1986. Named Cir. Ct. Judge of Yr. 1989, Judge of Yr. 1997. Mem. Utah Bar Assn. (named Cir. Ct. Judge of Yr. 1989, Judge of Yr. 1997), Weber County Bar Assn. (treas. 1977-79), Ogden Unit Contract Bridge League (dir. 1978-80,1987-89, pres. 1979-80, 1987-88, 1988-89). Avocations: golf, softball, bridge. Office: 2525 Grant Ave Ogden UT 84401-3101

WESTALL, OLIVER MARTIN, economic historian, educator; b. Ashburton, Eng.; s. Harry Martin and Doris (Oliver) W.; m. Karen Ann Harvey, Aug. 12, 1967; children: Rebecca Chloe, Rosina Ann. BSc in Econs., London Sch. Econs., 1966. Lectr., then sr. lectr. Lancaster (Eng.) U., 1969—. Author: The Provincial Insurance Company 1903-1938: Family, Markets and Competitive Growth, 1992 (Wadsworth prize 1992); contbr. articles to profl. jours. Recipient Cass prize for bus. history, 1994, 97. Mem. Econ. History Soc. (hon. treas. 1996—). Office: Lancaster U Sch Mgmt Dept, Econs, Lancaster LA1 4YX, England

WESTBERRY, JOHN ELLIOTT, mathematics educator; b. Knoxville, Tenn., Aug. 8, 1922; s. John Elliott and Annie (Richardson) W.; m. Gaynelle Hines, July 8, 1942 (dec. May 1992); 1 child, Larry; m. Maxine Willis, Mar. 18, 1993. BS, Livingstone Coll., 1941; MS, Atlanta U., 1949; MA, U. Mich., 1954. Asst. prof. Tex. Coll., Tyler, 1949-50, Tex. State U., Houston, 1950-54; registrar, dir. admissions Tex. So. U., Houston, 1954-94, assoc. prof., 1975—. Tech. sgt. U.S. Army, 1942-45, ETO. Named one of 100 Most Influential Blacks, Ebony mag., 1974, 75, 76, Am.'s Best Tchrs. Ednl. Comms., Inc., 1998. Mem. Am. Assn. Coll. Registrars and Admissions Officers (sec.-treas. 1980-83), Math. Assn. Am., Tex. Assn. Coll. Registrars and Admissions Officers (pres. 1982), Phi Beta Sigma (pres. 1974-76). Democrat. Avocations: reading, speaking. Home: 5306 Stuyvesant Ln Houston TX 77021-3145 Office: Tex So U 3100 Cleburne St Houston TX 77004-4501

WESTCOTT, BRIAN JOHN, manufacturing executive; b. Rexford, N.Y., June 19, 1957; s. John Campbell and Norma (Cornell) W.; m. Andrea Belrose, Apr. 23, 1988; children: Sarah Katharine, Paul Brian. BS, Lehigh U., 1979; MS, Stanford U., 1980, PhD, 1987. Engr. Combustion Engring., Windsor, Conn., 1980-81; rsch. engr. Gen. Electric Corp. Rsch., Niskayuna, N.Y., 1981-83; rsch. fellow Stanford (Calif.) Grad. Sch. Bus., 1987-88; mgr. Gen. Electric Corp. Mgmt., Bridgeport, Conn., 1988-89; prin. A.T. Kearney Tech. Inc., Redwood City, Calif., 1989—; chief exec. officer Westt, Inc., Menlo Park, Calif., 1990—; CEO e Innovate, 1999—. Author: (with others) Paradox and Transformation, 1988; contbr. articles to profl. jours.; inventor, patentee in field. Mem. Menlo Park Vitality Task Force, 1993-94. Recipient Tech 500 award Westt, Inc., 1996, 97, 98, Inc. 500 award, 1997, Silicon Valley Tech fast 50 award, 1997, 98; postdoctoral rsch. fellow Stanford U. Grad. Sch. Bus., 1987, 88; rsch. fellow Electric Power Rsch., Stanford, 1983-87. Mem. ASME. Avocations: sports, politics. Office: Westt Inc 1090 Obrien Dr Menlo Park CA 94025-1409

WESTENDORF, WOLFHART HEINRICH, Egyptologist; b. Schwiebus, Germany, Sept. 18, 1924; s. Otto and Charlotte (Mechler) W.; m. Marianne Harder, May 31, 1952; children: Beate, Andreas. PhD, Humboldt U., East Berlin, 1951, D Philosophy Habiliated, 1961; extraordinary prof. (hon.), U. Munich, 1965. Collaborator Acad. Wissenschften Inst. Orientforschung, Berlin, 1951-61; asst. prof. Egyptology U. Munich, 1962-67; ordinary prof. U. Göttingen, Fed. Republic Germany, 1967-89, prof. emeritus. Author, coauthor several books on Egyptology, 1953—; contbg. editor: (ency.) Lexikon der Ägyptologie, 1975-92; editor: (serial) Göttinger Orientforschungen, 1973—; contbr. numerous articles to profl. publs. Lt. German Air Force, 1942-45. Recipient Deutscher Nationalpreis, Acad. Wissenschaften Berlin, 1959. Mem. Deutsche Forschungsgemeinschaft (expert 1968-76, 84-91), Acad. Wissenschaften Göttingen, Deutsches Archäologisches Inst., Reinisch-Westfälische Acad. (coord.). Lutheran. Home: Über den Höfen 15, D-37077 Göttingen Germany Office: U Göttingen, Prinzenstrasse 21, D-37073 Göttingen Germany

WESTENDORP, IRIS C.D., cardiologist, epidemiologist; b. Durham, N.C., Oct. 10, 1967; d. Tjebbe A. Westendorp and Anne Meulenberg. MD, U. Amsterdam, The Netherlands, 1995; MSc, Netherlands Inst. Health Scis., Rotterdam, 1997; PhD, Erasmus U. Rotterdam, 1999. Rsch. assoc. dept. epidemiology and biostats. Erasmus U., 1995-99; resident in cardiology Onze Lieve Vrouwe Gasthuis, Amsterdam, 1999—. Contbr. articles to profl. jours. including The Lancet, Atherosclerosis, Thrombosis and Vascular Biology, Jour. Internal Medicine, Archives of Internal Medicine, Stroke, Atherosclerosis, Diabetologia Jour. Clin. Endocrinol Metab, Circulation. Mem. World Heart Fedn., Netherlands Assn. Epidemiology, Netherlands Assn. Cardiology. Home: Czaar Peterstraat 106, 1018 PS Amsterdam The Netherlands Office: Onze Lieve Vrouwe Gasthuis, 1st Oosterparkstraat 279, 1091 HA Amsterdam The Netherlands

WESTENDORP Y CABEZA, CARLOS, diplomat; b. Jan. 7, 1937; m. Amaya de Miguel; 3 children. Degrees in law and diplomatic studies. 1st class min. plenipotentiary; asst. consul Spanish Consulate, Sao Paulo, Brazil, 1966-69; head rels. with European Cmtys., sec. Spain-EEC Mixed Com., 1970-73; head tech. cabinet Ministry of Industry Govt. of Spain, 1974-75; econ. affairs adviser, dir. comml. office Spanish Embassy, The Hague, Netherlands, 1975-79; cons.-mem. head of cabinet Min. Rels. with European Cmtys., 1981; sec.- gen. Secretariat of State for European Cmtys., Ministry of Fgn. Affairs, 1981-85; Spanish amb. to European Cmtys., 1986-91; sec. state European Cmtys., Ministry of Fgn. Affairs Govt. of Spain, 1991-95, min. fgn. affairs, 1995-96; ambassador of Spain to UN, 1996-97; high rep. for Bosnia and Herzegovina, 1997—; mem. European Parliament, Brussels, Belgium, 1999-; chmn. free identity, fgn. trade, rsch., energy coms. Office: European Parliament, Rue Wiertz, ASP 11G302 Brussels B-1047, Belgium

WESTER, KEITH ALBERT, film and television recording engineer, real estate developer; b. Seattle, Feb. 21, 1940; s. Albert John and Evelyn Grayce (Nettell) W., m. Judith Elizabeth Jones, 1968 (div. Mar. 1974); 1 child, Wendy Elizabeth. AA, Am. River Coll., Sacramento, 1959; BA, Calif. State U., L.A., 1962; MA, UCLA, 1965. Lic. multi-engine rated pilot. Prodn. asst. Sta. KCRA-TV, Sacramento, 1956; announcer Sta. KSFM, Sacramento, 1960; film editor, sound rec. technician Urie & Assocs., Hollywood, Calif., 1963-66; co-owner Steckler-Wester Film Prodns., Hollywood, 1966-70; owner Profl. Sound Recorders, Studio City, Calif., 1970—, Aerocharter, Studio City, 1974—; owner Wester Devel., Sun Valley, Coeur d'Alene, Idaho, 1989—, also Studio City, 1989—; majority stockholder Channel 58 TV, Coeur d'Alene/Spokane, 1993-99. Prodn. sound mixer: (films) The Perfect Storm, 1999, Never Been Kissed, 1999, Runaway Bride, 1999, Armageddon, 1998 (Acad. award co-nominee 1999), Mouse Hunt, 1997, Air Force One, 1997 (Acad. award co-nominee for best sound 1998), Shadow Conspiracy, 1996, G.I. Jane, 1997, The Rock, 1996 (Acad. award co-nominee for best sound, 1997), Waterworld, 1995 (Acad. award co-nominee for best sound 1996), The Shadow, 1994, Wayne's World II, 1993, Coneheads, 1993, Body of Evidence, 1992, Indecent Proposal, 1992, School Ties, 1991, Frankie and Johnny, 1991, Another You, 1991, Thelma and Louise, 1990, Shattered, 1990, Desperate Hours, 1989, Joe vs. the Volcano, 1989, Black Rain, 1989 (Acad. award co-nominee 1990), Sea of Love, 1988, Real Men, 1985, Mask, 1984, Thief of Hearts, 1983, Young Doctors in Love, 1982, First Monday in October, 1981. Mem. NATAS (Emmy award An Early Frost 1986, Emmy nominations in 1982, 84, 85, 87), SAG, Acad. Motion Picture Arts and Scis. (Acad. award nomination for best sound Black Rain 1990, Waterworld 1996, The Rock 1997, Air Force One 1998, Armageddon 1999), Brit. Acad. Film and TV Arts (award nomination for The Rock 1997), Cinema Audio Soc. (sec. 1985-91, Sound award 1987), Soc. Motion Picture and TV Engrs., Internat. Sound Technicians, Local 695, Assn. Film Craftsmen (sec. 1967-73, treas. 1973-76), Aircraft Owners and Pilots Assn. (Confederate Air Force col.), Am. Radio Relay League (K6DGN). Home: 4146 Bellingham Ave Studio City CA 91604-1601 Office: Profl Sound Recorders 22440 Clarendon St Woodland Hills CA 91367-4467

WESTER, KNUT GUSTAV, physician, educator; b. Asker, Norway, Sept. 1, 1940; s. Gustav Arthur and Borghild Nancy (Joergensen) W.; m. Sidsel Eriksen, July 28, 1962; children: Kjerstin, Torjus. MD, U. Oslo, Norway, 1965, PhD, 1974. Rsch. fellow U. Oslo, 1968-70, asst. prof., 1973-74, tng. neurology and neurosurgery, 1975-86; rsch. fellow U. Calif., Irvine, 1971-72; cons. U. Bergen Med. Sch., Norway, 1986; prof. U. Bergen Med. Sch., 1989—, chmn. Dept. Neurosurgery, 1990—. Mem. Scandanavian Neurosurg. Assn. (chmn organizing com. ann. mtg. 1996), Norwegian Assn. Neurosurgeons (chmn. 1994-95, bd. dirs. 1995-98), Scandinavian Neurosurgical Soc. (chmn. 1998—). E-mail: knut.gustav.wester@haukeland.no. Office: Haukeland Hosp, Dept Neurosurgery, N-5021 Bergen Norway

WESTERBERG, LARS, automotive safety systems company executive; b. 1948. MBSS, Royal Instl Tech., Stockholm; MBA, U. Stockholm. With ASEA (now ABB), from 1972; various positions Esab AB, welding machine co.; pres. N.Am. subs. Esab AB welding machine co., 1984-87, pres., CEO; pres., CEO Granges AB, aluminum and plastics co., until 1999, Autoliv Inc., Stockholm, 1999—. Office: Autoliv Inc World Trade Ctr, Klarabergsviadukten 70, SE-10724 Stockholm Sweden

WESTERBERG, SIV ÖMAN, lawyer, physician; b. Borås, Sweden, June 11, 1932; d. Bror and Magda (Karlsson) Öman; m. Per G.S. Westerberg, June 19, 1964; children: Eva, Carl, Gösta. Medicine Kandidat, U. Uppsala, Sweden, 1954, Medicine Licentiat, 1960; Juris Kandidat, U. Lund, Sweden, 1982. Bar: Sweden 1982, European Commn. Human Rights 1983, European Ct. Human Rights 1987. Physician Univ. Clinics, Gothenburg, Sweden, 1960-64; physician, rschr. Clin. Labs., Univ. Hosp. Sahlgrenska Sjukhuset, Gothenburg, 1961-63; pvt. practice gen. medicine, Gothenburg, 1964-79, pvt. practice law,, 1982—. Author: Vaccination av utlandsresenärer, 1964, To Be a Physician, 1978, (with H.A. Hansen) A Handbook of Laboratory Work, 1962; contbr. articles on renal physiology to med. jours., articles on unnecessary taking of children into pub. care to Swedish and fgn. newspapers. Mem. bd. Nordic Com. for Human Rights. Lutheran. Achievements include bringing to and winning number of cases in The European Court of Human Rights, Strasbourg, France. Home and office: Skårsgatan 45, S-412 69 Göteborg Sweden

WESTERFIELD, HOLT BRADFORD, political scientist, educator; b. Rome, Italy, Mar. 7, 1928; s. Ray Bert and Mary Beatrice (Putney) W.; m. Carolyn Elizabeth Hess, Dec. 17, 1960; children: Pamela Bradford, Leland Avery. Grad., Choate Sch., 1944; BA, Yale U., 1947; MA, Harvard U., 1951, PhD, 1952. Instr. govt. Harvard U., 1952-56; asst. prof. polit. sci. U. Chgo., 1956-57; mem. faculty Yale U., 1957—, prof. polit. sci., 1965-2000, chmn. dept., 1970-72, Damon Wells prof. internat. studies, 1985-2000; prof. emeritus, 2000—; rsch. assoc. Washington Center Fgn. Policy Research, Johns Hopkins Sch. Advanced Internat. Studies, 1965-66; vis. prof. Wesleyan U., Middletown, Conn., 1967, 71; bd. visitors U.S. Joint Mil. Intelligence Coll., Washington, 1998—. Author: Foreign Policy and Party Politics: Pearl Harbor to Korea, 1955, The Instruments of America's Foreign Policy, 1963; editor: Inside CIA's Private World: Declassified Articles from the Agency's Internal Journal, 1955-92, 1995. Sheldon traveling fellow Harvard, 1951-52; Henry L. Stimson fellow Yale, 1962, 73; sr. Fulbright-Hays scholar, 1973; hon. vis. fellow Australian Nat. U., 1973. Mem. Am. Polit. Sci. Assn. (Congl. fellow 1953-54), Internat. Polit. Sci. Assn., Internat. Studies Assn. Home: 115 Rogers Rd Hamden CT 06517-3541 Office: Yale Univ Dept Polit Sci PO Box 208301 New Haven CT 06520-8301

WESTERHAUS, DOUGLAS BERNARD, lawyer; b. Marion, Kans., Jan. 11, 1951; s. Edwin Gerard and Bernadine (Ullman) W.; m. Susan Elizabeth Scott, Aug. 20, 1973 (div. Jan. 1979); m. Karen Sue Giersch, Sept. 20, 1980 (div. Aug. 1997); children: John Joseph, Jamie Lynn, Jeffrey Michael; m. Victoria Lee Ruhga, March, 1998. BSBA, Kans. U., 1973, JD, 1976. Bar: Kans. 1976, U.S. Dist. Kans. 1976, U.S. Supreme Ct. 1980. Assoc. Harper & Hornbaker, Junction City, Kans., 1976-78; prin. Harper & Hornbaker, Junction City, 1978-80; prin. Westerhaus Law Office, Marion, Kans., 1980-86; pres. Hydrogen Energy Corp., 1986-91, also bd. dirs.; staff atty. THORN Ams., Inc., dba Rent-A-Ctr., Wichita, Kans., 1991-95, chief counsel human resources, 1995-96, assoc. gen. counsel, 1996-97; dir. Field Human Resources, 1997-98; exec. v.p. Mr. Goodcents Franchise Sys., Inc., 1999—; atty. City of Grandview Plaza, Kans. 1977-80, City of Lehigh, Kans. 1980-86, Marion County, 1981-85; gen. counsel The Hydrogen Energy Corp., Kansas City, Mo. 1984-86, Marion Die & Fixture, 1980-86. Bd. dirs. St. Luke's Hosp., Marion, 1985-86. Mem. ABA, Kans. Bar Assn. (chmn. Lawyer Referral Commn. 1979-84, Outstanding Service award 1984), Marion County Bar Assn. (pres. 1985), Sedgwick County Bar Assn. Republican. Roman Catholic. Home: 12813 King St Overland Park KS 66213-4416

WESTERHOFF, HEINZ, thermodynamic engineer; b. Hagen, Fed. Republic Germany, May 12, 1928; s. August and Alma Westerhoff; m. Gertrud Keppler, May 30, 1954; children: Monika, Brigitte. Diploma in engring., Technische Hochschule, Aachen, Fed. Republic Germany, 1955. Engr. indsl. furnace system Siemens, Mülheim a d Ruhr, Fed. Republic Germany, 1955-56, 1957-60; engr. indsl. furnace system Power Plant Fortuna, Cologne, Fed. Republic Germany, 1956-57; engr. indsl. furnace system Reining Heisskühlung, Mülheim a d Ruhr, 1960-64, ptnr and exec. pres.

founder, 1965-94; cons. Reining Heisskühlung, 1994-2000, ret., 2000. Home: Jakobstr 36, D-45478 Mulheim an der Ruhr 1, Germany Office: Reining Heisskuhlung, Box 130245, D-45446 Mulheim an der Ruhr Germany

WESTERHOUT, GART, retired astronomer; b. The Hague, The Netherlands, June 15, 1927; came to U.S., 1962, naturalized, 1969; s. Gerrit and Magdalena (Foppe) W.; m. Judith Mary Monaghan, Nov. 14, 1956; children: Magda C., Gart T., Brigit M., Julian C., Anthony K. (dec.). Drs., Leiden U., Netherlands, 1954, Ph.D., 1958. Asst. Leiden U. Observatory, 1952-56, sci. officer, 1956-59, chief sci. officer, 1959-62; prof., dir. astronomy U. Md., 1962-73, chmn. div. math. and phys. scis. and engring., 1972-73, prof. astronomy, 1973-77; sci. dir. U.S. Naval Observatory, Washington, 1977-93; vis. astronomer Max Planck Inst. Radio Astronomy, Bonn, Germany, 1973-74, mem. adv. bd., 1976-79; mem. astronomy adv. bd. NSF, 1963-67; vice chmn. divsn. phys. sci. NRC, 1969-73; mem. com. on radio frequencies, 1971-92; trustee Assoc. Univs. Inc., 1971-74; mem. Intern Union Commn. on Allocation of Frequencies, 1974-82; mem. sci. coun. Stellar Data Ctr., Strasbourg, France, 1978-84, chmn., 1981; chmn. working group on astrometry, astronomy survey com. NAS, 1979-81; mem. adv. bd. Haystack-N.E. Radio Obs. Consortium, 1974-77; mem. Arecibo adv. bd. Nat. Astronomy and Ionosphere Ctr., 1977-80, chmn., 1979-80; mem. U.S. nat. com. CODATA, 1985-91. Contbr. on radio astronomy, spiral structure of our Galaxy and astrometry to profl. jours. Recipient citation for teaching excellence Washington Acad. Scis., 1972; U.S. Sr. Scientist award Alexander von Humboldt Stiftung, Ger., 1973; NATO fellow, 1959. Mem. Internat. Astron. Union (chmn. working group on astron. data 1985-91), Internat. Sci. Radio Union (pres. commn. on radio astronomy 1975-78), Am. Astron. Soc. (councillor 1975-78, v.p. 1985-87), Royal Astron. Soc. Roman Catholic. Home: 811 W 38th St Baltimore MD 21211-2203

WESTERMANN, MAARTEN HUIBERT JORIS, journalist, author; b. The Hague, May 28, 1953; s. Frederik Anthon Carl and Elisabeth Charlotte Augusta Maria (Hermans) W.; m. Emilie Cornélie Marguerite Koene, 1948; children: Emma Cora Elisabeth, Jeroen Joost Jolle. Editor Elseviers Weekblad, Amsterdam, 1978-86, Quote mag., Amsterdam, 1986-91; editor-in-chief Sponsoring mag., Amsterdam, 1991-92; freelance columnist, journalist, 1991-95, 99—; editor-in-chief Safe mag., Rotterdam, 1996-98; lectr. in field. Author: Volgens Vogels, 1989, John Block, Mijn Verhaal, 1992, Sponsoring als communicatie-instrument voor het bedrijfsleven, 1999. Chmn. congresses sponsoring and fundraising Nederlands Studie Centrum, Rotterdam; bd. dirs. Stichting W.F. Westermann Found. 1853-1953, 1985. Sgt. Dutch Royal Army, 1973-75. Mem. Aerdenhoutse Mixed Hockey Club Rood Wit (bd. dirs. 1993—, pres. 1994—), Illustrious Soc. E.R.A.S.M.V.S. (hon.). Avocations: collecting olympic paraphenalia, books and souvenirs. Email: presswes@wxs.nl. Home and Office: van Slingelandtlaan 4, 2101 BR Heemstede The Netherlands

WESTFALL, WAYNE LYNN, chemical engineer; b. Mechanicsburg, Pa., Jan. 9, 1941; s. Karl H. and Mae L. (Conrad) W.; m. Sharon L. Hillis, Aug. 10, 1966 (div. Dec. 1996); children: Amy, Wendy, Danielle, Kristian. AS, York (Pa.) Jr. Coll., 1960; BS in Chem. Engring., Pa. State U., 1965. Project engr. Avon Products, Inc., Suffern, N.Y., 1971-74; sr. project engr. H.J. Heinz Co., Pitts., 1974-77; plant engr. Witco Corp., Petrolia, Pa., 1977-79, mgr. ops., 1979-84; mgr. mfg. Witco Corp., Indpls., 1984-86; area supr Witco Corp., Blue Island, Ill., 1989-91; maintenance mgr. Witco Corp., Chgo., 1991-94; ins. agt., registered rep. Prudential Ins. Co., Lewistown, Pa., 1986-87; ops. mgr. Envirotrol, Inc., Sewickley, Pa., 1987-88; pres. Westfall Cons., Joliet, Ill., 1994—; plant mgr. Inolex Chem. Co., Chgo., 1995-96; site mgr. ETG Environ., Inc., Livingston, Mont., 1996-97; process ops. mgr. KFX Fuel Ptnrs. LP, Gillette, Wyo., 1998-99. With U.S. Army, 1960-63. Mem. AIChE, AAAS. Avocations: camping, hunting, fishing, hiking, photography.

WESTHAVER, LAWRENCE ALBERT, electronics engineer, consultant; b. Washington, Oct. 24, 1936; s. James Waldo and Hattie Virginia (Bush) W.; m. Jo Ann Turner, Jan. 5, 1957; children: Lawrence Albert Jr., Wendy Jo Westhaver Burke, Bonnie Jo. Cert. engring., U. Va., 1966. Electronic design, cons. Westhaver Assocs., Inc., Laurel, Md., 1971—; engring. draftsman Office Rsch. and Devel. Nat. Security Agy., Arlington Hall, Va., 1955-57; engring. technician Office Rsch. and Engring. Nat. Security Agy., Ft. G.G. Meade, Md., 1958-66, electronic engr. Office Rsch. and Engring., 1967-82, sr. engr. Office of Rsch. and Engring., 1982-84; sr. engr. Communications Systems Support Group, Laurel, Md., 1984-93. Patentee method for photographic aperture control, photographic light integrator, switching current regulator, photographic test equipment, electronic tuner for stringed musical instruments, microcomputer-based Ni-Cd battery charger, and color-correcting filter for underwater photography. Avocations: scuba diving, snorkeling, biking, hiking, bird watching. Home: 8609 Portsmouth Dr Laurel MD 20708-1819

WESTHEAD, JOHN MICHAEL, electronics executive; b. Bramhall, Cheshire, Eng., Nov. 13, 1928; s. Percy and Hilda Elizabeth (Wilson) W.; m. Portia Peters, June 14, 1958; children: Justin, Crispin. BA with 1st class honours in Physics, Oxford (Eng.) U., 1950, DPhil in Nuclear Physics, 1953; postgrad., Stanford U., 1963-64. Chartered engr., Eng. Gen. mgr. GEC-Henley, Kent, Eng., 1966-68; mng. dir. Pye Telecom. Ltd., Cambridge, Eng., 1968-74, Tye TMC Ltd., Malnesbury, Eng., 1974-78; mng. dir. Bowthorpe PLC, Crawley, Eng., 1979-99, chief exec., 1992-99; chmn. or bd. dirs. several Bowthorpe subs.; non-exec. dir. So. Water PLC, Sussex, Eng., T.R. Tech PLC, London, Tragen Fin. Co. Ltd., London. Mem. coun. Ctr. for Bus. Strategy, London Bus. Sch., 1983-99. Sloan fellow Stanford U. Bus. Sch., 1963-64. Fellow Instn. Elec. Engrs., Royal Soc. Arts; mem. Brit. Inst. Mgmt. (companion), Stanford U. Alumni Assn., Wine Soc., Chevaliers du Tastevin, Oxford and Cambridge Club, Riverside Club. Avocations: tennis, music, exploring, wine. Home: 6 Wetherby Mews, London SW5 0JG, England

WESTHEIMER, GERALD, optometrist, educator; b. Berlin, Germany, May 13, 1924; naturalized, 1944, came to U.S., 1951; s. Isaak and Ilse (Cohn) W. Optometry diploma, Sydney (Australia) Tech. Coll., 1943, fellowship diploma, 1950; BSc, U. Sydney, 1947; PhD, Ohio State U., 1953; DSc (hon.), U. NSW, Australia, 1988; ScD (hon.), SUNY, 1990. Practice optometry Sydney, 1945-51; research fellow Ohio State U., 1951-53; prof. physiol. optics U. Houston, 1953-54; asst. prof., then assoc. prof. physiol. optics Ohio State U., 1954-60; postdoctoral fellow neurophysiology Marine Biol. Lab., Woods Hole, Mass., 1957; vis. researcher Physiol. Lab., U. Cambridge, Eng., 1958-59; mem. faculty U. Calif. at Berkeley, 1960—, prof. physiol. optics, 1963-68, chmn. group physiol. optics, 1964-67, prof. physiology, 1968-89, prof. neurobiology, 1989—, head div. neurobiology, 1987-92; adj. prof. Rockefeller U., N.Y., 1992—; Sackler lectr. Tel Aviv U. Med. Sch., 1988, D.O. Hebb lectr. McGill U., 1991, Grass Found. lectr. U. Ill., 1991, Wertheimer lectr. U. Frankfort on the Main, 1998; mem. com. vision NRC, 1957-72; mem. visual scis. study sect. NIH, 1966-70, chmn. visual scis. B study sect., 1977-79; mem. vision, research and tng. com. Nat. Eye Inst., NIH, 1970-74, chmn. bd. sci. counselors, 1981-83; mem. exec. council com. vision NAS-NRC, 1969-72; mem. communicative scis. cluster Pres.'s Biomed. Rsch. Panel, 1975. Author rsch. papers; editor: Vision Rsch., 1972-79; editl. bd. Investigative Ophthalmology, 1973-77, Exptl. Brain Rsch., 1973-89, Optics Letters, 1977-78, Spatial Vision, 1985—, Ophthalmic and Physiological Optics, 1985—, Vision Rsch., 1985-92, Jour. of Physiology, 1987-94. Recipient Von Sallman prize Columbia U., 1986; Prentice medal Am. Acad. Optometry, 1986, Bicentennial medal Australian Optometric Assn., 1988. Fellow AAAS, Royal Soc. London (Ferrier lectr. 1992, editl. bd. procs. 1990-96, 2000—), Am. Acad. Arts and Scis., Optical Soc. Am. (Tillyer medal 1978, assoc. editor jour. 1980-83), Am. Acad. Optometry; mem. Royal Soc. New So. Wales, Soc. Neurosci., Assn. Rsch. in Vision and Ophthalmology (Proctor medal 1979), Internat. Brain Rsch. Orgn., Physiol. Soc. Gt. Britain, Sigma Xi. Home: 582 Santa Barbara Rd Berkeley CA 94707-1746

WEST-HILL, GWENDOLYN, poet, educator; b. Indpls., July 30, 1951; d. Wendell Waldon West and Joyce Moody Young; m. David Lee Spencer, March 12, 1972 (div. Mar. 1982); children: Hasan Abdul Spencer, Laila Marscia Spencer; m. David Lee Hill, July 25, 1985 (dec. July 1995). BA in Elem. Edn., Ind. U., 1973; Degree in Bus. Adminstrn., Butler U., 1983; degree in Commercial Art, Chas Wharton Sch. Art, 1984. Prin., owner T-shirt Haven, Atlanta, 1990—. Author: Poems for the Family, 1990, Prism of Thoughts, 1998, Giving It Back To You, 2000; contbr. poems to newspapers, mags., and anthologies. Missionary House of Refuge Prayer, Coll. Park, Ga., 1993—, Metro World Outreach Ctr., Stonemountain, Ga., 1998.; evangelist Metro World Outreach Ctr., The Potter's House, T.D. Jakes Ministries, Dallas, 1999. Recipient Eubie Blake award Ind. Black Expo, Indpls., 1985. Fellow Delta Sigma Theta (Gamma Nu chpt.). Pentecostal. Avocations: singing, drawing, writing, travel, teaching. Home: 4251 Parkview Ct Stone Mountain GA 30083-1294 Office: House of Refuge Prayer Mission 2523 Roosevelt Hwy College Park GA 30337-6243

WESTHOFF, VICTOR, vegetation ecologist; b. Sitoebondo, Java, Netherlands East Indies, Nov. 12, 1916; s. Joan Frederik and Petronella Maria (Schols) W.; m. Jeanette de Joncheere, July 22, 1942; children: Maja, Hugo Boudewyn, Iris Angelica, Edwin Arthur, Erna Rosalinde. MSc, U. Utrecht, The Netherlands, 1942, PhD, 1947. Asst. in botany U. Utrecht, 1938-43; head dept. Dutch Touring Club, The Hague, The Netherlands, 1943-47; sci. officer U. Wageningen, The Netherlands, 1947-56; sci. head officer State Inst. Nature Conservation Rsch., 1957-68; part-time prof. botany U. Nymegen, The Netherlands, 1967-68, prof. botany, 1968-81; sci. advisor Soc. for Promotion of Nature Reserves, The Netherlands, 1947-68; mem. State Coun. for Nature Conservation 1951-81. Author: A Detailed Vegetation Mapping of the Woodland Near Middachten, 1957, Flora and Vegetation of the National Park Veluwezoom, 1958; co-author: (with J. Meltzer) Introduction to Plant Sociology, 1944, (with J.W. Dujk & H. Passchier) Survey of the Plant Communities of the Netherlands, 1946, (with A.J. den Held) Plant Communities in the Netherlands, 1975, (with P.A. Bakker, C.G. van Leeuwen & E.E. van der Voo) Wild Plants, Flora and Vegetation of Our Natural Areas, Vol. 1, 1970, Vol. 2, 1971, Vol. 3, 1973, (with M.F. van Oosten) Flora and Vegetation of the Westfrisian Islands, 1991; editor: Landscape, Flora and Vegetation of the Botshol Near Abcoude, 1949, The Scientific Base of Nature Conservation, 1978; contbr. articles to profl. jours. Recipient Chevalier, Order of the Dutch Lion, 1978, Ridder, Order of Golden Ark, 1983, Silver medal City of The Hague, 1981. Fellow Royal Netherlands Acad. Arts and Scis. (life); mem. Brit. Ecol. Soc. (hon.), Internat. Assn. for Vegetation Sci. (hon.). Buddhist. Avocations: travel, gardening, music, writing poetry and essays. Home: PO Box 64, 6560 AB Groesbeek The Netherlands

WESTIN, DAVID LAWRENCE, broadcasting executive, lawyer; b. Flint, Mich., July 29, 1952; s. Lawrence Rae and Mary Louise (Holman) W.; m. Victoria Peters; children: Victoria, Elizabeth, Matthew. BA, U. Mich., 1974, JD, 1977. Bar: D.C. 1979. Law clk. U.S. Ct. Appeals (2d cir.), N.Y.C., 1977-78, U.S. Supreme Ct., Washington, 1979; assoc. Wilmer, Cutler & Pickering, Washington, 1979-84, ptnr., 1985-91; sr. v.p., gen. counsel Capital Cities/ABC, Inc., N.Y.C., 1991-93; pres. of prodn. ABC TV Network, N.Y.C., 1993-94, pres., 1994-97, pres. of news, 1997—; lectr. Harvard U. Law Sch., Cambridge, Mass., 1986; adj. prof. Georgetown U. Law Ctr., Washington, 1989-91. Bd. dirs. Lincoln Ctr. Film. Soc., 1994—, Am. Arbitration Assn., 1991—. Democrat. Presbyterian. Club: Chevy Chase (Md.). Office: ABC TV Network 47 W 66th St Fl 5 New York NY 10023-6201

WESTLAKE, MARTIN JEROME, government executive; b. Amersham, Eng., July 20, 1957; s. Bernard Russell and Teresa (Harrison) W.; m. Godelieve Marie Yolande Vandamme, May 10, 1986; children: Emily, Oliver. BA with honors, U. Coll. Oxford, Eng., 1979; Ma in internat. Studies, Johns Hopkins U., Bologna, Italy, 1981; PhD Polit. Sci., European Univ. Inst., Florence, 1992. Exec. coord. European Policy Unit, EUI, Florence, 1984-85; clk. Social Affairs and Migration, Refugees, Demography com. Parliamentary Assembly, Coun. Europe, Strasbourg, 1985-86; adminstr Directorate Gen. for Internal Mkt. Secretariat Gen., EC Coun. of Ministers, Brussels, 1986-87; adminstr., then prin. adminstr. Sec. Gen., European Commn., Brussels, 1987-95; head unit Dir. Gen. Info., Comm., Culture, Media European Commn., Brussels, 1995-99, head unit Dir. Gen. for Edn. and Culture, 1999—; assoc. mem. Ctr. for Legis. Studies, U. Hull, 1990—; vis. acad. Nuffield Coll., Oxford, 1994; prof. summer sch. on structure, decision-making processes of govts. in Europe, European Univ. Inst., Florence, 1996; lectr. W.G. Hart Legal Workshop on Lawmaking in European Union, 1996; prof. Coll. of Europe, Brugge, 1999—. Author: Britain's Emerging Euro-Elite? The British in the Directly-Elected European Parliament, 1979-92, 1994, The European Commission and the European Parliament: Partners and Rivals in the European Policy-Making Process, 1994, A Modern Guide to the European Parliament, 1994, British Politics and European Elections (with David Butler), 1994, The Council of the European Union, 1995, The European Union Beyond Amsterdam, 1998. Salzburg Seminar fellow, 1993. Avocations: literature, squash. Office: European Commn, DG EAC 120 Rue de Treves, 1040 Brussels Belgium

WESTLUND, HANS GUSTAV, researcher; b. Hallesjo, Jamtland, Sweden, June 22, 1957; s. Gustav Elser and Maria Birgitta (Hansson) W.; m. Loulou Louise Catharina Hasselquist, June 21, 1985; 1 child, Ellen. BA, Umea (Sweden) U., 1986, PhD, 1992. Ombudsman Jamtland Pupil Orgn., Ostersund, 1975-76; carpenter boss various, Jamtland, 1977-83; lectr. Umea U., 1987-92, Mid-Sweden U., Ostersund, 1992-93; comm. ofcl. Jamtland County Adminstrn., Ostersund, 1993-94; rsch. fellow Royal Inst. Tech., Stockholm, 1994-95; rsch. condr. Swedish Inst. for Regional Rsch., Ostersund, 1993—; evaluator Norwegian Inst. for Urban and Regional Rsch., Oslo, 1997-98. Contbr. articles to profl. jours. Chmn. Arbetarnas Bildningsförbund, Adult Ednl. Assn., Bracke, 1989—. Mem. European Regional Sci. Assn., Western Regional Sci. Assn., Swedish Hist. Assn. Avocations: fishing, moose hunting. E-mail: hans@westlund.pp.se and hans@sir.se. Fax: 46 696 40200. Home: Vallsjon 4552, SE-84064 Kalarne Sweden Office: SIR, Kyrkgatan 43b, SE-83134 Ostersund Sweden

WESTMACOTT, RICHARD KELSO, venture capitalist; b. Malta, Feb. 20, 1934; s. John Rowe and Ruth (Pharazyn) W.; m. Karen Husbands, June 30, 1965; children: Camilla Anne, John Richard. Student, Eton Coll., 1947-52. Chmn. Hoare Govt., London, 1975-90; dir. Martin Currie Moorgate Investment Trust, London, 1998—, Advanced Fluid Systems, London, 1993—, Prudential-Bache Internat. Bank Ltd. Lt. Royal Navy, 1952-55, U.K. Avocations: golf, sailing. Office: HW Assocs, 25 Thurloe St, London SW7 2LQ, England

WESTMAN, JAN OLOV, medical researcher and educator; b. Umeå, Sweden, Sept. 3, 1938; s. Rickard and Anna Elisabet (Öhman) W.; m. Siv Anne Marie Johansson, Sept. 17, 1966; children: Viktor, Mårten. MBBS, Uppsala (Sweden) U., 1964, MD, PhD, 1968. Med. diplomate. 1st amanuensis, dept. human anatomy Uppsala U., 1960-64, 1st asst., 1964-67, rsch. asst., 1967-69, asst. prof. dept. human anatomy, 1969-73, sr. lectr., 1973-85, 95-99, prof., 1985-95, 2000—, head dept. human anatomy, chmn. bd., 1983-89, 95-96. Editor: Information Processing in the Somatosensory System, 1991; Progress in Brain Research Series Brain Functions in Hot Environment, 1996. Avocations: badminton, Ju-jitsu, floor ball, tennis. Home: Ripv 7, S-756 53 Uppsala Sweden Office: Uppsala U, Dept Human Anatomy, Box 571, S-751 23 Uppsala Sweden

WESTMEYER, HANS, psychology educator; b. Vlotho, Germany, July 26, 1946; s. Bernhard and Erna (Priemer) W.; m. Hannelore Weber, Dec. 28, 1998; 1 child, Dirk. Diploma in psychology, U. Muenster, 1970; PhD, U. Munster, 1971; habilitation, Free U. of Berlin, 1975. Asst. prof. Free U. of Berlin, 1972-76, prof., 1976—, dean faculty ednl. studies, 1982-83, 1st v.p., 1983-85, mng. dir. Inst. Psychology. Author: Logic of Assessment, 1972, Critique of Psychological Unreason, 1973; co-author: Criteria of Psychological Research, 1975, Observation Procedures in Behavioral Assessment, 1987; editor: Psychological Theories from a Structuralist Point of View, 1989, The Structuralist Program in Psychology, 1992, Perspectives of Psychological Assessment, 1994; co-editor: Philosophy of Science on the Wrong Track?, 1973, Behavior Therapy, 1977, Psychological Methods and Social Systems, 1998; mng. editor Diagnostica, 1979-94; assoc. editor European Jour. Psychol. Assessment, 1992-98, Psychol. Rsch., 1997-2000; cons. editor Diagnostica, 1995—, Psychol. Assessment, 1997—, Methods of Psychol. Rsch., 1996—, European Jour. Psychol. Assessment, 1999—. Mem. APA (affiliate), European Assn. Psychol. Assessment (v.p. 1992-96), Internat. Soc. Theoretical Psychology, German Soc. Psychology, Internat. Assn. Applied Psychology, Philosophy of Sci. Assn., Soc. for Analytical Philosophy. Avocations: music, art. E-mail: hawest@zedat.fu-berlin.de. Office: Free U Berlin Dept Psychol, Habelschwerdter Allee 45, D-14195 Berlin Germany

WESTON, BRIAN GEORGE, defense industry executive; b. Ringwood, Victoria, Australia, May 24, 1945; s. William George and Joan Beryl (Mackay) W.; m. Renate Lotte Romaniuk, Dec. 16, 1969; children: Karla, Catherine. BSc, U. Melbourne, Australia, 1966; MBA, Auburn U., 1984. Served to air vice-marshal Australian Air Force, 1963-97; comdr. RAAF tactical fightr group Australian Air Force, Newcastle, Australia, 1990-93; with Royal Coll. Def. Studies Australian Air Force, London, 1994; asst. chief ops. Australian Def. Force, Canberra, 1995-97; cons. to def. industry Canberra, 1997-98; exec. dir. def. industries Australian Bus., Canberra, 1998—.

WESTON, DAWN THOMPSON, artist, researcher; b. Joliet, Ill., Apr. 15, 1919; d. Cyril C. and Vivian Grace Thompson; student (scholar) Penn Hall Jr. Coll., Chambersburg, Pa., 1937-38; BS, Northwestern U., 1942, postgrad. in reading and speech pathology, 1960-61, MA in Ednl. Adminstrn., 1970; postgrad. U. Ill., 1964; student Art Inst. Chgo., 1954, Pestalozzi-Froebel, Chgo., 1955, Phila. Inst. for Achievement Human Potential, 1963; m. Arthur Walter Weston, Sept. 10, 1940; children: Roger Lance, Randall Kent, Cynthia Brooke. Therapist, USN Hosp., Gt. Lakes, Ill., 1940-45; tchr. Holy Child and Waukegan (Ill.) High Schs., 1946-54, Lake Forest High Sch., 1966-69; elem. and jr. high art dir. Lake Bluff (Ill.) Schs., 1954-58; pioneer ednl. dir. Grove Sch. for Brain-Injured, Lake Forest, Ill., 1958-66, now life mem., treas. corp., chmn. bd., 1982-87. One woman shows include Evanston Woman's Club, Northwestern U., Deerpath Gallery, Lake Forest; The Hein Co., Waukegan; numerous group shows, 1939-76; represented in permanent collections: ARC, Victory Meml. Hosp., Waukegan, Sierra Assos., Chgo., numerous pvt. collections U.S., Can., Japan, Africa; works include: Poisonous Plants of Midwest set of etchings for Country Gentleman mag., 1956, Clouds mural, 1981; ind. researcher, lectr. on shifting visual imagery due to trauma, 1982-99; mem. 1st found. bd. for srs. in Lake Forest, Ill., 1999; chair Grove Sch. Inc., 1996-97; chmn. July 4th parade 100th Anniversary Child-Serve Greater Chgo., 1994. Mem. Presdl. Gold Chain, Trinity Coll., 1979; del. ann. conf. Meth. Ch., 1982-90; lay leader Grace United Methodist Ch., Lake Bluff, Ill., 1990-93. Named Citizen of Yr., Grove Sch., 1978, room at sch. named in her honor, 1982; cert. tchr./adminstr., Ill. Mem. Art Inst. Chgo., Penn Hall Alumni Assn. (Chgo. pres. 1938-40), Deerpath Art League (mem. bd. dirs.), Pi Lambda Theta. Research on uneven growth, 1969—. Home and Office: 349 Hilldale Pl Lake Forest IL 60045-3031

WESTON, FRANCINE EVANS, secondary education educator; b. Mt. Vernon, N.Y., Oct. 8, 1946; d. John Joseph and Frances (Fantino) Pisaniello. BA, Hunter Coll., 1968; MA, Lehman Coll., 1973; cert., Am. Acad. Dramatic Arts, N.Y.C., 1976; PhD, NYU, 1991. Cert. elem., secondary tchr., N.Y. Tchr. Yonkers (N.Y.) Bd. Edn., 1968—; aquatic dir. Woodlane Day Camp, Irvington-on-Hudson, N.Y., 1967-70, Yonkers Jewish Community Ctr., 1971-75; creative drama tchr. John Burroughs Jr. H.S., Yonkers, 1971-77; stage lighting designer Iona Summer Theatre Festival, New Rochelle, N.Y., 1980-81, Yonkers Male Glee Club, 1981-89, Roosevelt H.S., 1980-97; freelance, 1998—; rsch. specialist Scholarship Locating Svc., 1992-94, Yonkers Civil Def. Police Aux., 1994—; master electrician NYU Summer Mus. Theatre, 1979-80. Actress in numerous comty. theater plays including A Touch of the Poet, 1979; dir. stage prodns. including I Remember Mama, 1973, The Man Who Came to Dinner, 1975; author: A Descriptive Comparison of Computerized Stage Lighting Memory Systems With Non-Computerized Systems, 1991, (short stories) A Hat for Louise, 1984, Old Memories: Beautiful and Otherwise, 1984; lit. editor: (story and poetry collection) Beautifully Old, 1984; editor: Command Post Dispatch quar., 1997—. Steering com. chairperson Roosevelt H.S.-Middle States Assn. of Schs. and Colls. Self-Evaluation, 1985-88; mem. Yonkers Civil Def. Police Aux., 1994—, adminstrv. asst. to commanding officer, 1996—. Named Tchr. of Excellence, N.Y. State English Coun., 1990; recipient Monetary award for Teaching Excellence, Carter-Wallace Products, 1992, Educator of Excellence award N.Y. State English Coun., 1995; named to Arrid Tchrs. Honor Roll, 1992. Mem. U.S. Inst. for Theatre Tech., Nat. Coun. Tchrs. English, N.Y. State English Coun., N.Y. State United Tchrs. Assn., Westchester Coun. English Educators, Yonkers Fedn. Tchrs., Self Help for Hard of Hearing People, Port Chester Obedience Tng. Club, Inc., Therapy Dogs Internat., Am. Belgian Tervuren Club, Kappa Delta Pi. Republican. Roman Catholic. Avocations: swimming, animal related activities, anything theatrical. Office: Roosevelt High Sch Tuckahoe Rd Yonkers NY 10710

WESTON, JOHN, aerospace executive; b. Kendal, Aug. 16, 1951; married; two children. From undergrad. apprentice to engr. dynamics svcs. dept. Brit. Aircraft Corp., 1970-74; sales engr. Tornado and Jaguar projects Brit. Aircraft Corp., Weybridge, 1974-75; with Panavia Aircraft GmbH Brit. Aircraft Corp., Munich, 1975-78, area sales mgr., 1978-79, regional mktg. mgr., 1979-82; Middle Ea. sales mgr. Brit. Aerospace, Warton, 1985; project mgr. Al-Yamamah programme Brit. Aerospace, 1985-86, exec. dir. Saudi Arabian ops., 1986-87, dir. in charge Saudi Arabian ops., 1987, mem. divisional mgmt. com. Mil. Aircraft Divsn., 1986, bd. mem. Mil. Aircraft Co., 1989, mng. dir., 1990, chmn., mng. dir. Brit. Aerospace Def. Ltd.; CEO Brit. Aerospace plc (now called BAE Sys.), 1998, also bd. dirs.; chmn. Brit. Aerospace SEMA, Eurofighter GmbH, Def. Evaluation and Rsch. Agy., Nat. Mfg. Coun. of CBI. Avocations: skiing, photography, mountain walking. Office: Warwick House, PO Box 87, Famborough GU14 6YU, England*

WESTON, SIR (PHILIP) JOHN, communications executive, retired diplomat; b. Apr. 13, 1938; s. Philip George and Edith Alice Bray (Ansell) W.; m. Margaret Sally Ehlers, 1967; 3 children. Grad. with 1st class honors, Worcester Coll., Oxford (Eng.) U.; student Chinese lang., Hong Kong, 1964-66, Peking, China, 1967-68. Joined diplomatic svc. Govt. of Gt. Britain, 1962, served Fgn. Office, 1962-63, 69-71, with Treasure Ctr. for Adminstrv. Studies, 1964; permanent rep. to EEC Govt. of Gt. Britain, Brussels, 1972-74; asst. pvt. sec. to sec. state fgn. affairs and commonwealth affairs Govt. of Gt. Britain, 1974-76, counsellor, head EEC presidency secretariat Fgn. and Commonwealth Office, 1976-77; counsellor Brit. Embassy Govt. of Gt. Britain, Washington, 1978-81; head def. dept. Fgn. and Commonwealth Office Govt. of Gt. Britain, 1981-84, asst. under-sec. state Fgn. and Commonwealth Office, 1984-85; min. Brit. Embassy Govt. of Gt. Britain, Paris, 1985-88; dep. sec. to cabinet Cabinet Office Govt. of Gt. Britain, 1988-89, dep. under-sec. state def. Fgn. and Commonwealth Office, 1989-90, polit. dir. Fgn. and Commonwealth Office, 1990-92; amb., permanent rep. to NATO, also accredited to Western European Union Govt. of Gt. Britain, Brussels, 1992-95; U.K. amb. to UN, U.K. permanent rep. UN Security Coun., N.Y.C., 1995-98; non-exec. dir. Brit. Telecom, Rolls Royce plc, 1998—; vis. fellow Old Souls Coll., Oxford (Eng.) U., 1977-78; hon. pres. U.K. Cmty. Found. Network, 1998—. Served Royal Marines, 1956-58. Decorated knight comdr. St. Michael and St. George (Eng.); Order of Merit with star (Fed. Republic Germany). Address: 13 Denbigh Gardens, Richmond, Surrey TW10 6EN, England

WESTON, PETER HENRY, plant systematist, research scientist, curator; b. Lower Hutt, New Zealand, Oct. 22, 1956; came to Australia, 1957; s. Claude Warwick and Rosaline Winnifred (Moller) W.; m. Bridget Susan O'Donoghue, Nov. 26, 1988; children: Timothy, Caitlin, Nicholas. BS with honors, U. Sydney, Australia, 1979, PhD, 1985. Postgrad. rschr./tutor U. Sydney, 1979-82; sci. officer Royal Botanic Gardens, Sydney, 1982-89, rsch. scientist, 1989—. Author: (chpt.) Advances in Legume Systematics 3, 1987, (chpt.) Ontogeny and Systematics, 1988; mem. editl. bd. Soc. Systematic Biologists, 1992-95; contbr. articles to profl. jours. Recipient Rsch. grant Australian Rsch. Coun., 1991-92, Rsch. grant Wet Tropics Mgmt. Authority, 1993. Fellow Willi Hennig Soc. (coun. mem. 1999—); mem. Soc. Systematic Biologists , Australian Systematic Botany Soc. (coun. mem. 1996-99), Australian Systematic Botany (edt. adv. com. 1999—). Achievements include research in cladistic analysis of Fabaceae; extension of G.J. Nelson's direct method of character analysis; cladistic analysis, cladistic biogeography of Proteaceae. Office: Royal Botanic Gardens, Royal Botanic Gardens, Mrs Macquaries Rd, Sydney 2000, Australia

WESTON, RICHARD, adult education educator, researcher; b. Malmoe, Sweden; s. David Ernest and Agneta (Orndahl) W. Engring. degree, Pauliskolan, Malmoe, 1983; MS, Lund (Sweden) Inst. Tech., 1991, engring. lic., 1996. Tchr. Arbets-Marnadsutbildning, Eslov, Sweden, 1991; engr. Kronosept, Eslov, Sweden, 1991-92; tchr. Dept. Environ. and Energy Sys.

Studies, Lund, 1992-94, Dept. Materials and Products Engring., Lund, 1994—; cons. Numat, Lund. Contbr. articles to sci. jours. Grantee TFR, Sweden, 1996. Avocations: playing electric guitar, collecting guitar equipment. E-mail:richard.weston@mtov.lth.se. Office: Dept Materials & Product En, Ole Romers v 1, 221 00 Lund Sweden

WESTON, W. GALEN, SR., diversified holdings executive; b. Eng., Oct. 29, 1940; s. W. Garfield Weston and Reta L. Howard; m. Hilary Frayne, 1966; 2 children. BA, U. Western Ont., LLD (hon.). Chmn. bd. Wittington Investments, Ltd., George Weston Ltd., Toronto, Ont., Can., Holt, Renfrew & Co. Ltd., Loblaw Cos. Ltd., Weston Foods Ltd., Weston Resources Ltd.; vice chmn. bd. dirs. Fortnum and Mason PLC (U.K.); bd. dirs. Assoc. Brit. Foods PLC (U.K.), Can. Imperial Bank Commerce, Brown Thomas Group Ltd. (Ireland). Chmn. United World Colls.; bd. dirs. Lester B. Pearson Coll. Pacific; life mem. Royal Ont. Mus., Art Gallery Ont.; hon. trustee The Upper Can. Coll. Found.; mem. internat. adv. bd. Columbia U. Officer Order of Can. Mem. Badminton and Racquet Club, York Club, Toronto Club, Guards Polo Club, Lyford Cay Club, Windsor Club (Fla.), The Brook Club (N.Y.), White's Club (U.K.), Sunningdale Golf. (U.K.), Toronto Lawn Tennis, Windsor Club (Fla.). Office: George Weston Limited, 22 St Clair Ave E Ste 1900, Toronto, ON Canada M4T 2S7*

WESTON SMITH, JOHN HARRY, finance director; b. Gillingham, Kent, Eng., Feb. 3, 1932. Student, Fettes Coll., Edinburgh, Scotland, 1945-50; BA in Law, Cambridge U., 1954, MA in Law, 1958. Various positions Abbey Nat. plc, London, 1957-69, N. M. Rothschild & Sons Ltd., London, 1969-71; co. sec. The Brit. Land Co. PLC, London, 1971-73, co. sec., fin. dir., 1973-95, fin. dir., 1995—. Fellow Inst. Chartered Secs. and Adminstrs.; mem. Chartered Ins. Inst. (assoc.), Chartered Inst. Bankers (assoc.). Office: Brit Land Co PLC, 10 Cornwall Ter Regents Pk, London NW1 4QP, England

WESTPHAL, RUTH LILLY, educational media company; b. Glendale, Calif., July 27, 1931; d. Glen R. Lilly and Margaret Elizabeth John; m. H. Frederick Westphal, June 25, 1953. BA in Edn., UCLA, 1953; MA in Edn. Sys. Tech., Chapman Coll., 1968. Life tchg. credential, Calif. Pub. sch. tchr. L.A., Glendale,, Calif., East Whittier, 1953-65; edn. sys. analyst Litton Industries, Anaheim, Calif., 1965-67; dir. of devel. Trainex Corp., Garden Grove, Calif., 1967-69; CEO Concept Media Corp., Irvine, Calif., 1969—; pub. Westphal Pub., Irvine, 1980—. Author: (book) Plein Air Painters of California: The Southland, 1982 (Western Books award 1982), P.A.P.C.: The North, 1986; author, prodr. numerous ednl. films. Co-founder Friends of LaHabra (Calif.) Libr., 1960-65; mem. exec. com. Hist. Collections Coun., Orange County Mus. Art, 1996-99. Named one of Top 100 Prodrs., AV Video Multimedia Prodr. Mag., 1999. Republican/Libertarian. Avocations: art history, economics, boating. E-mail: info@conceptmedia.com. Office: Concept Media Corp 2493 DuBridge Ave Irvine CA 92606

WESTRÖM, LARS VILHELM, obstetrician, gynecologist, educator, researcher; b. Kristinehamn, Varmland, Sweden, Feb. 12, 1930; s. Fredrik and Edith Dagmar (Westerberg) W.; m. Ullacarin Jarlbrink, July 3, 1954; children: Anders, Johan. MD, U. Lund, Sweden, 1960, DMS, 1976. Cert. ob-gyn. specialist. Jr. rschr. ob-gyn. U. Lund, 1960-62; resident in surgery County Hosp., Simrishamn, Sweden, 1962-65; resident in ob-gyn. U. Hosp., Lund, 1965-70, head dept. ob-gyn., 1971-77, chief physician, 1978-96, ret., 1996; assoc. prof. U. Lund, 1978-96, ret., 1996. Author: Diagnosis, Aethiology and Prognosis of Acute Salpingitis, 1976; author and editor: Obstetrik och Gynekologi, 1977, Pelvic Inflammatory Disease, 1995; contbr. 200 articles to profl. jours. Temporary adviser WHO, Geneva, 1980, 82, 84, 86; expert NIH, Behtesda, Md., CDC, Atlanta. Recipient Glaxo award Internat. Union Against the Venereal Diseases and the Treponematoses, Bombay, 1985, Thomas Parran award Am. Venereal Disease Assn., Helsinki, 1993. Mem. Swedish Soc. Physicians, Swedish Gyn. Soc., Scandinavian Soc. Genitourin Medicine, Nordic Assn. Ob-Gyn. E-mail: lars.wes@swipnet.se. Home: N Promenaden 3 G, S 222 40 Lund Sweden

WESTROPE, MARTHA RANDOLPH, psychologist, consultant; b. Gaffney, S.C., May 19, 1922; d. Gordon Robert and Hannah (Brown) W.; 1 adopted child, Ashley Randolph. BS, Winthrop Coll., 1942; MA, U. N.C., 1944; PhD, State U. of Iowa, Iowa City, 1952. Lic. psychologist, S.C. Pvt. practice Greenville, S.C., 1960—, part-time pvt. practice, 1987-96; part-time staff mem. Spartanburg (S.C.) Mental Health Clinic, 1971-73, Greenville Mental Health Ctr., 1974-85, Patrick B. Harris Psychiat. Hosp., Anderson, S.C., 1985-87; med. cons. S.C. Vocat. Rehab. Dept., Greenville, 1987-91, part-time med. cons., 1993-99; cons. S.C. Parole Bd. for Psychol. Evaluation, S.C. Dept. Corrections, 1983-87. Mem. Am. Psychol. Assn., Southeastern Psychol. Assn., S.C. Psychol. Assn., Am. Assn. for Advancement of Psychology, Greenville County Mental Health Assn., Am. Group Psychotherapy Assn., Coun. for the Nat. Register of Health Svc. Providers in Psychology. Democrat. Presbyterian. Avocations: wildlife preservation, fine arts, collecting dolls, stamps. Home: 11 Darien Way Greenville SC 29615-3236

WESTRUM, HELEN JOSEPHINE, writer, retired educator; b. Mahnomen, Minn., Nov. 6, 1928; d. Roy Arthur and Bertha Florence (Smith) Dirl; m. Wesley Theodore Westrum. BS, Mont. State U., 1951, MS, 1966; EdD, Oreg. State U., 1974. Tchr. home econ. Libby (Mont.) H.S., 1950-52, Whitefish (Mont.) H.S., 1952-54; home economist Grant County Pub. Utility Dist., Wash., 1954-62, Pacific Power and Light Co., Roseberg, Oreg., 1964-65; mem. faculty Ea. Wash. U., Cheney, 1966-88, program dir. home econ., 1985-88, prof. emeritus, 1988—; vis. lectr. U. Mont., Missoula, 1963-64; adj. faculty Coll. Fin. Planning, Denver, 1983. Co-author: Competencies for Home Economics, 1978. Recipient Outstanding Tchr. award Wash. Vocat. Assn., 1986. Mem. PEO (chaplain 1993-94), Diaconia (v.p. 1991—), Eastern Star. Avocations: water color and oil painting, historical research. E-mail: piper@omnicast.

WESTVELD, BELINDA JOYCE, reliability and quality engineer, educator; b. Grand Rapids, Mich., Oct. 1, 1952; d. William Carl Maynard Sr. and Joyce Oliver Miller; m. Frank E. Westveld, July 30, 1983; children: Jered John, Gabrielle Lyn. Student, Grand Valley State Coll., Allendale, Mich., 1971-72, Grand Rapids C.C., 1983-90. Quality assurance insp. Holland (Mich.) Mold Engring., 1978-80; receiving insp. Grand Rapids Controls, Rockford, Mich., 1980-82, lead insp., 1982-86, asst. quality assurance dir., 1986-88, quality asurance dir., 1988-90; reliability/quality engr. Grand Rapids Controls, Rockford, 1990—; mgmt. rep. ISO9001/QS9000, ISO14001, 1999, dir. reliability control, 1999—; instr. Grand Rapids Controls, 1988—; pub. speaker. Mem. ASTM, Am. Soc. Quality Control (cert. quality tech., quality engr., quality auditor). Republican. Avocations: boating, photography, gardening, crafts, collectibles. Office: Grand Rapids Controls 825 Northland Dr Rockford MI 49341

WESTWOOD, LEE, professional golfer; b. Worksop, England, Apr. 24, 1973. Profl. golfer, 1993—. Winner Peter McEvoy Trophy, Brit. Youth's Championship; winner Volvo Scandinavian Master, 1996, Visa Taiheijo Masters, 1996; Volvo Masters, 1997; Australian Open, 1997; Loch Lomond Invitational, 1998; European TPC, 1998; English Open, 1998; Freeport-McDermott Classic, 1998, Deutsche Bank-SAP Open TPC of Europe, 2000. Avocations: films, snooker, cars. Office: care PGA 100 Avenue Of Champions Palm Bch Gdns FL 33418-3653*

WESTWOOD, MELVIN NEIL, horticulturist, pomologist; b. Hiawatha, Utah, Mar. 25, 1923; s. Neil and Ida (Blake) W.; m. Wanda Mae Shields, Oct. 12, 1946; children: Rose Dawn, Nancy Gwen, Robert Melvin, Kathryn Mae. Student, U. Utah, 1948-50; BS in Pomology, Utah State U., 1952; PhD in Pomology, Wash. State U., 1956. Field botanist Utah State U., Logan, 1951-52, supt. Howell Field Sta., 1952-53; rsch. asst. State Coll. Wash., 1953-55; rsch. horticulturist Agrl. Rsch. Svc. USDA, Wenatchee, Wash., 1955-60; assoc. prof. Oreg. State U., Corvallis, 1960-67, prof., 1967-80, prof. emeritus, 1986—; rsch. dir. Nat. Clonal Germplasm Repository, Corvallis, 1980-83, nat. tech. advisor, 1984-86. Author: Deciduous Fruit and Nut Production, 1976, Temperate-Zone Pomology: Physiology and Culture, 1978, 3d edit., 1993, Contract Military Air Transport: From the Ground Up, 1995, Pear Varieties and Species, 1996; co-author: Cherry Nutrition, 1966, Pear Rootstocks, 1987, Management and Utilization of Plant Germplasm, 1988, Maintenance and Storage: Clonal Germplasm, 1989, Genetic Resources of Malus, 1991; contbr. articles to profl. jours. With U.S. Air Transport Command, 1943-45, USAAF, 1946-47. Grantee NSF, 1966; recipient Hartman Cup award Oreg. Hort. Soc., 1989, Earl Price Excellence in Rsch. award Oreg. State U., 1983. Fellow Am. Soc. Hort. Sci. (bd. dirs. 1974-75, chmn. com. environ. quality 1971, adv. coun. 1974-79, mem. pomology sect. 1967-74, publs. com. 1971-74, pres. Western region 1974, Joseph Harvey Gourley award for Pomology 1958, 77, Stark award for Pomology 1969, 77, Outstanding Rschr. award 1986); mem. AAAS, Am. Soc. Plant Physiologists, Am. Pomological Soc. (mem. adv. bd. 1970-75, mem. exec. bd. 1980-84, Paul Howe Shepard award 1968, 82, Wilder medal 1980), UN Assn. USA, Ams. United for Separation of Ch. and State, Amnesty Internat., Phi Kappa Phi, Gamma Sigma Delta. Baptist. Achievements include patent for Autumn Blaze ornamental pear; research on Pyrus (pear), Malus (apple) and Prunus (plum, cherry, peach) and on the physiology of rootstock genera. Office: Oreg State U Dept Horticulture Corvallis OR 97331

WETENHALL, JOHN, museum director; b. June 1, 1957; s. Jack Wetenhall and Jane (Rinaud) Keating. AB cum laude, Dartmouth Coll., 1979; MA, Williams Coll., Williamstown, Mass., 1982, Stanford U., 1985; PhD, Stanford U., 1988; MBA, Vanderbilt U., 1999. Fellow Smithsonian Instn., Washington, 1986-87, 88-89; lectr. Santa Clara (Calif.) U., 1985, U. Minn., Mpls., 1988; curator painting and sculpture Birmingham (Ala.) Mus. Art, 1989-95; dir. Checkwood Mus. Art, Nashville, 1995—; founder Thomas Art Projects, Birmingham, 1992-95, Carell Woodland Sculpture Trail, Nashville, 1996-99; cons. Vietnam Women's Meml. Project, Washington, 1988-89, U. So. Calif. Pub. Art Program, 1991. Author: (with Karal Ann Marling) Iwo Jima: Monuments, Memories and the American Hero, 1991, (with David Cass) (catalogue) Italian Paintings, 1850-1910, 1982; editor: (catalogue) Splendors of the American West, 1990; contbr. articles to profl. jours.; appearance in Am. Masters: Alexander Calder, PBS, 1998. Chair livelier city ctr. com. Ops. New Birmingham, 1994-95, chair cultural dist. forum, 1992-94, nat. register peers, design excellence program Gen. Svcs. Adminstrn., 1998; chair Nashville Rotary Adopt-A-House Program. Recipient Award of Excellence Tenn. Assn. Mus., 1996, Gold and Silver medals for ednl. programming Southeastern Mus. Conf., 1999; B. Gerald Cantor fellow, 1986, Nat. Endowment for the Arts grantee, 1991, Lyndon Baines Johnson Found. Moody Travel grantee, 1986, John F. Kennedy Libr. Found. grantee, 1986. Mem. Am. Tchrs. Assn. of the Martial Arts (sensei), Rotary (Paul Harris fellow), Beta Gamma Sigma. Avocations: white water kayaking, flying, Aiki Ju Jitsu (blackbelt). Office: Cheekwood Mus of Art 1200 Forrest Park Dr Nashville TN 37205-4242

WETHERALL, ROBERT SHAW, librarian; b. Jesup, Ga., Aug. 18, 1944; s. Robert and Elizabeth (Shaw) W; m. Cynthia Jane Campbell, July 31, 1976; children—Robert G., Gerritt C. B.A. in History, U. Del., 1966, M.A. in History, 1968; M.L.S., Drexel U., 1973. Cert. profl. libr., N.J. Libr. Cumberland County Libr., Bridgeton, N.J., 1973-76; asst. dir., 1976-80, dir., 1981-89; dir. Dover (Del.) Pub. Libr., 1989—; mem. Cumberland County Audio-Visual Aids Commn., Bridgeton, 1981-89; pres. South Jersey Regional Libr. Coop., Inc., 1986-88, treas., 1988-89. Served with USAF, 1968-72. Mem. ALA, Del. Libr. Assn. (pres. 1992-93, action implementation com.). Office: Dover Pub Libr 45 S State St Dover DE 19901-7311

WETHERHORN, ARYEH (LEE MURRAY), computer analyst; b. Jacksonville, Fla., Jan. 8, 1940; arrived in Israel, 1972; s. Levi Lester and Gertrude (Weisman) W.; m. Madeline Donna Engberg, June 16, 1968; children: Talya Alina Shachar, Ronit Avishag Inbar, Micha Avram Oren, Elisha Reuven, David Goldberger. BA in History, U. Mich., 1962; postgrad., Hebrew U., 1966-67. Mem. Elazar Cooperative Settlement, Israel, 1979-90; computer specialist, 1974—. Author: (poetry) Where Dreams Begin, 1991; contbr. to U.S. Naval Inst. Procs., 1974, 79, 95; contbr. articles to profl. publs. Active local sch. bd., Gush Etzion, Israel, 1984-87, Cmty. Ctr. Directorate, Gush Etzion, 1987-90. Lt. USN, 1963-71; major Israeli Def. Forces, 1973-79. Decorated Navy Achievement medal. Mem. U.S. Naval Inst., Internat. Naval Rsch. Orgn. Jewish. Avocations: ship models, Scrabble, chess. Home: House 32, Elazar 90942, Israel Office: Systems Mgr Israel Lands, Authority Shamai 6, Jerusalem Israel

WETSCH, JOHN ROBERT, information systems specialist; b. Dickinson, N.D., Aug. 27, 1959; s. Joseph John and Florence Mae (Edwards) W.; m. Laura Jean Johnson, Aug. 29, 1981; children: Julie Elizabeth, Katherine Anne, John Michael. BS, U. State of N.Y.-Regents Coll., Albany, 1984; MA, Antioch U., 1989; PhD, Nova S.E. U., 1994. Radiation physics instr. Grand Forks (N.D.) Clinic, 1983-85; sr. programmer PRC, Inc., Cavalier Air Force Sta., N.D., 1987-91, PARCS project-SAFEGUARD sys.; pres. Dakota Sci. Inc., Langdon, N.D., 1988-95; instr. U. N.D.-Lake Region, Devils Lake, 1988-91; systems adminstr. U.S. Courts Nat. Fine Ctr., Raleigh, N.C., 1991-94; bus. project leader Raleigh (N.C.) Integrated Bus. Sys. Solution Ctr., 1994—; v.p. R & D HYTEC Consulting, Inc., 1997—; cons. on Wave Obs./N.D. Proposal, Gov.'s Office, Bismarck, 1991; founder, developer Dakota Sci., Inc., Langdon, 1988-95; instr. divsn. continuing edn. Wake Tech. C.C., 1993—; prin. tech. advisor Litton/PRC, 1997—; mem. adj. faculty computer info. systems N.C. Wesleyan Coll., 1997—, U. Phoenix; adj. faculty N.C. State U., 1999-2000, Capella U., Mpls., 2000—. Author: Distributed UNIX System Administration, 1998; (with others) COMPUTE!'s 2nd Book of Amiga, 1988; contbr. articles to COMPUTE! Jour. of Progressive Computing, 1987, other profl. jours. Program coord. Lake Region Outreach, U. N.D., Cavalier Air Force Sta., 1988-91; mem. bd. alumni trustees USNY-Regents Coll., Albany, 1995-2000, v.p., 1996-97, pres., 1997-2000, ex-officio mem. bd. overseers Regents Coll., 1997; pres. Zeta Rho chpt. Pi Kappa Alpha, Grand Forks, 1981, Alumni Assn. Regents Coll., 1999—; ex-officio voting Regents Coll. Bd. Trustees, 1999—. SMITS scholar N.D. Acad. Sci., 1990; Larimore-Mathews scholar U. N.D., Grand Forks, 1978, N.D. Acad. Sci. scholar, 1978; recipient Westinghouse Sci. Talent Search award, 1978; Sr. Tech. fellow Litton/PRC, 1997, Nova Southeastern U. Leadership award Internat. Alumni Assn., 1998. Mem. AAAS, IEEE, IEEE Computer Soc., Regents Coll. Degrees (grad. resource network), Assn. for Computing Machinery, Dakota Astron. Soc. (co-founder, pres. 1987-91). Republican. Roman Catholic. Achievements include missile simulation; microcomputer short range weather forecasting algorithm, study in astronomy and culture, and astronomy's impact on devel. on Western civilization, system administration assessment of U.S. Courts and establishment and assessment of information control systems for the U.S. Courts National Fine Center; established and manages TPML Lab, U.S. Postal Service. Office: RA IBSSC 4200 Wake Forest Rd Raleigh NC 27668-9000

WETTE, EDUARD WILHELM, mathematician; b. Radevormwald, Germany, Feb. 4, 1925; s. Eduard and Anna Auguste (Finkensieper) W.; m. Anna Maria Elisabeth Mohrhauer, Dec. 28, 1950; 1 dau., Adelheid Margaretha Elisabeth. Self-taught. Ind. rschr.; mem. adv. council Internat. Logic Rev., Bologna, Italy, 1975. Contbr. to profl. publs. in field; author articles on finite contradictions within pure arithmetic; anti-relativistic morphometric representation of the motions' totality; electronic ether-curvatures, rectifying a hydrogen atom; far-coherent monadometry confirms Tycho Brahe's immovability of earth; intrafinite recursive world calculus. With 405 Regt., 1944-45. Recipient prize Bonn U., 1968. Mem. Assn. Symbolic Logic, Am. Math. Soc., math. Assn. Am., History of Sci. Soc., N.Y. Acad. Scis., Centro Superiore di Logica e Scienze Comparate. Home: 26 Am Markt, D53773 Hennef Germany Office: PO Box 4115 Uckerath, D53767 Hennef Germany

WETTENHALL, ROGER LLEWELLYN, public administration educator; b. Hobart, Tasmania, Australia, Feb. 4, 1931; s. Ralph Henry and Dorothy Mabel (Rumbold) W.; m. Kathleen Lois Calvert (div. 1975); children: Irene, Lynn, Dean; m. Roslyn Avril Byrne. BA, U. Tasmania, Hobart, 1952, diploma in pub. adminstrn., 1954, MA, 1956; PhD, Australian Nat. U., Canberra, 1962. Pers. cadet/officer Australian Commonwealth Pub. Svc., Hobart and Adelaide, 1948-59; from lectr. to reader pub. adminstr. U. Tasmania, 1962-71; head Sch. of Adminstrv. Studies Canberra Coll. of Advanced Edn., Bruce, 1971-85, fellow in adminstrv. studies, 1985-89; prof. pub. adminstrn. U. Canberra, Bruce, 1990—. Author: Public Enterprise and National Development, 1987, Bushfire Disaster: An Australian Community in Crisis, 1975, Organizing Government: The Uses of Ministries and Departments, 1986; co-author: Reluctant Democrats-The Transistion to Self-Government in the Australian Capital Territory, 1996; editor Australian Jour. Pub. Adminstrn., 1989-95; co-editor: Public Enterprise Boards-What They Are and What They Do, 1994, A Decade of Self-Government in the Australian Capital Territory, 2000; contbr. numerous articles to profl. publs. Fellow Inst. Pub. Adminstrn. Australia (pres. Australian Capital Ter. divsn. 1973-75), Australian Inst. Mcpl. Adminstrn. (hon.); mem. Internat. Assn. Schs. and Insts. of Adminstrn. (regional v.p., working group project dir./co-chmn. 1985—), Ea. Regional Orgn. Pub. Adminstrn. Home: 12 Carmichael St, Deakin Australia 2600 Office: University of Canberra, Kirinari St, Bruce Australia 2616

WETTER, FRIEDRICH CARDINAL, archbishop; b. Landau, Germany, Feb. 20, 1928. ordained priest Roman Cath. Ch., 1953. Consecrated bishop Speyer, 1968; archbishop Munich and Freising, Fed. Republic Germany, 1982—; proclaimed cardinal, 1985. Address: Kardinal-Faulhaber-Str 7, D-8000 Munich 2, Germany also: Postfach 10 05 51, 80079 Munich Germany*

WETTERBERG, PER GUNNAR, professional society administrator; b. Malmoe, Skaane, Sweden, Jan. 18, 1953; s. S.A. Oerjan and S. Louise (Soerensson) W.; m. Maria Elisabet Desirée Johansson; children: Joergen Jon, Karin Klas. MA in History and Social Scis., U. Lund, Sweden. Diplomat Min. Affairs, Hanoi, Geneva, Stockholm, 1975-85; spl. advisor Min. Agr., Stockholm, 1986-87; gen. sec. Expert Group Pub. Fin., Stockholm, 1988-90; asst. under sec. Min. Fin., Stockholm, 1990-94; dir. Swedish Assn. Local Authorities, Stockholm, 1995-99; head policy dept. Swedish Confedn. Profl. Assns., 1999—; rep. coms. confs. UN, Orgn. for Econ. Cooperation and Devel. (OECD), European Union (EU), 1977-96; projet mgr. Nat. Audit Bur., Stockholm, 1979-82. Author: The New Society, 1991, 2d edit., 1995, History Never Repeats Itself, 1994, Local Self-Government, 1997, Next Sweden, 1998, What Every 50-Year Old Should Know About the Future, 2000; co-author: Medium Term Survey of the Swedish Economy, 1992, 95. Fellow Soc. Urban History. Avocations: history, gardening. Home: Soendagsvaegen, S 12360 Farsta Sweden Office: SACO, Box 2206, S 10315 Stockholm Sweden

WETTERWALD, AUDREY LYNN, dance educator; b. Chelmsford, Mass., Dec. 22, 1968; d. Edmund E. Jr. and Audrey Jane (Cooper) W. BFA, Lake Erie Coll., 1990. Cert. tchr. Ohio; registered dance educator. Dance educator Ashtabula (Ohio) Arts Ctr., 1990-92, Ashtabula City Schs., 1991-92, Phillips-Osborne Sch., Painesville, Ohio, 1990-96, Kirtland/Mentor (Ohio) Dances, 1991-96; dir. Dance Expressions Unltd., Mass., 1996—. Choreographer numerous dance concerts and musicals; appeared in Chorus Line, 1990, Tapestry, 1999, Nutcracker, 1999, Impulse Dance Co., 1999, Sleeping Beauty, 2000. Active World Wildlife Fund, Sponsor the Whales, United Cerebral Palsy Found., Am. Cancer Soc., Epilepsy Found, Sponsor the Wolves. Dance Tchrs.' Club of Boston scholar, 1983-85. Mem. AAH-PERD, Nat. Dance Edn. Assn., Nat. Dance Assn., Nat. Registry of Dance Educators, Internat. Tap Assn., Pythian Sisters, Arts Coun. Coop, Dance Tchr.'s Club Boston, Greater Lowell C. of C. Avocations: reading, sports, crafts, sewing. Office: 130 Middlesex Rd Ste 2 Tyngsboro MA 01879-2725

WETTSTEIN, HORST DIETER, data processing executive; b. Pforzheim, Fed. Republic Germany, Sept. 15, 1933; s. Otto Heinrich and Erna (Böhringer) W.; m. Ute Hiltrud Brunner, July 21, 1961; children: Matthias, Annette, Christine. Diploma Ing., U. Karlsruhe, 1962, PhD, 1966. Sys. programmer IBM, Yorktown Heights, N.Y., 1961-62; asst. prof. computer sci. U. Karlsruhe, 1962-72, prof. computer sci., 1972-98; ret., 1998; cons. in field. Author: Systemarchitektur, 1993, others; contbr. articles to profl. jours. Mem. ACM, IEEE Computer Soc., Gesellschaft für Informatik. Avocations: mountain climbing, antique clocks. Home: Ernst-Barlach-Strasse 50, D-76227 Karlsruhe Germany

WETZEL, FRANKLIN TODD, spinal surgeon, educator, researcher; b. Wilmington, Del., Mar. 7, 1955; s. Franklin Huff and Jean Hartman (Clouser) W.; m. Patricia Ann Cassanos, May 23, 1981 (div. June 1993); m. Cathleen Ann Myers, Nov. 21, 1993; 1 child, Colin Todd. AB, Harvard Coll., 1977; MD, U. Pa., 1981. Diplomate Am. Bd. Orthop. Surgery. Resident Yale U., New Haven, 1981-86, instr. Med. Sch., 1986-87; fellow S. Henry LaRocca, MD, New Orleans, 1987-88; asst. prof. Pa. State U., Hershey, 1988-91, assoc. prof., 1991-93; assoc. prof. U. Chgo., 1993—, dir. Spine Ctr., 1993—, vice chair dept. surgery; chief sect. orthopedic surgery L.A. Weiss Hosp., Chgo., 1998—; reviewer Clin. Orthops., Phila., 1993—. Assoc. editor Spine, 1990—; contbr. articles to profl. jours. Physician Armenian Gen. Benevolent, Hershey, 1988; mem. alumni coun. Wilmington Friends Sch., 1991—. Fellow Am. Acad. Orthop. Surgery; mem. Cervical Spine Rsch. Soc., N.Am. Spine Soc., Am. Neuromodulation Soc. (bd. dirs. 1994—), Acad. Orthop. Soc., Am. Pain Soc., Harvard Club (interviewer 1995—), Sigma Xi. Presbyterian. Avocations: vertebrate palentology, vintage cars, military history, baseball, tennis, squash. Office: U Chgo Spine Ctr 4646 N Marine Dr Chicago IL 60640-5759

WEUFFEN, WOLFGANG FRIEDRICH, pharmacist, microbiologist, hygienist, researcher; b. Schmiedeberg Schlesien, Germany, June 13, 1925; s. Gottfried and Maria (Radler) W.; m. Cathérine Höffler; children: Wolfgang, Norbert, Rainer, Gabriele, Angelika, Juliane. Grad. in pharmacy, U. Greifswald, Germany, 1952, MD, 1956, D Natural Scis., 1962, D Med. Habilitation, 1966. Pharmacist Adler-Apotheke, Vetschau, Germany, 1946-49; univ. lectr. Med. Faculty U. Greifswald, 1966, univ. prof., 1969, sr. asst. Inst. Pharmacy,, 1952-60, sr. physician Inst. Microbiology, 1960-67, dir. Univ. Inst. Hygiene, 1967-90; dir. Dist. Inst. Hygiene, Greifswald, 1967-92; prin. Lab. Microbiol. Diagnosis, Stralsund, Germany, 1992-2000. Author: Practice of Disinfection, 1973, Hospital Hygiene, 1977, 81 (Russian edit. Antiseptic, 8 vols., 1981-87, Microbial Environment and Antimicrobial Measures, 11 vols., 1975-88, Medical and Biological Importance of Thiocyanate (Rhodanide), 1982; contbr. over 500 articles to sci. jours.; over 50 patents in field med. and biochem. importance of thiocyanate, antimicrobial substances, hosp. hygiene, environ. medicine, toxicohygiene. Recipient Hufeland gold medal German Ministry Health, 1985, Ernst Moritz Arndt prize U. Greifswald, 1988. Mem. Soc. Microbiology (exec. com. 1967-90), German Soc. Microbiology. Avocations: animals, woodworking. Home: Ringstrasse 39, D-17498 Guest Germany Office: Riemser, An der Wiek 7, 17698 Insee Riems Germany

WEVER, CHRIS, child psychiatrist; b. Harlingen, The Netherlands, Dec. 22, 1957; s. Herman and Joan (Van de Zee) W. MBBS, U. Sydney, Australia, 1981. Intern Concord Hosp., Sydney, Australia, 1981, resident, 1982; registrar Prince of Wales Hosp., Sydney, Australia, 1982-89; psychiatrist Rivendell, Sydney, Australia, 1990-96; psychiatrist pvt. practice Sydney, Australia, 1997—; cons. Rural Health, Orange, 1991-95. Author: (book) The Secret Problem, 1993 (MHM Award 1994), The School Wobblies, 1994. Fellow Royal Australian and New Zealand Coll. Psychiatrists; mem. NSW Faculty of Child, Adolescent & Family Psychiatry (chmn. 1997—). Avocation: golf. Office: Delphis Anxiety Disorder, Clinic 31/103 Majors Bay Rd, Sydney 2137, Australia

WEVER, ULRICH ARNOLD, corporate communications executive; b. Wuppertal, Germany, Jan. 29, 1928; s. Eugen Karl and Marie (Kolb) W.; m. Dorothy Barnhouse (div. 1968); children: Stefan-Matthew, Kirsten-Ruth; m. Sigrid Gertrud Hohage, Aug. 28, 1969; 1 child, Pascal Marc. PhD, U. Marburg, 1957. Gen. sec. Studentenmission, Germany, 1957-60; program mgr. Am. House, Hannover, Germany, 1960-62; mgr. Wilh. Krah KG, Drolshagen, Germany, 1962-64; exec. mgr. Stätte der Begegnung, Vlotho, Germany, 1965-67; cons. Ministerpres. NRW, Düsseldorf, Germany, 1967-69; chief cons. IBM Germany, Stuttgart, 1969-78; dir. pers. devel. Hypo-Bank AG, Munich, 1978-89, with corp. communications dept., 1989-93; mgmt. cons. Munich, 1993—. Author: Unternehmenskultur in der Praxis, 1989, 3d edit., 1992, Unternehmens-Kommunikation als Lernprozess, 1995; contbr. articles to profl. jours. and chpts. to books. Avocations: sailing, hiking. Home and Office: Haydnstrasse 1, D-82327 Tutzing Germany

WEXLER, GEORGE, retired art educator, artist; b. Bklyn., Jan. 18, 1925; s. Morris and Sarah W.; m. Claire Seidner Wexler, Jan. 4, 1947; children: Andrew, James, Daniel. Diploma, The Cooper Union, N.Y.C., 1948; BA, NYU, 1950; MA, Mich. State U., 1954. Art instr. Mich. State U., E. Lansing, 1950-57; prof. art SUNY, New Paltz, 1957-87, prof. emeritus, 1987—; landscape painter. Cpl. U.S. Army, 1943-46.

WEXLER, JORGE SALOMON, geologist, writer; b. Santa Fe, Argentina, Mar. 2, 1952; s. Juan and Sara (Ritvo) W.; m. Susana Silvia Naishtat, July 24, 1975 (div. Sept. 1988); 1 child, Luis Rafael. Degree in Geology, Nat. U. Cordoba, Argentina, 1974. Tchr. secondary sch. Escuela Normal San Martin, Santa Fe, 1965-69; cons. in soil studies/hydrogeology and environ. geology Geologo Jorge Wexler y Asociados, Buenos Aires. Author: (poems) Del Tormento A la Libertad, 1984, Cancion Sudamericana, 1985, Un Amor de 120 Poesias, 1988, 200 Poemas de Amor, 1989, 250 Poemas de Un Amor Secreto, 1991, Argentina eres Hermosa-50 poesias, 2000, (novels) Ser Libre es Mi Bandera, 1986, Los Viajes y Relatos de Ramiro, 1987. Served with Argentine mil., 1975. Mem. AAAS, Consejo Superior Profl. de Geologia, Argentine Assn. Writers. Avocation: read. Home: Hidalgo 528 Piso 7, Dto B 1405 Capital Federal, 1405 Buenos Aires Argentina

WEYANDT, DANIEL SCOTT, naval officer, engineer, physicist; b. Altoona, Pa., Dec. 26, 1962; s. Blair Sherwood and Madolyn Rae (Dunmire) W. BS, Juniata Coll., Huntingdon, Pa., 1984; MS in Physics, Pa. State U., 1992; MBA, U. R.I., 1995. Commd. USN, 1984, advanced through grades to lt. comdr., 1996; divsn. officer USS John C. Calhoun, Charleston, S.C., 1987, USS Simon Bolivar, Charleston, 1986-89; rsch. officer Naval Undersea Warfare Ctr. Divsn., Newport, R.I., 1992-95; sr. engr., countermeasures mgr. Electronic Sensors and Sys. divsn. Northrop Grumman corp., Balt., 1995-99; fellow engr., leading engr. torpedo defense electronic sensors and sys. sector Northrop Grumman Corp., Annapolis, Md., 1999—; res. duty, tng. officer, adminstrv. officer COMSUBRON 8 Det 1106, 1995-98; asst. dep. comdr. COMSUBRON 8, 1995-98; ops. specialist COMSUBEASTLANT DET 1005, 1998—. Decorated Navy achievement medal, Navy commendation medal. Mem. Am. Soc. Naval Engrs., Am. Phys. Soc., Altoona Horseshoe Chorus (assoc. dir. 1978—), Sigma Pi Sigma. Republican. Methodist. Avocations: music, water sports, fitness. Home: PO Box 89 Hesston PA 16647-0089 Office: Northrop Grumman Corp PO Box 1693 Baltimore MD 21203-1693

WEYEL, VOLKER ALFRED, editor; b. Nebra, Sachsen-Anhalt, Germany, Oct. 2, 1944; s. Heinz and Rosa (Reuter) W.; m. Margaret Isahura, Apr. 6, 1973; children: Alfred, Angela. PhD in Social Anthropology, J.W. Goethe U., Frankfurt, Hesse, Germany, 1975. Freelance on devel.-related and African issues, 1974-76; editor-in-chief Vereinte Nationen, Bonn, Germany, 1977—; rsch. assoc. Makerere Inst. Social Rsch., 1970-73. Contbr. articles on Ugandan, African and internat. affairs to profl. jours. Mem. Inst. Internat. Politics, Wuppertal/Berlin, 1989—. With West German Army, 1964-65. Home: Stralsunder Weg 17, 53119 Bonn Germany Office: Redaktion Vereinte Nationen, Poppelsdorfer Allee 55, 53115 Bonn Germany

WEYERER, SIEGFRIED BERNHARD, epidemiologist; b. Traunstein, Bavaria, Germany, Aug. 20, 1947; s. Maximilian and Hedwig (Serger) W.; m. Betty (Berniece) Haire, Aug. 13, 1977; children: Margret Kathleen, Jan Curtis. PhD in Psychology and Sociology, U. Salzburg, Austria, 1976; Habilitation in Epidemiology, U. Heidelberg, Germany, 1994. Head dept. psychiat. case register Cen. Inst. Mental Health, Mannheim, Germany, 1985-87; head dept. psychogeriatric rsch. unit Cen. Inst. Mental Health, Mannheim, 1987—; expert in pub. health German Ministry Rsch. and Tech., Bonn, 1991—; mng. dir. Ctr. Epidemiology & Health Svcs. Rsch., 1998—; expert in pub. health German Ministry Rsch. and Tech., Bonn, 1991—. Author: Psychiatric Epidemiology, 1978, 84; editor: Unemployment, 1986; contbr. articles to profl. jours. Rsch. fellow U. Munich, psychiatric. dept., 1976-85; rsch. grantee German Ministry Rsch. and Tech., Bonn, 1986-89, 93—, rsch. grantee Found. of German Sci. Mem. Am. Pub. Health Assn., German Assn. Gerontology, Assn. European Psychiatrists (sec. gen. epidemiology and social psychiatry 1988—), Internat. Soc. Pharmacoepidemiology, N.Y. Acad. Scis., Soc. for Epidemiologic Rsch. Roman Catholic. Avocations: fishing, hiking, soccer, lit. Home: Zimmerbachstr 4, D-69469 Weinheim Baden-Wurtt Germany Office: Cen Inst Mental Health, J5 PO Box 122120, D-68072 Mannheim Germany

WEYERHAEUSER, GEORGE HUNT, retired forest products company executive; b. Seattle, July 8, 1926; s. John Philip and Helen (Walker) W.; m. Wendy Wagner, July 10, 1948; children: Virginia Lee, George Hunt, Susan W., Phyllis A., David M., Merrill W. BS with honors in Indsl. Engring., Yale U., 1949. With Weyerhaeuser Co., Tacoma, 1949-99, successively mill foreman, br. mgr., 1949-56, v.p., 1957-66, exec. v.p., 1966-88, pres., chief exec. officer, 1988, chmn. bd., chief exec. officer, 1988-91, chmn. bd., past CEO, 1988-99, also bd. dirs., 1960—; ret., 1999; bd. dirs. Boeing Co., SAFECO Corp., Chevron Corp.; mem. Bus. Coun., Bus. Roundtable, Wash. State Bus. Roundtable. *

WEYERS, WOLFGANG, dermatopathologist; b. Cologne, Germany, Nov. 13, 1958; s. Siegfried and Paula (Weber) W.; m. Imke Altekrueger, July 15, 1995. MD, U. Giessen, 1984, Doctor degree, 1989; degree in dermatology, Physician's Assn., Hesse, Germany, 1990. Resident Ctr. Dermatology and Andrology, Justus Liebig U., Giessen, 1984-90; asst. prof. Ctr. Dermatopathology and Andrology, Justus Liebig U., Giessen, 1990-97; attending physician Ctr. for Dermatopathology, Freiburg, Germany, 1997—. Author: Death of Medicine in Nazi Germany, Dermatology and Dermatopathology under the Swastika, 1998; contbr. articles to profl. jours.; editor Pink & Blue, 1997—; assoc. editor Dermatopathology: Practical and Conceptual, 1996—, Cutis, 1998—. Mem. German Dermatological Soc., Internat. Soc. Dermatopathology (historian 1996—). Office: Ctr Dermatopathology, Rosastr 9, 79098 Freiburg Germany

WEYHENMEYER, GESA ANTONIE, ecologist, researcher; b. Bonn, Germany, Nov. 4, 1969; d. Hans Paul and Ulrike Charlotte (Vogel) W. Diploma, Albert-Ludwigs U., Freiburg, Germany, 1991; BS, Trent U., Peterborough, Can., 1992; diploma, Uppsala (Sweden) U., 1995, PhD, 1996. Tchg. asst., rsch. asst. Uppsala U., 1992-97; rsch. asst. Erken Lab., Norrtälje, Sweden, 1997; rschr. Tech. U., Dresden, Germany, 1997-98; rschr., tchr. Uppsala U., 1998-99, Swedish U. Agrl. Scis., 1999—; rsch. asst. expedition to Amazon INPA, Manaus, Brazil, 1995, to Antarctica USGS, 1995, to Arctic Ocean AWI, 1997. Contbr. articles to profl. jours. Grantee Uppsala U., 1992, 93, 94, 97, Swedish Natural Sci. Rsch. Coun., Stockholm, 1994-95, State Ministry for Sci. and Culture, 1997. Mem. Am. Soc. Limnology and Oceanography, Am. Geophys. Union, Internat. Assn. Theoretical and Applied Limnology. Avocations: music (double-bass, clarinet), climbing, paragliding, traveling, photography. Home: Henry Saldes vag 17, 75643 Uppsala Sweden Office: Swedish U Dept Environ Assesment, PO Box 7050, 75007 Uppsala Sweden

WEYMAN, STEVEN ALOYSIUS, military officer, retired; b. Fort Thomas, Ky., May 31, 1957; s. Edward Joseph Weyman and Carol Jean (Steffen) Jackson; m. Kathleen Anne Bradford, June 2, 1990; 1 child, Jennifer Elizabeth. BS in Math., No. Ky. U., 1978; MS in Comm. Sys. Tech., Naval Postgrad. Sch., 1988. Commd. 2d lt. U.S. Army, 1978, advanced through grades to lt. col., 1995; bn. signal officer 8th Engr. Bn., 1st Cav. Divsn., Ft. Hood, Tex., 1979-81, 2nd M.I. Bn., Pirmasens, Germany, 1982-85; co. comdr. B Co., 307th M.I. Bn., Ludwigsburg, Germany, 1985-86; signal combat devel. project officer Combined Arms Command, Ft. Leavenworth, Kans., 1988-91; student U.S. Army Command Gen. Staff Coll., Ft. Leavenworth, 1991-92; bn. exec. officer 123rd Signal Bn., 3rd Inf. Divsn., Kitzingen, Germany, 1992-94; asst. divsn. signal officer 3rd Inf. Divsn., Wuerzburg, Germany, 1994-95; operational readiness evaluation team chief 5th U.S. Army (West), Ft. Lewis, Wash., 1995-97; def. info. sys. network deployed program mgmt. chief Def. Info. Sys. Agy., Arlington, Va., 1997-2000, ret., 2000; student Armed Forces Staff Coll., Norfolk, Va., 1998; tech. acct. mgr. Intel Online Svcs., 2000—. Decorated Legion of Merit. Mem. U.S. Signal Corps Assn. (Bronze Order of Mercury 1995), Armed Forces Comm. Electronics Assn. Avocations: computers, travel, reading, sports. Home: 43921 Felicity Pl Ashburn VA 20147-4860

WEYMULLER, BRUNO, oil and gas industry executive. Chief fin. officer Elf Aquitaine, Courbevoie, France; exec. v.p. fin. Elf Aquitaine. Office: 2 Pl de la Coupole, Paris 6 Courbevoie 92400, France*

WHALEN, JOHN PHILIP, retired educational administrator, clergyman, lawyer; b. Troy, N.Y., Jan. 4, 1928; s. Philip Joseph and Mary Catherine (Doyle) W. BA summa cum laude, St. Mary's Sem. and Univ., Balt., 1949; STL, Cath. U., 1953, MA, 1954, STD summa cum laude, 1965; JD, George Washington U., 1976; postgrad., Johns Hopkins U., 1959-60, U. Md., College Park, 1958-59, Fordham U., 1953-54; LHD (hon.), Marymount U., 1987. Ordained priest Roman Cath. Ch., 1953. Instr. Mater Christi Sem., Albany, 1953-58; asst. prof. Mt. St. Mary's Coll., Emmitsburg, Md., 1959-61; assoc. prof. Cath. U. Am., Washington, 1961-67, acting pres., 1968-69; pastor St. Mary's Ch., Oneonta, N.Y., 1970-72; pres. Consortium of Univs. of Washington area, 1972-88; mng. editor New Cath. Ency., 1963-67; pres., editor-in-chief Corpus Publs., 1967-94, ret., 1994; cons. 12 colls. and univs.; founder, chmn. Univ. Support Svcs., Inc., 1986-94, pres., CEO, founder; cons. student loans, capital access trust, capital loans to colls.; bd. dirs. U.S. Fund for Improvement Postsecondary Edn., 1988-91. Mem. editl. bd. Law and Edn.; weekly columnist Evangelist, Albany; contbr. to Nat. Geog. mag.; contbr. articles to ednl. and theol. jours. Bd. dirs. Sta. WETA-TV, 1968-69, Washington Ctr. for Met. Studies, 1968-69, Met. Bd. Trade, D.C., 1975-90, sec. bd. dirs., 1983-85; bd. dirs. Cath. U. Am., 1968-69, Nat. Shrine of Immaculate Conception, 1968-69, Dumbarton Coll., 1970-72, Trinity Coll., 1969-72, St. Mary's Coll., South Bend, Ind., 1970-74, St. Anselm's, 1979-85, Mt. Vernon Coll., 1982-84; pres. Univ. Extension Ednl. Corp., 1974-94; mem. Fed. City Coun., 1982—; mem. Coun. for Ct. Excellence, 1984-90; chmn. Ctr. Advanced Studies of the Ams., 1984-90. Named Man of the Yr., 1984; recipient Disting. Alumnus award George Washington U., 1988. Mem. Nat. Cath. Edn. Assn., Cath. Theol. Soc. Am. (dir. 1966-68), Higher Edn. Group Washington (pres. 1974-75), Tired Hands Club (pres. 1982-84), Cosmos Club (Washington), City Club, Rotary. Office: 1614 Parham Rd Silver Spring MD 20903-2256

WHALEN, MARY ROMANCE, library director; b. Rabat, Morocco, June 20, 1957; d. Francis Joseph and Ann Pickert (Romance); m. Kevin John Whalen, Oct. 7, 1995. BA in Orgnl. Comms. and Mgmt., U. Mich., Ann Arbor, 1979; MLS, Rutgers U., New Brunswick, N.J., 1992. Libr. coord. Bernardsville (N.J.) Pub. Libr., 1991-93; libr. dir. Rockaway (N.J.) Borough Pub. Libr., 1993-94, Lincoln Park (N.J.) Pub. Libr., 1994-97, Roslary Twp. Pub. Libr., Succasunna, N.J., 1997—; v.p., 1998, pres., 1999, M.A.I.N. Inc. Planning Coun.. Mem. Roxbury Area C. of C. Office: Rosbury Public Library 103 Main St Succasunna NJ 07876-1417

WHALLEY, RALPH DERWYN BROUGHTON, grassland ecologist; b. Macksville, Australia, July 9, 1933; s. Ralph Parker and Marjorie Eileen (Broughton) W.; m. Pamela May Robison, Mar. 22, 1958; children: Claevewen Frances, Catherine Louise, David William. BSc in Agrl., U. Sydney, 1956; PhD, U. Calif., 1965. Agronomist NSW Agrl., Trangie, Australia, 1956-62; rsch. asst. dept. agronomy U. Calif., Riverside, 1962-65; lectr. dept. botany UNE, Armidale, Australia, 1965-68, sr. lectr. dept. botany, 1969-89, head dept. botany, 1990-94, assoc. prof. dept. botany, 1990-98, head sch. rural sci. & natural resources, 1997-98, hon. fellow dept. botany, 1999—; postdoctoral fellow dept. range sci. Utah State U., Logan, 1972, vis. scientist 1988; vis. fellow dept. environ. biol. Australian Nat. U., Canberra, 1979; mem. continuing com. Internat. Rangeland Congress, 1988-95. Editor Australian Rangeland Jour., 1976-78; assoc. editor The Rangeland Jour., 1990-98, editor, 1999—; contbr. articles to profl. jours. Postgrad. travel grant Fulbright Found., 1962-65, sr. travel grant Australian-Am. Edn. Found., 1972; Quinney vis. rsch. fellow Quinney Found., 1988. Mem. Australian Inst. of Agrl. Sci. and Tech., Australian Ecol. Soc., Australian Rangeland Soc. Office: Dept Botany U New England, Armidale NSW 2351, Australia

WHALLON, WILLIAM, literature educator; b. Richmond, Ind., Sept. 24, 1928; s. Arthur J. and Adelaide (Wheeler) W.; m. Joanne Holland, Aug. 22, 1957; children: Andrew, Nicholas. B.A., McGill U., 1950; Ph.D., Yale U., 1957. From asst. prof. to prof. Mich. State U., East Lansing, 1963—. Author: Formula, Character, and Context, 1969, Problem and Spectacle, 1980, Inconsistencies, 1983, (poetry) A Book of Time, 1990, (scenarios) The Oresteia / Apollo & Bacchus, 1997. Fellow Center for Hellenic Studies, 1962-63; Fulbright prof. comparative lit., U. Bayreuth, 1984-85. Home: 1655 Walnut Heights Dr East Lansing MI 48823-2943

WHAM, WILLIAM NEIL, publisher; b. N.Y.C., Dec. 28, 1934; s. William and Jessie (Neill) W.; m. Lynn McCorvie, Mar. 6, 1966; children: McCorvie, Avery. B.S., Syracuse U., 1956. Salesman Mut. N.Y., N.Y.C., 1959-61; regional sales mgr. Doubleday Pub. Co., N.Y.C., 1961-64, Reinhold Pub. Co., N.Y.C., 1964-68; sales mgr. United Bus. Publs., N.Y.C., 1968; pres., pub. jours. Internat. Scientific Communications, Inc., Shelton, Conn., 1968—. Founder: sci. jours. Am. Lab., Internat. Lab., Am. Biotech. Lab., Am. Clin. Lab., Internat. Biotech. Lab., Lab. Products Tech., Am. Lab. News, European Clin. Lab., Internat. Lab. News, Internat. Biotech. News, European Clin. Lab. News, Am. Environ. Lab. Served with AUS, 1956-58. Home: 157 Pinewood Trl Trumbull CT 06611-3312 Office: Internat Sci Communications Inc 30 Control Dr Shelton CT 06484-6111

WHANG, KYU-KWANG, medical educator; b. Seoul, June 30, 1957; s. Hyun-Soo and Soon-Young (Lee) W.; m. Eun-Sun Choi, Nov. 25, 1989; children: Jieun, Jisung. MD, Yonsei U., Seoul, 1983; MS, Yonsei U., 1986, PhD, 1990. Lic. specialist in dermatology. Resident in dermatology Severance Hosp., Yonsei U., Seoul, 1984-87; head dermatology Nat. Sorokdo Leprosy Hosp., Korea, 1987-88; instr. dermatology Coll. Medicine Yonsei U., Seoul, 1990-91; head, asst. dermatology Coll. Medicine Konkuk U., Korea, 1991-93; assoc. prof. dermatology Coll. Medicine Ewha Womans U., Seoul, 1993-98, assoc. prof. dermatology, 1998—. Author: (book) Dermatology, 3d edit., 1994; mem. editl. bd. Annals of Dermatology, 1999; contbr. articles to profl. jours. Consulting dermatologist 121 Hosp., U.S. Army, Seoul, 1998—. Recipient Dong-A Acad. award, 1990; Perry Robins scholar Internat. Soc. Dermatol. Surgery, 1993. Fellow Internat. Soc. for Dermatology; mem. Korean Soc. Dermatologic Surgery (sec. gen. 1995-98), Am. Acad. Dermatology, Korean Dermatol. Assn., Korean Soc. Investigative Dermatology. Avocations: golf, tennis. Home: 105-305 Hyundai, Apkujung-dong, Kangnamku, Seoul Korea Office: Ewha Womans U Hosp, 70 Chongro-6ga Chongroku, Seoul 110-126, Korea

WHARTON, RALPH NATHANIEL, psychiatrist, educator; b. Boston, June 15, 1932; s. Nathaniel Philip and Deeda (Levine) W.; children: Naida, Philip, Laura. AB cum laude, Harvard U., 1953; MD, Columbia U., 1957, degree in psychoanalysis, 1970. Intern Cornell divsn. Bellevue Hosp., N.Y.C., 1957-58; resident Columbia-Presbyn. Med. Ctr., N.Y.C., 1961-64; practice medicine specializing in psychiatry/pharamcology N.Y.C., 1964—; assoc. psychiatry Coll. Physicians and Surgeons, N.Y.C., 1964-69, asst. prof. clin. psychiatry, 1969-72, assoc. prof., 1972-83, prof., 1984—; sr. rsch. psychiatrist N.Y. State Psychiat. Inst., N.Y.C., 1964-70; assoc. attending psychiatry Columbia-Presbyn. Hosp., 1970—; ex-officio mem. bd. trustees, pres. Soc. Practitioners Columbia-Presbyn. Med. Center, 1980-82, attending psychiatrist, 1984—; exec. dir. Wharton Fund for Brain Rsch.; med. dir. Black Sea project Macalester Coll., 1994-98. Author: Landmark Papers, Lithium Carbonate for Affective Disorders, 1966; contbr. numerous papers and publs. in profl. jours. With M.C., U.S. Army, 1958-61. Named one of Best Drs. N.Y. mag. Fellow N.Y. Acad. Medicine, Am. Psychiat. Assn., Am. Coll. Psychoanalysts (pres. 1996), Internat. Assn. Study of Pain (founder); mem. AMA (mem. legis. action com.), Soc. Biol. Psychiatry, Royal Soc. Medicine, Lotos Club, Salon de Virtuosi (founding bd. mem.), Harvard Club, Harmonie Club. Office: Columbia Presbyn Med Ctr Atchley Pavilion # 322 161 Fort Washington Ave New York NY 10032-3713 also: 1070 Park Ave Ste 1D New York NY 10128-1000

WHATELEY, TONY LOUIS, pharmaceutical science educator; b. Birmingham, Eng., May 14, 1938; s. Frank Louis and Gladys Elizabeth (Britten) W.; m. Maisie Anne Roberts, Sept. 6, 1967 (div. 1981); children: Judith Elizabeth Mary, Philippa Anne Louise; m. Diane Grace Godfrey, Apr. 16, 1988; 1 child, Isla Rosemary. BA with honors, Oxford (Eng.) U., 1962, MA, 1966; MSc, U. NSW, Australia, 1967; PhD, Cambridge (Eng.) U., 1972. Chartered chemist. Lectr. dept. pharm. scis. U. Strathclyde, Glasgow, Scotland, 1972—; expert witness patent disputes. Editor: Microencapsulation of Drugs, 1992; editor-in-chief Jour. Microencapsulation, 1994—, Drug Delivery, 1996—; contbr. over 100 articles to profl. jours. Mem. Com. Brit. Pharmacoepia Com., 1976—. Served with Royal Air Force, 1956-58. Fellow Royal Soc. Chemistry; mem. Internat. Microencapsulation Soc. (sec., treas. 1993—). Avocations: golf, skiing, bridge. Office: Dept Pharm Scis, U Strathclyde, SBS Glasgow G4 0NR, Scotland

WHEATLEY, CHARLES HENRY, III, lawyer, biomedical technology company executive; b. Balt., Aug. 11, 1932; s. Charles Henry Jr. and Rebecca W. (Cloud) W.; m. Charlotte Beryl Davis, June 11, 1955; children: Charles H. IV, Craig A., Cheryl L. W. Jackson. BA in Polit. Sci. with hons., Western Md. Coll., 1954; JD with hons., U. Md., 1959. Bar: Md. 1960, D.C. 1981, U.S. Supreme Ct. 1964. Tchr. Carroll County Pub. Schs., Westminster, Md., 1955-56; officer, judge advocate U.S. Army, 1957-62; law clk. assoc. judge William R. Horney Md. Ct. Appeals, Annapolis, 1959-60; pvt. practice Md. and Washington, 1960—; mem. Md. legislature Ho. of Dels., Annapolis, 1962-66; pres., COO Cell Works, Inc., Balt., 1997—; real estate, ins. exec. AID Realty & Ins. Co., Balt., 1960—; adj. coll. instr. Western Md. coll., Westminster, 1963-65, Villa Julie Coll., 1980-86, Balt. Cmty. Col., 1966-72; mem. adv. bd. Fleet Bus. Sch., Annapolis, Md., 1986—, Balt. Cmty. Col., 1986—; chmn. bd., ceo Regional Mfg. Inst., Balt., 1993-96; nat. del. White House Conf. on Small Bus., Washington, 1985. Contbr., editor: (weekly newspaper) Maryland Teacher, 1974-77; guest News Makers program WJZ-TV, 1985; contbr. articles to profl. jours. Md. del. Md. State Constitutional Convention, Annapolis, 1967-68; councilman Balt. City Coun., 1971-74. 1st lt. JAG U.S. Army, 1957-62. Received Cell Works Co. Computerworld-Smithsonian Science Innovation laureate award, 1999. Mem. Md. Commn. Mfg. Competitiveness, Md. State Bar Assn., Dist. Columbia Bar. Assn., Md. State Tchrs. Assn. (exec. sec. 1974-77), Order of the Coif, Pi Gamma Mu. Democrat. Methodist. Avocations: education, music, writing, basketball, skiing. Office: Cell Works Inc 5202 Westland Blvd Baltimore MD 21227-2349

WHEATLEY, JOSEPH KEVIN, physician, urologist; b. N.Y.C., Jan. 5, 1946; s. Patrick Owen and Catherine (Malloy) W.; m. Anne Johanna Foody, Aug. 22, 1970; children: Joseph, Thomas. BSChemE, Manhattan Coll., 1967; MSChemE, U. Del., 1969; MD, N.J. U. of Medicine, 1974. Diplomate Am. Bd. Urology. Rsch. engr. NASA, Houston, 1965, 66, Exxon, Florham Park, N.J., 1968-69; urology resident Emory Univ., Atlanta, 1975-79, assoc. prof. urology, 1979—; clin. urology practice Urology Assocs., Atlanta, 1986—; chief of urology Kennestone Hosp., Marietta, Ga., 1990-93; medicare care cons. Ga. Found. med. Care, Atlanta, 1982—; tchr. Atlanta VA Med. Ctr., Atlanta, 1979—; mem. hosp. exec. com. Kennestone Hosp., Marietta, 1990-93. Contbr. chpts. to books and articles to profl. jours. Active various Rep. actitives, 1992—. Named Top Drs. in Atlanta Atlanta Mag., 1995-96. Fellow ACS; mem. AMA, Urol. Assn., Urodynamics Soc., Am. Fertility Soc., Soc. of Reproductive Surgeons, Lithotripsy Soc. Roman Catholic. Avocations: skiing, hiking, biking trips, tennis, computers. Home: 692 N Saint Marys Ln NW Marietta GA 30064-1454 Office: Urology Assocs 55 Whitcher St NE Ste 250 Marietta GA 30060-1169

WHEATLEY, WILLIAM ARTHUR, architect, musician; b. Knoxville, Tenn., Sept. 23, 1944; s. Arthur Cornwallis and Inda Mary (Benway) W.; m. Celeste Ann George, Mar. 25, 1970 (div.); children: Charles Arthur, James Harris Giddings; m. Rosaria Giovanna Cilia, June 10, 1995. Student, Rice U., 1962-66; BA, U. St. Thomas, 1972. Registered architect, Pa., Md., N.J. Design draftsman W.W. Alexander, Houston, 1966-70; chief of prodn. W.W. Scarborough, Houston, 1970-74; project architect Ronald H. Waldie & Assocs., Houston, 1972-74; pres. Wheatley & Assocs., Houston, 1974-81; project architect Brooks Assn., Houston, 1977-79; mgr. design Stone Bldg. Systems, Inc., Houston, 1979-81; project architect Bechtel, Houston, 1981-84; prin. Wheatley & Assocs., Houston, 1984-87; project mgr. STV/Sanders & Thomas, Pottstown, Pa., 1987-88, MDC Sys. (divsn. Day & Zimmermann Internat., Inc.), Phila., 1988-97; prin., exec. v.p. MDC Sys., Inc., 1997—; chmn. MDC Sys. UK Ltd., 1999—. Composer piano solos, chorales, oratorio and cantata, 1961—; co-contbr. articles to profl. jours. Del. Tex. Rep. Convs., 1980, 82, 84; mem. vestry Ch. of the Good Shepherd, Rosemont; bd. dirs. Found. for Anglican Christian Tchg. Mem. AIA (Phila. chpt.), ABA (assoc.), Am. Coll. Forensic Examiners, Royal Archtl. Inst. of Can., Am. Arbitration Assn., Pa. Soc. Architects, Bldg. Ofcls. and Code Adminstrs. Internat., Forest Products Soc., The Mastersingers (bd. dirs. 1989-92, treas. 1990-91), Archeol. Inst. Am., Choral Soc. Montgomery County (bd. dirs. 1990-96, pres. 1992-95). Episcopalian. Avocations: writing poetry and fiction, drawing, painting, sculpture. Office: MDC Systems Inc 55 West Ave Wayne PA 19087-3255

WHEELER, DAVID MICHAEL, financial executive; b. Oxford City, Eng., Mar. 20, 1940; s. Antony and Edith (Dawkins) W.; m. Margita Vanneck, Oct. 21, 1961; children: Andrew, James. Student, Eton Coll., Windsor, Berkshire, U.K. Mem. Securities Inst., London. Ptnr. Strauss Turnbull & Co., to 1974; non-exec. dir. Sotheby's, London, 1989-93; dep. chmn. Harris & Dixon Group, 1984-95; chmn., founder Ermitage Group, 1974-00; bd. dirs. Liberty Armitage Group Funds, Le Masurier James Uchinn, Western Que. Mings, Edinburgh Pacific Fund. Mem. Whites Club London, Travelers Club Paris.

WHEELER, FRANK KNOWLES BLASDELL, retired military officer, business consultant; b. Mpls., Oct. 29, 1912; s. Walter Hall and Eva Maude (Blasdell) W.; widowed, Oct. 1991; children: Mary Ann Wheeler Masher, Frances Blasdell Wheeler Kindle, Charles Knowles. BSME, U.S. Naval Acad., 1935, PhD (Equivalent) Electronics, 1944. Registered profl. engr., Calif. Commd. ensign USN, 1935, advanced through grades to capt., 1954; commdg. officer U.S.S. Kearney, 1944-46; mem. various fleets/electronics staffs USN, 1946-60, ret., 1960; mfg. mgr. Hewlett Packard Co., Palo Alto, Calif., 1960-70; co. mfg. mgr. Fairchild, 1970-72; pres., bus. cons. Wheeler & Assocs., Los Altos Hills, Calif., 1972—. Mem. IEEE. Republican. Presbyterian. Avocations: electronics, preparing historical video productions. Home and Office: 27174 Elena Rd Los Altos Hills CA 94022-3343

WHEELER, GERALDINE HARTSHORN, historian; b. Pomona, Calif., Feb. 5, 1919; d. Albion True and Beatrice Osa (Barnes) Hartshorn; m. Lloyd Franklyn Wheeler, Dec. 2, 1938 (dec. Mar. 1996); children: Russell Lloyd, Robert Gerald. AA, Santa Barbara (Calif.) C.C., 1950's. Co-owner Atheling's, Santa Barbara, Calif., 1971-76, Pomona, 1976-90; chmn. bd. trustees Atheling Heritage Trust, Claremont, Calif., 1994—. Pub., editor (mag.) Atheling's, 1974-75; pub. editor (newsletter) Grand Priory of America Order of St. Lazarus, 1974-86; editor, founder St. Margaret's Jour., 1975—. Vol. PTA, Fontana and Santa Barbara, 1945-60; active Hist. Soc. Pomona Valley, 1950—; mem. various coms. and choir First Congl. Ch., Santa Barbara, 1952-72; leader Cub Scouts Am., Santa Barbara, 1953-56; grey lady unit chmn. Santa Barbara chpt.-ARC, 1958-62; women's project bd. v.p., activities chmn., active various coms. Santa Barbara Hist. Soc., 1960-74; exec. sec. 1960 Nixon for Pres. Campaign, Santa Barbara, 1960; mem. spkrs. bur. Nixon for Gov. Campaign, Santa Barbara, 1962; mem. Rep. state ctrl. com. State of Calif., 1962-64; blitz chmn. Rockefeller for Pres. Campaign, Santa Barbara, 1964; coord. vol. svcs. Office of Civil Def., City of Santa Barbara, 1965-76; coord. tv series on earthquakes Sta. KEYT, Office of Civil Def., Santa Barbara, 1968; bd. dirs. Calif. Ctrl. Coast Area, U.S.O., 1968-76, treas. bd., 1970-76; supporter Vis. Nurses and Hospice Assn., 1994—; others. Decorated Dame of Grace, Mil. and Hospitaller Order of St. Lazarus of Jerusalem, Cert. of Merit, 1973, The Alan Weaver Hazelton award; recipient Cert. of Merit, Santa Barbara Jr. Coll., 1954-55, Medal of Appreciation SAR, 1972, Cert. of Award Nat. Soc. Daus. of Founders and Patriots of Am., 1977. Mem. Calif. Hist. Soc., New Eng. Hist. and Geneal. Soc., The Pomona Ebell (pres. 1998-2000), Wilson Ctr. Assocs., Smithsonian Assocs., Nat. Trust for Hist. Preservation, Am. Farmland Trust. Republican. Avocations: book collecting, reading, genealogy, classical music, needlework. Home: 1047 E Baseline Rd Claremont CA 91711-1577

WHEELER, JOHN STUART, bookmaking company executive; b. London, Jan. 30, 1935; s. Alexander Hamilton and Betty Lydia (Gibbons) W.; m. Teresa Anne Codrington, July 9, 1979; children: Sarah Rose, Jacquetta Lydia, Charlotte Mary. Grad., Oxford U., England, 1958. Barrister London, 1959-62; with Mill Samuel & Co., London, 1962-68; mgr. J.H. Vavasseur & Co., London, 1968-73; mng. dir. I.C. Index, London, 1974—. 2d lt. Welsh Guards, 1953-55. Mem. Whites, Portland Club, Queen's Club. Avocations: bridge, tennis. Home: 73 The Chase, London SW4 0NP, England Office: 157-168 Blackfriars Rd, London SE1 8EZ, England

WHEELER, MARK ANDREW, SR., lawyer; b. Pitts., Feb. 14, 1963; s. Andrew Mate Wheeler and Anna Ruth (Whitfield) W.; m. Darla Jo Fusselman, May 10, 1993; children: Mark Andrew Jr., Lauren Anna, Layne Allison, Livia Arden. BA in Philosophy, Hampden-Sydney Coll., 1985; JD,

W.Va. U., 1991. Bar: Pa. 1992, U.S. Dist. Ct. (we. dist.) Pa. 1993; ordained to ministry Lighthouse Ch., 1997. Staff litigator W.Va. U. Coll. Law Legal Clinic, Morgantown, 1991-92; jud. clk. Mahoning County, Youngstown, Ohio, 1991-92; pvt. practice Reynoldsville, Pa., 1993—, Clarion, Pa., 1994—; legal cons. S.T. & E., Inc., Punxsutawney, Pa., 1993—, Jefferson County Gun Owners Assn., Brookville, Pa., 1994—, Crimestoppers of Jefferson County, Brookville, 1993-94, Five Star Homes, Inc., 1995-97, Bembeng Cons., Inc., 1994—. Bd. dirs. Reynoldsville Area Indsl. Bd., 1993-96; mem. exec. dist. com. Boy Scouts Am., Dubois, Pa., 1993—; bd. dirs. Reynoldsville Pub. Libr. Assn., 1993-96; mem. Dubois Christian and Missionary Alliance Ch., mem. choir, 1995—. Mem. ABA, ATLA, Internat. Platform Assn., Pa. Bar Assn. (young lawyers divsn., chair zone 7), Am. Ctr. for Law and Justice, Pa. Trial Lawyers Assn., Pa. Assn. Notaries, Jefferson County Bar Assn., Western Pa. Trial Lawyers Assn., Clarion County Bar Assn., Nat. Eagle Scout Assn. Republican. Avocations: songwriting, public speaking, home renovation, car restoration. Office: PO Box 176 512 Main St Reynoldsville PA 15851-1335 also: PO Box 770 Clarion PA 16214-0770

WHEELER, RICHARD LEWIS, psychologist; b. Christchurch, Canterbury, New Zealand, Aug. 24, 1939; s. Benjamin and Nora Isabelle (Fanthorpe) W.; m. Margaret Stubbs, Dec. 20, 1969; children: Benjamin, Christopher. BA, U. Canterbury, 1975, MA with honors, 1978, diploma clin. psychology, 1980. Probation officer Justice Dept. Christchurch, 1968-74; asst. clin. psychologist Sunnyside Hosp., Christchurch, 1977-78; dir. Family Health Counseling Ctr. Bishopdale, Christchurch, 1978-83; clin. psychologist Christchurch, 1983—; probation officer Brixton Prison, London, 1973-74; prodr., presenter Plain Talk, radio 1996—, tv 1997—. Bd. dirs. Plain Talk Trust. Mem. New Zealand Coll. Clin. Psychologists, New Zealand Psychol. Soc. Avocations: painting, tramping, growing native trees, working on radio and tv. E-mail: wheeler.r@netaccess.co.nz. Home and Office: Woodlands Ctr, 309 Johns Rd, Christchurch 8005, New Zealand

WHEELER, SEAN M., management consultant; b. Conn., Apr. 3, 1966. BS, Babson Coll., 1989; MBA, Boston U., 1994. Fin. analyst Bank of New England, Boston, 1989-90, State St. Bank, Boston, 1990-91; mgmt. cons. Ernst & Young, London, 1994—. Chair young mems. com., English Spkg. Union, London, 1998; mem. Ernst & Young sailing team. Office: Ernst & Young Becket House, 1 Lambeth Palace Rd, London SE1 7EU, England

WHEELER, SUSIE WEEMS, retired educator; b. Cassville, Ga., Feb. 24, 1917; d. Percy Weems and Cora (Smith) Weems-Canty; m. Dan W. Wheeler Sr., June 7, 1941; 1 child, Dan Jr. BS, Fort Valley (Ga.) State U., 1945; MEd, Atlanta U., 1947, EdD, 1978; postgrad., U. Ky., 1959-60; EdS, U. Ga., 1977. Tchr. Bartow County Schs., Cartersville (Ga.) City Schs., 1938-44, Jeanes supr., 1946-58; supr., curriculum dir. Paulding Sch. Sys.-Stephens Sch., Calhoun City, 1958-64; summer sch. tchr. Atlanta U., 1961-63; curriculum dir. Bartow County Schs., 1963-79; ret., 1979; pres., co-owner Wheeler-Morris Svc. Ctr., 1990—; mem. Ga. Commn. on Student Fin., 1985-95. Coord. Noble Hill-Wheeler Meml. Ctr. Project, 1983—. Recipient Oscar W. Canty Cmty. Svc. award, 1991, Woman in History award Fedn. Bus. and Profl. Women, 1995, New Frontiers Cmty. Svc. award, 1997. Mem. AAUW (v.p. membership 1989-91, Ga. Achievement award 1993, Edn. Found. award Cartersville-Bartow br.), Ga. Assn. Curriculum and Supervision (pres.-elect 1973-74, pres. 1974-75, Johnnye V. Cox award 1975), Delta Sigma Theta (pres. Rome alumnae chpt. 1978-80, mem. nat. bd. 1984, planning com. 1988—, Dynamic Delta award 1967, 78), Ga. Jeanes Assn. (pres. 1968-70). Home: 105 Fite St Cartersville GA 30120-3410

WHEELOCK, KENNETH STEVEN, chemist; b. Kansas City, Mo., Sept. 18, 1943; s. Kenneth Lewis and Clara Mae (Hanenkratt) W.; m. Mary Corinne Percy, June 30, 1972; children: Michael Steven, Celeste Marie. BSc, U. Mo., Kansas City, 1965; PhD, Tulane U., New Orleans, 1970; J.D. magna cum laude, Western New Eng. Coll., 1998. Bar: Mass.; registered patent atty. Chemist Exxon Rsch. & Devel. Labs., Baton Rouge, La., 1969-72, rsch. chemist, 1972-77, staff chemist, 1977-83, sr. staff chemist, 1983-86; assoc. prof. physics La. State U., Baton Rouge, 1987; sr. rsch. chemist Phillips Petroleum Co., Bartlesville, Okla., 1987-91; chmn. Prakti Katalysts, Bartlesville, Okla., 1992-93; patent agt. GE Plastics, Pittsfield, Mass., 1993-98, counsel intellectual property, 1998—; cons. dept. chemistry Tulane U., New Orleans, 1970-75. Advisor Jr. Achievement, Baton Rouge, 1971; sec. Baton Rouge Orchid Soc., 1983, Bartlesville Gifted and Talented, 1989; vestry St. Stephen's, Pittsfield, 1999—. NDEA trainee, Tulane U., New Orleans, 1965-67, NASA fellow, 1967-69. Fellow Am. Inst. Chemists (profl. rels. com. 1991, 92, patents com. 1992); mem. Am. Chem. Soc. (program chmn. petroleum div. 1976-77, Snyder award Legal Ethics 1998), Licensing Execs. Soc., Assn. Univ. Tech. Mgrs., N.Y. Acad. Sci., Sigma Xi. Episcopalian. Achievements include 20 patents; preparation and determination of crystal structure of (211) phase of 123 superconductors; invention of randomly cross-linked smectites, of high surface area supported perovskite catalysts and method for preparation; selective auto exhaust catalysts; theory of finely divided metals; bonding model for zerovalent acetylene and olefin complexes; fluidized catalytic cracking catalysts, sulfur tolerant catalytic reforming. Office: GE Plastics One Plastics Ave Pittsfield MA 01201

WHELAN, JAMES ROBERT, communications executive, international trade and investment consultant, author, educator, mining executive; b. Buffalo, July 27, 1933; s. Robert and Margaret (Southard) W.; children from previous marriage: Robert J., Heather Elizabeth; m. Guadalupe Aguirre, 1990. Student, U. Buffalo, 1951-53, U. R.I., 1955-57; BA, Fla. Internat. U., 1974. Staff corr., fgn. corr., country mgr., divsn. mgr. UPI, Buffalo, 1952-53; staff corr., fgn. corr., country mgr., div. mgr. UPI, Providence, 1955-57, Boston, 1957-58, Buenos Aires, Argentina, 1958-61, Caracas, Venezuela, 1961-66, San Juan, P.R., 1966, 68; regional dir. corp. rels., then v.p. ops. ITT World Directories, ITT, San Juan, 1968-70; Latin Am. corr. Scripps-Howard Newspaper Alliance, Washington, 1970-71; mng. editor Miami (Fla.) News, 1971-73; free-lance writer, 1973-74; pres., editor, pub. Hialeah (Fla.) Pub. Co., 1975-77; v.p., editl. dir. Panax Corp., Washington, 1977-80; v.p., editor Sacramento Union, 1980-82; editor, pub. Washington Times, 1982-84; mng. dir. CBN News, 1985-86; pres. Capital Comm. Internat., 1986—; editor-in-chief Conservative Digest, 1988-89; vice chmn. Inter-Am. Found., Arlington, Va., 1991-94; external affairs advisor Inter-Am. Investment Corp., 1992-93; dir. strategic planning Cocetel Holding, Santiago, Chile, 1993-94; pres. Minera Silver Standard S.A., 1994—, Silver Std., Mex., 1995—; free-lance writer; scholar World Assn. Internat. Studies, Stanford U., 1999—; vis. prof. Polit. Sci. Inst., U. Chile, 1993-95; assoc. prof. Finis Terrae U., 1993—; adj. prof. U. Md., 1992-93; guest lectr. ednl. instns., including Boston U., U. Miami, Ctrl. U. Venezuela, Cath. U., Andrés Bello U., Chile, U. Chile, U. Tex., Austin, U. Concepcion, U. Santiago; guest prof. U. Fla., 1973. Author: Through the American Looking Glass; Central America's Crisis, 1980, Allende: Death of a Marxist Dream, 1981, Catastrophe in the Caribbean: The Failure of America's Human Rights Policy in Central America, 1984, The Soviet Assault on America's Southern Flank, 1988, Out of the Ashes: Life, Death and Transfiguration of Democracy in Chile, 1833-1988, 1989, Hunters in the Sky, 1991, Desde las Cenizas: Vida, Muerte y Transfiguracion de la Democracia en Chile, 1833-1988, 1993, 2nd edit., 1995. Bd. dirs. Christian Community Service Agy., Miami, 1973, Hialeah-Miami Springs (Fla.) C. of C., 1976-77, Wolf Trap Found., 1984-87; bd. dirs. Nat. Council for Better Edn.; chmn. print media div. United Way campaign, Sacramento, 1981; bd. govs. Council on Nat. Policy, Washington, 1981-87; del. Commn. of Californias, 1981; chmn. Council for Inter-Am. Security Ednl. Inst., 1986-90; mem. spl. task force on pub. safety Greater Washington Bd. Trade; mem. Nat. Commn. on Free and Responsible Media, 1983-84; bd. dirs. Nat. Bus. Consortium for Gifted and Talented Children, 1985-87; bd. govs. Internat. Policy Forum, 1985—; mem. Presdl. Bd. Fgn. Scholarships (Fulbright Commn.), 1986-92, exec. planning com., 1987-92. With Signal Corps U.S. Army, 1953-55. Nieman fellow Harvard U., 1966-67; recipient citation of excellence Overseas Press Club, 1971, Unity award Lincoln U., 1976, Golden Press award Am. Legion Aux., 1977, Freedom award Valley Forge Found., 1981, Bernardo O'Higgins award Chilean Govt., 1990, presented at Chilean Embassy by Amb. Octavio Errazuriz. Mem. Nat. Press Club, Overseas Press Club, Univ. Club (Washington), Georgetown Club, Cosmos Club, Harvard Club (N.Y.C.), Club de Ofcls. de Fuerza Aerea (Santiago), Club Militar Lo Curro (Santiago), Instituto O'Higginiano de Chile. Home: Orquideas 163-Bugambilias, Saltillo Coahuila 25296, Mexico

WHELAN, RAYMOND E., educator, researcher; b. Syracuse, N.Y., July 8, 1941; s. Maurice P. Whelan and Anne J. King; m. Chantal Le Sage, Dec. 30, 1979. MA in Eng., Pitts. State U., 1970; MA in French, U. Kans., 1977, PhD in French, 1985. Asst. vis. prof. Ind. Purdue U., Fort Wayne, Ind., 1985-86; asst. prof. Barton Coll., Wilson, N.C., 1986-90; assoc. prof. Barton Coll., Wilson, 1990—; dir. academics U. Colo., Bordeaux, France, 1983-84, Academic Alliance, Wilson, N.C., 1987-93; bd. mem. Aid to Haitian Immigrants, Wilson, 1987-89. Editor Chimères, 1979-85. Mem. Crawford County Comprehensive Health Planning Commn., Pitts., Kans., 1968-75; gov. bd. Crawford County Mental Health Coun., Pitts., Kans., 1971-75. Burzle fellow U. Kans., Lawrence, 1983; scholar U. Kans., 1976, U. Clermont-Ferrand, France, 1977-78. Mem. AAUP, Am. Assn. Tchrs. French, Sigma Tau Delta, Pi Delta Phi. Avocations: tennis, boating, skiing, opera. E-mail: rwhelan@barton.edu. Home: 504 Monticello Dr NW Wilson NC 27893-1638 Office: Barton Coll College Station Wilson NC 27893

WHELESS, JAMES WARREN, neurologist; b. Glens Falls, N.Y., Apr. 18, 1956; s. True and Adelphine Ada (Bump) W.; m. Annette Carolyn Hyland, Apr. 7, 1984; children: Catherine Elizabeth, Margaret Caroline. BS, U. Okla., Oklahoma City, 1978, MD, 1982. Diplomate Am. Bd. Pediatrics, Am. Bd. Psychiatry and Neurology with spl. qualification in child neurology, with spl. qualification in clin. neurophysiology. Intern, then pediatric resident U. Okla.-Tulsa Med. Coll., 1982-85; fellow in child neurology Northwestern U., Chgo., 1985-88; fellow in clin. neurophysiology/epilepsy Med. Coll. Ga., Augusta, 1988-89; asst. prof. neurology and pediatrics U. Tex., Houston, 1989-95, dir. epilepsy monitoring unit, 1989—, assoc. prof. neurology and pediatrics, 1995-2000, prof. neurology in pediats., 2000—; dir., dir. pedia. epilepsy sect., head clin. EEG Tex. Comprehensive Epilepsy Program, 1998—; exec. bd. internat. epilepsy consortium Nat. Tuberous Sclerosis Assn. Contbr. articles to profl. jours., chpt. to book; mem. editl. bd.: Jour. of Child Neurology, The Stroke Interventionalist, Formulary. Camp physician Kamp Kleidoscope, Livingston, Tex., 1995—; mem. profl. bd. Nat. Tuberous Sclerosis Assn., Citizens United for Rsch. in Epilepsy; mem. exec. bd. Internat. Epilepsy Consortium. Pres.'s Fund grantee U. Tex.-Houston, 1990, Children's Miracle Network Telethon grantee Hermann Children's Hosp.; rsch. grantee NIH. Fellow Am. Acad. Neurology, Child Neurology Soc.; mem. AMA, Am. Epilepsy Soc., Am. Acad. Pediatrics, Epilepsy Assn. of Houston/Gulf Coast (chmn. profl. adv. bd. 1992-94). Avocations: running, camping, hiking, travel, reading. Office: U Tex-Houston Dept Neurology 6431 Fannin St Ste 7044 Houston TX 77030-1501

WHELPTON, JOHN FRANCIS, English language educator; b. Nottingham, Eng., Mar. 24, 1950; s. John Herbert and Florence Elizabeth (Cook) W.; m. Rita Shuk Fun Chui, Dec. 19, 1992. BA with honors, Trinity Coll., Oxford, Eng., 1972, MA, 1975; Diploma Teaching English Overseas, Manchester (Eng.) U., 1986; PhD, Sch. Oriental/African Studies, London, 1987; MA, U. Hong Kong, 1998. Lectr. English Tribhuvan U., Kathmandu, Nepal, 1972-74; adminstrn. trainee Ministry of Def., London, 1975-78, higher exec. officer, 1978-81; tchr. English Kiangsu-Chekiang Coll., Hong Kong, 1987-91, Cheung Sha Wan Cath. Sec. Sch., Hong Kong, 1991-96; lectr. English, Hong Kong Tech. Coll., 1996-97; tchr. English, Bapt. Lui Ming Choi Secondary Sch., Hong Kong, 1997—. Author: Kings, Soldiers and Priests: Nepalese Politics and the Rise of Jang Bahadur Rana, 1830-1857, 1991; co-author: People, Politics and Ideology: Democracy and Social Change in Nepal, 1999; translator/editor: Jang Bahadur in Europe, 1983; compiler (annotated bibliography) Nepal, 1990; editor, contbr.: Nationalism and Ethnicity in a Hindu Kingdom, 1997; editor South Asia Rsch., 1982-87, corres. editor, 1987—; corr. European Bull. of Himalayan Rsch., 1995—. Asst. field officer Vol. Svc., Nepal, 1974. Mem. Assn. Asian Studies, Nepal Studies Assn., Britain-Nepal Soc. Avocations: reading, music, hill walking. Home and Office: Flat D 18/F Block 5, Sceneway Garden, Lam Tin Kowloon, Hong Kong

WHETTEN, JOHN D., food products executive; b. Chgo., June 8, 1940; s. Lester and Kate (Allred) W.; m. Becky Pearse; children: Carma, Rebecca, Mary Coza. BS, Brigham Young U., 1965; MBA, U. Calif., Berkeley, 1967. Advt. and mktg. mgr. The Clorox Corp., Oakland, Calif., 1967-79; pres., CEO Challenge Dairy Products, Inc., Dublin, Calif., 1982—; CEO Dairy-America, Inc., Dublin, Calif., 1995-98; U.S. rep. Internat. Dairy Mktg. and Promotion Ann. Meeting, 1996. Co-chair U.S. Butter Task Force, 1990-97; bd. dirs. U.S. Diry Export Coun., 1995-98, Epidermolysis Bullosa Med. Rsch. Found., 1991—; mem. nat. steering com. Brigham Young U. Sch. Mgmt., 1992-95. Mem. Am. Butter Inst. (bd. dirs. 1982—, v.p. 1995-99, pres. 1999—, Pres.'s Disting. Svc. award 1991), Am. Dairy Products Inst. (bd. dirs. 1982-98, hon. life dir. 1999—), Dairy Export Incentive Program Coalition (pres. 1994—), Dairy Mktg. Coop. Fedn. (pres. 1992—), Barbecue Industry Assn. (dir. 1974-79, pres. 1977-78), Western Assn. Milk Mktg. Coop. (bd. dirs. 1992—, sec. 1994—). Office: Challenge Dairy Products Inc 11875 Dublin Blvd Ste B230 Dublin CA 94568-2818

WHILDIN, LEONORA PORRECA, nurse midwife, nursing; b. Boston, Mass., Dec. 7, 1926; d. John and Anna (Annunziata) Porreca; m. William Miller Whildin; children: Susan Lee, Robert Miller, Walter Thomas. BS, Boston U., 1954; MS, Columbia U., 1971. RN, Mass., N.Y., N.J.; cert. nurse midwife, N.Y. Cadet nurse corps. Boston City Hosp., 1943-46, staff, asst. head nurse neurology, neurosurgery, 1946-48, scrub nurse neurosurgery, 1948-50; civilian nurse Dept. of Army, Bremerhaven, Germany, 1948; pub. health nurse Bklyn. Vis. Nurse Assn., 1954-56; instr. Helene Fulde Sch. of Practical Nursing, N.Y.C., 1956-57; pub. health nurse V.N.A. Morris Co., Morristown, N.J., 1967; instr. All Souls Hosp. Sch. of Nursing, Morristown, N.J., 1968-69; guest lectr. Seton Hall U., South Orange, N.J., 1978; del. Am. Nurses Assn, Mass., 1954; By-Laws Com. Am. Coll. Nurse Midwives, N.Y., 1972, By-Laws Com. Am. Coll. Nurse Midwives (N.J. chpt.), 1980; bd. mem. V.N.A. Morris Co., Morristown, N.J., 1977-78; v.p. bd. health, Randolph Twp., Randolph, N.J., 1972-74. Coun. woman Randolph Twp., 1972-78; mayor (1st woman mayor) Randolph Twp., 1977; Dem. party county com., Morris Co., Morristown, N.J., 1972-96; Dem. party state com., N.J., 1992-98; vol. United Way of Morris County. Mem. APHA, ANA, LWV, Mass., N.Y., N.J. (bd. mem. 1964-66), Sigma Theta Tau. Democrat. Avocations: ice skating, knitting, crafts, baking. Home: 82 Radtke Rd Randolph NJ 07869-3815

WHINERY, MICHAEL ALBERT, physician; b. Watsford, Eng., June 30, 1951; s. Leo Howard and Doris Eileene W. and Alma Piper; m. Tatijana Dunnebier, 1976 (dec. Jan. 1981); m. Judy Renee Wright, Apr. 30, 1982; children: Rhiannon Daire Eileene, Terron Rae Lee. BS, Okla. U., 1976; D of Osteopathy, Okla. State U., 1980. Bd. cert. physician in gen. practice & family practice. Intern Hillcrest Health Ctr., Oklahoma City, Okla., 1980-81; with McLoud Clinic, McLoud, Okla., 1981-98; staff physician Okla. Vets. Ctr., Claremont, Okla., 2000—; house physician McLoud Nursing Ctr., 1988—; med. examiner Pottawatomie County Health, McLoud, 1983—; staff physician Claremore divsn. Okla. Vet.'s Ctr., 2000. Author: Poetic Voices of America, 1991; composer (recorded song) At Stella Gospel, 1993. Mem. Presdl. Order Merit Nat. Repub. Senatorial Com., Washington, 1991, Presdl. Task Force, 1983—, Senatorial Commn. Repub. Senatorial Inner Circle, Washington, 1991; mem. U.S. Congrl. Adv. Bd., 1993. With USMC, Vietnam. Recipient Acknowledgement of Outstanding Contbn. in Clin. Rsch. award SANDOZ Labs., 1992, Rep. Presdl. Legion of Merit, 1994, Rep. Majority medal, U.S. Senate, 1997, Rep. Task Force medal of merit, 1997. Mem. Am. Legion, C. of C., Jr. C. of C., U.S. Senatorial Club (preferred mem.), U.S. Congressional Act Bd. (state advisor 1990-91). Baptist. Avocations: fishing, music, composing. Office: PO Box 988 3001 W Bluestarr Claremont OK 74018

WHIPPLE, WILLIAM, JR., engineering consultant, writer; b. Cinclare, La., Feb. 4, 1909; s. William and Genevieve (Randolph) W.; m. Dixie Ancrum, Mar. 30, 1935 (dec. Oct. 1955); children: Anne Calhoun, William III, Claire Randolph; m. Renée Pauline Exiga, July 21, 1956 (div. May 1974); 1 child, Philip; m. Frances Edith Cheek, June 1, 1974 (dec. July 1983); m. Alice Terry Goodloe, Dec. 1, 1984. BS, U.S. Mil. Acad., 1930; BA, Oxford (Eng.) U., 1933, MA, 1937; Civil Engr., Princeton U., 1936. Registered profl. engr., N.J. Commd. 2d lt. Corps Engrs., U.S. Army, 1930, advanced through grades to brig. gen., ret., 1960; chief engr. N.Y. World's Fair Corp., Flushing Meadow, N.Y., 1960-64; pvt. practice cons. engr. N.Y.C., 1964-65; dir. Water Resources Rsch. Inst. Rutgers U., New Brunswick, N.J., 1965-79, rsch. prof. Coastal and Environ. Inst., 1979-81; asst. dir. divsn. water resources Dept. Environ. Protection, Trenton, N.J., 1981-89, coord. nonpoint cource control program divsn. water resource, 1989-90; prin. Greeley Polhemus Group, Chester, Pa., 1990-2000; pvt. practice cons. Princeton, N.J., 1999—. Author: New Perspectives on Water Supply, 1994, Comprehensive Water Planning and Regulation, 1996, Water Resource: A New Era for Coordination, 1998; contbr. articles to publs. on water resources. Chmn. Flood Control Com., Princeton, N.J., 1975-81. Recipient Trustees award N.J. inst. Tech., 1985, govt. award Water Resource Assn. of Delaware River Basin, 1987, Toulmin award for best articles Mil. Engr., 1975, Formal Commendation from Pres. of U.S., 1971. Fellow AAAS, ASCE (life, chmn. urban water resources rsch. coun. 1973-75), Soc. Am. Mil. Engrs. (life), Am. Water Resources Assn. (pres. 1993, Icko Iben award 1978, William Ackerman medal 1989, Boggess award); mem. Am. Acad. Environ. Engrs. (diplomate), Univs. Coun. on Water Resources (chmn. 1976-78), Sigma Xi. Avocations: tennis, walking with dog, history and biography. Home and Office: 395 Mercer Rd Princeton NJ 08540-4805

WHIPPLE, WILLIAM PERRY, foundation administrator; b. Cedar Rapids, Iowa, Nov. 1, 1913; s. Robert Milo and Jeanette (Fry) W.; m. Gayle Schroeder, Sept. 18, 1937; children: John William, Robert Milo. BA, Coe Coll., 1935, hon. doctorate, 1996. Prin. Whipple Ins. Agy., Cedar Rapids, 1935-57; pres. Whipple and Winterberg, Cedar Rapids, 1957-71; chmn. Frank B. Hall of Iowa, Inc., Cedar Rapids, 1971-74; pres. Hall Found., Inc., Cedar Rapids, 1974-95, also bd. dirs.; chair Hall-Perrine Found., Cedar Rapids, 1995—; exec. in residence Colo. State U., Fort Collins, 1973; bd. dirs. Fire Mark Cir. of Ams., Chamblee, Ga., Interocean Reins. Corp., Cedar Rapids, 1st Fed. Savs. and Loan, Cedar Rapids, Nissen Corp., Cedar Rapids, 1966-72, Banks of Iowa, Inc., Des Moines, 1982-85. Trustee Cedar Rapids Pub. Library, Coe Coll., chmn.; hon. bd. dirs. Methwick Manor, Cedar Rapids, Linn County ARC, Greater Cedar Rapids Found. Recipient Outstanding Layman award YMCA, Cedar Rapids, 1986, Alumni Achievement award, Coe Coll., 1990, First Community Svc. award, Cedar Rapids Rotary, 1993. Mem. Rotary (Paul Harris fellow 1987), Elks. Republican. Presbyterian. Avocations: signevierist, stamp collecting. Home: 1224 13th St NW Cedar Rapids IA 52405-2404 Office: Hall-Perrine Found 115 3d St SE Cedar Rapids IA 52401-1222

WHISHER, BRADLEY EDWARD, insurance company executive; b. Plattsburg, N.Y., Nov. 4, 1954; s. Floyd Edward and Angeline (Molinero) W.; children: Lindsay L., Kimberly A., Bradley E. Jr. BSBA, Ithaca Coll., 1976; student, Am. Coll., Bryn Mawr, Pa., 1991—. CLU, chartered fin. cons. Asst. mgr., sales rep. Prudential Ins. Co., Albany, N.Y., 1976-80; asst. mgr., cons. Home Life Ins. Co., Albany, N.Y., 1980-86; mgr. life and fin. svcs. Jardine Ins. Brokers Inc., Schenectady, N.Y., 1986; pres. Bradley E. Whisher Co., Albany, N.Y., 1992—; mem. pension adv. com., St. Clare's Hosp. Found., Schnectady; registered rep. Nothen & Lewis Securities, 1986—. Bd. dirs. St. Clare's Hosp. Found., Schenectady, 1989—; past pres. Schenectady chpt. Am. Cancer Soc., sec., 1996—. Mem. Nat. Assn. Life Unerwriters, Am. Soc. CLU, Internat. Assn. Fin. Planners, Million Dollar Round Table (honor roll), Rotary (chmn. Niskayuna Hank Whisher track meet 1991—). Avocations: skiing, hunting, fishing, boating. Home: 209 Stoker Ridge Dr Niskayuna NY 12309 Office: 3 Wembley Sq Ste 104 Albany NY 12205-3836

WHISNAND, REX JAMES, association executive; b. Van Nuys, Calif., Jan. 2, 1948; s. Harold Theodore Whisnand and Laura Fay Brigham Whisnand Brown; m. Cathy Ladeane Bennett, Apr. 1, 1978; 1 child, Bryce James. BS in Agrl. Bus. Mgmt., Calif. Poly State U., San Luis Obispo, 1970; BSBA, Calif. State U., Sacramento, 1976; MPA in Housing Adminstrn., U. San Francisco, 1985; grad., U.S. Naval Submarine Sch., New London, Conn., 1972, Stanford U., 1992; EdD, U. San Francisco, 2000. Generalist W & W Hardware Store, Orcutt, Calif., 1964-70; state park ranger Calif. Dept. Parks and Recreation, Lompoc and Sacramento, 1969-75; exec. asst. Constrn. Industry Legis. Coun., Sacramento, 1974-75; dir. assn. svcs. Bldg. Industry Assn. Superior Calif., Sacramento, 1976-79; exec. v.p. West Bay divsn. Bldg. Industry Assn. No. Calif., Redwood City, 1980-84; exec. v.p. Bldg. Industry Assn., Tacoma/Pierce County, 1984-86; supr. Lumberjack Store, Lodi, Calif., 1988-90; exec. v.p. Rental Housing Owners Assn. of So. Alameda County, Hayward, Calif., 1990-96; field rep. Am. Housing Survey, 1997-98, crew leader Census 2000, 1999; exec. peninsula dist. Boy Scouts Am., 1999—; mem. com. Calif. Bldg. Industry Assn., Sacramento, 1976-84; mem. exec. officers coun., local govt. com. Calif. Apt. Assn., 1991-96; mem. Alameda County Housing Rsch. Adv. Bd., Hayward, Calif., 1990-93; bd. dirs. Pacific Bay Fed. Credit Union, 1993-96, Credit Union Execs. Soc., Internat. Credit Assn., Pronet; adj. faculty U. San Francisco; guest svc. rep. Oakland Athletics, Oakland Raiders, Golden State Warriors, 1997-00; field ops. supr. Census 2000. Editor Pierce County Builder, 1984-86 (Assn. Achievement awards Nat. Assn. Home Builders 1984, 85), Superior California Builder Mag., 1978-80. Active 20-30 Club Internat. #1, Sacramento, 1976-80, officer, 1981-82; mem. South Sacramento Area Cmty. Planning Adv. Bd., 1978-79; grad. Pleasanton Leadership, 1995; chmn. Coastside Coalition for Safe Hwys., Half Moon Bay, 1983-84; bd. congregations Family Emergency Shelter Coalition Alameda County, 1995-96; mem. Pleasanton Gen. Plan Econ./Fiscal Growth Com., 1994-96, Bay Area Indsl. Edn. Coun., 1995-96, Hayward Coalition for Youth, 1995-96; officer Half Moon Bay C. of C., 1982-84; cert. basketball coach Nat. Youth Sports Assn., 1994-97. With USNR, 1970-76 , U.S. Army, N.G., 1990-92. Named Outstanding Young Man in Am., Jr. C. of C., Foster City, Calif., 1983. Mem. Internat. Assn. Bus. Communicators (pres. Sacramento chpt. 1979, pres. Peninsula chpt. 1981), Am. Soc. Assn. Execs. (cert.), No. Calif. Soc. Assn. Execs. (bd. dirs. 1994-97, com. chmn. 1993-95), Pleasanton C. of C. (econ. devel. com. 1990-96), Wash. State Home Builders Assn. (pres. exec. officers coun. 1985), Western Conf. Assn. Execs. (mem. com. 1995-96), Hayward C. of C. (govt. rels. coun. 1990-95), Calif. Vocat. Indsl. Clubs Am. (bd. dirs. 1977-80), Calif. Polytech. Alumni Assn., World Future Soc., Alpha Gamma Rho (charter, com. chair 1969-99). Episcopalian. Avocation: dog training, genealogy, coaching Little League baseball. Home: 5435 Black Ave Ste 3 Pleasanton CA 94566-5966

WHITACRE, EDWARD E., JR., telecommunications executive; b. Ennis, Tex., Nov. 4, 1941. BS in Indsl. Engring., Tex. Tech U., 1964. With Southwestern Bell Telephone Co., 1963-85; various positions in ops. depts. Tex., Ark., Kans.; pres. Kans. divsn. Topeka, 1982-85; group pres. Southwestern Bell Corp., 1985-86; v.p. revenues and pub. affairs, vice-chmn., chief fin. officer Southwestern Bell Corp., St. Louis, 1986-88, pres., COO, 1988-89, chmn., CEO, 1990—, also bd. dirs.; bd. dirs. Anheuser-Busch Cos., Inc., May Dept. Stores Co., Emerson Electric Co., Burlington No. Santa Fe, Inc.; with Learning Nat. Adv. Bd. Bd. regents Tex. Tech. U. and Health Scis., Lubbock; nat. pres. Boy Scouts Am.; trustee com. econ. devel. State N.Y., S.W. Rsch. Inst.; bd. govs. S.W. Found. Biomed. Rsch.; mem. govs. bus. coun. State of Tex.; chmn. campaign United Way, San Antonio, 1998. Recipient Internat. Citizen of Yr. award World Affairs Coun. San Antonio, 1997, Spirit of Achievement award Nat. Jewish Med. and Rsch. Ctr., 1998, Freeman award San Antonio C. of C., 1998; named to Tex. Bus. Hall of Fame, 1997. Presbyterian. Office: SBC Communications Inc 175 E Houston St San Antonio TX 78205-2255

WHITAKER, C. BRUCE, postal worker; b. Asheville, N.C., Oct. 28, 1953; s. Clyde Maskel and Elizabeth (Ingle) W. BA, U. N.C., 1974. Machine operator Beacon Mfg. Co., Swannanoa, N.C., 1974-76; coord. Eaton-Cutler Hammer, Arden, N.C., 1976-81; customer svc. rep. U.S. Postal Svc., Asheville, 1981—; bd. dirs. Cane Creek Cemetery, Fairview, N.C. Author: The Whitaker Family NC, 1989; newspaper columnist The Fairview Town Crier, 1999—; contbr. articles to profl. jours. Registrar Buncombe County Bd. Election, Swannanoa, 1977-85; election supervisor Swannanoa Fire Dept., 1980-83; libr. vol. Old Buncombe County Genealog. Soc., Asheville, 1981-89; dept. sec. First Bapt. Ch., Swannanoa, 1974-80, 86—; Sunday sch. dir. 1st Bapt. Ch., Swannanoa, 1999—; vice chmn. Fairview Rep. Party, 1999—. Recipient Family History Book award N.C. Soc. of Historians, 1989, Foster Sondley award Old Buncombe County Genealog. Soc., 1989. Mem. Cane Creek Cemetery Assn. (treas. 1985—), Blue Ridge N.C. SAR (chpt. genealogist 1998—). Republican. Southern Baptist. Avocations: genealogy, stamp collecting, antique collecting, travel, gardening. Home: 661 Old Fort Rd Fairview NC 28730-9522 Office: US Postal Svc 1302 Patton Ave Asheville NC 28806-2604

WHITAKER, CYNTHIA ELLEN, managed healthcare consultant; b. Dearborn, Mich., June 15, 1948; d. John Harold and Marion Violet (Malmsten) Fields; m. Elbert Charles Whitaker, Sept. 7, 1968; children: Shannon Kaye, Kaycee Susan. ADN, Oakland C.C., Union Lake, Mich., 1982; BSN, U. Mich., 1985. RN, Calif.; cert. case mgr. Nurse Wheelock Meml. Hosp., Goodrich, Mich., 1982-86; clin. nursing instr. Oakland C.C., Union Lake, Mich., 1985-86; rehab. nurse Continental Ins.-UAC, Southfield, Mich., 1987-88; med. mgmt. cons. Continental Rehab. Resources, Sacramento, 1988-89; founder, former pres. RNS Healthcare Cons., Inc., Sacramento, 1989-99; prin. C. Whitaker & Assoc., 1999—; spkr. in field; mem. core task force Coun. for Case Mgmt. Accountability; vice chair case mgmt. adv. bd. Am. Accreditation Healthcare Commn./Utilization Rev. Accreditation Commn., Washington, 1998-99. Co-author: (book) Infectious Disease Handbook, 1981, (booklet) Standards of Practice for Case Management, 1995; contbr. articles to profl. jours. Mem. adv. bd. grad. sch. nursing San Francisco State U., 1994-99; mem. cmty. adv. bd. Mercy Healthcare Sacramento, 1993-95, Kentfield (Calif.) Rehab. Hosp., 1993-96, North Valley Rehab. Hosp., Chico, Calif., 1991-93. Dean's Fellow Scholarship awardee U. Mich., 1986. Mem. Am. Assn. Legal Nurse Cons., Case Mgmt. Soc. Am. (co-founder No. Calif. chpt., affiliate dir. 1993-95, affiliate pres. 1992-93, nat. sec. 1995-96, nat. pres. 1997-98), Case Mgmt. Soc. Internat. (bd. dirs. 1996-98). Republican. Avocations: international travel, swimming, snow skiing, reading, hiking. Fax: 508-302-0247. E-mail: cwhitrns@aol.com. Address: 1601 NW 97th Ave PO Box 25216 Miami FL 33102-5216

WHITAKER, FOREST, actor, director, producer; b. Longview, Tex., July 15, 1961. Student voice, U. So. Calif. Pres. Spirit Dance Entertainment. Stage appearances (London) Swan, Romeo and Juliet, Hamlet, Ring Around the Moon, Craig's Wife, Whose Life Is It Anyway?, The Greeks; other stage appearances include Patchwork Shakespeare, Beggar's Opera, Jesus Christ Superstar; TV appearances include Amazing Stories, Hill Street Blues, Cagney and Lacey, Trapper John, M.D., The Fall Guy, Different Strokes; TV movies Hands of a Stranger, 1987, Criminal Justice, 1990, Last Light, 1993, Rebound: The Legend of Earl "The Great" Manigault, 1996, The Split, 1998, (TV) Witness Protection, 1999, Light It Up, 1999, Ghost Dog, 1999, Four Dogs Playing Poker, 1999; mini-series North & South, Parts I and II; films: Fast Times at Ridgemont High, 1982, Vision Quest, 1985, The Color of Money, 1986, Platoon, 1986, Stakeout, 1987, Good Morning, Vietnam, 1987, Bloodsport, 1988, Bird, 1988 (best actor Cannes Festival 1988), Johnny Handsome, 1989, Downtown, 1990, (also co-prodr.) Rage in Harlem, 1991, Article 99, 1992, Diary of a Hit Man, 1992, Consenting Adults, 1992, Body Snatchers, 1993, The Crying Game, 1993, Blown Away, 1994, Jason's Lyric, 1994, Prêt-à-Porter, 1994, Species, 1995, Smoke, 1995, Phenomenon, 1996, The Split, 1997, Four Dogs Playing Poker, 1999, Battlefield Earth, 2000; dir.: (films) Strapped (Toronto Film Festival award for best new dir.), Waiting to Exhale, 1995, Hope Floats, 1998; dir., exec. prodr.: (TV pilot) Black Jaq, 1998. Office: care DGA 7920 W Sunset Blvd Los Angeles CA 90046-3300

WHITAKER, HEIDI SUE, accountant, auditor, information systems specialist; b. Framingham, Mass., Sept. 21, 1964; d. Charles Harvey and Judith R. (Reich) Whitaker; m. Raymond Severian, Oct. 8, 1988 (div. Dec. 1997); 1 child, William Michael. BS in Acctg., BS in Mgmt. Info. Sys., U. Ariz., 1987; Master Cert. in Info. Tech. Project Mgmt, George Washington U., 1999. Acctg. clk. Inventory Auditors, Inc., Denver, 1984; leasing and adminstrv. asst. James Presley Co., Tucson, 1985-86; office mgr. Sid's Appliance and TV, Tucson, 1986; assoc. acct., acct. GTE Calif., Thousand Oaks, Calif., 1987-89; auditor I and II GTE Svc. Corp., Westlake Village, Calif., 1989-91, sr. auditor, 1991-94; staff acct., staff adminstr. regulatory acctg. GTE Telephone Ops., Irving, Tex., 1994-96; bus. process specialist sys. GTE Long Distance, Irving, 1996-97; program mgr. info. tech. GTE Bus. Devel. and Integration, Irving, 1997-99; IT audit mgr. EXCEL Comms., Inc., 1999-2000, sr. IT audit mgr., 2000—; mem. Project Mgmt. Inst., 1996—. Sec. bd. dirs. Congregation Kol Ami, 1997-98, sisterhood pres., 1997-99, chmn. reengring. com., 1997-99, treas. bd. dirs., 1999—; chair Highland Village Balloon Fest Stage Entertainment, 1998-99. Mem. Inst. Mgmt. Accts. (CMA), Inst. Internal Auditors, Lions (Lionette 1990-95, tail twister Flower Mound 1996-98, pres. Highland Village 1999-2000). Avocations: arts and crafts, word puzzles, reading. Office: Excel Comms Inc 8750 N Central Expy Ste 1600 Dallas TX 75231-6436

WHITAKER, MARSHA JONES, author, educator; b. Balt., Nov. 12, 1959; d. Arthur John Jones Jr. and Joyce Irene Jones Smith; m. Marvin J. Whitaker Sr., May 31, 1991; 1 child, Marvin J. Jr. AA, U. Md., 1985, BS, 1996. Coord., legal writer State of Md., Office of State's Atty., Balt., 1986—; owner, prin. Learning By Reading Inc., Balt., 1998—. Author, editor: Marvin's Adventure in the Owl, 1997, Marvin's Adventures in the Talking, 1997, Marvin's Adventures in the Universe, 1998, Marvin's Adventures in Learning About Cells, 2000. Recipient Editor's Choice award Nat. Libr. of Poetry, 1995, 96, 97, 98, Golden Apple award Balt. Pub. Schs., 1998. Democrat. Avocations: writing poetry, books, lyrics, music.

WHITAKER, PERNELL (SWEET PEA WHITAKER), professional boxer; b. Jan. 2, 1964. Olympic Gold Medalist, boxing, lightweight divsn. L.A., 1984; lightweight champion Internat. Boxing Fedn., 1989; jr. lightweight champion World Boxing Coun., welterweight champion, 1993-97; lightweight champion World Boxing Assn., 1990, middleweight champion, 1995. Recipient Gold medal boxing lightweight divsn. Olympics, 1984; named pound for pound best boxer in the world Ring Mag., 1995, winner record 6 world championship titles in 4 weight classes, 1995. Office: care Main Events 390 Murray Hill Pkwy East Rutherford NJ 07073-2109*

WHITAKER, REGINALD PERCY, educator; b. Bristol, England, Oct. 17, 1943; s. Percy Reginald and Ethel Ada (Renee) W. B in Technology, Loughborough U., 1968; BA, Open U., 1994. Arch. asst. N.J. Garner, Jersey, Eng., 1966-67; handicraft tchr. Inner London Ednl. Authority, 1971; horticulturist Jersey, Eng, 1979-83; math. tchr. Columberie House, Jersey, 1980-81; ret., 1985. Traffic warden Parish of St. Helier, Jersey, England, 1964; civil servant States of Jersey, 1973. With Brit. Mil., 1964. Grantee States of Jersey, 1963-68, Dept. of Edn. and Sci., 1969-70; Howard Davis scholar, 1971-72. Mem. Brit. Legion, Jersey Swimming Club (Bronze award 1979), Caesarean Cycling Club. Labour Party. Mem. Ch. of England. Avocations: studying mathematics, current affairs. Home: Val Plaisant, 3 Caesara Ct Windsor Rd, Saint Helier Jersey JE2 3YG, Channel Islands

WHITAKER, RUTH REED, retired newspaper editor; b. Blytheville, Ark., Dec. 13, 1936; d. Lawrence Neill and Ruth Shipton (Weidemeyer) Reed; m. Thomas Jefferson Whitaker, dec. 29, 1961; children: Steven Bryan, Alicia Morrow. BA, Hendrix Coll., 1958. Copywriter, weather person KTVE TV, El Dorado, Ark., 1958-59; nat. bridal cons. Treasure House, El Dorado, 1959; bridal cons. Pfeifers of Ark., Little Rock, 1959-60; dir. of continuity S. M. Brooks Advt. Agy., Little Rock, 1960-61; layout artist C. V. Mosby Co., St. Louis, 1961-62; editor, owner Razorback Am. Newspaper, Ft. Smith, Ark., 1979-81; ret., 1981. Host Crawford Conversations TV show; contbr. author indsl. catalog, 1979 (Addy award). State sec. Rep. Party of Ark., 1992-94, mem. Ark. Electoral Coll., 1996, del. Rep. Nat. Conv., 1996; mem. Ben Geren Regional Park Commn., Sebastian County, Ark., 1984-89, pres., 1990; past pres. Jr. Civic League; mem. Ft. Smith Orchid Com.; mem. com. of 21 United Way; publicity chmn. Sebastian County Rep. Com., 1983-84; state press officer Reagan-Bush Campaign, 1984; exec. dir. Ark. Dole for Pres., 1995-96; pres. Women's Aux. Sebastian County Med. Soc., 1974; mem. Razorback Scholarship Fund; class agt. alumni fund Hendrix Coll., 1990, 91, 92; mem. Sparks Woman's Bd.; 1st vice chmn. 3d Dist. Rep. Party; state committeewoman Rep. Party Ark.; chmn. Crawford County Rep. Com.; apptd. by Gov. of Ark. to Commr. Ark. Ednl. TV Network Commn., sec. 1998-99; mem. city coun., City of Cedarville, Ark., 1998. Recipient Disting. Vol. Leadership award Nat. Found. March of Dimes, 1973, Appreciation award Ft. Smith Advt. Fedn., 1977, 78, Hon. Parents of Yr. award U. Ark., 1984, Recognition award United Cerebral Palsy, 1980. Mem. AAUW, Alden Soc. Am. (life), Ft. Smith C. of C., Ark. Nature Conservancy, Am. Legion Aux., Frontier Rschrs. Soc. (pres. 1995-96), Daus. Union Vets. Presbyterian. Avocations: philanthropy, genealogy, writing, photography, ornithology. Home: PO Box 349 Cedarville AR 72932-0349

WHITAKER, SHIRLEY ANN, telecommunications company marketing executive; b. Asmara, Eritea, Ethiopia, Oct. 13, 1955; (parents Am. citizens); d. Calvin Randall and Ruth (Ganeles) Peck; m. John Marshall Whitaker, June 16, 1973; 1 child, Kathryn Ann. AA, Tacoma Community Coll., 1974; BA, Wash. State U., 1977, MBA, 1978. Planning adminstr. for econ. rsch. GTE NW, Everett, Wash., 1978-80; specialist in demand analysis western region GTE Svc. Corp., Los Gatos, Calif., 1980-81; fin. analyst GTE Svc. Corp., Stamford, Conn., 1981-83, staff specialist demand analysis and forecasting, 1983-84; group mgr. for rate devel. Nat. Exch. Carrier Assn., Whippany, N.J., 1984-87; mgr. pricing strategy and migration GTE Calif., Thousand Oaks, 1987-88; mgr. market forecasting GTE Telephone Ops. Hdqrs., Irving, Tex., 1989-90, dir. revenue analysis, 1990-92, dir. market rsch., 1992-93, dir. process re-engring., 1993-94, dir. network and resource mgmt., 1994-97; gen. sales mgr. customer contact GTE Network Svcs., Victorville, Calif., 1997—. Mem. Am. Mktg. Assn. (membership com. 1984), Beta Gamma Sigma, Phi Kappa Phi, Rotary (sec. Victorville chpt.). Avocation: sailing.

WHITAKER, THOMAS KENNETH, former university chancellor; b. Rostrevor, Ireland, Dec. 8, 1916; s. Edward and Jane (O'Connor) W.; m. Nora Fogarty; children: Kenneth, Gerald, Raymond, David, Catherine (dec.), Brian. MS in Econs., U. London, 1953; DEconSc, Nat. U. Ireland, Dublin, 1962; LLD (hon.), U. Dublin, 1976, Queen's U., Belfast, 1981; DSc (hon.), U. Ulster, 1983. Sec. irish Dept. Fin., 1956-69; gov. Ctrl. Bank Ireland, 1969-76; mem. Senate of Republic of Ireland, 1977-82, Coun. of State, 1991-98; dir. A. Guinness & Sons, 1976-84, Bank of Ireland, 1976-96; chancellor Nat. U. Ireland, Dublin, 1976-96; pres.Constitution Review Group, 1995-96. Author: Financing by Credit Creation, 1947, Interests, 1983; editor, contbg. author: Economic Development, 1958. Decorated Freeman of Drogheda (Ireland); comdr. Legion of Honor (France). Mem. Royal Irish Acad. (pres. 1985-87), Econ. and Social Rsch. Inst. (pres. 1970-87), Dublin Inst. Advaneed Studies (chmn. coun. 1980-95). Roman Catholic. Avocation: fishing.

WHITE, ALASDAIR ANTONY KENNETH, management consultant; b. Shifnal, Eng., May 24, 1952; s. Antony Hubert and Alexandrina Hilda Maclean (Earl) W.; m. Fiona Gillian MacLean, July 5, 1980; children: Riba Frances, Siobhan Diana. Diploma in engring., Farnborough Coll. Tech., Eng., 1971; cert. edn., King Alfred's Univ. Coll., Winchester, Eng., 1975. Mng. dir. Somos Deva Ltd., Eng., 1976-87; bus. devel. cons. Overseas Fin. Svcs., The Hague, The Netherlands, 1987-89; bus. devel. mgr. Citibank IPB, Amsterdam, The Netherlands, 1989-92; sr. exec. cons. Performance Mgmt. Solutions Ltd., St. Helier, Jersey, Channel Islands, 1992—; spkr. IBM European Tng. Ctr., La Hulpe, Belgium; lectr. Henley Mgmt. Coll.; faculty Am. Mgmt. Assn. Internat., Belgium; editor Hart Observer, Hampshire, Eng., 1984-85. Author: Managing for Performance, 1995, Continuous Quality Improvement, 1996, The Essential Guide to Developing Your Staff, 1998. Fellow Internat. Napoleonic Soc.; mem. Inst Dirs. (chmn. Belgium chpt. 1995—). Avocations: fly fishing, history, Battle of Waterloo. E-mail: alasdair.white@pm-solutions.com. Office: Performance Mgmt Solutions, 12 Hill St, Saint Helier Jersey, Channel Islands

WHITE, ALICE JUNE, retired educator; b. Oasis, Wis., June 22, 1905; d. Alfred Leroy and Florence Edna (Wilson) Leavitt; m. Gabriel Otto Anderson, July 8, 1933 (dec. 1972); children: Adeline Daniels, Alice Wilhyde, Amy Biggins; m. John Orville White, Feb. 28, 1987 (dec. 1997). BA, U. Oreg., 1965, MA, 1972. Missions tchr. Liberia, 1929-32; tchr. B.I.A. Chemawa Indian Sch., Salem, Oreg., 1966-81. Composer ballads and hymns like The Star That Shone; author, composer poems; contbr. articles to profl. publs. Mem. Oreg. Fedn. Rep. Women, 1983—. Mem. Oreg. State Poets' Assn. (Salem chpt., treas., mem. editorial bd. quarterly publ. 1985). Home: 2285 Rogers Ln NW Salem OR 97304-1004

WHITE, BONNIE HAVANA, retired federal agency official; b. Trammel, Va., Nov. 18, 1926; d. John Clark and Cordella (Burke) Holbrook; divorced; children: Jonnie, James, Sheila. BS, U. Md., 1988; postgrad., U. D.C., 1990. From libr. aide to examiner SEC, Washington, 1981-95, ret., 1995. Art docent Hirshhorn Mus., 1990; history docent Nat. Mus. Am. History, 1992—; mem. Commn. on People with Disabilities Program Under Montgomery County, 1999—. Mem. U. Md. Alumni Assn. Republican. Lutheran. Home: 10201 Grosvenor Pl Apt 1027 N Bethesda MD 20852-4696

WHITE, BRUCE DAVID, law and ethics educator, consultant; b. Elizabethton, Tenn., Jan. 10, 1951; s. Darold S. and Anna Ruth (Lewis) W.; m. Sarah Jo Pugh, Dec. 28, 1974; children: Sarah Elizabeth, Meredith Ruth, Rebecca Mae. BS in Pharmacy, U. Tenn., 1974, JD, 1976; DO, North Tex. State U., Tex. Coll. Osteo. Medicine, 1985. Bar: Tenn. 1977, U.S. Dist. Ct. (we. dist.) Tenn. 1979; diplomate Am. Bd. Pediats. Asst. prof. U. Tenn. Health Scis. Ctr., Memphis, 1977-81, assoc. prof., 1981; lectr. U. Miss., Oxford, 1980-81; asst. prof. North Tex. State U., Tex. Coll. Osteo. Medicine, Ft. Worth, 1981-85; ptnr. Swafford & White, Memphis, 1979-81; resident in pediats. U. Louisville, 1985-88; asst. prof. pediatrics. Meharry Med. Coll., 1988-93; asst. prof., asst. dir. Ctr. Clin. Rsch. Ethics, Vanderbilt U. Med. Ctr., 1988-94; fellow clin. med. ethics U. Chgo., 1989-91; dir. Clin. Ethics Ctr. St. Thomas Hosp., Nashville, 1993-98; prof. McWhorter Sch. Pharmacy, Samford U., Birmingham, Ala., 1994—; of counsel Moody Whitfield & Castellarin, 1999—; v.p. Integrity Svcs., L.L.C., Nashville, 1998-99; of counsel Moody Whitfield & Castellarin, 1999—; dir. Healthcare Ethics and Law Inst. Samford U., Birmingham, 1998—. Author: (with H. Wetherbee) Cases and Mateials on Pharmacy Law, 1980; (with W.B. Swafford) Tennessee Pharmacy Law Handbook, 1980, Mississipi Pharmacy Law Handbook, 1981. Fellow Am. Soc. Pharmacy Law, Am. Coll. Legal Medicine, Masons. Office: 95 White Bridge Rd Ste 509 Nashville TN 37205-1490

WHITE, CALVIN LAMONT, engineer; b. Chico, Calif., Nov. 14, 1947; s. Calvin Hardy White and Jean Elizabeth (Detree) Hardy; m. Elsie Jean, June 28, 1968; 1 child: Calvin Frederick. BS in Mech. Engr., U. Calif., Davis, 1969; MS in Mater. Sci., U. Minn., 1971; PhD, Mich. Tech. U., Houghton, 1974. Research staff Oak Ridge Nat. Lab., 1974-86; prof. Mich. Tech. U., Houghton, 1986—, chair dept. metall. and materials engring., 1996—. Recipient Material Sci. Rsch. award U.S. Dept. of Energy, 1984. Fellow ASM Internat.; mem. AAAS, Am. Welding Soc., Materials Rsch. Soc., The Metall. Soc. Inc. (bd. dirs. 1988-91), Am. Soc. Engring. Edn., Sigma Xi. Avocations: hunting, fishing. Office: Mich Tech U Dept Metall and Materials Engring Houghton MI 49931

WHITE, CECIL RAY, librarian, consultant; b. Hammond, Ind., Oct. 15, 1937; s. Cecil Valentine and Vesta Ivern (Bradley) W.; m. Frances Ann Gee, Dec. 23, 1960 (div. 1987); children—Timothy Wayne, Stephen Patrick. B.S. in Edn., So. Ill. U., 1959; cert. in Czech., Syracuse, U., 1961; M. Div., Southwestern Bapt. Sem., 1969; M.L.S., N. Tex. State U., 1970, Ph.D., 1984. Librarian, Herrin High Sch. (Ill.), 1964-66; acting reference librarian Southwestern Sem., Ft. Worth, 1968-70, asst. librarian, 1970-80; head librarian Golden Gate Bapt. Sem., Mill Valley, Calif., 1980-88; head librarian West Oahu Coll., Pearl City, Hawaii, 1988-89; dir. spl. projects North State Coop. Library System, Yreka, Calif., 1989-90; dir. library St. Patrick's Sem., Menlo Park, Calif., 1990—; library cons. Hist. Commn., So. Bapt. Conv., Nashville, 1983-84, Internat. Bapt. Sem., Prague, Czech Republic, 1996; mem. Thesaurus Com., 1974-84; mem. adv. bd. Cath. Periodical and Lit. Index, 1995—. Bd. dirs. Hope and Help Ctr., 1986-88, vice chmn. 1987-88. With USAF, 1960-64. Lilly Found. grantee Am. Theol. Library Assn., 1969. Mem. Am. Theol. Library Assn. (coord. consultation svc. 1973-78, program planning com. 1985-88, chmn., 1986-88), Nat. Assn. Profs. Hebrew (archivist 1985—), ALA, Assn. Coll. and Rsch. Librarians, Cath. Libr. Assn. (mem. exec. bd. 1999—), Phi Kappa Phi, Beta Phi Mu. Democrat. Baptist. Home: 40509 Ambar Pl Fremont CA 94539-3630 Office: St Patricks Sem 320 Middlefield Rd Menlo Park CA 94025-3563

WHITE, CHARLES OLDS, aeronautical engineer; b. Beirut, Apr. 2, 1931; s. Frank Laurence and Dorothy Alice (Olds) W.; m. Mary Carolyn Liechty, Sept. 3, 1955; children—Charles Cameron, Bruce Blair. B.S. in Aero. Engring., MIT, 1953, M.S., 1954. Aero. engr. Douglas Aircraft Long Beach, 1954-60, aero. engr. Ford Aerospace & Communication Corp., Calif., 1960-79, sr. engr. specialist, 1979-80, staff office of gen. mgr. DIVAD div., 1980-81, tech. mgr. DIVAD Fuzes, 1981-82, supr. design and analysis DIVAD div., 1982-85; tech. mgr. Advanced Ordnance Programs, 1985-87, PREDATOR Missile, 1987-90, cons. 1990-93; engring. tech. prin. Aerojet Corp., 1993-94; tech. prin. OCSW Ammunition Olin Ordinance, 1994-97, cons., 1997—. Mem. AIAA, AAAS, Nat. Mgmt. Assn., Am. Aviation Hist. Soc., Sigma Gamma Tau. Republican. Presbyterian. Clubs: Masters Swimming, Newport Beach Tennis. Contbr. articles to profl. jours.

WHITE, DAVID HODGE, agricultural scientist, consultant, researcher; b. Dunedin, Otago, New Zealand, June 8, 1941; s. James Hodge and Sally Violet (Roy) W.; m. Clare Daly, Mar. 21, 1969; children: Karl Jason, Alexander James, Martin David. M in Agrl. Sci., Canterbury U., Christchurch, New Zealand, 1965; grad. diploma in electronic computing, Bendigo (Australia) Inst. Tech, 1970; PhD, U. NSW, Sydney, Australia, 1975. Sci. liaison officer Ruakura Agrl. Rsch. Ctr. New Zealand Dept. Agr., Hamilton, 1966; sci. svcs. officer CSIRO Divsn. Plant Industry, Canberra, 1967; sheep industry officer Victorian Dept. Agr., Bendigo, 1967-70; sr. prodn. sys. officer Animal Rsch. Inst. Victorian Dept. Agr., Werribee, 1975-83, sr. rsch. scientist Animal Rsch. Inst., 1983-88; prin. rsch. scientist Bur. Rural Resources, Canberra, 1988-91, sr. prin. rsch. scientist, 1991-96; dir. ASIT Consulting, Canberra, 1996—; vis. lectr. U. Melbourne, 1979-88. Guest editor, author: Climate Change: Significance for Agriculture and Forestry, 1994; author: (with others) Ecosystems of the World: Managed Grasslands, 1987; guest editor, author Agrl. Sys.: Drought Policy, Assessment and Declaration, 1998; contbr. over 200 articles to profl. jours. Recipient sr. scholarship Australian Wool corp., 1971-74, Sec.'s award Dept. Primary Industries and Energy, 1997. Fellow Australian Inst. Agrl. Sci. and Tech. (cert.; pres. Victoria chpt., nat. treas. 1967—), Modelling and Simulation Soc. Australia and New Zealand (comms. officer 1987, Gen. Sys. medal 1999); mem. Australian Assn. Agrl. Consultants (accredited cons.), New Zealand Inst. Agrl. Sci. Avocations: bush walking, swimming, photography, scuba diving, skiing. E-mail: dwhite@acslink.aone.net.au. Office: ASIT Consulting, 15 Bambridge St, Weetangera ACT 2614, Australia

WHITE, DORIS GNAUCK, science educator, biochemical and biophysics researcher; b. Milw., Dec. 24, 1926; d. Paul Benjamin and Johanna (Syring) Gnauck; m. Donald Lawrence White Sr., Oct. 9, 1954 (div. Jan. 1986); children: Stanley, Dean, Victor, Donald Lawrence Jr. BS with honors, U. Wis., 1947, MS, 1949, PhD, 1956. Cert. tchr., Wis. Tchr. agr., chemistry, biology, gen. sci., math. U.S. Army Disciplinary Barracks, Milw., 1946-50; chairperson dept. sci. Waunakee (Wis.) High Sch., 1950-51; 4-H leader extension div. USDA, Wis., 1950-56; tchr. prof. U. Wis. Lab. High Sch., Madison, 1951-56; grad. teaching asst. health, rural, adult edn. U. Wis., Madison, 1951-56; prof. sci. edn., curriculum and instrn. William Paterson U., Wayne, N.J., 1957—; sci. teaching specialist Frankford (N.J.) Twp. Schs., 1962; steering com. N.J. Sci. Conv., 1977—; coll. liaison, N.J. Acad. Sci. liaison N.J. Sci. Suprs., 1979—; sr. faculty and grand marshal William Paterson U., 1992—; NSF Statewide Systemic Initiatives for N.J., 1992—, Eisenhower Profl. Devel. program Belleville (N.J.) Pub. Schs., 1992-94, Vernon (N.J.) Pub. Schs., Elmwood Park (N.J.) Pub. Schs.; participant N.J. Sci. and Math. Coalition NSF grant, 1993—; judge Seiko Youth Challenge, 1994, Hudson Co. Sci. Fair, 1994-96; R&D judge 100 top internat. inventions, 1994; mentor for handicapped scientists AAAS, 1995—; active N.J. Sci. Core Curriculum Stds., Trenton, 1997, N.J. Agrl. Edn. Core Curriculum Stds., Trenton, 1998. Mem. nat. sci. tchrs. manuscript rev. panel Jour. Coll. Sci. Teaching, 1991-94. Active 4-H Club Leadership, Morristown, N.J., 1968— (N.J. 4-H Club Alumni award 1991), Geraldine Rockefeller Dodge Found. Animal Shelter, Madison, N.J., 1968—, St. Hubert's Giralda; vol. for poor and homeless of Paterson, N.J., 1971—; lic. blood tester for salmonella/fowl typhoid USDA, 1987—; mem. panel on curriculum improvement N.J. Commr. Edn., 1990-91, program com. N.J. Sci. Conv., 1978—, sex equality com. N.J. Dept. Edn., 1987, Sci. Core Proficiencies Panel, 1994-97, N.J. Sci. Coalition, 1989—; judge presdl. candidates for N.J. schs. N.J. Dept. Edn., Trenton, 1985-88; judge sci. fairs Carteret, N.J., 1991, 92, N.J. Sci. Olympiad, 1993, 95—, SEER Morristown, 1986-92, Haledon, N.J., 1957-60, Atlantic County 4-H, N.J., 1995-96, Hudson County Sci. Fair, N.J., 1994-96, numerous other local, county and state fairs; trustee N.J. Sci. Suprs. Assn. Recipient Silver medals Nat. Garden Inst., 1947, 48, Liberty Hyde Bailey Hort. medal Cornell U., Ithaca, N.Y., 1947, Gen. Douglas McArthur Hort. medal Nat. Garden Inst., 1947, Educator award Am. Cancer Soc., N.J., 1967, Meth. Layleader award, 1995; Dyes Rsch. grantee William Paterson U. Alumni Found., 1989-90; grantee NSF. Fellow N.J. Sci. Tchrs. Assn. (exec. bd. 1978—, indsl. liaison com. 1990-92); mem. Am. Poultry Assn. (life, lic. judge 1948—), Am. Chem. Soc. (Poster Contest judge 1993—), Am. Mus. Natural History, Nat. Sci. Tchrs. Assn., Nat. Sci. Suprs. Assn., Nat. Sci. Leadership Assn., N.J. Acad. Sci. (chair sci. edn. divsn. 1990-95, liaison to sci. tchrs. 1992—, judge 1990—), N.J. Earth Sci. Edn. Assn., N.J. Sci. Edn. Leadership Assn., N.J. Sci. Suprs. Assn. (exec. bd. 1979—, pres. 1981, Outstanding Sci. Supr. award 1986, Pres.'s award 1992), Coun. Elem. Sci. N.J., N.J. Sci. Tchrs. Assn., N.J. Earth Sci. Tchrs. Assn., N.J. Marine Edn. Assn., Franklin-Ogdensburg Mineral. Soc., Sterling Hill Mining Mus., Liberty Sci. Mus. (charter). Republican. Methodist. Achievements include research in chromosome mapping of domestic fowl; development of 2 new varieties of winter squash which are now commercial varieties; development of penguin-like ducks, research in poultry genetics, genetics of Cucurbitaceae, ultrasound treatment of seeds concerning effects on seed germination and plant growth; using helium-neon lasers for holographic interferometry to measure plant growth occurring in seconds measured in wavelengths of light, growth regulators on flowers for parthenogenesis and for polyploidy; development of new variety of cat, herpes virus research with fowl, experiments with leaf berms for highway sound barriers; recycling waste tires stuffed with grass clippings for highway median strips covered with leaf compost; investigation of turkey head ornament colors as indicators of contentment or stress, turkey head color ornament color changes during courtship and copulation, catatonic effects in domestic fowl; design of portable methane generator, design of wave action and tidal pumps to transport glacial melt; suggested uses for incinerator ash, pollution caused by fireworks, Bernoulli's theorem as applied to bird flight, plausibility of human virgin births by cloning; improved cellular phone communication, global warming, greenhouse effect, effect of ocean floor heat vents as cause of El Nino. Home: PO Box 236 Hardwick MA 01037-0236 Office: William Paterson U 408 Raubinger Hall 300 Pompton Rd Wayne NJ 07470-2152

WHITE, DOUGLAS ALLAN, legislative aide, data archivist; b. Madison, Wis., May 14, 1970; s. Mathew James and Anna Mae (Schuette) W. BA in Polit. Sci. with honors, U. Hawaii at Manoa, Honolulu, 1997, MA in Polit. Sci., 1999. Data archivist Hawaii Mapping Rsch. Group, Honolulu, 1996—; legis. aide Hawaii Ho. of Reps., Honolulu, 1997—. Cpl. USMC, 1988-93. Mem. Am. Polit. Sci. Assn., Am. Radio Relay League, Phi Beta Kappa. Avocations: offshore yacht racing, inshore yacht racing, amateur radio.

WHITE, EDWARD ALFRED, lawyer; b. Elizabeth, N.J., Nov. 23, 1934. BS in Indsl. Engring., U. Mich., 1957, JD, 1963. Bar: Fla. 1963, U.S. Ct. Appeals (5th cir.) 1971, U.S. Ct. Appeals (11th cir.) 1981, U.S. Supreme Ct. 1976. Assoc. Jennings, Watts, Clarke & Hamilton, Jacksonville, Fla., 1963-66, ptnr., 1966-69; ptnr. Wayman & White, Jacksonville, Fla., 1969-72; pvt. practice Jacksonville, Fla., 1972—; mem. aviation law com. Fla. Bar, 1972-94, chmn., 1979-81, bd. govs., 1984-88, admiralty com., 1984—, chmn., 1990-91, chmn. pub. relations com., 1986-88, exec. coun. trial lawyers sect., 1986-91, chmn. admiralty cert. com., 1995-97. Fellow Am. Bar Found.; mem. ABA (vice chmn. admiralty law com. 1995—), Fla. Bar Assn. (bd. cert. civil trial lawyer, bd. cert. admiralty lawyer), Jacksonville Bar Assn. (chmn. legal ethics com. 1975-76, bd. govs. 1976-78, pres. 1979-80), Assn. Trial Lawyers Am. (sustaining mem. 1984—), Acad. Fla. Trial Lawyers (diplomate), Fla. Coun. Bar Assn. Pres.'s, Lawyer-Pilots Bar Assn., Am. Judicature Soc., Maritime Law Assn. (proctor in admiralty), Southeastern Admiralty Law Inst. (bd. dirs. 1982-084, chmn., pres. 1994). Fax: 904-356-6508. Home: 1959 Largo Rd Jacksonville FL 32207-3926 Office: 901 Blackstone Bldg 233 E Bay St Jacksonville FL 32202-3452

WHITE, ELMER, physicist, researcher; b. Atlanta, June 22, 1926; s. William Tallahasee and Gladys W.; m. Louise Turner, June 18, 1960; children: Allisa Michele, Derek Elmer. BS, Ohio State U., 1952; student, Air Force Inst. Tech., 1961-63; PhD in Mgmt., LaJolla U., 1982. Engring. designer GE, Evendale, Ohio, 1954-56; physicist Wright-Patterson AFB, Dayton, Ohio, 1960-67, Lawrence Livermore Lab., Livermore, Calif., 1967-71, Naval Ocean Syss., San Diego, 1972-86; physicist Naval Rsch. Lab. Stennis Space Ctr., Miss., 1986-94; ret., 1994. Contbr. articles to profl. jours. Served in USN, 1943-45. Mem. Acoustic Soc. Am. Home: 130 Moonraker Dr Slidell LA 70458-5521

WHITE, ELSIE PEARL, nurse, retired; b. Gause, Tex., Jan. 13, 1925; d. Conaway and Pearl Ella Moore; m. Chester A. White, Nov. 27, 1941; children: Arthur R., Harold Lynn. Degree in nursing, Sch. Nursing, Chgo., 1961. With Harris County (Tex.) Health Dept., Houston, City of Houston Dept. Health; now ret.; instr. Houston C.C., Sch. Law and Criminology, 1975-77; past owner ENCO Svc. Sta., Houston; seamstress, Houston, 1940-95. Active Harris County Dems., 1941-97. Mem. LWV, Concerned Women of Am., Toastmasters, Order of Mayans, Order Eastern Star. Methodist. Avocations: fitness, Christian sr. citizen groups. Home: 1509 Euel St Houston TX 77009-1605

WHITE, EMMET, JR., retirement community administrator; b. Newark, Oct. 18, 1946; s. Emmet Sr. and June (Howlett) W.; m. Betty Orr, June 7, 1970; children: Benjamin, Suzanne, George. BA, Lafayette Coll., 1968; JD, Coll. of William and Mary, 1971. Bar: Hawaii 1972; cert. nursing home adminstr., Hawaii. Law ptnr. Mau & White AAL, Honolulu, 1975-83, White & Tom AAL, Honolulu, 1983-95; CEO, adminstr. Arcadia Retirement Residence, Honolulu, 1996—. Bd. trustees Ctrl. Union Ch., Honolulu, 1980-84, chmn. 1983-84, moderator, 1987. Col. USAR, 1968-94. Mem. Hawaii Bar Assn., Hawaii Long Term Care Assn. Avocations: family activities, physical activities. Office: Arcadia Retirement Residence 1434 Punahou St Honolulu HI 96822-4754

WHITE, FAITH See ABRAMS, FAITH

WHITE, GARY RICHARD, electrical engineer, plant operator; b. Detroit, Nov. 15, 1962; s. Thomas Richard and Davene (Reynolds) W. BSEE, Wayne State U., 1986. Electronics engr. U.S. Army Info. Sys. Engring. Command, Ft. Belvoir, Va., 1987-88, Ft. Shafter, Hawaii, 1988-92; elec. worker U.S. Navy Pub. Works Ctr., Pearl Harbor, Hawaii, 1992-96; plant operator helper U.S. Navy Pub. Works Ctr., Pearl Harbor, 1996—. Mem. IEEE, NRA, NSPE, Assn. Computing Machinery, Am. Assn. Individual Investors, Am. Mgmt. Assn. Avocations: weightlifting, biking, hardware and software, rock concerts, movies. Office: PO Box 19055 Honolulu HI 96817-8055

WHITE, GEORGE EDWARD, pedodontist, educator; b. Jamestown, N.Y., July 31, 1941; s. Gordon Ennis and Margaret (Appleyard) W. AB, Colgate U., 1963; DDS, SUNY, Buffalo, 1967; PhD, MIT, 1973; DBA, Century U., 1982. Intern, then resident Children's Hosp., Buffalo, 1967-69; prof., chmn. dept. pediat. dentistry Tufts U. Sch. Dental Medicine, Boston, 1973—; chief dept. oral pediat. New Eng. Med. Center Hosp., Boston, 1973-80; pvt. practice pedodontics, Boston, 1974—; lectr. MIT, 1975-80; cons. Abcor, Inc.; nat., internat. lectr. Nat. Inst. Dental Rsch. grantee, 1973—. Author: Dental Caries: A Multifactorial Disease, 1975, To Stand Alone, 1979; co-author: Maxillofacial Orthopedics: For the Growing Child, 1983; founder, editor-in-chief Jour. Pedodontics, 1976, now named Jour. Clin. Pediat. Dentistry; editor: Clin. Oral Pediatrics, 1979, founder, editor-in-chief Mastering Clin. Pediat. Dentistry, 1993-98; editor-in-chief Protocols for Clin. Pediat. Dentistry; contbr. articles to profl. jours. Master Acad. Gen. Dentistry; fellow Am. Acad. Pediat. Dentistry, Internat. Coll. Dentistry, Am. Coll. Dentistry; mem. Am. Assn. Dental Editors, Fedn. Dentaire Internationale, Sigma Xi, Omicron Kappa Upsilon. Office: Tufts U Sch Dental Medicine Dept Pediat Dentistry 1 Kneeland St Boston MA 02111-1527

WHITE, GEORGE WASHINGTON, automotive consultant; b. Monticello, Ga., June 18, 1918; s. George W. and Julia A. (Preston) W.; m. Annie L. White, Mar. 18, 1938 (div. July 1944); m. Fannie C. White, Nov. 1, 1944 (dec.); children: Walter A. Martin, Patricia Ann, Ernest George. Grad. high sch., Rome, Ga., 1935. Aircraft engine maintenance worker Allison Engring. Autonautical div, GM, Indpls., 1940-43; aircraft engine maintenance worker Wright Patterson AFB, Ohio, 1943-47, with rsch. and devel., 1947-57, with engines rsch. devel., 1949-57; salesman Davis Buick Co., Dayton, Ohio, 1957-73; pres. George White Olds Inc., Cin., 1973-80; cons. Ernest White Ford-Lincoln-Mercury, Delaware, Ohio, 1980-86; pres., cons. G.W. Cons. Inc., Worthington, Ohio, 1983—. Pres. Frontiers Internat. Inc., Dayton, 1947-68; mem. Pres.'s Club, Dayton, 1967-72, NAACP, 1946-73. Democrat. Christian Methodist. Avocations: bowling, golfing, sr. citizen activities. Home: 354 Bear Woods Dr Powell OH 43065-7744

WHITE, GLADYS HOPE FRANKLIN, reading specialist; b. Elizabeth City, N.C., Mar. 22; d. Elbert and Pearl (Smithwick) Franklin; m. Frank Hollowell White, Apr. 12, 1941; children: Johnese Armelda, Sharon Faye. BS, Hampton Inst. U., 1939; MA, Columbia U., 1949; EdD, U. Sarasota, 1978. Elem. tchr. and music Brawley H.S., Scotland Neck, N.C., 1939-41; elem. critic tchr. Elizabeth City Pub. Schs., elem. tchr., music tchr. P.W. Moore H.S.; coll. edn. reading specialist Tex. Coll., Tyler; Jeanes supr. Currituck/Camden Pub. Schs., elem. supr.; elem. supr. Wake County Pub. Schs., Raleigh, N.C.; assoc. prof. edn. and reading N.C. Agrl. and Tech. U., Greensboro, N.C., 1962-82; founder, dir. project CARE Episcopal Ch. of the Redeemer, Greensboro, 1983—; dir. tchr. tng. inst. Nat. Def. Edn. Inst., Greensboro, 1965-68; tech. asst. reading lang. U.S. Right to Read Program, U.S. Edn. Dept., Wilmington, Del.; cons., workshop founder. Project Care exec. bd. Episcopal Ch. of Redeemer, Greensboro, N.C., 1982—; mem. Pres. Clinton's Exec. Coun. com., 1996-98; mem. Dem. Congrl. Campaign com., Washington, 1998; mem. Friends Chavis Learning Libr., Greensboro, 1982—. Mem. Internat. Reading Assn. (life, chair paraprofls., reading com.), Nat. Assn. of Bus. Profl. Womens Clubs (corr. sec., chair archives, chair scholarship com. 1960-92), Hampton U. Alumni Assn. (pres. emeritus 1990—, Greensboro chpt. past pres., Trendsetter award 1995), Lady Sertoma (life), Delta Sigma Theta (Delta Diamond award 1988, Leadership award 1991), Kappa Delta Phi. Democrat. Episcopalian. Avocations: tutoring, mentoring, sewing, crafts, reading. Home: 1206 E Side Dr Greensboro NC 27406-2149 Office: Episcopal Ch of the Redeemer 901 E Friendly Ave Greensboro NC 27401-3103

WHITE, GREGG KENNETH, writer; b. N.Y., May 1, 1949; s. Donald Anthony and Jimmie (Messex) W.; m. Andrea Maria Agee, 1969. High school diploma, Gen. Douglas MacArthur, Levittown, N.Y., 1967. Farm hand Booth Ranch, RIdgeview, S.D., 1969-70, Scarborough Farm, Stanley Co., S.D., 1970-71; factory laborer Utah/Idaho Sugar Co., Moses Lake, Wash., 1971-72; laborer Handy Andy, Denver, 1973-74; cashier, stocker, clerk Sunrise Gas Mart, Moses Lake, 1974; worker Sister Hazel Rescue Mission, Gainesville, Fla., 1976-77. Author: Prose & Cons, 1990, Prose & Cons Expanded, 2000. Sr. vice acting commander Everett Bundette, Evansville, Ind., 1982, sr. vice commander DAU, Evansville, 1981, 92. With U.S. Navy, 1967-68. Mem. Nat. Geo. Soc., S.C.A. Avocations: stamp collecting, reading. Home: PO Box 34 Kiln MS 39556-0034

WHITE, HALBERT LYNN, JR., economist, educator, consultant; b. Kansas City, Mo., Nov. 19, 1950; s. H. Lynn and Emily (Roach) W.; m. Kim A. Titensor, Oct. 25, 1986; children: Richard H. Weeks, Rachel A. Weeks. AB, Princeton U., 1972; PhD, MIT, 1976. Asst. prof. U. Rochester, N.Y., 1976-80; assoc. prof. U. Calif., San Diego, 1980-84, prof., 1984-95, prof. above scale, 1995—; vis. assoc. prof. MIT, Cambridge, 1984; mem. adv. bd. Merrill Lynch Acad., 1994-95; mem. sci. adv. bd. Stone Analytics, Inc.; chmn. LaJolla (Calif.) Data Sys., 1988-91, NeuralNet R&D Assocs., 1992—; commodity trading advisor, 1993—; pres. QuantMetrics Corp., 1998—; chmn. Bates & White, LLC, 1999—; cons. in field. Author: Asymptotic Theory for Econometricians, 1984, Estimation, Inference and Specification Analysis, 1994; co-author: Artificial Neural Networks - Approximation and Learning Theory, 1992, A Unified Theory of Estimation and Inference for Nonlinear Dynamic Models, 1988, Advances in Econometric Theory, 1998; editor: Abstracts of Working Papers in Economics, 1985—; contbr. articles to profl. jours.; patentee in field. Recipient Best Article award Internat. Jour. Forecasting, 1996-97, Multa Scripsit award Econometric Theory jour., 1997; Guggenheim fellow Guggenheim Found., 1988-89; NSF grantee, 1980—; Jour. Econometrics fellow, 1995. Fellow Econometric Soc., Am. Acad. Arts and Scis.; mem. IEEE (sr.), Internat. Assn. Fin. Engrs., Am. Fin. Assn., Internat. Inst. of Forecasters, Am. Math. Soc., Am. Statis. Assn., Internat. Neural Network Soc., Nat. Futures Assn., Big Band and Jazz Hall of Fame (bd. dirs. 1997—), Friends of Tiger Band (bd. dirs. 1998—), Jazz Soc. L.A., Jazz Soc. Lower So. Calif. (treas. 1988). Avocations: music performance and composition, antiques. Office: U Calif San Diego Dept Econs # 0508 La Jolla CA 92093

WHITE, IAN FRANK, chemical engineer; b. Leamington, England, Feb. 27, 1942; s. Harold Thomas and Norah Constance (Redgrove) W.; m. Wieslawa Barbara Klekowska, May 31, 1970; children: Izabela, Paul, Arthur, Norah, Zuzanna. BS, Bristol U., England, 1963; MS, Loughborough U., England, 1965, PhD, 1968. Grad. trainee BP Refineries, Llandarcy, Wales, 1963-64; plant mgr. ICI Ltd., Wilton, England, 1967-70; process engr. Catalytic Internat., London, 1970-80; tech. dir. Raytheon, New Malden, England, 1980-2000, Washington Group Internat., New Malden, 2000—. Co-author: (chpts.) Modern Chlor-Alkali Technology, vol. 3, 1986, vol. 4, 1990, vol. 5, 1992, vol. 6, 1995, vol. 7, 1998, vol. 8, 2000. Gov. Chevening Sch., Sevenoaks, England, 1984-90. Fellow Inst. Petroleum; mem. Internat. Soc. Pharm. Engring. Mem. Ch. of England. Avocations: dinghy sailing, badminton, classical music, chess. Office: Washington Group Internat, CI Tower St Georges Sq, New Malden KT3 4HH, England

WHITE, JAMES, JR., psychiatric, mental health nurse, consultant; b. Muskogee, Okla., Nov. 24, 1944; s. James Sr. and Mary Bd. (Brassfield) W.; children: Stacie R., Stephen W. BA, Northeastern State U., 1969; MS, Pittsburg State U., 1972, BSN, 1982; PhD, Columbia Pacific U., 1984. Diplomate Am. Bd. Forensic Examiners, Soc. for Study of Neuronal Regulation; CSW, advance register nurse practitioner, cert. rehab. counselor, limited license psychologist, nationally bd. cer. counselor. Exec. dir. Sanilac County Mental Health, Sandusky, Mich., 1975-78, Crawford County Mental Health, Pittsburg, 1978-80; psychologist Psychol. and Ednl. Svcs., Pittsburg, 1980-81; dialysis nurse St. John Med. Ctr., Joplin, Mo., 1982-84; psychiatric practitioner Family Counseling and Resource Ctr., Joplin, 1983-86; pvt. practice Joplin, 1986-88; med. sociologist Mich. Health Ctr., Detroit, 1988-91; psychiatric practitioner Wayne County Sheriff and Sinai Hosp. Psychiatry, Detroit, 1990—; clin. coord. Detroit Health Care for Homeless, 1991—; chmn. recipient right com. Lafayette Clinic, Detroit, 1991—, coun. mem., 1990—. Lt. U.S. Army, 1969-82. Mem. ANA for Nurses in Advanced Practice, Am. Psychatric Nurses Assn., Am. Acad. Nurse Practitioners (Mich. State Rep. 1991—), Am. Bd. Med. Psychotherapists (cert., clin. assoc.), Coun. Psychiatric and Mental Health Nursing, Am. Acad. Pain Mgmt. Avocations: biking, swimming, boating. Home: 42029 Utah Dr Sterling Heights MI 48313-2965 Office: Inst for Inner Resource 75 W Square Lake Rd Troy MI 48098-2929

WHITE, JAMES RICHARD, lawyer; b. McKinney, Tex., Jan. 22, 1948; s. James Ray and Maxine (Brown) W.; children: Nicole Olivia, Mandi Leigh, James Derek. BBA, So. Meth. U., 1969, MBA, 1970, JD, 1973, LLM, 1977. Bar: Tex. 1973, U.S. Tax Ct. 1975, U.S. Supreme Ct. 1989, U.S. Ct. Appeals (5th cir.) 1989); cert. Comml. Real Estate Law Tex. Bd. Legal Specialization. Assoc. Elliot, Meer, Vetter, Denton & Bates, Dallas, 1973-74, Atwell, Cain & Davenport, Dallas, 1974-75; atty. Sabine Corp., Dallas, 1975-77; assoc. Brice & Barron, Dallas, 1977-79; ptnr. Millard & Olson, Dallas, 1979-82, Johnson & Swanson, Dallas, 1982-83; ptnr. Winstead, Sechrest & Minick P.C., Dallas, 1983—, hiring ptnr., 1987—, exec. com., 2000—; mem. staff Southwestern Law Jour., Dallas, 1971-73; mem. So. Meth. U. Moot Ct. Bd., Order Barristers, Dallas, 1972-73; prof. North Lake Coll., Dallas, 1985; bd. dirs. Tex. Assn. Young Lawyers, Austin, 1980-82; sec. bd. dirs. Dallas Assn. Young Lawyers, 1976-80. Contbr. articles to profl. jours. Chmn. bd. dirs. Tex. Lawyers Credit Union, Austin, 1980-82; pres. North Tex. Premier Soccer Assn., Dallas, 1979-81; v.p. Lake Highlands Soccer Assn., 1995-96, pres., 1996—; mem. regional mobility task force Real Estate Coun., City of Dallas, 1991-92, mem. downtown revitalization com., 1995-97; mem. Dallas Indsl. Devel. Bd., 1992-93, Dallas Higher Edn. Authority Bd., 1994-96; spkr.'s bur. and accreditation divsn. World Cup USA '94. Mem. ABA (mem. title ins. and survey, mortgage loan origination and structure com., mortgage financing and opinion, non-traditional comml. real estate fin. coms.), Tex. Bar Assn. (cert. 1973, mem. mortgage loan opinion com.), Tex. Coll. Real Estate Attys., Coll. State Bar Tex. Methodist. Avocations: soccer, golf, skiing, racquetball. E-mail: jrwhite@winstead.com. Home: 8003 Hundley Ct Dallas TX 75231-4728 Office: Winstead Sechrest & Minick 5400 Renaissance Tower 1201 Elm St Ste 5400 Dallas TX 75270-2199

WHITE, JAN TUTTLE (MRS. BENJAMIN WINTHROP WHITE), information systems executive; b. Bridgeport, Conn., Nov. 5, 1943; d. Michael and Jennie Agnes (Leko) Soltis; m. David Dustin Tuttle, Oct. 7, 1972 (div. Apr. 1988); m. Benjamin Winthrop White, May 6, 1989. BS in Math., Bates Coll., 1965; MBA in Mktg. and Ops. Rsch., Columbia U., 1967. Cert. comml. real estate broker, Mass. With corp. staff IBM Corp., Armonk, N.Y., 1966; systems engr. IBM Corp., N.Y.C., 1967-69; mktg. rep. to Harvard U., corp. staff, sys. engr., Harvard U. account mgr. IBM Corp., Cambridge, Mass., 1969-72; asst. to dir. info. processing svcs. MIT, Cambridge, Mass., 1972-75; mng. dir. Tuttle Family Trust, Cambridge, Mass., 1975-81; VAX product mktg. mgr., then sr. product mgr. Digital Equipment Corp., Marlborough, Mass., 1981-86, artificial intelligence market devel. mgr., 1986-87, fin. systems group market devel. mgr., 1987-90, market devel. mgr. banking/investments group, 1990; program mgr. MIT Internat. Fin. Svc. Rsch. Ctr., Hudson; med. systems mgr. Beth Israel Deaconess Med. Ctr., Boston, 1990—; Spkr. in field; founder Boston Opera House (now Wang Ctr.); sponsor Harvard Host Family Program. Appeared in Disney channel documentary film Silver Men, 1987, Boston Mus. Sci. introductory film for opening of Mugar Omni Theatre, 1987; contbr. (books) An Olde Concord Christmas, 1980, Boston Symphony Orch. Cookbook, 1983, Boston Cooks, 1991. Chmn. Concord Coun. Boston Symphony Orch., assoc. assn. vols., supporter Tanglewood scholarship programs, capt. Centennial Major Gifts campaign; active guild bd. Opera Co. Boston, patron Fledrmaus Ball; life mem., chmn. Emerson Hosp. Aux.; trustee, mem. mgmt. rev. com. Women's Ednl. and Indsl. Union; edn. com. chmn. Ladies Assn.; life mem., bd. Concord Antiquarian Mus., nom. com. edn. long-range planning com., chmn. edn. com., costumes and textiles com., exhbt. designer An Old Concorde Christmas, established family meml. fund; bd. adv. Sci. Mus. Exhibit Collaborative, Garden Club Concord, Boston Mus. Sci.; life mem. Mus. of Fine Arts, Boston, Nat. Trust for Scotland, Friends of Loch Lomond, Mus. Fine Arts, Boston, Friends of the Beth Israel Med. Ctr, Harvard Neighbors.; mem. fin. com. Trinitarian Congl. Ch.; trustee, life mem. Women's Ednl. and Indsl. Union; bd. dirs., life mem. Hannah Duston Garrison House Assn., Mus. Fine Arts, Boston; life mem. Friends of the New Eng. Deaconess Hosp., Boston, Friends of the Beth Israel Deaconess Med. Ctr., Boston; patron mem. Friends of Music at the Mus. of Fine Arts, Boston; mem. Isabella Stewart Gardner Mus.; invitational alumni Hurricane Island (Maine) Outward Bound Sch., underwriter Silver Anniversary video 1987; water safety instr., sr. life saving instr., First Aid instr. Red Cross Nat. Aquatic Sch., 1964. Recipient numerous industry achievement awards; nominated White House fellow, 1971. Mem. NAFE, Am. Assn. Artificial Intelligence, Inst. for Mgmt. Scis., Ops. Rsch. Soc. Am., Hannah Duston Garrison house Assn. (life, bd.), Harwich Hist. Assn. (life), Stratford Hist. Soc. (life), Cambridge Hist. Soc., Internat. Platform Assn., Bates Coll. Class 1965 (sec., treas., reunion chmn., com. chmn. 25th reunion major gifts), Columbia U. Grad. Sch. Bus. Alumni Assn. (nat. chmn. membership, bd. dirs.), Mass. Hort. Soc., Conn. Soc. Genealogists, Nat. Assn. Underwater Instrs. (cert. scuba diver), So. Mass. Yacht Racing Assn., Columbia Bus. Club Boston (founding dir., bd. dirs.), Columbia U. Club New Eng. (founding dir.), Columbia Club N.Y., Concord Country Club, Harvard Club (Boston, N.Y.C.), Harvard Neighbors, Harvard U. art Mus., Harvard Faculty Club, Stone Horse Yacht Club, Women's City Club (com. membership), Royal Scottish Automobile Club, So. Mass. Yacht Racing Assn., Friends of Loch Lomond (life), Mass. Horticultural Soc., Arnold Arboretum Harvard U., Housatonic Boat Club. Republican. Avocations: the arts, sports, horticulture, environ. preservation, geneology. Fax: (617) 277-5724. E-mail: jwhite1@caregroup.harvard.edu. Home: 20 Chapel St Ste C101 Brookline MA 02446-5445 Office: Beth Israel Deaconess Med Ctr 110 Francis St Ste 9-C Boston MA 02215-5501

WHITE, JEFFERY HOWELL, lawyer; b. Tyler, Tex., Aug. 4, 1959; s. Bluford D. and Tempie R. (Tunnell) W.; m. Michael Anne Mackley, May 21, 1989; children: Kristin, Alex. BS in History, So. Ark. U., 1983; JD, Oklahoma City U., 1986. Bar: Tex. 1987. Assoc. Dean White, Canton, Tex., 1986-90; asst. dist. atty. Van Zandt Co., Canton, 1991-94; ptnr. Elliott Elliott & White, Canton, 1994-97; pvt. practice Canton, Tex., 1997—. Mem. Van Zandt County Bar Assn. (v.p. 1999—), Tex. Criminal Def. Lawyers Assn., Tex. State Bar (dist. 1-A grievance com. 1996—). Democrat. United Methodist. Avocations: golf, tennis, spectator sports. Home: PO Box 1200 Van TX 75790-1200 Office: 157 N Buffalo St Canton TX 75103-1353

WHITE, JEFFREY LLOYD, radiotherapy physicist; b. Vienna, W.Va.; s. Ralph Lloyd and Mary Virginia (Little) W.; 1 child, Jeffrey Lloyd II. BA in Chemistry, W.Va. U., 1980; MS in Radiol. Health Physics, San Diego State U., 1988. Diplomate in therapeutic radiol. physics Am. Bd. Radiology. Exploration oil/gas well testing specialist Otis Engring. Corp. subs. Halliburton Corp., Wyo., Calif., 1980-86; med. physicist Bapt. Med. Ctr., Jacksonville, Fla., 1988-93; cons. physicist Comp Health Inc., Atlanta, 1993; radiotherapy physicist Sarasota (Fla.) Oncology Ctr., 1993—; with B&O Railroad, C&P Telephone Cos. With U.S. Army Res., 1982-88. Mem. Am. Assn. Physicists in Medicine, Am. Soc. Therapeutic Radiology and Oncology, Am. Coll. Radiology, Inst. of Physics and Engring. in Medicine (U.K.). Office: Sarasota Oncology Ctr 3663 Bee Ridge Rd Sarasota FL 34233-1003

WHITE, JOHN JAMESON, solicitor; b. Leigh-on-Sea, Essex, Eng., July 6, 1938; s. Jameson Richard and Betty Annette (Payne) W.; m. Carolyn Helen Morgan (dec. Aug. 1991); children: Sarah Michelle, Matthew Jameson, Amanda Claire; m. Carolyn Margery Walton, May 22, 1992. Cert. solicitor. Articled clk. Cameron Kemm, London, 1957-62, asst. solicitor, 1962-64; ptnr. Cameron McKenna (formerly Cameron Kemm), London, 1964—. Mem. editl. bd. Jour. Internat. Banking Law. Fellow Chartered Inst. Banking; mem. Law Soc., Internat. Bar Assn., Insolvency Lawyers Assn., Soc. of Practitioners in Insolvency, European Assn. Profls., The Athenaeum, West Herts Sports Club. Avocations: cricket, hockey, port. Office: Cameron McKenna, Mitre House 160 Aldersgate, London EC1A 4DD, England

WHITE, JOHN WILLIAM, chemistry educator; b. Newcastle, N.S.W., Australia, Apr. 25, 1937; s. George Alexander John and Jean Florence White; m. Ailsa Barbara White, July 24, 1966; children: Sarah, Catherine, David, Rachel. BSc with honors, U. Sydney, Australia, 1957, MSc, 1959; MA, PhD, Oxford (Eng.) U., 1962. Lectr. Oxford U., 1963; assessor, 1981-82; fellow St. John's Coll.; neutron beam coord., exec. cons. AERA Harwell, 1973-74; adjoint dir. Inst. Laue-Langevin, Grenoble, France, 1974-77, dir., 1977-80; sci. coord., cons. Hulme sch. projects Los Alamos (N.Mex.) Nat. U., 1982-84; prof. phys. and theoretical chemistry Australian Nat. U., Canberra, 1985—, dean Rsch. Sch. Chemistry, 1995-98; Argonne fellow U. Chgo., 1985-90; Hinshelwood lectr. Oxford U., 1992; pro-vice chancellor, chmn. bd. Inst. Advanced Studies; hon. fellow St. Johns Coll. Oxford U., 1996; Hudnall Cars Disting. lectr. U. Chgo., 1998. Mem. editorial bd. Advances in Physics, 1989—. Christensen fellow St. Catherine's Coll., 1991. Fellow Australian Acad. Sci. (sci. policy sec. 1997), Royal Soc.; mem. Soc. Crystallographers in Australia (pres. 1989-91), Assn. Asian Chem. Socs. (found. lectr. 1991), Ryal Australian Chem. Inst. (pres.-elect 2000). Home: 2 Spencer St, Turner ACT 2601, Australia Office: Australian Nat U, Rsch Sch Chemistry, Canberra 0200, Australia

WHITE, JOYCE LOUISE, librarian; b. Phila., June 7, 1927; d. George William and Louisa (Adams) W. BA, U. Pa., 1949; MLS, Drexel U., 1963; MA in Religion, Episc. Sem. S.W., 1978. Head libr. Penniman Libr. Edn. U. Pa., Phila., 1960-76; archivist St. Francis Boys' Home, Salina, Kans., 1982-84; libr. Brown Mackie Coll., Salina, 1983-86; libr., dir. St. Thomas Theol. Sem., Denver, 1986-95; libr., dir. Archbishop Vehr Theol. Libr. Archdiocese of Denver, 1995-96. Author: Biographical and Historial Yarnall Library, 1979; asst. editor: Women Religious History Sources, 1983; contbr. articles to profl. jours. and chpts. to books. Vol. libr. St. John's Cath., Denver, 1993—. Mem. Ch. and Synagogue Libr. Assn. (life, founding, pres. 1969-70, exec. sec. 1970-72, exec. bd. 1967-76, ann. conf. chair 1996). Avocations: gardening, cats, church libraries. Office: St John's Cathedral Libr 1313 Clarkson St Denver CO 80218-1806

WHITE, LANA JOYCE, English language educator; b. Canyon, Tex.; d. Orva Odis and Leona Estelle (Dawdy) Henry; m. Billy Gene White, Feb. 19, 1960; 1 child, Denise. BA, West Tex. State U., 1960, MA, 1964; PhD, Tex. Christian U., 1983. Cert. tchr., Tex. Tchr. Kelton (Tex.) Ind. Schs., 1960-61, Gruver (Tex.) Ind. Schs., 1961-62, Farwell (Tex.) Ind. Schs., 1962-64, Amarillo (Tex.) Ind. Schs., 1964-81; assoc. prof. English West Tex. State U., Canyon, 1983-92; prof. English West Tex. A&M U., 1992—. Contbr. articles to profl. jours. Recipient accolade Amarillo Globe-News, 1972; fellow Tex. Christian U., 1981-83. Mem. MLA, Internat. Assn. Improvement Mother Tongue Edn., Nat. Coun. Tchrs. English. Democrat. Presbyterian. Avocation: gardening. E-mail: lwhite@wtamu.edu. Office: West Tex A&M Wt Sta Canyon TX 79016-0001

WHITE, LERRILL JAMES, clinical pastoral educator; b. Lafayette, Ind., Mar. 13, 1948; s. Joe Lloyd and Wanita Irene (Robertson) W.; m. Deborah June Brown, Dec. 27, 1969; children: Krister Colin Brant, Kourtney Cassidy Benay. BA, Abilene Christian U., 1970, MS, 1973; MDiv, Princeton Theol. Sem., 1975; postgrad., Pa. State U., 1980-89. Ordained to ministry Ch. of Christ, 1975. Clin. chaplain Ft. Logan Mental Health Ctr., Denver, 1975-76, Meml. Med. Ctr., Corpus Christi, Tex., 1976-78; sr. pastor Centre Community Ch. of Christ, State Coll., Pa., 1978-87; assoc. dir. pastoral care Geisinger Med. Ctr., Danville, Pa., 1983-87; dir. pastoral care Yuma (Ariz.) Regional Med. Ctr., 1987-95; pastor Mohawk Valley Cmty. Ch., Roll, Ariz., 1995-99; asst. dir. clin. pastoral edn. St. Luke's Episcopal Hosp., Houston, 2000—; pres. well i b enterprises inc., 1995—; author, presenter tng. courses, 1987—. Contbr. articles to profl. jours.; creator interview instrument P.C. Ranking Instrument, 1981. Bd. dirs. Behavioral Health Svcs., Yuma, 1991-96; mem., coach Yuma Youth Soccer Assn., 1987-93; mem., treas. Internat. Pastoral Care Network for Social Responsibility, Inc., 1987—. Mem. Assn. Clin. Pastoral Edn. (supr. 1983—), Assn. Profl Chaplains (bd. cert.), Ariz. Chaplain's Assn. (exec. com. 1988-93, pres. 1989-90), Cola-Gila Kiwanis (pres. 1995-2000).

WHITE, LESLIE, paediatric oncologist, clinician, researcher, hospital executive; b. Satu-mare, Rumania, Feb. 13, 1948; arrived in Australia, 1961; s. Rudolph and Rose (Straussman) W.; m. Jacqueline Marie Fitzgerald, Sept. 20, 1992; children: Lucinda, Harrison. MB, BS, U. Sydney, Australia, 1972; DSc, U. New S. Wales, Sydney, 1991, MHA, 1998. Registered med. practitioner in NSW, Queensland, Australian Capital Territory and UK. Intern Royal Brisbane Hosp., Australia, 1972; chief resident Prince of Wales Children's Hosp., Randwick, NSW, Australia, 1978-79; rsch. fellow Children's Hosp., L.A., 1981-83; assoc. prof. faculty of medicine U. New South Wales, Sydney, 1991—, full prof., 1997—; sr. staff specialist and head oncology program Sydney Children's Hosp., Randwick, 1992—, clin. dir., 1995-96, exec. dir., 1996—; pres. Children's Hosps. Australasia, 1999—; chmn. Brain Tumour Steering Ctr., Australia, 1987-95, Solid Tumour Studies, Australia, 1991-95; exec. Australia and New Zealand Childhood Cancer Group, 1994-95; dir. rsch. program Sch. of Paediatrics, Sydney, 1992-95; mem. editl. bd. Cancer Forum, 1991—, Am Jour. of Pediatric Hematology-Oncology, 1993—. Editor of book; contbr. more than 80 articles to profl. jours, 10 chpts. to books; also conf. abstracts. Pres. Ronald McDonald House, Randwick, Australia, 1993-95; bd. dirs. Sydney Children's Hosp. Found., Randwick, 1995—, Starlight Found., Australia, 1995—, Malcom Sargent Fund, Australia, 1995—. Recipient Hematology Rsch. award U. New South Wales, Sydney, 1989; grantee Nat. Health and Med. Rsch. Coun., Australia, 1991, Brain Found., Australia, 1994. Mem. Am. Assn. for Cancer Rsch., Internat. Soc. Haematology, Clin. Oncolog. Soc. Australia. Office: Sydney Childrens Hosp, High St, Randwick 2031 NSW, Australia

WHITE, LORAY BETTY, public relations executive, writer, actress, producer; b. Houston, Nov. 27, 1934; d. Harold White and Joyce Mae (Jenkins) Mills; m. Sammy Davis Jr., 1957 (div. 1958); 1 child, Deborah R. DeHart. Student, UCLA, 1948-50, 90-91, Nichiren Shoshu Acad., 1988-92; AA in Bus., Sayer Bus. Sch., 1970; study div. mem. dept. L.A., Soka U., Japan, 1970-86. Editor, entertainment writer L.A. Community New, 1970-81; exec. sec. guest rels. KNBC Prodns., Burbank, Calif., 1969-75; security specialist Xerox X10 Think Tank, L.A., 1975-80; exec. asst. Ralph Powell & Assocs., L.A., 1980-82; pres., owner, producer LBW & Assocs. Pub. Rels., L.A., 1980—; owner, producer, writer, host TV prodn. co. Pub. Pub. Rels., L.A., 1987—; dir., producer L.B.W. Prodn. "Yesterday, Today, Tomorrow, L.A., 1981—; with CBS news dept./Bogey's Corner, The Vol. Brigade Corps, KCBS News, 1999. Actress (film) Ten Commandments, 1956, (TV) L.A., 1981—, (Broadway) Joy Ride; appeared in the following endorsements including Budweiser Beer, Old Gold Cigarettes, Salem Cigarettes, TV comls. including Cheer, Puffs Tissue, Coca Cola, Buffern, others; entertainment editor L.A. Community News, 1970-73; writer (column) Balance News,

1980-82. Vol. ARC, 1995, L.B.W. & Assocs., Ltd. Ann. Prodn. of Mother and Daughter of the Yr. Tribute, 1999, L.B.W. & Assocs., United Peace and Cultural Exch. Dinner and Awards Show, 1999; mem. Habitat for Humanity Internat, Nat. Com. Preserve Soc. Sec. and Medicare, 1998-99, Nat. Black Network Assn., AARP, So. Calif. Com. Sr. Citizens, re-elect Scott Wildmen Rep. campaign; mem. Com. to Reelect Ted McConkey to Burbank City Coun., 1999; bd. dirs. Chabmlee Found. of Calif., 1998-99; exec. prodr. The Fifth L.B.W. and Assocs. Internat. Ann. Achievement Awards Show, 1999. Recipient Cert. of Honor, ARC, 1984, Internat. Orgn. Soka Gakkai Internat. of Japan, Cmty. Vols. of Am. award, 1994; named Performer of Yr. Cardella Demillo, 1976-77. Mem. ARC (planning, mktg., prodn. event com. 1995), UCLA Alumni Assn., Lupus Found. Am. (So. Calif. chpt.), Nat. Fedn. Blind, Myohoji-Hokkeko Internat., Libr. of Congress Assocs. (charter). Buddhist. Avocations: singing, acting, TV writing and producing.

WHITE, LYNDA GAYLE MELTON, reading specialist, educational diagnostician; b. Gatesville, Tex., Mar. 11, 1943; d. Dee and Myrtle (Dunlap) White; divorced; children: Melanie Gayle, William Matthew. BS, U. Tex., 1964; MA, U. North Tex., 1979, PhD, 1983, postgrad., 1993, 94; postgrad., Tex. Womans U., 1983. Cert. elem. tchr., spl. edn. tchr., supervision, spl. edn. supr., learning disabilities tchr., orthpedically handicapped tchr., reading specialist, Tex., adminstrs., ednl. diagnostician. Tchr. 2d and 4th grades, spl. edn. tchr. Irving (Tex.) Ind. Sch. Dist., 1964-79, tchr., 1982-83; 4th grade tchr. Northwest Ind. Sch. Dist., Justin, Tex., 1980-81; asst. prin. Grapevine-Colleyville Ind. Sch. Dist., Tex., 1983-87; tchr. reading improvement Carrollton (Tex.)-Farmers Branch Ind. Sch. Dist., 1988-89; cons. lang. arts Edn. Svc. Ctr. Region 10, Richardson, Tex., 1989-91; pvt. practice diagnostic reading and ednl. diagnostician Trophy Club, Tex., 1991—; reading clinician N.Tex. State U., Denton, 1980; instr. spl. edn. U. Tex., Dallas, 1983, U Tex., Arlington, 1988; vis. prof. Tex. Women's U., Denton, 1983, 84, 87-88; h.s. resource tchr., 1997-98; diagnostician, Hillsboro, Tex., 1999; tchr. homebound handicapped, Hillsboro, 1999-2000; tchr. spl. edn. Irving ISD, 2000—. Author: Matt's Cats; contbr. Reading Rsch. Revisited, also revs. to Case Mgmt. Monthly Confs., Scottish Rite Hosp. and profl. jours. Facilitator Helping One Student To Succeed Reading Program, Copperas Cove, Tex. Mem. ASCD, Internat. Reading Assn. (North Tex. coun.), Learning Disabilities of Tex., Orton Disability Soc., Coun. for Exceptional Children, Phi Delta Kappa. Home: 725 Cowboys Pkwy # 3072 Irving TX 75063-5261

WHITE, MARGIT TRISKA, financial advisor; b. Greenport, N.Y.; d. Joseph A. and Esther M. (Olstad) Triska; m. Robert Lamar Cannon (div. 1971); children: Catherine Margit, Sandra Leigh, Robert Milchrist II. BA, Duke U. CFP. Adminstr. Washington Opportunities for Women, 1971-80; account exec. Merrill Lynch, Bethesda, Md., 1980-82; v.p. investments, fin. planner Prudential Securities, Washington, 1982-94, Morgan Stanley Dean Witter, Washington, 1994—; mem. fin. adv. bd. Bus. Women Internat., Women of Washington. Mem. Internat. Assn. Fin. Planning, Inst. Cert. Fin. Planners, Women in Housing and Fin., Fin. Women's Assn., The Internat. Alliance, Zeta Tau Alpha. Office: Morgan Stanley Dean Witter 1775 Eye St NW Ste 200 Washington DC 20006-2409

WHITE, MARTHA VETTER, allergy and immunology physician, researcher; b. Richmond, Va., Oct. 23, 1951; d. Robert Joseph and Miriam Ernestine (Thomas) Vetter; m. Frederick Joseph Kozub, Oct. 11, 1975 (div. June 1982); m. John Irving White, Feb. 18, 1984; children: Josh, Christie. Student, Vanderbilt U., Nashville, 1969-71; BA, U. Richmond, 1973; MD, Va. Commonwealth U., Richmond, 1978. Cert. m. Bd. Pediatrics, Am. Bd. Allergy and Immunology. Pediatric intern and resident Va. Commonwealth U., Richmond, 1978-81; locum tenans Pub. Health, Richmond, Va., 1981-82; fellow Allergy and Immunology U. Southern Calif., L.A., 1983-84, Georgetown U., 1983-84; sr. staff fellow Food and Drug Adminstrn., Bethesda, Md., 1984-85; NSRA fellow Nat. Inst. Allergy and Infectious Diseases, Bethesda, Md., 1985-88; sr. staff fellow, 1988-93; rsch. dir. Inst. for Asthma and Allergy, Washington, 1993—; cons. Sandoz Pharms., Marion Merrell Dow, Glaxo, Boehringer Ingleheim, Ciba-Geigy, Miles Genentech; rschr. Glaxo, Abbott, Pfizer, Marion Merrell Dow, Miles, Rhône Poulenc Rhoen, Sanofi, Adams, Astra, Merck, Neurbiol. Techs., 3M, Zeneca, Wyeth, Smith-Kline Beecham; bd. dirs. Allery & Asthma Network/Mothers of Asthmatics, 1987—; med. editor MA Report, 1986—; assoc. editor Allergy, Asthma and Immunology Guide, 1989-90. Contbr. numerous scientific papers, abstracts, chpts. and reviews in field. Recipient Norwich Eaton Rsch. award, 1987; Merrell Dow scholar in allergy, 1989; Geigy fellow, 1984. Mem. Am. Assn. Immunologists, Am. Acad. Pediatrics, Adm. Acad. Allergy and Immunology, Am. Coll. Allergy and Immunology, Am. Thoracic Soc., Beta Beta Beta, Psi Chi, Gamma Sigma Epsilon. Office: Inst Asthma and Allergy 106 Irving St NW Ste 108 Washington DC 20010-2994

WHITE, MARY RUTH WATHEN, social services administrator; b. Athens, Tex., Dec. 27, 1927; d. Benedict Hudson and Sara Elizabeth (Evans) W.; m. Robert M. White, Nov. 10, 1946; children: Martha Elizabeth, Robert Miles, Jr., William Benedict, Mary Ruth, Jesse Wathen, Margaret Fay, Maureen Adele, Thomas Evan. BA, Stephen F. Austin State U., Nacogdoches, Tex., 1948. Chmn. Regional Drug Abuse Com., San Antonio, 1975-81, Met. Youth Coun., San Antonio, 1976-78; state chmn. Citizens United for Rehab. Errants, San Antonio, 1978-91; sec. Bexar County Detention Ministries, San Antonio, 1979-88; chmn. Bexar County (Tex.) Jail Commn., 1980-82; chmn. com. on role of family in reducing recidivism Tex. Dept. Criminal Justice, Austin, 1985—; chmn. Met. Cmty. Corrections Com., San Antonio, 1986-90; bd. dirs. Tex. Coalition for Juvenile Justice, 1975-93, Target 90 Youth Coordinating Coun., San Antonio, 1986-89; local chmn. vol. adv. bd. Tex. Youth Commn., 1986-87. Pres. San Antonio City Coun. PTA, 1976-78, Rep. Bus. Women Bexar County, San Antonio, 1984-86, North Urban Deanery, San Antonio Alliance Mental Illness, 1995-96, also legis. chmn.; bd. dirs. CURE, 1978-92; legis. chmn. Archdiocese of San Antonio Coun. Cath. Women; mem. allocation com. United Way, San Antonio, 1986-91; founder chmn. South Tex. Consumer and Family Support Consortium, 1996-97. Named Today's Woman, San Antonio Light newspaper, 1985, Outstanding Rep. Woman, Rep. Bus. Women Bexar County, 1987; honoree Rep. Women Stars over Tex., 1992. Mem. Am. Corrections Assn., Assn. Criminal Justice Planners, LWV (pres. San Antonio chpt. 1984-86), Conservation Soc., Fedn. Women (bd. dirs. 1984-90), DAR (regent), Colonial Dames (pres.), Cath. Daus. Am. (profl. registered parliamentarian, past regent Ct. of St. Anthony), Tex. Cath. Daus. Am. (state legis. chair), San Antonio Alliance for Mentally Ill (pres. 1996-97). Home: 701 E Sunshine Dr San Antonio TX 78228-2516 Office: 5372 Fredericksburg Rd Ste 114 San Antonio TX 78229-3559

WHITE, NELSON HENRY, writer, publisher, realtor; b. Balt., Oct. 29, 1938; s. Thomas Robert and Edith Eyre W.; m. Sergei Saint-Germain, Aug. 29, 1972 (div. Dec. 30, 1992); m. Sheila Ann Emery White, Apr. 1, 1994. BA in History, U. Redlands, Calif., 1968; D in Divinity, Light of Truth Ch., Pasadena, Calif., 1971; D in Theology, Pasadena Inst., Pasadena, Calif., 1973. Teaching cert., Calif. 1969. Opr. Religious Supply and Book Store, Pasadena, Calif.; sr. calibration lab. technician NASA Ames Rsch. Ctr., Moffet Field, Calif., 1991-96; ret., 1996; estate conservator Superior Ct., Martinez, Calif., 1997. Author over 130 books; contbr. articles to profl. jours. Deputy sheriff San Bernardino County, 1959-61; import specialist U.S. Customs Svc., Terminal Island, Calif., 1970. Named Knight and officer Alter Souveraner Templer Orden, Vienna, Austria, 1989. Mem. Mensa, The Richmond Chor, Pro-Constitution Polit. Action Group. Avocations: private pilot, amateur radio, 4-wheel drive enthusiast, photography, camping, hiking. E-mail address: whtmagick@aol.com. Home: PO Box 21172 El Sobrante CA 94820-1172 Office: Assist 2 Sell Emery Realty 5069 Appian Way El Sobrante CA 94803-1901

WHITE, RAYMOND BURTON, former insurance executive; b. Clarksburg, W.Va., Jan. 22, 1943; s. Joseph C. and Glendine Agnes (Saucer) W.; children: D. Andrew, Christopher B.; m. Cherry Semple; children: Fraser M., H. Hollyday. BS in Fin., U. W.Va., 1965; grad., Coll. of Ins., N.Y.C., 1970; postgrad., Columbia U., 1992. Lic. casualty, property broker. With U.S. Fidelity & Guaranty Co., Charleston, W.Va., 1965-66, Travelers Indemnity Co., Pitts., 1966-69; surety underwriter Travelers Indemnity Co., Hartford, Conn., 1969-70; trainee Johnson & Higgins, N.Y.C., 1970-71; mgr. fin. svcs. Johnson & Higgins, Pitts., 1971-76, mgr. sales dept., 1976-79, mgr. mid. market dept., 1979-83, mgr. benefits dept., 1983-85; mgr. nat. assn. dept. Johnson & Higgins, Washington, 1985-86; sr. acct. mgr., mgr. health group Johnson & Higgins, Pitts., 1986-95, sr. v.p., 1991, prin., 1991; CEO The Watson Inst., 1999; pres. Margaret H. W. Watson Found., 1998. Bd. dirs. Craig House, Pitts., 1987-93, pres., 1992-93, Boyd Cmty. Ctr., Pitts., 1988-89; vestryman local Episcopal Ch., Pitts., 1975-78; mem. Calvary Episcopal Ch.; pres. Pitts. Philharm. Soc., 1987-88; bd. dirs. Pitts. Symphony Soc., 1994—, D.T. Watson Health Svcs., 1994-98; active visiting com. W.Va. U. Coll. Bus. & Econs. With USAR, 1965-70. Mem. W.Va. U. Alumni (pres. 1978-81), Duquesne Club, Allegheny Country Club, Rolling Rock Club. Republican. Avocations: golf, travel, civic involvement.

WHITE, RENEE ALLYN, judge; b. Bronx, N.Y., Sept. 22, 1945; d. Lawrence and Ann (Kaufman) W.; m. Michael W. Moore, Oct. 23, 1993. BA, Hofstra U., 1966; JD, Bklyn. Law Sch., 1969. Bar: N.Y. 1969, U.S. Dist. Ct. (ea. and so. dists.) N.Y. 1977, U.S. Supreme Ct. 1978. Trial atty. Criminal Def. divsn. The Legal Aid Soc., N.Y.C., 1969-74; atty. in charge Criminal Justice sect. Office of Projects Devel. Appealate divsn. First Dept., N.Y.C., 1974-78; adminstrv. law judge City N.Y. Office Adminstrv. Trials and Hearings, 1978-84; judge N.Y.C. Civil Ct., 1984, Criminal Ct. City of N.Y., 1985-88; acting supreme ct. justice, supervising judge of N.Y. County Criminal Ct., 1988-90; acting supreme ct. justice, criminal term, 1990—; lectr. in field, mem. criminal procedure law com. of the office of ct. adminstrn. Editor: Criminal Trial Advocacy, 1977; contbr. in field. Mem. ABA, N.Y. State Bar Assn. (chmn. criminal justice sect. 1985-87, mem. house of dels. 1985-88, 91-95, elected nominating com. 1989-90, co-chair, spl. com. on AIDS and the law 1992-95, chair CLE com. on jud. sect., 1994-99, task force on ct. reorgn. 1997-2000), Assn. of Bar of City of N.Y. (coun. on jud. adminstrn. 1990-94), N.Y. Women's Bar Assn.

WHITE, RICHARD THOMAS, radiologist; b. Binghamton, N.Y., May 10, 1941; s. William Joseph and Winifred (Murphy) W.; 1 child by previous marriage, Kevin Michael; m. Rory Lynn Leyman. BS, SUNY, Binghamton, 1967; DO, Chgo. Coll. Osteo. Medicine, 1972. Intern Bi County Hosp., Warren, Mich.; staff radiologist Bi-County Hosp., 1977-79; resident Detroit Hosp., Children's Hosp., Detroit, 1973-76; fellow Johns Hopkins Hosp., Balt., 1976; asst. prof. radiology Mich. State U., East Lansing, 1980-84, cons. ultra-sound rsch., 1980-83, cons. nuclear magnetic rsch., 1982-83; asst. prof. radiology U. Tex., Houston, 1984-85, U. Ill., Chgo., 1985-88; chief radiology VA Med. Ctr., Bath, N.Y., 1988—; clin. prof. radiology U. Rochester (N.Y.) Sch. Medicine and Dentistry, 1989—; cons. varsity sports, 1980-84, handicapped athletes Spl. Olympics, Washington, 1978-84, Detroit Red Wings hockey team, 1977-84; cons. in radiology St. James Hosp., Hornell, N.Y., 1989—. Med. dir. Mich. Spl. Olympics Ctrl. Mich. U., Mt. Pleasant, 1977-84; bd. dirs. Spl. Olympics, Mich., 1980-84, N.Y. Spl. Olympics, 1996-2000; med. advisor Amateur Hockey Assn. USA, Colorado Springs, Colo., 1980-84. With U.S. Army, 1960-66; lt. col. USAR, 1990-96, ret. Recipient Outstanding Contbn. award Spl. Olympics, 1980; named Team Physician U.S. Nat. Hockey Team, Mich. Amateur Hockey Assn., 1979, 81, 83. Mem. AMA, Am. Osteo. Assn., Am. Osteo. Coll. Radiology, Assn. Mil. Physicians and Surgeons, Am. Osteopath Assn., Radiol. Soc. N.Am., Am. Coll. Radiology, Am. Inst. Ultrasound in Medicine, Am. Acad. Sci., Soc. Med. Cons. to U.S. Armed Forces, Kiwanis, Am. Legion.

WHITE, ROBERT MAYER, meteorologist; b. Boston, Feb. 13, 1923; s. David and Mary (Winkeller) W.; m. Mavis Seagle, Apr. 18, 1948; children—Richard Harry, Edwina Janet. B.A., Harvard, 1944; M.S., Mass. Inst. Tech., 1949, Sc.D., 1950; D.Sc. (hon.), L.I. U., 1976, Rensselaer Poly. Inst., 1977, U. Wis., Milw., 1978; ScD (hon.), U. Bridgeport, 1984, U. R.I., 1986, Clarkson U.; PhD (hon.), Johns Hopkins U., 1982, Drexel U., 1985, Ill. Inst. Tech., 1994. Project scientist Air Force Cambridge Research Center, 1950-58, chief meteorol. devel. lab., 1958-59; asso. dir. research dept. Travelers Ins. Co., 1959-60; pres. Travelers Research Center, Inc., 1960-63; chief U.S. Weather Bur., 1963-65; adminstr. Environ. Sci. Services Adminstrn., 1965-70, NOAA, 1970-77; pres. Joint Oceanographic Inst., Inc., 1977-79; chmn. Climate Research Bd., exec. officer Nat. Acad. Scis., 1977-79; Washington; adminstr. Nat. Research Council, 1979-80; pres. Univ. Corp. Atmospheric Research, 1980-83, Nat. Acad. Eng., 1983-95; Karl T. Compton lectr. MIT, Cambridge, 1995-96; sr. fellow Univ. Corp. Atmospheric Rsch., 1995—; sr. fellow H. John Heinz III Ctr. for Sci., Econs. and Environ., 1996—; pres. Wash. Adv. Group, 1996-98. Author articles in field; mem. editl. bd. Am. Soc. Engring. Edn. jour. Bd. overseers Harvard U., 1977-79; vis. com. meteorology and planetary sci. Mass. Inst. Tech.; Mem. vis. com. Kennedy Sch. Govt., Harvard U.; bd. dirs. Resources for Future, 1980—. Served to capt. USAAF, World War II. Decorated Legion of Honor France; recipient Jesse L. Rosenberger medal U. Chgo., 1971; Cleveland Abbe award Am. Meteorol. Soc., 1969; Godfrey L. Cabot award Aero Club Boston, 1966; Rockefeller Pub. Service award, 1974; David B. Stone award New Eng. Aquarium, 1975; Neptune award Am. Oceanic Orgn., 1977; Matthew Fontaine Maury award Smithsonian Instn., 1976; Internat. Conservation award Nat. Wildlife Fedn., 1976; Internat. Meteorol. Orgn. prize, 1980, Tyler prize for Environ. Achievement U. Calif., 1992, Vannevar Bush award Nat. Sci. Bd., 1998. Fellow AAAS, Am. Meterol. Soc. (coun. 1965-67, 77—, Charles Franklin Brooks award 1978, pres. 1980), Am. Geophys. Union, World Acad. Art and Scis., Australian Acad. Tech. Scis. and Engring., Am. Acad. Arts and Scis., UCAR (sr.); mem. NAE (coun. 1977, pres. 1983-95), Marine Tech. Soc., Coun. Fgn. Rels., Nat. Action Coun. Minorities in Engring. Inc., Finnish Acad. Tech. (fgn. mem. 1991—), Am. Philos. Soc., Engring. Acad. Japan (fgn. assoc. 1988—), Russian Acad. Engring., Royal Acad. Engring. (U.K.) (hon.), Cosmos Club (Washington). Home: Somerset House II 5610 Wisconsin Ave Apt 1506 Bethesda MD 20815-4439 Office: 1275 K St NW Ste 1025 Washington DC 20005-4089

WHITE, ROBERTA LEE, financial analyst; b. Denver, Sept. 18, 1946; d. Harold Tindall and Araminta (Campbell) Bangs; m. Lewis Paul White, Jr., Jan. 23, 1973 (div. Sept. 1974). BA cum laude, Linfield Coll., 1976; postgrad., Lewis and Clark Coll. Lic. tax preparer, Oreg. Office mgr. Multnomah County Auditor, Portland, Oreg., 1977-81; rsch. asst. Dan Goldy and Assocs., Portland, 1981-83; regional asst. Vocat. Rehab., Eugene, Oreg., 1983-85; internal auditor Multnomah County, Portland, 1985-89; cons. Portland, 1989-91; fin. analyst City of Portland, 1991-93; comptroller Wordsmith Svcs., Portland, 1993-97; fin. analyst City of Portland, 1997—; mem. Com. for Implementation of the ADA, Portland, 1991-93. Treas. Mary Wendy Roberts for Sec. of State, Portland, 1992, Re-Elect Mary Wendy Roberts, Portland, 1990, Elect Hank Miggins Com., 1994; mem. Oreg. Women's Polit. Caucus, Portland, 1982-85, City Club, Portland, 1978-81. Democrat. Mem. Disciples of Christ. Avocations: reading, hiking, opera, symphony, ballet. Home: 1620 NE Irving St Apt 80 Portland OR 97232-2244 Office: City of Portland Office of Mgmt and Fin Rm 1250 1120 SW 5th Ave Portland OR 97204-1912

WHITE, RODERICK DOUGLAS THIRKELL, editor, advertising and marketing consultant; b. Ottery St. Mary, Devon, Eng., Mar. 27, 1939; s. Noel Thirkell and Margaret Douglas Thirkell (Robertson) W.; m. Stephanie Frances Powell, Apr. 1964; children: Jestyn, Benedict. BA, Oxford (Eng.) U., 1961, MA, 1964. Various positions with J. Walter Thompson, London, 1962-78; planning dir. Conquest, London, 1979-96, head rsch., 1996—; editor Admap, Henley on Thames, Eng., 1996—. Author: Consumer Product Development, 1974, Advertising—What It Is and How To Do It, 1980, 4th edit., 1999; editor: Digital Media Review, 1999; contbr. numerous articles to profl. jours. Fellow Inst. Practitioners in Advt. Home: 28 Wilmington Ave, London W4 3HA, England Office: Lansdown Conquest Ltd, 4 Flitcroft St, London WC2H 8DJ, England

WHITE, ROGER L., JR., graphic designer, art director; b. Ft. Lauderdale, Fla., Feb. 16, 1961; s. Roger Lee and Bonnie Sue (Ratcliffe) W. Cert. in Art History, Am. Coll. Paris, 1982; BFA, Parsons Sch. of Design, 1983. Designer, art dir. Late Show with David Letterman, N.Y.C., 1985—; art dir. Late Night with David Letterman, N.Y.C., 1993—; illustrator Saturday Night Live, N.Y.C., 1987-94, N.Y. Times, 1993; designer Between the Lions PBS, N.Y.C., 1999—, Court TV, N.Y.C., 1999; illustrator Newsweek Mag., N.Y.C., 1999—; web designer Uproar.com, N.Y.C., 1997-98; instr. Assn. Graphic Comms.,N.Y.C., 1997-99, Tony Randal's Nat. Actors Theatre, N.Y.C., 1997-99. Prin. works include theater marquee Ed Sullivan Theater, 1993, logo design Late Show with David Letterman, 1993, Internet Game, Puzzle A-Go-Go, uproar.com, 1998. Recipient Emmy Contribution award Acad. TV Arts & Scis., 1986, 87; nominee Emmy award, 1994. Mem. Assn. for Computing Machinery, Art Students League, Broadcast Designers Assn. Avocations: painting, skiing. Office: White Lie Design 160 W End Ave Apt 3K New York NY 10023-5603

WHITE, SAXON WILLIAM, physiology educator; b. Sydney, Australia, Mar. 9, 1934; s. William Ernest and Enid Beatrice (Newton) W.; m. Julie Ann Mountain, Dec. 2, 1959; children: Mathew Saxon, Lisa Jane, Jessica Ann. MB, BS, U. Sydney, 1961; MD, U. New South Wales, Australia, 1967. Sr. tutor surgery U. New South Wales, 1964-65; Chapman fellow in cardiology U. Sydney, 1972-74; sr. lectr. human physiology Flinders U., Australia, 1975; found. chmn. human physiology U. Newcastle, Australia, 1976—; rsch. fellow Nat. Heart Found., Australia, 1966-67; sr. rsch. fellow Life Ins. Med. Rsch. Fund, Australia and New Zealand, 1971, O'Seas rsch. fellow, 1968-70; bd. dirs. Heart Rsch. Inst., U. Sydney, 1988—. Editor, co-author The Socio-Ethical and Med. Issues of Drugs in Sport, 1991; contbr. articles to sci. and profl. jours. Chmn. Hunter Acad. Sport, Newcastle, 1987-91; gov. Australian Postgrad. Fedn. Medicine, 1988; Australian rugby rep. in 7 test matches against Eng., Ireland, Scotland, South Africa and New Zealand Maoris. Grantee Nat. Health Med. Rsch. Coun. Australia, Nat. Heart Found., others, 1972—. Fellow Royal Australasian Coll. Surgeons (bd. examiners 1988—); mem. Australian Physiology and Pharm. Soc. (coun. 1978-81), Cardiac Soc. Australia and New Zealand, Internat. Soc. Hypertension, Am. Physiol. Soc. Avocations: cross country running, current affairs cartooning. Office: U Newcastle Med/Health Scis, Human Physiology, Callaghan 2308, Australia

WHITE, STEPHANIE DARLEEN, dancer; b. Richmond, Va., July 20, 1963; d. Stanley Curtis and Barbara Lucille (Logan) W. BFA, N.C. Sch. of the Arts, 1984. Dancer The Richmond (Va.) Ballet, 1984-87, Ballet Met., Columbus, Ohio, 1987-90, The Atlanta Ballet, 1990-91, Basel (Switzerland) Ballet/Stadttheater Basel, 1991-95, The Really Useful Group, 1996-97; tech. and front of house staff Musical Theater, Basel, 1997-98, Stadttheater Basel/Opera, 2000. Avocations: reading, travel, cooking, ice skating, consulting.

WHITE, STEPHEN HALLEY, biophysicist, educator; b. Wewoka, Okla., May 14, 1940; s. James Halley and Gertrude June (Wyatt) W.; m. Buff Ertl, Aug. 20, 1961 (div. 1982); children: Saill, Shell, Storn, Sharr, Skye, Sunde; m. Jackie Marie Dooley, Apr. 14, 1984. BS in Physics, U. Colo., 1963; MS in Physics, U. Wash., 1965, PhD in Physiology and Biophysics, 1969. USPHS postdoctoral fellow biochemistry U. Va., Charlottesville, 1971-72; asst. prof. physiology and biophysics U. Calif., Irvine, 1972-75, assoc. prof. physiology and biophysics, 1975-78, prof. physiology and biophysics, 1978—, vice chmn. physiology and biophysics, 1974-75, chmn. physiology and biophysics, 1977-89; guest biophysicist Brookhaven Nat. Lab., Upton, L.I., N.Y., 1977-99. Contbr. numerous articles to profl. jours. Served to capt. USAR, 1969-71. Recipient Research Career Devel. award USPHS, 1975-80, Kaiser-Permanente award, 1975, 92; grantee NIH, 1971—, NSF, 1971—. Mem. NSF (adv. panel for molecular biology 1982-85, mem. nat. steering com. advanced neutron source 1992-95), Internat. Union Pure and Applied Biophysics (U.S. nat. com. 1997—, chmn. 2000—), Fedn. Am. Soc. for Exptl. Biology (bd. mem. 1998—), Biophys. Soc. (chmn. membrane biophysics subgroup 1977-78, acting sec., treas. 1979-80, coun. 1981-84, exec. bd. 1981-83, program chmn. 1985, ann. meeting sec. 1987-95, pres. 1996-97, Disting. Svc. award 1999), Am. Physiol. Soc. (editl. bd. 1981-93, membership com. 1985-86, publ. com. 1987-91), Assn. Chmn. Depts. Physiology (rep. to coun. acad. scos. 1981-82, councilor 1982-83, pres. 1986-87), Soc. Gen. Physiologists (treas. 1985-88, The Protein Soc. (electronic pub. coord. 1993—). Avocations: sky diving, cooking, travel. Office: U Calif Dept Physiology & Biophysics Med Sci I-D346 Irvine CA 92697-4560

WHITE, W. ROBIN, writer; b. Kodaikanal, Madras, India, July 12, 1928; came to U.S., 1944; s. Emmons Eaton and Ruth Esther (Parker) W.; m. Marian Lucille Biesterfield, Feb. 3, 1948 (dec. Mar. 1983); children: Christopher, Parker, Shelley. BA, Yale U., 1950; MA, Calif. State Poly. U., 1991. Instr. writers program UCLA, 1985-93; lectr. Calif. State Poly. U., Pomona, 1985-93; exec. officer Calif. State Regional Ctrs., Ukiah, Calif., 1973-79. Author: Elephant Hill, 1959 (Harper prize), House of Many Rooms, 1958, Men and Angels, 1961, Foreign Soil, 1962, All in Favor Say No, 1964, His Own Kind, 1967, Be Not Afraid, 1972, The Special Child, 1978, The Troll of Crazy Mule Camp, 1979, Moses the Man, 1981, The Winning Writer: Studies in the Art of Self-Expression, 1997; anthologies include: Best American Stories, O. Henry Prize Stories, Best Modern Short Stories, Seventeen's Stories, others; contbr. numerous mags. including Harper's, The New Yorker, New York Times, L.A. Times, Harper's Bazaar, Saturday Evening Post, Ladies' Home Jour., Seventeen, Nat. Wildlife, Mademoiselle, The Reporter; author poetry (Poetry award 1993, 94, 95); editor-in-chief Per/Se Internat. Quar., 1965-69; fiction editor UCLA West/Word, 1989-90. Class rep. Kodai-Woodstock Found., 1986-2000; elder Presbyn. Session, Claremont, Calif., 1988-91; mem. libr. commn. Pasadena Presbyn. Ch., 1996-99. Recipient Disting. Achievement award Ednl. Press Assn., 1974, North Coast Regional Ctr., Ukiah, 1978, Harper prize Harper & Bros., 1959, O. Henry award Doubleday, 1960; Bread Loaf fellow Middlebury Coll., 1956, Stegner fellow Stanford U., 1956-57. Mem. Calif. State Poetry Soc., Authors Guild. Democrat. Presbyterian. Avocations: backpacking, gardening, photography, birds. Home: 1940 Fletcher Ave South Pasadena CA 91030-4625

WHITE, WALTER HIAWATHA, JR., lawyer; b. Milw., Aug. 21, 1954; s. Walter H. and Winifred (Parker) W.; m. Sonja Athene Rein, Dec. 30, 1977. Student, Leningrad Pedagogical Inst., USSR, 1976; BA, Amherst Coll., 1977; JD, U. Calif., Berkeley, 1980. Bar: Wis. 1980, U.S. Dist. Ct. (ea. dist.) Wis. 1980, U.S. Ct. Appeals (7th cir.) 1980, U.S. Supreme Ct. 1983. Assoc. Michael, Best & Friedrich, Milw., 1980-88; commr. securities State of Wis., 1988-91; ptnr. Quarles & Brady, Milw., 1991-94; mng. dir. Steptoe & Johnson Internat., Moscow, 1994-99; ptnr. Bryan Cave, London, 1999—; trustee Milw. Found., 1992—; vice chmn. dist. com. Bd. Attys. Profl. Responsibility, Milw., 1984-87; bd. dirs. Wis. Trust Found., Madison, Church Mut. Ins. Co., Merrill, Wis., Ctrl. Asian Am. Enterprise Fund. Editor Black Law Jour., 1978-80; mem. editorial bd. Barrister Mag.; contbr. articles to profl. jours. Mem. Cardinal Stritch Coll. Bus. Adv. Bd., Milw., 1982-85, health law com. Wis. Civil Liberties Union, Milw., 1985—, Gov.'s Adv. Bd. to Legal Services Corp., Madison, 1982-87; sec. Milw. Forum Inc., 1982—; pres. Milw. Urban League, 1985; bd. dirs. WUWM Pub. Radio Sta., Milw., 1983-86, Family Service Milw., Inc., 1987-89, Neighborhood House of Milw., Inc., 1987—. John Woodruff Simpson fellow, 1977; Named one of the 86 most interesting people in Milw., Milw. Mag., 1986. Mem. ABA (chair young lawyers div. 1989-90, commn. on opportunities for minorities in the profession, del. assn. Soviet lawyers, co-chair commonwealth of ind. states law com. of internat. law and practice sect. 1990-91), Nat. Bar Assn., Assn. Internat. des Jeunes Avocats, Milw. Bar Assn., Wis. Black Lawyers Assn. (bd. dirs. 1982-83), Milw. Young Lawyers Assn. (pres. 1984-85, pres.'s award 1985), Bd. Bar Examiners, Milw. Found. Avocations: Russian lit., rowing, squash. Office: Bryan Cave LLP, 33 Cannon St, London EC4M 5TE, England*

WHITE, WARREN TRAVIS, educational consultant firm executive; b. Thrift, Tex., Apr. 28, 1926; s. Warren Travis and Leika (Clark) W.; m. Genevieve Greer; children: Warren Travis, Grady Spruce, Robert Coulter, Carroll Greer; m. Elizabeth Jean Dinkmeyer, June 12, 1964; children: Naomi Kimberly, Stacey Michèle. BA, U. Tex., 1949, MA, 1955; EdD, Vanderbilt U., 1968. Cert. pub. sch. teaching and adminstrn., Tex. Tchr. Ft. Worth (Tex.) Ind. Sch. Dist., 1952-56, adminstr., 1971-89; prin. Midland (Tex.) Sch. Dist., 1956-61, Riverview Gardens Sch. Dist., St. Louis, 1963-64; adminstr. Richmond (Va.) Pub. Schs., 1964-68; supt. Caesar Rodney Sch. Dist., Camden, Del., 1968-71; v.p. White and White, Ft. Worth, 1989—; cons. Office of Indian Edn., Region VI; adj. prof. U. Va., 1964-68, U. Del., 1968-71. Contbr. articles to profl. jours. Mem. ushers com. Univ. Christian Ch.; mem. steering com. Ft. Worth Mayor's Adv. Com. on Energy Conservation; trustee Masonic Temple Assn., Ft. Worth Masonic Libr. and Mus., Ft. Worth Scottish Rite Found., Inc.; bd. dirs. Knights Templar Edn. Found. With U.S. Army, 1944-46, ATO. Mem. NRA, Tex. Assn. Sch. Adminstrs. (chmn. Tex. Pub. Schs. Week com.), Masons (chmn. pub. edn. com. Grand Lodge of Tex., past master Ft. Worth lodge 148, past high priest Ft. Worth chpt. 58, past master Ft. Worth coun. 42), Order of DeMolay (dist. gov., Legion of Honor), Knights Templar (past comdr. Worth Commandery 19),

Shriners, Scottish Rite (33-Degree IGH). Avocations: traveling, camping, hunting, reading. Home: 4109 Wedgworth Rd S Fort Worth TX 76133-3614 Office: White and White PO Box 330936 Fort Worth TX 76163-0936

WHITE, WILLIAM CHARLES, physicist; b. May 12, 1922; married. BA in Astronomy and Physics, Ohio Wesleyan U., 1948; MS in Astrophysics and Physics, Ohio State U., 1950; postgrad., U. Utah, 1951-52, Calif. State U. Physicist Naval Weapons Ctr., China Lake, Calif., 1950-71, project engr., 1971-73, ops. rsch. analyst, 1973-80, rsch. analyst, 1978-81. Bd. dirs. WSU Extension Beach Watchers, 1992—, Maxwelton Creek Restoration, 1992-97; mem. restoration-adv. bd. Naval Air Sta., Whidbey Island, Wash., 1996—; mem. tech. adv. com. Marine Resources Commn., Island County, Washington. Fellow Naval Ordnance Test Sta., 1951-52. Mem. AAAS, Am. Inst. Physics, Nature Conservancy, Am. Astronomical Soc., Smithsonian Assn., N.Y. Acad. Sci., Sigma Xi. Methodist. Avocations: skiing, fishing, hiking, coins, stamps. E-mail: wwoth@Whidbey.com.

WHITE, WILLIAM DEAKINS, economics educator; b. Phila., July 13, 1945; s. Gilbert F. and Anne (Underwood) W.;m. Olivia Peabody Murray, Aug. 24, 1985; children: Lydia Bayard, Gilbert Edward. BA, Haverford Coll., 1967; PhD, Harvard U., 1975. Asst. prof. econs. U. Ill., Chgo., 1975-82, assoc. prof. econs. and Inst. Govt. and Pub. Affairs,, 1982-92, prof., 1992-98, assoc. dir. Inst. Govt. and Pub. Affairs, 1989-92; assoc. prof., head health mgmt. program Med. Sch. Yale U., New Haven, 1998—. Author: Public Health and Private Gain, 1979. Vis. Rsch. scholar Yale U., New Haven, 1979-80; recipient Health Care Rsch. award Nat. Inst. for Health Care Mgmt., 1998, Article of Yr. award Assn. for Health Svcs. Rsch., 1999, Faculty Publ. of Yr. award Am. Acad. Med. Adminstrs., 1999. Democrat. Office: Dept Epidemiology and Public Health Yale U Sch of Medicine 60 College St PO Box 208034 New Haven CT 06520-8034

WHITE, WILLIAM DUDLEY, safety engineer; b. Birmingham, Mich., June 11, 1958; s. Paul Richard and Annetta Carole (Manhart) W.; m. Tamara Jean Wishon, Mar. 13, 1992; 1 child, Stacy Michelle; 1 stepchild, Royce Edward Vorel. BS cum laude, U. Ctrl. Okla., 1994. Chief maintenance engr. First Union Mgmt., Oklahoma City, 1984-89; safety rep., chmn. safety and suggestion coms. E-Systems, Inc., Greenville, Tex., 1994—; creator curriculum for various safety programs, 1994, 96. Pack master Boy Scouts Am., Edmond, Okla., 1991-92; CPR instr., std. first aid instr. ARC, Hunt County, Tex., 1993—. Mem. Am. Soc. Safety Engrs., Alpha Chi. Roman Catholic. Achievements include development of safety certification/O-J-T checklist tng. program to meet OSHA, Air Force Occupational Safety and Health and Department of Defense standards regarding task proficiency for aircraft servicing, maintenance and daily ops. powered aircraft ground and mobile equipment; restructured indsl. hygiene program in accordance with American Conference of Governmental Industrial Hygienists guidelines. Home: 10203 Blanch Ln Edmond OK 73003-1107

WHITE, WILLIAM SAMUEL, foundation executive; b. Cin., May 8, 1937; s. Nathaniel Ridgway and Mary (Loundes) W.; m. Claire Mott, July 1, 1961; children: Tiffany Loundes, Ridgway Harding. BA, Dartmouth Coll., 1959, MBA, 1960; LL.D. (hon.), Eastern Mich. U., 1975; hon. degree, GMI Engring. & Mgmt. Inst., 1996. With Barrett & Williams, N.Y.C., 1961-62; sr. assoc. Bruce Payne & Assos., N.Y.C., 1962-71; v.p. C. S. Mott Found., Flint, Mich., 1971-75; pres. C. S. Mott Found., 1976—, trustee, 1971—, also chmn. bd. dirs.; bd. dirs. Am. Water Works; chmn. bd. dirs. U.S. Sugar Corp. Mem. exec. com. Daycroft Sch., Greenwich, Conn., 1966-70; bd. dirs. Flint Area Conf., 1971-84, Coun. on Founds., 1985-90, Independent Sector, 1994—, European Found. Centre, 1994—, Civicus, 1995—; mem. citizens adv. task force U. Mich., Flint, 1974-79; chmn. Coun. of Mich. Founds., 1979-81, Flint Area Focus Coun., 1988—; mem. Pres.'s Task Force on Pvt. Sector Initiatives, 1982; trustee GMI Engring. and Mgmt. Inst., 1982-86. Served with U.S. Army, 1960-62. Office: C S Mott Foundation 1200 Mott Foundation Bldg Flint MI 48502-1807

WHITEHEAD, JOHN CUNNINGHAM, bank executive, diplomat, philanthropist; b. Evanston, Ill., Apr. 2, 1922; s. Eugene C. and Winifred W.; m. Helene E. Shannon, Sept. 28, 1946 (div. Dec. 1971); children: Anne Elizabeth, John Gregory; m. Jaan W. Chartener, Oct. 22, 1972 (div. 1986); 1 child, Sarah; m. Nancy Dickerson, 1989 (dec. 1997). BA, Haverford Coll., 1943; MBA, Harvard U., 1947; LLD (hon.), Pace. U., Rutgers U., Haverford Coll., Harvard U., Amherst Coll., Seton Hall U. With Goldman, Sachs & Co., N.Y.C., 1947-84, ptnr., 1956-76, sr. ptnr., co-chmn., 1976-84; dep. sec. Dept. State, Washington, 1985-89; past chmn. Fed. Res. Bank of N.Y. Trustee Haverford Coll., Rockefeller U., Lincoln Ctr. Theater; past pres. bd. overseers Harvard U.; past chmn. trustees coun. Nat. Gallery Art; co-chmn. greater N.Y. coun. Boy Scouts Am.; past chmn. Internat. Rescue Com., UN Assn. U.S.A.; chmn. emeritus Internat. House, Brookings Inst., Youth for Understanding, Andrew Mellon Found. With USNR, 1943-46. Mem. Coun. on Fgn. Rels., Links Club, Univ. Club. Office: 65 E 55th St New York NY 10022-3219

WHITEHEAD, MAURICE, education educator; b. Liverpool, England, Feb. 11, 1952; s. Francis and Mary (Kenolty) W.; m. Janet Helen Druce, Aug. 15, 1987; two children. BA, U. Durham, 1975; PhD, U. Hull, 1984. Tchr. Wimbledon Coll., London, 1976-87; from lectr. to sr. lectr. edn. U. Hull, Eng., 1987-2000; prof. edn. U. Wales, Swansea, 2000—. Author: The Academies of the Reverend Bartholomew Booth in Georgian England and Revolutionary America: Enlightening the Curriculum, 1996; editor-in-chief: European Jour. of Tchr. Edn., 1998—; contbr. articles to profl. jours. Trustee, adminstr. Andrew C. Duncan Cath. History Trust, 1999—. Grantee Spencer Found., Chgo., 1999—. Office: U Wales Swansea, Dept Edn Hendrefoelan, Swansea SA2 7NB, Wales/United Kingdom

WHITEHEAD, PAUL FELTON, landscape consultant; b. Liverpool, Eng.; s. William James and Muriel Lilian (Wood) W.; m. Joan Harris, Apr. 1, 1972; children: Emma Louise, James Anthony. Diploma in arboriculture, horticulture, Pershore Coll., Worcestershire, England, 1970. Prin. J&P Whitehead, Worcestershire, 1970—; cons. Friends of Ionian Greece, 1990—, Kemerton Trustees, Worcestershire, 1992—, English Nature, Eng., 1994—, Peoples Trust for Endangered Species, 1998—; invited lectr. Slovak Acad. Scis., 1995, 99; editor, pub.: 2000: The Little Comberton Millennium Text. Contbr. over 200 articles to profl. jours. Grantee Oleg Polunin Meml. Fund, 1989, Kemerton Trustees, 1994. Mem. Bot. Soc. Brit. Isles, Plantlife, Assn. Europaea de Coleopterologia. Avocations: photography, architecture, music, bibliophily, human culture. Address: Moor Leys Wick Rd, Little Comberton, Pershore Worcs WR10 3EH, England

WHITEHOUSE, FRANK, JR., microbiologist; b. Ann Arbor, Mich., Nov. 20, 1924; s. Frank and May Belle (MacIntire) W.; m. Helen Alice Schimkat Whitehouse; children: Lynne, Beth Ann, Frank Scott, Kim Elaine. BA, U. Mich., Ann Arbor, 1949; MD, 1953. Faculty U. Mich. Med. Sch., Ann Arbor, 1954-95. Contbr. over 65 articles and abstracts to profl. jours.; secular and religious mus. compositions performed in concert and in church. Scoutmaster Boy Scouts Am. 1st Lt. USAF, 1942-46. Decorated Air medal, 1945; recipient Univ. Hopwood Literary award, Ann Arbor, 1947, Undergrad. & Med. Sch. Curriculum Devel. award; Sr. Fulbright lectr. Bahrain, 1979-80. Mem. Am. Soc. Microbiology, Nat. Assn. Advisors for the Health Professions (founder, first exec. dir.), Gilbert and Sullivan Soc. and Choral Union. Avocations: secular and religous musical compositions and their public presentations, philately. Home: 3411 Woodland Rd Ann Arbor MI 48104-4257 Office: Dept Microbiology & Immunology Univ Michigan PO Box 620 Ann Arbor MI 48106-0620

WHITEHOUSE, JOHN HARLAN, JR., systems software consultant, diagnostician; b. Lakewood, Ohio, Sept. 12, 1951; s. John Harlan and Frances Elizabeth (Nation) W.; divorced; 1 child, John Harlan III. BA magna cum laude, Ohio Wesleyan U., 1973; MBA, Cleve. State U., 1976; PhD, Columbia Pacific U., San Rafael, Calif., 1988; postgrad., U. Chgo., 1974, Vedic U. of Am., 1996—. Cert. computing profl.; cert. info. sys. auditor. Programmer San Antonio Express-News, 1977; programming mgr. S.W. Info. Mgmt. Sys., San Antonio, 1977, Utility Data Corp., Houston, 1978; sr. data sys. auditor Nat. City Corp., Cleve., 1978-81; sys. programmer Standard Oil Co., Cleve., 1981-84; adv. sys. engr. IBM, Cleve., 1984-92; pres. Semiotica Corp., 1992—; mem. exams. editl. coun. Inst. for Cert. Computer Profls., Des Plaines, 1990—, test deployment mgr., 1996—, dir. certification, 1999—. Author: CICS Problem Determination Workshop, 1990; co-author: ICCP Guidelines for Recertification, 1990, ICCP Official Study Guide, 1991-95; editor Clifton-Gaston Allen Light, 1994—; also numerous articles, columnist. Mem. Assn. for Computing Machinery (chmn. Greater Cleve. chpt. 1982-83, Svc. Recognition award 1984), Assn. of Inst. for Cert. Computer Profls. (regional dir. 1989-93, nominating com. 1991), Masons, Philalethes Soc., Scottish Rite, York Rite, Phi Beta Kappa. Unitarian. Home: 22291 Berry Dr Rocky River OH 44116-2013 Office: Semiotica Corp PMB 241 25935 Detroit Rd Westlake OH 44145-2452

WHITEHOUSE, MARK EDWARD, communications executive, small business owner; b. Birmingham, England, Mar. 23, 1959; arrived in West Australia, 1969; s. Philip Edward and Denise (Fenton) W.; m. Carol Ann Fry, Oct. 12, 1985. Student, U. West Australia, Perth, 1977-78; diploma radio and TV service, Mt. Lawley Coll., Perth, 1983; diploma, Coll. Recording Arts, 1985. Technician Kosmic Electronic Industries, Perth, 1980-84; recording engr. Planet Sound Studios, Perth, 1985—; owner, mgr. Pro-Copy, 1989—. Patentee "Pro-Copy" system. Mem. Audio Engring. Soc. (assoc.). Avocations: music, golf, cycling. Office: 10-12 Dewar St Ste 3, Morley 6062, Western Australia

WHITEHURST, BROOKS MORRIS, chemical engineer; b. Apr. 9, 1930; s. David Brooks and Bessie Ann (Lowry) W.; m. Carolyn Sue Boyer, July 4, 1951; children: Garnett, Anita, Robert. BS, Va. Poly. Inst. and State U., 1951. Registered profl. engr., N.C. Sr. process asst. Am. Enka Corp., Lowland, Tenn., 1951-56; sr. process devel. engr. Va.-Carolina Chem. Corp., Richmond, Va., 1956-63; project engr. Texaco Inc., Richmond, 1963-66; mgr. engring. svcs. Texasgulf, Inc., Aurora, N.C., 1967-80, mgr. spl. projects, long range planning, 1980-81; pres. Whitehurst Assocs., Inc., New Bern, N.C., 1981—; instr., lectr., cons. alt. sources of energy comty. colls. and univs.; presenter paper Solar World Forum, Brighton, Eng., 1981. Co-chmn. N.C. state supt. task force on secondary edn., 1974—; mem. N.C. state adv. com. on trade and indsl. edn. 1971-77; chmn. Gov.'s Task Force Vols. in Workplace, 1981; chmn. State Adv. Coun. Career Edn., 1977—; gov.'s liaison for edn. and bus., 1978-79. Recipient commendation Pres. U.S., 1981. Mem. AIChE, Am. Inst. Chemists (cert., bd. dirs. 1980-84), N.C. Inst. Chemists (pres. 1975-77), Nat. Soc. Profl. Engrs., N.C. Soc. Profl. Engrs., Royal Soc. Chemistry. Achievements include patents and current work on biodegradable chelate systems, municipal yard waste disposal, micronutrients for agriculture, waste rubber recycling, conversion of industrial by-products containing manganese and phosphorous to useful non-toxic materials for use in agriculture for environmental clean-up; development of environmentally friendly products for forest fertilization. Home: 1983 Hoods Creek Rd New Bern NC 28562-9103 Office: PO Box 3335 New Bern NC 28564-3335

WHITELAW, IAIN EDWIN BAXTER, operations engineer; b. Carshalton, Surrey, England, July 4, 1954; immigrated to Australia, 1962; s. William and Jeanne Anne (Ludovici) W.; m. Rosemary Ann Harrison, Nov. 28, 1976; children: Leanne, Alison. BA Engring., U. West Australia, 1977; grad. dip.chem. engring., West Australia Inst. of Tech., 1986. Chartered profl. engr. Proj. engr. BHP Petroleum, Perth, Australia, 1982-85; prod. and maint. engr. Woodside Offshore Petroleum, Perth, 1985-87, prod. shift supvr., 1987-88, sr. safety advisor, 1989-90, platform ops. superintendent, 1990-95, princ. dev. engr.-ops., 1995-97; ops. engr. Tritech Cons., Perth, 1997-98; prodn. and offtake planner Woodside Energy, Ltd., Perth, 1998—. Mem. Inst. of Engrs., Australia, 1982—, Soc. of Petroleum Engrs., 1985—. Office: Woodside Energy Ltd, GPO Box D188, 6840 Perth Western Australia

WHITELAW, KEVIN JOHN, journalist; b. London, Mar. 28, 1973; s. John David and Susan (Johnson) W. B, Princeton U., 1995. Reporter U.S. News & World Report, Washington, 1995-96, assoc. editor world sect., 1996—. Contbr. numerous articles on world affairs. E-mail: kwhitelaw@usnews.com. Office: US News and World Report Ste 1 1050 Thomas Jefferson St NW Washington DC 20007-3837

WHITELEY, MARK STEVEN, consultant vascular surgeon; b. Bristol, Somerset, Eng., Dec. 5, 1962; s. Michael George and Rosemary Christine (Bogie) W.; m. Zofia Janina Lender, May 20, 1989; children: Emily, Alice, Lucy. M.B.B.S., St. Bartholomews Hosp. Med.Sch, London, 1986; MB, BChir, U. Bath, 1998. Demonstrator in human anatomy St. Bartholomew's Hosp. Med. Sch., London, 1987-88; sr. house officer, registrar in surgery Bristol and Weston, Bristol, Eng., 1989-91; registrar in surgery Queen Alexandra Hosp., Portsmouth, Eng., 1991-92; rsch. fellow Dept. Surgery, Bath, Eng., 1992-93, hon. lectr., 1993-95; clin. lectr. surgery Nuffield Dept. Surgery, 1995-98, U. Oxford, 1995—; cons. vascular surgeon Royal Surrey County Hosp., Guildford, Eng., 1998—; vis. sr. fellow vascular surgery U. Surrey, 1998—. Contbr. articles to profl. jours. Wessex Regional Rsch. grantee Wessex Regional Health Authority, 1993-94, European Soc. for Vascular Surgery European Ednl. Travel grantee, 1996. Fellow Royal Coll. Surgeons Edinburgh, Royal Coll. Surgeons; mem. Vascular Surg. Soc. Gt. Britain and Ireland (affiliate rep. coun. 1996-98), Rouleaux Club (sec. 1994-97). Office: Royal Surrey County Hosp, Dept Vasc Surg Egerton Rd, Guildford GU2 5XX, England

WHITELEY, ROSE MARIE, city clerk, treasurer; b. Benkelman, Nebr., Mar. 26, 1942; d. Alvin James and Grace Rebecca (Alsbury) W. BS, Nebr. State U., Kearney, 1963; MS, Colo. State U., 1968. Cert. home cons./bus. secondary tchr. Home econs. instr. Deuel County H.S., Chappell, Nebr., 1963-66; adult ednl. cons. McCalls Patterns, N.Y.C., 1967-70; exec. dir. Nebr./Iowa chpt. Nat. Multiple Sclerosis Soc., Omaha, 1971-78; grant writer, fundraising dir. Omaha Theatre, 1978-94; city clk., treas. City of Benkelman, 1994—; cons. Fundraising/Grantwriting, Omaha, 1982-94, 94—. Contbr.: The Harvest Gardener, 1992. Treas. Prevention Policy Bd., 1994—, Dundy County Resource Ctr., 1994—; mem. Benkelman Tree Bd., 1994—. Mem. S.W. Clks. Assn., Nebr. Mcpl. Clks. Assn., Internat. Inst. of Mcpl. Clks., Kappa Omicron Phi. Avocations: gardening, gourmet cooking. Home: HC 64 Box 58 Benkelman NE 69021-9156 Office: City of Benkelman PO Box 347 Benkelman NE 69021-0347

WHITEMAN, JOSEPH HILARY MICHAEL, writer, researcher; b. London, Nov. 2, 1906; arrived in South Africa, 1937; s. Frederick Carl and Emily (Brown) W.; m. Dorothy Saye Eavestaff, Dec. 24, 1936; 1 child, Sibyl. BA, Cambridge (Eng.) U., 1929, MA, 1934; BMus, U. South Africa, 1943; PhD, U. Cape Town, 1943, MMus, 1947; HLM, U. South Africa, 1994. Acad. head Staffords Sch., Harrow Weald, Eng., 1933-36; class tchr. Diocesan Coll., Rondebosch, South Africa, 1937-38; lectr. U. Cape Town, South Africa, 1939-43, Rhodes Univ. Coll., Grahamstown, South Africa, 1944-45; lectr., sr. lectr. U. Cape Town, 1946-61, assoc. prof., 1962-71, emeritus assoc. prof., 1972—. Author: The Mystical Life, 1961, Philosophy of Space and Time, 1967, The Meaning of Life, Vol. 1, 1986, Aphorisms on Spiritual Method, 1993; author/lectr. six broadcast lectures for Univ. of the Air, 1974; editor The South African Music Tchr., 1941-95. Mem. South African Soc. Music Tchrs. (coun., past pres.), South African Soc. for Psychical Rsch. (v.p. 1981-85, Valkhoff medal 1968), Am. Soc. for Psychical Rsch., Soc. for Psychical Rsch. Home: 20 Erica Pl, Bergvliet 7945, South Africa

WHITEN, ANDREW, psychologist, educator; m. Susie Challoner; children: Kirsty, Amy. BSc with 1st class honours, U. Sheffield, Eng., 1969; PhD, U. Bristol, Eng., 1973. Rsch. fellow Oxford (Eng.) U., 1972-75; lectr. U. St. Andrews, Scotland, 1975-90; reader U. St. Andrews, 1990-97, prof., 1997—; vis. prof. U. Zurich, Switzerland, 1992; F.M. Bird prof. Emory U., 1996; rsch. reader Brit. Acad., 1999—. Editor: Machiavellian Intelligence, 1988, Vol. II, 1997, Natural Theories of Mind, 1991, Foraging Strategies and Natural Diet of Monkeys, Apes and Humans, 1992. Leverhulme fellow U. St. Andrews, 1997. Fellow Brit. Psychol. Soc., Brit. Acad. E-mail: a.whiten@st-and.ac.uk. Office: U St Andrews, St Andrews KY16 9JU, Scotland

WHITENER, CAROLYN RAYE, artist; b. Corpus Christi, Tex., Feb. 2, 1941; d. Rayburn N. and Alice G. Hamilton; m. Howard Dwain Whitener; children: Mark Dwain, Rynn Rayna. Student, U. Sci. and Arts Okla., 1981-85. Co-owner Honk'n'Holler's, Stillwater, Okla., 1962-75; owner Clynn's Designs, Stillwater, 1969—; co-owner W&W Cattle Ranch, Ninnekah, Okla., 1973—; comml. artist, co-owner Colorvision, Inc., Okla. and Tex., 1979—; cons. Tele-Weight, Buena Vista, Colo., 1985-92, Craig Versus Boren, 1972-76; design cons. Rynn's Svcs., Oklahoma City, 1997—. Active Grady County Environ. Coalition, 1991-92. Recipient Outstanding Cmty. Svc. award, 1992, One Person Who Made a Difference LWVOK, 1997, Pres. Prestigious award Okla. State U., 1996; named Woman of Yr. Okla. City Coun. of Beta Sigma Phi, 1997-98, other awards. Mem. Okla. Assn. Family Cmty. and Edn., Grady County Ext. Homemakers, Oklahoma City Newcomer's Club, Beta Sigma Phi (Woman of Yr. award 1997-98, Outstanding Svc. award 1992, Evening Lions Homecoming Window Design awards, 1966-68). Democrat. Methodist. Avocations: art, sewing, cooking, travel, meeting new people. Home: 10400 Mantle Dr Oklahoma City OK 73162-4522

WHITENER, LAWRENCE BRUCE, political consultant, consumer advocate, educator, paralegal; b. Alexandria, Va., Mar. 5, 1952; s. Ralph Verly and Alice Lee W.; m. Deborah Susan Koons, Dec. 7, 1985; 1 foster child. BA in History and Polit. Sci., Va. Commonwealth U., 1975; diploma, Nat. Inst. Real Estate, 1986; AA in Sci., No. Va. C.C., Annandale, 1987, student, 1995—. Tchr. Fairfax (Va.) County Pub. Schs., 1975-96, Arlington (Va.) Pub. Schs., 1998—; wholesaler Consignment Auto, Falls Church, Va., 1975-77; coach Groveton High Sch. Wrestling Team, Alexandria, 1975-77; senate aide Va. Gen. Assembly, Richmond, 1978; pres. Whitener Cons., Springfield, Va., 1977-86, Real Estate Fin. Svcs., Springfield, 1986-90; U.S. Postal Svc., 1989-97; pres. Amicus Curiae, Springfield, 1992—; coach wrestling team Langley H.S., McLean, 1991-93, J.E.B. Stuart H.S., Falls Church, 1993-95, Mt. Vernon Wrestling Club, 1997—; panelist Am. Arbitration Assn., Washington; automotive and banking specialist, 1994—. Author poetry, 1975, 76, 94, 97, screenplays Sorrow, 1993, Saro, 1996; photographer landscapes; subject of article in The Postal Record, 1996. Mem. Athletic Coun., Fairfax County, 1975-84; appointee Housing Assistance Adv. Com., Fairfax County, 1990; commr. Indsl. Devel. Authority, Fairfax County, 1985-93; candidate Fairfax County Bd. Suprs., Springfield Dist., 1991, Fairfax County Sch. Bd., 1995; chmn. vol. rev. com. Fairfax County Access Cable Ch. 10, 1994—; chmn. W.T. Woodson High Sch.'s Class of '70 25th Reunion, 1995; umpire Am. Softball Assn., 1996—; v.p. Newington Forest Cmty. Assn., 1989-90, bd. dirs., 1998-99; chmn. W.t. Woodson H.S. Class of 1970 30th Reunion, 2000. Recipient Cert. of Appreciation, Fairfax County Bd. of Suprs., 1990, Cert. of Appreciation, Nat. Ctr. for Missing and Exploited Children, 1990. Mem. Am. Arbitration Assn. (panel 1994—), Mortgage Bankers Assn. (legis. com. 1985-90, edn. com. 1986-89), No. Va. Bd. Realtors (pub. rels. com. 1985-90, Cert. of Appreciation, Am. Home Week 1986, 90), No. Va. Wrestling Assn. (treas. 1999—). Avocations: Tae Kwon Do (Black Belt), scuba diving, skydiving, mountaineer, skiing.

WHITENER, WILLIAM GARNETT, dancer, choreographer; b. Seattle, Aug. 17, 1951; s. Warren G. and Virginia Louise (Garnett) W. Student, Cornish Sch. Allied Arts, Seattle, 1958-69. Dancer N.Y.C. Opera, 1969, Joffrey Ballet, N.Y.C., 1969-77, Twyla Tharp Dance, N.Y.C., 1978-87; asst. to choreographer Jerome Robbins for Robbins' Broadway, N.Y.C., 1988; artistic dir. Les Ballets Jazz de Montréal, 1991-93, Royal Winnipeg Ballet, 1993-95, Kansas City Ballet, 1996—; coord. dance dept. Concord Acad., Mass., 1988; vis. artist U. Wash., 1989-91; tchr. Harvard U. Summer Dance, 1989-90, NYU, 1985. Appeared in original Broadway cast Dancin', 1978; choreographer for Princeton Ballet, Joffrey II, John Curry Ice Theatre, Ballet Hispanico of N.Y., Boston Ballet Internat. Choreography Competition, Tommy Tune, Martine Van Hamel/Kevin McKenzie, Ann Reinking, Seattle Repertory Theatre, Am. Ballroom Theater, N.Y.C., Hartford (Conn.) Ballet, On the Boards, (with Bill Irwin) Alive From Off Center (PBS-TV), (opera ensemble of N.Y.) A Little Night Music, Pacific Northwest Ballet, (Seattle Opera) Rusalka, Aida; dancer (films) Amadeus, Zelig, (TV shows) The Catherine Wheel, Dance in America; performer Garden of Earthly Delights, 1988. Bd. trustees DanceUSA, 2000—. Ford Found. scholar, 1963-64. Mem. Actor's Equity, Am. Guild Mus. Artists. Office: Kansas City Ballet 1601 Broadway St Kansas City MO 64108-1207

WHITESIDE, WILLIAM ANTHONY, JR., lawyer; b. Phila., Feb. 23, 1929; s. William Anthony and Ellen T. (Hensler) W.; m. Eileen Ann Ferrick, Feb. 27, 1954; children: William Anthony III, Michael P., Eileen A., Richard F., Christopher J., Mary P. BS, Notre Dame U., 1951; LLB, U. Pa., 1954. Bar: Pa. 1955. Assoc. Speiser, Satinsky, Gilliland & Packel, Phila., 1956-58, ptnr., 1958-61; ptnr. Fox, Rothschild, O'Brien & Frankel, Phila., 1961—. Trustee Am. Coll. Mgmt. and Tech., Dubrovnik, Croatia; chmn. emeritus bd. trustees and exec. com., emeritus trustee, Rochester Inst. of Tech.; mem. pres. adv. coun. U. Notre Dame; bd. dirs. PAL, mem. exec. com.; emeritus trustee Germantown Acad., past pres. 1st lt. USAF, 1954-56. Named Man of Yr. Notre Dame club Phila, 1967. Mem. ABA, Pa. Bar Assn., Phila. Bar Assn., N.Y. Union League Club, Pyramid Club, Wissahickon Skating Club, Pa Soc. Republican. Roman Catholic. Home: 7808 Cobden Rd Laverock PA 19038-7256 also: 901 Gardens Plz Ocean City NJ 08226-4719 Office: Fox Rothschild O'Brien & Frankel 2000 Market St Ste 10 Philadelphia PA 19103-3231

WHITING, GORDON JAMES, investment banker; b. Bronxville, N.Y., Nov. 17, 1965; s. William Gordon Whiting and Doris (Chubb) Whiting Simmons. BS, Cornell U., 1988; MBA, Columbia U., 1994. Sales and mktg. mgr. Epcot Ltd., Tsim Sha Tsui, Kowloon, Hong Kong, 1989-90; mng. dir. Stapenhurst Ltd., Victoria, Hong Kong, 1990-92; acquisitions assoc. W. P. Carey & Co., LLC, N.Y.C., 1993-94; 2d v.p. W. P. Carey & Co., Inc., N.Y.C., 1994-95, v.p., 1995-97, 1st v.p., 1997-98, sr. v.p., 1998-2000, dep. dir. of acquistions, 1999—, exec. dir., 2000—; exec. v.p. and portfolio mgr. Corp. Property Assocs.: 14, Inc., N.Y.C., 1998-2000, pres., portfolio mgr., 2000—. Local bd. mem. Selective Svc. Sys.; mem. Hon. Order Ky. Cols.; active Eagle Scouts. Named to Hon. Order Ky. Cols. Mem. Profl. Assn. Diving Instrs., Bronxville Field Club, Constant Spring Golf Club (Jamaica), Holland Lodge No. 8 F&AM, Leander Club (U.K.), Mashomack Preserve Club (Pine Plains, N.Y.), The Order of St. John, The Pilgrims, Racquet and Tennis Club, Royal Hong Kong Yacht Club, Sigma Chi. Republican. Episcopalian. Avocations: fly fishing, golf, scuba diving, skiing, squash. Home: 136 E 55th St Apt 3P New York NY 10022-4518 Office: W P Carey & Co LLC 50 Rockefeller Plz New York NY 10020-1605

WHITLOCK, BRENT KEVIN, electrical engineer; b. Rockford, Ill., Aug. 21, 1967; s. James Robert and Barbara Kay Whitlock; m. Ellen Sue Cochran, May 26, 1990. BS, U. Ill., 1990, MS, 1993, PhD, 1996. Co-op engr. IBM Fed. Systems Divsn., Manassas, Va., 1986, Sundstrand Corp., Rockford, Ill., 1987-89; summer intern engr. Motorola Comms. Sector, Schaumburg, Ill., 1990, Motorola Land Mobile Products, Schaumburg, 1991; tchg. asst. U. Ill., Urbana, 1990, rsch. asst., 1991-96; summer intern rschr. IBM Watson Rsch. Ctr., Yorktown Heights, N.Y., 1993; sr. CAD engr. Cypress Semiconductor, San Jose, Calif., 1996-98; sr. scientist RSoft, Inc., Ossining, N.Y., 1998—; mem. tech. planning com. Internat. Soc. Optical Engring. Optoelectronics 2000 Symposium. Author: (software) iFROST Fiber-Optics Simulator, 1996; contbr. articles to profl. jours.; reviewer jour. articles in field. Sec., co-founder U. Ill. studnet chpt. Optical Soc. Am., Urbana, 1994-95; chmn. U. Ill. Elec. and Computer Engring. Student Adv. Com., Urbana, 1992-94. Recipient fellowship NSF, 1991-94, univ. fellowship U. Ill., 1990-91. Mem. IEEE, Optical Soc. Am., U. Ill. Alumni Assn. Avocations: photography, jazz music, piano, saxophone, bicycling, SCUBA diving. Office: RSoft Inc 200 Executive Blvd Ossining NY 10562-2560

WHITLOW, WILLIAM LA FOND, minister, theology school planter; b. Mpls., Oct. 20, 1932; s. George Lester and Wanona Nadine (Ridgeway) W.; m. Donna Mae Magnuson, June 13, 1953; children: Debra, Cathleen, Lisa Mae. Ministerial diploma, Eugene (Oreg.) Bible Coll., 1953; postgrad., Seattle Pacific U., 1961; BTh, ThM, Internat. Sem., Orlando, Fla., 1981, ThD summa cum laude, 1986, DD (hon.), 1984; LittD, Evangel Christian U. Am., 1992. Ordained to ministry Open Bible Standard Chs., 1954, Biltmore Bible Ch., 1988. Asst. and pastor Oreg. chs., 1949-55; dean pers. Calif. Open Bible Inst., Pasadena, 1957-58; pres., island supt. Bible Inst., Montego Bay, Jamaica, 1958-59, San Fernando, Trinidad, 1960-65; sr. pastor Biltmore Bible Ch., Phoenix, 1967—; pres. Biltmore Bible Sch. Theology, Phoenix, 1982-86; extension sch. rep. Internat. Sem., Orlando, 1984-91; adj. faculty mem. Evang. Theol. Sem., Dixon, Mo., 1989-91; affiliate prof. Vision Christian U., Ramona, Calif., 1991. Author, compiler: Basic Bible School Builder, 1986—;

also numerous Bible tng. courses. Recipient Outstanding Acad. Achievement award Internat. Sem., 1987. Office: Biltmore Bible Christian Ctr 3330 E Camelback Rd Phoenix AZ 85018-2310

WHITMAN, KATHY VELMA ROSE (ELK WOMAN WHITMAN), artist, sculptor, art educator; b. Bismarck, N.D., Aug. 12, 1952; d. Carl Jr. and Edith Geneva (Lykken) W.; m. Robert Paul Luger, Feb. 21, 1971 (div. Jan. 1982); children: Shannon, Lakota, Cannupa, Palani; m. Dean P. Fox (div. 1985); 1 child, Otgadahe. Student, Standing Rock C.C., Ft. Yates, N.D., 1973-74, Sinte Gleska Coll., Rosebud, S.D., 1975-77, U. S.D., 1977, Ariz. State U., 1992-93. Instr. art Sinte Gleska Coll., 1975-77, Standing Rock C.C., 1977-78; co-mgr. Four Bears Motor Lodge, New Town, N.D., 1981-82; store owner Nux-Baga Lodge, New Town, 1982-85; jeweler, painter Phoenix; artist-in-residence N.D. Coun. on Arts, Bismarck, 1983-84, bd. dirs., 1985; artist-in-residence Evanston Twp. H.S., Ill., 1996; cultural cons. movie prodn., Phoenix, Ariz., 1994. One woman shows include Mus. of Am. Indian, N.Y.C., 1983, Charleroi Internat. Fair, Belgium, 1984, Heard Mus., Phoenix, 1987-92, Phoenix Gallery, Nurnburg, Germany, 1990-96, Lovena Ohl Gallery, Phoenix, 1990-94, Phoenix Gallery, Coeur d'Alene, Idaho, 1992, Turquoise Tortoise Gallery, Tubac, Ariz., 1992-93, Yah-ta-hey Gallery, New London, Conn., 1992-93, Silver Sun Gallery, Santa Fe, N.Mex., 1992-96, Tribal Expessions Gallery, Arlington Heights, Ill., 1994-96, others; represented in permanent collections at Mus. of the Am. Indian, N.Y.C., Mesa (Ariz.) C.C. Bd. dirs. Ft. Berthold C.C., New Town, 1983-85; pres. Cannonball (N.D.) Pow-Wow Com., 1978; parent rep. Head Start, Ft. Yates, 1974. Recipient best craftsman spl. award Bullock's Indian Arts and Crafts, 1986, best of fine arts award No. Plains Tribal Arts, Sioux Falls, S.D., 1988, best of show award Pasadena Western Relic and Native Am. Show, 1991, 2 1st place awards Santa Fe Indian Market, 1993, 2 2nd place awards, 1994, 2 3rd place awards, 1994, 74th Ann. SWAIA Santa Fe Indian Mkt. 1st place award, 1995, 2d place award, 1995, 97, 2 3rd place awards, 1995, 2 Honorable Mentions in sculpture N.Mex. State Fair, 1996. Mem. Indian Arts and Crafts Assn., S.W. Assn. on Indian Affairs (life, 1st and 2nd place awards Santa Fe Indian Market 1995, 2 3rd place awards 1995, 1st place and 2nd place awards Santa Fe Indian Market 1996). Avocations: native American crafts, furniture building, running and hiking, dancing, singing. Home and Studio: 2717 E Victor Hugo Ave Phoenix AZ 85032-5935

WHITMAN, MARINA VON NEUMANN, economist, educator; b. N.Y.C., Mar. 6, 1935; d. John and Mariette (Kovesi) von Neumann; m. Robert Freeman Whitman, June 23, 1956; children: Malcolm Russell, Laura Mariette. BA summa cum laude, Radcliffe Coll., 1956; MA, Columbia U., 1959, PhD, 1962; LHD (hon.), Russell Sage Coll., 1972; LLD (hon.), Cedar Crest Coll., 1973, Hobart and William Smith Coll., 1973; LHD (hon.), U. Mass., 1975, N.Y. Poly. Inst., 1975; LLD (hon.), Coe Coll., 1975, Marietta Coll., 1976. Mem. faculty U. Pitts., 1962-79, prof. econs., 1971-73, disting. pub. svc. prof. econs., 1973-79; v.p., chief economist Gen. Motors Corp., N.Y.C., 1979-85, group v.p. pub. affairs, 1985-92; disting. vis. prof. bus. adminstrn., pub. policy U. Mich., Ann Arbor, 1992-94, prof. bus. adminstrn., pub. policy, 1994—; bd. dirs. Chase Manhattan Corp., Alcoa, Procter & Gamble Co., Unocal; mem. Trilateral Commn., 1973-84, 88-95; mem. Pres. Adv. Com. on Trade Policy and Negotiations, 1987-93; mem. tech. assessment adv. coun. U.S. Congress Office of Tech. Assessment, 1990-95; mem. Consultative Group on Internat. Econs. and Monetary Affairs, 1979—; mem. U.S. Price Commn., 1971-72, Coun. Econ. Advisers, Exec. Office of Pres., 1972-73. Author: Government Risk-Sharing in Foreign Investment, 1965, International and Interregional Payments Adjustment, 1967, Economic Goals and Policy Instruments, 1970, Reflections of Interdependence: Issues for Economic Theory and U.S. Policy, 1979, New World, New Rules: The Changing Role of the American Corporation, 1999; bd. editors: Am. Econ. Rev., 1974-77; mem. editl. bd.: Fgn. Policy; contbr. articles to profl. jours. Trustee Nat. Bur. Econ. Rsch., 1993—, Princeton U., 1980-90, Inst. Advanced Study, 1999—; bd. dirs. Inst. for Internat. Econs., 1986—, Salzburg Seminar, 1994—, Eurasia Found., 1992-95; bd. overseers Harvard U., 1972-78, mem. vis. com. Kennedy Sch., 1992-98. Fellow Earhart Found., 1959-60, AAUW, 1960-61, NSF, 1968-70, Social Security Rsch. Coun.; recipient Columbia medal for excellence, 1973, George Washington award Am. Hungarian Found., 1975. Mem. Am. Econ. Assn. (exec. com. 1977-80), AAAS, Coun. Fgn. Rels. (dir. 1977-87), Phi Beta Kappa. Office: U Mich Gerald Ford Sch Pub Policy 411 Lorch Hall Ann Arbor MI 48109-1220

WHITMAN, MICHAEL EDWARD, information systems educator; b. Ozark, Ala., Sept. 28, 1964; s. Frankie Joe and Jennifer Jackson Whitman; m. Rhonda Hake Whitman, Sept. 10, 1995; children: Rachel Lee, Alexander James Truman. BSBA in Mgmt., Auburn U., 1986, MBA, 1991, PhD in Info. Systems, 1994. Asst. prof. MIS U. Nev., Las Vegas, 1994-98; assoc. prof. info. systems Kennesaw (Ga.) State U., 1998—; rschr. Kennesaw State U., 1998—, U. Nev., 1994-98. Contbr. articles to profl. jours. Capt. U.S. Army, 1986-90. Mem. IEEE, Assn. of Computing Machinery, Decision Scis. Inst., Assn. for Info. Systems, Assn. of Info. Tech. Profls. Avocations: golf, home improvement, woodworking. Office: CSIS Dept Kennesaw State U 1000 Chastain Rd NW Kennesaw GA 30144-5588

WHITMORE, RAYMOND LESLIE, retired mining-metallurgical engineering educator; b. Luton, Eng., Sept. 13, 1920; arrived in Australia, 1967; m. Ruth H. Franklin, Oct. 23, 1947; children: John, Mark. BSc with honours in Physics, U. London, 1942; PhD, U. Birmingham, Eng., 1959, DSc, 1969. Chartered engr. and physicist, U.K.; chartered profl. engr., Australia. Lab. asst. mining dept. U. Birmingham, 1938-42, rsch. fellow chem. engring. dept., lectr., 1948-51; project engr. Simon-Carves Ltd., Cheadle Heath, Cheshire, Eng., 1946-48; rsch. mgr. Ferodo Ltd., Chapel-en-le-Frith, Eng., 1951-53; reader dept. mining engring. U. Nottingham, Eng., 1953-67; prof. mining and metall. engring. U. Queensland, Brisbane, Australia, 1967-85, prof. emeritus, 1985—, dean engring., 1974-76, established Julius Kruttschnitt Mineral Rsch. Ctr., hon. rsch. cons. dept. anthropology and sociology, 1991; mining, edn. and heritage cons., Brisbane, 1985—; mem. Australian Rsch. Grants Com., 1970-74; mem. coun. Australian Mineral Found., 1975-80; mem. project team econ. recycling and conservation structurs Warren Ctr., U. Sydney, Australia, 1989; hon. cons. Ipswich Mining Mus. and Bot. Gardens, 1989-91, Queensland Mus., 1994; advisor on mining edn., established dept. mining engring. Papua New Guinea U. Tech., Lae, 1989-99; Sir Raphael Cilento orator Nat. Trust Queensland, 1990; lectr. in Gt. Britain, Germany, Sweden, Japan, Can., U.S.; spkr. on indsl. archaeol. subjects. Author: Rheology of the Circulation, 1968, Riding the Minerals Boom, 1969, Coal in Queensland, Vol. 1, 1981, Vol. 2, 1985, Vol. 3, 1991, Queensland's Early Waterworks, 1997; editor 4 books; contbr. over 150 articles on fluid and particle mechanics with spl. reference to their application to mining, mineral processing and biol. sys., history and heritage of engring. in Australia, particularly Queensland, to profl. jours., chpts. to books. Mem. Internat. Com. for Conservation Indsl. Heritage, 1980-90; mem. adv. com. Landscapes Queensland, 1987-89; bd. dirs. Queensland Mus. Sciencentre, 1989—; mem. State Heritage Com., 1990-92; mem. heritage adv. com. Ipswich City Coun., 1991—, Bisbane City Coun., 1991—; mem. Queensland Heritage Coun., 1992-95. With Royal Air Force, 1942-46. Decorated mem. Order of Australia; rsch. grantee Dept. Sci. and Indsl. Rsch., Gt. Britain, Nat. Coal Bd., Gt. Britain, Nuffield Found., Gt. Britain, Australian Heritage Commn., Utah Found., Australia, Australian Coal Assn., pvt. cos. Fellow Instn. Engrs. Australia (hon., chmn. engring. heritage panel Queensland divsn. 1977-91, nat. engring. heritage panel 1980-82, mem. gen. coll. bd. 1980-82, chmn. Queensland divsn. 1982, mem. coun. 1982-85, chmn. nat. com. on engring. in mining 1985-87, John Monash medal 1990, Hawken Address spkr. 1993), Inst. Energy (London) (sr.), Instn. Mining Engrs. (London) (Overseas award 1981), Instn. Mining and Metallurgy (London), Inst. Physics (London), Australasian Inst. Mining and Metallurgy (chmn. South Queensland br. 1976); mem. Australian Soc. Hist. Archaeology, Assn. Indsl. Archaeologists (Gt. Britain), Queensland Historians Inst. (founder mem.), Brisbane History Group (patron, pres. 1987-89). Avocations: mountain climbing, travel. Fax: (07) 3372 7537. E-mail: R.Whitmore@mailbox.uq.edu.au. Home and Office: R4/356 Blunder Rd, Durack, Brisbane Qld 4077, Australia

WHITNEY, PAUL MICHAEL, publisher, import/export executive; b. Portland, Oreg., Jan. 9, 1969; s. Hartwell Herbert Whitney and Rosalie Mary Czapszys. BA with honors, Occidental Coll., L.A., 1992. V.p. Japan Publicity, Inc., Gardena, Calif.; co-founder MWM Trading Co., Portland; cons. Kyowa Kozai, Tokyo. Editor: Telephone Guide-The Japanese Telephone Directory and Guide of Southern California, 1993-2000 (APPY Silver-Mktg. Innovation award 1997), SF Telephone Guide-The Japanese Business Directory and Guide of Northern California, 1993-2000 (APPY Bronze-Innovation in Print Materials awad 1996); translator: Flowers Without Mouths, 1991. Avocations: music, soccer. E-mail: paul1198@japanpub.com. Fax: 310-515-7188.

WHITNEY, WILLIAM GORDON, investment management company executive; b. Rochester, N.Y., Oct. 12, 1922; s. William N. and Marguerite (Gordon) W.; m. Margaret M. Deis, Mar. 16, 1971; children: Carol Joy, Lance A., Valerie A., Fredericka A., William A. BS in Adminstrv. Engring., Cornell U., 1943; MBA with distinction, Harvard U., 1951. Field engr. Norma Hoffman Bearings Corp., Stanford, Conn., 1946-49; cons. McKinsey & Co., N.Y.C., 1951-54; v.p. Am. Airlines, Inc., N.Y.C., 1954-62; gen. mgr. Martin Marietta Corp., Balt., 1963-68; chmn. Whitney & Co., Inc., Rochester, 1969—, Whitney Holdings, Ltd., N.Y.C., 1984—. With USN, 1944-46. Mem. Delta Upsilon. Office: Whitney and Co Inc 311 Alexander St Rochester NY 14604-2613

WHITSELL, JOHN CRAWFORD, II, retired general surgeon; b. St. Joseph, Mo., Dec. 21, 1929; s. Ora Earl and Lorena (Spratt) W. AB, Grinnell Coll., 1950; MD, Washington U., St. Louis, 1954. Diplomate Am. Bd. Surgery, Am. Bd. Thoracic Surgery. From instr. to clin. prof. surgery Cornell U. Med. Ctr., N.Y.C., 1963-70; from asst. attending to attending in surgery N.Y. Hosp., N.Y.C., 1964-70; surg. dir. Rogosin Kidney Ctr. N.Y. Hosp.-Cornell Med. Ctr., N.Y.C., 1973-75; attending in surgery N.Y. Hosp., 1970-98; clin. prof. surgery Cornell Med. Coll., 1970-98, clin. prof. surgery emeritus, 1998; surg. cons. Rogosin Kidney Ctr., 1975—, Sharon (Conn.) Hosp., 1976—. Contbr. articles to profl. jours. Capt. USAF, 1961-63, Eng. Fellow ACS; mem. Transplantation Soc., N.Y. Surg. Soc., Am. Soc. Transplant Surgeons, N.Y. Soc. for Thoracic Surgery, Soc. Thoracic Surgeons, N.Y. Acad. Medicine, N.Y. Soc. Cardiovascular Surgery, Harvey Soc., Union Club of N.Y., Phi Beta Kappa. Avocations: golf, fishing, auto racing, antique cars.

WHITSON, KEITH R., business executive. With Hongkong and Shanghai Banking Corp., from 1961, HSBC Group, U.K., U.S., Germany, Hong Kong, Malaysia and Indonesia, 1978—; asst. gen. mgr. fin. area mgmt. office HongkongBank, 1984-87; CEO then gen. mgr. HongkongBank, London, 1987-90; exec. dir. Marine Midland Banks, Inc. (now HSBC Bank USA), U.S., 1990-92; CEO Midland Bank plc (now HSBC Bank plc), 1994-98, dep. chmn., 1998—; dir. HSBC Holdings, P.L.C., London, 1994, group CEO, 1998—; chmn. shareholders com., dep. chmn. supervisory bd. HSBC Trinkaus & Burkhardt KGaA, Düsseldorf; bd. dirs. HSBC Bank Can., HSBC Bank Argentina, HSBC Bank USA; non-exec. dir. Fin. Svcs. Authority, 1998—; chmn. Meryll Lynch HSBC, 2000—. Fellow Chartered Inst. Bankers. Office: HSBC Holdings, 10 Lower Thames St, London EC3R 6AE, England

WHITSON, LISH, lawyer; b. Washington, Oct. 13, 1942; s. I. Lish and Clytie B. (Collier) W.; m. Barbara Lee Sullivan, Sept. 16, 1965; children: L. Richard, Kimberly S. BA in Philosophy, Pa. State U., 1965; JD, U. Wash., 1972. Bar: Wash. 1973, U.S. Dist. Ct. (we. dist.) 1973, U.S. Dist. Ct. (ea. dist.) 1977, U.S. Supreme Ct. 1977. Assoc. Seattle-King County Pub. Defender Assn., 1972-76; assoc. Helsell, Fetterman, Martin, Todd & Hokanson, Seattle, 1976-81, ptnr., 1981-98; of counsel Badgley Mullins, Seattle, 1998—. Bd. dirs., past chmn. Downtown Emergency Svc. Ctr., Seattle, 1981-97; bd. dirs. Allied Arts, 1988-96, pres., 1994-96; mem. Allied Arts Found., 1997—; trustee Seattle Youth Symphony Orch., bd. dirs., 1986-95; mem. alumni bd. U. Wash. Law Sch., 1993—, treas., 1997-99, pres., 1999—. Fellow Am. Bar Found., Am. Coll. Trial Lawyers; mem. ABA (young lawyers divsn. rep. to exec. coun. 1979, mem. standing com. on lawyer referral svc. 1990-96, chmn. 1992-96, commn. on women in the profn. 1998—), ATLA, Am. Bd. Trial Advocates (assoc.), Wash. State Bar Assn. (gov. 1995-98), King County Bar Found. (mem. pres. coun.), King County Bar Assn. (pro bono com. chmn. 1981-84, bd. dirs. 1988-91, young lawyers sect. 1977-79, chmn. 1979, Pro Bono Svc. award 1993, Atty. of Yr. 2000), Fed. Bar Assn., Am. Judicature Soc. (bd. dirs. 1981-86), Seattle Pub. Def. Assn. (bd. dirs. 1982-86), Wash. Athletic Club. Office: Lish Whitson Pllc Ste 3800 999 3d Ave Seattle WA 98104

WHITTELL, POLLY (MARY) KAYE, editor, journalist; b. Washington, Oct. 20; d. Alfred Whittell Jr. and Mary Halsey (Patchin) Hopper. BA in English, U. Calif., Berkeley; postgrad., Radcliffe Coll.; postgrad. in journalism, Columbia U. Rschr. Nat. Rev. Mag., N.Y.C., 1970-71; asst. to presdl. speech writer The White House, Washington, 1971-72; asst. editor Travel Age Mag., Dun & Bradstreet Publs., N.Y.C., 1973-75; copy editor Ski Mag. Skier's Guides, Times-Mirror Mags. and Am. Express, N.Y.C., 1975-76; asst. editor to sr. editor Hearsts Mags., Motor Boating & Sailing Mag., N.Y.C., 1977-2000; contbg. editor Powerboat Mag., Nordskog Pub., Ventura, Calif., 2000—. Contbg. author: (anthology) Against the Sea, 1998; contbr. articles to nat. and internat. consumer mags. Mem. charity benefit com. Youth Counseling League, N.Y.C., 1975-85, Am. Cancer Soc., 1998-99, and others; v.p. Knickerbocker Rep. Club, N.Y.C., 1979-80; elected mem. N.Y. Rep. County Com., N.Y.C., 1980-84. Mem. Boating Writers Internat. (award for environ. article 1995), Soc. Profl. Journalists, Social Register Assn., Princeton Club (N.Y.), SandBar Beach Club (v.p. membership 1980-82). Episcopalian. Avocations: photography, travel, boating, skiing.

WHITTEMORE, LINDA GENEVIEVE, clinical psychologist; b. Ft. Bragg, N.C., Nov. 1, 1948; d. James and Nancy (Caudill) White; children: Trevor Johnson, Dylan Lane. BA in Anthropology, East Carolina U., 1972, MA in Clin. Psychology, 1980. Rehab. svcs. coord. Social Center, Fairfax, Va., 1978-79; site coord. Mental Health Assn. of N. Va., Annandale, 1979-80; program asst. Alliance to Save Energy, Washington, 1981-82; ednl. psychology officer APA, Washington, 1984-88; exec. mktg. dir. I.D.N., Provo, Utah, 1989-93; supr. 24th Dist. Ct. Svcs. Unit, Lynchburg, Va., 1994-96; psychologist Ctrl. Va. Tng. Ctr., Lynchburg, 1996—; prof. Benjamin Franklin U., Washington, 1986-87. Editor: Activities Handbook for the Teaching of Psychology, Vol. 2, 1987, Vol. 3, 1990. Mem. Noetic Soc., Assn. of Employee Assistance Counselors, Toastmasters Internat. Avocations: culinary arts, poetry, opera, travel, herb gardening. Home: Villa Mozart 517 Washington St Lynchburg VA 24504-2619

WHITTEMORE, RONALD PAUL, hospital administrator, retired army officer, nursing educator; b. Saco, Maine, Aug. 10, 1946; s. Ronald B. and Pauline L. (Larson) W.; m. Judy D. McDonald, Feb. 17, 1967; 1 child, Leicia Michelle. BGS, U. S.C., 1974, MEd, 1977; BSN, Med. Coll. Ga., 1975. Enlisted U.S. Army, 1968, advanced through ranks to maj., 1985, ret., 1991; adult/oncology nurse practitioner Martin Army Cmty. Hosp.; asst. head nurse SICU, infection control practitioner Moncrief Army Cmty. Hosp.; infection control practitioner U.S. Army Hosp., Seoul, Republic of Korea; chief nurse 2nd Combat Support Hosp., Ft. Benning, Ga.; cmty. health nurse Brooke Army Med. Ctr., Ft. Sam Houston, Tex.; cmty. health nurse Giessen (Germany) Mil. Cmty.; clin. instr. Eisenhower Army Med. Ctr., Ft. Gordon, Ga.; chief nursing adminstrn. E/N Frankfurt (Germany) Army Med. Ctr.; adminstr., dir. quality improvement Gracewood (Ga.) State Sch. and Hosp., 1995—; instr. Augusta (Ga.) Tech. Inst.; nurse epidemiologist Med. Coll. Ga., Augusta. Mem. ANA, Ga. ANA (3rd Dist. honoree, pres. 1983-85), Assn. Practitioners in Infection Control, Am. Holistic Nurses Assn., Nat. Assn. Health Care Quality Profls., Assn. for Profls. in Infection Control and Epidemiology, Sigma Theta Tau. Home: 352 Stagecoach Way Martinez GA 30907-3326 Office: Med Coll Ga Office Nurse Mgr/Infec Ctrl Augusta GA 30912

WHITTEN, RUTH ANN, mathematician; b. Washington, Oct. 1, 1952; d. Maynard Richmond and Ruth Marie (Gomes) Wilbur; m. Gregory Fogg Whitten, Jan. 8, 1983. BS in Math., Coll. of William and Mary, 1974; MBA, PhD in Bus. Adminstrn., U. Wash., 1993. Ops. rsch. analyst U.S. EPA, Washington, 1974-80, environ. scientist, 1980-82. Mem. Nat. Environ. Leadership Coun. of League of Conservation Voters, Wash., 1990; treas. Project Outreach of St. Thomas, St. Thomas Episc. Ch. in Medina, 1991. Recipient Silver Medal Group award, EPA, 1976; William E. Cox dissertation fellow, 1985. Mem. Beta Gamma Sigma. Episcopalian. Avocation: art collecting. Home: PO Box 329 Medina WA 98039-0329

WHITTINGHAM, WAYNE, chiropractor; b. Strasbourg, France, Feb. 1, 1967; s. Kenneth and Elisabeth Hedwig (Clare) W.; m. Melissa Anne Healey, Apr. 11, 1993; children: Bonnie Elisabeth, Isaac Francis, Alexander Brian Ken. B Applied Sci. in Chiropractic, Phillip Inst. of Tech., Melbourne, Australia, 1992; PhD, Royal Melbourne Inst. Tech. U., Melbourne, 1998. Tertiory acad. RMIT, 1989-91, rschr., 1990-95; chiropractor Plymouth (Eng.) Chiropractic Clinic, 1995—. Contbr. articles to profl. publs. Rsch. fellow Austalian Spinal Rsch. Found., 1993-96. Fellow Coll. Chiropractors; mem. Scottish Chiropractic Assn., Internat. Chiropractic Assn. Avocations: headache research, chiropractic philosophy, art, motorcycling, fitness. Home: 27 Thornhill Rd, Mannamead, Plymouth Devon PL3 5NF, England Office: Plymouth Chiropractic Clin, 152 Mannamead Rd Hartley, Plymouth Devon PL3 5QL, England

WHITTINGTON, CATHY DEE, chemist; b. Upland, Pa., Oct. 29, 1955; d. Frank Adam and Virginia Helen (Keil) W. AA in biology, Widenen Univ., 1984, BA, 1996. Asst. mgr. McDonald's, Brookhaven, Pa., 1973-75; blood lab. tech. CCMC, Chester, Pa., 1976-77; environmental tech. Scott Paper Internat., Chester, Pa., 1979-83; paramedic V AmbulCare Ambulance, Phila., 1984-96; sr. rsch. assoc. Scott Paper Corp. R&D, Phila., 1996-97; rsch. cons. Kimberly Clark Corp., Chester, Pa., 1997; process specialist HIA Cons., Chester, 1997-99; chemist Novell Inc., Provo, Utah, 1999—; network engr. Novell, Inc., Provo, Utah, Scott Paper House of Quality, team orgn. Scott Paper R&D. Amb. lt. Parkside Vol. Fire Co., Parkside, Pa., 1977—. Recipient Military History Excellence award Daughter's of Founders & Patriots of Am., 1977, tech. excellence award, 1987-91. Mem. Tech. Orgn. of Pulp & Paper Ins., Nat. Archieves (assoc.). Republican. Baptist. Avocations: walking, hiking, reading. Home: 139 W Roland Rd Brookhaven PA 19015-3217 Office: Novell Inc 301 W Germantown Pike Bldg 1 Norristown PA 19403-4227

WHITTINGTON, GEOFFREY, accountant, educator; b. Warsop, Eng., Sept. 21, 1938; s. Bruce and Dorothy Gwendoline (Gent) W.; m. Joyce Enid Smith, Sept. 7, 1963; children: Alan Geoffrey, Richard John. BSc in Econs., London Sch. Econs., 1959; MA, Cambridge U., 1964, PhD, 1971; DSc in Social Sci. (hon.), Edinburgh U., 1998. Rsch. officer Cambridge U., 1962-72; fellow Fitzwilliam Coll., Cambridge, Eng., 1966-72, 88—; prof. U. Edinburgh, Scotland, 1972-75, U. Bristol, Eng., 1975-88, U. Cambridge, Eng., 1988—; mem. U.K. Acctg. Standards Bd., 1994—, U.K. Monopolies and Mergers Commn., 1987-96; econ. adviser Office of Fair Trading, Eng., 1978-83; mem. Adv. Body on Fair Trading in Telecomms., 1997-98. Author: Inflation Accounting, 1983, The Elements of Accounting, 1992, the Prediction of Profitability, 1971; co-author: The Debate on Inflation Accounting, 1984. Profl. rsch. fellow Inst. Chartered Accts. of Scotland, 1996—. Fellow Inst. Chartered Accts. in Eng. and Wales. Avocations: music, walking, squash. Office: Faculty Econs and Politics, Sidgwick Ave, Cambridge CB3 9DD, England

WHITTINGTON, IAN DAVID, parasitologist; b. Birmingham, Eng., Sept. 19, 1960; arrived in Australia, 1987; s. Andrew Gordon and Eleanor Margaret (Waddington) W. BSc with honors, U. East Anglia, Norwich, Eng., 1982, PhD, 1986. Postdoctoral fellow U. Queensland, Brisbane, Australia, 1987-89, Queen Elizabeth II fellow, 1990-92, lectr. parasitology, 1993-97; dir. Heron Island Rsch. Sta., U. Queensland, Gt. Barrier Reef, 1996-99, sr. lectr. parasitology, 1998—; com. for 4th Internat. Symposium on Monogerea, 1999—. Sect. editor book revs. Internat. Jour. Parasitology, Brisbane, 1993-95, invited revs., 1995-97; co-editor: Systematic Parasitology, 1999—; mem. editl. bd. Folia Parasitologica, 2000—; contbr. articles to profl. jours. Rsch. grantee Australian Rsch. Coun., 1988—. Mem. Australian Soc. Parasitology, Brit. Soc. Parasitology. Office: U Queensland, Dept Microbiol/Parasitology, Brisbane 4072, Australia

WHITTINGTON-BROWN, VANESSA ELIZABETH, educator; b. Boston, Apr. 15, 1960; d. Samuel Wall and Ernestine (Brazand Hundley) W; m. July, 1992. BS, Bridgewater State U., 1978; postgrad., Cambridge Coll., 1992—. Elem. tchr. Boston (Mass.) Pub. Schs., 1983—, Pauline A. Shaw, Dorchester, Mass., 1987-92; tchr. The Josiah Quincy Sch., Boston, 1992—; adult edn. sec. Boston Pub. Schs., 1982, 83, mem. graphic learning com., 1983, impact II tchr. adaptor; musician cable TV program Gospel Expressions Prodns.; tutor Metco (after sch. program); mem. Primary Summer Source Inst., 1991; local pres. Sunshine Band, 1986, state pres., 1989-92. Mem. local Sunshine Band, 1985, state pres., 1989—; composer: Lord I'm Coming Home, 1986. Mem. Children's Mus. and the Mus. Sci., Women's Heritage Trail, 3 Regent St. Young Adult Choir, Women's Choir, Boston Writing Project, Professional Dev. Program; co-dir. Specially Trained Youth Leadership in Excellence (STYLE), 1997; church musician Church of God in Christ Church, 1976-92. With USAR, 1979-91. Mem. Assn. Supervision and Curriculum Devel., Greater Boston Reading Coun., Boston Tchrs. Union, Black Educators Alliance of Mass., Nat. Coun. Tchrs. English, Women's Heritage Trail, African Meeting House. Democrat. Avocations: music, bowling, racquetball, basketball.

WHITTLE, JOSEPH F., JR., engineering executive, consultant; b. N.Y.C., Mar. 5, 1943; s. Joseph F. and Margaret M. (Murphy) W.; m. Dorothy M. Baker-Dickinson, June 30, 1985; children: Gina, Karla, Alyssa. BS in Geology, Rensselaer Poly. Inst., 1967; MSCE, Mass. Inst. Tech., 1974. Registered profl. engr., profl. geologist, environ. assessor, spl. bldg. inspector. Asst. geologist Dames & Moore, N.Y.C., 1967-68; sr. instr. U.S. Army Engr. Sch., Ft. Belvoir, Va., 1968-69; geologist Haley & Aldrich, Cambridge, Mass., 1970-74; geotech. engr. Law Engring., Tampa, Fla., 1974-81; sr. engr. PSI/Fla. Testing Labs., Tampa, 1981-84; div. mgr. Profl. Svc. Industry, Tampa, 1984-87; sr. div. mgr. Profl. Svc. Industry, Clearwater, Fla., 1987-90; br. mgr., sr. tech. cons. Profl. Svc. Industry, Lombard, Ill., 1990-97; engring. mgr. Robert B. Balter Co., 1997—. Author: Construction and Quarry Blasting, 1969, Consolidation Behavior of an Embankment, 1974. 1st Lt. U.S. Army, 1968-70. Decorated Bronze Star, U.S. Army, Vietnam, 1970; recipient Svc. award, Suffolk (N.Y.) Police Dept., 1970. Mem. ASCE, Assn. Engring. Geologists, Soc. Am. Mil. Engrs., Assn. Groundwater Scientists & Engrs., Phi Kappa Theta, Sigma Xi. Home: 640 Buckhorn Rd Sykesville MD 21784-9003

WHITTLE, MARTIN JOHN, obstetrician; b. London, July 6, 1944; s. Bruce and Evelyn Emma (Hughes) W.; m. Lindsay Hall Jones, July 12, 1967; 1 child, Nicolas John. MB, ChB, U. Manchester, Eng., 1972, MD, 1980. Cert. obstetrician and gynecologist, specialist in maternal and fetal medicine. Houseman Manchester Royal Infirmary, 1972-73; sr. house officer, tutor U. Manchester, 1975-77; rsch. fellow L.A. County-U. So. Calif. Med. Ctr., 1978-79; lectr. Queen Mother's Hosp., Glasgow, Scotland, 1979-82, cons., 1982-91; prof. U. Birmingham, Eng., 1991; obstetrician Birmingham Women's Hosp., 1991—. Author: Prenatal Diagnosis in Obstetric Practice; co-author: Fetal Medicine, Basic Science and Clinical Practice. Fellow Royal Coll. Obstetricians and Gynecologists, Royal Coll. Physicians and Surgeons Glasgow. Avocations: flying, sailing, art, music. Office: Birmingham Womens Hosp, Edgbaston, Birmingham B15 2TS, England

WHITWORTH, HORACE ALGERNON, mechanical engineer; b. Kingston, Jamaica, W.I., Mar. 24, 1953; came to U.S., 1967; s. Egbert Leopold and Violet Cecilia (Trouth) W. BSME, U. Mass., 1975; MS, George Washington U., 1977, DSc, 1983. Asst. prof. Howard U., Washington, 1983-89, dir. grad. studies dept. mech. engring., 1988-96, assoc. prof. mech. engring., 1989—. Contbr. numerous articles to profl. publs. Bd. dirs. Jamaica Support Found., Washington, 1991-95. Recipient Sr. Fellows Found. award Pacific Telesis Found., 1988, Prof. Acad. award Honeywell Corp., 1992; rsch. grantee in field. Mem. ASME (bd. dirs. Washington chpt. 1994—, Instr. of Yr. student chpt. 1985-86, 87-89), Am. Soc. Metals, Soc. for Exptl. Mechanics. Democrat. Methodist. Achievements include development of mathematical models to evaluate fatigue damage development in fibrous composite materials. Avocations: chess, soccer, checkers. Office: Howard U 2300 6th St NW Washington DC 20001-2323

WHITWORTH, JUDITH ANN, medical educator; b. Melbourne, Australia, Apr. 1, 1944; d. Arthur Howard and Margaret Edith (Wilson Dobbs) W.; m. John Ludbrook, Aug. 24, 1981 (div. 1992); 1 child, Emma. MBBS, U. Melbourne, 1967, MD, 1974, PhD, 1978, DSc, 1992. Resident Royal Melbourne (Australia) Hosp., 1968-71, Etranger du Coll. de Medicine des Hosp., Paris, 1973-74; physician Royal Melbourne Hosp., 1978-81, asst.,

deputy dir. dept. Nephrology, 1979-91; prof. medicine U. New South Wales, St. George Hosp., 1991-97; chief med. officer Commonwealth Govt. of Australia, 1997-99; dir. John Curtin Sch. Med. Rsch., Australian Nat. U., Canberra, 1999—; chair med. rsch. com. Nat. Health and Med. Rsch. Coun. of Australia, 1994-97; leader Australian del. World Health Assembly, 1997-99. Co-author: Dictionary of Medical Eponyms, 2nd edit., 1996, Textbook of Renal Disease, 2d edit., 1994, The Kidney, 1987, Clinical Nephrology in Medical Practice, 1992. Winthrop travel fellow Royal Australian Coll. Physicians, 1973, Coun. high Blood Pressure Rsch. U.S.A. fellow, 1991; Howard Florey Inst. scholar, Melbourne, 1975-77. Fellow Royal Australasian Coll. Physicians; mem. Australian Soc. Med. Rsch. (pres. 1984), Internat. Soc. Hypertension (coun. mem. 1992—, sec. 1996, v.p. 1998-2000, mem. WHO regional com. Western Pacific chpt. 1996-98). Fax: 61 2 62492337. Avocations: skiing, reading, film, cricket, Australian football. Office: John Curtin Sch Med Rsch, Australian Nat U Mills Rd, Canberra 2601, Australia

WHITWORTH, KERNAN BRADLEY, III, corporate communications executive; b. Santa Monica, Calif., Dec. 4, 1953; s. Kernan Bradley Jr. and Carolyn Harkins (McGill) W.; m. Karen Elizabeth Nakano, July 10, 1982; children: Kernan Bradley IV, Joseph Taro. BA, BJ, U. Mo., 1975; MBA, Santa Clara U., 1988. Advt. dir. OGR Service Corp., Springfield, Ill., 1976-78; mgr. employee communications Horace Mann Ins. Co., Springfield, Ill., 1978-80; mgr. internal communications Hewlett-Packard Co., Palo Alto, Calif., 1980-91, mgr. internat. pub. affairs, 1991-2000, mgr. computing sys. comms., 2000—. Mem. Internat. Assn. Bus. Communicators (bd. dirs. 1984-91, Gold Quill award 1985, 86, 88, 97, 2000, chmn. 1989-1990, fellow 1996). Home: 1463 Ormsby Dr Sunnyvale CA 94087-4246 Office: Hewlett-Packard Co 10955 Tantau Ave Cupertino CA 95014-0770

WHYATT, ANTHONY STEWART, oil company executive; b. Hong Kong, Apr. 7, 1937; arrived in the U.K., 1973; s. Sir John and Maili Cecilia (Stewart) W.; m. Nancy Ruth Wilkins, June 27, 1964; children: Adrian, John Paul, Antonia, Nicholas. BA with honors, Oxford (Eng.) U., 1960, MA, 1965; MBA, Harvard U., 1964. Treas. Gulfoil Co. South Asia, Singapore, 1970-71; mgr. spl. projects Gulf Oil Corp., Pitts., 1971-73; asst. treas. I.T.T. Europe, Brussels, 1973; v.p., treas. Occidental Fin. Svcs. Inc., London, 1973-91; CFO Hardy Oil & Gas plc, London, 1991-95, JKX Oil & Gas plc, Guildford, Eng., 1996—; lectr. in field. Contbr. articles to profl. jours. Dir. Birch Island Cmty. Assn., Ontario, Can.; com. mem. Harvard Bus. Sch. European Alumni Assn., 1978-82. Sub-lt. Royal Navy, 1955-57. Fellow Assn. Corp. Treas.; mem. Harvard Bus. Sch. Club London, Travellers Club London, Naval Club London, Harvard Club N.Y. Roman Catholic. Avocations: Canadian wilderness, gourmandise, skiing. Home: 8 Aubrey Walk, London W8 7JG, England

WHYBROW, JOHN WILLIAM, electronics company executive; b. Hatfield, Eng., Mar. 11, 1947; s. Charles Earnest James and Doris Beatrice (Abbott) W.; m. Pauline Miriam Hobart, Oct. 19, 1968; children: Mark Charles, Andrea Patricia. BSc (hons.), Imperial Coll., London, 1968; MBA, Manchester Bus. Sch., England, 1973. Plant dir. Philips Components, Eng., 1983-86, Philips SemiConductors, Eng., 1986-88; mng. dir. TDS Circuits PLC, Eng., 1988-90; tech. dir. Philips Components UK, Eng., 1990-93; chmn., mng. dir. Philips Elect. U.K., Eng., 1993-95; pres., CEO Philips Lighting Holding BV, The Netherlands, 1995—; v.p. Philips Electronics N.V., 1998—; dir. Teletext Holding, Eng., 1993-95; non-exec. dir. Wolseley Plc, 1997—; chmn. lumileds Lighting BV, 1997-99. Mem. Inst. of Dirs., East India Club. Avocation: sailing. Home: Rapleys Bashurst Hill NR Horsham, RH 137TA Sussex England Office: Philips Lighting Holding BV Bldg Ed 5, PO Box 80020, 5600 JM Eindhoven The Netherlands

WHYBROW, PETER CHARLES, psychiatrist, educator, author; b. Hertforshire, Eng., June 13, 1939; U.S. citizenship, 1975; s. Charles Ernest and Doris Beatrice (Abbott) W.; children: Katherine, Helen. Student, Univ. Coll., London, 1956-59; MB BS, Univ. Coll., 1962; diploma psychol. medicine, Conjoint Bd., London, 1968; MA (hon.), Dartmouth Coll., 1974, U. Pa., 1984. House officer endocrinology Univ. Coll. Hosp., 1962, sr. house physician psychiatry, 1963-64; house surgeon St. Helier Hosp., Surrey, Eng., 1963; house officer pediatrics Prince of Wales Hosp., London, 1964; resident psychiatry U. N.C. Hosp., 1965-67, instr., research fellow, 1967-68; mem. sci. staff neuropsychiat. research unit Charshalton, Surrey, 1968-69; dir. residency tng. psychiatry Dartmouth Med. Sch., Hanover, N.H., 1969-71; prof. psychiatry Dartmouth Med. Sch., 1970-84, chmn. dept., 1970-78, exec. dean, 1980-83; prof., chmn. dept. psychiatry U. Pa., Phila., 1984-96, Ruth Meltzer prof. psychiatry, 1992; psychiatrist-in-chief Hosp. U. Pa., 1984-96; prof. psychiatry and biobehavioral scis., chmn. dept. psychiatry Sch. Medicine UCLA, 1996—, dir. Neuropsychiatric Inst., 1996—, physician-in-chief Neuropsychiatric Hosp., 1996-99, Judson Brown Prof. of Psychiatry, 1999—; dir. psychiatry Dartmouth Hitchock Affiliated Hosp., 1970-78; vis. scientist NIMH, 1978-79; cons. VA, 1970—, NIMH, 1972— ; chmn. test com. Nat. Bd. Med. Examiners, 1977-84; researcher psychoendrocrinology. Author: Mood Disorders: Toward a New Psychobiology, 1984, The Hibernation Response, 1988, A Mood Apart, 1997; editor: Psychosomatic Medicine, 1977; mem. editl. bd. Cmty. Psychiatry, Psychiat. Times, Directions in Psychiatry, Neuropsychopharmacology, Depression; contbr. articles to profl. jours. Recipient Anclote Manor award psychiat. rsch. U. N.C., 1967, Sr. Investigator award nat. Alliance for Rsch. into Schizophrenia and Depression, 1989; Josiah Macy Jr. Found. scholar, 1978-79; fellow Cen. for Advanced Studies in Behavioral Sci., Stanford, 1993-94; recipient Lifetime Investigator award NDMDA, 1996; decorated Knight of Merit, Sovereign Order of St. John of Jerusalem, 1993. Fellow AAAS, Am. Psychiat. Assn., Royal Coll. Psychiatrist (founding mem.), Am. Coll. Psychiatrists, Ctr. Advanced Study of Behavioral Scis. (hon.), Soc. Psychosomatic Rsch. London (hon.); mem. Am. Assn. Chmn. Depts. Psychiatry (pres. 1977-78), Royal Soc. Medicine, Am. Psychopath Assn., Am. Coll. Neuropsychopharmacology, Soc. Biol. Psychiatry, N.Y. Acad. Scis., Soc. Neurosci., Sigma Xi, Alpha Omega Alpha. Office: UCLA Sch Medicine Neuropsychiat Rsch Inst 760 Westwood Plz Los Angeles CA 90095-8353

WHYMAN, GENNADIY EVSEEVITCH, physicist, researcher, educator; b. Kiev, Ukraine, May 8, 1947; s. Evsey Abramovith Vaiman and Huma Davidovna Kolodnaya; m. Inna Ravillievna Chanysheva, Apr. 29, 1978; children: Olga, Eugene. PhD in Theoretical and Math. Physics, St. Petersburg, Russia, 1977. Sr. scientist Inst. Phys. Organic and Coal Chemistry, Donetsk, Ukraine; head chair physics Donetsk Coll., 1995—. Author: Spin-Extended Hartree-Fock Method and Application to Molecules, 1983; contbr. articles to profl. jours. Mem. N.Y. Acad. Scis. Home: 30 Universitetskaya fl. 74, 340050 Donetsk Ukraine

WHYTE, LESLEY CRAIG, data processing executive; b. Falkirk, Scotland, Feb. 8, 1958; d. James and Sarah (Leiper) W.; m. Duncan James Rae, May 23, 1987; children: Cameron James, Lachlan Duncan. BA with honors, U. Stirling, Scotland, 1980; Diploma in Libr. and Info. Studies, Univ. Coll. London, 1982. Editor Libr. Resources Coord. Com. U. London, 1982-83; head tech. svcs. Kings Coll., London, 1983-85, 86-87; vis. prof. Skidmore Coll., Saratoga Springs, N.Y., 1985-86; bibliographic svcs. mgr. T C Farries & Co. Ltd., Dumfries, Scotland, 1987-95; mng. dir. Bibliographic Data Svcs. Ltd., Dumfries, 1995—. Avocations: gardening, horticulture, literature, the Arts. Fax: 44-1387-702-259. E-mail: lesley.whyte@bibdsl.co.uk. Office: Annandale Ho The Crichton, Bankend Rd, Dumfries DG1 4TA, Scotland

WHYTE, NANCY MARIE, performing arts educator; b. Myrtlepoint, Oreg., Mar. 12, 1948; d. Lawrence Edward and Carol Elizabeth (Johnson) Guderian; m. Anthony John Whyte, Aug. 7, 1967 (div. Sept. 1968); 1 child, Charles Lawrence; m. Douglas Brian Graff, June 27, 1971 (div. Oct. 1974); m. Lawrence Hanson, Mar. 12, 1976 (div. Aug. 1984); m. Joseph Paul Deacon, Aug. 10, 1985; 1 child, Nina Alexandra. Student, U. Wash., 1969-72, Am. Sch. Dance, 1972; BA, Evergreen State Coll., 1987. Owner, dir. Nancy Whyte Sch. Ballet, Bellingham, Wash., 1969—; artistic dir. Garden Street Dance Players, Bellingham, 1969-72, MT Baker Ballet, Bellingham, 1975—; co-dir. Exptl. Performance Workshop, Bellingham, 1975-77; instr. creative dance St. Paul's Primary Sch., Bellingham, 1993-97; facilitator dance workshop Allied Arts/Whatcom Co., Bellingham, 1995—; guest lectr. Western Wash. U., Bellingham, 1976-83, 96—; guest faculty Dance Theatre Northwest, Tacoma, Wash., 1995—. Author: Memoirs of a Child of Theatre Street, 1993; soloist Raduga Folk Ballet/N.Y. Character Ballet, N.Y.C., 1978-79; choreographer numerous ballets, 1972—. Mem. Nat. Dance Assn., Regional Dance Am. (assoc.). Democrat. Avocations: voice, writing. Office: MT Baker Ballet 1412 Cornwall Ave PO Box 2393 Bellingham WA 98227-2393

WIATR, JERZY JOZEF, sociology educator, parliamentarian; b. Warsaw, Poland, Sept. 17, 1931; s. Wilhelm Zygmunt and Zofia Wanda (Jankowska) W.; m. Ewa Paulina Zurowska, Oct. 25, 1980; 1 child, Slawomir. MA, U. Warsaw, 1954, PhD, 1957. Asst. U. Warsaw, 1951-58, asst. prof., 1958-59, prof. sociology, 1969—; assoc. prof. U. Cracow, Poland, 1959-65, Mil. Polit. Coll., Warsaw, 1958-68; dir. Inst. Marxism-Leninism, Warsaw, 1981-84; vis. prof. U. Mich., 1967, 74, 76, U. Manchester, Eng., 1968-69, Boston U., 1973, So. Ill. U., Carbondale, 1985, UCLA, 1978, 80, 88, U. B.C., 1973, 81, 83, Cath. U. Leuven, Belgium, 1977, 80; mem. editl. bd. Internat. Polit. Sci. Rev., 1980—; editor-in-chief MYSL Socialdemokratyczna, 1991—; mem. parliament, Warsaw, 1991-97; min. of edn., Warsaw, 1996-97; dir. Inst. Social and Internat. Studies, Warsaw, 1998—. Author numerous books including The Soldier and the Nation: The Role of Military in Polish Politics, 1918-1985, 1988, Four Essays on East European Democratic Transformation, 1992, Education for and in the 21st Century, 1997; contbr. numerous articles to profl. jours. Mem. Polish Assn. Polit. Scis. (hon. 1985—; v.p. 1962-64, 67-76, pres. 1964-67, 76-79), Internat. Studies Assn. (v.p. 1980-81), Jacob Internat. Soc. Collaborative Rsch. (pres. 1996-97). Social Democrat. Avocations: White Arms collection, chess, swimming, traveling. Home: Sosnowskieo 2 #1, 02784 Warsaw Poland Office: U Warsaw Inst Sociology, Karowa 18, 00 322 Warsaw Poland

WIBERG, KRISTER NILS GUNNAR, architect, educator, dean; b. Stockholm, Oct. 21, 1937; s. Gunnar Georg Fredrik and Stina (Guttormsen) W.; m. Britt-Marie Siw Tinghammar; children: Karin, Bella, Anna, Hanna, Lotta, David, Björn. Arch., Chalmers Tech. H.S., Göteborg, Sweden, 1967; D in Tech., Lund (Sweden) Tech. H.S., 1981, prof., 1996. Pvt. practice arch. Lund, 1967-82, 93-96; ecol. design staff Sac, Malmö, Sweden, 1982-89, FFNS Arkitekter, Malmö, 1990-93; head dept. Lund U., 1996—; eco-design arch. ptnr. Ecoscape, Lund, 1995—. Named 5 time Swedish tennis champion for men over 45; recipient 1st prize for Habitat in Oregro, 1st Choice prize for internat. competition Green Bldg. in Vancouver, 1998, others. Fellow Amb. Club, Lucas Gillet. Avocation: tennis. Home: Nationsgatan 7, 22460 Lund Sweden Office: Lund U Dept Arch 1, PO Box 118, 22100SE Lund Sweden

WIBERG, LARS-ERIK, occupational compatibility consultant; b. Wakefield, Mass., June 1, 1928; s. Sverker Claesson and Ingrid (Heurlin) W.; m. Elizabeth Margaret Allenbrook, Oct. 18, 1957; children: Kirsten, Margaret, Brenda. BS in Geology, MIT, 1950; MA in Teaching, Harvard U., 1952. From engr. to dir. corp. communications EG&G Inc., Boston and Bedford, Mass., 1956-69; from asst. v.p. to v.p. compensation and orgnl. planning First Nat. Bank of Boston, 1969-81; cons. Rockport, Mass., 1981—; lectr. human resources mgmt. Boston U., 1988-92; lectr. job search and career planning U. Karlstad, Sweden, 1992. Author: It's Your Move, 1991; inventor in field. Mem. Gov. John A. Volpe's Mgmt. Engring. Task Force, 1965; mem. Planning Bd., Rockport, 1965-72, chmn., 1969-72; pres. ch. coun. Swedenborg Chapel, Cambridge, Mass., 1984—; dir. Mass. New Ch. Union, 1990—; mem. Zoning Bd. Appeals, Rockport, 1986—; mem. Site Rev. com., Rockport, 1999. 1st lt. USAF, 1953-55. Mem. Affiliated New Eng. Cons. (founder Lexington, Mass. 1985-95), Koussevitzky Recs. Soc., Heritage Found., Swedenborg Sci. Assn. Avocations: church work, home repairs, music, cooking, reading. Home and Office: 90 South St Rockport MA 01966-1916

WIBERG, NILS EGON, inorganic chemist; b. Karlsruhe, Baden, Germany, Oct. 6, 1934; s. Egon Gustaf Martin and Dora Margaretha (Schneider) W.; m. Christa Schapitz, July 7, 1963; children: Anja, Sylvia, Björn. Diploma in chemistry, U. Munich, Germany, 1959, Doctorate, 1961, Habilitation, 1966. Prof. U. Munich, 1972—. Author: Textbook of Inorganic Chemistry, 1985, rev., 1995; contbr. over 200 articles to profl. jours. Recipient Wacker Silicon award Wacker Chemistry, Burghausen, 1988, Frederic Stanley Kipping award, Amer. Chemical Soc., 1992. Mem. Academia Scientiarium et Artium Europaea, Gesellschaft Deutscher Chemiker. Home: Lerchenauerstrasse 39, 80809 Munich Germany Office: U Munich Dept Chemie, Butenandtstr 5-13 House D, D81377 Munich Germany*

WIBERG-JORGENSEN, FINN, anesthesiologist; b. Copenhagen, Apr. 3, 1942; s. Aage and Tove Cathrine (Jensen) W.-J.; m. Everdina Kaptein, June 27, 1967; children: Erik, Paul. MD, U. Copenhagen, 1967. Registrar Univ. Hosp., Copenhagen, 1967-68, 72-78, rschr., 1968-72, sr. registrar, 1981-82, mem. med. coun., 1975-77; sr. registrar Sundby Hosp., Copenhagen, 1978-79, Herlev Hosp., Copenhagen, 1979-81; cons. anesthesiologist Hillerod Hosp., 1982—. Contbr. articles to profl. jours. Lt. M.C. Danish Navy, 1968-70. Dutch Soc. for Hospitality scholar, 1963. Mem. Danish Soc. Anesthesiology (mem. coun. 1985-87, chmn. 1987-89), Danish Soc. Emergency Medicine, European Soc. Intensive Care Medicine. Lutheran. Avocations: yachting, cross-country skiing. Office: Hillerod Hospital, Dept Anesthesia Helsevej 2, 3400 Hillerød Denmark

WIBISONO, MAKARIM, diplomat; b. Mataram, Indonesia, May 8, 1948; married; 3 children. Degree in internatl rels., Gajahmada U., Jogjakarata, Indonesia, 1970; MS in Internat. Studies, Johns Hopkins U., 1984; MA in Polit. Economy, Ohio State U., 1986, PhD, 1987. Editor Express News Mag., Jakarta, Indonesia, 1970-72; head U.S. desk Dept. Fgn. Affairs, Indonesia, 1972-76, head N.Am. sect., 1976-77; head info. and cultural divsn. Indonesian Embassy, Brasilia, Brazil, 1977-81; dep. dir. trade and exhbns. Fgn. Affairs Dept., Indonesia, 1977-81, dep. dir. info. affairs, 1987-88; head info. divsn. Indonesian Embassy, Washington, 1988-91; min. counsellor, head econ. divsn. Indonesia UN Mission, 1991-93; dir. multilateral econ. coop. Dept. Fgn. Affairs, Indonesia, 1993-94; dep. permanent rep. from Indonesia UN, 1994-97; permanent rep. to UN Govt. Indonesia, N.Y.C., 1997—. Office: Permanent Mission Rep Indonesia to UN 325 E 38th St New York NY 10016-2745*

WIBLE, JAMES ORAM, plastics company executive; b. Pitts., June 30, 1949; s. Lewis Alfred and Wilda (Boa) W.; m. Norma Joan Klaus, Sept. 20, 1975; children: Judson F., Jerald L., Leslie K. BA, Allegheny Coll., 1971; MBA, Xavier U., 1974. Sales rep. Pitts. Paint & Glass Industries, Cin., 1971-72, Detroit, 1973-75; pres. Am. Colors, Inc., Sandusky, Ohio, 1975—. Pres. Montessori Parents Assn., Huron, Ohio, 1986; bd. dirs. Montessori Child Enrichment Ctr., 1986-91, pres., 1989-91; pres. bd. trustees 1st Presbyn. Ch., Sandusky, 1981; bd. session 1st Presbyn. Ch., 1994-99; trustees Fireland Com. Hosp., 2000—. Recipient Disting. Alumni award Fox Chapel Area Sch. Dist., 1989. Mem. Composites Fabrication Assn. (bd. dirs. 1989-92), Plum Brook Country Club (Sandusky), Longue Vue Club (Verona, Pa.). Republican. Avocation: golf. Home: 2509 Fairway Ln Sandusky OH 44870-6016 Office: Am Colors Inc 1321 1st St Sandusky OH 44870-3901

WICHMANN, HENRY, JR., accounting educator, researcher; b. Bemidji, Minn., Sept. 14, 1939; s. Henry and Bethel (Wells) W.; m. Nilda Oca, May 25, 1990; children: Holly Brittany, Henry William. BSBA in Mktg., U. Denver, 1962; MA in Bus. Edn., Colo. State Coll., 1965; PhD in Bus. Tchg., U. No. Colo., 1972. CPA, Wis. Asst. buyer May Co. Dept. Stores, Colo., 1962-63; distbrutive edn. coord. Newburgh (N.Y.) Free Acad., 1963-64; instr. in bus. adminstrn. and mid-mgmt. Dawson Coll., Mont., 1964-68; tchg. asst. acctg. U. No. Colo., Greeley, 1969-71; instr. mid. mgmt. Casper (Wyo.) Coll., 1971-72; asst. prof. acctg. U. Wis., Eau Claire, 1972-77, U. Wyo., Laramie, 1977-80; assoc. prof. U. Alaska, Anchorage, 1980-85; prof. U. Alaska, Fairbanks, 1986-96, head acctg. & info. sys. dept., 1996—; advisor Mktg. Club, Glendive, Mont., 1964-68; advisor Christmas promotion Laramie C. of C., 1978-80; dir. small bus. inst. U. Alaska, Anchorage, 1980-85; manuscript dir. Nat. Acctg. Assn., Anchorage, 1980-85; bd. dirs. JW Trading Co., Taichung, Taiwan; presenter in field. Contbr. articles to profl. jours. Recipient Keller Trophy, Nat. Assn. Acctg., 1981-82, Pres.'s award Nat. Assn. Acctg., 1985-86, At-Large Achiever Rsch. award Assn. of Govt. Accts., 1991-92, Disting. Theoretical Paper award Inst. Decision Sci., 1982. Mem. AICPA, Am. Acctg. Assn., Nat. Soc. Pub. Accts., Wis. Soc. CPAs, Assn. Govt. Accts., Inst. Mgmt. Accts. (bd. dirs.), Beta Alpha Psi, Beta Gamma Sigma, Alpha Kappa Psi (historian, dist. dir. 1978-80). Lutheran. Avocations: hunting, fishing, camping. E-mail:FFHW@Fortune.SOM.UNF.edu. Home: 1965 Weston Dr Fairbanks AK 99709-6535 Office: U Alaska Sch Mgmt PO Box 756080 Fairbanks AK 99775-6080

WICHMANN, H.-ERICH, epidemiologist, researcher; b. Elmshorn, Germany, Apr. 20, 1946; s. Heinz and Edith (Hell) W.; m. Margarett Fischer, May 2, 1980; children: René, Caroline, Stephanie, Christoph. PhD, U. Köln, Germany, 1976, MD, 1983, habilitation, 1983. Asst. prof. U. Köln, Germany, 1973-83; assoc. prof. U. Düsseldorf, Germany, 1983-88; prof. U. Wuppertal, Germany, 1988—; dir. GSF Inst. Epidemiology, Neuherberg, Germany, 1991—; prof. U. München, Germany, 1995—. Editor: Mathematical Modeling of Cell Proliferation, 1985, Handbuch der Umweltmedizin, 1992. Spkr. German Epidemiol. Assn., 1993—. Recipient Ludwig Heilmeyer Silver medal, 1984. Home: Waldhorn Str 54a, D80997 München Germany Office: GSF-Inst Epidemiology, Ingolstaedter Land Str 1, D85764 Oberschleissheim Germany

WICHMANN, JÜRGEN, chemist, researcher; b. Stadtoldendorf, Germany, Oct. 24, 1963; s. Robert and Gerda (Bock) W.; m. Angelika Dölle, May 22, 1993; children: Melanie, Natalie. Diploma, U. Göttingen, Germany, 1988, PhD, 1991. Asst. U. Göttingen, 1989-92; rsch. chemist, sr. scientist F. Hoffmann-La Roche Ltd., Basel, Switzerland, 1992—. Contbr. articles to profl. jours.; 13 patents in field. Funds of Chem. Industry grant, 1992. Mem. German Chem. Soc. Home: Im Wolfischbuhl 32, 79585 Steinen Germany Office: F Hoffmann La Roche Ltd, Grenzacher str 124, 4070 Basel Switzerland

WICHMANN, MATTHIAS WILHELM, surgeon, researcher; b. Munster, Germany, Apr. 1, 1968; s. Antonius and Inga (Schulze Schencking) W.; m. Juliane Maria Haisken, Jan. 4, 1994; children: Antoinette Sophia, Jakobus Ferdinand, Evangelia Therese. MD, Julius Maximilians U., Würzburg, Germany, 1994. Vis. rsch. assoc. Mich. State U., East Lansing, 1994-96; surg. rsch. assoc. Brown U., Providence, 1996; intern, then surg. resident Ludwig-Maximilians U., Munich, 1996-97; capt. Med. Acad. German Army, Munich, 1997-98. Guest editor Shock Jour., Providence, 1995-96. Mem. Shock Soc. Roman Catholic. Avocations: bike riding, hiking. Home: Wettersteinstr 28D, 82515 Wolfratshausen Bavaria, Germany Office: Ludwig Maximilians U, Marchioninistr 15, 81377 Munich Bavaria, Germany

WICHMANN, SØREN, linguist; b. Copenhagen, Mar. 12, 1964; s. Palle and Elisabeth (Poder) W.; 1 child, Teresa Ulrikke. MA in Comparative Lit., U. Copenhagen, 1992, PhD in Am. Indian Langs. and Cultures, 1995. Vis. scholar linguistics dept. U. Calif., Santa Barbara, 1995; asst. prof. dept. native Am. langs. and cultures U. Copenhagen, 1996-2000; sr. rschr. Danish Inst. for Advanced Studies in the Humanities, Denmark, 2000—; cons. NSF, 1994—. Author: The Relationship Among the Mixe-Zoquean Languages of Mexico, 1995, Cuentos y Colorados en Popoluca de Texistepec, 1996. Office: Danish Inst Adv Studies, in Hum Vimmelskaftet 41A 2, DK-1161 København K, Denmark

WICHRZYCKA-LANCASTER, ELZBIETA JADWIGA, pathology educator; b. Łódź, Poland, Jan. 11, 1933; arrived in South Africa, 1984; d. Kazimierz and Maria (Wisniewska) Krakowski; m. Andrzej Wichrzycki (div.); children: Alexander, Michał; m. Bryn Lancaster, 1972 (dec. 1990). MB, BChir, Med. Acad., Warsaw, Poland, 1957, PhD, 1964; M in Medicine in Anatomic Pathology, PG Ctr., Warsaw, Poland, 1972. Demonstrator dept. histology and embryology Med. Acad., Warsaw, 1952-57; asst. Inst. Hematology, Warsaw, 1957-68; fellow Postgrad. Med. Ctr., Warsaw, 1969-71; ho. officer hematology lab. Inst. Pediat., Warsaw, 1971-72, asst. prof., 1974-78; asst., sr. asst. Med. Acad., Warsaw, 1972-74; prof. HOD, UniJos, Nigeria, 1979-84; asst., sr. asst., asst. prof., prof. HOD, Medunsa, South Africa, 1985-98; sr. asst., acting HOD, Medunsa, 1998-99; cons. hematology Med. Acad. O&G, Warsaw, 1965-72; presenter in field. Contbr. articles to profl. jours. Mem. Medunsa Telemedicine Com. Avocations: gardening, embroidery, memoir writing. Home: PO Box 42601, 31 Maroela Ave, Boordfontein 0201, South Africa Office: Med Univ So Africa, Dept Anatomic Pathology, Medunsa 0204, South Africa

WICK, HANS JOACHIM, process automation engineer, consultant; b. Hornstorf, Germany, Aug. 26, 1934; arrived in Can., 1962; s. Paul and Else (Utecht) W.; m. Helga Krumke, Dec. 20, 1962; children: Claudia, Monica. Diploma in engring., U. Berlin, 1957; MSc, Oxford (Eng.) U., 1973; DSc, Aachen (Germany) U., 1977. Registered profl. engr., Ont., Can. Devel. engr. AEG, Berlin, 1957-62; analytical engr. Can. Gen. Elec., Peterborough, Ont., 1962-67; systems mgr. AEG-Telefunken, Berlin, 1967-73; scientific adviser Hoesch Steel AG, Dortmund, Germany, 1973-94; process automation cons. Dortmund, Germany, 1994—; mem. Citizen Amb. Del. to China, Spokane, 1987, mem. De. to Poland, Hungary, 1991; session chair IEEE Conf. on Control, Brighton, Eng., 1991. Contbr. articles to profl. jours.; patentee in field. Mem. IEEE (sr. mem.), German Iron & Steel Assn. Home: Von-der-Mark-Str 1A, D-44141 Dortmund Germany

WICK, LAWRENCE SCOTT, lawyer; b. San Diego, Oct. 1, 1945; s. Kenneth Lawrence and Lorrayne (Scott) W.; m. Beverly Ann DeRoss, Aug. 26, 1972 (div.); children: Ryan Scott, Andrew Taylor, Hayley Lauren. BA, Northwestern U., Evanston, Ill., 1967; JD, Columbia U., 1970. Atty. Leydig Voit & Mayer Ltd., Chgo., 1978-84, shareholder, 1984-98; ptnr. Wildman, Harrold, Allen & Dixon, Chgo., 1998—; v.p., sec., gen. counsel Lionheart Prodns., Ltd., 1995—. Contbr. articles to profl. jours. and encys. Bd. govs., lectr. Brand Names Edn. Found., 1994-95; exec. dir. Lefkowitz Internat. Trademark Moot Ct., 1994-95; bd. dirs. Tangley Oaks Homeowners Assn., 1997-2000, treas., 1998-99, pres., 1999—. Mem. ABA, Internat. Trademark Assn. (mem. treaties com.), Assn. Internat. Protection de la Propriete Industrielle, Copyright Soc. U.S., Pharm. Trade Marks Group (London), Am. Film Inst., Chgo. Bar Assn. (mem. fin. com.). Republican. Presbyterian. Avocations: international travel, film, swimming. Home: 317 Rothbury Ct Lake Bluff IL 60044-1927 Office: Wildman Harrold Allen and Dixon 225 W Wacker Dr Ste 3000 Chicago IL 60606-1224

WICK, LAWRENCE WAYNE, clergyman; b. Sterling, Ill., Aug. 13, 1939; s. Maurice L. Wick and Alice C. Johannsen; m. Sherrill A. Carlson, June 28, 1969; children: Anders Christopher, Annika Christina. BA, Wartburg Coll., 1961; MDiv, Lutheran Sch. Theology, 1966; MS, Purdue U., 1973; DMin, Chgo. Theological Seminary, 1976. Pastor Grace Luth. Ch., Richmond, Ill., 1966-70; sr. pastor Grace Luth. Ch., Woodstock, Ill., 1997—; pastor House of Prayer Luth. Ch., Country Club Hills, Ill., 1970-74; sr. pastor Wilmette (Ill.) Luth. Ch., 1974-84, St. Mark's Luth. Ch., Charlotte, N.C., 1984-86, Kountze Meml. Luth. Ch., Omaha, Nebr., 1986-97; adv. bd. Evangelical Luth. Ch., Chgo., 1990-94; bd. trustees Augustana Coll., Rock Island, Ill., 1991—, bd. of pensions Evangelical Luth. Ch., 1999—. bd. dirs. Wilmette (Ill.) Pub. Libr., 1976-84, Wartburg Coll. Alumni, Waverly, Iowa, 1986-91, AIDS Interfaith Network, Omaha, Nebr., 1989-92. E-mail: grace@owc.net. Home: 8503 Mason Hill Rd Woodstock IL 60098-7969 Office: Grace Lutheran Church 1300 Kishwaukee Valley Rd Woodstock IL 60098-2103

WICK, TAMARA, photographer, artist, writer; b. July 15, 1966; d. James Alan and Maxine Evelyn (Tankersley) W.; m. John E. Kulukundis, 1986. BA in Comm./Broadcasting, Ariz. State U., 1984; grad., Am. Acad. Dramatic Arts, N.Y.C. Asst. to exec. prodr. video devel. Columbia Pictures Industries, N.Y.C., 1986-87; pub. rels. coord., asst. to Estée Lauder Estée Lauder Cos., N.Y.C., 1987-90; founder, creative dir. Imagination Enterprises, Inc., N.Y.C., 1993—; founder, photographer Santa Paws, N.Y.C., 1993—. Active Met. Mus. Art, N.Y.C. Merit scholar U. Ariz., 1976. Mem. NAFE, U.S. Equestrian Team, N.Y. Women in Comm., N.Y. Zool. Soc., N.Y. Young Reps. Club, Ariz. State U. Alumni, Kappa Kappa Gamma Alumnae. Episcopalian. Avocations: showed horses on English circuit, tennis, snow skiing, watercolor painting, photography. Home: 150 W 56th St Apt 3010 New York NY 10019-3842

WICKBOM, KAJ STEN ERIK, media education scientist; b. Kalmar, Sweden, July 5, 1943; s. Sten-Erik and Brita Wickbom; m. Iris Kristina Persson, Aug. 12, 1977. BA, U. Lund, Sweden, 1969, MA, 1971, cert. tchr. tng., 1972. Lectr. polit. sci. Växjö (Sweden) Katedralskola, 1972—; media ednl. specialist, ednl. specialist U. Lund, 1980—; cons. on media edn. for govt., Sweden, Norway, Finland, Germany and France; UNESCO, FN, Coun. of Europe; dir. Kawis, Växjö, 1974; internat. critic jury of Berlin Film

Festival, 1979-81, film critic, 1966; with Guldbaggejury, 1979, 96—(Nat. Bd. Edn. projects: Democracy and Modern Media, 1999—, Student Influence and Power of Learning, 1996-2001). Author: Media Education, 1981, Media Education in Sweden, 1990, What is Media Education, 1992; contbr. articles to profl. jours. Recipient Golden Pen award for Best Film Critic of Yr., Swedish Film Prodrs., 1980, Honor award Swedish Film Studio, 1982, grantee Swedish Film Inst., Nat. Bd. Edn., 1989, 92, 97. Mem. Orgn. for Mass Media Rsrchrs., (Swedish filmcritic). Conservative. Avocations: reading, music, film, animals, swimming. Home: Högstorpsvägen 113, S-35242 Växjö 970515, Sweden Office: Växjö Katedralskola, Samuel Ödmans väg 1, 35239 Växjö Sweden

WICKER, FRANKLIN MICHAEL, financial consultant; b. St. Paul, June 3, 1924; s. Franklin Oscar and Florence Ruth (Corcoran) W.; m. Alice Mildred Parker, Jan. 23, 1954 (div. Jan., 1984), remarried Feb., 1994; m. Betty Jean Holden, May 27, 1988 (div. Dec., 1993). BA in Econs., Macalester Coll., 1948. Comml. property owner, ind. contractor, fin. cons., marketing specialist, 1948-53; credit analyst Swift & Co., St. Paul, 1953-60; fin. cons., ind. contractor various firms including fin. and constrn., St. Paul, 1960-64; rep., sr. acct. exec. Waddell & Reed, Kans. City & Bloomington, Minn., 1964-97, sr. fin. advisor, 1997—; apt. house and comml. property owner, pvt. investor, entrepreneur, 1953—; conductor seminars and adult edn. on You and Your Money, 1977-98; SBA counselor, 1979—; bus. cons., investment advisor. Ind. activist, St. Paul; sr. investment trustee St. James Luth. Ch., St. Paul, 1974-86; advisor vol. Condo Constrn. and Warranty, 1999—. With NAS, 1943-46. Lutheran. Office: Waddell & Reed 9801 Dupont Ave S Ste 420 Bloomington MN 55431-3199

WICKER, R. DAVID, JR., lawyer; b. Greensboro, N.C., Apr. 11, 1960; s. Ralph D. and Judith (Wade) W.; m. Susan Medders, June 5, 1982; children: Whitney L., Colby D., Lance D. BA in History, U.N.C., Greensboro, 1982; JD, N.C. Ctrl. U., Durham, 1985. Pvt. practice Durham, 1985-92; ptnr. Roberti, Wittenberg, Lauffer & Wicker, Durham, 1992—. Mem. Masons, Shriner. E-mail: dwicker@rwhl.com. Office: Robert Wittenberg Lauffer & Wicker 100 E Parrish St Ste 200 Durham NC 27701-3345

WICKER, THOMAS CAREY, JR., judge; b. New Orleans, Aug. 1, 1923; s. Thomas Carey and Mary (Taylor) W.; children: Thomas Carey III, Catherine Anne; m. Jane Anne Trepanier, Dec. 29, 1995. BBA, Tulane U., 1944, LLB, 1949, JD, 1969. Bar: La. 1949. Law clk. La. Supreme Ct., New Orleans, 1949-50; asst. U.S. Atty., 1950-53; practiced in New Orleans, 1953-72; mem. firm Simon, Wicker & Wiedemann, 1953-67; partner firm Wicker, Wiedemann & Fransen, 1967-72; dist. judge Jefferson Parish (La.), 1972-85, judge, Ct. of Appeals 5th cir., 1985-98, mem. faculty Nat. Jud. Coll., 1979-93, Tulane U. Sch. Law, 1978-83. Past bd. visitors Tulane U.; bd. dirs. La. Jud. Coll.; past pres. Sugar Bowl. Author: (with others) Judicial Ethics, 1982, (with others) Modern Judicial Ethics, 1992; editor Tulane Law Review, 1949. Lt. (j.g.), USNR, 1944-46. Mem. ABA (jud. div. council), La. (chmn. jr. bar sect. 1958-59, gov. 1958, mem. ho. of dels. 1960-72), Jefferson Parish, bar assns., Tulane U. Alumni Assn. (past pres.), Am. Judicature Soc., La. Dist. Judges Assn. (past pres.), Order of Coif, Beta Gamma Sigma, Pi Kappa Alpha. Episcopalian. Clubs: Rotary (pres. 1971-72), Metairie (La.) Country. Avocations: golf, photography, military history. Home: 500 Rue Saint Ann Apt 127 Metairie LA 70005-4639 Office: La Ct Appeal 5th Cir Gretna Courthouse Fl 4 Gretna LA 70053

WICKHAM, ROBERT JOSEPH JOHNSTONE, leasing company executive; b. Dornoch, Sutherland, Scotland, Mar. 25, 1934; s. Joseph Alexander and Elsie Muriel (Johnstone) W.; m. Isabella Margaret Walls, Apr. 1, 1959; children: Elizabeth Muriel Wilson, Margaret Sandra Hope. Mgr. Bank of Scotland, London, 1968-73, gen. mgrs. asst., 1974-77, chief mgr., 1977-85, divsn. gen. mgr., 1985-89, gen. mgr., mem. mgmt. bd., 1989-93; dir. Secure Trust Group Plc., Birmingham, Eng., 1993—; bd. dirs. Northern Leisure Plc, London, Rutland Trust Plc, London, Brough Fame Ltd., Sevenoaks, Eng.; chmn. Leased Hotels Ltd., London, 1994—. Sr. craftsman Royal Air Force, 1952-54. Fellow Chartered Inst. Bankers Scotland; mem. Bankers Club, Caledonian Club. Avocations: sailing, reading. Home: 77 Manor Rd South, Esher Surrey KT10 0QB, England Office: Brough Fame Ltd, 115A St Johns Hill, Sevenoaks Kent TN13 3PE, England

WICKI, JODOK EUGEN, lawyer; b. Zurich, Switzerland, July 20, 1966; s. André A. and Maja Wicki. Cert. in Law, U. Zurich, 1992; Atty.-at-Law degree, High Ct. of Canton of Zurich, 1994. Bar: Zurich, Zug, Aargau. Jr. assoc. Homburger Rechtsanwälte, Zurich, 1992-93; assoc. Henrici, Wicki & Guggisberg, Attys.-at-Law, Zurich, 1994-96, ptnr., 2000—; intern Kronish, Lieb, Weiner & Hellman, Attys. at Law, N.Y.C., 1996-97, Hunt & Hunt Solicitors, Sydney, Australia, 1997. Lt. Switzerland Artillery, 1989-94, capt. Switzerland Mil. Justice, 1999. Mem. Internat. Assn. Young Lawyers, Swiss Bar Assn. Avocations: sailing (World Champion 1985, European Champion 1996), skiing. Office: Henrici Wicki & Guggisberg, Hottingerstrasse 21, 8032 Zurich Switzerland

WICKLIN, BRIAN REINZIE, economist, statistician; b. Colombo, Sri Lanka, Apr. 18, 1939; arrived in Sweden, 1960; s. Basil Oscar and Rene Irangini (Aramasinghe) Wickremesinghe; m. Inger Margeretha Hietala, Dec. 31, 1965; children: Alexis, Martin, Sara. BSc, U. Uppsala, Sweden, 1965, MS, 1966. Statistican, economist Stats. Sweden, 1966-68, sr. statistician, economist, 1968-78, project coord., 1978-86; mktg. exec. Super Pros AB, Sweden, 1978-85; cons. Wicklin & Assocs., Sweden, 1997—, sr. cons., project coord.; project coord. Royal Commn. on Gambling, Stockholm, 1994-95. Author: Statistics of Sports, 1989 (Yearbook award), (report) Tobacco Consumption in the Nordic Countries 1970-98; author, editor: Proceedings From ISI, 1993, 95. Mem. Internat. Statis. Inst., Statis. Soc. Sweden (Statistician of Yr. 1989). Mem. Anglican Ch. Avocations: squash, tennis, skiing. Home: Knäckepilsgränd 92, S-16576 Hasselby Stockholm Sweden

WICKLUND, DAVID WAYNE, lawyer; b. St. Paul, Aug. 7, 1949; s. Wayne Glenwood and Elna Katherine (Buresh) W.; m. Susan Marie Bubenko, Nov. 17, 1973; children: David Jr., Kurt, Edward. BA cum laude, Williams Coll., 1971; JD cum laude, U. Toledo, 1974. Bar: Ohio 1974. Assoc. Shumaker, Loop & Kendrick, Toledo, 1974-80, ptnr., 1981—; adj. instr. law, U. Toledo, 1988. Editor-in-chief U. Toledo Law Rev. 1973-74. Mem. ABA, Ohio State Bar Assn. (mem. bd. govs. antitrust sect.), Toledo Bar Assn., U. Toledo Coll. of Law Alumni Assn. (pres. 1999-2000), Inverness Club, Toledo Club. Office: Shumaker Loop & Kendrick N Courthouse Sq 1000 Jackson St Toledo OH 43624-1573

WICKNER, FRAN S., psychotherapist, educator; b. Passaic, N.J., June 2, 1956; m. Larry E. Harris, June 11, 1983; children: Andrew, Jacob. BA in Psychology, SUNY, New Paltz, 1978; MA in Counseling Psychology, U. San Francisco, 1981; PhD in Clin. Psychology, Calif. Grad. Sch. Psychology, 1989. Co-dir. drug program Pyramid Alternatives, Pacifica, Calif., 1981-84; outpatient dir. St. Mary's, San Francisco, 1985-87; pvt. practice Albany, Calif., 1984—; prof. John F. Kennedy U., Orinda, Calif., 1988—; cons., Albany, 1985—. Mem. Am. Assn. Marraige and Family Therapy, Calif. Assn. Marriage and Family Therapists (nat., E. Bay chpt., San Francisco chpt.), Assn. Family Therapists No. Calif. Office: 902 Carmel Ave # 8 Albany CA 94706-2106

WICKREMASINGHE, RANIL, former prime minister of Sri Lanka, lawyer; b. Mar. 24, 1949. Student, Royal Coll. Colombo, Sri Lanka, U. Colombo, Sri Lanka Law Coll. Atty. Supreme Ct.; M.P. Parliament, 1977—; dep. min. fgn. affairs Govt. of Sri Lanka, 1977-79, min. youth affairs and employment, 1978-89, min. edn., 1980-89, min. industries, 1989-90, min. industries, sci. and tech., 1990-94, prime min., 1993-94. Leader of Opposition; leader of United. Nat. Party, 1994—. Mem. United Nat. Party.

WICKS, DAVID O., JR., communications executive; b. Boston, May 17, 1941; s. David O. and Elizabeth L. Wicks; m. Joan Gagnebin, Sept. 7, 1963; children: Perrin, Sara. BA, Trinity Coll., Hartford, Conn., 1963; MBA, U. Va., 1968. With nat. divsn. Chem. Bank, 1963-66; specialist in venture capital and cable TV Warburg Paribas Becker, N.Y.C., 1968-83, mng. dir., 1979-83; gen. ptnr. Becker Venture Assocs., Becker Comms. Assocs. II; sr. ptng. Criterion Venture Ptnrs., Houston, 1983-88; mng. dir. Criterion Investments, Inc., 1983-88; pres. Criterion Investments, Inc., 1985-88; v.p. Cablevision Sys. Corp., Bethpage, N.Y., 1996—; exec. NASA Mid Continent Tech. Transfer Ctr., 1992-95; bd. dirs. Matrix Enterprises Inc.; expert witness on cable TV, U.S. Congress and state regulatory bodies. Contbr. articles to profl. jours. Bd. dirs. Soc. for Performing Arts, Space Found., Adult Literacy Media Alliance. Recipient Vanguard award Nat. Cable TV Assn., 1978. Mem. Houston Venture Capital Assn. (bd. dirs.), Univ. Club (N.Y.C.). Office: Cablevision Sys Corp 1111 Stewart Ave Bethpage NY 11714-3581

WICKWIRE, PATRICIA JOANNE NELLOR, psychologist, educator; b. Sioux City, Iowa; d. William McKinley and Clara Rose (Pautsch) Nellor; m. Robert James Wickwire, Sept. 7, 1957; 1 child, William James. BA cum laude, U. No. Iowa, 1951; MA, U. Iowa, 1959; PhD, U. Tex., Austin, 1971; postgrad. U. So. Calif., UCLA, Calif. State U., Long Beach, 1951-66. Tchr., Ricketts Ind. Schs., Iowa, 1946-48; tchr., counselor Waverly-Shell Rock Ind. Schs., Iowa, 1951-55; reading cons., head dormitory counselor U. Iowa, Iowa City, 1955-57; tchr., sch. psychologist, adminstr. S. Bay Union High Sch. Dist., Redondo Beach, Calif., 1962-82, dir. student svcs. and spl. edn.; cons. mgmt. and edn.; pres. Nellor Wickwire Group, 1981—; mem. exec. bd. Calif. Interagency Mental Health Coun., 1968-72, Beach Cities Symphony Assn., 1970-82; chmn. Friends of Dominguez Hills (Calif.), 1981-85. Lic. ednl. psychologist, marriage, family and child counselor, Calif.; pres. Calif. Women's Caucus, 1993-95. Mem. APA, AAUW (exec. bd., chpt. pres. 1962-72), Nat. Career Devel. Assn. (media chair 1992-98), Am. Assn. Career Edn. (pres. 1991—), L.A. County Dirs. Pupil Svcs. (chmn. 1974-79), L.A. County Personnel and Guidance Assn. (pres. 1977-78), Assn. Calif. Sch. Adminstrs. (dir. 1977-81), L.A. County SW Bd. Dist. Adminstrs. for Spl. Edn. (chmn. 1976-81), Calif. Assn. Sch. Psychologists (bd. dirs. 1981-83), Am. Assn. Sch. Adminstrs., Calif. Assn. for Measurement and Evaluation in Guidance (dir. 1981, pres. 1984-85, 98—), ACA (chmn. Coun. Newsletter Editors 1989-91, mem. com. on women 1989-92, mem. com. on rsch. and knowledge, 1994—, chmn. 1995—, chmn. 1996—, mem. and chmn. bylaws com. 1998—), Assn. Measurement and Eval. in Guidance (Western regional editor 1985-87, conv. chair 1986, editor 1987-90, exec. bd. dirs. 1987-91), Calif. Assn. Counseling and Devel. (exec. bd. 1984—, pres. 1988-89, jour. editor 1990—), Internat. Career Assn. Network (chair 1985—), Pi Lambda Theta, Alpha Phi Gamma, Psi Chi, Kappa Delta Pi, Sigma Alpha Iota. Contbr. articles in field to profl. jours. Office: The Nellor Wickwire Group 2900 Amby Pl Hermosa Beach CA 90254-2216

WIDDER, JOACHIM, radio-oncologist, researcher; b. Graz, Austria, Feb. 15, 1962. MD, Vienna U., Austria, 1987; PhD, Nijmegen U., The Netherlands, 1999. Rsch. asst. Inst. Exptl. Pathology Vienna U., 1988-89, asst. Inst. History Medicine, 1993-96, resident Dept. Radiooncology, 1997—; vis. fellow Kennedy Inst. Ethics Georgetown U., Washington, 1990. Author: Das Vergessene Leben, 1999. Mem. ESPMH. Avocation: music. Office: Dept Radiotherapy, Allgemeines Krankenhaus, A-1090 Vienna Austria

WIDDISON, ADAM LEWIS, surgeon, consultant; b. Ruddington, Eng., Oct. 7, 1959; s. Ivor Kenneth and Gill June (Ashford) W.; m. Susan Elizabeth Taylor; children: Nicholas, Natasha. BA, Oxford (Eng.) U., 1981, MB, BChir, 1984, MA, 1985, D Medicine, 1991. Registrar Princess of Wales Hosp., Bridgend, 1989, Norfolk and Norwich (U.K.) Hosp., 1989-92, Frenchay Hosp., Bristol, U.K., 1992-93; sr. registrar Royal Devon and Exeter (U.K.) Hosp., 1993-94, Bristol Royal Infirmary, 1994-95; cons. surgeon Royal Cornwall Hosp., Truro, Eng., 1995—; edn. supr. Royal Cornwall Hosp., Truro, 1996—, clin. lead hosp. clin. computer project, 1996—, chmn. hosp. audit com., 1997-99; external examiner Imperial Col., London, 1999—. Jour. referee Brit. Jour. Surgery, Annals of Royal Coll. Surgeons, Pancreas, Med. Sci. Rsch.; contbr. chpts. to books and articles to profl. jours. Rsch. fellow NIH, UCLA, 1989-91. Fellow Royal Coll. Surgeons Eng. (Hunterian prof. 1995), Assn. Surgeons; mem. Brit. Soc. Gastroenterologists, Am. Soc. Gastroenterologists. Avocations: badminton, cricket, gardening, walking. Office: Dept Surgery, Royal Cornwall Hosp, Truro Cornwall TR1 3LJ, England

WIDELL, SUSANNE CHRISTINA MARIE-LOUISE, laboratory technologist; b. Stockholm, Dec. 21, 1945; d. Sven-Erik and Marie-Louise (Nilsson) Åberg; m. Bengt-Erik Widell; children: Peter, Jan-Erik, Robert. Degree, U. Med. Lab. Tech., Stockholm, 1978; D of Med. Sci./PhD, Karolinska Inst., Stockholm, 1994; diploma, Swedish Inst. Biomed. Lab. Sci., 1997. Med. lab. technologist Inst. Legal Chemistry, Stockholm, 1962-76; sr. med. lab. technologist hematology lab. Karolinska Hosp., Stockholm, 1978-94, sr. med. lab. technologist/dr. med. sci. divsn. hematology, 1994—; rschr. Karolinska Hosp., 1994—; postdoctoral fellow divsn. cellular and molecular tumorpathology, dept. oncology and pathology, Cancer Ctr. Karolinska Inst., 1994—; cons. CellaVision AB, Lund, Sweden, 1998-99; instr. morphologic hematology Inst. Biomed. Lab. Sci., 1997-99. Contbr. articles to profl. jours. Recipient award Swedish Hematology Patients Union, Stockholm, 1993. Mem. Swedish Assn. Health Sci. (treas. 1997-99), Swedish Assn. Med. Lab. Technologists, Internat. Assn. Med. Lab. Technologists, Swedish Assn. Hematology, Swedish Assn. Health Profls., Swedish Soc. Medicine. Avocations: golf, art, antiques, opera, travel. Home: Knektvägen 9, 17675 Järfälla Sweden

WIDHALM, KURT MARIA, pediatrician, researcher; b. Linz, Austria, Feb. 2, 1946; s. Kurt Maria and Gertraud A. (Mader) W.; m. Renate Widhalm, Sept. 7, 1974; children: George, Harald K., Kurt M.A. MD, U. Vienna, 1971. Diplomate Austrian Physicians Bd. Asst. prof. dept. physiology U. Vienna, 1971-73, asst. prof. dept. pediatrics, 1973-81, assoc. prof., 1986, prof. pediatrics, 1994, prof. clin. chemistry, 1992-94, prof. pediats. dept. pediats.; chmn. dir. Mautner Children's Hosp., Vienna, 1995—. Author: Lipids and Lipoproteins in Childhood, 1985. Mem. Health Bd., City of Vienna, 1990-97. Recipient Pirquet award Austrian Soc. Pediatrics, 1980, Konrad Lang award Deutsche Gesellschaft fuer Ernahrung, 1986. Mem. Soc. Pediatric Rsch. (pres. 1990), Austrian Soc. Nutrition (v.p.), Rotary. Roman Catholic. Achievements include research on age dependency of lipoproteins. Avocations: tennis, skiing, sailing. Home: Potzleinsdorfer Hohe 25, Vienna Austria Office: Univ Vienna Dept Ped, Wahringer Gurtel 18-20, A-1090 Vienna Austria

WIDHOLM, OLOF ERIC BERNHARD, obstetrician, gynecologist, educator; b. Helsinki, Finland, June 30, 1923; s. Eric and Saimi (Laakkonen) W.; m. Kerstin Stadigh; children: Mikael, Claes. MD, U. Helsinki, 1950, MD, PhD, 1953. Resident dept. ob-gyn Maria Hosp. Inst. Serobacteriology, Helsinki, 1949-58; sr. lectr. Helsinki U. Ctr. Hosp., 1959-63, asst. prof., 1963-69, assoc. prof., 1969-75, prof. chmn. dept. ob-gyn., 1975-87; cons. Finland Nat. Med. Bd., 1970—; adminstrv. chief physician dept. ob-gyn HUCH, Helsinki, 1976-82, 85—, mem. adminstrv. bd., 1977—; mem. liability com. physicians, Finland, 1982—. Contbr. over 200 articles on obgyn. to profl. jours. Decorated comdr. Order of Lion (Finland), 1981, comdr. Order of North Star (Sweden); recipient Civil Svc. medal of merit State of Finland, 1982. Mem. Finnish Gynecol. Assn. (hon. mem., pres. 1978-80), Scandinavian Assn. Ob-Gyn. (hon. mem., pres. 1980-82), Finnish Cancer Assn., Finnish Cancer Found. (bd. dirs.), Soc. Adolescent Medicine. Home: Westendintie 11, 02160 Espoo, Finland Office: Helsinki U Central Hosp, Dept Ob-Gyn, Haarmaninkatu 2,, 00290 Helsinki,, Finland

WIDIGSSON, OLLE, transport company executive; b. Gavle, Sweden, May 12, 1947; s. Sven and Marianne (Davidsson) W.; m. Maria Björnstam (div.); 1 child, Carl; m. Eva Månsson, Jan. 6, 1998; children: Emma, Eric. Master mariner, Nautical Coll., Stockholm, 1970, marine chief engr., 1973. Ship's officer Johnson Line, Sweden, 1970-71, Broström Group, Sweden, 1971-73; shore capt. Salen Group, Sweden, 1973-80; ops. mgr. Combi Shipping, Sweden, 1980-84; chief purchaser Stora, Sweden, 1984-86, purchasing mgr., 1986-89, transport devel. mgr., 1989-94; tech. dir. Stora, Falun, 1994—. Mem. IMD (mem. E2R3 1996), European Shippers Coun. (vice chmn. 1997). Lutheran. Avocations: family life, classical music, walking, golf. Home: Solvägen 13, S-18352 Täby Sweden

WIDÍMSKY, JIRI, cardiologist, medical educator; b. Pilsen, Czechoslovakia, Mar. 31, 1925; s. Bohus and Marie (Breiska) W.; m. Dagmar Petrovicka; children: Petr, Jiri Jr. MD, Charles U., Prague, Czechoslovakia, 1950, PhD, 1956, cert. prof., 1976, DSC, 1971. Intern Karlovy Vary, 1950-51; resident Inst. Cardiovascular Diseases, Prague, 1951-56; cardiologist, rschr. Inst. Cardiovascular Disease, Prague, 1951-61, chief cardiopulmonary lab., 1962-70; head dept. cardiology Inst. Clin. and Exptl. Medicine, Prague, 1970-83; head dept. cardiology Postgrad. Med. Sch., Prague, 1983-93, prof. cardiology, 1993—; cons. WHO, Geneva, 1975-85, Novartis, Prague, 1989—. Contbr. articles to profl. jours.; chief editor Jour. of AMA, Prague, 1993—. Fellow Swedish Cardiol. Soc., Gothenburg, 1961-62. Fellow European Soc. Cardiology (v.p. 1980-84, hon.); mem. Czech Med. Soc. (hon.), Czech Cardiol. Soc. (hon.), Czech Soc. Internal Medicine (hon.), Internat. Soc. Hypertension, European Soc. Hypertension. Roman Catholic. Fax: 420-2-4713439. Home: 7 Lukesova, 142 00 Prague 4, Czech Republic Office: IKEM Dept Cardiology, 800 Videnska, 142 00 Prague 4, Czech Republic

WIDIMSKY, JIŘÍ, JR., internist, educator; b. Prague, Czech Republic, May 10, 1956; s. Jiri and Dagmar (Petrovická) W.; m. Marcela Císarová, Oct. 20, 1984; children: Julie, Jiri. MD, Charles U., Prague, 1981. House physician U. Nemocnice, Prague, 1981-87, with hypertension dept., 1996—, assoc. prof. medicine, 1987-89; rsch. fellow CRIM, Montreal, Can., 1987-89. Contbr. over 80 articles to profl. jours. Recipient 1st prize Internat. Sch. Young Cardiologists, Berlin, 1986. Mem. Internat. Soc. Hypertension, Czech Urol. Soc., Czech. Neurol. Soc. Office: III Internal Dept, Nemocnice 1, 12808 Prague Czech Republic

WIDJAJA, INDRAJUWANA KOMALA, accountant, consultant; b. Pati, Indonesia, Sept. 19, 1965; s. Putranta and Astuti (Wardhani) W. Degree, UNPAR, Bandung, Indonesia, 1989. Registered CPA, Indonesia. Staff acct. Arthur Andersen, Jakarta, Indonesia, 1988-89, semi-sr. acct., 1989-90, sr. acct., 1990-91, supr., 1991-93, assoc. mgr., 1993-94, mgr., 1994-98, ptnr., 1998—. Mem. Indonesian Inst. Accts. Avocations: reading, swimming, watching movies. Office: Arthur Andersen, Wisma 46 Kotabni Level 25, Jakarta 10220, Indonesia

WIDMANN, WOLFGANG, engineering executive; b. Salzburg, Austria, Sept. 25, 1956; s. Richard and Olga (Mittersakechmoeller) W.; m. Sabine Wegener, July 31, 1982; children: Bernahrd, Bettina, Michael, Eva. Diploma, U. Innsbruck, Austria, 1982. Chartered civil engr. Design engr. ILF Consulting Engrs., Innsbruck, 1983-86, project mgr., 1986-89, dir., 1989—, also bd. dirs. Contbr. articles to profl. jours. Elder Bapt. Ch., Innsbruck, 1985—. Mem. WEF. Avocations: skiing, mountaineering, reading, music. Home: General-Teursteinstr. 15, A-6020 Innsbruck Austria Office: ILF Consulting Engrs, Framsweg 16, A-6020 Innsbruck Austria

WIDMAYER, WARREN J., lawyer; b. Detroit, Mar. 20, 1956; s. Warren Widmayer; m. Elizabeth A. Widmayer, Sept. 3, 1982; children: David J., Katherine R., Christine J. BA with high distinction, U. Mich., 1978, JD, 1982. Bar: Mich. 1983, U.S. Dist. Ct. (ea. dist.) Mich. 1983. Atty. Dobson, Griffin & Westerman, P.C., Ann Arbor, Mich., 1983-85, Dobson, Griffin, Austin & Berman, P.C., Ann Arbor, 1985-86, Ellis, Talcott, Ohlgren & Ferguson, P.C., Ann Arbor, 1986-89, Joscelyn & Treat, P.C., Ann Arbor, 1989-91; atty., prin. Ferguson & Widmayer, P.C., Ann Arbor, 1991—. Contbr. articles to law jours. Mem. ABA (mem. labor and employment sect., forum on health law), State Bar of Mich. (mem. taxation sect.), Washtenaw County Bar Assn. (chmn. tax law sect. 1991-93, mem. labor and employment law sect.), Washtewnaw County Estate Planning Coun. (mem., bd. dirs. 1986-87), Nat. Health Lawyer Assn. Avocations: musician, gardening. E-mail: warren@fergusonwidmayer.com. Office: Ferguson & Widmayer PC 538 N Division St Ann Arbor MI 48104-1136

WIEBE, BURCKHARD, public relations executive; b. Berlin, Mar. 13, 1941; s. Hans-Joachim and Amély (Kolb) W. BA, Luther Coll., Decorah, Iowa, 1962; MA, Free U., Berlin, 1966. Instr. Folkuniversitetet, Sweden, 1966-68; reader Fackelträger Publ. House, Hanover, Germany, 1969-71; press officer Volkswagen Found., Hanover, 1972-81; head press and info. dept. Social Sci. Rsch. Ctr., Berlin, 1982—; editor-in-chief WZB-Mitteilungen quarterly, 1982—. Editor, author: Zwischen Marktplatz und Elfenbeinturm, 1988; contbr. articles o profl. jours. Avocation: English and Swedish languages. Office: Wissenschaftszentrum Berlin, Reichpietschufer 50, D-10785 Berlin Germany

WIEBE, MICHAEL EUGENE, microbiologist, cell biologist; b. Newton, Kans., Oct. 1, 1942; s. Austin Roy and Ruth Fern (Stucky) W.; m. Rebecca Ann Doak, June 12, 1965; children: Brandon Clark, Thomas Huntington. BS, Sterling Coll., 1965; PhD, U. Kansas, 1971. Rsch. assoc. Duke U. Med. Ctr., Durham, N.C., 1971-73; asst. prof. Cornell U. Med. Coll., N.Y.C., 1973-81, assoc. prof., 1981-85; assoc. dir. rsch. and devel. N.Y. Blood Ctr., N.Y.C., 1980-83, dir. Leukocyte products, 1983-84; sr. scientist Genentech Inc., South San Francisco, Calif., 1984-88, assoc. dir. medicinal and analytical chemistry, 1988-90, dir. quality control, 1990-96, sr. dir. quality control, 1996-98; v.p., chief sci. officer BioReliance Corp., Rockville, Md., 1998—; mem. biol. scis. alumni adv. bd. U. Kans., 1994-99. Contbr. articles to profl. jours. Mem. bd. trustees Sterling Coll., 1990—, chmn., 1994-99. Postdoctoral fellow NIH, 1971-73. Mem. AAAS, Am. Soc. for Microbiology, Am. Soc. Virology, Parenteral Drug Assn. Presbyterian. Avocations: travel, photography. Home: 15200 Arminio Ct Darnestown MD 20874-3633 Office: BioReliance 14920 Broschart Rd Rockville MD 20850-3304

WIEBE, RICHARD HERBERT, reproductive endocrinologist, educator; b. Herbert, Sask., Can., Dec. 28, 1937; came to U.S., 1971; s. Herbert and Olga Maragratha (Jahnke) W.; m. Jacquelyn Dee Yancy, Aug. 30, 1975; 1 child, Richard Herbert, Jr. MD, U. Sask., 1962. Resident Queen's Univ., Kingston, Ont., Can., 1970; asst. to assoc. prof. Duke U., Durham, N.C., 1972-81; assoc. prof. to prof. U. So. Ala., Mobile, 1981-88; chmn. and prof. Dept. Ob-Gyn. U. S.D., Sioux Falls, 1988-95; chmn., prof. dept. ob-gyn. East Tenn. State U., Johnson City, 1996-98; editorial cons., Fertility/Sterility, Birmingham, Ala., 1978—; sec., Univ. Physicians, Sioux Falls, 1991-93. Contbr. numerous articles to profl. jours. Recipient, Rsch. Grant, NIH, Ala., 1981-89, Edn./Svc. Grant, USPHS, S.D., 1989-95. Mem. ACOG, Assn. Profs. of Ob-Gyn., Am. Soc. Primatologists, Soc. for Gynecol. Investigation, Soc. for Study of Reproduction, Am. Soc. Reproductive Medicine, Endocrine Soc. Home: 316 Settler Ln Kure Beach NC 28449-4835

WIECHERT, ALLEN LEROY, educational planning consultant, architect; b. Independence, Kans., Oct. 25, 1938; s. Norman Henry and Serena Johanna (Steinke) W.; m. Sandra Swanson, Aug. 19, 1961; children: Kristin Nan, Brendan Swanson, Megan Ann. BArch, Kans. State U., 1962. Lic. arch., Kans.; cert. Nat. Coun. Archtl. Registration Bds. Arch. in tng. McVey, Peddie, Schmidt & Allen, Wichita, Kans., 1962-63; arch. Kivett & Myers, Kansas City, Mo., 1963-68; asst. to vice chancellor plant planning and devel. U. Kans., Lawrence, 1968-74, assoc. dir. facilities planning, 1974-78, univ. dir. facilities planning, 1978-92, univ. arch., 1993-95; campus planner Gould Evans Assocs., Lawrence, 1995-96; code enforcement officer City of Prairie Village, Kans., 1997—; mem. long range phys. planning com. Kans. Bd. Regents, 1971-95; designer, archtl. programmer ednl. facilities; bd. dirs. Kans. U. Fed. Credit Union, 1972-81, pres. bd., 1974. Editor, contbr.: Physical Development Planning Work Book, 1973. Chmn. horizons com. Lawrence Bicentennial Commn.; designer Kaw River Trail, 1976; mem. Action 80 Com., 1980-81, Lawrence-Douglas County Horizon 2020 Task Group, 1993-95; mem. standing com. Kans. Episcopal Diocese, 1976-80, pres. com., 1981, mem. diocesan coun., 1982-84, chmn. coll. work com., 1982-84, commn. on ch. arch. and allied arts, 1986-99, long range planning com., 1988; sr. warden Trinity Episc. Ch., Lawrence, 1978-80, mem. vestry, 1997-99; trustee Kans. Sch. Religion, 1973-80, 82-95, v.p., 1984-85, pres., 1986-92, trustee friends of the dept. of religious studies, 1995—; mem. adv. bd. Salvation Army, 1990—; bd. dirs. Trinity Group Care Home, 1973-79; advancement chmn. troop com. Boy Scouts Am., 1981-87, dist. com. Pelathe dist., 1984—, vice chmn., 1984, chmn., 1985-87; exec. bd. Heart of Am. Coun., 1985-87. 1st lt. Kans. Air N.G., 1961-67. Recipient Dist. Award of Merit, Boy Scouts Am., 1988, Silver Beaver award, 1991. Mem. AIA, Assn. Univ. Archs. (sec.-treas. 1986-87, v.p. 1987-88, pres. 1998-99), Nat. Hist. Trust, Kans. U. Endowment Assn. (sec. 1981-85, founder, exec. bd. Hist. Mt. Oread Fund divsn.), Nat. Cathedral Assn. (regional co-chairperson 1993—). Home: 813 Highland Dr Lawrence KS 66044-2431

WIECKO, CRISTINA MARÍA, physicist; b. Warsaw, Poland, Mar. 25, 1948; arrived in Argentina, 1960; d. Czeslaw and Wanda Leokadia (Sieminska) W.; m. Néstor Omar Parga, Oct. 27, 1972 (div. Mar. 1992). Lic. in Physics, Nat. U de Cuyo, Bariloche, Argentina, 1973, D Physics, 1977.

Scholarship fellow CONICET, Bariloche, Argentina, 1974-78, Santa Barbara, 1978-80; rsch. fellow CONICET, Bariloche, 1981—; assoc. prof. ICTP, Trieste, Italy, 1984-90; dir. PhD thesis Nat. U. de Cuyo, Bariloche, 1989-93. Contbr. articles to profl. jours. Mem. Majnu, Rosario, Argentina, 1965-67. Vis. scholar ICTP, Trieste, 1986-91. Avocations: literature, paddle, yoga, drawing. Office: Centro Atómico, 8400 Bariloche, Rio Negro Argentina

WIECZOREK, NORBERT GEORG WALTER, government official, banker; b. Kassel, Hessen, Fed. Republic Germany, Dec. 12, 1940; s. Walter and Luise (Schweinebraten) W.; m. Heidemarie Zeul, Nov. 25, 1965 (div. 1980); m. Gerlinde Strauss, Sept. 18, 1981. Dr. rer. pol., U. Bremen, Fed. Republic Germany, 1980. Mktg. researcher Carl Freudenberg KG aA, Weinheim, Fed. Republic Germany, 1966-68; asst. lectr. mktg. U. Gottingen, Fed. Republic Germany, 1968-71; chmn. commn. social scis. U. Bremen, 1971-72; asst. lectr. econs. RWTH, Aachen, Fed. Republic Germany, 1972-76; dir. Bank fur Gemeinwirtschaft AG, Frankfurt, Fed. Republic Germany, 1976-91; mem. parliament Deutscher Bundestag, Bonn, Fed. Republic Germany, 1980-83, 84—. Author: Wirtschaftsplanung in Grossbritannien, 1945-70, 1980; contbr. articles to profl. publs. City councillor City of Russelsheim, Fed. Republic Germany, 1972-81; county councillor County of Gross Gerau, Fed. Republic Germany, 1976-93; mem. exec. coun. parliamentary group SPD, 1989—, dep. chmn., 2000—. Mem. Trilateral Commn., Deutsche Atlantische Gesellschaft, Atlantik-Brü cke e.v. Mem. Socialdemokratische Partei Deutsclands. Avocations: reading, hiking. Office: Deutscher Bundestag, Platz des Republik 1, 77077 Berlin Germany

WIECZOREK, PIOTR PAWEL, chemistry educator; b. Czarnowasy, Silesia, Poland, Aug. 21, 1953; s. Ryszard and Hildegard (Sikora) W.; m. Elżbieta Giejc, Oct. 25, 1974; children: Dorota, Krzysztof, Anna. MS in Chemistry, Tech. U., Wroclaw, Poland, 1978, PhD, 1982. Rsch. asst. Pedagogical U., Opole, Poland, 1981-85; asst. prof. U. Opole, 1985—; vis. rschr. Lund (Sweden) U., 1994, 96-97; docent Tech. U., Munich, 1995. Author: (with P. Kafarski) Laboratory Experiments of Bioorganic Chemistry, 1987 (award Polish Ministry Edn. 1989); contbr. articles to profl. jours. Councillor People's Town Coun., Dabrowa, 1990—; pres. Solidarnosc Trade U., U. Opole, 1995—. Recipient Sci. award Polish Ministry Edn., 1983; DAAD fellow, 1995, fellow Swedish Inst., 1996-97; INCO-Copernicus Joint Rsch. grantee European Cmty., Brussels, 1998; scholar Czechoslovak Acad. Sci., Prague, 1980. Mem. Internat. Assn. Environ. Analytical Chemistry, European Membrane Soc., Am. Chem. Soc., Polish Chem. Soc. (Kemula's award 1998). Roman Catholic. Avocations: dancing, listening to music, cycling, playing bridge. E-mail: Piotr.Wieczorek@uni.opole.pl. Home: ul Opolska 19a, PL46-086 Opole Sławice Silesia, Poland Office: Univ Opole, ul Oleska 48, PL45-052 Opole Silesia, Poland

WIECZOREK, ULRICH FRANZ JOSEF, geography educator; b. Munich, June 20, 1945; s. Josef Alfred and Franziska (Maier) W.; m. Elisabeth Antonie Schuhböck, Mar. 30, 1974; children: Andreas, Barbara. Exam., U. Munich, 1969, Doctorate, 1972, Habilitation, 1980. Asst. lectr., chair phys. geography and geog. remote sensing U. Munich, 1973-80; tchr. math., geography, physics Gymnasium Pfaffenhofen, Germany, 1980-86; prof. U. Augsburg, Germany, 1986—; chmn. commn. tchr. tng. U. Augsburg, 1989—. Contbr. articles to profl. jours. Office: U Augsburg, Universitätsstrasse 10, D-86159 Augsburg Germany

WIECZOREK-ZEUL, HEIDEMARIE, German government official. Mem. fed. parliament Govt. of Germany, 1987-98; now min. econ. cooperation and devel. Govt. of Germany, Berlin, 1998—. Office: Min Econ Coop and Devel, Stresemannstrasse 92, 10963 Berlin Germany*

WIED, GEORGE LUDWIG, physician; b. Carlsbad, Czechoslovakia, Feb. 7, 1921; came to U.S., 1953, naturalized, 1960; s. Ernst George and Anna (Travnicek) W.; m. Daga M. Graaz, Mar. 19, 1949 (dec. Aug. 1977); m. Kayoko Y. Yamauchi, Nov. 1, 1990. MD, Charles U., Prague, 1945, Hon. Med. Degree, 1995. Intern County Hosp., Carlsbad, Czechoslovakia, 1945; intern U. Chgo. Hosps., 1955; resident in ob-gyn U. Munich, Fed. Republic Germany, 1946-48; practice medicine specializing in ob-gyn West Berlin, 1948-53; asst. ob-gyn Free U., West Berlin, 1948-52; assoc. chmn. dept. ob-gyn Moabit Hosp., Free U., West Berlin, 1953; asst. prof., dir. cytology U. Chgo., 1954-59, assoc. prof., 1959-65, prof., 1965-91, mem. bd. adult edn., 1964-68, prof. pathology, 1967-91, Blum-Riese prof. ob-gyn, 1968-91, acting chmn. dept. ob-gyn, 1974-75. Editor-in-chief Jour. Reproductive Medicine, Acta Cytologica, Analytical and Quantitative Cytology, Clinical Cytology; editor: Introduction to Quantitative Cytochemistry, Automated Cell Identification and Cell Sorting, Compendium on Clinical Cytology, Compendium on the Computerized Cytology and Histology Laboratory, Compendium on Quality Assurance in Clinical Cytology; sr. editor Gen. and Diagnostic Pathology. Hon. dir. Chgo. Cancer Prevention Ctr., 1959-83; chmn. jury Maurice Goldblatt Cytology award, 1963-92. Recipient Cert. of Merit, U.S. Surgeon Gen., 1952, Maurice Goldblatt Cytology award, 1961, George N. Papanicolaou Cytology award, 1970, Masubuchi Gold Medal award 13th Internat. Cytology Congress, 1998, Kazumsa Masubuchi Lifetime Achievement award, 1998. Mem. Am. Soc. Cytology (pres. 1965-66), Mex. Soc. Cytology (hon.), Spanish Soc. Cytology (hon.), Brazilian Soc. Cytology (fgn. corr.), Indian Acad. Cytology (hon., Lifetime Achievement award 1998), Latin-Am. Soc. Cytology (hon.), Japanese Soc. Cytology (hon.), Internat. Acad. Cytology (pres. 1977-80), German Soc. Cytology (hon.), Ctrl. Soc. Clin. Rsch., Chgo. Path. Soc., Chgo. Gynecol. Soc. (hon.), Am. Soc. Cell Biology, German Soc. Ob-Gyn, Bavarian Soc. Ob-Gyn, German Soc. Endocrinology, Russian Assn. Cytologists (hon.), Swedish Soc. Medicine (hon.), Austrian Soc. Clin. Cytology (hon.), Sigma Xi. Home and Office: 1640 E 50th St Chicago IL 60615-3161

WIEDEBUSCH, MARY KATHRYNE, dance educator; b. Clarksburg, W.Va.; d. Danton Leon and Mary Margaret (Dixon) Caussin; m. Charles Edward Wiedebusch, July 12, 1952 (dec.); children: Carole Jean, Charles Edward II. BS, W.Va. U., 1951, MA, 1974; postgrad., Radford Coll., 1975, Am. U., 1979, Duke U., 1980. Tchr., choreographer Morgantown (W.Va.) H.S., 1951; asst. prof., choreographer Orchesis Modern Dance Ensemble W.Va. U., Morgantown, 1955-90, assoc. prof., dir., choreographer, 1990-93, prof. dance, coord. dance program, 1993—, dir. Orchesis Dance Ensemble, 1993—; mem. faculty fine arts music camp W.Va. U., 1976, dir. fund raiser project/residency program, 1978—, founder, dir. dance artist-in-residence program, 1978—; mem. faculty Governors Honor Acad., Morgantown, 1997. Choreographer gala performances W.Va. State Dance Festivals, 1975-95; choreographer, dir. theatrical dance prodns. W.Va. U. Creative ARts Ctr., 1976—. Bd. dirs. Betty Puskar Breast Care Ctr., Morgantown, 1993—, chair Golf Classic, 1993-95. Named to Hall of Fame, Sch. of Phys. Edn., W.Va. U., 1994. Mem. Am. Coll. Dance Festival Assn. (founding bd. dirs. 1973-87, nat. awards 1990-91). Avocations: golf, boating. Office: WVA U Coll Creative Arts PO Box 6111 Morgantown WV 26506-6111

WIEDEKING, WENDELIN, automotive executive; b. Ahlen, Westphalia, Germany, Aug. 28, 1952. Matriculated, Albertus-úMagnus H.S., Beckum/Westphalia, Germany, 1972; Diploma Mech. Engring., Aachen (Germany) U. Tech., 1978, D in Engring. with distinction, 1983. Rsch. asst. Lab. Machine Tools and Prodn. Engring. Aachen (Germany) U., 1978-83; asst. to dir. bd. prodn. materials mgmt. Dr. Ing. h.c. Porsche F AG, Stuttgart, Germany, 1983-88; project mgr. new paint works, body shop Porsche AG, Stuttgart, Germany, 1988, mem. exec. bd. prodn., material econs., 1991, spokesman bd. dirs., 1992, also chmn. bd. dirs., pres., CEO; dir. divsn. engring. GLYCO Metallwerke KG, Weisbaden, 1988, mem. mgmt. divsn. engring., 1989, mgmt. chmn., 1990, appted. mem. exec. bd. tech. sector; chmn. . bd. dirs. GLYCO AG, Wiesbaden, GLYCO Metallwerke KG, Wiesbaden. Recipient Borchers prize Aachen U. Tech., 1984. Office: Dr Ing hc F Porsche AG, Porscheplatz 42, D-70435 Stuttgart Germany*

WIEDEMANN, CHARLES LOUIS, dentist; b. Belvidere, N.J., May 6, 1936; s. Charles and Clothilde Paulina (Fischer) W.; m. Jacqueline Burdzy, June 11, 1960; children: Lorraine Carol, Julie Patricia. BA, Rutgers U., 1957; DDS with honors, Fairleigh Dickinson U., 1962; postgrad. student, Inst. for Grad. Dentists, 1968-69, Northwest Covenant Hosp. Continuing Edn., N.J., 1972—, U. Pa., 1974-75, Boston U. Sch. Grad. Dentistry, 1991. Pvt. practice dentistry Hackettstown, N.J., 1966—; mem., founder dental sect. staff dept. surgery Hackettstown Cmty. Hosp., chief dentistry, 1973-75, 77-78, chief of staff dental sect. dept. surgery, 1974, 80, 85; dental health dir. Clarence W. Sickles Med. Ctr., Hachettstown, 1970-90; co-dir. Stargazer, Bd. of Ed, Online Mag. telecomms. sys., 1985-86; pres. Rexxcom Sys. Electronic Pub. and Computer Software, Co., 1990—; lectr. Morris County Coll., dental socs.; designer giant talking toothbrush, talking molar. Author: The Now Philosophy for Dentistry, 1972, Fantastic Facts About Dental Health, 1975; (computer software) The Format Machine, 1987, Autofont, 1990, rev. edit., 1996, The Magic font Machine (Magifont, Magivue, Magishow), 1990, News 1, 1991, Digipad, 1993, The Autofont Titler (for electronic books), 1994; co-author: (computer software) Autodoc, 1990, rev. edit., 1993, Font Mania, 1991, rev. edit., 1996, XL100, 1993, XL2000, 1993, XL2001, 1994, rev. edit. (the XL book edit.), 1995, E-Z Book, 1995, Autofont Titler, 1995; author, designer (electronic publishing software) Rexxcom., 1987—; co-inventor Electronic Pub., 1990; designer computer fonts, modules, graphics simulations; pioneer in electronic publishing software; inventor Rexxcom character set, 1992; editl. adv. panel Dental Econs. Jour., 1979-80; editor DPA News, 1993-95; contbr. articles to profl. jours. and mags.; editor of electronic books, 1995—; columnist Hackettstown Gazette, 1983-85. Chmn. Bd. of Health, Washington Twp., Morris County, N.J., 1975-78; co-dir. telecomm. sys. Hunterdon Ctrl. Regional H.S., 1989-98; presentations to Morris, Warren, and Sussex Counties, N.J. elem. schs. ann., 1966-93. Capt. Dental Corps., U.S. Army, 1962-65. Recipient cert. Stuart L. Isler Found. for Preventive Dentistry, 1986. Fellow Acad. Gen. Dentistry, Am. Endodontic Soc. (Harold Katz Meml. award 1983); mem. ADA (panel on quarterly survey of pvt. practitioners 1990-93), Digital Pub. Assn. (founding mem., bd. dirs.), Am. Analgesia Soc., Internat. Analgesia Soc., N.J. Dental Assn., Warren-Sussex Dental Soc., Tri-County Dental Soc. (tchr. dental practice adminstrn. 1970-71), Hackettstown Dental Study Group (co-founder 1974—), Found. for Motivation in Dentistry (founder, chmn., bd. dirs. 1973—), Digital Pub. Assn. (bd. dirs. 1993-95). Republican. Office: 110 Mill St Hackettstown NJ 07840-2343

WIEDEMANN, RAMONA DIANE, occupational therapist; b. Topeka, Kans., Oct. 1, 1962; d. John Daniel Fay and Sue Ann Strotman; m. William Newell Wiedemann, Aug. 9, 1986; children: William Jr., Meaghan, Nathaniel, Emily, Daniel. BS in Occupl. Therapy, Tex. Woman's U., 1988. Occupl. therapist Healthcare Staff Resources, Dallas, 1988-91, Associated Rehab. Svcs., Greenville, Tex., 1991-96, 97-99, 1st Rehab., Ft. Worth, 1996, Cmty. Rehab. Svcs., Dallas, 1996-97. Mem. Am. Occupl. Therapy Assn. Republican. Methodist. Avocations: reading, travel, bicycling. Home: PO Box 1114 Paris TN 38242-1114

WIEDENMANN, BERTRAM, physician, internist, gastroenterologist; b. Bamberg, Germany, Dec. 21, 1953; s. Karl Helmut and Ilse (Kampf-Emden) W.; m. Stacy Anne Ehrlich Wiedenmann, May 15, 1988; children: Robert, Erik, Leah. MD, Tech. U., Munich, Germany, 1980. Rsch. fellow A. Einstein Coll. Medicine, N.Y.C., 1980-82; rsch. assoc. Harvard U., Cambridge, Mass., 1982-83, German Cancer Rsch. Ctr., Heidelberg, Germany, 1983-84; internist in tng. Heidelberg (Germany) U. Med. Sch., 1984-89, habilitation, gastroenterologist, 1990; prof. med. B. Franklin Med. Ctr., Berlin, 1990-97; chmn. dept. internal medicine divsn hepatology and gastroenterology U. Charité Humboldt-U. Berlin, 1997—. Recipient European prize in gastroenterology Eli Lilly Co., London, 1990; named Boehringer Mannheim young investigator, Heidelberg, Germany, 1988, Creutzfeldt Rsch. award, 1996. Mem. German Soc. Gastroenterology, Am. Gastroenterol. Soc., Am. Soc. Cell Biology. Avocations: sports, piano. Home: Kommandantenstr 96A, D-12205 Berlin Germany Office: U Charité Med Fakultät Humboldt U, Augustenburger Platz 1, D-13353 Berlin Germany

WIEDER, BRUCE TERRILL, lawyer, electrical engineer; b. Cleve., Dec. 9, 1955; s. Ira J. and Judith M. (Marx) W. BSEE, Cornell U., 1978; MBA, U. Tex., 1980, JD with honors, 1988. Bar: Tex. 1988, U.S. Dist. Ct. (we. dist.) Tex. 1989, U.S. Patent and Trademark Office 1989, U.S. Ct. Appeals (fed. cir.) 1990, D.C. 1991, U.S. Supreme Ct. 1992, U.S. Dist. Ct. (no. dist.) Tex. 1995, Va. 1997, U.S. Dist. Ct. (ea. dist.) Va. 1997. Engr. Motorola, Inc., Austin, Tex., 1979-85; assoc. Arnold, White & Durkee, Austin, 1988-90; law clk. U.S. Ct. Appeals (Fed. cir.), Washington, 1990-91; assoc. Burns, Doane, Swecker & Mathis, Alexandria, Va., 1991-97, ptnr., 1998—; adj. prof. Georgetown U. Law Ctr., 1998—. Mem. IEEE, ABA, Am. Intellectual Property Law Assn., Alpha Phi Omega (life), Beta Gamma Sigma (life). Office: Burns Doane Swecker & Mathis 1737 King St Ste 500 Alexandria VA 22314-2727

WIEDER, JUDY SARA, editor-in-chief; b. N.Y.C., Mar. 22, 1944; d. Jack E and Paula (Rosenberg) W. BA, Univ. Calif., Berkeley, 1966. Editor, creater Right On! Mag., Hollywood, Calif., 1969-72; songwriter L.A., 1976—; editor BLAST, Encino, Calif., 1987-88; contbr. editor RIP Mag., L.A., 1988-89; assoc. editor Creem Mag., L.A., 1989-90; editor Genre Mag., L.A., 1991-93; art and entertainment editor The Advocate, L.A., 1993-94, sr. arts & entertainment editor, 1995, exec. editor, 1996, editor-in-chief, 1996—. Author: 100 Soul Stars, 1971, How To Make A Record Deal, 1970. Recipient 3 Gold Albums, 1977, 78, Grammy award, 1978, Platinum Album award, 1990; named #1 dance hit song Billboard Mag., 1997. Mem. Nat. Acad. of Recording Arts & Scis., Human Rights Campaign. Avocation: tiling. Office: The Advocate 6922 Hollywood Blvd Los Angeles CA 90028-6117

WIEDERMANN, ALEXANDER RICHARD, engineer, educator; b. Hannover, Lower Saxony, Germany, July 17, 1956; s. Richard and Alice (Wientzek) W.; m. Mami Kano, Dec. 28, 1998. BS, U. Hannover, Germany, 1981; PhD, U. Hannover, 1985, U. Hannover, 1991. Rsch. fellow U. Hannover, Germany, 1981-85; asst. lectr. U. Hannover, 1985-92; sr. rsch. engr. Mitsubishi Heavy Industries, Takasago, Japan, 1992-99; mgr. R & D MAN Turbomaschinen AG GHH-BORSIG, Oberhausen, Germany, 1999—; guest lectr. Tokyo Denki U., 1991; lectr. dept. mech. engring. Tokyo Denki U., 1994-99. Author: Uber Die Numerische Erfassung Des Stromungsfeldes in Kanalen und Leitradgittern, 1991; contbr. articles to profl. jours. With German Fed. Army, 1975-76. Rsch. fellow Japan Soc. for Promotion Scis., Tokyo, 1991. Fellow NYAS, Soc. Applied Math. and Mechanics. Avocations: music, theater, fine arts, sports. Home: Zur Iangen Brucke 42, D-46569 Hunxe Germany Office: MAN Turbomashinen AG GHH BO, Bahnhofstrasse 66, D-46145 Oberhausen Germany

WIEDERUH, ECKHARDT MARTIN, educator; b. Bolkenhain, Germany, Oct. 15, 1945; s. Martin and Frieda W.; m. Edeltraud Kriegler, Mar. 23, 1973; 1 child, Carmen. Dipl.-Ing., U. Karlsruhe, Germany, 1973, Dr.-Ing., 1979. Scientific employee U. Karlsruhe, 1973-79; with Mannesmann-Demag, Germany, 1979-85, head dept., 1983-85; prof. engring. Fachhochschule Giessen, Germany, 1985—. Co-author: Heat Transfer and Fluid Flow Data Books, 1995, Taschenbuch der Technischen Formeln, 1996, Handbook of Technical Formulas, 1996. Lt. German Mil., 1968. Mem. VDI Lahn-Dill (pres. 1992-98). Home: Breslauerstrasse 20, D-35435 Wettenberg Germany Office: Fachhochschule Giessen-Friedberg, Wiesenstrasse 14, D-35390 Giessen Germany

WIEDOW, OLIVER, dermatologist, researcher; b. Heidelberg, Germany, May 15, 1957; s. Eberhard and Ingeborg (Randermann) W. Approbation, U. Kiel, Germany, 1985, MD, 1987; Diploma in Tchg., U. Kiel, 1994. Diplomate German Bd. Dermatology and Allergy. Resident in dermatology U. Kiel, 1987-94, univ. lectr. dept. dermatology, 1994-99; prof. dermatology, venenology, and allengology, 1999—. Served with Germany Navy, 1976-77. Mem. European Soc. Dermatol. Rsch., German Dermatol. Assn., N.Y. Acad. Scis. Mem. Evangelian Ch. Avocations: sailing, skiing. Home: Fonstweg 55, D-24105 Kiel Germany Office: Univ Kiel Dept Dermatology, Schittenhelmstr 7, D-24105 Kiel Germany

WIEGAND, RONALD, sociologist; b. Berlin, Mar. 17, 1937; m. Rosemarie Weisbrodt; 1 child, Irene. Diplom-Soziologe, Free U. Berlin, 1963, DrRerPol, 1967, Privatdozent, 1971. Qualified indsl. mcht. Prof. sociology Free U. Berlin, 1972—. Author: Gesellschaft und Charakter, 1973, Der Mitmensch als Aergernis, 1977, Sinndeutung als Wissenschaft, 1981, Gemeinschaft gegen Gesellschaft, 1986, Alfred Adler und danach, 1990, Individualitaet und Verantwortung, 1998. Mem. Deutsche Gesellschaft fuer Individual Psychologie (chmn. sci. group 1983—). Avocations: hiking, writing. Office: Inst for Sociology Free Univ, Babelsberger Strasse 16, D-10715 Berlin Germany

WIEGANDT, RICHARD, mathematician, educator; b. Budapest, Sept. 19, 1932; s. Arthur and Julianna (Oszwald) W.; m. Ilona Pusztai; children: Peter, Thomas. D Rerum Naturalium, L. Eötvös U., Budapest, 1967; D of Math. Scis., Hungarian Acad. Scis., 1975. Cert. tchr. high sch. math. and physics. Tchr. M. Tancsics High Sch., Oroshaza, Hungary, 1955-61; sci. co-worker Math. Inst., Budapest, 1964-72, sci. chief co-worker, 1972-78, sci. advisor, 1978—, head dept. algebra, 1982-96; vis. prof. UNESCO, U. Islamabad, Pakistan, 1970-72, U. Alexandria, Egypt, 1976-77, Tech. U. Clausthal, Fed. Republic Germany, 1978, U. B.C., Vancouver, 1982, U. Fla., Gainesville, 1986, Nat. Cheng Kung U., Taiwan, 1991-92, U. La., Lafayette, 1995, U. Linz, Austria, 1997-98. Author: Radical and Semisimple Classes of Rings, 1974; contbr. numerous articles to profl. jours. Mem. J Bolyai Math. Soc., Am. Math. Soc. Home: Orso Utca 50, H-1026 Budapest Hungary Office: Math Inst Hungarian Acad Sci, Math Inst Hungarian Acad, Realtanoda utca 13-15, H-1053 Budapest Hungary

WIEGEL, MARKUS, engineer; b. Siegen, Germany, May 25, 1965; m. Liang-Yu Dai. Diploma, Stuttgart (Germany) U., 1992; MS, IIT, 1993; PhD, Hannover (Germany) U., 1996. Rsch. asst. Stuttgart U., 1988-91, IIT, Chgo., 1991-92; scientist NASA-Langley, Hampton, 1992-93, Deutsches Zentrum fuer Luft-und Raumfahrttechnik, Goettingen, Germany, 1993-98, Ford Werke AG, Koeln, Germany, 1997—. Author: VDI Fortschritt Berichte, 1997. Rsch. grant Flughafen Frankfurt Main Stiftung, 1992. Office: Ford AG, Spessartstrasse, Cologne 50725, Germany

WIEGERSMA, SIES, psychologist; b. Zevenaar, Gelderland, The Netherlands, May 29, 1919; s. Wieger and Hinke (Bosga) W.; m. Elisabeth Christina Immina van den Heuvel; children: Harm, Marianne. Cand., U. Utrecht, The Netherlands, 1940; MS, U. Groningen, The Netherlands, 1946; PhD, U. Amsterdam, 1959. Registered psychologist Netherlands Inst. of Psychologists. Psychologist Psych. Inst., The Hague, The Netherlands, 1946-50; dir. Inst. Mental Health, Leeuwarden, The Netherlands, 1950-53; sr. rsch. worker Inst. Preventive Medicine, Leiden, The Netherlands, 1953-61; dir. Nat. Fedn. for Mental Health, Amsterdam, 1962-67; prof. U. Amsterdam, 1964-67, 68-89, vice-rector, 1968-72, dean of faculty, 1978-88; chmn. com. on reform Univ., The Hague, 1973-82; vice-chmn. Acad. Coun., The Hague, 1978-85; mem. bd. appeals Netherland Inst. of Psychologists, 1975-99. Author: (book) Vocational Interest Test, 1959, Vocational Psychology, 1961, rev. 1965, Social Industrial Psychology, 1972, rev. 1982, The Innovation of Higher Edn., 1989. Chmn. Nat. Vocat. Guidance Orgn., 1961-78; sec. Dutch Nat. Mental Health Fund, 1962-89; mem. bd. dirs. Cen. Bur. of Statis., 1978-85. Knight Order of the Dutch Lion, 1972, Knight-commdr. Order of Orange Nassau, 1989. Avocations: studying law, reading, walking. Home: van der Waalssingel 31, 7327 JM Apeldoorn The Netherlands

WIEGMAN, LENORE HO, chemist; b. Shanghai, China, Aug. 18, 1931; came to U.S., 1951; d. Molin and Wan Chuck Ho; m. Hans Wiegman, Mar. 17, 1961; 1 child, Elkan Douglas. BS, Mich. State U., 1955, MS, 1958; PhD, U. Amsterdam, 1979. Rsch. asst. U. Wash., Seattle, 1960-61; rsch. chemist Columbia U., N.Y.C., 1961-62, Am. Cyanamid, Princeton, N.J., 1962-65, AKZO Chem. Co., Amsterdam, The Netherlands, 1969-71, U. Amsterdam, 1971—; mem. Netherland Corrosion Centrum, The Netherlands, 1984—; mem. discussion group Electro Chem., The Netherlands, 1974—. Contbr. articles to profl. jours. including Jour. of Dental Rsch., Jour. of Dentistry, Jour. of Dental Assn. of South Africa; patentee in field. Mem. Am. Chem. Soc., Am. Womens Club Amsterdam, Women's Internat. Network, Iota Sigma Pi, Sigma Delta Epsilon, Pi Mu Epsilon. Achievements include patents for method of manufacturing ammonium polyphosphates, method to increase the expansion of plaster of Paris for casting purposes, method to improve dental stone. Home: Bosplaat 22, 1025AT Amsterdam The Netherlands Office: U Amsterdam, U Amsterdam, Nwe Achtergracht 166, Amsterdam The Netherlands

WIELAND, CARL, non-profit organization executive; b. Ostheim, Germany, Jan. 13, 1950; arrived in Australia, 1951; s. Paul Hugo Walter and Marie Magdalene (Steiger) W.; m. Victoria Pliczkowski, June 6, 1972; children: Lara Marie, Lisa Daria. M.B.B.S., Adelaide U., South Australia, 1973. Registered med. practitioner, Australia. Pvt. med. practice, Pooraka, S.A., Australia, 1974-86; mng. dir. Amswers in Genesis, Brisbane, Australia, 1987—; dir. Creation Sci. Found. (UK), Swindon, U.K., 1993—, Answers In Genesis, Florence, Ky., 1995—. Author: Stones and Bones: Powerful Evidence Against Evolution, 1994; co-author: The Answers Book, 1991; founder, initiator, founding editor Creation Ex Nihilo, 1978—. Mem. N.Y. Acad. Scis. Baptist. Office: Answers in Genesis, PO Box 6302 Acacia Ridge, Brisbane Qld 4110, Australia

WIELAND, PAUL OTTO, environmental control systems engineer; b. Louisville, Apr. 9, 1954; s. Otto George and Flora Carolyn (Wolf) W. BS in Botany, U. Louisville, 1982, BS in Applied Sci., 1985, M. in Engring., 1987. Lic. profl. engr., Ala., Va.; cert. indoor air quality profl. Assn. of Energy Engrs. Paper carrier Courier-Jour., Louisville, 1976-77; youth program dir. UNICORN, Louisville, 1978; recreation worker Met. Parks Dept., Louisville, 1978-80; retail sales clk. Lose Bros. Lawn and Garden, Louisville, 1980-82; trainee engr. Sealand Svc., Inc., Elizabeth, N.J., 1982; engr. NASA Marshall Space Flight Ctr., Huntsville, Ala., 1983—; pres. Wiseland Svcs., 1996—. Author: Designing for Human Presence in Space: An Introduction to Environmental Control and Life Support Systems, 1994, Living Together in Space: The Design and Operation of the Life Support Systems on the International Space Station, 1996, rev. edit., 1998, A Guidebook to a Healthier House, 1999; contbr. articles to profl. jours. Vol. advocate R.A.P.E. Relief Ctr., Louisville, 1977-80; vol. tutor Adult Basic Edn. Program, Huntsville, 1988-89; vol. projectionist Film Co-op., Huntsville, 1990-91; vol. tech. advisor Am. Lung Assn. Health House '96, Huntsville. Mem. ASME, ASHRAE, AIAA (chmn. student chpt. 1984-85), NSPE (mathcounts vol. 1990-91), Inst. for Advanced Studies in Life Support (treas. 1990-92). Avocations: appreciation of nature, creating visual arts, dancing. Home: 4212 9th Ave SW Huntsville AL 35805-3408 Office: NASA/MSFC/FD21 Marshall Space Flight Ctr Huntsville AL 35812

WIELAND, WOLFGANG, philosophy educator, physician; b. Heidenheim, Germany, June 29, 1933; m. Wieslawa Wolfram; 1 child, Aglaia. PhD, U. Heidelberg, Fed. Republic Germany, 1955, D Phil. Habil., 1960. Asst. U. Hamburg (Fed. Republic Germany), 1957-60, prof. philosophy, 1961-64; prof. philosophy U. Marburg (Fed. Republic Germany), 1964-68, U. Göttingen (Fed. Republic Germany), 1968-79, U. Freiburg (Fed. Republic Germany), 1979-83; asst. U. Heidelberg, 1956-57; prof. philosophy, 1983—. Author books on Schelling, 1956, Aristotle, 1962, med. diagnosis, 1975, Plato, 1982, med. ethics, 1986, moral responsibility, 1999; contbr. articles to profl. jours. Mem. Heidelberg Acad. Scis. and Humanities (sec. 1986—). Home: Augustinergasse 15, D-69117 Heidelberg Germany Office: U Heidelberg Philosophy Sem, U Heidelberg Philosophy Sem, Marsiliusplatz 1, D-6900 Heidelberg Germany

WIELEMANS, WILLY, education educator; b. 1939. Cert. Philosophy, Rome, 1963; M Ednl. Scis., Cath. U. of Leuven, 1967, PhD Ednl. Scis., 1973. Expert ednl. planning UNESCO-IIEP, Paris, 1974-75; chmn. dept. ednl. scis., prof. Cath. U. of Louvain, Belgium, 1979-82, prof., 1979—. Editl. bd.: Jour. for Ednl. Law & Policy, Brescia - Italy, Jour. for Edn. and Tng.; contbr. articles to profl. jours. Mem. Comparative Edn. Soc. in Europe (v.p.), Dutch Speaking Soc. for Comparative Edn. Office: Cath U Louvain/Ednl Scis, Vesaliusstraat 2, B-3000 Leuven Belgium

WIELONDEK, MIROSLAW, gastroenterologist; b. Mysliborz, Poland, Jan. 23, 1960; s. Stefan and Anna (Maliczewska) W.; m. Iwona Kolodzinska, Sept. 3, 1983; children: Milosz Stefan, Michal Maria. MD, Pomeraniam Med. Sch., Szczecin, Poland, 1995. From house officer to cons. Gastroenterol. Clinic, Szczecin, 1985—; pvt. prac., 2000—. Mem. Polish Assn. Internal Medicine, Polish Soc. Gastroenterology. Avocations: classical music, philosophy, football. E-mail: dr-mw@poczta.wp.pl. Home: Warszawska 2c/4, 78-400 Szczecinek Poland

WIEMANN, MARION RUSSELL, JR. (BARON OF CAMSTER), biologist; b. Sept. 7, 1929; s. Marion Russell and Verda (Peek) W.; 1 child from previous marriage, Tamara Lee (Mrs. Donald D. Kelley). BS, Ind. U., 1959; PhD (hon.), World U. Roundtable, 1991; ScD (hon.), The London Inst. Applied Rsch., England, 1994, The London Inst. Applied Rsch., England,

1995, World Acad., Germany, 1995. Ordained hon. min., 1998; cert. hypnotist. Histo-rsch. technician U. Chgo., 1959, rsch. asst., 1959-62, rsch. technician, 1962-64; tchr. sci. Westchester Twp. Sch., Chesterton, Ind., 1964-66; with U. Chgo., 1965-79, sr. rsch. technician, 1967-70, rsch. technologist, 1970-79; prin. Marion Wiemann & Assocs., cons. R&D, Chesterton, Ind., 1979-89; advisor Porter County Health Bd., 1989-91; mem. consultive faculty World U., 1991—, SkyWarn, Nat. Weather Svc., 1993—. Author: Tooth Decay, Its Cause and Prevention Through Controlled Soil Composition, 1985, The Mechanism of Tooth Decay, 1985; contbr. articles to profl. jours. and newspapers. Vice-chmn. The Duneland 4th of July Com., 1987-91; v.p. State Microscopical Soc. Ill., 1969-70, pres., 1970-71. With USN, 1951-53. Recipient Disting. Tech. Communicator award Soc. for Tech. Communication, 1974, Internat. Order Merit (Eng.), 1991; ennobled Royal Coll. Heraldry, Australia, 1991, Highland Laird, Scotland, 1995; named Sagamore of the Wabash Gov. Ind., 1985; McCrone Rsch. Inst. scholar, 1968; named Prof. of Sci. Australian Inst. for Co-Ordinated Rsch., Australia, 1995, knight corps Diplomatique The Sovereign Military Templar Order, 1994; recipient Scouters Key award Boy Scouts Am., 1968, Arrowhead honor, 1968, Albert Einstein Silver medal, Huguenin, Le Locke, Switzerland, Henri Dunant Silver medal with silver bars, 1995, Henri Dunant Silver medal, 1995, medal of honor, England, 1996. Fellow Australian Inst. for Co-Ordinated Rsch., World Lit. Acad.; mem. Internat. Soc. Soil Sci., Assn. of Masters of the Univers, World Acad., Order Internat. Fellowship, Internat. Graphoanalysis Soc., Maison Internat. des Intellectuels and Akademie MIDI, VFW (charter mem., bd. dirs., post judge adv. 1986—, apptd. post adj. 1986—, Cross of Malta 1986), Govs. Club. Achievements include demostration that radiation does not produce dental caries; proved that soil calcium, magnesium, potassium and phosphorous, with soil PH, controls population size and longevity of earthworms and humans and the incidence of dental caries; demonstrated that flouride neither reduces or prevents dental caries. Address: PO Box 1016 Chesterton IN 46304-0016

WIENEKE, PAUL, medical technologist; b. Dülmen, Germany, Oct. 1, 1960; s. Josef and Elisabeth (Bade) W.; m. Eva-Maria Schwochert, Sept. 22, 1986; children: Anna-Christina, Paul-Thomas, Ludger. MD, U. Münster, Germany, 1988, diploma in physics, 1990. Physician U. Clinic Anesthesiology, Münster, Germany, 1989-90; mgr. rsch. and devel. Aesculap, Tuttlingen, Germany, 1991-98; mgr. clin. rsch. Braun, Kronberg, Germany, 1998—; coord. joint project Microsystem Technique for Use of Minimally Invasive Neurosurg. Operative Technique, Germany and Hungary, 1993-96; chair adv. bd. RoMed-project Fraunhofer-Soc., 1999—. Co-author: Minimally Invasive Techniques for Neurosurgery, 1997; patentee in field. Cusanuswerk scholar, Bonn, Germany, 1983. Roman Catholic. Home: Bergstrasse 13, 78604 Rietheim-Weilheim Germany Office: Braun, Frankfurter Str 145, 61476 Kronberg Germany

WIENER, HESH (HAROLD FREDERIC WIENER), publisher, editor, consultant; b. Bklyn., July 20, 1946; s. Jesse Leonard and Regina (Rappaport) W. B.S. in Polit. Sci., MIT, 1969. Mem. staff systems devel. Data Gen. Corp., Southboro, Mass., 1969-70; dir. computer edn. project U. Calif., Berkeley, 1970-72; editor Computer Decisions Mag., Rochelle Park, N.J., 1973-78; editor, pub. Tech. News Am., N.Y.C., 1976-88; pres. Tech. News of Am. Co., Inc., N.Y.C., 1982—; mng. dir. Tech. News Ltd., London, 1992—; webmaster, tech-news.com, 1996—, primrosehill.com, 1998—, luminum.com, 2000—; pub. Computer and Comms. Buyer Newsletter, 1979-95, Mainstream Newsletter, 1980-82, Infoperspectives Newsletter, 1982—, Storage Tech. Monitor, 1984-87, Infoperspectives Internat. (U.K.), 1989—, (Mid. East), 1991—, The Four Hundred Newsletter (U.K.), 1990-97, The Four Hundred Newsletter (U.S.), 1990-97; editor Infoperspectives Internat. (Italy), 1991-98, The Four Hundred Newsletter (Italy), 1995—; pub. U.S. edit. Computergram Internat. Newsletter, 1985-90; corr. Processeurs mag., 1989-99; cons. Hewlett-Packard Co. (Paris), 1971-72, Xerox Corp., 1972-73; advisor NSF, 1975. Author: Big Blue and You, The IBM Atlas, The Mainframe; corr. Computer Weekly, U.K., 1975-81, Computable, Amsterdam, 1976-87, Computing Can., 1977-78, Ordinateurs, Paris, 1977-89, Data News, Brussels, 1979-86, Informatics, U.K., 1981-85, Datanytt, Copenhagen, 1982-89, Mgmt. Tech. mag., 1983-85; editor BusinessWeek Newsletter for Info. Execs., 1987-90, Datamation Mag., 1983-90, Infoperspectives Internat. (Milan), 1991—; contbg. editor Bus. and Soc. Rev., 1978-85; contbr. N.Y. Times Syndicate, Los Angeles Times Syndicate, N.Am. Newspaper Alliance Wireservice, Newsday, Manhattan, Inc., Rom Mag., Informatique (Paris), The Economist (London), Dun's Bus. Month, Software News, Intermedia, Digital News, Data Communications, Bus. Week Newsletter for Info. Execs., Bus. Strategy Internat., Nikkei Watcher on IBM (Tokyo), 1989-96. Club: Overseas Press. Home: 246 6th Ave Brooklyn NY 11215-2103 Office: Tech News Am 123 7th Ave Brooklyn NY 11215-1383

WIENER, SOLOMON, writer, consultant, former city official; b. N.Y.C., Mar. 5, 1915; s. Morris David and Anna (Pinchuk) W.; m. Gertrude Klings, Feb. 24, 1946; children: Marjorie Diane, Willa Kay Ehrlich. BS, Cornell, 1936; MPA, NYU, 1946. Exam. asst. N.Y.C. Dept. Pers., 1937-42, civil svc. examiner, 1946-55, asst. divsn. chief, 1955-59, divsn. chief, 1959-67, asst. dir. exams, 1967-70, dir. exams, 1970-72, asst. dir. exams, 1972-75; author, cons., 1975—; tchr. Washington Irving Evening Adult Sch., N.Y.C., 1949-60, tchr.-in-charge, 1960-67. Author: A Handy Book of Commonly Used American Idioms, rev. edit., 1981, Manual de Modismos Americanos Más Comunes, rev. edit., 1981, A handy Guide to Irregular Verbs and the Use and Formation of Tenses, 1959, Guia Completa de Los Verbos Irregulares en Inglès yel uso y Formación de los Tiempos, 1959, Questions and Answers on American Citizenship, rev. edit., 1982, Clear and Simple Guide to Business Letter Writing, rev. edit., 1978, The College Graduate Guide for Scoring High on Employment Tests, 1981, The High School Graduate Guide for Scoring High on Civil Service Tests, 1981, How to Take and Pass Simple Tests for Civil Service Jobs, 1981, Officer Candidate Tests, 5th edit., 2000, Military Flight Aptitude Tests, 4th edit., 2000; co-author Practice for the Armed Forces Test, ASVAB, 16th edit., 1999, Practica para el Examen de las Fuerzas Armadas, ASVAB en Español, 1989; contbr. to ARCO ROTC Coll. Guide, 1988. Served with AUS, 1942-46, PTO. Decorated Bronze Star. Mem. Am. Soc. Pub. Adminstrn., Internat. Pers. Mgmt. Assn., Authors Guild, Res. Officers Assn., Ret. Officers Assn., Assn. of U.S. Army, Nat. Def. Indsl. Assn., Marines Meml. Assn. Home: 523 E 14th St Apt 4F New York NY 10009-2931

WIENERT, PETER, physician; b. Konstanz, Baden, Germany, Nov. 28, 1964; s. Paul and Elisabeth (Nagel) W.; m. Anja Christine Luettke, Aug. 15, 1998; 1 child, Valerie-Elisabeth. MD, Albert-Ludwigs U., Freiburg, 1993. Physician dept. pathology Friedrich-Schiller U., Jena, Germany, 1994—; physician dept. surgery Albert-Ludwigs U., Freiburg, 1994-95, Kantonsspital Basel U. Kliniken, Switzerland, 1995-97; physician dept. anesthesiology Kantonsspital Basel U. Kliniken, Liniken, 1996, Chirurgische Klinik Dr. Rinecker, Germany, 1997—. Co-chmn. KDSTV Hohenstaufen, Freiburg, 1991. 2d lt. German Army Artillery, 1984-86. Mem. Deutsche Gesellschaft Chirurgie, Cath. German Students Corp. Hohenstaufen. Roman Catholic. Avocations: skiing, soccer, swimming, classical literature. Home: Alfred-Schmidt-Str 12, D-81379 Munich Bavaria, Germany Office: Surg Clinic, Am Isarkanal 30, D81379 Munich Bavaria, Germany

WIERCIGROCH, MARIAN, engineering educator; b. Rajcza, Poland, July 14, 1960; s. Karol and Ludwika (Krzepina) W. MEng, Silesian Tech. U., Gliwice, Poland, 1985, PhD, 1989. Rsch. asst. Silesian Tech. U., 1985, rsch. assoc., 1987-89, sr. lectr., 1990-91; rsch. fellow Aberdeen (Scotland) U., 1990-91, lectr., 1993-98, sr. lectr., 1999—; Fulbright scholar U. Del., Newark, 1994-95; mem. Faculty Coun., Gliwice, 1992-93; chmn. Young Faculty Assn., Gliwice, 1991-92, Advanced Rsch. Workshop, Aberdeen, 1995. Author: Dynamics of Discrete Mechanical Systems, 1994; editor: Applied Nonlinear Dynamics and Chaos in Mechanical Systems, 2000; contbr. articles to profl. jours. European Cmty. fellow, 1993; Sr. Fulbright scholar, 1994; grantee Office Naval Rsch., U.K., 1995, British Coun., 1997, Royal Soc. London, 1997-99, EPSRC, 1999-2000, LMS, 1999. Mem. ASME, Soc. Indsl. Applied Math., N.Y. Acad. Scis., Stowarzyszenie Inzynierow Mechanikow Polskich (Polish Soc. Mech. Engrs). Avocations: skiing, hiking, tennis, table tennis. Office: U Aberdeen, Dept Engring, Aberdeen AB24 3UE, Scotland

WIERCZINSKI, BIRGIT, radiochemist, researcher; b. Freiburg, Germany, July 13, 1967; d. Hans Juergen and Ingeborg Martina (Schlegel) W. Diploma in chemistry, Eidgenossische Tech. Hochschul, Zurich, 1991; D of Natural Scis., U. Mainz, Germany, 1994. Rschr. Lawrence Berkeley Nat. Lab., Berkeley, Calif., 1994-95, Chalmers U. Tech., Gothenburg, Sweden, 1996-97; sr. rsch. assoc. U. Tech. Delft, The Netherlands, 1998—. Mem. Am. Chem. Soc., Union of Pure and Applied Chemistry, German Chem. Soc., Am. Nuc. Soc., Soc. Nuc. Medicine. Avocations: reading, music, rowing, cooking. Office: Interfaculty Reactor Inst, Mekelweg 15, 2629 JB Delft The Netherlands

WIERENGA, JEFFREY BRENT, manufacturing executive, entrepreneur; b. Moline, Ill., Mar. 31, 1957; s. Robert Louis and Joan Darlene Wierenga; m. Susan Marie Parmley, Jan. 22, 1977 (div. Sept. 1989); children: Lisa Elaine, Christine Marie. AA, Black Hawke Coll., Moline, Ill., 1977; BA, Marycrest Internat. U., 1988; MBA, U. Iowa, 1996. Svc. technician Lerch & Thonn, Inc., Rock Island, Ill., 1983-87; assembler Deere & Co., East Moline, Ill., 1977-83; svc. technician LSG, Rock Island, Ill., 1987-90; spl. account mgr. Kartidg Pak Co., Davenport, Ill., 1990-91; sales rep. KP Aerofill, Davenport, Ill., 1991-96; aftermarket mgr. BWI Packaging Tech., Davenport, Ill., 1996-99; v.p. aftermarket Packaging Technologies, Davenport, Ill., 1999—. Mem. Rep. Nat. Com., Washington, 1996—. Mem. Sol. Aerosol Tech. Assnb., Aerosol Industry Devel. Assn., Profl. Pricing Soc. Presbyterian. Home: 2920 24th Avenue A Moline IL 61265-4203 Office: Packaging Technologies 807 W Kimberly Rd Davenport IA 52806-5706

WIERNIK, PETER HARRIS, oncologist, educator; b. Crocket, Tex., June 16, 1939; s. Harris and Molly (Emmerman) W.; m. Roberta Joan Fuller, Sept. 6, 1961; children: Julie Anne, Lisa Britt, Peter Harrison. BA with distinction, U. Va., 1961, MD, 1965; Dr. h.c., U. of Republic, Montevideo, Uruguay, 1982. Diplomate Am. Bd. Internal Medicine, Am. Bd. Med. Oncology (mem. writing com. 1981-87). Intern Cleve. Met. Gen. Hosp., 1965-66, resident, 1969-70; resident Osler Svc. Johns Hopkins Hosp., Balt., 1970-71; sr. asst. surgeon USPHS, 1966, advanced through grades to med. dir., 1976; sr. staff assoc. Balt. Cancer Rsch. Ctr., 1966-71, chief sect. med. oncology, 1971-76, chief clin. oncology br., 1976-82, dir., 1976-82; assoc. dir. div. cancer treatment Nat. Cancer Inst., 1976-82; assoc. dir. Albert Einstein Cancer Ctr., Bronx, 1982-98, prof. medicine, 1983-98, prof. radiation oncology, 1996-98, head divsn. med. oncology; asst. prof. medicine U. Md. Sch. Medicine, Balt., 1971-74, assoc. prof., 1974-76, prof., 1976-82; prof. medicine and radiation oncology N.Y. Med. Coll., 1998—; cons. hematology and med. oncology Union Meml. Hosp., Greater Balt. Med. Ctr., Franklin Sq. Hosp.; bd. dirs. Balt. City unit Am. Cancer Soc., 1971-78; chmn. patient care com., 1972-75, mem. profl. edn. and grants com., N.Y.C. divsn., 1983-90, mem. nat. clin. fellowship com., 1984-96; mem. med. adv. com. Nat. Leukemia Assn., 1976-88, chmn. med. adv. com., 1989—; chmn. adult leukemia com. Cancer and Leukemia Group B, 1976-83; prin. investigator Ea. Coop. Oncology Group, 1982-94, 96—; chmn. gynecol. oncology com., 1986-88, chmn. leukemia com., 1988-94; sci. cons. Vt. Regional Cancer Ctr., 1987—; dir. OLM Comprehensive Cancer Ctr., N.Y. Med. Coll., 1998—. Editor: Controversies in Oncology, 1982, Supportive Care of the Cancer Patient, 1983, Neoplastic Diseases of the Blood, 1985, 2d edit., 1991, 3d edit. 1996; assoc. editor Medical Oncology and Tumor Pharmacotherapy, 1987-91, sr. editor, 1991—; assoc. editor onoclogy Am. Jour. Therapeutics, 1994—; co-editor: Year Book of Hematology, 1986-98, Handbook of Hematologic and Oncologic Emergencies, 1988, Bone Marrow Transplantation (textbook), 1995, Am. Jour. Med. Scis., 1976-81; N.Am. editor Jour. Cancer Rsch. and Clin. Oncology, 1986-89; mem. editorial bd. Cancer Treatment Reports, 1972-76, Leukemia Rsch., 1977-86, 91—, Leukemia, 1986—, Cancer Clin. Trials, 1977—, Jour. Therapeutic Rsch., 1994—, Hosp. Practice, 1979—, Jour. Clin. Oncology, 1989-91, PDQ Nat. Cancer Inst., 1987-94; sect. editor antineoplastic drugs Jour. Clin. Pharmacology, 1985—; editor-in-chief Medical Oncology, 1993—; assoc. editor Cancer Investigation, 1998—; also articles, chpt. in books. Recipient Z Soc. award U. Va., 1961, Byrd S. Leavell Hematology award U. Va. Sch. Medicine, 1965. Fellow AAAS, ACP, Am. Coll. Clin. Pharmacology (awards com. 1999—), Internat. Soc. Hematology, Royal Soc. Medicine (London), N.Y. Acad. Medicine; mem. Am. Soc. Clin. Investigation (instl. rep. 1997—), Am. Soc. Clin. Oncology (chmn. edn. and tng. com. 1976-79, 84, subcom. on clin. investigation 1980-82, program com. 1990, pub. issues com., 1990-95, com. on rsch. awards 1996-2000, com. on health svcs. rsch. 2000—), Am. Assn. Cancer Rsch., Am. Soc. Hematology, Am. Fedn. Clin. Rsch., Am. Acad. Clin. Toxicology, Internat. Soc. Exptl. Hematology, N.Y. Acad. Sci., Am. Soc. Hosp. Pharmacy, Am. Soc. Clin. Pharmacology and Therapeutics, Am. Radium Soc. (program com. 1987-93, exec. com. 1988-95, publ. com. 1988-92, sec. 1990-91, pres.-elect, 1992-93; pres. 1993-94, Janeway medalist, 1996), Polish Oncology Soc. (hon.), Harvey Soc., Uruguan Hematology Soc. (hon.), Acad. Medicine Uruguay (corr.), European Assn. Cancer Rsch., European Soc. for Hematology, Phi Beta Kappa (assoc. 1991—), Sigma Xi, Alpha Omega Alpha, Phi Sigma (award 1961). Office: Comprehensive Cancer Ctr Our Lady Mercy Med Ctr 600 E 233rd St Bronx NY 10466-2604

WIERS, REINOUT WILLEM, psychologist, researcher, writer; b. Groningen, The Netherlands, Mar. 3, 1966; s. Jan Willem Wiers and Cécile Latooy; children: Joaquim Wonderling, Zovey Florian Thomas. Grad. in chemistry, U. Amsterdam, The Netherlands, grad. in philosophy, MA in Psychology(cum laude); PhD of Psychology (cum laude), U. Amsterdam, 1998. Rsch. asst. in devel. psychology U. Amsterdam, 1989-91, rsch. asst. in psychonomics, 1991-94, rschr. in clin. psychology, 1994-98; asst. prof. U. Maastricht, The Netherlands, 1998—. Author: Donker Bewaren, 1991, Bad Expectations? Cognitive and Neuropsychological Indicators of Enhanced Risks for Addiction, 1998. Office: U Maastricht, PB 616, 6200 MD Maastricht The Netherlands

WIERSBITZKY, SIEGFRIED KARL WILHELM, pediatrician; b. Neuruppin, Germany, Jan. 2, 1940; s. Siegfried W. and Sofia M. (Kuhnert) W.; m. Helga Kurzbein, Dec. 31, 1959; children: Mark Siegfried Kurt, Claudia Sofia Helga. MD, U. Greifswald, 1963, MS, 1973. Pediatrician Germany, 1968—, pediatric bronchopneumologist, 1983—, pediatric infectiologist, 1983—, neonatologist, 1993—; dir. Children's Hosp. of the Univ., Greifswald, 1991—; cons. allergologist Landesärztekammer Prov. Med. Assn., Mecklenburg-Vorpommern, 1991—; leader Gesellschaft für Allergologie M/V, Germany, 1993-95. Author, editor 32 books; contbr. over 390 articles to profl. jours. Mem. Deutsche Gesellschaft für Kinder-und Jugendheilkunde, Deutsche Gesellsch. zur Bekaempfung d. Mukoviszidose, Ärzteverband Deutscher Allergologen, Deutsche Gesellschaft für Paediatr. Infekt., Gesellschaft für Paediatr. Pneumology. Office: U Klinik, Soldtmannstrasse 15, 17487 Greifswald Germany

WIERUP, OLA, financial analyst; b. Stockholm, Sept. 9, 1973; s. Marlin and Marianne (Molmfors) W. MS, Stockholm Sch. Econs., 1997. Analyst Handelsbanten Markets, Stockholm, 1997—. Office: Handelsbanten Morhels, 114 37 Stockholm Sweden

WIERUSZ-KOWALSKI, MARTIN PETER, business consultant; b. Warsaw, Poland, Jan. 7, 1960; s. Tadeusz Maciej and Elzbieta Joanna (Kokczynska) K. MSc, Warsaw Sch. Econs., 1985, U. Warsaw, 1985. Officer Big -M Co., Warsaw, 1991, Internat. Bank in Poland, Warsaw, 1992; project officer, mgmt. cons. World Bank/Internat. Fin. Corp./European Bank R&D, Warsaw, 1992-94; sales mgr. MBI Internat., Warsaw, 1994-95; key account mgr. CIC Holding, Warsaw, 1996—; advisor to mgmt. bd. Daewoo Ins., 1999—. E-mail: mwk2@qdnet.pl.

WIERZBIETA, WOJCIECH, anesthesiologist, medical facility administrator; b. Warsaw, Poland, Dec. 20, 1948; s. Wincenty Maciej and Janina (Wolkanowska) W.; m. Joanna Wroblewska, Dec. 23, 1971; 1 child, Bartosz. MD, Med. Acad., Warsaw, 1974, 1st degree specialization, 1977, 2d degree specialization, 1979. Head anesthesia and intensive care dept. Ctrl. Children Traumatology Hosp., Warsaw, 1978-82; cons. in anesthesia and intensive care M.O.H., Benghazi, Libya, 1982-87, Ctrl. Railway Hosp., Warsaw, 1987-88; scientific coord. Upjohn, Warsaw, 1988-93, med. dir., 1993-96; med. dir. Pharmacia & Upjohn, Warsaw, 1996; gen. mgr. Innovex/Quintiles, Warsaw, 1997; mgr. clin. ops. ctrl. ea. Europe Parexel, Warsaw, 1998—; Lectr. 3d Internat. Congress of Anesthesiologists, Poland, 1979. Contbr. articles to med. jours. Mem. Polish Soc. Anaesthesiology and Intensive Care, Drug Info. Assn., Nat. Geographic Soc. Roman Catholic. Avocations: diving, skiing, ancient archaeology.

WIERZCHOS, JACEK, geobiologist, researcher; b. Szczuczyn, Poland, Sept. 11, 1957; arrived in Spain, 1979; s. Witold and Jadwiga (Szczemirska) W.; m. Janina Krupa, Sept. 1, 1979; 1 child Kacper. MS in Chemistry, U. M. Sklodowska-Curie, Lublin, Poland, 1981; PhD in Chemistry, Inst. Agrophysics, Lublin, Poland, 1989. Rsch. asst. Inst. Agrophysic, Lublin, Poland, 1982-88; sr. rsch. asst. Inst. Agrophysic, Lublin, 1988-90; rsch. fellow Ministry Edn. and Sci., Madrid, 1990-93; head electron microscopy svc. U. Lerida (Spain), 1993—. Mem. Polish Soc. Soil Sci., Spanish Soc. Electron Microscopy, Planetary Soc. Avocation: underwater archaeology. E-mail: jacekw@suic-me.udl.es. Office: Svc Microscopia Electron, UdL Av Rovira Roure 44, 25196 Lerida Catalunya, Spain

WIERZCHOWSKI, KAZIMIERZ LECH, biophysicist, researcher; b. Pulawy, Poland, Dec. 4, 1929; s. Zenon and Janina (Obuchowska) W.; m. Wieslawa Marianna Kostrzynska Wierzchowska, May 7, 1955; children: Tomasz, Jacek. MPhil in Chemistry, Warsaw (Poland) U., 1952; PhD in Natural Scis., Nencki Inst. Experimental Biol, Warsaw, Poland, 1960, D in Natural Scis., 1965. Asst. Chair of Inorganic Chemistry, Warsaw U., Poland, 1951-55; sr. asst., adjunct Inst. Biochemistry and Biophysics, Polish Acad. Scis., Warsaw, Poland, 1955-65, assoc. prof., 1965-71, 71-76, prof., 1976—; assoc. prof., contract Chair of Biophysics, Faculty of Physics, Warsaw U., Poland, 1965-69; rsch. fellow dept. chemistry Harvard U., Cambridge, Mass., 1960-61; prof., head dept. biophysics Inst. Biochemistry and Biophysics, Polish Acad. Scis., Warsaw, 1973-99; dir. Inst. Biochemistry and Biophysics, Polish Acad. Scis., Warsaw, Poland, 1972-80, Ctrl. Rsch. & Devel. Project on Molecular Principles of Biotechnology, State Com. on Sci. and Tech., Warsaw, Poland, 1986-90; mem. adv. edtl. bd. Biophysical Chemistry, 1984-97. Editor-in-chief: KOSMOS, 1992—; co-editor: Acta Biochemica Polonica, 1985—; contbr. over 100 articles to profl. jours. Recipient Leon Marchlewski Medal for Achievement in Sci., Com. on Biochemistry and Biophysics, Polish Acad. Scis., Warsaw, Poland, 1995, Officer Cross of the Polonia Restituta Order, Pres. of Poland, Warsaw, 1988, Annual Scientific prizes Polish Acad. Scis., 1965, 76, 92. Mem. Polish Acad. Scis., Polish Acad. Knowledge, N.Y. Acad. Scis. Avocation: tourism. E-mail: klw@ibb.waw.pl. Fax: (48)(22) 6584636. Office: Inst Biochem & Biophysics, Pawinskiego 5A, 02-106 Warsaw Poland

WIESBECK, WERNER, electronics educator; b. Bavaria, Germany, June 8, 1942; s. Werner Paul and Zenta (Ritter) W.; m. Renate Sailer, Dec. 23, 1970; children: Gregory, Mathey, Ferdinand. Diploma in engring., Tech. U. Munich, 1969, DEng, 1972. Rsch. assoc. Tech. U. Munich, 1969-72; lab. head AEG-Telefunken, Ulm, Germany, 1972-74, dep. head, 1974-77; dir. mktg. and sales AEG-Telefunken, Ulm, Fed. Republic Germany, 1981-83; dir. R & D AEG-Telefunken, Flensburg, Germany, 1977-81; prof. electronics, head dept. U. Karlsruhe, Germany, 1983—, dir. Microwave and Electronics Inst., 1983—; cons. SHR Shuttgant, Germany, 1984—, Astrium GmbH, Immenstadt, Germany, 1985—, German Aerospace, 1991, Govt. of State of Baden-Württemberg, 1992-94, German Rsch. Coun., 1992—. Editor conf. proc. Heinrich Hertz Centennial, 1988; contbr. over 350 papers and books on microwave metrology, radar, electromagnetics and wave propagation. Mem. Schrobenhausen (Fed. Republic Germany) City Coun., 1974-78. Recipient Alcatel SEL Tech. Com. award, 1996. Fellow IEEE (ad com. 1992—, chmn. GRS, exec. v.p. GRS-S 1998-99, pres. GRS-S 2000—, mem. awards com. 1994—, Millennium medal 2000); mem. Verband Deutscher Elektronics (VDE ITG award 2000). Roman Catholic. Avocations: golf, art, skiing. E-mail: werner@wiesbeck-net.de. Office: U Karlsruhe, Kaiserstrasse 12, D-76128 Karlsruhe Germany

WIESCHAUS, ERIC F., molecular biologist, educator; b. June 8, 1947. BS, U. Notre Dame, 1969; PhD in Biology, Yale U., 1974. Rsch. fellow Zool. Inst., U. Zurich, Switzerland, 1975-78; group leader European Molecular Biol. Lab., Germany, 1978-81; from asst. prof. to assoc. prof. Princeton (N.J.) U., 1981-87, prof. molecular biology, 1987—; fellow Lab. de Genetique Moleculaire, France, 1976; vis. rschr. Ctr. Pathobiology, U. Calif., Irvine, 1977; mem. sci. adv. coun. Damon Runyon-Walter Winchell Cancer Fund, 1987-92. Contbr. articles to profl. jours. Recipient Nobel Prize in Medicine, 1995. Fellow Am. Acad. Arts and Scis.; mem. NAS. Office: Princeton U HMMI Dept Molecular Biology Washington Rd Princeton NJ 08544-0001

WIESE, HANNS-PETER, administrator; b. Hamburg, Germany, July 3, 1959. Dipl.Kfm., U. Hamburg, Germany, 1986. Night auditor Hotel Vier Jahreszeiten, Hamburg, Germany, 1982-83; asst. to mgr. bd. Steigenberger Hotel AG, Frankfurt, Germany, 1987-88; investment mgr. 3i plc, Frankfurt, Germany, 1989-93; dir. Bayerische Vereinsbank, Munich, Germany, 1993-96, Euro Synergies Mgmt., Paris, 1993-95; mng. dir. Life Scis. Ventures, Munich, 1996—. With German Air Force. Avocations: sports, reading, travel, hunting. Office: Life Sci Ventures, Von der Tann Str 3, 80539 Munich Germany

WIESEL, ELIE, writer, educator; b. Sighet, Romania, Sept. 30, 1928; arrived in Paris, 1945; came to U.S., 1956, naturalized, 1963; s. Shlomo and Sarah (Feig) W.; m. Marion Erster, 1969; 1 child, Shlomo Elisha. Student, The Sorbonne, Paris, 1948-51; LittD (hon.), Jewish Theol. Sem., N.Y.C., 1967, Marquette U., 1975, Simmons Coll., 1976, Anna Maria Coll., 1980, Yale U., 1981, Wake Forest U., 1985, Haverford Coll., 1985, Capital U., 1986, L.I. U., 1986, U. Paris, 1987, U. Conn., 1988, U. Cen. Fla., 1988, Wittenberg U., 1989, Wheeling Jesuit Coll., 1989, Fairleigh Dickenson U., 1993; LHD (hon.), Hebrew Union Coll., 1968, Manhattanville Coll., 1972, Yeshiva U., 1973, Boston U., 1974, Coll. of St. Scholastica, 1978, Wesleyan U., 1979, Brandeis U., 1980, Kenyon Coll., 1982, Hobart/William Smith Coll., 1982, Emory U., 1983, Fla. Internat. U., 1983, Siena Heights Coll., 1983, Fairfield U., 1983, Dropsie Coll., 1983, Moravian Coll., 1983, Colgate U., 1984, SUNY, Binghamton, 1985, Lehigh U., 1985, Coll. of New Rochelle, 1986, Tufts U., 1986, Georgetown U., 1986, Hamilton Coll., 1986, Rockford Coll., 1986, Villanova U., 1987, Coll. of St. Thomas, 1987, U. Denver, 1987, Walsh Coll., 1987, Loyola Coll., 1987, Ohio U., 1988, Concordia Coll., 1990, N.Y.U., 1990, Fordham U., 1990, Conn. Coll., 1990, Upsala Coll., 1991, Duquesne U., 1991, Roosevelt U., 1991; PhD (hon.), Bar-Ilan U., 1973, U. Haifa, 1986, Ben Gurion U., 1988; LLD (hon.), Hofstra U., 1975, Talmudic U. Fla., 1979, U. Notre Dame, 1980, La Salle U., 1988, Bates Coll., 1995; HHD (hon.), U. Hartford, 1985, Lycoming Coll., 1987, U. Miami, 1988, Brigham Young U., 1989; D of Hebrew Letters, Spertus Coll. Judaica, 1973; DSc (hon.), U. Health Scis./Chgo. Med. Sch., 1989; ThD, U. Åbo Akadem, 1990; LHD (hon.), Hunter Coll., 1992, Susquehanna U., 1992, Am. U., 1992, Millersville U., 1993; hon. degree, U. Dayton, 1993, U. Mich., 1993; LHD (hon.), U. Bordeaux, 1993, Gustavus Adolphus Coll., 1994, McGill U., 1994, Mt. Sinai Med. Sch., 1994, Spelman Coll., 1995; Doctorat (hon.), U. Catholique de Louvain, 1995; LHD (hon.), Sacred Heart U., 1995; D (hon.), U. Buenos Aires, 1995; Docteur (hon.), U. de Picardie Jules Verne, Amiens, France, 1996; LHD (hon.), Briar Cliff Coll., 1996, Clark U., 1996, Phila. Coll. Textiles, 1996, U. Mass., Dartmouth, 1997, U. South Fla., 1997, Fla. Atlantic U., 1997, U. R.I., 1997, U. Mass., Lowell, 1997; LLD (hon.), U. Guelph, 1997; LHD (hon.), De Paul U., 1997, Seton Hall U., 1998; LittD (hon.), St. John's U., 1998; LHD (hon.), Eckerd Coll., 1998, Appalachian State U., 1998, Merrimack U., 1998; D. in Pub. Svc. (hon.), Cedar Crest Coll., 1998; LHD (hon.), Gettysburg Coll., 1998, Loyola U., Chgo., 1999; HHD (hon.), Mich. State U., 1999; Doutor (hon.), U. do Estado do Rio de Janeiro, 1999; Docteur (hon.), U. Montreal, 1999; LHD (hon.), St. Norbert Coll., 1999, St. Joseph's U., 2000; PhD (hon.), Hebrew U., 2000. Disting. prof. Judaic studies CCNY, 1972-76; prof. religious studies and univ. prof. Boston U., 1976—, prof. philosophy, 1988—; now prof. relig. studies, univ. prof., prof. philosophy, now Andrew W. Mellon prof. in the humanities; Disting. vis. prof. Henry Luce, 1982-83, Yale U.; lectr. Andrew W. Mellon Ann. Lecture Series Boston U., 92d St. YMHA, YWHA Ann. Lectr. Series, ann. radio broadcast series Eternal Light for Jewish Theol. Sem. Am., advisory bd. Rena Costa Ctr. for Yiddish Studies at Bar-Ilan U., 1994, advisory coun. Carnegie Commn. on Preventing Deadly Conflict, 1994; chmn. U.S. Pres.'s Commn. on the Holocaust, 1979-80, U.S. Holocaust Meml. Coun., 1980-86; hon. chmn. Holocaust Studies Ctr. of Bronx H.S. Sci., Nat. Jewish Resource Ctr., N.Y.C., 1983, Holocaust Meml. Commn., Vancouver Holocaust Ctr. Soc., 1992—, Ctr. Christian-Jewish Understanding, Sacred Heart U., Am. Friends of Ghetto Fighter's House; co-chmn. Children of Chernobyl/Children at Heart, 1995—; steering com. The Balkan Inst., 1996—; mem. Nat. hon. com. Darius Milhaud Soc.; mem. coun. Ethic Accord Project on Ethic Rels., (hon.) Am. Friends of Neve Shalom/Wahat al-Salam, 1996—; leadership coun. Tanenbsum Ctr. Interreligious Understanding, 1997—; founder Elie Wiesel Found. for Humanity, 1987; founding pres. Paris-based Universal Acad. Cultures, 1993; pres. Am. Friends Kiryat Ungvar-Jerusalem, 1990—; hon. pres. Comité

Français Pour "Yad Vashem," Am. Gathering of Jewish Holocaust Survivors, 1985, Am. Kurdish Info. Network, 1997, adv. bd., 1997; v.p. Internat. Rescue Com., 1985—; adv. bd. The Raoul Wallenberg Commn. of U.S., 1981—, Friends of LeChambon, 1982, Boston U. Inst. for Philosophy & Religion, 1986, Boston U. Students for a Free Tibet, Nat. Inst. Against Prejudice & Violence, Internat. Ctr. in N.Y., 1986—, Friends of Akim USA, 1991, Sholom Aleichem Meml. Found., Nat. Jewish Law Students Assn., 1995—, AmeriCares, 1995, React Take Action Awards, 1996—, No Greater Love, 1996—, Inst. Study of Violence, 1996—, Global Lawyers and Physicians: Working Together for Human Rights, 1997; internat. adv. bd. Elmhurst Coll. Holocaust Edn. Project, 1996—; Am. bd. adv. The Moscow Ctr.; adv. coun. U.S. Com. Refugees, 1996—, Nat. Endowmet for Democracy, 1996—; Helsinki adv. com. Human Rights Watch; bd. govs. Haifa U., (mem. emeritus) Tel Aviv U. 1976—, Massuah - Inst. Study of Holocaust, Israel; bd. dirs. Nat. Com. on Am. Fgn. Policy, Elaine Kaufman Cultural Ctr., Humanitas, Am. Assocs. Ben-Gurion U. of the Negev, Mut. of Am., France Libertés; hon. dir. HIAS; bd. trustees Annenberg Rsch. Inst., 1983-89, Am. Jour. World Svc., 1985—, Haifa U., Tel-Aviv U., Yeshiva U., 1977—, Am. Jewish Heritage Ctr., Mus. Jewish Heritage, N.Y.; patron Internat. Peace U., Berlin, 1995—; colleague Cathedral St. John the Divine, 1975—; mem. jury Neustadt Internat. Prize Lit., 1984; mem. Task Force Apprehending Indicted War Criminals, 1998—. Author: Night, 1960, Dawn, 1961, The Accident, 1962, The Town Beyond the Wall, 1964, The Gates of the Forest, 1966, The Jews of Silence, 1966, Legends of Our Time, 1968, A Beggar in Jerusalem, 1970, One Generation After, 1970, Souls on Fire, 1972, The Oath, 1973, Ani Maamin, 1973, Zalmen, or the Madness of God, 1974, Messengers of God, 1976, A Jew Today, 1978, Four Hasidic Masters, 1978, The Trial of God, 1979, The Testament, 1980, Le Testament D'Un Poète Juif Assassiné (France's Prix Livre-Inter 1980, Bourse Goncourt, 1980, Prix des Bibliothécaires, 1981), 1985, Images from the Bible, 1980, Five Biblical Portraits, 1981, Somewhere A Master, 1982, Paroles d'Étranger, 1982, The Golem, 1983, The Fifth Son (Grand Prix de la Littérature, City of Paris), 1985, Signes d'Exode, 1985, Against Silence (3 vols., ed. Irving Abrahamson), 1985, Job ou Dieu dans la Tempête, 1986, A Song for Hope, 1987, The Nobel Address, 1987, Twilight, 1988; (essays) Silences et Mémoire d'hommes, 1989, L'Oublié, 1989, From the Kingdom of Memory, 1990, Célébration Talmudique, 1991, Sages and Dreamers, 1991, The Forgotten, 1992, (with John Cardinal O'Connor) A Journey of Faith, 1990, (with Albert Friedlander) The Six Days of Destruction, 1988, (dialogues with Philippe-Michaël Saint-Cheron) Evil and Exile, 1990, commentaries to A Passover Haggadah, 1993, All Rivers Run To The Sea (a memoir), 1995, (with Jorge Semprun) Setaire est Impossible, 1995, (with François Mitterand) Memoir in Two Voices, 1996, Et la Mer N'est Pas Remplie, Memoirs II, 1996, Célébration Prophétique, Portraits et Légendes, 1998, Les juges, 1999, King Solomon and His Magic Ring, 1999, And the Sea is Never Full (English transl. of Et la mer n'est pas remplie, Memoirs II 1999), (dialogues with Michael de Saint Cheron) Le Mal et L'Exil/Dix ans après, 1999; editorial and adv. bds. Midstream, Religion and Lit. (U. Notre Dame), Sh'ma: Jour. of Responsibility, Hadassah Mag., Acad. of the Air for Jewish Studies, Holocaust and Genocide Studies: An Internat. Jour., Passages, Religion and the Arts; subject of 44 books; journalist Israeli, French and Am. newspapers. Chmn. adv. bd. World Union Jewish Students, 1985—; comité d'Honneur Ligue International Contre le Racisme et l'Antisemitisme, 1985—; founder Nat. Jewish Ctr. Learning and Leadership, 1974; mem. soc. fellows Ctr. Judaic Studies, U. Denver, 1980, bd. overseer Bar-Ilan U., 1970—. Recipient Prix Rivarol, 1963, Prix de l'Universite de la langue Francaise, 1963, Ingram Merrill award, 1964, Jewish Heritage award, Haifa U., 1975, Remembrance award, 1965, Prix du Souvenir, 1965, Nat. Jewish Book Council award, 1965, 73, Prix Médicis, 1968, Prix Bordin French Acad., 1972, Eleanor Roosevelt Meml. award, N.Y. United Jewish Appeal, 1972, Am. Liberties medallion Am. Jewish Com., 1972, Martin Luther King Jr. medallion, CCNY, 1973, Annual award for Disting. Service to Am. Jewry, Nat. Fedn. of Jewish Men's Clubs, 1973, Faculty Disting. Scholar award Hofstra U., 1974, Rambam award Am. Mizrachi Women, 1974, Meml. award N.Y. Soc. Clin. Psychologists, 1975, First Spertus Internat. award, 1976, Myrtle Wreath award Hadassah, 1977, King Solomon award, 1977, Liberty award HIAS, 1977, Jewish Heritage award, B'nai B'rith, 1966, Avodah award, Jewish Tchrs. Assn., 1972, Humanitarian award, B'rith Sholom, 1978, Joseph Prize for Human Rights, Anti-Defamation League, 1978, Zalman Shazar award State of Israel, 1979, Presdl. Citation, NYU, 1979, Inaugural award for Lit., Israel Bonds Prime Minister's Com., 1979, Jabotinsky medal, S.Y. Agnon medal, State of Israel, 1980, Rabbanit Sarah Herzog award Emunah Women of Am., 1981, Le Grand Prix Littéraire du Festival Internat. Deauville, 1983, Internat. Lit. prize for Peace, Royal Acad. Belgium, 1983, Lit. Lions award N.Y. Pub. Library, 1983, Jordan Davidson Humanitarian award Fla. Internat. U., 1983, Anatoly Scharansky Humanitarian award, 1983, Grand Officer, Legion of Honor, France, Congressional gold medal, 1985, Voice of Conscience award Am. Jewish Congress, 1985, Remembrance award, Israel Bonds, 1985, Anne Frank award, 1985, 4 Freedoms award FDR 4 Freedoms Found., 1985, Medal of Liberty award Statue of Liberty Presentation, 1986, Nobel Peace Prize, 1986, First Herzl Lit. award, First David Ben-Gurion award, Nat. UJA, Gov.'s award, Shaarei Tzedek, Internat. Kaplun Found. award Hebrew U. Jerusalem, Scopus award, 1974, Am.-Israeli Friendship award, Disting. Writers award Lincolnwood Library, 1984, First Chancellor Joseph H. Lookstein award Bar-Ilan U., 1984, Sam Levenson Meml. award Jewish Community Relations Council, 1985, Comenius award Moravian Coll., 1985, Henrietta Szold award Hadassah, 1985, Disting. Community Service award Mut. Am., 1985, Covenant Peace award Synagogue Council Am., 1985, Jacob Pat award World Congress Jewish Culture, 1985, Humanitarian award Internat. League Human Rights, 1985, Disting. Foreign-Born Am. award Internat. Ctr. N.Y., Inc., 1986, Freedom Cup award Women's League Israel, 1986, First Jacob Javits Humanitarian award UJA Young Leadership, 1986, Boston City Coun. Commendation, 1986, medal of Jerusalem, 1986, Freedom award Internat. Rescue Com., 1987, Achievement award Artist and Writers for Peace in the Middle East, 1987, La Grande Médaille de Vermeil de la Ville de Paris, 1987, La Médaille de la Chancellerie de l'Université de Paris, 1987, La Médaille de l'Université de Paris, 1987, First Eitinger Prize, U. Oslo, 1987, Lifetime Achievment award Present Tense mag., 1987, Spl. Christopher award The Christophers, 1987, Achievement award State Israel, 1987, Sem. medal Jewish Theol. Sem. Am., 1987, Metcalf Cup and Prize for Excellence in Teaching, Boston U., 1987, Spl. award Nat. Com. on Am. Fgn. Policy, 1987, Grã-Cruz da Ordem Nacional do Cruzeiro do Sul, Brazil's highest distinction, 1987, Profiles in Courage award B'nai B'rith, 1987, Centennial medal U. Scranton, 1987, Citation from Religious Edn. Assn., 1987, Golda Meir Sr. Humanitarian award, 1987, Spl. Christopher award The Christophers, 1987, Profiles in Courage award B'nai B'rith, 1987, Presdl. medal Hofstra U., 1988, Human Rights Law award Internat. Human Rights Law Group, 1988, Bicentennial medal Georgetown U., 1988, Hofstra U. Presdl. medal, 1988, Human Rights Law award Internat. Human Rights Law Group, 1988, Janus Korczak Humanitarian award INTERPHIL, 1989, Count Sforza award in Philanthropy Am. Hungarian Found., 1989, Lily Edelman award for Excellence in Continuing Jewish Edn. B'nai B'rith Internat., 1989, George Washington award NAHE, Kent State U., 1989, Bicentennial medal N.Y.U., 1989, Humanitarian award Human Rights Campaign Fund, 1989, Internat. Brotherhood award C.O.R.E., 1990, Frank Weil award for Disting. Contbn. to Adv. of N.Am. Jewish Culture Jewish Community Ctrs. Assn. N.Am., 1990, 1st Raoul Wallenberg medal U. Mich., 1990, Award of Highest Honor Soka U., 1991, Facing History and Ourselves Humanity award, 1991, La Médaille de la Ville de Toulouse, 1991, 5th Centennial Christopher Columbus medal City of Genoa, 1992, 1st Internat. Primo Levi award, 1992, Lit. Arts award Nat. Found. for Jewish Culture, 1992, Ellis Island Medal of Honor, 1992, Guardian of the Children award AKIM USA, 1992, Bishop Francis J. Mugavero award for religious and racial harmony Cath. Newman Ctr. Queens Coll., 1994, Golden Slipper Humanitarian award, 1994, Interfaith Coun. on the Holocaust Humanitarian award, 1994, Crystal award Davos World Economic Forum, 1995, First Niebuhr award, Elmhurst Coll., 1995; named Humanitarian of the Century Coun. Jewish Orgns., Presdl. medal Freedom, 1992; Beth Hatefutsoth hon. fellow, 1988; honors established in his name: Elie Wiesel award for Holocaust Rsch., U. Haifa, Elie Wiesel Chair in Holocaust Studies, Bar-Ilan U., Elie Wiesel Endowment Fund for Jewish Culture, U. Denver, 1987, Elie Wiesel Disting. Svc. award, U. Fla., 1988, Elie Wiesel awards for Jewish Arts and Culture B'nai B'rith Hillel Founds., 1988, Elie Wiesel Chair in Judaic Studies Conn. Coll., 1990, Disting. Libery award N.Y.C. Refugee Employment Project, 1995, Freedom award Nat. Civil Rights Mus., 1995, Humanitarian award Queensborough Comty. Coll./Holocaust Resource Ctr. Archives, 1995, Socio Honorario de la Sociedad Hebrai ca Argentina, 1995, Pres. award Quinnipac Coll., 1996, Golden Plate award Am. Acad. Achievement, 1996, Lotos medal of Merit, The Lotos Club, 1996, Guardian of Zion award Ingeborg Rennert Ctr. Jerusalem Studies, Bar-Ilan U., 1997, Eisenhower Leadership prize Eisenhower World Affairs Inst. Gettysburg Coll., 1997, Canterbury medalist Becket Fund for Religious Liberty, 1998, ABA ann. award, 1998, Rabbi Marc H. Tanenbaum award for Advancement Interreligious Understanding, 1998, Yitzhak Rabin Peacemaker award Merrimack Coll., 1998, Aesop prize Children's Am. Folklore Soc. for King Solomon and His Magic Ring (Children's Folklore sect. 1999), Raoul Wallenberg Internat. Humanitarian award The Am. Jewish Joint Distbn. Com., 1999. Fellow Jewish Acad. Arts and Scis., Am. Acad. Arts and Letters (dept. lit.), Am. Acad. Arts & Scis., Modern Lang. Assn. Am. (hon.), Timothy Dwight Coll., Yale U.; mem. Fgn. Press Assn. (hon. life), Amnesty Internat., PEN (New England coun.1993—), Writers & Artists for Peace in Middle East, Writers Guild of Am. East, The Author's Guild, Royal Norwegian Soc. Scis. and Letters, Soc. des auteurs Paris, European Acad. of Arts, Sci. and Humanities, Albert Einstein Soc. (hon., Phila.), Phi Beta Kappa (Assocs. award 1994). Office: Boston U Univ Profs Program 745 Commonwealth Ave Boston MA 02215-1401

WIESEL, FRITS-AXEL TAGE, psychiatrist, educator, researcher; b. Stockholm, Nov. 14, 1944; s. Frits Samuel and Greta Sofia (Svensson) W.; m. Maj-Britt Inga Alterfors, May 11, 1972; 1 child, Fredrika. MB, Karolinska Inst., Stockholm, 1968, PhD in Pharmacology, 1976. Register doctor, specialty in psychiatry. Rsch. asst. Karolinska Inst., Stockholm, 1969-75, lectr. in pharmacology, 1975-76; physician Karolinska and Sankt Görans Hosps., Stockholm, 1977-78; resident in psychiatry Karolinska Hosp., Stockholm, 1978-83, assoc. prof. pharmacology, 1978, assoc. prof. psychiatry, 1983, lectr. in psychiatry, 1984-89; prof. psychiatry, dept. head Uppsala (Sweden) U., 1989—; head psychiatry Uppsala Univ. Hosp., 1994—; rschr. in psychiatry Med. Rsch. Coun., Stockholm, 1984-89, priority com. in psychiatry; rsch.-edn. com. Uppsala U., 1989-93. Contbr. over 200 articles to profl. jours. Grantee Bank of Sweden Tercentenary Found., 1984-89, Med. Rsch. Coun., 1988—. Mem. N.Y. Acad. Scis., Am. Neurosci. Assn., European Neurosci. Assn., Assn. European Psychiatrists, Scandinavian Soc. for Psychopharmacology, Am. Psychiat. Assn. Office: Uppsala Univ Hosp, Dept Neurosci/Psychiatry, SE750 17 Uppsala Sweden

WIESEL, TORSTEN NILS, neurobiologist, educator; b. Upsala, Sweden, June 3, 1924; came to U.S., 1955; s. Fritz Samuel and Anna-Lisa Elisabet (Bentzer) W.; 1 dau., Sara Elisabet. MD, Karolinska Inst., Stockholm, 1954; D Medicine (hon.), Karolinska Inst, Stockholm, 1989; AM (hon.), Harvard U., 1967; ScD (hon.), NYU, 1987, U. Bergen, 1987. Instr. physiology Karolinska Inst., 1954-55; asst. dept. child psychiatry Karolinska Hosp., 1954-55; fellow in ophthalmology Johns Hopkins U., 1955-58, asst. prof. ophthalmic physiology, 1958-59; assoc. in neurophysiology and neuropharmacology Harvard U. Med. Sch., Boston, 1959-60; asst. prof. neurophysiology and neuropharmacology Harvard U. Med. Sch., 1960-64, asst. prof. neurophysiology, dept. psychiatry, 1964-67, prof. physiology, 1967-68, prof. neurobiology, 1968-74, Robert Winthrop prof. neurobiology, 1974-83, chmn. dept. neurobiology, 1973-82; Vincent and Brooke Astor prof. neurobiology, head lab. Rockefeller U., N.Y.C., 1983—, pres., 1992-98, pres. emeritus, 1998—, dir. Leon Levy and Shelby White Ctr. for Mind, Brain & Behavior, 1998—; Ferrier lectr. Royal Soc. London, 1972; NIH lectr., 1975; Grass lectr. Soc. Neurosci., 1976; lectr. Coll. de France, 1977; Hitchcock prof. U. Calif.-Berkeley, 1980; Sharpey-Schafer lectr. Phys. Soc. London; George Cotzias lectr. Am. Acad. Neurology, 1983. Contbr. numerous articles to profl. jours. Recipient Jules Stein award Trustees for Prevention of Blindness, 1971, Lewis S. Rosenstiel prize Brandeis U., 1972, Friedenwald award Assn. Rsch. in Vision and Ophthalmology, 1975, Karl Spencer Lashley prize Am. Philos. Soc., 1977, Louisa Gross Horwitz prize Columbia U., 1978, Dickson prize U. Pitts., 1979, Nobel prize in physiology and medicine, 1981, W.H. Helmerich III award 1989. Mem. Am. Physiol. Soc., Am. Philos. Soc., AAAS, Am. Acad. Arts and Scis., Nat. Acad. Arts and Scis., Swedish Physiol. Soc., Soc. Neurosci. (pres. 1978-79), Royal Soc. (fgn. mem.), Physiol. Soc. (Eng.) (hon. mem.). Office: Rockefeller U 1230 York Ave New York NY 10021-6399

WIESENBERG, JACQUELINE LEONARDI, lecturer; b. West Haven, Conn., May 4; d. Curzio and Filomena Olga (Turrinziani) Leonardi; m. Russel John Wiesenberg, Nov. 23; children: James Wynne, Deborann Donna. BA, SUNY, Buffalo, 1970; postgrad., 1970-73, 80—. Interviewer, examiner U.S. Dept. Labor, New Haven, 1948-52; sec. W.I. Clark Co., Hamden, Conn., 1952-55; acct. VA Hosp., West Haven, 1956-60; acct.-commissary USAF Missle Site, Niagara Falls, N.Y., 1961-62; tchr. Buffalo City Schs., 1970-73, 79; acct. Erie County Social Svcs., Buffalo, 1971-73; lectr., 1973—. Contbr. articles to CAP, USAF mag. Capt., Nat. Found. March of Dimes, 1969—, com. mem. telethon, 1983-86; vol. VA, 1973—; den mother Boy Scouts Am., 1961-68; chmn. Meals on Wheels, Town of Amherst, 1975-76; leader, travel chmn. Girl Scouts U.S., 1968-77; mem. Nat. Congress Parents and Tchrs., 1957—; heart fund vol. Heart Assn., 1960-86; rep. Am. Diabetes Assn., 1994—, vol. diabetes collection, 1994-95; mem. Humane Soc. U.S., ASPCA, N.Y. Srs. Coalition. Mem. AAUW, NAFE, Internat. Platform Assn., Nat. Pks. and Conservation Assn., Am. Astrol. Assn., Nat. Arbor Day Found., Western N.Y. Conf. Aging, Nat. Geog. Soc., Wilderness Soc., Nat. Wildlife Fedn., Nat. Trust for Hist. Preservation, Nature Conservancy, Ctr. for Marine Conservation, Internat. Funds Animal Welfare, North Shore Animal League, The Nature Conservancy, The Libr. Congress, U. Buffalo Found., U. Buffalo Alumni Assn., Epsilon Delta Chi, Alpha Iota. Home: 14 Norman Pl Amherst NY 14226-4233

WIESENBERG, RUSSEL JOHN, statistician; b. Kaukauna, Wis., Apr. 9, 1924; s. Emil Martin and Josephine (Appelbaker) W.; m. Jacqueline Leonardi, Nov. 23; children: James Wynne, Deborann Donna. BS, U. Wis., 1951; postgrad. Cornell U., 1960-61, U. Mich., 1969, George Washington U., 1976. Analyst, Gen. Electric Co., West Lynn, Mass., 1951-56; specialist Internat. Gen. Electric Co., Rio de Janeiro, Brazil, 1956-59; statistician Gen. Motors Corp., Lockport, N.Y., 1959-65, sr. statistician, Harrison Radiator div., 1965-78, sr. reliability engr., 1978-82, sr. reliability statistician, 1982-87. Auditor, Community Chest Fund, 1952-55; umpire Little League Baseball, 1962-65; committeeman Buffalo Area council Boy Scouts Am., 1962—, Cub Scout committeeman, 1962-64, Webelos cubmaster, 1963-64; mem. Nat. Congress Parents and Tchrs., 1963—; heart fund Vol. Heart Assn., 1968; tournament dir. Am. Legion Baseball, 1975; vol. United Way campaign, 1983, nat. telethon March of Dimes, 1983-84. Served with AUS, 1943-46. Decorated Bronze Star. Mem. AAAS, Am. Statis. Assn., Nat. Register Sci. and Tech. Pers., U. Wis. Alumni Assn., Artus, Internat. Platform Assn., Phi Kappa Phi. Lutheran. com.). Contbr. articles to profl. jours. Home: 14 Norman Pl Buffalo NY 14226-4233

WIESENTHAL, SIMON, cultural association executive, engineer; b. Dec. 31, 1908; s. Hans and Rosa (Rapp) W.; m. Cyla Muller, 1935. Grad. engr., Prague, Czechoslovakia; Dr. h.c., Hebrew Union Coll., N.Y.C., 1974, Hebrew Theol. Coll., Chgo., 1976, Wash. U., St. Louis, 1981, Colby Coll., Waterville, Maine, 1982, John Jay Coll., N.Y.C., 1982, U. Vienna, 1990, Wesleyan U. Ohio, Del., 1991, U. Vienna, 1991, Am. U. Paris, 1993, U. Libre de Bruxelles, 1994, U. (Austria) Innsbruck, 1994, Jagiellonian U., Cracow, Poland, 1994, Komenius U., Pressburg, Slovakia, 1995, Ben Gurion U. Negev, Israel, 1996, Webster U., Vienna, Austria, 1996, Palacky U., Olominc, Czech Republic, 1996, U. Sarajevo, Bosnia and Herzegovina, 1996, Karls U., Prague, 1997. individual practice architecture; head Jewish Documentation Ctr.; chmn. Jewish Ctrl. Com. U.S.A. Zone; chmn. Assn. Jews Persecuted by Nazi Regime; v.p. Union Internationale des Resistants et Deportes, Brussels. Author: KZ Mauthausen, 1946, Head Mufti Head-Agent of the Axis, 1947, I Hunted Eichmann, 1961, Limitation, 1964, The Murderers Among Us, 1967, The Sunflower, 1969, 97, Sails of Hope, 1973, The Case of Krystyna Jaworska, 1975, Max and Helen, 1982, Every Day Remembrance Day, 1986, Justice, Not Vengeance, 1989, For They Knew What They Were Doing, 1995. Decorated medal of Freedom (Netherlands, Luxembourg), Silver medal Bosnian Coat of Arms, 1998; Gt. Medal of Merit (W. Ger.), Grand Cross of Merit; diploma of honor Resistance, UN, City of L.A., State of Calif., Orgn. Jewish War Vets. U.S.A.; needle of honor Austrian Resistance; Merit award Decalogue Soc. Lawyers, Chgo., 1978; Jean-Moulin-Medaille, French Resistance; Kaj-Munk medal, Denmark; comdr. Order of Oranje Nassau (Netherlands); comdr. Order of Republic (Italy); named hon. citizen of Dallas, 1979, of Louisville, 1979, of Miami Beach, 1983, of Shelby County and Memphis, 1984, Hon. Citizen City of Vienna, 1995, Prof. Govt. of Austria, 1997; Henrietta Szold award, 1979; Justice Louis D. Brandeis award, 1980; Gold medal of Am. Congress, Pres. Carter, 1980, Jerusalem medal, 1980, medal of Honor, Found. Yad Vashem, Jerusalem; proclamation City of N.Y., 1981, Franklin D. Roosevelt Four Freedoms medal, 1990; comdr. Order of Merit (Luxembourg); David award Diaspora Jewry, 1981; Simon Wiesenthal Ctr. for Holocaust Studies, Yeshiva U., L.A. established, Apr. 1977; recipient Gold medal Union Jewish Congregations in Austria, Gt. medal Pres. of Fed. Republic of Germany, 1985, Grand Silver Hon. medal Mayor of Vienna, Austria, 1985, Otto Hahn Peace medal German Soc. U.N., Berlin, 1991, Human Rights award Karl Franzens U., Graz, Austria, 1994, Austrian Book Sellers Assn. award, 1995; created Knight of Hon. Legion of France Pres. of France, 1986; Spl. Erasmus prize, 1992, LAPID award, Jerusalem, 1993, Austrian Cross of Hon. of the Scis. and Arts, Vienna, 1993, Comdr.'s Cross of Order Polonia Restituta, 1994, Comdr.'s Cross of Order of Merit, 1995, Ring of Honor City of Linz, Austria, 1995. Mem. Inst. Recherches de Psychotherapie (hon., France), Dutch Resistance, Danish Assn. Freedom Fighters, Vienna U. Applied Arts, Internat. Coun. Yad Vashem (Jerusalem), Austrian League for Human Rights (hon. pres. 1991), Acad. Sci. (hon. mem.). Fax: 1-5350397. Office: Jewish Documentation Ctr, Salztorgasse 6, 1010 Vienna Austria

WIESLANDER, LARS E. I., biology educator; b. Norrhoping, Sweden, Nov. 13, 1950; s. Bergt K. H. and Carin E. (Silvfander) W.; life ptnr. Gunilla Antuin; children: Magnus, Anna, Bjorn. Med. degree, Karolinska Inst., 1975, MD, 1980. Rsch. asst. Nat. Sci. Rsch. Coun., Stockholm, 1980-85; rsch. fellow Swedish Med. Rsch. Coun., Stockholm, 1985-97; assoc. prof. Karolinska Inst., Stockholm, 1996-97; prof. Stockholm U., 1996—; scientific sec. Swedish Cancer Fund, Stockholm, 1993—; cons. to Astra Draco, Lund, Sweden, 1996-97; mem. biology com. Swedish Nat. Sci. Rsch. Coun., 1997-99. Author: Our Genome, 1986. Mem. RNA Soc., Royal Swedish Acad. of Scis. (biology com. 1997). Avocations: sports, outdoor activities, art. Office: Dept Molecular Genome Rsch, Stockholm U, S-10697 Stockholm Sweden

WIESMANN, KLAUS, NATO official; b. Lemgo, Germany, Aug. 13, 1940. Commd. 2d lt. Belgium Armed Forces, 1962, advanced through grades to lt. gen., 1995, tng. officer, instr., then comdr. hdqrs. and support battery, 1960-71; staff officer ops. divsn. HQ CENTAG, NATO Belgium Armed Forces, Mannheim, 1973-74; staff officer polit.-mil. affairs br., Armed Forces Staff Belgium Armed Forces, Bonn, 1974-78; comdr. 135 armoured arty. bn. Belgium Armed Forces, 1978-90; with mechanized infantry divsn. Belgium Armed Forces, Oldenburg, 1980-81; staff officer, chief nuclear planning br. Plans & Policy Divsn. Internat. Mil. Staff, NATO Hdqrs., Brussels, 1981-84; br. chief politico-mil. affairs Armed Forces staff Bonn, 1984-86; comdr. 11 mechanized infantry brigade Belgium Armed Forces, Bogen, 1986-90; asst. chief of staff policy, Hdqrs. NATO Belgium Armed Forces, Brunssum, The Netherlands, 1990-92; asst. chief of staff politico-mil. affairs and ops. Armed Forces Staff, Bonn, 1992-95; German mil. rep. to NATO Mil. Com. NATO, Brussels, 1995—, German mil. del. in Permanent Coun. Western European Union, 1995—. Office: NATO Hdqrs, Blvd Leopold III, 1110 Brussels Belgium*

WIESNER, ANATOL, signals intelligence specialist, researcher; b. Orsha, Russia, Feb. 20, 1948; s. Adolf and Elena (Sebastian) W.; m. Tamara Sawitschewa, Sept. 9, 1969; 1 child, Stella. BS, U. Radioelectronics, Minsk, Russia, 1970, MS, 1972; PhD in Info. Processing, Inst. Electronics, Minsk, Russia, 1987. Rsch. engr. Radio Instrumentation Labs., Minsk, 1972-76; rsch. scientist Inst. Electronics, 1976-85, sr. staff scientist, 1985-90; signal intelligence systems rschr. Westminster Comm., Berlin, 1990-93; signal intelligence R&D scientist Selectronic Corp., Werder, Germany, 1993—. Co-author: Photo Electrical Transucers for Optical Processing Systems, 1990; holder 27 patents; contbr. over 55 articles to profl. jours. Mem. IEEE, Armed Forces Comm. and Electronics Assn., W-Com. Cons. Avocations: Ham radio, jazz music (playing piano and classical guitar). Home: Berliner Str 109 Werder Havel, D-14542 Berlin Germany

WIESNER, LOUIS ARNOLD, social welfare organization executive; b. Apr. 14, 1916; m. Elizabeth Quincy Phenix, June 3, 1950; children: Jonathan Louis, Elizabeth Quincy, Margaret Bolles, Andrew Christopher. BS, Mich. State Coll., 1937; AM, Harvard U., 1938, postgrad., 1938-42. Rsch. sec. Coun. on Fgn. Rels., N.Y.C., 1942-43; rsch. analyst Office of Strategic Svcs., Washington, 1943-44; fgn. svc. officer Dept. of State, Washington, 1944-75, dir. office refugee and migration affairs, 1973-75; counselor and adminstr. Internat. Rescue Com., Washington, 1975-84; mem. bd., exec. com. Internat. Rescue Com., N.Y.C., 1985-96, mem. of corp., 1996—. Author: Victims and Survivors: Displaced Persons and Other War Victims in Viet-Nam 1954-75, 1988. Home and Office: PO Box 76 Chocorua NH 03817-0076

WIESNER, STEPHEN JAY, physicist researcher; b. Cambridge, Mass., Aug. 30, 1942; s. Jerome Bert and Laya (Wanger) W.; m. Beverly Belfer, Aug. 15, 1987; 1 child, Chaya Sarah. BA, Brandeis U., 1968; PhD, Columbia U., 1973. Physicist, rschr. Tel Aviv U., Ramat-Aviv, Israel, 1995—, Mizpeh Ramon (Israel) Yishiva. Jewish. Avocation: solar engring. Home: Box 432, 80600 Mizpeh Ramon Israel

WIETING, GARY LEE, federal agency executive; b. Huron, S.D., Apr. 24, 1937; s. LeRoy Charles and Edna Lorraine (Crawley) W.; m. Nancy Lou Clark, July 9, 1961 (div. 1991); children: Kevin Clark, Brian David; m. Julia Gladys Eli, Dec. 31, 1998. BA, U. Ill., 1961; MBA, Lake Forest Sch. Mgmt., 1983; travel and tourism diploma, Heritage Coll., Las Vegas, Nev., 1997. Logistics mgr. U.S. Army, Vietnam, 1967-68, NATO/Shape Support Group, Belgium, 1968-72, 8th U.S. Army, Korea, 1972-73, U.S. Army Readiness Region, Ft. Sheridan, Ill., 1973-77, U.S. Army Recruiting Command, Ft. Sheridan, Ill., 1977-83; rsch. and devel. logistics mgr. Belvoir Rsch. and Devel. Ctr., Ft. Belvoir, Va., 1983-85, 88-90; personal svcs. logistics mgr. Hdqrs. Dept. of Army, Washington, 1985-88; logistics mgr., assoc. program mgr. for adv. automation FAA, Washington, 1990-94; ret., 1994. Travel counselor, 1997; mem. So. Nev. Area Mil. Retiree Coun., 1998. Capt. U.S. Army, 1957-77, ret. lt. col., 1986. Decorated Army Commendation medal, Bronze Star medal; recipient Comdr. Award for Civilian Svc., U.S. Army, 1988. Avocations: collecting art, U.S. and internat. travel, playing bridge. Home: 2421 Flower Spring St Las Vegas NV 89134-1822

WIGAN, MARCUS RAMSAY, transportation research scientist; b. Horsham, Sussex, Eng., Sept. 3, 1941; s. Edmund Ramsay and Eileen (Power) W.; m. Jane Frances Geiringer, July 4, 1964 (dec. 1981); m. Christina Elger, Sept. 4, 1984; 1 child, Rebecca Jane. BA, Oxford U., 1963, MA, D.Phil, 1967; MBA, Monash U., 1993, MA in Asian Studies, 1994; grad. diploma in orgnl. psychology, Victoria U. Tech., 1999. Scientist Nat. Coal Bd. Operational Research Group, London, 1963-64, Dept. Nuclear Physics and Atomic Energy Research Establishment Oxford U., Harwell, Eng., 1964-67; prin. sci. officer Transport and Rd. Research Lab., Crowthorne, Eng., 1967-74; prin. planner Greater London Council, 1974-76; chief scientist Australian Rd. Research Bd., Vermont, Victoria, 1976-90; head computing and quantitative methods dept. Bowater Faculty of Bus., Deakin U., Burwood, Victoria, 1990-92; chmn. motorcycle helmet-visor com. Stds. Assn. Australia, Sydney, 1982-92; expert advisor standing com. on rd. safety Ho. of Reps., Canberra, Australia, 1977-78; mem. State Bicycle Com., Victoria, 1979-89; mem. coms. NSF Transp. Rsch. Bd., Washington, 1976—, others coms. include bicycle, freight data, urban data and info. sys., telecoms. and travel behavior, internat. activities; chmn. urban meta data subcom.; vis. prof. of Mgmt. Grad. Sch. Bus., U. Sydney, Newtown, Australia, 1992-95; assoc. dir. FMF Mgmt., 1996-99; vis. fellow dept. civil engring., 1992, hon. sr. rsch. fellow geography and environ. scis. Monash U., 1992—; vis. lectr. orgnl. psychology Victoria U. Tech., 1998; mem. Victorian Motorcycle adv. com. Minister of Roads, Australia, 1998—; prof. transport sys. Napier U., Edinburgh, Scotland, 1999—. Author: New Techniques for Transport Systems Analysis, 1977, Australian Personal Travel Characteristics, 1987, Knowledge Engineering Tools on Microsystems, 1987, Transport Policies for a New Millenium, 1994; contbr. articles to profl. jours.; assoc. editor Transp. Research, 1979-89; area editor transport revs., 1980-85. Tech. advisor Autocycle Union Australia, 1979-80; mem. com. social or econ. implications Australian Computer Soc., 1986—; ACS Ethics Taskforce, 1999—. Served with RAFVR, 1963-67. Sr. vis. fellow U.K. Sci. and Engring. Rsch. Coun., Leeds, Eng., 1982-83. Fellow Inst. Engrs. Australia, Inst. Traffic Planning and Mgmt. (pres. Victorian chpt. 1998-2000), Chartered Inst. Transport.; mem. Inst. Physics, Brit. Computer Soc. Instn. Civil Engrs. Avocations: microcomputer systems, science fiction, motorcycle racing, cycling, organ and choral music. E-mail: mwigan@vaxc.cc.monash.edu.du. Home: 68 Castle St, Eaglemont VIC 3084, Australia Office: Oxford Systematics, GPO 126, Heidelberg VIC 3084, Australia

WIGART, STURE BENGT, publishing company executive; b. Stockholm, May 11, 1934; arrived in Eng., 1983; s. Bengt Eric and Elsa Magarata (Westberg) W.; m. Anne Outram Mott (div. 1973); children: Bengt Eric,Karl Hans, Hans Sture; m. Julia Collbran Cokayne. Student, U. Munich, 1956-57, U. Stockholm, 1957-58. Gen. mgr. Byggfakta, Stockholm, 1969-88, chmn., 1988; chmn. Dodge Europe, London, 1989-93, Bau-Data, London, 1993-94, Sub-Contract, Basingstoke, Eng., 1992—. Avocations: sailing, skiing. Home: 38 Smith St, London SW3 4EP, England Office: Wigart Mgmt Ltd, The Square Basing View, Basingtoke RG21 4EB, England

WIGGER, JARREL L., lawyer; b. Wiesbaden, Germany, May 12, 1963; s. Philip Lee and Ervinetta (Maxey) W.; m. Rose Marie Riley, Aug. 1, 1987; children: Amy Elizabeth, Jordan Lee. BA in English, The Citadel, 1985; JD, Wake Forest U., 1988. Bar: S.C. 1988, U.S. Dist. Ct. S.C. 1993, U.S. Ct. Mil. Appeals 1991, U.S. Supreme Ct. 1998. Student prosecutor Forsyth County Dist. Atty. Office, Winston-Salem, N.C., 1988; assoc. Drose, Davidson & Bennett, Charleston, S.C., 1992-94, jr. ptnr., 1995-98; ptnr. Davidson, Bennett & Wigger, Charleston, 1999—; real estate cons. Co-editor, author: U.S. Navy Mass Casualty Handbook, 1991; co-editor: Law School for Nonlawyers Handbook, 1995. Lt. USN, 1986-92. Mem. ABA, ATLA, S.C. Trial Lawyers Assn., S.C. Bar Assn., Charleston County Bar Assn., Claimant Assn. for Workers Compensation (bd. govs.), Assn. Citadel Men (life), Citadel Brigadier Found., Charleston Area Citadel Club, Citadel Old Timers Wrestling Club (pres. 1996—), Sigma Tau Delta. Avocations: running, guitar, wrestling, coaching. Office: 8086 Rivers Ave N Charleston SC 29406-9235

WIGGERING, HUBERT, geologist, researcher; b. Freren, Germany, June 25, 1956; s. Hermann and Paula (Hegge) W.; m. Karola Hoogen, Nov. 5, 1981; children: Lukas, Benedikt. Diploma in Geology, U. Muenster, 1981; D in Natural Scis., U. Essen, 1984. Asst. prof. U. Essen, Nordrhein-Westfalen, 1981-92, prof., 1992-93; dir., prof., sec. gen. German Coun. Environ. Advisors, Wiesbaden, 1993—. Grantee Kommunalverband Ruhrgebiet, 1984, Ministerium fuer Wissenschaft und Forschung, 1986. Mem. Soc. Environ. Geology (pres. 1993-96), German Geol.Soc., Geol.Assn., Occupational Assn. German Geologists. Home: Greifstrasse 32, 65199 Wiesbaden Germany Office: Sachverstendigenrat fur Umweltfragen, Postfach 5528, 65180 Wiesbaden Germany

WIGGINS, DAVID, philosophy educator; b. London, Mar. 8, 1933. Student, St. Paul's Sch., London, 1946-51; degree in classics, history & philosophy, Brasenose Coll., Oxford, Eng., 1951055. Asst. prin. Home Civil Svc., 1957-58; Jane Eliza Proctor vis. fellow Princeton U., 1958-59; fellow New Coll. Oxford, 1960-67; prof. philosophy Bedford Coll. U. London, 1967-80; fellow, praelector in philosophy Univ. Coll., Oxford, 1981-89; prof. philosophy Birkbeck Coll. U. London, 1989-94; Wykeham prof. Logic U. Oxford, 1993-00; vis. prof. Stanford (Calif.) U., 1962-63, 63-64; vis. fellow All Souls Coll., Oxford, 1973; vis. prof. Harvard U., Cambridge, Mass., 1968; James Loeb vis. fellow in classical philosophy, 1972; Meyer prof. Sch. of Law NYU, 1989; vis. lectr. Istituto della Storia della Filosofia, U. Padua, Italy, 1983; John Locke lectr. in philosophy of medicine Soc. Apothecaries, City of London, 1982; chmn. Transport Users Consultative Com. for South East, 1978-81. Author: Sameness and Substance, 1980, Needs, Values, Truth: Essays in the Philosophy of Value, 1987, 2d edit., 1991, 3d edit., 1998; contbr. numerous articles to profl. publs. Fellow Ctr. for Advanced Study in Behavioral Scis., Stanford, 1984-85. Fellow Brit. Acad.; mem. AAAS (hon. fgn. mem.), Inst. Internat. Philosophy.

WIGGINS, MARY ANN WISE, small business owner, educator; b. Coushatta, La., Dec. 25, 1940; d. George Wilkinson and Maitland (Allums) Wise; m. Gerald D. Paul (div. Nov. 1977); children: John Barron, James Gordon, Brenda Michelle; m. Billy J. Wiggins, Oct. 3, 1981; children: Marshall Wade, Brian David, William Joshua, George Justin; stepchildren: Joseph James, Winona Gail. BA, Northwestern State U., Natchitoches, La., 1964, postgrad., 1994; postgrad., Weaterford Coll., 1967, North Tex. State U., 1968. Lic. ins. agt., real estate agt., La., pvt. pilot. Tchr. U.S. Army Schs., Nuremberg, Germany, 1964-66, Mineral Wells (Tex.) Ind. Sch. Dist., 1967-70; bookkeeper Wise Dept. Store, Coushatta, 1966-67; amb. of good will South Vietnam, 1971; owner, mgr. Mary Ann's Furniture & Hardware, Coushatta, 1977-97; tchr. Springville Mid. Sch., Coushatta, 1994-96, Red River Parish Alternative Sch., Coushatta, 1996—; com. mem. Instrn. and Profl. Devel. Com. La. Assn. Educators, 1998—, vice chmn. 1999—; v.p. La. Juvenile Detention Tchrs. Assn., 1999—. Chmn. Am. Cancer Soc., Conway, Ark., 1972, Red River Parish United Way, Coushatta, 1985; treas., bd. dirs. Hall Summit United Meth. Ch.; pres. Red River Parish Assn. Educators Polit. Action Com. Recipient German-Am. hospitality award Orgn. German-Am. Women, Nuremberg, 1965. Mem. NEA, La. Assn. Educators, Red River Assn. Educators (v.p. 1994, pres. 1998—), U.S. C. of C., Coushatta-Red River C. of C. (charter), Pi Kappa Sigma, Sigma Kappa. Democrat. Methodist. Avocations: gardening/landscaping, swimming, horseback riding, computers, week-enders with family. Home: 2217 E Carrol St Coushatta LA 71019-8567

WIGGINS, NANCY BOWEN, real estate broker, market research consultant; b. Richmond, Va., Oct. 9, 1948; d. William Roy and Mary Virginia (Colson) Bowen; m. Samuel Spence Saunders, Aug. 16, 1969 (div. 1977); m. Edwin Lindsey Wiggins, Jr., Apr. 16, 1983 (div. 1999); children: Neal Bowen, Mark Edwin. AA, St. Mary's Coll., Raleigh, N.C., 1968; postgrad., Trinity U., 1968-69; BA, U.S. Internat. U., San Diego, 1970; MA, U. Tex., Arlington, 1975; postgrad., Tulane U., 1976-77. Cert. comml. investment mem. Bank teller Bank of Am., San Diego, 1971-72; lectr. U. Tex., Arlington, 1974-76; instr. Johnson C. Smith U., Charlotte, N.C., 1977-78; human svcs. planner Centralina Coun. of Govt., Charlotte, 1978-80; mktg. rsch. analyst First Union Nat. Bank, Charlotte, 1980-81; mktg. rep. Burroughs Corp., Charlotte, 1981-83; ptnr., mktg. researcher George Selden & Assocs., Charlotte, 1983-84; pres., broker Bowen Wiggins Co., Charlotte, 1984-92; pres. WRB, Inc. (merger Bowen Wiggins Co. and W. Roy Bowen Co., Inc.), Charlotte, 1992-96; mgr., prin. Nancy Wiggins, LLC, Charlotte, 1996—; ptnr. Buster & Wiggins Internat., Myrtle Beach, S.C.; instr. U. N.C., Charlotte, 1984-85, 87-90, Winthrop U., Rock Hill, S.C., 1985-86, 91-92; bd. dirs. Roy Bowen, Inc., Frogmore, S.C., v.p., sec., 1990. Contbr. articles to profl. jours. Vice chmn. United Cerebral Palsy Coun., Charlotte, 1984; chmn. bd. dirs. Carriage House Condominium Assn., Charlotte, 1980-82; mem. Charlotte Mayor's Budget Adv. Com., 1980-81, Charlotte-Mecklenburg Planning Commn., 1994-99, mem. planning com., 1994-95, zoning com., 1995-97, vice-chmn. zoning com., 1997, planning com. 1998, vice chmn. planning com. 1998—, exec. com., 1997—; pres. Mecklenburg Dem. Women's Club, 1990; mem. state exec. com. N.C. Dem. Party, 1991-95, 99-2000; mem. Mecklenburg County Solid Waste Adv. Bd., 1991-92, chmn. recycling com., 1991-94, 95-96; mem. Comml. Investment Real Estate Inst., 1997-98, bd. dirs. N.C. chpg., 1999. Mem. AAUW, Charlotte Region Comml. Bd. Realtors, N.C. Assn. Appraisers (bd. dirs., pres. 1989-90), Internat. Coun. Shopping Ctrs., Internat. Real Estate Fedn. (Paris, U.S. del. Retail Conf. at World Congress 1998, U.S. vice chair trade missions, sec.-gen. exch. com. 1999-2000), Am. Planning Assn., Charlotte C. of C. (bd. advisors 1997), Multimillion Dollar Club, Tournament Players Club Piper Glen, Rose Soc., Good Friends, Nat. Assn. Realtors, FIABCI, Paris, Internat. Trade Mission Com. (sec. gen. internat. exch. com.), N.C. Citizens for Bus. and Industry, NAR Charlotte (region comml. bd.), CCIM (N.C. chpt. bd. dirs.), Pi Sigma Alpha. Democrat. Episcopalian. Avocations: gardening, art collecting. Home: 6919 Seton House Ln Charlotte NC 28277-4517 Office: Ste 300 501 N Church St Charlotte NC 28202-2207

WIGGLESWORTH, GILLIAN, linguist, educator; b. London, Aug. 19, 1951; d. George and Ruth (Latham) W.; m. Jeff Lynn Pressing, June 21, 1986; children: Adam, Rebecca. BA, La Trobe U., 1981, PhD, 1993. ESL tchr. La Trobe U., Melbourne, Australia, 1983-86; tutor Melbourne U., 1988-89, La Trobe U., 1990-91; lectr. Melbourne U., 1992-95; sr. lectr. Macquarie U., Sydney, Australia, 1995—. Editor: Access: Issues in Language Test Design and Delivery, The Language Testing Cycle: From Inception to Washback. Mem. Internat. Assn. Study Child Lang., Am. Assn. Applied Linguistics, Applied Linguistics Assn. Australia.

WIGINTON, MORRIS S., III, data processing executive; b. Austin, Tex., June 13, 1950; s. Morris S. Wiginton Jr. and Bernice (Moreland) Lilley; m. Deborah Joyce, Aug. 8, 1978 (dec. Aug. 1984); m. Gerry, Feb. 7, 1987 (div. Aug. 1995). U. Houston, 1972. Mgr. transit dept. 1st City Bank, Houston, 1973-76; br. mgr. Univ. Computer Svcs., San Antonio, 1976-80; gen. mgr. Universal Computer Forms, Inc., Houston, 1980-87; regional mgr., Western U.S. Universal Computer Systems, Houston, 1983-87, v.p. tng. and installations, 1982-87, v.p. mktg., 1984-87. Pres. Netcom Bus. Technologies, 1988-93; pres., CEO Summit Consulting, 1996—. Mem. Mensa, Rocky Mt. Elk Found. Republican. Avocations: flying (pvt. pilot), hunting, skiing, billiards, writing. Home: 2989 S Olympia Cir Evergreen CO 80439-8833

WIGUM, BØRGE JOHANNES, geologist, consultant; b. Trondheim, Norway, Jan. 20, 1963; arrived in Iceland, 1996; s. Odd and Marta (Kobberrød) W.; m. Margret Kristin Sigurdardottir, Aug. 10, 1985. BSc in Geology, Iceland U., Reykjavik, 1988; MSc in Engring., Norwegian Inst. Tech., Trondheim, 1990, PhD in Engring. Geology, 1995. Scientific asst. Norwegian Inst. Tech., Trondheim, 1990-93; tech. mgr. Norwegian Approval Body for Concrete Aggregates, Oslo, 1995-96; mgr. ERGO Engring. Geology, Reykjavik, Iceland, 1996—; scientific advisor SINTEF, Trondheim, 1990-92. Contbr. articles to profl. jours. Sgt. inf. Norwegian Army, 1982-83. Avocation: athletics. Home and Office: ERGO-Engring Geology, Grundarstigur 2, 101 Reykjavik Iceland

WIIG, KARL MARTIN, knowledge management expert and consultant; b. Karasjok, Norway, Feb. 8, 1934; came to U.S., 1957; s. Alf Kristian and Margarethe (Soylann) W.; Elisabeth Hemmersam Nielsen, June 10, 1958; children: Charlotte Elisabeth, Erik Daniel (dec.). BS, Case Inst. Tech., 1959, MS, 1964. Rschr. Chr. Michelsen Inst., Bergen, Norway, 1960-64; sys. engr. GE, Cleve., 1964-66; mgr. sys. engring. Dundee (Mich.) Cement Co., 1966-70; chmn. bd. Abacus Alpha, Inc., Newton, Mass., 1980-81; mgr. sys. and policy analysis Arthur D. Little, Inc., Cambridge, Mass., 1970-80, dir. artificial intelligence, 1981-87; ptnr. Coopers & Lybrand, Dallas, 1987-89; mng. ptnr. The Wiig Group, Arlington, Tex., 1989-95; chmn. bd., CEO Knowledge Rsch. Inst., Inc., Arlington, Tex., 1995—; presenter, cons. in field; co-founder Internat. Knowledge Mgmt. Network; spk. U.S. Info. Agy., Australia, 1998; lectr. U. Sao Paulo, Brazil, 1999, 2000; keynote spkr. Johannesburg, 1999, Prague, 2000, New Delhi, 2000, Taipei, 2000, Seoul, 2000. Author: The Economics of Offshore Oil and Gas Supplies, 1977, Expert Systems: A Manager's Guide, 1990, Knowledge Management Foundations: Thinking About Thinking - How People and Organizations Create, Represent and Use Knowledge, 1993, Knowledge Management: The Central Management Focus for Intelligent-Acting Organizations, 1994, Knowledge Management Methods: Practical Approaches to Manage Knowledge, 1995, Approaching Knowledge Management in Practice, 1996, Leveraging Knowledge for Business Performance, 1997; (publs.) Managing Knowledge: Executive Perspectives, 1989, Knowledge-Based Systems and Issues of Integration, 1988, Management of Knowledge: A New Opportunity, 1988, Knowledge Management Goals at Different Levels of Society and the Enterprise, 1996, Knowledge Management: Where Did It Come From--and Where Will it Go?, 1997, Knowledge Management: An Introductory Perspective, 1998, What Future Knowledge Management Users May Expect, 1999, (with Elisabeth H. Wiig) On Conceptual Learning, 1999, Introducting Knowledge Management into the Enterprise, 1999, What Future Knowledge Management Users May Expect, 1999, Knowledge Management in Innovation and R&D, 2000, Application of Knowledge Management in Public Administration, 2000; contbr. 12 chpts. to books, over 50 articles to profl. publs. With Norwegian Army, 1953-54. Achievements include patent in variable ratio power steering. E-mail: kmwiig@kri-i.com. Home and Office: 7101 Lake Powell Dr Arlington TX 76016-3517

WIJAYA, CHRISTOFORA HANNY, food chemist, educator; b. Semarang, Indonesia, Apr. 22, 1960; d. Willibrodus Kwik and Maria Magdalena (Tan) Herlina Wijaya; m. Jimmy Hariantono, Oct. 10, 1982; children: Randy, Enrikko, Elizabeth. BSc, Bogor Agrl. U., 1982; M in Agriculture Chemistry, Hokkaido U., 1987, DSc, 1990. From tchr. to assoc. prof. Bogor Agrl. U., Indonesia, 1982—; vis. prof. U. Wis., Madison, 1996; invited rschr. Hokkaido U., Sapporo, 1998; rsch. & devel. cons. Foodtech Utama Internat., Jakarta, 1993. Named outstanding woman scientist Assn. Univ. Women of Japan, 1989, Woman of Yr., 1999. Mem. Japan Soc. Promotion Sci. (area coord. 1991—), Indonesian Assn. Food Technologists, Inst. Food Technologists, Am. Chem. Soc. Roman Catholic. Avocations: reading, slow music, traveling. Home: Taman Cibalagung Blok N, No 10, 16610 Bogor Indonesia Office: TPG-Fateta Bogor Agrl U, Darmaga Campus PO Box 220, 16002 Bogor Indonesia

WIJAYARATHNA, PATHIRAGE GAMINI, computer scientist; b. Polonnaruwa, Sri Lanka, Sept. 5, 1961; parents Pathirage J. Wijayarathna and Leelawathie Heeralugedara; m. Champika Dilrukshi Wickramaarachchi, Dec. 31, 1992; 1 child, Puranjana. D in Engring., U. Electro-Comms., 1998; BSc, U. Kelaniya, 1984; M in Engring., U. Electro-Comms., 1995. Asst. lectr. U. Kelaniya, Sri Lanka, 1985; analyst/programmer Coopers & Lybrand, Colombo, Sri Lanka, 1985-90; sr. exec. computer svcs. Nat. Devel. Bank, Colombo, 1990-91; rsch. assoc. U. Electro-Comms., Tokyo, 1999—. Mem. IEEE, Assn. Computing Machinery, Nat. Geographic Soc. Office: U ElectroComms, 1-5-1 Chofugaoka, Chofushi Tokyo 182-8585, Japan

WIJDENBOSCH, JULES ALBERT, president of Suriname; b. 1942. D in Polit. Sci. & Pub. Adminstrn. Adviser to Gen. Desi Bouterse; v.p. Govt. Suriname, Paramaribo, 1980-87; fin. min. Govt. Suriname, Parmaribo, 1990, pres., 1996—. Mem. Nat. Dem. Party. Office: Office of President, Kleine Combeweg 2-4, Paramaribo Suriname*

WIJNS, PHILIPPE VICTOR CLEMENT, business executive; b. Ninove, Belgium, Mar. 14, 1964; s. Joseph and Frida (Renders) W.; m. Ann Imelda Meulepas, Sept. 28, 1991; children: Eline, Tine, Julie. Student, Cath. U. Leuven, Belgium, 1986, 88; MBA, U. Maastricht, 1996. Sales and mktg. exec. Mgr. Polarcup, The Netherlands, 1990-95; bus. mgr. Veiatec, Belgium, 1995-98; mng. dir. BBA Belgium, 1998—. Contbr. articles to profl. jours. V.p. Sports Counsel, Ternat, Belgium, 1996-98. Avocations: opera, classical music, gastronomy, sports. Home: Terlindenstraat 106, B-1740 Ternat Brabant, Belgium Office: BBA Belgium BVBA, Lozenberg 18, B-1932 Zaventem Brabaut, Belgium

WIK, TORSTEN ERIK INGEMAR, chemical engineer, researcher; b. Umeå, Sweden, Mar. 12, 1968; s. Ingemar Lars Haraldsson and Berit Maria Margareta (Bäckman) W. Elec. engr., Dragonskolan, 1987; MSc, Chalmers U. of Tech., 1994, PhD in Contol Engring., 1999. Rschr. Waterloo Fast Pyrolysis Group U. Waterloo, Ont., Can., 1993-94; rschr. Control Engring. Lab., Chalmers U. of Tech., 1994—, tchr., 1994—; mng. dir., pres. UMA Gen. Improvements and Cons. Inc., Stockholm, 1997—. Contbr. articles to profl. jours. Sgt. Swedish Navy, 1987-88. Grant, scholarship Adlebertska stiftelsen, 1991, 92, 93. Office: Control Automation Lab, Chalmers Univ Tech, 412 96 Göteborg Sweden

WIKLE, THOMAS ADAMS, geography educator, researcher; b. Pasadena, Calif., Jan. 26, 1962; s. John William and Ellen Cecil (Betts) W.; m. Michelle Ann Hist, Oct. 7, 1989; children: Paige Kathryn, Garrett Adams. BA, U. Calif., Santa Barbara, 1983; MA, Calif. State U., Fullerton, 1985; PhD, So. Ill. U., 1989. Staff cartographer, dept. geography Calif. State U., Fullerton, 1983-85; rsch. and tchg. asst. dept. geography So. Ill. U., Carbondale, 1986-89; asst. prof. dept. geography Okla. State U., Stillwater, 1989-93, assoc. prof., 1993—, head dept. geography, 1994-2000, prof., 1998—, assoc. dean Coll. Arts and Scis. Mem. bd. cons. editors McGraw Hill Encyclopedia of Sci. and Technology, 1998—; contbr. articles to profl. jours. Recipient Regents Disting. Tchg. award, 1996; Nat. Geog. Soc. grantee, 1993, 98, NSF grantee, 1991, 94, 98. Mem. Okla. Acad. Scis. (sect. chair 1990-91), Assn. Am. Geographers, Soc. for Photogrammetric Engring. and Remote Sensing (cert. mapping scientist), Nat. Coun. Geographic Edn. (media editor, Disting. Tchg. award 1997), Gamma Theta Upsilon (S.W. regional coord. 1994-99), Phi Kappa Phi. Democrat. Avocations: canoeing, backpacking, bicycling. Home: 12 N Canyon Rim Dr Stillwater OK 74075-6901 Office: Okla State U Dept Geography Stillwater OK 74078-0001

WIKLUND, NILS ALBIN, psychologist; b. Upplands Väsby, Mar. 1, 1947; s. Enar Daniel and Signe Viktoria (Friborg) W. PhD, Lund U., 1978. Diplomated psychologist. Asst. Lund U., 1971-79; psychologist Dept. Social and Forensic Psychiatry, Huddinge, Sweden, 1982-89; assoc. prof., docent Karolinska Inst., 1985—; mgr. Rättspsykologisk Konsult AB, Stockholm, 1991—; sr. lectr. Orbro U., 1999—. Author: The Icarus Complex, 1978, The Motives of Fire Setting, 1983; contbr. articles to profl. jours. Mem. APA. Avocation: languages. Office: Rättspsykologisk Konsult, Vanadisvägen 36, 113 46 Stockholm Sweden

WIKMAN, GEORG KARL, institution administrator; b. Helsingborg, Sweden, Aug. 15, 1943; s. Folke Karl and Hanna Linnea (Pramberg) W.; matriculation exam. Ulricehamn Coll., 1963; BSc in Math., U. Gothenburg, 1968, MSc, 1970, MSc in Physics, 1972. Lectr. dept. math. U. Gothenburg, 1965-66; lectr. Uddevalla Coll., 1970-72; lectr. dept. theoretical physics U. Lund, 1973-74; dir. Swedish Herbal Inst., Gotenburg, 1975—. Mem. Am. Soc. Pharmacognosy, Inst. for Advanced Rsch. in Asian Sci. and Medicine, Inst. Noetic Scis., Gesellschaft für Arzneipflanzenforschung. Office: Swedish Herbal Inst, Kronhusgatan 11, Gothenburg Sweden

WIKNER, JOHAN NILS PONTUS, physician, researcher; b. Stockholm, Sweden, June 18, 1956; s. Nils and Essie (Henden) W.; m. Birgitta Norstedt, June 22, 1985; children: Cecilia, Axel, Gustav. MD, Karolinska Inst., Stockholm, 1982, PHD, 1998. Resident in internal medicine and cardiology Karolinska Hosp., Stockholm, 1985-91; resident in internal medicine and cardiology Stockholm Söder Hosp., 1985-91, cons. dept. internal medicine, 1991—. Contbr. articles to profl. jours. Named Tutor of the Yr., Student Union, Sch. medicine, Karolinska Inst., 1997. Mem. Swedish Soc. Cardiology, Swedish Soc. Endocrinology. E-mail: johan.wikner@medklin.sos.sll.se. Office: Stockholm Söder Hosp, Dept Internal Medicine, 11883 Stockholm Sweden

WIKSTRÖM, ARNE KARL, dermatologist, researcher; b. Luleå, Sweden, Apr. 11, 1960; s. Sune Karl and Majken Margareta (Pettersson) W. Med. degree, U. Umeå, Sweden, 1985; MD, Nat. Bd. Health and Welfare, Stockholm, 1987; PhD, Karolinska Inst., Stockholm, 1995. Registrar Karolinska Hosp. and Inst., Stockholm, 1987-91, sr. registrar, 1991-96, cons., 1996—. Med. officer arty. Swedish Armed Forces. Recipient Lennmalms prize Nat. Swedish Med. Soc., 1993, award in venereology Glaxo Wellcome, 1997. Fellow Swedish Soc. Dermatology and Venereology, Swedish Soc. Sexually Transmitted Diseases, Internat. Union Against Venereal Diseases and Treponematoses, European Acad. Dermatology and Venerelogy, Am. Acad. Dermatology. Avocations: literature, film, wine tasting, skiing. Office: Karolinska Hosp, Dept Dermatovenereology, SE-171 76 Stockholm Sweden

WIKTOR, ZBIGNIEW BOLESLAW, political scientist, educator; b. Radomysl, Poland, June 9, 1942; s. Boleslaw and Maria (Rybak) W.; m. Ilona Ewa Biernacka, July 19, 1969; children: Adrian, Aleksandra, Elisabeth, Krzysztof. M, Bierut U., 1965, D, 1972; M, Lomonosow U., 1973; PhD, Karl Marx U., 1988. Asst. Wroclaw (Poland) U., 1965-72, asst. prof., 1973-76; asst. prof. Inst. Polit. Scis., Wroclaw, 1973-89, Faculty Social Scis., Wroclaw, 1990—; vis. prof. Ill. U., Chgo., 1991. Author: Illinois: An Outline of Social and Political System, 1994, The Political Science and the Scientific Socialism, 1990, The Theory of Scientific Communism, 1986; editor: Plebeian Socialism, 1995. Mem. Assn. Polit. Scis., Polish Tchrs. Trade Union, League Polish Communists (chmn. 1993—). Avocations: jogging, mountain touring, country music, swimming. Home: Rapackiego 4 m 2, 53-021 Wrocław Poland Office: Wrocław Univ, Pl Uniwersytecki 1, 50-137 Wrocław Poland

WIKTORCZYK, TADEUSZ, physicist, educator, researcher; b. Pszczyna, Poland, Feb. 13, 1950; s. Edward and Cecylia (Patyk) W.; m. Helena Kołodziej, July 3, 1976; children: Wojciech, Joanna. MSc in Physics, Tech. U., Wroclaw, Poland, 1974, PhD in Solid State Physics, 1982. Asst. Tech. U., Wroclaw, 1974-77, asst. lectr., 1977-82, rschr., lectr., 1982—, head thin film lab., 1984—. Mem. Polish Phys. Soc. Roman Catholic. Avocation: traveling. E-mail: wikt@rainbow.if.pwr.wroc.pl. Office: Inst Physics Wrocław U Tech, Wybrzeze Wyspianskiego 27, 50-370 Wrocław Poland

WILAILAK, SARIKAPAN, physician, researcher; b. Hatyai, Songkla, Thailand, Mar. 7, 1961; d. Sutin and Wacharee (Sathirakul) Pongpanich; m. Somkid Wilailak; 1 child, Kade-Chanya. BSc, Chulalongkorn U., Bangkok, 1982, MD, 1984. Diplomate Thai Bd. Ob-Gyn., Thai Sub-Bd. Gynecologic Oncology. Rotating intern Rajavithi Hosp., Bangkok, 1984-85; gen. practitioner Songklanakarin Hosp., Songkla, Thailand, 1985-87; resident Ramathibodi Hosp., Bangkok, 1987-90, fellow, 1990-92, mem. staff, assoc. prof., 1991—; vis. fellow Johns Hopkins Hosp., Balt., 1993-94. Author: Principles of Obstetrics, 1991, Population/Family Planning and Contraceptive Technology, 1992, Endometrial Cancer, 1996, Gynecology, 1996, Cervical Cancer, 1998, Textbook of Gynecologic Oncology, 1999; mem. editorial bd. Thai Jour. Ob-Gyn., 1996—. Grantee Faculty of Medicine, 1990, 96. Mem. Med. Coun. Thailand, Royal Coll. Ob-Gyn. Thailand, Internat. Gynecologic Cancer Soc., Thai Med. Assn., Thai Gynecologic Oncology Group. Home: 335/1 Rama VI Rd, Rajtaewee Bangkok 10400, Thailand Office: Ramathibodi Hosp Ob/Gyn Dept, Rama VI Rd, Rajtaewee Bangkok 10400, Thailand

WILAIRAT, PRAPON, biochemistry educator, researcher; b. Bangkok, June 30, 1944; s. Nibhon and Sadapin (Chantanasiri) W.; m. Mullika Bhongsvej, 1974 (dec. 1997). BSc with honors, Australian Nat. U., 1966; PhD, U. Oreg., 1974. Lectr. Faculty of Sci. Mahidol U., Bangkok, 1974-77, asst. prof., 1977-81, assoc. prof., 1981—, chmn. dept. biochemistry, 1988-92. Co-author: Biochemistry, 1987; co-editor: Application of Genetic Engineering to Research on Tropical Disease Pathogens with Special Reference to Plasmodia, 1985; editor Jour. Sci. Soc. Thailand, 1990-91. Recipient rsch. prize Mahidol U., 1987, Tchg. prize, 1993, Arts and Scis. Alumni Fellows award U. Oreg., 1998; named Outstanding Rschr. Nat. Rsch. Coun. of Thailand, 1996, Found. for Promotion of Sci. and Tech. Outstanding Scientist of Thailand award, 1997; sr. rsch. fellow Thailand Rsch. Fund, 1996, 2000, Outstanding Rsch. award Nat. Rsch. Coun. of Thailand, 1995, 1st prize for invention, 1996. Mem. Sci. Soc. Thailand (life, chmn. biochemistry sect. 1988-89), Thailand Acad. Sci. and Tech. (founding mem. 1997). Office: Mahidol U Faculty of Sci, Dept Biochemistry Rama 6 Rd, Bangkok 10400, Thailand

WILANSKY, ALEKSANDR NEAL, director, actor, choreographer; b. St. John's, Can., Sept. 5, 1960; arrived in Switzerland, 1991; s. Samuel B. and Sylvia Rose (Shapiro) W.; m. Claudia Bisagno, Sept. 5, 1994. Founder, dir. The Magic Light Co., 1974—; artistic dir. Nova Ballet Theatre, Montreal, Can., 1984-85, Theatre dela Diligence, Montreal, Can., 1985-87; freelance dir., actor, 1990—; co-organizer Nijinsky Centenary Celebrations, 1989; co-organizer, curator Nijinsky Exposition, Paris, 1990; lectr. La Sorbonne, Paris, 1989. Co-author: Ecrits sur Nijinsky, 1994; choreographer (musical) Little Mary Sunshine, 1987; dir., actor (stage play) Cyrano de Bergerac, 1986 (Dir. Circle award 1987); actor, choreographer (stage, TV) The Pirates of Penzance, 1985 (Best Actor award 1986, Best Musical award 1986). Recipient Nijinsky medal Govt. Poland, Polish Arts Ministry, 1996. Mem. Assn. Internat. des Amis de Vaslav Nijinsky (officer 1991—), Com. Internat. Nijinsky (officer 1988-91), Newfoundland Ind. Film-makers Coop. (founding mem.). Buddhist. Avocations: music, wood working, reading. Home and Office: Schaffhauserstr 360, CH 8050 Zurich Switzerland

WILBUR, ANDREW CLAYTON, radiologist, educator; b. Phila., May 30, 1952; s. Richard Sloan and Betty Lou (Fannin) W.; m. Debra Jean Jones, June 29, 1996; 1 child, Curtis Richard. AB in Human Biology, Stanford U., 1974; MD, George Washington U., 1978. Diplomate Am. Bd. Radiology. Extern in diagnostic radiology Palo Alto (Calif.) Med. Found., 1978-79; resident in diagnostic radiology U. Ill. Hosp., Chgo., 1979-83, fellow in body imaging, 1983-84; asst. prof. radiology U. Ill. Coll. Medicine, Chgo., 1984-90, assoc. prof., 1990—, dir. body imaging dept. radiology, 1988—, dir. radiology residency program, 1989—. Contbr. articles to profl. jours. Mem. Radiol. Soc. N.Am., Am. Coll. Radiology, Am. Roentgen Ray Soc., Chgo. Radiol. Soc. (trustee 1996—). Office: Univ of Illinois Hosp M/C 931 1740 W Taylor St Chicago IL 60612-7232

WILBUR, BARBARA MARIE, elementary education educator; b. Homer City, Pa., Dec. 1, 1945; d. Nicholas and Ann (Bender) Hrebik; m. Samuel Scime, Nov. 21, 1970 (div. Jan. 1974); m. Frederick Layton Wilbur, June 21, 1986 (dec. June 1989). BS in Elem. Edn., SUNY, Buffalo, 1967, EdM in

Guidance Counseling, 1971; postgrad., Harvard U., 1969; grad., John Robert Powers Modeling Sch., Buffalo, 1974. Cert. permanent elem. sch. tchr., N.Y. Elem. tchr. Buffalo Pub. Schs., 1967-70, 94—, Diocese of Ft. Lauderdale, Fla., 1971-72, Diocese of Buffalo, 1973-94. Mem. Internat. Platform Assn., State U. Buffalo Alumni Assn., State U. Coll. Buffalo Alumni Assn. (Outstanding Svc. award 1982), Buffalo State Coll. Alumni Assn. (bd. dirs. 1980-87, active various coms.). Republican. Roman Catholic. Avocations: modeling, volleyball, ice skating, tennis. Home: 301 Lowell Rd Tonawanda NY 14217-1236 Office: Buffalo Pub Schs Sch # 40 89 Clare St Buffalo NY 14206-2020

WILBUR, RICHARD PURDY, writer, educator; b. N.Y.C., Mar. 1, 1921; s. Lawrence L. and Helen (Purdy) W.; m. Mary Charlotte Hayes Ward, June 20, 1942; children: Ellen Dickinson, Christopher Hayes, Nathan Lord, Aaron Hammond. AB, Amherst Coll., 1942, AM, 1952, DLitt (hon.), 1967; AM, Harvard U., 1947; LHD (hon.), Lawrence Coll., Washington U., Williams Coll., U. Rochester, SUNY, Potsdam, 1986, Skidmore Coll., 1987, U. Lowell, 1990; DLitt (hon.), Clark U.; DLitt, Am. Internat. Coll., Marquette U., Wesleyan U., Carnegie-Mellon U.; D.Litt. (hon.), Lake Forest Coll., 1982, Smith Coll., 1996; LittD (hon.), Sewanee U., 1996. Jr. fellow Harvard U., Cambridge, Mass., 1947-50, Asst. prof. English, 1950-54; assoc. prof. Wellesley Coll., 1955-57; prof. Wesleyan U., 1957-77; writer in residence Smith Coll., 1977-86. Author: The Beautiful Changes, 1947, Ceremony, 1950, A Bestiary, 1955, reprint, 1993, Things of This World, 1956, Poems 1943-56, 1957, Advice to a Prophet, 1961, Poems of Richard Wilbur, 1963, Walking to Sleep, 1969, The Mind-Reader, 1976, Seven Poems, 1981, The Whale, 1982, New and Collected Poems, 1988 (Pulitzer prize for poetry 1989), Bone Key and Other Poems, 1998, Mayflies: New Poems and Translations, 2000; (children's books) Loudmouse, 1963, Opposites, 1973, More Opposites, 1991, A Game of Catch, 1994, Runaway Opposites, 1995, The Disappearing Alphabet, 1998, Opposites, More Opposites and Some Differences, 2000, The Pig in the Spigot, 2000; (criticism) Responses, 1976, expanded edit., 2000, (prose pieces) The Catbird's Song, 1997; co-author: (comic opera, with Lillian Hellman) Candide, 1957, (cantata, with William Schuman) On Freedom's Ground, 1986; translator: (Moliere) The Misanthrope, 1955, Tartuffe, 1963 (co-recipient Bollingen Translation prize 1963), The School for Wives, 1971, The Learned Ladies, 1978, Four Comedies, 1982, (Racine) Andromache, 1982, Phaedra, 1986, Molière's The School for Husbands, 1992, Imaginary Cuckold, 1993, Molière's Amphitryon, 1995, Don Juan, 1998, Molière's The Bungler, 2000; editor: Complete Poems of Poe, 1959, Poems of Shakespeare, 1966, Selected Poems of Witter Bynner, 1978. Decorated chevalier Ordre des Palmes Academiques; recipient Harriet Monroe prize Poetry mag., 1948, Oscar Blumenthal prize, 1950, Prix de Rome, Am. Acad. Arts and Letters, 1954, Edna St. Vincent Millay Meml. award, 1957, Nat. Book award, 1957, Pulitzer prize, 1957, Sarah Josepha Hale award, 1968, Bollingen prize, 1971, Brandeis U. Creative Arts award, 1971, Prix Henri Desfeuilles, 1971, Shelley Meml. award, 1973, Harriet Monroe Poetry award, 1978, St. Botolph's Club Found. award, 1983, Drama Desk award, 1983, Aiken-Taylor award, 1988, Bunn award, 1988, Washington Coll. Lit. award, 1988, St. Louis Lit. award, 1989, Grand Master award Birmingham-So. Coll., 1989, Gold Medal for Poetry, Am. Acad. Inst. Arts and Letters, 1991, Edward MacDowell medal, 1992, Nat. Arts Club Medal of Honor for Lit., 1994, PEN/Manheim Medal for Translation, 1994, Milton Ctr. prize, 1995, Acad. Am. Achievement award, 1995, Robert Frost medal Poetry Soc. of Am., 1996, T.S. Eliot award, 1996; Guggenheim fellow, 1952-53, 63, Ford fellow, 1960-61, Camargo Found. fellow, 1985; named U.S. Poet Laureate, Libr. Congress, 1987, Nat. Medal of the Arts, 1994. Fellow MLA (hon.); mem. AAAL (pres. 1974-76, chancellor 1976-78, 80-81), ASCAP, PEN (Transl. award 1983), Am. Acad. Arts and Scis., Acad. Am. Poets (chancellor emeritus), Dramatists Guild, Century Club. Home: 87 Dodwells Rd Cummington MA 01026-9705 also (winter): 715R Windsor Ln Key West FL 33040-6430

WILCHEK, MEIR, biochemist; b. Warsaw, Poland, Oct. 17, 1935; arrived in Israel, 1949; s. Eliezer Nechemia and Rachel (Zaidenberg) W.; m. Esther Edlis, Mar. 14, 1960; children: Eliezer Yizhak, Yael Zvia, Hagit Zipora. BS, Bar-Ilan U., Ramat Gan, Israel, 1960; PhD, Weizmann Inst., Rehovot, Israel, 1965; DSc (hon.), U. Waterloo, Can., 1989; PhD (hon.), Bar-Ilan U., Ramat Gan, Israel, 1995, U. Jyvaskyla, Finland, 2000, Ben-Gurion U., Beer-Sheva, Israel, 2000. Chief chemist Yeda Co., Rehovot, 1960-62; rsch. assoc. Dept. Biophysics, Weizmann Inst., Rehovot, 1965-66, sr. scientist, 1968-71, assoc. prof., 1971-74, prof., 1974—, head, 1977-78, 83-87; vis. fellow NIH, Bethesda, Md., 1966-67, rsch. assoc., 1967-68; vis. scientist NIH, 1972, 74-75, Fogarty scholar, 1981-82; chief cons. Miles-Yeda (Bio Makor), Rehovot, 1960-87; mem. Israeli Acad. of Scis., 1988. Editor: Biochemical and Biophysical Methods, 1975—, Applied Biochemistry and Biotechnology, 1975—, Methods in Enzymology vols. 34 and 46, 1974, 77, 184, 1990, Affinity Chromatography and Biological Recognition, 1983; contbr. articles to profl. jours. Recipient Rothschild prize for chemistry, Israel, 1984, Wolf prize for medicine, Israel, 1987, Pierce prize, Rockford, Ill., 1987, Israel prize in biotech. Govt. Israel, 1990, Sarstedt prize for analytical biochemistry, 1990, Disting. Clin. Chemist award Internat. Fedn. Clin. Chemistry, 1996. Mem. Am. Soc. Biol. Chemists (hon.), Am. Chem. Soc., Inst. Medicine Nat. Acad. Sci: (fgn. assoc.), European Molecular Biology Orgn., Israel Biochem. Soc., Israel Chem. Soc., Israel Immunological Soc., Israeli Acad. Scis. Office: Weizmann Inst Sci, Rehovot Israel

WILCKENS, HENRICH, utility company executive; b. Freiburg, Germany, Jan. 27, 1948; s. Johann Heinrich and Irmgard (Flohr) W.; m. Brigitte Wassermeyer, Dec. 30, 1977; children: Georg, Natalie, Vanessa. Assessor, U. Freiburg, 1975, D of Law, 1976; MBA, INSEAD, France, 1979. Trainee Deutsche Bank AG, Duesseldorf, Germany, 1976-78; asst., controller Dr. August Oetker, Bielefeld, Germany, 1979-84; sr. contr. Milupa AG, Germany, 1984-85; bd. officer Veba Group, 1985—, bd. dirs., 1991—. Mem. Rotary. Avocations: golf, skiing. Home: Inselwall 6, 38114 Braunschweig L Saxony, Germany Office: BKB AG, Schoeninger Str 2-3, 38350 Helmstedt L Saxony, Germany

WILCOX, IAN, medical research scientist, cardiology consultant; b. Melbourne, Victoria, Australia, Mar. 19, 1955; s. Max and Patricia Lorraine (Young) W.; m. Christa Ursula Boehm, Nov. 6, 1977; 1 child, Chloe Ursula. B Med. Sci. with honors, U. Newcastle, Eng., 1976, MB, BS, 1979; PhD, U. Sydney, Australia, 1991. House officer Royal Victoria Infirmary, Newcastle, 1980-81; resident med. officer Royal Prince Alfred Hosp., Sydney, NSW, Australia, 1981-83, med. registrar, 1983-84, cardiology registrar, 1984-86, cardiologist Sleep Disorders Unit, 1990—; rsch. fellow Hallstrom Inst. Cardiology U. Sydney, 1986-90, sr. rsch. officer Nat. Health and Med. Rsch. Coun., 1990-96, assoc. peof. dept. medicine, 1999—; chmn. dept. medicine Strathfield Pvt. Hosp., Sydney, 1996—; sr. rsch. assoc. Inst. Respiratory Medicine, Sydney, 1998—; cons. cardiologist Shoalhaven Dist. Hosp., Nowra, NSW, 1988-96, Royal Prince Alfred Hosp., Sydney, 1997—; cons. ResMed Inc., 1995—; clin. assoc. prof. dept. medicine Sydney U., 1999—. Contbr. articles to profl. jours. Grantee Nat. Health and Med. Rsch. Coun., 1990-96; med. rsch. scholar Med. Rsch. Coun., Newcastle (Eng.), 1975, postgrad. med. rsch. scholar Nat. Heart Found., Sydney, 1986-89; Bayer Travelling fellow Cardiac Soc., Australia, 1990. Fellow Am. Coll. Chest Physicians, Royal Australian Coll. Physicians; mem. Am. Heart Assn., Cardiac Soc. Australia and New Zealand, Med. Defence Union (NSW). Presbyterian. Avocations: oenology, architectural restoration, music. Home: 53 Wycombe Rd, Neutral Bay, Sydney NSW 2089, Australia Office: RPAH Med Ctr, 100 Carillon Ave Ste 407, Newtown NSW 2042, Australia

WILCOX, MARK DEAN, lawyer; b. May 25, 1952; s. Fabian Joseph and Zeryle Lucille (Tase) W.; m. Catherine J. Wertjes, Mar. 12, 1983; children: Glenna Lynn, Joanna Tessie, Andrew Fabian Joseph. BBA, U. Notre Dame, 1973; JD, Northwestern U., 1976. Bar: Ill. 1976, U.S. Dist. Ct. (no. dist.) Ill. 1976, Trial Bar 1982, U.S. Ct. Appeals (7th cir.) 1987, U.S. Supreme Ct. 1989; CLU, ChFC. Staff asst. Nat. Dist. Attys. Assn., Chgo., 1974-75; trial asst. Cook County States Atty., Chgo., 1975; intern U.S. Atty. No. Dist. Ill., Chgo., 1975-76; assoc. Lord, Bissell & Brook, Chgo., 1976-85, ptnr., 1986—. Bd. mgrs. YMCA Met. Chgo., Internat. Spl. Olympics; trustee Trinity United Meth. Ch. Mem. ABA (tort and ins. practice sect.), Am. Soc. CLU and ChFC, Chgo. Bar Assn. (ins. law com.), Nat. Assn. Ins. and Fin. Advisors, Def. Rsch. Inst., Soc. Fin. Svc. Profls., Trial Lawyers Club Chgo., Notre Dame Nat. Monogram Club, Union League Club, Beta Gamma Sigma. Office: Lord Bissell & Brook 115 S La Salle St Ste 3200 Chicago IL 60603-3902

WILCOX, ROBERTA MOAT, music educator; b. Santa Monica, Oct. 20, 1933; d. John Edlington and Ethel Dorothy (Bautz) M.; m. Omer Divers, June 1, 1964; 1 child, Timothy Divers; m. David Henry Smith Wilcox, Dec. 16, 1973. BA in Music, UCLA, 1959; MA in Music Edn., Calif. State U., Los Angeles, 1963. Cert. in secondary music edn., Calif. Freelance violinist Dunes Hotel, Las Vegas, 1963-66; violinist Pasadena (Calif.) Symphony Orch., 1963-73; music tchr. Eldorado Sch. for Gifted, Orange, Calif., 1970-79; strolling violinist The Strolling Two, Pasadena, 1970—; pvt. violin, viola tchr. Pasadena, 1958—; violin, viola tchr. Pasadena City Coll., 1972-77; music tchr. Pasadena Unified Schs., 1986—; founder, mgr. Pasadena Summer Youth Chamber Orch., Pasadena, 1986—; dir. Music to Go chamber music, 1989; mgr. Pasadena Young Musicians Orch., 1994—. Mem. Music Educators Nat. Conf., So. Calif. Sch. Band and Orch. Assn., The Tuesday Musicale (pres. 1980-82, Gold Crown award for Art in Edn. 1995), Mu Phi Epsilon. Republican. Christian Sci. Avocations: collecting antiques, musical instruments, statues and stuffed animals. Home: 734 N Wilson Ave Pasadena CA 91104-4652

WILCOX, WILMA BLANCHE, English language educator; b. Goodland, Kans., Oct. 18, 1942; d. James P. and Rita Shelton; m. John D. Wilcox; 1 child, David. BS in Home Econs. cum laude, Kans. State U., 1963; MA in TESOL curriculum and instrn., U. Kans., 1991, PhD in TESOL curriculum and instrn., 1995. Cert. family and consumer scientist Am. Assn. Family and Consumer Scis. Tchr. 8th grade home econs. Abilene (Kans.) Pub. Schs., 1963-64; tchr. jr. and sr. h.s. home econs. and sci. Thompson Dist. Pub. Schs., Loveland, Colo., 1964-69; tchr. English and home econs. Pescadero (Calif.) H.S., 1969-73; tchr. English, sci. and home econs. Global Assocs., Kwajalein (Marshall Islands) Secondary Sch., 1973-75; tchr. 8th grade English West Jr. H.S., Muscatine (Iowa) Pub. Schs., 1975-77; tchr. 9th grade sci. Saudi Arabian Internat. Sch. at Am. Consulate, Dhahran, 1978-79; supervising instr. intensive English continuing edn. program Johnson County C.C., Overland Park, Kans., 1989-92; instr., supr. fgn. student practicum tchrs. in TESOL, Applied English Ctr., U. Kans., 1990-92; supr. Sch. Edn., U. Kans., 1992-94; lectr. intensive English program So. Ill. U. Carbondale in Niigata, Japan, 1995-96, curriculum coord. intensive English program, 1996-97, acting dir. intensive English program, 1997-98, dir. intensive English program, 1998-99; intensive English lang. specialist Johnson County C.C., 2000—; supr. Writing Ctr. and Grammar Hotline, Johnson County C.C., 1991; asst. instr. C&I 806 methods of TESOL and fgn. lang. in secondary schs., 1993-94; instr. C&I 351 methods of tchg. reading in content areas for secondary tchrs., 1994-95; presenter profl. confs., including 5th Ann. Tchg. Acad. Survival Skills Conf., Cin., 1994, 48th Ann. Ky. Fgn. Lang. conf., U. Ky., Lexington, 1995, 22nd Japanese Assn. Lang. Tchg. conf., Hiroshima, Japan, 1996, 1st Pan-Asian Conf. and 17th Ann. Thai TESOL Internat. Conf., Bangkok, 1997, Info. Tech. in English Lang. Learning conf., Singapore, 1997, others. Author: Video Captions in the ESOL Classroom: A Sourcebook for Johnson County, 1991, Community Development at the Lao American Refugee Center: English for Speakers of Other Languages (ESOL) Practicum in Community Development, 1991; editor writer Arabian Sun, Arabian Am. Oil Co., Dhahran, 1979-87. Pres. Lyric Opera Guild of Kansas City, 1991-93; N. Ctrl. regional dir. Opera Guilds Internat., 1993-95; mem. cmty. opera chorus Shibata Sänger Ründe; mem. Sister Cities com. City of Olathe, Kans. Mem. TESOL (presenter conf. 1998), Nat. Assn. Fgn. Student Advisors, Am. Ednl. Rsch. Assn., Japanese Assn. Lang. Tchg. (program chair Niigata chpt., presenter nat. conf. 1996), Rotary (Nakajo-Tainai chpt., chair internat. com., internat. com. Olathe Santa Fe trail). Republican. Roman Catholic. Avocations: opera, singing, skiing, travel. Fax: (913) 469-2586. E-mail: wwilcox@jccc.net. Office: Johnson County C C 12345 College Blvd Overland Park KS 66210-1283

WILCZEK, HANUS, internist, researcher; b. Praha, Czech Republic, Feb. 12, 1935; s. Karel and Kamila (Steinova) W.; m. Alena Wittikova, June 7, 1961 (div.); children: Michal, Daniela. MD, Charles U., Praha, 1961, PhD, 1980. Med. doctor Teplice, Praha, 1961-74; home officer 3d Med. Clinic-Charles U., Praha, 1974, head med. dept., 1980-90, assoc. prof., 1990, dep. dir., 1990. Author: (book) Vitamin D and Metabolism, 1978; contbr. more than 140 articles on osteology and calcium metabolism to profl. jours. Lt. Health Corps., 1961-95. Mem. Czech Med. Soc. Roman Catholic. Achievements include research in medical care for addicts. E-mail: wil@volny.cz.

WILCZOK, TADEUSZ MARIAN, biochemist, educator; b. Katowice, Poland, June 22, 1934; s. Pawel and Roza Rozanska W.; m. Gizela Brezezina, Mar. 17, 1956; 1 child, Adam. BS in Chemistry, U, 1952; MS in Chemistry, Higher Pedag Sch., 1955; PhD in Biochemistry, U, 1960, DS in Biochemistry, 1962. Asst. Higher Pedagog Sch., Katowice, Poland, 1955; researcher Acad. Sci., Moscow, 1956-58; dozent Inst. Oncology, Gliwice, Poland, 1958; from asst. prof. to prof. Med. Acad., Katowice, 1966—; vis. prof. Gutenberg U., Mainz, 1959, Sloan Kettering Inst., N.Y.C., 1964, EPA Gulf Breeze, Fla., 1978; mem. Com. Biochemistry, Biophysics Polish Acad. Sci., Warsaw, 1968; chmn. Com. Med. Physics, Warsaw; pres. Polish Biophysics Soc., 1985; dean Pharm. faculty, 1984-96; v.p. Silesian Med. Acad., 1996—; rector U. Med. of Silesia, 1999—. Editor Atlas of Metabolic Pathways, 1993; contbr. over 200 scientific articles to profl. jours. Mem. Acad. Sci. Pharm. (France). Avocation: hunting. Office: Dept Mol Biol Biochem Biopharmacy, Jagiellonska 4, 41-200 Sosnowiec Poland

WILD, BONITA MARIE, healthcare company executive; b. Chgo., Jan. 14, 1949; d. Edward and Veronica (Hlad) Orzechowski; m. Forrest Wild; 1 child, Monica. Student, U. Chgo., 1973-75; BS, Roosevelt U., 1977; MA, U. Ariz., 1984. Sales rep. and dist. trainer Ortho Pharm. Corp., Raritan, N.J., 1978-82; v.p. and mktg. dir. Golden Era, Phoenix, 1982-84; sales rep. Surgikos, Arlington, Tex., 1984-88, Johnson & Johnson Med., Inc., Arlington, 1988-90; profl. products mgr. Johnson & Johnson Internat., Johnson & Johnson Poland, Warsaw, 1991-92; account bus. mgr. Johnson & Johnson Hosp. Svcs., New Brunswick, N.J., 1990-91, corp. bus. mgr., 1993—; corp. dir. Johnson & Johnson Health Care Sys., 1995—; counsellor Mariposa Women's Ctr., Orange, Calif., 1984-89. Mem. Franklin Honor Soc. at Roosevelt U. Republican. Roman Catholic. Avocations: skiing, travel, hiking, golf. Home: 16 Yankee Hl Oakland CA 94618-2332

WILD, HANS, physicist; b. Straubing, Germany, Aug. 24, 1939; s. Hans and Regina (Schreyer) W.; m. Hedwig Luise Becher, July 29, 1967; children: Mechthild, Hubert. Student, U. Munich, 1961; Main Diploma, U. Bonn, Germany, 1966. Lab. leader Dr. Kern, Indsl. Co., Göttingen, Germany, 1967; phys. scientist Rsch. Ctr., Karlsruhe, Germany, 1968-91, 93—, Ministerium for Umwelt, Stuttgart, 1991-93. Contbr. 70 articles to profl. jours. Mem. Nuclear Tech. Soc., Radaspona Cartell Verband. Christian Democrat Party. Roman Catholic. Avocation: music. Home: Albert-Einstein-Str 46B, 76646 Bruchsal-Buechenau Germany

WILD, HANS JOCHEN, former systems engineering executive; b. Leipzig, Sachsen, Germany, Apr. 19, 1935; s. Hans Bruno and Annelise (Maurer) W.; m. Ute Brigitta Eberle, Mar. 4, 1961; children: Barbara, Anne, Hans. Diploma, Bonn U., Germany, 1958. Asst. researcher Bonn U., Germany, 1958-62; systems engr. IBM Germany, Stuttgart, 1962-66; dist. systems engring. mgr. IBM Germany, Essen, Duesseldorf, Stuttgart, 1967-93; ret. IBM Germany, 1994. Co-author: Endogene Process Systematik, 1964; contbr. articles to profl. jours. Mem. Internat. Neural Soc. Avocations: neural network research, recreational computing, jogging, 19th century impressionists. Home: Im Heinental 61, 72218 Wildberg Germany

WILD, JOHN JULIAN, surgeon, director medical research institute; b. Sydenham, Kent, Eng., Aug. 11, 1914; came to U.S., 1946; s. Ovid Frederick and Ellen Louise (Cuttance) W.; m. Nancy Wallace, Nov. 14, 1949 (div. 1966); children: John O., Douglas J.; m. Valerie Claudia Grosenick, Aug. 9, 1968; 1 child, Ellen Louise. BA, U. Cambridge, Eng., 1936, MA, 1940, MD, 1942, PhD, 1971. Intern, resident U. Coll. Hosp., London, 1938-42; intern U. College Hosp., London, 1938-42; staff surgeon Miller Gen., St. Charles and North Middlesex Hosps., London, 1942-44; venereologist Royal Army Med. Corps, 1944-45; rsch. fellow, instr. depts. surgery and elec. engring., prin. investigator U. Minn., Mpls., 1946-51; dir. rsch. Medico.-Technol. Rsch. Dept. St. Barnabas Hosp., Mpls., 1953-60; dir. Medico-Technol. Rsch. Unit Minn. Found., St. Paul, 1960-63; pvt. practice Mpls., 1966—; dir. Medico-Technol. Rsch. Inst. Mpls., St. Louis Park, Minn., 1965—; lectr. in field of medical instruments, ultrasound. Contbr. articles to profl. jours. Recipient Japan prize in Medical Imaging, Sci. and Tech. Found. Japan, 1991, 1st Frank Annunzio award Christopher Columbus Fellowship Found., 1998, lifetime achievement award U. Minn. Med. Sch., 2000. Fellow Am. Inst. Ultrasound in Medicine (Pioneer award 1978); mem. AMA, World Fedn. Ultrasound in Medicine and Biology, Minn. State Med. Assn., Hennepin County Med. Soc., N.Am. Alvis Owners Club; hon. mem. British Inst. of Radiology, Japan Soc. of Ultrasound in Medicine. Achievements include patents in field; origination of ultrasonic medical imaging instruments and diagnostic techniques; origination of the field of pulse-echo ultrasonic diagnostic medicine. Avocations: automobile restoration, antique collecting and restoration. Home and Office: Medico-Technol Rsch Inst 4262 Alabama Ave S Minneapolis MN 55416-3105

WILD, JOHN PAUL, radio astronomer; b. Sheffield, Eng., 1923; s. Bessie Arnold and Alwyn H. Wild; m. Elaine Poole Hull, 1948 (dec.); 3 children; m. Margaret Lyndon, 1991. Educated Whitgift Sch., Croydon, Eng. and Peterhouse, Cambridge. Researcher in radio astronomy, especially of the sun, Radiophysics Div. of Commonwealth Sci. and Indsl. Research Orgn., CSIRO, Australia, 1947-77, chief of div., 1971-77, chmn. CSIRO, chief exec., 1978-85; pres. Radio Astronomy Commn. of Internat. Astron. Union, 1967-70. Contbr. articles to profl. jours. Served as radar officer Royal Navy, 1943-47. Recipient Edgeworth David medal, 1968, Hendryk Arctowski Gold medal Nat. Acad. Sci., 1969, Balthasar van der Pol Gold medal Internat. Union Radio Sci., 1969, Herschel medal Royal Astron. Soc., 1974, Thomas Rankin Lyle medal Australian Acad. Sci., 1975, Hale prize for solar astronomy Am. Astron. Soc., 1980, Royal medal Royal Soc. London, 1980, Hartnett medal Royal Soc. Arts, 1988, Anzaas medal, 1984. Fellow Royal Soc., Australian Acad. Sci., Australian Acad. Tech. Sci. and Engring.; mem. Am. Philos. Soc. (fgn.), Am. Acad. Arts and Scis. (fgn. hon.), Royal Soc. Sci. Liege (corr.). Home: 4/1 Grant Crescent, Griffith ACT 2603, Australia also: 800 Avon Rd Ann Arbor MI 48104-2738

WILD, RAY, academic administrator; b. Hayfield, Derby, United Kingdom, Dec. 24, 1940; s. Frank and Alice Wild; m. Carol Ann Mellor, Sept. 25, 1965; children: Duncan Francis, Virginia Kate. MSc in Mgmt., Bradford (U.K.) U., 1966, PhD in Mgmt., 1970, MSc in Engring., 1972; DSc, Brunel U., London, 1988. C.Eng. Apprentice engr., designer, R&D engr. Crossley Bros. Ltd., Manchester, Eng., 1957-65; rsch. fellow, sr. rsch. fellow U. Bradford, U.K., 1967-72; prof., pro-vice chancellor Brunel U., London, 1977-89; prin. Henley (U.K.) Mgmt. Coll., 1990—; coll. gov. Tertiary Coll., Oxford. Author 14 text books and 4 children's books; contbr. articles to profl. jours. Named Whitworth fellow Dept. Edn., U.K., 1971. Fellow Royal Soc. Arts, Inst. Elec. Engrs., Inst. Mech. Engrs. Avocations: painting, writing, sport, theatre, music, travel. Office: Henley Mgmt Coll, Greenlands, Henley RG9 3AU, England

WILD, THOMAS FABIAN, virologist, researcher; b. Chester, Eng., Sept. 30, 1942; arrived in France; s. Ernest and Irene Patricia (Hardy) W.; m. Christine Rosemary Fisher, Oct. 30, 1965; children: Andrew, Sarah, Sophie. BSc in Biochemistry, U. Cardiff, Wales, 1964; PhD in Microbiology, U. Reading, Eng., 1968. Scientific sr. officer Animal Virus Rsch. Inst., Pirbright, Eng., 1964-74; postdoc. Med. Ctr., Denver, 1968-69; scientist Inst. Nat. de la Santé et de la Recherche Médicale, Lyon, France, 1974—; dir. rsch. IPL, Lyon, 1993-95; dir. Inst. Nat. Déla Santé et de la Rsch. Médicale, Lyon, 1994—. Contbr. over 100 articles to profl. jours. Mem. steering com. WHO, Geneva, 1992—. Recipient Hallonen medal Med. Sch. Turku, 1993. Mem. Soc. Gen. Microbiology. Office: INSERM u 404, Ave Tony-Garnier, 69365 Lyon France

WILD, WERNER, software company executive; b. Innsbruck, Tyrol, Austria, July 27, 1958; s. Peter and Annemarie (Liegerer) W. Matura, Adolf-Pichler-Platz, Innsbruck, Austria, 1977. Cert. computer cons. Cons. Joaneum Rsch. Ctr., Graz, Austria, 1981-84, UNESCO, Paris, 1984-85, Nat. Inst. Oceanography, Panjim, India, 1984-85, U. Innsbruck, Austria, 1985-91, Austrian C. of C., Vienna, 1991-95; pres., CEO Evolution R, Innsbruck, 1993-97; pres. UBS Zurich, Warburg-Dillon-Read, 1997—; cons. Krankenhaus Der Barmherzigen Brüder, Graz, 1989-93, Gesellschaft fur Info. & Documentation, Heidelberg, Germany, 1982-86. Mem. IEEE, C. of C., Ballroom Dancing Club (pres. 1983-88). Avocations: flying, hiking, travel. Home: Weiherburgg 41, A 6020 Innsbruck Tyrol, Austria Office: Evolution R, Jahnstr 26 2, A 6020 Innsbruck Tyrol, Austria

WILDE, ALAN CONRAD, mathematician; b. Balt., Mar. 30, 1946; s. Walter Samuel and Mary Katherine (Koehler) W. BS, U. Mich., 1970, MA in Math., 1973. Ind. study tchr. Extension Svc. U. Mich., 1972-87; pvt. practice Ann Arbor, Mich., 1992—. Contbr. articles to profl. jours. including Am. Math. Monthly, Jour. of Undergrad. Math., Notre Dame Jour. of Formal Logic, Procs. of the Am. Math. Soc. Co-chair com. Aid Disabled Students, U. Mich., 1972-73, chair disabled student svcs. program policy bd., 1973; mem. Homeless Action Com., Ann Arbor, 1990-97. Mem. AAAS, N.Y. Acad. Sci. Home: 601 Pearl Ypsilanti MI 48197-2616 Office: U Mich Dept Math Ann Arbor MI 48109

WILDE, JAMES DALE, archaeologist, educator; b. Las Vegas, N.Mex., May 9, 1950; s. Ralph M. and Joyce (Anderson) W.; m. Deborah Thompson, Oct. 6, 1973 (div. 1979); 1 child, Colin James Post; m. Deborah E. Newman, June 4, 1983; children: Matthew Catlow, Russell James. BA, U. N.Mex., 1972; MA, U. Oreg., 1978, PhD, 1985. Registered profl. archaeologist. Archaeologist Deerlodge Nat. Forest, U.S. Forest Svc., Butte, Mont., 1977, Earth Tech. Corp., Seattle, 1981-82, Geo-Recon Internat., Ltd., Seattle, 1982-84; asst. dir. office pub. archaeology Brigham Young U., Provo, Utah, 1984-88, dir., 1988-95, adj. prof. dept. anthropology, 1985-95; archaeologist Hdqrs. USAF Ctr. for Environ. Excellence, San Antonio, 1995—; mem. com. on archaeology Brigham Young U., 1986-90, mem. mus. adv. com., 1990-95; mem. subcom. on antiquities legis. Utah Legislature, Salt Lake City, 1988-90. Author: Utah Avocational Archaeologist Certification Program: Teaching Guide (vols. I-III), 1988, Utah Avocational Archaeologist Certification Program: Student Handbook (vols. I-III), 1988, Baker Village Nevada: Report of Investigations, 1990-94, 1999; co-author: Archaeological Surveys and Limited Excavations, Clear Creek Canyon, 1998, Excavations at Icicle Bench, Radford Roost and Lott's Farm, 1999; contbr. articles to profl. publs., encys. and books. Mem. vestry St. Mary's Episc. Ch., Provo, 1992-95. Mem. Am. Anthropol. Assn., Soc. Am. Archaeology, Utah Profl. Archaeol. Coun. (treas. 1986-88, pres. 1988-90), Sigma Xi. Democrat. Avocations: reading, golf, tennis, fishing, hiking. Home: 7923 Moon Walk San Antonio TX 78250-6605 Office: HQ AFCEE/ECC 3207 North Rd Brooks AFB TX 78235-5363

WILDE, PATRICIA, retired artistic director; b. Ottawa, Ont., Can., July 16, 1928; m. George Bardyguine; children: Anya, Youri. Dancer Am. Concert Ballet, Marquis de Cuevas Ballet Internat., N.Y.C., 1944-45, Ballet Russe de Monte Carlo, N.Y.C., 1945-49, Roland Petit's Ballet Paris, Met. Ballet Britain, London, 1949-50; prin. ballerina N.Y.C. Ballet, 1950-65; dir. Harkness Sch. Ballet, N.Y.C., 1965-67; ballet mistress, tchr. Am. Ballet Theatre, N.Y.C., 1969-77; dir. Am. Ballet Theatre Sch., N.Y.C., 1977-82; artistic dir. Pitts. Ballet Theatre, 1982-97, artistic adviser, master tchr., 1997—; tchr. Am. Ballet Theatre, 1969-77, Joffrey scholarship program, N.Y.C. Ballet, 1968-69; established Sch. of Grand Theatre of Geneva, 1968-69; adjudicator Regional Ballet in Am. S.E. and S.W., 1969-82; choreographer N.Y. Philharmonic; guest tchr. various ballet cos. and colls.; trustee Dance U.S.A.; panelist Nat. Choreographic Project. Recipient Leadership award in Arts and Letters YWCA, 1990, Pitts. Woman of Yr. in Arts award, 1993, Cultural award for outstanding contbns. to cultural climate of region Pitts. Ctr. for Arts, 1997, History Makers award in arts and letters Sen. John Heinz History Ctr. and the Hist. Soc. Western Pa., 1999. Office: Pitts Ballet Theatre 2900 Liberty Ave Pittsburgh PA 15201-1511

WILDE, PATRICK JOSEPH, administrator; b. Decatur, Tex., July 21, 1959; s. Joseph Leroy and Alice Jean (Pennartz) W.; m. Donna Sue Stephenson, Mar. 28, 1981; children: Michael Patrick, Nicholas Everad, Gregory Allen, Johnathan Paul. BS in Physics, U. North Tex., 1983. Physics lab. trainer North Tex. State U., Denton, 1977-82; rsch. tech. InkJet Tech. (Xerox Corp.), Dallas, 1979-82; process engr. Tex. Instruments, Dallas, 1984-88, product mgr., 1989—. Patentee in field. Dir. religious edn. Wise & Jack County Cath. Chs., Decatur, Tex., 1984—. Republican. Roman Catholic. Avocations: hiking, welding, fishing, computers. Home:

1600 N Business 81/287 Decatur TX 76234 Office: Raytheon TI Systems 13510 N Central Expy Dallas TX 75243-1108

WILDE, SIMON ALEXANDER, geologist, educator; b. Telford, Eng., Aug. 10, 1945; arrived in Australia, 1972; s. Clarence William and Joan Mary (Jeffrey) W.; m. Irene Patricia Hill, Jan. 6, 1968 (div. 1980); children: Helen Louise, Caroline Maria; m. Antoinette Kanaris, Dec. 10, 1983. BS with honors, Exeter (Devon, Eng.) U., 1967, PhD in Geology, 1971. Geologist level 1 Geol. Survey, Perth, Australia, 1972-76; geologist level 2 Geol. Survey, Perth, 1976-81; lectr. Curtin U., Perth, 1981-88, sr. lectr., 1988-91, head of sch., 1991-97, assoc. prof., 1993-99, prof., 99—; discoverer largest goldmine in Australia, Boddington, 1976; co-discoverer world's oldest crystals, Jack Hills, Australia, 1986. Contbr. papers to profl. publs.; singer, songwriter: (album) Wilde Thoughts/Wilde Dreams, 1985, On the Edge, 1990. Mem. Geol. Soc. Australia (chmn. West Australia br. 1989-91). Avocations: tennis, music. Office: Curtin U Tech, Kent St, Perth 6102, Australia

WILDE, WILLIAM RICHARD, lawyer; b. Markesan, Wis., Mar. 1, 1953; s. Leslie Maurice and Elaine Margaret (Schweder) W.; m. Carolyn Margaret Zieman, July 17, 1981 (div. 1987); 1 child, Leah Marie; m. Barbara Joan Rohlf, Jan. 6, 1990. BA, U. Wis., Milw., 1975; JD, Marquette U., 1980. Bar: Wis. 1980, U.S. Dist. Ct. (ea. and we. dists.) Wis. 1980. Dist. atty. Green Lake County, Green Lake, Wis., 1980-83, corp.counsel, 1981; ptnr. Curtis, Wilde and Neal, Oshkosh, Wis., 1983-97, Wilde Law Offices, Oshkosh, 1997—. Mem. Assn. Trial Lawyers Am., Wis. Bar Assn., Wis. Acad. Trial Lawyers (Amicus Curiae Brief com. 1987-92, bd. dirs., assoc. editor The Verdict, treas. 1993, sec. 1994, v.p. 1995, pres.-elect 1996, pres. 1997), Wis. Assn. Criminal Def. Lawyers (bd. dirs. 1987-91), Winnebbago County Bar Assn., Green Lake County Bar Assn. Office: Wilde Law Offices 1901 S Washburn PO Box 3422 Oshkosh WI 54903-3422 also: PO Box 282 Markesan WI 53946-0282

WILDENTHAL, C(LAUD) KERN, physician, educator; b. San Marcos, Tex., July 1, 1941; s. Bryan and Doris (Kellam) W.; m. Margaret Dehlinger, Oct. 15, 1964; children—Pamela, Catharine. B.A., Sul Ross Coll., 1960; M.D., U. Tex. Southwestern Med. Ctr., Dallas, 1964; Ph.D., U. Cambridge, Eng., 1970. Intern Bellevue Hosp., N.Y.C., 1964-65; resident in medicine, fellow cardiology Parkland Hosp., Dallas, 1965-67; research fellow Nat. Heart Inst., Bethesda, Md., 1967-68; vis. research fellow Strangeways Research Lab., Cambridge, 1968-70; asst. prof. to prof. internal medicine and physiology U. Tex. Southwestern Med. Ctr., Dallas, 1970-76, prof., dean grad. sch., 1976-80, prof., dean Southwestern Med. Sch., 1980-86, prof., pres., 1986—; hon. fellow Hughes Hall, U. Cambridge, 1994—. Author: Regulation of Cardiac Metabolism, 1976, Degradative Processes in Heart and Skeletal Muscle, 1980; contbr. articles to profl. jours. Bd. dirs. Dallas Symphony, Dallas Opera, Dallas Mus. Art, S.W. Mus. Sci. and Tech., Dallas Citizen's Coun., Am. Friends Cambridge U., Hoblitzelle Found., Southwestern Med. Found. Recipient rsch. career devel. award NIH, 1972; spl. rsch. fellow USPHS, 1968-70; Guggenheim fellow, 1975-76. Mem. AMA, Inst. Medicine/NAS, Am. Soc. Clin. Investigation, Am. Coll. Cardiology, Royal Soc. Medicine Gt. Britain, Am. Physiol. Soc., Internat. Soc. Heart Rsch. (past pres. Am. sect.), Am. Fedn. Clin. Rsch., Assn. Am. Med Colls., Assn. Am. Physicians, Am. Heart Assn. (past chmn. sci. policy com.), Assn. Acad. Health Ctrs. (past chmn. sci. policy com.), British N.Am. Com. Home: 4001 Hanover Ave Dallas TX 75225-7010 Office: U Tex Southwestern Med Ctr 5323 Harry Hines Blvd Dallas TX 75390-7208

WILDER, AMOS TAPPAN, literary executor; b. Boston, Feb. 6, 1940; s. Amos Niven and Catharine (Kerlin) W.; m. Robin Gibbs, June 15, 1968; 1 child, Jenney Gibbs Wilder. BA, Yale U., 1962, M in Philosophy, 1976; MA, U. Wis., 1967. Adminstr. Yale U., New Haven, 1968-79; sr. assoc. Ptnr. for Livable Pls., Washington, 1979-81; freelance cons. Washington, 1982-84; dir. corp. planning and comms. Capital Care, Inc., Vienna, Va., 1984-90; cons. Chevy Chase, Md., 1991—; sr. rsch. fellow and ptnr. Livable Comtys., Washington, 1994—; mng. mem. Wilder Family LLC. Bd. dirs. Long Wharf Theater, New Haven, 1970-79, hon trustee, 1995—; bd. dirs. Student Conservation Assn., Charlestown, N.H., 1980-88, 97—. Rockefeller Bros. Found. fellow, 1962-63. Mem. Yale Club of N.Y.C., Elizabethan Club, Cosmos Club, Washington), Delta Psi. Home: 5535 Warwick Pl Chevy Chase MD 20815-5505

WILDER, ROBERT ALLEN, finance and leasing company executive, leasing broker, investment consultant; b. Memphis, Feb. 13, 1944; s. Donald Byrd and Marion S. (Brown) W.; m. Betty Michael, Apr. 23, 1977; 1 child, Elizabeth Michael. BS, Memphis State U. Sch. Engring., 1967, MS, 1973. Regional sales mgr. Hertz Corp. Truck div., Atlanta, 1974-77; regional dir. Itel Corp., Atlanta, 1978, 79, 90, 91, 92; pres. Interstate Systems, Inc., Atlanta, 1979-81; dir. corp. lease programs, 1981-83, dir PBX sales, 1983-87, dir., gen. mgr. distbr. sales, 1988-90, No. Telecom Fin. Corp., Atlanta and Nashville, 1981-90; cons.; sr. v.p. First Tenn. Equipment Fin. Corp., Nashville, 1990-91; investment cons. Am. Wealth Mgmt., Inc., Atlanta, 1992—. With U.S. Army, 1967-72. Mem. Am. Assn. Equipment Lessors (speaker 1988 conf.), Memphis State U. Alumni. Ga. (pres. 1986-88). Methodist. Home: 955 River Overlook Ct NW Atlanta GA 30328-3501 Office: 3525 Piedmont Rd NE Bldg 7 Atlanta GA 30305

WILDER, ROBERT DAVID, publishing executive; b. New Brunswick, N.J., June 4, 1948; s. Louis K. Wilder and Shirley (Schwartz) Pratt; m. Dorothy Corenna Slivocka, June 29, 1969; children: Paul Louis, Lauren Beth. BA in Econs., Rutgers U., 1970; MBA in Acctg., Fordham U., 1977. Cert. Internal Auditor. Sect. chief AT&T Lucent Techs., Kearny, N.J., 1970-74; sr. audit supr. Joseph E. Seagram & Sons, N.Y.C., 1974-77, mgmt. cons., 1977-79; audit dir. John Wiley & Sons, N.Y.C., 1979-85, gen. mgr., fin. adminstr., 1985-87, CFO, 1987-88, v.p. pub. fin. adminstr., 1987-90, sr. v.p., CFO, 1990-96, exec. v.p., CFO, COO, 1996—. With U.S. Army Reserves, 1970. Mem. Inst. Internal Auditors. Avocations: global travel, classic automobiles, photography. Home: 10 Cobblestone Ct Howell NJ 07731-1604 Office: John Wiley & Sons 605 3rd Ave Fl 6 New York NY 10158-0012

WILDER, ROLAND PERCIVAL, JR., lawyer; b. Malden, Mass., June 21, 1940; s. Roland Percival and Clarissa (Hunting) W.; m. Susan McAra Randell, Sept. 3, 1965; children: Roland Percival III, William Randell. BA, Washington and Jefferson Coll., 1963; JD, Vanderbilt U., 1966. Bar: D.C. 1967, U.S. Dist. Ct. D.C. 1967, U.S. Ct. Appeals (D.C. cir.) 1967, U.S. Supreme Ct. 1972, U.S. Ct. Appeals (4th, 5th and 6th cirs.) 1976, U.S. Ct. Appeals (8th and 9th cirs.) 1977, U.S. Ct. Appeals (2d cir.) 1978, U.S. Ct. Appeals (11th cir.) 1981, U.S. Dist. Ct. Md. 1994, U.S. Ct. Appeals (3d cir.) 1997, U.S. Dist. Ct. Colo. 1997, U.S. Dist. Ct. (ea. dist.) Mich. 1999. Atty. Office of Solicitor U.S. Dept. Labor, Washington, 1967-69; asst. counsel civil rights office of solicitor U.S. Dept. Labor, Washington, 1969-70, counsel civil rights office of solicitor, 1970-71; supr. atty. office gen. counsel NLRB, Washington, 1972-74; assoc. gen. counsel Internat. Brotherhood Teamsters, Washington, 1974-85; sr. mem. Baptiste & Wilder P.C., Washington, 1985—; lectr. numerous continuing legal edn. programs various states, 1970—. Mng. editor Vanderbilt U. Law Rev., 1965-66; contbr. articles to profl. jours. V.p. Arlington (Va.) Cubs Youth Club, Inc., 1975-81; coach Fairfax (Va.) Hockey Club, 1979-83. Mem. ABA, D.C. Bar Assn., Assn. Trial Lawyers Am., Phi Delta Phi, Pi Sigma Alpha, Phi Alpha Theta, Roosevelt Soc., Joint Council Flight Attendant Unions (hon. flight attendant 1985). Democrat. Avocations: history, tennis, skiing. Office: Baptiste & Wilder PC 1150 Connecticut Ave NW Ste 500 Washington DC 20036-4194

WILDER, VALERIE, ballet company administrator; b. Pasadena, Calif., Aug. 5, 1947; d. Douglas Wilder and Helen Marie (Wilson) Morrill; m. Geoffrey Duer Perry, Nov. 24, 1973; children: Stuart Whittier, Sabina Woodman. Student, Butler U., Indpls., 1966-68, U. Toronto, 1969-75. Dancer Nat. Ballet Can., Toronto, 1970-78; ptnr. Perry & Wilder Inc., Toronto, 1976-83; artistic adminstr. Nat. Ballet Can., Toronto, 1983-86, assoc. artistic dir., 1986-87, co-artistic dir., 1987-89, assoc. dir., 1989-96, exec. dir., 1996—; mem. adv. bd. Dancer Transition Ctr., Toronto, 1986—; mem. dance adv. com. Can. Coun., 1984-89, 97—, Ont. Arts. Coun., 1985-90; bd. dirs. Dance U.S.A. Bd. dirs. Toronto Arts Coun., 1990-94, Dance U.S.A., 1997—. Mem. Dance in Can. Assn., Can. Assn. Profl. Dance Orgns. Avocations: competitive running, triathlon. Office: Nat Ballet of Can, 470 Queens Quay West, Toronto, ON Canada M5V 3K4

WILDERER, PETER ADOLF, engineering educator; b. Karlsruhe, Baden, Germany, Mar. 8, 1939; s. Kuno and Emma Maria (Schmidt) W.; m. Jaroslava Janeckova, Aug. 29, 1970; children: Martin, Michael, Mirka. Diploma engring., U. Karlsruhe, Germany, 1965, D in Engring., 1969, D in Engring. Habilitation, 1976; D (honoris causa), Prague Inst. Chem. Tech., 1997. Prof. C2 U. Karlsruhe, Germany, 1980-81; prof. C3 Tech. U. Hamburg-Harburg, Germany, 1982-90; prof. C4 Tech. U. Munich, Germany, 1991—; v.p. Tech. U. Hamburg-Harburg, Germany, 1989-90; dir. Testing Lab. for Water Quality Control, Munich, 1991—, Bavarian Ctr. for Waste Minimization Rsch., Munich, 1992—. Regional editor Jour. Water Rsch., 1992—; editor Berichte aus Wassergute und Abfallwirtschaft, 1991—. Mem. Internat. Assn. on Water Quality (sci. and tech. com. 1989-93), Abwassertechnische Vereinigung, Deutsche Gesellschaft fuer Chemie-und Anlagentechnik, Bavarian Chamber Engring., European Acad. Sci. and Art. Lutheran. Office: TU Muenchen, Wasserguetewirtschaft, D-85748 Garching Germany

WILDERMUTH, KARL, physicist, educator; b. Stuttgart, Württemberg, Germany, July 25, 1921; s. Karl and Gertrud (Hole) W.; m. Erika Stahnke, May 30, 1947; children: Annette Wildermuth-Helmer, Stephan, Eberhard. PhD, GÖttingen U., 1949; habilitation, Munich, 1954; D (hon.), Graz U., Austria, 1989. Asst. M.P.I. of Physics, GÖttingen, 1949-53; asst. prof. U. Munich, 1953-56; researcher Kopenhagen and Genf, Cern, 1956-59; prof. Fla. State U., Tallahassee, 1959-64, Tübingen U., 1964—. Co-author (with McClure): Cluster Representations of Nuclei, 1966, (with Tang) A Unified Theory of the Nucleus, 1977. Home: Wolfgant-Stock-Str 27, 7400 Tübingen Württemberg Germany Office: Dept Theory Physics, Morgenstelle 14, 7400 Tübingen Bad-Württemburg Germany

WILDING, DIANE, marketing, financial and information systems executive; b. Chicago Heights, Ill., Nov. 7, 1942; d. Michael Edward and Katherine Surian; m. Manfred Georg Wilding, May 7, 1975 (div. 1980). BSBA in Acctg. magna cum laude, No. Ill. U., 1963; postgrad., U. Chgo., 1972-74; cert. in German lang., Goethe Inst., Rothenburg, Germany, 1984; cert. in internat. bus. German, Goethe Inst., Atlanta, 1994; cert. in Web page design, Kennesaw State U., 2000. Lic. cosmetologist. Systems engr. IBM, Chgo., 1963-68; data processing mgr. Am. Res. Corp., Chgo., 1969-72; system R & D project mgr. Continental Bank, Chgo., 1972-75; fin. industry mktg. rep. IBM Can., Ltd., Toronto, Ont., 1976-79; regional telecom. mktg. exec. Control Data Corp., Atlanta, 1980-84; gen. mgr. The Plant Plant, Atlanta, 1985-92; SAP cons. IBM, Atlanta, 1993—; pioneer installer on-line Automatic Teller Machines, Pos Equipment. Author: The Canadian Payment System: An International Perspective, 1977. Mem. Chgo. Coun. on Fgn. Rels.; bd. dirs. Easter House Adoption Agy., Chgo., 1974-76. Mem. Internat. Brass Soc., Goethe Inst., Mensa. Clubs: Ponte Verde (Fla.); Royal Ont. Yacht, Libertyville Racquet. Avocations: horticulture, travel, dancing, gourmet cooking, foreign languages. E-mail: wilding@usa.com. Home: PO Box 723055 Atlanta GA 31139-0055 Office: IBM 1600 Riveredge Pkwy NW Atlanta GA 30328-4697

WILDING, MICHAEL, writer, English and Australian literature educator; b. Worcester, Eng., 1942; s. Richard and Dorothy (Bull) W.; m. Lyndy Helen Abraham, 1986; 1 child, Sunny. BA, Oxford (Eng.) U., 1963, MA, 1968; DLitt, U. Sydney, 1996. Lectr. English, U. Sydney, 1963-66; lectr. English U. Birmingham (England), 1967-68; sr. lectr. English U. Sydney, 1969-72, reader English, 1973-92, prof. English and Australian literature, 1993—; vis. prof. U. Calif., Santa Barbara, 1987. Author: (non-fiction) Milton's Paradise Lost, 1969, Marcus Clarke, 1977, Political Fictions, 1980, Dragons Teeth: Literature in the English Revolution, 1987, The Radical Tradition, 1993, Social Visions, 1993, Studies in Classic Australian Fiction, 1997, (with Michael Green) Cultural Policy in Great Britain, 1970, (fiction) Aspects of the Dying Process, 1972, Living Together, 1974, The West Midland Underground, 1975, The Short Story Embassy, 1975, Scenic Drive, 1976, The Phallic Forest, 1978, Pacific Highway, 1982, Reading the Signs, 1984, The Paraguayan Experiment, 1985, The Man of Slow Feeling, 1986, Under Saturn, 1988, Great Climate, 1990, Her Most Bizarre Sexual Experience, 1991, This is for You, 1994, Book of the Reading, 1994, Somewhere New, 1996, Wildest Dreams, 1998, Raising Spirits, Making Gold and Swapping Wives-The True Adventures of Dr. John Dee and Sir Edward Kelly, 1999; editor: Three Tales (Henry James), 1967, Australians Abroad, 1967, Marvell: Modern Judgements, 1970, Julius Caesar and Marcus Brutus, 1970, We Took Their Order and Are Dead, 1971, Marcus Clarke, 1976, 2d edit., 1988, The Radical Reader, 1977, The Tabloid Story Pocket Book, 1978, The Workingman's Paradise, 1980, Stories by Marcus Clarke, 1983, Air Mail From Down Under, 1990, The Oxford Book of Australian Short Stories, 1994. Mem. Lit. Bd. Australia Coun., Sydney, 1974-76; chmn. NSW Lit. Awards Panel, Sydney, 1994; chair NSW Writers' Ctr., Sydney, 1997. Sr. fellow lit. bd. Australian Coun., 1978. Fellow Australian Acad. Humanities. Office: U Sydney, Dept English, Sydney 2006, Australia

WILDNAUER, RICHARD HARRY, pharmaceutical company executive; b. New Kensington, Pa., Feb. 14, 1940; s. Richard Michael and Rosemary Elizabeth (Moore) W.; BS in Chemistry, St. Vincent Coll., 1962; PhD in Biochemistry, W.Va. U., 1966; postgrad. (NSF fellow) U. Kans., 1967; MBA in Mgmt., Rider Coll., 1974; m. Sharon Ann Novick, Jan. 22, 1966; 1 dau., Tara Lynne. NIH trainee W.Va. U., 1963-66; sr. rsch. assoc. in skin biology, exploratory rsch. divsn. Johnson and Johnson Domestic Operating Co., New Brunswick, N.J., 1975, assoc. mgr. tech. planning, exploratory rsch. divsn., 1975-77; sr. project coord., new products, pharm. divsn. McNeil Labs., Ft. Washington, Pa., 1977-79; dir. new product devel. Janssen Pharmaceutica Inc., New Brunswick, N.J., 1979-82, v.p. research and devel., 1982-88; v.p. tech. and bus. devel., Johnson & Johnson Corp., New Brunswick, N.J., 1988-92; pres. Baker Cummins Dermatologicals, Inc., Lakewood, N.J., 1992-95; pres., CEO NeoStrata Co., Inc., Princeton, N.J., 1995—. Trustee, bd. dirs. United Way Cen. N.J., 1988-95, pres. 1991-93. Mem. N.Y. Acad. Scis., Soc. Investigative Dermatology, Am. Mgmt. Assn., Med. Mycology Soc., Am. Acad. Dermatology, Pharm. Advt. Club, Soc. Cos. Chemists, Sigma Xi. Roman Catholic. Contbr. articles to profl. jours. Office: NeoStrata Co Inc 4 Research Way Princeton NJ 08540-6618

WILDT, LUDWIG, gynecologist, endocrinologist; b. Zweibrücken, Germany, Mar. 20, 1949. MD, U. Bonn, Germany, 1977. Asst. U. Bonn, 1977, resident, 1980-84, sr. physician, 1984-86; postdoc. fellow U. Pitts., 1977-80; head divsn. U. Erlange, Germany, 1987—. With German Mil., 1975-77. Recipient Thesis award Faculty of Medicine, U. Bonn, 1977, Schöller-Junkmann awrd German Soc. Endocrinology, 1983, award Menopausengesellschaft Deutschsprachiger Lander, 1994. Office: U Frauenklinik, Universitatsstr 21-23, 91054 Erlangen Germany

WILENIUS, REIJO VALFRID, philosophy educator; b. Helsinki, Finland, Apr. 22, 1930; s. Väinö Valfrid and Evi Maria (Höijer) W.; m. Aijami Ritva Ant-Wuorinen, June 5, 1953; children: Helena, Jaakko, Markku, Henrik. MA, U. Helsinki, 1952, Lic. Polit. Scis., 1957, PhD, 1963. Chief editor Cultural Rev. Katsaus, 1957-68; lectr. philosophy U. Helsinki, 1966-72; prof. philosophy U. Jyväskylä, 1973—; ctrl. bd. Acad. Finland, 1975-80; pres. Rsch. Coun. for Humanities, 1975-80, Autroposophical Soc. Finland, 1966-96, European Forum for Freedom in Edn., 1997—; chmn. bd. Cultural Found. Ahtola, 1980—. Author: The Social and Political Theory of Fr. Suarez, 1963. Mem., chmn. several state coms., 1967—. Recipient State prize for the publ. of New Knowledge, Ministry of Edn., 1977, Medaille of the Order White Rose Finland, Pres. of the Republic, 1989. Mem. Philos. Soc. Finland. Lutheran. Avocations: skiing, gardening, literature. Home: Mäntypaadentie 7, Mäntypaadentie 7, 00830 Helsinki Finland

WILENSKY, ROBERT J., plastic surgeon, historian; b. N.Y.C., Oct. 2, 1941; s. Thomas and Gertrude Wilensky; m. Gail R. Roggin Aug. 4, 1963; children: Peter, Sara. BA, U. Mich., 1962, MD, 1966; PhD in History, Am. U., 2000. Diplomate Am. Bd. Surgery, Am. Bd. Plastic Surgery. Resident in gen. surgery U. Md., Balt., 1969-73; resident in plastic surgery U. Mich., Ann Arbor, 1973-75; pvt. practice, Washington, 1975-99; historian Am. U., Washington, 2000—; chmn. sect. plastic surgery Columbia Hosp. for Women, Washington, 1983-93. Contbr. articles to med. jours., including Am. Jour. Ob-Gyn., Jour. Plastic and Reconstructive Surgery, Clin. Procs. Children's Hosp.; also chpts. to books. Capt. M.C., U.S. Army, 1967-69, Vietnam. Decorated Bronze Star. Fellow ACS; mem. Am. Soc. Plastic Surgery, Am. Soc. Aesthetic Surgery, Nat. Capital Soc. Plastic Surgery (pres. 1992). Jewish. Avocations: biking, skiing, photography. E-mail: robertjwilensky@erols.com. Home and Office: 2807 Battery Pl NW Washington DC 20016-3439

WILEY, DAVID COLE, producer; b. Long Beach, Calif., Sept. 12, 1948; s. Norman Cole and Bettigene Rosamond W. Ind. prodr., 1987—. Prodr. Abduction - the UFO Soap, 1987, Speak-Out, 1988-89, Coal Canyon BMX, 1989, PC 101 - Computer Repair, 1989, Young Lives, 1990, A Slice of Life, 1990, 91, Hidden Talents, 1992, Rock Talk, 1992—, History of the Santa Ana Canyon, 1994—, Buena Park Journal, 1994—; (documentaries) In Search of the Butterfield Trail, 1990, George Key Ranch - Centennial Celebration, 1993, Visitors from Catalan, 1996, History of the Santa Ana River, 1997, The Steam Kalliope, 1998, Plan 10 from Outer Space, 1998. Recipient Western Access Video Excellence award Nat. Fedn. Local Cable Programmers, 1992, CABY Comcast Cablevision, 1996. Mem. Santa Ana Canyon Hist. Coun. (v.p., 1995—), Alliance Cmty. Media. Address: PO Box 6481 Fullerton CA 92834-6481

WILEY, DIANNE ELIZABETH, chemical engineering educator, researcher; b. Ceduna, Australia, May 30, 1957; d. Vincent C. and Roma M. (Nuske) Klingberg; m. Colin J. Wiley, Apr. 23, 1984; children: Timothy, Rebecca. B of Applied Sci. in Chemistry, Darling Downs Inst. Adv. Edn., Australia, 1978; diploma in edn., Armidale Coll. Advanced Edn., Australia, 1980; PhD, U. New South Wales, Australia, 1991. Tchr. primary sch. Adelaide, Australia, 1980; tchr. St. Paul's Coll., Walla Walla, Australia, 1980-81; tutor Sch. Chem. Engring. and Indsl. Chemistry-U. New South Wales, Sydney, 1986-90, lectr., 1990-95, sr. lectr., 1996—; assoc. dean Fac. Engrg., Univ. New South Wales, 2000—. Mem. bd. mgmt. Kanga's House Child Care Ctr., Kensington, New South Wales, Australia, 1990-96. Mem. Instn. Chem. Engrs. (com. mem. Sydney divsn. 1995-96), Royal Australian Chem. Inst. Lutheran. Office: U NSW, Sch Chem Engring Indsl Chem, Sydney NSW 2052, Australia

WILEY, WILLIAM T., artist; b. Beford, Ind., Oct. 21, 1937. BFA, San Francisco Art Inst., 1961, MFA, 1962. asoc. prof. U. Calif., Davis, 1962-73; instr. San Francisco Art Inst., 1963, 66-67, U. Nev., Reno, 1967, Wash. State Coll., Pullman, 1967, U. Calif., Berkeley, 1967, Sch. Visual Art, N.Y.C., 1968, U. Colo., Boulder, 1968.

WILFLING, BERND, economist, researcher; b. Bad Salzuflen, Germany, Mar. 26, 1965; s. Franz Joseph and Helga (Heinrich) W.; m. Corinna Mantaj, May 12, 1995. Diploma in stats., U. Dortmund, Germany, 1990, PhD in Natural Scis., 1993. Ind. sys. analyst Waltrop, Germany, 1990-94; sci. asst. U. Hamburg, Germany, 1994—; ind. sci. cons., Dortmund, 1990-94. Contbr. articles to profl. jours. Mem. Soc. for Social Politics. Avocations: bicycling, squash, literature, travel. Home: Max Brauer Allee 184C, 22765 Hamburg Germany Office: U Hamburg, Von Melle Park 5, Inst Aussenhdl u Wirtschft, 20146 Hamburg Germany

WILHELM, CHRISTIAN, biologist; b. Speyer, Pfalz, Germany, May 5, 1953; s. Hans and Gretel (Eifler) W.; married, Mar. 12, 1986; children: Frauziska, Johannes. Diploma, U. Mainz, 1980, PhD, 1983, habil., 1989. Asst. U. Mainz, 1983-89, lectr., 1990-94; prof. U. Leipzig, 1994—. Editor in chief Jour. Plant Physiology. Office: U Leipzig, Johannisallee 21, 04103 Leipzig Germany

WILHELM, EMMERICH, physical chemist, educator; b. Vienna, Nov. 25, 1941; s. Emmerich and Rosa Wilhelm; m. Olga Wilhelm, Sept. 28, 1968; 1 child, Katja Dagmar. PhD, U. Vienna, 1969, Habilitation, 1979. Sr. Fulbright rsch. assoc. Wright State U., Dayton, Ohio, 1969-71, assoc. prof., 1979-80; asst. prof. U. Vienna, 1971-78, assoc. prof., 1980—, head Inst. Phys. Chemistry, 2000—; v.p. Eurostar, Freiburg, Germany, 1992-95. Editor spl. issues Fluid Phase Equilibria Vols. 48 and 49, 1989, Thermochimica Acta Vol. 259, No. 1, 1995; mem. editl. bd. Fluid Phase Equilibria, Amsterdam, 1977-95, Internat. Data Series, Tex., 1990-93, Thermochimica Acta, Amsterdam, 1993—, ELDATA: The Internat. Electronic Jour. Physico-Chemical Data, 1995—; contbr. more than 150 articles to profl. jours. Recipient Felix-Kuschenitz award Austrian Acad. Scis., 1991. Mem. Chemisch-Physikalische Gesellschaft (sec. 1971-75), Gesellschaft Österreichischer Chemiker, Deutsche Bunsengesellschaft, N.Y. Acad. Scis., Sigma Xi. Roman Catholic. Avocation: philately. Office: U Vienna Inst Phys Chemistry, Währingerstrasse 42, Vienna A-1090, Austria

WILHELM, HANS RUDOLF, medical historian, researcher; b. Thusis, Switzerland, Dec. 21, 1952; s. Leonhard and Hedwig (Klotz) W. Contbr. articles to profl. jours. Home: Winkelriedstrasse 25, CH-8006 Zürich Switzerland

WILHELM, JANE T., physical therapist; b. El Paso, Tex., Mar. 26, 1958; d. Olin Edward Thayer and Frances Edwinell Bragdon; m. James Lee Wilhelm, Dec. 15, 1984; children: Nicholas Ernest, Zachary James. BS in Phys. Therapy, U. Tex., San Antonio, 1984. Phys. therapist Tex. Heart Inst.-Tex. Children's Hosp., Houston, 1984-85; pvt. practice Canyon Lake area, Tex., 1991-94; phys. therapist TheraTx, San Antonio, 1994-96; phys. therapist Easter Seal Rehab. Ctr., San Antonio, 1985-87, 94—, founder, prodr. Therapeutic Ice Skating program, 1997—. Tchr. CCD class St. Thomas Ch., Canyon Lake, Tex., 1997—. Fellow Am. Acad. Cerebral Palsy and Devel. Medicine; mem. Am. Phys. Therapy Assn., San Antonio Figure Skating Club. Roman Catholic. Avocations: figure skating, music, skiing, tennis, swimming. E-mail: jjnz@gvtc.com. Home: 1962 Colleen Dr Canyon Lake TX 78133-5318 Office: Easter Seal Rehab Ctr 2203 Babcock Rd San Antonio TX 78229-4412

WILHELM, JOHANNES PAUL, physics educator; b. Gadderbaum, Germany, July 30, 1926; s. Rudolf Karl and Frieda Ida (Biedermann) W.; m. Waltraud Helga Arndt, oct. 29, 1954 (dec. 1977); m. Sigrid Christa Pitschner, Dec. 23, 1980. BSc in Math., E.M. Arndt U., Greifswald, Germany, 1950, PhD in Physics, 1952; habilitation in physics, Humboldt U., Berlin, 1960. Vice dir. Inst. for Physics, Acad. Scis. at Berlin, Greifswald, 1963-69; dir. Inst. Theoretical Physics, E.M. Arndt-Univ., Greifswald, 1966-68; rsch. dir. for plasma physics Cen. Inst. for Electron-Physics, Acad. Scis., Berlin, 1969-78, dept. dir., 1978-88; head of theoretical physics dept. Cen. Inst. for Electron-Physics, Acad. Scis., Greifswald, 1989-91; lectr., docent E.M. Arndt U., Greifswald, 1954-61, prof., 1962—; prof. Acad. Scis. Berlin, 1983—. Editor-in-chief Contbns. to Plasma Physics Jour., 1980-93, science editor; contbr. over 220 articles to profl. jours. With German Air Force, 1943-44. Recipient Rsch. prize of 1st rank E.M. Arndt U., 1983, Max von Laue-medal, Acad. Scis. Berlin, 1986. Mem. Acad. Scis. Berlin (corres. mem., 1980). Avocations: music, literature. Home: Peter-Warschow-Str 38, D-17489 Greifswald Germany Office: Inst Low-Temp Plasma Physics, Friedrich-Ludwig-Jahn Str19, D-17489 Greifswald Germany

WILHELM, KLAUS F.H.K., physicist, space researcher; b. Hannover, Germany, Feb. 12, 1937; s. Friedrich and Helene (Krull) W.; m. Ingrid Nietsch, Aug. 19, 1959; children: Harald, Horst, Ricarda. Diploma in physics, U. Göttingen, Germany, 1962, PhD, 1966. Rsch. scientist Max Planck Inst. for Aeronomy, Katlenburg-Lindau, Germany, 1962-69; sr. scientist European Space Rsch. Orgn., Paris-Neuilly, 1970-72, Max Planck Inst. for Aeronomy, Katlenburg-Lindau, 1973—; mem. ad hoc group extraterrestrial rsch. German Ministry for Rsch. and Tech., 1973-74; mem. solar sys. working group European Space Agy., Paris, 1974-77; mem. atmosphere, magnetosphere, and plasmas-in-space sci. working group NASA, Washington, 1974-78; cons. GEOS, ISEE, ROSAT, ROCSAT, other spacecraft, 1973—; chmn. adv. group extraterrestrial rsch. Deutsche Forschungsanstalt für Luft-und Raumfahrt, Cologne, Germany, 1987-91; project scientist for auroral physics sounding rocket programs Deutsche Agentur für Raumfahrtangelegenheiten, 1977-83; prin. investigator electron spectrometer and fluxgate magnetometer experiments Spacelab I, 1983; co-investigator Halley Multicolor Camera, Giotto to Comet Halley, 1986; prin. investigator Solar Ultraviolet Measurements of Emitted Radiation Spectrograph on Solar and Heliospheric Obs., 1995—. Referee sci. jours., 1984—; contbr. rsch. articles to sci. jours. Mem. Am. Geophys. Union, German Geophys. Soc.,

German Phys. Soc. Avocation: beekeeping. Office: Max Planck Inst Aeronomy, Max Planck Strasse 2, D-37191 Katlenburg-Lindau Germany

WILHELM, KLAUS PETER, dermatologist, consultant; b. Bremen, Germany, Mar. 3, 1960; s. Alfred and Annette (Geissler) W.; m. Dorothea Schmidt, Mar. 7, 1986; children: Jan-Sebastian, Florian-Alexander, Antonia-Sophie. MD, Med. U. Lübeck, Germany, 1986, PhD, 1995. Cert. dermatologist, allergologist. Resident in dermatology Med. U. Lübeck, 1990-93, sr. dermatologist, 1993-94; pres., med. dir. proDERM, Schenefeld, Germany, 1994—; vis. postdoctoral fellow U. Calif. Med. Sch., San Francisco, 1988-90. Co-editor: (handbooks) Bioengineering of the Skin-Methods and Instrumentation, 1996, Bioengineering of the Skin-Surface Imaging and Analysis, 1997. Capt. M.C. German Army, 1986-88. Rsch. grantee Deutsche Forschungsgemeinschaft, 1990-92, 92-94, postdoctoral stipend, 1988-90. Mem. Internat. Soc. for Bioengring. and the Skin (mem. exec. bd. 1994—), Am. Acad. Dermatology. Home: Hein-Meyer-Str 41, 25495 Kummerfeld Germany Office: proDERM, Industriestr 1, 22869 Schenefeld Germany

WILHELM, NORBERT EDWIN, industrial engineer, structural engineer; b. Idar-Oberstein, Germany, Sept. 11, 1945; s. Paul and Klara F. (Schott) W.; m. Siegrun J. Wildhagen, July 31, 1972; children: Johanne, Eva-Sophie, Lorenz. Engring. diploma, Tech. U., Darmstadt, Germany, 1972, D in Engring., 1983. Rsch. asst. Tech. U., Darmstadt, 1972-73, 76-82; structural engr. Consulting Engr. Lemcke, Darmstadt, 1973-76; overseas mgr. Consulting Engrs. Schröder, Darmstadt, 1983-89; head indsl. engrs. divsn. CES Consulting Engrs. Salzgitter (Germany) GmbH, 1989-96; overseas mgr. Haas Consult, Hannover, Germany, 1997-99; mgr. overseas projects BGS, Frankfurt/Main, Hannover, 1999—; collaborator Eurocode 3 European Com. for Steel Constrn., Paris and Brussels, 1976-82; mem. steel constrn. com. Internat. Standards Orgn., 1977-82. Contbr. articles to profl. jours. Recipient scholarship of studies Cusanus-Werk, Bonn, Germany, 1967-72. Roman Catholic. Office: BGS Consulting Engrs, Schiffgraben 22, 30175 Hannover Germany

WILHELMI, BERND WERNER, physicist, researcher; b. Erfurt, Thueringen, Germany, Jan. 6, 1938; s. Gerhard and Liselotte (Tesch) W.; m. Edeltraud Lorenz, Apr. 16, 1960; children: Simon Dagmar, Lembeck Ute. BS, Jena (Germany) U., 1961, D Rerum Naturalium, 1966, D Rerum Naturalium Habilitation, 1972; Pochetnaya Gramata, Minsk (Belorussia) U., 1988. Asst. Jena U., 1961-70, asst. prof., 1970-73, prof., 1973-89, pres., 1983-88; sec. physics Acad. Scis., Berlin, 1989-91; rschr. Jenoptik AG, Jena, 1991—; cons. Carl Zeiss Co., Jena, 1973-90. Co-author: Introduction Nonlinear Optics, 1971, Nonlinear Optics, 1986, Laser for Ultrashort Light Pulses, 1987, Pulse Compression, 1989. Recipient Ernst Abbe award Carl Zeiss Found., 1979, Nat. Sci. award Govt. Germany, 1981; Eotvos Lorand medal Budapest U., 1987, Ernst Haeckel medal Urania, 1988. Mem. German Optical Soc., German Phys. Soc., European Phys. Soc. (bd. dirs. 1980-83), European Optical Soc. (bd. dirs., head indsl. com. 1992-98), Acad. Scis. (sec. physics 1989-91), Soc. History Tech., Soc. Natural Scis., Leopoldina Acad., Leibniz Soc. Avocations: history, arts, environment. Home: Ziegenhainer 74, D-07749 Jena Thuering, Germany Office: Jenoptik AG, Carl-Zeiss Str 1, D-07739 Jena Thuering, Germany

WILHELMSSON, MATS ANDERS, marketing executive; b. Ostersund, Jamtland, Sweden, Aug. 11, 1957; s. Karl Anders and Elna Katarina (Horneij) W.; m. Eva Karin Engelhart, May 14, 1985 (div. June 1999); children: Camilla, Linda, Mattias; m. Erica Christine Brown. Grad. h.s., Ostersund, Sweden, 1976. Trader SwedBank, Stockholm, 1983-86, Nordbanken, Stockholm, 1986-91, Carnegie Fondkommission, Stockholm, 1991-94, Ohman Fondkommission, Stockholm, 1994-96; head market surveillance Stockholm Stock Exch., Stockholm, 1996—. Sgt. Swedish Army and UNEF, 1976-78. Mem. Swedish Stockbrokers Golf Club (sec. 1989—). Avocations: golf, baseball, guitar, cigars, single Malt Whisky. Office: Stockholm Stock Exch, Kallargrand 2, SE 10578 Stockholm Sweden

WILHOIT, DARREL LOEL, chemical engineer; b. Portland, Oreg., May 8, 1938; s. D. Irvan and Vivian Eloise (Piepgrass) W.; m. Lana Renee Carpenter, Sept. 10, 1963; children: Michele, Renee, April, Ryan. BS, Brigham Young U., 1965; PhD, Wash. State U., 1990. Project leader pioneering R & D Crown Zellerbach, Camas, Wash., 1965-81; mgr. nonwoven R & D Am. Hosp. Supply, Evanston, Ill., 1981-82; cons. nonwoven products and processes Estech Corp., Neenah, Wis., 1982-87; sr. rsch. engr. Viskase Corp., Chgo., 1987-96; exploratory R&D leader Tredegar Film Products, Terre Haute, Ind., 1996—. Author: Improvements in Design and Control of the Drying Process in French Fry Manufacturing. Sch. bd. dir. Washougal (Wash.) Sch. Dist., 1975-77; county planning commr. Skamania (Wash.) County, 1979-81. Mem. AIChE, Instrument Soc. Am., Tech. Assn. Pulp and Paper Industry, Soc. Plastics Engrs. Achievements include patents for New Paper Making Headbox, Paper Softening Method, Splice for Cellulosic Food Casing, Antimicrobial Treatment for Food Surfaces, Biaxially Oriented Shrinkable Film, Cook-in Plastic Casing; conception and commercial implementation of advanced heat transfer methods in the manufacture of biaxially oriented polythylene film; developed commercial processes for making short fibers from PE and for making dry formed paper, unique algorithm for optimal control of cellulose substrate during drying operation, advanced process for adhering short fibers to apertured films. Home: 10163 N Limberlost Ct Terre Haute IN 47803-9637 Office: Tredegar Film Products 3400 Fort Harrison Rd Terre Haute IN 47804-1799

WILHOIT, SUSAN CASSIDY, artist; b. Detroit, Mar. 17, 1948; d. Robert Jean and Elizabeth Virgina Pace-Cassidy; m. Melvin-Ross Wilhoit, May 27, 1970; children: Robert Christian (dec.), Christina Elizabeth, Angela Noel. BA, Bob Jones U., 1971; postgrad., U. Tenn., 1983, U. Mich., 1985. Graphic designer Hiott Printing, Greenville, S.C., 1968-69, Keys Printing, Greenville, 1970-71; art designer Jostens Graphics Divsn., Owatonna, Minn., 1972-74; affil. broker Dayton (Tenn.) Real Estate, 1984-89; dir. pub. rels./ publs. Bryan Coll., Dayton, 1989-91; owner Pleasant Places Watercolours, Dayton, 1990—; adj. art faculty Pillsbury Bapt. Bible Coll., Owatonna, 1971-76, Bryan Coll., 1984-87; pres. Rhea County Bd. Realtors, Dayton, 1989-90; exec. bd. Rhea Arts Coun., Dayton, 1994—. Exhibited in shows at Rhea County Courthouse, Dayton, 1991—, Cumberland County Courthouse, Crossville, Tenn., 1992—, Bledsoe County Courthouse, Pikeville, Tenn., 1994, Hamilton County Courthouse, Chattanooga, 1996, War Meml. Bldg.-Capitol, Nashville; included in collection at Tenn. State U., Nashville. Exec. bd. Rhea County Coun. of Svcs., Inc., Dayton, 1994-96, Rhea County United Way, 1994-96, Rhea Arts Coun., v.p. 1994-96; mem. Dayton C. of C., 1989-91. Presbyterian. Avocations: travel, ch. choir, hiking. E-mail: swilhoit@volstate.net. Office: Pleasant Places Watercolour 537 Evergreen Dr Dayton TN 37321-6236

WILK, ANDRZEJ JAN, international consultant, journalist, educator; b. Witowo, Poznań, Poland, Mar. 7, 1938; s. Stanislaw and Janina (Lewicka) W.; m. Barbara Maria Mieczykowska, Dec. 29, 1962; 1 child, Karol Krzysztof. MS in Mech. Engring., Poznań Polytechnics, 1960; postgrad., U. Minn., Mpls., 1961-62; cert., Diplomatic Sch., Warsaw, Poland, 1977; PhD in Internat. Rels., Poznań U., 1983. Adviser Ministry Higher Edn., Warsaw, 1962-65; head dept. Polish Standards Com., Warsaw, 1965-67; expert COMECON Secretariat, Moscow, 1967-72; expert Ministry Fgn. Affairs, Warsaw, 1972-77, counselor to minister, 1983-88; indsl. devel. officer P-4 UNIDO Secretariat, Vienna, Austria, 1977-83; dep. dir. internat. dept. State Office for Tech., Warsaw, 1988-90, Ministry Internat Market, Warsaw, 1990-91; owner, dir. Transearch Poland (now Polsearch), Warsaw, 1991-99; prof. sch. mgmt. and mktg. Warsaw U., 1999—. Author: Na Zakrecie Czasu, 1970, Poland in the World, 1985, Bertrand Russell Biografia Polityczna, 1999; contbr. articles to profl. jours. Mem. head coun. Polish Student Assn., Warsaw, 1960-63; hon. pres. The Friendship Force, Atlanta, 1998. Recipient Poznań Golden Badge, City of Poznań, 1985, Golden Cross of Merit, Coun. of State, Warsaw, 1985; named Hon. Citizen State of Okla., 1992. Mem. Polish Authors' Assn. (sec. gen. 1990—), Polish Journalists' Assn., Bertrand Russell Soc., Nat. Geographic Soc., Phi Beta Delta. Avocations: reading, languages, travel, wine, songs. Home: ul Zielona 17 Osiedle, Curtis-Davis dom 24, 05-500 Piaseczno k Warsaw Poland Office: Polsearch, ul Madalinskiego 15 m 16, 02-513 Warsaw Poland

WILKE, ALFRED WALTER, language educator; b. Detroit, Mar. 12, 1952; s. Alfred Walter and Marilyn Sue (Miller) W.; 1 child, Kristoffer. BA, Kalamazoo Coll., 1973. Tchr. Gymnasium Syke, Germany, 1974—; cons., translator. Author: (poetry collection) No One Could Call You Pretty, 1975. Avocation: travel. Office: Gymnasium Syke, La-Chartre-Str, Syke 28857, Germany

WILKE, CONSTANCE REGINA, elementary education educator; b. Camden, N.J., Mar. 20, 1944; d. Matthew Stanley Sr. and Regina Rita (Przeradzki) Wojtkowiak; m. Alvin Frank Wilke Jr., Apr. 20, 1968; children: Joseph Alvin, Suzanne Renee. BA in Elem. Edn., Glassboro State U., 1967, MA in Reading and Supervision, 1979. Cert. tchr. and reading specialist, N.J. Tchr. 5th grade Bellmawr (N.J.) Bd. Edn., 1967-70; tchr. 2d grade Ethel M. Burke Sch., Bellmawr, N.J., 1970-97; tchr. 5th grade Bell Oaks Sch., Bellmawr, 1997—. Author: Wojtkowiak Family History, 1992. Vol. Gloucester (N.J.) City Libr., 1972-75, Vet.'s Standdown, Meals on Wheels, Cathedral Soup Kitchen; contact reassurance vol. Am. Heart Assn. Walk; sec. E.M. Burke Sch. PTA, Bellmawr, 1973-78, publicity person, 1980-85, pres., 1982-85, author and editor publicity book, 1980-83, rec. sec., 1995-97; advisor Cmty. Edn. Bd., Gloucester City, 1973-74; eucharistic minster St. Mary's Ch., Gloucester City, 1990—, 150 yr. Jubilee com., renew com., lector, parish coun.; dir., founder of Internat. Day at E.M. Burke Sch., dir. and founder Vet.'s Day Program, MS Read-a-thon, Jump Rope for Heart, Book It programs, Reading is the Ticket program. Named Citizen of Yr., Polish-Am. Congress, 1983. Mem. NEA, N.J. Epilepsy Found., N.J. Edn. Assn., West Jersey Reading Assn., Bellmawr Edn. Assn. (faculty rep.), Asthma Assn. Roman Catholic. Avocations: needle crafts, reading, gardening, family historian. Office: Bell Oaks Sch 256 Anderson Ave Bellmawr NJ 08031-1199

WILKE, INGRID, physicist; b. Offenbach, Hessen, Germany, Mar. 31, 1963. MSc, SUNY, Albany, 1986; diploma, U. Würzburg, Germany, 1988; PhD, ETH, Zürich, Switzerland, 1993. Post-doctoral staff Lawrence Berkeley (Calif.) Lab., 1993-94, Tokyo U., 1994-95; Cl U. Hamburg, Germany, 1995—. Editor: Kiss The Future!, 1999. Avocation: rowing.

WILKENS, LEONARD RANDOLPH, JR. (LENNY WILKENS), professional basketball coach; b. Bklyn., Oct. 28, 1937; s. Leonard Randolph Sr. and Henrietta (Cross) W.; m. Marilyn J. Reed, July 28, 1962; children: Leesha Marie, Leonard Randolph III, Jamée McGregor. BS in Econs., Providence Coll., 1960, HHD (hon.), 1980. Counselor Jewish Employment Vocat. Services, 1962-63; salesman packaging div. Monsanto Co., 1966; profl. basketball player St. Louis Hawks, 1960-68; player-coach Seattle SuperSonics, 1969-72, head coach, 1977-85, gen. mgr., 1985-86; profl. basketball player Cleve. Cavaliers, 1972-74, player NBA All-Star Game, 1973, head coach, 1986-93; player-coach Portland (Oreg.) Trail Blazers, 1974-76; head coach Atlanta Hawks, 1993-99, Toronto Raptors, 2000—; coach 4 NBA All-Star Teams including Ea. Conf. team All-Star game, Mpls., 1994, World Champion basketball team, 1979, IBM NBA Coach of the Year, 1994; winningest coach of all time, 1995, coach 1996 Olympic Basketball Team, asst. coach 1992 Olympic Basketball. Author: The Lenny Wilkens Story, 1974. Bd. regents Gonzaga U., Spokane; bd. dirs. Seattle Ctr., Big Bros. Seattle, Bellevue (Wash.) Boys Club, Seattle Opportunities Industrialization Ctr., Seattle U.; co-chmn. UN Internat. Yr. of Child program, 1979; organizer Lenny Wilkens Celebrity Golf Tournament for Spl. Olympics. 2d lt. U.S. Army, 1961-62. Recipient Whitney Young Jr. award N.Y. Urban League, 1979, Disting. Citizens award Boy Scouts Am., 1980; named MVP in NBA All-Star Game, 1971, Man of Yr., Boys High Alumni chpt. L.A., 1979, Sportsman of Yr., Seattle chpt. City of Hope, 1979, Congl. Black Caucus Coach of Yr., 1979, CBA Coach of Yr., 1979, Coach of Yr., Black Pubs. Assn., 1979, NBA Coach of Yr., 1994; named to NIT-NIKE Hall of Fame, 1988; named to 9 NBA All-Star Teams, elected to Naismith Memorial Basketball. Office: c/o Toronto Raptors, 40 Bay St Ste 300, Toronto, ON Canada M5J 2X2*

WILKENS, LUDWIG BERNHARD, physician; b. Friesoythe, Lower Saxony, Germany, Aug. 2, 1963; s. Ludwig and Lucia (Ollendieck) W.; m. Claudia Nachreiner, May 9, 1994; children: Ida, Gesa. MD, Hannover Med. Sch., 1990. Asst./resident MHH, Hannover, Germany, 1990—. Contbr. articles to profl. jours. With German Army, 1983-84. Office: Med Sch Hannover, Inst of Pathology, 30625 Hannover Germany

WILKERSON, THEODORE L., electrician, county commissioner; b. Baxley, Ga., Mar. 15, 1958; s. Mary Lee Wilkerson; married, Oct. 24, 1981; children: Tessie, Kim, Ashley. Student, Ft. Valley State Coll., So. Utah State Coll. Journeyman electrician So. Co., Baxley, 1982—; county commr. Appling County Bd. Commrs., Baxley, 1997—. Advisor Appling County Recreation Bd., Baxley; mem. Appling County vocat. adv. bd. Appling County H.S., Baxley, 1998—. Mem. IBEW. Democrat. Methodist. Fax: 912-367-5172. Home: 445 Middlewood Dr Baxley GA 31513-7711 Office: Appling County Commrs 100 Oak St Baxley GA 31513

WILKES, ANGELA BIGGS, mental health consultant; b. Reynolds, Ga., Nov. 6, 1952; d. George William and Biease Annetta (Grice) Biggs; m. Linster Bryant Jr., Feb. 22, 1979 (div. Mar. 1983); m. Gary M. Wilkes, June 25, 1983; children: Stephen Alexander, David Alan. BA, Clark Atlanta U., 1974; MA, U. Cin., 1980. Program coord. Alice Paul House battered women's shelter, Cin., 1977-80; dir. cmty. svcs. Mental Health Svcs. N.W., Cin., 1981-82; dir. devel. Community Guidance, Inc., Cleve., 1983-84; mktg. and cmty. svcs. cons. CIT Mental Health Svcs., University Heights, Ohio, 1984-88; v.p., dir. tng. Wilkes Mental Health Cons., Shaker Heights, Ohio, 1985—; guest lectr. Mendel Sch. Applied Social Scis., 1996—. Trustee Citizens Mental Health Assembly, Cleve., 1989-90, Women Together, Inc., Cleve., 1986-87, League Park Ctr., Cleve., 1984-86; mem. Action Ohio-Battered Women, Columbus, Ohio, 1979-84; dep. registrar Cuyahoga County Bd. Elections, Cleve., 1988-89; mem. Guild of St. Dominic, Shaker Heights, 1982—; tchr. parish sch. religion St. Dominic Cath. Ch., 1992—; trustee Orange Schs. Found., 2000—, Ursuline Sophia Ctr., 1999—; mem. Ohio State Med. Assn. Aux., 1990-96, bd. dirs., 1992-94. Recipient Vol. award Whitney Young Sch., 1987, cert. of recognition State of Ohio Voter Registration Program, 1988, Disting. Alumni Citation of Yr. Clark Atlanta U. Mem. ASTD, Acad. Medicine Cleve. Aux. (pres. 1993-94, bd. dirs. 1987-88, 90-97), AMA Aux., NAACP, Nat. Assn. Equal Opportunity in Higher Edn., Diabetes Assn. Gtr. Cleve. (bd. dirs. 1993—, Trustee of Yr. 1999), Clark Atlanta U. Alumni Assn., U. Cin. Alumni Assn., Zonta Internat. Democrat. Roman Catholic. Avocations: collecting china, Black folk art. Fax: 216-765-0448. Office: Wilkes Mental Health Cons 27600 Chagrin Blvd Ste 270 Woodmere OH 44118

WILKES, BRENT AMES, management consultant; b. Melrose, Mass., Sept. 30, 1952; s. Gordon Borthwick and Frances (Ames) W.; 1 child, Erin; m. Linda Dadourian, Oct. 18, 1998. Bachelor, U. Mass., 1974; M of Pub. Affairs, U. Conn., 1977. Cert. assn. exec., 1998, assoc. risk mgmt., 1998. Adminstrv. asst. Town of Tolland, Conn., 1975-76; mgmt. specialist Mass. Dept. Community Affairs, Boston, 1976-79; adminstrv.. asst. to mayor City of Gloucester, Mass., 1979-80; assoc. dir., dir. of field svcs. Mass. Mcpl. Assn., Boston, 1980-89; v.p., treas. Mass. Interlocal Ins. Assn., Boston, 1984-89; pres. MMA Consulting Group, Inc., Boston, 1989-94, MMA Mgmt. Svcs. Inc., Boston, 1995-98, N.E. Pub. Risk, Inc., Boston, 1998, N.E. Assn. Mgmt., Inc., Boston, 1999—; v.p., treas. Pub. Employer Risk Mgmt. Assn., Albany, N.Y., 1989-97, pres., 1997—; adj. prof. Suffolk U. Grad. Sch. Mgmt., Boston, 1980-82; lectr. numerous regional and nat. trade assns. Author and editor: Managing Small Towns, 1986; contbr. articles to profl. jours. Mem. fin. com. Town of Acton, Mass., 1977-79; mem. town meeting Town of Reading, Mass., 1987-89; pres. Unitarian Universalist Ch. of Reading, 1990-93. Mem. Internat. City Mgmt. Assn. (cert. in mgmt.), Mass. Mcpl. Mgmt. Assn. Democrat. Unitarian Universalist. Avocations: golf, tennis, volleyball, reading. E-mail: bwilkes@neami.com. Office: NE Assn Mgmt Inc 100 Conifer Hill Dr Ste 307 Danvers MA 01923-1168

WILKES, CLEM CABELL, JR., stockbroker; b. Johnson City, Tenn., Apr. 5, 1953; s. Clem Cabell Sr. and Dorothy Jane (Miller) W.; m. Tonya Jean McCall, July 20, 1974; children: Elizabeth Layne, Clem Cabell III. BS, East Tenn. State U., 1975; postgrad., Med. Coll. Pa., 1978, Owen Sch. Mgmt., Nashville, 1984. Salesman Beecham Labs., Bristol, Tenn., 1975-78, Smith Kline & French Labs., Phila., 1978-81; stockbroker J.C. Bradford & Co., Johnson City, 1981-85; stockbroker, ptnr. Raymond James Fin. Svcs., Inc., Johnson City, 1985-99; dir. Johnson City Med. Ctr. Hosp., 1997—; fin. advisor, v.p. Citizens Investment Svcs. Inc., 1999—, vice chmn., 1999-2000; vice chmn. bd. dirs. Mountain States Health Alliance, vice chmn., bd. dirs. Vestry mem. St. John's Epis. Ch., 1986-89, treas., 1986—, sr. warden, 1989; mem. com. Am. Cancer Soc., Johnson City, 1986-87, 2d v.p., 1989—; treas. Johnson City Ties for the Blind Found. (award, 1989), 1998—; mem. Johnson City Parks and recreation Bd.; v.p. Citizens Investment Svcs., 1999—; vice chmn. Mountain States Health Alliance; mem. adv. bd. City of Johnson City Parks and Recreation, 1999—. Mem. Johnson City C. of C. (membership chmn. 1987), Robert Thomas Securities Pres. Club, Raymond James Fin. Svcs. Leaders Coun., Lions (v.p. Johnson City 1986-88, pres. 1989-90, Lion of Yr. award 1985, Lion of Decade award 1992, Melvin Jones fellow 1989), Johnson City Parks and Recreation Bd., Kappa Alpha. Office: Citizens Investment Svcs Inc 901 N Roan St Johnson City TN 37601-4604

WILKES, DAVID ROSS, therapist, social worker; b. Springfield, Ohio, Sept. 4, 1951; s. Carol Monroe and Margaret (Perdi) W.; m. Donna Marie Roach, Apr. 11, 1987; children: Andrew David, Lauren Rose. AAS in Community Mental Health Tech., Borough Manhattan C.C., 1980; BA in Psychology, Queens Coll., 1985; postgrad., Ctr. Modern Psychoanalytic Studies, 1986-89; PhD in Clin. Psychology, Union Inst., 1999. Admission interviewer, referral counselor Westside Social Setting/Manhattan Bowery Project, N.Y.C., 1978-79; with dept. psychiatry City Hosp. Elmhurst, 1980-83; behavioral counselor Assn. Children with Retarded Mental Devel., 1985-87; therapist, social worker West Lawrence Care Ctr., 1987-90; case mgr. Nassau Case Mgmt. Program Nassau County Dept. Mental Health, Hempstead, N.Y., 1990—. Recipient Note of Commendation from Commr. Nassau County Dept. Mental Health and Devel. Disabilities, 1992. Mem. Am. Counseling Assn., Am. Psychol. Assn., Nat. Psychology Adv. Assn., Nat. Assn. Advancement of Psychoanalysis (assoc.), Phi Theta Kappa. Avocations: history of jazz, jazz musician. E-mail: serendip@mail.matav.hu. Office: Nassau Case Mgmt 175 Fulton Ave Ste 1 Hempstead NY 11550-3702

WILKES, DELANO ANGUS, architect; b. Panama City, Fla., Jan. 25, 1935; s. Burnice Angus and Flora Mae (Scott) W.; m. Dona Jean Murren, June 25, 1960. BArch, U. Fla., 1958. Cert. Nat. Coun. Archtl.; registration bds. cert. personal trainer, older adult specialty cert. Am. Coun. on Exercise. Designer Perkins & Will Partnership, Chgo., 1960-63; designer, job capt. Harry Weese, Ltd., Chgo., 1963-66; project arch. Fitch Larocca Carrington, Chgo., 1967-69; arch. Mittelbusher & Tourtelot, Chgo., 1970-71; assoc. Bank Bldg. Corp., Chgo., 1972-75; sr. assoc. Charles Edward Stade & Assocs., Park Ridge, Ill., 1975-77; sr. arch. Consoer Morgan Arch., Chgo., 1977-83, mktg. coord., 1980-83; design cons. Chamlin & Assocs., Peru and Morris, Ill., 1969-82; dir. arch. Chamlin & Assocs., Peru and Morris, 1983-86, v.p. arch., 1986—; archtl. cons. Sweet's divsn. McGraw Hill, Inc., Chgo., 1984-90; ptnr. Deri Wilkes Assocs., 1990-95; trainer Fitness Barn, 1995-96, Q Sports Club, 1997-98. Author: Colonel Ebenezer Folsom, 1778-1789, North Carolina Patriot and Tory Scourge, 1975; editor Folsom Bull., 1977-80; prodr. documentary film The Angry Minority, Menninger Found., 1978. Mem. coord. com. Dune Acres Plan Commn. (Ind.), 1983-91; bldg. commr. City of Dune Acres, 1984-89, Arch. Rev. Bd. Marsh Creek Country Club, St. Augustine, Fla., 1988—; chmn. Ind. party Dune Acres, 1987; elected trustee Dune Acres Town Bd., 1988-91, pres., 1988-89; mem. Dune Acres Civic Improvement Found., 1988-91 (leadership recognition for drive to restore Dune Acres Clubhouse); cons. Inst. of Crippled and Disabled, N.Y.C., 1978-83; guest lectr. field trip guide Coll. DuPage, Glen Ellyn, Ill., 1968-76; guest arch. med. adv. com. to Pres.'s Com. for Handicapped, 1977, 78; vice chmn. Westchester County Dem. Precinct, Porter County, Ind., 1986; chmn. selection com. Dem. Hdqrs., Porter County, 1986; treas. Com. to Elect Kovach to Coun., Porter County, 1986; vice chmn. Duneland Dems., 1988-92; pres. Ocean House Condominium Assn., St. Augustine, Fla., 1993-94. Mem. Businessmen for Pub. Interest, Folsom Family Assn. Am. (prse. 19780 82, v.p. 1982—, nominating chmn. 1983, host ann. meeting, Chgo. 1981), AIA, Chgo. AIA (chmn. design awards display com. 1978-79, prodr. New Mem. Show 1979, chmn. pub. rels. com. 1980), Art Inst. Chgo., Chgo. Lyric Opera Guild, Chgo. Assn. Commerce and Industry (display dir. 1979 meeting), Am. Soc. Interior Design (coord. Info. Fair 1979), N.C. Geneal. Soc., New Eng. Hist. Geneal. Soc., Putnam County Hist. Soc., Cook County Hist. Soc., Soc. Colonial Wars, Gargoyle, German Shorthaired Pointer Club North Fla. Democrat. Unitarian. Home: 332 Marsh Point Cir Saint Augustine FL 32080-5858

WILKES, E.M., III, judge; b. Hazlehurst, Ga., Mar. 27, 1946; s. E.M. Jr. and Beatrice McDuffie Wilkes; m. Patricia Elyse Edwards, Aug. 30, 1967; children: Thomas McLangton, Andrew McLean. BS in Gen. Mgmt., Ga. Inst. Tech., 1972; JD, Mercer U., 1975. Bar: Ga. 1975. Atty., pres. Wilkes, Johnson, Smith & Knox, P.A., Hazlehurst, 1975-93; judge Mcpl. Ct. City Hazlehurst, 1977-84, city atty., 1984-87; judge Juvenile Ct. Jeff Davis County State Ga., Hazlehurst, 1979-93, judge State Ct. Jeff Davis County, 1984-93, judge Superior Cts. Ga., Brunswick Jud. Cir., 1993—; bd. dirs. Jeff Davis Hosp., Hazlehurst, Bank Hazlehurst. Pres. Lions Club, Hazlehurst, 1977-78, Jeff Davis Athletic Booster Club, Hazlehurst, 1990-92; dir., sec. Jeff Davis Athletic Assn., Inc., Hazlehurst, 1977—. 1st lt. U.S. Army, 1967-70. Named Profl. of the Yr., Hazlehurst-Jeff Davis C. of C., 1978. Mem. ABA, State Bar Ga., Coun. Superior Ct. Judges Ga., Hazlehurst-Baxley Bar Assn. (pres.). Methodist. Avocations: hunting, fishing, golfing, gardening. E-mail: EMWilkes.CSCJ@hotoffice.net. Fax: 912-375-6634. Office: Jeff Davis Superior Ct Jeff Davis Cty Courthouse PO Box 1540 Hazlehurst GA 31539-1540

WILKEY, MALCOLM RICHARD, retired ambassador, former federal judge; b. Murfreesboro, Tenn., Dec. 6, 1918; s. Malcolm Newton and Elizabeth (Gilbert) W.; m. Emma Secul Depolo, Dec. 21, 1959. AB magna cum laude, Harvard U., 1940, LLB, 1948; LLD (hon.), Rose-Hulman Inst. Tech., 1984. Bar: Tex. 1948, N.Y. 1963, U.S. Supreme Ct. 1952, D.C. 1970. U.S. atty. So. Dist. Tex., 1954-58; asst. atty. gen. U.S., 1958-61; ptnr. Butler Binion Rice & Cook, 1961-63; gen. counsel, sec. Kennecott Copper Corp., 1963-70; judge U.S. Ct. Appeals D.C. Circuit, 1970-85; U.S. amb. to Uruguay, 1985-90; official in charge fed. forces at Little Rock Sch. Crisis, Dept. Justice, 1958; mem. U.S.-Chile Arbitration Commn., 1991-97; lectr. internat. constl. and adminstrv. law London Poly., 1979, 80; lectr. Tulane U. Law Summer Sch., Grenoble, France, 1981, 83, San Diego Law Summer Sch., Oxford, Eng., 1983, Brigham Young Law Sch., 1984, 93; vis. fellow Wolfson Coll., Cambridge U., 1985; chmn. Pres.'s Commn. on Revision Fed. Ethics Laws, 1989; spl. counsel to Atty. Gen. for inquiry into the House Banking Facility, 1992. Author: Is It Time For A Second Constitutional Convention, 1995. Del. Republican Nat. Conv., 1960. Served from 2d lt. to lt. col. AUS, 1941-45. Hon. fellow Wolfson Coll., Cambridge. Fellow Am. Bar Found.; mem. Am. Law Inst. (adv. com. restatement fgn. rels. law of U.S.), Jud. Conf. U.S. (com. on standards for admission to fed. cts. 1976-79), Phi Beta Kappa, Delta Sigma Rho, Phi Delta Phi (hon.). Address: Av El Bosque 379, Providencia, Santiago Chile

WILKIE, ANDREW OLIVER MUNGO, clinical geneticist; b. London, Sept. 14, 1959; s. Douglas Robert and June Rosalind (Hill) W.; m. Jane Elizabeth Martin, June 24, 1989; children: Oscar, Fergus. BA, Cambridge (Eng.) U., 1980; B Medicine B Surgery, Oxford (Eng.) U., 1983, DM, 1992. MRC tng. fellow Inst. Molecular Medicine, Oxford, 1987-90; sr. registrar Inst. Child Health, London, 1990-91, Inst. Med. Genetics, Cardiff, Wales, 1992-93; rsch. fellow, cons. Inst. Molecular Medicine, Oxford, 1993—; prof. genetics Oxford U., 2000—. Mem. editl. bd. Jour. Med. Genetics, 1994-99, Human Genetics, 1998—; contbr. numerous articles to profl. jours. Sr. rsch. fellow in clin. sci. Wellcome Trust, 1995. Fellow Royal Coll. Physicians, Genetical Soc. (mem. com. 1996-00), Brit. Soc. Human Genetics, Assn. of Physicians. Avocations: ornithology, mountaineering. Office: John Radcliffe Hosp, Inst Molecular Medicine, Oxford OX3 9DS, England

WILKINS, ADAM STANLEY, editor; b. Columbus, Ohio, Mar. 18, 1945; s. Alvin Francis and Sophie Clara (Meyer) W.; m. Jean Marr, Sept. 3, 1971 (div. Oct. 1995); 1 child, Isaac; m. Louise Holland, Mar. 17, 2000. BA, Reed Coll., 1965; PhD in Genetics, U. Wash., 1969. Postdoctoral fellow MIT, Cambridge, 1969-73, U. Wis., Madison, 1973-76; lectr. in genetics Massey U., Palmerston North, New Zealand, 1976-82, sr. lectr. in genetics, 1982-83; staff editor BioEssays Cambridge (U.K.) U. Press, 1984-89; editor BioEssays Co. of Biologists, Cambridge, 1990-97, John Wiley & Sons,

N.Y.C., 1998—; vis. lectr. Nat. U., Singapore, 1994; vis. prof. U. Wis., Madison, 1993, 87, U. Wash., Seattle, 1985. Co-editor: Molecular Evolution, 1984, Molecular Model Systems in the Lepidoptera, 1995; author: Genetic Analysis of Animal Development, 1986, 2d edit., 1993. Exec. bd. ACLU, Seattle, 1965-69; mem. Labor Party, New Zealand, 1978-82, European Dialogue, London, 1993—, Liberal Dems., Cambridge, 1997—. Fellowship Am. Cancer Soc., 1972-73; grantee NSF; hon. rsch. fellow, U. Coll. London, 1999—. Mem. Genetics Soc. of Am., British Soc. of Developmental Biology, Genetical Soc., Soc. Study Evolution, Clare Hall U. Cambridge (life). Avocations: photography, reading, travel, walking, visiting art museums and galleries. Office: BioEssays Editl Office, 10/11 Tredgold Ln Napier St, Cambridge CB1 1HN, England

WILKINS, DENIS CHARLES, surgeon, consultant, educator; b. Newcastle, Durham, Eng., Apr. 28; s. Francis Gerald and Catherine (Gavin) W.; m. Geraldine Janice Stevenson, July 6, 1976; children: Johanna, Claire, Helen, Jessica. MB, ChB, U. Liverpool, Eng., 1966, MD, 1975. Cert. in gen. and vascular surgery Royal Coll. Surgeons, Eng. House physician, surgeon Royal So. Hosp., Liverpool, Eng., 1966-67; med. officer Brit. Antarctic Survey, 1968-70; sci. officer Nat. Inst. for Med. Rsch., London, 1970-71; registrar in surgery Addenbrooke's Hosp., Cambridge, Eng., 1971-74; sr. registrar in surgery, asst. dir. rsch. Addenbrooke's Hosp., Cambridge, 1974-76; supr. in anatomy Jesus Coll., Cambridge, Eng., 1976-79; cons. surgeon Derriford Hosp., Plymouth, 1979—; lectr. Plymouth Postgrad. Med. Sch., 1991—; external examiner U. Cambridge, 1988-92; chmn. Plymouth Postgrad. Med. Sch., 1991-95, S.W. Regional Tng. Com. in Surgery, 1995—; ship's capt. med. certifier, Bd. of Trade examiner, 1993—; adv. com. gen. surgery Roy Coll. Surgeons, 1998; bd. dirs. Brit. Antarctic Survey Med. Unit, 1997—. Author (with others) Polar Human Biology, 1973, Textbook of Surgery, 1980, 2d rev. edit. 1997; also articles in profl. jours. Trustee, founder Plymouth and S.W. Med. Rsch. Found., 1995—; bd. dirs. Plymouth Health Authority Sports Ctr., 1988-94. Recipient WSA Griffith Travel Scholarship, St. Bartholomew's Hosp., 1978, Higher award S.W. Regional Health Authority, 1988. Fellow Royal Coll. Surgeons of Eng. (examiner 1996—, Named Regional Advisor for S.W., 1995—, chmn. clin. rev. group 1999—), Brit. Transplantation Soc., Vascular Surg. Soc. Great Britain (coun. 1996-99), Assn. Endocrine Surgeons. Avocations: private pilot, woodturning. Office: Derriford Hosp, Derriford, Plymouth PL6 8DH, England

WILKINS, (JACQUES) DOMINIQUE, retired professional basketball player; b. Orléans, France, Jan. 12, 1960; came to U.S., 1964; s. John and Geraldine Wilkins; m. Nicole Berry, Sept. 26, 1992; children: Iyisha, Chloe. BBA, U. Ga., 1982. Basketball player Atlanta Hawks, 1982-94, Los Angeles Clippers, 1994, Boston Celtics, 1994-95, Panathinaikos-Athens, Athens, Greece, 1995-96, San Antonio Spurs, 1996-97, Team System, Bologna, Spain, 1997-98; forward Orlando Magic, 1998-99, Anaheim Roadrunners, 2000S. Mem. NBA All-Star team, 1986-91, 93-94; NBA scoring leader, 1986; mem. All-NBA first team, 1986; mem. NBA All-Rookie team, 1983; Sporting News NCAA All-American, 1981, 82; mem. Dream Team II; slam dunk champion NBA, 1985, 90; mem. Panathinaikos-Athens european championship team, 1996. Achievements include holding a single game record for most free throws without a miss-23, 1992; currently 6th all-time leading scorer in NBA history. Office: Anaheim Roadrunners Arrowhead Pond of Anaheim 2695 East Katella Anaheim CA 92806*

WILKINS, H. ANDREW, artist; b. Reidsville, N.C., Aug. 6, 1950; s. Harry Bethel and Emma Louise (Hall) W. BS in Art, Barton Coll., Wilson, N.C., 1972; MEd, The Citadel, 1981. Art instr. Charleston County S.C. Schs., 1972-88; profl. artist Ruth & Green's Little Art Gallery, Raleigh, N.C., 1986—, Pine Tree Gallery, Troy, Ala., 1988—, Miss West and Sister, South Boston, Va., 1988—, Tony Sanders Gallery, Penzance, Eng., 1990—, Agora Gallery, N.Y.C., 1994—, Gallery Alexie, N.Y.C., 2000—; design instr. Trident Tech. Coll., Charleston, S.C., 1981-88; art instr. Dept. Def. Dependents Sch., Bamberg, Fed. Republic Germany, 1988—; owner Trilby's Antiques, Charleston; graphic arts advisor Bamberg Performing Arts Club, 1994; bd. dirs. Kolb Cons., Nurnberg, Germany; pres. Arasira Imports. One-man shows include Parsons Bruce Art Assn., 1985—, City Art Gallery Charleston, 1985-88, Charleston Pub. Libr., 1985, South Boston Mus. Art and History, 1999, The Prizery, 1999; exhibited in numerous group shows through U.S. and Europe, 1984—, also pvt., pub. and corp. collections in Europe, U.S. and Middle East. Nat. trustee Help Encourage Landmark Presvervation, Richmond, Va., 1975; mem. art edn. forum Gibbes ARt Mus., 1986. Mem. Parsons Bruce Art Assn., Nat. Art Edn. Assn., Historic Ansonborough Neighborhood Assn., Carolina Art Assn., Carolina Yacht Club, Phi Delta Kappa. Avocation: art antique collector.

WILKINS, MALCOLM BARRETT, botany educator, consultant; b. Cardiff, Wales, Feb. 27, 1933; s. Barrett Charles and Eleanor Mary (Jenkins) W.; m. Mary Patricia Maltby; children: Nigel Edward Barrett Wilkins, Fiona Louise Emma Barrett Wilkins (dec.). BS, Kings Coll.-London U., 1954, Kings Coll.-London U., 1955; PhD, Kings Coll.-London U., 1958, DSc, 1972. Lectr. botany Kings Coll., 1958-64; lectr. biology U. East Anglia, U.K., 1964-65, prof. biology, 1965-67; prof. plant physiology Nottingham (Eng.) U., 1967-70; Regius prof. botany Glasgow (Scotland) U., 1970-2000. Author: Plant Watching, 1988; editor: (textbooks) Advanced Plant Physiology, 1977, Plant Growth and Development, 1969; contbr. over 100 articles to sci. jours. Chmn. bd. trustees Royal Botanic Garden, Edinburgh, Scotland, 1994-99, Lifesci. Working Group-European Space Agy., Paris, 1985-87. Fellow Rockefeller Found., Yale U., 1961-62, rsch. fellow Harvard U., 1962-63. Fellow Royal Soc. Edinburgh (v.p. 1994-97); mem. Am. Soc. Plant Physiologists (hon. corr.), Caledonian Club London, New Club Edinburgh. Avocations: fishing, model engineering. Home: 5 Hughenden Dr, Glasgow G12 9XS, Scotland Office: IBLS Bower Bldg, Glasgow U, Glasgow G12 8QQ, Scotland

WILKINS, MAURICE HUGH FREDERICK, biophysicist; b. Pongaroa, New Zealand, Dec. 15, 1916; s. Edgar Henry and Eveline (Whittaker) W.; m. Patricia Ann Chidgey, Mar. 12, 1959; children: Sarah Fenella, George Hugh, Emily Lucy Una, William Henry. PhD, U. Birmingham, Cambridge, 1940; LLD, U. Glasgow, 1972; DSc, Birmingham U., 1992, Trinity Coll., Dublin, 1992. Research with Manhattan Project, U. Calif., Berkeley, 1944; lectr. St. Andrews U., 1945; mem. faculty Kings Coll., London, 1946—, dep. dir. biophysics unit Med. Research Council,, 1955-70, dir. biophysics unit, 1970-72, dir. neurobiology unit, 1972-74, prof. molecular biology, 1962-70, prof. biophysics, 1970-81, also dir. MRC cell biophysics unit (formerly Med. Research Council neurobiology unit), 1974-80, prof. emeritus, 1981—. Decorated comdr. Brit. Empire; recipient Albert Lasker award Am. Pub. Health Assn., 1960, Nobel prize for physiology and medicine (with F.H.C. Crick and J.D. Watson), 1962; fellow King's Coll., 1973—. Fellow Royal Soc.; mem. Brit. Biophys. Soc. (past chmn.), Am. Soc. Biol. Chemists (hon.), Brit. Soc. for Social Responsibility in Sci. (pres. 1969), Am. Acad. Arts and Scis. (fgn. hon.). Avocation: research publs. on structure of nerve membranes and X-ray diffraction analysis of structure of DNA, devel. of electron trap theory of phosphorescence and thermo-luminescence, light microscopy techniques for cyto-chem. research, including use of interference microscope for dry mass determination in cells.

WILKINS, MCCOWAN DAVID, management consultant; b. Melksham, Wiltshire, Eng., Aug. 30, 1945; s. Howard Joseph Hunt and Doris Mary Helen (Wilkins) Withers; m. Veronica Jean Regan, Mar. 25, 1967; children: Philip David, Mark Alan, Claire Louise. Diploma in Welding and Metallurgy, Inst. Welding, London, 1969; diploma bus. excellence, Newcastle U., 1999. Registered european engr., 1989. Welding engr. Robert Cort and Sons, Reading, Eng., 1966-73; inspecting engr. Foster Wheeler Internat., London, 1973-75; chief inspecting engr. The Ralph M. Parsons Co. Ltd., London, 1975-78; sr. engr. Exon Rsch. & Engring., Florham Park, N.J., 1978-83; area supr. Exon Rsch. & Engring., Huston, 1978-79; sr. engr. Ere Liasion, Inc., Tokyo, 1978-83, area mgmt., 1979-83; dir. cons., chief exec. Macron Cons., Hungerford, Eng., 1983—; pres. Macron USA, 1995—; cons. Macron Cons., Japan, Italy, 1983-86. Author: Quality Management in Japan, 1987, Macron Management Methods, 1990, Project Management Planning for Major Construction Projects, 1993, Quality Management in Petrochemical and Civil Construction, 1994. Fellow Royal Society, Inst. Mgmt. Specialists (life), Inst. Profl. and Tech. Mgmt. (founder fellow), Inst. Welding and Metallurgy; mem. Inst. Non. Destructive Testing, Inst. Quality Assurance (assoc.), Internat. MENSA. Avocations: foreign languages, deep sea fishing. Home: 1 Chilton Way, Hungerford RG17 0JR, England Office: Macron Cons, Croft Hall, Hungerford RG17 0HY, England

WILKINS, PETER IVAN, career officer, helicopter pilot; b. Eshowe, South Africa, Oct. 29, 1946; s. William Thomas and Katherine Agnes Mary (McLannahan) W.; m. Valerie Susan Mary Heath, Jan. 24, 1970; children: Bryan, Roan. BS in Aero. Sci., Maritzburg Coll., Pietermaritzburg, South Africa, 1963; student, South African Air Force Coll., 1983, South African Def. Coll., 1990. Cert. air force pilot. Joined South African Air Force, 1964, advanced through grades to brig. gen., 1999; officer commdg. 16 Squadron, Cape Town, South Africa, 1980, 22 Squadron, Cape Town, 1981-83, CLiskei Airwing, Bishno, 1984-85; sr. staff officer battlefield support Pretoria, South Africa, 1985-86; comdg. officer Durban AFB, South Africa, 1987-91; def. and air attaché South African Nat. Def. Force, Washington, 1992-94; dir. long term planning Pretoria, 1995-98; searchmaster Joint Task Force W., Cape Town, 1999—. Contbr. chpt. to book, articles to profl. jours. Mem. Metro, Cape Town, 1980-83; mem. Keep Durban Beautiful Orgn., 1987-91. Decorated U.S. Legion Merit; recipient Citizens Humanitarian award Lions, 1987-91, Igor Sikorsky Humanitarian award Helicopter Assn. Internat., 1992. Mem. South African Air Force Assn. (mem. exec. com. 1987-91). Baptist. Avocations: reading, travel, sketching, helicopter flying. Home: 374 Jan Smuts Ave, Wynberg Cape Town 7800, South Africa Office: Regional Joint Task Force W, Silvermine, Pvt Bag x8, Tokai Cape Town 7966, South Africa

WILKINS, PETER WILLIAM, plant breeder, researcher; b. Simla, India, Aug. 4, 1947; arrived in U.K., 1948; s. Patrick Noel and Margot (Williams) W.; m. Christine Kavanagh, July 12, 1969; children: Nicholas John, Claire Louise. BSc with Honors, U. Wales, Aberystwyth, 1968, PhD, 1977. Rsch. scientist Welsh Plant Breeding Sta., Aberystwyth, 1968-80; group leader Inst. Grassland and Environ. Rsch. (IGER), Aberystwyth, 1980—; hon. lectr. U. Wales, 1985—. Contbr. articles to profl. jours.; breeder new variety Aberdart, 1998, AberAvon, 2000. Sec. Aber Kayakers, 1998. Mem. Brit. Soc. Plant Breedres (group convenor, Ely, 1996—). Avocations: white water kayaking, hill walking. Office: IGER, Aberystwyth SY23 3EB, Wales

WILKINSON, ALBERT MIMS, JR., lawyer; b. Nashville, June 29, 1925; s. Albert Mims and Mary Nelle (Derryberry) W.; m. Edythe Bush, Mar. 27, 1953 (div.); children: William Terry, Elizabeth Ann, David Bush; m. Dolores Jean Attard, Oct. 22, 1971 (div.); 1 child, Mary Dolores. Student, Emory U., 1942-43; JD, U. Ga., 1949. Bar: Ga. 1948. Pvt. practice law Atlanta, 1950-85; gen. counsel GEC-Marconi Avionics Inc., Atlanta, 1985-98; hon. legal adviser to Brit. Consul Gen. at Atlanta. Author: The Winning of the Revolutionary War in the South, 1976, The Rights of Unsecured Creditors-The Law in Georgia, 1979. Mem. DeKalb County Bd. Elections, 1966-72; chmn. 4th Congl. Dist. Republican Exec. Com., 1968-70, Ga. State Rep. Exec. Com., 1968-74; 1st vice chmn. Ga. Rep. Party, 1972-74, asst. gen. counsel, 1974-75; vice chmn., trustee Atlanta Counseling Center, Inc., 1960-83. Served with USCGR, 1943-46. Decorated Order Brit. Empire. Fellow Comml. Law Found.; mem. BA, Ga. Bar Assn., Atlanta Bar Assn., Ga. Soc. (pres. 1962-63), SAR, Southeastern Mem.'s Assn. (pres. 1960-61), Comml. Law League Am., Ga. Soc. Colonial Wars, Old Guard of Gate City Guard (comdt. 1986), N.C. Soc. of Cincinnati, Sphinx Club, Gridiron Club, Commerce Club, Civitan, Masons, Blue Key, Omicron Delta Kappa. Baptist. Home and Office: 66 Demorest Ln # 333 Dillard GA 30537-2581

WILKINSON, CHRIS D. W., engineering educator; b. Blackburn, Lancashire, Eng., Jan. 9, 1940; s. Charles N. and Doris M. (Wicks) W.; m. Judy A. H. Hughes, June 25, 1962; children: Rona, Kit, Maggie. MA, Oxford (Eng.) U., 1962; PhD, Stanford U., 1968. Engr. English Electric Valve Co., Chelmford, 1968-69; lectr. dept. electronics and elec. engring. Glasgow (Scotland) U., 1969-75, sr. lectr. dept. electronics and elec. engring., 1975-79, reader dept. electronics and elec. engring., 1979-82, titular prof. dept. electronics and elec. engring., 1982-92, James Watt prof. dept. electronics and elec. engring., 1992—. Contbr. numerous papers to scholarly jours. Fellow Royal Soc. Edinburgh. Avocations: hill walking, allotment holder. Office: U Glasgow, Dept Electronics/Elec Engrg, G12 8QQ Glasgow Scotland

WILKINSON, GORDON THOMAS, retired chemical engineer, consultant; b. Gillingham, Kent, Eng., June 12, 1940; arrived in Australia, 1948; s. Thomas and Sarah Melissa (Morrow) W.; m. Nereda Patricia Milne, Aug. 14, 1965; children: Andrew Thomas, Ian David. BE in Chem. Engring., Melbourne U., 1962; PhDChemE, U. NSW, 1967. Chartered profl. chemist, Australia; chartered engr., U.K., registered eng. (Aust):. Tchg. fellow U. NSW, 1963-66; project engr. Lyell Mining and Railway Co. Ltd., Tasmania, 1967, sr. rsch. officer, 1968, rsch. metallurgist, 1968-69; lectr. U. South Australia (formerly South Australian Inst. Tech.), 1970-74, sr. lectr., 1974-90, prin. lectr., 1990-96, adjunct sen. rsch. fell., 1997—. Editor: Energy and Liquid Fuels, 1975; asst. editor Chem. Engring. in Australia, 1984-95; contbr. articles to profl. jours.; patentee flavor enhancement of low-alcohol wines. Fellow Instn. Chem. Engrs. (chmn. South Australia chpt. 1982-84, 92-93), Royal Australian Chem. Inst. (indsl. chemistry divsn. chair 1990-98, exec. councillor 1996-98); mem. Rotary Internat. (pres. Burnside chpt. 1990-91, Cmty. Svc. award PHF, 1995). Anglican. Avocations: golf, travel, community service.

WILKINSON, HARRY EDWARD, management educator and consultant; b. Richmond Heights, Mo., June 30, 1930; s. Harry Edward and Virginia Flo (Shelton) W.; m. Sara Beth Kikendall, Aug. 30, 1958; children: Linda Beth, Cheryl Susan. BA in Physics, Princeton U., 1952; MBA, Washington U., St. Louis, 1957; D Bus. Adminstrn., Harvard U., 1960. Lic. psychologist, Mass. Staff engr. Southwestern Bell Tel. Co., St. Louis, 1954-57; traffic engr. New Eng. Tel. & Telegraph Co., Boston, 1957-60; sr. mgmt. cons. Harbridge House Inc., Boston, 1961-65; dean bus. adminstrn., dir. Mgmt. Inst., Northeastern U., Boston, 1965-67; pres., chmn. bd. Univ. Affiliates Inc., North Port, Fla., 1967-2000; vis. prof. mgmt. Rice U., Houston, 1990-94, 97—, dir. office of exec. devel., 1993-97; cons. to various industries and govt., 1961—. Author: Influencing People in Organizations, 1993; contbr. articles to mgmt. jours. Lt. (j.g.) USN, 1952-54, Korea. Mem. APA, Acad. Mgmt., N.Am. Case Rsch. Assn., S.W. Case Rsch. Assn., Harvard Bus. Sch. Assn. Office: Jones Grad Sch Rice U 6100 Main St Houston TX 77005-1827

WILKINSON, JOHN ERIC, education educator, broadcaster; b. Blackburn, Lancashire, Eng., May 22, 1944; s. Richard Bell and Edith (Lomax) W.; m. Sandra Clegg Millar, Apr. 2, 1968 (div. Sept. 4, 1989); children: Neil, Adrian, Lynn. BS, U. St. Andrews, Scotland, 1966; MEd, U. Dundee, Scotland, 1968; PhD, U. Glasgow, Scotland, 1993. Chartered psychologist, Brit. Psychol. Soc. Asst. master Brockenhurst Sixth Form Coll., Hants, Eng., 1968-70; rsch. fellow U. Nottingham, Eng., 1970-72; lectr. U. Glasgow, 1973-91, sr. lectr., 1992-98, prof. edn., 1998—; broadcaster BBC, Glasgow, 1990—; dir. Glasgow Print Studio, 1998—; cons. Ctr. Brit. Tchrs., Reading, 1999—. Author: (chpt.) The Assessment of Quality in Early Education, 1994, (chpt.) Pre-School Education in the UK, 1999; contbr. articles to profl. jours. Recipient Rsch. grant Strathclyde Regional Coun., Glasgow, 1986, Rsch. grant Scottish Office Edn. and Industry Dept., 1997, Rsch. grant Ctr. Brit. Tchrs., 1998. Fellow Brit. Psychol. Soc. (assoc.), Royal Soc. Arts; mem. Scottish Ednl. Rsch. Assn. (pres. 1988-90). Avocations: ballet, art collecting, socialising, swimming, organ playing. Office: U Glasgow Dept Ednl Studies, 8 University Gardens, Glasgow G12 8QH, Scotland United Kingdom

WILKINSON, JOHN FREDERICK, geology educator, researcher; b. Bundaberg, Australia, Oct. 10, 1927; s. John and Amelia Augusta (Janke) W.; m. Margaret Anne Stark, July 31, 1957; children: Jan Louise, Leanne Lisa. BS, U. Queensland, Australia, 1949; MS, 1951; PhD, U. Cambridge, U.K., 1954; DSc, U. Queensland, Australia, 1971. Lectr. U. New England, Australia, 1951-52; Royal Dutch Shell scholar Cambridge U., U.K., 1952-54; sr. lectr. U. New England, Australia, 1955-64; vis. prof. Princeton U., 1959-60; prof. Geology U. New England, Australia, 1965-87; sr. fellow Nat. Sci. Found., 1968-69. Author 60 research papers on volcanic petrology. Recipient Gold medal U. Queensland, Australia, 1950. Mem. N.Y. Acad. Scis. Avocations: fishing, tennis. Home: 14/18-20 Burrawan St, Port Macquarie 2444, Australia

WILKINSON, LAURA, Olympic athlete; b. Houston, Dec. 17, 1977. Student, U. Tex. Placed 5th World Championships, 1998, winner platform Gold Medal Goodwill Games, 1998; winner nat. title summer nats. Tex., 1999; winner Gold Medal 10 meter platform Sydney, 2000. Office: US Diving Inc 201 S Capitol Ave Ste 430 Indianapolis IN 46225*

WILKINSON, PAUL, political scientist, educator; b. Harrow, Middlesex, Eng., May 9, 1937; s. Walter Ross and Joan Rosemary (Paul) W.; m. Susan Flook, Mar. 19, 1960; children: Rachel Margaret, John Paul, Charles Ross. BA in Politics and Modern History, Univ. Coll., Swansea, Wales, 1959; MA in History, U. Wales, Cardiff, 1968. Asst. lectr. in politics Univ. Coll., Cardiff, 1966-68, lectr., 1968-75, sr. lectr., 1975-78; vis. prof. Simon Fraser U., B.C., Can., 1973; reader U. Wales, 1978-79; prof. internat. rels., head dept. politics/internat. rels. U. Aberdeen (Scotland), 1979-89; prof. internat. rels. U. St. Andrews, Scotland, 1990—; head Sch. History Internat. Rels., 1994-96; vis. fellow Trinity Hall, Cambridge, 1997—; dir. Ctr. Study of Terrorism and Polit. Violence, U. St. Andrews, 1998—; chmn. Rsch. Found. for Study of Conflict and Terrorism, 1989-94; hon. fellow Univ. Coll. Swansea, 1986; mem. security adv. bd. Internat. Found. Airline Passengers Assn., 1988—. Author: Social Movement, 1971, Political Terrorism, 1974, Terrorism and the Liberal State, 1977, rev. edit., 1986, Terrorism vs. Liberal Democracy: The Problems of Response, 1976, Terrorism: Theory and Practice, 1979, Defence of the West, 1983, British Perspectives on Terrorism, 1981, The New Fascists, 1981, rev. edit., 1983, Terrorism and International Order, 1986, Lessons of Lockerbie, 1989, Terrorist Targets and Tactics: New Risks to World Order, 1990; editor: Contemporary Research on Terrorism, 1987, Terrorism: British Perspectives, 1993, Technology and Terrorism, 1994, Inquiry into Legislation Against Terrorism, vol. II, 1996, Aviation Terrorism and Security, 1998, Terrorism and Liberal Democracy: The Problem of Response, 2000; mem. editorial bd. Studies in Conflict and Terrorism Quar.; editor: Key Concepts in International Relations series, 1979—, History of Political Violence series, 1979—, Terrorism and Political Violence, 1989—, Cass Series on Political Violence, 1996—. Served with RAF, 1959-65. Fellow Royal Soc. Promotion Arts, Industry & Commerce; mem. Brit. Internat. Studies Assn., Polit. Studies Assn., Internat. Inst. Strategic Studies. Scottish Episcopalian. Office: U St Andrews, North St, Saint Andrews Fife KY169AJ, Scotland

WILKINSON, ROSEMARY REGINA CHALLONER, poet, writer; b. New Orleans, Feb. 21, 1924; d. William Lindsay Challoner Jr. and Julia Regina (Sellen) Challoner/Schillo; m. Henry Bertram Wilkinson, Oct. 15, 1949; children: Denis James, Marian Regina, Paul Francis, Richard Challoner. Lifetime credential to teach poetry, San Francisco State U., 1978; LHD (hon.), Livre U., Pakistan, 1975; DLitt (hon.), World Acad. Arts & Culture, Rep. of China, 1981. lectr./reader of poetry. Author: (poetry books) A Girl's Will, 1973, California Poet, 1976, Earth's Compromise, 1977, It Happened to Me, 1978, I Am Earth Woman, 1979, The Poet and the Painter, 1981, Poetry and Arte, 1982, Gems Within, 1984, Nature's Guest, 1984, In the Pines, 1985, Longing For You, 1986, Purify the Earth, 1988, Sacred in Nature, 1988, Earth's Children, 1990, New Seed, 1991, Angels and Poetry, 1992, Cambrian Zephyr, 1993, Collected Poems, 1994, Poetry: Nature, 1996, Poetry: Spiritual, 1997, Poetry Calendar 2000, 1999; (epic) An Historical Epic, 1974. Founder Poetry-Fine Arts Div. of San Mateo (Calif.) County Fair, 1977, Dr. Williams Poetry Workshop, Burlingame H.S., 1985; founder USA World Acad. Arts and Culture-USA, San Francisco, 1985, sec.-gen., 1985-95, pres., 1995—. Mem. World Congress of Poets (Taipei, Taiwan bd. dirs. 1973—, San Francisco pres. 1981, sec.-gen. 1985-95, pres. 1995—), World Acad. of Arts and Culture/World Congress of Poets, Nat. League Am. Pen Women Inc. (Washington 4th and 5th v.p. 1986-90, Berkeley, Calif. pres. 1988-90), Poetry Soc. of Am., Acad. Am. Poets, The Authors Guild, Authors League Am., Soroptomist Internat. (hon.). Democrat. Roman Catholic. Avocations: reading, research, brush painting. Home: World Congress of Poets 3146 Buckeye Ct Placerville CA 95667-8334

WILKINSON, RUPERT HUGH, educator; b. Hindhead, England; s. Gerald Hugh and Lorna Mary (Davies) W.; m. Mary Pulman, Sept. 11, 1965; children: Matthew Paul, Camilla Dorothy, Clara Mary. AB, Harvard U., 1961; PhD, Stanford U., 1970. Rsch. cons. Addiction Rsch. Found., Ont., Can.; lectr. U. Sussex, Brighton, England, 1966-74, reader, 1974-89, prof., 1989—. Author: The Prefects, 1964, American Tough, 1984, Pursuit of American Character, 1988; editor: American Social Character, 1992. Home: 44 Guildford Rd, London SW8 2BU, England Office: U Sussex, Falmer, Brighton BN1 9QN, England

WILKINSON, TIMOTHY JAMES, geriatric physician; b. Rakaia, Canterbury, New Zealand, Oct. 9, 1960; s. Arthur Hugh and Joan Rhoda Wilkinson; m. Lynette Mary Murdoch; children: Tom, Max. MB BChir, U. Otago, Dunedin, New Zealand, 1984. Sr. lectr. Christchurch Sch. Medicine, 1994—; cons., physician Princess Margaret Hosp., 1994—; assoc. dean Christchurch Sch. Medicine, 1996—. Fellow Royal Australasian Coll. Physicians; mem. Am. Geriatrics Soc., Australian and New Zealand Assn. Med. Edn.

WILKOMIRSKY, IGOR A.E., chemical and metallurgical engineer, educator; b. Angol, Chile, Oct. 13, 1937; s. Andres M.J. and Amalia M. (Fuica-Strube) W.; m. Pola Larrahona, Jan. 9, 1965; children: Karin, Kathy. BSChE, U. Concepcion, 1962; MS in Metall. Engring., Colo. Sch. Mines, 1966; PhD, U. British Columbia, Can., 1974. Registered profl. engr. Rsch. asst. U. Concepcion, Chile, 1961-64, asst. prof., 1968-71, prof., 1979—; metallurgist Cia Acero Pacifico, Talcahuano, Chile, 1965-68; sr. metallurgist R.P.C., Fredericton, N.B., Canada, 1975-76, chief metallurgist, 1977-78; cons. to engring. orgns., Chile, Canada, 1980—. Author: Fundamental of Metallurgical Process, 1980-86; contbr. articles to profl. jours.; patentee in field. Scholar Kennecott Copper Corp., 1963, O.A.S., 1966. Fellow TMS; mem. CIM Can., CIM Chile. Roman Catholic. Avocations: bicycling, squash, fishing. Fax: (56) (41) 220045. Home: Casilla 2186, Concepción Chile Office: U Concepción, Casilla 53-C, Concepción Chile

WILL, FRITZ G., physical chemist, consultant; b. Breslau, Germany, Jan. 12, 1931; came to U.S., 1959; s. Fritz and Adele M. (Schmidt) W.; m. Hertha M. Will, May 24, 1958; children: Heike, Christian, Helen. BS in Physics, Tech. U., Munich, 1954, MS in Physics, 1956, PhD in Phys. Chemistry, 1959. Coord. fuel cell program Engring. R&D Labs., Ft. Belvoir, 1959-60; mem. rsch. staff GE R&D Ctr., Schenectady, N.Y., 1960-90, mgr. electrochemistry, 1969-73; dir. Cold Fusion Inst. U. Utah, Salt Lake City, 1990-91, rsch. prof., 1991-93; vis. scientist Electric Power Rsch. Inst., Palo Alto, Calif., 1993-94, mgr. electrochem. sci. and tech., 1994-98; pres., owner Battery Vision, Consulting, Santa Barbara, Calif., 1998—. Contbr. articles to profl. jours. Recipient Indsl. Rsch. award Indsl. Rsch. Inc., 1975, Citation Classic award Inst. Sci. Info., 1984. Mem. Electrochem. Soc. (divsn. editor of jour. 1974-84, chmn. phys. chemistry divsn. 1983-84, chmn. honors and awards com. 1984-85, pres. 1987-88, 4th Battery Rsch. award battery divsn. 1964). Achievements include patents in field, including for nickel/metalhydride batteries employing AB5 compounds. Avocations: tennis, skiing, sailing, opera, classical music.

WILLADSEN, MICHAEL CHRIS, marketing professional, sales executive; b. Cheboygan, Mich., Sept. 18, 1946; s. Chris Jens and Helen Margaret (Barr) W.; m. Kay Ann Brooks, Dec. 10, 1964, (div. Dec. 10, 1989); children: Michael Jr., Erik; m. Linda Sue Degroff, Apr. 4, 1992; children: Stephanie, Gretchen, Ross. Student, Delta Coll., 1964-66; A in Bus. Mgmt., Northwood Inst., 1968, BA in Bus. Mgmt., 1969. Mktg. rep. Detroit dist. Petemco, Inc., 1970-73, mktg. rep. Indpls. Dist., 1973-74; dist. mgr. Petemco Inc.-Ind. Ohio Mich., Ind., Ohio, Mich., 1974-76, Consolidated Stas. Marathon Oil, Oshkosh, Wis., 1976-79; sales mgr. Champaign (Ill.) Dist. Marathon Oil, 1981-82; supr. Credit Card Ctr. Marathon Oil, Findlay, Ohio, 1982-84; wholesale mktg. profl. Marathon Brand Mktg./Ohio, Mich., Ky., 1982-84; jobber sales Marathon Oil/Ohio, Pa., W.Va., Ohio, Pa., W. Va., 1984-92, Marathon Oil/Ill., Wisc., Chgo., Chgo., 1992—. Named to Nat. Assn. Intercollegiate Athletes Sml. Coll. All-State Football Team/Dist. 23, 1968. Mem. Cleve. Petroleum Club (v.p. 1988-91), Chgo. Oilmens. Republican. Presbyterian. Avocations: camping, softball, basketball, physical work out. Office: Marathon Ashland Petroleum LLC PO Box 1635 Bolingbrook IL 60440-7356

WILLANS, JEAN STONE, bishop, religious organization executive; b. Hillsboro, Ohio, Oct. 3, 1924; d. Homer and Ella (Keys) Hammond; m.

Richard James Willans, Mar. 28, 1966; 1 dau., Suzanne Jeanne. Student, San Diego Jr. Coll.; DD (hon.), Am. Coll. Sems., 1996. Ordained archdeacon, 1996, ordained priest 1997, consecrated bishop 1998, Ch. of the East. Asst. to v.p. Family Loan Co., Miami, Fla., 1946-49; civilian supr. USAF, Washington, 1953-55; founder, dir. Blessed Trinity Soc.; editor Trinity mag., L.A., 1960-66; co-founder, exec. v.p., dir. Soc. of Stephen, Altadena, Calif., 1967—; exec. dir. Hong Kong, 1975-81; lectr. in field. Author: The Acts of the Green Apples, 1974, rev. edit. 1995; co-editor: Charisma in Hong Kong, 1970, Spiritual Songs, 1970, The People Who Walked in Darkness, 1977, The People Who Waled in Darkness II, 1992. Recipient Achievement award Nat. Assn. Pentecostal Women, 1964; monument erected in her honor Kowloon Walled City Park, Hong Kong Govt., 1996. Republican. Office: Soc of Stephen PO Box 6225 Altadena CA 91003-6225

WILLANS, RICHARD JAMES, bishop, religious organization executive; b. Detroit, July 24, 1943; s. James Cyril and Georgie Agnes (Ray) W.; m. Jean Stone, Mar. 28, 1966; 1 child, Suzanne Jeanne. Student, Dartmouth Coll., 1960-63; BS in Orgnl. Behavior, U. San Francisco, 1984; DD (hon.), Am. Coll. Seminarians, Santa Cruz, Calif., 1996. Ordained priest Ch. of the East/St. Thomas Tradition, 1996, consecrated as bishop, 1997. Assoc. editor Trinity Mag., Van Nuys, Calif., 1963-66; co-founder, pres., chmn. Soc. of Stephen, Altadena, Calif., 1967—; missionary pastor Soc. of Stephen, Hong Kong, 1968-81; tchr. Hong Kong Christian Coll., Caineway English Coll., Hong Kong, 1968-71; ops. mgr. RCM Svcs., Hong Kong, 1972-74; dir. exec. selection Peat, Marwick, Mitchell & Co., Hong Kong, 1974-81; pers. dir. Gen. Bank, L.A., 1982-83; dir. human resources Calif. Commerce Bank, L.A., 1984-88; mgr. human resources info. ctr. Union Bank of Calif., Monterey Pk., 1988-96; lectr. in field. Co-editor: (collection of personal stories) Charisma in Hong Kong, 1970, (song book) Spiritual Songs, 1970, (book series) The People Who Walked in Darkness, Vol. I, 1977, Vol. II, 1992, (book) The Acts of the Green Apples, 1995. Monument in his honor for drug addict rehab. work Kowloon Walled City Pk., Hong Kong, 1996. Republican. Office: PO Box 6225 Altadena CA 91003-6225

WILLARD, JOHN GERARD, consultant, author, lecturer; b. Pitts., Nov. 20, 1952; s. Cornelius Merle and May E. (Hinds) W.; m. Lorraine L. Franze, Sept. 2, 1978; children: Mary Elizabeth, Kristen Anne, Lisa Lorraine, Jessica Kathleen. BA in Journalism, Duquesne U., 1974. Producer, dir. air talent Sta. WDUQ-FM, Pitts., 1971-73; master control tech. dir. Sta. KDKA-TV, Pitts., 1973; cons. comms. Better Bus. Bur., Pitts., 1974; asst. account exec. Marc & Co. Advt., Pitts., 1975; adminstr., employee benefit adminstrn. Rockwell Internat. Corp., Pitts., 1975-80, adminstr. relocation and corp. personnel procedures, 1980-81, mgr. corp. policy, 1981-82; pres. John G. Willard Cons., 1982—. Contbr. articles to profl. jours. Mem. Am. Mensa Ltd., Internat. Platform Assn., Smithsonian Nat. Instn., NRA (marksmanship instr.), Stage 62, Kappa Tau Alpha, Alpha Tau Omega. Office: 360 Middlegate Dr Bethel Park PA 15102-1438

WILLARD, RALPH LAWRENCE, surgery educator, physician, former college president; b. Manchester, Iowa, Apr. 6, 1922; s. Hosea B. and Ruth A. (Hazelrigg) W.; m. Margaret Dyer Dennis, Sept. 26, 1969; children: Laurie, Jane, Ann, H. Thomas. Student, Cornell Coll., 1940-42, Coe Coll., 1945; D.O., Kirksville Coll. Osteo. Medicine, 1949; EdD (hon.), U. North Tex., 1985; ScD (hon.), W.Va. Sch. Osteo. Medicine, 1993. Intern Kirksville Osteo. Hosp., 1949-50, resident in surgery, 1954-57; chmn. dept. surgery Davenport Osteo. Hosp., 1957-68; dean, prof. surgery Kirksville Coll. Osteo. Medicine, 1969-73; asso. dean acad. affairs, prof. surgery Mich. State U. Coll. Osteo. Medicine, 1974-75; dean Tex. Coll. Osteopathic Medicine, 1975-76, pres., 1981-85, prof. surgery, 1985-87; v.p. med. affairs North Tex. State U., Denton, 1976-81; assoc. dean W.Va. Sch. Osteo. Medicine, Lewisburg, 1988-91; mem. Nat. Adv. Council Edn. for Health Professions, 1971-73, Iowa Gov.'s Council Hosps. and Health Related Facilities, 1965-68; chmn. council deans Am. Assn. Colls. Osteo. Medicine, 1970-73, pres., 1979-80. Served with USAAF, 1942-45; Served with USAF, 1952-53; col. USAFR, ret. Decorated D.F.C., Air medal with 4 oak leaf clusters, Meritorious Svc. medal, Legion of Merit; recipient Robert A. Kistner Educator award Am. Assn. Colls. Osteo. Medicine, 1989; named Disting. scholar Acad. Osteo. Medicine Nat. Acads. Practice, 2000. Fellow Am. Coll. Physician Execs., Am. Coll. Osteo. Surgeons; mem. Am. Osteo. Assn. (Disting. Svc. cert. 1992), Tex. Osteo. Assn., W.Va. Soc. Osteo. Medicine, Am. Acad. Osteopathy, Acad. Osteo. Dirs. Med. Edn., Aerospace Med. Assn., Flying Physicians Assn., Quiet Birdmen, Davis-Monthan Officers Club, Masons, Shriners, Lewisburg Rotary (Paul Harris fellow), Internat. Comanche Soc., Order of Daedalians. Democrat. Episcopalian. Home: PO Box 749 Lewisburg WV 24901-0749 Office: WVa Sch Osteo Medicine 400 N Lee St Lewisburg WV 24901-1128

WILLAUER, GEORGE JACOB, English literature educator; b. Oct. 30, 1935; s. George Jacob and Mary Catherine (Eshleman) W.; m. Cynthia Cameron Thun, June 11, 1966; children: George Jacob III, Elizabeth Christian. BA, Wesleyan U., 1957; MA, U. Pa., 1959, PhD, 1965. Asst. instr. U. Pa., Phila., 1958-62; instr. Conn. Coll., New London, 1962-66, asst. prof., 1966-72, assoc. prof., 1972-78, prof., 1978—, chair dept. English, 1972-77, 91-94, 2000—; Charles J. MacCurdy prof. of Am. Studies, 2000; coll. marshal, dean of acad. programs, 1997-2000; instr. Williams Coll.-Mystic Seaport Program in Maritime Studies, 1986-88; vis. prof. lit. U. Dar es Salaam, Tanzania, 1995; trustee MacCurdy-Salisbury Ednl. Found. Author: A Lyme Miscellany: 1776-1976, 1977; contbr. articles to profl. jours. Trustee; Lyme Hist. Soc., Florence Griswold Mus., pres. 1983-88, Lyme Land Conservation Trust, Lyme Pub. Libr., Cmty. Found. Southeastern Conn. (pres.), Lyman Allyn Art Mus. English-Speaking Union fellow, 1969, 72. Mem. AAUP, MLA, Century Assn. Home: 55-1 Beaver Brook Rd Old Lyme CT 06371-3219 Office: Conn Coll New London CT 06320

WILLAUSCHUS, WOLFGANG GUENTER, orthopedic surgeon; b. Berlin, Aug. 25, 1961; s. Guenter Albert and Berta (Rossocha) W.; m. Gudrun Berta Elisabeth Binder, Sept. 28, 1992; children: Maximilian Pascal, Maria Josefine, Katharina. Ed., U. München. Cert. orthopedic surgeon, 1996, rheumatologist, 1997. Intern orthopedics dept. Univ. Erlangen, 1989-90, 93-96, sr., 1996-97, establishment, 1997—; intern Pegnitz Hosp., 1990-92, Traumatol Hosp., Nurnberg, 1992. Mem. Internat. Soc. Orthopedic Surgery. Office: Orthopedic Praxis-Klinik, Am Sportplatz 26, D 96103 Hallstadt Germany

WILLBOLD, DIETER, structural biochemist, researcher; b. Gerlenhofen, Bavaria, Germany, Feb. 5, 1965; s. Josef and Franziska (Bosch) W.; m. Sabine Yvonne Kundler. Diploma in biochemistry, U. Bayreuth, Germany, 1991, D Natural Scis., 1994. Sci. asst. U. Bayreuth, Bavaria, Germany, 1994-95, rsch. group leader, 1995-98; ind. rsch. group leader Inst. for Molecular Biotech., Jena, Germany, 1998—. Contbr. articles to sci. jours., including Sci. Mem. Protein Soc., Gesellschaft Biochemie und Molekularbiologie, Gesellschaft Deutscher Chemiker. Office: Inst for Molecular Biotech, Beutenbergstrasse 11, D-07745 Jena Germany

WILLCOTT, EARLINE FAY, social worker; b. San Juan, Tex., Aug. 26, 1936; d. William Earl and Autie (Phillips) Hinkle; m. Mark Robert Willcott III, June 4, 1955; children: Julie Willcott Bell, June Derby, Mark Robert III, Ashley. BA in English, U. Houston, 1972, MSW, 1982. Lic. master social worker; advanced clin. pracititioner; accredited cert. social worker. Regulatory affairs officer NMR Imaging, Inc., Houston, 1983-89; coord. of social work Alive Hospice, Inc., Nashville, 1990-94; coord. of social svcs. Hospice Galveston County, Texas City, Tex., 1995-98; psychotherapist Samaritan Counseling & Edn., Houston, 1998—; pvt. practice psychotherapy, 2000—; sec. Mid. Cumberland Coun. of Health Care Social Workers, 1990-94; mem. selection com. Nat. Hospice Orgn., Arlington, 1993; facilitator White House Conf. on Aging, Houston, 1995. Mem. adv. bd. Tenn CARE: Population at Risk, Nashville, Tenn., 1993-94. Named Notable Women of Tex. State of Tex., 1984. Mem. NASW. Presbyterian. Avocations: gardening, traveling, needlepoint, theater, opera.

WILLE, ROSANNE LOUISE, higher education administrator; b. Hackensack, N.J., Aug. 4, 1941; d. Albert Wille and Rose Marie (Rock) Eberhardt; m. George B. Jacobs, Mar. 12, 1980; children: Leigh, Steven, Alexander, Jeffrey. M Pub. Adminstrn., Rutgers U., 1986; PhD, N.Y.U., 1980. Dept. chair Rutgers U., Newark, N.J., 1978-84, Lehman Col., Bronx, N.Y., 1984-87; dean Lehman Col., 1987-92, provost, sr. v.p., 1992—. Contbr. articles to profl. jours. Bd. dirs. Family Support Svcs., Bronx, N.Y., 1994—, bd. dirs. South Bronx Overall Economic Devel., Inc., Bronx, 1991—. Recipient Vision award Family Support Svcs., Bronx, 1996, Thousand Points of Light award Pres. George Bush, Washington, 1991. Mem. N.Y. Acad. Scis., N.Y. Acad. Medicine, Am. Assn. Higher Edn. Avocations: aviation, golf. Office: Lehman Col City U Bedford Pk Blvd W Bronx NY 10468

WILLE, VOLKER, publishing executive; b. Karlsruhe, Germany, Mar. 16, 1941; s. Bruno Johannes Wille and Lina (Müller) Munser; m. Barbara Dorthea Fett, 1969; children: Christina, Almut Martina, Gudrun Vera. Dipl. geography, U. Saarbrücken, 1968, Dr. phil., 1971. Researcher Deutsche Gesellschaft for Landentwicklung, Bad Homburg, 1969-72; cons., pub. mgr. Acad. for Raumforschung and Landesplanung, Hannover, 1989—. Mem., sec. Arbeitskreis der Landschaftsanwälte, Inst. fur Auslands beziehungen (ifa) GEDOK Rhein-Main-Taunus, Itneressen gemeinschaft deutschsprachiger Autoren. Avocations: writing, photography, traveling. Office: Acad for Raumforschung & Landesplanung, Hohenzollernstr 11, 30161 Hannover Germany

WILLEMS, KLAAS BJÖRN, Belgian language researcher; b. Bruges, W Flanders, Belgium, Aug. 28, 1965; s. Marcus A.A. and Christa (Lampe) W. MA, U. Ghent, Belgium, 1987, PhD, 1992; postgrad. studies, Deutscher Akad. Austauschdienst, Germany, 1987-88. Rsch. asst. Belgian Nat. Fund for Sci. Rsch., Brussels, 1988-94, rsch. fellow, 1994-97; prof. gen. linguistics U. Ghent, 1997—; rschr. U. Ghent, Belgium, 1994. Author: (books) Meta, Kritik der Erkenntnis des Sprachlichen, 1990, Sprache, Sprachreflexion und Erkenntniskritik, 1994, Eigenname und Bedeutung, 1996, Kasus, grammatische Bedeutung und kognitive Linguistik, 1997, (with J. Van Pottelberge) Geschichte und Systematik des adverbalen Dativs im Deutschen, 1998. Grantee Deutscher Akad. Austauschdienst Deutschland, 1987-88. Office: U Ghent Dept Gen Linguistic, Blandijnberg 2, B-9000 Ghent Flanders, Belgium

WILLEMSE, HEINRICH STEPHEN, humanities educator, journalist; b. Ladismith, South Africa, Sept. 18, 1957; s. Stephanus Jacobus and Catherine Dorothy (Samuels) W.; m. Carol-Ann Patricia Mohamed, Aug. 12, 1989. BA, U. Western Cape, 1978, BA with honors, 1979, MA, 1984, DLitt, 1995. Jr. lectr. U. Western Cape, Bellville, South Africa, 1981-84, lectr., 1984-86, sr. lectr., 1987-90, assoc. prof., 1991-95; exec. dir. OLM Pubs., 1996-2000; prof. U. Pretoria, South Africa, 2000—. Author: Angsland, 1981; editor: Die Trojaanse Perd, 1986, I Qabane Labantu, 1989, Vernuwing in die Afrikaanse Letterkunde, 1995, Die reis na Paternoster, 1997, Die Stukke wat ons sny, 1999, More than Brothers, 2000. Spl. rep. Congress of South African Writers, Athens, 1988; sec. United Dem. Front, Kraafontein, South Africa, 1984; spl. rep. Writers Forum, Johannesburg, 1987; lang. specialist African Nat. Congress, Johannesburg, 1990-94; trustee Youth Theatre, Cape Town, 1990—. Mem. Maatschappij Der Lettere, Afrikaans Lit. Soc. (chair publs. 1994-96, chair Nat. Lang. Project, Cape Town, South Africa, 1991-94, Western Cape Cultural Commn., vice chairperson Welkom Trust), Shoma Endl. Trust. Avocations: gardening, mountaineering, video production and photography, reading. E-mail: mowil@mweb.co.za.

WILLEN, ROGER, pathology consultant; b. Stockholm, Sept. 6, 1939; s. Sven and Siv Hervor Elisabeth (Jeppson) W.; m. Barbro Gunilla Nisbeth, May 20, 1962 (div. 1975); children: Gina, Ylva, Kristina; m. Helena Křivinková, May 27, 1976; 1 child, Linda. B of Medicine, U. Uppsala, Sweden, 1964, PhD, 1971, M of Medicine, 1973, MD, 1973. Asst., rsch. asst. dept. pathology Uppsala U., Sweden, 1964-71, 72-75; assoc. prof. U. Uppsala, 1973; resident Karolinska Hosp., Sweden, 1971-72; jr. cons. Ctrl. Hosp., Falun, Sweden, 1975-81; sr. cons. pathology U. Hosp., Lund, Sweden, 1981-98; prof. II pathology U. Trondheim, Norway, 1998-99; sr. cons. pathology U Hosp. Sahlgrenskn, Goteborg, 1999—; cons. King Faisal Hosp., Saudi Arabia, 1987; vice chmn. dept. pathology U. Hosp., Lund, 1989-95. Co-author: Oral Cancer, Epidemiology, Ethiology and Pathology, 1990, Urinary Diversion, 1995, Alimentary Tract Radiology, 1994; contbr. articles to profl. jours. Mem. Swedish Physian Soc., Swedish Soc. Pathology. Avocations: wood working, sailing, flying, travel, art.

WILLETT, ANNA HART, composer; b. Bartlesville, Okla., June 18, 1931; d. Thomas Kellogg and Mary Kathryn (Feist) Willett Dalferes; m. Roger Garland Horn, Aug. 1956 (div. June 1962). B in Music Edn., Southwestern La. Inst., 1954; MA, La. State U., 1964, postgrad. in piano, voice majors, 1976-87. Lifetime tchr. cert., La. Pub. sch. vocal music tchr. Iberville Parish, Plaquemine, La., 1954-55, Orleans Parish, New Orleans, 1966-71; elem. music pedagogy tchr. St. Mary's Dominican Coll., New Orleans, 1972. Composer: Dances for Solo Violin, 1981, Weaving Song, 1982, Entertainer's Song, (from the opera Omar), 1983, Hercules Piano Variations, 1986, En Ivrez Solo Song, 1989, Solo Songson Poems of Alfieri, 1996, 2000, Variations on a Southern Folk Hymn for piano, Memories of New Orleans, variations for piano, voice Recital at Fest For All, Baton Rouge, La., (operas) How to Murder Mother, Who Murdered Mother, Omar, 1982, Cellini the Opera, Lines on Wine, Caught, Druid Installation, 1997, Seven Gables, 1998, The Icey Road, 1999. Mem. ch. choir St. Albans Episcopalian chapel, 1976—. Scholar Loyola U. of the South, New Orleans, 1972-73. Mem. AAUW, Alpha Sigma Alpha, Sigma Alpha Iota. Episcopalian. Avocations: gardening, bridge, local archeology. Home: 2244 Ferndale Ave Baton Rouge LA 70808-2830

WILLETTS, NEIL STANLEY, biotechnologist, consultant; b. Norton Canes, Eng., Oct. 4, 1939; arrived in Australia, 1982; s. Stanley George and Iris May (Jackson) W.; m. Ruth Linda Litzky, Apr. 10, 1968; children: Karen Eve, Juliet Rebecca Mary, Sarah Lynne. BA with honors, Cambridge U., Eng., 1961, MA, PhD, 1965. Postdoctoral fellow ENCB, IPN, Mexico City, Mex., 1965-67; postdoctoral fellow dept. molecular biology U. Calif., Berkeley, 1967-68; staff mem. MRC Molecular Genetics Unit, Edinburgh, Scotland, 1968-74; lectr., reader in molecular biology Edinburgh U., 1974-82, prof. molecular genetics, 1982-84; dir. of R&D Biotech Australia, Sydney, 1982-97; vis. prof. biol. scis. Sydney U., 1985-97; chmn. faculty of sci. vis. com. U. Wollongong, 1996-98. Mem. editl. bd.: Genetical Rsch., 1972-86, Genes & Devel., 1986-89; contbr. numerous articles to sci. publs. and chpts. to 5 books in field of molecular genetics. Fellow Australian Acad. of Technol. Scis. and Engring.; mem. Australian Biotech. Assn. (bd. dirs. 1988-94, 98—, pres. 1992-93). Avocations: scuba diving, underwater photography, bush walking, classical music. Home: 113 Bent St, Sydney 2070, Australia

WILLEY, CHARLES WAYNE, lawyer; b. Dillon, Mont., Oct. 7, 1932; s. Asa Charles and Elizabeth Ellen Willey; m. Helene D., July 21, 1962 (div.); children: Stephen Charles, Heather Helene, Brent David, Scott D.; m. Alexis W. Grant, Jan. 26, 1986. BS with honors, Mont. State U., 1954; JD with high honors, U. Mont., 1959. Bar: Mont. 1959, Calif. 1960, U.S. Ct. Claims 1975, U.S. Tax Ct. 1975, U.S. Ct. Appeals (9th cir.) 1959, U.S. Ct. Appeals (Fed. cir.) 1983, U.S. Supreme Ct. 1972. Law clk. to presiding judge U.S. Ct. Appeals (9th cir.), 1959-60; ptnr. Price, Postel & Parma, Santa Barbara, Calif., 1960-77; pvt. practice Santa Barbara, 1977-97; shareholder Hollister & Brace, Santa Barbara, 1998—; prof. law corp.; instr. Santa Barbara City Coll., 1961-63, U. Calif., Santa Barbara, 1963-64; lectr. Mont. Tax Inst., 1990, 92, Am. Agr. Law Assn., 1993, 96. Chief editor Mont. Law Rev., 1958-59. Pres. Legal Aid Found. Santa Barbara, 1970; mem. Laguna Blanca Sch. Bd., pres. 1980-81; v.p. Phoenix of Santa Barbara. Served to capt. USAF, 1954-56. Mem. Santa Barbara County Bar Assn. (pres. 1972-73), Phi Kappa Phi, Phi Eta Sigma, Phi Delta Phi. Republican. Episcopalian. Lodge: Kiwanis. Avocations: reading, writing, traveling. Office: 1126 Santa Barbara St Santa Barbara CA 93101-2008

WILLGOOSE, GARRY RAYMOND, environmental engineer, researcher; b. Sydney, May 13, 1958; s. Colin Henry and Edna Almeda (Durham) W.; m. Veronica Ruth Antcliff, Oct. 10, 1983. BS, U. Newcastle, 1981, B in Engring. with honors, 1981; MS, MIT, 1987, PhD, 1989. Design engr. Dept. Main Rds., Sydney, 1980-81; hydrologist Croft and Assocs., Newcastle, Australia, 1981-82, Snowy Mountains Engring. Corp., Cooma, Australia, 1982-84; rsch. fellow U. Newcastle, Australia, 1989-91, lectr., 1991-98, sr. lectr. then assoc. prof., 1999—. Recipient Lorenz Straub award U. Minn., 1989. Mem. Am. Geophys. Union, Australian Inst. of Mining and Metallurgy, Sigma Xi. Avocations: woodworking, model railways. Office: U Newcastle Dept Civil Surveying and Environ Engring, University Dr, Callaghan NSW 2308, Australia

WILLI, ANDREA, Liechtenstein government official; b. 1955. PhD in Philosophy, U. Zurich, Switzerland. With Swiss Cultural Found., 1982-87; joined Diplomatic Svc., Liechtenstein, 1987; mem. European Union Negotiating Commn., 1989-91; rep. of Liechtenstein European Free Trade Assn., 1991-92, UN, Geneva, 1992-93; govt. councillor fgn. affairs Govt. Liechtenstein, Vaduz, 1993—, govt. councillor culture, youth and sport, 1993—, govt. councilor family and equality matters, 1997—. Mem. Patriotic Union. Office: Regierungsgebäude, FL-9490 Vaduz Liechtenstein*

WILLIAMES, LEE JOHN, university official, history educator; b. Phila., July 4, 1942; m. Frances Gray, Feb. 24, 1968; children: Elizabeth Jamerlan, Lee D., David. BA in Pre-Law and Liberal Arts, LaSalle U., 1964; MA in European History, Niagara U., 1966, ACS in Soviet Studies, 1966; PhD in History, SUNY, Binghamton, 1981. Prof., honors dir. Coll. Misericordia, Dallas, Pa., 1966-86; asst. provost, prof. U. Scranton, Pa., 1987-92; v.p. acad. affairs, prof. history U. St. Thomas, 1992—, now emeritus v.p. acad. affairs; sec. gen. internat. coun. U. St. Thomas, 1995-97. Author: Anton Chekov: Iconoclast, 1989; (curriculum exercises) Odyssey of the Mind, 1988-96. Cons. Penn's Woods coun. Girl Scouts U.S.A., 1986-90; commr. Northeastern Pa. coun. Boy Scouts Am., 1988-92, v.p., 1984-88; mem. water safety bd. ARC, N.E. Pa., 1988-91; chair steering com. St. Thomas/Shell Oil/Helms Collaboration, 1997—. Fellow Med. History Soc. Baylor U. Coll. Medicine, 1997; recipient Silver Beaver medal Boy Scouts Am., 1984, St. George medal Cath. Com. on Scouting, 1986, Jubalarian medal La Salle U., Phila., Centennial medal U. Scranton. Fellow Am. Coun. on Edn. (exec. com. coun. fellows 1989-92); mem. Mid. Atlantic Hist. Assn. of Cath. Colls. and Univs. (editor jour. 1985-92), Am. Assn. for Advancement of Slavic Studies. Roman Catholic. Avocations: swimming, canoeing, martial arts, stained glass, antique restoration. Office: U St Thomas 3800 Montrose Blvd Houston TX 77006-4626

WILLIAMS, ADAIR L., artist; b. Jackson, Tenn., Apr. 18, 1928; d. Horace Adair and Mary Elizabeth (Nelson) Lovin; m. Thomas Schuyler Williams Jr., June 13, 1950; children: Thomas Schuyler III, Elizabeth Leigh, Nelson Lovin. BA in Art, Randolph Macon Women's Coll., 1950; postgrad., Atlanta Sch. of Art. Home studio art tchr. Atlanta, 1960s-70s; co-op. owner Golden Easel Art Gallery, Atlanta; spkr. Emory U., Atlanta, 1978; demonstrator Roswell Fine Arts Assn., 2000; spkr. in field. One woman shows at Ga. Tech. Student Ctr. Art Gallery, 1971, The Tea Room, Nashville, 1977, Kennesaw Coll. Art Gallery, 1984, Ch. of Atonement, 1970, 90, 96, Houston lake Country Club, Perry, Ga., 1996, Barnes and Noble, North Point Mall, 1998; exhibited in group shows at DeKalb Fed Atlanta Artists Ctr. Show, 1980, 81, Atlanta Artists Ctr., 1980, 81, 82, 83, Jan Gallery, 1983, Patron's Watercolor Gala, Okla., 1984, Winter Arts Festival, 1985 (MGAA award), Coker Creek Artists, Brasstown, N.C., 1987, Marietta Gallery, 1987, Albany Mus. Art, 1989, Roswell Fine Arts City Show, 1991, 92, 93, Valdosta State Fine Arts Gallery, 1984, 87, 91, Roswell Visual Arts Ctr., 1993, 94, 99, Ctrl. South at Parthenon, Nashville, 1993 (Nations Bank award), Grandview Gallery, 1995, Gwinnett Fine Arts Ctr., 1996, Ga. Watercolor Soc., 1996, 98, Atlanta Bot. Gardens, 1996, North Fulton Invitational, 2000, numerous others. Mem. Atlanta Arts Coun., 1970s; art tchr. Meth. Settlement House, Atlanta, 1960s-70s; painter scenery Sandy Springs Players, North Springs H.S., Atlanta, 1960-70; vol. Girl Scouts U.S., Sr. Citizens, Northside Meth. Ch., Atlanta, 1960-70. Mem. Ga. Watercolor Soc. (signature mem., bd. dirs.), So. Watercolor Soc. (signature mem.), Atlanta Arts Ctr. (pres.), Tenn. Art League, Atlanta Athletic Club (chmn.), Alpha Omicron Pi. Republican. Episcopalian.

WILLIAMS, ALFRED BLYTHE, management consultant, educator; b. Oakland City, Ind., Sept. 17, 1940; s. Ross Merl and Jesse Adell (Helsley) W. BS cum laude, Oakland City U., 1963; MS, Ind. U., 1964; PhD, Ga. State U., 1974. Tchr. Arlington H.S., Indpls., 1964-65, Oakland City (Ind.) U., 1965-69; editor Southwestern Pub. Co., Cin., 1969-72, cons., 1981-93; adj. prof. Ga. State U., Atlanta, 1972-74; prof. mgmt. and bus. comm. U. La., Lafayette, 1975—, chmn. dept., 1986-96; cons. John Wiley Pub. Co., N.Y., 1988-89, Irwin Pub., 1989. Author study guides; editor Info. Systems Bus. Comm. Jour., 1983, 93. Patron Lafayette Cmty. Concerts, 1984—; contbr. La. and Nat. Rep. parties, Baton Rouge, Washington, 1983—. Mem. AAUP, Assn. Bus. Communicators (bd. dirs. 1986-90, Francis W. Weeks Merit award 1984), La. Assn. Higher Edn., Sierra Club, Kiwanis, Phi Delta Kappa, Phi Kappa Phi, Delta Pi Epsilon, Beta Gamma Sigma. Methodist.

WILLIAMS, BENJAMIN HAYDEN, JR., orthodontist; b. Davenport, Iowa, Dec. 18, 1921; s. Benjamin Hayden Williams and Margaret Ethyl (Grant) Williams-Glick; children: Benjamin, Kenneth, Camilla, Nanette, Grant. DDS, Ohio State U., 1946, MS, 1949; MS, U. Ill., Chgo., 1951. Diplomate Am. Bd. Orthodontics. Rsch. fellow U. Ill., Chgo., 1949-51; grad. teaching asst. Ohio State U., Columbus, 1946, 48-49; pvt. practice Worthington, Ohio, 1951-97; from instr. to prof. Ohio State U., Columbus, 1951-85, prof. emeritus, 1985—; cons. Dept. Human Svcs., City of Columbus, 1985—, Bur. Children's Med. Handicap, Columbus, 1988—; rsch. advisor numerous grad. students, 1951-96. Contbr. articles to profl. publs. Mem. ADA, Am. Assn. Orthodontists, Great Lakes Assn. Orthodontists (historian 1989-96), Ohio Dental Assn., Columbus Dental Soc., E.H. Amgle Soc. Orthodontists (pres. midwest area 1988). Avocations: travel, photography. Home: 2204 Partlow Dr Columbus OH 43220-2927

WILLIAMS, BERNABE FIGUEROA, professional baseball player; b. San Juan, P.R., Sept. 13, 1968. Outfielder New York Yankees, 1991—. Named Am. League Championship Series MVP, 1996; won World Series with best win record ever 127 games, 1998. Office: New York Yankees Yankee Stadium E 161 St and River Ave Bronx NY 10451

WILLIAMS, BERNARD, Olympic athlete; b. Balt., Jan. 19, 1978. Student, Barton County C.C., Great Bend, Kans., U. Fla., 2000—. Co-winner Gold Medal 4X100 meter relay U.S.A. Track and Field Team, Sydney, 2000. Office: USA Track and Field Team One RCA Dome Ste 140 Indianapolis IN 46225*

WILLIAMS, BETTY, peace activist; b. Belfast, Northern Ireland, May 22, 1943; m. Ralph Williams, 1961 (div.); 2 children; m. James T. Perkins, 1983. LL.D. (hon.), Yale U.; L.H.D. (hon.), Coll. Siera Heights, 1977. Co-organizer (with Mairead Corrigan) of movement Women for Peace (now Community of Peace People), Belfast, 1976-80. co-founder (with Mairead Corrigan) mag. Peace by Peace. Co-recipient Nobel Prize for Peace for 1976 (awarded 1977), Norwegian People's Peace Prize, 1976, Carl von Ossietzky prize German Fed. Republic, 1976. Roman Catholic. Address: 208 Camelia St Gulf Breeze FL 32561-4228 also: PO Box 725 Valparaiso FL 32580-0725

WILLIAMS, CALVIT HERNDON, environmental chemist; b. Houston, Dec. 28, 1936; s. Calvit Herndon and Julia Eloise (Tybor) W.; children: Sabina, Terence, Russel, Damon. BA in Chemistry, U. St. Thomas, Houston, 1958; PhD in Phys. Chemistry, Brown U., 1965. Cert. indsl. hygienist, safety profl.; qualified environ. profl. Postdoctoral fellow Rice U., Houston, 1964-66; rsch. scientist Sandia Labs., Albuquerque, 1966-70; prof. chemistry U. Estadual De Sao Paulo En Campinas, Brazil, 1971-76; lab. dir. Aer-Aqua Labs. Inc., Houston, 1976-77; prin. scientist Radian Corp., Austin, Tex., 1977—. Author: Chlorinated Dioxins and Furans, 1985; contbg. author: Principles of Environmental Sampling, 1996. Fellow Am. Indsl. Hygiene Assn. (com. chair-elect 1994, chmn. 1995, bd. dirs. 1992-93, 94-99, chmn. bd. 1990-92), Am. Inst. Chemists; mem. Am. Chem. Soc. (chmn. ctrl. Tex. chpt. 1980-82), Austin C. of C. (Leadership Austin 1992-93), N.Y. Acad. Sci., Am. Soc. Safety Engrs., Sigma Xi, Delta Epsilon Sigma. Achievements include development of numerous strategies and methods for environmental health monitoring, especially for ambient, indoor and workplace air. Avocations: backpacking, racquetball, skiing, coffee, sailing. Office: Radian Internat LLC PO Box 201088 Austin TX 78720-1088

WILLIAMS, CAROL MARIE, secondary school educator; b. Kansas City, Kans., June 10, 1939; d. Leonard Cropley and Minnie Marie (Wass) Nichol-

son; m. Howard Dean Williams, Dec. 29, 1961; children: Jeffrey Allen, Gregory Scott,. AA, Kansas City (Mo.) Jr. Coll., 1959; BS in Edn., Ctrl. Mo. State U., 1962. English tchr. Raytown (Mo.) H.S., 1961-62; English tchr., coord. dist. lang. arts Ruskin H.S., Kansas City, Mo., 1964-66; English tchr. Hickman Mills H.S., Kansas City, 1969-70; English/debate/history/student govt. tchr. Andover (Kans.) H.S., 1982-95, dist. lang. arts coord., dept. chair, 1982-95; English tchr. Olathe (Kans.) H.S., 1996—; coord., debate and forensics coach Andover Sch. Dist., 1982-85, chair North Ctrl. Accreditation, 1983-84, supt., prin. adv. couns., 1983-95, dist. curriculum coun., 1983-95. Publicity editor The Lamp mag., 1969 (Nat. Recognition award 1969); contbg. editor Topeka mag., 1977-79; co-editor Andover Rsch. jour., 1993. Recipient Outstanding Tchr. and Mentor Recognition award U. Kans., Outstanding H.S. Edn. Recognition award Kans. Newman Coll. Mem. NEA, Kans. NEA, Nat. Coun. Tchrs. of English, Kans. Assn. Tchrs. of English. Republican. Episcopalian. Avocations: reading, music, tennis, travel, writing. Home: 1204 W 63d St Kansas City MO 64113 Office: Olathe South HS 1640 E 151st St Olathe KS 66062-2851

WILLIAMS, CAROLE ANN, retired cytotechnologist; b. Duquesne, Pa., Apr. 14, 1934; d. Theodore Wylie and Dorothy Belle (Mehrmann) Williams. BS, Chatham Coll., 1956; postgrad., Case-Western Res. U., 1956-57; MS, Calif. State U., 1989. Cytotechnologist Clin. Path. Lab. of Paul Gross, Pitts., 1957-59; chief cytotechnologist, tchg. supr. Presbyn. U. Hosp., Pitts., 1959-63; staff Pathology Lab. of Drs. Armanini & Wegner, Stockton, Calif., 1964; chief cytotechnologist, tchg. supr. Hosp. of Good Samaritan, L.A., 1964-89; dir. cytotechnology tng. program UCLA Med. Ctr., 1989-99; condr. workshops in field. Mem. Am. Soc. Clin. Pathologists (cytotech exam. com. bd. registry 1978-84, mem. bd. govs. 1990-95), Calif. Assn. Cytotechnologists (pres. 1967-68, 72-73), Internat. Acad. Cytology, Am. Soc. Cytopathology (Technologist of Yr. award 1981, Excellence in Edn. award 1998). Democrat. Presbyterian. Home: 2460 Stoner Ave Los Angeles CA 90064-1326 Office: Pathology Assocs Lab 11915 La Grange Los Angeles CA 90025

WILLIAMS, CHARLES JUDSON, lawyer; b. San Mateo, Calif., Nov. 23, 1930; s. John Augustus and Edith (Babcock) W.; children: Patrick, Victoria, Apphia. AB, U. Calif., Berkeley, 1952, LLB, 1955. Bar: Calif. 1955, U.S. Supreme Ct., 1970. Assoc. Kirkbride, Wilson, Harzfeld and Wallace, San Mateo County, Calif., 1956-59; sole practice Solano County, Calif., 1959-64, Martinez, Calif., 1964—, Benicia, Calif., 1981-88; city atty. Pleasant Hill, Calif., 1962-80, Yountville, Calif., 1965-68, Benicia, 1968-76, 80-82, Lafayette, Calif., 1968—, Moraga, Calif., 1974-92, Danville, Calif., 1982-88, Pittsburg, Calif., 1984-93, Orinda, Calif., 1985-97; lectr. Calif. Continuing Edn. Bar 1964-65, U. Calif. Extension 1974-76, John F. Kennedy U. Sch. Law 1966-69; spl. counsel to various Calif. cities; legal advisor Alaska Legis. Council 1959-61; advisor Alaska sup. ct. 1960-61; advisor on revision Alaska statues 1960-62; atty. Pleasant Hill Redevel. Agy. 1978-82; sec., bd. dirs. Vintage Savs. & Loan Assn., Napa County, Calif., 1974-82; bd. dirs. 23d Agrl. Dist. Assn., Contra Costa County, 1968-70. Author: California Code Comments to West's Annotated California Codes, 3 vols., 1965, West' California Code Forms, Commercial, 2 vols., 1965, West's California Government Code Forms, 3 vols., 1971, Supplement to California Zoning Practice, 1978, 80, 82, 84, 85, 87, 89, 91, 94, 95, 96, 97, 98, 99, 2000; contbr. articles to legal jours. Mem. ABA, Calif. Bar Assn., Contra Costa County Bar Assn. Office: 1330 Arnold Dr Ste 149 Martinez CA 94553-6538

WILLIAMS, CHERYL A., secondary education educator; b. Neosho, Mo., July 7, 1957; d. Travestine Williams. BS in Math., Tex A&M U., 1978, postgrad., 1978-79; postgrad., Rose State Coll., 1980-81, Sheppard Tech. Tng. Ctr., 1980-81; MS in Math., U. Tex., 1997. Computer scientist Tinker AFB, Oklahoma City, 1980-81, Defense Comm. Agy., Washington, 1986; tchr. Parent Child Inc., San Antonio, 1989; asst. sec. Antioch Bapt. Ch., San Antonio, 1989-92; substitute tchr. San Antonio Ind. Sch. Dist., 1990-93; instrnl. asst. Northside Ind. Sch. Dist., San Antonio, 1995-96, asst. tchr., 1994-95; asst. tchr. North East Ind. Sch. Dist., San Antonio, 1996—; rep. West Telemarketing, 1998-99; math. tutor St. Philips Coll., 1998-99, instr. math., 1998—; instr. math. Alamo C.C. Dist., 1998—; math. tutor Trave and G.G.'s Tutorial Svc., 1999—; indep. beauty cons., Mary Kay Cosmetics, 1999—; asst. mgr. Fashion Place, San Antonio, 1994-95; distbr. Avon, 1999—. Counselor YMCA, San Antonio, 1989-91; active Girl Scouts U.S., 1964-86; mem. choir, asst. sec. area ch., 1972, tutor, 1970—, tchr. Sunday Sch., 1973-86, asst. sec. Sunday Sch., 1973-86, 88—, asst. ch. sec., 1988-91; mem. Dorcas Circle, Lupus Found. Am., Biomed. Rsch. U. Tex., 1995—; mem. Epilepsy Found. Am., Tex. Head Injury Assn., Nat. Head Injury Assn., Smithsonian Instn. Mem. NEA, Tex. Edn. Assn., Mu. Alpha Theta. Avocations: jigsaw puzzles, bowling.

WILLIAMS, CHRISTOPHER MAXWELL J., agricultural scientist; b. Sydney, Australia, Sept. 25, 1948; s. Maxwell Frederick and Vera Mary (Borzell) W.; m. Judith Barbara Spall, Dec. 20, 1980; 1 child, Michelle Susan. BSc in Agr. with honors, U. Sydney, 1970; PhD in Agronomy, U. Adelaide, Australia, 1978. Sr. rsch. officer South Australian Dept., Naracoorte, 1975-79; sr. lectr. Seed Tech. Ctr., Palmerston North, New Zealand, 1979-81; sr. agronomist Dept. Agr., Walpeup, Victoria, Australia, 1981-82; sr. rsch. scientist South Australian R&D Inst., Adelaide, 1982—; convenor, chmn. organizing com. Australian Potatoes 2000 Rsch. Conf., Adelaide, 2000. Expert, author/co-author, over 100 articles on potato and horticulture crop agronomy; author: Potato Diseases in South Australia, Potato Varieties in South Australia. Recipient Howard Meml. Trust award, 1977, Best Paper award Australian Potato Industry Conf., 1990. Mem. Australian Rotary, Australian Inst. Agrl. Sci. and Tech., Internat. Soc, Horticultural Sci. Avocations: cricket, rugby, swimming, Olympics. E-mail: williams.chrism@saugov.sa.gov.au. Fax: 61 8 8389 8899. Office: SA Rsch & Devel Inst, Swamp Rd, Lenswood 5240, Australia

WILLIAMS, CLAY RULE, lawyer; b. Milw., Sept. 25, 1935; s. George Laverne and Marguerite Mae (Rule) W.; m. Jeanne Lee Huber, Jan. 18, 1986; children: Gwynne, Amy, Daniel, Sarah. BA, Lawrence U., 1957; LLB, U. Mich., 1960. Bar: Wis. 1960, U.S. Dist. Ct. (ea. and we. dists.) Wis. 1964, U.S. Ct. Appeals (7th cir.) 1965, U.S. Ct. Mil. Appeals 1963, U.S. Supreme Ct. 1963. Assoc. Gibbs, Roper & Fifield, Milw., 1963-67; ptnr., shareholder Von Briesen, Purtell & Roper, S.C., Milw., 1967-99, of counsel, 1999—; mem. Gov.'s Task Force Creation Bus. Ct., 1994-99; instr. profl. seminars. Author: Berry, Davis, Deguire and Williams, Wisconsin Business Corporation Law, 1992; contbr. articles to profl. publs. Mem. Shorewood (Wis.) Sch. Bd., 1976-79. Capt. USAF, Judge Adv. Corps., 1960-63. Fellow Wis. Bar Found.; mem. ABA (sect. antitrust law, corp. counseling com., task force on Uniform Securities Act, com. on securities litigation), Wis. Bar Assn. (co-chmn. com. to revise corp. laws 1986-90, chmn. standing com. on bus. corp. law 1990-97, Pres.'s Award of Excellence 1990, 97), Milw. Bar Assn. (probate and real property sect., joint bench-bar com. Ct. Appeals, 1986-88, long-range planning com. 1987), 7th Cir. Bar Assn., Fedn. Ins. and Corp. Counsel, Def. Rsch. Inst., Am. Law Inst., Assn. Bar City N.Y., Milw. Club, Univ. Club. Republican. Episcopalian. Avocations: hunting, fishing, skiing, reading. E-mail: cwilliam@vonbriesen.com. Office: von Briesen Purtell & Roper SC 735 N Water St Milwaukee WI 53202-4100 also: 126 S Albany St Spring Green WI 53588-8809

WILLIAMS, CRAIG LESTER CRANAGE, microbiologist, educator; b. Lancaster, Eng., Apr. 24. B Medicine B Surgery, Liverpool (Eng.) U., 1982. Sr. registrar Western Infirmary, Glasgow, Scotland, 1989-93; cons. microbiologist Scunthorpe (U.K.) Gen. Hosp.; cons. microbiologist Royal Alexandra Hosp., Paisley, Scotland, 1995—, clin. dir. diagnostic svcs., 1996—; hon. sr. lectr. U. Glasgow, 1997—; sec. West of Scotland Microbiology Group; rschr. in field. Contbr. articles to profl. jours., chpt. to book. Grantee N.W. Regional Health Authority, 1997, Scottish Office, 1997, Children's Rsch. Found., 1998, Bayer U.K., 1999,. Fellow Royal Coll. Physicians Edinburgh; mem. Royal Coll. Pathology. E-mail: craig.williams@rah.scot.nhs.uk. Office: Royal Alexandra Hosp, Corsebar Rd, Paisley Renfrewshire PA2 9PN, Scotland

WILLIAMS, DAN EDWARD, music company owner; b. Tyler, Tex., July 31, 1950; s. Harry O. and Juanita (Whitaker) W.; m. Deborah P. Smith, Sept. 25, 1970; children: Jennifer, Dan II, Kindle. AA, Tyler Jr. Coll. Prin. Dan Williams Music, Nashville, 1984—; co-owner Creative Recording Studios, Nashville, clients include The Judds, Kenny Rogers. Co-author: (song) Don't You Know How Much I Love You, 1983; composer: (commls.), Red Lobster Seafood Lover, 1980, Reach for Sprite, 1981., Mama Clorox 2, 1986, also KMart, Folgers, Toyota, BellSouth and Mattel; assoc. producer, composer (top ten single) Sexual Power performed by the Pointer Sisters; composer, producer for Quincy Jones; producer commls. for Amoco featuring Gatlin Brothers, Busch featuring Ronnie Milsap, Budweiser featuring Leon Russell, George Jones, The Bellamy Brothers, Clint Black, Hank Williams Jr., Patty Loveless, Kathy Mattea, and Doug Stone, Coors Light featuring Restless Heart, Marty Stuart, T. Graham Brown, and Kelly Willis, Taco Bell featuring T. Graham Brown, Clorox featuring Dobie Gray, and Miller Genuine Draft featuring Vince Gill. Acad. scholar Daus. Confederacy, Texas 1969; recipient Clio awards, Mobius awards, IBA awards, Telly awards, Addy awrads. Mem. BMI, CMA, NARAS, SAG, AFTRA, AFM. Avocation: sports. Office: Dan Williams Music 2806 Azalea Pl Nashville TN 37204-3118

WILLIAMS, DANIEL, government official. Gov. gen. Grenada. Author: A Synopsis of the Public Service, Office and Duties of the Governor General of Grenada. Named Knight Grand Cross of the Most Disting. Order of Saint Michael and Saint George Queen's Counsel. Office: Office of the Gov Gen, Upper Lucas St, Saint Georges Grenada

WILLIAMS, DAVE HARRELL, investment executive; b. Beaumont, Tex., Oct. 5, 1932; s. George Davis and Mary (Hardin) W.; m. Reba White, Mar. 15, 1975. B.S. in Chem. Engring, U. Tex., 1956; M.B.A. (Baker scholar, Teagle fellow), Harvard U., 1961. Chartered fin. analyst. Chem. engr. Exxon Corp., Baton Rouge, 1959; security analyst deVegh & Co., N.Y.C., 1961-64; dir. research Waddell & Reed, Kansas City, Mo., 1964-67; exec. v.p. Mitchell Hutchins, Inc., N.Y.C., 1967-77; chmn. bd. Alliance Capital Mgmt. Corp., N.Y.C., 1977—; bd. dirs. AXA Fin., Inc. Contbr.: articles to Fin. Analysts Jour. Trustee Fgn. Policy Assn, Metropolitan Mus. of Art. Served with USNR, 1956-59. Mem. Fin. Analysts Fedn. (past officer, dir.), N.Y. Soc. Security Analysts (past pres.), Bond Club N.Y., Econ. Club N.Y., Knickerbocker Club, Century Assn., Grolier Club. Presbyterian. Office: Alliance Capital Mgmt Corp Ste 31R 1345 Avenue Of The Americas New York NY 10105-0302

WILLIAMS, DAVID, French language educator; b. Birmingham, England, May 22, 1938; s. Wilfred Richard and Edith May (Strong) W.; m. Eileen Colette Nelson, March 31, 1964; children: Richard, Victoria. BA, U. Birmingham, 1959, PhD, 1963, DLitt, 1999; D de l'univ. (hon.), Le Mans, France, 1984. Lectr. U. Southampton, England, 1962-69; assoc. prof. McMaster U., Canada, 1969-74, prof., 1974-76; prof. Sheffield U., England, 1976—, dean arts, 1994-97; selector Civil Svc. Commn., England, 1981—; mem. exec. com. Voltaire Found., Oxford, England; v.p. editl. coms. Voltaire Complete Works, Oxford, 1968—. Author: Voltaire: Literary Critic, 1966; editor: Commentaires sur Corneille, 1974-75, Voltaire's Essay on Epic Poetry, 1996; translator: Voltaire: Political Writings, 1994. Recipient Chevalier dans l'ordre des Palmes Academiques French Govt., 1998. Mem. Brit. Soc. for 18th Century Studies (pres. 1992-94), Assn. Profs. of French (pres. 1987-90), Soc. French Studies. Avocations: theatre, opera, baroque music. Home: 17 Stumperlowe Hall Rd, Sheffield S10 3QR, England Office: U Sheffield, Sheffield S10 2TN, England Address: U Sheffield French Dept, Western Bank, Sheffield S10 2TN, England

WILLIAMS, DAVID ALEXANDER, retired chief pilot; b. Helena, Mont., May 29, 1939; s. Daniel samuel and Dorothy (Alexander) W.; m. Jacquoline anders, Feb. 14, 1964 (div. Mar. 1988); children: Daniel Alexander, Darryl Jackson. BA, U. So. Calif., L.A., 1962. Lic. airline transport pilot, FAA. Commd. ensign USNR, 1963, advanced through grades to capt., 1985; tng. and test pilot McDonnel Douglas, Long Beach, Calif., 1980-87, chief pilot flight stds. and safety, 1987-97; chief pilot flight stds. and safety Douglas Products divsn. Boeing, Long Beach, 1997-99; ret., 1999; mem. internat. adv. com. Flight Safety Found., Washington, 1987-99; mem. windshear tng. aid task force FAA/industry, Washington, 1985-87; mem. CFIT tng. com. Flight Safety Found./FAA, 1992-96, joint safety analysis team FAA Industry, 1997-99. Author: Turbulence Education and Training Aid FAA/Industry, 1996-97. Mem. Naval Res. Assn., catalina Conservancy. Republican. Avocations: scuba diving, sailing. Home: 2135 Beebee St San Luis Obispo CA 93401-5004

WILLIAMS, DAVID ARNOLD, astronomy; b. Nottingham, England, Sept. 9, 1937; s. James Arnold and Frances Barbara (Begg) W.; m. Doreen Jane Bell, Apr. 3, 1964; children: Richard John, Alan Edward. BSc, Queen's U., Belfast, No. Ireland, 1959, BSc (hon.), 1960, PhD, 1963; DSc, U. Manchester, Eng., 1982. Asst. lectr. Coll. Sci. & Tech., Manchester, 1963-65; rsch. assoc. Goddard Space Flight Ctr., 1965-67; lectr., reader, prof. UMIST, Manchester, 1967-94; prof. Univ. Coll., London, 1994—; chmn. astronomy com. PPARC, Swindon, Eng., 1995-98. Co-author: The Chemically Controlled Cosmos, 1995, The Physics of the Interstellar Medium, 1997, Intesterllar Chemistry, 1980; co-editor: The Molecular Astrophysics of Stars and Galaxies, 1998. Fellow Inst. of Physics, Royal Astronomical Soc. (pres. 1998-2000). Office: Univ Coll London Dep Physic, Gower St, WC1E 6BT London England

WILLIAMS, DAVID RAYMOND, chemist, educator; b. Wrexham, Wales, Mar. 20, 1941; s. Eric Thomas and Amy Gwendoline (Baseley) W.; m. Gillian Kirkpatrick Murray, Aug. 20, 1964; children: Caroline Susan, Kerstin Jane. BSc with honors, U. Wales, Bangor, 1962; PhD, U. Wales, 1965; DSc, U. St. Andrews, Scotland, 1975. Lectr. chemistry U. St. Andrews, Scotland, 1966-77; prof. chemistry U. Wales, Cardiff, 1977—; mem. adv. com. Radioactive Waste Mgmt., 1980-95, Safety Nuclear Installations, 1985-87; mem. com. Radioactive Rsch. Environ. Monitoring, 1986-95, Med. Aspects Radiation in Environment, 1985-89. Author: The Metals of Life, 1970; co-author: The Principles of Bio-inorganic Chemistry, 1977, Analysis Using Glass Electrodes, 1984, Chemistry of Complex Equilibria, 1990, Trace Elements in Man and Medicines, 1995, What is Safe?, 1998, others; contbr. 15 rev. and chpts. to books, 400 articles to profl. jours.; lectr. in field. Fellow Royal Soc. Chemistry (devel. com. 1984-90, internat. com. 1990-95, Jeyes Silver medal 1986); mem. British Coun. Sci. (chmn. adv. com. 1986-94); Order British Empire (officer 1993). Home: Cerrig Llwydion, 12 St Fagans Dr, Cardiff CF5 6EF, Wales Office: Dept Chemistry, U Wales Cardiff PO Box 912, Cardiff CF10 3TB, Wales

WILLIAMS, SIR DENYS AMBROSE, chief justice; b. Barbados, Oct. 12, 1929; s. George Cuthbert Williams and Violet Irene Williams Gilkes; m. Carmel Mary Coleman, 1954; 6 children. Student, Worcester Coll., Oxford U., Eng. Asst. legal draftsman, asst. to atty. gen. Govt. of Barbados, sr. parliamentary counsel, supreme ct. judge, 1967-86, chief justice, 1987—; asst. legal draftsman Fedn. West Indies. Decorated Knight Comdr. Saint Michael and Saint George, Gold Crown of Merit. Avocations: horse-racing, tennis, gardening, walking. Office: Supreme Ct, Office of Chief Justice, Bridgetown Barbados

WILLIAMS, DEWAYNE ARTHUR, JR., artist, fish and wildlife biologist; b. San Diego, Aug. 20, 1943; s. DeWayne Arthur Sr. and Mary Elizabeth (Cardell) W.; m. Suelynn D. Davison, Jan. 18, 1964; children: Regan Lane, Rani Chellane Garcia, DeWayne Arthur III. BA in Biol. Sci., Fla. State U., 1966; MA in Interdisciplinary Studies, Oreg. State U., 1974; postgrad., U. Idaho, 1997-99, Clayton Coll. Natural Health, 2000—. Aquatic biologist Oreg. Game Commn., Corvallis, 1966-72; biol. technician (plants) EPA, Corvallis, 1974-75; crafts shop dir., instr. U.S.Army, Ft. Gulick, Canal Zone, 1975-79; artist/mus. curator U. Mont., Missoula, 1980-88; artist, author, editor, photographer Artistwork, Missoula, 1988-93; biol. technician (fish) Nat. Marine Fisheries Svc., Honolulu, 1994; exhibit specialist Nat. Pk. Svc., Homestead, Fla., 1994-96; environ. protection asst. U.S. Army Corps of Engrs., Boise, Idaho, 1996-2000; fish and wildlife biologist U.S. Fish and Wildlife Svc., Sacramento, 2000—; fine arts dir. student union Oreg. State U., Corvallis. Author, editor, photographer, pub.: Montana Tribute, 1990 (Mont. Offcl. Centennial book); Erotic Art by Living Artists, 1988, Photographs in Center for Creative Photography, Montana Historical Soc., Idaho State U., Oreg. State U.; designed Missoula County seal, 1982; creator of the Correlatia Composite Photograph. Boy Scout leader, 1967-93. Democrat. Episcopalian. Avocations: hunting, fishing, camping. Fax: 916-414-6710. Home: 2229 Edison Ave Apt 59 Sacramento CA 95821-1641 Office: US Fish & Wildlife Svc 2800 Cottage Way Ste W 2605 Sacramento CA 95825-1846

WILLIAMS, DIANE, psychologist, educator; b. Tacoma, Wash., June 30, 1950; d. Angus DeWitt and Olga K Williams; m. Mark Cameron Dumas (div. Apr. 1998); m. Rick Alan Shacket, June 21, 1998; children: Kara Shacket, Heather Shacket, Cory Shacket, Alison Shacket. BS in Math., U. Wash., 1973, BS in Psychology, 1976; MA in Psychology, U. Calif., San Diego, 1978, PhD in Cognitive Psychology, 1982. Software engr. The Boeing Co., Seattle, 1973-75; rsch. assoc. U. Calif., San Diego, 1976-81; postdoctoral fellow in neuropsychology Boston VA Med. Ctr., 1982-84; postdoctoral fellow in electrophysiology U. Calif., San Diego, 1985-87; rsch. psychologist Navy Personnel Rsch. & Devel. Ctr., San Diego, 1987-90; adj. prof. Calif. Sch. Profl. Psychology, San Diego, 1988—; rsch. psychologist Navy Health Rsch. Ctr., San Diego, 1990—; adj. prof. U. San Diego, 1989-92; ergonomics cons. Naval Med. Ctr., San Diego, 2000. Mem. APA, Human Factors and Ergonomics Soc., Psychonomics Soc. Democrat. Office: Naval Health Rsch Ctr PO Box 85122 San Diego CA 92186-5122

WILLIAMS, DONALD JOHN, research physicist; b. Fitchburg, Mass., Dec. 25, 1933; s. Toivo John and Ina (Kokkinen) W.; m. Priscilla Mary Gagnon, July 4, 1953; children: Steven John, Craig Mitchell, Eino Stenroos. BS, Yale U., 1955, MS, 1958, PhD, 1962. Sr. staff physicist Johns Hopkins U. Applied Physics Lab., 1961-65; head particle physics br. Goddard Space Flight Center, NASA, 1965-70; dir. Space Environ. Lab., NOAA, Boulder, Colo., 1970-82; prin. investigator Energetic Particles expt. NASA Galileo Mission, 1977—; prin. staff physicist Johns Hopkins U. Applied Physics Lab., 1982-89, dir. Milton S. Eisenhower Rsch. Ctr., 1990-96, chief scientist rsch. ctr., 1996-99, ret., 1999; nat. and internat. sci. planning coms.; chmn. NAS com. on solar-terrestrial rsch., 1989-93; sci. adv. bd. USAF, 1993-97. Author: (with L.R. Lyons) Quantitative Aspects of Magnetospheric Physics, 1983; assoc. editor Jour. Geophys. Rsch., 1967-69, Revs. of Geophysics and Space Rsch., 1984-86; editor: (with G.D. Mead) Physics of the Magnetosphere, 1969, Physics of Solar-Planetary Environments, 1976; mem. editl. bd. Space Sci. Revs., 1975-85; contbr. articles to profl. jours. Mem. USAF Sci. Adv. Bd., 1994-98. Lt. USAF, 1955-57. Recipient Sci. Rsch. award NOAA, 1974, Disting. Authorship award NOAA and Johns Hopkins Applied Physics Lab., 1976, 85, 97. Fellow Am. Geophys. Soc.; mem. Am. Phys. Soc., Internat. Assn. Geomagnetism and Aeronomy (pres. 1991-95), Internat. Acad. Astronautics, Sigma Xi. Home: 14870 Triadelphia Rd Glenelg MD 21737-9408

WILLIAMS, DREW DAVIS, surgeon; b. San Augustine, Tex., Jan. 18, 1935; s. Floyd Everett and Villamae (Morehead) W.; m. Marilyn Raus, June 27, 1958; children: Leslie, Cynthia, Matthew, Jennifer, Amelia. BS, Tex. A&M Coll., 1957; MD, U. Tex., 1960; grad., naval flight surgeon, U.S. Naval Sch. Aviation Medicine, 1963. Diplomate Am. Bd. Surgery, Am. Bd. Quality Assurance and Utilization Rev. Physicians. Intern USPHS Hosp., Seattle, 1960-61; resident in gen. surgery U. Tex. Med. Br., Galveston, 1961-62, 64-68; resident in pulmonary svc. M.D. Anderson Hosp., Houston, 1968; pvt. practice Baytown, Tex., 1968—; active staff San Jacinto (Tex.) Meth. Hosp., 1968-95, chief of surgery, 1972, 73, pres. med. staff, 1976; mem. courtesy staff Bay Coast Hosp., Baytown, 1968-95; cons. staff Baytown Med. Ctr. Hosp., 1972-95; 1st chmn. dept. surgery in devel. of family practice residency program affiliated with Tex. Med. Sch., Houston, 1977; mem. Tex. State Bd. Med. Examiners, 1983-89, sec.-treas., 1984-88, pres., 1988-89; unit med. dir., clin. instr. dept. preventive medicine and cmty. health U. Tex. Med. Br., Galveston, 1995-99. Contbr. chpt. to book and articles to profl. jours. Flight surgeon USN, 1962-64; lt. comdr. USNR, ret., 1967. Am. Cancer Soc. Clin. fellow, 1966-67. Fellow ACS, AMA (Physicians Recognition award), Tex. Med. Assn.; mem. Tex. Med. Found. (fed. peer rev. group), Houston Surg. Soc. (pres. 1994), Southwestern Surg. Congress, Tex. Surg. Soc., Singleton Surg. Soc. (past pres.), Harris County Med. Soc. (chmn. coun. med. splty., mem. exec. bd. 1994), East Harris County Med. Soc. (pres. 1982), Baytown Surg. Soc., Sir William Osler Soc., Am. Cancer Soc. (pres. Baytown chpt. 1970-71), Sons of Republic Tex. (at large life), SAR (past pres. local chpt.), Soc. Descendents of Colonial Clergy, Magna Carta Barons (Somerset chpt.), Colonial Order of the Crown, Sovereign Colonial Soc.-Ams. of Royal Descent, Masons (32 degree), Shriners, KT, Gideons Internat., Phi Beta Pi. Democrat. Mem. Ch. of Christ. Avocations: gardening, hunting, fishing, genealogy, golf. Home and Office: 1217 Kilgore Rd Baytown TX 77520-3912

WILLIAMS, EARL PATRICK, JR., editor, freelance writer; b. Washington, May 14, 1950; s. Earl Patrick Sr. and Charlie Mae (Wright) W.; m. Susan Miller Day, July 20, 1985. BA, U. Md., 1973; postgrad., Cath. U., 1974. Duplication machine operator Applied Physics Lab. Johns Hopkins U., Silver Spring, Md., 1968-74; substitute tchr. Fairfax County Va. Schs., 1974-75; clk. U.S. Govt. Printing Office, Washington, 1975-76; editor U.S. GAO, Washington, 1976—; freelance writer, Washington, 1974—. Author: Amtrak's Washington-New York Corridor, 1977, What You Should Know About the American Flag, 1987, What You Should Know About Flags of the Confederacy, 1993; contbr. articles to mags. and newspapers. Active in efforts to achieve recognition of Francis Hopkinson, the designer of first ofcl. U.S. flag; lectr. to sch. groups and civic orgns. on the history of the U.S. flag; discussed history of U.S. flag on radio broadcasts nationwide; mem. N.J. Coun. for Social Studies. Recipient Cert. of Appreciation Mil. Order of World Wars, Bronze Good Citizenship medal Nat. Soc. of Sons of Am. Revolution. Mem. Nat. Cathedral Assn., N.Am. Vexillological Assn., Nat. Flag Found, Star Spangled Banner Flag House Assn. Democrat. Methodist. Avocations: railroad buff, history buff, singing folk music. Home: 2323 40th Pl NW Apt 201 Washington DC 20007-1617

WILLIAMS, EDWARD MACON, poet; b. Rose Hill, N.C., Feb. 11, 1931; s. Samuel Paul and Laura Alethia (Murray) W. Author poems: Angels of Mercy, 1995, Beautiful Rose of Sharon, 1996, The Sacrificial Lamb, 1996, Heaven Rejoices, 1996, The Sweet Spirit of Yahweh, 1996, The Birth of Messiah, 1998, The Christ, 2000. Mem. Internat. Soc. Poets. Home: PO Box 1541 1201 Cheyenne Blvd Apt 613 Madison TN 37116-1541

WILLIAMS, ELLIS KEITH, broadcast executive; b. Birmingham, Ala., May 26, 1927; s. Christopher Ellis and Carrie Enfield (Watson) W.; m. Maxine Roberta Ellenberger, June 27, 1953; children: Mary, Christopher, Katherine, Kimberly. BA, U. Ala., 1949. Film dir. Sta. WAFM-TV, Birmingham, 1949-51; film dir. Sta. WBRC-TV, Birmingham, 1951-52, program dir., 1952-54, sales rep., 1954-68, local sales mgr., 1969-82, acct. exec., 1982-94; ind. TV cons., 1994—; guest lectr. U. Ala., 1990-97. Elder South Highland Presbyn. Ch., Birmingham. Recipinet Disting. Alumni award U. Ala. Radio and TV Broadcasting Sch., 1990, Outstanding Alumnus award Jefferson County Alumni Assn., U. Ala., 1996-97. Mem. Birmingham Area C. of C. (life), City Salesmen's Club (pres. 1962-63, Man of Yr. 1986), The Club (Birmingham), Met. Dinner Club (pres. 1987). Presbyterian. Avocation: family. Office: 2736 Cherokee Dr Birmingham AL 35216-1008

WILLIAMS, ERIC JOSEPH, transportation executive; b. Havana, Cuba, Nov. 15, 1945; came to U.S., 1961; s. Ereic and Frances (Waterhouse) W.; m. Maria Julia Williams, Mar. 30, 1984; children: Jason, Natasha. BS in Fgn. Svc., Georgetown U., 1968. With Emery Worldwide, 1970-88; regional mgr. S.Am. Emery Worldwide, Miami, 1977-81, dist. mgr. L.Am.-Caribbean, 1984-86, dir. L.Am.-Caribbean sector, 1986-88; dir. L.Am.-Caribbean sector LEP Internat., Miami, 1988-90, dir. L.Am.-Caribbean region, 1988-90; mng. dir. sales L.Am. divsn. Fed. Express, 1990-96; sr. mgr. L.Am. sales Fritz Co., 1996-98; v.p. internat. Pilot Air, 1999—; adult edn. tchr., Miami, 1973-75; chmn. Air Cargo Ams., 1999. Exec. bd. Hist. Mus. South Fla.; mem. mem. Miami Beacon Coun., 1995-97. 1st lt. U.S. Army, 1968-70. Mem. Soc. Ams., Coral Gables C. of C., Georgetown U. Alumni Assn. (com.), Coconut Grove Sailing Club (com. 1975-76). Episcopalian. Home: 501 Raven Ave Miami FL 33166-3950

WILLIAMS, EVELYN LOIS, chemical company executive, safety consultant; b. Richmond, Va., Sept. 20, 1954; d. Kenneth R. and Ardis M. (Paul) W. AB, Brown U., 1977. Engr. tech. svc. DuPont Co., Wilmington, Del., 1976-79; area engr. DuPont Co., Gibbstown, N.J., 1979-83; sr. supr. DuPont Co., Deepwater, N.J., 1983-85; prodn. asst. DuPont Co., Wilmington, 1985-87; unit mgr. DuPont Co., Memphis, 1987-88; plant mgr. DuPont Co., Montague, Mich., 1988-92, Antioch, Calif., 1992-96; sr. cons., project mgr., sr. devel. cons. DuPont Safety REsources Bus., Wilmington, 1996—; dir. FMB-Lumberman's Bank, Muskegon, Mich., 1990-92.

Campaign cabinet United Way, Muskegan, 1989-91, Concord, Calif., 1993-94; trustee Delta Meml. Hosp., Antioch, 1994-96. Named One of 100 Women to Watch in Corp. Am., Bus. Monthly Mag., 1989. Mem. AAAS, AAUW, ASM Internat., Soc. Women Engrs. Home: 4 Barley Mill Dr Wilmington DE 19807-2218 Office: EI DuPont de Nemours Co Inc Christiana Exec Campus 131 Continental Dr Ste 307 Newark DE 19713-4324

WILLIAMS, FELTON CARL, college administrator; b. L.A., Mar. 30, 1946; s. Abraham and Lula Mae (Johnson) W.; m. Maryetta Baldwin, July 3, 1966; children: Sonia Yvette, Felton Jr. AA, L.A. Harbor Coll., Wilmington, Calif., 1970; BA, Calif. State U., Long Beach, 1972, MBA, 1975; PhD, Claremont Grad. Sch., 1985. Jr. staff analyst Calif. State U., Long Beach, 1972-73, adminstrv. asst., 1973-74, supr., 1974-79; coord. Calif. State U. Dominguez Hills, Carson, Calif., 1979-84; asst. to pres. Calif. State U. Dominguez Hills, Carson, 1984-85, acting dir. learning assistance ctr., 1985-91; acting dir. student program Calif. State U., Dominguez Hills, 1991-93; dean counseling svcs. Sacramento City Coll., 1993-96; dean sch. bus. and tech. Long Beach City Coll., 1996-97, dean sch. bus. and social scis., 1997—; cons. U. So. Calif. Physician's Asst., L.A., 1983—, physician's asst. program Drew Med. Sch. Martin Luther King Hosp., Calif., 1981—, chair curriculum com., leadership Long Beach, 2000, bd. dirs.; bd. dirs. Employee Readiness Support Svcs., Carson, Alumni Assn. Calif. State Univ., Long Beach; mem. Long Beach Claims Adjudication Bd. Pres. San Pedro/Wilmington NAACP, San Pedro, Calif., 1974—, So. Area Cons. NAACP, L.A., 1979-80; chmn. region I, NAACP, San Francisco, 1979-80. With U.S. Army, 1966-68. Named Outstanding Young Man Am., U.S. Jaycees, 1977, in resolution-community contributions Calif. State Assembly, 1980; recipient cert. appreciation women's div. San Pedro C. of C., 1980, Outstanding Alumnus award L.A. Harbor Coll., 1989, Frederick Douglass Outstanding Alumnus award, 1989. Mem. Western Coll. Reading/Learning Assn., Nat. Assn. for Devel. Edn., Am. Mgmt. Assn., Am. Assn. Higher Edn., Pi Lambda Theta. E-mail: fwilliams@lbcc.cc.ca.us. Home: 2126 Daisy Ave Long Beach CA 90806-4109 Office: Long Beach City Coll Liberal Arts Campus 4901 E Carson St Long Beach CA 90808-1706

WILLIAMS, FRANCIS JOHN, chemist, researcher; b. N.Y.C., July 30, 1951; s. Harold James Williams and Mercedes Rodon Madriguera; m. Eulalia Cirici Villarino, Aug. 7, 1981; children: Elisenda, Gerard. BS, Ausies Marc, Barcelona, Spain, 1967; MS in Chemistry, U. Autonoma Barcelona, 1974. Chemist H.Q. Houhton, Barcelona, 1974-75; rsch. chemist Resisa, Sant Celoni, Spain, 1976-78, Polyvinyl, Parets, Spain, 1978; lab. chief Hooker, Sactellbisbal, Spain, 1979-83; rsch. mgr. Cray Valley, Sant Celoni, 1983—. Contbr. articles to profl. jours. Recipient Best Paper award Assn. Spanish de Fabricaûtes de Pintup/Union de Technicians ce la culture mediterraneee, 1998. Mem. Assn. Spainish de Técnicosen Pintro, Baruices and Adhesivos, Am. Chem. Soc. Avocations: music, lecture, cinema, tennis, soccer. Home: Collsabadell 54-B, 08450 Llinars Del Valles Spain Office: Cray Valley Iberica, Crtra Olzinellas s/n, 08470 Sant Celoni Spain

WILLIAMS, FREDERIC WARD, structural engineering educator; b. Romiley, Cheshire, Eng., Mar. 4, 1940; s. Frederic Calland and Gladys (Ward) W.; m. Jessie Anne Hope Wilson, Apr. 11, 1964; children: Frederic John Wilson, David Ward. BA, U. Cambridge, Eng., 1961, ScD, 1985; PhD, U. Bristol, Eng., 1964. Asst. engr. Freeman Fox and Ptnrs., London, 1964; lectr. Ahmadu Bello U., Zaria, Nigeria, 1964-67, U. Birmingham, Eng., 1967-75; prof. U. Wales Inst. Sci. and Tech., Cardiff, 1975-88, head dept. civil engrng. and bldg. tech., 1986-87; prof. structural engrng. U. Wales Cardiff (now Cardiff U.), 1988—, head divsn., 1988-98; founder, chmn. Cardiff Advanced Chinese Engrng. Ctr., 1993—; cons. NASA, Langley Rsch. Ctr., Va., 1981-98; guest prof. Shanghai Jiao Tong U., 1998—, U. Sci. and Tech. China, 1999—. Developer major computer program Viconopt for stiffened plate structures; contbr. articles to profl. jours. Recipient George Taylor prize Royal Aero. Soc., 1973; grantee Royal Soc., U.K. Sci. and Engrng. Rsch. Coun., others. Fellow Royal Acad. Engrng., Instn. Civil Engrs., Instn. Structural Engrs., Royal Aero. Soc. Conservative. Mem. Ch. of Wales. Avocations: hill walking, jogging, international travel. Home: 12 Ridgeway Lisvane, Cardiff CF14 0RS, Wales Office: Cardiff U, PO Box 925, Cardiff CF24 0YF, Wales

WILLIAMS, GILBERT THOMAS, systems engineer, consultant; b. New Bern, N.C., Dec. 29, 1956; s. Clayton Olan and Dawn Vernice (Hart) W. BS, Jacksonville State U., 1977; postgrad., Case Western Res. U., 1990—. Programmer Computer Sci. Corp., Huntsville, Ala., 1978-81; engr. Nat. Aeronautics & Space Adminstrn., Huntsville, 1981-83, Honeywell, Inc., Hopkins, Minn., 1983-86; systems engr. Westinghouse Electric Co., Cleve., 1986-95; founder 4C cons., Richmond Heights, Ohio, 1994—; propr. Williams Oil and Gas, Richmond Heights, 1989—. Inventor in field; contvr. articles to profl. jours. Mem. Heritage Found., Wilderness Soc. Recipient Snoopy award NASA, Huntsville, 1980, cert. of appreciation NASA, 1983. Mem. IEEE, Am. Motorcycle Assn., Assn. for Computing Machinery. Avocations: playing in blues bands, motorcycling, fishing, golf. Office: 4C Cons 25101 Chardon Rd Richmond Heights OH 44143-1340

WILLIAMS, GLANMOR, history educator, retired; b. Merthyr Tydfil, U.K., May 5, 1920; s. Daniel and Ceinwen (Evans) W.; m. Margaret Fay Davies, Apr. 6, 1946; children: Margaret Nest, Jonathan Huw. BA, Aberystwyth, U.K., 1940, MA, 1947, DLitt, 1962, LLD (honoris causa), 1998. Lectr. U. Coll. of Swansea, U.K., 1945-52, sr. lectr., 1952-57, prof., 1957-82, vice-prin., 1975-78; gov. BBC, U.K., 1965-71. Author: (books) The Welsh Church, 1962, Wales, 1415-1642, 1987, Wales and the Reformation, 1997; editor: (book) County History of Glamorgan (6 vols.) 1971-84. Chmn. Royal Commn. on Ancient and Hist. Monuments, 1986-91; chmn. Ancient Monuments Bd., Wales, 1954-94; chmn. Welsh Nat. Folk-Mus., 1984-90; vice-chmn. Hist. Bldgs. Commn., Wales, 1963-90. Decorated CBE, 1981, Knighthood, 1995. Fellow Brit. Acad., Soc. of Antiquaries, Royal Hist. Soc. Home: 11 Grosvenor Rd, SA2 OSP Swansea United Kingdom

WILLIAMS, GREGORY KEITH, accountant; b. Elizabethtown, Ky., Mar. 20, 1958; s. James Marion and Shirley Catherine (Yates) W.; m. Diana Lynn McGuffin, May 26, 1979; 1 child, Kathryn May. BA in Pub. Mgmt., U. Ky., Lexington, 1985; BSBA, U. Louisville, 1987; MPA, Ball State U., 1996. Cert. mgmt. acct., info. sys. auditor, govt. fin. mgr. Supervisory staff acct. Fin. Acctg. Off., Fort Knox, Ky., 1983-85, internal auditor, 1985-89, sys. acct., 1989-93; sys. acct. Def. Fin. and Acctg. Svc. Indpls. Ctr., 1993-95, electronic commerce/data interchange coord., 1995-97; dep. project mgr. corp. database Def. Fin. and Acctg. Svc. Hdqrs., 1997-98, project mgr. corp. database, 1998—. Mem. Inst. Cert. Mgmt. Acct., Info. Sys. Audit and Control Assn., Am. Soc. Mil. Comptr., Assn. Govt. Acct., Phi Beta Kappa, Beta Gamma Sigma, Phi Kappa Phi. Fax: 317-510-7250. E-mail: gkwdlw@msn.com. Home: 136 Lake Dr Greenwood IN 46142-9182 Office: Def Fin Acctg Svc 8899 E 56th St Indianapolis IN 46249-0002

WILLIAMS, HOWARD RUSSELL, lawyer, educator; b. Evansville, Ind., Sept. 26, 1915; s. Clyde Alfred and Grace (Preston) W.; m. Virginia Merle Thompson, Nov. 3, 1942; 1 son, Frederick S.T. AB, Washington U., St. Louis, 1937; LLB, Columbia U., 1940. Bar: N.Y. 1941. With firm Root, Clark, Buckner & Ballantine, N.Y.C., 1940-41; prof. law, asst. dean U. Tex. Law Sch., Austin, 1946-51; prof. law Columbia U. Law Sch., N.Y.C., 1951-63; Dwight prof. Columbia Law Sch., 1959-63; prof. law Stanford U., 1963-85, Stella W. and Ira S. Lillick prof., 1968-82, prof. emeritus, 1982, Robert E. Paradise prof. natural resources, 1983-85, prof. emeritus, 1985—; Oil and gas cons. President's Materials Policy Commn., 1951; mem. Calif. Law Revision Commn., 1971-79, vice chmn., 1976-77, chmn., 1978-79. Author or co-author: Cases on Property, 1954, Cases on Oil and Gas, 1956, 5th edit., 1987, Decedents' Estates and Trusts, 1968, Future Interests, 1970, Oil and Gas Law, 8 vols., 1959-64 (with ann. supplements/rev. 1964-95), abridged edit., 1973, Manual of Oil and Gas Terms, 1957, 10th edit., 1997. Bd. regents Berkeley Bapt. Divinity Sch., 1966-67; trustee Rocky Mountain Mineral Law Found., 1964-66, 68-85. With U.S. Army, 1941-46. Recipient Clyde O. Martz Tchg. award Rocky Mountain Mineral Law Found., 1994. Mem. Phi Beta Kappa. Democrat. Home: 360 Everett Ave Apt 4B Palo Alto CA 94301-1422 Office: Stanford U Sch Law Nathan Abbott Way Stanford CA 94305

WILLIAMS, IRVING LAURENCE, physics educator; b. Newport, R.I., Dec. 3, 1935; s. Leroy Payton and Alberta Helen (Troy) W.; m. Carrie Mae Graves, Aug. 26, 1967; children: Cheryl Anita, Carla Chantrase. EdB, R.I. Coll., 1957; MA in Teaching, Brown U., 1962; PhD, NYU, 1975. Cert. teaching, R.I. Classroom tchr. Newport (R.I.) Sch. Dept., 1962-63; prof. physics Morgan State U., Balt., 1963-67, Nassau Community Coll., Garden City, N.Y., 1967-97; prof. emeritus Nassau Community Coll., Garden City, 1998; asst. to pres. Nassau Community Coll., Garden City, N.Y., 1980-85, prof. emeritus, 1998—; adj. prof. Hofstra U., Hempstead, N.Y., 1980-87; adj. instr. physics Guilford Tech. C.C., Greensboro, N.C.; dist. clk. Roosevelt (N.Y.) Sch. Bd., 1989-91; instr. physics Guilford Tech. C.C., Greensboro, N.C., 1999—. Co-author: (lab. workbook) Meterology Lab. Exercises, 1975, 76. Treas. Econ. Opportunity Commn., Nassau County, N.Y., 1984; trustee Grace Lutheran Ch., Malverne, N.Y., 1987, Roosevelt Bd. Edn., 1988; active Roosevelt Rep. Club, 1989; mem. sch. bd. Grace Lutheran Sch., Malverne, 1991. With U.S. Army, 1957-60. Recipient Chancellor's award SUNY, 1975, Citzen's award EOC Nassau County, Hempstead, 1987, Roosevelt Educator's award, Roosevelt Coun., 1989; NSF Weather Svc. grantee, Washington, 1989. Mem. AAUP, Nat. Sci. Tchrs. Assn., Am. Assn. Physics Tchrs., Soc. Coll. Sci. Tchrs., N.Y. Acad. Sci., Am. Assn. Higher Edn., N.Y. Assn. Two Yr. Colls. Republican. Avocation: piano. Home: 2 Leeward Ct Greensboro NC 27455-0812

WILLIAMS, JACK RAYMOND, civil engineer; b. Barberton, Ohio, Mar. 14, 1923; s. Charles Baird and Mary Williams; m. Mary Berneice Jones, Mar. 5, 1947 (dec.); children: Jacqueline Rae, Drew Alan; m. Betty Ruth Scholfield, Nov. 9, 1990. Student, Colo. Sch. Mines, 1942043, Purdue U., 1944-45; BS, U. Colo., 1946. Gravity and seismograph engr. Carter Oil Co., Western U.S. and Venezuela, 1946-50; with Rock Island R.R., Chgo., 1950-80, structural designer, asst. to engr. bridges, asst. engr., 1980-82, engr. bridges system, 1963-80; sr. bridge engr. thomas K. Dyer Inc., 1980-82; v.p. Alfred Benesch & Co., 1982-96. Served with USMCR, 1943-45. Fellow ASCE (life); mem. Am. Concrete Inst., Am. Ry. Bridge and Bldg. Assn. (past pres.), Am. Ry. Engrng. Assn. (hon. mem., past chmn. com. 8, Concrete and Foundations, past chmn. com. 10 concrete ties). Home: 293 Minocqua St Park Forest IL 60466-1942

WILLIAMS, JAMES FRANCIS, physics educator; b. Newcastle, New South Wales, Australia, Nov. 24, 1935; s. Henry James and Constance Anne (Casley) W.; m. Barbara Anne Woods, Jan. 9, 1961; children: Robert James, Jennifer Kim, David Stuart, Allyson Anne. MSc, U. New Eng., NSW, Australia, 1958, Dip. Ed., 1959, BSc, 1956; PhD, Australian Nat. U., 1965, DSc, 1983. Rsch. asst. U. New England, 1958; sr. demonstrator Australian Nat. U., 1960-64; rsch. scientist Gulf Gen. Atomic, San Diego, 1967-70; lectr. Queens U., Belfast, No. Ireland, 1970-73, sr. lectr., 1973-76, reader, 1976-80; prof., physics U. Western Australia, Perth, 1980—, dept. head, physics, 1980-90, dean faculty of sci., 1992, head divsn. agr. and sci., 1993; mem. physics com. Sci. Rsch. Coun., 1977-80; mem. internat. editl. adv. bd. Jour. Physics B: Atomic, Molecular and Optical Physics, 1992—. Co-author: Progress on Atomic Spectroscopy, 1978; editor: Coherence and Correlations in Atomic Collisions, 1980; contbr. articles to profl. jours. Chmn. scientific adv. com. Perth Observatory, 1982-86; pres. Students Rep. Coun., U. New England, 1956-59. Recipient Boas medal Australian Inst. Physics, 1989; Commonwealth scholar Govt. of Australia, 1954-56; rsch. fellow Australian Atomic Energy Establishment, 1965, sr. vis. fellow Sci. Rsch. Coun., U.K., 1978, fellow Can. Nat. Rsch. Coun., 1965-67. Fellow Am. Inst. Physics, Australian Inst. Physics, Australian Acad. Scis., Inst. Physics (U.K.); mem. IEEE (sr.), Internat. Union Pure and Applied Physics (Australian rep. 1984-90), N.Y. Acad. Scis. Avocations: swimming, gardening, reading, chess, writing. Office: U Western Australia, Physics Dept, Nedlands Perth 6907, Australia

WILLIAMS, JAMES FRANKLIN, II, university dean, librarian; b. Montgomery, Ala., Jan. 22, 1944; s. James Franklin and Anne (Wester) W.; m. Madeline McClellan, Jan. 1966 (div. May 1988); 1 child, Madeline Marie; m. Nancy Allen, Aug. 1989; 1 child, Audrey Grace. BA, Morehouse Coll., 1966; MLS, Atlanta U., 1967. Reference libr. Wayne State U. Sci. Libr., Detroit, 1968-69; document delivery libr. Wayne State U. Med. Libr., Detroit, 1969-70, head of reference, 1971-72, dir. med. libr. and regional med. libr. network, 1972-81, regional dir., 1975-82; assoc. dir. of librs. Wayne State U., 1981-88; dean librs. U. Colo., Boulder, 1988—; bd. regents Nat. Libr. Medicine, Bethesda, Md., 1978-81; bd. dirs. Denver Art Mus., 1997—, pres. elect 1999—; bd. dirs. Ctr. Rsch. Librs., 1998—; pres.-elect Big Twelve Plus Libr. Consortium, 2000. Mem. editl. bd. ACRL Publications in Librarianship, College and Research Libraries; contbr. articles to profl. jours., chpts. to books; book editor and author. Bd. dirs. Educom, 1997-98, Boulder Cmty. Hosp., 2000—. Subject of feature interview in centennial issue Am. Librs. jour., 1976. Mem. ALA (Visionary Leader award 1988), Coll. and Rsch. Librs. (editl. bd.), Assn. Rsch. Librs. (bd. dirs. 1994-96), Boulder C. of C. (bd. dirs.). Avocations: cycling, travel, fishing. Office: U Colo Office Dean Librs PO Box 184 Boulder CO 80309-0184

WILLIAMS, JAMES JOSEPH, environmental scientist, researcher; b. Akron, Ohio, Jan. 12, 1954; s. Joseph Chester and Fawnabelle (Taylor) W. BS in Biology, U. Cin., 1976, MS in Environ. Sci., 1990; Exec. MBA, Ohio U., 1995. Chemist, plant operator Delaware (Ohio) WWTP, 1977-81; chemist CLC Lab., Columbus, Ohio, 1979-80; lab. supr. Burgess & Niple Ltd., Columbus, 1981-83; chemist, supr. Nestle QAL, Marysville, 1983-85; rsch. assoc. Roxanne Labs., Columbus, 1985-87; mgr. O&M manual div. OCS, Inc., Mason, Ohio, 1987-91; R & D assoc. Martin Marietta Energy Systems, Piketon, Ohio, 1991-93; supr. organic analytical svcs. Lockheed Martin Utility Svcs., Piketon, 1993-95; sect. mgr. for chem. technology U.S. Enrichment Corp., Piketon, Ohio, 1995—. Leader 4-H Club, Mechanicsburg, Ohio, 1965-74; singer, soloist Cantari Singers, Columbus, 1983-87; tenor soloist Trinity Episcopal Ch., Columbus, 1987-92; soloist Opera Columbus, 1981-90, Second Ch. of Christ Scientist, 1992—. Recipient Leadership award Nat. 4-H Found., 1972; U. Cin. grad. minority scholar, 1988, 89. Mem. Am. Chem. Soc., Water Pollution Control Fedn., Am. Water Works Assn., Sigma Xi (assoc.). Democrat. Baptist. Home: 550 Terrace Ln Chillicothe OH 45601-2948

WILLIAMS, JAMES KENDRICK, bishop. Ed., St. Mary's Coll., St. Mary's, Ky., St. Maur's Sch. Theology, South Union, Ky. Ordained priest Roman Catholic Ch., 1963; ordained titular bishop Catula and aux. bishop of Covington, 1984; ordained first bishop of Lexington, Ky., installed 1988. Office: Bishop of Lexington 1310 W Main St Lexington KY 40508-2048

WILLIAMS, JOAN ELAINE, podiatric surgeon, educator; b. La Mesa, Calif.; d. William E. and Dottie B. Williams; m. Edward Homewood Miller, 1987; children: Carol Martins, William Baerg, Michael Baerg. BS, Calif. Coll. Podiatric Med., 1978, D of Podiatric Medicine, 1981; MS, Pepperdine U., 1979. Diplomate Am. Bd. Podiatric Surgery, Am. Bd. Podiatric Orthopedics and Primary Podiatric Medicine. Chief podiatric medicine and surgery dept. vets. affairs Puget Sound Health Care System, Seattle, 1982—; clin. asst. prof. podiatric medicine Calif. Coll. Podiatric Medicine, San Francisco, 1982—, U. Osteo. Medicine and Health Sci., Des Moines, Iowa, 1982-90; clin. assoc. prof. U. Osteo. Medicine and Health Scis., Des Moines, Iowa, 1990—; oral bd. examiner Am. Bd. Podiatric Orthopedics, Chgo., 1988; reviewer merit rev. grant Vets. Affairs Ctrl. Office, Washington, 1989; lic. exam reviewer Nat. Bd. Podiatric Med. Examiners, State College, Pa., 1993—. Editor: Preferred Practice Guidelines, 1992-94; contbr. articles to profl. jours. County del. Wash. State Rep. Party, Seattle, 1994. Recipient Acad. scholarship Pepperdine U., 1979. Fellow Am. Coll. Foot and Ankle Surgeons, Am. Coll. Foot and Ankle Orthopedics. Presbyterian. Avocations: classical music, playing cello. Office: Puget Sound Health Care Sys Dept Vets Affairs 1660 S Columbian Way Seattle WA 98108-1532

WILLIAMS, JODY, political organization administrator; b. Rutland, Vt., Oct. 9, 1950. BA, U. Vt.; MA, Sch. Internat. Tng., Johns Hopkins Sch. Past English tchr. Washington, Mex.; former coord. Nicaragua-Honduras Edn. Project, Washington; assoc. dir. Children's Project Med. Aid El Salvador, L.A./El Salvador, 1986; founder Internat. Campaign to Ban Landmines Vietnam Vet. Found. Am., Washington, 1991—; amb. Internat. Campaign to Ban Landmines, Alexandria, VA, 1997—; spkr. in field. Contbr. articles to profl. jours. Past vol. El Salvadoran rescue group. Recipient Nobel Peace prize, 1997. Office: ICBL 110 Maryland Ave NE # 6 Washington DC 20002-5626

WILLIAMS, JOHN CHARLES, II, data processing executive; b. Dayton, Ohio, Jan. 29, 1955; s. John Charles and Frances Jerline (McKean) W.; m. Diane Catherine Busch, Feb. 11, 1978; 1 child, Tabitha Anne. Programmer Kino Starr, Tucson, 1977-78, City of Boise (Idaho), 1978; data processing mgr. Nat. Assn. Ind. Businesses, Inc., Boise, 1978-79; chief exec. officer Williams Rsch. Assoc., Boise, 1979-80, MRW Data Systems, Inc., Tucson, 1981-82, Computer Security, Tucson, 1983-86, Modern Magic, Tucson, 1986-88; tech. support dir. Program Sources, Inc., Tucson, 1988-89; chief exec. officer Cactus Explosives Corp., 1989-90, Systems Cons. Assocs., Tucson, 1990-94; sr. systems analyst Desert Diamond Casino, 1994-97; program analyst Muscular Dystrophy Assn., Tuscon, 1997—. Area coord. Kolbe For Congress Campaign, Tucson, 1984; Ariz. Rep. State Committeeman, 1986—; mem. Ariz. Sonora Desert Mus., Tucson, 1983—. Republican. Avocations: leather crafting, horsemanship, numismatics. Address: PO Box 64203 Tucson AZ 85728-4203

WILLIAMS, JOHN MARK GRUFFYDD, clinical psychology educator; b. Hawarden, North Wales, July 23, 1952; s. John Howard and Anna Barbara (Wright) W.; m. Phyllis Patricia Simpson, Oct. 6, 1973; children: John Robert Gareth, Jennifer Ruth Phyllis, Anne Marie Bethsian. BA, Oxford U., Eng., 1973, MSc, 1976, MA, 1977, DPhil, 1979, DSc, 1998. Cert. clin. psychologist; ordained Anglican priest, 1990. Lectr. applied psychology Newcastle U., Eng., 1979-82; scientist Med. Rsch. Coun., Cambridge, Eng., 1982-91; prof. clin. psychology U. Wales, Bangor, 1991-97, dir. Inst. Med. Scial Care Rsch., 1997—, pro-vice-chancellor, 1997—; cons. Unilever, Eng., 1994—. Author: Psychological Treatment of Depression, 1984, 2d edit., 1992, Cognitive Psychology and Emotional Disorders, 1988, 2d edit., 1997, The Psychology of Religious Knowing, 1989, Cry of Pain: Understanding Suicide and Self Harm, 1997. Recipient Publ. award Mental Health Found., 1993. Fellow Brit. Psychol. Soc. (May Davidson award 1987, Shapiro award 1999); mem. Internat. Assn. Suicide Prevention. Labour Party. Avocations: music, walking.

WILLIAMS, JOHN MICHAEL, physical therapist, sports medicine educator; b. Columbus, Ohio, Oct. 19, 1951; s. James Hutchison and Helen Lucille (Knight) W.; m. Karen Sue Eaglen, June 23, 1973; children: Michelle Rene, Elizabeth Ann. BS in Phys. Therapy, Ohio State U., 1975, MS in Allied Medicine, 1983. Lic. phys. therapist, Ohio. Asst. dir. phys. therapy Licking Meml. Hosp., Newark, Ohio, 1975-80; pvt. practice Westerville, Ohio, 1977-80; asst. dir. rehab. St. Anthony Hosp., Columbus, 1980-88; from chief phys. therapist to dir. phys. and sports medicine St. Ann's Hosp., Westerville, 1988-95; mgr. Nova Care Rehab., 1995-97; clin. instr. Ohio State U., Columbus, 1984—, faculty instr., 1997—; adj. faculty sports medicine Otterbein Coll., Westerville, 1989-96; cons. Licking County Arthritis Found., Newark, 1978-80; phys. therapy adv. bd. Ctrl. Ohio Tech. Coll., Newark, 1978—; bd. dirs. SAHCU Credit Union, Westerville; asst. prof. phys. and occupl. therapy programs U. Findlay, Ohio, 1996—. Author monograph. Med. team capt. Columbus Marathon, 1989—, U.S. Men's Olympic Marathon Trials, Columbus, 1992, U.S. Men's Nat. Marathon Championships, 1991, 92. Lt. col. USAR, 1969—; exec. officer 914th Combat Support Hosp., 2000—. Decorated Army Commendation medal with 2 oak leaf clusters, Meritorious Svc. medal; recipient Mayor's award for vol. svc. City of Columbus, 1993. Mem. Am. Acad. Med. Adminstrs., Am. Phys. Therapy Assn. (rep. to state assembly 1987—, state of Ohio faculty liaison to state bd. dirs.). Episcopalian. Avocations: volleyball, golf, sailing. Home: 132 Ormsbee Ave Westerville OH 43081-1151

WILLIAMS, JOHN MICHAEL, solicitor; b. Buxton, Derbyshire, Eng., Oct. 15, 1942; s. George Keith and Joan Doreen (Selby) W. BA, Oxford U., 1964, MA, 1968. Solicitor Supreme Ct. Eng. Solicitor Cooper Sons Hartley & Williams, Eng., 1967—. Condr. Buxton (Eng.) Mus. Soc., 1967—; vice chmn. Buxton Opera House, 1978—; organist St. John's Ch., Buxton, 1985—; mem. panel music advisers N.W. Arts, Eng., 1995—. Decorated mem. Order Brit. Empire. Mem. Buxton and High Peak Law Soc. (sec. 1984-97, pres. 1997—), East Midlands Assn. of Law Socs. (pres. 1996-97). Mem. Anglican Ch. Avocations: music, cricket, theater. Home: 143 Lightwood Rd Buxton, Derbyshire SK17 6RW, England Office: Cooper Sons Hartley & Williams, 25 Market St Chapel Frith, High Peak Derbyshire SK23 0HS, England

WILLIAMS, JOHN TROY, librarian, educator; b. Oak Park, Ill., Mar. 11, 1924; s. Michael Daniel and Donna Marie (Shaffer) W.; B.A., Central Mich. U., 1949; M.A. in Libr. Sci., U. Mich., 1951, M.A., 1954; Ph.D., Mich. State U., 1973. Reference libr. U. Mich., Ann Arbor, 1955-59; instr. Bowling Green (Ohio) State U., 1959-60; reference librarian Mich. State U., East Lansing, 1960-62; 1st asst. reference dept. Flint (Mich.) Pub. Library, 1962-65; head reference svcs., Purdue U., West Lafayette, Ind., 1965-72; head pub. svcs. No. Ill. U., Dekalb, 1972-75; asst. dean, asst. univ. libr. Wright State U., Dayton, Ohio, 1975-80; vis. scholar U. Mich., Ann Arbor, 1980—; cons. in field. Served with U.S. Army, 1943-46. Mich. State fellow, 1963-64; HEW fellow, 1971-72. Mem. Am. Libr. Assn., Spl. Libraries Assn., Am. Soc. for Info. Scis., Am. Sociol. Assn., AAUP, Coun. on Fgn. Rels. Contbr. articles to profl. jours. Home: PO Box 7531 Ann Arbor MI 48107-7531

WILLIAMS, JOSEPH SCOTT, energy and natural resources company executive, city commissioner; b. Chgo., Nov. 10, 1951; s. Hagle Eugene and Helen Elizabeth (Mellon) W.; m. Tamalou Mitchell, June 10, 1972 (dec. Apr. 2000); children: Troy Scott, Ari Layne. Welding Cert., John A. Logan Coll., Carterville, Ill., 1971; Cert. in Mining Tech., Rend Lake Coll., Ina, Ill., 1975. Dealer S&S Motors, West Frankfort, Ill., 1970-74; coal mine laborer Peabody Coal Co., Freeburg, Ill., 1973; coal mine electrician Old Ben Coal Co., Sesser, Ill., 1973-76; alt. energy cons. Helios Devel. Co., West Frankfort, Ill., 1977-83; instr. Rend Lake Coll., Ina, 1979-82; coal mine repairman Freeman United Coal Co., Pittsburg, Ill., 1979-87; mgr. ops. Royal Talon Co., West Frankfort, 1989—, pres., 2000—; pres. Egyptian Energies, Inc., West Frankfort, 1987—, Horn Dimond Coal Co., West Frankfort, 1991-99; commr. of public health and safety City of West Frankfort, Ill., 1999—; mem. Ill. State Mining Bd., Springfield, 1993—, sec., 1996—; pres. United Mine Workers Labor Union 9878, West Frankfort, 1990—. Precinct committeeman Rep. Party, Franklin County, 1988-94; reg. coord. Citizens for Sue Suter, 1990, Citizens for Jim Ryan, 1994; transition adv. com. mem. Jim Ryan Ill. Atty. Gen., Chgo., 1995; advisor, dir. Ill. YMCA Youth and Govt., 1992—. Mem. Ill. Oil and Gas Assn., West Frankfort C. of C. (dir. 1988—), Moose, Masons (32 deg.), Shriner (Krazy Klown unit dir. 1997-99), Lions (pres. 1992-93). Avocations: motorcycling, collecting old automobiles and memorabilia. Office: Egyptian Energies Inc 107 S Van Buren St PO Box 127 West Frankfort IL 62896-0127

WILLIAMS, JOY RHONDA, publishing and entertainment company executive; b. Ipswich, Australia, May 30, 1945; came to U.S., 1954; d. Francis Leon and Ailsa Mary (Bailey) W.; m. Raymond Joel Bennett, Feb. 12, 1962 (div. 1974); 1 child, Melissa Anne Tryon. AA in Psychology, DeAnza Coll., Cupertino, Calif., 1974. Exec. sec. Cobilt divsn. Computervision, Sunnyvale, Calif., 1972-74; tracking sys. analyst Memorex, Inc., Santa Clara, Calif., 1974-77; computer operator LCS Inc., Sunnyvale, 1977-78; project libr. Logisticon Inc., Sunnyvale, 1978-79, programmer-analyst, 1979-82; sr. programmer-analyst Microvertics, Inc., Mountain View, Calif., 1982-83; sr. sys. analyst Data Architects, Inc., San Francisco, 1983-84; tech. editor Sci. Applications Internat. Inc., Los Altos, Calif., 1985-92, Electric Power Rsch. Inst., Palo Alto, Calif., 1985-90; owner, pres. Artist Publs. Inc., Queensland, Australia, 1983—; west coast corr. MTV Music News, 1985-93; U.S. corr. Gosteleradio USSR, 1990-91, Komsomolskaya Pravda, Moscow, 1990-91, U.S. rep. Clearwater Rock, Moscow, 1992-93, SNC Radio, Moscow, 1992-93, KTR Corp., Moscow, 1992-93; Austrian corr. APB News, 1999-2000; staff writer Rock Hard mag., Germany, 1990-93, Jazz Forum Internat, 1988-93, RockAde mag., Moscow, 1990-94, Tournee mag., Moscow, 1992-94, Iron March mag., Moscow, 1992-93; owner Artist Web Designs Co., 1999—. Contbg. editor Thrash Metal mag., 1988-91, Metal mag., 1989-91; writer BAM mag, 1990-92; publicist BIZ Enterprises, Moscow, 1991; TV presenter, radio programmer Russian State TV & Radio Broadcasting Co., Moscow, 1990-93; news corr. Delovaya Volna (Bus. Wave Radio), Moscow, 1992-93; corr. Ogonyok Video and Mag., Moscow, 1990-91, Melodiya Mag., Moscow, 1993-95, Moskovsky Komsomolets, Moscow, 1993—, Mir Zvezd (World of Stars), Moscow, 1993-94, Russia Gazetta, Moscow, 1993, Novaya Yezhednevnaya Gazetta, Moscow, 1993-95, Moscow News, 1993—, APB News.com, 1999-2000; English lang. editor Diplomat Mag., Moscow, 1993;

author San Mateo Sch. Dist. white papers, 1992; editor: Country Music in Russia and the Former Soviet Union, 1993, Quick Fix Help Desk User Guide, 1996; author: Policy and Procedure Manual for Crime Reporting Information System for Police Queensland Police Svc., 1995; contbg. editor Music Box Mag., Moscow, 1996-99. Tech. support officer, expert svcs. sect. Queensland Police, 1996-99, rsch. and evaluation officer ethical stds. command, 2000—. E-mail: joyzine@zip.com.au. Office: Artist Publs & Web Design, 4/253 Riding Rd, Balmoral 4171, Australia

WILLIAMS, JULIUS PENSON, composer, conductor; b. Bronx, N.Y., June 22, 1954. BS, CUNY, 1977; MusM, Hartt Sch. Music, 1980; postgrad., Aspen Music Sch., 1984. Music dir. CPTV, 1984-85; asst. condr. Aspen (Colo.) Music Festival, 1985; condr., composer-in-residence Nutmeg Ballet, Bristol, Conn., 1986-88; music dir. Washington Symphony Orch., 1998—; artist-in-residence U. Vt., 1988-90; choral artistic dir. N.Y. State Summer Sch. of the Arts, Saratoga; music dir., prin. condr. Royal Ethiopian Philharm.; prof. music Berklee Coll. Music; edn. cons. Norwalk Symphony, 1997-98; mem. artistic adv. com. Queens Symphony, 1997—;. Composer: A Norman Overture, Tocatinna for Strings, Incommendation of Music, Meditation, Easter Celebration, Cantata for Orch., Chorus, Concerto for Harmonica and Orch., Rise Up Shepherd and Follow; (movie) My Heart Beats Loud; (off-Broadway) The Balm Yard; condr. Symphony Saint Paulia, Carnegie Hall; guest condr. New Haven Symphony, 1987, Savannah Symphony Orch., Dallas Symphony Orch., Norwalk Symphony Orch., Dubrovnik Symphony Orch., Yugoslavia, Knoxville Symphony, Okla. Symphony, Voldanska Philharm., Yugoslavia, Tulsa Philharm., Brno State Philharm, Czechoslavakia, Sacramento Symphony, 1995-96, Hartford Symphony, 1994, Bohuslau Martinu Philharm., Norfolk Symphony, 1997; appearances on CBS Sunday Morning, CBS Night Watch; recs. include Symphonic Brotherhood, 1994; contbr. articles to profl. jours. Named Hon. Disting. Alumnus Langston U., Disting. Alumn Herbert H. Lehman Coll.; recipient Nat. Cultural Through the Arts award, medal of artistic merit Found. Ecuador; Eminent Dupont scholar, Va. Mem. ASCPA (award 1979-—), NARAS, Am. Symphony Orch. League, Am. Choral Dirs. Assn., Music Educators Nat. Conf. Office: Julius Penson Williams Music Ste 293 35-31 Tacottville Rd Vernon Rockville CT 06066

WILLIAMS, KENYON DONALD, inventor; b. Grants Pass, Oreg., July 1, 1959; s. James D. and Darline Ruby (Witters) W. Grad. h.s., Grants Pass. Sr. technician Cable & Wireless Comm., Vienna, Va., 1983-97. Patentee in field. Sgt. USAF, 1978-84. Decorated Air Force Commendation medal. Mem. Phila. Ch. of God. Avocation: developing magnetic engine. E-Mail: Kenyon13@juno.com. Home and Office: 8322 Rolling Rd Manassas VA 20110-3625

WILLIAMS, LARRY ROSS, surgeon; b. Murphysboro, Ill., July 20, 1952; s. Laurel Ross and Mary Elizabeth (Blankinship) W.; m. Sarah Elizabeth Hecht, June 17, 1978; children: Gretchen Elizabeth, Noelle Louisa. BS, So. Ill. U., 1974; MD, U. Ill., Chgo., 1978, MS, 1982. Resident in surgery U. Ill., Chgo., 1978-83, fellow in surgery, 1983-84; fellow in vascular surgery Northwestern U., Chgo., 1984-85; asst. prof. U. South Fla., Tampa, 1985-92, clin. asst. prof., 1992—; chief vascular surgery Bay Pines VA Hosp., St. Petersburg, Fla., 1985-89; pvt. practice St. Anthony's Hosp., St. Petersburg, 1985—, chief of surgery, 1993-95, pres.-elect med. staff, 1993-95, pres. med. staff, 1996-97; bd. govs. Physician-Hosp. Orgn., 1994—. Contbr. articles to profl. jours. Active First United Meth. Ch., St. Petersburg, 1985—, Polywogs, St. Petersburg, 1989—. Fellow ACS; mem. Internat. Soc. Cardiovascular Surgery, Soc. Non-Invasive Vascular Technology, Assn. for Acad. Surgery, Pinellas County Med. Soc. (bd. govs. 1994-97), Fla. Med. Assn. (splty. soc. rep. 1994-96), Am. Inst. Ultrasound in Medicine, Fla. Assn. Gen. Surgeons, Peripheral Vascular Surg. Assn., Warren Cole Surg. Soc., So. Assn. for Vascular Surgery, Fla. Vascular Soc. (sec. 1991-94, pres. 1994-95), Fla. Surg. Soc., Southeastern Surg. Congress, Acad. Med. Arts and Scis., Frederick A. Coller Surg. Soc., Soc. for Clin. Vascular Surgery, Fla. Assn. Cardiovascular and Pulmonary Rehab., Phi Eta Sigma, Phi Kappa Phi, Phi Beta Kappa. Avocations: family activities, golf, tennis. Office: 1111 7th Ave N Saint Petersburg FL 33705-1348

WILLIAMS, LLOYD JOHN, entertainment company executive; b. Melbourne, Australia, May 7, 1940; s. Francis Ernest and Enid Betty (Temple) W.; m. Margaret Mavis Lord (div.); 1 child, Nick; m. Suzanne Jean Irwin, Aug. 14, 1981; children: Sara, John. Student, Xavier Coll. Chief exec. Hudson Conway Group, Melbourne, 1987—; exec. chmn. Crown Ltd., Melbourne, 1994—; dir. Australian Consolidated Press, Sydney, 1991—. Mem. Victoria Racing Club (com. mem. 1990-95), Melbroune Cricket Club, Victoria Amateur Turf Club, Lawn Tennis Assn. Victoria, Kingston Heath Golf, Greenacres Golf, Nat. Golf, Portsea Golf. Avocations: thoroughbred horse racing, golf. Home: 1 Albert Rd Apt 201, Melbourne VIC 3004, Australia Office: Hudson Conway, 250 Sturt St, Southbank VIC 3006, Australia

WILLIAMS, MARSHA KAY, data processing executive; b. Norman, Okla., Oct. 26, 1963; d. Charles Michael and Marilyn Louise (Bauman) Williams; m. Dale Lee Carabetta, Dec. 13, 1981. BS in Computer Mgmt. and Sci., Met. State Coll., Denver, 1996; postgrad., U. Denver, 1998—. Data processing supr. Rose Mfg. Co., Englewood, Colo., 1981-84, Mile High Equip. Co., Denver, 1984-88; mgr. info. tech. Ohmeda Monitoring Sys., Louisville, Colo., 1988-97; dir. info. tech. Cobe Cardiovasc., Inc., Arvada, Colo., 1997—. Mem. info. tech. adv. bd. Warren Tech. Sch., 1994-98, chairperson, 1996-98. Mem. Bus. and Profl. Women's Assn. (Young Careerist 1991). Home: 4700 Yates Ct Broomfield CO 80020-5622 Office: Cobe Cardiovasc 14401 W 65th Way Arvada CO 80004-3524

WILLIAMS, MARSHA RHEA, computer scientist, educator, researcher, consultant; b. Memphis, Aug. 4, 1948; d. James Edward and Velma Lee (Jenkins) W. Cert., Schiller Coll., West Berlin, Germany, 1968; BS in Physics, Beloit Coll., 1969; MS in Physics, U. Mich., 1971; MS in Sys. and Info. Sci., Vanderbilt U., 1976, PhD in Computer Sci., 1982. Cert. data processor. Engrng. coop. student Lockheed Missiles & Space Co., Sunnyvale, Calif., 1967-68; asst. transmission engr. Ind. Bell Tel. Co., Indpls., 1971-72; sys. analyst, instr. physics Memphis State U., 1972-74; computer-assisted instrn. project programmer Fisk U., 1974-76; mem. tech. staff Hughes Rsch. Labs., Malibu, Calif., 1976-78; assoc. sys. engr. IBM, Nashville, 1978-80; rsch. and tchg. asst. Vanderbilt U., Nashville, 1980-82, spl. asst. to dean Grad. Sch., spring 1981, minority engr. advisor, 1975-76; cons. computer-assisted instrn. project Meharry Med. Coll., Nashville, summer 1982; assoc. prof. computer sci. Tenn. State U., Nashville, 1982-83, 84-90, full tenured prof., 1990—, univ. marshal, 1992-97; assoc. prof. U. Miss., Oxford, 1983-84, faculty senator; assoc. program dir. Applications of Advanced Techs. Sci. and Engrng. Edn., NSF, 1987-88, apptd. USRA Sci. and Engrng. Edn. Coun., Advanced Design Program, 1992-94; cons. on minority scientists and engrs. Univ. Space Rsch. Assn., Washington, 1988; vis. scientist CSNET-Minority Instn. Networking Project Bolt, Beranek & Newman, Cambridge, Mass., 1989; mem. tech. staff Bell Comm. Rsch., Red Bank, N.J., 1990; presenter papers profl. meetings. Editor-in-chief newspaper Pilgrim Emanuel Bapt. Ch., 1975-76. Advisr Chi Rho Youth Fellowship, Temple Bapt. Ch., 1975-81, adv. com. Golden Outreach Sr. Citizens Fellowship, 1979-80, 86-87, 89-93, Women's Day spkr., 1979-81, Ebenezer Missionary Bapt. Ch., 1993; adviser Nat. Soc. Black Engrng. Students, 1983-84; founder, coord. Tenn. State U. Assn. for Excellence in Computer Sci., Math. and Physics (AE-COMP), 1986-87, coord. Tech. Opportunities Fair, 1986, 87; dir. Tenn. State U. Minorities in Sci., Engrng. and Tech. Rsch. Project-MISET, 1989—; child sponsor World Vision, 1981—; mem., newsletter staff Lake Providence Missionary Bapt. Ch. Recipient Disting. Instr. award, 1984, Disting. Svc. citation Beloit Coll. Alumni Assn., 1994; grantee Digital Equipment Corp., 1989-92; faculty rsch. grantee Tenn. State U., 1993, 94. Mem. AAUP, NAACP (nat. judge ACT-SO sci. olympics 1992), Assn. Computing Machinery, Assn. Info. Tech. Profls. (formerly Data Processing Mgmt. Assn.) (edn. chmn., bd. dirs. 1986), Tenn. Acad. Sci., Am. Assn. of Univ. Profs., Phi Kappa Phi. Achievements include research in developing a formerly complete model information/support system (database, network and human-computer interfacing), for minority scientists, especially African American science students, and for providing/locating technical resources for developing countries. Home: PO Box 270545 Nashville TN 37227-0545 Office: Tenn State U Dept Computer Sci PO Box 136 Nashville TN 37202-0136

WILLIAMS, MELVIN DONALD, anthropologist, educator; b. Pitts., Feb. 3, 1933; s. Aaron and Gladys Virginia (Barnes) W.; m. Faye Wanda Strawder, June 20, 1958; children: Aaron Ellsworth, Steven Rodney, Craig Haywood. A.B., U. Pitts., 1955, M.A., 1969, Ph.D., 1973. Owner, operator Wholesale Periodical Distbn. Co., Pitts., 1955-66; instr. dept. sociology and anthropology Carlow Coll., 1969-71, asst. prof., 1971-75, chmn. dept. sociology and anthropology, 1973-75; assoc. prof. anthropology U. Pitts., 1976-79, adj. prof., 1979-82; prof. anthropology Purdue U., 1979-83, U. Md., College Park, 1983-88, U. Mich., Ann Arbor, 1988—; Olie B. O'Connor prof. Am. instns. Colgate U., 1976-77. Author: On the Street Where I Lived, Community in a Black Pentecostal Church, The Human Dilemma, The Black Middle Class, An Academic Village, Race for Theory; editor: Selected Readings in Afro-American Anthropology; contbr. articles to profl. publs. Co-chmn. project area com. Urban Redevel. Authority, Pitts., 1972—; co-dir. interdisciplinary family community project Western Psychiat. Inst. and Clinic, 1973-76; bd. dirs. Cath. Social Svc. of Allegheny County, Pa., 1973-76; coll. ombudsman, 1991-93, faculty senate, 1993-96. NSF field tng. fellow in anthropology, 1967; grantee, 1969-72; Community Action Pitts. grantee, 1969-71; Social Sci. Research Council grantee, 1974-75; Lilly Endowment grantee, 1980-83, 85-86; NDEA Title IV fellow, 1969. Fellow Am. Anthrop. Assn.; mem. African Studies Assn., AAAS, AAUP, Am. Sociol. Assn., Assn. Study Afro-Am. Life and History, Soc. for Psychol. Anthropology. Home: 520 W Washington St Ann Arbor MI 48103-4232

WILLIAMS, MICHAEL ALAN, psychologist; b. Cin., May 20, 1948; s. Chester and Gentry Mae (Canada) W.; m. Linda Ann Presswood, Aug. 8, 1970; children: Michael Alan II, Derrick Alexander. BA, U. Cin., 1970, MA, 1971, EdD, 1980. Instr. U. Cin., 1972-75; sch. psychologist Dayton Bd. Edn., Ohio, 1975-78; assoc. prof. Wright State U., Dayton, 1978-99, coord. spl. edn. program, 1992-99; prof. emeritus Montgomery County Children's Services, Dayton, 1999—, 1999; clin. psychologist Profl. Psychol. Services, Dayton, 1981—; psychol. services coordinator Montgomery County Children's Services, Dayton, 1983-88; psychol. cons. Diversion Alternative for Youth, Dayton, 1990—; program mgr. Head Start Supplementary Tng. Program, Cin., 1973-74; cons. Ohio Luth. Synod, Dayton, 1981-83, Blacks in Govt., Dayton, 1982-85, Montgomery County, Stillwater Health Ctr., Dayton, 1982-86. Co-editor (book): Teaching in a Multicultural Pluralistic Society, 1982, 2d edit., 1987. Treas. Dayton Free Clinic and Counseling Ctr., Dayton, 1983; bd. dirs. Planned Parenthood Assn., Dayton, 1983, Miami Valley Literacy Coun., Dayton, 1990-97, Dayton Mediation Ctr., 1995-98, S. Cmty., Inc., 1996. Recipient Faculty Excellence award Wright State U., 1997, Disting. Prof. award Wright State U., 1997; named Outstanding Young Man Am., Jaycees, 1984, Top Ten African-Am. Males, Dayton chpt. Urban League, 1995; McCall Scholarship, 1966-70. Mem. Am. Psychol. Assn., Nat. Assn. Black Psychologists, Nat. Assn. Sch. Psychologists, Dayton Assn. Black Psychologists (v.p. 1986-88, pres. 1988-89), Mental Health Assn. (bd. dirs. 1985), Assn. Tchr. Educators. Avocations: bible student, music, handiwork, writing. Home: 4830 Old Hickory Pl Dayton OH 45426-2149 Office: Profl Psychol Svcs 4130 Linden Ave Ste 309 Dayton OH 45432-3034

WILLIAMS, MICHAEL JAMES, health care services consultant; b. Royal Oak, Mich., Sept. 23, 1951; s. Robert Burgett and Elizabeth (McGuire) W.; m. Juliana Caitlin. BA in Police Adminstrn., Wayne State U., 1974, BS in Psychology, 1974; MPA, Calif. State U., Fullerton, 1978. Asst. mgr. Suburban Ambulance Co., Royal Oak, 1970-74; dir. Emergency Med. Services Imperial County, El Centro, Calif., 1974-76, Orange County, Santa Ana, Calif., 1976-80; pres. EMS Systems Design, Irvine, Calif., 1980-89, The Abaris Group, Tustin, 1989—; instr., trainer ACLS, Am. Heart Assn., 1978-80, CPr, 1989—; spl. cons. Hosp. Coun. So. Calif., Calif. Assn. Hosps. and Health Systems; EMS med. coord. trauma emergencies Pyramid Films, Santa Monica, Calif., 1989 (Am. Film Inst. Blue Ribbon award). Contbr. numerous articles to profl. jours. Recipient Recognition award Orange County Emergency Care Commn., 1980, Appreciation award UCI Med. Ctr., Orange, Calif., 1980, Orange County Fire Chiefs Assn., 1980. Mem. Healthcare Fin. Mgmt. Assn., Am. Trauma Soc., Am. Heart Assn. (bd. dirs. Orange County chpt., 1976-82), No. Calif. Healthcare Execs., Orange County Trauma Soc. (bd. dirs. 1981-89, program achievement award, 1987), Internat. Assn. Fire Chiefs (EMS sect.), EMS Adminstrs. Assn. Calif. (founding). Democrat. Avocations: jogging, racquetball, fishing. Office: 700 Ygnacio Valley Rd Ste 250 Walnut Creek CA 94596-3871

WILLIAMS, MILLER, poet, translator; b. Hoxie, Ark., Apr. 8, 1930; s. Ernest Burdette and Ann Jeanette (Miller) W.; m. Lucille Day, Dec. 29, 1951 (div.); m. Rebecca Jordan Hall, Apr. 11, 1969; children: Lucinda, Robert, Karyn. BS, Ark. State Coll., 1951; MS, U. Ark., 1952; postgrad., La. State U., 1951, U. Miss., 1957; HHD (hon.), Lander Coll., 1983; DHL, Hendrix Coll., 1995. Instr. in English La. State U., 1962-63, asst. prof., 1964-66; vis. prof. U. Chile, Santiago, 1963-64; assoc. prof. Loyola U., New Orleans, 1966-70; Fulbright prof. Nat. U. Mex., Mexico City, 1970; co-dir. grad. program in creative writing U. Ark., 1970-84, assoc. prof., 1971-73, prof. English and fgn. langs., dir. program in transl., 1973-87, univ. prof., 1987—, dir. poetry-in-the prisons programs div. continuing edn., 1974-79, chmn. program in comparative lit., 1978-80; fellow Am. Acad. in Rome, 1976—, mem. adv. coun. Sch. Classical Studies, 1985-91; first U.S. del. Pan Am. Conf. Univ. Artists and Writers, Concepcion, Chile, 1964; invited del. Internat. Assembly Univ. Press Dirs., Guadalajara, Mex., 1991; mem. poetry staff Bread Loaf Writers Conf., 1967-72; founder, exec. dir. Ark. Poetry Cir., 1975; founding dir. U. Ark. Press, 1980-97; participant Assn. Am. Univ. Presses Soviet Mission, 1989. Author: (poems) A Circle of Stone, 1964, Recital, 1965, So Long At the Fair, 1968, The Only World There Is, 1971; (criticism) The Achievement of John Ciardi, 1968, The Poetry of John Crowe Ransom, 1971; (with John Ciardi) (criticism) How Does a Poem Mean?, 1974; (poems) Halfway From Hoxie: New & Selected Poems, 1973, Why God Permits Evil, 1977, Distractions, 1981, The Boys on Their Bony Mules, 1983; translator: (poems) Poems & Antipoems (Nicanor Parra), 1967, Emergency Poems (Nicanor Parra), 1972, Sonnets of Giuseppe Belli, 1981; editor: (poems) 19 Poetas de Hoy en Los Estados Unidos, 1966, (with John William Corrington) Southern Writing in the Sixties: Poetry, 1967, Southern Writing in the Sixties: Fiction, 1966, Chile: An Anthology of New Writing, 1968, Contemporary Poetry in America, 1972, (with James A. McPherson) Railroad: Trains and Train People in American Culture, 1976, A Roman Collection: An Anthology of Writing about Rome and Italy, 1980, Ozark, Ozark: A Hillside Reader, 1981, (criticism) Patterns of Poetry, 1986, (poetry) Imperfect Love, 1986, Living on the Surface: New and Selected Poems, 1989, Adjusting to the Light, 1992, Points of Departure, 1995, The Ways We Touch, 1997, Some Jazz A While: The Collected Poems, 1999; poetry editor La. State U. Press, 1966-68; contbr. articles to profl. publs. Mem. ACLU. Recipient Henry Bellaman Poetry award, 1957, award in poetry Arts Fund, 1973, Prix de Rome, Am. Acad. Arts and Letters, 1976, Nat. Poets prize, 1990, Charity Randall citation Internat. Poetry Forum, 1993, John William Corrington award for excellence in lit., Centenary Coll., Shreveport, La., 1994, Acad. Lit. award AAAL, 1995, Presdl. Inaugural Poet, 1997; named Bread Loaf fellow in poetry, 1963. Mem. MLA, PEN, AAUP, South Ctrl. MLA, Am. Lit. Translators Assn. (v.p. 1978-79, pres. 1979-81), Authors' Guild, Soc. Benemerito dell'Assn. Centro Romanesco Trilussa (Rome). Home: 1111 Valley View Dr Fayetteville AR 72701-1603

WILLIAMS, MORGAN HOWARD, computer science educator, researcher; b. Durban, South Africa, Dec. 15, 1944; s. Morgan and Ellen Frances (Reid) W.; m. Jean Doe, Dec. 13, 1969; children: Christopher M., Michael J. BSc, Rhodes U., Grahamstown, South Africa, 1965, BSc with honors, 1966, PhD, 1971, DSc, 1994. Chartered Engr. Physicist Antarctic expedition, 1967-69; lectr. Rhodes U., 1970-72, sr. lectr., 1972-77, prof. computer sci., head of dept., 1977-80; prof. computer sci., head of dept. Heriot-Watt U., Edinburgh, Scotland, 1980-88, prof. computer sci., 1988—; mem. Sci. and Engrng. Rsch. Coun., Engrng. and Phys. Scis. Rsch. Coun., European Union, and other cmtys.; mem. over 12 conf. program and organizing coms. Author 1 book, editor 3 books, contbr. over 170 articles to profl. jours. and conf. procs.; editor Jour. Quaestiones Informaticae, 1978-80; mem. editl. bd. 2 jours. Rsch. grantee SERC/EPSRC and European Union; travel grantee Brit. Coun., NATO, European Union. Fellow Brit. Computer Soc., Royal Soc. Arts. Home: 3 House O'Hill, Brae, Edinburgh EH4 5DQ, Scotland Office: Heriot-Watt U Comp Elec Eng, Riccarton, Edinburgh EH14 4AS, Scotland

WILLIAMS, MUKESH KUMAR, humanities educator, researcher; b. Allahabad, India, Aug. 2, 1953; s. Stephen and Persis Gloria Williams; m. Ritu Java, July 15, 1988. BA, U. Allahabad, 1972, MA, 1974; PhD in Contemporary Jewish Am. Fiction, Indian Inst. Tech., 1982. English lectr. Ewing Christian Coll., Allahabad, 1975, Indian Inst. Tech., Madras, 1981-82, St. Stephen's Coll., New Delhi, 1982—; vis. prof. English Soka U., Tokyo, 1994-96. Editor: Charles Dickens: Hard Times, 1999; editor-in-cief The Stephanian, 1984-94; contbr. articles to profl. jours. including Contemporary Jewish Am. Fiction, Studies in English Lang. and Lit., Contemporary Am. Fiction, Studies in English Lang. and Lit. Dist. leader Bharat Soka Gakkai, Delhi, 1984—. Recipient Acad. and Cultural Contbn. award Soká Gakkai Internat., 1993, highest honor Sec. Multi-Ethnic Lits. U.S.; grantee USIA, 1997. Mem. English Lang. and Lit. Soc., Am. Studies Assn., Mombusho Scholars Assn. India. Mem. Soka Gakkai Internat. Avocations: skiing, Japanese paintings, leather work, fiction writing. Office: St Stephens Coll, U Delhi, New Delhi 110007, India

WILLIAMS, NEVILLE, international solar energy corporation executive; b. Muncie, Ind., Mar. 28, 1943; s. Donald Charles and Rose Eileen (Boughton) W. Student, U. Colo., 1964-66, U. Neuchatel, Switzerland, 1967. Freelance corr. Vietnam, 1968-69; freelance journalist Montreal, Que., Can., 1970-71, London, 1971-73; writer, producer Sta. WNBC-TV News, N.Y.C., 1973-74; freelance writer Telluride, Colo., 1975-79; media liaison Office of Solar Energy U.S. Dept. Energy, Washington, 1979-80; dir. of mktg. Telluride Ski Resort, Inc., 1981-83; owner, operator Hist. Sheridan Opera Ho., Telluride, 1983-85; nat. media dir. Greenpeace U.S.A., Washington, 1987-89; chmn., pres. Solar Electric Light Fund, Washington, 1990-97; also, bd. dirs.; chmn. Solar Electric Light Co., SELCO-India, SELCO-Vietnam, SELCO-Sri Lanka. Author: The New Exiles, 1971, (monograph) Great Telluride Strike, 1977; contbr. articles to N.Y. Times mag., Penthouse, Outside, New Times, The Nation, The New Republic, Nature, others. Apptd. mem. Adv. Com. for Commerce and Devel., State of Colo., 1980-85; apptd. mem. Gov.'s Motion Picture & TV Commn., 1981-85. Fellow Internat. Solar Energy Soc. Avocations: mountaineering, hiking, history, metaphysics. Office: Solar Electric Light Co 35 Wisconsin Cir Chevy Chase MD 20815-7015

WILLIAMS, PAUL ROBERT, school system administrator; b. Portsmouth, Ohio, Aug. 30, 1937; s. Jesse Clinton and Lola Ethel (Harden) W.; m. Catherine Wilson, Sept. 4, 1959; children: Jacqueline Joy, John Scott. BS, Taylor U., 1961; MA, Mich. State U., 1969, PhD, 1980. Tchr. Chesaning (Mich.) Union Schs., 1961-70, curriculum coord., 1970-74; asst. supt. Durand (Mich.) Area Schs., 1974-75; supt. Caledonia (Mich.) Pub. Schs., 1975-80, Lakeview Sch. Dist., Battle Creek, Mich., 1980-94, Beachwood (Ohio) City Sch. Dist., 1994—; adj. prof. Western Mich. U., 1983—, Mich. State U., 1988—, U. Mich., 1991—; presenter Japanese Langs. Advs. for Langs., San Francisco, Japanese Saturday Sch., N.E. Conf. Teaching Fgn. Langs., Coun. State Univs. Mich., Nat. Invitational Conf. Sch. Health Programs, Pacific Rim Conf., Comparative Internat. Edn. Soc. Ann Conf., Mich. Congress Parents, Tchrs. and Students, Am. Assn. Sch. Adminstrs., Video on Voluntarism, Mich. Non-Profit Forum, Alternatives for Excellence Mich. State U., 1991, other profl. confs.; mem. mission to Japan Japanese Sat. Sch., recruiting and trade missions to Japan, extern seminars Mich. State U.; presenter Quality in Edn. Am. Assn. Sch. Svc. Agencies, Battle Creek Chamber Eye Opener, Traverse City Seminar Quality, Mich. Dept. Social Svcs., Am. Assn. Sch. Adminstrs. Ann. Conf., 1994, Ednl. Insights Group, Mich. Gov.'s Conf. on Quality in Edn., 1997, Ednl. mission to Israel, AACD conf., 2000, others. Editor: A Beacon of Hope; contbr. articles to profl. jours. Trustee Irving Gilmore Internat. Keyboard Festival, 1989-94, emeritus mem., 1994—; mem. exec. bd. Jr. Achievement of Greater Cleveland; chmn. exec. bd. Cuyahoga Spl. Edn. Svc. Ctr.; mem. Mohican Inst.; v.p., exec. bd. mem. Mich. State Nat. Alumni, 2000—; nat. adv. bd. mem. Mich. State U. Coll. of Edn., 2000—. Recipient Ednl. Divsn. award Kent County United Way, 1979, Disting. Svc. award Mich. PTA, 1985, Campaign Chairperson award United Way of Greater Battle Creek, 1986, Econ. Fund. Devel. award Battle Creek Unltd., 1986, Good Egg award Binder Park Zoo, Svc. award 1986, Winners Circle award 1990 Mich. Assn. Sch. Adminstrs. Mem. Buckeye Assn. Sch. Adminstrs. (legis. com.), Kent County Supt. Assn. (Disting. Svc. award 1980), Educators Task Force (exec. bd. dirs., chmn. 1988-91), Beachwood C. of C. (bd. dirs., v.p. 2000—). Republican. Avocations: golf, jogging, backpacking, reading. Home: 24675 Hilltop Dr Beachwood OH 44122-1345 Office: Beachwood City Sch Dist 24601 Fairmount Blvd Beachwood OH 44122-2239

WILLIAMS, PEARL See GOOD-BLACK, EDITH ELISSA

WILLIAMS, PHILIP GLADSTONE, research mycologist; b. Sydney, Australia, Mar. 31, 1932; s. Percy Gladstone and Ida Maude (Tear) W.; m. Maria Paula Wilma Kappenstein, Dec. 17, 1962; children: Karen, Peter, Glynn. BS in Agr., U. Sydney, 1954, MS in Agr., 1959; PhD, U. Wis., 1960. Asst. plant pathologist Dept. Agr., Hobart, Tasmania, 1955-57; rsch. asst. U. Wis., Madison, 1957-60; rsch. assoc. U. Saskatchewan, 1962-64; lectr. U. Sydney (Australia), 1965-67; vis. fellow U. New South Wales, Sydney, 1985—; cons. in field. Contbr. articles to profl. jours. Nat. pres. Scientists Against Nuclear Arms, Sydney, 1984; mem. dept. fgn. affairs Consultative Com. Peace and Disarmament, 1982-87; sec. mgmt. com. Total Environ. Ctr., Sydney, 1992-96. Postdoctoral fellow Prairie Regional Lab., Saskatoon, 1960-62, Rsch. fellow U. Sydney, 1967-77, Sr. Rsch. fellow, 1977-85. Mem. Australian Inst. Agrl. Sci. (pres. New South Wales br. 1983-84), Australian Plant Pathology Soc. (councillor 1981-85). Avocations: swimming, gardening, reading. Home: 6 Undercliff St, Neutral Bay, NSW 2089, Australia Office: U NSW, U NSW, Sch Biol Sci, Sydney NSW 2052, Australia

WILLIAMS, PHILLIP WAYNE, former state official and army officer, securities and diversified company executive, consultant; b. Birmingham, Ala., Nov. 1, 1939; s. Louie Alfred and A. Banks (Osborn) W.; divorced; children: Phillip Wayne, Christopher N., Charles Marion, William; m. Ramsey Waddell, Mar. 19, 1988. BS in Math. and Physics, Florence (Ala.) State Coll., 1961; M in Adminstrv. Sci., U. Ala., Huntsville, 1977; D in Pub. Adminstrn., Nova U., 1978. Dep. sheriff Lauderdale County, Florence, 1960-61; commd. 2d lt. U.S. Army, 1961, advanced through grades to lt. col., 1977; comdr., staff officer, project mgr. laser designators Redstone Arsenal, Ala., 1973-74; ret. U.S. Army, 1982; chmn., pres. COMTEL-South, Inc., Huntsville, 1982-85, Joint Capital Securities, Inc., Joint Capital Svcs., 1983-95; cons. def. industry, 1983-95, 96—; dir. fin. State of Ala., 1995-96; Rep. candidate for Gov. of Ala., 1998. Bd. dirs. BBB No. Ala., 1985. Decorated Legion of Merit, Bronze Star with V and 5 oak leaf clusters, Air medal with V, Army Commendation medal with VII and 3 oak leaf clusters. Mem. U.S. Armor Assn., Assn. U.S. Army, Blackhorse Assn., Am. Def. Preparedness Assn. (dir. 1982-84, regional v.p. 1985-97), Am. Soc. Pub. Adminstrn. (pres. 1982-84), Rotary Club (pres. 1993-94, dist. gov. group rep. 1994-95, dist. gov. 2001-02). Office: PO Box 2319 Huntsville AL 35804-2319

WILLIAMS, RHYS, minister; b. San Francisco, Feb. 27, 1929; s. Albert Rhys and Lucita (Squier) W.; m. Eleanor Hoyle Barnhart, Sept. 22, 1956; children: Rhys Hoyle, Eleanor Pierce. AB, St. Lawrence U., 1951, BD, MDiv, 1953, DD, 1966; postgrad., Union Sem., summer 1956; LLD (hon.), Emerson Coll., 1962. Ordained to ministry Unitarian Ch., 1954. Min. Unitarian Ch., Charleston, S.C., 1953-60; min. 1st and 2d Ch., Boston, 1960-00, min. emeritus, 2000—; mem. faculty, field edn. supr. Harvard U., 1969—; Russell lectr. Tufts U., 1965, Minns lectr., 1986. Pres. Edward Everett Hale House, 1987—, Soc. of Cincinnati, State of N.H., 1986-89; v.p. Franklin Inst., 1960-99, , sec., 1990-96, trustee, 1999—; v.p. Benevolent Frat. Unitarian Universalist Chs., 1982-93; pres. Unitarian Universalist Urban Ministry, 1991-99, pres. emeritus, 1999—; sec. bd. trustees Emerson Coll., 1961-94, trustee, 1994—; chaplain Gen. Soc. Cin., Washington, 1977—, Founders and Patriots of Mass., SR; chmn. Festival Fund, Inc., Am.-Soviet Cultural Exch., 1989-91; trustee Opera Co. Boston, 1970—; trustee Meadville Lombard Theol. Sch., Chgo., 1971-77, mem. ministerial fellowship com., 1961-69, chmn., 1968-69; fin. chmn. Ch. Larger Fellowship, 1968-86; bd. dirs. Peter Faneuil Housing Corp., AIDS Housing, 1995, clk. 1996—; trustee Franklin Square House, 1993—; chmn. Franklin Found., 1997; mem. pres. coun. U. Va., 1999—, mem. adv. com. New Horizons - U.S.-Russia students. Mem. Unitarian Universalist Mins. Assn. (pres. 1968-70), Unitarian Hist. Soc. (pres. 1960-75), Evang. Missionary Soc. (pres. 1965-80, v.p. 1980—), Soc. for Propagation Gospel Among Indians and Others in N.Am. (v.p. 1975-99, pres. 1999—), Unitarian Svc. Pension Soc. (pres.

1973—), Soc. Ministerial Relief (pres. 1973—, mem. com. for ch. staff fin.), Mass. Hist. Soc., Colonial Soc. Mass., Union Club (Boston), Union Boat Club (Boston), Unitarian Universalist Assn., Beta Theta Pi (pres. New Eng. 1964-66). Office: Hale-Bannard 273 Clarendon St Boston MA 02116-1404

WILLIAMS, RICHARD GLYN, singer, educator; b. Edmonton, Alta., Can., Apr. 6, 1955; s. Edward Glyn and Betty Mae (Smith) W.; m. Lynn Ellis, Apr. 30, 1982; 1 child, Elizabeth Anne. Student, Royal No. Coll. Music, Manchester, Eng., 1974-75, U. Mont., 1979. Cultural attaché Gen. Consulate of Belize, Geneva, 1995—; spl. cons. Gov. Gen. Belize, 1995; prin. Penrhyn Acad. Singing, Vancouver, 1997—; condr. North Shore Light Opera, Vancouver; condr. N.W. Opera, Christchurch Cathedral, Vancouver; music dir. Maple Ridge Choral Soc., St. David's Male Voice Choir; founding condr. SummerChor Vancouver; leader various workshops. Operatic performances include Curlew River, Festival de la Cite, Lausanne, Switzerland, Festivale Semana Santa, Cuenca, Spain, Le Cachet Rouge, Reinisches Symphonie/Opera de Bienne, Idomeneo, Festival Mulhouse, France, Gianni Schicchi, U. Mont., H.M.S. Pinafore, U. Mont.; oratorio performances include St. John Passion, Evanglist-Orfeo Chor, Frankfurt, Mass in B Minor, Choeur Orphee de Geneve, Lauda per la Nativitas Choeur Calliope, Lausanne, Les Sept Dernieres Paroles Choeur Bis Echalens, Switzerland, others; concert performances include Serenade for Tenor, Bernex, Switzerland, Choral Fantasia, Fribourg, Switzerland, Ninth Symphony, Vancouver, Can., Les Nuits d'Ete, Kamloops, Can., Rinaldo Compesieres, Switzerland; recitals include Dichterliebe, Hundred Mile House, Can., Sieben Fruhe Lieder, Compesieres, Switzerland, Songs of Travel, Montreaux, Switzerland, Vier Ernste Gesaenge, Geneva, others. Recipient 2d pl. award Nat. Festival of Can., 1981.

WILLIAMS, ROBERT HENRY, oil company executive; b. El Paso, Jan. 12, 1946; s. William Frederick and Mary (Page) W.; m. Joanne Marie Mudd, Oct. 22, 1967; children: Lara, Michael, Suzanne, Jennifer. BS in Physics, U. Tex., El Paso, 1968; PhD in Physics, U. Tex., Austin, 1973; MS in Physics, Va. Poly. Inst., 1971. Dir. Gulf Oil R&D, Houston, 1978-81; tech. mgr. Gulf Oil Internat., Houston, 1981-83; exploration mgr. Gulf Oil Co., Houston, 1983-85; mgr. geophys. rsch. Tenneco Oil Co., Houston, 1985-87, mgr., chief geophysicist, 1987-88; founder, mng. dir. Dover Energy, Houston, 1988—; exec. v.p. Tatham Offshore Inc, Houston, 1989-95, also bd. dirs.; chmn., CEO Dover Tech. Inc., Houston, 1989—; cons. Tenneco Inc., Houston, 1989—; DeepTech Internat., 1992-95; Ukraine Acad. Sci., 1993; bd. dirs., exec. v.p. DeepTech Inc., 1991-95; founder, pres. Westway tech. Assocs., 1986—; co-founder, chmn. CEO Castaway Graphite Rods, Inc., 1990—; owner, CEO Team Tex. Inc., 1993—; Bulldog Lures, Inc., 1994—; founder, CEO Houston Books Inc., 1994—; founder, CEO, chmn. Dover Energy Exploration, 1995—; pres. Westway Interests; chmn., CEO, bd. dirs. W.B. Oil & Gas Inc., 1997—, Dover (Belize), 1996—; bd. dirs. Tatham Offshore, Swep, Inc.; CEO Norman Lures, 1997—; founder, bd. dirs., CEO Win Leisure Products, 1997—. Contbr. articles to profl. jours. Mem. coun. Boy Scouts Am., Houston, 1989—; patron Mus. Fine Arts, Houston, 1990-2000, Houston Zool. Soc., 1990-2000; leader Girl Scouts U.S., Houston, 1989—, life mem. Mem. Soc. Exploration Geophysics, Am. Assn. Petroleum Geologists, Am. Geophys. Union. Republican. Avocations: scuba diving, book collecting, fishing. Office: Dover Group 11767 Katy Fwy Ste 1000 Houston TX 77079-1730

WILLIAMS, ROBERT JOSEPH, museum director, educator; b. Bennington, Vt., June 21, 1944; s. Joseph and Ruthe Allison (Moody) W. BS in Edn., U. Vt., 1970; MA in Interdisciplinary Social Sci., San Francisco State U., 1981. Tchr. adult edn. Mt. Anthony Union High Sch., Bennington, Vt., 1972-74; columnist Bennington Banner, 1972-77; tchr. San Francisco State U., 1976-79; founder, dir. NORRAD Drug Rehab. Ctr., San Francisco, 1986-88; museum curator Shaftsbury (Vt.) Historical Soc., 1989—; founder, dir. Bennington Tutorial Ctr., 1971-74. Author: Toward Humanness in Education, 1981, Chalice of Leaves: Selected Essays and Poems, 1988, Modern Salvation: Guidelines from Cosmology, 1994; author: (with others) Intimacy, 1985. Recipient Edmunds Essay medal Vt. Historical Soc., Montpelier, 1961, award of the League of Vt. Writers, 1972, Golden Poet award World of Poetry, Sacramento, Calif., 1990. Democrat. Avocation: cosmology. Home: 102 Putnam St Bennington VT 05201-2348 Office: Shaftsbury Hist Soc PO Box 401 Shaftsbury VT 05262-0401

WILLIAMS, ROBERT JOSEPH PATON, science educator. DSc (hon.), U. Keele, Eng., U. Leicester, Eng., U. East Anglia, Eng., U. Lisbon, Protugal. Fellow Wadham Coll., Oxford (Eng.) U., now fellow emeritus. Recipient Royal medal Royal Soc., 1995. Fellow European Acad. Sci., Royal Soc. U.K.; mem. Acad. Sci. Portugal (fgn.), Royal Acad. Sci. Sweden (fgn.), Acad. Sci. Czech Republic (fgn.), Acad. Sci. Belgium (fgn.). Home: 115 Victoria Rd, Oxford OX2 7QG, England Office: Inorganic Chemistry Lab, South Parks Rd, Oxford OX1 3QR, England

WILLIAMS, RONALD DAVID, telecommunications executive; b. Marshall, Ark., Mar. 15, 1944; s. Noble Kentucky and Elizabeth (Karns) W.; m. Beth L. Williams, Nov. 1977; children: Stephanie Noble, Keith Michael. BA, Columbia U., 1966, BS, 1967, MBA, 1973. Process engr. DuPont, Deepwater, N.J., 1966; design engr. Combustion Engring. Co., Hartford, 1971; cons. Arthur Andersen & Co., N.Y.C., 1973-76; corp. planner Amax Inc., Greenwich, Conn., 1976-77, group planning adminstr., 1978-80, mgr. corp. planning and analysis, 1980-94, dir. fin. analysis, 1984-86; project mgr. Olin Corp., Stamford, Conn., 1977-78; mgr. ops. planning and analysis Savin Corp., Stamford, 1986-88; dir. fin. Bandgap Tech. Corp., Broomfield, Colo., 1988-90, v.p. fin. and adminstrn., 1990-93; v.p., gen. mgr. Bandgap Chem. Corp., 1992-94; contr. Heraeus PMR, Inc., Alden, N.Y., 1994-95, v.p. fin. and adminstrn., 1995-96; gen. mgr. Acoustiflo, Boulder, Colo., 1996-97; sr. fin. staff analyst Energy Corp., New Orleans, 1998-99; mgr. fin. planning Energy Tech. Co., 1999—. Served with USN, 1967-70, Vietnam. NASA trainee, 1971; S.W. Mudd scholar, 1971. Mem. AAAS, Am. Chem. Soc., Am. Mgmt. Assn., Ark. Hist. Assn., Westport Hist. Soc., Colo. Hist. Soc., Appalachian Mountain Club, Boulder Road Runners, Checkers Running Club, Chalmette Track Club, Green Mountain Club, New Orleans Track Club, Gulf Coast Running Club, Pine Belt Pacers. Home: 7361 S Meadow Ct Boulder CO 80301-3951 Office: 639 Loyola Ave New Orleans LA 70113-3125

WILLIAMS, RONALD DOHERTY, lawyer; b. New Haven, Conn., Apr. 6, 1927; s. Richard Hugh nd Ethel W. (Nelson) w.; m. Laura Costarelli, Aug. 25, 1951; children: Craig F., Ronald D., Ellen A., Jane E. BA, U. Va., 1951; LLB, 1954. Bar: Conn. 1954. Assoc. Pullman, Comley, Bradley & Reeves, Bridgeport, Conn., 1954-60; ptnr., 1960-88, Williams, Cooney & Sheehy, 1989—; mem. Fed. Jud. Com., 1988-91, com. unauthorized practice law, 1988-94, com. to study rules civil practice & procedure, 1984-86; atty. state trial referee, 1984-90. Selectman Town of Easton (Conn.), 1975-85, justice of the peace, 1977—, town atty., 1985-2000; mem. Bridgeport Area Found., 1971-90, adv. com. U. Bridgeport Law Sch., 1982-92; mem. statewide grievance com., 1985-91, chmn., 1989-91; mem. exec. bd. Sch. Law Quinnipiac Coll., 1994—. Served with U.S. Army, 1945-46. Fellow Am. Coll. Trial Lawyers; mem. ABA, Am. Bd. Trial Advs., Conn. Bar Assn. (bd. govs. 1975-78), Bridgeport Bar Assn. (pres. 1975), Conn. Def. Lawyers Assn. (pres. 1984-85), Trial Attys. Am. Republican. Roman Catholic. Home: 14 Newman Dr Easton CT 06612-1915 Office: 1 Lafayette Cir Bridgeport CT 06604-6021

WILLIAMS, RONALD OSCAR, systems engineer; b. Denver, May 10, 1940; s. Oscar H. and Evelyn (Johnson) W. BS in Applied Math. Coll. Engring., U. Colo., 1964; postgrad, U. Colo., U. Denver, George Washington U. Computer programmer Apollo Sys. dept. Missile and Space div. Gen. Electric Co., Kennedy Space Ctr., Fla., 1965-67, Manned Spacecraft Ctr., Houston, 1967-68; computer programmer U. Colo., Boulder, 1968-73; computer programmer analyst Def. Sys. divsn. Sys. Devel. Corp. for NORAD, Colo. Springs, 1974-75; engr. def. sys. and command-and-info. sys. Martin Marietta Aerospace, Denver, 1976-80; sys. engr. space and comm. group, def. info. sys. divsn. Hughes Aircraft Co., Aurora, Colo., 1980-89; rsch. analyst Math. Rsch. Ctr., Littleton, Colo., 1990—, dir., sr. rsch. mathematician, 1996—. Vol. fireman Clear Lake City (Tex.) Fire Dept., 1968; officer Boulder Emergency Squad, 1969-76, rescue squadman, 1969-76, liaison to cadets, 1971, pers. officer, 1971-76, exec. bd., 1971-76, award of merit, 1971, 72, emergency med. technician, 1973—; spl. police officer Boulder Police Dept., 1970-75; spl. dep. sheriff Boulder County Sheriff's Dept., 1970-71; mem. nat. adv. bd. Am. Security Coun., 1979-91, Coalition of Peace Through Strength, 1979-91. Served with USMCR, 1958-66. Decorated Organized Res. medal. Mem. AAAS, AIAA (sr.), Math. Assn. Am., Am. Math Soc., Soc. Indsl. and Applied Math., Math. Study Unit of Am. Topical Assn., Armed Forces Comm. and Electronics Assn., Assn. Old Crows, Nat. Def. Indsl. Assn., Marine Corps Assn., Air Force Assn., U.S. Naval Inst., Nat. Geog. Soc., Smithsonian Inst., Nat. Space Soc., Soc. Amateur Radio Astronomers, Met. Opera Guild, Colo. Hist. Soc., Hist. Denver Inc., Historic Boulder Inc., Hawaiian Hist Soc., Denver Bot. Gardens, Denver Mus. Nature and Sci., Denver Zool. Found. Inc., Mensa. Lutheran.

WILLIAMS, ROSS ALAN, dean, educator; b. Inglewood, Victoria, Australia, Mar. 2, 1943; s. Harold Arthur and Joyce Ella (Cooke) W.; m. Lynne Susanna Tennant, Mar. 26, 1977; children: Kylie Jo, Gregory Mark. B of Commerce, U. Melbourne, Australia, 1963; MSc in Econs., London Sch. of Econs., 1966, PhD, 1969. Lectr. Monash U., Australia, 1969-74; economist World Bank, Washington, 1973-74; sr. rsch. fellow Australian Nat. U., Canberra, 1982-83; prof. of econometrics U. Melbourne, 1975—, dean faculty of econs. and commerce, 1994—. Joint author: (book) Patterns of Household Demand and Saving, 1977; editor: Economic Record, 1990-97. Fellow Acad. Social Scis. Australia. Office: U Melbourne, Faculty of Econs & Commerce, 3010 Parkville Victoria, Australia

WILLIAMS, RYNN MOBLEY, community health nurse; b. Georgetown, S.C., Aug. 2, 1950; d. Ralph Edward and Pearl (Hill) Mobley; m. C. Rogers Jr., July 3, 1971 (div. Mar. 1992); 1 child, Julie Pearl; m. L. Benton Williams, May 2, 1998. Student, Georgetown County Sch. Nursing, 1970; AS, SUNY, Albany, 1982; AS in Criminal Justice, Georgetown Tech. Coll., 1992; BS in Health Adminstrn., Calif. Coll. Health Scis., 1999. Cert. community nurse, med. asst., gerontology Am. Nurses Credentialing Ctr. Mem. staff Georgetown Meml. Hosp., 1969-71; office nurse Dr. L. Benton Williams, Georgetown, 1971—; jail nurse Georgetown County Detention Ctr., 1991-92; staff devel. nurse Prince George Village, 1992—. Mem. ANA, Am. Assn. Office Nurses, Nat. Assn. Physicians Nurses, S.C. Nurses Assn., Order Ea. Star. Baptist. Avocations: crafts, cross stitch, photography, fabric painting, wedding photography. Home: 2221 Pringle Ferry Rd Georgetown SC 29440-6086 Office: 1743 N Fraser St Georgetown SC 29440-6407 also: Prince George Village 901 Maple St Georgetown SC 29440-4377

WILLIAMS, SAMUEL JEYAKUMAR, venerologist; b. Madurai, Tamilnadu, India, Oct. 6, 1948; s. M. Williams and Anne (Parker) S.; m. N. Jemima Stella, Jan. 27, 1977; children: J. Immanuel, J. Gabriel. BSc in Zoology, Madura Coll., Madurai, India, 1969; MBBS, Madurai Kamaraj U., 1975, MD in venereology, 1980. Med. diplomate. Tutor in sexually transmitted diseases Govt. Rajaji Hosp., Madurai Med. Coll., 1981-82, asst. prof. sexually transmitted diseases, 1982-91; tutor in biochemistry Madurai Med. Coll., 1991-98; civil surgeon thoracic medicine Madurai Med. Coll., Govt. Rajaji Hosp., MDU, 1998—; postgrad. examiner Madurai Kamaraj U., 1984, 86; pharm. industry cons. in antibiotics, London, 1996. Reference author: Textbook of Dermatology, 1992; contbr. articles to profl. jours. Mem. Nat. Acad. Med. Scis., N.Y. Acad. Scis., Indian Assn. Sexually Transmitted Diseases (life). Avocations: book reading, screening HIV/AIDS/Tb. Home: 154 Immanuel Cottage, Tasildharnagar, Madurai 625 020, India Office: Govt Rajaji Hosp, Madurai Med Coll, Madurai 625 020, India

WILLIAMS, SERENA, professional tennis player; b. Saginaw, Mich., Sept. 26. Defeated 6th seed in 1st round Australian Open, 2d seed Sudney, 1998; ranked # 27 WTA Tour, 1998, #6 in 1999; finalist Roland Garros Mixed Doubles, 1998; winner doubles, Oklahoma City, 1998, French Open (wth Venus Williams), 1999, Hannover (with Venus Williams), 1999; singles semifinalist, Sydney, 1997, Chgo., 1998; singles winner U.S. Open, 1999, Paris Indoors, 1999, Indian Wells, 1999, L.A., 1999. Office: c/o USTA 70 W Red Oak Ln White Plains NY 10604-3602 Office: ATP Tour 201 Atp Tour Blvd Ponte Vedra Beach FL 32082-3211*

WILLIAMS, SIMON CHRISTOPHER, science educator; b. Dublin, Ireland, Jan. 31, 1961; s. Norman Victor Williams and Jean Mills Campbell; m. Alisa Anne Blackledge, Sept. 25, 1993 (div. Nov. 1997). BA, Trinity Coll., Dublin, 1983; PhD, SUNY, Buffalo, 1990. Postdoctoral fellow Advanced Bioscis. Lab.-Frederick (Md.) Cancer R&D Ctr., 1989-95; asst. prof. Tex. Tech. U. Health Scis. Ctr., Lubbock, 1995—; mem. S.W. Cancer Ctr., Lubbock, 1996—. Scientist Devel. grantee Am. Heart Assn., 1998. Mem. AAAS, Am. Soc. for Biochemistry and Molecular Biology, Am. Soc. for Hematology, Soc. for the Study of Reproduction. E-mail: simon.williams@ttmc.ttuhsc.edu. Fax: 805-743-2990. Home: 6615 Brentwood Ave Lubbock TX 79424-1509 Office: TTUHSC Dept Cell Biology & Biochem 3601 4th St Lubbock TX 79430-0001

WILLIAMS, STEPHEN MEREDITH, psychologist, writer; b. London, Feb. 2, 1950; s. Peter Meredith and Bettina Primrose (Hyams) W.; m. Brigitte Johanna Strater, July 4, 1980; children: Conrad Meredith, Stella Gael. BA with honours in Psychology-Philosophy, Cambridge (Eng.) U., 1972, MA in Psychology, 1977; DPhil in Exptl. Psychology, U. Sussex, Eng., 1980. Chartered psychologist. Rsch. cons. Open U., Milton Keynes, Eng., 1978-79; lectr. psychology U. Ulster, Coleraine, Eng., 1979-90, N.E. Essex Health Authority, Colchester, Eng., 1990-94; pvt. practice psychology, Colchester, 1994—. Author: Psychology on the Couch, 1988, Environment and Mental Health, 1994, Psychology: The Study of Mind, 1996, Key Articles in Psychology, 1997; contbr. over 50 articles to sci. jours. Mem. coun. Social Dem. Party, 1989; gov. Myland Sch., Colchester, 1992-96. Scholar Trinity Coll., Cambridge U., 1968, sr. scholar, 1970. Fellow Brit. Psychol. Soc. (assoc.); mem. Brit. Postal Chess Fedn. (sec. 1996-2000), Brit. Chess Fedn. (minutes sec. 1995-97). Unitarian. Avocations: books, chess, number theory, computing, writing. Home and Office: 43 Church Ln, Colchester CO3 4AE, England

WILLIAMS, SUSAN A., broadcast executive; b. N.Y.C.; d. Arthur G. and Mavourmeen (O'Brien) W.; 2 children. BA in Psychology, Syracuse U. With WAQX, Syracuse, N.Y., WPYX, Albany, N.Y.; pres., CEO S.A.W Broadcasting Inc., Springhouse, Pa. Prodr. various radio and TV commls. Nominated amb. team gov. Tom Ridge Pa. amb. program. Named one of top female voiceovers in the U.S.; recipient Gold, Silver, Bronze medals London Acad. Dramatic Arts. Mem. Phila. Ad Club, Phila., North Penn. C. of C., Screen Actors Guild, Subscriber Arbitron, Subscriber Nielson, Am. Advertising Fedn.. Fax: 215-643-7901. E-mail: saw0660@aol.com. Office: S A W Broadcasting PO Box 199 Spring House PA 19477-0199

WILLIAMS, TED VAUGHNELL, physical education educator; b. Bronx, N.Y., Apr. 1, 1952; s. Joseph Alexander and Annie (Canady) W. BS, Springfield Coll., 1977. Cert. tchr., N.Y. Substitute tchr. Valhalla (N.Y.) High Sch., 1977; tchr. aide for handicapped children, tchr. spl. edn. Rye Lake Campus, Valhalla, 1978; supr. recreation activities Springfield (Mass.) Girl's Club Family Ctr., 1979; assoc. dir. boy's and men's phys. edn. dept. Trenton YMCA, 1979—; house supr. Cardinal McCloskey's Group Home, Tappan, N.Y., 1980-81; phys. edn. tchr. Our Lady of Refuge Sch., Bronx, N.Y., 1982-83; tchr. phys. edn. various Cath. elem. schs. Yonkers, N.Y., 1983—; with ops. dept. Hudson Valley Nat. Bank, 1990-92. Active Walk Am. for Healthier Babies, March of Dimes, 1990-93. Recipient Ed Steitz award Basketball Hall of Fame, 1975, Capitol award Nat. Leadership Coun., 1991. Mem. ASCD, AAHPERD, Am. Assn. Leisure and Recreation, Hudson Valley Leisure Svcs. Assn. Democrat. Baptist. Home: 49 Bradford Ave White Plains NY 10603-2143 Office: Saint Denis Sch 73 Lawrence Ave Yonkers NY 10709-5417

WILLIAMS, THELMA JEAN, social worker; b. Blytheville, Ark., Nov. 2, 1934; d. Willie Louis and Louise (Witherspoon) Morgan; m. Raymond Augustus Williams, Sr., July 22, 1955 (div. Jan. 1961); children: Ronald Duane, Derrick Lamont, Raymond Augustus Jr. BA, U. Mo., St. Louis, 1971; MPA, U. Mo., Kansas City, 1994. Caseworker Mo. Divsn. Welfare, St. Louis, 1959-69, casework supr., 1969-73; quality assurance specialist Dept. Health, Edn. and Welfare, Kansas City, Mo., 1973-74, program integrity specialist, 1974-82; supervisory quality control specialist Dept. Health Human Svcs., Kansas City, Mo., 1982-88, sr. quality control specialist, 1988-90, children and families program specialist, 1990—; del. Citizen Ambassador Program, Russia, Estonia, 1994, China, Hong Kong, 1995, Australia, New Zealand, 1996, India 1997. Tutor Deramus Br. YMCA, Kansas City, 1994; mem. U. Mo. Coordinating Bd. on Diversity, 1995—; mem. U. Mo. Minority Affairs Com., 1995—; project leader Focus Kansas City, 1996; del. Citizen Ambassador Program, 1994-97. Recipient Pres.'s 1000 Points of Light award, 1991, Sec. Health and Human Svcs.' Disting. Vol. Svcs. award, 1991, Cert. of Appreciation Interagency Coun. on Homeless, 1992, Spl. Act of Svc., Dept. Health and Human Svcs. Dept., Family Support Administrn., 1989 (all Washington). Mem. ASPA, AAUW, People to People Internat. Methodist. Avocations: travel, reading, professional studies, classical music, continuing education. Office: Dept Health Human Svcs Children & Families Admins 601 E 12th St Ste 276 Kansas City MO 64106-2826

WILLIAMS, THOMAS ARTHUR, biomedical computing consultant, psychiatrist; b. Racine, Wis., May 11, 1936; s. Robert Klinkert and Marion Anne (Wisneski) W.; m. Rexanne Louise Smith, Aug. 8, 1988; children: Jennifer, Thomas, Ted, Susan, Hailey, Renate, Alexa. BA, Harvard Coll., 1958; MD, Columbia U., 1963; postgrad., NIH, 1967-68. Diplomate Nat. Bd. Med. Examiners, Am. Bd. Psychiatry and Neurology. Intern in surgery Columbia Presbyn. Med. Ctr., N.Y.C., 1963-64; resident in psychiatry Columbia Presbyterian Med. Ctr., N.Y. State Psychiat. Inst., N.Y.C., 1964-67; chief depression sect. NIMH, Bethesda, Rockville, Md., 1967-71; asst. prof. U. Pitts., 1969-70; assoc. prof. U. Utah, Salt Lake City, 1971-77; prof., chmn. dept. psychiatry Eastern Va. Med. Sch., Norfolk, Va., 1977-78; clin. dir. Sheppard & Enoch Pratt Hosp., Towson, Md., 1978-80; prof. U. South Fla., Tampa, 1980-83; practitioner psychiat. medicine, med. dir. St. Augustine (Fla.) Psychiat. Ctr., 1983-89, 89-90; prin. Williams & Assocs., Tampa, 1990—; dir., treas., pres. Klinkart Realty Co., Inc., Racine, Wis., 1960-85; dir., CEO Psych Systems, Inc., Norfolk, Va., 1977-78. Chief editor: Psychobiology of Depression, 1972, Mental Health in the 21st Century, 1979; contbr. numerous articles to profl. jours. and chpts. to books. Mem. Gov.'s Adv. Com. on Mental Health, Salt Lake City, 1971-77, Gov.'s Adv. Com. on Penal Code, Richmond, Va., 1978, Dist. Mental Health Bd., Tampa, 1980-83; mem. U.S. Govt. Mission on Psychiatry to USSR, 1974; sponsor, coach Forest Hills Little League Baseball, Tampa, 1980-83. Sr. surgeon USPHS, 1958-67. Recipient Predoctoral fellowship NIMH, 1960-61, Alumni Rsch. award N.Y. State Psychiat. Inst., 1964, Rush Bronze Medal award Am. Psychiat. Assn., 1973, Rsch. grants VA, 1971-77. Mem. AMA, Fla. Med. Assn., Hillsborough County Med. Assn., Columbia U. Alumni Club (dir. 1995—), Harvard Club of the West Coast of Fla. Avocations: personal computing, classical music, opera, profl. basketball. E-mail: tawmd@worldnet.att.net. Home: 831 S Delaware Ave Tampa FL 33606-2914

WILLIAMS, THOMAS B., secondary school educator; b. Bryn Mawr, Pa., Sept. 6, 1947; s. Thomas Beverly and Joyce Marie (Brittingham) W.; m. Margaret Kane, July 23, 1985. BS in Edn., West Chester (Pa.) U., 1969; MA in Theater, Villanova (Pa.) U., 1974. Cert. tchr. secondary sch. English, spl. edn. K-12. Tchr. Tredyffrin-Easttown Schs., Berwyn, Pa., 1969-72; grad. asst. dept. theater Villanova U., 1972-74; tchr. Marple Newtown Schs., Newtown Square, Pa., 1974—; tchr. advanced creative writing Eastern U. Wayne, Pa., 1979; tchr. poetry on Internet at Alien Flower Poetry Workshop, 1996-99. Author: Alive Beyond Blue, 1996, Talking About Life After America, 1998, (chapbooks) In The New Cairo, 1994, The Rustbelt Adventures, 1995; contbr. poetry and fiction to pubs. Recipient 1st place 22d Miss. Valley Poetry Competition, Calif. State Poetry Soc., New Spirit Press Chapbook Competition, New Press Lit. Quar. 1995 Poetry Contest, Nat. League Am. Pen Women, Palomar br., Internat. Poetry Contest, 1997, Prize for Excellence, Itoen Internat. Haiku competetion, 1998, Hon. Mention Mainichi Internat. Haiku Competition, 1998, Haiku Courage award Itoen Internat. Haiku Competition, 1999; winner 2d Kayfa Roshi award for enlightened tchg. Eastern U., numerous others; Delco Intermediate Unit Impact grantee, 1989. Mem. NEA, Poetry Soc. Am., Haiku Soc. of Am., British Haiku Soc., Calif. State Poetry Soc., New Eng. Poetry Club.

WILLIAMS, THOMAS LLOYD, psychiatrist; b. Mt. Carmel, Pa., May 8, 1925; s. Thomas Lloyd and Anna (Roberts) W.; m. Lucille H. Held, June 23, 1993; children: Scott, Michael, Thomas Held. BS, U. Pitts., 1949, MD, 1952. Diplomate Am. Bd. Neurology and Psychiatry. Intern Allegheny Gen. Hosp., Pitts., 1952-53; family practice Gilbert, Pa., 1953-59; resident Mental Health Hosp. affiliated with U. Iowa, Cherokee, 1959-62, mem. staff, 1962-63; pvt. practice Bethlehem, Pa., 1963—; chief of psychiatry St. Lukes Hosp., Bethlehem, Pa., 1976-88, mem. staff emeritus, 1988—. 1st lt. navigator, U.S. Army Air Corps, 1943-45, ETO. Decorated 7 Battle Stars, Air medal with 3 clusters, Disting. Flying Cross. Fellow Am. Psychiat. Assn. (life). Republican. Avocations: hunting, fishing, carving.

WILLIAMS, THOMAS STAFFORD CARDINAL, archbishop; b. Wellington, N.Z., Mar. 20, 1930; s. Thomas Stafford and Lillian Maude (Kelly) Williams. STL, Pontifical U., Rome, 1960; B Social Sci., Nat. U. Ireland, Dublin, 1962. Ordained priest Roman Cath. Ch., 1959. Archbishop of Wellington, 1979—, elevated to Sacred Coll. Cardinals, 1983, admitted to Order of New Zealand, 2000.

WILLIAMS, VENUS, professional tennis player; b. Lynwood, Calif., June 17. Profl. debut Bank of West Classic, Oakland, Calif., 1994; tennis player Bausch & Lomb Championships, 1996. Ranked No. 64 Am. tennis player, ranked 3d, 1999; winner 7 singles titles WTA Tour including Oklahome City, 1998, 99, Lipton, 1998, 99, Hamburg, 1999, Italian Open, 1999, Gland Slam Cup, 1998, 4 doubles titles, 1 doubles Grand Slam title, 2 mixed doubles; mixed doubles quarterfinalist Wimbledon, 1999; named TENNIS Mag. Most Improved Player, WTA Tour, 1998, Most Impressive Network Newcomer award, 1997; winner (with Serena Williams) French Open, 1999, Hannover, 1999. Office: US Tennis Assn 70 W Red Oak Ln White Plains NY 10604-3602*

WILLIAMS, VIVIAN LEWIE, college counselor; b. Columbia, S.C., Jan. 23, 1923; d. Lemuel Arthur Sr. and Ophelia V. (McDaniel) Lewie; m. Charles Warren Williams, Apr. 4, 1947 (div. 1967); children: Pamela Ann Williams-Coote, Charles Warren Jr. (dec.). BA, Allen U., 1942; MA in Psychology, U. Mich., 1946, postgrad., 1946, 48; MS, U. So. Calif., 1971, postgrad., 1971-72. Cert. marriage and family therapist, Calif.; cert. Calif. C.C. counselor. Asst. prof. psychology Tenn. State Agrl. and Indsl. U., Nashville, 1946-47; asst. prof. edn. Winston-Salem (N.C.) State U., 1947-50; asst. prof. edn., dir. tchr. edn. Allen U., Columbia, S.C., 1951-53; specialist reading, coord. lang. arts Charlotte (N.C.) Mecklenburg Schs., 1963-67, cons. comprehensive sch. improvement project, 1967-69; asst. prof. edn., psychology Johnson C. Smith U., Charlotte, 1967-69; counselor, team leader Centennial, U. So. Calif. Tchr. Corps, L.A., 1970-73; counselor Compton (Calif.) C.C., 1973—, adv. fgn. student, 1975-85; co-developer Hyde Park Estates and The Moors, Charlotte, N.C., 1960-63. Pres. bd. dirs. Charlotte Day Nursery, 1956-59; bd. dirs. Taylor St. USO, Columbia, S.C., 1951-53; sec. southwest region Nat. Alliance Family Life, 1973-74; sec. bd. dirs. NCCJ, Charlotte, 1959-62. Recipient Faculty Audit Program award Ford/Carnegie Found., Harvard U., Cambridge, Mass., 1968, Pub. Svc. Achievement award WSOC Broadcasting Co.; fellow U. Mich., 1946. Mem. NAACP (life, Golden Heritage mem. 1992), AAUW (life), NEA (life), Am. Fedn. Tchrs., Faculty Assn. Calif. C.C., Nat. Acad. Counselors and Family Therapists (life, clin. mem., pres. S.W. region 1989), C.C. Counselors Assn., The Links, Inc. (Harbor area chpt. historian 1985-87, chaplain 1990-94, 96-98), Jack and Jill Am. (charter mem., organizer Charlotte chpt., pres. 1954-56), Women on Target, Calif. Tchrs. Assn., Delta Sigma Theta, Alpha Gamma Sigma (Golden Apple award 1981). Democrat. Methodist. Avocations: sewing, crafts, photography. Home: 6621 Caro St Paramount CA 90723-4755 Office: Compton Community Coll 1111 E Artesia Blvd Compton CA 90221-5314

WILLIAMS, WALKER RICHARD, JR., social services administrator; b. Dayton, Ohio, July 11, 1928; s. Walker Richard Sr. and Addie Mary (Smith) W.; m. Eddora L. Saunders, Aug. 6, 1949 (dec. Sept. 1966); 1 child, Yvette R.; m. Emma Jean Griffin, Sept. 4, 1971; children: Timotny E., Walker R. III. Student, U. Dayton, 1946-48. Commd. 2d lt. U.S. Army, 1952; advanced through grades to capt. USAF, Wright Patterson AFB, Ohio, 1963, employee rels. specialist, pers. mgmt. specialist, 1966-71; EEO investigator and grievance examiner Army and Air N.G., Wright Patterson AFB,

Ohio, 1971-88; retired USAR, 1988; program dir. Youth Svc. U.S.A.-Dayton, 1988-89; pvt. contractor Dayton, 1989—. Mem. Adjutant Gen. Ohio Minority Recruiting Adv. Com., 1988—; bd. dirs. Dayton Opportunities Industrialization Ctr., 1976—, Wright Patterson Domestic Action Programs, Inc., 1984—; pres. Jefferson Twp. Bd. Edn., 1980—; mem. Nat. Black Caucus of Black Sch. Bd. Mems., 1980—, Nat. Black Caucus Local Elected Officials, Gov.'s Com. to Preserve Statue of Liberty, 1987, Citywide Vocat. Ednl. Com., 1986—, adv. com. Dayton Bd. Edn., 1980—, Miami Valley Mil. Affairs Assn., Black Elected Democrats of Ohio. Recipient Air Force Civilian Svc. award, Dayton C. of C., Internat. Personnel Mgmt. Assn. Employee of the Yr., Blacks in Govt. Pres.'s award, Federally Employed Women's Supr. of the Yr. runner up, Hispanic Heritage Wk. Spl. award, NAACP Humanitarian award, Community Svc. award, Dayton Bd. Edn., James W. Cisco award , Vocat. Ednl. award Wilberforce U., Urban League Humanitarian award, Svc. to Youth award Girl Scouts U.S., Spl. award United Negro Coll. Fund, Jack & Jill, 7 Air Force Logistics Command Significant Achievement awards, AG of Ohio award, Ohio State U. award, Black Studies Group award, Russell Lyle award Wright Patterson AFB Quarter Century Club, Student Intervention Program Radcliff Sch., others; a day named in his honor, Dayton, 1987, 88, Svc. award Jefferson Township Bd. Edn. Mem. Miami Valley Pers. Assn., Internat. Pers. Mgmt. Assn., Retired Officers Assn., Air Force Assn., NAACP, Urban League, Blacks in Govt. (Medallion award), Dayton Intergovt. EEO Coun. (chmn., historian 1967—), Miami Valley Mil. Affairs Assn., Wright Patterson Quarter Century Club (past pres.). Democrat. Avocations: reading, photography. Home: 5050 Fortman Dr Dayton OH 45418-2233

WILLIAMS, WALTER DAVID, aerospace executive, consultant; b. Chgo., July 22, 1931; s. Walter William and Theresa Barbara (Gilman) W.; m. Joan Haven Armstrong, Oct. 22, 1960; children: Latham Lloyd, Clayton Chapell, William Haven. BS, Ohio U., 1951; MBA, Harvard U., 1955; MS, MIT, 1972. Supr. fin. policy and systems Hughes Aircraft Co., Culver City, Calif., 1955-57; staff mem. Rand Corp. and SDC, Santa Monica, Calif., 1957-60; mgr. adminstrn. and fin. Microwave Div. TRW Inc., Canoga Park, Calif., 1960-63; exec. asst. Space Labs. Northrop Corp., Hawthorne, Calif., 1963-66; fin. mgr. comml. group Aircraft Div. Northrop Corp., Hawthorne, Calif., 1966-72; dir. internat. plans Northrop Corp., L.A., 1972-74, dir. internat. mkt. devel., 1974-77, exec. dir. internat., 1977-93; pres. Williams Internat. Assocs., L.A., 1994—; export advisor U.S. Sec. Commerce, Washington, 1986-98. Author (study/lect. series) Internat. Def. Mktg., 1982. Dir. KCET Men's Coun., L.A., 1970; pres. Westwood Rep. Club, L.A., 1970; assoc. mem. Rep. State Ctrl. Com., Calif., 1968; div. chmn. Rep. Ctrl. Com., L.A. County, 1968. Served to capt. U.S. Army, 1951-53. Recipient fellowship Alfred P. Sloan Found., 1971-72. Mem. AIAA, Soc. Sloan Fellows, MIT Club, Harvard Bus. Sch. Assn., Newcomen Soc., Chaine des Rotisseurs, L.A. Country Club, Harvard Club, Soc. Bacchus Am., Order of Malta, Delta Sigma Pi, Pi Kappa Alpha. Avocations: golf, tennis, paddle tennis. Office: Williams Internat Assocs PO Box 491178 Los Angeles CA 90049-9178

WILLIAMS, WILLIAM ANTHONY, language and classics educator; b. Manchester, Eng., Nov. 6, 1941; s. William Norman and Doris (Jeffrey) W.; m. Patricia Kathleen Youngfir, Aug. 11, 1973; children: Desmond Francis, Helen Victoria, Matthew David. MA with honours 1st class, St. Andrews U., Scotland, 1964; MLitt in Ancient Philosophy, Edinburgh U., 1966; postgrad., Bristol (Eng.) U., 1966-67. Tchr. classics Godalming County Sch., Surrey, Eng., 1966-69, head of classics, 1969-74; prin. lectr. in classics Jordanhill Coll. Edn., Glasgow, 1974-90, head div. lang. and lit., head of classics, 1990-93; head of lang. edn., head of classics Faculty of Edn., Strathclyde U., Glasgow, 1993—; classics panel rep. Scottish Exam. Bd., Dalkeith, Scotland, 1978-87, 93—; sec. 1st consultative panel on classics Scottish Consultative Com. on the Curriculum, Dundee, 1980-86, nat. devel. officer for Latin and Greek, Edinburgh, 1983-92; in-svc. cons. on all aspects of classics and tchr. edn., Scotland, Eng. and No. Ireland, 1974—; mem. Nat. Com. on Mentoring (Partnership in Edn.); mem. specialist group for classical langs. Higher Still Edn. Program Scotland, 1996-97. Author, chair publ.: New Greek Course for Schools, 6 books, 1977-85; author publs. on teaching translation and interpretation, 1985-87, lang. and translation course, 1988-90, others; contbr. chpt. to book. Mus. dir. Godalming Theatre Group, 1968-74; ch. organist Baldernock Parish Ch., Glasgow, 1979—. Mem. Joint Assn. for Classics Tchrs., Classical Assn., Assn. of Classics Tchrs. Avocations: classical music, playing piano, theatre/acting, travel. Home: 9 Baird Dr Bearsden, Glasgow G61 4BJ, Scotland Office: Strathclyde U Faculty Edn, Jordanhill Campus 76 Southbrae Dr, Glasgow G12 1PP, Scotland

WILLIAMS, WILLIAM GWYN, librarian; b. St. Asaph, Clwyd, Wales, U.K., Sept. 1, 1941; s. Trevor and Grace Eirweh (Roberts) W.; m. Sandra Christina Cartwright-Williams, 1967 (div. 1978); 1 child, Urien Gwyn. Dep. county libr. Flintshire County Coun., Wales, 1969-74; dep. county libr. Clwyd County Coun. Libr. and Info. Svc., Wales, 1974-82, dir., 1982-96; head cultural svcs. Denbigshire County Coun., Wales, 1996-2000, acting dir. edn., culture and info., 2000—. Decorated Order Brit. Empire. Fellow Royal Soc. Arts, Libr. Assn. (hon.); mem. Inst. Adminstrv. Mgmt., Soc. Chief Librs. (pres. 1997—). Avocations: horseback riding, rugby. Office: Denbighshire County Coun, YR Hen Garchar Clwyd St, Ruthin LL15 1HP, Wales

WILLIAMS, WILLIAM HENRY, II, publisher; b. Birmingham, Ala., Oct. 21, 1931; s. Calvin Thomas and Lillian Elizabeth (Levey) W.; m. Lewis Mozelle Hensley, Feb. 28, 1959; 1 child, William Henry III. Student, Baylor U., 1952-55. Printer Waco (Tex.) Tribune-Herald, 1950-59; internat. rep. Internat. Typog. Union, Colorado Springs, Colo., 1960-68; editor, gen. mgr. Colorado Springs Free Press, 1969-70; dir. labor relations The Morning Telegraph, N.Y.C., 1970-72; gen. mgr. Daily Racing Form, Hightstown, N.J., 1972-89, nat. gen. mgr. for U.S. and Can., 1990-91, pub., 1991-92; ret., 1992; pub. Kerrville (Tex.) Mountain Sun, 1993-96; mem. adv. council journalsim dept. Baylor U., Waco, 1970-72. Chmn. CentraState Med. Ctr., Freehold, N.J., 1982-83, CentraState Health Affiliates, Freehold, 1987-94; vice chmn. Ctr. for Aging, Inc., Freehold, 1985-90; dep. mayor Freehold Twp. Com., 1987, mayor, 1989-90, 93, committeeman, 1985-94; county commr. Kerr County, 1999—; chmn. Freehold Mayor's Task Force on Substance Abuse, 1987-91; mem. Upper Guadalupe River Authority, 1995-99, Kerr Econ. Devel. Found.; mem. devel. bd. Alamo Area Workforce, 1997-99. Named an Hon. Trustee Freehold Area Hosp., 1985—. Mem. Tex. Press Assn. (bd. dirs. 1995-96), NCCJ (Brotherhood award 1986), Exch. Club (Hightstown; carter pres.), Masons (32 deg.), Shriners, Optimists (charter mem. Freehold chpt.), Lions Club (host, pres. 1998-99). Republican. Lutheran. Club: Optimists (charter mem. Freehold chpt.). Avocations: music, golf, football, skiing. Home and Office: 172 Saint Andrews Loop Kerrville TX 78028-6441

WILLIAMS, WILLIAM LOUIS, JR. See AS-SALAAM, JAMAAL

WILLIAMS MADDOX-BROWN, JANICE HELEN, nurse; b. Boston; d. Arthur Hamilton Wade and Edith Josephine (Weekes) Williams; m. Larry Maddox, May 21, 1977 (dec.); m. Brown, Mar. 11, 2000. BS in Nursing, Boston U., 1957; MA, Atlanta U. Sch. Edn., 1971; MPH, Emory U., 1976; PhD, Union Inst., Cin., 1998. Staff nurse Beth Israel Hosp., Boston, 1958, N.Y. Hosp.-Cornell U. Med. Ctr., N.Y.C., 1958-59; ward supr. Jewish Meml. Hosp., Boston, 1959-61; staff and pvt. duty nurse Mass. Gen.Hosp., Boston, 1961-63; pub. health nurse Boston Health Dept., 1963-64; intravenous nurse Hughes Spalding Hosp., Atlanta, 1964-66; pub. health nurse Fulton County (Ga.) Health Dept., 1966-69; sr. tchr. Atlanta Southside Comprehensive Health Ctr., 1970-73, acting dir. edn., 1973-74, assoc. dir. clin. nursing, 1974-76; assoc. dir. mental health planning project So. Region Edn. Bd., Atlanta, 1976-78; nursing cons. Dept. Health and Human Svcs., Atlanta, 1978-81; head nurse VA Med. Ctr., Atlanta, 1982-85; br. mgr. Am. Home Health Care of Ga., Inc., Jonesboro, 1985-86; mem. staff Med. Emergency Clinic-Grady Meml. Hosp., 1986-91; project dir. Morehouse Sch. Medicine Initiative, W.K. Kellogg Found., 1991-95; evening coordinator, instr. for innovative practical nursing program for health para-profl. Atlanta Area Tech Sch., 1971-81; mem. admissions com. M. Pub. Health program Emory U. Sch. Medicine, 1979-91. Mem. coms., including Women's Day com. Ctrl. United Meth. Ch., Atlanta, Beh Hill United Meth. Ch. (mem.). Recipient spl. recognition Am. Cancer Soc., 1975.

WILLIAMSON, BRIAN DAVID, information systems executive, consultant; b. Danbury, Conn., May 14, 1973; s. Robert Garth and Celeste Marie (D'Alessio) W. AA in Specialized Bus., Art Inst. Phila., 1993; BS in Gen. Studies, Teikyo Post U., 1994; postgrad. in Tech. Mgmt., Polytech. U., 1997. Asst. mgr. The New Milford (Conn.) Music Ctr., 1991-93; prodn. asst. Med. Broadcasting Co., Conshohocken, Pa., 1993; CIO Custom Designs, Inc., Danbury, Conn., 1991—; info. systems and telecomms. analyst Datahr Rehab. Inst., Brookfield, Conn., 1996-97; LAN adminstr. Praxair, Inc., Danbury, Conn., 1998—; video technician Danbury Corp., Bethel, Conn., 1992-97. Author, writer (film script) The Senior, 1994. Republican. Roman Catholic. Avocations: tennis, computer graphics, movies, music, hiking. Home: 34 Lindencrest Dr Danbury CT 06811-4232 Office: Praxair Inc 39 Old Ridgebury Rd Ste 7 Danbury CT 06810-5109

WILLIAMSON, BRUCE LOOMIS, writer, retired journalist; b. New London, Conn., Aug. 8, 1921; s. Clyde Loomis Williamson and Gertrude Marion White; m. Leda Bess Palmer, Sept. 4, 1946 (div. 1971); m. Audrey Marie Powell, May 31, 1977; children: Bruce Loomis Jr., Blaine Williamson Kaercher. Student, Brown U. News dir. Radio Sta. WHIM, Providence, 1947-59; v.p., gen. mgr. Radio Sta. WRVM, Rochester, N.Y., 1959-60; news dir., anchor TV Sta. WTEN, Albany, N.Y., 1960-73; news dir. Radio Sta. WABY, Albany, N.Y., 1973-77; media rels. mgr. N.Y. State Sch. Bds. Assn., Albany, N.Y., 1977-88; real estate salesman Welbourne & Purdy, Clifton Park, N.Y., 1988-90; columnist, politics and media, Albany Knickerbocker News, 1973; legis. corr. N.Y. state govt., Albany, 1960-73. Author: Verse Things I Ever Did, 1994, That Rocky Fella, 1999. Active St. Peter's Episc. Ch., Albany, 39 yrs. Republican. Episcopalian. Avocations: horseback riding, chess, acting. Home: Sitterly Rd Twin Lakes Apt 25C Clifton Park NY 12065

WILLIAMSON, DOUGLAS FRANKLIN, JR., lawyer; b. Anniston, Ala., Mar. 23, 1930; s. Douglas Franklin and Elizabeth Louise (Connor) W.; m. Barbara Tuerk, Dec. 28, 1957; children: Mary Leyden, Douglas Franklin III, Bruce Reynolds. AB summa cum laude, Amherst Coll., 1952; LLB, Yale U., 1955. Bar: N.Y. 1958, Fla. 1976. Assoc. Breed, Abbott & Morgan, N.Y.C., 1957-63, ptnr., 1963-72; ptnr. Williamson & Hess and predecessor firm, N.Y.C., 1972-79; of counsel Winthrop, Stimson, Putnam & Roberts, N.Y.C., 1979-81, ptnr., 1982-95, sr. counsel, 1996—. Bd. dirs. World Wildlife Fund, Washington, 1979-88, treas., 1986-88, mem. nat. coun., 1988—; bd. dirs. Conservation Found., Washington, 1985-88, treas., 1986-88; bd. dirs. Lower Hudson chpt. Nature Conservancy, Katonah, N.Y., 1976-87, 93-97, sec., 1976-87, hon. dir., 1987—, chmn., 1993-94; bd. dirs. Oblong Land Conservancy, Pawling, N.Y., 1990-98, chmn. 1996-98; bd. dirs. Quaker Hill CIvic Assn., Pawling, 1974-2000, past pres.; chmn. Pawling Assessment Rev. Bd., 1976-2000. With U.S. Army, 1955-57. Fellow N.Y. State Bar Found.; mem. Assn. Bar City N.Y. (com. on trusts, estates and surrogate cts. 1973-78, chmn. 1975-78), English Spkg. Union, Old Guard Soc. Palm Beach Golfers, Everglades Club, Quaker Hill Country Club (pres. 1980-81), Phi Beta Kappa, Phi Beta Kappa Soc. (sec. 1975-77, v.p. 1977-79). Office: Winthrop Stimson Putnam & Roberts One Battery Park Plz New York NY 10004

WILLIAMSON, FLETCHER PHILLIPS, real estate executive; b. Cambridge, Md., Dec. 16, 1923; s. William Fletcher and Florence M. (Phillips) W.; m. Betty June (Stoker), Apr., 6, 1943; 1 child, Jeffrey Phillips; m. Helen M. Stumberg, Aug. 28, 1972. Student, U. Md., 1941-42. Test engr. engring. lab. Glen Martin Co., 1942-43; salesman Corkran Ice Cream Co., Cambridge, 1946-50; real estate broker, 1950—; chmn. bd. Williamson Real Estate, Dorchester Corp., 1963-72; vice-chmn. bd., dir. Nat. Bank of Cambridge, 1979—; dir. Cam-Storage Inc., Dorchester Indsl. Devel. Corp., Delmarva Bank Data Processing Ctr.; co-receiver White & Nelson, Inc. Bd. dirs. Delmarva coun. Boy Scouts Am., Dorchester County Pub. Libr.; past pres. Cambridge Hosp., United Fund Dorchester County; bd. dirs., v.p. Game Conservation Internat., Del. Mus. Natural History. With AUS, 1943-46, ETO. Mem. NRA, Md. Real Estate Assn. (gov. 1956-66), Outdoor Writers Assn., Nat. Def. Preparedness Assn., Cambridge Dorchester C. of C. (bd. dirs. 1955—), Power Squadron (comdr. 1954-56), Dorchester County Bd. Realtors (pres.), Scandinavian Atlantic Salmon Group, Explorers Club, Soc. South Pole, Rolling Rock Club, Shikar Safari Club, Anglers Club, Chesapeake Bay Yacht Club, Camp Fire Club, Md. Club, Georgetown Club, Masons, Shriners. Methodist.

WILLIAMSON, GARY, biochemist, researcher; b. Margate, Kent, Eng., July 7, 1958. BSc, Sheffield U., 1979, PhD, 1983. Postdoctoral fellow Emory U., Atlanta, 1983-85; sr. rsch. scientist Inst. Food Rsch., Norwich, Eng., 1985-88, head cellular metabolism and enzymology, 1988—. Contbr. more than 140 articles to profl. jours. Mem. Royal Soc. Chemistry, Biochem. Soc. Avocations: photography, badminton. Office: Inst Food Rsch, Norwich Rsch Park Colney, Norwich NR4 7UA, England

WILLIAMSON, IAN PHILIP, surveying and land information educator; b. Sydney, Australia, Sept. 29, 1947; s. Philip McKay and Violet Edith (Woodhead) W.; m. Munlika Thongdethsri, Sept. 29, 1972; children: Mark, Kim. B Surveying with honors, U. NSWs, Australia, 1970; M of Surveying Sci., U. NSW, Australia, 1974, PhD, 1983; D (hon.), Olsztyn U. Agr. and Tech., Poland, 1998. Cert. Bd. of Surveyors, New South Wales; lic. Surveyors' Bd. of Victoria. Cadet surveyor Dept. Main Roads, NSW, 1965-71; staff surveyor, project mgr. R.M. Towill Corp., Honolulu, 1971-73; ptnr. Cons. surveyor, NSW, 1973-76; lectr., sr. lectr. U. NSW, 1976-86; Found. prof. surveying and land info. U. Melbourne, Parkville, Australia, 1986—, head dept. geomatics, 1986-93, 96—, pro-vice-chancellor, 1991-94, pres. acad. bd., 1993-94, dir. Melbourne Bus. Sch., 1993-94; cons. Australian Agy. for Internat. Devel., 1978—, World Bank, Washington, 1989—, UN, 1992-94. Councillor, Camberwell Anglican Girls' Grammar Sch., Melbourne, 1994-99. Sr. acad. Fulbright fellow Australian-Am. Ednl. Found., 1989. Fellow Inst. of Surveyors Australia, Inst. Engrs. Australia, Mapping Scis. Inst. Australia (hon.), Australian Acad. Technol. Scis. and Engring. Avocations: fly-fishing, fly-tying, camping, swimming, theatre. Office: U Melbourne Dept Geomatics, Grattan St, Parkville Vic 3010, Australia

WILLIAMSON, JOHN, economist; b. Hereford, Eng., June 7, 1937; s. Harry and Eileen (Heap) W.; m. Denise Rausch de Souza, Mar. 30, 1974; children: Andre, Daniel, Theresa. BSc in Econs., London Sch. of Econ., 1958; PhD, Princeton U., 1963. Lectr. U. of York, Eng., 1963-68; cons. UK Treasury, London, 1968-70; prof. U. Warwick, Eng., 1970-77; advisor IMF, Washington, 1972-74; prof. Pontificia Universidade Catolica, Rio de Janeiro, Brazil, 1978-81; sr. fellow Inst. for Internat. Econs., Washington, 1981—; specialist advisor House of Commons Select Com. on Treasury, London, 1982-83; chief economist South Asia region World Bank, 1996-99. Author: Failure of World Monetary Reform, 1977; Political Economy and International Money, 1987. Pres. U. London Liberal Fedn., London, 1957-58. Mem. Royal Econ. Soc. (coun. 1976-77), Am. Econ. Assn. Avocation: birding. E-mail: jwilliamson@iie.com. Office: Inst for Internat Econ 11 Dupont Cir NW Washington DC 20036-1207

WILLIAMSON, JOHN JACOB, metaphysician, researcher; b. Norwich, Norfolk, Eng., Apr. 24, 1918; s. George and Alice Maria Williamson; m. Alice Rose Bilverstone; children: Carol, Heather, Nona, Paula. Student, Cify Guilds of London, 1947; DSc, Internat. Acad., Eng., 1954, U. Can., 1954. Editor, founder, pres. Soc. Metaphysicians, 1944—; Cranwell lectr. on neometaphysics. Originator infinitely based gen. sys. Sgt. instr. Royal Air Force, 1940-46. Fellow Soc. Metaphysicians; mem. Brit. Assn. Radio Engrs., British Inst. Radio Engrs. Avocations: yachting, pianoforte, gardening, electronics experiments in consciousness, lecturing. Home and Office: Archers Ct Stonestile Ln, The Ridge, Hastings, East Sussex TN35 4PG, England

WILLIAMSON, NICOL, actor; b. Hamilton, Scotland, Sept. 14, 1938; s. Hugh and Mary (Storrie) W.; m. K. Jill Townsend, July 17, 1971 (div. 1977); 1 son. Student, Central Grammar Sch., Birmingham, Eng. Appeared with Dundee Repertory Theatre, 1960-61, Royal Ct. tour in Arden of Faversham, 1961, That's Us; joined Royal Shakespeare Co., 1962; appeared in Nil Carborundum, The Lower Depths, Women Beware Women, Ginger Man, London, 1963, A Cuckoo in the Nest, 1963, Waiting for Godot, London, 1964, Inadmissible Evidence (N.Y. Drama Critics award), London, N.Y.C., 1964-65, 81 (Evening Standard award), Diary of a Madman, London, 1967, Hamlet, London, N.Y.C., 1968-69, Uncle Vanya, 1971, Corialanus, 1973, Nicol Williamson's Late Show, 1973, Midwinter Spring, 1973-74, Twelfth Night, 1974-75, Macbeth, 1974, 82, also TV film, 1982; plays Rex, 1976, The Entertainer, N.Y.C., 1983, The Real Thing, 1985, I Hate Hamlet, 1991, others; dir. (plays) The Lark, Edmonton, Ont., Can., 1983; motion pictures include Six-Sided Triangle, Inadmissible Evidence, 1967, The Bofors Gun, 1967, Laughter in the Dark, 1968, The Reckoning, 1968, Hamlet, 1969 (Evening Standard Drama award), Jerusalem File, 1972, I Know What I Meant, 1974, The Wilby Conspiracy, 1974, Robin and Marion, 1975, The Seven-Per-Cent-Solution, 1979, Excalibur, 1980, Venom, 1980, I'm Dancing as Fast as I Can, 1981, Return to Oz, 1985, Passion Flower, 1985, Black Widow, 1987, The Exorcist III, 1990, The Advocate, 1994; appeared in TV prodn. Arturo VI, 1972, Lord Mountbatten - The Last Viceroy, 1984, Christopher Columbus, 1985, (films) The Heur of the Pig, 1993, The Wind in the Willows, 1996, Spawn, 1997; wrote and appeared in play Jack, 1993. Address: Singel 56, 101SAB Amsterdam Holland

WILLIAMSON, ROBERT CHARLES, marketing executive; b. West Chester, Pa., Jan. 3, 1925; s. Herman Gideon and Grace (Faddis) W.; m. Frances Yvonne Ishmael, Apr. 10, 1945 (div. July 1969); children: Robert C. Jr., Edward H., Richard F., Kathryn G.; m. Mary Elizabeth Bogle, Oct. 1, 1983. BS, Naval Sci. Sch., Monterey, Calif., 1959; postgrad. in Internat. Rels., Naval War Coll., Newport, R.I., 1960. Commd. ensign, designated naval aviator USN, 1944, advanced through grades to comdr., 1963, ret., 1966; gen. mgr. Springfield (Va.) Assocs., 1966-69; v.p. CCC Corp., Rosslyn, Va., 1969-70; pres. WILCO Assocs., Mt. Vernon, Va., 1970-73; dir. mktg. Documail Systems, Lenexa, Kans., 1973-80; N.Am. mktg. mgr. Leigh Instruments, Waterloo, Ont., Can., 1981-83; v.p. Tabs Assocs., Abingdon, Md., 1983-87; pres. WILLMAR Assocs. Internat., Valrico, Fla., 1987—; exec. dir. nat. assn., 1985-98. Mem. Ret. Officers' Assn., Assn. Former Intelligence Officers, Assn. Naval Aviation. Club: Army and Navy. Home and Office: 2529 Regal River Rd Valrico FL 33594-8307

WILLIAMSON, SAMUEL CHRIS, research ecologist; b. New Braunfels, Tex., Nov. 1, 1946; s. Jens Christian Jr. and Dorothy Marie (Marbach) W.; m. Kathryn Laverne Rutherford, Dec. 28, 1971; children: James Ray, Mark Travis. MS, Tex. Arts and Industries U., 1973; PhD, Colo. State U., 1983. Stats. programmer Tex. Parks and Wildlife Dept., Austin, 1973-77; computer specialist U.S. Fish and Wildlife Svc., Ft. Collins, Colo., 1980-82, rsch. ecologist, 1982-93; rsch. ecologist Nat. Biol. Svc., Ft. Collins, Colo., 1993-96, U.S. Geol. Survey, Ft. Collins, Colo., 1996—; statis. cons. U. Wyo., Baidoa, Somalia, 1988, LGL Alaska Rsch., Inc., Anchorage, 1991; mem. adv. bd. EPA, Las Vegas, Nev., 1989-90; participant confs. and symposia. Contbr. articles to profl. jours., chpt. to manual. With U.S. Army, 1968-70, Vietnam. Decorated Bronze Star medal; scholar Caesar Kleberg Wildlife Found., 1971-73. Mem. Ecol. Soc. Am., Am. Statis. Assn., Am. Fisheries Soc., Range Soc., Wildlife Soc. Achievements include research, development and improvement of a nationally recognized capability (Instream Flow Incremental Methodology) concentrating on the mathematics and computer modeling of flow-oriented water management related to restoring salmonid population and habitat; development of a conceptual framework and structural design of a cumulative impacts assessment process based on ecological systems analysis and problem solving; research on application of statistics and logic to ecological problems. Office: US Geol Survey 4512 McMurry Ave Fort Collins CO 80525-3400

WILLIAMSON, STEPHEN, electrical engineer; b. Manchester, Eng., Dec. 15, 1948; s. Donald and Patricia Kathleen Mary (Leyland) W.; m. Zita Mellor, Dec. 19, 1970; children: Samuel Thurston, Rebecca Anne, Lucy Frances. BSc, Imperial Coll., London, 1970, PhD, 1973; DSc in Engring., London U., 1989. Lectr. U. Aberdeen, Scotland, 1973-81; sr. lectr., reader Imperial Coll., London, 1981-89; prof. Cambridge (Eng.) U., 1989-97; tech. dir. Brook Hansen, Huddersfield, Eng., 1997-2000; prof. U. Manchester Inst. Sci. and Tech., 2000—. Contbr. numerous articles to profl. jours. Fellow IEE (hon. editor procs. 1996—, chmn. power divsn. 1996-97, mem. coun. 1993-98, 99—), IEEE, Royal Acad. Engring. Home: 5 James Ct, Almondbury HD4 6SA, England Office: U Manchester Inst Sci/Tech, PO Box 88, Manchester M60 1QD, England

WILLIAMSON, THOMAS MICHAEL, pastor, civil servant; b. N.Y.C., Jan. 4, 1954; s. Hassan and Dorothy (Romlein) Abtahi. BA, Ill. Wesleyan U., 1974; ThM, Bethany Theol. Seminary, 1987, PhD, 1989. Civil servant U.S. Dept. Housing and Urban Devel., Chgo., 1979—; editor Illinois-Indiana Missionary Baptist newspaper, 1995—; asst. pastor Metro. Bapt. Tabernacle, Chgo., 1997-2000. Author: Universal Church Theory, 1987, Waldenses Were Independent Baptists, 1996. Mem. Bapt. Missionary Assn. Ill. and Ind. (clk. 1995—), Bapt. Missionary Assn. Am. Home: 3131 S Archer Ave Chicago IL 60608-6223

WILLIAMSON, WILLIAM ALLEN, retired optometrist; b. Dossville, Miss., July 29, 1933; s. Donald Wodsworth and Ruth Beatrice (Doss) W.; m. Martha Pearl Taylor, Mar. 28, 1959; children: Lamar Arthur, William Allen, Donna Taylor. AA, Northwest Jr. Coll., Senatobia, Miss., 1952; OD, So. Coll. Optometry, Memphis, 1956. Pvt. practice optometry Greenville, Miss., 1959-97; ret.; chmn. Adv. Com. to Medicaid, Miss., 1972-75. Mem. Miss. Blind & Deaf Bd. Trustees, 1974-76; charter mem. Optimist Club, Greenville, Miss., 1964; pres. Wash. County Assn. Retarded Citizens, Greenville, 1981-83, S.O.S. Retarded Workshop, Inc., Greenville, 1985-87, Christian Mission Concerns of Miss., Greenville, 1987-89. 1st lt. U.S. Army, 1956-59. Mem. Am. Optometric Assn. (legis. keyman 1971-72), Miss. Optometric Assn. (legis. chmn. 1973-74), Masons (32 degree), Shriners, Elks. Presbyterian. Avocations: The Bible, history, genealogy research, politics, fishing.

WILLIAMSON, WILLIAM JAMES, electronics professional; b. Yell, Shetland, U.K., June 7, 1938; s. William James and Tamar Jane (Mann) W. Registered technician. Marine electronic technician H. Williamson & Sons, Scalloway, 1968-72; freelance technician Yell, 1972-75; elec. and electronic technician Shetland Islands Coun., 1975-94; freelance technician and writer Yell, 1994—; video cons. Manpowers Svcs., Shetland, 1981-83; advisor North Isles Ferries, Shetland, 1990-92. Contbr. articles to profl. jours.; designer remote control system for ferry ramps, digitised speech system for recorded pub. announcements. Mem. Yell Comm. Coun., 1977-81; chmn. Yell Br. Shetland-Norwegian Friendship Soc. Mem. Brit. Astron. Assn., Inst. Inc. Engrs. (assoc. mem.). Avocations: astronomy, vintage radio restoration, music, reading, languages. Home: Leeskol Camb Yell, Shetland ZE2 9DA, United Kingdom

WILLIAMS-STEINWENDER, KARIN MAE, artist; b. Santa Monica, Calif., Oct. 14, 1948; d. Marion Glen and Margaret Grace (Long) Williams; m. Helmut Adolf Ludwig Steinwender, Aug. 17, 1985. BA with hons., Calif. State U., Dominguez Hills, Carson, 1983. Cert. tchr. art-dance, Calif.; cert. hypnotist; cert. Shiat-su therapist; cert. Cecchetti Ballet instr. Chmn. bd. South Bay (Calif.) Ballet Co., 1977-78, choreographer, 1976-77; gallery coord. F.O.T.A., Hermosa Beach, Calif., 1978-79; ballet instr. Act III Acad., Redondo Beach, Calif., 1976-83; self-employed ballet instr. South Bay, 1972-93; artist, painter Calif., N.Y., Oreg., 1972—; ballet instr. Banks, Oreg., 1994, Pendleton, Oreg., 1995—; owner, operator, dir. Acad. Classical Ballet, Pendleton, 1996—; owner Body Moves Dancewear, Pendleton, 1998—; owner Body Moves Dancewear, Pendleton; exhbns. include Art of 80's Gallery, Hermosa Beach, Calif., Barnsdale Mcpl. Gallery, L.A., Community galleries, South Bay, Calif., Ambiente', Redondo Beach, Calif., Everson Mus. exhbn., Syracuse, N.Y., Gallery Syracuse, 1972—; one-woman show Crackerjack Prodns.; interview and art filming South Bay News, Redondo Beach, Calif.; studio opening/exhbn., 1992. Author: Technique in Balance and Turning, 1985; writer, producer, choreographer (ballets) Woodcutter's Daughter, 1977, Power Plays, 1978; choreographer Midsummer Nights Dream, 1975, Danses for Danses' Sake, 1978, Grand Allegro, 1999, holiday and community programs, 1975-83. Vol. Rep. Party, Syracuse, 1988-89, Park Assn., Syracuse, 1990; mem. Rep. Women, Pendleton, 1996—. Mem. ASPCA, Rodale Inst., Arbor Day Found., Nat. Wildlife Fedn., Greenpeace, Wilderness Soc., Rosicrucians, In Def. of Animals. Avocations: gardening, herbology, reading, dancing, hiking. Office: Body Moves Dancewear 423 1/2 Main St Pendleton OR 97801 Studio: 421 1/2 S Main St Pendleton OR 97801-2247

WILLIE, CHARLES VERT, sociology educator; b. Dallas, Oct. 8, 1927; s. Louis James and Carrie (Sykes) W.; m. Mary Susannah Conklin, Mar. 31, 1962; children: Sarah Susannah, Martin Charles, James Theodore. BA, Morehouse Coll., 1948, DHL (hon.), 1983; MA, Atlanta U., 1949; PhD, Syracuse U., 1957, DHL (hon.), 1992; DD (hon.), Gen. Sem., 1974; DHL (hon.), Berkeley Div. Sch., Yale U., 1972, R.I. Coll., 1983, Johnson C. Smith U., Charlotte N.C., 1991; MA (hon.), Harvard U., 1974; DL (hon.), Framingham (Mass.) State Coll., 1992; DHL (hon.), Franklin Pierce Coll., Rindge, N.H., 1996; D of Engring. Tech. (hon.), Wentworth Inst. Tech., 1996. Instr. to asst. prof. sociology Syracuse (N.Y.) U., 1952-63, assoc. prof., 1964-67, prof., 1968-74, chmn. dept. sociology, 1967-71, v.p., 1972-74; prof. edn. and urban studies Grad. Sch. Edn. Harvard U., Cambridge, Mass., 1974-98, Charles William Eliot prof. edn. Sch. Edn., 1998-99, prof. emeritus Grad. Sch. Edn., 1999—; instr. dept. preventive medicine SUNY Upstate Med. Center, Syracuse, 1955-60; research dir. Washington Action for Youth delinquency prevention project, Pres.' Com. on Juvenile Delinquency and Youth Crime, Washington, 1962-64; vis. lectr. Lab. Community Psychiatry, Harvard U. Med. Sch., Boston, Mass., 1966-67; vis. lectr. ch. and soc. Episcopal Div. Sch., Cambridge, Mass., 1966-67; commr. Pres.'s Commn. on Mental Health, 1977-78; mem. tech. adv. bd. Maurice Falk Med. Fund, 1968-99; bd. dirs. Social Sci. Rsch. Coun., 1969-75; master Boston Sch. Desegregation case, Fed. Dist. Ct., 1975; mem. nat. adv. com. Maxwell Sch. Syracuse U., 1992—, Hogg Found. for Mental Health, 1998—, Morehouse Rsch. Inst., 1997—; bd. overseers Boston Sci. Mus., 1997—; corporator Emerson Hosp., Concord, Mass., 1998—; bd. dirs. Judge Baker Children's Ctr., 1998—. Author: Church Action in the World, 1969, Black Students at White Colleges, 1972, Race Mixing in the Public Schools, 1973, Oreo, 1975, A New Look at Black Families, 1976, 2d edit., 1981, 3d edit., 1988, 4th edit., 1991, The Sociology of Urban Education, 1978, The Caste and Class Controversy on Race and Poverty, 1979, 2d edit., 1989, The Ivory and Ebony Towers, 1981, Race, Ethnicity and Socioeconomic Status, 1983, School Desegregation Plans That Work, 1984, Black and White Families, 1985, Five Black Scholars, 1986, (with Michael Grady) Metropolitan School Desegregation, 1986, Effective Education, 1987, (with Michael Grady and Richard Hope) African-Americans and the Doctoral Experience, 1991, Theories of Human Social Action, 1994, (with Michael Alves) Controlled Choice, 1996, (with Ralph Edwards) Black Power/White Power in Public Education, 1998; editor: The Family Life of Black People, 1970, (with B. Brown and B. Kramer) Racism and Mental Health, 1973, Black/Brown/White Relations, 1977, (with R. Edmonds) Black Colleges in America, 1978, (with S. Greenblatt) Community Politics and Educational Change, 1981, (with Inabeth Miller) Social Goals and Educational Reforms, 1988, (with A. Garibaldi and W. Reed), The Education of African-Americans, 1991, (with P. Rieker, B. Kramer and B. Brown) Mental Health, Racism and Sexism, 1995. Hon. trustee Episcopal Div. Sch., Cambridge; mem. United Negro Coll. Fund, 1983-90; mem. nat. exec. coun. Episcopal ch., 1967-74, v.p. gen. conv., 1970-74; host Inner City Beat nat. pub. affairs weekly TV program, monitor channel, 1991-92. Recipient faculty svc. award Nat. Univ. Ext. Assn., 1969, 50th Anniversary Disting. Alumnus award Syracuse U. Maxwell Sch., 1974; Lee-Founders award Soc. for Study Social Problems, 1983, Family Scholar award, 1986; Disting. Career Contbn. award com. on role and status minorities in ednl. R & D, Am. Ednl. Rsch. Assn., 1990, Benjamin E. Mays Svc. award Morehouse Coll., 1994, Father John LaFarge, S.J. award Fairfield U., 1995, Disting. Career award Assn. Black Sociologists, 1996, Outstanding Book award for mental health, racism and sexism Myers Ctr. for Study of Human Rights, 1996, Arents Alumni award Syracuse U., 2000. Mem. Am. Ednl. Rsch. Assn., Am. Sociol. Assn. (coun. 1980-83, 95-98, v.p. 1996-97, DuBois-Johnson-Frazier award 1994), Phi Beta Kappa, Alpha Phi Alpha. Episcopalian. Home: 41 Hillcrest Rd Concord MA 01742-4615 Office: Harvard U Grad Sch Edn 457 Gutman Libr 6 Appian Way Cambridge MA 02138-3704

WILLIES, WALTER HARRY, language educator, arts/medicine specialist; b. Cape Town, S. Africa, Jan. 18, 1956; s. Harry George and Irma (Hachler-Richner) W. BA, U. Cape Town, 1976, BEd, 1983; DAL, U. Fort Hare, S. Africa, 1991; DLit, Knightsbridge U., U.K., 1993. Tchr. Sr. Secondary Sch., Keetmanshoop, Nambia, 1978-79, Maitlan H.S., Cape Town, 1980-88; vice-prin. Dale Coll., King William's Town, S. Africa, 1989-94; assoc. prof., dir. Potchestroom U., Vanderbijl Park, 1995—; presenter workshops in field. Contbr. articles to profl. jours and publs. Mem. adv. coun. Vaal Cmty. Radio, 1995. Office: Potchefstroom U for CHE, PO Box 1174, 1900 Vanderbijlpark South Africa

WILLIG, ROBERT DANIEL, economics educator; b. Bklyn., Jan. 16, 1947; s. Jack David and Meg W.; m. Virginia Mason, July 8, 1973; children: Jared Mason, Scott Mason, Brent Mason, Alexandra Mason. BA, Harvard U., 1967; MS in Ops. Rsch., Stanford U., 1968, PhD in Econs, 1973. Lectr. Stanford U., Palo Alto, Calif., 1971-73; mem. tech. staff Bell Labs., Holmdel, N.J., 1973-77; supr. dept. econs. rsch. Bell Labs., 1977-78; prof. econs. and pub. affairs Princeton U., 1978—; mem. Aspen Inst. Task Force on Future of Postal Svc., 1978-80; dep. asst. atty. gen. U.S. Dept. Justice, Washington, 1989-91; cons. in field; rsch. fellow U. Warwick, Eng., 1977; mem. organizing com. Telecom Policy Rsch. Conf., 1977-78; mem. rsch. adv. bd. Am. Enterprise Inst., 1980-88; mem. N.J. Gov.'s Task Force on Market-Based Pricing of Electricity, 1987; bd. dirs. Consultants in Industry Econs., Inc., 1983—; mem. Def. Sci. Bd. Task Force on Antitrust for the Def. Industry, 1993-94, Transp. Rsch. Bd. Task Force, 1995-96; advisor Inter-Am. Devel. Bank, 1997—. Author: Welfare Analysis of Policies Affecting Prices and Products, 1973, Contestable Markets and the Theory of Industry Structure, 1982; editor: Handbook of Industrial Organization, 1986, Can Privatization Deliver: Infrastructure for Latin America, 1999; contbr. articles to profl. jours. mem. editorial bd.: M.I.T. Press Series on Govt. Regulation, 1978—, Am. Econ. Rev., 1980-83, Jour. Indsl. Econs., 1985-89, Utility Policy, 1989—. Mem. adv. bd. B'nai B'rith Hillel Found., Princeton U., 1978—. NSF grantee, 1979-85. Fellow Econometric Soc. (program com. 1978-81); mem. Am. Econ. Assn. (nominating com. 1980-81). Office: Princeton Univ Economics Dept Princeton NJ 08540

WILLIGMANN, INGO HELGE, natural products chemist, researcher; b. Lingen, Germany, Mar. 19, 1960; s. Johannes and Ingrid (Heyer) W.; m. Marion Steinkemper, June 1995. Diplom Chemist, Westfaelische Wilhelms U., Muenster, Germany, 1987; Dr.rer.nat., Westfalische Wilhelms U., Muenster, Germany, 1990. Mgr. sect. natural products of the R&D dept. Schaper & Brümmer, Salzgitter, Germany, 1990—, project mgr., 1995—. Contbr. articles to Planta Medica; holder German, European and American patents. Served with German Air Force, 1979-81. Mem. Soc. German Chemists, Soc. for Medicinal Plant Rsch., Dechema e.V. Soc., German Soc. for Applied Chemistry, Phytochem. Soc. Europe. Evangelical Christian. Avocations: philately, soccer, minerals and fossils. Home: Geschwister-Scholl str 5, 38642 Goslar Germany Office: Schaper & Brummer, Bahnhofstr, 38259 Salzgitter Germany

WILLINGHAM, CLARK SUTTLES, lawyer; b. Houston, Nov. 29, 1944; s. Paul Suttles and Elsie Dell (Clark) W.; m. Jane Joyce Hitch, Aug. 16, 1969; children: Meredith Moores, James Barrett. BBA, Tex. Tech U., 1967; JD, So. Meth. U., 1971, LLM, 1984. Bar: Tex. 1971. Ptnr. Kasmir, Willingham & Krage, Dallas, 1972-86, Finley, Kumble et al, Dallas, 1986-87, Brice & Mankoff, Dallas, 1988-98, Moseley & Standerfer, PC, Dallas, 1999—. Contbr. articles to profl. jours. Exec. com. Dallas Summer Musicals, 1979-93, pres., 1994-95. Mem. ABA (chmn. agrl. com. tax sect. 1984-86), State Bar Tex. (chmn. agrl. tax com. 1985-87), Dallas Bar Assn., Am. Law Inst., Nat. Cattlemen's Beef Assn. (bd. dirs., pres. 1998), U.S. Meat Export Fedn. (exec. com. 1991-93), Beef Industry Coun. (exec. com. 1990-91, promotion chmn. 1992-94), Tex. Cattle Feeders Assn. (bd. dirs., pres. 1988), Tex. Bd. Vet. Med. Examiners (pres. 1994), Tex. Beef Coun. (bd. dirs., pres. 1989), Dallas County Club. Republican. Episcopalian. Home: 3824 Shenandoah St Dallas TX 75205-1702 Office: Moseley & Standerfer 3878 Oak Lawn Ave Ste 400 Dallas TX 75219-4469

WILLINGHAM, EDWARD BACON, JR., ecumenical minister, administrator; b. St. Louis, July 27, 1934; s. Edward and Harriet (Sharon) W.; m. Angeline Walton Pettit, June 14, 1957; children: Katie, Carol. BS in Physics, U. Richmond, 1956; postgrad., U. Rochester, 1958-59; MDiv., Colgate Rochester Div. Sch., 1960. Ordained to ministry Am. Bapt. Ch., 1960. Min. Christian edn. Delaware Ave. Bapt. Ch., Buffalo, N.Y., 1960-62; dir. radio and TV Met. Detroit Coun. Chs., 1962-75; exec. dir. Christian Communication Coun. Met. Detroit Chs., 1976-98; chmn. N.Am. Broadcast sect. World Assn. for Christian Comm., 1970-71, bus. mgr., 1972-98, archivist, 1999—; broadcast cons. Mich. Coun. Chs., 1965-75; guest cons. religious broadcasting Germany, 1968; mem. coord. com. Mich. Ecumenical Forum, 1986, 90-92, chmn., 1991-92. Bd. mgrs. Broadcasting and Film Commn., Nat. Coun. Chs., 1965-73; mem. Muslim-Christian-Jewish Leadership Forum, 1987—; bd. deacons 1st Bapt. Ch. Birmingham, chmn., 1994. Recipient Gabriel award Cath. Broadcasting Assn., 1972, 1st Ann. Ecumenical award Am. Bapt. Chs. of Mich., 1992, Race Rels. award Booker T. Washington Bus. Assn. of Detroit, 1983. Mem. Assn. Regional Religious Communicators (pres. 1969-71), World Assn. Christian Comm. (ctrl. com. 1973-78), Phi Gamma Delta, Sigma Pi Sigma. Office: 21440 Lathrup St Southfield MI 48075-4218

WILLINGHAM, WELBORN KIEFER, psychologist, educator; b. Rotan, Tex., Mar. 12, 1928; s. W.B. and Juanita Madge (Eason) W.; m. Mary Maxine McCollum, Aug. 14, 1950; children: Sharon, Douglas, Sheila. BA, Tex. Tech U., 1949; MEd, U. Tex., 1956; PhD, Tex. Tech U., 1964. Diplomate Am. Bd. Psychol. Specialties. Tchr., prin. elem. sch. Hale Center, Tex., 1951-53; edn. and tng. officer USAF, Brookley Air Force Base, Ala., 1953-55; tchr., coach Hutchinson Jr. High Sch., Lubbock, Tex., 1955-57; counselor Monterey High Sch., Lubbock, 1957-60; asst. dean students Tex. Tech U., Lubbock, 1963-64; clin. psychologist South Plains Guidance Ctr., Lubbock, 1964-66; from asst. prof. to prof. emeritus Tex. Tech U., Lubbock, 1966—; clin. prof. neuropsychiatry and behavioral scis. Tex. Tech. U. Health Scis. Ctr., 1983—; cons. psychologist Big Spring (Tex.) VA Med. Ctr., 1990—; mem. allied health staff psychology Meth. Hosp., Lubbock, 1990. Cons. editor Individual Psychology, 1989—; tech. reviewer Tex. Dental Jour., 1989—; contbr. articles to profl. jours. Lt. col. USAFR, 1949-77. Paul Harris fellow Rotary Internat., 1985. Fellow Am. Bd. Forensic Examiners (diplomate), Am. Bd. Forensic Medicine (diplomate); mem. N.Am. Soc. Adlerian Psychology (del. assembly 1983-89, chmn. publs. com. 1986-89). Avocations: travel, study, reading. Home: 1605 56th St Lubbock TX 79412-2803

WILLIS, ANDRÉ MAURICE, electrical engineer, computing service executive; b. Fairfield, Ala., Oct. 16, 1957; s. Lamar and Marie (Davis) W.; m. Selene Yvette Lowe, Mar. 4, 1958. BSEE, Tuskegee U., 1981; postgrad., Focus Automation, 1993-94. Cert. in elec. sys. FAA, network engr. Novell. Project engr. Arco, Port Arthur, Tex., 1980; sys. engr. Dictaphone Corp., Milford, Conn., 1982-86, project engr., 1986; mgr. avionic flight test McDonnell Douglas Corp., Long Beach, Calif., 1987-93; info. sys. cons. EDP, L.A., 1994, So. Calif. Presbyn. Homes, Glendale, Calif., 1994; network sys. analyst Weyerhauser Mortgage, Woodland Hills, Calif., 1995; sr. network engr. CB Comml. Real Estate, Torrance, Calif., 1995—, project mgr., 1997—; tech. customer adv. bd. Cheyenne divsn. Intel & Computer Assocs., 1998; corp. mgr. tng. McDonnell Douglas, 1990; info. sys. cons. EDP/Contract Svcs., L.A., 1994-95; pres., owner Datronics, L.A., 1996—. Vol. Going to Coll. program UCLA, 1997-98. Tuskegee U. Sch. Engring. scholar, 1976-80; recipient CB Comml Real Estate Project award IT, 1997. Mem. IEEE, ASME. Avocations: tennis, swimming, reading, chess, camping.

WILLIS, ARTHUR JOHN, botany educator, researcher; b. Sherborne, England, Jan. 11, 1922; s. John Henry Arthur and Lillie (Cobb) W.; m. Dorothy Powell Bees, Aug. 5, 1948; children: Hilary Ruth, Elizabeth Pamela. BS, U. Bristol (England), 1947, PhD, 1951, DS, 1966. Demonstrator U. Bristol, 1947-50, lectr. botany, 1951-66, reader, 1966-69; prof. botany, head dept. U. Sheffield, Eng., 1969-87; hon. dir. unit comparative plant ecology U. Sheffield, 1969-87; prof. botany emeritus U. Sheffield, Eng., 1987—, dean, 1982-84; mem. grant awarding com. Royal Soc. London, 1974-78, Natural Environ. Rsch. Coun., 1973-79, Leverhulme Trust, 1988-92, Yorkshire Cancer Rsch., 1973-87. Author: Introduction to Plant Ecology, 1973, The Vegetation of Egypt, 1992, Ecology of Sd Dunes, SaltMarsh and Shingle, 1997, Encyclopedia of Ecology and Environmental Management, 1998; editor 25 books in contemporary biology series, 1966-85, Biol. Flora of the Brit. Isles, 1969—; contbr. chpts. to books and articles to profl. jours. Mem. com. Nat Trust, WestMidlands, England, 1976-87, Peak Park Planning Bd., England, 1973-81. Recipient rsch. awards Natural Environ. Rsch. Coun., London, 1960-87; jr. fellow physiol. ecology U. Bristol, 1950-51; emeritus fellow Leverhulme Trust, 1988-90. Fellow Inst. Biology, Linnean Soc.; mem. Brit. Ecol. Soc. (v.p., coun. mem.), Internat. Assn. Plant Taxonomy, European Soc. Life Editors, Soc. Exptl. Biology, Brit. Bryological Soc., Bot. Soc. Brit. Isles, Bristol Naturalists Soc. (hon.). Avocations: bridge, flora. Home: 61 Clarkegrove Rd, Sheffield S10 2NH, England Office: U Sheffield, Dept Animal and Plant Scis, Sheffield S10 2TN, England

WILLIS, CLIFFORD LEON, geologist; b. Chanute, Kans., Feb. 20, 1913; s. Arthur Edward and Flossie Duckworth (Fouts) W.; m. Serreta Margaret Thiel, Aug. 21, 1947 (dec.); 1 child, David Gerard. BS in Mining Engring., U. Kans., 1939; PhD, U. Wash., 1950. Geophysicist The Carter Oil Co. (Exxon), Tulsa, 1939-42; instr. U. Wash., Seattle, 1946-50, asst. prof., 1950-54; cons. geologist Harza Engring. Co., Chgo., 1952-54, 80-82, chief geologist, 1954-57, assoc. and chief geologist, 1957-67, v.p., chief geologist, 1967-80; pvt. practice cons. geologist Tucson, Ariz., 1982—; cons. on major dam projects in Iran, Iraq, Pakistan, Greece, Turkey, Ethiopia, Argentina, Venezuela, Colombia, Honduras, El Salvador, Iceland, U.S. Lt. USCG, 1942-46. Recipient Haworth Disting. Alumnus award U. Kans., 1963. Fellow Geol. Soc. Am., Geol. Soc. London; mem. Am. Assn. Petroleum Geologists, Soc. Mining, Metallurgy and Exploration Inc., Assn. Engring. Geologists, Sigma Xi, Tau Beta Pi, Sigma Tau, Theta Tau. Republican. Roman Catholic. Avocations: travel, reading. Home: 4795 E Quail Creek Dr Tucson AZ 85718-2630

WILLIS, GLADDEN WILLIAMS, pathologist; b. Minden, La., Mar. 26, 1939; s. John Stillmon and Virgie Williams Willis; m. Lydia Hall, May 14, 1966; children: Charles Austin, Loye Stillmon. BS, Centenary Coll., 1960; MD, Tulane U., 1964. Intern La. State U. Med. Ctr., Shreveport, 1964-65, resident, 1965-69; fellow Meml. Sloan-Kettering Med. Ctr., N.Y.C., 1969-71; pathologist St. Luke's Hosp., Houston, 1971-72, St. Mary's Hosp., Roswell, N.Mex., 1972-73, Ochsner Clinic, New Orleans, 1973-76; dir. anatomic pathology Ochsner Med. Instns., New Orleans, 1976—, vice chmn. lab. medicine, 1996—. Contbr. numerous sci. papers to profl. jours., over 600 sci. photographs to encys., books in field. Pres. Jefferson Performing Arts Soc., Metairie, La. Capt. USAF, 1966-72. Recipient George Washington Honor medal Valley Forge Found., 1996. Fellow Arthur Purdy Stout Soc., Royal Microscopical Soc.; mem. Assn. Dirs. of Anatomic Pathology, Internat. Acad. Pathology, Am. Soc. Media Photographers, N.Y. Acad. Scis. Democrat. Methodist. Avocation: photography. E-mail: gwillis@ochsner.org. Home: 62 Verde St Kenner LA 70065-1029 Office: Ochsner Med Instns 1516 Jefferson Hwy New Orleans LA 70121-2429

WILLIS, HAROLD WENDT, SR., real estate developer; b. Marion, Ala., Mar. 7, 1927; s. Robert James and Della (Wendt) W.; m. Patsy Gay Bacon, Aug. 2, 1947 (div. Jan. 1975); children: Harold Wendt II, Timothy Gay, April Ann, Brian Tad, Suzanne Gail; m. Vernette Jacobson Osborne, Mar. 30, 1980 (div. 1984); m. Ofelia Alvarez, Sept. 23, 1984; children: Ryan Robert, Samantha Ofelia. Student, Loma Linda U., 1950, San Bernardino Valley Coll. Ptnr. Victoria Guernsey, San Bernardino, Calif., 1950-63, co-pres., 1963-74, pres., 1974—; owner Quik-Save, 9th & Waterman shopping ctr., 1966—, Ninth and Waterman Shopping Ctr., San Bernardino, 1969—; pres. Energy Delivery Systems, Food and Fuel, Inc. San Bernardino City water commr., 1964-98, pres. bd. water commrs., 1964-98; bd. councillors Loma Linda (Calif.) U., 1968-85, pres., 1971-74; mem. So. Calif. Strider's Relay Team (set indoor Am. and World record in 4x800 1992, sec distance medley relay U.S. and World record for 60 yr. old 1992). With U.S. Mcht. Marine, 1945-46. Mem. Calif. Dairy Industries Assn. (pres. 1963, 64), Liga Internat. (2d v.p. 1978, pres. 1982, 83). Seventh-day Adventist (deacon 1950-67). Avocation: lic. pvt. pilot. Office: PO Box 5607 San Bernardino CA 92412-5607

WILLIS, ISAAC, dermatologist, educator; b. Albany, Ga., July 13, 1940; s. R.L. and Susie M. (Miller) W.; m. Alliene Horne, June 12, 1965; children: Isaac Horne, Alliric Isaac. BS, Morehouse Coll., 1961, DSc (hon.), 1989; MD, Howard U., 1965. Diplomate Am. Bd. Dermatology. Intern Phila. Gen. Hosp., 1965-66; fellow Howard U., Washington, 1966-67; resident, fellow U. Pa., Phila., 1967-69, assoc. in dermatology, 1969-70; mem. staff Phila. Gen. Hosp., 1969-70; instr. dept. dermatology U. Pa., Phila., 1970-72; mem. staff Moffit Hosp. U. Calif., San Francisco, 1970-72; asst. prof. Johns Hopkins U., Johns Hopkins Hosp., Balt., 1972-73; mem. staff Johns Hopkins Hosp., Balt. City Hosp., Good Samaritan Hosp., Balt., 1972-72; asst. prof. Emory U., Atlanta, 1973-77; mem. staff Crawford W. Long Meml. Hosp., Atlanta, 1974—, West Paces Ferry Hosp., Atlanta, 1974—; assoc. prof. Emory U., Atlanta, 1977-82; prof. Morehouse Sch. Medicine, Atlanta, 1982—, chief dermatology, 1991—; dep. commdr. of 3297th USA Hosp. (1000B), 1990—; mem. gen. medicine group IA study sect., NIH, 1985—; mem. grants review panel EPA, 1986—; adv. bd. Arthritis and Musculoskeletal and Skin Diseases, 1991—, U. Pa. Sch. Medicine, 1995—, Emory U., 1994—; chmn. inst. review bd., mem. pharmacy and therapeutic com.; bd. dirs. Comml. Bank Gwinnett, Heritage Bank, Comml. Bank of Ga. (chmn. audit review com. 2000—), Landmark Bank Fla., 1999—, Learning Framework, West Paces Med. Ctr., Lupus Specialists, Inc., InterVu, Inc., Lupus Erythematosus Found., Jacquelyn McClure Lupus Erythematosus Clinic, Skin Cancer Found.; mem. med. staff Piedmont Hosp., 2000—; cons. in field. Author: Textbook of Dermatology, 1971; contbr. articles to profl. jours. Trustee Friendship Bapt. Ch., Atlanta, 1980-82; mem. gov.'s commn. on effectiveness and economy in govt. State og Ga. Human Resources Task Force, 1991—, Ga. State Bd. of worker's Compensation Med. subcom., 1997—. Col. USAR, 1983-95. EPA grantee, 1980—. Fellow Am. Acad. Dermatology, Am. Dermtol. Assn.; mem. AAAS, AMA, Nat. Cancer Inst., Soc. Investigative Dermatology, Nat. Med. Assn., Internat. Soc. Tropical Dermatology, Pan Am. Med. Assn., Am. Fedn. Clin. Rsch., Am. Soc. Photobiology, U. Pa. Nat. Alumni Adv. Coun., State of Ga. Dermatology Found., Frontiers Internat., Sportsman Internat., Phi Beta Kappa, Omicron Delta Kappa. Achievements include a patent for the development of a shaving composition and method for preventing Pseudofolliohtip Barbae, 1999; subspecialties in the areas of dermatology and cancer research (medicine). Home: 1141 Regency Rd NW Atlanta GA 30327-2719 Office: NW Med Ctr 3280 Howell Mill Rd NW Ste 342 Atlanta GA 30327-4109

WILLIS, JOHN, retired research scientist, consultant; b. Birkenhead, Eng., July 22, 1922; arrived in Australia, 1935; s. Alec Gee and Lucy Hilda (Weaver) W.; m. Amy Bettina Fletcher, Jan. 3, 1953 (dec. July 2000); children: Anthony Charles, Penelope Margaret. BSc in Chemistry with 1st class honors, U. Sydney, Australia, 1943, MSc in Chemistry, 1945; PhD, Univ. Coll., London, 1948, DSc, 1961. Demonstrator U. Sydney, 1944-46; rsch. student Univ. Coll., 1946-48; rsch. scientist Commonwealth Sci. and Indsl. Rsch. Orgn., Australia, 1948-78, asst. chief divsn. chem. physics, 1978-86; rsch. fellow Ames Lab. Iowa State U., 1967-68; cons. spectroscopist Varian Australia Pty Ltd., Mulgrave, Victoria, 1987—; sec. 5th Internat. Conf. on Atomic Absorption Spectroscopy, 1975; mem. spectroscopy com. Standards Assn. Australia, 1969-90; working group on atomic absorption and flame spectroscopy Internat. Standards Orgn., 1969-90. Formerly mem. editl. bd. J. Analytical Atomic Spectroscopy, Analytica Chimica Acta, ICP Info. Newsletter, Can. Jour. Spectroscopy; contbr. numerous articles to profl. jours., chpts. to books. Masson Meml. scholar; recipient Rennie Meml. medal Royal Australian Chem. Inst., 1949, Analytical Divsn. medal, 1983. Fellow Royal Australian Chem. Inst.; mem. CSIRO Officers' Assn. (hon. life, pres. 1970-72), Victorian Bookbinders' Guild (hon. life). Mem. Anglican Ch. Avocations: music, bookbinding. Home: 211 Orrong Rd, East Saint Kilda VIC 3183, Australia

WILLIS, JOHN ALVIN, editor; b. Morristown, Tenn., Oct. 16, 1916; s. John Bradford and George Ann (Myers) W.; m. Claire Olivier, Sept. 25, 1960 (div.); m. Marina Sarda, Jan. 26, 1978 (div.). BA cum laude, Milligan Coll., 1938; MA, U. Tenn., 1941; postgrad., Ind U., Harvard U. Asst. editor Theatre World, N.Y.C., 1945-65, editor, 1965—; asst. editor Screen World, N.Y.C., 1948-65, editor, 1965—; tchr. pub. high schs., N.Y.C., 1950-76; editor Dance World, 1966-80; asst. editor Opera World, 1952-54, Great Stars of Am. Stage, 1952, Pictorial History of Silent Screen, 1953, Pictorial History of Opera in America, 1959, Pictorial History of the American Theatre, 1950, 60, 70, 80, 85; mem. Tony Theatre Awards Com. Nat. bd. dirs. U. Tenn. Theatre; mem. com. to select recipients for Mus. Theatre Hall of Fame, NYU. Lt. USNR, 1943-45. Recipient Lucille Lortel Lifetime Achievement award, 1993, Drama Desk Lifetime Achievement award, 1994, Nat. Bd. Rev. Lifetime Achievement Film History award, 1999, Profl. Excellence award Milligan Coll., 1999; high sch. auditorium renamed John Willis Performing Arts Ctr. in his honor, Morristown, 1993. Mem. Actors Equity Assn., Nat. Bd. Rev. Motion Pictures (past bd. dirs.). Home and Office: 190 Riverside Dr New York NY 10024-1008

WILLIS, LAUREL EILEEN (ANNA LIVIA PLULAURELBELLE), publishing executive; b. Portage la Prairie, Manitoba, Canada, May 10, 1947; arrived in Japan, 1979; d. Charles and Thelma Mary (Durward) Willis; m. Glenn Charles Sicks, Aug. 31, 1970 (div. 1984). BA in English, U. Hawaii, 1975; postgrad., Sophia U., 1983-85; MA, Somerset U., England, 1996. Dir. The Abiko Quar. with James Joyce Studies, 1988—. Author: Growing Up in Canada, 1979, White Trash, 1980, The Long Ride, 1995, Going Home, 1995; featured as one of Joyce's Women in the James Joyce Quarterly. Curator James Joyce Parlor, Japan. Mem. James Joyce Found., Small Press Ctr. Presbyterian. Home: 8-1-8 Namiki, Abiko-shi Chiba-ken 2170-1165, Japan

WILLIS, PAUL ALLEN, librarian; b. Floyd County, Ind., Oct. 1, 1941; s. Clarence Charles and Dorothy Jane (Harritt) W.; m. Barbara Marcum, June 15, 1963; children: Mark, Sally. AB, U. Ky., 1963, JD, 1969; MLS, U. Md., 1966. Cataloger Libr. of Congress, Washington, 1963; head descriptive cataloging br. Sci. and Tech. Info. Facility NASA, College Park, Md., 1963-66; law libr., prof. law U. Ky., Lexington, 1966-73; dir. librs. U. Ky., 1973—, acting dean Coll. Libr. Sci., 1975-76, 88; exec. sec. Ky. Jud. Retirement and Removal Commn., 1977-81; mem. adv. com. Ctr. for Jud. Conduct Orgns., Am. Judicature Soc., Chgo., 1979-81; bd. dirs. Southea. Libr. Network, Atlanta, 1980-83, 96-2000, chair, 1998-99; mem. exec. com. Ky. Hist. Soc., 1984-88; mem. Ky. Adv. Coun. on Librs., 1985—, adv. com. Online Computer Libr. Ctr., 1986-90; cons. S.E. Consortium for Internat. Devel., U. Sriwijaya, Palembang, Sumatera, Indonesia, 1987-88, Hanoi U. Tech., 1999, Vietnam Nat. U., Ho Chi Minh City, 1999. Sr. fellow UCLA, summer 1982. Mem. Assn. Southea. Rsch. Librs. (chair 1986-88). E-mail: willis@pop.uky.edu. Home: 2140 Fort Harrods Dr Apt 12 Lexington KY 40513-1095 Office: U Ky Libr Office Of Dir Lexington KY 40506-0001

WILLIS, RALPH HOUSTON, mathematics educator; b. McMinnville, Tenn., Dec. 26, 1942; s. Carl Houston and Carrie Lee (Hill) W.; m. Gayle Catherine Celestin, June 29, 1973 (div. Apr. 1985); m. Velma Inez Church, Aug. 10, 1985; stepchild, Bobbie Lynn White. BS in Math., Mid. Tenn. State U., 1964, MA in Math., 1966. Cert. secondary edn. Instr. depts. math. & computer sci. Western Carolina U., Cullowhee, N.C., 1968-73, asst. prof., 1973-83, assoc. prof., 1983—; co-founder N.C. State Math. Contest & Contest Network, 1977-78, state maths. contest com., 1977-78, western regional rep. exec. steering com., 1978—, recording sec., 1978—; co-founder N.C. Math. League, 1981-82, mem. problem writing com., 1981-84. Editor: (newsletters) Abelian Grapevine-Secondary Math, 1970-88, The Child of Mathematics-Elementary-Middle Grade Math., 1972-78; mem. editl. bd. The Centroid, 1995—; contbr. articles to profl. jours. Founder, dir., coord. High Sch. Math. Contest, Western Carolina U., 1970—, solicitor-coord. Math. Contest Scholarship Program, 1971-82, founder, coord. math dept. student awards program, 1970—, initiator-coord. math. dept.'s Vis. Speaker Program, 1974-77; faculty sponsor N.C. Coun. Tchrs. Math. Student Affiliate, Cullowhee, 1988—; coord. state road paving project Univ. Heights Cmty. Devel. Orgn., 1974-76, chmn., founder cmty. watch., 1978-79, coord. public water sys. upgrade project, 1980-84; coord., bd. dirs., trustee Hunerwadle Cmty. Cemetery Assn., Beersheba, Tenn., 1983—; co-founder N.C. State Math Contest and Contest Network, 1977-78. Recipient Paul A. Reid Disting. Svc. award Western Carolina U., 1991, hon. mention N.C. Gov.'s Award for Excellence, 1991, Innovator award N.C. Coun. Tchrs. in Math., 1994; Exemplary Site award State Math. Contest Com., 1990. Mem. Nat. Coun. Tchrs. Math., Math. Assn. Am., N.C. Coun. Tchrs. Math. (historian 1993-98, Innovator award 1994. editl. bd. Centroid 1995—), Phi Kappa Phi, Kappa Mu Epsilon. Avocations: genealogy, gardening, military history, model building, carpentry. Office: Western Carolina U Math Dept Stillwell Bldg Cullowhee NC 28723

WILLIS, RALPH WALKER, retired firefighter; b. Redondo Beach, Calif., Nov. 21, 1921; s. Achatius Walker and Elizabeth Margaret (Dehm) W.; m.

Helen Elizabeth Willis, May 18, 1946; 1 child, Ron Lee. Grad. h.s., San Diego. Firefighter Richmond (Calif.) Fire Dept., 1946-67. Author: (books) The Eternal Regiment, 1995, My Life as a Jarhead, 1999 (The Ernie Pyle WWII Roundtable award), War and Rememberance Revisted, 1988. Sgt. USMC, 1941-45. Mem. VFW (life). American Independent Party. Avocations: travel, painting, writing, gardening. Home: 866 Camino De Oro San Jacinto CA 92583-6807

WILLIS, WALTER BRUCE, actor, singer; b. Fed. Republic Germany, Mar. 19, 1955; came to U.S., 1957; s. David and Marlene Willis; m. Demi Moore; children: Rumer Glenn, Scout Larue, Tallulah Belle. Student, Montclair State Coll.; studied with Stella Adler. mem. First Amendment Comedy Theatre. Actor: (off-Broadway prodns.) Heaven and Earth, 1977, Fool for Love, 1984, The Bullpen, The Bayside Boys, The Ballad of Railroad William, (TV film) Trackdown, (feature films) Prince of the City, 1981, The Verdict, 1982, Blind Date, 1987, Sunset, 1988, Die Hard, 1988, In Country, 1989 (Golden Globe nomination 1990), Look Who's Talking (voice), 1989, Die Hard 2: Die Harder, 1990, Bonfire of the Vanities, 1990, Mortal Thoughts, 1991, Hudson Hawk, 1991, Billy Bathgate, 1991, The Last Boy Scout, 1991, Death Becomes Her, 1992, Striking Distance, 1993, Color of Night, 1994, North, 1994, Pulp Fiction, 1994, Nobody's Fool, 1994, Die Hard With a Vengeance, 1995, 12 Monkeys, 1995, Four Rooms, 1995, Last Man Standing, 1996, The Jackal, 1997, The Fifth Element, 1997, Mercury Rising, 1998, Armageddon, 1998, The Siege, 1998, Breakfast of Champions, 1999, The Sixth Sense, 1999, The Story of US, 1999, The Whole Nine Yards, 2000, The Kid, 2000; guest star (TV series) Miami Vice, The Twilight Zone; regular (TV series) Moonlighting, 1985-89 (People's Choice award 1986, Emmy award 1987, Golden Globe award 1987), musician (TV spl.) The Return of Bruno, 1986; rec. artist (album) The Return of Bruno, 1987, If It Don't Kill You, It Just Makes You Stronger, 1989; appeared in numerous commls. Named Internat. Broadcasting Man of Yr. Hollywood Radio and TV Soc.; recipient Star on Walk of Fame, 1998, People Choice award, 2000. Office: William Morris Agency c/o Arnold Rifkin 151 S El Camino Dr Beverly Hills CA 90212-2775

WILLIS, WILLIAM HARRIS, internist, cardiologist; b. St. Augustine, Fla., June 26, 1943; m. Jan Willis; children: Brandon, Patrick. BA in Biology, So. Coll., 1961-65; MD, Loma Linda U., 1969. MD, Fla., Calif., Ala., Tex.; Diplomate Am. Bd. Internal Medicine, Am. Bd. Cardiovascular Diseases, Nat. Bd. Med. Examiners. Intern U. Ala. Hosp. and Clinics, Birmingham, 1969-70, resident, 1970-72; fellowship U. Ala. Med. Ctr., Birmingham, 1972-74, chief fellow of cardiology, 1973-74, instr. in medicine, 1973-74; staff cardiologist USAF Med. Ctr., San Antonio, 1974-76; asst. clin. prof. medicine U. Tex., San Antonio, 1975-76; asst. prof. medicine Loma Linda (Calif.) U. Sch. of Medicine, 1976-78, co-dir. Cardiovascular Labs., 1976-80, assoc. prof. medicine, 1978-84; dir. Cardiology Fellowship Program Loma Linda U. Med. Ctr., 1978-88, dir. Cardiovascular Labs., 1980-89; prof. medicine Loma Linda (Calif.) U. Sch. Medicine, 1984-89; asst. chief cardiology Loma Linda U. Med. Ctr., 1986; med. dir. Loma Linda (Calif.) Internat. Heart Inst., 1988; co-dir. cardiac catheterization lab. Fla. Hosp., Orlando, 1990-96, dir. CCU, 1992-96. Mem. editorial bd. Catheterization and Cardiovascular Diagnosis, 1987-95; reviewer Am. Coll. Cardiology, 1988—. Fellow ACP, Am. Coll. Cardiology, Soc. Cardiac Angiography and Interventions (chmn. program com. 1980-88); mem. Soc. Cardiog Angiography and Intervention (bd. dirs. 1989-92). Avocations: golf, fishing, skiing, scuba diving. Office: Fla Heart Group PA 1613 N Mills Ave Orlando FL 32803-1849

WILLMER, RALPH ROBERT, environmental planner, consultant; b. Bronx, N.Y., Mar. 12, 1955; s. Charles Fred and Helga Willmer; m. Colleen Mae Walters, June 14, 1980; 1 child, Rebecca Caitlin. BS in Enciron. Resources Mgmt., SUNY, Syracuse, 1977; MA in Urban and Environ. Policy, Tufts U., 1986. Cert. planner Am. Inst. Cert. Planners. Project coord. N.Y. Pub. Interest Rsch. Group, Syracuse, 1977-80; energy and consumer edn. project dir. Cambridge (Mass.) Econ. Opportunity Com., 1980-82; dir. planning Cambridge Econ. Opportunity Com., 1982-83; mem. faculty legal assistance program Boston U. Met. Coll., 1990-93; dir. environ. planning McGregor & Assocs., Boston, 1983—; instr. Harvard U. Grad. Sch. Design, Cambridge, summes 1999-00; mem. Solid Waste Adv. Com., Boston, Legis. Subcom. on Impact Fees, Boston. Pres., v.p., treas., clk., bd. dirs. Boston Oil Consumers Alliance, Jamaica Plain, Mass., 1982-91. Mem. Am. Planning Assn. (bd. dirs. 1998-02, Disting. Svc. award Mass. chpt. 1995, Merit award for cost of cmty. svcs. project 1996, planning award for cost of cmty. svcs. project R.I. chpt. 1997, Nat. Disting. Contbn. award 1998), New Eng. Assn. Environ. Profls. (bd. dirs.), Mass. Assn. Cons. Planners (pres.). Democrat. Avocations: bicycling, skiing, hiking, bonsai. Fax: 617-338-0737. E-mail: rwillmer@mcgregorlaw.com. Home: 17 Walnut Ct Arlington MA 02476-6101 Office: McGregor & Assocs 60 Temple Pl Ste 410 Boston MA 02111-1306

WILLMES, BERND, religious studies educator; b. Wanne-Eickel, Germany, July 30, 1952; s. Wilhelm and Katharina (Schröer) W. Diplom-Theologe, Ruhr U., Bochum, Germany, 1977, Magister Artium, 1979, ThD, 1983; PhD, Rh.F. Wilhelms U., Bonn, Germany, 1996. Ordained priest Roman Cath. Ch., 1984. Chaplain Diocese Essen, Duisburg, Germany, 1984-87; univ. asst. U. Osnabrück, Germany, 1987-89, Katholische U., Eichstätt, Germany, 1989-91; prof. O.T., Theologische Fakultät, Fulda, Germany, 1991—; vice-chancellor Theologische Fakultät, Fulda, 1994-2000, chancellor, 2000—. Author: Die sogenannte Hirtenallegorie Ez 34, 1984, Bibelauslegung-genau genommen, 1990, Alttestamentliche Weisheit und Jahweglaube, 1992, Freude über die Vergebung der Sünden, 1996, Fachwissen im Schulunterricht, 1997, Jahwe-ein schlummernder Beschützer?, 1998, Menschliches Schicksal und ironische Weisheitskritik im Koheletbuch, 2000; co-author: Gott als Vater in Bibel und Liturgie, 2000; co-editor: Ich bewirke das Heil und erschaffe das Unheil, 1998. Office: Theologische Fakultät Fulda, Domplatz 2, D-36037 Fulda Hessen, Germany

WILLOCH, KÅRE, former prime minister of Norway; b. Oslo, Oct. 3, 1928; s. Haakon and Agnes (Saure) W.; m. Anne Marie Jörgensen, 1954; 3 children. Grad. in econs., U. Oslo, 1953; LLD (hon.), St. Olaf Coll., 1982. Counsellor Fedn. Norwegian Industries, 1954-63; mem. Oslo City Coun., 1952-59, Storting (Norwegian Parliament), 1957-89; chmn. Conservative Party Group in Storting, 1970-81; dir. Fridtjof Nausen Inst., Lysaker, Norway, 1999—; minister of Trade and Shipping, 1963, 65-70; sec.-gen. Conservative Party, 1963-65, chmn., 1970-74; prime minister of Norway, 1981-86; mem. Nordic Coun., 1970-86, pres., 1973; past mem. Norwegian del. to UN Gen. Assembly, 1961; chmn. Internat. Dem. Union, 1987-89; chmn. Fgn. Affairs Com. Parliament, 1986-89; gov. Oslo and Akershus County, 1989-98; chmn. Norwegian Def. Commn., 1990-92; chmn. supervisory bd. Dennorske Bank, 1989-96; chmn. bd. Norwegian Broadcasting Corp., 1998—.

WILLOUGHBY, JOHN WALLACE, former college dean, provost; b. Brumanna, Lebanon, July 30, 1932; s. James Wallace and Ida Cecilia (Frost) W.; m. Joanne Arnoldt DeWitt, Sept. 2, 1959; children—James Wallace, David Frost. B.A., Yale U., 1952; B.A., M.A., Oxford U., Eng., 1954; Ph.D., U. Rochester, 1959. Instr. English U. N.Mex., Albuquerque, 1959-60; instr. U. Chgo., 1960-63; from asst. prof. to prof., dean faculty Southampton Coll. Long Island, N.Y., 1963-73; v.p. for acad. affairs S.W. Minn. State Coll., Marshall, 1973-74, St. Francis Coll., Loretto, Pa., 1974-83; provost, dean of faculty, dir. continuing edn. Southwestern Coll., Winfield, Kans., 1983-92; distributor Success Motivation Inst., 1988—, dir. region VII (Kans., Mo., Iowa, Nebr.), 2000—. Editor: English: Selected Readings, 1963; assoc. editor Brownings Correspondence Wedgestone Press, 1993-99; contbr. articles to profl. jours. Treas. Cambria-Somerset Coun. for Health Edn., Johnstown, Pa., 1976-83; v.p. for scouting Penns Woods Coun. Boy Scouts Am., 1978-82; mem. com. on preparation for ministry South Kans. Presbytery, 1989-95, 97—; pres. Winfield (Kans.) Lions Club, 1996-97. Rhodes scholar, Oxford, 1952-54. Mem. Am. Assn. Rhodes Scholars. Democrat. Presbyterian. Avocations: bicycling; camping; philately; gardening; singing. Home: 24 Braid Hills Dr Winfield KS 67156-6304

WILLOUGHBY, WILLIAM FRANKLIN, II, physician, researcher; b. Washington, Feb. 4, 1936; s. William Westel and Patricia (DeZychlinska) W.; m. Mary Scott Fishburne, 1963 (div. 1974); children: Westel Woodbury, William Franklin III, Laura Fishburne, Mary Scott; m. Judith Eleanor Barbaras, Oct. 25, 1975; 1 child, Robert Alexander Willoughby. AB, Johns Hopkins U., 1957, MD, 1965, PhD in Microbiology, 1965; grad. with distinction, USAF War Coll., 1985. Diplomate Am. Bd. Pathology. Intern then resident in pathology Johns Hopkins Hosp., 1965-67; asst. prof. depts. pathology and microbiology Case Western Res. U., Cleve.; dir. Virginia Mason Rsch. Ctr., Seattle, 1972-75; assoc. prof. dept. pathology Sch. Medicine, Johns Hopkins U., Balt., 1975-87; prof., chmn. dept. pathology Sch. Medicine, U. S.C., Columbia, 1987-92; dir. labs. Cook County Hosp., Chgo., 1992-98, interim med. dir., 1994-96; cons. NIH, Bethesda, Md., 1979-98, mem. pathology A study sect., 1982-86; cons. NRC, Washington, 1981-84; mem. Res. Component Med. Coun., Dept. Def., Pentagon, 1991-93; dep. surgeon gen. for res. affairs USAF, Bolling AFB, D.C., 1993-95; asst. surg. gen. USAF, Operation Desert Storm/Desert Shield, 1990-91. Mem. editorial bd. Am. Rev. Respiratory Disease, 1978-84; contbr. articles to profl. jours., reviewer numerous sci. manuscripts. Vestryman Trinity Episcopal Ch., Long Green, Md., 1984-87; bd. dirs. Ctrl. S.C. chpt. ARC, Columbia, 1989-92; bd. fellow Norwich U., 1992-95. Maj. USAFR, 1975-95, advanced through grades to maj. gen., 1992-95. Decorated D.S.M., Legion of Merit, Meritorious Svc. medal; recipient Edwin E. Osgood prize Va. Mason Rsch. Ctr., 1973; Arthritis Found. fellow Scripps Clinic and Rsch. Found., 1967-69; Poncine scholar Poncine Found., 1972-74; NIH rsch. grantee, 1976-91. Fellow Coll. Am. Pathologists; mem. AAAS, Am. Soc. Investigative Pathology, Am. Assn. Immunologists, Am. Soc. Cell Biologists, Chgo. Coun. Fgn. Rels., Internat. Acad. Pathology, Assn. Pathology Chmns., Aerospace Med. Assn., Soc. USAF Flight Surgeons (bd. govs. 1993-96), Soc. Cons. to Armed Forces, Am. Thoracic Soc., Assn. Mil. Surgeons U.S., Army Navy Club (Washington), Air Force Assn., Midtown Tennis Club (Chgo.). Avocations: aviation, music, tennis, genealogy. Home: 1416A S Federal St Chicago IL 60605-2739

WILLOUGHBY-MELLORS, DEBRA LYNN, human resources and equal opportunities specialist; b. Eastbourne, England, Dec. 8, 1957; d. Dennis Lionel and Diane Elizabeth (Strudwick) W.; m. Richard John Mellors; stepchildren: Rachael, Emilie, Luke. MEd, U. Hull, Eng., 1995; postgrad., U. Nottingham, Eng., 1997—. From police officer to rank of inspector Sussex (Eng.) Police, 1974-91; dir. studies Nat. Police Training, Harrogate, Eng., 1991-95; dir. Individual Orgnl. Devel. and Assessment, 1995—; cons. child abuse investigation Sussex Police, 1987-89; cons. equal opportunities Nat. Police Training, 1991-95; con. police training Communal Police, Rwanda, 1996—. Author: Conflict Management and Assertiveness, 1992, Sex Bias and Sex Discrimination, Implications for Police Training, 1996, (with Richard Johnson) Cross Cultural Transference of Training Methodologies from Britain to Africa, 1999. Recipient Testimony Disting. Conduct award Soc. Protection Life from Fire, 1970, First Aid award Assn. Chief Police Officers, 1989. Mem. Inst. Personnel Devel., City and Guilds Assn. (internat. affairs com.), Inst. Supvsn. Mgmt. Office: ioda House, Lower Rd, Beeston Nottingham NG9 2GL, England

WILLS, JEAN MARIE, professional association executive; b. Chgo., Feb. 21, 1956; d. Richard Robert Bremer and Harriet Marie Rhodes; m. Bart F. Wills, June 16, 1990; 1 child, Rachel. BA, Western Ill. U., 1978; BS, Nat. Lewis U., 1987; EdD, U. Ill., 2000. Course editor DELTAK, Oak Brook, Ill., 1978-81; designation coord. Realtors Nat. Mktg. Inst., Chgo., 1981-83; curriculum mgr. Inst. Real Estate Mgmt., Chgo., 1983-85; edn. programs mgr. Comml. Investment Real Estate Coun., Chgo., 1985-88; assoc. exec. v.p. Am. Oil Chemists' Soc., Champaign, Ill., 1988—. E-mail: jeanw@aocs.org.

WILLS, JOERG MICHAEL, mathematician; b. Berlin, Mar. 5, 1937; s. Franz Hermann and Helene (Osthoff) W.; m. Barbara Piecha, Feb. 14, 1971; children: Nina, Julia, Anna. Diploma in maths., Technische U., Berlin, 1962, Dr. rer.nat., 1965. Prof. math. Technische U., Berlin, 1969-70, 71-74, U. Marburg, Germany, 1970-71; prof. math. U. Siegen, Germany, 1974—, Prorektor, 1975-76. Co-editor: Contributions to Geometry, 1978, Handbook of Convex Geometry, 1993, Convexity and its Applications, 1983. Mem. Am. Math. Soc., Deutsche Math. Vereinigung, Osterreichische Math. Gesellschaft. Home: Eichlingsborn 6, D-57076 Siegen Germany Office: U Siegen Math Dept, Emmy-Noether-Campus, D-57068 Siegen Germany

WILLS, LOIS ELAINE, religious education educator; b. Dayton, Ohio, Feb. 26, 1939; d. Harold Otto and Marjorie Elizabeth (Schmidt) Wallen; m. David P. Wills, Sept. 26, 1960 (dec.); children: Marianne, Melody, Michele. Degree, Coll. of Mount St. Joseph, Cin. Cert. catechist. Educator, substitute various schs., 1985-90; gallery dir. Studio San Giuseppe, Cin., 1987-90; curator Murdock Art and Antiques, Cin., 1990-92; mgr. Cin. Antique Mall, 1992-93; dir. religious edn. St. John the Bapt., Dover, Ind., 1993-96, Blessed Sacrament, Ft. Mitchell, Ky., 1996—. Group exhibits include Clermont County Libr., Batavia, Ohio, 1990, Murdock Gallery, Cin., 1990, Studio San Giusseppe, Mount St. Joseph Coll., Cin., 1990, Milford Libr., Cin., 1991, Cathedral Fresh Art Exhibit, Covington, Ky., 1998 (1st pl.); represented in pvt. collections. Mem. Youth Encouragement Svcs., Aurora, Ind., 1985—; active Dearborn Highland Arts Coun., Lawrenceburg, Ind., 1990-95; mem. Rev. Club, Lawrenceburg, 1985—; dir. religious edn. Blessed Sacrament Parish, Ft. Mitchell, Ky., 1996—. Mem. Greendale Garden Club. Avocations: art, reading, traveling, gardening, swimming. Home: 1286 Indian Woods Trl Lawrenceburg IN 47025-8678 Office: 2407 Dixie Hwy Fort Mitchell KY 41017-2936

WILLS, RANDY SCOTT, management consultant; b. N.Y.C., July 30, 1973; s. Steven Howard and Helaine Wills. BS, Syracuse (N.Y.) U., 1995. Mgr. Andersen Consulting, Hartford, Conn., 1995—; sr. v.p. dot Something.com, Washington, 1999—; mem. recruiting team, mentoring team Andersen Consulting, Hartford, 1995—. Author: (website) Space Travel in Y2K, 1999. Mem. Am. Mgmt. Assn., Earthwatch Rsch. Orgn. Avocations: archaeological research expeditions, hiking, astronomy.

WILLS, RONALD BADEN HOWE, food technology educator; b. Sydney, Australia, July 23, 1939; s. Baden Powell and Cissie Elizabeth (Gum) W.; children: Denise, Karen, David, Stephen, Jennifer; m. Margarita Brown, Feb. 2, 1988. BS with honors, U. NSW, Australia, 1965; PhD, Macquarie U., Australia, 1970. Exptl. officer CSIRO, Sydney, Australia, 1965-72; sr. lectr. U. Otago, Dunedin, New Zealand, 1972-75; prof. food sci. U. NSW, 1975-90; dir. Acad. Grain Tech., Melbourne, Australia, 1990-95; prof. food tech. U. Newcastle, Ourimbah, Australia, 1995—; cons. FAO, Asia, 1986-92. Author 10 books; contbr. over 250 articles to profl. jours. Fellow Australian Acad. Tech. Scis. and Engring., Royal Australian Chem. Inst., Australian Inst. Food Sci. and Tech. Home: 5/15 Woonona Ave, Wahroonga NSW 2076, Australia Office: Univ Newcastle, PO Box 127, Ourimbah NSW 2258, Australia

WILLSON, DAVID ALLEN, reference librarian, writer; b. Seattle, June 30, 1942; s. Robert Richard and Alice Hansine (Aspen) W.; m. Penelope Poeschl, Dec. 13, 1972 (div. Mar. 1986); children: Mungo Park, Darcy Monroe; m. Michele Geraldine DeBruyne, Mar. 8, 1986; children: Joaquin Sandoval, Alice Maria. BA, U. Wash., 1964, MLS, 1970. Reference libr. Green River C.C., Auburn, Wash., 1970—; archivist Joe Hooper Collection of Vietnam War Lit. at Green River C.C., 1987—. Author: (novels) REMF Diary, 1988, The REMF Returns, 1992, In the Army Now, 1995; co-editor: (bibliography) Vietnam War Literature, 1996. With U.S. Army, 1966-67. Recipient Disting. Faculty award Puget Power, 1996, Vietnam Vets. Am. Contbn. to Am. Culture award, 1997. Mem. Popular Culture Assn., Vietnam Vets. Am. Democrat. Lutheran. Avocations: movies; listening to the blues, especially Fred McDowell. Home: 23630 201st Ave SE Maple Valley WA 98038-8633 Office: Green River CC 12401 SE 320th St Auburn WA 98092-3622

WILLSON, JOHN MICHAEL, mining company executive; b. Sheffield, England, Feb. 21, 1940; s. Jack Desmond and Cicely Rosamond (Long Price) W.; m. Susan Mary Partridge, Aug. 26, 1942; children: Marcus J., Carolyn A. BSc in Mining Engring. with honors, Imperial Coll., London, 1962, MSc in Mining Engring., 1985. With Cominco Ltd., 1966-74; v.p. No. Group Cominco Ltd., Vancouver, B.C., Can., 1981-84; pres. Garaventa (Canada) Ltd., Vancouver, 1974-81; pres., CEO Western Can. Steel Ltd., Vancouver, 1985-88, Pegasus Gold Inc., Spokane, Wash., 1989-92, Placer Dome, Inc., Vancouver, B.C., Can., 1993-2000; bd. dirs. Can. Occidental Petroleum Ltd., Finning Internat. Inc. Pres. N.W.T. Chamber Mines, Yellowknife, Can., 1982-84; chmn. bd. dirs. Western States Pub. Lands Coalition, Pueblo, Colo., 1990-91; bd. dirs. World Gold Coun. Mem. AIME, Can. Inst. Mining and Metallurgy, Inst. Mining and Metallurgy (London), Assn. Profl. Engrs. B.C., Assn. Profl. Engrs. and Geologists N.W.T., N.W. Mining Assn. (bd. dirs. Corp. Leadership award 1991), World Gold Coun. (chmn.). Avocations: cycling, tennis, squash, sailing, skiing. Fax: 604-228-9664. Home: 4722 Drummond Dr, Vancouver, BC Canada V6T 1B4 Office: Placer Dome Inc, 1055 W Dunsmuir St Ste 1600, Vancouver, BC Canada V7X 1P1

WILLWEBER, MARTIN, marketing consultant, musician; b. Ashiya, Hyogo, Japan, Dec. 15, 1951; s. Herbert Rudolf and En (Kishimoto) W.; m. Kazuko Hoshi, Apr. 7, 1992. BA in Polit. Sci., Sophia U., Tokyo, 1973, postgrad. polit. sci., 1974-75; student, Berklee Coll. Music, 1975-76. Concert, studio musician Tokyo, 1969—; endorser, cons. Yamaha Corp., Tokyo, 1977—; adv. Koyo Kanri Co., Ltd., Osaka, Japan, 1994—. Co-founder Orquesta del Sol, Tokyo, 1978-90; percussionist triangle sessions (album) Brecker Bros. & Fukamachi, 1977, (album) Matsuoka Naoya Live at Montreux, 1980. Dir., hon. sec. Internat. Hosp. and Med. Svcs. Assn., Kobe, 1998—; councillor Kobe Kaisei Hosp. Med. Found., 1993—; dir. Kobe Kaisei Nursing Home, 1997—. Mem. Tokyo Club, Internat. House Japan, Wash. Athletic Club (Seattle), Century Club (Osaka), Yokohama Country and Athletic Club (dir., hon. sec. 1995—), Kobe Club (pres. 1995-97), Suma Yacht Club. Avocations: sailing, travel. Home: 9-96 Koyoen Higashiyamacho, Nishinomiya 662-0012, Japan

WILLY, ALEXANDER KENNETH, controller, consultant; b. Rio de Janeiro, Nov. 28, 1969; s. Kenneth Alfred and Katalin W.; m. Claudia Lucia Balhestero, July 25, 1996. BA in Bus. Adminstrn., Fundacao Getulio Vargas, São Paulo, Brazil, 1994. Trader Banco Pactual S.A., São Paulo, 1991-93; fin. analyst Ford Motor Co., São Paulo, 1994-96; sr. cons. Roland Berger & Ptnr., São Paulo, 1996-98; contr. HBO Brazil, São Paulo, 1999—; cons. Roland Berger & Ptnr., São Paulo. Avocations: diving, swimming. Home: Rua Francisca Biriba 549, 02451040 Sao Paulo apt 83, Brazil Office: HBO Brazil Ltda, Av Dr Arnaldo 2180, 01255000 Sao Paulo Brazil

WILMER, HARRY ARON, psychiatrist; b. New Orleans, Mar. 5, 1917; s. Harry Aron and Leona (Schlenker) W.; m. Jane Harris, Oct. 31, 1944; children: Harry, John, Thomas, James, Mary. BS, U. Minn., 1938, MB, 1940, MS, 1940, MD, 1941, PhD, 1944. Intern Gorgas Hosp., Ancon, C.Z., 1940-41; resident in neurology and psychiatry Mayo Clin., Rochester, Minn., 1945-49, cons. in psychiatry, 1957-58; physician Palo Alto (Calif.) Clinic, 1949-51; pvt. practice medicine, Palo Alto, 1951-55, 58-64; prof. psychiatry U. Calif. Med. Sch., San Francisco, 1964-69; sr. psychiatrist Scott & White Clin., Temple, Tex., 1969-74; emeritus prof. psychiatry U. Tex. Health Sci. Ctr., San Antonio, 1974-87; staff mem.(part-time) Audie Murphy VA Hosp., San Antonio, 1974-82; founder, dir. Internat. Film Festivals on Culture and Psychiatry, U. Tex. Health and Sci. Ctr., 1972-80; founder, emeritus pres., dir. Inst. Humanities, Salado, TX, 1980—; pvt. practice, Salado, 1980—. Author: Huber the Tuber, 1942, COrky the Killer, 1945, This is Your World, 1952, Social Psychiatry in Action, 1958, First Book for the Mind, 1963, Vietnam in remission, 1985, Practical Jung, 1987, Closeness: A Dictionary of Ideas, Vol. I, 1989, Father Mother, 1989; (film) People Need People, 1961, Facing Evil, 1988, Evil, 1989, Creativity, 1990, Creativity Paradoxes and Reflections, 1991, Closeness: Personal and Professional Relations, 1992, Understandable Jung, 1994, How Dreams Help, 1999, Quest for Silence, 2000. Served to capt. M.C., USNR, 1955-57; Guggenheim fell., Zurich, 1969-70; NRC fell., Johns Hopkins Hosp., 1944-45. Fell. Am. Pscyhiatry Assn. (life, emeritus), Am. Coll. Psychiatrists, Am. Acad. Psychoanalysis; mem. AAAS, Internat. Assn. Analytical Pscyhology. Home: 1202 S Ridge Rd Mill Creek PO Box 528 Salado TX 76571-0528

WILMERS, FRITZ, retired climatologist; b. Gadderbaum, Germany, July 16, 1930; s. Johannes Friedrich and Sophie K. (Boehmlaender) W.; m. Ursula Adele Witt, Dec. 10, 1959; children: Elisabeth, Dorothea. Diploma engring., U. Hanover, 1959, D, 1966. From instr. to acad. dir. climatology U. Hanover, Germany, 1967-95. Mem. Internat. Soc. Biometeorology. Lutheran. Avocations: photography, music, travel. Office: Univ Inst Meteorology, Herrenhaeuserstr 2, Hannover 30419, Germany

WILMOT, JACK BOTWE, diplomat. Permanent rep. Ghana UN, N.Y.C., 1996-99. Office: Perm Mission of Ghana to UN 19 E 47th St New York NY 10017-1901

WILMOTS, MARC, soccer player; b. Dongelberg, Feb. 22, 1969. Midfielder Schalke 04, Germany, Belgian Nat. Team, Brussels. Recipient Belgian League Title, 1989, Belgian cup, 1993, UEFA cup, 1997. Address: Belgian Football Assn, Ave Houba de Strooper 145, 1020 Brussels Belgium*

WILMUT, IAN, biologist; b. Hampton, Eng., July 7, 1944; s. Jack and Eileen Mary (Dalgleish) W.; m. Vivienne Mary Craven, Sept. 9, 1967; children: Helen, Naomi, Dean. BS, Nottingham U., Eng., 1967, DS, 1998; PhD, Cambridge (Eng.) U., 1971. Sr. scientist ABRO, Edinburgh, Scotland, 1973-93; prin. investigator Roslin Inst., Midlothian, Scotland, 1993—, also mem. sr. mgmt. Editor Jour. Reproduction Fertility, 1993—; contbr. articles to profl. jours. Hon. fellow U. Edinburgh, 1993. Mem. Internat. Embryo Transfer Soc. (pres. 1994). Avocations: hill walking, photography, curling, gardening. Office: Roslin Inst, Roslin, Midlothian EH25 9PS, Scotland*

WILPERT, BERNHARD OTTMAR, educator; b. Breslau, Germany, Mar. 1, 1936; s. Johannes Gregor and Emma (Breitkopf) W.; m. Czarina Ann Huerta, Apr. 4, 1964; children: Gregory, Karin. Diploma in psychology, Tübingen (Germany) U., 1961, PhD, 1965. Editl. asst. Kreuz/Matthias Grunewald Pub., Bonn, Germany, 1962-63; del. Internat. Secretariat Vol. Svcs., Washington, 1965; dir. divsn. programs German Vol. Svc., Bonn, 1966-67; lectr. German Inst. Devel., Berlin, 1967-68; prof. Pädagogische Hochschule Berlin, 1978-80, Berlin U. Tech., 1980—; guest prof. Inst. d'Etudes Polit., Paris, 1980, U. Osaka, Japan, 1983; guest rschr. U. Calif., Berkeley, 1988; guest prof. U. Renee Descartes, Paris, 1990; hon. prof. indsl. and organizational psychology Inst. of Psychology Chinese Acad. of Sci., 1999. Author: Führung in Deutschen Unternehmen, 1977; co-author: Industrial Democracy in Europe, 1981, Industrial Democracy in Europe Revisited, 1993, Sicherheitskultur - Konzept und Analyse-methoden, 1999; co-editor: Reliability and Safety in Hazardous Work Systems, 1993, After the Event, 1997, Nuclear Safety - A Human Factors Perspective, 1999. Mem. German Reactor Safety Commn., Bonn, 1993-98; chair Internat. Coun. Work and Orgn. Rsch. Ctr., Tilburg, The Netherlands, 1990-96. Rsch. fellow Sci. Ctr. Berlin, 1969-77; study grantee Fulbright Commn., 1957-58, Volkswagen Found. grantee, Germany, 1963-64. Mem. Internat. Assn. Applied Psychology (pres. 1994-98). Avocations: music, cooking, hiking. Home: Douglasstr 11, 14193 Berlin Germany Office: Inst Psychology, Franklinstr 28 FR 3-8, 10587 Berlin Germany

WILSDON, THOMAS ARTHUR, product development engineer, administrator; b. Waterbury, Conn., Aug. 18, 1942; s. Arthur and Ruth (Wellington) W.; m. Yvonne Jeanne Pettit, June 19, 1964 (div. Apr. 1986); children: Thomas Charles, Beth Jeanne; m. Sharon Diann Culbertson, Feb. 14, 1988; children: Vandee Hyder, Jacklynn Hyder. BSEE, U. Conn., 1964; MBA, SUNY, Buffalo, 1978. Product design engr. Westinghouse Gen. Control Divsn., Buffalo, 1964-78; mgr. product devel. Westinghouse Control Divsn., Asheville, N.C., 1978-87; mgr. Advantage engring. Westinghouse Elec. Components Divsn., Asheville, 1987-94; mgr. logic control products devel. engring. Eaton/Cutler Hammer, Milw., 1994—. Mem. IEEE, NSPE, Am. Mgmt. Assn. Methodist. Achievements include development of low voltage AC and DC motor starters, Ampgard 7200V motor starter components, solid state controlled Advantage motor starters, PLC, DCI, sensor development, pushbuttons, limit switch, electronic product engineering. Home: PO Box 250 Pewaukee WI 53072-0250 Office: Eaton/Cutler Hammer 4201 N 27th St Milwaukee WI 53216-1897

WILSKE, STEPHAN, lawyer; b. Ebingen, Germany, July 16, 1962; came to U.S., 1995; s. Manfred and Irmgard (Schwarz) W. Grad., U. Aix-Marseille III, Aix-en-Provence, France, 1987; JD, U. Tübingen (Germany), 1990, MA in Polit. Sci., 1991; LLM, U. Chgo., 1996; Dr.iur, U. Tübingen, 1998. Bar:

N.Y. 1997, Germany 1997. Law clk. Higher Regional Ct., Stuttgart, Germany, 1990-93; rschr., tchg. fellow faculty of law U. Tübingen, 1990-96; assoc. Rogers & Wells, N.Y.C., 1996-97, Gleiss Lutz Hootz Hirsch, Stuttgart, Germany, 1997—; mem. faculty law coun. U. Tübingen, 1994-95. Co-editor: The United Nations System, 2 vols., 1996; contbr. articles to profl. jours. Bd. dirs., gen. counsel, Culture Ctr. Kupferhammer, Tübingen, 1988—. Recipient Caspar Platt award U. Chgo. Law Sch., 1996. Mem. ABA, Am. Soc. Internat. Law, Internat. Bar Assn., N.Y. State Bar Assn. Avocations: music performances, coaching soccer team. Home: Fritz Elsas Str 40, 70174 Stuttgart Germany Office: Gleiss Lutz Hootz Hirsch, Maybach str 6, 70469 Stuttgart Germany

WILSMAN, JAMES MICHAEL, lawyer; b. Port Huron, Mich., Oct. 7, 1939; s. Leo George and Fay P. Wilsman; m. Sandra Keith, June 28, 1962 (div. Sept. 1988); children: Sarah, David. BA, Hiram (Ohio) Coll., 1961; JD, U. Mich., 1964. Bar: Ohio 1964, U.S. Dist. Ct. Ohio 1965, U.S. Ct. Appeals (6th cir.) 1965. Assoc. Squire, Sanders & Dempsey, Cleve., 1964-66; ptnr. Parks, Eisele, Bates & Wilsman, Cleve., 1966-86, Hahn Loeser & Parks, Cleve., 1986-90, Kelley, McCann & Livingstone, Cleve., 1990-93, Wilsman & Schoonover, Cleve., 1993—. Pres. Citizens League of Greater Cleve., 1974-76. Mem. ABA, Ohio Bar Assn. (family law sect. Cleve. chpt. 1986—), Cleve. Bar Assn. (chmn. family law sect. 1986—), Shaker Heights Country Club. Avocation: golf. Home: 19801 Van Aken Blvd Apt 210F Cleveland OH 44122-3651 Office: Wilsman & Schoonover 1420 The Tower at Erieview 1300 E 9th St Cleveland OH 44114-1503

WILSON, ADEL MICHEL, plastic surgeon; b. Cairo, Egypt, Dec. 2, 1965; s. Michel and Soad Jimmy (Tadros) W. MD, Cairo U., 1988, M in Surgery, 1992, PhD, 1997. Registrar in surgery Cairo U., 1990-93, lectr. in plastic surgery, 1996—; registrar in plastic surgery U. Coll., London, 1994-95; cons. plastic surgery Ministry of Health, Cairo, 1997—, Al-Salam Hosp., Cairo, 1996—; dir. Infection Control com., Cairo, 1997-98, Microsurgery Unit, Cairo, 1996-98; mem. Environ. Care com., 1998—. Author: Case Presentations for MRCS, 1997; contbr. articles to profl. jours. Mem. bd. Gezira Sporting Club, Cairo, 1996. Fellow Royal Coll. Surgeons; mem. Royal Soc. of Medicine (hon.), British Assn. of Plastic Surgeons. Avocations: reading, table tennis, chess. Home: 37 Batal Ahmed Abdel-Aziz, Giza 12411, Egypt Office: 42 Dokki St Flat 132, Dokki 12311, Egypt

WILSON, ALAN MARTIN, veterinary educator and researcher, consultant; b. Glasgow, Scotland, Mar. 3, 1964; s. Henry Wallace and Fiona McPherson (Martin) W.; m. Anna Rose Wyn-Jones, Aug. 3, 1997; children: Ella, Callum, Sophie. BSc, Glasgow U., 1986, BVMS, 1987; PhD, Bristol (Eng.) U., 1991. Cert. vet. surgeon. Lectr. U. Bristol, Eng., 1992-96, dir. Equine Sports Medicine Ctr., 1993-96, pre-clin. dean Vet. Sch., 1995—; lectr. Royal Vet. Coll., London, 1996—; mem. coun. Brit. Schs. Exploring Society, London, 1991—. Contbr. numerous articles to profl. jours.; patentee in field. Grantee Horseracing Betting Levy Bd., 1987—, Home of Rest for Horses, 1992—, also various indsl. orgns. Fellow Royal Geog. Soc. Avocations: mountaineering, athletics. Office: Royal Vet Coll, North Mymms, Hatfield Herts AL9 7TA, England

WILSON, ALICE BLAND, sales manager; b. Rainelle, W.Va., Apr. 1, 1938; d. Brady Floyd and Mildred Martha (George) Bland; m. Louis William Groves, Jr., Apr. 20, 1957 (div. 1981); children: Martha Rachel, Leonora Jayne; m. Glen Parten Wilson, Dec. 11, 1982 (div. 1996). AB, W.Va. U., 1959, postgrad. in microbiology, 1975-78. Contract adminstr. Washington Plate Glass Co., Washington, 1979-80; mem. acctg. staff Forbes Co., Washington, 1981; customer relations rep. Stern's Co., Washington, 1982; real estate assoc. Prudential Preferred Properties, Washington, 1985—. Contbr. articles to Jour. Parasitology. Vol. coord. John Glenn for Pres. campaign, Washington, 1983-84; co-chmn. hospitality com. Women's Nat. Dem. Club, Washington, 1985—; mem. internat. adv. coun. ARC, Washington, 1985—; mem. exec. com. Nat. Symphony Orch., 1990—. Mem. Washington Assn. Realtors (mem. residential sales com. 1985—), Leading Edge Soc., Million Dollar Club. Avocations: flying, aerobatics, nature study. Home: 641 1/2 E Capitol St SE Washington DC 20003-1234 Office: Antique & Contemporary Leasing & Sales Inc 709 12th St SE Washington DC 20003-2962

WILSON, ARTHUR THEODORE, education consultant; b. Newark, July 2, 1945; s. Elmer and Dorothy May (Outlaw-Sloan) W. BA in Humanities, New Sch., 1971, MA in Philosophy, 1974; PhD in Program History, NYU, 1980. Cert. tchr., N.Y., N.J. Rschr. African Studies, N.Y.C., 1972; tchr. Teaneck Alternative High Sch., N.J., 1979-80, Hunter Coll., N.Y.C., 1980-81; gifted and talented program curriculum cons. Bd. Cooperative Ednl. Svcs., SUNY, Farmingdale, 1983—; apptd. arts & edn. acad. artist N.J. Performing Arts Ctr., Newark, 1996—; advisor, tutor Master's Degree Program in Acting, New Actors Workshop, Antioch U., N.Y., 1995—; workshop leader Young Playwright's Festival, N.Y.C., 1981—; adj. prof. drama Drew U., Madison, N.J.; co-founder, workshop leader N.J. Young Playwrights Festival, 1983; project dir., playwright Am. Folk Theater Young Co.'s exch. program, London, 1984-85; theater workshop cons. Milneck Sch. for Deaf, L.I., 1984; literature workshop cons. Orion Gifted and Talented Program, Lindenhurst, N.Y., 1984—; artistic dir. exch. program Manhattan Empire and Tukak Theater, Denmark; dir. playwriting in sch. project N.Y. Shakespeare Festival, 1986—; instr. N.Y. Lit. Assn., N.Y.C., 1984—; poetry reading and workshop with Poet Laureate Gwendolyn Brooks, Union Coll., 1985, guest poet for Mother Hale of Hale House, 1987; dir. playwriting in edn. dept. schs. N.Y. Shakespeare Festival, dir./prodr. Live! (radio edn. program), cons. arts edn. New Dance Group Ctr., N.Y., 1987—. Editor, writer, publisher Dance Giant Steps, Inc., Bklyn., 1981—; author: (play) The Extended Family, 1987; dir. Daddy Say, 1987, Children of Dahomey and Spirit Ensemble, 1986; dance editor; Feet Mag., 1969-72, Blacj Creations Mag., 1970-72; editor, pub.: Attitude: The Dancers' Monthly, 1982; contbr. poetry to Open Mag., Other Countries, New Rain, A Taste of Salt; producer: (plays) Life Sea Treasures, 1989-90, Guns Like Candy, 1991, Red High Heels Snap Back, 1995. Workshop leader N.J. Teen Program, 1983-84; advisor, workshop leader, founder N.J. Young Playwrights Festival, 1964-68; rsch. asst. Weeksville Project, Bjlyn., 1969-70; theater dir. local orgns. Recipient numerous scholars, 1970-79; grantee Bklyn. Art and Cultural Assn., 1983, N.Y. Dept. Cultural Affairs, 1983-84, N.Y. State Coun. on Arts, 1982-84, BECA Capezio Found., Heart grant Union County Bd. Freeholders, 1998-00; N.J. State Coun. Arts fellow, 1985-86. Mem. Black Writers Union, Dramatists Guild, Inc., ASSITEJ, Internat. Assn. Children's Theater Professionals. Office: Dance Giant Steps Inc 1040 Park Place Ste 5C Brooklyn NY 11213

WILSON, BLAIR MANSFIELD, architect; b. Brisbane, Queensland, Australia, Oct. 8, 1930; s. Ronald Martin and Olga Esme Mansfield (Wallis) W.; m. Elizabeth Ann Moxon, Jan. 12, 1958; children: Ross, Hamilton, Andrew, Elizabeth. BArch, U. Queensland, Brisbane, 1955. Registered arch., Queensland, RIBA, LFRAIA. Arch. Clifford Tee & Gale, London, 1955-56, R. Martin Wilson & Son, Brisbane, 1956-67; prin. Blair M. Wilson & Assocs., Brisbane, 1967-76; dir. Blair M. Wilson & Assocs. Pty Ltd., Brisbane, 1976—; pres. Royal Australian Inst. Archs., 1976-77; chmn. bd. dirs. Wilson Archs., 1990—. Prin. works include La Baite Theatre (Clay Brick award Queensland Brick Mfrs. 1973), John Kindler Theatre, (Bronze medal Royal Australian Inst. Archs.). Pres. Brisbane Repertory Theatre, 1974-77, Rotary Club of Hamilton, Brisbane, 1983-84; mem. Nat. Capital Planning Com., Canberra, Australia, 1976-82; senator U. Queensland, 1980-86. Served with Royal Australian Air Force Active Res., 1954-59. Fellow Royal Australasian Inst. Archs. (life); mem. Royal Inst. British Archs., Royal Queensland Yacht Squadron, Brisbane Club (sr.), United Svc. Club (sr.). Presbyterian. Avocations: painting, sailing. Home: 24 Ormond St Ascot, Brisbane QLD 4007, Australia Office: 564 Boundary St, Spring Hill 1, Brisbane QLD 4000, Australia

WILSON, BRIAN EUGENE, computer scientist; b. Dayton, Ohio, Dec. 19, 1963; s. Homer Eugene and Shirley Ann (Orth) W.; m. Donna Wimmer, Feb. 18, 1989; children: Lyndsey Marie, Brandy Lee. Student, Sinclair C.C., Dayton, 1982-85, Sage Evening Coll., Albany, N.Y. IBM cert. OS/2 Warp V4 Engr., AIX Specialist-Sys. Adminstrn., MQ Series. Programmer Sinclair C.C., Dayton, 1983-85; editor-in-chief, writer, v.p. Advanced Computer Enterprises, Englewood, Ohio, 1985-86; computer operator Albany (N.Y.) Savs. Bank, 1986-88; sr. computer programmer, analyst N.Y. State Dept. Tax and Fin., Albany, 1988-89, sys. programmer, 1990-94, database programmer/analyst, 1994-97, mgr. Internet technologies, 1997-2000; sr. info. tech. specialist IBM, Albany, 2000—; computer programmer Pub. Domain, Inc., West Milton, Ohio, 1984-86, Ledex, Inc., Vandalia, Ohio, 1984-86; cons. WKB Software, Union, Ohio, 1982-85; cons., owner Wilson Software and Solutions, Rensselaer, N.Y., 1992—; v.p. Advanced Computer Enterprises Ltd. Partnership, Englewood, 1995-96. Author: Using Model 204, 1990; editor Commodore Users Bull. Jour., 1985-86, contbr.; editor-in-chief, writer, v.p. Commodore Users Bull. Coach Westland Hills Little League, Albany, 1990-94, Rensselaer Little League, 1995—; vol. Hudson Valley coun. Girl Scouts U.S.; trombonist Capitaland Bigband. Mem. Internat. Model 204 Users Group (libr. 1989—), Nat. Fedn. Interscholastic Ofcls. Assn., Northeast Model 204 Users Group (bd. dirs.), N.Y. Assn. Cert. Football Ofcls. (Capital dist. chpt.), Pub. Employees Fedn. Methodist. Avocations: music, computers, woodworking, model railroading. Home: 1244 2nd St Rensselaer NY 12144-1816 Office: IBM 80 State St Ste 17 Albany NY 12207-2588

WILSON, BRUCE KEITH, men's health nurse; b. Alton, Ill., Aug. 18, 1946; s. Lewis Philip and Ruth Caroline Wilson; m. Karen Loughrey, Aug. 14, 1977; children: Sarah Ann, Andrew James. BSN, U. Tex., San Antonio, 1975, MSN, 1977; PhD, North Tex. State U., Denton, 1987. Cert. in nursing informatics Am. Nurses Credentialing Ctr. Coord. Pan Am. U., Edinburg, Tex., 1982-83; house supr. HCA Rio Grande Regional Hosp., McAllen, Tex., 1986-87; program dir. Tex. Southmost Coll., Brownsville, 1983-86; mem. faculty U. Tex.-Pan Am., Edinburg, 1986—. Author: Logical Nursing Math., 1987. With U.S. Army, 1966-68. Mem. ANA, Nat. League for Nursing, Am. Assembly for Men in Nursing (bd. dirs. 1997—), Tex. League for Nursing (bd. dirs. 1993-97). Avocations: photography, computer. Home: 1702 Ivy Ln Edinburg TX 78539-5367 Office: U Tex-Pan Am Dept Nursing Edinburg TX 78539

WILSON, C. DANIEL, JR., library director; b. Middletown, Conn., Nov. 8, 1941; s. Clyde D. and Dorothy M. (Neal) W.; m. M. April Jackson, Apr. 1986; children: Christine, Cindy, Clyde, Ben. BA, Elmhurst Coll., 1967; MA, Dominican U., 1968; MPA, U. New Orleans, 1995. Trainee Chgo. Pub. Libr., 1967-68; instr. U. Ill., 1968-70; asst. dir. Perrot Meml. Libr., Greenwich, Conn., 1970-76; dir. Wilton Pub. Libr., Wilton, Conn., 1976-79; assoc. dir. Birmingham Pub. Libr., Birmingham, Ala., 1979-83; dir. Davenport (Iowa) Pub. Libr., 1983-85, New Orleans Pub. Libr., 1985-97, St. Louis County Libr., 1997—. With USMC, 1962-65. Mem. ALA, Internat. Assn. Met. Librs. (pres. 1998—), Mo. Libr. Assn., Am. Soc. Pub. Adminstrs., Rotary, Pi Gamma Mu. Episcopalian.

WILSON, CARL WELDON, JR., construction company executive, civil engineer; b. Norfolk, Va., Sept. 4, 1933; s. Carl Weldon and Janie Marie (Ludford) W.; m. Jean Roberts, Feb. 13, 1960; children: Lisa Ann, Carl Weldon III. BCE, Tex. A&M U., 1954. Registered profl. engr., Tex. Engr. Magnolia Petroleum Co., Morgan City, La., 1954-55, Brown & Root, Houston, 1957-60; project mgr. Claude Everett Constrn. Co., Houston, 1960-62; pres. Falcon Constrn. Co., Houston, 1962-63; pres., owner Wilson Engring. and Constrn. Co., Houston, 1963-68; v.p. Divcon, Inc., Houston, 1968-71, Wilson Industries, Inc., Houston, 1971-81; pres., prin. owner BS&B Engring. Co., Inc., Houston, 1981-86; chmn., majority shareholder Task Internat., Inc., Houston, 1986—. Served to 1st lt. U.S. Army, 1955-57. Republican. Episcopalian. Avocations: tennis, running, painting. Home: 750 Bison Dr Houston TX 77079-4401 Office: Task Internat Inc PO Box 940121 Houston TX 77094-7121

WILSON, COLIN HENRY, writer; b. Leicester, Eng., June 26, 1931; s. Arthur and Anetta W.; m. Joy Stewart; children: Sally, Damon, Rowan; 1 child from previous marriage, Roderick. writer in residence Hollins (Va.) Coll., 1966-67; vis. prof. U. Wash., Seattle, 1967, Rutgers U., New Brunswick, N.J., 1974. Author (numerous books including novels): The Outsider, 1956, The Glass Cage, 1967, The Occult, 1971, The Black Room, 1971, The Space Vampires, 1975, Mysteries, 1978; 6 critical studies in the Outsider series; non-fiction: Access to Inner Worlds, 1982, A Criminal History of Mankind, 1983, (with Donald Seaman) Modern Encyclopedia of Murder, 1983, The Essential Colin Wilson, 1984, The Personality Surgeon, 1986, (with Damon Wilson) Encyclopedia of Unsolved Mysteries, 1987, Spiderworld, 1987, The Misfits, 1988, Beyond The Occult, 1988, Written in Blood, 1989, (with Donald Seaman) The Serial Killers, 1990; (play) Mozart's Journey to Prague, 1991, Spiderworld: The Magician, 1992, The Strange Life of P.D. Ouspensky, 1993, Unsolved Mysteries Past and Present (with Damon Wilson), 1993, From Atlantis To The Sphinx, 1996, Atlas of Holy Places and Sacred Sites, 1996, Alien Dawn, 1998, The Books in My Life, 1998, The Devil's Party, 2000; (with Rand Fle'math) Atlantis Blueprint, 2000. Club: Savage.

WILSON, DAVID CLIVE (BARON WILSON OF TILLYORN), utilities executive, former British diplomat; b. Alloa, Scotland, Feb. 14, 1935; s. William Skinner and Enid (Sanders) W.; m. Natasha Helen Mary Alexander, Apr. 1, 1967; children: Peter Michael Alexander, Andrew Marcus William. Student, Trinity Coll., Glenalmond, Scotland, 1948-53; MA, Oxford U., Eng., 1958; PhD, London U., 1974. Served with Brit. Diplomatic Svc., 1958-68; cabinet office Brit. Govt., London, 1974-77; polit. advisor Brit. Diplomatic Svc., Hong Kong, London, 1977-81; editor The China Quarterly, London, 1968-74; gov. Hong Kong, Hong Kong, 1987-92; with Fgn. and Commonwealth Office, London, 1981-87; chmn. Scottish and So. Energy plc (Scottish Hydro-Electric), Perth, Scotland, 1993—; vis. scholar Columbia U., N.Y.C., 1972; chmn. Scottish com. Brit. Coun., 1993—; chancellor U. Aberdeen, Scotland, 1997—. Trustee Mus. of Scotland, 1999—. Served as 2d lt. with Brit. military, 1953-55. Mem. Royal Scottish Geog. Soc. (v.p. 1996—), Bhutan Soc. U.K. (pres. 1993—), Hong Kong Soc. (pres. 1994—), Hong Kong Assn. (pres. 1994—). Office: The House of Lords, London SW1A OPW, England also: Scottish and So Energy plc, 200 Dunkeld Rd Inveralmond House, Perth Tayside PH1 3AQ, United Kingdom*

WILSON, DAVID LEE, clinical psychologist; b. Mooresville, N.C., July 5, 1941; s. William John Mack and Joyce Evelyn (Evans) W.; m. Barbara Ann Klepfer, Apr. 22, 1960 (div. Jan. 1982); children: Cheryl, Lisa, David; m. Cheryl Andersen, May 22, 1983 (div. Jan. 1992); m. Gail Grace, Aug. 31, 1997. Student, Auburn U., 1959-60; AB in Psychology, Davidson Coll., 1963; PhD in Clin. Psychology, U. N.C., 1967. Tchg. fellow U. N.C., Chapel Hill, 1964; psychology intern Letterman Hosp., San Francisco, 1966-67, supr., 1967-70; sr. psychologist Kaiser Hosp., Hayward, Calif., 1970-72; pvt. practice psychology San Francisco, 1970-72; mem. staff Far No. Regional Ctr., Redding, Calif., 1970-74; dir. Redding Psychotherapy Group, 1974—, Vietnam Vets. Readjustment Program, Shasta and Tehama, 1984—; cons. in field. Author: (play) The Moon Cannot Be Stolen, 1985; contbr. articles to profl. jours.; patentee in field. Chmn. Shasta Dam P.U.D. Com., Shasta County, 1981-82, Shasta County Headstart Bd., 1982-85, Criminal Justice Adv. Bd. Shasta County, 1982-87, Youth and Family Counseling Ctr., Shasta County, 1986-89. Capt. U.S. Army, 1965-70. Recipient Danforth award Danforth Found., 1959; Woodrow Wilson Found. fellow, 1963; Smith Fund grantee, 1966; Dana scholar, 1960-63. Fellow Am. Bd. Med. Psychotherapy; mem. APA, Calif. State Psychol. Assn. (chpt. rep. 1990-95, bd. dirs. 1990-95, 98-99, chair membership com. 1993-95, exec. com. 1993-95, 98-99, chair publs. com. 1994-95, chair divsn. VI 1996, chair divsn. I 1997, Silver PSI award 1995), Shasta Cascade Psychol. Assn. (pres. 1990-91, mem. bd. dirs. 1990—, Outstanding Psychologist 1993), Eye Movement Desensitization and Reprocessing Network (Outstanding Rsch. award 1994), Eye Movement Desensitization and Reprocessing Internat. Assn. (bd. dirs. 1995—, chair 1996-97, pres.-elect 1998, pres. 1999-2000, Outstanding svc. award 1997). Democrat. Avocations: fly fishing, backpacking, camping, white water rafting. Office: Redding Psychotherapy Group 616 Azalea Ave Redding CA 96002-0217

WILSON, SIR DAVID MACKENZIE, retired museum director; b. Oct. 30, 1931; s. Joseph W.; m. Eva Sjogren, 1955. Litt.D., St. John's Coll., Cambridge, Eng., 1950; postgrad., Lund U., Sweden, 1953-54. Research asst. Cambridge U., 1954; asst. keeper Brit. Mus., London, 1954-64, dir., 1977-92; reader archaeology Anglo Saxon period London U., 1964-71, prof. medieval archaeology, 1971-76; joint head dept. Scandinavian studies Univ. Coll. London, 1973-76; retired museum director; b. Oct. 30, 1931; s. Joseph W.; Litt.D., St. John's Coll., Cambridge, Eng., 1950; postgrad. Lund U., Sweden, 1953-54; m. Eva Sjogren, 1955. Research asst. Cambridge U., 1954; asst. keeper Brit. Mus., London, 1954-64, dir., 1977-92; reader archaeology Anglo Saxon period London U., 1964-71, prof. medieval archaelogy, 1971-76; joint head dept. Scandinavian studies Univ. Coll. London, 1973-76. Home: The Lifeboat House, Castletown Isle of Man 1M9 1LD

WILSON, DORIS H., volunteer; b. Akron, Ohio, Jan. 26, 1921; d. Charles Peter and Emma Clara (Howald) Huff; m. Angus Francis Wilson, June 14, 1952; children: Ann Wilson Lambertus, Lea Wilson MacInnis. BS, U. Akron, 1945; postgrad., Framingham State Coll., 1965, Salem State Coll., 1968. Adminstrv. asst. divsn. comml. engr. Ohio Bell Telephone Co., Akron, 1941-52; adminstr. Framingham Ctr. Kindergarten and Nursery Sch., 1965-68. Author: A History of Great Neck, Ipswich, 1984, 96. Vol. nurse's aide ARC, Akron, 1940s; mem. Gov.'s Coun. Civilian Def., Boston, 1960-66; co-founder, charter mem. Hospice at Home, Wayland, Weston, Natick, Sudbury, Mass., 1978; chmn. West Suburban Area Boston Symphony Orch. Coun. of Friends, 1978-81; docent The Great House at Castle Hill, Ipswich, 1984—, The Whipple House, Ipswich, 1985—; treas. Nuclear Freeze Coun., Ipswich, 1986-87; charter mem., bd. dirs. Aplastic Anemia Found. of Am. New Eng. region, Brookline, Mass., 1987-92; vol. office asst. Habitat for Humanity, St. Petersburg, Fla., 1988. Recipient Election Poll Officer citation Gov. of Mass., 1980. Mem. AAUW (charter mem., pres. Framingham-Wellesley Br., North Shore Br., grantee 1974), Boston Symphony Assn. of Vols., Peace Action, Ipswich Hist. Soc., Ipswich Woman's Club, Ipswich Bay Yacht Club (dir. 1981-82), Friends of Glen Magna (Danvers, Mass. dir. 1991-93), Wayland Woman's Club (hon. mem., pres.). Democrat. Roman Catholic. Home: 8 Bowdoin Rd Ipswich MA 01938-2807

WILSON, EDWARD OSBORNE, biologist, educator, writer; b. Birmingham, Ala., June 10, 1929; s. Edward Osborne and Inez (Freeman) W.; m. Irene Kelley, Oct. 30, 1955; 1 child, Catherine Irene. BS, U. Ala., 1949, MS, 1950, LHD (hon.), 1980; PhD, Harvard U., 1955; DPhil, Uppsala (Sweden) U.; DS (hon.), Duke U., 1978, Grinnell Coll., 1978, U. West Fla., 1979, Lawrence U., 1979, Fitchburg State Coll., 1989, Macalester Coll., 1990, U. Mass., 1990, Oxford U., 1993, Ripon Coll., 1994, U. Conn., 1995, Ohio U., 1996, Bates Coll., 1996, Coll. Wooster, 1997, U. Guelph, 1997, U. Portland, 1997; LHD (hon.), Hofstra U., 1986, Muhlenburg Coll., 1998, Yale U., 1998, Pa. State U., Bradford Coll., 1997, Conn. Coll., 2000; DHC, U. Madrid Complutense, 1995, Conn. Coll., 2000; LLD, Simon Fraser U.; Drernat, U. Würzburg, 2000. Jr. fellow Soc. Fellows, Harvard U., 1953-56, mem. faculty, 1956—, Baird prof. sci., 1976-94, Pellegrino U. prof., 1994-97, univ. rsch. prof., 1997—, curator entomology, 1971-97, hon. curator entomology, 1997—; mem. selection com. Guggenheim Found., 1982-89; bd. dirs. World Wildlife Fund, 1983-94, Orgn. Tropical Studies, 1984-91, N.Y. Bot. Garden, 1991-95, Am. Mus. Natural History, 1992—, Am. Acad. Liberal Edn., 1993—, Nature Conservancy, 1994—, Conservation Internat., 1997—. Author: The Insect Societies, 1971, Sociobiology: The New Synthesis, 1975, On Human Nature, 1978 (Pulitzer prize for non-fiction 1979), (with C.J. Lumsden) Promethean Fire, 1983, Biophilia, 1984, (with Bert Holldobler) The Ants, 1990 (Pulitzer prize for non-fiction 1991), Success and Dominance in Ecosystems, 1990, The Diversity of Life, 1992 (Nat. Wildlife Assn. award, Deutsche Umweltstiftung Book award, Sir Peter Kent Conservation prize), (with Bert Holldobler) Journey to the Ants, 1994 (Phi Beta Kappa prize sci. 1995), Naturalist, 1994 (L.A. Times Book prize sci. 1995), In Search of Nature, 1996, Consilience: The Unity of Knowledge, 1998 (Forkosch award Internat. Acad. Humanism 2000), Biological Diversity: The Oldest Human Heritage, 1999. Recipient Cleve.-AAAS rsch. prize, 1967, Nat. Medal Sci., 1976, Leidy medal Acad. Natural Sci., Phila., 1979, Disting. Svc. award Am. Inst. Biol. Scis., 1976, Mercer award Ecol. Soc. Am., 1971, Founders Meml. award and L.O. Howard award Entomol. Soc. Am., 1972, 85, Archie Carr medal U. Fla., 1978, Disting. Svc. award Am. Humanist Soc., 1982, Tyler ecology prize, 1984, Silver medal Nat. Zool. Park, German Ecol. Inst. prize, 1987, Weaver award scholarly letters Ingersoll Found., 1989, Crafoord prize Royal Swedish Acad. Scis., 1990, Prix d'Inst. de la Vie, Paris, 1990, Revelle medal, 1990, Gold medal Worldwide Fund for Nature, 1990, Achievement award Nat. Wildlife Fedn., 1992, Shaw medal Mo. Bot. Garden, 1993, Internat. prize Biology Govt. of Japan, 1993, Eminent Ecologist award, 1994, Audubon medal Audubon Soc., 1995, AAAS Pub. Understanding Sci. award, 1995, John Hay award Orion Soc., 1995, Schubert prize, Germany, 1996, Washburn award Mus. Sci., 1996, Hutchinson Medal Garden Club Am., 1997, Stone award New Eng. Aquarium, 1999, Nonino prize Letters and Sci., Italy, 2000, King Faisal Prize for Sci., 2000, Kistler prize Found. for the Future, 2000, others; Guggenheim fellow, 1978. Fellow Am. Acad. Arts and Scis., Am. Philos. Soc. (Franklin medal 1998), Deutsche Akad. Naturforsch; mem. NAS, Am. Genetics Assn. (hon. life), Brit. Ecol. Soc. (hon. life), Entomol. Soc. Am. (hon. life), Zool. Soc. London (hon. life), Am. Humanist Assn. (hon. life, Humanist of Yr.), Acad. Humanism (hon. life), Netherlands Entomol. Soc. (hon. life), Royal Soc. London, Finnish Acad. Sci. and Letters, Russian Acad. Nat. Sci., Royal Soc. Sci. Uppsala (Sweden), others. Home: 9 Foster Rd Lexington MA 02421-5505 Office: Harvard U Mus Comparative Zoology Cambridge MA 02138

WILSON, ELDON RAY, minister; b. Tieton, Wash., Apr. 16, 1931; s. Frank Madison and Beatrice Jane (Snider) W.; m. LouCelle Charlotte Seward, Aug. 3, 1957; children: Randall Wayne, Gary Ray. BTh, Internat. Bible Coll., San Antonio, 1967; PhD, Sussex Coll., Hayward's Heath, Eng., 1972. Ordained to ministry Emmanuel Ch., 1956. Founder, pastor Emmanuel Tabernacle, Port Arthur, Tex., 1958-63; evangelist U.S., Can., 1963-65; founder, pastor Gospel Tabernacle, Ilion, N.Y., 1965-70; pastor Full Gospel Ch., Halifax, N.S., Can., 1970-72; missionary Europe, Africa, 1972-77; founder, pastor New Covenant Ch., Columbus, Ohio, 1977-84; missionary New Covenant Ministries, Columbus, 1984-97; acad. dean City Bible Coll., Utica, N.Y., 1998—; bd. dirs. Good News Mission, Bogota, Colombia, 1985—; trustee Team Missions, Internat., Elkton, Md., 1989—. Author: The New Creation, 1975. Bd. dirs. Kuyahoora Valley Libr., Newport, N.Y., 1985—; overseer Shekinah Ministries, Amsterdam, The Netherlands, Bread of Life Ministries, Bastogne, Belgium. With USN, 1951-55. Republican. Home: 7417 West St Newport NY 13416

WILSON, ELEANOR MCELROY, county official; b. Lancaster, Pa., Sept. 10, 1938; d. Hartford Ford and Jane Ann (Bowker) McElroy; m. Frank Eugene Wilson, July 17, 1976 (dec. Jan. 1980). AA, Monterey Peninsula Jr. Coll., Monterey, Calif., 1959; BA in Edn., San Jose State U., 1963; MA in Bus. Adminstrn./Mgmt., Webster U., St. Louis, 1981; MA in Internat. Rels., Salve Regina Coll., Newport, R.I., 1990; MA in Nat. Security/Strategic Studies, Naval War Coll., Newport, 1991. Sec. Geo. Dovolis Real Estate, Monterey, 1957-59; legal sec. Thompson & Thompson Attys., Monterey, 1959-61; legal asst., supr. Thomson J. Hudson, Atty., Monterey, 1963-68, legal asst., 1972-74. Mem. Orange County Grand Jury, Superior Ct., Santa Ana, Calif., 1982-83; citizen mem. Orange County Parole Bd., Santa Ana, 1993-96, 99—; mem. Orange County Juvenile Justice Commn., Orange, 1992—, chair, 1995. Col. USMCR, 1968-98. Decorated Legion of Merit, Meritorious Svc. medal, Navy Commendation medal, others. Mem. Marine Corps Heritage Found. (bd. dirs. 1992-98), Marine Corps Aviation Assn. (bd. dirs. 1980-94, bd. advisers 1994—), Sloan Found. (bd. dirs. 1996-98). Republican. Episcopalian. Avocations: reading, golf, tennis, travel. Home: 22476 Alcudia Mission Viejo CA 92692-1157

WILSON, ESTHER ELINORE, technical college educator; b. Uehling, Nebr., Nov. 4, 1921; d. Lorenz John and Dorothea Emma Rosena (Schmidt) Paulsen; m. Billy LeRoy Wilson, Nov. 14, 1919; 1 child, Frances Ann Wilson Dellar. BS, Morningside Coll., 1950; postgrad., U. Nebr., 1947-80, U. S.D., 1954-83; MS, U. Minn., 1963. Cert. postsecondary tchr., Iowa. Tchr. Irvington (Nebr.) Pub. Schs., 1942-44, Immanuel Luth. Schs., Wichita, Kans., 1944-45, Winnebago (Nebr.) Pub. Schs., 1946-50, Nat. Bus. Coll., Sioux City, Iowa, 1950-51; tchr., asst. prin. Liberty Consol. Sch., Merrill, Iowa, 1951-55; mktg. tchr. coord. South Sioux City (Nebr.) Community Schs., 1955-86; adj. faculty prof. adult basic edn. Western Iowa Tech. Coll., Sioux City, 1989-94; mgr. rental properties Sioux City, 1950-2000; real estate assoc. State Nat., Dakota City, Nebr., 1988-92, Century 21 Marketplace, Sioux City, 1987-88; advt. sales mgr. Auto Hotline, South Sioux City, 1986-87. Author: I Said I Would, 1995; contbg. author: Siouxland Anthology, 1995, Capturing Our Heritage, 1996, The Lutheran Message, 1999. Vol. tchr. N.E. Nebr. C.C., South Sioux City, 1987-90; supt. St. Paul's Luth. Sunday Sch., Sioux City, 1972-76; treas. Hope Luth. Ch., 1989-95, historian 1995-97, nursing home lamplighter 1987-92, 95—; lamplighter, vol. nursing

homes Walker Colonial Village and Regency Square Care Ctr., 1987—; co-pres. Friends of Libr., South Sioux City, 1986-88; fundraiser South Sioux City Pub. Libr., 1984-85; pres. Am. Cancer Soc., Dakota County, Nebr., 1979-88; sponsor South Sioux City Distributive Club of Am., 1956-86; state pres. Nebr. Bus. Edn. Assn., 1979, Distributive Edn. Tchrs. Assn., 1980. Recipient Outstanding Svc. to State Orgns., Nebr. Vocat. Edn. Assn., 1976, Woman of the Yr. Am. Bus. Women Assn., 1972. Mem. Nebr. State Edn. Assn. (sec., treas., v.p., pres., Dedicated Svc. award 1986, Women of Excellence awards 1997), NEA, South Sioux City Chamberettes (sec., v.p., pres. 1972-89, 1st v.p. 1996-97, pres. 1998-99), Am. Federated Women's Club (sec., v.p., pres.), Svc. Corps Ret. Execs. (historian 1995-00, sec. 1997-98, sec.-treas. 1998-00), Am. Bus. Women's Assn. (sec., Sr. SOOS 1998-99). Avocations: reading, political and economic studies, internet, gardening, evangelism. Home and Office: 435 Dixon Path South Sioux City NE 68776-5300

WILSON, EVELYN L., legal educator; b. Parkersburg, W.Va., July 7, 1949; m. Charles A. Shropshire, Oct. 15, 1983; children: Charles A. II, Jeremy D. AB, Oberlin Coll., 1971; MS, U. Utah, 1975; JD, Paul M. Hebert Law Ctr., Baton Rouge, La., 1983. Bar: La. 1983. Sr. budget examiner N.Y. Dept. Budget, Albany, 1977-80; jud. law clk. Supreme Ct. La., New Orleans, 1983-84; atty. Losavio & Weinstein, Baton Rouge, 1984-86; prof. law So. U. Law Ctr., Baton Rouge, 1986—. Author: Louis Berry--A Man Among Men, 1993; contbr. chpt. to book, articles to profl. jours. Bd. dirs. Capital Area Legal Svcs. Coun., Baton Rouge, 1984-88; legal advisor Woodland Cmty. Ctr., Inc., Clinton, La., 1985—; v.p. PTO, clinton, 1999-2000. Mem. Feliciana Bar Assn. (pres. 1993-94). E-mail: Ewilson@sus.edu. Office: So U Law Ctr PO Box 9294 Baton Rouge LA 70813-9294

WILSON, FREDERIC SANDFORD, pharmaceutical company executive; b. Schenectady, NY, Mar. 28, 1944; s. Robert Omer and Isabel May (Sandford) W.; children: Amy Kathleen, Adrienne Ann; m. Judith Ann Goettsche, Feb. 7, 1973; children: Marla Ann, Brian Bennett, Jessica Lea, Jennifer Lynn. BS, Syracuse U., 1968. Acct. exec. Mastropaul Design Inc., Syracuse, N.Y., 1969-70; copy editor Norwich Eaton Pharms., Norwich, N.Y., 1970-72; sales rep. Norwich Eaton Pharms., Gary, Ind., 1972-73; asst. product mgr. Norwich Eaton Pharms., Norwich, 1974-75, mktg. svcs. mgr., 1975-76, product mgr., 1977-81, bus. devel. mgr., 1981-83, sr. product mgr., 1983-85, mgr. med. foods, 1986-89; assoc. mktg. mgr. P&G Pharms., Norwich, 1989-92; dir. profl. rels. P & G Pharms., Cin., 1993-96; mgr. mktg. svcs. P&G, Cin., 1997-98; mgr. CME P&G, Cin., 1998—; cons. Sandoz Nutrition Corp., Mpls., 1992. Inventor Jejunostomy Kit, 1981, Vivonex T.E.N. med. food, 1983, Tolerex med. food, 1987. Bd. dirs. Syracuse U. Minority Access Program, 1989-91; bd. dirs., sec., vice chair found. adv. bd. Am. Osteo. Found.; mem. Alliance for Continuing Med. Edn.; mem. Nat. Task Force on CME Provider/Industry Collaboration. Mem. Global Alliance Med. Edn. (bd. dirs., treas.), Pharms. Alliance for Continuing Med. Edn. Office: Procter & Gamble (SB2-3B5) 8700 Mason-Montgomery Rd Mason OH 45040-9462

WILSON, HENRY ARTHUR, JR., management consultant; b. Detroit, June 12, 1939; s. Henry Arthur and Ruth (Scott) W.; m. Mildred Rendell, June 17, 1961; 1 child, Suzanne. B.S., Mich. Luth. Coll., 1968; M.A., U. Detroit, 1976. Police officer Grosse Pointe Park Police Dept., Mich., 1960-68; v.p. Uniflight, Inc., St. Clare Shore, Mich., 1968-73; coordinator Criminal Justice Inst., Detroit, 1973-76; ptnr. Grant Thorton (formerly Alexander Grant & Co.), Detroit, 1976-92; pres., owner Thunderboat Racing, Inc., 1998; grand sec., CEO Grand Lodge F & A.M., Mich.; CEO Mich. Masonic Home; pres., CEO, Mich. Masonic Home Charitably Found., 1996-97. Author: Masonic Etiquette and Protocol, 1985; sr. warden St. Columba Episcopal Ch., Detroit, 1976—; bd. dirs. Grosse Pointe Yacht Club, 1997—. Served with USAF, 1957-60. Mem. Certified Data Processing Auditors Assn., Masons (grand master Mich. 1984-85). Republican. Avocation: boating. Office: 1022 Nottingham Rd Grosse Pointe Park MI 48230-1332

WILSON, HUGH STEVEN, lawyer; b. Paducah, Ky., Nov. 27, 1947; s. Hugh Gipson and Rebekah (Dunn) W.; m. Clare Maloney, Apr. 28, 1973; children: Morgan Elizabeth, Zachary Hunter, Samuel Gipson. BS, Ind. U., 1968; JD, U. Chgo., 1971; LLM, Harvard U., 1972. Bar: Calif. 1972, U.S. Dist. Ct. (cen. dist.) Calif. 1972, U.S. Dist. Ct. (so. dist.) Calif. 1973, U.S. Ct. Appeals (9th cir.) 1975, U.S. Dist. Ct. (no. dist.) Calif. 1977, U.S. Supreme Ct. 1978, U.S. Dist. Ct. (ea. dist.) 1980. Assoc. Latham & Watkins, Los Angeles, 1972-78, ptnr., 1978—. Recipient Jerome N. Frank prize U. Chgo. Law Sch., 1971. Mem. ABA, Los Angeles County Bar Assn., Order of Coif, Calif. Club., Coronado Yacht Club. Republican. Avocations: lit., zoology.

WILSON, IMOGENE R., counselor; b. Atlanta, Feb. 29, 1944; d. Henry and Edna Pope; m. June 9, 1979 (dec. Mar. 1980); 1 child, Bejide. BS in Elem. Edn., W.Va. State Coll., 1968; MA in Tchg., Trinity Coll., 1973; cert. advanced studies, Howard U., 1983, PhD, 1995. Cert. counseling, elem. edn., D.C. Elem. tchr. D.C. Schs., Washington, 1968-95, counselor, 1995—; counselor Washington Mental Health Counseling Ctr., 1987-89. Home: 11005 Willow Bottom Dr Columbia MD 21044-1065

WILSON, JAMES MILLER, IV, cardiovascular surgeon, educator; b. Atlanta, Mar. 11, 1946; s. James Miller Wilson III and Sara Sharp; m. Lisa VanLandingham; children: James Miller V, Robert Paul, Michael Simpson, Sara Ann. Student, Emory U.; MD, Duke U., 1971. Diplomate Am. Bd. Surgery, Am. Bd. Thoracic Surgery. Intern N.Y. Hosp., 1971-72; resident N.Y. Hosp.-Cornell Med. Ctr., 1972-73, U. Calif., San Francisco, 1975-80; attending staff Christ Hosp., Cin., 1980—, Bethesda Hosp., Cin., 1980—, Jewish Hosp., Cin., 1980—, Univ. Hosp., Cin., 1982—, Deaconess Hosp, Cin., 1982—; chmn. dept. cardiovasc. surgery Deaconess Hosp., Cin., 1985—; attending staff VA Med Ctr., Cin., 1983—, Children's Hosp., Cin., 1984—, Good Samaritan Hosp., Cin., 1994—; assoc. prof. clin. surgery U. Cin. Coll. Med., 1985—; open heart surgery adv. com., Ohio, 1995—: lectr. in field. Contbr. articles to profl. jours. Lt. Comdr. submarine svc. USN, 1973-75. Fellow ACS, Am. Coll. Cardiology; mem. AMA, U.S. Naval Submarine League, Am. Assn. Thoracic Surgery, Assn. Acad. Surgery, Soc. Thoracic Surgeons, Am. Heart Assn. (mem. cardiovasc. coun.), Ohio State Med. Assn., Cin. Acad. Medicine, Howard C. Nafziger Soc. Avocations: music, diving, hiking, skiing, horses. Office: 311 Straight St Cincinnati OH 45219-1018

WILSON, JAMES NOEL, orthopaedic surgeon; b. Coventry, England, Dec. 25, 1919; s. Alexander and Isobel Barbara (Fairweather) W.; m. Patricia Norah McCullough, Sept. 3, 1945; 4 children. Resident Birmingham (Eng.) Gen. Hosp., England, 1943, Birmingham & Coventry, England, 1947-52; cons. orthopaedic surgeon Cardiff United Hosps., Wales, 1952-55, Royal Nat. Orthopaedic Hosp., London, 1955-84, Hosp. Nervous Diseases, London, 1962-84; prof. orthopaedics Addis Ababa, 1985-2000. Editor: Fractures and Joint Injuries, 5th edit., 1976, 6th edit., 1982; contbr. articles to profl. jours. Vice-chmn. Impact Found., U.K., 1988—. Capt. Royal Army Med. Corps., 1943-46. Decorated Order Brit. Empire. Fellow Royal Soc. Medicine (pres. orthop. sect. 1982, hon. fellow 1998); World Orthop. Concern (pres. 1979-84, newsletter editor 1988—), Brit. Orthop. Assn. (travelling fellow 1954, editl. sec. 1972-76), Egyptian Orthop. Assn. (hon.), Bangladesh Orthop. Soc. (life). Mem. Ch. of England. Avocations: golf, photography, gardening. Home: The Chequers, Waterdell, Near Watford Herts WD2 7LP, England

WILSON, JAMES REID, JR., publishing executive; b. Phila., Aug. 5, 1934; s. James Reid Wilson and Florence Dunn; m. Eve-Ann Jones; children: Suzanne Winters, Diantha Curtis. BS in Econs., U. Pa., 1956. Assoc. dir. western hemisphere promotion The N.Y. Times, N.Y.C., 1966-69, mgr. indsl. advt., 1969-74; mgr. corp. advt. U.S. News & World Report, N.Y.C., 1974-79, advt. mgr., 1979-85, mktg. mgr., 1985-86; sr. v.p. Newspaper Advt. Bur., N.Y.C., 1986-93; dir. Izvestia/Hearst, WeMbl, N.Y.C. and Moscow, 1993-94; pres. Media Ptnr., N.Y.C., 1995-97; ad sales dir. Forbes SIP, N.Y.C., 1997-2000, v.p., 2000—. Pres. Pa. Assn. Retarded Citizens, 1969-71; sr. v.p. Assn. Retarded Citizens U.S., Arlington, Tex., 1975-77, pres. 1977-79. Mem. St. Nicholas Soc., Union League, Scarsdale Golf Club, Penn Club, N.Y. Sons of the Revolution. Republican. Presbyterian. Office: Forbes SIP 28 W 23rd St New York NY 10010-5204

WILSON, JOHN ERIC, biochemistry educator; b. Champaign, Ill., Dec. 13, 1919; s. William Courtney and Marie Winette (Lytle) W.; m. Marion Ruth Heaton, June 7, 1947; children: Kenneth Heaton, Douglas Courtney, Richard Mosher. SB, U. Chgo., 1941; MS, U. Ill., 1944; PhD, Cornell U., 1948. Rsch. asst. Pyroxylin Products, Inc., Chgo., summers 1941-42, Gen. Foods Corp., Hoboken, N.J., summer, 1943; asst. in chemistry U. Ill., 1941-44; asst. in biochemistry Cornell U. Med. Coll., N.Y.C., 1944-48, rsch. assoc., 1948-50; asst. prof. biochemistry U. N.C., Chapel Hill, 1950-60, assoc. prof., 1960-65, prof., 1965-90, prof. emeritus, 1990—, dir. grad. studies, dept. biochemistry, 1965-71, acting dir. neurobiology program, 1968-69, assoc. dir., 1969-72, dir., 1972-73; Kenan prof. U. Utrecht, The Netherlands, 1978. Mem. editl. bd. Jour. Neurochemistry, 1987-94; contbr. numerous articles on biochemistry and neurochemistry to profl. publs. Scoutmaster Occoneechee coun. Boy Scouts Am., 1959-66; mem. Chapel Hill Twp. Adv. Coun., 1978-85, Orange County (N.C.) Planning Bd., 1979-85. Fellow AAAS; mem. Am. Chem. Soc., Am. Soc. for Biochemistry and Molecular Biology, Am. Soc. Neurochemistry, Internat. Soc. for Neurochemistry, Internat. Brain Rsch. Orgn., Soc. Neurosci. (coun. 1969-70, chmn. fin. com. 1973-78, organizer and mem. exec. com. N.C. chpt. 1974-75), Harvey Soc., Sigma Xi, Phi Lambda Upsilon, Alpha Chi Sigma, Beta Theta Pi. Home: 214 Spring Ln Chapel Hill NC 27514-3540

WILSON, JOHN PASLEY, law educator; b. Newark, Apr. 7, 1933; s. Richard Henry and Susan Agnes (Pasley) W.; m. Elizabeth Ann Reed, Sept 10, 1955 (div.); children: David Cables, John, Jr., Cicely Reed. AB, Princeton U., 1955; LLB, Harvard U., 1962. Bar: N.J. 1962, U.S. Dist. Ct. N.J. 1962, Mass. 1963, U.S. Dist. Ct. Mass. 1963. Budget examiner Exec. Office of Pres., Bur. of Budget, Washington, 1955-56; assoc. Riker, Danzig, Scherer & Brown, Newark, 1962-63; asst. dean Harvard U. Law Sch., Cambridge, Mass., 1963-67; assoc. dean Boston U. Law Sch., 1968-82; dean Golden Gate U. Sch. Law, San Francisco, 1982-88, prof., 1988—; vis. prof. dept. health policy and mgmt. Harvard U., 1988; cons. Nat. Commn. for the Protection of Human Subjects of Biomed. and Behavioral Rsch.; mem. Mass. Gov's. Commn. on Civil and Legal Rights of Developmentally Disabled; former chmn. adv. com. Ctr for Community Legal Edn., San Francisco. Author: The Rights of Adolescents in the Mental Health System. Contbr. chpts. to books, articles to profl. jours. Bd. dirs. Greater Boston Legal Svcs., Chewonki Found.; mem. Health Facilities Appeals Bd., Commonwealth of Mass.; assoc. mem. Democratic Town Com., Concord; chmn. Bd. Assessors, Concord; bd. overseers Boston Hosp. for Women, past chmn. med. affairs com.; past mem. instl. rev. bd. Calif. Pacific Hosp., San Francisco. Served to lt. (j.g.) USNR, 1956-59. NIMH grantee, 1973. Mem. Nat. Assn. Securities Dealers (arbitrator). Office: Golden Gate U Sch Law 536 Mission St San Francisco CA 94105-2967

WILSON, JOHNNIE LOU, social work educator, retired; b. Moscow, Tex., Sept. 27, 1928; d. John Wesley and Hattie Idelle (Mitchell) Sprayberry; m. William Hayden Greene Wilson Sr., Apr. 23, 1950 (div.); children: William H. Greene Jr., John Beverly Greene, Lynn Greene Wilson Goodrum, David Greene, Diane Greene Wilson Hawk. AA in Bus. Adminstrn., Lee Coll., 1948; BA, Tex. Woman's U., 1980. Sec. Exxon-Humble, Baytown, Tex., 1947-50; social work lab. supr. Tex. Woman's U., Denton, 1974-94, ret., 1994; owner Abbey Demo Svcs., Bowie, Tex., 1998—. Author poetry. Mem. Cancer Soc. Denton, 1990-94, Cystic Fibrosis, Denton, 1990-94, Heart Assn., Denton, 1990-94, Mimbres Arts Coun., Silver City, N.Mex., 1996-99, Cmty. Concert Assn., Silver City, 1996-99; sec.-treas. Daus. of King, 1990—; mem. altar guild Episcopal Ch., 1990—, fellowship com., 1990-95, vestry, 1992-94, chair food com., 1994-99; mem. Environ. Com., Silver City, 1995-99. Recognition award Famous Poet for 1995, 1995, Editor's Choice award Nat. Libr. Poetry, 1996. Mem. Internat. Soc. Poets (Disting. Mem. award 1996). Democrat. Avocations: poetry, physical fitness, community help projects, church related activities. E-mail: Johnn88062@Juno.com. Home: PO Box 890 503 Malachite Ave Tyrone NM 88065

WILSON, JOHNNY LEE, group publisher; b. Santa Maria, Calif., Oct. 20, 1950; s. John Henry and Bobbie Lou (Henson) W.; m. Susan Lynne Leavelle, Aug. 28, 1970 (div. 1998); children: Jennifer Lynne, Jonathan Lee; m. Wai Lam Chu, May 21, 1999; children: William Chu, Talyn Chu. BA, Calif. Bapt. Coll., Riverside, 1972; MDiv, Golden Gate Bapt. Seminary, Mill Valley, Calif., 1975; ThM, So. Bapt. Theol. Seminary, Louisville, 1978, PhD, 1981. Pastor Rollingwood Bapt. Ch., San Pablo, Calif., 1974-75, Temple Bapt. Ch., Sacramento, Calif., 1975-77, Hermosa-Redondo Beach (Calif.) Ministries, 1981-82, Immanuel. Bapt. Ch., La Puente, Calif., 1982-86; asst. editor Computer Gaming World, Anaheim, Calif., 1986-89, editor, 1989-94; editor-in-chief Computer Gaming World, San Francisco, 1993-99; group pub. Wizards of the Coast, Renton, Wash., 1999—; pres. and prof. of Old Testament Calif. Korean Bapt. Seminary, Walnut, 1990-93; adj. prof. O.T. studies So. Calif. Ctr., Garden Grove, Calif., 1981-86; mem. com. Software Pub. Assn. Ratings Group, Washington, 1994; mem. adv. coun. Recreation Software Adv. Coun., 1995; bd. govs. Acad. Interactive Arts and Scis., 1995; bd. dirs. Turbine Entertainment. Author: The Sim City Planning Commission Handbook, 1990, The Sim Earth Bible, 1991; co-author: The Mercer Dictionary of Bible, 1990, Sid Meier's Civilization: Rome on 640K A Day, 1992, Civilization: Call to Power Official Strategy Guide, 1999. Named to Outstanding Young Men of Am., Jaycees, Ala., 1977, Best Software Reviewer, Software Pubs. Assn., Washington, 1990. Mem. Sci. Fiction and Fantasy Writers Am. (assoc.). Avocations: drama, miniatures gaming, writing. Home: 4664 144th Pl SE Bellevue WA 98006-3158 Office: Wizards of the Coast 1801 Lind Ave SW Renton WA 98055-4068

WILSON, JOSEPH CHARLES, IV, ambassador; b. Bridgeport, Conn., Nov. 6, 1949; s. Joseph Charles III and Phyllis (Finnell) W.; m. Susan Dale Otchis, Apr. 27, 1973 (div. 1986); m. Valerie Elise Plame, Apr. 3, 1998; children: Sabrina Cecile, Joseph Charles, Trevor Rolph, Samantha Finnell Diana. BA in History, U. Calif., Santa Barbara, 1972. Fgn. svc. officer Dept. of State, Washington, 1976-98; congl. fellow Am. Polit. Sci. Assn., Washington, 1985-86; dep. chief of mission Am. Embassy, Bujumbura, Burundi, 1982-85, Brazzaville, Congo, 1986-88, Baghdad, Iraq, 1988-91; amb. Gabon, Sao Tome and Principe, 1992-95; polit. adv. to Commdr. in Chief U.S. Armed Forces Europe, 1995-97; spl. asst. to pres., sr. dir. for African affairs Nat. Security Coun., Washington, 1997-98; pres. JC Wilson Internat. Ventures, Washington, 1998—. Recipient Disting. Alumni award U. Calif. Santa Barbara, 1991, Comdr. Order of Equatorial Star govt. Gabon award, 1995, Disting. Def. Dept. Civilian award, 1997; named hon. adm. County Commr., El Paso, Tex., 1991. Mem. Am. Polit. Sci. Assn., Am. Fgn. Svc. Assn. (William R. Rivkin award 1987), U. Calif. Santa Barbara Alumni Assn., San Onofre Surfing Club. Avocations: golf, bicycling, fitness. Office: 1717 Pennsylvania Ave NW Washington DC 20006-4619

WILSON, JOSEPH MORRIS, III, lawyer; b. Milw., July 26, 1945; s. Joseph Morris Jr. and Phyllis Elizabeth (Cresson) W.; children: Elizabeth J., Eric M.; m. Dixie Lee Brock, Mar. 23, 1984. BA, Calif. State U., Chico, 1967; MA, U. Washington, 1968; JD summa cum laude, Ohio State U., 1976. Bar: Alaska 1976, U.S. Dist. Ct. Alaska 1976, U.S. Ct. Appeals (9th cir.) 1986. Recruiter and vol. U.S. Peace Corps, People's Republic of Benin, 1969-73; legal intern U.S. Ho. of Reps., Washington, 1975; ptnr. Guess & Rudd P.C., Anchorage, 1976-88, chmn. comml. dept., 1981-82, ptnr. compensation com., 1982-84; mgr. Alaska taxes, sr. tax atty. BP Exploration Inc., Alaska, 1990-99; bus. law instr. U. Alaska, Anchorage, 1977-78. Mem. ABA, Alaska Bar Assn. Democrat. Club: World Affairs Coun. Avocations: music, sports, travel. Home and Office: 2556 Palmera Cir Las Vegas NV 89121-4016

WILSON, JULIA ANN YOTHER, lawyer; b. Dallas, Sept. 6, 1958; d. Julian White and Mary Ann (Estes) Yother; m. Eugene Richard Wilson, 1983. BA, East Ctrl. U., Ada, Okla., 1980; JD, U. Okla., 1983. Bar: Okla. 1990, Calif. 1993, D.C. 1995; U.S. Ct. Appeals (9th cir.) Calif. 1993, U.S. Supreme Ct. 1993, U.S. Dist. Ct. (ctrl. dist.) Calif. 1993, U.S. Dist. Ct. (we. dist.) Okla., 1997. Assoc. Law Office of George Rodda Jr., Newport Beach, Calif., 1984-96; sole practice law Oklahoma City, 1996-97; assoc. Coldiron, Wilson & Assocs., Oklahoma City, 1997—. Served to 1st lt. USAR, 1980-86. Mem. ABA, D.C. Bar Assn., Calif. Bar Assn., Oklahoma County Bar Assn., Okla. Bar Assn. (litigation sect.), Orange County Bar Assn. Office: Coldiron Wilson & Assocs 1800 E Memorial Rd Ste 106 Oklahoma City OK 73131-1827

WILSON, KAREN JEANINE, education educator; b. Houston, Feb. 21, 1957; d. Calvin Coolidge and Carrie Alice Wilson. Student, U. Houston, 1974-75; BA, Tex. A&M U., 1978, MS, 1985, EdD, 1992. Tng. program coord. New Dimensions tng. program Tex. A&M U., College Station, 1978-79; sr. tng. specialist Tex. Energy Extension Svc./Tex. A&M U., College Station, 1988-91; program coord. Tex. Energy Extension Svc./U. Tex.-Pan Am., Edinberg, 1991-92; dir. tng. SafePlace: A Sexual Assault & Domestic Violence Survival Ctr, Austin, Tex., 1992—; mem. adv. bd. Tex. Energy Devel. Project, Austin, 1988-92; cons. Tex. Coun. on Family Violence, Austin, 1996-98, Ft. Hays (Kans.) State U., 1997, SAHELI: Support Orgn. for Asian Women, Austin, 1998—. Author: When Violence Begins at Home, 1997. Mem. nat. awards nominating com. Resourceful Women, 1997-98; mem. adv. bd. Everywoman's Self-Def., 1998—; vol. OUT Youth, Austin, 1998 Children's Shelter of Tex., Austin, 1995-96; vol. advocate Brazos County Rape Crisis Ctr., Bryan, Tex., 1986-88, Shelter for Battered Women, Bryan, 1984-85; co-founder Tex. Energy and Aging Consortium, 1990; co-chair Austin Met. Ministries Task Force on Family Violence, 1999—. Recipient Cert. of Appreciation, State of Tex. Ho. of Reps., 1979. Mem. ASTD (co-founder Brazos County chpt., v.p. comms. 1990-91), Tex. Coun. on Family Violence, Golden Key Nat. Honor Soc. (hon.). Avocations: reading, drawing, writing. Office: SafePlace PO Box 19454 Austin TX 78760-9454

WILSON, KEITH DUDLEY, retired media and music educator, consultant; b. Windermere, July 13, 1936; s. Charles Alexander and Fanny (Shaw) W.; 1 child, Nicholas. BA with honors, Kings Coll., Cambridge, 1957, MA, 1960; LittD (hon.), Salford Coll. Tech., 2000. Lectr. Brit. Coun./Zagreb Univ., Croatia, 1957-58; assoc. prof., dir. TV Brit. Coun. Tehran U., Iran, 1958-64; reader Brit. Coun. Osmania U., Hyderabad, India, 1964-66; head of liberal edn. Salford Coll. of Tech., U.K., 1967-72, head of humanities, 1972-85; head of performing arts and media U. Coll. Salford, 1985-90; dir. ctr. for media performance and comm. U. Salford, 1990-96, founding chief exec. internat. media ctr., 1993-99; dean faculty of media, music and performance Salford U., 1996-99; tutor, counsellor Open U., 1972-90; dir. TVUK, Adelphi Prodns., Salford, 1988-99, Channel M, 1997-2000; chair PRS John Lennon awards, 1990-93; co-chair NYNEX Cable TV, Manchester, 1993-95; vis. acad. The Brit. Coun., Korea, 1992; founder over 30 higher edn. courses in music, media, drama, recording, entertainment orgns., media and science, new media; European edn. advisor/cons. media, music and rec. industries, 2000—. Contbr. articles to profl. jours. and nat. papers; concert tours to Brazil, Belgium, Holland, Iceland, Norway, Denmark, Greece, Ecuador, Russia and Hungary; residencies at Edinburgh Internat. Festival, broadcasts and recordings, 1986-97. Mem. U. Salford Centenary Com., 1994-96, City of Salford LS Lowry Centenary, 1988, The Lowry, The Nat. Landmark Millennium Project for the Arts, The Digital World Ctr.; founder Salford U. Brass Band, Wind Band, Big Band, Soundworks, Jazz Ensembles, Groove Machine, Aspects Theatre; mem. City Pride Initiative, Manchester, 1993-97, Fellowship Gt. Britain Sasakawa Found., Japan, 1991. Fellow Royal Soc. of Arts; mem. Royal TV Soc., British Film Inst., British Acad. of Film and TV., Prodrs. Assn. Cinema and TV. Avocations: nordic lands and culture, wines of the world, walking. Home and Office: 60 Central Rd, Didsbury, Manchester M204 ZA, England

WILSON, KELCE STEVEN, air force officer, electrical engineer; b. Orange, N.J., Oct. 14, 1966; s. Edward Arthur and Elinor Irene Wilson; m. Robyn Lee Wilson, Sept. 19, 1992; children: Kalyn Ashlee, Kristine Amanda. BSEE, U. Ariz., 1988; MBA, Chapman U., Orange, Calif., 1993; MSEE, Air Force Inst. Tech., 1994, PhD in Electromagnetic Field Theory, 1998. Commd. 2d lt. USAF, 1988, advanced through grades to major, 1989; elec. engr. Consol. Space Ops. Ctr., L.A., 1989-93, Air Force Rsch. Lab. Target Signatures, Wright-Patterson AFB, Ohio, 1998—. Contbr. articles to conf. procs. Tchr. AWANA, Grace Cmty. Ch., Huber Heights, Ohio, 1994—. Mem. Eta Kappa Nu, Tau Beta Pi. Avocation: woodworking.

WILSON, KENNETH GEDDES, physics research administrator, educator; b. Waltham, Mass., June 8, 1936; s. E. Bright and Emily Fisher (Buckingham) W.; m. Alison Brown, 1982. A.B., Harvard U., 1956, DSc hon., 1981; Ph.D., Calif. Tech. Inst., 1961; Ph.D. (hon.), U. Chgo., 1976. From asst. prof. to prof. physics Cornell U., Ithaca, N.Y., 1963-88, James A. Weeks prof. in phys. sci., 1974-87; Hazel C. Youngberg Trustees Disting prof. The Ohio State U., Columbus, 1988—. Co-author: Redesigning Education, 1974. Recipient Nobel prize in physics, 1982, Dannie Heinemann prize, 1973, Boltzmann medal, 1975, Wolf prize, 1980, A.C. Eringen medal, 1984, Franklin medal, 1982, Aneesur Rahman prize, 1993. Mem. NAS, Am. Philos. Soc., Am. Phys. Soc., Am. Acad. Arts and Scis.

WILSON, LANFORD, playwright; b. Lebanon, Mo., Apr. 13, 1937; s. Ralph E(ugene) and Violetta (Tate) W. Student, San Diego State Coll., 1955-56; PhD in Humanities (hon.), U. Mo., 1985, Grinnell Coll., 1994; PhD in Lit. (hon.), Southampton Coll., 1995. Playwright, 1962—; resident playwright, dir., co-founder Circle Repertory Co., N.Y.C., 1969-95. Author: (plays) So Long at the Fair, 1963, Home Free!, 1964, No Trespassing, 1964, The Sandcastle, 1964, The Madness of Lady Bright, 1964, Ludlow Fair, 1965, Balm in Gilead, 1965, This is the Rill Speaking, 1965, Days Ahead, 1965, Sex is Between Two People, 1965, The Gingham Dog, 1966, The Rimers of Eldritch, 1966, Wandering, 1966, Lemon Sky, 1969, Serenading Louie, 1970, The Great Nebula in Orion, 1970, The Hot L Baltimore, 1972, The Family Continues, 1972, The Mound Builders, 1975, Fifth of July, 1978, Brontasaurus, 1978, Talley's Folly, 1979, A Tale Told, 1981, Angels Fall, 1983, A Betrothal, 1984, Talley & Son, 1985, Burn This, 1987, A Poster of the Cosmos, 1987, The Moonshot Tape, 1990, Redwood Curtain, 1991, Trinity, 1993, I'm Not the Ocean, 1995, Sympathetic Magic, 1996, A Sense of Place (Virgil is Still the Frogboy), 1997, Your Everyday Ghost Story, 1997, Book of Days, 1998, Rain Dance, 1999; translator Three Sisters, 1984; author: (books) Balm in Gilead and Other Plays, 1966, The Rimers of Eldritch and Other Plays, 1968, The Gingham Dog, 1969, Lemon Sky, 1970, The Hot L Baltimore, 1973, The Mound Builders, 1976, Fifth of July, 1979, Talley's Folly, 1980, Angels Fall, 1983, Serenading Louie, 1985, Talley & Son, 1986, Burn This, 1988, Redwood Curtain, 1992, 21 Short Plays, 1994, By the Sea, 1996, Collected Plays, Vol. I, 1997, Vol. II, 1999, Vol. III, 1999, A Sense of Place, 1999, Book of Days, 2000. ABC Yale fellow, 1969; Rockefeller grantee, 1967, 73, Guggenheim grantee, 1970, NEA grantee, 1990; recipient Vernon Rice award, 1966-67, Inst. Arts and Letters award, 1970, Obie award, 1972, 75, 84, 97, Outer Critics Circle award, 1973, Drama Critics Circle award, 1973, 80, Pulitzer prize, 1980, Brandeis award, 1981, John Steinbeck award, 1990, Edward Albee Last Frontier award, 1994, Am. Acad. of Achievement award, 1995, Am. Assn. Theatre Critics Best Play award, 1998; inducted into Theater Hall of Fame, 1996, Mo. Writers Hall of Fame, 1998. Mem. Dramatists Guild Council.

WILSON, LEVON EDWARD, law educator, lawyer; b. Charlotte, N.C., Apr. 2, 1954; s. James A. and Thomasina Wilson. BSBA, Western Carolina U., 1976; JD, N.C. Ctrl. U., 1979. Bar: N.C. 1981, U.S. Dist. Ct. (mid. dist.) N.C. 1981, U.S. Tax Ct. 1981, U.S. Ct. Appeals (4th cir.) 1982, U.S. Supreme Ct. 1984; lic. real estate broker, N.C.; cert. mediator N.C. Alternative Dispute Resolution Commn. Pvt. practice Greensboro, N.C., 1981-85; asst. county atty. Guilford County, Greensboro, 1985-88; asst. prof. N.C. Agrl. & Tech. State U., Greensboro, 1988-91; asst. prof. Western Carolina U., Cullowhee, N.C., 1991-96, assoc. prof., head dept. bus. adminstrn., law and mktg., 1996—; pres. Trade Brokers Cons.; legal counsel, bd. dirs. Rhodes Assocs., Inc., Greensboro, 1982—; legal counsel Guilford County Sheriff's Dept., Greensboro, 1985-88; bd. dirs. Webster Enterprises, Inc. Contbr. articles to profl. jours. Bd. dirs. Post Advocacy Detention Program; active mem. Prison Litigation Study Task Force, Adminstrn. Justice Study Com. Recipient Svc. award Blacks in Mgmt., 1980, Excellence in Tchg. award Jay I. Kneedler Found. of Western Carolina U., 1994-95; Student in Free Enterprise fellow. Mem. ABA, N.C. Bar Assn., Acad. Legal Studies in Bus., Southeastern Acad. Legal Studies in Bus. (former editor-in-chief Jour. of Legal Studies in Bus., mng. editor), N.C. Assn. Police Attys., N.C. Real Estate Eudcators Assn., So. Acad. Legal Studies in Bus., Phi Delta Phi, Beta Gamma Sigma. Democrat. Methodist. Home: PO Box 620 Cullowhee NC 28723-0620 Office: Western Carolina U Coll of Bus Cullowhee NC 28723

WILSON, LYNTON RONALD, telecommunications company executive; b. Port Colborne, Ont., Can., Apr. 3, 1940; s. Ronald Alfred and Blanche Evelyn (Matthews) W.; m. Brenda Jean Black, Dec. 23, 1968; children:

Edward Ronald, Margot Jean, Jennifer Lyn. BA, McMaster U., 1962, LLD, 1995; MA, Cornell U., 1967; D honoris causa, U. Montreal, 1995; D in Civil Law, Bishop's U., Lennoxville, Que., Can., 1997; LLD, Univ. Coll. Cape Breton, 1998, Mount Allison U., 2000. Dep. minister Ministry Industry and Tourism, Ont., 1978-81; pres., CEO Redpath Industries, Ltd., Toronto, 1981-88; mng. dir. N.Am. Tate & Lyle, PLC, 1986-89; chmn. bd. Redpath Industries, Ltd., 1988-89; vice chmn. Bank of N.S., Toronto, 1989-90; pres., chief operating officer BCE, Inc., Montreal, 1990-92; pres., CEO BCE Inc., Montreal, 1992-93, chmn., pres. CEO, 1993-96, chmn., CEO, 1996-98, chmn. bd. dirs., 1998-2000; chmn. bd. dirs. CAE Inc.; bd. dirs. BCE, Inc., Nortel Networks Corp., Imperial Oil Ltd.; chmn. bd. Bell Can. Internat., Ont. Power Generation, Inc., Daimler Chrysler Can. Inc., Daimler-Chrysler Ag, mem. supervisory bd. and shareholders com.; mem. internat. coun. J.P. Morgan and Co., N.Y.C. Mem. Trilateral Commn.; chmn. HISTOR!CA Found. of Can. Decorated officer Order of Can. Mem. The Mount Royal Club of Montreal, York Club, Toronto Club, Toronto Golf Club, Rideau Club, Mount Bruno Country Club. Home: 2038 Lakeshore Rd East, Oakville, ON Canada L6J 1M3 Office: BCE Place, 181 Bay Ste Ste 4700, Toronto, ON Canada M5J 2T3

WILSON, MARC FRASER, art museum director; b. Akron, Ohio, Sept. 12, 1941; s. Fraser Eugene and Pauline Christine (Hoff) W.; m. Elizabeth Marie Fulder, Aug. 2, 1975. BA, Yale U., 1963, MA, 1967. Departmental asst. Cleve. Mus. Art, 1964; translator, project cons. Nat. Palace Mus., Taipei, Taiwan, 1968-71; assoc. curator of Chinese art Nelson Gallery-Atkins Mus., Kansas City, Mo., 1971-73, curator of Oriental art, 1973—, interim dir., 1982; curator Oriental art Nelson-Atkins Mus. Art, Kansas City, 1982-99, dir./CEO, 1999—; mem., rapporteur Indo-US Subcom. on Edn. and Culture, Washington, 1976-79; mem. adv. com. Asia Soc. Galleries, N.Y.C., 1984—, China Inst. in Am., 1985—. Mem. adv. com. Muni-Art Commn. on Urban Sculpture, Kansas City, 1984-87; com. mem. Kansas City-Xi'an, China, Sister City program, 1986—; mem. humanities coun. Johnson County Cmty. Coll., 1976-79; commr. Japan-U.S. Friendship Commn., Washington, 1986-88; panelist Japan-U.S. Cultural and Edn. Cooperation, Washington, 1986-88; mem. mayor's task force on race relations, 1996—; mem. indemnity adv. panel, 1995—; v.p. Brush Creek Ptnrs. 1995—. Recipient The William Yates Medallion Civic Svc. award William Jewell Coll., 1995, Disting. Svc. award Baker U., 1997. Mem. Assn. Art Mus. Dirs. (treas., trustee 1988-90, chmn. works of art com. 1986-90), Mo. China Coun., Fed. Coun. Arts and Humanities (chmn. arts and artifacts indemnity adv. panel 1986-89, 1995-98). Office: Nelson-Atkins Mus Art 4525 Oak St Kansas City MO 64111-1818

WILSON, MARY ELIZABETH, physician, educator; b. Indpls., Nov. 19, 1942; d. Ralph Richard and Catheryn Rebecca (Kurtz) Lausch; m. Harvey Vernon Fineberg, May 16, 1975. AB, Ind. U., 1963; MD, U. Wis., 1971. Diplomate Am. Bd. Internal Medicine, Am. Bd. Infectious Diseases. Tchr. of French and English Marquette Sch., Madison, Wis., 1963-66; intern in medicine Beth Israel Hosp., Boston, 1971-72, resident in medicine, 1972-73, fellow in infectious diseases, 1973-75; physician Albert Schweitzer Hosp., Deschapelles, Haiti, 1974-75, Harvard Health Svcs., Cambridge, Mass., 1974-75; asst. physician Cambridge Hosp., 1975-78; hosp. epidemiologist Mt. Auburn Hosp., Cambridge, 1975-79, chief of infectious diseases, 1978—, dir. Travel Resource Ctr., 1996—; adv. com. immunization practices Ctrs. for Disease Control, Atlanta, 1988-92; acad. adv. com. Nat. Inst. Pub. Health, Mex., 1989-91; cons. Ford Found., 1988; site dir. GeoSentinel network, 1999—; instr. in medicine Harvard Med. Sch., Boston, 1975-93, asst. clin. prof., 1994-99, assoc. prof. medicine, 1999—, assoc. Ctr. Health & Global Environ., 1996-2000; asst. prof. depts. epidemiology and population and internat. health Harvard Sch. Pub. Health, 1994-99, assoc. prof. population and internat. health, 1999—; lectr. Sultan Qaboos U., Oman, 1991; chair Woods Hole Workshop, Emerging Infectious Diseases, 1993. Author: A World Guide to Infections: Diseases, Distribution, Diagnosis, 1991; co-editor: (with Richard Levins and Andrew Spielman) Disease in Evolution: Global Changes and Emergence of Infectious Diseases, 1994; mem. editl. bd. Current Issues in Pub. Health, Emerging Infectious Diseases, Global Change and Human Health; sect. editor, travel medicine and tropical diseases, editl. bd. Infectious Diseases in Clin. Practice; assoc. editor Jour. Watch Infectious Diseases; editl. adv. bd. Clinical Infectious Diseases. Mem. Cambridge Task Force on AIDS, 1987-90, Earthwatch, Watertown, Mass., Cultural Survival, Inc., Cambridge; bd. dirs. Horizon Communications, West Cornwall, Conn., 1990-97. Recipient Lewis E. and Edith Phillips award U. Wis. Med. Sch., 1969, Cora M. and Edward Van Liere award, 1971, Mosby Scholarship Book award, 1971, Leo Blacklow teaching award, 1999; scholar in residence Bellagio (Italy) Study Ctr., Rockefeller Found., 1996. Fellow ACP, Infectious Diseases Soc. Am., Royal Soc. Tropical Medicine and Hygiene; mem. Am. Soc. Microbiology, N.Y. Acad. Scis., Am. Soc. Tropical Medicine and Hygiene, Mass. Infectious Diseases Soc., Peabody Soc., Internat. Soc. Travel Medicine, Wilderness Med. Soc., Soc. for Vector Ecology, Internat. Union Against Tuberculosis and Lung Disease, Soc. for Epidemiol. Rsch., Asculapian Club, Sigma Sigma, Phi Sigma Iota, Alpha Omega Alpha. Avocations: playing the flute, hiking, reading, travel. Office: Mt Auburn Hosp 330 Mount Auburn St Cambridge MA 02138-5597

WILSON, MELVIN EDMOND, civil engineer; b. Bremerton, Wash., Aug. 3, 1935; s. Edmond Curt and Madeline Rose (Deal) W.; m. Deanna May Stevens, Nov. 22, 1957 (div. Mar. 1971); children: Kathleen, Debra Wilson Frank. BSCE, U. Wash., 1957, MSCE, 1958. Registered profl. engr., Wash. Asst. civil engr. City of Seattle, 1958-60, assoc. civil engr., 1960-64, sr. civil engr., 1964-66, supervising civil engr., 1966-75, sr. civil engr., 1975-77, mgr. X, 1977-88; owner Wilson Cons. Svcs., Seattle, 1988-89; transp. sys. dir. City of Renton, Wash., 1989-96, ret., 1996; owner Mel Wilson Photographer, Seattle, 1975-84. Contbr. reports to profl. jours. Rep. Renton transp. work group King County (Wash.) Growth Mgmt. Policy Com.; rep. Renton tech. adv. com. South County Area Transp. Bd., King County, 1992-96, developer svc. policy (adopted by Puget Sound Govtl. Conf.) to encourage travel by transit. successfuly led effort to make Renton first suburban city to receive direct transit svc. under Met. King County Plan, 1994; vol. personal trainer, 1988—; vol. trainer for medical patients, 1988—. Mem. ASCE, Am. Pub. Works Assn., Inst. Transp. Engrs., Tau Beta Pi, Sigma Xi. Avocations: photography, weight lifting, hiking.

WILSON, MICHAEL GERALD, solicitor; b. London, Dec. 6, 1942; s. John Charles and Dorothy Beatrice (Harmer) W.; m. Maureen Brenda Hiron, Aug. 22, 1964; children: Sarah Michelle, James Michael. Solicitor of Supreme Ct. of Judicature for England and Wales. Articled clk. Slaughter & May, London, 1972-75, solicitor, 1975-77; now with Barlow Lyde & Gilbert, London; freeman City of London, Worshipful Co. of Slrs. Fellow Royal Soc. Art; mem. Law Soc., Internat. Bar Assn., So. Western Legal Found., Asia Pacific Lawyers Assn., Inter Pacific Bar Assn., Brit. Ins. Law Assn., RAC Club; assoc. mem. Lloyds of London. Avocations: tennis, squash, swimming, travel, reading, music, golf. Home: Lantern Cottage, Chalk Ln, Ashtead Surrey KT21 1DH, England Office: Barlow Lyde & Gilbert, 15 St Botolph St Beaufort, London EC3A 7NJ, England

WILSON, MICHAEL GREGG, film producer, writer; b. N.Y.C., Jan. 21, 1942; s. Lewis Gilbert Wilson and Dana (Natol) Broccoli; m. Coila Jane Hurley; children: David, Gregg. BS, Harvey Mudd Coll., 1963; JD, Stanford U., 1966. Bar: D.C., Calif., N.Y. Legal advisor FAA-DOT, Washington, 1966-67; assoc. Surrey, Karasik, Gould, Green, Washington, 1967-71; ptnr. Surrey and Morse, Washington and N.Y.C., 1971-74; legal advisor Eon Prodns., London, 1974-78, producer, mng. dir., 1978—. Writer/prodr.: For Your Eyes Only, 1981, Octopussy, 1983, View to a Kill, 1985, The Living Daylights, 1987, Licence to Kill, 1989, tomorrow Never Dies, 1977, The World Is Not Enough, 1999; prodr.: Goldeneye, 1995; author: Pictorialism in California, Getty Museum, 1994. Avocation: 19th and 20th century photograph collecting.

WILSON, MICHAEL HOLCOMBE, investment banker, former Canadian government official; b. Toronto, Ont., Can., Nov. 4, 1937; s. Harry Holcombe and Constance L. (Davies) W.; m. Margaret Catherine Smellie, Oct. 17, 1964; children: Cameron (dec.), Geoffrey, Lara. Student, Upper Can. Coll.; B. Comm., U. Toronto, 1959. With Harris & Partners Ltd., Toronto, 1961-63, 65-73; v.p. Harris & Partners Ltd., 1972; exec. v.p. following merger with Dominion Securities Ltd., 1973-79; mem. Can. Ho. of Commons, Ottawa, 1979-93; minister of state for internat. trade Govt. Can., Ottawa, 1979-80; minister of fin. Govt. Can., 1984-91, min. of industry, sci. & tech., min. internat. trade, 1991-93; bus. advisor Michael Wilson Internat., Toronto, 1993—; vice chmn. RBC Dominion Securities Inc., 1995-2000; chmn., CEO RT Capital Mgmt., Inc., 2000—; mem. bd. Ctr. for Addiction and Mental Health Found., Comty. Found. for Greater Toronto; mem. bd. dirs., bd. trustees Inst. Ams., Aspen Inst., Can. Club of Toronto; mem. bd. govs. Upper Can. Coll.; bd. dirs. BP Amoco pLc, Manulife Fin., Rio Algom Ltd., Office Splty. Ltd. Mem. Kappa Alpha. Progressive Conservative. Anglican. Clubs: Toronto, Albany, Toronto Golf, Badminton and Racquet, Osler Bluff Ski, Mad River Golf. Office: RT Capital Mgmt Inc, 77 King St W PO Box 85, Toronto, ON Canada M5K 1G8

WILSON, MICHAEL MOUREAU, lawyer, physician; b. Cheverly, Md., Dec. 30, 1952; s. Kenneth Moureau and Helen (Rice) Smith. BS, MIT, 1974; JD, Georgetown U., 1977, MD, 1986. Bar: D.C. 1977, N.Y. 1980, U.S. Dist. Ct. D.C. 1980, U.S. Dist. Ct. Md. 1992, U.S. Ct. Appeals (D.C. cir.) 1980, U.S. Supreme Ct. 1981. Law clk. Hon. John B. Hannum U.S. Dist. Ct., Phila., 1977-78; assoc. Cravath Swaine & Moore, N.Y.C., 1978-79; asst. to gen. counsel NSF, Washington, 1979-82; resident in psychiatry St. Elizabeth Hosp., Washington, 1986-89; pvt. practice med. malpractice litigation Washington, 1989—. Notes editor Am. Criminal Law Rev., 1976-77. Mem. ABA, Assn. Trial Lawyers Am., D.C. Trial Lawyers Assn., Phi Beta Kappa. Office: 1700 K St NW Ste 1007 Washington DC 20006-3815

WILSON, MYRON ROBERT, JR., retired psychiatrist; b. Helena, Mont., Sept. 21, 1932; s. Myron Robert Sr. and Constance Ernestine (Bultman) W. BA, Stanford U., 1954, MD, 1957. Diplomate Am. Bd. Psychiatry and Neurology. Dir. adolescent psychiatry Mayo Clinc, Rochester, Minn., 1965-71; pres. and psychiatrist in chief Wilson Ctr., Faribault, Minn., 1971-86; ret., 1986; chmn. Wilson Ctr., 1986-90; ret., 1990; assoc. clin. prof. psychiatry UCLA, 1985-99. Contbr. articles to profl. jours. Chmn., CEO C.B. Wilson Found., L.A., 1972—; mem. bd. dirs. Pasadena Symphony Orchestra Assn., Calif., 1987; vestryman, treas. St. Thomas' Parish, L.A., 1993-96. Lt. comdr., 1958-60. Fellow Mayo Grad. Sch. Medicine, Rochester, 1960-65. Fellow Am. Psychiat. Assn., Am. Soc. for Adolescent Psychiatry, Internat. Soc. for Adolescent Psychiatry (founder, treas. 1985-88, sec. 1985-88, treas. 1988-92); mem. Soc. Sigma Xi (Mayo Found. chpt.). Episcopalian. Office: Wilson Found 2565 Zorada Dr Los Angeles CA 90046-1747

WILSON, PAUL LOWELL, mortgage company executive, lawyer; b. May 12, 1951; s. James Joseph and Edna Vivian (Halterman) W.; children: Meredith Elaine, Taylor Halterman. AB, W.Va. U., 1973; JD, Coll. of William of Mary, 1976. Bar: W.Va., 1976, U.S. Dist. Ct. (so. dist.) W.Va. 1976, U.S. Dist. Ct. (ea. dist.) Va. 1991. Assoc. Brown & Peyton, Charleston, W.Va., 1976-78; title atty. Lawyers Title Ins. Corp., Williamsburg, Va., 1978-80; assoc. S.J. Baker, Williamsburg, 1981-83; counsel edn. com. W.Va. Legislature, Charleston, 1977-78; gen. counsel A J & L Corp., Williamsburg, 1983-85, v.p., gen. counsel, 1985-91; prin. First Capital Comml. Funding, Inc., 1997—; bd. dirs. 503 Cert. Devel. Co., Richmond, Sta. WHRO-TV. Mem. York County Sch. Bd., 1986-94, chmn., 1992-94; pres. Nat. Housing Corp., 1986-93, The Preservation Group, Inc., 1991-97. Mem. W.Va. State Bar, EconoLodges Am. Franchisee Assn. (sec., treas. 1986-90), Kiwanis, Sigma Phi Epsilon. Methodist. Office: 161 John Jefferson Rd Ste 103 Williamsburg VA 23185-5640

WILSON, PAUL WAYNE, retired real estate developer; b. Kokomo, Ind., June 13, 1933; s. Floyd Wayne Wilson and Stella (Dugan) Emry; m. Dixie Lee Cooprider, Feb. 23, 1952; children: Michael Wayne, Susan Jo Wilson-Broadus, Marci Ann, Paul Wayne II. Student, Ind. Bus. Coll., 1957-59. Cert. environ. inspector, environ. specialist,. constrn. inspector. Salesperson Kothe, Wells & Bauer, Indpls., 1956-60; owner, founder Pickin Chicken, Kokomo, 1958-60; broker Wayne Wilson Realty, Inc., Kokomo, 1963-98; owner Wayne Wilson Constrn. Co., Kokomo, 1960-78; apartment developer, 1998-2000, retired, 2000; v.p. Pyramid Inc., Kokomo, 1967-72, Mi-Su-Mar, Inc., Kokomo, 1967-78; founder, pres. Able Alarm Co., Inc., Kokomo, 1976-83; mgr. Honeywell Protection Svcs., Kokomo, 1983-97, ret.; pres., founder Midwest Organics, Inc., Kokomo, 1989—. Sch. bd. Taylor Community Schs., Center, Ind., 1963-73, pres., 1971; del. Dem. State Conv., Indpls., 1972; pres. Ind. Burglar & Fire Alarm Assn., 1982. Staff sgt. USAF, 1951-55. Recipient Beautification award Kokomo C. of C., 1979. Mem. Elks, Rotary. Roman Catholic. Avocations: flying, organic gardening. Home: 3400 Tally Ho Dr Kokomo IN 46902-3961 Office: Honeywell Protection Svcs 200 N Washington St Kokomo IN 46901-4508

WILSON, PETER, architect, civil engineer, management consultant; b. Wendover, United Kingdom, Dec. 22, 1938; s. Leonard Donald and Marion Forest (McLorg) W.; m. Esther Greaves, Mar. 16, 1963; children: Amanda Jane, Julia Ann. Diploma in Arch., Sch. of Art, Brighton, Eng., 1961; cert. in Civil Engring., Brixton Sch. Bldg., London, 1965; MBA, Internat. Mgmt. Ctr., U.K., 1990, D of Bus. Adminstrn., 1993. Chartered architect; incorporated engr. Architect London County Coun., 1961-73; head of tech. svcs. London Borough of Lambeth, 1973-90; cons., dir. Peter Wilson Cons. Ltd., London, 1990—; problem solving rschr. for engring. projects in the U.K. and West Indies., 1990—. Editor jour. Engring. World, 1994; patentee in field; prin. works include Poly. of Ctrl. London, 1962, Housing at Haverhill, U.K., 1965, sch., Greenwich, U.K., 1968. Mem. Soc. Engrs. (dir., coun. mem. 1988—, v.p. 1998-2000), Royal Inst. Brit. Architects (rsch. steering group 1991-94), Inst. Mgmt., Constrn. Industry Rsch. and Info. Assn. (rsch. steering group 1992-94), Sussex Yacht Club (reg. organizer for sailability 1998—). Avocations: sailing, sketching, yoga. Other: Rue du Vallon Rouxmesnil, Boutailles Normandy, France

WILSON, PETER WYMAN, internist, cardiovascular, metabolic epidemiology; b. New Haven, Conn., Oct. 13, 1948; m. Peggy Susan Lindsey. BS, Yale U., 1970; MD, U. Tex., 1974. Diplomate Am. Bd. Internal Medicine, Am. Bd. Endocrinology. Resident Duke U., Durham, N.C., 1974-78; med. officer Nat. Heart, Lung and Blood Inst./NIH, Bethesda, Md., 1978-98; dir. labs. Framingham Heart Study, 1983—; prof. medicine Boston U. Med. Sch., 2000—. Contbr. over 230 articles to profl. jours. Office: Framingham Heart Study 5 Thurber St Framingham MA 01702-6334

WILSON, R. DALE, marketing educator, consultant; b. Ironton, Ohio, July 16, 1949; s. Robert J. and Treva L. (Shively) W.; m. Emily J. Ray, June 19, 1971; 1 child, Travis Ray. BBA cum laude, Ohio U., 1971; MBA, U. Toledo, 1972; PhD, U. Iowa, 1977. Asst. prof. mktg. Pa. State U., University Park, 1976-80; v.p., dir. mktg. scis. Batten, Barton, Durstine & Osborn, Inc., N.Y.C., 1980-83; vis. prof. Cornell U., Ithaca, N.Y., 1983-84; assoc. prof. Mich. State U., East Lansing, 1984-87, prof., 1987—; cons. in field. Contbr. articles to profl. jours. Youth baseball and basketball coach, East Lansing, 1989-98. Faculty research grantee Pa. State U., Mich. State U. Mem. Am. Acad. Advt., Am. Mktg. Assn., Inst. Ops. Rsch. and Mgmt. Scis. (assoc. editor Interfaces, cert. recognition 1983), Product Devel. and Mgmt. Assn., Beta Gamma Sigma. Home: 859 Audubon Rd East Lansing MI 48823-3003 Office: Mich State U Eli Broad Grad Sch Mgmt Dept Mktg/ Supply Chain Mgmt N322 N Business Complex East Lansing MI 48824-1122

WILSON, RICHARD LEE, political science educator; b. Worthington, Minn., Dec. 20, 1944; s. G. Roy and Dorothy Eileen (Johnson) W.; m. Carolyn Ann Dirks, Aug. 24, 1968 (div.); 1 child, Kevin Richard. BA, U. Chgo., 1966, postgrad., 1966-67; PhD, Johns Hopkins U., 1971; postgrad., Columbia U., 1988, Stanford U., 1992. Congl. aide 4th Congl. Dist. Md., 1971; asst. prof. polit. sci. U. Tenn., Chattanooga, 1971-76, assoc. prof., 1976-87, prof., 1988—; registrar-at-large Hamilton County Election Commn., 1977-84; lectr. Robert A. Taft Inst. Govt., U. Tenn., Nashville, 1978, 79, 81; supr. state legis. and met. internship program U. Chattanooga, 1972-86; vis. prof. Govt. Fgn. Affairs Coll., Beijing, 1986-87; Fulbright prof. govt. Beijing U., 1988-89, Samford U., Birmingham, Ala., 1991-93. Author: Tennessee Politics, 1976, American Government, 1993, 2d edit., 1995; co-editor: Ready Reference: Censorship, 1997 (named Outstanding Ref. Source 1998 ALA), Encyclopedia of the Supreme Court, 2000; contbr. chpts. to books. Chmn. Hamilton County Health Planning Adv. Council, 1975-79; bd. dirs. Ga.-Tenn. Regional Health Commn., 1978-82; active Tenn. State Health Coordinating Council, 1977-81; exec. com. State Health Coordinating Council, 1979-81. Named Outstanding Educator of Yr., Signal Mountain (Tenn.) Jaycees, 1973, Outstanding Prof. of Yr., SGA, 1985-86; recipient Polit. Edn. award NAACP, 1980, Excellent Prof. award Fgn. Affairs Coll., Beijing, 1987, UTC Exceptional Merit award, 1990, 94; NEH grantee, 1988, 92. Mem. So. Polit. Sci. Assn., Midwest Polit. Sci. Assn., Am. Polit. Sci. Assn. (nat. rsch. grant 1995), Nat. Soc. Internships and Exptl. Edn., SAR, China People's Friendship Assn., Aircraft Owners and Pilots Assn. Methodist. Office: Univ of Tenn Dept Political Sci Fletcher Hall 417 Chattanooga TN 37403

WILSON, ROBERT FOSTER, lawyer; b. Windsor, Colo., Apr. 6, 1926; s. Foster W. and Anne Lucille (Svedman) W.; m. Mary Elizabeth Clark, Mar. 4, 1951 (div. Feb. 1972); children: Robert F., Katharine A.; m. Sally Anne Nemec, June 8, 1982. BA in Econs., U. Iowa, 1950, JD, 1951. Bar: Iowa 1951, U.S. Dist. Ct. (no. and so. dists.) Iowa 1956, U.S. Ct. Appeals (8th cir.) 1967. Atty., FTC, Chgo., 1951-55; pvt. practice, Cedar Rapids, Iowa, 1955—; pres. Lawyer Forms, Inc.; dir. Lawyers Forms, Inc. Democratic state rep. Iowa Legislature, Linn County, 1959-60; mem. Iowa Reapportionment Com., 1968; pres. Linn County Day Care, Cedar Repids, 1968-70; del. to U.S. and Japan Bilateral Session on Legal and Econ. Rels. Conf., Tokyo, 1988, Moscow Conf. on Law and Bilateral Rels., Moscow, 1990; U.S. del. to Moscow conf. on legal and econ. rels., 1990. Sgt. U.S. Army, 1944-46. Mem. ATLA, Am. Arbitration Assn. (mem. panel arbitrators), Am. Legion (judge advocate 1970-75, 1987-93), Iowa Trial Lawyers Assn., Iowa Bar Assn., Linn County Bar Assn., Delta Theta Phi. Club: Cedar View Country. Lodges: Elks, Eagles. Home: 100 1st Ave NE Cedar Rapids IA 52401-1128 Office: 810 Dows Bldg Cedar Rapids IA 52403-7010

WILSON, ROBERT GODFREY, radiologist; b. Montgomery, Ala., Mar. 18, 1937; s. Robert Woodridge and Lucille (Godfrey) W.; m. Dorothy June Waters, Aug. 31, 1957; children: Amy Lucille, Robert Darwin, Robert Woodridge II, Lucy Elizabeth. B.A., Huntingdon Coll., 1957; M.D., Med. Coll. Ala., 1961. Diplomate Nat. Bd. Med. Examiners, Am. Bd. Radiology, Am. Bd. Nuclear Medicine. Intern Letterman Gen. Hosp., San Francisco, 1961-62; resident in radiology U. Okla. Med. Center, Oklahoma City, 1965-68, clin. instr. in radiology, 1968—; practice medicine specializing in diagnostic and therapeutic radiology, nuclear medicine Shawnee, Okla., 1968—; mem. med. staff Shawnee Med. Center, Mission Hill Meml. Hosp., Shawnee, 1968—. Served to capt. M.C., USAF, 1960-65. Mem. AMA, Okla., Pottawatomie County med. socs., Okla., Greater Oklahoma City radiol. socs., Am. Coll. Radiology, Soc. Nuclear Medicine, Radiol. Soc. N.Am. Methodist. Home: 26 Sequoyah Blvd Shawnee OK 74801-5570 Office: 5606 Aquarius Shawnee OK 74804-9387

WILSON, ROBERT GORDON, civil and mechanical engineer; b. Covina, Calif., Jan. 27, 1946; s. Robert Kenneth and Margaret Ellen (Gordon) W.; m. Barbara Ann Poole, June 15, 1968; children: Mark Gordon, Kristen Leigh. BS in Civil Engring., San Jose (Calif.) State U., 1968; AA in Bus. Adminstrn., Saddleback C.C., Mission Viejo, Calif., 1979; MBA, Calif. State U., Fullerton, 1983. Registered profl. engr., Calif. Constrn. field engr. Bechtel Power Corp., Calvert County, Md., 1968-72; asst. project mgr. Bechtel Power Corp., Norwalk, Calif., 1972-73; nuclear engr. supr. Bechtel Power Corp., Madrid, 1973-76; site engr. supr. Bechtel Power Corp., San Onofre, Calif., 1976-78; constrn. supt. Bechtel Power Corp., San Onofre, 1978-85; maintenance supr. So. Calif. Edison, San Onofre, 1985-94, project mgr., 1994—; consulting engr. Wilson Engring., Dana Point, Calif., 1976—. Democrat. Avocations: sports, genealogy, computers. Home: 24361 Timothy Dr Dana Point CA 92629-1070 Office: So Calif Edison PO Box 128 San Clemente CA 92674-0128

WILSON, ROBERT M., financial executive; b. St. Louis, Aug. 10, 1952; s. William H. and Mary E. (Sacksteder) W.; m. Joli S. Schneeberger, Oct. 7, 1978; 1 child, William Wilcox. BS, Miami U., Oxford, Ohio, 1974; JD, Cleve. State U., 1977. Bar: Ohio; CPA, Ohio. Ptnr. Touche Ross & Co., Dayton, Ohio, 1972-88; ptnr. Roberds, Inc., Dayton, 1988-2000, pres., 1998—. Chmn. Dayton Ballet Assn., 1979-91; trustee Carillon Park, 1988-94, City-Wide Devl. Corp., 1991—, Cath. Social Svcs., 1995—; assoc. bd. Dayton Art Inst., 1989-95. Mem. ABA (com. chmn. 1990-92), Ohio Soc. CPAs (pres. 1985-86). Republican. Roman Catholic. Office: Roberds Inc 1100 E Central Ave Ste 6 Dayton OH 45449-1812

WILSON, ROBERT MICHAEL ALAN, writer; b. Jamestown, N.Y., June 19, 1944; s. Harry Garfield and Hazel Virginia (Groscost) W.; m. Ursula Lieselotte Frank, May 14, 1987; 1 child, Jeffrey Aryan. BS, Calif. State U., 1974; MPA, U. So. Calif., 1976; JD, Western State U., 1983. Deputy sheriff L.A. County Sheriff's Dept., 1968-92; traffic safety advocate San Bernardino (Calif.) Police Dept., 1992-94; free-lance writer, Moreno Valley, Calif., 1992—. Author: History of Masonry in Moreno Valley, California, 1991, 2d edit., 1996, Bad Wimpfen, 1994, Nolocaust, 1995, The Only Good Indian..., 1996, Drenched in Blood, Rigid in Death, The True Story of the Wickenburg Massacre, 2000. Creator, mgr. 999 Run for Abused Kids, Industry, Calif., 1988-91; creator, chmn. Masonic Essay Contest Against Drugs, Moreno Valley, 1991-99. Sgt. USAF, 1964-67. Recipient award of merit Calif. Peace Officers Assn., 1991, Disting. Svc. award Nat. Commn. Against Drunk Drivers, Washington, 1991. Mem. Masons (Hiram award 1992), Shriners, York Rite. Republican. Avocations: boating, fishing. Home: 8170 S Eastern Ave Ste 4 291 Las Vegas NV 89123

WILSON, ROBERT ROSS, engineering manufacturing executive; b. Glasgow, Scotland, Mar. 13, 1947; s. Robert and Ann Stuart (Caldwell) W.; m. Margaret Ann Upson; children: Robert James, John Ross. BSc, Glasgow U., 1968; PhD, Con. for Nat. Acad. Awards, 1972. Chartered physicist Inst. Physics. Head vibration group Ctrl. Electricity Generating Bd., Leatherhead, Surrey, Eng., 1968-73; head design audit Brit. Steel, London, 1973-76; design mgr. James Howden & Co. Ltd., Renfrew, Scotland, 1976-81, tech. dir., 1981-92, mng. dir., 1992—; CEO Howden Process Compressors, 1998; dir. Howden Group Tech., Renfrew, Scotland, 1998—; mem. panel Renfrewshire Bus. Growth Fund, 1996—; vis. prof. Strathclyde U., Glasgow, 1986-92; bd. dirs. Scottish Enterprise Renfrewshire, With (UK) Ltd., Burton Corblin S.A. France. Co-author: Vibreation of Engineering Structures, 1984, also articles; co-patentee fans and wind turbines. Mem. Inst. Physics, Brit. Wind Energy Assn. (bd. dirs. 1984-90, chmn. 1986-87, Pioneer of Wind Energy award 1996). Avocations: collecting Penguin paperback books. Home: Riversdale Lochwinnoch Rd, Kilmacolm Renfrewshire PA13 4DZ, Scotland

WILSON, ROBERT RUTHERFORD, religious studies educator; b. Louisville, Mar. 29, 1942; s. Ralph Elmer and Dorothy May (Rutherford) W.; m. Sharyn Elaine Beck, July 28, 1967. AB, Transylvania U., 1964; BD, Yale U., 1967, MA, 1969, PhD, 1972. Ordained to ministry Disciples of Christ, 1967. Instr. old testament Union Theol. Sem., N.Y.C., 1971-72; asst. prof. old testament Yale Univ., New Haven, Conn., 1972-76, assoc. prof. old testament, 1976-83, prof. old testament, 1983—, Hoober prof. religious studies, 1991—, chair dept. religious studies, 1986-92, 95-96. Author: Genealogy and History in the Biblical World, 1977, Prophecy and Society in Ancient Israel, 1980, Sociological Approaches to the Old Testament, 1984; editor (book): Canon, Theology, and Old Testament Interpretation, 1988. Mem. Civic Orch. of New Haven, 1975—. Dir. summer seminar for coll. tchrs. NEH, Washington, 1981; Danforth Grad. fellow Danforth Found., St. Louis, 1964; fellow Am. Coun. Learned Socs., Wash., 1975. Mem. Soc. Bibl. Lit. (coun. mem. 1977-79), Columbia Univ. Seminar Study Hebrew Bible (chair 1978-81), Am. Acad. Religion, Am. Oriental Soc., Am. Soc. for Study Religion, Am. Schs. Oriental Rsch. Avocations: music. Office: Yale Univ 409 Prospect St New Haven CT 06511-2167

WILSON, ROBERT WOODROW, radio astronomer; b. Houston, Tex., Jan. 10, 1936; s. Ralph Woodrow and Fannie May (Willis) W.; m. Elizabeth Rhoads Sawin, Sept. 4, 1958; children—Philip Garrett, Suzanne Katherine, Randal Woodrow. B.A. with honors in Physics, Rice U., 1957; Ph.D., Calif. Inst. Tech., 1962. Research fellow Calif. Inst. Tech., Pasadena, 1962-63; mem. tech. staff AT&T Bell Labs., Holmdel, N.J., 1963-76; head wireless tech. rsch. dept. AT&T Bell Labs., 1976-94; sr. sci. Harvard-Smithsonian Ctr. for Astrophysics, Cambridge, Mass., 1994—. Discoverer 3 deg. k microwave background radiation, 1965; discoverer CO and other molecules in interstellar space using their millimeter wavelength radiation. Recipient Henry Draper medal Royal Astron. Soc., London, 1977, Herschel medal Nat. Acad. Scis., 1977; named Fairchild Disting. scholar Caltech., 1987; Nobel prize in physics, 1978; NSF fellow, 1958-61, Cole fellow, 1957-58. Mem. Am. Astron. Soc., Internat. Astron. Union, Am. Phys. Soc., Internat.

Sci. Radio Union, Nat. Acad. Scis., Phi Beta Kappa, Sigma Xi. Home: 9 Valley Point Dr Holmdel NJ 07733-1320 Office: Harvard-Smithsonian Ctr Astrophysics 160 Concord Ave # M309 Cambridge MA 02138-2306

WILSON, RONALD GENE, physician; b. Hemet, Calif., Jan. 23, 1941; s. John Arthur and Inez Mary Wilson. BA, U. Colo., 1962; MD, George Washington U., 1966; DTMH, Mahidol U., Bangkok, Thailand, 1971; MPH, U. Hawaii, 1972. Diplomate Am. Bd. Preventive Medicine. Staff physician USPHS U.S. Peace Corps, Thailand, 1967-69, staff physician U.S. State Dept., 1969-71; assoc. dir. MEDEX/Micronesia Program, Hawaii and Micronesia, 1972-74; project mgr. Lampang Health Devel. Project Ministry Pub. Health, Thailand, 1974-81; health program officer Aga Khan Found., Geneva, 1982-85, dir. health programs, 1985-96; health systems and mgmt. cons., 1996—. Editor: Lampang Health Development Project Series (7 vols.), 1981, Planning and Managing Primary Health Care Programs, 1984, Primary Health Care Technologies, 1986, Management Information Systems and Microcomputers in Primary Health Care, 1988, Primary Health Care Management Advancement Programme Series (22 vols.), 1993; author chpts. in books. Recipient Most Honorable Order of the Crown of Thailand, His Majesty Bhumibol Adulyadej, 1978. Mem. Global Health Coun. (internat. assoc.), Am. Coll. Preventive Medicine, Am. Soc. Tropical Medicine and Hygiene, Internet Soc. Avocations: skiing, scuba diving, biking, bird watching, gardening. Home: Route des Sendys, Chalet Alt 927, CH-1273 Arzier Switzerland also: 55540 Howland Dr PO Box 3233 Idyllwild CA 92549-3233

WILSON, RONALD JACK, insurance company executive; b. Wyandotte, Mich., Oct. 19, 1939; s. Donald Lorenzo Wilson and Vedah Verla Kobel; m. Margaret Alice Young, Aug. 31, 1957; children: Ronald Jeffery, Garry Lee, Angela Joy. Student, United Wesleyan Coll., 1959-60; D in Bus. Mgmt. (hon.), Ind. Wesleyan U. CLU; ChFC. MIC mgr. Met. Life, Richmond, Va., 1970-73; dist. mgr. Hartford Life, Towson, Md., 1973-74; v.p., pres. Canton Agy. Inc., Balt., 1974-80, pres., owner, 1983—; pres., owner R.J. Wilson & Assocs. Ltd., Abingdon, Md., 1978—, Med. Benefits Adminstrn. Md., Abingdon, 1990—; dir., owner N.Am. Ins. Co., Madison, Wis., 1987-93; owner, gen. ptnr. Wilson Properties, Abingdon, 1985—, Mims Properties PA, Abingdon, 1987—; owner, pres. Good Samaritan Agy. LLC, Indpls., 1999—. Author: Cooperative Self Funded Method, 1979; contbr. articles to profl. jours. Mem. Profl. Ins. Agts., Soc. Fin. Profls., Consol. Transp. Ins. Trust (adminstr. 1976-99), Nat. Surplus Lines Offices, Am. Short Line R.R. Assn. (trustee 1978-99), GSA Employee Welfare Trust (adminstr. 1999). Avocations: history, genealogy, collecting rare books, travel. E-mail: mrjga@aol.com. Office: Canton Agy Inc 3103 Emmorton Rd Abingdon MD 21009-2021

WILSON, ROSINA, writer, editor; b. N.Y.C., Mar. 10, 1948; d. Louis John and Marie Chericone Tinari; m. Wayne Pastorius Wilson, Aug. 10, 1968 (div. Mar. 1998); 1 child, Siri Noel. BA, Sarah Lawrence Coll., 1967. Tchr. Calif. Culinary Acad., San Francisco, 1989—; editor Palate and Spirit mag., San Francisco, 1992-96; sr. editor Wine X Mag., Santa Rosa, Calif., 1996—; cons. Ctr. for Culinary Devel., San Francisco, 1996—. Author: (book) Seafood Pasta and Noodles: The New Classics, 1992; contbr. articles to cooking mags. Mem. Internat. Assn. Culinary Profls., Am. Inst. Wine and Food, San Francisco Profl. Food Soc. Avocations: photography, gardening. E-mail: rosinatw@sirius.com. Office: Wine X Mag 880 2nd St Santa Rosa CA 95404-4611

WILSON, SAMUEL ERIC, vascular and general surgeon; b. Lisburn, County Antrim, Ireland, Oct. 17, 1941; m. Sandra Wilson; children: Andrea, Brian Alexander. Student, Henry Ford Coll., 1958-59; BA, Wayne State U., 19631, MD, 1965. Diplomate Nat. Bd. Med. Examiners, Am. Bd. Surgery, Am. Bd. Gen. Vascular Surgery. Intern U. So. Calif., L.A., 1965-66; resident in surgery UCLA/Wadsworth VA Med. Ctr., 1966-70; chief and attending surgeon vascular sect. VA Med. Ctr., L.A., 1972-92, asst. chief surg. svc., 1978-82; asst. prof. surgery UCLA Sch. Medicine, 1972-76, assoc. prof. surgery, 1976-81, attending staff mem., 1972-92, prof. surgery, 1981-92; chmn. dept. surgery Harbor-UCLA Med. Ctr., Torrance, 1982-92; attending staff VA Med. Ctr., Long Beach, Calif., 1992—; prof. surgery U. Calif., Irvine, 1992—; chmn. dept. surgery U. Calif.-Irvine Med. Ctr., Orange, 1992—; McIlrath guest prof. Royal Prince Alfred Hosp., U. Sydney, Australia, 1991; 25th anniversary guest prof. Japanese Soc. for Vascular Surgery, 1993; Ira M. Teicher meml. lectr., vis. prof. Albert Einstein Coll. Medicine, L.I. Jewish Med. Ctr., 1994; lectr., cons. in field. Editor 12 textbooks; mem. editl. bd. Host/Pathogen Ne3ws, 1984-85, Infectious Disease Alert, 1989-91Internat. Vascular Surgery, 1991-93, Postgrad. Medicine, 1988-94, Dialysis and Transplantation, 1988-94, Vascular Forum, 1993-94, Advances in Therapy, 1990—, Postgrad. Gen. Surgery, 1991-97, Surg. Infections: Index and Revs., 1993-98, Antibiotics for the Clinician, 1996—, Surg. Infections, 1998—; reviewer various jours.; contbr. numerous articles to profl. jours. Bd. govs. L.A. Transplant Found., 1974-75;. Recipient Hon. Mention award AMA, 1975, Shed the Light on Cancer award Am. Cancer Soc., 1982, Disting. Alumni award Wayne State U. Sch. Medicine, 1990. Fellow ACS (young surg. del. 1977, standing com. on oper. rm. environ. 1981-90, chmn. exec. com. 1986-87, bd. govs. 1996-99, mem. gov.'s com. on surg. practice in hosps. 1998-99); mem. Am. Surg. Assn., Assn. VA Surgeons, Halsted Soc., Internat. Cardiovascular Soc., L.A. Surg. Soc. (pres. 1988), Pacific Coast Surg. Soc. (program chmn. 1997—), Soc. for Clin. Vascular Surgery, Soc. Univ. Surgeons, Soc. Vascular Surgery, So. Calif. Vascular Surg. Soc. (pres. 1994), Southwestern Surg. Congress (councilor 1992-97, program com. 1995-96, exec. com. 1996-97, nominating com. 1996-97), Surg. Infection Soc., Western Vascular Soc. Office: U Calif Irvine Dept Surgery Med Ctr 101 City Dr Orange CA 92868

WILSON, SANNA BETH, managing editor, writer religious magazine; b. Cannonsburg, Pa., Aug. 17, 1950; arrived in Australia, 1976; d. Elliott Donton Canonge and Viola Marguerite (Fuller) Frew; m. Peter Gordon Wilson, May 14, 1977; children: Jeremy Raymond, Kerryn Renee. BS, Phila. Coll. of Bible, 1972; grad. diploma in editing and pub., Macquarie U., 1998. Missionary Wycliff Bible Translators, Huntington Beach, Calif., 1972-76; promotions officer The Missions to Seamen, Sydney, Australia, 1977-80; mng. editor Christian Woman, Punchbowl, NSW, Australia, 1988—. Columnist My Soapbox in Christian Woman, 1988—; also contributes feature articles. Mem. bd. St. George Christian Sch., Allawah, NSW, Australia, 1995—, convenor enrollment com., 1996-98. Baptist. Avocations: needlework, reading. E-mail: cweditor@cwciaus.org.au.

WILSON, SONJA MARY, secondary education educator, consultant, poet; b. Lake Charles, La., Mar. 28, 1938; d. Albert Ronald and Annelia (DeVille) Molless; m. Willie McKinley Williams, Apr. 28, 1956 (div. May 1969); children: William P., Dwayne L., Rachelle A., Devon A., Lisa M., Ricardo Soto; m. Howard Brooks Wilson, Nov. 12, 1982 (div. Dec. 1999); stepchildren: Howard N. Wilson, Yvonne Wilson. AA in Social and Behavioral Scis., Mt. St. Jacinto Jr. Coll., 1992; Designated Subjects Credential, U. Calif., San Bernardino, 1983; student, Calif. State Poly. U., 1986; BS in Behavior Sci., Laverne U., 1985; BS in Edn., So. Ill. U., 1995; student, Riverside (Calif.) City Coll., 1988-89, 94. Prin.'s sec. Elsinore (Calif.) H.S., Elsinore Jr. H.S., 1974-83, tchr. bus. and adult vocat. edn. coord., 1979-88, notary pub., 1981-85, class adviser, 1983-88; long-term substitute tchr. Perris H.S. Dist., 1991-94; spkr. in field. Clk. Lake Elsinore Unified Sch. Dist. Bd., 19885, 1st pres., 1988, 98; clk., mem. Lake Elsinore Elem. Sch. Bd., 1979-88; pres., sec. treas., v.p. Riverside County Sch. Bds. Assn., 1979-98; assoc. sponsor, advisor Black Student Union/Future Leaders of Am., 1984-90; svc. unit rep., leader Girl Scouts U.S.A., bd. dirs. San Gorgonio coun., 19965, mem. nominating com., 1998, 99; den mother Boy Scouts Am.; mem. Ctrl. Dem. Com., 1989-91; del. PTSA, 1991-93. Tribute in her honor Black Student Union/Future Leaders Am., 1989; recipient Excellence in Edn. award Hilltop Community Ctr. Club, 1989, Leadership award Black Art and Social Club, 1989, Svc. award Sojourner Truth Media Network, 1989, Proclamation award City of Elsinore, 1989, County of Riverside, 1984; named Outstanding Poet, Nat. Libr. of Congress, 1994, 95; recipient Golden Leaf award PTSA. Mem. NAACP (charter mem.; treas. 1998-2000, Lake Elsinore affiliate, plaque, pres. 2000), Calif. Sch. Bds. Assn. (regional dir. 1988-92, conf. planning com. 1989, legis. com. 1981-97, nominations com. 1988, media com., dir. at large black 1993-95, audit com. 1993, dir./del. trainer 1993, alt. del., sgt. at arms 1994, 95, Fed. Rels. Network del. 1992, 95), Calif. Elected Women Ofcls. Assn., Calif. Sch. Employees Assn. (pres., treas., regional rep. asst., state negotiation com., del. to conf.), Internat. Soc. Poets, Lake Elsinore C. of C., Calif. Coalition Black Sch. Bd. Mems. (v.p. 1989, pres. 1990, program liaison 1989), Nat. Sch. Bds. Assn. (alt. del. 1994, 95), Nat. Coalition Black Sch. Bd. Mems. (dir. 1989-94, v.p. 1995-2000, sec.-treas. 1998—), Nat. Coun. Negro Women (charter, Willa Mae Taylor sect.), Black Art and Social Club, Lake Elsinore Black Art Culture Club (treas. 1997-2000, Vol. of Yr. 1999-2000, RTA com.), Hilltop Cmty. Club (plaque), Sojourner Truth Media Network (plaque), Eta Phi Beta (all offices Gamma Alpha chpt., pres. 1992-94, Western region dir. 1997—, plaque, Resurrection choir 1998—). Avocations: travel, writing poetry, winemaking, gardening, childcare. Home: 30402 Jernigan St Lake Elsinore CA 92530-5045

WILSON, STACY, hockey player; b. Moncton, Can., May 12, 1965. EdB. Tchr. phys. edn.; forward Maritime Sports Blades, 1973—, Team New Brunswick, 1986-87, 92-93, Olympic Oval, 1997. Recipient ice hockey Silver medal Olympic Games, Nagano, Japan, 1998. Avocations: guitar, badminton. Office: Can Olympic Assn. Av Pierre Dupuy 2380, Montreal, PQ Canada H3C 3R4*

WILSON, STANLEY LEIF, small business owner; b. Zanesville, Ohio, Jan. 13, 1961; s. Jack Clarence and Janet W.; m. Dana Venable, July 5, 1996; children: Alica Nicle Venable. AAS in Pre-Engring., Muskingum Area Jt. Tech. Coll., Zanesville, 1979; AAS, U. Tex., 1981, BS in Geology, 1983. Cert. legal asst., Profl. Paralegal Inst. Ga. Geologist/data analyst Tex. Electro-Seise, Ft. Worth, 1979-84; co-owner Wilson Collision & Coatings Techs., Zanesville, 1984-86; adminstr. Auto Collision Specialist Inc., Ft. Worth, 1987-91; founder, CEO Ft. Worth Body & Paint Works Corp., 1992—; founder, chmn., dir. The Faith Found., Dallas, 1997—; owner Dawson Exploration, Dallas, 1997—. Contbr. articles to profl. jours.; patentee in field. Lic. min. Assn. of Evangel. Gospel Assemblies, Monroe, La., 1999—; founder, dir. The Internat. Drinking Water for Children, Dallas, 1998—. Mem. The Nature Conservancy, The Planetary Soc., Am. Bible Soc., I Car USA. Avocations: flying, racing, scuba diving, photography, reading. Home: PO Box 5 Hull TX 77564-0005 Address: 1201 E Cubolo Rd Edinburg TX 78539

WILSON, STEPHEN RIP, public policy consultant; b. Twin Falls, ID, Apr. 26, 1948; s. Jerome P. and Epsy Jane (Griggs) W.; m. Judith Ann Newcomb, June 2, 1972 (dec. Nov. 16, 1977); children: Paul, Sloan; m. Judith E. Allen, Apr. 11, 1992. BA, Columbia U., 1970. Editor Sta. KABC TV, Los Angeles, 1970-72; owner, mgr. Oro Verde Farms, Hagerman, ID, 1972-77; new dir. Sta. KAET TV, Phoenix, 1978-83; adminstrv. aide U.S. Senator Dennis DeConcini, Phoenix, 1983-89; chief exec. officer Flatt & Assocs., Mesa, Ariz., 1989-90; exec. asst. to Gov. Rose Mofford State of Ariz., Phoenix, 1990-91; pres. SRW Cos., Phoenix, Ariz., 1991—; commr. Gov.'s Coun. Phys. Fitness, Phoenix, 1988-90; bd. dirs. Crime Victim Found., Phoenix, 1984; mem. Jefferson Forum. Mem. Nucleus Club, Com. on Fgn. Relations. Democrat. Avocations: scuba diving, skiing, tennis, fly fishing, golf, writing. Home: 2017 E Marshall Ave Phoenix AZ 85016-3110

WILSON, SUSAN RUTH, statistician; b. Sydney, NSW, Australia, Mar. 19, 1948; d. Albert Bowman and Mabel Constance (Speed) W.; 1 child, Jonathan Bruce. BSc, U. Sydney, 1968; PhD, Australian Nat. U., Canberra, 1972. Lectr. U. Sheffield, Eng., 1972-74; rsch. fellow Australian Nat. U., 1974-76, fellow, 1976-84, sr. fellow centre math. and its applications, 1984-94, prof., 1994—. Contbr. numerous articles to profl. jours. Fellow Am. Statis. Soc., 1991, Inst. Math. Stats., 1995. Fellow Royal Statis. Soc.; mem. Internat. Biometric Soc. (pres. and v.p. 1997-2000), Statis. Soc. Australia (mem. coun. Australian Capital Territory br. 1976-78, 85-90), Inst. Math. Stats. (editor bull. 1993-97), Human Genetics Soc. Australia (hon. treas. 1985-88), Internat. Statis. Inst. (Membership award 1979). Office: Australian Nat U Ctr Math, Dedman Bldg, Canberra ACT 0200, Australia

WILSON, TAMAR DIANA, anthropology, researcher; b. Lewisburg, Pa., Sept. 29, 1943; arrived in Mexico, 1988; d. Henry Seth Wilson and Gloralie Collier; m. Leif Johan Elvsaas, 1974 (div. 1981); m. José Alberto Garcia-Millan, Mar. 14, 1995. MA in Sociology, UCLA, 1981, MA in Anthropology, 1986, Masters in L.Am. Studies, 1987, PhD in Anthropology, 1992. Rsch. affiliate UCLA, 1993-95; rsch. officer U. Mo., St. Louis, 1997—. Editor: L.Am. Perspectives, 1990—; contbr. articles to profl. jours. Recipient Harold K. Schneider prize Supply for Econ. Anthropology. Fellow Royal Anthropol. Inst., Am. Anthropol. Assn., Am. Sociol. Assn. Home: Condominums Aloha 301-E, 23448 San Jose del Cabos Mexico

WILSON, THOMAS LEON, physicist; b. Alpine, Tex., May 21, 1942; s. Homer Marvin and Ogarita Maude (Bailey) W.; m. Joyce Ann Krevosky, May 7, 1978; children: Kenneth Edward Byron, Bailey Elizabeth Victoria. BA, Rice U., 1964, BS, 1965, MA, 1974, PhD, 1976. With NASA, Houston, 1965—, astronaut instr., 1965-74, high-energy theoretical physicist, 1969—. Author of two books on cosmic dust and astrophysics; contbr. articles in field to profl. jours. including Phys. Rev. Recipient Hugo Gernsback award IEEE, 1964; NASA fellow, 1969-76. Mem. AAAS, Am. Phys. Soc., N.Y. Acad. Scis., Am. Assn. Physicists in Medicine. Research on grand unified field theory, relativistic quantum field theory, quantum chromodynamics, quantum probability theory, supergravity, quantum cosmology, astrophysics, deep inelastic scattering, neutrino astronomy, neutrino tomography, discoverer classical uncertainty principle; subspecialty: relativity and gravitation. Patentee in field; contributor to design of NASA's proposed lunar base; originator olive branch as symbol of man's 1st landing on moon (on Susan B. Anthony and Eisenhower dollars); and manual Saturn takeover for Apollo moon program. Home: 206 Woodcombe Dr Houston TX 77062-2538 Office: NASA Johnson Space Ctr Houston TX 77058

WILSON, THOMAS MATTHEW, III, lawyer; b. Ware, Mass., Feb. 22, 1936; s. Thomas Matthew Jr. and Ann Veronica (Shea) W.; m. Deborah Ord Lockhart, Feb. 10, 1962; children: Deborah Veronica, Leslie Lockhart, Thomas Matthew IV. BA, Brown U., 1958; JD, U. Md., 1971. Bar: Md. 1972, U.S. Ct. Appeals (4th cir.) 1976, U.S. Supreme Ct. 1977. Sales mgr. Mid-Ea. Box Mfg. Co., Balt., 1966-74; asst. atty. gen., chief antitrust divsn. State of Md., Balt., 1974-79; ptnr. Tydings & Rosenberg, LLP, Balt., 1979—. Author: Defending an Antitrust Action Brought by a State, 1987, The Spectre of Double Recovery in Antitrust Federalism, 1989; co-author: Reciprocity and the Private Plaintiff, 1972; mem. editl. adv. bd. Bur. of Nat. Affairs Antitrust and Trade Regulation Report, 1979—. Mem. ABA (sect. on antitrust law 1974—, chmn. state antitrust enforcement com. 1986-89, antitrust sect. coun. 1990-93, coord. com. on legal edn. 1993—), Md. Bar Assn. (antitrust subcom. 1975-78), Internat. Bar Assn. (sect. on bus. law, antitrust law and monopolies com. 1983—), Churchwarden's Chess Club. Republican. Home: Baobab Farm Hampstead MD 21074 Office: Tydings & Rosenberg LLP 100 E Pratt St Baltimore MD 21202-1009

WILSON, THOMAS WOODROW, III, research scientist, consultant; b. Greensboro, N.C., Mar. 29, 1956; s. Thomas Woodrow Jr. and Ruth Hanes (Friddle) W. BS in Textile Chemistry with honors, N.C. State U., 1978, MS in Textile Chemistry, 1981, PhD in Fiber and Polymer Sci., 1986. Registered patent agent. Polymer scientist Rsch. Triangle Inst., Research Triangle Park, N.C., 1989-91; rsch. scientist Family Health Internat., Research Triangle Park, N.C., 1991-93, sr. rsch. scientist, 1993-94, assoc. dir., 1994-95; mgr. intellectual property and regulatory affairs Mayer Labs., Oakland, Calif., 1996-97; materials rschr. Nike, Beaverton, Oreg., 1997-99; advanced chemistry rsch. mgr. Nike, Taichung, Taiwan, 1999—; cons. IPAS, Carrboro, N.C., 1991-94. Patentee med. devices; contbr. articles to profl. jours. Grantee USDA, NASA, NIH/Nat. Inst. Dental Rsch., 1986. Mem. AAAS, Am. Chem. Soc. (polymeric materials sci. and engring. divsn., polymer divsn., rubber divsn., chemistry and law divsn.), ASTM, Sigma Xi. Avocations: leatherworking, woodworking, writing fiction. Office: Nike, 447 Wen Hsin Rd 28th Fl, Taichung ROC, Taiwan

WILSON, TREVOR GORDON, historian, educator; b. Auckland, New Zealand, Dec. 24, 1928; arrived in Australia, 1960; s. Andrew Gordon and Winifred Annie (Banyard) W.; m. (Mary) Jane Verney, Sept. 7, 1957; children: Jennifer Lynn, Sara Jane. MA, U. Auckland, 1951; PhD, U. Oxford, 1959. Asst. lectr. history Auckland U., Canterbury U., New Zealand, 1952-55; rsch. asst. govt. Manchester U., Eng., 1957-59; lectr., prof. history Adelaide U., Australia, 1960—; Commonwealth fellow St. John's Coll., Cambridge, Eng., 1972; vis. prof. Marshall U., W. Va., 1989. Author: The Downfall of the Liberal Party, 1914-1935, 1966, The Myriad Faces of War, 1986, (Adelaide Festival of Arts Lit. award 1988); co-author (with Robin Prior): Command on the Western Front 1914-1918, 1992, Passchendaele: The Untold Story, 1996, The First World War (Cassell History of Warfare), 1999; editor: The Political Diaries of C.P. Scott, 1970. Recipient Higby prize Am. Hist. Assn., 1965, Gilbert Campion award Hansard Soc., 1960. Fellow Royal Hist. Soc., Australian Acad. Humanities; mem. Hist. de la Grand Guerre (com.), Staff Club U. Adelaide. Australian Labour Party. Avocations: table tennis, jazz, studying Broadway and Hollywood musicals. Office: Univ Adelaide Dept History, Adelaide SA 5005, Australia

WILSON, WANDA LEE DAVIS, entertainment promotions professional, casting director; b. Pitts., May 15, 1950; d. James A. Davis, Jr. and Dorothy (Love) Davis Anselmi; m. Kirby L. Wilson Sr., Apr. 23, 1976 (div. July 1984); children: Le Chon Kirb, Lia Shawnyea. Student, Connelly Tech. Sch., Pitts., 1968-71, Allegheny Community Coll., Pitts., 1968-71, U. Pitts., 1984, 86. Stand-in co-host The Together Show Sta. KDKA-TV, CBS, Pitts., 1971; adminstrv. sec. GE, Pitts., 1971-78; sec., notary public Sta. WPCB-TV, Wall, Pa., 1979-80; producer, host The Wanda Wilson Show Am. Cablevision Co., Monroeville, Pa., 1981-84, Warner Cable Co. and Pitts. Telecommunications, Inc., 1984-87; mktg. mgr. The Informer newspaper Homewood Brushton Revitalization and Devel., Pitts., 1984-87; pres. local, nat. internat. pub. rels. W-W Prodns./Wanda Wilson Enterprises, Pitts., 1984—; sr. clk./chemical monitor Gencorp Aerojet Tech. Systems, Rancho Cordova, Calif., 1987-90; publicist, cons. Easy Internat., Pitts., 1990—; studio camera operator Sta. WPXI-TV, Pitts., 1990-92; casting dir. for commls., film, print media-theatre Wanda Wilson Enterprises, Pitts., 1992—; scout Modelsearch Am.; occasional writer, copywriter, announcer local radio shows, Pitts., 1972-85; radio show co-host, announcer Internat. People's Radio and TV, Sacramento, 1987; promoter concerts, screenplays, sound tracke Wan Mar Prodns., 1991—. Author (poetry) Love Traces on My Mind, 1972, (songs lyrics) The First Time I Saw You, 1982; performer poetry recitals, Pitts., 1973, (TV movies) $10,000,000 Getaway, 1990, Bump in the Night, 1990, Dead and Alive, 1991, (feature film) Lorenzo's Oil, 1991, Roommates, 1993; producer, hostess WanMar Info. and Talent Showcase Cable TV, Pitts., 1991—; line prodr., casting dir. With Abandon, 1999; casting dir. The Family Tree, 1999. Active Citizen Action for Reduction of Toxic Chems. in Product Packaging, 1990; organizer civic and community events, energy conservation, 1984-87; mem. Pitts. History and Landmarks Found., Smithsonian Assocs., 1991. Mem. AFTRA, NAFE, Pitts. Film Workers Assn., bd. dirs., Pittsburgh Film Workers Assn., Pitts. Models Assn., Pitts. Media Fedn. (bd. dirs.), Smithsonian Assocs. Democrat. Avocations: swimming, photography, art, interior decorating. Office: 2d Fl 547 Lincoln Ave Apt 1 Pittsburgh PA 15202-3534

WILSON, WESLEY WARREN, economics educator; b. Fargo, N.D., Feb. 7, 1958; children: Kelsey Gray, Regina Gray. BSBA, U. N.D., 1980; postgrad., N.D. State U., 1980-81; MA, Washington State U., 1984, PhD, 1986. Rsch. asst./assoc. Upper Great Plains Inst., N.D. State U., Fargo, 1980-81; rsch./teaching asst. dept. econs. Washington State U., Pullman, 1981-86, asst. prof. dept. agrl. econs., 1986-89; asst. prof. dept. econs. U. Oreg., Eugene, 1989-94, assoc. prof. dept. econs., 1995-2000, prof., 2000—; cons. Upper Great Plains Transp. Inst., 1982; presenter in field. Contbr. articles to profl. jours. Grantee Washington State U., 1989, USDA Agrl. coop. Svc., 1988-90, USDA Office Transp., 1987, Washington State U., 1985. Mem. Am. Agrl. Econs. Assn., Western Agrl. Econs. Assn., Am. Econ. Assn. (pres. TRPN and pub. utility group), Econometrics Soc., Indsl. Orgn. Soc., World Conf. on Transp. Rsch., Ctr. for Asian and Pacific Studies, Transp. Rsch. Forum (pres. agrl. and rural transp. chpt.). Democrat. Methodist. Avocations: golf, tennis, backpacking. Home: 4820 Larkwood St Eugene OR 97405-4014 Office: U Oreg Dept Econs Eugene OR 97405

WILSON, WILLIAM ALEXANDER, manufacturing engineer, consultant; b. Cleve., Sept. 8, 1959; s. Raymond and Lydia (Lima) W. Student, Cuyahoga C.C.; BME, Cleve. State U., 1986. Mfg. engr. Physics Internat., Wadsworth, Ohio, 1986-88; sr. mfg. engr. Lucas Aerospace, Broadview Heights, Ohio, 1988-89; mfg. engr. Siemens Energy and Automation, Inc., Norwood, Ohio, 1989—; prin. Wilson Engring., Cin., 1994—; cons. in field. Mem. SME (5 Yr. award 1992). Avocation: competitive swimming. Office: Wilson Engring 8605 Constitution Dr Cincinnati OH 45215-5301 also: Lemforder Corp 1100 Aviation Blvd Hebron KY 41048-9332

WILSON, WILLIAM JAMES, healthcare executive; b. Racine, Wis., Oct. 9, 1948; s. William Henry and Eileen (Tate) W.; m. Deborah Ann Leon, Nov. 14, 1987; children: Jacob Leon, James Tate. Degree in adminstrn. of justice summa cum laude, Am. U., 1972. Asst. dir. promotions Jerry Lewis Telthon, Richmond, Va., 1975; dir. mktg. Mile High Publs., N.Y.C., 1975-76; dir. bur. Travel Communicatiions, Honolulu, 1976-78; founder Hawaii 800, 1979—; v.p. mktg. Video Vacations, N.Y.C., 1982-84; founder Infovision, Los Angeles, 1984-87; chmn. bd. Visitor Cable Network, Honolulu, 1978—; pres. Comcor, Honolulu, 1976—; pres. bus. devel. 3HO Superhealth Hollistic Treatment Ctr., Tucson, 1990-93; pres. Educational Discovery, 1993-94; CEO Advanced Learning Inst., 1994—; mng. dir. Vet. Inst. Integrated Medicine, 1996—; founder Japan Am. News Network. Avocations: skiing, rugby. Home: 1109 Quince Ave Boulder CO 80304-0785 Office: PO Box 88377 Honolulu HI 96830-8377

WILSON, WILLIAM JAMES, marketing professional; b. Mpls., May 8, 1936; s. Elmo C. Wilson and Harriett (Ellis) Russo; m. Julie Steers, Sept. 24, 1960 (div. 1983); children: Amanda Jane, Heather May; m. Gabi Coatsworth, Aug. 4, 1983. AB, Yale U., 1958; MA, Cambridge U., Eng., 1964; postgrad., U. Vienna, summer 1964. Internat. advt. devel. mgr. Reader's Digest, London, 1964-67; exec. v.p., dir. Internat. Rsch. Assn., N.Y.C., 1968-71; chair, chief exec. officer Roper Starch Worldwide, Harrison, N.Y., 1971—; bd. dirs. Roper Ctr. Storrs Ct.; U.S. rep. ESOMAR, The Netherlands 1982-88; chmn. Coun. of Am. Survey Rsch. Orgn., 1994, Coun. for Mktg. and Opinion Rsch., 1996—; past dir. Market Rsch. Coun; mem. bd. advisors MSMR program U. Tex., Arlington, A.C. Nielsen Ctr. for Market Rsch. U. Wis., Madison, Baruch Coll., N.Y.C.; mem. bd. dirs. Intersections Inc. Contbr. articles to profl. jours. Mem. Am. Mktg. Assn., Internat. Advt. Assn., Am. Assn. Pub. Opinion Rsch., World Assn. Pub. Opinion Rsch., European Soc. Opinion & Mktg. Rsch. Avocations: gardening, golfing, reading, walking. Office: Roper Starch Worldwide Inc 500 Mamaroneck Ave Ste 103 Harrison NY 10528-1608

WILSON, WILLIAM ROBERT, surgeon; b. Norwich, Conn., June 2, 1954; s. William Robert and Margaret Mary (Sullivan) W.; m. Joan Marie Wilson, Apr. 6, 1985; children: William Robert III, Brandon David, Alaina Victoria. AB cum laude, Kenyon Coll., 1976; MD, U. Conn., 1982. Instr. U. Conn., Farmington, 1977-78; resident in gen. surgery U. Vt., Burlington, 1982-87; resident in thoracic surgery Case Western Res. U., Cleve., Ill., 1987-89; assoc. staff surgeon Hennepin County Med. Ctr., Mpls., 1989-90; fellow in pediat. cardiac surgery The Heart Inst. for Children, Oak Lawn, Ill., 1990-91; asst. prof. surgery and pediat. Med. Coll. Ohio, Toledo, 1991-97, chief pediat. cardiac surgery, 1991-97; assoc. prof. surgery & child health, chief pediat. cardiac The Children's Hosp. U. Mo., Columbia, 1997—; dir. ECMO program Med. Coll. Ohio, 1991—. Contbr. articles to profl. jours. and chpts. to books. Fellow ACS; mem. AMA, Soc. Thoracic Surgeons, Am. Heart Assn., Midwest Pediat. Cardiology Soc. Episcopalian. Avocations: skiing, golf. Office: Divsn Cardiothoracic Surgery Dept Surgery MA 312 1 Hospital Dr Columbia MO 65201-5276

WILSON-ALLEN, TAWANA BELINDA, community and political organizer, consultant; b. Mooresville, N.C., Dec. 16, 1949; d. Jehu Nivens and Ruby (Henderson) Alexander; m. Emmanuel Allen; children: Niki, Bruce, Tamia. BA in Sociology, N.C. Ctrl. U., 1972; postgrad. in Urban Adminstrn., U. N.C., Charlotte, 1979-81; Cert. Profl. Orgn., Midwest Acad., Chgo., 1984; Cert. in Polit. Campaign Mgmt., Kent State U., 1985. Tchr., dir. pre-kindergarten Pub. Schs./Dept. Human Resources, Prince George County, Md., 1972-77; organizer Coun. Sr. Citizens, Mecklenburg County, N.C., 1983-85; exec. dir. North Carolinians for Effective Citizenship, Charlotte, 1983-86; assoc. dir. Carolina Cmty. Project, Charlotte, 1986-90; devel. dir. Rural Advancement Fund, Charlotte, 1989-90; congl. liaison U.S. Rep. Melvin Watt, 12th Dist., Charlotte, 1993—; founder, pres. Inst. Cmty. Resources, Charlotte, 1990-92; trainer leadership devel. Charlotte Presbytery, 1990—; regional field dir. Harvey Gantt for U.S. Senate Campaign,

Charlotte, 1990, Mel Watt for Congress Campaign, Charlotte, 1992. Founder/trainer Electoral Skills Program Cmty. Based Campaigns, 1990—; program design/trainer leadership devel. program Miss/Mr. Black Teenage World, 1986-92, Leadership Coalition of So. Black Youth, 1986-92. Mem. Nat. Dem. Com., Washington, 1996; 1st v.p. Black Polit. Caucus, Charlotte-Mecklenburg, 1996—; mem. Black Women's Caucus, Charlotte-Mecklenburg, 1995—; coord. Mecklenburg Voter Coalition, Charlotte, 1996—; mem. Emily's List, Washington, 1996—; bd. dirs. Charlotte Sister Cities, Com., 1996; session mem., elder Eastfield Presbyn. Ch., 1996; mem. Presbyn. Women; organizer Charlotte/Kumasi, Ghana Sister Cities Com., 1994—. Recipient Bd. Dirs. Svc. award Cmty. Rels. Com., Charlotte, 1995. Mem. Focus on Leadership (v.p. program chair 1991-95, trainer 1996, Svc. awards 1989-95, Pres.'s award 1995, v.p. emeritus 1995), Delta Sigma Theta. Avocations: piano, flute, water color art, African art and artifacts collector. Home: 6921 Folger Dr Charlotte NC 28270-5947 Office: Congressman Melvin Watt 324 N College St Charlotte NC 28202-2150

WILSON OF TILLYORN, BARON See WILSON, DAVID CLIVE

WILSON-WEBB, NANCY LOU, adult education administrator; b. Maypearl, Tex., Jan. 20, 1932; d. Madison Grady Wise and Mary Nancy Pearson-Bedford (Haney) Wilson; m. John Crawford Webb, July 29, 1972. BS magna cum laude, Abilene (Tex.) Christian U., 1953; MEd with high honors, Tex. Christian U., 1985. Cert. tchr., mid-mgmt., sch. adminstr., Tex. Tchr. elem. grades Ft. Worth Ind. Sch. Dist., 1953-67, adult edn. tchr., 1967-73; dir. adult edn. consortium for 38 sch. dists. Tex. Edn. Agy., 1973—; pres. Nat. Commn. on Adult Basic Edn., 1994-95; pres. Tex. Adult Edn. Adminstrn., 1994; apptd. mem. Tex. State Literacy Coun., 1987-94, Tex. State Sch. Bd. Commn., 1994-99; exec. bd. Tex. Coun. Co-op Dirs., 1989-99, pres., 1994—; apptd. to Gov. Ann Richard's Task Force for Edn. Cons. to textbooks, 1994-98; editor textbooks, 1999. Pres. Jr. Womans Club, Ft. Worth, 1969, Fine Arts Guild, Tex. Christian U., Ft. Worth, 1970-72, Ft. Worth Womens Civic Club Coun., 1970; active Exec. Libr. Bd., Ft. Worth, 1990—, Jewel Charity Ball, 1988-2000; apptd. bd. dirs. Literacy Plus in North Tex., 1988-99, Greater Ft. Worth Literacy Coun., 1976-88; commr. Ed-16 Task Forces Tex. Edn. Agy., 1985-94; literacy bd. dirs. Friends of Libr., 1967-2000, Opera Guild Bd. Ft. Worth, 1965—, Fort Worth Ballet Guild, Johnson County (Tex.) Corrs. Bd., 1990-2000; bd. dirs. Salvation Army, 1991-99; mem. Tarrant County Bd. on Aging, 1997-98; mem. Tex. Workforce Coun., 1997-98; mem. Commn. Status of Women, Ft. Worth, 1973-99; mem. Southside Ch. of Christ. Recipient Bevy award Jr. Womans Club, 1968, Proclamation Commrs. Ct. Outstanding 43 Yr. Literacy Svc. to Tarrant County Com. Ctr., 1994, Tarrant County Woman of Yr. award, Fort Worth Star Telegram, 1995, Outstanding Leadership award Ft. Worth ISD Sch. Bd., 1985, 95; named one of Most Outstanding Educators in U.S. Nat. Assn. Adult Edn., 1983, Most Outstanding Woman Edn., City of Ft. Worth, 1991, others; nominated to Tex. Hall of Fame for Women, 1991; named to Ft. Worth Hall of Fame, 1992; scholar Germany, 1983. Mem. NEA, DAR (Mary Isham Keith chpt. 1985-2000, Nat. Most Outstanding Literacy award 1992, Leadership Literacy award 1985-87, 89, 94), AAUW, Am. Assn. Adult and Cont. Edn. (v.p. 1987-89, chair 1993 internat. conv. 1992, Nat. Adminstr. of Yr. in Adult Edn. 1998, Most Outstanding Adminstr. Adult Edn. in U.S. 1999), Tex. Assn. Adult and Cont. Edn. (pres. 1985-86, Most Outstanding Adult Adminstr. in Tex. 1984), Tex. Coun. Adult Edn. Dirs. (pres.), Coun. World Affairs (bd. dirs. 1980-92), Am. Bus. Women's Assn., Ft. Worth C. of C., Lecture Found., Internat. Reading Assn. (Literacy Challenge award 1991), Ft. Worth Adminstrv. Assn., Zonta, Tanglewood Garden Club, Ft. Worth Garden Club, Woman's Club, Ft. Worth Petroleum Club, Carousel Dance Club, Optimist Club (Ft. Worth), Met. Dinner Dance Club, Ridglea Country Club, Crescent Club (Dallas), Alpha Delta Kappa (Nat. Literacy award 1992), Phi Delta Kappa. Home: 3716 Fox Hollow St Fort Worth TX 76109-2616 Office: 100 N University Dr Fort Worth TX 76107-1360

WILTSHIRE, KENNETH WILLIAM, political science educator; b. Brisbane, Queensland, Australia, Dec. 11, 1944; s. Harry William and Beryl Muriel (Burdeu) W.; m. Gail Jocelyn Raymond, Apr. 27, 1968; 1 child, Christopher James. B in Econs. with honors, U. Queensland, Brisbane, 1968, PhD, 1981; MSc in Politics, London Sch. Econs., 1972. Rsch. economist Queensland Govt., Brisbane, 1962-70; sr. lectr. U. Queensland, 1972-83, prof. polit. sci., 1983—; chmn. Australian Heritage Commn., Canberra, 1982-85; chmn. UNESCO Nat. Com., 1992—; mem. exec. bd. UNESCO, 1999—. Author: An Introduction to Australian Public Administration, 1974, Formulating Government Budgets, 1976, Administrative Federalism, 1977, Planning and Federalism, 1986, Privatisation: The British Experience, 1987, The History of the Professional Officers Association, 1987, People, Places and Politics, 1996. Broadcaster Australian Broadcasting Commn., 1973—; polit. analyst Ten TV Network Australia, 1974—; mem. Inquiry Into Efficiency and Effectiveness of Brisbane City Coun., 1979. Recipient Order of Australia for contbn. to pub. policy and adminstrn. and UNESCO, 1998. Fellow Inst. Pub. Adminstrn. Australia; mem. Inst. Pub. Adminstrn. Can., Royal Inst. Pub. Adminstrn. (U.K.), Convocation London Sch. Econs. (life). Office: U Queensland Ctr Pub Admin, Lucia St, Brisbane QLD 4072, Australia

WILTSHIRE, WILLIAM HARRISON FLICK, lawyer; b. Martinsburg, W.Va., Dec. 29, 1930; s. Harrison Flick and Virginia Faulkner (White) W.; m. Edith Hayward, Nov. 13, 1954; children: Ashley Wiltshire Spotswood, Winn Wiltshire Crockard, William Harrison Flick Jr., Ashton Hayward. BA, Shepherd Coll., 1952; JD, U. Fla., 1960. Bar: Fla. 1960, U.S. Ct. Appeals (5th cir.) 1960, U.S. Dist. Ct. (no. dist.) Fla. 1960, U.S. Dist. Ct. (so. dist.) La. 1975, U.S. Dist. Ct. (so. dist.) Ala. 1978, U.S. Dist. Ct. (so. dist.) Fla. 1980, U.S. Ct. Appeals (11th cir.) 1982, U.S. Supreme Ct. 1987; cert. in civil trial Nat. Bd. Trial Advocacy and Fla. Bar Assn. With Jones & Harrell, Pensacola, Fla., 1960-62; ptnr. Harrell, Wiltshire, Stone, Swearingen, Wilson & Harrell and predecessor firms, Pensacola, 1962—; pres. Bayou Tex. Assn., 1967-71; dir. Fiesta Five Flags, 1968-82, pres. 1976-77. Contbr. articles to profl. jours. and textbooks. Trustee, gen. counsel Naval Aviation Mus. Found., 1989—; trustee Episcopal Day Sch., 1965-69; bd. dirs. Pensacola Acad. Arts and Scis., 1970-75, pres. 1973-74; bd. dirs. Gul Goast Coun. Boy Scouts Am., 1982—. Served with USN, 1952-57. Fellow Am. Coll. Trial Lawyers, Nat. Bd. Trial Advocacy; mem. ABA, Fla. Bar Assn., Am. Trial Lawyers Assn., Acad. Fla. Trial Lawyers, State Bar Fla. (chmn. trial lawyers sect. 1973-74, chmn. appellate rules com. 1974-78), Def. Rsch. Inst., Am. Judicature Soc., Rotary Club. Republican. Address: PO Box 1832 Pensacola FL 32598-1832

WIMBROW, PETER AYERS, III, lawyer; b. Salisbury, Md., Apr. 11, 1947; s. Peter Ayers Jr. and Margaret (Johnson) W. BS, East Tenn. State U., 1970; JD, Washington and Lee U., 1973. Bar: Md. 1973, U.S. Dist. Ct. Md. 1974, U.S. Ct. Appeals (4th cir.) 1979, U.S. Supreme Ct. 1979, U.S. Tax Ct. 1981, U.S. Ct. Appeals (D.C. cir.) 1981, U.S. Ct. Appeals (3d cir.) 1985. Sole practice Ocean City, Md., 1974—. Photographer, cast mem.: (film) Clear and Present Danger; contbg. editor Coconut Times. Mem. ACLU, City Solicitor Feasibility Study Com., Ocean City; mem. WWII com. Berlin Heritage Found. Mem. ABA, ATLA, Md. State Bar Assn. (bd. govs., program com., membership com., centennial com., mem. coun. solo & small firm practice sect.), Worcester County Bar Assn. (sec., treas., v.p., pres., chmn. com. on athletic endeavors), Md. Trial Lawyers Assn., Md. Criminal Def. Attys. Assn., Appellate Jud. Nominating Commn., Nat. Criminal Def. Attys. Assn., 29th Divsn. Assn., Terrapin Club. Democrat. Home: Seatime Condominium 136 St 502-n Ocean City MD 21842 Office: PO Box 56 4100 Coastal Hwy Ocean City MD 21843

WIMMEL, WALTER ERWIN, philologist; b. Krofdorf-Gleiberg, Hesse, Germany, Sept. 27, 1922; s. Wilhelm Maximilian and Else Louise (Hoffmann) W.; m. Johanna Maria Haefele, July 22, 1953; children: Conrad Hermann, Elsa Maria. PhD, U. Freiburg, Germany, 1950; Habilitation, U. Freiburg, 1957. Asst. U. Freiburg, 1951-57, univ. lectr., 1957-62, prof. extraord., 1962-63; prof. ord. philology U. Marburg, 1963—. Author: Kallimachos in Rom, 1960, Zur Form der Horazischen Diatribensatire, 1962, Der frühe Tibull, 1968, Hirtenkrieg und arkadisches Rom, 1972, Tibull und Delia I, 1976, II, 1983, Die Kultur holt uns ein, 1981, Der Tragische Dichter L. Varius Rufus, 1981, Collectanea Augusteertum und späte Republik, 1987, Die Bacchusode des Horaz, 1993, Sprachliche Ambiguitat bei Horaz, 1994; contbr. 140 articles to profl. jours. Fellow Marburger Gelehrte Gesellschaft. Avocation: history of technics. Home: Renthof 39 Marburg, D-35037 Hesse Germany Office: Philological Inst Philipps U, Wilhelm Röpke Str 6D Marburg, D-35039 Hesse Germany

WIMMER, CLEMENS ALEXANDER, garden historian; b. Berlin, Mar. 6, 1959; s. Dietrich and Edith (Langer) Krüger. Diploma in Landscape Architecture, Berlin Tech. U., 1982; Dr.rer.hort., U. Hannover, 1985. Architect Berlin, 1984-93, Potsdam, Germany, 1993—. Author: History of Garden Theory, 1989; editor Zandera: Report of German Horticulture Library, 1990—. Mem. Bücherei d. Deutschen Gartenbaues (mng. dir.), Pückler Gesellschaft (advisor) Garden History Soc. Home and Office: Thaerstr 7, 14469 Potsdam Germany

WIN, MYO, nutritionist, biochemist; b. Yangon, Burma; s. Aladdeen and Tin Aye Win; m. Mie Mie Tun. M.B.B.S., Inst. Medicine, Yangon, Myanmar, 1976; DFT, Rangoon Inst. Tech., 1978; M.Profl. Studies, U. of The Philippines, 1985. Asst. surgeon Dept. Health, Yangon, 1981-83; demonstrator Dept. Med. Scis., Inst. of Medicine, Yangon, 1983-88, asst. lectr., 1988-92, lectr., 1992—, chmn. R&D sect., 1985—; joint sec. Med. Edn. Unit, Yangon, 1986-96. Contbr. articles to profl. jours. Nuffic fellow Netherlands Govt. and FAO, 1985. Mem. Myanmar Med. Assn. Fax: 95-1-690265. Home: #9 148 St 6th Fl Tamwe, Yangon Myanmar Office: Inst of Medicine 2, Dept Biochemistry, Yangon Myanmar

WINAI-STROM, GABRIELE, political scientist; b. Karlsruhe, Germany, May 22, 1944; arrived in Sweden, 1949; d. Herman and Marta (Arnell) W.; m. Arne Gustav Tord Strom, Feb. 1, 1969; children: Niklas, Martin. BA, U. Stockholm, 1969; PhD, U. Uppsala, Sweden, 1978. Sec. Expert Group Migration & Ethnicity, Stockholm, 1981-87; head of divsn. Ministry Labor, Stockholm, 1981-96; rsch. program leader U. Uppsala, Sweden, 1987-92; prof., rschr. U. Dar-es-Salaam, Tanzania, 1988-91; program leader OSCE, Stockholm, 1994-96; spl. advisor Ministry Fgn. Affairs, Stockholm, 1996—. Home: Orrspelsv 17, S-16766 Stockholm Sweden Office: Ministry Fgn Affairs, S-11139 Stockholm Sweden

WINAND, RENÉ FERNAND PAUL, metallurgy educator emeritus; b. Ixelles, Belgium, Nov. 15, 1932; s. Fernand and Malvina (Lelievre) W.; m. Christiane Hauer, Mar. 25, 1961; children: Pascaline, Jean-Marc, Henri. BS, Free U. Brussels, 1949, MS in Electromech. Engring., 1954, PhD in Metallurgy, 1960. Engr. Ateliers de Constructions Electriques de Charleroi, Belgium, 1954-55, Brit. Petroleum Belgium, Antwerp, 1956-57; rsch. asst. Free U. Brussels, 1957-61, lectr., 1961-67, prof., 1967-98, head dept. metallurgy and electrochemistry, 1968-98, chmn. Faculty Applied Scis., 1977-80, chmn. Ctr. Indsl. Rsch., 1979-98, vice-rector, 1993-98, prof. emeritus, 1998—; Gollick lectr., U. Mo., Rolla, 1985. Patentee in field; contbr. articles to sci. jours. Comdr. Order of Couronne, Belgium; recipient East Surface Treatment Sci. and Tech. award, 1995, Electrodeposition Sect. Electrochem. Soc. award, 1999. Mem. Minerals Metals and Materials Soc. U.S., Electrochem. soc. U.S., Inst. Mining and Metallurgy U.K., Iron and steel Inst. Japan, Can. Inst. Mining and Metallurgy, French Soc. Metallurgy, Robotics Assn. Belgium (hon. chmn. 1988). Avocation: flying. Office: Univ Libre Brussels CP165, 50 ave F D Roosevelt, B 1050 Brussels Belgium also: Mgr CHEMETCONSULT SPRL, 24 Ave Jean XXIII, B 1330 Rixensart Belgium

WINATA, KEN OMAR, small business owner; b. Jakarta, West Java, Indonesia, May 10, 1944; s. Ignatius Bong and Maria (Lim) W.; m. Lily Bogar, June 18, 1971 (div. June 1993); children: Steve, Felix, Irinna; m. Jenna Rosana Chen, Mar. 27, 1994; children: Liang, Chien, Yen. Student, Canisius Coll., Jakarta, 1960-63; grad. civil engr. cum laude, ITB, Bandung, 1967; grad. in mech. engring., Stuttgart-Untertürkheim, Germany, 1971. Civil engr. Daimler-Beni AG, Germany, 1971-73; prodn. and quality control supr. Star Motors Indonesia, Jakarta, 1973-79; sales and field svc. asst. mgr. Maschinen Bau Makindo, Jakarta, 1979-82; instrumentation and turbochargers sales and svc. mgr. P.T. Mega Daya, Jakarta, 1982-85; asst. sales mgr. Nalco & Teledyne USA, Jakarta, 1985-88; sales and supply mgr. Dhanan Jaya Trading Co., Jakarta, 1988-92; asst. mktg. mgr. KHD Cement Plant, 1990-93; sales and tech. asst. mgr. PT Lerindo Internat., Jakarta, 1993-94; Indonsia country mgr. Kim Seng Hardware & Oil Field Supply PTE, Ltd., Jakarta, 1993-97; owner Jewelry & Goldsmith, Jakarta, 1994—. Roman Catholic. Avocations: jogging, fitness, tennis, golfing. Home: JL Kebon Pala I/15, 13320 Jakarta Indonesia

WINBERG, MARGARETA, Swedish government official; b. Sjuntorp, Sweden, 1947. Tchg. cert., Karistad Tchrs. Tng. Coll., 1969. Tchr. Krokom, Sweden, 1969; active mcpl. politics Krokom, 1970-79; with County Coun., Krokom, 1979-81; chmn. Fedn. Social Dem. Party Women, Stockholm, 1984-90; min. agr. Swedish Govt., Stockholm, 1994-96, 2000, min. labor, 1996—; chmn. Parliamentary Com. on Agr., 1992—, mem. various bds. and polit. com. Office: Min Agr, Drottninggatan 21, S-103 33 Stockholm Sweden*

WINCHELL, GEORGE WILLIAM, curriculum and technology educator; b. Coldwater, Mich., Nov. 12, 1948; s. Elwood F. and Ethel L. (DeBray) W.; m. Marcia A. Hersh, June 7, 1969 (dec.); 1 child, Paul Michael. BA, Mich. State U., 1969; diploma, Leningrad (USSR) State U., 1967; MA, Mich. State U., 1973; EdS, Cen. Mich. U., 1982. Cert. elem., secondary, Russian, lang. arts and social sci. tchr.; cert. adminstr., supt., elem. prin. Elem. tchr. Silverton (Colo.) Pub. Schs.; tech. edn. cons. Stanton, Mich.; off-campus instr. Cen. Mich. U., Mt. Pleasant; life-long learning instr. Mich. State U.; profl. devel. coord., facilitator strategic planning, dir. instrnl. tech. Montcalm Area Intermediate Sch. Dist., Stanton; dir. tech. edn. Cen. Montcalm Pub. Sch., Stanton; grants coord. Crystal Automation Sys., Inc. Mem. ASCD, Internat. Soc. Tech. Edn., Am. Soc. Distance Learning, Am. Soc. Quality, Mich. Assn. Computer Users in Learning, Nat. Staff Devel. Coun. Office: Crystal Automation Sys Inc 617 E Lake St Stanton MI 48888-8902

WINCHESTER, HILARY PATIENCE MARY, geographer, educator; b. Ilkeston, Eng., Mar. 22, 1954; arrived in Australia, 1987; 1 child, Richard. BA with honors, Oxford U., Eng., 1974, DPhil, 1980. Lectr. geography U. Plymouth, Eng., 1984-87, U. Wollongong, Australia, 1988-90; rsch. fellow U. New Eng., Australia, 1987-88; sr. lectr. U. Newcastle, Australia, 1991-95, head dept. geography, 1996—, pres. acad. senate, 1997—, mem. coun.; mem. social scis. and humanities panel Australian Rsch. Coun. Author: Contemporary France, 1993; co-author: Agricultural Change: France and the EEC, 1988; editor: Australian Geographical Studies; contbr. articles to profl. jours. Coun. mem. The Univ. Newcastle, 1996. Mem. Inst. Australian Geographers (coun.), Inst. Brit. Geographers. Avocation: distance running. Office: U Newcastle, University Dr, Callaghan NSW 2308, Australia

WINDER, RICHARD EARNEST, legal foundation administrator, writer, consultant; b. Vernal, Utah, Sept. 23, 1950; s. William Wallace and Winnifred (Jenkins) W.; m. Janice Fay Walker, Apr. 19, 1975; children: Scott Christian, Eric John, Brian Geoffrey, Laura Jeanne, Amy Elizabeth. BA magna cum laude, Brigham Young U., 1974, JD cum laude, 1978; MBA with honors, U. Michigan, Flint, 1988. Bar: Utah 1978, U.S. Dist. Ct. Utah 1978, Mich. 1979, U.S. Dist. Ct. (ea. and we. dists.) Mich. 1979. Tchg. asst., grad. instr. Brigham Young U., Provo, Utah, 1976-78; law clk. Willingham & Coté, E. Lansing, Mich., 1978-79, atty., 1979-87; exec. v.p. Mgmt. Leasing, Inc., Battle Creek, Mich., 1987-88, Mgmt. Options, Inc., Lansing, Mich., 1988-91; fin. mgr. Mich. State Bar Found., Lansing, Mich., 1991-94, dep. dir., fin. mgr., 1994—; panelist 9th Nat. Legis. Conf. Small Bus., San Antonio, 1987; adj. prof. Davenport Coll. Bus., Lansing, 1990-92, mgmt. adv. com., 1993-96; mem. founding steering com. Capital Quality Initiative, Lansing, 1992-96; liaison State Bar Mich. Long Range Planning Process, 1996-97; co-founder, rsch. prin. Quality Dynamics Rsch. Inst., Haslett, Mich., 1994-97; rsch. prin. Leadership Dynamics Rsch. Inst., Haslett, 1998—. Author: (with others) Value Sharing: Value Building, 1990, Corporate Orienteering, 1995; contbr., bd. editors: Summary of Utah Real Property Law, 1978. Vol. leader Boy Scouts Am., Chief Okemos Coun., Lansing, 1978—. Fellow Mich. State Bar Found.; mem. ABA, Am. Soc. Quality Control (chmn. Lansing-Jackson sect. 1994-95, spkr. and writer 1992—), Mich. Bar Assn., Utah Bar Assn., Lansing Regional C. of C. (small bus. coun., MBA task force Bus. and Edn. com. 1988-92, recipient Chmn.'s award 1992), Beta Gamma Sigma. Republican. Mem. LDS Ch. Avocations: writing, speaking, computer technology, research, teaching. Office: Mich State Bar Found 306 Townsend St Lansing MI 48933-2012

WINDGASSE V WENDORFF, GABRIELE, environmental scientist; b. Bonn, Germany, June 19, 1962; d. Heinz and Herta (Leissnig) Windgasse; m. Bernd-Eckhard von Wendorff, Aug. 25, 1994; children: Felix, Anna. Diploma, Tech. U. Berlin, 1982-86; MS, N.J. Inst. Tech., Newark, 1988; DrPH, Columbia U., 1993. Cert. occupl. safety and health officer, Germany. Adj. prof. N.J. Inst. Tech., 1988-96; asst. prof. Columbia U., N.Y.C., 1994—; sr. rsch. assoc. Hazardous Substance Mgmt. Rsch. Ctr., Newark, 1993-96, prin. investigator. Mem. AAAS, Am. Chem. Soc., Internat. Microwave Power Inst. Avocations: gardening, hiking, painting. Office: Columbia U SPH Divsn Environ Health Scis 60 Haven Ave New York NY 10032-2604

WINDHOLZ, LAURENTIUS, physicist; b. Ratten, Austria, July 9, 1949; s. Lorenz and Johanna (Gruden) W.; m. Eva Lex, Feb. 25, 1975; children: Sabine, Maria, Julia, Susanne. Diploma in Engring., Tech. U. Graz, Austria, 1974, D of Tech., 1980. From asst. to assoc. prof. Tech. U. Graz, 1974-94, prof., 1994—. Guest editor Physica Scripta, 1989, 96; contbr. articles to profl. jours. Office: Tech Univ Graz Inst fr Exptl Physics, Petersgasse 16, A-8010 Graz Austria

WINDHORST, ROBERT DENNIS, II, aerospace engineer; b. Redondo Beach, Calif., Jan. 25, 1971; s. Robert Dennis Windhorst and Norine Farrar. BS, U. Calif., Davis, 1993; MS, Santa Clara U., 1997, PhD, 1999. R&D engr. Space Sys. Loral, Palo Alto, Calif., 1993-96; adj. lectr. Santa Clara (Calif.) U., 1998-99; aerospace engr. NASA Ames Rsch. Ctr., Moffett Field, Calif., 1999—. Bible study coord. 20 Something Christian Fellowship Peace Luth. Ch., Santa Clara, 1997. Mem. AIAA, Tau Beta Pi. Avocations: swimming, running, mountain bike, scuba, skiing. E-mail: rwindhorst@mail.arc.nasa.gov. Home: 928 Maria Ln Apt D Sunnyvale CA 94086-8929 Office: NASA Ames Rsch Ctr Mail Stop 210 10 Moffett Field CA 94035

WINDLER, EBERHARD ERNST THEODOR, internist; b. Bremen, Germany, Dec. 4, 1950; s. Ernst and Gertraut Gesine (Garbade) W.; m. Friederike Luise Lempp, Dec. 4, 1985; children: Anne Margarete, Johannes Simon, Dorothea Christine. MD, U. Heidelberg, Germany, 1977. Bd. cert. internist, gastroenterologist, endocrinclogist. Postdoctoral fellow U. Calif., San Francisco, 1977-80; resident internal medicine U. Heidelberg, 1980; resident internal medicine U. Hamburg, Germany, 1981-86, cons. internal medicine, 1987-89, prof. medicine, cons., 1990-91, prof. medicine, 1992—. Editor: Hepatic Endocytosis of Lipids and Proteins, 1992, Hepatic Protein and Lipid Metabolism, 1996, Lipid Therapy in the Prevention and Treatment of Coronary Artery Disease, 1999. Lt. German Army, 1969-71. Recipient awards Dr. Martini-Stiftung Found., 1985, Werner Otto Found., 1991. Mem. German Soc. Internal Medicine (Theodor-Frerichs prize 1984), German Soc. Digestive and Metabolic Diseases, Am. Heart Assn. (Coun. Arteroscleresis). Avocations: pictorial arts, sports, skiing, riding. Office: U Hamburg-Eppendorf, Martinistr 52, D-20246 Hamburg Germany

WINDMILL, STEVEN MICHAEL, business strategy professional; b. London, Feb. 26, 1957; s. Ronald Alfred and Patricia (Bacon) W.; m. Virginia Anne Judge, May 1, 1956; children: Dominique A.V., Roger Stefan. BA with honors, London U., 1987; MBA, Brunel U., Eng., 1993; PhD, Pacific Western U., 1998. Cert. mil. engr. Bus. strategist Civil Svc., Eng., 1976-91; dir. Sun Alliance, Eng., 1991-94; head strategic planning Thames Valley Enterprise, Ltd., Eng., 1994—; part-time dir. C.A.L.E., Ltd., Eng., 1994-96, Trident Motor Co., Ltd., 1994-96; cons. The Hambleden Group Ltd., London, 1986—; chief exec., chief knowledge officer South East Eng. Devel. Agy., 1999-00. Author: Leadership & Growth in SME Companies, 1996, UK Business Performance 1986-96, 1996, Thames Valley: A Economic Assessment, 1998. Town crier South London C. of C., 1993-97. Maj. U.K. Army, 1976-96, NATO. Recipient Hon. Freedom of Crowborough, Her Majesty, 1987, Her Majesties Territorial Decoration, Buckingham Palace, 1994, Nigmegan medal Mayor Nigmegan Town Hall, 1989. Fellow Royal Soc. Arts. Anglican. Avocations: shooting, riding, hill climbing. Home: 149 St Andrews Rd, Surrey Coulsdon CR5 3HL, England

WINDSOR, COLIN GEORGE, physicist; b. Beckenham, Kent, U.K., June 28, 1938; s. George Thomas and Mabel (Rayment) W.; m. Margaret Elizabeth Lee, July 13, 1963; children: Jonathan, Elizabeth, Jane. BA in Physics with honors, Oxford (Eng.) U., 1960, PhD, 1963. Rsch. assoc. Yale U., New Haven, Conn., 1963-64; scientist U.K. Atomic Energy Authority, Harwell, U.K., 1964-96, Culham, U.K., 1996—; sr. cons. PENOP Ltd., 1998—; vis. fellow Japanese Soc. for Promotion of Sci., Sendaii, 1980; hon. prof. physics Birmingham U., U.K., 1990. Author: Pulsed Neutron Scattering, 1981, Four Computer Models, 1983, Solid State Science, Past, Present and Predicted, 1987; co-organizer (exhbn.) History of the Neutron, 1982; contbr. articles to profl. jours. Recipient Duddell medal Inst. Physics, U.K., 1986. Fellow Royal Soc. U.K., Brit. Inst. Nondestructive Testing, Inst. Physics U.K. Avocations: singing, art, cycling, naturism. Office: UKAEA Fusion, D3 Culham Lab, Abingdon OX14 3DB, United Kingdom

WINEBRENNER, SUSAN KAY, writer, educational consultant; b. Milw., Mar. 11, 1939; d. Samuel Bernard and Lillian (Ginsberg) Schuckit; m. Neil T. Winebrenner, Feb. 11, 1981 (dec.); children: Stacy Lynne Naimon, Kari Beth Naimon. BS, U. Wis., 1956; MS, U. Wis., Milw., 1979. Cert. tchr., Ill., Wis. Tchr. Shorewood (Wis.) Pub. Sch., 1961-81, River Forest (Ill.) Sch. Dist. 90, 1981-83; gifted coord. Forest Park (Ill.) Sch. Dist. 91, Ill., 1983-86; cons. Self-Edn. Cons. Svcs., Brooklyn, Mich., 1986—; steering com. Nat. Staff Devel. Coun., Chgo., 1986—. Author: Super Sentences Activity Book, 1987, Cluster Grouping Fact Sheet, 1996, Teaching Gifted Kids in the Regular Classroom, 2nd edit., 2000, Teaching Kids with Learning Difficulties in the Regular Classroom, 1996; contbr. numerous articles on differentiating instruction for atypical learners. Recipient Outstanding Tchr. award Joint Coun. on Econ. Edn., Wis., 1979. Mem. ASCD (presenter), Nat. Assn. Gifted Children (presenter). Home and Office: 160 Riviera Dr Brooklyn MI 49230-9795

WINEBRENNER, WILLIAM PATRICK, writer; b. West Columbia, W.Va., Sept. 26, 1933; s. Richard Arthur Winebrenner and Lucy Ethel Riley; children: Rita Jean Hreha, William Patrick II, Tonya Michelle Noel. Grad. h.s., Mason, W.Va. Journeyman Internat. Brotherhood Elec. Workers, Toledo, 1968-95; ret.; mem. adv. bd. Muskingum Area Tech. Coll., Zanesville, Ohio, 1998; owner Valley Enterprises Pub., Stockport, Ohio, 1993-98. Author: (books) The Woodwalkers, 1993, Smoke in the Valley, 1995, Narrowbackin', 1997, From Out of the Forest, 1998, A Place of Evil, 1999. Mem. Elec. Workers Retirement. Democrat. Avocations: hunting, fishing, writing and promoting books. Home: 2300 State Route 376 Stockport OH 43787-9570

WINEFIELD, HELEN RUSSELL, psychology educator; b. Adelaide, Australia, Feb. 26, 1946; d. George Russell and Jessie (Miller) Cowley; m. Anthony Harold Winefield, Oct. 25, 1968; children: Matthew James, Julia Louise. B.A. with 1st class honors, U. Adelaide, 1967, Ph.D., 1974. Registered psychologist S. Australian Psychol. Bd. Psychologist Mental Health Services, S. Australia, 1967-69; postgrad. award Australian Commonwealth Govt., Adelaide, 1970-71; lectr. psychiatry U. Adelaide, 1972-80, sr. lectr., 1981-93, assoc. prof., 1994—; coord. Masters Clin. Psychology, 1999—. Contbg. author book in field, also articles to profl. jours. Mem. Australian Psychol. Soc., South Australian Children's Interests Bur. Avocations: literature, theatre. Office: Dept Psychiatry, U Adelaide, Adelaide SA 5005, Australia

WINELAND, DESIREE CLAIRE ANN, career military officer; b. Linkoping, Sweden, Aug. 15, 1965; d. Jean H. and Beata S. Losier; m. Calvin D. Wineland Sr., Oct. 22, 1994; children: Calvin Jr., Austin J. BFA, Syracuse U., 1987; MBA, St. Mary's U., 2000. Commd. 2d lt. U.S. Army, 1987, advanced through grades to maj., 2000. Recipient MacArthur Leadership award, 2000. Mem. Am. Bus. Women's Assn., VFW, Reserve Officers Assn. Avocations: sailing, golf, travel, music.

WINER, CONRAD EDWARD ROBERT, osteopath, rehabilitation medicine physician; b. Westcliff-on-Sea, Eng., Jan. 1, 1931; arrived in Australia, 1967; s. Arthur Leon and Ellen Josephine (Evans) W.; m. Marguerita Anne Dutton, Apr. 13, 1957; children: Nicholas, Jeremy, Christopher. LLB, U. Coll., London, 1953; BS, 1960; MB, BChir, U. Coll., London, 1960; diploma in physical and rehab. medicine, U. Sydney, Australia, 1969; diploma in osteo. medicine, London Coll., London, 1964; diploma in homeopathy, Faculty Homeopathic Medicine, London, 1965. Capt. Royal Army Med. Corps, 1960-63; vis. specialist Clinic of London Coll. Osteopathy, 1964-67; vis. med. officer Royal London Homeopathic Hosp., London, 1964-67; vis. sr. specialist dept. rehab. medicine Royal Prince Alfred Hosp., Sydney, Australia, 1967-79, clin. dir. dept. rehab. medicine, 1980-98, hon. cons., 1998—; supr. postgrad. course spinal manipulation U. Sydney, 1974-91. Co-author: Manual Medicine, 1984; editor: Back Pain, 2000; editor Newsletter of Australian Assn. Manipulative Medicine, 1979-81; contbr. articles to profl. jours., chpts. to books. Edn. subcom. Chiropractic and Osteo. Registration Bd., Govt. NSW, 1977-79, Physiotheraphy Registration Bd., 1980-89; med. advisor Nat. Assn. for Tng. Disabled in Office Work, Sydney, 1968-75; med. com. Motor Traffic Accident Authority Govt. NSW, 1999—. Travel fellow L'inst. Nat. de la Rsch./Ciba Med. Found., 1965; Travel grant Postgrad. Com. in Medicine U. Sydney, 1969. Fellow Australian Faculty Rehab. Medicine (chair com. on guides to assessment of disability 1992); mem. Australian Coll. Rehab. Medicine (pres. 1983-85, chair edn. com. on muscoloskeletal medicine 1986-88), Australian Assn. Musculoskeletal Medicine (pres. 1984-86, hon. sec. 1974-84, hon. life), Australian Assn. Phys. Medicine and Rehab. Medicine (pres. 1979-81), Osteo. and Naturopathic Rsch. Soc. (hon. life), Childbirth Edn. Assn. (hon. life), Vertebro-Neurology Assn. Russia (hon.), Internat. Fedn. Manual Medicine (co-editor jour. 1984-95), Brit. Osteo. Assn., Australian Rheumatism Assn., Australian Med. Assn., The Spine Soc., The Stroke Soc., Medico-Legal Soc. Avocations: boating, skiing, horse riding. Home: 64 Finlay Rd, Turramurra NSW 2074, Australia Office: Royal Prince Alfred Hosp, 100 Carillon Ave, Newtown Sydney NSW 2042, Australia

WINER, JESSICA DARYL, artist; b. N.Y.C., Aug. 29, 1962; d. Nahum J. and Toba (Brill) W. BA, Swarthmore Coll., 1984; postgrad., Nat. Acad. Sch. Fine Arts, 1987-89. One woman shows include Saks 5th Ave., N.Y.C., 1991, Westport (Conn.) Artists Gallery, 1992, Art Insights Gallery, N.Y.C., 1993, Lincoln Ctr. Gallery, N.Y.C, 1994, 95, Nat. Arts Club, N.Y.C., 1997, The Silo Gallery, New Milford, Ct., 1999; group shows include List Gallery, Swarthmore (Pa.) Coll., 1994,, Cannondale Gallery (Conn.), 1996, 99, William Doyle Russian Tea Rm Auction, N.Y.C., 1996, Christies Benefit, N.Y.C., 1992, 94, 95; executed murals at White Barn Theatre, 1984, Times Square Visitors Ctr./Embassy Theater, N.Y.C., 1998; permanent collections at Mus. of the City of N.Y.; set designer The Little Foxes at WCT Theatre, 1990; designer boxed sets cards, poster, T-shirts for Met. Opera, 1993-94, book covers for Simon & Schuster, 1995, 96; portrait illustrator New Yorker Mag., 1996—. Mem. Nat. Arts Club, Artists Equity, Nat. Soc. Mural Painters. Studio: 1199 Park Ave New York NY 10128-1711

WINER, WARD OTIS, mechanical engineer, educator; b. Grand Rapids, Mich., June 27, 1936; s. Mervin Augustus and Ina Katherine (Wood) W.; m. Mary Jo Wielinga, June 15, 1957; children: Mathew Owen, James Edward, Paul Andrew, Mary Margaret. Asso., Grand Rapids Jr. Coll., 1956; BS, U. Mich., 1958, MS, 1959, PhD, 1961; PhD (Cavendish Lab. fellow), Cambridge (Eng.) U., 1961-63. Asst. prof. dept. mech. engring. U. Mich., Ann Arbor, 1963-66, assoc. prof., 1966-69; assoc. prof. mech. engring. Ga. Inst. Tech., 1969-71, prof., 1971-84, Regents' prof., 1984—, chair George W. Woodruff Sch. Mech. Engring., 1988—, Eugne C. Gwaltney Jr. chair mfg. sys., 1998—, mem. exec. bd., 1983-88, chmn., 1984-86; chmn. Gordon Research Conf. on Friction, Lubrication and Wear, 1980; mem. NRC, 1980-88; chmn. Com. on Recommendations for U.S. Army Basic Sci. Research, 1985-87; mem. div. mech., structural, materials engring. adv. bd. NSF Engring. Directorate, 1984-89. Co-editor: Wear Control Handbook, 1980; tech. editor: Jour. Lubrication Tech., 1980-84, Jour. of Tribology, 1984-87; contbr. articles to profl. jours. Democratic precinct chmn., 1967-68; Mem. exec. bd. Horace H. Rackham Sch. Grad. Studies, U. Mich., 1968. Recipient Disting. Faculty Svc. award Coll. Engring. U. Mich., 1967, Alumni Merit award, 1998, Cert. Recognition, NASA, 1977, Clarence E. Earle Meml. award Nat. Grease Lubricating Inst., 1979, Disting. Prof. award Ga. Inst. Tech., 1987. Fellow AAAS, ASME (bd. comms. 1987-81, v.p. rsch. 1989-93, Melville medal 1975, Centennial medallion 1980, Mayor D. Hersey award 1986, Charles Russ Richards Meml. award 1988), Soc. Tribologists and Lubrication Engrs. (bd. dirs. 1983-86, Internat. award 1997), Brit. Tribology Trust (gold medal 1987); mem. Am. Soc. Engring. Educators (Benjamin Garver Lamme award 1995, Donald Marlowe award 1996), NAE, Metro Atlanta Engring. Soc. (Engr. of Yr. 1989), Am. Acad. Mechanics, Soc. Rheology, Soc. Engring. Sci. (dir. 1980-84), AAUP (pres. Ga. Tech. chpt. 1972-74, v.p. state conf. 1973-75), Sigma Xi (chpt. pres. 1982-83, Sustained Rsch. in Engring. award 1975), Tau Beta Pi, Pi Tau Sigma, Phi Kappa Phi. Home: 1025 Mountain Creek Trl NW Atlanta GA 30328-3535

WINFIELD, RICHARD CHARLES, management consultancy company executive; b. Birmingham, W.Midlands, Eng., Apr. 15, 1947; s. Frederick James and Eileen Dorothy (Wilson) W.; m. Samantha White, Apr. 3, 1971; 1 child, Dafydd Huw Lewis. BSc in Civil Engring., U. Nottingham, 1969; MSc in Hwys. and Transp. Engring., U. Salford, 1970; MSc in Mgmt. and Tech., U. Wales, Cardiff, 1982. Rsch. engr. Marconi Co., Chelmsford, Eng., 1970-73; sr. cons. Hans B. Barbe & Assocs., Winchester, Eng., 1973-75; chief asst. transp. Dyfed County Coun., 1975-81; mng. dir. Brefi Group Ltd., Tregaron, Wales, 1981—; mng. orgn. devel. Haden Maclellan Holdings, Plc, Egham, 1995-98; dir. Landor Holdings Ltd., London, 1986—, Drumport Ltd., London; chmn. bd. Kennington Pub. Svcs., London, 1999—. Fellow Chartered Inst. Transport (Internat. Silver medal); mem. Inst. of Mgmt., Inst. of Dirs. Anglican Ch. Avocations: property and landscape development, reading, walking, choral singing.

WINFORD, MARIA, audit executive; b. Salonika, Greece, Apr. 5, 1945; arrived in Australia, 1949; d. Dusan Zey and Danae Georgiades. BS, U. Melbourne, 1968; diploma in teaching, Associated Teachers Tng. Inst., Victoria, Australia, 1972; MA, U. Calif., Berkeley, 1979. High sch. tchr. various states and pvt. schs., Victoria, Australia, 1968-72; lectr. Associated Tchrs. Tng. Inst., Victoria, 1972-74; ednl. planner Edn. Dept., Victoria, 1977-80; industry trainer Commonwealth Dept. Employment & Indsl. Relations, 1980-81; ednl. planner Commonwealth Tertiary Edn. Commn., 1981-83; pub. adminstr. Commonwealth Dept. Adminstrv. Svcs., 1983-89; risk mgr. and internal auditor Australian Agy. Internat. Devel., 1989-91; strategic planner Nat. Mus. of Australia, 1991; program evaluator, internal auditor, accredited comml. mediator Australian Agy. Internat. Devel., 1991—; vis. prof. sch. mgmt. Beijing U. Sci. and Tech., 1994, 95; cons. Victorian Employers' Fedn., 1978-80; chair corp. governance panel, mem. pub. sector accountants com. Australian Soc. Cert. Practising Accountants. Mem. Inst. Internal Auditors (gov. (former pres.), Australian Coll. Edn., AAAS, Australian and N.Z. Assn. for Advancement of Sci., Royal Inst. Pub. Adminstrn. Australia, Inst. Arbitrators and Mediators Australia, Environment Studies Assn. Victoria (bd. dirs. 1973-76), Tech. and Further Edn. Planning Officers Assn. (exec. mem. 1978-80). Avocations: bridge, environ. protection, music, gardening, spoken Mandarin. Office: Australian Agy Internat Devel, 62 Northbourne Ave, Canberra 2601, Australia

WINFREY, MARION LEE, television critic; b. Knoxville, Tenn., July 7, 1932; s. Charles Houston and Norma Elsa (Wesenberg) W.; m. Mary Anne Hight, Sept. 5, 1958 (div. 1977); 1 son, David Dylan; m. Kiki Olson, Aug. 24, 1978 (div. 1982). B.S., U. Tenn., 1966; M.F.A., U. Iowa, 1968. Reporter Nashville Tennessean, 1957-58, Knoxville News-Sentinel, 1958-60, Miami bur. UPI, 1960-62, Miami Herald, 1962-63, Washington bur. Knight Newspapers, 1963-66, Detroit Free Press, 1968-71; reporter Phila. Inquirer, 1971-74, TV critic, 1974—; instr. journalism U. Iowa, 1966-68; Bernard Kilgore journalism counselor DePauw U., 1971. Author: Kent State Report, The President's Commission on Campus Unrest, 1970; included in Best Sports Stories (edited by Marsh and Ehre), 1963. Served with U.S. Army, 1954-56. Nieman fellow Harvard U., 1971-72. Mem. TV Critics Assn. (founding pres. 1978-79), Sigma Delta Chi, Phi Gamma Delta. Baptist. Clubs: Harvard (Phila.); Pen and Pencil; Nat. Press (Washington). Home: 117 N 15th St Philadelphia PA 19102-1516

WING, JAMES DAVID, lawyer; b. Milw., May 4, 1943; s. William H. and Elaine E. (Koehler) W.; m. Marilyn Lee Walsh, Aug. 21, 1965 (div. June 1980); children: Benjamin, Tracy, Nathaniel, John; m. Eunide Valcin, Nov. 28, 1980. BA, Beloit (Wis.) Coll., 1965; MA, U. Chgo., 1966, JD, 1969. Bar: Wis. 1969, Fla. 1975, U.S. Ct. Appeals (7th cir.) 1973, U.S. Dist. Ct. (mid. dist.) Fla. 1975, U.S. Ct. Appeals (5th cir.) 1978, U.S. Dist. Ct. (so. dist.) Fla. 1981, U.S. Ct. Appeals (11th cir.) 1981, U.S. Supreme Ct. 1979. Assoc. Whyte, Hirschboeck, Minahan, Harding & Harland, Milw., 1969-75, Carlton, Fields, Ward, Emmanuel, Smith & Cutler, Tampa, Fla., 1975-85, Myers, Kenin, Levinson & Richards/Shea & Gould, Miami, Fla., 1985-88, Fine, Jacobson, Schwartz, Nash & Block, Miami, 1988-94, Holland & Knight, Miami, 1994—. Mem. Phi Beta Kappa, Phi Eta Sigma, Omicron Delta Kappa. Avocation: Germanistics, tennis. *

WING, LORNA, psychiatrist, consultant, researcher; b. Gillingham, Kent, Eng., Oct. 7, 1928; d. Bernard and Gladys (Whittall) Tolchard; m. John Wing, May 15, 1950; 1 child, Susan. MB BS, Univ. Coll., London, 1952; MD, U. London, 1965. Psychiat. registrar Netherne Hosp., Coulsdon, Eng., 1953-56; rsch. asst. Univ. Coll., 1958-64; mem. sci. staff Med. Rsch. Coun., London, 1964-90; hon. cons. Maudsley Hosp., London, 1972-90; hon. sr. lectr. Inst. Psychiatry, London, 1974-90; cons. psychiatrist Nat. Autistic Soc., U.K., 1990—. Author: The Autistic Spectrum, 1996; editor: Aspects of Autism-Biological Research, 1988; contbr. papers to profl. publs. V.p. Nat. Autistic Soc., London; bd. dirs. Sussex (Eng.) Autistic Soc. Recipient award for work in field of mental retardation Internat. Assn. for Study of Mental deficiency, 1988; named to Order of the British Empire, Brit. Govt., 1995. Fellow Royal Coll. Psychiatrists. Avocations: gardening, reading, walking. Office: Elliot House, 113 Masons Hill, Bromley Kent BR2 9HT, England

WINGENBACH, GREGORY CHARLES, priest, religious-ecumenical agency director; b. Washington, Feb. 1, 1938; s. Charles Edward and Pearl Adeline (Stanton) W.; m. MaryAnn Pearce, Sept. 16, 1961; children: Mary-Adele, Karl Eduard, John Clair, Evgenia Kisa Maria. Student, Georgetown U., 1958-62; BA, Goddard Coll., 1972; postgrad., U. Thessalonike, Greece, 1973-74; MDiv, Louisville Presbyn. Theol. Sem., 1976, D of Ministry in Pastoral and Ecumenical Theology, 1982. Ordained to ministry Greek Orthodox Archdiocese North and South Am. as deacon, 1971, assoc. priest, 1973. Editl. asst., mem. staff Washington Star and N.Y. Herald-Tribune, 1957-62; rsch. and legis. asst. U.S. Senator Clair Engle, Calif., 1962-63; cmty. rels. programs mgr. U.S. Exec. OEO, Washington, 1965-69; regional program devel. officer AEC-Oak Ridge (Tenn.) Associated Univs., 1970-73; assoc. St. George's Ch., Knoxville, Tenn., 1971-73; chaplain St. John Chrysostomos Ch. and Vlatadon Monastery, Thessalonike, 1973-74; named steward/oikonomos, preacher Met. Archdiocese of Thessalonike, 1974; pastor Assumption of Virgin Mary Ch., Louisville, 1974-79, Holy Trinity Ch., Nashville, 1979-82, St. Spyridon's Ch., Monessen, Pa., 1983-86; nat. dir. family life/pastoral ministries Greek Orthodox Archdiocese North and South Am., N.Y.C. and Brookline (Mass.), 1986-90; exec. dir. Kentuckiana Interfaith Community, Louisville, 1990-97; Pan-Orthodox missionary pastor Northwestern Mont. and Ch. of Annunciation, Missoula, 1997-98; exec. dir. Christian Assocs. S.W. Pa., 1999—; spl. asst. Metro Maximos Greek Orthodox Diocese, Pitts., 1999—; Orthodox del. Louisville Area Interch. Coun. and Ecumedia Com., 1974-79; pres., exec. adminstr. LAIOS-Kentuckiana Interfaith Coun., 1977-79; diocesan rep. Archdiocese Nat. Presbyters Coun., 1982-85; archdiocese del. Nat. Coun. Chs., Orthodox/Luth. Dialogues Consultation, 1986—, Orthodox Nat. Missions Bd., 1981-90; named protopresbyter Greek Orthodox Archdiocese, 1980, Pitts. Diocese, 1983, Detroit Diocese, 1986, 95; ecumenical officer Greek Orthodox Diocese Pitts., 1983-86. Author: The Peace Corps, 1961, Guide to the Peace Corps, 1965, Broken...Yet Never Sundered: The Ecumenical Tradition, 1987, Two, Yet One in Christ: A Handbook for InterChurch/InterCultural Couples, 1989; editl. rschr.: Richard Nixon, 1959, Duel at the Brink, 1960, The Floating Revolution, 1962. Mem. Fellowship St. Alban and St. Sergius, Orthodox Theol. Soc. Am. (exec. bd.), N.Am. Acad. Ecumenists. Address: 1356 Simona Dr Pittsburgh PA 15201-2002

WINGENDER, PERDITA ALEXANDRA, economist researcher; b. Trier, Germany, Dec. 17, 1959; d. Karl-Rudolf and Luise (Anderie) W.; children: Anthea, Atemar. Studies of Econs., U. Bochum, Germany, 1983, PhD, 1988. Asst. U. Bochum, Germany, 1984-89; scholarship Deutsche Forschungsgemeinschaft, Bochum, Germany, 1989-90; chief asst. U. Duisburg, Germany, 1990—. Author: (book) Westdevisen und Devisenschwarzmärkte in sozialistischen Planwirtschaften, 1989; editor: (book) Polens Integration in die Weltwirtschaft, 1992. Mem. List-Verein, Verein für Socialpolitik. Avocations: literature, theatre, travel. Office: Gerhard-Mercator U Gesamthochsch Duisburg, Fachbereich 5, D-47048 Duisburg Germany

WINGERT, HANNELORE CHRISTIANE, real estate agent, chemical company executive; b. Karlsbad, Czechoslavakia; came to U.S., 1962, naturalized, 1967; d. Andreas and Gisela Maria (Ciharz) Zwickel; m. Rudolf Wingert, Feb. 9, 1963; children: Angela Helene, Christopher Rudolf. I.B.A., Stadt. Berufsschule, Fed. Republic Germany, 1961; postgrad. in mgmt., Bergen Community Coll., 1983. Lic. real estate, N.J. Clk. various cos., N.J., 1963, bilingual sec., 1963-78; exec. sec., adminstrv. asst. Lurgi Corp., Hasbrouck Heights, N.J., 1978-81; sr. exec. sec. Degussa Corp., Teterboro, N.J., 1981-83, asst. product mgr. silica, 1983-85, asst. product mgr. H202, 1985-87, sales promotion coord., 1987; sales assoc. Schlott Realtors, Kinnelon, N.J., 1987-90; Caldwell Banker, 1990—; million dollar club, 1988, multimillion dollar club, 1990—, AR Million Dollar Club, 1992, 98. Author real estate newsletter, 1992—, community newsletter, 1977-79. Mem. Bd. Realtors Morris County; mem. Garden State Multiple Listing Svc.; chmn. master planning com. High Crest Lake, West Milford, N.J., 1974-75; advisor Jr. Woman's Club Kinnelon-Butler (N.J.), 1973-74; techr. computer classes Bd. Realtors, Passaic County, 1989-92. Mem. N.J. Fed. of Woman's Clubs (past pres.), High Crest Lake Woman's Club (pres. 1972-73) (West Milford, N.J.). Republican. Roman Catholic. Home: 204 High Crest Dr West Milford NJ 07480-3710 Office: Caldwell Banker Realtors Kinnelon 1450 State Rt 23 Butler NJ 07405-1624

WINGFIELD, THOMAS CHRISTOPHER, lawyer; b. N.Y.C., July 29, 1962; s. Samuel Griffin III and Maryann Margaret (Frost) W. BA, Ga. State U., 1987; JD, Georgetown U., 1996, LLM, 1999. Bar: Ga. 1996, D.C. 1997. Commd. officer USN, 1987, advanced through grades to lt., 1991; squadron intelligence officer USS Midway, Atsugi, Japan, 1988-90; desk officer Office of Naval Intelligence, Suitland, Md., 1990-93; intelligence officer Ctr. for Naval Analysis, Alexandria, Va., 1993-97; resigned USN, 1997; counsel, prin. nat. security analyst Aegis Rsch. Corp., Falls Church, Va., 1997—. Contbr. articles to profl. jours. With USNR, 1997—. Republican. Roman Cath. E-mail: wingtom@worldnet.att.net. Home: 4702 English Ct Suitland MD 20746-3783 Office: Aegis Rsch Corp 7799 Leesburg Pike Ste 1100 Falls Church VA 22043-2413

WINK, MICHAEL, biologist, educator, scientist; b. Esch Bad Münstereifel, Fed. Republic Germany, Apr. 10, 1951; s. Alfred and Johanna (Remmen) W.; m. Coralie Oberhoffer, Mar. 11, 1978; children: Leonie, Charlotte, Lucie, Adrian. Diploma in Biology, U. Bonn., Fed. Republic Germany, 1977; Dr. rer. nat., U. Braunschweig, Fed. Republic Germany, 1980, Habilitation, 1985. Scientist U. Braunschweig, 1980-85; Heisenberg fellow U. Munich, 1986-88; assoc. prof. U. Mainz, Fed. Republic Germany, 1988-89; prof. faculty pharmacy and faculty biology U. Heidelberg, Fed. Republic Germany, 1989—; dir. Inst. Pharm. Biology, Heidelberg, 1989—, vice dean, 1990-91, 93-97, dean faculty pharmacy, 1991-93, 97—; vis. prof. U. Nanhing, China, 1988, U. Cordoba, Argentina, 1996. Author four books on ornithology and Lupinen, 1991, Forschung, Anbau und Verwertung, 1992, PCR im Medizinischen und Biologischen Labor, 1994, Fortschritte in der Lupinenforschung und im Lupinenaubau, 1995, Rheumatherapie mit Phytopharmaka, 1998, Alkaloids: Biochemistry, Ecology and Medicinal Applications, 1998, Lupinen in Forschung und Praxis, 1998, Phytopharmaka bei Störungen und Erkrankungen des Nervensystems, 1998, Biochemistry of Plant Secondary Metabolism, 1999, Function of Plant Secondary Metabolites and their Exploitation in Biotechnology, 1999; contbr. over 375 articles on natural products, chem. ecology, molecular evolution, ornithology, medicinal plants and plant physiology to profl. jours. Recipient Rheinlandtaler award Cultural Achievements Landschaftsverband Rheinland, Köln, 1988, G. Niethammer award for ornithology. Mem. AAAS, N.Y. Acad. Scis., Brit. Ornithologist's Union, Deutsche Ornithologen Gesellschaft, Gesellschaft fur Biologische Chemie, Internat. Soc. Molecular Evolution, Internat. Soc. Chem. Ecology, Phytochemical Soc. Europe, other sci. socs., Rotary. Office: Inst Pharm Biology, Univ Heidelberg, Im Neuenheimer Feld 364, 69120 Heidelberg Germany

WINKEL, ELAINE MARIE, physician, transplant cardiologist; b. Milw., Sept. 21, 1948; d. Joseph James and Catherine Helen Strharsky; m. Jan Edward, Oct. 13, 1973. BS, DePaul U., 1979; MD, Loyola Stritch Sch. Medicine, 1987. Diplomate Am. Bd. Internal Medicine. Asst. prof. medicine Rush Med. Coll., Chgo., 1994—; attending cardiologist Rush Presbyn., Chgo., St. Luke's Med. Ctr., Chgo., Heart Failure and Cardiac Transplant Program, Chgo., 1994—. Assoc. editor Jour. Heart and Lung Transplantation, 1994—. Fellow Am. Coll. Cardiology (councillor 1998—); mem. ACP, Internat. Soc. Heart and Lung Transplantation, Am. Soc. Transplantation, Am. Heart Assn., Heart Failure Soc. Roman Catholic. E-mail: ewinkel@rush.edu. Home: 699 Glendale Dr Prospect Heights IL 60070-1121 Office: Rush Presbyn St Lukes Med Ctr 1725 W Harrison St Ste 439 Chicago IL 60612-3836

WINKEL, PER, clinical chemist, laboratory director; b. Copenhagen, Sept. 2, 1935; s. Poul and Grethe (Hald) W.; m. Gudny Jonsdottir (div. May 1976); children: Jon, Poul; m. Hanne Ciljeso (div. 1993); m. Lisa Trolle Jacobsen. MD, U. Copenhagen, 1963, D in Med. Scis., 1976. Cert. clin. chemist, 1976. Rsch. fellow U. So. Calif., 1967-69, U. Copenhagen, 1969-71; resident Univ. Hosp. Copenhagen, 1971-74; registrar Finsen Inst., Copenhagen, 1974-77, cons., 1977-85; cons. Univ. Hosp. Copenhagen, 1985-95; dir. hosp. labs. Cen. Hosp., Nykøping Falster, 1996—; vis. scientist Dept. Hosp. Lab., U. N.C., Chapel Hill, 1976-77; vis. prof. Dept. Hosp. Lab., Univ. Hosp. Boston Med. Ctr., 1982-83; chmn. Danish Soc. Med. Data Processing, 1975-76; assoc. prof. med. data processing U. Copenhagen, 1989-94. Author: (textbook) Clinical Diagnosis by Laboratory Methods, 1979, 84, 91; contbr. over 150 articles to med. jours. Grantee Danish Rsch. Coun., 1987. Avocation: chess. Office: Cen Hosp, Fjordvej 15, 4800 Nykøbing Falster, Denmark

WINKEL, WOLFGANG, ornithologist; b. Danzig, Germany, June 15, 1941; s. Hans and Elisabeth (Naumann) W.; m. Doris Laux, Jan. 29, 1965; 1 child, Renate. D Natural Sci., U. Brunswick, 1968. Sci. asst. Inst. Avian Rsch., Wilhelmshaven, Germany, 1970-77, head Brunswick Rsch. Sta., 1978—. Co-author: (with R. Berndt) Eco-ornithological Glossary, 1983, (with R. Nerlich) Die Vogelfamilien der Westpaläarktis, 1995; editor in chief Die Vogelwelt, 1971-87; co-editor Die Vogelwarte, 1972—. Recipient Silberne Ehrennadel, Deutscher Bund Vogelschutz, 1984. Mem. Deutsche Ornithologen-Gesellschaft, Brit. Ornithologists' Union, Am. Ornithologists' Union, Animal Behavior Soc. Office: Aussenstation Braunschweig, Bauernstr 14, D-38162 Cremlingen Germany

WINKELHUIS, FREDERICUS BASTIANUS, electronics executive, consultant; b. Badhoevedorp, The Netherlands, June 8, 1956; s. Francsicus Bernardus J. de Vries and Johny Winkelhuis; m. Marion Bernadette Beneken genamnd Kolmer; children: Roderick Pieter, Anne-Aimeé. MBA. Sales rep. Armstrong World Internat., 1986-89; asst. mgr. tech. svcs. Armstrong World Internat., Germany, 1989-92; field svcs. mgr. Armstrong World Industries, Benelux, 1992-94; divsn. sales and mktg. mgr. N.W. European Armstrong World Industries, 1994-96; mng. dir. Stago BV, 1996—, Sandas Montag, 1996—; chmn. GSVB, 1999—; cons. Installers, 1999—. Contbr. articles to profl. jours. Mem. Comml. Club Alhmaar. Avocations: golf, family. Home: Sperwer 11, NL-1752 Zuid-Scharwoude The Netherlands Office: Stago BV, Electronwg 1, 1627 LB Hoorn The Netherlands

WINKELMANS, WILLY, economics educator; b. Antwerp, Belgium, Jan. 6, 1941; m. Josiane Devis, June 3, 1989; children: Alex, Indra. M in Econs., U. Antwerp, 1963; PhD in Econs., U. Ghent, 1972. Prof. RUCA, Belgium, 1978-87, full prof., 1988—, dean of faculty applied econs., 1995-99; chmn. ednl. bd. UA RUCA; chmn. exec. bd. Inst. of Transport and Maritime Mgmt., 1996—; dir. U. Antwerp, 1996—; vis. prof. Erasmus U., Rotterdam, 1983-92; econ. advisor Hydronamics, The Netherlands, 1973-75; chmn. Flemish Port Commn., Brussels, 1989—; dir. Flemish Aviation Co., Deurne, 1993-95; dir. European DataCom., St. Niklaas, 1996—. Author: (book) Socio-Economic Evaluation of Transport Investments, 1997; editor: (book) Post Reforms in Belgium, 1991; contbr. articles to profl. jours. Sec. BNL Interuniv. Group of Transport Econs., Brussels, 1977—; advisor Flemish Minister of Transport of Pub. Works, 1988-89; spl. advisor of Transport commrs. K. Van Miert, EC, 1991-92. Recipient Maritime award Count D. Le Grelle European Shipping Press Assn., 1973. Mem. Econ. Commn. of Nat. Found. for Scientific Rsch. (chmn. 1995-97), World Conf. on Transport Rsch. Soc. (mem. scientific com. 1996-98). Avocations: gymnastics, tennis, biking, music. Home: Riverside Lepelstraat 81/C, B 9140 Steendorp Belgium Office: U Antwerp RUCA, Middelheimlaan 1, B2020 Antwerp Belgium

WINKLER, CHARLES HOWARD, lawyer, investment management company executive; b. N.Y.C., Aug. 4, 1954; s. Joseph Conrad and Geraldine Miriam (Borok) W.; m. Joni S. Taylor, Aug. 28, 1993. BBA with highest distinction, Emory U., 1976; JD, Northwestern U., 1979. Bar: Ill. 1979, U.S. Dist. Ct (no. dist.) Ill. 1979. Assoc. Levenfeld & Kanter, Chgo., 1979-80; assoc. Kanter & Eisenberg, Chgo., 1980-84, ptnr., 1985-86; ptnr. Neal Gerber & Eisenberg, Chgo., 1986-96; sr. mng. dir., COO Citadel Investment Group, LLC, Chgo., 1996—; sr. mng. dir. Citadel Trading Group, Chgo., 1996—, Aragon Investments Ltd., Chgo., 1996—; bd. dirs. Kensington Global Strategies Fund, Ltd., Antaeus Internat. Investments, Ltd., Jackson Investment Fund Ltd., Citadel Investment Group (Europe) Ltd. Author: (with others) Basic Tax Shelters, 1982, Limited Liability Companies: The Entity of Choice, 1995; mng. editor Northwestern Jour. Internat. Law and Bus., 1979. Mem. ABA (mem. sect. on taxation), Beta Gamma Sigma. Home: 50 E Bellevue Pl Chicago IL 60611-1129 Office: Citadel Investment Group LLC 225 W Washington St Fl 9 Chicago IL 60606-2418

WINKLER, FRANZ, mathematics educator, researcher; b. Salzburg, Austria, Oct. 24, 1955; s. Franz and Anna (Bahn) W.; m. Eva Maria Polesofsky, July 13, 1979; children: Stephan M., Georg W., Christoph B. Diploma in Math., J. Kepler U., Linz, Austria, 1979, D in Tech., 1984. Asst. prof. Inst. for Maths. J. Kepler U., Linz, Austria, 1986-92, univ. dozent, 1990, assoc. prof. Inst. for Math., 1992-97, assoc. prof. RISC-Linz, 1997—; vis. asst. prof. dept. computer and info. scis. U. Del., Newark, 1984-86; vis. scientist Inst. Phys. and Chem. Rsch., Tokyo, 1988; vis. prof. dept. math. Universidad Alcala Henares, Madrid, Spain, 1991, 94, 96; dir. RISC-LINZ summer sch. in computer algebra, 1990, 92. Author: (with B. Kutzler and F. Lichtenberger) Softwaresysteme zur Formelmanipulation, 1990, Polynomial Algorithms in Computer Algebra, 1996; editor SIGSAM Bull., 1986-91, (with H. Hong, D. Wang) Algebraic Approaches to Geometric Reasoning, 1995, (with C.M. Hoffmann, J.R. Sendra) Parametric Algebraic Curves and Applications, 1997 (with B. Buchberger) Grobner Bases and Applications, 1998; contbr. articles to profl. jours. Osterreichische Forschungsgemeinschaft grantee, 1986-88, Austrian Fonds zur Forderung der Wissenschaftlichen Forschung grantee, 1988—. Mem. Am. Math. Soc., Math. Assn. Am., Assn. Computing Machinery, Soc. for Indsl. and Applied Math., Osterr. Mathematische Gesellschaft. Office: J Kepler U Inst for Math, Altenbergerstr. 69, A-4040 Linz Austria

WINKLER, IGOR, chemistry researcher, educator; b. Chernovtsy, Ukraine, Dec. 15, 1967; s. Aaron and Nina (Kopilovich) W.; m. Nataliya Burkun, Mar. 8, 1969; 1 child, Margarita. Grad. in Chemistry, Chernovtsy U., 1991, PhD in Chemistry, Phys. Chemistry, 1996. Engr. analyst Inst. Ecol. Rsch., Chernovtsy, 1990-92; asst. rschr. Chernovtsy U., 1991-94, sr. rschr., 1994—. Contbr. articles to profl. jours. Lt. Ukraine Army, 1986-88. Mem. Am. Chem. Soc. Avocations: music, stamps, coins, Internet walking. Office: Univ, Kotsybinsky str 2, 274012 Chernovtsy Ukraine

WINKLER, ROSITA ALICE, research scientist; b. Reghin, Romania, Sept. 29, 1946; arrived in Belgium, 1964; d. Maximilien Winkler and Adele Buchsenspanner; m. Jean John Gol (div. June 1994); 1 child, Gol Deborah. BSc, U. Liege, Belgium, 1968, M of Biology, 1970, PhD, 1977. Asst. U. Liege, 1969-70, 1970-77; Royal Soc. fellow London, 1972; chef de travaux U. Liege, 1977-80; postdoctoral fellow NIH, Bethesda, Md., 1981-83; rsch. asst. U. Liege, 1983-85; chercheur qualifie Fonds Nat. Scientific Rsch., Belgian

Found. Scientific Rsch., Brussels, 1985—; cons. Fond Nat. De La Recherche Scientifique, Brussels, 1998—, FRIA, Brussels, 1985—. Contbr. articles to sci. jours. Mem. exec. com. Friends of Opera Royal de Wallonie, Liege, 1990—; mem. Nat. Consultative Com. on Bioethics, Brussels, 1995—; mem. exec. com. Grand Liege, 1997—. Fogharty fellow, 1981-83. Mem. Am. Assn. for Rsch. on Cancer (corr. mem.), Belgian Biochem. Soc., Belgian Assn. for Rsch. on Cancer, Soroptomist Internat. (v.p. 1995). Jewish. Avocations: opera, swimming, literature, treaking. Fax: 32/4/3662922. E-mail: rwinkler@ulg.ac.be. Home: rue Belle Jardiniere 337, 4031 Liege Belgium Office: U Liege, Tour de Pathologie B23, B4000 Liege Belgium

WINKLER, ULRICH HORST, gynecologist, researcher, consultant; b. Stuttgart, Fed. Republic Germany, June 3, 1954; s. Werner and Heide (Münster) W.; m. Christiane Volles; 1 child, Lukas. MD, U. Hannover, Germany, 1981; Pvt. Dozent, U. Essen, Germany, 1998. Sr. ob/gyn. U. Hosp., Munster, Germany, 1984-87, Essen, Germany, 1987-98; chief dept. ob-gyn. Friedrich Ebert Hosp., Neumünster, Germany, 1998—. Reviewer Geb Fra, 1993—, Fertil Sterie; editl. bd. European Jour. Contraception & Reproductive Health. Recipient Martin Tausk prize, 1992, Fritz Karl Beller prize, 1997. Office: Friedrich Ebert Hosp, Dept Ob-Gyn Friesenstr 11, 24534 Neumönster Germany

WINKLER, WOLFGANG GEORG, engineering educator, researcher; b. Gmünd, Austria, Jan. 24, 1949; arrived in Germany, 1978; s. Helmut and Helmtraut (Langer) W.; m. Beate J'a'ger, Apr. 30, 1981; children: Brigitte, Wolf-Christian. Diploma in engring., TH Wien, Vienna, Austria, 1974, D of Tech., 1977. Project leader Deutsche Babcock, Oberhausen, Germany, 1978-82; mgr. TÜV Rheinland, Cologne, Germany, 1982-86; chief engr. Progas, Dortmund, Germany, 1986-87; mgr. Akzo Engring., Arnheim, The Netherlands, 1987-89; prof. U. of Applied Scis., Hamburg, Germany, 1990—; mem. acad. senate U. Applied Scis., 1993—; bd. dirs. VDI Hamburg; advisor European Fuel Cell Forum, Luzerne, Switzerland, 1998—; dep. dir. working group fuel cells VDI-GET, Düsseldorf, Germany, 1999—. Contbr. articles to profl. jours.; patentee in field. Pres. Hochschullehrerbund, Hamburg, 1993-95. Served with Austrian mil., 1977-78. Grantee Ministry of Rsch., Bonn, Germany, 1998, HEW, Hamburg, 1993—. Mem. Lions (pres. Hamburg Uhlenhorst chpt. 1998-99). Avocations: science, history, politics. Office: U of Applied Sci, Berliner Tor 21, D 20099 Hamburg Germany

WINKLER, ZORAN, company executive; b. Zagreb, Croatia, Feb. 19, 1944; s. Zlatko Winkler and Stefania Dvorscak; m. Ani Winkler; children: Darko, Vesna. MS, U. Zagreb, Croatia, 1968. Engr. Sulzer Bros., Winterthur, 1969-70; project mgr. V.L. Shipyard, Rijeka, Croatia, 1971-77, project sales mgr., 1977-87; mng. dir. ATC Marine S.A., Lugano, 1987-90; exec. dir. Enico S.A., Lugano, 1990-95; mng. dir. MACK Project Engring. Sagl, Lugano, 1995—; v.p. Penntec, Phila., 1995—. Office: Mack Sagl, MACK Project Engring Sagl, 22 Corso Elvezia, 6900 Lugano Switzerland

WINLAND, DENISE LYNN, physician; b. Elizabeth, N.J., Aug. 9, 1951; d. James Edward and Audrey Anna (Hansen) W.; m. Charles F. Francke III, May 30, 1982; children: Shannon W. Francke, Eric W. Francke. BS with honors, Rutgers U., 1973; M in Phys. Therapy with honors, Baylor U., 1975; MD, U. Louisville, 1982. Resident in psychiatry U. Louisville, 1982-83, 90-93, staff physician student health svc., 1983-89; pvt. practice psychiatry Louisville, 1993—; emergency room physician North Clark Community Hosp., Charlestown, Ind., 1983-87; physician Immediate Care Ctrs., Louisville, 1983-86. With U.S. Army, 1974-77, lt. col. Res., 1977-96, ret. 1996.. Teagle Found. scholar, 1978-82; named Outstanding Young Women Am., 1983, 84. Mem. Ky. Psychiat. Assn., Ky. Med. Assn., Jefferson County Med. Assn., Res. Officers Assn., Ret. Officers Assn. (meritous svc award). Democrat. Mem. Unity Christian Ch. Avocations: walking miniature Schnauzers, music, reading. Home: 1103 Holly Springs Dr Louisville KY 40242-7762 Office: 8135 New Lagrange Rd Louisville KY 40222-4682

WIN MRA, ambassador. Permanent rep. Myanmar UN, N.Y.C., 1994—. Office: Permanent Mission Myanmar to UN 10 E 77th St New York NY 10021-1704*

WINN, ANTHONY W., chess player, poet, screenwriter; b. Topeka, Aug. 14, 1958; s. Paul Winn and Ruby Green; m. Rhonda Guyle; 1 child, Samuel Harris. AA, St. Mary's Coll., Leavenworth, Kans., 1988. Contbr. poetry to lit. publs. Recipient Golden Poet award, award of merit and hon. mention World of Poetry, 1990. Mem. Internat. Poetry Soc., U.S. Chess Fedn. Home: PO Box 156 Hazelton KS 67061-0156

WINN, C(OLMAN) BYRON, former mechanical engineering educator; b. Canton, Mo., Nov. 21, 1933; s. Colman Kersey and Kiula Elmeda (Ingold) W.; m. Donna Sue Taylor, Aug. 25, 1957; children: Byron, Derek, Julie. BS in Aeronautics, U. Ill., 1958; MS in Aeronautics, Stanford U., 1960, PhD, 1967. Engr. Lockheed Missiles & Space Co., Palo Alto, Calif., 1958-60, sr. engr., 1962-64; rsch. scientist Martin-Marietta, Denver, 1960-62; lectr. Santa Clara (Calif.) U., 1963-65; assoc. prof. Colo. State U., Ft. Collins, 1966-74, prof. mech. engring., 1974—, prof., head dept., 1982-95, assoc. dean, 1995—; cons. Space Rsch. Corp., North Troy, Vt., 1969-73; pres. Solar Environ. Engring. Co., 1973-85. Author: Controls in Solar Energy Systems, 1982, Controls in Solar Energy Systems, 1993; assoc. editor Jour. Solar Energy Engring., 1982-89, Passive Solar Jour., 1987, Advances in Solar Energy, 1996—. Loaned exec. United Way, Ft. Collins, 1992. With U.S. Army, 1953-55. Named Disting. Alumnus U. Ill., 1984, J.E. Cermak Adv. award, 1986, EPPEC award Platte River Power Authority, 1992, ABELL Svc. award, 1997. Fellow ASME; mem. AIAA (Energy Systems award 1991), Internat. Solar Energy Soc. (bd. dirs. 1980-89), Am. Solar Energy Soc. (bd. dirs. 1979-86, solar action com. 1991-93), Tau Beta Pi. Achievements include development of controllers for solar energy systems; design and development of the reconfigurable passive evaluation analysis and test facility; founding of the Energy Analysis and Diagnostic Center, The Waste Minimization Assessment Center, The Industrial Assessment Center and Manufacturing Excellence Center at Colo. State U. Office: Colo State U Dept Mech Engring Fort Collins CO 80523-0001*

WINN, FRANCIS JOHN, JR., medical educator; b. Detroit, Aug. 12, 1946; s. Francis John and Margaret (Aubuchon) W.; m. Cathy Mannion, Aug. 24, 1974 (div. Dec. 1980); m. Gloria Elizabeth Morrow, Feb. 6, 1981; children: Francis John III, Paige Whitney. BS in Psychology, Mich. State U., 1968; MA in Physiol. Psychology, Cen. Mich. U., 1974; PhD in Psychology and Stats., Tex. Tech U., 1977. Commd. USPHS, 1978, advanced through grades to comdr., 1984, ret., 1997; chief mental health svcs. and Atlantic area psychiat. screening unit USCG Outpatient Clinic, Governor's Island, N.Y., 1978-83; staff rsch. psychologist, cons. to chief psychiatry br. USCG Tng. Ctr., Cape May, N.J., 1983-86; sr. scientist psychophysiology & biomechanics sect. Nat. Inst. Occupational Safety and Health, Cin., 1986-91; sr. rsch. support scientist officer Nat. Inst. Drug Abuse, 1991-92; sr. rsch. support scientist officer Substance Abuse and Mental Health Svc. Adminstrn., 1992-95, sr. health statistician, 1995-97; clin. asst. prof. E. Carolina U., Greenville, N.C., 1997—; cons. assoc. Duke U. Sch. Nursing, 1998—; program evaluation cons. New Bold Assocs., 1998—; asst. adj. prof. Med. Coll. Ga., 1995—; bd. collaborators N.C. Agro-Med. Inst., 1998—, exec. com., 2000-2001; vis. asst. prof. dept. psychology U. Tex., El Paso, 1977-78; adj. assoc. prof. dept. human svcs., counseling St. John's U., Jamaica, N.Y., 1980-82; lectr. Stockton State Coll., Pomona, N.J., 1985-86, U. Cin., 1989-91; mem. adv. bd. Conf. Engring. and Aging, Stein Gerontol. Inst., Drexel U., 1990-91; mem. sci. program com. 2d Internat. Conf. on Aging and Work, Danish working Environ. Fund, 1998; program chair tech. group on aging X10th Triennial Congress of Internat. Ergonomics Assn., 2000. Assoc. editor Exptl. Aging Rsch.; contbr. article to profl. jours. Mem. DAV, Res. Officers Assn. (v.p. Cin. Navy chpt. 1990, pres. 1991), Assn. Physician Assist Programs, Am. Psychol. Soc., Soc. for Exptl. Biology and Medicine, Gerontol. Soc. Am., Soc. Air Force Clin. Psychologists, Sigma Xi. E-mail: winnf@mail.ecu.edu. Home: 3401 Cutler Ct Greenville NC 27834-7621 Office: E Carolina U Dept Physician Assist Studies Sch Allied Health Sci Greenville NC 27858-4353

WINN, KYAW, geologist; b. Mahlaing, Meiktila, Myanmar, Oct. 19, 1941; arrived in Germany, 1978; naturalized, 1988; s. Min Han and Emma Dawson; m. Kathleen Khin Aye Mu, Oct. 29, 1965; children: Le Mu, Toe Mu, Ye Thuya. BS, Rangoon U., 1961, MS, 1970; D, Christian-Albrechts U., Kiel, Germany, 1974. Geologist Burma Oil Co. Ltd., Rangoon, 1961-65, People's Oil Industry, Rangoon, 1965-70; exploration geologist, field mgr. Myanmar Oil Corp., Rangoon, 1970-78; staff scientist Christian-Albrechts U., Kiel, Germany, 1978—; mem. earth scis. rsch. divsn. Govt. Burma, Rangoon, 1968-76. Editor Meyniana, 1993—; contbr. articles to profl. jours. Grantee Deutsche Forschungsgemeinschaft, 1994-97; recipient scholarship Edn. Ministry Govt. Burma, 1957-61, Deutsche Akademischer Austauschdienst, 1972-74. Mem. Internat. Assn. Sedimentologists, Geologische Vereinigung, Am. Geophys. Union. Buddhist. Achievements include acoustical imaging system for sea floor mapping, empirical relationship between productivity, water depth and organic carbon accumulation rates, mapping of glacial-interglacial oceanic water masses with oxygen and carbon isotopes of Cibicides wuellerstorfi, sea-level changes in the Baltic and German Bight regions. Office: Inst Geoscis, Olshausenstrasse 40, 24098 Kiel Germany

WINN, U TIN, diplomat; b. May 22, 1942; m. Daw Khin Nu; 3 children. BA, Yangon U., 1962. Registered lawyer advocate. Tutor dept. philosophy U. Yangon, 1962-65; lt. col. Myanmar Tatmadaw, 1965-89; AE & P Union Myanmar, Republic of Korea, 1990-94; amb. extraordinary, plenipotentiary Union Myanmar, Kingdom of Thailand, 1994-96; amb. extraordinary and plenipotentiary Union Myanmar to U.S., 1996—. Avocations: reading, golf. Office: Embassy of Myanmar 2300 S St NW Washington DC 20008-4089

WINN, WALTER GARNETT, JR., marketing strategist, advertising executive; b. Wilmington, N.C., Dec. 1, 1941; s. Walter Garnett and Pamela Weber (Bradham) W.; m. Linda Ann Irvin, July 1, 1964; children: Walter Welborn, Katie Hillary. BFA, U. Ga., 1966, MS with honors, 1968. Account exec. Sudler & Hennessey Advt., N.Y.C., 1968-69, Dean Burdick & Assocs. Inc., N.Y.C., 1969-70; v.p., creative dir. Buntin & Assocs. Inc., Nashville, 1970-72; pres. Smith & Winn Advt. Inc., Jacksonville, Fla., 1972-77; mktg. mgr. Standard Telephone Co., Cornelia, Ga., 1977-79; mktg., sales mgr. Commonwealth Telephone Co., Dallas, Pa., 1979-83; advt. dir. CTE Corp., Wilkes Barre, Pa., 1983-84; dir. mktg. North State Telephone Inc., High Point, N.C., 1984—. Creator, designer bus. strategy game Merchants and Movers, 1990, Air Mogul, 2000. Bd. dirs., chair com. High Point Area Arts Coun., 1989-96; bd. dirs. Back Mountain Arts Guild, Dallas, 1980, Misericordia Coll. Arts Endowment, 1982-84; pres. Civitan Found., 1998-2000. Named Advt. Person of Yr. Am. Advt. Fedn., Northeastern Pa., 1983. Mem. N.C. Tel. Assn. (chmn. mktg. 1989-91, 95-97), Civitan (pres. High Point 1994-95, Civitan of Yr. 1996). Republican. Avocations: strategy games, model railroading, woodworking. Home: 381 Hunters Pt Lexington NC 27295-0339 Office: North State Telephone Co 111 N Main St High Point NC 27260-5007

WINNACKER, ALBRECHT, physicist; b. Frankfurt, Germany, Aug. 31, 1942; s. Karl and Gertrud (Deitenbeck) W.; m. Eva Hubner, 1978; children: Malte, Maren, Marlis. Student, U. Freiburg, 1961-67; PhD, U. Heidelberg, 1970; postgrad., U. Calif. Berkeley, 1970-72. Prof. exptl. physics U. Heidelberg, Germany, 1980-86; with Siemens Rsch. Labs., Erlangen, Germany, 1986-91; prof. materials sci., dir. materials sci. dept. U. Erlangen, 1991—; vis. scientist IBM Rsch. Labs., San Jose, Calif., 1984-85; supervisory bd. mem. SiCrystal AG, 1991—. Author: Physics of Masers and Lasers, 1984; co-editor: Atomic Physics, 1974.

WINNER, MICHAEL ROBERT, film director, writer, producer; b. London, Oct. 30, 1935; s. George Joseph and Helen (Zloty) W. Degree in law and econs. with honors, Cambridge (Eng.) U., 1956. Writer Fleet St. (newspapers), London, 1956-58; columnist London Sunday Times, 19905, London News of the World, 19955. Engaged in film prodn., 19565; dir. films Play it Cool, 1962, West 11, 1963, The Mechanic, 1972, Death Wish II, 1981; dir., writer The Cool Mikado, 1962, You Must be Joking, 1965, The Wicked Lady, 1982; producer, dir. The System, 1963, I'll Never Forget What's 'isname, 1967, The Games, 1969, Lawman, 1970, The Nightcomers, 1971, Chato's Land, 1971, Scorpio, 1972, The Stone Killer, 1973, Death Wish, 1974, Won Ton Ton The Dog Who Saved Hollywood, 1975, Firepower, 1978, Scream for Help, 1983, Death Wish III, 1985; producer, writer, dir. films The Jokers, 1966, Hannibal Brooks, 1968, The Sentinel, 1976, The Big Sleep, 1977, Appointment With Death, 1987, A Chorus of Disapproval, 1988, Bullseye!, 1989, Dirty Weekend, 1992, Parting Shots, 1997; producer plays Nights at the Comedy, Comedy Theatre, London, 1960, The Silence of St. Just, Gardner Centre, Brighton, 1971, The Tempest, Wyndhams Theatre, London, 1974, A Day in Hollywood, A Night in the Ukraine, Mayfair Theatre, London, 1978, (TV series London Weekend TV) Michael Winner's True Crimes, 1990, 91, 92, 93, 94; author: Winner's Dinners, 1999, rev. edit., 2000. Founder, chmn. Police Meml. Trust, 1984. Mem. Dirs. Guild Gt. Britain (coun., trustee, chief censorship officer 1983). Office: Scimitar Films Ltd, 6-8 Sackville St, London W1X 1DD, England

WINNING, THOMAS J. CARDINAL, archbishop. DD (hon.), U. Glasgow; D, Univ. Strathclyde, 1992; professorship (hon.), U. Glasgow, 1996; LLD (hon.), U. Aderdeen, 1996; D.Univ. (hon.), U. Strathclyde, 1992. Ordained priest Roman Cath. Ch., 1948. Parish priest St. Luke; auxiliary bishop Glasgow, Scotland, 1971-74; parish priest Our Holy Redeemer's, Clydebank, 1972-74; archbishop Glasgow, 1974—, cardinal, 1994—; pres. Bishops Conf. of Scotland, 1985—; active Pontifical Coun. for Family, Pontifical Coun. for Promotion of Christian Unity. Named Grand Prior Scottish Lieutenancy of Equestrian Order of Holy Sepulchre of Jerusalem, 1989—; hon. fellow Ednl. Inst. Scotland, 1986. Home: 40 Newlands Rd, Glasgow G43 2JD, Scotland Office: Archdiocese Glasgow Curial Offices, 196 Clyde St, Glasgow G1 4JY, Scotland

WINNINGTON, G. PETER, English educator, editor; b. Nottingham, England, Aug. 15, 1944; s. George Edward and Nancy (Winder) W.; m. Martine Aubort, 1973 (div., 1996); children: Mark, Eric. MA, U. Lausanne, 1970. Tchr. Gymnase de la Cite, Lausanne, 1965-72; lectr. English dept. U. Lausanne, 1972—; dir. lang. ctr. U. Lausanne, 1989-73. Editor: Titus Groan, 1981, Titus Alone, 1981, Peake's Progress, 1981, Gormenghast, 1982; editor Mervyn Peake Rev., 1975-84, Book People, 1985-93, NLP World, 1994—; editor, publisher Peake Studies, 1988—; author: Vast Alchemies, 2000; contbr. articles to profl. jours. Mem. Soc. Authors. Avocations: walking, photography (solo exhibition, Lausanne, 1998). Home: Les 3 Chasseurs, 1413 Orzens Switzerland

WINSHIP, BLAINE H., lawyer; b. Ithaca, N.Y., Apr. 3, 1951; s. Hershell F. and June M. (Nickless) W.; m. Karin M. Byrne, Dec. 21, 1979. AB magna cum laude, Dartmouth Coll., 1973; JD, Cornell U., 1976. Bar: Ill. 1976, Fla. 1982. Assoc. Sonnenschein, Nath & Rosenthal, Chgo., 1976-82; ptnr. Winship & Byrne, Miami, Fla., 1983—. Contbg. author: ABA Criminal Antitrust Manual, 1982. Mem. bd. trustees StageWorks, Tampa, Fla., 1984-86, pres., 1986. Rufus Choate scholar Dartmouth Coll., 1972-73. Mem. Miami City Club, Fla. Bar Assn. (vice chmn., antitrust and trade regulation com., exec. com. bus. law sect.), Phi Beta Kappa. Home: 1014 Hardee Rd Coral Gables FL 33146-3330 Office: Winship & Byrne 200 S Biscayne Blvd Ste 1870 Miami FL 33131-2329

WINSKEL, GLYNN, computer science educator, researcher; b. Lancaster, Eng., May 23, 1953; s. Thomas Francis and Helen Juanita (McCall) W.; m. Kirsten Jensen, July 24, 1982; children: Sofie, Stine. BA in Math., Cambridge (Eng.) U., 1975, ScD, 1995; MSc in Math., Oxford (Eng.) U., 1976; PhD in Computer Sci., Edinburgh (Scotland) U., 1980. Rsch. scientist Carnegie-Mellon U., Pitts., 1982-83; lectr. Cambridge U., 1984-87, reader, 1987-88, fellow King's Coll., 1985-88; prof. computer sci. Aarhus (Denmark) U., 1988—, dir. basic rsch. in computer sci., 1994-2000; prof. computer sci. Cambridge U., Eng., 2000—. Author: Formal Semantics of Programming Languages, 1993; contbg. author: Handbook of Logic in Computer Sci. IV, 1994; editor: Math. Structures in Computer Sci., 1989—. Fellow Emmanuel Coll.

WINSLET, KATE, actress; b. Reading, Berkshire, Eng., Oct. 5, 1975. Appeared in plays including Peter Pan, What the Butler Saw (Manchester Evening News award for Best Supporting Actress), A Game of Soldiers, (musical) Adrian Mole; appeared in TV shows including Anglo-Saxon Attitudes, Shrinks, Dark Season, Casualty, Get Back; appeared in films including Heavenly Creatures, 1994 (Best Fgn. Actress award New Zealand Film and TV Awards), Sense and Sensibility, 1995 (SAG award, Brit. Acad. of Film and TV award for Best Supporting Actress, Golden Globe nominee, Am. Acad. of Motion Picture Arts and Scis. nominee), A Kid in King Arthur's Court, 1995, Jude, 1996, Hamlet, 1996, Titanic, 1997 (nominated for Acad. award for Best Actress), Hideous Kinky, 1998, Plunge, 1999, Holy Smoke, 1999; appeared in various TV comms. Office: The William Morris Agy care Hilda Quealy 151 S El Camino Dr Beverly Hills CA 90212-2775 also: c/o Peters Fraser & Dunlop, 503 The Chambers, Chelsea Harbour SW14 CXF, England

WINSLOW, DAVID ALLEN, chaplain, retired naval officer; b. Dexter, Iowa, July 12, 1944; s. Franklin E. and Inez Maude (McPherson) W.; m. Frances Lavinia Edwards, June 6, 1970; children: Frances, David. BA, So. Nazarene U., 1968; MDiv, Drew U., 1971, STM, 1973; cert. of achievement, Emergency Mgmt. Inst., FEMA, 1997. Ordained to ministry United Meth. Ch. Detroit Annual Conf., 1969; cert. FEMA instr. Clergyman, 1969—; assoc. minister All Sts. Episcopal. Ch., Millington, N.J., 1969-70; asst. minister Marble Collegiate Ch., N.Y.C., 1970-71; min. No. N.J. Conf. United Meth. Ch., 1971-75; joined chaplain corps USN, 1974, advanced through grades to lt. comdr., 1980, ret., 1995; with Oak Knoll Naval Med. Ctr., Oakland, Calif., 1993-95; disaster cons. Ch. World Svc., Cupertino, Calif., 1997—; NDMS/DMAT, CA-6, Contra/Costa County, Calif., 1997—. Author: The Utmost for the Highest, 1993, Epiphany: God Still Speaks, 1994, Be Thou My Vision, 1994, Evening Prayers At Sea, 1995, Wiseman Still Adore Him, 1995, God's Power At Work, 1996; (with Walsh) A Year of Promise: Meditations, 1995, editor: The Road to Bethlehem: Advent, 1993, Preparation for Resurrecton: Lent, 1994, God's Promise: Advent, 1994, The Way of the Cross: Lent, 1995; contbr. articles to profl. jours. Bd. dirs. disaster svcs. and family svcs. ARC, Santa Ana, Calif., 1988-91, Child Abuse Prevention Ctr., Orange, Calif., 1990-91; bd. dirs. Santa Clara County Coun. Chs., 1993-94, del., 1995-98; bd. dirs. Salvation Army Adult Rehab. Ctr. Adv. Coun., San Jose, Calif; bd. dirs. emergency svcs. Santa Clara Valley chpt. ARC, San Jose, 1995-98; bd. dirs. disaster svcs. Interfaith Svc., Inc., San Jose Internat. Airport. Fellow Am. Acad. Experts in Traumatic Stress (cert. expert); mem. ACA, USN League (hon.), Sunrise Exch. Club (chaplain 1989-91), Dick Richards Breakfast Club (chaplain 1988-91), Kiwanis, Masons (charter), Shriners, Scottish Rite. Avocations: golf, skiing, sailing. Home: 20405 Via Volante Cupertino CA 95014-6318

WINSLOW, NORMAN ELDON, business executive; b. Oakland, Calif., Apr. 4, 1938; s. Merton Conrad and Roberta Eilene (Drennen) W.; m. Betty June Cady, Jan. 14, 1962 (div. Aug. 1971); 1 child, Todd Kenelm; m. Ilene Ruth Jackson, Feb. 3, 1979. BS, Fresno (Calif.) State U., 1959. Asst. mgr. Proctors Jewelers, Fresno, 1959-62; from agt. to dist. mgr. Allstate Ins. Co., Fresno, 1962-69; ins. agt. Fidelity Union Life Ins., Dallas, 1969-71; dist. and zone mgr. The Southland Corp., Dallas, 1971-78; owner Ser-Vis-Etc., Goleta, Calif., 1978—; expert witness, cons. Am. Arbitration/Calif. Superior Cts. Pub./editor FranchiserviceNews; author: Hands in Your Pockets, 1992; contbr. numerous articles to profl. jours. With USAFNG, 1961-67. Mem. Nat. Coalition of Assn. of 7-11 Franchises (affiliate, mem. adv. bd. Glendale, Calif. chpt. 1984-90). Republican. Methodist. Avocations: gardening, photography, traveling, model railroading. Home: 1179 N Patterson Ave Santa Barbara CA 93117-1813 Office: Ser-Vis-Etc PO Box 8276 Goleta CA 93118-8276

WINSTANLEY, DEREK, water resource executive; b. Wigan, England, May 19, 1945; s. Thomas and Bessie W.; m. Betty Lon, Jan. 30, 1982; children: Deborah Lon, Stuart Neil, Kay Dee. BA, Oxford Univ., England, 1966; MA, Oxford Univ., 1970, DPhil, 1970. Dir. Nat. Acid Precipitation Assessment Program, Washington, 1992-94; deputy chief scientist Nat. Oceanic and Atmospheric Adminstrn., Washington, 1994-97; chief Ill. State Water Survey, Champaign, Ill., 1997—; adj. prof. geography Univ. Ill., Champaign, 1997; editor Environ. Sci. and Policy Jour., 1998—. Contbr. articles to profl. jours. Chair Ill. Global Climate Change Task Force, Springfield, Ill., 1999—; mem. sci. adv. com. Ill. River Coordination Coun., Springfield, 1998—. Mem. Am. Meterological Soc., Am. Geophysical Union. Avocations: wood sculpture, photography. E-mail: dwinstan@uiuc.edu. Office: 2204 Griffith Dr Champaign IL 61820-7463

WINSTANLY, DEREK MILES, medical practitioner, company executive; b. Pretoria, S. Africa, June 25, 1946; s. Miles Winstanly and Gwen Cathrine Christie Gibbings; m. Heather Bucke (div. 1978); 1 child, Janet Hilary Winstanly; m. Louise Marie Teichler, Jan. 31, 1997. MB ChB, U. Pretoria, 1972. Cert. med. practitioner, aviation and space medicine. Gen. practitioner Pretoria, 1976-80; med. adviser clin. devel., regulatory, and med. affairs Glaxo Pty Ltd., S. Africa, 1984-87, dir. mktg. and sales, 1987-89, dir. strategy and new bus. devel., 1989-90, chief exec., 1990-93, chmn., chief exec., 1993-94; dir. migraine and new therapy areas Glaxo Pty Ltd., U.K., 1994-95; dir. emerging diseases Glaxo Wellcome Plc, U.K., 1995-97; pres. Nippon Wellcome KK, Japan, 1997-99; 1st gov. Med. U. South Africa, 1992-93, now trustee; prin. med. officer Inst. Aviation Medicine; apptd. Pres. of Quintiles K.K., Japan, 1999. With S. African Def. Force, 1980-84. Mem. S. African Aerospace Med. Soc. (past pres.). Avocations: tennis, golfing, yachting, reading, wild life.

WINSTEAD, GEORGE ALVIS, law librarian, biochemist, educator, consultant; b. Owensboro, Ky., Jan. 14, 1916; s. Robert Lee and Mary Oma (Dempsey) W.; m. Elisabeth Donelson Weaver, July 18, 1943. BS, We. Ky. U., 1938; MA, George Peabody Coll., 1940, MLS, 1957, MEd, 1958. Head chemistry and biology dept. Belmont Coll., Nashville, 1952-56; head chemistry dept. George Peabody Coll., Vanderbilt U., Nashville, 1956-58; assoc. law librarian Vanderbilt U., Nashville, 1958-76; dir. Tenn. State Supreme Ct. Law Libraries, Nashville, 1976—; law cons. Tenn. Youth Legis., Nashville, 1976—; cons. civic clubs, local colls., 1976—, Tenn. State Govt. Depts. Archives, Nashville, 1976—. Author: Tenn. State Law Library Progress Reports, 1975, Supreme Court Library Personnel Guide, 1981, Designing Future Law Libraries' Growth and Expansion, 1982, Problem Identification and Solutions in Law Libraries, Tenn. Supreme Courts, 1985; mem. editl. bd. A Dictionary of Chemical Equations, 1952—. Mem. Col. Tenn. Gov.'s staff, Nashville, 1978. With USAAF, 1943-46. Named to Gov.'s Staff of Ky. Cols., Lexington, 1988. Fellow Am. Inst. Chemists, SAR. Baptist. Avocations: camping, hiking, traveling, crafts, antique cars. Home: 3819 Gallatin Pike Nashville TN 37216-2609 Office: Tenn Supreme Ct Libr Nashville TN 37219

WINSTON, HAROLD RONALD, lawyer; b. Atlantic, Iowa, Feb. 7, 1932; s. Louis D. and Leta B. (Carter) W.; m. Carol J. Sundeen, June 11, 1955; children: Leslie Winston Yannetti, Lisa Winston Shaw, Laura Winston Moritz. BA, U. Iowa, 1954, JD, 1958. Bar: Iowa 1958, U.S. District Ct. (no. and so. dists.) Iowa 1962, U.S. Tax Ct. 1962, U.S. Ct. Appeals (8th cir.) 1970, U.S. Supreme Ct. 1969. Trust Officer United Home Bank & Trust Co., Mason City, Iowa, 1958-59; mem. Breese & Cornwell, 1960-62, Breese, Cornwell, Winston & Reuber, 1963-73, Winston, Schroeder & Reuber, 1974-79, Winston, Reuber, Swanson & Byrne, P.C., Mason City, 1980-92, Winston, Reuber & Byrne, 1992-96, Winston & Byrne P.C., 1996—. Police judge, Mason City, 1961-73. Contbr. articles to profl. jours. Past pres. Family YMCA, Mason City, Cerro Gordo County Estate Planning Coun.; active local charitable orgns. Capt. USAF, 1955-57. Fellow Am. Coll. Trust and Estate Counsel, Am. Bar Found. (life), Iowa Bar Found. (life); mem. ABA, Iowa Bar Assn. (gov., lectr. ann. meeting 1977-79), 2d Jud. Dist. Bar Assn. (lectr. meeting 1981-82), Cerro Gordo County Bar Assn. (past pres.), Am. Judicature Soc., Assn. Trial Lawyers Am., Mason City Country Club, Kiwanis, Masons. Republican. Presbyterian (elder). Office: Winston & Byrne 119 2d St NW Mason City IA 50401-3105

WINSTON, MICHAEL G., corporate executive; b. Jan. 23, 1951; s. Ralph and Irene (Sochrin) W.; children: Chelsie Blair, David Robert. BA cum laude, Ohio U., 1972; MA, U. Notre Dame, 1975; PhD, U. Ill., 1977; post grad. exec. program, Stanford U., U. Pa. Instr. psychology U. Ill., 1975-77; cons. Mgmt., Health and Devel. Corp., L.A., 1977-78, sr. psychologist, 1978, v.p. orgnl. devel., 1978-79; v.p. ortn. devel. Creative Mgmt. Systems, Encino, Calif., 1980-81; dir. orgn devel. Lockheed Corp., Burbank, Calif., 1981-85; dir. human resources devel. McDonnell-Douglas Corp., Huntington Beach, Calif., 1985-87, sr. dir. orgn. devel., 1987-88; dir. orgn. devel. Motorola, Inc., Rolling Meadows, Ill., 1988-90, v.p., dir. orgn. devel., 1990-98; sr. v.p. Orgn. Strategy and Mgmt. Resources Rockwell Internat., 1998-99; sr. v.p. global leadership and orgn. devel. Merrill Lynch, 1999—; adj. prof. Grad. Sch. Bus.

and Mgmt., Pepperdine U., 1981, Golden Gate U., San Francisco, 1982, U. San Francisco, 1982, U. Calif., Irvine, 1986; keynote spkr. World Acad. Mgmt. Conf., The Hague, The Netherlands, 1987, 91, SW Productivity Conf., 1987, Am. Productivity Conf., 1987, 88, Internat. Conf. Strategic Mgmt., 1993; guest lectr. de Baak Mgmt. Ctr., Noodwijk, The Netherlands, 1987—; diplomate spkr., 1988—; spl. advisor European Cmty., 1990—, Asia-Pacific Mgmt. Inst., 1993—; mem. exec. devel. adv. coun. U. Calif. Author: Executive Excellence, 1990, 3d edit., 1996. Mem. Human Resources Planning Soc. (keynote spkr. annual conv. 1985), Internat. Soc. Strategic Mgmt. (keynote spkr. 1991, 93, internat. conf. bus. strategy, Venice 1994, Monte Carlo 1996, top mgmt. forum, Tokyo 1994), Phi Kappa Phi, Kappa Delta Phi, Phi Delta Kappa.

WINTER, ALAN THOMAS, university official, physicist; b. Harrogate, Yorkshire, Eng., Sept. 26, 1949; s. Alan and Maggie (Thwaites) W.; m. Marjorie Blake Batchelor, Sept. 23, 1978; children: William Thomas, Roger Thwaite, Dale Alan. BA, Cambridge (Eng.) U., 1970, PhD, 1974. Chartered physicist, Eng. Rsch. fellow Christ's Coll., Cambridge U., 1975-76; rsch. assoc. Bell Tel. Labs., Murray Hill, N.J., 1977, Brookhaven Nat. Lab., Upton, N.Y., 1978; demonstrator Cambridge U., 1979-84, univ. lectr. physics, 1984-93, sec. chemistry dept., 1993-97, sec. Sch. Phys. Scis., 1997—. Gen. sec. Cly Diocesan Assn. Ch. Bellringers, 1984-89; treas. Cambridgeshire Children's Holiday Orch., 1990—. Fellow Inst. Physics. Anglican. Avocations: music, running, bell ringing. Office: Cambridge U Sch Phys Scis, 19 Trumpington St, Cambridge CB2 1QA, England

WINTER, EDWIN THOMAS, JR., accountant, treasurer; b. Darby, Pa., July 28, 1962; s. Edwin Thomas and Christa K. (Mang) W.; m. Patricia Anne Ott; children: Elizabeth Anne, Stephanie Marie, Edwin Thomas III, Matthew Dominic. BS in Acctg. and Fin., Drexel U., 1985, MBA in Fin. cum laude, 1993; M in Taxation, Villanova U., 1994. CPA, Pa. Auditor, rev. officer IRS, Phila., 1983, 84; acct. Cogen Sklar Levick, Bala Cynwyd, Pa., 1984-87, Shotz Miller & Glusman, Phila., 1987-88; acctg./office mgr. Bachmann Industries, Inc., Phila., 1988—; treas. Cyrax Fed. Credit Union, Upper Darby, Pa., 1996—; tchr. Delaware County C.C. Bd. dirs., v.p. sch. bd. Upper Darby, 1996—; bd. dirs. Upper Darby Ednl. Cultural Found. Mem. Nat. Holy Name Soc. (exec. dir., treas. 1996—, fin. sec. 1995—), Phila. Archdiocesan Holy Name Union (exec. dir., pres. 1995-97). Republican. Roman Catholic. Avocations: reading, outdoor activities. Fax: 610-394-2862. Home: 347 Congress Ave Lansdowne PA 19050-1003 Office: E T Winter & Assocs PO Box 2266 Upper Darby PA 19082-0766

WINTER, HANS, veterinary pathologist; b. Vienna, Austria, Dec. 1, 1922; arrived in Australia, 1954; s. Rudolf and Rosina (Kozler) W.; m. Jean Isobel McRae, Dec. 18, 1962; children: Christopher, Alexander, Richard, Harold. Degree in vet., Vet. U., Vienna, 1950, DVM, 1951; D Vet Sci, U. Queensland, Brisbane, Australia, 1966. Diplomate Am. Coll. Vet. Pathologists. Asst. dept. vet. pathology Vet. U., Vienna, 1950-54; pathologist Vet. Sch., U. Queensland, Brisbane, 1954-87, head dept. vet. pathology, 1980-85, rsch. cons., 1986—; cons. FAO/UN, Rongoon, Burma, 1966-67; sr. cons. in vet. pathology FAO/UN, Iran, Iraq, India, Bhutan, 1970-85; sr. cons. Asian Developing Bank, Bhutan, 1988-91; sr. fgn. scientist U.S. Nat. Sci. Found., Mich. State U., East Lansing, 1968; hon. vet. Brookfield Show Soc., Brisbane, 1970—; pres. Australian Assn. Vet. Pathologists, 1974-82, World Assn. Vet. Pathologists, 1979-87. Author: Postmortem Examinations of Ruminants, 1966, Spanish edit., 1968, Burmese edit., 1968, Farsi edit., 1970, Arabic edit., 1980; contbr. articles to profl. jours. Fulbright fellow Cornell U., Ithaca, N.Y., 1951-52; sr. scientist fellow Deutscher-Akademischer Austausch Dienst, Munich, 1973, 78. Mem. Australian Coll. Vet. Scientists, Royal Coll. Vet. Surgeons, Australian Vet. Assn. (coun. mem. 1974-83), European Soc. Vet. Pathology, Royal Queensland Yacht Squadron, Phi Zeta, Sigma Xi. Avocations: equestrian, sailing. Home: 175 Boscombe Rd Brookfield, Brisbane QLD 4069, Australia Office: Univ Queensland, Brisbane QLD 4072, Australia

WINTER, JOAN ELIZABETH, psychotherapist; b. Aiken, S.C., Feb. 24, 1947; d. John S. and Mary Elizabeth (Caldwell) Winter. BS, Ariz. State U., 1970; MSW, Va. Commonwealth U., 1977; EdS, Coll. William and Mary, 1989, EdD, 1993. Lic. marriage and family therapist, lic. clin. social worker, AAMFT bd. approved supr., clin. group worker. Va. Counselor Child Psychiatry Hosp., Phoenix, 1969-70, Ariz. Job Coll., Casa Grande, 1970-71; dir. Halfway House, Richmond, Va., 1971-73; state supr. resdl. treatment, Richmond, 1973-75; psycotherapist Med. Coll. Va., Richmond, 1975-76, Va. Commonwealth U., 1976-77; adj. prof., exec. dir. Family Rsch. Project, Coll. of William and Mary, Richmond, Va., 1979—; dir. Family Inst. Va., Richmond, 1980—; examiner, approved supr. Bd. Behavioral Scis., Commonwealth of Va., 1982—; faculty dept. psychiatry Med. Coll. of Va., Commonwealth U.; mem. adj. faculty dept. psychology Coll. William & Mary, Med. Coll. Va.; mem. Avanta Network, Exec. Coun. and Faculty, Nat. Inst. of Drug Abuse, Rsch. Adv. Com. Author: The Phenomenon of Incest, 1977, The Use of Self in Therapy: The Person and Practice of the Therapist, 1987, Family Life of Psychotherapists, 1987 Enhancing the Marital Relationship: Virginia Satir's Parts Party, 1990, Enhancing the Marital Relationship: Virginia Satir's Parts Party, Satir Theory, 1991, Family Therapy Research Outcomes: Bowen, Haley and Satir; editor Jour. Couple Therapy; contbr. articles to profl. jours. Diplomate Nat. Assn. Social Workers; mem. Am. Soc. Cert. Social Workers, Am. Family Therapy Assn., Am. Assn. Marriage and Family Therapy (approved supr.), Avanta Network Faculty. Address: 2910 Monument Ave Richmond VA 23221-1404

WINTER, MARK ANTHONY, graphic designer, educator, filmmaker; b. Invercargill, Southland, New Zealand, Apr. 10, 1958; m. Senga White (div. 1992); 1 child, Benjamin Mark. BA, Massey U., New Zealand, 1983, MEd with first class honors, 1993. Graphics tutor Southland Poly. Art Faculty, Invercargill, 1988—; mgr. Movieland 5 Multiplex, Invercargill; founder, ptnr. Think In Ink Film, 1989—; founder Chicane Pictures Ltd., 1999. City councillor Invercargill City Coun., 1983—, dep. mayor, 1986-89, 96-98. Recipient The Christopher Columbus award Columbus Internat. Film and Video Festival, Ohio, 1991, The Gold Camera award U.S. Internat. Film and Video Festival, Chgo., 1993, numerous others; Winston Churchill fellow Winston Churchill Trust, Wellington, 1993.

WINTER, MARTIN, physician, ophthalmologist; b. Goettingen, Germany, Nov. 9, 1964; s. Burkhard and Renate (Bartels) W.; m. Christine Fehrmann, July 21, 1994; children: Wiebke, Katrin. MD, U. Kiel, Germany, 1992. Postdoctoral fellow Inst. Anatomy, Kiel, 1992-94; resident U. Eye Hosp., Kiel, 1994-97, house officer, 1997-99; pvt. practice, 1999—. Office: Waller Heerstr 154a, 28219 Bremen Germany

WINTER, RICHARD LAWRENCE, financial and health care company executive; b. St. Louis, Dec. 17, 1945; s. Melvin Lawrence and Kathleen Jane (O'Leary) W.; children from previous marriage: Leigh Ellen, Jessica Marie, George Bradford; m. Kathryn Ann Geppert, Dec. 4, 1993. BS in Math., St. Louis U., 1967, MS in Math. (fellow), 1969; MBA, U. Mo., St. Louis, 1976. Rsch. analyst Mo. Pacific R.R., St. Louis, 1971-73; dir. fin. rels. Linclay Corp., St. Louis, 1973-74; asst. v.p. 1st Nat. Bank in St. Louis (now Centerre Bank, NA) subs. Boatmen's Nat. Bank, 1974-79; v.p. fin. UDE Corp., St. Louis, 1979-81; pres. Health Care Investments, Ltd., St. Louis, 1981—, Larus Corp., St. Louis, 1981—, Garden View Care Ctr., Inc., O'Fallon, Mo., 1987—; exec. bd. Duchesne Bank, St. Peters, Mo., 1989-97; lectr. math. U. Mo., St. Louis, 1972-74, St. Louis U., 1982-90. Fundraising staff St. Louis Symphony, Jr. Achievement, United Way St. Louis, Arts and Edn. Fund, St. Louis, 1974-79; bd. dirs. Dance St. Louis, 1998—. With U.S. Army, 1969-71. Mem. Nat. Health Lawyers Assn., Mo. Athletic Club (St. Louis), Pi Mu Epsilon. Roman Catholic. Home: 1321 Green Tree Ln Saint Louis MO 63122-4744 Office: Ste 175 12412 Powerscourt Dr Saint Louis MO 63131-3659

WINTER, RICHARD SAMUEL, JR., computer training company owner, writer; b. Denver, Mar. 17, 1958; s. Richard Samuel and Jerryl Dene (Gano) W.; m. Karen Annette Hansen, May 27, 1989. Student, Griffith U., Brisbane, Australia, 1979; BA in Internat. Environment, Colo. Coll., 1981; MA in Pub. Adminstrn., U. Colo., Denver, 1989. Range aide U.S. Forest Svc., Desert Exptl. Station, Utah, 1976-77; pub. health investigator, lab. technician Denver Health Dept., 1982-84; projects mgr. Colo. Statesman, Denver, 1984-85; editor Mile Hi Prep, Denver, 1985; fin. analyst Pan Am. World Airways, N.Y.C., 1985-88; sr. ptnr., owner PRW, Denver, 1988—; tng. mgr. Qwest, 2000—; pres. info. systems Trainers, Denver, 1994. Co-author, revisor: MicroRef Quick Reference Bd. Lotus 1-2-3 Rel. 3.0, 1990, MicroRef Quick Reference Gd. Lotus 1-2-3 Rel. 2.2, 1990, Que Q&A QueCards, 1991, Que 123 Release 2.3 QuickStart, 1991, Que 123 Release 2.4 QuickStart, 1992, Que Look Your Best with Excel, 1992, Que Excel for Windows Sure Steps, 1993, Que Using Lotus 123 Release 4, 1994, Que Using Excel 5, 1994, Que Using Microsoft Office, 1994, Que Using Microsoft Office 95, 1995, Que Special Edition Using Microsoft Office Professional for Windows 95, 1996, Que Special Edition Using Microsoft Office 97 Professional, 1997, Que Microsoft Access 97 Quick Reference Guide, 1997, Que Using Microsoft Office 95, 1998, Que Microsoft Office 97 User Manual, 1998, Que Microsoft Excel 2000, Cheat Sheet, 1999, DDC Learning Office 2000, 1999, DDC Learning Access 2000, 1999, DDC One Day Office, Excel, Access, Word, Power Point (1999-00), Rising Moon, Dirty Birdy Feet, 2000. Chmn. N.Y. Victims for Victims, N.Y.C., 1986-87; bd. dirs. Colo. Common Cause, Denver, 1984-85; steering com. Voter Registration "Motor Voter" Amendment, Denver, 1983-84; pres. Broadway Commons Homeowners Assn., Denver, 1982-84; pres. Info. Systems Trainers, 1994, bd. dirs. 1990-96; Dist. Accountability Adv. Com. budget chair Clear Creek Sch. Dist., 1996-98; chair Clear Creek Imagine Ednl. Excellence, 1997-98, Citizens for Improved Edn., 1999-00. Recipient Vigil Honor, Order of the Arrow, 1976, Disting. Svc. award Info. Sys. Trainers, 1996. Mem. Phi Beta Kappa, Alpha Lambda Delta.

WINTER, STEFAN MANFRED, physicist; b. Jena, Germany, Jan. 13, 1960; s. Manfred Max and Ingrid Erna (Fuchs) W.; m. Martina Uta Ziechner, May 28, 1982; children: Cathleen, Norman. BS in Physics, F. Schiller U., Jena, 1985; PhD, Martin Luther U., Halle, Germany, 1990. Postdoc. Acad. Agrl. Scis., Berlin, 1990-91; rsch. asst., head fluorescence lab. Inst. Molecular Biotech., Jena, 1992-98; project mgr. CyBio Inc., Jena, 1998—. Contbr. articles to profl. jours. With German Mil., 1978-80. Avocations: photography. Home: Steinweg 9, D-07778 Dorndorf Germany Office: CyBio AG, Goeschwitzer Strasse 40, D-07745 Jena Germany

WINTER, STEVEN, internist, cardiologist; b. Bklyn., July 25, 1950; s. Nathan Harold and Magda (Markowitz) W.; m. Florence Stein, Aug. 20, 1972; children: Amy R., Daniel. BA, Yeshiva U., 1972; MD, U. Med./Dentistry of N.J., 1976. Diplomate Am. Bd. Internal Medicine with subspecialty in cardiovascular disease. Intern North Shore Univ. Hosp., Manhasset, N.Y., 1976-77, resident in medicine, 1977-79; fellow in cardiology R.I. Hosp.-Brown U., Providence, 1979-81; pvt. practice S.I., N.Y.; attending in medicine and cardiology S.I. U. Hosp., 1981—, St. Vincent's Med. Ctr., Richmond, 1985—; asst. clin. prof. SUNY, Bklyn., 1985—. Fellow ACP, Am. Coll. Cardiology; mem. AMA, Am. Heart Assn. Office: 2627B Hylan Blvd Staten Island NY 10306-4353

WINTER, WERNER, linguistics educator; b. Haselau, Fed. Republic Germany, Oct. 25, 1923; s. Carl and Anna (Lienau) W.; m. Ingrid Anders, Dec. 13, 1952; 1 child, Christian Anders. PhD, U. Bern, Switzerland, 1949; LittD (hon.), U. Poznan, Poland, 1984, U. Kaliningrad, Russia, 2000. Asst. prof. U. Kans., Lawrence, 1953-57; assoc. prof. U. Tex., Austin, 1957-61, prof., 1961-65; prof., dept. head U. Kiel, Fed. Republic Germany, 1964-92, dean, 1971-72; vis. prof. various univs., 1956—. Author: Studien zum "Prothetischen Vokal" im Griechischen, 1950, Studia Tocharica, 1984, Materials Toward a Dictionary of Chamling, 1985, Walapai (Hualapai) texts, 1998. Mem. Acad. Europaea, Societas Scientiarum Fennica, Linguistic Soc. Am. (hon.), Linguistic Soc. Nepal (hon.), Societas Linguistica Europaea (sec. 1966). Lutheran. Home: von Liliencronstr 2, D 24211 Preetz Germany

WINTER, WILLIAM PAUL, JR., ministry director; b. Arkansas City, Kans., Apr. 27, 1942; s. Paul William and Dessie Marie (Francis) W.; m. Sharon Ruth Fells, Dec. 26, 1964; children: Todd William, Heidi Reneé. BA, Ashland (Ohio) Coll., 1965; Cert. Electronics Cirs. and Systems Program, RCA Inst., N.Y.C., 1970; MDiv, Ashland Theol. Sem., 1986. Chief engr. radio/TV dept. Ashland Coll., 1967-72; electronic technician CAVEA Studio, Buenos Aires, 1972-74, tech. dir., 1974-93; exec. dir. Open Arms Ministry, Denver, 2000—; exec. bd. dirs. Evang. Found. of Argentina, Buenos Aires, 1979-93; tech. cons. various evang. orgns. in Argentina, Paraguay, Uruguay; bd. dirs. Trans World Radio, Buenos Aires, Interdenominational Theol. Sem., Buenos Aires. Contbr. articles to profl. jours. Baptist. Avocations: travel, camping, car restoration, amateur radio, photography. Home: 11957 Keough Dr Northglenn CO 80233-1223

WINTERER, PHILIP STEELE, lawyer; b. San Francisco, July 8, 1931; s. Steele Leland and Esther (Hardy) W.; m. Patricia Dowling, June 15, 1955; children: Edward J., Amey W. Marrella. BA, Amherst Coll., 1953; LLB, Harvard U., 1956. Bar: N.Y. 1957, Republic of Korea 1958. Assoc., then ptnr. Debevoise & Plimpton, N.Y.C., 1956-93, ret. ptnr., 1993, of counsel, 1994-96; dir. Am. Savs. Bank, 1972-92. Contbr. articles to profl. publs. Trustee Amherst Coll., Adelphi U.; chmn. emeritus Sch. of Am. Ballet; mem. Com. on the Folger Shakespeare Libr.; past pres. Am. Italy Soc.; chmn. exec. com. Phipps Houses; hon. trustee N.Y. State Bd. Nature Conservancy; trustee, past chmn. Austen Riggs Ctr.; bd. dirs. Adirondack Trail Improvement Soc., Phi Beta Kappa Assocs. Recipient Amherst Coll. medal for Eminent Svc., 1980. Mem. Coun. on Fgn. Rels., Am. Law Inst., Citizens Housing and Planning Coun. N.Y., N.Y. Acad. Scis., Tax Forum, Am. Coll. Tax Counsel, Ausuable Club (trustee). Home: East Hill Rd Keene NY 12942 also: 1165 5th Ave New York NY 10029-6931 Office: Debevoise & Plimpton 875 3rd Ave Fl 23 New York NY 10022-6225

WINTERER-SCHULZ, BARBARA JEAN, designer, author; b. Manchester, N.H., Apr. 1, 1938; d. John Edward and Elizabeth Virginia Grace; m. Allen George Winterer, Mar. 30, 1959 (div. 1977); children: Audrey Lyn Winterer, Amy Jo Winterer DeNoble; m. James Robert Schulz, May 28, 1983 (div. May 1999). AA, Mesa (Ariz.) C.C., 1980; BS summa cum laude, U. Md., Heidelberg, Germany, 1996. Art designer Morningstar Art Design Studio, Cortez, Colo., 1988—; interpreter Colo. State Park; U.S. rail ranger Durango-Sivlerton R.R.; master gardener Colo. State U. Contbr. articles to newspapers and jours. Ofcl. U.S. reporter at World Eskimo Indian Olympics, Faribanks, Alaska, 1994; asst. dir. Ariz. Myasthenia Gravis Found., 1977-80; mem. ARC Disaster Response Team, Cortez, Colo. Recipient Humanitarian award Phila. Inst. Human Potential, 1972, Chancellor of Germany award for acad. achievement, 1986, Citation of Meritorious Achievement award in the arts and humanitarianism Internat. Biograph. Ctr., 1997. Mem. AAUW, Libr. of Congress (assoc.), Alpha Sigma Lambda, Phi Theta Kappa. Avocations: gardening, gourmet cooking. Office: Morningstar Art Design Studio 247 Davis Cup Dr Unit 4212 Pagosa Springs CO 81147-8338

WINTERFELDT, EKKEHARD, chemistry educator; b. Danzig, Germany, May 13, 1932; s. Herbert and Herta (Krieschen) W.; m. Marianne Heinemann, Sept. 30, 1958; children: Thomas, Susanne. Diploma in Chemistry, Tech. U. Braunschweig, Germany, 1956, D Natural Scis., 1958; Habilitation, U. Berlin, 1963; Dr. h.c., U. Liège, Belgium, 1991. Dozent Tech. U. Berlin, 1963-67, assoc. prof., 1967-70; prof. chemistry U. Hannover, Germany, 1970—. Author: Chemistry of Acetylenes, 1969; editor: Comprehensive Organic Synthesis (vol. V), 1991. Recipient Adolf Windaus medal U. Gottingen, 1993. Mem. Acad. Wissenschaften, Göttinger Akademie, Braunschweigische Wissenschaft Gesellschaft, Gesellschaft Deutscher Chemiker (Emil Fischer medal 1990, Richard Kuhn medal 1995), Deutsche Akademie der Naturforscher Leopoldina. Home: Sieversdamm 34, D 30916 Isernhagen Germany Office: Univ Hannover, Schneiderberg 1 B, D 30167 Hannover Germany

WINTERHALTER, BERND RAINER, internist, pharmaceutical company administrator; b. Freiburg, Germany, Oct. 22, 1958; s. Josef and Maria (Maier) W.; m. Ute Dentler, May 1988; children: Felix, Julia. MD, Albert Ludwigs U., Freiburg, Germany, 1986. Diplomate German Bd. Internal Medicine. Resident and fellowship in internal medicine Albert Ludwigs U., 1986-93; dept. head tumor testing lab. dept. med. oncology/hematology U. Hosp. Freiburg, head computer dept. dept. med. oncology/hematology; sr. clin. rsch. mgr. bus. unit Oncology Farmitalia Carlo Erba/Pharmacia, 1993-94; head clin. rsch. bus. unit Oncology Pharmacia Germany, 1994; head med. affairs Oncology/Immunology Pharmacia Germany, 1994-97; med. and scientific dir. Pharmacia and Upjohn, 1997-2000; v.p. med., sci. and health econs. Pharmacia and Upjohn, Germany, 2000—. Contbr. chpts. to books and over 60 articles to profl. jours. Mem. Am. Assn. for Cancer Rsch., Arbeitsgemeinschaft internistische Onkologie, Am. Soc. for Hematology, Am. Soc. Clin. Oncology, European Soc. Med. Oncology, German Cancer Soc., German Assn. Hematology and Oncology. Avocations: high end music reproduction, photography, travelling. Office: Pharmacia & Upjohn Germany, Am Wolfsmantel 46, 91058 Erlangen Germany

WINTER-NEIGHBORS, GWEN CAROLE, special education/art educator, consultant; b. Greenville, S.C., July 14, 1938; d. James Edward and Evelyn (Lee) Walters; m. David M. Winter Jr., Aug., 1963 (dec. Feb. 1982); children: Robin Carole Winter, Charles G. McCuen, Dustin Winter TeBrugge; m. Thomas Frederick Neighbors, Mar. 24, 1989. BA in Edn. and Art, Furman U., 1960, MA in Psychology, 1967; cert. in guidance/pers., Clemson U., 1981; EdD in Youth and Mid. Childhood Edn., Nova Southeastern U., 1988; postgrad., U. S.C., Spartanburg, 1981-89; cert. clear specialist instrn., Calif. State U., Northridge, 1991; art edn. cert., Calif. State U., L.A., 1991; JD, Glendale U., 1999. Cert. tchr. art, elem. edn., psychology, secondary guidance, S.C. Tchr. 7th grade Greenville Jr. H.S., 1960-63; art tchr. Wade Hampton H.S., Greenville, 1963-67; prin. adult edn. Woodmont H.S., Piedmont, S.C., 1983-85, Mauldin H.S., Greenville and Mauldin, S.C., 1981; tchr. ednl. psychology edn. dept. Allen U., Columbia, S.C., 1969; activity therapist edn. dept. S.C. Dept. of Corrections, Columbia, 1973-76; art specialist gifted edn. Westcliffe Elem. Sch., Greenville, 1976-89; tchr. self-contained spl. day class Elysian Heights Elem. Sch., Echo Park and L.A., Calif., 1989-91; art tchr. medh. drawing Sch. Dist. Greenville County Blue Ridge Mid. Sch., Greer, S.C., 1991-95; participant nat. conf. U.S. Dept. Edn./So. Bell, Columbia, 1989; com. mem. nat. exec. com. Nova Southeastern U., 1988-89. Illustrator: Mozart Book, 1988; author: (drama) Let's Sing a Song About America, 1988 (1st pl. Nat. Music award 1990). Life mem. Rep. Presdl. Task Force, 1970—; mem. voter registration com. Lexington County Rep. Party, 1970-80; grand jury participant 13th Jud. Ct. Sys., Greenville, 1986-88, guardian ad litem, 1988-89. Tchr. Incentive grantee Sch. Dist. Greenville County, 1986-88, Project Earth grantee Bell South, 1988-89, 94-95, Edn. Improvement Act/Nat. Dissimination Network grantee S.C. State Dept. Edn., 1987-88, Targett 2,000 Arts in Curricular grantee S.C. Dept. Edn., 1994-95, Alliance grantee Bus. Cmty. Greenville, 1992-95, Greer Art Rsch. grantee, 1993-94, S.C. Govs. Sch. Study grantee, 1994, Edn. Improvement Act Competitive Tchr. grantee S.C. Dept. Edn., 1994-95, Alliance Grand grant, 1995-96; recipient Am. Jurisprudence Bancroft-Whitney award Glendale U. Sch. Law, 1997, 98, Excellence Recognition in Real Property award Glendale Law Faculty, 1997, Excellence in Art of Appellate Advocacy, Glendale U. Sch. Law, 1998, Am. Jurisprudence Bancroft-Whitney award Constl. Law I, 1998. Mem. NEA, ABA (student orgn.), Nat. Art Edn. Assn., Nat. Mus. Women in Arts, S.C. Arts Alliance, S.C. Art Edn. Assn., Phi Delta Kappa (com. mem. 1976-90), Upstate IBM-PC Users Group. Baptist/Lutheran. Avocations: computers, art, writing, music composition, law. Home: 26 Charterhouse Ave Piedmont SC 29673-9139 Office: Neighbors Enterprises 3075 Foothill Blvd Unit 138 La Crescenta CA 91214-2742

WINTERS, RICHARD ALLEN, mineral economist; b. Butte, Mont., Feb. 19, 1963; s. Allen S. and Doris Ellen (Taylor) W. BS in Fin. and Econs., U. Mont., 1986; MS in Mineral Econs., Colo. Sch. Mines, 1990, postgrad., 1991-93. Office engr. Morrison Knudsen Engrs., Richland, Wash., 1986-88; project acct. Morrison Knudsen Engrs., Richland, 1987-88; ops. analyst Echo Bay Mines, Denver, 1989; instr. Colo. Sch. Mines, Golden, Colo., 1991-92; cons. Coors Brewing Co., Golden, 1991-92; sr. rsch. engr. Phelps Dodge Mining Co., Morenci, Ariz., 1992-94; gold analyst Robertson, Stephens and Co., San Francisco, 1994-95; v.p. corp. devel. Golden Star Resources Ltd., Denver, 1995-99; v.p. RMB Resources, 2000—. Pres. Mineral Econ. Grad. Student Assn., 1989-90. Mem. Soc. Mining, Metallurgy and Exploration, Assn. Environ. Resource Economists, Mineral, Econs. and Mgmt. Soc. Avocations: outdoors, jewelry craft. Office: 303 E 17th Ave Ste 700 Denver CO 80203-1260

WINTERSTEIN, JAMES FREDRICK, academic administrator; b. Copperas Cove, Tex., Apr. 8, 1943; s. Arno Fredrick Herman and Ada Amanda Johanna (Wagnr) W.; m. Diane Marie Bochmann, July 13, 1963; children: Russell, Lisa, Steven, Amy. Student, U. N.M., 1962; D of Chiropractic cum laude, Nat. Coll. Chiropractic, 1968; cert., Harvard Inst. for Ednl. Mgmt., 1988. Diplomate Am. Chiropractic Bd. Radiology; lic. chiropractic, Ill., Fla., S.D., Md. Night supr. x-ray dept. DuPage Meml. Hosp., Elmhurst, Ill., 1964-66; x-ray technologist Lombard (Ill.) Chiropractic Clinic, 1966-68, asst. dir., 1968-71; chmn. dept. diagnostic imaging Nat. Coll. Chiropractic, Lombard, Ill., 1971-73, chief of staff, 1985-86, pres., 1986—; pvt. practice West Chicago, Ill., 1968-73, Fla., 1973-85; faculty Nat.-Lincoln Sch. Postgrad. Edn., 1967—; chmn. x-ray test com. Nat. Bd. Chiropractic Examiners, 1971-73; govs. adv. panel on coal worker's pneumoconiosis and chiropractic State of Pa., 1979; v.p. Am. Chiropractic Coll. Radiology, 1981-83; mem. adv. coun. on radiation protection Dept. Health and Rehabilitative Svcs. State of Fla., 1984-85; cons. to bd. examiners State of S.C., 1983-84, State of Fla., 1980-85; cons. to peer review bd. State of Fla., 1980-84; trustee Chiropractic Centennial Found., 1989-90; mem. adv. com. Aids Alternative Health Ptnrs., 1996—, CCCR, 1998—; bd. dirs. FIICU, 1995—; bd. trustees Alternative Medicine, Inc., 1999—; spkr. in field. Pub. Outreach, monthly Nat. Coll. Chiropractic; author numerous monographs on chiropractic edn. and practice; inventor composite shielding and mounting means for x-ray machines; contbr. articles to profl. jours. Chmn., bd. dirs. Trinity Luth. Ch., West Chgo., 1970-72, Luth. High Sch., Pinellas County, Fla., 1979-82, St. John Luth. Ch., Lombard, 1988; chmn. bd. edn. First Luth. Sch., 1975-79; chmn. First Luth. Congregation, Clearwater, Fla., 1979-82; chmn. bldg. planning com. Grace Luth. Ch. and Sch., St. Petersburg, Fla., 1984-85; bldg. planning com. ch. expansion, new elem. sch., First Luth. Sch., 1975-79; stewardship adv. coun. Fla./Ga. dist. Luth. Ch. Mo. Synod, 1983-85; trustee West Suburban Regional Acad. Consortium, 1993—. With U.S. Army, 1961-64. Recipient Cert. Meritorious Svc. Am. Chiropractic Registry of Radiologic Technologists, Cert. Recognition for Inspiration, Guidance, and Support Delta Tau Alpha, 1989, Cert. Appreciation Chiropractic Assn. South Africa, 1988, 1st pl. Fund Raiser Ride for Kids award Pediat. Brain Tumor Found. U.S., 1997, Cert. Appreciation Ill. Chiropractic Soc., 1997, Hope and Support award AAHP, 1998. Mem. APHA, Am. Chiropractic Assn., Am. Chiropractic Coll. Radiology (pres. 1983-85, exec. com. 1985-86), Am. Chiropractic Coun. on Diagnostic Imaging, Am. Chiropractic Coun. on Diagnosis and Internal Disorders, Am. Chiropractic Coun. on Nutrition, Nat. Coll. Alumni Assn., Am. Acad. Chiropractic Physicians (sec.), Assn. Chiropractic Colls. (sec.-treas. 1986-91), Coun. Chiropractic Edn. (sec.-treas. 1988-90, v.p. 1990-92, pres. 1992-94, immediate past pres. 1994), Fla. Chiropractic Assn. (chmn. radiol. health com. 1977—, Disting. Svc. award 1999). Republican. Lutheran. Avocations: reading, automobile rehabilitation, Harley-Davidson motorcycles, fishing.

WINTER-SWITZ, CHERYL DONNA, travel company executive; b. Jacksonville, Fla., Dec. 6, 1947; d. Jacqueline Marie (Carroll) Winter; m. Frank C. Snedaker, June 24, 1974 (div. May 1976); m. Robert William Switz, July 1, 1981. AA, City Coll. of San Francisco, 1986; BS, Golden Gate U., 1990, MBA, 1992. Bookkeeper, agt. McQuade Tours, Ft. Lauderdale, Fla., 1967-69; mgr. Boca Raton (Fla.) Travel, 1969-76; owner, mgr. Ocean Travel, Boca Raton, 1976-79; ind. contractor Far Horizons Travel, Boca Raton, 1979-80; mgr. Tara/BPF Travel, San Francisco, 1981-84; mgr. travel. dept. Ernst & Whinney/Lifeco Travel, San Francisco, 1984-86; travel cons. Golden Gate U., San Francisco, 1986-99, Siemer & Hand Travel, San Francisco, 1989-99, Ravenel Travel, Charleton, S.C., 1999—; instr. Golden Gate U., 1986-99, U. San Francisco. Mem. Amateur Trapshooting Assn., Hotel and Restaurant Mgmt. Club. Republican. Episcopalian. Avocations: trap shooting, gardening, cooking, travelling, reading. Home: 1189 W Park View Pl Mount Pleasant SC 29466-7910 Office: Ravenel Travel 480 E Bay St Charleston SC 29403-6356

WINTHER, GORM, economist and social scientist; b. Aalborg, Jutland, Denmark, Apr. 9, 1951; s. Hans Jorgen and Ellen Brandt (Christensen) W.; m. Susanne Bramsen, Apr. 9, 1977; 1 child, Louise. M, U. Aalborg, 1981, PhD, 1990. Asst. prof. U. Aalborg, Denmark, 1982-83; vis. fellow Cornell U., Ithaca, N.Y., 1984-85, 90-91; rschr. U. Aalborg, 1986-89; asst. prof. Copenhagen Bus. Sch., 1989-92; sr. rschr. U. Aalborg, 1992—, assoc. prof. econs., 1996-99; prof. U. Greenland, 1999—, head dept. adminstrn., 1999—; course dir. Interuniversity Ctr., Dubrovnik., Yugoslavia, 1986-90, 96—. Author: Den Gronlandske Okonomi, 1988, Erhvervsudvikling i Gronland,

1988, Employee Ownership - A Comparative Analysis of Growth Performance, 1995; contbr. articles in Danish to internat. jours. Bd. dirs. Assn. for Studies in Coop. Socs., 1987-89; chmn. Greenland Com. for Competition, 1999—; bd. mem. Stats. Greenland, 2000—, European Fedn. Employed Shareholders, 1999—. Scholar Danish Social Sci. Rsch. Coun., 1984, 85, 88, 90, 94, Am. Coun. Learned Socs., 1990, Fulbright Commn., 1994, Commn. for Sci. Rsch. in Greenland, 1995, 96. Mem. Am. Econ. Assn. Home: Niels Hammekensvej 21, GR-3900 Nuuk Greenland Office: U Greenland Dept Adminstrn, PO Box 279, GR-3900 Nuuk Greenland

WINTHER, KASPAR TOBIAS, materials scientist, geologist; b. Frederiksberg, Denmark, Apr. 6, 1963; came to U.S., 1994; s. Richard Ludvig Philip Weibull and Judith (Stigaard) W. MS, Københavns U., Copenhagen, 1986; PhD, U. Chgo., 1990; MBA, RPI, Troy, N.Y., 2000. Cons. Winther's Internat. Consultancy, Skillingsfors, Sweden, 1991-92; mus. trainee U. Bergen, Norway, 1993; project leader U. Bergen, 1994; vis. scientist dept. earth and environ. scis. Rensselaer Poly. Inst., Troy, N.Y., 1994-96, vis. scientist dept. materials sci. and engring., 1996, vis. scientist N.Y. State Ctr. Advanced Tech. in Automation, Robotics, and Mfg., 1996-97; sr. rsch. scientist N.Y. State Ctr. Advanced Tech., 1997—. Scholar Carlsbergfondet, Copenhagen, 1985; grantee Danish Natural Sci. Rsch. Coun., 1987-89. Mem. Am. Geophys. Union. Office: Rensselaer Poly Inst Ctr for Advanced Tech 110 8th St # Cii8015 Troy NY 12180-3522

WINTHROP, KENNETH RAY, insurance executive; b. N.Y.C., Dec. 29, 1950; s. Ralph and Lore (Bruck) W.; m. Sharon Swinnich, 1976 (div. 1978); m. Diane Louise Denney, June 27, 1981; children: Alyssa Louise, Matthew Lawrence, Andrew Lee. BA in English, SUNY, Buffalo, 1972. CLU. Agt. Northwestern Mut. Life Ins., Woodland Hills, Calif., 1975-78, Nat. Life of Vermont, L.A., 1978-93; mgr. Mass Mut., L.A., 1993-97, agt., 1997—. Referee Am. Youth Soccer Orgn., L.A., 1996—. Mem. Million Dollar Round Table (life). Avocations: racquetball, snow skiing, trout fishing, gardening. E-mail: kwinthrop@finsvcs.com. Home: 1404 5th St Manhattan Beach CA 90266-6338 Office: 4601 Wilshire Blvd Fl 3 Los Angeles CA 90010-3880

WINTHROP, SHERMAN, lawyer; b. Duluth, Minn., Feb. 3, 1931; s. George E. and Mary (Tesler) W.; m. Barbara Cowan, Dec. 16, 1956; children: Susan Winthrop Crist, Bradley T., Douglas A. BBA, U. Minn., 1952; JD, Harvard U., 1955. Bar: Minn. 1955, U.S. Dist. Ct. Minn. 1955, U.S. Tax Ct. Law clk. to chief justice Minn. Supreme Ct., St. Paul, 1955-56; ptnr. Oppenheimer, Wolff & Donnelly, St. Paul, 1956-79; chmn. Winthrop & Weinstine P.A., St. Paul, 1979—; bd. dirs. Bremer Fin. Corp., St. Paul, Minn.; bd. dirs., sec. St. Paul Progress Corp. Mem. ABA, Minn. Bar Assn. (chair exec. coun., bus. law sect. 1992-93), Ramsey County Bar Assn. Avocations: tennis, travel, family. Home: 1672 Pinehurst Ave Saint Paul MN 55116-2158 Office: Winthrop & Weinstine PA 3200 Minn World Trade Ctr 30 7th St E Saint Paul MN 55101-4914

WIN TIN, Burmese government official; b. Mawlamyaing, Burma, July 5, 1935. BS in Mech. Engring. Min. of fin. and revenue Govt. of Burma (now Myanmar), Yangon, 1992-97; min. comms., post and telegraph Ministry of Telecomms, Post and Telegraphs, Yangon, 1997—. Office: 80 Corner Merchant, and Theinbyu Rd, Botahtaung Twp Yangon, Myanmar*

WINTON, CALHOUN, literature educator; b. Ft. Benning, Ga., Jan. 21, 1927; s. George Peterson and Dorothy (Calhoun) W.; m. Elizabeth Jefferys Myers, June 30, 1948; children: Jefferys Hobart, William Calhoun. Student, Ga. Inst. Tech., 1944-46; BA, U. of the South, 1948; MA, Vanderbilt U., 1950, Princeton U., 1954; PhD, Princeton U., 1955. Instr. Dartmouth Coll., Hanover, N.H., 1954-57; asst. prof. U. Va., Charlottesville, 1957-60; asst. prof. then assoc. prof., asst. dean Grad. Sch. U. Del., 1960-67; prof. dept. English U. S.C., Columbia, 1967-75, chmn. dept., 1970-73; prof. U. Md., College Park, 1975-97, dir. Rsch. Ctr. for Humanities, 1988-90; prof. emeritus U. Md., 1997—; del. Jt. Nat. Com. on Langs., Washington, 1986-90, 95-99. Author: (biography) Captain Steele, 1964, Sir Richard Steele, 1970; editor: Plays of Aaron Hill, 1981, John Gay and the London Theatre, 1993; author (with others) Colonial Book in the Atlantic World, 1999. Pres. faculty guild U. Md., 1986-89; bd. dirs. Md. Fedn. Tchrs., Balt., 1986-89. Capt. USN, 1944-47, 50-52. Am. Philos. Soc. grantee, 1960; Guggenheim Found. fellow, 1965-66, Folger Shakespeare Libr. fellow, Washington, 1970, John Carter Brown Libr. fellow, Providence, 1995; Fulbright Commn. lectureship, Ankara, Turkey, 1979-80. Mem. MLA (exec. com. South Atlantic chpt. 1977-80), Am. Soc. 18th-Century Studies (founder 1970—), East Cen. Soc. 18th Century Studies (pres. 1987), Assn. Princeton Grad. Alumni (exec. bd. 1986-90), Cosmos Club Washington, Princeton Club (N.Y. and Washington), Am. Antiquarian Soc. Democrat. Episcopalian. Avocations: swimming, book collecting. Home: 8201 16th St Apt 1025 Silver Spring MD 20910-3252 Office: U Md Dept English College Park MD 20742-0001

WINTON, HOWARD PHILLIP, retired optometrist; b. Springfield, Mo., June 23, 1925; s. George Lecoumpt and Emma Pearl (Schoonover) W.; m. Frances Jeanne Zellweger, June 29, 1946; children: Susan, James, Stephen, Gary, Carolyn. Student, Northern Ill. Coll. of Optometry, Midwest Sch. of Optics; LHD, Ill. Coll. of Optometry, 1965. Diplomate Am. Bd. Optometry. Pvt. practice optometry Melbourne, Fla.; nat. cons. to Surgeon Gen. USAF, 1979. Pres. Melbourne C. of C.; pres., chmn. bd. dirs. Brevard Econ. Devel. Coun., Brevard County, 1970-79. With USN, 1943-46, PTO. Named Optometrist of the Yr., Fla. Optometric Assn., 1972. Fellow Am. Acad. Optometry; mem. Fla. Optometric Assn. (pres. 1965), Am. Optometric Assn. (pres. 1975-76, mem. coun.), So. Coun. Optometrics (pres. 1968), Brevard Optometric Assn. (founder, pres. 1973), Rotary (founder 1st Interact Club 1962, pres. Melbourne 1962).

WINTZEK, BERNHARD CHRISTIAN, publisher; b. Trachenberg, Germany, Aug. 9, 1943; s. Paul-Anton and Elsa (Vogel) W.; m. Hilke Zempel, Sept. 30, 1967; children: Germar, Gesa. Diploma, Akademie für Musische Bildung, Remscheid, Germany, 1966. Licensed social worker. Founder, head MUT Pub. House, Asendorf, Germany, 1965—. Mem. German Assocs. of the Ben-Gurion U. of the Negev. Office: MUT-Verlag, Bahnhofstr 1, 27330 Asendorf Lower Saxony, Germany

WINZENREID, JAMES ERNEST, lawyer, entrepreneur; b. Wheeling, W.Va., June 9, 1951; s. Ernest Christian and Dorothy Emma (Wolf) W.; m. Rebecca Lee Rice, Aug. 11, 1979; children: Diana Lee, Lauren Rice. AB, W. Liberty State Coll., 1973; MBA, W.Va. U., 1979; JD, Duquesne U., 1987; LLM, Wayne State U., 1989. Bar: Pa. 1987, U.S. Dist. Ct. (we. dist.) Pa. 1987. Staff asst. Wheeling Pitts. Steel Corp., Wheeling, 1974-78, supr. indl. relations, 1978; mgr. profl. planning and devel. Copperweld Corp., Pitts., 1978-79; mgr. human resources Copperweld Corp., Glassport, Pa., 1979-81; plant mgr. Copperweld Corp., Glassport, 1981-83; group mgr. human resources Copperweld Corp., Pitts., 1984-85, market program mgr., 1986-87; with lab. and employment dept. Eckert, Seamans, Cherin & Mellott, Pitts., 1986-87; corp. staff rep. Tecumseh (Mich.) Products Co., 1987-89; v.p. human resources devel. Lafarge (Va.) Corp., 1989-94; v.p. human resources western region Lafarge Constrn. Materials, Calgary, Alta., Can., 1994-96, Lafarge Can. Inc., Calgary, 1996-99; mgr. union rels. GE, Bloomington, Ind., 2000—. Mng. editor Juris mag., 1986. Bd. dirs. Wheeling Symphony Soc., 1977-86, Wheeling Jaycees, 1976-78; mem. adv. bd. Jr. Achievement Southwestern Pa., 1981-83. Named Outstanding Young Men Am. U.S. Jaycees, 1979. Mem. ASTD, ABA, Pa. Bar Assn., Allegheny Bar Assn., Am. Soc. Human Resources Mgmt., Human Resource Planning Soc., Phi Alpha Delta. Republican. Lutheran. Avocations: golf, reading. Home: 4647 Fox Moor Ln Greenwood IN 46143-9279 Office: GE 301 N Curry Pike Bloomington IN 47404-2502

WINZENRIED, ARTHUR PAUL, library administrator, historian; b. Melbourne, Victoria, Australia, Oct. 3, 1949; s. Paul Henry and Marjory Joyce (Druber) W.; m. Jillienne Eve Madigan, Nov. 20, 1973; children: Matthew G. A., Andrew D. A. Diploma of tchg., Burwood State Coll., Melbourne, 1968; BA with honors, Melbourne U., 1972; PhD in History, Monash U., Melbourne, 1993; postgrad., Charles Sturt U., 1996—. Lectr. Burwood State Coll., Melbourne, 1970-72; tchr. primary edn. Dept. Edn., Victoria, 1972-77, tchr. secondary edn., 1978-91; tchr. libr. Seventh-Day Adventist Ch., Victoria, 1992-97; head libr. and info. sys. Eltham Coll., Victoria, 1998—; cons. historian Bicentennial Com., Victoria Govt., 1987-89, Seymour Water Bd., Victoria, 1988-89, Burnley Horticultural Coll., Melbourne, 1989-91; presenter Learned Info, Europe, London, 1996, 99, Hong Kong, 1997, Internat. Libr. Assn., Vancouver, 1997; presenter Isis 2000 online info. conf. Author 13 books; author, co-designer: (book) Hills of Home, 1988 (Nom-Gally award 1988); editor: (periodical) Narrow Gauge, 1987-93; prodr., dir. 2 videotapes. Mem. Profl. Historians Assn., Internat. Assn. Sch. Librarianship, Assn. Seventh-Day Adventist Librs., Sch. Libr. Assn. Victoria, Australian Curriculum Studies Assn., Light Rwys. Rsch. Soc. Australia, Nat. Trust Australia (founding pres. Dandenong Ranges br.), History Inst., Knowledge Mgmt. Group (chair 1998—), Eastern Region Librs. Assn. (chair). Seventh-Day Adventist. Avocations: railway history, industrial archaeology. Office: Eltham Coll, 1660 Main Rd, 3179 Eltham Victoria, Australia

WIO, HORACIO SERGIO, physicist; b. Buenos Aires, Nov. 14, 1946; s. Welka and Sofia (Beitelmajer) W.; m. Maria Luz Martinez Perez, Feb. 16, 1973; children: Marcelo Gabriel, Mayra Cecilia, Nicolas Bernardo. Tech. Bachellor, Otto Krausse, Buenos Aires, 1965; MSc, Inst. Balseiro, 1972; PhD in Physics, U. Nac. Cuyo, 1977. Rsch. scholar Nat. Rsch. Coun., S.C. Bariloche, 1973-77; asst. researcher Nat. Atomic Energy Commn., S.C. Bariloche, 1977-79; vis. scientist Technischen U., Munich, 1979-80, 87-88; assoc. researcher Nat. Atomic Energy Commn., S.C. Bariloche, 1980-85; invited prof. U. Baleares, Palma de Mallorca, Spain, 1988-89; vis. prof. FAMAF, U.N. Cordoba, Argentina, 1989; full prof. Instituto Balseiro, S.C. Bariloche, 1995—; ind. researcher Centro At. Bariloche, S.C. Bariloche, 1986-90, sr. rschr., 1990—; vis. prof. U. Cantabria, Spain, 1990, 92, U. Mar del Plata, Argentina, 1991, 92, 93, 95, U. Chile, 1995, U. Freiburg, Germany, 1992, Fritz-Haber Inst., 1994, Max Planck Inst., Dresden, 1995, U. Libre, Brussels, 1998, U. Arica, 2000, U. Navarra, 2000, U. New Mexico, 2000, U. Tarapacá, Chile, 2000, U. Autónoma Mex., 2000; cons. INVAP S.E., S.C. Bariloche, 1977; head stat. physics group Centro Atomico Bariloche, 1986—, head theoretical physics divsn., 1992-94; adv. editor, Physica A, mem. organizing com. Latin Am. Sch. Physics, La Plata, 1987, MEDYFINOL Conf., Mar del Plata, 1991—; chmn. 4th Work Nonlinear Phenomena, Bariloche, 1995, workshop on pattern formation, ICTP, Ineste, 1997, workshop on sparsely connected sys., Bariloche, 2000. Editor: Connections among..., 1988, Stochastic Processes and Nonequilibrium Statistical Physics Process MEDYFINOL Conf., 1991, Proc. WSCS, 2000; author: Introduction to Path Integrals, 1990, An Introduction to Stochastic Processes and Nonequilibrium Statistical Physics, 1994; referee Phys. Rev. Letters, 1993—; adv. editor: Physica A; contbr. more than 150 articles to profl. jours. Nat. AEC scholar, 1969-72, Nat. Rsch. Coun. scholar, 1973-77, fellow, 1977—, grantee, 1984, 85, 90, 93, 97; Inst. Coop. Iberoam. Spain joint rsch. grantee, 1990, 92, 93, 94, grantee Found. Antorchas, 1991, ANPCyT, 1998, SECyT, 2000, SECyT-CAPES, 2000. Fellow Nat. Rsch. Coun.; mem. ICTP Italy (assoc. 1992-99), Am. Phys. Soc., Argentine Phys. Soc. (treas. 1983-86, com. 1986-88). Avocations: chess, swiming, go, judo. E-mail: wio@cab.cnea.gov.ar. Office: Centro Atomico Bariloche, E Bustillo Km 9 1/2, Bariloche Argentina 8400

WIPPERN, RONALD FRANK, financial and corporate consultant; b. Huntington, W.Va., June 28, 1933; s. Virgil V. and Lucille (Hotzfield) W.; m. Jill Kathleen Nelson, June 20, 1982; children: Christopher, Mitchell, Stacy, Joscelyn. BS, U. Colo., 1955, MBA, 1961; PhD, Stanford U., 1964; MA (hon.), Yale U., 1979. Asst. prof. U. Minn., Mpls., 1964-66; assoc. dean, assoc. prof. Dartmouth Coll., Hanover, N.H., 1966-71; prof. IMEDE Mgmt. Devel. Inst., Lausanne, Switzerland, 1971-73; assoc. prof. Harvard U. Bus. Sch., Boston, 1973-76; prof. Yale U., New Haven, 1976-87; pres. Ronald F. Wippern, Inc., New Canaan, Conn., 1987—; mng. ptnr. Derivatives Advisories, Inc., 1993—; bd. dirs. Super D Corp., N.Y.C., Big V Holdings, Inc., N.Y.C.; cons. McKinsey & Co., Inc., N.Y.C., 1st Boston Corp., N.Y.C., Bankers Trust Co., N.Y.C. Author: Shipping Investments, 1975, Cases in Modern Financial Management, 1980; contbr. numerous articles in profl. jours. Expert witness U.S. Ho. of Reps., 1975; cons. Ford Found., N.Y.C. and Latin Am., 1967-71. Served to lt. USN, 1956-59. Ford Found. fellow, 1961-64. Mem. Am. Econ. Assn., Am. Fin. Assn. Democrat. Avocations: music, cabinet making. Office: 815 Silvermine Rd New Canaan CT 06840-4330

WIRANTO, GEN., federal official; b. 1947. Min. def. and comdr.-in-chief Armed Forces, 1998—. Office: Ministry of Defense, Jl Merdeka Barat 13-14, Jakarta Pusat 10110, Indonesia*

WIRASINHA, ROHAN MAHENDRA, electrical engineering consultant; b. Gampola, Sri Lanka, Oct. 25, 1946; arrived in Australia, 1990; s. Alpheus Henry and Olive Gladys (Gooneratne) W.; m. Charmanie Shiranika Gunaratne, Sept. 21, 1971 (div. 1978); m. Maesri Collette Gooneratne, Sept. 28, 1984; children: Chanaka, Shavindra. BSc in Engring., U. Ceylon, Peradeniya, Sri Lanka, 1969; MSc, U. Manchester, Eng., 1984. Chartered profl. engr. Field engr. IBM, Colombo, Sri Lanka, 1970-71; comms. engr. Ceylon Electricity Bd., Colombo, 1971-72, rural electrification engr., 1975-82, chief engr., 1984-89, dep. gen. mgr., 1989-90; sr. cons. power sys. Hydro Electric Corp., Hobart, Tasmania, Australia, 1991—; project mgr. rural electrification Ceylon Electricity Bd., Colombo, 1978-82; cons., project dir., Ceylon Electricity Bd., Lahmeyer GmbH, Colombo, 1984-89; cons., distbn. planner UNCDF, Da Nang, Vietnam, 1993; team leader, cons. World Bank, Phnom Penh, Cambodia, 1996-97. Contbr. articles to profl. jours. and procs. Sec. Havelock Sports Club, Colombo, 1987-88; co-organizer Regional Symposium on Power Sys. Planning, Colombo, 1989; sr. v.p. Ethnic Comtys. Coun. of Tasmania, Hobart, 1996. Fellow Inst. Elec. Engrs. U.K.; mem. Inst. Engrs. Australia, Cigre Australian Panel 33, mem. St. George Lodge 217OEC (w. master 1989). Anglican. Avocations: cricket, rugby football, snooker, billiards, reading. E-mail: rohan.wirasinha@hydro.com.au. Home: 32 Garnett St, Blackmans Bay TAS 7052, Australia Office: Hydro Elec Corp, 4 Elizabeth St, Hobart TAS 7000, Australia

WIRE, DONALD RICHARD, II, college administrator; b. Danville, Ill., July 16, 1940; s. Donald Richard and Margaret Louise (Main) W.; 1 child by a previous marriage: Donald Richard III; m. Kay Lynn Sivills, Feb. 18, 1999. BA, So. Ill. U., 1964, MA, 1965; PhD, Walden U., 1978. Instr. politics N.C. State U., Raleigh, 1965-71; tchr. Fayetteville (N.C.) City Schs., 1971-72; dean coll. Lafayette Coll., Fayetteville, 1973-76; dir. instl. rsch. Durham (N.C.) Coll., 1977-78, acad. dean, dir. mastery learning program, 1978-80; dir. high sch. dipl. program Rowan Tech. Coll., Concord, N.C., 1980-82; dean evening and weekend coll. Bladen Community Coll., Dublin, N.C., 1982-99; instr. history and polit. sci. Fayetteville (N.C.) Tech. C. C., 1999—; instr. East Asia studies Campbell U., Ft. Bragg, N.C., 1999 ; cons., pollster Com. for Dem. Processes, 7th Congl. Dist., Fayetteville, 1969-70; sci. fair judge Bladen County Schs., 1988-90, coll. bowl judge, 1991. Author: Mathematics Competency Study Guide, 1981; contbr. articles to profl. edn. and polit. jours., fiction and poetry to newspapers and Am. Indian jours. Recipient U. Ky. Grad. assistantship; named Walden U. scholar, 1977-78. Mem. N.C. Community Coll. Instrl. Adminstrs. Assn., Adult Edn. Assn. Top One Percent Soc., Phi Theta Pi. Pentecostal. Avocations: archaeology, writing, mathematics, philosophy, swimming. Home and Office: 540 Nottingham Dr Fayetteville NC 28311-1334 Office: Bladen Community Coll Hwy 41 Dublin NC 28332-9999

WIRÉN, MARCO, strategic planning executive; b. Rauma, Finland, Jan. 14, 1966; s. Jarmo and Kirsti (Mäkelä) W. BSc, U. Örebro, Sweden, 1991; MSc in Bus. Adminstrn., U. Uppsala, Sweden, 1996. Auditor RSV, Stockholm, 1991-95; bus. contr. NCC Group, Stockholm, 1995-96, bus. analyst, 1996-98, strategies planning v.p., 1998—. Avocations: mountaineering, skiing, running. Office: NCC Group, Vallgaten 3, 170 80 Solna Sweden

WIRGIN, JAN CHRISTER, educator, museum director emeritus; b. Stockholm, Sweden, June 15, 1932; s. Nils Allan Christer and Margit Alma Louise (Gyllenberg) W.; m. Signe Margareta Brunnberg, May 24, 1958; children: Claes Christer, Jeanette Louise. MA, U. Stockholm, 1955, degree in philosophy, 1959, PhD, 1970. Asst. curator to dir. Mus. Far Eastern Antiquities, Stockholm, 1957-98, dir. emeritus; dep. dir. Swedish Nat. Art Mus., Stockholm, 1989-98; prof. art U. Hawaii, Honolulu, 1966-67; assoc. prof. U. Stockholm, 1970—, censor U. Copenhagen, 1969—, U. Arhus, 1983—. Author: Sung Ceramic Designs, 1970, The Georg von Bekesy Collection, 1974, The Ernest Erickson Collection in Swedish Museums, 1989, Från Kina till Europa (From China to Europe), 1998. Grantee Fulbright Found., 1966; named commdr. most noble order crown of Thailand, Thai Govt., 1984, order of the rising sun gold rays with rosette Govt. Japan, 1994; named Prof. Swedish Govt., 1998. Mem. China Com. (sec.), Sweden-Japan Soc. (vice chmn.), Swedish-Thai Soc. (dir. 1974-98), Friends Assn. Mus. Far Eastern Antiquities (dir. 1960-98), Swedish Archaeol. Soc., Swedish Assn. Mus. Curators, Swedish Mus. Assn., Oriental Ceramic Soc., Travellers Club. Home: Furusangsvagen 1, 167 67 Bromma Sweden Office: Mus Far Eastern Antiquities, Tyghusplan Box 16176, 103 24 Stockholm Sweden

WIRNARDI, LIE, travel company executive; b. Pematang Siantar, Indonesia, Oct. 28, 1957; m. Natalia Sylvia Joyce; children: Indra Wibisono, Arlia Vivian Roseline, Arienne Natasha Mercelyn. B in Bus. Mgmt., Nomenssen U., Medan, Indonesia, 1981; MBA, Western U., Boise, Idaho, 1995. Dir. PT. Trophy Tour, Famba Group, Medan, 1981—, dir. PT. BTS Internat., 1985—, dir. PT. Indoma Citra Agung., 1987—, dir. PT. Indocitra Harta Berkah., 1988—, dir. PT. Wimana Nardika Utama., 1989—; dir. PT Citylink Transindo, Famba Group, Jakarta, Indonesia, 1990—; dir. PT. Mandala Nusantara Transiedo Utama, Famba Group, Medan, 1987—, dir. APOTIK ROSI., 1987—; lectr. in field of bus. Mem. Internat. Air Transp. Assn., Assn. Indonesian Travel Agys., Japan Assn. Travel Agys., Pacific Asia Travel Assocs., Soc. Indonesian Profl. Conv. Organizers, Kamar Dagang Indonesia, Exch. Club, Lions. E-mail: pttrophy@indosat.net.id. Office: PT Trophy Tour & Travel Svc, Jl Brigjend Katamso No 33DE, NSumatra Medan 20151, Indonesia

WIRSCHING, MICHAEL HILMAR, medical educator; b. Berlin, May 26, 1947; s. Arnold and Helene (Waldhecker) W.; m. Barbara Ute Single (div.); children: Max, Hans-Georg, Paul, Carla. MD, Free U., Berlin, 1971; Pvt. Dozent, Ruprecht-Karls U., Heidelberg, Fed. Republic Germany, 1978. From resident to lectr. Ruprecht-Karls U., 1971-81; dir., prof. Justus-Liebig U., Giessen, Fed. Republic Germany, 1981-89, Albert-Ludwig U. Freiburg, Fed. Republic Germany, 1989—. Home: Carl-Maria-en-v-Webstr 3, D 79104 Freiburg Germany Office: U Freiburg, Hauptstr 8, D 79104 Freiburg Germany

WIRSIG, WOODROW, magazine editor, trade organization executive, business executive; b. Spokane, Wash., June 28, 1916; s. Otto Alan and Beulah Juliet (Marohn) W.; m. Jane Barbara Dealy, Dec. 11, 1942; children: Alan Robert, Guy Rodney, Paul Harold. Student, Kearney (Nebr.) State Tchrs. Coll., Los Angeles City Coll., UCLA, 1933-39; B.A., Occidental Coll., 1941; M.S., Columbia Grad. Sch. Journalism, 1942. Dir. Occidental Coll. News Bur., 1939-41; radio newswriter WQXR, N.Y.C., 1941-42; news writer, propaganda analyst CBS, 1942-43; rewrite man Los Angeles Times, 1943-44; asst. editor This Week mag., 1944-45; staff writer Look mag., 1946, asst. mng. editor, 1946-49, exec. editor, 1950-52; mng. editor Quick mag., 1949-50; asso. editor Newsweek mag., Ladies' Home Jour., 1952; editor Woman's Home Companion, 1952-56; editorial cons. Ednl. Testing Service, Princeton, 1957-67; TV cons. NBC-TV, ABC-TV; creator Nat. Daytime Radio Programs, 1957-60; radio documentary Companion; pres. communications firm Wirsig, Gordon and O'Connor, Inc., 1956-58; editor Printers' Ink mag., N.Y.C., 1958-65, Salesweek mag., 1959-60; editorial dir. Overseas Press Club ann. mag. Dateline, 1961, 62; creator, editorial dir. Calif. Life mag.; pres. Better Bus. Bur. Met. N.Y., Inc., 1966-77; also pres. Edn. Research Found.; pres. Bus. Advocacy Center, Inc., 1977—; creator Corp. Social Accountability Audit and Customer Services/Consumer Affairs Audit.; Cons. to Office Sec. HEW, 1965-66. Author: I Love You, Too., 1990; editor, contbr.: Your Diabetes (Dr. Herbert Pollack), 1951; editor: Advertising: Today-Yesterday-Tomorrow; New Products Marketing; cons. editor: Principles of Advertising; contbr. nat. mags.; lectr.; syndicated columnist: other newspapers L.A. Times, 1964-65. Recipient gold medal Benjamin Franklin Mag. Awards, 1956. Mem. Soc. Consumer Affairs Profls. (pres. 1983), Newcomen Soc., Archons, Players Club, Overseas Press Club, Nat. Press Club, N.Y. Advt. Club, N.Y.C. Club, Springdale Country Club, Evergreen Country Club (v.p.), Nassau Club, Century Assn., Families for Alzheimers Rights Assn. (pres. 1994—), Univ. Club, Sigma Delta Chi, Phi Gamma Delta, Gamma Delta Upsilon. Democrat. Presbyterian. Home and Office: Sandhill Cove 1459 SW Shoreline Dr Palm City FL 34990-4533

WIRSING, ROLF LORENZ, public health educator, researcher; b. Chemnitz, Germany, Dec. 2, 1942; 1 child, Mara. Grad., Engring. Sch., Berlin, 1961; PhD, SUNY, Buffalo, 1974; MPH, U. Calif., Berkeley, 1981; postgrad. studies with pvt. docent, U. Leipzig, Germany, 1990. Engr. Tech. U. Berlin, 1964-65; educator U. Konstanz, Germany, 1973-80; rschr Gesellschaft fur Strahlen und Umweltforschung, Munich, Germany, 1981-82; prof. U. Hamburg, Germany, 1987-92, Hochschule fur Technik, Wirtschaft und Sozialwesen, Görlitz, Germany, 1993—; vis. prof. Instituto Venezolano de Investigaciones Cientificas, Caracas, Venezuela, 1977, 80; post doctoral fellow U. Calif., Berkeley, 1978, U. Calif. San Francisco, 1983-84; field rschr., Feke, Turkey, 1984-85; nat. coord. Rsch. on Children with Asthma, 1995-99. Mem. Am. Anthrop. Assn. Home: Wilhelmsplatz 9, D-02826 Görlitz Germany Office: HTWS FB Sozialwesen, Goethestr 5, D-02826 Görlitz Germany

WIRSZUP, IZAAK, mathematician, educator; b. Wilno, Poland, Jan. 5, 1915; came to U.S., 1949, naturalized, 1955; s. Samuel and Pera (Golomb) W.; m. Pola Ofman, July 19, 1940 (dec. 1943); 1 son, Vladimir (dec. 1943); m. Pera Poswianska, Apr. 23, 1949; 1 dau., Marina (Mrs. Arn 'd M. Tatar). Magister of Philosophy in Math, U. Wilno, 1939; Ph.D. in Math, U. Chgo., 1955. Lectr. math. Tech. Inst. Wilno, 1939-41; dir. Bur. d'Études et de Statistiques Spéciales, Société Centrale d'Achat-Société Anonyme des Monoprix, Paris, 1946-49; mem. faculty U. Chgo., 1949—, prof. math., 1965-85, prof. math. emeritus, 1985—, prin. investigator U. Chgo. Sch. Math. Project (sponsored by Amoco Found., also dir. resource devel. component), 1983—, dir. Internat. Math. Edn. Resource Ctr., 1988—; dir. NSF Survey Applied Soviet Rsch. in Math. Edn., 1985-91; cons. Ford Found., Colombia, Peru, 1965-66, Sch. Math Study Group, 1960, 61, 66-68; participant, writer tchr. tng. material African Math. Program, Entebbe, Uganda, summer 1964, Mombasa, Kenya, summers 1965-66; assoc. dir. Survey Recent Ea. European Math. Lit., 1956-68, dir., 1968-84; dir. NSF program application computers to mgmt., 1976-83; cons. NSF-AID Sci. Edn. Program, India, 1969; mem. U.S. Commn. on Math. Instn., 1969-73. Contbr. articles to profl. jours.; Editor Math. books, transls., adaptions from Russian.; Adviser math.: Ency. Brit., 1971—. Recipient Lewellyn John and Harriet Manchester Quantrell award U. Chgo., 1958, Univ. Alumni Svc. medal, U. Chgo., 1994; resident master Woodward Ct., U. Chgo., 1971-85; endowed Wirszup Lecture Series, U. Chgo., 1986. Mem. N.Y. Acad. Scis., Am. Math. Soc., Math. Assn. Am., AAAS, Nat. Council Tchrs. Math. (chmn. com. internat. math. edn. 1967-69, Lifetime Achievement medal for Leadership, Tchg., and Svc. in Math. Edn. 1996). Home: 5750 S Kenwood Ave Chicago IL 60637-1744 Office: U Chgo Dept Math 5734 S University Ave Chicago IL 60637-1514

WIRT, SHERWOOD ELIOT, minister, writer; b. Oakland, Calif., Mar. 12, 1911; s. Loyal Lincoln and Harriet Eliot (Benton) W.; m. Helen Winola Wells, July 2, 1940 (dec. Sept. 1986); 1 child, Alexander Wells; m. Ruth Evelyn Love, Aug. 29, 1987. BA, U. Calif., Berkeley, 1932; BD, Pacific Sch. Religion, Berkeley, 1943; PhD, Edinburgh (Scotland) U., 1951. Ordained to ministry, 1943. Pastor 1st Congl. Ch., Collinsville, Conn., 1943-44, Knox Presbyn Ch., Berkeley, 1951-55, Hillside Presbyn. Ch., Oakland, Calif., 1955-59; editor Decision mag. Billy Graham Evangelistic Assn., 1959-76; min. to students U. Wash., 1946-49; chmn. San Diego Jesus 2000. Author 28 books including Crusade at the Golden Gate, 1959, Not Me, God, 1966, Social Conscience of the Evangelical, 1968, Translation, Confessions of Augustine, 1971, Jesus Power, 1972, Topical Encyclopedia of Living Quotations, 1974, Afterglow, 1975, A Thirst for God, 1980, The Doomsday Connection, 1986, The Making of a Writer, 1987, The Book of Joy, 1994, Billy, 1997, Spiritual Awakening, 1987 (Gold Medallion Book award Evang. Christian Pub. Assn.), Jesus, Man of Joy, 1999; editor 7 books. Pres. San Diego Gilbert and Sullivan Soc., 1980-81; scoutmaster Boy Scouts Am., 1936. Capt. USAAF, 1944-46. Recipient Freedom of Valley Forge Found. award, 1968; named Hon. Col., State of Tenn. Mem. Associated Ch. Press (life), Evang. Press Assn. (life, pres. 1969-71), San Diego County Christian Writers Guild (founder/convener 1977-96), Theta Chi, Sigma Delta Chi. Republican. Avocations: hiking, swimming, tennis, golf. Home: 14140 Mazatlan Ct Poway CA 92064-3964

WIRTH, DAVID EUGENE, software designer, consultant; b. Norfolk, Va., Oct. 20, 1951; s. Eugene Ross and Darlene (Worley) W. BA, Luther Coll.,

1975. Systems analyst ASI Computer Systems, Cedar Falls, Iowa, 1974-87, v.p. ops., 1987—. Avocations: basketball, softball, fishing, hunting. Office: ASI Computer Systems Inc PO Box 338 Cedar Falls IA 50613-0338

WIRTH, DYANN FERGUS, public health educator, microbiologist; b. Racine, Wis., Jan. 31, 1951; d. Russell and Phyllis Rose (Muratone) Fergus; m. Peter Wirth, Aug. 25, 1973. BA with highest honors, U. Wis., 1972; PhD, MIT, 1978; AM (hon.), Harvard U., 1990. Instr. Marine Biol. Lab., Woods Hole, Mass., 1980-84; asst. prof. Sch. Pub. Health Harvard U., Boston, 1981-86, assoc. prof., 1986-90, prof., 1990—, dir. Harvard Malaria Initiative, 1997—; editor-in-chief Acad. Press Exptl. Parasitology, Boston, 1987—; NIH study sect. mem. tropical medicine and parasitology NIH, Bethesda, 1987-91; chmn. steering com. on chemotherapy of Malaria WHO, Geneva, 1986-91, 91—, chair steering com. on drug devel., mem. rsch. capacity strengthening, mem. strategic rsch. com., 1997—; mem. sci. adv. bd. Edna McConnell Clark Found.; chair sci. adv. com. Burroughs Wellcome Fund Career Awards, 1994—. Contbr. numerous articles to profl. jours. Fellowship Fulbright Found., 1972-73, Predoctoral fellowship NIH, 1973-78, Helen Hay Whitney fellowship, 1978-81; recipient Burroughs-Wellcome award in Molecular Parasitology, 1982, 85-90. Mem. AAAS, Am. Soc. Microbiology, Am. Soc. Tropical Medicine and Hygiene (pres. 1999, Bailey K. Ashford award 1995), Am. Soc. Virology, Phi Beta Kappa. Office: Harvard U Sch Pub Health 665 Huntington Ave Boston MA 02115-6021

WIRTH, EUGEN, geography scientist; b. Würzburg, Germany, May 12, 1925; s. Eugen and Anna (Dienstbier) W.; m. Ingeborg Holland, May 12, 1958; children: Gisela, Volkmar, Ulrike, Raimund. MA, U. Erlangen, Germany, 1949; PhD, U. Freiburg, Germany, 1952; Habilitation, U. Hamburg, Germany, 1959. Asst. prof. U. Hamburg, 1953-59, assoc. prof., 1959-64; prof. geography U. Erlangen, 1964-91, prof. emeritus, 1991—, dean faculty sci., 1965-66, head dept., 1964-90. Author 8 books and 10 monographs on geography and Mid. East, 1955-99; contbr. over 200 articles to sci. jours., 11 maps of Mid. Ea. cities. Lt. German Army, 1943-45. Decorated Order of Merit (Bavaria); H.A.R. Gibb fellow Harvard U., 1982. Mem. Acad. Europea, Austrian Acad. Sci. (corr.), German Archaeol. Inst. Lutheran. Home: Membacher Weg 41, D-91056 Erlangen Germany Office: U Erlangen Inst Geography, Kochstrasse 4, D-91054 Erlangen Germany

WIRTHENSOHN, MICHELLE GABRIELLE, botany researcher; b. Adelaide, Australia, Feb. 22, 1963; d. Alfred Josef and Barbara (Oexle) W.; m. Leigh Sierp (div. Jan. 1995); children: Angus Joseph Sierp, Ingrid Michelle Sierp; m. Kimberley John Anderson; 1 child, Grace Kimberley Anderson. B in Agrl. Sci., U. Adelaide, 1988, PhD, 1999. Rsch. officer U. Adelaide, 1988-93, postdoctoral fellow, 1999—. Mem. Internat. Soc. for Horticultural Soc., Australian Soc. Horticultural Sci., Soc. for Growing Australian Plants, Royal Australian Chem. Inst. Avocations: trail riding, volleyball, philately, motorcycling, gardening. Office: U Adelaide, Waite Campus PMB 1, Dept Hort, Viticul & Oenology, Glen Osmond SA 5064, Australia

WIRTSCHAFTER, IRENE NEROVE, tax consultant; b. Elgin, Ill., Aug. 5; d. David A. and Ethel G. Nerove; m. Burton Wirtschafter, June 2, 1945 (dec. 1966). BCS, Columbus U., 1942. Cert. tax profl.; enrolled agt. IRS. Commd. ensign Supply Corps, USN, 1944, advanced through grades to capt., 1975; commdg. officer Res. Supply Unit, 1974-75; ret., 1976; agt. Office Internat. Ops., IRS, 1967-75; internat. banking specialist, real estate profl., appraiser,, 1976-80; now pvt. practice tax cons., Cocoa Beach, Fla.; hon. sec. agr., La., 1975; sr. intern program U.S. Senate, 1981; mem. Sec. Navy's Adv. Com. Ret. Pers., 1984-86, VA Adv. Com. for Women Vets., 1987-90. Past troop leader Girl Scouts U.S.A.; cons. Jr. Achievement, 1989-94; lt. col. and mission pilot CAP, 21 air races; comml. instrument pilot land and sea; founder Sr. Action Com. Brevard County, 1981; chmn. College Park Airport Johnny Horizon Day, 1975; Navy liaison officer Commd.'s Retiree Coun., Patrick AFB, 1985-89; elected dir. Fla. Space Coast Philharm., 1985—, treas., 1986-92; bd. dirs., adv. mgr. Cocoa Beach Citizens League, 1990-92; co-chmn. Internat. Women's Yr. Take Off Dinner, Washington, 1976; mem. Nat. Com. Internat. Forest of Friendship, Atchison, Kans., 1976—; 1st v.p. Friends of Cocoa Beach Libr., 1988-90, pres., 1990-92, bd. dirs., 1993—, apptd. to Cocoa Beach Libr. Br., 1996—; mem. Cocoa Beach Bus. Improvement Coun.; elected senator Silver Haired Legislature, Fla., 1985—; elected silver rep. Nat. Silver Haired Congress, 1977-2000; trustee Internat. Women's Air and Space Mus., 1993—, bd. dirs., 1999—; vol., founding mem. Brevard Zoo; chmn. Cocoa Beach Code Enforement Bd., 1989-96; mem. sr. adv. com. Cape Canaveral Hosp., co-chmn. 1994—; state rep. Nat. Soc. to Preserve Social Security and Medicare, 1999; bd. dirs. Honor Am., 2000. Named hon. citizen of Winnipeg, Man., Can., 1966, Atchison, 1989, New Orleans, 1988; hon. dep. state fire marshal, Fla., 1987; recipient Svc. Above Self award Rotary, 1998; named Ky. col., La. col. Mem. AAUW, Naval Res Assn. (nat. treas. 1975-77, nat. adv. com. 1985—, Nat. award of Merit 1992), Ninety Nines (past chpt. sect. and nat. officer, 99 achievement awards), Naval Order U.S. (treas. nat. capitol commandry), Assn. Naval Aviation (nat. trustee 1988—), Banana River Squadron (founder, comptr. 1984—), Assn. Enrolled Agts., Cocoa Beach Area C. of C., Internat. Platform Assn. (life), Silver Wings (bd. dirs. 1990—, nat. sec. 1986, Woman of Yr. award 1985), WAVES Nat. (bd. dirs. chpt. 75 1989—, Tailhook Assn., Patrick Women's Golf Assn. (treas. 1996—), Jazz Soc. Brevard, Rotary. Achievements include being first female Navy Supply Corps officer to be assigned sea duty, 1956. Avocations: aviation, golf, music. Home: 1825 Minutemen Cswy Apt 301 Cocoa Beach FL 32931-2033

WISCHMEYER, ERHARD, neurobiologist, researcher; b. Melle, Germany, Sept. 26, 1960; s. Adolf and Paula (Meiners) W.; m. Elke Dissmann, Oct. 18, 1996; 1 child, Thilo. Diploma, U. Bielefeld, Germany, 1988, PhD, 1993. Biol. diplomate. Stipendiate Max-Planck Soc., Goettingen, Germany, 1993-96, asst., 1996—. Contbr. articles to sci. jours. Mem. Neurobiol. Soc., Westfalian Ornithol. Soc. Avocations: ornithology, historical motorcycles, philosophy. Home: Am Hirtenberg 1, 37136 Waake Germany Office: MPI for Biophys Chemistry, Am Fassberg 11, 37070 Göttingen Germany

WISCHNIK, ARTHUR, physician; b. Munich, Germany, May 30, 1952; s. Emil and Franziska (Werkmuelle) W.; m. Brigitte Susanne Holz, Nov. 18, 1977; children: Ariane Sandra, Susanne Maximilliane Ingeborg. Dr.med., Ludwig-Maximilians U., Munich, Germany, 1977. Resident Hosp., Donauworth, Germany, 1977-80, Red Cross Hosp., Munich, Germany, 1980-86; chief physician U. Hosp., Mannheim, Germany, 1986-94; med. supt. Ctrl. Clinik, Augsburg, Germany, 1994—; lectr. U. Munich, 1983-86, U. Heidelberg, Germany, 1986—. Author: Treatment of Premature Labor, 1985; inventor computerized childbirth simulation. Mem. Rotary. Roman Catholic. Office: Zentralklinikum Augsburg, Stenglinstrasse 2, D-86156 Augsburg Germany

WISDOM, PEGGY J., neurologist; b. OKeene, OKla., Nov. 4, 1947; d. Clarence W. and Grace V. Wisdom. BS in Biology/Chemistry, Northwestern State Coll., 1968; MD, U. Okla., 1972. Diplomate Am. Bd. Psychiatry and Neurology. Resident in neurology U. Fla., 1972-76; asst. prof. neurology U. Okla., Oklahoma City, 1976-90, assoc. prof. neurology, 1990—, vice chair dept. neurology, 1981—; med. dir. neurologic rehab. O'Donoghue Rehab. Inst., Oklahoma City, 1981-89, chief of staff, 1986-90; chief neurology VA Med. Ctr., Oklahoma City, 1994-97, chief neuorlogy/rehab., 1997—; cons. Commn. on Accreditation of Rehab. Facilities, Tuscon, 1990—, Okla. Dept. Rehab. Svcs., Oklahoma City, 1993-96. Scientific adv. bd. Omniplex Mus., Oklahoma City, 1994—. Mem. Am. Acad. Neurology, Am. Acad. Neurology (chmn. women issues in neurology sect. 1999—), Assn. of VA Neurologists, Am. Epilepsy Soc. Republican. Presbyterian. E-mail: Wisdom.peggy@oklahoma.va.gov. Office: U Okla Health Scis Ctr # 215 711 Stanton L Young Blvd Oklahoma City OK 73104-5021

WISE, AARON NOAH, lawyer; b. Hartford, Conn., Feb. 14, 1940; s. Joseph J. and Ethel (Sklar) W.; m. Genevieve Ehrlich, Dec. 17. 1966; children: Haywood Martin, Paul Russell, Renee Alicia. AB, Boston U., 1962; JD, Boston Coll., 1965; LLM in Comparative/Internat. Law, NYU, 1971; certificat de Doctorate, d' Université en Droit, U. Paris Law Sch., 1970. Bar: N.Y., U.S. Dist. Ct. (so. dist.) N.Y. Internat. atty. Schering-Plough, Kenilworth, N.J., 1969-74; ptnr. Conboy Hewitt O'Brien & Boardman, N.Y.C., 1974-80, Wise Lerman & Katz P.C. (formerly Rosenbaum Wise Lerman & Katz), N.Y.C., 1981-95, Klepner & Cayea, N.Y.C., 1995-98, Brand, Cayea & Brand, LLC, 1998-2000, Siller Wilk LLP, N.Y.C., 2000—; lectr. bus. and legal groups U.S., Europe, Latin Am. Author: International Sports Law and Business (Kluwer Law Internat., 1997, 3 vols.), Foreign Businessman's Guide to U.S. Law-Practice-Taxation; contbr. articles to pubs. in U.S. and Europe. Mem. ABA, N.Y. State Bar Assn. Avocations: multilingual including French, Spanish, Portuguese, Italian, Russian, Japanese and German. Home: 38 Cummings Cir West Orange NJ 07052-2264 Office: Siller Wiilk LLP 747 3rd Ave New York NY 10017-2803

WISE, ROBERT, film producer, director; b. Winchester, Ind., Sept. 10, 1914. Student, Franklin Coll., D.F.A. (hon.), 1968. Staff cutting dept. R.K.O., 1933, became sound cutter, asst. editor, film editor, 1939-43, dir., 1943-49; with 20th Century-Fox, 1949-52, M.G.M., 1954-57; free-lance, 1958—, ptnr. ind. film co., 1970-2000; Past mem. Nat. Council of Arts. Ind. producer/dir. various studios; motion pictures include The Curse of the Cat People, 1944, Mademoiselle Fifi, 1944, The Body Snatcher, 1945, A Game of Death, 1945, Criminal Court, 1946, Born to Kill, 1947, Mystery in Mexico, 1948, Blood on the Moon, 1948, The Set-Up, 1949, Two Flags West, 1950, Three Secrets, 1950, The House on Telegraph Hill, 1951, The Day the Earth Stood Still, 1951, The Captive City, 1952, Something For the Birds, 1952, The Desert Rats, 1953, Destination Gobi, 1953, So Big, 1953, Executive Suite, 1954, Helen of Troy, 1955, Tribute to a Bad Man, 1956, Somebody Up There Likes Me, 1957, This Could Be the Night, 1957, Until They Sail, 1957, Run Silent, Run Deep, 1958, I Want to Live, 1958, Odds Against Tomorrow, 1959, West Side Story (Acad. awards best dir. with Jerome Robbins, and best picture), 1961, Two For the Seasaw, 1962, The Haunting, 1963, The Sound of Music, 1965 (Acad. award best dir., best picture), The Sand Pebbles, 1966, Star!, 1968, The Andromeda Strain, 1971, Two People, 1973, The Hindenburg, 1975, Audrey Rose, 1977, Star Trek-The Motion Picture, 1979, Rooftops, 1989, A Storm in Summer, 2000; appeared in The Stupids (acting debut), 1996. Recipient Nat. Medal of Arts award, 1992,Life Achievement award Am. Film Inst., 1998. Mem. Dirs. Guild (pres. 1971-74), Acad. Motion Picture Arts and Scis. (pres. 1985-87). Office: Robert Wise Prodns 222 Ave of Stars Ste 105E Los Angeles CA 90067

WISE, WILLIAM HARVEY, IV, human service executive; b. Alexandria, Va., Apr. 28, 1948; s. William Harvey III and Emily Virginia (Miller) W.; m. Susana Andrea Joublanc, July 28, 1973; children: Adam J., Andrea Susana, Virginia Elizabeth. BS, Washington & Lee U., 1970; postgrad, George Washington U., 1972. Acct. Arthur Andersen & Co., Washington, 1970-71; contr. Joint Action in Community Svc., Inc., Washington, 1971-79, dep. dir., 1979-87, exec. dir., 1987—; mem. Ind. Sector, Washington, 1987—, Nat. Assembly of Nat. Voluntary Health and Social Welfare Orgns., Washington, 1989—. V.p. Whittier Woods Civic Assn., Bethesda, Md., 1983-86; cubmaster Boy Scouts Am., Bethesda, 1984-85; fin. com. chmn. Concord-St.-Andrew's United Meth. Ch., Bethesda, 1983-86, chmn. adminstrv. bd., 1995-2000, bd. trustees, 2000—; bd. dirs. Ridgeleigh Homes Assn., Potomac, Md., 1988-99, Pax World Svc., 1995—, treas., 1996-2000; del. Balt. Ann. Conf. United Meth. Ch., 1996-99. Mem. Mensa, Kenwood Golf and Country Club. Avocations: tennis, gardening, genealogy. Home: 8229 Gainsborough Ct W Potomac MD 20854-4273 Office: Joint Action Community Svc 5225 Wisconsin Ave NW Washington DC 20015-2014

WISEMAN, CARTER STERLING, editor, author; b. N.Y.C., Oct. 8, 1945; s. Mark Huntington Wiseman and Eleanor Carter Wood; m. Eileen Condon, Oct. 19, 1985; children: Emma, Owen, Damian. BA, Yale U., 1968; MA, Columbia U., 1972. Newsman Associated Press, N.Y.C., 1972-74; assoc. editor Newsweek Mag., N.Y.C., 1974-77; sr. editor Horizon Mag., N.Y.C., 1977-79; mng. editor Portfolio Mag., N.Y.C., 1979-80; archtl. critic N.Y. Mag., N.Y.C., 1980-96; editor Yale Alumni Mag., New Haven, Conn., 1986—; bd. dirs. MacDowell Colony, Peterborough, N.H., pres., 1999—. Author: I.M. Pei, 1990, Shaping a Nation, 1998; contbg. editor Artnews, 1996—. Co-chair Loeb Fellowship Assn. Harvard U., 1986-95. With U.S. Army, 1968-71. Loeb Fellow Harvard U., 1985; Recipient Special Citation award Am. Inst. Archs., N.Y.C., 1984, Interpretive Writing award Soc. Silurians, N.Y.C., 1985, Inst. Honor award Am. Inst. Archs., N.Y.C., 1987, Roger Starr award Citizens Housing and Planning Coun., N.Y.C., 1987, 90. Mem. Century Assn., Yale Club of N.Y., Elizabethan Club. E-mail: carter.wiseman@yale.edu. Office: Yale Alumni Magazine PO Box 1905 New Haven CT 06509-1905

WISEMAN, HOWARD MARK, physicist; b. Brisbane, Queensland, Australia, June 19, 1968; married Apr. 4, 1992. BS with honors, U. Queensland, 1991, PhD, 1994. Postdoct. rsch. fellow U. Auckland (New Zealand), 1994-96, U. Queensland, 1996-99; rsch. fellow Griffith U., Queensland, 1999—. Contbr. articles to profl. jours. Recipient Bragg medal Australian Inst. Physics, 1995. Avocation: Arthurian history. Office: Griffith U, Nathan Campus, Brisbane Queensland 4111, Australia

WISEMARK, EVA MARIA, management executive; b. Gothenborg, Sweden, Feb. 21, 1948; d. Kurt Erik Stig and Inga Victoria Kullberg W.; m. John David Wertheim; children: Jenny, Paul. Mech. Engring., Norrkoping, Sweden, 1968; MBA, Rutgers U., 1980. Turbine engr., adminstrn. mgr. GEC Turbine Generators, Sweden, 1971-75; sr. cost engr., project mgr. Union Carbide, Eng., U.S., 1975-78; mgr. acquisitions AlliedSignal Inc., Morristown, N.J., 1980-86, dir. bus. devel., 1986-92; bus. devel. dir. N.W. Water plc, Warrington, Eng., 1992-95; mng. dir. Optima Mgmt. Svcs. Ltd., Tarporley, Cheshire, Eng., 1996—; non exec. dir. Kingfisher Wood Products Ltd., Storrington, U.K., 2000—. chmn. Bus. in the Arts: N.W., Eng., 1994—; mem. U.K. and U.S. Fulbright Commn., 1999—, Turning Pt. Regional Com. North, 1999—. Mem. Inst. Dirs. (ednl. liaison 1996-97, chmn. Manchester 1997-99, N.W. region 1999—).

WISKICH, JOSEPH TONY, botany educator, researcher; b. Tully, Queensland, Australia, July 21, 1935; s. Joseph Tony and Vera (Piglic) W.; m. Diane Lesley, Apr. 20, 1968; children: Peter Joseph, Anthony David, Robert Leslie. BSc with honors, U. Sydney (Australia), 1956, PhD, 1960; PhD, U. Adelaide (Australia), 1964. Spl. investigator status. Rsch. assoc. U. Pa., Phila., 1961, UCLA, 1962; rsch. assoc. U. Adelaide, 1963-64, lectr. botany, 1964-71, sr. lectr., 1972-78, assoc. prof., 1979-95, prof., 1995—, mem. univ. coun., 1985-96. Mem. editorial bd.: Australian Jour. Plant Physiology, 1975-88, Plant Physiology, 1983-92; contbr. over 100 articles to sci. jours. Chmn. Anzaas Inc., Adelaide, 1985-91. Elected fellow Australian Acad. Scis., 1994. Fellow Royal Soc. South Australia, Australian Inst. Biology; mem. Biochem. Soc. (London), Am. Soc. Plant Physiologists, Australian Biochem. Soc., Scandinavian Soc. Plant Physiologists, Australian Soc. Plant Physiologists (chmn. 1996-98), N.Y. Acad. Scis., Soc. Francaise Physiol. Vegetable, Japanese Soc. Plant Physiologists. Achievements include research in bioenergetics and plant metabolic biochemistry. Office: U Adelaide Botany Dept, North TCE, Adelaide 5005, Australia

WISMAR, GREGORY JUST, minister; b. Jersey City, Jan. 9, 1946; s. Adolph Harold and Norma Adela (Just) W.; m. Priscilla Emily Ames, June 7, 1969; children: Eric Andrew, Sarah Emily, Elizabeth Victoria, Jessica Eve. BA, Concordia Sr. Coll., Ft. Wayne, Ind., 1967; MDiv, Concordia Sem., St. Louis, 1971; MS, So. Conn. State U., 1977; D of Ministry, Hartford Sem., 1990. Ordained to ministry Luth. Ch.-Mo. Synod, 1971. Asst. pastor Immanuel Luth. Ch., Danbury, Conn., 1971-72; pastor St. Paul's Luth. Ch., Naugatuck, Conn., 1972-78, Redeemer Luth. Ch., Cape Elizabeth, Maine, 1978-83, Messiah Luth. Ch., Lynnfield, Mass., 1983-87, Christ the King Luth. Ch., Newtown, Conn., 1987—; v.p. New Eng. dist. Luth.-Mo. Synod, Springfield, Mass., 1979-83, mem. nominations com., St. Louis, 1985-86, archivist New Eng. dist., 1989—, mem. commn. on worship, St. Louis, 1990-95; rsch. fellow Yale Inst. Sacred Music, Liturgy and Arts, 1991. Author: A Parish Portrait, 1990, Saints and Angels All Around, 1995; editor: Prayers for Worship, 1993. Mem. CT-5 Congl. Adv. Bd., Waterbury, Conn., 1975-78, Ft. Williams Com., Cape Elizabeth, 1981-83, Newtown Family Life Ctr., 1988-90; guest chaplain U.S. Ho. of Reps., Washington, 1977, U.S. Senate, Washington, 1982; chmn. Lynnfield Arts Commn., 1985-87; sec. bd. regents Concordia Coll., Bronxville, N.Y., 1998—. Recipient Svc. award NED Youth Commn., 1987, award Kodak Internat., 1988. Mem. New Eng. Luth. Hist. Soc. Home: 81 Mount Pleasant Rd Newtown CT 06470-1545 Office: Christ the King Luth Ch 85 Mount Pleasant Rd Newtown CT 06470-1535

WISNICKI, JEFFREY LEONARD, plastic surgeon; b. N.Y.C., May 15, 1957; s. Joseph and Lorraine (Justman) W.; m. Rebecca Lynn O'Shields, Feb. 2, 1997; 1 child, Justin Robert. BS summa cum laude, Rensselaer Poly. Inst., 1976; MD cum laude with honors, Union U., 1980. Diplomate Am. Bd. Plastic Surgery. Intern in surgery Stanford (Calif.) U. Med. Ctr., 1980-81, resident in gen., plastic and reconstructive surgery, 1981-84, chief resident in plastic and reconstructive surgery, 1985-86; fellow in plastic and reconstructive surgery Dartmouth-Hitchcock Med. Ctr., Hanover, N.H., 1984; active staff Good Samaritan Hosp., West Palm Beach, Fla., 1986—, Wellington Regional Hosp., West Palm Beach, 1986—; chief divsn. plastic surgery John F. Kennedy Meml. Hosp., West Palm Beach, 1990-93; chmn. dept. surgery Palms West Hosp., West Palm Beach, 1991-93, chief med. staff, 1994-97, chmn. bd. trustees, 1997—; chief divsn. of plastic surgery Good Samaritan and St. Mary's Hosp., West Palm Beach, 1997—; clin. instr. surgery U. Calif., San Francisco, 1985; bd. dirs. Interplast, 1985-86, clin. faculty, 1986—; presenter in field. Contbr. chpts. to books and articles to profl. jours. Fellow ACS; mem. Am. Soc. Plastic & Reconstructive Surgeons, Alpha Omega Alpha. Office: 2047 Palm Beach Lakes Blvd West Palm Beach FL 33409-6501

WIŚNIEWSKI, ADAM BOGUSŁAW, scientist; b. Muszyna, Poland, Oct. 13, 1947; s. Wawrzyniec and Zofia (Duda) W.; m. Teresa Elżbieta Urbańczyk, July 17, 1971; children: Olimpia, Diana. MS, Mil. Tech. Acad., Warsaw, Poland, 1972, Doctorate, 1976; Dr.hab., U. Mining and Metallurgy, Cracow, Poland, 1999. Commd. lt. Mil. Inst. Armament Tech., Zielonka, Poland, 1976; advanced through grades to lt. col. Mil. Inst. Armament Tech., Zielonka, 1986, chief dept. armour and ammunition, 1993—, chief dept. armor, ammunition and materials tech., 2000—. Author: Ceramic Materials in Protective Layers, 1999. Named First Inventor of Polish Army, 1997. Mem. Soc. Polish Engrs. (armour expert 1998—). Avocations: yachting, doing diy. Office: Mil Inst Armament Tech, Wyszyńskiego 7, 05-220 Zielonka Poland

WISNIEWSKI, BOHDAN, philologie educator, researcher; b. Lazin, Lowics, Poland, May 4, 1926; s. Felix Wisniewski and Emilia Crynska; m. Jolanta Freyer, Feb. 1, 1956; 1 child, Sophia. Magister, U. Warsaw, Poland, 1948, doctor, 1965. Lector of Latin U. of Toch, Poland, 1950-70, reader of classical philology, 1971-86, prof. extraordinary of classical philology, 1986-90, prof. ordinanus of classical philology, 1990-96; dir. Inst. Classical Philology, 1976-96. Author: Philo von Larissa, 1982, Karneader Text and Commentar, 1970. Mem. Am. Inst. for Life, Scientific Soc., Philolog. Soc. Roman Catholic. Home: Aleje Kosciushe 52/2, Toch Poland Office: Wolczanska 90, Toch Poland

WISNIEWSKI, ZBIGNIEW, geodesist, educator; b. Lisie-Katy, Torun, Poland, Mar. 30, 1952; s. Jozef and Zofia (Wilewska) W.; m. Malgorzata Wasilewska, July 16, 1983; children: Justyna, Anna. Grad. in Engring., U. Agr. and Tech., Olsztyn, Poland, 1976, D of Engring., 1980; D of Habilitation, U. Mining and Metallurgy, Cracow, Poland, 1987. Asst. U. Agr. and Tech., 1976-80, sr. asst., 1980-87, prof. asst., 1987-92, prof., 1992-95, prof. ordinary, 1995—. Author: Matrix Algebra for Geodesist, 1986, Matrix Algebra and Statistics in Adjustment Computation, 1999; contbr. articles to profl. jours. Mem. Internat. Assn. Geodesy. Home: ul Sikiryckiego 12/5, 10-691 Olsztyn Poland Office: Olsztyn U Agr and Tech, ul Oczapowskiego 1, !0-957 Olsztyn Poland

WISNOM, MICHAEL ROBERT, aerospace engineer, educator; b. London, Eng., Sept. 6, 1955; s. William McLachlan and Dorothy Clare (Pillers) W.; m. Ilaina Tatiana Smerekovska, Nov. 23, 1981; 1 child, Laura Selena. BSc in Engring., Imperial Coll., London, 1977; PhD in Aerospace Engring., U. Bristol, 1991. Engr. Brit. Aerospace Civil Aircraft Divsn., Hatfield, 1977-78; cons. SDRC Engring., Hitchin, 1978-81, Cin., 1981-82; tech. dir. SDRC Engring., Paris, 1982-83, Hitchin, 1983-87; aerospace engring. lectr. U. Bristol, 1987-92, reader, 1992-95, prof. aerospace structures, 1995—; cons. numerous orgns. including Brit. Aerospace, Westland. Contbr. more than 100 articles on mechanics and failure of fiber reinforced composites to jour. including Composites, Composites Sci. and Tech., Jour. Composite Materials, and Jour. Reinforced Plastics and Composites. Mem. Instn. Mech. Engrs. (chartered engr.). Office: U Bristol Dept Aero Engring, University Walk, Bristol BS8 1TR, England

WISOTSKY, SERGE SIDOROVICH, engineering executive; b. Chelsea, Mass., Oct. 19, 1919; s. Sidor Radionovich and Anna Epatiovna (Fariba) W.; m. Marion Ellen Ramsdell, Aug. 10, 1952; children: Serge S. Jr. (dec.), Tanya Lloyd, Stephan, John and Alexander (twins), Phillip. Student, Boston Trade Sch., 1933-37, Lowell Inst. Sch., 1937-43; BS in Physics, MIT, 1950; MS in Physics, Brown U., 1952. Registered profl. mech. engr., Mass., Okla.; lic. electrician, Mass. Elec. motor mech./armature winder United Motors Corp., Boston, 1937-40; machinist apprentice, mfg. methods, steam turbine test GE River Works, Lynn, Mass., 1940-44; engr. R & D Ultrasonics Corp., Cambridge, Mass., 1952-53; instrument engr. Control Engring. Corp., Canton and Norwood, Mass., 1953-57; staff engr. MIT/Draper Lab., Cambridge, Mass., 1957-59; hydroacoustic transducer sect. head Raytheon/Submarine Signal Divsn., Portsmouth, R.I., 1959-70; MSR engr. Raytheon Equipment Divsn. North Dighton, Mass. and Kwajalein Atoll, 1958; v.p. engring. ORB Inc., Sharon, Mass. and Tulsa, 1970—; chief engr. Indsl. Vehicles, Internat., (geophys. prospecting vehicles using VIBROSEIS, worldwide), Tulsa, 1974-84; cons. Amoco Prodn. Rsch. Ctr. (geophys. prospecting sound sources), Tulsa, 1985-86, 93. Contbr. articles to profl. jours. including Jour. Underwater Acoustics, Jour. Geophys. Rsch., Jour. Inst. Navigation, ONR, Jour. Acoustical Soc. Am., Offshore Tech. Conf., Soc. Exptl. Geophys., Sea Tech.; appeared on Dave Garroway's morning TV show, 1953. Brass band clarinetist Stoughton VFW, 1937-42, Bklyn. Armed Guard Ctr., 1945, Brockton Cosmopolitan, 1951-65, Aleppo Shrine, 1965—, Lawrence Colonial, 1989—, Canton/Am. Legion, 1992—. With USNR, 1944-46. Mem. ASME, Acoustical Soc. Am., Am. Soc. Materials, Soc. Exploration Geophysicists (life), Masons, Am. Legion. Russian Orthodox, Congregationalist and Baptist. Achievements include patents for Electro/Syn Pressure Gauge, Electro-HydroSonic Transducer, 6 Water Hammer Piledrivers, and WastePile, also numerous related patents. Home and Office: PO Box 422 89 Bullard St Sharon MA 02067-1007

WISSE, BILLY, writer; b. Montreal, Que., Can., Dec. 19, 1962; s. Leonard H. and Ruth (Roskies) W. BA, McGill U., Montreal, 1984, MA, 1994. Assoc. mgr. Bibliophile Bookstore, Montreal, 1985-88; proofreader Reader's Digest, Montreal, 1985-88; editor BB Comm., Santa Monica, Calif., 1989; proofreader The Workbook, L.A., 1989-90; rschr. Jeopardy!, L.A., 1990-96; writer Jeopardy!, Culver City, Calif., 1996—. Author: Defrosting, 1996, Poems from the Archive of the Pearl Roth Institute, 1999; co-prodr. Rev. Kirk Prodns., 1990-91; grip Gen. Frolic Prodns., 1990-92. Coord. Miracle Mile Neighborhood Watch, L.A., 1994-97. Recipient Emmy award Acad. TV Arts and Scis., 1997. Mem. Writers Guild Am. West, Tea Club. Jewish. E-mail: billywisse@aol.com. Office: Jeopardy! 10202 Washington Blvd Culver City CA 90232-3119

WISSMANN, MATTHIAS, German government official, lawyer; b. Ludwigsburg, Germany, Apr. 15, 1949; s. Paul and Margaret (Kalcker) W. Grad. in Law, U. Bonn., 1974. Polit. asst. Fed. Bundestag (Lower House of Parliament), Bonn., 1970-71, fed. chmn. Junge Union, 1973-83, elected, 1976; pres. European Union of Youth Christian Dems., 1976-82; chmn. enquiry commn. Fed. Bundestag, mem., spokesman Christian Dem. Party econ. working com., 1983; mem. presidium, chmn. Christian Dem. Party, Baden-Württemberg, 1985, mem. faction's exec. com., 1991—, dep. chmn., 1993; Fed. Min. of Rsch. and Tech. Fed. Bundestag, 1993, Fed. Min. Transport, 1993-98; chmn. com. economy and tech. German Parliament, 1998—; spokesman Christian Dem. Party econ. working com., then treas. Christian Dem. Party, 1998-2000; mem. presidium Christian Dem. Party, chmn., exec. com. Fed. Bundestag, 1998-2000; ptnr. Wilmer, Cutler and Pickering, Berlin. Author: Social Market Economy, 1998; contbr. articles to profl. jours. Spokesman econ. working com. Christian Dem. Party, 1983-93. Office: Deutsches Bundestag, Platz der Republik, 11011 Berlin Germany

WIST, PAUL GABRIEL, accountant; b. Balt., July 25, 1929; s. George John and Regina Marie (Ward) W.; m. Mary Lee Vaeth, Oct. 23, 1954; children: Paul Gabriel, Timothy V., Matthew W., Ami A. ABA, U. Balt., 1951. CPA; cert. fin. planner. Assoc. C.W. Amos & Co., Balt., 1952-56, ptnr., 1956-69, mng. ptnr., 1969-85, sr. ptnr., 1985-91, ret., 1991. Bd. dirs. Md. Blue Cross, 1965-73, Assoc. Cath. Charities, 1976-88, pres. 1985-88; mem. adv. bd. St. Joseph Hosp., 1964-88, Stella Maris Hospice, 1969-73;

trustee Cardinal Shehan Ctr. for Aging, 1977-97, Marian House, Inc., 1982-89, McAuley Inst., Inc., 1987-93, St. Joseph Hosp. Found., 1988-95; trustee Am. Inst. CPAs Benevolent Fund, 1977-83, pres. 1980-83; bd. visitors U. Balt., 1984-88, 94-97, trustee ednl. found., 1984-97; trustee Children's Fund, Inc., 1986-95, pres., 1987-95; trustee New Cathedral Cemetary, 1994—, pres. 1996—; trustee Cherry Hill Town Ctr., Inc., 1997—, pres. 1997—; trustee Stella Maris, Inc., 1997-99. With USNR, 1948-49. Recipient Cardinal Gibbons medal, 1973, Papal medal, 1982, U. Balt. Disting. Svc. award, 1990; named Alumnus of Yr. U. Balt., 1982, Disting. Alumnus award Mt. St. Joseph H.S., 1999. Mem. AICPAs (coun. 1974-75, 77-80), Md. Assn. CPAs (pres. 1975-76, Pub. Svc. award 1990), Fin. Planners Assn., Internat. Exec. Svc. Corps (vol. svc. Guatemala, Poland, Egypt, Lithuania, Russia, Republic of Georgia), Towson (Md.) Golf and Country Club, Rotary (pres. 1986-87). Roman Catholic. Home: 523 Saint Francis Rd Baltimore MD 21286-1327 Office: 2 N Charles St Ste 210 Baltimore MD 21201-3754

WISTRAND, RICHARD RHODE, electric and gas utility executive; b. Colorado City, Tex., June 17, 1951; s. Gwen Carter Wistrand; m. Natalie Susan Wistrand, Dec. 29, 1979; children: Andra Renae, Michael Hunter. BSCE, Tex. A&M U., 1973. Registered profl. engr., Tex. Engr. Tex. Utilities Bus. Svcs., Colorado City, Tex., 1973-77; ops. engr. Tex. Utilities Bus. Svcs., Glen Rose, Tex., 1977-81, adminstrv. supt., 1981-85, ops. mgr., 1985-87; project mgr. Tex. Utilities Bus. Svcs., Dallas, 1987-91, regulatory engring. mgr., 1991-94, purchasing mgr., 1994-96, dir. procurement, 1996-97, v.p., 1997—. Adv. bd. Richardson (Tex.) Boys and Girls Club, 1997-99; campaign leader Boy Scouts Am., Dallas, 1996-99. Named Outstanding Men of MBD Minority Bus. News, 1996, Outstanding Young Man of Am. U.S. Jaycees, 1984, Optimist of Yr. Granbury Optimist Club, 1985. Mem. Dallas Electric Club, Utility Purchasing Mgrs. Group (sec.-treas. 1994—), Nat. Assn. of Purchasing Mgrs. Avocations: golf, children. Office: Tex Utilities Bus Svcs 1601 Bryan St Dallas TX 75201-3401

WISWALL, FRANK LAWRENCE, JR., lawyer, educator; b. Albany, N.Y., Sept. 21, 1939; s. Frank Lawrence and Clara Elizabeth (Chapman) W.; m. Elizabeth Curtiss Nelson, Aug. 9, 1975; children by previous marriage: Anne W. Kowalski, Frank Lawrence III. BA, Colby Coll., 1962; JD, Cornell U., 1965; PhD in Law, Cambridge U., 1967. Bar: Maine 1965, N.Y. 1968, U.S. Supreme Ct. 1968, D.C. 1975; lic. master near coastal steam and motor vessels, 1960—. Assoc. Burlingham, Underwood, Barron, Wright & White, N.Y.C., 1967-73; maritime legal adviser Rep. of Liberia, 1968-88; v.p. com. Internat. Maritime Com. (CMI), 1997—, intern, 1999; prof. (ad honorem) internat. maritime law Internat. Maritime Inst., 1999; mem. legal com. Internat. Maritime Orgn., London, 1972-74, vice chmn. 1974-79, chmn., 1980-84; tutorial supr. internat. law Clare Coll., Cambridge, Eng., 1966-67; vis. lectr. Cornell Law Sch., 1969-76, 82; lectr. U. Va. Law Sch. and Ctr. for Oceans Law and Policy, 1978-82; prof. law Cornell U., 1984; Johnsen prof. maritime law Tulane U., 1985; vis. prof. law World Maritime U., Malmo, Sweden, 1986—; prof. Internat. Maritime Law Inst., Malta, 1991—, mem. governing bd., 1992—; prof. admiralty law Maine Maritime Acad., 1993-94; del. Internat. Conf. Marine Pollution, London, 1973; del., chmn. drafting com. Internat. Conf. Carriage of Passengers and Luggage by Sea, Athens, 1974; del. Internat. Conf. on Safety of Life at Sea, London, 1974, 3d UN Conf. on Law of Sea, Caracas, Venezuela, 1974, 3d UN Conf. on Law of Sea (all subsequent sessions); del., chmn. com. final clauses Internat. Conf. on Limitation of Liability for Maritime Claims, London, 1976; del. UN Conf. Carriage of Goods by Sea, Hamburg, 1978, XIII Diplomatic Conf. on Maritime Law, Brussels, 1979; chmn. com. of the whole Internat. Conf. Carriage of Hazardous Substances by Sea, 1984; del. internat. conf. on Maritime Terrorism, Rome, 1988; counsel various marine casualty bds. of investigation, 1970—, harbormaster, Port of Castine, 1960-62; prof. internat. maritime law (hon.) Maritime Law Inst., 1999. Author: The Development of Admiralty Jurisdiction and Practice Since 1800, 1970; editor-in-chief Benedict on Admiralty, Vols. 6, 6A-6F (Internat. Maritime Law), 19925; contbr. articles to profl. jours. Ofcl. prin. Diocese of Mid-Atlantic States, 1988—, Diocese of the U.K., 1997—, Anglican Cath. Ch.; chancellor Missionary Diocese of N.E., 19935, Diocese Australia, 19985; spkr. assembly laity Anglican Cath. Ch., 19955. Recipient Yorke prize U. Cambridge, 1968-69. Fellow Royal Hist. Soc.; mem. Nat. Lawyers Assn., I.M.O., Comité Maritime Internat. (exec. councillor 1989-96, v.p. 19975), Maritime Law Assn. U.S. (chmn. com. on intergovtl. orgns. 1983-87, chmn. com. on CMI 1987-95), Ecclesiastical Law Soc., Selden Soc., Nat. Lawyers Assn., Am. Soc. Legal History, U.K. Assn. Average Adjusters, U.S. Assn. Average Adjusters, Maine Bar Assn., U.S. Navy League (pres. Penobscot coun. 1997), United Oxford and Cambridge U. Club (London), Century Assn., Alpha Delta Phi, Phi Delta Phi. Office: PO Box 201 Castine ME 04421-0201

WISZNIEWSKI, ANDRZEJ JÒZEF, electrical engineer; b. Warsaw, Poland, Feb. 15, 1935; s. Tadeusz and Ewa Maria (Ciechomska) W.; m. Ewa Maria Lutoslawska, Nov. 21, 1958; 1 child, Barbara Borzymowska. MSc, Tech. U., Wroclaw, Poland, 1957, PhD, 1961, DSc, 1966; D. Honoris Causa, Ctr. Conn. State U., 1993, Lviv (Ukrain) Tech. U., 1999. From tchg. asst. to prof. elec. engring. Tech. U., Wroclaw, 1957-72, prof., 1972—; min. sci., chmn. Com. for Sci. Rsch., Warsaw, 1997—; dept. head U. Benghazi, Libya, 1977-79; v.p. Tech. U., Wroclaw, 1981, pres., 1990-96. Author: Measuring Transformers, 1982, 2d edit. 1992, Digital Measuring Algorithms, 1989, Protection Techniques in Power Systems, 1995, Perswasive Speaking and Speech Making, 1994, 2d edit., 1996. Recipient City of Wroclaw prize, 1996. Fellow IEE (hon., com. head 1986-89, Golden Badge 1996), CIGRE (hon., nat. com. head 1990—). Roman Catholic. Avocations: modern literature, skiing, living creatures. Home: Krasickiego 18, 51-144 Wroclaw Poland Office: Com for Scientific Rsch, Wspolna 1/3, 00-921 Warszawa Poland

WIT, DAVID EDMUND, software and test preparation company executive; b. N.Y.C., Feb. 25, 1962; s. Harold Maurice W. and Joan Leta (Rosenthal) Sovern; m. Kathleen Mary Bentley, Sept. 9, 1989. BA summa cum laude, Hamilton Coll., 1985. Rsch. assoc. E.M. Warburg Pincus and Co., N.Y.C., 1985-86; CEO Logicat Inc., N.Y.C. Mem. N.Y. Software Industry Assn., Phi Beta Kappa. Avocation: exercise. Home: 3 Stratford Rd Larchmont NY 10538-1341 Office: Logicat Inc 201 E 16th St New York NY 10003-3706

WITCOSKI, JOHN ROBERT, social studies educator; b. Shenandoah, Pa., Aug. 7, 1944; s. Francis B. and Anna (Volousky) W.; m. Mary Ann Miscannon, Aug. 20, 1966; 1 child: John Christopher. BS, Bloomsburg U., 1966; MA, Coll. N.J., 1972. Cert. secondary edn. tchr., Pa. Tchr. Anne Arundel County, Annapolis, Md., 1966-67, Neshaminy Sch. Dist., Langhorne, Pa., 1967—; chair dept. social studies Neshaminy H.S., Langhorne, 1986—. Chair com. Boy Scouts Am., Levittown, Pa., 1980-87. Mem. Am. Fedn. Tchrs., Nat. Coun. Social Studies. Democrat. Roman Catholic. Avocation: gardening. Office: Neshaminy HS 2001 Old Lincoln Hwy Langhorne PA 19047-3295

WITHEROW, PETER KENT, geographic information systems analyst; b. Torrance, Calif., June 17, 1969; s. James Vernon and Linda Mae W.; children: Andrew, Kyrsten. BS in Urban and Regional Planning, Calif. Poly. U., 1997. Geographic info. sys. intern City of Ontario (Calif.), 1990-93, geographic info. sys. analyst, 1993—; self-employed PW Enterprises, Upland, Calif.; instr. U. Calif., Riverside, 1996—. Programmer (ArcView program) Land Use Module, 1995; contbr. article to El Nino Hotline, 1998. Recipient 2nd Place in Customizing Arc View with Avenue award Environ. Sys. Rsch. Inst.'s Internation User Conf., 1995. Avocations: classic car restoration, softball. Fax: (909) 395-2411. E-mail: pwithero@ci.ontario.ca.us. Home: 1850 w Arrow Rte # 134 Upland CA 91786 Office: City of Ontario 303 E B St Ontario CA 91764-4196

WITHERS, CARL RAYMOND, lawyer; b. Reading, Pa., Jan. 26, 1924; s. Stuart Snable Withers and Edith Garman; m. Jenny Constance Cory, Sept. 2, 1950; children: Wren, Jill, Bradford. AB, Wittenberg U., 1950; JD, U. Mich., 1953. Bar: Ohio 1954. Pvt. practice Cleve., 1954—. Former pres. mus. Shaker Hist. Soc., Shaker Heights, Ohio, 1970—; former trustee, treas. N.E. Inter Mus. Coun., Cleve., 1980—; exec. com. Cuyahoga County Rep. Party, Cleve., 1984-94. 1st lt. U.S. Army Air Force, 1942-46. Mem. Ohio State Bar Assn. (former coun. of dels. 1955), Cleve. Bar Assn., Am. Legion (Army-Navy Shaker post 54, former commander, adjutant), Gt. Lakes Curling Assn. (treas., pres. 1985-96), Cleve. Grays, Estate Planning Coun. of Cleve., Cleve. Rotary Club, Cleve. City Club, Cleve. Skating Club (former trustee), Beta Theta Pi (former pres.), Delta Theta Phi. Republican. Presbyterian. Avocation: curling, genealogy, American lithographs. Home: 3419 Courtland Rd Pepper Pike OH 44122-4280 Office: Van Aken Withers & Webster 629 Euclid Ave Cleveland OH 44114-3003

WITHERS, PHILIP JOHN, materials science educator; b. Cwymbran, Wales, May 11, 1963; s. David Charles Withers and Shirley Mary (Stone) Davis; m. Lindsey Jayne Owen, July 28, 1990; children: Chloe Elizabeth, David Alexander, Peter Samuel. BA, Cambridge (Eng.) U., 1985, MA, 1988, PhD, 1989. Univ. asst. lectr. Cambridge (Eng.) U., 1989-94, lectr., 1994-98, prof., 1998—; cons. Alcan Internat., Banbury, Eng., 1996—. Author: An Introduction to Metal Matrix Composites, 1993. Recipient Outstanding Paper award Acta Metallurgica, 1989, Materials Sci. & Tech. Prize Fedn. European Materials Socs., 1999. Mem. Inst. Materials. Avocations: cricket, football, rugby, golf, photography. Office: Manchester Materials Sci Ct, Grosvenor St, Manchester MI 7HS, England

WITHERS, ROBERT THOMAS, exercise physiologist, educator; b. Birmingham, Eng., Aug. 26, 1938; arrived in Australia, 1974; s. Thomas and Ada (Ingram) W.; m. Pamela Sue Peridier, July 5, 1974. Cert. in edn., Alsager Coll. of Edn., Eng., 1961; diploma in phys. edn., St. Luke's Coll., Eng., 1962; MSc, Washington State U., 1967; PhD, U. Md., 1974. Prof. phys. edn. Flinders U., Bedford Park, Australia; mem. Nat. Lab. Accreditation Com., Australian Sports Commn., 1990-96, chmn., 1997—. Assoc. editor Australian Jour. Sci. and Medicine in Sport, 1985—; mem. editl. bd. Internat. Jour. Sports Medicine, 1994—; contbr. over 80 articles to profl. jours. Fellow Australian Sports Medicine Fedn., Am. Coll. Sports Medicine; mem. Australian Physiol. and Pharmacol. Soc. Avocations: reading, weight-training, jogging, spectator sports. Office: Exerc Phys Lab Flinders U, Bedford Park, South Australia 5042, Australia

WITHERSPOON, JOHN PATTERSON, retired communications educator, consultant; b. Chgo., July 5, 1929; s. Walter Edward and Helen Frances (Couch) W.; m. Mercedes Witherspoon, June 19, 1950; children: Leslie W., Lynn M. BA, U. of Pacific, 1951; MA, Stanford U., 1960. Gen. mgr. Sta. KPBS-TV-FM Pub. Broadcasting, San Diego, 1967-70; dir. TV Corp. for Pub. Broadcasting, Washington, 1970-73; pres. Pub. Svc. Satellite Consortium, San Diego and Washington, 1975-79; prof., dir. Ctr. for Comm. San Diego State U., 1979-90, chair telecom. and film, 1990-92, prof. emeritus Sch. Comm., 1992—; ind. cons. in field, 1973-75, 92—; Founding chair Nat. Pub. Radio, Washington, 1970; sr. advisor Western Coop. for Ednl. Telecom., Boulder, Colo., 1993—. Author: Distance Education: A Planner's Case Book, 1997. Bd. dirs. Pub. Svc. Satellite Consortium Legacy Fund, San Diego, 1992—. Lt. USNR, 1952-55. Named Disting. Alumnus, Modesto (Calif.) Jr. Coll., 1971; recipient spl. citation Ednl. TV Stas., Washington, 1972. Mem. Coronado Yacht Club (bd. dirs., sec. 1997—). E-mail: withersj@aol.com.

WITHERSPOON, JOHN THOMAS, water treatment company executive; b. Springfield, Mo., June 25, 1947; s. Warren Thomas and Kathryn (Corbus) w.; m. C. Frances Teter, June 12, 1971. BS, S.W. Mo. State U., 1969, MA, 1971; PhD, U. Mont., 1975. Water control inspector City of Springfield, Mo., 1976-78; dir. labs. City Utilities, Springfield, 1978-91, mgr. water treatment and supply, 1991—; mem. safe drinking water commn. Mo. State Dept. Natural Resources, Jefferson City, 1992—, now chair; bd. dirs. James River Basin Partnership, Nixa, Mo., 1996; tech. advisor Watershed Com. of the Ozarks, Springfield, 1983—. Pres. Univ. Club Springfield, 1989. Mem. Am. Water Works Assn. (chair, Boyd Utility Mgr. award 1996, Fuller award 1999), Kiwanis. Avocations: golf, reading, guitar, travel. Home: 1927 E Lark St Springfield MO 65804-4345 Office: City Utilities PO Box 551 Springfield MO 65801-0551

WITHERSPOON, WALTER PENNINGTON, JR., orthodontist, philanthropist; b. Sept. 3, 1938; s. Walter P. and Florence Evelyn (Jones) W.; m. Joyce Ann Smith, Sept. 6, 1970; 1 child, Annie Melissa. BS, U. S.C., 1960; DDS, U. N.C., 1964, MSO, 1969. Bd. qualified Am. Bd. Orthodontics. Pvt. practice Columbia, 1969—; med. staff Bapt. Med. Ctr., Columbia, 1970—, Lexington County Hosp., West Columbia, 1974—. Host Nite Line Broadcasting Co. Adv. bd. 1st Palmetto Bank and Trust, West Columbia, 1982; mem. adv. bd. 1st Citizens Bank; candidate S.C. Ho. of Reps., 1994; del. S.C. Rep. Com., 1989—; mem. platform com. S.C. Rep. Party Conv., poll com., 1992; del. Rep. Nat. Conv., Houston, 1992, rules com., task force on edn.; Rep. nat. committeeman, 1996—, rules com., rep. nat. com.; pres. Rep. Electoral Coll., 1996; bd. dirs. Southeastern Coll. Assemblies of God, Lakeland, Fla., 1984, Brookland Plantation Home for Boys, Orangeburg, S.C.; pres. Friends of Irmo Libr.; bd. dirs. Irmo-St. Andrew's Coalition of Neighborhood Home Owners' Assns.; chmn. Lexington County Rep. Party; commr. Richland/Lexington Counties Commn. for Tech. Edn., S.C. Commn. on Alcohol and Drug Abuse; bd. dirs. Centerplace for Homeless; mem. Presdl. Visit-Ticket Com.; amb. Irmo C. of C.; vol. lockup telethon Muscular Dystrophy Assn. Lt. USN, 1964-66. Recipient Century Mem. award Boy Scouts Am., 1984. Mem. ADA, Greater Columbia Dental Assn. (pres. 1975-76), U. N.C. Dental Alumni Assn. (bd. dirs.), S.C. Dental Assn. (ho. of dels. 1971-73, 91-96, legis. com. 1993), S.C. Orthodontic Assn. (cen. dist. dir.), Am. Assn. Orthodontists, Sertoma (pres. 1975-76), Am. Legion (mem. baseball com.), So. Assn. Orthodontists, Cen. Dist. Dental Soc. Home: 250 Lancer Dr Columbia SC 29212-1216 Office: 205 Med Cir W Columbia SC 29169

WITHERSPOON, WILLIAM, investment economist; b. St. Louis, Nov. 21, 1909; s. William Conner and Mary Louise (Houston) W.; student Washington U. Evening Sch., 1928-47; m. Margaret Telford Johanson, June 25, 1938; children: James Tomlin, Jane Telford, Elizabeth Witherspoon Vodra. Rsch. dept. A. G. Edwards & Sons, 1928-31; pres. Witherspoon Investment Co., 1931-34; head rsch. dept. Newhard Cook & Co., 1934-43; chief price analysis St. Louis Ordnance Dist., 1943-45; head rsch. dept. Newhard Cook & Co., 1945-53; owner Witherspoon Investment Counsel, 1953-64; ltd. ptnr. Newhard Cook & Co., economist, investment analyst, 1965-68; v.p. rsch. Stifel, Nicolaus & Co., 1968-81; lectr. on investments Washington U., 1948-67. Mem. Clayton Bd. of Edn., 1955-68, treas., 1956-68, pres., 1966-67; mem. Clayton Park and Recreation Commn., 1959-60; trustee Ednl. TV, KETC, 1963-64; mem. investment com. Gen. Assembly Mission Bd. Presbyn. Ch. (USA), Atlanta, 1976-79, mem. permanent com. ordination exams, 1979-85; cons. to investment com. Ctr. Theol. Inquiry, Princeton, N.J., 1995-97. Served as civilian Ordnance Dept., AUS, 1943-45. Chartered fin. analyst. Mem. St. Louis Soc. Fin. Analysts (pres. 1949-50). Club: Mo. Athletic (St. Louis). Home: 6401 Ellenwood Ave Saint Louis MO 63105-2228

WITHERSPOON, WILLIAM TOM, company executive; b. Dallas, Feb. 1, 1949; s. Vernon Howard and Mary Ruth (Coffee) W.; m. Sandra Stein, June 10, 1970; children: Mary Jacqueline, Stephen Thomas. BS in Civil Engring., So. Meth. U., 1971; MS in Mgmt. and Adminstrv. Sci., U. Tex., Dallas, 1979; postgrad., So. Meth. U., 1979-81. Registered profl. engr., Tex.; lic. irrigator, Tex.; registered surveyor, Tex., sanitarian, Tex. Field engr. Robert E. McKee Constrn. Co., Dallas, 1971-73; supt. Batson Cook Co., Dallas, 1973-77; project mgr. Rucker Constrn. Co., Dallas, 1977-81; v.p. Wynn Oil Co., Dallas, 1981-85; pres. Sandco Petroleum Corp., Dallas, 1985-87, S&W Found. Contractors, Richardson, Tex., 1986—; pres. U.S. Weightlifting-North Tex., Dallas, 1975-95; bd. dirs. Internat. Assn. Found. Drilling, Dallas; pres. Found. Repair Assn. Tex., 1997-2000. Author: Residential Found. Performance, 1999; patentee in field. With USN, 1971-80. State champion U.S. Weightlifting, 1984, 87, 89, 90, 94; recipient Contractor of Yr. award Internat. Assn. Found. Drilling, 1997. Mem. Am. Assn. Civil Engrs., Am. Assn. Petroleum Engrs., Am. Assn. Petroleum Geologists, Am. Weightlifting Assn., Richardson C. of C. Republican. Avocations: weightlifting, golf, writing, ranching. E-mail: tomw5@ix.netcom.com. Office: S&W Found Contractors 1030 E Belt Line Rd Richardson TX 75081-3703

WITHERWAX, CHARLES HALSEY, lawyer, arbitrator, mediator; b. Schroon Lake, N.Y., July 24, 1934; s. Halsey Jerome and Elizabeth Daisy (Bingham) W.; m. Marianne Jehander, June 24, 1980. BS in Marine Transp., N.Y. State Maritime Coll., 1956; LLB, Union U., 1959. Bar: N.Y. 1962, U.S. Dist. Ct. (so. dist.) N.Y. 1962, U.S. Supreme Ct. 1968, Hawaii 1971, U.S. Dist. Ct. Hawaii 1971, U.S. Ct. Appeals (9th cir.) 1984, U.S. Tax Ct. 1984, Nev. 1991, D.C. 1993, U.S. Ct. Appeals (2d cir.) 1995. Assoc. prof. N.Y. State Maritime Coll., Fort Schuyler, N.Y., 1963-64; asst. v.p., bond claims atty. Chubb Ins. Group, N.Y.C., 1961-70; v.p., gen. counsel Hawaiian Ins. Group, Honolulu, 1970-74; ptnr. Davis, Witherwax, Playdon & Gerson, Honolulu, 1974-78; prin. atty. Witherwax, Pottenger & Nishioka, Honolulu, 1978-91; of counsel D'Amato & Lynch, N.Y.C., 1992—. Author: (manual) Hawaii Construction Law, Mechanics Liens and Bond Claims, 1985, co-author, 1987. Bronx county chmn. N.Y. State Conservative Party, 1962-67; state sec. N.Y. State Conservative Party, 1967-70. Lt. comdr. USNR, 1959-79. Mem. ABA (vice chair fidelity and surety com. 1978-83), Internat. Assn. Def. Counsel. Roman Catholic. Avocations: sailing, travel, golf. Office: D'Amato & Lynch 37th Flr 70 Pine St Fl 37 New York NY 10270-0002

WITHROW, LUCILLE MONNOT, nursing home administrator; b. Alliance, Ohio, July 28, 1923; d. Charles Edward Monnot and Freda Aldine (Guy) Monnot Cameron; m. Alvin Robert Withrow, June 6, 1945 (dec. 1984); children: Cindi Withrow Johnson, Nancy Withrow Townley, Sharon Withrow Hodgkins, Wendel Alvin. AA in Health Adminstrn., Eastfield Coll., 1976. Lic. nursing home adminstr., Tex.; cert. nursing home ombudsman. Held various clerical positions Dallas, 1950-72; office mgr., asst. adminstr. Christian Care Ctr. Nursing Home, Mesquite, Tex., 1972-76; head adminstr. Christian Care Ctr. Nursing Home and Retirement Complex, Mesquite, 1976-91; nursing home ombudsman Tex. Dept. Aging and Tex. Dept. Health, Dallas, 1991-93; legal asst. Law Offices of Wendel A. Withrow, Carrollton, Tex., 1993—; mem. con. on geriatric curriculum devel. Eastfield Coll., Mesquite, 1979, 87; mem. ombudsman adv. com. Sr. Citizens Greater Dallas; nursing home cons.; notary pub., 1995—. Vol. Dallas Arboretum and Bot. Soc., Dallas Summer Musicals Guild; mem. Ombudsman adv. com. Sr. Citizens of Greater Dallas, Health Svcs. Speakers Bur.; charter mem. Stage Show Prodns. Recipient Volunteerism awards Tex. Atty. Gen., 1987, Tex. Gov., 1992. Mem. Tex. Assn. Homes for Aging, Am. Assn. Homes for Aging, Health Svcs. Speakers Bur., White Rock Kiwanis. Mem. Ch. of Christ. Avocations: reading, travel, theater. Home: 11344 Lippitt Ave Dallas TX 75218-1922 Office: Law Office of W A Withrow 1120 Metrocrest Dr Ste 200 Carrollton TX 75006-5872

WITKIN, ERIC DOUGLAS, lawyer; b. Trenton, N.J., May 14, 1948; s. Nathan and Norma Shirley (Stein) W.; m. Regina Ann Bilotta, June 8, 1980; children: Daniel Robert, Sarah Ann. AB magna cum laude, Columbia U., 1969; JD, Harvard U., 1972. Bar: N.Y. 1973, D.C. 1989, U.S. Dist. Ct. (so. and ea. dists.) N.Y. 1974, U.S. Ct. Appeals (2d and D.C. cirs.) 1974, U.S. Supreme Ct. 1977, U.S. Dist. Ct. D.C. 1989. Assoc. Poletti, Freidin, Prashker & Gartner, N.Y.C., 1972-80, ptnr., 1980-85; sr. atty. labor Kaye, Scholer, Fierman, Hays & Handler, N.Y.C., 1985-88; of counsel Akin, Gump, Strauss, Hauer & Feld, Washington, 1988-90; counsel Benetar, Bernstein, Schair & Stein, N.Y.C., 1990-99; ptnr. Roberts & Finger, LLP, N.Y.C., 1999—. treas., founder Property Owners Against Unfair Taxation, N.Y.C., 1983-90; trustee Congregation Emanu-El of Westchester, 1996—. Lawrence Chamberlain scholar Columbia U., N.Y.C., 1968; recipient Alumni medal Alumni Fedn. Columbia U., 1982. Mem. ABA (labor and employment law sect.), N.Y. State Bar Assn. (labor and employment law sect., com. on equal employment opportunity law), Assn. of Bar of City of N.Y. (spl. com. on sex and law 1975-82, com. on labor and employment law 1982-85, 92-94), Westchester County Bar Assn., Columbia Coll. Alumni Assn. (pres. 1988-90, bd. dirs. 1974—, Robert Lincoln Carey prize, Alumni prize 1969, Lions award 1990), Alumni Fedn. Columbia U. (alumni trustee nominating com. 1990-97, pres. 1997-99), Am. Soc. Pers. Adminstrn. (contbr. monthly newsletter 1986-88), Soc. Human Resource Mgmt., Soc. Columbia Grads. (bd. dirs. 1994-97), Human Resources Assn. N.Y., Phi Beta Kappa. Club: Harvard (N.Y.C.). Avocations: piano, sailing. Home: 103 Wendover Rd Rye NY 10580-1939 Office: Roberts & Finger LLP 767 3rd Ave Fl 12 New York NY 10017-2023

WITKOWSKI, RYSZARD, test pilot, consultant; b. Milanowek, Masovia, Poland, May 9, 1926; s. Josef and Felicja (Brodowska) W.; m. Teresa Ryszkowska, Oct. 28, 1961; 1 child, Grazyna. BSc in Engring., Wawelberg/Rotwand Sch. Engr., Warsaw, 1949; MSc in Aeronautics, Warsaw Inst. Tech., 1962. Designer Aviation Inst., Warsaw, 1949-50, flight tester, 1956-88; quality inspector ZWAO-Works, Warsaw, 1951-55; cons. Ministry of Transport, Warsaw, 1989-92; cons. EER Sys. Corp., Vienna, 1991-92; court expert in air accidents, Poland, 1979-97. Author; Helicopters, 1958, Design and Piloting of Helicopters, 1980, 2d edit., 1986, Six Degrees of Freedom, 1980, 2d edit., 1998, Rotorcraft in Poland, 1986, Introduction to the Knowledge on Helicopters, 1998. Recipient Paul Tissandier diploma Internat. Aviation Fedn. (Paris), 1972, Righteous Among the Nations award Yad Vashem Inst. (Jerusalem), 1993, Hon. Citizen of Israel, 1994. Mem. Exptl. Test Pilots Club (pres. 1990—), Warsaw Aviation Srs. Club (v.p. 1992—). Roman Catholic. Avocations: translations, history of rotorcraft, stamp collection. Home: Al Krakowska 268/25, 02-210 Warsaw Poland Office: SIMP Exptl Test Pilots Club, ul Czackiego 3/5, 00-043 Warsaw Poland

WITMAN, LAURA KATHLEEN, writer, security professional; b. Pottstown, Pa., Mar. 4, 1957; d. William Tedford and Kathleen (Nieman) W. Student, San Bernardino Valley Coll., 1976-79; Degree in Actg. magna cum laude, Adelphi Bus. Coll., San Bernardino, Calif., 1985. Cert. acctg. bookkeeper. Silent alarm monitor, payroll acct. Comml. Security Alliance, San Bernardino, Calif., 1985—. Author: The Sun, 1994; (poetry) World of Poetry, 1990, National Library of Poetry, 1992, 94, 95, 96, 98, Sparrowgrass, 1993; (short story) Antivivesection Soc., 1993, Animal Voice, 1994, Paws Newsletter, 1993, 94, 96, A Dogs Day Newsletter, 1994, House Rabbit Soc., 1994, 95, songs. Mem. Gay and Lesbian Cmty. Ctr. Inland Empire, Heartland Christian Fellowship Met. Cmty. Ch., Inland Empire Pride Coun. Mem. People for Ethical Treatment of Animals, House Rabbit Soc. Democrat. Home: 2001 N Rancho Ave Apt A27 Colton CA 92324-1211

WITMEYER, JOHN JACOB, III, lawyer; b. New Orleans, Dec. 18, 1946; s. John J. and Thais Audrey (Dolese) W. BS, Tulane U., 1968; JD with distinction, Duke U., 1971. Bar: N.Y. Assoc. Mudge Rose Guthrie & Alexander, N.Y.C., 1971-76; ptnr. Ford Marrin Esposito & Wittmeyer (now Ford, Marrin, Esposito, Witmeyer & Gleser LLP), N.Y.C., 1976—. Bd. trustees Gregorian U. Found., 1999—; adv. coun. Paul Tulane Coll., Tulane U., 1998—. Col. U.S. Army; ret. Office: Ford Marrin Esposito Witmeyer & Gleser LLP Wall St Plz New York NY 10005-1875

WITORSCH, PHILIP, internist, educator; b. N.Y.C., July 11, 1937; s. Benjamin and Sarah (Etkin) W.; m. Joan Linda Pellman, June 7, 1959; children: Beth Joy, Jeffrey Lee. AB, N.Y. U., 1958, MD, 1962. Diplomate Am. Bd. Internal Medicine and subsplty. pulmonary disease. Intern, residentin internal medicine Yale U.-New Haven Hosp., 1962-64; clin. assoc., clin. investigator Nat. Inst. Allergy and Infectious Diseases NIH, Bethesda, Md., 1964-67; resident, chief resident in internal medicine, fellow pulmonary diseases VA. Hosp., Washington, 1967-69; chmn. pulmonary and critical care medicine, dir. med. intensive care unit, med. dir. respiratory therapy Washington Hosp. Ctr., 1969-82, sr. attending in medicine, 1969—; prof. medicine and physiology, dir. sect. environ. medicine and toxicology, divsn. pulmonary diseases and allergy, med. dir. for respiratory care George Washington U., 1983-95; prin. Internat. Ctr. Toxicology and Medicine; prof. medicine and pharmacology, clin. dir. toxicology and applied pharmakinetics program, dir. environ. occupl. toxicology assessment clinic Georgetown U., 1995—; adj. prof. pharmacology Georgetown U., 1986-95; cons. pulmonary diseases, Va. Hosp. NIH, Dept. State, Andrews AFB, Dept. Justice, Dept. Labor. Contbr. articles to profl. med. jours. Served with USPHS, 1964-67. Fellow ACP, Am. Coll. Chest Physicians (gov. Washington chpt. 1995-97), Am. Geriatric Soc., Royal Soc. Medicine; mem. AMA (physicians recognition awards 1972, 75, 78, 81, 84, 87, 90, 93, 96), Soc. Critical Care Medicine, Am. Thoracic Soc., D.C. Thoracic Soc., Med. soc. D.C., Am. Fedn. Clin. Rsch., So. Med. Assn., Am. Assn. Respiratory Therapy, Am. Heart Assn., Am. Soc. Internal Medicine, Am. coll. Toxicology, Am. Coll. Occupl. and Environ. Medicine, Phi Beta Kappa, Alpha Omega Alpha. Office: 6001 Montrose Rd Ste 400 Rockville MD 20852-4882

WITT, ALAN MICHAEL, lawyer, accountant; b. Chgo., Apr. 13, 1952; m. Pamela Beth Ander, Dec. 29, 1976; children: Caryn, Kenneth, Amy. BS in Acctg., U. Ill., 1974, JD. Bar: Ill. 1977. Tax and audit cons. Weisbard, Strauss & Snider, Chgo., 1977-81; sole practice Wheeling, Ill., 1977—; tax mgr. Laventhol & Horwath, Chgo., 1981-83; tax ptnr. Ostrow, Reisin, Berk & Abrams, Ltd., 1983—; mng. dir., 1992-95; lectr. law Lewis Coll. Law,

Glen Ellyn, Ill., 1980, Kent Coll. Law, Chgo., 1981—. Co-author: Year End Tax Planning, 1982, 3rd rev. edit., 1986; editor: The Tax Advisor Tax Clinic, 1990-96; co-editor: Callaghan's Legal Checklists, 1985-96; contbg. editor: Hanbook for Tax Advisors, 1990—. Mem. ABA, AICPAs (accredited personal fin. splst.), Ill. State Bar Assn., Chgo. Bar Assn., Ill. CPAs Soc., Beta Gamma Sigma, Tau Kappa Epsilon. Home: 1155 Wayne Ave Deerfield IL 60015-2824 Office: Ste 2600 455 N Cityfront Plaza Dr Chicago IL 60611-5506

WITTBERGER, STEVEN DUANE, nursing educator; b. Brize Norton, U.K., Apr. 17, 1953; s. Russell Grant and Patricia Elizabeth (Bradley) W.; m. Jean Ann Moody, Apr. 20, 1974 (div. Nov. 1979); 1 child, Tammy Michelle; m. Melinda Santos, May 24, 1993. BA in Psychology, U. Wales, 1980. Registered mental health nurse, U.K., registered gen. nurse, U.K. Staff nurse Salisbury (U.K.) Health Authority, 1983-84, charge nurse, 1984-86; sr. nursing officer YANPET, Yanbu Al-Sinaiyah, 1986-88; nursing supr. Saudi ARAMCO, Yanbu Al-Sinaiyah, 1988-91; nursing instr. Saudi ARAMCO, Hofuf, Saudi Arabia, 1991-96, Dhahran, Saudi Arabia, 1996—. Students Union pres. U. Coll.-Cardiff, 1980; county coun. candidate Wiltshire County Coun., 1985. Social Democrat. Avocations: amateur dramatics, snorkeling, country walking, folk singing. Office: Saudi ARAMCO, Box 10816, Dhahran 31311, Saudi Arabia

WITTE, HARTMUT FRIEDRICH, anatomist, biomedical engineer; b. Wanne-Eickel, Germany, Jan. 4, 1961; s. Günter and Annemarie (Strelow) W.; m. Birgit Tewes, Apr. 10, 1992; children: Kirsten Elisabeth, Phillipp Sebastian. Diploma in engring., U. Dortmund, Germany, 1984; ARZT, Ruhr U., Bochum, Germany, 1990, MD, 1992. Lectr. Ruhr U., Bochum, 1990-97, specialist in anatomy, 1995; asst. prof. U. Jena, Germany, 1997—. Mem. VDI, Anatomische Assn., DGBMT, DG Biomechanik, DZG. Avocation: rowing. Office: Inst Spezielle Zoologie, FSU Jena, D-07740 Jena Germany

WITTE, HERMANN, economist, researcher; b. Schleswig, Germany, Mar. 30, 1947; s. Hermann Hartwig and Emilie (Rossmann) W.; m. Renate Böttcher, July 23, 1947; children: Inga, Julia. Diplom-Volkswirt, U. Bonn, Germany, 1973, Dr.rer.pol., 1976; Dr.Hab.(PL), U. Stettin, Poland, 1995. Rschr. U. Bonn, 1973-84, sr. rschr., 1989-91; sr. rschr. U. Cologne, Germany, 1985-88; prof. FH Osnabrueck, Germany, 1992—; vis. prof. U. Innsbruck, Austria, 1995-96; cons. Kaist/World Bank, Seoul, Korea, 1983, U. Bahia-Blanca, Argentina, 1983, Bank for Internat. Devel.; sr. rschr. U. fukuoka, Japan, 1990. Mem. Verein für Socialpolitik, Arbeitskreis Europaische Integration. Avocations: sailing, tennis, jogging. Office: FH Osnabrueck, Albrechtstr 30, D-49076 Osnabrück Germany

WITTE, KLAUS JUERGEN, research physicist, educator; b. Bromberg, Jan. 27, 1939; s. Erich and Emilie (Hullmann) W.; m. Christel Elisabeth Reinke, Apr. 4, 1975; 1 child, Benedikt. Diploma in mech. engring., Tech. Hochschule, Darmstadt, Germany, 1964, D in Engring., 1968, habilitation, 1985, Ausserordenlicher prof., 1991. Wissensch asst. Inst. für Flugtechnik der Technischen Hochschule, Darmstadt, 1964-68; postdoctoral staff MIT Dept. Aero. and Astronautics, Cambridge, Mass., 1969-70; scientist Inst. for Plasmaphysik der Max-Planck-Gesellschaft, Garching, Germany, 1971-75, Projektgruppe fuer Laserforschung der Max-Planck-Gesellschaft, Garching, 1976-80; sr. scientist Inst. fuer Quantenoptik der MPG, Garching, 1981-94; head of laser plasma group Inst. fuer Quantenophik der MPG, Garching, 1994—; cons. in field, Germany, 1985—. Co-author: The High-Power-Iodine Laser, 1983; co-editor Jour. Applied Physics B/Springer-V., 1990; contbr. articles to profl. jours. Mem. Deutsche Physikalische Gesellschaft. Roman Catholic. Achievements include three patents on lasers. Avocations: reading newspapers, music, tennis. Home: Sultenstrasse 10, D-85586 Poing b Muenchen Germany Office: Max-Planck-Inst fuer Quantenoptik, Hans-Kopfermann-Str 1, D-85748 Garching Germany

WITTE, OTTO WILHELM, neurologist, physiologist; b. Dorpen, Germany, Nov. 19, 1956; s. Bernhard and Elisabeth Witte; m. Ursula M. Witte, Nov. 19, 1982; children: Jan Hendrik, Christina, Robert. Med. diploma, U. Muenster, Germany, 1982, MD, 1983; habilitation, U. Duesseldorf, Germany, 1991. Rsch. asst. Dept. Physiology, U. Muenster, 1982-85; rsch. asst. Dept. Neurology, U. Duesseldorf, 1985-90, asst. prof., 1990—; head experimental neurophysiology study group, Duesseldorf, 1987—. Author: Neurophysiologie, 1992; contbr. articles to profl. jours. Recipient Gerhard Hess award German Rsch. Found., 1990, Alfred Hauptmann Epilepsie Kuratorium, 1988. Mem. German Physiol. Soc., German EEG Soc. (Kornmueller award 1989), European Neurosci. Assn., Soc. for Neurosci., Neurol. Soc., Neurosci. Soc. Office: Heinrich Heine U Dept Neurology, Moorenstr 5, D-40225 Duesseldorf Germany

WITTE-BAKKEN, JAN KAREN, clinical psychologist; b. Waynesboro, Pa., Nov. 12, 1957; d. Louis William and Margee Lee (Johnson) Witte; m. Luther P. Aadland, May 26, 1979 (div. 1991); 1 child: Alison; m. Joel T. Bakken, Aug. 16, 1991; children: Andrea, Andrew, Adam. BA in Psychology, Concordia Coll., Moorhead, Minn., 1980; MS in Clin. Psychology, N.D. State U., 1983; PhD in Clin. Psychology, U N.D., 1997. Diplomate Am. Bd. Psychol. Specialties; licensed psychologist, N.D., Minn. Behavior analyst, psychologist Grafton (N.D.) State Sch., 1983-85, psychologist, 1985-86; lectr. dept. psychology N.D. State Univ., Fargo, 1988-89; psychologist S.E. Human Svc. Ctr., Fargo, 1986-96; clin. psychologist, supr. S.E. Human Svc. Ctr., Nebr., 1996-98; psychology intern Norfolk (Nebr.) Regional Ctr., 1995-96; psychologist Lakeland Mental Health Ctr., Moorhead, 1997-2000; clin. psychologist Solutions Behavioral Healthcare Profls., Inc., 2000—; sec., bd. dirs. Great Beginnings, Moorhead; chair Region V Behavior Intervention Com., Fargo, 1996-98, Individual Justice Planning Com. Region V, Fargo, 1993-96. Contbr. articles to profl. jours., numerous paper to profl. med. confs. Bd. dirs. Gooseberry Park Players, Moorhead, 1999—. Mem. APA, Minn. Psychol. Assn., Am. Coll. Forensic Examiners, Nat. Register Health Svc. Providers in Psychology, Soc. Clin. Psychology, Am. Psychology-Law Soc. Avocations: playing organ, composing music. E-mail: jbakken3@juno.com. Office: Solutions Behav Healthcare Profls 1606 30th Ave S Moorhead MN 56560-5152 Address: RR 2 Box 6 Glyndon MN 56547-9604

WITTELS, BARNABY CAESAR, lawyer; b. Phila., Mar. 28, 1948; s. David G. and Beatrice Tanya (Graitcr) W.; m. Heidi Jo Linsk, Sept. 8, 1974 (div. Aug. 1997); children: Kate Sophie, William David; m. Mary M. Labaree, Sept. 20, 1998. BA cum laude, Temple U., 1970; MA in Pol. Sci., Boston U., 1972, JD, 1975. Bar: Pa. 1975, U.S. Dist. Ct. (ea. dist.) Pa. 1985, U.S. Ct. Appeals (2d, 3d and 4th cir.) 1986. Asst. defender Defender Assn. of Phila., 1975-80; law clk. to Hon. Stanley Kubacki Ct. Common Pleas Phila. County, 1980-84; ptnr. Wittels, Newman & Bomstein, Phila., 1980-82; assoc. LaCheen & Alva, Phila., 1982-86; ptnr. LaCheen & Assoc., Phila., 1986—. Contbr. column to newspapers. Chair Northwest Victim Svcs., Phila., 1981-84, mem. counsel, 1984-90, mem. bd. dirs., 1983-90, chair, 1997— (outstanding svc. & leadership 1990), founding mem.; com. man 21st Divsn. Dem. Party, Phila., 1985-90, various polit. and jud. campaigns, 1980—; baseball coach Chestnut Hill Fathers Club, 1985-98, commr. 1991-93, 92-98; mem. exec. com. Northwest Interfaith Movement, 1985-86. Mem. NACDL, Pa. Assn. Criminal Def. Lawyers, Phila. Bar Assn. (fee dispute com. 1996—, mem. com. to elect good judges 1987-88, Pa. Bar Assn., Phila. Bar Found. (Apothaker award 1983). Democratic. Jewish. Avocations: writing, baseball, football, reading, woodworking. Office: LaCheen & Assoc 3100 Lewis Tower Bldg Philadelphia PA 19102

WITTENBERG, JON ALBERT, accountant; b. Valparaiso, Ind., Mar. 22, 1939; s. Fred E. and Elizabeth (DeWaal) W.; m. Joann S. Zachwieja, May 13, 1967; children: Brad, Glen, Pam. BS, Ind. U., 1961. CPA, Ill. Auditor Ernst & Young, Chgo., 1961-66; fin. analyst Amoco Chems., Chgo., 1966-69; contr. Nat. Van Lines, Broadview, Ill., 1969-76, Consol. Millinerey, Chgo., 1976—. Mem. Am. Inst. CPA's, Ill. Soc. CPA's, Inst. Mgmt. Accts. Home: 1297 W New Britton Dr Hoffman Estates IL 60195-1764 Office: Consol Millinerey Co 18 S Michigan Ave Ste 605 Chicago IL 60603-3283

WITTENBERG, RALF HERMANN, orthopaedic surgeon, educator; b. Delmenhorst, Germany, Apr. 1, 1956; s. Helmut H. and Danuta (Wingert) W.; m. Ann Bailly, Oct. 1, 1988; children: Jana Michelle, Kira Annik. Student, Ruhr U., Bochum, Germany, 1978-80, MD, 1984. Cert. orthopaedic surgeon. Asst. prof. surgery U. Clinic, Bochum, 1984-87, Orthopaedic U. Clinic, Bochum, 1987-90; assoc. prof. Ruhr Univ., Bochum, 1991-96, prof., 1997—; cons. Implant Design, Germany, 1989—. Author, editor: Instrumented Spinal Fusion, 1994, Chemomucleolysis and Related Intradiscal Therapies, 1994; author: Intradiskale Therapie, 1996. Scholar German Nat. Scholarship Found., Bonn, Germany, 1980-84. Mem. Rotary Club. Avocations: hunting, bicycling, tennis. Fax: 0049 (0)2366 153899. E-mail: Ralf.Wittenberg@ruhr-uni-bochum.de. Office: St Elisabeth Hosp Herten, Ort Abteilung Im Schlosspark 12, 45699 Herten Germany

WITTENBRINK, BONIFACE LEO, priest; b. Evansville, Ill., June 30, 1914; s. Max C. and Catherine Rose (Pautler) W. PhL, Gregorian U., Rome, 1939; STL, Ottawa (Can.) U., 1943; MA, Cath. U. Am., 1947. Ordained priest Oblates of Mary Immaculate, Roman Cath. Ch., 1941. Instr. Latin, logic, history and religion St. Henry's Coll., Belleville, Ill., 1943-48; instr., registrar, prin. high sch. dept. Coll. of Our Lady of the Ozarks, Carthage, Mo., 1948-52; founding dir. King's House of Retreats, Buffalo, Minn., 1952-53; mission procurator Roman Cath. Ch., St. Paul, 1955-56, 59-62; prin. Alemany High Sch. for Boys, Oblate Western Province, San Fernando, Calif., 1956-59; permanent sec. Conf. Maj. Superiors of Men, Washington, 1963-69; exec. dir., sec. Found. for Community Creativity, Washington, 1970-71; founder, dir., then dir. devel. Radio Info. Svc. for Blind and Handicapped, Belleville, 1972-84; pres., then local dir. Friends of Eye Rsch., Boston, 1983-87; exec. v.p. Citizens for Eye Rsch., Belleville, 1987—; pres. Oblate Ednl. Assn., St. Paul, 1961-62; sci. adv. bd. Nat. Acad. Child Devel., 1984-86; mem. com. Eye Experience St. Louis, 1984; adv. bd. Welfare of the Blind, Inc., 1984—; adv. coun. svcs. for print-handicapped Nat. Pub. Radio, 1976-77; active Internat. Christian Leadership, 1968-72; bd. dirs. LOGOS Translators; ptnr. CBMI. Bd. dirs. Technoserve, 1968-72, Internat. Book Svc., 1969-72; vol. Ill. Literacy Project, 1989-90; founding charter mem., bd. dirs. Washington Workshops Found. Recipient RPI Internat. Vision award, 27th Annual Vision Awards, Agrama Harmony Gold and Light award, 2000, Beverly Hills, Calif. Mem. Madison County Assn. Blind, Mo. Coun. Blind, Am. Coun. of Blind (ednl. radio com. 1974-76), Am. Found. for Blind (radio talking book com. 1973-76), Inst. for Study of Econ. Systems (bd. dirs. 1971-72), Ednl. Communications Assn., Coun. for Dept. of Peace, Wycliffe Bible Translators Assn., Vols. for Internat. Tech. Assistance, Ill. Radio Info. Svc., Soc. Internat. Devel., UN Assn., Rotary Internat., Belleville Econ. Progress, Eagles, KC, Press Club St. Louis, Am. Assn. Ret. Persons. Avocations: reading, travel. Home: 200 N 60th St Belleville IL 62223-3951

WITTFOHT, HANS HEINRICH HERMANN, construction consultant; b. Wittingen, Germany, Nov. 26, 1924; s. Johann and Anna (Kleineberg) W.; Dipl.-Ing., Tech. Hochschule Karlsruhe, 1951, Dr.-Ing., 1963; Dr.-Ing. E.h., Tech. U. Stuttgart, 1979; m. Irma Redmann, July 29, 1950; children: Dörte, Jens. With Polensky & Zöllner Gesellschaft mbH & Co., Frankfurt am Main, Fed. Republic Germany, 1951—, dept. dir., 1959-68, mng. dir., 1968-93, ptnr., 1970-93, pres., 1980-87; pres. German Concrete Assn., 1985-91; lectr., nat. and internat. congresses. Served with tank, arty. corps. German Army, 1942-45. Decorated Iron Cross I; recipient nat. Ehrenzeichen des VDI, 1977; internat. medal FIP, 1978, 94; with Emil-Mörsch Denkmünze des Deutschen Beton-Vereins, 1981—; Golden medaille Gustave Magnel, 1984, Silver medal Ville de Paris, 1987, Kerensky medal, 1988; recipient International award of Merit Internat. Assn. for Bridge and Structural Engring., 1989, Fressinet Medaille, 1994, hon. fellow The Inst. pf Structural Engrs., 1986; also awards for bridge constrn. in nat., internat. competitions. Mem. German Concrete Soc. (hon.), Rsch. Assn. Underground Transp. Facilities (hon.), Internat. Assn. Bridge and Structural Engring. (v.p.), Fédération Internationale de la Précontrainte (hon. pres., mem. presidium). Author: Kreisfoermig gekruemmte Träger, 1964; Triumph der Spannweiten, 1972; Building Bridges, 1984; contbr. numerous articles to profl. lit. Patentee in field of bridge bldg. Home: 20 Am Kiekeberg, 22587 Hamburg Germany

WITTIG, RAYMOND SHAFFER, lawyer, technology transfer advisor; b. Allentown, Pa., Dec. 13, 1944; s. Raymond Battie and Alice (Shaffer) W.; m. Beth Glover, June 21, 1975; children: Meaghan G., Allison G. BA, Pa. State U., 1966, MEd, 1968; JD, Dickinson Sch. Law, 1974. Bar: Pa. 1974, U.S. Ct. Appeals (D.C. cir.) 1978. Rsch. psychologist Intext Corp., Scranton, Pa., 1968; minority counsel Small Bus. Com., U.S. Ho. Reps., Washington, 1975-84; pvt. practice Washington, 1984-92; tech. mgmt. group leader Geo-Ctrs., Inc., Newton Ctr., Mass., 1992—. Capt. U.S. Army, 1969-71. Mem. AAAS, ABA, Nat. Order Barristers, Tech. Transfer Soc., Fed. Lab. Consortium.

WITTIG, SIGMAR, academic administrator, researcher; b. Nimptsch, Germany, Feb. 25, 1940. MS in Engring., Technical U., Aachen, Germany, 1964, DSc, 1967; Dr (hon.), U. Thessaloniki, Greece, 1998, U. Ufa, Russia, 1999; Dr-Ing E.h, U. Darmstadt, Germany, 2000; Dr (hon.), Purdue U. Asst. Univ. Aachen, Germany, 1964-67; asst. prof. Purdue U., West LaFayette, Ind., 1967-71; assoc. prof., 1971-76; rsch. engr. part time Westinghouse Elec. Corp., 1971-76; dir., prof. U. Karlruhe, 1976—; v.p., 1989-94, pres., 1994—; v.p. German Rsch. Assn., 1989-95. Author, co-author of more than 200 articles to profl. jours. Recipient Isromac award Hawaii, 1990, Karl-Heinz Beckurts award large Rsch. Ctr., 1992, Korean Soc. Mech. Engrs.. award, 1995. Mem. Acad. Scis. Heidelberg, Leopoldina. Avocation: sports. Home: Heinrich-Weitz Str, D76228 Karlsruhe Germany Office: University of Karlsruhe, D-76128 Karlsruhe Germany

WITTING, CHRIS J., electrical manufacturing executive; b. Cranford, N.J., Apr. 7, 1915; s. Nicholas and Anne (Begasse) W.; B.S., N.Y. U., 1941; grad. Am. Inst. Banking; student Fordham Law Sch.; D.Eng. (hon.), Clarkson Coll. Tech.; m. Grace Orrok, Oct. 8, 1938 (dec. 1993); children—Leland James, Anne Kristin, Nancy Jane, Chris J.; m. Marshia K. Pullman, Nov. 15, 1997. Exec. asst. Guaranty Trust Co., 1933-36, N.Y. Trust Co., 1936-39; mgr. Price Waterhouse & Co., 1939-41; comptroller, treas. U.S.O. Camp Shows, Inc., 1941-46; mng. dir. Allen B. DuMont Labs., Inc., 1946-53; pres. Westinghouse Broadcasting Co., 1953-54, group v.p. and gen. mgr. consumer products group, Westinghouse Electric Corp., 1954-64; v.p. exec. asst. to chmn. and pres. Internat. Tel.& Tel. Corp., 1964-65; pres., chief exec. officer, dir. Crouse-Hinds Co., Syracuse, N.Y., 1965-75, chmn., chief exec. officer, 1975-82; vice chmn. bd. Cooper Industries Inc., Houston. Chmn. Pub. Auditorium Authority of Pitts. and Allegheny County, 1963-64; chmn. bd. trustees Syracuse U., 1975-93. Mem. Nat. Electric Mfrs. Assn. (chmn. bd. govs., bd. dirs.), Electronic Industries Assn. (bd. govs. 1961-62, dir. 1960-63), Nat. Planning Assn. (nat. council), Am. Mgmt. Assn. (mem. mktg. planning council), Elec. Mfrs. Club, Met. Devel. Assn. Syracuse and Onondaga County, N.Y. (dir.). Clubs: Athletic, Union League, Century, Onondaga Country, Athletic (Syracuse). Office: 518 Bradford Pky Syracuse NY 13224-1804

WITTKE, WALTER KARL, geotechnical engineer; b. Hamburg, Germany, Mar. 28, 1934. MSc, Tech. U. Hanover, 1959; PhD, U. Karlsruhe, 1962; D in Engring., U. Hannover, 1998. From rsch. asst. to assoc. prof. Tech. U. Karlsruhe, Germany, 1959-74; head inst. for geotech. engring. U. Aachen, Germany, 1974-99; pres. WBI, 1980—; vis. prof. rock mechs., Northwestern U., Evanston, Ill., 1971, Purdue U., West Lafayette, Ind., 1983. Author: Rock Mechanics: Basics for Economic Construction in Rock, 1984, Stability Analysis for Tunnels, Fundamentals, 2000, Verlag Glückauf, Essen; editor: Geotechnik in Forschung und Praxis-WBI-Print, Verlag, Glückauf, Essen. Mem. Am. Inst. Mining, Metallurgical and Petroleum Engrs. (rock mech. award 1977), Deutsche Gesellschaft fuer Geotechnik (pres.), Deutscher Ausschuss fuer Unterirdisches Bauen, Deutsches Talsperren Komitee. Office: WBI, Henricistrasse 50, 52072 Aachen Germany

WITTMAACK, RALF, physicist; b. Dortmund, Germany, June 24, 1958; s. Rolf and Margret (Kaempfert) W. Diploma, U. Hamburg, 1988; D in Engring., U. Karlsruhe, 1998. Trainee AWST, Gluckstadt, Germany, 1978-79; tchg. asst. U. Hamburg, Germany, 1983-86; physicist Siemens AG, Erlangen, Germany, 1988-99, Muelheim/Ruhr, Germany, 2000—. Avocations: theoretical physics, motorcycles, cycling, karate. Fax: 49-208-456-3376. E-mail: Ralf.wittmaack@erl11.siemens.de. Home: Sperlingstr 7, D-91056 Erlangen Germany Office: Siemens AG KWU G221T, Weisenstr 35, D-45473 Muelheim/Ruhr Germany

WITTMANN, FOLKER HELFRID, physicist, educator, consultant; b. Karlsruhe, Germany, Apr. 20, 1936; arrived in Switzerland, 1980; s. Alfred and Angela (Eder) W.; m. Xinhua Zhang, Dec. 7, 1987; children: Marc, Stephanie, Roland, Angela. Vordiplom, U. Karlsruhe, 1958; Diplom, U. Munich, 1961; PhD, U. Tech., Munich, 1964, Habilitation, 1969; DEng (hon.), U. Essen, Germany, 1998. Head bldg. materials physics lab. U. Tech., Munich, 1966-76; prof. U. Delft, The Netherlands, 1976-80, U. Tech., Lausanne, Switzerland, 1980-88, Swiss Fed. Inst. Tech., Zurich, 1988—; cons. to engring. co., 1989Ô, to govt. agys., 1988Ô; hon. adv. prof. Tsinghua U., Beijing, China, 1995Ô. Author: The Munich Model, 1976 (L'Hermite medal 1976); editor 25 sci. books; editor Internat. Jour. Restoration, 1995; contbr. more than 250 articles to profl. jours. Fellow Am. Ceramic Soc.; mem. Am. Concrete Inst.; mem. Réunion Internationale des Laboratoires d'Essais et de Recherches sur les Matériaux (past pres.), Internat. Assn. Sci. and Technology of Restoration and Protection of Monuments (hon.). Roman Catholic. Avocations: playing piano, collecting paintings. Home: Rietstr 33, 8103 Unterengstringen Switzerland Office: Swiss Fed Inst Tech, 8093 Zurich Switzerland

WITTNER, MICHAL, physiology educator; b. Karlovy Vary, Czechoslovakia, Jan. 29, 1968; parents: Vaclav and Milena (Fibichova) W. MD, Charles U., Prague, 1993. Asst. prof. Faculty Medicine 1 Charles U., Prague, 1993—; guest rschr. U. Kuopio (Finland), 1995-96. Fax: 420-2-24918816. E-mail: wittner@cesnet.cz. Home: Kurzova 2199, CZ-15500 Prague 5, Czech Republic Office: Charles U Dept Physiology, Albertov 5, CZ-12800 Prague 2, Czech Republic

WITTROCK, MERLIN CARL, educational psychologist; b. Twin Falls, Idaho, Jan. 3, 1931; s. Herman C. and Mary Ellen (Baumann) W.; m. Nancy McNulty, Apr. 3, 1953; children: Steven, Catherine, Rebecca. BS in Biology, U. Mo., Columbia, 1953, MS in Ednl. Psychology, 1956; PhD in Ednl. Psychology, U. Ill., Urbana, 1960. Prof. grad. sch. edn. UCLA, 1960—, founder Ctr. Study Evaluation, chmn. divsn. ednl. psychology, chmn. faculty, exec. com.; univ. com. on outstanding teaching; dir. math. and humanities program, 1997; co-founder Urban Tchr. Edn. Program, 1996; co-dir. Imagination Project, 1998; fellow Ctr. for Advanced Study in Behavioral Scis., 1967-68; vis. prof. U. Wis., U. Ill., Ind. U., Monash U., Australia; bd. dirs. Far West Labs., San Francisco; chmn. com. on evaluation and assessment L.A. Unified Sch. Dist.; mem. nat. adv. panel for math. scis. NRC of NAS, 1988-89; chmn. nat. bd. Nat. Ctr. for Rsch. in Math. Scis. Edn., chmn. charges com. UCLA; adv. bd. Kauffman Found., Kansas City, Mo., 1995—; bd. dirs. Western Edn. Lab. for Edn. Rsch., Far West Lab. Author, editor: The Evaluation of Instruction, 1970, Changing Education, 1973, Learning and Instruction, 1977, The Human Brain, 1977, Danish transl., 1980, Spanish transl., 1982, The Brain and Psychology, 1980, Instructional Psychology: Education and Cognitive Processes of the Brain, Neuropsychological and Cognitive Processes of Reading, 1981, Handbook of Research on Teaching, 3d edit., 1986, The Future of Educational Psychology, 1989, Research in Learning and Teaching, 1990, Testing and Cognition, 1991, Generative Science Teaching, 1994, Metacognitiion 1995, Problem-Solving Transfer, 1996. Mentor Edn. Leadership Program. Capt. USAF, 1953-55. Recipient Thorndike award for outstanding psychol. rsch., 1987, Disting. Tchr. of Univ. award UCLA, 1990, Greenfield award for rsch. in learning UCLA Grad. Sch. Edn., 1988; Ford Found. grantee. Fellow AAAS, APA (pres. divsn. ednl. psychology 1984-85, assn. coun. 1988-91, award for Outstanding Svc. to Ednl. Psychology 1991, 93, Disting. Svc. award for svc. to sci. adv. coun.), Am. Psychol. Soc., (charter fellow), Am. Ednl. Rsch. Assn. (chmn. ann. conv., chmn. publs. 1980-83, assn. coun. 1986-89, bd. dirs. 1987-89, chmn. com. on ednl. TV 1989—, Outstanding Contbns. award 1986, Outstanding Svc. award 1989), Phi Delta Kappa. Office: UCLA 3339 Moore Hl Los Angeles CA 90095-0001

WITTRUP, HANS HECHMANN, cardiologist; b. Elsinore, Denmark, Aug. 17, 1963; s. Palle and Irene (Hechmann) W.; m. Catherine Elizabeth Cox, Feb. 1, 1986; children: Nicolas, Lucas. MD, U. Copenhagen, 1992. Intern U. Copenhagen Hosp. Sys., 1992-93; resident Frederiksberg Univ. Hosp., Copenhagen, 1993-94; sr. registrar Herlev Univ. Hosp., Copenhagen, 1994—; bd. dirs. MedPro, Inc., Tingvoll, Norway, NetIntelligence Inc., Copenhagen. Mem. Am. Heart Assn. Lutheran. Avocations: tennis, windsurfing, golf. Home: 73 Gammel Strandvej, DK-3050 Humlebaek Denmark Office: Herlev U Hosp Dept Biochem, 75 Herlev Ringvej, DK-2730 Herlev Denmark

WITTSTADT, THOMAS PETER, economic expert, media specialist, entrepreneur; b. Muenster, Wetphalia, Germany, Sept. 21, 1967; s. Klaus and Brigitte (Effmert) W. BA, U. Münster, Germany, 1989; student, U. Münster, 1987-90. Ptnr. Pan Logon, Münster, 1993-2000; initiator Ecclesia Pro Albania, 1993—; ptnr. Kastrioti Co., Tirana, Albania, 1993—, Media Forum, Munich, 1994; chief adv. Internat. Hilfsfonds, Brussels, 1993-2000; cons. chrome industry Govt. Albania, 1993, Teled Internat., Virginia Beach, 1994-99, various East European, African Govts.; mng. dir. Universal Tolerance Düsseldorf, 1995-96, Welthilfe e.V., Münster, 1994-99; founding mem. German-Albanian Econ. Soc. (DAW), 1995; CEO, ptnr. Highlight GmbH, Münster, 1995—; head task force Green African Bank, Johannesburg, 1995—; initiator Green Cross Germany, 1997; ptnr. Resource Devel. Internat., 1997—; rep. Germany Robinco Mining, 1998—; gen. mgr. Hazy Investments GmbH, 1998—; ptnr., gen. mgr. Airgomomics GmbH, 1998—, rep. Germany Lev. Co., 2000—; ptnr., gen. mgr. Mediax GmbH, 2000—. Author (TV program) German TV, Australian TV; contbr. ariticles to popular publs. Roman Catholic. Avocations: travel, reading. Office: Personal Office, Angelstrasse 22, D-48167 Münster Germany

WITTSTOCK, GUNTHER JÜRGEN ULLRICH, chemist, researcher; b. Schwerin, Germany, Sept. 12, 1965; s. Gerhard Joachim and Jutta Agnes Gertrud (Preuss) W.; m. Marion Schaefer, Mar. 2, 1998; 1 child, Alena W. Diploma in chemistry, U. Leipzig, Germany, 1991, PhD, 1994. Sci. coworker Tech. U., Munich, 1994; sci. co-worker U. Leipzig, 1994-96, sci. asst., 1996—; rsch. asst. U. Cin., 1992, rsch. asst., 1993; guest rschr. Tech. U., Munich, 1995, 96, 97. Contbr. articles to profl. jours. Grantee German Nat. Scholarship Found., 1991, A.V. Humboldt Found., 1995. Mem. Soc. German Chemists (Fachgruppenpreis 1996). Office: U Leipzig W Ostwald Inst, Phys Chem Linnéstr 2, D-04103 Leipzig Germany

WITTY, CHRISTINE (CHRIS WITTY), speed skater; b. West Allis, Wis., June 23, 1975. Student, Carroll Coll. Speed skater, 1985—; mem. U.S. nat. team, 1988—. Recipient 1000 meter Silver medal Olympic Games, Nagano, Japan, 1998, 1500 meter Bronze medal, 1998; finished 2nd U.S. Olympic Team Trials, 2000. Avocations: cycling, movies, mountain biking. Fax: (719) 578-4628 and (719) 578-4596. Home: PO Box 564 Park City UT 84060-0564*

WITTY, THOMAS EZEKIEL, III, psychologist, researcher; b. Greensboro, N.C., Oct. 11, 1955; s. Thomas Ezekiel Jr. and Peggy (Coggins) W.; m. Ginger Lynell Kissee, June 28, 1997; 1 child, Ezekiel Thomas. BA in English, U. N.C., Greensboro, 1980; MS, Va. Commonwealth U., 1989; PhD, U. Mo., 1995. Lic. psychologist, Mo.; lic. health svcs. provider, Mo. Tchr. secondary English, debate and cross-country coach Henry County Pub. Schs., Collinsville, Va., 1981-87; fin. aid. counselor asst. Va. Commonwealth U., Richmond, 1987-89; substance abuse counselor Dist. 19 Alcoholism Svcs., Petersburg, Va., 1990; grad. rsch. asst. U. Mo., Columbia, 1990-94, grad. instr., 1992-94; postdoctoral fellow Rusk Rehab. Ctr., Columbia, 1995-98; clin. asst. prof., chief psychology Mo. Rehab. Ctr., Mt. Vernon, 1998—; rsch. cons. Coun. on Rehab. Edn., Inc., Champaign, Ill., 1991; ad hoc reviewer Jour. Rehab. Psychology, 1995—; internship selection com. U. Mo. Health Svcs. Consortium, Columbia, 1996—. Contbr. articles to profl. jours. NIH postdoctoral fellow in rehab. rsch., 1995-98, Walter Scott Monroe rsch. fellow U. Mo., 1992-95; rsch. grantee U. Mo. Rsch. Bd., 1997. Mem. APA (divsn. 17, 22, 38, 50, program rev. com. divsn. 22 1996—, Student Rsch. Travel award 1994), Mo. Psychol. Assn., Am. Pain Soc., Nat. Rehab. Counseling Assn., Sierra Club, KC, Kappa Delta Pi. Democrat. Roman Catholic. Avocations: running, swimming, cycling, hiking, camping. Office: Mo Rehab Ctr Dept PM&R/Psychology Svcs 600 N Main St Mount Vernon MO 65712-1004 Home: 616 Main Mount Vernon MO 65712

WITZEL, LOTHAR GUSTAV, physician, gastroenterologist; b. Mannheim, Fed. Republic Germany, July 27, 1939; s. Gustav and Martha (Pilger) W. MD, U. Freiburg, Fed. Republic of Germany, 1965; PhD, U. Berlin,

1983. Substitute medicine supt. U. Bern (Switzerland) Med. Sch., 1973-77; dir., med. supt. German Red Cross Hosp., Berlin, 1978-93. Contbr. articles to profl. jours.; patentee in field. Mem. Indian Soc. Gastroenterology (hon.), European Congress Endoscopy (sec. gen. 1981), Swiss Soc. Gastroenterology (corr. mem. 1989, Award of Gastroenterology 1981). Avocation: jazz music. Office: Koloniestrasse 21, 13359 Berlin Germany

WIZARD, BRIAN, publisher, author; b. Newburyport, Mass., June 24, 1949; s. Russell and Ruth (Hidden) Willard. BA, Sonoma (Calif.) State U., 1976; D of Metaphysics, Universal Life Ch., 1997. Ordained to ministry Universal Life Ch., 1997. Pvt. practice as jeweler, sculptor and craftsman Calif., 1974-79; Wallowa, Oreg., 1991—; prin. The Starquill Pub., Port Douglas, Queensland, Australia, 1981-86; owner Starquill Internat., Wallowa, Oreg. Author: (trilogy) The Will He Make it Saga (nominee Pulitzer prize), Permission to Kill, 1985, Permission to Live, 1992, Back in the World, 1995; (novels) Shindara, 1990, Heaven on Earth, 1998, Coming of Age, 1990, Pollution IV, 1993, Nigerian 419 Scam "Game Over!", 2000; (short stories) Tropical Pair, 1986, Metempsychosis, 1988 (In Search of) The Silver Lining, 1994, The Moon Whistling By on a Cloud, 1994, (The Princess of the) Wildflowers, 1995, Mushroom Magic, 1996, Vietnam 1999! Make Friends Not War; contbr. to Smithsonian Inst.'s The Vietnam War Generation; contbr. to SpaceArc; prodr. (video documentary) Thunderhawks, 1987, Swift Action Newsteam, Tope Creek Lookout, 1995; songwriter, prodr. (cassette) Brian Wizard Sings for His Supper, 1989 (cert. of achievement Billboard 1993); songwriter, singer, prodr. (I Don't Want) Permission to Kill, 1989, Busker's Theme Song, Living in North Queensland, Circus Act, Hitch Hiking Man, Self-Portrait, The Love We Share Will Never End, 1994, Never Met a Girl Like You, Folk-Rock Opera: A Cover Story: After That Ugly Saloon Incident; contbr. to America's Finest Songwriter and Lyricists CD, 1997, (novels, video and music) Brian Wizard's 20th Century Anthology, 1998 (nominee Nobel Prize in Lit. 2000), (video) Vietnam '99, Make Friends Not War, 1999; contbr. to TV documentary History of the Machine Gun, 2000. Renovator hist. landmark The Tope Creek Lookout (Skyship); mem. Nat. Hist. Lookout Register; sponsor Adopt A Hwy., 1995; min. Universal Life Ch. With U.S. Army, 1967-70. Decorated Air medals (26), Aviator Flight Wings; recipient Cert. of Appreciation, Pres. Richard M. Nixon. Mem. Vietnam Helicopter Crewmember Assn., 145th Combat Aviation Bn. Assn., Vietnam Combat Vets. Assn., Vietnam Vets. Am., Vietnam Vets. Australia Assn. E-mail: bwizard@eoni.com. Office: PO Box 42 Wallowa OR 97885-0042

WLOSOK, ANTONIE ELISABETH, classics educator; b. Rokietnica, Poland, Nov. 17, 1930; d. Vinzenz and Elisabeth (Meister) W. PhD, U. Heidelberg, Germany, 1958, Habilitation, 1964. Asst. scholar U. Heidelberg, 1958-64, lectr., 1964-67; prof. ordinarius, dir. inst. U. Kiel, Germany, 1968-73; full prof. classics U. Mainz, Germany, 1974—. Author: Lactantius and Gnosis, 1961, Venus in Vergil's Aeneid, 1967, On Human and Divine Things (Collected Acad. Papers), 1990; editor: Roman Imperial Cult, 1978; co-editor: Augustinus-Lexikon, 1986—. Mem. Inst. for Advanced Study, Princeton, N.J., 1972-73. Mem. Heidelberg Acad. Sci. Home: Elsa Braendstroem Str 19, 55124 Mainz Germany Office: Saarstr 21, Johannes Gutenberg U, 55099 Mainz Germany

WOBUS, ULRICH, biology researcher; b. Niesky, Germany, Mar. 5, 1942; s. Ernst and Gertrud (Posselt) W.; m. Anna Magdalene Knietsch, May 17, 1970; children: Christiane, Friedemann. Diploma, Humboldt U., Berlin, 1965, PhD, 1969. Rschr. Inst. Crop Plant Rsch., Gatersleben, Germany, 1966-82; sr. scientist Inst. Genetics and Crop Plant Rsch., Gatersleben, Germany, 1982-86, group leader, 1986-90, dept. head, 1990—; acting dir. Inst. Plant Genetics and Crop Plant Rsch., Gatersleben, 1992—; prof. genetics Halle U., 1994—. Author: Isolation...of Nucleic Acids, 1981, others; contbr. articles to profl. jours. Recipient Leibniz-Preis, GDR Acad. Scis., 1974, Friedrich-medal, 1984. Mem. Deutsche Akademie der Naturforscher LEOPLODINA, Berlin-Brandenburgische Acad. der Wissenschaften, Nordrhein-Westfal Acad. Wissenschaften. Home: Liebigweg 7, D-06466 Gatersleben Germany Office: Inst Plant Genetics & Crop Plant Rsch, Corrensstr 3, D-06466 Gatersleben Germany

WÖCKEL, WERNER FRIEDRICH, pathologist; b. Langenwetzendorf, Thuringia, Germany, Mar. 2, 1930; s. Friedrich Ernst and Liesbeth Maria (Rothe) W.; m. Edith Ingrid Prestin, Aug. 8, 1952; children: Klaus, Dietrich. Student, F. Schiller U., Jena, German Dem. Repub., 1948-54; MD, Med. Acad., Erfurt, German Dem. Repub., 1957; D in Med. Habilitation, Med. Acad., Erfurt, 1965. Vice dir. Inst. Pathology of the Med. Acad., Erfurt, 1964-84, Inst. Pathology of the U. Saarland, Homburg, Saar, Fed. Republic of Germany, 1984-86; med. supt. Inst. Pathology Cen. Hosp. of the Land Ins. Instn. High Bavaria, Gauting, Fed. Republic of Germany, 1987-95; prof. medicine Univ. of the Saarland, Homburg, 1985. Author: Non-Chromaffine Paragangliomas, 1969; contbr. articles to profl. jours. Mem. German Assn. Pathology. Home: 30 Hans-Fitz-Weg, D-81476 Munich Germany Office: Asklepios-Fachkliniken, Robert Koch Allee 2, 82131 Gauting Germany

WODE, HENNING, education educator; b. Elmshorn, Schleswig, Holstein, Germany, Feb. 19, 1937; s. Heinrich and Johanna (Erhorn) W.; m. Barbara Fuchs, Sept. 26, 1965; children: Heiko, Birgit, Lars, Inga. Staatsexamen, Freiburg U., 1962, PhD, 1965, Habilitation, 1968. Prof. Kiel U., Germany, 1969—. Author: Linguistische Untersuchungen zum Parkinsonismus, 1970, Learning a Second Language, Vol. 1, 1981, Einführung in die Psycholinguistik, 1988, Bilinguale Unterrichtserprobung in Schleswig-Holstein, 1994, Lernen in der Fremdsprache: Grundzüge von Immersion und bilingualem Unterricht, 1995. Chmn. Amerika Gesellschaft Schlewig-Holstein, 1993. Mem. Deutscher Anglisten Verband,, Gesellschaft fuer Angewandte Linguistik, Soc. Linguistica Europea, Deutsche Gesellschaft für Freudsprachenforschung, Gesellschaft für Kanada-Studien, European Inst. Immersion Tchg. (founder). Avocations: tennis, skiing, biking. Home: Am Reff 2, 24226 Heikendorf Germany Office: Kiel Univ English Dept, Olshausenstrasse 40-60, 24098 Kiel Germany

WODNIECKI, PAWEL, physicist, researcher; b. Cracow, Poland, Jan. 20, 1946; s. Joseph and Sophia (Lipska) W.; m. Krystyna Kamińska, June 6, 1970 (dec. Aug. 1970); m. Barbara Ingarden, May 8, 1977; 1 child, Katarzyna. M in Physics, degree in elec. engring., Acad. Mine and Metallurgy, Cracow, 1969; D in Physics, Inst. Nuc. Physics, Cracow, 1984. Engr. Inst. Nuc. Physics, Cracow, 1969-70, asst., 1970-81, 83-84; asst. II Physikalisches Inst., Göttingen, Germany, 1981-83; asst. prof. Inst. Nuc. Physics, Göttingen, 1984—; mem. internat. adv. com. Hyperfine Interaction Conf., 1997. Contbr. articles to jours. in field. Mem. Solidarity trade union, 1980—. Grantee Polish Com. Sci. Rsch., 1994-97, 2000—. Roman Catholic. Avocations: skiing, sailing, touring, hiking, photography. Home: Wielopole 6/3, PL-31072 Cracow Poland Office: Inst Nuc Physics, Radzikowskiego 152, PL31-342 Cracow Poland

WODRASCHKE, GEORG STEPHAN, communications educator; b. Bratislava, Slovakia, May 11, 1934; s. Peter and Maria (Schreiter) W.; m. Angela Hanke; children: Stephan, Ann-Kathrin, Susann-Marie, Tim, Susan. PhD, U. Munich, 1964. Prof. Pedagogical U., Freiburg, Germany, 1968-99. Recipient Cross Federal Rep. Germany, 1994, Gold medal Caritas Soc., 1994. Mem. Deutsche Gesellschaft Erziehungswissenschaft, Deutsche Gesellschaft Publiztik and Kommunikationswissenschaft. Home: Am Forsthaus 5, D-87490 Börwang Germany

WODZINSKI, PIOTR, mechanical engineering educator, researcher; b. Pabianice, Poland, June 29, 1946; 1; s. Wacław and Julita (Pawelczyk) W.; m. Hanna Wodzinski, Jan. 10, 1976; 1 child, Jagoda. BSc, Tech. U. Lodz, Poland, 1965, PhD, 1975, DSc, 1982; MSc, Moscow Tech. Inst., 1968. Cert. process engr. Rschr. Moscow Tech. Inst., 1966-68; sr. asst. Tech. U. Lodz, Poland, 1968-75, lectr., 1975-85, assoc. prof., 1985-91, prof., 1991—. Author papers. Home: Kochanowski 3/9-31, 95-200 Pabianice Poland Office: Tech Univ Lodz, Zwirki 36, 90-924 Łódź Poland

WOELFEL, ROBERT WILLIAM, broadcast executive, mayor; b. L.A., Nov. 5, 1944; s. William Herman and Mary Jane (Hiatt) W. AA, Mt. San Antonio Coll., 1965; BS in Bus., Calif. State U., L.A., 1969; MBA, U. So. Calif., 1972. Salesman Burroughs Corp., El Monte, Calif., 1969-71; sales mgr., announcer Sta. KMFB/KPMO, Mendocino, Calif., 1973-81; gen. mgr. Sta. KOZT, Ft. Bragg, 1981-85, Sta. KBLC, Lakeport, Calif., 1984-85; v.p., sales mgr. Sta. KZOZ/KKAL, San Luis Obispo, Calif., 1985-86; corp. gen. mgr. Visionary Radio Euphonics, Santa Rosa, Calif., 1986-87; dir. mktg., gen. sales mgr. Sta. KUBA/KXEX, Yuba City, Calif., 1987-88; gen. mgr. Sta. KMRJ, Ukiah, Calif., 1988-91; prin. ptnr. Electoral Target Advt., 1988-91; broadcast cons. Lahaina, Hawaii, Hamilton, New Zealand, Hobart, Tasmania, 1991-93; gen. mgr. radio divsn. Mendocino Broadcasting Co., 1993—; instr. advt. and mktg. community coll.; bd. dirs. Mendocino Soda Pop Co. Appeared in film Racing with the Moon, 1984. Advt. cons., vice mayor City of Ft. Bragg, 1982-84, mayor, 1984-85; mem. City Coun., 1979-85; v.p. bd. dirs. Mendocino Coast Ednl. TV Assn., 1983-85; Ft. Bragg planning commr., 1996—; mem. Coll. of the Redwoods Endowment Bd., 1996—. With USN, 1966-68. Mem. Ukiah C. of C. (bd. dirs. 1990-91). Home: PO Box 2538 Mendocino CA 95460-2538

WOELFLE, PETER KLAUS, physicist, educator; b. Munich, Germany, Mar. 24, 1942; s. Luitpold and Maria (Wirth) W.; m. Ursula M. Gergler, July 24, 1969; children: Andrea, Stephanie, Rebecca. Dipl. Physics, Tech. U., Munich, Germany, 1966, Dr. rer. nat., 1969, Dr. habil., 1974. Postdoctoral researcher Max-Planck Inst. Physik, Munich, Germany, 1969-71, 73-75, Cornell U., Ithaca, N.Y., 1971-73; asst. prof. Tech. U., Munich, 1975-78, assoc. prof., 1978-86; prof. U. Fla., Gainesville, 1986-89, U. Karlsruhe, Germany, 1989—. Author: Superfluid Phases of Helium 3, 1990; contbr. over 100 articles to profl. jours.; mem. editl. bd. Springer Tracts in Modern Physics, Jour. Low Temperature Physics, Jour. Physics C, Phys. Rev. Letters. Recipient Physics prize Goettingen Acad. Scis., 1975. Fellow Inst. Physics (London); mem. German Phys. Soc., Am. Phys. Soc. Roman Catholic.

WOELK, KLAUS HUBERT, chemist; b. Aachen, Germany, Aug. 25, 1961; s. Günther Egbert Valerian and Marianne Luzia (Schnaas) W.; m. Madonna Lynn Bychowski, Sept. 24, 1994; children: Marlena Elisabeth, Christina Nicole. PhD, U. Bonn (Germany), 1991. Diplomate physical chemistry. Postdoctoral fellow Argonne (Ill.) Nat. Lab., 1992-94; asst. lectr. U. Bonn, 1994-99, assoc. lectr., 1999—; vis. scientist Argonne Nat. Lab., 1995, 97, 98, 99. Inventor: Toroid Cavity Imager, 1992 (R & D 100 award 1994). Mem. Catholic Student Soc. Ripuaria CV, Bonn, 1980—, Soc. of Friends and Patrons of the U. Bonn (Geffrub), 1994—, Alumni Konrad-Adenauer Found., St. Augustin, Germany, 1992—. Grantee Konrad-Adenauer-Fellowship, 1989-91. Mem. Soc. of German Chemists. Roman Catholic. Avocations: craftsmanship, biking, sailing. Office: U. Bonn Inst. Phys. Chem., Wegelerstr 12, 53115 Bonn 1, Germany

WOELKERLING, WILLIAM JAMES, botanist, educator; b. Milw., Dec. 2, 1941; arrived in Australia, 1966; m. Jean Marie Jungton, Apr. 17, 1965; children: Mark, Eric. BSc, U. Wis., Milw., 1964, MSc, 1966; PhD, U. Adelaide, Australia, 1969, DSc, 1986. NSF postdoctoral rsch. fellow Marine Biol. Lab., Woods Hole, Mass., 1969-71; asst. prof. botany U. Wis., Madison, 1971-76; lectr. botany La Trobe U., Melbourne, Australia, 1976-77; sr. lectr. botany La Trobe U., Melbourne, 1977-83, reader/assoc. prof. botany, 1983—; mem. com. on algae Internat. Assn. Plant Taxonomists, 1981—; co-conveneer Third Internat. Phycological Congress, Melbourne, 1988; chair organizing com. Internat. Phycological Congresses, China, 1994, The Netherlands, 1997. Author: M.H. Foslie and the Corallinaceae, 1984, The Coralline Red Algae, 1998 (Gerald W. Prescott award Phycological Soc. Am., 1989), Collections of Corallinales (Rhodophyta) in the Foslie Herbarium, 1991, (with D. Lamy) Non-geniculate Coralline Red Algae and the Paris Museum: Systematics and Scientific History, 1998; editor Phycologia, 1983-89 (with B. de Reviers) Cryptogamie, Algologie, 1998—; bd. mem. CSIRO Australian Jours. Sci. Rsch., 1994-99; mem. adv. com. Australian Systematic Botany Jour., 1991-99, chair, 1994-99; contbr. articles to profl. jours. Mem. Internat. Phycological Soc. (hon. life, v.p./pres.-elect 1998-99, pres. 2000—), Brit. Phycological Soc., Korea Soc. Phycology, Seaweed Rsch. and Utilization Assn. India. Fax: 61-3-94-79-11-88. E-mail: W.Woelkerling@latrobe.edu.au. Home: 84 Spencer Rd, Woodend VIC 3442, Australia Office: Dept Botany La Trobe Univ, Kingsbury Dr, Bundoora VIC 3083, Australia

WOESSNER, MARK MATTHIAS, business executive; b. Berlin, Oct. 14, 1938; married; 2 children. D Engring., Studium TH, Karlsruhe, Germany. Mgmt. asst. Bertelsmann AG, Gütersloh, Germany, 1968-72, mem. exec. bd., pres. printing and mfg. divsn., 1976-83, pres., CEO, 1983-98, chair supervisory bd., 1998—; tech. mgr. Mohndruck Printing Co., 1972-74, CEO, 1974-76; chair exec. bd. Bertelsmann Found., 1998—. Office: Bertelsmann Stiftung, Carl-Bertelsmann-Str 256, 33311 Gütersloh Germany

WOESTE, ALBRECHT HUGO, chemistry company executive; b. Dusseldorf, Germany, Oct. 30, 1935; married; 4 children. Diploma, Tech. U. Berlin, 1961. Head prodn. and tech. R. Woeste & Co., Dusseldorf, 1963-73; mem. supervisory bd. Henkel KGaA, Dusseldorf, 1973-75, mem. shareholder's com., 1975; sole shareholder, chmn. mgmt. bd. R. Woeste & Co., Dusseldorf, 1976-78; mng. dir. Rochusclub Tournament GmbH, Dusseldorf, 1978-88; vice chmn. shareholder's com., mem. supervisory bd. Henkel KGaA, Dusseldorf, 1988-90, chmn. supervisory bd. and shareholders' com., 1990—; mem. adv. bd. Allianz Lebensverischerung, AG, Stuttgart, Deutsche Bank AG, Frankfurt; mem. bd. dirs. Ecolab Inc., St. Paul; mem. internat. adv. bd. IESE, U. Navarra, Barcelona, Spain. Mem. Dusseldorf Chamber Industry and Commerce (pres.), Rochus Tennis club (past chmn. bd.), Rotary Club, Dusseldorf Horse Racing Club, Dusseldorf C. of C. (mem. gen. assembly, pres.), Industry Club (bd. mem.), German Foundry Assn. (coun. mem. Ductile Iron br.), Dusseldorf Dist. Iron Metal Industry Assn. (chmn.), others. Avocations: forestry, hunting, hiking, tennis. Office: Henkel KGaA, Henkel Strasse 67, 40191 Düsseldorf Germany*

WOESTMANN, HERIBERT, theologian, university administrator; b. Recklinghausen, Germany, July 21, 1942; s. Antonius and Johanna (Münch) W.; m. Marianne Deppe, Aug. 2, 1969; children: Johannes, Markus, Burkhard, Barbara-Maria. Diploma in Theology, U. Münster, Germany, 1967; Asst. Master Secondary Sch., Tchrs. Tng. Sem., Münster, 1972. Asst. U. Münster, 1967-71; tchr. trainee Sem. Münster, 1971-72; lectr. Tchr. Tng. Coll., Münster, 1972-79; lectr. U. Münster, 1980-92, acad. dir., 1992—; dir. Ctr. Sci. and Practice, Münster, 1992—. E-mail: woestmann@uni-muenster.de. Home: Schleiderweg 9, D-48249 Dülmen Germany Office: U Münster, Schlossplatz 2, D-48149 Münster NRW, Germany

WOGAMAN, GEORGE ELSWORTH, insurance executive, financial consultant; b. Mikado, Mich., May 29, 1937; s. Edgar R. and Leah Katherine (McGuire) W.; m. Sandra Lee Jensen, Apr. 10, 1965; children: Jennifer, Christopher. Grad. various ins. courses. CLU; ChFC. With Blair Transit Co., Dun & Bradstreet, Chrysler Engring. Co., 1955-61; exec. chef Westward Ho!, 1961-68; owner, mgr. George Wogaman Ins. Agy., Grand Forks, N.D., 1969—; mem. pres. coun. Farmers Ins. Group, 1988; alderman East Grand Forks (Minn.) City Coun., 1979-00, v.p., 1982-00. Corp. mem. United Hosp., Grand Forks, 1982—; mem. Nat. Rep. Congl. Com., Rep. Presdl. Task Force; mem. Red River Valley Estate Planning Coun.; mem. Wesley United Meth. Ch., Grand Forks. Recipient Pub. Svc. award East Grand Forks City Coun., 1979. Mem. Am. Soc. CLU's, North Valley Life Underwriters Assn. (Life Underwriter of Yr. 1988), Farmers Ins. Group Pres.'s Coun. Home: 1703 20th St NW East Grand Forks MN 56721-1013 Office: 2612 Gateway Dr Grand Forks ND 58203-1406

WOIE, MAREN, social worker educator, consultant; b. Arendal, Norway, Sept. 30, 1924; d. Lars Theodor and Borghild (Floistad) W. BS, Concordia Coll., Moorhead, Minn., 1964; MS, U. Wis., Madison, 1966. Lectr. Sch. Social Work, Stavanger, Norway, 1966-74; prof. U. Trondheim, Norway, 1974-91; mem. Coun. of Social Work Edn., Oslo, Norway, 1967-80; dir. Grad. Sch. Social Work, Trondheim, Norway, 1979-82, 84-87. Mem. Church Coun., Trondheim, 1976-82; pres. Ctr. for Elderly, Arendal, Norway, 1993—. Recipient Travelling grant European Coun., 1974; Fulbright Assn., 1983-84. Avocation: voluntary work with elderly. Home: Noroddvein 66, 4800 Arendal Norway

WOIKE, LYNNE ANN, computer scientist; b. Torrance, Calif., Oct. 20, 1960; d. Stephen J. and Virginia (Ursich) Shane; m. Thomas W. Woike, Feb. 13, 1988; 1 child, Karla. BSc in Computer Sci. cum laude, Calif. State U., Dominguez Hills, 1994. Computer cons. Unocal Oil Co., Wilmington, Calif., 1992-94; x-window/motif software developer Logican Inc., San Pedro, Calif., 1994-95; reticle engr. TRW, Inc., Redondo Beach, Calif., 1982-88, sr. mem. tech. staff product data mgmt. database adminstr., 1995-98, chmn. product data mgmt. change control bd., 1995—; staff engr. TRW, Inc., Redondo Beach, 1999-99, sr. Unix/NT system adminstr., 1999; tech. lead, subscriber database DIRECTV, Inc., El Segundo, Calif., 1999—. Mem. IEEE, IEEE Computer Sci., Assn. for Computing Machinery (chmn. student chpt. 1993-94), Calif. State U. Sci. Soc. (computer sci. rep. 1993-95). Office: DIRECTV Inc 200 N Sepulveda Blvd El Segundo CA 90245-4340

WOINAROSCHY, ALEXANDRU ELIGIU, engineering educator, researcher; b. Bucharest, Romania, Aug. 29, 1947; s. Alexandru and Valeria (Georgescu) W.; m. Tanta Woinaroschy David, Dec. 8, 1972; 1 child, Kristina. Degree in chem. engring., Politechnica U. Bucharest, 1970, PhD, 1985. Design engr. Iprosin, Bucharest, 1970-73; sys. engr. Computer Ctr. Romanian Chem. Industry, Bucharest, 1973-74; assoc. asst. Politechnica U. Bucharest, 1970-74, asst., 1980-90, assoc. prof., 1990-94, prof., 1994—, mem. faculty coun., 1996—; mem. adminstrn. bd. Colorom, S.A., Codlea, Romania, 1999. Co-author: Optimization of Chemical Engineering Processes, 1978, Applications to Optimization of Chemical Engineering Processes, 1990, System Engineering and Chemical Process Optimization, 1983, Applications to Chemical Reactors Design, 1984. Recipient Nicolae Teclu award Romanian Acad., 1996. Mem. Romanian Soc. Chem. Engring. (v.p. 1995—). Avocations: computers, skiing, mountain trips, travel. E-mail: a woinaroschy@chim.upb.ro. Office: Politechnica U Bucharest, Str Polizu NR 1-5, 78126 Bucharest Romania

WOJCIECHOWICZ, BOLESLAW, machinery educator; b. Postawy, Poland, Jan. 2, 1927; s. Bronislaw and Anna (Osinska) W.; m. Irena Wolk-Karaczewska, Dec. 2, 1950; children: Joanna, Dorota. BSc in Engring., Poznan U. Tech., Poland, 1950; Dsc in Engring., U. Tech., Cracow, 1962; Post Doctoral Degree, Cracow U. Tech., 1968. Asst. prof. Poznan U. Tch., 1950-68, assoc. prof., 1968-72, prof., 1972—, vice rector, 1969-72, rector, 1972-81; head Inst. Machines, Poznan, 1972-90; cons. in field. Contbr. numerous articles to sci. publs. Recipient Commandor Cross Polonia Restituta Warsaw Pres. Rep. Poland, 1990. Mem. Poznan Assn. Science Funs, Polish Tribological Assn., Assn. Polish Mech. Engrs. Roman Catholic. Avocations: tourism, fishing, spending time with grandsons. Home: Bonin 16/10, 60-658 Poznań Poland Office: Poznań U Tech, 5 Maria Sklodowska Sq, 60-965 Poznań Poland

WOJCIECHOWSKI, JACEK M., electrical engineering educator; b. Karczew, Poland, Dec. 24, 1942; s. Roman and Zofia (Maruszewska) W.; m. Halina E. Lenartowicz, Aug. 30, 1969; children: Olga, Zofia, Anna. MS in Electronics, Warsaw U. Tech., 1966; MS in Mathematics, U. Warsaw, 1974; PhD with honors, Warsaw U. Tech., 1976, DSc in Habilitation, 1989. Rsch. engr. Inst. Elec. Computers, Warsaw, 1966-70; from asst. prof. to prof. Warsaw U. Tech., 1970—; post-doctoral fellow McMaster U., Hamilton, Canada, 1981-83; visiting assoc. prof. Wash. State U., Pullman, 1984-86; visiting prof. U. Waterloo, Canada, 1990-91; cons. Wydawnictwo Komunikacji i Lacznosci, Warsaw, 1994—, Inst. Français du Pétrole, 1996—; mem. Sup. Coun. Gdansk (Poland) Refinery, 1991-95; chmn. Supv. Coun. Byfuch, Poland, 1996-98. Author (with others) Topological Analysis of Electrical Networks, 1983, Bicycle, 1985. Recipient Nat. Com. for Sci. and Tech. award, 1968, award Ministry Higher Edn., 1984-90. Mem. IEEE, Inst. Radioelectronics (head radiocomm. group). Office: Inst RadElec Warsaw U Tech, Nowowiejska 15/19, 00-665 Warsaw Poland

WOJCIECHOWSKI, PIOTR KAZIMIERZ, pediatric surgeon; b. Poznan, Poland, Oct. 16, 1959; s. Kazimierz and Aleksandra Paulus W.; m. Katarzyna Maria Adamska, July 19, 1991; children: Maria, Zosia. Doctor, Med. Acad. Poznan, Poland, 1984; MD, Jagiellonian U., Cracow, Poland, 1993. FRCS Edinburgh. House officer Szpital Miejski im J. Strusia, Poznan, 1984-85; resident Szpital Dziecięcy im. Sw. Jozefa, Poznan, 1985-88, asst., 1988-89; asst. Jagiellonian U. Cracow/Polish-Am. Inst. Pediatrics, 1989-97, sr. lectr., 1997—; chief of pediat. surgery Faculty of Medicine, Cracow, 1996—; v.p. Liver Assn., Cracow, 1990—. Co-author: Management of Esophageal Atresia, 1990, Functional Diseases of Desophageal Atresia, 1991, Important Problems in Paediatric Surgery, 1998, Pediatric Surgery-Operative Book, 1999, also others. Mem. Polish Assn. Pediat. Surgeons, Brit. Assn. Pediat. Surgeon, Asian Assn. Pediat. Surgeons. Mem. Polish Conservative Party. Roman Catholic. Avocations: gardening, skiing, tennis, sailing, cycling. Home: Sabały 55, PL-31479 Cracow 73, Poland Office: Polish-Am Inst Pediatrics, Wielicka 265 Fac Medicine, PL-30663 Cracow Poland

WOJCIECHOWSKI, RYSZARD JOZEF, physicist; b. Sroda, Poland, Jan. 17, 1952; s. Witold and Stanislawa (Czernak) W.; m. Ewa Elzbieta Jankowska, Apr. 21, 1952; children: Juliusz, Grzegorz. MSc, A. Mickiewicz U., 1976, PhD, 1983. From asst. to prof. A. Mickiewicz U., Poznan, Poland, 1976—. Grantee Sci. & Engring. Rsch. Coun., Sheffield, U.K., 1990. Avocations: mountain tourism, music. Home: Os Rusa 46, 61-245 Poznan Russia

WOJCIK, CASS, decorative supply company executive, former city official; b. Rochester, N.Y., Dec. 3, 1920; s. Emil M. and Casimira C. (Krawiecz) W.; student Lawrence Inst. Tech., 1941-43, Yale U., 1943-44, U.S. Sch. for European Personnel, Czechoslovakia, 1945; m. Lilliam Leocadia Lendzion, Sept. 25, 1948; 1 child, Robert Cass. Owner, Nat. Florists Supply Co., Detroit, 1948-88, Nat. Decorative, Detroit, 1950-89; co-owner Creation Ctr., Detroit, 1955-60; cons.-contractor hort.-bot. design auto show displays, TV prodrs., designers and decorators. Mem. Regional Planning and Evaluation Coun., 1969-75; city-wide mem. Detroit Bd. Edn., 1970-75; commr. Detroit Public Schs. Employees Retirement Commn., until 1975; mem. Area Occupl. Ednl. Commn., Ednl. Task Force; chmn., grand marshal Ann. Gen. Pulaski Day Parade, Detroit, 1970, 71; mem. Friends of Belle Isle; mem. Nat. Arboretum Adv. Coun., U.S. Dept. Agr., 1982-83; mem. pastoral coun. Archidiocese of Detroit, 1983-86, 88-92; v.p. rsch. Barna Coll., Ft. Lauderdale, Fla., 1989-94; vice chmn. 13th Congl. Dist. Rep. Party Mich., 1987-91; elected to 1988 electoral coll. With U.S. Army, 1944-46. Decorated Bronze Star; recipient citation Polish-Am. Congress, 1971, Art in Park 3d prize City of Oakland Park, Fla. Mem. S.E. Mich. Coun. Govts., Mich., Nat. sch. bd. assns., Big Cities Sch. Bd. Com., Nat. Coun. Great Cities Schs., Mcpl. Fin. Officers Assn. U.S., Nat. Coun. Tchr. Retirement, Ctrl. Citizens Com. Detroit, Internat. Platform Assn., Mich. Heritage Coun., Nat. Geog. Soc., Polish Century Club. Home: 1729 SW 14th Ct Fort Lauderdale FL 33312-4109

WOJCIULEWITSCH, EGON SERVAZ, aeronautical engineer, astrophysicist; b. Deggendorf, Germany, May 13, 1945; s. Alexander and Wladyslawa W.; m. Rita Hendrika Deruytter, July 8, 1947; children: Sven, Anja. BS, Rijks U. Centrum Antwerpen, Belgium, 1967; MSc, Katholieke U Leuven, Belgium, 1970; postgrad., Cracow (Poland) U., 1976, 77. From dir. to pres. Urania Obs., Hove, Belgium, 1973—; dir. Nat. Planetarium, Brussels, 1985-90; adj. dir. Sabena Flight Acad., Brussels, 1990—. Recipient Govt. prize in violin (Belgium), 1964. Mem. AIAA.

WOJCZYS, ROMUALDA MARIA, surgeon, researcher; b. Bystrzyca Kłodzka, Poland, Aug. 26, 1958; d. Wacław and Genowefa (Pierzecka) W. MB, Med. U., Wroclaw, Poland, 1983, MD, 1990. Intern U. Clinic, Wroclaw, Poland, 1983-84; asst. dept. anatomy Med. U., Wroclaw, 1984-87; attending surgeon 1st Dept. Surgery, Wroclaw, 1984-87, asst., 1987-97; vis. fellow Dept. Surgery, Malmö, Sweden, 1992, Herlev U. Hosp., Copenhagen, Denmark, 1993, 97; clin. fellow Dept. G.I. Surgery, Poznan, Poland, 1992; postgrad. tchg. term St. Mark's Hosp., Stefan Batory Found., 1994; presenter in field. Contbr. articles to profl. jours. Scholar Danish Govt., 1993, 97; grantee Swedi. Mem. Polish Surg. Soc., Internat. Gastro-Surg. Club, Assn. Women Surgeons. Avocations: classical music, art, horseback riding. Office: U Medicine 1st Dept Surgery, 2 Poniatowski Str, 50-326 Wroclaw Poland

WOJNECKI, STEFAN, photographer; b. Poznań, Poland, Apr. 6, 1929; s. Edward and Zofia (Ziawinska) W.; m. Barbara Malinowska, Nov. 5, 1955; 1 child, Ryszard. MS, Poznan U., 1952. Dean faculty Acad. Fine Arts, Poznan, 1987-93, dir. extramural studies, 1994—; expert Coun. Higher Ednl. Sys., Warsaw, Poland, 1993—. Author: Impulsegraphic, 1979; exhibited at Polish Intermedial Photography, 1988; one-man show Faces, 1969; author,

curator I Biennale of Polish Photography, 1998. Recipient Josef Sudek medal Min. Culture Czechia, 1989, 1st prize Culture and Art Min. Poland, 1992. Mem. Union Polish Artists-Photographers (Gold Croise 1986). Office: Acad Fine Arts, Al Marcinkowskiego 29, 60-967 Poznań Poland

WOJTILLA, GYULA, ancient history educator; b. Budapest, Hungary, June 13, 1945; s. Gyula Wojtilla and Etelka Isztin; m. Agnes Salgó, Dec. 27, 1971; children: Gergely, Kinga. MA in History, MA in Indology, Budapest U., 1969; PhD in Linguistics, Acad. Sci., Budapest, 1972. Mem. rsch. staff Hungarian Acad., Budapest, 1970-80; lectr. U. Delhi, India, 1980-83; head archives Hungarian Acad. Scis., Budapest, 1983—; chmn. Oriental com. Hungarian Acad. Scis.; prof., head dept. ancient history U. Szeged, Hungary, 1992—; chmn. Oriental com. Hungarian Sci. Fund. Author: R. Tagore in Hungary, 1983, A List of Words in Sanskrit and Hungarian, 1984, A mesés India/The Fabulous India, 1988, History of Krsisastra, 1999; contbr. articles to profl. jours. Research fellow Banaras Hindu U., Benares, India, 1973-74. Mem. Linguistic Soc. India (life), Asiatic Soc. Bengal, Hungarian Soc. Ancient Studies, Internat. Assn. Sanskrit Studies (adv. bd.), Körösi Csoma Soc. Budapest (mem. exec. com.). Home: Pannonia 3, H-1205 Budapest Hungary

WOJTYLA, KAROL JOZEF See JOHN PAUL, HIS HOLINESS POPE, II

WOJTYNA, VINCENT JOHN, scientist; b. Butler, Pa., July 12, 1956; s. Stanley Joseph and Valeria W.; m. Teresa Pichardo, Aug. 29, 1981; children: Oliver, Sarah, Alexander, Emily. BS in Biology, Pa. State U., 1978; BS in Chemistry, U. Pitts., 1982. Lab. tech. Koppers Co., Inc., Monroeville, Pa., 1979-82, chemist, 1982-88, process devel. mgr., 1988-90; sr. chemist Thermal Products Internat., Pitts., 1990-92, project cons., 1992-93; sr. scientist Penn CHamp, Inc., East Butler, Pa., 1993-96, Syndicate Sales, Inc., Kokomo, Ind., 1996—. Mem. Am. Chem. Soc., Royal Soc. Chemistry, Soc. Plastics Engrs., Profl. Plant Growers Assn. Achievements include patents (3) on closed cell phenolic foam and resin technology, (1) on reducing shrinkage of phenolic foam; invented formula for Aquafoam, second largest selling floral foam in U.S., formula for aquafoam media for growing seedlings and plant cuttings. Avocations: drawing, painting, chess, home remodelling, fishing. Home: 7211 Lands End Cir Noblesville IN 46060-9416 Office: Syndicate Sales Inc PO Box 756 Kokomo IN 46903-0756

WOLBACH, ALBERT BOGH, JR., family practice physician; b. Allentown, Pa., Sept. 6, 1932; s. Albert Bogh and Gertrude Lillian (Mitchell) W.; m. Shirley Ann Mentzer, Dec. 21, 1957; children: Sheryl Ann, Wendy Sue, Ann Mentzer. AB, U. Pa., 1954; MD, Jefferson Med. Coll., 1958. Diplomate Am. Bd. Family Practice. Intern Lancaster (Pa.) Gen. Hosp., 1958-59; pvt. practice, Ephrata, Pa., 1961—; ret., 1997; mem. med. staff Ephrata C.C., 1961—; pres. med. staff Ephrata Hosp., 1969-70, bd. dirs., 1971-86. Contbr. articles to med. jours. Dir. Ephrata Sch. Dist., 1971-83; mem. Ephrata Rep. Com., 1983—. Lt. comdr. USPHS, 1959-61. Mem. Train Collectors Assn. (life, treas. Keystone divsn. 1990—), Masons, Shriners, Nat. Honor Soc., Phi Beta Kappa, Alpha Epsilon Delta. Mem. Ch. of Brethren. Avocation: model railroading. Office: 923 W Main St Ephrata PA 17522-1329

WOLBERSEN, JOACHIM ERIC, consulting company executive; b. Giessen, Hessen, Germany, July 9, 1964; s. Karl Heinrich and Hermine (Bannert) W.; m. Maren Bruemmer, Dec. 5, 1992; 1 child, Merle. BBA, U. Lueneburg, Germany, 1992. Project mgr. Tchibo AG, Hamburg, Germany, 1989-90; premier cons. Bertelsmann AG, Guetersloh, Germany, 1991-93; pres., CEO WHS Consulting Group, Hamburg, 1993-2000; chmn. bd. Wolbersen Assocs. Mgmt. Cons. AG, 2000—. Author, co-author: PC-Organisations Handbook, 1997, Project Management, 1998; contbr. articles to profl. jours.; pub. Service Report mag., 1995—. Bd. dirs. Found. Absalom, Hamburg, 1996—, spkr., 1995—. Served with German Air Force, 1983-87. Mem. Help Desk Inst. Germany (pres. 1993—), German Assn. Info. Tech. Consultants, Project Mgmt. Inst. Avocations: golf, horsemanship, hunting. Office: Wolbersen Assocs AG, Dubbenwinkel 7, 21147 Hamburg Germany

WOLCOTT, HUGH DIXON, obstetrics and gynecology educator; b. N.Y.C., Jan. 12, 1946; s. Charles Edmund and Joan Degrau (Loveland) W.; m. Jane Jarrell Smith; children: Allison, James. BS, U.S. Naval Acad., 1967; MSE, Princeton U., 1969; MD, Northwestern U., Chgo., 1979. Diplomate Am. Bd. Ob-Gyn, Am. Bd. Med. Examiners. Commd. ensign USN, 1967, advanced through grades to capt., 1990; aviator, Fighter Squadron 14 Naval Air Station, Oceana, Va., 1971-74; test pilot Naval Air Test Ctr., Patuxent River, Md., 1974-76; staff physician Naval Hosp., Portsmouth, Va., 1984, Jacksonville, Fla., 1984-86; dir. colposcopy and laser clins. Naval Hosp., Portsmouth, Va., 1986-89; dir. ob-gyn. residency program Naval Hosp., Portsmouth, 1989-91, acting chmn. dept. ob-gyn., 1990-91; ret., 1991; asst. prof. Med. Coll. Hampton Roads, Norfolk, Va., 1991—; chmn. dept. ob-gyn. Sentara Hosps., Norfolk, 1996—, mem. med. exec. com.; ob-gyn. splty. advisor Sentara Health Mgmt. Corp., 2000—; mem. Maternal Care Futurists Adv. Bd., Hill-Rom Corp., 1998—; chmn. C-section rate reduction task force, Sentara Hosps., 1998—; bd. mgrs. Mid-Atlantic Women's Care, LLC, 1999—; ob-gyn. specialty advisor Sentara Health Mgmt. Contbr. articles profl. jours. Awarded 1st prize scientific paper by resident physician Am. Coll. Obstetricans and Gynecologists; recipient Guggenheim fellowship Princeton U., 1967-68; Trident scholar U.S. Naval Acad., 1966-67. Fellow Am. Coll. Ob.-Gyns. (chmn. Navy sect. armed forces dist. 1989-91), Assn. Profs. Ob.-Gyns. (assoc.); mem. Am. Assn. Gynecol. Laparoscopists. Episcopalian. Home: 835 Botetourt Gdns Norfolk VA 23507-1814 Office: Woman Care Ctrs 811 Med Tower 400 Gresham Dr Norfolk VA 23507-1901

WOLD, MARGARET BARTH, religion educator, author; b. Chgo., Mar. 6, 1919; d. Frank Philip and Esther Sophie (Pedersen) Barth; m. Erling Henry Wold, Oct. 4, 1942; children: John, Michael, Kristi Wold de Merlier, Stephen Ganzkow-Wold, Erling Jr. BA, Luther Coll., 1941; MA, Luther Sch. Theology, Chgo., 1950; DD (hon.), Luther Coll., 1986; LittD (hon.), Calif. Luth. U., 1973; DD (hon.), Wartburg Sem., 1985. Exec. bd. Am. Luth. Ch. Women, Mpls., 1966-73, exec. dir., 1973-74; dir. for ministry in changing communities So. Pacific dist., Am. Luth. Ch., 1977-84; assoc. prof. N.T. Calif. Luth. U., Thousand Oaks, 1985-89, coord. sr. mentor program, 1986-99; organizer, dir. preschs., Calif. and N.D., 1960-72; cons. Pub. Welfare Bd., Bismarck, N.D., 1967-68; v.p. So. Calif. West Synod, Evang. Luth. Ch. in Am., 1987-90; keynote speaker Luth. World Fedn. Assembly, Budapest, Hungary, 1984; C.C. Hein Meml. lectr., 1985; study leader student conf. Sun-Moon Lake Edn. Ctr., U. Taiwan, 1977; spkr. in field. Author: The Shalom Woman, 1975, The Critical Moment, 1978, Women of Faith and Spirit, 1987, The Power of Ordinary Christians, 1988; also 5 books co-authored with Erling H. Wold. Bd. dirs. Grand Forks (N.D.) Unified Sch. Dist., 1968-70; bd. dirs. Pacific Luth. Theol. Sem., Berkeley, Calif., 1974-86, pres. bd. dirs., 1978-84, bd. dirs., Calif. Lutheran Homes, 1996-2000, mem. adv. bd., Ctr. for Spirituality and Ethics, Walnut Manor, Anaheim, 1999—. Recipient Martin Luther 450th Anniversary award Luth. Brotherhood, 1967, Disting. Svc. award Luther Coll., 1968, 125th Anniversary award Augustana Coll., S.D., 1968, Hon. Alumna award Pacific Luth. Theol. Sem., 2000. Mem. Am. Acad. Religion, Soc. for Bibl. Lit. Democrat.

WOLDAY, DAWIT, immunologist; b. Aug. 1, 1961; parents Fitiwi Wolday and Tedla Zenebech; m. Zewdi Debessay, Nov. 16, 1989; children: Benhur, Merry. MD, Gondar Coll. Med. Scis., Ethiopia, 1987; MSc in Med. Microbiology, Addis Ababa U., Ethiopia, 1993; PhD, Karolinska Inst., Stockholm, 1999. Cert. in medicine. Jr. med. officer St. Mary Hosp., Axum, Ethiopia, 1987-89; jr. med. officer Black Lion Tchg. Hosp., Addis Ababa, 1989-90, rschr., 1995—; med. officer Am. Joint Distbn. Com., Addis Ababa and Rwanda, 1994-95; African rsch. fellow Armauer Hanson Rsch. Inst., Addis Ababa, 1998-99; rsch. fellow Karolinska Inst., Stockholm, 1999. Contbr. numerous papers to profl. jours. Mem. Am. Soc. Tropical Medicine and Hygiene (travel grantee 1997). Mem. Coptic Ch. Avocations: music, traveling, walking, art. E-mail: dawit@enarp.com. Office: Ethio-Netherlands AIDS, Rsch Project PO Box 8297, Addis Ababa Ethiopia

WOLDE, MILLON, Olympic athlete. Winner Gold medal 5000 meter Sydney, 2000. Office: Ethiopian Athletic Fedn, PO Box 3241, Addis Ababa Stadium Addis Adaba Ethiopia*

WOLDRING, HENDRIK EGBERT SIPKE, political philosophy educator; b. Leeuwarden, The Netherlands, July 25, 1943; s. Reinder Harke and Grietje (Sipkes) W.; m. Anna Cornelia Van der Weele, Dec. 9, 1976; 3 children. M Sociology, State U. Groningen, The Netherlands, 1968; M Philosophy, Free U., Amsterdam, 1971, PhD in Philosophy, 1976. Asst. prof. social philosophy Free U., Amsterdam, 1969-76, assoc. prof., 1976-86, prof., 1986—; rsch. fellow Calvin Coll., Grand Rapids, Mich., 1981-82, U. Chgo., 1982; Fulbright fellow U. Notre Dame, 1990-91; lectr. U. Berkeley, 1991, St. John's U., 1991, Clark U., Worerster, 1991. Author: Karl Mannheim. The Development of His Thought, 1986, History of Friendship, 1994, Political Philosophy of Christian Democracy, 1996; mem. editl. bd. Christen Democratische Verkenningen, 1989-97. Mem. bd. Christian Dem. party, Netherlands, 1995-97; mem. Dutch Parliament, 1999—. Home: Burg Haspelslaan 382, 1181 NG Amstelveen The Netherlands Office: Free U Dept Philosophy, De Boelelaan 1105, 1081 HV Amsterdam The Netherlands

WOLDT, HAROLD FREDERICK, JR., newspaper publishing executive; b. Atlanta, July 4, 1947; s. Harold Frederick and Dorothy Rose (Lansdowne) W.; m. Lisa Diane Neves; children: Lauren Rae, Katherine Neves, Caroline Neves. BS in Journalism, So. Ill. U., 1969. Classified advt. rep. Chgo. Tribune, 1969-70, classified automobile staff mgr., 1970-72; nat. advt. sales rep. Chgo. Tribune newspapers, N.Y.C., 1972-74, city circulation mgr., 1974-77; nat. circulation mgr. Chgo. Tribune, 1977-80, circulation mgr., 1980-84; v.p., circulation dir. News & Sun Sentinel Co., Ft. Lauderdale, Fla., 1985; circulation mgr. Newsday, Inc., L.I., N.Y., 1985-86; circulation dir. Newsday, Inc., Melville and L.I., N.Y., 1986-88, v.p., circulation dir., 1988-94; pres., sr. v.p. circulation Newsday Distbn. Systems. Am. subs. of Newsday, Inc., 1988-94; v.p. sales circulation mktg. The N.Y. Times, Melville, 1998; dir. circulation Omaha World-Herald, 1999—, Omaha, 1999—; speaker, participant Am. Press Inst.; bd. dirs. Abilities Health and Rehab. Svcs. (Nat. Ctr. for Disability Svcs.), Albertson, L.I., N.Y., 1992-94. Bd. dirs. Robert R. McCormick Boys Club, Chgo., 1980-81; chmn. United Way campaign, Chgo. Tribune, 1980. Mem. Am. Pubs. Newspaper Assn. (circulation and readership com. 1988-93), Internat. Circulation Mgrs. Assn. (pres. 1991-92), Alpha Delta Sigma, Tau Kappa Epsilon. Office: Omaha World-Herald World Herald Sq Omaha NE 68102-1138

WOLENSKY, JOAN, occupational therapist, interfaith minister; b. Wilkes Barre, Pa., Mar. 4, 1954; d. Paul and Anna (Havrilla) W.; children: Maurisa Ann Fela, Jennifer Andrea Fela. BS, Coll. Misericordia, Dallas, Pa., 1985; DDiv (hon.), New Theol. Sem., N.Y.C., 1992. Cert. interfaith minister; cert. minister Order of Melchizedek, 1992; ordained minister Order of Holy Spirit, 1998; Reiki master, USUI and Karuna Sys.; cert. nat. and internat. spiritual response therapy counselor/tchr.; cert. master tchr. magnified healing. Founder, adminstr. N.E. Pa. Interfaith Ministries/Celestial Pathways Ctr., Harveys Lake, Pa., 1988; founder, dir., adminstr. Occupational Therapy Cons. Svcs., Harveys Lake, 1989; traveling occupational therapist; dean, mem. adv. bd. Sage Inst., Shokan, N.Y.; mem. adv. bd. and quality assurance bd. At Home Health Care, Wilkes-Barre; mem., spkr. Am. Congress Rehab. Medicine, 1995. Contbr. articles to profl. jours. Recipient Supr.'s award City of Richmond Nursing Home, 1989; Mary K. Minglin scholar Am. Occupational Therapy Assn., 1984. Mem. Assn. for Interfaith Mins., Holistic Consortium of N.E. Pa., Inst. for Higher Healing/Wellness, Spiritual Response Assn., Universal Holistic Healers Assn. Avocations: martial arts, yoga, angels, guitar. Home: PO Box 197 Harveys Lake PA 18618-0197

WOLF, ALOIS, educator; b. Micheldorf, Austria, Sept. 12, 1929; s. Gratian and Maria (Hany) W.; m. Marie-Antoinette Siret, Aug. 20, 1966; children: Bernadette, David. PhD, U. Innsbruck, Austria, 1953; habilitation, U. Salzburg, Austria, 1965. Lectr. U. Hull, Eng., 1955-57, U. Strasbourg, France, 1957-59; asst. lectr. U. Innsbruck, Austria, 1959-64, U. Salzburg, Austria, 1964-65; prof. U. Kiel, Germany, 1966-73, U. Freiburg, Germany, 1973—. Author: Gregorius bei Hartmann von Aue und Thomas Mann, 1964, Gestaltungskerne und Gestaltungsweisen in der altgermanischen Heldendichtung, 1965, Variation und Integration Tagelieder, 1979, Deutsche Kultur im Hochmittel-alter, 1986, Gottfried v. Strassburg und die Mythe v. Tristan und Isolde, 1989, Heldensage und Epos, 1995, Erzahjlkunst des Mittelalters, 1999; contbr. articles to profl. jours. Mem. Austrian Acad. Sci. Roman Catholic. Home: Lorettostrasse 60, D-79100 Freiburg Breisgau, Germany Office: Dept German U Freiburg, Werthmanunplatz, D-79085 Freiburg Breisgau, Germany

WOLF, BERNHARD ANTON, polymer chemistry educator; b. Linz, Austria, Aug. 8, 1936; arrived in Fed. Republic Germany, 1969; s. Karl and Frida (Panhuber) W.; m. Gerda F. Zach, 1960; children: Wilfried, Rupert, Dagmar. PhD, U. Vienna (Austria), 1965; venia legendi, U. Mainz, Fed. Republic Germany, 1972. Hochschulassistent U. Vienna, 1965-69; hochschulassistent U. Mainz, 1969-72, prof., 1972—. Contbr. articles to profl. jours.; author books; patentee in field. Office: U Mainz, Welder Weg 13, 55099 Mainz Germany Home: Fontanestr 84, 55127 Mainz 31, Germany

WOLF, CHRISTOPHER ROBIN, technology executive; b. Richmond, Va., Apr. 29, 1954; s. Rene Arthur and Charlotte Elizabeth W.; m. Lise Holt Honoré; children: Eleonor Charlotte, Elyssa Harriet. BA summa cum laude, univ. honors, Ohio Wesleyan U., 1978; MBA, Yale U., 1983. Pres. Computer Data Designs Co., San Francisco, 1978-81; v.p. investment banking Kidder, Peabody & Co. Inc., N.Y.C., 1983-88; sr. v.p., ptnr. mergers and acquisitions Oppenheimer & Co., Inc., N.Y.C., 1989-91; mng. ptnr. The Georgica Group, Inc., N.Y.C., 1991-96; sr. v.p., group head investment banking Fahnestock & Co., Inc., N.Y.C., 1996; exec. v.p., CFO Hyseq, Inc., Sunnyvale, Calif., 1996-99; pres., CEO Protogene Labs., Inc., Palo Alto, Calif., 1999—; adj. prof. Columbia U. Grad. Sch. Bus. Trustee Arneson Inst., Delaware, Ohio; ptnr. Blue Hill Ptnrs., N.Y.C., 604 Ptnrs., San Francisco, Rock Creek Ptnrs., Boulder, Colo. Mem. Knickerbocker Club, River Club, St. Francis Yacht Club, Yale Club, Phi Beta Kappa. Episcopalian. Avocations: expedition trekking, tennis, collecting antiquities, sailing. E-mail: wolf@protogene.com. Office: Protogene Labs Inc 303 Constitution Dr Menlo Park CA 94025-1110

WOLF, CYD BETH, lawyer, entrepreneur; b. N.Y.C., Oct. 6, 1957; d. Aaron Joseph and Sally (Marcus) W.; m. Germano Fabio Fabiani, Nov. 18, 1990; children: Alessandra Julia Fabiani, Francesca Isabella Fabiani. BA in Urban Studies with honors, U. Pa., 1977; JD, U. Balt., 1983. Bar: Md. 1983, U.S. Dist. Ct. Md. 1983, U.S. Ct. Appeals (6th and 11th cir.) 1986, U.S. Ct. Appeals (4th and 5th cir.) 1989. Assoc. Weinberger, Weinstock, Sagner, Stevan & Harris, Balt., 1983-86, Semmes, Bowen & Semmes, Balt., 1986-90, Piper & Marbury, Balt., 1990-95; private practice Balt., 1995-98, Owings Mills, Md., 1998—. Contbr. articles to profl. jours. Leadership com. Univ. Balt. Ednl. Found. 1983—, fundraiser 1983—, mentor 1983—. Mem. ABA, Am. Bankruptcy Inst., Md. State Bar Assn. (banking sect., bus. sect.), Bankruptcy Bar Assn. Md., Comml. Law League Am. (bankruptcy and insolvency sect.), Bar Assn. Balt. City (banking sect., bankruptcy sect., bus. sect.). Avocations: tennis, swimming, painting, drawing, fiction and nonfiction reading and writing. Home: 5 Hillchase Ct Baltimore MD 21208-6306 Office: Cyd Beth Wolf Atty at Law 6 Park Center Ct Ste 202 Owings Mills MD 21117-5604

WOLF, DALE EDWARD, state official; b. Kearney, Nebr., Sept. 6, 1924. BSc, U. Nebr., 1945; PhD in Agronomy and Weed Control, Rutgers U., 1949. With Dept. Agr., 1946; assoc. prof. agronomy Rutgers U., 1949; with E.I. duPont de Nemours & Co., Inc., from 1950, dir. agrichem. mktg., then gen. mgr. biochem. dept., 1972-79; v.p. biochems., also chmn. bd. subs. Endo Labs., Inc., Wilmington, Del., from 1979; group v.p. Agrl. Products, Wilmington, Del., from 1983; dir. Del. Devel. Office, Dover, 1987-89; lt. gov. of Del. Dover, 1989-93; gov. State of Del., Dover, 1993; sr. internat. cons. Mezzullo & McCandlish Law Firm, 1993—; chmn. Daynel Internat. Inc., Wilmington, Del., 1996—; vice chmn. WSFS Bank, 1998. Co-author: Principles of Weed Control, 1951. Bd. dirs. Del. chpt. ARC, 1975; gen. campaign chmn. United Way Del., 1978, also bd. dirs.; gen. campaign chmn. Girls Club Del., 1987; chmn. Del. Found. for Literacy, 1993-98. 1st lt. AUS, 1943-46. Decorated Bronze Star, Purple Heart. Mem. Nat. Agrl. Chem. Assn. (chmn. 1981-83), Pharm. Mfrs. Assn. (dir.), Masons, Sigma Xi, Alpha Zeta.

WOLF, DAVID BRIAN, social worker, writer; b. Phila., Dec. 3, 1960; s. Julius and Nancy (Bank) W.; m. Miriam Yocheved Wolf, Dec. 26, 1987; children: Sita, Abhimanyu David. BS in Psychology, Penn State U., State College, Pa., 1983; MSW, Fla. State U., Tallahassee, 1997, PhD in Social Work, 1999. Crisis-intervention and short term counselor On Drugs, Inc., State College, Pa., 1981-83, dir. counselor tng., 1981-83; pres. Internat. Soc. for Krishna Consciousness, Tel-Aviv, Israel, 1987—; dir. arabic ednl. programs Internat. Soc. Krishna Consciousness, Rama, Israel, 1988-90; coll. campus dir. Fla. Vedic Coll., Zephyrhills, Fla., 1991-92; counselor State of Fla., Live Oak, 1994-95; dir. ctrl. office of child protection Internat. Soc. Krishna Consciousness, Alachua, Fla., 1998—; program mgr. Dept. Health State of Fla., Gainesville, 1995—, social worker svcs. program mgr., 1995—; mem. bd. dirs. Multi-disciplinary Assessment Team, Starke, Fla., 1995—, Palatka, Fla., 1995—, Trenton, Fla., 1995—, Lake City, Fla., 1995—, Gainesville, Fla., 1995—, Svc. Assessment Team, Gainesville, Fla., 1995—, Family Svc. Planning Team, Trenton, Fla., 1995—, Gainesville, Fla., 1995—, Alachua Learning Ctr., 1999—; chmn. bd. dirs. Free U. Pa. State U, 1978-83, Vaisnava Acad. Day Sch., Alachua, Fla., 1996-98, Internat. Soc. Krishna Consciousness, Alachua. Fla., 1997—. Author: Krsna, Israel, and the Druze-An Interreligious Odyssey, 1994, Effects of the Hare Krsna Maha Mantra on Stress, Depression and the Three Gunas, 1999; editor: Fortunate Souls, 1996, North American Sankirtana Newsletter, 1991-92; contbr. articles to profl. jours. Recipient Fellowships Fla. State U., 1996-97, 1997-98. Mem. NASW, Phi Kappa Phi. E-mail: dgovinda@aol.com. Fax: 904-418-0982. Home: 17303 NW 112th Blvd Alachua FL 32615-4537 Office: Children's Med Svcs 1701 SW 16th Ave Gainesville FL 32608-1153

WOLF, DAVID CARY, gastroenterologist, medical educator; b. Scarsdale, N.Y., June 11, 1959; married; two children. BA, Yale U., 1981; MD, Columbia U., 1985. Resident Presbyn. Hosp., N.Y.C., 1985-88; gastroenterology fellow Albert Einstein Coll. Medicine, Bronx, 1988-91; asst. prof. medicine U. Cin. Coll. Medicine, 1991-93, Mt. Sinai Sch. Medicine, N.Y.C., 1993-96; assoc. prof. medicine N.Y. Med. Coll., Valhalla, 1996—; med. dir. liver transplantation Westchester Med. Ctr., Valhalla, 1996—. Contbr. articles to profl. jours. Fellow ACP, Am. Coll. Gastroenterology. Avocation: race walking. Office: NY Medical Coll Hunger Pavilion Rm 206 Valhalla NY 10595

WOLF, DIETER HEINRICH, chemistry educator, dean; b. Frankfurt, Hessen, Germany, Sept. 18, 1941; s. Reinhard and Lieselotte (Schmalz) W.; m. Irmhilt Beate Guzinski, June 18, 1966; children: Birgit, Andreas, Thomas, Marcus. Diploma in chemistry, Tech. U., Munich, Germany, 1968; PhD, U. Freiburg, Germany, 1972. Cert. biochemistry. Rsch. assoc. Cornell U., Ithaca, N.Y., 1973-75; rsch. assoc. U. Freiburg, Germany, 1975-80, prof., 1980-89; prof., dir. Inst. Biochemistry U. Stuttgart, Germany, 1989—, faculty dean chemistry, 1994-95. Editor: (with W. Holt) Proteasomes: The World of Regulatory Proteolysis, 2000. Recipient Alexander von Humboldt-J.C. Mutis award Govt. Spain, 1991, City of Clermont-Ferrand medal, 1995. Mem. AAAS, German Chem. Soc., Soc. for Biol. Chemistry, Am. Soc. for Microbiology, Am. Soc. for Biology, Am. Soc. for Biochemistry and Molecular Biology, Genetics Soc. Am. Avocation: tennis. Office: U Stuttgart Inst Biochemie, Pfaffenwaldring 55, 70569 Stuttgart Germany

WOLF, E. DAN, veterinary ophthalmologist; b. Xenia, Ohio, July 28, 1943; s. Elmer Marcus and Wanda Jeanne (Hess) W.; m. Marja Elina Nieminen, Dec. 31, 1992; children: Adam Benjamin, Aida Elina. DVM, Ohio State U., 1968. Diplomate Am. Coll. Vet. Ophthalmologists. Rsch. assoc. U. Ill. Coll. Medicine, Chgo., 1973-79; asst. prof. Coll. Vet. Medicine U. Fla., Gainesville, 1979-84; med. cons. Animal Eye Clinic, Denver, 1984-86; asst. prof. Ohio State U., Columbus, 1986-92; med. cons. Animal Eye Clinic, Tampa, Fla., 1992—; pres., owner So. Eye. Clin. for Animals, Southwest, Fla., 1996—; cons. Wil Rsch. Lab., Ashland, Ohio, 1988-92, Bushy Run Rsch. Lab., Export, Pa., 1986-92. Mem. AVMA, Fla. Vet. Med. Assn., Hillsborough County Vet. Med. Assn. (chmn.). Avocations: environmentalism, diversity tolerance, social equity, photography. Office: Animal Eye Clinic 8008 W Waters Ave Tampa FL 33615-1800

WOLF, FRANCES MARY GUTHRIE, music therapist, teacher of the disabled; b. Hemel Hempstead, Eng., Dec. 2, 1906; arrived in Argentina, 1937; d. James and Elizabeth (Coldwells) Guthrie; m. Ernst Wolf, Apr. 25, 1936 (dec. 1977); children: Frank, Rose. Grad., Montessori Coll., London, 1927. Tchr. Montessori House, Harpenden, Eng., 1927-30; dir. English dept. Escuela Plurilingue, Madrid, 193-134; founding mem. Collegium Musicum, Buenos Aires, Argentina, 1946, founding dir. childrens dept., 1949-58; tchr. Nat. Inst. for the Disabled, Buenos Aires, 1958-59; founder, pres. Argentine Assn. Music Therapy, Buenos Aires, 1966-87; music therapist R. Rossell Inst. for the Blind, San Isidro, Argentina, 1960-91; founder blind children's choir Los Cantates del Rossell, ca. 1970; lectr. at internat. congresses Internat. Soc. Music Edn.; lectr. music theory Salvador U., Buenos Aires, 1994-96; visitor to schs. for the blind in Germany, U.S., Poland, Guatemala, Brazil, Ecuador. Author: Viva La Musica, 2 vols.; (with Susana Alemany) Conversations on Music Therapy, 1988; contbr. articles to mags. and newspapers. Recipient Gold medal I.S.M.E. Congress, Warsaw, Poland, 1980, Mecenas prize for cultural achievements, 1999. Mem. Argentine Assn. Music Therapy (hon. pres.), Latin Am. Found. for Music Edn. (hon.), Assn. Dem. Women of Argentina, Argentine Rotary Club (hon.). Avocations: teaching English and music to children and adults, gardening, vocational counseling for students, animal behavior. Home: Ayacucho 1336, 1602 Las Flores Buenos Aires, Argentina

WOLF, FRANK, business educator, consulting executive; b. Dessau, Germany, Jan. 16, 1933; came to U.S., 1952; s. Erwin and Else Wolf; m. Sandra Lance; 1 child, Amelia. BS, Davis and Elkins Coll., 1960; MS, Poly. Inst. N.Y., 1965; D in Bus. Adminstrn., Nova U., Ft. Lauderdale, Fla., 1997. Dir. info. tech./MIS Am. Can. Corp., Greenwich, Conn., 1967-80; v.p. mktg. Marketronics, N.Y.C., 1980-81; pres. On Line Rsch., Greenwich, 1980-93, SB Software, Savannah, Ga., 1986—; adj. prof. bus. Nova State U., 1997—; spkr. in field. Contbr. articles to profl. pubs. Chmn. Inland Wetlands Agy., Town of Greenwich, 1975-86; non-govtl. orgn. rep. UN, N.Y., 1994—. White Ho. fellow Presdl. Interchange, Washington, 1972-77. Mem. Acad. Internat. Bus. Republican. Avocations: swimming, diving, flying glider. E-mail: wolff@nova.edu.

WOLF, FREDERICK GEORGE, environmental scientist; b. Paterson, N.J., Aug. 30, 1952; s. Frederick George and Doris (Miller) W. BS, U. S.C., 1974; postgrad., Clemson U., 1976-77; MS in Environ. Health, East Tenn. State U., 1978; MS in Sys. Mgmt., U. Denver, 1990; DBA in Mgmt., Nova Southeastern U., 2000. Phys. scientist U.S. Army Environ. Hygiene Agy., Edgewood, Md., 1974-75, S.C. Dept. Health and Environ. Control, Columbia, 1977-78; environ. scientist EPA, Atlanta, 1978-79; hydrologist Boston, 1979-81; regional hydrogeologist Seattle, 1981-86; mgr. hazardous waste sect. Parametrix Inc., Bellevue, Wash., 1986-88; regional mgr. environ. affairs Atofina Chems., Inc., Tacoma, 1988—. Lt. USNR, 1974-87. Recipient Spl. Svc. award EPA, 1982; decorated Bronze medal, 1983. Mem. Am. Inst. Profl. Geologists (cert. profl. geol. scientist), Acad. of Hazardous Materials Mgmt. (cert. hazardous materials mgr. master level), Soaring Soc. Am. (Bronze badge number 338), Sigma Xi, Epsilon Nu Eta. Office: Atofina Chems Inc 2901 Taylor Way Tacoma WA 98421-4330

WOLF, HANS JOACHIM, medical microbiology educator; b. Kronach, Bavaria, Germany, Mar. 9, 1945; s. Franz Seraph and Lina Helene (Dietlmeier) W.; m. Anita Irene, May 23, 1969; children: Dominik Stefan, Sebastian Tobias, Maximilian Michael. Abitur, Gymnasium, Kronach, 1966; state's exam in chemistry and biology, Julius-Maximilians U., Wurzburg, Germany, 1970, Dr. rer. nat., 1974; MD habilitation, Ludwig-Maximilians U., Munich, 1979. Rsch. assoc. Julius-Maximiliaus U., Wurzburg, 1971-72, U. Erlangen, Germany, 1972-74; rsch. fellow U. Chgo., Ill., 1974-77; rsch. assoc. Ludwig-Maximilians U., Munich, 1977-82, prof. sect. chief, 1982-90; dir. dept. med. microbiology and hygiene U. Regensburg, Germany, 1990—. Recipient Curt-Bohnewand-Preis, Munich, 1983; named Hon. Prof., Chinese Acad. Preventive Medicine, 1983, Inst. Medical Biology of Chinese Acad. Medical Scis., Peking Union Medical Coll., 1996. Mem. Deutsche Ges. f. Hygiene u. Mikrobiologie, Deutsche Ges. f. Chemiker, Am. Soc. for Microbiology, European Group Rapid Viral Diagnosis, Assn. for Biol. Chemistry, German Assn. Virology. Home: Josef Jägerhuber Str 9, 82319 Starnberg Germany Office: Inst Med Microbiology & Hygiene, Franz-Josef-Strauss Allee 11, 93053 Regensburg Germany

WOLF, HANS-CHRISTOPH, physicist educator; b. Karlsruhe, Germany, July 16, 1929; s. K. Lothar and Anneliese (Michel) W.; children: Peter, Caroline, Ulrich. Diploma in Physics, Univ., Tübingen, Germany, 1951, Doctor for Natural Scis., 1953; Habilitation, Tech. Hochschule, Stuttgart, Germany, 1958. Prof. Univ., Stuttgart, Germany, 1964—. Author: Atom- und Quatenphysik, 1996, 6th edit., 1996, Physics of Atoms and Quanta, 5th edit., 1995, Molekülphysik und Quantenchemie, 3d edit., 1997; assoc. editor Jour. of Luminescence, Chem. Physics, Chem. Physics Letters. Mem. Deutsche Physikalische Gesellschaft (bd. dirs. 1989—). Avocations: horse riding, skiing. Home: Umgelterweg 19 a, D-70195 Stuttgart Germany Office: U Stuttgart 3 Phys Inst, Pfaffenwaldring 57, D-70550 Stuttgart Germany

WOLF, HELLMUT RUDOLF D., internal medicine educator; b. Giessen, Germany, May 6, 1946; s. Rudolf G. and Gertrud H.O. W.; m. Evelyn Cornelia Beck, Oct. 8, 1982; 1 child, Sascha René. MD, U. Giessen, 1973. Scientific mem. in clin. chemistry U. Giessen, 1972-74, scientific resident in internal medicine, 1974-85; team leader in internal medicine U. Freiburg, 1985-92; head dept. internal medicine Diakonie Krankenhaus, Kreuznach, Germany, 1992—. Mem. FLugsportverein Giessen (pres. 1981-85), Dt. Ges. Haemorheologie, Internat. Soc. Biorheology. Office: Diakonie Krankenhaus, Ring Str 64, D-55543 Bad Kreuznach Germany

WOLF, JEAN-PIERRE, physics educator, researcher; b. Lausanne, July 14, 1960. Degree in physics, Swiss Fed. Inst. Tech., Lausanne, 1984, PhD in Physics, 1987; Habilitation, U. Lyon I, France, 1991. Asst. Swiss Fed. Inst. Tech., 1984-87, project mgr., 1987-89; asst. prof. Free U., Berlin, 1989-92; prof. U. Lyon I, 1992—; assoc. prof. Yale U., 1999; founder Elight, Inc., Berlin, 1991; mem. Nat. Coun. Univs., Paris, 1996—. Contbr. articles to profl. jours.; rschr., metal clusters, aerosols, femtosecond spectroscopy, non-linear optics and atmospheric scis.; inventor in the field of laser applications; innovator in field of environ. scis. Mem. Inst. Univ. de France. Avocations: piano, photography, writing. E-mail: wolf@hplasim2.univ-lyon1.fr. Office: U Claude Bernard Lyon I, Bd Du 11 Novembre 1918, 69622 Villeurbanne France

WOLF, JOHN HOWELL, retired publisher; b. Narberth, Pa., Mar. 19, 1918; s. W. Dale and Ruth Coryell (Howell) W.; m. Jane Belmeur, May 18, 1946 (div. Dec. 16, 1969); children: John B., Wendy J.; m. Emily West Asbury, Dec. 21, 1969. Student, DePauw U., Greencastle, Ind., 1935-39, Xavier U., Cin., 1940-41. Pub. Cin. Suburban Newspapers, Inc., 1946-73; pres., pub. Cin. Suburban Newspapers, Inc./Clermont Newspapers, Inc., 1973-82; chmn. Nat. Better Newspaper Contests, Washington, 1957-58; adv. bd. U.S. Suburban Press, Inc., Chgo., 1970-75. Dir. Suburban Press Found., Chgo., 1972; del. 5th UNESCO Conf., 1956; chmn. Police Media Adv. Com., Cin., 1968; chmn. small media com. United Appeal, Cin., 1965; mem. com. of mgmt. YMCA, Norwood, Ohio, 1947—; pres. Y Men's Club, Norwood, 1952, Carlisle (Ky.) Nicholas County Indsl. Authority, 1984-89, chmn., 1988-89. Maj. U.S. Army, 1942-46. Recipient Silver medal Advertisers Club, Cin., 1973. Mem. Soc. Profl. Journalists, Suburban Newspapers of Am. (pres. 1973, pres. suburban newspapers sect. 1968), Nat. Newspaper Assn. (dir. 1978-83, exec. com. 1980-83, fin. com. 1980-83, Outstanding Dir. 1980), Accredited Home Newspapers of Am. (dir. 1972), Norwood Club (pres. 1950), Masons. Presbyterian. Avocations: reading, travel. Home: 244 Azalea Ct Carlisle KY 40311-9053

WOLF, JÖRN HENNING, medical historian, educator; b. Hannover, Germany, Sept. 26, 1937; s. Kurt and Ellen (Fricke) W.; m. Telse Timm, Apr. 25, 1969; children: Friederike, Mareike, Friedemann. Student, U. Göttingen, Germany, 1966; Doctorate, U. Munich, 1970, postdoctoral qualification univ. lectr., 1974. Nat. dr.'s cert. Asst. Inst. History of Medicine, U. Munich, 1969-75, lectr., 1975-78, prof., 1978-82; chair history of medicine U. Kiel, Germany, 1982—; dir. Inst. History of Medicine and Pharmacy, Kiel, 1982—, U. Mus. History of Medicine and Pharmacy, Kiel, 1987—. Author, editor numerous sci. publs. Pres. Museumsverband Schleswig-Holstein, 1999—. Maj. doctor M.C. German Armed Forces Res. Fellow Joachim Jungius Gesellschaft Wissenschaften; mem. several sci. socs. Lutheran. Avocation: classical music. Home: An den Eichen 67, 24248 Mönkeberg Germany Office: Christian Albrechts U Inst History of Medicine and Pharmacy, Brunswiker Strasse 2, 24105 Kiel Germany

WOLF, JOSEF, anthropologist; b. Prague, Czech Republic, Mar. 20, 1927; s. Joseph and Marie (Simkova) W.; m. Zora Wolfova, May 23, 1953 (div. June 1971); m. Eva Boskova, Dec. 23, 1971; children: George, Radka, Thomas. BA, Charles U., Prague, 1951, PhD, 1969. Asst. anthropology Charles U., 1950-59, asst. prof., 1960-73, vis. prof., 1990-98, prof., 1999—; senator Internat. Parliament for Safety and Peace, 1988—; expert in cultural anthropology Inst. Psychology, Czech Acad. Sci., Prague, 1976-90, Charles U. Prague, 1990-2000. Author: Introduction to the Study of Man, Culture and Society, 1965-70, Integral Anthropology, 1971, Last Witnesses of Prehistory, 1972, Ency. of Man, 1977, The Dawn of Man, 1978, Peoples of Five Continents,1979, The Prehistory of Mankind, 1980, Anthropology of Aging, 1982, Ency. of Nations, Past and Present, 1984, Dictionary of Nations, 1984, Man in the World of Religion and Magic, 1992, Man and his World, 1993, Early People, 1994, Cultural Heritage of Humankind, 1996, ABC of Man Dictionary, 1997, Humanology-Integral Anthropology of 21st Century, 2000, Human Races and Racism, 2000, Anthropology for Everyday, 2001. Recipient medal J.A. Comenius, 1970, awards Czechoslovak Sci. Tech. Soc., 1981, Czechoslovak Acad. Arts, 1999. Mem. Soc. Anthropology Prague, Soc. Sociology Prague, Sci. Tech. Soc. Home: v Cibulkach 5, 15000 Prague 5, Czech Republic

WOLF, MAREK, physicist; b. Nowa Ruda, Wroctawski, Poland, July 10, 1956; s. Antoni and Krystyna (Mehera) W.; m. Małgorzata Trendak, Mar. 5, 1992; children: Magdalena, Marta. MSc, U. Wroclaw, 1978, PhD, 1982, Habil., 1993. Asst. U. Wroclaw, 1981-83, adj. prof. physics, 1983—; asst. prof. Sch. Mgmt. and Fin., Wroclaw. Co-editor: Chaos - The Interplay Between Stochastic and Deterministic Behavior, 1995; contbr. articles to profl. jours. Mem. Solidarity Party, Poland, 1981-89. Recipient Smolvchowski award Polish Acad. Scis., 1978, Min. of Edn. award, 1983. Mem. Polish Phys. Soc. Avocations: jazz, photography. Home: Działkowa 22/9, 50-583 Wrocław Poland Office: U Wrocław, Inst Theoretical Physics, 50-204 Wrocław Poland Office: Sch Mgmt and Fin, Pabianicka 2, PL-53339 Wroclaw Poland

WOLF, MARILYN, freelance writer; b. Muncie, Ind., June 12, 1950; d. Richard D. and Jessie Clair; m. Dan Edward Wilson, June 13, 1970 (div. May 1982); children: Jorja Rae, Jacob Vincent; m. Burton Charles Weitzman, July 30, 1988. BS in Comms., U. Md., Rockville, 1999; AA, Montgomery Coll., Rockville, 1997. Office mgr., bookkeeper Dr. James L. Shoot, Indpls., 1982-85; budget asst. U.S. Mil. Acad., West Point, N.Y., 1985-87; mgmt. analyst FDA, Rockville, Md., 1987-95, consumer safety officer, 1995-99; freelance writer, 2000—; chief steward Nat. Treasury Employees' Union chpt. 282, 1999; GSA Interagy. Telecommuting Ctr. Pilot Project, 1993. Trustee Montgomery Coll., 1992. Mem. Women's Exec. Leadership Program, Federally Employed Women (Parklawn chpt. pres. 1991-92, regional bd. 1991-92, Parklawn exec. com. 1992-94), Pub. Health Svc. Women's Network (one of founding mem.), Am. Mensa Soc. (Met. Washington Mensa scholarship chair 1993-96, bus. mgr. 1998), Phi Theta Kappa. Avocations: writing, reading. Home: 9452 Conservation Dr New Port Richey FL 34655-6020

WOLF, MARTIN EUGENE, lawyer; b. Balt., Sept. 9, 1958; s. Eugene Bernard and Mary Anna (O'Neil) W.; m. Nancy Ann Reinsfelder, May 9, 1980; children: Matthew Adam, Allison Maria, Emily Elizabeth. BA, Johns Hopkins U., 1980; JD, U. Md., 1991. Bar: Md. 1991, U.S. Dist. Ct. Md. 1992, U.S. Ct. Appeals (4th cir.) 1992, U.S. Ct. Appeals (2d cir.) 1993, U.S. Ct. Appeals (3d cir.) 1998, U.S. Ct. Appeals (3d cir.) 1999. Mgmt. trainee Giant Foods, Inc., Landover, Md., 1980-82, dept. mgr., 1982-83, ops. analyst, 1983-86, fin. coord., 1986-89; law clk. Piper & Marbury, L.L.P., Balt., 1989-91, assoc., 1991-96; prin. Law Office of Martin E. Wolf, Abingdon, Md., 1996-99; ptnr. Quinn, Gordon & Wolf LLP, Towson, Md., 2000—; dir. Giant Food Fed. Credit Union, Landover, 1984-89; pres. Stalagmite Properties, Ltd., Abingdon, Md., 1995-96; tchg. asst. U. Md. Sch. Law, Balt., 1992-94, adj. prof., 1996—. Mem. ABA, Md. State Bar Assn., Harford County Bar Assn., Harford County Bar Found. (Vol. Svc. award 1992, 94). Republican. Roman Catholic. Avocations: Lacrosse, hockey. Home: 11 Mitchell Dr Abingdon MD 21009-1628

WOLF, MILTON ALBERT, economist, former ambassador, investor; b. Cleve., May 29, 1924; s. Sam and Sylvia (Davis) W.; m. Roslyn C. Zehman, June 23, 1948; children: Leslie Eric, Caryn Sue, Nancy Gail, Sherri Hope. BA in Chemistry and Biology, Ohio State U., 1948; BS in Civil Engring. summa cum laude, Case Inst. Tech., 1954; MA in Econs., Case Western Res. U., 1973, PhD in Econs., 1993, LHD (hon.), 1980; LLD (hon.), Cleve. State U., 1980; D in Diplomacy (hon.), Ohio State U., 1997. Pres. Zehman-Wolf Constrn. Co., Cleve., 1948-76; U.S. ambassador to Austria, 1977-80; disting. professorial lectr. in econs. Case Western Res. U., 1981-87; chmn. Milton A. Wolf Investors, 1980—; bd. dirs. Town and Country Trust; U.S. del. UN conf. on Sci. and Tech. for Devel., 1979; U.S. del. dedication of UN Internat. Ctr., Vienna, 1979; host Salt II Summit, Vienna, 1979; trustee Cleve. Clinic; chmn. Fulbright Commn. for Austria, 1977-80. Trustee emeritus Ohio State U., 1986-96, chair, 1995-96; hon. trustee Case Western Res. U., Cleve. Orch.; chmn. Coun. Am. Ambs.; chmn. Am. Austrian Found.; chmn. Am. Jewish Joint Distbn. Com.; mem. econ. adv. task force Carter Presdl. Campaign, 1976; mem. Carter Inauguration Com.; nat. trustee United Israel Appeal, United Jewish Appeal, Coun. Jewish Fedns.; trustee United Way Svcs.; life trustee Park Synagogue, Cleve.; past pres., life trustee Jewish Cmty. Fedn., Cleve.; bd. dirs. Grad. Sch. Internat. Econs. and Fin., Brandeis U. With USAAF 1943-48. Recipient Austrian-Am. medal of honor, 1999, Austrian Cross of Honor for Sci. and Art 1st Class, 1997, Gt. Gold medal of honor with sash Republic of Austria, 1980, Gt. Gold medal of State Province of Salzburg, Republic of Austria, 1979, Eisenman award Jewish Cmty. Fedn. Cleve., 1990, Internat. Humanitarian award Raoul Wallenberg Com., 1995. Mem. Am. Econ. Assn., Cleve. Engring. Soc., Cleve. Builders Assn., Coun. Fgn. Rels., Fgn. Policy Assn., Acad. Polit. Sci., Cleve. Com. World Affairs, UN Assn.- U.S. (bd. govs.), Tau Beta Pi. Home: 19200 S Park Blvd Shaker Hts OH 44122-1857 Office: 25700 Science Park Dr Beachwood OH 44122-7319

WOLF, MONICA THERESIA, small business owner, inventor; b. Germany, Apr. 26, 1943; came to U.S., 1953, naturalized, 1959; d. Otto and Hildegard Maria (Heim) Bellemann; children: Clinton, Danielle. BBA, U. Albuquerque, 1986. Developer Word Processing Ctr. Pub. Svc. of N.Mex., Albuquerque, 1971-74, word processing supr., 1974-78, budget coord., 1978-80, lead procedures analyst, 1980-88; owner Monika's Woodworks, 1988-91; founder Monidan Blue, 1992—; ind. dir. Royal Body Care, 1999—; bd. dirs. Pub. Svc. Co. of N.Mex. Retirees; adv. bd., former student trainer APS Career Enrichment Ctr.; instr. firearm safety and pistol competition. Animal rights activist. Mem. Internat. Word Processing Assn. (founder N.Mex. chpt.), Nat. Assn. Female Execs., NRA, N.Mex. Shooting Sports Assn., Sandia Gun Club (adv. bd., coach), N.Mex. Inventors Club. Democrat. Home and Office: 305 Alamosa Rd NW Albuquerque NM 87107-5312

WOLF, NORMAN SANFORD, cell biologist; b. Kansas City, Mo., July 22, 1927; s. Edward J. and Sadie H. Wolf; m. Susan Herring, May 1995; 1 child, Jeremy R. BS, Kansas State U., 1953, DVM, 1953; PhD, Northwestern U., 1960. Diplomate Am. Coll. Lab. Animal Medicine. Dir. vivarium Northwestern U. Med. Sch., Chgo., 1953-58, postdoctoral fellow, 1953-60; NSF postdoctoral fellow Pasteur Inst., Paris, 1960-61; cons. Biology div. Oak Ridge (Tenn.) Nat. Lab., 1962-63; rsch. asst. prof. Div. Experimental Cell Biology Baylor Coll. Medicine, Houston, 1963-68; assoc. prof. Dept. Experimental Animal Medicine U. Wash. Med. Sch., Seattle, 1968-72; assoc. prof. Dept. Pathology U. Wash. Med. Sch., Seattle, 1968-90, prof., 1990—; adj. prof. dept. comparative medicine U. Wash., Seattle, 1990—; vis. scientist Cell Biology, Peter MacCallum Cancer Inst., Melbourne, Australia, 1988, 92, 93, 94; chmn. animal care com. U. Wash., Seattle, 1987, 90-91. Contbr. articles to profl. jours. With U.S. Army, 1945-47. Postdoctoral Rsch. grant Nat. Inst. Scis., 1960-61; grantee NIH, 1969—. Mem. AAUP (exec. com. 1989—), Internat. Soc. for Exptl. Hematology, Soc. for Investigative Pathology, Gerontology Soc. of Am., Am. Coll. Lab. Animal Medicine, ACLU, Common Cause, Amnesty Internat. Avocations: skiing, hiking. Office: U Wash Dept Pathology 357470 Seattle WA 98195-0001

WOLF, PETER TRAUGOTT, epileptologist, researcher; b. Winnenden, Germany, Dec. 21, 1938; s. Ernst F. and Elisabeth (Krull) W.; m. Jytte K. Jepsen, Apr. 9, 1966; children: Kerstin, Sigrid. Dr.med., U. Heidelberg, Germany, 1968; venia legendi, Free U., Berlin, 1978. Asst. U. Heidelberg, 1966-73; asst. prof. U. Berlin, 1973-79; assoc. prof. Free U., Berlin, 1979-85; med. dir. Epilepsy Ctr. Bethel, Bielefeld, Germany, 1985—; affiliated prof. U. Münster, Germany, 1986—; prof. Sch. Pub. Health, U. Bielefeld, 1994. Author and editor of books; co-editor, mem. editl. bd. various nat. and internat. jours.; contbr. over 250 articles to profl. jours. Named Amb. for Epilepsy, Epilepsy Internat., 1982. Mem. Internat. League Against Epilepsy (sec.-gen. 1993—), Deutsche Gesellschaft für Klin. Neurophysiologie (pres. 1994-95), Epilepsie Kuratorium (chmn. 1992—), European Epilepsy Acad. (chmn. 1996—). Avocations: literature, music, arts. Office: Klinik Mara, Maraweg 21, D-33617 Bielefeld Germany

WOLF, STEPHEN M., airline executive; b. Oakland, Calif., Aug. 7, 1941. BA, San Francisco State U., 1965. Various positions Am. Airlines, Los Angeles, 1965-79, v.p. western div., 1979-81; sr. v.p. mktg. Pan Am. World Airlines, N.Y.C., 1981-82; pres., chief operating officer Continental Airlines, Houston, 1982-83; pres. Republic Airlines, Mpls., 1984-85, pres., chief exec. officer, 1985-86; chmn., pres., chief exec. officer Tiger Internat., Los Angeles, 1986-87; chmn., pres., chief exec. officer UAL Corp. and United Airlines, Chgo., 1987-92, chmn., CEO, 1992-94, former pres., dir.; adviser Air France, 1994-96; chmn., CEO USAIR Inc, Arlington, Va., 1996-98; chmn. USAIR Inc, Arlington, 1998—; bd. dirs. Air Transport Assn., Bus. Roundtable, Washington, conf. bd. N.Y. Internat. Air Transport Assn., Geneva, World Travel and Tourism Coun., London. Bd. dirs. Alzheimer's Disease and Related Disorders Assn., Chgo., Art Inst., Chgo., Chgo. Symphony Orch., Muscular Dystrophy Assn., Rush-Presbyn.-St. Luke's Med. Ctr., Chgo., J.L. Kellogg Sch. Bus. Adv. Coun., Northwestern U. Trustee Northwestern U., mem. bus. adv. com. Transportation Ctr. Office: USAIR Inc 2345 Crystal Dr Ste 1 Arlington VA 22227-0001

WOLF, STEWART GEORGE, JR., physician, medical educator; b. Balt., Jan. 12, 1914; s. Stewart George and Angeline (Griffing) W.; m. Virginia Danforth, Aug. 1, 1942; children: Stewart George III, Angeline Griffing, Thomas Danforth. Student, Phillips Acad., 1927-31, Yale U., 1931-33; A.B., Johns Hopkins U., 1934, M.D., 1938; M.D. (hon.), U. Göteborg, Sweden, 1968. Intern N.Y. Hosp., 1938-39, resident medicine, 1939-42, NRC fellow, 1941-42; rsch. fellow Bellevue Hosp., 1939-42, clin. assoc. vis. neuropsychiatrist, 1946-52; rsch. head injury and motion sickness Harvard neurol. unit Boston City Hosp., 1942-43; asst., then assoc. prof. medicine Cornell U., 1946-52; prof., head dept. medicine U. Okla., 1952-67, Regents prof. medicine, psychiatry and behavioral scis., 1967—, prof. physiology, 1967-69; dir. Marine Biomed. Inst., U. Tex. Med. Br., Galveston, 1969-78; dir. emeritus Marine Biomed. Inst., U. Tex. Med. Br., 1978—, prof. medicine univ., also prof. internal medicine and physiology med. br., 1970-77; prof. medicine Temple U., Phila., 1977—; v.p. med. affairs St. Luke's Hosp., Bethlehem, Pa., 1977-82; dir. Totts Gap Inst., Bangor, Pa., 1958—; supr. clin. activities Okla. Med. Rsch. Found., 1953-55, head psychosomatic and neuromuscular sect., 1952-67, head neuroscis. sect., 1967-69; adv. com. Space Medicine and Behavioral Scis., NASA, 1960-61; cons. internal medicine VA Hosp., Oklahoma City, 1952-69; cons. (European Office), Paris, Office Internat. Rsch., NIH, 1963-64; mem. edn. and supply panel Nat. Adv. Commn. on Health Manpower, 1966-67; mem. Nat. Adv. Heart Coun., 1961-65, U.S. Phamacopeia Scope Panel on Gastroenterology, Regent Nat. Libr. Medicine, 1965-69; chmn., 1968-69; mem. Nat. Adv. Environ. Health Scis. Coun., 1978-82; exec. v.p. Frontiers Sci. Found., 1967-69; mem. sci. adv. bd. Muscular Dystrophy Assns. Am., Inc., 1974-91, chmn., 1980-89; mem. gastrointestinal drug adv. com. FDA, 1974-77; bd. Internat. Cardiology Fedn.; mem. bd. visitors dept. biology Boston U., 1978-88; mem. vis. com. Ctr. for Social Rsch., Lehigh U., 1980-90; chmn. adv. com. Wood Inst. on History of Medicine, Coll. Physicians, Phila., 1980-90, mem. program com. Coll. Physicians, 1990-91; dir. Inst. for Advanced Studies in Immunology and Aging, 1988—. Author: Human Gastric Function, 1943, The Stomach, 1965, Social Environment and Health, 1981, others; adv. editor Internat. Dictionary Biology and Medicine, 1978—; editor in chief Integrative Physiol & Behavioral Sci.: The Official Jour. of Pavlovian Soc., 1990—. Pres. Okla. City Symphony Soc., 1956-61; mem. Okla. Sch. of Sci. and Math. Found., 1961—. Recipient Disting. Svc. Citation U. Okla., 1968, Dean's award for disting. med. svc., 1992; Horsley Gantt medal Pavlovian Soc., 1987, Hans Selye award Am. Inst. Stress, 1988, Rsch. award Carolinska Inst., Stockholm, 1994, Wilém Laufberger medal Acad. Scis. of Czech Republic, Citation for sci. and humanitarian achievement The J.E. Purkynê Bohemian Med. Assn. Fellow Am. Psychiat. Assn. (disting., trustee 1992—, Hofheimer prize for rsch. 1952); mem. AMA (coun. mental health 1960-64), Am. Soc. Clin. Investigation, Am. Clin. and Climatol. Assn. (pres. 1975-76), Assn. Am. Physicians, Am. Psychosomatic Soc. (pres. 1961-62), Am. Gastroent. Assn. (rsch. award 1943, pres. 1969-70), Am. Heart Assn. (chmn. com. profl. edn., com. internat. program, awards), Romanian Acad. Med. Sci. (hon.), Coll. Physicians Phila., Collegium Internat. Activitas Nervosae Superioris (exec. com. 1992—, pres. 1994), Philos. Soc. Tex., Sigma Xi, Alpha Omega Alpha, Omicron Delta Kappa. Club: Cosmos (Washington). Home: 1430 Totts Gap Rd Bangor PA 18013-5632 Office: Totts Med Rsch Labs Bangor PA 18013

WOLF, WERNER WINFRIED, English and general literature educator; b. Munich, Germany, Mar. 11, 1955; s. Friedrich and Emma (Karger) W.; m. Gertrud Brosch, Oct. 11, 1980; children: Sophia, Theresia. MA, Ludwig-Maximilians-U., Munich, 1982, DrPhil, 1984, DrPhilHabil, 1991. Grammar sch. tchr. Munich and Icking, Germany, 1983-85; asst. prof. English lit. Ludwig-Maximilians-U., Munich, 1985-91, sr. asst. prof. English lit., 1991-94; chair English and gen. lit. Karl-Franzens-U., Graz, Austria, 1994—. Author: Ursprünge und Formen der Empfindsamkeit im französischen Drama, 1984, Ästhetische Illusion und Illusionsdurchbrechung in der Erzählkunst, 1993, The Musicalization of Fiction, A Study in the Theory and History of Intermediality, 1999; co-editor jour. AAA. Grantee in field. Mem. Internat. Assn. Word and Music Studies, Deutscher Anglistentag, Austrian Assn. Univ. Tchrs. of English, Deutscher Hochschulverband. Roman Catholic. Avocations: music, church organ, hiking. Home: Hans-Dolf-Weg 11, A-8042 Graz Austria Office: U Graz Inst Anglistik, Heinrichstr 36, 8010 Graz Austria

WOLFE, DEBORAH ANN, lawyer; b. Detroit, May 4, 1955; d. Adam and Mary A. (Smyth) Wolfe; m. Lester D. McDonald, May 23, 1987; children: Molly, Thomas. Student, Ariz. State U., Tempe, 1973-76; BA in Polit. Sci., Bus., Tex. Christian U., Ft. Worth, 1977; postgrad., So. Meth. U., 1977-78; JD, U. San Diego, 1980; grad., Gerry Spence's Trial Lawyers, 1999. Bar: Calif. 1981, Ariz. 1982. Sole practice San Diego, 1981-83; ptnr. Kremer & Wolfe, San Diego, 1983-86; assoc. D. Dwight Worden, Solana Beach, Calif., 1986-89; pvt. practice San Diego, 1989-91; owner Wolfe & McDonald, 1991-96; shareholder Nugent & Newnham, San Diego, 1996—; instr. San Diego Inn of Ct. Evidence, 1988-95. Floutist San Diego City Guard Band, 1981-93, Grossmont Sinfonia, La Mesa, 1982-83, Classical/Chamber Music Quartet, San Diego, 1983-87, Foothills United Meth. Ch. band, 1997—; leader Girl Scouts. Named one of Lawyers of the Yr. Calif. Lawyer Mag., 1996. Mem. Assn. Trial Lawyers Am., Consumer Attys. Calif., Consumer Attys. San Diego (pres. 1996, Outstanding Trial Lawyer award 1996, 2000, Trial Lawyer of Yr. award 1996), Lawyers Club (San Diego), San Diego Trial Lawyers Assn. (Outstanding Trial Lawyers award 1987), Am. Inns of Ct. (master), Nat. Bd. Trial Advocates. Office: Nugent & Newnham 1010 2nd Ave Ste 2200 San Diego CA 92101-4911

WOLFE, DEBORAH CANNON PARTRIDGE, government education consultant, educator, clergy; b. Cranford, N.J.; d. David Wadsworth and Gertrude (Moody) Cannon; 1 son, Roy Partridge. BS, N.J. State Coll.; MA, EdD, Tchrs. Coll., Columbia U.; postgrad., Vassar Coll., U. Pa., Union Theol. Sem., Jewish Sem. Am.; hon. doctorates, Seton Hall U., 1963, Coll. New Rochelle, 1963, Morris Brown U., 1964, Glassboro/Rowan Coll., 1965, Bloomfield Coll., 1988, Monmouth Coll., 1988, William Paterson Coll., 1988; LLD (hon.), Kean Coll., 1981; LHD (hon.), Stockton State Coll., 1982; LLD (hon.), Jersey City State Coll., 1987, Centenary Coll., William Paterson Coll., 1989, Tuskegee U., 1989, Glassboro State Coll., 1985, Tuskegee U., 1989, St. Peter's Coll., 1989, Rider Coll., 1989, Georgian Court Coll., 1990; DSc (hon.), Stevens Inst. Tech., 1991; LLD (hon.), Rutgers U., 1992, Thomas Edison Coll., 1992; DSc, U. Med. and Dentistry N.J., 1989. Former prin., tchr. pub. schs. Cranford, also Tuskegee, Ala.; faculty Tuskegee Inst., Grambling Coll., NYU, Fordham U., U. Mich., Tex. Coll., Columbia U.; supervision and adminstrn. curriculum devel., social studies U. Ill., summers; prof. edn., affirmative action officer Queens Coll.; prof. edn. and children's lit. Wayne State U.; edn. chief U.S. Ho. of Reps. Com. on Edn. and Labor, 1962—; Fulbright prof. Am. lit. NYU; U.S. rep. 1st World Conf. on Women in Politics; chair non-govtl. reps. to UN (NGO/DPI exec. com.), 1983—; editl. cons. Macmillan Pub. Co.; cons. Ency. Brit.; adv. bd. Ednl. Testing Svc.; mem. State Bd. Edn., 1964-94; chairperson N.J. Bd. Higher Edn., 1967-94; mem. nat. adv. panel on vocat. edn. HEW; mem. citizen's adv. com. to Bd. Edn., Cranford; mem. Citizen's Adv. Com. on Youth Fitness, Pres.'s Adv. Com. on Youth Fitness, White House Conf. Edn., 1955, White House Conf. Aging, 1960, White House Conf. Civil Rights, 1966, White House Conf. on Children, 1970, Adv. Coun. for Innovations in Edn.; v.p. Nat. Alliance for Safer Cities; cons. Vista Corps, OEO; vis. scholar Princeton Theol. Sem., 1989—; chairperson Human Rels. Coun., N.J., 1994—; vis. prof. U. Ill., U. N.C., Wayne State U.; theologian-in-residence Duke U.; mem. trustee bd. Sci. Svc.; mem. N.J. Commn. on Holocaust Edn., 1996. Contbr. articles to ednl. publs. Bd. dirs. Cranford Welfare Assn., Cmty. Ctr., 1st Bapt. Ch., Cranford Cmty. Ctr. Migratory Laborers, Hurlock, Md.; trustee Sci. Svc., Seton Hall U., bd. regents; mem. Pub. Broadcasting Authority, N.J. Commn. on Holocaust Edn., 1996—, Tuskegee U. Alumni, 1995; mem. N.J. Conv. of Progressive Baptists, 1995, v.p., 1996—; parliamentarian Progressive nat. Bapt. Conv.; sec. Kappa Delta Pi Ednl. Found.; mem. adv. com. Elizabeth and Arthur Schlesinger Libr., Radcliffe Coll., trustee Edn. Devel. Ctr., 1965—; assoc. min. 1st Bapt. Ch.; chair Human Rels. Commn., Monroe, 1995; v.p., then pres. N.J. Conv. Progressive Bapt., 1996—; parliamentarian Progressive Nat. Baptist Conv.; mem. exec. com. Nat. Coun. Agrl. Rsch., Ext. and Teaching, 1997—; mem. N.J. Holocaust Commn., 1996—;. Recipient Woman of Yr. award Delta Beta Zeta, Woman of Yr. award Morgan State Coll., Medal of Honor, DAR, 1990, Disting. Svc. medal Nat. Top Ladies of Distinction, 1991, Disting. Svc. award Nat. Assn. State Bds. Edn., 1992, 94, Disting. Svc. to Edn. award N.J. Commn. on Status of Women, 1993, Svc. to Children award N.J. Assn. Sch. Psychologists, 1993, Disting. Medal award U. Medicine and Dentistry N.J., Union Coll., citation N.J. State Coun. on Vacat. Edn., 1994, citation N.J. State Bd. Edn., 1994, Svc. award for 50 Yrs., Cranford Bd. Edn., 1995, Women Who Count award Zonta Internat., 1996, Minister's Appreciation award Progressive Nat. Baptist Convention, 1996, Edn. award Tuskegge U. Alumni, 1996, Women Whom Make a Difference award Zonta Internat., 1995, Dr. George Washington Carver award Pa. Acad. Sci., 1998; named to NABSE Hall of Fame, Lifetime Svc. award William Patterson U., 1999. Mem. NEA (life), ASCD (rev. coun.), AAAS (chmn. tchr. edn. com.), LWV, NCCJ, AAUW (nat. edn. chmn.), AAUP, NAACP (Medal of Honor 1994), Coun. Nat. Orgns. Children and Youth, Am. Coun. Human Rights (v.p.), Nat. Panhellenic Coun. (dir.), Nat. Assn. Negro Bus. and Profl. Women (chmn. spkrs. bur., Nat. Achievement award 1958), Nat. Assn. Black Educators (pres.), N.Y. Tchrs. Assn., Am. Tchrs. Assn., Fellowship So. Churchmen, Internat. Reading Assn., Comparative Edn. Soc., Am. Acad. Polit. and Social Sci., Internat. Assn. Childhood Edn., Nat. Soc. Study Edn., Am. Coun. Edn. (mem. commn. fed. rels.), Nat. Alliance Black Sch. Educators (pres.), Internat. Platform Assn., Ch. Women United (UN rep., mem. exec. com.), UN Assn.-U.S.A. (mem. exec. com.), N.J. Fedn. Colored Women's Clubs, N.J. Holocaust Commn., 1996, Nat. Assn. State Univs. and Colls. and Land Grant Colls. (mem. exec. bd. 1996, mem. coun. on agr. extension and tchg.), N.J. Commn. Holocaust Edn., Alliance of Black Clegywomen (pres.), N.J. Conv. of Progressive Baptists (1st woman elected pres. 1999). Home: 326 Nantuckett Ln Jamesburg NJ 08831-1704

WOLFE, JAMES RONALD, lawyer; b. Pitts., Dec. 10, 1932; s. James Thaddeus and Helen Matilda (Corey) W.; m. Anne Lisbeth Dahle Eriksen, May 28, 1960 (dec. 1996); children: Ronald, Christopher, Geoffrey; m. Patricia D. Yoder, Oct. 30, 1999. B.A. summa cum laude, Duquesne U., 1954, DHL (hon.), 1997; LL.B. cum laude, NYU, 1959. Bar: N.Y. 1959. Assoc. Simpson Thacher & Bartlett, N.Y.C., 1959-69, ptnr., 1969-95, counsel, 1996-99. Co-editor: West's McKinney's Forms, Uniform Commercial Code, 1965. Served to 1st lt. U.S. Army, 1955-57. Mem. ABA, Assn. Bar City N.Y., Am. Judicature Soc. Roman Catholic. Home: 500 SE 5th Ave Apt 601

Boca Raton FL 33432-5510 Office: Simpson Thacher & Bartlett 425 Lexington Ave New York NY 10017-3954

WOLFE, JON M, glass artist; b. Urbana, Ill., Mar. 19, 1955; s. Ralph Stoner and Gretka (Young) W.; m. Karen Zoot, Aug. 2, 1983; children: Madeline, Zoe. AA, Parkland Coll., Champaign, Ill., 1976; BFA, U. Ill., 1981, MFA, 1984. Ind. studio artist, Philo, Ill., 1082-98; dir. Hot Glass Studio, Kokomo (Ind.) Opalescent Glass Co., 1998—; vis. asst. prof. U. Ill., Champaign, 1985, 98. Work represented in Contemporary Glass, 1990; mus. collections include Renwick Gallery, Smithsonian Instn., Washington, Corning (N.Y.) Mus. Glass, Yokohama (Japan) City Mus., High Mus., Atlanta, Huntington (W.Va.) Mus., Ill. State Mus., Springfield, Rockford (Ill.) Mus. Art, Wheaton Mus. Am. Glass, Millville, N.J., Hunter Mus., Chattanooga, Evansville (Ind.) Mus. Arts and Sci. Glass fellow Creative Glass Ctr. Am., Millville, N.J., 1984, artist fellow Ill. Arts Coun., 1987, 97. Mem. Am. Craft Coun., Internat. Sculpture Ctr. Office: Kog Hot Glass Studio 1310 S Market St Kokomo IN 46902-1633

WOLFE, MILDRED NUNGESTER, artist; b. Celina, Ohio, Aug. 23, 1912; d. Roy Clifford and Augusta Wilhelmina (Hoenie) Nungester; widowed; children: Karl Michael, Elizabeth Hoenie. AB, U. Monte Vallo, 1932; MA, Colo. Coll., 1944. Tchr. Decatur (Ala.) City Schs., 1933-42; tchr. art and art history Millsaps Coll., Jackson, Miss., 1960-70; artist Wolfe Fine Art Studio, Jackson, 1945—. Artist 4 lithographs of So. scene, 1940s, lithographs displayed in Montgomery Mus. of Art, 1940, Libr. of Congress, London, Warsaw, Coventry, 1944; oil portrait of Eudora Welty, Nat. Portrait Gallery, Washington, 1989; represented in permanent collections at Miss. Mus. of Art, 1995, Huntsville Mus. of Art, 1996, Ga. Mus. of Art, 1996. Recipient 1st prize oil painting, Ala. Art League, Montgomery, 1935, 1st prize watercolor Miss. Art League, Jackson, 1949, award of merit, Grumbacher Internat., Lakeland, Fla., 1952, Visual Arts award Miss. Inst. of Arts and Letters, Jackson, 1989. Mem. Miss. Mus. of Art, Miss. Watercolor Soc. Office: Wolfe Fine Art Studio 4308 Old Canton Rd Jackson MS 39211-5920

WOLFE, RALPH STONER, microbiology educator; b. Windsor, Md., July 18, 1921; s. Marshall Richard and Jennie Naomi (Weybright) W.; m. Gretka Margaret Young, Sept. 9, 1950; children: Daniel Binns, Jon Marshall, Sylvia Suzanne. Mem. faculty U. Ill., Urbana, 1953—, prof. microbiology, 1961—; cons. USPHS, Nat. Inst. Gen. Med. Scis. Contbr. microbial physiology rsch. papers to profl. jours. Guggenheim fellow, 1961, 75, USPHS spl. postdoctoral fellow, 1967; recipient Pasteur award Ill. Soc. for Microbiology, 1974, Selman A Waksman Award in Microbiology Nat. Acad. of Sciences, 1995, Applied Environ. Microbiology award Procter & Gamble, 1999. Mem. NAS (Selman Waksman award in microbiology 1995), Am. Acad. Arts and Scis., Am. Soc. Microbiology (Carski Disting. Teaching award 1971, Abbott Lifetime Achievement award 1996, hon. mem.), Am. Soc. Biol. Chemists. Office: U Ill Dept Microbiology B103 Chem & Life Scis Bldg 601 S Goodwin Ave Urbana IL 61801-3709

WOLFE, ROSE, academic administrator; b. Toronto, Ont., Can.; m. Ray D. Wolfe, July 5, 1940 (dec.); children: Jonathan, Elizabeth. BA, U. Toronto, 1938, diploma in Social Work, 1939. Chancellor U. Toronto; case worker, supr., bd. dirs., mem. exec. com., life mem. Jewish Family & Child Svcs.; case worker, supr. Protestant Children's Home, Young Men's Hebrew Assn. Trustee Bantine Rsch. Inst., Lester Pearson Coll. of the Pacific, McMichael Can. Art Collection; mem. endowment com. Women's Legal Edn. & Action Fund Found.; v.p. Ont. region Can. Jewish Congress; mem. exec. com. nat. Can. Jewish Congress; dir. Mt. Sinai Hosp.; mem exec com., bd. dirs., mem. advt. com. Can. Jewish News. Decorated Order of Can., Order of Ont. Avocations: tennis, golf, swimming, theatre. Home: 89 Bayview Ridge, Willowdale, ON Canada M2L 1E3

WOLFE, THOMAS KENNERLY, JR., writer, journalist; b. Richmond, Va., Mar. 2, 1931; s. Thomas Kennerly and Helen (Hughes) W.; m. Sheila Berger; children: Alexandra, Thomas. AB, Washington and Lee U., 1951, DLitt (hon.), 1974; PhD in Am. Studies, Yale U., 1957; DFA (hon.), Mpls. Coll. Art, 1971, Sch. of Visual Arts, 1987; LHD (hon.), Va. Commonwealth U., 1983, Southampton Coll. (N.Y.), 1984, Randolph-Macon Coll., 1988, Manhattanville Coll., 1988, Longwood Coll., 1989; DLitt (hon.), St. Andrews Presbyn. Coll., 1990, Johns Hopkins U., 1990, U. Richmond, 1993. Reporter Springfield (Mass.) Union, 1956-59; reporter, Latin Am. corr. Washington Post, 1959-62; city reporter N.Y. Herald Tribune, 1962-66; mag. writer N.Y. World Jour. Tribune, 1966-67; contbg. editor New York mag., 1968-76, Esquire Mag., N.Y.C., from 1977; writer N.Y. Sunday Mag., 1962-66; contbg. artist Harper's Mag., N.Y.C., 1978-81. One-man show of drawings include Maynard Walker Gallery, N.Y.C., 1965, Tunnel Gallery, N.Y.C., 1974; author: The Kandy-Kolored Tangerine-Flake Streamline Baby, 1965, The Electric Kool-Aid Acid Test, 1968, The Pump House Gang, 1968, Radical Chic and Mau-mauing the Flak Catchers, 1970, The Painted Word, 1975, Mauve Gloves and Madmen, Clutter and Vine, 1976, The Right Stuff, 1979 (Am. Book award 1980), In Our Time, 1980, From Bauhaus to Our House, 1981, The Purple Decades: A Reader, 1982, The Bonfire of the Vanities, 1987, A Man in Full, 1998, (audio) Ambush at Fort Bragg, 1997; editor, contbr. The New Journalism, 1973; contbr. articles to Esquire Mag., others. Recipient Front Page awards for humor and fgn. news reporting Washington Newspaper Guild, 1961, Soc. Mag. Writers award for excellence, 1970, Frank Luther Mott Rsch. award, 1973, Harold D. Vursell Meml. award Am. Acad. and Inst. Arts and Letters, 1980, Columbia Journalism award, 1980, Nat. Sculpture Soc. citation for art history, 1980, John Dos Passos award, 1984, Gari Melchers medal, 1986, Benjamin Pierce Cheney medal Ea. Wash. U., 1986, Washington Irving medal St. Nicholas Soc., 1986, Theodore Roosevelt medal Theodore Roosevelt Assn., 1990, Wilbur Cross medal Yale Grad. Sch. Alumni Assn., 1990, St. Louis Literary award, 1990, Quinnipiac Coll. Pres. award, 1993; named Va. Laureate for Lit., 1977. Office: Farrar Straus & Giroux Inc 19 Union Sq W 11th Fl New York NY 10003-3304

WOLFENDALE, SIR ARNOLD (WHITTAKER), physicist, educator; b. June 25, 1927; m. Audrey Darby, 1951; 2 children (twins). BS with honors, U. Manchester, 1948, PhD, 1953, DSc, 1970; DSc (hon.), U. Potchestroom, Lodz, Poland, Bucharest, Romania, Ctrl. Lancaster, Teeside, Newcastle upon Tyne, Eng., Open U., Lancaster, Paisley. Asst. lectr. in physics U. Manchester, 1951-53, lectr. in physics, 1954-55; lectr. in physics U. Durham, 1956-58, sr. lectr. in physics, 1959-62, reader in physics, 1963-64, personal professorship in physics, 1965-72, head dept. physics, 1973-77, 80-83, 86-89; prof. exptl. physics Royal Instn. Gt. Britain, 1996—; chmn. No. region action com. Manpower Svcs. Commn., 1975-78, Cosmic Ray Commn. of the Internat. Union of Pure and Applied Physics, 1982-84; Astronomer Royal for the U.K., 1991-95. Fellow Tata Inst. Fund Rsch. Bombay, 1996. Fellow NAS India (fgn.), Indian Nat. Sci. Acad. (fgn.), Inst. Physics (pres. 1994-96), Royal Astron. Soc. (coun. mem. 1976-84, v.p. 1978-79, 82-83, pres. 1981-83), Royal Soc. (coun. mem. 1980-82), Durham Soc. Fellows (pres. 1988-94), Royal Soc. South Africa (fgn. assoc. mem.), Antiquarian Horological Soc. (pres. 1993—), European Physics Soc. (pres. 1999-2001), Acad. Europe. Home: Ansford Potters Bank, Durham DH1 3RR, England Office: U Durham, Physics Dept, Durham DH1 3LE, England

WOLFENSBERGER, CHRISTOPH, plastic and reconstructive surgeon; b. Zurich, Jan. 19, 1940; s. Christoph and Susie (Haessig) W.; m. Petra Elisabeth Leuzinger, Oct. 24, 1975. MB ChB, U. Zurich, 1965, MD, 1971. Cert. in plastic and reconstructive surgery Swiss Med. Fedn. Fellow and resident dept. surgery U. Lucerne, Switzerland, 1969-74; resident orthopedic dept. Kantonshospital, St. Gallen, Switzerland, 1975; resident in hand and plastic surgery U. Hamburg, Bermany, 1976-77; resident in plastic surgery Tech. U., Munich, Germany, 1978-79; chief resident dept. plastic surgery Aarau U., Zurich, 1980-83; pvt. practice plastic surgery, Zurich, 1984—. Editor: Gottfried Lemperle, MD, 1998; contbr. chpt. to book. Fellow World Scout Found., 1996. Served with Swiss Army, 1961-62. Mem. Internat. Soc. Aesthetic Plastic Surgery, Swiss Soc. for Plastic Surgery, Am. Soc. Plastic and Reconstructive Surgeons (corr.), German Soc. Anti-Aging Medicine. Avocations: music (playing jazz trumpet and classical piano), golf, skiing. Home: Hornlistrasse 4, CH-8702 Zollikon, Zurich Switzerland Office: Bodmerstrasse 2, CH-8002 Zurich Switzerland

WOLFENSOHN, JAMES DAVID, finance company executive; b. Sydney, Australia, Dec. 1, 1933; naturalized, 1980.; s. Hyman and Dora (Weinbaum) W.; m. Elaine Ruth Botwinick, Nov. 26, 1961; children: Sara, Naomi, Adam. BA, U. Sydney, 1954, LLB, 1957; MBA, Harvard U., 1959. Bar: Supreme Ct. of Australia 1957. Ptnr. Ord Minnett (brokers), Australia, 1963-65; mng. dir. Darling & Co. (investment bankers), Australia, 1965-67, J. Henry Schroder Wagg, London, 1968-70; pres. J. Henry Schroder Banking Corp., N.Y.C., 1970-76; exec. dep. chmn., dir. Schroders Ltd., London; prin. exec. officer Schroder Group, London, 1974-77; exec. ptnr. Salomon Bros., N.Y.C., 1977-81; chmn. Salomon Bros. Internat., London, 1977-81; pres., CEO James D. Wolfensohn, Inc., 1981-95; pres. World Bank, 1995—; vis. lectr. fin. U. New South Wales, 1963-66. Contbr. articles to profl. jours. Mem. Australian Olympic Team, 1956; chmn. bd. dirs. John F. Kennedy Ctr. for the Performing Arts, Washington, 1990-95, chmn. emeritus, 1995—; bd. dirs. Met. Opera Assn., 1977-93, Joint Ctr. for Polit. Studies, 1978-88, mem. emeritus, 1988—; trustee Rockefeller Found., 1979-85, Population Coun., 1977-84; trustee Inst. for Advanced Study, Princeton, N.J., 1978—, chmn., 1986—; trustee Brookings Inst., 1983-90, hon., 1990—; trustee Rockefeller U., 1985-94, Howard Hughes Med. Inst., 1987-96; steering com. Bilderberg mtgs., treas. Am. Friends of Bilderberg, Inc., 1985—; pres. Internat. Fedn. Multiple Sclerosis Socs., 1977-83, Carnegie Hall, 1972—, bd. dirs., chmn., 1980-91, chmn. emeritus, 1991; bd. dirs. Nat. Multiple Sclerosis Soc., 1977-82. With Royal Australian Air Force, 1952-57. Recipient Business Com. for the Arts Leadership award, 1994; decorated by govts. of Australia, Germany, France; honored by HM Queen Elizabeth of Eng. with KBE and HM. King of Morocco. Fellow Am. Acad. Arts and Scis.; mem. Coun. on Fgn. Rels., Century Assn., Harvard Club (N.Y.C.), Australian Club (Sydney). Office: The World Bank 1818 H St NW Washington DC 20433-0001

WOLFF, ARNOLD, architect, scholarly writer; b. Wevelinghoven, Germany, July 26, 1932; s. Wilhelm and Anna (Hahn) W.; m. Gerta Ramjoué; 4 children. Diploma in archtl. engring., T.H. Aachen, Germany, 1961, DEng, 1968; prof., 1986. Cert. arch. Labor contractor Cologne (Germany) Cathedral, 1958-62, architect, 1962-72, chief architect, 1972-98. Author over 300 books, articles and reports on Cologne Cathedral, 1963—.

WOLFF, BIRGITTA ANNE MARIA, economist, educator; b. Muenster, Westphalia, Germany, July 14, 1965; d. Theodor and Elisabeth (Esser) W. Diploma in econs., Witten/Herdecke (Germany) U., 1991; D in Bus. Econs., U. Munich, 1994, habil. in bus. econs., 1999. Apprentice in banking Westdeutsche Landesbank, Muenster, 1984-86; part-time cons. Bur. for Mktg. Svc., Wuppertal, Germany, 1987-91; lectr. U. Munich, 1991-94, asst. prof., 1994-99; prof. U. Magdeburg, Germany, 1999—; vis. fellow Harvard U., Cambridge, Mass., 1995-96; vis. prof. Georgetown U., 1999-2000. Author: Organization by Contracts, 1995, Incentive-Compatible Change Management, 1999; co-author: (with Edward P. Lawern) Introduction to Personnel Economics, 2000. Recipient Bayerischer Habilitations-Foerderpreis, Bavaria, 1995, Best Paper award VHB, 1999; J.F. Kennedy Meml. fellow Harvard U., 1995-96. Mem. Am. Econ. Assn., Acad. of Mgmt., Verband der Hochschullehrer Fuer Betriebswirtschaft, Bund Junger Unternehmer. Roman Catholic. Avocation: horseback riding. Office: Univ Munich Inst for Orgn, Ludwigstr 28, 80539 Munich Germany

WOLFF, BRIAN RICHARD, metal manufacturing company executive; b. L.A., Dec. 11, 1955; s. Arthur Richard and Dorothy Virginia (Johnson) W.; divorced; children: Ashley Rachael, Taryn Nicole. BSBA, Calif. State U., Chico, 1980; postgrad., U. Phoenix, 1990—. Registered counseling practitioner, Calif., 1996, guidance practitioner, Calif., 1996; ordained min. Progressive Universal Life Ch., 1996. Sales rep. Federated Metals Corp./ASARCO, Long Beach, Calif., 1980-82, dist. sales mgr., 1983-84; sales mgr. Copper Alloys Corp., Beverly Hills, Calif., 1982-83; dir. mktg. Federated-Fry Metals/Cookson, Long Beach, Industry and Paramount, Calif., 1984-87; regional sales mgr. Colonial Metals Co., L.A., 1987-91; nat. sales mgr. Calif. Metal X/Metal Briquetting Co., L.A., 1991-93; sales engr. Ervin Industries, Inc., Ann Arbor, Mich., 1993-95; tech. sales mgr. GSP Metals & Chems. Co., 1987-91; cons. sales Calif. Metal Exch., L.A., 1987-91, Atlas Pacific Inc., Bloomington, Calif., 1993—. Mem. citizens adv. com. on bus. Calif. Legis., 1983; ordained min. Universal Life, 1996. Mem. Non Ferrous Founders Soc., Am. Foundrymen Soc., Calif. Cast Metals Assn., Steel Structures Painting Coun., Am. Electroplaters Soc., Soc. Die Cast Engrs., NRA. Republican. Presbyterian. Avocations: scuba diving, tennis, freshwater fishing, trap shooting, hunting.

WOLFF, DIANE PATRICIA, author, journalist, producer; b. N.Y.C., Oct. 12, 1945; d. Irving Mark and Catherine Halkett (Grossman); m. Wallace Gorell (div.). BS, Columbia U., 1968; postgrad., U. Calif., Berkeley, 1977-78, Stanford U., 1978-79; student, Interuniv. Ctr., Tokyo. Prodr. Sta. KRON-TV, San Francisco, 1983-87; prodr. ind. films, 1990-92; prodr. CD-ROM Exec. Prodrs., 1994-96; contbg. editor New Asia Pacific Review, Westport, Conn., 1996-98; journalist Far Ea. Econ. Rev., Nat. Interest, N.Y. Times, San Francisco Chronicle, others. Author: Chinese Writing: An Introduction, 1975, Ghenghis Khan: Blue Sky, Golden Swords: A Novel of the Mongol Empire, 1999, Ogodei, Guyug and Mongilg the Khagans, Khubilai Khan: Conquest of China, 2000, others; contbr. Persimmon: A Jour. of Asian Culture. Nat. def. fgn. lang. fellow Columbia U., 1967; recipient Most Notable Book award Am. Libr. Assn., 1975. Mem. Author's Guild, Am. Soc. Journalists & Authors, Assn. For Asian Studies, Asia Soc. Avocations: sailing, swimming, fitness, cooking. E-mail: wuwolff@msn.com. Home: 1250 W Marion Ave Apt 143 Punta Gorda FL 33950-5388

WOLFF, EDWIN RAY, retired construction engineer, consultant; b. Continental, Ohio, Mar. 24, 1933; s. Ray Simeon and Datha Ruth (Donaldson) W.; m. Elizabeth I. Sutterlin, Feb. 16, 1963; children: Sandra Jean, Donald Scott. BSME, U. Toledo, 1969. Registered profl. engr., Ohio. Mem. design staff City of Ft. Lauderdale, Fla., 1965-67; mem. design/spl. orders staff Devilbliss Co., Toledo, 1967-69; engineer, mem. R & D staff Toledo Scale, 1969-70; design/constrn. engr. Lucas County Engr., Toledo, 1970-98, ret., 1998; cons. G.A.F., Inc., Oregon, Ohio, 1980—. Vol. Spl. Olympics, Lucas County, 1989—; trustee, bd. elders Fairgreen Ch., Toledo, 1975—; trustee Beneficial Union Pittsburg, 1986—; bd. dirs. Lucas County ARC. With Combat Engrs. Corps, 1956-58. Mem. Phi Kappa Chi, Pi Kappa Alpha. Democrat. Presbyterian. Home: 4312 Grantley Rd Toledo OH 43613-3738

WOLFF, ELROY HARRIS, lawyer; b. N.Y.C., May 20, 1935; s. Samuel and Rose Marian (Katz) W.; children: Ethan, Anna Louise. A.B., Columbia U., 1957, LL.B., 1963. Bar: N.Y. 1963, D.C. 1969. Assoc. Kaye, Scholer, Fierman, Hays & Handler, N.Y.C., 1963-65; atty.-adviser to commr. FTC, Washington, 1965-67; sr. trial atty. Dept. Transp., 1967-69; assoc. Leibman, Williams, Bennett, Baird & Minow, Washington, 1969-70, ptnr., 1970-72; ptnr. Sidley & Austin, Washington, 1972—; mem. adv. com. on practice and procedure FTC, 1969-71; chmn. adv. com. on procedural reform CAB, 1975. Served to 1st lt. USAF, 1957-60. Mem. ABA (chmn. spring meeting program 1992-94, coun. 1995-98), Union Internationale des advocats (chmn. competition law com. 1994-98), Army and Navy Club. Office: Sidley & Austin 1722 I St NW Washington DC 20006-3795

WOLFF, HANS-JOACHIM, construction executive; b. Berlin, June 12, 1939; s. Horst and Johanna Wolff; m. Mareile Laves; children: Anika, Franziska, Katharina. Student, TU, Hannover, Germany, 1960-66, postgrad., 1966-71; Doctorate, 1971. Joined Dyckerhoff & Widmann AG, Munich, 1971; authorized signatory and br. mgr. Dyckerhoff & Widmann AG, Bremen, Germany, 1983; mgr. Wiesbaden br., dep. br. mgr. Frankfurt am Main Dyckerhoff & Widmann AG, 1985-88, head Frankfurt am Main br., 1988-90, apptd. dep. mem. exec. bd., 1990, apptd. full mem. exec. bd., 1991; CEO Dyckerhoff & Widmann Aktiengesellschaft, Munich, 1992—, chmn. bd., pres.; chmn. supervisory bd. Union-Bau AG. Contbr. articles to profl. jours. Mem. Tiefbau Berufsgenossenschaft (exec. com.), Bayerischer Bauindustrie-Verband (exec. com.), Hauptverband der Deutschen Bauindustrie (expert com.). Avocations: tennis, sailing. Office: Dyckerhoff & Widmann, Erdinger Landstr 1, D-81902 Munich Germany*

WOLFF, HANS-ULRICH, management consultant; b. Zurich, Switzerland, Jan. 23, 1953; m. Margrit M. Spaeni; children: Michael, Stefanie. BSChemE, Basle Engring. Coll., Muttenz, Switzerland, 1978; Economical Engr. STV, Swiss Tech. Asn., Zurich, 1982. Devel. and plant mgr. Swiss Insulating Works/United Technologies, Breitenbach, Switzerland, 1978-84; mgmt. cons. Swiss Auditing and Fiduciary Co., Zurich, 1984-88; product mgr. Zentrum fuer Unternehmensfuehrung AG, Kilchberg, Switzerland, 1988-90; sr. cons. Zuehlke Engring. AG, Schlieren, Switzerland, 1990-94; bd. dirs. K. Winzeler & Ptnr. AG Mgmt. Consultants, Zurich, 1994—. Capt. artillery, Swiss Army, 1983-99. Mem. Swiss Tech. Assn., Knowledge Group Economic Engrs. Home: Wannenstr 78, 8610 Uster Switzerland Office: K Winzeler & Ptnr AG, Fliederstr 16, 8006 Zurich Switzerland

WOLFF, HEINRICH EKKEHARD, linguist, educator; b. Stolp, Pommerania, Germany, Aug. 25, 1944; s. Heinrich Otto Karl and Hildegard Erna (Gnuschke) W.; m. Raina Tuulia Ottila, Sept. 4, 1971; children: Per-Erik, Patrick. PhD, U. Hamburg, Germany, 1972, habil., 1980. Asst. to dean Oriental Studies U. Hamburg, Germany, 1971-72; rschr. linguistic fieldwork Nigeria, Cameroon, 1973-74; asst. prof. Dept. African Langs. and Cultures U. Hamburg, 1976-83, prof. Dept. African Langs. and Cultures, 1983-94; sr. lectr. Dept. Langs. and Linguistics U. Maiduguri, Nigeria, 1980-82; prof. Dept. of Linguistics U. Niamey, Niger, 1987-89; prof., chair Inst. African Studies U. Leipzig, Germany, 1994—. Editor: (monograph series) Afrikanistische Forschungen, Beiträge zur Afrikanistik; author and editor several books on African langs., lit., and linguistics; contbr. articles to jours. and collective works. Grantee U. Hamburg, 1968, 70-71, 86-87, DAAD, 1968-69, 97-99, DFG, 1974-76, 85-88, 87-89, 90-92, 95-98, U. Maiduguri, 1981-82. Mem. West African Linguistic Soc. (coun. mem. 1990—). Office: U Leipzig Inst Afrikanistik, Burgstr 21, D-04109 Leipzig Germany

WOLFF, HENNING OTTO AUGUST, private public school administrator; b. Berlin, Jan. 9, 1928; s. Gunther E. W. and Andrea Elisabeth (Kûhne) W.; m. Lieselotte K. C. Gerlach, Sept. 6, 1958; children: Cord-Michael, Daniela. Diploma in engring., Tech. U. Munich, Germany, 1954. Cert. in chem. engring. Co-owner Wolff & Co. KGaA, Walsrode, Germany, 1961-65; tech. mgr. Wolff Walsrode AG, Walsrode, 1965-77; mng. owner Henning Wolff GmbH & Co KG, Walsrode, 1989—; mgr. Otto-Kûhne-Schule Godesberg GmbH, Bonn, 1980—; mng. ptnr. Paedagogium Godesberg GmbH, Bonn, 1980—. Fellow Rotary Club; mem. Rotary Internat. (dist. gov. 1986-87). Avocation: golf. Office: Paedagogium Godesberg, Otto-Kuhne-Platz 1, 53173 Bonn Germany

WOLFF, KLAUS, dermatologist, educator, researcher; b. Hermannstadt, Romania, Dec. 4, 1935; arrived in Austria, 1947; s. Helmut Konrad and Hedwig (Orendi) W.; m. Marilies von Artens, June 12, 1962 (div. Dec. 12, 1970); m. Elisabeth Christine Schreiner, July 7, 1971 (div. Dec. 1998); children: Philippa, Eva, Bernhard; m. Gabriele Robitschek, Jan. 8, 1999. MD, U. Vienna, 1962; MD (hon.), U. Keil. Med. diplomate; diplomate dermatology. Prof. U. Vienna, 1974-76, 81—, head divsn. exptl. dermatology, 1974-78; prof., chmn. dept. dermatology U. Innsbruck, Austria, 1976-81; chmn. dept. dermatology U. Vienna Gen. Hosp., 1981—. Editor: Dermatology in General Medicine, 1979, 87, 93, 99, Vasculitis, 1979, Color Atlas and Synopsis of Clinical Dermatology, 1992, 2d edit., 1997; contbr. 380 articles to profl. jours. Fellow Royal Coll. Physicians; mem. Internat. League of Dermatol. Socs. (pres. 1987-92), European Soc. Dermatol. Rsch. (pres. 1975-76), Austrian Acad. Scis., German Acad. Natural Scis., 16 internat. scientific socs. (hon.). Avocations: literature, opera, tennis, skiing. Home: Günthergasse 1, A-1090 Vienna Austria Office: Vienna Gen Hosp Dept Dermat, 18-20 Währinger Gürte, A-1090 Vienna Austria

WOLFF, RICHARD CARL, financial planner, insurance agency and pension planning company executive; b. Boston, July 17, 1933. Student, Boston U., 1957-60. CLU. Pres. Richard C. Wolff Ins. Agy., Swanpscott, Mass., 1960—, Fiscal Planning Corp., Swanpscott, 1978—, Multi Pension Planning Co., Swanpscott, 1979—; mem. adv. bd. para-actuary program Bentley Coll., Waltham, Mass., 1979-90; past chmn. adv. bd. Elite Club of Western Life, St. Paul; lectr. on fringe benefits. Author: Measure of Success, 1987. Pres. Temple Israel, Swampscott, 1981-83, pres. Bortherhood, 1987-89. Recipient Legion of Honor, DeMolay, 1978, Man of Yr. award, Temple Israel, 1989. Mem. Top of Table (charter), Million Dollar Round Table (life), Mass. Assn. Accident/Health Underwriters (pres. 1965-66), Essex County Estate Planning Assn. (founder, pres. 1975-76), Boston Life Underwriters Assn. (founder, pres. North Shore br. 1979-80), Swampscott Bus. Council (pres. 1980), Lynn C. of C. (v.p. 1982-85, disting. svc. award 1984, community leader award 1985), Peabody C. of C. (bd. dirs. 1985-86, 96-97), Masons (master 1974), K.P., Rotary (Peabody award, Paul Harris fellow, pres. 1975-76), B'nai B'rith (pres. 1962-63, bd. dirs. 1991, Jewish family svc.), Kernwood Country Club (membership com., house com.). Avocations: golf, boating. Office: Fiscal Planning Corp PO Box 182 Swampscott MA 01907-0382

WOLFF-KING, SALLY, college administrator, educator; b. Little Rock, Aug. 21, 1954; d. Haskell and Elaine Wolff; m. Frederick A. King, July 2, 1991; stepchildren: Alex King, Lizzie King. BA in English, Vanderbilt U., 1976; MA in English, Emory U., 1979, PhD in English, 1983. Asst. prof. English Ark. State U., State University, 1988-89; asst. dean Emory U., Atlanta, 1989-99, assoc. dean, 1999—; advisor Freshman Advising and Mentoring, Atlanta; dir. First Yr. Orientation, Atlanta. Author: Talking About William Faulkner, 1996, Southern Mothers, 1999. Mem. MLA, Soc. for Study of So. Lit., South Atlantic MLA. E-mail: swolff@emory.edu. Office: Emory Univ Atlanta GA 30322

WOLFFSOHN, JAMES STUART WILLIAM, optometrist; b. Wilbledon, England, Oct. 5, 1972; s. Hervyn and Monica (Contreras) W. BS in Ophthalmic Optics, UMIST, Manchester, England, 1993; PhD, Cardiff U., England. Pre-reg optometrist Moorfields Eye Hosp., London, 1993-94; rschr. Cardiff U., England, 1994-97; clin. rsch. optometrist Victorian Coll. Optometry, Melbourne, Australia, 1997-99; lectr. Aston U., Birmingham, England, 2000—. Contbr. articles to profl. jours. Grantee Vision Australia Found., Melbourne, 1998-99. Fellow Am. Acad. Optometry. Avocations: hill walking, first aid, skiing. Office: Aston U, Aston Triangle, Birmingham B4 7ET, England

WOLFF VON NATTERMOELLER, HANS JÜERGEN, film director, script writer, producer; b. Dresden, Germany, June 23, 1921; s. Hans Conrad Wolff and Maria (Weber) Wolff Von N.; m. Ingeborg Dorothea Bruhn, 1960; children by previous marriage: Daniela, Mario. Grad. high sch., Berlin; dipl. Maestro di Pittura (hon.), Seminario Internat. d'Arte Moderna e Contemporanea, 1982. Journalist Wiesbaden and Frankfurt, Germany, 1946; script writer Curt Oertel Film Studios, Wiesbaden, 1948; dir., script writer UFA Universum Film AG, 1953-62; head of prodns., 1st dir. ZDF, Germany, 1963; prodn. head ZDF, Mainz, Germany, 1969, prodn. head of staff, 1972-85; chief Internat. Film Union, Remagen, Germany, 1966; media cons., 1986—. Author 37 film scripts, dir. 43 films. Served to lt., Naval Reserve, 1941-46. Recipient Film prize Fed. German Rep., 1956, Grand Prix award Internat. Film Festival, Brussels, 1956, Internat. Film Festival award, Harrogate, Eng., 1957, Cultural Film award Fed. German Rep., 1957, Internat. Film Fair award, Hollywood, Calif., 1964, VIP award Ency. Corp., U.S.A., 1979, Gold medal Acad. of Art of Italy, 1980, Merit award Services to the Arts, 1981, Golden Centaur award Italian Acad., 1982, Gold medal Internat. Parliament, U.S.A., 1983, Grand prize of the Nations, Italy, 1983, Victory Statue of the World prize of Culture, Italy, 1984. Mem. Italian Acad. of Arts, Marquis Giuseppe Scicluna Internat. U. Found. Avocations: art, antiques, interior design, books, wines. Home and Office: 32 Tiergartenstr, 40237 Duesseldorf Germany

WOLFGRUBER, MATTHIAS LUDWIG, specialty chemical company executive; b. Anger, Germany, Jan. 24, 1954; m. Susanne Christine Stuerzl, July 27, 1990; children: Lena, Hannah. Grad. in chemistry, Tech. U. Munich, 1981, D Natural Scis., 1983; postgrad., U. Calif., Berkeley, 1985. Bus. mgr. Wacker Silicones Corp., 1990-94, v.p. ops., 1994-96; R & D chemist Wacker Chemie GmbH, Burghausen, Germany, 1985-88, process developer, 1988-89, with mktg. dept., 1989-90, mgr. bus. unit/v.p. silicones divsn., 1996—. Office: Wacker Chemie GmbH, Johannes Hess Strasse 24, 84489 Burghausen Germany

WOLFHAGEN, FRANCISCUS HUBERTUS JOSEPH, internist, researcher; b. Spaubeek, Limburg, Netherlands, Jan. 13, 1964; s. Joseph C.H. and Elisabeth (Schreurs) W.; m. Harriet Maria Theodora Van Dongen, Aug. 14, 1992; children: Laura, Eefje, Femke. MD, U. Maastricht, Netherlands, 1990; PhD, U Rotterdam, Netherlands, 1995. Sentinel physician St.

Gregorius Hosp., Brunssum, Netherlands, 1991; rschr. Dijkzigt Hosp., Rotterdam, 1991-94; fellow internist Ikazia Hosp., Rotterdam, 1995-98, Dykzigt Hosp., Rotterdam, 1998-2000; internist Albert Schweitzer Hosp., Zwyndrecht, The Netherlands, 2000—; med. advisor Stichting Wetswinkel Geleen, Netherlands, 1991—. Author: Bile Acid and Immunosuppressive Therapy in Primary Biliary Cirrhosis; contbr. articles to profl. jours. Col., Med. Forces Netherlands, 1983-84. Netherlands Digestive Disease Found. rsch. grantee, 1991; Mayo Found. travel grantee, 1994; EASL Travel bursary, Copenhagen, 1995. Mem. Dutch Internists Soc., Dutch Soc. for Gastroenterology. Avocations: tennis, motorcycle riding, composing and playing music, skiing. Home: Muiderslotstraat 87, 4834 KM Breda, Brabant Netherlands

WOLFHARD, HANS GEORG, research scientist; b. Basel, Switzerland, Apr. 2, 1912; came to U.S., 1956, naturalized, 1961; s. Albert Georg and Helen (Buerck) W.; m. Adelheid Rohde, Jan. 18, 1940 (dec. 1995); children: George, John, Bernie; m. Clara Ralston, Jan. 4, 1997. Student, U. Berlin, 1934-35; D.Rer.Nat., U. Goettingen, 1938. Scientist Aero. Rsch. Sta., Brunswick, Germany, 1939-46; rsch. scientist Imperial Coll., London, Aircraft Establishment, Eng., 1946-56, Bur. Mines, Pitts., 1956-59; head dept. physics reaction motors divsn. Thiokol Chem. corp., Denville, N.J., 1959-63; mem. sr. rsch. staff Inst. Def. Analyses, Alexandria, Va., 1963-96; cons. Sverdrup Tech., AEDC-Arnold AFB, Tenn. Co-author: Flames, 4th edit., 1979, Chinese transl., 1990. Recipient 1st Gen. Goodpastor award for Excellence in Rsch., 1983. Fellow Am. Optical Soc., Mil. Sensor Symposium (First Jamieson award); mem. AIAA, Combustion Inst. Presbyterian. Home: 711 Bright Ave Fayetteville TN 37334-2255

WOLF-KLEIN, GISELE PATRICIA, geriatrician; b. Geneva, June 11, 1951; came to U.S., 1976; d. Francis and Patricia (Johnston) Wolf; m. Allen Klein. MD, Geneva U., 1975. Diplomate Am. Bd. Internal Medicine. Intern., resident L.I. Jewish Med. Ctr., 1976-78; fellow in geriatric medicine L.I. Jewish Med. Ctr., New Hyde Park, N.Y., 1978-80, chief geriatric medicine, 1991—; assoc. prof. medicine Albert Einstein Coll. of Medicine, N.Y. Author: Keys to Alzheimers Disease, 1992; contbr. numerous articles to profl. jours. Recipient 1 of Best Drs. in USA award Woodward-White, 1992-93. Fellow ACP, Am. Geriatric Soc.; mem. Gerontol. Soc. Am., Met. Area Geriatric Soc. (bd. dirs. 1991—), Sigma Xi. Avocations: skiing, mountain climbing, sculpture. Office: Parker Jewish Geriatric Inst 27111 76th Ave New Hyde Park NY 11040-1436

WOLFOVÁ, EVA, humanities educator; b. Prague, Czech Republic, Aug. 27, 1948; d. Alfred and Emilie Bošek; m. Josef Wolf, Dec., 1971; 1 child, Thomas. BA, Charles U., Prague, 1973, PhD, 1975. Asst. Libr. of Nat. Mus., 1975-83, head dept. lit. culture, 1983-91; dir. Mus. Czech Lit., Prague, 1991—; head Assn. Mus. and Galleries in Prague, 1993; mem. Internat. Com. of Mus., 1993. Author: ABCs of Man, 1977, History of Prague Culture and Art Doc., 1996. Home: V Cibulkach 5, 150 00 Prague 5, Czech Republic

WOLFRAM, STEPHEN, physicist, computer company executive; b. London, Aug. 29, 1959; came to U.S., 1978; Degree, Eton Coll., 1976, Oxford U., 1978; PhD in Theoretical Physics, Calif. Inst. Tech., 1979. With Calif. Inst. Tech., Pasadena, 1979-82, Inst. for Advanced Study, Princeton, N.J., 1983-86; prof. physics, math, computer sci. U. Ill., Champaign, 1986-90; pres., CEO Wolfram Rsch. Inc., Champaign, 1987—. Author: Theory and Applications of Cellular Automata, 1986, Mathematica: A System for Doing Mathematics by Computer, 1998, 2d edit., 1991, Mathematica Reference Guide, 1992, Mathematica: The Student Book, 1994, The Mathematica Book, 4th edit., 1999, Cellular Automata and Complexity, 1994; editor jour. Complex Systems, 1987—. Fellow MacArthur Found., 1981. E-mail: s.wolfram@wolfram.com. Office: Wolfram Rsch Inc 100 Trade Centre Dr Champaign IL 61820-7237

WOLFRUM, JÜRGEN MANFRED, physical chemist; b. Jena, Germany, Sept. 23, 1939; s. Erich and Christa (Otto) W.; m. Ilse-Verena Löwen; children: Tobias, Fabian. PhD, U. Göttingen, Germany, 1968, Habilitation, 1975. Rsch. asst. Ruhr-U., Bochum, Germany, 1968-70; rsch. group leader Max-Planck Soc., Germany, 1970-82; dir. Inst. for Phys. Chemistry U. Heidelberg, Germany, 1982—. Contbr. numerous articles to sci. jours. Recipient Bodenstein prize Deutsche Bunsengesellschaft, 1978, Philip Morris prize, 1987, Max Planck prize, 1993, Karl Heinz Beckurts prize, 1998, Michael Polanyi medal, 2000. Achievements include 14 patents on Lasers in Chemistry and Life Scis. Office: Inst Phys Chemistry, Im Neuenheimer Feld 253, 69120 Heidelberg Germany

WOLFSON, DAVID JOHN, pharmacist, researcher; b. Liverpool, Merseyside, U.K., Feb. 21, 1946; s. Myer and Sara (Chmielnicki) W.; m. Eunice Florence Inestone, Mar. 3, 1974; children: Sara, Rebecca, Deborah, Eliot, Nadia. BSc, Liverpool John Moores U., 1969, PhD in Mgmt. Studies, 1985. Pharmacist/sr. pharmacist Walton & Fazakerley Hosps., U.K., 1970-71; dep. chief pharmacist Alder Hey Children's Hosp., U.K., 1971-73; prin. pharmacist Whiston Hosp., Prescot, U.K., 1973-90; dir. Mersey Acad. Pharmacy Practice Unit, Liverpool, 1990-99; module leader U. Liverpool, 1994-98; module leader/rsch. project liaison officer Liverpool John Moores U., 1991-99; advisor WHO, 1991—; mem. East Cheshire Prescribing Interface Working Group, 1992-95, St. Helens & Knowsley Drug and Therapeutics Com., 1974-96; organising com. Nat. Drug Info. Conf., 1993-94; mem. Med. Benefit/Risk Found., 1994-96. Editor: Adverse Drug Reactions, 1994; co-editor: Medicines Management for Clinical Nurses, 1999; author/pub.: Alder Hey Book of Children's Doses, 1st edit., 1973; contbr. articles to profl. jours. Recipient Nicholas award Guild Hosp. Pharmacists, 1980, Ciba Geigy award, 1990; hon. rsch. assoc., hon. lectr. U. Liverpool, 1994-99. Fellow Royal Pharm. Soc. Gr. Britain (mem. BPC Pharmacy Practice Adjudicating Panel 1988-97, vice chmn. BPC Pharmacy Practice Adjudicating Panel 1994-97). Jewish. Avocations: choir singing, classical music, reading, current affairs, voluntary welfare work. Home and Office: 18 Cavendish Rd, Salford M7 4WW, England

WOLINSKY, FREDRIC DAVID, health services research educator; b. Chgo., Sept. 22, 1950; s. Morris and Anne Malinda Wolinsky; m. Sally Rae Hunt, June 11, 1972; 1 child, Michael Collin. BA, Friends U., 1972; MA, Drake U., 1974; PhD, So. Ill. U., 1977. Asst. prof. East Carolina U., Greenville, N.C., 1977-79; sr. rsch. scientist AMA, Chgo., 1979-81; assoc. prof. St. Louis U., 1981-85, prof. health svcs. rsch., 1996—; assoc. prof., then prof. Tex. A&M U., College Station, 1985-90; prof. medicine Ind. U., Indpls., 1990-96; mem. initial rev. groups NIH, Washington, 1988—. Author: The Sociology of Health: Principles, Professions and Issues, 2d edit., 1988; contbr. articles to profl. jours. Fellow Gerontol. Soc. Am. (editor Jour. Gerontology: Social Scis. 1998—), Assn. Health Svcs. Rsch.; mem. APHA (dep. editor Med. Care 1987-97), Am. Sociol. Assn. (chair med. sociology sect. 1993). Mem. Soc. of Friends. Avocations: writing, reading, carpentry. Fax: (314) 977-8150. E-mail: wolinsky@slu.edu. Home: 481 E Jackson Rd Webster Grvs MO 63119-4127 Office: St Louis U Sch Pub Health 3663 Lindell Blvd Ste 240 Saint Louis MO 63108-3342

WOLKERSDORFER, CHRISTIAN, geologist; b. Schwabach, Germany, Feb. 17, 1964; s. Horst Fritz Emil and Roswitha Ruth (Steiner) W.; m. Ulrike Marianne Margot Biller, June 30, 1990; children: Karoline, Franziska. Diploma, Tech. U., 1989, PhD, 1995. Scientific employee Tech. U., Clausthal, Germany, 1991-96; exec. Ingenieurbüro für Geotechnik, Freiberg, Germany, 1996-99; postdoctoral specialist in mine water hydrogeology Tech. U. Bergakademie, Freiberg, Germany, 1999—. Contbr. articles to profl. jours. Recipient Award Tryolian Govt., 1989, Hanns-Seidel Found., 1993-94, German Sci. Found., 1999-00. Mem. Deutsche Geologische Gesellschaft, Berufsverband Deutscher Geologen, Internat. Mine Water Assn. (gen. sec.). Home: Leipziger Str 20, D-09599 Freiberg/Sa Germany Office: Bergakademie Freiberg, Lehrstuhl für Hydrogeologie, D-09596 Freiberg Germany

WOLKOFF, PEDER, occupational health research scientist; b. Copenhagen, Jan. 13, 1946; m. Anne Rode-Møller, Apr. 11, 1981; children: Nikolaj, Christian. MSc, U. Copenhagen, 1972, PhD, 1976, DMS, 1996. Rsch. assoc. Brock U., adr., Can., 1972-74; NATO sci. fellow U. Amsterdam, The Netherlands, 1976; postdoctoral fellow U. Ottawa, Ont., 1976-78; sr. scholar U. Copenhagen, 1979-81; scientist Nat. Inst. Occupl. Health, Copenhagen, 1982-89, sr. rsch. scientist, 1990—. Author: Volatile Organic Compounds, 1995; contbr. articles to sci. jours. Recipient Scandinavian Indoor Climate award ISS Denmark, 1998. Mem. Internat. Soc. Indoor Air Quality and Climate, Internat. Acad. Indoor Air Scis. Office: Nat Inst Occupl Health, Lersø Parkallé 105, 2100 Copenhagen Ø, Denmark

WOLKOV, HARVEY BRIAN, radiation oncologist, researcher; b. Cleve., Feb. 8, 1953; s. Sidney and Norma (Levin) W.; m. Lauren Cronin, Jan. 9, 1993; 1 child, Nicole. BSc, Purdue U., 1975, MSc, 1977; MD, Medical Coll. Ohio, 1979. Diplomate Am. Bd. Radiology. Intern U. Calif., San Francisco, 1979-80; res. Stanford Med. Ctr., Stanford, Calif., 1980-83; rsch. asst. Stanford (Calif.) U., 1982; from asst. clin. prof. to assoc. clin. prof. U. Calif., Davis, 1983-97, assoc. clin. prof., 1997—; medical dir. Mercy Hosps., Sacramento, Calif., 1987-90; med. dir. Sutter Cancer Ctr. Dept. Radiation Oncology, Sacramento, Calif., 1990—; co-prin. investigator Pediat. Oncology Group, Chgo., 1989—; adv. bd. Nat. Graves Disease Found., Jacksonville, Fla., 1993—; bd. dirs. Sutter Hosps. Found., Sacramento. Author: (with others) Intraoperative Radiation, 1989, Frontiers in Radiation, 1991, Textbook Radiation Oncology, 1998; contbr. 30 articles to profl. jours. Fellow Am. Cancer Soc., 1978, 1983, Am. Coll. Radiology, 1997; recipient Travel award Am. Soc. Therapeutic Radiology Oncology, Reston, Va., 1987. Mem. Am. Coll. Radiolgy (chmn. standards accreditation com. 1997—, councilor at large 1999), Am. Cancer Soc. (reviewer 1990—), Assn. Residents Radiation Oncology (exec. com. 1997—), Council Affiliated Radiation Oncology Soc. (pres. 1999—), No. Calif. Radiation Oncology Soc. (pres. 1999—), Radiation Therapy Oncology Group (com. chair 1986—), Am. Soc. Therapeutic Radiology and Oncology (vice chair outcome rsch., fin. com., bd. dirs. 2000—), Calif. Radiation Oncology Soc. (pres.-elect 1999, pres. 2000). Jewish. Avocations: oil painting, sculpture, travel. Office: Sutter Cancer Ctr 2800 L St Ste 10 Sacramento CA 95816-5616

WOLLAN, CURTIS NOEL, theatrical producer and director; b. St. Paul, Nov. 10, 1951; s. Curtis Berdins and Lorraine Alice (Walser) W.; m. Jane Ellen Deter, May 17, 1980; children: Alexis Lorraine, Chet Curtis. BA in Speech and Theatre, Luther Coll., Decorah, Iowa, 1973; MFA in Directing, U. Iowa, 1976. Ptnr., artistic dir. Stage Two Prodns., Mpls., 1977-85; artistic dir. Chimera Theatre Co., St. Paul, 1985-87; ptnr., artistic dir. T.C.C. Prodns., Mpls., 1990-92; pres., prodr., dir. Troupe Am., Inc., Mpls., 1987—; past sec., bd. dirs. Midwest Citizens for Arts, Mpls., 1985-87; dir., asst. prodr. Sheehan Prodns. Medora Mus., Mpls., 1987-91; prodr., dir. Medora Musical, 1992—; guest dir. Circa 21 Prodns., Rock Island, Ill., 1983, Big League Theatricals, N.Y.C., 1988-93, Ryman Auditorium, Nashville, 1999, 2000. Creator, dir. mus. concept revue: The Lovely Liebowitz Sisters, 1986—; dir. nat. tour: Pump Boys and Dinettes, 1987-88, 95, 2000, Big River, 1988-89, Oil City Symphony, 1989-90, Gifts of the Magi, 1990, Driving Miss Daisy, 1991-92, Steel Magnolias, 1992-93, Steven King's Ghost Stories, 1993, 94, On Golden Pond, 1994, A Christmas Carol, 1996, 97, 98, 99, 2000, The Odd Couple, 1997, Moon over Buffalo, 1998/99, Lost Highway, 2000; co-author, dir. nat. tour: Mr. Pickwick's Christmas, 1987, 88, 89, 90, 91, 92; prodr., dir. nat. tour: 1940's Radio Hour, 1988, 90; prodr. nat. tour: A Child's Christmas in Wales, 1988, 89, Forbidden Broadway, 1990, 91, 94, Babes In Toyland, 1992, 93, 94, 95, 96, Tap Dance Kid, 1995, Mahalia, 1996, Miracle on 34th St...The Musical, 1997, 98, Schoolhouse Rock Live!, 1997/98, 98/99, 2000, Here's Love, 1999; actor film Bix, 1990, The Childhood Friend, 1993. Recipient Best Prodn. award, Best Direction award Twin Cities Critics Circle, Mpls., St. Paul, 1981, Patriotism award Am. Legion, 1995. Mem. Southeastern Theatre Conf. Lutheran. Avocations: movies, restaurants, travel, history, horseback riding. E-Mail: cwollan@mninter.net. Office: Troupe Am Inc 528 Hennepin Ave Ste 206 Minneapolis MN 55403-1810

WOLLENBERG, JÖRG, university educator; b. Ahrensbök, Holstein, Germany, Jan. 30, 1937; s. Fritz and Heta (Grimm) W.; m. Ilse Grefe, July 24, 1966; 1 child, Anna. Cert., U. Göttingen, Germany, 1965, PhD, 1976. Ednl. leader Working and Living, Hannover, Germany, 1966-71; dir. Volkschochschule, Bielefed, Germany, 1971-78; prof. U. Bremen, Germany, 1978—; dir. Bildungszentrum, Nürnberg, Germany, 1985-92. Author: Richelieu, 1977, French translation 1992, Von der Krise zum Faschismus, 1983, Den Blick Schärfen Gegen das Verdrängen und Entsorgen Bremen, 1998, Ahrensbök Eine Kleinstadt in National-Socialines, Bremen, 2000; editor: Judenverfolgung, 1988, Licht in die Schatten der Vergangenheit. Zur Enttabuisierung der Nürnberger Kriegsverbrecher-prozesse, Frankfurt, 1987, Menetekel Das Gesicht des Zweiten Weltkrieges, Krakau, 1991, Von der Hoffnung aller Deutschen, Wie die BRD entstand., 1945-49, Köln, 1991, Theodor Lessing, Ausgewählte Schikften, Bd. 1, 1995, Bd. 2, 1997, Völkervesohmung oder Völksveröhnung, 1918-1933, 1998. Evangilican Lutheran. Home: Fesenfeld 136, D 28203 Bremen Germany Office: U Bremen, Postfach 330440, 28334 Breman Germany

WOLLENHAUPT, JURGEN H., rheumatologist; b. Neuss, Germany, June 4, 1957; s. Karl-Heinz and Elfriede (Abstoss) W.; m. Katharina B. Krauch, 1987; children: Hannah Sophie, Charlotte Marie, Carl Christian. MD, U. Dusseldorf, Germany, 1983; PhD, Hannover (Germany) Med. Sch., 1998. Diplomate German Bd. Internal Medicine, German Bd. Rheumatology, German Bd. Phys. and Rehab. Medicine. Rsch. fellow divsn. immunology U. Heidelberg, Germany, 1985-86; rsch. assoc. U. Dusseldorf, 1986-89; staff mem. Hannover Med. Sch., 1989-92, sr. lectr., 1992-98, assoc. prof., 1998—, head dept. rheumatology, 1999—. Assoc. editor Aktuelle Rheumatologie. Maj. German Air Force, 1984-85. Office: Eilbek Hosp, 60 Friedrichsberger Str, D-22081 Hamburg Germany

WOLLER, JAMES ALAN, lawyer; b. Adrian, Mich., Dec. 27, 1946; s. Robert Arthur and Florence Emma (Jacob) W.; m. Jill Ann Samis, Aug. 18, 1968 (div. Aug. 1978); 1 child, Emily Erin; m. Elizabeth Julia Frey, May 22, 1982 (div. Apr. 1999); m. Carol Pierini, Oct. 29, 1999. BA, U. Mich., 1969; JD, Columbia U., 1974. Bar: N.J. 1974, U.S. Dist. Ct. N.J. 1974, U.S. Tax Ct. 1976, U.S. Supreme Ct. 1995. Assoc. McCarter & English, Newark, 1974-79; v.p. Pfaltz & Woller, PA, Summit, N.J., 1979-86, pres., 1987—. Editor Columbia U. Human Rights Law Rev., 1973-74. Mem. ABA, N.J. Bar Assn., Union County Bar Assn., Summit Bar Assn. (pres. 1987-88), Downtown Club (trustee 1997-99, treas. 1999, v.p. 2000), Raritan Yacht Club (fin. sec. Perth Amboy, N.J. 1988-89, treas. 1989-92, vice commodore 1993-94, commodore 1994-95), Columbia Law Sch. Assn. N.J. (trustee 1992-97, v.p. 1997—). Republican. Methodist. Avocation: sailing. Home: I-4 80 Audrey Zapp Dr # I4 Jersey City NJ 07305-4127 Office: Pfaltz & Woller PA 382 Springfield Ave Ste 217 Summit NJ 07901-2780

WOLLMAN, JUNE ROSE, clothing executive; b. Bklyn., June 14, 1929; d. Louis and Ella (Klein) Nierenberg; m. Howard Louis Wollman, Sept. 29, 1922; children: Jodi Ann (dec.), Randi Sue. Interior designer June Rose Decors Ltd., Valley Stream, N.Y., 1951—; with Louella Realty, N.Y.C., 1956-85; designer Lou Nierenberg Corp., N.Y.C., 1956-80; with Lou Nierenberg Internat., N.Y.C., 1974-85; with Lou Nierenberg Ltd., N.Y.C., 1985—, real estate pres., 1985—; cons. fake furs, jackets, coats, N.Y.C., 1985—. Trustee Green Acres Civic Co., Valley Stream, 1951—; bd. dirs. Mill Brov Civic Assn., 1990—; presenter Meml. Jodi Ann Wollman Scholarship Ann., South High Sch., Valley Stream, 1969—; life mem. Temple Emanu-El, Lynbrook, 1969—, asst. to chair Long Island (N.Y.) inter temple networking caring cmtys., 1989—, bd. dirs. sisterhood, 1990—; founding sponsor Mt. Sinai Med. Ctr., past v.p.; pres. Sam & Rose Klein Family Inc., 1975-85, CEO, 1985—; pres. Jodi Ann Wollman Glioblastomn Rsch. Fund, 1970-90. Recipient L.I.J.H. Med. Ctr. award Ladies Svc. Guild, New Hyde Park, N.Y., 1965-85, Mt. Sinai Med. Ctr. award, N.Y.C., 1969-89. Mem. Am. Jewish Congress (pres. South Shore chpt. 1957-63). Republican. Jewish. Avocations: reading, golf, tennis, swimming, travel. Home and Office: June Rose Decors Ltd 13 Cloverfield Rd Valley Stream NY 11581-2421

WOLLPERT, SANDRA COX, horse breeder; b. Phila., July 8, 1950; d. Robert Miller and Audrey Olive (Fullam) Cox; m. Worth Alan Wollpert, Sept. 29, 1973; children: Worth Douglas, Shaunna Lee. BA, Pa. State U., 1971, BS, 1971. Cert. secondary sch. tchr., Pa. Tchr. Cheltenham (Pa.) High Sch., 1972-73; officer Four Seasons Devel. Inc., Ohio, 1975-86; pres. SW Acquisitions and SW Realty Inc., Chardon, Ohio, Blythswood Farm, Inc., Chardon; bd. dirs. CW Holding Co., Wilmington, Del., Spruco Investment Co., Wilmington, Diamondtech Inc., Chardon; chmn. Arabian Race Com., Ohio, 1990-95. Author: Cerissa, 1976, Rebel's Honor, 1980, Winter Roses, 1983, Rapture's Fury, 1988; contbg. editor (pedigrees) Arabian, 1996—; contbr. articles to profl. jours. including Finish Line. Contbr. WWF, NRDC. Mem. Nat. Trust for Scotland, Arabian Jockey Club, Deep Springs Trout Club, Concord Country Club, Union League Phila., EARA, The Baronial Order of Magna Carta, Phi Kappa Phi (hon.). Avocations: horseback riding, fishing, horse racing, reading, traveling. Office: Blythswood Inc 401 South St Chardon OH 44024-2805

WOLOZIN, BENJAMIN LABE, biomedical researcher; b. Washington, May 27, 1958; s. Harold Wolozin and Ruth Leah Schwartz; m. Danielle Murstein, May 20, 1984; children: Rebecca Ruth, Jacqueline Murstein. BA, Wesleyan U., 1980; MD, PhD, Albert Einstein Coll. Medicine, 1988. Postdoctoral fellow Mt. Sinai Med. Ctr., N.Y.C., 1988-89; staff fellow NIH, Bethesda, Md., 1989-90; commd. offoicer NIH/USPHS, Bethesda, 1990-96; assoc. prof. pharmacology Loyola U. Med. Ctr., Maywood, Ill., 1996—; rschr. Parkinson's disease and Alzheimer's disease. Mem. Soc. Neurosci. (pres. Chgo. chpt. 1999—, Donald B. Lindlay prize 1988), AAAS. Democrat. Jewish. Avocations: soccer, tennis, hiking. Home: 215 S Monroe St Hinsdale IL 60521-3921 Office: Loyola U Med Ctr 2160 S 1st Ave Maywood IL 60153-3304

WOLPIN, MILES D., political science educator; b. Mt. Vernon, N.Y., Dec. 4, 1937; s. Arthur A. and Sylva Wolpin; m. Natasha S. Shuaeva, Apr. 17, 1992. JD, Columbia U., 1962, MA, 1964, PhD, 1968. Instr. CUNY, N.Y.C., 1965-66; jr. faculty Marlboro (Vt.) Coll., 1968-70; asst. prof. St. Francis Xavier U., Antigonish, N.S., Can., 1970-72; vis. asst. prof. U. N.Mex., Albuquerque, 1972-73; assoc. prof. SUNY, Potsdam, 1973-84, prof., 1984—; vis. rschr. Internat. Peace Rsch. Inst., Oslo, 1980-81, 89-90. Mem. editl. adv. bd. Internat. Jour. Peace Rsch., 1998—; contbr. articles to profl. jours. Town justice Town Ct., Hopkinton, N.Y., 1992-99. Mem. Nat. Assn. Scholars. Avocation: organic agriculture. E-mail: wolpin@northnet.org. Fax: 315-265-9421. Home: RR 3 Fletcher Rd 346 Potsdam NY 13676-9803 Office: Dept Politics State Univ Coll Potsdam NY 13676

WOLSCHIN, GEORG, physicist, journalist, consultant; b. Bremerhaven, Germany, Nov. 8, 1948; s. Karl and Irmgard (Runge) W.; m. Sabine Maria Assmann, July 6, 1971; children: Meike, Florian. Diploma in physics, U. Freiburg, Germany, 1973; PhD, Tech. U. Darmstadt, Germany, 1976; habilitation, U. Heidelberg, Germany, 1982. Scientist Lawrence Berkeley (Calif.) Lab., 1974-76, U. Heidelberg, 1976-81, Max-Planck-Inst., Heidelberg, 1981-83; editor Spektrum d. Wissenschaft (German edit. Scientific American), Heidelberg, 1983-90; editor, pub. J. Springer Verlag, Heidelberg, 1990-91, J.A. Barth-A. Hüthig Verlag, Leipzig-Heidelberg, Germany, 1991-93; freelance scientist and journalist Heidelberg, 1993—; cons. editor W. Kohlhammer Verlag, Stuttgart, Germany, 1994; cons. MVV, Mannheim, Germany, 1996, GSI, Darmstadt, 1999—. Author: Elementare Materie, Vakuum und Felder, 1986, 2d edit., 1994, Spektrum der Physik, 1992; contbr. over 100 articles to Spektrum d. Wissenschaft, 1983-93, 98—, 80 articles to Lexikon d. Nobelpreisträger, 1988, and over 40 articles to internat. profl. physics jours. With Bundeswehr, 1967-68, Bad Reichenhall, Germany. Mem. Germany Physics Assn. Avocations: mountaineering, skiing, badminton, Tai-Chi.

WOLTER, ANNA, astrophysicist; b. Milan, Apr. 29, 1960; 1 child, Martina. Diploma in physics, U. Milan, 1985. Physicist Smithsonian Astrophys. Obs., Cambridge, Mass., 1986-90; astronomer Astronomical Obs. in Brera, Milan, 1991—. Contbr. articles to profl. jours. Mem. Internat. Astron. Union, Am. Astron. Soc. Office: Via Brera, 28, 20121 Milan Italy

WOLTERS, CURT CORNELIS FREDERIK, foreign service officer; b. Nymegen, The Netherlands, Mar. 13, 1938; came to U.S., 1957; s. Frederik and Cornelia Johanna (Jansen) W.; m. Sara J. Daughters, June 10, 1962 (div. 1980); children: Gwyneth, Chad; m. Charlotte Cooper, Sept. 22, 1980 (div. 1988); children: Lottena, Cicely; m. Sylvana K. Perry, Apr. 1989; 1 child, Roger. Student, Wash. State U., 1958-61, U. Bonn, Fed. Republic Germany, 1962-63; BA, U. Oreg., 1964, MA, 1966; MBA, U. Washington, 1976; PhD, Pacific Western U., 1989. Asst. sec. Rep. Botswana Govt., Gaborone, 1966-68; program advisor The Ford Found., N.Y.C., 1968-74; sr. rsch. analyst Seattle C. of C., 1974-76; sr. assoc. Inst. Pub. Adminstrn. N.Y., N.Y.C., 1976-78; freelance economist Africa, 1978-79; econ. program officer, diplomat (AID) Dept. State, Washington, 1979—; cons. Inst. for Puget Sound Needs, Seattle, 1975-76, Pacific Cons., Washington, 1976; chair Am. Cmty. Assoc., U.S. Embassy, Lusaka, Zambia, 1998—. Contbr. numerous articles to profl. jours.; author project evaluations. Mem. civic action com. Congress of Racial Equality, Eugene, Oreg., 1965-66; vol. campaign Dixie Lee Ray Gubernatorial Campaign, Seattle, 1976; treas., chmn. fin. com. Internat. Sch. Islamabad, 1989-92. Carnegie Found. fellow, 1964-65, Africa-Asia pub. svc. fellow Maxwell Sch., 1966-68, fellow German Govt., U. Bonn, 1962-63; recipient Air Def. Command Outstanding Achievement award USAF, 1960, Cmty. Svc. award U.S. Embassy, Islamabad, 1992-93, 93-94, Meml. Order of Tin Hats, Kabaw Valley Shellhole chpt. Lusaka, Zambia, 1997—. Mem. Am. Econ. Assn., Air Force Assn., Wilson Ctr. (assoc. of Smithsonian Instn.), Am. Fgn. Svc. Assn., Holland Am. Club (treas. Greater Seattle area 1975-76), Am. Legion. Office: USAID/Zambia Lusaka Dept Of State Washington DC 20521-0001

WOLTERS, KARA, basketball player; b. Aug. 15, 1976. Office: 179 Allyn St Ste 403 Hartford CT 06103-1421

WOLTERS, MENNO, political science educator; b. The Hague, The Netherlands, Sept. 23, 1948; s. Hendrik A.J. Wolters and Wilhelmina H.M.M. Peijpers; a child, Vincent. MA, U. Leiden, The Netherlands, 1972, PhD, 1984. Radio reporter VARA, Hilversum, The Netherlands, 1973; with polit. sci. dept. U. Iowa, Iowa City, 1974; mem. faculty dept. data theory U. Leiden, 1974-78; mem. faculty dept. sociology U. Utrecht, The Netherlands, 1978-85; mem. faculty dept. bus., polit. and social sci. Open U., The Netherlands, 1984-88; mem. faculty dept. polit. sci. U. Nijmegen, The Netherlands, 1984-86; mem. faculty U. Twente Faculty Pub. Adminstrn. and Pub. Policy, Enschede, The Netherlands, 1987-97; ind. cons. European integration policies Enschede and Brussels, 1998—; info. tech. cons. OECD, Paris, 1988-92; cons. on cross-border coop. between Finnish and Russian local authorities, 1996-98; cons. on cross-border coop. among subnat. authorities in So. Africa to UN-CRD, 1996-98. Author: Interspace Politics, 1984; editor: (with Coffey) The Netherlands and EC Membership Evaluated, 1990, (with Frissen, Bekkers, Brussaard and Sneller) European Public Administration and Informatization, 1992; Democracy and Policy in the European Community, 1992. Councillor Town of Nijkerk, The Netherlands, 1974-78, Village Coun. of Ugchelen, Apeldoorn, The Netherlands, 1984-96. Mem. European Group for Pub. Adminstrn. Mem. Groenlinks Party. Avocations: genealogy, hiking. E-mail: MennoWolters@yahoo.com. Home: De Akker 19, 7552 EX Hengelo Twente Twente, The Netherlands

WOLTERS, ULRICH, physician, educator; b. Kleve, Germany, Feb. 20, 1959; s. Ernst and Therese (Bongers) W.; m. Stefanie Theissen, May 1986; children: Christopher, Johannes, Katherina, Theresa. MD, U. Cologne, 1987, habilitation, 1995. Resident dept. surgery U. Cologne, 1987-92, assoc. prof. dept. surgery, 1992-95, prof., attending physician, 1996—. Author: Handbook for Quality Assurance, 1996. Served with mil., 1978-81. Grantee Sanofi, 1998. Mem. German Surg. Soc., Cmty. for Quality Assurance, Soc. for Vascular and Endoscopic Surgery. Roman Catholic. Avocations: sailing, marathons. Office: Univ Cologne Surg Dept, J Stelzmanustr 9, 50931 Cologne Germany

WOLYNIES, EVELYN See GRADO-WOLYNIES, EVELYN

WOMER, CHARLES BERRY, retired hospital executive, management consultant; b. Cleve., Mar. 30, 1926; s. Porter Blake and Margaret (Berry) W.; m. Elizabeth Benson, Oct. 7, 1950; children: Richard B., Carol E., John C. MS in Hosp. Adminstrn., Columbia U., 1953; BS in Mech. Engring., Case Inst. Tech., 1949. Asst. dir. Univ. Hosps., Cleve., 1957-61; assoc. dir. Univ. Hosps., 1961-65, pres., 1976-82; mgmt. cons., 1982-90, ret., 1990; adminstr. Yale-New Haven Hosp., 1965-67, dir., 1968-76, pres., 1976; lectr. Yale U., 1965-78, 87-91; adj. asst. prof. Case Western Res. U., 1976-83; mem. Conn. Commn. on Hosps. and Health Care, 1973-76; bd. dirs. New Haven Savings Bank, 1969-76. Bd. govs. U. New Haven, 1972-76. Served with AUS, 1944-46. Fellow Am. Coll. Healthcare Execs. (life); mem. Am.

Hosp. Assn. (chmn. coun. on mgmt. and planning 1977-79), Conn. Hosp. Assn. (trustee 1970-74, pres. 1972-73, Disting. Svc. award 1976), Assn. Am. Med. Colls. (exec. coun. 1974-77, 78-80, treas. 1975-76, chmn. 1979-80, adminstrv. bd. coun. tchg. hosps. 1972-77, chmn. 1975-76, Disting. Svc. Mem. 1982—). Home: 88 Notch Hill Rd Apt 382 North Branford CT 06471-1861

WON, YOUKYUNG, business administration educator; b. Injae, Kangwon-do, South Korea, July 12, 1957; s. Bongsik Won and Kinam Yoon; m. Soonoak Kim, Jan. 11, 1993; 1 child, Seokjae. BBA, Sung Kyun Kwan U., Seoul, South Korea, 1981; MBA, Seoul Nat. U., Seoul, South Korea, 1983; PhD, Korea Advanced Inst. Sci./Tech, Taejon, South Korea, 1994. Instr. Sang Ji Jr. Coll., Wonju, South Korea, 1984-89, Jeonju U., Chonju, South Korea, 1995—. Contbr. articles to profl. jours. Avocations: badook, stamp collecting. Office: Jeonju U 1200, 3 Ga Hyoja-dong Wansan-gu, Chonju Chonbuk 560-759, South Korea

WONDRAZEK, FRITZ, physicist; b. Pfaffenhofen, Fed. Republic Germany, Nov. 14, 1953; s. Fritz and Anna (Wirzmueller) W. Diploma in Physics, Tech. U. Munich, 1980, Dr. rer. nat., 1983. Sci. asst. physics dept. Tech. Univ. Munich, 1980-83; laser physicist MBB-Medizintechnik GmbH, Munich, 1983-88, sect. mgr., 1989-91, project mgr., 1991-92; prof. applied physics Fachhochschule Munich, 1992—; scientific adviser Solid-State-Laser Ctr., Berlin, 1990-91. Author: Laser Lithotripsy, 1988; contbr. articles to profl. jours. Achievements include 13 U.S. and internat. patents. Home: Tannenstrasse 21, 85276 Pfaffenhofen Bavaria, Germany

WONG, ALBERT KOON-SIU, mechanical engineer, research scientist; b. Hong Kong, Nov. 19, 1957; arrived in Australia, 1969; s. Yuen and Choi-Yen (Lee) Wong; m. Alicia Szeto, May 25, 1985; 1 child, Natasha-Claire. B in Engring. with 1st class honors, U. NSW, Australia, 1981, PhD, 1985. Tchg. fellow Sch. Mech. Engring. U. NSW, 1982-84, resident tutor Basser Coll., 1982-85; rsch. scientist Def. Sci. and Tech. Orgn., Victoria, Australia, 1985-91, sr. rsch. scientist, 1991-95, prin. rsch. scientist, 1995—, head Machine Dynamics Group, 1997—; PhD supr. Free U. Brussels, 1991-92, Monash U., Victoria, 1992-95. Contbr. chpt. to ref. book, numerous articles to profl. jours.; patentee in field; contbr. 3d Supplement Encyclopedia of Materials Science and Engineering, 1992. Recipient Australia Day medal, Australia Day Coun., Victoria, 1991, Ministers award Min. Def., 1995. Avocations: collecting and restoring antiques, listening to classical music. Office: Defence Sci & Tech Orgn, 506 Lorimer St, Fishermans Bend VIC 3207, Australia

WONG, ALLAN WAI HOONG, civil engineer, consultant; b. Kowloon, Hong Kong, Apr. 17, 1957; s. Hoi Wah and Yin Yu (Au-Yeung) W.; m. Kwai Kuen Ng, Dec. 23, 1982; children: Odeon, Simpson. BSCE, U. Wash., 1978; Diploma Structural Steel Design, Imperial Coll. of Sci. Tech., London, 1980; MS in Structural Steel Design, U. London, 1980. Chartered engr., U.K.; chartered profl. engr., Australia; registered structural engr., Hong Kong, China. Grad. engr. W. Szeto & Ptnrs., Cons. Engrs., Hong Kong, 1980-82; asst. project mgr. Kuen Lee Constrn. Co. Ltd., Hong Kong, 1983; project engr. John C. Lo Cons. Engrs. and Architects, Hong Kong, 1984; civil and structural engr. RSP Architects, Planners & Engrs., Singapore, 1985-87; sr. engr./resident engr. Harris & Sutherland Cons. Engrs., Hong Kong, 1988-95; prin. engr. Halcrow Cons. Engrs., Hong Kong, 1996-97; chief civil engr. KCRC West Rail, 1998; sr. resident engr. Cyber Port Devel. Bldg. and Found. Contracts, 2000; cons. design engr. Garden Hotel Guangzhou, China, 1980-82; quality assurance team leader Phase 2A Mass Rapid transit, Singapore, 1985-87; resident engr. for 1st suspension bridge in China, Shantou, 1994-96; cons. NENT Landfill, Hong Kong, 1996, KCRC West Rail, Hong Kong, 1997; master degree course tutor computer-aided design, on-line edn. U. Paisley, U.K., 1994. Profl. engr. witness in ct. Hong Kong Govt., 1992. Fellow ASCE, Geol. Soc. London; mem. Instn. Engrs. Australia, Hong Kong Instn. Engrs., European Fedn. of Nat. Engring. Assn., Australian Computer Soc., Instn. Structural Engrs. U.K., Chartered Instn. of Water and Environ. Mgmt., Instn. Environ. Scientists U.K. Mem. Australian Chinese Evang. Ch. Achievements include quality assurance of first suspension bridge in China and deepest landfill in the world and checking all civil engineering designs for KCRC West Rail 34 km of heavy rails. Home: 127 Fiddens Wharf Rd, Killara NSW 2071, Australia Office: L12 Peninsula Ctr, 67 Mody Rd TST East, Kowloon Hong Kong China

WONG, ANDREW WAI BUN, marketing professional; b. Hong Kong, Nov. 1955; s. N. and Y. (Ng) Wong. Diploma, UCLA; BSME, RPI, 1980; diploma, UCLA, 1988. Gen. mgr. Telecom Ltd., Hong Kong, Spantum Ltd., Hong Kong; sr. mem. TV Ltd., Hong Kong; gen. mgr. Sigm Ltd., N.Y.C.; regional dir. Mite Ltd., Can.; with HK Telecom, 1997-99, EVHEV, 1999—; cons. Inpac Ltd.; mktg. advisor Hanasonic; media cons. Lotus Group. Author: Guerilla Warfare Tactics in Marketing. Mem. Hong Kong Mktg. Assn., Hong Kong Jaycees, HKPC. Office: PO Box 47283 Morrison Hill, Hong Kong China

WONG, CHESNEY TAK-KEUNG, internet analyst; b. Hoi Nam, China, Feb. 15, 1974; s. Wei Yin Wong and Chun Wa Fung; m. Lui Iris Kai-Wai. BEng with honors, Hong Kong U. Sci. & Tech., 1996. Analyst, cons. Andersen Consulting, Hong Kong, 1996-97; internet analyst, cons. Modem Media.Poppe Tyson, Hong Kong, 1999—; asst. computer office Cyberspace Ctr., Hong Kong U. Sci. and Tech., 1997-99. Mem. Assn. Computing Machinery (student, winner Internat. Programming Contest 1996, Regional Programming Contest 1995). Avocations: religion, internet business, travel, family. Office: Rm 2604-2605 Sino Plaza, 256 Gloucester Rd, Causeway Bay Hong Kong

WONG, CHEUK WAH, neurosurgeon; b. Canton, China, Aug. 19, 1951; s. Pak Sun and Wong Hing (Lee) W.; m. Chun Chun Chan, Jan. 9, 1976; children: Ching Yat Philip, Ting Yat Patrick. MB, Nat. Taiwan U., 1978. Resident in internal medicine Chang Gung Meml. Hosp., Taiwan, 1978-80, neurosurgeon, 1990-97; extern Med. Coun. Hong Kong, 1980-82; med. officer Kwong Wah Hosp., Hong Kong, 1982-89, Prince of Wales Hosp.-Chinese U. Hong Kong, 1998-99; pvt. practice Hong Kong, 2000—; chief divsn. neurosurgery Chang Gung Meml. Hosp., Keelung, 1995-97; lectr. Chang Gung Med. Coll., Taiwan, 1994-96, assoc. prof., 1996-97; spkr. Asian-Australasian Congress Neurol. Surgery, Taipei, 1995. Contbr. articles to profl. jours. Fellow Coll. Surgeons Hong Kong; mem. Neurosurg. Soc., N.Am. Skull Base Soc., Am. Assn. Neurol. Surgeons (assoc.). Avocations: walking, reading, music. Home: 213-221 Yu Chau St, Flat B 4/F Chiat Hing Bldg, 213-221 Kowloon Hong Kong Office: Taiwai Shatin, 92B Hin Tin Village, Hong Kong China

WONG, CHIH-SHUNG, anesthesiologist; b. Pen-Hu, Taiwan, Aug. 25, 1956; s. Ser and Yu-Lien (Wu) W.; m. Yen-Yen Chou; children: Pei-Yi, Sei-Yung. MD, Nat. Def. Med. Ctr., Taipei, Taiwan, 1981; PhD, Duke U., 1992. From resident dept. anesthesiology to att. physician Nat. Def. Med. Ctr., 1981-97, prof., 1997—; assoc. prof. Nat. Def. Med. Ctr., 1992—, dir. edn. anesthesiology, 1992-94, acting chmn. dept. anesthesiology, 1995-96, dir. clin. anesthesia, 1996—, chmn., 1999—; cons. anesthesiology tng. and edn. Taipei Dept. Health, 1992—; editl. com. Acta Anesthesiology Sinica, 1992—, editor-in-chief, 1994—; reviewer Chinese Jour. Pain, 1992—, Chinese Jour. Medicine, 1992-94. Grantee Nat. Sci. Coun., Taipei, 1992, Dept. Health, Taipei, 1993, Inst. Physics Acad. Sinica, Taipei, 1995. Mem. Soc. Anesthesiology (sec. gen. 1994—, exec. editor newsletter 1994—), Chinese Bd. Pain Clinicians. Avocations: travel, music, tennis, reading, gardening. Office: Nat Def Med Ctr Anesthesia, #8 Sec 3 Ting-Chow Rd, Taipei Taiwan

WONG, CHIN WAH, quantity surveyor; b. Singapore, Mar. 4, 1954; s. Joon Kai and Jee Lan (Kam) W.; m. Edna Teo Beng Kuan, Oct. 28, 1986. BS in Bldg. with honors, U. Singapore, 1979. Contracts cons. Jurong Town Corp., Singapore, 1977—; quantity surveyor Mass Rapid Transit Corp., Singapore, 1985-88. Served to lt. arty. Singapore Armed Forces, 1972-75. Recipient Good Svc. medal Singapore Armed Forces, Gold medal Singapore Inst. of Surveyors. Mem. Singapore Inst. Surveyors and Valuers, Jurong Country Club. Home: Gloriosa Block Parc Oasis 20-06, 41 Jurong East Ave 1, Singapore 609777, Singapore Office: Jurong Town Corp, Singapore Singapore

WONG, DENNIS KA-CHEONG, physician, physical therapist; b. Hong Kong, Hong Kong, Jan. 23, 1954. BA, Columbia U., 1977, cert. in phys. therapy, 1978, MS in Phys. Therapy, 1982; MD, Am. U. of the Caribbean, Montserrat, Brit. West Indies, 1988. Intern internal medicine dept. SUNY Health Sci. Ctr., Bklyn., 1988-89; Nat. Inst. on Disability and Rehab. Rsch. fellow Harvard-MIT Rehab. Engring. Ctr., Cambridge, Mass., 1989-90; resident rehab. medicine dept Kingsbrook Jewish Med. Ctr., Bklyn., 1990-92, chief resident rehab. medicine dept., 1992—; instr., attending physician dept. rehab. medicine Mt. Sinai Med. Ctr., N.Y.C., 1993-94, pvt. practice, 1994—. Fellow Am. Acad. Phys. Medicine and Rehab.

WONG, ELIZABETH, financial controller; b. Singapore, Nov. 1950; m. Calvin Chua; children: Joshua, Janice. B of Accountancy, U. Curtin, 1991; diploma in human resource mgmt., Singapore Inst. Human Resource, 1995. Nurse Drs. Oh and Lim Clinic, Singapore, 1968-74; accounts clk., asst. Matsushita Greatwall Corp., Singapore, 1974-82; asst. contr. Sears Buying Svcs. Inc., Singapore, 1982-88; acct. Premier Computer Coop., Singapore, 1988-90; fin. and adminstrv. mgr. Pilling Weck (Asia) Pte Ltd., Singapore, 1991-95; acct. Pilling Weck, Singapore, 1995-97, fin. contr., dir., 1997—. Mem. Singapore Human Resource Inst. (assoc.). Presbyterian. Office: Pilling Weck Asia P/L, 21 Moonstone Ln, Singapore 328462, Singapore

WONG, FELIX WU-SHUN, obstetrics and gynecology educator; b. Hong Kong, China, Apr. 28, 1951; arrived in Australia, 1992; s. Pui and King Dai (Wong) W.; m. Lam Angela, Oct. 28, 1984; children: Nicholas, Gregory. MBBS, Hong Kong U., 1976; M of Medicine, Singapore U., 1981; MD, Chinese U. Hong Kong, 1991. Med. officer Queen Mary Hosp., Hong Kong, 1976-87; sr. lectr. Prince of Wales Hosp., Hong Kong, 1988-92; prof. Liverpool (Australia) Hosp., 1992—; hon. prof. Sun Yat Sen U., Guangzhou, China, 1990—, Yang Med. Coll., China, 1991—, Peking Union Med. Coll., Beijing, 1995; dir. ob-gyn. South Western Health Svc., Australia, 1990—. Contbr. articles to profl. jours. Rsch. grantee Hong Kong Govt., 1986-92; rsch. fellow Croucher Found., 1986—. Mem. Royal Soc. Medicine, Royal College O & G, Royal Australian Coll. O & G, Hong Kong Acad. Medicine. Office: Liverpool Hosp, Dept Ob-Gyn, Liverpool 2170, Australia

WONG, HENRY HOK-YONG, retired aerospace engineering educator; b. Hong Kong, May 23, 1922; arrived in Eng., 1948; s. Shao Ping and De Fang (Guo) W.; m. Joan Mary Anstey, Aug. 16, 1952; children: Andrew, Philip, Sarah. BSc, Jiao-Tong U., Shanghai, 1947; diploma Imperial Coll., London U., 1952; PhD, Glasgow (Scotland) U., 1967. Chartered engr. Asst. lectr. Jiao-Tong U., Shanghai, 1947-48; engr. Armstrong Siddeley Co., Coventry, Eng., 1949; structural engr. Hunting Percival Aircraft Co., Luton, Eng., 1949-51; sr. structural engr. de Havilland Aircraft Co., Hatfield, Eng., 1952-57; sr. lectr. Hatfield Poly. (now Hertfordshire U.), 1957-59; from lectr. sr. lectr. reader to prof. aeronautics and fluid mechanics Glasgow U., 1960-87, prof. emeritus, sr. rsch. fellow, 1987—; part-time lectr. Hertforshire U., 1954-57; tng. lectr. aeronautics de Havilland Aircraft Co., 1955-57; lectr. Brit. Assn. for Advancement of Sci., 1974-87; advisor on Chinese affairs Glasgow U., 1986—, lectr. engring. heat transfer, 1973-81; advisor on aviation matters Glasgow Herald, 1978—; advisor on Chinese affairs Glasgow City Coun., 1986-96, Strathclyde Regional Coun., 1986-96; advisor Glasgow Airport Noise Abatement Group, 1980-85, adv., Guangdong (China) Higher Edn. Bur., 1985; cons. on econ. and technol. matters Shantou (China) Spl. Econ. Zone, 1988; cons. Ministry of Def., Eng., 1969, 70, 72, Dept. Energy, Eng., 1978, Nat. Engring. Lab., Scotland, 1973, South of Scotland Electricity Bd., 1982, Edinburgh Crown Ct., 1984, 87, Lothian Health Bd., Scotland, 1975-77, cons. Brit. Gas Corp., Scottish Aviation, Ferranti Ltd. Scotland, Rolls Royce, Scotland, Halliburton Svcs., U.S., FMC Corp. Ltd., John Brown Engring., Barr & Stroud, Ltd., and others, 1979-88. Author: Handbook on Heat Transfer for Engineers, 1977, Russian edit., 1979, Spanish edit., 1981, Hungarian edit., 1983; contbr. chpts. to: Thermal Conductivity, 1968, Practical Experiences with Flow Induced Vibration, 1979; contbr. articles to profl. jours. and procs.; patentee devices for suppression vortex excitation, thermal insulation for windows, vibration damping devices, devices for wave suppression, devices for reducing drag on road vehicles. Past treas., vice chmn. Kilmardinny Music Cir.; chmn. Glasgow Summer Sch., 1979-95. Hon. prof. Nanjing (China) U. Aeronautics and Astronautics, 1987, Nat. U. Def. Tech., Changsha, China, 1989; hon. prin. Ming Sheng Sch., Shantou, China, 1985; recipient Lord Provost's award City of Glasgow, 1988. Fellow Royal Aero. Soc. Avocations: reading, music, painting, swimming. Home: 77 Antonine Rd, Beardsden, Glasgow G61 4DS, Scotland Office: Glasgow Univ, University Ave, Glasgow G12 8QQ, Scotland

WONG, JAMES BOK, economist, engineer, technologist; b. Canton, China, Dec. 9, 1922; came to U.S., 1938, naturalized, 1962; s. Gen Ham and Chen (Yee) W.; m. Wai Ping Lim, Aug. 3, 1946; children: John, Jane Doris, Julia Ann. BS in Agr., U. Md., 1949, BS in Chem. Engring., 1950; MS, U. Ill., 1951, PhD, 1954. Rsch. asst. U. Ill., Champaign-Urbana, 1950-53; chem. engr. Standard Oil of Ind., Whiting, 1953-55; process design engr., rsch. engr. Shell Devel. Co., Emeryville, Calif., 1955-61; sr. planning engr., prin. planning engr. Chem. Plastics Group, Dart Industries, Inc. (formerly Rexall Drug & Chem. Co.), L.A., 1961-66, supr. planning and econs., 1966-67, mgr. long range planning and econs., 1967, chief economist, 1967-72, dir. econs. and ops. analysis, 1972-78, dir. internat. techs., 1978-81; pres. James B. Wong Assocs., L.A., 1981—; chmn. bd. dirs. United Pacific Bank, 1988—; tech. cons. various corps. Author: Jade Eagle, 2000; contbr. articles to profl. jours. Bd. dirs., pres. Chinese Am. Citizens Alliance Found.; mem. Asian Am. Edn. Commn., 1971-81. Served with USAAF, 1943-46. Recipient Los Angeles Outstanding Vol. Service award, 1977. Mem. Am. Inst. Chem. Engrs., Am. Chem. Soc., VFW (vice comdr. 1959), Commodores (named to exec. order 1982), Sigma Xi, Tau Beta Pi, Phi Kappa Phi, Pi Mu Epsilon, Phi Lambda Upsilon, Phi Eta Sigma. Home: 2460 Venus Dr Los Angeles CA 90046-1646

WONG, JAMES ROBERT, oncologist, educator. BA in Biochemistry summa cum laude, Harvard Coll., 1981, MD cum laude, 1986. Bd. cert. radiation oncology. Rsch. fellow, assoc. Dana-Farber Cancer Inst., Harvard Med. Sch., 1986-87; intern internal medicine New Eng. Deaconess Hosp., Harvard Med. Sch., 1987-88; resident Harvard Joint Ctr. for Radiation Therapy, Harvard Med. Sch., 1988-92; asst. prof. dept. radiology Cornell U. Med. Coll., 1992-97; chmn. dept. radiation oncology AHS/Morristown (N.J.) Meml. Hosp., 1997—; tchg. asst. introductory biology Harvard Coll., 1980; organizer, lectr. tumor biology course for health professions program Harvard U., 1982-83; assoc. clin. prof. radiation oncology Columbia U., Coll. Physicians and Surgeons, 1998—; co-dir. dept. radiation oncology N.Y. Downtown Hosp., 1992-94, dir. Nasopharyngeal Cancer Ctr., 1993-95, dir. dept. radiation oncology, 1994-95; asst. attending dept. radiation oncology N.Y. Hosp./Cornell U. Med. Ctr., 1992-97, radiation oncology fellowship program dir. dept. radiation oncology, 1996-97, dir. brain tumor and stereotactic radiosurgery dept. radiation oncology, 1996-97, dir. radiation oncology rsch., 1996-97; presenter, lectr. in field. Contbr. articles to profl. jours. Recipient Essay Nat. Grand Prize awad Boehringer-Ingelheim Pharmacology, 1985, Physician's Rsch. Tng. Fellowship award Am. Cancer Soc., 1987, Young Oncologist Essay award Am. Radium Soc., 1992; Harvard Club scholar, 1978-81, Edward Wetmore scholar, 1979-81; Betty Lea Stone fellow Am. Cancer Soc., 1983. Mem. Am. Soc. for Therapeutic Radiology and Oncology (Traveling award 1990), Chinese Am. Med. Soc. (bd. dirs. 1995-98), Am. Coll. Radiology, Radiol. Soc. N.J., Oncology Soc. N.J., Phi Beta Kappa. Office: Morristown Meml Hosp 100 Madison Ave Morristown NJ 07960-6095

WONG, JOSEPH CHEE-HOE, nuclear medicine physician; b. Seremban, Negeri, Malaysia; arrived in Australia, 1982; MBBS with honors, U. Queensland, Brisbane, 1988; Fellowship, Australasian Coll. Physicians, 1995; postgrad., U. Queensland, Brisbane, Australia, 1998—. Registrar Wellington Area Health Bd., Timaru, New Zealand, 1990, Princess Margaret Hosp., Christchurch, New Zealand, 1991, Christchurch Hosp., 1992, Prince of Wales Hosp., Sydney, 1993-94; clin. rsch. assoc. Guy's and St. Thomas Hosps., London, 1995-96; staff physician Royal Brisbane Hosp., 1996—; mem. rsch. sub-com. Royal Brisbane Hosp., 1998, 99; invited spkrs. Australasian Doctors Assn., Gold Coast, Australia, 1998, 99, European Sch. of Nuclear Medicine, Warsaw, 1995. Contbr. articles to profl. jours.; contbg. author: Critical Care Nephrology, 1998. Fellow Royal Australasian Coll. Physicians; mem. Australian and New Zealand Soc. of Nuclear Medicine (treas. 1997-99, pres. 1999—), Australian and New Zealand Assn. of Physicians in Nuclear Medicine, Soc. Nuclear Medicine. Avocations: cycling, photography. Office: Nuclear Med Dept, Royal Brisbane Hosp/Herston, 4029 Brisbane Australia

WONG, KAN SENG, Singapore government official; b. Sept. 8, 1946; m. Lee Hong Geok; two children. BA, U. Singapore; MS, U. London. Tchr. Ministry of Edn., 1964-67; with adminstrv. svc., 1970-81; pers. man Hewlett Packard Singapore, 1981-85; M.P. Kuo Chuan, Singapore, 1984, Thomson GR C, Singapore; min. state, home affairs and cmty. devel. Govt. of Singapore, 1985, min. state cmty. devel. and comm. and info., 1985, acting min. for cmty. devel., min. of state (comm. and info.), 1986, min. cmty. devel., 2d min. for fgn. affairs, 1987, min. cmty. devel., 1988-91, min. fgn. affairs, 1991-93, min. home affairs, 1994—. Office: Ministry Home Affairs, Phoenix Park, Tanglin Rd, Singapore 247904, Singapore*

WONG, KIN-LU, engineering educator, electrical engineer; b. Tainan, Taiwan, Aug. 14, 1959; s. Be-Gee and Be-Lien (Tsai) W.; m. Ruey-Tsai Lin, Sept. 13, 1986; children: Wei-Der, Lee-Gia. BSEE, Nat. Taiwan U., Taipei, 1981; MSEE, Tex. Tech. U., 1984, PhD in Elec. Engring., 1986. Vis. scientist Max-Planck Inst. Plasma Physics, Munich, Germany, 1986-87; assoc. prof. Nat. Sun Yat-sen U., Kaohsiung, Taiwan, 1987-90, prof., 1991—, chmn. Elec. Engring. Dept., 1994—. Recipient Outstanding Rsch. award Nat. Sci. Coun. Republic of China, 1993. Mem. IEEE, Microwave Soc. Republic of China (directorate 1995—), Internat. Union Radio Sci. (mem. com. Republic of China 1991—, Outstanding Rsch. award 1993, Young Scientist award 1993). Avocations: basketball, swimming, mountain climbing. Home: No 109 Ta-Rong St, 804 Kaohsiung Taiwan Office: Dept Elec Engring Nat Sun-, Yat-sen U #70 Lien-Hai Rd, 804 Kaohsiung Taiwan

WONG, KON MAX, electrical engineer educator; b. Macau, China, June 11, 1945; arrived in Can., 1976; s. Ho Ting and Sin Hung (Yung) Wong; m. Margaret Ellen Rumsey, Aug. 25, 1984; children: An Zhong Alexander, Hui Zhong Richard. BSc in Engring., U. London, 1969; DIC, Imperial Coll., London, 1972; PhD, U. London, 1974, DSc, 1995. Rsch. engr. Plessey Telecom Rsch., Taplow, 1969-76; assoc. prof. Tech. U. Nova Scotia, Halifax, Can., 1976-81; prof. McMaster U., Hamilton, China, 1981—, Mitel Prof. signal processing, 1999—; chmn. Dept. Elec. Engring. McMaster U., Hamilton, 1985-86, 88-94; hon. prof. South East U., Nanjing, China, 1995—; vis. prof. Chinese U. Hong Kong, Hong Kong, 1997—; cons. Defence Rsch. Establishments, Can., 1986—, Mitel Corp., Ottawa, Can., 1993—, Lockheed-Martin, Ottawa, 1993-94, Canadian Marconi, Ottawa, 1995-97; assoc. editor IEEE Transaction on Signal Processing, 1997—. Contbr. articles to textbooks and to profl. jours. Fellow Inst. Elec. Engrs., Inst. Physics, Royal Statistics Soc. Avocations: table tennis, swimming, squash, piano playing, painting. Office: Dept Elec & Computer Engring, McMaster U, Hamilton, ON Canada

WONG, KWOK-YIN, chemistry educator; b. Hong Kong, Oct. 9, 1958; s. Yan-Fai and Lai-Ming (Yeung) W. BSc with honors, U. Hong Kong, 1981, PhD, 1986. Postdoctoral rsch. fellow Calif. Inst. Tech., Pasadena, 1986-87; chemist Govt. Lab., Hong Kong, 1987-90; lectr. The Hong Kong Poly. U., Hunghom Kowloon, 1990-94, assoc. prof., 1994-95, prof., 1995—; coun. mem. Hong Kong Chem. Soc., 1994-95. Contbr. articles to profl. jours. Rch. Grants Coun. grantee Hong Kong, 1991, 92, 93, 96, 2000, Croucher Found. grantee Hong Kong, 1993. Mem. AAAS, Am. Chem. Soc. (sec. Hong Kong Internat. Chem. Scis. chpt. 1998-2000, Rsch. Grants Coun. (panel mem. 1999—), Royal Soc. Chemistry. Office: Hong Kong Poly U, Dept Applied Biology & Chem Tech, Hunghom Kowloon Hong Kong

WONG, LILY LIM, interior design company executive, architect; b. Hong Kong, China, June 30, 1962; d. James and Shio Cho Go (Lim) Limpio; m. Billy Wong, Apr. 29, 1990; children: Sarah, Jesurun, Gracie. BS in Architecture, UST, The Philippines, 1985. Architect Leo A. Daly (Pacific) Ltd., Hong Kong, 1986-89; architect (resident) P&T Architects Ltd., Hong Kong, 1989-90; architect Leigh & Orange, Ltd., Hong Kong, 1990-91; pres. Kangotic Phils., Inc., Pasig City, The Philippines, 1991—; v.p. Cosmos Resources, Inc., Pasig City, The Philippines, 1992—; pres. Limex Phils., Inc., Pasig City, The Philippines, 1993—; bd. dirs. Midpark Ltd. Hong Kong, J&S Canada Co, Liz Design Ltd., Can., Sorpresa Can. Ltd. Recipient Cert. of Merit Asia Pacific Interior Design, IDA, Hong Kong and F Pal. Mem. Can. C. of C. in The Philippines. Avocations: golf, travel, reading, tennis, swimming. Office: Limex Phils Inc Ste 1605, 16/F Phil Stck Exch W Twr, Ort Ctr Pasig City 1605, The Philippines

WONG, LING WAH, investment company executive; b. Nien Do, Kiangsi, China, July 1, 1946; s. I-Ting and Shing Teh (Wu) W.; m. May L. Lo, Oct. 23, 1992. BS in Econs., So. Ill. U., 1969. V.p. mktg. Blyth Eastman, Dillon, N.Y., 1976-81; exec. v.p. Sun Hung Kai-Bear Stearns, Hong Kong, 1981-83; mng. dir. Security Pacific Pvt. Capital (subs. Security Pacific Bank), 1983-89, Spremberg, Hong Kong, 1989-94; exec. dir. Warburg Asset Mgmt., Hong Kong, 1994-95; chmn. Spremberg, Hong Kong, 1995—; cons. Intrados Group, Washington, 1995—; Asia coord. Am. Stock Exch., N.Y.C., 1981—. Author: Marketing Manual for Unit Investment Fund, 1996. Mem. The Am. Club, Jockey Club. Republican. Avocations: tennis, climbing, photography, animal science, travel. Office: Spremberg Co Ltd Blissful Bldg, 247 Des Voeux Rd Ctrl Ste 1103, Hong Kong Hong Kong

WONG, MARY, financial executive; b. Ipoh, Perak, Malaysia, Nov. 20, 1956; m. Yam. B in Accountancy, U. Singapore, 1978. CPA, Singapore. Credit officer, sr. fin. exec. Sing Investments & Fin./Sing Bullion Pte. Ltd., 1978-80; acct. Clemco Internat., Singapore, 1980-83; acctg. and adminstrv. mgr. Mark Controls/Crane Ltd., Singapore, 1984-95; fin. and adminstrv. mgr. Wattyl-Dimet, Singapore, 1996-97, 98—; fin. ops. mgr. Hewlett Packard, Singapore, 1996-97, 98—; corp. sec. Wattyl-Dimet, Singapore. Exec. coun. Luth. and Meth. Chs., Singapore. Mem. Inst. Cert. Accts. Singapore. Methodist. Avocation: reading. E-mail: yammary@hotmail.com and wattylsf@pacific.net.sg. Home: 487 Clementi Rd, Singapore 599480, Singapore Office: Wattyl-Dimet Singapore Ltd, 24 Gul Dr, Singapore 629472, Singapore

WONG, MING HUNG, biology educator, environmentalist, consultant; b. Hong Kong, May 16, 1946; s. Kai Wing and Wan Yin (Wu) W.; m. Ursula Absalom, June 5, 1975; children: Adrian Nga-jing, Dominic Ming-Ming. BSc, Chinese U., Hong Kong, 1968; MSc, Durham (Eng.) U., 1969, PhD, 1973, DSc, 1992; MBA, Strathclyde (Scotland) U., 1992. Biology lectr. Chinese U., Hong Kong, 1973-81, sr. lectr., 1981-85; reader, head in biology Hong Kong Bapt. U., 1986-89, chair, prof., head, 1990—, dir. Centre for Waste Recycling and Environ. Biotech., 1990-97; dir. Inst. for Natural Resources and Waste Mgmt., 1997—; sr. rsch. fellow Croucher Found., 1997—. Mem. editl. bd. Resources, Conservation and Recycling, Environ. Sci., Acta Scientiae Circumstantiae, Internat. Jour. Phytoremediation, Environ. Geochemistry and Health, Environ. Mgmt.; contbr. more than 200 articles to profl. jours. Fellow Inst. Biology (U.K.; chmn. Hong Kong chpt.), Instn. Waste and Environ. Mgmt. (U.K.). Avocation: travelling. Office: Hong Kong Bapt U, 224 Waterloo Rd, Kowloon China

WONG, OLIVIER, physician, educator; b. Paris, June 6, 1961; s. Ming and Christiane (Berge) W.; m. Catherine Goutierre, July 1, 1988; children: Marine, Nathalie, Heloise, Nicolas. Baccalaureat C, Coll. Stanislas, France, 1979; CESAM, U. Paris VI, 1992; MD, Faculte Necker, Paris, 1992; B of Statistics, Faculte Bicetre, Paris, 1998. Registrar Drass Ile de France, Paris, 1989-91; pvt. practice Reims, France, 1992-93; clin. rsch. assoc. Hoecht Ag, Paris, 1994—; pvt. practice Paris, 1994, 95; legist physician Mairie de Paris, 1994-96; cons. Le Generaliste, Paris, 1996—; tchr. Faculte/Necker, Paris, 1995—; physician Hosp. Nursery, Paris, 1995—. Contbr. articles to profl. jours. Cons. Drug Nat. Agy., St. Denis, France, 1996—; cons. regulatory affairs Commn. Transparence, 1998—. Medecin Capitaine de Res. Svc. de Sante des Armees, 1992—. Recipinet G d'or, 2000. Fellow Parisian Coll. of Family Doctors. Avocations: recreational activites with my children, traveling. Office: Cabinet Med, 45 Rue Saint Lambert, 75015 Paris France

WONG, OTTO, epidemiologist; b. Canton, China, Nov. 14, 1947; came to U.S., 1967, naturalized, 1976; m. Betty Yeung, Feb. 14, 1970; children: Elaine, Jonathan. BS, U. Ariz., 1970; MS, Carnegie Mellon U., 1972, U. Pitts., 1973; ScD, U. Pitts., 1975. Cert. epidemsiologist Am. Coll. Epidemi-

ology, 1982. USPHS fellow U. Pitts., 1972-75; asst. prof. epidemiology Georgetown U. Med. Sch., 1975-78; mgr. epidemiology Equitable Environ. Health Inc., Rockville, Md., 1977-78; dir. epidemiology Tabershaw Occuopational Med. Assocs., Rockville, 1978-80; dir. occupational rsch. Biometric Rsch. Inst., Washington, 1980-81; exec. v.p., chief epidemiologist ENSR Health Scis., Alameda, Calif., 1981-90; chief epidemiologist, pres. Applied Health Scis., San Mateo, Calif., 1991—; adj. prof. epidemiology and biostats. Tulane U. Med. Ctr., New Orleans; vis. prof. epidemiology and occupl. health Nat. Def. Med. Ctr., Taipei, Taiwan, Shanghai Med. U.; vis. prof. dept. cmty. & family medicine Chinese U. Hong Kong; cons. WHO, Nat. Cancer Inst., Nat. Inst. Occupl. Safety and Health, Occupl. Safety and Health Adminstrn., Nat. Heart, Lung and Blood Inst., Internat. Agy. for Rsch. on Cancer, U.S. EPA, Ford Motors Co., Gen. Electric, Mobil, Chevron, Union Carbide, Fairfax (Va.) Hosp., Agy. for Toxic Substances and Disease Registry, U. Ariz. scholar, 1967-68. Assoc. editor Annals Epidemiology; contbr. articles to profl. jours. Fellow Am. Coll. Epidemiology, Human Biology Council; mem. Am. Pub. Health Assn., Biometric Soc., Soc. Epidemiologic Rsch., Phi Beta Kappa, Pi Mu Epsilon. Republican. Office: Applied Health Scis PO Box 2078 181 2nd Ave Ste 628 San Mateo CA 94401-3812

WONG, PATRICIA JIA-YIING, mathematician, educator; b. Singapore, Aug. 21, 1962; d. William and Liew-Hong (Phuah) W. BSc with 1st class honors, Nat. U. Singapore, 1985, diploma in edn., 1986, MSc, 1988, PhD, 1992. Tchr. Ministry of Edn., Singapore, 1986-91; tchg. fellow Nanyang Tech. U., Singapore, 1991, lectr., 1992-97, sr. lectr., 1998—; assoc. Nat. Inst. Edn. Ctr. Edn. Rsch., Singapore, 1996—. Author: Error Inequalities in Polynomial Interpolation and their Applications, 1993, Advanced Topics in Difference Equations, 1997, Positive Solutions of Differential Difference and Integral Equations, 1999; contbr. chpts. to books, numerous articles to profl. jours. Asst. treas. sch. adv. com. Juying Primary Sch., Singapore, 1995-97; sec. Nanyang Civil Def. Exec. Com., 1998—. Mem. Internat. Fedn. Nonlinear Analysts, Assn. Math. Educators, Nanyang Cmty. Club (mem. mgmt. com. 1994—). Office: Nanyang Tech U Sch Elec & Elec Engring, 50 Nanyang Ave, Singapore 639798, Singapore

WONG, PHILLIP ALLEN, osteopathic physician; b. Oakland, Calif., Dec. 8, 1956; s. Timothy Him and Lillian (Lee) W.; m. Lisa Perreautt, Apr. 30, 1983; children: Ashley, Heather. BS in Microbiology and Chemistry, No. Ariz. U., 1979; DO, Kirksville Coll. Osteo. Med., 1983. Intern Kirksville Osteo. Health Ctr., 1983-84; staff family physician USAF, Kirtland AFB, N.Mex., 1984-87; CEO, pvt. practice Albuquerque, 1987—. Capt. USAF, 1984-87. Mem. Am. Acad. Osteopathy (bd. cert. in osteo. manipulative medicine), Am. Osteo. Assn., Am. Coll. Osteo. Family Physicians (bd. cert. family practice), N.Mex. Osteo. Med. Assn. (bd. mem.), Ariz. Acad. Osteopathy (bd. mem.), Cranial Acad. (bd. cert. in cranial in the osteo. field). Office: 10211 Montgomery Blvd NE Ste A Albuquerque NM 87111-3608

WONG, PO-KEUNG, environmental microbiologist, toxicologist; b. Hong Kong, Aug. 17, 1954; s. Cheung-Sung and Ngau (Mok) Wong; m. Lai-Hor Lee, 1977; children: Carmine, Carol, Carson. BSc in Biology, Chinese U. Hong Kong, 1977, MPhil in Microbiology, 1979; PhD in Microbiology, U. Calif., Davis, 1983. Lectr. Chinese U. Hong Kong, 1986-94; assoc. dir. Ctr. Environ. Studies, Hong Kong, 1991-2000; sr. lectr. Chinese U. Hong Kong, 1994-96, assoc. prof., 1996-97, prof., 1997—; vis. rsch. scientist, U. Calif., Davis, 1993; mem. ISO14000 Tech. Com., Hong Kong, 1997—. Editor-in-chief Jour. Environ. Scis. (Chinese Acad. Scis.), 1995—. Mem. Am. Soc. Microbiology, Soc. Toxicology, Soc. Environ. Toxicology and Chemistry, Chartered Instn. Water and Environ. Mgmt. Office: Chinese U Hong Kong, Dept Biology Shatin NT, Hong Kong SAR, China

WONG, RODERICK SUE-CHEUN, mathematics educator; b. Shanghai, People's Republic of China, Oct. 2, 1944; s. Chu-Chai and May-Chaun (Yu) W.; m. Edwina Ching-Yee Nee, June 26, 1976; children: Priscilla Mae, Letitia Leigh. BA, San Deigo State Coll., 1965; PhD, U. Alberta, Edmonton, Can., 1969. Asst. prof. U. Manitoba, Winnipeg, Can., 1969-73, assoc. prof., 1973-79, prof. math., 1979-86, prof., head applied math., 1986-93; prof., head City U. of Hong Kong, Kowloon, 1994-97, prof. math. dean faculty sci. and engring., 1997—; mem. grant selection com. for pure and applied math. Nat. Sci. and Engring. Rsch. Coun. of Can., Ottawa, 1988-91; math. cons. Schlumberger-Doll Rsch. Ctr., Conn., 1979; math. cons. Integrated Engring. Software Inc., Winnipeg, 1989-90, Atomic Energy of Can. Ltd., Pinawa, Can., 1991-93. Author: Asymptotic Approximations of Integrals, 1989; editor: Asymptotic and Computational Analysis, 1990; co-editor-in-chief Methods and Applications of Analysis, 1993-99. Killam Rsch. fellowship Can. Coun., 1982-84. Fellow Royal Soc. of Can.; mem. Can. Applied Math. Soc. (pres. 1989, 90), Can. Math. Soc. (v.p. 1991-93), Hong Kong Math. Soc. (pres. 1996-98). Office: City Unv of Hong Kong Dpt of Math, Tat Chee Ave, Kowloon Hong Kong

WONG, SIU KOU, electronic engineer; b. Hong Kong, Oct. 10, 1960; s. King Kwong W. and Yun Wah Lam; m. Lai Tim Man, Apr. 24, 1993; 1 child, Cheuk Ying Charlie. AP (HK), Hong Kong Poly. U., 1983. Registered profl. engr., Hong Kong. Engr. Hong Kong Jockey Club, 1983-88, Cable & Wireless HKT, 1988—. Mem. IEEE, Instn. Elec. Engr., Hong Kong Instn. Engrs. Avocations: reading, hiking. Home: Flat 14 5/F Block Q Telford Gardens, 33 Wai Yip St, Kowloon Hong Kong Office: Pacific Century Cyberworks, PO Box 9896 GPO, Hong Kong Hong Kong

WONG, STEPHEN T.C., radiology, neurology, computer scientist, and bioengineer educator; b. Hong Kong, Sept. 8, 1959; came to U.S., 1985; s. Cheuk and Sam Kuk (Lam) W.; m. Sandie P.K. Ho, Jan. 26, 1960; children: Solomon, Gabriella. B of Engring., U. Western Australia, Perth, 1983; MSc in Computer Sci., Lehigh U., 1989, PhD in Computer Sci., 1991. Registered profl. engr., Pa. Mech. engr. Mass. Engring. Co., Manila, Philippines, 1977-78; rsch. assoc. Australian Nat. U., Canberra, 1982-83; elec. engr. Hewlett Packard Co., Singapore, 1984-85; tech. staff AT&T Bell Labs., Allentown, Pa., 1985-87; rsch. assoc. NSF Engring. Rsch. Ctr., Lehigh Valley, Pa., 1988-91; rschr. Japan MITI ICOT Lab., Tokyo, 1992-93; asst. prof. U. Calif., San Francisco, 1993—; sr. tech. staff Philips Rsch. Lab., Palo Alto, Calif., 1996-97; chief arch., dir., dir. engring. Philips Med. Sys., Best, The Netherlands, 1999-2000; v.p. info. tech. Charles Schwab & Co., 2000—; grant rev. com. NSF, Washington, 1995—, NIH, Bethesda, 1997—; tech. adv. com. Intenrat. Conf. Computer Assay Radiology, Berlin, 1996—. Editor: Medical Image Databases, 1997; mem. editl. bd. Jour. Computer Med. Imaging, 1997—; editor Digital Librs. in Medicine, 1998. Australian Nat. U. scholar, 1982, Gleddon Tour scholar, 1983; NSF fellow, 1987-91; Japan Sci. and Tech. grant, 1992-93. Mem. IEEE (chpt. chmn. 1984—), Am. Assn. Med. Physicists. Achievements include patent disclosures and product devel. in biometrics on the World Wide Web; digital trust center of medical imaging; broadcasting model of electronic medical record; personalization of electronic medical record; development of the first working prototype of optical time domain reflectometer and hospital-wide PACS in U.S. Academic Medical Centers, and product development of radiology information systems PACS, computerized patient record and Healthcare systems and on-line global trading systems. Office: UC San Francisco Sch Medicine Dept Radiology 505 Parnassus Ave # 628 San Francisco CA 94122-2722

WONG, TIN HONG, finance administrator, accountant; b. Malaysia, Apr. 17, 1954; arrived in Eng., 1977; s. Onn Nan Wong and Kit Fong Poon; m. Evelyn Maria Jenkinson Dorothea, Aug. 15, 1988; children: Sophie, Aimee, Annie. BS in Acctg., Stockport, Manchester, Eng., 1980; postgrad in fin., London, 1984. CPA U.K. Ptnr. Arif Wang and Co., London, 1985-90, Wang and Co., London, 1985—; fin. officer Immigration Adv. Svc., London, 1992-99; CEO, Wang Enterprise, London, 1997—. Fellow Taxation and Mgmt. Accts. (Australia), Inst. Cost and Exec. Accts. (U.K.). Avocations: collecting watches, reading, table tennis, traveling, financial research. Home: 94 Malpas Rd, London SE4 1BU, England

WONG, TOMMY SAI-WAI, civil engineering educator; b. Hong Kong, Dec. 14, 1952; arrived in Singapore, 1985; naturalized, 1990; s. Sze-Fong and En-Yueh (Woo) W.; m. Christina Lai-Lin Sum, July 24, 1982; children: Alston Jun-Ngai, Lester Jun-Long, Hanson Jun-Chuen. BS, Leeds U., 1974; MS, Birmingham U., 1976; PhD, Nat. U. Singapore, 1994. Registered profl. engr., Singapore. Author: An Introduction to Kinematic Wave Method for Storm Drainage Design, 1992; contbr. articles to sci. jours., including Jour. Hydrology, Jour. Hydraulic Engring., Water Sci. and Tech., Advances in Water Resources, Hydrological Sci. and Tech., Hydrological Scis. Jour., Jour. of Irrigation and Drainage Engring, Jour. Hydrologic Engring., Jour. Hydraulic Rsch., Hydrological Processes. Fellow ASCE; mem. Internat. Assn. Hydraulic Rsch., Internat. Assn. Hydrological Scis., Singapore Inst. Mgmt., Hong Kong Mgmt. Assn. Achievements include research in time of concentration and peak discharge formulas for drainage design. Home: 135 Sunset Way # 06-13, Singapore 597158, Singapore Office: Nanyang Tech U Sch Civil & Struc, Engring, Nanyang Ave, Singapore 639798, Singapore

WONG, WA PENG, engineering educator; b. Macau, Aug. 17, 1964. B in Engring., U. Essex, 1992; MSc, City Univ. Hong Kong, 1996. Engr. H.K. Telecomms., Hong Kong, 1993-98; lectr. City Univ. Hong Kong, 2000—. Mem. IEEE, Internat. Soc. Optical Engring. Office: City Univ Hong Kong, 83 Tat Chee Ave, Hong Kong China

WONG, WAI MING OTIS, editor-in-chief; b. Hong Kong, Aug. 21, 1954; m. Shu Hing Lee, Mar. 6, 1976; children: Wong Man Hon, Wong Man To, Wong Man Yin. Diploma in English Lang. and Lit., Shue Yan Coll., Hong Kong, 1981; MA in Chinese Lang. and Literature, Su Zhou U., 2000. Civil servant Hong Kong Govt., 1973—. Editor-in-chief Poetry, 1976-84, Shi Bi-Monthly, 1989-94, 97-98, Modern Poetry - East and West, 1981, Aesculus Chinensis, 1991, Modern Chinese Poetry Anthology, 1995, On Poets and Poetry, 1999. Recipient first prize open sect. Astronomical Project Competition Essay Hong Kong Urban Coun., 1977, Internat. Order of Merit Internat. Biog. Centre, Cambridge, 1993. Mem. Shih Feng Assn., Shi Bi-Monthly Assn., Hong Kong Archaeol. Soc., Hong Kong Ex-Libris Assn. Avocations: art collecting, travel. Office: Sai Ying Pun Post Office, PO Box 50431, Hong Kong Hong Kong

WONG, WAI ON, mechanical engineer, educator; b. Hong Kong, Apr. 13, 1964; s. Tin Po and Kit Ling (Hung) W.; m. Vivian Wong, Sept. 5, 1993. B of Engring. with honors, Hong Kong Poly., 1987, MSc in Precision Engring., 1992, PhD, 1997. Engring. trainee Hong Kong Productivity Ctr., 1985-86; mech. engr. Schick Ltd., Hong Kong, 1987-89, Miti Rsch. Ltd., Hong Kong, 1989-90, Philips (Hong Kong) Ltd., 1990; lectr. Hong Kong Poly., 1990-99, asst. prof., 1999—; cons. Kowloon-Canton Ry. Corp., Hong Kong, 1992, Jebsen & Co. Ltd., Hong Kong, 1995. Contbr. articles to profl. jours. Rsch. Grants Coun. Hong Kong grantee, 1998, Univ. Rsch. grantee, 1998. Mem. AAAS, Hong Kong Profl. Tchrs. Union. Avocations: swimming, reading, hiking. Home: Flat 1003 Blk E Glaxia, 3 Lung Poon St Diamond Hill, Taikoktsui Kowloon China Office: Hong Kong Poly U, Dept Mech Engring, Hung Hom, Kowloon China

WONG, WALTER FOO, county official; b. San Francisco, Apr. 11, 1930; s. Harry Yee and Grace (Won) W. AA, Hartnell Coll., 1952; BS, U. Calif., Berkeley, 1955; MPH, U. Hawaii, 1968. Registered sanitarian, Calif. Sanitarian Stanislaus County Health Dept., Modesto, Calif., 1955-56; sanitarian Monterey County Health Dept., Salinas, Calif., 1956-67, sr. sanitarian, 1968-69, supervising sanitarian, 1969-70, dir. environ. health, 1971—; sec. Monterey County Solid Waste Mgmt. Com., 1976—, Monterey County Hazardous Waste Mgmt. Com., 1987—; coord. Monterey County Genetic Engring. Rev. Com., 1987—; mem. Monterey County Genetic Engring. Experiment Permit Rev. Panel, 1995; mem. Monterey County Hazardous Materials Response Task Force, 1988—; mem. tech. adv. com. Monterey Peninsula Water Mgmt. Dist., 1985—, Monterey Regional Water Pollution Control Agy., 1985—; chmn. task force Monterey Regional Wastewater Reclamation Study for Agr., EPA and State of Calif. Chmn. Salinas Bicentennial Internat. Day Celebration, 1974, Pollution Clean-up Com. of Fort Ord Task Force, 1992; mem. Calif. Bare Closure Environ. adv. com., 1993. Recipient Community Svc. award Monterey County Med. Soc., 1998. Mem. Calif. Conf. Dirs. Environ. Health (pres. 1982-83), Assn. Environ. Health Adminstrs. (pres. 1982-83), Salinas C. of C. (Mem. of Yr. award 1971), U. Calif. Berkeley Alumni Assn., U. Hawaii Alumni Assn. (Disting. Alumni award 1992), Monterey County Hist. Soc. (pres. 1995-96), Ethnic Cultural Coun. (chmn. 1995). Republican. Presbyterian. Avocations: sports, music, outdoor recreation. Home: 234 Cherry Dr Salinas CA 93901-2807 Office: Monterey County Health Dept 1270 Natividad Rd Rm 301 Salinas CA 93906-3198

WONG, WING KEUNG, trading and electronics company executive, physician; b. Hong Kong, Jan. 5, 1933; s. Lai Cho Wong and Sut Mui Chung; m. Ban Cho, May 28, 1957; children: Hoi Ling, Hoi Yin. MB, BS, Beijing Med. Coll., 1955. Lic. Med. Coun. Hong Kong. Physician lst Hosp. of Beijing Med. Coll., 1955-69; with Hosp., Ganshu, China, 1970-73; pvt. practice Hong Kong, 1979-94; dir. Cheung Tai Hong Ltd., Hong Kong, 1974-86; chmn. bd. dirs. Computime Ltd., Hong Kong, 1979-93; dir. Computime Internat. Ltd., Brit. V.I., 1993-95; dep. chmn. Cheung Tai Hong Holdings Ltd., Bermuda, 1994-95; exec. dir. Cheung Tai Hong Ltd., Hong Kong, 1987-96. Mem. Hong Kong Med. Assn., Dynasty Club. Avocations: travel, music, diving, photography.

WONGCHAROEN, TIPARATANA, engineering educator; b. Tapanhin, Phicit, Thailand; d. Boonying and Chumnong (Ohmmakup) W.; m. Surapong Pinitglang, July 22, 1985. BSc in Physics, Silpakorn U., Nakornpathom, Thailand, 1983; MSc in Applied Math., Mahidol U., Bangkok, 1986; PhD in Engring., City U., London, 1995. Postdoctoral rsch. fellow City U., U.K.; lectr. physics dept. Bumrung Vitaya Sch., Thailand, 1980-82, Satree Patheonvitaya Sch., Thailand, 1983-85; tutor Mahidol U., Bangkok, 1985-86; lectr. Satit of Kasetsart U., Thailand, 1986-87, Civil Aviation Tng. Ctr., Thailand, 1987-89; rschr. King Mongkut's Inst. of Tech., Thonburi, Thailand, 1989-91; lectr. Bangkok U., 1987-92. Author: (books) Mechanical Physics, 1988, Nuclear Physics, 1988; contbr. tech. jours. Recipient scholarship, John F. Kennedy Found., Bangkok, 1979-83, Dr. Tab Found., Bangkok, 1984-85, PhD scholarship, Bangkok U., 1992-96, Gold medal award Buddhism Soc. Thailand, 1982, Dr. Tab Found., 1986; grantee The Royal Soc. U.K. Acad. Sci., 1998, 2000. Mem. IEEE, Sci. Soc. Thailand, Math. Soc. Thailand, Optical Soc. Am. Buddhist. Avocations: music, badminton, reading, walking. Office: Bangkok U, Sch of Engring, Klonglaung Pathum Thani 12120, Thailand

WONG-DIAZ, FRANCISCO RAIMUNDO, lawyer, educator; b. Havana, Cuba, Oct. 29, 1944; came to U.S., 1961; s. Juan and Teresa (Diaz de Villegas) Wong; m. Elena Wong, 1997; 1 child, Richard Alan. BA with honors, No. Mich. U., 1965; MA with highest honors, U. Detroit, 1967; PhD, MA, U. Mich., 1974; JD, U. Calif., Berkeley, 1976. Bar: Calif. 1980, U.S. Dist. Ct. (no. dist.) Calif. 1990, Fla. 1987. Prof. City Coll. San Francisco, 1975—, dept. chmn., 1978-85; rsch. atty. Marin Superior Ct., 1980-81; ct. arbitrator Marin Mcpl. Ct., 1985; atty. pvt. practice, Kentfield, Calif., 1980—; adj. asst. prof. San Francisco State U., 1977; assoc. dean Miami-Dade Coll., 1986; dir. Cutcliffe Cons., Inc., Hawthorne, LaFamila Ctr., Inc., San Rafael, Calif., 1980-85, Small Bus. Inst., Kentfield, 1982-86; cons. ICC Internat., San Francisco, 1980-82. Author: American Politics in a Changing World, 1999; bd. editors Indsl. Rels. Law Jour., 1975-76; mem. editl. bd. Calif. Lawyer, 1991-93; editor American Politics in A Changing World, 1999. Lector St. Sebastian's Ch., 1984—, parish coun., 1995; bd. dirs. Am. Cancer Soc., 1999—. Vis. scholar U. Calif., Berkeley Sch. Bus., 1983-84, U.S. Dept. State scholar, Washington, 1976; Horace C. Rackham fellow U. Mich., 1970, summer fellow U. Calif. Berkeley, 1995, Nat. Security Law Ctr. U. Va., 1996; named Best New Vol. of Yr., Am. Cancer Soc., 2000. Mem. ABA, Am. Polit. Sci. assn., Latino Ednl. Assn. (treas. 1985), Cuban Am. Nat. Coun., World Affairs Coun. (sem. leader San Francisco 1980), Commonwealth Club. Roman Catholic.

WONGWISES, SOMCHAI, mechanical engineering educator; b. Bangkok, Oct. 3, 1959; s. Sombun and Buppha Wongwises; m. Veena Wongprasert, Sept. 22, 1996. B in Engring. with honors, King Mongkut's Tech. U., 1982; M in Engring., Asian Inst. Tech., 1984; D in Engring., U. Hannover, 1994. Engr. Jalaprathan Cement, Bangkok, 1985; lectr. King Mongkut's Tech. Thonburi, Bangkok, 1987-90, asst. prof., 1990-96, assoc. prof., 1996—. Author: Design and Optimization of Thermal System, 1997; contbr. articles to profl. jours. Sgt. Thai Def. Dept., 1975-78. Master scholar Asian Inst. Tech., 1983-84, doctoral scholar U. Hannover, 1990-94. Mem. Thailand Engring. Inst. Office: King Mongkuts Univ, Thonburi, Radburana Bangkok 10140, Thailand

WONNACOTT, JAMES BRIAN, physician; b. Charlottetown, P.E.I., Can., Feb. 24, 1945; came to U.S., 1978, naturalized, 1984; s. Earl Lepage and Eunice Deborah (Eaton) W. Honors diploma, Prince of Wales Coll., 1964; BSc with honors in biology, Dalhousie U., 1966, MD, 1972. Diplomate Am. Bd. Family Practice, Coll. Family Physicians Can. Intern Victoria Gen. Hosp., Halifax, N.S., Can., 1971-72; gen. practice medicine Summerside, P.E.I., 1975-78; med. dir. alcoholism treatment unit Raleigh Hills Hosp., 1981-83; preceptor tchg. staff U. Tex. Med. Sch., Baylor Coll. Medicine, Houston, 1984-95; exec. med. dir. Oak Forest Med. Ctr., 1990-95, Vis. Nurse Assn., Hospice, Houston, 1991-95; pvt. practice family medicine rural Kans., 1996-2000; med. dir. Rural Health Clinic, Spearman, Tex., 2000—; mem. med. adv. bd. Med. World News, 1983-90. Served as flight surgeon RCAF, 1967-75. Fellow Am. Acad. Family Physicians; mem. AMA, Kans. Med. Assn., Univ. Lodge Halifax. Methodist. Office: PO Box 8 Spearman TX 79081-0008

WONNEBERGER, REINHARD, theology educator, computer scientist; b. Forchheim, Germany, Sept. 30, 1946; s. Arthur and Elfriede (Blasig) W.; m. Brigitte Goecke, Apr. 25, 1980; children: Sigrun, Henrike. I. Theol. Exam., Bayrische Landeskirche, Munich, 1970; II. Theol. Exam., Badische Landeskirche, Karlsruhe, Germany, 1975; ThD, U. Heidelberg, Germany, 1975; Habilitation, U. Mainz, Germany, 1991. Asst. prof. theology and EDP, U. Heidelberg, 1972-76, U. Hamburg, Germany, 1977-86; computer scientist Electronic Data Sys., Rüsselsheim, Germany, 1986—; lectr. U. Mainz, 1991—; quality auditor EOQ, 1993—. Author: Syntax und Exegese, 1979, Understanding BHS (Biblica Hebraica Stuttgartensia), 1990, German version, 1986, Japanese version, 1990, Verheissung und Versprechen, 1986, Kompaktführer LaTeX, 1988, Redaktion, 1992; also numerous articles; expert in linguistics and on ethics of EDP. Office: EDS, Eisenstrasse 56, 65428 Rüsselsheim Germany

WOO, ALEX, process engineer; b. Hong Kong, Aug. 20, 1975; came to U.S., 1990; s. S. C. and K. W. Woo. BSChemE, Rensselaer Poly. Inst., 1996. Coop. engr. G.E. Silicones, Waterford, N.Y., 1995-96; process engr. Masonite Corp., Towanda, Pa., 1997—. Mem. AIChE, Internat. Mgmt. Coun. (key rep. 1997—). Avocations: traveling, outdoor activities. Home: 48 Hemlock Rd Sayre PA 18840-1442 Office: Masonite Corp PO Box 311 Towanda PA 18848-0311

WOO, CHIA-WEI, academic administrator. BS in Physics and Math., Georgetown Coll., 1956; MA in Physics, Washington U., 1961, PhD, 1966. Applied mathematician Monsanto Co., 1958-62; rsch. assoc. Washington U., 1966; asst. rsch. physicist U. Calif., San Diego, 1966-68; from asst. prof. to assoc. prof. physics Northwestern U., 1968-73, chmn., prof. dept. physics and astronomy, 1973-79; provost, prof. physics U. Calif., San Diego, 1979-83; pres., prof. physics San Francisco State U., 1983-88, Hong Kong U. Sci. & Tech., 1988—; vis. assoc. prof. U. Ill., Champaign, 1970-71. Office: Hong Kong U Sci & Tech, Clear Water Bay, Kowloon Hong Kong

WOO, CHUNH-HO, materials engineering educator, researcher; b. Hong Kong, Sept. 7, 1943; arrived in Can., 1967; s. Wai-Sang Woo and Yuen-Mei Cheung; m. Helen Lam, June, 1968; 1 child, Winston Baw-Yen. BSc with honors, Hong Kong U., 1966, Hong Kong U., 1967; MSc, Calgary (Can.) U., 1969; PhD, Waterloo (Can.) U., 1973; DSc, Hong Kong U., 2000. Asst. rsch. officer Atomic Energy of Can., Ltd., Pinawa, Chalk River, 1975-77, assoc. rsch. officer, 1977-79, rsch. officer, 1979-86, sr. rsch. officer, 1986-95, sr. scientist (SE 6), 1995-96; prof. dept. mech. engring. Hong Kong Poly. U., 1996-98, chair mech. engring., 1998—; adj. prof. U. Man., Winnepeg, Can., 1975-96; vis. scientist Max-Planck-Inst., Stuttgart, Germany, 1984-85, Rosario (Argentina) U., 1993, U.K. Atomic Energy Authority Harwell, U.K., 1978. Editor spl. jour. issue Fundamental Mechanisms of Radiation Induced Energy and Growth, 1988; contbr. articles to profl. jours. Rsch. grantee Rsch. Grant Coun. Hong Kong, 1997-99. Fellow Hong Kong Instn. Engrs. (chmn. nuc. divsn. 1998-2000). Office: Hong Kong Poly U, Dept Mech Engring, Hung Hom Kowloon Hong Kong

WOO, HEE-GWEON, chemistry educator; b. Seoul, Republic of Korea, Apr. 18, 1956; s. Hang-Sik and Young-Ja Park; m. Jennifer Mihee Choi, July 10, 1983; children: Grace B., Laura S., Sarah H. BS in Chemistry, Yonsei U., Seoul, Korea, 1979; MS in Polymer Chemistry, Korea Advanced Inst. Sci. Tech, Seoul, Korea, 1981; MA in Inorganic Chemistry, Harvard U., 1985; PhD in Inorganic Chemistry, U. Calif., La Jolla, 1990. Instr. Inha U., Incheon, Korea, 1981-83; postdoctoral assoc. MIT, Cambridge, Mass., 1991; postdoctoral fellow McGill U., Montreal, Can., 1992-93; asst. prof. Chonnam Nat. U., Kwangju, Korea, 1993-97; assoc. prof. Chonnam Nat. U., Kwangju, 1998—; vis. rsch. prof. U. Wis., Madison, 1997, Tokyo U., 1998, McGill U., Montreal, 1998, Oxford (Eng.) U., 1998, Calif. Inst. Tech., 1999, Cambridge (Eng.) U., 1999. Contbr. articles to profl. jours. Pvt. soldier Korean Army, 1981-85. Mem. Am. Chem. Soc. (life), Korean Chem. Soc. (life, mem. exec. com. 1998—, Sci. Appreciation medal 1994, Sci. and Advancement award 1996, Disting. Svc. medal 1998), Yonsei U. Alumni Assn. (life, Disting. Svc. medal 1998), Phi Beta Delta. Avocations: stamp collecting, hiking, fishing, golfing, painting. Office: Chemistry Dept, Chonnam Nat Univ, Kwangju 500-757, Republic of Korea

WOO, JEAN, medical educator; b. Hong Kong, Apr. 14, 1949; d. Hing Tak and Chiu Wah Lam; m. Chi Ming Wong, Aug. 15, 1975; children: Rebecca, Jennifer. BA, Cambridge U., U.K., 1971, MBBChir, 1974; MD, Cambridge U., 1988; MRCP, Royal Coll. Physicians, U.K., 1976. Lectr. dept. medicine The Chinese U. of Hong Kong, 1985-89, sr. lectr., 1989-91, reader, 1991-94, prof., 1994—, chmn. dept. medicine, 1993-99; hon. cons. geriatrician, Hosp. Authority, Hong Kong, 1991—, chief of svc. Shatin Hosp., Hong Kong, 1994—. Fellow Royal Coll. Physicians, Hong Kong Coll. of Physicians (coun. mem. 1991-95), Hong Kong Acad. Medicine. Office: Dept Medicine, Chinese U of Hong Kong, Shatin NT Hong Kong

WOO, JOHN See WU, YUSEN

WOO, JONATHAN C. G., chemist, management consultant; b. San Francisco, Oct. 22, 1968; s. Gar Lok and Julia Y. P. Woo. AB, U. Calif., Berkeley, 1990; MS, Northwestern U., 1992, PhD, 1994. Res. fellow Memorial Sloan Kettering Ctr., N.Y.C., 1994-97, Mitchell Madison Group, 1997-99, Bristol-Myers Squibb, 1999—. Contbr. articles to profl. jours. Fellow NIH, 1995. Mem. Am. Chem. Soc.

WOO, KWANG-SUNG, civil engineering educator; b. Seoul, South Korea, June 26, 1960; s. Hee-Chang and Gui-Boon (Eum) W.; m. Doug-Oh Rhee, Aug. 25, 1984; 1 child, Dong-Joon. BS, Seoul Nat. U., 1981, MS, 1983; PhD, Vanderbilt U., 1988. Cert. civil engr., South Korea. Tchg. asst. Seoul Nat. U., 1981-83; rsch. asst. Vanderbilt U., Nashville, 1985-88, rsch. asst. prof., 1988-89; asst. prof. Chonnam U., Kwangju, South Korea, 1989-94; assoc. prof. Yeungnam U., Kyongsan, South Korea, 1995—; cons. prof. Ministry of Constrn., Seoul, 1996—. Contbr. articles to profl. jours. V.p. Korean Assn., Nashville, 1986-87. Sub-lt. South Korean armed forces, 1983-84. Recipient Best Paper award Korean Fedn. Sci. and Tech. Socs., 1993. Fellow Computational Structural Engring. Inst. Korea (prime editor, Best Paper award 1996); mem. Korean Soc. Civil Engrs. (Best Paper award 1995). Mem. Grand Nat. Party Korea. Roman Catholic. Avocations: tennis, oriental chess, travel, reading, movies. Office: Yeungnam U, 214-1 Daedong, Kyongsan 712-749, South Korea

WOO, MI-HEE, pharmacy educator; b. Daegu, Republic of Korea, Nov. 10, 1957; d. Keung-Sik Kim and Yun-Soon Kwak; m. Tae-Kwon Kim, Dec. 7, 1985; children: Ji-Won, Seo-Young, Soo-Young. BS, Cath. U. of Daegu-Hyosung, Republic of Korea, 1980, MS, 1982; PhD, Yeungnam U., Republic of Korea, 1991. Part-time instr. Cath. U. Daegu-Hyosung, 1982-83, instr., 1983-86, asst. prof., 1986-91, assoc. prof., 1991-96, prof., 1996—; vis. prof. Purdue U., Lafayette, Ind., 1994-95. Contbr. articles to profl. jours. Mem. Pharm. Soc. Korea, Korean Soc. Medicinal Crop Sci., Korean Soc. Pharmacognosy, Korean Soc. Applied Pharmacology. Roman Catholic. Office: Cath U Daegu-Hyosung, 330 Geumnak 1 Ri, Hayang Gyeongbuk 712-702, Republic of Korea

WOO, NORMAN YING SHIU, zoologist, educator; b. Hong Kong, Oct. 1, 1950; m. Man Bun and Wai Ching (Chan) W.; m. Teresa Siu Lee Yu, Dec. 9,

1975 (div. Mar. 1987); 1 child, Derek Kevin; m. Amy Ngar Yee Cheung, Nov. 20, 1988; 1 child, Clement Ka Shui. BSc, U. Hong Kong, 1973, PhD, 1976. Postdoctoral rsch. zoologist U. Calif., Berkeley, 1976-77; lectr. in biology Chinese U. of Hong Kong, 1977-84, sr. lectr. in biology, 1985-92, reader in biology, 1993-94, prof. biology, 1995—; rsch. fellow U. Calgary, Canada, 1983; vis. scientist U. Paul Sabatier, Toulouse, France, 1980, 95; mem. bd. trustees Shaw Coll., Chinese U. Hong Kong, 1992—; dir. Marine Science Lab., 1994-96; chmn biology dept, 1994-96/. Author: (book) Recent Advances in Biotechnology & Applied Biology; contbr. articles to profl. jours. Chmn. Pacific Congress on Marine Sci. & Technology, Hong Kong, 1997. Recipient Rsch. grant United Nations U., 1987, Earmarked Rsch. grant Rsch. Grants Coun., 1991, 94, 97; fellow Internat. Union of Biochemistry, 1982. Avocations: paintings, sculpture. Home: 3A Casas Domingo, Kwu Tung-Sheung Shui Hong Kong China Office: Biology Dept, Chinese U Hong Kong, Shatin Hong Kong China

WOO, PATRICIA, pediatric rheumatologist; b. Hong Kong, Feb. 12, 1948; arrived in U.K., 1961; d. Hing Tak and Chiu Wah (Lam) W. BSc, U. London, 1969, M.B.B.S., 1972; PhD, U. Cambridge, U.K., 1979. Tng. fellow U. Cambridge, 1976-79; registrar Northwick Park Hosp., London, 1979-81; sr. registrar Guy's Hosp., London, 1981-83; rsch. fellow Boston Children's Hosp., 1983-85; MRC cons. rheumatologist, hon. cons. physician Northwick Park and Great Ormond St. Hosps., London, 1985-94; prof. pediatric rheumatology U. Coll. London, 1994—, Royal Postgrad. Med. Sch., 1994-95; cons. physician Great Ormond St., UCLHS, 1994—; house officer Charing Cross Hosp., London, 1973-74, sr. house officer Brompton Hosp., London, 1974-75, Northwick Park Hosp., 1975-76; mem. ILAR and WHO task force on paediatric rheumatology, 1993—. Editor: Oxford Textbook of Rheumatology, 1993, 98, Paediatric Rheumatology Update, 1989; assoc. editor Rheumatology, 1992—; contbr. articles to profl. jours. Fellow Royal Coll. Physicians U.K., Royal Coll. Pediat. and Child Health; mem. Assn. Physicians U.K., Brit. Paediatric Rheumatology Group (convenor 1993-96), European Pediat. Rheumatology Soc. (pres.). Achievements include research on acute phase gene regulation by cytokines, cytokine network in paediatric rheumatology and clinical research in juvenile arthritis. Avocations: playing piano, music, drama, skiing, tennis. Office: Univ Coll London Med Sch, 46 Cleveland St, London W1P 6DB, England

WOO, PETER WING KEE, organic chemist; b. Canton, China, June 22, 1934; came to U.S., 1950; s. Yu Chang and Lim Tsing (Poon) W.; m. Katherine Liang, Aug. 27, 1966; children: Karen H.W., Lena H.A., Nelson H.Y. BS with great distinction, Stanford U., 1955; PhD, U. Ill., 1958. From assoc. rsch. chemist to sr. rsch. chemist Parke Davis & Co., Detroit, 1958-71; from rsch. scientist to sr. rsch. assoc. Parke Davis Pharm. Rsch. (divsn. Warner-Lambert Co.), Ann Arbor, Mich., 1971-2000; chemist Pfizer Global Rsch. & Devel., Ann Arbor Labs. Pfizer, Inc., 2000—. Co-inventor antileukemia drug (pentostatin); contbr. to devel. lipid-modifying drug (atorvastatin, lowering cholesterol) and anti-arrhythmia drug (pirmenol); patentee in field; reviewer in field; contbr. articles to profl. jours. Mem. AAAS, Am. Chem. Soc. (excellence in indsl. chem. rsch. award 1983, Huron Valley sect.), Internat. Isotope Soc., Sigma Xi, Phi Beta Kappa. Avocations: tennis, table tennis, swimming, soccer, piano. Office: Pfizer Global Rsch & Devel 2800 Plymouth Rd Ann Arbor MI 48105-2495

WOO, SEONG IHL, chemical engineering educator; b. Seoul, Korea, May 19, 1951; s. Sae Young and Duck Chul (Lee) W.; m. Youn-Shin Lee, Aug. 28, 1978; children: Jessica, Everlyn, Rosemary. BSChemE, Seoul Nat. U., 1973; MSChemE, Korea Advanced Inst. Sci., Seoul, 1975; PhD in Chem. Engring., U. Wis., 1983. Rsch. engr. KIST, Seoul, 1975-78; fellow 3M Co., Toronto, Ont., Can., 1983-85; vis. prof. Tokyo Inst. Tech., 1989; Humboldt rsch. prof. Fritz-Haber Inst., Berlin, 1990-91; prof. dept. chem. engring. Korea Advanced Inst. Sci. and Tech., Taejon, Korea, 1985—; cons. Catalyst Cons. Inc., Springfield, Pa., 1992—; dir. Consortium for Organometallic Polymerization Catalysis, Taejon, Korea, 1992—; co-chmn. 1st, 2nd and 3rd Pacific Rim Conf. on Application of Femoelectric Materials. Contbr. over 150 articles to profl. jours.; patentee in area of catalysis, polymer, surface sci. and semicondr. materials; mem. editl. bd. Catalysis Letter, 2000—. Recipient Excellent Rsch. award Korean Advanced Inst. Sci., 1988, 92, 94, Excellent Rsch. Paper award Korean Sci. Assn., 1994, 25th Anniversary Rsch. award KAIST, 1996. Mem. AIChE, Am. Chem. Soc., Japan Soc. Catalysis, Korean Acad. Sci. and Tech., Nat. Acad. Engring. Korea, Korean Inst. Chem. Engrs. (divsn. sec. 1989-91, editor staff 1989-91, editor-in-chief 1996-98, v.p. Chung-Nam br., Acad. Rsch. award 1997), Korea Advanced Inst. Sci. Alumni Assn. (pres. 1995-96). Avocations: tennis, golf, music. Home: 219-601 Family Apt, Mun-Jung-Dong Song-Pa-Ku, Seoul Republic of Korea Office: Korea Advanced Inst Sci & Tech, Dept Chem Engring, Yusong-Gu, 301 701 Taejon Republic of Korea

WOOD, ALEXANDER SANDFORD, retired urologist; b. Melbourne, Australia, July 9, 1927; s. Carlyle Sandford and Ruth Nellie Layton (Millar) W.; m. Jennifer Maddern, June 2, 1956; children: Peter Sandford, John Alexander, Katherine. MB BS, Melbourne U., 1951. Urologist Bethlehem Hosp., Melbourne, 1965-95; hon. sr. lectr. urololgy Monash U., Melbourne, 1993-98; urologist Royal Southern Meml. Hops., Melbourne, 1977-85; dir. continence svc. Maroondah Hosp., Ringwood, Australia, 1992-95; vis. urologist Cabrini Hosp., Melbourne, 1962-98; asst. surgeon nephrology Royal Melbourne Hosp., 1976-78; asst. urologist Alfred Hosp., Melbourne, 1959-76; asst. surgeon Austin Hosp., Melbourne, 1959-63; urologist Mental Health Dept., Melbourne, 1969-73, 88-91; chmn. med. staff Bethelehem Hosp., Melbourne, 1987-95, Royal Southern Meml. Hosp., Melbourne, 1983. Contbr. articles to profl. jours. Civilian Surg. team, Vietnam, 1966; chmn. Victorian Com. State of Australia. Fellow Royal Coll. Surgeons (Eng.), Royal Australisian Coll. Surgeons; mem. Australian Assn. of Surgeons (chmn. com., fed. com.), Urol. Assn. of Australsia, Melbourne Cricket Club. Avocations: bush walking, birds, theatre, reading. Home: 108 Burke Rd East Malvern, Melbourne VIC 3145, Australia

WOOD, ANDRÉE ROBITAILLE, archaeologist, researcher; b. Chgo., Feb. 10, 1929; d. Andrew George and Alice Marie (Fortier) Robitaille; m. Richard Lawrence Wood, Jan. 14, 1956; children: Mary Wood Molo, Matthew William Wood, Melissa Irene Wood, Elizabeth Wood Wesel, John Andrew Wood. BA, No. Ill. Univ., DeKalb, 1977, MA, 1982. Freelance archaeologist, 1981-84; rsch. asst. Prehistoric Project Oriental Inst., Univ. Chgo., Ill., 1984—; rsch., discovery, removal, analysis and identification of ancient blood residues on lithic material excavated at ten millenium old site, Çayönü in Ergani, Turkey. Contbr. articles to profl. jours. Avocations: writing poetry, boating, tennis, golf. Home: 356 Old Sutton Rd Barrington IL 60010-9113 also: 8735 Midnight Pass Rd Apt 604B Sarasota FL 34242-2892

WOOD, BENJAMIN CARROLL, JR., safety professional; b. Leonardtown, Md., June 16, 1956; s. Benjamin C. Sr. and Ethel M. (Cole) W.; m. Sheilaann P. Manibog; May 26, 1977; children: Dreamer K., Cinnamon K.; stepchildren: Reynaldo K. Yumul, Angelica K. Yumul. AGS, Chaminade U., Honolulu, 1984; BS in Fire Sci., U. Md., 1997; BA in environmental studies, U. Nev., Las Vegas. Cert. criminal justice instr., food svc./sanitation mgr., environ. health and safety law profl., Va.; notary pub., Va. Aviation ordnanceman USMC, 1974-90; non-nuclear safety officer USMC, El Toro, Calif., 1990-94; ret., 1994; safety spec. Office of the Sheriff, Arlington, Va., 1995-98; safety coord. Monte Carlo Resort & Casino, Las Vegas, Nev., 1998-99; safety/loss prevention officer Monte Carlo Resort & Casino, Las Vegas, 1999, Econ. Opportunity Bd., North Las Vegas, 1999-2000; loss prevention cons. Employers Ins. Co. Nev., Las Vegas, 2000—. Recipient Excellence in Pub. Svc. award, Arlington (Va.) County Govt., 1997, 98, Naval Commendation medal, Sec. Navy, Washington, 1982, Humanitarian Svc. medal CMA, Washington, 1984. Mem. Am. Soc. Investigative Specialists, Am. Soc. Safety Engrs., Soc. for Advancement of Safety and Health, Nat. Safety. Coun., Va. Safety Coun., Nev. Safety Coun., Am. Legion, Employers for Workers Compensation, Nat. Fire Protection Assn. E-mail: bwood@eicn.com. Home: 7305 Hospitality Pl Las Vegas NV 89131-4588 Office: Employers Ins Co Nev 7180 Pollock Dr Las Vegas NV 89119-9003

WOOD, CHARLES TUTTLE, history educator; b. St. Paul, Oct. 29, 1933; s. Harold Eaton and Margaret (Frisbie) W.; m. Susan Danielson, July 9, 1955; children: Lucy Eaton, Timothy Walker, Martha Augusta, Mary Frisbie. AB, Harvard, 1955, AM, 1957, PhD, 1962. Investment analyst, trader Harold E. Wood & Co., St. Paul, 1955-56; teaching fellow gen. edn. Harvard, 1959-61, instr. history, 1961-64; mem. faculty Dartmouth, 1964-96, prof. history, 1971-80, Daniel Webster prof. history, 1980-91, Daniel Webster prof. history and comparative lit., 1991-96, Daniel Webster prof. emeritus, 1996—, chmn. dept. history, 1976-79, chmn. dept. comparative lit., 1977; vis. Keeney prof. of history Brown U., 1992-93; vis. prof. U. Coll. London, 1996. Author: The French Apanages and the Capetian Monarchy, 1223-1328, 1966, Philip the Fair and Boniface VIII, 2d edit., 1971, reprint, 1976, Felipe el Hermoso y Bonifacio VIII: Mexico: UTEHA, 1968, The age of Chivalry: Manners and Morals 1000-1450, 1970, The Quest for Eternity, reprint edit., 1983, Joan of Arc and Richard III, 1988, The Trial of Charles I, 1989, Fresh Verdicts on Joan of Arc, 1996; also articles. Chmn. Dresden Bd. Sch. Dirs., 1972-74. Guggenheim fellow, 1986-87; recipient Disting. Service award N.H. Sch. Bds. Assn., 1975; Am. Council Learned Socs. fellow, 1980-81; Am. Bar Found. fellow, 1981-82. Fellow Medieval Acad. Am. (treas. 1989—, fin. com. 1979—, council 1985-87); mem. Am. Hist. Assn. (chmn. nominating com. 1977, Adams prize com. 1976-78), Conf. Brit. Studies, Soc. for French Hist. Studies, N.H. Sch. Bds. Assn. (2d v.p. 1974-75), New Eng. Medieval Conf. (pres. 1978-79), Am. Soc. Legal History, Phi Beta Kappa (pres. Alpha of N.H. 1997-99). Club: St. Botolph (Boston). Home: 7 N Balch St Hanover NH 03755-1502

WOOD, DAVID BRUCE, naturopathic physician; b. Fayetteville, N.C., Jan. 21, 1954; s. Marvin James and Rachel Elenor (Thom) W.; m. Wendy Ann McKiernan, Aug. 1974 (div. Aug. 1976); m. Cheryl Lynn Garbarino, Aug. 17, 1980. BS in Microbiology, U. Wash., 1977; D in Naturopathic Medicine, Bastyr U., Seattle, 1983. Pres., co-founder Trinity Family Health Clinic, Inc., P.S., Lynnwood, Wash., 1984—; CMO, co-founder BioGenesis Nutraceuticals Inc., Bothel, Wash., 2000—; Spkr. local and nat. TV programs; host Health Hope and Healing radio show, KGNW-AM, 1998—. Singer Sound of Praise Choir, Overlake Christian Ch., Kirkland, Wash., 1987-92; narrator Easter Pagent, 1989; mem. Cedar Park Assembly of God, Bothel, Wash. Mem. Am. Assn. Nutritional Cons., Nat. Health Fedn., Am. Assn. Naturopathic Physicians, Wash. Assn. Naturopathic Physicians (trustee, exec. bd. 1989-92). Avocations: singing, snow skiing, snorkeling, bicycling, travel. Home: 20724 121st Ave SE Snohomish WA 98296-3935

WOOD, DIRK GREGORY, surgeon, physician, forensic consultant; b. Springfield, Ohio, Sept. 19, 1953; s. Carlos Paul and Evelyn Cecelia (Bird) W.; m. LaShanda R. Daniels, Dec. 10, 1996. BA magna cum laude, Urbana (Ohio) U., 1973; postgrad., Ohio State U., 1973-75; MD, UAG Facultad de Medicina, Guadalajara, Mexico, 1980; mini pupilage, Inns of Court School of Law, London, 1990; JD, Capital Law Sch., Columbus, Ohio, 1991. Diplomate Am. Bd. Ob-Gyn, Am. Bd. Forensic Medicine. Intern Bronx (N.Y.) Lebanon Hosp., 1981-82; resident William Beaumont Hosp., Royal Oak, Mich., 1982-86; physician, surgeon Her Care, Inc., Springfield, 1986—; CEO Just What the Doctor Ordered, Springfield, 1992—; dir. of obstetrics Mercy Med. Ctr., Springfield, Ohio, 1999—; chief collaborative physician Nurse Midwives Ctr., 1999—. Coroner Clark County, Ohio, 1991-97; mem. Clark County Rep. Ctrl. Com., Clark County Dist. 14, 1992—. Named Ky. col., Ala. col. Fellow ACS, Am. Coll. Ob-Gyn., Internat. Coll. Surgeons, Am. Coll. Legal Medicine, Am. Coll. Forensic Examiners, Royal Soc. Medicine (London), Interam. Coll. Physicians and Surgeons; mem. SAR, Am. Soc. Law and Medicine, Phi Delta Epsilon (past chpt. pres.), Phi Alpha Delta. Republican. Avocations: scuba diving, bibliophilia, travel. Home: 202 Tuttle Rd Springfield OH 45503-5236 Office: Her Care Inc 2029 E High St Springfield OH 45505-1315

WOOD, DONALD CRAIG, retired marketing professional; b. Wilmington, Del., June 24, 1937; s. Thomas Henry and Madelyn (Brehm) W.; m. Elizabeth Haring, Apr. 28, 1962; children: Craig Standish, Allison Jean. BA, U. Del., 1959; MBA, Northwestern U., 1967. Sales engr. NVF Corp., Broadview, Ill., 1960-62, Synthane Corp., Morton Grove, Ill., 1962-68; account exec., mgr. sales Donnelley Mktg. subs. Dun and Bradstreet Corp., Oakbrook, Ill., 1968-76; from dir. to v.p. market devel. to v.p. mktg. Donnelley Mktg. subs. Dun and Bradstreet Corp., Stamford, Conn., 1977-1980; from v.p., gen. mgr. to pres. Donnelley Mktg. Info. Svcs. subs. Dun and Bradstreet Corp., Stamford, 1980-86; sr. v.p. Donnelley Mktg. Inc. subs. Dun and Bradstreet Corp., Stamford, 1987-90; v.p., gen. mgr. info. svcs. Triad Systems Corp., Livermore, Calif., 1990-96; ret., 1996. Served to 1st lt. U.S. Army, 1959-60. Home: 6312 Providence CC Dr Charlotte NC 28277

WOOD, EDWIN CARLYLE, gynecologist; b. Melbourne, Australia, May 28, 1929; s. Carlyle Sandford and Ruth Nellie Wood; m. Judith Badger, Sept. 17, 1957 (div.); children: Gavin Carlyle, Caroline Archer, Simon Alexander; m. Marie Counsel, Oct. 12, 1990. MB BS, Melbourne U., 1952. Resident Royal Women's Hosp., Melbourne, 1954-56, Queen Charlottes and Chelsea Hosp., London, 1957-58; lectr., sr. lectr. Queen Charlotte's & Chelsea Hosp., London, 1959-64; rsch. assoc. Rockefeller Inst., N.Y.C., 1961; chmn. dept. ob.-gyn. Monash U., Melbourne, 1965—; dir. Infertility Med. Ctr., Melbourne, 1978—; chmn. reproductive biology unit Queen Vic Med. Ctr., Melbourne, 1984—, IVF program Monash U., 1978—; found. chmn. med. adv. com. Family Planning Assn., Victoria, Australia, 1970—; dir. Melbourne Gynoscopy Ctr. Author 14 books; contbr. chpts. to books and articles to profl. jours. Decorated comdr. Brit. Empire; comdr. of Australia; recipient award European Soc. Human Reproductive Endocrinology. Fellow Royal Australian Coll. Ob-Gyns., Royal Coll. Ob-Gyns., Royal Coll. Surgeons (Axel Munthe award for reproductive sci. 1988). Avocations: windsurfing, swimming, tennis. Office: 19 Simpson St, Melbourne 3002, Australia

WOOD, FRANCES DIANE, medical secretary, artist; b. Caddo, Okla., Mar. 7, 1950; d. Clovis Lynn and Hilda Dee (Guthrie) Wood; m. Samuel Dante Wolfe, Aug. 20, 1990 (div. Mar. 1992). BA, Southeastern Okla. State U., 1972; student, Grayson County Coll., 1984-87. Ins. clk. Sherman Cmty. Hosp., Tex., 1973-74; med. sec. Essin Clinic, Sherman, Tex., 1980-83; med. transcriptionist Texoma Med. Ctr., Denison, Tex., 1983-88, Wilson N. Jones Meml. Hosp., Sherman, Tex., 1989-95; CEO Designs by Diane, Caddo, Okla., 1995—; conv. del. Blue Cross-Blue Shield Tex., Dallas, 1980-83; v.p. Jett Transcription, Denison, Tex., 1988. Exhibited paintings in cmty. art shows; Native Am. craft work in permanent collections Bryan County Nat. Bank, Caddo, Indian Terr. Mus., Caddo. Charter mem. Caddo Edn. Found., Okla., 1993-95; sponsor Save the Children, Philippines, 1995. Mem. Am. Soc. Prevention Cruelty to Animals, The Nature Conservancy, Physicians Com. for Responsible Medicine, Nat. Trust Historic Preservation, Okla. Sheriffs Assn. (hon.), Arts Coun. Co-op (life), Nat. Arbor Day Found., Sierra Club, Sacred Heart Auto League, People for the Ethical Treatment of Animals, So. Poverty Law Ctr. Supporters. Democrat. Avocations: pet care, interior decorating, astronomy, folk medicine, gardening.

WOOD, JEANNE CLARKE, charitable organization executive; b. Pitts., Dec. 21, 1916; d. Joseph Calvitt and Helen Caroline (Mattson) Clarke; m. Herman Eugene Wood, Jr., May 6, 1936 (dec.); children: Helen Hamilton (Mrs. John Harry Mortenson), Herman Eugene III. Student, Collegiate Sch. for Girls, Richmond, Va., 1932-33. Asst. to Dr. and Mrs. J. Calvitt Clarke, Christian Children's Fund, Inc., Richmond, 1938-64; founder Children, Inc., Richmond, 1964; pres., internat. dir. Children, Inc., 1964—. Author: (with Helen C. Clarke) In Appreciation: A Story in Pictures of the World-Wide Family of Christian Children's Fund, Inc, 1958, Children's Christmastime Around the World, 1962, Children's Games Around the World, 1962, Children-Hope of the World-Their Needs, 1965, Children-Hope of the World-Their Friends, 1966; Editor: CI News, 1964. Recipient citation Eastern Council Navajo Tribe, 1970, citations Mayor of Pusan (Korea), 1971, citations Mayor of Seoul, 1971, citations Gov. of Kanagawa Prefecture (Japan), 1972, commendation Pres. of U.S., 1972, citation Stephen Philibosian Found., 1975, citation Santa Ana (El Salvador) Dept. Edn., 1975, citation Nat. Sch. for Blind, Dominican Republic, 1982, citation Navajo Tribal Council of Navajo Nation, Window Rock, Ariz., 1982. Home and Office: Children Inc PO Box 5381 1000 Westover Rd Richmond VA 23220-6624

WOOD, JULIE DIANE, family therapist; b. New Orleans, May 29, 1964; d. Jack Owen Wood and Jeanne Diane Matheson; m. Richard Arvey, Nov. 24, 1979 (div. May 1991); children: Aaron, Sarah. BA, U. Wash., 1983; MA, Seattle U., 1992. Therapist in tng. Eastside Mental Health, Bellevue, Wash., 1990-91; family therapist Youth Eastside Svcs., Bellevue, 1991-92, Kindering Ctr., Bellevue, 1992—; pvt. practice Bellevue, 1996—; cons. Early Head Start, Washington and Oreg., 1998-99. Mem. Am. Assn. Marriage and Family Therapy (clin. mem.), Wash. Assn. for Marriage and Family Therapy (ethics com. 1998, editor 1999—), Phi Beta Kappa. Avocations: hiking, gardening, kayaking, reading. E-mail: woodjulied@aol.com. Office: Kindering Ctr 16120 NE 8th St Bellevue WA 98008-3937

WOOD, KENNETH ANDERSON, artist, designer, consultant; b. Cleve., May 11, 1913; s. George Robert and Leonore (Anderson) W.; m. Ruth Eleanor Diehm, Sept. 14, 1937 (dec. May 1999). Student, Fenn Coll., Cleve., 1932-34, Cleve. Inst. Art, 1935-45. Artist Patterson Displays, Cleve., 1934-35; art dir. Bailey Meter Co., Wickliffe, Ohio, 1936-71; owner Kenwood Designers, Chesterland, Ohio, 1971—; designer of stained glass windows, 1979—; pres. Artist and Craftsman Assocs., Cleve., 1940-44, Geauga Artists Assn., Geauga County, Ohio, 1950-53. Exhibited in over 80 nat., regional and local juried exhibits, 1939-97; represented in permanent collections Butler Mus. Am. Art, Youngstown, Ohio, Inlander Collection of Gt. Lakes Regional Paintings, Cleve. Mus. Art, numerous pvt. collections; holder patents for product designs. Mem. Indsl. Designers Soc. Am. (life). Republican. Seventh-day Adventist. Avocation: travel. Office: Kenwood Designers 11950 Sperry Rd Chesterland OH 44026-2225

WOOD, LEIGHTON LLOYD, events chief executive; b. Wangaratta, Australia, Feb. 2, 1960; s. Lloyd and Lyn (Robinson) W.; m. Leisha Simone Browning, Oct. 17, 1998. B in Applied Sci. (P.E.), Victoria U., Melbourne, Australia, 1981; MBA, Bond U., Robina, Australia, 1998. Entertainment mgr. Tooleybuc Sporting Club, Australia, 1982-87; exercise physiologist Pindara Sports Clin., Benowa, Australia, 1988-89; mgr. Bond U. Sport and Recreation, Robina, Australia, 1990-94; cons. Strategic Sports and Recreation, Melbourne, Australia, 1995-96; chief exec. Melbourne Major Events Co., 1997-98, Melbourne 2006 Commonwealth Games Bid, 1999; chief exec. Melbourne 2006 Commonwealth Games (organizing com.) 1999—; organising com. mem. 1999 World Sailing Championship, Victorian Yachting Fedn., 1997-99, mktg. com. mem. Australian U. Sport, Brisbane, 1998-99. Office: Melbourne 2006 Commonwealth Games, 65 Palmerston Cres, South Melbourne VIC 3205, Australia

WOOD, LESLIE ANN, retail administrator; b. Chgo., Apr. 9, 1957; d. Howard Arnold and Anita Eleanor (Andler) W. AA, Harper Coll., 1977; BS in Comm. Scis., Ill. State U., 1979; MBA, Olivet Nazarene U., 1998. Advt. asst. Harry Alter Co., Chgo., 1979-80; clk. typist Career Guild, Evanston, Ill., 1980-81; reporter Aparacor, Evanston, Ill., 1981-82; sales mgmt. trainee Prudential Ins. Co. Am., Millburn, N.J., 1983-84; fin. cons. Summit Fin. Resources, Livingston, N.J., 1984; mgr. Chgo. area Renault Inc. div. AMC/Jeep/Renault, Elk Grove Village, Ill., 1985-87; customer relations specialist Chrysler Motors, Lisle, Ill., 1987-88; dist. svc. and parts mgr. Chrysler, Lisle; dist. parts mgr. Subaru of Am., Addison, Ill., 1989-91, dist. fixed ops. mgr., 1992-95; univ. rep. Olivet Nazarene U., Schaumburg, Ill., 1996-97; mktg. cons. WZSR STAR 105.5, Crystal Lake, Ill., 1997-99; parts cons. Am. Isuzu Motors, Cerritos, Calif., 1999—. Mem. ch. choir, rainbows coord. First Presbyn. Ch., Libertyville, Ill. Avocations: aerobics, circuit weight training, sewing, stained glass crafts. Home and Office: 230 Brett Cir Unit D Wauconda IL 60084-1587

WOOD, MALCOLM JAMES, lawyer; b. Aberdeen, Scotland, Sept. 12, 1955; s. James and Doris Agnes Elizabeth Wood; m. Nicola Ross, Sept. 13, 1980; children: Rachel, Caroline. LLB, U. Edinburgh, Scotland, 1977. Vis. scholar U. Calif., Berkeley, 1977; apprentice Brodies W.S., Edinburgh, 1978-80, asst., 1980-81, 82-83; asst. Herbert Smith & Co., London, 1981-82; asst. W & J Burness W.S., Edinburgh, 1983-85, ptnr., 1985—; notary pub., 1981—; diploma tutor U. Edinburgh, 1984-89. Mem. Scottish com. Marie Curie Cancer Care, London, 1987—; trustee Ch. Hymnary Trust, Edinburgh, 1991—. Rotary Internat. fellow, 1977. Mem. Soc. Writers to H.M. Signet, Securities Inst., Law Soc. Scotland, von Poser Soc. Scotland (grand treas. 1994—). Avocations: music, real tennis, dry stone walling, silviculture. Office: Burness, 50 Lothian Rd Festival Sq, Edinburgh EH3 9WJ, Scotland

WOOD, NEIL RODERICK, real estate development company executive; b. Winnipeg, Man., Can., Aug. 22, 1931; s. Reginald and Pearl (Beake) W.; m. Jean Mitchell Hume, Aug. 10, 1957; children: Barbara, David, John, Brian. B.Com., U. Man., 1952; M.B.A., Harvard U., 1955. Asst. mgr. Ont. real estate investment office Gt. West Life Assurance Co., 1955-59; with Cadillac Fairview Corp. Ltd. (and predecessor), Willowdale, Ont., 1959-61, 63-81; exec. v.p. Cadillac Fairview Corp. Ltd. (and predecessor), 1968-71, pres., 1971-81, vice chmn., 1980-81; pres. N.R. Wood Devel. Co. Ltd., 1982—; exec. v.p., dir. Campeau Corp., 1985-86; pres., CEO, dir. Markborough Properties Inc., 1986-95; bd. dirs. Gentra Inc., Dorsay Devel. Corp.; past pres., trustee Internat. Coun. of Shopping Ctrs., U. Guelph Heritage Trust. Mem. Toronto Club, Rosedale Golf Club, Craigleith Ski Club, Beaumaris Club, Lost Tree Club, Loxahatchee Golf Club, Beacon Hall Club. Home and Office: RR # 3, Newmarket, ON Canada L3Y 4W1

WOOD, NICHOLAS, clinical psychologist, researcher; b. Kitwe, Zambia, June 4, 1961; came to South Africa, 1970; s. Peter Derek and Maxine Elizabeth (Meyrick-Clarke) W.; m. Glenda Joy Ericksen, Nov. 17, 1990; children: Nicole Sasha, Natasha Alexis. BA, Univ. Cape Town, 1981; BA (hons.), Univ. Natal, South Africa, 1984, MA, 1987; postgrad., Univ. London, 1996—. Cmty. worker Health Dept. City Coun., Cape Town, South Africa, 1982-83; intern clinical psychologist Midlands Hosp., Pietermaritzburg, South Africa, 1986-87; clinical psychologist Lentegeur Hosp., Cape Town, 1988-93; sr. clinical psychologist, lectr. dept. psychiatry Univ. Cape Town, 1994-95; unit mgr. substance abuse unit Lentegeur Hosp., 1990-91, clinical supr. Lentegeur Valkenberg Hosp., 1992-95, sr. specialist mgr., 1992-93. Contbr. articles to profl. jours.; author short stories. Active mem. Orgn. for Appropriate Social Svcs. South Africa, Pietermaritzburg, Cape Town, 1987-91; crisis counsellor Life Line, Cape Town, 1981-83; pres. William Gooderough Nursery, London, 1996—. Recipient scholarship Centre for Sci. Devel., South Africa, 1997, Wingate scholarship Harold Hyam WIngate Found., Eng., 1996. Mem. Am. Psychological Assn. (fgn. affiliate), British Psychological Soc. (chartered mem.), Soc. for Rsch. in Child Devel. Avocations: creative writing, astronomy, squash, birding, youth work. Office: Donald Winnicott Coate St, London E2 9AG, England Home: 22 Victoria Rd Mill Hill, NW7 4SB London England

WOOD, PETER JOHN, small business owner; b. Melbourne, Australia, Nov. 11, 1939; s. Maurice and Helen (Lehne) W.; m. Barbara Ashford Maughan, Sept, 2, 1961; children: Susan, Michael. B of Applied Sci. Hort., Melbourne U., 1998. Nurseryman Woodlyn Nurseries, Melbourne, 1954-97; prin. cons. Oakford Horticultural Cons., 1998—; sr. cons. Oakford Horticultural Cons. Ltd., 1997—. Mem. Nurserymen's Assn. Victoria (exec. mem. 1967-70, v.p. 1970-77, pres. 1977-83), Australian Nurserymen's Assn. (pres. 1983-85, exec. mem. 1981-83), Victorian Coll. Agrl. & Hort. (v.p. 1982-84, pres. 1984-86). Avocations: Victorian football league, foster parenting.

WOOD, SANDRA SYNHOFF, psychotherapist, corporate trainer, seminar leader; b. Dec. 9, 1956. BA in Psychology, U. North Fla., Jacksonville, 1989, MA in Counseling Psychology, 1991. Licensed Mental Health Couns., cert. clin. sexologist, 1996. Psychotherapist in pvt. practice, Jacksonville, 1991—; mem. faculty, counselor Fla. C.C. at Jacksonville, 1992—. Office: 9250 Cypress Green Dr Ste 101 Jacksonville FL 32256-7798

WOOD, THOMAS WESLEY, humanities educator, editor; b. Hugo, Okla., Mar. 16, 1920; s. Thomas Wesley Wood Sr. and Alma Elora (Rogers) Daniel; m. L. Deloris Gray, May 31, 1968; m. Doreen Anderson, June, 1950 (div. 1966); children: John William, Thomas Wakefield. BA in History and Journalism, Tulsa U., 1951, MA in History, 1952; MS in Journalism, Northwestern U., 1953; PhD in European History, U. Okla., 1966. Reporter City News Bur. Chgo., 1952-54; prof. Tulsa (Okla.) U., 1954-73, So. Ill. U., Carbondale, 1973-76; vis. prof. Am. U., Cairo, Egypt, 1976-78, U. Ark., Little Rock, 1978-80; prof. Temple U., Phila., 1980-90, emeritus prof., 1990—; reporter, corr. Tulsa World, 1954-84; editor, pub., founder Lost Generation Jour., Salem, Mo., 1973—. Author: Tulsa U. Editing Hankbook, 1956, 60, Tulsa U. Reporting Handbook, 1958, 60, 69, Outline History of American Journalism, 1961, Influence of the Paris Herald on the Lost Generation Writers, 1966; sub.-editor Egyptian Gazette, 1977-78. Recipient

editing and writing award Mo. Press Women, 1985, writing award Pa. Press Club, 1983, writing award Ark. Press Women, 1979, 80, photography award Soc. Profl. Journalists, 1972. Mem. Overseas Press Club Am., Assn. Edn. Journalism and Mass Comm., Hemingway Soc., Soc. Scholar Editors, Coun. Editors Learned Journals, Pi Alpha Mu (nat. pres. 1956-60). Republican. Baptist. Avocation: fly fishing, traveling, interviewing expatriate 20's Americans. Home: RR 5 Box 134 Salem MO 65560-9008 Office: Lost Generation Jour RR 3 Box 387 Salem MO 65560-9315

WOOD, VIVIAN POATES, mezzo soprano, educator, writer; b. Washington, Aug. 19, 1923; d. Harold Poates and Mildred Georgette (Patterson) W. Studies with Walter Anderson, Antioch Coll., 1953-55; Denise Restout, Saint-Leu-La-Fôret, France and Lakeville, Conn., 1960-62, 64-70, Paul A. Pisk, 1968-71; Paul Ulanowsky, N.Y.C., 1958-68; Elemer Nagy, 1965-68, Vyautas Marijosius, 1967-68; MusB, Hartt Coll. Music, 1968; postgrad. (fellow), Yale U., 1968; MusM (fellow), Washington U., St. Louis, 1971, PhD (fellow), 1973. Debut in recital series Internat. Jeunesse Musicals Arts Festival, 1953; solo fellowship Boston Symphony Orch., Berkshire Music Ctr., Tanglewood, 1964, St. Louis Symphony Orch., 1969, Washington Orch., 1949, Bach Cantata Series Berkshire Chamber Orch., 1964, Yale Symphony Orch., 1968; appearances in U.S. and European recitals, oratorios, operas, radio and TV, 1953-68; appeared as soloist in Internat. Harpsichord Festival, Westminister Choir Coll., Princeton, N.J., 1973; appeared as soloist in meml. concert, Landowska Ctr., Lakeville, 1969; prof. voice U. So. Miss., Hattiesburg, 1971-2000, ret. 2000; asst. dean Coll. Fine Arts, 1974-76, acting dean, 1976-77; guest prof. Hochschule für Musik, Munich, 1978-79; prof. Italian Internat. Studies Program, Rome, 1986; Miss. coord. Alliance for Arts Edn., Kennedy Ctr. Performing Arts, 1974—; mem. Miss. Gov.'s Adv. Panel for Gifted and Talented Children, 1974—; mem. 1st Miss. Gov.'s Conf. on the Arts, 1974—. Author: Polenc's Songs: An Analysis of Style, 1971. Recipient Young Am. Artists Concert award N.Y.C., 1955; Wanda Landowska fellow 1961-68. Mem. Miss. Music Tchrs. Assn., Nat. Assn. Tchrs. of Singing, Music Tchrs. Nat. Assn., Am. Musicology Soc., Golden Key, Mu Phi Epsilon, Delta Kappa Gamma, Tau Beta Kappa (hon.), Pi Kappa Lambda. Democrat. Episcopalian.

WOOD, WILLIS BOWNE, JR., retired utility holding company executive; b. Kansas City, Mo., Sept. 15, 1934; s. Willis Bowne Sr. and Mina (Henderson) W.; m. Dixie Gravel, Aug. 31, 1955; children: Bradley, William, Josh. BS in Petroleum Engring., U. Tulsa, 1957; grad. advanced mgmt. program, Harvard U., 1983; JD (hon.), Pepperdine U., 1996. With So. Calif. Gas Co., L.A., 1960-74, from v.p. to sr. v.p., 1975-80, exec. v.p., 1983-84; pres., CEO Pacific Lighting Gas Supply Co., L.A., 1981-83; from sr. v.p. to chmn., pres., CEO, Pacific Enterprises, L.A., 1984-93, chmn., CEO, 1993-98; ret., 1998; bd. dirs. Washington Mut., Seattle, Automobile Club Soc. Calif., Am. Automobile Assn.; trustee U. So. Calif. Trustee, vice-chmn. Harvey Mudd Coll., Claremont, Calif., 1984—; trustee, past chmn. Calif. Med. Ctr. Found., L.A., 1983-2000; trustee, past pres. S.W. Mus., L.A., trustee emeritus, 2000—; trustee John and Dora Haynes Found., 1998—; past bd. dirs. L.A. World Affairs Coun.; past dir., past chmn. bus. coun. for Sustainable Energy Future, 1994—; past dir. Pacific Coun. for Internat. Affairs. Recipient Disting. Alumni U. Tulsa, 1995. Mem. Soc. Petroleum Energy Engrs., Am. Gas Assn., Pacific Coast Gas Assn. (past bd. dirs.), Pacific Energy Assn., Calif. State C. of C. (past bd. dirs.), Nat. Assn. of Mfrs. (past bd. dirs.), Hacienda Golf CLub, Ctr. Club, Calif. Club. Republican.

WOODAHL, BRIAN ARVID, theoretical physicist; b. Choteau, Mont., Mar. 16, 1965; s. Robert Lee and Arlene Rae (Depner) W.; m. Gaylene Marie Robertson, Aug. 26, 1989; 1 child, Lysny Marie. BS in Elec. Engring., Wash. State U., 1987, MS in Mech. Engring., 1993; PhD in Theoretical Physics, Purdue U., 1999. Elec. engr. Boeing Co., Seattle, 1987-90; rsch. engr. Battelle-PNL, Richland, Wash., 1991-93; rsch. asst. dept. physics Purdue U., West Lafayette, Ind., 1993-99, vis. prof. dept. physics, 1999—. Mem. Am. Phys. Soc. Home: 2416 Depauw Dr West Lafayette IN 47906-6809 Office: Purdue Univ Dept Physics 1396 Physics Building West Lafayette IN 47907-1396

WOODARD, CARL GARY, file company employee, independent distributor; b. Cullman, Ala., Mar. 15, 1950; s. Carl Jubal and Martha Louise Woodard; m. Peggy Gail Eady, May 24, 1973 (div. Mar. 1990); 1 child, Shawn Paul. Student, St. Bernard Coll., Cullman, 1968-71, U. Ala., 1971-73. Handyman Buettner Bros., Cullman, 1975; shipping clk. Teague Warehouse, Birmingham, Ala., 1975; stocking clk. Giant Foods Groceries, Cullman, 1975-76; egg insp. Ala. Egg, Cullman, 1976-77; plant svc. attendant Nicholson File, Cullman, 1977—, mem. newspaper staff, 1985-91, sec. quality cirs., 1985-95; indep. distbr. NIKKEN, Cullman, 1999—. Author: Inspirational Poetry, 2000. Asst. scoutmaster Boy Scouts Am., Cullman, 1987-93. Recipient recognition Ala. Soil and Water Conservation, Cullman, 1996, Vol. Spirit award Cooper Industries, Cullman, 1996. Assoc. mem. Mus. Natural History, Acad. Am. Poets, Libr. Congress; mem. Internat. Soc. Poets (disting. mem.). Republican. Lutheran. Avocations: reading, writing poetry, crafts, woodworking. Home: 1541 County Road 702 Cullman AL 35055-9546

WOODARD, CHARLES GARRARD, political scientist; b. Adelaide, S. Australia, July 3, 1929; m. Helen Cameron (dec.); children: Andrew Cameron, Alastair Charles. LLB, Adelaide U. Ambassador to Burma, China, Malaysia Dept. Fgn. Affairs and Trade, Canberra, 1952-86; sr. assoc. in polit. sci. East Asian affairs Melbourne U., 1986—, mem. adminstrv. appeal tribunal, 1986—; internat. adv. bd. Wright Investors Svc. Ct. Nat. pres. Australian Inst. of Internat. Affairs, Canberra, 1991—. Office: Melbourne U, Parkville VIC 3053, Australia

WOODARD, H. TOM, entertainment company executive; b. Lebanon, Ind., May 5, 1948; s. Edgar Clifford and Edna Anne (Yaryan) W. AS in Music and Theater, Vincennes U., 1985; BA in Communication, Calif. State U., Sacramento, 1986, MA in Communication, 1988; postgrad. in comm., U. Nebr., 1989; postgrad. in edn., U. Tenn., 1990. Actor TV series Timothy Churchmouse Indpls., 1967-68; entertainer stage and TV L.A., 1969-71; tchr. dance Arthur Murray Sch. Dance, Fresno, Calif., 1973-75; tchr. dance, choreographer Dance Palace Studios, Tacoma, 1976-80; lectr. Purdue U., West Lafayette, Ind., 1987; producer, tchr. Aba-Daba Prodns., Lincoln, Nebr., 1988-90; lectr. U. Tenn., Knoxville, 1990-91, Pellissippi State Coll., Knoxville, 1991-96; pres. Pharaoh Records, Knoxville, 1993—; promoter Saddle Talent Prodns., Knoxville, 1995-99; pub. trade mag. Country Note Connection, 1993-97, Steinwood Publishing, 1993—, Goliath Alliance Group, 1999—; personal mgr. Grand Trunk Talent Mgmt., 1999—. Author: To See the Sun Shine, 1997, George Fruits: Last Survivor of the American Revolution, 1999; producer dance videos Learning to Dance Vols. 1-12, 1989; exec. prodr. (CD series) Gold Rush Country, vol. 1-6, 1995-99, Alamo George: Last of the Original Frontiersmen. With USAF, 1966-67. Recipient Gold Double Honors Ballroom Dance award, 1979, First Place Forensic Speaking, West Coast Championship, 1980, Indie Record Lab of Yr. Country Music Assn. Am., 1995, Album of Yr., 1995, Trade Publ. of Yr., 1995. Mem. ASCAP, SAR, European Country Music Assn. (Tenn. rep. 1996-97), Broadcast Music Inc., Aircraft Owners and Pilots Assn. Democrat. Avocations: music, aviation, writing, computers, genealogy. E-mail: tsmith3@conc.tds.net. Home and Office: Pharaoh Internat Records 433 Gallaher View Rd Knoxville TN 37919-5350

WOODARD, NINA ELIZABETH, banker; b. L.A., Apr. 3, 1947; d. Alexander Rhodes and Harriette Jane (Powers) Matthews; divorced; children: Regina M., James. D. Grad., Pacific Coast Banking Sch., 1987; BS in Mgmt., Calif. Coast U., 1993; postgrad., Ctr. for Creative Leadership, 1994. Lifetime cert. sr. profl. in human resources. Dental asst. Donald R. Shire DDS, L.A., 1965-66; with Security Pacific Nat. Bank, Marina Del Rey, Calif., 1968-69; with First Interstate Bank, Casper, Wyo., 1971—, adminstr. asst. pers., 1975-78, asst. v.p., asst. mgr. pers., 1978-82, v.p., dir. mktg. and pers., 1982-84, v.p., mgr. human resources, 1984-88; v.p., mgr. employee rels. First Interstate Bank Ltd., L.A., 1988-93; v.p., mgr. employee rels. Ams. region Standard Chartered Bank, 1993-95, sr. v.p. human resources, 1995-99; sr. v.p. advisor cultural integration and employee comm. Standard Chartered Bank, Thailand, 1999-2000; sr. v.p., mgr. cultural integration Standard Chartered Bank, Dubai, UAE, 2000—; instr. mktg. Am. Inst. Banking, 1983, Casper Coll., 1982. Mem. Civil Svc. Commn., City of Casper, 1983-88; bd. dirs. YMCA, 1984-87, Downtown Devel. Assn.; pres. Downtown Casper Assn.; instr. St. Patrick's Parish Religious Edn., 1991-92, mem. parish coun., 1993-94; advisor to the parish coun. Parish of the Resurrection, Jersey City, 1999. Named Bus. Woman of Yr., Bus. and Profl. Women, 198, Young Career Woman, 1975. Mem. Nat. Assn. Bank Women, Bus. and Profl. Women (dist. dir.), Am. Soc. Pers. Adminstrn. (regional v.p., state coun. Wyo. 1987-88), Pers. and Indsl. Rels. Assn. (chmn. govt. affairs com. 1989-90, Fast Track award 1991, Pres.'s Achievement award 1993, conf. chmn. 1991, 92, dist. chair 1993, 2d v.p. 1994), Fin. Women Internat. (Wyo. state chair 1986, regional edn. and tng. chair 1987, dist. coord. L.A. 1993, L.A. group chair 1994, nat. bd. dirs.), Soc. Human Resource Mgmt. (area I v.p. 1996-99). Republican. Roman Catholic. Office: Standard Chartered Bank, 2d Fl 23-25 MG Rd, Fort Mumbai 400 100 Mumbai, India

WOODBRIDGE, JOHN DUNNING, history and church history educator; b. Salisbury, N.C., May 24, 1941; s. Charles Jahleel and Ruth (Dunning) W.; m. Susan Jane Frerichs, June 28, 1970; children: Elisabeth Anne, Joshua, David. BA in History, Wheaton Coll., 1963; MA in History, Mich. State U., 1965; Doctorat de Troisième Cycle, U. Toulouse, France, 1969; MDiv, Trinity Evang. Div. Sch., Deerfield, Ill., 1971. Vis. prof. history U. Toulouse, 1968-69; asst. prof. history Trinity Coll., Deerfield, 1970-74; prof. ch. history Trinity Evang. Div. Sch., Deerfield, 1970—; vis. prof. history Northwestern U., Evanston, Ill., 1988-95; vis. prof. religion Hautes Etudes, Sorbonne, U. Paris, 1996, 99. Author: Biblical Authority, 1982, Revolt in Pre-revolutionary France, 1995; editor: Great Leaders of the Christian Church, 1988; co-editor: Historische Kritik und biblischer kanon, 1988; sr. editor Christianity Today, 1997-99. NEH fellow, 1973-74, Herzog August Bibliothek fellow, 1982, ACLS fellow, Paris, 1976-77; NEH summer grant, Chgo., 1995. Mem. Am. Soc. Eighteenth Century Studies, Soc. French History. Mem. Evangelical Free Ch. Avocation: composing music. Office: Trinity Evangel Div Sch Deerfield IL 60015

WOODCOCK, BARRIE, accountant, consultant; b. Flintshire, Wales, Dec. 8, 1946; s. Ronald and Harriet Annie (Mellor) W.; m. Rosemary Hughes, Nov. 26, 1947; children: James Vaughan, Edward Owen. Diploma in mgmt. studies, Leicester (Eng.) Poly., 1977. Chartered pub. fin. acct., cert. chartered acct.; Diploma in Mcpl. Adminstrn.; cert. mgmt. cons. Asst. chief exec. Leicestershire County Coun., Leicester, Eng., 1974-77; asst. county treas. W. Glamorgan County Coun., Swansea, Wales, 1977-79; dep. county treas. Nottinghamshire County Coun., Nottingham, Eng., 1979-84; from sr. mgr. to ptnr. Klynveld Peak Marwick Goerdeler, Birmingham, Eng., 1984-95; mng. dir. RBW Assocs., Nottingham, Eng., 1995—. Author: Managing Cash-A Practical Approach, 1995, Making the Right Choices-A Practical Guide to Project Appraisal, 1996, Appointing and Managing Advisors and Providers of Professional Services, 1996, Measuring Up - Theories and Concepts of Performance Measurement, 1998, Achieving Excellence in Financial Management, 1998, Developing the Financial Manager, 1999. Mem. ind. rev. panels Nat. Health Svc., Eng. Fellow Chartered Assn. Cert Accts.; mem. Inst. Mgmt., Chartered Inst. of Pub. Fin. and Accountancy (fin. mgmt. panel 1994—). Methodist. Avocations: skiing, squash, tennis. Office: RBW Assocs Parkside Ctr, 6 Oxford St, NG1 5BH Nottingham England

WOODCOCK, RICHARD WESLEY, educational psychologist; b. Portland, Oreg., Jan. 29, 1928; s. Carol Wesley and Captola Winifred (Catterlin) W.; m. Annie Lee Plant, Aug. 16, 1951; children: Donna, Dianne, Judy, Wayne; m. Ana Felicia Muñoz-Sandoval, June 14, 1991. BS, U. Oreg., 1949, MEd, 1953, EdD, 1956. Diplomate of Am. Bd. of Profl. Psychol. Lt. USN, 1945-46, 50-51; elem. tchr. Arago Schs., Oreg., 1951-52; dir. spl. edn. Coos County Sch., Coquille, Oreg., 1952-54, Corvallis (Oreg.) Pub. Schs., 1955-57; asst. prof. psychology Western Oreg. U., 1957-61; assoc. prof. spl. edn. Univ. No. Colo., Greeley, 1961-63; prof. spl. edn., Peabody Coll. Vanderbilt Univ., 1963-68; editor, dir. rsch. Am. Guidance Svc., 1968-72; dir. Measurement Learning Cons., Tenn., Oreg., 1972—; vis. scholar Univ. of Ariz., 1985-88, Univ. So. Calif., L.A., 1988-91; rsch. prof. psychology U. Va., 1993-97; cons. NCAA, 1989-94. Author: (battery tests) Mini-Battery of Achievement, 1994, Woodcock Language Proficiency Battery English and Spanish forms, 1991, 95, Woodcock-Muñoz Language Surveys, 1993, W-J Psycho-Edn. Battery, 1977, 89, Bateria Woodcock Psico-Educativa en Español, 1982, 96, Woodcock Reading Mastery Tests, 1973-87, Scales of Independent Behavior, 1984, 95, G-F-W Auditory Skills Battery, 1976, The Peabody Rebus Reading Program, 1967, The Colorado Braille Battery, 1966, Woodcock Diagnostic Reading Battery, 1997, Mather-Woodcock Group Writing Tests, 1997; contbr. numerous articles to profl. jours. Fellow Am. Acad. Sch. Psychology.

WOODFILL, CHRISTOPHER C., secondary school educator; b. Racine, Wis., Nov. 13, 1974; s. William Alan and Louisa Ann Woodfill. BA in History and Spanish, Gallaudet U., 1997; MA in L.Am. Studise, George Washington U., 1999. Elem. tchr. Ofelia Tancredi Corredor Sch. for the Deaf, Merida, Venezuela, 1992-93; ESL tchr. Gallaudet U., Washington, 1996-99; freelance ESL tchr. Delavan, Wis., 1999—; h.s. social studies tchr. Wis. Sch. for the Deaf, Delavan, Wis., 1999—. sponsor, vol. Deaf People in Nazi Europe Conf., Washington, 1998, World Deaf History Conf., Washington, summer 2000. Vol. Habitat for Humanity, Dallas, summer 1995; instr. Deaf Action Ctr., Dallas, summer 1995; campaign vol. Bob Dole for Pres., Washington, 1996. Recipient Vol. of Yr. award Cosmopolitan Club, 1997. Mem. Fgn. Lang. Hon. Soc., Gallaudet U. Alumni Assn., George Washington U. Alumni Assn., Phi Alpha Pi (sec. 1999—), Sigma Phi Iota. Republican. Roman Catholic. Avocations: reading, debating, world travel, food tasting. Home: 215 Franklin St Unit D Delavan WI 53115-1013 Office: Wis Sch for the Deaf 309 W Walworth Ave Delavan WI 53115-1099

WOODFORD, F. PETER, scientific editor; b. Portland, Oreg., Nov. 8, 1930; arrived in U.K., 1931; s. Wilfrid Charles and Mabel Rose (Scarff) W.; m. Susan Silberman, Dec. 18, 1964; 1 child, Julia. BA, Oxford U., 1952, MA, 1955; PhD, U. Leeds, 1955; DSc (hon.), U. Salford, 1993. Chartered chemist. Rsch. fellow U. Leiden, The Netherlands, 1958-63; guest investigator Rockefeller U., N.Y.C., 1963-71; sci. historian Ciba Found., London, 1971-74; exec. dir. Inst. for rsch. in Mental and Multiple Handicap, 1974-77; prin. to chief sci. officer Dept. of Health, London, 1977-93; editor of publs. Camden History Soc., London, 1994—; vis. lectr. Inst. Pharmacol. Scis., Milan, Italy, 1995-96; disting. visitor Royal Free Sch. Medicine, London, 1995—. Author: Scientific Writing for Graduate Students, 1969, The Ciba Foundation 1949-74: An Analytic History, 1974, A Constant Vigil (100 Years of Heath and Old Hampstead Soc.), 1997, Streets of Bloomsbury & Fitzrovia, 1997, How to Teach Scientific Communication, 1999, Streets of Old Holborn, 1999, The Streets of Hampstead, 3d edit., 2000, Streets of St. Giles, 2000, Hampstead Cemetery, Fortune Green, 2000, 36 others; editor conf. procs. in cardiology, 1995, 98; exec. editor: Jour. of Atherosclerosis Rsch., 1960-63, Jour. of Lipid Rsch., 1963-69; mng. editor: Procs. Nat. Acad. Scis., U.S., 1970-71, Camden History Rev., 1995—. Chmn. London Sch. Prosthetics, 1992-93. Officer RAF, 1956-57. Fellow Royal Coll. Pathologists, Royal Soc. Chemistry, Inst. Physics and Engring. in Medicine, Royal Coll. Physicians (assoc., founder), Hampstead Music Club (chmn. 1996-99). Avocations: playing chamber music, local history. E-mail: woodford@dircon.co.uk. Home and Office: 1 Akenside Rd, London NW3 5BS, England

WOODHOUSE, JOHN FREDERICK, food distribution company executive; b. Wilmington, Del., Nov. 30, 1930; s. John Crawford and Anna (Houth) W.; m. Marilyn Ruth Morrow, June 18, 1955; children: John Crawford II, Marjorie Ann Woodhouse Purdy. BA, Wesleyan U., 1953; DHL, 1997; MBA, Harvard U., 1955. Bus. devel. officer Can. Imperial Bank of Commerce, Toronto, Ont., 1955-59; various fin. positions Ford Motor Co., Dearborn, Mich., 1959-64, Cooper Industries, Inc., Mount Vernon, Ohio, 1964-67; treas. Houston, 1967-69, Crescent-Niagara Corp., Buffalo, 1968-69; exec. v.p., CFO Sysco Corp., Houston, 1969-71, pres., COO, 1972-83, pres., CEO, 1983-85, chmn., CEO, 1985-96, mem. exec. and fin. coms., 1996-98, chmn. bd. dirs., chmn. exec. com., 1998-2000, sr. chmn., 2000—; bd. dirs., mem. exec. com. Shell Oil Co.; bd. dirs., mem. exec. com. Winrock Internat., 1993-2000; dir. Harvard Bus. Sch. Assocs., 1995—. Chmn. Mich. 16th dist. rep. Club, 1962-64; treas. Cooper Industries Found., 1967-69; trustee Wesleyan U., 1976-92, vice-chmn., 1986-92, chmn. comprehensive capital campaign, 1998—; ruling elder Presbyn.. Ch.; trustee, chmn. audit com., mem. exec. com. Mt. Holyoke Coll., South Hadley, Mass., 1996—; bd. dirs. Winrock Internat. Inst. for Agrl. Devel., 1993-2000, mem. fin. com., mem. exec. com., chmn. investment com.; bd. advisors The Retail Food Industry Ctr., U. Minn. Recipient Herbert Hoover award for disting. svc. to food industry, 2000. Mem. Nat. Am. Wholesale Grocer's Assn. (bd. dirs. 1990—, vice chmn. 1992, chmn. 1994-96), Internat. Foodservice Distbrs. Assn. (Herbert Hoover award 2000), Houston Soc. Fin. Analysts, Fin. Execs. Inst., Harvard Bus. Sch. Club, Sigma Chi. Avocations: backpacking, canoeing, tennis. Office: Sysco Corp 1390 Enclave Pkwy Houston TX 77077-2099

WOODHOUSE, STAN PETER, cardiology educator; b. New Delhi, Oct. 9, 1936; s. William John and Tristina Mary (Burton) W.; m. Anne Mackay Walker, 1963 (div. 1984); children: Damian, Marcus, Tara; ptnr. Craig Lollback, 1982. MBChB, U. Otago, New Zealand, 1962. Jr. house surgeon Timaru Pub. Hosp., New Zealand, 1962-63; registrar Dunedin Pub. Hosp., New Zealand, 1963-66; cardiologist pvt. practice, Sydney, 1982-83; dir. cardiology Princess Alexandra Hosp., Brisbane, Australia, 1983-93; assoc. prof. medicine U. Queensland, Brisbane, Australia, 1992—. Editor: Eating for Health, 1975; contbr. articles to profl. jours. Rsch. fellow U. Otago, 1967-68, McGill U., Montreal, Can., 1967-70, Johns Hopkins U., Balt., 1970-71. Fellow Royal Australian Coll. Physicians; mem. Internat. Soc. Heart Rsch., Internat. Fedn. Epidemiology, Am. Soc. Echocardiography. Home: GPO Box 172 New Farm, Brisbane Q4005, Australia Office: Taylor Med Ctr, 12/40 Annerley Rd, Brisbane Q4102, Australia

WOODHOUSE, THOMAS EDWIN, lawyer; b. Cedar Rapids, IA, Apr. 30, 1940; s. Keith Wallace and Elinor Julia (Cherny) W.; m. Kiyoko Fujiie, May 29, 1965; children: Miya, Keith, Leighton. AB cum laude, Amherst Coll., 1962; JD, Harvard U., 1965. Bar: N.Y. 1966, U.S. Supreme Ct. 1969, Calif. 1975. Assoc. Chadbourne, Parke, Whiteside & Wolff, N.Y.C., 1965-68; atty./adviser AID, Washington, 1968-69; counsel Pvt. Investment Co. for Asia S.A., Tokyo, 1969-72; ptnr. Woodhouse Lee & Davis, Singapore, 1972-74; assoc. Graham & James, San Francisco, 1974-75; asst. gen. counsel Natomas Co., San Francisco, 1975-81; mem. Lasky, Haas, Cohler & Munter, San Francisco, 1982-90; trust adminstr. Ronald Family Trust A, 1989—, Gordon P. Getty Family Trust, 1994—; sole practice Berkeley, 1990—; of counsel Wilson, Sonsini, Goodrich & Rosati, Palo Alto, Calif., 1992-95; instr. law faculty U. Singapore, 1972-74; CEO, Vallejo Investments, 1997—. chmn. Police Rev. Com. of Berkeley (Calif.), 1980-84; mem. Berkeley Police Res., 1986—; bd. dirs. Friends Assn. of Svcs. for Elderly, 1979-84; clk. fin. com. Am. Friends Svc. Com. of No. Calif., 1979-83; pres. Zyzzyva Inc., lit. quar., 1985-87. Trustee Freedom from Hunger, 1989-99, Coun. of Friends Bancroft Libr., 1997—, Dominican Sch. of Philosophy and Theology, 1998—. With U.S. Army, 1958. Fellow Am. Bar Found. (life); mem. Calif. Bar Assn., Assn. Internat. de Bibliophilie, Harvard Club, Univ. Club, Book Club Calif., Roxburghe Club, Travellers Club, Grolier Club, Faculty Club U. Calif.-Berkeley, Mira Vista Golf and Country Club. Republican. Roman Catholic. Home and Office: 1800 San Antonio Ave Berkeley CA 94707-1618

WOODIES, LESLIE, choreographer, dancer; b. Boston, Nov. 19, 1952; d. Richard and Mary(Kinoian) W.; m. Brian Leo Kennedy, June 8, 1974 (div. 1980). Grad. high sch., Needham, Mass., 1970. Soloist Boston Ballet Co., 1970-79, Dennis Wayne's Dancers, N.Y.C., 1979-80; prin. N.Y. Shakespeare Festival, Cassie in A Chorus Line, 1980-82; prin. cover On Your Toes, N.Y.C., 1982-84; tchr. Boston Ballet Co., Boston Ballet Ctr. for Dance Edn., Harvard U. Office for Arts, Boston Conservatory, Brown U. Guest artist N.Y. Dance Theatre, Boston Opera Co., Chgo. Lyric Opera, Boston POPS Youth Concert Series, Cen. Wis. Ballet Found., Walnut Hill Sch. of Performing Arts, Children's Ballet Theater, (TV) Move Out!, Sta. WQTV, Boston, George's House, PBS (Emmy award), The Kennedy Ctr. Honors, 1982, CBS, (films) Echoes, A Chorus Line-The Movie; (advertisements) prin. player New Eng. Telephone/AT&T, (live) I Love New York Industrials, Alfred Fiandaca's Spring & Summer Collections, Smirnoff-Black Velvet Rep., N.Y. Italian Shoe Show; choreographer: mems. of Kirov Ballet for Fred's Jewelers, Beverly Hills, episodes of Old MacDonald's Farm for Lifetime TV, episode of Adventures in Wonderland for Disney TV Channel, The Wonderful World of Barbie for EPCOT Ctr., Disney, Mattel. Scholar Sch. of Am. Ballet, Boston Sch. Ballet, Studio Ballet of Wellesley, Jacob's Pillow Dance Festival, 1969, Dramalogue, Robby awards for choreography On the Town, Calif. Music Theater, 1990. Mem. Actors Equity Assn., Am. Guild Musical Artists.

WOOD KAHARI, BRENDA MARIE, lawyer; b. Washington, Jan. 29, 1951; d. Sylvester and Laverne Morris; m. Muzanenhamo Eric Kahari, June 13, 1981; children: Brent, Morris. BA, U. Dayton, 1972; JD, Howard U., 1975; LLM, Georgetown U., 1982. Bar: Ohio 1975, D.C. 1977. Legal intern Dept. State/U.S. AID, Washington, 1974-75; assoc. atty. Squire, Sanders & Dempsey, Cleve., 1975-78; assoc. counsel Pepco, Washington, 1978-81; legal advisor Ministry of Justice, Harare, Zimbabwe, 1981-86; pvt. practice B.W. Kahari Law Office, Harare/Washington, 1986; office affil. Soble Internat. Law, 1996; bd. dirs. Olmur Investments, Harare; trustee Zimbabwe Health Care Trust, 1996—; bd. dirs. Nat. Anglican Theol. Colls., Zimbabwe, 1996. Author, reporter and spkr. in field of trademarks. Fellow Chartered Inst. Internat. Arbitrators; mem. Ohio Bar Assn., D.C. Bar Assn., Law Soc. Zimbabwe. Home: 96 Montgomery Rd Highlands, Harare Zimbabwe Office: BW Kahari, 38 Samora Machel Ave, Harare Zimbabwe

WOODLAND, ALAN DONALD, economics educator; b. Dorrigo, NSW, Australia, Oct. 4, 1943; s. Cecil James and Elsie (Shephard) W.; m. Narelle Barbara Todd, Dec. 9, 1966; children: Lisa, Nicole, Todd. BA with honors, U. New Eng., Armidale, Australia, 1965, PhD, 1970. Lectr. econ. U. New Eng., 1967-69; asst. prof. econ. U. B.C., Vancouver, Can., 1969-74, assoc. prof. econ., 1974-77, prof. econ., 1978-81; prof. econometrics U. Sydney, Australia, 1982—. Author: International Trade and Resource Allocation, 1982; contbr. articles to profl. jours. Fellow Econometric Soc. (chair Australasian standing com. 1984—), Acad. Social Scis. Australia. Avocations: tennis, bridge. Office: Univ Sydney, Dept Econometrics, Sydney NSW 2006, Australia

WOODLE, E. STEVE, transplant surgeon; b. Texarkana, Ark., Jan. 7, 1954; three children. BS summa cum laude, Tex. A&M U., 1976; MD magna cum laude, U. Tex., 1980. Diplomate Am. Bd. Surgery, Am. Coll. Surgeons. Asst. prof. surgery Washington U. Sch. Medicine, St. Louis, 1990-92; asst. prof. surgery & immunology U. Chgo., 1992-98, assoc. prof. surgery & immunology, 1998-99; prof. surgery, pediat. & pathology U. Cin., 1999—, chief, divsn. transplantation, 1999—; com. mem. Ctr. for Biol. Evaluation and Rsch., FDA, Washington, 1994-97. Contbr. more than 130 articles to med. and sci. jours., also chpts. to books. Mem. Am. Soc. Transplant Surgeons (bd. dirs.), Am. Soc. Transplantation, Internat. Transplantation Soc., Soc. Univ. Surgeons, Ctrl. Surg. Assn., Western Surg. Assn., Mensa. Office: U Cin Dept Surgery ML 4567-0558 231 Bethesda Ave Cincinnati OH 45267-0001

WOODLEY, ANN E., lawyer, educator; b. Greenville, S.C., July 23, 1956; d. Donald Robert Woodley and Elizabeth Van Dyke. BA in Polit. Sci. and Journalism summa cum laude, U. Ariz., 1978; JD cum laude, Ariz. State U., 1981. Bar: Ariz. 1981, U.S. Dist. Ct. Ariz. 1981, D.C. 1983, U.S. Dist. Ct. D.C. 1984, U.S. Ct. Appeals (D.C. and 9th cirs.) 1984, U.S. Ct. Appeals (7th cir.) 1986, U.S. Supreme Ct. 1987, Ohio 1991, Calif. 1992. Law clk. to chief judge U.S. Dist. Ct. Ariz., Phoenix, 1981-83; assoc. Winston & Strawn, Washington, 1983-88; asst. prof. law U. Akron (Ohio) Sch. Law, 1988-95, assoc. prof. law, 1995-2000; dir. Lodestar Mediation Clinic, clin. prof. law Ariz. State U. Coll. Law, 2000—. Mem. ABA, Am. Trial Lawyers Assn., Ariz. Bar Assn., D.C. Womens Bar Assn., Soc. Profls. in Dispute Resolution (assoc.), Nat. Inst. Dispute Resolution. Democrat. Presbyterian. E-mail: woodley@uakron.edu. Office: U Akron Sch Law Akron OH 44325-0001

WOODMAN, ARTHUR TULLIS, architect, consultant; b. Kans. City, Mo., Mar. 21, 1926; s. Clyde E. and Esther M. W.; m. Frances G., Sept. 15, 1946; children: Susan, Jo Ann, Scott, Sherry, Julie, Janet, Tom, Rebecca. Student in Engring., Washburn U., 1946; BS in Archl. Engring., U. Kans., 1948. Registered profl. architect, Kans. Mem. staff Overend & Boucher, Wichita, Kans., 1948-49, Thomas & Harris, Wichita, Kans., 1950-52; assoc. arch. John M. Hickman and Arthur T. Woodman Archs. Associated, Wichita, Kans., 1953-59; prin., owner Arthur T. Woodman Arch., Wichita, Kans., 1959-62; sr. ptnr., architect Woodman Van Doren, Wichita, Kans., 1962-82; prin., owner Woodman Archs., Wichita, Kans., 1982—; commr. for Kans., Okla., Ark. River Commn., 1990, 96; cons. Wichita Art

Mus., 1973-75, Wichita State U., 1970-83. Architect Hyperbolic Parabaloid Vickers Petroleum, 1957, First Nat. Bank, Wichita, 1965 (design award AIA 1967), Lincoln Park Cmty. Ctr., Wichita, 1975 (design award 1978). Mem. vestry St. Andrew's Episcopal Ch., Derby, Kans., 1964-94; environ. chair Water Resources, Wichita, 1975-95. With USN, 1944-46. Recipient Cert. of Appreciation Kans. Water Authority, Topeka, 1997; named to Hall of Fame Ark. River Histories Soc., Tulsa, Okla., 1998. Mem. AIA, Ark. River Devel. Assn. (chmn.), Wichita C. of C. (environ. chair), Phi Delta Theta. Republican. Avocations: golf, tennis, classic cars.

WOODRING, JOHN OLMER, JR., financial planner and advisor; b. York, Pa., Feb. 4, 1947; s. John Olmer and Louise Romaine (Mummert) W.; Ph.D., Am. U., 1982; m. Carolyn Sue Henry, Mar. 30, 1969; children—John A., Rachel Sue. Sec., Govt. Employees Assn., Inc., Washington, 1971-76; pres. N.Am. Mint, Bird-in-Hand, Pa., 1973-76, Keystone Mint, Bird-in-Hand, 1973-76; adminstr. Little People Day Care Schs., York, 1976-85; mem. accreditation com. United Pvt. Acad. Schs. Assn. Pa., 1979-85; mem. founders group Luth. Ednl. Assn. York County, 1979-85; with Fin. & Managerial Services of York, 1972—, MONY Fin. Services, 1985-95. Served with USMC, 1966-70. Decorated Navy Achievement medal; recipient Letter of Appreciation for United Fund dr., 1973. Registered fin. planner. Mem. York C. of C., U.S. Pvt. Acad. Schs. Assn. Pa., Internat. Assn. Registered Fin. Planners, Inc., VFW, Nat. Rifle Assn., York Hist. Soc. Democrat. Lutheran. Home: 221 Silver Spur Dr York PA 17402-2732

WOODRING, MARGARET DALEY, architect, planner; b. N.Y.C., Mar. 29, 1933; d. Joseph Michael and Mary (Barron) Daley; m. Francis Woodring, Oct. 25, 1954 (div. 1962); m. Robert Bell, Dec. 20, 1971 (dec.); children: Ward, Gabrielle, Phaedra. Student, NYU, 1959-60; BArch, Columbia U., 1966; MArch, Princeton U., 1971. Registered architect; cert. planner. Architect, planner various firms, N.Y.C.; environ. design specialist Rutgers U., New Brunswick, N.J., 1966-68; programming cons. Davis & Brody, N.Y.C., 1968-71; planning cons. William H. Liskamm, San Francisco, 1971-74; mgr. planning Met. Transp. Commn., Oakland, Calif., 1974-81; dir. Internat. Program for Housing and Urban Devel. Ofcls. Ctr. for Environ. Design Rsch. U. Calif., Berkeley, 1981-89; prin. Woodring & Assocs., San Rafael, Calif., 1989—; adj. lectr. dept. architecture U. Calif., Berkeley, 1974-84; founder New Horizons Savs. Assn., San Rafael, 1977-79; cons. U.S. Agy. for Internat. Devel., Washington, 1981-89; mem. jury Nat. Endowment Arts, others. Chair Bicentennial Com., San Rafael, 1976; bd. dirs. Displaced Homemakers Ctr., Oakland, 1981-84; pres. Environ Design Found., San Francisco, 1984-90. William Kinne Travel fellow Columbia U., 1965-66; Richard King Mellon fellow Princeton U., 1968-71. Mem. AIA (chair urban design com. San Francisco chpt. 1980-81), Am. Inst. Cert. Planners, Urban Land Inst., Soc. for Internat. Devel. (pres. San Francisco chpt. 1980-83), World Affairs Coun., Internat. World Congress on Land Policy. Avocations: hiking, gardening, reading, race walking.

WOODRUFF, MARK REED, magazine editor; b. Roanoke, Va., Jan. 3, 1957; s. James Moses and Elizabeth (Reed) W. BFA, Va. Commonwealth U., 1981; postgrad., San Francisco State U., 1983-84. Freelance writer N.Y.C., 1984-88; features editor Tasty Mag., N.Y.C., 1988-90; mng. editor Spin Mag., N.Y.C., 1990-95; sr. editor Rolling Stone, N.Y.C., 1995-97, asst. mng. editor, 1997-98; editor-in-chief Tennis mag., N.Y.C., 1998—. Mem. Am. Soc. Mag. Editors. Democrat. Avocation: tennis. Home: 118 Glendale Rd Ossining NY 10562-1619 Office: Tennis Mag 810 7th Ave 4th Fl New York NY 10019-5818

WOODRUM, ROBERT LEE, executive search consultant; b. Merkel, Tex., Mar. 3, 1945; s. Bill and Norma (Shea) W.; m. Linda Mary Larkin, July 20, 1968; children: Jennifer, Michael. BA, Calif. State U., Northridge, 1967; postgrad., U. Okla., 1974. Press sec. U.S. Senate, Washington, 1977-78; dir. pub. affairs U.S. Office Personnel Mgmt., Washington, 1979-80; pres. Corp. Communications, Washington, 1980-82; v.p. Norton Simon Inc., N.Y.C., 1982-83; spl. asst. to the commr. NFL, N.Y.C., 1983-84; exec. dir. Ritz Paris Hemingway Award, 1984-87; pres. Ritz Paris Internat., 1984-86; sr. v.p. AmBase Corp., 1986-91; mng. dir. Korn/Ferry Internat., N.Y.C., 1991—; advisor USIA, Washington, 1980-93, ARC, 1983, White House Vets. Com., 1979-80. Trustee N.Y.C. Meals on Wheels, Inc. Lt. comdr. USN, 1968-77. Decorated Navy Achievement medal (2). Mem. N.Y. Sky Club. Office: 6 Plumbridge Ln Hilton Head Island SC 29928-3360

WOODS, DAVID BRIAN, soil scientist, consultant; b. Van Der Bijl Park, South Africa, Nov. 26, 1955; s. Brian John and Ruth Lorraine (Shuter) W.; m. Sharon Lee Fowair, Dec. 7, 1985; children: Wendy Leigh, Mark David. BSc in Agr., U. Natal, Pretoria, South Africa, 1980, MSC in Agr., 1991; MBL, U. South Africa, Pretoria, 1996. Soil scientist Sortvedr Farms, South Africa, 1979-80, 1980-81; dep. mgr. Outspan Labs., South Africa, 1981-99; soils specialist Outspan Internat., 1996-99; owner Ferti Plan, 1999—. E-mail: dwoods@mweb.co.za. Address: PO Box 21246, Nelspruit 1200, South Africa

WOODS, GREGORY, liberal studies educator, literary critic, poet; b. Cairo, Jan. 4, 1953; s. Frederick and Charmion (Crocombe) W. BA with honours, U. East Anglia, Norwich, Eng., 1974, MA, 1975, PhD, 1983. Lectr. U. Salerno, Italy, 1980-84, Crewe and Alsager (Eng.) Coll. Higher Edn., 1985-90, Nottingham Trent (Eng.) U., 1990-95; reader lesbian and gay studies Nottingham (Eng.) U., 1995-98, prof. lesbian and gay studies, 1998—. Author: Articulate Flesh: Male Homo-Eroticism and Modern Poetry, 1987, We Have the Melon, 1992, This Is No Book: a Gay Reader, 1994, A History of Gay Literature: The Male Tradition, 1998, May I Say Nothing, 1998. Office: Nottingham Trent U, Fac Humanities, Clifton Ln, Nottingham NG11 8NS, England

WOODS, GWENDOLYN LENAR, parole program administrator; b. Cin., Jan. 6, 1962; d. Ike and Jessie L. (Warren) Everson; m. Robert Anthony Woods, Aug. 19, 1961; 1 child, Brandon Antonio. BA, Ohio U., 1984; MS, Xavier U., Cin., 1986. Cert. fitness instr. Receptionist, adminstrv. asst. Chester C. Pryor II, MD, Cin., 1978-86; diversion officer Montgomery County Prosecutor, Dayton, Ohio, 1986-91; mediator Cin. Prosecutor's Office, 1984-86; fitness instr. Holiday/Bally's Fitness, Dayton and Columbus, Ohio, 1989—; instr. Sinclair C.C., Dayton, 1989-91; supr. U.S. Census Bur., Dayton, 1990; parole officer Ohio Dept. Rehab. and Corrections, Columbus, 1992-93, parole program specialist, 1993-95, dep. superintendent, 1995-99, exec. asst. to chief, 1999—. Mem. Am. Fitness Assn., Am. Probation/Parole Assn., Am. Correctional Assn., Nat. Coun. Negro Women, Alliance of Women in Cmty. Rels., Delta Sigma Theta. Avocations: aerobics, music, reading, interior decorating. Office: Ohio Dept Rehab/Corrections 1050 Freeway Dr N Columbus OH 43229-5411

WOODS, IVAN K.J., financial executive; b. Pa., June 13, 1970; arrived in England, 1978; s. James Austin and Geraldine Mary (Meade) W ; m. Clare Denise Arnold, July 3, 1999. Degree in econs., Bristol U., 1991. Analyst Baring Securities, London, 1990, Coopers & Lybrand, London, 1991-94; assoc. dir. European Capital, London, 1995—; cons. in field. Office: European Capital, 3 Lombard St, London EC3V 9JN, England

WOODS, J. P., minister; b. Houston, June 22, 1950; s. William Oliver and Lilly Virginia (Hetherington) W. Student, Blinn Coll., Brenham, Tex., 1968-69; BA, Ft. Lewis Coll., Durango, Colo., 1971. Ordained to ministry, Life Bible Coll., 1996. Div. mgr. Gateway Sporting Goods, Denver, 1971-74; dist. mgr. Super X Drug, Inc., Cin., 1974-77; v.p. sales Bon Ton, Inc., Dallas, 1977-80; regional sales mgr. John O. Butler Co., Chgo., 1980-81; sales mgr. Fox Meyer, Inc., Oklahoma City, 1981-82; sales cons., trainer Rugby Labs., Inc., N.Y.C., 1982-83; nat. dir. key accounts United Rsch. Labs., Inc., Mut. Pharm., Inc., Phila., 1983-88; v.p. Western div. Barr Labs., Pomona, N.Y., 1988-94; pres., CEO J. P. Woods Ministries, Inc., 1996—; pastor Aspen Christian World Outreach, 1996—; elected to Tex. State Bd. Pharmacy, 1992. Author, editor: Sales and Marketing Techniques, 1984. Mem. Rep. Presdl. Task Force, Washington, 1982—, life membership honor roll; mem. Presdl. Commn., 1988; sustaining mem. Rep. Nat. Com., Washington, 1983—, cert. recognition, 1991-92; preferred mem. Nat. Conservative Polit. Action Com., Washington, 1983—; elected mem. Rep. Campaign Coun. Com., 1992—; elected del. State Tex. Rep. Party, 1992; founding mem. CBN Founders, Virginia Beach, Va., 1986—; active Christian Coalition, 1992—, Kenneth Copeland Ptnrs. Ministries, 1992. Recipient Medal of Merit, Ronald Reagan, Pres., Washington, 1985, Presdl. Commn. from Ronald Reagan, 1986, Cert. of Recognition Rep. Nat. Com., 1991-92; named to Rep. Presdl. Task Force Life Membership Honor Roll. Mem. Nat. Assn. Chain Druggists, Nat. Wholesale Drug Assn., Nat. Assn. Retail Druggists, Tex. Pharm. Assn. (com. mem. 1991-92), DAV Comdrs., U.S. Senatorial Club (founder). Mem. Full Gospel Ch. Avocations: collecting Southwestern art, golf, tennis, snow skiing, traveling.

WOODS, MICHAEL, government official; b. Dec. 8, 1935; married; 5 children. MS in Agrl., U. Coll. Dublin, PhD, DS. Elected to Dial, 1977; min. Ministry State Dept. Prime Min. & Govt. Chief Whip, 1979, Ministry Health & Social Welfare, 1979-81, 82, 89-91, 91, 93-94, opposition spokesman justice, 1983-87; min. Ministry AGrl. & Food, 1991-92; min. Ministry Health, 1994, opposition spokesman social welfare, 1997; min. Dept. Marine & Natural Resources, Dublin, 1992, 97—, Dept. Edn., Sci. and Tech., Dublin. Office: Dept Marine & Nat Resources, Lesson Ln, Dublin 2, Ireland*

WOODS, PENDLETON, college director, author; b. Ft. Smith, Ark., Dec. 18, 1923; s. John Powell and Mable (Hon) W.; m. Lois Robin Freeman, Apr. 3, 1948; children: Margaret, Paul Pendleton, Nancy Cox. BA in Journalism, U. Ark., 1948. Editor, asst. pub. mgr. Okla. Gas & Electric Co., Oklahoma City, 1948-69; dir. Living Legends of Okla., Okla. Christian U., Oklahoma City, 1969-82; project, promotion dir. Enterprise Square and Am. Citizenship Ctr., 1982-92, dir. Nat. Edn. Program and Am. Citizenship Ctr., 1992; arbitrator BBB; leader youth seminars in field. Author: You and Your Company Magazine, 1950, Church of Tomorrow, 1964, Myriad of Sports, 1971, This Was Oklahoma, 1979; recorded Sounds of Scouting, 1969, Born Grown, 1974 (Western Heritage award Nat. Cowboy Hall of Fame), One of a Kind, 1977, Countdown to Statehood, 1982, The Thunderbird Tradition, 1989, A Glimpse at Oklahoma, 1990; editor Libertas, The War Chief. Bd. dirs. Campfire Girls Coun., Okla. Jr. Symphony, past pres., Boy Scout Coun., Zoo Amphitheater of Oklahoma City, Will Rogers Centennial Commn., Greater Oklahoma City Tree Bank Found.; bd. dirs., co-founder Ctrl. Park Neighborhood Assn.; dir. Okla. for Resource Preservation; chmn. State Directional Signage Task Force; vol. reader Okla. Libr. for the Blind; past pres. Okla. Assn. Epilepsy; past pres. Keep Okla. Beautiful, Oklahoma City Mental Health Clin.; pub. rels. chmn. Oklahoma County chpt. A.R.C.; past chmn. Western Heritage award Nat. Cowboy Hall of Fame; past pres., hon. lifetime dir. Variety Health Ctr.; dir. Am. Freedom Coun.; state pres. SAR; exec. dir. Oklahoma City Bicentennial Commn.; mem. Okla. Disabilities Coun.; charter dir. Okla. Vets. Med. Rsch. Found.; cons. Exec. Svc. Corps; mem. Coun. Pub. Affairs; vol. Oklahoma City VA Hosp. With AUS, WWII and Korean War; ret. col.; state historian Okla. N.G.; chmn. Oklahoma City Independence Day Parade; exec. com. Oklahoma City Centennial Commn. Named Outstanding Young Man of Yr., Oklahoma City Jr. C. of C., 1953; recipient Silver Beaver award Boy Scouts Am., 1963, Wokan award Okla. City Coun. Camp Fire girls, 1968, Silver medal award Advt. Fedn. Am., Disting. Cmty. Svc. award Neighborhood Devel. and Conservation Ctr., Gold and Silver Patrick Henry Patriotism medals Mil. Order of the World Wars, 2 Commendation awards Am. Assn. for State and Local History, 4 honor medals Freedoms Found., Jefferson Davis medal United Daus. of the Confederacy, Okla. Disting. Svc. medal (2), Outstanding Contbn. to Okla. Mus., Okla. Mus. Assn., 1987, Outstanding Contbn. to Okla. Tourism award Okla. Dept. Tourism, 1989, Cmty. Svc. award U. Ark. Alumni Assn., 1992, Citizenship and Patriot award SAR, 1992, 5 Who Care award KOCO-TV, 1993, Jefferson award Am. Inst. for Pub. Svc., 1993, Mayor's award in Beautification, 1994, George Washington award Youth Leadership Found., St. Augustine, Fla., 1993, Golden Rule award J.C. Penney Found., 1999, Lifetime Achievement award Keep Okla. Beautiful. Mem. DAV, Soc. Assoc. Indsl. Editors (past v.p.), Advt. Fedn. Am. (past dist. dir.), Ctrl. Okla. Bus. Communicators (past pres., hon. life mem.), Okla. Jr. C. of C. (hon. life, past internat. dir.), Okla. Distributive Edn. Clubs (hon. life), Oklahoma City Advt. Club (past pres. hon. life mem.), Words of Jesus Found. (pres.), Okla. Zool. Soc., Okla. Geneal. Soc. (past pres.), Okla. County Sr. Nutrition Found. (sec., bd. dirs.), Nat. Eagle Scout Assn. (Okla. chmn.), U. Ark. Alumni Assn. (charter pres. Oklahoma City chpt.), Okla. Lung Assn. (pub. rels. com.), Am. Cancer Soc. (dir. Okla. County chpt.), Okla. Travel Industries Assn., Okla. Hist. Soc. (publ. editor), Okla. Heritage Assn. (publ. editor), Oklahoma City Beautiful (publ. editor), Okla. Safety Coun. (publ. editor), Oklahoma County Hist. Soc. (dir., past pres.), 45th Inf. Div. Assn. (past pres.), Korean War Vets Assn., Am. Legion, VFW, Mus. Unassigned Lands (chmn.), Mil. Order World Wars (regional comdr., Okla. City comdr., nat. staff), Oklahoma City Hist. Preservation Commn., Oklahoma City Clean and Green Coalition, Sigma Delta Chi, Kappa Sigma (nat. commr. publs.), Lincoln Park Country (pres.), Am. Ex-Prisoners of War (state comdr.), Okla. Vets. Coun. (chmn.). Home: 541 NW 31st St Oklahoma City OK 73118-7334

WOODS, PHYLLIS MICHALIK, retired elementary school educator; b. New Orleans, Sept. 12, 1937; d. Philip John and Thelma Alice (Carey) Michalik; 1 child, Tara Lynn Woods. BA, Southea. La. U., 1967. Cert. speech and English tchr., libr. sci., La. Tchr. speech, English and drama St. Charles Parish Pub. Schs., Luling, La., elem. tchr., secondary tchr. remedial reading, Chpt. I reading specialist; Wicat tchr. coord. St. Charles Parish Pub. Schs., Luling, ret.; tchr. cons. St. Charles parish writing project La. State U. Writing Project. Author: Egbert, the Egret, Egbert's Picnic, Egbert Visits Sammy, Angel Without Wings, The Necklace and Egbert's Calf, The Hurricane, The Cleanup Day, The Rainbow, The Fair, The Tornado; songwriter; musical compositions include The Fruits of the Spirit, Father's Day Song, Mother's Day Song; contbr. articles and poems to River Parish Guide, St. Charles Herald. Sch. rep. United Fund, St. Charles Parish Reading Assn.; parish com. mem. Young Authors, Tchrs. Who Write; active 4-H leader; bd. trustees Michalik Scholarship Trust. Mem. ASCD, Internat. Platform Assn., Internat. Reading Assn., St. Charles Parish Reading Coun., Newspaper in Edn. (chmn., historian), La. Assn. Newspapers in Edn. (state com.).

WOODS, RICHARD DALE, lawyer; b. Kansas City, Mo., May 20, 1950; s. Willard Dale and Betty Sue (Duncan) W.; m. Cecelia Ann Thompson, Aug. 11, 1973 (div. July 1996); children: Duncan Warren, Shannon Cecelia; m. Mary Linna Lash, June 6, 1999. BA, U. Kans., 1972; JD, U. Mo., 1975. Bar: Mo. 1975, U.S. Dist. Ct. (we. dist.) Mo. 1975. Assoc. Shook, Hardy & Bacon L.L.P., Kansas City, Mo., 1975-79, ptnr., 1980-2000; gen. chmn. Estate Planning Symposium, Kansas City, 1985-86; chair Northland Coalition, 1993. Chmn. fin. com. North Woods Ch., Kansas City, 1986-88, 93-96; mem. sch. bd. N. Kansas City Sch. Dist., 1990-97, treas., 1992-97; mem. North Kansas City Ednl. Found., 1998—, pres., 1999-2000; mem. planned giving com. Truman Med. Ctr., 1992—, chmn., 1992-98; mem. Clay County Tax Increment Fin. Commn., 1990-99; bd. dirs. Heart of Am. Family Svcs., 1998—, sec., 2000—. Fellow Am. Coll. Trust and Estate Counsel; mem. ABA, KC, Mo. Bar Assn., Kans. City Met. Bar Assn., Lawyers Assn. Kans. City (sec., v.p., pres. young lawyers sect. 1981-84), Kans. City Estate Planning Soc. (bd. dirs. 1985-88, 93-95). Democrat. E-mail: rwoods@shb.com. Office: Shook Hardy & Bacon LLP 1010 Grand Blvd Fl 5 Kansas City MO 64106-2220

WOODS, ROSALIE KAREN, dietitian, researcher; b. Melbourne, Australia, Oct. 4, 1962; d. Walter Raymond and Florence Fay (Morris) W.; m. Mark Anthony Griffiths, Feb. 1, 1997; 1 child, Zoë Rebecca. BS, Deakin U., Victoria, 1983, diploma, 1984; MPH, Monash U., Victoria, 1994, PhD, 1997. Dietitian Cooma Hosp. & Area Health Svc., Cooma, Australia, 1985-86; dietitian Alfred Hosp., Victoria, 1986-89, sr. dietitian, 1989-90; deputy chief dietitian Mornington Peninsula Hosp., Frankston, Australia, 1990-94; rsch. scholar, dietitian Alfred Hosp. Monash U., 1994-97; Nat. Health and Med. Rsch. Coun. postdoctoral rsch. fellow dept. epidemiology and preventive medicine Monash U., Prahran, Austaralia, 1998—; cons. dietitian St. Kilda Football Club, Australia, 1989-90, Olive Miller Nursing Home, Malvern, 1991-92. Contbr. articles to profl. jours. Tech. pers. All Australian Netball Assn., 1994—. Janssen-Cilag scholar, 1989, Australian Postgrad. award Commonwealth Gov., 1995-97; Lillian Roxon Travel grant Lillian Roxon Meml. Trust, 1997; Nat. Health and Med. Rsch. Coun. Rsch. fellow, 1998. Mem. Dietitians Assn. of Australia, Thoracic Soc. of Australia & New Zealand, Phoenix Netball Club (bd. dirs. 1999—). Avocations: sports, travel. E-mail: rosalie.woods@med.monash.edu.au. Office: Monash Med Sch Dept Epidemiology & Preve, Commercial Rd, Prahran VIC 3181, Australia

WOODS, ROSS ANDREW, hydrologist, researcher; b. Lincoln, Canterbury, New Zealand, May 25, 1963; s. Neville Andrew and Neroli Jean (Dunlop) W.; m. Deirdre Michelle Wright, Jan. 26, 1985; children: Constance, Benjamin. BSc with honors, U. Canterbury, Christchurch, New Zealand, 1983, M in Comm. with honors, 1985; PhD, U. Western Australia, Perth, 1998. Hydrologist Ministry of Works and Devel., Christchurch, 1986-88, Dept. Sci. and Indsl. Rsch., Christchurch, 1988-92, Nat. Inst. for Water and Atmosphere, Christchurch, 1992—. Author: (with others) Floods and Droughts--The New Zealand Experience, 1997; contbr. articles to profl. jours. including Hydrol. Processes, Jour. Hydrology, and Water Resources Rsch. Recipient Prince and Princess of Wales travel award Royal Soc. New Zealand, 1989, travel award Brit. Coun., 1991. Mem. New Zealand Hydrol. Soc., Am. Geophys. Union. Avocations: music, reading, bridge, tramping. Office: Nat Inst for Water & Atmos, 10 Kyle St PO Box 8602, Christchurch New Zealand

WOODS, TIGER (ELDRICK WOODS), professional golfer; b. Cypress, Calif., Dec. 30, 1975; s. Earl and Kultida W. Student, Stanford U. Winner U.S. Jr. Amateur titles, 1991, 92, 93, U.S. Amateur titles, 1994, 95, 96, U.S. Amateur Championship, 1995, 96, Walt Disney World Classic, 1996, Las Vegas Invitational, 1996, NCAA Tournament, 1996, Masters Tournament, 1997, Asian Honda Classic, 1997, Bell South Classic, 1998, Meml., 1999, PGA Championship, 1999; Winner Buick Invitational, 1999, Motorola Western Open, 1999, WGC NEC Invitational, 1999, Nat. Car Rental Golf Classic, 1999, The Tour Championship, 1999, WGC Am. Express Championship, 1999, Mercedes Championship, 2000, AT&T Pebble Beach Nat. Pro-Am, 2000, Bay Hill Invitational, 2000. Winner Masters tournament, 1997. Achievements include being the youngest, first African Am., first Asian Am., and first to win Masters by largest margin of 12 strokes, 1997. Office: PGA PO Box 109601 100 Avenue Of Champions Palm Beach Gardens FL 33418-3665*

WOODS, WINTON D., law educator; b. Balt., Jan. 11, 1938; s. W.D. and Nancy N. W.; m. Barbara Lewis; children: Tad, Adam, Brooke, Lindsy, Jessica. AB Econ./Gov., Ind. U., 1961, JD with distinction, 1965. Bar: Ind., Ariz.; U.S. Supreme Ct. Law clk. U.S. Dist. Ct. (no. dist.) Calif., Sacramento, 1965-67; prof. law U. Ariz., Tucson, 1967—; reporter U.S. Dist. Ariz. Civil Justice Reform Act Com., 1992—; pres. Law Office Computing, Inc., 1990—; dir. Courtroom of the Future Project, U. Ariz., 1993—. Contbr. articles to profl. jours; author: The Lawyers Computer Book, 1990. Mem. bio-ethics com. UMC, Tucson, 1984-96. Recipient Fulbright award, 1979, Educator of Yr. award Internat. Comm. Industry Assn., 1996-97; fellow NEH, 1972, Nat. Inst. for Dispute Resolution, 1982. Fellow Coll. Law Practice Mgmt; mem. ABA, Ariz. State Bar Assn. Jewish. Avocations: computers, automobiles, photography. Office: U Ariz Coll Of Law Tucson AZ 85721-0001

WOODSIDE, JOHN MOFFATT, marine geology educator; b. Toronto, Ont., Can., Jan. 23, 1941; s. Moffatt St. Andrew and Eleanor Agnes (Barton) W.; m. Melinda Ann Siemen, Sept. 2, 1967; children: Sven, Drum. BSc, Queens U., Kingston, Can., 1964; SM, MIT, 1968; PHD, Cambridge (Eng.) U., 1975. Marine geophysicist Geol. Survey Can., Dartmouth, Can., 1968-71, 76-79, 1981-89; post-doctoral fellow Cambridge U., 1975-76; sr. marine geophysicist Com. Coord. Joint Prospecting Mineral Resources Asia, Bangkok, 1979-81; prof. Free U., Amsterdam, The Netherlands, 1989—. Office: Ctr for Marine Earth Scis, De Boelelaan 1085, 1081 HV Amsterdam The Netherlands

WOOD-SMITH, DONALD, plastic surgeon; b. Sydney, Australia, June 30, 1931; s. William Frederick and Vera Mary; children: Christina Margaret, Donald William, Phillip Raynor. MB, BS, Sydney U., 1954. Diplomate Am. Bd. Plastic Surgury. Surg. resident Lewisham Hosp., Sydney, 1954-56, Royal Marsden Hosp., 1957-58; resident plastic surgery N.Y. U. Hosp. Med. Center, 1960-64, asst., assoc. and attending surgeon, 1964-92; vis. surgeon Bellevue Hosp., 1964-92; chmn. plastic surgery Manhattan Eye Ear and Throat Hosp., 1975-77; assoc. prof. plastic surgery NYU, 1977-84, prof., 1984-92; surgeon, dir. plastic surgery Manhattan Eye Ear and Throat Hosp., 1977-84; cons. plastic surgeon N.Y. Eye and Ear Infirmary, chmn. dept. plastic and reconstructive surgery, 1984—; prof. plastic surgery Columbia Presbyn. Med. Ctr., 1991—. Author: Nursing Care of the Plastic Surgery Patient, 1967, Cosmetic Facial Surgery, 1973; contbr. articles to med. jours. Fellow ACS, Royal Coll. Surgeons of Edinburgh; mem. Am. Assn. Plastic Surgeons, Am. Soc. Plastic Surgeons, Am. Soc. Maxillofacial Surgeons, N.Y. Acad. Medicine, Brit. Assn. Plastic Surgeons, N.Y. Athletic Club. Republican. Office: 830 Park Ave New York NY 10021-2757

WOODWARD, CLIFFORD EDWARD, chemical engineer; b. Richmond, Va., Jan. 17, 1941; s. Clifford Rawlings and Myrtis (Wilson) W.; m. Katherine Roberts, June 1, 1967; children: Ted, Robert, Christopher, John. BSChemE, Va. Poly. Inst. and State U., 1962, MS in Nuclear Sci. and Engr., 1963; MSChemE, U. Houston, 1975. Registered profl. engr., Tex. Devel. engr. Olin Corp., 1963-65; supervising engr. Monsanto Co., 1965-72; lead engr. Brown & Root Inc., Houston, 1972-74; process mgr. Kvaerner Process Inc., Houston, 1974-77, 1979-81, process dir., 1983-88, process mgr., 1992—; prin. engr. Jacobs Engring. Group, Inc., Houston, 1977-79; process mgr. M.W. Kellogg, Amsterdam, N.C., 1981-83; sr. engr. mgr. M.W. Kellogg, Houston, 1988-89; process dept. mgr. BE&K, Houston, 1989-92; pres. Process Resources, Houston, 1975-77. Mem. planning comm. City of Alvin, Tex., 1970-72; founder Cypress Creek Emergency Med. Svcs. Assn., 1975; pres. Klein (Tex.) Sch. Bd., 1979-90. Mem. AIChE, Engrs. Coun. of Houston (v.p., sec. 1991). Achievements include electrodeposition of polymers from latex solutions and surface kinetics and direct contact heat transfer. Home: 4114 Oxhill Rd Spring TX 77388-9705 Office: Kvaerner Process 7909 Parkwood Circle Dr Houston TX 77036-6565

WOODWARD, SIR (ALBERT) EDWARD, academic administrator, retired judge; b. Ballarat, Victoria, Australia, Aug. 6, 1928; s. Eric Winslow and Amy Freame (Weller) W.; m. Lois Thorpe, Sept. 20, 1950; children: Meredyth, Penelope, Kathleen, Elisabeth, Edward Winslow, Alison, Patricia. LLD (hon.), U. NSW, 1986; LLM, U. Melbourne, 1950; D Litt (hon.), U. Ballar, 1998. Barrister, 1951-72; judge Australian Indsl. Ct., 1972-90, Supreme Ct. Not Ter., 1972-79, Supreme Ct. Australia Capital Terr., 1972-90, Fed. Ct. Australia, 1977-90; chancellor U. Melbourne, 1990—; pres. Trade Practices Tribunal of Australia, 1974-76, dir. gen. security, 1976-81; chmn. Armed Svc. Pay Inquiry, 1972; royal commr. Aboriginal Land Rights, 1973-74, Australian Meat Industry, 1981-82; pres. Def. Force Discipline Appeal Tribunal, 1988-90. Chmn. Victoria Dried Fruits Bd., 1963-72, Stevedoring Industry Coun., 1970-72, Coun. Camberwell Grammar Sch., Melbourne, 1983-87, Schizophrenia Australia Found., 1985-97, Coun. Australian Def. Force Acad., 1982-99, Australian Banking Ombudsman Coun., 1997—. Named Queens Counsel, 1965, Officer Order of Brit. Empire, 1969, Knight Bachelor, 1982. Avocations: birdwatching, bush walking. Office: U Melbourne, Grattan St, Victoria 3010, Australia

WOODWARD, FRANK IAN, botany educator, ecologist; b. Sheffield, Eng., Dec. 15, 1948; s. Frank Clement and Gwenda Agnes (Allen) W.; m. Pearl May Chambers, Aug. 5, 1972; children: Helen Marie, David Ian. BA in Botany, U. Oxford, Eng., 1970; PhD, U. Lancaster, Eng., 1973; MA, U. Cambridge, Eng., 1979. Nat. Environ. Rsch. Coun. rsch. fellow U. Lancaster, 1973-75; higher sci. officer Grassland Rsch. Inst., Hurley, Berkshire, Eng., 1975-76; lectr. dept. plant sci. U. Wales, Cardiff, 1976-79; lectr. dept. plant sci. U. Cambridge, 1979-91, fellow Trinity Hall, 1981-91; prof. dept. animal and plant scis. U. Sheffield, Eng., 1991—; vis. lectr. U. Innsbruck, Austria, 1984, Duke U., 1996; rsch. scholar Inst. Applied Sys. Analysis, Vienna, Austria, 1989. Author: Climate and Plant Distribution, 1987 (WS Cooper award Ecol. Soc. Am. 1991); contbr. articles to profl. jours. Fellow Linnean Soc., London, 1990. Mem. Brit. Ecol. Soc., Soc. Exptl. Biology. Avocations: woodturning, music. E-mail: f.i.woodward@sheffield.ac.uk. Fax: 44 0 114 222 0002. Office: Univ Sheffield, Western Bank, Sheffield S10 2TN, England

WOODWARD, JOANNE GIGNILLIAT, actress; b. Thomasville, Ga., Feb. 27, 1930; d. Wade and Elinor (Trimmier) W.; m. Paul Newman, Jan. 29, 1958; children: Elinor Terese, Melissa Stewart, Clea Olivia. Student, La. State U., 1947-49; grad., Neighborhood Playhouse Dramatic Sch., N.Y.C. First TV appearance in Penny, Robert Montgomery Presents, 1952; under-

study broadway play Picnic, 1953; appeared in plays Baby Want a Kiss, 1964, Candida, 1982, The Glass Menagerie, Williamstown Theatré Festival, 1985, Sweet Bird of Youth, Toronto, 1988; motion pictures include Three Faces of Eve, 1957 (Acad. award Best Actress, Nat. Bd. Rev. award, Fgn. Press award), Count Three and Pray, 1955, Long Hot Summer, 1958, No Down Payment, 1957, Sound and the Fury, 1959, A Kiss Before Dying, 1956, Rally Round the Flag Boys, 1958, The Fugitive Kind, 1960, Paris Blues, 1961, The Stripper, 1963, A New Kind of Love, 1963, A Big Hand for the Little Lady, 1965, A Fine Madness, 1965, Rachel, Rachel, 1968, Winning, 1969, WUSA, 1970, They Might Be Giants, 1971, The Effect of Gamma Rays on Man-in-the-Moon Marigolds, 1972 (Cannes Film Festival award), Summer Wishes, Winter Dreams, 1973 (N.Y. Film Critics award), The Drowning Pool, 1975, The End, 1978, Harry and Son, 1984, Glass Menagerie, 1987, Mr. & Mrs. Bridge, 1990, Philadelphia, 1993, My KNees Were Jumping: Remembering the Kindertransports, (voice) 1998; TV appearances include All the Way Home; TV-film appearances in Sybil, 1976, Come Back, Little Sheba, 1977, See How She Runs, 1978 (Emmy award), Streets of L.A., 1979, The Shadow Box, 1980, Crisis at Central High, 1981, Do You Remember Love?, 1985 (Emmy award), Blind Spot, 1993 (Emmy nomination, Lead Actress - Miniseries, 1993); The Age of Innocence (voice), 1993; Blind Spot, 1993; Breathing Lessons, 1994 (Emmy nomination, Lead Actress - Special, 1994, Golden Globe award, Best Actress), James Dean: A Portrait, 1996; narrator film documentary Angel Dust, TV documentary on Group Theatre, 1989. Co-recipient (with Paul Newman) Kennedy Ctr. Honors for Lifetime Achievement in the Performing Arts. Democrat. Episcopalian. Office: ICM 40 W 57th St Fl 16 New York NY 10019-4098

WOODWARD, JOHN FRANK, educator, consultant; b. London, June 23, 1933; s. Frank Thomas and Lucy Agnes (Ffortune) W.; m. Marjorie Isobel Fenwick; children: Jane Frances, Patricia Ann, Fiona Mairi, Susan Katrina. BSc, U. Glasgow, 1954; DLitt, Paisley, 1997. Engr. Taylor Woodrow, U.K., 1956-67; reader U. Stirling, U.K., 1968-81; head civil enging. Paisley Coll., U.K., 1982-87; vice prin. U. Paisley, Scotlan, 1987-92; prof. emeritus U. Paisley, Scotland, 1992—; fellow Trinity Hall, Cambridge, 1992-93; ptnr., cons. bus. pvt. practice U.K., 1993—. Author: Construction Management, 1975, Science in Industry, Science of Industry, 1982, Construction Project Management--Right First Time, 1997; also some 20 tech. papers. Decorated Order of Brit. Empire; emeritus fellow Leverhulme, 1993-94. Fellow Inst. Civil Engrs., Assn. Project Mgmt. Home and Office: Holly Cottage/The Fairstead, near Holt, NR25 7RJ Cley/Norfolk NR25 7RJ, England

WOODWARD, MICHAEL CLIFFORD, geriatrician, researcher; b. Melbourne, Victoria, Australia, Jan. 6, 1955; s. William John and Sue Mary (Hirning) W.; m. Anne Julie Dickins, Nov. 26, 1976; children: Sophy K., Erin C.S., Tess M. MB, BCHir, Melbourne U., 1979. Intern, resident med. officer, registrar Royal Melbourne Hosp., 1980-83; registrar Mount Royal Hosp., Victoria, 1984-85; Victoria; specialist physician Repatriation Gen. Hosp., Heidelberg, Victoria, 1988-95; dir. Aged Care Svcs. Austin Repatriation Ctr., Heidelberg, 1995—; chmn. med. adv. coun. MacLeod Hosp., Victoria, 1990-93; mem. Repatriation Pharm. Ref. Com., Canberra, Australia, 1990—; mem. patient care com. Heidelberg Repatriation Hosp., 1990-91. Co-author: Geriatric Medicine, 2000; contbr. chpts. to books, articles to profl. jours. Fellow Royal Australasian Coll. Physicians (chair com. for physician tng. 2000—, bd. censors 1996—); mem. Australian Assn. Gerontology (pres. Victoria divsn. 1990-94), Australian Soc. for Geriatric Medicine (chairperson edn. & tng. subcom. 1992-97) Brit. Geriatrics Soc., Am. Geriatrics Soc. Avocations: teaching, meditation, gardening, photography, bushwalking. Home: 23 McAuley Dr, Rosanna 3084, Australia Office: Austin Repatriation Med Ctr, Aged Care Svcs Banksia St, Heidelberg West 3081, Australia

WOODWARD, RICHARD H. (WOODY WOODWARD), electric power industry executive; b. Las Vegas, Nev., June 4, 1952; s. Harold R. and Mercedus Marie (Gollhardt) W.; m. Tary Lorainne Kalisbeck, Nov. 8, 1988; children: Angela, Wayne, Christy, Kevin. Grad. H.S., Las Vegas. Cert. utility theft investigator Associated Corp. Cons. and Western States Energy Theft Assn. Meter reader Nev. Power Co., Las Vegas, 1973-76, field svc. rep., 1976-80, field svc. investigator, 1980-85, lead person meter validity, 1985-94, team leader meter validity, 1994-99, team leader revenue protection, 1999—; dir. emeritus, past pres. Western States Energy Theft Assn.; internet web master, bd. mem. Internat. Utilities Revenue Protection Assn.; internet web master Radio Emergency Associated Comm. Teams, Las Vegas, 1999. Active Las Vegas Met. Police Dept. Vol. Program, 1999, County Multi-Agy. Response Team, Las Vegas. Recipient Pres. Nat. medal of patriotism Am. Police Hall of Fame, Fla., 1994; hon. fellow Acad. Law Enforcement, Nat. Law Enforcement Acad., Washington, 1993. Mem. Am. Fedn. Police. Avocations: computers, Internet, electronics. E-mail: RWoodward@nevp.com. Fax: 702-657-4141. Home: PO Box 33846 Las Vegas NV 89133-3846 Office: Nev Power Co Sta 97 2215 E Lone Mountain Rd North Las Vegas NV 89031-2607

WOODY, DONALD EUGENE, lawyer; b. Springfield, Mo., Mar. 10, 1948; s. Raymond D. and Elizabeth Ellen (Bushnell) W.; m. Ann Louise Ruhl, June 5, 1971; children: Marshall Wittmann, Catherine Elizabeth. BA in Polit. Sci. with honors, U. Mo., 1970, JD, 1973. Bar: Mo. 1973, U.S. Dist. Ct. (we. dist.) Mo. 1973, U.S. Ct. Appeals (8th cir.) 1973, U.S. Supreme Ct. 1987. Assoc. Neale, Newman & Bradshaw, Springfield, 1973-74; ptnr. Taylor, Stafford & Woody, Springfield, 1974-82, Taylor, Stafford, Woody, Cowherd & Clithero, Springfield, 1983-93, Taylor, Stafford, Woody, Clithero & Fitzgerald, Springfield, 1993—. Editor U. Mo. Law Rev., 1973. Chmn. county campaign U.S. senator Thomas Eagleton, Springfield, 1980; committeeman Greene County Dem. Party, Springfield, 1984-86; cons. Children's Home Mayors commn., Springfield, 1985. Mem. ABA, Springfield Metro Bar Assn. (sec. 1977-80, precedure com. 1986, bd. dirs. 1991-93, pres.-elect 1995, pres. 1996), Assn. Trial Lawyers Am., Springfield C. of C. (chmn. performing arts com. 1980-84), Order of Coif, Phi Delta Phi. Avocations: fishing, growing roses, bicycling, running. Home: 1421 S Ginger Blue Ave Springfield MO 65809-2260 Office: Taylor Stafford Woody Clithero & Fitzgerald 3315 E Ridgeview St Ste 1000 Springfield MO 65804-4083

WOOLARD, CONNIE WARD, artist, retired art gallery manager; b. Wilkes-Barre, Pa., Mar. 25, 1931; d. Harold Walton and Betty Bertha (Mandeville) Ward; m. Maurice Emmett Woolard, Oct. 25, 1952; children: Karin Elise Woolard Snoots. Student, U. Md., 1949-50, Abbott Art Sch., 1951-52. Comml. artist Rex Engraving Co., Silver Spring, Md., 1953-60, art dir., 1959-60; mgr. Town Ctr. Gallery, Rockville, Md., 1978-99; mgr. Town Ctr. Gallery, Bethesda, Md., 1960-99, ret., 1999; freelance artist, fine artist, 1965—. One-person shows include Town Ctr. Gallery, 1984, 86, 89, 91, 93, 96, Art Contemporary, Bethesda, 1982, Sugar & Frichtl Gallery, 1993, Blue Skies Gallery, Hampton, Va., Hughes Network Sys., 1999; exhibited in group shows at Cumberland Valley Artists Exhbn. (Purchase award), (annually) Salmagundi Club, N.Y.C.; paintings selected for Art in Embassies program U.S. State Dept., Havana, Cuba, El Salvador, Tanzania; permanent collection Montgomery County Dept. Recreation, Washington County Mus. Fine Arts; commissioned by U.S. Info. Agency, AMVETS, City of Rockville, Md., NAS, Georgetown Prep. Sch. Recipient Salmagundi Non-Member award Salmagundi Club, N.Y.C., 1983, Judges Choice award Nat. League Am. Penwomen, 1996, Juror's award Miniature Painters Sculptors and Gravors Washington, 1997, awards Cider Painters Am. Mem. Rockville Art League (past pres.), Washington Watercolor Assn. (past pres.), Phila. Watercolor Soc., So. Watercolor Soc. (signature mem.), Nat. League Am. Penwomen (past sec., current pres., named Women Yr. 1984), Miniature Painters, Sculptors & Engravers Soc. Washington, Balt. Watercolor Soc. (Mid Atlantic Regional award 1985), Potomac Valley Watercolorists, Nat. Soc. Painters in Casein and Acrylic, Salmagundi Club. Avocations: gardening, reading, photography. Home: 3922 Havard St Silver Spring MD 20906-4311

WOOLARD, EDGAR S., JR., chemical company executive; b. Washington, N.C., Apr. 15, 1934; s. Edgar Smith and Mamie (Boone) W.; m. Peggy Harrell, 1956; children: Annette, Lynda. BS, N.C. State U., 1956. Indsl. engr. DuPont, Kinston, N.C., 1957-59, group supr. indsl. engring., 1959-62, supr. mfg. sect., 1962-64, planning supr., 1964-65; staff asst to prodn. mgr. DuPont, Wilmington, Del., 1965-66; product supr. DuPont, Old Hickory, Tenn., 1966-69, engring. supt., 1969-70; asst. plant mgr. DuPont, Camden, S.C., 1970-71; plant mgr. DuPont, Kinston, S.C., 1971-73; dir. products mktg. div. DuPont, Wilmington, Del., 1973-75, mng. dir. textile mktg. div., 1975-76, mgr. corp. plans dept., 1976-77, gen. dir. products and planning div., 1977-78, gen. mgr. textile fibers, 1978-81, v.p. textile fibers, 1981-83, exec. v.p., 1983-85, vice chmn., 1985-87, pres., COO, 1987-89, chmn., CEO, 1989-96, chmn., 1998-97, also bd. dirs., 1996—; bd. dirs. N.C. Textile Found., Citicorp. Trustee Med. Ctr. Del., N.C. State U., Winterthur Mus. Lt. U.S. Army. Recipient Internat. Palladium medal Soc. Chimie Industrille (Am. sect.), 1995. Office: DuPont 1007 Market St Wilmington DE 19898-0001

WOOLCOCK, ANN JANET, physician; b. Adelaide, South Australia, Dec. 11, 1937; d. Angus Norval and Dulcie Annie (Woodroffe) W.; m. Charles Ruthven Bickerton Blackburn, Sept. 1, 1968; children: Simon, Angus. MB, BS, U. Adelaide, 1961; MD, U. Sydney, Australia, 1967. Sr. lectr. U. Sydney, 1973-76, assoc. prof., 1976-84, prof. respiratory medicine, 1984—; dir. Inst. Respiratory Medicine, 1985-2000; Sims C'weath Travelling prof., 1992; exec. global strategy for asthma mgmt. WHO, 1993; prin. scientist CRC Asthma, 1999—. Contbr. over 250 articles to profl. jours., chpts. to books. Life gov. Asthma Found. NSW, Sydney, 1992; chmn. Cmty. Health & Anti-TB Assn., NSW, 1995—. Named to Order of Australia, Govt. Australia, 1989. Fellow Royal Australian Coll. Physicians, Australian Acad. Sci. (coun. 1992), Royal Australasian Coll. Physicians, Am. Coll. Chest Physicians; mem. Internat. Union Against Tb and Lung Disease (at large 1985), Asian Pacific Soc. Respirology (pres. 1999—), French Acad. Medicine (corr. 1994), Com. Health and Anti-Tb Assn. NSW (chmn. 1995-99), Thoracic Soc. of Australian and New Zealand (Soc. medal 1998), Am. Thoracic Soc. (Disting. Achievement award 1998), Inst. of Respiratory Medicine. Office: Royal Prince Alfred Hosp, Level 8 Bldg 82, Camperdown NSW 2050, Australia

WOOLCOTT, PETER RICHARD, diplomat, lawyer; b. Berlin, Germany, Oct. 19, 1953; s. Richard and Birgit Woolcott; m. Tanya Woolcott; children: Charles, Nicholas, Isabella. BA, LLB, Australian Nat. U., Canberra, 1976; MA, Fletcher Sch. Law/Diplomacy, Boston, 1980. Barrister at law Sydney, Australia, 1977-81; officer Dept. Fgn. Affairs and Trade, Australia, 1987-88; leader of the opposition Australia, 1984-86; internat. advisor Bond Corp. Holdings, Perth, Australia, 1989-90; dir. sea law and ocean policy Dept. Fgn. Affairs and Trade, Australia, 1990-91; exec. mgr. internat. bid rels. Sydney Olympics 2000 Bid, 1991-92; dir. human rights Dept. Fgn. Affairs and Trade, Australia, 1992-95; DCM Australian Embassy, Manila, 1994-97; asst. sec. spl. projects Dept. Fgn. Affairs and Trade, Australia, 1997; consul gen. of Australia, rep. to CINCPAC Dept. Fgn. Affairs and Trade, Canberra, 1998—. Author: (book) Australian Human Rights Manual, 1994. E-mail: peter.woolcott@dfat.gov.au. Office: Dept Fgn Affairs, R G Lasey Bldg, Canberra ACT 0221, Australia

WOOLDRIDGE, MICHAEL, politician; b. Nov. 7, 1956; married; 2 children. BS, Scotch Coll.; B of Medicine, Monash U., Melbourne, Australia, MBA. Resident Alfred Hosp., Australia, 1982-85; elected mem. Chisholm, Ho. of Reps., Australia, 1987; shadow min. Aboriginal and Torres Strait Islander Affairs, Australia, 1990-93, Assisting Min. Leader on Youth Affairs, Australia, 1992-93; deputy leader opposition, shadow min. Dept. Edn., Employment & Tng., Australia; shadow min. AIDS/HIIV matters Australia; shadow min. Dept. Cmty. Svcs., Sr. Citizens & Aged Care, Australia, 1994-95, Min. Health & Family Svcs., Australia, 1995-98; min. Health and Aged Care, Canberra, Australia, 1998—; chmn. UNAIDS pcb, 1997-98, WHO Western Pacific Region, 1997-98. Elected mem. Casey, Ho. of Reps., 1998. Office: Dept Health & Aged Care, Parliament Ho Ste MG48, Canberra ACT 2600, Australia

WOOLDRIDGE, PATRICE MARIE, marketing professional, martial arts and meditation educator; b. Chgo., June 3, 1954; d. Charles E. and Marlys E. (Kuehn) Reardon; m. Patrick Wooldridge, June 27, 1981. AS, Moraine Valley Coll., 1974; BA, Govs. State U., 1976, MA, 1977; MBA, Loyola U., Chgo., 1983. Community prof. Govs. State U., University Park, Ill., 1977-78; counselor, social worker Bloom Twp. High Sch., Chicago Heights, Ill., 1977-78; market analyst Dr. Scholl Footcare, Chgo., 1978-79; supr. consumer rsch. Unocal, Schaumburg, Ill., 1979-84; group rsch. dir. Tatham-Laird & Kudner, Chgo., 1984-87; v.p., assoc. dir. strategic planning & rsch. Bayer Bess Vanderwarker Advt., Chgo., 1987-90; v.p. dir. qualitative svcs. Goldring/MIL Rsch., 1990-91; pres. Wooldridge Assocs., Inc., Chgo., 1991—; instr. dancing, 1969-89; instr. T'ai Chi the Sch. of T'ai Chi Chuan, N.Y.C., 1986—; instr. Arica the Arica Inst., N.Y.C., 1978—. Performer The Anawim Players, Chgo., 1985-97; treas. Karma Thegsum Choling, Chgo., 1987-97; bd. dirs. Illustrated Theatre Co., Chgo., 1987, The Human Process, Chgo., 1992—, Tai Chi Found., Inc., 1994-97; adv. bd. N.W. Suburban Boy Scouts, Schaumburg, 1984; participant White House Conf. on Small Bus., 1996; team mem. Gold ARF Ogilvy award Kraft Singles, 2000. Recipient Gold Medallion 2000 Ogilvy Awards. Mem. Am. Mktg. Assn., Qualitative Rsch. Cons. Assn., Union of Concerned Scientists, The Planetary Soc. Home and Office: 1717 W Rascher Ave Chicago IL 60640-1117

WOOLDRIDGE, WILLIAM CHARLES, lawyer; b. Miami, Fla., Feb. 24, 1943; s. Clarence Edward and Easter Marguerite (Souders) W.; m. Joyce L. Norton, June 15, 1968; children: William Charles, John Michael. BA, Harvard U., 1965; LLB, U. Va., 1969. Bar: Va. 1969. Atty. Norfolk and Western Ry. Co., 1973-82; with Norfolk So. Corp., 1982-2000, v.p. dept. law, 1996-2000. Pres. John Marshall Found., Richmond, Va., 1992-94; pres. Norfolk Hist. Soc., 1995-96; chair Friends of Chrysler Mus. Hist. Houses, 1997-99; bd. dirs Sta. WHRO (FM and TV), 1997-2000. Capt. JAGC, U.S. Army, 1969-73. Mem. ABA, Va. Bar Assn. Republican.

WOOLEY, GERALDINE HAMILTON, writer, poet; b. Idlewild, Mich., Feb. 15, 1942; d. Charles Loren and Alice (Smith) Hamilton; m. David Wooley, June 11, 1961 (div. 1983); children: Vickie Wooley Houston, Monica Wooley Roberts, Deborah Wooley Williams. GED, Flint, Mich. Cosmetologist pvt. practice, Flint, Mich., 1967-70; tchr's. aide Flint Cmty. Schs., 1969-71; nurse's aide Clara Barton Home, Flint, 1972; factory worker GM AC Plant, Flint, 1973-76; child care worker Beecher Cmty. Schs., Flint, 1987-89; poet, songwriter Flint, 1994—; songwriter Hilltop Records, Hollywood, Calif., 1996—. Author: (poems) Between The Raindrops, 1995 (Editor's Choice 1995), At Water's Edge, 1995 (Editor's Choice 1995), Tapestry, 1996 (Editor's Choice 1996), Memories of Tomorrow, 1996 (Editor's Choice 1996). Mem. PTA Flint Sch. Dist., 1969-70. Named to Internat. Poetry Hall of Fame, 1996. Mem. Internat. Soc. Of Poets, Nat. Writers Assn., Internat. Black Writers. Democrat. Avocations: camping, playing organ, exploring old houses, writing. Home: 2176 Flamingo Dr Mount Morris MI 48458-2610

WOOLF, ANTHONY DEREK, consulting rheumatologist; b. London, June 12, 1951; s. Douglas Langston and Kathorn Beth (Pearce) W.; m. Hilary Ann Ruddock-West, Dec. 4, 1975; children: Sarah Louise, Richard Thomas. BSc with honours, London Hosp. Med. Coll., 1972, MB, BS, 1975. House physician and surgeon London Hosp., 1976; sr. house officer Hammersmith Hosp., Brompton Hosp. and Nat. Hosp. for Nervous Diseases Queen Square, London, 1977-78; registrar Guy's Hosp., London, 1979-83; sr. registrar Royal Nat. Hosp. for Rheumatic Diseases, Bath, Eng., 1983-87, Bristol (Eng.) Royal Infirmary, 1983-87; cons. rheumatologist Royal Cornwall Hosp., Truro, Eng., 1987—; hon. lectr. King's Coll., London, 1994—; hon. prof. U. Plymouth Postgrad. Med. Sch., 1999—. Author: Avoiding Osteoporosis, 1989, Osteoporosis: A Clinical Guide, 1990, 1998, Osteoporosis, 1994; editor Balliere's Clin. Rheumatology, 1996—; assoc. editor Annals Rheumatic Diseases. Chmn. Nat. Osteoporosis Soc., Bath, 1987; sec., trustee Cornwall Arthritis Trust, 1991; chmn., Eular Standing Com. for Edn. and Tng., Zurich, Switzerland, 1994. Recipient various rsch. grants. Fellow Royal Coll. Physicians; mem. Hunterian Soc., Brit. Soc. for Rheumatology, Brit. Med. Assn, Steering Com. Bone & Joint Decade, Internat. League Assns. for Rheumatology (exec. bd.). Home: Rope House, Point, Devoran, Truro TR3 6NS, England Office: Royal Cornwall Hosp, Infirmary Hill, Truro TR1 2HZ, England

WOOLF, HAROLD, judge; b. Newcastle upon Tyne, England; s. Alexander and Leah (Cussins) W.; m. Marguerite; 3 children. Student, Fettes Coll., Eng., U. Coll. London. Practice in pub. law, 1956, Treasury Devil, Revenue Devil, Master of the Rolls, 1996-2000; lord chief justice Ho. of Lords, London. Served with 15th/19th Royal Hussars. Avocations: swimming, cycling, tennis, classical music, opera. Office: Lord Chief Justice, House of Lords, London England SW1*

WOOLHOUSE, MARK EDWARD JOHN, research scientist; b. Shrewsbury, Eng., Apr. 25, 1959; s. John George and Ruth Carolyn (Harrison) W. BA in Zoology, Oxford U., Eng., 1980; MSc in Biol. Computation, U. York, Eng., 1981; PhD in Biology, Queen's U., Can., 1985. Rsch. fellow U. Zimbabwe, 1985-86, Imperial Coll., London, 1986-89, U. Oxford, Eng., 1989-97; chair vet. pub. health and quantitative epidemiology U. Edinburg, Scotland, 1997—; lectr. Hertford Coll., Oxford, 1992-93, St. Peter's Coll., Oxford, 1995-97. Contbr. articles to sci. jours., chpts. to books. Recipient Beit Meml. fellowship for med. rsch., 1989-92, univ. rsch. fellowship Royal Soc., 1992-97. Mem. Brit. Soc. Parasitology, Brit. Ecol. Soc., Soc. Vet. Epidemiology and Preventive Medicine. Avocations: walking, tennis, flyfishing. Office: Ctr Tropical Vet Med, U Edinburgh Easter Bush, Roslin EH25 9RG, Scotland

WOOLLEY, BRYAN (LOWELL BRYAN WOOLLEY), author, journalist; b. Gorman, Tex., Aug. 22, 1937; s. G.L. Jr. and Beatrice Voleta (Gibson) W.; m. Julianne Nelson, Aug. 31, 1958 (div. 1968); m. Margaret Ray Hilpert, July 13, 1968 (div. 1978); children: Bryan Edward, John Patrick; m. Isabel Catherine Rickert, Apr. 14, 1979. BA, U. Tex., El Paso, 1958; BDiv, Tex. Christian U., 1963; MTh, Harvard U., 1966. Reporter El Paso Times, 1955-58; tchr. Bel Air H.S., El Paso, 1958-59; bank teller Ft. Davis (Tex.) State Bank, 1959-60; corr. AP, Tulsa, 1967-68; city editor The Anniston (Ala.) Star, 1968-69; reporter, editl. writer The Courier-Jour., Louisville, 1969-76; sr. writer, columnist The Dallas Times Herald, 1976-89; sr. writer The Dallas Morning News, 1989—. Author: Some Sweet Day, 1974, We Be Here When the Morning Comes, 1975, Time and Place, 1977, November 22, 1981, Sam Bass, 1983 (Spur award 1984), The Time of My Life, 1984, Where Texas Meets the Sea, 1985, The Edge of the West, 1990, The Bride Wore Crimson, 1993, Generations, 1995, Mythic Texas, 1999. Recipient Tex. Headliner award, 1977, 81, 83, 90, Lit. award in journalism PEN West, 1993, U. Mo. Lifestyle Journalism award in arts and entertainment, 1995; named to Authors of the Pass: El Paso Writers Hall of Fame, 1989; Bernard DeVoto fellow Bread Loaf Writers Conf., 1975. Mem. Tex. Inst. Letters (pres. 1993-94, Stanley Walker Journalism award 1981, 83, 99, O. Henry awrd for mag. journalism 1991), Tex. State Hist. Assn., Tex. AP Mng. Editors Assn. (Sweepstakes award 1999), West Tex. Hist. Assn., Tex. Folklore Soc., PEN West. Democrat. E-mail: lbwoolley@aol.com. Home: 18040 Midway Rd Apt 215 Dallas TX 75287-6503 Office: Dallas Morning News 508 Young St Dallas TX 75202-4828

WOOLLEY, DONNA PEARL, timber and lumber company executive; b. Drain, Oreg., Jan. 3, 1926; d. Chester A. and Mona B. (Cheever) Rydell; m. Harold Woolley, Dec. 27, 1952 (dec. Sept. 1970); children: Daniel, Debra, Donald. Diploma, Drain High Sch. Sec. No Life Ins. Co., Eugene, Oreg., 1943-44; sec., bookkeeper D & W Lumber Co., Sutherlin, Oreg., 1944, Woolley Logging Co. & Earl Harris Lumber Co., Drain, 1944-70; pres. Woolley Logging Co., 1970—, Smith River Lumber Co., 1970—, Mt. Baldy Mill, 1970-81, Drain Plywood Co., 1970-81, Woolley Enterprises, Inc., Drain, 1973—, Eagle's View Mgmt. Co., Inc., Eugene, 1981—. Bd. dirs. Wildlife Safari, Winston, 1991, Oreg. Cmty. Found., Portland, 1990-99, chairperson, 1997-99; bd. trustees Linfield Coll., McMinnville, U. Oreg. Found., Eugene, Oreg. Trl. Coun., Boy Scouts Am., 1980—. Recipient Pioneer award U. Oreg., 1982, Econ. and Social Devel. award Soroptimist Club, 1991. Mem. Oreg. Women's Forum, Pacific Internat. Trapshooting Assn., Amateur Trapshooting Assn., Eugene C. of C. (bd. dirs. 1989-92), Arlington Club, Town Club (bd. dirs., pres.), Sunnydale Grange, Cottage Grove/Eugene Rod & Gun Club. Republican. Avocations: golf, travel. Office: Eagle's View Mgmt Co Inc 1399 Franklin Blvd Eugene OR 97403-1979

WOOLLING, KENNETH RAU, vascular internist; b. Indpls., Mar. 6, 1918; s. Kenneth Kaarta and Marie May (Rau) W.; m. Catherine Margaret McColl, Mar. 20, 1948; children: Kenneth Rau Jr., Mary Catherine. BA magna cum laude, Butler U., 1939; postgrad., Harvard U., 1939-40; MD, Ind. U., 1943; MS in Medicine, U. Minn., 1951. Diplomate Nat. Bd. Med. Examiners, Am. Bd. Internal Medicine, Am. Bd. Cardiovascular Disease. Intern Indpls. City Hosp. (now Wishard Meml.), Indpls., 1943-44; resident in internal medicine Marion County Gen. Hosp., Indpls., 1947; fellow, first asst. internal medicine Mayo Found., Rochester, Minn., 1948-52; mem. med. staff, mem. tchg. staff postgrad. med. edn. Marion County Gen. Hosp. (name now Wishard Meml. Hosp.), Indpls., 1952—; founder, dir., peripheral vascular diseases clinic Indpls City & Marion County Gen. Hosp. (now Wishard Meml.), Indpls., 1952-68; pvt. practice internal medicine and cardiovascular diseases Indpls, 1952—; founder, dir. peripheral vascular diseases clinic Meth. Hosp., Indpls., 1967-72, founder, dir. vascular lab., 1970-73, mem. med. staff, tchr. staff postgrad. med. edn., 1952—; mem. med. staff St. Vincent Hosp., St. Francis Hosp. and Winona Meml. Hosp., Indpls., 1952—; charter mem. med. staff Cmty. Hosp., Indpls., 1952—; charter mem. med. adv. com. Butler U., Indpls, 1956—. Contbr. articles to profl. jours., 1950—. Capt. Med. Corps U.S. Army, 1944-46. Fellow ACP, Am. Coll. Chest Physicians, Coun. on Cardiology Am. Heart Assn., Am. Coll. Angiology (gov. state of Ind. 1979-80); mem. AMA (50 Yr. award 1993), SAR, Internat. Union Angiology, Am. Soc. Internal Medicine, Am. Diabetes Assn., Ind. State Med. Soc., Ind. Diabetes Assn., Am. Fedn. for Clin. Rsch., N.Y. Acad. Med. Scis., North Ctrl. Clin. Soc., Mayo Cardiovascular Soc., Ind. Hist. Soc., Res. Officers Assn., Indpls. Med. Soc., Am. Legion, Shriners, Masons (Scottish Rite and Mystic Tie Lodge, 50 yr. award 1989), Contemporary Club of Indpls., Indpls. Athletic Club, Highland Golf and Country Club, Phi Delta Theta (50 yr. award 1985), Phi Kappa Phi, Phi Chi. Presbyterian. Office: PO Box 80192 Indianapolis IN 46280-0192

WOOLSEY, ROY BLAKENEY, electronics company executive; b. Norfolk, Va., June 12, 1945; s. Roy B. and Louise Stookey (Jones) W.; m. Patricia Bernadine Elkins, Apr. 17, 1988. Student, Calif. Inst. Tech., 1962-64; BS with distinction, Stanford U., 1966, MS, 1967, PhD, 1970. Sr. physicist Tech. for Communications Internat., Mountain View, Calif., 1970-75; mgr. radio direction finding systems Tech. for Communications Internat., Mountain View, 1975-80, program mgr., 1980-83, dir. strategic systems, 1983-88, dir. research and devel., 1988-91, v.p. engring., 1991-92; v.p. programs Tech. for Communications Internat., Fremont, Calif., 1992—; bd. dirs. Merit Software Corp., Menlo Park, 1990-96. Author: (with others) Applications of Artificial Intelligence to Command and Control Systems, 1988, Antenna Engineering Handbook, 1993; contbr. articles to profl. jours. Active YMCA, Palo Alto, Calif., Los Altos Hills com. rels. com., 1994—. Fellow NSF, 1966-70. Mem. Stanford Club of Palo Alto, Sequoia Yacht Club, Sigma Xi, Phi Beta Kappa. Republican. Presbyterian. Avocations: sailing, tennis, racquetball, skiing, contract bridge, travel. Home: 26649 Snell Ln Los Altos Hills CA 94022-2039 Office: Tech Comm Internat 47300 Kato Rd Fremont CA 94538-7334

WOOLSTON-CATLIN, MARIAN, psychiatrist; b. Seattle, Jan. 20, 1931; d. Howard Brown and Katharine Nichols (Dally) Woolston; m. Randolph Catlin Jr., July 5, 1959; children: Laura Louise, Jennifer Woolston, Randolph III. BA cum laude, Vassar Coll., 1951; MD, Harvard U., 1955. Diplomate Nat. Bd. Med. Examiners. Intern in pediat. medicine Children's Hosp., Boston, 1956, asst. resident in pediat. medicine, 1956; resident in psychiatry Mass. Mental Health Ctr., Boston, 1957-59; fellow in child psychiatry Tavistock Clin., London, 1960; commonwealth fellow in child psychiatry Harvard U. at Gaebler Children's Unit, Waltham, Mass., 1975-78, clin. instr. psychiatry, 1978-79; pvt. practice Wellesley Hills, Mass., 1978-91, Medfield, Mass., 1991—; clin. instr. psychiatry Harvard U. at Mass. Mental Health Ctr., Boston, 1957-59, 78-82, Tufts U. at Mass. Mental Health Ctr., 1957-59; mem. exec. bd. Parents' and Children's Svcs., Boston, 1983-86. Designer H.H. Hunnewell Meml. Garden for New England Flower Show Mass. Hort. Soc., 1975 (Ames Cup award). Mem. exec. bd. Ext. Divsn. New Eng. Conservatory Music., 1972-75; charter mem. reuse com. Medfield State Hosp., 1992—. Fellow Am. Acad. Child and Adolescent Psychiatry; mem. AMA, Am. Psychiat. Assn. (life mem.), Mass. Psychiat. Assn., Mass. Med. Soc., Boston Vassar Club (exec. bd. 1963-75), Hills Garden Club Wellesley (exec. bd. and design chief 1973-75). Episcopalian. Avocations: landscape design, sculpting. Home and Office: 314 North St Medfield MA 02052-1204

WOOLWORTH, SUSAN VALK, primary school educator; b. Toledo, Ohio, Apr. 24, 1954; d. Robert Earl and Alice (Melick) Valk; m. Andrew Baker Woolworth, June 26, 1976; children: Alison Valk, Andrew Baker. BA, Pine Manor Jr. Coll., Chestnut Hill, Mass., 1974; BS, Boston U., 1976. Tchr. kindergarten Lancaster (Pa.) Country Day Sch., 1986—. Past bd. dirs. Planned Parenthood, Vis. Nurse Assn.; bd. mem. Hands-on House; mem. Fulton Opera House. Mem. Jr. League (sustainer), Sigma Gamma. Republican. Episcopalian. Avocations: walking, gardening, tennis, decorating.

WOON, TAI HO, broadcasting executive; b. Singapore, Singapore, July 26, 1958. BA, Nat. U. Singapore, 1982, degree in polit. sci. with honors, 1983. Prodr. current affairs divsn. Sinapore Broadcasting Corp., 1983-87, editor current affairs divsn., 1987-90, sr. exec. editor current affairs divsn., 1990-92, dir. current affairs divsn., 1992-94; v.p. current affairs divsn. TV Corp. Singapore, 1994-98, v.p. channel NewsAsia, 1998-99; COO Singapore TV Twelve Pte. Ltd., 1999—. Mem. filming faclitation sub-com.) Singapore Film Commn., 1998—. Recipient Cert. Excellence in Prodn. of Pres. George Bush's The Singapore Lecture, White House, 1992, Internat. Grand Prix for Creative Documenatary, 1990. Office: 12 Prince Edward Rd, #05 00 Bestway Bldg, Singapore 079212, Singapore

WOOSNAM, IAN HAROLD, professional golfer; b. St. Martins, Shropshire, U.K., Mar. 2, 1958; s. Harold and Joan Woosnam; m. Glendryth Mervyn Pugh, Nov. 12, 1983; children: Daniel Ian, Rebecca Louise, Ami Victoria. Ed., St. Martins Modern Sch. Profl. golfer, 1976—; tournament winner News of the World under 23 match-play, 1979, Cacharel under 25 Championship, 1982, Swiss Open, 1982, Silk Cut Masters, 1983, Scandinavian Enterprise Open, 1984, Zambian Open, 1985, Lawrence Batley TPC, 1986, 555 Kenya Open, 1986, Hong Kong Open, 1987, Jersey Open, 1987, Cepsa Madrid Open, 1987, Bell's Scottish Open, 1987, 90, Lancome Trophy, 1987, 93, Suntory World Match-Play Championship, 1987, 90, World Cup (Wales) Team and Individual, 1987, Million Dollar Challenge, 1987, Welsh Pro Championship, 1988, Volvo PGA Championship, 1988, Panasonic European Open, 1988, Carrolls Irish Open, 1988, 89, AmEx Med Open, 1990, Epson Grand Prix, 1990, Torras Monte Carlo Open, 1990, 91, Fujistu Mediterranean Open, 1991, U.S. Masters, 1991, USF&G Classic, 1991, PGA Grand Slam of Golf, 1991, World Cup Individual, 1991, European Montecarlo Open, 1992, Murphy's English Open, 1993, Air France Cannes Open, 1994, Brit. Masters, 1994, Johnnie Walker Classic, 1996, Scottish Open, 1996, German Open, 1996, Heineken Classic, 1996, Volvo PGA Championship, 1997, Hyundai Motor Masters, 1997; ranked 1st Sony world rankings, 1991, Ryder Cup Team Mem., 1983, 85 (winners), 87 (winners), 89, 91, 93, 95 (winners), 97 (winners). Avocations: snooker, sports, water skiing.

WOOTEN, AUSTIN FRANKLIN, lobbyist, educator, writer; b. Washington, May 14, 1951; s. Julius Jr. and Doris Issabelle (Abbott) W.; m. Diane Elizabeth Carelock, Dec. 26, 1981; 1 child, Austing Franklin Jr. BA, Howard U., Washington, 1973, MEd, 1980; postgrad., Southeastern U., 2000—. Cert. spl. edn. provisional tchr., D.C.; cert. tchr. secondary social studies, Va. Collection specialist Libr. of Congress, Washington, 1980-86; instrnl. svc. specialist D.C. Pub. Schs., Washington, 1986-91, inclusion specialist, 1997-98; assessment specialist Potomac Job Corps, Washington, 1992-95; residential advisor, tutor Grafton Sch./D.C. Tutors, Washington and Rockville, Md., 1995-97; spl. edn. tchr. Leary Sch., Oxon Hill, Md., 1996-97; lobbyist Bonner and Assocs., Washington, 1999—. Author: (poems) Precious Pieces (The Nameless People), 1995 (Mark Waxman Archives 1996); (novels) The Deprogrammer, 1983, Blind Luck, 1994; author, lyricist: What Shall We Do?, 1999; author instrnl. TV guides for first instrnl. fixed TV sys. D.C. Pub. Schs. Chief election judge P.G. County Bd. Elections, Oxon Hill, Md., 1991-95; fundraiser Dem. Nat. Com., Washington, summer 1996. Recipient cert. of appreciation U.S. Ho. of Reps. Page Sch., Washington, 1997. Mem. Washington Tchrs. Union, K.C. (2nd degree). Roman Catholic. Avocations: writing, poetry, chess, stamp collection, coin collecting.

WOOTEN, JOHN J., artistic director, playwright; b. Las Cruces, N.Mex., Oct. 11, 1965; s. Ralph Cleon Wooten and Doris Ann (Werner) Mozer; m. Andrea Bianchi, Oct. 26, 1996. BA in Theatre, Montclair State U., 1990. Artistic dir. Life Repertory Co., N.Y.C., 1990-92; playwright Off Broadway & regional, 1990—, freelance dir., 1992—; artistic dir. Theatrefest, Upper Montclair, N.J., 1992—; instr. various univs., 1994—; bd. dirs. N.J. Theatre Group, Madison, N.J. Author plays Dover Won't Get Out, 1992, Trophies, 1994, Kiss The Bride, 1995, Uncivil War, 1996, The Role of Della, 1996, Hannah Senesh — The Mission Home, 1998; plays pub. by Dramatist's Play Svc., Dramatic Pub., Inc., various scene and monologue books. Fellow State of N.J. Arts Coun., 1995. Mem. Dramatists Guild, Actors Equity Assn. Democrat. Avocations: Civil War research, traveling, games, sports, carpentry. Office: Theatrefest Montclair State U Montclair NJ 07043

WOOTSON, GERRY LEVON, preschool teacher, writer; b. Mar. 30, 1973. Tchr. Creations Acad. Daycare, Goldsboro, N.C., 1997—. Home: PO Box 11544 3100 Cashwell Dr Goldsboro NC 27532-1544

WORACH-KARDAS, HALINA, demographer, educator; b. Stuzno, Kielce, Poland, Apr. 15, 1941; d. Jan and Genowefa (Zasowska) Worach; m. Edward Kardas, July 1, 1965; 1 child, Przemysław. BA, U. Lodz, Poland, 1965, PhD, 1971. Asst. dept. demographics Polish Acad. Scis., Warsaw, 1966-70, rschr. Inst. Philosophy and Sociology, 1971-91; assoc. prof. WHO Inst. Occupl. Medicine, Lodz, 1992-99; prof. Acad. of Humanities and Econs., Lodz, 1999—; expert rschr. and prospects com. Poland 2000, Warsaw, 1972-76; cons. Ministry of Health and Social Affairs, Warsaw, 1976; vis. lectr. Norwegian Inst. Gerontology, Oslo, 1986. Author: Teachers and Retirement, 1973, Age and Social Roles, 1984, Phases of the Professional and Family Life, 1988; co-author: Retirement in Industrialized Societies, 1987. Expert UN World Assembly on Aging, Vienna, 1982. Mem. Polish Assn. Gerontology (co-founder), Polish Demograph. Assn. (bd. dirs. 1987—), European Assn. Population Studies, Polish Assn. Pub. Health. Democrat. Roman Catholic. Avocations: history, recreational activities, flowers. Home: Murarska 9/5, 91-465 Łódź Poland Office: Acad Humanities and Econs, Reuolucji 1905 no 64 str, 90-222 Łódź Poland

WORDEN, KATHARINE COLE, sculptor; b. N.Y.C., May 4, 1925; d. Philip Gillette and Katharine (Pyle) Cole; m. Frederic G. Worden, Jan. 8, 1944; children: Fred, Dwight, Philip, Barbara, Katharine. Student, Potters Ch., Tucson, 1940-42, Sarah Lawrence Coll., 1942-44. Exhibited in group shows at Royce Galleries, Galerie Francoise Besnard, Paris, Cooling Gallery, London, Galerie Schumacher, Munich, Selected Artists Gallery, N.Y.C., Art Inst. Boston, Reid Gallery, Nashville, Weiner Gallery, N.Y.C., Boston Athanaeum, House of Humor and Satire, Gabrovo, Bulgaria, 1983, Newport Bay Club, 1984; pvt. collections Grand Palais, Paris, Dakar and Bathurst, Africa. Dir. Stride Rite Corp., 1980-85; occpl. therapist psychopathic ward L.A. County Gen. Hosp., 1953-57; Headstart vol., Watts, Calif., 1965-67; tchr. sculpture Watts Towers Art Ctr., 1967-69; participant White House Women Doers Luncheon meeting, 1968; dir. Cambridgeport Problem Ctr., Cambridge, Mass., 1969-71; mem. Jud. Nominating Commn., 1976-79; bd. overseers Boston Mus. Fine Arts, 1980-83; bd. govs. Newport Seamens Ch. Inst., 1989-91; tustee Comm. Rsch., Miami, Fla., 1960-69, chmn. bd., 1966-69; trustee Newport Art Mus., 1984-86, 92-94, Jamestown Cmty. Theatre, 1994-97, 99—, Newport Health Found., 1986-91, Hawthorne Sea Fund, 1990-93; bd. dirs. Boston Ctr. for Arts, 1976-80, Child and Family Svcs. of Newport County, 1983-97, 99—. Mem. Common Cause (Mass adv. bd. 1971-72, dir. 1974-75), Mass. Civil Liberties Union (exec. bd. 1973-74, dir. 1976-77). Home: 24 Fort Wetherill Rd Jamestown RI 02835-2908

WORDEN, MARNY, artist, musician; b. Williamsport, Pa., Sept. 23, 1926; d. Harold Ernest and Marion Francis (Tillinghast) W.; m. Richard Dean Blair, Sept. 9, 1949 (div. 1957); 1 child, Brian Eric; m. John Riley Olson, Dec. 19, 1957. BA, U. Toledo, 1946; MAT, Ind. U., 1968. English tchr. Tex. Sch. for Deaf, Austin, 1954-62, Ind. Sch. for Deaf, Indpls., 1962-65; French, Spanish tchr. Indpls. City Schs., 1965-70; curriculum projects dir. Ind. Sch. for the Deaf, Indpls., 1970-71, tchr. English, Latin, 1972-79; symphony musician and pvt. tchr. flute, piccolo, 1942—; dir. Tillinghast Early Music Consort; adjudicator Ind. Sch. Music Competitions. Author: (textbooks) 1,2,3 Language Series, 1970, (adaptations for the deaf) Beowulf, 1973, Song of Roland, 1974. Recipient of craftsman's rating in lapidary work, silversmithing; stone sculptures. Mem. Internat. Porcelain Artists & Tchrs., Inc. Avocations: oil paintings, watercolors, porcelain painting, performing. Home: 178 Ladd Ridge Cir Kingston TN 37763-6964

WORDEN, WILLIAM PATRICK, deacon; b. Chgo., July 23, 1933; s. Shannon Gerard and Florence Marie (Chouinard) W.; m. Shirley Ann Poerio, Apr. 1, 1956; children: Mary Patricia Maloney, Judith Ann Laverdiere, Ellen Jean. BEE, Ill. Inst. Tech., 1955; MA in Pastoral Studies, Loyola U., Chgo., 1986; D Ministry, Grad. Theol. Found., Bristol, Ind., 1991. Deacon St. Peter and Paul Parish, Naperville, Ill., 1980-85, St. Thomas the Apostle Parish, Naperville, 1985—; chaplain DuPage County Jail, Wheaton, Ill., 1991-96; mem. reactor safety rev. com. Argonne Nat. Lab., Darien, Ill., 1989-97; dir. Diaconate for the Diocese of Joliet, 1997—; del. Region VII Deaconal Orgn., 1981-84. Author: (with others) Decontamination and Decommissioning of Nuclear Facilities, 1980; contbr. articles to religious column in newspaper, jours. in field. Bd. dirs. Interfaith Counseling Svc., Naperville, 1980-85, Just of DuPage Jail Ministry, Wheaton, 1986-90. Office: St Thomas the Apostle Ch 1500 Brookdale Rd Naperville IL 60563-2129

WORDSMAN, ELIZABETH SCHMITT (BETSY WORDSMAN), senior manager print production; b. Milw., Mar. 1, 1955; d. Paul E. and Dorothy A. (Rehmer) Schmitt; m. Arthur Wordsman, Dec. 29, 1986. BFA, Boston U., 1981. Advt. mgr. Brills Inc., Milw., 1983-85; prodn. mgr. in tng. Allied Graphics Arts, N.Y.C., 1985-87; acct. supr. Bel-Aire Assoc., N.Y.C., 1987-88; cons. Bloomingdale's, N.Y.C., 1988-89; sales promotion prodn. dir. Lord & Taylor, N.Y.C., 1989-95; sr. mgr. global print prodn. Avon Products, N.Y.C., 1995—; judge Gravure Assn. of Am. Golden Cylinder awards, 1998, 99; spkr. PIRA Internat. Catalog Conf., 1999. Judge Gold Ink Awards, 1998, 99. Recipient Gold Ink award Printing & Pub. Exec., 1992, 93, 96, 97, 98, Rose Achievement award Lord & Taylor, 1993, Avon Chmn.'s Achievement award, 1999. Mem. Direct Mktg. Assn., Gravure Assn. of Am.

WORDSWORTH, BARRY, conductor; b. Eng., 1948. Student, Royal Coll. Music, London; studied conducting, Adrian Boult, London; studied harpsichord, Gustav Leonhardt, Amsterdam. Debut as soloist Frank Martin's Harpsichord Concerto, Royal Opera House for Kenneth Macmillan's ballet Las Hermanas; freelance condr. Royal Ballet, Australian Ballet, Nat. Ballet Can.; music dir. BBC Concert Orch. and Brighton Philharm., 1989, Royal Ballet and Birmingham Royal Ballet, 1991; debut with Royal Opera at Covent Gardens with Carmen, 1991; condr. BBC Concert Orch., 1991 Promenade Concerts: Piano Concerto by Bliss, Malcolm Arnold's Guitar Concerto, Vaughan Williams 8th Symphony, Act 3 of Sleeping Beauty; condr. Last Night of the Proms, with BBC Symphony Orch., 1993; recs. include Series of British music with BBC Concerto Orch., 1990-91. Avocations: walking, cooking, photography, swimming, tennis. Office: Brighton Philharm Orch, 50 Grand Parade, Brighton BN2 2QA, England*

WORENKLEIN, JACOB JOSHUA, lawyer; b. N.Y.C., Oct. 1, 1948; s. Abraham and Cela (Zyskind) W.; divorced; children: David, Daniel, Laura; m. Cindy Sternkler, Feb. 26, 1995. BA, Columbia U., 1969; MBA, JD, NYU, 1973. Bar: N.Y. 1974. From assoc. to ptnr. Milbank, Tweed, Hadley & McCloy, N.Y.C., 1973-93, chmn. firm planning com., 1988-90, exec. com., 1990-93, sr. advisor to exec. com., 1993-94; mng. dir., group head of global project fin. group Lehman Bros., N.Y.C., 1993-96; mng. dir., head project fin, commodity fin., export fin. Soc. Gen., N.Y.C., 1996-98; mng. dir., global head project and sector fin. Soc. Gen., Paris and N.Y.C., 1998—; mem. investment banking mgmt. com. Lehman Bros., 1993-96; mem. adv. coun. Amoco Power Resources Corp., 1995—; adj. prof. fin. NYU Stern Sch. of Bus. Mem. editl. bd. Jour. Project Fin., 1996—; contbr. articles to profl. jours. Pres. Old Broadway Synagogue, N.Y.C., 1978—; trustee Fedn. Jewish Philanthropies, N.Y.C., 1984-86; bd. overseers United Jewish Appeal-Fedn. Jewish Philanthropies, 1987, chmn. lawyers divsn. major gifts, 1989-91, chmn. lawyers divsn., 1991-93, bd. dirs., 1991-97; trustee Jewish Cmty. Rels. Coun. N.Y., 1995-98, mem. coun. on fgn. rels., 1998—. Mem. Coun. on Fgn. Rels. Office: Soc Gen 1221 Avenue Of The Americas New York NY 10020-1001

WORKMAN, GEORGE HENRY, engineering consultant; b. Muskegon, Mich., Sept. 18, 1939; s. Harvey Merton and Bettie Jane (Meyers) W.; Asso. Sci., Muskegon Community Coll., 1960; B.S.E., U. Mich., 1966, M.S.E., 1966, Ph.D., 1969; m. Vicki Sue Hanish, June 17, 1967; children—Mark, Larry. Prin. engr. Battelle Meml. Inst., Columbus, Ohio, 1969-76; pres. Applied Mechanics Inc., Longboat Key, Fla., 1976—; instr. dept. civil engring. Ohio State U., 1973, 82. Served with USN, 1961-64. Named Outstanding Undergrad. Student, Engring. Mechanics dept. U. Mich., 1965-66, Outstanding Grad. Student, Civil Engring. dept., 1968-69. Registered profl. engr., Ohio. Mem. Am. Acad. of Mechanics, ASME, Sigma Xi, Chi Epsilon, Phi Kappa Phi, Phi Theta Kappa. Congregationalist. Contbr. tech. papers to nat. and internat. confs. Home and Office: 3431 Bayou Ct Longboat Key FL 34228-3028

WORKMAN, JAMES E., retired school psychologist; b. Hillsboro, Ohio, Mar. 19, 1938; s. Russell Cochran and Stella Mae W.; m. Brenda Lee Staats, Oct. 8, 1960; children: Jennifer Nakayama, Loretta Workman. AB, Cin. Bible Sem., 1961; postgrad., Cin. Bible Grad. Sch., 1961-63; MEd, U. Cin., 1969; postgrad., 1969-72, Gestalt Inst. of Cleve., 1975. Lic. psychologist, Ohio. English tchr. Clermont Northeastern Local Schs., Owensville, Ohio, 1964-66; social worker Clermont County Human Svcs., Batavia, Ohio, 1966-69; dir. Regional Spl. Edn. Ctr., Wilmington, Ohio, 1969-71; intern Hamilton County Office Edn., Ohio, 1971-72; psychologist Zanesville (Ohio) City Schs., 1972-97. Bd. dirs. SCI, Inc., Zanesville, 1975—, chairperson FY92, FY93; bd. dirs., v.p. Residential Resources, Inc., Zanesville, 1992—; bd. dirs. Southeastern Ohio Symphony, New Concord, Ohio, 1980—, Friends of the Libr., Zanesville, 1995—, pres., 2000. Mem. Ohio Sch. Psychologists assn., East Cen. Ohio Sch. Psychologists Assn. (pres. 1974). Avocations: flying, sailing, reading, writing, motorcycling. Home: 1450 Lectric Ln Zanesville OH 43701-6928

WORKMAN, JOHN MITCHELL, chemist; b. Uniontown, Pa., Oct. 25, 1949; s. Hugh Lawrence and Mary Louise (Mitchell) W.; m. Gayle Sue Zappin, Nov. 20, 1987. BA in Psychology, Miami U., Oxford, Ohio, 1971; MS in Edn., Kans. State U., 1976; MS in Chemistry, U. Cin., 1985, PhD in Chemistry, 1987; MBA in Fin., Wright State U., Dayton, Ohio, 1995. Teaching and rsch. asst. dept. chemistry Wright State U., Dayton, Ohio, 1977-81; grad. teaching asst. U. Cin., 1982-83, grad. rsch. asst., 1983-86; sr. scientist Chemsys Inc., Fairborn, Ohio, 1986-89, dir. elemental analysis, 1989—; lab. dir., 1994—. Contbr. articles to jours. Analytical Chemistry, Applied Spectroscopy. With U.S. Army, 1972-75. Mem. Am. Chem. Soc., Am. Phys. Soc., Sigma Xi, Sigma Pi Sigma, Sigma Iota Epsilon. Roman Catholic. Achievements include rsch. in spectroscopic studies of fundamental plasma characteristics; trace and compositional analysis of aerospace materials including metals and metal alloys by optical emission spectrometry; chem. analysis of failed components in mil. aircraft accident investigations. Office: Chemsys Inc PO Box 427 Fairborn OH 45324-0427

WORKMAN, NORMAN ALLAN, accountant, graphic arts consultant; b. Boston, Apr. 20, 1918; s. William Horace and Estelle Emily (Hanlon) W.; m. Harriet Patricia Banfield, Aug. 1, 1946; children: Stephen, Mark, Brian, Patricia. Student, Coll. William and Mary, 1938-39; BS in Econs. magna cum laude, Bowdoin Coll., 1941. CPA, Oreg. Staff acct. Lybrand Ross Bros. & Montgomery, Boston, 1941-43, Whitfield Stratford & Co., Portland, Oreg., 1946-51; ptnr. Workman, Shephard & Co., CPAs, Portland, 1951-60; sole practitioner Portland, 1961-96. Newsletter columnist Good Impressions, 1993-98. Chmn. bd. Sylvan Sch., Portland, 1956-57; pres. Doernbecher Children's Hosp. Found., Portland, 1963-85, Bowdoin Club Oreg., Portland, 1963—; trustee Oreg. Episcopal Schs., Portland, 1974-76. Lt. (j.g.) Supply Corps, USNR, 1944-46. Mem. AICPA, Inst. Mgmt. Accts. (pres. Portland chpt. 1954-55), Oreg. Soc. CPA's, Pacific Printing and Imaging Assn., Arlington Club, Multnomah Athletic Club, Phi Beta Kappa. Avocations: bird hunting, fishing, horticulture. Home: 4381 SW Fairview Blvd Portland OR 97221-2709 Office: 1750 SW Skyline Blvd Portland OR 97221-2533

WORKMAN, WILLIAM GATEWOOD, JR., educator; b. Valdosta, Ga., Feb. 4, 1940; s. William Gatewood and Mildred (Turnbull) Workman; m. Elizabeth Parker, Apr. 5, 1975; children: Anne Parker, William Gatewood III, William Buchanan. AB, Davidson Coll., 1963, MusD, 1983; diploma, Curtis Inst. Music, 1965. Prof. singing Hochschule fuer Musik und Theater, Hamburg, Germany, 1987—; dept. chair Hochschule fuer Musik und Theater, 1997—. Baritone soloist Hamburg State Opera, 1965-90; prin. baritone Frankfurt (Germany) Opera Co., 1973-90; guest soloist Met. Opera Co., Royal Opera Covent Garden, Paris Opera, Teatro Colòn, Buenos Aires, Vienna State Opera, others; concert, recital and appearances on radio, TV and recs. Europe, U.S. and Australia. Mem. Rotary. Avocations: horses, gardening, dog breeding. Home: Heisterender Ch 28, 25358 Horst Germany

WORLD, MICHAEL JOHN, military medicine educator; b. Croydon, Surrey, Eng., Oct. 31, 1947; s. John Victor and Joyce Eleanor (Parker) W.; m. Patricia Jean Erdmann, July 27, 1995; children by previous marriage: James Richard, David Andrew. BSc with 1st class honors in Physiology, U. London, 1969, MBBS, 1972, MD, 1981. House physician Royal Free Hosp., London, 1973; sr. house officer London Hosp., 1974; lectr. medicine London Hosp. Med. Coll., 1974-77; asst. prof. U. Riyadh, Saudi Arabia, 1977-81; prof. mil. medicine Brit. Army, London, 1992-96, Def. Med. Svcs., London, 1996—; cons. physician nephrologist Royal Hosp. Haslar, Gosport, 1996—. Contbr. articles to profl. jours. Lt. col. Brit. Army. Fellow Royal Coll. Physicians London; mem. Renal Assn. Mem. Ch. of England. Avocations: motorcycling, running, computing. Office: Royal Hosp Haslar, Gosport Portsmouth PO12 2AA, England

WORLEY, NOELLE FRANCES, poet; b. Blackburn, Victoria, Australia, Oct. 1, 1939; d. Frank and Eliza Doreen (Dubois) O'Connor; m. Allen Robert Worley, Nov. 16, 1960 (div. 1980). Grad. H.S. Nurse Williamstown Gen. Hosp., Melbourne, Australia, 1958-59; sales Darrods Dept. Store, Melbourne, Australia, 1959; nurses aide Melbourne, Australia, 1959-60. Author: Shades of The Orient and Other Poems, 1995; author numerous poems. Fellow Victoria Writers Ctr., Australian Writers; mem. Fellowship Australian Writers (Victoria br.), Writers Ctr., Victoria. Avocations: films, reading, drawing, picnics.

WÖRMAN, ANDERS LARS EDVARD, civil engineering educator; b. Stockholm, Mar. 19, 1961; s. Lars-Erik and Charlotte (Thunberg) W.; m. Ulrike Elisabeth Melin, Oct. 7, 1989; children: Johannes, Oscar, Jacob. MSc in Civil Engring., Royal Inst. Tech., Stockholm, 1985, PhD in Hydraulic Engring., 1991. Asst. prof. engring. Royal Inst. Tech., Stockholm, 1988-91; rsch. engr. Swedish State Power Co., Sweden, 1991-93; assoc. prof. engring. Uppsala (Sweden) U., 1992—; coord. aquatic and environ. engring. programs, Uppsala U., 1993—; dir. of studies, 1993—. Contbr. articles to profl. jours. Recipient Thernwall prize Royal Acad. Engring. Sci., Sweden, 1992. Mem. Internat. Assn. Hydraulic Rsch., N.Y. Acad. Sci., Am. Geophys. Union. Avocation: climbing. Office: Uppsala U Inst Earth Sci, Norbyvagen 18B, 75236 Uppsala Sweden

WORMER, EBERHARD JUERGEN, science writer, medical historian; b. Frankfurt/Main, Germany, Aug. 22, 1951; s. Helmut and Zita (Metzger) W. Staatsexamen, Ludwig-Maximilian U., Muenchen, 1978; Med. Diploma, Technische U., Muenchen, 1985, DrMed, 1986. Asst. Praxis fuer Allgemeinmedizin, Nuernberg, Germany, 1987-88; redakteur Medikon-Verlag, Munich, 1988-89; lektor Urban & Schwarzenberg Verlag, Munich, 1989; freelance writer and journalist Munich, 1989—; biographer Bayerische Akademie der Wissenschaften, Muenchen, 1990—; journalist Gesellschaft fuer medizinische Information, Muenchen, 1990—. Author: History of Cardiology, 1989, History of Angiology, 1991, Bavarian History 18th and 19th Centuries, Lexikon Angiologie Phlebologie, 1993, Hormones, 1994, Salt in Medicine, 1995, Home Toxicants, 1996, Psoriasis, 1997, Atopic Dermatitis, 1998, Handbook Selfdiagnosis, 1998, Prostate Diseases, 1998, 2000, Handbook Laboratory Findings, 1999, Hair Problems, 2000; editor: Lexikon Herz-Kreislauf, 1994; contbr. articles to profl. jours. Mem. Internat. Physicians for Prevention of Nuclear War, Deutsche Gesellschaft fuer Geschichte der Medizin, Naturwissenschaften und Technik. Avocations: musical composing, playing jazz piano, photography. Home: Leonrodstrasse 32, Munich 80636, Germany

WORMS, JEANNINE ELIANE, writer; b. Buenos Aires, Apr. 19, 1923; d. Lucien and Marcelle (Ulmann) Metzger; m. Gérard Worms; children: Danielle Worms Bouvier, Laurent. MA in Sociology and Philosophy, U. Buenos Aires, 1945, MA in Spanish Lit., 1956. Author: Album de L-202-Bas, 1974, 30 plays including With or Without Trees, 1985, La Boutique, 1990, Vies de la Mort, 6 essays including Five Philosophic Essays, 1992, also 30 theater plays; translations from Spanish and Portuguese. Home: 70 Fq St Honoré, 75008 Paris France

WORNER, THERESA MARIE, internist, educator; b. Breckenridge, Minn., Feb. 19, 1948; d. William Daniel and Elizabeth (Stelten) W.; m. Martin Herbst, Mar. 24, 1979. AB, St. Theresa Coll., 1970; MD, U. Minn., 1974. Diplomate Am. Bd. Internal Medicine. Rotating intern Kings County Hosp., Bklyn., 1974-75, resident medicine, 1975-77; fellow VA Med. Ctr., Bronx, N.Y., 1977-78; chief med. sect. Alcoholism treatment program VA Med. Ctr., Bronx, 1978-87; asst. prof. medicine Mt. Sinai Sch. Medicine, N.Y.C., 1984-87; mem. faculty Postgrad. Ctr., 1985-90; physician in charge alcoholism svcs. L.I. Coll. Hosp., Bkyn., 1987-92; assoc. prof. clin. medicine SUNY, Health Sci. Ctr., Bkyn., 1988—; dir. rsch. 32BJ Health Fund, 1992-99; clin. assoc. prof. Pub. Health Cornell U. Med. Coll., 1996—; pres. Menachem Publ., Bethlehem, N.H., 1999—; pres./founder Alcohol. Info. 1995-97; advisor Patient Care Mag., 1984—; cons. REA, 1996—. Referee Hepatology, 1986, Jour. Study Alcohol, 1984—, Substance Abuse, 1992—, Alcoholism: Clinical and Exptl. Rsch., 1992—, Drug and Alcohol Dependence, 1993—, Drug Therapy, 1994—, Addiction, 1996—; contbr. numerous articles to profl. jours. Active Bronx Bot. Garden, Mus. Modern Art, Met. Mus. Art, Mus. Natural History, Bklyn. Mus. Art, Turtle Bay Civic Assn., Bklyn. Lyric Opera, Empire State Opera, Amato Opera. Grantee Child Welfare Adminstrn., 1991, 92, 93; recipient Physicians Recognition award AMA, 1984, 89, 91, 96, Cert. of Merit Govt. Employees Ins. Co., 1986, PACT Intern Site award, 1991, 92. Fellow ACP, N.Y. Acad. Medicine; mem. AAAS, Am. Med. Soc. on Alcoholism and Other Drug Dependence, Am. Soc. Internal Medicine, Am. Assn. for Study Liver Diseases (Travel award 1978), N.Y. Acad. Scis., Rsch. Soc. on Alcoholism, Internat. Soc. Biologic Rsch. in Alcoholism. Home: PO Box 256 Bethlehem NH 03574-0256 Office: 322 E 50th St New York NY 10022-7902

WORONOFF, GEORGES D., engineer; b. Brussels, Belgium, May 12, 1948; s. Andre and Marie-Therese (Jooris) W.; m. Armelle de Broqueville, May 10, 1975; children: Alexandre, Venceslas, Constantin, Maroussia. MS in Engring., U. Catholique de Louvain, Belgium, 1972; BA, Manchester Bus. Sch., U.K., 1973. Mining engr. Kempense, Steenkolenmyen, Belgium, 1974-84, dep. comml. dir., 1984-88; gen. mgr. STEP, Brussels, 1989-92; advisor fgn. trade Brussels Regional Devel. Agy., 1992-95; sr. engr. Techniirail S.A., Brussels, 1995—; mng. dir. Bur. SOFIE, Brussels, 1991-92, Ecopub., Brussels, 1992—. Author: Rock Movements Around Underground Excavations, 1974 (recipient prize of travel grants Belgian Ministry of Edn. 1974). Chmn. energy com. Belgian Union of Mgrs., 1979-82. Mem. Soc. Royale Belge des Ingeniurs and Indsls., Cercle Royal Gaulois. Christian Democratic Party. Roman Catholic. Avocations: choral singing, horseback riding, fgn. langs. (7), history. Office: Ecopublic sprl, PO Box 59, B-3080 Tervuren Belgium

WORRALL, JOHN DENNIS, economics educator, consultant, writer; b. Wildwood, N.J., July 29, 1942; s. John and Adele Veronica (McKenna) W.; m. Suzanne Elizabeth Hopkins; children: Heather, John; m. Janet Priscilla Moran; 1 child, Kevin. BA, Rutgers U., 1969, MA, 1972, PhD, 1976. Asst. dir. Rutgers Bur. Econ. Rsch., New Brunswick, N.J., 1974-77; dir. rsch. Nat. Ctr. for Employment Handicapped-Human Resources Ctr., L.I., N.Y., 1977-78; v.p., dir. econ. rsch. NCCI, N.Y.C., 1979-83; prof. econs. Rutgers U., Camden, N.J., 1983—; asst. dir. Bur. Econ. Rsch. Rutgers U., New Brunswick, 1983—; advisor Courier Post newspaper, Camden, 1994-97; John R. Commons lectr. U. Wis. Bus. Sch., Madison, 1991. Co-author: An Evaluation of Policy Related Rehabilitation Research, 1975; co-editor: Placement in Rehabilitation, 1979, Benefit Issues in Workers' Compensation, 1985; editor: Safety and the Workforce, 1983; assoc. editor Jour. Ins.: Math. and Econs., 1990—, Jour. Risk and Ins., 1992—. Del. White House Conf. on Handi-

capped, Washington, 1977; pres. South Jersey Irish Am. Unity Conf., Fedn. Irish Am. Socs., Phila., 1996-98; bd. dirs. St. Patrick's Day Observance Com., Phila., 1996-98, Phila. Immigration Resource Ctr., 1999—. Sgt. U.S. Army, 1960-66. Named Outstanding Faculty Mem. Rutgers U. Alumni Assn., 1991; honoree Gaelic Ball, Ladies Ancient Order Hibernians, Phila., 1998. Fellow Risk Theory Soc. (sec. 1990, pres. 1991); mem. Nat. Acad. Social Ins., Am. Econs. Assn., Am. Risk and Ins. Assn., Commodore John Barry Soc. (pres. 1996-98). Roman Catholic. Avocations: golf, fishing. Fax: 609-354-3274. E-mail: jworrall@crab.rutgers.edu. Office: Rutgers U Armitage Hall Camden NJ 08102

WORRELL, ERNST, energy and environmental analyst, researcher; b. Goor, Netherlands, Feb. 22, 1964; s. Cornelis Wijnandus and Marijke (Schets) W.; m. Antoinette Françoise Van Der Haagen, Dec. 5, 1997. MSc in Chemistry, Utrecht (Netherlands) U., 1989, PhD in Chemistry, 1994. Asst. tchr. Utrecht U., 1986-89, sci. rschr., 1988-94, sr. scientist, 1995-98; scientist Princeton (N.J.) U., 1994-95; staff scientist Lawrence Berkeley (Calif) Nat. Lab., 1998—; vis. prof. U. Sao Paulo, 1996; mem. roster of experts African Energy Policy Rsch. Network, 1996—. Author: Potentials for Improved Use of Industrial Energy and Materials, 1994; assoc. editor Energy, the Internat. Jour., 1995—; editor-in-chief Resources, Cons. and Recycling, 1998—; contbr. chpts. to books, articles to profl. jours. Office: Lawrence Berkeley Nat Lab MS 90-4000 1 Cyclotron Rd Berkeley CA 94720-0001

WORTH, GARY JAMES, communications executive; b. Berkeley Township, N.J., Dec. 13, 1940; s. Melvin Raymond and Viola Vista (Landis) W. Student, Trenton State Coll., 1964, Palm Beach Jr. Coll., 1958-59. Dir. sta. relations MBS, Inc., N.Y.C., 1972; v.p. sta. relations MBS, Inc., 1972; exec. v.p. MBS, Inc., Washington, 1972-79; mem. exec. com. MBS, Inc., 1978-79; v.p. Mut. Reports, Inc., Washington, 1972-79; dir. Mut. Reports, Inc., 1972-79; v.p., dir. WCFL, Inc., Chgo., 1979, Mut. Radio N.Y., Inc., N.Y.C., 1979; pres., dir. Robert Wold Co. Inc. and subs. Wold Communications, Inc., L.A., 1980-85; pres., chief exec. officer, dir. WesternWorld Inc. and subs. WesternWorld TV, L.A., 1986-93, The Video Tape Co., North Hollywood, Calif., 1987-93; sec. dir. WesternWorld Video Inc., L.A., 1986-87; CEO Starcom Television Svcs., Inc., 1993—96; chmn., CEO Starcom Entertainment, Inc., 1993—; CEO Starcom Mgmt. Svcs. Inc., 1993—, New Age Conversions, Inc., 1996—. Producer, dir.: USAF movie Assignment McGuire. Served to capt. USAF, 1960-66, Vietnam. Decorated Air Force Commendation medal, Armed Forces Expeditionary medal.; recipient Chief Herbert H. Almers Meml. award Bergen County (N.J.) Police Acad., 1972. Mem. Nat. Assn. Broadcasters, Nat. Assn. TV Program Execs., Nat. Informercial Mktg. Assn. Methodist.

WORTH, MARY PAGE, mayor; b. Balt., Jan. 23, 1924; d. Christian Allen and Margaret Pennington (Holbein) Schwarzwaelder; m. William James Worth, Nov. 4, 1947 (dec. May 1986); children: Margaret Page, William Allen, John David III. Student, Ladycliff Coll., Highland Falls, N.Y., 1941-42, Abbott Sch. Art, Washington, 1942-44; grad., Packer Coll. Inst., Brooklyn. Selectman Town of Searsport, Maine, 1973-75; mayor City of Belfast, Maine, 1986—; recreation chmn. Town of Searsport, 1970-72. Del. Rep. State Conv., Maine, 1970-94; pres. Searsport Reps., 1974-76; active ARC Overseas Assn., 1976—; pres. Searsport C. of C., 1976-79; mem. exec. bd. Waldo County Com. for Social Action, Belfast, 1986—; mem. Abnacki coun. Girl Scouts U.S.; tutor Literacy Vols. Am.; recreation specialist ARC, Camp Haugen, Japan, 1946-47; bd. dirs. RSVP-Walto County, Heat Start Waldo County; vol. tchr. Sch. for Blind, Cholon, Republic Vietnam, 1959-61, Am. Sch. at Saigon, Republic Vietnam, 1959-61; club dir. USAF Spl. Svcs., Ft. Meyer, Va., 1962-63, U.S. Army Spl. Svcs., Ft. Belvoir, Va., 1963-64; mem. Congresswoman Olympia Snow's Mpcl. Adv. Bd.; town chair Rep. Party; mem. adv. Belfast History Project. Mem. Gibson Island Club, 1938-73, mem. DAR (officer Maine 1986—), Internat. Platform Assn., Ret. Officers Assn. (life), 11th Airborne Assn./511th Parachute Infantry Regiment Korea War Vets. Assn., Waldo County Humane Soc. (pres. 1990—), Waldo County Law Enforcement (v.p. 1990—), VFW Aux., Am. Legion Aux., Belfast Garden Club (parliamentarian 1984—), Rotary (bd. govs. com. Maine St. '90), ARC Overseas Assoc.. Avocations: Great Dane breeding, antiques. Home: 5 Seaside Dr Belfast ME 04915-6039 Office: City of Belfast Mayor's Office 71 Church St Belfast ME 04915-6208

WORTH, PETER HERMAN LOUIS, consultant surgeon; b. London, Nov. 17, 1935; s. L.H. and R.M. (Niemeyer) W.; m. Judith Katherine Frances Girling, Feb. 8, 1969; children: Hugo Francis, Anna Louise. MB BChir, Cambridge (England) U., 1960, MA, 1961. Urologist cons. U. Coll. London Hosp., 1975—; cons. King Edward VII Hosp., London, 1992—. Contbr. articles to profl. jours. Fellow Royal Soc. Medicine; mem. British Soc. Urological Surgery. Avocations: music, gardening, skiing, food & wine. Home: Broad Eaves Mill Ln, Broxbourne EN10 7AZ, England Office: 31 Wimpole St, London W1M 7AZ, England

WORTHAM, CHRISTOPHER JOHN, literature educator; b. Zebedela, Transvaal, South Africa, Nov. 11, 1940; s. Leonard Willem and Violet Vivien (Daniell) W.; m. Maryanne Courtenay Osborne, Jan. 15, 1966; children: Miranda Vivienne, Nicholas Matthew. BA in Law, Rhodes U., Grahamstown, South Africa, 1962, BA with honors, 1964, MA, 1967; PhD, London U., 1974. Lectr. U. Rhodesia, Salisbury, 1967-76; assoc. prof. lit. U. Western Australia, Perth, 1976—. Author: Everyman, 1980, Marlowe's Dr. Faustus, 1985, 2nd edit., 1989, Andrew Marvell, 2000; contbr. articles to lit. publs. Recipient Roma Gill prize Marlowe Soc. Am., 1988, U. Western Australia rsch. award ULM, Perth, 1995; Australian Rsch. Coun. grantee, 1996. Mem. Australian and New Zealand Assn. for Medieval and Renaissance Studies (pres. 1984-85, editor jour. Parergon 1996—), Australian and New Zealand Shakespeare Assn. (sec. 1992-94). Avocations: golf, tennis. Home: 12 Boreham St, W Austr Perth 6011, Australia Office: Univ Western Aust, Dept English, W Austr Crawley Australia

WORTHINGTON, CAROLE YARD LYNCH, lawyer; b. Knoxville, Tenn., Aug. 29, 1951; d. Charles R. and Alma (Allred) Yard; m. Robert F. Worthington Jr., Sept. 14, 1996; 1 child, Allison Kathleen. BA, U. Tenn., 1972, JD, 1977. Bar: Tenn. 1977, Ga. 1982. Assoc. Thomas, Leitner, Mann, Warner & Owens, Chattanooga, 1977-78; assoc. Thomas, Mann & Gossett, Chattanooga, 1978-81, ptnr., v.p., 1981-86; ptnr. Grant, Konvalinka & Harrison, P.C., Chattanooga, 1987-96, Carole Lynch Worthington, Atty. at Law, Knoxville, 1996—; sec. Nat. Transp. Rsch. Ctr., Inc.; bd. dirs. U. Tenn. Alliance of Women Philanthropists. Author: Estate Planning Tennessee Practice, 1992; asst. editor Tenn. Law Rev., 1976-77. Vice chmn. allocations United Way of Chattanooga, 1985, pilot campaign, 1986; active Jr. League of Chattanooga, 1981-92; mem. alumnae adv. coun. U. Tenn. Coll. Law, 1983-92, dean's cir., 1989—; bd. dirs. Mental Health Assn. Chattanooga Inc., 1986-92, 1st v.p., 1988-89, sec., 1989-92; trustee St. Nicholas Sch., 1992-95. Recipient Alumni Leadership award U. Tenn. Coll. Law, 1988, 92. Fellow Am. Bar Found., Tenn. Bar Found., Chattanooga Bar Found.; mem. ABA (assembly del. 1991-97, 98-2001, com. on legal aid and indigent defendants 1994-95, select com. of house 1994-96, standing com. on charter and by laws 1999-2000, standing com. on credentials and admissions 1999-2000, standing com. on credentials and admissions 1999-2000, com. on client rels. 2000-2002), Chattanooga Bar Assn. (bd. govs. 1982-89, sec.-treas. 1985-86, pres. 1987-88), Tenn. Bar Assn. (vice chair comml. law, banking and bankruptcy 1988-90, unified bar study com. 1990-91, chair bar leadership conf. 1990, editl. bd. Tenn. Bar Jour. 1991-94, Tenn. Bar Assn. long range planning com. 1992-95, 97-99, bd. govs. 1994-96, chair long range planning com. 1995-96, future of bar com. 1998-2001), Ga. Bar Assn., Nat. Conf. Lawyers and Realtors (ABA del. 1990-92), Nat. Conf. Bar Pres.'s (exec. coun. 1989-92, treas. 1992-93, sec. 1993-94, pres.-elect 1994-95, pres. 1995-96), Tenn. Bd. Profl. Responsibility, Phi Alpha Delta. Home: 7618 Cherokee Springs Way Knoxville TN 37919-9033

WORTHINGTON, PAUL FRANCIS, engineering geoscientist, educator; b. Preston, Lancashire, Eng., Aug. 8, 1945; s. James Gerard and Mary Linda Worthington; m. Catherine Irene Osborne, Mar. 31, 1973; children: Michelle Frances, Mark Alexander, Timothy John. BSc, U. Hull, Eng., 1966; MSc, U. Durham, Eng., 1967; PhD, U. Birmingham, Eng., 1970; DSc, U. Pretoria, South Africa, 1979. Chartered engr. U.K.; chartered geologist U.K. Postdoctoral rsch. fellow U. Birmingham, Eng., 1970-73; chief rsch. officer CSIR, Pretoria, 1973-78; sr. engr. Howard Humphreys & Ptnrs., Reading, Eng., 1978-79; sr. rsch. assoc. petroleum engring. Brit. Petroleum Co., London, 1980-92; prin. cons. engring. geosci. Gaffney, Cline & Assocs., Alton, U.K., 1992—; spl. prof. geology U. Nottingham, U.K., 1987-90; vis. prof. geology U. Leicester, U.K., 1989-92; vis. rsch. prof. earth scis. Columbia U., N.Y.C., 1990-97; vis. prof. engring. geosci., U. London, 1997—, hon. rsch. fellow geology, 1993-96; keynote spkr. Internat. Conf. on Sci. Ocean Drilling, Strasbourg, France, 1987, Geol. Socs. of the Brit. Isles, London, 1988, Internat. Conf. on Reservoir Characterization, Dallas, 1989. Editor: Advances in Core Evaluation, 1990; co-editor: Advances in Core Evaluation II, 1991, III, 1993, Geological Applications of Wireline Logs II, 1992; mem. editl. bd. The Log Analyst, 1982-89, 96—, Marine & Petroleum Geology, 1984—, Formation Evaluation, 1986-89, Basin Rsch., 1988-94, Petroleum Geosci., 1994—; contbr. over 70 articles to profl. jours. Chmn. downhole measurements panel Ocean Drilling Program, Washington, 1987-92; rsch. adviser ocean sci. Nat. Govts., U.K., Australia, USA, 1989-92; chmn. working group on lab. practices for measurement permeability Am. Petroleum Inst., Washington, 1990-92; ind. mem. U.K. Earth Sci. Nat. Com., 1991-94. Fellow Geol. Soc. London (mem. coun. 1991-94), mem. London Petrophys. Soc. (pres. 1982-84), Soc. Prof. Well Log Analysts (pres. 1985-86, Disting. Svc. award 1996), Soc. Petroleum Engrs. (disting. lectr. 1985-86). Avocations: writing, theatre, travel, soccer. Office: Gaffney Cline & Assocs, Bentley Hall Blacknest, Alton Hampshire GU34 4PU, United Kingdom

WORTHINGTON, SANDRA BOULTON, lawyer; b. Phila., July 12, 1956. BA with high distinction, U. Va., 1978; JD, Temple U., 1983. Bar: Pa. 1983, U.S. Dist. Ct. (ea. dist.) Pa. 1984. Summer clk. Ct. of Common Pleas Montgomery County, Pa., summer 1981; legal intern Peruto, Ryan & Vitullo, Phila., 1982-83; assoc. Michael D. Fioretti Law Office, Phila., 1983-84; founding ptnr. Stocker & Worthington Law Office, Jenkintown, Pa., 1984—; legal counsel Phila. Women's Squash Racquets Assn., 1985—. Mem. Pa. Trial Lawyers Assn., Phila. Trial Lawyers Assn., Pa. Bar Assn., Montgomery County Bar Assn. Avocations: small business consulting, squash, tennis. Office: Stocker & Worthington Law Offices 820 Homestead Rd Jenkintown PA 19046-2840

WORTMANN, HILDEGARD MARIA, global media executive; b. Muenster, Germany, Sept. 27, 1966; d. Felix Anton and Gertrud (Naischall) W. Diploma in Bus. Studies, U. Muenster, Germany, 1989; MBA with distinction, London U., 1995. Owner franchise bus. World of Cotton, 1988-91; product mgr. Unilever, Duesseldorf, Germany, 1990-92; internat. mgr. Unilever, London, 1992-95; mktg. dir. Unilever, Wiesbaden, Germany, 1995-98; head global media BMW Group, Munich, 1998—. Author: (book) Franchising, 1990. Recipient Fashion Industry award. Mem. European Women Mgmt. Devel. Network. Home: Cosimastrasse 46, 81927 Munich Germany

WOSCOFF, ALBERTO, dermatologist; b. Rosario, Argentina, Nov. 26, 1934; s. Salvador and Frida (Casak) W.; m. Marta Beatriz Raskin, Mar. 6, 1938; children: Leonardo Guillermo, Mariana Sandra. MD, U. Buenos Aires, 1959, D in Medicine, 1963. Chief Program Against Venereal Diseases, Argentina, 1969-73; dir. sch. dermatology Buenos Aires U., 1991-94; dir. dept. dermatology Hosp. de Clinicas, Buenos Aires, 1993; head prof. dermatology U. Buenos Aires; dir. Argentine sect. Internat. Herpe Mgmt. Forum, London, 1997; cons., prof. Naval Hosp.; dir. Dermatolgia Argentina. Author: Dermatologia Geriatrica, 1963, Sexually Transmitted Diseases, 1977, 2nd edit., 1999, Urticaria, 1981, 2nd edit., 1999, Dermatologia, 1996; contbr. articles to profl. jours. Med. asst. mil. hosp., 1955-56. Recipient Ragusin award Argentine Dermatologic Assn., 1962, Xavier Vilanova award Argentine Dermatologic Soc., 1994, Jose Uribur award, 1981. Mem. Uruguayan Dermatologic Soc., Internat. Soc. Tropical Diseases, Brasilian Dermatologic Soc., Am. Acad. Dermatology, Investigative Dermatology Sec., Spain Acad. Dermatology. Avocation: sailing. E-mail: awoscoff@intramed.net.ar. Office: M T de Alvear 2127, 1122 Buenos Aires Argentina

WOSK, MIRIAM, artist; b. Vancouver, B.C., Can., Aug. 17, 1947; d. Morris J. and Dena W.; 1 child, Adam. Student, U. B.C., Can., 1966; AAS, Fashion Inst. Tech., N.Y.C., 1969; postgrad., Sch. Visual Arts, New Sch. Social Rsch., N.Y.C., 1969-74. lectr. Fashion Inst. Tech., N.Y.C., Sch. Visual Arts, N.Y.C., Art Ctr. Sch. Design, Pasadena, Calif., Woman's Bldg. Graphic Ctr., L.A., Otis Parsons Sch. Design, L.A., Ctr. Early Edn., L.A., Crossroads Sch., Santa Monica, Calif., UCLA Ext., L.A., Folk Art Soc., L.A.; freelance illustrator N.Y.C. mags., 1970s-1980s, including 1st cover of Ms., Mademoiselle, N.Y. Times, Esquire, Vogue, N.Y. Mag., Viva, McCalls, Saturday Rev., Sesame St., New West, Psychology Today, 1969-79; curator group show The Inner Lives of Women: Psyche, Spirit and Soul, Spring St. Gallery, L.A., 1996; art bd. dirs. Santa Monica Museum, 1998—. One woman shows include Transam. Ctr., L.A., 1983, West Beach, L.A., 1988, Wilshire Pacific Bldg., L.A., 1990, Robert Berman Gallery, Santa Monica, Calif., 1991, Drago, Santa Monica, 1992, Jazz, Pacific Design Ctr., West Hollywood, Calif., 1995; exhibited in group shows at Harkness House Gallery, N.Y.C., 1979-80, Dist. 1199 Cultural Ctr. Inc., N.Y., 1981, Smithsonian Inst., Washington, 1981, Transam. Pyramid, San Francisco, 1983, Barnsdall Art Gallery, L.A., 1983, Functional Art Gallery, L.A., 1985, One Market Plaza, San Francisco, 1986, Laforet Mus., Tokyo, 1986, Art et Industrie Gallery, N.Y.C., 1986, Otis Parsons Sch. Design, L.A 1987, B1 Gallery, Santa Monica, 1987, Katharina Rich Perlow Gallery, N.Y.C., 1988, Sam Francis Studio, Santa Monica, 1988, Gallery Functional Art, Santa Monica, 1989, 91, Santa Monica Mus. Art, 1990, 99, 2000, Getty Mus., Malibu, Calif., 1990, James Corcoran Gallery, Santa Monica, 1990, Joan Robey Gallery, Denver, 1992, Cultural Ctr., Eureka, Calif., Calif. State U., Long Beach, 1992, Pacific Design Ctr., L.A., 1992, U. Art Mus., Long Beach, 1992, L.A. County Mus. Art, 1992, 96, Helander Gallery, Palm Beach, Fla., 1993, Spring Street Gallery, L.A., 1994, 96, Anderson Ranch Art Ctr., Aspen, Colo., 1995, Park Ave. Armory, N.Y.C., 1997, 98, 2000, Adam Baumgold Gallery, N.Y.C., 1997, Pub. Corp. Arts, Long Beach Arts, 1998, Boritzer Gray Hamano, Santa Monica, 1999, Santa Monica Fine Arts Studio, 1999, Jan Baum Gallery, L.A., 2000; pub. in nat. and internat. mags., books and newspapers including The Golden Age of Magazine Illustration: The Sixties and Seventies New Feminist Criticism-Art-Identity Action, Los Angeles Times, Washington Post, Casa Vogue, L'Express Paris and Idea Internat. (Japan). Recipient Merit award Art Dirs. Club N.Y., cert. of merit Soc. Illustrators, cert. excellence Am. Inst. Graphic Artists; named guest editor Maedmoiselle Mag. Studio: 436 Adelaide Dr Santa Monica CA 90402-1354

WOSKOW, CATHERINE ROSE, artist; b. Ukiah, Calif., Jan. 21, 1958; d. Donald Thomas and Mary Jane Woskow; m. Bruce Robert Farrelly, July 16, 1983. Student, Bradford Liberal Arts Coll., 1976-77, Sonoma State U., 1978-79, Koningkijke Acad. Kunsten Vormgeving, The Netherlands, 1980-81. One-woman shows include Eleonore Austerer Gallery, San Francisco, 1996, 98, Kimzey Miller Gallery, Seattle, 1998; group exhbns. include Gallery Marckant, Langelo, The Netherlands, 1992, San Francisco Mus. Modern Art Rental Gallery, 1992, William Zimmer Gallery, Mendocino, Calif., 1992—, Solomon Dubnick Gallery, Sacramento, 1994, Eleonore Austerer Gallery, San Francisco, 1996—, Tercera Gallery, Palo Alto, Calif., 1996-99, Kimzey Miller Gallery, Seattle, 1997-99, Gwenda Jay Addington, Chgo., 1998-99. Grantee Rotary Internat., The Netherlands, 1980-81. Avocations: whitewater kayaking, gardening, dancing.

WOSNITZA, JOACHIM, physicist; b. Grevenbroich, Germany, Dec. 15, 1959; s. Max and Christina (Monissen) W. Diploma, Aachen U., Germany, 1985; Doctor rerum naturalium, U. Karlsruhe (Germany), 1988, habilitation, 1995. Sci. employee RWTH Aachen, 1985-86; sci. employee U. Karlsruhe, 1986-93, sci. asst., 1993-99; lectr. physics, 1999—. Mem. Am. Phys. Soc., Deutsche Physikalische Gesellschaft. Avocations: volleyball, badminton, sailing. Office: U Karlsruhe, Engesserstrasse 7, 76128 Karlsruhe Germany

WÖSSNER, MARK MATTHIAS, retired publishing company executive; b. Berlin, Oct. 14, 1938. DEng, Tech. U. Stuggart, Germany. Asst. to top mgr. Bertelsmann AG, Gütersloh, Germany, 1968-70, prodn. mgr. Mohndruck unit, offset printing operation, 1970-72, tech. mgr. Mohndruck unit, 1972-74, mng. dir. Mohndruck unit, 1974-76, mem. exec. bd. in charge corp. divsn. for printing and mfg., 1976-81, dep chmn. exec. bd., 1981-82, CEO, chmn. exec. bd., 1982-98, chmn. supervisory bd., 1998-99; chmn. bd. Bertelsmann Found., 1999; ret., 1999. Exec. bd. dirs. Bertelsmann Found., 1996-99, chmn., CEO, 1999—. Office: Bertelsmann AG 1540 Broadway New York NY 10036-4039

WOSTREL, NANCY JO A.W.S., painter, illustrator; b. San Diego, Feb. 21; d. George Jerome Wostrel and Imogene Marie Nelson. BFA, Famous Artists Schs., 1972. Staff artist Marikle & Kelly Advertising, San Diego, 1960-61; illustrator San Diego, 1961-62, 66-67; art dir., illustrator J. Jessop & Sons, San Diego, 1962-66; v.p., art dir. Concept Advt. Inc., San Diego, 1967-68; advt. mgr. Streicher & Seaman Inc., San Diego, 1968-70; painter, illustrator San Diego, 1970—; bd. dirs. publicity Watercolor West, Riverside, Calif., 1980-82. Represented in over 10 solo, invitational exhbns. Recipient First award for watercolor S.D. Art Inst., 1975, Lloyd award for watercolor SDWS Nat. Exhbn., 1980, 2nd prize watercolor So. Calif. Expo, 1979. Mem. Am. Watercolor Soc. (signature mem.), Watercolor West (bd. dirs. 1980-82). Avocations: writing, golf, gardening, collecting blue and white porcelain. Studio: 2505 Montclair St San Diego CA 92104-5348

WOUK, HERMAN, writer; b. N.Y.C., May 27, 1915; s. Abraham Isaac and Esther (Levine) W.; m. Betty Sarah Brown, Dec. 9, 1945; children: Abraham Isaac (dec.), Nathaniel, Joseph. AB with gen. honors, Columbia U., 1934; LHD (hon.), Yeshiva U., 1954; LLD (hon.), Clark U., 1960; LittD (hon.), Am. Internat. Coll., 1979; PhD (hon.), Bar-Ilan U., 1990, Hebrew U., 1997; DLitt (hon), Trinity Coll., 1998. Writer radio programs for various comedians N.Y.C., 1935; asst. writer weekly radio scripts comedian Fred Allen, 1936-41; Presdl. cons. to U.S. Treasury, 1941; vis. prof. English Yeshiva U., 1952-57; scholar-in-residence Aspen Inst. Humanistic Studies, 1973-74. Author: novels: Aurora Dawn, 1947, The City Boy, 1948, Slattery's Hurricane, 1949, The Caine Mutiny, 1951 (Pulitzer Prize award for fiction 1952), Marjorie Morningstar, 1955, Youngblood Hawke, 1962, Don't Stop the Carnival, 1965, The Winds of War, 1971, War and Remembrance, 1978, Inside, Outside, 1985 (Washingtonian Book award 1986), The Hope, 1993, The Glory, 1994; dramas: The Traitor, 1949, The Caine Mutiny Court-Martial, 1953; comedy: Nature's Way, 1957; non-fiction: This is My God, 1959, This Will to Live On, 2000; screenplays for TV serials: The Winds of War, 1983, War and Remembrance, 1986. Trustee Coll. of V.I., 1961-69; bd. dirs. Washington Nat. Symphony, 1969-71, Kennedy Ctr. Prodns., 1974-75. Exec. officer U.S.S. Southard USNR, 1942-46, PTO. Recipient Richard H. Fox prize, 1934, Columbia U. medal for Excellence, 1952, Alexander Hamilton medal, 1980, U. Calif.-Berkeley medal, 1984, Golden Plate award Am. Acad. Achievement, 1986, USN Meml. Found. 'Lone Sailor' award, 1987, Yad Vashem KaZetnik award, 1990, Bar Ilan U. Guardian of Zion award, 1998, USCD medal U. Calif.-San Diego, 1998. Mem. Naval Res. Assn., Dramatists Guild, Authors Guild, Internat. Platform Assn. (Ralph Waldo Emerson award 1981), PEN. Jewish. Clubs: Bohemian (San Francisco); Cosmos, Metropolitan (Washington); Century Assn. (N.Y.C.). Office: care BSW Literary Agy 3255 N St NW Washington DC 20007-2845

WOUTERS, CHRIS, banker; b. Belgium, Mar. 26, 1959; m. Beatrice Suykens; 1 child, Michael. Degree in Applied Econs., U. Antwerp, Belgium; student, U. Aix-Marseille, France. Mgr. relationship banking Generale Bank, Ghent, Belgium, 1989-96; mgr. credit Generale Bank, Antwerp, 1996-98; mgr. bus. line Generale Bank, 1998-99; mgr. bus. line medium-sized enterprises and corp. Fortis Bank, Belgium, 1999—. Home: Niedernhausenlaan 15, 2610 Antwerp Belgium Office: Fortis Bank NV, Warandeborz 1QA1A, 1000 Brussels Belgium

WOUTERS, DIRK CONSTANTIA, network management and software development administrator; b. Duffel, Antwerp, Belgium, July 29, 1955; s. Paul C. and Emma (Van Noten) W.; m. Brigitte J. T'Jampens, Apr. 24, 1982; children: Stef, Carl. Grad. in Classical Langs., Onze-Lieve-Vrouw Coll., Boom, Belgium, 1973; grad. in Mech. Engring., Province Tech. H.S., Boom, Belgium, 1978; grad. in Indsl. Engring., Indsl. H.S. Antwerp/Mechelen, Antwerp, 1979. Team leader mech. design space divsn. Bell Telephone MFGC, Antwerp, 1980-84, team leader mech. design mobile radio, 1984-86; sect. head software devel. network mgmt. Alcatel Telecom, Antwerp, 1986-99, software project leader classic products, 1999—. Chmn. Parents' Orgn. OLV Coll., Boom, 1995-99, mem. Parents' Orgn., 1999—. Avocations: airplanes, biking, football, power kiting. Office: Alcatel Telecom WD27, Prins Boudewijnlaan 49, 2650 Edegem Belgium

WOUTERS, JAN T. M., microbiologist; b. 1936. Doctorate, U. Amsterdam. Asst. microbiology lab. U. Amsterdam, 1960-68, assoc. prof., 1969-86; dir. biol. and chem. rsch. NIZO Food Rsch., Ede, 1986-2000, consultative dir., 2000—; prof. dairy sci. Wageningen Agrl. U., 1997—; rsch. mgr. Wageningen Ctr. Food Scis., 1997-2000. Mem. editl. bd. Jour. Antonie van Leeuwenhoek, 1975—, Jour. Gen. Microbiology, 1983-84, editor, 1984-87; mem. editl. bd. Netherlands Milk and Dairy Jour., 1984-89, editor, 1989-96; editor Internat. Dairy Jour., 1996—. Fellow Inst. of Microbiology, Rutgers U., 1968-69. Mem. Am. Soc. Microbiology, Netherlands Soc. Microbiology, Soc. Gen. Microbiology, Royal Netherlands Chemistry Soc. Office: NIZO Food Rsch, Kernhemseweg 2 Postbus 20, 6710 BA Ede The Netherlands

WOUTERS, JOHAN, research scientist; b. Huy, Belgium, May 10, 1969; s. Roger Wouters and Maryse Deprez; m. Dominique Warnant, Nov. 15, 1995. PhD in Chemistry. Rsch. asst. F.N.R.S., Namur, Belgium, 1991-94, rsch. assoc., 1995-97; lectr. U. Namur, 1998—. Recipient Prix Stass, Acad. Royal Scis., 1991. Mem. Royal Chemistry Soc. (End-Years Work award 1991). Avocation: swimming. Fax: 32 0 81 724530. E-mail: johan.wouters@fundp.ac.be. Office: U Namur, 61 rue de Bruxelles, 5000 Namur Belgium

WOXENIUS, JOHAN, engineering educator; b. Gothenburg, Sweden, Mar. 3, 1967; s. Åke and Torborg (Lundquist) W.; m. Anna Persson, July 5, 1997. Degree in Computer Sci., U. Lund, Sweden, 1987; degree in history of econs., U. Gothenburg, Sweden, 1992; MSc in Indsl. Engring., Chalmers U. Tech., Gothenburg, 1991, Lic. Engring., 1994, PhD in Transp., 1998. Tchr., rschr. Chalmers U. Tech., Gothenburg, 1991—, dir. studies internat. master programme mgmt. of transp., 1994-97, lectr., head dept., 2000—; cons. Woxkonsult, Gothenburg, 1991—; guest lectr. U. Gothenburg, 1995-99; expert evaluator of rsch. proposals European Commn., Brussels, 1996, 97, 99; educator for Russian transport experts World Bank, Helsinki; advisor technol. devel. project Swedish State Rwy. and tech. survey for The Internat. Rd. Transport Union. Author: Modelling European Combined Transport as an Industrial System, 1994, Development of Small-Scale Intermodal Freight Transportation in a Systems Context, 1998; contbr. articles to profl. jours. Student union leader Vedeby H.S., Karlskrona, 1982-83. 1st lt. Air Def., Sweden, 1986—. Curt Nicolin's CN70 grantee Internat. C. of C., 1995, 97, 99. Mem. Intermodal Transport Rschrs., Internat. Assn. Avocation: golf. E-mail: johan.woxenius@mot.chalmers.se. Home: Rävbergsgatan 7, SE-43133 Mölndal Sweden Office: Chalmers Univ of Tech, Dept Transp and Logistics, SE-41296 Göteborg Sweden

WOŹNIAK, MARIAN FELIKS, organic chemistry educator; b. Cracow, Dec. 9, 1936; s. Feliks and Anna (Bilska) W.; m. Magdalena Treit, July 4, 1964; children: Marta, Mirosław. MSc in Chemistry, Jagiellonia U., Cracow, 1958, Doctorate, 1973, DSc habilitation, 1981, chemistry diploma, 1958. Tchr. chemistry Secondary Sch., Cracow, 1959-66; rsch. asst. Cracow U. Tech., 1966-73, adj., 1973-83, docent, 1983-91, prof., 1991-96, full prof., 1996—, head dept. organic chemistry, 1983—, dir. Inst. Chemistry and Tech., 1990-97. Contbr. chpt. to book and articles to profl. jours. Recipient award for rsch. results Ministry of Edn. and Rsch., Poland, 1984. Mem. Internat. Soc. Heterocyclic Chemistry. Avocations: gardening, playing the clarinet, philatelistic, military books, music. Home: Stradom 15/9, 31-068 Cracow Poland Office: Cracow U Tech, Warszawska 24, 31-155 Cracow Poland

WOZNIAK, RICHARD ANTHONY, computer engineer; b. Buffalo, Aug. 24, 1959; s. Richard Anthony and Julia Marie (Cefaratti) W. BA, U. Buffalo, 1981, MS, 1983. Software engr. Sierra Rsch., Buffalo, 1983-85; sr. analyst Marine Midland Bank, Buffalo, 1985-91, project mgr., 1991-93, tech. specialist, 1993—. Pres. South Cheektowaga Baseball Assn., Cheektowaga, N.Y., 1984—. Recipient award Cheektowaga C. of C., 1992. Home: 33 Grand Prix Dr Cheektowaga NY 14227-3613 Office: HSBC 241 Main St Fl 5 Buffalo NY 14203-2703

WOZNIAK, WITOLD STANISLAW, anatomist, researcher; b. Krasne, Molodeczno, Poland, July 22, 1934; s. Wladyslaw S. and Anna (Menke) W.; m. Ewa Wanda Matuszkiewicz, Sept. 29, 1959; children: Witold, Tomasz. MD, U. Poznan, Poland, 1960. Diplomate in medicine. Asst. dept. anatomy St. Louis U., 1967-68; asst. dept. anatomy U. Poznan, 1960-70, 70-76, assoc. prof. dept. anatomy, 1977-84, chmn. dept. anatomy, 1975—, prof., 1984—, vice dean med. faculty, 1975-82, dean med. faculty, 1982-84; v.p. Univ. Med. Sch., Poznan, 1987-90; cons. in neurobiology U. Calif., Davis, 1975-81; vis. prof. Georgetown Univ. Medical Ctr., Washington, 1995, 98, 99. Author: Neuroanatomy, 1970; editor: Human Topographic Anatomy, 1996, Human Anatomy, 2000; editor Folia Morphologica, 1983, Annales Medicorum Posnanienses, 1981. Decorated Cross of Polonia Restituta; recipient medal Nat. Edn. Com., Coun. of State, Warsaw, 1981, Sci. award Polish Ministry Health, 1990, 96, Innovative Excellence award in Tchg., Learning, and Tech., 2000. Mem. Polish Anat. Soc. (pres. 1996—), Am. Assn. Anatomists, Anatomische Gesellschaft, N.Y. Acad. Sci., Romanian Anat. Soc. Avocations: history of medicine and anatomy, gardening, driving. Home: 31 Porazinskiej, 60-195 Poznań Poland Office: Dept Anatomy, 6 Swiecicki, 60-781 Poznań Poland

WRAGA, WILLIAM G., educator; b. Teaneck, N.J., Mar. 21, 1957; s. William Francis and Maryjane M. (Conlon) W.; m. Amy Jeanne Schneider, June 26, 1982; children: William Frederic, Ian Thomas. AB, Rutgers Coll., 1979; MAT, U. Chgo., 1980; EdD, Rutgers U., 1991. Tchr. Hillsborough H.S., Belle Mead, N.J., 1980-81, Green Brook (N.J.) H.S., 1981-84, Mendham (N.J.) H.S., 1984-86; dept. supr. Freehold (N.J.) Twp. H.S., 1986-87; dist. supr. K-12 Bernards Twp. Pub. Schs., Basking Ridge, N.J., 1987-94; adj. asst. prof. Rider U., Lawrenceville, 1994; asst. prof. dept. edn. leadership U. Ga., Athens, 1995-99, assoc. prof., 1999—; chmn. civics com. N.J. State Dept. Edn., 1988-90, mem. social studies core course proficiencies panel, 1989-91; bd. dirs. N.J. Coun. for Social Studies, 1988-90, chmn. publ. com., 1988-89; mem. exec. bd. N.J. ASCD, 1992-93; mem. adv. com. N.J. Vietnam Vets. Meml. Ednl. Ctr., 1993-94; presenter in field. Author: Democracy's High Sch., 1994; contbg. author: Readings in Middle Sch. Curriculum, 1993, Curriculum Issues and the New Century, 1995, Handbook on Teaching Social Issues, 1996; exec. editor Focus on Edn. Jour., N.J. ASCD, 1993 edit.; co-editor Rsch. Rev. for Sch. Leaders, 1996, 98, 00; guest co-editor Social Edn., 1990; contbr. articles and book revs. to profl. jours. Grad. Merit scholar Rutgers U., 1984-85, 85-86; recipient Excellence in Dissertation award Rutgers Grad. Sch. Edn. Alumni Assn., 1992. Fellow John Dewey Soc. (bd. dirs. 2000—); mem. Am. Ednl. Rsch. Assn., Profs. of Curriculum (Factotum 1989-99), Soc. Study Curriculum History (pres. elect 2000—), Phi Delta Kappa, Pi Lambda Theta, Kappa Delta Pi. Office: U Ga Coll Edn Dept Ednl Leadership 850 College Station Rd Athens GA 30605-2718

WRAY, GERALDINE SMITHERMAN (JERRY WRAY), artist; b. Shreveport, La., Dec. 15, 1925; d. David Ewart and Mary Virginia (Hoss) Smitherman; m. George Downing Wray, June 24, 1947; children: Mary Virginia Hill, Deanie Galloway, George D. Wray III, Nancy Armistead. BFA with honors, Newcomb Art Sch., Tulane U., 1946. tchr. children's art. One woman shows include Don Batman Gallery, Kansas City, Mo., 1982, Gallery II, Baton Rouge, 1985, McNeese Coll., Lake Charles, La., 1987, Dragonfly Gallery, Shreveport, La., 1987, Barnwell Garden and Art Ctr., Shreveport, 1988, 95, Southdown Mus., Houma, La., 1989, La. State U., Shreveport, 1991, WTN Radio Station, Shreveport, 1993, The Cambridge Club, Shreveport, 1993, Centenary Coll., 1993, Northwestern State U., Natchitoches, La., 1995, Goddard Mus., Ardmore, Okla., 1996, Art Buyers Caravan, Atlanta, 1996, Lockhaven (Pa.) U., 1996, Billingsley Gallery, Pensacola, Fla., 1996, Casa D'Arte, Shreveport, La., 1996, N.E. State U., Monroe, La., 1997, Art Expo, N.Y.C., 1997, Palmer Gallery, Hot Springs Ark., 1998, Tower Art Gallery, Shreveport, La., 1999; Group shows include Watercolor USA Springfield., Mo., 1988, Waddell's Gallery, Shreveport, 1988, 91, Water Works Gallery, Dallas, 1990, Southwestern Watercolor Show, 1991 (D'Arches award, Creative Artist award 1997), Masur Mus. Exhibition (honorable mention 91, 92), , Bossier Art Ctr., Bossier City, La., 1992, Irving Art Assn. (honorable mention), 1992, Leon Loard Gallery, Montgomery, Ala., 1993, Ward-Nasse Gallery, N.Y.C., 1993, 97, Soc. Experimental Artists Internat. (1st. place, honorable mention), 1993, Palmer Gallery, Hot Springs, Ark., 1994, Nat. Watercolor Soc. Ann., 1994-96, 98, Art Expo, N.Y.C., 1996, Casa D'Arte, Shreveport, 1996, Art Buyers Caravan, Atlanta, 1996, Off The Wall Gallery, Savannah, Ga., 1997, Art Effects Gallery, Merian, Pa., Boulevard Art Gallery, Macon, Ga., 1997, Visual Inspirations, Newton, N.J., 1997, Mossey Brake Gallery, Tex., 1997, Barnwell Ctr. (with children & grandchildren), Shreveport LA, 1998, Manhattan Arts Mag. Showcase Award, Nat. Assn. Women Artist Traveling Show; permanent collections include NAWA, Zimmerli Mus., Rutgers Univ., N.J.-Meir Mus., Lynchburg, Va., Goddard Mus. Ardmore, Okla., Bibl. Arts Ctr., Dallas, La. State Capitol Bldg., Lockhaven Univ. Penn., LSUS Med. Ctr., Shreveport, LA. Art chmn. Jr. League, Shreveport, 1955-60; bd. dirs. Holiday-in-Dixie Cotillion, Shreveport, 1974-76. Inducted into Visual Artists Hall of Fame, Shreveport, La., 1998. Mem. Nat. Assn. Women Artists, Nat. Watercolor Soc. (signature mem. 1994, 96), Southwestern Watercolor Soc. (signature mem. 1991), La. Watercolor Soc. (signature mem. 1990), La. Artists Inc. (elected mem.), Internat. Soc. Exptl. Artists (signature mem.), Western Fedn. Soc. Artists (signature mem.). Episcopalian. Avocation: tennis. E-mail: jwray@softdisk.com. Home: 573 Spring Lake Dr Shreveport LA 71106-4603

WRAY, ROBERT, lawyer; s. George and Ann (Moriarty) W.; m. Lila Keogh (dec.); children: Jennifer, Edward, Hillary. BS, Loyola U., 1957; JD, U. Mich., 1960. Bar: D.C., Ill. 1960. Assoc. Hopkins & Sutter, Chgo., 1964-69; gen. counsel Agy. for Internat. Devel., 1969-71; sr. counsel TRW, Inc., 1972-73, Export-Import Bank of the U.S., 1974-79; prin. Robert Wray Assocs., 1979-86; internat. ptnr. Pierson, Ball & Dowd, 1986-87; prin. Robert Wray Assocs., 1988—; spec. counsel Graham & James, 1988-97; ptnr. Holland & Knight, Washington, 1997—. Recipient medal of superior honor Dept. of State. Mem. ABA, Fed. Bar Assn., Am. Soc. Internat. Law, Internat. Bar Assn., Bretton Woods Com., Met. Club, Talbot Country Club, Annapolis Yacht Club. Office: Holland & Knight 2100 Pennsylvania Ave NW Washington DC 20037-3295

WREDE, RABBE KENNETH, lawyer; b. Turku, Finland, July 13, 1944; s. Rabbe Casper and Ebba Elisabeth (Reuter) W.; m. Christina Elisabeth Reincke, Oct. 5, 1968; children: Catharina, Antoinette, Natascha. Student, Classicum, Turku, 1962; BBA, Econ. Sch., Turku, 1963; LLM, U. Helsinki, Helsinki, Finland, 1969. Assoc. law Palotie law firm, Helsinki, 1969-75; mem. Palotie law firm, 1975-78; pvt. practice law Helsinki, 1978-80; ptnr. Nordic Law Consultants, Helsinki, 1980-82; pvt. practice law Helsinki, 1982-88; mng. ptnr. Wrede & Furstenborg, Helsinki, 1989-91, Wrede & Co., Helsinki, 1991—. Co-author: Tax Incentives in Developed and Development Countries, The Lawyers Guide to Transnational Corporate Acquisitions, Mergers and Acquisitions, Meeting the Challenges in Europe and America After 1992, Corporate Insolvency and Rescue, The International Dimension; contbr. articles to profl. jours. Named Hon. Consul of Jamaica. Mem. Finnish Bar Assn., Internat. Bar Assn., Assn. Internat. Protection Property Indsl., Licensing Exec. Soc.-Scandinavia, EEC-Soc. Finland, Stock Exchange Club, Rotary. E-mail: kenneth.wrede@wredeco.fi. Office: Wrede & Co, P Kasarmikatu 27, 00130 Helsinki Finland

WREGE, JULIA BOUCHELLE, tennis professional, physics educator; b. Charleston, W.Va., Apr. 11, 1944; d. Dallas Payne and Mary Louise (Hagan) Bouchelle; m. Douglas Ewart Wrege, July 13, 1968; children: Dallas Ewart, Shannon Bouchelle. B.S. in Physics, Ga. Inst. Tech., 1965, M.S. in Physics, 1967. Systems analyst GE Apollo Systems, Daytona Beach, Fla., 1967-68; med. scientist Space Instruments Research, Atlanta, 1968-70; head tennis profl. Riverside Tennis Club, Atlanta, 1971-72, Am. Adventures, Roswell, Ga., 1972-75, Hampton Farms Tennis Club, Marietta, Ga., 1975-79; head women's tennis coach Ga. Inst. Tech., Atlanta, Ga., 1979-86, 91-92; v.p. Sirius Software, Inc., 1988—; instr. physics So. Coll. Tech., 1990-98; stadium chmn., umpire, referee USTA, Atlanta, 1977—; sec. Tennis Techs., Inc., 1997—. Author: Tournament Manual, 1977, 3d edit., 1989; co-developer software TMS Tennis Tournament, 1989. Pres. Dickerson Mid. Sch. Parent-Tchr.-Student Assn., Marietta, Ga., 1982-85. Named Umpire of Yr., Ga. Tennis Assn., 1978, So. Tennis Assn., 1978; Ga. Tennis Coach of Yr., Assn. Intercollegiate Athletics for Women-Ga. Tennis Coaches Assn., 1981, 82, 83; named to Ga. Tech. Athletic Hall of Fame, 1997. Mem. U.S. Profl. Tennis Assn. (pres. 1980), U.S. Tennis Assn. (mem. tennis rules com. 1999—), Intercollegiate Tennis Coaches Assn., Ga. Tennis Assn. (pres. 1976-81, 94—, v.p. 1974-76, 91-92), Atlanta Lawn Tennis Assn., Atlanta Profl. Tennis Assn., Alpha Xi Delta, Sigma Pi Sigma. Republican. Episcopalian. Home: 1366 Little Willeo Rd Marietta GA 30068-2135

WREN, BARRY GEORGE, gynecological endocrinologist, educator, researcher, consultant; b. Canowindra, NSW, Australia, Apr. 8, 1932; s. George Brien and Violet Ada (Bird) W.; m. Loloma Anne Cochrane, Jan. 2, 1957; children: Grahame, David, Michael. MB, BS, Sydney U., Australia, 1956; MD, U. NSW, 1972, M in Health Pers. Edn., 1978. Registrar KEMH, Perth, W. Australia, 1957-61, Hammersmith Hosp., London, 1961-62; dir. Maternity Svcs., We. Nigeria, 1963-64; assoc. prof. ob-gyn U. NSW, Australia, 1964-87; dir. Sydney Menopause Ctr. Royal Hosp. Women, Sydney, 1978-97, cons. Sydney Menopause Ctr., 1998—; pres. Australian Amarant Found., 1990-92. Author: Handbook of Obstetrics and Gynecology, 1978, 83, 87, 95, Your Choice, 1995; author, editor: Clinical Management of Menopause, 1996; editor: Proceedings 8th International Congress on Menopause, 1997. Decorated Order of Australia, 1999; recipient Inaugural Distinction award Australian Menopause Soc., 1995; Fotheringham fellow Royal Australian Coll. Ob-gyn, 1959. Fellow Royal Australian Coll. Obgyn., Royal Coll. Ob-gyn., Internat. Gynecol. Endocrinology Soc., Internat. Menopause Soc. (mem. sci. com. 1993-96, mem. exec. com. 1993-99), Australian Med. Assn., Australasian Menopause Soc. (1st pres. 1988-89). Avocations: golf, exploration. Home: 78 John St, Woollahra NSW 2025, Australia Office: 506/180 Ocean St, Edgecliff NSW 2027, Australia

WRIGHT, ALFRED GEORGE JAMES, band symphony orchestra conductor, educator; b. London, June 23, 1916; came to U.S., 1922, naturalized, 1936; s. Alfred Francis and Elizabeth (Chapman) W.; m. Bertha Marie Farmer, Aug. 6, 1938; children: Adele Marie Wright Needham, Cynthia Elaine Wright Williams; m. Gladys Violet Stone, June 28, 1953. BA, U. Miami, 1937, MEd, 1947; PhD (hon.), Troy State U., 1980. Dir. music Miami Sr. High Sch., 1938-54; prof., head dept. bands Purdue U., Lafayette, Ind., 1954-85; founder, condr. U.S. Coll. Wind Band Tours, 1971—; pres. Internat. Music Tours, Inc.; v.p., exec. sec. Music Tour Svcs., Inc.; dir. pre-race pageant Indpls. 500 Mile Automobile Race, 1957-82; mem. adv. coun. Performing Arts Abroad, 1972—; chmn. N.Am. Band Dirs. Coordinating Commn., 1974-75, Nat. H.S. Honors Band, 1975-76, 77—; jury World Music Contest, Holland, 1974, 70, 81, 85; bd. dirs. 500 Festival Assocs., 1961-81; founder, chmn. bd. dirs. Hall of Fame Disting. Band Condrs.; pres. All Am. Hall of Fame Band Found.; chmn. bd., CEO John Philip Sousa Meml. Found., 1979—. Founding condr., Purdue U. Symphony Orch., 1971-81; Author: The Show Band, 1957, Marching Band Fundamentals, 1963, Bands of the World, 1970; marching band editor: Instrumentalist mag, 1953-81; contbr. articles to profl. mags. Mem. bd. advisors Internat. Music Festivals, 1989; bd. dirs. World Assn. Wind Bands and Ensembles Found., 1991-94. Decorated Star of the Order John Philip Sousa; recipient Disting. Svc. award Purdue U., 1993. Mem. Nat. Band Assn. (founder, pres. 1960-63, hon. life pres. 1973), Coll. Band Dirs. Nat. Assn., Am. Sch. Band Dirs. Nat. Assn., Japan Marching Band Assn. (hon. bd. dirs. 1971-77), Big Ten Band Dirs. Assn. (pres. 1977), Am. Bandmasters Found. (bd. dirs. 1987-89), Am. Bandmasters Assn. (pres. 1979-80), Nat. Acad. Wind and Percussive Arts (founder, chmn. 1961-81), Phi Mu Alpha, Kappa Kappa Psi (Disting. Svc. award 1981), Phi Beta Mu. Home and Office: 345 Overlook Dr West Lafayette IN 47906-1249

WRIGHT, BARBARA, foreign language educator; b. Dublin, Ireland, Mar. 8, 1935; d. William Edward and Rosaleen Hilda (Hoskin) Robinson; m. William Wright, July 14, 1961; 1 child, Jonathan Hetherington. BA, LLB, Trinity Coll., Dublin, 1956, LittD, 1995; PhD, Cambridge (Eng.) U., 1962. Asst. lectr. Manchester (Eng.) U., 1960-61; lectr. Exeter U., 1963-65; lectr. to assoc. prof. Trinity Coll., Dublin, 1965-78, personal chair French lit., 1978—, dean faculty arts, 1983-86, 90-96. Editor: Eugène Fromentin: Correspondance Génerale, 1995; author: Eugène Fromentin: A Life in Art and Letters, 2000—; contbr. articles to profl. jours. Mem. Royal Irish Acad., Academia Europaea. Avocation: music. Office: Trinity Coll Arts bldg, Dept French, Dublin 2, Ireland

WRIGHT, BETH SEGAL, art historian, educator; b. N.Y.C., July 23, 1949; d. Ben and Ella (Litvack) Segal; m. Woodring Erik J. Wright, Sept. 5, 1971; children: Benjamin, Joshua. AB cum laude, Brandeis U., 1970; MA, U. Calif., Berkeley, 1972, PhD, 1978. Instr. Mountain View Coll., Dallas, 1978-82; lectr. U. Tex., Dallas, 1980-81, Tex. Christian U., Ft. Worth, 1981; asst. prof. U. Tex., Arlington, 1984-88, assoc. prof., 1988-98, prof., 1998—; adj. and vis. asst. prof. art history U. Tex., Arlington, 1981-84. Author: Painting and History During the French Restoration. Abandoned by the Past, 1997; contbr. articles to Art Bull., Arts Mag., Word & Image, Oxford Art Jour., Nouvelles de l'Estampe, Clio, others. Kress Found. hon. traveling fellow, 1975-76; NEH Travel to Collections grantee, Paris, 1987, 93; U. Tex. Arlington Rsch. Enhancement grantee, Paris, 1990, 93, 99, Coll. Art Assoc. Meiss grant, 1996; recipient Dallas Mus. Art Vasari award Painting and History, 1998. Mem. Soc. Histoire Art Français (contbr. articles to bull.), Am. Soc. for 18th-Century Studies, Coll. Art Assn., Midwest Art History Soc. (bd. dirs. 1990-93).

WRIGHT, C. T. ENUS, former academic administrator; b. Social Circle, Ga., Oct. 4, 1942; s. George and Carrie Mae (Enus) W.; m. Mary Stephens, Aug. 9, 1974. BS, Fort Valley State U. (Ga.), Ga., 1964; MA, Atlanta U., 1967; PhD, Boston U., 1977; LHD, Mary Holmes Coll., 2000. Tchr. Ga. Pub. Schs., Social Circle, 1965-67; mem. faculty Morris Brown Coll., Atlanta, 1967-73, divsn. chmn., 1973-77; program dir., asst. provost Eastern Wash. U., Cheney, 1977-81; v.p. acad. affairs Talladega Coll. (Ala.), 1981-82; pres. Cheyney U. Pa., Cheyney, 1982-85; v.p. and provost Fla. Meml. Coll., 1985-89; exec. dir. Internat. Found. and Coord. African-African Am. Summit, 1989—; cons. and lectr. in field; bd. dirs. IFESH, England, Leow Sullivan Trust, So. Africa, Peoples Investment Fund for Africa. Author: (booklet) The History of Black Historical Mythology, 1980; contbr. articles to profl. jours. Commnr., Wash. Pub. Broadcasting, Olympia, 1980-84; exec. com. Boy Scouts Am., Phila., 1982—; Goodwill Amb. State of Ga., 1997—. Human Rels. scholar, 1969, Nat. Tchg. fellow Boston U., 1971. Mem. Am. Assn. Colls. and Univs. (coms. 1982—), Am. Hist. Assn. (coms. 1970—), Assn. Study Afro-Am. Life & History (coms. 1965—), Nat. Assn. Equal Opportunity in Higher Edn. (coms. 1982—), NEA (coms. 1965—). Am. Baptist. Clubs: Lions (Cheyney, Wash. (v.p. 1979-81), Tuscan, Fountain Hills Times, Atlanta Constitution. Address: 17420 E Dull Knife Dr Fountain Hls AZ 85268-3218

WRIGHT, CAROLE DEAN, reading specialist; b. Mt. Clemens, Mich., Aug. 18, 1943; d. Edward Lawrence and Alice Agnes Hundt; m. David John Wright, Dec. 20, 1964 (div. Sept. 1984); 1 child, Amy Elizabeth. BA, Mich. State U., 1964, MA, 1967. Reading specialist Holt (Mich.) Pub. Schs., 1965-70, Ypsilanti (Mich.) Pub. Schs., 1970-71, Aurora (Colo.) Pub. Schs., 1972—; pres. Aurora Edn. Assn., 1978-80, Colo. Edn. Assn., Denver, 1982; mem. adv. com. Nat. Assessment of Ednl. Progress, Denver, 1975; chair unit accreditation bd. Nat. Coun. Accreditation of Tchr. Edn., Washington, 1990-99; trustee Pub. Employees Retirement Assn. Colo., 1993 . Contbg. author to Idea's for Children's Literature, 1976. Mem. Colo. Commn. on Tchr. Edn. and Accreditation, Denver, 1976-82; vice chair Gov.'s Chpt. 2 Adv. Com., Denver, 1987-93. Named Outstanding Educator, Fed. Programs Adminstr. Coun. U.S. Dept. Edn., 1991. Mem. NEA (bd. dirs. 1984-87), Internat. Reading Assn., Colo. Edn. Assn. (v.p. 1980-81, 83-84, pres. 1982, award 1999), Phi Delta Kappa (Leadership award 1998). Home: 2268 Clermont St Denver CO 80207-3740

WRIGHT, CHARLES ALAN, law educator, author; b. Phila., Sept. 3, 1927; s. Charles Adshead and Helen (McCormack) W.; m. Mary Joan Herriott, July 8, 1950 (div. Jan. 1955); 1 child, Charles Edward; m. Eleanor Custis Broyles Clarke, Dec. 17, 1955; children: Henrietta, Cecily; stepchildren: Eleanor Custis Clarke, Margot Clarke. BA, Wesleyan U., Middletown, Conn., 1947; LL.B., Yale U., 1949; LHD (hon.), Episcopal Theol. Sem. S.W., 1992. Bar: Minn. 1951, Tex. 1959. Law clk. to Hon. Charles E. Clark, U.S. Ct. Appeals (2d cir.), New Haven, 1949-50; asst. prof. law U. Minn., Mpls., 1950-53, assoc. prof., 1953-55; assoc. prof. law U. Tex., Austin, 1955-58, prof., 1958-65, McCormick prof., 1965-80, Bates prof., 1980-97; Arthur Goodhart vis. prof. legal sci. Cambridge (Eng.) U., 1990-91, Hayden W. Head regents chair, 1990-91; Charles Alan Wright chair in Fed. Cts. U. Tex., Austin, 1997-2000; vis. prof. U. Pa., 1959-60. Harvard U., 1964-65, Yale U., 1968-69; vis. fellow Wolfson Coll., Cambridge U., 1984; reporter study div. of jurisdiction between state and fed. cts. Am. Law Inst., 1963-69; mem. adv. com. on civil rules Jud. Conf. U.S., 1961-64, standing com. on rules of practice and proc., 1964-76, 87-93; cons., counsel for Pres., 1973-74; mem. com. on infractions NCAA, 1973-83, chmn., 1978-83, chmn. adminstrv. rev. panel, 1993-94; mem. permanent com for Oliver Wendell Holmes Devise, 1975-83; mem. Commn. on Bicentennial of U.S. Constn., 1985-92; U. Tex. faculty athletics rep. NCAA, Big 12 Confs., 1999—. Author: Wright's Minnesota Rules, 1954, Cases on Remedies, 1955; (with C.T. McCormick and J.H. Chadbourn) Cases on Federal Courts, 9th edit., 1992, 10th edit. (with John B. Oakley), 1999, Handbook of the Law of Federal Courts, 5th edit., 1994; (with H.M. Reasoner) Procedure-The Handmaid of Justice, 1965, Federal Practice and Procedure: Criminal, 3d edit., 1997; (with A.R. Miller) Federal Practice and Procedure: Civil, 1969-99, 3d edit. (with Miller and E.H. Cooper), 1999, Federal Practice and Procedure: Jurisdiction and Related Matters, 1975-82, 3rd edit., 1998; (with V.J. Gold) Federal Practice and Procedure: Evidence, 1977—; mem. editl. bd. Supreme Ct. Hist. Soc. Yearbook, 1987-93—. Trustee St. Stephen's Episc. Sch., Austin, Tex., 1962-66, St. Andrew's Episc. Sch., Austin, 1971-74, 77-80, 81-84, chmn. bd., 1973-74, 79-80; trustee Capitol Broadcasting Assn., Austin, 1966—, chmn. bd., 1969-90; trustee Austin Symphony Orch., 1966—, mem. exec. com., 1966-70, 72-83, 86—; trustee Austin Choral Union, 1984-90, Austin Lyric Opera Soc., 1986—; bd. dirs. Am. Friends of Cambridge (Eng.) U., 1994—; corr. fellow British Acad., 1999. Recipient Fordham-Stein prize Fordham U., 1997, Learned Hand medal Fed. Bar Co., 1998, Lifetime Achievement award U. Tex. Law Sch. Alumni Assn., 2000; hon. fellow Wolfson Coll. Cambridge U., 1986—. Mem. ABA (commn. on standards jud. adminstrn. 1970-77, ho. of dels. 1993—), AAAS, Am. Law Inst. (coun. 1969—, 2d v.p. 1987-88, 1st v.p. 1988-92, pres. 1993—), Am. Bar Found. (Rsch. award 1989), Inst. Jud. Adminstrn., Am. Judicature Soc., Philos. Soc. Tex., Am. Friends Cambridge U. (bd. dirs. 1994—), Country Club, Tarry House Club, Headliners Club, Ridge Harbor Yacht Club, Barton Creek Lakeside Club (Austin), Century Club, Yale Club (N.Y.C.), Mid Ocean Club (Bermuda), Oxford Club, Cambridge Club (England). Republican. Episcopalian. Avocations: reading and reviewing mysteries, railroads, fishing, coaching Legal Eagles (intramural touch football team). Home: 5304 Western Hills Dr Austin TX 78731-4822 Office: U Tex Sch Law 727 Dean E Keeton St Austin TX 78705-3224 *Died July 7, 2000.*

WRIGHT, DANIEL BROOKS, psychology educator, researcher; b. L.A., Nov. 25, 1965; s. Kenneth Brooks and Sandra Beryl (Smith) W.; m. Rachel George, Aug. 13, 1993. BA in Math., Pomona Coll., Claremont, Calif., 1987; MSc in Econ., London Sch. Econ., 1988, PhD in Psychology, 1992. Rsch. officer London Sch. Econ., 1991-93; British Acad. rsch. fellow City U., London, 1994-96; lectr. Bristol (Eng.) U., 1996—; reader in psychology, 2000—. Author: Understanding Statistics, 1997, also papers; co-editor: Surveying Memory Processes, 1998. Mem. Am. Psychol. Soc., British Psychology Soc. (chmn. math., stats., and computing sect. 1996-99, mem. coun. 1997—), Psychonomics Soc. Office: Cognitive/Computing Scis, U Sussex Falmer, Brighton BN1 9QH, England

WRIGHT, DAVID, diplomat; b. Montreal, Can.; m. Ilze Skuja; 1 child, Julian. BSc in Math. and Econs., McGill U., 1966; MBA in Internat. Finance, Columbia U., 1968. Fgn. svc. officer Ottawa, Can., 1968-69; 2d sec. Can. Embassy, Rome, 1969-72; 1st sec., Can. Perm. Mission to UN N.Y.C., 1972-75; with external affairs, Econ. Bur. Govt. of Can., Ottawa, 1975-78; econ. counsellor Can. Embassy, Tokyo, 1978-82; dir. Policy Planning Bur., external affairs Govt. of Can., Ottawa, 1982-85, dir. gen. Econ. Policy Bur., 1985-87; minister plenipotentiary Can. Embassy, Paris, 1987-90; asst. dep. minister Fgn. Affairs for Europe Govt. of Can., 1990-94; Can. amb. to Spain Can. Embassy, 1994-97; amb., perm. rep. of Can. to NATO, 1997—. Contbr. articles to profl. jours. Office: NATO Hdqrs, Blvd Leopold III, 1110 Brussels Belgium*

WRIGHT, DAVID FREDERICK, religious studies educator; b. Hayes, Kent, Eng., Oct. 2, 1937; s. Harry George Durie and Dorothy Emily (Forster) W.; m. Anne-Marie MacDonald, Mar. 27, 1967; children: Andrew, Jenny. MA, U. Cambridge, Eng., 1961; DD, U. Edinburgh, Scotland, 1997. Lectr. in ecclesiastical history U. Edinburgh, 1964-73, sr. lectr., 1973-99, prof. patristic and reformed Christianity, 1999—; dean faculty of divinity U. Edinburgh, 1988-92; mem. Ctr. of Theol. Inquiry, Princeton, N.J., 1988—; vis. fellow Hill Monastic Manuscript Libr., Collegeville, Minn., 1980; chmn. bd. dirs. Handsel Press, Edinburgh, 1990—; sec. praesidium Internat. Congress on Calvin Rsch., 2000—. Chief gen. editor, contbr.: Dictionary of Scottish Church History and Theology, 1993; joint editor, contbr.: Disruption to Diversity: Edinburgh Divinity 1846-1996, 1996; editor, contbr.: Martin Bucer: Reforming Church and Community, 1994; trans., editor: Common Places of Martin Bucer, 1972. Chair Tyndale Fellowship for Biblical and Theol. Rsch., U.K., 1987-99; bd. dirs. Internat. Christian Coll., Glasgow, Scotland, 1984—; mem. coun. Whitefield Inst., Oxford, 1988-2000, Keston (Eng.) Coll., 1975-91. Fellow Royal Hist. Soc.; mem. Assn. Internat. d'Etudes Patristiques, N.Am. Patristics Soc., Ecclesiastical History Soc., Scottish Ch. History Soc. Mem. Ch. of Scotland. Avocations: gardening, walking, reading. Home: 3 Camus Rd E, Edinburgh EH10 6RE, Scotland Office: New Coll, Mound Pl, Edinburgh EH1 2LX, Scotland

WRIGHT, DAVID JOHN, telecommunications systems specialist, educator; b. London, June 20, 1947; arrived in Canada, 1981; s. John William and Doreen Mary W.; m. Mina Wright; children: Leila, Ramin. BA with honors, Cambridge U., 1968, PhD, 1972. Sr. scientific officer Dept. Environment, London, 1972-76; lectr. Ahmadu Bello U., Zaria, Nigeria, 1976-78, Sussex U., Brighton, United Kingdom, 1978-81; assoc. prof. U. Ottawa, Canada, 1981-87, prof., 1987—; vis. rschr. Nortel Networks, Ottawa, 1988-89; provider tng. to telecomms. industry with specialty in ATM, packet voice and electronic commerce. Author: Broadband: Business Services, Technologies and Strategic Impact, 1993 (translated into Japanese, 1994), Telelearning via the Internet, 1999, The Business Base for the Web Based Training, 2000; contbr. articles to profl. jours. and chpts. to books; editor-in-chief INFOR, 1985—. Mem. IEEE, Assn. for Computing Machinery. Avocation: piano.

WRIGHT, DONALD GENE, accountant; b. Grand Junction, Tenn., June 7, 1950; s. Ernest Young and Frances Irene (Reeder) W.; children: Richard Benjamin, Jacqueline; m. Helen "Vicki" Elizabeth Holt Wright, Oct. 1, 1988; step children: Veronica Reynolds Garcia, Mindy Reynolds Barrett. A Engring. (equivalent), U. Tenn., Martin, 1970; BBA in Acctg., Lambeth U., 1995. Cost acctg. clk. Harman Automotive, Inc., Bolivar, Tenn., 1975-79, sr. acct., 1979-85, budget & spl. projects mgr., 1985-92, acctg., estimating mgr., 1992-95; contr. Hutchinson Sealing Sys., Inc., Wytheville, Va., 1995—, Hutchinson Rubber Mixing Tech. Ctr., Wytheville, Va., 1995-99; bd. dirs. West Tenn. Chpt. NAA, Jackson, Tenn., 1987-95. Editor: VP Communications Monthly Newsletter, 1991, Director of Newsletter Monthly Newsletter, 1989. Mem. Nat. Assn. Accts. (pres. West Tenn. chpt.), Gideon's Internat. Methodist. Avocations: martial arts, home improvement, travel. Home: 235 S 10th St Wytheville VA 24382-3703 Office: Hutchinson Sealing Sys Inc 1150 S 3rd St Wytheville VA 24382-3925 also: Rubbu Mixing Tech Ctr 455 Industry Rd Wytheville VA 24382-3491

WRIGHT, DONALD IAN, history educator; b. Aldgate, Australia, Oct. 22, 1934; s. Cyril Noel and Florence (Lemaistre) W.; m. Janice Melva Gambling, Feb. 9, 1937; children: David Arthur, Alan Michael, Ian Mark. BA with honors, Adelaide U., 1965; PhD, Australian Nat. U., 1968. Tchr. South Australian Edn. Dept., Murray Bridge, 1956-63; sr. master Westminster Sch., Adelaide, Australia, 1963-65; from lectr. to assoc. prof. history U. Newcastle, Newcastle, N.S.W., Australia, 1968-93; head history dept. U. Newcastle, 1984-88, pres. staff assn., 1982-85, dean faculty arts, 1988. Author: Shadow of Dispute, 1970, Mantle of Christ, 1984, Looking Back, 1992, The Methodists, 1993, Dalmar-A Century of Caring, 1993, Alan Walker: Conscience of the Nation, 1997; editor: The French Revolution, 1974; editor, co-author: Federalism in Canada and Australia, 1978; contbr. articles to profl. jours. Pres. Specific Learning Difficulties Assn., Newcastle, 1973-76; mem. founding bd. Pacific Coll. Evangelism, Sydney, Australia, 1987-97; mem. Coun. of U. Newcastle, 1982-88. Mem. Uniting Church Hist. Soc. N.S.W. Mem. Uniting Church in Australia. Avocations: driving, lay preaching, walking. Office: U Newcastle, University Dr, Newcastle NSW, Australia 2308

WRIGHT, FRANCES JANE, educational psychologist; b. L.A., Dec. 22, 1943; d. step-father John David and Evelyn Jane (Dale) Brinegar. BA, Long Beach State U., 1965; MA, Brigham Young U., 1968, EdD, 1980; postgrad., U. Nev., 1970, U. Utah, 1972-73; postdoctoral, Utah State U., 1985-86. Cert. secondary tchr., adminstr., Utah. Asst. dir. Teenpost Project, San Pedro, Calif., 1966; caseworker Los Angeles County, 1966-67; self-care inservice dir. Utah State Tng. Sch., American Fork, Utah, 1968, vocat. project designer, 1968; tchr. mentally handicapped Santa Ana Unified Schs., Calif., 1968-69; state specialist intellectually handicapped State Office Edn., Salt Lake City, 1969-70; vocat. counselor Manpower, Salt Lake City, 1970-71; tchr. severely handicapped Davis County Schs., Farmington, Utah, 1971-73, diagnostician, 1973-74, resource elem. tchr., 1974-78; instr. Brigham Young U., Salt Lake City, 1976-83; resource tchr. jr. high Davis County Schs., Farmington, 1978-90; ednl. cons. Murray, Utah, 1973-90; chief ednl. diagnostician Ctr. for Evaluation of Learning and Devel., Layton, Utah, 1989-90; clin. dir. assessment and observation program Idaho Youth Ranch, 1990-95, clin. dir. intake program, 1992-94, supr. family preservation svc./aftercare teams, 1993-95, co-ranch treatment dir. and placement officer, 1995; cons. juvenile correctional dist. 5, 1996—; clin. cons. Magic Hot Springs Youth Camp, 1996-97; mem. cmty. accountability bd. McNeil Assn., 1996—, Dist. 5 Juvenile Justice Coun., 1997—, parent project facilitator, 1998—; trainer Detour prison prevention programfor adolescents, 1997—; cons. Northstar Family Preservation, 1997—; acting chmn . Dist. 5 Juvenile Justice Coun., 1998-99, chmn. 1999—; mem. Ida ho Juvenile Justice Commn., 1999—; adv. bd. So. Central Learning Ctr., 1999—; mem. oversight bd., evaluator Status Offender prog. 1997—; lectr. in field. Named Profl. of Yr. Utah Assn. for Children with Learning Disabilities, 1985. Mem. Assn. Children/Adults with Learning Disabilities (del. 1979-85, 87, nat. nominating com., 1985-86, nat. bd. dirs. 1988-91), Utah Assn. Children/Adults with Learning Disabilities (exec. bd. 1978-84, profl. adv. bd. 1985-90, coord. LDA orgn. Idaho 1991—), Coun. Exceptional Children (div. learning disabilities, ednl. diagnostics, behavioral disorders), Coun. Learning Disabilities, ASCD (regional adv.), Windstar Found., Nat. Wildlife Found., World Wildlife Fedn., Best Friends Animal Sanctuary, Cousteau Soc., Nat. Assn. Sch. Adminstrs., Job's Daughters. Democrat. Mormon. Avocations: geneaology research, horseback riding, sketching, crafts, reading. Home: 2176 Julie Ln Twin Falls ID 83301-8361 Office: Youth Ctr Juvenile Corrections 2469 Wright Ave Twin Falls ID 83301-7972

WRIGHT, FRANK BEVERLEY, law educator; b. Leeds, Yorkshire, Eng., Oct. 7, 1947; s. Frank and Edith Anne (Foster) W.; m. Dorothy Jean Hannant, Oct. 6, 1973; children: Evelyn, Elizabeth, Adrian. LLB, Leeds U., Eng., 1977; postgrad. diploma, U. Nice, France, 1984; LLM, Leicester U., Eng., 1989, PhD, 1995. Pub. health diplomate. Local govt. officer City of Westminster, London, 1971-79; lectr. law Leeds Poly., 1979-83, sr. lectr. law, 1983-87; lectr. law U. Salford, Eng., 1988-92, sr. lectr. law, 1992-97, prof. law, 1997—; advisor Internat. Thomson Pub., Can., 1993-99; expert Internat. Labour Orgn., Geneva, 1992—, European Commn., Brussels, 1989-92; cons. John Mowlem Group of Cos., London, 1992—. Author: Law of Health and Safety at Work, 1997, Guide to the Noise at Work Regulations, 1990; author/editor: (CD-ROM) European Communities' Health and Safety Legislation, 1997, Occupational Health and Safety Law in the United Kingdom; contbr. Ency. Occupl. Health and Safety, 4th edit., 1998. Dep. chmn. Royal Soc. Health, London, 1997; mem. Internat. Coun. of Environ. Law, 1980—; mem. ct., coun. and senate U. Leeds, 1975-76; reader The Queen's Anniversary Prizes for Higher and Further Edn., Nat. Awards Scheme, Royal Anniversary Trust, 1994—. Fellow Royal Inst. Pub. Health and Hygiene, Royal Soc. Health, Chartered Inst. Environ. Health. Avocations: chess, bridge, travel, music, gardening. Office: Univ of Salford, The Crescent, Salford M5 4WT, England

WRIGHT, GAVIN, economics educator; b. New Haven, Sept. 30, 1943; s. Charles F. and Agnita Marie Greisen W.; m. Cathe Winn Wright, Sept. 4, 1965; children: Anders, Nicholas. BA, Swarthmore Coll., 1965; PhD, Yale U., 1969. Asst. prof. Yale U., New Haven, 1969-71; asst. prof. U. Mich., Ann Arbor, 1971-74, assoc. prof., 1974-79, prof., 1979-82; prof. Sanford (Calif.) U., 1982—, William Robertson Coe prof. Am. econ. history, 1994—; Pitt prof. Am. history and instns. U. Cambridge, Eng., 1994-95; vis. fellow All Souls Coll., Oxford, Eng., 1999. Author: The Political Economy of the Cotton South, 1978, Old South, New South, 1986. Recipient Owsley prize So. Hist. Assn. Mem. Am. Econ. Assn. (mem. exec. com. 1992-95), Econ. History Assn. (pres. 1997-98). E-mail: write@leland.stanford.edu. Office: Stanford U Dept Econ Stanford CA 94305

WRIGHT, GLADYS STONE, music educator, composer, writer; b. Wasco, Oreg., Mar. 8, 1925; d. Murvel Stuart and Daisy Violet (Warren) Stone; m. Alfred George Wright, June 28, 1953. BS, U. Oreg., 1948, MS, 1953. Dir. bands Elmira (Oreg.) U-4 High Sch., 1948-53, Otterbein (Ind.) High Sch., 1954-61, Klondike High Sch., West Lafayette, Ind., 1962-70, Harrison High Sch., West Lafayette, 1970-84; organizer, condr. Musical Friendship Tours, Cen. Am., 1967-79; v.p., condr. U.S. Collegiate Wind Band, 1975—; bd. dirs. John Philip Sousa Found. 1984—; chmn. Sudler Cup, 1986—, Sudler Flag, 1982; pres. Internat. Music Tours, 1984—, Key to the City, Taxco, Mex., 1975. Editor: Woman Conductor, 1986—; composer: marches Big Bowl and Trumpets and Tabards, 1987; contbg. editor: Informusica (Spain). Bd. dirs. N. Am. Wildlife Park, Battleground, Ind. 1985. Recipient Medal of the order John Philip Sousa Found., 1988, Star of Order, 1991; 1st woman guest conductor U.S. Navy Band, Washington D.C., 1961, Goldman Band, N.Y.C., 1958, Kneller Hall Band, London, 1975, Tri-State Music Festival Massed Orch., Band, Choir, 1985; elected to Women Bd. Dirs. Hall of Fame of Disting. Women Conductor, 1994; inductee Hall of Fame Disting. Condrs., Nat. Band Assn., 1999. Mem. Am. Bandmasters Assn. (bd. dirs. 1993, 1st woman mem.), Women Band Dirs. Nat. Assn. (founding pres. 1967, sec. 1985, recipient Silver Baton 1974, Golden Rose 1990, Hall of Fame 1995), Am. Sch. Band Dirs. Assn., Nat. Band Assn. (Citation excellence 1970), Tippecoanoe Arts Fedn. (bd. dirs. 1986-90), Tippecanoe Fife and Drum Corps. (bd. dirs. 1984), Daughters of Am. Revolution, Col. Dames-Pre Quitanen Chpt., New England Women, Tau Beta Sigma (Outstanding Svc. to Music award 1970), Phi Beta Mu (1st hon. women mem. 1972), North Am. Wildlife Park (bd dirs, 1990—). Avocations: historic preservation, environ. activities.

WRIGHT, HELEN CLARE, physical education educator, researcher; b. London, Jan. 3, 1956; arrived in Singapore, 1987; d. Francis Edmund and Eileen Mary (Matthews) W.; m. Daniel Guillaume Soucie. B in Edn. with honors, U. London, 1979; MSc, U. Loughborough, Eng., 1987; PhD, U. Leeds, Eng., 1996. Cert. in edn. (with distinction), U. London, 1977. Tchr. Abbotsford H.S., London, 1979-80, Hillside H.S., Liverpool, Eng., 1980-81, Woodchurch H.S., Liverpool, Eng., 1981-82; lectr. Hugh Baird Coll., Liverpool, Eng., 1983-84; tchr. Amman (Jordan) Baccalaureate Sch., 1984-86; univ. lectr. Nanyang Technol. U., Singapore, 1987—. Co-author: Motor Coordination Disorders in Children, Physical Education for All; contbr. chpt. to books, articles to profl. jours; reviewer Human Movement Scis., 1997, Brit. Jour. Ednl. Psychology, 1996, European Jour. Phys. Edn., 1996, 98, Jour. Disability, Devel. and Edn. Rsch. grantee Nanyang Technol. U., 1992. Mem. Brit. Assn. Sport and Exercise Scis. (Best Student Presentation award 1994), Phys. Edn. Assn. U.K., Singapore Phys. Edn. Assn. Avocations: tennis, squash, swimming, cinema, classical music. Office: Nanyang Technol U, 469 Bukit Timah Rd, S259756 Singapore Singapore

WRIGHT, HELEN KENNEDY, retired professional association administrator, publisher, editor, librarian; b. Indpls., Sept. 23, 1927; d. William Henry and Ida Louise (Crosby) Kennedy; m. Samuel A. Wright, Sept. 5, 1970 (dec. 1998); 1 child, Carl F. Prince II (dec.). BA, Butler U., 1945, MS, 1950; MS, Columbia U., 1952. Reference libr. N.Y. Pub. Libr., N.Y.C., 1952-53, Bklyn. Pub. Libr., 1953-54; reference libr., cataloger U. Utah, 1954-57; libr. Chgo. Pub. Libr.; asst. dir. pub. svcs. ALA, Chgo., 1958-62, editor Reference Books Bull., 1962-65, asst. dir. for new product planning, pub. svcs., 1985-89, dir. office for libr. outreach svcs., 1987-90, mng. editor yearbook, 1988-89. Contbr. to Ency. of Careers, Ency. of Libr. and Info. Sci., New Book of Knowledge Ency., Bull. of Bibliography, New Golden Book Ency. Recipient Louis Shores/Oryx award, 1991. Mem. Phi Kappa Phi, Kappa Delta Pi, Sigma Gamma Rho. Roman Catholic. Home: 1138 W 111th St Chicago IL 60643-4508

WRIGHT, HELEN PATTON, professional society administrator; b. Washington, Jan. 15, 1919; d. Raymond Stanton and Virginia (Mitchell) Patton; m. James Skelly Wright, Feb. 1, 1945 (dec. 1988); 1 son, James Skelly; m. John H. Pickering, Feb. 3, 1990. Student, Sweet Briar Coll., 1936-38; grad., Washington Sch. Secretaries, 1939, Am. U., 1989. Tchr. Washington Sch. Secs., N.Y.C., 1939-40; sec. The White House, 1941-43, Am. Embassy, London, 1943-45; asst. to exec. dir. Senate Atomic Energy Com., 1946-47. Author: My Journey Recollections of the First Seventy Years, 1995. V.p., mem. budget and admissions com. United Fund New Orleans, 1960-62; chmn. met. div., campaign; v.p. Dept. Pub. Welfare, Orleans Parish and City New Orleans, 1960-62, Milne Asylum for Destitute Orphan Boys, New Orleans, 1958-62; mem. bd. New Orleans Social Welfare Planning Coun., 1954-62, New Orleans Cancer Soc., 1958-60; v.p. Juvenile Ct. Adv. Com. New Orleans, 1961; successively sec., v.p., pres. Parents' Assn. Metairie Park Country Day Sch., 1956-59; v.p. La. Assn. Mental Health, 1960-62; del. dir. to Nat. Assn. Mental Health, 1960-62; bd. mem. Washington Health and Welfare Coun., 1962-64, Hillcrest Children's Ctr., Washington, 1963-69, D.C. Mental Health Assn., 1962-72, 73-76; bd. dirs. Hospice Care of D.C., 1981-88, 90-96, pres., 1986-88; mem. adv. bd. civil commitment project Nat. Ctr. for State Cts., 1981; bd. dirs. Nat. Assn. Mental Health, 1960-66, 67-74, sec., 1968-70, pres.-elect, 1970-71, pres., 1972-73, cons. on assn. film, 1972; mem. commn. on mentally disabled ABA, 1973-80, commn. on legal problems of elderly, 1997; mem. adv. bd. Alzheimer's Assn. Greater Washington chpt., 1996; chmn. altar guild Christ Ch. Cathedral, New Orleans, 1960, Little Sanctuary of St. Albans Sch., Washington, 1965; pres. Altar Guild, St. Alban's Ch., 1976, 77; chmn. Washington com. Nat. Cathedral Assn., 1976-79, trustee, 1976-90, sec., 1977, v.p., 1980-83, trustee emeritae, 1997; bd. dirs. Nat. Ctr. Voluntary Action; mem. task panel Mental Health Problems, Scope and Boundaries, Pres.'s Commn. Mental Health, 1977; mem. tech. rev. com. Md. Psychiat. Rsch. Ctr., 1979-81. Mem. ABA (commn. on legal problems of the elderly 1997-99). Address: 5317 Blackistone Rd Bethesda MD 20816-1822

WRIGHT, JOHN SPENCER, school system administrator; b. Washington, May 8, 1948; s. Clarence S. and Florence (Nagel) W.; m. Debra Kim Buck, Aug. 4, 1973; 1 child, Deanna Michelle. BA in Econs., U. Va., 1969, MEd in Secondary Adminstrn., 1971, EdD in Adminstrn. and Supervision, 1976. Cert. social studies tchr., prin., supt., fin. officer, N.C.; registered sch. bus. adminstr. Tchr. govt. and social studies Lane H.S., Charlottesville, Va., 1969-72, spl. asst. to prin., 1972-74; supr. Sch. Gen. Learning Charlottesville H.S., 1974-75; exec. dir. Va. Assn. Sch. Execs., Charlottesville, 1976-78; prin. E.C. Glass H.S., Lynchburg, Va., 1978-82; dir. bus. svcs. Lynchburg Pub. Schs., 1982-86, dir. fin. and planning svcs., 1986; asst. supt. bus. and fin. svcs. Greensboro (N.C.) Pub. Schs., 1986-90, assoc. supt. human and fin. resources, 1990-93; assoc. supt. adminstrv. svcs. Guilford County (N.C.) Schs., 1993—; investigating probation officer 8th Regional Juvenile and Domestic Rels. Ct., Charlottesville, 1970-71; grad. asst., teaching asst. Sch. Edn., U. Va., 1975-76; rsch. asst. Tayloe Murphy Inst., U. Va., 1975-76; asst. prof. Grad. Sch. Edn., U. Va., 1976-78; part time asst. prof. Grad. Sch. Edn., U. Va., 1978-80; adj. prof. U. Va., Sch. Continuing Edn., 1983, 86. Co-author: Charlottesville Change Project: Year End Report, 1974; editor: Developments in School Law, 1976-78; contbr. articles and reviews to profl. jours. Former bd. dirs. Triad Sickle Cell Anemia Found.; former bd. dirs. Presbyn. Home and Family Svcs., Inc.; past v.p. deductible fund Local Govt. Ins. Funds, Greensboro, Guilford, N.C., past pres. liability fund; former mem. N.C. Profl. Rev. Com., 1993-98; former mem. N.C. Profl. Practices Commn., 1996-98; mem. Com. 100, Greensboro Human Rels. Commn.; Former mem. dean's coun. U. Va. Sch. Edn. Found. Mem. ASCD, Am. Assn. Sch. Adminstrs., Am. Assn. Sch. Pers. Adminstrs., Assn. Sch. Bus. Officials, Southeastern Assn. Sch. Bus. Officials, N.C. Assn. Sch. Bus. Officials (past region chmn., vice-chair and mem. state exec. com.), Edn. Law Assn., Distributive Edn. Clubs Am. (hon. life), Greensboro C. of C. (govtl. affairs coun., former minority/women bus. devel. coun.), U. Va. Alumni Assn. (former class agt.), Va. Student Aid Found., Greensboro Civitans (v.p. 1993-94, bd. dirs. 1994-96), Human Resources Mgmt. Assn. Greensboro (bd. dirs. 1997-98), Phi Delta Kappa (former chpt. treas.), Kappa Delta Pi, others. Presbyterian. Home: 4610 Charlottesville Rd Greensboro NC 27410-3655 Office: Guilford County Schools PO Box 880 Greensboro NC 27402-0880

WRIGHT, JOHN WILLIAM, psychology educator; b. Seattle, June 12, 1944; m. Donna Elene W.; children: Timothy William, Shonna Ann. BA, We. Wash. U., 1966, MS, 1968; PhD, Mich. State U. Asst. prof. psychology Fordham U., N.Y.C., 1972-75; asst. prof. psychology Wash. State U., Pullman, 1975-78, assoc. prof. psychology, 1978-83, prof. psychology, 1983—, chair psychology dept., 1994-99, dir. neurosci. program, 1998—; pres. Pacific Northwest Biotech., Pullman, 1994—. Co-author: Hypertension and Blood Pressure, 1988; contbr. over 150 articles to profl. jours. Cmty. aide, Pullman Disaster Response, 1996—. Mem. Soc. Neurosci., Am. Heart Assn., Am. Psychol. Soc., Internat. Behavioral Neurosci. Soc. Avocation: private pilot (single engine land certified). E-mail: wrightjw@wsu.edu. Office: Wash State U Dept Psychology Pullman WA 99164-0001

WRIGHT, KATIE HARPER, educational administrator, journalist; b. Crawfordsville, Ark., Oct. 5, 1923; d. James Hale and Connie Mary (Locke) Harper; m. Marvin Wright, Mar. 21, 1952; 1 child, Virginia K. Jordan. BA, U. Ill., 1944, MEd, 1959; EdD, St. Louis U., 1979. Elem. and spl. edn. tchr. East St. Louis (Ill.) Pub. Schs., 1944-65, dir. Dist. 189 Instrnl. Materials Program, 1965-71, dir. spl. edn. Dists. 188, 189, 1971-77, asst. supt. programs, 1977-79; interim supt. East St. Louis Sch. Dist, 189, 1993-94; adj. faculty Harris/Stowe State Coll., 1980; mem. staff St. Louis U., 1989—; interim supt. Dist. 189 Schs., 1994—; cons. numerous workshops, seminars in field; mem. study tour People's Republic of China, 1984. Author: Delta Sigma Theta/East St. Louis Chapter History, 1992; contbr. articles to profl. jours.; feature writer St. Louis Argus Newspaper, 1979—. Mem. Ill. Commn. on Children, 1973-85, East St. Louis Bd. Election Comms., East St. Louis Fin. Adv. Authority, 1999—; pres. bd. dirs. St. Clair County Mental Health Ctr., 1970-72, 87—; bd. dirs. River Bluff coun. Girl Scouts USA, 1979—, nat. bd. dirs., 1981-84; bd. dirs. Jackie Joyner-Kersee Youth Ctr. Found., 1991—, United Way, 1979—, Urban League, 1979—, Provident Counseling Ctr., 1995-98; pres. bd. trustees East St. Louis Pub. Libr., 1972-77; pres., bd. dirs. St. Clair County Mental Health Ctrs., 1987; mem. adv. bd. Magna Bank; charter mem. Coalition of 100 Black Women; mem. coord. coun. ethnic affairs Synod of Mid-Am., Presbyn. Ch. U.S.A.; mem. Ill. Dept. Corrections Sch. Bd., 1995—; charter mem. Metro East Links Group, Gateway chpt. The Links, Inc.; mem. Ill. Minority/Female Bus. Coun., 1991—; del. Nat. Republican Convention, 2000. Recipient of more than 150 awards including Lamp of Learning award East St. Louis Jr. Wednesday Club, 1965, Outstanding Working Woman award Downtown St. Louis, Inc., 1967, Ill. State citation for ednl. document Love is Not Enough, 1974, Delta Sigma Theta citation for document Good Works, 1979, Girl Scout Thanks badge, 1982, award Nat. Coun. Negro Women, 1983, Cmty. Svc. award Met. East Bar Assn., 1983, Journalist award Sigma Gamma Rho, Spelman Coll. Alumni award, 1990, A World of Difference award, 1990, 92, Edn. award St. Louis, YWCA, 1991, SIU-E-Kimmel award, 1991, St. Clair County Mental Health award, 1992, Gateway East Met. Ministry Dr. M.L. King award, 1993, Nat. Coun. Negro Women Black Leader of Yr., 1995, Disting. Alumni award U. Ill., 1996, Pioneer award Mosque 28B, 2000; named Woman of Achievement, St. Louis Globe Democrat, 1974, Outstanding Adminstr. So. region III Office Edn., 1975, Woman of Yr. in Edn. St. Clair County YWCA, 1987, Nat. Top Lady of Yr., 1988, Disting. Alumnus U. Ill., 1996, Vashon H.S. Hall of Fame, 1989, Citizen Amb., South Africa, 1996, Sr. Illinoisan Hall of Fame, 1997. Mem. Am. Librs. Trustees Assn. (regional v.p. 1978-79, 92, nat. sec. 1979-80), Ill. Commn. on Children, Mensa, Coun. for Exceptional Children, Top Ladies of Distinction (pres. 1987-91, nat. editor 1991—, Journalism award 1992, Media award 1992), Delta Sigma Theta (chpt. pres. 1960-62, Letters award 2000), Kappa Delta Pi (pres. So. Ill. U. chpt. 1973-74), Phi Delta Kappa (Svc. Key award 1984, chpt. pres. 1984-85), Iota Phi Lambda, Phi Lambda Theta (chpt. pres. 1985-87), East St. Louis Women's Club (pres. 1973-75). Republican. Home: 733 N 40th St East Saint Louis IL 62205-2138

WRIGHT, KIRBY MICHAEL, writer, editor; b. Honolulu, Sept. 1, 1955; s. Harold Stanley and June Gertrude (McCormack) W.; m. Darcy Laureen Mobraaten, Dec. 28, 1991. BA, U. Calif., San Diego, 1983; MFA, San Francisco State U., 1994. Pub. rels. dir. Winners Circle Resorts, Carlsbad, Calif., 1987-90; instr. Palo Alto (Calif.) Adult Sch., 1994-95; writer GT Prodn. Co., Palo Alto, 1995-96, editor, 1997—. Author: The Rainbow Warrior, 1998; (screenplay) Gordon & Al, 1996; (dramatic monologue) Blue Mesa Review, 1994 (1st pl. award Browning Soc. 1993, 94); (play) Houdini, 1999, (novel) Ulua Lines, 2000. Rschr. Ctr. for Auto Safety, Washington, 1980; advisor SAT Success, Palo Alto, 1998. Recipient Poetry prize Ann Fields Trust, San Francisco, 1993, 1st pl. Poets award Acad. Am. Poets, San Francisco, 1993. Fellow Arts Coun. Santa Clara County, Arts Coun. Silicon Valley. Democrat. Roman Catholic. Avocations: boxing, surfing, gourmet cooking. Office: GT Prodn Co 3259 Alma St Palo Alto CA 94306-2925

WRIGHT, MALCOLM STURTEVANT, nuclear facility manager, retired career officer; b. Orange, N.J., Sept. 2, 1941; s. Malcolm Everett and Margaret Sommer (Kohler) W.; m. Barbara Jean Larsen, June 5, 1963 (div. Aug., 1988); children: Tracy Ann, Karen Elizabeth; m. Lya Hanfri Baughman, Nov. 5, 1988; children: Zachary Seth, Sara Ann. BS in Engring., U.S. Naval Acad., 1963; MA in Polit. Sci., Villanova U., 1974. Commd. ensign USN, 1963, advanced through grades to capt., 1983, retired, 1993; dir. tactical tng. dept. US Naval Submarine Sch., Groton, Conn., 1982-84; commanding officer USS Alabama, Silverdale, Wash., 1984-87; planner polit.-mil. strategy Staff of Chmn. Joint Chiefs of Staff, Pentagon, Washington, 1987-90; comdr. Submarine Squadron Seventeen, Silverdale, Wash., 1990-92; chief of staff to comdr. Naval Base Seattle, 1992-93; mgr. waste and decontamination plant Westinghouse Hanford Co., Richland, Wash., 1993-96; mgr. 324/327 facility stabilization project Babcock and Wilcox Hanford Co., Richland, 1996-99; dir. 324 bldg. deactiviation project Fluor Hanford Co., Richland, 1999—; tech. advisor Disney Studios, Burbank, Calif., 1994-95. Vol. ARC, East Orange, N.J., 1957-59. Decorated Legion of Merit, USN, 1982, 86, 92, 93, Meritorious Svc. medal 1984, Defense Superior Svc. medal, 1990. Mem. U.S. Naval Inst., U.S. Naval Submarine League, U.S. Naval Acad. Alumni Assn. Republican. Presbyterian. Avocations; military history, civil war, Scottish culture, golf. Home: 3512 W 30th Ave Kennewick WA 99337-2500 Office: Flour Hanford Inc PO Box 1000 Richland WA 99352-1000

WRIGHT, MARIE BEULAH BATTEY, retired advertising executive; b. Cordell, Okla., Jan. 12, 1917; d. John William and Mary (Yoder) Battey; m. Joseph Barney Gifford, Sept. 3, 1948 (dec. 1960); m. Harold Arthur Wright, May 18, 1979. BFA, U. Okla., 1937; posgrad., Oklahoma City Symphony, 1940; postgrad., Baylor U., 1943-44, Oklahoma City Symphony, 1939-40. Host 15-minute daily piano show U. Okla. Radio Sta., 1935; supt. music Woodward (Okla.) Pub. Schs., 1937-38; sales and promotion mgr. KOME, Tulsa, 1940-43; instr. Sch. Radio Baylor U., Waco, Tex., 1943-45; asst. program mgr. KWKH, Shveveport, La., 1945-47; salesman KTBS Radio, Shveveport, 1947-55; comml. mgr. KTBS-TV, Shveveport, 1955-57; comml. mgr. KEEL Radio, Shveveport, 1957-62, v.p., gen. mgr., 1963-75; v.p. Lin Broadcasting, Shreveport, 1963-75; gen. mgr. KEEL/AM and KMBO/FM, Shreveport, 1968-80; v.p. Multimedia Broadcasting, Shreveport, 1975-80. Freelance mus. in arrangements Okla. City radio stas., 1938-39; editl. writer radio stas.; author: The Killing of the Presidency, 1974 (RTNDA Best Editl. 1973). Mem. publicity com. United Fund, 1955-62, exec. com. Shreveport Symphony, 1976-82, Strand Theatre of Shreveport Corp., 1977-94; bd. dirs. Downtown Devel. Corp., 1975-81; La. rep. So. Growth Policies Bd., 1985-96; mem. La. State Arts Coun., 1992-96; bd dirs. Caddo-Bossier Cmty. Action, 1969-71; mem. housing com. Caddo Parish, Shreveport, 1969; mem. City Charter Com., Shreveport, 1970; bd. dirs. Amb. Club, Shreveport, 1971-74; bd. dirs. David Raines Assn., Shreveport, 1969; mem. Com. of 500 March of Dimes, Shreveport, 1969; exec. asst. Shreveport Summer Theatre, 1950-60. Named Broadcaster of Yr., La. Assn. Broadcasters, Shreveport, 1970, Women Who Have Made a Differnce, YWCA, Shreveport, 1988; recipient Humanitarian award Shreveport Negro C. of C., 1969, Humanitarian award for outstanding contbn. to the arts, 1995. Mem. Shreveport C. of C. (bd. dirs. 1968-71, 1st woman mem.). Democrat. Avocations: theatre, symphony, reading, politics. Home: 701 Livingston Ave Shreveport LA 71107-3914

WRIGHT, MAX, information processing executive, consultant, youth leadership corporate training executive; b. Windsor, England, June 14, 1954; came to the U.S., 1989; s. Harold Edwin and Sheila Doreen (Young) W.; 2 children: Robyn, Devan Lucien. Electronics tech. Electricity Supply Commn., Germiston, South Africa, 1972-74, R. Muller, Johannesburg, South Africa, 1974-75; svc. mgr., sr. technician OKTV, George, South Africa, 1975-77; field engr. Burroughs Machines, Johannesburg, 1978-79; systems analyst Sidha Assocs. (Pty.) Ltd., Johannesburg, 1980-84, mng. dir., 1984-88; v.p. Arisoft, Inc., Fairfield, Iowa, 1989-97, pres., 1997—. Contbr. articles to profl. jours. Tchr. Transcendental meditation, 1979—; treas. South African Assn. Age of Enlightenment, 1980-87; founder, pres. Life Force, Inc., 1994—. Mem. T'ai Chi Assn. South Africa, Fairfield T'ai Chi Assn. (founding instr. and dir. 1992—). Avocations: Transcendental meditation, T'ai Chi Ch'uan, peaceful warrior training. Office: Arisoft Software PO Box 2198 Fairfield IA 52556-0037

WRIGHT, MICHAEL KEARNEY, retired public relations executive; b. Durham, N.C., Apr. 23, 1928; s. Wilburn Kearney and Roberta Audrey (Lee) W. BS, N.C. Cen. U., 1951; MS, Columbia U., 1954. Actor, singer, dancer Broadway and TV, 1951-60; dir. edn. Am. Cancer Soc., N.Y.C., 1960-69; dir. audio/visual edn. Media Medica, Inc., N.Y.C., 1969; dir. N.Y. office McFadden, Strauss & Irwin Inc., N.Y.C., 1970-75; v.p. ICPR, N.Y.C., 1975-77; sr. v.p. Stone Assocs., N.Y.C., 1977-85; pres. The Wright Co., N.Y.C., 1985; v.p. The Lippin Group, N.Y.C., 1985, 99; ret., 1999, actor, pub. rels. cons., 1999—; pub. rels. cons. Nuc. Rsch. Assocs., New Hyde Park, N.Y., 1967-69. Bd. dirs. CSC Repertory Co., N.Y.C., 1988-89; counsellor 1st Ch. of Religious Sci., N.Y.C., 1981-96, Alcoholics Anonymous, N.Y.C., 1970—; lectr. Sci. of Mind, N.Y.C., 1988-96; supporter ASPCA, Humane Soc., Morris Dees and others. With U.S. Army, 1946-47. Mem. NATAS, SAG, Smithsonian Assocs., Actors' Equity Assn., N.Y. City Ctr., Alpha Kappa Mu, Beta Kappa Chi. Avocations: collector old movies on videos, weightlifting. Home: 200 E 36th St Apt 11G New York NY 10016-3648

WRIGHT, MICHAEL WILLIAM, wholesale distribution and retail executive; b. Mpls., June 13, 1938; s. Thomas W. and Winifred M. W. BA, U. Minn., 1961, JD with honors, 1963. Ptnr. Dorsey & Whitney, Mpls., 1966-77; sr. v.p. Supervalu Inc., Mpls., 1977-78; pres., COO, Super Valu Stores, Inc., Mpls., 1978-82, CEO, 1981-82; chmn., pres., CEO Supervalu Inc., Mpls., 1982—; bd. dirs., past chmn. Fed. Res. Bank, Mpls.; bd. dirs. Norwest Corp., Honeywell, Inc., The Musicland Group, Shopko, Inc., S.C. Johnson & Co., Inc., Cargill, Inc., Internat. Ctr. for Cos. of the Food Trade and Industry, Food Mktg. Inst., Nat. Am. Wholesale Grocers Assn., Inc.; vice chmn. Food Mktg. Inst. 1st lt. U.S. Army, 1964-66. Office: Supervalu Inc PO Box 990 Minneapolis MN 55440-0990

WRIGHT, NINA HORNBUCKLE, police official; b. Augsburg, Germany, Feb. 14, 1961; d. John Allen and Clarice J. Hornbuckle; 1 child, Monica LaReisha Davis. Cert. law enforcement tech., Ctrl. Piedmont C.C., Charlotte, N.C., 1990; degree in criminal justice, Pfeiffer U., 1993. Advanced law enforcement cert. N.C. Dept. Justice. Reconciler So. Nat. Bank, Charlotte; computer operator 1st Citizen's Bank, Charlotte; proof encoder N.C. Nat. Bank, Charlotte; police capt. Charlotte-Mecklenburg Police Dept., Charlotte, 1986—; mem. cmty. child fatality prevention and protection team, Charlotte, 1999; advisor restorative justice task force, Charlotte, 1999. Bd. dirs. Nat. Conf. Cmty. and Justice, Charlotte, 1999; mgr. Unity Women's Basketball Team, Charlotte, 1999. Named Outstanding Police Officer of Yr., Charlotte Jaycees, 1990. Mem. Nat. Orgn. Black Police Execs., Police Exec. Rsch. Forum. Democrat. Baptist. Avocations: travel, reading, women's basketball, comedy. Fax: 704-336-4529. E-mail: mwright@cmpd.ci.charlotte.nc.us.

WRIGHT, PAMELA JEAN, administrator; b. Flint, Mich., Mar. 7, 1947; d. Richard Dardine and Mary Louise Smith; m. Arnold Freeman Wright, Dec. 11, 1972; 1 child, Jason Freeman. AA in Edn., Harford C.C., 1969; BA in Edn., Augusta Coll., 1972; MEd of Guidance Counseling, U. S.C., 1975. Employment counselor Fla. State Employment Svcs., Miami, 1975-79, area counseling supr., 1979-80; cons. Tradcom Internat., Miami, 1986-87; dir. student employment and career svcs. and One Stop Ctr. Miami-Dade C.C., 1981—. Mem. Fla. Assn. C.C. (pres., v.p., membership chair, region V dep. dir.), Coral Gables C. of C., South Dade C. of C., Fla. Coll. Placement Assn. (bd. dirs. 1994-97). Roman Catholic. Avocations: sailing, camping,

skiing. Office: Miami-Dade Cmty Coll 11011 SW 104th St Rm 3105 Miami FL 33176-3393

WRIGHT, PATRICK RICHARD HENRY (LORD WRIGHT OF RICHMOND), diplomat, retired; b. Reading, Berks., Eng., June 28, 1931; s. Herbert Henry Stafford and Rachel Mary (Green) W.; m. Virginia Anne Gaffney, June 14, 1958; children: Marcus, Olivia, Angus. MA, Merton Coll., Oxford, Eng., 1955. With Brit. Diplomatic Svc., 1955-91; pvt. sec. to Prime Minister Overseas Affairs, London, 1974-77, Brit. amb. to Luxembourg, 1977-79, Brit. amb. to Syria, 1979-81, Brit. amb. to Saudi Arabia, 1984-86; permanent under-sec. and head British Diplomatic Svc., London, 1986-91; chmn. Royal Inst. Internat. Affairs, London, 1995-99; non-exec. dir. Brit. Petroleum, Delarue plc, 1991—; adv. dir. Unilever, 1991-99; non-exec. dir. Barclays plc, 1991-96, BAA plc, 1992-98. Cross-bench mem. Ho. of Lords, 1994. Lt. Royal Arty., 1950-51. Decorated Grand Knight Comdr. Order of St. Michael and St. George, Knight of Order of St. John; hon. fellow Merton Coll., 1987. Fellow Royal Coll. Music (coun. mem.); mem. United Oxford and Cambridge Univ. Club. Ch. of Eng. Avocations: music, philately, walking, travel. Office: House of Lords, Westminster, London SW1A 0PW, England

WRIGHT, RICHARD KIRK, physicist, materials researcher, consultant; b. Portland, Oreg., May 24, 1945; s. Roscoe Kirk and Esther Agnes (Hobbs) W.; m. Judie Kay Patterson, June 9, 1969; children: Kimberlee, Jamie, Ashlee, Lindsay. BS, Ariz. State U., 1975; DSc, Eurotech. Rsch. U., Palo Alto, Calif., 1989. Engr. Motorola Semicondr., Phoenix, 1973-77, Tektronix Inc., Beaverton, Oreg., 1977-83; sr. engr. Amdahl Corp., Sunnyvale, Calif., 1983-90; mfg. engr. TAQ Comms., Santa Clara, Calif., 1990-93; cons. Loral Fairchild, Milpitas, Calif., 1993-94; sr. mem. tech. staff Infineon Techs. Corp. (formerly Siemens Microelectronics), Cupertino, Calif., 1994—; cons. Ultra Fine Assembly Co., Fremont, 1990—. Author articles and procs. Served with U.S. Army, 1966-68, Germany. Mem. Am. Phys. Soc. Achievements include research in thermal fatigue in semiconductor packaging; room temperature re-crystallization of tin; Brownian motion of tin whiskers; also patents applied for in micro electronic assembly. Avocations: fishing, hunting, private pilot. Home: 6632 Catamaran St San Jose CA 95119-1706 Office: Siemens Microelectonics 19000 Homestead Rd Cupertino CA 95014-0799

WRIGHT, RICHARD OSCAR, III, pathologist, educator; b. La Junta, Colo., Aug. 9, 1944; s. Richard O. Jr. and Frances R. (Curtiss) W.; m. Bernale Trout, May 31, 1969; children: Lauren Diane, Richard O. IV. BS in Biology, Midwestern State U., 1966; MS in Biology, U. Houston, 1968; DO, U. Health Sci., 1972. Cert. anatomic pathology and lab. medicine Am. Osteo. Bd. Pathology. Sr. attending pathologist Normandy Met. Hosps., St. Louis, 1977-81; sr. attending pathologist Phoenix (Ariz.) Gen. Hosps., 1981-97, dir. med. edn., 1989-92, 96—; clin. asst. prof. pathology Coll. Osteo. Medicine, Western U., Pomona, Calif., 1985—; dir. labs., chmn. dept. John C. Lincoln Hosp., Deer Valley, 1997—; dir. med. edn., dir. labs. John C. Lincoln Hosp., Deer Valley, Ariz., 1997—; v.p. Osteo. Postdoctoral Tng. Inst., Kirksville, Mo., 1998—; clin. instr. pathology Ohio U. Coll. Osteo. Medicine, Athens, 1976-77; clin. asst. prof. pathology Kirksville Coll. Osteo. Medicine, 1985-87; vis. lectr. pathology New Eng. Coll. Osteo. Medicine, Biddeford, Maine, 1989-92; clin. asst. prof. pathology Midwestern U. Ariz. Coll. Osteo. Medicine, 1997—; cons. pathologist Phoenix Indian Med. Ctr., 1992-94; adv. bd. Inter Soc. Coun. Pathology, Chgo., 1992—; sec. med. staff John C. Lincoln Hosp.-Deer Valley, 1997-99, v.p. med. staff, 2000—. Active Ariz. Rep. Party, Phoenix, Rep. Nat. Coun., Washington; precinctman Dist. 18 Maricopa County, Ariz., 1996-98, Madison Heights Precinct, 1996-98; chmn. bd. trustees Phoenix (Ariz.) Gen. Hosp., 1994-95; ex-officio, trustee, 1995-97; dir. John C. Lincoln Health Network Guild, 1997—; mem. found. adv. coun. Lincoln Health Found.-Phoenix Gen. Hosp. Osteo. Endowment Fund. Recipient Mead-Johnson award Nat. Osteo. Assn., 1975. Fellow Am. Osteo. Coll. Pathologists (disting., pres. 1989-90, bd. govs. 1984-91), Coll. Pathologists, Coll. Am. Pathologists, Am. Soc. Clin. Pathologists; mem. Ariz. Osteo. Med. Assn. (del. dist. 2 ho. of dels. 1998), Ariz. Soc. Pathologists, Century Club Alumni Assn., AAAS, Alpha Phi Omega, Rho Sigma Chi, Psi Sigma Alpha. Presbyterian. Office: Anatomic Pathology Assoc 19829 N 27th Ave Phoenix AZ 85027-4001

WRIGHT, ROBERT JOHN, mathematics educator, researcher; b. Brisbane, Queensland, Australia, May 13, 1948; s. John Ernest and Monica Mary (Chicken) W.; m. Rebecca Janet Solly, Dec. 27, 1974; children: Anna Jane, Sally Rebecca. BS, U. Queensland (Australia), Brisbane, 1974, MS, 1976; EdD, U. Ga., 1989. Tchg. Tchr. Queensland Dept. Edn., Gold Coast, Australia, 1967-69, St. Columbian's Sch., Brisbane, Queensland, Australia, 1969-71; lectr. No. Rivers Coll. Advanced Edn., Lismore, Australia, 1976-89; sr. lectr. So. Cross U., Lismore, Australia, 1990-94, prof. math. edn., 1994—; cons. Oconee County Sch. Dist., Walhalla, S.C., 1994-97, N.C. State Dept. Edn., Raleigh, 1996-97, Wigan (Eng.) Edn. Authority, 1996-97; developer Maths. Recovery Program, Australia, U.S., Eng., 1992-97. Author: (monograph with Jim Martland and Ann Stafford) Early Numeracy: Assessment for Teaching and Intervention, 2000; contbr. articles to profl. jours. Collaborative rsch. grantee Australian Rsch. Coun., 1992, large rsch. grantee, 1992, small rsch. grantee, 1995. Mem. Nat. Coun. Tchrs. Math., Am. Edn. Rsch. Assn., Australian Assn. Rsch. Edn. Avocations: reading, squash, surfing, music, art appreciation. Office: So Cross U, Military Rd, 2480 Lismore NSW, Australia

WRIGHT, ROBERT JOSEPH, lawyer; b. Rome, Ga., Dec. 13, 1949; s. Arthur Arley and Maude T. (Lacey) W.; m. Donna Ruth Bishop, Feb. 18, 1972; children: Cynthia Ashley, Laura Christine. BA cum laude, Ga. State U., 1979; JD cum laude, U. Ga., 1983. Bar: GA. 1983, U.S. Dist. Ct. (no. dist.) Ga. 1983, U.S. Dist. Ct. (mid. dist.) Ga. 1985. Assoc. Craig & Gainer, Covington, Ga., 1983-84, Heard, Leverett & Adams, Elberton, Ga., 1984-86; gen. counsel Group Underwriters, Inc., Elberton, 1987—. Editorial staff Ga. Jour. Internat. and Comparative Law, 1981-82. Mem. State Bar Ga. (sec. legal econs. sect. 1987-88, chmn. legal econs. sect. 1988-90), Order of the Coif, Masons, Phi Alpha Delta. Baptist. Home: 1030 E Canyon Creek Ct Watkinsville GA 30677-1500

WRIGHT, ROBERT ROSS, III, law educator; b. Ft. Worth, Nov. 20, 1931; m. Susan Webber; children: Robert Ross IV, John, David, Robin. BA cum laude, U. Ark., 1953, JD, 1956; MA (grad. fellow), Duke U., 1954; SJD (law fellow), U. Wis., 1967. Bar: Ark. 1956, U.S. Supreme Ct. 1968, Okla. 1970. Instr. polit. sci. U. Ark., 1955-56; mem. firm Forrest City, Ark., 1956-58; partner firm Norton, Norton & Wright, Forrest City, 1959; asst. gen. counsel, asst. sec. Crossett Co., Ark.; atty. Crossett div. Ga.-Pacific Corp., 1960-63; asst. sec. Pub. Utilities Co., Crossett, Triangle Bag Co., Covington, Ky., 1960-62; mem. faculty law sch. U. Ark., 1963-70; asst. prof., dir. continuing legal edn. and research, then asst. dean U. Ark. (Little Rock div.), 1965-66, prof. law, 1967-70; vis. prof. law U. Iowa, 1969-70; prof. U. Okla., 1970-77; dean U. Okla. (Coll. Law); dir. U. Okla. (Law Center), 1970-76; vis. prof. U. Ark., Little Rock, 1976-77; Donaghey Disting. prof. U. Ark, 1977-99, Donaghey disting. prof. emeritus, 1999—; vis. disting. prof. U. Cin., 1983; Ark. commr. Nat. Conf. Commrs. Uniform State Laws, 1967-70; past chmn. Com. Uniform Eminent Domain Code; past mem. Com. Uniform Probate Code, Ark. Gov.'s Ins. Study Commn.; chmn. Gov. Commn. on Uniform Probate Code; chmn. task force joint devel. Hwy. Research Bd.; vice chmn. Okla. Jud. Council, 1970-72, chmn., 1972-75; chmn. Okla. Center Criminal Justice, 1971-76. Author: Arkansas Eminent Domain Digest, 1964, Arkansas Probate Practice System, 1965, The Law of Airspace, 1968, Emerging Concepts in the Law of Airspace, 1969, Cases and Materials on Land Use, 3d edit., 1982, supplement, 1987, 5th edit., 1997, Uniform Probate Code Practice Manual, 1972, Model Airspace Code, 1973, Land Use in a Nutshell, 1978, 4th edit., 2000, The Arkansas Form Book, 1979, 2d edit., 1988, Zoning Law in Arkansas: A Comparative Analysis, 1980; contbr. numerous articles to legal jours. Mem. Little Rock Planning Commn., 1978-82, chmn., 1982. Named Ark. Man of Year Kappa Sigma, 1958. Fellow Am. Law Inst., Am. Coll. Trust and Estate Counsel (acad.); mem. ABA (past chmn., exec. coun. gen. practice, solo and small firm sect., former chmn. new pubs. editl. bd., sect. officers conf., ho. of dels. 1994-2000, standing com. fed. jud. improvements 1998—), Ark. Bar Assn. (exec. coun. 1985-88, ho. of dels., life mem., chmn. eminent domain code com., past mem. com. new bar ctr., past chmn. preceptorship com., exec. com. young laywers sect.), Okla. Bar Assn. (past vice-chmn. legal internship com., former vice-chmn. gen. practice sect.), Pulaski County Bar Assn., Ark. Bar Found., U. Wis. Alumni Assn., Duke U. Alumni Assn., U. Ark. Alumni Assn., Order of Coif, Phi Beta Kappa, Phi Alpha Delta, Omicron Delta Kappa. Episcopalian. Home: 249 Pleasant Valley Dr Little Rock AR 72212-3170 Office: U Ark Law Sch 1201 McMath St Little Rock AR 72202-5142

WRIGHT, ROBERT THOMAS, JR., lawyer; b. Detroit, Oct. 4, 1946; s. Robert Thomas and Jane Ellen (Blandin) W.; m. Diana Feltman, June 8, 1994; children: Sarah Allison, Jonathan Brian. BA in History and Polit. Sci., U. N.C., 1968; JD, Columbia U., 1974. Bar: Fla. 1974. Assoc. Paul & Thomson, Miami, Fla., 1974-77; assoc. Mershon, Sawyer, Johnston, Dunwoody & Cole, Miami, 1977-81, ptnr., 1981-95; ptnr. Shutts & Bowen, Miami, 1995-98; ptnr. Verner, Liipfert, Berhhard, McPherson & Hand, Miami, 1998—, also bd. dirs. 1st lt. U.S. Army, 1968-71. Mem. ABA, Fla. Bar, Dade County Bar Assn. Avocations: golf, rugby, African cichlids. Home: 11095 SW 84th Ct Miami FL 33156-4311 Office: Verner Lippfert et al 200 S Biscayne Blvd Ste 3100 Miami FL 33131-5324

WRIGHT, THEODORE OTIS, forensic engineer; b. Gillette, Wyo., Jan. 17, 1921; s. James Otis and Gladys Mary (Marquiss) W.; m. Phyllis Mae Reeves, June 21, 1942 (div. 1968); children: Mary Suzanne, Theodore Otis Jr., Barbara Joan; m. Edith Marjorie Jewett, May 22, 1968; children: Marjorie Jane, Elizabeth Carter. BSEE, U. Ill., 1951, MS in Engring., 1952; postgrad., Air Command and Staff Coll., 1956-57, UCLA, 1958. Registered profl. engr. Wash. 2d lt. U.S. Air Force, 1942-65, advanced through grades to lt. col., 1957, ret., 1965; dep. for engring. Titan SPO, USAF Sys. Command, L.A., 1957-65; rsch. engr. The Boeing Co., Seattle, 1965-81; pres. The Pretzelwich, Inc., Seattle, 1981—; cons., forensic engr. in pvt. practice Bellevue, Wash., 1988—; adj. prof. U. Wash., Greenriver Jr. Coll., both 1967-68. Contbr. articles to nat. and internat. profl. jours. Decorated Purple Heart, Air medal. Mem. NSPE (v.p. western region 1985-87), ASTM (com. E-43 metric practice 1988—), Nat. Coun. Weights and Measures, Wash. Soc. Profl. Engrs. (state pres. 1981-82, Disting. Svc. award 1980, Engr. of Yr. 1996, Columbia award 1996), U.S. Metric Assn. (life, cert. advanced metrication speciallist), Am. Nat. Metric Coun. (bd. dirs. 1978-94), Air Force Assn. (charter life, state pres. 1974-76, 90-91, Jimmy Doolittle fellow 1975), Order of Daedalians (life), Eta Kappa Nu, Pi Mu Epsilon, Tau Beta Pi. Democrat. Presbyterian. Avocations: flying, photography, classical music, archaeology. Home: 141 140th Pl NE Bellevue WA 98007-6939

WRIGHT, WILLIAM GORDON, foundation executive; b. Big Spring, Tex., Feb. 13, 1955; s. Emmett Gordon and Marilyn June (Ellis) W. BS in Adminstrv. Mgmt., Clemson U., 1978; JD, Western New England Col., 1981, MBA, 1981; LLM in Taxation, Boston U., 1982. Bar: Mass., D.C., N.J., U.S. Tax Ct., U.S. Ct. Appeals (1st cir.). Staff atty. Touche Ross & Co., Boston, 1982-84; atty. Womble, Carlyle, Sandridge & Rice, Winston-Salem, N.C., 1984-86; sr. atty. advisor U.S. Tax Ct., Washington, 1986-88; atty. Hannoch Weisman, Roseland, N.J., 1988-93, Proskauer Rose, LLP, N.Y.C., 1993-96; chmn., exec. dir. Teresa G. Wright Promise Found., Randolph, N.J., 1996—; co-founder, exec. com. mem. N.J. .08 Coalition, 1996—; delegate Lifesavers Hwy. Safety Conf., New Mexico, Fla., 1996, 97; alcohol/drug countermeasures rep. Morris County (N.J.) Hwy. Traffic Safety Com., 1996—. Contbr. chpts. to books, articles to profl. jours; spkr. in field. Minister, Fund-raising com. mem. St. Matthew's Ch., Randolph, N.J., 1994—; co-founder Family & Friends of Teresa Wright Orgn., Randolph, N.J., 1995-96. Recipient N.J. Equal Justice award N.J. Assn. of Crime Victim Advocates, 1996. Mem. D.C. Bar Assn., Mass. Bar Assn., N.J. Bar Assn., N.J. Assn. Crime Victim Advocates, Mothers Against Drunk Driving (pub. policy liason, state rep., youth com. co-chair). Roman Catholic. Avocations: running, racing, scuba diving, biking, music. Home: 24 Whitehall Dr Orinda CA 94563-4226

WRIGHT-PASCOE, ROSEMARIE ANGELA, endocrinologist; b. Kingston, Jamaica, Oct. 1, 1958; d. Wilbur Wright and Beville (Burke) Clark; 1 child, Dwayne. MBBS, U. W.I., 1982, DM, 1990. Med. officer of health Ministry of Health, Kingston, 1985-86; med. resident Kingston Pub. Hosp., Jamaica, 1986, U. Hosp. of W.I., Jamaica, 1986-90; acting cons. physician KPH, Jamaica, 1991, cons. physician, 1991-93; cons. physician U. W.I., Jamaica, 1992—; lectr. U. W.I., Jamaica, 1992—. Cons. physician Diabetic Assn. of Jamaica, 1992—. Recipient commonwealth fellowship in endocrinology, U.K., 1995-96, govt. scholarship, Israel Jamaican, 1992. Mem. Endocrine Soc., Royal Coll. Physicians, Am. Coll. Physicians, Assn. Cons. Physicians, Med. Assn. of Jamaica, Am. Diabetes Assn., Internat. Diabetes Fedn. Avocation: reading. Office: Dept Medicine, U of the West Indies, Kingston 6, Jamaica

WRIGHT-RIGGINS, AIDSAND F., III, religious organization executive. Exec. dir. ABC Bd. of Nat. Ministries, Valley Forge, Pa., 1991. Office: ABC Bd of Nat Ministries PO Box 851 Valley Forge PA 19482-0851

WRIGHTSON, KEITH EDWIN, historian; b. Croxdale, England, Mar. 22, 1948; s. Robert and Evelyn (Atkinson) W.; m. Eva Mikusovä, Aug. 19, 1972; children: Nicholas Mikus, Eliska Anne. BA, U. Cambridge, 1970, MA, 1974, PhD, 1974. Rsch. fellow Fitzwilliam Coll., Cambridge, 1972-75; univ. lectr. U. St. Andrews, United Kingdom, 1975-84; Can. commonwealth fellow U. Toronto, Can., 1983-84; univ. lectr. U. Cambridge, Eng., 1984-93, reader in English social history, 1993-98, prof. social history, 1998-99; prof. history Yale U., New Haven, Conn., 1999—; fellow Jesus Coll., Cambridge, 1984-99, dir. studies in history, 1990-98; vis. prof. U. Alberta, 1988, U. Toronto, 1992. Author: English Society 1580-1680, 1982, Earthly Necessities, Economic Lives in Early modern Britain, 2000; co-editor: The World We Have Gained, 1986; co-author: (with D. Levine) Poverty and Piety in an English Village, 1979, The Making of an Industrial Society, 1991; contbr. articles to profl. jours. Fellow, British Acad., Royal Hist. Soc.; mem. Social History Soc., Econ. History Soc. Avocations: modern jazz, contemporary literature. Office: Yale U Dept History PO Box 208324 New Haven CT 06520-8324

WROBLE, LISA ANN, writer, educator; b. Dearborn, Mich., June 17, 1963; d. Robert Frank and Ruth Marie (Schiller) W. Diploma, Inst. Children's Lit., 1983; BA cum laude, Ea. Mich. U., Ypsilanti, 1985. Cert. ESL tchr., ltd. profl. class B, Libr. Mich. Asst. editor cmty. rels. Vets. Adminstrn., Ann Arbor, Mich., 1983-85; prodn. coord. Cmty. Crier Newspaper/COMMA Graphics, Plymouth, Mich., 1985-86; proofreader Valassis Inserts, Livonia, Mich., 1986-89; tech. writer Nat. TechTeam, Dearborn, Mich., 1989-90; freelance writer Plymouth, 1990—; publicist Garden City (Mich.) Osteopathic Hosp., 1990-91; creative writing instr. Cmty. Edn. Plymouth (Mich.)-Canton Schs., 1992-93, 97—. Author: (12 book series) Kids Throughout History, 1997, 98, The Oceans, 1998, How Things Work, Childcraft, vol. 9, 1999; contbg. editor Metroparent, 1991-93; contbg. tech. writer Cleaner Times, 1992-95, Facilities Planning News, 1993-96, FM Data Monthly, 1997-2000, Mich. Learning, 1998—; book rev. editor Parenting Today's Teens, 1998—; book reviewer BookPage Promotions, 1997—, The ALAN Rev., 1993—, Christian Libr. Jour., 1997—; software reviewer Compute Publs., 1989-92, Falsoft Inc., 1991-94; contbr. articles, essays and sects. to reference books, multi-media CD ROMs and textbooks; contbg. writer Eye on the Web, 1998, Bridges CX, 1999-2000, Career Explorer, 1999—, Teach-Michigan Found., 1999—. Tutor Cmty. Literacy Coun., Plymouth, 1989-93; vol. spkr. in schs. Recipient Reading Tutor award Cmty. Literacy Coun., 1991-93. Mem. Soc. Childrens Book Writers and Illustrators (adv. com. Mich. chpt. 1993-94, 98—, workshop facilitator 1990, 97—), Nat. Writers Assn. (vol. critiquer 1989-93), Childrens Lit. Assn., Mich. Reading Assn., Womens Nat. Book Assn., Text and Acad. Authors Assn., Peninsula Writers, Livonia Writers Group. Republican. Roman Catholic. Avocations: swimming, photography, crafting, cross country skiing, cooking. Home: 14344 Princeton Dr Plymouth MI 48170-3178

WROBLESKI, JEANNE PAULINE, lawyer; b. Phila., Feb. 14, 1942; d. Edward Joseph and Pauline (Popelak) W.; m. Robert J. Klein, Dec. 3, 1979. BA, Immaculata Coll., 1964; MA, U. Pa., 1966; JD, Temple U., 1975. Bar: Pa. 1975. Pvt. practice law Phila., 1975—; pres., shareholder Jeanne Wrobleski & Assocs., LLC, Phila., 1999—; lectr. on bus. law Wharton Sch., Phila. Mem. Commn. on Women and the Legal Profession, 1986-89; v.p. Center City Residents' Assn.; Eisenhower Citizen Amb. del. to Soviet Union. Bd. dirs. Wilma Theater, South St. Dance Co., Women in Transition; bd. dirs., mem. exec. com. Temple Law Alumni; del. to Moscow Conf. on Law and Econ. Coop., 1990; del. to jud. conf. 3d Cir. U.S. Ct. Appeals, 1991; mediator U.S. Dist. Ct. (ea. dist.) Pa., 1996. Rhea Liebman scholar, 1974. Mem. AAUW, ABA, Pa. Bar Assn., Phila. Bar Assn. (chmn. women's rights com. 1986, com. on jud. selection and retention, 1986-87, chmn. appellate cts. com. 1992, bus. cts. task force, com. on bus. litigation), Pa. Acad. Fine Arts, Nat. Mus. Women in the Arts, Am. Judicature Soc., Jagiellonian Law Soc., Lawyers Club, Founders Club, The Cosmopolitan Club, Penn Club, Alpha Psi Omega, Lambda Iota Tau. Democrat. Office: Jeanne Wrobleski & Assocs LLC 1845 Walnut St Fl 24 Philadelphia PA 19103-4708

WROBLOWA, HALINA STEFANIA, electrochemist; b. Gdansk, Poland, July 5, 1925; came to U.S., 1958, naturalized, 1970; 1 child: Krystyna Wrobel-Knight, grandson Christopher E. Knight. MSc, U. Lodz, Poland, 1949; PhD, Warsaw Inst. Tech., 1958. Chmn. dept. prep. studies U. Lodz, 1950-53; adj. Inst. for Phys., Chemistry Acad. Scis., Warsaw, Poland, 1958-60; dept. dir. electrochemistry lab. energy inst. U. Pa., Phila., 1960-67; dir. electrochemistry lab., 1968-75; prin. research scientist Ford Motor Co., Dearborn, Mich., 1976-91; pvt. practice cons., 1991; chmn. Gordon Rsch. Conf. on Electrochemistry, 1983. Contbr. chpts. to books, articles to profl. jours., patent lit. Served with Polish Undeground Army, 1943-45, decorated Mil. Silver Cross of Merit with Swords. Mem. Electrochem. Soc., Internat. Electrochem. Soc., Mensa, Sigma Xi.

WRONSKI, IAN, physician, educator; b. Tel-Aviv, Apr. 10, 1951; arrived in Australia, 1951; s. Chaskel and Genia (Borek) W.; m. Maggie Al Grant, Nov. 25, 1983; children: Daniel, Miriam. MB, BChir, Monash U., Melbourne, Australia, 1976; diploma, Liverpool (U.K.) U., 1984; MPH, Harvard U., 1989, SM in Epidemiology, 1990. Resident med. officer Victorian Hosp., Melbourne, 1977-79; fellow Victorian Acad. Gen. Practice, Melbourne, 1980; med. dir. Broome (Australia) Regional Aboriginal Med. Svc., 1981-86; dir. health svcs. Kimberley Aboriginal Med. Svcs. Coun., Broome, 1986-92; dir. Anton Breine Ctr. for Tropical Medicine, Townsville, Australia, 1992—; found. prof., head dept. pub. health and tropical medicine James Cook U., Townsville, 1994—, exec. dean faculty health and molecular scis., 1997—; communicable diseases adv. com. Aboriginal and Torres Strait Islander Commn., 1987-91. Design author: (software) Healthplanner, 1987; contbr. articles to profl. jours. Fellow Australasian Coll. Tropical Medicine (coun. mem. 1994—), Australasian Faculty of Pub. Health Medicine, Royal Australian Coll. Gen. Practitioners, Australian Coll. Rural and Remote Medicine; mem. Royal Australasian Coll. Physicians (aboriginal health com. 1991—), Rural Drs. Assn. Queensland (aboriginal and Torres Strait Island health com. 1993). Avocations: piano, stamp collecting. Office: James Cook Univ, Fac Health Life & Molec Sci, Townsville 4811 QLD, Australia

WROSCH, CARSTEN, psychologist; b. Berlin, Oct. 19, 1965; s. Wolfgang Wrosch and Helga (Seils) Mueller. MA, Free U. of Berlin, 1994, PhD, 1997. Predoctoral fellow Max-Planck Inst. for Human Devel., Berlin, 1994-97, postdoctoral fellow, 1997-99; vis. scientist U. Pitts., 1998, Carnegie Mellon U., Pitts., 1999—. Mem. Am. Psychol. Assn. Office: Carnegie Mell U Dept of Psychology Pittsburgh PA 15213

WRUKOWSKI, KRZYSZTOF WŁADYSŁAW, engineering executive; b. Torun, Poland, May 22, 1949; s. Aleksander and Helena (Brettschneider) W.; m. Hanna Wanda Górczyńska, Jan. 25, 1975; chlildren: Piotr, Malgorzata. High, Mil. Acad. Tech., Warsaw, 1972. Technologist Mil. Aircraft Works No. 3, Deblin, Poland, 1972-80; tech. mgr. Mil. Aircraft Works No. 3, Deblin, 1981-96; spls. in standardization Bur. Mil. Standardization Svcs., Warsaw, 1996-97; mgr. organizational group Mil. Codification Bur., Warsaw, 1997—. Author: (procedures for maintenance of aircraft) Technologies of Maintenance, 1996, User's Manual, 1996; editor: Polish Version of Allied Codification Publication, 1999, manuals for teaching codification, 1998. Col. Polish Mil. Codification Bur., 1996—. Office: Orgnl Group Mil Codif Bur, Aleje Niepodległości 218, 00-911 Warsaw Poland

WU, BRUCE CHUNG DAN (BRUCE CHUNG DAN NG), steamship company executive, investor; b. Shanghai, Kiangsu, China, June 17, 1937; s. T.Y. and S.Y. (Shen) Wu; m. Victoria Yang NG, Jan. 11, 1968; children: Alvin Chi Hai, Christina Shieu Yeing, Shrah Shieu Wen. BSEE, U. Notre Dame, 1958, MSEE, 1960, PhD in Engring. Sci., 1965. Asst. prof. U. Hong Kong, 1965-67; dir. Teh Hu Steamship Co. (H.K.) Ltd., Hong Kong, 1965-75, v.p., 1975-85, sr. v.p., 1985—; Bd. dirs. S.E. Soda Mfg. Co., Ltd., 1985—. Mem. ASME, IEEE, Assn. Computing Machinery, Optical Soc. Am., Internat. Soc. Optical Engring., N.Y. Acad. Scis. Home: Apt 10 Block A Bellevue Ct, 41 Stubbs Rd, Hong Kong China Office: Teh Hu Steamship Co Ltd, 77-79 Gloucester Rd Fl 15 unit B, Wan Chai Hong Kong

WU, CHANG-CHUN, mechanical engineering educator; b. Bengbu, Anhui, China, July 7, 1946; s. Ke-ben and Kuan-ron (Zhang) W.; m. Xue-ying Chen, Aug. 11, 1974; children: Xiao-wen, Dan. Grad., Hefei Poly. U., 1973; MSc, U. Sci. and Tech. of China, Hefei, 1982, PhD, 1987. With Co. of Civil Constrn., Bengbu, 1964-70; teaching asst. Hefei Poly. U., 1974-78; instr. U. Sci. and Tech. of China, 1982-90; Alexander von Humboldt rsch. fellow U. Stuttgart, Fed. Republic of Germany, 1988-89, 99; assoc. prof. U. Sci. and Tech. of China, 1990-92, prof., head of computer mechanics lab, 1993—; vis. scholar U. Hong Kong, 1989-90, 91-92, 1994, 98. Editor Jour. Engring. Mechanics, 1984-91. Recipient Natural Sci. prize Chinese Acad. Sci., 1988, 93, honour medal Nat. Edn. Com. China, 1991, T.H.H. Pian medal ICES'92 Hong Kong, 1992, Nat. Nature Sci. award 1997. Fellow East China Network of Solid Mechanics (sec. gen. 1984-88), mem. of GAMM, council of Chinese Soc. Theo. Appl. Mech. Avocation: art. Office: U Sci and Tech of China, Dept Modern Mech, Hefei Anhui 230026, China

WU, CHENGBIN, biologist, researcher; b. Huainan, China, Oct. 15, 1967; came to U.S., 1991; s. Youqi and Peizhu (Zhang) W.; m. Jenny Zhi Jin, June 28, 1994; 1 child, Daniel Yilen. BS, East China U., Shanghai, 1989; MS, S.D. State U., 1993; PhD, U. Ga., 1997. Rschr. Harvard Med. Sch., Boston, 1997—. Recipient fellowship grant Cancer Rsch. Inst., N.Y.C., 1999, Robert Anderson award U. Ga., 1999. Mem. AAAS, The Endocrine Soc., Am. Assn. Immunologists. Avocations: painting, travel. E-mail: dcbwu@email.com. Home: 76 Desoto Rd West Roxbury MA 02132-6033 Office: Beth Israel Deaconess Med Ctr Harvard Med Sch 330 Brookline Ave Boston MA 02215-5400

WU, CHENG-WEN, biochemist, researcher; b. Taipei, Taiwan, June 19, 1938; came to U.S., 1965; s. Hai-Chu and Fan-Po (Chen) W.; m. Felicia Ying-Hsiueh Chen, Nov. 10, 1963; children: David, Faith, Albert. MD, Nat. Taiwan U., Taipei, 1964; PhD in Biochemistry, Case Western Reserve U., 1969. Med. Licensure, China; cert. AMA. Postdoctoral assoc. Cornell U., Ithaca, N.Y., 1969-70; fellow Yale Y., New Haven, Conn., 1971-72; from asst. prof. to prof. Albert Einstein Coll. Medicine, 1972-78, prof., 1978-80; prof. SUNY, Stony Brook, N.Y., 1980-90; dir. planning office Nat. Health Rsch. Inst., Taipei, 1991-95, pres., disting. investigator, 1996—; vis. prof. Inst. Pasteur, France, 1979-80; adj. prof. Nat. Taiwan U. Coll. Medicine, 1988-96, U. Calif., San Francisco, 1991-96, Nat. Taiwan U., 1996—; dir. prep. office Inst. Biomed. Scis., Acad. sinica, Taipei, Taiwan, 1988-92, founding dir. 1992-95, rsch. fellow 1992—; trustee numerous orgs.; adv. com. Nat. Sci. Coun., 1989—, Ministry Edn., 1989—, Inst. Molecular Biology, Academia Sinica, 1984—, Nat. Yang-Ming U., 1990—, Nat. Taiwan U. Coll. Medicine, 1992—, Nat. Sun Yat-Sen U., 1993—, Nat. Chiao-Tung U., 1993—, Nat. Tsing-Hua U., 1994—; coun. mem. NSF, Internat. Union for Pure and Applied Biophysics. Editor: Biochemical and Structural Dynamics of the Cell Nucleus, 1990, Structure and Function of Nucleic Acids and Proteins, 1990; mem. editl. bd. Jour. Formosan Med. Assn., 1994—, Biochemistry, Biomed. Jour., Archives of Biochemistry and Biophysics, Biology of the Cell, Cell Rsch.; adv. cons. editl. bd. Jour. Genetics and Molecular Biology; reviewer Jour. Biological Chem., Biochemistry, Jour. Molecular Biology, Cell, Biochim. et Biophysics, Acta, others; mem. review com. Internat. Human Frontier Sci. Orgn., France; patentee in field; contbr. over 150 articles to profl. jours. Recipient NIH Career Devel. award, 1972, Irma T. Hirschl Scientific award 1977, Philippe Found. award 1978, Catacosinos Prof. award 1980, Sci. and Tech. award Taiwanese-Am. Found., 1993, Outstanding Scientific Achievement award Chinese Am. Profl. Assn., 1998; fellow NIH, 1972, John Simon Guggenheim Meml. Found., 1988; cancer rsch. scholar Am. Cancer Soc., 1988, French-Am. 1979. Fellow Am. Inst. Chemists; mem. ACS, Asian-Pacific Orgn. Cell Biology (trustee 1991-94, sec. 1995-98), Asian Conf. Transcription (founding mem.), Asian Pacific Soc. Biologists (founding mem., pres. 1998-2002), Asian Molecular Biology Orgn.

(founding mem.), Internat. Union Pure and Applied Biophysics (chmn. nat. com. Rep. China), Am. Soc. Advancement Sci., Am. Soc. Biochemistry Molecular Biology, Am. Soc. Cell Biology, Am. Soc. Microbiology, Am. Soc. Pharmacology and Experimental Therapeutics, Biophys. Soc., N.Y. Acad. Scis., Soc. Chinese Bioscientists in Am. (lifetime achievement award 1997), Biophys. Soc. Rep. China (pres. 1996-98), Chinese Soc. Cell and Molecular Biology (pres. Taipei 1992-97), Formosan Med. Assn., Chinese Biochemical Soc., Chinese Oncology Soc., Chinese Soc. Genetics, Sigma Xi. Avocations: reading, hiking. Home: No 9 Alley 1 Lane 61, Yen-Chiu-Yuan Rd Sec 11, Taipei 115, China Office: Nat Health Rsch Inst No 128, Yen-Chiu-Yuan Rd Sec II, Taipei 115, China

WU, CHI, chemistry educator; b. Wuhu, Anhui, China, Mar. 17, 1955; s. Guoan and Chuixia (Cheng) W.; m. Yueyuan Huang, Jan. 28, 1984; children: David, Jennifer. BS, China U. Sci. and Tech., 1982; MPh, SUNY, Stony Brook, 1984, PhD, 1987. Tchr. The 20th High Sch., Wuhu, China, 1973-78; rsch. asst. SUNY, Stony Brook, 1984-87, rsch. assoc., 1987-89; rschr. BASF, Ludwigshafen, Germany, 1989-92; prof. Chinese U. of Hong Kong, 1992—; adj. prof. physics and chemistry dept. Anhui Normal U., Wuhu, China, China U. of Sci. and Tech., Hefei, China. Editor Jour. of Polymer Blends and Networks, 1996—; contbr. numerous articles to profl. jours. Alexander von Humboldt fellow, 1989-90, Guo Mo-re fellow, 1982; recipient Young scholar award Pacific Basin Socs., 1996, Nat. Disting. Young Investigator award 1996, Qiu shi Disting. Young scholar award, 1997. Fellow Am. Phys. Soc.; mem. Hong Kong Chem. Soc. (coun. mem.), The Internat. Polymer Network Group (com. mem.), Internat. Conf. of Polymer Characterization (sci. com.). Home: M-2-12 Fairview Garden, Yuen Long NT, Hong Kong China Office: Dept Chemistry, The Chinese U of Hong Kong, Shatin Hong Kong

WU, CHIA-JU, engineering educator; b. Kaohsiung, Taiwan, Sept. 10, 1958; s. Kuen-Lin Wu and Ming-Hwa Yang; m. Ching-Ya Yang, Nov. 24, 1985. BS, Nat. Chiao-Tung U., Hsin-Chu, Taiwan, 1980, MS, 1985; PhD, U. Ky., 1990. Lectr. dept. elec. engring. Nat. Hu-Wei Inst. Tech., Taiwan, 1985-87; assoc. prof. dept. elec. engring. Nat. Ocean U., Taiwan, 1990-91, Nat. Yunlin U. Sci. and Tech., Taiwan, 1991-95; prof. dept. elec. engring. Nat. Yunlin U. Sci. and Tech., 1995—, chmn. dept. elec. engring., 1996-98; patent reviewer intellectual property office Ministry Econs., 1992-96; counselor champion team Nat. Micro-Robot Contest, Taiwan, 1986. Author 2 books; co-author 1 book; contbr. over 30 articles to profl. jours., 30 tech. and conf. papers. 2nd lt. Army, 1980-82. Recipient Rsch. Award Nat. Sci. Coun., 1993, 94, 96, 97, 98;. Mem. Chinese Inst. Engrs. (sr.), Automatic Control Soc. (bd. dirs. 1998—). Office: Nat Yunlin U Sci and Tech, Dept Elec Engring, Touliu Yunlin 640, Taiwan

WU, CHIH-YANG, mechanical engineering educator; b. Changhua, Taiwan, June 16, 1955; s. Kai-Di and Suan (Shih) W. BS, Nat. Cheng-Kung U., Taiwan, 1977, MS, 1981; PhD, U. Okla., 1986. Teaching asst. Nat. Cheng-Kung U., Taiwan, 1980-81, instr., 1981-83, assoc. prof., 1986-90, prof., 1990—; vis. scholar U. Ill., Champaign-Urbana, 1992-93. 2d lt. Chinese Army, 1977-79. Recipient Excellence Rsch. award Nat. Sci. Coun., Taipei, 1989-93. Mem. ASME. Avocation: classical music. Office: Nat Cheng Kung U Dept Mech Engring, 1 Ta Hsueh Rd, Tainan Taiwan

WU, CHING-MU, mathematician; b. Tainan, Taiwan, Republic of China, May 16, 1929; s. Wen-kuei and Bii (Lin) W.; m. Nuan Shy, Dec. 26, 1954; children: Huey-jen, Huey-lee, Huey-daw, Huey-shen. BS, Nat. Taiwan U., 1953; DSc, Osaka City U., Japan, 1971. Asst. instr. to assoc. prof. Nat. Cheng-kung U., Tainan, 1953-65; assoc. prof., prof. Tunghai U., Taichung, Taiwan, 1965-72; research fellow Rsch. Inst. Math. Scis. Nat. Kyoto U., Japan, 1969-71; prof., dir. Grad. Sch. Math. Tamkang U., Tamsui, Taiwan, 1972-78; vis. prof. U. West Fla., Pensacola, 1978-80; chair prof. Tamkang U., Tamsui, 1980-95 (ret.); vis. prof. Teikyo U., Japan, 1993-94. Served to 2d lt. Republic of China Army. Recipient Decoration for Disting. Educator Ministry Edn., 1983, 93. Home: 2F No 6 Alley 18 Ln 250 Sect 5, Nanking East Rd, Taipei 105, Taiwan

WU, CHUAN KUN, cryptographer, mathematician; b. Yishui, China, July 2, 1964; arrived in Australia, 1995; s. Jinglu and Dongmei (Li) W.; m. Hong Zhang, Dec. 20, 1988; children: Yugian, Helen. BS, Qufu (China) Normal U., 1985; MS, Xidian U., Xian, China, 1988, PhD in Engring., 1994. Tchg. asst. Xidian U., 1988-90, lectr., 1990-92, assoc. prof., 1992-95, prof., 1995; postdoctoral fellow Queensland U. Tech., Brisbane, Australia, 1995-97, U. Western Sydney, Australia, 1997-2000; lectr. Australian Nat. U., 2000—; head tchg. and rsch. sect. dept. math. Xidian U., 1992-95. Contbr. articles to profl. jours. Recipient Rsch. award China Edn. Com., 1989, 93, Excellent Sci. Youth of Yr. award Dept. Machinery and Electronic Industry China, 1991, subsidy State Coun. China, 1993. Mem. IEEE, IACR, China Math. Assn., China Assn. Sci. Founds. Avocations: fishing, bush walking, tasty math problems collection. Office: Dept Computer Sci, Australian Nat U, Canberra 0200, Australia

WU, CHU-HSIA PATRICIA, foreign language educator, linguistics educator; b. Hsinchu, Taiwan, Nov. 3, 1953; d. Lan-fang and Hsiu-yin (Kuo). BA, Nat. Kaohshung Formal U., Taiwan, 1976; MS, Georgetown U., 1989, PhD, 1992. Sr. translator World Translation Svc., Inc., Taiwan, 1992-93; prof. Nat. Cheng Kung U., Tainan, Taiwan, 1993—; chair Alumni Admission Program, Georgetown U., 1994-99. Recipient grad. scholarship, Georgetown U., 1989-90, grad. fellowship, 1990-92, The Barons Presidential award. Mem. Computational Linguistic Assn., Internat. Chinese Language Computer Soc., Internat. Assn. Intercultural Comm. Studies. Avocations: music, mountain hiking, arts, gardening. Office: Dept Foreign Languages Lit, Nat Cheng Kung U, Tainan Taiwan

WU, DAGUAN, aeroengine design engineer; b. Zhenjiang, Jainsu, Peoples Republic of China, Nov. 13, 1916; s. Jainfei and Jimei (Wang) W.; m. Guo Hua, July 19, 1942; 1 child, Xiaoyun. BS, S.W. United Univ., Kuanming, China, 1942. Pres. and chief designer Rsch. Inst. for Shenyang (China) Aeroengine Design, 1957-78; chief engr. Shenyang Aeroengine Factory, 1973-76; vice chmn. Xian (China) Aeroengine Factory, 1978-82; mem. standing bd. Sci. and Tech. Com. Ministry of Aerospace Industry (MAS), Beijing, 1982-93, 1993-99; mem. standing bd. sci. and tech. com. China Aviation Industry Corp. I, 1999—. Editor: Study of Performance of Turbofon Engine and Its Systems, 1986, The Performance Study and Failure Analysis of Gas Turbine Engine in Testing, 1987. Mem. Nat. Com. Chinese Peoples' Consultative Conf., Beijing, 1978-93; standing coun. Chinese Soc. of Engrs. of Thermal Physics, Beijing, 1982—. Named Outstanding Contribution Expert, State Coun., 1990, Ministry of Aerospace Industry, 1992. Mem. AIAA. Achievements include pioneering and organizing design and devel. of first type of aerogas turbine engine in China, 1958—. Home: PO Box 761, Beijing 100012, China Office: China Aviation Industry Corp 1, Sci & Tech Com Box 761, Beijing 100012, China

WU, DONGPING (DON WU), optical and electrical engineer; b. Shi-jiazhuang, Hebei, China, Apr. 21, 1960; came to U.S., 1992; s. Hongquan and Shujian Wu; m. Helen Hongwei Zhu, July 30, 1988; children: Yue, Eric Z. BS, Harbin Inst. Elec. Tech., Heilongjiang, China, 1982; MS, Beijing U. Posts & Telecomms., 1987, U. Cin., 1996. Nat. profl. tng. in integrated optics, China. Tchr. Ma'anshan 2d H.S., Anhui, China, 1977-78; asst. engr. Shanghai Electric. Cable Rsch. Inst., 1982-84; asst. prof. S.E. U., Nanjing, Jiangsu, China, 1987-92; engr. Nanometrics, Inc., Sunnyvale, Calif., 1996-98; sr. engr. JDS Uniphase Corp., San Jose, Calif., 1998—; vice-sec. gen. Jiangsu Inst. Electronics, Nanjing, 1989-91; dept. sec. for rsch. and acad. affairs S.E. U., Nanjing, 1989-91. Contbr. articles to Beijing U. of Posts and Telecomms. jour., Procs. of IEEE-EMC Symposium, others. Recipient 2d prize sci. and tech. progress China Ministry Machinery Industry, 1986. Mem. IEEE Electromagnetic Compatibility Soc., Electron Devices Soc., China Inst. Electronics, Jiangsu Inst. Electronics. Achievements include E-M theory of anisotropic optical fibers; unified formula for E-M effects of power lines on telecommunication lines; processing and characterization of PCD and DLC semiconductor materials; anisotropic ellipsometry and reflectometry; optical characterization of copolymers; semiconductor lasers with waveguide-cavity combined structure; Argon Laser R&D and product development and manufacturing; precision cleaning chemistry and precious metal brazing; correction to Marcatili's model of channel waveguides. Avocations: American history, reading, classical music, Chinese classical literature, language learning. Office: JDS Uniphase-Comml Lasers 163 Baypointe Pkwy San Jose CA 95134-1623

WU, FU-CHUN, environmental engineer; b. Taipei, Taiwan, Aug. 24, 1963; s. Chang-Peng Wu and Jane Chuang; m. Diana Yu Ma; 1 child, Harrison. BS, Nat. Taiwan U., 1986; MS, U. Calif., Berkeley, 1989, PhD, 1993. Postdoctoral rschr. Nat. Taiwan U., Taipei, 1994-96, asst. prof., 1996—; asst. engr. Natural Resources Consulting Engrs., Berkeley, 1991-93. Contbr. rsch. papers to profl. jours. Recipient Rsch. award Nat. Sci. Coun., 1998, 99,, Rsch. Paper award Chinese Soc. Agrl. Engrs., 1995, 2000. Mem. ASCE, Internat. Assn. Hydraulic Engring. and Rsch., Am. Geophys. Union.

WU, GANG, telecommunications researcher; b. Shanghai, China, Aug. 20, 1962; s. Liang Wu and Xinmei Chen; m. Gangzhu Chen, Dec. 26, 1989; 1 child, Nanette. BE, Xian Jiaotong U., 1984; MSEE, Xidian U., 1987; PhD, Shizuoka U., Hamamatsu, Japan, 1994. Tchg. asst. Xidian U., Xian, China, 1987-88; lectr. Xidian U., 1989-90; rschr. High Tech Rsch., Inc., Matsudo, Japan, 1994; rschr. Comms. Rsch. Lab., Tokyo, 1994-95, sr. rschr., 1995—; vis. scholar Rutgers U. of N.J., Piscataway, 1998-99; rsch. fellow Telecomm. Advanced Org., 2000—. Mem. IEEE (sr.). Avocation: soccer. Office: YRC Comms Rsch Lab, MPT 3-4 Hikarino-Oka, Yokosuka 239-0847, Japan

WU, GUANG, research scientist; b. Tianjin, China, Sept. 26, 1956; s. Qing-He Wu and He-Qing Zhou; m. Shao-Min Yan, Sept. 5, 1984; 1 child, Tian-Yu. MD, Tianjin Med. U., 1984; PhD, Russian State Med. U., Moscow, 1992. Worker Tianjin 1st Machine Plant, 1976-79; tchr. Tianjin Med. Workers' Coll., 1984-86; postdoctoral fellow U. Udine, Italy, 1992-93, 94-99; Sci. and Tech. Agy. fellow Nat. Inst. for Minamata Disease, Japan, 1993-94; postdoctoral fellow U. Mediterranean Aix-Marseille II, Marseilles, France, 2000—. Contbr. articles to profl. jours. Recipient PhD studentship Chinese and Russian govts., 1988-92. Avocations: marathon, swimming, volleyball, skating.

WU, HAI-PING, science educator, consultant; b. Tai-Chung, Taiwan, China, June 22, 1947; d. Sun-Win and Sean-Er Wu; m. Shih-Jeing Un; 1 child. BS, Nat. Taiwan U., China, 1969; MA, Yeshiva U., 1970; MS, CUNY, 1984, PhD, 1988. Cert. assoc. prof. Ministry Edn., Taiwan, environ. mgmt. occupl. safety and health counselor. Lectr. Hunter Coll. Bellune Nursing Sch., N.Y.C., 1971-74; assoc. scientist CIBA-GEIGY Co., 1974-77; sr. scientist Ortho Diagnostics Inc., Rariton, 1977-80; stability project mgr. J.B. Williams Inc., Cranford, 1980-83; group supr. Berlex Lab. Inc., Wayne, 1983-88; assoc. prof. Ming-Hsin Inst. Tech., Hsin-Chu, Taiwan, China, 1990—; cons. Bayer Taiwan Co., Tapei, Taiwan, 1988-97, Ministry Econ. Affairs, Tapei, 1989-98; cons., trainer Chinese Dept. Health, Tapei, 1988-98; advisor EPA, Tapei and Hsin-Chu, 1988-97, Chinese OSHA and Labor Dept., Taiwan, 1990-99. Author: Life operation via food, drug and Environment, 1999; editor: Regulations and Finger-prints Developing of Chinese Herbal Medicine/Instrumental Analysis, 1990-99, Environmental and Technology Management targeting Sustainability, 2000. Avocations: reading and writing books, teaching, traveling. Office: Ming-Hsin Inst Tech CE Dept, Ming-Hsin Inst Tech CE Dept, 1 Hsin-Sing Rd, Hsin-Fong Hsin-Chu Taiwan, Republic of China

WU, HAI-SHAN, electrical engineering educator; b. Pengze, Jiangxi, China; came to U.S., 1992; s. Guihua and Jinyun W.; m. Juanjuan; children: Raymond, Daniel. BSEE, Shanghai Jiaotong U., 1982, MSEE, 1985, PhD, 1988. Lectr. Shanghai Jiaotong U., 1988-91; vis. rschr. Imperial Coll. Sci. & Tech., London, 1991-92; vis. asst. prof. CCNY, 1992-95; asst. prof. Mt. Sinai Sch. Medicine, N.Y.C., 1995—. Contbr. articles to profl. jours. Fellow Royal Soc., U.K., 1991. Mem. IEEE. Avocation: chess. Office: Mt Sinai Sch Medicine PO Box 1194 1 Gustave Levy Pl New York NY 10029

WU, HONG REN, computer science and engineering educator; b. Beijing, Oct. 4, 1956; arrived in Australia, 1986; s. Yun Nan and Su Wu; m. Mei Mei, Feb. 17, 1986. BEng, Beijing U. Iron & Steel Tech., 1982, MEng., 1985; PhD, U. Wollongong, Australia, 1990. Tchr. physics #132 H.S., Beijing, 1975-78; asst. lectr. Beijing U. Iron and Steel Tech., 1982-86; tutor U. Wollongong, 1986-87; lectr. Chisholm Inst. Tech., Melbourne, Australia, 1990; lectr. Monash U., Melbourne, 1990-92, sr. lectr., 1992-96, assoc. prof. sch. computer sci. & software engring., 1997—; rsch. cons. U. Wollongong, 1989-90. Contbr. articles to profl. jours. U. Wollongong Tchg. fellow, 1986, Postgrad. Rsch. scholar, 1987-90. Avocations: bush walking, reading ancient Chinese literature. Office: Monash Univ, Wellington Rd, Clayton VIC 3168, Australia

WU, HONGMIN, research scientist; b. Shanghai, Apr. 22, 1966; d. Zhaoji and Fengying (Li) Wu; m. Xiaodong Zheng, June 30, 1991; 1 child, Junwen. B in Engring., Harbin (China) Engring. U., 1988, M in Engring., 1991; PhD, Tokyo Inst. Tech., 1999. Asst. Underwater Acoustics Lab., Harbin, 1991-94; engr. Fukuda Denshi Co. Ltd., Japan, 1999—. Recipient 2nd class award for sci. and tech. in advancing China State Shipbuilding Corp., 1996. Mem. Internat. Cardiac Doppler Soc. (Daniel Kalmanson Meml. award 1997), Acoustical Soc. Japan, N.Y. Acad. Scis. Avocations: computer programming, swimming, music. Home: 51-1 Tigusadai, Hills Tigusadai 1-406, Aoba-ku Yokohama 227-0051, Japan Office: Fukuda Denshi Co Ltd, 6-7 Hongo-3-Chome Bunkyo-ku, Bunkyo-Ku Tokyo 113-0033, Japan

WU, HSIEN-JUNG, researcher; b. Taipei, Taiwan, June 13, 1962; s. A-Tien Wu and Tsui-Wan Lin; m. Hsu-Heng Pi, July 19, 1991; 1 child, Yu-chen. MS, U. Mo., 1989; PhD, Pa. State U., 1994. Prodn. engr. Patent Master Internat. Corp., Taipei, 1987-88. Contbr. articles to profl. jours. Mem. IEEE, Soc. Mfg. Engrs., N.Y. Acad. Scis., Internat. Neural Network Soc., Inst. Indusl. Engrs. Office: Tung-Hai U, Tung-Hai U Dept Indsl Desig, Box 965, Taichung Taiwan

WU, JAMES KWAN MIN, hotel management company executive; b. Hong Kong, Oct. 9, 1949; s. John C.T. and Annie (Ho) W.; m. Karen Pui Yee Chau, Mar. 22, 1981; 1 child, Jessica. Tchrs. cert., 1969, diploma in mgmt. studies, 1977, cert. hotel adminstr., 1981, MBA, 1987. Tchr. St. Joseph's Coll., Hong Kong, 1969-73; pers. adminstr. Hong Kong Airport Security, 1973-77; pers. mgr. Hong Kong Hotel, 1978-81; exec. asst. mgr. Jianguo Hotel, Beijing, 1981-83; exec. gen. mgr. Hotel Beijing Toronto, 1984-87; gen. mgr. projects and devel. Ansett Transport Industries, Australia, 1987-90; gen. mgr. Hong Kong Parkview, 1990-97; v.p. Parkview Hotels Resorts Ltd., Hong Kong, 1994—; pres., mng. dir. Jiangsu Parkview Hotels & Resorts, Ltd., 1996; dir. project and devel. Hutchison Internat. Hotels, Hong Kong, 1997—. Cadet tng. commr. Scout Assn., Hong Kong, 1970; tng. officer Hong Kong Red Cross, 1968, gen. sec. Hong Kong Cath. Youth Coun., 1968. Mem. Assn. Constrn. Inspectors (cert. constrn. project mgr.), Brit. Inst. Mgmt., Australian Inst. Mgmt., Inst. Tng. and Devel., Inst. Indsl. Mgrs., Inst. Supervisory Mgmt., Chartered Inst. of Transport, Inst. Traffic Adminstrn., Inst. Housing, Hotel Catering Instl. Mgmt. Assn., Royal Soc. Health. Roman Catholic. Avocations: travel, driving. Office: Hutchison Internat Hotels, 20 Tak Fung St Hung Hom, Kowloon Hong Kong Hong Kong

WU, JICHUAN, Chinese government official; b. Changning County, Hunan, People's Republic of China, 1937. Lectr. Beijing Inst. Posts and Telecomms., 1959-62; dep. dir. Bur. Materials and Equipment, Ministry of Posts/Telecomms., 1978-83; dept. dir. Planning Bur., Ministry of Posts/Telecomms., 1983-84; vice-min. Ministry of Posts/Telecomms., 1984-90, min., 1993—; min. info. industry. Mem. The Communist Party. Office: 13 West Chang An Ave, 100804 Beijing People's Republic of China*

WU, JIHUAI, dean, chemical engineer; b. Quanzhou, Fujian, China, Mar. 25, 1958; s. Jisheng and Qiying (Xu) W.; m. Yuyong Nai, Jan. 16, 1989; 1 child, Xiaoyang. PhD, Fuzhou U., Fujian, China, 1999. Dean Huaqiao U. Chem. Engring. Coll., Quanzhou, China, 1998—; dir. Inst. Material Phys. Chem. Huaqiao U., Quanzhou, 1995—; gen. mgr. High Tech. Co. Inst. Material Phys. Chem., Quanzhou, 1995—; dir. PhD China Geol. U., Wuhang, 1999—. Author: The Foundations of Materials Science, 1997; contbr. articles to profl. jours. Recipient Excellent Youth Chemistry prize Chinese Chemistry Soc., 1992. Mem. Chinese Materials Rsch. Soc. (sr. mem.), China Composite Soc. (com. mem., vice-chmn. 1998), Chinese Minerals Rocks Soc. (vice-chmn. mineral materials com., vice-chmn. minerals physics and structure com.). Avocations: reading, music, TV, internet. Home: No 29 West Ave Licheng Area, 362000 Quanzhou China Office: Huaqiao Univ, Inst Material Phys Chem, 362011 Quanzhou China

WU, JING LONG, electrical engineer; b. Jiutai, China, Aug. 4, 1958; s. Wu Zheng Kai and Yin Shu Xiang; m. Nie Li, July 8, 1987; children: Hao, Yu. B in Engring., Jilin Profl. Vocat. Coll., Changchun, China, 1984; M in Engring., Kyoto (Japan) U., 1991, D in Engring., 1994. Asst. prof. Jilin Vocat. Tchr.'s Coll., Changchun, 1984-88, Ritsumeikan U., Kyoto, Japan, 1994-97; prof. Yamaguchi U., Ube, Japan, 1997-99, Kagawa U., Takamatsu, Japan, 1999—; advisor Mystar Engring., Inc., Osaka, Japan, 1995, Oriental Electronics, Inc., Tanabe, Japan, 1994. Mem. IEEE, Soc. Instrument & Control Engrs., Robotics Soc. Japan. Avocations: tennis, fishing, reading, music. Fax: 81-87-864-2369. E-mail: wu@eng.kagawa-u.ac.jp. Office: Kagawa U Faculty Engring, Hayashi-cho 2217-20, Takamatsu 761-0396, Japan

WU, JUNE HSIEH, biochemist, educator; b. Taipei, Taiwan, Jan. 28, 1944; came to U.S., 1967; d. Pin-Ho and Tsai-Lian (Tsai) H.; m. Albert Ming-Tao, July 1, 1972. BS, Nat. Taiwan U., 1966; MS, U. Mo., 1971; PhD, Tex. A&M U., 1986. Cert. med. technologist. Med. technologist Drs. Hosp. and Hazel Hosp., Detroit, 1968-69, Boone County Hosp., Columbia, Mo., 1969-72, No. Westchester Hosp., Mt. Kisco, N.Y., 1972-73; biochemist Westchester County Med. Ctr., Valhalla, N.Y., 1973-83; rsch. asst. Tex. A&M U., College Station, 1983-86, rsch. assoc., 1986-88; rsch. assoc. Baylor Coll. of Medicine, Houston, 1988-89; assoc. prof. Chang-Gung U., Coll. Medicine, Tao-Yuan, Taiwan, 1989—. Rsch. grants Chang-Gung U., Coll. Medicine, 1990—, Nat. Sci. Coun. Mem. Am. Soc. for Cell Biology, Am. Soc. for Microbiology, Am. Heart Assn. Avocations: classical music, cooking, horticulture, jogging. Office: Chang-Gung U Coll Medicine, 259 Wen Hua 1 Rd, Kwei-San Tao Yuan 333, Taiwan

WU, JUNG-SHYR, electrical engineering educator; b. Ping-Tong, Taiwan, Rep. of China, Aug. 6, 1956; s. Yue-Dong and Min-Jing (Chen) W.; m. Tsui-Feng Tsai, Aug. 31, 1983; children: James, Helene, Sam. BS, Nat. Chiao-Tung U., Hsin-Chu, Taiwan, 1979, MSc, 1981; PhD, U. Calgary, Can., 1989. Assoc. prof. Nat. Cen. U., Taiwan, 1989-96, prof., 1996—. Contbr. articles to profl. jours. Mem. IEEE. Avocations: swimming, reading, basketball. Office: Nat Cen Univ, Dept Elect Engring, 32054 Chung-Li Republic of China

WU, KEGANG, geographer, trade consultant; b. Huilai, Guangdong, China, Aug. 16, 1961; s. Kunxiang Wu and Huiwen Wang; m. Ludi He, June 26, 1987; children: Yichen, John Yipu. BS, Zhongshan U., Guangzhou, China, 1982; MS, South China Normal U., Guangzhou, China, 1985; PhD, U. London, 1996. Tchg. asst. South China Normal U., 1983-85, univ. asst. lectr., 1985-87, univ. lectr., 1987-91; tchg. asst. King's Coll. U. London, 1991-94; univ. lectr. U. Liverpool, Eng., 1994—; dir. ChinaLink, Liverpool C. of C. and Industry, Eng., 1999—; vis. scholar U. Toronto, Can., 1986-87; dep. dir. Youth Chinese Geographers, Guangzhou, 1989-91; sr. advisor Silk Road News, Liverpool, 1995—. Co-author: (book) Research on the Landforms of the Wind Drift Sand in South China Coast, 1995; contbr. articles to profl. jours. Grantee rsch. devel. fund U. Liverpool, 1996, Cen. Rsch. Fund, U. London, 1991, Natural Sci. Fund, Nat. Natural Sci. Found., Beijing, 1988. Fellow Royal Geograph. Soc.; mem. Assn. Chinese Geography (England chpt., pres. 1996—), Brit. Geomorphol. Rsch. Group; mem. Liverpool C. of C. and Industry (mem. Liverpool China com. 1995—, chmn., 1997-99). Avocations: Chinese calligraphy, Chinese studies, reading, travel, tea. Office: Dept Geography/U Liverpool, PO Box 147, L69 3BX Liverpool Merseyside, England

WU, LAWRENCE MG HLA MYIN, physician; b. Rangoon, Burma, May 12, 1937; arrived in U.S., 1964; s. John and Maria (Wong) W.; m. Margaret Perez, June 1968. MBBS, U. Rangoon, Burma, 1961. Internship Knickerbocker Hosp., N.Y.C., residency, chief residency; house phys. (fell.) St. Mary's Hosp., Bklyn.; surgeon Harrison Cmty. Hosp., Cadiz, Ohio, Harris Walker Clin., S. Williamsoms, Ky.; priv. prac. Boenger Clin., Edgerton, Ohio; med. dir., Boenger Clin., Edgerton, Ohio, 1991—; bd. govs., Community Meml. Hosp., Hicksville, Ohio, 1996—. Mem. C. of C., Edgerton, Ohio. Fellow Am. Coll. Emergency Medicine (life, charter); mem. AMA, Am. Coll. Gen. Practice (life, charter), Ohio St. Med. Assn., Williams Co. Med. Assn., Am. Coll. Internal Phys., Midwest Burma Med. Assn. Republican. Roman Catholic. Home: 3804 Lake Rd Edgerton OH 43517-9536 Office: 104 N West St Edgerton OH 43517-9697

WU, LIAN-AO, physics educator; b. Jilin City, China, Apr. 3, 1961; s. Bing-Yu and Hui-Xin (Ma) W.; m. Jing Sun, Dec. 30, 1985; 1 child, Sun. BSc, Jilin U., 1983, PhD, 1989. Lectr. Jilan U., Changchun, China, 1991-93, assoc. prof., 1993-96, prof., 1996—; rsch. prof. Osaka (Japan) U., 1996-97. Contbr. articles to profl. jours. Home: Yihe Road No 10, Jilin 130023, People's Republic China Office: Dept Physics, Jie Fang Rd No 119, Jilin 130023, People's Republic of China

WU, MIN, cell biologist, researcher, educator; b. Qixian, China, Oct. 4, 1958; s.. Han Zhang Wu and Su Bi Cheng; m. Yun Zeng, July 12, 1985; 1 child, Lu-shen. BSc in Medicine, Luzhou (China) Med. U., 1983; MD, Shanghai Second Med. U., 1988; PhD, Leeds (Eng.) U., 1997. Lectr. Luzhou (China) Med. Sch., 1988-91, assoc. prof., 1992—, rsch. asst., 1993-94; rsch. officer Leeds (Eng.) U., 1994-97; rsch. assoc. pulmonary divsn. Ind. U./Purdue U., Indpls., 1998—; sr. scientist Synvirion, Ltd., Leeds, 1988—; hon. prof. Tsinghua U., Beijing, 1988—; vis. scientist Peking U., Beijing, 1994-95, Tohoku U., Sendai, Japan, 1991-92. Author: Medical Microbiology, 1990; contbr. articles to profl. jours. Mem. Life Sci. Soc. for Chinese Bioscientists in U.K. (v.p. 1995-96, pres. 1996-97), Drug Delivery System Soc., chinese Immunology Soc., Biochem. Soc., Chinese Scholars Assn. (exec. mem. 1993-94), Leeds Chinese Scholars Assn. (pres. 1994-95). Avocations: football, painting, singing. Home: 123 Beachway Dr Indianapolis IN 46224-8503 Office: Res Asso Pulmonary Divsn IUPU 1 1001 W 10th St # St425 Indianapolis IN 46202-2859

WU, MING-YEN, Republic of China diplomat; b. Republic of China, Oct. 3, 1939; s. Shu and Yen (Lin) W.; m. Mei-shiue Lin, Jan. 14, 1965; children: Michelle, Julie, Catherine. LLB, Nat. Chengchi U., Taipei, Republic of China, 1962, postgrad. in diplomacy, 1963-65. Cert. in fgn. svc. and journalism. Second sec. Chinese Embassy, N.Z., 1967-73; 1st sec. Chinese Embassy, Seoul, 1978-84; sect. chief Ministry Fgn. Affairs, Taipei, 1973-75, dep. dir. consular affairs, 1984-87; sect. chief Republic of China Rep.'s Office in Thailand, Bangkok, 1975-78; Republic of China rep. to Sweden, Taipei Trade Tourism and Info. Office, Stockholm, 1987-90; ROC rep. Fiji Trade Mission of the Republic of China, 1990-93; dir. gen. Records and Data Processing Min. Fgn. Affairs, Taipei, 1993-96; ROC amb. to Commonwealth of Bahamas, 1997; counsellor and acting sec. gen. Min. Fgn. Affairs, Taipei, 1997-98, dir. gen. Telecomms. Svcs., 1998; dir. Secretariat Nat. Security Coun., Republic of China, 1998; China rep. to the Republic of Finland Taipei Econ. and Cultural Office, Helsinki, 1999—. 2d lt. Chinese Army, 1962-63. Recipient Civil Servant award Exec. Yuan. Mem. Formosa First Golf Club, Fiji Golf Club, Helsinki Golf Club. Mem. Nationalist Party. Roman Catholic. Avocation: golf. Home: Vuorimiehenkatu 11 A 7, FIN00140 Helsinki Finland Office: Taipei Econ/Cultural Office, WTC PO Box 800, FIN00101 Helsinki Finland

WU, MIN-KAI, dentist, researcher; b. Shanghai, Oct. 19, 1946; s. Mao-Sun and Feng (Wang) W.; m. Xiao-Fan Jiang, Nov. 25, 1982; 1 child, XiDi. MSD, Beijing Med. U., 1982; PhD, U. Amsterdam, 1993. Gen. dentist gen. hosps., China, 1973-79; lectr. Beijing Med. U., 1982-87; vis. rschr. Baylor Coll. Dentistry, Dallas, 1988; vis. rschr. U. Amsterdam, 1987-88, 89-94, lectr., sr. rschr., 1994—. Contbr. chpt. to book, numerous articles to profl. jours. Mem. Nat. Med. Assn. China, Dutch Soc. Endodontics, European Soc. Endodontics. Avocation: soccer. Office: Acad Ctr for Dentistry, Amsterdam, Louwesweg 1, 1066 EA Amsterdam The Netherlands

WU, NAE-LIH, chemical engineering educator; b. Taipei, Taiwan, China, Sept. 26, 1958; parents: Keh-Sarn and Fon-Mei (Liu) W.; m. Chung-Huei Jowin Liu, Oct. 27, 1991; children: Yih-Chyng, Yi-Ping. BSChemE, Nat. Taiwan U., Taipei, 1980; PhD in Chem. Engring., Pa. State U., 1987.

Postdoctoral fellow SUNY at Buffalo, 1987-88; assoc. prof. chem. engring. dept. Nat. Taiwan U., 1988-92, prof., 1992—; vis. prof. Tex. Ctr. Superconductivity, U. Houston, 1996—. Patentee method for preparing monolith tin oxide. 2d lt. Chinese Marines, 1980-82. Mem. AIChE, Chinese Inst. Chem. Engring. (Outstanding Young Investigator award 1993), Materials Rsch. Soc. Avocations: traveling, swimming, music. Office: Nat Taiwan U, Dept Chemical Engineering, Taipei Taiwan

WU, RONGLING, geneticist, researcher; b. Rugao, Jiangsu, China, Jan. 27, 1964; s. Youpeng Wu and Xiuying Zhang; m. Helen Rong Chen, Mar. 12, 1989; 1 child, Louie. BS, Nanjing (China) Forestry U., 1984, MS, 1987; PhD, U. Wash., 1995. Assoc. prof. Nanjing Forestry U., 1987-90; postdoctoral rsch. assoc. U. Wash., Seattle, 1995-96; postdoctoral rsch. assoc. N.C. State U., Raleigh, 1996-98, rsch. assoc., 1998—; advisor Chinese Acad. Forestry, Beijing, 1997—, Nanjing Forestry U., 1997—. Contbr. articles to profl. jours. Recipient Rsch. Excellence prize State Economy Commn. and State Sci. and Tech., China, 1990, 2d Sci. and Ext. prize Ministry of Forestry, China, 1991, 3d Sci. Invention prize State Sci. and Tech. Commn. of China, 1994. Avocations: running, swimming, camping, movies. Home: 4229 NW 43rd St # S147 Gainesville FL 32606-2510 Office: NC State U 2501 Founders Dr Raleigh NC 27695-0001

WU, RUDOLF SHIU-SUN, biology educator; b. Hong Kong, Nov. 29, 1949; s. Kon Choy and Shiu Kee (Yuen) W.; m. Oi-Lee Chong, July 15, 1974; children: Karen Kar-Yan, Cassandra Kar-Chit. BS with hons., Chinese U. Hong Kong, 1971, BS with spl. hons., 1972; MPhil, U. Hong Kong, 1974; PhD, U. B.C., Vancouver, Can., 1978. Rsch. scientist Agr. and Fisheries Dept., Hong Kong, 1978-83, head marine pollution sect., 1983-85, acting head Fisheries Rsch. Sta., 1985-88; prin. lectr. City Polytechnic of Hong Kong, 1988-90; prof., head Victoria U. of Technology, Melbourne, Australia, 1990-93, City U. of Hong Kong, 1993—. Contbr. articles to profl. jours. Recipient ann. award Can. Soc. Zoologists, 1976, award for excellence AAAS, 1977, commonwealth scholarship, Commonwealth Assn., 1974-77. Mem. Charter Inst. Water and Environ. Mgmt., Marine Biol. Assn. of Hong Kong (vice chmn. 1982-90). Office: City U Dept Biology & Chem, Tat Chee Ave, Kowloon Hong Kong China

WU, SHAOZU, Chinese government official; b. Xi'an City, Hunan, Republic of China, 1939. Grad., Qinghua U., 1964. Dep. for Guangdong Province to 3rd Nat. People's Congress, to 1967, reactivated, 1979; mem. CCP 12th 13th Cen. Coms., 1985; vice minister State Commn. of Sci., Technology and Industry for Nat. Def., 1983-88; minister in charge State Commn. of Phys. Culture and Sports, 1988—. Pres. Chinese Olympic com., 1994, All-China Sports Fedn., 1996; polit. commr. State Commn. for Sci., Tech. and Industry of Nat. Def., 1985; mem. Chinese Communist Party, 12th, 13th, 14th and 15th ctrl. com. Mem. Students' Fedn. (chmn. 1965-67, 79-82), Youth Fedn. (vice-chmn. 1979-83), Nuclear Soc. (v.p. 1984). Office: State Phys Culture Sports Commn, 9 Tiyuguan Lu, 100763 Beijing China*

WU, SHIMING, materials scientist, researcher; b. Shanghai, Oct. 1, 1957; d. Dongdi Wu and Manjun He; m. Dufei Fang; 1 child, Eileen. BS, U. Sci. Tech. China, Hefei, 1982; MS, Chinese Acad. Sci., Shanghai, 1987; PhD, U. Ill., Urbana, 1994. Rsch. asst. Chinese Acad. Sci., Shanghai, 1982-87; asst. prof. Fudan U., Shanghai, 1987-90; guest scientist Nat. Inst. Standard Tech., Gaithersburg, Md., 1990; rsch. asst. U. Ill., Urbana, 1991-94; rsch. fellow U. Southampton, Eng., 1994; rsch. assoc. U. Cambridge, Eng., 1995-97; sr. engr. Philips Lighting Co., 1998—. Mem. Materials Rsch. Soc. Office: 7265 Rte 54 Bath NY 14810

WU, SHI-QI (SAMUEL WU), medical geneticist; b. Anhuei, China, Oct. 14, 1945; s. Wu Qi-Qiang and Xu Yi-Fang. MD, Shanghai First Med. Coll., China, 1971. Diplomate Am. Bd. Med. Genetics. Internist Xian 52 Hosp., China, 1972-73, res. gen. surgery, 1973-78; res. hematololgy Zhongshang Hosp., Shanghai, China, 1979-84; fellowship clin. cytogenetics U. Wis., 1985-88; fellowship cytogenetics U. British Columbia, Vancouver, Canada, 1988-90; co-dir. cytogenetics. rsch. lab Comp. Cancer Ctr. U. Wisc., Madison, Wis., 1993-98; cons. cytogenetics Wis. State Lab Hygiene, Madison, Wis., 1993-98; assoc. scientist human oncol. U. Wis. Med. Sch., Madison, 1990-92, sr. scientist human oncology, 1992-98; assoc. prof. dept pediat. U. So. Calif., 1998—; dir. cytogenetics lab Children's Hosp., L.A., 1998—; program dir. Am. Bd. Med. Genetics program in CHLA, Chiildren's Hosp., U. So. Calif. Med. Sch., 1999—. Mem. ACMG, Am. Assn. Cancer Rsch., Am. Soc. Med. Gene. Office: Children's Hosp Cytogenetics Lab Mailstop 11 4650 W Sunset Blvd Los Angeles CA 90027-6062

WU, SHU YII, chemistry educator; b. Ping-Tong, Taiwan, Feb. 8, 1956; s. Chia Lee and Liu (Liao) W.; m. Chiung Si Chang, Aug. 30, 1981; 1 child, Yeh Min. BSc, Feng Chia U., Taichung, Taiwan, 1978, MSc, 1984; PhD, Katholieke U. Leuven, Belgium, 1990. Asst. Feng Chia U., 1980-84, lectr., 1984-87, assoc. prof., 1990—; cons. Indsl. Tech. Rsch. Inst., Hsinchu, Taiwan, 1996-97. Co-author: (with J. Baeyens) Powder Technology, 1991, Advanced Powder Technology, 1992, (with J. Baeyens and D. Geldart) Powder Technology, 1992, (with Y.Y. Chen, D. Liou and J. Baeyens) Powder Handling and Processing, 1997. Served with Taiwanese Army, 1978-80. Mem. Chinese Inst. Chem. Engring., Chinese Chem. Soc. Confucianist. Avocations: swimming, badminton, global travel. Office: Feng Chia U, 100 Wenhwa Rd, Seatwen Taichung 407, Taiwan

WU, SUH-CHIN, science educator; b. Ping-tung, Taiwan, Jan. 15, 1962; s. M.-J. Wu and K.-S. Wang; m. Yu-Min Cheng; children: Jesse, Gigi. BS, Nat. Cheng-Kung U., Tainan, Taiwan, 1985, MS, 1987; PhD, Tex. A&M U., 1993. Vis. fellow NIH, Bethesda, Md., 1994-95; assoc. investigator Nat. Inst. Preventive Medicine, Taipei, Taiwan, 1995-97; asst. prof. Nat. Tsing-Hua U., Hsinchu, Taiwan, 1997—. Contbr. articles to profl. jours. Recipient rsch. award Nat. Sci. Coun., Taiwan, 1997, 98. Mem. AIChE, Am. Chemistry Soc., Internat. Soc. Vaccines,. Office: Nat Tsing Hua U, Dept Life Sci, Hsinghu 30043, Taiwan

WU, THOMAS XINZHANG, engineering educator, researcher; b. Urumuqi, Xinjiang, China, Nov. 21, 1968; came to U.S., 1995; m. Nadine Xiufang Guo, June 15, 1992; 1 child, Lucy. BS in Engring., U. Sci. and Tech., Hefei, Anhui, China, 1988, MS in Engring., 1991; MS in Engring., U. Pa., 1997, PhD, 1999. Asst. U. Sci. and Tech., Hefei, 1991-93, lectr., 1993-95; asst. prof. Sch. Elec. Engring./Computer Sci. U. Cen. Fla., Orlando, 2000; presenter in field. Contbr. articles to profl. jours. Rsch. fellow U. Pa., 1995-99; recipient Pres. award Chinese Acad. Scis., 1991, Excellent Papers award China Microwave Soc., 1993, Young Scientist Found. award U. Sci. and Tech., 1994-95. Mem. IEEE (reviewer 1996—), Optical Soc. Am. (reviewer 1999—). Achievements include rsch. in chaotic electromagnetics, discontinuities in chirowaveguide, China C-band satellite beam forming network design using rectangular coaxial waveguide technology; invention of omni-directional leaky wave antenna. Avocations: Bible reading, music, travel, sports, friends. Fax: 407-823-5835. E-mail: tomwu@mail.ucf.edu. Office: U Central Fla Sch Elec Engring Orlando FL 32817

WU, TUNG-CHUAN, mechanical engineer; b. Chia-Yi, Taiwan, Republic of China, Sept. 20, 1949; parents Cheng-Wen Wu and Mei-Chi Chang; m. Mei-Hua Lin, Mar. 4, 1976; children: Chien-Te, Chien-Hui. BS, Nat. Cheng-Kung U., 1973; MS, Nat. Tsing-Hua U., 1983; PhD, Chiba U., 1993. From mgr. ultra-precision machining to deputy gen. dir. Mech. Industry Rsch. Labs/Indsl. Technology Rsch., Hsinchu, Taiwan, 1976—. patentee in field. Mem. Chinese Soc. Abrasive Machining (exec. dir. 1995—), Chinese Mech. Engring. Soc. (bd. dirs. 1998—), Chinese Inst. Engrs. (outstanding young engr. 1986), Micromachine Ctr. Buddhist. Avocations: reading, jogging, exercise, meditation.

WU, WAYNE WEN-YAU, artist; b. Tachia, Taiwan, Republic of China, Oct. 5, 1935; s. K.C. Kau and Chin-Fong (Chen) W.; m. Amy Hsueh, Dec. 25, 1961; children: Ingrid, Judy, David. BA in Fine Arts, Taiwan Normal U., 1959. Supr. art edn. ctr. Taichung (Taiwan) Libr., 1970-74; instr. fine arts dept. Taiwan Normal U., Taipei, 1973-74; instr. paintings Hunter Mus. of Art, Chatanooga, Tenn., 1980-92; artist, painting instr. Wayne Wu's Art Studio, Atlanta, 1994-2000, San Jose, Calif., 2000—. Represented in 22 solo shows including Taiwan Mus. of Art, 1995, Hunter Mus. of Am. Art, 1980, 98, and over 100 group shows. Mem. Am. Watercolor Soc. Home: 6232 Yeadon Way San Jose CA 95119-1230

WU, WEI, cardiologist, educator; b. Guangzhou, Canton, China, Oct. 11, 1957; s. Jin Cheng and Xing Wei (Deng) W. BM, Sun Yat-sen U. Med. Scis., Guangzhou, 1982, MD, 1991. Diplomate in medicine. Resident dept. internal medicine Sun Yat-sen Meml. Hosp., Sun Yat-sen. U. Med. Scis., Guangzhou, 1982-91, lectr., attending cardiologist, 1991-93, assoc. prof. divsn. cardiology, 1993-97, prof., 1997—, vice dir. divsn. cardiology, 1996—; Contbr. Practice of Cardiac Pacing and Cardioversion, 1994 (China Ministry Pub. Health 3d award for excellent books 1996), Temporary Cardiac Pacing for Emergency in Clinical Practice (China Guangdong Province 3rd award for progress in sci. and tech. 1994, China Ministry Edn. 3rd award 1998), Clinical and Experimental Studies of Arrhythmias (China Guangdong Province 3rd award for progress in sci. and tech. 1996); contbr. articles to Acta Pharmacologia Sinica, Cardiovascular Drugs and Therapy, others. Mem. Chinese Assn. for Medicine, Chinese Med. Assn. (com. mem. Guangdong br. cardiovasc. com.).

WU, WEN-FANG, mechanical engineer, educator; b. Taipei, Taiwan, Nov. 22, 1954; s. Wan-Yen and Chen-Suifei (Chen) Wu; m. Shin-Pey Tina Yuan, June 20, 1982; 1 child, JoAnn. BSCE, Nat. Taiwan U., 1977; MS, U. Ill., 1983, PhD, 1985. Field surveyor Surveying and Mapping Bur., Taipei, 1977-79; asst. tchg. and rsch. Nat. Taiwan U., Taipei, 1979-80; rsch. asst. U. Ill., Urbana, 1981-84, Fla. Atlantic U., Boca Raton, 1984-85; rsch. scientist Columbia U., N.Y.C., 1985-88; assoc. prof. Nat. Taiwan U., Taipei, 1988—; patent reviewer Ministry of Econs., Taipei, 1994—. Assoc. editor Chinese Jour. Mechanics, 1994—; contbr. articles to profl. jours. Mem. Chinese Soc. Mech. Engrs. (exec. editor jour. 1991-95, Best Paper award 1990), Soc. Theoretical and Applied Mechanics (Best Paper award 1992). Avocations: jogging, camping, reading, sports. Office: Dept Mech Engring, Nat Taiwan Univ, Taipei 10617, Taiwan

WU, WILLIAM CHIEN LIN, cardiologist; b. Bac Lieu, Vietnam, July 24, 1955; came to U.S., 1983.; s. Ban Ngo and Hue Lien; m. Crystal Hwang, 1983; children: Albert, James. MD, Kao Hsiung (Taiwan) Med. Coll., 1982; MPH, Johns Hopkins U., 1984. Cert. in internal medicine and cardiovasc. disease. Staff physician U. Ark. for Med. Scis., Little Rock, 1990-91; clin. instr. U. Tex., San Antonio, 1995-99, clin. assistance prof., 1999—; pvt. practice San Antonio, 1990—; pres., CEO Ctrl. Cardiovasc. Inst., San Antonio, 1998; cons. in cardiology. Fellow Am. Coll. Cardiology, Am. Coll. Physicians, Soc. Cardiac Angiography and Intervention; mem. ACP. Home: 13910 Bluff Wind San Antonio TX 78216-7915 Office: Ctrl Cardiovascular Inst San Antonio 927 Mccullough Ave San Antonio TX 78215-1630

WU, XI-JUN, government official, chemistry educator; b. Wuxi, Jiangsu, China, Aug. 5, 1933; d. Bai-on Wu and Wan-jin Kuo. Grad., East China Sci. and Tech. U., Shanghai, 1955. Engr. Jilin (People's Republic China) Chem. Industry Co., 1955-56; sr. engr., pres. Nanjing (People's Republic China) Rsch. Inst. of Chem. Tech., 1956-83; from assoc. prof. to prof. East China Sci. and Tech. U., Shanghai, 1982—; chmn. Sci. and Tech. Commn. of Jiangsu Province, Nanjing, 1983—; prof. Nanjing Inst. Chem. Tech., 1984—; vice gov. Jiangsu Province, Nanjing, 1987-93, vice speaker, 1993—; leader Sequential Method Project, 1978 (Nat. award 1981), Evolutionary Optimization Project, 1981 (Nat. award 1983), Process Optimization Project, 1981 (Nat. award 1984). Author: Series of High Technology, vols. 1-9, 1992 (Nat. award 1996); co-author: Synthetic Ammonia, 1976. Del. Nat. People's Congress, Beijing, 1982—; chmn. Assn. Friendship with Fgn. Countries, Nanjing, 1984—. Mem. Chinese Chem. Engring. Soc. (exec. 1978—), Chinese Sci. and Tech. Assn., Chinese Acad. Sci. and Tech. Devel. (chair Jiangsu br. 1998—). Avocations: basketball, guitar. Office: Jiangsu Provincial People's Congress, 32 N Zhong Shan, Nanjing Jiangsu 210028, China

WU, XIN BAO, engineering educator, researcher; b. Xiaoxian, Anhui, China, Jan. 25, 1965; s. Xiaoti Wu and Lanying Zhu; m. Xiaomei Li, Aug. 20, 1989; 1 child, Fei. BS, Fuyang (China) Normal Coll., 1986; M in Engring., China Rsch. Inst. Radiowave Propogation, Xinxiang, 1988; PhD, U. Electronic Sci. Tech. China, Chengdu, 1992. Engr. China Rsch. Inst. Radiowave Propagation, Xinxiang, 1991-92, sr. engr., 1993-95, rsch. prof., dep. dir. gen., 1996—; vis. fellow Kyushu U., Fukuoko, Japan, 1996-97, Macquarie U., Sydney, Australia, 1997-98. Dep. chief editor Chinese Jour. Radio Sci., 1997—; contbr. articles to profl. jours. Recipient subsidy Min. Electronics Industry China, 1992-96, Excellent Young People award Xinxiang City, 1995. Fellow Henan Geophys. Soc.; mem. IEEE (sr.), Chinese Inst. Electronics.

WU, XIYING, mechanical engineering educator; b. Wuxi, JiangSu, China, Aug. 25, 1931; s. Bingtai Wu and Huifen Zheng; m. Zhifang Xu; 1 child, Rong. Grad., Tianjin (China) U., 1956. Asst. Tianjin (China) U., 1956-57; asst. Nanjing (China) Inst. Tech., 1957-78, lectr., 1978-83, assoc. prof., 1983-90; prof. S.E. Univ., Nanjing, 1990—; gen. designer of CIMS for Beijing No. 1 Machine Tool Plant, 1990—; cons. Guizhou Inst. Tech., Guiyang, China, 1992-94; part-time prof. Anhui Inst. Mech. and Elec. Engring., Wuhu, China, 1993—, East China Shipbuilding Inst., Zhengjian, China, 1993—, Yangzhou U., 1996—. Author: Computer Aided Manufacturing, 1990, 92, Manufacturing System Automation, 1992, Computer Integrated Manufacturing Technology, 1996, Handbook of Mechatronics Design, 1996. Recipient Industry LEAD award, 1995, CASA/SME. Mem. Am. Soc. Mech. Engring., Chinese Mech. Engring. Soc. (sr.), Bd. Chinses Inst. and Univ. (vice chmn. 1986—), Soc. Mfgs. Engrs. (sr.). Avocations: classical music, table tennis, watching spot match. Home: 14-404 #2 West Beijing Rd, Nanjing Jiangsu 210008, China Office: Dept Mech Engr Southeast U, #2 Si Pai Lou, Nanjing Jiangsu 210096, China

WU, XIZHEN, physicist; b. Hebei, China, July 3, 1940; s. Zexin and Shi (Li) W.; m. Zhuxia Li, Mar. 10, 1968; 1 child, Kaiyu. BS, Chinese U. Sci. & Tech., Beijing, 1964; MS, Inst. Atomic Energy, Beijing, 1968. Asst. rschr. China Inst. Atomic Energy, Beijing, 1972-78, rsch. assoc., 1979-88, sr. scientist, 1989-96, prof., 1997—. Contbr. articles to profl. jours. Humboldt fellow, Bonn, Germany, 1984, Sci. & Tech. Agy. fellow, Tokyo, 1997. Mem. Chinese Phys. Soc., Chinese Nuclear Physics Soc., Chinese High Energy Physics Soc. Avocation: chess. Office: China Inst Atomic Energy, PO Box 275 (18), Beijing China

WU, YING, economics educator, researcher; b. Beijing, Sept. 22, 1955; s. Dazhi and Chengying (Mao) W.; m. Hong Yao, Jan. 20, 1987; children: Danke, Danlei. BA in Econs., Peking (China) U., 1984, MA in Econs., 1987; PhD in Econs., U. Oreg., 1992. Instr. Peking U., 1986-87; grad. tchg. fellow U. Oreg., 1987-92; asst. prof. U. Portland, 1992-93; instr. Lane C.C., 1993-94; lectr. Nanyang Technol. U., Singapore, 1994-98; asst. prof. Salisbury State U., 1998—; guest prof. Peking U., 1995; guest commentator Asia Bus. News, Singapore, 1996-97, Brit. Broadcasting Corp., 1997. Author: An Analysis of Credit and Equilibrium Credit Rationing, 1994; jour. referee Journ. Macroecons., 1996; contbr. articles to profl. jours. Libr. svc. coord. Nanyang Techol. U., 1997-98. Recipient 20th Century Achievement award Internat. Biog. Ctr., U.K., 1998, 2000 Millennium medal, Am. Biog. Inst., 1999. Mem. Am. Econ. Assn., Western Econ. Assn., Pi Gamma Mu. Avocations: table tennis, jogging, swimming, hiking, movies. Office: Salisbury State U Franklin P Perdue Sch Bus 1101 Camden Ave Salisbury MD 21801-6860

WU, YU-CHI, engineering educator, consultant, researcher; b. Fengshan, Kaohsiung, Republic of China, July 19, 1964; s. Shih-Dar and Shang-Feng (Wang) W.; m. Suhua Ho; 1 child, Yi-Hong. PhD in Elec. Engring., Ga. Tech., Atlanta, 1993, MS in Elec. Engring., 1993. Rsch. asst. Ga. Tech., Atlanta, 1989-92; cons. PG&E, San Francisco, 1990; assoc. analyst EDS/EMA, Atlanta, 1992-93, analyst, 1993-94; assoc. prof. dept. elec. engring. Lien Ho Inst. Tech., Miao-Li, Taiwan, 1994—; chmn. Lien Ho Coll. Tech. and Commerce, Miao-Li, Taiwan, 1995-98; cons. EDS/CMS, Taipei, Taiwan, 1994-95; project prin. investigator, NSC, Taiwan, 1995—. Inventor: IPM-OPF Software, 1993, PHS Software, 1992; contbr. articles to profl. jours. Mem. Youth Goodwill Mission Group, Taiwan, 1983. 2nd Lt. Army, 1984-86, Taiwan. Recipient Acad. award Nat. Kaohsiung Inst. Tech., 1984, Straight A's in MS work, Ga. Tech., 1990. Mem. IEEE (sr.), IEEE/PES, IEEE Power Elec., Gamma Beta Phi, Pi Mu Epsilon. Avocations: reading, movies, golf, sports.

WU, YUSEN (JOHN WOO), film director; b. Guangzhou, Canton, China, 1948. Asst. dir. Shaw Bros. Studios, 1969. Dir. (films) A Better Tomorrow, 1986, The Killer, 1989, Bullet in the Head, Hard Boiled, Hard Target, 1993, Broken Arrow, 1996, Face/Off, 1997 (Acad. Sci. Fiction, Horror and Fantasy Films Saturn award Best Dir.), Black Jack, 1998, Kings Ransom, 1998, Mission Impossible 2, 1999. Recipient CineAsia Lifetime Achievement award, 1996. Office: William Morris Agency c/o Mike Simpson 151 S El Camino Dr Beverly Hills CA 90212-2775

WU, ZHEN, opto-electronic engineering educator; b. Dongyang, Zhejiang, China, Sept. 2, 1943; s. Fu-Qi Wu and Baocou Lou; m. Ping Zhang, Dec. 25, 1968; 1 child, Jun. BS, Zhejiang U., Hangzhou, China, 1966; English diploma, Zhong Shang U., Guangzhou, China, 1981. Engr. Jiangnan Optical Factory, Nanjing, China, 1966-74; tchg. asst. Huazhong U. Sci. & Tech., Wuhan, China, 1974-78; lectr. Huazhong U. Sci. & Tech., Wuhan, 1978-81, assoc. prof., 1986-92, prof., 1993—; vis. scholar Reading (Eng.) U., 1981-83; prof. Hubei Inst. Tech., Wuhan, 1995—; vice dir. Libr. and Info. Com. for Univs. and Colls., Hubei, 1994—. Author: Interference Testing Tech., 1995; co-author: (handbook) Handbook of Optical Technology, 1994; chief editor Internat. Acad. Devels., 1996. Visitor Del. of State Edn. Commn.-Sony Co., Tokyo, 1985. Recipient 2nd prize for outstanding paper Hubei Province, 1986, 2nd prize for outstanding rsch. achievements Hubei Province, 1992, 3rd prize for outstanding rsch. achievements State Edn. Commn., 1993. Mem. Info. Soc. Hubei Province (standing dir. 1995—), Nat. Soc. for Optical Testing (dir. 1984—). Avocations: Chinese calligraphy, volleyball, basketball. Office: Dept Optoelectronic Engring, Huazhong U Sci & Tech, Wuhan Hubei 430074, China

WU, ZHEN YANG, engineering educator; b. Wuxi, China, Jan. 20, 1949; s. Qi Ming and Fong Ming (Gu) W.; m. Man Qin Dai; 1 child, Zhi Kai. Ms in Engring., Nanjing Inst. Tech., China, 1982; postgrad., U. Wis., 1992-95, Hong Kong U., 1995. Farmer Yangzhou, China, 1969-74; lectr. Nanjing Inst. Tech., China, 1982-87; assoc. prof. Southeast U., Nanjing, 1987-97, prof., 1998—; cons. in field. Author: Principle and Implementation of Digital Signal Processing, 1997. Vis. scholar U. Wis., Madison, 1992-94. Mem. Chinese Inst. Elecs. (sr.). Avocations: swimming, biking. Office: Southeast U Dept Radio Engr, Si Pai Lou #2, Nanjing 210018, China

WU, ZHISHEN, engineering educator; b. Zhenjiang, Jiangsu, China, June 12, 1961; s. Zhongan Wu; m. Qian Shi, Feb. 2, 1986; 1 child, Xiqing. B in Engring., S.E. U., Nanjing, China, 1983, M in Engring., 1986; D in Engring., Nagoya (Japan) U., 1990. Rsch. assoc. Nagoya U., 1990-93; asst. prof. Saitama U., Urawa, Japan, 1993-94; assoc. prof. Saitama U., Urawa, 1994-95, Ibaraki U., Hitachi, Japan, 1995—; prof. Nanjing U., 1995—; prof. S.E. U., Nanjing, 1997—; rschr. Geol. Survey Japan, Tsukubu, 1997—; dir. Advanced Computational Engring., Inst. Nanjing U., 1998—; overseas assessor Chinese Acad. Scis. Contbr. over 100 articles to profl. jours.; patentee in field. Recipient Sci. Rsch. Program award Ministry Edn., Culture and Sci. of Japan, 1995, 96-98, 99-2000, Internat. Sci. Rsch. Program award Ministry Edn., Culture and Sci. of Japan, 1997-98; named rep. State Coun. Peoples Republic China, Beijing, 1999. Mem. Japanese Soc. Civil Engrs. (Rsch. prize 1990), Infrastructure Devel. Soc. (pres. 1991-96), Chinese Acad. Sci. and Engring. Japan (pres. 1999). Buddhist. Avocations: calligraphy, Chinese painting. E-mail: zswu@ipc.ibaraki.ac.jp. Fax: 81 294 38 5268. Home: Mikanohara-cho 1-9-1, Hitachi Ibaraki 316-0026, Japan Offfice: Ibaraki Univ, Nakanarusawa-cho 4-12-1, Hitachi Ibaraki 316-8511, Japan

WU, ZHONGHU, reserach scientist; b. Yilian, Heilongjng, China, Dec. 27, 1941; s. Xianting Wu and Yufang Xiao; m. Yi Zhang, Dec. 22, 1981; 1 child, Yihan. Grad., Electricity Power U., Beijing, 1966. Engr. Power Plant, Shizhuishan, China, 1968-80; rschr. Energy Rsch. Inst., Beijing, 1981-88, assoc. fellow, 1988-93, dir. of divsn., 1988—, prof., 1994—; sr. cons. China's Electricity Coun., Beijing, 1995—. Author: (law of energy/law vol.) Great Encyclopedia of China, 1984; chief editor/author: (books) Study on Electricity Industry Reform in China, 1988, Establishment of China's Energy Law System, 1992; mem. editl. commn., dep. chief editor of energy and economy/author: Energy Great Encyclopedia of China, 1997. Mem. China Energy Rsch. Soc. (mem. coun. 1992—), China Law Soc. (sec. gen. acad. of energy law 1997—), Internat. Assn. for Energy Econs. Avocations: reading books, movies, Chinese painting, collecting stamps. Office: Energy Rsch Inst SDPC, Zhansi Men Lu Sha he, 102206 Beijing China

WU, ZONGMIN, mathematics educator and researcher; b. Shanghai, China, June 25, 1957; s. Dade and Fengying (Liu) W.; m. Huiyong Jiang, Mar. 2, 2000; 1 child, Yanjung. B degree, Fudan U., Shanghai, 1982; PhD, Georg August U., Göttingen, Fed. Republic of Germany, 1986. Asst. prof. Fudan U., Shanghai, 1987-90, assoc. prof., 1991-96, prof., vice dean dept. math., 1996—. Contbr. articles to profl. jours. Fellow Am. Math. Soc. Avocations: literature, philosophy, music, touring. Office: Fudan U, Dept Math, Handan Rd 220, Shanghai 200433, China

WU, ZU-WANG, science educator; b. Shanghai, China, Apr. 21, 1934; s. Sui-Fang Wu and Xi-Chun Huang; m. Yu-Ling Wei, Nov. 16, 1957; children: Zhi-Dong, Zhi-Ning. BS, Dalian Inst. Tech., China, 1955. Chartered colourist, U.K. Instr. Dalian Inst. Tech., 1955-63, lectr., 1963-81, assoc. prof., 1981-86, prof., 1986—; inventor in field. Contbr. articles to profl. jours. Fellow SDC; mem. AAAS, Nat. Dyestuff Standard Com. (vice dir. 1988—), Chinese Dyestuff Soc. (exec. mem. 1993-98). Avocations: table tennis, Chinese music. Home: Room 14-14, 1 Congshan St, Dalian 116011, China Office: Dalian U Tech, 158 Zhongshan Rd, 116012 Dalian China

WUBAH, DANIEL ASUA, microbiologist, educator, dean; b. Accra, Ghana, Nov. 6, 1960; came to U.S., 1984; s. Daniel Asua and Elizabeth Bruba (Appoe) W.; m. Judith A. Dadson, Dec. 17, 1993; children: Vera, Araba. BSc with honors, DipEd, U. Cape Coast, Ghana, 1984; MS, U. Akron, 1988; PhD, U. Ga., 1990. Cert. in hazardous waste site ops. and emergency response health and safety. Postdoctoral fellow U.S. EPA Rsch. Lab., Athens, Ga., 1991-92; asst. prof. dept. microbiology Towson (Md.) U., 1992-97, assoc. prof., 1997-2000, dept. chair, 1998-2000; assoc. dean Coll. Sci. and Math. James Madison U., 2000—; councillor Coun. Undergrad. Rsch. Assoc. editor: Mycologia; contbr. articles to profl. publs. Sr. warden Sherwood Episcopal Ch., Cockeysville, Md., 1998-2000; bd. govs. Nat. Aquarium Balt. Recipient Paul Acquarone award U. Akron, 1985, Palfrey award U. Ga., 1989, Ruska award Southeastern Electron Microscopy Soc., 1989; Faculty Rsch. grantee Towson State U., 1992, 94, 97; grantee NSF, 1993, 98—, USDA, 1994, Univ. Sys. Md., 1998, 99, 2000, NIH, 2000-02. Mem. AAAS, Mycological Soc. of Am., Am. Soc. Microbiology, Med. Mycological Soc. of Am., Internat. Soc. for Human and Animal Mycology, CUR (councilor biology divsn.), Sigma Xi (pres. Towson chpt. 1996-97), Coun. on Undergrad. Rsch. (listserver adminstr. Project Kaleidoscope F21). Episcopalian. Achievements include first description of the resting stage of anaerobic zoosporic fungi from rumen; first isolation of rumen zoosporic fungi from nature; description of a novel morphological development in rumen fungus; demonstration that hitherto fungi belonging to different species were the same. Home: 415 Confederacy Dr Penn Laird VA 22846-9625 Office: James Madison U Office Dean Coll Sci And Math Harrisonburg VA 22807-0001

WU CHENG-CHUNG, JOHN BAPTIST CARDINAL, bishop; b. Ng Wah County, Kwangtung, China, Mar. 26, 1925; s. Wu Shing Sing and Mary Chow. Degrees in philosophy and theology, South China Regional Sem., Hong Kong; D Canon Law summa cum laude, Pontifical U., Rome, 1956. Ordained priest Roman Cath. Ch., 1952; ordained bishop, 1975. Priest Cath. Ch., Hong Kong, 1952-53; pastor parishes N.Y.C., Boston, Chgo., 1956-57, Republic of China, 1957-75; bishop of Hong Kong, 1975—; cardinal Hong Kong, 1988—. Mem. (apptd.) Congregation for Evangelization of Peoples, Pontifical Coun. Interreligious Dialogue, Pontifical Coun. Culture, Pontifical Coun. Social Communications. Address: Carltas House, 2 Caine Rd, Hong Kong China*

WUCHERER-HULDENFELD, AUGUSTINUS KARL, philosopher; b. Gleinstatten, Austria, July 1, 1929; s. Otto Reichsfreiherr and Rosa (Alt-

grafin Salm-Reiferscheidt) Wucherer von Huldenfeld. DrPhil, U. Vienna, 1954; Absolutorium theologiae, U. Innsbruck, Austria, 1961; Habil Phil, U. Vienna, 1974, Prof., 1997. Chaplain St. Norbert-Fathers, Stift Geras, Austria, 1961-64; prof. theol.-philos. coll. Augustiner-Regular-Cannons, Klosterneuburg, Austria, 1954-55, 64-69; asst. Inst. for Atheism Rsch. U. Vienna, 1967-74, prof., dir. Inst. for Christian Philosophy, 1974-97. Author: Die Gegensatzphilosophie R. Guardinis, 1968, Personales Wort und Sein (Ferdinand Ebner), 1985, Ursprungliche Erfahrung und personales Sein, Philosophische Studien I, 1994, II, 1997. Mem. Soc. for Daseinsanalysis (pres. 1990—), Inst. for Psychotherapy, Psychosomatic and Basic Rsch. (v.p. 1995), Soc. for Ferdinand Ebner (pres. 1996—). Home: Ramperstorffergasse 65, A-1050 Vienna Austria

WUELLNER, ULLRICH, neurologist; b. Minden, Germany, July 7, 1962; s. H. and E. W.; m. Heike Gratz, Nov. 20, 1988; children: Tobias, Marlene. MD, U. Goettingen, 1989. Rsch. fellow in neurology Mass. Gen. Hosp., Boston, 1991-93; resident in neurology U. Tubingen, Germany, 1994-98; asst. prof. neurology U. Bonn (Germany), 1999—. Office: Univ Bonn, Sigmund Freud Str 25, 53105 Bonn Germany

WUEST, LARRY CARL, tax examiner; b. Blue Ash, Ohio, Oct. 14, 1940; s. Carl William and Billie Asalee (Lanham) W. AA in Acctg., Long Beach City Coll., 1961; BS in Acctg., Miami U., Oxford, Ohio, 1969; MBA, Xavier U., 1977. Acct. Ohio River Co., Cin., 1969-79; computer programmer Bertke Electric, Cin., 1979-81, Great Am. Ins., Cin., 1982, Belcan Svcs., Cin., 1983-84, PDR Svcs., Cin., 1985; retail shop owner Raven's Records, Harrison, Ohio, 1986-87; tax examiner IRS, Covington, Ky., 1988—. Mem. Mensa, World Affairs Coun. of Greater Cin. Avocations: travel, music collecting, art, computer programming. Home: 217 S Vine St Harrison OH 45030-1354

WULF, HANS CHRISTIAN, dermatology educator; b. Haderslev, Denmark, Aug. 18, 1943; s. Jens and Esther (Olsen) W.; m. Benedicte Maria Elisabeth Bronnum Scavenius, June 26, 1971; children: Casper Jens, Nicholas Henrik. MD, U. Copenhagen, 1973, D Pharmacy, 1989. Rsch. prof. in photobiology Skin and Cancer Inst., Phila., 1987-88; cons. in photodermatology, 1991-94; prof. in skin and venereal diseases dept. dermatology Nat. U. Hosp./U. Copenhagen, 1994; chief cons., prof. dermatology Bispebjerg Hosp./U. Copenhagen, 1996—; established a photobiol. lab. at Finsen Inst., 1975; lectr. in field. Contbr. more than 300 articles to profl. jours. Office: Bispebjerg Hosp/Dept Dermat, Bispebjerg Bakke 23, 2400 Copenhagen NV, Denmark

WULF, HERWIG, language educator. Prof. Pädagogische Hochschule Freiburg, Germany; chmn. langs. dept., 1987-89; mem. commn. for English tchg. curriculum revision Realschule, Baden-Württemberg, 1992-93; freelance advisor to sch. adminstrn., Baden-Württemberg, 1994-98. Contbr. articles and books to profl. publs. Chmn. local chpt. Social Democrats., 1986-94. Avocations: fossil collecting, tennis. Home: Alte Sage 11, 79199 Kirchzarten-Burg Germany

WULF, SHARON ANN, management consultant; b. New Bedford, Mass., Aug. 23, 1954; d. Daniel Thomas and Norma Dorothy (McCabe) Vieira; m. Stanley A. Wulf, 1983. BS in Acctg. cum laude, Providence Coll., 1976; MBA, Northeastern U., 1977; PhD, Columbia Pacific U., 1984. Staff acct., intern Laventhol & Horwath, Providence, 1977; jr. fin. analyst Polaroid Corp., Waltham, Mass., 1977-78; fin. analyst Polaroid Corp., Freetown, Mass., 1978-79, Cambridge, Mass., 1979-81; sr. fin. cons., mktg. strategic planner Digital Equipment Corp., Stow, Mass., 1981-82; sr. fin. cons., mktg. strategic planner Digital Equipment Corp., Maynard, Mass., 1982-83, mgr. fin. devel. program, 1983-84, strategic fin. cons. engring. divsn., 1984-86; group mgr. planning & strategic ops. Digital Equipment Corp., Hudson, Mass., 1986-87, group mgr. strategic bus. planning, 1987-89; mktg. planning mgr. Digital Equipment Corp., Marlboro, Mass., 1989-90, new ventures bus. devel. mgr., 1990-92; pres. Enterprise Sytems, Framingham, Mass., 1993—; prof. Cambridge Coll., 1998—; lectr. fin. acctg. Southeastern Mass. U., 1979-81; adj. prof. acctg., mgmt. & fin. Northeastern U., Boston, 1980—; instr. Nat. Tech. U., 1991—, Framingham State Coll., 1999—; sr. instr. Cambridge Coll., 1997—, Framingham State Coll., 1999—; exec. com. enterprise forum MIT, 1987-92; prin. Work Systems Assocs., Inc., Marlborough, Mass., 1992-93; bd. advisors Spaceball Tech., Inc., Lowell, Mass., Terasys, Inc.; cons. in field. Author: Building Performance Values, 1996, Customer Service Action Plans, 1997, LEadership in Action: The Way It Is Cersus The Way It Should Be, 1997. Chair pub. support and fund raising ARC, New Bedford, 1974-84; bd. dirs. Vets. Outreach Ctr., Metrowest, Framingham, 1989-93; v.p. MIT Leadership Found., Cambridge, 1991-93; mem. exec. com. MIT Enterprise Forum, also co-chair stant up clinics, 1986-92. Mem. Black Alumni of MIT (bd. advisors 1989-92), Univ. Coll. Faculty Soc., Phi Sigma Tau. Fax: 508-626-9038. E-mail: sharonw@enters.com. Home: 902 Salem End Rd Framingham MA 01702-5532 Office: Enterprise Systems 1257 Worcester Rd Ste 301 Framingham MA 01701-5217

WULF, STANLEY ARTHUR, engineering executive; b. Adrian, Minn., Aug. 14, 1943; s. Arthur Harry and Dena (Huisenga) W.; m. Sharon A. Vieira Wulf, Oct. 1, 1983. BSME, Mass. Inst. Tech., Cambridge, 1965; PhD, Northwestern, Evanston, Ill., 1970. Rsch. engr. Argonne (Ill.) Labs., 1971-73; dir. Materials Testing Lab. Brewer Engring. Labs., Marion, Mass., 1973-81; v.p. AMPS Ltd., Marion, 1981-92; OEM sales mgr. HBM, Inc., Marlborough, Mass., 1982-90; mktg. dir. NMB Tech., Chatsworth, Calif., 1990-93; pres. Enterprise Sys., ž, 1993—; dir. Psi Delta Corp., Boston, 1996, Marine Biotech Inc., Beverly, Mass. Mem. Internat. Soc. Weighing and Measurements, Soc. for Experimental Mechanics, Soc. of Automotive Engrs. Home: 902 Salem End Rd Framingham MA 01702-5532 Office: Enterprise Systems 1257 Worcester Rd Ste 301 Framingham MA 01701-5217

WULFF, DANIEL LEWIS, molecular biologist, educator; b. Santa Barbara, Calif., Mar. 29, 1937; s. Daniel Reid and Mary (Lewis) W.; m. Bonnie Taylor, Dec. 30, 1957; children: Melissa, Mark, Elise. BS in Chemistry, Calif. Inst. Tech., 1958, PhD in Chemistry, 1962. Postdoctoral fellow Inst. Genetics U. Cologne, Germany, 1962-63; postdoctoral fellow dept. biology Harvard U., Cambridge, Mass., 1963-65; asst. prof. molecular biology U. Calif., Irvine, 1965-68, assoc. prof., 1968-74, prof., 1974-79, assoc. dean biol. scis., 1975-79; dean Coll. Sci. and Math. SUNY, Albany, 1980-93, prof. biol. scis., 1980—. Mem. AAAS, Am. Soc. Microbiology, Genetics Soc. Am., Am. Soc. Biochemistry and Molecular Biology. Office: SUNY Biology Albany NY 12222

WULFF, GERHARD, mathematician; b. Herrenberg, Germany, Oct. 2, 1939; s. Otto and Hildegard Wulff; m. Frieda Ursula Bornemann, Apr. 11, 1970; children: Petra, Karen. Diploma in math., U. Tübingen, Germany, 1967. Scientist ops. rsch. br. DLR Inst. Flight Rsch., Braunschweig, Germany, 1968-77, scientist math. methods and data handling br., 1977—, group leader statis. data analysis group, 1983—; lectr. analysis and stochastics Inst. Flight Mechanics, Braunschweig, Germany, 1972-97. Contbr. articles to profl. jours. Mem. AIAA, Am. Math. Soc., Deutsche Gesellschaft fuer Luft-und Raumfahrt, European Math. Soc., Soc. for Indsl. and Applied Math., Deutsche Mathematiker Vereinigung. Home: Schulring 37, D-38108 Braunschweig Germany Office: DLR Inst Flight Rsch, Lilienthalplatz 7, D-38108 Braunschweig Germany

WULFF, GUENTER, chemistry educator, researcher, university dean; b. Hamburg, Germany, Feb. 19, 1935; s. Georg and Kaete Wulff; m. Gertraud Ida Zaake, May 11, 1962; children: Marianne, Wolfgang, Gerhard. Diploma in chemistry, U. Hamburg, 1960; DSc, U. Bonn, Germany, 1963, Habilitation, 1970. Rsch. asst. U. Bonn, 1963-70, lectr., 1971-72, assoc. prof., 1972-79; prof. chemistry U. Düsseldorf, Germany, 1979—, dean sci. faculty, 1991-92; guest prof. Ateneo de Manila U., 1970. Contbr. over 200 articles to sci. jours.; patentee in field. Recipient Dozenten prize Fonds Chemischen Industrie, 1973, Prix Cerealier, European prize for achievements in field of renewable resources, 1996, Havinga medal Royal Netherlands Chem. Soc., 1997. Mem. German Chem. Soc. (br. chmn. 1977-78), Am. Chem. Soc. Avocations: sports, gardening. Office: Heinrich Heine U, Organic & Macromol Chem, 40225 Düsseldorf Germany

WULKER, LAURENCE JOSEPH, portfolio manager, educator, financial planner; b. Cin., Apr. 6, 1945; s. Joseph Laurence and Dorothea Clare (Link) W. BS, Xavier U., Cin., 1967, MA, 1971; cert. fin. planner, Coll. Fin. Planner, 1985. Instr. Lloyd High Sch., Erlanger, Ky., 1967-68, Elder High Sch., Cin., 1968-73, Peoples High Sch., Cin., 1973-74, Regina High Sch., Cin. Tech. U., Cin., 1974-75; stockbroker Harrison-Bache, Cin., 1976-78; portfolio mgr., fin. planner, v.p. investments Paine Webber, Cin., 1978—, formed Wulker Group, 1997; instr. U. Cin., 1981-98, Nat. Inst. Fin., South Plainfield, N.J., 1986-88; systems operator, Fin. Planning Forum Tristate Online, Cin., 1991-97; speaker at numerous seminars 1984—; systems operator Investor Forum, Compuserve, 1985-86. Author column Japanese-Am. League Newsletter, 1985-96; contbr. articles to Cin. Enquirer, Cin. Post, Cin. Bus. Courier. Bd. dirs., v.p., pres. No. Ky. Symphony, 1993-99; mem. Greater Cin. Planned Giving Coun.; bd. dirs. Friends of Findley Market, Findley Market Assn., 1999—. Fulbright scholar Dept. Health, Edn. and Welfare, 1972; named 1 of best 200 Stockbrokers Country Money mag., 1987. Mem. Stock and Bond Club, Fulbright Soc., Order Ky. Cols., Updowntowners Club. Roman Catholic. Avocations: computers, tennis, golf, volleyball, reading. Fax: 513-369-4184. Home: 558 Davenport Ave Apt 11 Cincinnati OH 45204-1362

WULLAERTS, LODE RENE ELISABETH, finance executive; b. Louvain, Belgium, May 14, 1959; s. Marcel Wullaerts and Cecile Willemyns; m. Frieda Van Steenbergen, Feb. 14, 1983; 1 child, Isabelle. Licentiate in Law magna cum laude, U. Louvain, 1984, Licentiate in Philosophy magna cum laude, 1984, Licentiate in Econs. magna cum laude, 1985. Cert. tax cons., lawyer, fin. analyst. Mgmt. trainee G-Bank, Belgium, 1984-85; head fin. engring. G-Bank, Brussels, 1985-88; asst. gen. mgr. Bankers' Assn., Brussels, 1988-89; head of mergers and acquisitions Paribas, The Netherlands/Belgium, 1989-91; dir. corp. fin./investment banking Societé Générale, Paris and Brussels, 1991-94; exec. dir. corp. fin./investment banking Societé Générale Benelux, Paris/Brussels/Amsterdam, 1995—; prof. Banking Sch., Brussels, 1988-93; spkr. numerous seminars and confs. in field of corp. fin., 1988—. Co-author: Merger Control in Europe, 1987; contbr. articles to profl. jours. and books. Fellow Philosophy Sch.; mem. Law Econ. Ancient Studies. Home: Heidestraat 45, 1755 Kester Belgium Office: Soc Générale, Place du Champs de Mars 5, 1050 Brussels Belgium

WUNDERER, ROLF FRIEDRICH, human resources educator; b. Meiningen, Germany, Oct. 21, 1937; arrived in Switzerland, 1983; s. Erwin and Ursula (Löhe) W.; m. Barbara Johanne Kind, Sept. 30, 1962; children: Jörg, Ulrike, Felix. Diploma fin., U. Munich, Germany, 1962, D in Oceanomiae Publicae, 1967. Lectr. U. Munich, Germany, 1966-74, U. German Armed Forces, Munich, 1973-74; prof. U. Essen, Germany, 1974-83, U. St. Gallen, Switzerland, 1983—; dean, 1987-88; vis. prof. UCLA, Berkeley, 1981, U. Munich, 1995-97, Hitotsubashi U., Tokyo, 1998. Author: Leadership and Cooperation, 1993, rev. 3d edit., 2000; (with A. Jaritz) Controlling of Human Resources, 1999; (with P. Dick) HR-Management-Quo vadis?, 2000; editor Handwörterbuch der Führung, 2d rev. edit. 1995, Implementation Competence, 2000, others. Mem. Am. Mgmt. Assn., Assn. Univ. Profs. Mgmt., Rotary Club, Inst. Leadership and Human Resource Mgmt. E-mail: rolf.wunderer@unisg.ch. Home: Hardungstr 22, CH 9011 Saint Gallen Switzerland Office: U St Gallen Ldrshp Hmn Mgmt, Inst. Dufourstr 48, 9000 St Gallen Switzerland

WUNDERLI, PETER FRANZ ALBERT, romance linguistics educator; b. Zürich, Switzerland, May 30, 1938; s. Hans K. and Berta (Funk) W.; m. Susann Amberg, July 1, 1963 (div. 1978); children: Martin, Monica. PhD, U. Zürich, Switzerland, 1963, Dr. habil., 1968. Asst. U. Zürich, Switzerland, 1963-67; Gymnasiallerer OR Winfertnur, Switzerland, 1967-70; pvt. dozent U. Zürich, Switzerland, 1968-70; prof. U. Freiburg, Germany, 1970-76, U. Düsseldorf, Germany, 1976—. Avocations: tennis, horse riding, music. Office: U Dusseldorf, U Dusseldorf Romanistik IV, Universitatstr 1, D-40225 Düsseldorf Germany

WUNDERLICH, HERMANN, diversified corporation executive. Vice chmn. bd. mgmt. Bayer AG, Leverkusen, Fed. Republic Germany; chmn. bd. Miles Inc. (subs. Bayer AG), Pitts.; mem. supervisory bd. Bayer AG, Leverkusen, Fed. Republic Germany. Office: Bayer Group, Bayer AG, D-51368 Leverkusen Germany*

WUNDERLICH, PETER, retired pediatrician, educator; b. Rostock-Mecklenburg, Germany, May 8, 1935; s. Felix Adolf Ernst and Magda W.; m. Christa Elisabeth Froelich, Aug. 4, 1959; children: Christian, Ulrike. MD, Med. Acad., Dresden, Germany, 1959. Asst. Children's Hosp. Dresden, 1961-65, sr. asst., 1965-78, asst. prof., 1978-84, assoc. prof., 1984-92, full prof., 1992-2000; ret., 2000. Co-author (with M. Gahr): (textbook) Pediatric Differential Diagnostics, 1977, 3d edit. 1997; co-author 5 medical books; contbr. articles to profl. jours. Student's Dean Med. Acad. C.G. Carus, Dresden, 1991-93. Mem. Freundes-Kreis der Carus-Fakultät (dir. 1996-99). Evangelist. Avocations: walking, climbing, arts, classical music. Home: Boettger Str 47, D-01129 Dresden Saxony, Germany Office: Tech U-Med Faculty, Fetscher str 74, D-01307 Dresden Saxony, Germany

WÜNSCH, VOLKMAR NORBERT, mathematics educator; b. Hohenwiese, Silsea, Germany, Apr. 10, 1941; s. Robert Fritz and Liesbeth (Lätsch) W.; 1 child, Christiane. Diploma in Math., U. Leipzig, Germany, 1966, D Natural Sci., 1969, Habilitation, 1977. Asst. U. Leipzig, 1969-77, docent, 1977-81; prof. math. Pedagogical Coll., Erfurt, Germany, 1981-96, prorector, 1990-93; prof. math. U. Jena, Germany, 1996—. Author: Differentialgeometrie, 1997; contbr. articles to profl. jours. Mem. Akademie Gemeinnütziger Wissenschaften zu Erfurt. Home: Ligusterweg 24, D-99097 Erfurt Germany Office: Pedagogical Coll PSU Jena Math Inst, FSU Jena Math Inst, Ernst-Abbe-Platz 4, D-07743 Jena Germany

WUNSTELL, ERIK JAMES, non-profit organization administrator, communications consultant; b. Fresno, Calif., Dec. 24, 1951; s. John Wunstell and Rose Soldorian. Grad. comml. law, Dept. U.S. Treas., 1976; grad., N.Am. Sch. Acctg., 1978. Owner Camden Comm., Fresno, Calif., 1974—; founder, dir. Earth Ecology Found., Fresno, Calif., 1980—. Author: Earthology - The Physics of Solar Relativity, 1990, The Geometric Progression of Space and Time, 1979, The Binary Duality of the Universe, 1996, Ecological Civilization 2020, 1985, Earth's Unified Solar Field Pattern, 2000. Office: Earth Ecology Found PMB 303 6120 W Tropicana Ave Las Vegas NV 89103-4694

WUOLIJOKI, ERKKI ENSIO FREDRIK, pharmacologist; b. Tampere, Finland, Jan. 8, 1948; s. Jaakko Robert and Pirkko Helena (Holmström) W.; m. Maria Suoma Renée Silfverhjelm, June 16, 1973; children: Kirsti Katariina, Väinö Sakari Fredrik. MS, Helsinki (Finland) U., 1973, Licentiate of Sci., 1977, DSc, PhD, 1981. Rsch. scientist Acad. Finland, 1973-78; project mgr. Ciba-Geigy Oy, 1978-85; project coord. Orion-Pharma, 1985-88; head of dept. Meda Oy Helsinki, 1988-93; bus. group rep. Bayer, Finland, Estland, Latvia,, Lithuania, 1993-97; rsch. dir. Finn-Medi Rsch. Oy, Tampere, 1997—; lectr. Tampere Tech. H.S., 1976-77; dir. resp. for radioisotopes Meda Ltd., 1993-96; dir. responsible for health svcs. Finn-Medi, 1998—. Author: (book) Työsuojelufysiologia, 1977; contbr. numerous monographs, papers, and articles to profl. publs. Columnist Kangasalan Sanomat, Tampere, 1998—; mem. steering com. Hauko Mcpl. Ch., 1997—; sec. Finnish Hakka Peliitta Assn., 1997—; patron European Championship Competition for Dressage Riding, Helsinki, 1995. Recipient Medal of Merit, Finnish Equestrian Soc., 1988, Finnish Armoury History, 1999, Finnish Phys. Edn. and Sports, 1998, 1st J. Jauhiainen Meml. award Finnish Soc. Med. Tech., 1978; rsch. grantee Acad. Finland, 1975-77. Mem. Finnish Soc. for Pharmacology, Finnish Soc. Helsinki, Helsinki Equestrian Soc. (pres. 1985—), Roineentausta Hunting Club (pres. 1996—). Home: Niskavuorentie 315, FIN17400 Hauho Finland Office: Finn-Medi Rsch Ltd, Lenkkeilijänkatu 8, FIN33529 Tampere Finland

WUORI, MATTI OSSIAN, lawyer, environmental affairs consultant; b. Helsinki, July 15, 1945; s. Ossi Valdemar and Toini (Tjaga) W. LLM, Helsinki U., 1979. Lic. advocate, Finland. Jr. lawyer Asianajotoimisto Erhard Galle, Kerava, Finland, 1967-68; sr. ptnr. Asianajotoimisto Matti Wuori Ky, Helsinki, 1970—; ombudsman, arbitrator Helsinki Journalists Assn., Helsinki, 1970-83; chmn., internat. bd. dirs. Greenpeace Internat., 1991-93; mem. various state coms. in Finland. Contbr. articles to various publs. Founder, v.p. Suomen Varusmiesliitto, Helsinki, 1970-73; v.p. Am. Field Svc.-Finland, Helsinki, 1966-67; spl. advisor Truth and Reconciliation Commn. South Africa, 1996-98; mem. European Parliament, 1999—. Mem. Finnish Bar Assn., Internat. Bar Assn., Internat. Commn. Jurists (pres. Helsinki chpt. 1988—), Union Internat. Avocats Human Rights Commn. Avocation: history. Office: Arkadiankatu 12 B 48, SF-00100 Helsinki Finland

WUORI, PAUL ADOLF, engineering educator; b. Kauniainen, Finland, Aug. 1, 1933; s. Bruno Adolf and Anna Maria (Nyberg) W.; m. Anne Mari Pihlström, Aug. 17, 1963; children: Eva Maria, Johan Henrik. MS in Engring., Helsinki U. of Tech., Espoo, Finland, 1960, Lic. of Tech., 1969, D in Tech., 1972. Lab engr. Helsinki U. of Tech., Espoo, 1960-67, acting prof., 1967-73, prof. in hydraulic machines, 1973-76, 85—, dean dept. mech. engring., 1976-79, pres., 1979-85; cons. in field. Contbr. articles to profl. jours.; patentee in field. Served to lt. Finnish Air Force Res., 1959-60. Named Commdr. of the Order of the white rose of Finland, 1983. Mem. European Soc. for Engring. Edn. (adminstrv. coun. 1979-87, pres. 1985-86), Finnish Acad. Tech. Scis., Nyländska Jaktklubben, Ind. Order Odd Fellows, 5 Grankulla (chmn. 1974-75). Avocation: yachting. Home: Tallbackavägen 12, 02700 Grankulla Finland Office: Helsinki Univ of Tech, Otakaari 4 A, 02150 Espoo Finland

WÜRFEL, WOLFGANG JOHANN, gynecologist; b. Munich, Mar. 3, 1955; s. Erich and Gretchen (Weiss) W.; m. Gerda Philomena Kimmerle, May 8, 1985; 2 children. Dr. med., 1981. Asst. Frauenklinik Dr. Wilhelm Krüsmann, oberarzt, chefarzt, now dir.; asst. arzt Univ. Klinik, Würzburg; oberarzt Univ. Klinik, 1990; prof. U. Würzburg, Germany, 1998—; bd. dirs. Deutsche Gesellschaft für Gynäkologische Endokrinologie und Fortpflanzungemedizin, Deutsche Gesselschaft für Reproduktions Medizin, Internat. Assn. Pvt. Reproductive Insts. Editor: Frauenheilkuncle, 1996; contbr. articles to profl. jours. Mem. Deutsche Gesellschaft für Gynäkologie und Geburtsh, Bayerische Gesellschaft für Frauenheilkunde und Geburtsch, Deutsche Gesellschaft für Perinatalmedizin, European Soc. for Human Reproduction and Embryology, Deutsche Gesellschaft für Gynäkologische Psychosomatik. Office: Bodenseestr 7, D-81241 Munich Germany

WURSTER, DALE ERWIN, pharmacy educator, university dean emeritus; b. Sparta, Wis., Apr. 10, 1918; s. Edward Emil and Emma Sophia (Steingraeber) W.; m. June Margaret Peterson, June 16, 1944; children: Dale Eric, Susan Gay. BS, U. Wis., 1942, PhD, 1947. U. Wis. Sch. Pharmacy, Madison, 1958-71, Mem. faculty, 1947-71; prof., dean N.D. State U. Coll. Pharmacy, 1971-72; prof. U. Iowa Coll. Pharmacy, Iowa City, 1972—, dean, 1972-84, dean emeritus, 1984—; George B. Kaufman Meml. lectr. Ohio State U., 1968; Hancher Finkbine Medallion prof. U. Iowa, 1984; Joseph V. Swintosky disting. lectr. U. Ky., 2000; cons. in field; phys. sci. adminstr. USN, 1960-63; sci. advisor U. Wis. Alumni Rsch. Found., 1968-72; mem. revision com. U.S. Pharmacopoeia, 1961-70; mem. pharmacy rev. com. USPHS, 1966-72; mem. tech. adv. com. contraceptive R & D program Ea. Va. Med. Sch., 1989—, rsch., U. Wis. Contbr. articles to profl. jours., chpts. to books; patentee in field. With USNR, 1944-46. Recipient Superior Achievement citation Navy Dept., 1964, merit citation U. Wis., 1976, Disting. Alumni award U. Wis. Sch. Pharmacy, 1984. Fellow Am. Assn. Pharm. Scientists (founder, sponsor Dale E. Wurster rsch. award 1990—, Disting. Pharm. Scientist award 1991); mem. Am. Assn. Colls. Pharmacy (exec. com. 1964-66, chmn. conf. tchrs. 1960-61, vis. scientist 1963-70, Disting. Educator award 1983), Acad. Pharm. Scis. (exec. com. 1967-70, chmn. basic pharmaceutics sect. 1965-67, pres. 1975, Indsl. Pharm. Tech. award 1980), Am. Pharm. Assn. (chmn. sci. sect. 1964-65, rsch. achievement award 1965, Wis. Disting. Svc. award 1971), Iowa Pharmacists Assn. (Robert G. Gibbs award 1983), Wis. Acad. Scis., Arts and Letters, Soc. Investigative Dermatology, Rumanian Soc. Med. Sci. (hon.), Am. Found. Pharm. Edn. (bd. grants 1987-92), Sigma Xi, Kappa Psi (past officer), Rho Chi, Phi Lambda Upsilon, Phi Sigma. Home: 16 Brickwood Cir NE Iowa City IA 52240-9129

WURTZBURG, SUSAN JANE, anthropologist, educator; b. Toronto, Ont., Can., Jan. 29, 1960; arrived in New Zealand, 1994; d. Chris Bryan and Diana Jane (Cook) W.; m. Lyle Richard Campbell, Jan. 2, 1988. BS with honors, Trent U., Can., 1984; MA, U. Albany, 1988, PhD, 1991. Regional archaeologist Mus. Geosci., La. State U., Baton Rouge, 1991-92, lect. dept. geography and anthropology, 1993; lectr. dept. sociology Southeastern La. U., Hammond, 1994; lectr. dept. geography U. Canterbury, Christchurch, New Zealand, 1995, lectr. dept. Am. studies, 1996, rsch. scholar Macmillan Brown Ctr. Pacific Studies,, 1997; lectr. divsn. human scis. Lincoln U., New Zealand, 1999-2000. Contbr. to book: Women in Archeology, 1994, American Indians, 1995, Women in the Biological Sciences, 1997, Encyclopedia of Multiculturalism, 1998, The Sixties in America, 1999, Encyclopedia of Women's Studies, 2000; contbr. articles to profl. jours. including Internat. Jour. Am. Linguists, Devel. Bulletin, Mexicon, Procs. New Zealand Geog. Advocate Christchurch Women's Refuge, 1994-99, mem. gov. com., 1996-99. Rsch. grantee Sigma Xi, 1989. Fellow Am. Anthrop. Assn.; mem. Royal Soc. New Zealand, Soc. Rsch. Women (mem. exec. com. Christchurch br. 1995-97). Avocations: hiking, scuba diving, kayaking.

WURZ, ALEXANDER, race car driver; b. Waidhofen, Austria, Feb. 15, 1974. Race car driver, 1991—. BMX World Champion, 1986, 2d pl. Austrian Formula Ford 1600, 1991, champion German and Austrian Formula Ford 1600, 1992, winner 24 Hours of Nürburgring Group B, 1992, champion Austrian Formula 3, 1993, 2d pl. German Formula 3, 1994, winner 24 Hours of Le Mans, 1996. Office: Benetton Formula Ltd, Whiteways Tech Ctr, Enstone Chipping Norton Oxfordshire OX7 4EE, England*

WURZBERGER, BEZALEL, psychiatrist; b. Medias, Romania, June 28, 1945; came to U.S., 1967; s. Joshua and Isabella Wurzberger; m. Gladys Schmidt, Mar. 19, 1971; children: Tamar, David. BA, Columbia U., 1972; MD, Nat. U., Tegucigalpa, Honduras, 1982. Diplomate, Am. Bd. Psychiatry and Neurology. Intern North Gen. Hosp., N.Y.C., 1982-83; resident in psychiatry Creedmoor Psychiat. Ctr., Queens Village, N.Y., 1983-86; clin. psychiat. fellow N.Y. Med. Coll., Valhala, N.Y., 1986-87; staff psychiatrist Glens Falls (N.Y.) Hosp., 1987-92, chmn. dept. psychiatry, 1993-98; med. dir., Samaritan Counseling Ctr., Keene, N.Y., 1987—; psychiat. cons., Uihlein Mercy Ctr., Lake Placid, N.Y., 1988—, Psychol. Assocs., Queensbury, N.Y., 1998—; forensic psychiatry cons. Fed. Bur. Prisons, 1999—. V.p. Jewish Community Tegucigalpa, 1978-80; bd. dirs. Congregation Shaarey Tefily, Glens Falls, 1989—, v.p., 1993-96, pres., 1996-97. Sgt. Israeli Air Force, 1964-67. Mem. AMA, Am. Psychiat. Assn., Soc. Liaison Psychiatry, Acad. Psychosomatic Medicine, Honduran Coll. Physicians. Office; PO Box 794 Glens Falls NY 12801-0794

WUSSING, HANS, historian of science; b. Waldheim, Sachsen, Germany, Oct. 15, 1927; s. Hans and Lucie (Altmann) W.; m. Gerlinde Walter, Oct. 25, 1952; 1 child, Petra. Dr. rer. nat., U. Leipzig, Germany, 1957; Habilitation, U. Leipzig, 1967. Asst. U. Leipzig, 1957-67, docent, 1967-68, prof., 1968-92. Author: Über Einbettungen endlicher Gruppen, 1958, Mathematik in der Antike, 1962, 2d edit., 1965, Nicolaus Copernicus, 1963, Die Genesis des abstrakten Gruppenbegriffes, 1969, Am. edit., 1984, Carl Friedrich Gauss, 1974, 5th edit., 1989, Isaac Newton, 1977, 4th edit., 1990, Adam Ries, 1989, 2d edit., 1992, Vom Zählstein zur Computer, 1999; co-author: Wissenschaftsgeschichte en miniature, 1989; author, editor: Biographien bedeutender Mathematiker, 1975, 3d edit., 1983, Vorlesungen zur Geschichte der Mathematik, 1979, 2d edit., 1989, Spanish edit., 1999, Geschichte der Naturwissenschaften, 1983, 2d edit., 1987; co-editor: Adam Ries: Coss, 1992, ABC Fachlexikon Forscher und Erfinder, 1992; co-author: Produktivkräfte in Deutschland, 3 vols., 1990; editor: J.C. Poggendorffs Biographisch-literarisches Handwörterbuch der exakten Naturwissenschaften; co-editor Ostwalds Klassiker der exakten Wissenschaften, to 1990, NTM: Schriftenreihe zur Geschichte der Naturwissenschaften, Technik und Medizin, 1967-98, Sci. Networks to 1998. Mem. Saxonian Acad. Scis., Internat. Acad. History Sci., Internat. Union History of Sci. (asst. sec., v.p. 1981-94, Kenneth O. May prize 1993). Home: Braunschweiger Str 39, D 04157 Leipzig Germany Office: Saxonian Acad Scis, Karl Tauchnitz Str 1, D 04107 Leipzig Germany

WÜTHRICH, KURT, molecular biologist, biophysical chemist, educator; b. Oct. 4, 1938. BS in Chemistry and Physics, U. Bern, Switzerland, 1962;

Eidenössisches Turn-und Sportlehrerdiplom, U. Basel, Switzerland, 1964, PhD in Chemistry, 1964; D Chem (hon.), U. Siena, Italy, 1997; PhD (hon.), U. Zürich, Switzerland, 1997. Postdoctoral tng. U. Basel, U. Calif., Berkeley, Bell Telephone Labs., Murray Hill, N.J., 1964-69; prof. biophysics Swiss Fed. Inst. Tech., Zürich, 1972—, chmn. dept. biology, 1995-2000; mem. coun. Internat. Union Pure and Applied Biophysics, 1975-78, 87-90, sec. gen., 1978-84, v.p., 1984-87; mem. gen. com. Internat. Coun. Sci. Unions, 1980-86, standing com. on free circulation of scientists, 1982-90. Editor Jour. Biomolecular NMR, Quar. Rev. Biophysics, Macromolecular Structures; contbr. articles to profl. jours. Recipient Friedrich Miescher prize Schweizerische Biochemische Gesellschaft, 1974, shield of faculty of medicine Tokyo U., 1983, P. Bruylants medal Cath. U. Louvain, 1986, Stein and Moore award Protein Soc., U.S., 1990, Louisa Gross Horowitz prize Columbia U., 1991, Gilbert N. Lewis medal U. Calif., Berkeley, 1991, Marcel Benoist prize Swiss Confederation, 1992, Disting. Svc. award Miami Winter Symposia, 1993, Prix Louis Jeantet de Médecine, Geneva, 1993, Kaj Linderstrøm-Lang prize Kaj Linderstrøm-Lang Found., Copenhagen, 1996, Eminent Scientist of RIKEN (Tokyo), 1997, Kyoto prize in Advanced Tech., 1998, Guenther Laukien prize Exptl. Nuclear Magnetic Resonance Conf., 1999, Otto Warburg medal Soc. for Biochemistry and Molecular Biology, Germany, 1999; Fgn. fellow Indian Nat. Sci. Acad.; hon. fellow NAS India. Fellow AAAS; mem. U.S. Nat. Acad. Sci. (fgn. assoc.), Deutsche Acad. der Naturforscher Leopoldina, European Molecular Biology Orgn., Academia Europea, Am. Acad. Arts and Scis. (fgn. hon.), Acad. Scis., Inst. France (fgn. assoc.), Japanese Biochem. Soc. (hon.), Nat. Magnetic Resonance Soc. India (hon.). Office: Inst Molecular Biology & Biophysics, ETH Hönggerberg, 8093 Zurich Switzerland

WUTTKE, DIETER, philology and art history educator; b. Fuerstenwalde, Germany, Oct. 12, 1929; s. Walther Gustav Hugo and Charlotte (Weichert) W.; m. Helga Anna Geller, Nov 2, 1965; children: Carolin, Henrike. PhD, U. Tuebingen, Fed. Republic Germany, 1958; habilitation, U. Goettingen, Fed. Republic Germany, 1971. Tchr. Altes Gymnasium, Bremen, Fed. Republic Germany, 1957-62; postgrad. scholar, lectr. U. Bonn, Fed. Republic Germany, 1962-66; oberstudienrat i.h. U. Goettingen, 1966-71; prof. U. Goettingen, Fed. Republic Germany, 1971-79; prof. emeritus U. Bamberg, Fed. Republic of Germany, 1995—; dir. Seminar fuer Deutsche Philologie U. Goettingen, 1972-79; holder of chair Deutsche Philologie des Mittelalters und der Fruehen Neuzeit U. Bamberg, 1979-95; vis. prof. U. Hamburg, 1975, 76. Author: Die Historia Herculis, 1964, Deutsche Germanistik und Renaissanceforschung, 1968, Von der Geschichtlichkeit der Literatur, 1984, Humanismus als integrative Kraft, 1985, Nuremberg: Focal Point of German Culture and History, 2d edit., 1988, Sebastian-Brant-Bibliographie, 1990, Aby M. Warburgs Methode, 4th edit., 1991, Der Humanist Willibald Pirckheimer, 1994, Das Institut: Eine Einführung, 1995, Dazwischen: Kulturwissenschaft auf Warburgs Spuren, 1996, Aby M. Warburg-Bibliographie 1866-1995, 1998; author, editor: Aby M. Warburg, 3d edit., 1992, Caritas Pirckheimer 1467-1532, 1982, Commedia dell'arte, 2d edit., 1983, E.R. Curtius und das Warburg Inst., 1989, W. Pirckheimers Briefwechsel, Vol. III, 1989, Fastnachtspiele, 6th edit., 1998, E. Panofsky: Hercules am Scheidewege, 1997; editor: Das Verhältnis der Humanisten zum Buch, 1976, Gratia, 1977—, Probleme der Edition mittel- und neulateinischer Texte, 1978, Ethik im Humanismus, 1979, Saecula Spiritalia, 1979—, From Wolfram and Petrarch to Goethe and Grass: Festschrift L. Forster, 1982, Philologie als Kulturwissenschaft, 1987, S. Brant: Das Narrenschiff, 1994, Festschrift: Poesis et Pictura, 1989, Artibus, 1994, Schimpf und Ernst, 1995. Fellow The Warburg Inst. U. London, Westfield Coll. U. London, Ctr. Advanced Study in Visual Arts Nat. Gallery (Washington), Volkswagenstiftung, Getty Ctr. History of Art and the Humanities, Prague Acad.; mem. Inst. Advanced Study, Inst. Germanic Studies (corr.). Lutheran. Home: Obere Seelgasse 8, D-96049 Bamberg Germany Office: Univ Bamberg, D-96045 Bamberg Germany

WU YI, Chinese government official, engineer; b. Wuhan City, Hubei, China, 1938. Technician, then sec., polit. office Lanzhou Oil Refinery, from 1962; technician prodn. dept. Ministry of Petroleum Industry; dep. chief to chief, tech. dep. engr., dep. dir. Dongfang Hong Oil Refinery; dep. pres., party sec. Beijing Yanshan Petrochems. Corp., 1984; vice mayor Beijing Municipality, 1988; dep. min. fgn. trade and econ. cooperation Beijing People's Govt., 1991-93, min. fgn. trade and econ. cooperation, 1993—; alternate mem. CPC CC Politburo, 1997—; state councilor State Coun. Mem. Communist Party of China, 1962—, alternate mem. Ctrl. Com., 1987, mem. Ctrl. Com. 1992—. Office: Office of Premier, Zhong Nan Hi, Beijing 100731, China*

WUYTS, KOENRAAD MARIA, lawyer; b. Beveren-Waas, Belgium, Jan. 11, 1964; m. Godelieve A. Van Camp, July 1, 1988. PhB, U. Leuven, Belgium, 1992; PhD in Physics, U. Leuven, 1992. Rschr. U. Leuven, Belgium, 1986-92, sr. rschr., 1992-93; indsl. advisor Interuniv. Micro Electronics Ctr., Leuven, 1993-94, patents and licensing exec., 1994-2000; licensing exec. Royal KPN Telecom., The Hague, The Netherlands, 2000—. Contbr. articles to profl. jours.; inventor in field. Office: Royal KPN Telecom, Maanplein 5, 2516 CK The Hague The Netherlands

WYATT, BRETT MICHAEL, secondary school educator; b. Toledo, Dec. 31, 1958; s. Warren Dale and Jacqueline Elizabeth (Angelides) W.; 1 child, Adrian. BA in Geography, Calif. State U., San Bernardino, 1981; MA in Geography, U. Calif., Davis, 1985. Elem. tchr. Sacramento City Unified Sch. Dist., 1987-89, tech. resource tchr., 1989-91; ednl. cons. IBM, Sacramento, 1989-92; asst. editor Computers in the Schs., Reno, Nev., 1991-93; media specialist L.A. Unified Sch. Dist., 1998—. Author: Jewish Settlement in Sacramento, A Pictorial History, 1987; prodr.: (video) Sacramento Educational Cable Consortium, 1991, 92; contbg. poet: Nevada High Desert Rev., 1997, 98; contbr. articles to profl. jours. Advisor Tech. Preparation Com., Sacramento, 1991; founding dir. Nev. Schs. Network, Reno, 1992; advisor WCSD Internet Task Force, Reno, 1994—; archivist Temple B'hai Israel, Sacramento, 1986-87; computer technician vol. Ptnrs. in Edn., Sparks, Nev., 1994—. Named Vol. of the Yr., Ptnrs. in Edn., Sparks, 1995; recipient award for outstanding ednl. video Sacramento Ednl. Cable Consortium, 1991, 92. Democrat. Home: 2614 S Harcourt Ave Los Angeles CA 90016-2827

WYATT, EDWARD AVERY, V, city manager; b. Petersburg, Va., Nov. 1, 1941; s. Edward Avery and Martha Vaughan (Seabury) W.; m. Regina Helen Stec, Aug. 23, 1969; children: Edward Avery VI, Stephen Alexander, Kent Seabury. AS in Bus., Bluefield Coll.; BS in Bus., Pub. Adminstrn., Va. Poly. Inst. and State U., 1964; M.Commerce, U. Richmond, 1969; MA in Polit. Sci., Appalachian State U., 1977. Chief gen. svc. City of Petersburg, Va., 1966-67, asst. to city mgr., 1967-70; city mgr. City of Washington, N.C., 1970-73, City of Morganton, N.C., 1973-78, City of Greenville, N.C., 1978-82, City of Fairfax, Va., 1982-91, City of Wilson, N.C., 1991—; adj. lectr. George E. Mason U. Bus. Sch., 1985-86; bd. dirs., sec. Electricities of N.C.; commr. N.C. Ea. Mcpl. Power Agy. Contbr. numerous articles to profl. jours. and newsletters. Chmn. N.C. Code Ofcls. Qualification Bd., 1980-82; mem. adv. bd. Wilson Salvation Army, 1992—; bd. dirs. N.C. League of Municipalities; mem. adv. com. Wilson Boys and Girls Club. Served with USNG and USAR, 1964-70. Paul Harris fellow Rotary Internat.; Dennis Duffey Meml. award Fairfax Police Youth Club. Mem. ASPA (ea. N.C. chpt.), Internat. City Mgmt. Assn. (endowment com., chair 1991-92, coun. mgr. plan task force 1993-94), Va. Local Govt. Mgmt. Assn. (pres. 1989-90), N.C. City/County Mgmt. Assn. (pres.), Soc. Cincinnati in Va., Descendants of Francis Epes of Va. (pres., past v.p.), Wilson Rotary (dir.). Home: 1307 Waverly Rd NW Wilson NC 27896-1483 Office: City of Wilson PO Box 10 Wilson NC 27894-0010

WYATT, HAROLD VIVIAN, medical researcher; b. Devonport, Eng., June 11, 1926; s. Fred and Emily (Phillips) W.; m. Joan Wilkinson Jones, Feb. 23, 1956; children: Tristram Dick, Ben Timothy. BSc, U. London, 1951, BSc with honors, 1952, PhD, 1957. Chartered biologist. Rsch. asst. St. Bartholomew's Hosp., London, 1954-57; postdoctoral fellow Johns Hopkins Hosp., Balt., 1957-59; ICI fellow U. of Leeds, 1959-62, hon. rsch. fellow, 1986—; reader in microbiology U. Bradford, 1962-82; vis. scientist Nat. Cancer Inst., Bethesda, 1969-71; hon. rsch. assoc. U. Manchester, 1980-81; dir. sch. of sci. Coll. of Med. Scis., West Bank, 1982-83; guest rsch. worker Indian Inst. Chem. Biology, Calcutta, India, 1985; cons. for legal actions for compensation for vaccine damaged children. Author: AIDS Information, 1988; editor: Information Sources in the Life Sciences, 4th edit., 1997, Poliomyelitis in India, 1998; contbr. over 250 articles to profl. publs. Sgt. Army, 1944-48, U.K. Grantee Royal Soc., 1987, British Libr., Wellcome Trust, 1993, 94. Fellow Inst. of Biology. Achievements include discovery of aggravation of paralytic poliomyelitis by injections and susceptibility of hypo-gamma-globulinemics to oral polio vaccine, incidence and case-fatality of neonatal poliomyelitis. Home: 1 Hollyshaw Terr, Leeds LS15 7BG, England

WYATT, KENNETH MARK, veterinarian, consultant; b. Perth, Australia, May 19, 1968; s. Kenneth George and Margaret Mary Wyatt; m. Gemma Lisa Brunini, Oct. 1, 1995. BS, Murdoch U., Australia, 1988, B Vet. Medicine and Surgery, 1990. Gen. vet. practice Perth, Australia, 1991-95; resident in small animal medicine Murdoch U. Vet. Hosp., Western Australia, 1996-98, registrar in small animal medicine, 1999—; referral veterinarian in oncology Perth Animal Referral Clinic, 1999—; cons. Murdoch Animal Cancer Care Unit, Western Australia, 1999—. Contbr. articles to Australian Vet. Jour., Australian Vet. Practitioner. Mem. Australian Coll. Vet. Scientists. Avocation: triathlon. E-mail: wy-att@numbat.murdoch.edu.au. Office: Murdoch U Vet Hosp, Murdoch Dr, Murdoch 6150, Australia

WYATT, OSCAR SHERMAN, JR., retired energy company executive; b. Beaumont, Tex., July 11, 1924; s. Oscar Sherman Sr. and Eva (Coday) W.; m. Lynn Sakowitz; children: Steven, Douglas, Oscar Sherman III, Brad. BS in Mech. Engring., Tex. A&M U., 1949. With Kerr-McGee Co., 1949, Reed Roller Bit Co., 1949-51; ptnr. Wymore Oil Co., 1951-55; founder Coastal Corp., Corpus Christi, Tex., 1955; now chmn. exec. com. Coastal Corp., Houston. Trustee DeBakey Med. Found., 1987—; founding mem., bd. stewards Tex. Aviation Hall of Fame, 1997—. Served with USAAF, World War II. Office: 8 E Greenway Plz Ste 930 Houston TX 77046-0892

WYATT, PHILIP RICHARD, geneticist, physician, researcher; b. St. Louis, Oct. 22, 1951; s. John Poyner and Isabel (Gillespie) W.; m. Sharon Lorraine Parker, June 23, 1978; children: Geoffrey, Kathryn. BS, U. Man., 1972; PhD, U. Man., Winnipeg, Man., Can., 1976; MD, U. Ky., 1980. Lic. Med. Coun. Can. Chief genetics dept. North York Gen. Hosp., Toronto, 1983—, chair instnl. rev. bd.; advisor Ministry Health, Toronto, 1984-90; mem. Mins. Adv. Com. on Genetics, Ont., 2000; chmn. Maternal Serum Screening Com., Ont., 2000. Recipient Karger prize Karger Pub., Switzerland, 1976. Fellow Human Biology Coun.; mem. Am. Soc. Human Genetics, Ont. Med. Assn. (sect. chmn. genetics 1995-98, rev. bd. 1998—). Office: Genetics North York, 4001 Leslie St, North York, ON Canada M2K 1E1

WYATT, ROBERT LEE, IV, lawyer; b. Las Cruces, N.Mex., Mar. 9, 1964; s. Robert Lee III and Louise Carole (Bard) W.; m. Vicki Harris Wyatt. BS, Southeastern Okla. State U., 1986; JD, U. Okla., 1989. Bar: Okla. 1989, U.S. Dist. Ct. (we. dist.) Okla. 1990, U.S. Ct. Appeals (10th cir.) 1990, U.S. Dist. Ct. (no. dist.) Okla. 1991, U.S. Ct. Appeals (8th cir.) 1991, U.S. Supreme Ct. 1993. Intern Okla. State Bur. Investigation, Oklahoma City, 1988-89, guest lectr., 1989; dep. spl. counsel Gov. of Okla., 1995; atty. Jones & Wyatt, Enid, Okla., 1989-2000; mem. criminal justice panel atty. We. Dist. Okla. Contbg. author: Vernon's forms Oklahoma, Criminal Law and Procedure, 1999. counsel to Fire Civil Svc. Commn. City of Enid, 1998-2000. Mem. ABA (mem. criminal & litigation sects.), Okla. Bar Assn. (mem. ins., family sect., mem. crimial law com.), Oklahoma County Bar Assn., Okla. Criminal Def. Lawyers Assn., Nat. Inst. for Trial Advocacy, Nat. Assn. Criminal Defense Lawyers, Luther Bohanon Am. Inn of Ct. (barrister), Phi Delta Phi, Alpha Chi. Democrat. Baptist. Home: 2430 Sherwood Dr Enid OK 73703-1512 Office: Wyatt Law Office 311 N Harvey Ave Ste 103 Oklahoma City OK 73102-3420

WYATT, ROSE MARIE, clinical social worker; b. San Angelo, Tex., Feb. 16; d. James Odis and Annie LaVernia (Lott) W. BA, Fisk U., 1957; MS, U. So. Calif., 1963; MA, MSW, U. Chgo., 1972; postgrad., Ill. Inst. Tech., 1976—. Elem. tchr. Chgo. Bd. Edn., 1959-63, clin. social worker, 1979—; adult program dir. Chgo. YWCA, 1963-64; youth counselor Chgo. Commn. on Youth Welfare, 1964-66; supervising social worker for Head Start, Chgo. Com. on Urban Opportunity, 1966; social worker Chgo. Commn. on Youth Welfare, 1966-68, Jewish Vocat. Svc., 1968; social worker Sch. Community Rels., Detroit Pub. Schs., 1968-70; social worker United Charities, 1972-74; clin. social worker Rosman-Wyatt and Assocs., Chgo., 1980—, pres., 1981—; instr. dept. corrections Chgo. State U., 1972—; adj. instr. Chgo. State U. Mem. adv. bd. United Charities, Calumet area, program com. chmn., 1974-80; vol. Assn. of Comty. Agts. 1968-70, Southside Sr. Citizens Coalition, Chgo., 1963-66, Roseland Health Planning Com., 1974-76, Teen Pregnancy Caucus, 1978-82; mem. social work adv. coun. Chgo. Bd. Edn., 1976. Recipient Outstanding Employee award for med.-social work svcs. Maternal and Child Health Svcs. div. HEW; 1971; Ford Found. scholar Fisk U., 1953-57, U. Chgo. scholar, 1970-72, United Charities scholar, 1970-72. Mem. Nat. Assn. Social Workers (Tx. unit), Acad. Cert. Social Workers, Ill. Cert. Social Workers, Chgo. Psychol. Club, Ill Acad. Criminology, NEA, Ill. Assn. Sch. Social Workers, Am. Assn. Mental Deficiency, Qualified Mental Retardation Profls., Fisk U. Alumni Assn., Am. Bridge Assn., Alpha Kappa Alpha.

WYATT, WILSON WATKINS, JR., communications and public affairs executive; b. Louisville, Dec. 3, 1943; s. Wilson Watkins Sr. and Anne (Duncan) W.; m. Jane Clay, Aug. 15, 1964 (dec. 1975); children: Carol, Wilson III, Sarah Wyatt; m. Kathleen Valonis, June 14, 1998. Student, U. of the South, 1961-65. Reporter The Courier-Jour., Louisville, 1965-67; pub. rels. account exec. Doe-Anderson Advt., Louisville, 1967-68; account exec. Zimmer-McClaskey-Lewis (McCann-Ericksn Advtsg.), Louisville, 1968-70; ptnr. Bennett & Wyatt Pub. Rels., Louisville, 1970-71; state rep., vice chair appropriations and revenue com. Ky. Gen. Assembly, Frankfort, 1969-71; exec. dir. Louisville Cen. Area Inc., 1971-77; dir. corp. affairs and communications Brown & Williamson Tobacco Corp., Louisville, 1977-82; v.p. pub. policy BATUS Inc., Washington, 1982-86; v.p. corp. affairs BATUS Inc., Louisville, 1986-90; sr. v.p. corp. affairs PNC Fin. Corp., Pitts., 1990-92; sr. v.p. corp. comm. and govt. rels. The Travelers Cos., Hartford, 1992-94; exec. dir., CEO Am. Acad. of Actuaries, Washington, 1995-98; CEO Wyatt Comm. Cons., 1998—; lead U.S. def. pub. rels. activities against hostile takeover for B.A.T. Industries, U.K., 1989-90; chmn. Travelers Found., 1991-94, Travelers Good Govt. Com., 1992-94. Mem. youth adv. com. Atlantic Inst., 1967-68; del. North Atlantic Treaty Assn. Young Leaders Conf., 1967; chmn. Leadership Effort for All Dems., Ky., 1967-68; regional campaign coord. for Robert F. Kennedy, Ky.-Ind., 1968; mem. Pres.'s Forum, Washington, 1988-91; trustee Conn. Policy Econ. Commn., 1992-95; mem. exec. com. Hartford Downtown Coun., 1992-94; mem. adv. bd. Dem. Leadership Coun., Washington; mem. Am. Savings Edn. Campaign U.S. Dept. Labor, 1996. Named one of Outstanding Young Men in Am., Ky. Jaycees, 1973. Mem. The Pres.'s Forum, Pub. Affairs Rsch. Coun. (conf. bd. 1986-95), Forum I, Assn. Chief Execs. Coun., Pub. Affairs Coun. (bd. dirs. 1982—, exec. com. 1982-86), Speakers Club (Washington), Greater Hartford C. of C. (exec. com. 1992-94), Hartford Stage (bd. dirs. 1993-95), Louisville Country Club, Congl. Country Club (Bethesda, Md.), University Club (Washington), Louisville Country Club. Avocations: boating, photography, writing. Home and Office: PO Box 298 7291 Bozman-Neavitt Rd Bozman MD 21612

WYBER, RONALD JOHN, acoustic consultant; b. Sydney, Jan. 26; s. Robert and Nancy Jessie (Vaughan) W.; m. Charlotte Stephanie Pring, Jan. 22, 1972; children: Kirsten Elizabeth, Amy Kathleen, Tristan Robert. BSc, Sydney U., 1968, B Engring. with honors, 1970, PhD, 1974. Registered elec. engr. Rsch. scientist Def. Sci. & Tech. Orgn., Canberra, Australia, 1973-78, Sydney, 1978-87; vis. scientist Applied Rsch. Lab., Austin, Tex., 1987-89; dir. Midspar Systems, Sydney, 1989—. Contbr. articles to profl. jours.; patentee in field. Chmn. Coronation Bay Protectin Assn., Sydney, 1994—. Mem. IEEE, Acoustical Soc. Am. Avocations: golf, surfing. Office: Midspar Systems, 24 Farrer Pl, Oyster Bay NSW 2225, Australia

WYCHERLEY, PAUL RENODEN, retired botanist; b. Bromley, Kent, Eng., June 17, 1928; arrived in Australia, 1971; s. Harry John and Ivy Annie (Shepstone) W.; m. Jennifer Gek-Kin Yeap, Sept. 21, 1968; children: Eleanor Ann, Sheryl Ruth, Giles Renoden. BSc in Botany with honors, U. London, 1949, PhD, 1952. Botanist Rubber Rsch. Inst. of Malaya, 1953-65; head botany divsn. Rubber Inst. of Malaya, 1965-71; dir. Kings Park and Bot. Garden, Perth, Australia, 1971-92. Contbr. aticles to profl. jours. Decorated officer Order Brit. Empire, 1972; recipient Queen's Silver Jubilee medal, 1977. Fellow Linnean Soc. London, Inc. Soc. Planters Kuala Lumpur, Royal Australian Inst. Parks and Recreation (hon. life, pres. 1982, councillor 1977-89); mem. Malayan Nature Soc. (hon. life; pres. 1963, 71), Royal Soc. Western Australia (pres. 1977). Anglican. Avocations: conservation, natural history.

WYCOFF, CHARLES COLEMAN, writer, retired anesthesiologist; b. Glazier, Tex., Sept. 2, 1918; s. James Garfield and Ada Sharpe (Braden) W.; m. Gene Marie Henry, May 16, 1942; children: Michelle, Geoffrey, Brian, Roger, Daniel, Norman, Irene, Teresa. AB, U. Calif., Berkeley, 1941; MD, U. Calif., San Francisco, 1943; postgrad., U. London, 1954-55. Diplomate Am. Bd. Anesthesiology. Intern San Francisco County Hosp., 1943-44; resident in anesthesiology U. Calif. Hosp., San Francisco, 1944-45; tng. in anesthesiology Walter Reed Genl. Hosp., 1945; founder The Wycoff Group of Anesthesiology, San Francisco, 1947-53; chief of anesthesia St. Joseph's Hosp., San Francisco, 1947-52, organizer residency tng. program in anesthesiology, 1950; organizer residency tng. program in anesthesiology San Francisco County Hosp., 1954, chief anesthesia, 1953-54; tchr. practice anesthesiology Presbyn. Med. Ctr., N.Y.C., 1955-63; asst. prof. anesthesiology Columbia U., N.Y.C., 1955-63; clin. practice anesthesiology St. Francis Meml. Hosp., San Francisco, 1963-84. Producer, dir. films on regional anesthesia; contbr. articles to sci. jours. Scoutmaster Boy Scouts Am., San Francisco, 1953-55. Capt. M.C., U.S. Army, 1945-47. Mem. Alumni Faculty Assn. Sch. Medicine U. Calif.-San Francisco (councilor-at-large 1979-80). Democrat. Avocations: research in evolution of human behavior, freelance writing, Sierra hiking, gardening, pigeon breeding. E-mail: ccwycoff@pacbell.net. Home: Unit 133 1400 Carpentier St Apt 133 San Leandro CA 94577-3655

WYDRA, FRANK THOMAS, healthcare executive; b. Republic, Pa., May 11, 1939; s. Frank T. and Anne M. (Kois) W.; m. Karen Branch, June 24, 1961; children: Denise Lee, Sheryl Lynn, Frank Thomas III. BS in Mgmt., U. Ill., 1961. V.p. Allied Supermarkets, Inc., Detroit, 1967-75; sr. v.p. HGH Health System, Detroit, 1975-85; pres. Radius Health Care Sysytems, Inc., Detroit, 1983-85; cons. Birmingham, Mich., 1985-88; exec. v.p. The Chi Group, Ann Arbor, Mich., 1988-91; owner IRI, Mgmt. Cons., Detroit, 1991—; lectr. various profl. groups; bd. dirs. Mich. Health Systems Inc., Saber-Salisbury Assocs. Inc., Midwestern Health Ctr., MultiCare Med. Inc., RHS Inc. Author: Learner Controlled Instruction, 1980, (with others) Hospital Survival Guide, 1984, The Cure, 1992; creator 2 mgmt. games Performulations, 1978, The Dynamics of Power and Authority, 1981; contbr. articles to profl. jours. Personnel program advisor Mich. State U. Sch. Labor Relations, 1979-83; chmn. new programs Wayne County Community Coll., Detroit, 1979-80; bd. dirs. Detroit Metro Youth Found., 1980-83, State Mich. Health Occupations Council, Lansing, 1982-85. Capt. U.S. Army, 1961-63. Recipient numerous awards ASTD, Nat. Soc. Performance and Instrn., Mich. SOc. Instructional Tech., Supermarket Inst. Mem. Am. Hosp. Assn., Planning Soc. of Am. Hosp. Assn., Hosp. Personnel Adminstrs. Assn. (pres. 1981-82, numerous awards), Am. Mgmt. Assn., Am. Soc. Hosp. Pers.Adminstrs. (bd. dirs. 1981-83), Mich. Soc. Instrnl. Tech. (life, pres. 1973-74), Mich. Hosp. Assn., Employers Assn. Detroit (bd. dirs. 1982-85), Detroit Athletic Club. Avocations: writing, sailing. Home: 1001 W Glengarry Cir Bloomfield Hills MI 48301-2223

WYKE, JOHN ANTHONY, cancer researcher, research institute official; b. Cleethorpes, Eng., Apr. 5, 1942; m. Anne Wynne Mitchell, Sept. 14, 1968; 1 child, Robert Andrew. BA, Cambridge (Eng.) U., 1964, MA, Vet. MB, 1967; PhD, U. London, 1970. Postdoctoral rschr. U. Wash., Seattle, 1970-71, U. So. Calif., L.A., 1971-72; mem. sci. staff Imperial Cancer Rsch. Fund Labs., London, 1972-76, head Tumor Virology Lab., 1976-83; head Imperial Cancer Rsch. Fund Labs., St. Bartholomew's Hosp., London, 1983-87; asst. dir. Imperial Cancer Rsch. Fund, London, 1985-87; dir. Beatson Inst. for Cancer Rsch., Glasgow, Scotland, 1987—; chmn. or mem. numerous nat. and internat. adv. coms. on cancer R & D, U.K., Denmark, Czech Republic, 1983—; gov. Inst. for Animal Health, U.K., 1984-95. Editor 9 sci. jours., 1975—; contbr. over 100 articles to sci. jours. Fellow Royal Soc. Edinburgh; mem. Royal Coll. Vet. Surgeons. Avocations: mountain climbing, skiing, gardening. Office: Beatson Inst Cancer Rsch, Garscube Est, Switchback Rd, Glasgow G61 1BD, Scotland

WYLDER, DELBERT E(UGENE), English educator; b. Jerseyville, Ill., Oct. 5, 1923; s. Robert Maines and (Alice) Blanche (Coulthard) W.; m. Jean Williams, June 5, 1950 (div. July 1965); children: Stephen John, William Creighton; m. Edith Beverly Perry, July 15, 1965; stepchildren: Paul Greenwood Stamm, Philip Baldridge Stamm (dec.). BA, U. Iowa, 1948, MFA, 1950, PhD, 1968; student, U. Nacional de Mex. Asst. prof. English, Utah State U., Logan, 1965-66, Colo. State U., Ft. Collins, 1966-68; assoc. prof. Bemidji (Minn.) State U., 1968-69; prof. English S.W. State U., Marshall, Minn., 1969-77, Murray (Ky.) State U., 1977-89; tech. writer Sandia Corp., Albuquerque, 1958-61. Co-author: Toward Better Writing, 1958; author: Hemingway's Heroes, 1968, Emerson Hough, 1981, also articles and short stories; exec. editor Western Am. Lit., 1966-69; mng. editor Crazy Horse, 1978-82; editor Ky. Philol. Assn. Bull., 1984. Served to 2d lt. USAAC, 1942-45, MTO. NEH grantee, 1976; grantee Colo. State U., S.W. State U., Murray State. U. Mem. AAUP (chpt. pres. 1978-81, Western Lit. Assn. (pres. 1966-67), Minn.-Dakotas Am. Studies Assn. (pres. 1974-75), Ky. Assn. Depts. English (pres. 1979-81), Hemingway Soc. (book rev. editor 1983-86). Democrat. Avocation: writing. Home: # 114 4312 S 31st St Apt 114 Temple TX 76502-3360

WYLE, NOAH, actor; b. Hollywood, Calif., June 4, 1971. Represented by IFA Talent Agy., L.A. Appeared in films, including Blind Faith, 1990, Crooked Hearts, 1991, A Few Good Men, 1992, Swing Kids, 1993, There Goes My Baby, 1994, The Myth of Fingerprints, 1997, Can't Stop Dancing, 1999, Fail Safe, 2000; TV appearances include: ER, 1994-, Guinevere, 1994, Pirates of Silicon Valley, 1999; prodr. Myth of Fingerprings, 1997. Recipient SAG awards, 1998, 99.

WYLIE, JAMES MALCOLM, educator; b. N.Y.C., Mar. 16, 1938; s. James M. and Nancy Beatrice (Worthy) W. BS, Boston U., 1960. Columnist Mexico City Times, 1964; assoc. prof. The Cooper Union Coll., N.Y.C., 1986—. Author: The Lost Rebellion, 1971, The Homestead Grays, 1977, The Sign of Dawn, 1981. Office: 51 Astor Pl New York NY 10003-7132

WYLIE, JOHN ANGUS, business executive, consultant; b. Birmingham, Eng., Mar. 15, 1937; s. Clarke and Ada May (Greensmith) W.; m. Margaret Gilkison Gow, Sept. 7, 1962; children: Morag, Aileen. BS in Chemistry, U. Strathclyde, 1963; HNC Chemistry, Paisley Coll., 1958. Chartered chemist. Analytical chemist Singer Mfg. Ltd., Clydebank, Scotland, 1954-59; sr. analyst British Rayophone Ltd., Wigton, Combria, Eng., 1961-66; chief chemist British Sidal Ltd., Wigton, 1966-67; indsl. liaison officer U. Paisley, Scotland, 1968-83, dir. tech. and bus. ctr., 1984-90, dir. external rels., 1993-96, bus. adviser, 1996—. Pres. Paisley C. of C., 1995-96. Named MBE Buckingham Palace/Order of the British Empire, 1994; hon. fellowship U. Paisley, 1999. Mem. Royal Soc. of Chemistry. Home: 10 Mar Ave, Bishopton PA7 5BS, Scotland Office: U Paisley, Paisley PA1 2BE, Scotland

WYLIE, RICHARD THORNTON, aerospace engineer; b. Long Beach, Calif., July 11, 1956; s. Howard Hance and Marcella Dart (Metcalf) W. BS, Calif. State Poly. U., Pomona, 1978; MS, U. Calif., Berkeley, 1979. Registered profl. engr., Calif. Engr. Aerocraft Heat Treating, Paramount, Calif., 1991-94, TRW, Inc., Redondo Beach, Calif., 1980-91, 94—. Vol. tutor TRW Bootstrap, 1981—. Mem. Mensa (scholarship chmn. Harbor area 1995—, editor Harbor area newsletter 1996-99). Avocation: Graphoanalysis. Home: 1005 Kornblum Ave Torrance CA 90503-5113

WYLLIE, STANLEY CLARKE, retired librarian; b. Clearwater, Fla., Nov. 19, 1935; s. Stanley Clarke and Euginia Lee (Tison) W.; m. Martha Ann Thomason, June 14, 1963; children: Stanley Clarke Jr., Susan Lynne DeHerder, Patricia Anne. BS in History and Social Scis., Fla. So. Coll., 1958; MS in Libr. Sci., Fla. State U., 1963. Tchr. civics and English Lakeland (Fla.) Jr. H.S., 1960-61; libr. I Tampa (Fla.) Pub. Libr., 1962; dir. Chestatee Reg. Libr. Sys., Gainesville, Ga., 1963-64; ind. and sci. ref. libr.

Dayton and Montgomery County Pub. Libr., Dayton, Ohio, 1964-66, collection libr., 1967-73, social scis. and genealogy ref. libr., 1973-90; ret. Editor Mad River Currents newsletter, 1996-97, Bits, 1964-66. Corr. sec. Montgomery County Geneal. Soc., 1990-91, rec. sec., 1997-98; pres. Dayton and Montgomery County Pub. Libr. Staff Assn.; pres. Men's Rep. Club, Lakeland, 1960-61; mem. tV cable commn. City of Riverside, Ohio, 1997-98; presiding judge Riverside, Montgomery County Bd. Elections, 1992—. Recipient Edward M. Selby award Ohio Chpt. of Rsch., 1991-92, Alumnus Disting. svc. award Fla. So. Coll., 1991; Knight York Cross of Honor, Ohio Priory #18, KYCH, 1983; named Ky. Col. Mem. Pub. Employee Retirees Inc. (chpt. pres. 1998, dist. 3 rep. 1999—), Am. Assn. Ret. Persons (dist. coord. 1997-99, del. 2000 Nat. Conv.), Lions (pres. 1996-97, zone chmn. 1996-98, Pres. Excellence award 1997), Odd Fellows (Noble grand 1996-98, grand lodge rep. 1998—, chief patriarch Mad River Encampment # 16 1998-99, jr. grand warden Grand Encampment Ohio 2000, lt. occidental Canton patriarchs militant 1999—), KP (chancellor comdr. Red Star Lodge 2000), United Ancient Order of Druids (vice arch Franklin Grove # 2, 2000), Elks, Toastmasters (area 3 gov. 1995, v.p. edn. 1997), Nat. Wildlife Fedn., Audubon Soc., Mensa, Order of DeMolay (adv. bd. 3d dist. 1996—, Cross of Honor, Legion of Honor), Order Rainbow for Girls (Grand Cross of Color), Dayton High Twelve (pres. 1998), Far Hills High Twelve Club (pres.), SAR (pres. Richard Montgomery chpt. 1990-91, Silver Good Citizenship medal 1997), Masons, Shriners, KP (chancellor comdr. Red Star Lodge 2000—) , Fla. Geneal. Soc., Fla. State Geneal. Soc., Pres.'s Club of Dayton (pres. 2000—), United Ancient Order of Druids (vice arch Franklin Grove # 2), Elks. Anglican Catholic. Avocations: reading, stamp collecting. Home: 4960 Franlou Ave Riverside OH 45432-3120

WYMAN, RICHARD VAUGHN, engineering educator, exploration company executive; b. Painesville, Ohio, Feb. 22, 1927; s. Vaughn Ely and Melinda (Ward) W.; m. Anne Fenton, Dec. 27, 1947; 1 son, William Fenton. BS, Case Western Res. U., 1948; MS, U. Mich., 1949; PhD, U. Ariz., 1974. Registered profl. engr., Nev., Ariz.; registered geologist, Ariz., Calif.; lic. water right surveyor, Nev. Geologist N.J. Zinc Co., 1949, 52-53, Cerro de Pasco Corp., 1950-52; chief geologist Western Gold & Uranium, Inc., St. George, Utah, 1953-55, gen. supt., 1955-57, v.p., 1957-59; pres. Intermountain Exploration Co., Boulder City, Nev., 1959-93; tunnel supt. Reynolds Electric & Engring. Co., 1961-63, mining engr., 1965-67; asst. mgr. ops. Reynolds Electric and & Engring. Co., 1967-69; constrn. supt. engr. Sunshine Mining Co., 1963-65; lectr. U. Nev., Las Vegas, 1969-73, assoc. prof., 1973-80, dept. chmn., 1976-80, prof., 1980-92, prof. emeritus, 1992—, chmn. dept. civil and mech. engring., 1984-90, chmn. dept. civil and environ. engring., 1990-91; mineral rep. Ariz. Strip Adv. Bd., 1976-80, U.S.B.L.M.; mem. peer rev. com. Nuclear Waste Site, Dept. Energy, Las Vegas, 1978-82; pres. Ariz. Juno Resources, Boulder City, 1980-87, v.p., 1990-97; pres. Wyman Engring. Cons., 1987—; cons. Corp. Andina de Fomento, Caracas, Venezuela, 1977-78; v.p. Comstock Gold, Inc., 1984-93; program evaluator Accreditation Bd. for Engring. and Tech., 1995—. Contbr. articles to profl. jours. Sec. Washington County Republican Party, Utah, 1958-60; del. Utah Rep. Conv., 1958-60; scoutmaster Boy Scouts Am., 1959-69; mem. Citizens Adv. Com., Tech. Adv. Com. Regional Flood Control Dist., 1998—. Served with USN, 1944-46. Recipient Order of Engr. award, 2000. Fellow ASCE (life; edn. divsn. 1990, local rep. nat. conv. Las Vegas), Soc. Econ. Geologists (life); mem. AIME/SME (chmn. So. Nev. sect. 1971-72, dir. 1968—, sec.-treas. 1974-92, chmn. Pacific S.W. Minerals Conf. 1972, gen. chmn. nat. conv. 1980, Disting. Mem. award 1989, Legion of Honor 1999), Assn. Engring. Geologists (dir. S.W. sect. 1989-91), Am. Inst. Minerals Appraisers, Nev. Mining Assn. (assoc.), Assn. Ground Water Scientists and Engrs., Arctic Inst. N.Am. (life), Am. Soc. Engring. Edn., Soc. for History of Discoveries, Am. Philatelic Soc., SAR, Am. Legion, Kiwanis, Sigma Xi (pres. Las Vegas sect. 1986-91), Phi Kappa Phi (pres. U. Nev. Las Vegas chpt. 100 1982-83), Sigma Gamma Epsilon, Tau Beta Pi (hon.). Congregationalist. Home: 610 Bryant Ct Boulder City NV 89005-3017 Office: Wyman Engring PO Box 60473 Boulder City NV 89006-0473

WYNALDA, ERIC, professional soccer player; b. Fullerton, June 9, 1969; m. Amy. Student, San Diego State U. Forward FC Saarbruecken, Vfl Bochum Football Club, San Jose Clash, Calif., 1996-99; with U.S. Nat. Team, 1990—; forward Miami Fusion, 1999—. Named to All-Copa Am. Team, 1995; named U.S. Soccer Male Athlete of Yr., 1996. Office: Miami Fusion 2200 Commercial Blvd Ste 104 Fort Lauderdale FL 33309

WYNBERG, INGE DAGMAR, veterinarian; b. Leeuwarden, Friesland, The Netherlands, Oct. 28, 1965. DVM, U. Utrecht, The Netherlands, 1990, specialization in equine internal med., 1999. Pvt. practice veterinarian Warden, The Netherlands, 1990-92, Marrum, The Netherlands, 1992-94; rschr., veterinarian RIVM, Bilthaen, The Netherlands, 1992; resident, jr. docent U. Utrecht, 1994-99, rschr., specialist, 1999—. Contbr. articles to sci. jours., including Vet. Quarterly, Vet. Record. Office: U Utrecht Fac Vet Medicine, PO Box 80-152, 3508 TD Utrecht The Netherlands

WYNMAALEN, HANS ALEXANDER, retired government official; b. Banjoewangi, Java, Indonesia, Apr. 24, 1931; s. Henk Johannus and Maria (Kouwenhoven) W.; m. Atie Petronella Anema, Dec. 17, 1960; children: Mirthe, Pieter, Elizabeth. MA, Free U., 1957. Internat. sec. Dutch Nat. Farmers Orgn., The Netherlands, 1958-64; agrl. counselor, permanent rep. of The Netherlands to European Commn., Brussels, 1964-69, chief of staff to mem., 1973-78, 86-93; dep. gen. dir. Ministry of Agriculture, The Hague, The Netherlands, 1969-73; exec. dir. of bd. Dutch Sugar Co., Amsterdam, 1979-85. Active European Movement, The Netherlands, mem. bd., 1972-92. Capt. Dutch Military, 1952-54. Named Officeur de Merite Agricole Govt. of France, 1978, Comdr. in Order of Merit Govt. of Austria, 1979, Officer in Ordre Orange Naussau, Govt. of The Netherlands, 1986, Knight in Ordre Nederlandse, Leeuw, 1993. Mem. European Movement (mem. bd. 1972-92), Acad. Agriculture of France. Mem. Christian Democrat Party. Mem. Dutch Reformed Ch. Home: Baarnseweg 69, 3734 CA Den Dolder The Netherlands

WYNN, ROBERT RAYMOND, retired engineer, consultant; b. Omaha, Mar. 4, 1929; s. Horace Oscar and Yvonne Cecil (Witters) W.; m. Joann Elizabeth Swicegood, June 28, 1974; children: Kay, William, Frederick, Andrew, Emma, Lawrence, Robert. Diploma in Nuclear Engring., Capitol Radio Engring. Inst., 1964; BSEE, Pacific Internat. Coll. Arts and Scis., 1964; AA in Bus. Adminstrn., Allen Hancock Coll., 1969; MSEE, Pacific Internat. Coll. Arts and Scis., 1971; MSMS, West Coast U., 1975, ASCS, 1985; BSCS, U. State of N.Y., 1985. Registered profl. engr., Calif. Meteorologist United Air Lines, Calif., 1949-53; engring. planner Aircraft Tools Inc., Inglewood, Calif., 1953-55; field service engr. N. Am. Aviation, Inglewood, Calif., 1955-59; R&D engr. Carstedt Research Inc., N. Long Beach, Calif., 1959-60; test engr. Martin Marrietta Corp., Vandenburg AFB, Calif., 1960-64; project engr. Fed. Electric Corp., Vandenburg AFB, Calif., 1965-69; systems engr. Aeronutronic Ford Corp., Pasadena, Calif., 1970-75; MTS Jet Propulsion Lab., Pasadena, Calif., 1975-83; engring. mgr. Space Com., Redondo Beach, Calif., 1983-84; engring. specialist Boeing Service Inc., Pasadena, 1984-86; cons., mem. tech. staff Jet Propulsion Lab., Pasadena, 1986-96; ret., 1996; instr. computer sci. and CAD, Jet Propulsion Lab., 1980-82. With USAAF, 1946. Mem. Calif. Soc. Profl. Engrs., Exptl. Aircraft Assn. (pres. Lompoc chpt. 1968), Am. Legion Rep. (life), W. Coast U. Alumni Assn. Republican. Avocations: model airplane design and constrn., flying, camping. Home: PO Box 26316 Prescott Valley AZ 86312-6316

WYNN, STANFORD ALAN, lawyer; b. Milw., May 9, 1950; s. Sherburn and Marjory (Tarrant) W. BBA, U. Wis., Milw., 1972; JD, Case Western Res. U., 1975; LLM in Taxation, U. Miami, 1976. Bar: Wis. 1975, Fla. 1976. Assoc. Walsh and Simon, Milw., 1976-78; atty., asst. dir. advanced mktg. Northwestern Mut. Life Ins. Co., Milw., 1978—. Author: The Insurance Counselor-Split Dollar Life Insurance, 1991; cons. editor: The Insurance Counselor-The Irrevocable Life Insurance Trust, 1995. Bd. dirs. Waukesha Estate Planning Coun., 1985-86. Office: Northwestern Mut Life Ins Co 720 E Wisconsin Ave Milwaukee WI 53202-4703

WYNNE, MEREDITH W., musician, writer; m. Chase B. Coleman. AB, Vassar Coll., 1984; MusM, Boston Conservatory, 1991. Adminstr. Harvard U., Cambridge, Mass., 1988-94; classical recital artist on cruise ships, 1995-97; music critic, arts critic Flagstaff (Ariz.) Live, 1999—; prin., co-owner Coleman Wynne Music, Flagstaff, 1998—; instr. No. Ariz. U., Flagstaff, 1998—. Contbr. articles to profl. jours. Active Girl Scouts USA, N.J. Mem. Nat. Assn. Tchrs. of Singing, Coll. Music Soc. E-mail: roxolana@bigfoot.com. Office: Coleman Wynne Music 1235 W Saturn Way Flagstaff AZ 86001-1154

WYNSTRA, NANCY ANN, lawyer; b. Seattle, June 25, 1941; d. Walter S. and Gaile E. (Cogley) W. BA cum laude, Whitman Coll., 1963; LLB cum laude, Colulmbia U., 1966. Bar: Wash. 1966, D.C. 1969, Ill. 1979, Pa. 1984. With appellate sect., civil divsn. U. S. Dept. Justice, Washington, 1966-67; TV corr. legal news Stas. WRC, NBC and Stas. WTOP, CBS, Washington, 1967-68; spl. asst. Corp. Counsel Washington, 1968-70; dir. planning and rsch. D.C. Superior Ct., Washington, 1970-78; sp. advisor White house Spl. Action, Office for Drug Abuse Prevention, Washington, 1973-74; fellow Drug Abuse Coun., 1974-75; chief counsel Michael Reese Hosp. and Med. Ctr., Chgo., 1978-83; exec. v.p., gen. counsel Allegheny Health Edn. and Rsch. Found., Pitts., 1983-98; pres., CEO Allegheny Health Svcs. Provider's Ins. CO., Pitts., 1989-98; health law cons., 1998—; assoc. prof. Carnegie Mellon U., Sch. Urban and Pub. Affairs, 1985—, Allegheny U. Health Scis., 1991—; cons. to various drug abuse programs, 1971-78; health law cons., 1998—. Author: Fundamentals of Health Law, others; contbr. articles to profl. jours. Mem. bd. overseers Whitman Coll., 1993—; mem. bd. deacons East Liberty Presbyn. Ch., 2000—; elder East Liberty Presbyn. Ch., 2000—. Mem. ABA, Nat. Health Lawyers Assn. (bd. dirs. 1985-91, 92-97, 97-99, chair publs. com. 1989-91, audit com. 1991-92, treas. 1992-93, 95-96, exec. com. 1992-99, edn. fund com. 1992-93, mem. nominating com. 1992-93, sec. 1993-95, treas. 1995-96, pres.-elect 1996-97, pres. 1997-98), Am. Health Lawyers Assn. (pres. 1997-98, exec. com. 1997-99, immediate past pres. 1998-99), Am. Soc. Hosp. Attys., others.

WYNTER, CORAL VERN ANN, biochemist; b. Sydney, Australia, Mar. 14, 1945; d. Henry Adam Channells and Thelma Marshall; children: Chantal Georgina Channells-Wynter, Katrina Zoe Clara Channells. BSc, U. Sydney, 1963; PhD, U. London, 1973. Tutor U. New South Wales, Sydney, 1977-79; rsch. officer Queensland Workers Health Ctr., 1987-89, U. Queensland, Brisbane, Australia, 1990-92, 95—; mgr. Brisbane Ctr. Protein & Nucleic Acid Rsch., Brisbane, 1992-94. Contbr. articles to profl. jours. Mem. Dem. Socialist Party, Brisbane, 1978—; candidate Brisbane City Coun., 1997, fed. election, Brisbane, 1996; sec. Coms. Solidarity Latin Am. & Caribbean, Brisbane, 1986-98. Sir Edward Dunlop Rsch. Found. grantee, Melbourne, Australia, 1997. Avocations: squash, tennis, bushwalking, science fiction. Office: U Queensland, Dept Biochemistry, St Lucia PC 4072, Australia

WYRICK, PRISCILLA BLAKENEY, microbiologist; b. Greensboro, N.C., Apr. 28, 1940; d. Carnie Lee and Prestine (Blakeney) W. BS in Med. Tech., U. N.C., Chapel Hill, 1962; MS in Bacteriology, U. N.C., 1967, PhD in Bacteriology, 1971. Technologist Clin. Microbiology Lab., N.C. Meml. Hosp., Chapel Hill, 1962-64; asst. supr. Clin. Microbiology Lab., N.C. Meml. Hosp., 1964-65, supr., 1965-66; sci. staff fellow Nat. Inst. Med. Rsch., Mill Hill, London, 1971-73; asst. prof. dept. microbiology U. N.C. Sch. Medicine, Chapel Hill, 1973-79; assoc. prof. U. N.C. Sch. Medicine, 1979-88, prof., 1988-2000; prof. dept. microbiology James H. Quillen Coll. Medicine, East Tenn. State U., Johnson City, 2000—; chair dept microbiology, 2000—. Grantee, NIH. Mem. Am. Acad. Microbiology, Am. Soc. Microbiology (pres. N.C. br. 1981-82, chmn. div. gen. med. microbiology 1981-82), AAAS, Soc. Infectious Diseases, Sigma Xi. Office: East Tenn State U Box 70579 VA # 1-41 Johnson City TN 37614

WYROBISZ, ANDRZEJ, historian, educator; b. Cracow, Poland, Nov. 10, 1931; s. Stanisław and Janina (Tarnowicz) W. MA, U. Warsaw, Poland, 1955; PhD, Polish Acad. Scis., 1961. Rschr. inst. history material culture Polish Acad. Scis., 1955-69; asst. prof. U. Warsaw, 1969-78, prof., 1978—. Author: Glass in Poland in the 14th-17th Centuries, 1968; editor: Studies on the History of Society and Economy of Podlasie Region, 16th-18th c., 1981, (jour.) Polish Hist. Rev., 1954—; mem. editl. bd. Quar. Rev. History Material Culture, 1990—; overseas corr. Urban Hsitory. Mem. Warsaw Sci. Assn., Polish Sci. Soc. AIDS, Polish Hist. Soc. Avocations: theatre, opera, ballet. Home: Uniwersytecka 4 m 25, 02 036 Warsaw Poland Office: Inst History Art U Warsaw, Krakowskie Przedmiescie 26/28, 00 927 Warsaw Poland

WYROST, PIOTR, anatomist, educator, researcher; b. Sandomierz, Poland, June 28, 1925; s. Aleksy and Zubrzycka Rozalia Wyrost; m. Czesława Madziarz, Aug. 2, 1954; 1 child, Aleksandra. Vet. surgeon, U. Wrocław, 1952; DVM, Agrl. U., 1960, DSc, 1967. Asst. Dept. of Animal Anatomy, Wrocław, 1950-57, adj., 1957-69, assoc. prof., 1969-78, extraordinary officer, 1978-89, full prof., 1989-95, ret., 1995; head dept. of animal anatomy Agrl. U. of Wrocł, 1969-95; prodean Faculty of Vet. Medicine, 1972-81. Co-author: Polish Veterinary Anatomical Nomenclature, 1978, Outline of History of Polish Veterinary Medicine, 1990; co-author, editor: Veterinary Old Prints in the Polish Libraries, 1996, The Fauna of Ancient Silesia, 1985; editor-in-chief Archivum Veterinarium Polonicum, 1988-97. Mem. Internat. Coun. for Archaeozoology, 1971-98. Recipient Knight Cross Order Revival of Poland Pres. of Poland, 1978, Medal of Commn. Nat. Edn., Min. of Edn., 1980, Order Educator of Merit, Pres. of Poland, 1984. Mem. Polish Anatomical Soc. (hon. mem., bd. dirs.), Polish Soc. of Vet. Scis. (hon. mem., bd. dirs., sect. for history of vet. medicine, 1987-98), Polish Acad. of Scis. (com. vet. scis. 1987-98). Roman Catholic. Avocations: bibliography of old prints, philately, numismatics. Home: Pl Grunwaldzki 17 m 41, 50-378 Wroclaw Poland Office: Dept Anim Anat Fac Vet Med, ul Kozuchowska 1-3, 51-631 Wroclaw Poland

WYRWICKA, WANDA, research anatomist; b. Pabianice, Poland, Sept. 8, 1912; came to U.S., 1966; d. Jacob and Veronica (Rytwinska) W.; m. Leszek Kolodziejczyk, Dec. 26, 1946; 1 child, Joanna. MS, Poznan U., 1937, PhD, 1947. From asst. researcher to prof. extraordinaire Nencki Inst. of Exptl. Biology, Warsaw, Poland, 1947-66; from asst. researcher to full researcher UCLA, 1966-79, rsch. anatomist, 1980—; cons. neuropsychology lab. VA Med. Ctr., Sepulveda, Calif., 1967-72; key investigator Ctr. for Ulcer Rsch. and Edn., VA Med. Ctr., Wadsworth, Calif., 1974-78. Author: The Mechanisms of Conditioned Behavior, 1972, The Development of Food Preferences, 1981, Brain and Feeding Behavior, 1988, Imitation in Human and Animal Behavior, 1996, Conditioning: Situation vs. Intermittent Stimulus, 2000. Recipient Pavlovian Soc. award, 1977. Achievements include research on conditional reflexes (mostly those related to feeding), brain structures related to regulation of feeding, gastric acid secretion and its brain substrates, role of situation in conditioning. Office: UCLA Sch Medicine Dept Neurobiology Los Angeles CA 90095-0001

WYSEMAN, ROBIN, industrialist, consultant; b. Nottingham, Eng., Oct. 10, 1951; m. Karen Lorry Asplu, Feb. 17, 1987; 1 child, Meryl Veronica. BA with honors, U. London, 1973, PhD, 1978. Cons. Burton Group, London, 1974-82, ICI, London, 1983-93, R.J. Whiteman Inc., Nottingham, 1993-98; chief exec. Wyeth Pharms. Europe and U.K., 1999—; econ. adviser MidLand Bank PLC; chief econ. cons. Wyeth Pharms., Europe and U.K., 1998; cons. to numerous cos., Europe and U.K., 1997; mem. adv. com. to Chancellor of the Exchequer, U.K. Author: Invasion From Earth, 1997, Planet X, 1998; contbr. articles to profl. jours. Beneficiary, trustee various cos., U.K. and Europe, 2000—. Mem. adv. com. to Chancellor of Exchequer U.K. Fax: 01623 6602076. Home: 54 Albert St, Mansfield Woodhouse, NG19 8BH Nottingham England

WYSOCKI, BOGDAN JOSEPH, marketing manager; b. Cieszyn, Silesia, Poland, Nov. 1, 1946; s. Joseph and Franciszka (Woynar) W.; m. Halina Krzepinski, Jan. 21, 1972; children: Marcin, Ursula. M of Computer Sci., Tech. Mil. Acad., Warsaw, 1970; D of Econ. Sci., Mil. Acad., Warsaw, 1976. Sys. designer Govtl. Computer Ctr., Warsaw, 1979-81; project mgr. Cenzin, Warsaw, 1981-87; comml. attache Embassy of Poland, Lagos, Nigeria, 1987-91; comml. dir. Vigo Sensor, Warsaw, Poland, 1991-93; dir. dept. Cenzin, Warsaw, 1993-96; sr. mktg. mgr. PCO, Warsaw, 1996—. Lt. col. Computer Sci., 1970-91. Avocations: tennis, skiing, bridge, golf, history.

WYSOCKI, JAROSŁAW, otolaryngologist; b. Warsaw, Apr. 13, 1964; s. Jerzy and Wiestawa (Ratajczyk) W.; m. Agnieszka Czerwonka, June 6, 1992; 1 child, Martyna. MD, U. Med. Sch., Warsaw, 1988, PhD, 1995. Sci. worker normal anatomy dept. U. Med. Sch., Warsaw, 1988—; ear, nose and throat specialist Clin. Hosp. No. 3, Warsaw, 1996—. Author, editor: Temporal Bone Injuries, 1999; contbr. articles to profl. jours. Recipient Prof. Miodonski award Polish Ear, Nose and Throat Surgeons Orgn., 1996. Fellow Polish Anatom. Soc.; mem. Polish Ear, Nose and Throat Surg. Soc. Mem. Union of Freedom. Avocations: history, tourism. Home: 21 Skierniewicka Ap 58, 01-230 Warsaw Poland Office: Normal Anatomy Dept, Chałubinskiego 5, 02-004 Warsaw Poland

WYSOCZANSKI, DARIUSZ, science educator; b. Kyrnica, Poland, Dec. 10, 1968. MSc, Wroclaw (Poland) U. Tech., 1992, Grad. Engr. of Electronics, 1992, PhD, 1996; PhD, U. Rouen, France, 1996. Cert. engring. Asst., chair electronic and photonic metrology Wroclaw U. Tech., 1992-97, adj., chair electronic and photonic metrology, 1997—. Avocations: electronics, physics, informatics, dancing. E-mail: wysoczanski@kmeif.pwr.wroc.pl. Fax: 48 71 321 42 77. Office: Wroclaw U Tech, ul B Prusa 53/55, 50317 Wroclaw Poland

WYSS, DAVID ALEN, financial service executive; b. Ft. Wayne, Ind., Nov. 14, 1944; s. Alen G. and Anne W. (Winicker) W.; m. Grace H. Hawes, June 11, 1966; children: Sarah J., Alen D. BS, MIT, 1966; PhD, Harvard U., 1971. Economist Fed. Res., Washington, 1970-74, sr. economist, 1975-77; advisor Bank Eng., London, 1974-75; sr. staff economist Council Econ. Advisers, Washington, 1977-79; v.p. DRI Ltd., London, 1979-83; rsch. dir. DRI/McGraw Hill, Lexington, Mass., 1983-97; chief economist Std. & Poor's/DRI, Lexington, 1997-99, Std. & Poor's, N.Y.C., 2000—. Contbr. numerous articles to profl. jours. Mem. Am. Econ. Assn., Am. Statis. Assn., Nat. Assn. Bus. Economists. Office: Std & Poors 55 Water St Ste Concl2 New York NY 10041-0003

WYSS, RAMON ALEXANDER, educational administrator; b. Heidelberg, Germany, Mar. 1, 1952; arrived in Sweden, 1967; s. Dieter Heinrich Eduard J. and Ursula (Daecke) W.; m. Josefin Dorota Irena Gorczak, June 6, 1973; children: Katja Tora, Björn Anatol. MSCE, Royal Inst. Tech., Sweden, 1985, PhD, 1990, docent, 1993. High precision grinding Atlas Copco, Stockholm, 1972-80; rsch. asst. Oak Ridge Nat. Lab., Tenn., 1990-92; rsch. asst. Royal Inst. Tech., Stockholm, 1992-97, asst. prof., 1993—, dir. of studies, 1996—; chmn. internat. symposium New Nuclear Structure Phenomena in the Vicinity of Closed Shells, Stockholm, 1995, nuc. physics sect. Swedish Physical Soc., 2000. Editor: Physica Scripta, vol. T56, 1995; contbr. numerous articles to profl. jours. Avocations: reading, history, skating, swimming, diving. Home: Värmdöv 238, S-13142 Nacka Sweden Office: Royal Inst Tech, Fysik I, 100 44 Stockholm Sweden

WYZAN, MICHAEL LOUIS, economist, researcher; b. Albany, N.Y., Feb. 3, 1955; s. Henry S. and Marjorie Hope (Burger) W.; m. Kie Min Tang, July 30, 1985; 1 child, Rebecca Ling. AB, Miami U., Oxford, Ohio, 1975; PhD, U. N.C., 1979. Assoc. prof. econs. Ill. State U., Normal, 1982-91; vis. staff economist planning and econ. analysis staff U.S. Dept. State, Washington, 1990-91; advisor to Bulgarian Fin. Ministry U.S. Treas. Dept., Sofia, Bulgaria, 1994-95; sr. economist Open Media Rsch. Inst., Prague, 1995-97; assoc. prof. Stockholm Sch. Econs., 1993—; rsch. scholar Internat. Inst. for Applied Sys. Analysis, Laxenburg, Austria, 1997-2000; econ. advisor USAID, Yerevan, Armenia, 2000—. Editor: The Political Economy of Ethnic Discrimination and Affirmative Action: A Comparative Perspective, 1990, First Steps Toward Economic Independence: New States of the Post-Communist World, 1995; co-editor: Economic Change in the Balkan States: Albania, Bulgaria, Romania and Yugoslavia, 1991, The Mixed Blessing of Financial Inflows: Transition Countries in Comparative Perspective, 1999. Mem. Am. Assn. for Advancement of Slavic Studies, Assn. Comparative Econ. Studies, European Assn. for Comparative Econ. Studies. Jewish. Avocations: travel, fiction, horseback riding. Home: Usaid Armenia 7020 Washington DC 20523-0001 Office: IIASA, Schlossplatz 1, A-2361 Laxenburg Austria

WYZNER, EUGENIUSZ, diplomat; b. Chelmno, Poland, Oct. 31, 1931; s. Henryk and Janina (Czaplicka) W.; m. Elzbieta Laudanska, June 27, 1961; 1 child, Jaroslaw. Student, U. Warsaw, Poland, 1952; LLM, U. Warsaw, 1954; postgrad., Hague (The Netherlands) Acad. of Internat. Law, 1958. With Ministry Fgn. Affairs, Poland, 1952-54; sec. of the neutral supervisory com. Korea, 1954-55; mem. staff Ministry Fgn. Affairs, Warsaw, 1956-61; ambassador to Geneva, 1973-78; dir. dept. internat. orgns. Ministry Fgn. Affairs, Warsaw, 1978-81; chmn. UN Disarmament Commn., 1982; under-sec. gen. conf. services and spl. assignments UN Disarmament Commn., N.Y.C., 1982-92; undersec. gen. pub. info. UN, N.Y.C., 1992-94; dep. min. for fgn. affairs Republic of Poland, Warsaw, 1994-95; 1st dep. min. for fgn. affairs, sec. of state Republic of Poland, Warsaw, Poland, 1996-97; permanent rep. amb. to UN N.Y.C., 1998-99; vice-chmn. Internat. Civil Svc. Commn., N.Y.C., 1999—. Vice-chmn. preparatory com. Internat. Conf. on Human Rights, chmn. com. on periodic reports on human rights, 1965-68; chmn. sub-com. of UN Com. on Peaceful Uses of Outer Space, 1967-82; pres. Rev. Conf. of Parties to Treaty on Prohibition of Nuclear Weapons, 1977; mem. Polish del. of UN Gen. Assembly, UN Programme Planing and Budgeting Bd., 1984-93; chmn. UN Publs. Bd., 1982-93; chmn. com. for 2000 review conf. of the parties to the treaty on the non-proliferation of nuclear weapons, 1998-99. Decorated Cross of Polonia Restituta Polish Council of State, 1969, 77, Golden Cross of Merit, 1964, Comdr.'s Cross with a star Order of Polonia Restituta, 1996, Comdr.'s Cross of the Legion d'Honneur, Pres. of France and Grand Comdr.'s Cross of the Order of the Phoenix, Pres. of Greece, 1996. Mem. Internat. Inst. Outer Space Law (bd. dirs. 1974—, Citation 1977), Internat. Peace Acad. (bd. dirs. 1983-91), Internat. Congress Inst. (bd. dirs. 1987-90), Internat. Congress Acad. (mem. senate 1990-95). Office: Internat Civil Svc Commn 2 United Nations Plz New York NY 10017-4403

XEIDAKIS, GEORGIOS STYLIANOS, civil engineering educator; b. Heraclion, Crete, Greece, June 24, 1940; s. Stylianos George and Kalliopi Mathaios (Farsaraki) X.; m. Eugenia George Varagouli, Dec. 24, 1979; children: Stylianos, Anastasios. BS, Physics-Maths., Thessaloniki, Greece, 1965; MS, Earth Scis., Leeds, Eng., 1976; PhD, Civil Engring., Leeds, Eng., 1979. Sci. tchr. Govt. Greece, 1965-80; univ. lectr. Democritos U. of Thrace, Xanthi, Greece, 1980-96, univ. prof., 1996—. Contbr. articles to profl. jours. Home: 53 Tsimiski Str, 67100 Xanthi Greece Office: Dept Civil Engring, Democritos U of Thrace, 67100 Xanthi Greece

XHOLI, ZIJA, philosopher; b. Korca, Albania, Apr. 25, 1923; s. Isuf and Behije (Mulla) X.; m. Tefta Cami, Nov. 29, 1954; children: Rudina, Melita. B, Lomonosou U., 1952; M, Tirana U., 1960. Editor-in-chief Rinia Newspaper, Tirana, Albania, 1946-47; lector Tirana U., 1952-73; dean Law and Philos. Faculty, Tirana, 1974-89; prof., 1994—. Author: Naim Frasheri-Life and Works, 1962, 2d edit., 1978; co-author: Albanian Encyclopedia, 1985, High School Philosophical Text Book, 1975. Mem. Acad. of Sci., Albanian Trade Union (mem. gen. coun. 1967-72, mem. presidium 1972-76, chmn. culture dept. 1977-90), Albanian Philos. Assn. (chmn. 1991). Avocations: tennis, jogging, classical music. Home: Rruga Emin Duraku, Pall 1 Sh 18 Ap 4, Tirana Albania Office: Sheshi Fan Noli 1, Tirana Albania

XI, CHANGCHANG, mathematician; b. Shaanxi, Peoples Republic of China, Feb. 20, 1960; s. Huibin and Yunxia (Ma) X.; m. Shuping Dong, 1986; 1 child, Ou. BS, Shaanxi Normal U., Xi'an, 1981, MS, 1984; D in Math., U. Bielefeld, Germany, 1989. Lectr. Shaanxi Normal U., Xi'an, 1984-85, U. Bielefeld, 1988-91; postdoctoral fellow Beijing Normal U., 1991-93, asst. prof., 1993-97, prof., 1997—, vice-dir. Mathematics Inst., 1995; vis. prof. U. Bielefeld, 1995-96. Editor: Acta Math. Sinica, 2000—; contbr. articles to profl. jours. including Jour. Algebra, Jour. Pure Applied Algebra, Jour. London Math. Soc., Math. Japanica, Advances in Math., Compositio Math., Comms. Math. Phys., Math. Annalen. Office: Beijing Normal U Dept Math, Hai Dian, Beijing 100875, China

XI, GUANG KANG, vacuum scientist, physics educator; b. Changsha, Hunan, China, Feb. 26, 1928; s. Bai Jie and Feng Chun (Wang) X.; m. Er Yi Xu, Jan. 28, 1959; children: Gang, Yan Ling. BS, Fudan U., Shanghai, 1953. Asst. Nankai U., Tianjin, China, 1953-60, lectr., 1961-80, assoc. prof., 1981-84, prof. physics and electronics, 1986—; vis. prof. Hamburg (Germany) U., 1985-86. Author: Solid Surfaces and Interfaces, 1996; contbr. articles to profl. jours.; inventor mass spectrometer, surface analysis apparatus. Recipient Sci. prize Tianjin Govt., 1986, Sci. prize Nat. Edn. Com., 1991. Mem. Chinese Vacuum Soc. (bd. dirs. 1981—), Tianjin Vacuum Soc.

(chmn. bd. dirs. 1991—), N.Y. Acad. Sci. Avocations: swimming, table tennis, tennis, television. Office: Nankai U Dept Elec Sci, 94 Weijin Rd Nankai Dist, Tianjin 300071, People's Republic of China

XI, JIANGTAO, telecommunications engineer, educator; b. Yiyang, China, June 2, 1962; p. Tianqi Xi and Wuyan Liang; m. Aidong Miao, Aug. 15, 1985; children: Cecily, Christopher. B of Engring., Beijing Inst. Tech., 1982; M of Engring., TsingHua U., Beijing, 1985; PhD, U. Wollongong, Australia, 1996. Lectr. Zhengzhou U., Henan, China, 1985-90, assoc. prof., 1990-91; assoc. lectr. U. Wollongong, Australia, 1992-95, lectr., 1998—; postdoctoral fellow McMaster U., Hamilton, Can., 1995-96; mem. tech. staff Bell Labs., Middletown, N.J., 1997-98. Contbr. articles to profl. jours. Mem. IEEE. Home: 10 Cochrane St, West Wollongong NSW 2500, Australia Office: Sch Elec Computer Telecomm, Northfields Ave, Wollongong NSW 2522, Australia

XI, JUN YANG, financial educator, academic advisor; b. Shanghai, China, Dec. 1, 1955; s. Xue and Ying (Wang) X.; m. Yu Zhen Zhu, May 1, 1985; 1 child, Linda. BA, Shanghai U. Fin. and Econs., 1982, MA, 1985; PhD in Econs., East-China Normal U., 1988. Pro-dir. Rsch. Ctr. on Econ. Reform, Shanghai, 1988-91; rsch. fellow London Sch. Econs., 1991-92; dir. Internat. Fin. Sect., SUFE, Shanghai, 1992—; acad. advisor Changsha (China) Securities Co., 1994-99, Bank of Shanghai. Author: A Study of International Reserves, 1998 (Zhongzhen Acad. Book prize 1998); co-author: Economic Reform: Flying Thought, 1985 (Young Economist prize 1985), Money, Banking and Financial Markets, 1990, Macro-supervision on National Economy, 1992, Operation of Financial Markets, 1994, An Analysis on International Financial Crisis, 1997. Recipient Excellent Paper prize North-East Internat. Fin. Mag., 1986, Silver Paper prize Shanghai Securities Jour., 1994; K.C. Wong fellow Brit. Acad., London, 1991. Mem. Shanghai Econ. Reform Assn., Shanghai Internat. Fin. Assn., Shanghai Fin. Assn. Avocations: stamp collecting, local opera acting. Home: 485/70/602 Sanmen Rd, 200439 Shanghai China Office: Internat Fin Sect, 777 Guoding Rd, 200433 Shanghai China

XI, NING, engineering educator, researcher; b. Beijing, Aug. 31, 1959; came to U.S., 1985; s. Fulin Xi and Guanling Wen; m. Li Liu, Nov. 22, 1995. MS, Northeastern U., Boston, 1987, Washington U., St. Louis, 1990; DSc, Washington U., St. Louis, 1993. Postdoctoral rschr. Washington U., St. Louis, 1993-94, asst. prof., 1994-97; assoc. prof. Mich. State U., E. Lansing, 1997—; pres. Xi Assocs., E. Lansing, 1996—. Editor: IEEE Transactions on Robotics and Automation, 1998. Recipient Career award NSF, 1997. Mem. IEEE (Acad. Career award 1999), ASME. Avocations: sports, fishing, travel. Office: Mich State U 2120 Engineering Bldg East Lansing MI 68824

XI, YUYAO, engineering educator; b. Shanghai, July 21, 1933; s. Gongshi Xi and Yunwu Yang; m. Chunyun Zhang, Sept. 1, 1957; 1 child, Shiyun Xi. Student, E. China Inst. Hydraulic, Engring., Nanjing, 1953, Dalian Inst. Tech., Dalian, Liaoning, China, 1956. Asst. lectr. East China Inst. Hydraulic Engring. (now Hohai U.), Nanjing, 1956-61, 61-81; assoc. prof. Hohai U., 1981-86, prof., 1986-98, dean dept. engring., 1984-94, dir. rsch. inst., 1986-94; vis. scholar Netherlands Ship Model Basin, Wageningen, The Netherlands, 1979-81. Chief editor: Layout of Harbour, Water Intake and Outlet for Guangdong Nuclear Power Station, 1988 (Nat. prize People's Rep. of China 1992). Recipient award for Outstanding Scientific and Technol. Worker, Ministry of Com., China, Beijing, 1991, Assn. of Sci. and Tech., Jiangsu Province, Nanjing, 1992. Mem. China Ocean Engring. Soc. (coun. mem. 1985—). Avocations: Chinese chess, contract bridge. Office: Hohai U, Xikang Rd 1, Nanjing Jiangsu 210024, China

XIA, AN BANG, computer engineering educator; b. Wuhan, China, June 15, 1945; s. Mu Ru Xia and Chang Hong Wang; m. Ling Zhang, Oct. 1, 1973; children: Xiyuan Xia, Yiyuan Xia. BA, Tsinghua U., Beijing, 1968; MA, S.E. U., Nanjing, China, 1982. Engr. Elec. Tools Factory, Xining, China, 1968-78; lectr. Automation Inst., Nanjing, 1982-86; assoc. prof. Mgmt. Sch., Nanjing, 1987-91; assoc. prof. engring. S.E. U., Nanjing, 1992-93, prof. engring., 1994—; cons. Office of Manpower Plan, Nanjing, 1985-88, Talent Rsch. Inst., Nanjing, 1991—; chief engr. Hua Bao Computer Integrated Mfg. Sys., Shunde, China, 1992-97, Sa Gang Computer Integrated Mfg. Sys., Zhangjiagang, China, 1994-98, Su Fa Computer Integrated Mfg. Sys., Suzhou, China, dir. Jiangsu Office, 1996—. Author: Manpower Forecasting and Education Planning, 1989, Manpower Planning, 1989, Systems Identification, 1991, Introduction to Decision Support Systems, 1991 (1st prize of Tongji press 1992), Introduction to Quantitative Forecast, 2000. Mem. Internat. Fedn. of Automatic Control, Soc. Mfg. Engrs., Jiangsu Talents Assn. (sec.-gen. 1988—). Avocations: reading, music, stamp collecting, golf. Home: Ninghai Rd, Hua Xin Lane 17-1-301, Nanjing 210024, China Office: Southeast Univ, Dept Elec Engring, Nanjing 210018, China

XIA, CHANG YU, mathematician; b. Jianli, Hubei, China, Oct. 17, 1962; s. Dao Fa and Mo Re (Dan) X.; m. Qiao Ling Wang, July 2, 1989; children: Yuan, Yuhao. BA, Hubei U., 1983; MS, Wuhan U., 1985; PhD, Fudan (Shanghai) U., 1989; postdoc., Tohoku U., Sendai, Japan, 1993-94, Inst. Math. Pura Aplicada, Rio de Janeiro, 1996-97. Assoc. prof. U. Brasilia, Brazil, 1998—. Contbr. articles to profl. jours. Office: Univ Brasilia, Dept Mathematics IE, 70910 Brasilia Brazil

XIA, CHAOYI, advertising company executive, painter, artist; b. Beijing, Aug. 15, 1958; s. Ruai and Xiaobing (Bin) X.; m. Hueilin Zhang, Apr. 24, 1984; 1 child, Xia Dongping. BA, China Ctrl. Coll. Arts and Crafts, 1984. Creative dir. China United Adv. Co., Beijing, 1984-90, pres., 1992—; vis. artist Paris Coll. of Decorative Arts, 1991-92. Solo exhbn. Eastern Arts Gallery, Lyon, France, 1991. Recipient Lyon Artists Salon City of Lyon, France, 1991. Mem. Am. Adv. Assn., Beijing Adv. Assn., Western N.Y. Adv. Assn. Avocations: bridge, music, swimming.

XIA, HARRY HUA-XIANG, medical researcher, microbiologist; b. Wuhan, Hubei, China, Oct. 21, 1962; arrived in Australia, 1993; s. Guang-zhen and Zai-zai (Liu) X.; m. Jihong Chen, Dec. 30, 1988; children: Mary Biwen, Patrick Aozhe. MB, Tongji Med. U., Wuhan, 1985, MSc, 1988; PhD, Dublin (Ireland) U., 1994. Physician Union Hosp., Wuhan, 1988-90; postdoctorate St. James's Hosp., Dublin, 1994-95; rsch. fellow Nepean Hosp., Sydney, 1995—; lectr. Tongji Med. U., Wuhan, 1988-90, Trinity Coll, Dublin U., 1994-95. Contbr. articles to profl. jours. and med. books. Recipient Sci. and Tech. awards Provincial Govt., Wuhan, 1989, City Govt., Wuhan, 1989, Invention award Invention Soc. Wuhan, 1990. Mem. Path. Soc. Gt. Britain and Ireland, N.Y. Acad. Scis. Office: Nepean Hosp GI Lab Clin Scis Bldg, Derby St PO Box 63, Penrith NSW 2751, Australia

XIA, JIDING, chemical engineering educator; b. Jiangyin, Jiangsu, China, Mar. 23, 1921; s. Baogen Xia; m. Ming Yu, Oct. 1, 1958; children: Wei, Men. BS, Zhejiang U., Hangzhou, China, 1945, MS, 1948. Assoc. prof. Haijiang U., Fujian, China, 1949-50, Nanjing (China) Normal U., 1953-54; dir. teaching and rsch. divsn. Southeast U. (China), 1954-58; assoc. prof. and dir. teaching/rsch. divsn. Wuxi (China) U. Light Industry, 1958-85; prof. chem. engring. Wuxi U. of Light Industry, 1985-92; rsch. chemist U. Wis., Madison, 1995-96; vis. prof. Wayne State U., Detroit, 1993-95; mem. expert group synthetic detergents and fatty acids, Ministry of Light Industry China, 1979-86; vis. prof. The VI Univ. of Paris, 1986; , evaluation com. acad. degree Authorized U., 1980-84, Jiangsu Light Industry Sr. Engrs., 1982-92; project evaluator China Nat. Natural Sci. Found. Surface Chemistry, 1985—; cons. Chemithon Co., Seattle, 1990-93, Aging Toilet Soap Factory, China, 1991—, Tianjin Rsch. Inst. Interface and Colloid Scis., 1993, Stepan Co., Chgo., 1994, Proctor & Gamble Co., Cin., 1994-95, Vista Chem. Co., Houston, 1994—;mem. adv. com. Internat. Symposium on Surfactants in Solution, 1993. Author: Synthetic Detergents, 1976, Chemistry and Technology of Surfactants and Detergents, 1997; author and editor: Protein-Based Surfactants, 2000; editor: Composite Soaps, 1987; translator: Comprehensive Refining of Sunflower Seed Oil, 1956, Chemistry of Oil and Fats, 1958, Manufacture of Detergents, 1986; mem. editl. bd. Jour. Surfactant Industry, 1982-90, Jour. Petro-Finechemicals, 1982, Chinese Ency. LIght Industry, 1987-91; contbr. more than 120 articles to acad. jours. Recipient award Ministry of Petroleum Industry for EOR Project, 1992, Outstanding Contbn. to Chinese Higher Edn. award State Coun., 1992, Ministry of Light Industry for rsch. on composite soaps, 1983, Remarkable Achievement in Sci. and Tech. Invention and Innovation, UN, 1994; Excellent Advanced Sci. Rsch. fellow Wuxi, 1990, 93. Mem. China Assn. Surfactants and Detergent Industry (hon. dir. 1992, standing dir. 1983-92), Jiangsu Soc. of Daily Chem. Industry (chmn. 1978-85), Am. Chem. Soc. Address: Wuxi U Light Industry, Box 66, Wuxi Jiangsu 214036, China

XIA, KANG, agronomy educator; b. Beijing, June 24, 1967; came to US, 1990; p. Xuezhi Xia and Lizhu Zhang. BS, Beijing Agrl. U., 1989; MS, La. State U., 1993; PhD, U. Wis., 1997. Postdoctoral rsch. assoc. dept. soil sci. U. Wis., Madison, 1997-98; asst. prof. dept. agronomy Kans. State U., Manhattan, 1998—. Mem. Am. Chem. Soc., Soil Sci. Soc. Am. (Emil Truog Soil Sci. award 1997). Avocation: outdoor activities. E-mail: kxia@ksu.edu. Office: Kans State U Dept Agronomy 2004 Throckmorton Plant Scienc Manhattan KS 66506-5500

XIA, RENJIE, civil engineer, researcher; b. Shanghai, China, Dec. 25, 1943; came to U.S., 1986; s. Yalun and Xizhu (Mao) X.; m. Aifang He, Aug. 25, 1988; children: Tao, Fangzhou. BS, U. Agrl. Engring., Beijing, 1968; ME, East China Tech. U. Water Resources, Nanjing, 1982; PhD, U. Ill., 1991. Registered profl. engr., Ill. Engr. East China Tech. U. Water Resources, 1979-86; rsch. asst. U. Ill., Urbana-Champaign, 1986-87; rsch. asst. U. Ill. State Water Survey, Champaign, 1987-91, assoc. profl. scientist, 1991-96, profl. scientist, 1996—. Contbr. articles to profl. jours. Mem. ASCE, Internat. Assn. for Hydraulic Rsch. Achievements include contribution to the discovery of significance of momentum and pressure coefficients on using Saint-Venant equations to solve unsteady flow problems; contribution to the detection of distribution of turbulent velocity fluctuations and relation between mean and maximum velocities in natural rivers. Avocations: playing piano, watching movies, travel. Office: Ill State Water Survey 2204 Griffith Dr Champaign IL 61820-7495

XIA, XIANG-GEN, electrical engineering educator; b. Nanjing, Jiangsu, China, Feb. 20, 1963; s Youmao Xia and Chunying Xu; m. Rong Zhang, June 5, 1990; children: Kevin, Lawrence. BS, Nanjing Normal U., 1983; MS, Nankai U., Tianjin, China, 1986; PhD, U. So. Calif., 1992. Lectr. Nankai U., 1986-88; tchg. asst. U. Cin., 1988-90; rsch. asst. U. So. Calif., L.A., 1990-92; rsch. scientist Air Force Inst. Tech., Wright-Patterson AFB, Ohio, 1993-94; mem. rsch. saff Hughes Rsch. Labs., Malibu, Calif., 1995-96; asst. prof. elec. engring. U. Del., Newark, 1996-99, assoc. prof., 1999—; cons. Hughes Network Sys., Germantown, Md., 1997-98. Contbr. articles to sci. jours., including IEEE Trans. on Signal Processing, IEEE Trans. on Info. Theory. Recipient young investigator award Nat. Nature Sci. Found., China, 1989, Office Naval Rsch., 1998, career award NSF, 1997. Mem. IEEE. E-mail: xxia@ec.udel.edu. Office: U Del 311 Evans Hall Newark DE 19716

XIA, XUHUA, biology educator; b. Yong-feng, China, Feb. 24, 1959; s. Jie and Wu-Ying (Yu) X.; m. Zheng Xie, Aug. 10, 1999; children: Catherine M., Kimberley H. BS, Jiangxi U., 1982; PhD, U. Western Ont., 1990. Instr. Jiangxi U., Nanchang, China, 1982-84; tchg. asst. U. Western Ont., London, Ont., Can., 1984-90; postdoctoral fellow U. Helsinki, Helsinki, Finland, 1990-91; NSERC postdoctoral fellow U. Toronto, Toronto, Ont., Can., 1991-93; mus. assoc. Mus. Natural Scis. La. State U., Baton Rouge, 1994-96; asst. prof. U. Hong Kong, 1996—. Author: (book) Data Analysis in Molecular Biology and Evolution, 2000; contbr. articles to profl. jours. Recipient Grad. Rsch. award U. Western Ont., 1989, postdoctoral fellowship Natural Sci. & Engring. Rsch. Coun. of Can., 1991-93, vis. fellowship in govt. labs. Natural Sci. & Engring. Rsch. Coun. of Can., 1994, rsch. grants in molecular biology Nat. Sci. Found., Rsch. Grants Coun. of Hong Kong, Com. on Rsch. and Conf. Grants, U. Hong Kong, 1996—. Avocations: table tennis, computer games. E-mail: xxia@hkusua.hku.hk. Home: 23F Blk 17 S Horizons Rd, Hong Kong China Office: Dept Ecology & Biodiversity, U Hong Kong, Hong Kong China

XIA, YIBEN, college dean; b. Shanghai, China, Dec. 4, 1942; s. Zhongdao and Renying (Xu) X.; m. Minhua Hou, Mar. 21, 1980; 1 child, Fuyan. B, Fudan U., Shanghai, 1965; MSc, Shanghai U. Sci. & Tech., 1981; DSc, Shanghai U., 1995. Engr. Beijing Electronic Tube Co., 1965-78; lectr. Shanghai U. Sci. & Tech., 1981-85; vis. scientist Wuerzburg U., West Germany, 1985-87; prof. Shanghai U., 1987—, chmn. inorganic dept., 1991—, dep. dean Coll. Materials Sci. & Engring., 1994—; guest prof. Fraunhofer Inst. Thin Films and Surface Engring., Braunschweig, Germany, 1996-97, guest prof., Inst. Materials Rsch., Tohoku U., Sendai, Japan, 1998-99. Contbr. articles to profl. jours.; patentee in field. Recipient First Rank for Electronic Products, Chinese Electronic Dept., 1977, First Rank for Sci. Rsch., Shanghai U., 1991. Fellow Chinese Electron Soc., Chinese Optical Soc.; mem. N.Y. Acad. Scis. Avocation: table tennis. Office: Shanghai U, Coll Materials Sci & Engrin, Shanghai 201800, China

XIADLAN, SONG, research fellow; b. Dongming County, Shandong, China, July 27, 1967; s. Song Boqin and Guiyun Wu; m. Jianguo Wang, Nov. 26, 1992. Bachelor's degree, Xi'an (China) Jiaotong U., 1987, Master's degree, 1990, PhD, 1993. Lectr. Xi'an Jiaotong U., 1993-96; postdoctoral fellow Nanyang Technol. U., Singapore, 1996-98, rsch. fellow, 1998—. Contbr. papers to profl. jours. Avocations: watching movies, listening to music, reading novels, jogging. E-mail: mxlsong@ntu.edu.sg. Office: Nanyang Technol U Sch MPE, Nanyang U, Singapore 639798, Singapore

XIANG, GUO BO, engineering cybernetic educator; b. Haikou, China, June 14, 1935; s. Xiang Bang Xiang and Chen Bao-Ying Ghen; m. Cheng Yun, July 21, 1961: children: Xiang Liang-Ji, Xiang Li-Qun, Xiang Liang-Jun. Diploma, Zhejiang U., Hangzhou, China, 1958. Mem. sch. bd., sec. electromech. dept. Xiamen (China) U., 1958-61; vice chmn. tech., rschr. automation Fuzhou (China) U., 1961-73, vice chmn. scientific rsch. group, 1973-78, vice chmn. Automation Rsch. Inst., 1978-89; head of automation dept. Wuhan (China) U. Tech., 1989-92, prof. automation engring., 1989—; part-time prof. Shandong U., Jinan, China, 1982-85, Zhejiang Coll. Tech., 1991-94, Jiangsu Coll. Tech., Zhenjiang, China, 1992—, Huazhong U. Sci. & Tech., Wuhan, 1993-96. Author: Parallel Operation of Diesel-Generator Sets and Its Stability, 1979 (2d prize 1981), Parallel Operation of Generator Sets and Its Stability, 1982, Optimum Control with ITAE Performance, 1986, Guo-Bo Xiang & Dei-Sen Lei (Automation and Social Development), 1987 (3d prize), Nonlinear System, 1991, Twice Optimum Control of System with Dead-Time, 1995, The Optimal Control for the Multi-Objective Control System with Clegg Integrator, 1998, X-Q Adaptive PID Controller and its Application in Multiobjective Control System with Satisfied Performance, 1999; mem. editl. bd.: Automatic Control & System Engineering, (vol. of Great Ency. of China) 1991. Mem. Fujian Com. Chinese People's Polit. Consultative Conf., 1983-90, Hubei com., 1989-97; mem. Ctr. Com. China Dem. League, 1986—. Recipient 3d prize for Automation of Tea with Flower, Fujian, 1981, 1st prize for Design for a kind of Ninlinearized System, Wuhan, 1993. Mem. Chinese Assn. Automation (coun. mem. 1978—). Mem. China Democratic League. Avocations: music, art, scientific research. Home: 2-103 Qin-Yang Bldg, Fuzhou Univ, Fuzhou Fujian 350002, China Office: Wuhan U Tech, Dept Automation, Wuhan 430070, China

XIANG, HUAICHENG, Chinese government official; b. Wujiang, Jiangsu, 1939. Grad., Chinese Dept. of Shandong U., 1960. Rschr. Inst. of Computing Tech., Chinese Acad. of Scis., 1960-63; dep. sect. chief of budgeting Dept. of Ministry of Fin., 1972-82, dep. divsn. chief, 1982-84; dep. dir. Ministry's Comprehensive Planning Dept., 1984-86; vice min. fin. Ministry of Fin., 1986—. Office: 3 San Li He Nan Jie, Fu Xing Men Wai, 100820 Beijing China*

XIANG, KAI-YAO, mathematician; b. Shanghai, China, Apr. 25, 1948; s. Shi-Xiao Xiang and Chun-Jiao Wu; m. Guang-Hua Li, Jan. 1, 1981; 1 child, Jia-Qing. Student, Shiyan (China) U., 1977; BSc in Math., Wuhan (China) U., 1980; postgrad., East China Normal U., Shanghai, 1985-87. Lectr. Shiyan U., 1980-92; assoc. prof. No. 1 H.S. Dongfeng Motor Corp., Shiyan, 1992—. Contbr. articles to profl. jours. Mem. Math. Soc. China. Avocation: music. Office: No 1 H S Dept Math, Dongfeng Motor Corp, 442008 Shiyan Hubei, China

XIANG, LIMIN, computer science researcher; b. Gaoyou, Jiangsu, China, Aug. 10, 1962; s. Bin Xiang and Ling Hu; m. Xin Yi; children: Cheng Yi, Wenqian Xiang. BSc, Nanjing (China) U., 1982; M Engring., U. Electronic Sci.-Tech. China, Chengdu, 1988; PhD, Kyushu U., Fukuoka, Japan, 1999. Assst. Sichuan U., Chengdu, 1982-87, lectr., 1987-93, assoc. prof., 1993-94; rschr. in computer sci. Kyushu U., 1994—. Author: (with C. Tang and M. Xiong) The Design and Implementation of DBMS, 1993; contbr. articles to sci. jours., inclduing IEEE Trans. Parallel Distbn. Sys., IEICE Trans. Info. and Sys., Computer Jour., Info. Processing Letters, Parallel Processing Letters. Recipient 3d class award for progress in sci. and tech. Sichuan Province, China, 1989; 2d class award for progress in sci. and tech. City of Chengdu, 1992, 3d class award, 1994. Avocations: music, movies, watching sports. Office: Kyushu U Dept Computer Sci, Higashi-ku, 6-10-1 Hakozaki, Fukuoka 812-8581, Japan

XIANG, YUN-YAN, molecular biologist, researcher; b. Wuhan, Hubei, China, July 31, 1957; d. Shi-Xiao Xiang and Chun-Jiao Wu; m. Dong-Yu Wang, July 13, 1985; 1 child. MD, Tongji Med. U., Wuhan, China, 1982, MSc, 1988; PhD, Hamamatsu U., Japan, 1997. Asst. Yunyang Med. Coll., Shiyan, 1982-85; lectr. Henan Med. U., Zhengzhou, China, 1987-92; rsch. asst. Hamamatsu U., 1992-97, rsch. fellow, 1997-98; rsch. fellow U. Toronto, Can., 1998—. Contbr. articles to profl. jours. Mem. AAAS, Chinese Med. Assn., Japanese Cancer Assn. Avocation: basketball. Office: Sunnybrook & Womens Coll Health Scis Ctr, 2075 Bayview Ave, Toronto, ON Canada M4N 3M5

XIANG, ZHONGGUI GORDON, research scientist; b. Suining, People's Republic of China, Sept. 1, 1961; arrived in Can., 1999; s. Xuecheng and Doazhi (Xi) Xiang; m. Jue Julie Zhang, June 19, 1989; children: Shang, Grace. BS, U. Elec. Sci./Tech. of China, 1983, MS, 1988; PhD, Nanyang Technol. U., 1998. Asst. lectr. U. Electronic Sci. and Tech. of China, Chengdu, 1983-85; rsch. engr. Sichuan Space, Chengdu, 1988-95; rsch. scholar Nanyang Technol. U., Singapore, 1995-97; mem. tech. staff DSO Nat. Labs., Singapore, 1997—; assoc. dir. Dept. Elec. and Computer Engring., Sichuan Space, Chengdu, 1990-95. Author: (with others) Progress in Electromagnetics Research, 1997; inventor in field. Recipient 2d. Ministerial Sci. and Tech. Achievement prize China Space, 1995; scholarship Nanyang Technol. U., 1995-97. Avocations: music, flute, chess, reading, table-tennis.

XIAO, CHUANGUO, urologist; b. Pugi, Hubei, China, Dec. 5, 1955; came to U.S., 1988; s. Zuoyuan Xiao and Gui Yu Xie; m. Wei Yuan, June 1985 (div. June 1993); children: Kate, David; m. Yan Xia, May 1999; 1 child, Angela. MD, Hubei (China) Med. U., 1975. Intern, resident Tongji Med. U. Hosp., Wuhan, China; attending, lectr. Tongji Med. U., Wuhan, China, 1981-84, assoc. prof., 1985-88, prof., chmn. urology, 1997—; instr., fellow Ea. Va. Med. Sch., Norfolk, Va., 1988-90; asst. prof. SUNY, Bklyn., 1991—; dir. rsch. L.I. Coll. Hosp., Bklyn., 1991—; rsch. adv. bd. L.I. Coll. Hosp., Bklyn., 1991—, institional rsch. bd., 1991—. Contbr. articles to profl. jours. Rsch. grant Paralyzed Vets. of Am., NIH, 1993-97, 1999—. Mem. Am. Urol. Assn., Internat. Paraplegian Assn. E-mail: cg xiao@yahoo.com. Office: LI Coll Hosp 340 Henry St Brooklyn NY 11201-5514

XIAO, JINGPING, plant biochemist, physiologist, scientist-educator; b. Beijing, Jan. 14, 1929; s. Zhiming Xiao and Yunsu Huang; m. Yulie Xi, June 27, 1956; children: Ming, Wei. Grad., Zhejiang U., Hangzhou, China, 1952. Sr. engr. diplomate, prof. qualification diplomate. Agronomist Chinese Min. Agr., Beijing, 1952-54; head rsch. group Chinese Acad. Tropical Crops, Hainan, 1955-60, head dept., 1961-75; prof. South China Agrl. U., Guangzhou, 1986—; cons. expert for Sci. and Tech. Devel. Program, European Cmty., Brussels, 1983-89. Inventor in field of plant physiology. Recipient spl. allowance, Chinese State Coun., Beijing, 1992, prize Chinese Nat. Assembly Sci., 1978. Mem. AAAS (internat.), Chinese Assn. Plant Physiology, Chinese Assn. Plant Growth Substances (dep. chmn. 1990-92), Chinese Assn. Agronomy (sr.). Office: South China Agrl Univ, Coll Biotechnology, Guangzhou 510642, China

XIAO, LUN, radiochemist, researcher; b. Pi Xian, Sichuan, China, Jan. 3, 1912; s. Ju Gao and Xiu Lan (Yu) X.; m. Louisa Jung-Chun Hsiao, Jan. 3, 1956; children: Dong, Guang. BS, Tsing Hua U., Kunming, China, 1939; MS, U. Ill., 1948, PhD, 1951. Dir. Great-China Alcohol Plant, Jintang, 1941-47; rsch. assoc. U. Ill., Urbana, 1951-52; phys. chemist Petroleum Exptl. Sta. Bur. Mines, Bartlesville, 1952-55; prof. Inst. Physics, Beijing, 1956-58, Inst. Atomic Energy, Beijing, 1958-84, China Inst. Atomic Energy, Beijing, 1984—; assoc. dir. No. 5 Lab., Inst. Physics, Beijing, 1956-58; dir. No. 16 Lab., Inst. Atomic Energy, Beijing, 1959-79, dept. isotopes, 1979-83, rsch. divsn. isotopes, 1981-83; prof. dept. tech. physics Peking U., Beijing, 1957; gen. chmn. 1st Internat. Conf. on Isotopes, Beijing, 1995. Editor-in-chief Jour. of Isotopes, 1988—, Radioisotope Technology, 2000; contbr. articles to profl. jours. Congressman 5th Nat. People's Congress, Beijing, 1978-83; hon. chmn. engring. and tech. com. Rsch. Ctr. State Lab. of Isotopes, Engring., and Tech., Beijing, 1996—. Recipient Hon. Cert. Nat. Def. Soc., Tech., and Indsl. Commn., 1988, Cert. of Appreciation Am. Nuclear Soc., 1991, Ho Leung Ho Lee Found. award, Hong Kong, 1997; grantee Nat. Natural Sci. Found. China, 1994. Mem. AAAS, Chinese Acad. Scis., N.Y. Acad. Scis., Chinese Nuclear and Radiochem. Soc. (vice chmn. 1979-83), Isotope Soc. China (pres. 1984-92), Phi Lambda Upsilon, Sigma Xi. Avocations: reading, jogging, listening to music, writing Chinese poetry. Home: 12 Yuetan Beijie Ste 206, Beijing 100045, China Office: China Inst Atomic Energy, PO Box 275-12, Beijing 102413, China

XIAO, MAO, physician, consultant; b. Sheyant County, China, Mar. 3, 1934; s. Xingwu Xiao and Yuzhen Wang; m. Yufen Hua, Dec. 22, 1967; children: Lan, Yang. B in Medicine, Nantong Med. Coll., Nantong City, China, 1955. Physician Yancheng Dist. People's Hosp., Yancheng City, China, 1955-79; vis. physician Wuxi Fifth People's Hosp., Wu Xi City, China, 1980-86, head dept. internal medicine, 1985-94, vice-chief physician, 1987-95, chief physician, 1996—; dir. Affiliated Hosp. Puyang Bronchitis Inst., Puyang City, China, 1996-98; cons. Shuixiu Hosp. Wu Xi City, 1999. Contbr. articles to profl. jours. Mil. surgeon Chinese People Liberation Army, 1947-54. Avocations: reading, Weiqi, swimming. Home: Apt 403, 18 Zhongqiao 1 Village, Wu Xi City 214073, China Office: Shuixiu Hosp Wu Xi City, Shuixiu St, Jiansu Province 214071, China

XIAO, PHILIP GENGMIN, pharmaceutical executive; b. Dangshan, China, Aug. 9, 1968; s. Zhipeng and Yizheng (Lu) X. MD, The 1st Mil. Med. Coll., Guargzhon, China, 1989; MIM, Am. Grad. Sch. Internat. Mgmt., Phoenix, 1991. Regional ops. mgr. Merck & Co., Inc., 1991-96; bus. unit dir. Schering-Plough, Shanghai, 1996-99; v.p. Bristol-Myers Squibb, Shanghai, 1999—. Office: Bristol Myers Squibb China, 100 Yan Dan Rd GF, 2000 20 Shanghai China

XIAO, YONGSHUN, biomathematician, animal population dynamicist, marine biologist; b. Yuguan Dist., Hebei, China, Dec. 4, 1956; s. Ruilin and Sulan (Wu) X.; m. Qiong Huang, Jan. 4, 1982; 1 child, Ying. BS, Shandong Coll. Oceanography, Qingdao, China, 1982; MS, Inst. Oceanography, Academia Sinica, Qingdao, China, 1984; PhD, U. Queensland, Brisbane, Australia, 1991. Tchr. Village Feng Secondary Sch., Funing, 1975-78; rsch. scientist Inst. of Oceanology Academia Sinica, Qingdao, 1982-87; tutor, demonstrator U. Queensland, Brisbane, 1987-90; rsch. scientist No. Territory Dept. Primary Industry and Fisheries, Darwin, Australia, 1991-94, CSIRO Divsn. Fisheries, Hobart, Tasmania, 1994-97, South Australian Aquatic Scis. Ctr., Adelaide, Australia, 1997—. Contbr. articles to profl. jours. including Can. Jour. Fisheries and Aquatic Scis., Fishery Bull., Oceanography and Marine Biology, An Annual Rev. Named Hon. Prof., Qingdao Ocean U., 1996. Mem. Australian Marine Sci. Assn. Avocations: running, reading, listening to classical music, gardening. Office: South Australian Aquatic Scis Ctr, 2 Hamra Ave, West Beach, Adelaide SA 5024, Australia

XIAO, ZHONGMIN, engineering educator; b. Lian-Yuan, China, Mar. 27, 1965; arrived in Singapore, 1991; s. Jiqiu and Jiahe (Deng) X.; m. Zhiqing Liu, Oct. 18, 1992; children: Eric, Daniel. B of Engring. with honors, U. Sci. & Tech., China, 1984, M of Engring. with honors, 1987; MS, Rutgers U., 1989, PhD, 1991. From rsch. fellow to sr. lectr. Nanyang Tech. U., Singapore, 1991-99, assoc. prof., 1999—; dir. strength of materials lab Nanyang Tech. U., 1996-98, tchg. area leader mechanics of materials, 1997—. Contbr. articles to profl. jours. Grantee Ministry Edn., Singapore, 1997-2000, Nat. Sci. and Tech. Bd., Singapore, 1998-2000; Excellence fellow Rutgers U., N.J., 1987-91. Mem. ASME, Internat. Microelectronics and Packaging Soc.

Avocations: bridge, tennis, jogging. Office: Nanyang Tech Univ, Sch Mech and Prodn Engring, 639798 Singapore Singapore

XIAO FENG, GUO, mathematics educator; b. Zhenjiang, Jiangsu, China, Nov. 6, 1945; s. Songxiang Guo and Jinying Zhang; m. Lizhen Jiang, Feb. 1, 1975; children: Yong, Bing. Grad., Beijing Post & Telecomm. Coll., China, 1968. Worker Post and Telecom. Factory, Yaan, China, 1970-75, Wulumuqi (Xinjiang, China) P.O., 1976-79; asst. engr. Xinjiang Post & Telecomm. Sci. Rsch. Inst., Wulumuqi, 1979-82, Xinjiang Post and Telecom. Factory, Wulumuqi, 1982-84; tchr. dept. math. Xinjiang U., Wulumuqi, 1984-88, assoc. prof., 1988-90, prof., 1991-93, prof. Inst. Math. and Physics, 1993—; vis. scholar U. Trondheim, Norway, 1991, Drake U., Des Moines, 1992-93, 98-99, U. Minn., Duluth, 2000. Author: Springer-Verlag, 1990; contbr. articles to profl. jours.; reviewer Math. Revs. Recipient Progressive Sci. and Tech. awards Xinjiang Govt., 1986, 96, Nat. Edn. Com., 1991. Mem. Chinese Math. Soc. (bd. dirs.), Am. Math. Soc., Internat. Soc. Math. Chemistry, Xinjiang Math. Soc. (dep. dir.). Avocation: music. Office: Xinjiang U, Inst Math and Physics, Wulumuqi 830046, China

XIAOHUA, YANG (WILLIAM XIAOHUA), underwriter; b. Shanghai, China, Nov. 30, 1961; s. Hai Ping Yang and Fei Wu; m. Shu Zhang, Oct. 28, 1993. BA, Nanjing (China) U., 1983; LLM, Dalin (China) Maritime U., 1988. Asst. gen. mgr. operation mgmt. dept. Ping An Ins. Co. of China, Shenzhen, China, 1991-92, dep. gen. mgr. internat. dept., 1993-94, gen. mgr. underwriting control dept., 1995, gen. mgr. claims dept., 1996-97, dep. mng. dir., 1997-99, mng. dir., 2000—; bd. dirs. China Ins. Inst. Mem. China Maritime Law Assn. (bd. dirs. 1994—). Avocations: golf, tennis, classical music, "Go" chess, reading. Home: Ever Happy Garden Rm 11-F, 4 Bai Hua Rd Tower C, Shenzhen China Office: 11/F Dah Sing Fin Ctr, 108 Gloucester Rd, Wanchai Hong Kong

XIAOJUN, HU, physicist; b. Giuyang, China, Sept. 6, 1938; s. Lu Jingxuan and Ge Yang; m. Bu Shuxian, Feb. 4, 1972; 1 child, Hu Ning. B in Engring., Beijing U. Iron Steel Tech., 1964; D in Engring., Beijing U. Sci. & Tech., 1993. Engr., sr. engr. Beijing Metallurgical Rsch. Inst., 1964-92; prof. Shougang Metallurgical Rsch. Inst., Beijing, 1993—. Mem. Chinese Soc. Metal, Chinese Soc. Physics. Avocations: painting, art, music. Home: # 1306, 31 Bldg Xibahe Zhongli, 100028 Beijing China Office: Shougang Metallurgical Rsch Inst, Qing he town, 100085 Beijing China

XIAOPENG, LI, Olympic athlete. Winner Gold medal gymnastics parallel bars team all around Sydney, 2000. Office: Chinese Gymnastics Assn, 9 Tiyuguan Rd, 100763 Beijing China*

XICAI, CAO, radiologist; b. Tianjin, China, Aug. 26, 1949; s. Yunming and Xiuqin Huo Cao; m. Zungai Qin; 1 child, Lei Cao. MD, Tianjin (China) Med. U., 1987. Chief doctor dept. radiology Tianjin Med. U. Gen. Hosp., 1987-94, v.p., 1994-99, prof., 1999—. Author: Imaging Study of Renal Vascular Hypertension, 1997 (Scientific award 1997), The Treatment of Hepatocellular Carcinoma with Yttrium Microspheres, 1999 (Scientific award 1999). Mem. Chinese Med. Assn. Office: Tianjin Med Gen Hosp, Dept Radio Anshan Rd, Tianjin 300052, China

XIE, AILIANG, medical scientist, writer; b. Xi'an, China, Nov. 15, 1948; arrived in Can. 1989; came to U.S. 1996; d. Jiazhen Xie and Yiqing Dong; m. Yanping Liu, Nov. 7, 1976; 1 child, Brandon Jiang Liu. MD, Shanxi (China) Med. U., Taiyuan, 1975; MS, Shanxi (China) Med. U., 1981; PhD, Toronto U., 1996. Resident First Tchg. Hosp. Shanxi Med. U., Taiyuan, 1981-83, asst. prof., staff physician, 1984-89; rsch. fellow U. Toronto, 1989-95; postdoct. fellow U. Wis., Madison, 1996-98, asst. scientist, 1998—; prof. (hon.) 1st Tchg. Hosp. Shanxi Med. U., 1999—. Contbr. articles to profl. jours., chpts. to books. Travel rsch. fellow High Edn. Bur. Shanxi Province, 1990, Canadian Thoracic Soc. fellow Canadian Lung Assn., 1991—, Am. Heart fellow AHA, 1995—; Ontario grad. scholar Ont. Ministry Edn. and Tng., 1992; recipient Young Rsch. Trainee award Canadian Soc. Clin. Investigation, 1990. Mem. AAAS, Chinese Med. Assn. Avocations: literature, watching the sunrise and sunset, travel. Home: 817 Eagle Hts Apt A Madison WI 53705-1573 Office: VA Hosp Pulmonary Lab 2500 Overlook Ter Madison WI 53705-2254

XIE, HONG QUAN, chemist, educator; b. Shanghai, Jan. 16, 1931; s. Yu Xiang Xie and Zhen Lian Huang; m. Jun Shi Guo, Feb. 18, 1959; children: Dong Xie, Ding Xie. B of Chemistry, U. Shanghai, 1952. Technician Inst. Applied Chemistry Academia Sinica, Changchun, China, 1952-56, asst. rschr., 1956-77; assoc. rschr. Hubei Rsch. Inst. Chemistry, Wuhan, China, 1978-85, sr. rschr., 1986-87; prof. dept. chemistry Huazhong U. Sci. and Tech., Wuhan, 1988—; mem. editorial bd. China Synthetic Rubber Industry, Lanzhou, China, 1975—, Chinese Jour. Applied Chemistry, Changchun, 1980—, Polymer Material Sci. and Engring., Chengdu, China, 1984—; cons. Hubei Rsch. Inst. Chemistry, Wuhan, 1988—. Author: Polyacetal, 1973; contbr. over 280 articles to profl. jours. Recipient 2 Sci. and Tech. Progress prizes Nat. Edn. Com., 1991, 97, 2 Sci. and Tech. Progress prizes Hubei Province, 1987, 93. Mem. Chinese Chem. Soc. (coun. 1978-86). Avocations: music, football, art. Home: West 1 Dist 23 Rm 201, Huazhong U Sci and Tech, Wuhan 430074, China Office: Dept Chemistry, Huazhong U Sci & Tech, Wuhan 430074, China

XIE, LIANGDI, physician, researcher; b. Zherong, Fujian, People's Republic of China, June 2, 1962; s. Maochang Xie and Jinyu Lin; m. Pinyun Guo, Sept. 16, 1985; 1 child, Xiaolu. Bachelor, Fujian Med. Coll., Fuzhou, People's Republic of China, 1984, M of Med. Sci., 1991. Intern Jianou Mcpl. Hosp., Fujian, 1983-84; resident Zherong County Hosp., Fujian, 1984-88; med. rschr. Fujian Hypertension Divsn., 1989-91; physician 1st Affiliated Hosp., Fujian Med. Coll., Fuzhou, People's Republic of China, 1991-95; cons. cardiologist 1st Affiliated Hosp., FMC, Fuzhou, People's Republic of China, 1996—; postdoctoral rsch. fellow St. Mary's Hosp. Med. Sch., London, 1995-96; dep. dir. Fujian Hypertension Rsch. Inst., 1998—; assoc. prof. Fujian Med. Coll., 1996-99, prof., 1999—. Mem. editl. bd. Jour. Fujian Med. Coll., Jour. Chinese Hypertension; contbr. articles to profl. publs. Com. mem. Fujian Provicial Sci. and Tech. Commn. of Chinese Dem. League, 1998. Named Trans-Century Scientist Pioneer Fujian Provicial Bur. of Pub. Health, 1997, Key Tchr. State Edn. Commn., 1999; scholarship British Coun., 1995; recipient Award of Sci. and Tech. Fujian Provincial Adminstrn., 1997, 98, Award of Provinciall Elite Young Scientist, 2000, State Coun. Special Allowance, 2000; travel grantee Am. Soc. of Hypertension, 1998. Mem. Chinese Assn. of Lab. Animal Sci. (com. mem. Fujian br. 1999—), Chinese Hypertension League, Chinese Med. Soc. (exec. mem. youth com. Fujian br.). Avocation: swimming. Home and Office: Fujian Med Coll, 1st Affiliated Hosp, Fuzhou 35005, People's Republic of China

XIE, LINZHEN, government executive; b. Changsha, China, June 23, 1940; s. Xuanang and Weijin (Zhu) X.; m. Yida Ta Xie, Feb. 4, 1967; children: Xiangjin, Wei. Student, Peking U., Beijing, China; U. Calif., Berkeley. Lectr. Peking U., Beijing, China, 1978-79; vis. scholar U. Calif., Berkeley, 1980-82; assoc. prof. Peking U., Beijing, China, 1985-89, prof., 1989—; deputy dir. gen. telecomms. dept. Min. Electronics Industry, Beijing, China, 1994-98; dir. China Nat. Lab. on Optical Transmission, Beijing, China, 1995—; dep. dir. gen. dept. of info. equipment adminstrn. Minn. Info. Industry, Beijing, 1998—; deputy dir. China High Tech. Program on Telecomms., Beijing, China, 1991-96. Patent All-optical Network Control System, 1997; contbr. over 100 papers in field. Recipient Sci. and Tech. award State Edn., Commn. of China, 1988. Avocation: tennis. Home: Dept Electronics, Peking U, Beijing 100871, China Office: Dept Telecomm MII, Wanshu Lu # 27, 100846 Beijing China

XIE, MIN, scientist, lecturer; b. Changsha, Hunan, China, Oct. 25, 1963; arrived in Singapore, 1991; m. Wenhong Zhu, Sept. 28, 1988; 1 child, Jessica. MS, Royal Inst. Tech., 1984; Lic. Engring., Linköping (Sweden) U., 1986, PhD, 1987. Rsch. fellow Linköping U., 1987-91; rsch. scientist Nat. U. Singapore, 1991-94, sr. lectr., 1994—. Author: Software Reliability Modelling, 1991, Application, 1993; contbr. articles to profl. jours.; editor Internat. Jour. Reliability, Quality and Safety Engring., 1994. Lee Kuan Yew fellow Nat. U. Singapore, 1991. Mem. IEEE (Internat. Symposium on Software Reliability Engring.), Internat. Assn. Sci. and Tech. for Devel. (Internat. Conf. on Reliability, Quality Control and Risk Assessment), Soc. Reliability Engrs., Am. Statis. Assn., Am. Soc. Quality Control. Office: Nat U Singapore, Dept Indsl Systems Engring, Singapore 0511, Singapore

XIE, RUI-HUA, physicist, researcher; b. Ganxian, Jiangxi, China, Sept. 21, 1969; s. Xiangan Xie and Yuying Yang; m. Qin Rao, Dec. 28, 1995; 1 child, Jianing. BS, Wuhan U., 1991; PhD, Nanjing U., 1996. Rsch. asst. Wuhan (China) U., 1991-93, Nanjing (China) U., 1993-96; postdoctoral rschr. CCAST, Beijing, 1996-97, U. Toronto, Ont., Can., 1997-98; Alexander von Humboldt fellow Max-Planck Inst. Ströngsforschung, Göttingen, Germany, 1998-2000; tchg., rsch. asst. Queen's U., Ont., 2000—. Contbr. articles to profl. jours. Avocation: philately. Home: 2-142 Colborne St, Kingston, ON Canada K7K 1E2 Office: Queen's U, Dept Chemistry, Kingston, ON Canada K7L 3N6

XIE, SHANG-PING, environmental studies educator; b. Quzhou, Zhejiang, China, Aug. 8, 1963; s. Chang-Tu Wang, Aug. 17, 1988; children: Weijiang Cordelia. BSc, Shangdong Coll., 1984; MSc, Tohoku U., 1988, DSc, 1991. Program scientist Princeton (N.J.) U., 1991-93; rsch. assoc. U. Washington, Seattle, 1993-94; assoc. prof. Hokkaido U., Sapporo, Japan, 1994-99, Univ. Hawaii, 1999—; session convenor Am. Geophys. Union, Washington, 1996; spkr. in field; vis. fellow Nat. Sci. Found. of China, 1996. Editor Jour. Meteorol. Soc. Japan; contbr. articles to profl. jours. Reciepient Young Investigator award Ministry of Edn., Culture and Sci. of Japan. Mem. Am. Geophys. Union, Oceanographical Soc. of Japan, Meteorol. Soc. Japan (Yamamoto-Shyono medal 1996). E-mail: xie@soest.hawaii.edu. Avocations: travel, swimming, reading. Office: Internat Pacific Rsch Ctr SOEST Univ Hawaii 1000 Pope Rd Honolulu HI 96822

XIE, SHI-LENG, consulting engineer, educator; b. Shanghai, China, May 20, 1935; s. Ji-Shan Xie and Yu-Hua Hu; m. Yu-Ru Zhang, Feb. 1, 1962; 1 child, Shan-Wen. Bachelor's degree, Dalian (China) U. Tech., 1956. Cert. prof. sr. engr. Ministry of Comms., China. Engr. Design Inst. for Water Transp., Beijing, 1956-58; engr. 1st Design Inst. of Navigation Engring., Tianjin, China, 1958-78, chief design dept., 1979; vis. scholar, rsch. fellow Delft (The Netherlands) U. Tech., 1979-81; dep. chief engr. 1st Design Inst. of Navigation Engring., Tianjin, 1981—; dir. Zhong Bei Harbor Engring. Supervision Corp., Tianjin, 1990-97; part-time prof. Qingdao (China) U. Oceanology, 1994—. Editor-in-chief: (design code) Harbor Hydrology and Hydraulics, 1978 (Nat. Sci. and Tech. prize 1985); chief engr.: (design) 100, 000 DWT Class Open Sea Coal Terminal, 1985 (Nat. Excellent Design prize 1990). Rep. Mcpl. People's Congress, Tianjin, 1983-87. Named Nat. Expert with Outstanding Contbn., Ministry Pers. Affairs, 1986, Nat. Design Master, Ministry Constrn., 1994, Design Expert for Coastal Engring., Tianjin Sci. & Tech. Commn., 1992. Mem. Internat. Assn. for Hydraulic Rsch. (com. mem. 1994-00), Chinese Ocean Engring. Soc. (exec. dir. 1999), Coastal Dynamics Com. (chmn. 1986—). Avocations: classical music, photography, stamp collecting. Office: 1st Design Inst Nav Engring, 1472 Dagu South Rd, 300222 Tianjin China

XIE, SHU-SEN (SHU-SEN HSIEH), economics and finance educator, consultant; b. Shanghai, China, July 7, 1919; s. Kwei-quan and (Yen) H.; m. Zing-sien Chen, Oct. 10, 1941 (dec. Apr. 1957); children: Dehong, Dehua Xie. BA with honors, St. John's U., Shanghai, People's Republic China, 1941; MA, Columbia U., 1948. Assoc. prof. econs. dept. St. John's U., Shanghai, 1949-52; assoc. prof. Fudan U., Shanghai, 1972-78; assoc. prof. econs. and fin. Shanghai Inst. Fin. and Econs., 1952-72, prof., 1979—; adj. prof. Shanghai Inst. Fgn. Trade, 1983—; vis. prof. De La Salle U., Manila, 1982, 84, 86-87, Erasmus U., Rotterdam, The Netherlands, Met. State U., St. Paul, 1990; exch. prof. Met. State U., Denver, 1989-90; cons. Shanghai Investment and Trust Corp., 1986—, Bank of Communication, 1988—. Author: Security Markets, 1989, Transnationals and China's Shenzhen, 1989; chief translator: International Economics, 1987; chief editor Survey of International Finance, 1982. Recipient plaque of appreciation De La Salle U., 1986. Mem. China Soc. Fin. (hon. bd. dirs. 1984—), China Soc. Internat. Fin. (bd. dirs. 1984—), Shanghai Soc. Fin. (bd. dirs. 1984—), Shanghai Soc. Internat. Fin. (bd. dirs. 1984—). Office: Shanghai U Fin and Econs, 777 Guoding Rd, Shanghai 200433, China

XIE, XIANYA, computer control and signal processing scientist; b. Suzhou, China, Sept. 17, 1934; s. Weiqi and Shiyan (Jin) X.; m. Huanrun Li, Jan. 24, 1963; 1 child, Binyun. Grad., Tsinghua U., 1959. Prof. Shanghai Univ. Sci. & Technology, China, 1963—. Mem. IEEE, N.Y. Acad. Sci. Office: Shanghai U Jiading Campus, Chengzhong Rd, Jiading, Shanghai 201800, China

XIE, YI-MIN, engineering educator; b. Zhenjiang, Jiangsu, China, Dec. 23, 1963; arrived in Australia, 1991; s. Hong-Jun Xie and Yun-Zhen Shao; m. Grace Lai-Hung Lam, Mar. 16, 1990; children: Sarah Jia-Yi, Victor Yang-Ming, Catherine Jia-Jing. BSc in Engring., Jiao Tong U., Shanghai, China, 1984; PhD, U. Wales, Swansea, 1991. Rsch. fellow U. Sydney, Australia, 1992-93; lectr. Victoria U. Tech., Melbourne, Australia, 1993-95; sr. lectr. Victoria U. Tech., Melbourne, 1995-97, assoc. prof., 1998—; proprietor Oxbridge Press, Melbourne, 1996—. Author: Evolutionary Structural Optimization, 1997; editor: Structural Optimization, 1998; editor, pub.: Who's Who in Structural Engineering in Australia, 1996. Grantee Australian Rsch. Coun., 1995—. Avocations: soccer, tennis. Office: Victoria U Tech Civil Engr, PO Box 14428 MCMC, Victoria 8001, Australia

XIE, YU JUN, mechanical engineering educator; b. Fushun, Liaoning, China, Feb. 8, 1960; s. Ji Lu Xie and Zhi Ming Mei; m. Xiao Hua Wang, Sept. 10, 1985; 1 child, Pei. BS, Fuxin (China) Mining Coll., 1982; MS, Chengdu (China) U. Sci./Tech., 1990; PhD, East China U. Sci. & Tech., Shanghai, 1996. Tchr. Xinyang (China) Normal Coll., 1982-85; tchr. Fushun (China) Petroleum Inst., 1985-96, dean, prof., 1996—. Contbr. articles to profl. jours. Mem. Chinese Soc. Composites, Chinese Soc. Mechanics. Office: Fushun Petroleum Inst, 1 W Dandong Rd, Fushun 113001, China

XIE, YUSHENG, foundation administrator, educator; b. Xiajiang County, China, Oct. 12, 1942; s. Chengen and Jinrun (Zou) X.; m. Beixin Sun, Aug. 1, 1968; 1 child, Yihai. BS, Shanghai Fudan U., 1966. Rsch. asst. Inst. Chem. Metallurgy, Beijing, 1966-78, rsch. assoc., 1982-86, assoc. prof., 1986-91, rsch. prof., 1991—; rsch. assoc. Nagoya (Japan) U., 1979-81. Author: Metallurgical Reaction Engineering, 1981; editor Computers and Applied Chemistry, 1988; chief editor Engring. Chem. Metall., 1996; patentee in field. Mem. Metal Soc. of China (mem. coun. 1991), Chinese Soc. of Particuology (mem. coun. 1986). Avocations: reading, films. Office: Inst Chemical Metallurgy, 1 Bei Er Tiao Zhongguancun, Haidian Dist Beijing 100080, China

XIE, YU-ZHANG, physicist, educator; b. Soochow, China, Feb. 18, 1915; s. He-Sheng and Yong-Min (Pan) X.; m. Shu-Qin Kou, Nov. 1, 1952; 1 child, Rose. BS, Tsinghua U., Peking, China, 1936; MS, Tsinghua U., Kunming, China, 1942; PhD, Vanderbilt U., 1950. Asst. prof. Ctrl. U., Nanking, China, 1945-48; vis. lectr. Purdue U., West Lafayette, Ind., 1950-51; assoc. prof. Hampton (Va.) Inst., 1951-52; rsch. assoc. Vanderbilt U., Nashville, 1952-55; asst. prof. Wichita (Kans.) U., 1955-57; prof. Tsinghua U., Peking, 1957—; guest rschr. Inst. Theoretical Physics, Peking, 1992—. Author: Liquid Crystal Physics, 1988; co-author: Geometric Methods in the Elastic Theory of Membranes in Liquid Crystal Phases, 1999. Recipient Natural Scis. award Chinese Acad. Scis., Peking, 1995, Nat. Nature Sci. award State Sci. and Tech. Commn., Peking, 1999. Mem. Chinese Phys. Soc. (councillor 1982-85), Chinese Liquid Crystal Soc. (rpes. 1980-86), Internat. Liquid Crystal Soc. Avocations: visiting scenic sites, music. Office: Dept of Physics, Tsinghua U, 100084 Beijing China

XIE, ZELIANG, metallurgist, researcher, educator; b. Ningziang, Hunan, China, Dec. 20, 1960; s. Zi-Pu and Yi-Fu (Ren) X.; m. Yong Liu, Nov. 16, 1987; children: Elina Wenxin, Susanna Xiangyi. BSc, Hunan U., 1982, MSc, 1988; Licentiate in Tech., Helsinki U. Tech., 1992, DTech, 1994. Tchr., engr. Inst. Electronic Equipment, Guilin, China, 1982-85, 88-89; rsch. asst. Inst. Metal Rsch., Chinese Acad. Scis., Shenyang, 1985-88; rschr. Helsinki U. Tech., Espoo, 1989-94; vis. rschr. U. Lulea, Sweden, 1990; postdoctoral rsch. fellow Cath. U. Leuven, Belgium, 1996-98; vis. scientist Lawrence Berkeley Nat. Lab., 1999; TEM liaison rsch. fellow Johns Hopkins U., Balt., 1998—. CIMO grantee, Finland, 1993, 94. Mem. Belgian Soc. for Microscopy, Microscopy Soc. Am. Avocations: reading, travel, cooking. Office: Johns Hopkins U 3400 N Charles St Baltimore MD 21218-2680

XIE, ZHIJUN, energy economist; b. Beijing, Jan. 13, 1962; came to U.S., 1993; d. Zhongmin Xie and Lixian Zhang; m. Qun Hao, Dec. 24, 1988; 1 child, Samantha. BS, Tsinghua U., Beijing, 1985; MA, Tsinghua U., 1988; PhD, Boston U., 2000. Asst. rsch. prof. Energy Rsch. Inst., Beijing, 1988-93; rsch. fellow Ariz. State U., Tempe, 1993-94; tchg. & rsch. asst. Boston U., 1995—. Author: Improving Energy Use Efficiency, 1998; contbr. articles to profl. jours. McNamara fellow The World Bank, 1993; recipient Applied Geography Best Project award Assn. Am. Geographers, 1993. Mem. Internat. Assn. Energy Econs. (fellow 1999), Inst. Operation Rsch. and Mgmt. Sci. (Edelman Mgmt. Sci. Achievement Finalist 1994), Am. Econ. Assn. Office: Ctr Energy and Environ Studies 675 Commonwealth Ave Boston MA 02215-1406

XIN, XIAN-KUN, physics educator; b. Shanghai, China, Jan. 28, 1944; s. Yuancai and Songmei (Yu) X.; m. Guangci Cao, Apr. 10, 1967; 1 child. BA, Shanghai Tchrs. U., 1965. Asst. prof. Shanghai Tchrs. U., 1965-81, lectr., 1981-88, assoc. prof., dir. modern physics lab., 1986—, prof., 1999—. Author: Semiconductor Physics and Devices, 1995, Modern Experimental Physics, 1998; contbr. mroe than 20 articles to profl. jours. Avocations: watching football, listening to classical music. Office: Shanghai Tchrs U Dept Physics, 100 Guilin Rd, Shanghai 200234, China

XING, QI YI, retired research chemist and chemistry educator; b. Tianjin, Hebei, China, Nov. 24, 1911; m. Cun Rou Qian, Aug. 26, 1942; children: Zutong, Zujian. BS, Furen U., Beijing, 1933; PhD, U. Ill., 1936; postgrad., U. Munich, 1937. Assoc. rschr. Inst. Chemistry Academia Sinica, Shanghai, China, 1937-38; rschr. Inst. Chemistry Academia Sinica, Kunming, China, 1938-42; prof. Mil. Med. U. Middle China, Tianchang, 1944-45; prof. Peking U., Beijing, 1946-88, prof. emeritus, 1988—; academician Acad. Scis., Beijing, 1980—; counselor Chem. Jour. Chinese Univs., Changchun, China, 1985—; group leader Nat. Natural Sci. Found. China, Beijing, 1986-91; chmn. spl. com. for edn. Chinese Chem. Soc., Beijing, 1986-90. Contbr. articles to profl. jours.; inventor in field of peptide chemistry and organic reactions. Mem. Chinese People's Polit. Consultation Conf., Beijing, 1982-92; counselor China Internat. Culture Exch. Ctr., Beijing, 1985—. Recipent 1st class prize State Commn. Natural Scis., Beijing, 1982, Excellent Tchg. Material prize State Commn. of Edn., Beijing, 1988.

XIONG, BING HENG, physicist, educator; b. Nanking, Jiangsu, China, Sept. 17, 1930; s. Qing Lai Xiong and Ju Yuan Jian; m. Zhong Hui Ding, Sept. 27, 1944; children: Youwen, Quan. BS in Physics, Yunnan U., 1961. Asst. Changsha (China) Railway Inst., 1961-78, lectr., 1978-81, assoc. prof., 1981-86; researcher French Nat. Sci. Rsch. Ctr., 1986; prof. Yunnan Poly. U., 1987—; vis. prof. Ecole Centrale de Paris, 1989. Contbr. articles to profl. jours. Mem. N.Y. Acad. of Sci., Optical Soc. China (mem. holography and optical info. processing com. 1984—), Internat. Soc. Optical Engring., China Holography Assn., Yunnan Assn. for Sci. and Tech., Kunming Soc. Non-Destructive Testing and Evaluating (v.p. 1993—). Avocations: drawing, photography. Home: 255 East Rd, 650051 Kunming Yunnan, China Office: Yunnan Poly U Laser Inst, 250 East Rd, 650051 Kunming Yunnan, China

XIONG, FUSHENG, biologist, researcher; b. Hefei, China, Mar. 21, 1957; s. Yisu Xiong and Shuzen Xiang; m. Yang Yang, June 23, 1987; 1 child, Chuan. BS, Anhui U., Hefei, 1981; MS, Yangzhou (China) U., 1984; PhD, South Bohemia U., Czech Republic, 1996. Rsch. assoc. Yangzhou U., 1985-87, asst. prof., 1987-93, assoc. prof., 1993—; rsch. assoc. Inst. Microbiology, Prague, Czech Republic, 1993-96, Ariz. State U., Tempe, 1996—. Contbr. sci. rsch. papers to profl. publs. (Outstanding Paper award 1992, 94). V.p. Jiangsu Soc. Young Physiologists, Nanjing, China, 1989-93; exec. com. Labor Union Yangzhou U., 1991-93. Recipient 3d prize for acad. achievement Jiangsu T&S Com., 1993. Fellow AAAS, Internat. Soc. Photosynthesis Rsch., Ecol. Soc. Am., Chinese Soc. Plant Physiology. Avocations: running, swimming, reading, gardening. E-mail: fxiong@imap3.asu.edu. Home: 1140 E Orange St Apt 16 Tempe AZ 85281-4183 Office: Ariz State U Dept Plant Biology PO Box 87-1601 Tempe AZ 85287-1601

XIONG, SHAOJUN, ecologist, educator; b. Hohhot, China, Dec. 16, 1957; m. Bo Xu; 1 child, Shuo Tom. BS, Lanzhou (China) U., 1982, MS, 1985; PhD, Umeå (Sweden) U., 1999. Asst. lectr. Liaoning Normal U., Dalian, China, 1985-88, lectr., 1988-92; guest rschr. Umeå U., 1992-93, rsch. fellow, 1993-99, rschr., 1999, 2000—; rschr. Neuchâtel (Switzerland) U., 1999-2000; dir. sect. botany Liaoning Normal U., 1988-92. Contbr. articles to profl. publs. Sec. Assn. Biology, Dalian, 1989-91; assoc. gen. sec. Youth League, Lanzhou, 1979-82; sec. br. com. Chinese Communist Party, Dalian, 1987-89. Mem. Brit. Ecol. Soc. Avocations: driving, cooking, carpenter work. Office: Umeå U Landscape Ecology, Uminova Sci Park, SE-90187 Umeå Sweden

XIONG, TOUSU SAYDANGNMVANG, minister; b. Xieng Khouang, Laos, June 23, 1966; came to U.S., 1976; s. Nhialue Saydang and May (Vang) X.; m. Zoua Pahoua Moua, Sept. 14, 1993; children: Chivkeeb Genesis Toupa, Naamonunas Ruth, Nujsimloob Hebrews. BA in Bibl. Studies, Simpson Coll., San Francisco, 1989; MA in Theology, Mennonite Brethren Bibl. Sem., Fresno, Calif., 1991; AS in Computerized Acctg., Phillips Jr. Coll., Fresno, Calif., 1993. Ordained to ministry Christian and Missionary Alliance, 1991. Assoc. min. Hmong San Raphael (Calif.) Bapt. Ch., 1986-88; youth min. Hmong Alliance Ch. of Santa Barbara, Goleta, Calif., 1984-85, Hmong Alliance Ch. of Fresno, 1989—. Scoutmaster Boy Scouts Am., 1984-85. Home: 874 Orienta Ave Apt C Altamonte Springs FL 32701-5656 Office: Hmong Alliance Ch Fresno 8234 E Belmont Ave Fresno CA 93727-9725

XOICULESCU, IONELIA, engineer, educator; b. Fetesti, Romania, Sept. 11, 1959; d. Aurel and Elena (Cretu) Voiculescu; divorced; 1 child, Marius. PhD in Engring., U. Poly., Bucharest, Romania, 1983, MD, 1998. Engr. Electroarges Enterprise, Curtea de Arges, Romania, 1983-85; asst. prof. U. Poly., Bucharest, 1985-91, lectr., 1991-99, prof., 1999—. Co-author: Welding and Connects Procedures, 1990, Designing and Testing of Welded Structures, 1993, Materials and Heat Treatment for Welded Structres, 1994; contbr. articles to profl. jours. Mem. The Inst. of Materials, Romanian Welding Assn., Gen. Romanian Assn. Engrs. Avocations: traveling, athletics, reading science fiction, playing Rebus. Home: Ileana Cosinzeana BL P7, Ap 87 SC III Sector 5, Bucharest Romania Office: U Politechnica, 313 Splaiul Independentei, 77206 Bucharest Romania

XU, ALEX S., real estate development company executive; came to U.S., 1987; m. Wei Wang; children: Ashley, Brian. MS in Math. and M. Computer Engring., U. So. Calif., L.A., 1989. Mgr. corp. data svcs./fin. ops. Carter Hawley Hales, Inc., L.A., 1990-94; dir. fin. Santa Anita Realty, Arcadia, Calif., 1994-95; COO Tone Yee Investment, Rancho Cucamonga, Calif., 1995-97; pres. Concordia Homes of So. Calif., Ontario, 1998—. Office: Concordia Homes of Southern Calif 1131 W 6th St Ste 110 Ontario CA 91762-1100

XU, CHANG-QING, electrical company researcher; b. Hefei, Anhui, China, Dec. 15, 1962; s. Quan-Zhang Xu and Ji-Xiang Wang; m. Ye Hu, Dec. 20, 1993; 1 child, Yi-Chen. BS, U. Sci. and Tech. of China, Hefei, 1985, MS, 1988; D of Engring., U. Tokyo, 1991. Rschr. Oki Electric Industry Co. Ltd., Tokyo, 1991-95, sr. rschr., 1995—. Contbr. articles to profl. jours. Scholarship The Edn. Ministry of Japan, 1987-91. Mem. IEEE, Optical Soc. of Am., Japan Soc. of Applied Physics. Avocations: reading, travel. Office: Oki Elec Industry Co Ltd, 550-5 Higashiasakawa-cho, Tokyo 193-8550, Japan

XU, CHAO-NAN, materials scientist, researcher; b. Shengyang, Liaonin, China, Oct. 21, 1963; arrived in Japan, 1987; d. Li-Qin and Chen (Nian-Shu) X.; m. Xu-Guang Zheng, Feb. 23, 1987; children: Mei-Jia, Li-Jia. BSc, Jiaotong U., Xi'an, China, 1984; MSc., Elec. Vac Tech. Inst., Beijing, China, 1986; D. in Engring., Kyushu U., Fukuoka, Japan, 1991. Asst. prof. Fukuoka (Japan) U., 1991-94; rsch. fellow Kyushu Nat. Indsl. Rsch. Inst., Tosu, Japan, 1995-98; sr. rschr. Kyushu Nat. Indsl. Rsch. Inst., Tosu, 1998—; dir. Nagasaki Ceramics Tech. Ctr., Japan, 1995-96; cons. Kumamoto (Japan) Indsl. Tech. Ctr., 1995-98, Fukuoka Indsl. Tech. Ctr., 1995-98, Saga

(Japan) Indsl. Tech. Ctr., 1995-96. Contbr. articles to profl. jours. Grantee Yazaki Meml. Fund for Sic. and Tech., Tokyo, 1996, Assn. Women Scientists, Tokyo, 1996, Agy. Indsl. Sci. Tech., Min. Internat. Trade Industry, Japan, Tokyo, 1997. Mem. Electrochem. Soc. (U.S.), Chemistry Soc. Japan, Applied Physics Soc. Japan. Avocations: reading, cooking, shopping, children, table tennis. Home: Futsu-hara 11-A3, Tosu 841-0053, Japan Office: Kyushu Nat Indsl Rsch Inst, Shuku 807-1, Tosu 841-0052, Japan

XU, CHENG, mechanical engineer, researcher; b. Shexian, Anhui, People's Republic of China, Apr. 11, 1964; came to U.S., 1998; s. Yingqiang Cao and Huixia Xu; m. Jiaenu Wang, July 22, 1991; 1 child, Shiliang Cao. B in Engring., Xian Coll. of Engring., 1989; M in Engring., Nanjiang U. Aero. and Astro., China, 1992; PhD, Nanyang Tech. U., 1997. Asst. prof. Nanjiang U. of Aeronautics and Astronautics, 1992-95; sr. officer Nat. Measurement Ctr., Singapore, 1997-98; rschr., instr. U. Wis., Milw., 1998—. Contbr. articles to profl. jours. Avocations: art design, reading, fishing, jogging, travel. Office: U Wis Dept Mech Engring Milwaukee WI 53201

XU, CHUNHUI, systems engineer, educator; b. Daye, China, Mar. 15, 1964; s. Ping Ding, 1990; 1 child, Zhouyuan. B in Engring., Huazhong U. Sci. & Technology, 1984, M in Engring., 1987, PhD, 1990; D in Engring., Tokyo Inst. Technology, 1995. Assoc. prof. Hiroshima Inst. Technology, Japan. Mem. IEEE, Ops. Rsch. Soc. Japan, Japan Soc. Mgmt. Info., Internat. Fedn. Automatic Control. Office: Hiroshima Inst Technology, 2-1-1 Miyake Saeki-ku, 731-5193 Hiroshima Japan

XU, DING-XIN, structural engineer, consultant, educator; b. Shanghai, May 11, 1928; s. Junshan Xu and Abao Wang; m. Yi Huang, Feb. 9, 1975; 1 child. BSc with honors, Da Tong U., Shanghai, 1949. State registered 1st grade structural engr.; Shanghai registered cons. expert. Trainee Shanghai Rlwy. Bur., 1950-51; structural engr. Qun An Design Inst. of Arch. and Engring., Shanghai, 1951-53; engr., design group leader, acting dept. chief engr., chief engr. project design, acting vice chief engr. East China Design Inst., Shanghai, 1954-79; sr. engr., prof., vice chief engr. Inst. Archtl. Design and Rsch. Tongji U., Shanghai, 1980-92, chief engr. 1st br. Inst. Archtl. Design and Rsch., 1984-87; chmn., chief engr. Jin Ding Group Inc., Shanghai, 1994—; state registered 1st grade structural engr. State Reg. 1st Grade, 1998—; reg. cons. exp. Shanghai, 1998—; expert 1st and 2d com. of experts Shanghai Investment Consulting Co., 1987-93, Com. Sci. and Tech. Shanghai Mcpl. Constrn. Bd., 1991-96; vice chief engr. Constrn. Project Mgmt. and Consulting Co. of Tong Ji U., 1992—; sr. advisor Haipo Group Inc., U.S.A., Shanghai, 1993—; sr. tech. advisor Shanghai Ye Jian House Property Devel., 1994-96; tech. advisor Si Tong Steel Fiber Factory, Ningbo, China, 1994—. Editor, compiler: Bent Structures and Frames, 1962; compiler: Design Handbook of R.C. Columns of Mono Storey Industrial Buildings, 1958, Design Handbook of Brick Shallow Shells, 1961; inventor in field. Recipient cert. of merit Nat. Congress of Sci. and Tech., Beijing, 1978. Mem. Shanghai Ctr. of Tech. Devel. for Space Structures (bd. dirs. 1991—), Shanghai Soc. of Civil Engrs., Shanghai Assn. Archs., Shanghai Assn. Mechanics, Shanghai Assn. Ret. Sr. Experts, Internat. Assn. for Bridge and Structural Engring. Avocations: music, swimming, movies, television, singing. Home and Office: 541/2 Tong Ji New Village, Zhang Wu Rd, 200092 Shanghai China

XU, DONG-SHENG, material scientist, educator; b. Heilongjiang, China, Apr. 1, 1964; s. Wei-zhen Xu and De-rong Miao; m. Yan Tong, May 14, 1989; 1 child, Xiang-Bo. BS, Northeastern U., Shenyang, China, 1985; MS, Liaoning U., Shenyang, China, 1988; PhD, Chinese Acad. Scis., Shenyang, China, 1994. Tchr. Shenyang Poly. U., 1988-90; postdoctoral fellow Northeastern U., Shenyang, 1994-96; assoc. prof. Inst. Metal Rsch., Chinese Acad. Scis., Shenyang, 1996—. Contbr. articles on computational alloy design to profl. jours. Fax: 86-24-23891320. E-mail: dsxu@imr.ac.cn. Office: Inst Metal Rsch Chinese Acad Scis, 72 Wenhua Rd, Shenyang 110015, China

XU, DU, mechanical engineer, educator; b. Chengdu, Sichan, People's Republic of China, Apr. 19, 1958; s. Liang and Quanzhen (Du) X.; m. Yongping Jiang, Apr. 5, 1985; 1 child, Jing. BS, Harbin Shipping Engring. Inst., 1982; MS, Chongquing U., 1989; postgrad., Sichan Inst. Fgn. Langs., Chongquing, 1989, U. Kans., 1991-92. Asst. engr. The 716th Inst. China, Wanxian, 1982-83; lectr. Chongquing U., 1983-93; assoc. prof. Shantou U., 1993-99, prof., 1999—; cons. engr. The Factory of Jinyan Gen. Elec. Equipment, Shantou, 1993—. Contbr. articles to profl. jours. including Modern Sci. Instruments, Practical Measurement Tech., Tool Engring., Mfg. Tech. and Machine Tool, Chinese Jour. Quantum Electronics, China Mech. Engring., Process Automation Instrumentation, Chinese Jour. Scientific Instrument, and Acad. Conf. Paper Index of China. Recipient 3d prize Nat. Achievements in Applying Microcomputer, Electron Developing Group of the State Coun., Beijing, 1986, 3d prize of Achievements in Sci. Rsch. of Chongqing U., 1987, Achievement in Sci. Rsch. Edn. Com. China 2d prize, 1995. Mem. Chinese Sci. Instruments Soc. (com. precision measurement 1991—, author proceedings), Chinese Optics Soc. (com. photoelectronci tech. and sys. 1999—), Young Academics Soc. Shantou U. Avocations: music, reading. Office: Shantou U, Dept Mechatronics Engring, Shantou Guangdong 515063, China

XU, FU-LUI, science educator; b. Lin-Quang, Anhui, China, Nov. 27, 1962; s. Guang-Ting Xu and Xiu-Zhen Wang; m. Fang Wang; 1 child, Rui-Xiang. BSc, Hefei (China) U. Tech., 1984; MSc, Xi-an (China) Geol. U., 1988; PhD, Royal Danish Sch. Pharmacy, Copenhagen, 1998. Technician Anhui Co. Coal-ore Exploration, Bangpu, China, 1984-85; engr., sr. engr. Anhui Inst. Environ. Scis., Hefei, 1988-94; assoc. prof. Peking U., Beijing, 1998—; rschr. in field. Mem. editl. bd. Ecol. Modelling, 1992—. Recipient award Sci. Found. for Chinese Scholars, 1998, Nat. Sci. Found., 1999. Mem. Internat. Soc. Ecol. Engring., N.Y. Acad. Scis. Avocations: Chinese gong-fu, badminton, running. Office: Peking U, Dept Urban & Environ Scis, Beijing 100871, China

XU, GANG, medical researcher, educator; b. Hefei, Anhui, China, Aug. 26, 1955; came to U.S., 1982; s. Xue-shou Xu and Jian Zhang. BA, Sichuan U., 1981; MS, Ohio U., 1984, PhD, 1989. Rsch. trainer Coll. Osteo. Medicine Ohio U., Athens, 1987-89; rsch. assoc. Jefferson Med. Coll., Phila., 1989-95, 96—; rsch. adminstr., assoc. prof. Ohio U., Athens, 1995—; adv. bd. mem. rsch. planning com. Ohio Acad. Family Physicians, Columbus, 1995—; sr. rsch. assoc., assoc. prof. Jefferson Med. Coll., Phila., 1996—. Author: Life in America-A Personal Perspective, 1996, The Procedures of Passing USMLE, 1999, How to Become A Medical Doctor in U.S., 1999; contbr. more than 100 articles to profl. jours. and newspapers. Mem. APA, Am. Edn. Rsch. Assn., N.Am. Primary Care Rsch., Asian-Am. Psychol. Assn. Avocations: swimming, table tennis, long distance running. Home: 139 Ashley Ct Cherry Hill NJ 08003-3743 Office: Jefferson Med Coll 1025 Walnut St Philadelphia PA 19107-5001

XU, GANG DA, physicist; b. Shashi, Hubei, China, Dec. 23, 1935; s. Qing Zheng and Xian Qing (Li) X.; m. Yu Shen, Jan. 26, 1964; 1 child, Yiding. B in Physics, Sichuan U., Chendu, China, 1958. Technician Nat. Inst. Metrology, Beijing, 1958-61, group leader, 1962-75, dir. lab., 1976-93, rschr., 1994-99. Author: Research on Laser Energy Standard at High Level, 1978, Quantities and Units of Light and Related E-M Radiations, 1982; inventor energy and power measurement system. Recipient Sci. Congress award, Beijing, 1978, 2nd Nat. prize Sci. and Tech. Progress, Chinese Sci. and Tech. Commn., Beijing, 1991, 3rd Nat. prize, 1997. Fellow Nat. Bur. Tech. Supervision (mem. Chinese com. quannitics units and symbols, award 1989); mem. Chinese Optical Soc. (mem. topical com. for laser), SPIE, Internat. Soc. Optical Engring. Avocations: reading, swimming, coin collecting, learning foreign languages. Home: 0304 Bldg 39, Dist 11, Hepinglo Beijing 100013, China Office: Nat Inst Metrology, 18 Bei San Huan Dong Lu, Beijing China

XU, GUANG-YIN, neuroscientist, researcher; b. Jingjiang, Jiangsu, China; s. Jialong Xu and Guifang Shi; m. Wen Wang, Oct 1, 1990; 1 child, Haotian. MD, Nantong (China) Med. Coll., 1986; MS, Suzhou (China) Med. Coll., 1992; PhD, Chinese Acad. Sci., Shanghai, 1998. Asst. prof. Nantong Med. Coll., 1986-89, lectr., 1992-95; asst. prof. Suzhou Med. Coll., 1989-92; PhD scholar Shanghai Brain Rsch. Inst., 1995-98; vis. scientist UI. Tex. Med. Br., Galveston, 1998—; former reviewer Acta Physiologica Sinica, Shanghai; former grad. student advisor Grad. Studnt Advising Com., Nantong. Contbr, articles to med. jours. Recipient Pres.'s award Chinese Acad. Scis., 1997, award Chinese Soc. for Neurosci., 1997; travel grantee Internat. Congress Physiol. Sci., 1997. Mem. Soc. for Neurosci., Sigma Xi. Avocations: sports, fishing, reading, collecting. Fax: 409-762-9382. E-mail: gyxu@utmb.edu. Home: 302 Holiday Dr Apt 2 Galveston TX 77550-5670 Office: U Tex Med Br 301 University Blvd Galveston TX 77555-5302

XU, GUANGYU, chemist; b. Chengdu, Sichuan, China, Apr. 1, 1969. BS, Sichuan U., 1990; MS, Brandeis U., 1995, PhD, 1999. Chemist S.W. Inst. Tech. Physics, Chengdu, Sichuan, China, 1990-93, Shipley Co., Marlboro, Mass., 1997—. Contbr. articles to sci. jours. Recipient 2d class Nat. Sci. Progress award China Nat. Sci. Found., 1994. Mem. Am. Chem. Soc. E-mail: gxu@shipley.com. Home: 59 School St Apt B14 Northborough MA 01532 Office: Shipley Co 455 Forest St Marlborough MA 01752

XU, GUO FANG, design engineer; b. Xiao Shan, China, Mar. 21, 1961; came to U.S., 1995; d. Jin-Kuan Xu and Yu-Zheng Ma; m. Cheng Hua, Dec. 25, 1986; children: Xin Hua, Jane Hua. BEE, Huazhong U. Sci. & Tech., Wuhan, China, 1983, MS, 1986; PhD, U. Colo., 1999. Instr. Zhejiang U., Huangzhou, China, 1986-93; scholar rschr. U. Adelade, Australia, 1993-95; rsch. asst. U. Colo., Denver, 1995-99; design engr. Tex. Instruments, Longmont, Colo., 1999—; cons. Hai-Teng Electronics Co., Huangzhou, 1990-93, Modulation Scis., Inc., Denver, 1997-98. Grantee Colo. Advanced Software Inst., 1997, IBM, 1998. Mem. IEEE. Avocations: reading, travel. Home: 3632 Wildrose Pl Longmont CO 80503-6402 Office: Tex Instruments 2600 Trade Center Ave Longmont CO 80503-7551

XU, GUOJIAN, lawyer, educator; b. Rudong County, China, Oct. 19, 1962; s. Shouyou and Lanfang (Hu) X.; m. Qiong Mei, Mar. 24, 1967; 1 child, Mengyao. BA, S.W. Inst. Politics and Law, 1984; M of Law, Wuhan U., 1986; Dr. juris, Hamburg U., 1994. Lectr. Wuhan (China) U., 1986-87; van Kalker scholar Swiss Inst. of Comparative Law, Lausanne, Switzerland, 1988; asst. lawyer Triebel Weil & Elsing, Düsseldorf, Germany, 1989-89; asst. lawyer Schulz Noack Barwinkel, Hamburg, Germany, 1992, rep., 1994-97; vis. scholar Max-Planck Inst. for Fgn. and Internat. Pvt. Law, Hamburg, 1989-92; mng. ptnr. Boss & Young, Shanghai, China, 1999—; hon. prof. Hunan Normal U., Changsha, 1993; assoc. prof. Law Sch., Shanghai U., 1996—. Author: Anwendungsprobleme des chinesischen internationalen kaufrechts, 1994, The Movement of International Unification of Private Law, 1993; contbr. numerous articles to profl. jours. Mem. Soc. of Internat. Law, Can. Study in China, Sino-German Assn. of Jurists. Avocations: reading, table tennis. Office: Ste BC 12th Fl, 379 Pudong South Rd, Pudong New Area Shanghai 200120, China

XU, HAO, tribologist, researcher; b. Tianquan, China, Feb. 3, 1962; arrived in Eng., 1983; s. Wenyan Xu and Folong Liu; m. Wen Dou, July 1, 1988; 1 child, Beatrice. BEng, Northeast Inst. Heavy Machiney, Qiqihar, China, 1982; PhD, Leeds U., Eng., 1988. Rsch. fellow U. Ctrl. Lancashire, Preston, Eng., 1987-90; sr. engr. T&N Tech. Ltd., Rugby, Eng., 1990-93, prin. engr., 1993-96, head hydraulics and tribology section, 1994-96, exec. engr., 1996-99; group cons. Glacier Vandervell Tech. Ctr., 1999—. Contbr. articles to profl. jours. and confs. Mem. ASME, Soc. Tribologists and Lubrication Engrs. Avocations: photography, walking, playing card games. Office: Glacier Vandervell Tech Ctr, Cawston House, Rugby CV22 7SD, England

XU, HONG QI, physicist, researcher; b. Dalian, Liaoning, China, Aug. 20, 1956; arrived in Sweden, 1985; s. Dianfu and Lianfang (Wang) X.; m. Min Lu, Feb. 4, 1983; 1 child, Can. BS, Dalian (China) U. Tech., 1982; PhD, Lund U., Sweden, 1991, docent, 1995. Tchr. Pingjia Sch., Wafangdian, Liaoning, China, 1975-78; asst. tchr. Dalian (China) U. Tech., 1982-85; postdoctoral fellow Linköping (Sweden) U., 1991-93; rsch. assoc. Lund (Sweden) U., 1993-95; asst. prof. Lund U., 1995—; referee Am. Inst. Physics., 1995—, Am. Phys. Soc., 1996—, Inst. Physics, U.K., 1998—; adj. prof. Inst. Semiconductors Chinese Acad. Scis., Beijing, 1998—, Dalian U. Tech., China, 1999—, prof., 2000—. Contbr. articles to profl. jours. including Phys. Rev., Applied Physics Letters, Jour. Applied Physics, Jour. Physics, Internat. Jour. Modern Physics, Semiconductor Sci. and Tech. Mem. AAAS, Am. Phys. Soc., N.Y. Acad. Sci. Fax: 46 46 222 3637. Office: Lund U Solid State Physics, Box 118, 22100 Lund Sweden

XU, HUA, engineering educator, researcher; b. Shangyao, Jiangxi, China, Dec. 24, 1959; s. Bingsong and Yuanying (Li) X.; m. Xining Zhong, July 28, 1985; 1 child, Jiaqi. B.Engring., Northeastern U., Shenyang, China, 1982, M.Engring., 1985; Dr.Engring., Hiroshima (Japan) U., 1993. Rsch. assoc. Northeastern U., Shenyang, 1985-87; rsch. assoc. Hiroshima U., 1993-96, assoc. prof. engring., 1996-98; assoc. prof. engring. U. Tsukuba, 1998—. Contbr. articles to profl. jours. Mem. Soc. Instrument Control Engring., Internat. Soc. Dynamic Games. Avocations: cycling, baseball, television. Home: 16-1007 Eichujima Ichome, 3 ban Koto-ku Tokyo 135-0044, Japan Office: 3-29-1 Otsuka Bunyko-ku, Tokyo 112-0012, Japan

XU, HUAI-SHU, microbiologist, educator; b. Zunhua, Hebei Prov, China, July 7, 1936; s. Rui-Qi and Ru-Zhi (Zhou) X.; m. Shou-Wen Jin, June 17, 1967; children: Jin, Fu-Jin. Diploma in biology, Nankai U., Tianjin, China, 1960. Tchg. asst. Shandong Coll. Oceanography, Qingdao, 1960-77, lectr., 1978-85; assoc. prof. Ocean U. qingdao, 1986-90, prof. microbiology, dept. marine biology, 1991—, PhD supr., 1995—; vis. scholar U. R.I., Kingston, 1980-81, U. Md., College Park, 1981-82, 86-87; advisor Adv. Bd. of High Tech., Qingdao Govt., 1988—; coop. scientist Inst. Ocean Scis., Sidney, Can., 1984. Editor Jour. Ocean U. Qingdao, 1996, Chinese Jour. Microbiology, 1996, Chinese Biodiversity, 1995; contbr. numerous articles to profl. jours. Named Outstanding Scientist, Shandong Province govt., 1992, Excellent Tchr., 1995; grantee UNESCO, 1986, 86-87, Chinese U. Hong Kong, 1986, Sci. and Tech. Commn. Shandong Province, 1985-86, Ocean U. Qingdao, 1988, Nat. Sci. Found. China, 1987-88, 90-92, 94-96, Sci. and Tech. Commn. Qingdao Municipality, 1989-91, State Dept. Agr., 1991-94, State Commn. Sci. and Tech., 1991-95, European Econ. Cmty., 1994-96, State Commn. of Edn., 1997—, others. Mem. Chinese Soc. Microbiology (coun. mem. 1996, bd. dirs. 1988), Chinese Soc. for Ecology (coun. 1991), Am. Soc. Microbiology, Chinese Soc. Microbial Ecology (coun. 1984—), Chinese Soc. Marine Ecology (coun. 1983—), Chinese Soc. Marine Biotech. (coun. 1988). Avocations: photography, travel. Home: 39 Hongdao Rd Apt 10, Qingdao 266003, People's Republic of China Office: Ocean U Qingdao Marine Life, 5 Yushan Rd, Qingdao 266003, People's Republic of China

XU, HUANG, olympic athlete; b. Nantong, China, Feb. 4, 1979. Mem. men's gymnastics team China; winner team gold World Championship, 1997, 99; winner gold medal team all-around Olympics, Sydney, Australia, 2000. Office: Chinese Gymnastics Assn, 9 Tiyuguan Rd, 100 763 Beijing China*

XU, HUI-LIAN, plant scientist; b. Cangshan, Shandong, China, Jan. 8, 1954; arrived in Can., 1991; s. Yu-rui Xu and Li-ying Tian Xu; m. Li-wei Zhang, June 22, 1987; children: Chieko Xu, Alexandre Cheyue Xu. BA in Agronomy, Laiyang (China) Agrl. U., 1982; MSc in Crop Physiology, U. Tokyo, 1986, PhD in Crop Physiology, 1989. Postdoctoral rschr. Nippon-Kayaku Co., Ltd., Tokyo, 1989-91; postdoctoral rschr. Laval U., Que., Can., 1991-93, assoc. prof. plant sci., 1993-96; sr. rschr., dep. dir. Internat. Farming Rsch. Ctr., Nagano, Japan, 1996—. Contbr. articles to profl. jours. Mem. Am. Soc. for Hort. Sci., Am. Soc. Agronomy, Crop Sci. Soc. Am., Soil Sci. Soc. Am., N.Y. Acad. Scis., Japan Soil Sci. Soc., Japan Hort. Sci. Soc. Avocations: poetry, classical art, travel. Office: Internat Nature Farm Rsch, 5632 Hata, Nagano 390-1401, Japan

XU, JIEFENG, industrial engineer; b. Shanghai, China, Dec. 11, 1965. Master's, Shanghai Jiaotong U., 1990; M of Applied Sci., U. Toronto, Ont., Can., 1993; PhD in Bus., U. Colo., 1997. Mem. tech. staff U.S. West Advanced Tech., Boulder, 1996; sr. developer Delta Tech. Inc., Atlanta, 1997—. Contbr. articles on optimization computing and computerized decision-making systems to profl. jours. Open fellow U. Toronto, 1992, Dean's Small grantee U. Colo., 1994, Hart Rsch. fellow, 1994-95. Mem. Inst. Ops. Rsch. and Mgmt. Sci. Avocation: reading. Home: 5185 Coacoochee Ter Alpharetta GA 30022-3106 Office: Delta Tech Inc Dept 709 1001 International Blvd Dept 709 Atlanta GA 30354-1802

XU, JINGDA, mining engineer; b. Shanghai, China, Oct. 27, 1935; s. Zhongkai and Zhique (Chu) X.; m. Rongfang Xu; children: Zhishi, Ge, Jiangmei. Med. technician, China Profl. Sch., 1952; mining engr., Mining Inst., U.S.S.R., 1960. Technician engr., dept. mgr. Daching Oil Field, China, 1960-69; dept. mgr. Jianhang Oil Field, Tsianjiang, China, 1970-73; co. exec. Gilling Oil Field, Songyian, China, 1973-82, Drilling Co., Zhangjiang, China, 1982-85, Prodn. Co., Zhangjiang, China, 1985; chief rep. in Chinese side ARCO chinca Inc., Zhangjiang and Shenzhen, 1985-96; mem. editors com. Oil Drilling and Prodn. Tech., Renqui, 1980-95; dir. PSC in Gilling Prov., Chuangchen, China, 1979-82, Petroleum Engring. Soc. of China, Beijing, 1980-82, PSC in Guangdong Prov., Guangzhou, China, 1984-94. Editor: Drilling Mechanism of the Insert Rock Bit (First Class award 1959); editor articles in profl. jours. Recipient Achievement award Petroleum Ministry, 1962, 63. Avocations: European classic music, singing, reading. Office: ARCO China Inc, ITF Finance Ctr, Shekou Shenzhen 518067, China

XU, JING-HUA, biophysicist; b. Beijing, China, Nov. 17, 1922; s. Zi-qiu and Zong-wen (Ma) X.; m. Li-jun Chen, Dec. 23, 1950; children: Lin, Nan. BSc, South-west Associated U., Kunming, 1944. Asst. Inst. of Medicine Academia Sinica, Shanghai, 1945-49, rsch. assoc. Inst. of Physiology and Biochemistry, 1949-56, assoc. prof., 1956-60, prof. Inst. of Biochemistry, 1960-76; prof. Shanghai Inst. of Biochemistry, 1976—; prof. Inst. Biophysics Academia Sinica, Beijing, 1979-87; prof. Zhejiang U., Hangzhou, 1987—; vis. prof. Inst. Theoretical Physics, Academia Sinica, Beijing, 1987-89. Contbr. articles to profl. jours. Mem. Chinese Biophys. Soc. (v.p. 1979-85), Shanghai Biophys. Soc. (pres. 1984-88, honorable pres. 1988—), Soc. of Math. Biology (U.S.). Home: Qing-zhen Rd 99-12/204, Shanghai 200032, China Office: Shanghai Inst Biochemistry, Yue-yang Rd 320, Shanghai 200031, China

XU, LIHAO, education educator. PhD, Calif. Inst. Technology, Pasadena, 1999. Lectr. Shanghai Jiao Tong U., China, 1991-94; rsch. asst. Calif. Inst. Tech., Pasadena, 1994-99, postdoctoral scholar, 1999; asst. prof. Washington U., St. Louis, 1999—. Mem. IEEE, IEEE Computer Soc. and Info. Theory Soc. E-mail: lihao@cs.wustl.edu. Office: Washington Univ One Brookings Dr Saint Louis MO

XU, LIXIN, research engineer; b. Jinhua, Zhejiang, China, 1966; came to U.S., 1994; BS, Zhejiang U., 1985; MS in Engring., Shanghai (China) Jiao Tong U., 1990, U. Mich., 1997; PhD, U. Mich., 1998. Naval arch. Shanghai Merchant Ship Design and Rsch. Inst., 1985-94; rsch. asst. U. Mich., Ann Arbor, 1994-98; rsch. engr. Am. Bur. Shipping, N.Y.C., 1998-99, Houston, 1999—; tech. in chief, cons. Minzhou Marine Engring, Ningbo, Zhejang, China, 1993-94. Reviewer Jour. Ship Rsch., 1998—, Jour. Waterways, Ports, Coastal and Ocean Divsn., 1998—; contbr. articles to profl. jours. Mem. ASME, Internat. Soc. Offshore and Polar Engrs., Am. Phys. Soc., Soc. Naval Arch. and Marine Engrs. E-mail: lxu@eagle.org. Office: Am Bur Shipping 16855 Northchase Dr Houston TX 77060-6006

XU, MIN, mechanical vibration diagnosis engineer, educator; b. Changzhou, Jiangzu, China, Sept. 15, 1928; s. Bo Xin and Yu Qing (Zhou) X.; m. Guang Ce Ru, Aug. 28, 1932; children: Ru, Yu Bing. B, Da Lian (China) U., 1954; M, Shanghai Jiao Tong U., 1957; postgrad., Shanghai Fgn. Lang. Inst., 1964-65. Assoc. prof. Shanghai Jiao Tong U., 1980-84, prof., 1984—, 1st seat exec. prof., 1994-98, dir. Inst. Vibration, Shock and Noise Rsch., 1978-87, dir. Nat. Key Lab. Inst. Vibration, Shock and Noise Rsch., 1988-92, establisher Nat. Key Lab. Inst. Vibration, Shock/Noise Rsch., 1988-92; vis. scholar Imperial Coll., London, 1965-67; vis. rschr. Ono Sokki Inst., Tokyo, 1983; appraisal expert Nat. Natural Sci. Found. China, Beijing, 1990-92; chmn. Fault Diagnosis Soc. China, 1986-94; early founder Machinery Condition Monitoring and Fault Diagnostics Tech. in China. Chief author: Signal Processing and Analysis Techniques, 1983; chief editor: Plant Diagnostics Handbook, 1996. Recipient Chinese Sci. and Tech. Progress award, 1986, 88, 96, Tech. Outstanding contbr. State Coun., China, 1991. Mem: IMEKO (Hungary), ISO (U.S.A.), Chinese Soc. Shipbuilding Engring. (fellow), Chinese Soc. Vibration Engring. Avocations: classic music, travel. Home and Office: Shanghai Jiao Tong U Inst Vibration Rsch, 1954 Hua Shan Rd, Shanghai 200030, China

XU, MINGHOU, thermophysics educator, researcher; b. Huangpi, Peoples Republic of China, June 25, 1966; s. Xinzhou and Xiaomei (Pan) X.; m. Lin Zhang Xu, June 25, 1990; one child. BS, Huazhong U. Sci. and Tech., Wuhan, China, 1986; MS, 1989, PhD, 1992. Lectr. Huazhong U. Sci. and Tech., Wuhan, China, 1992-94; assoc. prof., 1994—; cons. Internat. Energy Found., Regina, Can., 1995—. Ao-author: Progress in Science at Huazhong University of Science and Technology, 1993; contbr. articles to profl. jours. Recipient The Second Rank award Progress of Sci. and Tech., Hubei Province Govt., 1995, award Ministry of Edn. of People's Republic of China, 1999, award State Edn. Commn., 1998. Mem. Combustion Inst., Am. Chem. Soc., Chinese Soc. for Elec. Engring., Chinese Soc. for Engring. Thermophysics. Avocations: Chinese chess, football, basketball. Office: Nat Lab Coal Combustion, Huazhong U Sci and Tech, 430074 Wuhan China

XU, PENG SHOU, physicist; b. Taixing, China, Jan. 15, 1947; s. De Ming and Wen Hua (Sheng) X.; m. Fei Ping Lin, Feb. 5, 1976; 1 child, Lin Li. BS, U. Sci. and Tech., China, 1970. Asst. U. Sci. and Tech., China, 1973-79, lectr., 1980-88, assoc. prof., 1989-94, prof., 1995—; guest rschr. Brookhaven (N.Y.) Nat. Lab., 1986. Contbr. articles to profl. jours. Recipient 1st class Sci. and Tech. Progress prize Chinese Acad. Scis., 1992. Mem. Chinese Vacuum Soc. (Hayashi award 1995), Chinese Synchrotron Radiation Soc. Home: 96 Jinzhai Rd, Hefei 230026, China Office: NSRL, U Sci and Tech China, Hefei 230026, China

XU, PING, chemist; b. Shanghai, China, Apr. 29, 1957; came to U.S., 1985; s. Yuan Xu and Changfu Zhu; m. Shuhong Wang, Feb. 17, 1987; children: Helen W., Olivia W. BS, East China U. Chem. Tech., Shanghai, 1982, MS, 1984; MS, U. Cin., 1987, PhD, 1991. Asst. prof. East China U. Chem. Tech., 1984-85; Paul J. Flory meml. fellow U. Cin., 1990-92; sr. rsch. chemist Quantum Chem. Corp., Cin., 1991-94; polymer scientist W.L. Gore & Assocs., Inc., Elkton, Md., 1994—; vis. scientist Oak Ridge (Tenn.) Nat. Lab., 1998—; vis. scientist Nat. Inst. Stds. and Tech., Gaithersburg, Md., 1999—. Contbr. numerous articles to sci. jours. Mem. AAAS, Am. Chem. Soc., Material Rsch. Soc. Achievements include research in engineering, rubber elasticity, polymer morphology and polymer physics. Home: 22 Piersons Rdg Hockessin DE 19707-9291 Office: WL Gore & Assocs Inc 2401 Singerly Rd Elkton MD 21921-2733

XU, QI WU, neurosurgeon; b. Shanghai, Sept. 11, 1944; s. Han Jian Xu and Gui Zhen Gu; m. Wei Huan Chen, Oct. 1, 1975; 1 child, Qi. B Medicine, Shanghai 2d Med. U., 1967; M Neurosurgery, Shanghai Med. U., 1981. Neurosurg. resident Huashan Hosp., Shanghai, 1981-86, attending neurosurgeon, 1986-90, vice chmn. dept. neurosurgery, 1986—, assoc. prof., 1990-93, prof., 1993—, doctoral advisor, 1994—, vice chmn. Inst. Neurology, 1998—; vis. rsch. prof., vis. prof. U. Mich., An Arbor, 1995; cons. Legal Med. Identification Ctr. of Shanghai, Higher People's Ct., 1994—. Mem. editl. bd. Chinese Clin. Neurosci., 1993—, Chinese Gen. Practice, 1998—; prodr., dir. ednl. videos. Recipient 1st class prize Med. Colls. and Univs. of E. China, 1987, 2d class prize Health Ministry of the People's Republic of China, 1988, 3d class prize, 1997, edn. prize Higher Edn. Bur. of Shanghai, 1990, 2d class prize Shanghai Mcpl. Health Bur., 1993, 3d class prize Shanghai People's Govt., 1994, 98, Shanghai Mcpl. Health Bur., 1995. Mem. Chinese Assn. Neurol. Surgeons (mem. com. 1996—), Shanghai Assn. Neurol. Surgeons (mem. com. 1994—). Avocations: Chinese chess, table tennis. Fax: 86-21-62499412. Office: Huashan Hosp, 12 Wulumuqi Zhong Rd, Shanghai 200040, China

XU, QIANG, chemist, researcher; b. Yang Zhou, Jiang Su, China, July 23, 1964; s. Bing-Sheng and Shi-Mei (Gu) X.; m. Dai-Fei Fang, May 30, 1989; 1 child, Ke-Fang. DSc, Osaka (Japan) U., 1994. Rsch. scientist Osaka U., 1994-95, Osaka Nat. Rsch. Inst., 1995—; vis. lectr. Osaka U., 1996-97. Contbr. articles to profl. jours. Bd. dirs. Found. of Japan-China Juvenile Edn., Osaka, 1995—. Mem. Chem. Soc. Japan, Catalysis Soc. Japan, Soc. Synthetic Organic Chemistry Japan (Daicel award 1997). Office: Osaka Nat Rsch Inst, 1-8-31 Midorigaoka, Ikeda Osaka 563-8577, Japan

XU, RONGLIE, civil engineer; b. Shaoxing, Zhejiang, People's Republic China, May 21, 1931; s. Lanzhou Xu and Xianglian Jiang; m. Shiying Zhang, Apr. 12, 1954; 2 children. B.Eng., China State Nanjing Inst. Tech.; degree in rsch. engring., Acad. Architecture & Constrn. of USSR; DSc (hon.), U. Brighton, Hawaii, 1997. Technician North China Constrn. Bur., Beijing, 1953-56; engr. China Acad. Bldg. Rsch., Beijing, 1958-68; chief engr. Constrn. Co. # 101, Jinzhou, People's Republic China, 1968-72; div. chief State Constrn. Com., Beijing, 1972-79; dep. dir. Bur. Sci. and Tech. State Adminstrn. Bldg. Constrn., Beijing, 1979-82; dir. Bur. Sci. Tech. Ministry Urban and Rural Constrn. Environ. Protection, Beijing, 1982-86; ministerial chief engr. Ministry Constrn., Beijing, 1984-86; prof. Xi'an Inst. Metallurgy and Architecture, 1988—; guest prof. Tongji U., 1987—, Qiughua U., 1993—; mem. China subcom. UNESCO, Beijing; vice chmn. com. for sci. and tech. Ministry of Constrn., China, 1983—. Author: Technical Guide of Building in China, 1984 (1st grade Ministerial awards 1987); chief editor: Appropriate Technology Construction and Quality, 1988, China's Experimental Housing Estates, 1991, Theory and Practice of Piling and Deep Foundations in China-Papers Presented to the 4th International Conference on Piling and Deep Foundations, 1991, The Proceedings of China's Experimental Housing Estates, 1991, The Guide to China Civil Engineering, 1993. Fellow Inst. Civil Engrs. (U.K.), Hong Kong Inst. Engrs.; mem. Royal Swedish Acad. Engring. (fgn.), China Civil Engring. Soc. (exec. v.p. 1988-93, pres. 1993—), Archtl. Soc. China (exec. v.p. 1987—), China Deep Found. Inst. (pres. 1988-92), China Assn. Bldg. Manufacture (pres. 1984-90), China Assn. Constrn. Machines (pres. 1992—), fell. Chartered Inst. Bldg. (U.K.). Fax: 01068393711. Home: 1-1-301 Bldg 1 Housing Yard, Ministry Construction, Beijing 100037, China Office: 9 San Li He Rd, Beijing 100835, China

XU, RUO NING, mathematics educator; b. Puning, China, Dec. 22, 1957; s. Ri Xin Xu and Shu Ming Chen; m. Xiao Yan Zhai, Aug. 22, 1987; 1 child, Chao. BS, Beijing Normal U., 1984, MS, 1987. Lectr. Guangzhou (China) U., 1987-92, assoc. prof. math., 1992-98, prof. math., 1998—. Author: Fuzzy Mathematical Methods in Economic Information Analysis, 1997; contbr. articles to profl. jours. Avocation: table tennis. Home: No 21-703 Lu Jin Lu, Shi Dai Guang Xi, 510091 Guangzhou China Office: Guangzhou U, Inst Fuzzy Sys, Guangzhou 510091, China

XU, S. LIANG, pediatrics educator; b. Wuming, Guangxi, China, May 15, 1917; s. Liang Chan and Lu Zan (Guai) Hai; m. Lo Wan Chen, May 15, 1952 (dec. Aug., 1983); 1 child, Liang Yin. MD, Guangxi Med. Coll., Guailin, China, 1942; postgrad., Harvard U., 1947-48. Asst. prof., head dept. pediatrics Guangxi Med. Coll., Nanning, Guangxi, China, 1949-52, prof., dean, 1952-73, prof., head lab. of genetics, 1973—; com. mem. Pediatric Soc., Chinese Med. Assn., Beizing, China, 1952-91, Med. Genetic Soc., Chinese Med. Assn., Beizing, 1985-91, Chinese Assn. Genetics, 1985-91; vice-chmn. Rsch. Ctr. Chinese Pediatric Hematology, 1983—. Contbr. articles to profl. jours. Recipient Nat. Award of Sci., Nat. Congress of Sci., Beizing, 1978, Prize of Achievement in Sci., Chinese Com. of Sci., Beizing, 1983, medal Chinese Com. of Edn., Beizing, 1991. Mem. N.Y. Acad. Sics., Club of Chinese Pediatric Hematology (vice chmn. 1983—). Avocations: swimming, music. Office: Guangxi Med Coll, 6 Bin Hu Rd, Nanning Guangxi 530027, China

XU, SHANJIA, engineering educator; b. Zhejiang, China, July 9, 1939. Grad., U. Sci. and Tech. of China, 1965. Faculty U. Sci. and Tech. of China, Anhui Hefei, prof., chmn. dept. elec. engring. and info. science, 1993-99, vice dir. acad. com., v.p. High Technic Coll., vice dir. Acad. Com., 1993—; vis. scholar Poly. Inst. of N.Y. (Poly. U.), 1983-86; guest scientist and vis. prof. Wurzburg (Germany) U., 1991, 93; acad. visitor several univs. in U.S., Can., Japan, Germany, Korea, Hong Kong; vice dir. Chinese MTT Soc.; lectr. in field. Sub. assoc. editor IEEE MGWL; mem. editl. bd. Jour. China Inst. Comm., IEEE Trans. on MTT, Progress in Nat. Science, Jour. Infrared and Millimeter Wave, Jour. Electronics and Info., Chinese Jour. Radio Science, Jour. Microwave; contbr. over 300 articles to profl. jours. Recipient 1st award for the natural sci. Chinese Acad. Scis., 1st award for sci. and tech. Kwang-Hua Sci. and Tech. Found. Mem. IEEE (sr. mem.). Achievements include research in fields of microwave, millimeter and optical wave theory and techniques; non-uniform dielectric waveguides and applications, numerical techniques in electromagnetics and millimeter wave technology. Office: U Science & Tech-Dept Elec Engring & Info Sci, PO Box 4, Anhui Hefei 230027, China

XU, SHAOHONG, physics educator; b. Longhai, Fujian, China, Feb. 4, 1921; s. Hongtu and Peiying (Lin) X.; m. Wenman Zhu, May 31, 1952; children: Youwen Xu, Fangwen Zhu. BS, Nat. S.W. Associated U., Kunming, China, 1943; postgrad., Harvard U., 1948-49, Tex. A&M U., 1949-50. Asst. rsch. fellow Inst. of Physics, Academia Sinica, Beijing, 1950-56, rsch. fellow, 1956-65; rsch. fellow Changchun Inst. of Physics, Academia Sinica, Jilin, People's Rep. of China, 1965-83, sr. rsch. fellow, 1983-84; prof. Coll. Materials Sci. and Engring. Shanghai U. (formerly Shanghai U. Sci. Tech.), 1985—; head rsch.div. Inst. of Physics, Academia Sinica, Beijing, 1963-65, Changchun Inst. of Physics, Academica Sinica, 1965-80, vice dir., 1981-83; concurrent prof. U. Sci. & Tech. China, Hefei, Anhui, People's Republic of China, 1978-84, Xiamen U., Fujian, 1985—. Editor-in-chief: Solid State Luminescence, 1975, Chinese Jour. Luminescence, 1980-84; mem. editorial com. Chinese Jour. of Rare Earths, 1983—. Fellow Chinese Soc. of Rare Earths; mem. Am. Phys. Soc., Chinese Phys. Soc., Chinese Soc. Luminescence (vice chmn. 1980-92), Electrochem. Soc. Avocations: Go, bridge, classical music. Home: Tacheng Rd, Ln 440, #27 Apt 502, Jiading, Shanghai 201800, China Office: Shanghai U Jiading Campus, # 20 Chengzhong Rd, Jiading Shanghai 201800, China

XU, SHIZHONG, agricultural educator; b. Benxi, Laoning, China, June 6, 1958; s. Guangzhi and Zhen Fu X.; m. Yuhuan Wang, Jan. 6, 1985; children: Mumu, Nicole. BS, Shengyang Agrl. Coll., China, 1981; MS, N.E. Agrl. Coll., Harbin, China, 1984; PhD, Purdue U., 1989. Elem. sch. tchr. Wanli Elem. Sch., Benxi, Laoning, China, 1976-77; lectr. Northeast Agrl. Coll., Harbin, 1984-86; rsch. scientist Purdue U., West Lafayette, Ind., 1990-91; postdoctoral rsch. assoc. Rutgers U., New Brunswick, N.J., 1991-92, N.C. State U., Raleigh, 1992-95; asst. prof. U. Calif., Riverside, 1995-99, assoc. prof., 1999—. Recipient award USDA, 1995-97, 97-2000, NIH, 1997-2001. Office: U Calif Dept Botany Plant Scis Riverside CA 92521-0001

XU, TINGDONG, materials science scientist; b. Beijing, Jan. 1, 1944; s. Zongyuan Xu and Shuangyu Jing; m. Guohua Li, Aug. 12, 1973; 1 child, Heli. BS, Beijing U. Sci. and Tech., 1968, MS, 1982. Engr. Factory Qinghai Engring. Machine, China, 1968-78; assoc. prof. Wuhan Iron & Steel U., China, 1982-90; vis. prof. MPI fur Metallforschung, Stuttgart, Germany, 1990-93; prof. Ctrl. Iron and Steel Rsch. Inst., Beijing, 1993—. Contbr. articles to profl. jours. Alexander von Humboldt-Stiftung fellow, 1990-93. Mem. N.Y. Acad. Scis. Office: Ctrl Iron & Steel Rsch Inst, No 76 Xueyuan Nanlu, Beijing 100081, China

XU, XIAO JI, nuclear physicist; b. Cao County, Anhui, China, Feb. 16, 1936; s. Ke Qin and Guang Hui (Li) Xu; m. Zi Qun Wang; 1 child, Lian. Grad., Nanjing (China) U., 1965, English Tng. Sch., Chengdou, China, 1983. Technician Inst. Modern Physics, Chinese Acad. Scis., Lanzhou, 1965-76, asst. prof., 1977-87, assoc. prof., 1988-95, prof., 2000—; vis. scholar Oak Ridge (Tenn.) Nat. Lab., 1997-98, Lawrence Berkeley (Calif.) Nat. Lab., 1998—; leader rsch. group Inst. Modern Physics, Lanzhou, 1969-71, 87-96. Contbr. articles to profl. jours. Sr. rep. Staff Rep. Assembly, Lanzhou, 1988-95. Recipient 3rd prizes Nat. Natural Sci. Found. China, Lanzhou, 1979, Chinese Acad. Scis., Lanzhou, 1980, grants Nat. Natural Sci. Found. China, Lanzhou, 1987-97. Mem. Chinese Nuclear Physics Soc. Avocations: table tennis, swimming, hiking, travel, driving. Home: 102 Montelena Ct Mountain View CA 94040-1088 Office: Lawrence Berkeley Nat Lab 1 Cyclotron Rd Bldg 88 Berkeley CA 94720-0001

XU, XIAOMIN, remote sensing educator, lecturer, researcher; b. Jinan, Shandong, China, Jan. 9, 1964; s. Xuemeng and Xiangmei (Guan) X.; m. Qin Wei; 1 child, Ling. BSc, Shandong U., Jinan, China, 1985, MSc, 1988. Asst. Shandong U., 1988-91, lecvtr., 1991-97, adj. prof., 1997—. Contbr. articles to profl. jours.; patentee in field. Mem. SPIE, Nat. Fedn. Remote Sensing. Avocation: the game of Go. Office: Infrared/Remote Sensing Lab, Shandong U, 250100 Jinan, Shandong China

XU, XIN QING, plant biochemist, food scientist, educator; b. Changxing, China, Sept. 2, 1958; s. Lie Min Xu and Feng Yu Zheng; m. Xia Liu, Oct. 19, 1983 (div. Oct. 1995); 1 child, Hui; m. Yin Fong Evangeline Au, Feb. 28, 1996; children: Victoria Kai Lin, Edward Kai Jie. BS in Agronomy, Zhejiang Agrl. U., 1982, MS in Agronomy, 1987; PhD, Monash U., Australia, 1994. Asst. lectr. Zhejiang Agrl. U., 1982-87, lectr., 1987-89; rsch. officer Monash U., 1994; rsch. scientist Food Sci. Australia, 1994—. Contbr. articles to sci. and profl. jours. Mem. Am. Oil Chemists Soc., Australian Inst. of Food Sci. and Tech., Australasian Soc. for Aquatic Botany and Phycology, Australian Oils and Fats Specialists Group, Chinese Soc. of Tea Sci. Home: 17 Townville Ct, Hoppers Crossing VIC 3029, Australia Office: Food Sci Australia, Sneydes Rd, Werribee 3030, Australia

XU, XUE JUN, mathematician, researcher; b. Yixing, Jiang Su, People's Republic of China, Oct. 5, 1968; s. Xing Sheng Xu and Ting Lan Jiang; m. Jing Li. Bachelor, Suzhou U., People's Republic of China, 1990, master, 1993; doctor, Fudan U., Shanghai, People's Republic of China, 1997. Asst. prof. Suzhou U., 1993-94; postdoctoral Chinese Acad. of Scis., Beijing, 1997-99, assoc. prof., 1999—. Contbr. articles to profl. jours. Avocations: chess, music.

XU, XURONG, physicist, researcher; b. Jinan, Shandong, People's Republic of China, Apr. 23, 1922; s. Zhongang and Wangshi (Wang) X.; m. Yuying Liu, Feb. 13, 1950; children: Gang, Yan, Zheng. D degree, P.N. Lebedev Phys. Inst. Scis., Moscow, 1955. Asst., lectr. Beijing U., 1946-51; assoc. prof. Inst. Physics Chinese Acad. Scis., Beijing, 1955-65, prof. dir., 1966-85; dir., hon. prof. Changchun Inst. Physics, Chinese Acad. Scis., Changchun, 1985—; dir., prof. Tianjin Inst. Tech., 1987-96; prof. dir. Inst. Optoelectronics No. Jiaotong U., Beijing, 1996—. Author numerous chpts. in books; contbr. more than 200 articles to profl. jours. including Jour. Luminescence, Jour. Crystal Growth, Comm. Solid State Physics, Reports of Russian Acad. Scis., Optics and Spectroscopics, Jour. Chinese Found. Natural Scis., Chinese Jour. Luminescence, Ke Xue Tong Bao, and Functional Materials, among others. Rep. Tianjin Peoples Congress. Recipient Model Worker award Jilin Province Govt., 1983, Excellent Rschr. award Hotel of Tianjin, 1990, award for remarkable achievements in sci. and tech. Invention and Innovation by Technol. Promotion Info. Sys. UN, Nat. Bur. in China. Mem. Soc. Luminescence China (chmn. 1981-96), Soc. for Info. Display, Chinese Soc. for Physics. Avocations: sports, newspapers, program of focus events or common life in television. Office: No Jiaotong U, Inst Optoelectronics, Beijing 100044, China

XU, YANGGUANG, acoustical engineer, system analyst; b. Nanjing, China, Aug. 23, 1959; s. Zaixing Xu and Molan Yang. BS in Physics, Nanjing U., 1982, MS in Physics, 1984, PhD in Acoustics, 1988; MS in Computer Scis., CUNY, 1997. Prof. acoustical engring. Nanjing U., 1989—; sr. engr. IBM, Boulder, Colo., 1997-98, Bell Comms. Rsch., Piscataway, N.J., 1998—; sr. tech. cons. Lucent Techs., Allentown, Pa., 1997—. Contbr. articles to profl. jours. Recipient 1st award in sci. and tech. China Govt., 1991; NSF grantee, 1993, 95. Mem. Acoustical Soc. Am., Internat. Fedn. Nonlinear Analysts. Home: PO Box 525229 Flushing NY 11352-5229 Office: Bell Comms Rsch 444 Hoes Ln Piscataway NJ 08854-4104

XU, YOU-HENG, physiology educator, cellular biology researcher; b. Shanghai, Feb. 22, 1924; s. Shan-Zheng Xu and Jing-Ying Zhu; m. Guo Zhen Chen, Oct. 1, 1953; 2 children. MD, Hsiang-Ya Med. Sch., Changsha, China, 1950; diploma in human physiology, Shanghai Med. U., 1957. Vis. scientist U. Md., Balt., 1981-82; v.p. Hunan Med. U., Changsha, 1981-83, pres., 1983-87, prof. physiology, 1983—; dir. Rsch. Lab. Blood Physiology, Changsha, 1983-92; referee Chinese Nat. Fund for Natural Scis., Beijing, 1989—. Author: Textbook of Human Physiology, 4th edit., 1996 (Nat. prize 1997); contbr. articles to profl. jours.; editor: Physiology of Autonomic Nervous System, 1995, Physiology of Hematopoiesis, 1997, Bull. of Hunan Med. U., 1985-93; mem. editl. bd. Internat. Jour. Cell Cloning, Dayton, Ohio, 1987-92. Pres. Jiou-San Soc. Hunan Com., Changsha, 1987—; vice chmn. Chinese People's Polit. Consultative Com. in Hunan, Changsha, 1987—. Recipient prize for disting. acad. work Ministry of Pub. Health, Beijing, 1984, 97, citation for 40 yrs. disting. svc. in univ. edn. Chinese Nat. Ednl. Com., 1991. Mem. Chinese Assn. Physiol. Scis. (v.p. 1989-95), Internat. Soc. Exptl. Hematology. Avocations: reading novels, stamp collecting, Chinese calligraphy, classical music. Home: Hunan Med U, PO Box 357, Changsha 410078, China Office: Hunan Med U, Rsch Lab Blood Physiology, Changska Hunan 410078, China

XU, YOUSHENG, mineral physicist; b. Xinfeng, China, May 25, 1967; parents Jiabo Xu and Huixiang Huang; m. Xue Shen, Oct. 27, 1994. PhD, Chinese Acad. Scis., 1996. Guest scientist U. Bayreuth, Germany, 1996—. Mem. Am. Geophys. Union, Mineral. Soc. Am. Office: U Bayreuth, Universitaetstrasse 30, Bayreuth Bayern, Germany 95440

XU, ZHI-BIAO, physician, educator; b. Jiaxing, China, Oct. 31, 1930; s. Chi-Ping Xu and Jing-Wen Chen; m. Zhi-Bai Han, May 1, 1959; children: Jian-Xin, Jian-Min. MD, Beijing Med. Coll., 1954. Resident Tong-Ren Hosp., Beijing, 1954-59; vis. physician, then dep. chief Friendship Hosp., Beijing, 1959-87; vice dir., prof. Beijing Tropical Med. Rsch. Inst., 1987—; cons. Pharmanex, Brisbane, Calif., 1999—. Fellow Royal Soc. Tropical Medicine & Hygiene; mem. Chinese Med. Assn., Chinese Soc. Tropical Medicine and Parasitology. Avocation: Chinese chess. Office: Beijing Trop Med Rsch Inst, 94# Yong An Rd, Beijing China

XU, ZHIHONG, soil scientist; b. Nanchang, Jiangxi, People's Republic of China, May 19, 1960; arrived in Australia, 1986; s. Zheng-Wen X. and Su-Juan Wang; m. Xiao-Qi Zhao, Feb. 22, 1988; children: Jane, Geoffrey. BSc in Chemistry, Jiangxi Normal U., Nanchang, 1982; MSc in Soil Sci., Chinese Acad. Scis., Nanjing, 1984; PhD in Environ. Sci., Griffith U., Brisbane, Australia, 1991. Rsch. assoc. Chinese Acad. Scis., Nanjing, 1985-86; sr. rsch. officer South Australian Dept. Agr., Adelaide, 1990-93; rsch. scientist Queensland Dept. Primary Industries, Gympie, 1993-96, sr. rsch. scientist, 1996—. Contbr. articles to profl. jours. Acta Pedologica Sinica, Fertilizer Rsch., Plant and Soil, and Australian Jour. Soil Rsch. Recipient univ. gold medallist Jiangxi Normal U., 1981, scholarship Chinese Acad. Scis., 1982, Griffith U., 1986. Mem. Internat. Soil Sci. Soc., Australian Soc. Soil Sci., Australian Soil and Plant Analysis Coun. Avocations: basketball, table tennis, swimming, running, tennis. Office: Queensland Forestry Rsch, MS 483 Fraser Rd, Gympie QLD 4570, Australia

XU, ZHIXIANG, electronic engineering educator, consultant; b. Haining, Zhejiang, China, Dec. 30, 1937; s. Baokui and Yubao (Guo) X.; m. Xinzhen Liu, Jan. 22, 1963; children: Wenbaio, Wenfang. BS, East China U. Tech., Shanghai, 1961; MS, Shanghai Jiao Tong U., 1963. Lectr. Shanghai U. Tech., 1963-72; assoc. prof. Shanghai U. Sci. and Tech., 1972-83; vis. prof. U. Pitts., 1983-85; prof. Shanghai U. Sci. and Tech., 1986-94; prof. Shanghai U., 1994—, dir. electronic engring. divsn., 1994—; vis. prof. Nanyang Technol. U., Singapore, 1990, Honk Kong U. Poly., 1991, Hong Kong U., 1992, Yamaguchi (Japan) U., 1995. Author: Principles of Color TV IC, 1983 (award of excellent book 1987), Theory of Digital Television, 1996; editor TV Engring., 1978-99. Recipient award of Sci. of China, 1987, award of Guang Hua Sci., 1995, award of sci. China Acad. Inst., 1996. Fellow Shanghai Assn. Image and Graphics, Shanghai Assn. TV and Movies; mem. IEEE (sr.). Avocations: orchestra conducting, music. E-mail: xuzxiang@online.sh.cn. Home: Rm 1904 Lane 600 # 8, Liu-Zhou Rd, 200233 Shanghai China Office: Shanghai U (Jiading Campus), 20 Cheng Zhong Rd, Jiading, 201800 Shanghai China

XU, ZHONG, mechanical engineering educator; b. Shanghai, Sept. 15, 1937; s. Yutong and Shifang (Chen) X.; m. Caifen Ma, Aug. 25, 1963; 1 child, Hao. B of Engring., Jiaotong U., Xi'an, Shaanxi, China, 1959. Lectr. Xi'an Jiaotong U., 1959-82, assoc. prof. dept. power machinery engring., 1982-90, dep. dir. Fluid Machinery Lab., 1981-90, prof. dept. power machinery engring., 1990—, dir. Nat. Lab. Fluid Machinery, 1990-99; chair dept. fluid engring. Nat. Lab. Fluid Machinery, 1994-99; dir. Rsch. Inst. Gen. & Chem. Engring. Machinery, 1994-2000; vis. scholar dept. chem. engring. U. Del., Newark, 1984-86; advisor in tech. Shaanxi Blower Factory, Xi'an, 1992—. Author: Theory of Centrifugal Compressor (in Chinese), 1980, 90; contbr. articles to profl. jours. Dep., Nat. Congress of the Chinese Zhigong Party, Beijing, 1992, 97; mem. The Chinese People's Polit. Consultative Conf. Xi'an City 9th and 10th Com., 1996—, 9th com., 1998—; chmn. Xi'an City Com. Chinese Zhigong Party, 1996—. Recipient award for achievements in sci. rsch. Com. of Nat. Edn., Beijing, 1990, 92, honor in outstanding contbn. to higher edn. The State Coun., Beijing, 1992, Outstanding Publication award Ministry of Mech. Ind., others. Fellow Chinese Inst. Engring. Thermophysics (mem. engring. thermodynamics and energy com.), Shaanxi Inst. Engring. Thermophysics (mem. coun. 1989—), Chinese Mech. Engring. Soc. (editor Fan Tech. 1989—); mem. ASME. Avocations: calligraphy, classical literature, lisening to music, playing chess. Office: Xi'an Jiaotong U, Dept Power Machinery Engrs, Xi'an 710049, China

XU, ZHONG LING, mathematician, educator; b. Beijing, Mar. 6, 1937; came to U.S., 1984, naturalized; s. Chang L. and Ying (Yu) X.; m. Ling Wang, June 23, 1963; children: Nan, Rong. MS, U. Mass., 1987, PhD, 1990. Asst. prof. Acad. Scis. China, Beijing, 1978-84; assoc. prof. U. Tex. Pan Am., Brownsville, 1990-92; assoc. prof. U. Tex., Brownsville, 1992-99, prof., 1999—. Mem. AIAA, IEEE Soc. Control and Decision, Am. Math. Soc., Soc. Indsl. and Applied Maths. Achievements include research in Hoo control for attitude of spacecraft, control of flexible smart structures and robotic control by fuzz logic. Avocations: oil painting, water color, calligraphy. Office: U Tex 80 Fort Brown St Brownsville TX 78520-4956

XUAN, LIU, olympic athlete; b. Changsha, China, Mar. 12, 1979. Mem. men's gymnastics team China; winner team bronze World Championship, 1997, 99; winner individual all-around gold Asian Games, 1998, winner team gold, 1998; winner gold medal in beam Olympics, Sydney, Australia, 2000. Office: Chinese Gymnastics Assn, 9 Tiyuguan Rd, 100 763 Beijing China*

XUE, HUACHENG, information systems educator; b. Shijiajhuang, Hebei, China, Aug. 30; s. Dhangkun Xue and Xiying Chen; m. Manlin Yang, May 1, 1965; children: Hang, Ling. BS, N.W. Poly. U., Xian, China, 1956; MS, Tsingua U., Beijing, 1960. Lectr., head industry electronics Tsinghua U., 1960-70, lectr., assoc. prof., dir. automation instrument shop, 1970-80, assoc. prof., head MIS tchr. group econ. mgmt. dept., 1980-85; assoc. prof. Fudan U., Shanghai, 1985-86, prof., chair dept. mgmt. sci., 1987—; vis. prof. Auburn (Ala.) U., 1986-87; rschr. in field; expert Info. Decision Group, Beijing, 1992-96. Author: Management Information Systems, 1988, 3d edit., 1999 (state award 1996); contbr. articles to profl. jours. Office: Fudan U, Dept Mgmt Sci, 200433 Shanghai China

XUE, JUE, management science educator, consultant; b. Suzhou, Jiangsu, China, Apr. 1958; m. Xiaonong Liu; children: Lester, Gilbert. MSc, Acad. Sinica, China, 1985; MS, Carnegie Mellon U., 1987, PhD, 1991. Asst. prof. Clark U., Worcester, Mass., 1991-96; asst. prof. mgmt. sci. City U. Hong Kong, Kowloon, 1996-98, assoc. prof., 1998; cons. SCS, IGS, IBM, 1998-2000. Contbg. author: Ency. of Combinatorial Optimization, 1998, Handbook of Optimization, 1998; contbr. articles to sci. jours., including SIAM, Jour. Networks, Algorithmica. Mem. INFORMS. Fax: 240-358-2347. Home: 6505 Tipperary Ct Clarksville MD 21029-1547 Office: City U Hong Kong Dept Mgmt, Tat Chee Ave, Kowloon HK, China

XUE, LAN, engineering educator; b. Beijing, China, June 25, 1959; s. Futang and Jingmei (Yu) X.; m. Xiaoping Li, Apr. 3, 1985; 1 child, Dyland Mooching. BSME, Changchun Inst. Optics, 1982; MS in Tech. Systems Mgmt., SUNY, Stony Brook, 1986, MS in Policy and Mgmt., 1987; PhD in Engring. and Pub. Policy, Carnegie Mellon U., 1991. Instr., researcher Changchun (People's Republic of China) Inst. Optics, 1982-85; rsch. and teaching asst. SUNY, Stony Brook, 1985-87, Carnegie Mellon U., Pitts., 1987-91; asst. prof. George Washington U., Washington, 1991—; assoc. prof., prof., Devel. Rsch. Acad. 21st Century Tsinghua U., Beijing, 1996—, asst. dir., exec. dep. dir., 1996—; cons. Capital Iron & Steel Co., Beijing, 1993, Tangshan (China) Iron & Steel Co., 1993, The World Bank, 1994, NIST, 1994-95, Govt. of Bolivia, 1997; lectr. in field. Contbr. articles to profl. jours. Dilthy fellow George Washington U., 1993; recipient Pride award George Washington U., 1995, Stephen Lee award Carnegie Mellon U., 1991, Short Term Enrichment Program award AAAS, 1989, Chinese Econ. Rsch. fellowship Washington Ctr. for China Studies, 1996. Mem. IEEE Soc. on Engring. Mgmt., Chinese Econ. Soc., Chinese Profl. Forum (pres. 1993-94), Tech. Transfer Soc. (bd. dirs. 1994-95), Inst. Mgmt. Sci., Am. Soc. for Engring. Edn., Chinese Assn. for Sci. and Tech. (pres. Washington chpt. 1995-96). Avocations: reading, table tennis, tai-chi, travel. Office: Tsinghua U, Devel Rsch Acad, 100084 Beijing China

XUE, MIAO, dentistry educator, biomaterial scientist; b. Shanghai, China, June 24, 1929; s. Kai-Chang and Gui-zhen (Li) X.; m. Zong-Lan Shen, June 15, 1949; children: Jing-Fang, Jie-Fang. DDS, Shangai Med. U. #2, Peoples Republic China, 1953. Asst. prof. prosthetic dentistry sci. Shanghai Med. U. # 2, 1953-60; lectr., asst. prof. dental material rsch. lab. Shanghai Med. U. # 2, 1960-82, vice head, assoc. prof., 1982-87; vice head, assoc. prof. biomaterial rsch. lab. Shanghai Med. U. # 2, 1982-87; head, prof. dept. dental material sci. Shanghai Med. U. # 2, 1987-91, head, prof. dental material and biomaterial rsch. labs., 1988-91; sr. researcher Nat. Testing Ctr. for Med. Polymer, Shangdong, 1988-95; dir. Shanghai Biomaterial Rsch. & Testing Ctr., 1989—; hon. dir. Biomaterial Inst. of Jiamushi U., 1997—; dir. biomaterial lab. of key lab. Shanghai U., 1998—. Author: (with others) Science of Applied Dental Material, 1963, Material Science of Prosthetic Dentistry, 1987; editor: China Yearbook of Dentistry, 1984—; chief editor Jour. of Dental Materials and Devices, 1991—. Recipient Cert. of Merit medal China Ministry Pub. Health, 1960, Merit cert. Shanghai Sci. and Tech. Commn., 1984, 90, 92, State Edn. Commn., China, 1988, 92, 96, China Ministry Pub. Health, 1988, 95, Nat. Govt. Spl. Subsidy, 1992—, Shanghai Advanced Worker award, 1995, award Title Nat. Advanced Sci. & Tech. Rsch. of China, 1996. Mem. ASTM, China Dental Material Soc. (bd. dirs.), China Maxillo-facial Implant Soc. (bd. dirs.), China Biomaterial Com. (bd. vice dirs.), Nat. Med. Standard Technical Com. China, China Med. Devices Examination Com., Shanghai Biomaterial and Product Adminstrn. (bd. dirs.), Shanghai Biomaterial Com. (chief), China Shape Memory Alloy Com. (com. mem.), Internat. Biog. Inst. (hon. mem. adv. coun., Cert. Merit 1994), Am. Biog. Inst. (hon. mem. rsch. bd. advisors, 20th Century Achievement award 1994). Office: Shanghai Biomaterial Rsch Ctr, 716 Xie Tu Rd, Shanghai 200023, China

XUE, QI-MING, neurologist, educator, researcher; b. Zhenjiang, China, Dec. 28, 1928; s. Jie-san Hsueh and Yong-mei Ding; m. Zhong-xuan Wu, Jan. 31, 1959; 1 child, Victor. MD, Nat. Chekiang U., 1953. Asst. res., then vis. physician Beijing Med. Coll., China, 1953-60; from vis. physician to prof. Beijing Friendship Hosp., 1960—, Capital U. Med. Scis., 1960—. Author: Handbook of Chemical Industrial Toxicology, 1959, 2d edit., 1965, Geneteical Metabolic Diseases of the Nervous System, 1988; editor: Lectures on Neurochemistry, 1962, Physiological & Pathological Chemistry of the Nervous System, 1978, 2d edit., 1993. Mem. Internat. Soc. Devel. Neuroscience, Internat. Brain Rsch. Orgn., Chinese Soc. Neurochemistry, Beijing Neurosci. Soc., Asian-Pacific Soc. Neurochemistry, Internat. Soc. Neurochem. Avocations: classical music, collecting stamps. Home: 95 Yong-an Rd New Apt 1-3-1, 100050 Beijing China Office: Beijing Friendship Hosp Dept Neurology, 95 Yong-an Rd, 100050 Beijing China

XUE, SANG, Olympic athlete; b. Tianjin, China, Oct. 7, 1984. Winner World Cup title, 1999. Office: Swimming Assn People's Rep China, 9 Ti Yuguan Rd, Beijing 100061, China*

XUE, WEIMIN, mathematics educator, researcher; b. Jianning, Fujian, China, July 20, 1957; s. Jinmei Xue and Zhaoxian Bian; children: Jitian, Jixuan. Diploma, Fujian Normal U., Fuzhou, China, 1979; MS, U. Iowa, 1985, PhD, 1988. Assoc. prof. math. Fujian Normal U., 1990-94, prof., 1994—; vis. asst. prof. U. Maine, Orono, 1989, U. Iowa, Iowa City, fall 1992, U. Iowa, 1998. Author: Rings with Morita Duality, 1992; contbr. articles to Proc. Am. Math. Soc., Bull. Australian Math. Soc., Chinese Ann. Math., Jour. Algebra, Jour. Pure Applied Algebra, Comm. Algebra, Algebra Colloq., Can. Math. Bull., Chinese Sci. Bull, Sci. in China. Mem. Am. Math. Soc., Chinese Math. Soc. Office: Fujian Normal U, Dept Math, Fuzhou, Fujian 350007, China

XUE, YONGBIAO, plant molecular biologist; b. Taiyuan, Shanxi, China, Jan. 2, 1963; s. Shouzhoung Xue and Lingxiang Yin; m. Jungqing Wang,

Jan. 24, 1987; 1 child, Bo. BS, Lanzhou (China) U., 1983; MS, Inst. Devel. Biology, Beijing, China, 1986; PhD, U. East Anglia, Norwich, Eng., 1989. Rsch. asst. Inst. Devel. Biology Acad. Sinica, Beijing, 1986-87; postdoctoral rsch. fellow Oxford U. and John Innes Ctr., Oxford and Norwich, Eng., 1990-95; Gatsby rsch. scientist John Innes Ctr., Norwich, 1995—; prof. Inst. Devel. Biology Acad. Sinica, Beijing, 1995—, dir. lab. plant genetics and devel. Inst. Devel. Biology, 1995. Editor: Plant Reproductive Genetics, 1995; contbr. articles to sci. jours. including Plant Cell, Plant Jour., Plant Molecular Biology. K. C. Wong fellow K. C. Wong Edn. Found., Hong Kong, 1995, 96. Mem. Gentical Soc. Gt. Britain, Soc. Exptl. Biology. Avocations: playing soccer, running, collecting stamps. Office: Acad Sinica Inst Devel Biol, Zhongguangcun, Beijing 100080, China

XUE, YUSHENG, engineering educator; b. Wuxi, China, Feb. 7, 1941; s. Mingjian and Fuqian (Sun) X.; m. Zhengjue Pan, Aug. 4, 1970; children: Feng, Ying. BS, Shandong Inst. Tech., 1963; MS, Electric Power Rsch. Inst., China, 1981; PhD, U. Liege, 1987. Tech. Elec. Power Rsch. Inst., 1963-70; engr. Second Design Inst., China, 1970-78; dep. dir. Nanjing Automation Rsch. Inst., China, 1981-85, chief engr., 1987—; vis. researcher Hiroshima U., Japan, 1991; guest prof. Shanghai Jiaotong U., China, 1990—, Zhejiang U., China, 1992—, Shangdong U. Tech., China, 1994—, Wuhan U. Hydraulic, China, 1995—, Hohai U., China, 1996—; editor-in-chief: Automation of Electric Power Systems, 1999—. Author: Direct Methods for Power System Stability Assessment, 1995; contbr. articles to profl. jours. Recipient prize Nat. Sci. Com., Beijing, 1977, Min. Energy, 1991, Min. Elec. Power, 1994, Nat. Sci. 1st prize, 1996. Mem. Chinese Soc. Elec. Engring. (com. 1988—), Internat. Fedn. Automatic Control (com. 1990—), N.Y. Acad. Sci., Chinese Acad. Engring. Office: NARI, PO Box 323, 210003 Nanjing China

XUE, ZHONG TIAN, plant molecular biologist, educator; b. Wusi, Jiangsu, China, May 21, 1942; s. Gui Fang Xue and Wei Ging Wu; m. Shi-Gui Yu, Feb. 4, 1968; children: Wei-Chun, Wei-Feng. Diploma in biochemistry, Fudan U., Shanghai, China, 1965. Rsch. asst. Shanghai Inst. Plant Physiology, 1966-78, rsch. assoc., 1978-80; vis. scholar Roswell Park Meml. Inst., Buffalo, N.Y., 1980, Calif. Inst. Tech., Pasadena, 1980-81; assoc. prof. plant molecular biology Shanghai Inst. Plant Physiology, 1985—; vis. prof. dept. plant physiology and molecular biology Aarhus (Denmark) U., 1988; rsch. scientist Ctr. Plant Biotechnology, Aarhus, 1988-91; rsch. scientist, dept. plant biochemistry Lund (Sweden) U., 1991-95; rsch. scientist, dept. hort. sci. Swedish U. Agr. Sci., Alnarp, 1996—; group leader Molecular Genetics Lab., Shanghai Inst. Plant Physiology, 1972-79, 81-87; mem. Nat. Del. Scientists, Kyoto, Japan, 1983, U.S., 1984. Contbr. rsch. articles to scientific jours., including Scientia Sinica, Nuc. Acids Rsch., and Plant Molecular Biology. Recipient 1st award rsch. achievement Academia Sinica, 1980, 2d award 3d Nat. Natural Sci. Prizes, 1988, 2d award Sci. and Tech. Prizes, 1988. Mem. Phytochemistry Soc. Europea, Swedish Assn. Biochem. and Molecular Biology. Achievements include notable findings of (1) molecular evidence for the progenitor of cultivated soybean (Glycine max), (2) oxygen regulation of uricase and sucrose synthase in soybean callus tissue exerted at the mRNA level, (3) new genes isolated from different plant species. Home: Sångarevägen 10C, S-224-71 Lund Sweden Office: Swedish U Agr Sci, Dept Crop Sci Box 55, S-230 53 Alnarp Sweden

XUE-QIN, CAO, civil engineering educator; b. Shanghai, China, May 29, 1933; s. Cao and Zhang (Cui-e) Xing-Sheng; m. Xu Shi-Min, Oct. 2, 1959; three children. BS, Tong-Ji U., 1953, MS, 1966. Lectr. Tong-Ji U., Shanghai, 1956-78; assoc. prof. Shanghai Inst. Railway Tech., 1979-85; prof. Shangai Tie-Dao U., 1986—. Author: Dynamic Analysis of Bridge Structure, 1987, Lateral Vibration of Railway Truss Bridge, 1991. Avocation: Chinese opera. Home: No 551 Rm 4 Zhang-Wu Rd, 200092 Shanghai China Office: Dept Civil Engring, 450 Zhen-Nan Rd, 200331 Shanghai China

XUEXIAN, QIAN, cardiovascular physician; b. Shanghai, Jan. 11, 1934; m. Zhou Qinyun, May 21, 1936; children: Yunhang, Yujia. Grad., 4rh Mil. Med. U., Xian, China. Asst. 1st Affiliated Hosp., Four Mil. Med. U., Xian, 1956-74, vis. physician, lectr., 1974-84, vice chief physician, vice prof., 1984-88, chief physician, prof., 1988-89; chief physician, prof., dept. cardiology 2d Affiliated Hosp., 1st. Mil. Md. U., Guangzhou, China, 1989-90, doctorial dir., chief dept. cardiology, 1990-97, chief dept. internal medicine, 1997—. Editor-in-chief: Modern Coronary Care in Medicine, 1994—, Modern Cardiology, 1992-99; editor: Modern Diagnosis and Treatment of Heart Failure, Modern Handbook of Clinical Laboratory Diagnosis, Modern Diagnosis of Clinical Disease, Modern Clinical Medicine Dictionary, Modern Handbook of Diagnoses and Treatment of Internal Medicine, Modern Medicine Roution of Diagnosis and Treatment; contbr. articles to profl. jours., include Chinese Med. Jour., Chinese Jour. Interventional Cardiology, South China Jour. Cardiology, Chinese Jour. Internal Medicine, Chinese Jour. Hypertension. Mem. Soc. Cardiovascular Medicine of PLA (People Liberation Army), Rsch. Soc. Chinese Interventional Cardiology, CMA (Chinese Med. Assn.) Soc. Cardiovascular Medicine of Guangdong. Avocations: reading, walking, travel, television, chess. Office: Zhujiang Hosp 1st Mil Med U, 253 Industry Rd, Guangzhou 510282, China

XUN, YULONG, optics scientist; b. Nanping, Fujian, China, July 11, 1939; s. Menghan and Ze (Wang) X.; m. Juemin Wu, Mar. 6, 1970; children: Xiaodong, Shangpei. Student, Peking U., 1963; postgrad., Changchuan Inst. Optics/Mechs., China, 1966. Mem. staff CIOFM, Changchun, 1966-77; dep. dir. remote sensing divsn. Anhui Inst. Optics, Hefei, China, 1978-86, assoc. prof., dir. remote sensing divsn., 1986-91, prof., dir. remote sensing divsn., 1991—; vis. scholar U. Ariz., Tucson, 1983-85. Chief editor: Fundamental Experiments and Applications of Remote Sensing, 1991; editor: Applicable System of Airborne Remote Sensing at High Altitude, 1990; mem. editl. bd. Remote Sensing Tech. and Applications, 1986—. Recipient Top Grade award of Sci. and Tech. Progress, Academia Sinica, 1993, 2d Grade awards, 1987, 89, 91, 92, 95, Guanghua Sci. Found. award 3d degree, 1996; named Outstanding Scientist, Govt. of Anhui Province, 1988. Mem. Optical Soc. China, Oceanic Remote Sensing Soc. China (mem. coun.), Space Aviation Soc. China (vice chmn. remote sensing com.). Achievements include leadership in design and development of the first airborne spectroradiometer, laser fluorescent ridar and pattern recognition technique for detecting chemical vapor in China. Office: AIOFM Remote Sensing Divsn, PO Box 1125, 230031 Hefei China

YAACOBI, GAD, former Israeli ambassador; b. Moshav Kfar Vitkin, Israel, Jan. 18, 1935; s. Alexander and Sara Y.; m. Nela Yaacobi; 3 children. Grad. in Econs. and Polit. Sci., Tel Aviv U. Asst. to min. agr., head agrl. and settlement planning and devel. ctr. Govt. of Israel, 1960-66, dep. min. transport, 1971-74, min. transport, 1974-77, min. econs. and planning, 1984-88, min. comm., 1987-90, mem. Inner Cabinet, 1990; amb. to UN Govt. of Israel, N.Y.C., 1992-96; M.P. Knesset, 1969-92; mem. Moshavim Movement, 1960-67; chair econ. coun. Histadrut, Labor Union, Rafi Faction; mem. parliamentary fin. com. Knesset, 1969-70, mem. parliamentary def. and fgn. affairs com., 1974; chmn. bd. dirs. Israel Elec. Corp., 1996. Author: The Power of Quality, 1971, The Freedom to Choose, 1975, The Government, 1980, A Call for Change, 1983, On the Razor's Edge, 1990, (poems) Grace of Time, 1991, The New-York Diary, 1997, A Place Near-by, 1998; contbr. articles to profl. jours. Mem. Israel Authors Assn. Avocations: theatre, reading, writing. Home: 6 Hadassa St, Tel Aviv Israel

YAALON, DAN HARDY, soil scientist; b. Uh.Hradiste, Czechoslovakia, May 11, 1924; married 1952; 2 children. BSc, Royal Agrl. U., Copenhagen, 1947; PhD in Soil Sci., Hebrew U., Jerusalem, 1954; fellow, Rothamsted Exptl. Sta., Harpenden, Eng., 1954-55; UNESCO fellow in Soil Salinity, Hydroingeo Inst., Tashkent, Russia, 1962. Sr. lectr. Inst. Eart Scis. Hebrew U., Jerusalem, Israel, 1961-69, assoc. prof., 1970-77, prof. pedology, 1978-92, prof. emeritus, 1993—; vis. lectr. U. Melbourne, Australia, 1968, Johns Hopkins U., Balt., 1968-69; assoc. prof. Ben Gurion U. of the Negev, Beersheba, 1974-76; vis. prof. U. Ariz., 1977, U. Calif., Davis, 1987, U. Ghent, Belgium, 1993; vis. fellow Australian Nat. U., Canberra, 1981, U. Cambridge, Eng., 1992. Mem. editl. bd. Geoderma, 1967—, Catena, 1973-91, Palaeo-geography, -climatology, -ecology, 1973-98, Soil Sci., 1975—; co-editor: Catena, 1991—; contbr. over 130 articles to profl. jours. and numerous revs.; edited 7 books. Recipient George Sarton medal U. Ghent, 2000. Mem. Internat. Soc. Soil Sci., Israel Soil Sci. Soc. (past pres. 1980), Israel Geol. Soc. (past pres. 1959), Israel Pleistocene Assn. (past pres. 1976-83), Russian Soil Sci. Soc. (Dokuchaev Soil Sci. Medal). Office: Hebrew U Jerusalem, Givat Ram Campus, IL-91904 Jerusalem Israel

YABLOKOV, ALEXEY VLADYMIROVICH, biologist; b. Moscow, Russia, Oct. 3, 1933; s. Vladymir Sergeevich Yablokov and Tatyana Georgievna Sarycheva; m. Eleonora Dmitrievna Bakulina, Mar. 11, 1954 (dec. Nov. 1987); 1 child, Dmitryi; m. Dilbar Nikolaevna Klado, Feb. 10, 1990; 1 child, Sergey. MSc, Moscow State U., 1956; D in Biology, Inst. Animal Morphology, Moscow, 1959; DSc, USSR Acad. Sci., Novosibirsk, 1965; Dr. hon. causa, Free U., Brussels, 1991. Jr. scientific worker Inst. Animal Morphology, Moscow, 1956-65; sr. scientific worker Inst. Devel. Biology, Moscow, 1966-69, head lab., 1969-89; vice chair commn. ecology USSR Parliament, Moscow, 1989-91; spl. advisor to pres. Moscow, 1991-93; chair interagy. commn. environ. security Nat. Security Coun., Moscow, 1993-97; pres. Ctr. Russian Environ. Policy, Moscow, 1993—. Author: Beluga, 1964, 2d edit., 1969, Variability of Mammals, 1966, 2d edit., 1974, Whales and Dolphins, 1972, 2d edit., 1974, Phenetics, 1980, 3d edit., 1986, Population Biology, 1986, 2d edit., 1987, Level of Nature Protection, 1982, Problems/Prospect of Living Resources Conservation, 1988, 2d edit., 1991, Nuclear Mythology, 1996, 2d edit., 1997, others. Chair Youth Club Moscow Zoo., 1948-49, youth sect. All Russian Union Protection Nature, 1950-52, Ichthyological Commn. USSR Min. Fisheries, 1986-87; vice chair ecol. coun. Russian Parliament, 1996—. Recipient A.N. Severtzov award USSR Acad. Sci., 1976, WASA Environ. prize, Sweden, 1994, A. Karpinsky prize, Germany, 1996, Bask medal Royal Geog. Soc. Gt. Britain, 1996, Duke Edinburgh Conservation medal, 2000; Pew scholar, 1993-96. Mem. Am. Acad. Art Sci. (hon.), Russian Acad. Sci. (corr.), Russian Coun. Marine Mammals (vice chair 1996—), Internat. Socio-Ecol. Union (co-chair), Internat. Union Conservation Nature (Roll of Honor 1986). Avocations: carpentry, fishing. Office: Ctr Russian Environ Policy, Valilov Str 26, 117808 Moscow Russia

YABLONSKY, GRYGIORIY SEMJONOVICH, chemistry educator; b. Essentiky, Stavropol, USSR, Sept. 7, 1940; came to U.S., 1995; s. Semen Yakovlevich Yablonsky and Sophia L'vovna (Lazareva) Krichevskaya; m. Ekaterina Michailovna Platonova. BS in Chemistry, Kiev (Ukraine) Poly. Inst., 1962; PhD in Phys. Chemistry, Boreskov Inst. Catalysis, Novosibirsk, Russia, 1971, DSc in Phys. Chemistry, Kinetics, 1989. Chem. engr. Kiev Chem. Factory, 1962-64; postgrad. jr. rsch. assoc. Boreskov Inst. Catalysis, 1964-86, sr. rsch. assoc., 1986-91; chief lab., dep. dir. Tuvinian Tech. Inst., Kyzyl, USSR, 1986-91; prof. chem. engring. Nat. Tech. U., Kiev, 1991-95; v.p. Internat. Solomon U., Kiev, 1992-94; prof. chem. engring. Washington U., St. Louis, 1995—. Co-author: (with V. Bykov) Kinetic Models of Catalytic Reactions, 1991, (with A. Gorban) Skizzes on Chemical Relaxation, 1987, (with J. Gleaves) Tap-2: Interrogative Kinetics Approach, 1997. Bd. dirs. Soviet Union Scientist, Moscow, 1988-91, Russian Union Scientists, Moscow, 1991-92. Recipient Silver medal Exhbn. Nat. Econ. Acheivements of USSR, 1971, diploma Mendelejev's Chem. Soc., 1977, 79. Mem. AAAS, AAUP, AIChE. Achievements include development of theory of complex kinetic behavior of heterogeneous catalytic reactions; theory of pulse-response experiment in heterogeneous catalysis. Avocations: literature, history and methodology of science. Office: Washington U Dept Chem Engring Campus Box 1198 1 Brookings Dr Saint Louis MO 63130-4862

YABUKI, NOBUYOSHI, civil engineering educator; b. Tokyo, July 21, 1959; s. Kiyonobu and Kiyo (Okada) Y.; m. Tomoko Umiji, Mar. 15, 1986; children: Taro, Jiro. BE, U. Tokyo, 1982; MS, Stanford U., 1989, PhD, 1992. Registered profl. engr., Calif. Civil engr. Electric Power Devel. Co., Ltd., Tokyo, 1982-88, dep. mgr., 1992-99; assoc. prof. dept. civil engring. and arch. Muroran Inst. Tech., Muroran-shi, Japan, 1999—. Contbr. articles to profl. jours. Fulbright scholar, 1988. Mem. IEEE, ASCE, Am. Assn. for Artificial Intelligence, Japan Soc. Civil Engrs., Assn. for Computing Machinery, Electric Power Civil Engrs. Assn. Avocations: astronomy, keyboards, music, reading, photography. Office: Muroran Inst Tech, 27-1 Mizumoto-cho, Muroran-shi 050 8585, Japan

YABUNAKA, SATORU, educator; b. Sakai, Japan, Dec. 29, 1939; s. Shigeru and Hamako (Sakanaka) Y.; m. Yoshiko Tsuda, Mar. 26, 1967; children: Kazushige, Chika, Yoshinori. BA, Osaka U. Fgn. Studies, 1961. Asst. dir. SEIDO Lang. Inst., Ashiya, Japan, 1964-67; instr. Kyoto (Japan) Sangyo U., 1967-71, asst. prof., 1971-80, prof., 1980—; dir. student dept. Cen. Libr., lifelong edn., placement, extension lead, dir. adminstrn., mng. dir. of bd. dirs.1989-99; mem. com. Lic. Exam. Comml. English C. of C. and Industry, Tokyo, 1972—; lectr., cons. NHK Culture Ctr., Osaka/Kyoto, 1980—, Kyoto U., 1999—, Kobe City U. of Fgn. Studies, 1999—; cons. in field. Author: El Español de 20 Naciones, 2 vols., 1976, 77, La Presencia de la Madre Patria en Iberoamèrica, 1986; translator Fiestas, 1986, Venceslau de Morais; Notícias do Exílio Nipónico, 1993. Mem. com. Placement Office Kyoto City Hall, 1994-97. Mem. Hispanic Acad. Japan (bd. dirs. 1980-84, 86-94, auditor 1996-2000), Acad. Portugal and Brazil, Osaka Internat. Sci. Club. Roman Catholic. Avocations: pictorial art, music, poetry, travel. Home: 65-3 Yodonohara-cho, Takatsuki shi 569-0001, Japan Office: kyoto Sangyo U, Kamigamo Motoyama Kita-Ku, Kyoto shi 603 8555, Japan

YABUNO, HIROSHI, physicist; b. Sinagawa, Tokyo, Japan, Dec. 1, 1961; s. Jyun-Zo and Kuniko (Nishimura) Y. Rschr. Toshiba, Yokohama, Japan, 1986-87, Inst. Phys. and Chem. Rsch., Saitama, Japan, 1990-92; assoc. prof. U. Tsukuba, Ibaraki, Japan, 1992—. Contbr. articles to profl. jours. Mem. ASME, Japanese Soc. Mech. Engrs. Avocations: golf, tennis, baseball. Office: U Tsukuba Inst Engr Mech, Tenno-dai 1-1-1, Tsukuba-Science City 305-8573, Japan

YACKLE, ALBERT REUSTLE, aeronautical engineer; b. Willow Grove, Pa., May 13, 1922; s. Albert J. and Marion D. (Reustle) Y.; m. Ruth E. Everett, Sept. 18, 1948; children: Linda McCann, Tom, Brad. BS in Mech. Engring. Aeronautical Option, Pa. State U., 1943. Registered profl engr., Calif. Structures engr. Ea. Aircraft, 1944; structures engr. Kellett Aircraft Corp., 1946-48, chief structures engr., 1950-60; structures engr. Chase Aircraft, 1948-50; advanced design and program mgr. Lockheed Aircraft Corp., 1960-91; ret., 1991; cons. Huntington Med. Rsch. Inst., Pasadena, Calif., 1991-96. Contbr. tech. papers to profl. jours. Lt. (j.g.) USN, 1944-46. Recipient Lockheed Spl. Achievement awards, 1976, 77, 79, 87; inducted into H.S. Hall of Fame, 1996. Fellow (assoc.) AIAA; mem. Am. Helicopter Soc. Achievements include 2 patents in rigid rotor helicopters. Home: 5105 Quakertown Ave Woodland Hills CA 91364-3538

YACOUT, MAGED MAHMOUD, physiologist, educator, researcher; b. Cairo, Egypt, May 7, 1946; s. Fahmy Mahmoud and Bahera Mahmoud (El-Shayeb) Y. MB BCh, Ain Shams U., Cairo, 1969; DMSc, Al-Azhar U., Cairo, 1973, MD in Physiology, 1976. Demonstrator dept. physiology Faculty of Medicine, Al Azhar U., 1971-74, asst. lectr., 1974-76, lectr., 1976-80; asst. prof. Faculty of Medicine, Zagazig (Egypt) U., 1980-84, prof., head dept. physiology, 1984—; cons. rschr. Human Reprodn. Rsch. unit Internat. Islamic Ctr. for Population Studies and Rsch., Cairo, 1976-81; guest mem. Intrauterine Contraception Core Adv. Com. in U.S., IFRP, Washington, 1979; chmn. organizing com., sec.-gen. Zagazig U. Ann. Conf. on Med. Physiology, 1988-92; mem. scientific permanent com. for evaluation and promotion of physiologist Supreme Coun. of Egyptian Univs., 1985—. Author: Principles of Human Physiology, 5 vols., 6 edits., 1985-95; editor-in-chief Zagazig Jour. Med. Physiology, 1991—; contbr. chpts. to books, articles to profl. jours. WHO grantee, 1974. Mem. Egyptian Soc. for Physiol. Scis., Egyptian Soc. for Basic Med. Scis., Zagazig Clin. Med. Soc. Mem. Nat. Democratic Party. Moslem. Avocations: poetry, gardening and indoor plant care, flower arranging. Office: Dept Physiology, Zagazig U Faculty Medicine, Zagazig Egypt

YADAV, AVINASH, engineer, business educator; b. Banares, India, Nov. 30, 1962; s. Kris and Prabha Yadav; m. Sushma Singh, Jan. 21, 1991; 1 child, Neel. BS, Washington U., St. Louis, 1984, MS, 1989; MBA, So. Ill. U., Edwardsville, 1992. Engr. McDonnel Douglas, St. Louis, 1986-91; instr. So. Ill. U., 1992-93; campaign mgr. Gehl Group, St. Joseph, Mo., 1993; sr. engr., project mgr. Boeing, Long Beach, Calif., 1994-98; dept. mgr. Gen. Dynamics, Sterling Heights, Mich., 1998—; instr. Detroit Coll. Bus., Warren, Mich., 1999—. Crisis worker Life Crisis Svcs., St. Louis, 1989-90; pub. spkr. United Way, St. Louis, 1989, com. mem., 1990. Address: PO Box 452 Sterling Heights MI 48311-0452

YADAV, SUNIL, mechanical engineer; came to U.S., 1991; BS, Indian Inst. Tech., Kanpur, India, 1991; MS, Johns Hopkins U., 1994, PhD, 1996. Postdoctoral rsch. scholar Calif. Inst. Tech., Pasadena, 1996-98; engr. II Fermi Nat. Accelerator Lab., Batavia, Ill., 1998—. Contbr. papers to profl. jours. Mem. AAAS, ASME, Am. Acad. Mechanics, Sigma Xi.

YAFAROV, RAVIL KYASHSHAFOVICH, physicist, researcher, educator; b. Chita, Russia, June 18, 1948; s. Kyashashaf Zarifovich and Raisa Vasilievna (Zabirova) Y.; m. Larisa Ivanovna Sanzharevskaya, Dec. 5, 1971; children: Galina, Andrei. Candidate Engring. Sci., Inst. Electron Engring., Moscow, 1980, D in Engring. Sci., 1991. Engr. Rsch. Inst. Machine Bldg., Saratov, Russia, 1973-80; head lab. Inst. Radio Engring. and Electronics, Saratov, 1980—; prof. Tech. U., Saratov, 1981-99. Contbr. articles to profl. jours. Grantee Presidium of Russian Acad. Sci., Moscow, 1993, 96, Ministry Sci. and Tech. Russian Fedn., Moscow, 1993, 95, 97. Mem. Soc. Info. Display, N.Y. Acad. Sci. Achievements include author of regional program on electronics Saratov Region's Govt.; patent for set-up for MW vacuum plasma processing. Avocations: sports, theater, country. Home: PO Box 1072, 410009 Saratov Russia Office: IRE RAS Saratov Dept, Zelyonaya 38, 410019 Saratov Russia

YAFFA, ANDREW BRYAN, lawyer; b. Richmond, Va., May 26, 1966; s. Jack Ber and Phyllis P. Yaffa; m. Romy J. Yaffa, Aug. 17, 1991; children: Ryan, Garrett. BA, U. Richmond, 1988; JD, U. Miami, 1991. Bar: Fla. 1991, U.S. Dist. Ct. (so. dist.) Fla. 1992. Atty. Grossman & Roth, P.A., Miami, 1991—. Mem. ABA, Acad. Fla. Trial Lawyers. Avocations: sports, fishing. Office: Grossman and Roth PA 2665 S Bayshore Dr Ph 1 Miami FL 33133-5448

YAGER, THOMAS C., judge; b. L.A., Feb. 16, 1918; s. Thomas C. and May M. (McGowan) Y. AB in pol. sci., UCLA, 1939, gen. secondary lifetime tchg. credential, 1940; JD, USC, 1948; LLD, Western State U., Calif., 1972. Reader UCLA Philosophy Dept., 1940; atty. L.A., 1949-57; legal advisor Gov. Calif., 1957, 58; superior ct. sr. judge Calif.; founder Cmty. Betterment Svc., L.A. Author numerous legal and religious books; contbr. articles to profl. jours. Founder The Judge Thomas C. Yager Found., L.A., The Cmty. Betterment Svc., L.A.; Major U.S. Army, 1942-46. E-mail: pvtsecty@aol.com. Office: The Cmty Betterment Svc 108 N Gower St Los Angeles CA 90004-3828

YAGER, WILLIAM STEWART, sculptor; b. Albany, June 7, 1950; s. William Stewart and Mary Dorothy (Reynolds) Y.; m. Karen Sue Hokenson, Sept. 7, 1973 (div. Aug. 1995); children: William III, Natalie, Julia. AS, Hudson Valley C.C., 1970; BS, SUNY, Brockport, 1972; MFA, U. Buffalo, 1977. Assoc. prof. art, artist SUNY, Buffalo, 1976-77; tchr., artist Albion (N.Y.) Ctrl. High Sch., 1977-83, Rochester (N.Y.) Schs., 1993—. Pub. commissions include N.Y. Korean War Vets. Meml., 1996, Rochester (N.Y.) Vietnam Vets. Meml., 1997. N.Y. State Art grantee, 1978. Home and Studio: 274 Goodman St N Ste 66 Rochester NY 14607-1172

YAGHOUBI, MAHMOOD, mechanical engineering educator, researcher; b. Zahedan, Sistan-B., Iran, Oct. 17, 1945; s. Mohammad Hossien Yaghoubi and Shahpari Bolagh; m. Homa Babiri; children: Sepeher, Ali-Sina, Ehsan, Yassaman. BSME, Shiraz (Iran) U., 1970, MSME, 1972; PhD in Mech. Engring., Purdue U., 1978. Mem. faculty dept. mech. engring. Shiraz U., 1979—, prof., 1991—, chmn. dept., 1979-81, vice chancellor, 1981-82, 93, vice dean, 1985-86, dir. Computer Ctr., 1987-90, editor-in-chief, 1996—; vis. scholar Internat. Ctr. for Theoretical Physics, Italy, 1987; mem. adv. bd. Internat. Jour. Engring. Design, India, 1994-96; mem. editl. bd. Esfahan (Iran) U., 1996—; dir. Engring. Edn. Jour., Acad. Scis. Iran, 1999—. Editor Procs. Internat. Conf. on Computational Methods, 1993 (prize 1993). Recipient Abadi prize Iranian Ministry Bldgs., 1995. Fellow Iranian Acad. Scis. (head 1994—), Iranian Soc. Mech. Engrs. (Disting. Mech. Engring. Prof. award 1998); mem. ASME. Office: Shiraz U Engring Sch, Zand Ave, Shiraz Fars, Iran

YAGI, HAJIME, electronics company executive; b. Tokyo, Feb. 19, 1937; m. Yukiko Nagano, May 21, 1966; children: Yoko, Shigeru, Minoru. BS, Tokyo U., 1960. Gen. mgr. semicondr. R&D divsn. Sony Corp., Atsugi, Japan, 1978-85, gen. mgr. Memory div., 1986-87, dep. sr. gen. mgr. semicondr. group, 1988-91, sr. gen. mgr. ULSI Labs., 1991-94, rsch. fellow, gen. mgr. Rsch. Ctr., 1994-98; councillor Sony Corp., Atsugi, 1998—; mem. com. SEMI Tech. Symposium, Tokyo, 1982-90; mem. steering com. SORTEC Co., Tokyo, 1989-95; advisor Innotech Co., Yokohamma, Japan, 1998—, Fine Materials Corp., Miyagi, Japan, 1998—, OptoTech Corp., Hsinchu, Taiwan, 1998—; cons. ATMI Co., Danbury, Conn., 1999—, Genus Co., Sunnyvale, Calif., 1999—; vis. prof. JAIST, Ishikawa, Japan, 1999—. Patentee semicondr. devices. Bd. dirs. Found. for Promotion of Material Sci. and Tech., Tokyo, 1989-95. Recipient commendation Minister of State for Sci. and Tech., Japan, 1993, commendation Japan Invention Soc., 1972. Mem. IEEE. E-mail: hj-yagi@xb3.so-net.ne.jp. Home: 2-5-15 Kakinokizaka, Meguro, Tokyo Japan Office: Sony Corp, 4-13-1 Asahi, Atsugi Kanagawa, Japan

YAGI, HIROSHI, surgeon, hospital administrator; b. Fukuoka, Kyushu, Japan, Sept. 16, 1928; s. Kusuo and Kikuyo Y.; m. Ryoko Kasai Yagi, Oct. 12, 1956; children: Seiji, Yukiko, Shoko, Kenji. MD, Kyushu U., Fukuoka, Japan, 1953, PhD, 1959. Intern Sagamihara Nat. Hosp., Kanagawa, Japan, 1953-54; resident dept. 2d surgery faculty medicine Kyushu U., Fukuoka, Japan, 1954-58; instr. 2d dept. surgery Faculty of Medicine, Kyushu U., Fukuoka, Japan, 1958-66, asst. prof. 2d dept. surgery, 1966-68; assoc. prof. dept. surgery Inst. Balneotherapeutics, Kyushu U., Beppu, Japan, 1968-70; chmn. Yagi Kosei-kai Hosp., Fukuoka, Japan, 1970—. Author: Cerebral Infarct, 1984, Fat Embolism, 1987, Problem Wounds, 1990, Ileus, 1990. Bd. dirs. Fukuoka Pvt. Hosp. Assn., 1978—, v.p., 1991—; bd. dirs. Fukuoka Hosp. Assn., 1985—, v.p., bd. pres. 1997—. Boston Children's Hosp. rsch. fellow, 1964-65, Boston City Hosp. rsch. fellow, 1965-66; recipient Mayor's award Fukuoka City, 1985, Prefectural Gov.'s award Fukuoka Prefectura, 1990. Fellow Internat. Coll. Surgeons; mem. Japanese Soc. Surgeons, Japanese Soc. Angiology (councilor 1972—), Japanese Soc. Clin. Surgery (councilor 1980—), Japanese Soc. Hyperbaric Medicine (pres. 1985-86, bd. dirs. 1987—), Japanese Soc. for Acute Medicine (councilor 1987—), Japanese Soc. Low Temperature Medicine (pres. 1990—), Undersea and Hyperbaric Medicine in U.S.A., Fukuoka Jyonan Rotary Club. Avocations: photography, tennis. Home: 1-22-24 Oike Minami-ku, Kyushu, Fukuoka 815, Japan Office: Yagi Kosei-Kai Hospital, 2-21-25 Maidashi Higashi-ku, Fukuoka 812, Japan

YAGI, TAKASHI, physicist, researcher; b. Aomori, Japan, Apr. 20, 1951; s. Hikozo and Fumi Yagi; m. Hiroko Takahashi, Oct. 12, 1983; children: Tanana, Yukon. BS, U. Niigata, Japan, 1974, MS, 1977; PhD, LaTrobe U., Bundoora, Australia, 1983. Physics tchr. Kenyo Sr. High Sch., Kawaguchi, Japan, 1977-78; post-doctoral fellow SUNY, Albany, 1983-84, Geophys. Inst. U., Fairbanks, Alaska, 1984-85; knowledge engr. NTT Software Corp., Yokosuka, Japan, 1986-87; rsch. scientist Inst. Rsch. & Innovation, Kashiwa, Japan, 1987-97; assoc. prof. physics Tokai U., Hiratsuka, Japan, 1997-98, prof., 1998—; involved in nat. project on Excimer Laser, Femtosecond Tech., Japan, 1987—; vis. scientist Japan Atomic Energy Rsch. Inst., 1996-98. Inventor in field. Mem. Am. Phys. Soc., Phys. Soc. Japan, Japan Soc. Applied Physics, Optical soc. Am. Avocation: fishing. Office: Tokai U Dept Physics, 1117 Kita-kaname, Hiratsuka 259-1292, Japan

YAGIL, JOSEPH, finance educator; b. Haidan, Yemen, May 15, 1947; s. Moshe and Naama Ahron Y.; m. Nurit Beraha, May 29, 1985; children: Leeran, Nadav, Matan. BA, Hebrew U., Jerusalem, 1973; MBA, Hebrew U., 1975; PhD, U. Toronto, 1980. Prof. fin. Haifa U., Israel, 1983—, Columbia U., N.Y.C., 1993-95, NYU, N.Y.C., 1988-90, York U., Toronto, Can., 1981-82; economist Bank of Israel, Jerusalem, 1973-75; fin. cons. Israel, U.S., Can., 1980—; participant in scholarly confs., many countries, 1980—; referee for profl. jours. Author: (book) Financial Management, 1981. Capt. Israel Def. Army Res., 1965—. Jewish. Avocations: basketball, swimming, tennis. Office: Sch of Business, Haifa Univ, 31095 Haifa Israel

YAGIZ, OKTAY BORA, management consultant; b. Hozat, Turkey, Aug. 2, 1942; s. Cemal Huseyin and Munevver (Istemi) Y.; m. Esin Remziye

Akcakoyunlu, Sept. 14, 1996; 1 child, Bora. Student, Am. U. Beirut, 1961-63; BS, Middle East Tech. U., Ankara, 1968; postgrad. in internat. relations, Ankara U. Econ. planner State Planning Orgn., Ankara, 1969-72; gen. mgr. Viking Pulp and Paper Inc., Izmir, Turkey, 1973-82; mng. ptnr. Obey Mgmt. Cons. Inc., Istanbul, 1984—; mng. dir. Point Mgmt. Cons., Inc., Istanbul, 1993—; gen. mgr. DynaChange Mgmt. Cons. Inc., McLean, Va., 1995—; exec. dir., cons. Dedeman Group of Cos., Istanbul, 1993—; exec. dir. Std. Profil Inc., Istanbul, 1989—, Fox Printing Industries, Istanbul, 1995—, also 37 other cos.; led more than 90 corp. restructuring, instnl. devel. and change mgmt. projects. Mem. Econ. and Social Studies Found., Istanbul, 1992-95; mem. Taksim Round Table, Istanbul, 1991—. 2d lt. Turkish Army, 1972-73. Rockefeller scholar, 1961-63. Mem. Turkish Mgmt. Cons. Assn. (charter mem.; pres. 1994-96, chmn. emeritus 1996), Am. Mgmt. Assn., Talas/Tarsus Alumni Assn., Middle East Tech. U. Alumni Assn. Avocations: travel, horseback riding, chess, literature, essays in management. Office: DynaChange Mgmt Cons 6202 Stoneham Ln Mc Lean VA 22101-2342 also: OBEY Mgmt Cons, Selcuklar Sok 51-3 Levent, 80630 Istanbul Turkey

YAHALOM, SHAUL, government official; b. Tel Aviv, Israel, 1947; married; 4 children. BA in Edn. & Econs., Bar-Ilan U. Polit. sec. NRP, 1987-95; mem. Knesset, Israel, 1992—; chmn. Constitution, Law & Justice Com.; min. Ministry Transport, Jerusalem, 1998-99; dep. min. of edn. Knesset, Jerusalem, 1999-2000. Office: The Knesset, 91000 Jerusalem Israel*

YAHAYA, MOHAMED JAMIL, school system administrator; b. Kuala Nerang Kedah, Malaysia, Dec. 27, 1946; s. Hassan and Ariffin (Mariam) Yahaya; m. (div.); children: Mohd Johan, Mohd Hussein. Cert. in edn., Lang. Inst., Kuala Lumpur, 1969; BA, U. Malaya, Kuala Lumpur, 1975; postgrad., Nat. Inst. Publ. & Adminstrn., Malaysia, 1986. Tchr. Secondary Sch. Yuk Choy, Ipoh, Perak, Malaysia, 1975-93; supr. Secondary Sch. Idris Shah, Gopeng, Perak, Malaysia, 1994-98; asst. headmaster Secondary Sch. Sri Kampar, Malaysia, 1998—; prin. Sec. Sch. Kenering Gerik, Perak, 1998—; tech. chess chmn. Perak Sport Sch. Coun., 1976-86, Malaysia Sch. Sport Coun., Malaysia, 1985-95, Dist. Sport Coun., Kinta, 1980-95; chess chmn. Ednl. Sport & Cultural Kinta, 1990-97. Sec. Perak Chess Assn., 1984-86, 90-95, pres., 1987-89; v.p. Malaysian Malay Chess Fedn., 1990-92. Recipient Cert. Excellence, Ministry Edn., 1976; awarded Internat. Arbiter norm for being Deputy Chief Arbiter 1st Saturday Chess Championship, Budapest, Hungary, 1998. Mem. Coop. Soc. Avocations: chess, environment. Home: Taman Alkaff, 3 Jalan Kledang Raya 20, 30100 Ipoh Malaysia Office: Sec Sch Kenering, 33300 Gerik Malaysia

YAHYA, AARIF, marketing professional; b. Karachi, Sind, Pakistan, Sept. 19, 1969; s. Mohammad Yahya and Mehtab Suriyya; m. Shazia Jabbar Aarif, Jan. 20, 1995; children: Nyema Aarif, Anusha Aarif. B, Nat. Coll. Karachi, 1990; MBA, Punjab Coll. Bus. Adminstrn., 1992. From coord. sales to mgr. mktg. Ahmed Food Industry Ltd., Karachi, 1990-96; dir. mktg. Naurus (Pvt.) Ltd., Karachi, 1996—. Mem. Am. Mktg. Assn., Mktg. Assn. Pakistan, Mgmt. Assn. Pakistan. Avocations: travel, painting, reading. Home: 59A Bl 3 DACHS, 74800 Karachi Sind, Pakistan Office: Naurus (Pvt) Ltd, C 1B Manghopir Rd, 75700 Karachi Sind, Pakistan

YAHYA PETRA, ISMAIL PETRA, Sultan of Kelantan; b. 1949; s. Tuanku Yahya Petra; m. Tengku Anis, Dec. 4, 1966; 3 children. Student, Sultan Ismail Coll. Named Tengku Mahkota of Kelantan, 1967; named sultan State of Kelantan, 1979—. Address: Istana, Kota Bharu, Kelantan Malaysia Office: care Press Attache Malaysian Embassy 2401 Massachusetts Ave NW Washington DC 20008-2851*

YAJIMA, KYOSHIRO, social philosophy educator; b. Taipei, Taiwan, Dec. 11, 1929; arrived in Japan, 1938; s. Yunosuke and Fusa (Ogishima) Y.; m. Yuriko Tahara, Mar. 21, 1958. BA, U. Tokyo, 1953. Asst. prof. U. Tokyo, 1953-58; lectr. Tokai U., Tokyo, 1958-59, assoc. prof., 1959-63; assoc. prof. U. Tokyo, 1963-72, prof., 1972-90, prof. emeritus, 1990—; prof. Obirin U., Tokyo, 1990-2000, prof. emeritus, 2000—; vis. prof. U. Vienna, Austria, 1967-68, U. Heidelberg, Germany, 1976-78; chmn. Grad. Sch. Internat. Rels., U. Tokyo, 1979-81, 85-87; councilor Grad. Sch., U. Tokyo, 1985-87; dir. Inst. Internat. Studies, Obirin U., 1995-99. Author: (books) A Study of Dialectics—From the Viewpoint of Intellectual History, 1972, Spiritual Climate and Culture, 1973; contbr. articles to profl. jours. Recipient Austrian Erasmus prize in humanities, 1960. Mem. Internat. Assn. for Study of Dialectical Philosophy (exec. mem.), Japan Assn. Internat. Rels. (councilor 1996—), Japan Soc. for Ethics. Home: 2412-19 Ozenji, 215-0013 Asao Kawasaki Kanagawa, Japan Office: Obirin U, 3758 Tokiwa-machi, 194-0294 Machida Tokyo, Japan

YAKASAI, BASHIR ADAM, neuropsychiatrist, consultant; b. Kano, Nigeria, Dec. 29, 1953; s. Adam Muhammad and Khadija Adam (Ummahani Nuoh) Y.; m. Maimuna Hassana Musa, Sept. 22, 1977; children: Khadija, Yusuf, Maryam, Rukaiya, Abdullahi, Binta, Mustaph, Amina, Maimuna, Rabiat. MBBS, Ahmadu Bello U., Zaria, Nigeria, 1979; diploma in Psychiatry, U. London, 1985; diploma in Psychol. Medicine, Royal Coll. Physicians Ireland, Dublin, 1987; diploma in Clin. Neurology, Inst. Neurology, London, 1986. Registrar in psychogiriatrics Princess Alex Hosp., Harlow-Essex, Eng., 1985-86; registrar mental handicap Spencer House Epping, Essex, 1986-87; registrar drug dependancy unit Hackney Hosp., Eng., 1987-88; sr. registrar psychiatry dept. psychiatry Ahmadu Bello U., 1988-92; chief cons. neuropsychiatrist Nigerian Air Force, 1992—; dir. Fed. Neuropsychiat. Hosp., Kware-Sokoto, Nigeria, 1996—; hon. lectr., cons. neurologist dept. medicine Ahmadu Bello U., 1995—; assoc. sr. lectr. neurology and psychiatry Usmanu Danfodio U., Sokoto; faculty mem. U. Benin-Nigeria; rosource mem. Tng. Course on Psychotherapy, 1997—. Author: The Practice of Psychotherapy in Africa, 1995. Comdr. Nigerian Air Force Unit of Spl. Marshals, 195-97; vice-chmn. Spl. Marshals, Sokoto State, 1997—. Group capt. Nigerian Air Force, 1980—. Recipient merit awards Nigerian Air Force, Kaduna, 1997, Nat. Assn. Nigerian Nurses and Midwives, 1999, Ctr. for Campaign Against Drug Abuse/Trafficking, Sokoto, 1999. Mem. N.Y. Acad. Scis., Assn. Psychiatrists in Nigeria (auditor), Nigerian Soc. Psychotherapy (v.p. 1999), Federal Road Safety Code (spl. marshal, vice chmn. 1999). Avocations: travel, watching comedies, farming. Home: Balarabe Musa Close, PO Box 9110, Kaduna Nigeria Office: Fed Neuropsychiat Hosp, PMB 2196, Kware Sokoto, Nigeria

YAKIMANSKAYA, ĬRĬNA SERGEĬEVNA, psychologist, researcher; b. Astrayhan, Russia, Dec. 20, 1931; d. Sergeĭ Ilich and Lĭdĭa Yakimanskaya; m. Victor Fĭodorovich Zaĭtsev; 1 child, Zaĭtsev Sergeĭ Victorovich. Student, Moscow U., 1950-55, postgrad., 1955-58. Jr. rschr. Inst. Psychology, Moscow, 1958-63, sr. rschr., 1963-80, chief dept. ednl. psychology, 1980-90; chief dept. child-centered edn., prof. Inst. Ednl. Innovations, Moscow, 1990—; instr. postgrad. students, Moscow, 1970—; leader projects on child-centered edn.; trainer tchrs., 1965—. Author: Developing Teaching, 1979, Development of Thinking Through Imagination in School Age, 1980, Knowledge and Thinking of Student, 1985, Child-centered Ednucation in Contemporary School, 1996 and 6 other books; contbr. over 180 articles to profl. jours. Recipient award Russian Govt., 1990, Ushinskij medal Russian Acad. Edn., 1996, 850th Ann. of Moscow City medal Moscow Govt., 1997. Mem. Internat. Acad. Edn., Soc. Russian Psychologists. Avocations: visiting museums and theatres. Office: Inst Ednl Innovations, Vinocurova str 3(b), 117449 Moscow Russia

YAKIMENKO, IRINA, physicist, researcher; b. Kharkov, Ukraine, July 29, 1960; d. Ivan and Lidia (Zabashta) Y.; m. Sergey Tsikounov, July 2, 1981 (dec. Oct. 1985); 1 child, Victor; m. Alexander Onipko, June 18, 1996; children: Ivan, Alexander. MS, Kiev U., 1982; PhD, Inst. for Theoretical Physics, Kiev, 1991. Rschr. Inst. for Theoretical Physics, Kiev, 1982-92, 95-96, Centre d'Etudes Nucleaires, Saclay, France, 1993-94; rschr. Linköping (Sweden) U., 1997-98, invited prof., 1999—. Contbr. articles to profl. jours. including Jour. Appl. Phys., Phys. Rev. E., and Jour. Chem. Physics. Grantee Min. de la Recherche et de la Technology Commissariat Energie Atomique, France, 1993, 94, European Commn., 1998-99, Swedish Natural Sci. Rsch. Coun., 1999—. Mem. N.Y. Acad. Scis. Avocations: reading, travel, aerobics. Officer: Inst for Theoret Physics, Metrologicheskaya Str 14B, 03143 Kiev Ukraine

YAKIMENKO, ROMAN IVANOVICH, government agency administrator; b. Sverdlovsk, Russia, Oct. 1, 1953; s. Ivan Ivanovich and Vera Ivanivna (Mironyuk) Y. Degree in mech. engring., Moscow Aviation Inst., 1976, PhD, 1996. Engr. Moscow Aviation Inst., 1976-79; sr. engr., then leading engr. Design Bur. of Keldysh Rsch. Ctr., Moscow, 1979-93; head specialist Russian Aviation and Space Agy., Moscow, 1993—. Co-author reports in field. Avocations: reading, hunting. Home: 16-1-135 Lavochkina, 125499 Moscow Russia Office: Russian Aviation/Space Agy, 42 Shchepkina, 129090 Moscow Russia

YAKIMOV, ANDREW INNOKENT'EVICH, physicist, researcher; b. Berdsk, Russia, Apr. 11, 1964; s. Innokentii Pavlovich Yakimov and Valentina Alekseevna (Filatova) Ivanova; m. Natalia Nikolaevna Oshikhmina, May 8, 1982; children: Ksenia, Nikita. Specialization in physics and math., Novosibirsk, Russia, 1981; degree in physics, State U. Novosibirsk, 1986, PhD, 1991. Jr. rschr. Inst. Semiconductor Physics-Russian Acad. Scis., Novosibirsk, 1988-91, rschr., 1991-94, sr. rschr., 1994—; vis. rschr. Cavendish Lab., U. Cambridge, Eng., 1994, 96, 98. Recipient Soros award Internat. Sci. Found., 1995. Avocation: fishing. E-mail: yakimov@isp.nsc.ru. Fax: 7-3832-351771. Office: Inst Semiconductor Physics, prospekt Lavrent'eva 13, 630090 Novosibirsk Russia

YAKINTHOS, JOHN, physics educator; b. Drama, Greece, May 19, 1937; s. Kyriakos and Anna (Zerdalidou) Y.; m. Anna Athina Mescou, Dec. 26, 1966; children: Kyriakos, Marianne. Degree in French lit., French Institut, Thessaloniki, 1958; Degree in Physics, Aristote U., Thessaloniki, 1964; Degree in Solid State Physics, Univ., Grenoble, 1970, PhD, 1972. Rschr. Nuclear Rsch. Ctr., Grenoble, 1966-72; head Neutron Diffraction Lab., Nuclear Ctr., Athens, 1973-76; prof. U. Thrace, Xanthi, Greece, 1977—; dean Polytechnic Sch., Xanthi, 1980-81; dir. Physics and Applied Math. Sect., Xanthi, 1989-96; head Elec. & Computer Engring. Dept., Xanthi, 1989-92; mem. Accreditation Com. for Fgn. Drs. Degrees, 1981; mem. Exams. State Scholarship Found., 1981. Author: (books) Classical Mechanics-Interactions, Statistics-Wave Mechanics, Atomic and Nuclear Physics, Quantum Mechanics; contbr. over 100 articles to sci. jours. Sec.-gen. Democritos Internat. Found., 1980-82; chmn. D.U.t. profs. Assn., 1982-84. Mem. Macedonian Studies Found., Democritos Univ. Profs. (chmn. 1979-80). Avocations: classical music, swimming. E-mail: yakinthos@xanthi.cc.duth.gr. Home: Saranda Ekklission, 67100 Xanthi Greece Office: Democritos U Thrace Elec &, Comp Engring Dept Phys Lab, 67100 Xanthi Greece

YAKISICH, JUAN SEBASTIAN, medical researcher; b. Posadas, Argentina, Feb. 26, 1967; s. Juan Andres and Amanda (Laudonio) Y. MD, U. Buenos Aires, Argentina, 1994. Teaching asst. U. Buenos Aires, Argentina, 1990-96, U. Gral San Martin, Buenos Aires, Argentina, 1995-96; guest rschr. Karolinska Inst., Stockholm, 1997—; lectr. U. Buenos Aires, 1997, 98. Contbr. articles to profl. jours. Mem. Argentinian Soc. Neurochemistry. Avocations: music, movies, reading, Tae-kwon-do, computing. Office: Karolinska Inst, Huddinge Sjuykhus, S-14186 Huddinge Sweden

YAKOBSON, EMANUEL AHARON, research scientist; b. Riga, Latvia, Feb. 13, 1947; arrived in Israel, 1973; s. Aharon Mendel and Sarrah Mozes (Okliansky) Y.; m. Bracha Avsei Libshits, June 1969 (div. 1989); children: Miriam, Ronit. MSc, Latvian U., Riga, 1969; PhD, Moscow U., 1972, Weizmann Inst. Sci., Israel, 1979. Rschr. Imperial Cancer Rsch. Fund., London, 1979-80, U. Calif., San Diego, 1980-85, Weizmann Inst. Sci., Rehovot, Israel, 1986-88, Tel Aviv Med. Ctr., 1994—; cons. Ministry of Adsorption, State of Israel, 1988-91, Weizmann Inst. Sci., Rehovot, 1992—. Contbr. numerous articles to profl. jours. Fellow Feinberg Sch., 1978, European Molec. Biology Orgn., 1979-80, Cold Spring Harbor, 1984, Springer Verlag, 1981, Israel Cancer Assn., 1998. Mem. Human Genome Orgn. Avocations: sports, table tennis, swimming.

YAKOUN, MAURICE, surgeon, researcher; b. Algiers, Algeria, Dec. 30, 1948; s. Gaston and Renee (Moatti) Y.; m. Muriel Attali, Oct. 13, 1984. MD, U. Montpellier, France, 1975, surg. and oncology specialization, 1989. Intern in surgery U. Hosp. Montpelier; resident in surgery Montpelier Anti-Cancer Ctr.; chief dept. surgery Clinic St.-Jean, Montpellier, 1983—; asst. prof. Anticancer Ctr., Montpellier, 1979-83. Author: Digestive Failure, 1975 (award French Acad. Surgery 1976); editor Nutrition-Metabolism, 1981. With M.C., Tunis Anti-Cancer Ctr., 1975-76. Fellow Am. Soc. for Parenteral and Enteral Nutrition (young rsch. award 1981), N.Y. Acad. Scis. Office: Clinique St-Jean, 36 Ave Bouisson-Bertrand, 34090 Montpellier France

YAKOVLEV, VENIAMIN FEDOROVICH, judge; b. Petukhovo, Russia, Feb. 12, 1932; s. Fedor Kuzmich and Domna Pavlovna Yakovlev; m. Galina Ivanovna, 1956; 2 children. Student, Sverdlovsk Inst. Law. Tchr., dir. Yakut Sch. Law, 1953-56; asst. atty.-gen. Yakut Autonomous Republic, 1956-60; aspirant, tchr., docent, dean, pro-rector Sverdlovsky Inst. Law, 1960-87; dir. All-Union Rsch. Inst. Soviet Legis., 1987-89; dept. chair Pub. COm. Internat. Coop. Humanitarian Problems & Human Rights, 1988; min. justice Govt. of USSR, 1989-90; chair Supreme Arbitration Ct., USSR, 1991, 92—. Author: Civil Law Method of Regulation for Social Relations; contbr. articles to profl. jours. Avocations: skiing, sports. Office: 12 Malyi Kharitonievskiy, by-street, 101000 Moscow Russia*

YAKOVLEVA, EVGUENIA LEONIDOVNA, psychologist, researcher; b. Ufa, Baschkiria, USSR; d. Leonid Ivanovitsch and Ekaterina Fiodorovna (Amiliakina) Petrov; m. Viatsheslav Ivanovitch Zemskikh, Mar. 12, 1976 (div. Feb. 1994); 1 child, Leonid; m. Mikhail Romanovitsch Ginzburg, Mar. 4, 1995. M degree, Pedagogical Inst., Ulianovsk, 1969; PhD, Psychol. Inst. Moscow, 1975. Asst. rschr. Psychol. Inst., Moscow, 1972-83, sr. rschr., 1983—; cons. H.S., Moscow, 1985-95, sci. cons., 1985-95; lectr. Orgn. Knowledge, Moscow, 1972-95; cons. Union of Psychologists, Moscow, 1975-95. Author: The Psychology of the Development of the Creative Potential of the Personality, 1997; co-author: The Education and the Psychological Development of the Children 13-17 Years Old, 1988, The Development of the Creative Activity of the Children, 1991; contbr. articles to profl. jours. including Problems of Psychology. Recipient medal and diploma Nat. Exhbn., 1985., Nat. award Realm of Edn., 1998. Mem. Internat. Soc. for Study of Behavioral Devel., Assn. Humanistic Psychologists. Orthodox. Avocations: aikido, walking tours, theater, exhibitions, books. Home: Osenny Bulvar 12-2-199, 121614 Moscow Russia Office: Psychol Inst, Mokhovaya St 9 Block V, 703009 Moscow Russia

YAKUBOV, VLADIMIR PETROVICH, radiophysics educator, researcher; b. Chita, USSR, Feb. 8, 1948; s. Piter Nikitich and Nina Vasilievna (Samodurova) Y.; m. Valentina Nikolaevna Kovtun, Dec. 19, 1951; children: Andrei, Olga. Higher edn., Tomsk (USSR) State U., 1970, Candidate Sci., 1977; DSc, Tomsk (Russia) State U., 1992. Sr. sci. employee Siberian Physics and Tech Inst. Tomsk (USSR) State U., 1973-79, univ. reader, 1979-84, leading scientific employee SPhTI, 1984-91; prof. Tomsk (Russia) State U., 1991-94, chief of faculty, 1994—; univ. reader Higher Certification Commn., Moscow, 1983; prof. HCC, 1994. Author: Narrowband VLBI for Space Investigation, 1996, Doppler VLBI, 1997; contbr. articles to profl. jours. Recipient Silver Medal Exhbn. of Nat. Econ. Achievement of USSR, 1986, Gagarin Medal Fedn. Astronautics Russia, 1996. Mem. Metrology Acad. Russia (corr.), Natural Scis. Acad. Avocations: underwater swimming,, motoring, gardening. Home: Lytkina 22-100, 634034 Tomsk Tomsk, Russia Office: Tomsk State U, Lenina 36, 634050 Tomsk Tomsk, Russia

YAKUSHCHENKO, IGOR KONSTANTINOVICH, chemist, researcher; b. Baku, USSR, Dec. 18, 1952; s. Konstantin Michailovich and Valentina Petrovna (Sedak) Y.; m. Tatiana Nikolaevna Lobatcheva, Dec. 30, 1982; 1 child, Olga. Student, Moscow U., 1976; PhD, Moscow Agrl. Acad., 1980. Jr. rschr. Inst. Chem. Physics, Chernogolovka, Russia, 1981-86; rschr. Inst. Chem. Physics, Chernogolovka, 1987-93; sr. rschr. Inst. Problems Chem. Physics, Chernogolovka, 1994—. Office: Russian Acad Sci, Inst Problems Chem Physics, 142432 Chernogolovka Moscow, Russia

YAKUSHEVICH, LUDMILA VLADIMIROVNA, physicist, researcher; b. Chernovtsy, Ukraine, Oct. 20, 1947; d. Vladimir Lavrent'evich and Nina Romanovna (Chemolosova) Y. Diploma in physics, Moscow State U., 1971; PhD in Theoretical and Math. Physics, Joint Inst. for Nuc. Rsch., Dubna, Russia, 1978; DSc in Biophysics, Russian Acad. Scis., Pushchino, 1998. Postgrad. fellow Inst. Biol. Physics, Acad. Scis. USSR, Pushchino, Russia, 1971-73; jr. rschr. Inst. Biol. Physics, Acad. Scis. USSR, Pushchino, 1973-90; rschr. Inst. Cell Biophysics, Russian Acad. Scis., Pushchino, 1990-91, sr. rschr., 1991-98, leading rschr., 1998—. Author: Methods of Theoretical Physics and Their Applications to Biopolymer Science, 1990, English edit., 1996, Nonlinear Physics of DNA, 1998. Recipient medal 850th Anniversary of Moscow, 1997. Avocation: painting. E-mail: yakushev@ibfk.nifhi.ac.ru. Fax: 0967 790509. Office: RAS Inst Cell Biophysics, Institutskaya St, 142290 Pushchino Moscow, Russia

YAKUSHIN, VLADIMIR LEONIDOVICH, physics researcher, educator; b. Chkalovskoe, Russia, Mar. 26, 1952; s. Leonid Evdokimovich and Alexandra Petrovna (Sovina) Y.; m. Tatiana Fiedorovna Lipatova, May 12, 1978; children: Anastasiya, Elena. Degree in engring.-physics, Moscow State Engring. Physics Inst., 1975, DS, 1980. Engr. Moscow State Engring. Physics Inst., 1975-77, sr. engr., 1980-81, head lab., 1981-92, assoc. prof., 1992—, dep. head dept. phys. problems of materials sci., 1991—. Author: Problems in Selection of Materials for Fusion Reactors, 1985; author over 120 sci. works, including monography, 67 articles; patentee in field. Mem. Nuclear Soc. Russia, Interregion Materials Soc. Avocations: theater, travel, motoring. Home: 24-39 Vucheticha St, 125206 Moscow Russia Office: Moscow State Engring Phys Inst, 31 Kashirskoye sh, 115409 Moscow Russia

YAKUT, ATILLA, linguist; b. Ankara, Turkey, Mar. 24, 1945; s. Halit and Anakiz (Ozutemiz) Y.; m. Yvonne Gabriele Reck, Nov. 28, 1991; children: Toygar, Yelve. MA, U. Ankara, 1971; PhD, U. Konstanz, Germany, 1977. Lectr. U. Konstanz, 1974-77; rschr. U. Essen, Germany, 1978-80, U. Kassel, Germany, 1980-85, U. Giessen, Germany, 1985—; rschr. on bilingualism, German Coun. of Sci., 1992. Author: (books) Sprache der Familie, 1978, Muttersprachlicher Unterricht, 1986, Cultural Linguistics and Bilingualism, 1994, Sexualitat im Islam, 1995. Lt. Turkish Army, 1972-73. Mem. N.Y. Acad. Sci.

YALAMOV, YURI IVANOVICH, vice rector, educator; b. Novocherkask, Rostov, Russia, Apr. 20, 1932; s. Ivan Panayotovich Yalamov and Emma Vartanovna (Sarkisyan) Yalamova; m. Ludmila Vasilyevna Sumkova, May 6, 1962 (div. Dec. 1983); children: Georgiy, Karen; m. Yulia Vladimirovna Popova, April 11, 1987. Degree, Moscow Engring. Physical Inst., 1956, PhD, 1969. Tchr. Moscow Engring. Physical Inst., 1956-63; sr. rschr. Inst. Physical Chemistry Russian Acad. Scis., Moscow, 1963-67, lab. chief, 1967-73; chmn. Kalinin (Russia) State U. Dept. Physics, 1973-76; chmn., vice rector Moscow Pedagogical U. Dept. Theoretical Physics, 1976—. Co-author: (with B.V. Derjaguin) The Theory of Thermophoresis and Diffusiophoresis of Particles and their Experimental Testing, 1972, (with V.S. Galoyan) Dynamics of the Droplets in Nonuniform Viscos Mediums, 1985, (with E.I. Alekhin) Mathematical Foundations of the Solving the Boundary Problems of the Kinetic Theory of the Multicomponent Gases Near Condensed Phase, 1991. Mem. Internat. Acad. Info., Russian Acad. Nat. Scis. (P.L. Kapitsa award 1996, scientific achievement award 1997), N.Y. Acad. Scis. Avocations: playing chess, reading, music. Home: Tokmakov Lane, house 13/15 apt 128, 107066 Moscow Russia Office: Moscow Pedagogical Univ, St Radio 10A, 107005 Moscow Russia

YALÇINELI, MELIH, educational projects executive, physics educator; b. K. Maras, Turkey, July 8, 1965; s. Mehmet and Nilgün (Büyükavsar) Y.; m. Zehra Bakan, Dec. 6, 1992; children: Talha, Tarik. Grad. with 1st degree, Bosphorus U., Istanbul, Turkey, 1988. Tchr. diplomate. Physics tchr., Olympiad trainer Izmir (Turkey) Özel Yamanlar, 1988-96; writer Sürat A.S., Istanbul, 1997; co. exec. Genç Multimedya, Istanbul, 1997-99; ednl. cons. Ugur Koleji, Nema Egitim Kurumlari, Istanbul, 1998—; physics Olympiad trainer Istanbul Özel Fatih H.S., 1997—; info. tech. and sci. resource person Enka Schs., 1999—; physics Olympiad trainer Izmir Özel Malhatun Kiz Lisesi; physics project coord. Nizamiye Koleji, Aydin, 1995-96, Özel Malhatun Kiz Lidesi, Izmir, 1995-96; cons. family bus. INKA, Istanbul, 1999; patent cons. Huseyin Sepik, Istanbul, 1999; internat. trade cons. Reyyan Trade, Istanbul, 1999. Author 8 books on physics Olympiad. Recipient Success plate Karisiyaka Kaymakamligi, 1995, Coord. award Bursa Özel Nilufer Koleji, 1997, Tchr. award of medalists Internat. Physics Olympiad Orgn., 1992, 93, 94, 95, 96, 97. Mem. Am. Assn. Physics Tchrs., Özögretder. Muslim. Avocations: Web site authoring, multimedia, international trade, table tennis. Office: 23 Nisan Cad 67/2 Armaganevler, Umraniye-81240 Istanbul Turkey

YALE, JOHN PAUL, computer systems developer; b. Uhrichsville, Ohio, Sept. 4, 1945; s. Vernon Elna and Joan (Papworth) Y.; m. Mary Anne Hinkley, Feb. 9, 1966; children: John Vernon, Eric Kendall. AAS, Orange County C.C., 1968; BS, Ohio U., 1971. Dir. Pub. Broadcasting, Athens, Ohio, 1969-71; freelance prodr./dir. GGT, Niantic, Conn., 1971-79; dir. media svcs. L & M Hosps., New London, Conn., 1979-96; dir. sys. devel. C&E group MPTN, Ledyard, Conn., 1996—. Mem. Internat. TV Assn., Internat. Teleconf. Assn., Assn. fo Multimedia Internat., Internat. Internet Assn., Internat. Platform Assn. Home: 38 Sea Spray Ave Niantic CT 06357-3336 Office: 110 Pequot Trail PO Box 3180 Mashantucket CT 06339-3180

YALE, SEYMOUR HERSHEL, dental radiologist, educator, university dean, gerontologist; b. Chgo., Nov. 27, 1920; s. Henry and Dorothy (Kulwin) Y.; m. Muriel Jane Cohen, Nov. 6, 1943; children: Russell Steven, Patricia Ruth. B.S., U. Ill., 1944, D.D.S., 1945, postgrad., 1947-48; postgrad., Spertus Inst. Jewish Studies, 1995—. Pvt. practice of dentistry, 1945-54, 56—; asst. clin. dentistry U. Ill., 1948-49, instr. clin. dentistry, 1949-53, asst. prof. clin. dentistry, 1953-54, assoc. prof. dept. radiology Coll. Dentistry, 1956, prof., head dept. Coll. Dentistry, 1957-65, adminstrv. asst. to dean Coll. Dentistry, 1961-63, asst. dean Coll. Dentistry, 1963-64, acting dean Coll. Dentistry, 1964-65, dean, 1965-87, dean emeritus, 1987—; also mem. grad. faculty dept. radiology Coll. Medicine U. Ill., Chgo., prof. dentistry and health resources mgmt. Sch. Pub. Health, 1987—; sr. dental dir. Dental Care Plus Mgmt. Corp., Chgo.; pres., dir. dental edn. Dental Care Plus Mgmt. Ednl. Svcs., Ltd.; health care facilities planner; dir. tng. Dental Technicians Sch., U.S. Naval Tng. Ctr., Bainbridge, md., 1954-56; mem. subcom. 16 Nat. Com. on Radiation Protection; mem. Radiation Protection Adv. Bd., State of Ill., 1971, City of Chgo. Health Sys. Agy.; founder Ctr. for Rsch. in Periodontal Disease and Oral Molecular Biology, 1977; organizer, chmn. Nat. Conf. on Hepatitis-B in Dentistry, 1982; organizer, dir. Univ. Taskforce Primary Health Care Project, U. Ill., Chgo.; chmn. U. Ill.-U. Stockholm-U. Gothenberg Conf. on Geriatrics, 1985; dir. planning AMVETS/UIC Tchg. Nursing Home Project, 1987-91; co-sponsor 1st Egyptian Dental Congress, 1984; adj. prof. Ctr. for Exercise Sci. and Cardiovasc. Rsch., Northeastern Ill. U., Chgo., 1991, Northwestern U. Sch. Dentistry Divsn. Behavioural Scis., Evanston, Ill., 1996—. Editor-in-chief Dental Care Plus Mgmt. Digest, 1995—. Bd. dirs., co-benefactor (with wife) World Heritage Mus., U. Ill., Urbana, 1985; mem. Hillel Bd., U. Ill.-Chgo.; life mem. (with wife) Bronze Circle of Coll. Liberal Arts, U. Ill., Urbana; mem. (with wife) Pres.' Council, U. Ill. Recipient centennial research award Chgo. Dental Soc., 1959; Distinguished Alumnus award U. Ill., 1973; Harry Sicher Meml. Lecture award Am. Coll. Stomologic Surgeons, 1983. Fellow Acad. Gen. Dentistry (hon.), Am. Coll. Dentists; mem. Ill. Dental Soc. (mem. com. on radiology), Chgo. Dental Soc., Internat. Assn. Dental Rsch., Am. Acad. Oral Roentgenology, Am. Dental Assn., Odontographic Soc. Chgo. (Award of Merit 1982), Council Dental Deans State Ill. (chmn.), N.Y. Acad. Scis., Gerontol. Soc. Am., Pierre Fauchard Acad. (Man of Yr. award Ill. sect. 1988), Am. Pub. Health Assn., Gerontol. Soc. Am., Omicron Kappa Upsilon, Sigma Xi, Alpha Omega (hon.). Achievements include established (with wife) collection of Coins of Ottoman Empire and Related Mohammedan States and supplemental antique map collection at World Heritage Mus., U. of Ill.; established C. Muriel Yale Collection, antique maps of Holy Land collection at Spertus Inst. of Jewish Studies. Home: 155 N Harbor Dr Chicago IL 60601-7364 Office: 30 N Michigan Ave Chicago IL 60602-3402

YALOURIS, NICHOLAS, archaeologist; b. Smyrna, Asia Minor, Aug. 2, 1918; s. Philemon and Anastasia (Zormalia) Y.; grad. dept. philosophy U. Athens, 1940; Ph.D., U. Basel (Switzerland), 1950; m. Athanasia Bogri, May 4, 1963; children—Marc-Pierre, Helen-Anastasia. Researcher, Musé e d'Art et d'Histoire, Geneva, 1949-50; officer Greek Archaeol. Service, 1951-81; dir. antiquities Western Peloponnes, 1952-66, dir. Greek antiquities, 1970-71, dir. Nat. Archaeol. Mus., 1973-80, gen. insp. Service, 1977-81; prof. U. Athens, 1977-78; sr. research fellow Greek and Roman antiquities Met. Mus. Art,

N.Y.C., 1969; lectr. Coll. Year in Athens, 1964-94 ; excavations include ancient Elis, Temple of Apollo Epikourios at Bassae, also sites in Achaia, Elis, Messenia; mem. Inst. Advanced Studies, Princeton, N.J., 1968-69. Served with Greek Army, 1938-41, 45. Fulbright scholar, 1955-56; scholar Warburg Inst., London, 1958. Mem. Greek Archaeol. Soc., German Archaeol. Inst., Austrian Archaeol. Inst., Internat. Olympic Acad. (hon. v.p.), Lexicon Iconographicum Mythologiae Classicae (pres.), Archaeol. Inst. Am. (hon.). Author: Athena als Herrin der Pferde, 1950, The Sculptures of the Parthenon, 1960, The Sculptures of the Temple of Zeus in Olympia, 1967, Olympia, Altis and Museum, 1972, Pegasus, The Art of the Legend from Prehistoric to Modern Times, 1975, The Sculpture of the Temple of Asclepios in Epidanuros, 1989, The Olympic Games in Ancient Greece, 1982, Archaia Glypta (Ancient Sculptures) 1994, The City-State of Elis, The Crade of the Olympic Games, 1996; also guidebooks, articles in field.

YALOW, ROSALYN SUSSMAN, biophysicist; b. N.Y.C., N.Y., July 19, 1921; d. Simon and Clara (Zipper) Sussman; m. A. Aaron Yalow, June 6, 1943; children: Benjamin, Elanna. A.B., Hunter Coll., 1941; M.S., U. Ill., Urbana, 1942, Ph.D., 1945; D.Sc. (hon.), U. Ill., Chgo., 1974, Phila. Coll. Pharmacy and Sci., 1976, N.Y. Med. Coll., 1976, Med. Coll. Wis., Milw., 1977, Yeshiva U., 1977, Southampton (N.Y.) Coll., 1978, Bucknell U., 1978, Princeton U., 1978, Jersey City State Coll., 1979, Med. Coll. Pa., 1979, Manhattan Coll., 1979, U. Vt., 1980, U. Hartford, 1980, Rutgers U., 1980, Rensselaer Poly. Inst., 1980, Colgate U., 1981, U. So. Calif., 1981, Clarkson Coll., 1982, U. Miami, 1983, Washington U., St. Louis, 1983, Adelphi U., 1983, U. Alta. (Can.), 1983, SUNY, 1984, Tel Aviv U., 1985, Claremont (Calif.) U., 1986, Mills Coll., Oakland, Calif., 1986, Cedar Crest Coll., Allentown, Pa., 1988, Drew U., Madison, N.J., 1988, Lehigh U., 1988; L.H.D. (hon.), Hunter Coll., 1978; DSc. (hon.), San Francisco State U., 1989, Technion-Israel Inst. Tech., Haifa, 1989; DSc (hon.), Med. Coll. Ohio Toledo, 1991; L.H.D. (hon.), Sacred Heart U., Conn., 1978, St. Michael's Coll., Winooski Park, Vt., 1979, Johns Hopkins U., 1979, Coll. St. Rose, 1988, Spertus Coll. Judaica, Chgo., 1988; D. honoris causa, U. Rosario, Argentina, 1980, U. Ghent, Belgium, 1984; D. Humanities and Letters (hon.), Columbia U., 1984; DSc (hon.), Fairleigh Dickinson U., 1992, Conn. Coll., 1992, Smith Coll., Northampton, Mass., 1994, Union Coll., Schenectady, 1994. Diplomate: Am. Bd. Scis. Lectr., asst. prof. physics Hunter Coll., 1946-50; physicist, asst. chief radioisotope service VA Hosp., Bronx, N.Y., 1950-70, chief nuclear medicine, 1970-80, acting chief radioisotope service, 1968-70, sr. med. investigator emeritus; research prof. Mt. Sinai Sch. Medicine, CUNY, 1968-74, Disting. Service prof., 1974-79, Solomon A. Berson Disting. prof.-at-large, 1986—; Disting. prof.-at-large Albert Einstein Coll. Medicine, Yeshiva U., 1979-85, prof. emeritus, 1986—; chmn. dept. clin. scis. Montefiore Med. Ctr., Bronx, 1980-85; cons. Lenox Hill Hosp., N.Y.C., 1956-62, WHO, Bombay, 1978; sec. U.S. Nat. Com. on Med. Physics, 1963-67; mem. nat. com. Radiation Protection, Subcom. 13, 1957; mem. Pres.'s Study Group on Careers for Women, 1966-72; sr. med. investigator VA, 1972-92, sr. med. investigator emeritus, 1992—. Co-editor: Hormone and Metabolic Research, 1973-79; editorial adv. council: Acta Diabetologica Latina, 1975-77, Ency. Universalis, 1978—; editorial bd.: Mt. Sinai Jour. Medicine, 1976-79, Diabetes, 1976, Endocrinology, 1967-72; contbr. numerous articles to profl. jours. Bd. dirs. N.Y. Diabetes Assn., 1974. Recipient VA William S. Middleton Med. Research award, 1960; Eli Lilly award Am. Diabetes Assn., 1961; Van Slyke award N.Y. met. sect. Am. Assn. Clin. Chemists, 1968; award A.C.P., 1971; Dickson prize U. Pitts., 1971; Howard Taylor Ricketts award U. Chgo., 1971; Gairdner Found. Internat. award, 1971; Commemorative medallion Am. Diabetes Assn., 1972; Bernstein award Med. Soc. State N.Y., 1974; Boehringer-Mannheim Corp. award Am. Assn. Clin. Chemists, 1975; Sci. Achievement award AMA, 1975; Exceptional Service award VA, 1975; A. Cressy Morrison award N.Y. Acad. Scis., 1975; sustaining membership award Assn. Mil. Surgeons, 1975; Distinguished Achievement award Modern Medicine, 1976; Albert Lasker Basic Med. Research award, 1976; La Madonnina Internat. prize Milan, 1977; Golden Plate award Am. Acad. Achievement, 1977; Nobel prize for physiology/medicine, 1977; citation of esteem St. John's U., 1979; G. von Hevesy medal, 1978; Rosalyn S. Yalow Research and Devel. award established Am. Diabetes Assn., 1978; Banting medal, 1978; Torch of Learning award Am. Friends Hebrew U., 1978; Virchow gold medal Virchow-Pirquet Med. Soc., 1978; Gratum Genus Humanum gold medal World Fedn. Nuclear Medicine or Biology, 1978; Jacobi medallion Asso. Alumni Mt. Sinai Sch. Medicine, 1978; Jubilee medal Coll. of New Rochelle, 1978; VA Exceptional Service award, 1978; Fed. Woman's award, 1961; Harvey lectr., 1966; Am. Gastroenterol. Assn. Meml. lectr., 1972; Joslin lectr. New Eng. Diabetes Assn., 1972; Franklin I. Harris Meml. lectr., 1973; 1st Hagedorn Meml. lectr. Acta Endocrinologica Congress, 1973; Sarasota Med. award for achievement and excellence, 1979; gold medal Phi Lambda Kappa, 1980; Achievement in Life award Ency. Brit., 1980; Theobald Smith award, 1982; Pres.'s Cabinet award U. Detroit, 1982; John and Samuel Bard award in medicine and sci. Bard Coll., 1982; Disting. Research award Dallas Assn. Retarded Citizens, 1982, Nat. Medal Sci., 1988; Abram L. Sachar Silver Medallion Brandeis U., Waltham, Mass., 1989, Disting. Scientist of Yr. award ARCS, N.Y.C., 1989, Golden Scroll award The Jewish Advocate, Boston, 1989, spl. award Clin. Ligand Assay Soc., Washington, 1988, numerous others. Fellow N.Y. Acad. Scis. (chmn. biophysics div. 1964-65), Am. Coll. Radiology (asso. in physics), Clin. Soc. N.Y. Diabetes Assn.; mem. Nat. Acad. Scis., Am. Acad. Arts and Scis., Am. Phys. Soc., Radiation Research Soc., Am. Assn. Physicists in Medicine, Biophys. Soc., Soc. Nuclear Medicine, Endocrine Soc. (Koch award 1972, pres. 1978), Am. Physiol. Soc., (hon.) Harvey Soc., (hon.) Med. Assn. Argentina, (hon.) Diabetes Soc. Argentina, (hon.) Am. Coll. Nuclear Physicians, (hon.) The N.Y. Acad. Medicine, (hon.) Am. Gastroent. Assn., (hon.) N.Y. Roentgen Soc., (hon.) Soc. Nuclear Medicine, Phi Beta Kappa, Sigma Xi, Sigma Pi Sigma, Pi Mu Epsilon, Sigma Delta Epsilon, Tau Beta Pi. Office: Vet Affairs Med Ctr 130 W Kingsbridge Rd Bronx NY 10468-3904

YAM, CONSTANCE SHUK-CHEE, dermatologist; b. Hong Kong, July 19, 1940; d. Tung-Lam and Shuet-Ying (Chan) Y.; children: Christine, Monica. MBBS, U. Hong Kong, 1965. Diplomate Am. Bd. Dermatology. Resident in dermatology Cin. Gen. Hosp., 1969-71; vis. fellow Columbia-Presbyn. Med. Ctr., N.Y.C., 1971-72; pvt. practice Hong Kong, 1973-74, 80—; asst. clin. prof. dermatology U. Cin. Sch. Medicine, 1975-79; pvt. practice Cin., 1976-79; admitting privilege Hong Konh Adventist Hosp., Hong Kong Sanatorium Hosp., Canossa Hosp.; dermatology cons. H.K. Adventist Hosp., 1980-86. Author: Save Your Skin and Stay Young, 1986. Fellow Am. Acad. Dermatology, Am. Soc. for Dermatology Surgery, Hong Kong Acad. Medicine, Australian Coll. Cosmetic Surgery (hon.); mem. Internat. Soc. Dermatology Surgery, Asian Acad. of Cosmetic Surgery, Hong Kong Coll. Physicians, Hong Kong Surg. Laser Assn., Am. Acad. Cosmetic Surgery (corr.). Avocations: swimming, scuba diving, travel, reading, painting. Office: 1203 Melbourne Plz, 33 Queens Rd Ctrl, Hong Kong China

YAM, JOSEPH CHI-KWONG, financial executive; b. China, Sept. 9, 1948; s. Shun and Hook-chun (Shum) Y.; children: Denise W.Y., Lawrence T.Y. B in Social Scis., U. Hong Kong, 1970; diploma in stats. and nat. acctg., Inst. Social Studies, The Hague, 1974. Statistician Census and Stats. Dept. Hong Kong Govt., 1971-76, economist, prin. asst. sec. for econ. svc. Econ. Svcs. Br., 1976-82, prin. asst. sec., dep. sec. for monetary affairs, 1982-91, dir. Office of the Exch. Fund, 1991-93, chief exec. Hong Kong Monetary Authority, 1993—. Fellow Chartered Inst. Bankers, Hong Kong Inst. Bankers; mem. Hong Kong Jockey Club (steward, voting mem.), Hong Kong Bankers Club, Royal Hong Kong Golf Club. Avocations: golf, horse racing, swimming. Office: Hong Kong Monetary Auth, 30/F 3 Garden Rd Ctrl, Hong Kong China*

YAMADA, HIROAKI, engineering educator, chemist; b. Fukuyama, Hiroshima, Japan, Nov. 10, 1936; s. Tatsuo and Yasue (Takahashi) T.; m. Chizuko Shichijo, Sept. 1, 1995. B in Engring., Kinki U., Osaka, Japan, 1960; MSc, Osaka U., 1962, DSc, 1968. Rsch. assoc. Kobe (Japan) U., 1965-85, assoc. prof., 1985—. Contbr. articles to profl. jours., chpts. to books. Recipient grant in aid Itoh Sci. Found., 1986. Fellow Japan Soc. High Pressure Sci. and Tech.; mem. ACS, Chem. Soc. Japan. Avocations: high power rifle target shooting, car driving. Home: 117 13-20 2-chome, Nigawa-kita, Takarazuka 665-0061, Japan Office: Kobe U Dept Chem Fac Sci, Rokkodai-cho Nada-ku, Kobe 657-0013, Japan

YAMADA, JASON MASAYOSHI, periodontist, educator; b. Honolulu, Aug. 10, 1964; s. Shiro and Yoshiko (Watanabe) Y.; m. C. Janice Matsuyama, Sept. 23, 1995; 1 child, Jenna Mari. BS, U. So. Calif., 1986, DDS, 1990; MS, Northwestern U., 1992. Asst. prof. U. So. Calif., L.A., 1990; pvt. practice Torrance, Calif.; founder Ctr. for Advanced Dental Surgery, L.A., 1998—. Contbr. articles to profl. jours. including Am. Acad. Periodontology, Jour. Prosthodontics; inventor chem. used for periodontics. Mem., fundraiser WWI-442/MIS/100th, L.A., 1999. Mem. ADA, Calif. Dental Assn., Am. Acad. Implant Dentistry, Japanese Am. Dental Soc. (pres. 1995-97, mem. adv. bd. 1992—), Harbor Dental Soc. (pres.-elect, pres. 1999—, exec. bd. dirs. 1994—), Omicron Kappa Upsilon. Avocations: tennis, golf, basketball, skiing. Office: 2369 Torrance Blvd Torrance CA 90501-2541

YAMADA, KEIICHI, engineering educator, university official; b. Dec. 23, 1931. M in Engring., U. Tokyo, 1956; DSc, U. Göttingen, Germany, 1958, U. Freiburg, Germany, 1959; D in Engring., U. Tokyo, 1964. Asst. prof. U. Tokyo, 1959-68; assoc. prof. Tokyo Inst. Tech., 1968-75, prof., 1975-77; prof. U. Tsukuba, Ibaraki, 1977-95, prof. emeritus, 1995—, dir. Inst. Socio-Econ. Planning, 1984-86, dir. Rsch. Ctr. for Univ. Studies, 1986-90, provost of colls., 1991-93; vice-dir. Inst. for Policy Scis., Tokyo, 1984—. Author: Life Cycles of Scientific Research, 1986, The World Mountains from the Air, 1987; editor-in-chief Jour. Sci. Policy and Rsch. Mgmt., 1985-88; one-man syow includes Le Montagna del Cielo, Italy, 1989. Mem. Japan-China Soc. (councilor 1990—). Avocation: alpine aerial photography.

YAMADA, KOHEI, art educator; b. Osaka, Japan, Mar. 21, 1926; s. Tokujiro and Hisako Yamada; m. Sachiko Fujimoto, Dec. 1952; 1 child, Ruka Tamai. BA, Kyoto (Japan) U., 1950; LittD, Osaka U., 1994. Tchr. Hyogo Prefectural High Sch., Ashiya, Japan, 1950-53; fellow Kyoto U., 1953-62; lectr. Naniwa Jr. Coll., 1962-64, Osaka U. Arts, 1964-71; prof. Osaka U. of Arts, 1972, dean of faculty, 1975-90, prof. grad. sch., 1993—; lectr. grad. sch. Kansei Gakin U., Kobe, Japan, 1980—. Author: All of Dostoevsky's, 1973, The Lightning Flashes of Toledo, 1973, Science of Russian Arts, 1994, Dostoevsky and Chekhov, 1999. Mem. Japan Soc. Image Arts and Scis. (bd. dirs.), Japanese Soc. for Aesthetics. Home: Hashiridani 1-22-22, Hirakata City Japan Office: Osaka Univ of Arts, Minamigawachi Kanancho-Higashiyama, Osaka Japan

YAMADA, MAMORU, molecular biologist, researcher; b. Onoda, Japan, Dec. 24, 1954; s. Toshio and Chisayo (Sasaki) Y.; m. Yasue Ohno; 1 child, Kaoru. B, Yamaguchi Univ., Yamaguchi, Japan, M; PhD, Yamaguchi Univ., Ube, Japan; postgrad., Univ. Calif., 1985-87. Rsch. assoc. Yamaguchi Univ., Ube, 1984-85, 87-90; assoc. prof. Yamaguchi Univ., Yamaguchi, 1990—. Contbr. articles to profl. jours. Recipient Nakamura prize Yamaguchi Medical Sch. Soc., 1988, Koso-Ōyo symposium prize, 2000. Office: Yamaguchi Univ Dept Biol Ch, Yoshida 1677-1, Yamaguchi 753-8515, Japan

YAMADA, RYO, rheumatologist, researcher; b. Shiogama, Japan, Jan. 22, 1968; s.Koh andAyako (Itoh) Y.; m. Junko Nakayama, Mar. 13, 1993; children: Hana, Sato. MD, U. Tokyo, 1992. Am. Bd. Internal Medicine. Resident Nat. Med. Cen., Tokyo, 1992-93; house officer internal medicine U. Mich. Med. Cen., Ann Arbor, 1994-97; staff physician allergy and rheumatology U. Tokyo Hosp., 1997-99; postgrad. rheumatology U. Tokyo, 1999—. Mem Japan Rheumatism Assn., Japanese Soc. Internal Medicine. Avocation: badminton. Office: U Tokyo Hosp Rheum/IM, 7-3-1 Hongo, 113-8655 Tokyo Japan

YAMADA, RYOJI, economist; b. Tochigi-Ken, Japan, Sept. 29, 1928; s. Mamoru and Nami Y.; B.A., Aoyama Gakuin U., 1952; MA, Hitotsubashi U., 1955; Fulbright fellow, Stanford U., 1963-64; postgrad. Brookings Instn., 1964, Internat. Faculty Comparative Econs., Luxemburg, 1964; m. Sadayo Yamada, Aug. 26, 1956; children: Mika, Kazuto. Prof., Aoyama Gakuin U., Tokyo, 1955-69; lectr. Internat. Christian U., Tokyo, 1958-61, 67-70, 80-83, Tokyo Theol. Sem., 1961-63, 67-72, Seikei U., Tokyo, 1971-74; prof. econs. Tokyo Coll. Econs., 1970—, dean, v.p., 1974-76, bd. govs., 1974-76, pres. univ. libr., 1988-91; mem. rsch. com. fin. system in Japan, Fedn. Banker's Assn. in Japan, Tokyo, 1982-84; advanced research works for monetary policy Econ. Planning Bur., 1960-62. Mem. final screening com. grad. applicants Fulbright Com. in Japan, 1965-67, 69; final screening com. grad. applicants East-West Center, U. Hawaii, 1966. Mem. Japan Fin. Assn. (bd. dirs. 1994—, exec. dir. 1995—), Am. Econ. Assn., Can. Econ. Assn. Mem. Nihon Kiristo-Kyodan. Author: An Introduction to Finance, 1957; Financial Structure in Japan, 1967; Lectures on Keynesian Economics, 1970; A Study in International Finance, 1973; An Introduction to Theory of Finance, 1977; Banking in Future, 1983; A Theoretical Study on Financial Structure, 1984, Introduction to Economics, 1988; editor: International Finance, 1996. Home: 7-4 Kiyokawa-cho, Hachioji-shi Tokyo 193, Japan Office: 1-chome 7, Minami-cho, Kokubunji Tokyo 185, Japan

YAMADA, SHIGERU, engineering educator; b. Ono-cho, Hiroshima, Japan, July 6, 1952; s. Setsuo and Yasuko (Kawamoto) Y.; m. Sachiko Kameyama, June 17, 1959; children: Nozomi, Yu. BS in Engring., Hiroshima U., 1975, MS, 1977, PhD, 1985. Mem. Nippondenso Co., Ltd., Kariya-shi, Japan, 1977-80; asst. prof. Okayama (Japan) U., Japan, 1983-88; assoc. prof. Hiroshima U., 1988-93; prof. Tottori (Japan) U., Japan, 1993—; cons. NTT Software Labs., Japan, 1989-91, Info.-Tech. Promotion Agy., Japan, 1992-94, Mitsubishi Heavy Industries, Ltd., 1994—, Japan Soc. Mech. Engrs., 1995—, Quality Mgmt. Assn. in Chugoku Area, Japan, 1997—, Deming Prize Com., Union Japanese Scientists and Engrs., Japan, 1999—. Author: Software Reliability Assessment Technology, 1989, Fault Tolerant Computing, 1989, Software Reliability: Theory and Practical Application, 1990, Encyclopedia of Computer Software, 1990, Introduction to Software Management Model, 1993, Software Reliability Models, 1994, Reliability Handbook, 1997, Statistical Quality Control for Total Quality Management, 1998. Blood donation mem. Red Cross Soc. Japan. Recipient Telecom Sys. Tech. award Telecom. Advancement Found., 1993, grant-in-aid for sci. rsch. Ministry of Edn., Sci. and Culture, Japan, 1985—, citation of excellence-high quality rating ANBAR Electronic Intelligence, U.K. Mem. IEEE, Info. Processing Soc. Japan (Best Author award 1992), Inst. Electronics, Info. and Comm. Engrs. Japan, Ops. Rsch. Soc. Japan, Japan Indsl. Mgmt. Assn., Reliability Engring. Assn. Japan (Best Paper award 1999), Japan Soc. Indsl. and Applied Math., Japan Soc. Quality Control, Nat. Geog. Soc., Soc. Project Mgmt. Avocations: folklore music and dances, movies. Home: Nishi 1-570 Koyama-cho, Tottori-shi 680-0947, Japan Office: Tottori U Faculty Engring, Minami 4-101 Koyama-cho, Tottori-shi 680-8552, Japan

YAMADA, SHIN-ICHIRO, computer services company executive; b. Hakodate, Japan, Feb. 20, 1948; s. Shotaro and Shizue (Kondo) Y.; m. Kazuko Kameyama, May 2, 1971; children: Junya, Mizuho, Kenji. BSc, Muroran Inst. Technology, 1970. From sr. rsch. engr. to sr. mgr. NTT Musashino Lab., Tokyo, Japan, 1970-95; dir., v.p. Verisign, Tokyo, 1996; gen. mgr. NTT Electronics Tech., Tokyo, 1997; pres., CEO Exway Inc., Tokyo, 1998—. Author: LSIs and Certification Authority, 1996, Secure Electronic Commerce, 1998; contbr. articles to profl. jours. Mem. IEEE, Inst. Electronics Info. & Comm., Info. Processing Soc. Japan. Avocations: reading, badminton, bowling. E-mail: yamada@exway.co.jp. Home: 2-5-27 Unomori, 228-0801 Sagamihara Kanagawa, Japan Office: Exway Inc, 2-8-8 Kyobashi Chuo-ku, Tokyo 104-0031, Japan

YAMADA, SHOJI, electronics educator, administrator, retired; b. Hamamatsu, Japan, Jan. 2, 1929; s. Jiro and Hide (Kihira) Y.; m. Kazuko Hirano, May 15, 1955; children: Yukihiko, Yoko. BSc, Nagoya U., Japan, 1951, DSc, 1962. Lectr. Meijo U., Nagoya, 1951-52; lectr. Shizuoka U., Humamatsu, Japan, 1960-62, rsch. assoc., 1952-60, assoc. prof., 1962-65, prof., 1965-92; prof. Shizuoka Inst. Sci. & Tech., Fukuri, Japan, 1992-99, dean faculty, 1995-99; retired. Author: Large-Area Chromogenics, 1990, Optical Properties of Semiconductors, 1995; contbr. articles to profl. jours. Recipient Saitoh prize Saitoh Found., Shizuoka, 1976, Takayanagi prize Takayangi Found., Shizuoka, 1989. Mem. Japan Soc. Applied Physics, Chromogenics Part Japan (sec. 1980—), Japan Soc. Promotion Sci. (rsch. com. mem. 1965—). Avocations: Go, history.

YAMADA, TAKAO, educator, lawyer; b. Nagoya, Japan, Apr. 12, 1937; s. Katsuichi and Suzuko Yamada; m. Midori Itoh, Jan. 18, 1964; 1 child, Sumio. LLB, U. Tokyo, 1960, LLM, 1962; LLM, Harvard U., 1973. Rsch. assoc. U. Tokyo, 1962-67; lectr. Chuo U., Tokyo, 1967-68, assoc. prof., 1968-74, prof., 1974-80; prof. Yokohama (Japan) Nat. U., 1980-98, Nihon U., Tokyo, 1998—; chair Kanto Dist. Labor Rels. Commn. for Seafarers, Yokohama, 1994—. Author: Autonomy and Private Affairs, 1987; co-author: Introduction to Civil Law, 2d edit., 1995; editor: Studies in Tort Law, 6 vols., 1996-97. Rep. dir. Japan Civil Liberties Union, Tokyo, 1988-99. Mem. Japan Assn. Bioethics (dir. 1993—. Home: 6-9-19 Himonya, 152-0003 Meguro, Tokyo Japan Office: Nihon U Coll Law, 2-3-1 Misaki-Cho, 101-8375 Chiyoda, Tokyo 101-8375, Japan

YAMADA, TETSUJI, health economist, educator. M of Internat. Affairs, Columbia U., 1978; MPhil, CUNY, 1983, PhD in Econs., 1987. Instr. CUNY, N.Y.C., 1982-86; asst. prof. dept. econs. Rutgers U., Camden, N.J., 1987-91; assoc. prof. Ritsumeikan U., Kyoto, Japan, 1991-92; rsch. fellow NBER, 1987-90, rsch. assoc., 1991-94; health economist Internat. Leadership Ctr. Longevity and Society, 1993-94; rsch. assoc. Ctr. Pacific Basin Fed. Res. Bank, San Francisco, 1990—; assoc. prof. Rutgers U., 1992—, chair dept. econs., 1996-99; exec. bd. China East Inst. Soc. Ins., China, 1998—; rep. Japan Econ. Fedn., Ditchley, Oxford, Eng., 1994; vis. rsch. scholar Inst. Policy and Planning Scis., Tsukuba U., Japan, 1997, 99; temp. advisor WHO, 1999; faculty assoc. The Walter Rand Inst., 1999—; ctr. assoc. The Ctr. for Children and Childhood Studies, 2000—; reviewer and referee profl. jours. and books. Contbr. articles to profl. jours. Rsch. grantee Ministry of Edn., Japan, 1991, Iryo Kagaku Kenkyu Jo, Japan, 1991-92, 96-97, Pfizer Health Rsch. Found., Japan, 1992-93, 21st Century Cultural Rsch. Found., Japan, 1993, Ministry of Health and Welfare, Japan, 1993-94, Nomura Found., Japan, 1995-96, Iryo Keizai Kenkyu Kiko, Japan, 1997-98, Rutgers U., 1992-2000. Mem. Am. Econ. Assn., So. Econs. Assn., Western Econ. Assn., Internat. Health Econ. Assn., Japan Econ. Sem., Omicron Delta Epsilon (award). Fax: 212-297-0192. E-mail: ytetsuji@aol.com. Home: 300 E 40th St # 4M New York NY 10016-2147 Office: Dept Econs-CCAS Rutgers Univ State Univ NJ Camden NJ 08102

YAMADA, YASUHIKO, geographer, educator; b. Kakogawa, Hyogo, Japan, May 27, 1927; s. Takezo Yamada and Toyono Hata; m. Masue Matsumoto, May 6, 1955; children: Norihiro, Hirohisa. MA, Ritsumeikan U., Kyoto, Japan, 1954; DSc, Tokyo Kyoiku U., 1974. Asst. Ritsumeikan U., Kyoto, 1954-59; asst. prof. Iwate U., Morioka, Japan, 1959-70; prof. Iwate U., 1970-76; prof. Chiba (Japan) U., 1976-93, prof. emeritus, 1993-99; prof. Kōbe (Japan) Gakuin U., 1993-97. Author: The Ancient Frontier in Northeastern Japan, 1971, A Study for Correlation Between Faith of Azimuth and Regional Planning in Ancient Times, 1986, Roman Centures Land Allotments and Jori Land Allotment, 1999; editor: The Science of Region, 1984, The Historical Cities in all Japan, Vol. 1-12, 1989-97, Suggest to Hydrosphere Environment, 1993, The Science of Region Based on the Turning Point, 1993, Direction and Folk Customs and Industry, 1994, Dictionary on Relating to Azimuth, 2000, Dictionary of Rudiment and Disappearance Place Name, 2000. Mem. Assn. Japanese Geographers (coun. 1988-97), Assn. Hist. Geographers in Japan (coun. 1976-90, pres. 1990-93, coun. 1997—), Human Geog. Soc. Japan (conferee 1976-96). Home: Chiyoda 5 7 14, Yotsukaido, Chiba 284-0015, Japan Office: Kōbe Gakuin U, Ikawadani Arise 518, Nishi-ku Kōbe 651-2120, Japan

YAMAGATA, KANATO, neuroscientist, researcher; b. Shio-machi, Japan, Apr. 17, 1960; s. Shuhei and Hisako Yamagata; m. Shigemi Ishimoto, Mar. 13, 1988; 1 child, Tomosato Naoki. PhD, Kanazawa (Japan) U., 1989. Asst. prof. Osaka (Japan) U., 1989-90; postdoctoral fellow Johns Hopkins U., Balt., 1990-93; rsch. assoc. Howard Hughes Med. Inst., Balt., 1990-92; asst. prof. Osaka U., Suita, Japan, 1994-95; chief Tokyo Met. Inst. for Neurosci., Fuchu, Japan, 1995-98, dir., 1998—. Contbr. articles to profl. jours. Mem. Japanese Soc. for Neurochemistry (coun.), Japanese Pharmacol. Soc. Office: Tokyo Met Inst Neurosci, Molec Neuro/2-6 Musashidai, Fuchu 183-8526, Japan

YAMAGATA, KENJI, internist; b. Tokyo, Dec. 30, 1946; s. Kenkichi and Hiroko (Goto) Y.; m. Aiko Hirose, Aug. 31, 1975; children: Akira, Yuri, Hiroshi. BS, U. Tokyo, 1972; MD, Loma Linda U., 1976. Diplomate Am. Bd. Internal Medicine. Clin. asst. resident Loma Linda U., Calif., 1976-80; chmn. internal medicine Kobe Adventist Hosp., Japan, 1981—, chief of staffs, 1989—, v.p., 1996—; cons. Five-Day Plans Against Smoking, Kobe, 1980—. Author: SDA and Modern Japanese Society, 1972, SDA and Politics, 1973, The Meaning of Suffering, 1986, Dying as Human, 1996; contbr. articles to profl. jours. Mem. ACP, Japanese Soc. Internal Medicine, Japanese Soc. for Palliative Medicine, Am. Acad. for Hospice and Palliative Medicine, Japanese Med. Assn., Japan Chrisitan Med. Assn., Japan Xylophone Assn. Office: Kobe Adventist Hosp, 4-1 8 chome Arinodai Kita-ku, Kobe 651-1321, Japan

YAMAGUCHI, AKIRA, engineering educator; b. Ayabe Kyoto, Japan, Oct. 15, 1940; s. Tohzoh and Matsue Yamaguchi; m. Shunko Inoh, June 11, 1972. BS, Nagoya Inst. Tech., 1964; PhD, Nagoya U., 1977. Engr. Toshiba Co. Ltd., Kawasaki, Japan, 1964-65; asst. prof. Nagoya (Japan) Inst. Tech., 1965-72, lectr., 1972-78, assoc. prof., 1978-89, prof., 1989—. Author: How to Use Thermodynamics for High Temperature Materials, 1989, Usage of Phase Equilibria Daiagrams, 1997. Recipient New Tech. Devel. Found. award for tech. contbn., 1981, Tech. Assn. Refractories of Japan award for disting. contbn., 1993, Ceramic Soc. Japan award for acad. achievement in ceramic sci. and tech., 1995, award for excellent writings Japanese Soc. for Engring. Edn., 1994. Avocations: music, travel, golf. Home: 5-5-3 Iwanaridai, Kasugai 487-0033, Japan Office: Nagoya Inst Tech, Gokiso-cho, Showa-ku, Nagoya 466-8555, Japan

YAMAGUCHI, HARUHIKO, wood chemistry educator; b. Fukuoka, Japan, Jan. 21, 1943; s. Yasuzo and Aoyagi (Yachiyo) Y.; m. Kuniko Satake, May 6, 1978; children: Hidehiko, Youko. M, Kyushu U., 1969, D, 1991. Asst. prof. Kyushu U., Fukuoka, Japan, 1974-78, instr., 1978—. Achievements include patents on much-functional woody materials and their manufacturing process, porous spherical tannin resin and its manufacturing process, tannin and lignin adhesives and their manufacturing process, wood-inorganic complex compounds and their manufacturing process, and antifungal, antibacterial and fire-retardant woody materials. Office: Faculty Agrl Kyushu U, 6-10-1 Hakozaki Higashi-ku, Fukuoka 812, Japan

YAMAGUCHI, KAZUYUKI, history educator; b. Yokohama, Japan, June 10, 1928; s. Tokiharu and Kunie (Wada) Y.; m. Hiroko Ohtani, Mar. 21, 1965; children: Tokiko, Yuko. BA, Waseda U., Tokyo, 1952. Rsch. Ohkuma Inst., Waseda U., 1953-55, rschr. Inst. Social Scis., 1955-62, libr., 1962-73; instr. lit. Komazawa U., Tokyo, 1973-74, asst. prof., 1974-79, prof., 1979-95. Editor: Ohkuma Monjo, 5 vols., 1958-62; contbr. articles to profl. jours. Fellow Japan Assn. Internat. Rels. Avocation: bamboo flute. Home: 4-1-7 Zaimokuza, Kamakura Kanagawa-ken 248, Japan

YAMAGUCHI, KIYOTADA, food service executive; b. Yokohama, Kanagawa, Japan, Sept. 12, 1947; s. Torazo and Kuniko (Kojima) Y. BA, Nihon U., 1970; BS, Utah State U., 1977. Asst. v.p. Avco Fin. Svcs., Tokyo, 1977-87; sr. v.p. Assocs. Corp. of N.Am., Japan, 1987-97; rep. dir. K. Yamaguchi Corp., Tokyo, 1997—. Home: Parkheim Kotakemukaihara#111, 3-6-18 Komone Itabashi, Tokyo 173-0037, Japan

YAMAGUCHI, NOBUO, chemical company executive; b. Dec. 23, 1924; m. Yoshiko. Degree in commerce, Tokyo U., 1952. Chmn. bd. Asahi Chem. Industry, Chiyoda, Japan; chmn. ALC Assocs. Office: Asahi Chem Industry Co Ltd, Hibiya-Mitsui Bldg 1-2, Yurakucho 1 chome Chiyoda Tokyo 100, Japan*

YAMAGUCHI, SEIYA, environmental and occupational medicine consultant; b. Nagasaki-city, Japan, May 27, 1926; s. Ryousai and Suzuko (Kaharu) Y.; m. Keiko Azumi, May 3, 1955; children: Hisata Toshiko, Yamaguchi Kenya. MD, Kyushu U., 1951, PhD, 1956. Prof., dir. Dept. of Pub. Health, Kurume U., 1965-75, Inst. of Cmty. Medicine, Tsukuba U., 1975-90; prof., pres. Environ. and Occupl. Health Inst., Tokyo, 1990—; ILO expert, 1970; mem. expert com. WHO, 1973-91; cons. ICI Japan, Daiwa Inst. of Rsch. Ltd.; cons., expert Japan Internat. Cooperation Agy. and Overseas, Econ. Cooperation Fund, 1973—. Author 2 books; co-author 22 books; contbr. numerous articles to profl. jours. Recipient K. M. Bhansali award

Med. Assn. of India, 1988. Fellow Am. Coll. Occupl. and Environ. Medicine; mem. N.Y. Acad. of Sci., Collegium Ramazzini. Avocations: golf, Go. Office: Environ/Occupl Health Inst, Miyamae 2-21-10 Suginami-ku, Tokyo 168-0081, Japan

YAMAGUCHI, SHIGEHIRO, chemist; b. Nagasaki, Japan, July 22, 1961; s. Itsuo and Kazue (Matsuyama) Y. B Engring., Yokohama Nat. U., 1984, M Engring., 1988, DEng, 2000. Rsch. assoc. Teikyo Heisei U., Ichihara, Japan, 1989—. Mem. AAAS, Chem. Soc. Japan, Japan Oil Chemists' Soc., Am. Chem. Soc. Home: 5-6-9 Oyumino, Midori Ward, Chiba 266-0016, Japan Office: Teikyo Heisei U, 2289-23 Uruido, Ichihara Chiba 290-0193, Japan

YAMAGUCHI, SHIGERU, judge; b. Chiba, Japan, Nov. 4, 1932. Degree in Law, Kyoto U., 1955. Bar: Japan, 1954. Asst. judge Okayama Dist. Ct./Okayama Family Ct., 1957; judge Hakodate Dist. Ct./Hakodate Family Ct., 1967; dir. Secretariat of Rsch. and Tng. Inst. for Ct. Clks., 1969; judge (presiding judge of divsn.) Tokyo Dist. Ct., 1976-80; dir. Secretariat of Tokyo High Ct., 1980-83, Gen. affairs Bur. of Gen. Secretariat of Supreme Ct., 1983-88; pres. Kofu Dist. Ct./Kofu Family Ct., 1988-89; judge (presiding judge of divsn.) Tokyo High Ct., 1989-91; pres. Legal Tng. and Rsch. Inst., 1991-94, Fukuoka High Ct., 1994-97; justice Supreme Ct. of Japan, Tokyo, 1997, chief justice, 1997—. Office: Supreme Court of Japan, 4-2 Hayabusa-cho Chiyoda-ku, Tokyo 102-8651, Japan

YAMAGUCHI, SHOKO, journalist; b. Dairen, Japan, Sept. 5, 1940; arrived in France, 1990; s. Wataro and Tazuko (Nishijima) Y. Lic. Letters, Keio U., Tokyo, 1963. Cert. Ctr. Formation Journalists Paris. Journalist Sankei Shimbun, Tokyo, 1966—, dir. bur. Paris, 1991—; corr. Jour. Sankei Shimbun, Paris. Recipient prize Vaughn-UEDA, UPI, 1994. Avocation: music. Office: Sankui Shimbun, 51-53 Ave Champs Elysees, 75008 Paris France

YAMAGUCHI, TORU, internist; b. Kobe, Japan, Mar. 7, 1958. MD, Kobe U., 1982, PhD, 1989. Lic. physician, Japan. Resident internal medicine Kobe U. Hosp., 1982-83, Uwajima (Japan) City Hosp., 1983-85; sr. staff internal medicine Miki City Hosp., 1989, Seirankai Mima Hosp., 1989-91; clin. staff and asst. prof. medicine 3d divsn. Dept. Medicine, Kobe U., 1991-94, 99—; chief internal medicine Hattori Hosp., Hyogo, Japan, 1994-96; rsch. fellow Brigham & Women's Hosp., Boston, 1996-99. Contbr. articles to profl. jours. Rsch. grantee Yamanouchi Found., 1990, Smoking Rsch. Found., 1992, Japanese Ministry of Edn., Sci. and Culture, 1993, 94, Yamanouchi Found., 1996, Mochida Found., 1996. Fellow Japanese Soc. Internal Medicine; mem. Japan Endocrine Soc., Japanese Soc. Gastroenterology, Japanese Soc. Bone and Mineral Rsch., Am. Soc. Bone and Mineral Rsch., Endocrine Soc. Office: Kobe U 3d Div Dept Medicine, 7-5-1 Kusunoki-cho Chuo-ku, Kobe 650-0017, Japan

YAMAGUCHI, YURIKO FUJITA, artist; b. Japan, Jan. 25, 1948; came to the U.S., 1971; d. Alexander and Michi (Hirose) Fujita; m. Hiroyuki Yamaguchi, Mar. 25, 1975; children: Seiji, Mariko. BA, U. Calif., Berkeley, 1975; MFA, U. Md., 1979. Instr. U. Md., College Park, 1982-83; adj. faculty Corcoran Sch. Art, Washington, 1988-97; vis. artist Md. Inst. Art, Balt., 1991, 95, Mass. Coll. Art, Boston, 1994. Exhibited in shows including Koplin Gallery, L.A., 1991, 94, 96, 99, Penine Hart Gallery, N.Y., 1989, 94, L.A. County Mus., 1987, Hirshhorn Mus., 1984, Gallery Emon, Japan, 1997, 2000, Numark Gallery, 1999; commd. wall mural Atlanta Internat. Airport, 1998; represented in permanent collections at Hirshhorn Mus., Nat. Mus. Women in Arts, Nat. Mus. Am. Art, Smith Coll. Art Mus. Fellow Va. Mus. Fine Arts, 1988, 85, Mid-Atlantic Found., 1995; grantee Va. Commn. Arts, 1994, Salzburg Kunstlerhaus Residency grant, 1993. Home: 1517 Snughill Ct Vienna VA 22182-1724

YAMAKAWA, DAVID KIYOSHI, JR., lawyer; b. San Francisco, Jan. 25, 1936; s. David and Shizu (Negishi) Y. BS, U. Calif., Berkeley, 1958, JD, 1963. Bar: Calif. 1964, U.S. Supreme Ct. 1970. Prin. Law Offices David K. Yamakawa Jr., San Francisco, 1964—; dep. dir. Cmty. Action Agy., San Francisco, 1968-69; dir. City Demonsration Agy., San Francisco, 1969-70; mem. adv. coun. Calif. Senate Subcom. on the Disabled, 1982-83, Ctr. for Mental Health Svcs., Substance Abuse and Mental Health Svcs., Adminstrn. U.S. Dept. Health and Human Svcs., 1995-99; chmn. cmty. residential treatment system adv. com. Calif. Dept. Mental Health, 1980-85, San Francisco Human Rights Commn., 1977-80; pres. Legal Assistance to the Elderly, 1981-83; 2d v.p. Nat. Conf. Social Welfare, 1983-89; v.p. Region IX Nat. Mental Health Assn., 1981-83; mem. cmty. partnership bd. Sch. Social Welfare, U. Calif., Berkeley, 1999—. vice chmn. Mt. Zion Hosp. and Med. Ctr., 1986-88; bd. dirs. United Neighborhood Ctrs. of Am., 1977-83, ARC Bay Area, 1988-91, Goldman Inst. on Aging, 1993-99, v.p. 1994-96, vice-chmn. 1996-99, hon. lifetime dir., exec. com. mem., 1999—; trustee Mt. Zion Med. Ctr. U. Calif., San Francisco, 1993-97, UCSF/Mt. Zion, UCSF Stanford Health Care, 1997-2000; chmn. bd. trustees United Way Bay Area, 1983-85; CFO Action for Nature, Inc., 1987—; bd. dirs. Ind. sector, 1986-92; bd. dirs. Friends of the San Francisco Human Rights Commn., 1980—, CFO, 1980-85, 94—, vice chmn. 1985-94; bd. dirs. Father Alfred Boedeker's La Madre Found., 1982—, v.p. 1994—; bd. dirs. Hispanic Cmty. Found. of the Bay Area, 1989-98, legal counsel, 1989-98; bd. dirs. Kimochi Inc., 1999—, Goldman Inst., 1999—, San Francisco Sr. Ctr., 1999—; bd. dirs. Non-Profit Svcs., Inc., 1987—, sec. 1987-90; chmn. 1990—; pres. Coun. Internat. Programs, San Francisco, 1987-89, Internat. Inst. San Francisco, 1990-93; mem. citizens adv. com. San Francisco Hotel Tax Fund Grants for the Arts Program, 1991—. Recipient John B. Williams Outstanding Planning and Agy. Rels. vol. award United Way of the Bay Area, 1980, Mortimer Fleishhacker Jr. Outstanding Vol. award United Way, 1985, Spl. Recognition award Legal Assistance to the Elderly, 1983, Commendation award Bd. Suprs. City and County of San Francisco, 1983, cert. Honor, 1985, San Francisco Found. award, 1985, 1st Mental Health Awareness award Mental Health Assn., San Francisco, 1990, David Yamakawa Day proclaimed in San Francisco, 1985. Mem. ABA (Liberty Bell award 1986). Office: 582 Market St Ste 410 San Francisco CA 94104-5301

YAMAKAWA, TETSUFUMI, economist; b. Oumi-town, Niigata, Japan, Mar. 18, 1957; s. Michio and Naoko (Taniguchi) Y.; m. Satomi Fukiba, May 22, 1994. BA in Econs., Hitotsubashi U., Japan, 1979; MA in Econs., Brown U., Providence, 1984, PhD in Econs., 1992. Dir. econ. rsch. The Bank of Japan, Tokyo, 1979-94; dir. econ. rsch. Goldmnan Sachs (Japan) Ltd., 1995—, mng. dir., 1998—. Office: Goldman Sachs (Japan) Ltd, 1-12-32 Akasaka-Minato-ku, Tokyo Japan

YAMAKI, MASAO, dentist, educator; b. Osaka, Japan, June 14, 1934; s. Shigeji and Shige (Shirakawa) Y.; m. Hiromi Yamashita, Dec. 18, 1963; children: Hiroshi, Mariko. D.D.S., Tokyo Med. and Dental U., 1960; D. Med. Sci., Kyoto U., 1965. Research fellow Eastman Dental Ctr., Rochester, N.Y., 1965-66, research assoc., 1966-67; instr. Hiroshima U. (Japan), 1967-68, assoc. prof., 1968-77, prof., 1977-98, hon. prof., 1998—. Author: Standard Textbook of Dental Materials, 1995. Mem. Internat. Assn. Dental Rsch., Japanese Soc. Dental Materials and Devices. Home: 1362-129 Katsugi, Kabe-cho, Hiroshima 731-0235, Japan Office: Hiroshima U Sch Dentistry, Dept Dent Mats, 1-2-3 Kasumi-cho, Hiroshima 734, Japan

YAMAKURA, AKIHIRO, English educator; b. Tenri, Nara, Japan, May 28, 1952; s. Eiji Yamakura and Nobuko Kadota; m. Machiko Fukui. MA, U. Tex., 1983. Internat. planning staff Sharp Corp., Osaka, Japan, 1975-76; English tchr. Tenri H.S., 1976-92; assoc. prof. Tenri U., 1993—. Avocation: reading. E-mail: yamakura@sta.tenri-u.ac.jp. Fax: 0743-62-1965. Office: Tenri Univ, 1050 Somanouchi-cho, Tenri Nara 632-8510, Japan

YAMAMOTO, ERIKO, historian, educator; b. Mattoh, Japan, June 29, 1957; s. Tomiji and Yuriko Yamamoto. BA, Kobe (Japan) City U., 1980; MA, Claremont (Calif.) Grad. U., 1983; PhD, U. Hawaii-Manoa, Honolulu, 1988. From asst. prof. to assoc. prof. Sugiyama Jogakuen U., Nagoya, Japan, 1989-2000, prof., 2000—. Sankei Found. scholar, 1980-81; East-West Ctr. grantee, 1982-86, Fulbright grantee, 1998-99. Mem. Am. Studies Assn., Assn. for Asian Am. Studies, Oral History Assn. Office: Sugiyama Jogakuen U, 17-3 Hoshigaoka Motomachi, Chikusa Nagoya Aichi 464-8662, Japan

YAMAMOTO, HIDEO, computer science educator; b. Kochi-shi, Japan, May 9, 1940; s. Tohru and Fujiko (Ogawa) Y.; m. Sachiyo Takemoto, Sept. 30, 1966; children: Ichiro, Makiko. BSEE, Kyoto (Japan) U., 1963, MSEE, 1965, PhD, 1973. Mgr. lab., chief rsch. engr. KDD, Tokyo, 1965-86; dep. dir. R & D labs. KDD, Kamifukuoka, Japan, 1986-88; dir. R & D adminstrn. divsn. KDD, Tokyo, 1988-92; pres., CEO KDD Am., Inc., N.Y.C., 1992-96, KDD Comm., Inc., Tokyo, 1996-98; sr. v.p. KDD R & D Lab. Inc., Kamifukuoka, 1998-2000; prof. computer sci. Utsunomiya U., 2000—; chmn. WG-D/SG11, Consultative Com. Internat. de Radio Comm., Geneva, Switzerland, 1978-90; chmn. image engring. profl. group Inst. Electronics and Comm. Engrs. Japan, Tokyo, 1986-88; editor-in-chief Inst. TV Engrs. Japan, Tokyo, 1998-2000. Contbr. articles to profl. jours. and conf. procs. Recipient Excellent Achievement award Ministry Sci. and Tech., Tokyo, 1986, Maejima award Soc. Telecomm., Tokyo, 1986, Excellent Contbn. award Soc. Internat. Telecomms. Union, Japan, 1983. Mem. Inst. Image Electronics Engrs. Japan (v.p. 1998—).

YAMAMOTO, IRWIN TORAKI, editor, publisher investment newsletter; b. Wailuku, Maui, Hawaii, Apr. 5, 1955; s. Torao and Yukie (Urata) Y. B in Bus. Adminstrn., Mktg., Chaminade U., 1977. Pres., editor, publisher The Yamamoto Forecast, Kahului, Hawaii, 1977—. Author: (book) Profit Making in the Stock Market, 1983; columnist The Hawaii Herald, 1978—. Named Top Market Timer, Top Gold Timer, Top Bond Timer, and to Timer Digest Honor Roll by Timer Digest, also honored by Select Info. Exchange and Rating the Stock Selectors. Avocations: exercise, music, reading, philosophy. Home and Office: PO Box 573 Kahului HI 96733-7073

YAMAMOTO, MASAHIRO, hospital director; b. Wakayama City, Japan, Nov. 22, 1933; m. Kazuko Mio, 1963; 3 children. MD, Osaka (Japan) U., 1959, PhD, 1965. Fellow dept. medicine Osaka U., 1965-71; rsch. assoc. dept. biochemistry U. Pitts. and Mich. State U., 1966-68; lectr. dept. medicine Chiba (Japan) U., 1971-75, assoc. prof. dept. medicine, 1975-79; head dept. internal medicine Nissay Hosp., Osaka, 1979-90; vice dir. Nissay Hosp., 1988-90, dir., 1990-2000, dir. emeritus, 2000—. Author, editor: Ten Talks on Ginseng Research, 1987, Panax Ginseng Research, 1981, 85, 89, 95; contbr. numerous articles to profl. jours., books. Mem. Med. and Pharm. Soc. for Oriental Medicine (bd. dirs. 1983-85, 89-97, award 1995), Japan Endocrinology Soc., (councillor 1971—), Japan Soc. Internal Medicine (councillor Kinki br. 1979—), Sinojapanese Med. Assn. (councillor 1975—), Local Med. Assn. (v.p. 1994—). Avocations: fine arts, cultural pursuits, history. Office: Nissay Hosp, Nippon Life, 3-8 Itachibori-6-chome, Nishi-ku Osaka 550-0012, Japan

YAMAMOTO, MASANOBU, geochemist; b. Fukuno, Japan, Feb. 23, 1964. BS, Tohoku U., Sendai, Japan, 1986; MS, Tohoku U., 1988; PhD, Nagoya (Japan) U., 1995. Rschr. Geological Survey of Japan, Tsukuba, 1988-95, sr. rschr., 1995—, assoc. prof., 1995—. Mem. Japanese Assn. Organic Geochemists (bd. dirs., recipient Taguchi prize 1997). E-mail: yamamoto@gsj.go.jp. Office: Geological Survey of Japan, 1-1-3 Higashi, Tsukuba 305-8567, Japan

YAMAMOTO, MASANOBU, electronic company executive; b. Hitachi, Japan, June 27, 1949; s. Akira and Kuniko Yamamoto; m. Emiko Ohsaku, 1973; 3 children. BS, Tokyo U., 1973. Rschr. Sony Corp., Tokyo, 1973-85, mgr., 1986-94, gen. mgr., 1995—. Avocation: rowing. Home: B-203 313-1 Mutsuura-cho, Kanazawa-ku, Yokohama 236-0032, Japan Office: Sony Corp 6-7-35, Kitashinagawa Shinagawa-ku, Tokyo 141-0001, Japan

YAMAMOTO, RYOZABURO, meteorology educator; b. Kyoto, Japan, May 23, 1927; s. Ryotaro and Ima (Tanaka) Y.; m. Teiko Namekawa, Nov. 14, 1956; children: Masako, Satoko. BS, Kyoto (Japan) U., 1951, DSc, 1957. Prof. meteorology Kyoto U., 1965-91, prof. emeritus, 1991—; dir. Climate Change Rsch. Lab., Kyoto, 1981-91; chmn. Meterology Com. in Sci. Scoun., 1982-88, Panel on Climate Issue, Tokyo, 1991-95. Contbr. rsch. articles to sci. jours. Recipient Culture prize of transp. Min. of Transp., 1990. Mem. Meteorol. Soc. Japan (hon. mem., pres. 1984-88, Fujiwara prize 1993). Home: Tskisocho 111-1013 Sai in, 615-0054 Kyoto Japan

YAMAMOTO, SHOZO, biochemist; b. Osaka, Japan, May 12, 1933; s. Matsujiro and Teruko (Nakamura) Y.; m. Ikuko Tsubaki, May 12, 1963; children: Toshitaka, Yoritaka, Yukiko. MD, Osaka U., 1960; PhD, Kyoto U., 1967. Intern Osaka Univ. Hosp., 1960-61; rsch. assoc. Kyoto U., 1964-72, lectr., 1972-75, assoc. prof., 1975-78; rsch. fellow Harvard U., 1967-69; prof. Sch. Medicine Tokushima U., 1979-99, prof. emeritus, 1999—; corp. advisor Japan Tobacco Inc., Gen. Pharm. Rsch. Inst. Mem. editorial bd. FEBS Letters, Prostaglandins and Other Lipid Mediators, 1977—, co-editor Oxygenases and Oxygen Metabolism, 1982; co-editor: Advances in Prostaglandin, Thromboxane, and Leukotriene Research, vol. 15. Mem. Japanese Biochem. Soc. (hon.), Am. Soc. for Biochemistry and Molecular Biology, Vitamin Soc. Japan, Japan Soc. Clin. Chemistry, N.Y. Acad. Scis. Home: 4-14-8 Ankoji-cho, Takatsuki, Osaka 569-1029, Japan Office: 1-1 Murasaki-cho, Takatsuki, Osaka 569-1125, Japan

YAMAMOTO, TADASHI, pathologist, educator; b. Niigata, Japan, Nov. 27, 1949; s. Yukio and Masako (Takatsu) Y.; m. Keiko Harada, Mar. 30, 1983; children: Aya, Haruka. MD, Niigata U., 1974, PhD, 1982. Med. internship and residency Nagaoka Red Cross Hosp., Nagaoka/Niigata, 1974-75; asst. in pathology Sch. Medicine Niigata U., 1975-82, assoc. prof., 1982-99, prof., 1999—; councilor Japanese Soc. Nephrology, Japanese Soc. Allergy. Editor: Pathophysiology of Glomerular Epithelia Cell, 1993. Mem. Niigata Med. Assn. (Sci. award 1988), Soc. Cardiovascular Endocrinology and Metabolism. Avocations: game of Go, tennis, skiing. Home: 1-34-2 Kobari, Niigata 950-2022, Japan Office: Niigata U Sch Med Inst Neph, Niigata U Sch Med Inst Neph, 1-757 Asahimachi-dori, Niigata 951-8510, Japan

YAMAMOTO, TAKUMA, computer company executive; b. Kumamoto, Japan, Sept. 11, 1925. BEE, U. Tokyo, Japan, 1949; D Litt (hon.), U. Honolulu, HI, 1986. With Fujitsu Ltd., Tokyo, Japan, 1949—; bd. dirs Fujitsu Ltd., 1975—, mgn. dir., 1976-79, exec. dir., 1979-81, pres., rep. dir., 1981-90, chmn., rep. dir., 1990-97, chmn. emeritus, 1997—; vice chmn. Commn. Industries Assn. Japan, 1986; chair Japan Electronic Industry Devel. Assn., 1987-89, vice chair, 1989—; chair Com. Internat. Coord. of Econ. Policies, 1988—. Recipient Blue ribbon with medal of Honor, 1984, Grant Cordon of the Order of the Sacred Treasure, 1997; named Hon. Knight Comdr. of Most Excellent Order of Brit. Empire, 1997. Mem. Communication Industries Assn. Japan (vice chmn. 1986), Japan Electronic Industry Devel. Assn. (chmn. 1987-89). Avocations: river fishing, golf, gardening. Office: Fujitsu Ltd, 6-1 Marunouchi 1-chome, Chiyoda-ku Tokyo 100, Japan*

YAMAMOTO, TETSURO, pharmaceutical company executive; b. Beppu, Japan, Oct. 2, 1953; s. Fujikazu and Masu (Fukuda) Y.; m. Sahara Atsuko, Jan. 25, 1981; children: Etsushi, Keiji. B, Osaka U., Osaka, Japan, 1978, PhD, 1988. Rschr. Takara Shuzo Co. Ltd., Matsudo, Japan, 1978-81, Nat. Rsch. Inst. Brewing, Tokyo, 1981-84; rschr. immunology divsn. Jichi Medical Sch., Minamikawachi, 1984-85; rschr. Rsch. Ctr. for Medical Mycology Teikyo U., Hachioji, 1985-88; asst. chief Takara Shuzo Co. Ltd., Otsu, 1988-89, Takara Shuzo Co., Ltd., Otsu, 1990-92; fellow dept. biochemistry U. Rochester, Rochester, N.Y., 1989-90; dir. Nichinichi Pharm. Co. Ltd., Ohyamada, 1993-94, exec. dir., 1994—. Contbr. articles to profl. jours. Mem. AAAS, N.Y. Acad. Scis., The Planetary Soc., The Soc. Yeast Scis. Avocations; pastel painting, tennis, golf, baseball, collecting classical music recordings. Home: 1406-69 Entokuin, Ayama-tyo 518-13, Japan Office: Nichinichi Pharm Co Ltd, 239-1 Tominaga, Ohyamada 518-14, Japan

YAMAMOTO, YOSHIRO, bank executive. Pres., CEO Fuji Bank Ltd., Tokyo. Office: Fuji Bank Ltd, 5-5 Otemachi I-chome Chiyod, Tokyo Japan*

YAMAMOTO, YOUSUKE, electronics educator, scientist; b. Kyoto, Japan, Mar. 29, 1946; s. Teiichirou and Hisako Yamamoto; m. Izumi (Kawamura) Y., Mar. 26, 1984; children: Yoshihito, Hirofumi, Toshiharu. BS, Electro-Comm. U., Tokyo, 1969, MS, 1971; Dr degree, Shizuoka U., Shizuoka, Japan, 1986. Scientist large scale integration lab. Nippon Telegraph Tele. Corp., Kanagawa, Japan, 1971-94; prof. electronics Tamagawa U., Tokyo, 1994—. Office: Tamagawa U, 6-1-1 Tamagawa Gakuen, Machida-shi Tokyo 194-8610, Japan

YAMAMOTO, YUSHO, bank executive; b. Tokyo, Oct. 3, 1942; s. Kikuichiro and Yuukiko (Hoynden) Y.; m. Kiyoko Yamamoto. BA in Econs., Keio U., 1967. Postgrad. rschr. King's Coll., U. Cambridge, 1967-70; loan officer in charge of trading cos. Long-Term Credit Bank of Japan Ltd., 1971-73, internat. fin. divsn. head office in charge of bond issues and shipping fin., 1974-76, in charge bus. devel., 1977, internat. fin. divsn. head office in charge Am., 1978-80, dep. gen. mgr. Singapore br. in charge bus. devel., 1981-82, assoc. gen. mgr. internat. fin. divsn. in charge Europe/Am., 1983-84, gen. mgr. Mcht. Banking group mergers and acquistions, 1988-92, gen. mgr. corp. fin. divsn., 1993-94, exec. dir. Europe, Africa and Middle-East, gen. mgr. London, 1995, mng. dir. Europe, Africa and Middle-East, gen. mgr. London, 1996-98; in-charge Eng. and Euro syndicated loan Mfrs. Hanover Ltd., London, 1972-73; in charge bus. devel. Credit Lyonnais, Tokyo, 1977; exec. dir. in charge M&A adv. Peers & Co., 1985-87; CEO Willis Japan Ltd., 1999—. Mem. United Oxford's Cambridge Club (London). Office: 7-13-5 Tsukimino Yamato, Kangawa 242-0002, Japan

YAMAMURA, MITSUHIRO, cardiovascular surgeon; b. Ashiya City, Hyogo, Japan, Feb. 1, 1964; s. Sohei and Yasuko (Sakaue) Y.; m. Haruyo Miyata, July 28, 1996; children: Mitsuho Yamamura, Kaho Yamamura. MD, Hyogo Coll. Medicine, Nishinomiya City, Japan, 1988, postgrad., 1995-99. Lic. medical doctor Japanese Nat. Med. Bd. Resident Hyogo Coll. Medicine Cardiovasc. Inst. Kansai Rosai Hosp., 1988-94; clin. instr. Hyogo Coll. Medicine, Nishinomiya City, Japan, 1994-95; hon. fellow U. Wis., Madison, 1997-98, rsch. intern, 1998-99; clin. instr. Hyogo Coll. Medicine, Nishinomiya City, Japan, 1999—. Recipient Morimura's award Hyogo Coll. Medicine, 1988. Fellow Internat. Coll. Angiology (Prof. Albert Senn Young Investigator award 2000); mem. Internat. Soc. for Cardiovasc. Surgery, Japanese Soc. for Cardiovasc. Surgery, Japanese Assn. for Thoracic Surgery.

YAMANA, HIDEAKI, surgeon; b. Fukuoka, Japan, Jan. 5, 1949; s. Sansetsu and Mieko (Sadanaga) Y.; M.D., Kurume U., 1973, D.Med. Sci., 1980; m. Kazuko Takao, Mar. 16, 1976; 1 child, Hidekazu. Asst., first dept. of surgery, Kurume (Japan) U. Sch. Medicine, 1973—, asst. prof., 1986-96, assoc. prof., 1997—, prof. multidisciplinary treatment ctr., 2000—. Recipient honor rsch. prize, First Dept. Surgery, Kurume U. Sch. Medicine, 1980. Mem. Japan Surg. Soc., Japanese Assn. Thoracic Surgery, Japanese Soc. Gastroenterol. Surgery, Japanese Soc. Gastroenterology, N.Y. Acad. Scis., Collegium Internationale Chirurugiae Digestivae, Internat. Soc. Diseases Esophagus. Liberal. Buddhist. Clubs: Kokura High Sch. Rugby Old Boy. Contbr. articles to Japanese med. jour. Home: 190-11 Sasayamamaci, Kurume 830-0021, Japan Office: 67 Asahimachi, Kurume 830-0011, Japan

YAMANA, SHUKICHI, chemistry educator; b. Nichinan-cho, Tottori, Japan, May 28, 1917; s. Katsuji and Tada (Irisawa) Y.; m. Mitsu Fukui, Apr. 13, 1946; children: Hikaru, Manabu, Hajimu. BS, Hiroshima Bunrika U., 1942; DSc in Quantum Chemistry, Kyoto U., 1961. Tchr. Fukushima (Japan) Prefectural Women's Normal Sch., 1942-43; assoc. prof. Fukushima Normal Sch., 1943-47, prof., 1947-49; prof. Kyoto (Japan) Normal Sch., 1949; assoc. prof. Kyoto Gakugei U., 1949-62, prof., 1962-66; prof. Kyoto U. Edn., 1966-81, prof. emeritus, 1981—; prof. chemistry Kinki U., Higashi Osaka, Japan, 1981-90, lectr., 1990-93; hon. fellow U. Wis., Madison, 1967-68; cons. Colombo Plan, Govt. Thailand, Bangkok, 1972. Author: Stereochemical Models From Folded Envelopes, 1998; contbr. numerous articles to profl. jours. Recipient Rising Sun Third Order of Merit, Japan, 1991, Disting. Svc. medal Tojo-cho, 1995. Mem. Chem. Soc. Japan (award 1986), Am. Chem. Soc., Soc. Japan Sci. Teaching. Avocation: go (Japanese chess), origami. E-mail: s-yamana@mbox.kyoto-inet.or.jp. Home: 27-2 Momoyama Tsutsui, Iga Nishi-machi, Fushimi-ku, Kyoto 612-0073, Japan

YAMANAKA, CHIYOE, institute president; b. Osaka, Japan, Dec. 14, 1923; s. Kichibei and Mitsuko (Kakudoh) Y.; m. Tamiko Kashida, May 6, 1955; children: Kaoru, Chihiro. B Engring., Osaka U., 1948, D Engring., 1960. Rsch. assoc. Osaka U., 1953-55, assoc. prof., 1955-63, prof. elec. engring. dept., 1963-87, emeritus prof., 1987—; prof. Kinki U., Osaka, 1987-90; dir. Inst. Laser Tech., Osaka, 1987—; pres. Himeji (Japan) Inst. Tech., 1990-95; cons. Tech. Rsch. Inst. Def., Tokyo, 1987-92, Mitsubishi Electric Mfg. Co., Tokyo, 1987-92, Fuji Electric Mfg. Co., Tokyo, 1987-96, Kansai Electric Power Co., Osaka, 1987—; gen. chmn. Internat. Free Electron Laser Conf., Kobe, 1992; mem. Japan Nuclear Fusion Coun., Sci. and Tech. Agy., 1960-90. Editor: Laser Technology, 1982 (Laser Soc. award 1985); author: Introduction to Laser Fusion, 1992 (Edward Tellor award 1991); patentee in field. Recipient Leadership awards Fusion Power Assocs., Md., 1985, Purple medal Japanese Govt., 1992; named to Order of the Sacred Treasure, 2000. Fellow IEEE (life), Am. Phys. Soc., Inst. Elec. Engrs. Japan (life, pres. 1987-88, disting. career award 1993); mem. Phys. Soc. Japan, Inst. Atomic Energy Japan, Laser Soc. Japan (pres. 1974-87, Excellence in Laser Tech. award 1987), Rotary. Avocations: painting, hiking, swimming, golf, travel. Home: 11-1 Nishiyama, Ashiya 659-0083, Japan

YAMANAKA, MITSUYOSHI, literature educator; b. Shimonoseki, Yamaguchi, Japan, Mar. 24, 1942; s. Zenkichi and Mitsuko (Yamanaka) Masuda; m. Hisayo Nakashima, Sept. 4, 1994. BA, Kyushu U., Fukuoka, Japan, 1964, MA, 1966, PhD, 2000. Asst. lectr. Kobe (Japan) U. Commerce, 1966-69, lectr., 1969-70; lectr. Yamaguchi (Japan) U., 1970-74; asst. prof. Fukuoka Women's U., 1974-86, prof., 1986—, prof. grad. sch., 1993—; trustee Fukuoka Women's U., 1986-96, dir. univ. libr., 1990-92. Author: Traditional Ballads: An Appreciation, 1988; co-editor: Traditional and Literary Ballads, 1980; co-translator: A Book of Ballads--English and Scottish Folk Songs, 1978, Ballads--Love Songs under the Greenwood Trees, 1993. Fulbright grantee Japan-U.S. Ednl. Commn., 1966-67. Mem. English Literary Soc. Japan, Japan-Scotland Soc. Avocations: tennis, gardening. E-mail: handm@lib.bekkoame.ne.jp. Home: 3-36-7 Tagama Sawara-ku, Fukuoka-shi 814-0174, Japan Office: Fukuoka Women's Univ, 1-1-1 Kasumigaoka Higashi-ku, Fukuoka-shi 813-8529, Japan

YAMANAKA, NOBUHIKO, linguist; b. Warabi, Saitama, Japan, Nov. 26, 1960. BA, Tokyo U., 1983, MA, 1986. Asst. prof. Saitama U., Urawa, Japan, 1987-90; assoc. prof. Saitama U., 1990—. Contbr. articles to profl. jours. Mem. Internat. Pragmatics Assn., Linguistic Soc. of Japan, Soc. for Study of Japanese Lang. Office: Saitama U, 255 Simo-ookubo, Urawa 338-8570, Japan

YAMANE, NAOKO, composer, lyricist, pianist, educator; b. Iwakuni, Yamaguchi, Japan, Dec. 22, 1969; d. Katsuji and Midori (Nakano) Y.; m. Takeshi Hara. B in Music, Kunitachi Coll. Music, Tokyo, 1992. Tchr. Tokyo Comm. Art Coll., 1991-97; tchr., chief dept. Tokyo Inst. Computer Sci., 1993-99; tchr., founder Wings Sch. Music, Tokyo, 1996—; tchr., chief dept. music VANTAN Art Coll., Tokyo, 1997-99; founder Wings Music Prodn., Tokyo, 1999—. Composer, lyricist, arranger (CD) You, 1997; piano soloist charity concert for Asian and African children, 1997; music instr., actress Let's play with computer with Noppo-san, 1997; keyboard player Rikki, 1996. Mem. Japanese Soc. Rights Authors, Composers, Pub. Buddhist. Avocations: traveling, reading about aroma therapy and psychology. Office: Wings Music, Castle Mansion 301 13-8 Daikanyama-cho, Shibuya-ku Tokyo 150-0034, Japan

YAMANE, TAKASHI, biomedical engineer; b. Okayama, Japan, Mar. 4, 1953; m. Eriko Tsuda, Jan. 23, 1983; children: Hiroyuki, Mari. BA, U. Tokyo, 1975, MA, 1977, PhD, 1980. From rschr. to head biomimetics divsn. Mech. Engring. Lab., Tsukuba, Japan, 1980—; chair biofluid engring. com. Soc. Life Support Technology Japan, 1996—; rsch. & devel. com. implantable artificial heart Min. Internat. Trade & Industry, 1995—. Mem. Japan Soc. Mech. Engrs., Am. Soc. Artificial Internal Organs, Internat. Soc. Rotary Blood Pumps. Avocations: tennis, jogging. Office: Mech Engring Lab, Namiki 1-2, Tsukuba Ibaraki 305-8564, Japan

YAMANI, HASHIM BIN ABDALLAH BIN HASHIM, federal official. PhD in Physics, Harvard U., 1974. Prof. physics King Fahd U. Petroleum Minerals, chmn. dept. physics, dir. dept. energy and resources; v.p. King Abd al-Aziz City Sci. Tech.; min. Ministry Industry and Elec-

tricity, Riyadh, Saudi Arabia, 1995—. Office: PO Box 5729, Oman bin al-Khattab St, Riyadh Saudi Arabia*

YAMANOBE, YOSHIMASA, business educator; b. Mito, Ibaraki, Japan, July 9, 1928; m. Isuzu Yamanobe, Sept. 13, 1964. B of Econs., Tokyo U., 1952; MBA, Xavier U., 1962. Lectr. faculty econs. Ryutsu Keizai U., Ryugasaki, Japan, 1975-83, prof. faculty econs., 1984-95, prof. Grad. Sch., 1989—; prof. faculty distbn. and logistics sys. Ryutsu Keizai U., Ryugasaki, 1996—. Author: Management Comparison of Land Transport Enterprises, 1980, Knowledge of Air Transport, 1983, Air Transport Enterprises, 1990, Land Transport Enterprises, 1991, Basis of Logistics Management, 1991, Basic Knowledge of Logistics Enterprises, 1992. Mem. Japan Transp. Acad., Japan Soc. Comml. Sci., Japan Logistics Soc. Home: 369-1 Ireji, Ryugasaki Ibaraki 301-0046, Japan Office: Ryutsu Keizai U, 120 Hirahata, Ryugasaki Ibaraki 301-8555, Japan

YAMANOUCHI, TOYOTOSHI, civil engineer, educator; b. Fukuoka, Kyushu, Japan, Jan. 1, 1922; s. Toyota and Isoko (Tanaka) Y.; m. Teiko Suemitsu, Oct. 14, 1956 (dec. Jan. 1998); children: Akiko, Toyoaki. M in Engring., Kyushu U., 1950, D in Engring., 1961. Assoc. prof. Kyushu U., Fukuoka, 1953-68, prof., 1968-85; prof. Kyushu Sangyo U., Fukuoka, 1985-95, dean Faculty of Engring., 1988-90; prof. emeritus Kyushu U., Fukuoka, 1985—; hon. prof. Tianjin U., 1993—; vis. fellow MIT, Cambridge, 1954-55; vis. prof. U. N.S.W., Sydney, 1975; bd. dirs. Nakamura Ednl. Inst., Fukuoka, Engring. Acad. Japan, Tokyo, 1989-93, Yamanouchi Rsch. Lab., Fukuoka; mem. tech. com. U.S. Hwy. Rsch. Bd., Washington, 1970-75, Internat. Soc. Soil Mech. Found. and Geotextiles and Geomembranes Engring., London, 1983-94. Author: Soil Mechanics, 1983, Selected Papers of Toyotoshi Yamanouchi, 1985; editor, creator: Friendship through Chinese Poems, 1993, Matsukadai, 1995; mem. editl. bd. Jour. Geotextiles, 1983-94, Jour. Geosynthetics, 1984-95. Mem. tech. com. for preservation of old monuments Agy. for Cultural Affairs, Tokyo, 1970—. Recipient Cultural Merit award Fukuoka Prefecture, 1987, Fukuoka City, 1989. Fellow ASCE, Japanese Soc. Civil Engrs., Geotech. Soc., Japan Soc. Engring. Geology. Mem. Liberal Party. Buddhism. Achievements include research in geotextiles, brittle failures in steep cut slopes, soft-ground improvement techniques, and studies of clayey grounds subjected to repeated loads. Home: 4-3-9 Ropponmatsu Chuo-ku, Fukuoka 810, Japan Office: Yamanouchi Rsch Lab, 5-25-25 Morooka, Hakataku Fukuoka 816, Japan

YAMAOKA, MINORU, dentist; b. Okaya, Japan, Oct. 5, 1942; s. Setsuko and Satoru (Ohgochi) Y.; m. Miyoko Ema, May 29, 1973; children: Rieko, Hajime. DDS, Nippon Dental Coll., 1967; PhD, Osaka U., 1972. Staff Osaka (Japan) Police Hosp., 1972-73, Osaka U., 1973-74; asst. prof. Matsumoto Dental U., Shiojiri, Japan, 1974-75, assoc. prof., 1975-84, prof., 1984—. Contbr. articles to profl. jours. Fellow Internat. Assn. Oral and Maxillofacial Surgeons; mem. Am. Cleft Palate-Craniofacial Assn. Home: Tsukama 2-3-4, Okaya 394-0026, Japan Office: Matsumoto Dental U, Sch Dentistry, Shiojiri 399-0781, Japan

YAMASAKI, HIROYUKI, electrical engineer; b. Hyogo, Japan, Sept. 9, 1956; s. Motoyuki and Keiko (Watanabe) Y.; m. Kanae Nasu, June 7, 1986; children: Mari, Yumi. B in Engring., Shizuoka U., 1980, M in Engring., 1982, PhD, 1985. Chartered engr. Brit. Engring. Coun. Sr. engr. Mitsubishi Electric Corp., Hyogo, Japan, 1985-91; asst. mgr. strategic R&D planning Mitsubishi Electric Corp., Hyogo, 1991-93, asst. mgr. R&D planning office, 1993-95, mgr. strategic planning, 1995—; vis. lectr. Shizuoka U., 1991-92, vis. assoc. prof., 1996-97. Patentee in field; contbr. articles to profl. jours. Recipient Takayanagi Meml. award Hamamatsu Electronic Rsch. Found., 1986, Meritorious Person award Sanda City, 1993. Mem. IEEE (sr., awards com. Kansai sect. 2000—), Engring. Mgmt. Soc. (Japan chpt. founding sec.), N.Y. Acad. Sci., Internat. Assn. Mgmt. Tech. (liaison com. Far East), Instn. Elec. Engrs. U.K., Japan Soc. Sci. Policy and Rsch. Mgmt. (editl. com. 1991—, bd. dirs. 1995-97, counselor 1997—, exec. com. Kansai sect. 1995—), Japan Soc. Promotion Sci. (com. 149), Acad. Assn. Orgnl. Sci., Inst. Image Info. and TV Engrs. Japan, Sanda Internat. Assn. (chmn. pub. rels. 1991—, bd. dirs.), Japan-Brit. Soc. Tokyo, Japan-Brit. Soc. Kansai, Japan-Belgium Soc., Japan-Sweden Soc. Kansai (exec. com. 1994-96, 99—), Japan-Am. Soc. Osaka. Avocations: driving, golf, travel, reading, gourmet cooking. E-mail: hyamasaki@iee.org. Office: Mitsubishi Elec Corp, 4-1 Mizuhara, Itami Hyogo 664-8641, Japan

YAMASAKI, YUKUZO, lawyer; b. Yamaguchi, Japan, Oct. 12, 1924; s. Bunsaburo and Yasuko (Ueda) Y. m. Keiko Furubayashi, Aug. 15, 1961; children: Takao, Chiyo. BA, Tokyo U., 1952; M of Comparative Law, So. Meth. U., 1965. Assoc. Shozawa & Nagashima, Tokyo, 1961-72; trainee Kaye, Scholer, Fierman, Hayes & Handler, N.Y.C., 1965-66; sr. ptnr. Yamasaki Law & Patent Office, Tokyo, 1972—. Author: Digest of Japanese Patent Infringement Cases 1966-68, 1970; contbr. articles to Jour. of Assn. Internat. pour Protection Propriété Indsl. Mem. Indsl. Property Coun. of the Patent Office, Tokyo, 1991-96. Recipient commendation Ministry Internat. Trade and Industry. Mem. First Tokyo Bar Assn., Japanese Bar Assn. (chmn. intellectual property com. 1989-90), Patent Attys. Assn. of Japan, Inter-Pacific Bar Assn. (chmn. intellectual property com. 1991-93), Japanese Br. Assn. Internat. Protection Propriété Indsl. (councillor, commendation 1986). Home: 2-20-21 Higashi, Kunitachi Tokyo 186-0002, Japan Office: Yamasaki Law & Patent Office, 1-11-28 Nagatacho, Chiyoda-ku Tokyo 100-0014, Japan

YAMASHITA, JIRO, physicist, educator; b. Tokyo, Dec. 29, 1915; s. Kaneki and Roku (Kato) H.; m. Tugi Tukamoto, May 30, 1947; children: Ken, Sonoko, Mamoru. BA in Sci., Kyushu U., Fukuoka, Japan, 1941, D of Sci., 1947. Asst. prof. Inst. Solid State Physics U. Tokyo, 1947-58, prof., 1959-76, dir., 1973-76, prof. emeritus, 1976—; prof. dept. physics Nihon U., Tokyo, 1976-86, lectr. dept. physics, 1986-91. Contbr. articles to profl. jours. Mem. Am. Phys. Soc., Phys. Soc. Japan. Home: 2 33 7 Okamoto, Setagaya-ku Tokyo 157, Japan

YAMASHITA, KOTARO, financial executive; b. Amagasaki-shi, Hyogo, Japan, Nov. 16, 1947; s. Yoshitaro and Masayo (Watanabe) Y.; m. Sakae Matubara, Feb. 13, 1985; children: Yoko, Kumiko, Tatsuya. BBA, Waseda U., 1971, MBA, 1974. Rschr. Hitachi Sys. Devel. Lab., Kawasaki, 1974-93; sr. rschr. Hitachi Rsch. Inst., Tokyo, 1993-95; sr. mgr. Hitachi Bus. Sys. Devel. Ctr., Yokohama, 1995-96; COO Hitachi New Fin. Sys., Tokyo, 1996—. Author: Banking Strategies for the 21st Century, 1991, E-Cash That You Have to Know, 1996; contbr. articles to profl. jours.; developer Smart Card control method. Office: Hitachi Ltd New Fin Sys, Minami Oi 6-chome, Shinagawa-ku, Tokyo 140, Japan

YAMASHITA, TERUO, seismology educator; b. Shimonoseki, Japan, May 10, 1948; s. Yasuhiro and Misao (Hiasa) Y.; m. Chikako Nakajima, Oct. 25, 1978; children: Chisato, Maki. BS, U. Tokyo, 1971, MS, 1973, DSc, 1976. Rsch. assoc. U. Tokyo, 1976-86; vis. rschr. UCLA, 1983-85; assoc. prof. U. Tokyo, 1986-95, prof., 1995—. Mem. Seismol. Soc. of Japan (v.p. 1994-96), Am. Geophys. Union. Avocations: jogging, mountaineering. Office: Earthquake Rsch Inst, U Tokyo 1-1-1 Yayoi, Bunkyo-ku Tokyo Japan

YAMASHITA, YASUMASA, educator; b. Urawa, Japan, Aug. 23, 1931. BS, Hiroshima U., Japan, 1954; MS, U. Tokyo, 1956, PhD, 1963. Asst. U. Tokyo, 1956-63, assoc. prof., 1963-75, prof., 1975-88; prof. Nat. Astron. Observatory, Japan, 1988-92, prof. emeritus, 1992—; dir. Okayama Astrophys. Observatory, Japan, 1976-92. Author: The Reflecting Telescope, 1992, (with others) An Atlas of Representative Stellar Spectra, 1977. Postdoctoral fellow Dominion Astrophys. Observatory, Can., 1964-66. Home: 1-14-12 Asahigaoka, Hino, Tokyo 191-0065, Japan

YAMASHITA, YOSHIHARU, flour milling company executive; b. Imari, Saga, Japan, Oct. 22, 1933; s. Tokujiro and Nui (Furukawa) Y.; m. Michiko Torigoe, Jan. 28, 1959; children: Tokuko Kawara, Tetsu Torigoe. Grad. in Econs., Tokyo U., 1958. Dir. Torigoe Co., Ltd., Fukuoka, Japan, 1964-70, mng. dir., 1970-81, sr. mng. dir., 1981-83, v.p., 1983-86, pres., 1986—. Buddhist. Avocations: appreciation of arts, driving. Office: The Torigoe Co Ltd, 5-1 Hie-machi, Fukuoka 812-0014, Japan

YAMATAKA, HIROAKI, economist; b. Japan, Oct. 13, 1944; s. Yutoku and Masae (Yamataka) Y.; m. Harue Maruyama, Mar. 21, 1970; children: Miwa, Rena. BA, Tokyo Keizai U., 1968; postgrad., U. Wis., 1973-74. Sales exec. Nikko Securities Co. Ltd., Tokyo, 1968-72; mgr. Nikko Securities Co. (Asia) Ltd., Hong Kong, 1974-78; dir. Wako Internat. (Europe) Ltd., London, 1978-84, Grieveson Grant Pacific Ltd., London, 1984-87, Kleinwort Benson Securities Ltd., London, 1987-94, Covent Garden Pioneer Floral St. Prodn., 1992—. Author: True Causes of Economic Collapse, 1994, Farewell to Keynesianism, 1996. Bd. dirs., internat. v.p. London Symphony Orch. Ltd., 1987—, mem. adv. coun., 1996—. Mem. Naval and Mil. Club (London). Avocations: reading, classical music, opera.

YAMATO, KEI C., international business consultant; b. Honokaa, Hawaii, Sept. 21, 1921; s. Kango and Shizuka (Tanaka) Y.; children: Karen, Marla, Kei Tracy. BA, U. Hawaii, 1946; LLD, Yale, 1950; DD, World Christianship Ministries, 1994. Ordained to ministry Ind. Universal Ch. of God, 1994. Pres. Internat. Bus. Mgmt. Co., 1950; founder Pacific-Asia Bus. Council, 1950; pres. Orchids of Hawaii Internat., Inc., 1951, Polynesian Products, Inc., Holiday Promotions Internat., Inc., 1952, Orchawaii Internat. Travel Corp., 1962, Pacific Area Landscaping, Inc., 1970—, Hawaii Hort. Enterprises, Inc., 1970—, Agrisystems, Inc., 1971-95; minister Ind. Universal Ch. God, Honolulu, 1995—; v.p., dir. Sperry & Hutchison Travel Awards, Inc., 1964, Copley Internat. Corp., 1967; all N.Y.C.; pres. Internat. Cons. Co., 1968, Asia-Pacific Corp., 1968; chmn. Asia Internat. Group of Cos., Asia Internat. Cons.; mng. dir. Internat. Cons. Assocs., 1993; universal cons. svcs. God's Universal Ch. and Ministries. Bd. dirs. Internat. Execs. Assn., World Trade Club N.Y.C., Sales Execs. Club N.Y.C.; mem. Regional Export Expansion Council, U.S. Dept. Commerce; organizer Asia Pacific Inst.; pres. Saudi Arabia Pacific Asia Bus. Council, Arab Assian Assocs. Served to 1st lt. AUS, World War II, ETO. Decorated Silver Star, Purple Heart with 2 oak leaf clusters. Mem. Advt. Club N.Y.C., Nat. Indsl. Conf. Bd., Profl. Mgmt. Cons. Assn. Am., Sales Promotion Execs. Assn., Chgo. Execs. Club, Sales and Marketing Execs. Internat., N.Y. Hort. Soc., Asia Soc., Japan Soc., Am. Mgmt. Assn. (lectr.), 442d Regimental Combat Team Assn., Landscape Contractors Assn. Hawaii, Gen. Contractors Assn. Hawaii, Friends East-West Center, East-West Philosophers Conf., Hawaii Assn. Nurserymen, Hawaii Bot. Soc., Honolulu Execs. Assn., U. Hawaii Alumni Assn., Navy League, Nat. Fedn. Ind. Bus., Am. Assn. Nurserymen, Pacific Area Travel Assn., Assn. U.S. Army, Hawaii Visitors Bur., Hawaii C. of C., U.S. Arab C. of C., Saudi Arabia Bus. Council. Clubs: Rotary, Bankers. Home: PO Box 22564 Honolulu HI 96823-2564

YAMAUCHI, EDWIN MASAO, history educator; b. Hilo, Hawaii, Feb. 1, 1937; s. Shokyo Yamauchi and Haruko (Owan) Yamauchi Higa; m. Kimie Honda, Aug. 31, 1962; children: Brian, Gail. Student, U. Hawaii, 1957-58; BA, Shelton Coll., 1960; MA, Brandeis U., 1962, PhD, 1964. Instr. Greek lang. Shelton Coll., Ringwood, N.J., 1960-61; grad. asst. Brandeis U., Waltham, Mass., 1962-63; asst. prof. Rutgers U., New Brunswick, N.J., 1964-69; assoc. prof. Miami U., Oxford, Ohio, 1969-73, prof. dept. history, 1973—, dir. grad. studies, 1978-82. Author: Pre-Christian Gnosticism, 1973, World of the First Christians, 1981, Foes from the North Frontier, 1982, Persia and the Bible, 1990, 7 other books, 1966-99; sr. editor Christianity Today, 1992-94; co-author 2 books, co-editor 2 books. Fellow NEH, 1968, Inst. for Holy Land Studies, Jerusalem, 1968, Inst. for Advanced Christian Studies, 1974-75; grantee Am. Philos. Soc., 1970. Fellow Am. Sci. Affiliation (pres. 1983), Inst. Bibl. Rsch. (chair 1984-86, pres. 1987-89); mem. Conf. on Faith and History (pres. 1974-76), Near East Archaeol. Soc. (v.p. 1978-79), Archaeol. Inst. Am. (chpt. pres. 1973-74), Evang. Theol. Soc. (chair ea. sect. 1965-66). Office: Miami Univ Dept History Oxford OH 45056

YAMAUCHI, KUNIHIKO, hematologist; b. Kyoto, Japan, June 7, 1947; s. Masanori and Kazuko Y.; m. Naoko Inoue, Apr. 3, 1981; children: Keiko, Yuhya. MB, Osaka (Japan) Med. Coll., 1974, MD, 1981. Jr. resident Nat. Hosp. Med. Ctr., Tokyo, 1974-76; sr. resident Tokai U. Hosp., Isehara, Japan, 1976-79; asst. Tokai U. Sch. Medicine, Isehara, Japan, 1979-88, asst. prof., 1987—; chief internal medicine Nat. Tochigi Hosp., Utsunomiya, Japan, 1986-87; vice-dir. Kiyokawa Hosp., 1997—. Contbr. articles to profl. jours. Rsch. fellow Roswell Park Meml. Inst., Buffalo, N.Y., 1984-86. Fellow Japanese Soc. Internal Medicine, Japan Soc. for Occupl. Health, Japanese Soc. Clin. Hematology; mem. Japan Rheumatism Assn., Japanese Soc. Hematology. Avocations: jigsaw puzzles, igo, travel. Office: Tokai Univ Sch Medicine, Bohseidai, 259-11 Isehara shi, Japan

YAMAUCHI, OSAMU, chemistry educator; b. Nagoya, Aichi-Ken, Japan, Sept. 15, 1936; s. Kiyoji and Tomino (Sugiyama) Y.; m. Yoshimi Horikawa; children: Takahiro, Kimiko. B.Pharm.Sci., Kyoto (Japan) U., 1959, PhD, 1967. Assoc. prof. Osaka U., Toyonaka, Japan, 1967-80; prof. chemistry Kanazawa (Japan) U., 1980-87, Nagoya U., 1987-2000, Kansai U., 2000—; dean grad. sch. sci. Nagoya U., 1994-96; dir. Nagoya U. Rsch. Ctr. for Materials Sci., 1998-2000; prof. chemistry Kansai U., Suita, Japan, 2000—. Contbr. articles to profl. jours. Mem. AAAS, N.Y. Acad. Scis., Chem. Soc. of Japan, Am. Chem. Soc., Pharm. Soc. of Japan. Buddhist. Office fax: 81-52-789-2953. Office: Kansai U Faculty Engring, Yamate-cho, Yamate-cho Suita 564-8680, Japan

YAMAYEE, ZIA AHMAD, engineering educator, dean; b. Herat, Afghanistan, Feb. 2, 1948; came to U.S., 1974; s. Sayed and Merjan Ahmad. BSEE, Kabul (Afghanistan) U., 1972; MSEE, Purdue U., 1976, PhD, 1978. Registered profl. engr., Calif., Wash. Mem. faculty of engring. Kabul U., 1978; engr. Systems Control, Inc., Palo Alto, Calif., 1979-81; sr. engr. Pacific N.W. Utilities, Portland, Oreg., 1981-83; assoc. prof. elec. engring. Clarkson U., Potsdam, N.Y., 1983-85; assoc. prof. Gonzaga U., Spokane, 1985-87, dean Sch. Engring., 1988-96; prof., chair elec. engring. dept. U. New Orleans, 1987-88; part-time rsch. engr. La. Power and Light Co., New Orleans, 1987-88; sr. cons. Engring. and Cons. Svcs., Spokane, 1989-96. Contbr. articles, reports to profl. jours. Bd. dirs. Wash. State Math., Engring. Sci. Achievement, Seattle, 1989-96; mem. Spokane Intercollegiate Rsch. and Tech. Inst. Adv. Coun., 1990-96. NSF grantee. Mem. Am. Soc. Engring. Edn., IEEE (sr.). Office: University of Portland 5000 N Willamette Blvd Portland OR 97203-5798

YAMAZAKI, TOSHIMITSU, physicist, educator; b. Tokyo, Sept. 28, 1934. BSc, U. Tokyo, 1957, DSc, 1964. From assoc. prof. to prof. dept. physics U. Tokyo, 1967-86, prof., dir. Inst. Nuclear Study, 1986-95; supr. Japan Soc. for Promotion Sci., Tokyo, 1996-99; vis. prof. CERN, 1995-96. Recipient Imperial prize Japan Acad. Sci., 1987, Acad. prize, 1987, prize Nishina Meml. Found., 1975, prize Matsunaga Found., 1972, prize Fujiwara Found., 1994.

YAMAZAKI, YOSHIO, rail transportation executive; b. Hanno, Saitama, Japan, Sept. 7, 1953; s. Toshio and Kimiko (Machida) Y. Railman Seibu Rlwy. Co., Iruma-Shi Sta. Saitama-Ken Kitatama Sta., Tokyo, 1969, Eidan Subway Koishikawa Factory, Tokyo, 1970; various positions, 1970-73; railman Japanese Nat. Railway, Tokyo, 1973-87; chief railman East Japan Railway Co., Tokyo, 1987—; railman Sumidagawa Cargo Sta., Tokyo, 1973-84, Sinjiyuku Sta., Tokyo, 1984-85, Suido Bashi Sta., Tokyo, 1985-86, Okubo Sta., Tokyo, 1986—. Mem. East Japan Labor Union (Okubu Sta.), Internatl. Airline Passengers Assn. (Hong Kong), Nat. Geog. Soc., Highlander Club, Oxford Club, The Exec. Club Internat. (London). Fax: 81 3 3369 8556. Home: 7-18 Iwasawa, Hanno-shi Saitama-Ken 357-0023, Japan Office: East Japan Rlwy Okubo Sta, 1-17-1 Hiyakunin-Cho, Sinjiyuku Tokyo 169-0073, Japan

YAMBRUSIC, EDWARD SLAVKO, lawyer, consultant; b. Conway, Pa., Mar. 9, 1933; s. Michael Misko and Slavica Sylvia (Yambrusic) Y.; m. Natalie Visniak, 1990. *Second generation Croatian American. Father Misko and mother Slavica (Sylvia) born in Ruskovac, Croatia, arrived to the United States 1913 and 1931 respectively. Father, a boiler maker with PRR for 40 years. Mother, a farmer, blue-collar worker, housewife, a beautiful human being who instilled in me the love of God, Country and our beautiful Croatian cultural heritage* BA, Duquesne U., 1957; postgrad. Georgetown U. Law Ctr., 1959-61; JD, U. Balt., 1966; cert. The Hague (Netherlands) Acad. Internat. Law, 1967, 69, diploma Ctr. Study and Research of Internat. Law and Internat. Relations, 1970; PhD in Pub. Internat. Law, Cath. U. Am., 1984. Bar: Md. 1969, U.S. Ct. Customs and Patent Appeals 1972, U.S. Supreme Ct. 1972, U.S. Ct. Internat. Trade 1988. Copyright examiner U.S. Copyright Office, Library of Congress, Washington, 1960-69, atty. adviser Office Register of Copyrights, 1969-98; pvt. practice internat. and immigration law, 1969—; legal counsel Nat. Ethnic Studies Assembly, 1976—, Soc. Fed. Linguists, 1980; pres. AMCRO Internat. Cons., Inc., 1995. Pres. Nat. Confedn. Am. Ethnic Groups, Washington; nat. chmn. Croatian-Am. Bicentennial Com.; nat. chmn. Nat. Pilgrimage of Croatian-Ams. to Nat. Shrine of Immaculate Conception, Washington; v.p. Croatian Acad. Am. Served to capt. U.S. Army, 1957-59. Duquesne U. Tamburitzans scholar, 1953-57; Hague Acad. Internat. Law fellow, 1970. Mem. ABA, Md. Bar Assn., Internat. Law Assn., Internat. Fiscal Assn., Am. Soc. Internat. Law, Croatian Cath. Union Am., Croatian Frat. Union Am. Republican. Roman Catholic. Author: Treaty Interpretation: Theory and Reality, 1987, The Trade-Based Approaches to th Protection of Intellectual Property, 1990; contbr. articles to ofcl. newsletter Nat. Confedn. Am. Ethnic Groups, also legal jours. *Certificate issued by the Librarian of Congress in recognition of 40 years of distinguished service to the people of the United States of America, 1957-98* Home and Office: 4720 Massachusetts Ave NW Washington DC 20016-2346

YAMI, KAYO DEVI, microbiologist, researcher; b. Kathmandu, Nepal, Sept. 30, 1957; d. Dharma Ratna and Hira Devi (Kansakar) Yami; m. Madan Kumar Khatiwada, Apr. 21, 1985; 1 child. BSc, Amrit Sci. Campus, Kathmandu, 1975; MSc, Tribhuvan U., Kathmandu, 1979; PhD, Indian Agrl. Rsch. Inst., New Delhi, 1984. Lectr. dept. botany Tribhuvan U., 1983-84, lectr. dept. microbiology, 1984-85; program officer Royal Nepal Acad. Sci. and Tech., Kathmandu, 1984-85, rsch. officer, 1985-88, sr. sci. officer, 1988-91, chief sci. officer, 1992—; nat. coord. FAO Project of Royal Nepal Acad. Sci. and Tech., 1988-91, project investigator IFS Project, 1985-87, part time lectr. in Mocrobiol. for grad. and postgrad students, Tribhuven Univ. Author: Legume Inoculants and Their Use, 1994. Recipient Mahendra Vidyabhusan Gold medal, 1984; Internat. Found. Sci. grantee, 1985, 87. Mem. Women in Sci. and Tech. (gen. sec. 1996-2000), Third World Orgn. for Women in Sci., Bot. Soc. (treas. 1988-90). Buddhist. Avocations: music, floriculture. Office: Royal Nepal Acad Sci & Tech, New Baneshwor, 3323 Kathmandu Nepal

YAMIN, DIANNE ELIZABETH, judge; b. Danbury, Conn., June 4, 1961; d. Raymond Joseph and Linda May (Bucko) Goetz; m. Robert Joseph Yamin, Sept. 3, 1988; children: Samantha Blythe, Rebecca Anne. AB, Lehigh U., 1983; JD, Mercer U., 1986. Bar: Conn. 1986, U.S. Dist. Ct. Conn. 1989. Lawyer Gerald Hecht & Assocs., Danbury, 1986-92; judge State Conn., Danbury, 1991—; atty. Yamin & Yamin, Danbury, 1992—; chmn. ethics com. Conn. Probate Assembly, 1994—; mem. Conn. Coun. on Adoptions, 1992—, Conn. Probate Assembly, 1991—. Bd. dirs. Big Bros./Big Sisters, Danbury, 1987-94, Conn Brass Soc., Inc., 1991—, Lions Club Danbury, 1993-94, Friends of Tarrywile Park, Inc., Danbury, 1993-99, Danbury Music Ctr., 1996—, Hispanic Ctr. Greater Danbury, 1999—. Recipient outstanding young citizen award Conn. Jaycees, 1994, pro bono award Conn. Legal Svcs., 1993; named as one of 21 Young Lawyers Leading Us into the 21st Century, ABA Mag., 1995. Mem. ABA, Conn. Bar Assn., Conn. Health Lawyers Assn., Danbury Bar Assn, Omicron Delta Kappa. Republican. Roman Catholic. Avocations: ballet, volunteerism, travel, outdoor activities. Home: 66 Barnum Rd Danbury CT 06811-2938 Office: 155 Deer Hill Ave Danbury CT 06810-7726

YAMIN, MICHAEL GEOFFREY, lawyer; b. N.Y.C., Nov. 10, 1931; s. Michael and Ethel Yamin; m. Martina Schaap, Apr. 16, 1961; children: Michael Jeremy, Katrina. AB magna cum laude, Harvard U., 1953, LLB, 1958. Bar: N.Y. 1959, U.S. Dist. Ct. (so. and ea. dists.) N.Y., U.S. Ct. Appeals (2d cir.) 1966, U.S. Supreme Ct. 1967. Assoc. Weil, Gotshal & Manges, N.Y.C., 1958-65; sr. ptnr. Colton, Hartnick, Yamin & Sheresky, N.Y.C., 1966-93, Kaufmann, Feiner, Yamin, Gildin & Robbins, LLP, N.Y.C., 1993—. Trustee Gov.'s Com. Scholastic Achievement, 1976—, Rockland County Soc. Prevention of Cruelty to Children, 1979—; mem. Manhattan Cmty. Bd. 6, 1974-88, chmn., 1986-88. Lt. USNR, 1953-55, Korea. Mem. ABA, N.Y. State Bar Assn., Assn. Bar City N.Y., Fed. Bar Coun., Am Fgn. Law Assn. (Am. br.), Internat. Law Assn., Societe de Legislation Comparee, Internat. Bar Assn., Harvard Faculty Club (Cambridge, Mass.), Harvard Club of N.Y.C. (trustee N.Y. Found. 1981—, pres. 1999—, sub-chmn. schs. and scholarships com. 1972-93, bd. mgrs. 1985-88, 93-98, chair house com. 1992-95, v.p. 1995-98, chair comms. com. 1997-99, chair membership svcs. com. 1999-2000), Harvard Alumni Assn. (bd. dirs. 1995-98). Office: 777 3rd Ave New York NY 10017-1401

YAMMINE, RIAD NASSIF, retired oil company executive; b. Hammana, Lebanon, Apr. 12, 1934; came to U.S., 1952, naturalized, 1963; s. Nassib Nassif and Emilie (Daou) Y.; m. Beverly Ann Hosack, Sept. 14, 1954; children: Kathleen Yammine Gross, Cynthia Yammine Rotman, Michael. BS in Petroleum Engring., Pa. State U., 1956; postgrad. advanced mgmt. program, Harvard U., 1977. Registered profl. engr., Ohio. Engr. Trans-Arabian Pipe Line Co., Saudia Arabia, 1956-61; with Marathon Pipe Line Co., 1961-75; mgr. western divsn. Marathon Pipe Line Co., Casper, Wyo., 1971-74; mgr. Ea. divsn. Marathon Pipe Line Co., Martinsville, Ill., 1974-75; mktg. ops. divns. mgr. Marathon Pipe Line Co., 1975-83; pres. Marathon Pipeline Co., 1983-84; v.p. supply and transp. Marathon Petroleum Co., 1984-88, dir., 1984-90; pres. EMRO Mktg. Co., 1988-98; exec. v.p. Marathon Ashland Petroleum, 1998-99; ret.; bd. dirs. Marathon Oil Co.; also officer, bd. dirs. various subs. Patentee in field. Past trustee Wright State U. Found., Fisk U. Mem. ASME, Am. Petroleum Inst., Springfield and Clark C. of C. (bd. dirs.), Findlay Country Club. Republican. Home: 200 Penbrooke Dr Findlay OH 45840-8301

YAMOUT, HASSAN MOHAMMAD, engineering executive; b. Beirut, Mar. 18, 1943; s. Mohammad Abdel Qader and Afife Khalid (Dayye) Y.; m. Randa Hachoui, Feb. 23, 1978; children: Dania, Hala, Nadine. BSEE, Am. U. Beirut, 1966, BSCE, 1968, MSCE, 1978; postgrad., Brit. Tutorial Inst., 1972, 74. Site engr. Contracting and Trading Co., Nigeria, 1968-69; project engr. Contracting and Trading Co., Saudi Arabia, 1970-72, dep. project mgr., 1973-77, project mgr., 1978-82; project mgr. Contracting and Trading Co., Jordan and Malaysia, 1982-89; area mgr. Contracting and Trading Co., Saudi Arabia, 1992-98; group v.p. Contracting and Trading Co., Beirut, 1998—; gen. mgr. Target Constrn., Can., 1990-91. Mem. Lebanese Order of Engrs., Lebanese Syndicate of Engring. Avocations: music, reading, computers. Office: Contracting and Trading Co, Al-Arz St Saifi PO Box 11-1036, Beirut Lebanon

YAMPOLSKY, PHYLLIS, artist; b. Phila.; d. Louis Jacob Yampolsky and Bassia Yampolsky Green; m. Peter Forakis, June 12, 1959 (div. 1964); children: Gia, Jozeph Peter. Student, Phila. Mus. Sch. Arts, 1950-52, Inst. Allende, San Miguel de Allende, Mex., 1954-55, Ecole Beaux Arts, Fontainbleau, France, 1956, Hans Hofmann Atelier, N.Y.C., 1956-58. Founder, dir., tchr. Workshop Yampolsky, N.Y.C., 1956-66; art instr. 92d St. YMHA, N.Y.C., 1958-60; founder, dir. Hall of Issues, N.Y.C., 1960-61; 1st artist-in-residence N.Y.C., 1966-67; creator, dir. Portrait of Ten Towns N.Y. State Coun. Arts, 1967-70; founder, officer Northeast Windham Coun. Arts, Vt., 1978-79; instr. Vt. Acad., Saxton's River, 1979-81, Vt. C.C., Springfield, 1979-81; co-founder, instr. New Vt. Sch. Arts, 1981; founder, pres. Ind. Friends McCarren Pk., Inc., N.Y.C., 1988—; creator, dir., prodr. Hoving Happenings, 1966, 67; cons. Model Cities, Columbus, Ohio, 1968, Province Ont. Coun. Arts, 1968-70, Phila. Bicentennial Commn., Smithsonian Inst. Bicentennial Travelling Festival Kit; cons., panelist, performance artists Arcosanti, Ariz., 1977-78, 80, 81; facilitator NEA, 1970-75; cons., organizer, program dir. Habitat II CBO Host Com., N.Y.C., 1995-96; spl. events dir. Youth Pavilion, World's Fair, San Antonio, 1968; writer, dir. art curriculum Marylerose Acad., Albany, 1969, Bennett Coll., 1970; presenter Habitat II, UN conf., Istanbul, Turkey, 1996. One-woman shows include Phila. Art Alliance, 1953, Judson Gallery, N.Y.C., 1960, 62, Walker Gallery, N.Y.C., 1974, Kulicke Gallery, N.Y.C., 1975, Graham Gallery, N.Y.C., 1977, O.K. Harris and Susan Caldwell Galleries, N.Y.C., 1978, Stryke Gallery, N.Y.C., Windam Coll., Vt., 1978, Marlboro Coll., Vt., 1981, A Place Apart, N.Y.C., 1984, City Bank Gallery, Bklyn., 1986, Loft Lawyers, N.Y.C., 1987, 479 Gallery, N.Y.C., 1996; exhibited in group shows at Park Place Gallery, N.Y.C., Brata Gallery, Cornell U., Dallas Mus. Fine Arts, Mus. Erotic Art, San Francisco, Mus. Erotic Art, Stockholm, Whitney Mus., Weisner Gallery, N.Y.C., City Without Walls Gallery, Newark, Green Gallery, N.Y.C., Leo Castelli Gallery, N.Y.C., Allan Stone Gallery, N.Y.C., Franklin Furnace,

N.Y.C., Dorsky Gallery, N.Y.C., Bklyn. Terminal Show, N.Y.C., Food Stamp Gallery, N.Y.C., ABC No Rio, N.Y.C., Blue Mountain Gallery, N.Y.C., Boriqua Coll., N.Y.C., Phila. Mus. Art, Holland-Goldowsky, Chgo., Peter David, Mpls., Mc Nay Inst., San Antonio, Tex., Stephen Gang Gallery, N.Y.C., The Cave, Bklyn., Bklyn. Brewery; represented in permenant collections Am. Town Hall Wall Sys. used in Robert Kennedy Presdl. Primary, 1968, Clinton Presdl. Campaign and Inaugural Festivities, 1993, 97, UN Women's Conf., Beijing, 1995, UN 50th Celebration, N.Y.C., 1995, V.P. Gore's Reinvention Revolution Conf., Washington, 1996-97, March Against Cancer, Washington, 1998, W.A.F.E. Festival/Conf. on the Environment, Bklyn., 1998, The Hague (The Netherlands) Appeal Peace Conf., 1999, Main St. Millennium, Washington; contbr. articles to profl. jours. Recipient Cue Mag., 1967, Betsy Barlow Rogers award Ind. Friends McCarren Pk., 1995; Ecole Beaux Arts scholar, Hans Hofmann Atelier scholar; grantee Ind. Friends McCarren Pk., J.M. Kaplan Fund, Andy Warhol Found., N.Y. Found., Vincent Astor Found., Citizen's Com. N.Y.C. Inc., 1990—. Fax: 718-383-5785. E-mail: ifmp@earthlink.net.

YAN, GAO, power company executive; b. 1942. With CCP, 1965; vice gov. Jilin Province, 1988-92, gov., 1992-95; sec. CCP Com., Yunan Province, 1995-97; dir. polit. dept. Chinese People's Armed Police Force; sec. CPC 6th Yunan Province Com.; mem. 14th CCP Ctrl. Com., 1992-97, 15th CCP Ctrl. Com., 1997—; gen. mgr. State Elec. Power Corp., 1998—. Office: State Power Corp, 137 Fuyoe St, Beijing 100031, China*

YAN, HONG, university educator; b. Jiangsu, China, Aug. 8, 1959; m. Linda Song, June 12, 1986. BE, Nanking IP&T, China, 1982; MSE, U. Mich., 1984; PhD, Yale U., 1989. Rsch. asst. Tsinghua U., Beijing, 1982-83, Yale U., New Haven, Conn., 1984-89; rsch. scientist Gen. Network Corp., New Haven, Conn., 1987-89; lectr. Sydney U., Australia, 1989-91, sr. lectr., 1992-96, prof., 1997—; cons. DSP Engring., New Haven, Conn., 1988-89. Contbr. articles to profl. jours. Fellow Instn. Engrs. Australia; mem. IEEE (sr.), INNS, SPIE, SMRM, SMRI. Office: U Sydney J03, Sch Elec Engring, Sydney Australia 2006

YAN, HUA, microwave techniques educator; b. Changsha, Hunan, China, Oct. 10, 1930; d. Min Yan and Li Zhang; m. Sile Yu, Jan. 1, 1955; children: Ying Yu, Yan Yu. Grad. elec. dept., Wuhan (China) U., 1953; postgrad., Tianjin (China) U., 1957-60. Asst. Tianjin U., 1953-62, lectr. microwave techniques, 1962-79, assoc. prof., 1979-86, prof., 1986—; mem. Tianjin Commn. Sic. and Tech., 1992-97. Author: Microwave Solid-state Circuit, 1996. Exec. mem. Tianjin Women's Fedn., 1983-93. Recipient award Nat. Sci. Conf., Beijing, 1978, secondary award Electronic Industry Ministry, Beijing, 1980. Fellow China Inst. Comm. (councillor 1980-93); mem. China Electronic Inst. (sr.), Tianjin Inst. Comm. (v.p. 1984-98), Tianjin Inst. Electronics (councillor 1981-92). E-mail: slyu@tju.edu.cn. Home: Tianjin U, 12-2-402 North Village 5, Tianjin 300073, China Office: Tianjin U Coll Elec Info, Engring, 92 Weijin Rd, Tianjin 300072, China

YAN, JERRY JINYUE, scientist, educator, researcher; b. Datong, Shanxi, China, Nov. 10, 1959; arrived in Sweden, 1989; s. Renyan Yan and Yuewen Cai; m. Nikki Xiaoyan Yan, Jan. 24, 1986; children: Käthrine Diane, Björn Niclas Grant. BS, Taiyuan (China) U. Tech., 1983; PhD, Royal Inst. Tech., Stockholm, 1991. Rsch. asst. Tianjin (China) U., 1983-86, asst. prof., 1986-89; vis. scientist Royal Inst. Tech., Stockholm, 1989-92, asst. prof., 1992-97, assoc. prof., 1997—; Cheung Kong scholar prof. Shanghai Jiaotong U., 2000—. Editor (procs.) Efficient, Cost, Optimization, Simulation and Environmental Aspects of Energy Systems, 1996; guest editor (spl. issue) Energy Conversion and Mgmt., The Internat. Jour., 1997. Recipient awards Wenner-Gren Ctr. Found., Sweden, 1995, Ragnar and Signeuls Found., Sweden, 1996, Peter Klasons Found., Sweden, 1996. Mem. ASME, Internat. Gas Turbine Inst. (com. mem. 1996—), Chinese Acad. Scis. (overseas assessor 2000—). Home: Södervägen 28, S-18369 Täby Stockholm Sweden Office: Royal Inst Tech Chem Engr, Teknikringen 50, S-100 44 Stockholm Sweden

YAN, JIANPING, physicist, researcher; b. Zhejiang, Peoples Republic of China, Apr. 15, 1967; arrived in Germany, 1996; s. Shicheng and Xinbei (Wang) Y.; m. Xianghong Li, Sept. 29, 1994; 1 child, Julia Ziyi. BS, Zhejiang U., 1989, MS, 1992. Rsch. asst. Zhejiang U., 1992-94, Tech. U. Berlin, Germany, 1996. Contbr. articles to profl. jours. Office: Hermann-Fottinger Inst, Müller-Brelau Str 8, 10623 Berlin Germany

YAN, JI-MIN, chemist, educator; b. Shanghai, China, Feb. 9, 1934; s. Cai-Zhang Yan and Yu-Xiang Sun; m. Lan-Min Xing, May 28, 1934; children: Lin, Kun. BSc, Beijing U., 1957. Rsch. asst. Chinese Acad. Sci., Beijing, 1957-58; rsch. assoc. Inst. Chemistry Chinese Acad. Sci., 1958-78, assoc. prof., 1978-85, prof., 1985—. Author: Surface and Pore of Solid, 1982 (2d prizes The Chinese Acad. Sci.); authored numerous published, theoretical papers in chemistry. Recipient 2d prizes Chinese Acad. Sci., 1978, 99. Home: No 504 Apt 941, Zhong Guan Cun, Beijing 100086, China Office: Inst Chemistry, Chinese Acad Sci, Beijing 100080, China

YAN, SHANG-LUAN, social sciences educator; b. Hsinchu, Taiwan, Mar. 2, 1955; d. So-Chan Yan and Feng-Chiou Yan Tsai; m. Hsing-Chou Sung, Oct. 24, 1955; children: Sung, Kun-Ying H. BA in Law, Chinese Culture U., Taipei, Taiwan, 1977; MS in Sociology, N.C. State U., 1981; PhD in Sociology, Ariz. State U., 1990. Rsch. assoc. Ariz. State U., Tempe, 1984-90; lectr. Calif. State U., Bakersfield, 1990-91; assoc. prof. Chinese Culture U., Taipei, 1991-92, Hsingchu (Taiwan) Normal Coll., 1992-93, Chung-Cheng U., Chia-Yu, Taiwan, 1993—. Author: Studies of Social Structure in the USA and Taiwan, 1995, Qualitative Research Methods: Participant Observation, 1996; editor: Danger & Secrecy: Research Ethics, 1998; mem. editl. bd. Race, Gender and Class, 1995—. Councilor Taipei City Govt., 1998—; bd. dirs. Awakening Found., Taipei, 1998—. Recipient MacKay Can. Studies award Can. Office in Taipei, 1995. Mem. Sociologists Women in Soc., Am. Sociol. Assn., Taiwanese Sociol. Assn. Office: Chung-Cheng U Dept Labor Studies, 160 San-Hsing Ming-Hsiung, Chia-Yi 621, Taiwan

YAN, SHANGYAO, civil engineering executive; b. Taipei, Taiwan, Feb. 20, 1961; s. Ching-Chiang and Juan (Hon) Y.; m. Miaw-jane Chen, Dec. 22, 1989; children: Tzyy-Hao, Tzyy-Bin. BSc, Nat. Taiwan U., 1983, MSc, 1987; PhD, MIT, 1992. Rsch. asst. Nat. Taiwan U., Taipei, 1985-87, MIT, Cambridge, Mass., 1987-91; assoc. prof. Nat. Ctrl. U., Chungli, Taiwan, 1992-97, prof. civil engring., 1997—, head transp. divsn., 1998—; cons. Taiwan Inst. Economy, Taipei, 1994-95, Taipei Govt., 1997-98. Contbr. articles to profl. jours. 2d lt. Taiwanese Army, 1983-85. Mem. INFORMS, Chinese Inst. Civil and Hydrol. Engring. (Outstanding Paper award 1996), Chinese Inst. Transp. Avocations: swimming, softball, hiking. Office: Nat Ctrl U, Dept Civil Engring, 32054 Chungli Taiwan

YAN, WEI MON, mechanical engineering educator; b. Taichung, Taiwan, May 10, 1961; s. Chao and Chou Chen (Chou) Y.; m. Sue Fen Jen, Dec. 2, 1987; 3 children. BS, Taitung Inst. Tech., Taipei, Taiwan, 1983; MS, Nat. Chiao Tung U., Hsinchu, Taiwan, 1985, PhD, 1989. Postdoctoral fellow Nat. Chiao Tung U., 1989; assoc. prof. Huafan U., Taipei, Taiwan, 1991-95, prof. dept. mech. engring., 1995—, chmn. dept. mech. engring., 1994—; patent reviewer CNS, Taipei, 1990—. Contbr. articles to profl. jours. Lt. Republic of China Mil., 1989-91. Recipient award for outstanding teaching Dept. Edn., Taiepi, 1993, Huafan U., 1992, Book Coupon award Taitung, 1979-83. Mem. AIAA, China Soc. Mech. Engring. Mem. Kuo Ming Tan Party. Avocations: music, reading, basketball, jogging. Office: Huafan U, Dept Mech Engring, 22305 Taipei Taiwan

YAN, XIAOJUN, chemist, biologist; b. Qingdao, China, Aug. 6, 1968; s. Xingsheng and Juying (Sun) Y.; m. Chengxu Zho; 1 child, Xingjian. BSc, Fudan U., Shanghai, China, 1989; PhD, Inst. Oceanology/Acad. Scis., Qingdao, China, 1994. Asst. prof. Inst. Oceanology, Chinese Acad. Scis., Qingdao, 1994-95, assoc. prof., 1995-96, prof., 1999—; rschr. Nat. Food Rsch. Inst., Tsukuba, Japan, 1999—; cons. Huren Group Ltd., Qingdao. Author: Analytical Method in Seaweed Chemistry, 1996; editor: Advances in Marine Biotechnology, 1999; contbg. author: Marine Biotechnology, 1998, Marine Biotechnology, Principles and Applications, 1998. Recipient Sci. and Tech. Progress award Chinese Acad. Scis., 1996, Trace Element and Human Health award Wangxueying Fund, 1996; STA fellow, 1996. Mem. Fedn. Asian Chem. Soc., N.Y. Acad. Scis. Avocations: Igo, chess. E-mail: xjyan@ms.qdio.ac.cn. Office: Inst Oceanology/Ch Acad Sci, 7 Nanhai Rd, Qingdao, Shandong China 266071

YAN, YIMING, physics educator; b. Beijing, Dec. 31, 1933; m. Shuhua Lu, Dec. 31, 1960; children: Jianzhi, Meizhi. MA, Moscow U., 1960. Rschr. Beijing U., 1960-77; prof., vice dir. Inst. Low Energy Nuclear Physics Beijing Normal U., 1977—; head Chinese expert group Gongpencham (Cambodia) Royal U., 1966-68; vis. scholar Ohio U., Athens, 1980-81; vice chmn. acad. com. Joint Nuclear Rsch. Ctr. Beijing U., Tsinghua U. and Beijing Normal U., 1988—; prof. Changchun (China) Inst. Optics and Fine Mechnics, Chinese Acad. Scis., 1994—. Author: Nuclear Physics, 1990; contbr. numerous articles to profl. jours.; patentee in field. Recipient Second award Nat. Com. Edn., Beijing, 1989, 98, 1st award 1997, Third award Kwang-Hua Sci. and Tech. Found., Beijing, 1995; named Model Tchr., Beijing Local Govt., 1991. Mem. Phys. Soc. China (acad. exch. com.), Measure and Surveying Soc. China (com. of ionization and radiation). Office: Inst Low Energy Nuclear Phy, Beijing Normal Univ, Beijing 100875, China

YAN, ZHENGHUA, combustion and fire researcher, safety engineer; b. Lin Chuan, Jiang Xi, China, Jan. 14, 1968; s. Dong Quan and Pulan (Fu) Y.; m. Yan Liu, Oct. 7, 1993. BSc, U. Sci. and Tech., Hefei, China, 1990, MSc, 1992; PhD, Lund U., Sweden, 1999. Rschr. State Key Lab. Fire Sci., Hefei, 1992-93; vis. rschr. Fire Rsch. Sta., Eng., 1993-94; rschr. Lund U., Sweden, 1994—. Contbr. articles to profl. jours. Recipient Cinese Nat. Acad. Pres. award 1992, 2d class prize, 1993; 1st Class Excellent paper award Fire Safety Sci., 1994. Avocations: music, tennis, fishing, badminton, reading. Home: Kämnärsvagen 8C-116, 22645 Lund Sweden Office: Lund U, Fire Safety Engring Dept, 221 00 Lund Sweden

YAN, ZHONGSHU, surgeon; b. Liuyang, China, Dec. 25, 1932; s. Meishou Yan and Qiuyuan Song; m. Yanxian Zhang, Aug. 12, 1964; children: Xiangdong, Xianghui, Xianglan. MD, Hunan Med. Coll., 1954. Resident, attending surgeon Yichun City Hosp., China, 1955-70, dir. surg. oncology, 1971-80; from assoc. prof. to prof. surgery Xiangya Hosp. Hunan Med. U., Changsha, China, 1981—; dir. dept. internat. acad. exch. Hunan Med. U., 1988-93; cons. surgeon Hosp. Aged, Changsha, 1988—, Univ. Hosp. Nat. Def. Technology U., Changsha, 1985—; vis. scholar Monash Med. Sch., Melbourne, Australia, 1987-88. Author: Diseases of the Breast, 1988, Abdominal Operation, vol. 1, 1986, vol. 2, 1988; contbr. 8 chpts. to med. books and articles to profl. jours. Mem. China Med. Assn., China Anti-Cancer Assn., Assn. UICC Fellowships. Avocations: classical music, reading. E-mail: winman@public.cs.hn.cn. Office: Dept Surgery Xiangya Hosp, Hunan Med U, 410008 Changsha Hunan, China

YAN, ZI JUN, physicist, educator; b. Fuzhou, Fujian, China, Sept. 21, 1932; s. Zong Lian Yan and Xiao Gin Lin; m. Yu Mei Xu, Jan. 23, 1963; children: Ninrong, Hairong. Grad., Xiamen (China) U., 1956. Asst. dept. physics Xiamen U., 1956-62, lectr., 1963-80, assoc. prof., 1981-85, prof., 1986—; hon. mem. IBC Advisory Coun., Cambridge, Eng., 1992—; hon. advisor ABI Rsch. Bd. Advisors, N.C., 1992—. Contbr. numerous articles to profl. jours. and book series (numerous awards); assoc. editor-in-chief Jour. Progress Physics Chem. Mech., Beijing, 1991—. Recipient award Kwang-Hua Sci. Fund, 1993, Sci. and Tech. Advance prize and prize of excellent achievement in tchg. Nat. Edn. Commn., 1992, 93, 98; Best of the South scholar Xiamen U., 1992; Enjoy the State Spl. grantee State Coun., 1992. Mem. Physics Soc. (China, Xiamen coun. 1987—), China Ctr. Advance Sci. and Tech., Chinese Soc. Engring. Thermophysics, Internat. Order Merit. Office: Xiamen U Dept Physics, Fujian Xiamen 361005, China

YANABU, SATORU, electronics executive, engineering educator; b. Gotsucity, Shimane, Japan, July 15, 1941; s. Shiro and Shukuko Y.; m. Sanae Nishikawa, Sept. 28, 1965; 3 children. BE, U. Tokyo, 1964; PhD, U. Liverpool, Eng., 1981; D in Engring., U. Tokyo, 1990. Sect. mgr. High Power Lab., Kawasaki, Japan, 1976-84; sr. mgr. High Voltage and High Power Lab., Kawasaki, Japan, 1984-90, Transmission and Substation Engring. Dept., Tokyo, 1990-93; sr. fellow Heavy Apparatus Engring. Lab., Kawasaki, 1993-94, gen. mgr., 1994-97; tech. exec. power sys. Toshiba Corp., Tokyo, 1997-99, gen. mgr. tech. planning and coordination divsn., 1996-98; chief fellow Toshiba Corp., Kawasaki, 1998—; vis. prof. Nagoya (Japan) U., 1990—, U. Doshisha, Kyoto, Japan, 192-93, U. Liverpool, 1996—, Kushu U., 1997—; vis. fellow U. Tokyko, 1988—. Contbr. articles to scientific jours. Recipient Significant Devel. awards IEE of Japan, 1982, 88, Tech. Book award 1991, Tech. Paper awards, 1989, 92, Dyke award, 1998. Fellow IEEE, IEE of Japan; mem. Current Zero Club. Home: 1-2-28 Minami-Tsukushino, Machida, Machida Tokyo 194, Japan Office: Toshiba Corp Power & Indsl Syss R&D Ctr, 2-1 Ukishima-cho Karbusaku-ku, Kawasaki 210-0862, Japan

YANAGA, KATSUHIKO, surgeon, researcher; b. Mii-gun, Japan, Mar. 9, 1955; s. Masanori and Yoshiko (Kinoshita) Y.; m. Yuriko Yano, Jan. 13, 1956; 1 child, Eri. MD, Kyushu U., Fukuoka, 1979, PhD, 1991. Asst. prof. surgery Kyushu U. Faculty of Medicine, 1986, 89-91, assoc. prof. surgery, 1991-98, chief outpatient clinic, dept. surgery, 1991-92, chief of ward, dept. surgery, 1993-94, sec. gen., dept. surgery, 1995-96; dir. dept. surgery Matsuyama Red Cross Hosp., 1998-2000; assoc. prof. surgery Nagasaki (Japan) U. Sch. Medicine, 2000—; asst. prof. surgery U. Pitts. Sch. Medicine, 1988-89; vis. prof. surgery Mt. Sinai Med. Sch., 1998—. Recipient Morikazu Kaibara Rsch. award, 1992, Rsch. award Found. for Advancement of Clin. Medicine, 1991, Rsch. award Nakamura Harujiro Promotion Found., 1993. Fellow ACS; mem. Japanese Soc. Transplantation (councilor 1995—), Japanese Soc. Hepatobiliary-pancreatic Surgeons (councilor 1994—), Japanese Study Group of Liver Transplantation (bd. dirs. 1993—), Japanese Soc. Gastroenterol. Surg (councilor 1996—), Japanese Soc. Organ Preservation and Med. Biology (councilor 1998—), Japanese Soc. Endoscopic Surgery (councilor 1998—), Japanese Soc. Vascular Surgery (councilor 1999—), Japan Soc. Organ Preservation and Med. Biology (councilor). Office: Nagasaki U Sch Medicine, Dept Surgery II, Nagasaki 852-8501, Japan

YANAGAWA, TATSUO, internist; b. Tokyo, Japan, Apr. 4, 1956; s. Kikuji and Ruriko (Sugimoto) Y.; m. Mariko Shimazaki, May 18, 1986; children: Mayumi, Yurie. MD, Keio U., 1982, PhD, 1991. Resident internal medicine Keio U. Hosp., Tokyo, 1982-84, instr. internal medicine, 1986-91; staff internal medicine Saitama Chuo Hosp., 1984-86; rsch. assoc. U. Chgo., 1991-94; staff internal medicine Nerima Gen. Hosp., Tokyo, 1994—. Contbr. articles to profl. jours. Avocations: watching NBA basketball games. Office: Nerima Gen Hosp, 2-41-1 Asahigaoka, Nerima-ku 176-8530, Japan

YANAGAWA, TSUTOMU, technology transfer company engineer; b. Osaka, Japan, Nov. 29, 1956; s. Hazime and Hiroko (Konishi) Y.; m. Masami Kawabata, Oct. 16, 1983 children: Sakiko, Fumitoshi. B Engring., U. Osaka Prefecture, Sakai, Japan, 1980, M Engring., 1982; D Engring., Osaka U., Suita, Japan, 1993. Rschr. Nippon Telegraph and Telephone Pub. Corp., Musashino, Japan, 1982-85; rsch. scientist NTT Basic Rsch. Labs., Musashino, 1985-89, sr. rsch. scientist, 1989-91; sr. rsch. engr. NTT Opto-Electronics Labs., Atsugi-shi, Japan, 1991-97; mgr. NTT Affiliated Bus. Hdqrs., Tokyo, 1997-99; sr. rsch. engr. NTT Photonics Labs., Atsugi-shi, 1999-2000; mgr. NTT Advanced Tech. Corp., Atsugi-shi, Japan, 2000—. Author: Sensor Dictionary, 1991; patentee semiconductor laser equipment, waveguide, optical equipment; contbr. articles to profl. jours. Mem. Japanese Soc. Applied Physics, Phys. Soc. Japan, Internat. Soc. Life Info. Sci. Avocations: art, flower arrangement, tea ceremony. Home: Ishida 861-1-8-401, Isehara Kanagawa 259-1116, Japan Office: NTT Advanced Tech Corp, 3-1 Morinos, Atsugi-shi Kanagawa 243 0198, Japan

YANAGI, KENJIRO, mathematics educator; b. Hofu, Yamaguchi, Japan, Oct. 8, 1950; s. Minoru Inoue and Chieko Yanagi; m. Kumiko Sumida, Nov. 4, 1979; 2 children. Bachelor's degree, Tokyo Inst. Tech., 1974, Master's degree, 1976, Doctorate, 1983. From asst. to lectr. Yamaguchi U., 1976-89, assoc. prof., 1989-93, prof., 1993—. Author: Hilbert Spaces and Linear Operators, 1995. Office: Yamaguchi U, Tokiwadai 2-16-1, 755-8611 Ube Japan

YANAGIDA, SHOZO, chemist, educator; b. Kobe, Hyogo, Japan, Sept. 19, 1940; p. Giichi and Natsue Yanagida; m. Kinu Yanagida, Feb. 18, 1968; children: Masatoshi, Takako. B Engring. in Applied Chemistry, Osaka (Japan) U., 1964, M Engring. in Applied Chemistry, 1966, D Engring., 1970. Asst. prof. Osaka U., 1966-80, assoc. prof., 1980-87, prof., 1987—. Author: Advances in Chemical Conversions for Mitigating Carbon Dioxide, 1998; contbr. articles to profl. jours. Recipient prize Japan Oil Chemists' Soc., 1979, Yazaki Sci. and Tech. award Yazaki Meml. Found. for Sci. and Tech., 1998, award Asahi Glass Found., 1999, award Millennium Project Found., 2000. Avocation: golf. Fax: 81-6-6879-7875. E-mail: yanagida@chem.eng.osaka-u.ac.jp. Home: 2-10-13 Uguisudai, Kawanisishi Hyogo 666-0133, Japan Office: Osaka U, 2-1 Yamadaoka, Suitashi Osaka 565-0871, Japan

YANAGIOKA, HIROSHI, research company executive, consultant; b. Ichihana, Japan, Nov. 17, 1936; s. Haruo and Fumi (Hashimoto) Y.; m. Yoko Chiba Yanagioka, Mar. 30, 1969; children: Yasuhito, Masaki. BS, Tokyo U., 1960; MS, MIT, Cambridge, Mass., 1966. Mgr. Chiyoda Chem. Engr. and Constrn. Co., Japan, 1970-80, deputy gen. mgr., 1980-83, gen. mgr., 1983-90, chief engr., 1990-96; dir. U-Tech. Consulting Co., Japan, 1996-99; pres. Yanagioka Assocs., Japan, 1999—. Inventor: Flue Gas Desulfunization, 1969; author: Chemical Engineering Progress, 1978, Business and the Environment, 1995, Chemical Reaction and Reactor Design, 1998. Avocations: artistic drawing, athletic walking. Home phone: 81-45-783-4975. Home: 2-6-19 Kamariya nishi, Kanazawa ku, Yokohama Japan Office: Yanagioka & Assocs, 3366 Mashiko, Tochigiken Japan

YANAI, MICHIO, meteorologist, educator; b. Jan. 16, 1934; came to U.S., 1970; s. Kin (Watanabe) Y.; m. Yoko Miyazaki, Apr. 25, 1965; children: Takashi, Satoshi. BS, U. Tokyo, 1956, MS, 1958, DSc, 1961. Rsch. meteorologist Meteorol. Rsch. Inst. Japan Meteorol. Agy., Tokyo, 1961-65; asst. prof. U. Tokyo, 1965-70; from assoc. prof. to prof. UCLA, 1969—. Fellow Am. Meteorol. Soc. (awards com. 1992, assoc. editor Jour. Atomos. Scis. 1988-90, Jule Charney award 1986); mem. Am. Geophys. Union, Royal Meteorol. Soc., Meteorol. Soc. Japan (Soc. award 1962, Fujiwara award 1993). Achievements include discovery of a large-scale wave in the equatorial stratosphere called the Yanai wave; formulated a method of diagnosing mass flux in cumulus ensemble called Q1-Q2 diagnosis; revealed the role of the Tibetan Plateua in the onset of the Asian summer monsoon. E-mail: myanai@ucla.edu. Office: UCLA Dept Atmos Scis 405 Hilgard Ave Los Angeles CA 90095-9000

YANAI, SHUNJI, diplomat; b. Tokyo, 1937. Grad., U. Tokyo, 1961. Joined Ministry Fgn. Affairs Japan, 1961, dir. internat. convs. divsn. Treaties Bur., 1976, cabinet councilor Prime Mins. Office, 1977, dir. legal affairs divsn. Treaties Bur., 1977, dir. treaties divsn. Treaties Bur., 1978, french interpreter Imperial Household Agy., 1980, amb. Embassy of Japan Republic Korea, counselor min., 1981, dep. dir.-gen. Asian Affairs Bur., 1984, dep. dir.-gen. Treaties Bur., 1987; consul-gen. Japan Ministry Fgn. Affairs Japan, San Francisco, 1987; dir.-gen. Treaties Bur. Ministry Fgn. Affairs Japan, 1990, exec. sec. Internat. Peace Cooperation Hdqrs. Prime Mins., 1992, dir.-gen. Fgn. Policy Bur., 1993, dep. min. fgn. affairs, 1995, vice-min. fgn. affairs, 1997; amb. E.& P. U.S., 1999. Fax: 202-328-2187. Office: Embassy of Japan 2520 Massachusetts Ave NW Washington DC 20008-2869

YANAKA, AKINORI, medical researcher, educator; b. Mitsukaido, Ibaraki, Japan, Sept. 27, 1955. MD, U. Tsukuba, Japan, 1980, PhD, 1985. Jr. resident U. Tsukuba Hosp., 1980-81, sr. resident, 1985-86, chief resident, 1987-88, rsch. assoc., 1991-93, part-time instr., 1993-95, asst. prof. Inst. Clin. Medicine, 1995—; rsch. fellow Harvard Med. Sch., Boston, 1988-91. Contbr. articles to profl. jours. Avocations: travel, driving. Fax: 81-298-53-3124. E-mail: ynk-aki@md.tsukuba.ac.jp. Office: U Tsukuba Inst Clin Medicine, 1-1-1 Tennodai, Tsukuba Ibaraki 305-8575, Japan

YANCEY, CAROLYN DUNBAR, educational policy maker; b. Detroit, Feb. 10, 1921; d. Henry Steward and Annie Louise (Dye) Dunbar; m. Asa Greenwood Yancey Sr., Dec. 28, 1944; children: Arthur H. II, Carolyn L., Caren L., Asa Greenwood, Jr. BA, Wayne State U., 1941. Cert. tchr., Mich. Mem. Bd. Edn. Atlanta Pub. Schs., 1982-97, v.p. Bd. Edn., 1993; mem. bd. regents Univ. Sys. of Ga., 1985-92; trustee Spelman Coll., Atlanta, 1972—; bd. dirs. Women's C. of C. of Atlanta, 1972-74. Pres. PTA, Frank L. Stanton Sch., Atlanta, 1960; active in voter registration Atlanta Voters League, 1963. Recipient Daniel James Gen. Edn. award Tuskegee Airmen, Inc., 1993, Achievement award Atlanta Med. Assn., 1982, Leadership award NAACP, 1981. Mem. Links Inc. (pres. 1968), Delta Sigma Theta. Congregationalist. Avocations: sewing, homemaking. Home: 2845 Engle Rd NW Atlanta GA 30318-7216

YANCHEV, IVAN YANEV, physicist; b. Kardjali, Bulgaria, Apr. 10, 1943; s. Yani Ivanov and Petronka Rousseva Y.; m. Valeria Borissova Stoyanova, June 16, 1979; 1 child, Krassimir. MSc in Physics, Sofia U., Bulgaria, 1968; PhD in Physics, Ioffe Inst., St. Petersburg, Russia, 1974. Rshc. fellow Semiconductor Physics Inst., Sofia, 1975-81; assoc. prof. Sofia U., 1982—; vice dean Physics Dept., Sofia, 1991-95. Contbr. articles to sci. jours. Avocations: skiing, mountain climbing. Office: Physics Dept-Sofia U, 5 James Bourchier Blvd, BG 1126 Sofia Bulgaria

YANCY, WILLIAM SAMUEL, pediatrician; b. Pittsboro, Miss., Aug. 17, 1939; s. Lester Truman and Maxyne (Lindsey) Y.; m. Susan Elizabeth Guest, June 19, 1965; children: Amy Lynn Yancy, William Samuel Jr., James Michael. BA, Duke U., 1961, MD, 1965. Resident in pediatrics Duke U. Med. Ctr., Durham, N.C., 1965-66, 67-68; resident in pediatrics, then fellow in adolescent medicine U. Rochester (N.Y.) Med. Ctr., 1966-67, 70-71; pediatrician Durham Pediatrics, 1971—; dir. adolescent medicine tng. program Duke U. Med. Ctr., 1971-99, dir. behavioral pediat. tng. program, 1978-90, assoc. clin. prof. psychiatry, 1982—, clin. prof. pediatrics, 1984—; dir. pediat. tng. program Durham Regional Hosp., 1977-80, med. coun., 1980-86, chmn. dept. pediatrics, 1980-86, chmn. nursery com., 1986-96; pediatrician Duke U. Affiliated Physicians, 1995—; bd. mem. Am. Bd. Pediatrics, 1992—; chmn. Coalition for Healthy N.C. Youth, 1991-95; editl. bd. Jour. Devel. and Behavioral Pediatrics, 1984—. Bd. dirs. Child Advocacy Commn. Durham, 1973-76, 79-85, pres. 1973-74; bd. dirs. Durham Cmty. Guidance Clinic, 1974-76; N.C. State Coordinating Coun., Raleigh, 1994-95; vestry St. Stephen's Episcopal Ch., Durham, 1985-87, 95-98. Lt. cmdr. U.S. Navy, 1968-70. Fellow Am. Acad. Pediatrics (com. on adolescence), Soc. Adolescent Medicine (exec. sec.-treas. 1978-83, pres. 1985-86, chmn. fin. com. 1989-93); mem. AMA, Internat. Assn. Adolescent Health, Ambulatory Pediat. Assn., Soc. Devel. & Behavioral Pediatrics (pres. 1984-85), N.C. Pediat. Soc. (chmn. com. on adolescents 1989-96), Beta Omega Sigma, Omicron Delta Kappa. Avocations: stamp collecting, writing, golf. Home: 59 Kimberly Dr Durham NC 27707-5418 Office: Durham Pediatrics 2609 N Duke St Ste 1000 Durham NC 27704-3048

YANDLE, SYLVESTER ELWOOD, II, sales executive, inventor; b. Lafayette, La., Sept. 14, 1932; s. Arthur Ray and Marie (Delhomme) Y.; m. Gretchen Ehrensing, June 28, 1957; children: Gretchen Marie, Sylvester E. III, Gladys Anne, Henry Arthur. Student, Southwestern La. Inst. Well logger Core Labs., Lafayette, La., 1954-56; salesman Security Rock Bits, Lafayette, La., 1956-61, Orbit Valve, New Orleans, 1961-62, So. Engine & Pump, New Orleans, 1962-66; owner, pres. Indsl. Pump Sales, Inc., Belle Chasse, La., 1967—, Commodore Boat Stores, Belle Chasse, La., 1978—, Hydro Damp Inc., Belle Chasse, La., 1992—. Inventor: Air bag for airlines (patent 1991), Hydro Damp (patent 1989), Indicators Studs for Railroads (patent pending), 2 others pending. Active mem. Aurora Civic Assn., La. Sgt. 1st class, M.C., USAR, 1948-59. Mem. New Orleans C.C., Airplane Owners & Pilots Assn. Republican. Roman Catholic. Avocations: duck carving, knife making, painting, inventing, flying. Home: 5883 Rhodes Ave New Orleans LA 70131-3925 Office: Indsl Pump Sales Inc 2814 Engineers Rd Belle Chasse LA 70037-3153

YANEV, YOTZO YANKOV, geologist, researcher; b. Sofia, Bulgaria, Mar. 26, 1938; s. Yanko Panteleev and Maria Yotzova (Antova) Y.; m. Kunka Mincheva Ivanova; children: Maria, Kalin. MS, U. Mining and Geology, Sofia, 1960. Engr., geologist Rare Metal Soc., Sofia, 1960-65, sr. geologist, 1965-67; geologist Geol. Inst., Sofia, 1967-69, sci. rschr., 1973-90, head sect. to deputy dir., 1993—, 2000—; geologist Bur. Recherche et participation

minière, Rabat, Morocco, 1969-72; rsch. prof. Bulgarian Acad. Sci., Sofia, 1990; invited asst. U. Paris, Sud, 1983-84; cons. Rare Metal Soc., Bulgaria, 1975-77, 86-88; invited prof. U. St. Jerome, Marseille, France, 95, U. Paris, Sud, 1997; cons. Geol. & Geophys, Sofia, 1981-83, 86, 88. Geoingeniring, Asenovgrad, 1988-91. Co-author, co-editor: Geological Map df Bulgaria, 1994 (Acad. award Bulgarian Acad. Sci. 1994); co-author invention, 1975 (Acad. award Bulgarian Acad. Sci. 1982). Grantee Ministry of Tech. and Rsch. of France, U. Paris VI, 1991, NATO, U. Pisa, 1994, Inst. Physique du Globe, Paris, 1996; recipient Acad. award Bulgarian Acad. Sci., 2000. Mem. Bulgarian Geol. Soc., Bulgarian Scientist Union, Bulgarian Mineral. Soc. Home: Ravnetz Str 1-A, 1421 Sofia Bulgaria Office: Geol Inst, Acad G Boncev Str Bl 24, 1113 Sofia Bulgaria

YANG, AMANDA, real estate agent; b. Kaohsiung, Taiwan, Mar. 7, 1968; d. Yung-Shung Yang and Chiu-Jiu Yang-Huang; m. Ryne Yang; children: Andy, Jimmy. Grad. dept. acctg., Tamkang U., Taipei, Taiwan, '. Asst. to dir. Lai Lai Sheraton Hotel, Taipei, 1991-92, account mgr., 1992-93; mgr. Colliers Jardine Taiwan Ltd., Taipei, 1993—. Mem. Acctg. Club. Avocations: movies, reading. Fax: 886 2 25450048. E-mail: amanda yang@cj-group.com. Office: Colliers Jardine Taiwan Ltd, 8F # 261 Nanking E Rd Sec 3, Taipei 105, Taiwan

YANG, ANJA, lawyer; b. Taipei, China, July 15, 1957; d. Chun-fu and Pei-lian (Dwan) Y.; m. John Xavier Keenan, July 19, 1980 (div. Oct. 1986). LLB, Nat. Taiwan U., Taipei, 1979; MA, Ohio State U., 1984; LLM, NYU, 1986. Bar: N.Y. 1999. Legal assoc. Lee & Li, Taipei, 1979-81, Tsar & Tsai, Taipei, 1989-91; specialist Ministry of Fgn. Affairs, Taipei, 1991-95; lectr. Nat. Ching Hwa U., Hsin Chu, Taiwan, 1992; legal assoc. Ding & Ding, Taipei, 1995-96; mem. exec. legal staff Baker & McKenzie, Taipei, 1996-99; assoc. Shay and Ptnrs., Taipei, 1999-2000; asst. v.p. Chiao Tung Bank, Taipei, 2000—; exchange fellow Internat. Christian U., Tokyo, 1985. Co-author: International Tracing of Assets, 1997; translator (Japanese to Chinese) Theory and Practice of International Organizations, 1996. Observer Conf. of Parties of Montreal Protocol, Nairobi, Kenya, 1994, Conf. of Parties of Framework Convention on Climate Change, Berlin, 1995. Nat. Def. fellow Ohio State U., 1983-85. Mem. Am. C. of C., Chinese Soc. Internat. Law. Avocations: reading, listening to classical music. Fax: 2375-2176. Home: 32-5F Alley 53 Ln 220, Sect 2 Hsing Lung Rd 117, Taipei Taiwan Office: Shay and Ptnrs, 91 Heng Yang Rd, Taipei 100, Taiwan

YANG, BG LEE HSIEN, communications company executive. Degree in engrng. with 1st class honors, Cambridge (Eng.). Pres., CEO Singapore Telecomms. Ltd., 1994—. Brigadier gen. mil. service, Singapore. Fax: 65-732-8300. Office: 27th Fl Comcentre, 31 Exeter Rd, Singapore 239732, Republic of Singapore*

YANG, BO-SUK, mechanical engineering educator; b. Kangwon, Korea, Feb. 8, 1956; s. Jae-Yong and Duk-Ryu (Cho) Y.; m. Jung-Mi Um, Apr. 26, 1980; children: Sung-Ill, Sung-Wook. BS in Engring., Nat. Fisheries U. Pusan, Korea, 1978, MS in Engring., 1980; PhD in Engring., Kobe U., Japan, 1985. Teaching asst. Nat. Fisheries U. of Pusan, 1978-82, asst. prof., 1985-90, dept. chmn., 1990-92, assoc. prof., 1990-95, prof., 1995-96; prof. dept. mech. engring. Pukyong Nat. U. (formerly Nat. Fisheries U. of Pusan), Korea, 1996—; vis. prof. U. Va., Charlottesville, 1989-90; vis. scientist Kobe (Japan) U., 1990-91; cons. Korea Heavy Industries, Ltd., Changwon, 1994-98, LG Electronics Inc., Changwon, 1991-95, 2000—, Hyundai Heavy Industries, Ltd., Ulsan, 1995-99, Hyosung-Ebara Co. Ltd., Changwon, 1994—. Editor: Jour. of Korean Soc. of Lubrication Engrs., 1992-99, Jour. of Korean Soc. of Marine Engrs., 1991, Jour. Korean Soc. for Power Sys. Engring., 1999—; contbr. papers to profl. jours. Recipient Best Paper award Korean Fedn. Sci. and Tech., Socs., 1994. Mem. ASME (H.H. Jeffcott award 1987), Korean Soc. Mech. Engrs., Japan Soc. Mech. Engrs. (Disting. rsch. award 1988), Korean Soc. Marine Engrs. (best paper award 1994), Korean Soc. Noise and Vibration Engring. Presbyterian. Avocations: swimming, reading. E-mail: bsyang@dolphin.pknu.ac.kr. Office: Pukyong Nat U, San 100 Yongdang-dong, Nam-ku Pusan 608-739, Republic of Korea

YANG, C. C., biochemistry educator, researcher; b. Taipei, Taiwan, July 15, 1927; s. Ching-Chi and Chen Mei Yang; m. Lin Yeh Hsiang, Dec. 18, 1951; five children. MD, Nat. Taiwan U., Taipei, 1950; D Med. Sci., Tokyo Jikei U., 1956. Assoc. prof. Kaohsiung (Taiwan) Med. Coll., 1956-58, prof. biochemistry, 1958-73, pres., 1967-73; concurrent rsch. fellow Inst. Zoology Academia Sinica, Taipei, 1964-87; nat. rsch. chairprof. Nat. Sci. Coun., Republic of China, 1964-67; dir. Inst. Molecular Biology Nat. Tsing Hua U., Hsinchu, Taiwan, 1973-85, prof. Inst. Life Scis., 1985-94, disting. chair prof., 1994—; rsch. assoc. U. Wis., Madison, 1961-62; mem. coun. inquiry of divsn. life sci. Nat. Sci. Coun., 1971—; mem. com. inquiry of arts and sci. Ministry of Edn., Republic of China, 1972-97; academician Academia Sinica, Taipei, 1990—, bd. ctrl. adv. com., 1995—. Mem. editorial coun. Internat. Jour. Toxicon, 1973-90; contbr. more than 150 articles on snake venom proteins to profl. jours. Recipient Premir's award for the Outstanding Scientists, 1983, Outstanding Rsch. award Nat. Sci. Coun., 1985, 87, 89, 91, 93, named Disting. Rsch. Chair, 1997—; recipient Javits Neuroscience Investigator award NIH, 1987-94; named One of Ten Outstanding Young Men, Republic of China, 1965. Mem. AAAS (life), Internat. Soc. on Toxicology (coun. 1988-91), Am. Chem. Soc. (emeritus, life), Protein Soc., N.Y. Acad. Scis., Chinese Biochem. Soc. (life, pres. Taipei chpt. 1979-81, emeritus dir. 2000—), Chinese Chem. Soc. (life), Japanese Biochem. Soc., Formosan Med. Assn., Asia-Pacific Internat. Molecular Biology Network. Office: Nat Tsing Hua U, Dept Life Sci, Hsinchu 30013, Taiwan

YANG, CHEN NING, physicist, educator; b. Hofei, Anhwei, China, Sept. 22, 1922; naturalized, 1964; s. Ke Chuan and Meng Hwa Lo; m. Chih Li Tu, Aug. 26, 1950; children: Franklin, Gilbert, Eulee. BS, Nat. S.W. Assoc. U., China, 1942; PhD, U. Chgo., 1948; DSc (hon.), Princeton U., 1958, Bklyn. Poly. Inst., 1965, U. Wroclaw, Poland, 1974, Gustavus Adolphus Coll., 1975, U. Md., 1979, U. Durham, Eng., 1979, Fudan U., 1984, Swiss Fed. Inst. Tech., Switzerland, 1987, Moscow State U., 1992, Drexel U., 1995. Instr. U. Chgo., 1948-49; mem. Inst. Advanced Study, Princeton, N.J., 1949-55, prof., 1955-66; Albert Einstein prof. SUNY, Stony Brook, 1966-99, prof. emeritus, 1999—, dir. Inst. Theoretical Physics, 1966-99, dir. C.N.Yang Inst. Theoretical Physics; disting. prof.-at-large Chinese U., HOng Kong, 1986—. Trustee Rockefeller U., 1970-76, Salk Inst., 1978-89, Ben Gurion U., 1980—. Recipient Nobel prize for physics, 1957, Rumford prize, 1980, Nat. Medal of Sci., 1986, Benjamin Franklin medal, 1993, Bower prize, 1994. Mem. AAAS (bd. dirs. 1975-79), NAS, Am. Phys. Soc., Royal Soc. London (fgn.), Chinese Acad. Scis., Academia Sinica, Brazilian Acad. Scis., Veneuzuelan Acad. Scis., Royal Spanish Soc. Scis., Polish Acad. Scis., Russian Acad. Scis., Korean Acad. Sci. & Tech., Am. Philos. Soc., Pontifical Acad. Scis., Sigma Xi. Office: SUNY Inst Theoretical Physics Stony Brook NY 11794-0001*

YANG, CHIH-HUNG, academic administrator; b. Taipei, Taiwan, Oct. 5, 1953. BL in Sociology, SooChow U., Taipei, 1977; MA in Journalism, Nat. ChenChi U., Taipei, 1980, PhD in Mass Comm., 1992. Dir. Inst. Edn. for Mass Comm., Taipei, 1989-91; mng. dir. Young Generation Found., Taipei, 1990—; dean Sch. Comm. Ming Chuan U., Taipei, 1995—, dean sch. comm., 1999—; bd. dirs. Chinese TV Sta., 2000—; dir. Acad. Journalism, Taipei, 1993—; standing dir. Acad. Advt., Taipei, 1993—; chmn. dept. mass comm. Ming Chuan Coll., Taipei; reporter, vice editor-in-chief China Times, Taipei, 1979-83; cons. Chinese TV Sta., Taipei, 1988; prodr. Broadcasting Corp. China, Taipei, 1991-92; exec. com. Exec. Com. Golden Horse Award, Taipei, 1990-93. Author: The Investment Environment of Media Industry of Mainland China, 1994, Profile of Mass Media: A Media Worker's Observation, 1990. Founder, mgr. Found. for Open Space Taipei City, 1989-93. Mem. Assn. for Pub. Opinion (bd. dirs. 1990—). Office: Ming Chuan Univ, 250 Chung Shan N Rd Sec 5, Taipei Taiwan

YANG, CHIH-PING, medical products executive; b. Taipei, Taiwan, July 5, 1959; s. Ching-Tong and Yueh (Chou) Y.; m. Shir-Ly Huang, Nov. 7, 1992; 1 child, Szu-Min. BS, Nat. Taiwan U., 1982; PhD, U. Tex., 1990; Exec. MBA, Nat. Cheng-Chi U., 1999. Postdoctoral rsch. scientist Upjohn Co., Kalamazoo, Mich., 1990-92; assoc. rsch. fellow Devel. Ctr. for Biotech., Taipei, 1992-94, rsch. fellow, 1995-96; med. dir. Bayer Taiwan, 1996-99; dir. med. affairs Schering-Plough Taiwan, Taipei, 1999—; assoc. prof. Nat. Taiwan U., Nat. Yang Ming U. Contbr. articles to profl. jours. Recipient fellowship Robert A. Welch Found., 1984, Young Investigator grant Nat. Sci. Coun., Taipei, 1994. Mem. AAAS, Am. Chem. Soc., Chinese Soc. for Biophysics (mem. coun.), N.Y. Acad. Scis., Internat. Union Pure and Applied Biology (mem. coun.). Achievements include patents on anti-HIV drug; design and synthesis of U-96.988 as anti-HIV agents. Office: Schering-Plough Ltd, 7F 89 Nanking E Rd Sect 5, Taipei Taiwan 105

YANG, CHING-YU, mechanical engineer; b. Taoyuan City, Taiwan, July 4, 1959; s. Cheng-yi Yang and A-hsueh Lee; m. Mei-chun Sissy Lin, Feb. 5, 1991; children:Ya-hsuan Sylvia, Yun-shan Elizabeth. BS, Nat. Taiwan Inst. Technology, 1984; MS, Nat. Cheng-Kuang U., 1986; PhD, Colo. State U., 1992. Lectr. Lee-Ming Jr. Coll., Taipei, 1986-88; assoc. prof. Hua Fan Coll. Humanites & Technology, Taipei, 1993-96; prof. Nat. Kaohsiung U. Applied Scis., Kaohsiung City, Taiwan, 1996—. Office: Dept Mold & Die Engring, Nat Kaohsiung U Appl Scis, Kaohsiung 807, Taiwan ROC

YANG, CHUNG-CHUAN, communications educator; b. Chia-Yi, Taiwan, July 6, 1966; s. Wen-Fu Yang and Lung-Hsiu Lin. BA, Nat. Kaohsiung Normal U., 1990; MA, Ohio State U., 1990, PhD, 1994. Instr. Taipei Mcpl. Nan Kang Vocat. H.S., Taiwan, 1989-90; assoc. prof. World Coll. Journalism & Comm., Taipei, 1994-95, Yuan Ze Inst. Technology, Taiwan, 1995-96, Nat. Kaohsiung First U. Sci. and Tech., Taiwan, 1996—. Grantee Nat. Sci. Coun., Taiwan, 1996. Mem. Chinese Comm. Soc. (bd. dirs. 1996-98), Internat. Comm. Assn., Am. Advt. Acad., Am. Mktg. Assn. Avocations: travel, reading, music, internet surfing. E-mail: kyang@ccms.nkfu.edu.tw.

YANG, CHUNG-CHUN, mathematics educator; b. Wu-Xi, Kiang-Su, People's Republic China, Nov. 21, 1942; came to U.S., 1965; s. I-Sheng and Yu (Wu) Y.; m. Chwang-chia Huang, Dec. 2, 1966; children: David, Dwight, Philip. BS, Nat. Taiwan U., 1964; MS, U. Wis., 1966, PhD, 1969. Instr. U. Wis., Madison, 1969; rsch. assoc. Mich. State U., East Lansing, 1969-70; rsch. mathematician Naval Rsch. Lab., Washington, 1970-90; prof. math. Hong Kong U. Sci. and Tech., 1990—; vis. prof. Ill. Inst. Tech., Chgo., 1983-84. Author, co-author math. monographs in Chinese and English; author, co-author, editor, co-editor 25 books; also over 100 articles, chpts. to books. Recipient rsch. publ. award Naval Rsch. Lab., 1973, spl. achievement award, 1987. Mem. Am. Math. Soc. (com. on Chinese transl. 1985—), S.E. Asian Math. Soc., Hong Kong Math. Soc., Internat. Soc. Analysis, Applications and Compution (v.p.). Avocations: ping pong, Chinese chess. Office: Hong Kong U Tai Po Tsai, Clear Water Bay Rd, Kowloon Hong Kong

YANG, CHUNGHAI, chemist, researcher; b. Shanghai, Nov. 4, 1928; d. Zaizhi Yang and Julong Shi; m. Wenyou Sha, Feb. 10, 1959; 1 child, Jushi. BSc, Tangshan (China) Jiaotung U., 1952. Lectr. Anshan (China) Inst. Iron Steel, 1952-56, S.E. U., Nanjing, China, 1957-58; sr. rschr. Inst. Atomic Energy, Chinese Acad. Sci., Beijing, 1958-61, Nanjing, 1961-73; prof. Nanjing Inst. Chem. Tech., 1973—. Contbr. articles to Jour. Physical Chemistry, Chinese Jour. Chem. Physics, Jour. Colloid and Interface Sci., Chinese Soc. Corrosion Protection. Mem. AAAS, N.Y. Acad. Sci., Chinese Chem. Soc., Am. Chem. Soc. Achievements include invention of a statistical mechanical approach to the establishment of relationship between macroscopic behavior and microscopic properties for adsorption systems.

YANG, CHUN-YUH, medical educator; b. Tainan County, Taiwan, China, July 4, 1959; s. Lien-Yi Yang and Bi-Shya Chou; m. Hui-Fen Chiu, July 23, 1988; children: Tina, Nancy, William. BSc, Nat. Taiwan U., Taipei, 1982, MPH, 1984; PhD, Yale U., 1993. Lectr. Kaohsiung (Taiwan) Med. Coll., 1986-94, assoc. prof., 1994-99, prof., 1999—, dir. grad. studies, 1999—, dir. dept. pub. health, 2000—; cons. Bur. Environ. Protection, Kaohsiung, 1997—, Bur. of Health, 1999—. Contbr. articles to med. jours., including Environ. Rsch., Internat. Jour. Cancer, others; mem. editl. bd. Kaohsiung Jour. Med. Scis., 1999—. Founder Cmty. Healthcare Assn., Kaohsiung, 1999; mem. Parent Coun. Dung-kung Sch., Kaohsiung, 1996. Recipient Kung-Pei Cheng Meml. award Chinese Pub. Health Assn., Taipei, 1997, Excellent Rsch. award Nat. Sci. Coun., Taipei, 1998, 99. Mem. Soc. Epidemiologic Rsch., Internat. Soc. Indoor Air Quality and Climate, Internat. Soc. Environ. Epidemiology. Avocations: table tennis, basketball, history. Office: Inst Pub Health Kaoh Med U, 100 Shih-Chuan 1st Rd, Taiwan Kaohsiung 80708, China

YANG, CZAU-SIUNG, medical microbiologist, educator; b. Nan-Tou, Taiwan, Jan. 28, 1922; s. Mu-Kuei and Kuei (Liu) Y.; m. Pi-Yun Lin, Jan. 30, 1949; children: Chwen-Shi, Chwen-Jen, Ming-Chiang. MD, Taihoku (Japan) Imperial U., 1945; D in Med. Sci., Matsumoto (Japan) Med. Sch., 1960. Med. diplomate, ednl. diplomate. Fellow in virology and epidemiology Baylor Coll. Medicine, Houston, 1961-63; prof. bacteriology Coll. Medicine Nat. Taiwan U., Taipei, 1963-92, prof. emeritus Coll. Medicine, 1992—; dir. Grad. Inst. Microbiology Nat. Taiwan U., Taepei, 1969-75, dean academic affairs Coll. Medicine, 1984-85; dean Coll. Medicine Nat. Taiwan U., Taipei, 1985-87; dir. dept. of health medicine, health Nat. Inst. Preventive Medicine, Taipei, 1977-81; cons. USN Med. Rsch. Unit # 2, Taipei, 1974-77; mem. hepatitis control com. Dept. of Health, Taipei, 1981—. Co-editor: Human Tumor Immunology, 1984, Epstein-Barr Virus and Human Diseases, 1990; pub. Chinese Jour. Microbiology and Immunology, 1980-97; contbr. articles to profl. jours. Surgeon lt. M.C., Chinese Army, 1960. Fellow Internat. Union Against Cancer, 1972-73; recipient Disting. Scientists and Technologists award Cabinet China, 1982, Disting. Scientist Nat. Sci. Coun., 1986. Mem. Asia and Pacific Coun. Sci. and Tech., Jing Fu ALumni Assn. (pres. 2000—),Ching-Hsing Med. Found. (pres. 1988—). Avocation: Chinese boxing. Home: 2F # 38 Yun-ho St, Taipei 106, Taiwan Office: Nat Taiwan U Grad Inst Microbiology, 1-1 Jen-ai Rd, Taipei 100, Taiwan

YANG, DI, aerospace engineer, educator; b. Liaoning, Peoples Republic of China, Mar. 7, 1937; s. Weizhang and Yanan (Miao) Y.; m. Zhengshu He, Feb. 1, 1963; children: Hong, Kai, Xu. BS in Engring., Harbin Inst. Tech., 1961. Asst. prof. Harbin (Peoples Republic of China) Inst. Tech., 1961-78, lectr., 1978-82, assoc. prof., 1982-88, prof., 1988—; cons. Ministry of Chemistry, Beijing, Peoples Republic of China, 1973-78. Author: DDZ-III Electronic Regulator Instruments, 1978; contbr. articles to profl. jours. Recipient 2d prize Com. of Sci. and Tech. 1989, 91. Fellow Control Soc. Aerospace and Moving Objects. Office: Harbin Inst Tech, Po Box 137, 150001 Harbin China

YANG, DONG-SEOK, science educator, physicist; b. Sangju, Kyungbuk, Korea, Aug. 27, 1959; s. Kisung Yang and Sangyi Lee; m. Chunrim Lee, Apr. 24, 1988; children: Andrew, Isaac. BS, Chungbuk Nat. U., Cheongju, 1980; MS, Seoul Nat. U., 1988; PhD, Ill. Inst. Tech., Chgo., 1994. Lectr. Chungbuk Nat. U., Cheongju, 1995-96; rschr. Seoul Nat. U., 1996-98; instr. Kyungdong U., Khosung, 1998—. Sgt. Korean Army, 1983-85. Avocations: guitar, tennis, Korean chess. Fax: 82 392 631 9543. E-mail: dsyang@kyungdong.ac.kr. Home: Dongbu apt 106-1301, Sokcho Kangwon Korea Office: Kyungdong U, san 91-1 Thosung, Khosung Kangwon 219-830, Korea

YANG, EN ZE, electronics engineering educator; b. Raoping, Guangdong, China, Oct. 20, 1919; s. Shichong and Apai (Chen) Y.; m. Shulan Li, May 1, 1955; children: Jing, Shi, Jie. B in Telecomm. Engring., Wuhan (Hubei, China) U., 1941, M in Telecomm. Engring., 1943. Asst. Wuhan U., 1943-46; lectr. elec. engring. Zhongshan U., Guangzhou, Guangdong, 1946-47, Nankai U., Tianjin, China, 1948-52; asst. prof. Post and Telecom. U., Beijing, 1955-60; asst. prof. Post and Telecom. U., Wuhan, 1960-73, prof., chief engr. Rsch. Inst., 1974-85; asst. prof. Tianjin U., 1952-55, prof., 1985—; part-time prof. Shantou (Guangdong) U., 1988—. Author: Receiver of Digital Optical Communication, 1984; contbr. entry to ency., articles to profl. jours. Mem. Polit. Conf., Hubei, 1980-85. Recipient Hon. award Nat. Sci. and Tech. Conf., Beijing, 1978, 1st Rank award Ministry of Post and Telecom., Beijing, 1984, Govt. of Hubei Province, 1984. Mem. IEEE, Comm. Inst. China (hon., fellow, dep. chief fiber comm. group 1980-95). Avocations: tennis, bicycling, swimming, bridge, western classical music. Office: Tianjian U, Coll Elec and Info Engring, Tianjin 300072, China

YANG, FENGJIE, science educator; b. Jinan, China, Apr. 28, 1957; s. Bingyu and Danfeng (Zhang) Y.; m. Junlu Wang, Jan. 24, 1982; 1 child, Zhenyi. Doctor, Tongji U., Shanghai, China, 1999—. Tchr. Jiaozuo Tech. Inst., China, 1982-87; docent Shandong Inst. Mining and Tech., Taian, China, 1987-92; vis. scholar Monic U., Germany, 1992-94; assoc. prof. Shandong Inst. Mining and Tech., Taian, 1994-99, prof., 1999—; dir. geosci. dept., Shandong U., Taian, 1996-99. Mem. IEEE, SPIE. Avocation: taiji. Office: Shandong U Sci and Tech, Diazongdajie 223, Shandong 271019, China

YANG, FU-YU, biochemist; b. Shanghai, China, Oct. 30, 1927; m. Jin-lan Wang, Oct. 1, 1956; children: Zhong-gao, Zhong-qian, Zhong-shan. BS, Zhejiang U., Hangzhou, China, 1950; PhD, Moscow State U., 1960. Jr. rschr. Inst. Biophysics, Academia Sinica, Beijing, 1950-55, sr. rschr., 1960—, dep. dir., 1979-86, supr. PhD students, 1986—; chmn. acad. coun. Inst. Biophysics Nat. Lab. Biomacromolecules, Academia Sinica, Beijing, 1988—; prof. faculty biol. sci. and tech. Tsing Hua U., Beijing, 1985-96, faculty biol. sci. Wuhan (China) U., 1993—. Editor-in-chief: Acta Biophysica Sinica. Recipient prize for sci. and tech. progress, 2nd class Chinese Acad. Scis., Beijing, 1986, Nat. Natural Sci. prize 3rd class State Commn. Sci. and Tech., Beijing, 1989, Natural Sci. prize 2nd class Chinese Acad. Scis., Beijing, 1995. Mem. Chinese Soc. Biochemistry and Molecular Biology (v.p. 1993-97), Group Biogenetics and Biomembranes of Internat. Soc. Biochemistry and Molecular Biology (Chinese del.), Chinese Acad. Scis. Mem. Communist party. Avocation: classical music. Office: Inst Biophysics Academia Sinica, 15 Datun Rd Chaoyang Dist, Beijing 100101, China

YANG, GANG, physiology educator; b. Shanghai, China, Sept. 28, 1933; s. Jianpin and Baoling (Shan) Y.; m. Yilian Zhu; children: Lin, Dan. Grad., Jilin Med. U., Changchun, China, 1956, MSc, 1979; MD, Bethune Med. U., Changchun, China, 1982. Asst. Jilin Med. U., Changchun,, China, 1957-65; lectr. Jilin Med. U., Changchun,, 1965-80; assoc. prof. Bethune Med. U., Changchun,, 1980-90; prof. Hubei Med. U., Wuhan, China, 1990—. Author: Endocrine Physiology and Pathophysiology, 1981, 3d edit., 2000, Endocrinology Diagnosis and Atlas, 1988, Medical News Titbits, 1988, A Dictionary of Chinese Poems on Scenic Spots and Historical Sites, 1993, 2d edit., 2000; editor Jour. Bethune Med. U., 1975-82; contbr. articles to profl. jours. Mem. Chinese Assn. Physiology, Wuhan Assn. of Physiol Sci. (dir.), Hubei Assn. Physiol. Sci. (dir.). Avocations: reading Chinese lit. and poetry, writing poetry. Office: Hubei Med U Dept Physiology, Donghu Rd #39, 430071 Wuhan Hubei, China

YANG, HAI-YUAN, engineering educator; b. ShenYang, LiaoNing, China, Oct. 24, 1931; s. Dai-Lin and Yan-Rong (Zhan) Y.; m. Li-Duan Wang, Feb. 15, 1958; children: Jia-Hui, Zhi-Qi. BS, Tianjin U., 1952. Asst., lectr., assoc. prof. Tianjin U., 1952-83, prof. mechanics, 1983—, head dept. mechanics, 1984-88; lectr. Sch. Mechanics, Tsinghua U., beijing, 1957-59; vis. scholar U. Wyo., Laramie, 1981, Yale U., New Haven, 1982; vis. prof. U. N.Mex., Albuquerque, 1993-95; mem. instructing com. on courses of engring. mechanics in colls. and univs., China, 1987-95; rschr. in solid mechanics. Author: Numerical Method in Solid Mechanics, 1991; contbr. articles to profl. jours. Mem. Tianjin Assn. for Sci. and Tech., Tianjin Soc. Mechanics (chmn. coun. 1989—). Avocations: music, Chinese opera, table tennis. Office: Tianjin Univ, Dept Mechanics, Tianjin 300072, People's Republic of China

YANG, HENRY (HONG) S., metallurgist, materials engineer; b. Tai Xin, Jiang Su, China, Oct. 27, 1964; came to U.S., 1989; s. Xiao-Wen and Yan-Hua (Li) Y.; m. Xiao-Ping (Susan) Su, May 1, 1992; children: Jenny Su, Rachel Su. BS, Harbin (China) Inst. Tech., 1984; MPhil, U. Birmingham, Eng., 1987, PhD, 1989. Postdoctoral rsch. fellow U. Calif., Davis, 1989-92, staff rsch. assoc., 1992-93; staff rsch. metallurgist Kaiser Aluminum & Chem. Corp., Pleasanton, Calif., 1994-98; sr. metall. Kaiser Aluminum Engineered Products, L.A., 1999—; instr. Laney Coll., Oakland, Calif., 1994-95. Contbr. articles to internat. sci. jours. Recipient Emsley award Inst. Materials, London, 1988, Pfeil medal and prize Inst. of Materials, London, 1993, Buehler Tch. Paper Merit award Internat. Metallographic Soc., 1997. Mem. The Minerals, Metals and Materials Soc., Materials Rsch. Soc. Christian. Achievements include contributions to the understanding of superplasticity in aluminum alloys, titanium alloys, and intermetallics; study of physical and mechanical metallurgy problems of aluminum alloys. Avocations: inventions, table tennis, tennis. Office: Kaiser Aluminum Engrd Products 6250 Bandini Blvd Los Angeles CA 90040-3168

YANG, HONG-SHENG, electronics educator; b. Jiashan, Zhejiang, China, Jan. 21, 1938; s. Song-Yu Yang and Yin-Bao Ye; m. De-Kun Sun, May 4, 1968; children: Rong, Jun. Bachelor's degree, Nanjing (China) Inst. Tech., 1962. Cert. appointments as prof. and doctoral dir. Asst. prof. Nanjing Inst. Tech., 1962-78, lectr., 1978-85; assoc. prof. Nanjing Inst. Tech. (now Southeast U.), 1985-92; prof. Southeast U., Nanjing, 1992—, prof., doctoral dir., 1994—; vis. scholar U. Wis., Madison, 1981-83; dir. Divsn. Microwave and Millimeter Wave Electronics, Photonics, and Techniques, Nanjing, 1985—; mem. com. Nat. Key Lab. of Millimeter Wave, Nanjing, 1994—, Lab. of High Power Microwave and Electromagnetic Radiation, Inst. Electronics, Chinese Acad. Scis., Beijing, 1995—. Author: IEEE Transactions on Microwave Theory and Techniques, 1995; patentee in field; contbr. articles to profl. jours. Mem. IEEE (sr. mem.), Chinese Inst. Electronics (sr. mem., mem. com. vacuum electronics and optoelectronics of Jiangsu province 1994—), N.Y. Acad. Scis. Avocation: music.

YANG, HUA QUAN, chemistry educator; b. Gui Yang, Gui Zhou, China, Jan. 2, 1940; s. Da Shi and Xiu Yun (Miao) Y.; m. Xie An, Feb. 28, 1968; children: Xie, Li. Master, Peking U., Beijing, 1963. Technician China Acad. of Bldg. Rsch., Beijing, 1963-70; tchr. Peking U., Beijing, 1971-78, lectr., 1979-87, assoc. prof., 1988-95, prof. chemistry, 1996—; vis. scholar Free U. Berlin, 1989, Chinese U. of Hong Kong, 1994-95. Contbr. articles to profl. jours.; patentee in field. Mem. Chinese Chemistry Soc., Chinese Soc. Corrosion and Protection, Chinese Soc. of Fast Ionic Conductor. Avocations: reading, travel, Beijing opera, embroidery. Fax: (86 010) 62751708. Home: #108 Bldg 316 Yan Bei Yuan, Beijing 100091, People's Republic of China Office: Peking Univ, Dept of Chemistry, Beijing 100871, People's Republic of China

YANG, HYUNG-JAE, environmentalist; b. Koje, Kyungnam, Korea, Aug. 25, 1954; s. Yong-keun and Ki-Yeon (Yun) Y.; m. Young-Suk June, Jan. 21, 1983. BS, Dong-A U., Pusan, Korea, 1982; MS, Polytech. U., N.Y.C., 1987; PhD, Hanyang U., Seoul, Korea, 1998. Tchr. Dongby Mid. Sch., Kyungnam, Korea, 1982-84; environ. engr. Robert Rogers Engring., Ocal, 1987-90; sr. rschr. Nat. Inst. Environ. Rsch., Seoul, 1990—. Mem. editl. com. Geo-Spatial Info. Sys., 1994. Sgt. Korean mil., 1975-77. Recipient scholarship Polytech U., N.Y.C., 1986. Mem. Korean Soc. Environ. Impact Assessment, Korea Soc. Water Quality. Office: Nat Inst Environ Rsch, 613-2 Bulkwang-dong, Seoul 122-706, Korea

YANG, JIACHI, research scientist; b. Wujian, Jiangsu, China, July 16, 1919; s. Wucheng and Weisheng (Shen) Y.; m. Fei Hsu, Nov. 10, 1951; children: Xi Yang Wang, Rui. BS, Jiao-Tung U., 1941; MS, Harvard U., 1947, PhD, 1949. Rsch. assoc. U. Pa., Phila., 1950-54; sr. engr. Rockefeller Inst., N.Y.C., 1954-56; prof. Inst. Automation, Beijing, 1956-68, Chinese Acad. Space Tech., Beijing, 1956-68, 1968—, v.p., 1981-85; dir. Beijing Inst. Control Engring., 1968-81. Editor: IFAC Proceedings Series, 1986; contbr. articles to profl. jours. Rep. Nat. Peoples Congress, China, 1965-78. Recipient Nat. award P.S.T., Chinese Govt., 1985, 87, Tan Kah Kee prize in info. sci. Tan Kah Kee Found., 1995, award HLHL Tech. Sci. prize, 1999. Mem. IEEE (chmn. Beijing sect. 1988-89, sr.), Chinese Acad. Scis., Chinese Assn. Automation, China Instrument Soc., Internat. Acad. Astronautics. Avocations: bridges, touring, taiji. Home: Zhongquancun 13/304, Beijing 100080, China Office: Chinese Acad Space Tech, PO Box 2417, Beijing 100081, China

YANG, JIANWEN, earth science educator, researcher; b. Changshu, China, Dec. 1, 1962; s. Bingyuan and Xiujin Yang; m. Xing Feng, Jan. 17, 1990. B in Engring., Guilin (China) Inst. Tech., 1983; M in Engring., Ctrl.-South U. Tech., Changsha, China, 1986; MSc in Physics, Toronto (Can.) U., 1992, PhD in Physics, 1996. Lectr. Guilin Inst. Tech., 1986-91; rsch. scientist U. Toronto, 1996-99; asst. prof. earth scis. U. Tasmania, Hobart, Australia, 1999—. Contbr. articles to profl. jours. Grantee Waterloo (Can.) Ctr. Groundwater Rsch., 1997-99. Mem. Am. Geophys. Union. Avocations:

bush walking, fishing, tennis, music, travel. Office: U Tasmania Sch Earth Scis, GPO Box 252-79, Hobart TA 7001, Australia

YANG, JIAPING, structural engineering researcher; b. Shanghai, China, Dec. 27, 1960; arrived in Singapore, 1993; m. Bei Li, Apr. 1993; children: Zhenyan, Junyan. BS, Tongji U., Shanghai, 1983; M in Engring., Shanghai Jiaotong U., Shanghai, 1988; PhD, Nanyang Tech. U., Singapore, 1996. Engr. Inst. Transp. Engring., Shanghai, 1983-85; lectr. Shanghai Jiaotong U., 1988-93; rsch. scholar Nanyang Tech. U., Singapore, 1993-96, rsch. assoc., 1996-97; sr. rschr. data storage inst. Nat. U. Singapore, 1997—. Author: (book) Computational Mechanics in Structural Engineering, 1992; contbr. tech. papers to profl. jours. Recipient Best Paper award ASCE, Tech. Coun. on Computer Practices, 1997. Office: Data Storage Inst Nat Univ, 5 Engineering Dr 1, Singapore 117608, Singapore

YANG, JINGAN, science educator; b. Bengpu City, Anhui, China, Oct. 8, 1943; parents Dezhao Yang and Yangshi Peng; m. Guangzhi Wu, Jan. 1, 1974; 1 child, Ximing. BS, Hefei (Anhui) U. Tech., 1969; PhD, U. Rome, 1985; HPhD, Inst. Image Processing, Bari, Italy, 1986. From lectr. to assoc. prof. Hefei U. Tech., 1969-93, prof., 1993—; vis. prof. U. Rome, 1982-85, Australian U., Canberra, 1990-91; faculty prof. U. Md., College Park, 1992-93; sr. assoc. Internat. Ctr. for Theoretical Physics, Trieste, Italy, 1996; sr. scientist Italian Acad. Scis., Rome, 1998, 99; dir. Inst. Artificial Intelligence, Hefei, 1995—; v.p. Coll. Computer Scis., Hefei, 1998—. Author: (book) Three Dimensional Computer Vision, 1994 (2d prize of outstanding books 1997); contbr. papers to profl. jours. Recipient awards Italian Acad. Scis., 1985-86; fellow U. Rome, 1982-85, U. Md., 1992-93, Australian Nat. U., 1990. Fellow N.Y. Acad. Scis.; mem. IEEE (sr.), Chinese Computer Fedn., Anhui Computer Fedn. (dir. 1990—). Avocations: music, touring, table tennis, cooking. Fax: 86 551 2904517. E-mail: jayang@mail.hf.ah.cn. Home: Hefei U Tech, PO Box 466 South Campus, 230009 Hefei Anhui, China Office: Hefei U Tech Inst Artfl Int, # 193 Tunxi Rd, 230009 Hefei Anhui, China

YANG, JUNG PIL, engineer, researcher, consultant; b. Seoul, South Korea, July 21, 1964; s. Jae Ran Yang and Hyun Sook Yong; m. Mi Ja Chung, April 9, 1993; 1 child, Eun Jin Yang. BS, Yonsei U., Seoul, 1987; MS, Korea Advanced Inst. Sci. Tech, Seoul, 1989, PhD, 1992. Post doctoral Korea Advanced Inst. Sci. and Tech., Seoul, 1992; sr. rsch. engr. Halla Engring. and Heavy Industries Ltd., Eumsung-Kun, Korea, 1992-95, Mando Machinery Corp., Namyangju, Korea, 1995-98; cons. Advanced Materials Engring. Co., Seoul, 1998-99, Advanced Magnetic Materials Co., Ltd., Seoul, 2000—. Contbr. articles to profl. jours. Mem. IEEE, The Korean Inst. Metals and Materials, The Korean Magnetics Soc., Korean Powder Metallurgy Inst. Avocations: tennis, swimming, baseball. E-mail: jpyang@shinbiro.com. Fax: 82-2 591 9328. Home: 402 Daesung Bldg 110-1, Banpo 4 Dong Seocho-Gu, 137-044 Seoul South Korea Office: Rm 4006 Korea World Trade Ctr, 159 Samsun-dong Kangnam-ku, 135-729 Seoul South Korea

YANG, JUNG-SUNG, chemist, educator; b. Nonsan, Choongnam, Korea, Jan. 20, 1941; m. Ok-ja Park, Apr. 21, 1971; children: Soo-Jung, Yun-Soo, Woo-Je. BS, Yonsei U., Seoul, Korea, 1965; MED, Yonsei U., 1969; MS, Kunkoo U., Seoul, 1977; PhD, Dongkuk U., Seoul, 1983. Tchr. H.S. Seoul, 1965-79; prof. chemistry Kyungnam U., Masan, Korea, 1979—, dean coll. natural sci., 1990-92, dir. Environ. Inst., 1983-85; vis. prof. U. So. Calif., L.A., 1984-85, Calif. State U., L.A., 1986, Far Eastern State U., Vladivostok, Russia, 1995, Kyoto (Japan) U., 1997-98. Author: Man and Nature, 1994, Chemical History, 1995, Life of Mendeleef, 1997 (award Min. Culture and Info. 1997), Physical Chemistry, 1998. Standing mem. Adv. Coun. on Dem. and Peaceful Unification, Seoul, 1989—; v.p. Tchrs. Union Soc., Masan, 1990; mem. probation Dist. Pub. Prosecutor's Office, Changwon, Korea, 1993—. Cpl. Korean Inf., 1960-62. Recipient prize social svc. ACDPU, Seoul, 1994, presdl. citation, 1995, prize city culture Masan City, 1996, Nobel Laureate in Chemistry, 1998. Mem. Korean Chem. Soc. (dir. 1973—, presdl. citation 1994), Am. Chem. Soc., Russian Acad. Sci. Roman Catholic. Avocations: climbing, tennis, golf, collecting. E-mail: jsyang@Kyungnam.ac.kr. Home: Daedong Apt No 116, Yangduk Dong, Masan 631, Republic of Korea Office: Kyungnam U Dept Chemistry, Happo-ku, Wolyoung Dong, Masan 631-701, Republic of Korea

YANG, KAM SANG, electrical engineer; b. Bentong, Pahang, Malaysia, Dec. 31, 1939; s. Choy and Voon Ying (Chui) Y.; m. Kathy Chang, Aug. 26, 1966; children: Alan, Chris. Diploma, Faraday Ho. Engring. Coll., 1965. Registered chartered elec. engr., U.K., Australia, Malaysia. Sr. mgr. The State Electricity Supply Authority, Malaysia; engr. MM Cables, Melbourne; tech. mgr. Asia Pacific, Radox Calbe Divsn., 1995-98; tech. cons. in field; part-time lectr. Malaysia; lectr. Victoria U., Melbourne. Mem. Inst. of Elec. and Electronics Engrs., Instn. of Engrs. Australia, Instn. of Engrs. Malaysia, Instn. of Elec. Engrs. U.K. Home and Office: 5 Glendarragh Rd, Templestowe, Melbourne 3106, Australia

YANG, KE, materials science and optics researcher; b. Chengdu, China, July 3, 1964; came to U.S., 1993; s. Yuan Yang and Shuqiong Wan; m. Tao Yang, Feb. 18, 1992; 1 child, Tracy. BS, Peking U., 1985; MS, Tsinghua U., Beijing, 1988; PhD, U. Mass., Lowell, 1999. Tchg. asst. U. Electronic Sci. and Tech. of China, Chengdu, 1988-90, lectr., 1990-93; tchg. asst. Bowling Green (Ohio) State U., 1993-94; rsch. asst. U. Mass., Lowell, 1994-99, rsch. assoc., 1999—. Contbr. articles to profl. jours. Mem. AAAS, Am. Chem. Soc., Am. Phys. Soc., Optical Soc. Am. (travel grantee 1999), Materials Rsch. Soc. (finalist grad. student rsch. award 1997), Sigma Xi. Home: 48 Riverside St Apt 2 Lowell MA 01854-4801 Office: U Mass Lowell 1 University Ave Lowell MA 01854-5009

YANG, KELLY, applications engineer; b. Mandalay, Burma, Mar. 7, 1973; p. Patrick and Chen Yang. BS, Harvey Mudd Coll., 1995; MS, U. Calif., Berkeley, 1996. Design engr. TRW, Redondo Beach, Calif., 1997-98; applications engr. Teradyne, Agoura Hills, Calif., 1998—. Avocations: reading, Internet. E-mail: kelly yang@yahoo.com. Home: 2237 Richelieu Ave Los Angeles CA 90032-3213 Office: Teradyne 30801 Agoura Rd Agoura Hills CA 91301-4324

YANG, KUAN-HSIUNG, mechanical engineer, educator; b. Kaohsiung, Taiwan, Oct. 1, 1950; s. Tou and Hsu-Tsan Y.; m. Fen-Fwa Bao; children: Tung-Feng, Tung-Chieh. BS, Cheng Kung U., Tainan, Taiwan, 1972; MS, U. Ark., 1980; D in Engring., Lamar U., 1985. Dept. chief engr. S.E. Cement Corp., Kaohsiung, Taiwan, 1974-78; engr. Pacific Engring. Cons., Inc., Kaohsiung, Taiwan, 1980-81; prof. mech. engring. Nat. Sun Yat-Sen U., Kaohsiung, Taiwan, 1985—; tech. cons. China Engring. Cons., Taiwan, 1987—, Indsl. Tech. Rsch. Inst, Taiwan, 1996—; dir. edn. ASHRAE Taiwan chpt., 1990-91; mem. tech. com. Nat. Fire Protection Bur., Taiwan, 1995—; dir. energy rsch. ctr. Nat. Sun Yat-Sen U., 1995—. Author: The Anlalysis of Thermal Energy Storage Air-Conditioning Systems, 1991, Smoke Management Design Analysis for Building Fire Protection, 1996; contbr. over 120 articles to profl. jours.; patentee in field. Recipient Best Paper awards, 1986, 95, Outstanding Contributions Bldg. Energy Rsch. award, Taiwan, 1991, Tunnel Ventilation award China Rd. Fedn., 1995, TECO Tech. award Tungyen Elec. Co., 1997; named among Top Ten Outstanding Engring. Professors in Nation, Taiwan, 1993. Mem. ASHRAE (dir. edn. 1990-91). Avocations: sports, music, movies. Home: Chien Tsin Dist, 6 F 2 # 303 Sin Tien Rd, Kaohsiung 800, Taiwan Office: Dept Mech Engring, Nat Sun Yat Sen U, Kaohsiung 80424, Taiwan

YANG, LU, economist; b. Yantai, Shandong, China, Mar. 21, 1924; s. Yuezhou and Guixiang (Wang) Y.; m. Yan Jiang, July 7, 1943; children: Shaotong, Shaoqin, Shaohua. BS, Nankai U., Tianjin, China, 1947. Corres. and editor Dawn Daily, Peiking, China, 1947-49; staff, div. chief Communist Party Com. of Beijing Mcpl., 1949-64; exec. Price Commn. of Beijing Mcpl., 1964-67; dep. dir. Price Bur. of Beijing Mcpl., 1979-81; dir. gen. office Price Rsch. Ctr., The State Coun., Beijing, 1981-84, v.p., 1984-85; advisor, sr. rsch. fellow Devel. Rsch. Ctr., The State Coun., Beijing, 1985—. Chief editor: Strategic Option for the Development and Reform of Electricity Industry of China, 1991; author: Price Reform Research, 1992; co-author: Housing System Reform: Theoretical Thought and Practical Option, 1992. Fellow Acad. of Price Studies of China (exec.), Acad. Cost Studies of China (advisor). Communist Party of China. Avocation: opera. Home: 1-302 Bldg 2 Tuanjiehubeili, Beijing 100026, China Office: Devel Rsch Ctr State Coun, 22 Xianmen St, Beijing China 100017

YANG, LU, chemist, researcher; b. Shanghai, June 15, 1955; s. Lu Yinong and Sheng Xuanshuang; m. Zhu Yibing, Aug. 18, 1987; 1 child, Chen. BS, Anhui Chinese Trad. Med. Coll., Hefei, 1982; MS, Shanghai Med. U. 2, 1985; PhD, U. Paris, 1992. Technician Inst. Post and Tele Anhui, Hefei, 1985-88; lectr. Shanghai Med. U. 2, 1985-93, assoc. prof., dep. dir. dept. chem., 1993-96, prof., chief dept., 1996—, chief basic med. coll., 1999—; dep. dir. sect. natural products Shanghai Pharm. Soc., 1995—. Editor Chinese Traditional Herbal Drugs, 1996—; contbr. articles to Acta Shanghai Med. U. 2. Ecole Nat. Superiore Chem. Paris fellow, 1992-93; recipient Baogang prize, 1994, Honor of Excellent Lecture, Municipality Shanghai, 1995. Mem. AAAS, Chinese Chem. Soc. Office: Dept Chemistry, 280 S Chongqing Rd, Shanghai 200025, China

YANG, MIIN-SHEN, statistics educator; b. Pin-tong, Taiwan, Oct. 2, 1955; s. Yu-Lan and Sei-Sing (Yeh) Y.; m. In-Hwei Shei, Feb. 8, 1980; children: Ching-Tzu Amy, Gina, Wei-En Grace. BS in Math., Chung-Yuan Christian U., Chung-Li, Taiwan, 1977; MS in Applied Math., Nat. Chiao-Tung U., Hsinchu, Taiwan, 1980; PhD in Stats., U. S.C., 1989. Assoc. prof. Chung-Yuan Christian U., Chung-Li, 1989-94, prof., 1994—; vis. prof. U. Wash., Seattle. Contbr. articles to profl. jours. Recipient Rsch. award Nat. Sci. Coun., 1990-93, 95-99. Mem. Phi-Tao-Phi (hon.). Avocations: swimming, Christian music, biking, camping. Home: Jen-Ai Fl, #5 Chung-Yuan New Village, Chung-Li Taiwan Office: Chung-Yuan Christian U, Dept Math, 32023 Chung-Li Taiwan

YANG, NAIHENG, engineer; b. Zejiang, China, Feb. 6, 1942; s. Senyi and Wenhua (Sen) Y.; m. Lanhua Bai, May 1, 1968; children: Zeyan, Yang. Grad., U. Sci. and Tech. China. Technician Nanjing (China) Rsch. Inst. Elec. Tech., 1965-80, engr., 1980-86, sr. engr., 1986—; dep. dir. Nat. Key Lab. Antenna and Microwave Tech., China, 1994—. Editor: ABD for Method of Moments in Electromagnetics, 1983. Vis. scholar Syracuse (N.Y.) U., 1980-82; recipient Spl. award Defense and Scientific Com. China, 1984, First Sci. and Tech. Devel. award Ministry Mech. and Electronic Industry, 1992. Mem. IEEE (sr.) , Chinese Inst. Elecs. (sr.). Home: PO Box 1315-600, Nanjing 210013, China Office: Nanjing Res Inst Elec Tech, PO Box 1315, Nanjing 210013, China

YANG, NORRIS HONG-CHING, lawyer, consultant; b. Hong Kong, Mar. 13, 1951; s. Ching Ko Yang and Shirley Ming-Tseng Ko; divorced. Student, Vancouver (Can.) Coll., B.C., 1969; BS, U. Toronto, 1974; LLB, U. Windsor, Can., 1978. Solicitor, Hong Kong, Singapore, Eng., Wales; barrister, solicitor, Ontario, New South Wales, Australia; mediator Hong Kong, Australia; apptd. attesting officer Ministry of Justice China. Assoc. Baker & McKenzie, Solicitors & Notaries, Hong Kong, 1982-84; ptnr. Alan Lam & Norris, Solicitors, Hong Kong, 1984-95, Boughton Peterson Yang Anderson (in assn. with BPYA, B.C.), Hong Kong, China, 1995—. Legal advisor Hong Kong Eye Found. Ltd., 1993—; bd. gov. Hong Kong Kidney Found. Ltd., 1997—. Mem. Internat. Bar Assn., Law Soc. Upper Can., (practicing cert.), Law Soc. Hong Kong (practicing cert.), Royal Hong Kong Yacht Club, Royal Hong Kong Jockey Club, Kowloon Tong Club, Diocesan Sch. Old Boys' Assn. (pres. 1992-95, mem. com. 1982—), Kiangsu & Chekiang Residents (HK) Assn. (mem. com. 1982—). Avocations: racket sports, tai-chi, meditation, classical western and Chinese music. Home: 1702 Dina Ho Ruttonjee Ctr, 11 Duddell St Ctrl, Hong Kong China

YANG, PEIRAN, tribologist; b. Weihai, China, June 16, 1949; s. Jingqiu and Ruihong (Wang) Y.; m. Shuhua Wang, Dec. 29, 1976; 1 child, Xin. MS, Shandong Poly. U., 1982; PhD, Tsinghua U., 1989. Tchr. Weihai Univ. Workers, China, 1976-79; from lectr. to prof. Qingdao Inst. Arch. and Engring., China, 1983—; lab. dir. Qingdao Inst. Arch. & Engring., 1989-92, chmn. dept., 1992—; vis. prof. U. Alberta, Edmonton, Can., 1994. Author: Elastohydrodynamic Lubrication, 1992 (award Govt. China 1995); contbr. articles to profl. jours. Recipient sci. progress award Govt. Shandong Province, 1994, named outstanding scientist, 1993; named excellent tchr. Govt. China, 1995. Mem. Chinese Soc. Mech. Engrs., N.Y. Acad. Scis. Avocations: reading, travel, sports, chess, speech. Office: Qingdao Inst Arch & Engring, 11 Fushun Rd, Qingdao Shangdong 266033, China

YANG, PI PENG, chemistry educator; b. Chengdu, Sichuan, China, Mar. 20, 1938; s. Xiao Shan and Hui Fu (Xie) Y.; m. Ai Hua Tang, Dec., 1964; 1 child. Diploma in Chemistry, Yunnan U., Kunming, China, 1961. Chemistry educator Yunnan U., 1961—, Chemistry prof., 1993—. Contbr. articles to profl. jours. Mem. Chinese Chem. Soc. Office: Dept Chemistry, Yunnan U, 650091 Kunming China

YANG, PING, gastroenterologist; b. Tianjin, He-Bei, China, Dec. 6, 1962; s. Jia-Xiang and Shu-Fu (Wei) Y.; m. Xinyu Wang, Dec. 18, 1996; 1 child, Rui-Long Richard. B.Medicine, Tianjin Med. U., 1985, M.Medicine, 1992; MD, Linkoping (Sweden) U., 1998. Intern Tianjin Med. U. Hosp, China, resident; physician Tianjin Med. Univ. Hosp., 1985-92; rschr. Örebro Med. Ctr. Hosp., Sweden, 1992-98; gastroenterologist Karolinska Hosp., Stockholm, 1999—. Contbr. articles to profl. jours. Home: L=206g9964, Terapivägen 4F, 141 55 Huddinge Sweden Office: Karolinska Hosp, Dept Med/Div Gastroenterol, 171 76 Stockholm Sweden

YANG, POPLAR, consumer products executive; b. Beijing, May 13, 1971; p. Liu and Yang; m. Yue, June 17, 1997; 1 child, Bridge. BS, Nankai U., Tianjin, China, 1993, MS, 1996. Cert. comml. engring. Biochem. engr. Tianjin Co., 1994-96; product supply mgr. Procter & Gamble, Guangzhou, China, 1996—; cons. Tianjin Co., 1994-96. Scholar Nankai U., 1989-96. Mem. South Flight Club, Holiday Inn Club, Sheraton Club. Avocations: watching television, long distance running, barling, reading. E-mail: yang.po@pg.com. Fax: 862086683733. Office: Procter & Gamble, Aether SQ 986 Jie Fang Bei, Guangdong 510400, China

YANG, QING, physicist; b. Zibo, Shandong, China, Aug. 30, 1963. BSc, Shandong U., Jinan, China, 1984, MSc, 1987; PhD, U. Newcastle, NSW, Australia, 1994. Postdoctoral rsch. fellow U. Newcastle, 1994-95; sr. rsch. officer Royal Melbourne (Australia) Hosp. Rsch. Found., 1995-97; assoc. U. Melbourne, 1996-98, sr. fellow, 1998—; sr. fellow in radiology Royal Melbourne Hosp., 1997—. Contbr. articles to profl. jours. Scholar Dept. Edn., Employment and Tng., Australia, 1990-93, U. Newcastle, 1990-93, Shandong U., 1983, 84. Mem. Austrian Inst. Physics. Fax: 61-3-9342 8369. E-mail: qy@radior.medrmh.unimelb.edu.au. Office: Royal Melbourne Hosp, Grattan St Parkville, Melbourne VIC 3050, Australia

YANG, QUANBING, materials engineering educator, researcher; b. Shaowu, Fujian, China, Mar. 22, 1964; s. Chunsheng Yang and E-er Tang; m. Zongping He, Mar. 30, 1994; 1 child, Yi-chang. B, Zhejiang U., Hangzhou, China, 1985, M, 1988. Asst. tchr. Zhejiang U., Hangzhou, 1986-88; lectr. Shanghai Inst. Bldg. Materials, 1988-95; assoc. prof. Tongji U., Shanghai, 1996—. Author: Concrete in the Service of Mankind, 1996; contbr. articles to profl. jours. Named Outstanding Young Tchr., Shanghai Govt., 1997. Mem. Silicate Assn. of China, Shanghai Civil Engring. Soc. (engring. materials com.). Avocations: bridge, go, chess, badminton. Office: Tongji U Coll Mat Sci and E, 100 Wu Dong Rd, Shanghai 200433, China

YANG, RUI, materials scientist, researcher; b. Xiangfan, Hubei, China, Feb. 3, 1965; s. Bangbo and Zhilan (Dai) Y. BSc in Mech. Engring., Wuhan U., 1984; MSc, Chinese Acad. Scis., Shenyang, 1987; PhD, Cambridge (Eng.) U., 1992. Rsch. fellow St. John's Coll. Cambridge U., 1992-95; prof. Inst. Metal Rsch. Chinese Acad. Scis., Shenyang, 1995—, head Titanium Alloy Lab., Inst. Metal Rsch., 1997—. Assoc. editor Intermetallics, 2000—; mem. editl. bd. Intermetallics, 1998—; vice chmn. editl. com. Jour. Materials Sci. and Tech., 1997—; prin. editor Acta Metallurgica Sinica, 1988-93 (1st class award for Best Periodicals in China 1993). Mem. Am. Soc. for Metals. Achievements include discovery of alloying effects on titanium alloys. Avocations: climbing, literature. Office: Chinese Acad Scis Inst Met Rsch, 72 Wenhua Rd, Shenyang Liaoning 110015, China

YANG, RUIKANG, research scientist; b. Nei Monggol, China, July 9, 1963; s. Bingnan and Jiacheng (Hong) Y.; m. Li Song, Feb. 1989; 1 child, Betty. BSEE, U. Elec. Sci. and Tech., China, 1983, MSEE, 1986; D of Technology, Tampere U. of Tech., 1996. Asst. lectr. U. Elec. Sci. and Tech. of China, 1986-88, lectr., 1988-91; rsch. fellow Tampere U. of Tech., 1991-93; sr. rsch. engr. Nokia Rsch. Ctr., Tampere, 1994-96; mem. tech. staff Bell Labs Lucent Tech., Murray Hill, N.J., 1996—. Contbr. articles to profl. jours. including IEEE Trans. Signal Processing, IEEE Trans. Cirs. and Systems, IEEE Signal Processing Letters, Signal Processing; reviewer IEEE Trans. on Signal Processing, IEEE Trans. on Image Processing. Mem. IEEE, Internat. Soc. Optical Image, European Speech Comm. Assn., N.Y. Acad. Sci. Avocations: reading, sports. Home: 3 O Keefe Rd Bridgewater NJ 08807-5694

YANG, SAM YU-SHUANG, physicist, software engineer; b. Wutai County, China, Nov. 17, 1957; s. You-yuan and Shu-zhen (Yan) Y. DPh, Chinese Acad. Scis., Beijing, 1987; PhD, U. Melbourne, 1998. Lectr. Shanxi U., Shanxi, China, 1987-88; tech. cons. BHP Pty. Ltd., Melbourne, 1991-92; rsch. fellow U. Melbourne, 1989-90, 1993-95; rsch. fellow U. Melbourne/Telstra, Australia, 1996-98; software engr. CSIRO, 1998—; cons. Telstra Australia, Melbourne, 1994-95. Contbr. articles to profl. jours.; author software. Office: CSIRO Mfg Sci and Tech, Locked Bag 9, Preston VIC 3072, Australia

YANG, SAO-PING (DAISY YANG), accountant; b. Singapore, Feb. 26, 1959; d. Cher-Kern (Robert) Yeo and Ker-Mei (Helen) Chang. BSc in Econs., London Sch. Econs., 1982; cert. diploma in acctg. and fin., Singapore Inst. Mgmt., 1985. Bookkeeper Yang Investments P/L, Singapore, 1983-89; acct. Yeo Engring. Org. P/L, Singapore, 1983-89; exec. Harrimosa Materials P/L, Singapore, 1989—. Mem. Nat. U. Singapore Soc. Avocations: visiting libraries and bookshops, reading. Home: 4 Goldhill View, Singapore 3088 26, Singapore

YANG, SHANG-SHYNG, science educator, editor; b. Chang-hua, Taiwan, Aug. 7, 1944; s. Hsieh-Hua and Hsiu-Rian (Chiaung) Yang; m. Chuen-Ying Liu, Sept. 10, 1970; 3 children. BS, Nat. Taiwan U., Taipei, 1967, MS, 1970, PhD, 1975. Cert. in agr. and microbiology. Rsch. fellow dept. microbiology and molecular genetics Harvard Med. Sch., Boston, 1979-80; prof. Nat. Taiwan U., Taipei, 1981—, chmn. dept. agrl. chemistry, 1989-92, divsn. head Global Change Rsch. Ctr., 1993-98, dir. Agrl. Exhbn. Hall, 1998—; vis. prof. Inst. Nat. de la Rsch. Agronomique-Dijon (France) Sta. de Géne Microbiologique, 1982-83; vis. prof. dept. microbiology and biochemistry U. Orange Free State, Bloemfontein, South Africa, 1992; commr. Power Devel. Found., Taipei, 1995—; congress pres. 2d Internat. Congress of Biogeochemistry of Trace Elements. Contbr. rsch. articles to profl. publs. (Outstanding Rschr. award 1997—); patentee extraction of sweet potato starch (Dr. Sun-Yat-Shen Invention award 1986). Named one of Top Ten Young People, Taiwan Jr. Chamber, 1983; recipient Rsch. awards Nat. Sci. Coun., 1975-97, Outstanding Rsch. awards Taiwan Yourt Co., 1996-98. Mem. Chinese Soc. Microbiology (pres. 1996—), Chinese Agrl. Chem. Soc. (pres. 1993-95), Biomass Energy Soc. China (pres. 1991-93), Am. Soc. Microbiology. Avocations: bridge, fishing. E-mail: ssyang@ccms.ntu.edu.tw. Office: Nat Taiwan U Dept Agrl Chem, # 1 Sect 4 Roosevelt Rd, 10617 Taipei Taiwan

YANG, SHI-MING, engineering educator; b. Wuxi, Jiangsu, China, Jan. 5, 1925; s. Shou-Bo and Ren-Zhen (Chen) Y.; m. Ju-Nuan Lin, Jan. 6, 1954 (dec. Oct. 1981); children: Yang Ya-Yun, Yang Yun-Kai. BS, Jiaotong U., Shanghai, China, 1948; MS, Case Inst. Tech., Cleve., 1950; PhD, Ill. Inst. Tech., Chgo., 1953. Sr. engr. Tsen-Tai Rubber Co., Shanghai, 1954-56; tchg. staff Jiaotong U., Shanghai, 1956-57; assoc. prof. Xian (China) Jiaotong U., 1958-60, prof., 1980-84; prof. dept. power engring. Shanghai Jiaotong U., 1985—. Author: Heat Transfer, 1987 (Nat. Excellent Textbook award 1988), Fundamentals of Heat Transfer, 1991 (Nat. Achievement award on Edn. 1997); contbr. numerous articles to profl. jours.; mem. hon. editl. adv. bd. Internat. Jour. Heat and Mass Transfer, 1982—. Mem. Internat. Ctr. Heat and Mass Transfer (mem. sci. coun. 1987—), Chinese Soc. Engring. Thermophysics (hon., exec. com. 1999—). Avocations: novel reading, travel. Home: Rm 202 Bldg 10 Lane 50, Guangyuan Xi Rd, Shanghai 200030, China

YANG, SHU-CHIN, economist, consultant; b. Tieling, Liaoning, China, Nov. 20, 1917; came to U.S., 1946; s. Pei-chang and Shu-Fong (Wang) Y.; m. Nancy Shu-Teh Cheng, Dec. 23, 1947 (dec. Sept. 1985); 1 child, Catherine Tsai; m. Flora Kai-wah Quek, July 27, 1991. BA, Nat. Cheng-Chi U., Nanking, China, 1939; MA, Nankai Inst. Econs., Chung-King, China, 1943; PhD, U. Wis., Madison, 1954. Economist for joint head office of 4 nat. banks Chung-King, 1939-41; economist Cen. Planning Bd., Chung-King, 1943-46; econ. affairs officer, br. chief UN Econ. Commn. for Asia and the Far East, Bangkok, 1950-63; sr. economist The World Bank, Washington, 1963-82; econ. mission chief, mem. The World Bank Mission for Korea, Taiwan, Egypt, India, etc., various locations, 1968-80; coord., mgr. UN Devel. Program/The World Bank, Washington, Beijing, Shanghai, 1983-86; dir. Inst. Internat. Econs., Nankai U., Tianjin, China, 1987-97; pres., cons. Svcs. for Econs. and Trade, Chevy Chase, Md.; econ. advisor Nat. Econ. Coun. of The Philippine Govt., Manila, 1956; adv. prof. Fu-dan U., Shanghai, 1987—; cons. World Bank, Shanghai, 1987-91; hon. prof. Shanghai, Dongbei and Cen. Fin. and Econs. univs., Shanghai, Dalian, and Beijing, 1987—. Author: (books) A Multiple Exchange Rate System, 1957, Theories and Strategies of Economic Development, 2d edit., 1989, China: Economic Reform, Development and Stability, 2000; author, editor: (book) Manufactured Exports of East Asia, 1994. Mem. Am. Econ. Assn., Chinese Econ. Assn. in N.Am. Home and Office: # 2404-S 4515 Willard Ave Apt 2404S Chevy Chase MD 20815-3650

YANG, SONG-YU, research biochemist; b. Wu-Xi, Jiangsu, China, Oct. 27, 1938; came to U.S., 1981; s. Rong-Geng Zhong and Su-Fei Yang; m. Xue-Ying He, Jan. 1965; children: Ying-Zi, Yu-Xiao. MD, Beijing U., 1960; MS, CCNY, 1983; PhD, CUNY, 1984. Med. diplomate Peking Med. Coll. Instr. Peking Med. Coll./Beijing U. Med. Ctr., 1960-75; asst. prof. Acad. Sinica, Shanghai, China, 1975-80; tchg. asst. CCNY, 1981-84; rsch. assoc. Rsch. Found. of CUNY, 1984-88; rsch. scientist NYS OMRDD, 1988—; head med. biochem. lab. Inst. for Basic Rsch. in Devel. Disabilities, 1994—. Contbr. chpts. to books and articles to profl. jours. Investigator Am. Heart Assn., N.Y.C., 1991-94. Recipient L.J. Curtman prize CCNY, 1984, Wall Street Fellowship award, 1991, NIH Rsch. award, 1994. Mem. AAAS, Am. Chemistry Soc., Am. Soc. Biochemistry and Molecular Biology, N.Y. Acad. Scis., Sigma Xi. Office: NYS Inst Basic Rsch in Devel Disabilities Dept of Pharmacology 1050 Forest Hill Rd Staten Island NY 10314-6356

YANG, TEN-FANG, cardiologist, medical educator and researcher; b. Taichung, Taiwan, Dec. 28, 1956; s. Li-Hsien Yang and Tsui-Shiang Chang. MD, Taipei (Taiwan) Med. Coll., 1982; MSc, U. Glasgow, Scotland, 1987, PhD, 1994. Med. diplomate, Gen. Med. Coun. registration in cardiology, internist bd., critical care bd., Taiwan. Resident Taipei Med. Coll., 1982-84; registrar (hon.) Glasgow Royal Infirmary, 1985-87; rsch. fellow St. George Hosp., London, 1988; cons. cardiologist Tzu-Chi Gen. Hosp., Hua-Lien, Taiwan, 1988-89; rsch. fellow John-Radcliffe Hosp., Oxford, Eng., 1990; hon. med. officer, rsch. fellow Glasgow Royal Infirmary, 1991-94; assoc. prof., cardiologist Taipei Med. Coll., 1995—. Contbr. articles to profl. jours. Recipient Young Investigator award Internat. Soc. for Computerized ECG, 1994. Mem. Internat. Soc. Applied Cardiovasc. Biology (sr.), Internat. Congr. on Electrocardiology (Young Investigator award 1994), European Soc. Intensive Care Medicine. Avocations: coin and stamp collecting, astrology, fortune-telling, swimming. Home: 94 East Green River St, Taichung City 40001, Taiwan Office: Taipei Medical College, 252 Wu-Hsing St, Taipei 105, Taiwan

YANG, VICTOR TING HSUN, retired physician, gastroenterologist, educator; b. Peikang, Taiwan, Apr. 9, 1931; s. Luh Hoh and Chih (Chen) Y. BMed, Nat. Taiwan U., Taipei, 1957. Intern dept. medicine Nat. Taiwan U. Hosp., Taipei, 1959, resident dept. medicine, 1959-63, fellow in gastroenterology, 1963-66, staff physician, dept. medicine, 1966-92; fellow in gastroenterology, dept. medicine Hosp. U. Pa./U. Pa. Sch. Medicine, Phila., 1971-72; instr. medicine Nat. Taiwan U. Coll. Medicine, 1969-92. 2d lt. Army of Taiwan, 1957-59. Roman Catholic. Avocations: reading, listening to classical music, hospital work.

YANG, XI QIANG, medical association administrator, pediatrician; b. Chongqing, China, June 3, 1938; s. Can San Yang and Ming Qing Zhu; m. Kang Ru Zhou, Sept. 9, 1961; 1 child, Li. MD, Chongqing U. Med. Sci., 1961. Chmn., prof. Chongqing U. Med. Sci., 1989—; resident, attending physician Children's Hosp., Chongqing, 1961-82, assoc. prof., 1983, dir. dept. pediat., 1989—; vis. scholar U. Washington, Seattle, 1985-87; vis. prof. Hong Kong U., 1994. Co-editor: Pediatrics, National Health Publisher, 3d edit., 1992, Encyclopedia of Chinese and Western Medicine, 1994; assoc. editor in chief Chongqing Med. Jour., 1991—, Chinese Jour. Pediatric, 1993—; editl. bd. Jour. Applied Clin. Pedatric, 1992—; standing editor Jour. Applice Pediatric; contbr. articles to profl. jours. Cons. Sichuan Internat. Exchg. Promotion Assn. Med. Health Care, Chengdu, China, 1994, Sci. Tech. Com. Health, Bur. Sichuan, Chengdu, 1996; vice chair Nat. Assn. Pediatric Edn., Beijing, 1994—; chair Pediatrician Promotion Com. of Chongqing, 1997—. Grantee Nat. Natural Sci. Found. China, 1988, 92, 96. Mem. AAAS, Chinese Pediatrician Assn. (vice chair 1997—), Pediatric Assn. Sichuan (vice chair 1997—), Pediatric Assn. Chongqing (chair 1993—), Nat. Visuale Aural Edn. Com., Nat. Med. Exam Ctr., Nat. Med. Mgmt. Bur (evaluation of medication expert 1999—), N.Y. Acad. Scis. Avocations: swimming, running, reading, music, photography. Home: 136 Zhongsan 2nd Rd, Chongqing 400014, China Office: Children Hosp, Chongqing U Med Sci, Chongqing 400014, China

YANG, XIANHUA, systems engineer, researcher; b. Nanjing, Jiangsu, China, 1964; came to U.S., 1997; s. Shaoqi and Laomei (Li) Y.; m. Yan Zhang, 1990; children: Lianna, Rita. BSc in Elec. Engring., Southeast U., Nanjing, 1984, MSc in Elec. Engring., 1988; PhD in Elec. Engring., U. Man., Winnipeg, 1994. Systems engr. Raytheon/APT I, Washington, 1997—. NSERC indsl. fellow, Ottawa, 1995, 96. Sr. mem. IEEE (R.W.P. Ing award 1996). Office: APTI 1250 24th St NW Ste 850 Washington DC 20037-1224

YANG, XIAO QI, mathematician; b. Chongqing, China, Apr. 24, 1962; arrived in Australia, 1995; s. Hong Jun Yang and Cong Xiu Liu; m. Qiong Tang, July 31, 1985; children: Zoe Zhuo, Lucy Lu. BS, Chongqing Jianzhu U., China, 1982; MS, Chinese Acad. Scis., 1988; PhD, U. NSW, Australia, 1994. Asst. lectr. Chongqing Jianzhu U., 1982-85, lectr., 1988-89; assoc. lectr. U. NSW, 1992-94; rsch. assoc. U. Western Australia, 1994-96, Australian postdoctoral fellow, 1997, lectr., 1998-99; asst. prof. Hong Kong Poytechnic U., 1999—; vis. rsch. fellow U. Melbourne, Australia, 1989-90; vis. fellow, U. NSW, 1990-91. Contbr. articles to math. jours. Recipient Excellent Thesis award Sichuan Prov. Ops. Rsch., China, 1989, Glenden Travel award, 1996; Overseas Postgrad. Rsch. scholar, Australia, 1991, Australian Rsch. Coun. grantee, 1998-99; grantee rsch. com. Hong Kong Poly. U. Mem. Math. Programming Soc., Hong Kong Math. Soc. Avocations: soccer, classical music, basketball, go. Office: Hong Kong Polytechnic U, Dept of Applied Mathematics, Kowlon Hong Kong

YANG, XIAOPING, optics microelectronics scientist; b. Taiyuan, Peoples Republic of China, Oct. 7, 1963; arrived in Australia, 1990; s. Lin and Zhifen (Zhao) Y.; m. Xiping Zheng, Aug. 23, 1989. BS, Sichuan U., 1985; M in Optics, Shanxi U., 1990; PhD in Optical Sci., Australian Nat. U., 1994. Assoc. lectr. Shanxi U., Taiyuan, People's Rep. of China, 1985-90; sr. rsch. scientist Commonwealth Sci. and Indsl. Rsch. Office, Melbourne, Australia, 1994—. Contbr. articles to profl. jours.; patentee in field. Rsch. fellow Australian Rsch. Coun., 1994. Mem. Optical Soc. Am. Avocations: soccer, skating, swimming. Home: Edward Freeth Dr, Melbourne Australia Office: CSIRO Mfg Sci Tech Divsn, Clayton Pvt Bag 33, Melbourne 3168, Australia

YANG, XIAOPING, engineering researcher; b. Sichuan, People's Republic of China, 1966. BS with honors., S.W. Jiaotong U., Sichuan, People's Republic of China, 1986; MS, Dalian U. Tech., People's Republic of China, 1989; postgrad., Purdue U., 2000. Contbr. chpts. to books and rsch. articles to profl. jours. Dean's fellow U. Mo., 1995, Andrew's fellow Purdue U., 1996. Mem. Am. Soc. Mech. Engrs., Tau Beta Pi Nat. Honor. Soc.

YANG, XINGJIAN, computer software scientist, educator; b. Chongqing, Sichuan, China, Nov. 16, 1939; s. Lisan Yang and Youshi Xing; m. Wenjie Liu, Feb. 1966; 1 child, Dongning. BS, Northwestern Poly. U., Xian, China, 1962. Cert. prof. computer sci. Asst. engr. 630 Inst., China, 1962-65; engr. 623 Inst., China, 1965-70; sr. engr. 623 Inst., 1979-81; prof. Computing Tech. Inst., China, 1982—. Mem. IEEE. Avocations: Erhu, photography. Office: PO Box 90, Xian 710068, China

YANG, XIN-MEI, mycology educator, phytopathology researcher; b. Nanchang, Kiangsi, China, Oct. 16, 1911; s. Shu-Chang and (Cai) Y.; m. Yao-Qin Xu, June 14, 1936; children: Xiao-Yun, Gui-Yuan. BS, Chekiang U., Hangchow, China, 1931; PhD, U. London, 1950. Lectr. plant pathology Nat. Chekiang U. Agrl. Coll., 1936-44; assoc. prof. plant pathology and mycology Chekiang U., 1945-48; Brit. Coun. scholar U. London Imperial Coll. Sci. and Tech., 1948-50; prof. plant pathology Wuhan (Hubei, China) U., 1950-52; head dept. plant protection, prof. Huazhong Agrl. U., Wuhan, 1954-84, prof., dir. Hubei Mushroom Rsch. Inst., 1979-89. Editor-in-chief Edible Fungi of China, 1986-93, Research Methods of the Edible Mushroom, 1998, Ecologica; Plant Pathology, 2000, Mycological Imparts and Exploitations in China, 2000; chief editor: Mushroomology of China, 1988 (high quality book award Govt. of China 1988, 2d best award 1990); inventor Tremella fusiformis, 1959. Recipient hon. cert. Chinese Comm. Edn., Ministry Agr. and Ministry Forestry, 1989. Mem. Phytopath. Soc. China (adviser 1989), Mushroom Splty. Assn. China (hon. chmn. 1987), Mycol. Soc. Sinica (hon. pres. 1993). Avocations: shadow boxing, gardening. Office: Huazhong Agrl U Dept Pl Pr, Shizhisan, Wuhan 430070, China

YANG, XUN REN (HSUN JEN YANG), physics educator, researcher; b. Hangzhou, China, Aug. 22, 1929; s. Guang Han and Su Xia (Huang) Y.; m. Shu Zhuang Liang, Feb. 4, 1955; children: Chong Yi Yang, Howard C. Yang, Liu Liang. BS in Physics, Tsing Hua U., Beijing, 1952; PhD in Theoretic Acoustics, Academia Sinica, Beijing, 1964. Tchg. asst. physics Coll. Agrl. Engring., Beijing, 1953-54; tchg. asst. physics Normal Coll., Beijing, 1954-55, lectr. physics, 1956-57; asst. prof. physics Academia Sinica, Beijing, 1964-76, assoc. prof. physics, 1976-80, rsch. prof., 1980—. Author: Random Talk on Acoustics, 1994, Taiwan edit., 1995 (outstanding popular sci. book prize 1995), (monograph) Atmospheric Acoustics, 1997 (award 1997); contbr. articles to China's Grand Encyclopedia/Volume of Physics, China's Military Encyclopedia/Volume of Fundamental Theories, 1987 (award 1989), over 50 articles to prof. jours. Recipient significant sci. achievement prize Academia Sinica, 1978, sci.-tech. achievement prize Coun. Sci. & Tech. in Nat. Defense, China, 1980; invited acadademic lectures in U.K., 1985, Australia, 1988, Japan, 1990, U.S., 1991. Home: China Agrl Univ (East Dist), Bldg 31C -3-201, Beijing 100083, China Office: Acad Sinica Inst Acoustics, Zhong Guan Cun, Beijing 100080, China

YANG, YING-PING, geophysicist; b. Kunming, China; s. Gui-Gong and Chun Fang (Liu) Yang; m. Hong Qu, Apr. 20, 1976. BSc, Yunnan U., Kunming, 1982; PhD, Sydney (Australia) U., 1995. Lectr. Yunnan U., 1982-91; rsch. fellow, CRCAMET Macquarie U., Sydney, 1996—. Mem. Am. Soc. Exploration Geophysicists, Australian Soc. Exploration Geophysicists. Avocations: swimming, basketball. Fax: 61-2-98508366. E-mail: yyang@laurel.ocs.mq.edu.au. Office: CRCAMET, Macquarie U, Sydney NSW 2109, Australia

YANG, YINHUA, molecular biologist, researcher; b. Chongqing, China, Oct. 30, 1956; s. Jinfei Yang and Zhijun Xia; m. Baiquan Li, July 26, 1985; 1 child, Yang. MD, Shanghai First Med. U., 1983; MS, West China U. Med. Sci., Chengdu, 1986; PhD, U. Nice-Sophia Antipolis, France, 1997. Lectr. Third Med. U. Chongqing, China, 1986-89, asst. prof., 1989-91; rsch. scientist SUNY, Stony Brook, 1996-97; postdoctoral assoc. Yale U. Sch. Medicine, New Haven, 1998-99, rsch. scientist, 2000—. Contbr. articles to profl. jours. Internat. Exch. fellow Chinese Govt., 1992; Cancer rsch. fellow Assn. Cancer Rsch., France, 1994. Mem. AAAS. E-mail: yinhua.yang@usa.net Fax: (203) 737-2286. Office: Yale U Sch Medicine BCMM 331 295 Congress Ave New Haven CT 06519-1418

YANG, YONG YUAN, chemistry educator; b. Shaoxiog, China, June 9, 1938; s. Renyu and Lanzhew (Dong) Y.; m. Huizhu He, Sept. 30, 1967; children: Xiao Jun, Lei. BS, Peking U., Beijing, 1964. Rsch. assoc. Inst. Chemistry, Chinese Acad. Scis., Beijing, 1964-78; asst. prof. Inst. Photographic Chemistry, Chinese Acad. Scis., Beijing, 1978-86, assoc. prof., 1986-91, prof., 1991—; prof. grad. sch. U. Sci. & Tech. China, Beijing, 1994—. Author: Holographic Recording Materials and Application, 1997. Vis. scholar Royal Inst. Tech., Stockholm, 1980-81, CSIRO Australia, Melbourne, 1993-94, 96. Mew. Chinese Soc. Photographic Sci. & Engring. Avocations: singing, basketball. Home: Rm 310 Bldg 910, Zhongguan cun Haidian, Beijing 100086, China Office: Inst Phorographic Chemistry, Bei Sha Tan, Beijing 100101, China

YANG, YONGLIN, linguist, educator; b. Lanzhou, Gansu, China, Nov. 25, 1954; s. Baoming and Hanying (Ma) Y.; m. Yi Cheng, Oct. 1, 1981; children: Yang, Zhengli. BA, Northwest Normal U., Lanzhou, 1982, MA, 1986; MS, Ctrl. Conn. State U., New Britain, 1991; PhD, Peking (China) U., 1998. Asst. prof. fgn. lang. dept. Northwest Normal U., Lanzhou, 1982-85, lectr., 1985-89, assoc. prof., 1989-95, prof., 1995—, vice chmn. dept., 1993-95, supr. MA program in linguistics, 1993—; supr. PhD prog. in linguistics Northwest Normal U., Beijing, 1999—. Contbr. articles to profl. jours. Recipient spl. govt. fin. aid State Dept. China, 1992, Zeng Xianzi ednl. award State Ednl. Commn. China, 1993, award Ednl. Commn. Gansu Province, 1995. Mem. Gansu Assn. Sr. Intellectuals. Avocations: football, aquatic animals and plants. Office: Tsinghua U, Fgn Langs Dept, Beijing 100084, China

YANG, YUFENG, hydrobiologist, researcher; b. Linli, Hunan, China, Dec. 28, 1963; s. Yunwan and Lanying (Su) Y.; m. Shaohong He, Nov. 21, 1993; 1 child, Ziyi. BS, Hunan Normal U., 1986; MS, Chinese Acad. Scis., 1991, DS, 1997. Rsch. assoc. Inst. Hydrobiology, Chinese Acad. Scis., Wuhan, 1991-96, assoc. prof., 1997; assoc. prof. Shantou (China) U., 1997—; vis. scientist Inst. Limnology, Austrian Acad. Scis., Mondsee, 1993, Hydrobiol. Inst., Czech Acad. Scis., Budejovice, 1993, Zool. Inst., Russian Acad. Scis., St. Petersburg, 1993, Edinburgh (Eng.) Lab., Inst. Freshwater Ecology, 1996. Contbr. articles to profl. jours. Mem. Chinese Zool. Soc., Chinese Ecol. Soc. Avocations: tennis, tourism, badminton, swimming, table tennis. Office: Shantou U Sci Ctr, Marine Biol Lab, 515063 Shantou China

YANG, YUH-SHYONG, science educator; b. Taipei, Taiwan, Jan. 25, 1957; s. Tsai-I and Chiou-Tsan (Cheng) Y.; m. Juo-Wei Wu; children: Linyun, Jinny. BS, Nat. Taiwan U., Taipei, 1979; MS, U. Calif., Berkeley, 1983; PhD, U. Wis., Madison, 1987. Rsch. asst. Henchun (Taiwan) Tropical Garden, 1979-81; postdoctoral rsch. asst. Inst. Enzyme Rsch., Madison, 1988-89; vis. fellow NIH, Bethesda, Md., 1989-92, vis. assoc., 1992-94; assoc. prof. Nat. Chiao Tung U., Hsinchu, Taiwan, 1994—, chair dept. biol. sci. and tech., 1999—; cons. in field. Contbr. articles to profl. jours. Mem. Am. Soc. Biochemistry and Molecular Biology, Am. Chem. Soc. Office: Dept Biol Sci and Tech, 75 Po-Ai St, Hsinchu 30050, Taiwan

YANG, ZAIFU, management educator; b. Songtao, China, May 24, 1965; s. Xiu-Jian Yang and Yu-Xian Chen; m. Qing Yu, Nov. 26, 1993. BSc, NW Telecomms. Engring. Inst., Xian, China, 1986; MSc, Xidian U., 1989; PhD, Tilburg U., 1996. Asst. prof. Xidian U., Xian, 1989-91; rsch. asst. Tilburg U., The Netherlands, 1992-96; sr. rsch. fellow U. Tsukuba, Japan, 1996-98; assoc. prof. Yokohama Nat. U., Japan, 1998—. Author: Simplicial Fixed Point Algorithms and Applications, 1996, Computing Equilibria and Fixed Points, 1999; contbr. articles to profl. jours. Mem. European Soc. Econometrics. Avocations: chess, hiking, movies, classical music. Office: Yokohama Nat U, 79-4 Tokiwadai Hodogaya-ku, Yokohama 240-8501, Japan

YANG, ZANE (ZHIJIA), mechanical engineer; b. Shanghai, May 16, 1957. BSME, Huainan Inst. Mining and Tech., China, 1982; MSME, U. Ky., 1989, PhD in Mech. Engring., 1993. Mech. engr. Amatrol Inc., Jeffersonville, Ind., 1993-95; sr. mech. engr. Mallincrodt Inc., Cin., 1996-99; sr. design engr. Valeo, Auburn Hills, Mich., 1999—. Contbr. articles to profl. engrs., including Internat. Jour. Mechanisms and Machine Theory, ASME Transaction Jour. of Mech. Design. Mem. ASME. E-mail: zane.yang@valeo.com. Office: Valeo 3000 University Dr Auburn Hills MI 48326-2356

YANG, ZHICAI, chemical engineering educator; b. Tianjin, Hebei, China, Nov. 3, 1937; s. Yang Chufang and Sun Xiuru; m. Wang Hongli; children: Yang Zhaoxia, Yang Zhaoying. BS, Tianjin U., 1961, PhD, 1965. Instr. chem. engring. Tianjin U., 1965-83, assoc. prof., 1983-92, prof., 1992—. Coauthor: Chemical Engineering Handbook, 1989, 2d edit., 1996; contbr. articles to profl. jours., including Indsl. Engring. Chem. Rsch., Chem. Engring. Sci. Recipient tech. sci. prize Ednl. Commn. China, 1988, 89, spl. subvention award State Coun. China, 1993. Achievements include patents in field. Avocations: swimming, football, ping pong. Office: Tianjin U, Chem Engring Rsch Ctr, Hebei Tianjin 300072, China

YANG, ZHIHONG, computer scientist; b. Shihezi, Xinjiang, China, 1969; came to U.S., 1997; parents: Wenzhi and Mingsheng Yang; m. Haihang Sun, Feb. 22, 1995; 1 child, Siyuan. BS, U. Sci. & Tech. China, Hefei, Anhui, 1991, MS, 1994; postgrad., U. Conn., 1997—. Software engr. Legend Group Corp., Beijing, China, 1994-95, software engr., project mgr., 1995-97; rsch. asst. U. Conn., Storrs, 1997—. Mem. Assn. for Computing Machinery, IEEE. Avocation: Chinese calligraphy. Fax: 860-486-1273. E-mail: zhyang@engr.uconn.edu. Office: Booth Rsch Ctr U-1031 U Conn 369 Fairfield Rd Storrs Mansfield CT 06269-9016

YANITSKY, OLEG NIKOLAEVICH, sociologist; b. Moscow, Russia, Mar. 24, 1933; s. Nikolai Fedorovich and Elizaveta Fedorovna (Gordeenko) Y.; m. Galina Ivanovna Kouzina, Oct. 19, 1932; 1 child, Tatiana Olegovna. Arch., Moscow Archtl. Inst., 1957; M of Architecture, Inst. Pub. Bldgs., Moscow, 1964; PhD, Inst. Internat. Labor Movement, Moscow, 1978. Head dept. Inst. Pub. Bldgs., 1957-66; sr. rschr. Inst. History Architecture, Moscow, 1966-67, Inst. Internat. Labor Movement, 1967-94, Inst. Sociology-Russian Acad. Scis., Moscow, 1993—; part-time prof. Internat. U., Moscow, 1993-94; vis. prof. MIT, 1995; head nat. group UNESCO program, Moscow, 1976-92; head sect. sci. coun. on biosphere, Moscow, 1976-92; mem. sci. coun. global problems, Moscow, 1984-89, sci. coun. social problems of sci. and tech., Moscow, 1980-85; cons. European Bank Reconstrn. and Devel., 1993-94. Author: Urbanization & Social Contradictions of Capitalism, 1975, Urban Ecology, Interdisciplinary Concepts, 1984, Ecological Prospects of a City, 1987, Social Movements, 100 Interviews with Leaders, 1991, Russian Environmentalism. Leading Figures, Facts, Opinions, 1993, Environmental Movement in Russia. Critical Analysis, 1996; editor: Russia: Risks and Threats of a Transition Society, 1998, Russian Greens in a Risk Society, 2000; contbr. over 270 articles to profl. jours. Grantee UNESCO, Paris, 1989, Swiss Nat. Sci. Found., 1996, Soros Found., 1997, World Wide Fund for Nature, 1999; numerous others. Mem. Russian Sociol. Soc., Union Soviet Architects, Internat. Sociol. Assn. Avocations: painting, collecting oral life histories. Office: Inst Sociology RAS, Krzhizhanovskogo 24/35 B.5, 117259 Moscow Russia

YANIV, MOSHE, molecular biology educator; b. Petach-Tikva, Israel, Nov. 7, 1938; arrived in France, 1964; s. Zvi and Haya (Grodensky) Yanishesky; m. Josette Rouviere, Sept. 1968; children: Gil, Karine. MSc, Hebrew U., Jerusalem, 1961; PhD, Paris U., 1969. Prof. molecular biology Inst. Pasteur, Paris, 1987—, head unit, 1976—, chmn. dept. molecular biology, 1985-87, chmn. dept. biotech., 1993-95; vice chmn. Embo Coun., Heidelberg, Germany, 1991-95, chmn., 1996; mem. assembly GM Cancer Rsch. Found., N.Y., 1990-94. Mem. French Acad. Sci. (Charles-Leopold Mayer prize 1995), Academia Europaea. Recipient Rosen prize for Cancerology, Found. Med. Rsch., 1983. Fgn. hon. mem. Am. Acad. Arts and Scis. Home: 159 Rue Blomet, 75015 Paris France Office: Inst Pasteur, 25 Rue du Docteur Roux, 75724 Paris Cedex 15, France

YANKAH, ABRAHAM CHARLES, cardiothoracic and vascular surgeon, educator; b. Anomabu, Ghana, Apr. 15, 1942; arrived in Hungary, 1962; arrived in Germany, 1965, naturalized, 1993.; s. John Abram and Sophia (Quansah) Y.; m. Aug. 1, 1970 (div. Mar. 1995); children: Ato, Ekow, Ekua, Aba. MB, Med. U. Sch. Debrecen, Hungary, 1966; MD, U. Med. Sch., Kiel, Germany, 1969; PhD, Free U., Berlin, 1993. Resident in surgery U. Hosp., Kiel, 1970-79, sr. resident, 1977-79, cons., 1980-86; sr. registrar Hosp. Sick Children, London, 1976; cons. J.F.K. Med. Sch., Monrovia, Liberia, 1979-80, German Heart Inst., Berlin, 1986—; assoc. prof. Free U., Berlin, 1993-97; prof. Humboldt U., Berlin, 1998—. Contbr. articles to profl. jours. Recipient The Best Sci. Work award on allograft heart valve Com. for Advancement of Cardiac Bioprosthesis, Coronado, Calif., 1988. Mem. Soc. Supporting Impoverished Children with Heart Diseases (v.p. 1988-97), Kiwanis Club (contr. of treas. 1990-96), Internat. Club Berlin. Avocations: tennis, golfing, music. Office: German Heart Inst, Augustenburger Platz 1, 13353 Berlin Germany

YANKOV, ROSSEN ANGELOV, physicist, researcher; b. Archar, Montana, Bulgaria, Aug. 11, 1949; arrived in Germany, 1993; s. Angel Ivanov and Vera Dimitrova (Deneva) Y.; m. Lena Petrova Karagyaurova, Dec. 1, 1974; 1 child, Yankova Aglika. Student, Tech. U., St. Petersburg, Russia, 1967-70; BSc in Physics, U. Sofia, Bulgaria, 1973, MSc in Solid State Physics, 1974; PhD in Physics, Bulgarian Acad. Scis., Sofia, 1981. Physicist U. Sofia, Bulgaria, 1974-75, Inst. Nuclear Physics Bulgarian Acad. Scis., Sofia, 1977-81, Inst. Electronics Bulgarian Acad. Scis., Sofia, 1981-83; rsch. officer Inst. of Electronics, Bulgarian Acad. Scis., Sofia, 1985-93; rsch. fellow U. Surrey, Guilford, Eng., 1983-85; rschr. Rsch. Ctr. Rossendorf, Inc., Dresden, Germany, 1993-98; sr. scientist dept. R & D CCR GmbH Coating Tech., 1998—; project coord. State Com. Sci. and Tech., Sofia, 1985-87; exec. joint com. Royal Soc. London and Bulgarian Acad. Scis., 1985-88. Contbr. over 150 articles and papers to profl. jours. and sci. confs.; co-patentee, 9 patents including 1 U.S. patent, 1984; inventor Siltex novel dressing for burns (patent pending). Founder, mem. Kyupsfilm, Rousse, Bulgaria, 1966. Recipient fellowship Internat. Atomic Energy Agy., Vienna, Guildford, Eng., 1983. Mem. Bulgarian Phys. Soc., N.Y. Acad. Scis., Am. Phys. Soc. (sec. Bulgarian br. 1991-93), Nat. Geog. Soc., Material Rsch. Soc. Avocations; classical music, jazz, painting, bodybuilding, karate. E-mail: R.Yankov@ccrtechnology.de. Office: CCR GmbH Coating Tech, Maarweg 30, 53619 Rheinbreitbach Germany

YANNAKOU, GEORGE, management consultant; b. Thessaloniki, Greece, Apr. 25, 1957; s. Nikolaos and Efrosini (Karasimou) Y.; m. Despina Anagnostopoulou, June 8, 1997. BSEE, Aristotle U., Thessaloniki, 1980; MS in Power Electronics, Ecole Superieure D'Electricite, Paris, 1981; Diploma in Econs., Aristotle U. of Thessaloniki, 1985; Diploma/Quality Assessor, P-E Batalas, Eng., 1993. Project engr. CGEE Alsthom, Paris, 1984-85; project mgr. CGEE Alsthom, Athens, 1985-87; sales mgr., product mgr. of fork lift trucks Petros Petropoulos S.A., Thessaloniki, 1988-89, mktg. mgr. Profit Ctr., to gen. mgr. Matl. Handling Divsn., 1990-91; mktg. mgr. I. Boutaris S.A., Thessaloniki, 1992; quality assurance cons. H. & A. Vassaras S.A., Oli Rose S.A., Thessaloniki, 1993-94; sr. quality assurance cons., shareholder, gen. mgr. Group Y Consulting, Ltd., Thessaloniki, 1993—; quality assurance cons. Lamaplast S.A., Crystal S.A., Thessaloniki, 1995, Trophotechniki SA, Thessaloniki, 1996, Chaitoglou Bros., S.A., Morris S.A., Thessaloniki, 1997, G. Apostolou SA, Thessaloniki, 1997, Kreser-Serres, 1997, Agrl. Coop. Union of Serres, 1997, Novaknit Hellas SA, Thessaloniki, 1997, I. Elmaliotis SA "Santana", Thessaloniki, 1997, Interstoff Vasiliadis SA, Thessaloniki, 1997, Glass Cleaning SA, Thessaloniki, 1997, Bronze Art SA, Athens, 1997, B. Hatzikosmas & Sons SA, Komotini, 1997, Ath. Koukoutaris SA, Kozani, 1998, Olympia Electronics SA, Katerini, 1998, I. Pirpiris & Sons SA "Bildus", Xanthi, 1998, Macedonian Lime SA "Titan", Thessaloniki, 1998, E. Gouletsos, Thessaloniki, 1998, Group 'Y' Consulting Ltd., Thessaloniki, 1998; sr. assessor EFQM for the European Quality Award for SMES, 1998-2000. Contbr. articles to profl. jours. Mem. IEEE, Hellenic Quality Forum of Cen. and No. Greece, Chamber of Economists, Chamber of Engrs. in Greece. Avocations: tennis, philately, coin collecting. Home: Afendouli 8, Thessaloniki GR-54630, Greece Office: Group Y Cons Ltd, 30 El Venizelou Str, GR-54624 Thessaloniki Greece

YANNAS, IOANNIS VASSILIOS, polymer science and engineering educator; b. Athens, Apr. 14, 1935; s. Vassilios Pavlos and Thalia (Sarafoglou) Y.; m. Stamatia Frondistou (div. Oct. 1984); children: Tania, Alexis. AB, Harvard U., 1957; SM, MIT, 1959; MS, Princeton U., 1965, PhD, 1966. Asst. prof. mech. engring. MIT, Cambridge, 1966-68, duPont asst. prof., 1968-69, assoc. prof., 1969-78, prof. polymer sci. and engring. dept. mech. engring., 1978—, prof., dept. materials sci. and engring., 1983—; prof. Harvard-MIT Div. Health Scis. and Tech., Cambridge, 1978—; vis. prof. Royal Inst. Tech., Stockholm, 1974. Mem. editorial bd. Jour. Biomed. Materials Rsch., 1986—, Jour. Materials Sci. Materials Medicine, 1990—, Tissue Engineering, 1994—; contbr. over 100 tech. articles. to profl. jours.; 15 patents in field. Recipient awards for design of first successful artificial skin for treatment of massively burned patients and for identification of regeneration templates for dermis and peripheral nerves, including Founders award Soc. for Biomaterials, 1982, Clemson award Soc. for Biomaterials, 1992, Fred O. Conley award Soc. Plastics Engrs., 1982, award in medicine and genetics Sci. Digest/Cutty Sark, 1982, Doolittle award Am. Chem. Soc., 1988; fellow Pub. Health Svc., Princeton U., 1963, Shriners Burns Inst., Mass. Gen. Hosp., Boston, 1980-81. Fellow Am. Inst. Chemists, Am. Inst. Med. and Biol. Engrs. (founding mem.), Biomaterials Sci. and Engring.; mem. Inst. Medicine of Nat. Acad. Scis. Office: MIT Bldg 3-332 77 Mass Ave Cambridge MA 02139-4307

YANNOTTA, BERNARD JOSEPH, musician; b. Summit, N.J., Apr. 17, 1948; s. Bernard and Josephine (Damiano) Y. BFA, Carnegie-Mellon U., Pitts., 1970; MS, The Juilliard Sch., N.Y.C., 1971; Diplôme, Conservatoire de Rouen, Ronen, France, 1974; MMA, Yale U., 1979. Clarinetist Nielsen Woodwin Quintet, Paris, 1974-80, New American Music Ensemble, Paris, 1975-80; asst. condr. N.J. Youth Symphony, 1980-92; condr. The Mannes Coll. Orch., N.Y.C., 1981-87; artistic dir. Festival des Arcs, Paris, 1989—; mus. dir. nat. tour of opera: The Man Who Mistook His Wife for a Hat, 1996-98, Trouble in Tahiti, 1998—; mus. cons. Maison de la culture de Chambery, France, 1989—. Arranger (opera) Trouble in Tahiti, 1998; composer: (musical comedy) Les Enfants Gatés, 1997-98, (play) The Life of Galileo, 1999—, (theatre) Phaedre, Luna Park, Josephine, 1996—. Mem. AIDES, Paris, 1996—; bd. dirs. N.J. Youth Symphony, 1979-81. Martha Baird Rockefeller grantee, 1980; Fulbright Found. grantee, 1974-76. Avocations: tennis, bridge. Home: 34 rue Reaumur, 75003 Paris France

YANO, CHIAKI, lawyer; b. Kanonji-shi, Kagawa-ken, Japan, Sept. 24, 1947; s. Keizo and Miyoko (Mori) Y.; m. Yukie Sakaide, Mar. 21, 1984; 1 child, Akiko. B in Engring., U. Tokyo, 1971; LLM, Legal Tng. and Rsch. Inst., 1984. Ptnr. Sumio Takeuchi Law Offices, Tokyo, 1984-94, Takanawa Law Offices, Tokyo, 1995-97, Yano Sogo Law Offices, Tokyo, 1997—; counselor for Prof. Morota Hosei U., Tokyo, 1987—, Nippon SERC Inc., Osaka, 1993—, Oak Architects, Planners & Engrs., Tokyo, 1987—, Eijitsu Co. Ltd., Tokyo, 1989—, Human Co. Ltd., Tokyo, 1993—; lectr. Ryutsu Keizai U. Author: Explanation of Company Law, 1985, Explanation of Securities Law, 1985, Diagram of Company Law, 1986, Diagram of Securities Law, 1986, Basic Construction of Securities Law, 1994, Patent Right and Parallel Import, 1994. Waseda Seminar fellow; named chief editor of Intellectual Property. Mem. Diners Club Internat. Avocations: tennis, skiing, reading, writing. Home: 2612-78 Kanai-cho, Machida-shi Tokyo 195, Japan Office: Yano Sogo Law Offices, Yani Sogo Law Offices, 2-4-3 Nisahi-Shinbasi, Tokyo 05-0003, Japan

YANO, HIROAKI, automotive industry executive. Joined divsn. foods Mitsubishi Corp., 1963, gen. mgr. divsn. foods (comodities), dir., 1995—, mng. dir., 1997; with divsn. foods Mitsubishi Internat. Corp., N.Y.C., 1971-75, Honduras, 1975-80; exec. v.p. Mitsubishi Internat. Corp., 1996, pres., 1998—. Co-chmn. Carnegie Hall Corp. Fund; mem. bus. com. Mus. Modern Art. Sloan fellow 1981-82. Mem. Japanese C. of C. and Industry of New York, Inc. (chmn.).

YANO, HIRONORI, organization executive; b. Mito, Ibaragi, Japan, Jan. 1, 1941; s. Tsuneo and Motoko (Ohi) Y.; m. Keiko Yamagami, Nov. 15, 1964; children: Yasuhiro, Naoko, Yoshinori, Tomoko. LLB, U. Tokyo, 1963; postgrad., U. Wis., 1969-71. With Toshiba Corp., Tokyo, 1963—, mgr. labor rels., 1975-79, sr. mgr. adminstrn. several bus. divsns., 1979-87, gen. mgr. pub. comm., 1987-92, gen. mgr. Yokohama facility adminstrn. ctr., 1992-95, gen. mgr. internat. divsn., 1995-97; corp. rep. - Europe, pres., CEO Toshiba of Europe, Ltd., Tokyo, 1997-99; dir. internat. divsn. Nikkeinen (Japan Fedn. Employers' Assns.), Tokyo, 1999-2000, dep. dir. gen., 2000—; mem. Ilo com. Nikkeiren, Tokyo, 1979-89. Co-author: Behavior of Japanese

Multinational Corporations in Malaysia, 1975. Chmn. toshiba Philharm. Orch. Avocations: cello, Judo (5th degree) Igo (7th degree), tennis. Home: 3-10-6 Minamiogikubo, Suginami-ku Tokyo 167-0052, Japan

YANO, MICHITAMI, gastroenterologist, health facility administrator; b. Fukuoka, Japan, Dec. 3, 1936; s. Toshio and Kimiko Yano; m. Keiko Kawamura, Apr. 23, 1966; 1 child, Koji. MD, Nagasaki Genbaku Hosp., 1965; PhD, Hannover Med. Coll., 1973. Dir. gastroenterol. dept. Nagasaki (Japan) Chuo Nat. Hosp., 1973-97; dir. clin. rsch. dept. Nagasaki Chuo Nat. Hosp., 1984—; dir. Ctr. for Virus Hepatitis WHO, 1986—; prof. Nanjin (China) Med. Ry. Coll., 1990, Shanghai 2d Med. Coll., 1992, Nagasaki U., 2000; dir. Japanese Liver Soc., Tokyo, 1994; pres. Asia Pacific Study Liver Disease, 1996; v.p. Nagasaki Chuo Nat. Hosp., 1997-99, pres., 1999. Recipient award Min. Health and Welfare, 1986. Mem. N.Y. Acad. Sci., Asian Pacific Study of Liver Disease (pres. 1999), Japanese soc. Gastroenterology (pres. 1999). Avocations: yachting, golf, Go. Home: Kushima 2-294-2, Omura 856-0834, Japan Office: Nagasaki Chuo Nat Hosp, Kubara 2-1001-1, Omura 856-8562, Japan

YANOV, VITALY GEORGIEVITH, biologist, researcher; b. Moscow, Apr. 8, 1936; s. Georgi Petrovith and Reveka Kivovna (Shmois) Y.; m. Evgenia Michailovna Shmeleva, July 22, 1964 (div. May, 1978); children: Julia, Andrei; m. Kira Alekseevna Nikolskaya, July 28, 1984; 1 child, Sergey Nikolsky. Radio Engr., Moscow Power Inst., 1964; postgrad., Severo-Zapadny Poli. Inst., Leningrad, USSR, 1973-77; PhD in Biology, Russian Acad. Sci., 1996. Researcher engr. Acoustic Inst., Moscow, 1964-71; researcher engr., scientist A.N. Severtsov Inst. Problems of Ecology and Evolution Russian Acad. Scis., Moscow, 1971—; vice dir. seaside br. Russian-Vietnam Tropical Rsch. Ctr., Nha-Trang, Vietnam, 1998-99. Contbr. articlest to profl. jours. Avocations: mountain skiing. Home: 5 Koguhovskya str 32-1-22, 109193 Moscow Russia Office: Severtsov Inst Problems Ecology & Evolution, Russian Acad Sci Leninskii PR 33, 117071 Moscow Russia

YANOVSKY, FELIX J., radio-electronics and remote sensing scientist, educator, researcher; b. Kiev, Ukraine, Feb. 7, 1946; s. Joseph F. and Eugenia M. (Kaminker) Y.; m. Lilia G. Kanishcheva, Apr. 18, 1985; children: Gennady, Igor. MS in Radio and Electronic Engring., Kiev Inst. Civil Aviation Engrs., 1968; PhD in Radar and Radionavigation, Moscow Inst. Civil Aviation Engrs., 1979; DSc in Aviation Meteorology, Kiev Internat. U. Civil Aviation, 1992; DSc in Radar and Radionavigation, Moscow State Technical U. Civil Aviation, 1993. Asst. Kiev Inst. Civil Aviation Engrs., 1969-78, sr. lectr., 1978-81, assoc. prof., 1981-93; prof. Kiev Internat. U. Civil Aviation, 1993—, sr. scientist, 1989-96, dir. rsch. group, 1993—; top sci. rschr., vis. prof. Delft (The Netherlands) U. Tech., 1996—; sci. adviser Radar Rsch. Inst., Ukraine, 1989-96; academician Transport Acad. Ukraine, 1994; dir. European sub-regional Internat. Civil Aviation Orgn. Tng. Ctr., Kiev Internat. U. Civil Aviation, 1998-2000. Author: Airborne Weather Radar, 1982, Airborne Weather Radars. System Structure and Design Features, 1987, Localization of Dangerous Weather Phenomena from Airborne, 1991; contbr. articles to profl. jours.; inventor and patentee in field. Head Popov Soc. Radio-Electronics and Comm., Kiev, 1981-94; mem. coun. Ukrainian Popov Soc. Radio-Electronics and Comm., Kiev, 1985-94. Recipient State Prize Laureate in Sci. and Technol. Ukraine, Pres. and Govt. Ukraine, 1996; grantee Internat. Sci. Found., 1994, Civilian R&D Found., 1997, IEEE Geosci. and Remote Sensing Soc., 2000, European Space Agy., 2000. Mem. IEEE (sr.), European Geophysical Soc., N.Y. Acad. Sci., Electromagnetics Acad. Achievements include contbns. to design of airborne weather radars; Doppler and polarimetric signal processing; invention of methods for dangerous meterological phenomena detection, radar autonomous method to avoid aircraft collisions. Avocations: soccer, touring, swimming, tennis, bibliophile and book collector. E-mail: yanovsky@kiv-ca.kiev.ua and Ayanovsky@i.com.ua . Office: Kiev Internat U Civic Aviat, Prospect Komarova 1, 03058 Kiev Ukraine

YANOVSKY, SERGEY STEPANOVICH, psychiatrist, health facility administrator; b. Svetlogorsk, USSR, Nov. 30, 1953; s. Stepan Konstantinovich and Tatiana Stepanovna Yanovskaya; m. Olga Petrovna Volodchenko; 1 child, Taras Sergeevich. MD, Med. U., Vladivostok, USSR, 1977; PhD, Inst. Social & For. Psychiatry, Kiev, Ukraine, 1997. Psychiatrist City Hosp., Valdivostok, 1977-78, Zaparogie, 1978-82; psychiatrist Ctr. for Narcology, Simpheropol, 1982—. Author: Psychiatry Manual, 1998, Lectures on Psychiatry, 1999; co-author: Forensic Psychiatry, 1998; contbr. articles to profl. jours. Mem. orgn. com. Internat. Conf. 2000 Yrs. Christianity, 1995, 96, 97, 98, 99. Capt. USSR Res. Mem. N.Y. Acad. Scis., Rotary. Avocations: mountain hiking, mountain biking, swimming. Office: Ctr Narcology/Psychosom Med, 20/1 Sevastopolskaya Str, 95000 Simpheropol Crimea, Ukraine

YANOVSKY, YURI GRIGOREVICH, physicist, educator; b. Moscow, U.S.S.R., Sept. 26, 1937; s. Grigorii Dmitrievich and Irina (Arcadievna) Y.; m. Nina Yanovskaja Solov'eva, June 21, 1961 (div. 1979); 1 child, Alex; m. Julija Carnet, Sept. 19, 1986; 1 child, Julija. Diploma in engr., Power Engring. Inst., Moscow, 1961; PhD, Inst. Petrochem. Synthesis, Moscow, 1965, DSc, 1973. Registered profl. engr., U.S.S.R. Inferior rschr. Inst. Petrochem. Synthesis, 1961-64, fellow rschr., 1964-68, sr. rschr., 1969-72, head rheology group, 1973-89; head rheology and biomechanics dept. Inst. Applied Mechanics USSR Acad. Scis., Moscow, 1990-92, dep. dir., 1992-97; dir. Inst. Applied Mechanics Russian Acad. Scis., 1998—; prof. polymer physics and mechanics Inst. Applied Biotech., Moscow, 1982; sci. cons. Co. Olkon, Moscow, 1989. Author: Thermophysics and Rheophysics Polymer Materials, 1991, Polymer Rheology: Theory and Practice, 1992, Advances in Structure and Heterogenious Continua, 1995; editor in chief: Jour. on Composite Mechanics and Design, 1995—; inventor in field; contbr. numerous articles to profl. jours. Mem. Internat. Acad. Ecology, Man and Nature Protection Scis. Russian Acad. Knowledge, Soc. Rheology, British Soc. Rheology, Am. Acad. Mechanics, N.Y. Acad. Scis., Club of Scientists of Moscow. Avocations: sports, music, non-traditional medicine. Home: Okruznoi proezd 22/64-92, Moscow 105187, Russia Office: Inst Applied Mechanics, Leninsky Prospect 32 A, Moscow 117334, Russia

YANQUI MURILLO, CALIXTO, civil engineering educator, dean; b. Puquina, Moquegua, Peru, Oct. 14, 1954; s. Julian Yanqui and Hermelinda Murillo; m. Adela Llerena, Jan. 3, 1978; children: Hypatia Hermelinda, Nabor Calixto. P.E., geol. engr., San Agustin Nat. U., Arequipe, Perú, 1978, civil engr., 1995; MSCE, U. S.C., 1982; soil engr., Japan Internat. Coop. Agy., Tokyo, 1996. Mem. civil engring. faculty San Agustin Nat. U., Arequipa, 1978—, head civil engring. dept., 1996, dean Civil Engring. Sch., 1999; vis. prof. San Antonio Abad Nat. U., Cusco, PerU, 1986, Antenor Orrego U., Trujillo, Peru, 1995; cons. Technosynesis Str S.p.A., Italy, 1989, Gitec Consult GMBH, Germany, 1992, Ken Assn., Arequipa, 1993-94, Consulcont S.A., Lima, 1995, Constructora Marquisa, Arequipa, 1997, Constructora Manfer S.A., Arequipa, 1997, Coinpesa, Arequipa, 1997, So. Peru Copper Corp., Moquegua, 19987, Minera ubinas SAC, Italy, 1998, Construtora Queiroz Galvao, Brazil, 1999, Civsa, Arequipa, 1999. Author: Mechanics of Tectonic Deformation, 1981, Statics of Gravitating Discontinua, 1982, Seismic Analysis, 1989, Discontinuous Mechanics, 1996; contbr. articles to profl. jours. Recipient Emilio Le Roux, Peruvian Soc. Soil Mechanics, Lima, 1998; named Best Rschr., Peruvian Assn. Rds., Lima, 1999. Mem. AIME, Soc. Mining Engrs., Instn. Peruvian Engrs., Geol. Soc. Peru. Office: U Nat San Agustin, Arias Araguez 527, Arequipa Peru

YANSON, IGOR KINDRATOVICH, physicist, educator; b. Kharkiv, Ukraine, Mar. 18, 1938; s. Konrad Janson and Rosa Gurevich; m. Tatianna Iarovaia, Sept. 11, 1971; children: Olga, Maya, Alexei, Yurii. Degree in radio physics, Kharkiv State U., Ukraine, 1961; degree in piano, Leningrad (Russia) State Cons., 1963; Cand. Sci., DSc, Inst. Low Temp. Physics/Engr., 1976. Jr. scientist Inst. for Low Temperature Physics and Engring., Kharkiv, 1961-67, sr. scientist, 1967-70, head of divsn., 1970—; educator Kharkiv State U., 1978-93. Co-author: (books) Josephson Effect, 1970, Interactions of Biomolecules, 1985, Atlas of Point-Contact Spectra, 1986; contbr. numerous articles to profl. jours. Recipient State Prize in Physics, Ukraine, 1980, Hewlett-Packard prize European Phys. Soc., 1987, Alexander von Humboldt prize, Germany, 1995. Mem. NAS. Office: Inst Low Temp Physics & Eng, 47 Lenin's Prospekt, 310164 Kharkiv Ukraine

YANTS, SVETLANA VLADIMIROVNA, librarian, lecturer; b. Pavlovsk, Voronezh, Russia, Oct. 14, 1933; d. Vladimir Mikhailovich and Anastasiya Lavrent'evna (Gubanova) Bukovshina; m. Villi Yakovlevich Yants, Nov. 17, 1956; children: Vladimir, Andrei. Diploma of higher edn., Voronezh State U., 1956, excellence diploma, 1956. Librarianship diplomate Moscow Inst. Culture. Jr. mem. tchg. staff dept. of hydrology of land Voronezh State U., 1956-59; jr. libr. Voronezh State U. Sci. Libr., 1959-61, reference libr., 1961-64, head circulation dept., 1964-68, dir., 1968—. Author: The State & Prospects for Development of the Catalog System in the Libraries of Institutions of Higher Education, 1983; editor Catalogs of Russian and Fgn. Periodicals, 1969—. Chairperson Com. for Aesthetic Edn. of Young People Voronezh State U., 1973-83. Recipient Labour Prowess medal Supreme Soviet of USSR, Moscow, 1976, Honoured Culture Worker award Pres. of Russian Fedn., 1994. Mem. Regional Coun. Libr. Dirs. Edn. Insts. (chairperson), State Com. for Higher Edn. of Russian Fedn. (libr. and info commn. 1969—). Avocations: theatre, handicrafts, gardening. Office: Sci Libr, Pr Revolyutsii 24, Voronezh 394000, Russia

YAO, ANDY SHUNCHI, computer science educator; b. Toufen, Taiwan, Republic of China, Mar. 24, 1956; s. Weilu and Tinmay (Huang) Y.; m. Feng-Yi Chen Apr. 4, 1997; children: Wesley R., Addison R. AA in Elec. Engring., Ming Hsin Engring. Coll., Taiwan, Rebublic of China; BS in Computer Sci., Old Dominion U., MS in Computer Sci.; PhD in Computer Sci., Kennedy Western U. Sr. sys. analyst IMS, Rockville, Md., 1984-91; adj. prof Montgomery Coll., Rockville, 1985-92, prof., 1992—; prof. United Tech. Inst., 1998—; prof. Harmony Computer Inst., Rockville, 1995-97; assoc. prof. Univ. Coll. U. Md., College Park, 1990-96, adj. assoc. prof., 1997-99, prof. practice, 1999—; adj. assoc. prof. Shenandoah U., Winchester, Va., 1996—; cons. Info. Tech. Advanced Tng., Vienna, Va., 1997-98. Avocations: singing, writing. Home: 11619 Paramus Dr North Potomac MD 20878-4277 Office: Montgomery Coll 51 Mannakee St Rockville MD 20850-1101

YAO, CHUNG-CHIN, physician; b. Kaoshiung, Taiwan, Oct. 5, 1957; s. Shun and Kim-Kou (Chen) Y.; m. Huai-Ling Mu, Mar. 29, 1989; children: Tung, Jui. MD, Nat. Def. Med. Ctr., Taipei, Taiwan, 1982. Resident surgery Vet. Gen. Hosp., Taipei, 1982-86, chief resident surg. dept., 1986-87; vis. dept. surgery 804 Army Gen. Hosp., Tao-Yuan, Taiwan, 1987-89, head gen. surgery, 1989-92; vis. dept. surgery Min-Shen Gen. Hosp., Tao-Yuan, Taiwan, 1992-95, 98—, head dept. surgery, 1995-98; tchg. asst. Nat. Yang-Min Med. U., Taipai, 1982-87. Contbr. articles to profl. jours. Maj. Army Gen. Hosp., Taiwan, 1987-92. Avocations: playing golf and basketball, swimming, sight-seeing, reading. Home: No 1, 7th Flr, Lane 5, Rong-Wha 1st Rd, Pei-Tou, Taipei Taiwan Office: Min-Shen Gen Hosp, No 106, Sec 3, San Min Rd, Tao-Yuan Taiwan

YAO, DUANZHENG, physicist, educator; b. Wuhan, China, Aug. 1, 1946; s. Yizhai Yao and Mingzhen Yan; m. Guiguang Xiong, Jan. 27, 1973; 1 child, Duan Xiong. Grad., Wuhan (China) U., 1970. Asst. dept. physics Wuhan (China) U., 1970-82, lectr., 1983-93, assoc. prof., 1993-97, prof., 1997—. Author: Mathematical Methods in Physics, 1992 (Excellent Tchg. Material prize 1995), Mathematical Methods in Physics II, 1997. Fellow Chinese Phys. Soc.; mem. Chinese Soc. Computational Physics, Nat. Universities Soc. Math. Physics (dep. chmn. 1996—). Avocations: playing piano, Chinese lute. Home: 1 Gate 3 Bldg 2, West-3 Dist, Wuhan U, Wuhan 430072, China Office: Dept Physics Luojia Hill, Wuhan U, Wuhan 430072, China

YAO, HUEY-FEN FAY, English language educator; b. Kaohsiung, Taiwan, Aug. 15, 1964; d. Bing-Kwen and Ching-Kuay (Yen) Y. BA, Nat. Taiwan U., Taipei, 1987; MA, Ind. U., 1992. Tchg. asst. Nat. Taiwan U., Taipei, 1987-89; English sec. Chinese Taipei U. Sports Fedn., 1992-93; English instr. Tzu Chi Buddhist Coll. of Tech., Hualien, Taiwan, 1993—, Nat. Open U., 1995-98, Tzu Chi Buddhist Coll. of Medicine and Humanities, Hualien, 1997-99; dir. English sect. Tzu Chi Buddhist Coll. of Medicine and Humanities, 1997-99. Author: Prometheus, 1985, Tzu Chi, 1993, Bulletin of Tzu Chi Buddhist College of Technology, 1994, Ching Lien, 1995; translator: Taipei Fine Arts Mus. Internat. Conf., 1988. Chair Dist. Polit. Party Kuomintang of Nat. Taiwan, Taipei, 1986-87; mem. Tchrs. Dance Troup of Hualien. Mem. MLA, Keats Friends U.K., Wordsworth Friends U.K., Assn. Met. Mus. Art Am., Evergreen Club. Avocations: reading, fgn. travel, opera, art, classical music. Home: 880 Sec 2 Chien Kuo Rd, Tzu Chi Coll Tech, Hualien 970, Taiwan

YAO, JIN, engineering educator, researcher; b. Qianwei, Sichuan, China, Sept. 15, 1958; s. Zhong-Lu Yao and Su-nan Wang; m. Yang-ping Yang, Feb. 20, 1985; 1 child, Si-Ming. BS, Harbin Inst. Tech., China, 1982; MS, Chengdu U. Sci. and Tech., China, 1984; PhD, Sichuan U., China, 1999. Lectr. Chengdu (China) U. Sci. and Tech., 1985-90; vis. scholar Newcastle U., Eng., 1990-91; prof. Sichuan Union U., Chengdu, China, 1992—; vis. scholar McGill U., Canada, 1997-98. Contbr. articles to profl. jours. Science Advanced on Mechanisms and Robotics award State Edn. Commn. China, 1996, Excellent Tchg. award Sichuan Province (China) Govt., 1996. Mem. Chinese Soc. Mech. Engring. (sr.). Office: Sichuan U, Dept Mech Engring, 610065 Chengdu Sichuan, China

YAO, JOHN SEN, physician; b. Honolulu, Aug. 28, 1954; s. Hsin-Hung and Dorothy W. Yao; m. Pauline A. Mysliwiec, Oct. 16, 1993. MPH, Columbia U., 1978, MD, 1983; MBA, UCLA, 1998; MPA, Harvard U., 1999. Diplomate Am. Bd. Internal Medicine, Nat. Bd. Med. Examiners. Intern in internal medicine U. Calif.-San Francisco Med. Ctr., 1983-86, asst. clin. prof., 1988-94; chief med. officer USPHS, Calif., 1990-98; med. dir. Cigna Healthcare, inc., 1997-98; fellow in policy studies Harvard U., Cambridge, Mass., 1998—; mem. exec. com. State of Calif. TB Control, 1994—; mem. steering com. Breast and Cervical Cancer Prevention, Stte of Calif., 1991-94; med. advisor State of Calif. Medicaid Reform com., 1994-95. Contbr. articles to profl. jours. Med. advisor Gov.'s Coun. on Exercise and Health, Calif., 19945; mem. Calif. HIV-AIDS Commn., 1990-93. Fellow ACP. Avocations: golf, tennis, skiing, classical music, opera. E-mail: jyaomd@aol.com. Office: Box 14531 Benjamin Franklin Sta Washington DC 20044-4531

YAO, JOHN T.K., school system administrator; b. Loching, Chekiang, China, Jan. 24, 1918; s. Yao Barnaba and Yao Chang Maria. BTh, Paul's Coll. Theology, Chekiang, China; As. Thoma Aq. U. Rome; D Pontificia, Studiorum U., Rome; LLD (hon.), Cath. U., Fu Jen, 1991. Ordained Monseigneur, Pope, Holy Father/Priest, Roman Cath. Ch. Founder Sacred Heart Kindergarten, Keelung, Taiwan, 1962—, Sacred Heart Elem. Sch., Keelung, 1965—; founder day dept. Sacred Heart Advanced Vocat. Sch., Keelung, 1969—, founder night dept., 1972—; founder Sacred Heart Sr. H.S., Keelung, 1990—, Sacred Heart Jr. H.S., Keelung, 1995—; assoc. prof. Cath. U. Fu Jen, Taipei, 1978-86; rector Cardinal-Tyan Meml. Hosp., Taipei, 1985-90; organizer Med. Coll. of Cath. U., 1985-90; founder Sacred Heart Ch., Keelung, 1963—. Avocations: reading, preaching, writing, walking. Office: 166 Shi-ding Rd, 203 Keelung Taiwan

YAO, KAI-PING GRACE, psychology educator, researcher; b. I-Lan, Taiwan, Sept. 19, 1961; d. Ho-Nien and Ta-Hwa (Chu) Yao; m. Chan-De Lin, Jan. 2, 1999. BS in Occupl. Therapy, Nat. Taiwan U., 1984; MS in Therapeutic Sci., U. Wis., 1988; MS in Stats., U. Ill., 1992, MS in Psychology, 1993, PhD in Psychology, 1995. Registered occupl. therapist, U.S. Tchg. asst. Nat. Taiwan U., Taipei, 1984-86; rsch. asst., tchg. asst. U. Wis., Madison, 1986-88; rsch. asst. u. Ill., Urbana-Champaign, 1988-95, tchg. asst., 1990-94; lectr. Nat. Taiwan U., 1995-96, assoc. prof., 1996—; clin. supr. Nat. Taiwan U. Hosp., Taipei, 1984-86. Author: The Development of the World Health Organization Quality of Life Questionnaire, Taiwan Verson, 1999, also articles. Recipient Rsch. awards Nat. Sci. Coun., Taipei, 1995, 96, 98, 99, Outstanding Rsch. award in area of counseling Am. Ednl. Rsch. Assn., 1995, Dr. Robert Bohrer Meml. award in stats. U. Ill., Urbana-Champaign, 1995, Student Dissertation Rsch. award APA, 1995, Rsch. on Intelligence and Intellectual Giftness award Mensa Edn. and Rsch. Found., 1995. Mem. Psychometric Soc., Am. Statis. Assn. Christian. Avocations: playing violin and cello, oil painting. Office: Nat Taiwan U Dept Psych, No 1 Sect 4, Roosevelt Rd, 10660 Taipei Taiwan

YAO, LEEHTER, educator; b. Kaosiung, Taiwan, Sept. 24, 1962; s. Chi-tao Y. and Shupin Su; m. Fangfang Kuan; children: Albert, Jerry. BS, Nat. Taipei Inst. Tech., Taiwan, 1982; MS, U. Mo., 1987; PhD, U. Wis., 1992. Assoc. prof. Nat. Taipei U. Tech., Taiwan, 1992-97, prof., 1997—, dean Coll. Mech. & Elec. Tech., 1999—; cons. and spkr. in field. Inventor in field. Student liaison Min. Fgn. Affairs, Taiwan, Wis., 1988-92; sec. chief Kuoming Tang Party, Taipei, 1994-96; mem. parents com. Shin-An Primary Sch., Taipei, 1999—. 2d lt. Taiwan Mil., 1982-84. Recipient Disting. Rsch. award Taiwan Power Co., 1994, 96, 97, 98, 99, Nat. Sci. Coun. Taiwan, 1993, 94, 95, 96, 98. Mem. IEEE. Avocations: computers, painting, chess, biking, hiking. Office: Nat Taipei U Tech, 1 Sec 3 Chung-Hsiao E Rd, Taipei 106, Taiwan

YAO, SUSU, electronics professor, researcher; b. Nantong, Jiangsu, China, Nov. 29, 1962; s. Jianshi Huang and Jianqinq Yao; m. Honghui Zhu, Feb. 19, 1995; 1 child, Liran. BEng., Nanjing (China) Inst. Aeronaut, 1983; PhD, Nat. U. Def. Tech., Changsha, China, 1993. Asst. prof. Wuhan (China) Radar Coll., 1983-87; vis. scholar Heriot-Watt U., Edinburgh, U.K., 1991-93; postdoctoral fellow S.E. U., Nanjing, 1993-95; prof. electronics Tongyuan U., Nanjing, 1996—. Editor Jour. Data Acquisition and Processing, 1997; contbr. articles to profl. jours. Mem. IEEE, N.Y. Acad. Scis. Avocations: tourism, sports. Office: Tong Yuan U, Yudao St 2 Biao Ying PO Box 11, Jiangsu Nanjing 210016, China

YAO, TANDONG, glaciologist, paleoclimatologist; b. Tongwei, Gansu, China, July 26, 1954; s. Dianwua Yao and Yumei Chang; m. Hong Wang, Dec. 2, 1955; 1 child, Ruzhen. BS, Lanzhou (China) U., 1978, Master's degree, 1982; PhD, Inst. Geography, Beijing, China, 1986. Prof. climatology Lanzhou Inst. Glaciology, China Acad. Scis., 1988-90, assoc. prof., 1989-91, dep. pres., 1999—; dep. dir. environ. divsn. Lanzhou Inst. Glaciology, 1989-91, dep. dir. ice core lab., 1991-95; dir. Office of Western China Environment, Lanzhou, 1995-98. Contbr. articles to sci. jours. Rep. Nat. People's Congress, Beijing, 1998-2002. Recipient Award of Antarctic Gladiology Study, Chinese Govt., 1997. Mem. Internat. Glaciol. Soc. (corr.), Chinese Glaciol. Soc. (dep. chair 1996-2000, Basic Rsch. award 1998). Avocations: Ping Pong, basketball, Chinese chess. Office: Lanzhou Inst Glaciology, 260 W Donggang Rd, 730 000 Lanzhou Gansu, China

YAO, TITO GO, pediatrician; b. Manila, May 30, 1943; came to U.S., 1970, naturalized, 1984; s. Vincente and Sin Keng (Go) Y.; m. Lilia Ytem, July 3, 1976; children: Robert, James, Richard. MD, Far Ea. U., Manila, 1969. Diplomate Am. Bd. Pediatrics, Am. Bd. Quality Assurance. Intern Evang. Deaconess Hosp., Milw., 1970-71; resident in pediatrics T.C. Thompson Children's Hosp., Chattanooga, 1971-72, Meth. Hosp., Bklyn., 1972-73; fellow St. Christopher Hosp. Children, Phila., 1973-74, Cook County Children's Hosp., Chgo., 1974-75; dir. GSK Med. Ctr., Chgo., 1976—; chmn. dept. pediat. St. Anne's Hosp., Chgo., 1986-88, Loretto Hosp., Chgo., 1988—; dir. RJ Med. Center, Chgo., 1980—; mem. staff Norwegian Am. Hosp., St. Anthony's Hosp., St. Mary of Nazareth Hosp. Fellow Am. Acad. Pediatrics, Am. Coll. Utilization Rev. Physicians; mem. AMA (Physician Recognition award 1973—), Assn. Philippine Physicians Practicing in Am., Ill. Med. Assn., Am. Assn. Individual Investors, Chgo. Med. Soc., Chgo. Pediatric Soc. Office: 5351 W North Ave Chicago IL 60639-4350 also: 5140 W Chicago Ave Chicago IL 60651-2903

YAO, Y. LAWRENCE, engineering educator; b. Shanghai, China, May 25, 1953; came to U.S., 1982; s. Da-Jun Yao and Mei Fen Xu; m. Nancy Yao, June 24, 1984; children: David, Phillip. BE, Shanghai Jiao Tong U., China, 1982; MS, U. Wis., 1984, PhD, 1988. Grad. asst. U. Wis., Madison, 1983-87; lectr. U. NSW, Sydney, Australia, 1989-91, sr. lectr., 1991-94; assoc. prof. Columbia U., N.Y.C., 1994—; cons. Unisearch & CAMIA, Australia, 1989-94, Med. Devices Mfrs., N.Y. and N.J., 1994—. Assoc. editor: Jour. High Temperature Materials Processes, 1998—; contbr. tech. papers to profl. jours. and conf. procs. Rsch. grantee NSF, 1995—, Australian Rsch. Coun., 1990-95, collaborative rsch. grantee Commonwealth Sci. and Indsl. Rsch. Orgn., Australia, 1990-92. Mem. ASME, Soc. Mfg. Engrs. (sr. mem., assoc. editor Jour. Mfg. Processes 1998—), N.Am. Mfg. Rsch. Inst., Am. Soc. Engring. Edn. Avocations: traveling, movies, skiing, popular music. E-mail: yly1@columbia.edu. Office: Columbia U Dept Mech Engring 220 Mudd Bldg New York NY 10027

YAO, ZHENHAN, engineering mechanics educator; b. Changshu, Jiangsu, China, Apr. 10, 1939; s. Baohuang Yao and Xiuying Feng; m. Zhenqing Sun, Dec. 31, 1972; 1 child, Meng. BS, Tsinghua U., Beijing, 1962, MS, 1966; D Engring., Ruhr U.-Bochum, Germany, 1986. Tchr. Tsinghua U., 1967-78, lectr., 1978-88, asst. prof., 1988-89, prof., 1989—; Alexander von Humboldt rsch. fellow Ruhr-U. Bochum, 1984-86. Contbr. articles to profl. publs. (2d award of sci. and technol. progress Nat. Edn. Commn. of China, 1989, 1st award of sci. and technol. progress, 1991). Mem. Beijing Soc. of Mechanics (vice chmn., gen. sec.), Chinese Soc. Mechanics (mem. coun.), Chinese Soc. of Vibration Engring. Office: Dept Engring Mechanics, Tsinghua Univ, 100084 Beijing China

YAO, ZHINENG, publishing executive. Editor Sichuan Ribao. Office: Sichuan Ribao, 70 Hongxing Zhonglo, Chengdu 610017, China

YAO, ZUKANG, transportation engineering educator; b. Suzhou, Jiangsu, China, July 6, 1934; s. Yunshu and Yunyu (Li) Y.; m. Gongyu Fan, July 11, 1962; children: Xuechen, Xiaofan. Diploma, Tongji U., Shanghai, 1955, postgrad. diploma, 1959. Asst. Tongji U., Shanghai, 1959-60, lectr., 1960-80, assoc. prof., 1980-86, prof., 1986—, acting head dept. road and traffic engring., 1982-84, acting dir. Rsch. Inst. of Road and Traffic Engring., 1982-84; head dept. road and traffic engring., 1985-91; dir. Rsch. Isnt. Road and Traffic Engring., 1985-93. Author: Pavement Engineering, 1987, Pavement Management Systems, 1993, Highway Subgrade and Pavement Engineering, 1994, Planning and Design of Airports, 1994, Introduction to Transportation Engineering, 1996, Cement Concrete Pavement Design, 1999. Recipient 3d grade sci. rsch. prize State Edn. Commn., 1991, 92, 2d grade sci. rsch. prize, 1992, 96, 1st grade sci. resch. prize Ministry of Comm., 1993. Mem. China Civil Engring. Soc., China Hwy. and Transport Soc. Home: Tongji Xincun, 577/#9 Siping Rd, Shanghai 200092, China Office: Tongji U Dept Road/Traffic Engring, 1239 Siping Rd, Shanghai 200092, China

YAOBANG, CHEN, Chinese government official. Min. of agr. Govt. of China, Beijing, 1998—. Ofice: Ministry of Agr, 11 Nong Zhan Guan Nan Li, East Dist, Beijing China 100026*

YAOU, AISSATOU, government official; b. Tcheboa, Cameroon, Nov. 28, 1951; married; 4 children. BA in Macroecons., Rouen (France) U., 1975; MBA, Claremont Coll., 1979. Mgr. investigations and ops. Nat. Investment Instn., 1979-81, dir.-adjoint fins., 1981-84; minister of women's affairs Govt. Cameroon, 1984-88, minister of social and women's affairs, 1988—; min. women's affairs. Pres. Women's Orgn. People's Dem. Assembly of Cameroon, 1985—. Office: Ministry Social & Women's A, Yaoundé Cameroon*

YAP, JERRY, management consultant; b. Simpany Ampat, penang, Malaysia, Feb. 21, 1970; s. James Yap and Phuan Thicia; m. Wenny Tan, May 6, 1997; 1 child, Linda. Diploma in Mgmt. Specialist, U.K., 1992; Profl. Status, IMS, U.K., 1992; Diploma in Multi-Skill Mgr. Mgmt., U.K., 1994; MBA, Kensington U., 1998. Cert. profl. mgr.; cert. quality engr.; cert. profl. purchaser (CPP). Prodn. supr. Molex, Malaysia, 1989-90; asst. prodn. mgr. Tenong, Malaysia, 1990-93, factory mgr., 1994-95; gen. mgr. Tenong, Thailand, 1995-97; mktg. mgr. Gen. Electronics Component, Thailand, 1995-97; br. mgr. Utilux, Malaysia, 1997—; mng. dir. Magna-Thai Intertrade Co., Ltd., Thailand, 1993—; mng. dir. Pacvest Internat., Malaysia, 1992—; prin. Magna Mgmt. Consultantcy, Malaysia, 1994—; commr. Internat. Mgmt. execs. Acad., Malaysia Asean, 1994—. Fellow Inst. of Mgmt. Specialists; mem. WWF/Malaysia, Nat. Geographic Soc., Assn. Mouth & Footprinting Artists, Malaysia Chiness Assn. (treas. dist.), Acad. of Multi-Skilled Mgrs. and Adminstrs. (founder 1996), Am. Soc. Quality. Avocations: sports, travel, reading. E-mail: jerryyap@tm.net.my.

YAPIJAKIS, CONSTANTINE, environmental engineering educator, consultant; b. Drama, Macedonia, Greece, July 18, 1948; came to U.S., 1971; s.

Nikos and Stella (Voyagi) Y.; m. Lily Huang, July 10, 1993; 1 child, Nicole Isako. MS in Civil Engring., Nat. Tech. U., Athens, Greece, 1971; MS in Environ. Engring., NYU, 1973; PhD in Environ. Engring., Polytechnic U., N.Y.C., 1981. Registered profl. engr., N.Y.; civil engr., Tech. Chamber of Greece. Jr. engr. Dr. Panaghiotakis' Cons. Group, Athens, 1969-71; intern engr. Dutch Pub. Wks. Dept., Amsterdam, 1970; environ. lab. asst. NYU, N.Y.C., 1971-73; environ. engr. City Planning Dept., N.Y.C., 1972, John J. Kassner & Co., N.Y.C., 1973, Hazen and Sawyer, P.C., N.Y.C., 1973-78; adj. prof. CCNY/Polytechnic U., 1977—; assoc. prof. Pratt Inst., N.Y.C., 1980-86; prof. environ. engring., environ. rsch. lab dir. The Cooper Union, N.Y.C., 1986—; founding ptnr. Hellenic EnvironTech, Inc., Athens, 1991—; cons. N.Y.C. agencies, 1980—, various engring. firms and industries, 1978—. Co-author: Scale-up of Treatment Processes, 1983, Industrial Wastes Treatment Handbook, 1993, Hazardous Waste Site Remediation Management, 1999, Water Quality-Reflection of Land Use, 1999; contbr. over 125 articles to profl. jours. and conf. proceedings. Intern. Engr. scholar Internat. Assn. Students Tech. Edn., 1970; recipient Sr. Scholar award Fulbright Program, Greece, 1993-94, Earth Day award and medallion City Club of N.Y., 1995, Intern Engr. award Inst. Internat. Edn., N.Y.C., 1972; NSF grantee, 1988, 92. Mem. Water Environment Fedn. (VIP Circle 1994, Recruiters Recognition Club 1996), Am. Water Wks. Assn., Internat. Assn. Water Quality, N.Y. Acad. Scis. (judge h.s. sci. projects annual competition 1994—), N.Y. Water Environment Assn. (Met. chpt. bd. dirs. 1992-94, chmn. edn. com., Svc. award 1995, membership award 1996, 97, 98, 99), Environ. Law Inst. Achievements include development and design of pre-ozonation - D.E. filtration process for New York City's water supply; new design for rotating biological contactors for application to industrial and hazardous wastes; study that established extensive lead contamination in surface soil of parks and playgrounds in New York City, perc pollution prevention study for 2000 drycleaners in N.Y.C.; fast-rate bioremediation for protection of groundwater; enhanced solar evaporation for treatment of hazardous wastes. Avocations: travel, photography, reading, movies. Office: The Cooper Union Sch of Engring 51 Astor Pl New York NY 10003-7185

YAPP, MALCOLM EDWARD, historian; b. Birmingham, England, May 29, 1931; s. Arthur and Iris Ada Rose (Edwards) Y.; m. Jessie Kerr Gillespie, Dec. 31, 1955; children: Perry, Sally, Catherine, Margaret. BA in History, U. Birmingham, 1954; PhD in History, U. London, 1959. From asst. lectr. to prof. sch. Oriental and African studies U. London, 1957-93, prof. emeritus, 1993—; chmn. Ctr. for Near & Middle Eastern Studies, 1969-72, dean of studies, 1980-85, governing body, 1985-89. Author: Strategies of British India, 1980 (Trevor Reese meml. prize in imperial history 1982), The Making of the Modern Middle East, 1792-1923, 1987, The Near East Since the First World War, 1991, 2d edit., 1995; editor: Politics and Diplomacy in Egypt, 1997. Gov. St. Alban's Girls' Sch., England, 1968-88. Mem. Royal Soc. for Asian Affairs (coun., v.p. 1974-82). Avocations: reading, gardening, golf. Office: Sch Oriental & African Studies, Thornhaugh St Russell Sq, WC1H 0XG London England

YAQUB, BASIM ABDUL RAUF, neurologist, consultant; b. Jericho, Jordan, Apr. 6, 1948; s. Abdul Raul Mohammad Yaqub and Fardous Faris Abu Gazala; m. Ghada Najib Al Ahmad, Feb. 2, 1982; children: Rawan, Razan, Tamara. MB, BS, Alexandria (Egypt) U., 1972. Intern Alexandria U. Hosp., 1972-73; resident in neurology various hosps., Eng., 1976-80; neurologist King Khaled U. Hosp., Riyadh, Saudi Arabia, 1985-92; cons. neurologist Armed Forces Hosp., Riyadh, 1992-96, sr. cons. neurologist, 1997—, head neurophysiology unit, 1992—; asst. prof. King Saud U., Riyadh, 1986-90, assoc. prof., 1990-92, head neurology and neurophysiology unit, King Khalid U. Hosp., 1988-92. Fellow Royal Coll. Physicians (London), Am. Acad. Neurology; mem. World Fedn. Neurology, Pan-Arab Union Neurol. Scis., Internat. League Against Epilepsy (sec. gen. 1996—), Riyadh Neuroscis. Club (sec. 1987-91), also European neurol. socs. Avocations: swimming, tennis, travel, reading, music. Home: King Fahad St, Riyadh Saudi Arabia Office: Riyadh Armed Forces Hosp, PO Box 7897 (1006), Riyadh 11159, Saudi Arabia

YAQUB, MOHAMMED, educator; b. Karachi, Pakistan, Aug. 5, 1960; s. Abdul Rahim; m. Kausar Perveen, Sept. 5, 1991; children: Mohammed Umair, Wahhaj Ahmed, Nayeemah Perveen, Mubashshir Amhed. B of Engring., N.E.D., Karachi, Pakistan, 1984; MS, K.F.U.P.M., Dhahran, Saudi Arabia, 1991. Asst. engr. B.E.W.L., Karachi, Pakistan, 1984-87; rsch. asst. K.F.U.P.M., Dhahran, Saudi Arabia, 1987-91, lectr., 1991—. Mem. PEC, Inst. Engr. Avocations: games, reading. Home and Office: KFUPM, Box 767, Dhahran Saudi Arabia

YARAR, BAKI, mining and metallurgical engineering educator; b. Adana, Turkey, Feb. 28, 1941; came to U.S., 1980; s. Salih and Sidika Yarar; m. Ruth G. Yarar; children: Deniz, Defne. BSc in Chemistry, Mid. East Tech. U., Ankara, Turkey, 1965, MSc in Chemistry, 1966; PhD in Surface Chemistry, U. London, 1969; DIC in Mineral Tech., Imperial Coll. London, 1969. Instr. Mid. East Tech. U., 1970-71, asst. prof., 1971-76, assoc. prof., 1976-79; vis. prof. U. B.C., Vancouver, Can., 1979-80; assoc. prof. Colo. Sch. of Mines, Golden, 1980-86, prof., 1986—; pvt. practice cons. in mineral processing, worldwide, 1980—. Author chpts. to books, over 120 papers; editor books; mem. editl. bd. 4 jours. Lt. Turkish Army, 1970-71. Holder numerous awards and certificates of recognition. Mem. Soc. Mining Engrs. (chmn. fundamental com. 1989), Am. Chem. Soc., Materials Rsch. Soc., Sigma Xi (life, pres. CSM chpt.). Achievements include pioneering work in selective flocculation; invention of the gamma floation process; patent for superconductivity meter device. Home: 13260 Braun Rd Golden CO 80401-1643 Office: Colo Sch Mines Dept Mining Engring Golden CO 80401

YARBOROUGH, WILLIAM PELHAM, writer, lecturer, retired army officer, consultant; b. Seattle, May 12, 1912; s. Leroy W. and Addessia (Hooker) Y.; m. Norma Mae Tuttle, Dec. 26, 1936; children: Norma Kay (dec.), William Lee, Patricia Mae. BS, U.S. Mil. Acad., 1936; grad., Command and Gen. Staff Coll., 1944, Brit. Staff Coll., 1950, Army War Coll., 1953. Commd. 2nd lt. U.S. Army, 1936, advanced through grades to lt. gen., 1968, ret., 1971; various assignments U.S. Army, U.S., Philippines and ETO, 1936-42; exec. officer Paratroop Task Force, North Africa, 1942; comdr. 2d Bn., 504th Par. Inf. Regt., 82d Airborne Div., Sicily invasion, 1943, 509th Parachute Inf., Italy and France, 1943-44; comdg. officer 473 Inf., Italy, 1945; provost marshal 15th Army Group, ETO, 1945, Vienna Area Command and U.S. Forces, Austria, 1945-47; mem. staff, faculty U.S. Army Info. Sch., 1948-49; operations officer, gen. staff Joint Mil. Assistance Adv. Group, London, Eng., 1951-52; mem. faculty Army War Coll., 1953-56, 57; dep. chief Mil. Assistance and Adv. Group, Cambodia, 1956-57; comdg. officer 66th CIC Group, Stuttgart, Germany, 1958-60, 66th M.I. Group, Stuttgart, 1960; comdg. gen. U.S.A. Spl. Warfare Ctr.; also comdt. U.S. Army Spl. Warfare Sch., Ft. Bragg, 1961-65; sr. mem. UN Command Mil. Armistice Commn., Korea, 1965; asst. dep. chief staff DCSOPS for spl. operations Dept. Army, Washington; chmn. U.S. delegation Inter-Am. Def. Bd., Joint Brazil U.S. Def. Commn., Joint Mexican-U.S. Def. Commn.; Army mem. U.S. sect. permanent Joint Bd. on Def., Can.-U.S. Def. Commn., Washington, 1965; asst. chief of staff intelligence Dept. Army Washington, 1966-68; comdg. gen. I Corps Group, Korea, 1968-69; chief staff, also dep. comdr.-in-chief U.S. Army, Pacific, Hawaii, 1969-71. Contbr. Internat. Mil. and Def. Ency., 1993, MacMillan Ency. of the Am. Mil., 1994; William P. Yarborough collection papers and artifacts donated to Mugar Meml. Librs., Boston U. Decorated Disting. Svc. medal with three oak leaf clusters, Silver Star, Legion of Merit with three oak leaf clusters, Bronze Star, Joint Svc. Commendation medal with oak leaf clusters, Croix de Guerre with Palm (France), Cross for Valor and Diploma (Italy), Order of Merit Second Class (Korea), Order of Ulchi (Korea). Fellow Co. Mil. Historians, Explorers Club; mem. Kiwanis Club. Home: 160 Hillside Rd Southern Pines NC 28387-6727

YARBROUGH, ISABEL MILES, dentist, educator; b. Columbus, Ga., May 24, 1956; d. Wiley and Lillie Miles; m. David E. Yarbrough; children: Davida Elizabeth, David Earl Jr. BS, Ala. A&M U., 1978; DDS, Loyola U., 1982. Instr. endodontics Howard U. Sch. Dentistry, Washington, 1989-91; asst. prof. biology Ala. A&M U., Normal, 1991-94; dentist Drs. David and Isabel Yarbrough, Huntsville, Ala., 1993—. Mem. NAACP, Huntsville, 1996. Capt. U.S. Army, 1986-89. Mem. North Ala. Med. Assn., Huntsville-Madison Dental Soc., Delta Sigma Theta, Psi Omega. Avocations: reading, swimming, jogging. Home: 204 Cheswick Dr Madison AL 35757-8720 Office: 4530 Bonnell Dr NW Ste A Huntsville AL 35816-2002

YARBROUGH, TERRY PINCKNEY, physician; b. Columbia, S.C., Apr. 2, 1940; s. Dabney Randolph and Frances Horton (Colcock) Y.; m. Alexandra Mayo, Aug. 28, 1965; children: Alexandra, Laurens. MD, Med. Coll. of Va., 1965. Intern U. of Tex. Med. Br., Galveston, 1965-66; resident in internal medicine Med. Coll. Va., Richmond, 1968-71; pvt. practice Internal Medicine of Portsmouth Ltd., 1971—. Capt. USAR, 1966-68. Mem. ACP, Am. Coll. of Cardiology, Coun. Clin. Cardiology, Am. Heart Assn., Am. Soc. of Internal Medicine, Med. Soc. of Va. Episcopalian. Office: Internal Medicine of Portsmouth Ltd 3300 High St Portsmouth VA 23707-3321

YARGA, LARBA, government official; b. 1951. Instr. U. Ouagadougou-IUT, 1977-79, sec. gen., 1988-91; min. defense Govt. of Burkina Faso, Ouagadougou, 1992-94, min. justice and keeper of seals, 1994—. Mem. Orgn. for Popular Democracy/Labor Movement. Office: Ministry of Justice, 01 BP 526, Ouagadougou 01, Burkina Faso*

YARMOLA, ELENA GEORGIYEVNA, research scientist; b. Moscow, Feb. 11, 1958; came to the U.S., 1998; d. Georgiy Aleksandrovich and Galina Alekseevna Savchenko; m. Valeriy Vladimirovich Yarmola, Jan. 31, 1981; children: Tatiana Valeryevna, Andrew Valeryevich. MS in Biophysics, Moscow Inst. Physics & Tech., 1980, PhD in Biophysics, 1986. Rsch. scientist Engelhardt Inst. Molecular Biology, Moscow, 1985—; contractor rsch. in biophysics NIH, Bethesda, Md., 1994-98; postdoctoral assoc. U. Fla., 1998—. Sci. editor Molekuliathia Biologiia, Moscow, 1998; contbr. articles to profl. jours. Mem. Biophys. Soc. Avocation: kayaking. E-mail: yarmola@hotmail.com. Office: Univ Fla 303 NW 34th Ter Gainesville FL 32607-2431

YAROSLAVTSEV, ANDREW BORISOVICH, foundation administrator; b. Moscow, Mar. 19, 1956; s. Boris and Lenina Nicolavna (Kameneva) Y.; m. Elena Matvervena Rozneva, Oct. 27, 1980; children: Alexey, Sergey. Postgrad. Diploma Chemistry, Moscow State U., 1978, PhD in Chemistry, 1982, Dr. Chemistry, 1992. Postgrad. Moscow State U., 1978-81, sci. rschr., 1981-89, asst. prof., 1989-91; assoc. prof. Higher Coll. Material Sci., Moscow, 1991-94; prof., vice chmn. Higher Chem. Coll., Moscow, 1994-97; dir. dept. chemistry Russian Found. for Basic Rsch., Moscow, 1997, exec. sec., 1997—; leading sci. rschr. Kurnokov Inst. Gen. and Inorganic Chemistry, Moscow, 1994-96, head dept., 1996—; prof. Higher Chem. Coll., 1997—. Contbr. articles to profl. jours. Grantee Soros Found., 1994-96, Russian Found. for Basic Rsch., 1997. Avocations: canoeing, football, swimming. E-mail: yaroslav@rfBr.ru. Home: Nowoslobodskaya 54/56-110, 103055 Moscow Russia Office: Russian Found Basic Rsch, Leninsky Prospect 32a, 117334 Moscow Russia

YAROVOI, LEONID KONSTANTINOVICH, research scientist; b. Kiev, Ukraine, July 27, 1954; s. Constantin Nikitorovich and Florentina Leonidovna (Çarkusha) Y.; m. Irena Vasilievna Stepachno; 1 child, Polyna. Univ. diploma, Moscow State U., 1977; PhD in Tech. Sci., Kiev Poly. Inst., 1989. Cert. physicist and optical instrument engr. Engr. Tech. and Rsch. Inst. Optics, Kiev, 1977-79; sci. rschr. Kiev Poly. Inst., 1980-91, Kiev State U., 1991-93; head holography dept. Rsch. Ctr. Ometa-Optic, Kiev, 1993-95; sr. sci. rschr. Taras Schevchenkois Nat. U., Kiev, 1995—; chief engr. Rsch. Laser Ctr., Kiev, 1991-92. Recipient Silver medal Ctrl. Exhbn. USSR, Moscow, 1989. Mem. SPIE (Ukrainian chpt.), Ukrainian Optical Soc. (exec. dir. 1992—). E-mail: uos@gluk.org. Home: PO Box 164, 03191 Kyiv Ukraine Office: Kyiv U Mechanics & Math Sci & Tng Ctr, 64 Volodymyrska St, 01033 Kyiv Ukraine

YAROVOI, SERGE V., molecular biologist, researcher, interpreter, writer; b. Nov. 15, 1964; s. Victor S. and Laurissa A. Yarovoi; m. Helen V., Oct. 24, 1986; children: Eugene, Catherine, Andrew. MS in Chemistry, 1989, PhD in Chemistry cum laude, 1993. Cert. biochemist, tchr. Rschr. Hosp. Pitiè-Salpêtrière, Paris, 1994-96, Sidney Kimmel Cancer Ctr., La Jolla, Calif., 1996-97, UMMS/WFBR, Worcester, Shrewsbury, Mass., 1997-2000. Author: (poetry) La Pensée Russe, 2000. Galderma fellow Sophia-Antipolis, France, 1996-97. Mem. Am. Soc. Cell Biology, Am. Assn. Cancer Rsch., Soc. History Alchemy and Chemistry, N.Y. Acad. Scis. Avocations: mountain hiking, reading, history of sciences, writing poetry. Home: 11 Carver St Worcester MA 01604-6001 Office: WFBR/UMMS Biotech Four 377 Plantation St Rm 337 Worcester MA 01605-2300

YARROW, ANDREW LOUIS, writer, journalist, educator, international relations consultant; b. Washington, June 11, 1957; s. Leon Jay and Marian Jeannette (Radke) Y.; 1 child, Richard. BA, UCLA, 1979; MA, Princeton U., 1981; MPA, Harvard U., 1994. Reporter N.Y. Times, N.Y.C., 1981-92; prof. Am. U., Washington, 1994-97; spl. asst. to sec. labor U.S. Dept. Labor, Washington, 1995-99; speechwriter Export-Import Bank, 1999—; internat. rels. cons. World Bank, Washington, 1994-95, UNICEF, 1999—. Author: Latecomers: Children of Parents Over 35, 1991; contbr. articles to profl. jours. and popular mags. Inst. for Internat. Edn. fellow, Eng., 1979; recipient Visitors Program award European Union, Brussels, 1993; Rsch. grant Govt. France, 1992-93. Mem. Phi Beta Kappa. Democrat. Avocations: photography, creative writing. Home: 4122 Jenifer St NW Washington DC 20015-1952 Office: Export-Import Bank Washington DC 20571

YARYMOVYCH, MICHAEL IHOR, retired manufacturing company executive; b. Bialystok, Poland, Oct. 13, 1933; came to U.S., 1951, naturalized, 1956; s. Nicholas Joseph and Olga (Kruczowy) Y.; m. Roxolana Abramiuk, Nov. 21, 1951; children—Tatiana, Nicholas. B.Aero. Engring., NYU, 1955; M.S. in Engring. Mechanics, Columbia U., 1956, D. Engring. Sci., 1969. Dep. asst. sec. research and devel. U.S. Air Force, Washington, 1967-70; dir. AGARD, NATO, Paris, 1970-73; chief scientist U.S. Air Force, 1973-75; asst. adminstr. field ops. ERDA, 1975-77; v.p. engring. N.Am. aerospace ops. Rockwell Internat. Corp., Seal beach, Calif., 1977-81; v.p. advanced systems devel. Rockwell Internat. Corp., El Segundo, Calif., 1981-86, v.p., assoc. dir. Sys. Devel. Ctr., 1986-96; ret. Rockwell Internat. Corp., 1996; v.p. internat. tech. The Boeing Co., 1996-98; chief scientist ANSER Corp., 1998—; ret. The Boeing Co., 1998; mem. Air Force Sci. Adv. Bd., 1990-94; chmn. NATO Adv. Group for Aerospace R&D, 1994-97; chmn. NATO R&T Orgn., 1997-2000; cons. in field. Author papers in field. Recipient Exceptional Civilian Svc. award Dept. Air Force, 1968, 73, 75, 94, Disting. Svc. award ERDA, 1977; Guggenheim fellow, 1956-58. Fellow AIAA (dir., pres., gen. chmn. ann. meeting 1978); mem. Air Force Assn., Am. Astronautical Soc., Internat. Acad. Astronautics (v.p. sci. programs, pres.). Office: ANSER Ste 800 1215 Jefferson Davis Hwy Arlington VA 22202-3251

YARZÁBAL, LUIS, biomedical researcher, university educator; b. Melo, Uruguay, Feb. 1, 1938. MD, U. Uruguay, 1964; postgrad. in immunoparasitology, U. Lille, 1964. Assoc. prof. immunology Ctrl. U. Venezuela, Caracas, 1985—; dir. Regional Ctr. for Higher Edn. in Latin Am. and the Caribbean UNESCO, Caracas, 1994—; coord. Amazonian Essential Health Rsch. programme Assn. Amazonian Univs., 1992-97; mem. clin. immunology com. Internat. Union Immunol. Socs.; rep. U. Uruguay in Grupo Montevideo Internat. Assn. Univs., 1991—; cons. Inter-Am. Devel. Bank, 1992. Recipient Orden Francisco de Miranda, Venezuela, 1985, Orden Andres Bello, Venezuela, 1987, Nat. award CONICIT Venezuela, 1987. Mem. Uruguayan Soc. Microbiology, Venezuelan Soc. Parasitology, Venezuelan Assn. for Advancement Sci., Venezuelan Assn. Allergy and Immunology, Uruguayan Assn. Parasitology, Uruguayan Assn. Immunology. *

YASHIMI, TOSHIAKI, electric power industry executive. CEO Tohoku Electric Power, Sendai, Japan. Office: Tohoku Electric Power, 3-7-1 Ichiban-cho, Aoba-ku Sendai 980-8550, Japan*

YASHIRO, JUNJIRO, pharmaceutical executive, patent lawyer; b. Niigata, Japan, Sept. 5, 1940; m. Ikuko. Degree in pharmacy, Tohoku Pharm. U., Sendai, Japan, 1963; degree in patent law, Patent Acad., Tokyo, 1969. Mgr. licensing Eisai Co., Ltd., Tokyo, 1975-88, dir. licensing, 1988-93, dir. intellectual Property, 1993-2000; auditor Genox Rsch., Inc., Kawasaki-shi, Kanagawa, Japan, 2000—. Mem. Licensing Exec. Soc. Internat. (vice chair biotechnology com. 1999-2000), Japan Pharm. Mfrs. Assn. (chair intellectual property com. 1999-2000), Licensing Exec. Soc. Japan (healthcare com. 1995-97, trustee 1995-98, v.p. 1999—). Home: 10-17 Negishidai-7, Asaka 351 0005, Japan Office: Genox Rsch Inc, 907 Nogawa, Miyamae-ku, Kawasaki-shi Kanagawa, Japan

YASINZAI, MOHAMMAD MASOOM, biochemistry educator; b. Quetta, Pakistan, Oct. 1, 1958; s. Abdul Latif Yasinzai and Khadija Bibi Latif; m. Pari Gul Kausar, Oct. 14, 1981; children: Imran, Memoona, Adnan, Danial, Raneen. MS, U. Balochistan, Quetta, 1979; PhD, U. Hull, Eng., 1985; postgrad., Perugia (Italy) Med. Sch., 1988. Lectr. chemistry U. Balochistan, Quetta, 1980-85, asst. prof., 1985-93, assoc. prof., 1993-96, prof. biochemistry, 1996—; pres. acad. staff assn. U. Balochistan, Quetta; Food Agr. Orgn. cons. Health and Nutrition, Quetta, 1996-97; cons. incharge Masoom's Diagnostic Lab., Quetta, 1996—. Contbr. articles to profl. jours. Recipient Ibn Al-Hythum award Coun. for Sci. and Tech., Pakistan, 1995, Aizaz-i-Fazeelat award Pres. of Pakistan, 1999; named Young Scientist of Yr., Ministry of Sci. and Tech., Pakistan, 1998; Third World Acad. Scis. fellow Perugia Med. Sch., 1987-88; Fulbright fellow Chgo. Med. Sch., 1993. Mem. Biochem. Soc. U.K., Am. Soc. for Tropical Medicine, Pakistan Soc. for Biochemistry and Molecular Biology, Pakistan Sci. Found. (mem. tech. com. 1987—), Pakistan Atomic Energy Coun., Environ. Club (pres. 1995—). Office: Inst Biochemistry, U Balochistan Sariab Rd, Quetta Pakistan

YASKAWA, KATSUMI, university administrator; b. Nagano, Japan, Oct. 13, 1930; s. Hiroshi Miyajima and Mikiko Yaskawa; m. Misa Matsumura, Apr. 18, 1964; children: Shunsuke, Genta. BSc, Kyoto (Japan) U., 1955, MS, 1957, PhD, 1963. Lectr. Fukui (Japan) U., 1963-69; assoc. prof. Osaka (Japan) U., 1969-75; prof. Kobe (Japan) U., 1975-94, dean faculty sci., 1986-90, dir. univ. libr., 1990-94, prof. emeritus, 1994—; pres. Osaka Coll., 1994-2000, Southern Osaka U., 1998—; rsch. assoc. St. Louis U., 1965-66. Contbr. articles to profl. jours. Mem. expert com. Ministry Edn., Tokyo, 1981, 82; mem. judging com. Kyoto Prize, 1986, 90, 94; mem. environ. coun. Environ. Agy., Tokyo, 1989-94; mem. harbor coun. Hyogo Prefecture Govt., Kobe, 1995—. Recipient Hyogo Sci. award Hyogo Prefecture Govt., 1992. Mem. Am. Geophys. Union, Soc. Geomagnetic Earth, Planet and Space Sci. (Tanakadate award 1973), Royal Astron. Soc. Home: 2-1-32 Sone-Higashi-Machi, Toyonaka-shi Osaka 561-0802, Japan Office: Southern Osaka U, Hirao, Mihara-cho Osaka 587-8555, Japan

YASNYI, ALLAN DAVID, communications company executive; b. New Orleans, June 22, 1942; s. Ben Z. and Bertha R. (Michalove) Y.; m. Susan K. Manders; children: Benjamin Charles, Evelyn Judith, Brian Mallut. BBA, Tulane U., 1964. Free-lance exec. producer, producer, writer, actor, designer TV, motion picture and theatre, 1961-73; producer, performer the Second City; dir. fin. & adminstrn. Quinn Martin Prodns., Hollywood, Calif., 1973-76, v.p. fin., 1976-77, exec. v.p. fin. & corp. planning, 1977; vice chmn., CEO QM Prodns., Beverly Hills, Calif., 1977-78, chmn. bd., CEO, 1978-80; pres., CEO The Synapse Comm. Group, Inc., 1981—, ASI Entertainment, 1998-99; exec. dir., adj. prof. U. So. Calif. Entertainment Tech. Ctr., 1994-99, exec. dir. emeritus, 1999—; participant IC IS Forum, 1990-95; exec. prodr. first live broadcast combining Intelsat, Intersputnik, The Voice of Am., and The Moscow World Radio Svc., 1990; resource guest Aspen Inst. Exec. Seminars, 1990; chmn. bd. dirs. Found. of Global Broadcasting, Washington, 1987-93. Trustee Hollywood Arts Coun., 1980-83; exec. v.p., trustee Hollywood Hist. Trust, 1981-91; bd. dirs. Internat. Ctr. Intergative Studies, N.Y.C., 1988-92; bd. dirs. Asthma and Allergy Found. Am., 1981-85. With U.S. Army, 1964-66, Viet Nam. Named Tulane U. Hall of Fame. Mem. Acad. TV Arts and Scis., Inst. Moetic Scis., Hollywood Radio and TV Soc., Hollywood C. of C. (dir., vice chmn. 1978-93), Screen Actors Guild, Assn. Transpersonal Psychology (keynote spkr. 1988). Office: 4132 Fulton Ave Sherman Oaks CA 91423-4340

YASUDA, ISAMU, electrochemical researcher; b. Kyoto, Japan, May 4, 1962; s. Kenji and Etsuko (Bandoh) Y.; m. Hitomi Saitoh, May 23, 1987; children: Ayaka, Sachika. B Engring., U. Tokyo, 1985, M Engring., 1987, D in Engring., 1998. Rschr. Tokyo Gas Co., Ltd., 1987, sr. rschr., 1993—; instr. Tohoku U., Sendai, Japan, 1995. Contbr. articles to profl. jours., including Jour. Electrochem. Soc., Jour. Solid State Chemistry, Solid State Ionics, Jour. Materials Sci. Mem. Electrochem. Soc. Japan, Chem. Soc. Japan (editl. bd. Nippon Kagaku Kaishi 1996-97), Electrochem. Soc. (U.S.). Avocations: floriculture, reading. Office: Tokyo Gas Co Fund Tech Lab, 1-16-25 Shibaura, Minato-ku, Tokyo 105-0023, Japan

YASUDA, TAKAKO, literature educator; b. Toyohashi-shi, Aichi, Japan, Mar. 26, 1935; d. Hayato Kato and Tsurue Kato; m. Motoo Yasuda, Apr. 12, 1959; 1 child, Kumi. Student, Aichi Prefectural Jr. Coll., Nagoya, Japan, 1955; BS, Osaka (Japan) Prefectural U., 1957. Asst. Aichi Prefectural U., 1957-61, 63-66; instr. prof. Nagoya Jiyugakuin Coll., Aichi, 1966-69; instr. prof. Sugiyama Jogakuen U., Nagoya, 1969-71, assoc. prof., 1971-77, prof., 1977—. Author: Study on the Narrative Literature, 1997 (Govt. grant), The Method of Composition in Senjusho, 1997; annotator: Senjusho, 1987, Ujishuimonogatari: Shasekishu, 1987. Mem. Narrative Lit. Assn. (pres. 1987-89, mem. com. 1985—), Buddhism Lit. Assn. (mem. com. 1996—), Wakan Comparative Lit. Assn. (bd. dirs. 1991—). Avocation: visiting historic sites. Home: 391-3 Takama-cho Meito-ku, Nagoya Aichi-ken 465-0081, Japan

YASUDA, YUZURU, neurologist; b. Kyoto, Japan, May 7, 1949; S. Saburo and Shigeko (Kuriyama) Terada; m. Hiroko Suwa, Jan. 15, 1983; children: Ken, Noriko. MD, Kyoto U., 1983. Bd. cert. diplomate in neurology. Intern Kyoto Univ. Sch. Medicine, 1977-78, Kitano Hosp., Osaka, Japan, 1978-79; sub-chief dept. neurology Kyoto City Hosp., 1983-90; chief dept. neurology Otsu Red Cross Hosp., Japan, 1990—. Mem. Japanese Soc. Neurology, Japanese Soc. Internal Medicine, Japanese Soc. Neuropathology. Home: 62-4 Takenokaido-cho, Takehana Yamashina-ku Kyoto 607, Japan Office: Otsu Red Cross Hosp, Dept Neurology, 1-1-35 Nagara, Otsu 520, Japan

YASUHARA, MICHIRU, mechanical engineering educator; b. Kagi, Taiwan, Mar. 22, 1928; arrived in Japan, 1940.; s. Sentaro and Kazue (Kubota) Y.; m. Yumiko Shinohara, Mar. 30, 1959; 1 child, Shigeki. Bachelor's degree, U. Tokyo, 1951, D of Engring., 1962. Engr. Tahara Mfg., Tokyo, 1951-54; assoc. U. Tokyo, 1954-58; assoc. prof. Nagoya (Japan) U., 1958-67, prof., 1967-91; prof. emeritus, 1991—; assoc. prof. U. So. Calif., 1965; prof. Aichi Inst. Tech., Toyota, Japan, 1991—; rsch. assoc. Cornell U., Ithaca, N.Y., 1963-65; mng. com. mem. Inst. Space and Astronautical Sci., Sagamihara, Japan, 1987-91. Author: The Day Japanese Space Shuttle Flies, 1984; co-editor, author: Numerical Fluid Dynamics, 1992, Handbook of Flow Experiments, 1997; contbr. articles to profl. jours. Mem. Japan Soc. Aeronautical and Space Scis. (bd. dirs. 1984-85, dir. ctrl. br. 1987, paper award 1993, hon.), Japan Soc. Fluid Mechanics, Japan Soc. Mech. Engrs. Avocations: Go, driving, fishing, golf. Home: 34-18 Neura Iwasaki, 470-0131 Nissin Aichi, Japan Office: Aichi Inst Tech, 1247 Yachigusa Yagusa, 470-0131 Toyota Aichi, Japan

YASUI, KYUICHI, physicist; b. Tokyo, Sept. 12, 1967. BSc, Waseda U., Tokyo, 1991, MSc, 1993, PhD, 1996. Asst. Waseda U., Tokyo, 1995-98; rsch. fellow JSPS, Tokyo, 1998-99; rschr. Nat. Indsl. Rsch. Inst. of Nagoya, 1999—. Author: Why Is a Rotating Top Standing? (in Japanese), 1998. Fax: 81-52-916-2802. Office: Nat Indsl Rsch Inst Nagoya, 1 Hirate-cho Kita-ku, Nagoya 462-8510, Japan

YASUI, YUKIO, biologist; b. Osaka, Japan, Jan. 30, 1964; s. Tokuichi Yasui and Reiko (Fujimura) Y. BAS, Kyoto (Japan) Prefectural U., 1987, MAgr, 1989; DAgr, Hokkaido U., Sapporo, Japan, 1993. Fellow Hokkaido U., Sapporo, 1993-96, Kyoto U. Ctr. for Ecol. Rsch., 1997—. Mem. Ecol. Soc. Japan, Japan Ethological Soc. Home: 13-5 Doyama, 571-0059 Kadoma Japan Office: Kyoto Univ, Ctr Ecol Rsch, 606-01 Kyoto Japan

YASUKATA, TOSHIMASA, educator; b. Yonago, Tottori, Japan, Jan. 26, 1952; s. Kei and Sadako (Tanabe) Y.; m. Etsuko Maehara, July 1, 1982; children: Kuniki, Yuri, Kaori. BA, Kyoto (Japan) U., 1975, MA, 1977, LittD, 1997; PhD, Vanderbilt U., 1985. Jr. rsch. fellow Japan Soc. for Promotion of Sci., Kyoto, 1980, 85-87; assoc. prof. Morioka (Japan) Coll., 1987-93; assoc. prof. Seigakuin U., Ageo, Japan, 1993-96, prof., 1996—. Author: Ernst Troeltsch, 1986 (Japan Assn. for Religious Studies award 1987), Lessing and the German Enlightenment, 1998. Sci. rsch. grantee

Japan Ministry Edn., 1986, 86, 94, 98, 99; Exch. fellow Japan found., 1999. Mem. Am. Acad. Religion, Lessing Soc., Ernst-Troeltsch-Gesellschaft. Mem. United Ch. of Christ. Avocation: books. Home: 62-791 Nozawa, Takizawamura Iwate 020-0173, Japan Office: Seigakuin U, 1-1 Tozaki, Ageo Saitama 362-8585, Japan

YASUKAWA, ETSUKO, economist, educator; b. Yokohama, Kanagawa, Japan, Oct. 13, 1936; d. Masao and Emiko (Sobue) Ando; m. Juneosuke Yasukawa, Sept. 23, 1965. M of Econs., Nagoya (Japan) U., 1961, D of Econs., 1982. Prof. Nagoya City Women's Coll., 1975-95, pres., 1995-97; prof. Nagoya City U., 1997—. Author: British Working Classes' Movement and Socialism, 1982, Irish Question and British Socialism, 1993; co-author: History of Social Thought Against Women's Discrimination in Japan, 1995. Home: 5-22-2 Tohmeicho, Chikusa, Nagoya 464-0028, Japan Office: Nagoya City U, 1 Yamanohata, Nagoya 467-8501, Japan

YASUMI, SHINJIRO, nuclear physicist, physics educator; b. Kyoto, Japan, Feb. 3, 1924; s. Wasaburo and En (Morita) Y.; m. Yasuko Hirota, Mar. 30, 1952; 1 child, Mari Nakano. BS, Kyoto U., 1946, DSc, 1957. Asst. prof. Konan U., Kobe, Japan, 1951-57; asst. prof. Kyoto U., 1957-63, prof., 1963-71; prof. Nat. Lab. High Energy Physics KEK, Tsukuba, Japan, 1971-84, prof. emeritus, 1984—; prof. Teikyo U., Tokyo, 1984-99; dir. physics dept. Nat. Lab. High Energy Physics KEK, Tsukuba, 1971-76. Author: Beautiful Physics, 1995, (with B. Arakatsu et al) Modern Physics, Encyclopedia of Science and Technology, Vol. 8, Physics; contbr. articles and papers on the electron neutrino mass, and so on, to profl. jours. Mem. Phys. Soc. Japan. Avocations: tennis, skiing, listening to classical music, traveling. Home: 3-9-3 Kitano, Mitaka Tokyo 181-0003, Japan Office: Inst Particle/Nuc Studies High Energy Accelerator Rsch Orgn, 1-1 Oho Tsukuba, Ibaraki 305-0801, Japan

YASUMOTO, TAKESHI, chemistry educator; b. Naha, Okinawa, Japan, Feb. 22, 1935; s. Jitsuga and Kisako (Oshiro) Y.; m. Tomiko Hayashi, May 2, 1963; children: Ken-ichi, Sanehiro, Akiko. BS, Tokyo U., 1957, MS, 1959, PhD, 1966. Asst. prof. Tokyo U., 1960-69; assoc. prof. chemistry Tohoku U., Sendai, Japan, 1969-77, prof., 1977-97; prof. emeritus Tohoku U., Sendai, 1997—; cons. Japan Food Rsch. Labs., 1997—; cons. on food hygiene Japanese Ministry Health and Welfare, Tokyo, 1985—. Author: Marine Natural Products, 1987; editor: Bioactive Marine Products, 1987. Recipient award Symposium on Toxins, Tokyo, 1986, Internat. Conf. on Toxic Marine Phytoplanktons, 1989, P.J. Scheuer award for marine natural products, 1994, Naito Found. rsch. prize, 1994, Yomiuri prize for agrl. scis., 1997, Medal with purple ribbon, 1999, Okinawa Times award, 1999. Mem. AAAS, Japanese Soc. Sci. Fisheries (award 1977), Japan Soc. for Biosci., Biotech. and Agrochemistry (award 1992), N.Y. Acad. Sci., Fedn. Socs. Agrl. Scis. Home: 3-14-13 Nakayama, Aobaku Sendai 981, Japan Office: Japan Food Rsch Labs, 6-11-10 Nagayama, Tama Tokyo 206-0025, Japan

YASUOKA, OKIHARU, federal official. Min. of justice Japan. Office: Ministry of Justice 1-1-1, Kasumigaseki Chiyoduku, Tokyo 100, Japan*

YASUTAKE, SHIRO, commodities trader. CEO Nissho Iwai, Tokyo. Office: Nissho Iwai, 2-4-5 Akasaka, Minato-ku Tokyo 107-0052, Japan*

YASUYUKI, NAMBU, employment agency executive. CEO Pasona Group, Tokyo. Fax: 813-5223-6839. Office: Palace Side Bldg, 1-1-1 Hitotsubashi, Chiodaku Tokyo 100-8228, Japan

YATES, JOHN MELVIN, ambassador; b. Superior, Mont., Nov. 25, 1939; s. Leon Glen and Violet May (McPheeters) Y.; m. Peggy Maureen Simpson, Mar. 26, 1961 (dec. Apr. 1986); children: Catherine Diener, John Simpson, Maureen Cole, Paul Marion, Leon Gregory; m. Mary Barbara Carlin, Jan. 30, 1988. A.B., Stanford U., 1961; M.A., Fletcher Sch. Law and Diplomacy, 1962, M.A.L.D., 1963, Ph.D., 1972. Fgn. service officer U.S. Dept. State, Washington, 1964—, Algiers, Algeria, 1964-66, Blantyre, Malawi, 1967-68, Bamako, Mali, 1969-71, New Delhi, 1973-75, Ankara, Turkey, 1975-77, Libreville, Gabon, 1977-80, Washington, 1971-73, 80-82; amb. to Republic of Cape Verde, Am. Embassy, 1983-86; counselor for polit. affairs Am. Embassy, Manila, 1986-89; dep. chief of mission Am. Embassy, Lagos, Nigeria, 1989-91; dep. chief of mission Am. Embassy, Kinshasa, Zaire, 1991-93, chief of mission, 1993-95; amb. to Republic of Benin, Am. Embassy, Cotonou, 1995-98; amb. to Republic of Cameroon and Republic Equatorial Guinea, Am. Embassy, Yaounde, 1998—. Recipient Presdl. award for sustained superior accomplishment in conduct of fgn. policy. Mem. Am. Fgn. Service Assn. Office: Dept State 2520 Yaounde Pl Washington DC 20521-2520

YATES, KENNETH LEE, electro-optics engineer, flight instructor; b. Sagmihara, Japan, Nov. 14, 1959; s. John Thomas and Leokadia (Iwan) Y.; m. Conchita Delores Aarts, Sept. 8, 1984; 1 child, Jonathan. BS in Physics, Va. Mil. Inst., 1982; MBA, U. W. Fla., 1985; MS in Optical Scis., U. Ariz., 1987. Lic. pilot; cert. flight instr. Commd. capt. USAF, 1982; munitions test engr. USAF, Eglin AFB, Fla., 1982-84, electro-optics test engr., 1984-86, lab. program mgr., 1988-90, lead engr., 1990-94, program mgr., 1994-95; sr. engr. Sverdrop Techs., Niceville, Fla., 1995—. Mem. Soc. Photo Optical Instrumentation Engrs., Elctro-Magnetic Windows Working Group (chmn. 1989-90), Emerald Coast Optical Soc. (pres. 1997-98). Avocations: flying, flight instruction, boating. Home: 30 Newcastle Ct Niceville FL 32578-3933 Office: Sverdrup Techs 214 Government Ave Niceville FL 32578-1871

YATES, LINDA SNOW, communications and marketing executive; b. St. Louis, July 20, 1938; d. Robert Anthony Jerrue and June Alberta (Crowder) Armstrong; m. Charles Russell Snow, Nov. 26, 1958 (div. 1979); children: Cathryn Louise, Christopher Armstrong, Heather Highstone, Sean Webster; m. Alan Porter Yates, July 22, 1983. BBA, Auburn U., 1973, MEd, 1975, EdD, 1998. Cert. profl. sec. Div. head placement div. Solutions Group, Atlanta, 1981-83; employment coord. Fulton Fed. Savs., Atlanta, 1983-84; owner, recruiter Data One, Inc., Atlanta, 1984-85; ops. mgr. Talent Tree Temporaries, Atlanta, 1985-87; legal asst., sec. Rice & Keene, Atlanta, 1987-90; legal word processing asst. Kilpatrick & Cody, Atlanta, 1990-94; pres., owner Power Comm., Cashiers, N.C., 1994-98; regional coord. S.E. region, regional mktg. rep. WorldConnect Comms., Tulsa; adj. instr. DeKalb Coll., Atlanta, 1980-84, Mercer U., Atlanta, 1981-82; instr. bus. So. Union State Jr. Coll., Valley, Ala., 1974-75; legal sec. Swift, Currie, McGhee & Hiers, Atlanta, 1979-80, Samford, Torbert, Denson & Horsley, Opelika, Ala., 1969-71; chmn. edn. divsn., mem. part-time faculty in ednl. adminstrn. Monterrey Inst. Grad. Studies, Nuevo Leon, Mex. Columnist Neon News Flash, 1995. Mem. Paralegal Assn. Beaufort County (charter mem., sec. 1993-94), Women Bus. Owners, Nat. Assn. Pers. Cons., Internat. Soc. Poets (Disting. mem., Internat. Poet of Merit 1996, Internat. Poetry Hall of Fame 1996), Cashiers Writers Group, Phi Delta Kappa, Alpha Xi Delta. Republican. Episcopalian. Avocations: golf, writing, international travel. Office: PO Box 2441 Cashiers NC 28717-2441

YATES, MICHAEL FRANCIS, management consultant; b. N.Y.C., Feb. 9, 1946; s. John Berchmans and Jane Ann (Gretz) Y.; m. Christine Mary Dallos, Jan. 14, 1967; children: Erik Michael, Alison. BA, U. Buffalo, 1968. Mgmt. trainee, dept. mgr. Sears, Roebuck & Co., Buffalo, 1968-69; cons. Rothman & D'Alessandro, Inc., N.Y.C., 1969-71; sr. cons. Martin & Segal & Co., Inc., N.Y.C., 1971-75, A.S. Hansen, Inc., N.Y.C., 1975-78; exec. v.p. A.M. D'Alessandro & Co., Inc., North Haledon, N.J., 1978-81; mng. dir. Alexander & Alexander Cons. Group, Inc., Lyndhurst, N.J., 1981-97; pres. Michael F. Yates & Co., Inc., Hampton, N.J., 1997—. Pres. Lincoln Sch. PTA, 1975-77, Bethlehem Twp. Rep. Club, mem. Hunterdon County com.; chmn. Bethlehem Twp. Econ. and Indsl. Devel. Bd., 1980-83; active Rep. Nat. Com.; bd mem. Am. Intercon, Inc., 1998—. Mem. Am. Mgmt. Assn., Am. Compensation Assn., Soc. Human Resource Mgmt., Adminstrv. Mgmt. Soc., Aircraft Owners and Pilots Assn. Home: 519 Lannon Ln Glen Gardner NJ 08826-5217 Office: 3 Anor Dr Hampton NJ 08827-5409

YATES, MILDRED CAMPBELL, retired literature educator; b. Beaumont, Tex., Jan. 1, 1920; d. William Holland and Eula Mildred (Owens) Campbell; m. Reed Henry Yates, Jr., May 17, 1944; children: Reed Henry III, Mary Campbell Yates Kirkpatrick. BFA, U. Ga., 1940; MA in English, Lamar U., 1962. Cert. tchr. grades 5-12, Tex. Tchr. elem. lang. arts and music Beaumont (Tex.) Ind. Sch. Dist., 1953-67; asst. prof. elem. lang. arts edn. Lamar U., Beaumont, 1968-70; tchr. Am. lit. and world civilization French H.S., Beaumont, 1970-79; bd. dirs. Mental Health Assn., Austin, Tex., 1972-76; commr. Beaumont Landmark Corp., 1980-84; dir. of bd. Arts Related Curriculum, Beaumont, 1982-89; docent French Hist. House, Beaumont, 1979—. Co-author: (devel. reader) Images, 1971, Keystone, 1975; co-author, co-editor: With a Dome More Vast, 1986 (Kate Warnick award 1986); author: (essay) Beaumont Women, A Memoir, 1992. Pres. Beaumont Heritage Soc., 1980-82; genealogist Tex. Gulf Hist. Soc., Beaumont, 1986—; pres., sec. Tyrrell Hist. Libr. Assn., Beaumont, 1987—; tchr. adult classes First United Meth. Ch., Beaumont, 1998—; bd. dirs. Beaumont Music Commn., 1988—, chmn. Speaker's Bur., Jefferson Theatre Restoration, 1998—. Nominee for Jefferson award Beaumont Enterprise, 1996; recipient Preservation award Main St. Project, Beaumont, 1997. Mem. Art Mus. of Tex., Pi Beta Phi (sec.). Methodist. Avocations: reading, travel, hist. preservation, volunteering.

YATHIRAJAN, HEMMIGE SRINIVASAIYENGAR, chemist; b. June 8, 1956; m. Lakshmi N. Yathirajan; children: Ajay S., Bharath R., Arathi R. BS, U. Mysore, 1974, MS, 1976, PhD, 1981. Lectr. in phys. chemistry Mysore (India) U., 1976-92, reader in chemistry, 1992—; NSF postdoctoral rsch. assoc. dept. chemistry Washington U., St. Louis, 1990-93; dep. dir. Acad. Staff Coll. U. Mysore, 1997-98; examiner for Bangalore, Mangalore and Kuvempu Univs.; sec. chem. soc., U. Mysore. Contbr. articles to profl. jours. Fellow Indian Chem. Soc.; mem. IUPAC, Am. Chem. Soc. Home: 12 MIG New KR, URS Rd, Kuvempunagar Mysore 570023, India Office: Mysore U, Dept Studies Chem, Mysore 570 006, India

YATSALO, BORIS IVANOVICH, mathematician, researcher; b. Grechanovka, Russia, Feb. 10, 1959; s. Ivan Kupriyanovich and Olga Vladimirovna (Rosputko) Y.; m. Irina Alexeevna Pichugina, Sept. 27, 1980; children: Elena, Olga. Degree, Moscow State U., 1981, postgrad., 1984; DSc, Moscow Computer Ctr., 1985. Jr. rsch. worker Russian Inst. Agrl. Radiology and Agroecology, Obninsk, 1985-87, sr. rsch. worker, 1988-90, leading rsch. worker, 1991-93, head sector of computer and GIS sys., 1994-97; leading rschr., head GIS lab. Obninsk Inst. Nuc. Power Engring., 1998—; prin. rschr. RRC Kurchatov Inst., Moscow, 1997—. Contbr. papers to sci. publs. Grantee Internat. Sci. and Tech. Ctr., Moscow, 1995, 99. Mem. Nuc. Soc., N.Y. Acad. Sci., Internat. Union of Radioecology. Avocations: tennis, folk music, poetry. Fax: 08439-70822. E-mail: yatsalo@prana.obnisa. Office: OINPE, Studgorodok 1, 249020 Obninsk Kaluga, Russia

YATSENKO, NIKOLAI AFANASYEVICH, physics researcher, educator; b. Russia, Jan. 1, 1948; came to the U.S., 1996; s. Afanasii and Vera (Bogacheva) Y.; m. Lyudmila Yegorovna Fedyanina, May 6, 1972; 1 child, Marina. MS in Physics, Moscow Inst. Physics & Tech., 1973, PhD in Physics and Math., 1978; DSc in Physics and Math., Russian Acad. Scis., Moscow, 1992. Rschr. Zhukovsky Mil. Air Force Acad., Moscow, 1973-75; rschr., sr. rschr. Inst. for Problems in Mechanics, Russian Acad. Scis., Moscow, 1978-95, head rschr., 1995—; assoc. prof. physics Russian Inst. Textile and Light Industry, Moscow, 1980-93, full prof. physics, 1993—; project scientist Optical Engring., Inc., Santa Rosa, Calif., 1996-98, Macken Instruments, Inc., Santa Rosa, Calif., 1998—; referee Soviet Union State Com. for Inventions and Discoveries, Moscow, 1986-91; mem. sci. coun. Inst. for Problems in Mechanics, Moscow, 1992—; mem. spl. PhD coun. Moscow Inst. Physics and Tech., 1995—. Co-author: Thermal Plasma Diagnostics, 1994, Radio-Frequency Capacitive Discharges, 1995, Gas Lasers-Recent Developments and Future Prospects, 1996; mem. editl. bd: Jour. Edn. Experiment in U., 1997—; referee Jour. Physics D: Applied Physics, 1998—; contbr. articles to jours. on plasma physics and gas lasers. Decorated Medal of Hon. 850th Ann. Moscow, 1997; recipient 6 awards Inst. Problems in Mechanics, Russian Acad. Scis., 1984-90, Outstanding Achievement medal Internat. Biog. Ctr., Cambridge, Eng., 1999, 20th Century Achievement award Am. Biog. Inst., 1999; grantee Ministry of Edn., Moscow, 1992, 94, 95, 97, Internat. Sci. Found., Russia, 1993, 94, Joint Russian and Internat. Sci. Found., 1995. Fellow Internat. Biog. Assn., Am. Biog. Inst. (life), Inst. Physics (London); mem. IEEE (sr.), AAAS, Am. Phys. Soc., European Phys. Soc., Am. Vacuum Soc., Am. Assn. Physics Tchrs., Nat. Geog. Soc., Sigma Xi. Achievements include experimental discoveries relating to radio-frequency capacitive discharges at moderate pressures; invention and demonstration of a slab CO2 laser; 10 patents including laser apparatus utilizing a magnetically enhanced electrical discharge with transverse AC stabilization; Russian patent for gas-flow CO2 laser. Avocations: books, travel. E-mail: nyatsenko@ieee.org. Office: Macken Instruments Inc 3644 Airway Dr Santa Rosa CA 95403-1669

YAU, TIEN YAU, telecommunications products company executive; b. Taipei, Taiwan, Nov. 10, 1966; arrived in Hong Kong, 1971; s. Lai Kwan Yau and Chuk Ping Ng. B in Engring. (hons), City U. Hong Kong, 1993; MS in Elec. and Electronic Engring., Hong Kong U. Sci. and Tech., 1999. Electronic engr. Star Paging Mfg. Ltd., Hong Kong, 1989-90; electronic engr. Cirkisys Tech. Ltd., Hong Kong, 1993-95, sr. engr., 1995-97, project mgr., 1997-98; project mgr. Group Sense Ltd., Hong Kong, 1998—. Mem. IEEE. Avocations: travel, photography, reading. Home: 306C Ground Fl, Prince Edward Rd, Kowloon Hong Kong Office: Group Sense Ltd, 27/F Wu Chung House, Wanchai China

YAVARKOVSKY, JEROME HAROLD, library director; b. N.Y.C., May 12, 1940. B Mech. Engring., Rensselaer Poly. Inst., 1960; MS in Mgmt., MIT, 1962; M Libr. Sci., Columbia U., 1971. Lic. pub. libr. Adminstrv. specialist Bell Labs., Murray Hill, N.J., 1963-64; systems analyst J.C. Penney Co., N.Y.C., 1965-67; tech. cons. Auerbach Assocs., N.Y.C., 1967-68; head programming Columbia U., N.Y.C., 1969-71, chief systems, 1971-72, asst. univ. libr., 1972-83; dean librs. Adelphi U., Garden City, N.Y., 1983-85; dir. N.Y. State Libr., Albany, 1985-95; univ. libr. Boston Coll., Chestnut Hill, 1995—. Office: Thomas P O'Neill Libr Boston Coll Chestnut Hill MA 02467

YAVELOV, IGOR SEMENOVICH, cardiologist, researcher; b. Moscow, June 21, 1965; s. Samuil Abramovich and Larisa Nickolaevna (Yudina) Y. MD, Russian Med. U., Moscow, 1988; PhD, Nat. Cardiology Rsch. Ctr., Moscow, 1995; postgrad., Rsch. Inst. Phys. Chem. Med., Moscow, 1991-94. Med. diplomate cardiology Diplomate Internat. Sch. for Good Clin. Practice. Resident cardiology Sklifosovsky Rsch. Inst. Emergency Medicine, Moscow, 1988-90; cardiologist in the cardiac care unit City Hosp. # 6, Moscow, 1990-91; rschr. Rsch. Inst. Physico-Chem. Medicine, Moscow, 1994-98, sr. rschr., 1999—; cons. City Hosps. # 29, Moscow, 1995—. Contbr. articles to profl. jours. E-mail: yavelov@medscape.com. Home: Korp 2 Kv 26, Molostovikh St 13, 111555 Moscow Russia Office: Rsch Inst Physico-Chem Med, Malaya Pirogovskaya Str 1A, 119828 Moscow Russia

YAWATA, YOSHIHITO, hematologist, oncologist educator; b. Kamakura, Kanagawa, Japan, Feb. 7, 1936; s. Yoshio and Chieko (Kawaguchi) Y. MD, Yokohama U., Japan, 1961; PhD, U. Tokyo, Japan, 1967. Bd. cert. in internal medicine, hematology/oncology. Clin. fellow U. Tokyo, Japan, 1962-64, rsch. fellow, 1964-69; rsch. specialist UCLA, 1969-71; rsch. fellow U. Minn., Mpls., 1971-72, asst. prof., 1972-74; assoc. prof. Kawasaki Med. Sch., Kurashiki, Japan, 1974-77, prof. hematology/oncology, 1977—; com. mem. Idiopathic Disorders of Hematopoietic Organs for Japanese Ministry of Health and Welfare, 1974—; prin. investigator Japan-France Coop. Study by Japan Soc. for Promotion of Sci., 1992-94; prin. investigator Japan-Germany Coop. Study by Japan Soc. for Promotion of Sci., 1997-99. Author: Red Cell Enzymology, 1963-70, Red Cell Membrane Researches, 1971—; mem. editorial bd. Jour. of Lab. and Clin. Medicine Gene Function and Disease; editor-in-chief Kawasaki Med. Jour. Grantee Japanese Ministry of Edn., Sci. and Culture, 1970—. Mem. Am. Soc. Hematology, Internat. Soc. Hematology, Am. Fedn. Clin. Rsch., Japan Soc. Hematology (dir.), Japan Soc. Clin. Hematology (pres. 1999-2000), Japanese Soc. Internal Medicine. Avocation: landscape photography. Home: 1342-343 Nishizaka, Kurashiki 710-0004, Japan Office: Kawasaki Med Sch, 577 Matsushima, Kurashiki 701-0192, Japan

YAXING, WEI, agricultural engineer; b. Huangyuan, China, Dec. 21, 1969; s. Wei Zhao and Zhu Yulan; m. Wang Liwen, Sept. 8, 1996. B in Engring., Wuhan (China) Tech. U., 1991; M in Agriculture, Gansu Agrl. U., Lanzhou, China, 1998. GIS engr. Gansu Grassland Ecol. Rsch. Inst., Lanzhou, 1991-99; cons. Remote Sensing Tng. Course, Lanzhou, 1996; adviser GIS and Remote Sensing Tng. Course, 1998. Trainee Japanese Internat. Coop. Agy., Tokyo, 1998. Avocations: Qigong, swimming, table tennis, mountain climbing. Fax: 0086-0931-8497553. Office: Gansu Grassland Ecol Rsch Inst, PO Box 61, Lanzhou 730020, China

YAZAMI, RACHID, research scientist, consultant; b. Fez, Morocco, Apr. 16, 1953; arrived in France,; s. Abdelkader and Fatima (Attar) Y.; m. Michèle Dauriat, Oct. 3, 1992; 1 child, Jehane. Diploma in electrochemistry engring., U. Grenoble, France, 1978, PhD in Electrochemistry, 1985. Rsch. dir. CNRS, Grenoble, 1985—; cons. Grenoble, 1992—; sabbatical Calif. Tech. U., Jet Propulsion Lab., Pasadena, Calif., 2000—. Inventor of carbon-lithium for batteries. mem. Electrochem. Soc. (v.p.), Internat. Battery Assn. (chmn. European office IBA-ITE, Rsch. award 1999), French Group Carbon Studies. Avocations: sports, tennis, skiing, soccer. Office: Caltech Mail Code 138-78 1200 E California Blvd Pasadena CA 91125

YAZAN, YASEMIN, pharmaceutical technologist, cosmetic researcher; b. Nazilli, Aegean, Turkey, Apr. 11, 1953; d. Sevki and Yildiz (Türkoğlu) Sener; m. Kudret Yazan, Apr. 22, 1978; children: Elif, Merve. BA in Pharmacy, Hacettepe U., Ankara, Turkey, 1975, MSc, 1976; PhD, Anadolu U., Eskisehir, Turkey, 1987. Asst. rschr. Anadolu U., 1981-87, asst. prof. pharmacy, 1987-94, assoc. prof., 1994-00, prof., 2000—, exec. faculty pharmacy, 1987-00, vice dean, 1995-98, head dept. cosmetology, 1993—, exec. of Medicinal Plants and Drug Rsch. Ctr., 1993—; gen. sec. Sci. Internat. Cosmetics Symposium (biann.). Editor: Procs. 1st Internat. Cosmetics Symposium, 1993, Procs. 2d Internat. Cosmetics Symposium, 1995, Procs. 3d Internat. Cosmetics Symposium, 1997, 4th Internat. Cosmetics Symposium, 2000; referee Jour. Ankara Assn. Pharm. Scis., 1993—; contbr. articles to profl. jours. Founder Turkish Assn. Univ. Women, Eskisehir, 1987, head, 1989-91. Recipient rsch. grants Anadolu U., U. Paris-Sud, 1991, Rsch. Found., 1995-98. Mem. N.Y. Acad. Tech. Scientists, Turkish Soc. Cosmetic Scientists (founder, gen. sec. 1996—), Turkish Soc. Pharm. Tech. Scientists (founder). Home: Porsuk Bulvari, Ilgaz Sok No 57/A, D.17, 26020 Eskisehir Turkey Office: Anadolu U Fac Pharmacy, Dept Pharm Technology, 26470 Eskisehir Turkey

YAZGAN, ERDEM, electronic engineering educator; b. Ankara, Turkey, Sept. 10, 1949; d. Ahmet Fevzi and Melahat Cayman Kutlucan; m. Mehmet Kaya Yazgan, Oct. 24, 1973; children: Isil, Ufuk. BSc in Electronic Engring., Middle East Tech. U., Ankara, Turkey, 1971, MSc in Electronic Engring., 1973; PhD in Electronic Engring., Hacettepe U., Ankara, Turkey, 1980. Cert. electronics engr. Project engr. PTT-NATO Divsn., Ankara, Turkey, 1971-72; tchg. asst. Middle East Tech. U., Ankara, Turkey, 1972-77; lectr. Hacettepe U., Ankara, Turkey, 1977-80, asst. prof., 1980-84, assoc. prof., 1984-90, prof., 1990—; head radio-TV standardization, Ankara, Turkey, 1986—; expert World Bank Indsl. Project, Ankara, 1988-93; head TAFICS-NATO, Ankara, 1990-93; vis. prof. Ohio State U., Columbus, 1993-94. Designer microwave digital radio comm. sys.; contbr. articles to profl. jours. Recipient Brit. Coun. rsch. award, Essex, Eng., 1992, Fulbright rsch. award, Columbus, Ohio, 1993-94, sci. and encouragement award Prof. M. Parlar, Ankara, 1992. Mem. IEEE, Internat. Armed Forces Com. Assn., Chamber of Elec. Engring. Avocations: classical music, swimming, reading. Home: Mesa Koru Sitesi, Karanfil Blok No 42 Cayyolu, 06530 Ankara Turkey

YBARRA, EMILIO, bank company executive. CEO Banco Bilbao Vizcaya, Bilbao, Spain, 1996—. Office: Banco Bilbao Vizcaya, Banco Bilbao Vizcaya, Pla de San Nicolás 4, 48001 Bilbao Spain

YBARRA, KATHRYN WATROUS, systems engineer; b. Middletown, Conn., Aug. 7, 1943; d. Claude Philip Jr. and C. Lyle (Crook) Watrous; m. Norman L. Adams (div.); children: Cynthia Anne Leonard, Suzette Mae Gross, Daniel Joseph Adams; m. Raul M. Ybarra, Dec. 11, 1976; stepchildren: Esther Ingram, Yolanda Ybarra, Lisa Ybarra. BA in Computer Sci., U. Tex., 1985. Scientific programmer Tracor, Inc., Austin, 1978-86; tech. staff engr. Honeywell, Inc. Comml. Avionics, Phoenix, 1986—. Mem. Friends of Phoenix Libr., v.p. Juniper chpt., 1996-97, pres., 1998-99. Mem. RTCA (spl. com. # 147, Traffic Alert and Collision Avoidance Sys. II, chair requirements working group 1991—, leadership citation 1995, spl. com. 186, co-chair working group 4 1997-99, chair enhancement subgroup, Cert. Achievement 1998), Nat. Soc. of DAR (registrar Camelback chpt. 1998—). Roman Catholic. Achievements include 5 patents for algorithms related to aircraft tracking systems for collision avoidance. Home: PMB 418 7942 W Bell Rd Ste C5 Glendale AZ 85308-8710

YBERT, JEAN-PAUL GUSTAVE, occupational medicine physician, anthropologist; b. Angerville, L'Orcher, France, May 2, 1944; s. Paul Leon and Paulette Henriette (Cesarine) Y. MD, Faculty of Medicine, Rouen, France, 1974; qualified in agrl. medicine, U. Tours, France, 1988; qualified in occupl. medicine, U. Paris, 1994. Physician Com. Inter-entreprises de Mé du Tra vail dela Nièvre, Nevers, France, 1976-78, Svc. de Médecine du er-entreprises de Médecine de Travail de la Région d'Alencon, Rouen, 1978-83, Assn. Médico-sociale Inter-Enterprises dEvraux et de sa Région, Alençon, France, 1988-91, Service Médicosocial Inter Entreprises, Louviers, France, 1991, Ctr. de Recherches Archéologiques de Haute Normanie, St. Quentin, 1996-98, Assn. Medicosociale Vernon et Desa, Vernon, France, 2000—. Contbr. papers to conf. procs. Fellow Internat. Commn. Occupl. Health (adminstr. 1964—); mem. CIST-ICOH, AAAS, N.Y. Acad. Scis. Home: 25 Parc de Cerisy, Rue du Pays de Caux, 76730 Montsaint Aignan France

YE, BIQING, biomedical engineer, researcher; b. Wenzhou, Zhejiang, China, Dec. 16, 1938; came to the U.S., 1987; d. Jing Ye and Suxin Li; m. Wenda Shen, Aug. 3, 1962 (div. Nov. 1995); children: Jiong, Han, Lu. BS, Peking U., Beijing, 1960, MS, 1962. Asst. Inst. Electronics, Chinese Acad. Sci., Beijing, 1962-64; asst. prof. Shanghai Inst. Optics & Fine Mechanics, Chinese Acad. Sci., 1964-85, assoc. prof., 1985-89; rsch. fellow Coll. Medicine, U. Fla., Gainesville, 1987-89, asst., 1989-90; assoc. scientist N.E. Deaconess Hosp., Harvard Med. Sch., Boston, 1990-94; scientist R&D Instrumentation Lab., Lexington, Mass., 1994—. Co-author: Pulse and CW Lasers, 1977, Lasers in Cardiovascular Medicine and Surgery, 1990; contbr. over 40 articles to profl. jours. Recipient Outstanding Achievement award in sci. and tech. Shanghai City Govt., 1982; grantee A. Ward Ford Meml. Inst., 1990-94. Mem. Am. Assn. for Clin. Chemistry, Optical Soc. China, Laser Soc. Shanghai. Achievements include patents for optical fiber coupler and power supply for laser flashlamp; applications of laser to medical areas; improvements of related laser devices; optical and spectroscopic studies in animal models. Office: Instrumentation Lab 526 Route 303 Orangeburg NY 10962-1309

YE, GAO-XIANG, physicist, educator; b. Chang Xin, Zhejiang, China, July 25, 1958; s. Yin Ye and Sun-nan Zhang; m. Hui-li Wang, May 26, 1985; 1 child. Bachelor's degree, Hangzhou (China) U., 1982, Master's degree, 1988; PhD, Zhejiang U., 1994. Lectr. Hangzhou U., 1988-92, assoc. prof., 1993-94, prof., 1995—, vice dir. dept. physics, 1994-95, dir., 1996-99; vice dean Coll. Sci. Zhejiang U., 1999—. Contbr. articles to profl. jours. Named Excellent Young Scientist, Zhejiang Province Govt., 1997. Mem. Chinese Phys. Soc. Avocations: classical music, botany. Office: Zhejiang U, Dept Physics, 310028 Zhejiang China

YE, JIANQIAO, applied mechanics and structural engineering educator, researcher; b. Tongcheng, Anhui, China, Oct. 11, 1957; arrived in U.K., 1989; s. Tang and Ruyu Sun Ye; m. Qin Wang, Aug. 2, 1986; 1 child, Helen Xiaomeng. B of Engring., Hefei U. Tech., 1982, M of Engring., 1986; PhD, U. Wales, Cardiff, 1993. Chartered engr. Farm worker Nankou, Tongcheng, China, 1975-77; lectr. Hefei (China) U. Tech., 1982-89, Leeds (England) U., 1995—; vis. prof. Hefei U. Tech., 2000—; cons. aerospace industry. Contbr. articles to profl. jours. Rsch. fellow Aston U., Birmingham, England, 1989-90, U. Nottingham (Eng.), 1992-94; recipient Mech. and Manufactural Industry prize The Ministry of China, 1995, Petroleum Divsn. award ASME, 1996. Mem. Royal Aero. Soc., Chinese Soc. Theoretical and Applied Mechs., Inst. for Learning and Tchg. in High Edn. Office: U Leeds Sch Civil Engring, Leeds LS2 9JT, England

YE, MENG, engineer, materials researcher; b. Jinghua, Zhejiang, China, Dec. 30, 1964; s. Birong and Zhifang (Xu) Y.; m. Hangling Hu; 1 child, Hao. B, Jiangsu Inst. Tech., Zhenjiang, China, 1984; M, Shanghai Jiaotong U., 1987, Mie U., Tsu, Japan, 1996; PhD, Mie U., Tsu, Japan, 1999. Lectr. Zhejiang Inst. of Tech., Hangzhou, China, 1987-93; engr. Takayasu Indsl. Corp., Yokkaichi, Japan, 1999—; pres. CNJP Tech., Jinghua, Zhejiang, China, 2000—, Tsu, Japan, 2000—. Contbr. articles to profl. jours. Mem. SPIE (Best Student Paper 1998). Avocations: music, swimming. Home: Ishindencho 167 R2-13, Tsu 514-0114, Japan Office: Takayasu Indsl Corp, Kusucho Kitakomitsuka 397, Yokkaichi 510-0103, Japan

YE, MIN, researcher; b. Qianshan, China, June 19, 1960; s. Zaihe and Yehui (Zhang) Y.; m. Feng Jian; children: Feng, Feng Shuo. BS, Anhui U., Hefei, China, 1982; MS, U. Scis. & Tech, Hefei, China, 1986; DS, U. Libre, Brussels, 1994. Lectr. physics dept. Anhui U., Hefei, China, 1985-89; rschr. U. Libre, Brussels, 1995—. Contbr. articles to profl. jours. Vis. scholar U. Libre, 1990-94. Office: Industrial Chemistry, U Libre Bruxelles CP165/63, B-1050 Brussels Belgium

YE, RONGBIN, researcher; b. Wuwei, Anhui, China, Nov. 10, 1965; parents Shihua Ye and Meiji Zhuo; m. Qian Chen, May 9, 1999. BS, East China Normal U., Shanghai, 1989; M of Engring., Nanjing U. Aeronautics/Astro., Nanking, China, 1995; D of Engring., Iwate U., Morioka, Japan, 1999. Cert. engr. Asat. Shanghai Radio Ltd., Co., 1989-92; engr. Shenzhen (China) Telcom Ltd., Co., 1995-96; rschr. Iwate Prefecture Joint-Rsch. Project/Region Intensive Japan Sci. and Tech. Corp., Morioka, 1999—. Mem. Globe and Citizens, Morioka, 1996—. Mem. Japan Applied Physics Soc. Avocations: reading, bridge, China chess. Fax: 81 19 631 1610. E-mail: ye@iwate-techno.com. Home: 105 Yumikon, 10-11, Nishishitadai Cho, Morioka Iwate 020-0065, Japan Office: Iwate Adv Sci/Tech Rsch Ctr, 3-35-2 Iioka Shinden, Morioka Iwate 020-0852, Japan

YE, SANYU, software engineer; b. Zhouning, Fujian, China, Jan. 26, 1963; arrived in Norway, 1998; parents Xuexin Ye and Xiuyun Hu; m. Qinglan Wu, Feb. 7, 1987; children: Julie Yuqing, David Huawei. BSc, U. Sci. and Tech. China, Hefei, Anhui, 1983; MSc, Fed. Inst. Tech., Zurich, Switzerland, 1986, PhD, 1992. Rsch. asst. Fed. Inst. Tech., Zurich, 1987-92; rsch. scientist Rsch. Ctr. for Marine Geoscis. U. Kiel, Germany, 1992-98; sr. geophysicist Petroleum Geo-Svc., Oslo, Norway, 1998-99; sr. software engr. Accept Data Norge AS, Oslo, 1999—; cons. Petroleum Geo-Svc., Oslo. Author: (book) Crustal Structure Beneath the Central Swiss Alps Derived from Seismic Refraction Data, 1992; contbr. articles to profl. jours. Scholar Swiss Govt., 1985, Fed. Inst. Tech., 1987. Mem. Soc. Exploration Geophysicists, Am. Geophys. Union. Avocations: reading, badminton, bicycling.

YE, SHITAI, allergist, educator; b. Suzhou, Jiangsu, China, Nov. 17, 1926; s. Fengxian Ye and Huizhen Yen; m. YuQin Zhen, Nov. 10, 1954; children: Meng, Wei, Jing. BA, St. John's U., Shanghai, China, 1949, MD, 1952. Med. diplomate. Resident physician Peking Union Med. Coll. Hosp., Beijing, 1952-59, cons. physician, 1959-72, dep. dept. chief, 1972-82, dept. chief, 1982-93, assoc. prof., 1978-83, prof., 1983—. Author: Allergic Diseases, 1983; chief editor: Practical Allergy, 1987, Chinese Allergenic Pollen, 1988, An Atlas on Chinese Allergenic Pollen, 1989, China Allergenic Aromycology, 1992, A National Survey on Chinese Allergenic Pollens, 1991, A National Survey on Chinese Allergenic Molds, 1994, Allergology, 1997. Fellow Am. Acad. Allergy and Immunology (emeritus); mem. China Allergology Soc. (pres. 1986—), Am. Acad. Otolaryngologic Allergy (hon.). Avocations: reading, music, traveling. Office: Dept Allergy, PUMC Hosp, Beijing 100730, China

YE, WEICHUN, information scientist, educator; b. Shanghai, May 10, 1945; arrived in Singapore, 1994; s. Jiaju Ye and Junxuan Yuan; m. Meiping Wu, Feb. 4, 1970; 1 child, Xiaofeng. BSc, Fu-Dan U., Shanghai, 1967; MSc, Jiao Tong U., Shanghai, 1982. Engr. Shanghai Elec. Equipment Co., Shanghai, 1967-82; assoc. prof. Jiao Tong U., Shanghai, 1982—; mem. tech. staff Nat. U. Singapore, 1994—. Inventor in field. Office: Data Storage Inst, 10 Kent Ridge Crescent, Singapore 117608, Singapore

YE, XIU, mathematician, educator; b. Wuhan, China, May 17, 1957; s. Zizao and Guolin (Ye) Z.; m. Yijun Ding, Mar. 14, 1957; 1 child, Don. MS in Math., U. Pitts., 1987, MSME, 1991, PhD in Math., 1990. Lectr. U. Pitts., 1989-90, postdoctoral fellow, 1991; asst. prof. U. Ark., Little Rock, 1991-96; assoc. prof. U. Ark., 1996-99, prof., 1999—. Contbr. articles to profl. jours. Mem. Am. Math. Soc., Soc. of Indsl. Applied Math. Office: Dept Math U Ark 2801 S University Ave Little Rock AR 72204-1000

YE, XUDONG, electrical engineering educator; b. Quzhou, Zhejiang, China, Feb. 4, 1967; s. Youshun Ye and Ganqiu Jin; m. Qiong Lin. B Engring., Zhejiang U., China, 1989, M Engring., 1991, D Engring., 1994. Postdoctoral worker Zhejiang U., 1994-96, assoc. prof., 1996—. Contbr. articles to profl. jours. Avocations: reading, music, sports. Office: Dept Elec Engring, Yu Gu Rd # 20, Hangzhou Zhejiang 310027, China

YE, YIMIN, research scientist; b. Yiwu, Zhejiang, China, Nov. 21, 1958; s. Zhichang Ye and Jiangxiang Jing; m. Wei Zhang; 1 child, Qing Ye. BSc, Zhejiang (China) Fisheries U., 1982; PhD in Fisheries, U. London, 1994. Lectr. Zhejiang Fisheries U., 1982-87; prof. Shanghai (China) Fisheries U., 1994-96; rsch. scientist Kuwait Inst. for Sci. Rsch., Salmiya, 1996—. Mem. Asia Fisheries Soc., China Fisheries Soc. Office: Kuwait Inst Sci Rsch, PO Box 1638, 22017 Salmiya Kuwait

YE, YIMING, computer scientist, researcher; b. Xian, Shaanxi, China, Feb. 14, 1963; came to the U.S., 1997; s. Jizhong Ye and Chu Ying Wang. BS, Huazhong U. Sci. & Tech., Wuhan, China, 1985; MS, Chinese Acad. Sci., Beijing, 1988; PhD, U. Toronto, Ont., Can., 1997. Rschr. Chinese Acad. Sci., Beijing, 1988-91; postdoctoral rsch. fellow U. Toronto, 1996-97; rsch. staff mem. IBM T.J. Watson Rsch. Ctr., Yorktown Heights, N.Y., 1997—. Assoc. editor Electronic Commerce Rsch. Jour., 1999—; contbr. chpt. to book. Open fellow U. Toronto, 1991-93, rsch. fellow Ctr. for Advanced Studies IBM C. Achievements include provided a way of calculating length, area and volume of a geometric entity without analytical expression; provided a method for knowledge re-organization in machine translations; provided an object search algorithm; provided a people tracking algorithm. Avocation: travel. Office: IBM TJ Watson Rsch Ctr PO Box 704 Yorktown Heights NY 10598-0704

YE, YUNXIU, physics educator; b. Shanghai, Sept. 13, 1938; d. Yuheng Ye and Xuying Ting; m. Chenguo Xiao, Jan. 20, 1968; children: Yanyang Xiao, Beixing Ye. Grad., U. Sci. and Tech. of China, Beijing, 1965. Prof. U. Sci. and Tech. of China, Beijing, 1965—; vis. scholar U. Paris VI and VII, 1986, Ctr. Nuclear of Strasbourg, France, 1989, LBL, Berkeley, Calif., 1989-90, 91, CERN, Geneva, 1992. Contbr. articles to profl. jours. Recipient rsch. prize Acad. Cinica, Hefei, 1979, 81, Anhui Province, 1999. Mem. Nuclear Phys. Soc., High Energy Phys. Soc. Avocations: table tennis, Chinese writing, travel. Home: 96 Jin Zhai Rd Apt 59 #202, Anhui Hefei 230026, China Office: U Sci and Tech of China, Dept Modern Physics, Anhui Hefei 230026, China

YEADON, TAMMY PAMELA, information specialist; b. Bayonne, N.J., Feb. 3, 1967; d. Tom and Betty Yeadon. BS in Polymer and Plastics Engring., U. Detroit, 1989; MLS, Rutgers U., 1994. Engr. Whirlpool Corp., Benton Harbor, Mich., 1988, Ford Motor Co., Detroit, 1989-90, MedTech Group, South Plainfield, N.J., 1991; quality assurance analyst Block Drug, Jersey City, N.J., 1992-93; info. mgr. John Brown, Bridgewater, N.J., 1994-97; tech. knowledge specialist A.T. Kearney, N.Y.C., 1998—; computer cons. Tyrell the Collection, Linden, N.J., 1991—; libr. cons. The Penn of N.Y., 1998-99. Tutor Literacy Vols. of Am., Elizabeth, N.J., 1993; vol. Gay Men's Health Crisis, N.Y.C., 1993. Mem. ALA, Am. Soc. of Info. Scis., Spl. Libr. Assn.

YEAGER, ANSON ANDERS, writer, former columnist and newspaper editor; b. Salt Lake City, June 5, 1919; s. Charles Franklin and Elise Marie (Thingelstad) Y.; m. Ada May Bidwell, Sept. 10, 1944; children: Karen Ann, Anson Anders, Harry H., Terry Douglas, Ellen Elise. BS, S.D. State U., Brookings, 1947; LLD, Dakota State Coll., Madison, S.D., 1972; D of Pub. Svc. (hon.) S.D. State U., 1991. Printer's devil, linotype operator Faith Ind. and Gazette (S.D.), 1935-38; printer S.D. State U., 1940-41; staff writer Argus Leader, Sioux Falls, S.D., 1947-55, Sunday editor, 1955-60, exec. editor, 1961-77, assoc. editor, 1978-84, editor editorial page, 1961-84, columnist, 1984-98, author Travel articles and commentary; lectr. dept. journalism U. S.D., 1953-55. Contbr. World Book Ency., 1966-84. Bd. dirs. Sioux Falls Devel. Found., 1967; bd. dirs. S.D. State U. Found., 1987-99, chmn., 1988-89; dir. Sioux council Boy Scouts Am., Sioux Falls, 1967-72, v.p., 1970-72; bd. dirs. Boys' Club of Sioux Falls, 1966-68. Capt. U.S. Army, 1942-46, 50-52; lt. col. Res. (ret.). Decorated Army Commendation medal; recipient Editorial Excellence award William Allen White Found., 1976; Disting. Alumni award S.D. State U., 1980; Friend of Augustana Coll. award Augustana Coll. Alumni Assn., 1980; Ralph D. Casey Minn. award for Disting. Svc. in Journalism U. Minn., 1981, Eminent Service award East River Elec. Power Coop., 1984, Mass Communications award S.D. State U., 1985, Disting. Svc. award S.D. Press Assn., 1988, Les Helgeland Community Svc. award S.D. AP Mng. Editors, 1985, named to Newsman of Yr., 1978, South Dakota A.H. Pankow award, 1995; named to S.D. Newspaper Hall of Fame, 1994, South Dakota Hall of Fame, 1998; recipient Jerome J. Lohr award S.D. State U. Found. Mem. Sioux Falls Area C. of C. (dir. 1967-70), Am. Soc. Newspaper Editors, Soc. Profl. Journalists, Rotary. Republican. Methodist.

YEE, HENRY CHAN MYINT, cardiologist; b. Kyaukme, Burma, Dec. 26, 1961; s. Shaw Sing Yee and Kwan Yee Cho; m. Angela Dong Li Lii; 1 child, Stephanie. Diploma in biology, Mandalay Gen. Hosp., 1986; MBBS, Inst. Medicine, Mandalay, 1985. Intern Mandalay Gen. Hosp., 1985-86; pvt. practice Mandalay, 1986-92; rschr. in cardiology Albert Einstein Coll. Medicine, Bronx, N.Y., 1993-94; resident in internal medicine Seton Hall U. Grad. Sch. Med. Edn., Elizabeth, N.J., 1994-97; fellow in cardiology Kasier Permanente, L.A., 1997-2000. Mem. Am. Coll. Physicians, Am. Coll. Cardiology.

YEE, KUO CHIANG, neuroscientist, neurologist; b. Shanghai, Jan. 18, 1935; came to U.S., 1981; s. Hun and Wang J. Yee; m. Pei Ching Cai, Oct. 1, 1954; children: Hsiao Chiang, Hsiao Pei. MD, Zuzhen Med. Sch., Cheking, China, 1954; MS, U. Wash., 1983; PhD, U. B.C., Vancouver, Can., 1992. Prof. U. B.C., Vancouver, 1992-93; dir. Neurosci. Med. Ctr., Seattle, 1981—; pres. AmeriTek, Inc., Seattle, 1993—. Author: Biological Effects and Dosimetry of Nonionizing Radiation, 1982; contbr. numerous articles to profl. jours. Achievements include development of advanced rapid in-vitro immunodiagnostic and clinical chemical reagent systems diagnostic test kits. Home: 7338 23rd Ave NE Seattle WA 98115-5806 Office: Neurosci Med Ctr 7030 35th Ave NE Seattle WA 98115-5917

YEE, STEVE, artist; b. Sacramento, Jan. 22, 1953; s. J. Bok Yee. Art dir. Photo Design Studios, Sacramento, 1974-76, Griswold Advt., Sacramento, 1976-79, Hubbard Advt., Sacramento, 1979-82, Corcoran Co., Sacramento, 1982-84; artist State of Calif., Sacramento, 1984-88; tchr. Argonaunt Ctr., Sacramento, 1976; program advisor info. tech. and multimedia, U. Calif., Davis; mem. Calif. State Personnel Task Force for Graphic Artists. Author: The World Alters as We Walk in it, 1976, Art in the Third Century, 1976. Active Religious Community for Peace, Sacramento, Am. Soc. for Aesthetics, N.Y.C. Named Selected Artist Palais Des Congres, Paris, 1975, Centro De Arte y Commicacion, Buenos Aires, 1979, Bradford Mus., Yorkshire, Eng., 1982, U. Man., Winnipeg, 1984; recipient Nat. Sch. Pub. Rels. Assn. award for web site design, 1997, Am.'s Disting. Achievement award for electronic media, 1998, Nat. Sch. Pub. Rels. Assn. award for electronic media, 1998, CalSPRA award for web site design, 1998, 99. Democrat. Baptist. Home: PO Box 188499 Sacramento CA 95818-8499

YEGGE, ROBERT BERNARD, law educator, dean; b. Denver, June 17, 1934; s. Ronald Van Kirk and Fairy (Hill) Y. A.B. magna cum laude, Princeton U., 1956; M.A. in Sociology, U. Denver, 1958, J.D., 1959. Bar: Colo. 1959, D.C. 1978. Ptnr. Yegge, Hall and Evans, Denver, 1959-78; with Harding Shultz & Downs successor to Nelson and Harding, 1979—; prof. U. Denver Coll. Law, 1965—, dean, 1965-77, 97-98, dean emeritus, 1977—; asst. to pres. Denver Post, 1971-75; v.p., exec. dir. Nat. Ctr. Preventive Law, 1986-91. Author: Colorado Negotiable Instruments Law, 1960, Some Goals; Some Tasks, 1965, The American Lawyer: 1976, 1966, New Careers in Law, 1969, The Law Graduate, 1972, Tomorrow's Lawyer: A Shortage and Challenge, 1974, Declaration of Independence for Legal Education, 1976. Mng. trustee Denver Ctr. for Performing Arts, 1972-75; chmn. Colo. Coun. Arts and Humanities, 1968-80, chmn. emeritus, 1980—; mem. scholar selection com. Henry Luce Found., 1975—; Active nat. and local A.R.C., chmn. Denver region, 1985-88; trustee Denver Symphony Soc., Inst. of Ct. Mgmt., Denver Dumb Friends League, 1992—, chmn. 2000—, Met. Denver Legal Aid Soc., 1994-99, Colo. Legal Svcs., 2000—, Colo. Acad.; chmn. Colo. Prevention Ctr., 2000—; trustee, vice chmn. Nat. Assembly State Arts Agys.; vice chmn. Mexican-Am. Legal Edn. and Def. Fund, 1970-76. Recipient Disting. Svc. award Denver Jr. C. of C., 1965; Harrison Tweed award Am. Assn. Continuing Edn. Adminstrs., 1985, Alumni Faculty award U. Denver, 1993. Mem. ABA (chmn. lawyers conf. 1987-88, chmn. accreditation commn. for legal asst. programs 1980-90, standing com. legal assts. 1987-92, 98—, standing com. delivery legal svcs. 1992-95, com. on Gavel award 1995-98, del. to jud. adminstrn. coun. 1989-95, Robert B. Yegge award 1996), Law and Soc. Assn. (life, pres. 1965-70), Colo. Bar Assn. (bd. govs. 1965-77, 97-98), Denver Bar Assn., D.C. Bar Assn., Am. Law Inst., Am. Judicature Soc. (bd. dirs. 1968-72, 75-85, Herbert Harley award 1985), Am. Acad. Polit. and Social Sci., Am. Sociol. Soc., Assn. Am. Law Schs., Order St. Ives, Phi Beta Kappa, Beta Theta Pi, Phi Delta Phi, Alpha Kappa Keta, Omicron Delta Kappa. Home: 3472 S Race St Englewood CO 80110-3138 Office: U Denver Coll Law 1900 Olive St Denver CO 80220-1857

YEGOROV, VALERY PAVLOVICH, heraldic expert and artist; b. Sochi, Russia, Oct. 28, 1950; s. Paul Grigorievich and Nina Ivanovna (Volovikova) Y.; m. Anthonina Yegovov, 1973 (div. 1979); 1 child, Andrew; m. Larisa Yegorov, 1980 (div. 1986; 1 child, Anne; m. Natalie Rostislavovna Lenskaya, Jan. 24, 1989; 1 child, Ilya. MS in Nav., Rostov Marine Coll., 1973; MA in English Lang., Taganrog Tchrs. Tng. Inst., 1987. Seaman, navigator, chief mate, world-wide, 1968-80; various positions including tchr. English, 1980-90; head Collegium Heraldicum Russiae, Monino, Russia, 1990—; founder, keeper Matricula Armorum of CHR. Co-author: Civic Arms of Russia, 1997; contbr. numerous articles to heraldic publs.; co-editor Gerboved, Russian heraldic mag., 1991—; artist for numerous coats of arms;. Capt. Russian Navy Res. Decorated companion, chevalier, grand comdr. and grand prior of numerous internat. chivalric orders. Mem. Russian Heraldy Soc. (v.p.), also numerous heraldic socs. and instns. Russian Orthodox. Avocations: history, arts, foreign languages. Office: Collegium Heraldicum Russ, Sanatorium 5, 141152 Monino Russia

YEGOROV, YEGOR EUGENEVICH, biologist; b. Moscow, May 16, 1958; s. Eugeny Petrovich and Diana Petrovna (Dolotova) Y.; m. Irina Nikolaevna Nikitinskaya, Jan. 31, 1987; children: Anton, Alena. MS, Moscow Med. U., 1981; PhD, Engelhardt Inst. Molec. Biol., Moscow, 1986. Jr. rsch. fellow Engelhardt Inst. Molecular Biology, Moscow, 1984-87, rsch. fellow, 1987-96, sr. rsch. fellow, 1996—; postdoct. fellow Imperial Cancer Rsch. Fund, London, 1989; lectr. Physico-Tech. Inst., Moscow, 1990—. Contbr. articles to profl. jours. Grantee Internat. Sci. Found., 1992, 94; recipient Travel award Internat. Fedn. Cell Biology, 1996, diploma best jour. publ. Internat. Academical, 1997, Russian Ministry Sci. & Tech., 1999. Mem. Moscow Soc. Cell Biology. Office: Engelhardt Inst Molec Biol, 32 Vavilov Str, 117984 Moscow Russia

YEH, AN-I, food engineering educator, researcher; b. Hsin-Ying, Taiwan, Nov. 16, 1953; s. Chuin-Ming and Chun-Yu (Lu) Y.; m. Yueh-Ing Chang, Aug. 19, 1990; children: Sean T., Hana. BS, Chung-Hsing U., Taichung, Taiwan, 1977; MS, Mont. State U., Bozeman, 1983, PhD, 1986. Sales engr. Shei-Tai Co., Kaushiung, Taiwan, 1979-80; rschr. Pres. Co., Tainan, Taiwan, 1980-81; rsch. assoc. Rutgers U., Piscataway, N.J., 1986-87; assoc. prof. Nat. Taiwan U., Taipei, 1987-92, prof. food engring., 1992—; cons. U.S. Grain Coun., Taipai, 1992—, Fu-Sow Co., Taichung, 1993-94, Pres. Co., Tainan, 1996; reviewer Dept. Edn., Taipei, 1996. Author: Food Extrusion Science and Technology, 1992; contbr. articles to profl. jours. 2d lt. Chinese Army, 1977-79. Recipient Grad. Achievement award Mont. State U., 1983; named Outstanding Rschr., Nat. Sci. Coun., Taipei, 1994. Mem. Inst. for Food Technologists, Am. Assn. Cereal Chemists, Chinese Inst. for Food Technologists. Achievements include modernization of the process for producing traditional Chinese foods, including rice noodle and salted egg yolk; development method of selecting solvents for extractive distillation. Home: 2F No 60-5 Chang-Hsin St, 106 Taipei Taiwan Office: Nat Taiwan U, 59 Ln 144 Keelung Rd Sect 4, 106 Taipei Taiwan

YEH, CHANG-TUNG, government official; b. Foochow, Fukien, China, Aug. 2, 1929; s. Hsuan and Pei-Yin (Liu) Y.; m. Jung Chao, Oct. 10, 1935; children: Der-Lan, Der-Hwa, Der-Chuang. BS, Naval Acad., Taiwan, 1949; MS, Naval War Coll., U.S., 1967. Commd. Taiwanese Armed Forces, advanced through grades to admiral, 1986—; comdr. Destroyer 17, 1969-70; vice-chief of gen. staff Min. of Def., 1982-88; comdr. in chief Naval Forces, Taiwan, 1988-92; supt. Armed Forces U., 1992-94; strategics advisor Office of the Pres., Taipei, 1994—. Pub. Armed Forces Mo., 1992. Decorated Medal of Precious Tripod, Govt. of Taiwan, 1982, Medal of Cloud and Banner, 1986, Medal of Tai-Tung, 1988. Mem. Chinese Soc. for Mil. History Studies (chmn. bd. 1998—). Home: 3F #3 Lane 31, Wohlong St, Taipei Taiwan

YEH, CHUNG-HSING, business systems educator; b. Chiayi, Taiwan, July 19, 1955; arrived in Australia, 1985; s. Feng-Chun and Pei-Hua (Liu) Y.; m. Maggie Mei-Chu Chang, May 25, 1980; children: Paul Sung-Hao, Arthur Sung-Yang. BS, Nat. Cheng Kung U., Tainan, Taiwan, 1977, M in Mgmt. Sci., 1982; PhD, Monash U., Clayton, Australia, 1988. Cert. higher certification in mgmt.; cert. in water transp. mgmt. Engr. Nan Ya Plastic Corp., Taiwan, 1979-80; rsch. fellow Transp. Planning Bd., Taipei, 1982-83; sr. ofcl. Yangming Marine Transport Corp., Taiwan, 1983-85; tutor Monash U., Clayton, 1986-88, lectr., 1989-93, sr. lectr., 1994-99, prof., 2000—; vis. assoc. prof. Nat. Cheng Kung U., Tainan, 1992-93, vis. scholar, 1995-96; cons. Overseas Project Corp. Victoria, Melbourne, 1994, Corrs Chambers Westgarth, Melbourne, 1995-97; vis. prof., 1989-99. Contbr. articles to profl. jours. 2nd lt. Army Engring. Sch., 1977-79, Taipei. Rsch. grantee Nat. Sci. Coun., Taiwan, 1992, Spl. Project grantee Nat. Sci. Coun., Taiwan, 1995, 98, 99; Monash grad. scholar Monash U., Australia, 1985-88. Mem. IEEE Computer Soc., Australian Computer Soc., Australian Prodn. and Inventory Control Soc., Internat. Fuzzy Sys. Assn., Inst. for Ops. Rsch. and the Mgmt. Scis. Avocations: tennis, chess. Home: 39 Gordon Rd, Mount Waverley VIC 3149, Australia Office: Sch Bus Sys, Monash Univ, Clayton VIC 3168, Australia

YEH, JOHN SHO-JU, neurosurgeon, educator; b. Taipei, Taiwan, Feb. 16, 1964; s. Neng-Che Yeh and Verna (Lin) Y.; m. Nai-Yu Wang, Dec. 29, 1994. BA with honours, Cambridge (Eng.) U., 1987, MB, BChir, 1989, MA, 1991. House officer Addenbrookes Hosp., Cambridge, 1990-91; sr. house officer Royal Victoria Infirmary, Newcastle-upon-Tyne, Eng., 1991, North Staffordshire Royal Infirmary, Stoke-on-Trent, Eng., 1991-94, Frenchay Hosp., Bristol, Eng., 1994; rsch. registrar Mid. Ctr. for Neurosurgery and Neurology, Birmingham, Eng., 1994-97; specialist registrar Queen Elizabeth Neurosci. Ctr., Birmingham, 1997—; hon. clin. lectr. Birmingham U., 1994—. Contbr. articles to med. jours., including Brit. Med. Jour., Clin. Neurology and Neurosurgery, Brit. Jour. Neurosurgery, European Spine Jour. Fellow Royal Coll. Edinburgh; mem. Soc. Brit. Neurol. Surgeons (assoc.), Brit. Cervical pine Soc. Avocations: computing, music, squash, jogging. Home: 11 Metfield Croft, Birmingham B17 0NN, England Office: Queen Elizabeth Neurosci Ctr, Edgebaston, Birmingham B15 2TH, England

YEH, JUNG-HUA, senior mechanical engineer; b. Taipei, Taiwan, Nov. 3; parents Min-An and Hsiu-Ming Y.; m. Shu-Ting Tsai, Nov. 7, 1987; 4 children. BA, Nat. Taipei Inst. Technology, 1984; MS, U. Mo., 1993, PhD, 1997. Mech. engr. Lotun Technic Co., Taipei, 1986-87, Logitech, Inc., Taipei, 1987-88, YFY Paper Mfg. Co., Taipei, 1988-90, Pro-Tech. Engrs. & Constructors Co., Taipei, 1990-91; sr. mech. engr. prediction maintenance team Inteplast Group, Ltd., Lolita, Tex., 1997—; worked on equipment failure detection and performance by using advanced vibration techniques. Christian Fellowship chmn., deacon. Recipient Disting. Leadership award in field of System Failure Detection and Prevention. Mem. AAAS, Soc. Automotive Engrs., ASME, Sigma Xi. Discovered dominant frequency shift when a bolted connection is slightly loosened. Virtual spring element to model contact conditions. Expertise includes detection of machine and structure assemblies with bolt looseness, failure diagnosis for civil and mechanical structures, multi-body contact condition modeling, fixture clamping condition modeling and monitoring, mechanical drive and transmission component design, hybris control of seismic structures. Avocations: reading, research, jogging, hiking. E-mail: jyehtx@yahoo.com.

YEH, KUO HSING, bank executive; b. Taipei, Taiwan, Republic of China, Feb. 1, 1932; m. Hsiu-Mei Yeh Tsang. BA, Nat. Taiwan U., 1954. Exec. v.p. Hwa Nan Comml. Bank, Ltd., Taiwan, 1955-81; pres. Banking Inst. Republic China, 1981-88; CEO Fin. Info. System Group Ministery Fin., Taiwan, 1984-88; pres. Chang Hwa Comml. Bank Ltd., Taiwan, 1988-94; chmn. Taipeibank, Taipei, 1994-97, Taiwan First Investment & Trust Co Ltd, Taipei, 1998, Cathay United Bank Co Ltd., Tapei, Taiwan, 1998—. Author: Theory and Practice of Lending Management, 1980; editor: Practice of Bank's Consumer Loan, 1983. Recipient Disting. Fin. Staffer award Ministry Fin., Taipei, 1974. Mem. Banker's Assn. Taiwan (chmn. 1988-92), Banker's Assn. Taipei (chmn. 1992-97), Taiwan U. Alumni Assn. (mng. dir. Taipei chpt. 1994), Taiwan U. Alumni Club, Taipei Yuen-Shan Club. Home: 3 Fl No 432 Chi Lin Rd, Taipei 104, Taiwan Office: Cathay United Bank Co Ltd, 218 Sec 2 Tun Hwa S Rd, Taipei 104, Taiwan

YEH, LUN-SHU RAY, electrochemist; b. Taoyuan, Taiwan, Oct. 2, 1946; came to U.S., 1970; s. Ming-Ching and Lan-Kwei Yeh; m. Ming Mavis Lu; children: Leon Allen, Rick Norman. BS in Engring., Cheng-Kung U., Tainan, Taiwan, 1969; MS, U. Ky., 1972; PhD, U. Tex., 1976. Postdoctoral fellow Rice U., Houston, 1977; rsch. chemist Allied Chem. Corp., Morristown, N.J., 1978-83; sr. rsch. chemist Allied Signal Inc., Morristown, 1983-87; scientist Philips Electronic Instruments Co., Mahwah, N.J., 1988-92, sr. scientist, 1993-97; sr. scientist Edax Internat. Co. subs. Philips Electronics Instruments Co., Mahwah, 1993-97, Edax Inc., Mahwah, 1998—. Contbr. numerous articles to profl. pubs. Inventor award Allied Signal Inc., 1987. Mem. IEEE, Electrochem. Soc., Phi Kappa Phi, Phi Lambda Upsilon. Achievements include 5 patents in areas of bipolar batteries, solid state x-ray detectors, cryostat designs. Office: Edax Inc 85 Mckee Dr Mahwah NJ 07430-2121

YEH, MING-NENG, obstetrician, gynecologist; b. Taiwan, Oct. 13, 1938; came to U.S., 1966; s. Chao-Chieh and Pu-Tseng (Song) Y.; m. Lisa Lie-Yu Lin, Oct. 18, 1965; children: Angela, Rubina, Noreen, Janet. MD, Nat. Taiwan U., Taipei, 1964. Diplomate Am. Bd. Ob-Gyn. Intern Johnston-Willis Hosp., 1966-67; resident Bklyn.-Cumberland Hosp., 1967-68, St. Luke's Hosp. Ctr., N.Y.C., 1968-71; fellow fetal medicine Columbia-Presbyn. Med. Ctr., N.Y.C., 1971-73, attending obstetrician, 1987—; clin. prof. Columbia U., N.Y.C., 1987—. Fellow N.Y. Acad. Medicine, N.Y. Acad. Sci.; mem. Am. Fertility Soc., Am. Inst. Ultrasound Medicine, Am. Coll. Ob-Gyn., N.Y. Obstet. Soc., N.Y. Gyn. Soc. Office: Columbia-Presbyn Med Ctr 161 Fort Washington Ave New York NY 10032-3713

YEH, MING-YANG, immunology educator; b. Taipei, Taiwan, Republic of China, May 13, 1950; s. Chin-Chih and San Mei (Peng) Y.; m. Chen-Chen Dai, Aug. 7, 1975; children: Hui-Chen, Chun-Hung, Hsin-Hung. MD, Nat. Defense Med. Ctr., Taipei, 1975; PhD, U. Wash., Seattle, 1981. Intern Tri-Svc Gen. Hosp., Taipei, 1974-75; teaching asst. Nat. Defense Med. Ctr., Taipei, 1975-77, assoc. prof., 1981-89; assoc. investigator Academia Sinica, Taipei, 1987-89; prof. Nat. Defense Med. Ctr., Taipei, 1989—; chief cancer rsch. lab. Tri-Svc. Gen. Hosp., Taipei, 1982-98; chmn. dept. microbiology & immunology Nat. Defense Med. Ctr., Taipei, 1992-95; sec. gen. steering com. faculty Nat. Defense Med. Ctr., 1985-86; exec. sec. Med. Oncology Tng. Program Inst. Biomed. Scis., Academia Sinica, Taiwan, 1987-90; exec. sec. Nat. Health Rsch. Inst., 1994-95; dean of faculties Nat. Defense Med. Ctr., Taipei, 1995-96; dir. Inst. Preventive Medicine, Nat. Def. Med. Ctr., Taipei, 1996-98; sec. gen. Chinese Immunology Soc., 1995-97—; assoc. dir. Cheng Hsin Med. Ctr., 1998—. Contbr. articles to profl. jours. Pres Chinese Student Assn., U. Wash., 1980; bd. dirs. Taiwan Allergy Found., Taipei, 1983—; bd. trustees Chen Tzong-Jen Immunology Found., Taipei, 1986—;

bd. dirs. Health Sci. Found., Taipei, 1996—, Formosa Cancer Found., Taipei, 1997—. Rsch. fellow Swedish Hosp. Med. Ctr., Seattle, 1986-87, Sr. Rsch. fellow Nat. Health Rsch. Inst., 1991-95; recipient Outstanding Svc. award Ministry Defense, Taipei, 1991, Outstanding Rsch. award Nat. Sci. Coun., Taipei, 1991, 92. Mem. Chinese Med. Assn., AAAS, Am. Assn. Cancer Rsch., N.Y. Acad. Sci., Clin. Immunology Soc., NIH Alumni Assn. (exec. sec. Taiwan chpt. 1992-95). Avocations: reading, collecting stone sculpture, hiking, folk songs, travel.

YEH, PATRICE ALAIN, geneticist, researcher; b. Saint-Denis Sur Seine, France, Jan. 24, 1958; s. Claude and Denise (Bouffard) Y.; m. Rosemary Louise Sousa, June 30, 1989; children: Celine, Lauren, Chloé. Diploma in engrng., Inst. Nat. Agr. Paris-Grignon, Paris, 1984; PhD in Microbiology, U. Toulouse, 1988. Rsch. scientist Genetica SA, Joinville, France, 1988-89; rsch. scientist yeast genetics Rhône-Poulenc Rorer Vitry, Vitry, France, 1989-93; rsch. fellow Rhône-Poulenc Rorer Gencell, Vitry, France, 1993-97, sr. rsch. fellow, 1997-98; co-dir. UMR 1582 Gustave Roussy Inst. Aventis Gencell, Villejuif, France, 1998—; vis. scientist MIT, 1985-86, Pasteur Inst., 1987. Contbr. articles to profl. jours. Mem. Am. Soc. Gene Therapy, Soc. Francaise Microbiology. Avocation: volleyball. E-mail: patrice.yeh@aventis.com. Home: 48 Allee la Pointe Genete, 91190 Gif Sur Yvette France Office: Aventis Gencell, 13 Quai Jules Guesdes, 94403 Vitry/Seine France

YEH, WEN LING, orthopaedist, consultant; b. Taipei, Taiwan, Jan. 28, 1961; s. Chen Gia Yeh and Hung Tung Chen; M. Win Ying Chen, July 14, 1987 (div. 1991); m. Su Ru Lin, Jan. 19, 1995; 3 children. MD, Taipei Med. Coll., 1987. Intern Vet. Gen. Hosp., Taipei, 1986-87; resident Father Fox Meml. Hosp., Tainan, Taiwan, 1987-88; resident Chan-Gung Meml. Hosp., Taipei, 1988-93, attending staff, 1993—; leader of arthroscope Cang-Gung Meml. Hosp., 1997—; med. com. Football Assn. of Taiwan, Taipei, 1993—, Athletic Assn. of Hsin-Ghu and Chia-Yi of Taiwan, 1997—; team physician Nat. Team of Football, Taipei, 1992—; panel doctor med. com. Asian Football Conf., Kula Lumpur, Malaysia, 1998—. Contbr. articles to profl. publs. Mem. Assn. of Chinese-Speaking Orthopedics (cons. 1998—), Orthopedic Assn. of Taipei, Arthroscopic Assn. of Taipei. Avocations: football, research. Home: Chan-Gung Village 310 4F, Taoyuan 333, Taiwan Office: Chan-Gung Meml Hosp, Fu-Hsin St No 5, Tao-Yuan 333, Taiwan

YEH, YING CHIN, electrical engineer; b. Tainan, Taiwan, June 1, 1945; came to U.S., 1978; s. Tso Hsueh and Ai Lien (Yen) Y.; m. Su Chin Lee, Oct. 24, 1972; children: Karen Y.C., Cindy S.C. BSEE, Nat. Cheng Kung U., 1967; MSEE, Nat. Taiwan U., 1970; PhDEE, U. Ottawa, Can., 1973. Indsl. postdoctoral fellow RCA Ltd. R&D Lab., Montreal, Can., 1973-76; sr. engr. Canadair Ltd., Montreal, 1976-78; sr. mem. tech. staff Otis Elevator Co. R&D Ctr., Farmington, Conn., 1978-81; assoc. tech. fellow The Boeing Co., Comml. Airplane Group, Seattle, 1981—; mem. IRIP working group on Dependable Computing and Fault Tolerance. V.p. Taiwanese Am. Citizen League, Seattle, 1993-95. Mem. IEEE, Taiwanese Assn. for Greater Seattle (bd. dirs. 1998—). Achievements include development in 7J7 Control System Performance Study for synchronous PFC and Autonomous ARINC 629 operation; development 777 flight controls ARINC 629 Bus Requirement; design and validation testing of 777 PFC (primary flight computer) redundancy management. Office: Boeing Comml Airplane Group PO Box 3707 Seattle WA 98124-2207

YEHOSHUA, ABRAHAM B., writer, comparative literature educator; b. Jerusalem, Dec. 9, 1936; s. Yaakov and Malka (Rosolio) Y.; m. Rivka Karni, June 14, 1960; children: Sivan, Gideon, Nahum. Grad. in Philosophy and Hebrew Lit., Hebrew U., Jerusalem; doctorate (hon.), Hebrew Union Coll., 1990. Gen. sec. World Union Jewish Students, Paris, France, 1963-67; dean students Haifa U., Israel, 1967-72, prof. comparative lit., 1972—; guest writer Saint Cross Coll., Oxford, Eng., 1975-76; guest prof. Harvard U., Cambridge, Mass., 1977, U. Chgo., 1988, 97, Stanford (Calif.) U., 1990, Princeton (N.J.) U., 1992. Author: (short stories) The Death of the Old Man, 1962, Facing the Forest, 1968, (essays) Between Right and Right, 1980; (plays) A Night in May, Last Treatments, Possessions, Night's Babies; (novella) At the Beginning of Summer 1970; (novels) The Lover, 1976, A Late Divorce, 1982 (Premio Internat. Flaino 1996), Five Seasons, 1986 (Torino Cavour prize 1994), Mr. Mani, 1990 (Booker prize 1992, Jewish Quaterly prize 1993), Open Heart, 1994; (film or stage) Three Days and a Child, The Lover, Continuing Silence of a Poet, At the Beginning of Summer, 1970, Facing the Forests, (novel) A Journey to the End of the Millennium, 1997, (book literary essays) The Moral Context of the Literary Text, 1997; editorial bd. Siman Krea, Tel-Aviv Review, Mifgash; mem. editl. bd. Keshet, 1966-74; contbr. stories to Massa, Haaretz, Keshet; books translated into 20 langs. Mem. bd. art Haifa Mcpl. Theatre; mem. Kibbutz Chatzerim; activist Israeli Peace Movement. With Israeli Army, 1954-57. Recipient Akum prize, 1961, Municipality of Ramat-Gan prize, 1968, Prime Min. prize, 1972, Brenner prize, 1983, Alterman prize, 1986, Bialik prize, 1989, Am. Nat. award 1990, 93, Israeli prize, 1995, Koret prize AP, 2000. Office: Haifa U Dept Gen Lit, Mount Carmel, 31999 Haifa Israel

YEL'CHENKO, VOLODYMYR YU, diplomat; b. Kyiv, Ukraine, June 27, 1959; s. Yuri N. Yelchenko and Albina I. Tarassenko; m. Iryna V. Korniyaka, June 20, 1981; 1 child, Olga. Third sec. MFA of Ukraine, Kyiv, 1981-83, second sec. 1983-86; second sec. Permanent Mission of Ukraine, N.Y.C., 1986-92; head of polit. divsn. UN Dept. MFA of Ukraine, 1992-92; civil affairs officer UN Protection Force, Croatia, 1993; deir. dept. of internat. orgns. MFA of Ukraine, 1993-97; amb., permanent rep. of Ukraine to the UN MFA of Ukraine, N.Y.C., 1997—. Avocations: music, soccer, tennis.

YELENICK, MARY THERESE, lawyer; b. Denver, May 17, 1954; d. John Andrew and Maesel Joyce (Reed) Y. B.A. magna cum laude, Colo. Coll., 1976; J.D. cum laude, Georgetown U., 1979. Bar: D.C. 1979, U.S. Dist. Ct. D.C. 1980, U.S. Ct. Appeals (D.C. cir.) 1981, N.Y. 1982, U.S. Dist. Ct. (so. and ea. dists.) N.Y. 1982, U.S. Supreme Ct. 1992, U.S. Ct. Appeals (5th cir.) 1995. Law clk. to presiding justices Superior Ct. D.C., 1979-81; ptnr. Chadbourne & Parke, LLP, N.Y.C., 1981—. Editor Jour. of Law and Policy Internat. Bus., 1978-79. Mem. Phi Beta Kappa. Democrat. Roman Catholic. Home: 310 E 46th St New York NY 10017-3002 Office: Chadbourne & Parke LLP 30 Rockefeller Plz Fl 31 New York NY 10112-0129

YELIN, ROBERT BRUCE, musician, recording artist, composer, lyricist; b. Yonkers, N.Y., Sept. 25, 1944; s. Paul and Libby (Watinsky) Y.; m. Harriet Ann Hunter, Mar. 22, 1980. Student, NYU, 1962-65. Jazz guitarist, performer, educator N.Y., 1962-80, Colo., 1981-85; pres. Arbee Why Music Publs., Colo., Conn., 1981-87; prof. jazz guitar studies U. Colo., Denver, 1982; pres. Chord Master Records, Colo., Conn., 1983-88; jazz performer, educator Conn., 1985-88; pvt. guitar tchr., 1962-88. Jazz guitarist (solo guitar albums) Night Rain, 1981 (Reviewer's Choice 1982), Talents of the Heart, 1990, Robert Yelin Plays the Music of Jobim & Brazil, 1999; (jazz trio album) Song for My Wife, 1983; performer N.Y. Jazz Guitar Festival, 1976, Breckenridge (Colo.) Jazz Festival, 1982, Winter Park (Colo.) Jazz Festival, 1983; (CD recordings), Bossa, Ballads and Blues Vols. 1-5, 1997, Welcome to my World, 1999, Enchanted, The Beauty of the 14-String Guitar, 1999; jazz clubs, concerts nationwide, 1962—; author: (with others) The Tal Farlow Jazz Guitar Method Book, 1973-74; contbg. editor Guitar Player mag., 1968-82, Frets mag. 1978-80; Wes Montgomery's Book, 1984-85(newsletter) The Jazz Guitar Soc. We. Australia, 1989—; contbg. cons., article writer Just Jazz Guitar, 1994—; arranger also; co-prodr. (videos) Legends of Jazz Guitar, vols. 1-3, 1995-96; commd. 1st 14-string archtop guitar. Donates audio and video tape recordings to music schs., colls., univs. and guitar socs. all over the world. Mem. Broadcast Musician, Inc. Club: Jazz Guitar Record Library and Club (pres. 1981—). Home and Office: 17709 Fieldbrook Cir N Boca Raton FL 33496-1534

YELISEEV, ALEXEI ARKADIEVICH, biochemist, researcher; b. Moscow, Nov. 3, 1959; s. Arkadii Aleksandrovich and Tatiana Georgievna (Sokolova) E.; m. Elena Dmitrievna Polonnikova, Aug. 20, 1985; children: Ekaterina, Tatiana. MS in Chemistry, Moscow State U., 1981; PhD in Biochemistry, Russian Acad. Scis., 1987. From trainee rschr. to sr. rschr. A.N. Bakh Inst. Biochemistry, Russian Acad. Scis., Moscow, 1981-92, sr. rschr., 1992—; vis. rsch. scientist U. Tex., Houston, 1993-99; sr. rsch. scientist Roche Vitamins, Inc., 1999—. Author: (chpt.) Biosynthesis of Corrinoids, 1993, Control of Photosystem Formation in Rhodobacter sphaeroides, 1998; contbr. articles to profl. jours. Rsch. fellow Alexander von Humboldt Stiftung, 1989-92, Internat. Union Biochemistry, 1992, Royal Soc. London, 1993; grantee Internat. Sci. Found., 1994-95. Mem. AAAS, Am. Soc. Microbiology, Russian Biochem. Soc. (lectureship 1987). Avocations: travelling, music, books. Office: Roche Vitamins Inc 340 Kingsland St Bldg 102 Nutley NJ 07110-1150

YELTSIN, BORIS NIKOLAYEVICH, Russian government official; b. Butka, Sverdlovsk, USSR, Feb. 1, 1931; s. Nikolai Ignatycvich and Klavdiya (Vassilyevna) Y.; m. Naina Iosifovna Girina, 1956; children: Yelena, Tatyana. Grad., Urals Poly. Inst., 1955. Mem. Communist Party Soviet Union, 1961-90; foreman, supt., sr. engr., head constrn. bd. Yuzhgorstroi trust, 1955-63; chief engr., head Sverdlovsk House-Bldg. Factory, 1963-68; dep. head, sec. Sverdlovsk Regional Party Com., 1968-76, First Sec., 1976—; mem. Presidium USSR Supreme Soviet, 1976-85; mem. cen. com. Communist Party Soviet Union, 1985-87; first dep. chmn. State Constrn. Com., Moscow, 1987-89; pres. Russian Republic, 1991-99. Author: Against the Grain, 1990, The Struggle for Russia, 1994. Recipient Order Service to the Fatherland of 1st Degree, Order of Lenin, Order of Red Banner of Labour (2), Badge of Honour, Royal Order of Peace and Justice, UNESCo, Shield of Freedom for Selflessness and Courage, U.S., Order of Grand Cross, Italy, Order of Malta; named Man of Yr., 1996, German Press. Avocations: tennis, volleyball, hunting, the cinema. E-mail: president@gov.ru. *

YEMELYANOV, SVYATOSLAV IGOREVICH, aeronautical engineer, research; b. Kharkov, Ukraine, Apr. 2, 1928; s. Igor Fedorovich and Galina Vacilievna (Lastochkina) Y.; m. Ludmila Vacilievna Mikhailik, Oct. 17, 1953; children: Eugene, Vladimir. Cert. in engring., Inst. Aviation Industry, Kharkov, 1954. Turner's apprentice Ry. Repair Plant, Tashkent, USSR, 1942-44; lab. attendant Inst. Aviation Industry, 1948-49, prof.'s asst., 1954-56; engr., then sr. engr. aircraft design bur. Antonov ASTC, Kiev, Ukraine, 1956—; conf. participant, 1993. Contbr. articles to sci. jours., including T'Sagi Sci. Notes, Problems of Strength, Engring. Fracture Mechanics. Avocations: reading English and French novels, home carpentry. Home: Flat 30, Depoutatscaya ul 17/6, 03115 Kiev Ukraine Office: ANTONOV ASTC, Ac Toupolev ul 1, 03062 Kiev Ukraine

YEMELYANOVA, INNA SERGEEVNA, physics and mathematics educator; b. Gorky, Russia, June 24, 1938; d. Sergey Nickolayevich and Alexandra Mikhaylovna (Khayurkhina) Varypayev; m. Yevgeny Ilyich Yemelyanov, Apr. 12, 1960 (div. 1976); children: Dmitry, Alexander. BS, Gorky State U., 1959, MS, 1960, PhD in Physics and Math., 1974; Dr in Physics and Math., Moscow State U., 1990. Lectr. Gorky State U., 1960-72, sr. lectr., 1974-87; prof. Nizhny Novgorod State U., Russia, 1990—, dep. head calculating math. and cybernetics dept., 1974-87, 95-99; Author monograph and articles; editor-in-chief Procs. of Russian Assn. Women in Math., 1993-2000. Mem. Russian Assn. Women Mathematicians (pres. 1995-98), European Assn. Women in Math. (mem. standing com. 1997—), Russian Assn. Women in Sci. and Edn. (v.p. 1994—), Am. Assn. Women in Math., N.Y. Acad. Scis. Avocations: forest walking, Internet. Office: U Nizhny Novgorod, Gagarina Prospekt 23, 603600 Nizhny Novgorod Russia

YEN, BEN CHIE, water resources engineering educator; b. Canton, China, Apr. 14, 1935; came to U.S., 1958; s. George T. and Jun-Yu (Yeh) Y.; m. Ruth H. Chao, Mar. 6, 1993. BSCE, Nat. Taiwan U., Taipei, 1956; MS, U. Iowa, 1959, PhD, 1965. Registered profl. engr., Ill., Taiwan. Rsch. assoc. Hydraulics Inst. U. Iowa, Iowa City, 1960-64; rsch. assoc. Princeton (N.J.) U., 1964-66; from asst. prof. to prof. civil engring. U. Ill., Urbana, 1966—; prof. U. Va., Charlottesville, 1988-91; Gast. prof. U. Karlsruhe, Germany, 1974-75, U. Stuttgart, 1983, 84; vis. prof. East China Tech. U., Nanjing, China, 1982, Ecole Polytech Federale, Lausanne, Switzerland, 1982, Nat. Taiwan U., 1983, 91, Vrije U., Brussels, Belgium, 1983, U. New South Wales, Australia, 1988, Hong Kong U. Sci. and Tech., 1995-99; adv. bd. Chinese Inst. Water Works, Taiwan, 1985—; bd. dirs. Wang, Reidel and Assocs., Inc., Northbrook, Ill.; mem. CIES Fulbright Scholar Bd., 1996—; mem. Ctr. for Advanced Studies U. Va., Charlottesville, 1988-90. Author and editor 10 books, 1982, 86, 87, 89, 91, 93, 99; contbr. 220 articles to profl. jours.: author (computer software) ISS model, 1973, ILSD model, 1976-84. Recipient Fulbright Disting. Sr. Lectr., Disting. Lectr. Nat. Sci. Coun., Taiwan, 1989; U.K. Dept. Environment rsch. fellow, 1975, fellow Japan Soc. Promotion Sci., 1996; 27 fed. and state rsch. grantee, 1966—. Fellow ASCE (com. chairs 1976—, assoc. editor Jour. Hydraulic Engring. 1987-94, Best Hydraulics Tech. Note award 1994, Hunter Rouse Hydraulic Engring. award 1999), Internat. Water Resources Assn. (V.T. Chow Meml. award 1996); mem. Am. Geophys. Union (life, coms. 1972-76), Internat. Assn. Hydraulic Rsch. (com. chairs 1982-86), Chinese Am. Water Resources Assn. (founding pres. 1993-95), Sigma Xi (mem. at-large), Phi Tau Phi. Avocation: folk dancing. Office: Univ Ill Civil/Environ Engring Dept 205 N Mathews Ave Urbana IL 61801-2350

YEN, GILI, economics researcher; b. Taipei, Taiwan, Mar. 8, 1953; s. Tzeng-song and Yueh-yun Yen; m. Eva Chung-Chiung; 1 child, Bernard Chih-hsun. BA, Nat. Taiwan U., Taipei, 1975, MA, 1978; PhD, Wash. U., 1983. Assoc. rsch. fellow Chung-Hua Instn. for Econ. Rsch., Taipei, 1983-86; assoc. prof. Inst. Indsl. Econs. Nat. Ctrl. U., Chung-li, 1985-87, prof., then dir., 1987-89, prof., founding dir. Inst. Fin. Mgmt., 1989-92; sr. rsch. fellow, divsn. dir. Taiwan Inst. Econ. Rsch., Taipei, 1992-93; sr. rsch. fellow Taiwan Rsch. Inst., Taipei, 1994—; 1st v.p. China Devel. Bank (formerly China Devel. Corp.), Taipei, 1994-97; dir., supr. China Steel Corp., Kaohsiung, 1990-97; dean Sch. Mgmt. Chaoyang U. of Tech., 1998—; advisor Exec. Yuan Ctrl. Govt., Taipei, 1983-84, 89-90; adj. prof. Nat. Taiwan U., Taipei, 1987-93. Author: Empirical Studies on Business Finance and Government Policy in Taiwan, 1996; editor: New Directions in Regional Trade Liberalization and Investment Cooperation, 1994; mem. editl. bd. Advances Pacific Basin Bus., Econs., Fin., 1995—, Rev. Pacific Basin Fin. Markets and Policies, 1998—; contbr. more than 30 articles to profl. jours. including Jour. Health Econs., Jour. Econs. and Bus., Am. Jour. Econs. and Sociology, Rev. Quantitative Fin. and Acctg., Managerial and Decision Econs., Advances in Fin. Planning and Forecasting, Advances in Quantitative Fin. and Acctg., Advances in Pacific Basin Bus., Econs., and Fin., Jour. Developing Areas, Atlantic Econ. Jour., India Jour. Econs., Asian Econ. Rev., others. Recipient numerous rsch. awards Nat. Sci. Coun. Mem. Chinese Econ. Assn. (gov. 1991-94), Chinese Fin. Assn. (sec.-gen., exec. dir. 1992-96), Internat. Soc. for Instnl. Econs. (country rep. 1997). Avocations: reading, listening to music, playing table tennis, traveling, playing mahjong. Home: 6F No 233 Song-Der St, Taipai 110, Taiwan

YEN, JOSEPH CHEN-YING, artist, educator; b. Lai-Yang, Shan-Tung, China, July 14, 1940; arrived in Taiwan, 1949; s. Min-Sheng Yen and Min Tsu; m. Joy Shih-Min Liu, Oct. 16, 1967 (div. Aug. 1989); children: Ling-Yu, Ling-Hsi, Ling-Hsuan; m. Jui-Fen Fan, Jan. 16, 1990; children: Ling-Wan, Ling-Hu. BA, Soochow U., Taipei, Taiwan, 1963; MA, Chinese Cultural U., Taipei, 1967; PhD, Brigham Young U., 1973; ArtsD (hon.), Honan Normal U., Hsin-Shiang, China, 1995; EdD (hon.), Beijing P.E. Coll., 1995. Assoc. prof. Nat. Taiwan U., Taipei, 1973-75; chair, acad. dean Soochow U., Taipei, 1975-79; chair, dean Chinese Culture U., Taipei, 1979-87; dir., liberal arts dean Nat. Cheng-Kung U., Tainan, Taiwan, 1987-95, prof., univ. affairs adviser, 1995—; founder, proprietor Taipei Lab. for Arts & Lit., 1983—; prodr. Asian-Pacific Puppet Theatre Festival, Taipei, 1983-93; cons. Asian-Pacific Film Festival, Taipei, 1976-86, Nat. Civil Svc. Exam., Taipei, 1976-94, Cen. Films Prodn. Co., China TV, Fu-Sheng Radio Sta., other cultural and ednl. founds., Taipei, 1976—. Editor-in-chief 104 books, including Series of Literature and Arts, 1984-89; co-editor: Encyclopedia and Encyclopedic Dictionary, 1978-87; author 8 books and numerous articles; painter 21 solo shows; prodr., playwright, transl. numerous dramatic works. Recipient Golden medal for Young Poets, Republic of China Nat. Youth Fedn., 1963, Pres. Chiang Kai-Shek's Culture award for Most Disting. Writings, 1970, Golden medal for Lit. and Art, Republic of China Nat. Writers and Artists Fedns., 1978, Chung-Hsin award for Lit. and Art, Taiwan Writers Fedn. Fellow Republic of China Am. Studies Soc. (life, initiator), Republic of China Playwrights Assn. (life, hon.); mem. Century 21 Artists Assn. (life, initiator). Avocations: painting, antiques, arts and rocks collection. Office: Nat Cheng-Kung U, # 1 Ta-Hsueh Rd, Tainan Taiwan

YEN, SHIOW KANG, materials scientist, educator, consultant; b. Taichung, Taiwan, Republic of China, Mar. 15, 1957; s. Wu Quei and Tsai Man (Tsai) Y.; m. Yang Mei-Hwei Yang, Dec. 25, 1984; children: Chu-June, Chau-June, Mi-June. BS, Nat. Tsing Hua U., 1979, MS, 1983, PhD, 1990. Lectr. dept. mech. materials Nat. Fu-Wei (Taiwan) Inst. Tech., 1983-90; assoc. prof. Nat. Chung-Hsing U., Taichung, Taiwan, 1991-93; assoc. prof. Inst. of Materials Engring. Nat. Chung-Hsing U., Taichung, 1993—; dir. Inst. of Materials Engring., Nat. Chung-Hsing U., 1997-99; cons. Min-Sin Mech. Co., Taichung, Taiwan, 1999—. Patentee in field. Lt. Army, 1979-81. Recipient Intelligent Children award Town Govt., 1969, Tchg. Svc. award Ministry of Edn. Republic of China, 1995. Mem. Electrochem. Soc., Chinese Soc. for Materials Sci., Corrosion Engring. Assn. of Taiwan in Republic of China (Contbn. on corrosion prevention 1997). Avocations: swimming, talking, traveling, fishing, bicycling. Home: 2/3 16F 2 Nan-Her Rd, Taichung 402, Taiwan Office: Nat Chung Hsin U, Kuo-Kuang Rd 250, Taichung 80227, Taiwan

YEN, WEN LIANG, aerospace engineer; b. Taipei, Taiwan, Dec. 13, 1937; came to U.S., 1963; s. Ping Ting and Mei Yen; m. Fina H. Kuo, Mar. 9, 1966; 1 child, AnnFrances. BS, Nat. Taiwan U., 1960; MS, Nat. Tsinghua U., Taiwan, 1962; PhD, Purdue U., 1969. Asst. prof. Ind. U.-Purdue U., Indpls., 1968-73, assoc. prof., 1973-80; mem. sci. staff Deutsches Elektronen-Synchrotron, Hamburg, Germany, 1978-80; programmer/analyst Computer Scis. Corp., Greenbelt, Md., 1980-82; sys. specialist Lockheed Engring. and Mgmt. Svcs. Co., Inc., Greenbelt, Md., 1982-87; sr. analyst AlliedSignal Tech. Svcs. Corp., Greenbelt, Md., 1987—. Contbr. articles to profl. jours. Recipient Group Achievement award NASA, 1993. Mem. AIAA. Achievements include development of spacecraft battery model which predicts whether the battery of a spacecraft will support proposed loads. Office: AlliedSignal Tech Svcs Corp 7515 Mission Dr Lanham Seabrook MD 20706-2291

YEN, WEN-HSIUNG, language and music professional, educator; b. Tainan, Taiwan, June 26, 1934; came to U.S., 1969; m. Yuan-yuan Yen, Jan. 6, 1961; children: Tin-ju, Tin-jen, Tin-Tao. BA, Nat. Taiwan Normal U., 1960; MA, UCLA, 1971; PhD in Music, World U., 1988; Candidate Philosophy in Ethnomusicology, UCLA, 1995; cultural doctorate philosophy of music, The World Univ., 1988. Instr. Nat. Taichung Tchr. Coll., 1961-62; prof. Chinese Culture U., Taipei, 1964-69; lectr. West L.A. C.C., 1978-82; founder Chinese Culture Sch. L.A., 1976—; grad. tchg. asst. U. Md., 1982-83; instr. L.A. City Coll., 1983—, Calif. State U. L.A., 1984—, Pasadena City Coll., 1989—; prof. Chinese Santa Monica (Calif.) Coll., 1986—, Calif. State U. Northridge, 1986—; founder Wen Yen Piano Studio, 1972—; founder, dir. Chinese Mus. Orch. So. Calif., 1974—; founder, pres. Chinese-Amer. Musicians Assn. of So. Calif., 1990—; co-chairConf. Students of Chinese Lang. and Culture. Musical compositions include: Collection of Works by Mr. Yen, 1969; recordings: Art Songs and Chinese Folk Songs, 1982; author: Taiwan Folk Songs, 1967, vol. 2, 1969, A Dictionary of Chinese Music and Musicians, 1967, A Collection of Wen-hsiung Yen's Songs, 1968, vol. 2, 1987, vol. 3, 2000, Achievement and Methodology for Comparative Musicology, 1968; transl. Chinese Musical Culture and Folk Songs, 1989, Silk and Bamboo Expresses Emotion and Meaning, 2000; composer of 100 songs and instrumental music; exhibitor traditional Chinese musical instruments and publs. Chinese Culture Ctr., 1995, 96, Arcadia Pub. Libr., 1999; organizer concerts and conductor; contbr. to profl. jours. Bd. dirs. So. Calif. Coun. Chinese Sch., 1998—; bd. dirs. Chinese Studies Ctr., Calif. State U., L.A., 1990—. Mem. Chinese-Am. Musicians Assn. So. Calif. (pres.), Chinese Choral Soc. So. Calif. (music dir.), Chinese Performing Arts Assn. of Am. (CPAAA) (bd. dirs). Soc. Ethnomusicology, Coll. Music Soc., Internat. Coun. Traditional Music, Soc. Asian Music, Alumni Assn. Chinese Culture U. in USA, Taiwan Benevolent Assn. Am. (bd. dirs.), Taiwan Benevolent Assn. Calif. (bd. dirs., v.p. 1986, pres. 1987-89), Chinese Am. PTA So. Calif. (supr. 1985—), So. Calif. Coun. Chinese Schs. (chmn. exec. com., v.p. 2000—). Avocations: walking, table tennis, Tai Chi Chuan. Office: Chinese Culture Sch 615 Las Tunas Dr Ste B Arcadia CA 91007-8469

YENER, AYLIN, electrical engineer, researcher; b. Istanbul, Turkey, June 23, 1971; came to U.S., 1991; BSEE, BS in Physics, Bogazici U., Istanbul, 1991; MSEE, Rutgers U., 1994, PhD in Elec. Engring., 2000. Tchg. asst. Rutgers U., Piscataway, N.J., 1991-93, rsch. asst., 1993—. Reviewer jours., 1996—; contbr. articles to profl. jours. Mem. IEEE. E-mail: yener@ece.rutgers.edu. Office: WINLAB Rutgers Univ 73 Brett Rd Piscataway NJ 08854-8060

YEO, ALLEN CHIEW BENG, mechanical engineer, consultant; b. Singapore, Oct. 3, 1971; s. Thiam Seng and Siew Poh (Yap) Y. Student physics; BS in Engring. with honors, U. Glasgow, Scotland, 1995, PhD in Laser Microbiology, 1999. Rsch. scientist Laser & Optical Sys. Engring. Ctr., Glasgow, 1995—. Contbr. articles to profl. jours. Overseas Rsch. scholar Com. Vice-Chancellors and Principals of Us. of the U. Kingdom, London, 1995-96, 96-97. Mem. Instn. Mech. Engrs., Instn. Physics, Internat. Soc. Optical Engring, Nat. Geographic Soc., Glasgow U. Singapore Soc. (pres., 1994-95, sr. advisor, 1996—). Avocations: soccer, badminton, reading. Home: 2 Melrose St, St George's Cross Glasgow G4 9BJ, Scotland Office: Laser & Opt Sys Engring Ctr, James Watt Bldg Unv Glasgow, Glasgow G12 8QQ, Scotland

YEO, GEORGE YONG-BOON, Singapore government official; b. Singapore, Sept. 13, 1954; s. Eng-Song and Lee Hoon (Kan) Y.; m. Jennifer Lai-Peng Leong, June 17, 1984; children: Edwina Shi-En, Edward Shi-Ming, William Shi-Zhi, Frederick Shi-Hong. BA, Cambridge U., 1976; MBA, Harvard Bus. Sch., 1985. Mil. offcr. Singapore Armed Forces, 1972-88, chief-of-staff Air Staff, 1985-87, dir. joint ops. and planning, 1986-88, brigadier-gen., 1988; min. of state for fin. and fgn. affairs Singapore, 1988-90, min. for info. and arts, 2d min. fgn. affairs, 1991-93, min. info. and arts, min. health, 1994-97, min. info. and arts, 2d min. trade and industry, 1997-99, min. for trade and industry, 1999—. Chmn. Young People's Action Party, 1992-2000. Recipient scholarship Singapore Armed Forces, 1973, Pres.'s scholarship Govt. Singapore, 1973, Baker scholar, 1985. Roman Catholic. Avocations: reading, jogging, swimming, golf. Office: Ministry Trade & Industry, 100 High St 09-01 Treasury, Singapore 179434, Singapore

YEO, NING-HONG, Singapore industrialist; b. Singapore, Nov. 3, 1943; m. Janny Zee; children: Elaine, Elena. BS with honors, U. Singapore, 1966, MS, 1968; MA, PhD, Cambridge U., 1970. Rsch. assoc. Stanford U., 1970-71; lectr. U. Singapore, 1971-74; mgr. Internat. Pharm. Co., Singapore, 1974-80; def. min. of state, mem. parliament Singapore Govt., 1981-83, min. for comm., 1983-85, min. comms. and info., 1983-91, min. for def., 1991-94; chmn. Port of Singapore Authority, 1994-97, PSA Corp. Ltd., Singapore, 1997—; exec. chmn. Singapore Technologies, 1995-97; gov. Asia Europe Found., 1996-2000; bd. dirs. DBS Bank. Contbr. articles to profl. jours. Pres. Singapore Nat. Olympics Coun., 1991-98. Fellow Christ's Coll. Cambridge U., 1969-72, hon. fellow, 1998—. Avocations: golf, sailing, reading. Home: Cluny Hill, 259651 Singapore Singapore Office: PSA Corporation Ltd, 460 Alexandra Rd PSA Bldg, 119963 Singapore Singapore

YEO, SEUNG TAI, mechanical engineer, researcher; b. Seoul, Dec. 2, 1964; s. Chang Hoi Yeo and Won Sook Kim; m. Hee Sook Park, Oct. 26, 1991. BS, Seoul Nat. U, 1987; MS, Korea Adv. Inst. Sci.-Tech., Taejoa, 1989, PhD, 1997. Sr. rsch. Samsung Advanced Inst. Tech., Suwon, Korea, 1989-91, Agy. for Def. Devel., Taejon, Korea, 1997—; exec. cons. FEAsoft (Venture Group for Finite Element Analysis Software Devel.), Taejon, 1997—. Contbr. articles to profl. jours. including Internat. Jour. Numerical Method Engring. and Computer Methods Applied Mech. Engring. Scholar Seoul Nat. U., 1983-86, Korea Advanced Inst. Sci. and Tech., 1987-88, 92-96. Mem. Korean Soc. Mech. Engrs. Avocations: mountain climbing, swimming, bowling, meditation. E-mail: fyns@hananet.net. Home: Dungji Apt 111-905, Dunsan-dong, Seo-gu, Taejon 302-122, Republic of Korea Office: Agy for Def Devel, Yusung, PO Box 35-1 Yusung-gu, Taejon Republic of Korea

YEO, TAT-SOON, electrical engineer, educator; b. Singapore, June 29, 1954; s. Siu-Lam and Choy-Wah (Tan) Y.; m. Mui-Na Gooi, May 18, 1990; 1 child, Jun-Wei. BE, U. Singapore, 1979; ME, Nat. U. Singapore, 1981; PhD in Engring., U. Canterbury, New Zealand, 1985. Chartered engr., U.K. Sr. tutor Nat. U. Singapore, 1979-85, lectr., 1985-89, sr. lectr., 1989-96, dir. Radar and Signal Processing Lab., 1991—, mgr. synthetic aperture radar devel. program, 1992-96, assoc. prof., dir. ctr. microwave & radio frequency, 1996—, dir. antennas and scattering lab., 1996—. Contbr. articles to profl.

jours. Hon. advisor Chou Ann Civic Assn., Singapore, 1993—. Fellow Inst. Elec. Engrs. (U.K.), Inst. of Engrs. of Singapore; mem. IEEE (sr.). Office: Nat U Singapore, Dept Elec Engring, Singapore Singapore

YEO, YOUNG KEUN, biochemistry educator; b. Taegu, Republic of Korea, Nov. 18, 1950. BSc, Youngram U., Taegu, 1973; MSc, Seoul Nat. U., 1975; PhD, U. Tenn., 1982. Rsch. assoc. Seoul Nat. U., 1976-78; postdoctoral rschr. Ohio State U., Columbus, 1983-85; vis. prof. Cornell U., Ithaca, N.Y., 1987; adj. prof. U. Guelph, Ont., Can., 1987-89; vis. prof. U. Munich, 1991-92; prof. biochemistry Kyungpook Nat. U., Taegu, 1992—; expert-cons. FAO, WHO, UN, 1993, Korea Food and Drug Adminstrn, 1999. Contbr. articles to sci. jours., including Lipids, Neurochemistry Rsch., Jour. Biochemistry and Molecular Biology. Grantee Internat. Sci. Exch., 1988, Koreea Sanhak Found., 1998. Mem. Am. Soc. for Nutritional Scis., Fedn. Am. Socs. for Exptl. Biology, Am. Oil Chemists Soc. Office: Kyungpook Nat U Coll Agr, Lipid Chemistry Lab, Taegu 702-701, Republic of Korea

YEOM, CHOONG KYUN, chemical engineer, researcher; b. Ookcheon, Republic of Korea, Mar. 26, 1958; s. Chul Hoon and Duk Soon (Kim) Y.; m. Mi Kyong Jeon, Nov. 4, 1984; children: Joomin, Jooyoung. BA in Chem. Engring., Hanyang U., Seoul, 1982; M in Chem. Engring., Korea Advanced Inst Sci & Tech, Taejon, Republic of Korea, 1984; D Chem. Engring., U. Waterloo, Waterloo, Can., 1991. Rschr. SK Chem., Inc., Seoul, 1984-88; rsch. asst., tchg. asst. U. Waterloo, 1989-91; postdoctoral fellow U. Alta., Edmonton, Can., 1991-92, McMaster U., Hamilton, Can., 1992-94; sr. rschr. Korea Rsch. Inst. Chem. Tech., Taejon, 1994—; adj. exec. B.S. Chem., Inc., Taejon, 1999—. Rschr. in field. Recipient Republic of Korea scholarship, 1982-83, Faculty of Engring. scholarship, U. Waterloo, 1989-91, Ont. Grad. scholarship, 1990-91, Best Student Papers award, Bakish Materials Corp., Englewood, N.J., 1989. Mem. AAAS, N.Am. Membrane Soc. E-mail: ckyeom@pado.krict.re.kr. Home: #508-502 Expo Apt, Junmin-dong 305-390, Republic of Korea Office: Korea Rsch Inst Chem Tech, PO Box 107, Yusong, Taejon 305-606, Republic of Korea

YEOMANS, CHARLES MARGRAVE, software company executive; b. Khartoum, Sudan, June 2, 1952; s. John Leslie and Joan (Coleman) Y. BSc in Physics and Computing, Kent (Eng.) U., 1974. Project leader First Nat. Bank Chgo., London, 1974-80; Asia Pacific regional project leader First Nat. Bank Chgo., Hong Kong, 1980-84; regional head Internet Sys., Hong Kong, 1985-88; Asia Pacific regional sys. head DJ/Telerate, Hong Kong, 1988-92; mng. dir. Yes Ltd. (formerly Total Solutions Software), Hong Kong, 1992—, also bd. dirs.; pres. Yes Inc., The Philippines, 1992—; bd. dirs. Pacific Privilege Ltd., Hong Kong. Capt. Hong Kong Rugby 7's, 1983. Mem. Hong Kong Mgrs. Assn., Hong Kong Club, Landsdowne Club London. Avocations: rugby, golf, squash, tennis. Office: Yes Ltd, GPO Box 381, Hong Kong Hong Kong

YERGER, LINDA F., human resources administrator, educator; b. Checotah, Okla., Nov. 8, 1948; d. Henry W. and Mary L. (Cobb) McGee; m. Cardis L. Yerger, Sept. 4, 1973; children: Michael, Daniel, Jamiil. BS in Edn., Northeastern Okla. State U., Tahlequah, 1970; MS in Human Resource Mgmt. and Devel., Chapman U., Orange, Calif., 1991. Cert. sr. profl. in human resources. Eligibility worker Tex. State Dept. Welfare, Beeville, 1975-77; program mgt. Taft (Okla.) Pub. Schs., 1977-80; employee counselor Kitsap Cmty. Action Program, Bremerton, Wash., 1980-81; program mgr. Bremerton Bus. Coll., 1981-84; employment/career counselor Wash. State Dept. Employment Security, Bremerton, 1984-86; asst. dir. Met. Bus. Coll., Port Orchard, Wash., 1986-91; human resources dir. Olympic Coll., Bremerton, 1991—. Mem. mental health bd. Kitsap County Commrs., Port Orchard, 1992; mem. Wash. Cmty. and Tech. Colls. Human Resource Commn., 1995—; active Leadership Kitsap, Bremerton, 1995; mem. exec. bd. YWCA, Bremerton, 1999—; mem. adv. team Family Svc., Bremerton, 1997—; v.p. Black Hist. Soc., Bremerton, 1999—. Named Employee of Yr., U.S. Postal Svc., Oak Harbor, Wash., 1975; Outstanding Adminstr., Olympic Coll., 1996. Mem. Soc. for Human Resources Mgmt. (exec. bd. N.W. chpt. 1999—). Office: Olympic Coll 1600 Chester Ave Bremerton WA 98337-1600

YEROULANOS, MARINOS, environmentalist, consultant; b. Athens, Greece, May 13, 1930; s. Ioannis and Despina (Streit) Y.; m. Aimilia Kalliga, July 31, 1955; children: Despina, Irini, Pavlos, Marina. Civil engr., Swiss Fed. Inst. Tech., 1953. Civil engr. Royal Navy Arsenal, 1954-57; with Pub. Power Corp., Tavropos, Greece, 1957-60, Indsl. Devel. Bank, 1960-61; pvt. sec. King Paul of Hellenes, 1961-64; master ceremonies King Constantine, 1964-67; marshall queen's ct. Queen Anne-Marie, 1967-74; dir. gen., permanent sec. Nat. Environment Coun., Athens, 1976-81; cons. fish farming UN Envrion. Program, Greece, 1981-86; co-founder, chmn. Cephalonian Fisheries, Greece, 1982—; vis. prof. U. Guelph, Can., 1983. Bd. trustees Benaki Mus., Athens, 1975—, chmn. 1995—; bd. trustees Greek Anticancer Inst., 1975-95, Yeroulanos Found., 1965—; governing bd. Hellenic Animal Welfare Soc., 1984-88, Inst. Econ. and Indsl. Rsch., 1992-98; gen. coun. Greek Bd. Industry, 1990-96; chmn. Benaki Phytopathol. Inst., 1990-95. Recipient Global 500 award UN, 1987, Gold Cross, Orders George I and Phoenix, Order of Danneborg (comdr.), Crown Thailand, Order of Merit Italy, Tunisia. Mem. ASCE, Greek Tech. Chamber, Hellenic Soc. for Protection Nature, Boy Scouts Greece, Hellenic Yacht Club. Home and Office: 10 Lykiou St, 10674 Athens Greece

YERRID, C. STEVEN, lawyer; b. Charleston, W.Va., Sept. 30, 1949; s. Charles George and Audrey Faye Yerrid; m. Sharon Wainman, Feb. 13, 2000. BA in History and Polit. Sci., La. State U., 1971; JD, Georgetown U., 1975. Bar: Fla. 1975, Va. 1975, U.S. Supreme Ct. 1979, D.C. 1984; cert. civil trial advocate Nat. Bd. Trial Advocacy. Aide U.S. Senator Ellender, Washington, 1971-73; ptnr. Holland & Knight, Tampa, Fla., 1975-86; pres. Stagg, Hardy & Yerrid, Tampa, 1986-89, Yerrid, Knopik & Krieger PA, Tampa, 1990-2000; with The Yerrid Law Firm, Tampa, 2000—. Mediator and Cir. Ct. arbitrator Fla. and Fed. Cts. Mem. ABA, Va. Bar Assn., D.C. Bar Assn., Fla. Bar Assn. (chmn. admiralty law com. 1984-85, bd. cert. com. 1988-91, vice chmn. 1989-91, chmn. 1994-95, bd. cert. civil trial lawyer), Southeastern Admiralty Law Inst., Am. Judicature Soc., Assn. Trial Lawyers Am. (sustaining), Am. Bd. Trial Advocates (advocate), Maritime Law Assn. (proctor), Tex. Trial Lawyers Assn., Acad. Fla. Trial Lawyer (founder, designated continuing legal edn. speaker 1982—, bd. dirs. 1989-97 2000—), Inner Cir. Advocates, Internat. Soc. Barristers, Am. Inns. of Ct. (supporting fellow), Cousteau Soc., Harbour Island Athletic Club, Centre Club, Tampa Club, Univ. Club. Democrat. Avocations: fishing, tennis, boxing. Office: The Yerrid Law Firm 101 E Kennedy Blvd Ste 3910 Tampa FL 33602-5187

YERYOMIN, KONSTANTIN ISANOSICH, engineering educator, dean; b. Magnitogorsk, Russia, May 3, 1959; s. Ivan Nikolaevich and Alexandra Afanasyevna (Litvinova) Y.; m. Irina Alexandrovna Preekodko; children: Artyom, Gugeneya, Georg. Engr., Mining Inst., Magnitogorsk, 1981; PhD, Bldg. U., Moscow, 1987, DSc, 1996. Asst. Mining Inst., Magnitogorsk, 1981-83, tchr., 1987-90; dozent Metallurgy Acad., Moscow, 1990-93; vice dean engring. dept. Tech. U., Moscow, 1988-90, dean engring. dept., 1990—, prof., 1994—. Author: Cyclically Loaded Metal Structures, 1996, Metal Structures, 1998. Dep. Soviet of Sity, Magnitogorsk, 1990-93. Lt. Russian Mil., 1981. Mem. Russian Acad. Ecology, N.Y. Acad. Scis. Achievements include patentee in field. Avocation: traveling. Home: Metallurgov Av 6-66, 455005 Magnitogorsk Russia Office: State Tech Univ, 38 Lenin Av, 455000 Magnitogorsk Russia

YERYOMKA, VICTOR DANILOVICH, physicist; b. Shevchenko Village, The Ukraine, Mar. 2, 1938; s. Daniel Iosifovich and Yekaterina (Ivanovna) Y.; m. Antonina Ivanovna Anoricheva, June 17, 1987; children: Daniel, Dar'ya. Degree in elec. engring., Nat. Tech. U. Kiev, 1961; PhD in Physics and Math. of Scis., Karazin Nat. U., 1974. Rsch. engr. Inst. for Radiophysics and Electronics, Nat. Acad. Scis., Kharkiv, The Ukraine, 1961-68, rsch. scientist, 1971-77, sr. rsch. assoc., 1977-83, head of lab., 1982-96, head of dept., 1996—; chief designer Design Office Space Oriented Instrument Making Industry, Moscow, 1982-90, Istok Corp., Fryazino, Moscow, Russia, 1990-91. Contbr. articles to sci. and profl. jours. Grantee Found. for Fundamental Investigations by State-run Com. Sci. and Tech., Kiev, 1993, 95; recipient Outstanding Inventor medal, Investors Soc. of USSR, 1979. Mem. IEEE (electron devices sect. 1995-98), Internat. Soc. Optical Engring. Avocations: music, philosophy, inventing, skiing, viticulture. Office: Usikov Inst Radiophys NAS, 12 Academician Proskura St, Kharkiv 61085, Ukraine

YET, LARRY, organic chemist, researcher; b. Vancouver, B.C., Can., Dec. 18, 1964; came to U.S., 1987; s. Chew Henry and Helen Yet. BSc, U. B.C., Vancouver, 1987; MS, Ohio State U., 1990, PhD, 1995. Postdoctoral rsch. assoc. U. Del., Newark, 1994-96; sr. rsch. chemist Albany (N.Y.) Molecular Rsch., Inc., 1996—. Contbr. chpt. to book. E-mail: larryy@albmolecular.com. Office: Albany Molecular Rsch Inc 21 Corporate Cir Albany NY 12203-5154

YETIV, STEVE A., political science educator. Postdoctoral tchr., rschr. Harvard U.; polit. sci. prof. Old Dominion, 1993—. Author: America and the Persian Gulf: The Third Party Dimension in World Affairs, 1995, The Persian Gulf Crisis, 1998 (Choice award 1998); featured on CNN, C-SPAN, Nat. Pub. Radio, Voice of Am., CBC, and others. Recipient Sec.'s Open Forum Disting. Pub. Svc. award U.S. State Dept., 1996, Scholar award Va. Social Sci. Assn., 1988. E-mail: syetiv@odu.edu. Office: Old Dominion Univ Grad Program Int Studies Norfolk VA 23529

YETT, SALLY PUGH, elementary education educator, art specialist; b. St. Louis, Feb. 15, 1935; d. John D. and Esther Ruth P.; m. Donald Edward Yett, June 19, 1964; children: Stephen Edward, John Harold. BFA, Washington U., St. Louis, 1956; tchg. credential, Calif. State U., L.A., 1989. Cert. gen. clear multiple subject and art supplementary, Calif. Dept. Edn. Recreation therapist ARC, San Antonio, 1956-58; dir. recreation therapy dept. Jewish Hosp., St. Louis, 1958-64; tchr. art-gifted class Juan Cabrillo Elem., Malibu, Calif., 1975-78; educator pre-kindergarten Malibu Meth. Pre-Sch., 1979-81; educator grades 9-12 Santa Monica (Calif.) Sch. Dist., 1981-89; educator grades 1-6 art L.A. Unified Sch. Dist.-Visual and Performing Arts Magnet, 1990—. Works exhibited Malibu Art Festival, 1976 (3rd place award), Malibu Art Assn. Show, 1984 (3rd place award), Roberts Art Gallery, 1989; contbr. articles to profl. jours. PTA pres. Juan Cabrillo Elem., Malibu, 1976-78, Malibu Park Jr. H.S., 1981-82; pres. Santa Monica Jr. Programs, 1979-81; 2nd, 3rd and 4th v.p. Santa Monica/Malibu PTA Coun., 1982-85; pres. Malibu Art Assn., 1982-83. Honoree Bravo award L.A. Music Ctr. Mem. Nat. Art Edn. Assn., Tchrs. and Writers Collaborative, Soc. for Calligraphy (bd. dirs., pub. rels. 1987-91), Calif. Coun. for Social Studies, Calif. Art Edn. Assn., UCLA Fowler Mus. Cultural History, Armand Hammer Mus., L.A. County Art Mus., S.W. Mus., Mus. Contemporary Art, Mus. Natural History, Nat. Mus. Women, Smithsonian Inst., Shakespeare Festival/L.A., Americans for the Arts, Calif. Alliance for Arts Edn., Craft & Folk Mus., East West Players Orgs., Metro. Mus. Art, Pacific Asia Mus., People to People Internat. (Indigenous Art del. to New Zealand, Australia 1998), Internat. Studies Overseas Program, UCLA Book Club, Ams. for the Arts, East-West Players, Pacific Asia Mus., UCLA Tchrs. & Scholars Symposium. Avocations: traveling, reading, painting, calligraphy, hiking. Home: 2042 Hanscom Dr South Pasadena CA 91030-4012

YETTER, R. PAUL, lawyer; b. Milw., Aug. 5, 1958; s. Richard and Lobelia (Gutierrez) Y.; m. Patricia D. Yetter, May 6, 1983; children: Chris, Mark, Michael, Joseph, Thomas, Andrew, Daniel. BA, U. Tex., El Paso, 1980; JD, Columbia U., 1983. Bar: Tex. 1983, U.S. Dist. Ct. (so., ea., no. and we. dists.) Tex., U.S. Ct. Appeals (5th cir.). Bd. cert. in civil trial law and personal injury trial law Tex. Bd. Legal Specialization. Law clk. to Hon. John R. Brown U.S. Ct. Appeals (5th cir.), Houston, 1983-84; assoc. Baker & Botts, L.L.P., Houston, 1984-89, ptnr., 1990-97; name ptnr. Yetter & Warden, L.L.P., Houston, 1997—; chair state judiciary rels. com. State Bar, 1995-96; mem. Funding Parity Task Force, 1995-97; mem. ex officio Jud. Selection Task Force, 1995-97; chair Alliance for Jud. Funding, Inc., 1996—; mem. ex officio contbns. com. Tex. Ctr. for the Judiciary. Contbr. articles to profl. jours. Recipient Presdl. citation State Bar Tex., 1996; Southwestern Legal Found. rsch. fellow. Fellow Tex. Bar Foun., Houston Bar Found. Office: Yetter & Warden LLP 600 Travis St Ste 3800 Houston TX 77002-2912

YETTO, JOHN HENRY, company executive; b. N.Y.C., Apr. 25, 1928; s. Michael and Josephine Yetto; m. Nancy A. Cagliostro, June 9, 1957; children: Sheryl, Kay, Michelle. BSChemE, CCNY, 1950; postgrad., Bklyn. Poly., 1951, Rutgers U., 1952. Devel. engr. Materials Lab., N.Y. Naval Shipyard, Bklyn., 1951-52; process engr. Bakelite Co., Div. UCC, Bound Brook, N.J., 1953-57; asst. plant engr. Revlon, Inc., Passaic, N.J., 1957-59; dept. mgr. Aerojet, Inc., Sacramento, 1959-71; pres. Systemedics, Sacramento, 1971-85, Proserv, Inc., Sacramento, 1975—. Chmn. YMCA Bd. of Mgrs., San Juan, Sacramento, Calif., 1964; pres. Fairway Pines Homeowners Assn., 1989-99, Sunrise Knolls Townhouse Owners' Assn., 1995. 1st lt. USAF, 1952-53. Mem. Fair Oaks C. of C. (pres. 1984), Rotary (pres. Fair Oaks 1982). Avocations: computers, tennis.

YEUNG, ALLAN YUN-LEUN, accounting educator; m. Eppie Yau-kwan Wong; 2 children. BS in Bus. Adminstrn., The Chinese U. Hong Kong, 1973, MBA, 1975. Lectr. Hong Kong Polytech. Univ., Hong Kong, 1986-94, asst. prof., 1995-97; tng. dir. Arthur Anderson & Co., Hong Kong, 1997—. Fellow Chartered Assn. Cert. Accts. (mem. exec. com. Hong Kong br. 1990-96, chmn. China liaison subcom. 1995-96), Hong Kong Soc. Accts. Avocations: soccer, reading, research, table tennis. Office: Arthur Anderson & Co. 21/F Edinburgh 15 Queens Rd, Central Hong Kong

YEUNG, ERIC TSUN MAN, entrepreneur; b. Hong Kong, Apr. 8, 1946; s. Winston Wing Tong Yeung and Nora Yuk Ning Lau-Yeung; m. Anna; 1 child, Derek Emory Ting Lap. BA, Washington U., St. Louis, Mo., 1969, MBA, 1970, PhD, 1974. V.p. Perfekta Enterprises Ltd., Hong Kong, 1974—; mng. dir. Perfekta Toys Lda., Macau, 1976—, Manly Pacific Internat. Hotel Pty. Ltd., Sydney, Australia, 1986—; bd. dirs. Perfekta Internat. Ltd., Hong Kong; dir. Yau Lee Holdings Group, Hong Kong, 1993—; vice chmn. Macau Electro-Optics Instrument Lda., 1995—, Guangdong Yong Fen Agrl. Co. Ltd., Gaozhou, 1995—; dep. chmn. Hong Kong Bapt. U.; chmn. Tsinghua-Perfekta Devel. Ctr., Macau Productivity and Tech. Transfer Ctr., IJCM Logistics Lda, Macau, 1997—, Tianjin Hong Gang Horticultural Co. Ltd., Tianjin, 1994—, Pacific Concrete & Quarries Pty. Ltd., Sydney, Australia, 1993—; dir., 3CE Internat. Express Lda., Macau, 1999—; convenor econ. sub-com. Macau Spl. Adminstrv. Region Preparatory Com. Decorated Comdr., Order of Merit, Govt. of Portugal; recipient Medal of Merit Macau Govt. Fellow Hong Kong Mgmt. Assn. (mem. exec. coun.); v.p. Macau Gov. Econ. Coun.; mem. World Pres.'s Orgn., Chief Exec. Orgn., Chinese People's Polit. Consultative Conf. (nat. mem.). Office: Perfekta Enterprises Ltd, G/F 141 Connaught Rd W, Hong Kong China also: Perfekta Toys Lda, 188 Av Venceslau De Morais, Macau China

YEUNG, KWAN LAWRENCE, electronics engineer; b. ChengDu, China, Feb. 12, 1969; s. Chuen and Hei (Wong) Y. B in Engring., Chinese U. Hong Kong, 1992, PhD, 1995. Tech. staff AT&T Bell Labs., N.J., 1993; asst. prof. City U. Hong Kong, 1995-2000, U. Hong Kong, 2000—. Mem. IEEE (sr.). Office: U Hong Kong Elec Eng, Pokfulan Rd, Hong Kong China

YEUNG, WILLIAM WAI-HUNG, technology educator; b. Hong Kong, July 12, 1959; s. Wood-Kow and Lai-Wan (Ng) Y.; m. Michelle Bee-Hoon Goh, Nov. 15, 1996; 1 child, Celine Wing-See. BASc, U. B.C., Vancouver, Can., 1983, MASc, 1985, PhD, 1990. Assoc. prof. in tech. Nanyang Technol. U., Singapore, 1991—. Contbr. articles to Jour. Fluid Mechanics, Jour. Aircraft, ASME Jour. Applied Mechanics. NSERC postgrad. scholar, 1987. Mem. ASME, Canadian Aeronautics and Space Inst. Avocation: travel. Home: Blk 281, Choa Chu Kang Ave 3 #04-352, 680281 Singapore Singapore

YEUNG, YUE-MAN, geographer, educator; b. Hong Kong, Oct. 1, 1938; s. Tat Hing and Lai Wah (Ma) Y.; m. Ameda Lau, May 14, 1967; children: Tao-Ming, Sze-Mei. BA with honors, U. Hong Kong, 1962, diploma in edn., 1963; MA, U. Western Ontario, 1966; PhD, U. Chgo., 1972. Lectr. U. Singapore, 1969-75; sr. program officer, assoc. dir. Internat. Devel. Rsch. Ctr., Ottawa, Canada and Singapore, 1975-84; registrar Chinese U. Hong Kong, 1986-90, prof. geography, 1984—; dir. Hong Kong Inst. of Asia Pacific Studies, 1990—, head Shaw Coll., 1994—; cons. World Bank, UNDP, ADB, various other orgns., 1985-93; mem. Kowloon-Canton Ry. Corp., Hong Kong, 1991-95, Hong Kong Housing Authority, 1990-98, Town Planning Bd., Hong Kong, 1991-98; dir. Commonwealth Geog. Bur., 1992-96. Editor: Pacific Asia in 21st Century, 1993, A Place to Live, 1983; author: Changing Cities of Pacific Asia, 1990; co-editor: China's Coastal Cities, 1992, Shanghai, 1996, Guangdong, 1998, Fujian, 2000. Active Barrister Disciplinary Tribunal Panel, Hong Kong, 1993-98, Consultative com. in New Airport, Hong Kong, 1991-97, Hong Kong Com. for Pacific Econ. Cooperation Coun., 1990-98; dir. Joint Univ. and Poly. Admissions, Hong Kong, 1993-94. Govt. scholar, 1959-62, scholar Canadian Govt. Commonwealth, 1964-66; Univ. Endowment fellow U. Chgo., 1967-69. Mem. Assn. Am. Geographers. Islam. Avocations: tennis, music, photography. Office: Chinese U Hong Kong, Shatin Hong Kong China

YEVDAYEV, NOBERT, retired engineer, art historian; b. Baku, Azerbaidjan, Nov. 2, 1929; came to U.S., 1989; s. Michael and Basja (Beskina) Y.; Nelly Yevdayev, Nov. 4, 1956 (div. March 1989); children: Marina Berger, Michael Baskin. MS in Tech. Sci., Baku U., 1953, MS in Fgn. Lit., 1955. Engr. Mitsubishi, Moscow, 1967-77, ABB, Moscow, 1977-89; art historian N.Y.C., 1993—. Author: (books) ASEA Robots, 1984, ASEA and Gasostats, 1985, Onboard Equipment, 1986; contbr. articles to profl. jours. Home: 1925 Seagirt Blvd Apt 17-0 Far Rockaway NY 11691-3766

YEVI, GILBERT YAOVI, petroleum engineer; b. Cotonou, Benin, Feb. 4, 1965; came to U.S., 1992; s. Frederick A. and Cecile Amouzouvi (Fande) Y.; m. Cynthia Ann Summerlin, Dec. 30, 1994. BS in Drilling and Prodn., U. Mining & Geology, Sofia, Bulgaria, 1991; MS in Petroleum Engring., Miss. State U., 1994, PhD in Computational Engring., 1996; MBA in Fin., Tulane U., 2000. Asst. prodn. engr. Bulgarian Geol. Prospecting Co., Pleven, 1990; asst. well testing engr. Bulgarian Geol. Prospecting Co., 1991; rsch. asst. in Petroleum Engring. Miss. State U., Starkville, 1992-93; rsch. asst. NSF Ctr. for Computational Field Simulation, Starkville, 1994-96; reservoir engr. Shell Offshore Inc., New Orleans, 1996-99; sr. reservoir engr. Shell Internat. E&P Inc., Houston, 2000—. Contbr. articles to profl. jours.; patentee in field. Mem. Soc. Petroleum Engrs., Nat. Petroleum Engring. Honor Soc. Avocations: fishing, tennis, badminton, table tennis, travel. Office: 200 N Dairy Ashford St Houston TX 77079-1101

YEVTUSHENKO, ALEXANDER ALEXEJ, mathematician, researcher; b. Kolomyja, Ivano-Fran, Ukraine, Mar. 25, 1954; s. Alexej Andrej and Tatjana (Gulak) Y.; m. Helena Novikova, Aug. 1, 1980; 1 child, Andreij. MD, Lviv State U., Ukraine, 1976, PhD, 1981. Jr. sci. rschr. Lviv State U., 1981-83, sr. sci. rschr., 1983-86, chief of rsch. lab., 1986-99; prof. Tech. U. Lodz, Poland, 1999—; rschr. Warsaw U., 1987-88, 89. Contbr. articles to profl. jours. Avocation: classical music. Home: Sadova 27A, 290021 Lviv Ukraine Office: Lviv State Univ, Universitetska 1, 290602 Lviv Ukraine

YEW, DAVID T., anatomy educator; b. Hong Kong, July 8, 1947; s. Ping Chiu and Hok Fong Yew; m. Lily K., 1970; children: Jeanette O., Jason C. BS, Chinese U., Hong Kong, 1969; PhD, Wayne State U., 1974; DSc in Medicine, U. Rostock, Germany, 1988, Habilitation in Medicine, 1995. Rsch. assoc. Wayne State U., Detroit, 1974; lectr. U. Hong Kong, 1976-80; lectr. anatomy Chinese U., 1974-76, sr. lectr., 1981-90, reader, 1991-95, prof., dept. chair, 1995—; vis. scientist Hubrecht Lab., The Netherlands, 1980; vis. prof. Sun Yat Sen U. Med. Scis., China, 1991—, Jinan (China) U., 1994—, 1st Mil. Med. Sch., China, 1996—, Beijing Med. U., 1999—. Author: A Laboratory Manual of Neuroanatomy, 1986, Basic Neuroanatomy, 1996; editor: Vision-Structure and Function, 1988, Human Prenatal Brain Development, 1993; contbr. over 110 articles to sci. jours. Fellow Inst. of Biology U.K. Avocations: antiques, tennis. Office: Chinese U, Dept Anatomy, Shatin Hong Kong

YEW, LEE KUAN, government executive; b. Sept. 16, 1923; married; 3 children. Student, Raffles Coll., Singapore, Ftizwilliam Coll., Cambridge, England, 1946-49. Advocate, solicitor, legal adviser several trade unions, 1951; co-founder PAP, 1954, sec. gen., 1954-92; elected MP, 1955—; prime min., 1959-90; rep. Malaysian Parliament, 1963-65; sr. min., 1990—. Office: Office of Prime Min, Istana Annese Orchard Rd, Singapore 238823, Singapore*

YEW, MICHAEL MUN HONG, electronics company executive. Pres. Aztech Sys. Ltd., Singapore. Fax: 65-741-9713. Office: Aztech Bldg, 31 Ubi Rd 1, Singapore 408694, Republic of Singapore*

YEZERNITSKY, YITZHAK See SHAMIR, YITZHAK

YEZERSKI, DANNY, special event producer; b. Sydney, NSW, Australia, July 16, 1969; s. Sol and Ziva Yezerski. BSc, U. NSW, 1992. Dir. Event Factory, Sydney, 1992-94; prodn. mgr. Key Largo, Sydney, 1994-96; mng. dir. TP Events, Sydney, 1996—. Mem. Internat. Spl. Events Soc., Meetings Industry Assn. Australia (award for excellence 1997-98, Event Prodr. of Yr. 1998), Sydney Conv. and Visitors Bur., Young Entrepreneurs Orgn. Avocations: African drumming, yoga. Office: TP Events, 2/51 Spring St, Bondi Junction 2022, Australia

YGLESIAS, RAFAEL JOSE, novelist; b. N.Y.C., May 12, 1954; s. Jose and Helen (Bassine) Y.; m. Margaret Joskow, Oct. 15, 1977; children: Matthew, Nicholas. Author: Dr. Neruda's Cure for Evil, 1996, The Murderer Next Door, 1990, Only Children, 1988; screenwriter, author (film) Fearless, 1993; screenwriter (films) Death and the Maiden, 1995, Les Miserables, 1998. Mem. The Author's Guild, Writer's Guild of Am., Acad. Motion Picture Arts and Scis.

YI, JOON-JEONG, metallurgist, researcher; b. Chonju, Chonbuk, Korea, Feb. 11, 1952; s. Yeon-So Y. and Jung-Ju Song; m. Tong-Eun Kim, Aug. 24, 1983; children: You-Bin, You-Sun. BS, Sung Kyun Kwan U., Seoul, 1977; MS, Korea Advanced Inst. Sci. Tech, Seoul, 1977, PhD, 1983. Rsch. engr. POSCO, Pohang, Korea, 1979-82, rsch. mgr., 1983-87; rsch. mgr. RIST, Pohang, Korea, 1987-94, prin. researcher, 1994—; concurrent prof. Pohang (Korea) U. Sci. and Tech., 1995—; vis. researcher KIST, Seoul, 1979-82; cons. Ministry of Commerce and Industry, Seoul, 1988-94. Co-editor: Current and Future of Rolling Technology, 1996, Exploitation of Future Rolling Technologies, 1999; contbr. articles to profl. jours.; patentee in field. Mem. Korean Soc. Tech. of Plasticity (dir. 1995—), Korean Soc. Heat Treatment (dir. 1987—, editor jour. 1987-92), Korean Soc. Metals and Materials (mem. coun. 1992—, editor 1998—, Chung-Wung award 1996), N.Y. Acad. Scis. Avocations: driving, swimming, travel, collecting match boxes. Home: 5-504 Kyosu-Apt Jigok-dong, Nam-gu, 790-390 Pohang Kyungbuk, Republic of Korea Office: Rsch Inst Indsl Sci & Tech, San 32 Hyoja-dong Nam-gu, 790-330 Pohang Kyungbuk, Republic of Korea

YI, KYONGSU, mechanical engineer, educator; b. Seoul, Nov. 12, 1962; s. Chong-Pong and No-chon (Pak) Yi; m. Kyeonghi Kim, Mar. 19, 1988; children: Juheon, Juyeon. BS, Seoul Nat. U., 1985, MS, 1987; PhD, U. Calif., Berkeley, 1992. Rschr. U. Calif., Berkeley, 1992-93; assoc. prof. Hanyang U., Seoul, 1993—. Avocation: tennis. Home: Mido Apt 108-201, Daichi-Dong 511, Kangnam-ku Seoul 135-280, Republic of Korea Office: Hanyang U, Sch Mech Engring, Sungdong-ku Seoul 133-791, Republic of Korea

YIANNAKOPOULOS, YIANNIS, executive; b. Athens, May 8, 1964; s. Eyaggellos and Vasiliki (Maglara) Y ; m. Kiriaki, Aug. 12, 1965. BSBA, U. Macedonia, Greece, 1989. Acct. Artisti/Taliam S.A., Greece, 1989-90; controller J. Boutari & Son S.A., Greece, 1991; supr. MIDAS S.A., Greece, 1992-94; costing controller UD S.A., Greece, 1995-96; logistics, customer operating mgr. UDV S.A., Greece, 1996—; cons. in field. Mem. SOLE, Greek Comml. & Econs. Assn. Office: UDV HElla SA, 214 Kifisias Ave, 15232 Athens Greece

YIH, YUEHWERN, engineering educator; b. Keelung, Taiwan, Dec. 16, 1962; came to the U.S., 1984; p. Ren-Ku Yih and Guey-Ron Cheng. BS, Nat. Tsing Hua U., Hsin-Chung, Taiwan, 1984; PhD, U. Wis., 1988. Project asst. U. Wis., Madison, 1985, tchg. asst., 1985-88; asst. prof. Purdue U., West Lafayette, Ind., 1989-94; assoc. prof. Purdue U., West Lafayette, 1994—; vis. rschr. Nat. Inst. Stds. and Tech., Gaithersburg, Md., summer 1992-95; rsch. asst. U. Wis., Madison, summer 1992-95; cons. Heritage Environ. Svcs., Indpls., 1993-94. Editor: Manufacturing Cells - A System Engineering View, 1995; dept. editor IEE Trans., 1994—; contbr. articles to

profl. jours. Recipient Young Investigator award NSF, 1993, Dell K. Allen Outstanding Young Mfg. Engr. award Soc. Mfg.. Engrs., 1998; GE Faculty fellow GE Found., 1992, NEC Faculty fellow NEC Corp., 1993. Mem. Inst. Indsl. Engrs. (pres. Ctrl. Ind. chpt. 1993-94, dir. Ctrl. Ind. chpt. 1994-95), Coll. on Artificial Intelligence-Inst. for Ops. Rsch. and Mgmt. Sci. (v.p. 1996-99), Artificial Intelligence Com. Ind. Corp. for Sci. and Tech. Avocations: ballroom dancing, ballet, piano. E-mail: yih@ecn.purdue.edu. Fax: 765-494-1299. Office: Purdue Univ 1287 Grissom Hall West Lafayette IN 47907-1287

YI-JUN, QIU, electronic engineer; b. Shanghai, China, Nov. 8, 1936; s. Qiu Zi-Tong and Liang Xue-Xin; m. Wang HuiFang, Apr. 7, 1957; 2 children. Degree, Zhe-Jiang U., 1955. Technologist North China Radio Appliances Combine Factory, Beijing, 1955-64; engr. Beijing 3d Radio Appliances Factory, 1964-70; dir., chief engr. Baoji Jinshan Radio Elements Factory, China, 1970-85; vice chief engr. Changzhou Electronics Industry Corp., China, 1985-88; vice chmn. bd. dirs., chief engr., pres. Changzhou Electronics Industry & Commerce Corp., 1988-89; vice chief engr. Changzhou Electronics Indsl. Bur., 1989-97, tech. dir. gen., 1997—. Author: The Technology of Permanent Magnet Alloy, 1975; editor: The Technology of Permanent Magnet Alloy, 1985. Mem. IEEE (sr.), China Elec. Magnetic Material and Devices Industry Assn. (cons. 1986—), Chinese Electronic Inst. (sr.). Home: Rm 301 2d Unit 24 Bldg, Qing Liang Xin Cun, Changzhou China Office: Changzhou Jianli Elec Co Lt, #272 Qingtan Rd, Changzhou Jiangsu 213015, China

YILDIZ, BÜLENT OKAN, physician; b. Ankara, Turkey, May 19, 1971; s. Kamil and Müjgan Y. MD, Hacettepe U., Ankara, 1994. Cert. in internal medicine Ednl. Commn. Fgn. Med. Grads. Resident dept. internal medicine Faculty of Medicine Hacettepe U., Ankara, 1994-98, fellow dept. internal medicine Faculty of Medicine, 1998—; cons. Internal Medicine Clinic Hacettepe U. Hosp., Ankara, 1997-98, Endocrinology Clinic Hacettepe U. Hosp., 1998—. Mem. study group exch. team Pa. Rotary Internat., 1998. Mem. Turkish Med. Assn., Am. Diabetes Assn., Nat. Geographic Soc., Rotary Internat. (mem. study group exch. team Pa. 199). Avocations: football, table tennis. Home: Emekli Subayevleri 2 C 23, C Block No:15/3, Yücetepe Ankara, Turkey 06580 Office: Hacettepe U Faculty Medicin, Dept Medicine Endocrinology, Samanpazara Ankara, Turkey

YILMAZ, AYSE BAHAR, chemistry educator; b. Alpullu, Turkey, Apr. 9, 1954; d. Ihsan and Ilhan (Gumuloglu) Bahadirli; m. Mehmet Yilmaz, Jan. 30, 1977; 2 children. BS, U. Ankara, Turkey, 1975; PhD, U. Cukurova, Adana, Turkey, 1994. Mem. coun. mgmt. Tech. Coll. Iskenderun, Turkey, 1984-90, asst. dean faculty fisheries, head dept., 1995—. Mem. Rotary. Avocations: swimming, reading, classical music. Home: Lala Mustafa Pasa CD 41/6, 31200 Iskenderun Turkey Office: Mustafa Kemal U, Su Urunleri Fakultesi Pk 23, 31200 Iskenderun Turkey

YILMAZ, MESUT, political party administrator; b. Istanbul, Turkey, Nov. 6, 1947; s. Hasan and Güzide Y.; m. Berna Müren; 2 children. Student, faculty of polit. studies, U. Ankara, Turkey, U. Cologne, Germany. Dep. Rize, 1983—; former min. state Govt. of Turkey, min. culture and tourism, 1986-87, min. fgn. affairs, 1987-90, prime min., 1991-96, 97-99; chair Motherland Party; vice chair EDU. Office: Motherland Party, 13 Cad 3, Balgat, Ankara Turkey

YILMAZ, VEYSEL TURAN, chemist, educator; b. Carsibasi, Trabzon, Turkey, Oct. 1, 1961; s. Osman and Asiye Y.; m. Gonul Yazar Tuncer, Jan. 11, 1985; children: Attila, Canan. BS, Karadeniz Tech. U., Trabzon, 1982; MS, Ondokuz Mayis U., Samsun, Turkey, 1987; PhD, U. Aberdeen (Scotland), 1991. Rsch. asst. Ondokuz Mayis U., Samsun, 1985-88, asst. prof., 1988-93, assoc. prof., 1993-99, prof., 1999—; mem. adminstrn. bd. Samsun Fertilizer Factory, 1998—. Contbr. articles to profl. jours. Recipient award Scientific and Rsch. Coun. Turkey, 1996. Mem. Turkish Chem. Soc. Muslim. Office: Ondokuz Mayis U Chem Dept, Kurupelit, Samsun 55139, Turkey

YIM, ANTHONY PING-CHUEN, cardiothoracic surgeon; b. Hong Kong, July 6, 1958; s. Lai-Ying Yim and Pui-Hing Wong; m. Esther Yu; 1 child, Katrina. BA in Pathology with 1st class honors, U. Cambridge, Eng., 1981, MA, 1985; B Medicine and Surgery, U. Oxford, Eng., 1984, MA, 1985; M.D., Oxford, 2000. Diplomate Am. Bd. Surgery. House surgeon John Radcliffe Hosp., U. Oxford, 1985; sr. house officer Harefield Hosp., 1986; surg. resident U. Chgo. Med. Ctr., 1986-91; clin. surg. fellow Mass. Gen. Hosp., Harvard Med. Sch., 1991-92; lectr. surgery Chinese U. Hong Kong, 1992-95; prof. surgery, chief divsn. cardiothoracic surgery Chinese U. Hong Kong, Shatin, 1995—; vis. prof. cardiothoracic surgery Guangzhou Med. U., People's Republic of China, 199—, People Liberation Army Gen. Hosp., Beijing, 1994—; dir. 1st Asian Pacific Workshop on Minimally Invasive Thoracic Surgery, Hong Kong, 1996; adviser Tech. Transfer Assn. Asia Ltd.; mem. cardiovasc. and thoracic med. adv. coun. MedAscend Inc. Author: Course Manual on Video Thoracoscopic Surgery Workshop, 1993, Video Assisted Thoracic Surgery - A Course Manual), 1994, Video Assisted Thoracoscopic Surgery Workshop Course Manual, 1995; lead editor: (with others) Minimal Access Cardiothoracic Surgery, 1999; contbr. over 200 peer reviewed articles to profl. jours., chpts. to books; mem. editl. bd. Asia Pacific Jour. Thoracic and Cardiovascular Surgery, Annals of Thoracic Surgery Chest, Asia-Pacific Heart Jour.; mem. adv. editl. bd. Jour. Modern Clin. Med. Bioengring., Med. Updates on Therapy, Diagnosis and Prevention; past editor-in-chief ELSA, Jour. Endoscopic and Laparoscopic Surgeons Asia; guest editor Internat. Jour. Cardiology, World Jour. Surgery, Asian Jour. Surgery. Mem. Hong Kong Lung Found. Fellow Internat. Coll. Surgeons, Internat. Acad. Chest Physicians and Surgeons, Am. Coll. Chest Physicians (v.p. Hong Kong & Macau chpt. 1995-97), Hong Kong Coll. Surgeons, Royal Coll Surgeons (Eng.), Hong Kong Coll. Medicine, Royal Coll. Physicians and Surgeons (Glasgow), Royal Coll. Surgeons (Edinburgh), Hong Kong Acad. Medicine; mem. Soc. Thoracic Surgeons (internat. mem.), N.Y. Acad. Scis., U. Chgo. Surg. Soc. (life), Soc. Endoscopic and Laparoscopic Surgeons of Asia (sec.-gen. 1996-99), Hong Kong Surg. Laser Assn., Internat. Soc. for Minimally Invasive Cardiac Surgery (bd. dirs.). Roman Catholic. Avocations: swimming, squash, movies, golf. Home: Flat B3, Villa Castell Block 39, Tai Po Hong Kong NT, China Office: Chinese U Hong KongPrince of Wales Hosp, Dept Surg Div Cardthor Surg, Shatin Hong Kong NT, China

YIM, LOUIS WAI KEUNG, research scientist; b. Kowloon, Hong Kong, May 2, 1970; arrived in England, 1989; s. Hin Sau Yim and Mary Hau Yin Yip. B in Electronic and Elec. Engring., U. Strathclyde, Glasgow, Scotland, 1993; PhD in Engring., U. Cambridge, Eng., 1997. Croucher Rsch. fellow engring. dept. Cambridge U., 1996-98; Sr. Frederick Handley Page sr. rsch. fellow St. Catharine's Coll., Cambridge U., 1998—. Contbr. articles to profl. jours. Scholar Hong Kong and U.K. Govts., 1989-93, Croucher scholar, 1993-96. Avocations: music, reading, sports. E-mail: lwky100@eng.cam.ac.uk. Fax: 01223-332662.

YIM, WYSS WAI-SHU, earth scientist; b. Hong Kong, Oct. 14, 1947; s. George and Yau-Mui (Chau) Y.; m. Fiona Fung-Lan Chung, Aug. 10, 1976; children: Mark Man-hoi, Justin Man-Ching. BSc, U. London, 1970, MPhil, 1974; PhD, U. Tasmania, 1991; DSc, U. London, 1997. From asst. to assoc. prof. U. Hong Kong, 1974—; sec. Commn. on Quaternary Shorelines Internat. Union for Quaternary Rsch., 1991-95, pres. West Pacific SubCommn. on Quaternary Shorelines, 1995-99; cons. Geosvcs., Hong Kong, 1977-92; coleader Internat. Geo. Correlation Programme Project #396 UNESCO, 1996-2000; leader Shelf Working Group, Commn. on Global Carbon, Internat. Union for Quaternary Rsch., 1999—. Editor: Geology of Surficial Deposits of Hong Kong, 1984; contbr. articles to profl. jours. Fellow Geol. Soc.; mem. Geol. Soc. Hong Kong (vice chmn. 1983-85), Instn. Mining & Metallurgy, Hong Kong Instn. Engrs., Chinese Soc. Mineralogy, Petrology and Geochemistry (life mem.). Office: U Hong Kong Dept Earth Scis, Pokfulam Rd, 0 Hong Kong SAR, China

YIN, BAOLU, educator; b. Beijing, Aug. 15, 1936; s. ChangQing and CaoShi (Cao) Y.; m. Wen Shu Liu; children: Li, Lei. Cert., Beijing U., China, 1960; diploma, He R Bin Mil. Engring. Coll. Technician Nat. Def. Scientific and Tech. Com., Beijing, 1963-74; prof. Beijing Polytech. U., 1974—. Contbr. articles to profl. publs. Recipient awards Mcpl. Govt., 1992, 94, 96, 98. Avocations: playing, basketball, swimming. Home: Apt No 2 South Gate 4 Fl, No 41 DongDan BeiDaJJ, Beijing 100005, China Office: Beijing Polytech, Applied Phys Dept, Beijing 100022, China

YIN, BEATRICE WEI-TZE, medical researcher; b. Taipei, Taiwan, Mar. 9, 1959; came to U.S., 1970; d. Chuan Keun and Ming Hsien (Huang) Y. BS, CUNY, Flushing, 1982, MS, 1988. Rsch. asst. Meml. Sloan-Kettering Cancer Ctr., N.Y.C., 1982—. Inventor Monoclonal antibodies to human gastrointestinal cancers, 1992. Avocations: readings, travel, gardening. Office: Meml Sloan Kettering Cancer Ctr 1275 York Ave New York NY 10021-6094

YIN, CHANG-MIN, biology educator; b. Nanchang, Jiangxi, China, Oct. 4, 1923; d. Ren-Qing and Ya-Hui (Wu) Y.; m. Xiao-Liang Bei; children: Bei Xing-Ya, Bei Hua. B, Nat. Zhong-Zheng U., Taihuo, China, 1945. Prof. Hunan Normal U., Changsha, China, 1979—; alt. mem. ctrl. com. CCP, China, mem. ctrl. com., alt. mem. ctrl. com., 1987-92; vice chair Hunan com. CPPCC, Changsha, 1985-92, mem. standing com., 1983-85; pres., v.p. Hunan Tchrs. Coll., 1973-82. Author (with others): Textbook of Zoology, 1983, Spiders in China, 1990, Lycosids in China, 1997, Fauna Sinica: Araneidae, 1997. Named Nat. Red-Banner Pacesetter of Woman, Woman Assn. China, 1959, Mode Worker of Hunan Province, People's Govt. Hunan Province, 1960; recipient prizes Hunan Provincial Sci. and Tech. conf., Dept. Agr. and Forestry, Nat. Com. Sci. and Tech., 1979-86, improvement of sci. and tech. prize Nat. Com. Edn., 1992. Mem. Assn. Sci. and Tech. (vice chair 1981-85, hon. chair 1985—), Hunan Biology/Zoology Soc. (chair bd. dirs. 1981—). Avocations: literature, collecting postage stamps. Office: Hunan Normal U Dept Zoology, Coll Life Sci, Changsha 410081, China

YIN, CHUNYONG, metrology educator; b. Dalian, Liaoning, China, Mar. 8, 1937; m. Yuxian Xu, Jan. 27, 1967; children: Yuqi, Yuzhe. Grad., Tsinghua U., Beijing, 1961. Asst. Tsinghua U., 1961-79, lectr. dept. precision instruments, 1979-86, assoc. prof., 1986-88, prof., 1988—; mem. Com. Calibration Method for Measuring Instruments, 1983-87. Author: Fundamentals of Optical Information Processing, 1985, Contemporary Interferometry, 1997, Quality Engineering, 1998; inventor 2-frequency interferometer for measuring refractive index of air, attitude measurement method for magnetic head, measurement equipment for magnetic disk; principle, designer electro-optic instruments, 1996. Recipient 3d grade prize for invention Nat. Com. Sci. and Tech., 1981, 92, 3d grade prize for progress in sci. and tech., 1993. Mem. Soc. Photo-Optical Instrument Engrs., Soc. Metrologic Instruments of Chinese Soc. Metrology (vice bd. dirs. 1995—). Office: Tsinghua U, Dept Precision Instruments, Beijing 100084, China

YIN, KEWEN KAREN, chemical engineer, educator; b. Beijing, June 21, 1946; Came to U.S., 1985; d. Yixin Yin and Wanzhen Zhu. MSChemE, Beijing Inst. Chem. Tech., 1982; MA in Math., U. Md., 1990, PhD in Chem. Engring., 1991. Engr. Lanzhou (China) Chem. Industry Co., 1969-78; rsch. asst. Beijing Inst. Chem. Tech., 1978-82; engr. Chem. Industry Design Corp., Beijing, 1983-84; lectr. Wuhan Inst. Material Sci., Beijing, 1984-85; grad. asst. U. Md., College Park, 1986-91; asst. prof. chem. engring. U. Minn., Duluth, 1991-96, assoc. prof., 1996-98; assoc. prof. U. Minn., St. Paul, 1998—; mem. program com. The 1997 Am. Control Conf., Albuquerque, 1997. Contbr. numerous articles to profl. jours. Rsch. grantee NSF, 1994, Minn. Sea Grant, 1996, 98, Minn. Dept. Natural Resources, 1999. Mem. AIChE (vice-chair internat. meeting program 1997), Am. Stats. Soc. Avocation: classical music. Office: U Minn Dept Wood and Paper Sci 2004 Folwell Ave Saint Paul MN 55108-6128

YIN, LIXUE, cardiologist, physician, educator; b. Kumin, Yunan, People's Republic of China, Aug. 21, 1964; s. JiXan and GuiFang (Lou) Y.; m. Ying Lin, July 27, 1984; 1 child, YiLin. B in Medicine, ChongQing Med. (China) U., 1985, MD, 1988. Resident Sichuan Provincial Hosp., Chengdu, 1988-91, attending physician, 1991-96, vice chief physician, 1996-97, prof., chief physician, 1999—; rsch. fellow Mayo Clinic, Rochester, Minn., 1997-98; duty leader Med. Sci. and Tech. in Sichuan, Chengdu, 1997—; mem. Nat. Excellent Rsch. Diagnostic Ultrasound, China, 1998—. Editor: Jour. Clin. Ultrasound Medicine, 1999—; contbr. articles to profl. jours.; patentee in field. Grantee Nat. Nature Sci. & Tech. Found., Chinese Gov., 1996, 99, Mayo Found., 1998. Mem. Chinese Soc. Echocardiography (com. 1999—), Young Scientist Soc. (com. 1999—). Avocations: swimming, music, hiking, football. Office: Sichuan Provincial Hosp, 32 2d Sect/W 1st Round Rd, Chengdu Sichuan 610071, Peoples Republic of China

YIN, WEIPING, mathematics educator; b. Jiangyin, Peoples Republic China, Nov. 1, 1937; s. Jiuchou and Zexiang (Liu) Y.; m. Caihua Xue, Sept. 22, 1966; 1 child, Xiaolan. B, Peking U., 1960, M, 1962; D in Math., Acad. Sinica, Beijing, 1966. Asst. research fellow inst. math. Acad. Sinica, 1966-71; instr. U. Sci. and Tech. China, Hefei, Anhui, 1973-80; prof. U. Sci. and Tech. Peoples Republic China, Hefei, Anhui, 1981-85, full prof., 1985-93; dir. math. sci. rsch. inst. Capital Normal U., Beijing, China, 1994—; vis. prof. U. Poitiers, U. Notre Dame, Sophia U. Found. Natural Sci. China grantee, 1984-87, 88-91, 92—; U. Md. fellow, 1984. Mem. Am. Math. Soc., Chinese Math. Soc., Inst. Des Hautes Etudes Scientific, Internat. Ctr. for Theoretical Physics, Tata Inst. Fundamental Rsch., Math. Sci. Rsch. Inst. Office: Capital Normal U, Dept Math, Beijing 100037, China

YING, JACKIE, chemical engineering educator. St. Laurent assoc. prof. MIT, Cambridge, Mass. Mem. editl. bd. Advances in Chem. Engring., Jour. Metastable and Nanostructured Materials, Nanoparticle Sci. and Tech., Jour. of Electroceramics, Jour. of Porous Materials. David and Lucile Packard fellow, 1995; recipient Exxon Solid-State Chemistry Fellowship award Am. Chem. Soc., 1997, Camille Dreyfus Tchr.-Scholar award, 1996, Colburn award Am. Inst. Chem. Engrs., 2000.

YING, JOHN L., manufacturing executive; b. Shanghai, Chiang-Su, People's Republic of China, June 15, 1948; came to U.S., 1970; s. D.C. and W.T. (Ma) Y.; m. Cynthia C. Chen, Apr. 7, 1981; children: Janice, Jonathan. BS, Tatung Inst. Tech., Taipei, Taiwan, 1969; MS, Poly. Inst. Bklyn., 1972; Profl. Engrs. Degree, Columbia U., N.Y.C., 1974. Application engr. Summit Engring Co., Taipei, 1969-70; asst. to pres. James Betesh Import Co., N.Y.C., 1972-73; strategic planner GM, Detroit, 1973-79; asst. to pres. Lawless Detroit Diesel Corp., City of Industry, Calif., 1979-81; pres., chief exec. officer Cen. Power Products, Inc., Grandview, Mo., 1981—, also bd. dirs.; bd. dirs. Cen. Mfg., Inc., Grandview, Mo., USA-China C. of C. Dir. adv. bd. Mercantile Bank, Kansas City, Mo.; mem. Rep. Recipient Outstanding Minority Bus. Enterprise award Minority Bus. Devel. Agy., Kansas City/Washington, 1986. Mem. USA-China C. of C., Kansas City Club, Hallbrook Country Club.

YINGLING, GERALD PHILLIP, business executive; b. Pitts., Mar. 8, 1952; s. Roy Phillip and Mary Elvira (Lawall) Y.; 1 child, Jonathan Eric. BA, Calif. State U., San Francisco, 1977; cert. grad. rsch., Oita Nat. U., Japan, 1978-80. Asst. v.p. Denny's Internat., Inc., LaMirada, Calif., 1980-83; mgr. bus. devel., Asia-Pacific region Visa Internat., Tokyo, 1983-86; mng. dir. Asia-Pacific devel. State of Ga., Dept. Industry and Trade, Atlanta, 1986—; prin., owner Ga'ga Inc., Guam; exec. mgr. Guam Internat. Airport Authority. Mem. cabinet Gov. Carl T.C. Gutierrez, Guam. With USMC, 1969-71. Mem. Ga. Indsl. Developers, Red Cross of Constantine, Masons. Methodist. Avocations: scuba diving, golf, hiking. Home: PO Box 12788, 420 Farenholt Ave, Tamuning 96911, Guam

YINH, VICTOR MARIUS, electrical engineer; b. Panama, Dec. 19, 1946; came to U.S., 1988; s. Juan and Elena (Wong) Y.; m. Luz Aura Clop, Mar. 5, 1977; children: Victor, Daniel, Marius. BSEE, BSME, U. Panama, 1970, BS in Indsl. Engring., 1975. Cert. code enforcement and adminstrn. profl.; cert. bldg. ofcl. Elec. designer Amado's Engring., Inc., Panama, 1977-79; gen. mgr., project engr. Yinh & Assocs., Panama, 1979-88; mech. engr. AJT & Assocs., Inc., Cape Canaveral, Fla., 1989-90; substa. project engr. Fla. Power & Light Co., Juno Beach, 1990-93; plans examiner & inspector Town of Jupiter, Fla., 1994-2000, chief plans examiner, 2000—. Mem. Bldg. Ofcls. Assn. Fla. Mem. NSPE, IEEE, Fla. Assn. Plumbing, Gas, Mech. Inspectors (2d v.p. 1997), Bldg. Offcls. Assn. of Fla. Home: 5592 Eagle Lake Dr Palm Bch Gdns FL 33418-1550 Office: Town of Jupiter Bldg Divsn 210 Military Trl Jupiter FL 33458-5786

YIP, STEVE YUK-MAN, computer company executive, consultant; b. Hong Kong, Oct. 1, 1953; arrived in Australia, 1992; s. Yiu-Sun and Hing-Oi (Siu) Y.; m. Anissa Fung-King Ling, Dec. 6, 1985; 1 child, Wing Yip. BSc with honors, Portsmouth (Eng.) Poly. U., 1980; MS in Control Engring., Bradford (Eng.) U., 1981. Chartered engr., U.K. Engring. Coun. Technician Rediffusion (Hong Kong) Ltd., 1970-75; svc. engr. Rank Xerox, Hong Kong, 1975-78; designer engr. Chubb Electronics, Hong Kong, 1978; chief engr. Uni-Art, Hong Kong, 1982; supervising engr. Conic Semiconductor, Hong Kong, 1982-87; acting sr. lectr. Vocat. Tng. Coun., Hong Kong, 1987-92; mng. dir. Compucon, Adelaide, Australia, 1992—, Tech-Excel Distbn., Adelaide, Australia, 1997—. Mem. IEEE (sr.), Instn. Engrs. (Australia), Inst. Elec. Engrs. (corp., U.K.), Inst. Engrs. (H.K.), South Australia Jockey Club. Office: Compucon House, 79-81 Burbridge Rd, Hilton SA, Australia

YIP, TENNYSON SAU KING, management executive; b. Oct. 15, 1962. BA in French with honors, U. Saskatchewan, Can., 1985; postgrad. diploma in bus. adminstrn., Monash U., Australia, 1991; MA in Pub. and Social Adminstrn., City U. of Hong Kong, 1995; PGD in English with distinction, Hong Kong Polytech. U., 1997; tchrs. cert., HK Tech. Tchrs. Coll., 1994, City of Guilds of London Inst., 1994; continuing edn. cert. in Putonghua, City U. of Hong Kong, 1995-96. Sr. adminstrn. clk. Reliance Motors Ltd., Hong Kong, 1985-87; exec. Internat. Rendition House Ltd., Hong Kong, 1987-88; mgr. Comml. Radio Edn. Sect., Hong Kong, 1988-96; exec. officer I dept. of electronic engring. City U. of Hong Kong, 1991-95, adminstrv. officer faculty of sci. and tech., 1995-98; regional dir. adminstrn. Far East Regional Office Expeditors Internat. of Washington, Inc., San Po Kong, Hong Kong, 1998—. Home: Blk 24 1B Parc Versailles 2, 3 Mui Shu Hang Rd, Tai Po NT, Hong Kong Office: 26/F Stelux House, 698 Prince Edward Rd East, San Po Kong Kowloon, Hong Kong

YIP, WAI-HONG, music educator, composer, conductor; b. Canton, Republic of China, Dec. 31, 1930; s. Pui-Chor and Yeut-Yung (Lee) Y.; m. Ching-Yee Choi; children: Sincere, Wing-Sie, Nina. MCM, So. Bapt. Theol. Sem., Louisville, 1970; DMA, Southwestern Bapt. Theol. Sem., Ft. Worth, 1979; diploma, Beijing Cen. Conservatory Music, 1955. Resident composer Wuhan Opera Ho., Republic of China, 1955-56; lectr. Wuhan Conservatory Music, 1956-61; dir. music div., lectr. Hong Kong Bapt. Coll., Kowloon, 1963-73, founder and head dept. music and fine arts, 1973—, sr. lectr., 1976-86, prin. lectr., 1986-88, dean faculty of arts, 1980-84, reader, 1988-92; founder, condr. Pan Asia Symphony Orch., 1976—, Hong Kong Bapt. Coll. Girl's Choir, 1973-92, Hong Kong Bapt. Coll. Chamber Orch., 1973-87, Yip's Children's Choir, Hong Kong, 1983—, others; dir., condr. Hong Kong Children's Choir, 1969-83; presenter workshops and seminars including Internat. Soc. for Music Edn., Canberra, Australia, 1988, Am. Choral Dirs. Assn., Louisville, 1989, Brigham Young U., Salt Lake City, 1988, Assn. Brit. Choral Dirs., Oxford, Eng., 1996; various orgnl., adv. and juristic roles nat. and internat. piano competitions including Japan Nat. Piano Competition, 1987, Gina-Bachauer Internat. Piano Competition, 1988; advisor, cons. numerous musical groups and orgns. Author: A Treasury of Music, 1980, The Yip's Concepts for Children Music Education, 1991; author, composer: Hong Kong Children's Choir Song Book, vols. 1-9, 1970-80; composer choral songs including China Sea, 1967, March of the Christian Youth, 1972, Strive for a Bright Future, 1983, Happy Lo-Sor, 1986, others; composer Cello Concerto in A Minor, 1955, Symphony of Earth, 1969, symphonic poem Temptation for piano, mixed choir and orch., 1979, Symphony in E, 1990; composer and arranger numerous instrumental songs and solos; developer several computer programs in mus. edn., 1983—. Advisor Ednl. Publs., Ltd. Drug Awareness program Lions Clubs Internat., 1985. Scholarship recipient Am. So. Bapt. Fgn. Mission Bd., 1968-69; named an hon. citizen Ft. Worth, 1983, Dallas, 1987, 94, Tucson, 1991. Mem. Internat. Soc. Children's Choral and Perfoming Arts (chmn. 1983-87, 99—, permanent honours chmn. 1987-99, 99—). Home: 4A Block 8 16 LaSalle Rd, Kowloon Hong Kong Hong Kong Office: Yip's Children's Choral & Performing Arts Ctr, 1/Fl Wah Chi Mansion, 292 Temple St, Kowloon Hong Kong

YIP, WILLIAM CHIN-LING, pediatric cardiologist, consultant, educator; b. Singapore, Nov. 8, 1950; s. Chun-Houng Soo Yip and Chi-Yong Linly Lee; children: Annie Fong-Tzu, Julie; m. Ting-Fei Ho, Sept. 25, 1979; children: Benjamin Cherng-Hann, Vincent Cherng-Hui, Timothy Cheng-En. MBBS, U. Singapore, 1974, M in Medicine (Pediatrics), 1978; AM, Acad. Medicine Singapore, 1982; MD, Nat. U. Singapore, 1986; diploma in child health, Royal Coll. Physicians, London, 1980. House officer Singapore Gen. Hosp., 1974-75, univ. trainee dept. pediat., 1977-78, lectr. dept. pediat., 1978-82, sr. lectr., cons., 1982-87; assoc. prof. Nat. Univ. Hosp., Singapore, 1987-88, chief divsn. pediatric cardiology, 1998—; cons. pediat. cardiologist Gleneagles Hosp., Singapore, 1988—; vis. cons. Inst. Health Sch. Health Scis., Singapore, 1982-88, Ministry of Edn., Singapore, 1984, Nat. Univ. Hosp., Singapore, 1988—; dir. Singapore Baby and Child Clinic, Singapore, 1988—; adj. assoc. prof. Nat. U. Singapore, 1998—. Author, editor book chpts.; contbr. articles to profl. jours. Capt. Singapore Armed Forces, 1975-77; capt. Res.; capt. Sinapore Civil Def. Res., 1993—. Recipient Long Svc. medal St. John Ambulance Brigade, 1981. Fellow Acad. Medicine Singapore, Royal Coll. Physicians (Edinburgh), royal Soc. Medicine (London); mem. AAAS (internat.), Royal Coll. Physicians (U.K.), Singapore Pediat. Soc. (v.p., Haridas Meml. Lectr. gold medal 1983), Am. Inst. Ultrasound in Medicine, Singapore Med. Assn., Singapore Cardiac Soc., N.Y. Acad. Scis. Avocations: music, model train collecting, stamp collecting, reading, swimming. Office: Singapore Baby & Child Clin, 6 Napier Rd 07-01-03, Singapore 258499, Singapore

YIP, WING CHIU, electrical and electronic engineering researcher; b. Hong Kong, Hong Kong, June 11, 1966; s. Tai Leung Yip and Shek Kiu Lau. BEng in Electronic Engring. 1st honors, City U. Hong Kong, 1992; PhD in Elec. and Electronic Engring., Hong Kong U. Sci. and Tech., 1999. Rsch. asst. Hong Kong U. Sci. and Tech., 1993-99, rsch. assoc., 1999—. Mem. IEEE. Achievements include research on applied optics and information processing. Home: No 3909 Man Chak House, Hing Man Estate Chai Wan, Hong Kong Hong Kong Office: Hong Kong U Sci & Tech, Clear Water Bay Kowloon, Hong Kong Hong Kong

YIP, YU LAP, surgeon, medical administrator; b. Hong Kong, May 10, 1953; s. Sue Leong Yip. MBBS, Hong Kong U., 1977; FRCS, Royal Coll. Surgeon, Glasgow, Eng., 1981. Med. diplomate, Hong Kong. Intern, then resident; house obstetrician Nethersole Hosp., Hong Kong, 1977; house surgeon United Christian Hosp., Hong Kong, 1978; med. health officer Govt. Chest Service, Kowloon Hosp., Hong Kong, 1978-79; med. officer Surg. Dept. United Christian Hosp., Hong Kong, 1979-84; head dept. surgery Pok Oi Hosp., Hong Kong, 1984-90; hon. lectr. Hong Kong U. Med. Faculty, 1992—; divisional surgeon St. John's Ambulance, 1992—; hon. lectr. Nethersole Sch. Nursing, Hong Kong, 1979-84; hon. clin. asst. prof. Hong Kong U. Med. Faculty, 1998—; adj. clin. prof. Chinese U. Hong Kong, 1999—. Author: Hand Rehabilitation with Computer, 1985, Blood Gas Computer Analysis, Telephone Transmission, 1986, Endourology and Stone Surgery, 1988, Video Endoscopy, 1984; chief editor, Pok OI Hospital Gazette, 1984-90; contbr. articles to profl. jours. Graham scholar Hong Kong Govt., 1970. Fellow Royal Soc. Health, Internat. Coll. Surgeons, Am. Acad. Cosmetic Surgeons, Hong Kong Coll. Surgeons, Am. Coll. Chest Physicians, Hong Kong Acad. Medicine.

YIZHONG, LI, business executive. Grad., Beijing Petroleum Inst., 1966. Various mgmt. and sr. engr. positions; pres. Qilu Petrochem. Co., 1985-87; v.p. then mng. v.p. Old Sinopec, 1987-97; chmn., pres. China East United Petrochem. Group Ltd., 1997-98; chmn. Yizheng Chem. Fiber Co. Ltd.; pres. Sinopec Group Co., Beijing, 1998—, also bd. dirs. Office: Sinopec Corp, A6 Huixindong St, Beijing China*

YLI-JOKIPII, PENTTI OLAVI, geography educator; b. Jalasjarvi, Finland, Feb. 7, 1941; s. Väinö Gabriel and Laimi Susanna (Hakkola) Yli-J.; m. Hilkka Mirjami Pekonen, Mar. 2, 1969; children: Kaisa, Markus. BSc, U. Helsinki, Finland, 1964, MSc, 1965, PhD, 1967. Acting assoc. prof. U. Helsinki, 1968-69, 71-73; prof. econ. geography Turku (Finland) Sch. Econs., 1973-74; prof. geography U. Turku, 1974—, dean faculty sci., 1987-93; vis. scholar Mich. State U., 1970. Author papers, articles, books on econ. geography, geography and regional planning. Mem. Geog. Soc. Finland (pres. 1979), Finnish Nat. Com. Internat. Geog. Union (pres. 1983-88), Fin-

nish Acad. Sci. and Letters, Rsch. Coun. Acad. of Finland, 1995-2000. Office: U Turku, U Turku Dept Geography, 20014500 Turku Finland

YLINEN, JAAKKO KRISTIAN, architect; b. Helsinki, May 18, 1936; s. Arvo Albin and Lea Maria (Hietarinta) Ylinen; m. Maija Vappu Suomalainen, Dec. 4, 1967; 1 child, Kristian. MArch, Helsinki U. Tech., 1962, Licentiate Tech., 1968. Ptnr. Mansikka, Salonen & Ylinen, Architects, Helsinki, 1963-67, Salonen & Ylinen, Architects, Helsinki, 1967-68; ptnr. Kaupunkisuunnittelu Ltd., Helsinki, 1969—, pres., 1994—; sr. asst. architecture Helsinki U. Tech., 1964-69; lectr. architecture, 1971-77. Contbr. articles to profl. jours. Mem. State Council Architecture, Finland, 1968-71, chmn. 1971-73; vice-chmn. State Council for Arts, Finland, 1971-73; bd. dirs. Bldg. Info. Instn., Helsinki, 1975-78. Mem. Finnish Assn. Architects, Finnish Assn. Cons. Engrs. Avocation: photography. Home: Katajanokankatu 3A 6, FIN00160 Helsinki Finland Office: Kaupunkisunnittelu Ltd, Katajanokankatu 3F25, FIN00160 Helsinki Finland

YNGVE, VICTOR H., linguist, researcher; b. Niagara Falls, N.Y., July 5, 1920; s. Victor and Miriam (Huse) Y.; m. Jean Huber, Sept. 6, 1943; children: Marna, David, Alan. BS in Physics, Antioch Coll., Yellow Springs, Ohio, 1943; MS in Physics, U. Chgo., 1950, PhD in Physics, 1953. Staff mem., rsch. assoc. MIT, Cambridge, Mass., 1953-65; prof. linguistics U. Chgo., 1965-90, prof. emeritus, 1990—; co-founder, editor Mechanical Translation and Computational Linguistics, 1954-70; cons. Standardization of Am. Std. Code for Info. Interchange (ASCII); founder, editor, pub. Comms. of the Workshop for Sci. Linguistics, 1990—. Author: Computer Programming with Comit II, 1972, Linguistics as a Science, 1986, From Grammar to Science, 1996. Mem. Linguistic Soc. Am., Soc. Linguistica Europaea, Linguistic Assn. of Can. and the U.S. (v.p. 1984-85, pres. 1985-86), Assn. for Computational Linguistics (co-founder, 1st pres. 1962-63).

YODA, KENTARO, biomedical engineering educator; b. Wakakusa, Yamanashi, Japan, Feb. 13, 1939; s. Toshiyuki and Fumiko (Ueno) Y.; m. Junko Okuwaki, Nov. 17, 1968; children: Naoko, Shinichiro, Makiko. BSc in Chemistry, Sci. U., Tokyo, 1962; PhD in Engring., Kyoto (Japan) U., 1972. Rschr. Toyobo Co., Otsu, Japan, 1962-73, chief rschr., 1973-78, sr. rschr., 1978-83; dir. R & D Toyobo Co., Osaka, Japan, 1983-89; sr. v.p. Toyobo Am. Inc., N.Y.C., 1989-91; prof. biomed. engring. Tokai U., Numazu, Japan, 1991—; mem. ops. com. Bioreactor Sys. Resh. Orgn., Tokyo, 1984-88; mem. mgmt. com. Protein Engring. Rsch. Inst., Osaka, 1987-89; mem. standardization com. Japan Indsl. Stds., Tokyo, 1988-89; vis. scholar Stanford U., Palo Alto, Calif., 1989-90. Author: Chemical Sensors, 1983, Methods in Enzymology, Vol. 137, 1988; contbr. articles to med. jours., including Clin. Chemistry, Annals N.Y. Acad. Scis., Brain Rsch. Mem. adv. com. City of Numazu, 1991—, Shizuoka (Japan) Prefecture, 1994—. Recipient excellent invention award Japan Econ. Newspaper, 1984. Mem. Chem. Soc. Japan, Japanese Assn. Clin. Pathology, Am. Chem. Soc. Baptist. Achievements include development of new biosensors, high performance artificial kidney; elucidation of neuronal mechanism of pain allevation by laser irradiation. Office: Tokai U, 317 Nishino, Shizuoka Numazu 410-0321, Japan

YODA, MITSUHIRO, economist; b. Gunma, Japan, Oct. 15, 1958; s. Kunio and Sumiko (Matsumoto) Y. B in Econs., Tokyo U., 1982; MSBA, U. Ill., 1989. Bus. clk. Toyota Motor Corp., Tokyo, 1982-88; sr. economist Inst. for Internat. Econ. Studies, Tokyo, 1990—. Mem. Japan Assn. Bus. Analysis, Phi Kappa Phi. Avocations: tennis, skiing. Home: 1-27-1 Togoshi Shinagawa-ku, 142-0041 Tokyo Japan Office: Inst Internat Econ Studies, 2-3-18 Kudan-minami, Chiuoda-ku Tokyo 102-0074, Japan

YODA, NAOYA, research executive, educator, consultant; b. Tokyo, June 11, 1931; s. Shui'chi and Teru (Ozaki) Y.; m. Kazuko Hironaka, Apr. 7, 1960; children: Naohisa, Nobuhisa, Yoshihisa Emie. BA, Nagoya U., 1954, PhD, 1960; postgrad., Harvard U., 1954-57, U. Ariz., 1962-63. Sr. rsch. chemist basic rsch. lab. Toray Industries Inc., 1960-62, rsch. assoc., 1963-68, project leader, 1968-72, rsch. mgr. plastics rsch. labs., 1972-76, gen. mgr. R&D strategic planning dept., 1976-79; exec. v.p. Toray Industries (America) Inc., N.Y., 1979-85; pres., CEO Toray Corp. Bus. Rsch., Inc., Tokyo, 1990-96; exec. advisor Kansai Rsch. Inst., 1996—; prof. Keio U. Internat. Ctr., Tokyo; prof. bus. adminstrn. Rissho U., Tokyo, 1996—; cons. Maxdem Inc.; mem. com. Fedn. Mgmt. of Polymer Industry, Japan, 1978-79; postdoctoral assoc. U. Ariz., 1962-63. Fulbright scholar Harvard U., 1954-57; recipient Excellent Achievement of Polymer Sic. award Soc. High Polymers Japan, 1977. Mem. Engring. Acad. Japan, Chem. Soc. Japan, Am. Chem. Soc., Soc. Polymer Sci. Japan, Japanese Chem. Assn. N.Y. (pres. 1984—), Swedish Royal Acad. Engring. Sci., Harvard Club, Tokyo Club. Achievements include contbr. articles on phys. organic chemistry and polymer sci. to books, articles to ind. mgmt. study, plastics and indsl. chemistry to profl. jours.; research in new polymerization processes and high polymer syntheses. Home: 6-45-24 Hinominami Konan-ku, Yokohama Kanagawa 234-0055, Japan Office: Kansai Rsch Inst Rissho Univ, 4-2-16 Osaki Shinagama-ku, Tokyo Chiyoda 141-0032, Japan

YODER, HATTEN SCHUYLER, JR., petrologist; b. Cleve., Mar. 20, 1921; s. Hatten Schuyler and Elizabeth Katherine (Knieling) Y.; m. Elizabeth Marie Bruffey, Aug. 1, 1959; children: Hatten Schuyler III (dec.), Karen Marianne Yoder Wallace. AA, U. Chgo., 1940, SB, 1941; postgrad., U. Minn., 1941; PhD, Mass. Inst. Tech., 1948; D honoris causa, U. Paris VI, 1981; DEngring. (hon.), Colo. Sch. of Mines, 1995. Petrologist Geophys. Lab., Carnegie Instn., Washington, 1948-71, dir., 1971-86, dir. emeritus, 1986—; cons. Los Alamos (N.Mex.) Nat. Lab., 1972—, chmn. external adv. com. earth & environ. scis. divsn., 1991-97. Author: Generation of Basaltic Magma, 1976, Planned Invasion of Japan, 1945, The Siberian Weather Advantage, 1997; editor: The Evolution of the Igneous Rocks: Fiftieth Anniversary Perspectives, 1979; co-editor: Geochemical Transport and Kinetics, 1974; co-editor Jour. of Petrology, 1959-69; assoc. editor Am. Jour. Sci, 1972-90; mem. editl. bd. Earth Scis. History, 1993—; contbr. articles to sci. jours. Trustee The Cutler Trust, 1992—; bd. advisors Coll. of Democracy of the Nat. Grad. U., founders com. 1985, exec. com./sec.-treas. 1995—). Lt. comdr. USNR, 1942-58. Naval Expedition to Siberia, 1945-46. Recipient Bicentennial medal Columbia U., 1954, A.G. Werner medal German Mineral Soc., 1972, Profl. Achievement award U. Chgo. Club Washington, 2000; named to Disting. Alumni Hall of Fame, Lakewood (Ohio) H.S., 1990; mineral yoderite named in his honor. Fellow Geol. Soc. Am. (coun. 1966-68, A.L. Day medal 1962, History Geology award 1998), Geol. Soc. London (hon. Wollaston medal 1979), Geol. Soc. South Africa (du Toit lectr. 1987), Am. Acad. Arts and Scis., Mineral. Soc. Am. (coun. 1962-64, 69-73, pres. 1971-72, MSA award 1954, Roebling medal 1992), Am. Geophys. Union (pres. volcanology, geochemistry and petrology sect. 1962-64); mem. NAS (chmn. geology sect. 1973-76, A.L. Day prize and lectr. 1972), Mineral Soc. London (hon., Hallimond lectr. 1979), Geol. Soc. Finland, Russian Mineral Soc. (hon.), Geochem. Soc. (organizer, founding mem., coun. 1956-58), Am. Chem. Soc., Mineral Assn. Can., Washington Acad. Sci., Geol. Soc. Washington, Chem. Soc. Washington, French Soc. Mineralogy and Crystallography (hon.), Am. Philos. Soc. (coun. 1983-85, 94-2000), Pub. Mems. Assn. of Fgn. Svc. (bd. dirs. 1993-96, 97—, v.p. 1994, 98-2000, treas. 2000—), History of Earth Scis. Soc. (pres. 1995-96), History of Sci. Soc. (Forum lectr. 1998), SAR, Sigma Xi, Phi Delta Theta (Golden Legion award). Home: 6709 Melody Ln Bethesda MD 20817-3152 Office: Geophys Lab 5251 Broad Branch Rd NW Washington DC 20015-1305

YOELI, PINHAS (GUENTHER APTEKMANN), engineering educator; b. Bayreuth, Bavaria, Germany, July 1, 1920; s. Julius and Edith (Schindler) Aptekmann; m. Judith Donath (div.); 1 child, Dan; m. Agi Izsakova, 1949; 1 child, Raphael. Diploma in Engring., Eidgenossische Technische Hoch, Switzerland, 1956. Sr. lectr. Technion, Israel, 1957-64, assoc. prof., 1964-68; prof. Tel Aviv (Israel) U., 1968-91, prof. emeritus, 1991—; chief instr. mil. topography Hagana, Palestine, 1938-49. Author: Cartographic Drawing with Computers, 1982; contbr. articles to profl. jours. Comdr. map and photo intelligence svc. Israel Army, 1949-52. Lt. col. Israel Army, 1949-57. Mem. Israel Surveyors Assn., Assn. Engrs. and Archs., Israel Cartographic Assn. (pres. 1988-91). Avocations: gardening, painting. Home: 8 Haneviim, 64356 Tel Aviv Israel Office: Tel Aviv Univ, Ramat Aviv, Tel Aviv Israel

YOGESAN, KANAGASINGAM, telemedicine center director; b. Colombo, Sri Lanka, Mar. 18, 1963; arrived in Australia, 1996; s. Kanagasingam and Ratnambal (Velautham) T.; m. Saiyinthie Vijayarajah, Oct. 28, 1993. BS with honors, U. Oslo, 1988, MS, 1992, PhD, 1995. Rsch. asst. Kozo Keikahu Engring., Inc., Tokyo, 1988; programmer Multimedia Lab., Oslo, 1989-90; computer scientist The Norwegian Radium Hosp., Oslo, 1991-96; dir. Telemedicine Ctr. Lions Eye Inst., Perth, Australia, 1996—; cons. in field. Author: Textur Analysis as a Prognostic and Diagnostic Tool in Tumor Pathology, 1995; inventor/patentee in field. Recipient Astech prize Norwegian Urology Soc., Oslo, 1996, Wolf prize German Urology Soc., 1996; rsch. fellow The U. Oslo, 1992-96. Mem. IEEE (pres. Computer Soc. Wa. chpt.), Australian Pattern Recognition Soc. Avocations: photography, cycling, cricket, soccer, exercise. Office: Lions Eye Inst, 2 Verdun St, Nedlands 6009, Australia

YOH, SOO-DONG, chemistry educator; b. Sungjoo, Kyungpook, Korea, Feb. 5, 1937; s. Sang Woon Yoh and Kwan Yeol Doh; m. Young Nam Lee, June 7, 1961; children: Seong-Jin, Hae-Joo, Tae-Ho, Eon-Joo. BS, Kyungpook U., Taegu, Korea, 1961, MS, 1964; PhD, Osaka (Japan) U., 1973; postgrad., SUNY, Buffalo, 1976-77. Asst. prof. Youngnam Jr. Indsl. Coll., Taegu, 1964-69; prof. Kyungpook Nat. U., Taegu, 1969—, chmn. dept. chemistry Grad. Sch., 1985-87, chmn. Internat. Seminar of Chemistry, 1986-87, dir. Sci. Edn. Rsch. Inst., 1989-91; rschr. Osaka U., 1971-73; deliberative mem. Coun. R&D-Korea Sci. and Engring. Found., Daejon, Korea, 1991-93; vis. prof. Kyushu U. Japan, 1999. Author: Modern Organic Chemistry, 1987, Colloid and Surfactant, 1995, High School Chemistry, 1, 2, 1996; contbr. articles to profl. jours. Practical mem. Group to Evaluate for Univs., 1991. Soldier 15th Divsn., 1961-62. Mem. Korean Chem. Soc. (life, dir. Taegu-Kyungpook local chpt. 1990-92, Acad. Devel. v.p. 1999, award 1980), Chem. Soc. Japan, Korean Chem. Soc. (v.p. 1999). Avocations: tennis, mountain climbing. Home: 1382-62 SanKyug-dong Puk-ku, Taegu 702-014, Korea Office: Dept Chem Edn, Tchrs Coll Kyungpook Nat U, Taegu 702-701, Korea

YOKOBORI, TAKEO, materials and mechanical engineering scientist, educator; b. Tochigi-ken, Japan, Nov. 20, 1917; s. Syotaro and Yayoi (Kobori) Y.; B. Engring., U. Tokyo, 1941, Sc.D., 1956; m. Miyoko Uzuka, Aug. 20, 1945; 1 son, Toshimitsu. Asso. prof. mech. engring. Tohoku U., 1955-57, prof., 1957-81, prof. emeritus, 1981—; dean, prof. Sch. of Sci. and Engring. Teikyo U., 1989—. founder, dir. Rsch. Inst. Strength and Fracture for Materials, 1964-81; mem. Sci. Coun. Japan, 1966-85. Recipient Japan Acad. Sci. prize, 1971, Cross of Merit with Collar Ribbon, A. Einstein Internat. Acad. Found., 1993; decorated Second Order of Merit, Emperor of Japan, 1991; guest U.S.S.R. Acad. Scis., 1971. Mem. Internat. Congress on Fracture (pres. 1965-73, founder pres. 1973—), Japanese Soc. Strength and Fracture of Materials (pres. 1966—), Japan Acad. (Academician 1996—), Japan Soc. Mech. Engrs. (hon.), Japan Inst. Metals (hon.), Japan Soc. Biomaterials (founding pres. 1978—), Soc. Materials Sci. Japan (hon.), Nat. Acad. Engring. U.S. (fgn. assoc., 1981—), Author: The Strength, Fracture and Fatigue of Materials, 1965; An Interdisciplinary Approach to Fracture and Strength of Solids, 1968; Methodologies and Fundamentals of Fracture of Matter and Solids, 1978; editor in chief Internat. Jour. Biomed. Materials and Engring., 1991—; contbr. 450 articles to profl. jours. Home: 31-15 Aoyama 1 chome, Taihakuku Sendai 982, Japan

YOKOBORI, TOSHIMITSU, materials engineering researcher, educator; b. Tokyo, Mar. 29, 1951; s. Takeo and Miyoko Yokobori; m. Naoko Endo, Sept. 3, 1988; 1 child, Hanako. BA, Tohoku U., Sendai, Japan, 1973, MA, 1975, PhD, 1978. Rsch. assoc. Tohoku U., 1978-79, assoc. prof. materials engring., 1979—; mem. nat. com. on materials Sci. Coun. Japan, 1994—; mem. coun. Internat. Congress on Fracture, 1993—; mem. tech. working area Creep Crack, Versailles Advanced Materials and Stds. Project, 1988—. Exec. editor Biomed. Materials and Engring., 1990—. Mem. ASTM (sect. chmn. F-4-4-10 com. Phila. 1987-91, co-chmn. symposium biomaterials mech. properties Pitts. 1992, co-editor Biomaterials Mech. Properties STP1173 1994), Far East Oceanic Fracture Group (dir. 1993-98), Japan Soc. Mech. Engrs. (Promotion prize 1983), Japan Soc. for Strength and Fracture (dir. 1994—), Japan Soc. Biomaterials (dir. 1984-00), Soc. Materials Sci. Japan (bd. dirs. 1995-97, dir. 2000—). Home: Taihaku-ku, 31-15-1 chome, Aoyama, Sendai 982, Japan Office: Tohoku U Faculty Engring, Aoba Aramaki Aobaku, Sendai 980-77, Japan

YOKOE, TAKAO, medical educator; b. Chiba, Japan, Nov. 19, 1952; p. Yasuo and Akiko Yokoe; m. Machiko Yokoe, Nov. 23, 1981; children: Takamichi, Ayako. MD, Gunma U., Maebashi, Japan, 1977, D in Med. Sci., 1988. Med. diplomate. Asst. prof. second dept. surgery Gunma U. Hosp., Maebashi, 1986-91; assoc. prof. dept. emergency/critical care medicine Gunma U. Sch. Medicine, Maebashi, 1991—; assoc. dir. emergency room Gunma U. Hosp., Maebashi, 1991—; inspector Med. Reimbersement Found., Gunma, 1992—. Assoc. editor: Breast Cancer, 1998. Mem. Japan Surg. Soc. (instr. 1995—), Japanese Soc. for Clin. Surgery (councilor 1993—), Japanese Soc. for Cancer Therapy (councilor 1995—), Japanese Assn. Endocrine Surgery (councilor 1991—). E-mail: tyokoe@med.gunma-u.ac.jp. Fax: 27-220-8540. Office: Gunma U Sch Medicine, 3-39-15 Showa-machi, Maebashi 371-8511, Japan

YOKOI, TSUYOSHI, pharmaceutical educator; b. Nagoya, Japan, Mar. 3, 1956; s. Yutaka and Hisako Yokoi; m. Sanae Taniguchi, Nov. 2, 1980; children: Satoshi, Akira. BS, Gifu (Japan) Pharm. U., 1978, MSc, 1980, PhD in Pharmacology, 1989; PhD in Medicine, Tohoku U., Sendai, Japan, 1985. Rsch. assoc. Gifu U., 1980-84; rsch. assoc. Tohoku U., 1984-89, asst. prof., 1989-90; fellow Baylor Coll. Medicine, Houston, 1985-87; assoc. prof. Hokkaido U., Sapporo, Japan, 1990-97; prof. Kanazawa (Japan) U., 1997—. Mem. Japanese Assn. for Cancer Rsch., Japanese Soc. for Drug Metabolism and Disposition (award for promotion of rsch. 1996), Japanese Soc. for Toxicol. Sci. (Tanabe Meml. award 1995), Japanese Soc. for Pharmacology, Japanese Biochem. Soc., Internat. Soc. for Study of Xenobiotics. Home: Heiwamachi 3-20-10, Kanazawa 921-8105, Japan Office: Takara-Machi 13-1, Kanazawa U, Kanazawa 920-0934, Japan

YOKOI, YASUHARU, chemist; b. Tokyo, Sept. 4, 1966; s. Yasuaki Yokoi and Kazuko Shibata; m. Chikako Amano, Dec. 24, 1992; children: Nana, Masaharu, Kazushi. BS, Sci. U. Tokyo, 1990; MS, Waseda U., Tokyo, 1992. Rschr. Fundamental Tech. Rsch. Lab. Tokyo Gas Co., Ltd., 1992-99; rschr. Frontier Tech. Lab., Yokohama, Japan, 1999—. Mem. Chem. Soc. Japan, Am. Chem. Soc. Divsn. Fuel Chemistry. Achievements include Japanese patent. Office: Frontier Tech Lab, 1-7-7 Suehiro-Cho, Yokohama 230-0045, Japan

YOKOMIZU, YASUNOBU, engineering educator; b. Kozakai-town, Aichi, Japan, Oct. 13, 1962; m. Eiko Uchiyama, Oct. 11, 1992. BA, Nagoya (Japan) U., 1985, MA, 1987, D, 1991. Assoc. prof. Nagoya U., 1990—. Patentee in field. Mem. Inst. Elec. Engring. of Jaan (tech. com. on gas circuit breaker, excellent paper award 1991, 95, 97). Office: Nagoy U Dept Elec Engring, Furo-cho Chikusa-ku, Nagoya 464-8603, Japan

YOKOTA, FUMIHIKO, chemical engineer; b. Asahikawa, Japan, Nov. 3, 1961; s. Osamu and Emiko (Seto) Y.; m. Kei Takahashi, June 25, 1989; 1 child, Junichiro. BSc, Hirosaki U., 1984, MSc, 1987; D in Engring., Yamagata U., 1998. Engr. Tohoku Tosoh Chem. Co. Ltd., Sakata, Japan, 1987—. Mem. Japan Soc. Analytical Chemistry, Japan Railfan Club. Home: 129 Tatenosawa Soegawa, 999-7652 Fujishima Yamagata, Japan Office: Tohoku Tosoh Chem Co Ltd, 1-4-16 Ohama, 998-0064 Sakata Yamagata, Japan

YOKOTA, MITSUHIRO, cardiologist educator; b. Nagoya, Aichi, Japan, Apr. 3, 1942; s. Matao and Miyo (Suzuki) Y.; m. Saeko Yamada, Apr. 29, 1970; children: Yuri, Shigeki, Satoshi, Kazumi. MD, Nagoya U., 1969, PhD, 1978. Med. diplomate in cardiology. Intern Chuno Gen. Hosp., Gifu, Japan, 1969-70, resident, 1970-72; clin. fellow first dept. internal medicine Nagoya U. Sch. of Medicine, 1972-76; rsch. specialist U. Minn., Mpls., 1976-78; dir. dept. cardiology Chubu Nat. Hosp., Obu, Japan, 1978-87; asst. prof. medicine Nagoya U., 1987-89, assoc. prof., 1989-2000; chief circulatory physiology sect. Nagoya U. Hosp., 1989—, vice dir. dept. clin. lab. medicine, 1993—; assoc. prof. grad. sch. medicine Nagoya U., 2000—. Contbr. numerous articles to profl. jours. Fellow Am. Coll. Cardiology, Am. Heart Assn. Avocations: golf, music, travel. Home: 3-98 Kaminokura, Midori-ku Nagoya 458-0812, Japan Office: Nagoya U Sch Medicine, 65 Tsurumai-cho Showa-Ku, Nagoya 466-8550, Japan

YOKOTA, SHOUHEI, internist, researcher; b. Okazaki, Aichi, Japan, July 17, 1956; s. Hisashi and Sachiko (Aizu) Y.; m. Keiko Fujitani, Sept. 26, 1982; 1 child, Eriko. B Medicine, Kyoto Prefectural U Med, Japan, 1981, MD, 1988. Lic. internist. Intern Kyoto Prefectural U. Medicine, 1981-83; resident Otsu (Japan) Mcpl. Hosp., 1983-84; scholar U. Ulm, Germany, 1988-90; instr. Kyoto Prefectural U. Medicine, 1990—, dir. Fushimi br., 1995-97; head dept. internal medicine Kyoto Yosanoumi Hosp., Iwataki, Japan, 1991-95; dir. Kameoka Pub. Health Ctr., 1998—. Author: Atlas of Hematological Malignancies, 1990; editor: Case Method Approach for Subspeciality Training for Blood Diseases, 1995, Diagnostic Guide for Hematology/Oncology, 2000. Recipient scholarship Alexander von Humboldt Found., Bonn, Germany, 1988-90. Mem. Am. Soc. Hematology, Japanese Soc. Internal Medicine, Japanese Soc. Hematology. Buddhist. Avocation: photography. Home: 16-2 Kamiumenoki-cho, Shichiku, Kyoto 603-8179, Japan Office: Kyoto Pref U Medicine, Kawaramachi-Hirokoji, Kyoto 602-0841, Japan

YOKOYAMA, SHIGERU, science facility professional; b. Sendai, Japan, Mar. 5, 1947; s. Katsujiro and Toyoko Y.; m. Yoko Ogawa, May 30, 1976; 3 children. B of Engring., U. Tokyo, 1969, PhD, 1986. Rsch. engr. CRIEPI, Tokyo, Japan, 1969-80; sr. rsch. engr. CRIEPI, Tokyo, 1980-85, prin. rsch. engr., 1985-89, mgr., 1989-93, deputy dir., 1993-95, dir., 1995-98, assoc. v.p., 1998—. Author: Lighting-Damages and Protective MEthods, 1988 (IEE prize 1989); patentee in field. Recipient Assn. Found. Elec. Sci. and Engring. tech. award, 1986. Fellow IEEE; mem. Inst. Elec. Engrs., Soc. Atmospheric Electricity Japan (rsch. prize 1995). Avocations: soccer, yachting. Home: Ohsumidai 2-3-4, Kanagawa Isehara-shi 259-1109, Japan Office: Komae Rsch Lab CRIEPI, Iwadokita 2-11-1, Komae-shi Tokyo 201-8511, Japan

YOKOYAMA, SHOICHI, manufacturing executive; b. Niigata, Japan, Nov. 9, 1945; s. Tetsuzo and Ariko (Watanabe) Y.; m. Emi Hirase, Mar. 26, 1970; children: Gaku, Lena. BA, Keio U., 1969. Mid.-east rep. IHI Co., Beirut, Lebanon, 1972-75, Kuwait, 1975-77; asst. mgr. IHI Co., Tokyo, 1977-86, mgr. mid.-east, 1986; mng. dir., gen. mgr. IHI UAE Co., Abu Dhabi, United Arab Emirates, 1987—. Co-author: Asagiri, 1994. Mem. Abu Dhabi Mitakai (chmn.). Buddhist. Avocations: tennis, golf, skiing, classical music. Office: IHI UAE Co Ltd, PO Box 2374, Abu Dhabi United Arab Emirates

YONDA, ALFRED WILLIAM, mathematician; b. Cambridge, Mass., Aug. 10, 1919; s. Walter and Theophelia (Naruscewicz) Y.; B.S., U. Ala., 1952, M.A. in Math., 1954; m. Mary Jane McManus, Dec. 19, 1949 (dec.); children—Nancy, Kathryn, Elizabeth, John; m. Peggy A. Terrel, June 22, 1975. Mathematician rocket research Redstone Arsenal, Huntsville, Ala., 1953, U.S. Army Ballistic Research Labs., Aberdeen, Md., 1954-56; instr. math. U. Ala., Tuscaloosa, 1954, Temple U., Phila., 1956-57; asso. scientist, research and devel. div. Avco Corp., Wilmington, Mass., 1957-59; sr. mem. tech. staff RCA, Camden, N.J., 1959-66; mgr. computer analysis and programming dept. Raytheon Co. space and information systems div., Sudbury, Mass., 1966-70, mgr. software systems lab., 1969-70, prin. engr. missiles systems div., 1970-73; mgr. systems analysis and programming GTE Govt. Systems Corp., 1973-77, mgr. software engring. Atlantic ops., 1977-82, sr. mem. tech. staff Command Control & Communications Sector, 1983-91; software systems engr. Yonda Software Systems Cons., 1991—. Pres., Milford Area Assn. Retarded Children, 1970-74; vice-chmn. fin. com. Town of Medway, 1973; bd. dirs. Blackstone Valley Mental Health and Retardation Area , 1970-76; trustee Medway Libraries, 1973-82, chmn., 1974-81. Served with USAAF, 1943-46. Hon. fellow Advanced Level Telecommunications Tng. Center, Ghaziabad, India, 1981. Registered profl. engr. Mem. AAAS, IEEE, Math. Assn. Am., N.Y. Acad. Scis., Sigma Xi, Phi Eta Sigma, Pi Mu Epsilon (pres. Ala. chpt. 1953-54), Sigma Pi Sigma. Contbr. articles to profl. jours. Office: 12 Sunset Dr Medway MA 02053-2008

YONDEMLI, FUAT, medical educator; b. Nevsehir, Turkey, Mar. 24, 1951; s. Huseyin and Meliha (Gokturk) Y.; children: Hande, Emre; m. Lilya Kurtayeva, Sept. 24, 1993. MD, Ankara Med. Faculty, 1979; dipl. ear nose and throat, Hacettepe Med. Faculty, Ankara, 1979. Head clinician Ankara (Turkey) Emergency and Traffic Hosp., 1979-80, Social Security Ankara Hosp., 1981-82; asst. prof., assoc. prof. faculty medicine Selcuk U., Konya, Turkey, 1982-92; prof. faculty medicine Selcuk U., Konya, 1992—. Author: A Handbook of Ear, Nose, Throat, 1987; translator: Lectures on Ear, Nose, Throat Diseases, 1989. 2d lt. Turkish Army, 1980-81. Avocations: Islamic calligraphy (Hüsnü-Hat), gilding (Tezhip), marbling (Ebru). Hcme: Askan Cad Muge Sitesi 120/3, 42090 Konya Turkey Office: Dept Ear Nose Throat, Selcuk Univ, 42001 Konya Turkey

YONEDA, IKUO, anesthesiologist; b. Yatsushiro, Japan, Mar. 7, 1955; s. Noboru and Chizuko (Hashimoto) Y.; m. Motoko Miyazaki, May 2, 1982; children: Masafumi, Madoka, Shiori, Tsuyoshi. MD, Nat. Def. Med. Coll., 1981, PhD, 1992. Flight surgeon 5th wing Japan Air Self-Def. Force, Japan, 1983-85; staff med. sect. Air Staff Office Def. Agy., Japan, 1992-93; dir. 4th divsn. aeromed. lab. Air Self-Def. Force, Japan, 1994-97; assoc. prof. divsn. of behavioral scis. Nat. Def. Med. Coll. Rsch. Inst., Japan, 1997—. Contbr. articles to profl. jours. Mem. Am. Soc. of Anesthesiologists, Aerospace Med. Assn. Avocation: private pilot. Home: 4-403 3-2 Namiki Tokorozawa, Saitama 359-0042, Japan Office: Nat Def Med Coll Rsch Inst, 3-2 Namiki, Tokorozawa 359-8513, Japan

YONEDA, MASASHI, gastroenterologist, scientist, educator; b. Tokyo, Apr. 24, 1957; s. Masaya and Michiko (Tachioka) Y.; m. Eriko Yoshida, Apr. 17, 1990; 1 child, Lisa. BS, Hirosaki (Japan) U., 1979, MD, 1983, PhD, 1987. Diplomate Bd. Internal Medicine, Bd. Gastroenterology, Bd. Hepatology. Resident in internal medicine and gastroenterology Hirosaki U. Med. Ctr., 1983-87; mem. med. staff Hakodade (Japan) Chuo Hosp., 1987-88, Hachinohe (Japan) Mcpl. Hosp., 1988-89, Hirosaki U., 1992-93; vis. rschr. UCLA, 1989-92; mem. med. staff Asahikawa (Japan) Med. Coll., 1993-94, asst. prof. dept. medicine, 1994-98; assoc. prof. Internat. U. Health and Welfare, Japan, 1998—. Author: Liver Innervation, 1995; contbr. articles to med. jours., including Gastroenterology, Hepatology, Am. Jour. Physiology, Brit. Jour. Pharmacology. Recipient young investigator award World Soc. Gastroenterology, 1994; rsch. grantee Japan Rsch. Found. Clin. Pharmacology, 1993, Kanae Rsch. Found., 1995, Japanese Ministry Edn. and Sci., 1995, 96, 97, 98, 99. Mem. Japanese Soc. Gastroenterology, Am. Gastroenterol. Assn., Soc. for Neurosci. Avocations: tennis, skiing. Home: Horan Murasakizuka Maison, # 308, Murasakizuka 1-3-10, Otawara 324-0058, Japan Office: Internat U Health & Welfare, Kitakanamaru 2600, Otawara Tochigi 324-0011, Japan

YONEHARA, SHIN, cell biologist, educator; b. Kyoto, Japan, Dec. 2, 1952; s. Yoshio and Hisami (Uemura) Y.; m. Minako Takahashi, Apr. 5, 1981; children: Jun, Ryo. BS, Kyoto U., 1975, MS, 1977, DSc, 1982. Rsch. scientist Tokyo Met. Inst. Med. Sci., 1978-92; sr. rschr. Pharm. Basic Rsch. Lab., JT Inc., Yokohma, Japan, 1992-94; prof. Inst. Virus Rsch., Kyoto U., 1994—. Contbr. articles to profl. jours. Recipient Princess Takamatsu award Cancer Rsch. Found., 1998. Mem. AAAS, Japan Soc. Cell Biology, Japan Soc. Immunology, Japanese Cancer Assn. Avocations: art, reading. Office: Inst Virus Rsch Kyoto Univ, Sakyo ku, Kyoto 606-8507, Japan

YONEI, YOSHIKAZU, gastroenterologist; b. Tokyo, Jan. 18, 1958; s. Hidekazu and Chieko (Nakada) Y.; m. Keiko Nakatani, Dec. 15, 1985; children: Shoichiro, Lisa. MD, Keio U., Tokyo, 1982, PhD, 1986. Vis. rschr. Ctr. for Ulcer Rsch., L.A., 1986-89; attending physician Nippon Kokan Hosp., Kawasaki, Japan, 1989—; chmn. bd. dirs. Keiyo Kai Med. Found., Tokyo, 1997—; pres. Mind Works, Inc., Tokyo/Abuja, Lagos, Nigeria, 1999—, Cenegenics Japan, Tokyo, Las Vegas, 2000—; chmn. bd. dirs. Keiyo Kai Med. Found., Tokyo. Co-author: Mast Cell, 1990. Named Hon. Citizen Botucatu City, Sao Paulo, Brazil, 1981. Mem. Keio Sakura Reunion (pres. 1992—), Sympathy for H. Pylori Assn. (pres. 1999—), Keio Med. Sch. Yacht Club (bd. dirs. 1993-98). Avocation: sailing. Home: 5-21-26 Ryokuen, Izumi-ku, Yokohama Kanagawa 245-0002, Japan Office: Nippon Kokan Hosp, 1-2-1 Kokandori Kawasaki-ku, Kawasaki Kanagawa 210-0852, Japan also: Mind Works Inc, 3-15-10-3F Jingumae, Shibuya Tokyo 150-0001, Japan also: c/o Alvan Farooq & Assocs, Pl 109a Norman Williams St, SW Ikoyi Lagos Nigeria also: Cenegenics Japan, 4-15-30 Seta, Setagaya-ku Tokyo 158-0095, Japan

YONEKAWA, SATOSHI, agricultural engineering and agro-biology educator; b. Sekiyado Town, Japan, Feb. 8, 1958; s. Takeshi Someya and Kimiko Yonekawa.; m. Misako Itou, Apr. 29, 1986; children: Yukari, Tomotaka, Mai. B in Agr., U. Tokyo, 1981, M in Agr., 1983, PhD, 1988. Asst. prof. U. Tokyo, 1985-99, assoc. prof., 1999—. Contbr. articles to profl. jours. Adminstrv. cooperator Tokorozawa City, Saitama, 1991, Sekiyado Town, Chiba, 1993, 2000. Rsch. grant Ministry of Edn., Sci., Sports and Culture of Japan, 1986—, Minstry of Agrl., Forestry, and Fisheries of Japan, 1994-2000, Bio-oriented Tech. Rsch. Advancement Instn. of Japan, 1996-99. Mem. IEEE, Am. Soc. Agrl. Engrs., Japanese Soc. Farm Work Rsch. (mgr. 1995—, chair info. com. 1999—), Japanese Soc. Agrl. Machinery, Assn. Computing Machinery. Avocations: art, music, sports. Office: U Tokyo Univ Field Prod Sci Ctr, 1-1-1 Midori-cho, Tokyo Tanashi 188-0002, Japan

YONEKUBO, AKIE, food products company executive; b. Kanagawa, Japan, Dec. 20, 1947; s. Masashi and Sawa (Akahane) Y.; m. Tokiko Miyamoto, Nov. 10, 1974; children: Yuriko, Yumiko, Naoaki. BS, Nagoya U., 1970, MS, 1972, PhD, 1994. Gen. mgr. Nutrition Sci. Inst., Meiji Milk Products, Japan, 1988—. Fellow Japan Soc. for Lipid Nutrition; mem. Biosci. Biotech. Biochemistry, N.Y. Acad. Scis. Avocation: tennis. Home: 3-7-6 Honda, Kokubunji Tokyo 185-0011, Japan Office: Meiji Milk Products Co Nutr, Sci Inst 1-21-3 Sakaecho, Higashimuraymа 189, Japan

YONEYAMA, KOICHI, chemistry educator; b. Matsumoto, Nagano, Japan, Nov. 3, 1951; s. Heihachiro and Yoshimi (Maruyama) Y.; m. Chieko Hara, Oct. 3, 1977; children: Tsuyoshi, Ayako, Tsutomu. BA, U. Tokyo, 1976, MS, 1978, PhD, 1983. Asst. prof. Utsunomiya (Japan) U., 1978-87, assoc. prof. agrl. chemistry, 1987-98; prof. Utsunomiya (Japan) U., Canberra, 1998—; rsch. assoc. Australian Nat. U., Canberra, 1987—. Mem. Japan Soc. for Biosci., Biotech. and Agrochemistry (award for young scientists 1990), Japanese Soc. of Plant Biologists, Chem. Soc. of Japan, Soc. for Chem. Regulation of Plants. Avocations: golf, painting. Office: Utsunomiya Univ, 350 Mine-machi, Utsunomiya, Tochigi 321-8505, Japan

YONEYAMA, TSUKASA, electrical communications educator; b. Masuda, Akita, Japan, Dec. 26, 1935; s. Chuichi and Toshiko (Satoh) Y.; m. Yoko Fukushima, Feb. 16, 1963; children: Fumiya, Hisaki. B in Engring., Tohoku U., Sendai, Japan, 1959, M in Engring., 1961, D in Engring., 1964. Rsch. assoc. Tohoku U., 1964-65, assoc. prof., 1965-84, prof., 1986-99; prof. Ryukyu U., Naha, Japan, 1984-86, Tohoku Inst. of Tech., Sendai, Japan, 1999—; vis. rschr. Comms. Rsch. Lab., Tokyo, Japan, 1995-99; cons. Advantest Labs., Sendai, Japan, 1998—; com. mem. Japan Resources Observation System, Tokyo, 1999—; lectr. in field. Author: Electromagnetic Wave Transmission Engineering, 1981 (Best Publ. award 1984); inventor dielelectric waveguide (Achievement award 1997). Recipient Shida Rinzoburo Meml. award Assn. for the Promotion of Info-Comms., 1995, Achievement award Agy. of Sci. and Tech., 1998. Fellow IEEE (award 1990), IEICE of Japan (Inada Meml. award 1964, Career award 1998), IEE of Japan. Avocations: tennis, golf, gardening. Home: Taihaku Fukurdbara, Kodaira 12-17, Sendai 981-1102, Japan Office: Taihaku Yagiyama, Kasumicho 35-1, Sendai 982-8577, Japan

YONG, HE, Chinese government official. Minister of supervision Govt. of China, 1998—. Mem. Communist Party. Office: Ministry of Supervision, 4 Chao Jun Miao, Hai Dian, Beijing China 100081*

YONG, PUNG HOW, judge. Chief justice Supreme Ct. Singapore, Singapore. Office: Supreme Ct Bldg, St Andrew's Rd 1, Singapore 178957, Singapore*

YONG, WENG KWONG, biomedical scientist; b. Singapore, Republic of Singapore, Sept. 14, 1946; arrived in Australia, 1973; s. Mook Yee Yong and Mui Koen; m. Maria Hilda Girard, June 28, 1975; children: Michael, Mathew, Peter. BSc with honors, U. Otago, Dunedin, New Zealand, 1972; PhD, U. Queensland, Brisbane, 1976, GCertEd, 1994; PGDipMgmt, Deakin U., Geelong, Australia, 1991. Cert. internal auditor. Rsch. scientist Wallaceville Animal Rsch. Ctr., Upper Hutt, New Zealand, 1976-79; lectr. Internat. Immunol. Tng. and Rsch. Ctr., Amsterdam, The Netherlands, 1979-81; rsch. scientist U. Queensland, Brisbane, 1981-82, Victorian Dept. Agr., Hamilton, Australia, 1982-92, Greenslopes Repatriation Hosp., Brisbane, 1992-95, Commonwealth Dept. of Vets. Affairs, Brisbane, 1995—. Editor: Footrot and Foot Abscess of Ruminants, 1989, Control of Animal Parasites Utilising Biotechnology, 1992; patentee anthelmintic non-living vaccine; contbr. over 60 articles to sci. jours. Sec. First Hamilton Scout Group, 1985-88. Commonwealth fellow Australian Govt., 1973, Ross McKenzie fellow, 1989; recipient Leo Dintenfass trophy Rebecca L. Cooper Med. Rsch. Found., 1993. Mem. Australian Inst. Risk Mgmt., Australian Soc. Immunology, Assn. Profl. Engrs., Scientists, Mgrs. Australia, Inst. Internal Auditors-Australia (bd. govs. Queensland chpt.). Avocations: stamp collecting, reading historical novels, fishing.

YONG, ZHAO, engineer; b. Shen Yang, Liao Ni, China, May 17, 1973; parents Zhao Zhifu and Zhang Xiu Lan. BS, Harbin Inst. Tech., 1996, MS, 1998. Cert. in engring. Contbr. articles to profl. jours. V.p. Workshop of Young People of Harbin Inst. Tech., 1997; chmn. Culture Intercomm. Union of China and Abroad, Harbin, 1998. SMC scholar of Japan, 1997. Avocations: Ping-Pong, tennis, singing. E-mail: lps@hope.hit.edu.cn. Office: Harbin Inst Tech, Xidazhi 192#, Harbin 150001, China

YONG-DAL, SUH, accounting educator; b. Pusan, Republic of Korea, Mar. 30, 1933; arrived in Japan, 1942; s. Sung-Man Suh and Jong-Rae Hong; m. Hyun-Sin Park, Oct. 20, 1963; children: Kwi-Yong, Young-Soon, Kwi-Mi, Kwi-Hye. MBA, Kobe (Japan) U., 1960, postgrad., 1963. Dean dept. bus. adminstrn. St. Andrew's U., Osaka, Japan, 1964-66; councilor St. Andrew's U., Osaka, 1964-73, prof.; vis. prof. Frankfurt (Germany) U., 1986-87, Wien (Austria) U., 1995, Buckingham U., U.K., 2000, London U., 2000; adv. com. Dept. Fgn. Affairs, Republic of Korea, 1989-92. Author: Germann Accounting Theory, 1992, Current Bookkeeping, 1992; author, editor: Internationalization of University and Foreign Teachers in Japan, 1980, Asian Citizen and Koreans in Japan, 1993, Voting Rights in Local Election for One Community, 1995, Symbiotic Multicultural Society: A Perspektive, 2000. Mem. standing com. Nippon Urban Mgmt. Local Govt. Rsch. Assn., 1984-89; auditor rsch., promotion Korean Culture Found., Tokyo, 1989—; mem. adv. com. Coun. Dem. Peaceful Unification, Republic of Korea, 1991—; chief dir. Korean Scholarship Assn. in Japan, Osaka, 1994—. Recipient Nat. Decoration Second prize, 1996. Mem. Internat. Assn. Study Koreans in Japan (pres. 1987—), Korean-Japanese Assn. (corp. judicial person 1986—), Korean C. of C. and Industry Japan (adv. com. 1992—). Avocations: photography, mountain climbing, art. Fax: 81-742-45-5770. Home: 1-5-7 Higashi Tomigaoka, Nara City 631-0002, Japan Office: Korean Scholarship Assn, 2-4-2 Nakazaki, Kita-ku Osaka 530-0016, Japan

YONGUE, XY, Chinese government official. Minister state security Govt. of China, Beijing. Mem. Communist Party. Office: Ministry State Security, 14 Dong Chang/An Jie/East, Beijing China 100036*

YON-KAHN, JEANNINE MARIE LOUISE, biochemist, educator; b. Paris, Feb. 10, 1927; d. Charles Raymond and Germaine (Beal) Yon; m. Théophile Kahn, Sept. 13, 1977 (dec. Nov. 1986). B Philosophy and Math., U. Paris, 1945, PhD in Phys. Sci. (hon.), 1955; lic. in phys. sci., U. Sorbonne, Paris, 1948. Attachée rsch. Nat. Ctr. Sci. Rsch., France, 1951-55, chargé le rsch., 1955-61, maîtr rsch., 1961-66; dir. rsch. Nat. Ctr. Sci. Rsch., Orsay, France, 1966—. Author: Structure and Conformational Dynamics of Proteins, 1969, (with C. Ghélis) Protein Folding, 1982; contbr. over 200 articles to profl. publs. Mem. Conseil Supérieur de l'Edn. Nat., 1966-69, Comité Rsch. Vème PLAN, 1963-67, Nat. Com. Sci. Rsch., France, 1962-71, 75-83, 87-91, Sectorial Com. of Sci. Rsch., France, 1975-79. Mem. French Soc. Chem. Biology (v.p. 1975-77, pres.), Cercle Français de Biologie Cellulaire (pres. 1979-80), Chemistry Com. of Palais de la Découverte (pres. 1975-78), Brazilian Acad. Scis. (corr.), N.Y. Acad. Scis., Protein Soc. Office: U Paris-Sud Lab Enzymology, Physicochem Bldg 433, 91405 Orsay France

YONKMAN, FREDRICK ALBERS, lawyer, management consultant; b. Holland, Mich., Aug. 22, 1930; s. Fredrick Francis and Janet Dorothy (Albers) Y.; m. Kathleen VerMeulen, June 9, 1953 (div. Sept. 22, 1980); children: Sara, Margriet, Nina.; m. Barbara Anne Sullivan, Aug. 22, 1981 (div. Mar. 31, 1994); 1 child, Fredrick Ryan; m. Jewel Marie Humphrey, July 4, 1998. BA, Hope Coll., Holland, 1952; JD, U. Chgo., 1957. Bar: N.Y. 1958, Mass. 1968, D.C. 1984. With Winthrop, Stimson, Putnam & Roberts, N.Y.C., 1957-64; sec., gen. counsel Reuben H. Donnelley Corp., N.Y.C., 1964-66, Dun & Bradstreet, Inc., N.Y.C., 1966-68; ptnr. Sullivan & Worcester, Boston, 1968-72; gen. counsel Am. Express Co., N.Y.C., 1972-78; exec. v.p. Am. Express Co., 1975-80; pres. Buck Cons., N.Y.C., 1980-81; mgmt. cons., psychoanalyst, 1981—; counsel Peabody, Lambert & Myers, Washington, 1983-84; chmn. Outward Bound, Inc., Garrison, N.Y., 1980-81; mem. bd. and chmn. audit com. Kennecott Corp., 1978-81; adj. prof. law Georgetown U., 1976-78; chmn. Georgetown Internat. Law Inst., 1980-81; vis. com. U. Chgo. Law Sch., 1980-82; mem. exec. com. Warner-Amex, 1978-80. Bd. dirs. Washington Campus Program, 1976-81; bd. dirs. Young Audiences, 1978-83. With U.S.Army, 1952-54. Recipient Silver Anniversary award Nat. Coll. Athletic Assn., 1977. Mem. ABA, N.Y. State Bar Assn., Mass. Bar Assn., Rsch. Soc. for Process Oriented Psychology (Zurich) (diplomate). Methodist. Home: 925 Rock Rimmon Rd Stamford CT 06903-1213

YOO, BYUNG CHUL, internal medicine educator; b. Seoul, Republic of Korea, June 27, 1953; Home phone: 82-2-481-7447.; s. Jung Sik and Jong Nam (Lim) Y.; m. Hye Kyoung Lee, Oct. 6, 1976; children: Shin Jae, Yang Jae. MD, Seoul Nat. U., 1977, PhD, 1986. Diplomate Korean Bd. Internal Medicine. Resident dept. internal medicine Seoul Nat. U., 1978-82; rsch. fellow Fox Chase Cancer Ctr., Phila., 1989-91; clin. instr. internal medicine Chung-Ang U., Seoul, 1985, asst. prof., 1985-90, assoc. prof., 1990-95, prof., 1995—; chief sect. gastroenterology Chung-Ang U. Hosp., 1996—, dir. dept. internal medicine, 1997—. Contbr. articles to med. jours., including Virology, Korean Jour. Internal Medicine. Capt. Korean Army, 1982-85. Mem. Korean Assn. Gastroenterology (sec. Seoul 1999—, best sci. paper award 1985, acad. award 1995), Korean Assn. for Study Liver (sec. 1997-99). Home: Hyosung Villa 4-302, Sangildong 176 Kangdongku 134-090, Seoul 134-090, Republic of Korea Office: Chung-Ang U Hosp Dept IM, 82-1 Pildong 2ka, Chung-ku, Seoul 100-272, Republic of Korea

YOO, CHANGSIK, integrated circuit designer, researcher; b. Daejon, Korea, Dec. 15, 1969; s. Kwang-Joon Yoo and Hurn-Boon Lim. BSc with high honors, Seoul Nat. U., Korea, 1992, MSc, 1994, PhD, 1998. Intern Hyundai Electronics, Ichon, Korea, 1992; rsch. asst. Seoul Nat. U., 1992—; mem. postdoctoral rsch. staff ETH, Zurich, Switzerland, 1998-99; sr. rsch. staff Samsung Electronics, Korea, 2000—; lectr., cons. Samsung Electronics, Kiheung, Korea, 1995, ETRI, Daejon, 1995. Contbr. articles to profl. jours. Recipient bronze award Postech, 1987, silver award LG Semicon, 1996. Mem. IEEE (student), KITE. Avocation: reading. Home: Woo-Sung Apt 821-1004, Young-Tong-Dong Pal Dal Ku, Suwon 442-470, Korea Office: Samsung Electronics, Nongseo-Ri Kiheung-Eup, Yongin City Kyungki-Do 449-711, Republic of Korea

YOO, CHUL-IN, anthropology educator, museum administrator; b. Kwangju, Republic of Korea, Oct. 25, 1956; parents Won-Ho Yoo and Mun-Hi Kang; m. Sun-Ae Han, Mar. 12, 1981; children: Sang-Hyun, Sang-Pil. BA, Seoul Nat. U., 1979; MA in Anthropology, SUNY, Binghamton, N.Y., 1983; PhD in Anthropology, U. Ill., 1993. Rschr. Korea Rural Econs. Inst., Seoul, 1979-81, 83-84; prof. anthropology Cheju Nat. U., Cheju City, Korea, 1984—, dir. univ. mus., 1997-01; part-time lectr. Seoul Nat. U., 1983; vis. lectr. Pohang (Korea) U. Sci. and Tech., 1996-97; vice-dir. steering com. Coun. for Cheju History Studies, Cheju City, 1997—; advisor organizing com. World Festival for Island Cultures, Cheju City, 1997—. Co-editor: (book) Tastes of Cultural Anthropology, 1998; co-author: (book) Studies on Cheju Society, 2 vols., 1995, 98; contbr. articles to profl. jours. Dir. Cheju April 3rd Uprising Inst., Cheju City, 1995—; mem. Ombudsmen Coun. Cheju MBC TV, Cheju City, 1996-98. Recipient Grand Prix, Ministry of Edn., 1978; Fulbright-Hays grantee, 1986-90, Non-Directed Rsch. Fund grantee Korea Rsch. Found., 1991, 94, 96, 97, 98, 99. Mem. Am. Anthropol. Assn., Am. Ethnol. Soc., Soc. for Cheju Studies (editor-in-chief 1993-96), Korean Soc. for Cultural Anthropology (chair rsch. com. 1996-98). Fax: 82 64 7020645. E-mail: chulin@cheju.cheju.ac.kr. Home: 1398 Ara-2-dong, Daerim Villa 1-302, 690-122 Cheju City Cheju-do, Korea Office: Cheju Nat U Univ Mus, 1 Ara-dong, 690-756 Cheju City Cheju-do, Korea

YOO, HOSEON, mechanical engineer, educator; b. South Korea, Apr. 5, 1955; s. Cheoljae and Oksoo (Park) Y.; m. Miyoung Pak, May 25, 1986; 1 child, Hyebin. BS, Seoul Nat. U., 1977, MS, 1979, PhD, 1986. Rsch. assoc. Seoul Nat. U., 1983-86; rsch. scientist Korea Inst. of Sci. and Tech., Seoul, 1986-87; asst. and assoc. prof. Gyeongsang Nat. U., Chinju, 1987-93; assoc., full prof. dept. mech. engring. Soongsil U., Seoul, 1993—; vis. scholar Purdue U., West Lafayette, Ind., 1990-91. Contbr. articles to profl. jours. including Internat. Jour. Heat and Mass Transfer, Solar Energy, Numerical Heat transfer, Internat. Jour. Heat and Fluid Flow, others. Recipient Best Paper award Korean Fedn. of Sci. and Tech. Socs., 1996, Nam-Heon award Korean Soc. Mech. Engrs., 1996, KSME award, 1998. Avocations: tennis, golf, singing. Office: Soongsil Univ, Dept Mech Engring, Seoul 156-743, South Korea

YOO, JEONG-GEUN, electric company executive; b. Suwon, Kyungki-do, Korea, Dec. 31, 1966; p. Young-Tae and Hyun-Ok Kim; m. Sun-A Oh, Sept. 8, 1996; 1 child, Hyun-Se. BS, Yonsei U., Seoul, Korea, 1989; MS, KAIST, Seoul, Korea, 1991; PhD, KAIST, Taejon, Korea, 1998; postgrad., Tokyo Inst. Tech., 1996-97. Cert. phys. chemistry. Mgr. Samsung Display Devices, Suwon, Korea, 1991—. Contbr. articles to profl. jours. Mem. Internat. Liquid Crystal Soc. E-mail: jgyoo@114.co.kr and jgyoo@sdd.samsung.co.kr. Fax: 82-331-210-7798. Home: 859-2403 Sulak Apt, Sanbon-dong, Kunpo Kyungki-do 435-040, Korea Office: Samsung Display Devices, 575 shing-dong paldal-gu, Suwon Kyungki-do 442-391, Korea

YOO, JOO-SIK, mechanical engineer, engineering educator; b. Kyungnam, Rep. of Korea, Aug. 15, 1962; s. Hwan-Soo and Ho-Kyung Ro; married; 2 children. BS, Seoul (Rep. of Korea) Nat. U., 1984; MS, Korea Advanced Inst. Sci. and Tech., Seoul, 1986, PhD, 1991. Cert. engr. Sr. rschr. Daewoo Electronics Co. Ltd., Incheon, Rep. of Korea, 1992-94; asst. prof. dept. mech. engring. edn. Andong (Rep. of Korea) Nat. U., 1995—. Contbr. articles to sci. jours. including Internat. Jour. Heat and Mass Transfer, Numerical Heat Transfer, Part A, others. Office: Andong Nat U Mech Engr Edn, 388 Songchun-dong, Andong, Kyungpuk 760-749, Republic of Korea

YOO, SEONG-YEON, engineering educator; b. Kwang-ju, Korea, Oct. 28, 1953; s. Byung-Yoon Yoo and Soon-Duck Lee; m. Kyung Kim, June 20, 1980; children: In-Kyung, In-Seo. BS, Seoul Nat. U., Korea, 1977; MS, KAIST, Seoul, 1979, PhD, 1989. Lectr. Chungman Nat. U., Taejon, Korea, 1980-82, asst. prof., 1982-87, assoc. prof., 1987-93, prof., 1993—, dept. head, 1989-92, vice-dir. Rsch. Inst. Indsl. Tech., 1998—; cons. Korea Atomic Energy Rsch., Taejon, 1989—, Ministry Trade & Industry, Seoul, 1990-92, Korea Inst. Energy Rsch., Taejon, 1994-98; vis. fellow U. Minn., Mpls., 1986-88, U. Ottawa (Can.), 1994, U. Oxford (Eng.), 1995, Bldg. Rsch. Establishment, (Eng.), 1998, Luikov Heat and Mass Transfer Inst., (Belarus), 1998, Kyushu (Japan) U., 1999. Contbr. articles to profl. jours. Com. mem. Chungnam Province, Taejon, 1991—. Mem. Soc. Air-Conditioning and Refrigeration Engrs. Korea (rep. 1997—), Korean Solar Energy Soc. (editl. bd. 1991-93), Korean Soc. Mech. Engring. (editl. bd. 1997—). Achievements include patent for parallel type plate heat exchanger, heat exchanger for gas boiler. Office: Chungnam Nat U, Mech Design Engring, Taejon 305-764, Republic of Korea

YOO, VAK YEONG, health facility administrator; b. Seoul, Republic of Korea, June 28, 1947; d. Jang Mun Yoo and So Ran Choi. MA, Ewha Women's U., Seoul, 1974. Med. diplomate internal medicine. Founder pvt. med. exam. ctr., Seoul, 1981—; dir. Yoovakyeong Internal Medicine, Seoul, 1981-92; head Med. Examination Ctr., Seoul, 1981—; dir. Cheong-Vak P.B. Hosp., Seoul, 1992—; head Women's Health Dx & Climacteric, Seoul, 1992—; mem. menopause and osteoporosis unit, 1992—, YVY-QOL Inst., 1997, YVY-QOL osteoporosis leader NOF-PPN, 1997; mem. sci. com. Koran Soc. Menopause, 1997-99; creator, organizer YVY-QOL support group for meno/osteoporosis Nat. Osteoporosis Found., 1997. Editor Jour. Meno/Osteoporosis, 1998—; co-editor Jour. Menopause Soc. Korea, 1999—; inventor in field. Mem. N.Am. Menopause Soc., Internat. Menopause Soc., Korean Soc. Endoscopy, Christian Med. Assn. (planning dir. 1993-96), Am. Assn. Clin. Endocrinologists, AAAS, Am. Soc. for Microbiology, Korean Soc. Endocrinology, Korean Diabetes Assn., Korean Soc. Menopause (scientific com. 1996-98, editing com. 1999—), Korean Soc. Circulation, The Endocrine Soc., N.Y. Acad. Scis., NOF-Profl. Ptnr. Network, ASBMR. Avocations: traveling, listening to music, opera music. Home: 138-60 Yongdu Dong, Dongdaemun Ku, Seoul 130-072, Republic of Korea Office: Cheong-Vak PrimeBeyond Hosp, 582 Shinsa Dong Kangnam Ku, Seoul 135-120, Republic of Korea

YOO, YOUNG SOOK, research scientist, educator; b. Wonju, Kangwon-Do, Republic of Korea, May 29, 1955; d. Jin Won Yoo and Kee Yun Lee; m. ChoongHee Nam, May 11, 1980; 1 child, SangHyun Nam. BS, Ewha Women's U., Seoul, Korea, 1977, MS, 1979; PhD, Oreg. State U., 1987. Tchg. asst. Ewha Women's U., Seoul, 1977-79, rsch. asst., 1979-80; rsch. asst. Oreg. State U., Corvallis, 1982-86; post-doctoral fellow Stanford U. Sch. Medicine, Palo Alto, Calif., 1986-89; sr. rschr. Korea Inst. Sci. and Tech, Doping Control Ctr., Seoul, 1990-94, prin. rsch. scientist, 1994-97; prin. rsch. scientist Korea Inst. Sci. and Tech., Bioanalysis and Biotransformation Rsch. Ctr., Seoul, 1997—; vis. rsch. scientist NIH, Bethesda, Md., 1994; affiliate prof. Korea U., Seoul, 1995—, Han Yang U., Ansan, Korea, 1997—. Editor: Easy Internet for Biochemists, 1997; editl. sec. Jour. Biochemistry and Molecular Biology, 1995-96; mem. editl. bd. Jour. Biochemistry and Molecular Biology, 1997—. Mem. Korean Soc. for Molecular Biology (life), Assn. Korean Women Scientists and Engrs. (trustee 1993—), Biochem. Soc. Republic of Korea (trustee 1995—). Avocations: skiing, reading, aerobics. E-mail: ysyoo@kist.re.kr. Fax: 82-2-958-5170. Home: Chung-gu Apt 8-909, Nowon-gu Hagye-dong, Seoul 139-231, Republic of Korea Office: KIST BBRC, PO Box 131 Cheongryang, Seoul 130-650, Korea

YOOK, CHONG CHUL, engineering educator; b. Kyngbuk, Sunsan, Korea, Jan. 1, 1926; s. Jae Kyun Yook and Choi (Shoon) Ie; m. Sook Kae Chang, Aug. 15, 1949; children: Myung-Hi, Oak-Soo, Sun-Hi. BS in Engring., Seoul (Republic of Korea) Nat. U., 1950; postgrad., Oak Ridge Inst., Argonne Internat. Inst., 1961, U. Ill., 1962; PhD in Nuclear Engring., Hanyang U., Seoul, 1967. Prof. Chung-Nam Nat. U., Taejon, Republic of Korea, 1957-64, dean Engring. Coll., 1962-64; prof. Hanyang U., 1964-91, prof. emeritus, 1991—; mem. tech. adv. bd. Ministry of Sci. and Tech., Seoul, 1988-90; advisor inspection, testing and examination cons. ITEC Svc. Co., Ltd., Seoul, 1991—. Author: Radiation Safety Handling, 1982, East and West, 1991 (Panel award 1991); patent for applied measuring device of engine ring wear. Mem. energy and resources adv. com. Rep. of Korean Govt., Seoul, 1981-83. Mem. Korean Assn. for Radiation Protection (pres. Seoul chpt. 1977-79), Internat. Radiation Protection Assn. (rep. Netherlands chpt. 1977-80, adv. com. Fed. Republic of Germany 1978-81), Korean Atomic Energy Rsch. Inst. (standing com. Taejon chpt. 1989-90), Korean Radioisotapes Assn. (audit treas. Seoul chpt. 1985-91). Mem. Christian Ch. Avocations: reading, mountain climbing, swimming.

YOOL, GEORGE RICHARD, consultant; b. Orange, Calif., Apr. 16, 1969; s. George Malcolm and Norma Susan (Cravey) Follette; m. Megan Tiffaney Jackson, June 6, 1991 (div. Nov. 1997); children: Thor Alexander, Logan Anthony, Ashley Rene; m. Liliana Matilde Cuzzocrea, Mar. 13, 2000. BS in Criminal Justice, No. Ariz. U., Flagstaff, 1993, MEd in Ednl. Leadership, 1995. Cons. dir. Cons. Unltd., Apache Junction, Ariz., 1988—; co-founder Barbarian Corp., 1996. Author: The Blue Rose/Silence, 1986 (1st pl. art contest 1986), Silent Dreams, 1992, The Writer's Cookbook, 1992, An Introduction to Zen Thought, 1993, rünLi Ching (Classic of Ethic), 1994, LiJie Ching (Classic of Knowledge), 1997, Metamorphosis of the Flying Rose, 1997, Unified Field Theory, 1998, Survey of Information Systems Technologies, 1999, Introduction to Web Design, 2000; co-author: Handbook for Humanizing Higher Education, 1995; creator, author: (discovery) Problem Solving Using Paradology, 1995, Integrated Theory of Learning and Development, 1995; author, discoverer: (book, presentation, discovery) Mensonnomy: A New Unified Cosmology, 1994; inventor: Virtual Keyboard, 1995; contbr. articles to profl. jours. Recipient grad. scholarship No. Ariz. U., Flagstaff, 1995. Mem. Ariz. Grad. Student Assn. (del. 1995), Students and Tchrs. Instrnl. Needs Group (pres. 1995—), Grad. Student Assn. No. Ariz. U. (pres. 1995). Avocations: reading, research, writing, math, physics, guest lecturing. E-mail: god@barbaria. com.

YOON, E. YUL, retired career officer; b. Pyungyang, Korea, Feb. 10, 1927; s. Jung Soon and Jung Duk (Lee) Y.; m. Sun Sam Lee Yoon, Nov. 29, 1931; children: Kyung Ran, Kyung Im, Kwang Ho. Grad., Mil. Acad. Seoul, 1948; BS in Politics and Fgn. Policy, Dangook U., Seoul, Korea, 1955; grad., U.S. Air U., Montgomery, Ala., 1957. Squadron comdr. The 12th Fighter SQ F-51, Korea, 1952-53; armed force attache Korean Embassy, Paris, 1959-61; wing comdr. The 1st Combat Wing, The 10th Fighter Wing, Seoul, 1961-63; pres. Korean Air Force Coll., Seoul, 1963-64; supt. Korean Air Acad., Seoul, 1964-66; commanding gen. Combat Air Command, Korea, 1968-70; minister plenipotentiary Korean Embassy, France, Mexico, 1966-68; vice minister for def. devel. Ministry of Def., Seoul, 1970-73; pres., CEO Korea Tacoma Shipbuilding Indsl. Co., Korea, 1973-76, Buyeon Co., Ltd., Seoul, 1976-86; cons. United Tech./Martin Marieta, 1976-85. Mem. Korean Heavy Industrialization Com., Seoul, 1970-73. Recipient Eulchi and two Gold Stars, Chungmoo Meritorious Svc. medals, Korea, 1952, 53, Korean Disting. Svc. medal, 1955; decorated U.S. Disting. Flying Cross, U.S. Air medal, Repub. of China Disting. Svc. medal. Mem. The Disting. Flying Cross Soc. (life), U.C.S.D. Chancellor's Assoc., Ministry of Nat. Def. of Korea (rsch. assoc.). Avocations: photography, art collecting, golf.

YOON, HYUNG-SEOK, technology educator, consultant; b. Kwang-ju, South Korea, Sept. 18, 1957; s. Byung-ho Yoon and Soon-sun Ryu; m. Miyoung Kim, Apr. 30, 1988; children: Nara, Jaesang. B in Pub. Adminstrn., Dankuk U., Seoul, 1981, MBA, 1983. Pres. Data Rsch. & Comms., Seoul, 1991—; lectr. Korea Inst. New Tech. and New Info. Svc., Seoul, 1996-97, LG Distbn. Rsch. Inst., Seoul, 1998-99; prof. Induk Inst. Tech., Seoul, 1998—; v.p. Korea Info. Distbn. Assn., Seoul, 1998—; mem. com. Ministry of Info. and Comm., Seoul, 1998-99; chief Dr. Intelligence Net Inst., Seoul, 1998—; dir. Korea Orgn. Social Opinion and Mktg. Rsch., Seoul, 1998—; mem. exec. com. Consumer Protection Orgn., Seoul, 1989-91; rschr. Korea Rsch. Orgn. Pub. Benefit, 1987-89. Author: A Research Method Consumer Satisfaction. Pvt. 1st class Korean Army, 1983-85. Mem. Am. Mktg. Assn., Nat. Press Club. Avocations: tennis, swimming. Fax: 02 3487 1444. E-mail: narapapa@drch.co.kr. Office: Data Rsch, CPO Box 164, Seoul 100-601, Korea

YOON, ILL HEE, meteorologist; b. Miryang, Korea, Sept. 22, 1954; s. Moo Soo Yoon and Hyung Joo Park; m. Young Hee Lee, Mar. 28, 1982; children: Yesie, Susie. BS, Kyungpook Nat. U., Taegu, Korea, 1978; MS, Seoul Nat. U., 1983, PhD, 1991. Rsch. asst. Seoul Nat. U., 1982-90, asst., 1986-88; lectr. earth sci. Kyungpook Nat. U., 1990-92, asst. prof., 1992-96, assoc. prof., 1996—. Mem. AAAS, Am. Geophys. Union, Am. Meteorol. Soc., Royal Meteorol. Soc., Australian Meteorol. and Oceanographic Soc., Korean Meteorol. Soc., Clean Air Soc., Korean Earth Sci. Soc., Korean Environ. Sci. Soc. Home: 103-805 Nokwon Apt, Jisandong, 706-091 Taegu Republic of Korea Office: Kyungpook Nat U, 1370 Sankyukdong Bukku, 702-701 Taegu Republic of Korea

YOON, JAY MYOUNG, oncologist, hematologist, internist; b. Korea, Sept. 30, 1946; married. BA Coll. Liberal Arts & Sci. summa cum laude, Seoul Nat. U., 1967, MD summa cum laude, 1971. Diplomate Am. Bd. Internal Medicine, 1978, Am. Bd. Oncology, 1979, Am. Bd. Hematology, 1980. Intern in medicine Bklyn. Hosp. Ctr.-Cornell U., N.Y.C., 1974-75; resident in medicine Bronx-Lebanon Hosp.-Albert Einstein Coll. Medicine, N.Y.C., 1975-76; fellow in hematol. oncology Baystate Med. Ctr.-Tufts U. Sch. Medicine, Springfield, Mass., 1976-78; fellow in oncology Roswell Park Cancer Inst.-SUNY, Buffalo, 1978-79, rsch. clinician in oncology dept. surg. develop. oncology, 1979-80; attending physician, med. oncologist St. Francis Hosp. and Health Ctr., Meth. Hosp., Cmty. Hosp., Beech Grove and Indpls., 1980-98; prof. medicine Ulsan U. Med. Sch., Korea, 1998; CEO, pres. Yoon Clinic, P.C., Edmonds, Wash., 1999—; mem. med. staff Stevens Meml. Hosp., Edmonds, Wash., 1999—, Northwest Hosp., Seattle, 1999—. Contbr. articles to profl. jours. Mem. AAAS, AMA, ADA, AACR, Am. Assn. Blood Banks, Am. Soc. Clin. Oncology, Am. Soc. Hematology, N.Y.

Acad. Sci. Fax: 425-697-6222. E-mail: yoon@dnamail.com. Home: 11901 59th Ave W Mukilteo WA 98275-5569 Office: Yoon Clinic PC Edmonds Med and Profl Ctr 7631 212th St SW Ste 113C Edmonds WA 98026-7565

YOON, KI HYUN, electronic materials educator; b. Bullkyo, Chonam, Korea, May 29, 1939; s. Duksoo and Sonam (Lim) Y.; m. Josephine Kyoungjin Shim, June 7, 1971; children: Kathleen Lira, Kevin Eylhan. BS, Yonsei U., Seoul, Korea, 1962, MS, 1968; PhD, U. Mo., Rolla, 1975, postgrad., 1976-76. Sr. scientist Agy. for Def. Devel., Seoul, 1976-78; prof. Yonsei U., 1978—, chmn., dept. ceramic engring, 1982-88, 90-92; vis. prof. U. Calif., Berkeley, 1981-82, Sophia U., Tokyo, 1988; guest prof. Argonne (Ill.) Nat. Lab., 1991; adv. mem. Ministry of Edn., Seoul, 1987-92; coord. Korea Sci. and Engring. Found., Taejon, Korea, 1991-93; dir. Rsch. Inst. Advanced Materials, Seoul, 1997—; hon. prof. U. Auckland, New Zealand, 1996—. Author: (chpt.) Chemical Processing of Ceramics, 1994, Electronic Ceramic Materials, 1994; assoc. editor Jour. Korean Chem. Soc., 1979, Jour. Korean Ceramic Soc., 1988-89. 1st lt. Korean Air Force, 1963-67. Recipient Sci. award Yonsei U., 1979, 83. Fellow Korean Acad. Sci. and Tech., Koran Chem. Soc., Korean Ceramic Soc. (basic sci. divsn. head 1993-97, electronic divsn. head 1998—); mem. Am. Ceramic Soc., Acad. of Ceramics. Roman Catholic. Avocations: golf, travel. E-mail: khyoon@yonsei.ac.kr. Home: 1706-1601 Shinan Apt, Juyop-2 Dong Koyang, Kyunggi 411-372, Republic of Korea Office: Yonsei Univ, Dept Ceramic Engring, Seoul 120-749, Republic of Korea

YOON, NAE-HYUN, historian, educator; b. Haenam-kun, Korea, June 15, 1939; s. Jae-eyl Yoon and Yong-nam Yi; m. Jeong-oh Kim, Dec. 25, 1964; children: Jang-won, Jin-won, Juwon. BA, Dankook U., 1965, MA, 1975, LittD, 1978. Asst. prof. coll. lit. Dankook U., Seoul, 1978-81, prof., 1981—, chmn. dept. history, 1982-87, dir. mus., 1989-97, chmn. faculty coun., 1997-98, dean graduate sch. indsl. design, 1997-98, dean coll. liberal arts, 1998-99, v.p., 1999—; vis. scholar Harvard U., Cambridge, Mass., 1979-82; mem. com. cultural assets Ministry of Culture and Sport, Korea, 1993—; mem. commn. State Higher Exam. Fgn. Affairs, Korea; mem. com. Jud. Exam., Korea; mem. Ednl. Coun. Korean History (citation of Prime Minister of Republic of Korea 1998). Author: A Study on Shang Dynasty, 1978, Primitive Age of China, 1982, The History of Shang and Chou, 1984 (Ilsuk academic prize 1985), A New Interpretation of Ancient Korean History, 1986 (Book of Today prize 1986), A Study on Ko-Chosun, 1994 (Kumho Acad. prize 1995), The History of China, vol. 1, 1991, vol. 2, 1992, vol. 3, 1995, A Study on Multi-State Period of Korean History, 1999. Mem. Assn. for Asian Studies Inc., Soc. for Study of Early China, Korean Hist. Assn., Soc. for Asian Hist. Studies, Korea Study Soc., Korean Ancient Hist. Soc. Home: # 3101 Boramaenasan-Ste, 395-68 Shindaebang-2 dong, Dongjak-ku Seoul 156-710, Republic of Korea Office: Dankook U Dept History, 8 Hannam-dong Yongsan-ku, Seoul 140-714, Republic of Korea

YOON, SOON JONG, civil engineering educator; b. Seoul, Korea, Dec. 26, 1954; s. Jae Young and Napshim (Kim) Y.; m. Kyung Soon Kim, Apr. 10, 1983; children: Sungoh, Hyunoh. B oc Civil Engring., Hongik U., 1982, MSCE, 1987; DPhil, Ga. Inst. Tech., 1993. Civil engr. Daelim Indsl. Co., Seoul, Korea, 1981-85; rsch. engr. Hongik U., Seoul, 1987-88, rschr., instr., 1993-97; asst. prof. Hongik U., Seoul, Korea, 1994—. Contbr. articles to profl. jours. With Korean Army, 1978-80. Mem. ASCE, ASME, Korean Soc. Civil Engrs., Korean Concrete Inst., Korean Inst. Steel Constrn., Korean Soc. for Composite Materials, Korean Soc. for Mech. Engrs., Korean Soc. Wood Sci. and Tech., Earthquake Engring. Soc. Korea, Korea Inst. Structural Maint. Inspection, Computational Structural Engring. Inst. of Korea. Avocations: table tennis, soccer, fishing, travel. Office: Hongik U Dept Civil Engring, 72-1 Sangsoo-dong Mapo-Gu, Seoul 121-791, Republic of Korea

YOON, TAE-HO, materials science engineering educator; b. BorYong, ChungNam, Korea, Sept. 16, 1957; s. Dae-Sun and Soon-Han (Shin) Y.; m. Regina H. Kim, Aug. 1988; 2 children. BS, Chung Nam Nat. U., Dae-Jeon, Republic of Korea, 1980; MS, Va. Poly. Inst. and State U., 1987, PhD, 1991. Postdoctoral fellow NSF Ctr., Va. Poly. Inst. and State U., Blacksburg, 1991-94; asst. prof. materials sci. engring. Kwangju (Republic of Korea) Inst. Sci. and Tech., 1994-97, assoc. prof., 1997—. Contbr. articles to sci. jours., including Jour. Adhesion Sci. and Tech., Korea Polymer Jour. 1st lt. Korean Army, 1980-82. Mem. Am. Chem. Soc., Adhesion Soc. Achievements inlcude patent for washing of PE film from agricultural use by compressed air. Avocations: fishing, rock climbing, hiking. Home: 101-702 Bycksan-Apt, Kwangsan-gu Kwangju, Republic of Korea Office: Kwangju Inst Sci and Tech, 1 Oryong-dong Buk-gu, Kwangju 500-712, Republic of Korea

YOON, TAE-YOUNG, dermatologist, educator; b. Seoul, Korea, Sept. 18, 1956; s. Il-Byeong and Soon-Hee (Lee) Y.; m. Mi-Kyeong Kim, Mar. 9, 1985; children: Young-Sik, Jae Hong. B in Medicine, Seoul Nat. U., 1982, MM, 1985, PhD in Medicine, 1990. Intern Seoul Nat. U. Hosp., 1982-83, resident in dermatology, 1983-86; instr. Chungbuk Nat. U., 1990-92, asst. prof., 1992-97, assoc. prof., 1997—, dir. dept. dermatology, 1990—. Contbr. articles to profl. jours. including Brit. Jour. Dermatology, Jour. Am. Acad. Dermatology, Jour. Dermatology (Japan). Mem. Korean Derm. Assn. Avocations: travel, swimming. E-mail: tyyoon@med.chungbuk.ac.kr. Office: Chungbuk Nat U Dept Derm, Kaeshin dong, Cheongju Chungbuk 361-711, Korea

YOON, UNG CHAN, chemistry educator; b. Seoul, Korea, May 4, 1949; s. Choo Soo and Yang Ja (Cho) Y.; m. Jennifer Louise Koh, June 20, 1976; 1 child, Eileen Laurel. BS in Pharmacy, Seoul Nat. U., 1972, MS in Pharmacy, 1974; PhD in Chemistry, Fordham U., 1981. Cert. organic chemist, pharmacist. Rschr. Natural Products Rsch. Inst., Seoul Nat. U., 1974-75; postdoctoral rsch. assoc. dept. chemistry U. Md., College Park, 1981-83; asst. prof. dept. chemistry Pusan (Korea) Nat. U., 1983-86, assoc. prof., 1986-91, prof., 1991-92, chmn. dept. predentistry, 1992-95, assoc. dean Coll. Natural Scis., 1995-96, chmn. dept. chemistry, 1996-97. Contbr. articles to profl. jours. Mem. Korean Chem. Soc. (bd. dirs.), Korean Soc. Photosci. (editorial sec. 1994-97, gen. sec. 1999-00). Buddhist. Avocations: movies, reading, Zen. Office: Pusan Nat U Dept Chemistry, Keumjeong-Ku, Pusan 609-735, Republic of Korea

YOON, YONG-JIN, chemistry educator; b. Chochiwon, Chung-Nam, South Korea, May 10, 1950; s. Chang-Lim and Gui-Rae (Kim) Y.; m. Chong-Hee Kim, May 22, 1977; children: Hyeong-Jae, Hyo-Jae. BS in Chemistry, Sung Kyun Kwan U., 1976, PhD in Organic Chemistry, 1983. Instr. dept. chemistry Gyeongsang Nat. U., Chinju, Korea, 1980-82, asst. prof., 1982-86, assoc. prof., 1986-91, prof., 1991—; vis. prof. dept. med. chemistry U. Mich., Ann Arbor, 1984-85; vice dean acad. affairs Gyeongsang Nat. U., 1992-95. Contbr. articles to profl. jours. Mem. Korean Agrochem. Soc., Korean Chem. Soc. (div. organic chemistry and med. chemistry, Chem. Edn. prize 1987), Am. Chem. Soc. (div. med. chemistry), N.Y. Acad. Sci. Office: Gyeongsang Nat U, Dept Chemistry, Chinju 660-701, Republic of Korea

YORDANOVA, JULIANA, psychophysiologist; b. Belovo, Bulgaria, July 19, 1959; m. Roumen Kirov, 1985. MD, Med. U. Sofia, 1984; PhD, Bulgarian Acad. Scis., Sofia, 1991. Scientific fellow Brain Rsch. Inst. Bulgarian Acad. Sci., Sofia, 1985-95, scientific fellow Inst. Physiology, 1995—. Mem. Internat. Brain Rsch. Orgn., Soc. Psychophysiol. Rsch. Avocations: painting, psychology, mythology, art. E-mail: jyord@iph.bio.bas.bg. Office: Inst Physiology, Acad G Bonchev str bl 23, Sofia 1113, Bulgaria

YORIKAWA, HIROHARU, physicist, educator; b. Hyogo, Japan, Aug. 4, 1958; s. Mineo and Yaeko (Kobayashi) Y. BS, Sci. U. Tokyo, 1983, MS, 1985, DSc, 1989. Rsch. asst. Utsunomiya (Japan) U., 1989—. Contbr. articles to Phys. Rev. B, Solid State Comms., Synthetic Metals, Appl. Phys. Lett., others. Mem. Phys. Soc. Japan. Avocation: painting. Office: Utsunomiya U Faculty of Engring, 7-1-2 Youtou, Utsunomiya 321-8585, Japan

YORK, CHRISTOPHER RODNEY, finance company executive; b. Oxted, Surrey, Eng., Oct. 9, 1952; arrived in Switzerland, 1999; s. Alfred Edward and Doreen Ruth (Bicknell) Y.; m. Simone Rosita Zrieschling, Oct. 4, 1999; children: Noah Alexis, Joshua James. BA with Modern European Studies, Ealing Coll. Higher Edn., 1974. Support engr. ICL, U.K., 1977-79; supprt mgr. Redifon, U.K., 1979-84; mktg. mgr. London Stock Exch., 1984-88; data broadcast cons. Citibank, Australia, 1988-90; bus. devel. dir. Bocom, Europe, 1990-96, Ten Fore, Europe, 1996-99; gen. mgr., CEO Ten Fore Schweiz, Switzerland, 1999—. Inentor Market-Eye, 1987; founder Innovative Internet Co., Channelmoon.com, 2000. Avocations: cooking, reading, skiing, chess, running restaurants.

YORK, JAMES ORISON, real estate executive; b. Brush, Colo., June 27, 1927; s. M. Orison and Marie L. (Kibble) Y.; m. Janice Marie Sjoberg, Aug. 1, 1959; children: Douglas James, Robert Orison. Student, U. Calif. at Berkeley, 1945-46; B.A. cum laude, U. Wash., 1949. Teaching fellow U. Wash., Seattle, 1950-52; econ. research analyst Larry Smith & Co. (real estate), Seattle and N.Y.C., 1953-60; partner Larry Smith & Co. (real estate), Seattle, 1960-66; pres. Larry Smith & Co. (real estate), San Francisco, 1966-71; pres., chief exec. officer R.H. Macy Properties, N.Y.C., also sr. v.p. planning and devel., dir. R.H. Macy & Co., Inc., 1971-88; chmn. James York Assocs. (real estate), 1988—; dir. emeritus UBP Properties, Inc.; chmn., N.Y.C. retail div. Am. Cancer Soc. Contbg. author: Shopping Towns-USA, 1960. Trustee ICSC Ednl. and Rsch. Found. With USNR, 1945-47. Recipient Disting. Alumnus award U. Wash., 1989. Mem. Am. Soc. Real Estate Counselors, Urban Land Inst., Internat. Real Estate Fedn., Internat. Council Shopping Centers, Phi Beta Kappa, Lambda Alpha. Episcopalian. Clubs: Olympic (San Francisco); American Yacht (Rye, N.Y.); Corinthian Yacht (Seattle); Union League (N.Y.C.); Knights of Malta, Order St. John, Washington Athletic (Seattle), Royal Victoria (B.C.) Yacht. Home and Office: 4 Riverstone Laguna Niguel CA 92677-5309 also: Sunrise Country Club 6 Malaga Dr Rancho Mirage CA 92270-3820

YORK, JANET BREWSTER, nurse, family and sex therapist, sculptor; b. N.Y.C., Mar. 5, 1941; d. Edward Cox and Janet Stone Brewster; m. Albert Thompson York, Mar. 31, 1962 (dec.); children: Clifton Gaston, Torrance Brewster, 1 adopted child, Justin Brigham. AA with honors, Briarcliff Coll., 1961; RN with highest honors, U. Iowa, 1965; BA summa cum laude, Marymount Manhattan Coll., 1975; MA with honors, NYU, 1978. Nurse Manhattan Eye, Ear and Throat Hosp., N.Y.C., 1966-74; nurse, counselor Washington Free Clinic, 1969-71; family therapist Ackerman Family Inst., N.Y.C., 1976-80; sex therapist N.Y. Med. Coll., Flower Fifth Ave. Hosp., N.Y.C., 1976-80; pvt. practice pvt. practice, N.Y.C., 1978—; supervisory staff grad. edn. program in human sexuality N.Y.U. Med. Ctr., 1982—, sculptor, 1988—, operator Piccadil Kennel, breeder Cavalier King Charles Spaniels; bd. dirs. Manhattan Eye, Ear and Throat Hosp., Animal Med. Ctr. Represented in permanent collection The Dog Mus. of Am., St. Louis; author: Corneel the Cavalier; contbr. articles to profl. jours; author: (videotape) Death as a Part of Life. Named Vita fellow Internat. Coun. Sex Edn. and Parenthood, Am. U., 1981; recipient Evelyn Monte Sculpture award, 1988, 94, Ellsworth Howell Art Sculpture award Pen & Brush Club, 1991, 93, 96, 99, Dog Fanciers Club, 1999. Mem. Am. Soc. for Sex Therapy and Rsch., Am. Assn. Sex. Edn., Counseling and Therapy, Soc. For Sci. Study Sex, Sex Info. and Edn. Coun. U.S., Am. Assn. Marriage and Family Therapists, Nat. Assn. Women Artists, Am. Medallic Soc., Nantucket Art Assn., Walker Art Ctr., Nat. Mus. Women in Arts, Lawrence Beach Club, Rockaway Hunting Club, Millbrook Club. Home: 155 E 72nd St New York NY 10021-4371

YORKE, HAROLD W., astrophysicist; b. Riverside, Calif., Aug. 24, 1948; s. Harold W. and Wilda Mercedes (Bender) Y.; m. Ruth Barbara Rossbach, Nov. 7, 1969; children: Colleen Olivia, Vanessa Alexandra. BS, UCLA, 1970; Dipl. phys., U. Goettingen, Germany, 1972, Dr. rer. nat., 1974, Dr. habil., 1979. Rsch. asst. Calif. Inst. Tech., Pasadena, 1970-71; fellow, Fulbright scholar U. Goettingen, 1971-73, sci. asst., 1973-75; staff scientist Max Planck Inst. for Astrophysics, Munich, 1975-78; tenured scientist U. Goettingen, 1978-88; prof. Wuerzburg (Germany) U., 1988-98; sr. rsch. scientist Jet Propulsion Lab., Calif. Inst. Tech., Pasadena, 1998—; Co-author: Radiation in Moving Gaseous Media, 1988; contbr. articles to Astronomy & Astrophysics, Astrophysical Jour. Regents' scholar U. Calif., 1966, Fulbright scholar, 1971, Fulbright fellow, 1972, NSF fellow Calif. Inst. Tech., 1970. Mem. Internat. Astron. Union, Am. Astron. Soc., Astronomische Gesellschaft, Phi Beta Kappa. Office: Jet Propulsion Lab MS 169-506 4800 Oak Grove Dr Pasadena CA 91109-8001

YOROZU, ATSUNORI, physician; b. Tokyo, Nov. 13, 1960; s. Koichi and Chizuko (Iijima) Y.; m. Tomoko Awano, Apr. 27, 1988; children: Haruka, Alice. MD, Keio U., Tokyo, 1985, DSc, 1996. Intern Keio U. Hosp., Tokyo, 1985-89; med. asst. Tokyo Met. Hiroo Hosp., Tokyo, 1989-91; cons. Nat. Tokyo Med. Ctr., 1991-99; clin. tng. fellow Christie Hosp., Manchester, U.K., 1999—. Contbr. articles to profl. jours. Home: Flat 4 Hanover House, 6 Olive Shapley Av Didsbury, Manchester M20 6QG, England Office: Christie Hosp NHS Trust, Wilmslow Rd Worthington, Manchester M20 4BX, England

YOSHIDA, JUNICHI, surgeon; b. Nagoya, Japan, June 26, 1955; s. Shigeru and Ikuko (Masuda) Y.; m. Yukimi Izumi, Dec. 2, 1984; children: Masashi Christopher, Hiroki. MD, Kyushu U., Fukuoka, Japan, 1981; MS, U. Ill., Chgo., 1986. Bd. cert. in surgery. Resident Kyushu U., 1981-85; rsch. assoc. U. Ill., Chgo., 1985-88; house officer Kyushu U., 1988-93, asst. prof., 1993-96; divsn. chief Shimonoseki (Japan) City Hosp., 1996—. Contbr. articles to profl. jours. Fellow ACS. E-mail: info@yoshidaj.com. Office: Shimonoseki City Hosp Surg, 1-13-1 Koyo-cho, 750-8520 Shimonoseki Japan

YOSHIDA, KEIKO, linguist; b. Odawara, Kanagawa, Japan, Dec. 27, 1961; d. Mitsuo and Hinako (Ito) Kawakubo; m. Tomoyuki Yoshida, July 20, 1986. BA, Internat. Christian U., Tokyo, 1984; MEd, Tokyo Gakugei U., 1987; PhD, Cornell U., 1993. Assoc. prof. Waseda U., Tokyo, 1998—. Author: Syntax and Semantics of Wh-Quantifier Interactions, 1995; contbr. articles to profl. jours. Travel grantee The Mario Einaudi Ctr. for Internat. Studies, 1991, Cornell U., 1991. Mem. Phi Kappa Phi. Office: Waseda U, 1-6-1 Nishi-Waseda, 169 8050 Shinjuku-ku Japan

YOSHIDA, KENTARO (KENTAROH YOSHIDA), science educator; b. Kanazawa, Japan, Oct. 10, 1935; s. Zennichiro and Sotoko (Kiyokawa) Y.; m. Keiko Kubo, Dec. 19, 1964; children: Yumiko, Masanobu, Takeaki Kubo. BS, Kyoto (Japan) U., 1958, MS, 1960, DSc, 1973. Rschr. Toshiba Elec. Co. Ltd., Tokyo, 1960-63; rsch. asst. Kobe (Japan) U., 1963-75, assoc. prof., 1975-91, prof., 1991-99. Co-author: Collected Techniques of Electron Microscope Specimen Preparation, 1970, Thin Films Handbook, 1983; editor: Surface Interface X-Ray Scatterings and Diffractions of Industrial Metallic Materials, 1996. Recipient 12th award for Fundamental Rsch. Aids, Hyogo Invention and Devel. Assn., Kobe, 1988, 1st Coop. Rsch. Aid, 1993-96. Fellow New Industry Rsch. Assn.; mem. Japanese Soc. Electron Microscopy (councilor 1982-92, bd. dirs. 1992—), Jyōdoshinshuu-Buddhist Assn. (councilor 1994—). Avocations: fishing, travel. Office: Kobe U Fac Engring, Rokkodai 1 Nada, Hyogo Kobe 657 8501, Japan

YOSHIDA, KOICHI, insurance company executive. CEO, pres. Sumitomo Life Ins. Co., 1996—. Fax: 81-6-232-2349. Office: Sumitomo Life Ins Co, 2-2-5 Nakanoshima Kita-ku, Osaka 530, Japan*

YOSHIDA, MASAMI, university administrator, researcher; b. Sapporo, Japan, Mar. 31, 1963; s. Ken'ichi and Seiko (Hatayama) Y.; m. Ayako Tanno, Jan. 15, 1990; children: Mai, Naoto. BA, Hokusei Gakuen U., Sapporo, 1985. Salesman Hokusei Gakuen Co-op., Sapporo, 1985-87, Hokkaido U. Co-op., Sapporo, 1987-98; mem. merchandising and support staff Hokkaido Bus. Fedn. Univ. Co-op Assns., 1998—; dir. Hokusei Gakuen Co-op., Sapporo, 1982-83, U. Co-op Assn., Sapporo, 1983-84; mng. dir., 1983, dir., 1984. Mem. Japan Automobile Fedn., F&AM Hokkaido Centennial Lodge. Avocations: listening to world music, world broadcasts, travel. Office: Sodosha, CPO Box 293, Sapporo 060-8694, Japan

YOSHIDA, NORIHIRO PRINCE, mathematician; b. Fukuoka-Ken, Japan, Aug. 11, 1938; s. Yoshikatsu and Harue (Yamamoto) Y. Student, Tokyo U. Fgn. Studies, 1963-64; BSc, U. Tokyo, 1970. Exec. dir. Soc. Advancement of Culture U. Tokyo, 1964-68; promoter Interfield Edn. Dept., Tokyo, 1978-82; researcher Human Devel. Inst., Tokyo, 1982-84; phon-in dir., lectr. Borgnan Sci. Acad., Tokyo, 1984-86; mgr. Borgnan Human Devel. Inst., Tokyo, 1986-95; sr. cons. Career Network Co., Ltd., Tokyo, 1995—; dir. Ecotopia Co., Ltd., Tokyo, 1999—; exec. dir. HyperMedic Co., Ltd., Tokyo, 1999—; sec.-gen. Soc. Advancement of Sci., Tokyo, 1984-86; bd. dirs. DEN Sys. Co., Ltd. Mem. Accelerated Teaching and Ednl. Research Group, Soc. Reading Sci. Books, Am. Math. Soc., Soc. Teaching Japanese as Fgn. Lang. Avocation: philately. E-mail: yoshida@vinet.or.jp. Home: 2-15-2-206 Akabanekita, Kita-ku, Tokyo 115-0052, Japan Office: HyperMedic Co Ltd, 4-23-17 Higashi-Ikebukuro, Toshima-ku Tokyo 170-0013, Japan

YOSHIDA, TAKASHI, history researcher; b. Maebashi, Gunma, Japan, Oct. 28, 1963. BA in Pvt. Law, Aoyama Gakuin U., 1988; BA in Polit. Sci., U. Ill., 1989; M in Internat. Affairs, Columbia U., 1992, MA in History, 1996; advanced cert., CU East Asian Inst., 1997. Rsch. asst. Columbia U., 1995-98; vis. scholar Hitosubashi U., 1998-99; adj. prof. Marymount Manhattan U., N.Y., 1995-98, Pace U., N.Y., 1998. Contbr. articles to profl. jours.; author: The Nanjing Massacre in Japan in The Nanjing Massacre in History and Historiography, 2000. Fulbright-Hays DDRA fellow, 1998-99; Toyota Found. Rsch. grantee, 1999-2000. Mem. Am. Hist. Assn., Assn. for Asian Studies, Ctr. for Rsch. and Documentation of Japan's War Responsibility. E-mail: ty44A@Columbia.edu. Home: 501 W 123rd St Apt 6E New York NY 10027-5008

YOSHIDA, TAKEHITO, electric industrial company researcher; b. Tokyo, Minato-ku, Japan, Sept. 22, 1959; s. Kazunari and Yoshiko (Izumi) Y.; m. Tamayo Takakura, May 23, 1987. BS, Shinshu U., Nagano, Japan, 1982; MS, U. Tsukuba, Ibaragi, Japan, 1984, D of Engring., 1993. With Matsushita Elec. Corp., Tokyo, 1984-85; with Matsushita Elec. Indsl. Co., Osaka, Japan, 1985-91, mem. tech. staff, 1991-93; mem. tech. staff Matsushita Rsch. Inst., Tokyo, 1993-96, sr. staff rschr., 1996—; designing engr. Matsushita Elec. Corp., 1984-85, fabrication processing engr., 1985-93. Contbr. articles to profl. jours.; patentee in field. Mem. Materials Rsch. Soc., Japan Applied Physics Soc. Avocations: skiing, hiking, photography, reading. Office: Matsushita Rsch Inst, 3-10-1 Higashimita Tama-ku, Kawasaki 214-8501, Japan

YOSHIDA, TAKESHI, pharmaceutical executive, research scientist; b. Fukuoka, Japan, July 24, 1938; s. Kiyoshi and Yae (Miyama) Y.; m. Tomoko Tasaka, Nov. 7, 1964; children: Atsushi, Keiko. BS, Tokyo U., 1959, MD, 1963, D Med. Sci., 1970. Med. diplomate; lic. physician. Rsch. assoc. NIH, Tokyo, 1964-71; asst. prof. SUNY, Buffalo, 1971-74; asst. prof. U. Conn. Health Ctr., Farmington, 1974-75, assoc. prof., 1976-81, prof., 1981-83; exec. dir. Merck Sharp and Dohme Rsch. Labs., Tokyo, 1983-86; dir. Chugai Pharm. Co., Tokyo, 1986-91, exec. dir., 1991-97, mng. dir., 1997-98, sr. v.p., 1998—; pres. Tokyo Inst. Immunopharmacology Inc., Tokyo, 1987-95, Chugai Rsch. Inst. Molecular Medicine Inc., Ibaraki, Japan, 1995-96; clin. prof. U. Conn. Health Ctr., 1986-97; vis. lectr. Hokkaido U. Rsch. Inst. Immunology, Sapporo, Japan, 1992-99; spl. rsch. scientist Nat. Age program Tsukuba (Japan) U., 1984-89; cons. WHO Tb Program, Geneva, 1991-95. Co-editor: Basic and clinical Aspects of Granulomatous Diseases, 1980, Immunology of the eosinophil, 1983, New horizons of tumor immunotherapy, 1989, Basic mechanisms of granulomatous inflammation, 1989. Recipient Imai award Japanese Soc. for Tb, 1984; grantee U.S. NIAID/NCI/NIH, 1978-82. Mem. NIH Immunology Study Sect., Internat. Soc. Immunopharmacology (councilor 1992-95), Japan Soc. BRM (coun.), Japan Soc. Inflammation (coun.), Pluto Club, Japan Soc. Cancer. Office: Chugai Pharm Co Ltd, 2-1-9 Kyobashi Chuoku, Tokyo 104-8301, Japan

YOSHIDA, YOSHIO, dean, physical geography educator; b. Hara-Machi, Shizuoka, Japan, Dec. 18, 1930; s. Eijiro and Mioko (Egawa) Y.; m. Yuki Takeuchi, Nov. 27, 1963; children: Shin'ichi, Yosuke, Kei. BS, U. Tokyo, 1954, MS, 1956, DSc, 1980. Rsch. assoc. Tokyo Met. U., 1959-61; lectr. Ochano Mizu U., Tokyo, 1962-64; assoc. prof., prof. Hiroshima (Japan) U., 1964-76; prof., chief scientist Nat. Inst. Polar Rsch., Tokyo, 1976-94; prof. Rissho U., Tokyo, 1994-98; prof., dean Rissho U., Kumagaya, Japan, 1998—; mem. Antarctic Place-Names Com. Japan, 1973—, chmn., 1997—; mem., Japan rep. working group on geology Sci. Com. on Antarctic Rsch., 1986-94, alt. del. Japan, 1990-92. Author, editor: Nankyoku, 1973, Nankyoku No Kagaku-5, Chigaku, 1986, Recent Progress in Antarctic Earth Science, 1992. Alt. rep. Japanese Del. to Antarctic Treaty Consultative Meetings, 1977-92; mem., sub-com. chmn. Ednl. Textbook Examination Coun., Ministry Edn., Sci. and Culture, Tokyo, 1985-98; mem. Natural Environment Conservation Coun., Environmental Agy. Japan, Tokyo, 1997. Recipient Silver Cup prize for Antarctic rsch. Mininstry Edn., Sci. and Culture, Tokyo, 1977, Antarctic Svc. medal NSF U.S. Govt., Washington, 1978, Silver Crup for prize for internat. sci. coop. Ministry Fgn. Affairs, Tokyo, 1994. Mem. Internat. Glaciological Soc., Japan Polar Rsch. Assn. (dir., sec.-gen.), China Assn. for Sci. Expedition (hon.). Avocation: tennis. Home: 5-2-3-404 Nakaarai, Tokorozawa-shi 359-0041, Japan Office: Rissho U Fac Geo-Environ, 1700 Magechi, Kumagaya-shi 360-0194, Japan

YOSHIE, HISAYA, educator; b. Toyama Prefecture, Japan, July 5, 1917; s. Masajiro Shibata and Shizue Yoshie; m. Kazuko Inui, Mar. 24, 1961; children: Shihoko, Toyoaki, Kikuko.; BA, Tokyo Higher Normal Sch., 1940; MA, Tokyo Bunrika U., 1951; DLitt, Mukogawa Women's U., 1994. Tchr. Sapporo Daiichi Chugakko and other high schs., Japan, 1940-69; asst. prof. Bukkyo U., Kyoto, Japan, 1969-73, prof., 1973-88, nonregular prof., 1988-90; tchr. part time Osaka (Japan) U. of Fgn. Langs., 1980-81, Mukogawa Women's U., Nishinomiya, Hyogo, Japan, 1991-94; part-time tchr. various univs., 1969-94; lectr. Bukkyo U., 1965-69, Internat. Symposium Saikaku's 300th Birthday, 1993, Symposium Rabindranath Tagore and Miyazawa-Kenji, 1996. Author: A Study of Saikaku's Works, 1974, Poems, Dankyo, 1980, Akinari Ueda as a Poet, 1983, Saikaku's Works on Human Mind, 1988, Saikaku's Works and Those of His Contemporaries, 1990, Rabindranath Tagore and Kenji Miyazawa-Two True Poets' Religion and Literature, 1999. Chmn. Neighborhood Assn., Kyoto, 1976. Mem. Nippon Poets' Club (awards 1991, 92), Japan Edo Period Literature Assn., Tsukuba U. Lit. Assn., The Miyazawa-Kenji Assn. (Ihatobu ctr.). Avocations: viola, music, poetry, travel. Home: 43 Kamimidori-cho, Shichiku Kita-ku Kyoto 603, Japan

YOSHIHIKO, OHTSUKI, physicist, educator; b. Kakuda City, Miyagi, Japan, June 18, 1936; s. Ohtsuki Sato Sazou and Ohtsuki Takie; m. Ohtsuki Ogawa Kiyoko, Dec. 20, 1960; 1 child, Tomi. D in Physics, Tokyo U., 1961. Asst. Tokyo U., 1963-67, lectr., 1967-68; asst. prof. Waseda U., Tokyo, 1968-73, prof., 1973—; guest prof. Nagoya (Japan) U., 1975-77, München (Germany) U., 1979-80; dir. Japan Physical Soc., Tokyo, 1983-84. Editor Parity Monthly, 1985—. Avocations: hiking, mushroom gathering. Office: Dept Physics Waseda U, 4 1 Ohkubo 3 Chome, Shinjuku Tokyo 169 50, Japan

YOSHIKAWA, KENICHI, biophysicist, chemicalphysicist, researcher; b. Takarazuka, Hyogo, Japan, July 25, 1948; s. Takashi and Kazuko (Kojima) Y.; m. Yuko Ito, Nov. 7, 1976; children: Hiroshi, Eiko. PhD, Kyoto U., 1976. Asst. prof. Tokushima (Japan) U., 1976-78, assoc. prof., 1979-87; assoc. prof. Nagoya U., 1988-89, prof. biophysics, 1990-97; prof. physics Kyoto U., 1998—. Contbr. articles to profl. jours. Recipient Japan IBM award, 1991. Fax: 81-75-753-3819. Office: Kyoto Univ, Dept Physics, Kyoto 606-8502, Japan

YOSHIKAWA, KUNIHIKO, dermatologist, educator; b. Kyoto, Japan, May 16, 1939; s. Saburou and Yukiko (Nishino) Y.; m. Noriko Ohkido, Mar. 30, 1971; children: Momoko, Tadahiko, Yuko. BSc, Osaka (Japan) U., 1960, MD, 1964, PhD, 1978. Diplomate Japanese Dermatol. Assn., Japanese Nat. Bd. Instr. Sch. Medicine, Osaka (Japan) U., 1970-71, prof., chmn. dept. dermatology, 1985—; rsch. fellow dept. dermatology Sch. Medicine, U. Miami, Fla., 1972-75; assoc. prof. dept. dermatology Med. Sch., Nagoya (Japan) City Univ., 1975-85; vis. sci. Oreg. Regional Primate Rsch. Ctr., Beaverton, Oreg., 1971-72; expert panel mem. Rsch. Inst. Fragrance Materials, Hackensack, N.J., 1988-96; mem. exam. com. Japan Med. Bd., 1993-97. Editor-in-chief Jour. Dermatol. Sci., 1993-97, Photomedicine and Photobiology, 1995-97; co-editor Comprehensive Dermatology Series, 1986-90, Dermatology for non-Specialist Series, 1987—; mem. editl. bd. Environ. Dermatology, 1994—. Recipient Best Clin. Poster award 17th World Congress Dermatology, 1987. Mem. Japanese Med. Assn. (v.p. Osaka divsn.), Japanese Dermatol. Assn. (bd. dirs., head ctrl. divsn.), Japanese Soc. Investigative Dermatology (inspector), Japanese Soc. Dermatoallergology (bd. dirs.), Japanese Soc. Photomedicine and Photobiology, European Soc. for

Dermatology Rsch., Soc. Investigative Dermatology, Japanese Soc. Psoriasis Rsch. (bd. dirs.), Japanese Soc. Contact Dermatitis Rsch. (bd. dirs.), Japanese Soc. Connective Tissue Rsch. (auditor), Japan Allergy Found. (bd. dirs., head Kansai divsn.). Buddhist. Avocations: golf, driving, gardening, stone collecting, watching sports. Office: Osaka U Sch Med Dept Dermatology, 2-2 Yamada-oka, Suita, Osaka 565-0871, Japan

YOSHIKAWA, TOSHIKAZU, medical educator; b. Uji, Kyoto, Japan, Apr. 28, 1947; s. Satoshi and Hana (Nagano) Y.; m. Masako Yamamoto, May 3, 1974; 2 children. MD, Kyoto Pref. U. Medicine, 1973, PhD, 1983. Resident Kyoto Pref. U. of Medicine, 1973-75, sr. resident, 1976-83, asst. prof., 1985-86, assoc. prof., 1986—; vis. prof. La. State U., 1984, U. Tokyo, 1993-95. Editor: Free Radical Research, 1989-96, Free Radical Biology and Medicine, 1994, Redox Report, 1996; editor-in-chief Pathophysiology, 1993. Mem. European Surg. Club, N.Y. Acad. Sci. Avocations: golf, tennis. Office: 1st Dept Medicine, Kyoto Pref U of Medicine, Kamigyo-ku Kyoto 602, Japan

YOSHIMI, YOSHIAKI, geotechnical engineer, consultant; b. Taipei, Japan, Jan. 31, 1928; s. Masao and Sumiko Y.; m. Fumiko Yano Yoshimi, Aug. 21, 1957; children: Takashi , Kenji. BS, Tokyo Inst. Tech., 1950; MS in Engring., U. Washington, 1952; PhD, Northwestern U., Evanston, Ill., 1958. Structural engr. T. Yamashita Architects & Engrs., Tokyo, 1950-60; asst. prof. Carnegie Inst. Tech., Pitts., 1961-64; assoc. prof. Tokyo Inst. Tech., 1964-68, prof., 1968-88; sr. adv. Shimizu Corp., 1988-98; dean of students, 1984-86, dir. Inst. Libr., 1986-88, Tokyo Inst. Tech. Author: Liquefaction of Sandy ground, Tokyo, 1980; contbr. papers in field. Garioa grant Inst. for Internat. Edn., N.Y.C., 1950; recipient Technological Achievement award Japanese Soc. Soil Mechanics and Found. Engring., Tokyo, 1986. Mem. ASCE, Engring. Acad Japan, Japanese Geotech. Soc., Instn. Civil Engrs. (London). E-mail: yoshiaki.yoshimi@nifty.ne.jp. Home: 4074 Shimotsuruma, Yamato 242-0001, Japan

YOSHIMOTO, TETSUYUKI, neurosurgeon; b. Takikawa, Japan, Apr. 27, 1962; s. Kinnosuke and Kimiko Yoshimoto; m. Kumiko Sekiguchi, Sept. 3, 1988; 1 child, Arina. MD, Asahikawa Med. Coll., 1987; DMSc, Hokkaido U., 1996. Cert. Bd. Japanese Neurosurg. Soc. Physician Hokkaido U. of Medicine, Sapporo, Japan, 1987-92, rsch. fellow, 1992-96; physician Otaru Mcpl. 2d Hosp., 1996-98; asst. rschr. Queen's Med. Ctr., 1998—, Ctr. for Study of Neurol. Disease, Neurosci. Inst., 1998—. Contbr. articles to profl. jours.

YOSHIMURA, MASATAKA, engineering educator, mechanical engineer; b. Innami-cho, Japan, May 15, 1945; s. Gentaro and Saeko (Izawa) Y.; m. Machiko Suzuki, Oct. 25, 1975; children: Yukimitsu, Kazuhiro. B in Engring., Kyoto U., 1968, M in Engring., 1970, DSc in Engring., 1976. From instr. to prof. Kyoto U., Japan, 1973—. Author: Concurrent Engineering: Contemporary Issues and Modern Design Tools, 1993, Design for X: Concurrent Engineering Imperatives, 1996; editor, author: Principles of CIM, 1993; contbr. articles to profl. jours. Mem. ASME, AIAA, Japan Soc. Mech. Engring. Office: Kyoto U Grad Sch Engring, Dept Precision Engring, 606-8501 Kyoto Japan

YOSHINAGA, FUMIHIRO, microbiologist; b. Maebashi, Gunma, Japan, July 14, 1937; s. Kunihiro and Toshiko (Murata) Y.; m. Nozomi Shimizu, Apr. 18, 1964; children: Akashi, Eri. B of Agrl., Tokyo U., 1961, D of Agrl., 1970. Rschr. Ajinomoto Co. Inc., Kawasaki, Japan, 1961-72, chief microbiol. chemist, 1973-79, mgr., 1980-87, basic rsch. lab. dir., 1988-92; mng. dir. Bio-Polymer Rsch. Co. Ltd., Kawasaki, 1992-98, gen. lab. mgr., 1992-98, tech. adr., 1998—; prof. extraordinary Saga U., 1976; working com. mem. Ministry of Trade and Industry, Japanese Govt., 1981-86, Nat. Sci. Coun., Tokyo, 1983-84. Author: Amino Acids: Biosynthesis and Genetic Regulation, 1983, Biotechnology of Amino Acid Production, 1986; contbr. articles to profl. jours. Mem. Japan Soc. for Biosci., Biotech. and Agrochemistry (working com. mem. 1988-93), Japan Bioindustry Assn. Avocations: walking, hiking, famous tree watching, birdswatching, gardening, Haiku. Home: 4-13-6 Kataseyama, Fujisawa 251-0033, Japan Office: Bio-polymer Rsch Co Ltd, 1-15-1 Kyobashi Chuo ku, Tokyo 104-8115, Japan

YOSHINO, GEORGE, food products executive; b. Kennewick, Wash., June 25, 1928; s. Frank H. and Kazuye (Hada) Y.; m. Frances T. Kaku, Dec. 29, 1951 (div. 1979); children: Jean Frances, Frankie Jo, Michael Stanton, Harry Walter; m. Marguerite Shirley Mosley, Dec. 8, 1990. Grad. high sch., Weiser, Idaho. Owner Yoshino Farms, Quincy, Wash., 1948—; pres. Columbia Growers Inc, Quincy, 1956-62, Yoshino Western, Inc., Quincy, 1962—, Wyco, Inc., Seattle, 1968-74; asst. sr. v.p. U & I Inc., Pasco, Wash., 1974-79; dir., gen. mgr. Spad Distributing, Inc., Pasco, 1979-86; pres. Century 21 Products, Inc., Pasco, 1987-99; exec. bd. Benton-Franklin Govtl. Conf., 1993—; dir. Assoc. Wash. Bus. Mem. City Coun. Quincy, 1964-66; bd. dirs. Columbia Basin Commn., Olympia, Wash., 1964-68; dir. Associated Wash. Bus., 1994—; dir. exec. com. Benton Franklin Regional Coun., 1993—. Mem. Produce Mktg. Assn., Associated Wash. Bus. Republican. Office: Yoshino-Western Inc 1917 N 2nd Ave Pasco WA 99301-3722

YOSHINO, HAJIME, law educator, knowledge engineer; b. Matsuyama, Japan, Feb. 23, 1939; s. Akira and Yoshiko Yoshino; m. Kazuko Shigenobu, Apr. 2, 1968; children: Yoshikazu, Keiko, Shinichi, Aiko, Tomoko. LLB, Keio U., Tokyo, 1962, LLM, 1965. Asst. prof. law Meiji Gakuin U., Tokyo, 1973-76, assoc. prof. law, 1976-83, prof. law, 1983—; leader Legal Expert System Project, Tokyo, 1983-84, 86-87, 93-94, 94—. Author, editor: Foundation of Legal Expert Systems, 1986. Recipient Yomiuri prize Yomiuri Shimbun, Japan, 1983. Mem. Japanese Assn. Legal Philosophy (dir. 1986-91, mgr. 1991-92), Law and Computers Assn. Japan (dir. 1981—), Japanese Soc. for Artificial Intelligence (councilor 1988-90). Avocations: skiing, swimming, tennis, marathons. Office: Meiji Gakuin Univ Faculty of Law, 1-2-37 Shirokanedai, Minato Tokyo 108, Japan

YOSHINO, HIROYUKI, automotive industry executive; b. Nov. 2, 1939; m. Etsuko Yohino. Grad., Tokyo U., 1963. Pres. Honda of Am. Mfg.; CEO Honda Motor Co. Ltd., Tokyo. Avocations: go, reading. Office: 2-1-1 Minami Aoyama, Minato-ku, Tokyo 107-8556, Japan*

YOSHINO, TOSHIHIKO, education educator; b. Tokyo, Apr. 27, 1939; s. Shijemasa and Mie Y.; m. Noriko, Apr. 23, 1969; 2 children. BS, Tokyo U., 1963, MS, 1965, PhD, 1968. Asst. prof. Inst. Indsl. Sci. U. Tokyo, 1968-75, lectr. Inst. Indsl. Sci., 1975-88, assoc. prof. Inst. Indsl. Sci., 1988; prof. Gunman U., Kiryu, Japan, 1988—; chief dept. elec. engring. Gunman U., Kiryu, 1996; vis. rsch. Hannover (Germany) U., 1971-73; vis. prof. IBM, San Jose, Calif., 1985; consulting prof., Boden, China, 1997. Fellow IOP; mem. Soc. Lightwave Sensing Tech. (chmn. 1989-92), Japan Soc. Applied Physics (exec. com. 1982-85). Home: 3-11-9 Shoan, Suginamibu, Tokyo 162-0054, Japan Office: Gunman Univ, 1-5-1 Tenjin-Che, Kiryu 376-8515, Japan

YOSHINORI, MIYAMOTO, medical officer; b. Taga-cho, Shiga-Ken, Japan, Mar. 7, 1952; s. Miyamoto Fujimoto (Shizuko) Y.; m. Kobayashi Kimie, May 3, 1979; 2 children. B.Pharm., Kyoto Pharm. U., 1976; BS, Nat. Def. Acad., Kanagawa, Japan, 1981; PhD, Kyorin U., Tokyo, 1988. Commd. Japan Air Self-Def. Force, 1976—, advanced through grades to lt. col., 1993; med. officer Japan Air Self-Def. Force, Saitama and Shizuoka, 1976-79; chief pharmacochemistry sect. Aeromed. Lab. Japan Air Self-Def. Force, Tokyo, 1981-88, staff med. divsn. air staff office, 1988-90, chief pahrmacochemistry sect. Aeromed. Lab., 1990-97; comdr. med. squadron Komatsu Air Base Japan Air Self-Def. Force, Ishikawa, 1997-99; command surgeon Southwestern Composite Air Divsn./Japan Air Self-Def. Force, Okinawa-ken, 1999—. Contbr. articles to profl. jours. Window-on-Sci. Program grantee USAF, Asia Office of Aerospace R&D, Tokyo, 1995. Mem. Aerospace Med. Assn., Science. Avocations: fishing, orchids. Office: SW Composite Air Divsn, 301 Tohma Naha-shi, Okinawa-ken 901-0194, Japan

YOSHIOKA, MIEKO, hospital administrator, pediatrician, consultant; b. Nara, Japan, June 3, 1940; d. Toshi and Tadao (Hujita) Y. MD, Kyoto (Japan) U., 1965, DMS, 1977. Intern Kyoto U. Hosp., 1965-66, resident dept. pediat., 1966-67; med. staff dept. pediat. Kyoto Nat. Hosp., 1967-72; chief dept. pediat. Utano Nat. Hosp., Kyoto, 1972-78; staff dept. pediat. Sch. Medicine, Kyoto U., 1978-81; vis. assoc. dept. molecular, cellular and devel. biology U. Colo., Boulder, 1980-81; asst. prof. dept. pediat. Sch. Medicine, Kyoto U., 1981-82; chief dept. pediat. Kobe (Japan) Gen. Hosp., 1982-99; dir. Kobe City Pediatric and Gen. Rehab. Ctr. for Challenged, 1999—. Author: Congenital Muscular Dystrophies, 1997; contbr. articles to profl. jours. Mem. Internat. Child Neurology Assn., Japanese Child Neurology Assn., Japan-Pediat. Soc. (mem. bd.), Japanese Epilepsy Assn. Avocations: music, painting. Office: Kobe City Pediat & Gen Rehab Ctr for Challenged, 2-3-50 Maruyama-cho, Nagata-ku Kobe 653-0875, Japan

YOSHIOKA, SHOICHI, geophysicist; b. Okayama, Japan, Nov. 3, 1962; s. Tatsuji and Sumiko (Wake) Y. BS, Kobe (Japan) U., 1985, MS, 1987, DSc, 1990. Postdoctoral fellow Kyoto (Japan) U., 1990-91, Tokyo U., 1991-92, Utrecht (The Netherlands) U., 1992-94; asst. prof. Ehime U., Matsuyama, Japan, 1994-97; assoc. prof. Kyushu U., Fukuoka, Japan, 1997—. Contbr. articles to profl. jours. Avocations: music and art appreciation, saxophone. Home: Domile Wakamiya B-205, Wakamiya 4-12-9 Higashi-ku, Fukuoka 813-0036, Japan Office: Kyushu U Dept Earth/Plan Sc, Hakozaki 6-10-1 Higashi-ku, Fukuoka 812-8581, Japan

YOSHISE, AKIKO, mathematical programming researcher, educator; b. Machida, Tokyo, Japan, Aug. 19, 1962; d. Kouhei and Reiko (Totsuka) Y.; m. Takahito Kuno, Nov. 16, 1989; 1 child, Yoko. B in Engring., Tokyo Inst. Tech., 1985, M in Engring., 1987, D in Engring., 1990. Asst. prof. U. Tsukuba, Japan, 1991-93; assoc. prof. U. Tsukuba, 1993—. Co-author: A Unified Approach to Interior Point Algorithms for Linear Complementarity Problems, 1991 (Computer Sci. Tech. Sect. award Ops. Rsch. Soc. 1992). Mem. Ops. Rsch. Soc. Japan (Frederick W. Lanchester prize 1993), Soc. Indsl. and Applied Math. Avocations: illustrating, movies. Office: U Tsukuba, Inst Policy & Planning Scis, Tsukuba 305, Japan

YOSHIURA, KAZUNORI, oral radiologist, researcher; b. Fukuoka, Japan, Feb. 11, 1959; s. Kiyoshi and Michiko (Nakanishi) Y.; m. Junko Otsuka, Sept. 15, 1987; children: Saki, Yuki, Harunori. DDS, Kyushu U., Fukuoka, 1983, PhD, 1989. Diplomate oral radiology. Resident Kyushu U. Dental Hosp., Fukuoka, 1987-88; instr. Nagasaki (Japan) U., 1988-90; instr. Kyushu U., Fukuoka, 1990-91, asst. prof., 1991-99, assoc. prof., 1999—. Recipient Grant-in-aid Ministry Edn., Sci. and Culture, 1990, 92-93, 97-98, 99—. Mem. Internat. Assn. Dentomaxillofacial Radiology, Japanese Soc. Oral and Maxillofacial Radiology, Japanese Stomatological Soc., Japan Soc. Ultrasonics in Medicine. Home: Miwadai 1-18-5, Fukuoka 811-0212, Japan Office: Kyushu U Faculty Dentistry, Maidashi 3-1-1, Fukuoka 812-8582, Japan

YOSHIZAKI, MICHIYO, company executive; b. Oita, Kyushu, Japan, June 18, 1949; arrived in Eng., 1991; d. Bunzaburo and Takayo (Tanaka) Y.; m. Emmanuel Cassuto, 1979 (dec. Jan. 1994); 1 child, Ado Maximillian. Student, Bunka Gakuin Coll., Tokyo, Centro Sperim Entale Cinematografica, Rome. European rep. Nippon Herald, Tokyo, v.p.; CEO, pres. N.D.F. Internat., Inc., London, 1991—. Prodr. (film) The Crying Game, Basquiat, Kamasutra, 1995, Wilde, Chinese Box, 1998, Titus, 1999. E-mail: ndfiltd@aol.com.

YOSHIZAKI, SHIRO, research scientist, consultant; b. Komatsushima, Tokushima, Japan, Feb. 17, 1944; s. Yoshiyuki and Masu (Matsushima) Y.; m. Ayako Ohno, May 31, 1970; children: Masahiko, Tatsuo. B. Engring., Tokushima (Japan) U., 1966, M. Engring., 1968; PharmD, Osaka (Japan) U., 1981. Cert. cons. engr., Japan. Rschr. Otsuka Pharm. Co., Ltd., Tokushima, 1968-81, sr. rschr., 1982-89; sr. rschr. NKK Corp., Kawasaki, 1989-95, Maruho Co., Ltd., Kyoto, Japan, 1995-97; head Yoshizaki Engr. Office, Komatsusushima, Japan, 1997—. Contbr. articles to profl. jours.; inventor, patent for procaterol, carteolol, 250 other patents. Fellow Am. Chem. Soc.; mem. Pharm. Soc. Japan, Kinki Chem. Soc. (Kagaku Gijyutsu prize 1983). Buddhist. Avocations: fishing, Go game. Office: Yoshizaki Engr Office, 15-1 Azasotobiraki Komatsushima, Tokushima 773-0001, Japan

YOSHIZAWA, KIYOSHI, agricultural studies educator; b. Tokyo, Jan. 13, 1933; s. Masayoshi and Tamaki (Kobayashi) Y.; m. Sadako Hirashima, Oct. 25, 1957; children: Yuko, Akira, Yasuko Scher. B of Agr., U. Tokyo, 1955, PhD in Agr., 1966. Rsch. official Nat. Rsch. Inst. Brewing, Tokyo, 1955-67, chief rsch. official, 1967-72, dir., 1972-87, pres., 1987-89; prof. Tokyo U. Agr., 1989—; Researcher in field. Author: Culture and Civilization of Alcoholic Beverages, 1991; author, editor: Science of Alcoholic Beverages, 1995; inventor treatment for waste water using yeast, 1998. Recipient Prize of Minister of Sci. and Tech. Ministry Sci. and Tech., 1985. Mem. Agrl. Chem. Soc. (Prize of Tech. 1981), Agrl. Chem. Soc., Brewing Soc. Japan. Avocations: tennis, classical music. Office: Tokyo U Agr, 1-1-1 Sakuragaoka, 156-8502 Tokyo Japan

YOSHIZAWA, NOBUYUKI, medical educator, nephrologist; b. Kawasaki, Kanagawa, Japan, Nov. 28, 1940; s. Jirokichi and Sumi (Noda) Y.; m. Naoko Taniguchi, Dec. 22, 1984. MD, Nihon U., 1973. Rsch. fellow N.Y. Med. Coll., 1969-72; asst. prof. dept. medicine Nihon U., Tokyo, 1975-78, Nat. Def. Med. Coll., Saitama, Japan, 1978-96; prof. dept. pub. health Nat. Def. Med. Coll., Saitama, 1996—. Contbr. articles on clinical nephrology, nephritogenic streptococcal antigen to profl. jours. Mem. Japanese Soc. of Nephrology (councillor), Japanese Soc. of Allergology (councillor), Japanese Soc. of Clin. Immunology (councillor), Japan Soc. for Occupl. Health (councillor), Japan Epidemiol. Assn. (councillor), Internat. Soc. of Nephrology, Am. Soc. Nephrology. Avocations: jogging, movies, golf. Home: 2-325-157 Kohan, Higashiyamatoshi, Tokyo 207-0002, Japan Office: Nat Def Med Coll Pub Health, 3-2 Namiki Tokorozawa, Saitama 359-8513, Japan

YOSIPOVITCH, GIL, dermatologist, researcher; b. Jerusalem, Mar. 22, 1961; s. Zvi and Shifra (Rabinovitch) Y.; m. Galit Trupin, Nov. 2, 1993; children: Natalie, Dan. MD, Tel-Aviv (Israel) U., 1988, MSc, 1994. Bd. cert. internal medicine, Israel. Intern Ichilov Hosp, Tel-Aviv, 1988-89; resident internal medicine Beilinson Med. Ctr., Petah-Tiqva, Israel, 1990-94; resident dept. dermatology Beilinson Med. Ctr., Petah-Tiqva, 1995-98; rsch. fellow U. Calif. San Francisco Med. Ctr., 1994-95; lectr. dermatology Sackler Faculty Medicine, 1992—; cons. various drug cos., San Francisco, 1994—; cons. Nat. Skin Ctr., Singapore. Contbr. articles to profl. jours. Med. officer Israeli Def. Force, 1978—. Recipient Heinz Maurer prize Dermatol. Rsch., 1998; grantee Israel Cancer Assn., 1993, Rothschild Found., 1994. Avocations: swimming, basketball, tennis. Office: Nat Skin Ctr Dept Dermatology, 1 Mandalay Rd, 308205 Singapore Singapore

YOSKIN, JON WILLIAM, II, insurance company executive; b. Phila., Oct. 16, 1939; s. Lewis William and Louise (Houck) Y.; m. Dorothea James, Sept. 25, 1961 (div. Mar. 1992); children: Nicholas, Dorothea, Maurice P.; m. Elizabeth Anne Groves, Sept 26, 1992. Pvt. practice Phila., 1959-74; sr. v.p. Mid. Atlantic Gen. Investment Co., Phila., 1974-80; exec. v.p. Transatlantic Life Assurance Co., Phila., 1980-85, Meritor Life Ins. Co., Phila., 1985-88; owner, CEO Tri-Arc Fin. Svcs., Phila., 1988—; chmn., CEO Magellan Ins. Co. Ltd., Bermuda, 1996—; bd. dirs. Annuity and Life Re (Holdings), Ltd. Bd. dirs. Concerto Soloist, Phila., 1990-92, Nat. Media Corp., 1994-98, Phila. Commn. to End. Homelessness, 1995—; mem. Spl. Olympics Adv. Com. Mem. Nat. Assn. Life Underwriters, Coun. Ins. Agts. and Brokers (bd. dirs.), Profl. Assn. Ins. Agts., Sons of Am. Revolution, Mil. Order Loyal Legion of U.S. Republican. Episcopalian. Avocation: big game hunting. Home: 1606 Pine St Philadelphia PA 19103-6711 Office: Tri-Arc Fin Svcs PO Box 6745 983 Old Eagle School Rd Ste 616 Wayne PA 19087-1711

YOST, BERNICE, detective agency owner; b. Houston; d. Kenneth Wayne and Georgia (Sampson) Cox; m. Matthew Yost. Student, L.A. Trade Tech, 1968-70, Compton Coll., 1974-76, Ariz. State U., 1983-85. Staff acct. Moultrie, Liggens, Terrel CPA's, L.A., 1969-71; spl. agt. IRS, L.A., 1972-79; supervisory spl. agt. IRS, Phoenix, 1979-91; supervisory spl. agt. IRS, Washington, 1991-93; owner, operator Yost Detective Agy., Silver Spring, Md., 1995-2000, Culver City, Calif., 1998—. Recipient Albert Gallatin award for merit, 1993. Mem. Nat. Orgn. of Black Law Enforcement Execs. Democrat. Baptist. Avocations: tennis, jogging, sewing.

YOST, GERALD B., lawyer; b. Harvey, Ill., Dec. 21, 1954; s. Richard Dennis and Marilyn Patricia (Moore) Y.; m. Kay Lynn Benton, Apr. 16, 1977; children: Matthew Brian, Benjamin Gerald, Andrew Richard. BA in Journalsim, Drake U., 1973-76; student, Purdue U., 1975; JD, Hamline U., 1980. Bar: Minn. 1980, U.S. Dist. Ct. Minn. 1980, Wis. 1987. Assoc. Bergman, Street & Ulmen, Mpls., 1980-84; ptnr. Wasserman and Baill, Mpls., 1984-90, Yost, Stephenson & Sanford, Mpls., 1990-95, Yost & Baill LLP, Mpls., 1996—. Editor: Student Osteo. Med. Assn. Publ. mag., 1976; mem. Law Review Hamline U., 1978-80. Active YMCA, St. Paul. Recipient Am. Jurisprudence award, Lawyers Coop. Pub. Co., St. Paul, 1979. Mem. ABA, Minn. State Bar Assn., Wis. Bar Assn., Phi Alpha Delta, Sigma Delta Chi. Avocations: tennis, racquetball, boating and water skiing, jogging. Home: 1958 Bayard Ave Saint Paul MN 55116-1216 Office: Yost & Baill LLP 2350 One Fin Plz 120 S 6th St Minneapolis MN 55402-1803

YOST, NANCY RUNYON, artist, designer, art educator; b. Eaton, Ohio, July 16, 1933; d. Stanley Everett and Treva (Geeting) Runyon; m. Kenneth John Yost, Aug. 17, 1952 (div. Dec. 1962); 1 child, Debra Colleen Yost Mayne. BS in Art Edn., Miami U., Oxford, Ohio, 1966, MEd in Art, 1970. Cert. profl. permanent tchr., Ohio. Sec. N.Am. Aircraft, Columbus, Ohio, 1957; sec. Miami U., Oxford, 1957-61, textile instr., 1978; textile instr. Living Arts Ctr., Dayton, Ohio, 1972-73; coord. art, music and phys. edn. Stewart Jr. High Sch., Oxford, 1981-86; art instr. Talawanda Sch. System, Oxford, 1965-90, dist. coord., 1986-90; owner, creator Allegro Adornments Bus., 1988—; postgrad. Sem. Charles Jeffrey, Cleve., Inst. Art, Miami U., 1973, David Van Dommelen Penn State at U. Tenn., 1975, Bill Helwig, N.Y., 1975, Nik Krevitsky, N.Y., 1976, Tom Shafer, Columbus, Ohio, 1982; mem. curriculum coun. Talawanda Sch. Dist., 1982—; rep. Amway Corp., 1980-81, World Book Co., Chgo., 1986-88; lectr. Miami U., 1986; invited workshop speaker, presenter Nat. Art Edn. Assn. Conv., Phoenix, 1992. Contbg. artist: Wall Hangings, 1971, Knotting, 1973; one-woman exhibit at Creative Fibers Studio, Buffalo, 1974; exhibited group show Dayton Art Inst., Invitational Fiber Artists Am., Ball State U., 1974, Christkindl Markt, Canton Art Inst. 1994 (hon. mention); one-woman retrospective Preble County Art Ctr., 1998; designer Oxford Bicentennial Calender, 1976; guest jewelry designer Saks 5th Avenue. Supr. Community Artworks, 1986; mem. adv. bd. Miami U. Summer Theatre, 1991-93; mem. spl. events planning com. Miami U. Art Mus., 1993—. Recipient Winner Most Creative Costume Ohio Mart, 1992, 93, First Pl. awards Community Photo Contest, 3d Pl. and Hon. Mention award Oxford Audubon Photo Show, 1994, 1st Pl. 3D Design, Greater Hamilton Art Exhibit at Fitton Ctr, 1995, Cash award ribbon and Purchase award Wyo. Art Show, 1996, Cash award ribbon Minnetrista Arts Fair, 1996, Best in Show Preble Co. Arts Assn. Juried Show, 1997, First Pl. Sculpture, 1997, 2d Pl Ribbon cash award Christ Kindl Markt, Canton Art Inst., 1999, 1st Pl. 3D Design award, Greater Hamilton Art Exhibit, 2000. Mem. Southwestern Art Edn. Assn., Ohio Art Edn. Assn., Ohio Edn. Assn., Talawanda Edn. Assn., Ohio Designer Craftsmen, Ohio Arts and Crafts Guild, Oxford Arts Club, Kappa Delta Pi. Avocations: commissioned artwork, sculpture, wearable art, fabric, metal collages, limited edition prints, painted wood furniture. Home and Studio: 6674 Fairfield Rd Oxford OH 45056-8813

YOU, HONG, mathematics educator; b. Shanghai, China, Jan. 6, 1948; s. Shan-liang You and Fu-zen Wang; m. Feng-men Li, Jan. 10, 1979; 1 child, Ling-Ling. MS in Math., Northeast Normal U., 1981; PhD in Math., Jilin U., 1995. Vice chmn. dept. math. Northeast Normal U., Changchun, China, 1984-87, assoc. prof., 1986-90, prof., 1990—, head dept. math, 1993-94; prof. Harbin Inst. Tech., 1995—, dean; vis. fellow Cornell U., Ithaca, N.Y., 1987-89; vis. prof. Pa. State U., State Coll., 1992. Author: Chinese Annals of Math, 1993, Linear Algebra and Its Applications, 1994, Jour. Algebra, 1999, Comm. in Algebra, 1992-94, 95-98, 99—; reviewer Math. Revs. Grantee NSF of China, Beijing, 1987-90, 92-94, 95—. Mem. Am. Math. Soc. Office: Harbin Inst Tech, Dept Math, Harbin 150001, China

YOU, KE-WEI, educator; b. Dingzhou, China, Apr. 21, 1933; s. Guan-xian and Xian-kun (Yan) Y.; m. Qi-yun Wu, Jan. 16, 1966; children: Yong, Yu. B of Engring., Xian Jiaotong U., 1957. Faculty mem. Chengdu (China) U. Sci. & Tech., 1957—; vis. scholar SUNY, Stony Brook, 1981-83; dean internat. edn. program Chengdu U. Sci. & Tech., 1984-87, chmn. dept. CCE, 1987-93; vice chmn. editl. bd. Jour. A&I, Chengquing, China, 1980—; vis. prof. U. Dundee, Scotland, 1989. Author: Design Theory of Control Systems, 1981, An Introduction to Algebraic System Theory, 1984; mem. editl. bd. Jour. Human Nature Sci. Studies, 1995—; adv. editl. bd. Jour. Computer Applications, 1995—; contbr. papers to prof. publs. Mem. Acad. Degree Com. State Edn. Commn. China, Beijing, 1990. Rsch. grantee Natural Sci. Found. China, 1989, 91. Fellow Chengdu Soc. Sci. & Engring. (pres. 1990—), China Soc. Elec. Engring. (vice chmn. edn. com. 1991—); mem. Internat. Assn. ASME, (editor 1988—), Chinese Assn. Automation. Avocations: painting, traditional Chinese regiman. Office: Chengdu U Sci & Tech, Dept Computer and Control Engring, Chengdu 610065, China

YOU, SUNG-KEUN, philosophy educator, statesman; b. Seoul, Feb. 15, 1950; s. Ki-Joon You and Heung-Soo Lee; m. Mee-Young Song, May 2, 1981; children: Ji-Hoon, Da-Hyun. BA in Law with honors, Seoul Nat. U., 1973; MA in Philosophy, Sogang U., Seoul, 1987, PhD in Philosophy, 1993. Internat. fin banker Korea Devel. Bank, Seoul, 1976-84; lectr. philosophy Sogang U., 1988-95; lectr. medieval philosophy Seoul Nat. U., 1996—; elected mem. Parliament Hanam City Govt., 2000—; elected dep. fl. leader Hannara party, 2000—; vis. fellow in philosophy Harvard U., Cambridge, Mass., 1991-92; postdoctoral rschr. in philosophy Oxford (Eng.) U., 1993-94. Author: Ontological Elucidation of Augustine's Theory of Freedom, 1993; contbr. articles to profl. jours., including Internat. Jour. for Philosophy of Religion, Philosophy and Reality. Chief policy maker for Dem. Party pres., 1997, chmn. in Mapo-gab-gu, 1997; chmn. Hannara Party in Mapo-gab-gu, 1997-98. Mem. Korean Philos. Assn., Christian Philos. Assn. Avocation: travel. Home: #1801 116 Dong Eunheng, Ssang-young Apt Chang woo dong, Hanam City 465-120 Kyunggi-do, Republic of Korea Office: #708 Hanam livingel, Shinjang-dong, Hanam City Kyunggi-do, Republic of Korea

YOU, SUYA, computer scientist; b. Wuhan, Hubei, China, July 6, 1964; s. Zehan You and Guozhen Shen; m. Jing Yang, Dec. 1, 1986; 1 child, Sailun. BSc, Huazhong U. Sci. and Tech., Wuhan, China, 1985, MSc, 1991, PhD, 1994. Engr. China Maritime Inst., Wuhan, 1985-88; invited assoc. prof. Tianjing (China) Normal U., 1994-96; rschr. Huazhong U. Sci. and Tech., 1991-94; postdoctoral fellow Tsinghua U., Beijing, 1994-96; rsch. assoc. SUNY, Stony Brook, 1996-97; rsch. scientist U. So. Calif., L.A., 1997—. Contbr. over 30 articles to profl. jours. Recipient Royal Soc. Sino-Brit. Fellowship Trust award, 1996. Mem IEEE, ACM, SIGGRAPH, SPIE, CIA, SSC. Avocations: reading, sports, music, movies. Office: U So Calif IMSC/Computer Sci Los Angeles CA 90089-0781

YOU, YUZHU, oceanographer; b. Wuxi County, Jiangsu, China, Oct. 27, 1952; came to Japan, 1999; s. Qianfa You and Xianxie Shao; m. Lu Mi, May 1, 1979; 1 child, Jane. B in Oceanography, Ocean U. Qingdao, China, 1977; M in Math., U. NSW, Australia, 1989; PhD in Phys. Oceanography, U. Sydney, Australia, 1991. Tutor dept. oceanography and marine meteorology Ocean U. Qingdao, 1977-85, lectr., 1985-86; vis. scientist CSIRO Marine Lab., Hobart, Tasmania, Australia, 1986-89; rsch. asst. prof. geology and geophysics U. Sydney, 1989-91; postdoctoral visitor Sch. Space, Meteorology and Earth Scis. MIT, 1992; postdoctoral fellow Sch. Earth Scis. Flinders U. South Australia, Australia, 1992-94; vis. prof. lab. phys. oceanography Nat. Mus. Natural History, Paris, 1995; guest investigator Inst. Meereskunde U. Kiel, Germany, 1996, 98; vis. prof. Ctr. for Climate Sys. Rsch. U. Tokyo, 1997, 99. Contbr. articles to sci. jours. Mem. Am. Geophys. Union. Office: U Tokyo Ctr Climate Sys Rsc, 4-6-1 Komaba, 153-8904 Meguro-ku Tokyo, Japan

YOUAN, BI BOTTI CÉLESTIN, pharmacist, researcher; b. Anoumaba, Côte d'Ivoire, July 3, 1966; arrived in Belgium, 1994; s. Bi Youan Pierre Boli and Lou Boli Zamble. Degree in pharmacy, U. d'Abidjan, Côte d'Ivoire, 1993; MSc in Pharm. Engring., Cath. U. Louvain, Brussels, 1996, PhD in Pharmaceutics, 1999; MBA, United Bus. Inst., Brussels, 1998. Rschr. Project of Clin. Rsch./WHO, Daloa, Côte d'Ivoire, 1992-93; trainee Drug Dealer Co., Abidjan, 1993-94; rschr. Cath. U. Louvain, 1994—. Contbr. articles to profl. jours. Grantee Ministry of Edn. and Sci. Rsch., Côte d'Ivoire, 1986-93, Belgian Govt., 1994-98. Mem. Am. Assn. Pharm. Scien-

tists, Assn. Pharmacie Galenique Industrielle, N.Y. Acad. Scis. Roman Catholic. Avocations: reading, swimming, cinema, football, theater. Office: Cath U Louvain Sch Pharmacy, Ave E Mounier 7320, 1200 Brussels Belgium

YOUN, GAHYUN, psychology educator; b. Kwangju, Korea, Sept. 9, 1958; s. Jae-Kwan and Geum-Lim (Park) Y.; m. Hayrran Kwon, Aug. 29, 1987; children: Eunji, Susy. BA, Chonnam Nat. U., 1982; MS, U. Ga., 1986, PhD, 1988. Cert. gerontologist. Rsch. asst. U. Ga., Athens, 1986-88, rsch. assoc., 1988; prof. Chonnam Nat. U., Kwangju, 1989—; head psychology dept. Chonnam Nat. U., 1998-99; rschr. Japan Inst. of Labor, Tokyo, 1999; vis. prof. U. So. Calif., L.A., 1996-97, U. Ga., Athens, 1994. Author: Psychology and Culture of Sex, 1998, Psychology of Homosexuality, 1997, Understanding Psychology, 1993, 2d edit., 1997; editor-in-chief Korean Jour. of Rsch. in Gerontology, 1992—. Rsch. grant WHO, 1993, Korea Rsch. Found., 1996. Mem. Am. Psychol. Assn., Korean Soc. of Rsch. in Gerontology (exec. dir.), Sigma Xi. Avocations: tennis. Home: 59-20 Duamdong, Mirabo Apt 102-402, Kwangju 500-100, Korea Office: Chonam Nat U, 300 Yongbong-dong, Kwangju 500-757, Korea

YOUNES, NADIA, United Nations official. Chief of protocol Exec. Office Sec.- Gen., UN, N.Y.C. Office: UN Protocol & Liaison Svc Office of Sec-Gen Rm S-201A New York NY 10017

YOUNG, (ARTHUR) ALLEN, writer; b. Washington, July 4, 1918; s. Arthur N. and Nellie May Y.; m. Barbara Jean Young; children: Sarah Abigail, David Allen, Andrew Nichols, Elizabeth Corlett. Student, Occidental Coll., L.A., 1937-40, U. Chgo., 1940-41, 1946. Music columnist The Denver Post, 1948-57; arts editor Cervi's Jour., Denver, 1959-63; exec. dir. Young Audiences, Inc., Denver, 1963-70; asst. editor Rocky Mountain Med. Jour. (Colo. State Med. Soc.), Denver, 1972-80. Author: (book) Opera in Central City, 1993. Pres. Allied Arts, Inc., Denver, 1973-90; sec. Friends of Chamber Music, Denver, 1970-73, 1989-2001. T/5 U.S. Army Air Force, 1941-45. Democrat. Episcopalian. Avocations: piano, reading, writing. Home: 460 S Marion Pkwy Apt 451B Denver CO 80209-2507

YOUNG, BARNEY THORNTON, lawyer; b. Chillicothe, Tex., Aug. 10, 1934; s. Bayne and Helen Irene (Thornton) Y.; m. Sarah Elizabeth Taylor, Aug. 31, 1957; children: Jay Thornton, Sarah Elizabeth, Serena Taylor. BA, Yale U., 1955; LLB, U. Tex., 1958. Bar: Tex. 1958. Assoc. Thompson, Knight, Wright & Simmons, Dallas, 1958-65; ptnr. Rain, Harrell, Emery, Young & Doke, Dallas, 1965-87; mem. firm Locke Purnell Rain Harrell (A Profl. Corp.), 1987-98; of counsel Locke, Liddell & Sapp LLP, 1999—. Mem. adv. coun. Dallas Cmty. Chest Trust Fund, Inc., 1964-66; bd. dirs. Mental Health Assn. Dallas County, Inc., 1969-72, Trammell Crow Family Found., 1984-87; trustee Hockaday Sch., Dallas, 1971-77, 90—, chmn., 1994-96, Dallas Zool. Soc., 1986-92, Lamplighter Sch., Dallas, 1976-99, chmn., 1983-86, St. Mark's Sch., Dallas, 1970—, pres., 1976-78, The Found. for Callier Ctr. and Comm. Disorders, 1988-99, Friends of Ctr. for Human Nutrition, 1988—, Shelter Ministries of Dallas Found., 1993—, Dallas Hist. Soc., 1993—; bd. dirs. Susan G. Komen Breast Cancer Found., 2000—, Nat. Assn. Ind. Schs., 2000—; mem. Yale Devel. Bd., 1984-91, 1998—. Fellow Tex. Bar Found., Dallas Bar Found.; mem. ABA, Tex. Bar Assn., Dallas Bar Assn., Am. Judicature Soc., Order of Coif, Phi Beta Kappa, Pi Sigma Alpha, Phi Gamma Delta, Phi Delta Phi, Dallas Country Club., Petroleum Club (Dallas), Yale Club (Dallas, N.Y.C.). Home: 6901 Turtle Creek Blvd Dallas TX 75205-1251 Office: Locke Liddell & Sapp LLP 2200 Ross Ave Ste 2200 Dallas TX 75201-6776

YOUNG, BETTE ANN, writer; b. Columbus, Ohio, Jan. 9, 1937; d. Richard Jack Abel and Gussie Ruth Dean Seiden; m. robert David Roth Mar. 17, 1957 (div. Dec. 1980); children: Deborah Anne Fay, Diane Hope Helbig, Robert David Roth Jr.; m. Sheldon Mike Young, Nov. 11, 1988. BA in Sociology, Oakland U., 1971; MA in Am. Culture, U. Mich., 1974, postgrad., 1977. Dir. libr. Jewish Cmty. Ctr., Detroit, 1980-82; edn. dir. Jweish Parents' Inst., Detroit, 1980-82; lectr. Adult Coll. Jewish Studies, Columbus, Ohio, 1985-87; adminstrv. sec. Nat. Coun. Jewish Women, Columbus, 1985-90; cons., membership dir., grant writer Columbus Jewish Hist. Soc., Columbus, 1987-90, oral historian, 1990—. Author: Congregation Shaarey Zedek, 1981, The History of the Association of Jewish Community Organization Personnel, 1969-87, 1987, The Columbus Jewish Foundation, 1994, Emma Lazarus in Her World, 1995; book critic Jewish News, 1980-82, Ohio Jewish Chronicle, 1991—, Columbus Dispatch, 1992—. Cmty. cons. Anti-Defamation League, Detroit, 1982-83. Democrat. Home: 4776 Smoketalk Ln Westerville OH 43081-7838

YOUNG, BRUCE ARTHUR, animal production scientist, educator; b. Sydney, Australia, Jan. 16, 1939; s. Maxwell Arthur and Gwen Lyllian (Taylor) Y.; m. June Eleanor Scott, Feb. 4, 1995; children: Steven B., Michael R. BS, U. New England, Australia, 1963, MS, 1965, PhD, 1968. Tchg. fellow U. New England, 1962-65; rsch. scholar Commonwealth Scientific and Indsl. Rsch. Orgn. (CSIRO), Australia, 1965-68; asst. to assoc. prof. animal prodn. U. Alta., Can., 1968-91; sr. officer, seconded IAEA/FAO, Austria, 1979-81; prof. animal prodn. U. Queensland, Brisbane, Australia, 1991—; dir. Gounly Ltd., Australia, 1992—, Australasian PIC Inst., 1995-2000, Recycled Organics Consortium. Co-author: Effect of Environment on Nutrient Requirements of Domestic Animals, 1981, Cooling Hot Cows, 1991; contbr. 150 articles to scientific jours.; holder 5 scientific patents. Recipient Sr. Scholar award Australian Wool Bd., 1996, Appreciation for Rsch. award Alta. Cattle Commn., 1978, Outstanding Rsch. in Genetics and Physiology medal Can. Soc. Animal Sci., 1989, Japan Soc. Prodn. Sci. fellowship, 1991. Mem. Am. Soc. Animal Sci., Australian Soc. Animal Prodn. Office: Univ Queensland, Sch Animal Studies, Gatton QLD 4343, Australia

YOUNG, BRYAN KENDALL, radio announcer; b. Oswego, Kans., Feb. 10, 1960; s. John E. and Rachel H. (Pennington) Y.; m. Donna L. Patton, Aug. 1, 1987 (div. July 1990). Student, SE Mo. State U., 1978-82. Mgr. Pvt. D.J. Svc., Cape Girardeau, Mo., 1981—; entertainment dir. Foolish Pleasure, Cape Girardeau, 1984-85, Rumor's Night Club, Cape Girardeau, 1985-87; radio announcer Sta. KGMO Radio, Cape Girardeau, 1986—; TV announcer Sta. KBSI-TV, Cape Girardeau, 1988—; music editor, arranger Royal Ballet Dance, Cape Girardeau, 1989—; fashion show announcer local merchants, Cape Girardeau, 1986-88. Announcer (live satellite broadcast) Disney MGM Studios, 1990; co-host Children's Miracle Network Telethon, 1989, (cert. 1989); lead actor (operetta) H.M.S. Pinifore, 1979, (musical) Oklahoma, 1977. Recipient Cert. of Appreciation ARC, 1990. Mem. Am. Poolplayers Assn. Avocations: all terrain vehicles, billiards, boating, music library.

YOUNG, CELIA NOREEN, biologist, consultant; b. Seven Kings, Eng., Dec. 27, 1941; arrived in South Africa, 1974; d. Bertie Edward and Phyllis Gwendoline (Dilkes) Y. BS in Botany with honors, U. Sheffield, 1964; PhD, U. London, 1971; BS in Pharmacology with honors, U. Witwatersrand, 1989. Chartered biologist. Fellow Royal Coll. Pathologists, London. Lectr. med. mycology Inst. Dermatology, London, 1964-73; asst. Brompton Hosp., London, 1973; lectr., head dept. med. mycology SAIMR, U. Witwatersrand, Johannesburg, South Africa, 1974-81, sr. lectr. med. microbiology and head dept. med. mycology, 1981-84; med. advisor Wellcome (Pty.) Ltd., Johannesburg, 1984-95; cons. in med. microbiology and med. mycology, 1995—; Pfizer traveling fellow U. Rhodesia, Salisbury, 1977; vis. lectr. U. Pretoria, South Africa, 1989-92, U. Cape Town, South Africa, 1984; cons. to pvt. pathologists, Johannesburg, 1993—, S.A. Assn. Indsl. Editors, 1998. Reader Tape Aids for Blind, Johannesburg, 1991—. Grantee WHO, 1973-74. Mem. Fedn. South African Socs. Pathology (treas. 1982-89), Internat. Soc. Human and Animal Mycology, Am. Soc. Microbiology, Brit. Soc. Med. Mycology, Soroptimists (exec. com. Highveld br. 1998-2000). Avocations: singing, sculpting, modeling, gardening. E-mail: filbert@netactive.co.za.

YOUNG, CHAINLLIE, physician; b. Taipei, Taiwan, May 20, 1964. MD, Nat. Taiwan U., 1988, postgrad. Physician Nat. Taiwan U. Hosp., Taipei, 1994—; instr. Nat. Taiwan U., Taipei, 1994—. Office: Nat Taiwan Univ Hosp, Chung Shan S Rd, Taipei 100, Taiwan

YOUNG, CHARLES EDWARD, university chancellor emeritus; b. San Bernardino, Calif., Dec. 30, 1931; s. Clayton Charles and Eula May (Walters) Y. AA, San Bernardino Coll., 1954; AB, U. Calif., Riverside, 1955; MA, UCLA, 1957, PhD, 1960; DHL (hon.), U. Judaism, L.A., 1969, Occidental Coll., L.A., 1997. Congl. fellow Washington, 1958-59; adminstrv. analyst Office of the Pres., U. Calif., Berkeley, 1959-60; asst. prof. polit. sci. U. Calif., Davis, 1960; asst. prof. polit. sci. UCLA, 1960-66, assoc. prof., 1966-69, prof., 1969-97, asst. to chancellor, 1960-62, asst. chancellor, 1962-63, vice chancellor, adminstrn., 1963-68, chancellor, 1968-97; interim pres. U. Fla., Gainesville, 1999—; bd. dirs. Intel Corp., Acad. TV Arts and Sci. Found.; cons. Peace Corps., 1961-62, Ford Found. on Latin Am. Activities, 1964-66; mem. bd. govs. L.A. Met. Project. Mem. Knight Found. Commn. on Intercollegiate Athletics, Calif. Coun. on Sci. and Tech., Town Hall of Calif., Carnegie Comm. Task Force on Sci. and Tech. and the States, Pacific Coun. on Internat. Policy, NCAA Pres.'s Commn., Coun. for Govt.-Univ.-Industry Rsch. Roundtable and the Nat. Rsch. Coun. Adv. Bd.-Issues in Sci. and Tech., Nat. Com. on U.S.-China Rels., chancellor's assocs. UCLA, coun. trustees L.A. Ednl. Alliance for Restructuring Now; past chair. Assn. Am. Univs., Nat. Assn. State Univs. and Land-Grant Colls.; past co-chair Calif. Campus Compact; mem. adminstrv. bd. Internat. Assn. Univs.; bd. govs. Found. Internat. Exchange Sci. and Cultural Info. by Telecom.; bd. dirs. L.A. Internat. Visitors Coun., Greater L.A. Energy Coalition, L.A. World Affairs Coun.; trustee UCLA Found. With USAF, 1951-52. Named Young Man of Year Westwood Jr. C. of C., 1962; recipient Inter-Am. U. Cooperaton award Inter-Am. Orgn. Higher Edn., Neil H. Jacoby Internat. award UCLA Student Ctr., 1987, Edward A. Dickson Alumnus of Yr. award UCLA Alumni Assn., 1994, Disting. Svc. award U. Calif. Riverside Alumni Assn., 1996, Treasure of L.A. award L.A. Ctrl. City Assn., 1996, Albert Schweitzer Leadership award Hugh O'Brien Youth Found., 1996; hon. fellow UCLA Coll. Letters and Sci., 1996. Fellow AAAS. Office: U Fla 226 Tigert Hall PO Box 113150 Gainesville FL 32611-3150

YOUNG, CHARLES GRAHAM, chemistry educator; b. Deniliquin, NSW, Australia, Oct. 10, 1956; s. William David and Elizabeth Florence Young; m. Brooke Magen Morse, Aug. 21, 1987; children: Sigourney Rebeccah, Graham Kimball. BSc, Australian Nat. U., Canberra, 1979, PhD, 1983. Fellow U. B.C., Vancouver, 1982-84, U. Ariz., Tucson, 1984-86; lectr., sr. lectr. La Trobe U., Bundoora, Victoria, Australia, 1986-91; sr. lectr., reader U. Melbourne, Victoria, Australia, 1991—; coord. Internat. Devel. Program, Australia, 1993. Contbr. articles to profl. jours. and books. Mem. Am. Chem. Soc., Royal Australian Chem. Inst., Soc. Biol. Inorganic Chemistry. Avocations: rock climbing, mountaineering. Office: Sch of Chemistry, U Melbourne, Victoria 3010, Australia

YOUNG, CHESLEY VIRGINIA, writer, educator; b. Hamburg, Ark., Sept. 7, 1919; d. Lewis Chesley and Winifred (Massey) Barnes; m. Morris Nathan Young, Aug. 20, 1948; children: Cheryl Lesley, Charles Chesley. BA, Ark. U., 1947; MA, Columbia U., 1951. Cert. statistician; lic. N.Y. Dept. Edn.; lic. civilian pilot. Statistician Washington, 1942; tchr. N.Y.C. Dept. Edn., 1954-67; pres. Chesley Music Corp./Denton & Haskins Corp., 1969—; treas. Gem Music Corp. Composer: (songs) Have You, 1949, Come On, Come to the Fair, 1953; author: Magic of a Mighty Memory, 1971, Magic of a Powerful Memory, 1981; editor: Magic Tricks, 1952, Card Tricks, 1952; co-author: How to Read Faster & Remember More, 1965. Pres. Manhattan Bus. & Profl. Women's Club, 1949-51; pres. women's aux. N.Y. Polyclinic Hosp. & Med. Sch., 1969-72; mem. pres.'s coun. Finch Coll., N.Y.C., 1967-69; co-founder Libr. of Memory and Mnemonics, U. San Marino, Republic of San Marino, McManus-Young Libr. of Magic, Libr. of Congress, Washington, U. Tex., Austin, U. Calif., Berkeley, Libr. of Cryptography Houdini Hist. Ctr., Appleton, Wis., Meth. History and Hymnals Libr. John St. Meth. Ch., N.Y.C. WAC U.S. Army, 1943; capt. signal corps AUS, 1943-51, ret., inactive res. Named Dame of Honor, Knights of Malta. Mem. NEA, DAR (regent N.Y.C. chpt.), ASCAP (mem. as both composer and publisher), Mil. Order of World Wars, Order of Lafayette, Huguenot Soc., Greater N.Y. U. Ark. Alumni Assn. (charter), Horticultural Soc., Washington Sq. Art Exhibit, Women's Nat. Rep. Club of N.Y.C. Home: Apt 16M 2 Fifth Ave New York NY 10011

YOUNG, COLIN S., financial services executive; b. Bloemfontein, South Africa, Apr. 8, 1967; s. Allen A. and Elizabeth A. (Brooke) Y.; m. Beverley Lynne Jones, Jan. 23, 1988; children: Lauren, Dillon. BComm, U. Cape Town, South Africa, 1989, BComm (hons.), 1990, MBA cum laude, 1998; B of Computers, UNISA, Cape Town, 1992. Chartered Acct. Mgr. Ernst & Young, Cape Town, 1991-94; IT audit mgr. Woolworths, Cape Town, 1994, head of audit divsn., 1994-97, head fin. solutions group, 1998, ops. exec. fin. svcs., 1999—. Mem. com. Republic South Africa Credit Assn., 1999. With South African Army, 1985-86. Old Mut. scholar U. Cape Town, 1999. Mem. E&Y Toastmasters (treas. 1994, Villagers Rugby Club (treas. 1995), Mowbray Golf Club. Avocations: golf, gym, running, rugby, reading. Office: Woolworths Fin Svcs, 1 Mostert St, 8001 Cape Town South Africa

YOUNG, SIR COLVILLE, Belizean government official; b. Nov. 20, 1932; s. Henry Oswald and Adney Wilhelmina (Waite) Y.; m. Norma Eleanor Trapp, 1956; four children. BA in English, U. London, U. West Indies, 1961; PhD in Linguistics, U. York, 1971. Prin. St. Michael's Coll., Belize, 1974-76; lectr. English and gen. studies Belize Tech. Coll., 1976-86; pres. U. Coll. Belize, 1986-90, lectr., 1990-93; gov.-gen. Belize, 1993—. Author: Creole Proverbs of Belize, 1980, rev. edit., 1988, From One Caribbean Corner, 1983, Caribbean Corner Calling, 1988, Language and Education in Belize, 1989, Pataki Full, 1990; contbr. articles to profl. jours. Knighted Queen Elizabeth II. Avocations: composing, creative writing, playing and arranging steelband music. Office: Office of Gov-Gen, Belize House PO Box 174, Belmopan Belize*

YOUNG, DANIEL GREER, surgical pediatrics educator; b. Skipness, Scotland, Nov. 22, 1932; s. Gabriel and Julia McColl (McNair) Y.; m. Agnes Gilchrist, Aug. 3, 1957; children: Donald, Rhoda Agnes, Kenneth Donald. MB ChB, U. Glasgow, Scotland, 1956; diploma of tropical medicine and hygiene, U. Liverpool, Eng., 1959. Sr. registrar, resident asst. surgeon Hosp. for Sick Children, London, 1965-67; sr. lectr. Inst. Child Health, London, 1967-69; hon. cons. surgeon Gt. Ormand St. & Queen Elizabeth Hosps., London, 1967-69; head dept. surg. pediatrics U. Glasgow, 1969-98, reader in surg. pediatrics, 1983-92, prof. surg. pediatrics, 1992-98; hon. cons. surgeon Greater Glasgow Health Bd., 1979-98; chmn. nat. paramedic tng. bd. Scottish Ambulance Svc., 1990-98; profl. adv. group Scottish Ambulance Svc. Brit. Isles, 1988-98. Co-author: Pediatric Surgery, 1972, Children's Medicine and Surgery, 1995, Baby Surgery; editor Jour. Pediat. Surgery, 1987—. Hon. sec. Soc. for Rsch. in Hydrocephalus and Spina Bifida, 1980-85, trustee, 1995—, hon. mem., 1998—; elder Sherbrooks, St. Gilbert's Ch. of Scotland, 1975—; med. adviser Riding for the Disabled, Glasgow, 1984—. Recipient Denis Browne Gold medal, 1999. Fellow Royal Coll. Surgeons, Edinburgh, Royal Coll. Surgeons, Royal Coll. Physicians and Surgeons (mem. coun. 1987-91), Royal Coll. Pediats. and Child Health; mem. Brit. Med. Assn., Brit. Assn. Pediat. Surgeons (pres. 1990-92, hon. 1998—), Brit. Urol. Assn., Royal Soc. Medicine, West of Scotland Surg. Assn. (pres. 1993-94), Royal Med. Chirurgical Soc. of Glasgow (pres. 1988-89), Hungarian Pediatric Surg. Assn. (hon.), South African Pediat. Surg. Assn. (hon.), Am. Pediat. Assn. (hon.), Scottish Spina Bifida Assn. (hon. pres. 1976—). Presbyterian. Avocations: gardening, curling, fishing. Home: 49 Sherbrooke Ave, Glasgow G41 4SE, Scotland Office: Royal Hosp Sick Children, Yorkhill, Glasgow G3 8SJ, Scotland

YOUNG, DANSON, sanitary engineer, plumbing engineer, civil engineer, contractor; b. Guangzhou, China, Aug. 14, 1936; s. Yeung Chok Po and Yeung Liu Choy Shin; m. Judy Kant Young, Aug. 2, 1967; children: Merlin, Maggie, Michelle. BSc, Hong Kong Bapt. Coll., 1962; grad., Hong Kong Poly. U. Supr. Winsome Co. Ltd., Hong Kong, 1962-63; structural engr. C.C. Cheng, Architects and Engrs., Hong Kong, 1963-64; engr. Lee Yu Kee, Ltd., Hong Kong, 1964-74; chmn., mng. dir. Yue Sheng B.S. Co., Ltd., Hong Kong, 1975—; owner Far East Engring. Corp., Hong Kong, 1973—; chmn., mng. dir. Telford Engring., Co., Ltd., Hong Kong, 1979—; bd. dirs. Kai Huo Trading Ltd.; ptnr. The Evergreen Trading Co., Hong Kong, 1971—; dir. Grand Concourse Holding Ltd.; proprietor Kan Constrn. Co. Fellow ASCE; mem. Am. Soc. Plumbing Engrs., Hong Kong Inst. Engrs. (assoc.), Royal Soc. Health, Am. Welding Soc., Inst. British Engrs., Hong Kong Plumbing and Sanitary Trade Assn. Ltd., Royal Hong Kong Jockey Club, Craigengower Cricket Club, Chinese Gen. C. of C. (life). Avocations: arts of Chinese tea and paintings, collecting antiques. Office: Yue Sheng BS Co Ltd, Queen Victoria St Central, 402 Leelong Bldg Hong Kong Hong Kong

YOUNG, DAVID BRADLEY, lawyer; b. Delaware, Ohio, Aug. 1, 1970. BA, Ohio State U., 1993; JD, Willamette U., 1997; LLM, U. San Diego, 1998. Bar: Oreg. 1997, Calif. 1998. Staff counsel SANYO N.Am. Corp., San Diego, 1998—. Evans scholar Western Golf Assn., 1988. Avocations: golf, skiing. Office: SANYO N Am Corp 2055 Sanyo Ave San Diego CA 92154-6229

YOUNG, DEAN ANTHONY, solicitor; b. Edinburgh, Scotland, Sept. 21, 1954; came to Hong Kong, 1982; s. Kenneth Walls and Joyce Margaret (Brodie) Y.; m. Linda Vivian Wilhelm-Hansen, May 17, 1986; children: Holly Katrina Young, Matthew Douglas Young. LLB, Dundee U., 1976. Asst. solicitor Norton Rose, London, 1979-82; asst. solicitor Linklaters & Paines, Hong Kong, 1982-85; ptnr. Deacons, Hong Kong, 1985—. Mem. Hong Kong Law Soc., Hong Kong Shipowners Assn., Hong Kong Aerospace Forum, Hong Kong Equipment Leasing Assn., U.K. Law Soc. Avocations: sports, art, philately. Office: Deacons, 3-7 Fls Alexandra House, Hong Kong Hong Kong

YOUNG, DEIDRA JANE, educational researcher; b. Ottawa, Ont., Can., Nov. 19, 1955; came to Australia, 1970; d. Douglas Pedar and Elizabeth Alice (Allison) Holmberg; m. Stephen Young, Oct. 11, 1980; 1 child, Lauren. BS, U. Western Australia, Perth, 1977; diploma of edn., Murdoch U., Perth, 1988; M in Applied Sci., Curtin U., Perth, 1988, PhD, 1991. Postdoctoral rsch. fellow Curtin U. Tech., 1991-94, Australian rsch. fellow, 1995—; sec. Western Australian Inst. Ednl. Rsch., Perth, 1998—. Author: How to Use HLM2, 1993, A Comparison of Student Performance in Metropolitan, Rural and Remote Western Australian Government Schools, 1994; contbr. numerous articles to profl. jours. and conf. procs., chpt. to book; conf. presenter in field; assoc. editor Education in Rural Australia. Recipient Brce Chopin Meml. award Internat. Assn. Ednl. Achievement, 1994. Mem. Am. Ednl. Rsch. Assn. (divsns. D and H, various spl. interest groups), Internat. Congress Sch. Effectiveness and Improvement, Nat. Assn. Rsch. in Sci. Tching., Australian Assn. Rsch. in Edn., Western Australian Inst. Ednl. Rsch. (exec. mem.), Australian Rural Edn. Rsch. Assn. (exec. mem.). Avocations: quilting, cross-stitching, crafts, swimming, walking. Fax: 61 8 9440 0243. E-mail: d.young@curtin.edu.au. Home: 18 George St, Stirling 6021 WA, Australia Office: Curtin U Tech, GPO Box U1987, Perth WA 6845, Australia

YOUNG, DIANE S., social work educator; b. Flint, Mich., June 7, 1957; d. Richard Charles Graves and Sylvia Marie Jandacek; m. D. Peter Young, May 27, 1978; children: Daniel, Sara. BA, Spring Arbor Coll., 1979; MSW, U. Wash., 1993, PhD, 1997. Corrections counselor Snohomish County Jail, Everett, Wash., 1982-92; asst. prof. Syracuse (N.Y.) U. Sch. Social Work, 1997—. Contbr. articles to profl. jours. Scholar Magnuson Inst. for Biomed. Rsch. and Health Professions Tng., U. Wash., Seattle, 1995-96. Mem. Soc. for Social Work and Rsch., Coun. on Social Work Edn. Avocations: hiking, bicycling, traveling. E-mail: dsyoung@syr.edu. Office: Syracuse U Sch Social Work 417 Sims Hl Syracuse NY 13244-0001

YOUNG, SIR GEORGE, British government official; b. July 16, 1941; s. George and Elisabeth (Knatchbull-Hugessen) Y.; m. Aurelia Nemon-Stuart, 1964; 4 children. MA, Oxford U., MPhil. Economist NEDO, 1966-67; Kobler rsch. fellow U. Surrey, 1967-69; econ. adviser PO Corp., 1969-74; councillor London Borough of Lambeth, 1968-71; mem. BLC London Borough of Ealing, 1970-73; M.P. Brit. House of Commons, 1974—, opposition whip, 1976-79; parliamentary under sec. of state DHSS, 1979-81, Dept. Environment, 1981-86; comptr. Her Majesty's Household, 1990; min. of state Dept. Environment, 1990-94; fin. sec. Her Majesty's Treasury, 1994-95; sec. of state for transport Brit. Govt., 1995-97. Author: Accommodation Services in the UK, 1970-80, 1970, Tourism, Blessing or Blight?, 1973. Trustee Guinness Trust, 1986-90; chmn. Acton Housing Assn., 1972-79. Address: House of Commons, London SW1A 0AA, England

YOUNG, HARRISON, II, software development and marketing executive; b. Bklyn., Feb. 11, 1944; s. Harrison and Bobbie Aline (King) Y.; m. Shirley Gene Stanfield, Aug. 31, 1967 (div. Sept. 21, 1992); children: Melanie Marie, Tracy Lea; m. Emelie Martha Mannweiler, Dec. 18, 1993. BBA, Pacific Western U., L.A., 1990; MBA, U. Leicester, Eng., 1993. Cert. computer profl. Sr. systems rep. Info. Systems divsn. RCA, Houston, 1967-70; sr. scientist and program mgr. Tetra Tech Inc., San Diego, 1970-74; co-founder, dir., exec. v.p. and sr. program mgr. Atlantic Analysis Corp., Norfolk, Va., 1974-85; program mgr. Comarco Inc., Anaheim, Calif., 1985-86, v.p., divsn. gen. mgr., 1986-87; pres. Washington-based subs. Comarco Inc., 1987-88; pres., CEO, dir. Comarco Inc., Anaheim, 1985-90; pres., CEO Tetra Tech Systems Integration subsidiary Honeywell, San Diego, 1990-92; pres., COO JWK Internat. Corp., Annandale, Va., 1992-94; pres., CEO, chmn. Advanced Programming Concepts, Austin, Tex., 1994—. Bd. dirs. Blue Cross Blue Shield of Va., 1976-81. With USN, 1961-67. Mem. Am. Mgmt. Assn., Armed Forces Comms. and Electronics Assn., Nat. Contract Mgmt. Assn., IEEE, Instrumentation Soc. Am. Avocations: boating, computers, foreign travel. Home: 12633 Pony Ln Austin TX 78727-4628 Office: Advanced Programming Concepts 7004 Bee Caves Rd Austin TX 78746-5004

YOUNG, HERBERT G., ambassador. Min. fgn. affairs amd tourism Govt. St. Vincent and the Grenadines, Kingstown, 1989-94; permanent rep. of St. Vincent and the Grenadines UN, N.Y.C., 1994—. Office: Permanent Mission St Vincent and Grenadines to UN 801 2nd Ave Fl 21 New York NY 10017-4706*

YOUNG, IAN ROBERT, academic administrator, educator, researcher; b. Cunnamulla, Queensland, Australia, Jan. 1, 1957; s. Richard and Mary Stella (Groves) Y.; m. Heather Anne Beckwith, Apr. 23, 1985; 1 child, Katrina Maree. B Engring. with honours, James Cook U., Townsville, Australia, 1979, M Engring. Sci., 1982, PhD in Engring., 1984. Rsch. scientist Max Planck Inst., Germany, 1984-85; sr. tutor James Cook U., 1985-86; lectr. civil engring. U. NSW, Canberra, Australia, 1989-90, sr. lectr., 1990-94, prof., 1994-99; exec. dean faculty engring., computer and math. scis. U. Adelaide, S.A., Australia, 1999—. Humboldt fellow, Germany, 1992. Fellow Instn. Engrs.; mem. Am. Geophys. Union. Fax: 61-8-8303 4361. E-mail: ian.young@adelaide.edu.au. Office: U Adelaide Dept, Engring Computer & Math Sci, Adelaide SA 5005, Australia

YOUNG, IAN THEODORE, physics educator; b. Chgo., Dec. 15, 1943; s. Seymour and Ethel Y.; m. Maria Johanna Antoinette Taal, Jan. 30, 1977; children: Heather, Aaron, Michael. BS, MIT, 1965, MS, 1966, PhD, 1969. Asst. prof. elec. engring. MIT, Cambridge, 1969-73, assoc. prof. elec. engring., 1973-79; prof. applied physics Tech U. Delft, Netherlands, 1981—, chmn. dept. applied physics, 1998—; vis. prof. elec. engring. Tech. U. Delft, 1975-76, EPFL, Lausanne, Switzerland, 1979-80; group leader Lawrence Livermore Lab., Livermore, Calif., 1978-81; cons. NIH, Bethesda, Md., 1979-81, Govt. of The Netherlands, The Hague, 1985—, World Bank, Bandung, Indonesia, 1992. Author: Signals and Systems, 1983; editor: Bioimaging, 1992-99; contbr. articles to profl. jours.; patent for microscope devel. Recipient Tchg. prize Weisterdijk Funds, 1986, Rsch. prize Schlumberger Found., 1990, Leermeester Tchg. prize, 1999. Mem. IEEE (sr., editor EMB mag. 1972-76), Internat. Soc. for Analytical Cytology, Internat. Assn. for Pattern Recognition. Jewish. Avocations: skiing, diving, cooking, reading, classical and jazz music. Office: Faculty Applied Scis, Lorentzweg 1, 2628 CJ Delft Netherlands

YOUNG, INA WEINSTEIN, association administrator; b. New Haven, Aug. 28, 1939; d. Nathan and Sarah (Brown) Weinstein; m. Morton H. Halperin, June 19, 1960 (div.); children: David Halperin, Mark Halperin, Gary Halperin; m. Joseph Leslie Young, Mar. 19, 1988; step-children: Michal Fandel, Avigayl Young. AB, Barnard Coll., 1961; MEd, Am. U., 1975. Tchr. Little Sch., North Reading, Mass., 1961-62, cons., 1963-75; career counselor Am. U., Washington, 1976-79; exec. dir. Jewish War Vets. Aux., Washington, 1979-85; adminstr. The Brookings Instn., Washington, 1985-87; dir. career svcs. Am. U. Law Sch., Washington, 1987-93; exec. adminstr. Population Assn. Am., Washington, 1993-95; program mgr. U.S.

C. of C., Washington, 1995-98; mgr. continuing edn. Am. Indsl. Hygiene Assn., Fairfax, Va., 1999—. Mem. Greater Washington Soc. Assn. Execs., Barnard Club. Democrat. Jewish. Avocations: arts, theatre, film, lit., travel. Home: 4846 Montgomery Ln Bethesda MD 20814-5302 Office: Am Indsl Hygiene Assn 2700 Prosperity Ave Ste 250 Fairfax VA 22031-4320

YOUNG, IVEN HUNTER, physician, educator, researcher; b. Kempsey, NSW, Australia, Sept. 17, 1943; s. Roy Hunter and Dorothy Kendall (Barker) Y.; m. Kay Patricia Wood, Apr. 22, 1972; children: James Hunter, Alexander Robert. BSc in Medicine, U. Sydney, Australia, 1965, MB BS, 1968, PhD, 1978. Resident, med. officer Royal Prince Alfred Hosp., Sydney, 1969-73, vis. respiratory physician, 1978-85, sr. staff specialist physician, 1986—, head dept. respiratory medicine, clin. assoc. prof., 1991—; rsch. fellow in medicine U. Sydney, 1974-76, part-time rsch. fellow, 1980-83, clin. assoc. prof., rschr., 1992—; cons. respiratory physician Hornsby Ku-Ring-Gai Hosp., Sydney, 1983—; fellowship examiner Australian Colls. of Anesthetists and Physicians, Sydney, 1978—, postgrad. tchr., 1978—. Contbr. articles to profl. jours. including Jour. Applied Physiology, Thorax, and Am. Rev. of Respiratory Disease. Grantee Nat. Health and Med. Rsch. Coun. Australia, 1980, 83, 90, pharm. industries, 1988—. Fellow Royal Australasian Coll. Physicians; mem. Thoracic Soc. Australia and New Zealand, Am. Thoracic Soc. Avocations: music, reading, jogging, cycling, golf. Home: 9 Warrabina Ave, Saint Ives NSW 2075, Australia Office: Royal Prince Alfred Hosp-Dept Respiratory Medicine, Missenden Rd, Camperdown NSW 2050, Australia

YOUNG, JAMES E., business executive, engineer; b. Celina, Ohio, Sept. 1, 1941; s. Thomas D. and Margaret E. (Flora) Y.; m. Patricia C. Teare, June 13, 1964; children: Kathleen M., Peter C. BSME, Rose-Hulman Inst. Tech., 1963; MBA, Ind. U., 1965; EdS, Ind. State U., 1998. V.p. Citicorp, N.Y.C., 1965-73; pres. James E. Young & Assoc., Inc., Indpls., 1974-91, The Young Group, Angola, Ind., 1991—; vis. prof. guest lectr. Purdue U., Lafayette, Ind., 1986—; adv. bd. Purdue-Anderson, Inc., 1985—, Rsch. Inst. for Devel. of Interactive Learning Sys., Terre Haute, Ind., 1986—; pres. Remote Equipment Corp., Indpls., 1988-90; pres. Forum for Internat. Profl. Svcs., Inc., 1988-91, bd. dirs., 1988—; chmn. bd. WKJM, Inc., 1989-90; chmn. World Competitiveness Conf., 1990—; pres. G & G Angola, Inc., 1991-98, Ramco of Ind., 1992-98, Jaymer, Inc., 1996—. Author: Industrial Communications Networks, 1987, Load Rating Analysis For Steel Manhole Covers, 1995; Load Rating Analysis for Composite Manhole Covers, 1996, What Makes Steel Manhole Covers Unsafe?, 1999; Smart Choices for Composite Manhole Covers, 2000; patentee in field. Co-founder, chmn. bd. Ind. Amateur Baseball Assn., Inc., 1982—; mktg. chmn. Ind. Major League Baseball Commn., Indpls., 1982-86. Mem. ASME, Soc. Mfg. Engrs., Bus. Modernization and Tech. Corp. (chmn. telecom. 1984—), Rotary, Beta Gamma Sigma. Avocations: reading, boating, golf. Office: Young Group 406 Inglenook Pl Angola IN 46703-2223

YOUNG, JAMES HARVEY, historian, educator; b. Bklyn., Sept. 8, 1915; s. W. Harvey and Blanche (DeBra) Y.; m. Myrna Goode, Aug. 25, 1940; children: Harvey Galen, James Walter. B.A., Knox Coll., 1937, D.H.L., 1971; M.A., U. Ill., 1938, Ph.D., 1941; D.Sc., Rush U., 1976. Mem. faculty Emory U., 1941-84, prof. history, 1958-80, Charles Howard Candler prof. Am. social history, 1980-84, prof. emeritus, 1984—, chmn. dept., 1958-66; vis. assoc. prof. Columbia U., 1949-50; mem. nat. adv. food and drug council FDA, 1964-67; mem. Consumers Task Force, White House Conf. on Food, Nutrition and Health, 1969; mem. history life scis. study sect. NIH, 1970-73, 79-80, 91-93, chmn., 1992-93; vis. lectr. Am. Assn. Colls. Pharmacy Vis. Lectrs. Program, 1970-73; cons.-panelist NEH, 1970-83; cons. in history Centers for Disease Control; advisor Am. Coun. Sci. and Health; Logan Clendening lectr. U. Kans. Med. Ctr., 1973; Samuel X. Radbill lectr. Phila. Coll. Physicians, 1978; Beaumont lectr. Yale U., 1980; vis. hist. scholar Nat. Library Medicine, 1986; Harold J. Lawn lectr. U. Minn., 1990; David L. Cowen lectr. Rutgers U., 1990; James Campbell lectr. Rush U., 1992; Waring lectr. Med. U. S.C., 1993. Author: The Toadstool Millionaires, 1961, The Medical Messiahs, 1967, expanded edit., 1992, American Self-Dosage Medicines, An Historical Perspective, 1974, Pure Food: Securing the Federal Food and Drugs Act of 1906, 1989, American Health Quackery: Collected Essays, 1992; editor: (with W.A. Beardslee and T.J.J. Altizer) Truth, Myth and Symbol, 1962, (with T.L. Savitt) Disease and Distinctiveness in the American South, 1988. Served with AUS, 1943-45. Recipient Arts and Scis. award of distinction Emory U., 1999; FDA rsch. appointee, 1977-85; Carnegie rsch. grantee, 1947, USPHS grantee, 1960-65, Nat. Libr. Medicine grantee, 1990-94; Faculty fellow Fund Advancement Edn., 1954-55, Social Sci. Rsch. Coun. fellow, 1960-61, Guggenheim fellow, 1966-67. Mem. Am. Hist. Assn., So. Hist. Assn. (pres. 1982), Orgn. Am. Historians, Soc. Am. Historians, Am. Assn. History of Medicine (coun., Fielding H. Garrison lectr. 1979, William H. Welch medal 1982, Continuing Lifetime Achievement award 1992), Am. Inst. History of Pharmacy (coun., hon. pres. 1993-95, Edward Kremers award 1962), Phi Beta Kappa, Sigma Xi, Phi Kappa Phi, Omicron Delta Kappa, Phi Alpha Theta. Congregationalist. Home: 272 Heaton Park Dr Decatur GA 30030-1027

YOUNG, JONATHAN I.A., grain merchant, executive; b. Doncaster, Eng., Sept. 3, 1950; arrived in Switzerland, 1978; s. Ian S. and Glenda (Rabagliati) Y.; m. Louise Margaret Robertson, Mar. 1, 1980 (div. 1997); 1 child, Andrea; m. Christa Elizabeth Etienne-Fisher, March 31, 2000; children: Chantal, Laurent, Nicholas. BSc, Bristol (Eng.) U., 1971; MSc (MBA), U. London Bus. Sch., 1975. Grain trader Continental Grain Co., London, 1975-78, Geneva, 1978-80; grain trader Philipp Bros., Geneva, 1980-84; adminstrn. mgr. Conagra Internat., Geneva, 1989-93; fin. mgr. Romak S.A., Geneva, 1993-98; dir. Decom S.A., Geneva, 1998—; cons. Falmouth (Eng.) Oil Co., 1988-89. Religious adv. Geneva Hash House Harriers, 1998. Mem. Beaconsfield Golf Club, Ski Club of Great Britain, Geneva Squash Club, Seaview Yacht Club. Anglican. Avocations: skiing, golf, squash, mountain walking. Office: Decom SA, 4 Rue du Parc, CH-1207 Geneva Switzerland

YOUNG, JONATHAN PIERS, editor; b. Crediton, Eng., Sept. 23, 1959; s. Peter Alan George and Mavis Irene (Glossop) Y.; m. Caroline Margaret Bankes, June 5, 1993; children: Henrietta, Fergus. BA, U. Leicester, Eng., 1981. Editor Shooting Times and Country mag., London, 1986-90, editor-in-chief, 1997-99; editor The Field, London, 1991—; liveryman Worshipful Co. Gunmakers, 1992—. Editor: A Pattern of Wings, 1989. Freeman, City of London, 1992—. Mem. Flyfishers' Club. Avocations: shooting, fishing, church architecture, cooking. Office: The Field Kings Reach Tower, Stamford St, London SE1 9LS, England

YOUNG, JUDITH ANNE, animal conservationist; b. L.A., Feb. 11, 1953; d. John Mahlstedt Young and Cynthia Sheilds Tunnicciff. Grad. h.s., L.A. CEO Otter Conservation Ctr., Statesboro, Ga., 1983—. Copyright U.S. Govt., 1995. Republican. Avocations: animal keeping, water gardens, agriculture.

YOUNG, JULIA ANNE, librarian, elementary education educator; b. El Campo, Tex., July 25, 1958; d. Harold Lane and Marcella Jeanne (Payne) Y. BA in English and French, Sam Houston State U., Huntsville, Tex., 1979; MBA, Sam Houston State U., 1982; M in Libr. and Info. Sci., U. Tex., 1986. Cert. tchr. secondary bus., Elem. English 1-12, talented and gifted K-12, PK-12 learning resource ctrs., K-8 elem. gen., Tex. Cataloguer Sam Houston State U., 1976-85; mem. acquisitions and serials staff Tex. State Libr., Austin, 1985-86; cataloguer PCL Grad. Libr. U. Tex., Austin, 1985-86; libr., tchr. Dallas Ind. Sch. Dist., 1986—. Vol. voter registration, Huntsville, 1982-83; mem. Common Cause, Dallas, 1996-97; leader Girl Scouts Am., Huntsville and Dallas, 1976, 87-88; sec. PTA, 1998-2000; mem. fin. com. adminstrv. bd. Highland Pk. United Meth. Ch., 1995-97. Grantee Jr. League, Dallas, 1994, 96. Mem. Dallas Emmaus Cmty., Dallas Assn. Sch. Librs. Democrat. Avocations: swimming, reading, walking, needlework, writing. Home: PO Box 190403 Dallas TX 75219-0403

YOUNG, KUU-YOUNG, engineering educator; b. Kaohsiung, Taiwan, Dec. 22, 1961; s. Huang-Hwa Yang and Su-Chin Chen. BEE, Nat. Taiwan U., 1983; MEE, Northwestern U., 1987, PhD, 1990. Assoc. elec. and control engring. Nat. Chiao-Tung U., Hsinchu, Taiwan, 1990-98, prof., 1998—, vice chmn., 2000—. Contbg. author: Multiple Muscle Systems, 1990; author tech. papers in field. Ensign Taiwanese Navy, 1983-85. Recipient Outstanding Paper award Chinese Automatic Control Soc., Taiwan, 1995. Mem. IEEE. Buddhist. Avocations: movies, tennis, music, television. Office: Dept Elec/Control Engring, Nat Chiao-Tung U, 300 Hsinchu Taiwan

YOUNG, LAUREN SUE JONES, education educator; b. San Diego, July 21, 1947; d. Warren Calvin and Lola Esther (Rucker) Jones; 1 child, Forest McRay Young. AB, Occidental Coll., 1969; MS, San Diego State U., 1971; EdM, Harvard U., 1979, EdD, 1984. Adminstrv. asst. Child Devel. Research Unit, Nairobi, Kenya, 1969-70; asst. prof. San Diego State U., 1974-78, assoc. dir. tchr. corps., 1971-78; co-chmn. and mem. Harvard Ednl. Review, Cambridge, Mass., 1979-81; research assoc. The Huron Inst., Cambridge, 1980-82, Atari Cambridge Research Lab., Cambridge, 1982-84; policy analyst N.Y. State Dept. Social Services, Albany, 1984-85, spl. asst. to commr., 1985-87; assoc. prof. Mich. State U., East Lansing, 1987—; sr. program officer The Spencer Found., Chgo., 1998—; cons. Am. Insts. for Rsch., Cambridge, 1980, Tchr. Corps, Boston area, 1978-80, instr., Pago Pago, Am. Samoa, 1979; rsch. assoc. A Study of H.S.'s, Cambridge, 1980-82; disting. visitor John D. and Catherine T. MacArthur Found., 1995-96. Co-editor: Too Little, Too Late, 1988; mem. editorial bd. Evaluation Rev. Jour., L.A., 1984-88, Jour. Negro Edn. Team mem. Operation Crossroads for Africa, Morogoro, Tanzania, 1968; mem. program adv. bd. Spencer Found., 1992. Danforth Found. fellow, St. Louis, 1978-84. Mem. Am. Ednl. Research Assn., Phi Delta Kappa. Office: The Spender Found 875 N Michigan Ave Chicago IL 60611-1803

YOUNG, MARTIN FORD, barrister; b. Folkstone, Kent, Eng., Mar. 29, 1959; s. Gordon Mawson and Janet Rosemary (Ford) Y.; m. Lesley Patricia Manley, Oct. 1, 1988; children: Nathanael, Abagael. LLB, U. London, 1980, LLM, 1983. Barrister: Bar of Eng. and Wales. Barrister Middle Temple, 1984—; mem. Coun. of London Borough of Tower Hamlets, 1994—. Trustee Isle of Dogs Cmty. Found., London, 1994-99, Mudchute Assn., London, 1994—; pres. Queen Mary Coll., London, Students Union, 1980-81, U. London Union, 1981-82. Mem. Labour Party. Mem. Ch. of England. Avocations: local history, local life. E-mail: younge14@aol.com. Office: Chambers of Michael Ashe QC, 9 Stone Bldgs/Lincolns Inn, London WC2A 3NN, England

YOUNG, MICHAEL EDWARD, psychologist, educator; b. Rockford, Ill., Sept. 24, 1962; s. Walter Eldon Young and Viola Ethel Green; m. Carolyn Ann Noble, Oct. 19, 1985; children: Nathan, Matthew, Rachel. BS in Computer Sci., U. Ill., 1984; MS in Computer Sci., U. Minn., 1991, PhD in Psychology, 1995. With Constrn. Engring. Rsch. Lab., Champaign, Ill., 1983-94; sys. analyst Procter & Gamble, Cin., 1985-88; postdoctoral assoc. U. Iowa, Iowa City, 1995-2000; asst. prof. So. Ill. Univ., Carbondale, Ill., 2000—. Reviewer various jours.; contbr. articles to profl. jours. Grantee NSF, 1999. Mem. Am. Psychological Assn. (young investigator award 1997, 99), Soc. Judgement and Decision Making, Psychonomic Soc., Phi Kappa Phi, Sigma Xi. Mem. Evangelical Ch. Avocations: astronomy, geneaology, guitar playing. E-mail: meyoung@siu.edu.

YOUNG, MICHAEL JOHN, engineering executive; b. Bristol, Eng., Jan. 14, 1942; s. William Charles and Esme Joan (Down) Y.; m. Williamina K.C.R. Blair, May 26, 1965; children: Isobel Kelly, John. A in Mech. Engring., Bristol Coll. Tech., 1964. Trainee drilling supr. Shell Internat., Bangladesh, Brunei, and, North Sea, 1964-73; drilling supr. Shell Internat., 1973-79; drilling supt. Qatar and North Sea Shell Internat., Nigeria, 1973-79; drilling mgr. Nigeria and Thailand Shell Internat., 1979-85; tech. mgr. Strata-Bit, Aberdeen, Scotland, 1985-86; mng. dir. Ecodrill Ltd., Aberdeen, Scotland, 1986-95; CEO Keltec Petroleum Svcs., Aberdeen, Scotland, 1995-97; mng. dir. Cedar Internat., Aberdeen, 1997—. Mem. Soc. Petroleum Engrs., Inst. Dirs. and Petroleum Engrs. Conservative. Mem. Ch. of Eng. Avocations: golf, world affairs, gardening.

YOUNG, MICHAEL WARREN, geneticist, educator; b. Miami, Fla., Mar. 28, 1949; s. Lloyd George and Mildred (Tillery) Y.; m. Laurel Ann Eckhardt, Dec. 27, 1978; children: Natalie, Arissa. BA, U. Tex., 1971, PhD, 1975. NIH postdoctoral fellow Stanford (Calif.) U. Med. Sch., 1975-77; asst. prof. genetics The Rockefeller U., N.Y.C., 1978-83, assoc. prof., 1984-88, prof., 1988—; head Rockefeller unit NSF Sci. and Tech. Ctr. Biol. Timing, 1991—; investigator Howard Hughes Med. Inst., N.Y.C., 1987-96; adv. panel on genetic biology NSF, Washington, 1983-87; spl. advisor Am. Cancer Soc., N.Y.C., 1985—; spl. reviewer genetics study sect. NIH, Bethesda, Md., 1990—, cell biology study sect., 1993-97. Contbr. articles to profl. jours. Meyer Found. fellow, N.Y.C., 1978-83. Fellow N.Y. Soc. Fellows; mem. AAAS, Genetics Soc. Am., Am. Soc. Microbiologists, N.Y. Acad. Scis., Harvey Soc. Achievements include research on transposable DNA elements, molecular genetics of nerve and muscle development, biological clocks, molecular control of circadian rhythms. Home: 51 Greenwoods Rd Old Tappan NJ 07675-7018 Office: The Rockefeller Univ 1230 York Ave New York NY 10021-6399

YOUNG, NICHOLAS ANDREW, electrical engineering; s. Rodney Leo and Morag Briony (Morris) Y. BEE, Imperial Coll., 1993, MS in Engring. and Phys. Science in Medicine, 1994. Analyst, programmer Salomon Bros., London, 1994-96, UBS Warburg, London, 1996-98; v.p. Goldman, SAchs & Co., N.Y.C., 1998—. E-mail: nick young1@yahoo.com. Office: Goldman Sachs & Co 125 Broad St New York NY 10004-2400

YOUNG, PAULA ERNESS, corporate trainer; b. Memphis, Sept. 20, 1957; d. Erneest Leroy and Carrie Louise (Watson) Y. BS, Memphis State U., 1978; MPA, Atlanta U., 1981; EdD in Ednl Adminstrn., U. Cin., 1993. Asst. dir. grants and contracts Nat. Assn. for Equal Opportunity in Higher Edn., Washington, 1981-83, clearinghouse and conf. exhibits mgr., 1981-83; dir rsch. and proposal devel. Clark Coll., Atlanta, 1984-87; asst. v.p. for devel. Johnson C. Smith U., Charlotte, N.C., 1987-88; v.p. instl. advancement Bennett Coll., Greensboro, N.C., 1988-90; spl. asst. to dean Coll. Arts and Scis., N.C. Agrl. and Tech. State U., Greensboro, 1990-98; sr. instrl. design specialist Fed. Express Corp., 1998—. Mem. Women of Color Com., 1994; mem. Greensboro Minority/Women Bus. Enterprise Adv. Bd., 1993; mem. Greensboro Human Rels. Commn., 1990; founder African Am. Atelier Art Gallery; vol. Girl Scouts U.S.A., 1985-86; active YWCA, NAACP. Woodrow Wilson fellow, 1981-83, 85-87. Mem. Nat. Assn. Negro Bus. and Profl. Women's Clubs, Nat. Soc. Fund Raising Execs., Toastmasters Internat., Alpha Kappa Alpha. Avocations: ceramic artwork, reading. Address: 7617 Windsong Dr Memphis TN 38125-6513

YOUNG, PETER FRANCIS, investment banker; b. Brisbane, Queensland, Australia, Feb. 7, 1945; s. Frank Stanley and Muriel Heather (Watt) Y.; m. Susan Janette Halstead, Jan. 19, 1972; children: Elisabeth Jane, Emma Louise. BSc, U. Queensland, 1969; MBA, U. NSW, 1973. Cons. geologist Core Labs., Inc., Dallas, 1968-71; project mgr. Lend Lease Corp., Sydney, NSW, Australia, 1973-75; v.p. Citibank N.A., N.Y.C., 1975-85; exec. prin. A.C. Goode & Co., Ltd., Sydney, 1985-88; mng. dir. Burdett, Buckeridge & Young, Ltd., Sydney, 1988—; bd. dirs. Maratime Svcs. Bd., Sydney, 1988—. Commonwealth scholar Govt. Australia, Brisbane, 1963, Postgrad. scholar, Sydney, 1972. Avocations: golf, sailing, art collecting. Office: Burdett Buckeridge & Young, ABN Amro Australia, 255 George St, Sydney NSW 2000, Australia

YOUNG, ROBERT CRAIG, banker; b. N.Y.C., Mar. 15, 1960; s. Robert J. and Gloria L. (Sandhop) Y. BS cum laude, NYU, 1982, MBA, 1985. Asst. v.p. Chem. Bank, N.Y.C., 1982-86; project mgr. GE Credit Corp., Stamford, Conn., 1986-87; dir. Merrill Lynch & Co., N.Y.C., 1987-94; sr. v.p. Greenwich (Conn.) Capital Markets, Inc., 1994-97; mng. dir. Nomura Securities, N.Y.C., 1997—. Home: 98 Revere Rd Manhasset NY 11030-2733 Office: Nomura Securities Internat Inc Bldg B World Fin Ctr New York NY 10281

YOUNG, SANDRA, adult education executive; b. Kew, Melbourne Victoria, Australia, Dec. 26, 1944; d. Walwyn Gilmour Nicholls and Lorna May Harle; m. Barry Lionel Young, Aug. 29, 1964; children: Kim Maree, Mark Phillip. BA in Politics and Religious Studies, Deakin U., Australia, 1993. Cert. chaplain. Coord. Edn. Found. Student Exchange Program, Cardross, Australia, 1986—; dir. Ashera Corban Interior Plasterers Proprietry Ltd., Cardross, 1986—; coord. volunteer tutor program Adult Multicultural Edn. Svcs., Mildura, Australia, 1986—. Regional chmn. Australian Red Cross, 1988-90, 92-95, chmn. Red Cliffs unit, Victoria, Australia, 1995—, dep. regional chmn., 1999—; chmn. Irymple br. Liberal Party, Australia, 1997—; chmn. Sunraysig parish Uniting Ch. Australia, 1992-95, lay asst. elders parish coun; chaplain Mildura Base Hosp., 1994—. Recipient Long Svc. award Australian Red Cross, Spl. Svc. award Australian Red Cross, 1993, 98; awarded Life Governorship Mildura Base Hosp., 2000. Mem. Assn. Supervised Pastoral Edn. (Aus.), Deakin U. Alumni Assn. Avocations: arctophile (collecting teddy bears), reading, watching cricket, debating politics. Address: PO Box 269, Cardross Victoria Australia

YOUNG, SEAN (MARY SEAN YOUNG), actress; b. Louisville, Ky., Nov. 20, 1959. Appeared in films: Jane Austen in Manhattan, 1980, Stripes, 1981, Blade Runner, 1982, Young Doctors in Love, 1982, Dune, 1984, Baby-Secret of Lost Legend, 1985, Blood and Orchids, 1986, No Way Out, 1987, Wall Street, 1987, The Boost, 1988, Cousins, 1989, Fire Birds, 1990, A Kiss Before Dying, 1991, Once Upon a Crime, 1992, Love Crimes, 1992, Fatal Instinct, 1993, Ace Ventura Pet Detective, 1994, Witness to the Execution, 1994, Even Cowgirls Get the Blues, 1994, Blue Ice, 1994, Dr. Jekyll and Ms. Hyde, 1995, Mirage, 1995, The Proprietor, 1996, Motel Blue, 1997, Exception to the Rule, 1997, The Invader, 1997, Men, 1997, Out of Control, 1998, Special Delivery, 1999. Office: Met Talent Agy 4526 Wilshire Blvd Los Angeles CA 90010-3801

YOUNG, SHELDON MIKE, lawyer, author; b. Cleve., Aug. 27, 1926; s. Jack and Rae (Goldenberg) Y.; m. Margery Ann Polster, Dec. 25, 1948 (div. 1988); children: Jeffrey, Martin, Janet; m. Bette Abel Roth, Nov. 11, 1988. BA, Ohio State U., 1948, JD, 1951; LLM, Case Western Res. U., 1962. Bar: Ohio 1951, U.S. Dist. Ct. (no. dist.) Ohio. Gen. counsel Eugene M. Klein & Assocs., Actuaries, Cleve., 1952-72; assoc. Shapiro, Persky & Marken, Cleve., 1972-74; counsel pension tech. svcs. dept. CNA Ins., Chgo., 1974-76; ptnr. Weiss & Young, Cleve., 1976; of counsel Arter & Hadden, Cleve., 1977-85, Squire, Sanders & Dempsey, Cleve., 1985-87; pvt. practice Cleve., 1987-91, Columbus, Ohio, 1987-93; of counsel Walter & Haverfield, Columbus, Ohio, 1993—; instr. Case Western Res. U. Law Sch., 1962-82, 85, U. Akron Law Sch., 1984, 88. Author: Pension and Profit Sharing Plans, 7 vols., 1977-93; freelance writer for newspapers and mags.; contbr. articles to profl. jours. Served with USN, WWII. Recipient award Nathan Burkan Meml. Copyright Competition, 1951. Fellow Am. Coll. Employee Benefits Counsel (charter); mem. ABA (chair obsolete pension rev rul taskforce), Ohio Bar Assn., Cleve. Bar Assn., Columbus Bar Assn., Masons. Democrat. Jewish. Fax: 614-898-7190. E-mail: yomike@asacomp.com.

YOUNG, SONIA WINER, public relations director, educator; b. Aug. 20, 1934; d. Meyer D. and Rose (Demby) Winer; m. Melvin A. Young, Feb. 24, 1957; 1 child, Melanie Anne. BA, Sophie Newcomb Coll., 1956; M in Ednl. Psychology, U. Tenn.-Chattanooga, 1966. Cert. speech and hearing specialist Am. Speech and Hearing Assn. Speech therapist Chattanooga-Hamilton County Speech and Hearing Ctr., 1961-66, ednl. psychology, 1966-78; staff psychologist Chattanooga Testing and Counseling Svcs., 1978-80; ins. rep. Mut. Benefit Life Ins. Co., Chattanooga, 1980-84; columnist Chattanooga Times, 1982-84; comty. affairs reporter Sta. WRCB-TV, Chattanooga, 1983-84; pub. rels. and promotions dir. Purple Ladies, Inc., Chattanooga, 1984—; cons. psychology Ga. Dept. Human Resources, also Cheerhaven Sch., Dalton, 1970-78; adj. prof. psychology U. Tenn.-Chattanooga, 1971-80, adj. prof. dept. theatre and speech, 1988—; pres. Speak Out; bd. dirs. M. Young Comm., Vol. Ctr., 1995—, Arthritis Found., 1995-98; spl. projects dir. Chattanooga State Tech. C.C., 1995—. Contbg. editor: Chattanooga Life and Leisure Mag. Pres. Chattanooga Opera Guild, 1973-74, Chattanooga Opera Assn., 1979-80; bd. dirs., sec. Chattanooga-Hamilton County Bicentennial Libr., 1977-79; pres. Little Theatre of Chattanooga, 1984-90, bd. dirs., 1974—; v.p. Girls Club, Chattanooga, 1979-80; bd. dirs. March of Dimes, 1988, Chattanooga Symphony Guild, Mizpah Congregation, Chattanooga Area Literacy Coun., Chattanooga Cares, 1993—, Tourist Devel. Agy., 1990—; mem. alumni coun. U. Tenn.-Chattanooga; mem. selection com. Leadership Chattanooga, 1984-86; sec. Allied Arts Greater Chattanooga, 1978-80, residential campaign chmn., 1985; bd. dirs. Chattanooga Ctr. for the Dance, Ptnrs. for Acad. Excellence, 1987—, Chattanooga Mental Health Assn., 1988, Chattanooga Symphony Opera Assn., 1999—; chmn. March of Dimes Mother's March, 1988, One of a Kind-the Arts Against AIDS-Chattanooga Cares, 1993, 94; co-chair Am. Heart Assn. Gala, 1994, chmn., 1995; chair Little Theatre Capital Campaign, 1995; chmn. Galactic Gala fundraiser Chattanooga State Coll., 1996, Chattanooga Theatre Ctr. Endowment Campaign, 1998-99, April in Paris fundraiser, Chattanooga St. Coll., 1997, Chattanooga H.S. Ctr. for the Creative Arts fundraising, 1999, chmn. Broadway Lights Broadway Nights, 1999; adv. coun. Hamilton County Magnet Schs., 1999; bd. dirs. Chattanooga Symphony Opera Assn., 1999. Recipient Disting. Citizens award City of Chattanooga, 1975, Steakley award Little Theatre Chattanooga, 1982, Pres. award, 1991, 92, Vol. of Yr., 1995, Woman of Distinction award Am. Lung Assn., 1995, Vol. of Yr. award, 1995, Penney's Golden Rule award Chattanooga Cares, 1994, Vol. of Yr., 1995. Mem. Phi Beta Kappa (pers. Chattanooga chpt. 1978-79). Jewish. Home: 1025 River Hills Cir Chattanooga TN 37415-5611 Office: U Tenn Theatre & Speech Dept 615 Mccallie Ave Chattanooga TN 37403-2504

YOUNG, SUSAN BABSON, retired library director; b. Boston, June 22, 1939; d. David Leaveau and Katherine Lockhart (Allen) Babson; m. Thomas Herbert Young III, June 17, 1961; children: Thomas Herbert IV, Nathaniel Allen. BA, Vassar Coll., 1961; MLS, SUNY, Albany, 1983. Cert. sch. media specialist, Mass. English and history tchr. St. Anthony's H.S., Long Beach, Calif., 1962-63; asst. dir. Geier Libr. Berkshire Sch., Sheffield, Mass., 1968-72, dir., 1972-95. Contbr. articles to profl. jours. Chair Friends of the Bushnell-Sage Meml. Libr. Capital Fund, Sheffield, Mass., 1995—, trustee, 1994—; mem. Arts Coun., Sheffield, 1983-90, 95—; mem. So. Berkshire Regional Sch. Com., 1998—. Mem. Am. Needlepoint Guild (1st pl. Nat. Exhibit award 1980, 95, 2d Internat. Exhibit award 1982), Embroiders Guild Am., Sheffield Garden Club (pres. 1996-98), Phi Beta Mu. Republican.

YOUNG, VERA LEE HALL, educational administrator, association executive; b. Natchitoches, La., Jan. 9, 1944; d. Sidney and Gertrude (Bell) H.; m. Willie L. Young, Aug. 21, 1965 (div. June 1971). BS, Grambling State U., 1967; MS, Bank St. Coll., 1977; PhD with distinction, Century U., 1985. Cert. tchr., La., N.J., N.Y. Ednl. cons. family day care program N.Y.C. Community Sch. Dist. 6; ednl. dir. Leslie Freeman Daycare Ctr., Bklyn., 1973-74; tchr. West N.Y. Bd. of Edn., 1978—; exec. dir., founder Operation Super Inst., Ft. Lee, N.J., 1986—; lectr., tchr., panelist and cons. in field; participant Statewide Child Care Adv. Coun. Conf., N.J., 1980, State Ill. Tchrs. Conf., 1987, U. S.C. Tchrs. Conf., Georgetown, 1989; discussant Speaking for Schools radio program, N.J., N.Y.; program developer N.Y. Pub. Schs., 1996; del. 24th Internat. Congree Arts and Comms., 1997; instr. Funda C.C., Soweto, South Africa, 1998. Author: A Day Care Solution in America: The Learning Center, 1985; contbr. articles to field. Recipient Internat. Order of Merit award (# 320 of 500 world-wide), Internat. Biog. Ctr., Cambridge, Eng.; named Educator or Yr., Black Achievement and Awards, 1988; Dept. Labor grantee, Jerusalem, 1982-83. Mem. NEA, Nat. Alliance Bus., N.J. Edn. Assn. (conf. participant 1987), N.J. Women Bus. Ownership Orgn., Internat. Platform Assn., Internat. Reading Assn., Minority & Women Owned Bus. N.Y., Bank St. Coll. Alumni Assn., Gambling Coll. Alumni Assn. Mem. Dutch Reform Ch. Avocations: reading, travel, sports. Office: Operation Super 229 Main St # 1834 Fort Lee NJ 07024-5709

YOUNG, WARREN ARTHUR, state official, researcher; b. Auckland, New Zealand, Nov. 3, 1950; s. Lionel Arthur and Mary Doreen (Hutchinson) Y.; m. Robyn Janet Christopher, May 6, 1972; children: Paul Jeffrey, Christopher Mark. BA, Auckland U., 1971, LLB with honours, 1973; PhD, Cambridge (Eng.) U., 1978. Barrister. solicitor, New Zealand. Probation officer, Biggleswade, Eng., 1974; barrister, solicitor, Auckland, 1978-80; dir. Inst. Criminology, Wellington, New Zealand, 1980-92; asst. vice chancellor for rsch. Victoria U. Wellington, 1992-97, prof. law, 1993-2000; dep. sec. justice Ministry of Justice, Wellington, 2000—; policy and rsch. cons., 1989-91; mem. internat. editl. adv. bd. Brit. Jour. Criminology. Author: Community Service Orders, 1979; co-author: Dangerousness and Criminal Justice, 1981, The New Zealand National Survey of Crime Victims, 1997; also articles. Rsch. grantee Fulbright Found., 1985. Mem. Australian and New Zealand Soc. Criminology. Avocations: tennis, squash, running, skiing,

reading. Office: Ministry of Justice, Bower St PO Box 180, Wellington New Zealand

YOUNGBLOOD, DEBORAH SUE, lawyer; b. Fairview, Okla., July 29, 1954; d. G. Dean and Beatrice J. (Hiebert) White. BS with honors, Okla. State U., 1976, MA with honors, 1979; JD cum laude, Boston Coll. Law Sch., 1991; MPH in Health Care Mgmt., Harvard U., 1992. Bar: Colo., N.Mex., U.S. Ct. Appeals (10th cir.). Judicial law clk. Colo. Supreme Ct., 1992-94; assoc. atty. Patton Boggs, L.L.P., Denver, 1994-97, Vaglica & Meinhold, Colorado Springs, 1997-99; atty. pvt. practice, Conway, N.H., 1999—. Mem. ABA, Colo. Bar Assn., N.Mex. Bar Assn., Minoru Yasui Am. Inns of Ct. (exec. coun. 1995-97), Phi Kappa Phi. Avocation: travel. Office: SAU 9 19 Pine St North Conway NH 03860-5211

YOUNGDAHL, PAUL FREDERICK, mechanical engineer; b. Brockway, Pa., Oct. 8, 1921; s. Harry Ludwig and Esther Marie (Carlson) Y.; m. Elinor Louise Jensen, Nov. 27, 1943; children: Mark Erik, Marcia Linnea, Melinda Louise. Student Pa. State U., 1938-40; BS in Engring., U. Mich., 1942, MS in Engring., 1949, PhD, 1962. Indsl. and devel. engr. duPont, Bridgeport, Conn., 1942-43, Carneys Point, N.J., 1946-48; dir. research Mech. Handling Systems, Detroit, 1953-62; prof. U. Mich., Ann Arbor, 1962-74; cons. mech. engr., Palo Alto, Calif., 1974—; dir. Liquid Drive Corp., Holly, Mich. Contbr. articles to profl. jours. With USNR, 1943-46. Mem. Mich. Soc. Profl. Engrs., Nat. Soc. Profl. Engrs., ASME, Am. Soc. Engring. Edn., Mich. Assn. Professions, Sigma Xi, Tau Beta Pi, Phi Kappa Phi, Pi Tau Sigma. Methodist. Address: 501 Forest Ave Ph 4 Palo Alto CA 94301-2637

YOUNG-LYON, KAY LYNN, dance educator, small business owner; b. Decatur, Tex., Aug. 7, 1955; d. Cecil V. and Evelyn Jane (Cohron) Y. BS in Dance Edn., U. North Tex., 1977, MS in Dance Edn., 1981. Owner, dir. Kay Lynn's Studio of Dance, Carrollton, Tex., 1977—; choreographer, dir. in field; mem. Nat. Tap Dance Day com., Artists Helping Artists, 1994—; adv. bd. mem. dance and theatre arts dept. U. North Tex., 1997—. Hostess (cable TV) Kay Lynn's Aerobics, 1985-87, Dallas Dance News, 1989—. Mem. Civic League, Inc., 1997—, sec., 1998-99, asst. fundraising chair, 1999—; mentor Carrollton Farmers Branch; key communicator Carrollton Farmers Br. Ind. Sch. Dist., 1982—; vol. dancer, choreographer and hostess Nat. Svcs. Orgn. of Iwo Jima Battle Survivors, 1993—, C. of C. galas, 1985—. Named one of Outstanding Young Women of Am., 1983; recipient Alumna Honor award U. North Tex. Dance and Theatre Arts Dept., 2000. Mem. AAUW (edni. v.p. 1983-84, cultural v.p. 1987-88, membership v.p. 1991-93), Dallas Dance Coun. (social v.p. 1988-91, bd. dirs.), Nat. Assn. Dance and Affiliate Artists (sec., treas. 1988-91). Baptist. Avocation: travel. Office: 4339 S Capistrano Dr Dallas TX 75287-4012

YOUNGQUIST, CARL WILLIAM, environmental engineer; b. Des Moines, May 25, 1942; s. Carl Paul and Alice June Youngquist; m. Sharon Kay Beckman, June 6, 1964 (div. 1983); children: Billy Charles, Scott Alan; m. Nyoka June Y., Sept. 1, 1989. BS in Chem. Engring., Iowa State U., 1966. Engr. Brown Engring. Co., Des Moines, 1966-73; environ. engr. III State of Iowa Dept. Natural Resources, Des Moines, 1973-2000; environ. engr. Youngquist Environ., Des Moines, 2000—. Author instrnl. manuals, 1973, 87, 99. Avocations: photography, music, boating, waterskiing. E-mail: billscody@earthlink.net. Home: 3750 SE 11th St Des Moines IA 50315-2911

YOUNGQUIST, WALTER LEWELLYN, consulting geologist; b. Mpls., May 5, 1921; s. Walter Raymond and Selma Regina (Knock) Y.; m. Elizabeth Salome Pearson, Dec. 11, 1943; children: John, Karen, Louise, Robert. BA, Gustavus Adolphus Coll., St. Peter, Minn., 1942; MSc, U. Iowa, 1943, PhD, 1948. Registered profl. geologist, Oreg. Jr. geologist U.S. Geol. Survey, 1943-44; rsch. assoc. U. Iowa, Iowa City, 1945-48; asst. prof. geology U. Idaho, Moscow, 1948-51; sr. geologist Internat. Petroleum Co., Talara, Peru, 1951-54; prof. geology U. Kans., Lawrence, 1954-57, U. Oreg., Eugene, 1957-66; cons. geologist Minerals dept. Exxon Corp., Houston, 1968-73; geothermal cons. Eugene Water & Electric Bd., 1973-92; ind. cons. Eugene, 1992—. Author: Investing in Natural Resources, 1980, Mineral Resources and the Destinies of Nations, 1990, GeoDestinies, 1997; co-author: Ordovician Cephalopod Fauna of Baffin Island, 1954. Ensign, USNR, 1944-45. Recipient Lowden Prize in Geology, U. Iowa, 1943, Journalist award, Am. Assn. Petroleum Geology, 2000. Fellow AAAS, Geol. Soc. Am.; mem. Am. Assn. Petroleum Geologists, Geothermal Resources Coun., N.W. Energy Assn., N.Y. Acad. Scis., Sigma Xi. Lutheran. Avocations: fly-tying, photography, fishing. Office: PO Box 5501 Eugene OR 97405-0501

YOUNGS, ROBERT RIGGS, engineer; b. Riverside, Calif., Aug. 20, 1947; s. James Porter and Gwendolyn Gloria (Miller) Y.; m. Susan Ann Cohen, Feb. 10, 1974; children: Sarah Gwen Cohen Youngs, Noah James Cohen Youngs. BS, Calif. State Poly. Coll., 1967; MS, U. Calif., Berkeley, 1973, PhD, 1982. Staff engr. Pacific Found. Engrs., Bloomington, Calif., 1970-72; staff to project engr. Woodward Clyde Consultants, Oakland, Calif., 1974-84; sr. to prin. engr. Geometrix Consultants, Oakland, 1985—. Contbr. articles to profl. jours. Mem. Am. Soc. Engrs., Seismol. Soc. Am., Earthquake Engring. Rsch. Inst. Avocations: fishing, science fiction. Home: 1147 High Ct Berkeley CA 94708-1624 Office: Geomatrix Consultants 2101 Webster St Fl 12 Oakland CA 94612-3027

YOUSEF, FATHI SALAAMA, communication studies educator, management consultant; b. Cairo, Jan. 2, 1934; came to U.S., 1968; naturalized, 1973; s. Salaama and Rose (Tadros) Y.; m. Marjan-El-Faizy Lowies, June 24, 1994. BA, Ain Shams U., Cairo, 1955; MA, U. Minn., 1970, PhD, 1972. Svc. ctr. supt. Shell Oil Co., Cairo, 1955-61; indsl., mgmt. tng. instr. ARAMCO, Dhahran, Saudi Arabia, 1961-68; tchg. assoc. U. Minn., Mpls., 1968-72; comm. studies prof. emeritus Calif. State U., Long Beach, 1972—; with orgn. and indsl. engring. dept. ARAMCO, 1978-80. Co-author: An Introduction to Intercultural Communication, 1975, 85; contbr. articles to profl. jours. Grantee NSF, 1981, 82, 83. Mem. AAUP, ASTD, Am. Mgmt. Assn., Internat. Comm. Assn., Soc. Cross-Cultural Rsch., Nat. Comm. Assn., Internat. Soc. Intercultural Edn., Tng. and Rsch., World Comm. Assn., Western States Comm. Assn., Assn. Egyptian Am. Scholars. Democrat. Office: Calif State U Dept Comm Studies Long Beach CA 90840-0001

YOUSEFI, VALI OLLAH, occupational hygienist, environmentalist, mathematician, consultant, researcher; b. Alamout, Ghazvin, Iran, Sept. 11, 1939; s. Mohamad Hassan and Mahvash (Kiae) Y.; m. Nahid Maleki; 2 children. BS, U. Tehran, Iran, 1963, MS, 1968, MS in Pub. Health, 1968; MS, London Sch. Hygiene, 1973; MPhil, Aston U., Birmingham, Eng., 1981. Diplomate Brit. Examining Bd. in Occupl. Hygiene. Chief environ. officer Tehran Municipality, 1967-68; safety and sanitary engr. Iron Steel Plant, Esphehan, Iran, 1969-70; head dept. air quality Inst. Water Resources Tech., Tehran, 1970-71; rschr. Aston U., 1975-81; mng. dir. MIKH Constrn. Co., Tehran, 1981-83; chief air pollution control officer Dept. Health, Bophuthatswana, South Africa, 1984-87; specialist scientist occupl. hygienist, dep. dir., head of section Nat. Ctr. Occupl. Health, Johannesburg, South Africa, 1980—. Mem. Inst. Occupl. Hygiene, Occupl. Hygiene Assn. South Africe (coun. 1988-95), Am. Confs. Govtl. Indsl. Hygienists, Internat. Commn. on Occupl. Health. E-mail: vali@ncoh.pwv.gov.za. Office: Nat Ctr Occupl Health, PO Box 4788, Johannesburg 2000, South Africa

YOUSSEF, DIAA TOHAMY, pharmacist, researcher, educator; b. El-sharkia, Egypt, Dec. 24, 1961; s. Tohamy Ali Youssef and Amina I. Sayed; m. Lamiaa Ahmed Shaala; 1 child, Salma Diaa. B.Pharm., Assiut (Egypt) U., 1984, M.Pharm., 1988; PhD, Albert-Ludwigs-U., Freiburg, Germany, 1995. Cert. pharmacist, educator. Assoc. lectr. Assiut U., Egypt, 1988-1990; sci. asst. Albert-Ludwigs-U., Freiburg, 1995-1996; prof. Suez Canal U., Ismailia, Egypt, 1996—. Served med. svc., Govt. of Cairo, 1985-1986. Fulbright scholar, 1999-2000. Avocations: reading, swimming, diving, travel. E-mail: youssefdiaa@hotmail.com. Office: Suez Canal U, Faculty Pharmacy, Ismailia 41522, Egypt

YOUSSEF, HALA FOUAD, chemist, archaeologist; b. Kowady, Monufia, Egypt, Feb. 6, 1956; d. Fouad Abdel Fatah and Neamat Said Youssef. BSc, El Azher U., Egypt, 1979; Islamic studies diploma, Islamic Studies Inst., Egypt, 1981; Islamic archaeol. diploma, Cairo U., 1988, master's degree, 1992, PhD in Archaeology, 1998. Chemist Gen. Orgn. of Vaccines and Serums, Egypt, 1980-86; conservator Nat. Ctr. Fine Arts, Giza, Egypt, 1986-95, mem. data bank, 1995—. Author: (books) The Decorative Elements on the Coptic Sculptures, 1992, Planning of Monasteries' Cells, 1998. Mem. ICOMOS, IIWC, ICCROM, Nat. Geog. Soc., Planetary Soc. Muslim. Avocations: writing poems, painting. Home: 4 Sudan St, 12311 Cairo Dukie, Egypt

YOUSSEF, HAROUN ALI, veterinary surgery educator; b. Dir Mawas, El-Minia, Egypt, Apr. 1, 1953; s. Ali Youssef and Hussnah Abd (El-Mageed) H.; m. Dorreah Mostafa Taha, May 6, 1982; children Ali, Mohamed. B in Vet. Sci., Assiut (Egypt) U., 1976, M in Vet. Sci., 1980, PhD, 1984. Demonstrator Assiut U., 1977-80, asst. lectr., 1980-84, lectr., 1984-89, assoc. prof., 1989-94, prof., 1994—; prof. King Saud U., Saudi Arabia, 2000—; rsch. fellow Zurich (Switzerland) U., 1982-83, Ill. U., Urbana, 1989-90; cons. Faculty Vet. Medicine, Assiut, 1991—. Contbr. numerous articles to profl. jours. Mem. Egyptian Vet. Med. Assn., Egyptian Vet. Med. Syndicate, Egyptian Soc. Cattle Diseases, Assn. Arabic Horses. Avocations: photography, farming, playing football. Home: El-Zahraa Bldg, El-Galaa St, Assiut Egypt Office: Assiut U Dept Surgery, Faculty Vet Medicine, Assiut Egypt

YOUSSEF, MAHMOUD MOHAMED AHMED, nematologist, plant pathologist, researcher; b. Kousyia, Assiut, Egypt, Aug. 6, 1953; s. Mohamed Ahmed Youssef and Ganna Khamees Ibrahim; m. Kamar Shaaban Zeid Mahassab, Mar. 24, 1994; children: Manar, Mariem. BS, Cairo U., Giza, Egypt, 1978, MS, 1985, PhD, 1990. Tech. specialist Nat. Rsch. Ctr., Giza, 1981-85, rsch. asst., 1985, asst. lectr., 1985-90, rschr., 1990-95, assoc. rsch. prof., 1995-2000, rsch. prof., 2000—. Contbr. articles to profl. jours. Mem. Pakistan Soc. Nematologists, Egyptian Soc. Agrl. Nematology, Rsch. Staff Club. Muslim. Avocations: reading, listening to music. Home: 2 Mohamed Fadel St, Boulak El-Dakrour 12351, Egypt Office: Nat Rsch Ctr, Tahrir St, Dokki 12311, Egypt

YOUSSOUFI, ABDERRAHMANE, Moroccan politician; b. Tanger, Morocco; m. Hélène Youssoufi. Grad., U. Paris. Mem. Istiqlal, 1959; co-founder Union Nat. des Forces Populaires; co-founder Union Socialiste Forces Populaires, sec. gen., 1992-93, 1995-98; past asst. to Medhi Ben Barka; prime min. Govt. of Morocco, 1998—. Activist in union and independence movements; spokesman African and Arab nationalist campaigns and human rights. Office: Office Prime Min, Palais Royal, Rabat Morocco*

YOUTCHEFF, JOHN SHELDON, physicist; b. Newark, Apr. 16, 1925; s. Slav Joseph and Florence Catherine (Davidson) Y.; m. Elsie Marianne, June 17, 1950; children: Karen Janette, John Sheldon, Mark Allen, Heidi Mary Anne, Lisa Ellen. AB, Columbia U., 1949, BS, 1950; PhD, UCLA, 1953. Registered profl. engr., Calif., D.C. Ops. analyst Gen. Elec. Co., Ithaca, N.Y., 1953-56; cons., engr. missile & space divsn. Gen. Elec. Co., Phila., 1956-64, mgr. advanced reliability programs, 1964-72; mgr. reliability and maintainability Litton Industries, College Park, Md., 1972-73; program mgr. U.S. Postal Svc. Headquarters, Washington, 1973—; instr. U. Pa., 1965-66, Villanova U., 1957—. Lt. USAAF, 1943-46; to comdr. USNR, 1946—. Fellow AAAS, Br. Interplanetary Soc., AIAA, Explorers Club; mem. IEEE (sr.), Ops. Rsch. Soc., Rsch. Soc. Am., Am. Math. Soc., Am. Physics Soc., Am. Cehm. Soc., Am. Astron. Soc., Am. Geol. Socl., Nat. Soc. Profl. Engrs., Engring. and Tech. Socs., Coun. Del. Vly. (spkrs. bur.), USCG Aux. (flotilla comdr.), Res. Officers Assn., Am. Legion, Optimists Internat. (pres. Valley Forge chpt. 1970-71). Roman Catholic. Home: 1400 S Joyce St Apt 1406 Arlington VA 22202-1852 Office: L'Enfant Plz Washington DC 20260

YOVETICH, NANCY ANN, business executive, research scientist; b. Pitts., Oct. 31, 1965; d. George Yovetich and Frances Brant; m. Marty Stanly Kraut, June 11, 1994; 1 child, Hannah Elizabeth Kraut. BA, Allegheny Coll., 1987; PhD, U. N.C., 1997. Rsch. assoc. U. Pitts., 1987-88; psychology instr. U. N.C., Chapel Hill, 1989-92; rsch. asst. N.H.-Dartmouth Psychiat. Rsch. Ctr., Lebanon, 1994-95; SAS programmer analyst Rho, Inc., Chapel Hill, 1992-94, 95-97, sr. project mgr., 1997-99, dir. project ops., 1999—. Editor Representative Rsch. in Social Psychology, 1991-92. Recipient Nat. Rsch. Svc. award NIMH, 1993-94, Theodore and Vaida Stanley Rsch. award Theodore and Vaida Stanley Found., 1994-95. Mem. Drug Info. Assn., Phi Beta Kappa. E-mail: nyovetich@rhoworld.com. Office: Rho Inc 100 Eastowne Dr Chapel Hill NC 27514-2286

YPMA, ALPHONS FGVM, urologist, consultant; b. The Hague, The Netherlands, May 10, 1945; s. Alphons Maria and Mia Phh (Busch) Y.; m. Clementine Felice Thole, Oct. 11, 1969; children: Claartje, Renske. MD, U. Amsterdam, The Netherlands, 1974; Urologist, U. Nymegen, The Netherlands, 1981. Ednl. counsel for fgn. med. grads. exam. (ECFMG), 1974. Intern, resident U. Amsterdam, 1971-74; chef de clinique Dept. Urology, Nymegen, 1981-82; cons. urologist Deventer Hosp., 1983—, ednl. course dir. urology, 1987—; vis. lectr. uro-oncology, U.S.A., 1982, Internat. Coll. Surgeons, Indonesia, 1988; vis. prof. European Assn. Urology, Cluj, Romania, 1992, Spanish Urol. Assn., Valladolid, 1997. Editor Dutch Jour. Urology, 1994—, The Prostate Booklet, 1994—; editor in chief: Urological Examination, 1996. Mem. Internat. Rotary Doctors Bank, The Netherlands, 1996—; mem. Brit.-Dutch Soc., Deventer, 1995—; founding mem. Dr. Frog Soc., Diepenveen, The Netherlands, 1996. Lt. col. Dutch Army, 1974-95. Recipient Golden Eagle award, Deventer City, 1992, Josef award Med. Sci. Com., 1993. Mem. Dutch Urol. Assn. (pres. 1995-97, east-west liaison officer, Brongersma medal 1997), Internat. Coll. Surgeons (bd. mem.), Am. Urol. Assn. (corr. mem.). Liberal Democrat. Avocations: golf, skiing, sailing, travel, medical history. Home: Brinkerinckbaan 7, 7431 BX Diepenveen The Netherlands Office: Deventer Hosp Dept Urology, Postbox 5001, 7400 GC Deventer The Netherlands

YTTERSTAD, BØRGE, surgeon, educator, researcher; b. Harstad, Norway, Apr. 15, 1943; s. Rolf Lind and Astrid Malene (Ervik) Y.; m. Merethe Lange-Nielsen, Mar. 10, 1972; children: Andreas, Petter, Karianne. MD, U. Oslo, 1968; PhD, U. Tromsø, Norway, 1995. Resident in surgery Harstad Hosp.; resident in surgery, urology, gynecology and orthop. Tromsø U. Hosp.; cons. Harstad H, 1977-87, head surgeon, 1988-96; staff urol. dept. Trondheim U. Hosp., 1990; rsch. fellow Inst. Cmty. Medicine, U. Tromsø, 1992-94; assoc. prof. surgery U. Tromsø, 1996—; surgeon Norwegian Red Cross, Nigeria, 1972, Sahlgrenska Hosp., Gothenburg, Sweden, 1982; cons. WHO, United Arab Emirates, 1996; hon. rsch. fellow Injury Prevention Ctr., U. (New Zealand) Auckland, 1997-98; lectr. in field. Contbr. numerous articles on injury prevention to profl. jours. Recipient Traffic Safety Partnership award U.S. Dept. Transp./Na.t Hwy. Traffic Safety Assn., 2000. Home: Ervik, 9400 Harstad Norway Office: Harstad Hosp, Dept Surgery, 9400 Harstad Norway

YU, AI-BING, materials processing educator; b. Kaiping, Guandong, China, Jan. 18, 1963; s. Guan-Tan and Rui-Yao Y.; m. Rui-Ping Zou, Jan. 25, 1988; children, David Xiang, Elizabeth Yue. BEng, Northeastern U., Shenyang, China, 1982, MEng, 1985; PhD, U. Wollongong, Australia, 1990. Rsch. assoc. U. Wollongong, 1989; postdoctoral fellow CSIRO, Melbourne, Australia, 1990-91; lectr. U. New South Wales, Sydney, Australia, 1992-94, sr. lectr., 1995-97, assoc. prof., 1998—; adj. prof. Xi'an (China) U. Architecture and Tech., 1994—; concurrent prof. Northeastern Univ. (China), 1999—, vis. acad. U. Cambridge, Eng., 1995; dir. Ctr. Computer Simulation and Modelling of Particulate Systems, 2000—. Contbr. articles to profl. jours., including Indsl. and Engring. Chem. Rsch., Powder Tech., Jour. Am. Ceramic Soc., Chem. Engring. Sci., Physica A. CSIRO postdoctoral fellow, 1990; Queen Elizabeth II fellow Australian Rsch. Coun., 1993. Mem. AIChE, Am. Ceramic Soc., The Minerals, Metals and Materials Soc. Avocations: reading, sightseeing, table tennis, swimming. Office: U New South Wales, Sch Materials Sci Enging, 2052 Sydney NSW, Australia

YU, BENITA KA PO, solicitor; d. Yu Sai Hung and Yu Shiu So Har Shirley; m. Edmund King Yan Kwok; 1 child, Veronica Pui Yen Kwok. BA, U. Oxford, 1986, MA, 1991; law soc. finals 1st class, 1987. Solicitor: Supreme Ct., England, 1989, Wales, 1989, High Ct. Hong Kong Spl. Adminstv. Region, 1994. Articles clk. Norton Rode, London, 1987-89, asst. solicitor, 1989-93; asst. solicitor Slaughter and May, Hong Kong, 1994-96, ptnr., 1996—. Recipient Book prize St. Hugh's Coll., Oxford U., 1984; scholar Hong Kong Govt., 1976-81, Ho Leung Ho Lee, 1983. Mem. Law Soc. England, Law Soc. Hong Kong, The Oxford and Cambridge Soc. Hong Kong, Hong Kong Golf Assn. Avocations: piano, golf, classical music, jazz, arts. Office: Slaughter and May, 27th Flr 2 Exchange Sq, Hong Kong Hong Kong

YU, BINGZHONG, mechanical engineer; b. Fuzhou, China, June 1, 1931; s. Zongping and Wenqing (Pan) Y.; m. Xiuzhen Guan. BS, Tsing Hua U., 1953. Dir., dep. chief engring. Inst. of Petroleum Mech. Engring., Daqing, China, 1964-74; chief engr., dir. Inst. of Petroleum Exp. 8 Dept., Beijing, China, 1974-78; v.p. Inst. of Petroleum Exploration and Devel., Beijing, 1978-94; bd. dirs. China Petroleum Equipment and Material Std. Com., Beijing; dir. China Petroleum and Natural Gas Std. Com., Beijing, 1987-92. Chief editor: Russian-English-Chinese Petroleum Dictionary, 1997. Mem. China Petroleum Engring. Assn. (dir. 1982-90, quality and reliability com. 1995-96). Home: PO Box 910, Beijing China Office: Xue Yuan Rd 20, Beijing China

YU, CHACK YUNG, pediatrics educator; b. Guangdong, Ohio, People Republic of China, Dec. 24, 1957; s. Hung Ho and Shui-Wo (Kwok) Y.; m. Lai-Chu, Apr. 23, 1987; children: Gayang Heidi, Gakit Richard. BS, Chinese U. Hong Kong, 1981, MPhil, 1983; DPhil, Oxford U., England, 1988. Asst. prof. Ohio State U., Columbus, 1990-96, assoc. prof., 1996—. Contbr. articles to profl. jours. Grantee NIH, Bethesda, Md., 1994—, March of Dimes, 1992-94; postdoctoral fellow Med. Rsch. Coun. Lab. Molecular Biology, Cambridge, England, 1987-90. Mem. AAAS, Am. Assn. Immunologists, Am. Soc. Human Genetics, Am. Soc. Microbiology, Am. Soc. Biochem. & Molecular Biology. Office: Children's Rsch Inst 700 Childrens Dr Columbus OH 43205-2664

YU, CHANGTAI, engineering educator; b. Tengzhou, Shandong, China, Mar. 12, 1940; s. Dequan Yu and Zhenlan Zhang; m. Fengzhen Guo (dec. Dec. 1997); children: Hua, Xiang; m. Jiali Mi, Apr. 28, 1998. BS, Jinan U., Shandong, 1967. Engr. Optoelectronics Rsch. Inst., Chongqing, China, 1968-86; prof. Zheijiang U., Hangzhou, China, 1986—; prof. Osaka U., Japan, 1993, 98. Author: Fiberoptic Sensing Technology and Application, 1992. Recipient Sci. and Tech. Achievement award Sichuan Sci. Com., Chendu, 1978, award for rsch. Chongqing Optoelectronics Rsch. Inst., 1979, Achievement award Ministry Electronic Industry, 1986, awards for rsch. Nat. Natural Sci. Found. China, 1991, 97. Mem. Internat. Soc. Optical Engring. (prof. 1993, 98), Chinese Elec. Soc., Chinese Optical Soc. Avocations: collecting stamps, singing, swimming. Home: 21-412, Qiushi Residential Qtr, Hongzhou Zheijiang 310013, China Office: Zhejiang U, 20 Yugu Rd, Hangzhou Zhejiang 310027, China

YU, CHAO CHUAN, business educator, consultant; b. Taichung, Taiwan, Republic of China, Mar. 9, 1952; s. An Poe and In Hua Liao Yu; m. Chun Hua Wang; children: Nicola, Alexender. BS, Nat. Taiwan U., Taipei, 1974, MBA, 1978, DBA, 1984. Cert. security analyst, managerial acct. Sales mgr. Great Wall Corp., Taiwan, 1979-80; sec. Taipin City, Taichung, Taiwan, 1980-81; assoc. prof. Soochow U., Taipei, 1984-89, dir. grad. sch. of acctg., 1987-93, dean sch. of bus., 1996-99, prof. sch. of bus., 1999—; cons. UMC, Shin-zu, Taiwan, 1985; chief cons. Harvard Cons. Co., Taipei, 1988; dir. China Ship Building Corp., Taipei, 1995—, Sino-Pac Securities Investment, Taipei, 1999—. Author: Competetive Marketing, 1987 (Univ. textbook award 1988), Productivity System (Chia Shin award 1989), Marketing Management, 1990 (Ministry of Edn. award 1991). 2d lt. China Air Force, 1975-76. Recipient Young Rschr. award Ministry of Edn., 1984, Best Univ. prof., 1990. Mem. China Mgmt. Assn. (Paper award 1984), China Mangerial Acc. Assn. (mng. dir. 1989-99). Avocation: fishing. Home: 70-70 Lin-Shi Rd, Taipei Taiwan, Republic of China Office: Soochow U, 56 Kwei Yang St, Taipei Taiwan, Republic of China

YU, CHENG, radiation oncology educator, medical physicist; b. Gao County, Sichuan, China, Sept. 15, 1959; came to U.S., 1986; s. Songgsheng and Shufeng (Yan) Y.; m. Lin Chen; 1 child, Shawn Yu. BS in Physics, Chengdu (China) U. Sci.-Tech., 1982; MS in Applied Physics, Mich. Technol. U., 1989, PhD in Applied Physics, 1991. Rschr., instr. Chengdu U. Sci. and Tech., 1982-86; tchg. and rsch. asst. Mich. Technol. U., Houghton, 1986-91; postdoctoral fellow U. Chgo., 1991-94; asst. prof. clin. radiation oncology U. So. Calif., L.A., 1994—. Author: Enzymology and Molecular Biology of Carbonyl Metabolism 4, 1993; contbr. articles to sci. jours. Mem. Am. Assn. Physicists in Medicine, Am. Phys. Soc., Internat. Electron Paramagnetic Resonance Soc. Avocation: sports. Office: U So Calif Dept Radiation Oncology 1441 Eastlake Ave Los Angeles CA 90033-1048

YU, CHIA-PENG, health facility administrator; b. Chiayu, Taiwan, Apr. 1, 1966; s. Tse-Lung and Tsai-Chien Yu; m. Su-Chun Lin, Jan. 16, 1994; children: Wie-Ting, Lun-Ching. B, Nat. Defense Med. Ctr., 1994; M, Nat. Defense Med. Ctr., Taipei, 1997. Cert. environ. analyst. Staff Armed Forces Peitou Hosp., Taipei, Taiwan, 1997-98; lab. dir. Armed Forces Kaohsiung Hosp., Kaohsiung, Taiwan, 1999—. Maj. Army, Taiwan, 1989-2000. Mem. Chinese Soc. Microbiology, Nosocomial Infection Control Soc. Avocations: swimming, tennis. Home: 11F No 91-1 Yon-Shing Rd, Tainan 710, Taiwan Office: Armed Forces Kaohsiung Hosp, No 2 Chung-Cheng 1 Rd, Kaohsiung 802, Taiwan

YU, DAHAI, mathematics and engineering educator, researcher; b. Changyi, China, Dec. 8, 1964; came to U.S., 1992; s. Shengcheng Yu and Juqiu Li. BSc in Space Physics, U. Sci. and Tech. of China, 1985; MSc in Space Physics, Chinese Acad. Scis., 1992; PhD in Civil Engring., U. Notre Dame, 1998. Asst. rsch. fellow Chinese Acad. Scis., Beijing, 1990-92; rsch. asst. U. Notre Dame, Ind., 1992-97; postdoctoral State U. N.Y., Stony Brook, 1997-98, vis. asst. prof., 1998—. Contbr. articles to profl. jours. Ctr. for Applied Math. fellow U. Notre Dame, 1994-95; Rsch. grantee Chinese Nat. Sci. Found., Beijing, 1992-94. Avocation: table tennis. E-mail: dyu@ams.sunysb.edu. Office: Dept Applied Math and Stats State U New York Stony Brook NY 11794-0001

YU, DAO-YI, ophthalmologist; b. Hangzhoiu, Zhejiang, China, Aug. 4, 1943; arrived in Australia, 1987; s. Dan-Ban and Suxian (Wang) Y.; m. Erning Su, Aug. 6, 1967; children: Christine Yunxi, Ben Yunbei. MD, Zhejiang Med. U., Hangzhou, 1966, degree in ophthalmology, 1973; PhD, U. Western Australia, Perth, 1991. Ophthalmologist Zehjiang's Hosps., 1967-80, Zhejiang Chinese Med. Inst., Hangzhou, 1980-84, Zhejiang Provincial Hosp., Hangzhou, 1985-86; rsch. fellow U. Western Australia, Perth, 1985-86, U. Ill., Chgo., 1986-88; dir. Physiology and Pharmacology Ctr. Lions Eye Inst., Perth, 1993—, rsch. dir. McCusker Glaucoma Ctr., 1993—; prof. ophthalmology (hon.) Shanghai Med. U., 1998—; adj. prof. biomedicine Murdoch U., Perth, 1999—; hon. prof. ophthalmology Shanghai Med. U., 1998—; adj. prof. biomedicine Murdoch U., Perth, Australia, 1999—; adj. assoc. prof. ophthalomology U. Western Australia, 1999—. Contbr. more than 100 articles to profl. jours. including Am. Jour. Physiology, Investigative Ophthalmology and Visual Sci., among others. Recipient awards Ministry of Health in China, 1980, 83, 84; grantee Nat. Health and Med. Rsch. Coun. (Australia), 1990—. Mem. Assn. for Rsch. in Vision and Ophthalmology. Achievements include patents for a system for ocular ultrasurgery, method of penetrating tissue wall, ocular tonometer, and biological microfistula. Office: U Western Australia Ctr Ophthal and Vision Sci, 2 Verdun St, Nedlands WA 6009, Australia

YU, EIN-FEN, oceanographer; b. Taiwan, China, Aug. 30, 1960; parents I-Fei and Gon (Dai) Y. PhD, MIT, Cambridge, 1994. Rsch. asst. Inst. Earth Sci./Academica Sinica, Taiwan, 1985-88; asst. prof. dept. earth sci. Nat. Taiwan Normal U., Taipei, 1994—. Office: Nat Taiwan Normal Univ, Dept Earth Sci/Ting-Chou Rd, Taipei 117, Taiwan

YU, FUSHUN, physiologist, researcher; b. Changchun, Jilin, People's Republic of China, Sept. 30, 1960; d. Dongxiu and Shunsan (Li) Y.; m. Shengfu Piao; 1 child, Shi. MD, Norman Bethune U. Med. Scis., Changchun, 1984, MSc in Med. Biochemistry, 1989; PhD in Cellular and Molecular Muscle Physiology, Karolinska Inst., Stockholm, 1999. Lectr., rsch. assoc. dept. clin. biochemistry Hosp. Dalian Med. U., Liaoning Province, People's Republic of China, 1991-94; lectr. Noll Physiol. Rsch.

Ctr. Pa. State U., University Park, 1997-99; post-doctoral rschr. dept. pharmacology Ohio State U., Columbus, 1999-2000; rsch. scientist Noll Physiol. Rsch. Ctr. Pa. State U., University Park, 2000—. Fellow Karolinska Inst., Stockholm, 1994-97; Doktorand-tjänst scholar Karolinska Inst., 1994-97; recipient Outstanding Young Scientist awards Jilin Biochemistry Soc., People's Republic of China, 1989. Mem. Biophysical Soc., Am. Physiol. Soc., Sigma Xi. E-mail: fuy104@psu.edu. Office: Noll Physiol Rsch Ctr Pa State U University Park PA 16802-6900

YU, HAN QING, civil and structural engineer; b. Wuwei, Anhui, China, Oct. 23, 1966; s Jia Pei and Xiao Nan (Ding) Y.; m. Yu Xin Chen, June 10, 1991. BSc, Hefei (China) U. Tech., 1986; MSc, Tongji U., Shanghai, 1989, PhD, 1994. Lectr. Hefei U. Tech., 1989-91; postdoctoral fellow U. Newcastle, U.K., 1994-95, Nanyang Tech. U., Singapore, 1995-97; rsch. fellow Hong Kong U., 1997—. Recipient outstanding young scholar award Edn. Com., Anhui Province, China, 1991. Mem. Assn. Marie Curie Fellows European Union, Internat. Assn. Water Quality. Avocations: classical music, soccer, chess. Office: Hong Kong U Dept Civil Engr, Pokfulam Rd, Hong Kong Hong Kong

YU, HSIN-SU, dermatologist, educator; b. Chia-Yi, Taiwan, Sept. 3, 1946; s. Han-Chan and Chou-Cheu (Yamamoto) Y.; m. Mei-Chia Huang, July 26, 1973; children: Chu-Ling, Hsu-Sheng, Wei-Tai. MD, Kaohsiung (Taiwan) Med. Coll., 1972; PhD, U. Tokyo, 1980. Diplomate in dermatology, Taiwan, Japan. Resident Kaohsiung Med. Coll. Hosp., 1973-75; resident and rsch. fellow U. Tokyo, 1975-81; rsch. fellow Harvard Med. Sch., Boston, 1981; assoc. prof. Kaohsiung Med. Coll., 1981-85, prof. dermatology, 1985—, chmn. dept. dermatology, 1985—, dean sch. medicine, 1990-93, dir. grad. sch. medicine, 1992-94; NIH Fogarty fellow Rockefeller U., N.Y.C., 1984-86; lectr. in field. Contbr. articles to profl. jours. Vol. physician Rotary Club, Kaohsiung, 1986. Ensign, Chinese Marine Corps, 1972-73. Named Outstanding Scientist Nat. Sci. Coun., Taipei, 1993-95. Mem. Chinese Dermatol. Soc., Japanese Dermatol. Assn., Soc. for Investigative Dermatology. Avocations: music, pen and watch collection. Home: Sun-Min Dist, 159 Chi-Lin St, 80709 Kaohsiung Taiwan Office: Kaohsiung Med Coll, Dept Dermatology, 80708 Kaohsiung Taiwan

YU, HUIMING, computer scientist; b. Jinan, Shangtong, China, May 5, 1952; came to U.S., 1984; d. Tongyun and Guixiang (Shi) Y.; m. William L. Lawrence, Jr. BS, Xiamen (China) U., 1976; MS, Hefei (China) Poly. U., 1981; PhD, Stevens Inst. Tech., 1992. Instr. Hefei Poly. U., 1982-84; grad. rsch. asst. Stevens Inst. Tech., Hoboken, N.J., 1987-90, 91-92; assoc. engr. Syncsort Co., Woodcliff Lake, N.J., 1990-91; asst. prof. computer sci. N.C. A&T State U., Greensboro, 1992-97, assoc. prof., 1997—; mem. com. SigAda program com., 1998; judge Developers Competition and Conf., 1993—; mem. program com. IASTED Conf. on robotics and Mfg., 1998—. Author: Ada 95 Object-Oriented Programming, 1997; contbr. articles to profl. jours. Recipient grants in software engring., robotics and edn. Mem. Assn. for Computing Machinery, Spl. Interest Groups Ada, Triad Assn. for Computing Machinery (treas. 1994), Spl. Interest Groups Artificial Intelligence, Chinese Assn. Greensboro. Avocation: table tennis. Office: NC A&T State U 1601 E Market St Greensboro NC 27411-0001

YU, JACK CHUNGKAI, plastic surgeon, researcher; b. Taipei, Taiwan, Apr. 21, 1959; came to U.S., 1977; s. Lieh-Chun and Hsiao Yu; m. Marian Reed Lambert, June 5, 1988; children: Megan, Robert, Jaclyn. DMD, U. Pa., 1982, MSEd, 1984, MD, 1985. Diplomate Nat. Bd. Dental Examiners, N.E. Regional Bd. in Dentistry, Am. Bd. Surgery, Am. Bd. Plastic Surgery. Asst. isntr. surgery U. Pa., Phila., 1987-91, instr. surgery, 1991-94; assoc. prof. plastic surgery VA Med. Ctr., Augusta, Ga., 1994—; chief pediatric plastic surgery Children's Med. Ctr. at Med. Coll. Ga., Augusta, 1998—; assoc. prof. Med. Coll. Ga., Augusta, 1994—, dir. craniofacial ctr., 1996—. Recipient Robert H. Ivy award Soc. Plastica nd Reconstructive Surgery, 1991, 94, others; grantee Am. Soc. Maxillofacial Surgeons, 1995, Maxillofacial Surgeons Found., 1995, others. Fellow ACS, Acad. Dentistry Inernat., Am. Soc. for Laser Medicine and Surgery; mem. AAAS, AMA, Assn. for Surg. Edn., N.Y. Acad. Scis., Am. Soc. Maxillofacial Surgeons, Am Soc. for Plastic and Reconstructive Surgeons, Am. Soc. Craniofacial Surgery (assoc.), Plastic Surgery Rsch. Coun., Am. Cleft Palate-Craniofacial Assn., Med. Assn. Ga., Richmond County Med. Soc., Andrw Surg. Soc., Alpha Omega Alpha, Omicron Kappa Upsilon, Pi Mu Epsilon, Alpha Lambda Delta. E-mail: jyu@mail.mcg.edu. Office: Med Coll Ga 1467 Harper St # Hb5040 Augusta GA 30901-2600

YU, JANICE J., journalist. MA, U. Iowa, 1985, postgrad., 1985-88; postgrad., Stanford U., 1989. Internat. news editor CTV, Taipei, Taiwan, 1994—; Jefferson fellow East-West Ctr., 1998; columnist internat. politics Ctrl. Daily News, Taipei, 1995-99. Translator: The Joy Luck Club, 1991, The Alien Realm, 1996; author: Is There a Quarrel in Troy, 1993. E-mail: janiceyu@yahoo.com. Fax: 886-2-27260140. Office: CTV, 120 Chung Yang Rd, Nankang Taipei 115, Taiwan

YU, JEONG-SIK, physician; b. Iksan, S. Korea, Aug. 22, 1963; s. Young-Soo Yu and Jeong-Ja Ju; married; children: Hong-Seok, Hong-Min. MD, Yonsei U. Coll. of Medicine, Seoul, 1988. Intern YongDong Severance Hosp., Seoul, 1988-89, resident diagnostic radiology, 1989-92, rsch. fellow, 1995-97; instr. dept. diagnostic radiology Yonsei U. Coll. of Medicine, Seoul, 1997-99, asst. prof. diagnostic radiology, 1999—. Editl. bd.: Jour. of Korean Soc. of Med. Ultrasound, 1998—, Korean Jour. of Radiology, 1999—; manuscript reviewer Jour. of Magnetic Resonance in Medicine, 1999—, Jour. of Korean Radiol. Soc. Capt. Korean Air Force, 1992-95. Recipient Acad. Achievement award Yonsei Univ. Coll. of Medicine, Seoul, 1999. Mem. AAAS, Radiol. Soc. N.Am., Internat. Soc. Magnetic Resonance in Medicine, Korean Radiol. Soc. E-mail: yjsrad97@yumc.yonsei.ac.kr. Office: Dept Rad/YongDong Severance, Hosp/146-92 Dogog-Dong, Gangnam-Gu, Seoul 135-270, Korea

YU, JIANG W., research scientist; b. Beijing, Nov. 8, 1956; came to U.S., 1980; s. Daosheng Wu and Baoqing Shen. Student, Peking U., Beijing, 1978-80; BA, SUNY, Albany, 1983, PhD, 1990. Rsch. scientist N.Y. State Office of Alcoholism and Substance Abuse Svcs., Albany, N.Y., 1988-00; dir. Sci. Rsch. Consulting, Albany, 1991-99. Contbr. rsch. articles to profl. jours. Mem. APHA, Internat. Coun. on Alcohol, Drugs and Traffic Safety, Am. Sociol. Assn., Am. Soc. Criminology, Acad. Criminal Justice Scis., Rsch. Soc. on Alcoholism. Avocations: tennis, skiing, inline skating. Home: 173 Williamsburg Ct Albany NY 12203-5507 Office: N Y State Office Alcoholism and Substance Abuse Svcs 1450 Western Ave Albany NY 12203-3539

YU, JIA-RONG, mathematics educator; b. Hankow, Wuhan, Hubei, China, Nov. 16, 1920; s. Yu-pu and Jia-kun (Li) Y.; m. Kwang-chung Tu, Feb. 27, 1947; children: Jiu-ji, Jiu-jian, Jiu-man, Jiu-cheng. BS, Cen. U., Chungking, China, 1944; DSc in Math., U. Paris, 1950. Asst. dept. math. Cen. U., Chungking and Nanking, 1944-47; researcher Nat. Ctr. of Sci. Rsch., Paris, 1949-51; from assoc. prof. to prof. math. Wuhan (China) U., 1951—, dir. of Sino-French class of math., 1980-94, dir. Sino-French Ctr. of Math. and Computer Sci., 1985-94; reviewer Math. Revs., Am. Math. Soc., Providence, 1986—, Zentralblatt Mathematik und ihre Grenzgebiete, Heidelberger Akademie der Wissenschaften Fachinformationszentrum, Karlsruhe, 1991—. Author: Functions of a Complex Variable, 1979 (1st class prize Chinese Nat. Commn. of Edn. 1988), 3d edit., 2000, Dirichlet series and Rardm Dirichlet series (in Chinese), 1997; editor: Chinese Annals of Math., 1980-98; contbr. articles to profl. jours. in China, France, and U.S., 1949—. Named Officier dans l'Ordre Palmes Academiques, Govt. of France, 1990. Mem. Chinese Math. Soc., Am. Math. Soc. Avocations: Chinese history, classical literature, philosophy. E-mail: jryu@whu.edu.cn. Office: Wuhan U, Dept Math Wuhan Hubei, Wuhan 430072, China

YU, JIETAI, mathematician, educator; b. Tunxi, Anhui, China, Oct. 15, 1954; s. Yicheng Yu and Peiqin Wu. MSc, U. Sci. and Tech., Hefei, China, 1987, U. Notre Dame, Ind., 1991; PhD, U. Notre Dame, Ind., 1994. Tchr. Taiping (China) H.S., 1974-84; lectr. U. Sci. and Tech., Hefei, 1987-89; instr., tchg. asst. U. Notre Dame, 1989-93; asst. prof. U. Hong Kong, 1994-98, assoc. prof., 1998—; reviewer math. abstracts, Zentralblatt fur Mathematik, Berlin, 1994—; participant Congress of Math., Zurich, 1994. Contbr. numerous rsch. papers to profl. jours. and conf. procs. U. Notre Dame math. fellow, 1989-90, Nat. Sci. and Engring. Rsch. Coun. Can. internat. fellow, Ottawa, 1994-96; recipient U. Notre Dame grad. sch. award, 1994. Mem. Am. Math. Soc., Hong Kong Math. Soc., Math. Assn. of Am. Avocations: playing chess and ko, traveling, singing, bicycling, writing poetry. Home: PO Box 471 Notre Dame IN 46556-0471 Office: Univ of Hong Kong Dept of Math, Pokfulam Rd, Hong Kong Hong Kong

YU, JING QUAN, educator; b. Yiwu, China, Dec. 19, 1963; s. Guan Nai and Su Min (Wang) Y.; m. Wei Hua Ying, Aug. 8, 1988. BS, Zhejiang Agrl. U., Hangzhou, China, 1983; MS, Shimane U., Matsue, Japan, 1991; DS, Tottori (Japan) U., 1991. Rschr. Zhenjiang Acad. Agrl. Scis., Hangzhou, China, 1983-88, Tokushima Agrl. Rsch. Inst., Japan, 1985-86, Takeda Chem. Co., Tokyo, 1994-95; prof. Zhenjiang Agrl. U., 1995-98, Zhejiang U., Hangzhou, 1998—; cons. in field. Contbr. articles to profl. jours. Named Key Young Scientist Agrl., China. Mem. AAAS, Japanese Soc. Soil Sci. & Plant Nutrition, Japanese Soc. Phytopathoy Soc., Internat. Soc. Chem. Ecology, Inernat. Soc. Hort. Scis., Internat. Allelopathy Soc., Chinese Soc. Plant Physiology, Chinese Soc. Hort. Avocations: driving, music. Home: 3-104 Kaixuan St 258, Hangzhou China Office: Zhejiang U Hort Dept, Kaixuan Rd 268, Hangzhou 310029, China

YU, JOHN YUH-LIN, endocrinologist, veterinary medicine and zoology educator; b. Hsin-Chu, Republic of China, Dec. 1, 1937; s. Hsi-Tsing and Wei-Mei (Cheng) Y.; m. Siu-Yu Lo, May 10, 1970; children: Helen Chiayin, Linda Chiahui, Sophy Chiahsue. BS in Vet. Medicine, Nat. Taiwan U., Taipei, 1960; MS, U. Alta., Edmonton, Can., 1967; PhD, U. Man., Winnipeg, Can., 1972. Asst. instr. Nat. Chung-Hsing U., Taichung, Republic of China, 1961-64; rsch. assoc. U. Alta., 1967; wildlife biologist N.W. and Indian bur. Can. Wildlife Svc., Vancouver, B.C., 1967-68; rsch. fellow Can. Nat. Sci. Coun., Winnipeg, 1968-71; postdoctoral fellow U. Man., 1972-73; rsch. investigator U. Wash., Seattle, 1973-78, sr. fellow, 1979; rsch. scientist Inst. Zoology Acad. Sinica, Taipei, 1980—; dep. dir. Inst. Zoology Acad. Sinica, Taipei, 1990—; prof. Nat. Taiwan U., 1980—, Tunghai U., Taichung, 1981—; mem. coun. Taiwan Pig Rsch. Inst., Chu-Nan, 1983—; mem. adv. panels various livestock rsch. projects Taiwan Provincial Dept. Agr., Taichung, 1983—; mem. thesis dissertation coms. various ednl. instns., Republic of China and India, 1980—; mem. com. Internat. Symposium Avian Endocrinology, 1988—; mem. com. Internat. Symposium Comparative Endocrinology, 1985-89; mem. com. Internat. Symposium Hormones and the Environ., 1989; mem. bd. Internat. Fedn. Comparative Endocrinology Socs., 1993—, mem. coun. 1993-97; mem. bd. Internat. Symposium Amphibian Endocrinology, 1993, 97, Internat. Symposium Fish Endocrinology, 1993—. Mem. bd. editors. Gen. and Comparative Endocrinology, 1990—; assoc. editor Zool. Studies, 1993—; bd. editors Zoologica Taiwanica, Livestock Rsch. Mem. coun. Sino-Can. Cultural and Econ. Assn., Taipei, 1986—; bd. dirs. parents assn. Taipei 1st Girl High Sch., 1987—. 2nd lt. Republic of China Army, 1960-61. Recipient Outstanding Agrl. Rsch. award Coun. of Agriculture, Exec. Yuan, 1989, Outstanding Rsch. Scientist award Coun. Nat. Sci., 1989. Mem. AAAS,Asia and Oceania Soc., Comparative Endocrinology (sec., mem. coun. 1987—, mem. found. ad hoc com. 1987, pres. 1992-96, pres. internat. orgn. com. 2nd symposium Thailand 1993, 3d Cong. Australia 1996), Endocrine Soc. Republic of China (mem. coun. 1989—), Chinese Soc. Lab. Animal Sci. (mem. coun. ad hoc com. 1989, pres. 1995-99), Soc. Study Reprodn. Buddhist-Taoist. Avocations: travel, photography, reading. Home: 16 Subln 3 Ln 61 Sect 2, Yen-Chiu-Yuen Rd, Taipei 11529, Taiwan Office: Acad Sinica Inst Zoology, Yen-Chiu-Yueng Rd Sect 2, Taipei 11529, Taiwan

YU, JONG-SUNG, chemistry educator; b. Seoul, Korea, Aug. 19, 1959; s. Yong Woon Yu and Yang Soo Kim; m. Eun Hee Lee, Dec. 23, 1988; children: Jeong Min, Ji Hyae, Shin Young. BS cum laude, Sogang U., Seoul, 1983; PhD of Sci., U. Houston, 1990. Postdoctoral fellow Ohio State U., Columbus, 1990-91; assoc. prof. Sunchon (Korea) Nat. U., 1991-93, Han Nam U., Taejon, Korea, 1993—. Contbr. rsch. articles to profl. pubs. Mem. Korean Chem. Soc. Avocations: climbing mountains, travel. Office: Han Nam U Dept Chemistry, Ojeong-Dong, 306-791 Taejon Republic of Korea

YU, KUO TSUNG (GUOCONG), chemical engineer educator; b. Guangzhou, Guangdong, China, Nov. 18, 1922; s. Chi Ho and Shiao Sha (Chen) Y.; m. Man Chuan Liang, Aug. 21, 1951; children: Xiao Ming, Xiao Hua. BCE, Southwest Associated U., Kunming, China, 1943; MS, U. Mich., 1945; PhD, U. Pitts., 1947. Asst. engr. Nat. Inst. Indsl. Rsch., Chungking, China, 1943-44; asst. prof. U. Pitts., 1948-50; prof. North Chao-Tung U., Tangshan, China, 1950-52; prof. Tianjin (China) U., 1952—, dir., 1982—; tech. cons. Mcpl. Bur. Chem. Industry, Tianjin, 1983—, Daqing (China) Petroleum Adminstrn., 1988—. Editor: Chemical Engineering Dictionary and others; chief editor Chinese Jour. Chem. Engring.; contbr. articles to profl. jours. Recipient Nat. Sci. and Technol. Advancement prize State Commn. Sci. and Tech., 1985, 87, May First medal State Union of Workers, 1985. Mem. Chinese Acad. Scis., Chem. Industry and Engring. Soc. China (hon. dir. 1988—), Rsch. Soc. Am., Phi Lambda Upsilon, Sigma Xi. Avocations: classical music, stamp collecting. E-mail: ktyu@tju.edu.cn. Office: Tianjin Univ, Chem Engring Rsch Ctr, Tianjin 300072, China

YU, KWAN LUNG, trading company executive; b. Hong Kong, Mar. 3, 1962; m. Yuk Ming Lau. Ptnr. Macrology Group, Hong Kong, 1989—, MG and Co., Hong Kong, 1991—. Office: Macrology Group, GPO Box 4238, Central Hong Kong

YU, LONG, chemist, consultant; b. Beijing, Jan. 21, 1957; d. Jizeng Yu and Deyuan Luo; m. Di Pei, May 1, 1983; 1 child, Andy. B Engring., South China U. Tech., Contan, China, 1982; PhD, Monash U., Melbourne, Australia, 1993. Assoc. rschr. Inst. Chemistry, Zhengzhou, China, 1982-86, rschr., 1986-88; vis. rsch. fellow Royal Melbourne Inst. Technology, Australia, 1988-90; R&D mgr. Therma Rite Pty. Ltd., Gold Coast, Australia, 1992-93; rsch. fellow Coop. Rsch. Ctr. Polymer Blends, Melbourne, 1993-96; scientist, project leader Commonwealth Sci. Inc. Rsch. Orgn., Melbourne, 1997—; spkr. in field. Author: The Polymeric Materials Encyclopedia; contbr. articles to profl. jours. Recipient Sci. and Tech. award Henan Academia, China, 1986, Oversea Postgrad. Rsch. award Australian Govt., 1990, Monash Postgrad. scholar, 1990. Mem. RACI. Home: 10 Torbreck St, Glen Waverly VIC 3150, Australia Office: CSIRO Divsn Materials Sci, Gate 4 Normandy Rd, Clayton 3168, Australia

YU, LU-GANG, biochemist, lecturer; b. Linqu, Shandong, China, Sept. 16, 1961; arrived in England, 1991; s. Zhen-He Yu and Shu-Yuan Zhang; m. Jie Liu; children: Tony Bing, Jessie Ying. BS, Shandong U., 1982, MS, 1986; PhD, Liverpool (Eng.) U., 1996. Asst. rsch. scientist Shanghai Biochemistry Inst. Chinese Acad. Scis., 1982-83; rsch. scientist Inst. Pharmacology and Toxicology Chinese Acad. Med. Scis., Beijing, 1986-91; European Cmty. rsch. fellow Liverpool U., 1991-92, rsch. assoc., 1993-99, lectr., 2000—. Contbr. articles to sci. jours. Pres. Liverpool Chinese Students and Scholars Assn., Liverpool, 1993-94. Avocations: reading, hiking, sports. Office: U Liverpool, Dept Medicine, L69 3GA Liverpool England

YU, MAY HUANG, librarian, educator; b. Chengdu, Sichuan, China, June 24; came to the U.S., 1989; s. Dazhou Huang and Jiangzhen Yu; m. Lixin Yu; 1 child, Michael. Student, Beijing U., 1988; LLB, State Normal U. Sichuan, Chengdu, 1982; MLS, SUNY, Albany, 1996. Cert. pub. libr., N.Y. Tchr. Fuxing H.S., Qingcheng, Sichuan, China, 1975-78; asst. prof. State Normal U. Sichuan, Chengdu, 1982-89; govt. documents libr. Alcorn State U., Lorman, Miss., 1996-97; web developer, sr. libr. tech. asst. Fla. State U., Tallahassee, 1997-99; libr. Fla. Resources & Environ. Analysis Ctr., Fla. State U., Tallahassee, 2000—; media libr., instr. Alcorn State (Miss.) U., 2000—; spl. corr. Jour. Ethics, Chengdu, 1985-89; gen. sec. Sichuan State Ethics Assn., Chengdu, 1985-89. Editor: The Dictionary of Ethics, 1987. Named Outstanding Rschr., Assn. Philosophy and Social Scis. Sichuan Province, 1987. Mem. Am. Libr. Assn. Avocations: table tennis, movies, travel. E-mail: mhyu@lorman.alcorn.edu. Fax: 601-877-3885. Home: 2160 S Frontage Rd Apt 10A Vicksburg MS 39180-5256 Office: JD Boyd Libr 1000 Asu Dr Alcorn State MS 39096-7510

YU, MING LUN, physicist; b. Hong Kong, Aug. 21, 1945; came to U.S., 1969; s. Tat Chee and Ying (Lai) Y.; m. Lynne Alison Latham, Sept. 16, 1978; children: Joyce Ginger, Elaine Lee. BSc, U. Hong Kong, 1967; PhD, Calif. Inst. Tech., 1974. Rsch. assoc. Brookhaven Nat. Lab., Upton, N.Y., 1973-74, asst. physicist, 1974-76, assoc. physicist, 1976-78; rsch. staff mem. IBM, T.J. Watson Rsch. Ctr., Yorktown Heights, N.Y., 1978-96, mgr. analytical rsch., 1984-94; prof. physics, dir. materials characterization and prep. facility Hong Kong U. Sci. and Tech., Kowloon, Hong Kong, 1996-98; sr. scientist, mgr. microcolumn applications ETEC Systems, Inc., Hayward, CA, 1998—; vis. scientist State U. N.Y. Dept. Physics, Stony Brook, 1976-78. Fellow Am. Phys. Soc.; mem. Am. Vacuum Soc. Achievements include rsch. in superconductivity, in Josephson devices, in secondary ion mass spectrometry, in surface physics and chemistry in electron beam microcolumns. Office: ETEC Systems Inc 26460 Corporate Ave Hayward CA 94545-3914

YU, MING-HUEI, mechanical engineering educator; b. Taoyuan, Taiwan, Oct. 9, 1956; s. Ar-Bau and Su-Jane (Lin) Y.; m. Ling-Ing Gloria Lee, Aug. 6, 1987; children: Kevin, Timothy. BS, Nat. Tsing-Hua U., Tsingchu, Taiwan, 1979, MS, 1981; PhD, UCLA, 1990. Asst. rsch. scientist Chun Shan Inst. Sci. & Tech., Taiwan, 1983-84; rsch. asst. Ariz. State U., Tempe, 1984-86; grad. student rschr. UCLA, 1986-90, postdoctoral scholar, 1990-92; assoc. prof. mech. engring. Nat. Sun Yat-Sen U., Kaohsiung, 1992—. Contbr. articles to profl. jours. Recipient Nat. Sci. Coun. Rsch. award, 1993. Mem. ASME, Solar Energy Soc. (organizer for acad. affairs 1993-96). Avocations: tennis, painting, baseball. Home: Apt 9F-1, 438 Hwa Rong Rd, Kaohsiung Taiwan Office: National Sun Yat-Sen Univ, Dept Mech Engring, Kaohsiung 80424, Taiwan

YU, NAI-TENG, chemistry educator; m. Julia C. Clark, June 3, 1966; children: Christopher Min-Fu, Ramona Li-Wei. BS, National Taiwan U., Taipei, 1963; MS, New Mexico Highlands U., Las Vegas, 1966; PhD, MIT, Cambridge, 1969. Adj. prof. ophthalmology Peking Union Med. Coll., Beijing, 1985—, Emory U. Med. Sch., Atlanta, 1984—; asst. prof. chemistry Ga. Inst. Tech., Atlanta, 1970-75, assoc. prof. chemistry, 1975-80, prof. chemistry, 1980-90; founding head chemistry dept. Hong Kong U. Sci. & Tech., Hong Kong, 1990—; cons. SPECTRX Corp., Norcross, Ga., 1990—; mem. Metallobiochemistry Study Sect., U.S. National Inst. Health, 1982-86; mem. Rsch. Grant Coun., Hong Kong Govt., 1993-96; chmn. Internat. Steering Com. Internat. Conf. Raman Spectroscopy, 1996—. Editor: (book) Proc. XIVth Internat. Conf. on Raman Spectroscopy, 1994; inventor in field. Dir. Hong Kong Macua Taiwanese Assn., 1996. Recipient Rsch. grants U.S. NIH, 1971-90, Rsch. Grant Coun. Hong Kong Govt., 1990-96, CIBA-Vision Corp., 1987-90. Fellow MIT; mem. Sigma Xi. Avocations: photography, symphony, travel, arts. Office: Dept Chemistry-The HK UST, Clear Water Bay, Kowloon Hong Kong

YU, PEI-SAN, business educator, marketing consultant; b. Taipei, Taiwan, May 18, 1961; d. Kwang-Chung and Wo-Chan (Fan) Y. BA, Chinese U. Hong Kong, 1983; MA, Mich. State U., 1987; PhD, U. Cin., 1991. Reporter Sing Tao Daily News, Hong Kong, 1983-85; instr. No. Ky. U., 1990-91; advisor Contemporary Art Gallery, Taichung, Taiwan, 1994; prof. dept. bus. adminstrn. Coll. Mgmt., Tung-Hai U., Taichung, Taiwan, 1991—. Mem. AMA, SCP. Office: Tung-Hai U Coll Mgmt, Dept Bus Adminstrn, Taichung 407, Taiwan

YU, PETER KWAN-NGOK, physics educator; b. Hong Kong, July 25, 1963; s. K.Y. and Y.H. (Au) Y.; m. Rebecca Ching-Wa Kwok, Aug. 26, 1989. BSc, U. Hong Kong, 1985, PhD, 1988. Chartered physicist; chartered mathematician. Assoc. prof. City U. Hong Kong, 1988—. Author: A Search for Gamma Rays--A New Area in Astronomy, 1991, Radiation and Health, 1993, Modern Applications of EPR/ESR—From Biophysics to Materials Science, 1998, Stellar Astrophysics, 1998; contbr. articles to profl. jours. Fellow Royal Astron. Soc. U.K., Royal Statis. Soc. U.K., Royal Soc. Health U.K., Royal Inst. Pub. Health and Hygiene U.K., Gemmological Assn. and Gem Testing Lab of Gt. Britain. Avocations: gemmology. Office: City U HK Dept Physics/MS, Tat Chee Ave, Kowloon HK, China

YU, PETER LEGASPI, rehabilitation physician; b. Jan. 31, 1957. BS, U. Santo Tomas, Manila, 1975, MD, 1979. Intern Vets. Meml. Med. Ctr., Quezon City, Philippines, 1979-80; resident in gen. surgery St. Clare's Hosp., N.Y.C., 1982-84; resident in phys. medicine U. Ala., Birmingham, 1987; pvt. practice, Niles, Mich., Merrillville, Ind.; pvt. practice South Bend, Ind., 1988—; attending physiatrist Meth. Hosp., Gary, Ind., 1989—, Merrillville, 1989—, Porter Meml. Hosp., Ind., 1994—, Meml. Hosp., Ind., 1988—, Lakeland Med. Ctr., Niles, 1995—, St. Anthony Med. Ctr., Crown Point, Ind., 1992—, St. Mary's Med. Ctr., Hobart, Ind., 1994—, St. Catherines Hosp., East Chicago, Ind., 1994—; rehab. dir. Healthwyn Hosp., South Bend, 1999—, Cardinal Nursing and Rehab. Ctr., South Bend, 1999—, Silverbrook Manor, Niles, Mich., 1997—. Mem. AMA, No. Ind. Rehab. Med. (pres.); Philippine Am. Physiatry Assn., (pres.-elect 1999-01), Asian Am. Med. Soc. (bd. dirs. 1999-02), Am. Acad. Phys. Medicine and Rehab., Am. Congress Rehab. Medicine, Am. Acad. Electrodiagnostic Medicine, Am. Acad. Exec. Physicians, Ind. Soc. Phys. Medicine and Rehab. Address: 8127 Merrillville Rd Merrillville IN 46410-6158 also: 115 S Saint Joseph Ave Niles MI 49120-2848

YU, PUFAN, educational administrator; b. Shanghai, People's Republic of China, July 18, 1923; s. Victor Haw and Whachan (Shi) Y.; m. Wen Chow Yu, Apr. 4, 1952; 1 child, Lanchang. BS, U. Shanghai, 1945. Engr. China Electric Co., Shanghai, 1946-49; chief testing engr. Shanghai Wired Communication Factory, 1950-58; dept. head East China Inst. Computer Tech., Shanghai, 1958-78, dep. dir., 1979-84, adviser, 1985-93; adviser East China Magnetic Recording & Electronics Corp., 1994—; chmn. Shanghai Computer Soc., Shanghai, 1984-88, hon chmn., 1989—. Chief of designers computer design J-501 large scale computer system, 1964; designer computer design two most powerful computers in China, 1973, 79; inventor high speed electronic printer, 1964; author: Digital Magnetic Recording, Peripheral Devices, 1978, 85; chief editor Computer Engring., 1989-94. Recipient Gt. Achievement award Shanghai Mcpl. Govt., 1977, 1st class award Nat. Def. Sci. and Tech. Com., Beijing, 1973-79. Office: PO Box 800-209, Shanghai 201800, China

YU, QIFENG, optical mechanics educator; b. Fengshun, China, Apr. 13, 1958; s. Yunchang and Zhiyi (Xu) Y.; m. Xiaolin Liu; 1 child, Liuqing. BSc, Northwestern Poly U., Xian, China, 1981; MSc, Nat. U. Def. Tech., Changsha, China, 1984; DrIng, Bremen (Germany) U., 1996. Lectr. Changsha Inst. Tech., Nat. U. Def. Tech., 1986-90, assoc. prof., 1990-96, prof., 1996—; vis. scholar Tech. U. Braunschweig, Germany, 1990-92. Contbr. articles to Applied Optics, Optical Engring., others. Recipient 2d pl. Hunan award of sci. and tech. Sci. Com. Hunan Province, 1989, 95, 96, 2000. Office: Changsha Inst Tech, Dept Astronautics, 410073 Changsha China

YU, QILIAN, engineering educator; b. Jiaxing, Zhejiang, China, Feb. 16, 1938; s. Yehou Yu and Wenying Ma; m. Deming Ma, Jan. 19, 1963; children: Jiahui, Jiaxuan. BS, Zhejiang U., Hangzhou, China, 1960. Asst. prof. Tianjin (China) U., 1960-78, lectr., 1979-86, assoc. prof., 1986-92, prof., 1992—; v.p. Chinese Med. Optical Instrument Standardization Com., Hangzhou, 1994—; vis. scholar U. Calif.-San Diego and Ga. Inst. Tech., 1989-91; tech. advisor Shengyang (China) Med. Instrument Factory, 1986—; gen. engr. Tianjin China Yanbo Endoscop Co., 1996—. Author 5 books including Medical Optical Instruments, 1988; contbr. papers to profl. jours.; patentee in field. Recipient 3d Class Sci. Achievement award Tianjin Sci. and Technique Com., 1988; govtl. spl. allowance State Coun. China, 1993—. Mem. Internat. Soc. Optical Engring., Biomed. Engring. Soc. China, Audio-Visual Engring. Soc. China (v.p. 1981—). Avocations: reading, music, plants, collecting stamps, chess. Office: Tianjin U Coll Precision Instrument and Opto-elec Engring, Wei jin Rd 92 Nan Kai Dist, 300072 Tianjin China

YU, QINGCHANG, science educator; b. Yuanling, Hunan, China, Dec. 23, 1938; parents Liangfu Yu and Rong Wang; m. Yunan Du, Nov. 26, 1969; 1 child, Yan. Student, Tsinhua, Beijing, 1963. Asst. Inst. Atomic Energy, Beijing, 1963-78; lectr. Inst. High Energy Physics, Beijing, 1978-86, assoc. prof., 1986-93, prof., 1993—; cons. Shenzhen (China) OUR Internat. Tech. & Scis. Co. Ltd., 1997—. Author: (books) Principles of High-Current Ion Optics, 1982, Foundation of Proton Therapy Technology, 1999; contbr. articles to profl. jours. Recipient Govt. Spl. Subsidy, State Coun., 1997. Mem. Chinese Soc. Computational Physics (mem. coun. 1998—). Avocations: Chinese literature, Chinese calligraphy. Fax: 086 01068213374. E-

mail: yuqc@alpha02.ihep.ac.cn. Office: Inst High Energy Physics, 19 Yuquanlu Rd, Beijing 100039, China

YU, ROBERT KUAN-JEN, biochemistry educator; b. Chungking, China, Jan. 27, 1938; came to U.S., 1962; m. Helen Chow, July 1, 1972; children: David S., Jennifer S. BS, Tunghai U., Taiwan, 1960; PhD, U. Ill., 1967; Med.ScD. (hon.), Tokyo, 1980; MA (hon.), Yale U., 1985. Rsch. assoc., instr. Albert Einstein Coll. Medicine, Bronx, 1967-72; asst. prof. Yale U., New Haven, 1973-75, assoc. prof., 1975-82, prof., 1983-88; prof. biochemistry, chmn. dept. Med. Coll. Va. Va. Commonwealth U., Richmond, 1988-2000; dir. Inst. Mol. Med. Genetics Med. Coll., Augusta, Ga., 2000—; mem. study sect. NIH, Washington, 1980-84, 96—; mem. Bd. Lab. Svcs., Va., 1994-98. Editor: Gangioside Structure Function and Biomedical Potential, 1984, New Trends in Ganglioside Research, 1988; contbr. over 500 articles to profl. publs. Josiah Macy scholar, 1979; grantee NIH, 1975—; recipient Va. Outstanding Scientist of Yr. award, 1995, Jacob Javits award NIH, 1984-91, Alexander von Humboldt award, 1990, GRA Eminent scholar, 2000. Mem. AAAS, Am. Soc. Cell Biology, Am. Soc. Neurochemistry (mem. coun. 1983-86, 91-95), Internat. Soc. Neurochemistry, Soc. Neurosci., Am. Soc. Biochemistry and Molecular Biology, Am. Chem. Soc., N.Y. Acad. Sci. Home: 821 River Bluff Rd North Augusta SC 29841-6056 Office: IMMAG Med Coll Ga 1120 15th St Augusta GA 30912-0004

YU, ROGER HONG, physics educator; b. Shanghai, China, Apr. 19, 1960; came to U.S., 1987; s. Rei Qian and Wei-Zen (Zhang) Y.; m. Ting Shi, Sept. 8, 1990; children: William S., John S. BS, Shanghai U. Sci. & Tech., 1982; MS, U. Mo., 1987; PhD, Mont. State U., 1990. Lectr. physics Shanghai U. Sci., 1982-85; tchg. asst. U. Mo., Kansas City, 1985-86, rsch. asst., 1986-87; tchg. asst. Mont. State U., Bozeman, 1987-88, rsch. asst., 1988-90; prof. physics Ctrl. Wash. U., Ellensburg, 1990—, dist. prof. rsch., chmn. dept. physics, 1997—; dir. undergrad. rsch. program Ctrl. Wash. U., Ellensburg, 1998—. Contbr. articles to profl. jours.; referee Phys. Rev. B. Mem. Am. Phys. Soc., Acoustic Soc. Am., Coun. Undergrad. Rsch., Associated Western Univs. (rsch. and edn. com.). Office: Ctrl Wash U Dept Physics Ellensburg WA 98926

YU, SHIAW-SHIAN, computer engineer; b. Changhua, Taiwan, June 20, 1959. B in Computer Sci., Nat. Chiao Tung U., 1981, M in Computer Engring., 1983, D in Info. Sci. & Engring., 1990. From design engr. to project engr. Electronic Rsch. & Svc. Orgn. Indsl. Technology Rsch. Inst., Hsinchu, Taiwan, 1983-90; from rsch. mgr. to dir. Computer and Comm. Rsch. Labs. Indsl. Tech. Rsch. Inst., Hsinchu, Taiwan, 1990—; assoc. prof. Yuan-Ze Inst. Technology, Taoyuan, Taiwan, 1990-93; chmn. patent rev. bd. Computer and Comm. Rsch. Labs., 1992-94. Mem. IEEE. Avocation: chess. Office: Computer Comm Rsch Labs, E000 195-11 Sect 4, Chung Hsing Chutung Taiwan, China 31015

YU, SHI-GUI, biochemist; b. Bei-Dai-He, China, Jan. 17, 1939; d. Dong-Bi Yu and Xin-Yuan Zhao; m. Zhong-Tian Xue, Feb. 4, 1968; children: Wei-Chun, Wei-Feng. Diploma in biophysics, Moscow State U., 1965; PhD, U. Lund, 1994. Rsch. asst., then rsch. assoc. Shanghai Inst. Plant Physiology, China, 1966-87; guest rschr. U. Lund, Sweden, 1987-94, rsch. scientist dept. biochemistry, 1995—. Contbr. some 50 articles to sci. jours. Grantee Carl Trygger Found., 1996, 97, 98, 99, Kungl Fysiografiska Sallaskapet i Lund, 1997, 98. Mem. Phytochem. Soc. Europe, Swedish Assn. Biochemistry & Molecular Biology. Achievements include notable findings of the domain organization of photosynthetic membrane of chloroplast; two dimensional gel protein databases for thylakoid membrane proteins, positive and regulatory effects of ultraviolet-B radiation on the structure and the function of chloroplasts, others. Avocations: music, tai-chi, badminton. Home: Sångrevägen 10C, 224 71 Lund Sweden Office: Dept Biochem/Chem Centre, Lund U PO Box 124, 221 00 Lund Sweden

YU, SHIU-LAM, engineering educator; b. Hong Kong, July 10, 1952; s. Yuen-Fong and Yu-ho (Cheung) Y. Degree in mech. engring. with honors, U. Sunderland, Eng., 1978; M of Tech. in Engring. Design, Loughborough (Eng.) U. Tech., 1983. Design draftsman Otis Elevators (H.K.) Ltd., Hong Kong, 1971-73; head of drawing office Hong Kong Electric Co. Ltd., Hong Kong, 1973-75; asst. design engr. Coles Crane Ltd., Crown Works, Sunderland, 1977; design engr. G.E.C. Reactor Equipment Ltd., Whetstone, Leicester, Eng., 1978-80; lectr. engring. design dept. mech. engring. Hong Kong Polytechnic U., Kowloon, 1980—; cons. in field, Hong Kong and Eng., 1980—. Patentee multifunctional rule design, 1988. Cultural Exch. scholar l'Alliance Française de Hong Kong, 1987. Mem. ASME, European Fedn. of Nat. Assn. Engrs., Inst. Marine Engrs. U.K. Avocations: football, volleyball, basketball, hiking, linguistics. Office: Hong Kong Polytechnic U, Dept Mech Engring, Kowloon Hong Kong Hong Kong

YU, SHU-CHENG, mineralogist, materials scientist, educator; b. Hsin-chu, Taiwan, Republic of China, Aug. 8, 1942; came to U.S., 1968; s. Dean-Schon and Tram-May (Deng) Y.; m. Lee-Jen Chen, July 23, 1970; children: Tony, Sylvia. BS, Nat. Taiwan U., 1966; MS, U. Minn., 1971; PhD, Pa. State U., 1976. Postdoctoral rsch. assoc. U. Md. and Naval Rsch. Lab., Washington, 1976-79; rsch. assoc. Northeastern U., Boston, 1979-80; prof. Nat. Cheng-Kung U., Tainan, Taiwan, 1980—; dept. head Nat. Cheng Kung U. Dept. Earth Scis., Tainan, 1987-93. Author: (textbook) Structures and Property of Crystals, 1987; patentee in field. 2nd lt. Taiwan Army, 1967-68. Mem. Am. Crystallographic Assn., Mineralogical Soc. Am., Geological Soc. China (councilor 1989-95, pres. 1991-92), Chinese Soc. Materials Sci., Astron. Soc. China, Chinese Geoscience Union (councilor 1993-95), Phi Tau Phi. Buddhist. Avocations: hiking, reading, traveling. Office: Nat Cheng Kung U, 1 Ta-hsueh Rd, 700 Tainan Taiwan

YU, SHUKUN, biochemist; b. Wendeng, Shandong, China, Mar. 27, 1958; arrived in Sweden, 1987; s. Kai-Shan and Zhen-Hua (Liu) Y.; m. Julia Liu, Dec. 22, 1983; children: Roland Julius, Richard Eric. B of Biology, Qingdao U., China, 1981; M of Biology, Academia Sinica, China, 1985; PhD in Plant Physiology, U. Uppsala, Sweden, 1992. Rsch. scientist Danisco, Denmark, 1992-94, sr. scientist, 1994—; European Commn. expert in biotech., 1999—. Contbr. articles to profl. jours.; patentee in field. Achievements include discovery of new glycogen and starch degrading pathway. Avocation: photography. Home: G Hejdemansgatan 29, S212 40 Malmoe Sweden Office: Danisco A/S Biotech, Langebrogade 1, DK1001 Copenhagen Denmark

YU, SI LE, electronics educator; b. Suzhou, Jiangsu, China, Aug. 10, 1930; m. Hua Yan, Jan. 1, 1955; two children. Diploma Elec. Engring., Nankai U., Tianjin, 1952. Asst. various depts. Tianjin (China) U., 1952-62, lectr., dep. dir. divsn. cirs. and signals, 1962-79, assoc. prof., dir. Image Info. Lab. electronic engring. dept, 1979-83, prof., chmn. electronic engring. dept., 1983-91, prof., dir. Inst. TV and Image Info., 1991-2000, prof., hon. dir. Inst., 2000—. Author: (textbook) Fundamentals of Television, 1981, 84, 88, 94, 2000 (award for Nat. Superior Textbook 1987, 96); contbr. articles to profl. jours.; patentee. Named Advanced Sci. and Technol. Worker Tianjin City, 1977, Advanced Individual for Key Sci. and Tech. Projects of the Nat. Eighth Five-Year Plan, 1996; recipient award for superior achievement Electronic Industry Min. and Nat. Bur. Stds., 1981, award for advancement of sci. and tech. State Edn. Commn., 1987. Fellow Chinese Inst. Electronics (editl. bd. Acta Electronica Sinica 1988—); mem. IEEE (sr.), Broadcast Technol. Soc. of Chinese Inst. Electronics (exec. councillor). Office: Tianjin U Inst TV/Image Info, 92 Weijin Rd, Tianjin 300072, China

YU, TELING, telecommunications company executive; b. NanXian, Hunan, China, Jan. 12, 1938; s. Zhongshu Yu and Shizhen Jiang; m. Yulan Ma; two children. Grad., HuaZong Technol. Inst., China, 1964. From technician to rsch. fellow PSM FRI, Beijing, 1964—. Author: Modern Communications and Police Communications, 1981. Mem. IEEE, China Inst. Comms., China Inst. Electronics. Home: 2808 Box, 100044 Beijing China

YU, WANSIK, medical educator; b. Taegu, Korea, Apr. 19, 1953; parents Bongkwan Yu and Hyosoon Sohn; m. In Joo Choi, Feb. 3, 1977; children: Yongjee, Byunghyuk. MD, Kyungpook Nat. U., Taegu, 1977, PhD, 1984. Med. lic. Korean Bd. Gen. Surgery. From instr. to asst. prof. to assoc. prof. Kyungpook Nat. U., Sch. Medicine, Taegu, 1985-96, prof., 1996—; dir. Cancer Rsch. Inst., Kyungbook Nat. U., Taegu, 1997—. Contbr. articles to profl. jours. Fellow Am. Coll. Surgeons; mem. Internat. Gastric Cancer Assn. (Poster prize 1995), Internat. Soc. Surgery, Internat. Soc. Digestive Surgery. Fax: 82 53 421 0510. E-mail: wyu@knu.ac.kr. Office: Kyungpool Nat U Sch Med, 50 Samduk-dong, Taegu 700-721, Korea

YU, WEN, science educator; b. Shenyang, Liaoning, China, June 30, 1966; parents Pingzhang Yu and Jianming Liu; m. Xiaoou Li; children: Huijia, Lisa. PhD, Northeastern U., Shenyang, 1995. Prof. CINVESTAV-IPN, Mexico City, 1996—. Recipient Award of Sci. and Tech., Liaoning Province, China, 1995. E-mail: yuw@ctrl.cinvestav.mx. Office: CINVESTAV-INP, Av IPN 2508, Mexico City 07360, Mexico

YU, YONG, engineering educator, robotics researcher; b. Nanjing, Jiangsu, China, Jan. 29, 1957; arrived in Japan, 1988; s. Xing Mai Yu and Yong Lian Zeng; m. Qi Gong, Apr. 27, 1985; 1 child, Sheng Hai. B in Engring., Jiangsu Inst. Chem. Tech., Changzhou, China, 1982; postgrad., Suzhou Inst. Silk Tech., China, 1986-88; M in Engring., Kyoto (Japan) U., 1991, D in Engring., 1995. Clk. Sulun Spinning Industry Corp., Suzhou, 1975-78; asst. engr. Suzhou Mech. Inst., 1982-86; rschr. Kyoto U., 1988-95; asst. prof. Kagoshima (Japan) U., 1996-99, assoc. prof., 1999—; concurrent prof. Suzhou (China) U., 2000—. Contbr. articles to profl. jours. Recipient Sci. and Tech. award Suzhou City, 1986. Mem. IEEE Robotics and Automation Soc., Inst. Sys., Control and Info. Engrs., Robotics Soc. Japan. Home: 2-2-502, Higashikohrimotocho, Kagoshima 890-0068, Japan Office: Kagoshima Univ, 1-21-40 Kohrimoto, Kagoshima 890-0065, Japan

YU, YONG MING, physiological biochemist, surgeon; b. Beijing, China, June 20, 1945; came to U.S., 1980; s. Dah-Piao and Hwa-Tzi Hsu Y.; m. Pei-Ra (Bei-Lei) Ling, Sept. 10, 1971; 1 child, Yi-Qian. MD, Peking Union Med. Coll., Beijing, 1970; PhD, MIT, 1987. Surg. resident Minhe County Hosp., Qinghai, China, 1970-78; resident, rsch. student Peking Union Med. Coll. Hosp., Beijing, 1978-80; rsch. fellow, surgery Harvard U. at Mass. Gen. Hosp. and Shriners Hosp., Boston, 1980-88; assoc. biochemist Mass. Gen. Hosp. and Shriners Burns Hosp., Boston, 1988—; instr. in surgery Harvard U., 1990-95, asst. prof. in surgery, 1995—. Contbr. articles to profl. jours. Named Co-Prin. Investigator med. rsch. program Shriners Hosp., 1985-88, 89-91, Prin. Investigator, 1992-95. Mem. Am. Burn Assn., N.Y. Acad. Scis., Am. Inst. Nutrition, Sigma Xi. Achievements include development and application of stable isotope tracer techniques for quantitative evaluation of de novo synthesis of non-essential amino acids, their relationship with essential amino acids and the nutritional importance in health and after trauma; examination of the hypothesis of clinical application of branched-chain enriched nutritional support in surgical patients; establishment of an in vivo animal model for quantifying splanchnic region amino acid metabolism under different nutritional states and routes of feeding protein and amino acid metabolism in severely burned patients; use of positron emission tomograph in metabolism research, and research on metabolic regulation of glutathione and antioxidant activity in the critically ill patients. Office: Shriners Hosp 51 Blossom St Boston MA 02114-2601

YU, YUE QING, mechanical engineering educator, researcher; b. Beijing, Peoples Republic of China, Sept. 30, 1958; s. Bao Jun and Ning Liu; m. Hong Ying Zhang, Aug. 15, 1996; children, Yang and Han. BS, Beijing Polytechnic U., 1982, MS, 1984, PhD, 1990. Asst. prof. Beijing Polytechnic U., 1984-86, lectr., 1986-90, assoc. prof., 1990-93, prof., 1993—; postdoctoral fellow U. Newcastle, Eng., 1992-93; dir. State Edn. Commn. China, Beijing, 1995—. Contbr. articles to profl. jours. including Mechanism and Machine Theory. Recipient Outstanding Youth Educator award State Edn. Commn. China, 1992, Advanced Achievement award Beijing Sci. and Tech. Com., 1992, 93, 99. Mem. China Assn. for Sci. and Tech. (China Youth Scientist award 1990), Chinese Mech. Engring. Soc., Beijing Mech. Engring. Soc. Avocations: basketball, volleyball, running, table tennis. Office: Beijing Polytechnic U, Coll Mech Engring, Beijing 100022, China

YU, ZULIANG, physicist; b. Wuxi, Jiangsu, China, Oct. 2, 1942; s. Quanhai and Qiushi (Wu) Y.; m. Yuhua Yao, Oct. 3, 1973; children: Wei, Qing. B Engring., Qinghua U., Beijing, 1966, M Engring., 1982; PhD, U. Bremen, Germany, 1992. Diplomate engring. Rsch. scientist Inst. Applied Optics, Xian, China, 1967-78; asst. prof. Nanjing (China) U., 1982-85; assoc. prof. Nanjing (China) U., 1986-88; vis. scientist U. Bremen, 1988-91, U. Hannover, Germany, 1992—. Author: Computer - Generated Holography, 1984, Optical Information Processing, 1986; inventor in field. Home: Warstr 1, D-30167 Hannover Germany Office: U Hannover Lab Info Tech, Schneiderberg 32, D-30167 Hannover Germany

YUAN, (DAVID) AIDONG, cell biologist, researcher; b. Zhoukou, Henan, China, Nov. 26, 1963; came to the U.S., 1997; s. Zhenxiang Yuan and Yumei Xiao; m. Susan Shumin Liu, Dec. 29, 1987; children: Helen Lin, Jack Bin. MD, Hunan Med. U., Changsha, China, 1986; PhD, U. Otago, Dunedin, New Zealand, 1997. Physician Xuanwu Hosp., Beijing, 1988-93; rsch. fellow U. Otago, Dunedin, 1993-94; rsch. assoc. U. Nebr., Lincoln, 1997—. Author: Cardiology Q and R, 1990; contbr. articles to profl. jours. Recipient Math. Competition award Zhoukou City Coun., 1981; rsch. fellow Sandoz Found., Australia, 1992. Mem. Am. Soc. for Cell Biology (Travel award 1996), Physiol. Soc. New Zealand, Dunedin Co. Physiologists, Internat. Dictyostelium Soc. (Travel award 1999). Avocations: fishing, reading, ping-pong, travel. E-mail: dyuan@unlserve.unl.edu. Office: U Nebr Sch Biol Scis 348 Manter Hall Lincoln NE 68588

YUAN, CHENG-YE, chemistry educator; b. Shang-yu, Zhejiang, China, Aug. 14, 1924; s. Kai-Ji and Da-Quan (Zao) Y.; m. Zhen-Kun Wang, Feb. 2, 1949; children: Chun-Mei, Chun-Su. BS, Nat. Coll. Materia Medica, Nanjiang, China, 1948; PhD, All-Union Rsch. Inst. Pharm., Chemistry, Moscow, 1955. Rsch. chemist Shanghai No. 1 Pharm. Plant, 1948-51; dep. chief engr. Ministry of Chem. Industry, Beijiang, Peoples Republic of China, 1955-56; assoc. prof. Shanghai Inst. Organic Chemistry/Chinese Acad. Scis., 1956-60, prof., 1960—; vis. prof. Univ. of Nice, France, 1983, U. New South Wales, Australia, 1991, LCC, CNRS, U. So. Calif., L.A., 1993; mem. internat. sci. bd. Internat. Conf. on Phosphorous Chemistry, Nice, 1983, Bonn, Germany, 1986, Tallinn, USSR, 1989, Toulouse, France, 1992, Jerusalem, Israel, 1995, Cin., 1998; lectr. numerous univs. including U. Calif., Berkeley, 1990, U. So. Calif., L.A., 1990, S.D. State U., 1990, U. Mass., Amherst, 1990, U. Ariz., 1991, 83, 85, 90, Moscow State U., 1989, Tech. U., Tokyo, U. Sydney, U. New South Wales, U. Melbourne, 1991, Lab. Chime Coord., Ctr. Nat. Rsch. Sci., France, others. Author: Solvent Extraction of Rare Earth, 1987 (State award 1990); inventor solvent extractants, 1982 (State award 1989); editorial bd. Solvent Extractants Ion Exch., 1983—, Phosphorus and Sulfur and the Related Elements, 1986—, Heteroatom Chemistry, 1994—; dep. editor-in-chief Jour. of the Chinese Soc. of Rare Earth, 1981-91; contbr. over 295 articles to profl. jours./publs.; patentee in field. Recipient nat. awards State Coun. of Sci. and Tech. of China/Natural Scis. 1982, Creative Invention 1985, 87, 90, Progress in Sci. and Tech., 1985, 87. Mem. Chinese Acad. Scis., Chinese Chem. Soc. (bd. dirs. 1983-90), Am. Chem. Soc. (charter mem. sub-div. separation 1982—), Internat. Coun. on Main Group Chemistry. Avocations: travel, photography. Home: 1483 Huai Haizhong Rd Rm 202, 200031 Shanghai China Office: Shanghai Inst Organic Chem, 345 Lingling Lu, 200032 Shanghai China

YUAN, CHUAN RONG, educator, academic administrator; b. Shou County, An Hui, China, Feb. 15, 1937; s. Jia Xiang and Zhang Yuan; m. Xiao Rong Wang, July 23, 1967; children: Bin, Quan. B in Chemistry, Nanjing (China) U., 1962. Asst. Nanjing U., 1962-77, lectr., 1978-84, assoc. prof., 1985-91, prof., 1992—, dean chemistry dept., 1978-82, dean gen. affairs office, 1984-87, v.p., 1988—; dean Inst. Technol. Devel. and Rsch., Nanjing, 1987-95. Author: Systematic Project and Laboratory Management, 1992 (first prize 1995); chief editor: New Theory on Public Relations Management of Organization, 1990; translator: Physical Methods in Chemistry, 1991; inventor of software. Recipeint first prize excellent thesis Fang Zheng Cup, Indsl. Annual Meeting, Chinese Inst. High Learning, Beijing, 1997, Spl. allowance and cert. state coun. State Coun. Peoples Republic China, Beijing, 1998. Mem. Industry Chinese Inst. High Learning (vice chief councillor 1992-98), Lab. Rsch. Inst. (vice chief councillor 1988-95), Pub. Rels. Assn. Jiangsu Province (v.p. 1988-98). Avocations: basketball, table tennis, swimming. Home: 52-1 Hankou Rd, Nanjing 210008, China Office: Pres Office, 52 Hankou Rd, Nanjing 210008, China

YUAN, JASON XIAO-JIAN, medical researcher, educator; b. Xintian, Hunan, People's Republic of China, May 9, 1963; s. Tian-Lin Yuan and Li-Hua Chen. MD, Suzhou (China) Med. Coll., 1983; PhD in Physiology, Peking Union Med. Coll., Beijing, 1993; postgrad., U. Md., 1993. Intern Suzhou Med. Coll. Hosp., 1982-83; resident Lanzhou (China) Med. Coll. Hosp., 1983-84; mem. sci. cadre Office Sci. and Tech. Gansu Environ. Protection Bur., Lanzhou, 1984; rsch. asst. dept. environ. medicine Gansu Inst. Environ. Scis., Lanzhou, 1984-85; postdoctoral fellow dept. physiology and medicine U. Md. Sch. Medicine, Balt., 1988-93, rsch. asst. prof. dept. physiology, 1993-96, rsch. asst. prof. divsn. pulmonary and critical care med., 1993-96, asst. prof., 1996-98, assoc. prof., 1998-99; assoc. prof. U. Calif.-San Diego Sch. Medicine, 1999—; lectr. in field; ad hoc reviewer grant applications NIH, 1995—, study section mem. Am. Heart Assn., 1995-97, 98—, exec. com. mem., 1999—; ad hoc reviewer rsch. grant applications Wellcome Trust (London), 1995, 98, U.S. Dept. Vets. Affairs, 1995. Author: Olympic Complete Words, 1988; editorial asst. Gansu Assn. Environ. Scis., 1984-85; contbr. articles to profl. jours. Parker B. Francis fellow, 1994-97. Mem. AAAS, Am. Heart Assn. (Md. affiliate rsch. fellow 1990-92, exec. com. 1999—, grantee 1990-92, 93-95, 96-98, Cournand and Comroe Young Investigator award 1995, Best Abstract award 1996, Established Investigator award 1998), Am. Physiol. Soc. (Giles F. Filley Meml. award 1995, Rsch. Career Enhancement award 1995, Lamport award 1998), Am. Thoracic Soc., Biophys. Soc., Chinese Assn. Physiol. Sci. (editl. asst. 1987-88), Soc. Chinese Bioscientists in Am. (Dr. C.W. Dunker award 1993). Home: 3775 Georgia St Apt 301 San Diego CA 92103-7608 Office: U Calif San Diego Med Ctr Divsn Pulmonary CC Medicine 200 W Arbor Dr San Diego CA 92103-1911

YUAN, LIBO, physics educator; b. Tieli, People's Republic of China, Nov. 15, 1962; s. Sucheng Yuan and Caixia (Liu) Y.; m. Lirong Liu, Aug. 20, 1989; 1 child, Tingting. BS, Heilongjiang U., 1984; MS, Harbin Shipbuilding Engr. Inst, 1990. Asst. Harbin Shipbuilding Engring. Inst., China, 1984-91, asst. prof., 1991-92, assoc. prof., 1992-96, prof., 1996—; vis. rsch. fellow N.J. Inst. Tech., Newark, 1995-97. Contbr. articles to profl. jours. Recipient Sci. and Tech. Prize Heilongjiang Province for Youth, 1997, Disting. Allowance Prize China Govt., 1998; named Disting. Young and Middle-Aged Scientist, 1996. Fellow Phys. Soc. of Heilongjiang; mem. Phys. Soc. of China, Sci. Instrument Soc. of China. Avocations: music, table tennis, walking. Office: Harbin Engring Univ, No 11 Wenmiao St, Harbin 150001, People's Republic of China

YUAN, PU, engineering educator; b. Peking, China, Sept. 5, 1934; s. Thomas Li and Yu-Kun Zhao; m. Xiang-Ya Zhang, Oct. 1, 1964; children: Qingwen, Qingsheng. BS, Beijing Petroleum Inst., 1956; MS, Tsing-Hua U., Beijing, 1958. Lectr. Beijing Petroleum Inst., 1958-69, East China Petroleum Inst., Dong-Ying, China, 1970-78; assoc. prof. East China Petroleum Inst., 1978-86; prof. U. Petroleum, Beijing, 1986—; mem. Coun. of China Automation Assn., 1994—, CNPC Indsl. Automation Edn. Com., 1986—. Author: Process Dynamic Model and Its On-Line Applications, 1994; patentee in field; contbr. articles to profl. jours. Recipient Nat. Scientific and Technology awards China Nat. Awards Com., 1990, 98, Scientific and Technology award SINOPEC, 1989, 94, 97. Avocations: recreational activities. Office: Univ Petroleum Beijing, PO Box 902, 100083 Beijing China

YUAN, SHEN-CHUAN, civil and structural engineer, consultant; b. Hangchow, Chekiang, China, May 10, 1922; came to U.S., 1963; s. Cheng-Ten and Win-Chu (Chou) Y.; m. Hazel Chien, June 11, 1949; children: Alan Y., Brad H., Cary H., Dana I. BS, Nat. Chiao-Tung U., Chungking, China, 1945; MS, U. Colo., 1967. Registered profl. engr., China, Colo., Hawaii, Idaho. Engr. Taiwan Railway Adminstrn., China, 1948-56; chief civil engring. and constrn. Taiwan Fertilizer Plant #6, China, 1956-60; chief soil divsn. Shihmem Devel. Commn., China, 1960-63; project structural engr. Stearns-Roger Engring. Inc., Denver, 1964-85; pres. Y&Y Cons. Engrs., Denver, 1986-87; cons. structural engr. Stone & Webster Corp., Denver, 1987, 88, 90, 91, 93, 97, 99, ECI, Denver, 1998, 99. Contbr. articles to Jour. Irrigation and Drainage. Recipient Dist. Svc. award Rocky Mtn. Chinese Soc. Sci. and Engring., 1991. Fellow ASCE (life mem.). Home: 2766 S Otis St Denver CO 80227-3526

YUAN, XIAO JIE, high technology professional, researcher; b. Tianjin, People's Republic of China, Nov. 4, 1957; s. Shu Ji Yuan and Li Xia Guan; m. Fenghong Zhang, July 9, 1988; children: Peijia Yuan. B.Eng., Tianjin U., China, 1982, MSc, 1986; PhD, U. Liverpool, 1995. Engr. Inst. Sensors, Harbin, China, 1982-83; lectr. Tianjin U., China, 1986-91; rsch. assoc. U. Liverpool, 1991-95; sr. engr. Chartered Semiconductor Mfg., Singapore, 1995-96; mem. rsch. staff IMEC, Leuven, Belgium, 1996—. Contbr. articles to profl. jours. Mem. IEEE. Avocations: music, reading, travelling, sports. Home: 1101 E Grand Ave Apt 8 El Segundo CA 90245-4223 Office: Inter-Univ, Microelec. Ctr., Kapeldrzef 75, B-3001 Leuven Belgium

YUAN, XUE-MING, applied mathematics researcher and educator; b. Nantong, Jiangsu, China, May 10, 1965; parents Bu-Rong Yuan and Xiao-Yu Chen; m. Yu Zhang, July 25, 1990; 1 child, Jing. BSc, Nat. U. Def. Tech., Changsha, China, 1987; MSc, Chinese Acad. Scis., Beijing, 1990, PhD, 1993. Postdoctoral fellow Inst. Nat. de Rsch. en Info. et en Automatique and Chinese c, France and China, 1993-95; visiting scholar Hong Kong U. Sci. and Tech., Hong Kong, 1995-96, rsch. fellow, 1997-98; rsch. fellow Nanyang Technol. U., Singapore, 1998—; assoc. prof. Chinese Acad. Scis., Beijing, 1994—; cons. Siemens Nixdorf, Singapore, 1998—, SONY Precision Engring. Ctr., Singapore, 1998—, Parkway Group Healthcare, Singapore, 1998—, Fedex, Singapore, 1999—; mem. Queueing theory com., 1993—. Contbr. articles to profl. jours. Recipient first award of first invention competition Jiangsu Province Govt., 1981. Mem. Asian Pacific Ops. Rsch. Ctr. (acad. sec. 1995—), Ops. Rsch. Soc. China. Avocations: badminton, fitness, music, swimming. Office: Inst Applied Math, Chinese Acad Scis, 100080 Beijing China

YUAN, YI QUAN, physician; b. Wu Xi, China, July 27, 1938. B, Southeast U., Nanjing, China, 1961. Lectr. dept. radio engring. Southeast U., Nanjing, China, 1977-86, assoc. prof., 1987-91, prof., 1992—, dir. rsch. inst., 1995—. Author: Ultrasonic Transducer, 1992; patentee in field. Vis. rsch. fellow Shanghai Inst. Ceramics Chinese Acad. Sci., 1984-90, State Key-opening Lab. Sensor, 1990-94, Modern Acoustics Lab. Nanjing U., 1994-96. Mem. Chinas Assn. Tech. (electron inst., acoustics inst.), N.Y. Acad. Scis. Communist. Avocations: basketball, shooting, swimming, erhu, opera. Office: Southeast U, Si Pai Lou #2, Nanjing 210 018, China

YUAN, ZENG REN, computer science educator, researcher; b. Sushou, Jiangsu, China, Oct. 20, 1934; s. Shu Gong Yuan and Peng Hu Li; m. Li Ying Cai, Oct. 1, 1964; children: Feng, Jun. BSc in Engring., N.E. U., Shenyang, China, 1956. Sect. chief sci. rsch. dept. automatic control Tsinghua U., Beijing, 1964-66, computer sci. tchr., 1966—; presenter in field. Author: Computer Aided Design of Control Systems, 1988, Artificial Neural Networks and Their Applications, 1999; contbr. over 110 articles to profl. jours. Fellow Chinese Soc. Automatic Control, Chinese Assn. for Computing Machinery; mem. AAAS, N.Y. Acad. Scis. Office: Tsinghua U, Dept Computer Sci and Tech, Beijing 100084, China

YUAN, ZHONG-YI, biochemistry researcher; b. Sheng, Zhejiang, China, Mar. 15, 1938. Degree in biochemistry, Fudan U., Shanghai, China, 1961; postgrad. in Enzymology, Shanghai Inst. Biochemistry. Sr. postdoctoral rsch. Artificial Cells & Organs Rsch. Ctr., McGill U., Montreal, Can., 1983-84; vis. scholar dept. physiology U. Toronto, 1984-85; rsch. assoc. Shanghai Inst. Biochemistry, Acad. Sinica, 1966-82, assoc. prof. biochemistry, 1986-91, prof., 1991—, chief Lab. Enzyme Engring., 1986—; vis. prof. Lab. Molecular Genetic, NIH, 1992-93. Contbr. over 250 sci. articles to profl. jours. including Biochemistry, Chinese Jour. Biotech., Ann. N.Y. Acad. Scis., others. Mem. Chinese Soc. Enzyme Engring. (dep. dir. 1988—), Shanghai Union Life Sci. Socs. (bd. dirs. 1995—), Shanghai Soc. Biochemistry and Molecular Biology (bd. dirs. 1994—). Achievements include invention of a new process of immobilized 5'-phosphodiesterase for production of mononucleotides (Nat. Invention prize of Sci. & Tech., China, 1979); research in purification and immobilization of various enzymes, microb. cells and mammalian cells for bioconversions and biosensors, molecular cloning enzymes and enzyme catalysis in non-aqueous media. Office: Shanghai Inst Biochem AS, 320 Yueyang Rd, Shanghai 200031, China

YUASA, HIROSHI, pharmacologist; b. Shibata-city, Japan, Mar. 3, 1953; s. Youji and Shizuko Y.; m. Kazue Emori, Apr. 29, 1981; two children. B in Pharmacy, Tokyo U. Pharmacy & Life Sci., 1976; M in Pharmacy, Kitasato U., 1978; DSc in Pharmacy, Tokyo U. Pharmacy & Life Sci., 1981. From asst. to asst. prof. Tokyo U. Pharmacy & Life Sci., Hachioji, Japan, 1981—. Mem. Internat. Pharm. Fedn., Am. Assn. Pharm. Scientists, Pharm. Soc. Japan, Acad. Pharm. Sci. Tech. Japan, Soc. Powder Tech., Japan Soc. DDS, Soc. Polymer Sci., Japanesse Assn. Crystal Growth, Japan Soc. Pharm. Machinery and Engring. Office: Tokyo U Pharmacy & Life Sci, Horinouchi 1432-1, 192-0392 Hachioji-city Tokyo Japan

YUASA, TETSUYA, engineering educator; b. Sapporo, Hokkaido, Japan, June 25, 1961; s. Toshio and Ikuko (Mikami) Y. BS, U. Tokyo, 1986, M.Engring., 1991, PhD, 1997. Rschr. Fujitsu Labs., Atsugi, Japan, 1986-89; rsch. assoc. dept. elec./info. engring. Yamagata U., Yonezawa, Japan, 1991-99, assoc. prof. dept. biosystem engring., 1999—. Contbr. articles to profl. jours. Recipient Poster award Internat. Soc. Optical Engring., 1996. Mem. Japanese Soc. Med. Imaging Tech. (program com. 1997, Paper award 1997, 98). Avocations: jogging, skiing. Home: 3-5-22-611 Ekimae, Yonezawa 992, Japan Office: Yamagata U Dept Biosystem, 4-3-16 Jonan, Yonezawa 992-8510, Japan

YÜCEER, MÜMTAZ FARUK, automotive company executive; b. Manisa, Turkey, July 12, 1947; s. Necmettin and Nezahat (Egin) Y.; div. Mar. 1989. Lic. in polit. sci., U. Ankara, 1968. Salesman Egemak, Izmir, Turkey, 1968-70, coord., 1971-74, asst. gen. mgr., 1975-87, gen. mgr., 1987—. Lt., Turkish Armed Forces Infantry, 1968-70, Istanbul. Mem. Izmir C. of C., Aegean Chamber of Industry. Office: Egemak A/S, Ankara Asfalti 30, 35110 Izmir Turkey

YÜCEER, NURULLAH, neurosurgeon; b. Niöde, Turkey, Jan. 17, 1965; s. Celal and Meliha Yüceer; m. Dinçer Yüceer, July 29, 1995. MD, Ankara (Turkey) U., 1988. Resident dept. neurosurgery Ankara U. Sch. Medicine, 1989-93, chief resident, 1993-94, mem. staff dept. neurosurgery, 1994-95; asst. prof. dept. neurosurgery Yününcü Yyl U. Sch. Medicine, Van, Turkey, 1995-98, Dokuz Eylül U. Sch. Medicine, Yzmir, Turkey, 1998—. Fax: 90-232-278-8802. E-mail: nyuceer@hotmail.com. Home: Gayret St No 21, Güzelbahçe, 35100 Yzmir Turkey Office: Dokuz Eylül U Sch Med, Ynciralty, 35340 Yzmir Turkey

YÜCEL, YONCA FATMA, lawyer; b. Ankara, Turkey, July 15, 1971; d. Mustafa Tören and Sezen (Akyol) Y. Grad., Ankara Law Sch., 1992. Law diplomate, cert. of law in English and banking-comml. law Banking and Comml. Inst., Ankara; cert. patent and competence law Ctr. for Legal Studies, Austria. Atty.-at-law, counselor Devel. Bank Turkey, Ankara, 1994-99, sr. atty.-at-law, counselor, 1999—; mem., cons. fgn. rels. com. Turkish Union Bar, Ankara, 1998—, young lawyers com., 1995—; mem., cons. fgn. rels. editl. bd. Ankara Bar Assn., 1995. Editor: Turkish Criminal LAw, 1994, The Effectiveness of Justice in Turkish Law, 1991 (Sedat Smavi Found.'s award 1991). Scholar Ctr. for Internat. Legal Studies, 1996. Mem. Internat. Bar Assn. (grant scholar 1996), Turkish Law Assn., Ctr. for Internat. Legal Studies, Met. Rotary Club, Union Internat. des Avocats, Confédération des Femmes de la Mediterranée. Avocations: playing piano and guitar, writing poetry and stories, playing tennis. Office: Devel Bank Turkey, Izmir cad # 35, Ankara Turkey

YUCHUN, WANG, science educator; b. Jilin, China, Jan. 13, 1945; s. Wang Wunxiu and Chen Peixia; m. Chen Jingxun. B of Chem. Engring., Tsinghua U., Beijing, 1970; M of Engring., Chinese Acad. Scis., Beijing, 1982; PhD in Biosci. and Biotech., U. Strathclyde, Glasgow, Scotland, 1995. Tchr. Tsinghua U., Beijing, 1970-79; rsch. assoc. Chinese Acad. Scis., Beijing, 1989-91, assoc. prof., 1985-97, prof., PhD grad. supr., 1998—; vis. scientist U. Strathclyde, Glasgow, 1989-91. Editor: Engring. Chemistry and Metallurgy, 1996-98, vice-chief editor, 1998—; contbr. rsch. articles to profl. jours.; inventor in field. Office: Nat Lab Biochem Engring, Zhong-guan-cun PO Box 353, 100080 Beijing China

YUDILEVICH, ISAAC, engineering educator, management consultant, researcher; b. Santiago, Chile, Nov. 19, 1926; arrived in Israel, 1970; s. Elias and Matilde (Levy) Y.; m. Myriam Jaimovich, Sept. 18, 1949; children: Eduardo Eitan, Gloria Galit, Patricia Paty. Diploma in Indsl. Engring., U. Chile, 1951; postgrad. in stats., Interamerican Ctr. for, Stat. Studies, Santiago, 1953; postgrad. and prof., U. Chile, 1962-64. Registered profl. engr., Israel; cert. in robotics Mfg. Engrs. Cert. Inst., U.S. Asst. tchr. metalography U. Chile, 1949-51, asst. prof. materials tech., 1952-55, assoc. prof. indsl. systems mgmt., 1962-64, dir., sr. rschr. Ctr. for Rsch. in Indsl. Mgmt., 1962-70, prof. indsl. engring., 1965-70; ind. rschr. robotics FMS, CIM, Advanced Mfg. Techs., Israel, 1971—; prof. advanced techniques for feasibility analysis Ben Gurion U., Israel, 1983, prof. performance evaluation and mgmt. of computer systems, 1984; prof. and coord. advanced engring. courses for cert. MECI/Soc. Mfg. Engrs., Israel, 1985-90; founder, chmn. Forum of Robotics and FMS SME/Israel, 1990-97; assoc. rschr., ops. rsch. and project mgmt. U. Calif., Berkeley, 1966-67; cons. Mgmt. of Indsl. and Computer Sys., Advance Mfg. Techs., Israel, 1975—; sr. cons. Seker Ltd., Amit Ltd., Israel, 1971-74; internat. bus. cons. IBCON, Mex., 1956-58, Chile, 1959-62, Inst. Planing and Devel. of Israel, 1974, numerous others in indsl. engring., Advanced Mfg. Techs. and robotics fields. Editor, co-author: Industrial Engineering Reform at University of Chile, New Definition/Activities and Curriculum, 1969; co-author: Networking Programming of Pert, 4 edits., 1964-65, 67-69; co-editor/co-author: Robotic Systems and Advanced Manufacturing Technologies, 1990; contbr. articles to profl. jours. and publs. Founder, v.p. Chilean Inst. Productivity in Bldg. and Constrn., Santiago, 1967-70; founder Friends of the Technion-Israel, Santiago, 1970; pres. Bne' Brith "Negba", Santiago, 1969-70; past dir. Israeli Country Club, Santiago. Mem. Soc. Mfg. Engrs. (life; pres. award 1992, Israeli chpt. chmn. 1990-91, Engring. Cert. chmn. 1985-95), Robotic Internat. (sr.; life; World Recruiter award 1988), Forum of Robotics and Flexible Mfg. Sys. of SME Israel (founder, chmn. 1990-97), Israeli Soc. Mgmt. Cons. (sr., exec. com. 1978), Assn. Engrs. and Architects of Israel, Israel Soc. for Computer Aided Design and Mfg., Israel Soc. Quality, Israel Soc. Informatics, Israeli Ctr. Mgmt., Internet Soc. Israel. Jewish. Avocations: writing poems, listening to music, literature, swimming, research in robotics/Advanced Manufacturing Technologies/management. Office: Mgmt Indsl and Computer Sys, 45 Jabotinsky Ave, Ramat Gan 52511, Israel

YUE, DAIYUN, literature educator; b. Guiyang, Guizhou, China, Jan. 31, 1931; s. Jin Lu and Wen (Xu) Y.; m. Yijie Tang, Sept. 13, 1952; children: Dan Tang, Shuang Tang. BA, Peking U., Beijing, 1952; D Litterarum (hon.), McMaster U., Hamilton, Ont., Can., 1990. From asst. prof. to assoc. prof. Peking U., Beijing, 1952-85, prof., 1985—, dir. Inst. Comparative Lit., 1986—; vis. fellow Harvard U., Cambridge, Mass., 1981-82; vis. prof. Calif. U., Berkeley, 1982-84, McMaster U., Hamilton, 1986-87, 92-93, Melbourne U., Australia, Leiden U., The Netherlands, 1997-98, Tech. U. of Hong Kong, 1999-2000. Author: The Theory of Comparative Literature, 1987 (1st prize 1988), Intellectual in Chinese Fiction, 1986, Modern Chinese Literature and Comparative Literature, 1987, A Dictionary of World Poetics, 1992. Mem. Internat. Comparative Lit. Assn. (v.p. 1990-98), Chinese Comparative Lit. Assn. (pres. 1989—). E-mail: tyjydy@pku.edu.cn. Home: # 103 Apt 13 Lang Run Yuan, Beijing 100871, China Office: Peking U, Inst Comparative Lit, Beijing 100871, China

YUE, NORA YIK-LO, entrepreneur, researcher; b. Hong Kong, Hong Kong, Apr. 8, 1964; d. Cheung-Suen and Wong-Yiu (Wong) Y.; m. Raymond Ka-Hon Lung, Oct. 10, 1998. BSc in Engring. with 1st class honors, U. London, 1987, MSc, DIC, 1988; PhD, Imperial Coll., London, 1992. Sr. rsch. assoc. Goldsmith's Coll., London, 1993-96, Imperial Coll., London, 1996-98; nat. project coord. family learning millennium awards scheme Pre-sch. Learning Alliance, London, 1998-2000; founder Pinkpepper.co.uk, 2000—. Contbr. articles to profl. jours. Recipient Mae's Prize for Math., U.K., 1983, Overseas Rsch. Studentship award, London, 1989-92. Mem. IEEE, IEEE Computer Soc., Instn. Elec. Engrs. U.K., Assn. Computing Machinery.

YUE, YI, operations analyst, physicist, engineer; b. Urumqi, Xinjiang, China, Feb. 28, 1963; d. Guangren and Xiuru (Wang) Y.; m. Jun Wang, Apr. 21, 1987; children: Wang, Jiapei, Geoffrey. BS, U. Sci. & Tech. of China, 1985, MS, 1988; PhD, U. Sydney, 1997. Rsch. scientist cyrogenic lab. Chinese Acad. Scis., 1988-91; vis. scholar U. NSW, 1991-93; rsch. student U. Sydney, 1993-96, rsch. asst., 1997; rsch. scientist Def. Sci. and Tech. Orgn., Australia, 1997-2000; sr. rsch. scientist, 2000—. Contbr. articles to profl. jours. Mem. Australian Soc. Ops. Rsch. Office: Def Sci & Tech Orgn, Land Ops Divsn PO Box 1500, Salisbury 5108, Australia

YUE, ZHONG QI, civil engineer, educator, consultant; b. Xuan Cheng, Anhui, People's Republic of China, Jan. 15, 1962; s. Zhen Kai and Gui Zheng (Sun) Y.; m. Yao Xun, Aug. 15, 1992; children: Linda R., Wendal V. BSc, Peking U., Beijing, China, 1983, MSc, 1986; PhD, Carleton U., Ottawa, Can., 1992. Registered profl. engr., Hong Kong. Asst. engr. Ministry Constrn. China, Beijing, 1986-88; rschr. Nat. Rsch. Coun. Can., Ottawa, 1992-96; geotech. engr. Halcrow Asia Partnership Ltd., Hong Kong, 1996-98, sr. geotech. engr., 1998-99; asst. prof. U. Hong Kong, 1999—. Contbr. articles to profl. jours. including Can. Jour. Civil Engring., Jour. Engring. Sci., Can. Geotech. Jour., Internat. Jour. Applied Math. Modelling, Internat. Jour. Analytical and Numerical Methods for Geomechanics, ASCE, Jour. Elasticity, among others. Recipient Halcrow Tech. Paper award Halcrow Group (Eng.), 1997, Excellence Engring. Project award Min. Constrn. China's Comprehensive Inst. for Geotech. Engring. and Surveying (China), 1987; Nat. Sci. and Engring. Rsch. Coun. Can. fellow, 1992. Mem. ASTM, Assn. Profl. Engrs. Ont., Hong Kong Instn. Engrs., Can. Soc. for Civil Engring., Can. Geotech. Soc., Geo. Soc. Hong Kong (exec. mem. 1998-99). Avocations: tai-ji martial arts, swimming, fishing, travel. E-mail: yeuqzq@hkucc.hku.hk. Office: U Hong Kong/Dept Civil Engr, Pokfulam Rd, Hong Kong China

YUECHIMING, ROGER YUE YUEN SHING, mathematics educator; b. Mauritius, Feb. 25, 1937; s. James and Marie Yuechiming; m. Renée Bethery, Nov. 9, 1963; children: Françoise, Marianne, Isabelle. BSc with 1st class honours, U. Manchester, Eng., 1964, PhD, 1967. Asst. U. Strasbourg, France, 1967-69, lectr. math. U. Paris VII, 1970—; participant math. confs. and seminars in numerous countries; referee various math. jours. Contbr. over 80 articles on ring theory to sci. jours. of numerous countries. Mem. French Math. Soc., Am. Math. Soc., London Math. Soc., Belgian Math. Soc., Japan Math. Soc. Achievements include introduction of concept of p-injective modules and the more generalized notion of YJ-injectivity, new approaches in ring and module theory leading to a better understanding of von Neumann regular rings, V-rings, self-injective rings and generalizations. Home: 38 rue du Surmelin, 75020 Paris France Office: U Paris VII Unité Mixte de Rsch, 9994 CNRS 2 Pl Jussieu, 75251 Paris France

YUEN, SHIU YIN KELVIN, engineering educator; b. Hong Kong, May 9, 1963; s. Hong Keung and Kum Shan Diana (Dang) Y. Higher diploma dept. electronic engring., Hong Kong Polytech., 1984, MPhil dept. electronic engring., 1988; DPhil, Sch. Cognitive/Computing Scis., Sussex, U.K., 1992. Summer trainee Simmons Engineered Products Ltd., 1982; assoc. dept. electronic engring. Hong Kong Poly., 1985, rsch. asst. 1 dept. electronic engring., 1986-87, vis. lectr. dept. electronic engring., 1987-88; tutor U. Sussex, Hong Kong, 1989-90; lectr., univ. lectr., asst. prof. dept. electronic engring. City Univ., Hong Kong, 1992—; reviewer Image and Vision Computing, U.K., Pattern Recognition Letters, IEEE Procs, IEEE Trans. Pattern Analysis and Machine Intelligence. Contbr. articles to profl. jours. Croucher Found. scholar, 1990, 91; Sir Edward Youde Meml. fellow Sir Edward Youde Meml. Coun., 1988; strategic grantee City U., 1992, 93, 94, 98, direct allocation grantee City U., 1999, competitive earmarked rsch. grantee Rsch. Grants Coun., 2000. Mem. IEEE. Avocations: astronomy, seeing movies, cycling, hiking, badminton. Office: City U Dept Elec Engring, 83 Tat Chee Ave, Kowloon Hong Kong

YUFIK, YAN MARK, director research development; b. Jan. 22, 1946. MS, Odessa Poly. U., 1968; PhD, Kalinin U., 1973; postgrad, U. Calif., 1981. Sr. scientist General Atomic, Calif., 1981-83; sr. advisor, v.p. R&D NCR Co., Ohio, 1983-85; sr. scientist FMC Co., Calif., 1985-87; dir. R&D Inst. Med. Cybernetics, 1987—. Home: 12204 St Taures Rd Potomac MD 20854

YUH, IN-SUH, agricultural science educator; b. Hoing-Sung, Kangwondo, Korea, June 24, 1958; s. Yoon-Taek and Chae-Soon (Park) Y.; m. Jeong-Hyun Jung, Dec. 13, 1986; children: Ju Eun, Ju-Hae, Seong-Soo. BS, Kangwon Nat. U., Chuncheon, Korea, 1982; MS, Seoul Nat. U., Suwon, Korea, 1984; PhD, U. Wis., 1991. Rsch. asst. Nat. Livestock Rsch. Inst., RDA, Suwon, Korea, 1985-86, U. Wis., Madison, 1987-91; prof. Kangwon Nat. U., Chuncheon, 1991-93, asst. prof., 1993-97, assoc. prof., 1997—; dept. chmn. dept. of dairy sci. Kangwon Nat. U., 1999—. Editl. bd., coun. mem. Korean Jour. of Animal Reprodn., 1994—; editl. bd. Korean Jour. of Dairy Sci., 1998—. 2d lt. The Res. Mil. Acad., 1994-95. Mem. Endocrine Soc., Soc. for Exptl. Biology and Medicine. Home: Toigye Jugong Apt, 213 dong #802 Toigyedong, Chuncheon Korea Office: Coll Animal Resource Sci, Kangwon Nat U Hyozadong, Chuncheon 200-701, Korea

YUHAN, HAI, physicist; b. Luocheng QianWei, Sichan, China, May 30, 1939; s. Baozhang Hai and Wanhong Lin; m. Yang Yurong, may 13, 1972; 1 child, Hao Hai. BS, Nankai U., Tianjin, China, 1961. Prof. Inst. Electronics, Acad. Sinica, Beijing, 1961—. Inventor in field; contbr. numerous articles to profl. jours. Recipient Academia Sinica Achievement prize, Industry/Sci. Rsch., 1980, Golden prize, in nat. patent, 1993. Mem. IEEE (sr., Signigicant Achievement prize 1999), AAAS. Achievements include the devel. of the abnormal photoconduction response of a-SiH films, a-SiH target vidicon, a-SiH liquid crystal light valve, field-enhanced a-SiH photoemitter, nonlinear charge intensification effect in a-SiH and NC-SiH. Office: Inst Electronics/Acad Sinica, Zhong Guan Cun Rd 17#, 100080 Beijing China

YUHARA, TAKAMICHI, rheumatologist; b. Ryugasaki, Japan, Feb. 20, 1958; parents Katsumi Yuhara and Haruyo Yuhara; m. Kyoko, June 7, 1992; 1 child, Mikiko. MD, U. Tsukuba, 1982. Resident U. Tsubuka Hosp., 1982-88; physician Kitaibaraki Mcpl. Hosp., Japan, 1988-90, Mito Genl. Hosp., Hitachinaka, 1990-91, U. Tsukuba, 1991—. Author: Drugs of Today, 1997; contbr. articles to profl. jours. Mem. Japanese Soc. Internal Medicine, Japan Rheumatism Assn., Japanese Soc. Clin. Immunology. Office: U Tsukuba Clin Med, Tennodai 1-1-1 Tsukuba, Ibaraki 305-8575, Japan

YUI, DAIZABURO, educator; b. Kamakuro, Japan, Dec. 2, 1945; s. Hajime Y. and Yuriko (Suzuki) Arai; m. Mitsue Tamaki; children: Mikiko, Gentaro. BA, U. Tokyo, 1968, MA, 1970; PhD, Hititsubashi U., Tokyo, 1985. Asst. prof. Meiji U., Tokyo, 1974-79, assoc. prof., 1979; assoc. prof. Hitotsubashi U., Tokyo, 1980-87, prof., 1987-96; prof. U. Tokyo, 1996—; rsch. assoc. U. Calif., Berkeley, 1984-86, U. Md., College Park, 1995; dean student affairs Hititsubashi U., 1992-94l acting dir. Ctr. Am. Studies, U. Tokyo, 1998—. Author: The Formation of the Postwar World Order, 1985, The Unfinished Reform in the Occupied Japan, 1990 (Mainich Press award 1990), The Gap of War Memory Between Japan and the USA, 1995, Living with the Bomb, 1997. m. Coun. Learned Soc. fellow, N.Y.C., 1984-86, Abe fellow, Tokyo, 1995. Mem. Japanese Assn. Am. Studies (exec. dir. 1996—). Avocations: mountain climbing, skiing, music. Office: U Tokyo Grad Sch Arts & Sci, 3-8-1 Komaba Neguro, Tokyo 153, Japan

YUI, NOBUHIKO, science educator; b. Yamaguchi, Japan, Mar. 24, 1958; s. Isamu and Hisae (Nohara) Y.; m. Fumiko Yamashita, Jan. 9, 2000; children: Chiaki, Tomoaki. BS, Sophia U., Tokyo, 1981; MS, Sophia U., 1983, PhD, 1985. Asst. prof. Tokyo Women's Med. Coll., 1985-88, 89-93; doctoral rsch. fellow Univ. Twente, Enschede, The Netherlands, 1988-89; assoc. prof. Japan Advanced Inst. Sci. and Tech., Ishikawa, 1993-98; prof. Japan Adv. Inst. Sci. and Tech., Ishikawa, 1998—; bd. dirs. Japanese Soc. Artificial Organs, Tokyo. Author: Advances in Polymeric Systems for Drug Delivery, 1994; mem. editl. bd. Jour. Biomaterials Sci.; contbr. numerous articles to profl. jours. Recipient Outstanding Rsch. award Soc. Biomaterials U.S.A., 1985, Young Investigator award Japanese Soc. Biomaterials, 1993, 49th Worthy Invention award Sci. and Tech. Agy. Japan, 1990, Outstanding Paper award Japanese Soc. Artificial Organs, 1997, Cygnus Recognition award for excellence in guiding student rsch. Controlled Release Soc., 1997. Mem. Soc. Polymer Sci. Japan (mem. organizing com. Biomed. Polymer), Japan. Soc. Biomaterials (bd. dirs.), N.Y. Acad. Scis. Office: Japan Adv Inst Sci and Tech, Tatsunokuchi, Ishikawa 923-1292, Japan

YUKSELEN, ADIL MAHMUT, academic administrator; b. Kayseri, Turkey, Jan. 15, 1953; s. Mehmet Haci Yukselen and Emine (Basaran) Y.; m. Emine Colak, June 14, 1976; children: Ozlem, Alper Mehmet. BS, Istanbul (Turkey) Tech. U., Turkey, 1974; MS, Istanbul (Turkey) Tech. U., 1976, PhD, 1987; MS, ENSAE, Toulouse, France, 1988. Asst. aero. engring. dept. Istanbul Tech. U., 1976-87, lectr., 1987-88, assoc. prof., 1988-99, prof., 1999—. Contbr. numerous articles to profl. jours. Avocation: aircraft modelling. Office: Faculty Aeronautics & Aero, Istanbul Technical U, 80626 Istanbul Turkey

YULE, ALEXANDER, theologian; b. Melbourne, Victoria, Australia, Dec. 18, 1941; s. Alexander and Jean Russel (Ward) Y.; m. Dorothy Fay Bainbridge, Jan. 31, 1964; children: Rebecca, Martin. BA with 1st honors, U. Melbourne, Victoria, 1963; BD with 1st honors, Melbourne Coll. Divinity, 1965; ThD cum laude, Princeton Theol. Sem. Ordained to ministry, 1970. Tutor U. Melbourne, 1963; master in residence Princeton (N.J.) Theol. Seminary, 1966-68; tutor Ecumenical Inst., Chateau de Bossey, Celigny, Switzerland, 1969-70; gen. sec. Australian Student Christian Movement, Melbourne, 1970-75; lectr. Swinburne Coll. of Tech., Melbourne, 1975, U. Melbourne (previously Melbourne Coll. of Advanced Edn.), 1976-95; lectr. in theology Sia'atoutai Theol. Ctr., Nafualu, Tonga, 1997—. Author: Making Peace, Making Sense, 1988, (with Jen Glaser) Classroom Dialogue and the Teaching of Thinking, 1994; contbr. articles to profl. jours. Min. Uniting Ch. of Fitzroy, 1972-81; min. in assn. Ch. of All Nations, Carlton, Victoria, 1982-96. Home: Sia'atoutai Theol Coll, Nafualu Tonga

YULE, ANDREW MORRISON, broadcasting director; b. Edinburgh, Scotland, Dec. 27, 1972; s. Robert Morrison and Christene Robb (Webb) Y.; m. Sharon Margret Elizabeth Magill, Apr. 12, 1997. Grad. in Elec. and Electronic Engring., Canterbury U., Christchurch, New Zealand, 1994; B of Broadcasting Comm., Christchurch Poly., 1997. Technician Ctrl. Power, Palmerston North, New Zealand, 1992-93, Radio New Zealand, Palmerston North, New Zealand, 1993-94, New Zealand Broadcasting Sch., Christchurch, 1995-96; prodr., dir., technician various film/TV/video prodns., Holywood, Calif., and New Zealand, 1995—; editor/graphics numerous TV commls. Ruffell Films, Christchurch, New Zealand, 1997-99; tutor digital video post prodn. New Zealand Broadcasting Sch., 2000—. Prodr./dir. (film) Never Again, 1996 (Acad. TV Arts and Scis. summer internship 1996). Mem. creative/music team Spreydon Bapt. Ch., Christchurch, 1992—. Avocations: movies, music, concert/theatre lighting, motion graphics. Home: 43 Rahera St, Christchurch New Zealand

YU-LEE, REGINALD TOMAS, internet executive; b. Dayton, Ohio, May 3, 1964; s. Rudolph Mario and Winifred Earline (Webster) Lee; 1 child, Erin Jeong Mi. B in Engring., U. Dayton, 1987, M in Engring., 1994, PhD in Engring., 1997. Staff engr. Montgomery County, Dayton, 1987; devel. engr. IBM, Dayton, 1987-91; pres., chief oper. officer Bus. Dynamics & Rsch., Dayton, 1994-96; from asst. prof. to assoc. prof. Sinclair Coll., Dayton, 1991-96; sr. cons. Oracle Cons., 1996-97; from mgr. to sr. mgr. Ernst & Young LLP, Cin., 1997-99; dir., digital supply chair Sapient Corp., Atlanta, 1999—; cons. Sinclair Coll., 1991-94; mentor underpriviledged minority students; cons. Dayton Daily News, 1993-94; guest lectr. Black Leadership Dayton; developer Adopt-a-Class program. ontbr. articles to profl. jours. Mem. Parity 2000 Econ. Devel., Dayton, 1995. Mem. Inst. Indsl. Engrs., Soc. Mfg. Engrs., Am. Prodn. and Inventory Control Soc., Omega Psi Phi. Home: Apt 5416 1401 W Paces Ferry Rd NW Atlanta GA 30327-2460 Office: Sapient Corp 600 N Park Town Ctr 1200 Abernathy Rd NE Ste 1400 Atlanta GA 30328-5670

YULEK, MURAT ÂLI, economist, engineer; b. Ankara, Turkey, Jan. 15, 1968; s. Ertan Ibrahim and Gurcan Gurcu (Kaplanci) Y.; m. Elif Çakir, Feb. 8, 1992; children: N. Bera, Mehmet C. BSc in Mech. Engring., Bogazici U., Istanbul, Turkey, 1988; MS in Mgmt., Boston U., Brussels, 1989; MA in Econs., Bilkent U., Ankara, 1990, PhD in Econs., 1996; M Pub. and Pvt. Mgmt., Yale U., 1994. Expert State Planning Orgn., Prime Min. Turkey, Ankara, 1989-91; tchg. asst. Bilkent U., Ankara, 1991-92, instr., 1994-97; tchg. asst. Yale U., New Haven, 1993-94; mktg. and sales dir. Etibank Corp., Ankara, 1997; project officer Islamic Devel. Bank, Jeddah, 1998—; cons. The World Bank, Washington, 1993, 94. Author: Economic Policies of Singapore, 1991, Financial Liberalization and the Real Economy: The Turkish Experience, 1998, Financial Policy in a Repressed Market: Turkey (1950-79), 1998; contbr. articles to profl. jours. Mem. Am. Econ. Assn., European Econ. Assn. Islam. Avocation: pilot license for lightweight aircraft. E-mail: myulek@yahoo.com. Office: Islamic Development Bank, PO Box 5925, 21432 Jeddah Saudi Arabia

YULIANG HE, physics educator; b. Beijing, Feb. 28, 1934; s. Fengshu He and Genru Shi; m. Bangyui Gong, Feb. 20, 1961 (div. Feb. 1990); children: He Peiwei, He Piegi; m. Heining Peng, June 25, 1993 (div. May 19998); 1 child, Peng Cheng. Grad., Fudan U., Shanghai, 1955. Cert. prof. Asst. Nanjing U., China, 1956-64, lectr., 1964-85, assoc. prof., 1985-91, prof., 1991—; vis. prof. Beijing U. Aeronautics and Astronautics., 1992-98. Author: The Amorphous Semiconductor Physics, 1989; patentee in field. Sr. scholar Harvard U., 1985-87. Mem. Amorphous Physics Soc. China, Electronics Soc. China, Physics Soc. Am. Avocation: classical music. Home: Suogen 2 Village, Bldg 21 Rm 404, Nanjing 210042, China Office: Shanghai Wayon Adv Materials, 16 Kunming Rd, Shanghai 200082, China

YUMOTO, NOBUO, manufacturing company executive; b. Nishinomiya, Hyogo, Japan, Nov. 25, 1936; s. Toyokichi and Haru Y.; m. Tokiko Takemura, Mar. 24, 1967; children: Yoko, Natsuko. BEE, U. Tokyo, Japan, 1960. Gen. mgr. systems divsn. Sumitomo Electric Industries Ltd., Osaka, Japan, 1983-86, sr. gen. mgr. R & D and systems businesses, 1986-88, mem. bd. dirs., 1988-91, bd. mng. dirs. in charge R & D, IP, prodn. tech., 1991-96, sr. mng. dir., 1996-99, corp. advisor, 1999—. Mem. IEEE, Intelligent Transp. Soc. Am. (bd. dirs. 1991—), Vehicle, Road and Traffic Intelligence Soc. (bd. dirs. 1994—), Vehicle Info. and Comm. Sys. Assn. (vice-chmn. 1991-95, bd. dirs. 1995—). Achievements include contribution to deployment of Vehicle Information and Communication System. Home: 1-4-22 Nakayama-Dai, Takarazuka Hyogo 665-0876, Japan Office: Sumitomo Electric Ind Ltd, 1-1-3 Shimaya Konohana-ku, Osaka 554, Japan

YUMOTO, TAKAKAZU, tropical ecologist, educator; b. Ikeda, Japan, Mar. 11, 1959; s. Hitomu and Yuriko (Hori) Y.; m. Kayo Suzuki, Apr. 28, 1984; children: Yuki, Karin, Sinya, Genki. BS, Kyoto (Japan) U., 1982, MS, 1984, PhD in Ecology, 1987. Asst. Kobe (Japan) U., 1989-92, lectr., 1992-94; assoc. prof. Kyoto U., 1994—. Author: Yakushima Island, 1995, Tropical Rainforest, 1999. Office: Kyoto U Ctr Ecol Rsch, Kamitanokami-hirano, Shiga Otsu 520-2113, Japan

YUN, CHANG HEE, management association administrator, researcher; b. Chung Song County, Korea, Feb. 6, 1967; s. Sang Ho Yun and Sam Chun (Park) Y. Graduate, Hankuk U. of Fgn. Studies, 1993. Clk. Samsung Fire & Marine Ins. Co., Seoul, Korea, 1993-94; asst. mgr. Korea Mgmt. Assn., Seoul, 1995—; head internat. ops. Korea Fin. Planner Assn. Author publ.: Cook Grammar, Cooked is Complicated English. Vol. English interpreter Seoul Olympics Internat. Weightlifting Fedn., Seoul, Korea, 1988, English interpreter Boy Scouts 17th World Jamboree, Korea, 1991; chief of mgmt. for past Asian Boy Scout Jamboree, Mt. Sorak, 1996. With Korean Army, 1989-90. Avocations: swimming, travel, fgn. contacts. Office: Korea Mgmt Assn 3d Fl, Koryo Bldg 544 Dohwa 1 Dong, Mapo-ku Seoul 121-704, Korea

YUN, DANIEL DUWHAN, physician, foundation administrator; b. Chinjoo, Korea, Jan. 20, 1933; came to U.S., 1959; naturalized, 1972; s. Kapryong and Woo Im Yun; m. Rebecca Sungja Choi, Apr. 13, 1959; children: Samuel, Lois, Caroline, Judith. BS Coll. Sci. and Engring., Yon-Sei U., 1954, MD, 1958; student, U. Pa., 1963; PhD, Barrington U., 1995. Intern Quincy (Mass.) City Hosp., 1960; resident and fellow Presbyn.-U. Pa. Med. Ctr., Phila., 1961-65; med. dir. Paddon Meml. Hosp., Newfoundland, Labrador, Can., 1965-66; dir. spl. care unit Elkins Park (Pa.) Hosp., 1967-79; founder, pres. Philip Jaisohn Meml. Found., Inc., Elkins Park, Pa., 1975-85, also med. dir., trustee; clin. prof. medicine U. Xochicalco, 1978; faculty Allegheny U. Health Scis., Phila.; bd. dirs. Elkins Park Hosp. Mem. Bd. Asian Studies Found., U.S. Senatorial Bus. Adv. Bd.; mem. home safety com. Mayor's Commn. on Svcs. to Aging, Phila.; trustee United Way of Southeastern Pa., co-founder Rep. Presdl. Task Force; mem. U.S. Congl.

Adv. Bd.; cons. on Korean affairs Phila. City Coun.; hon. mem. adv. coun. Peaceful Unification Policy of Korea; trustee Albright Coll., Reading, Pa., 1997—; chmn. bd. Korean-Am. Christian Broadcasting of Phila.; mem. Phila. Internat. City Coord. Com.; commr. Pa. Human Rels. Commn., 1991—; founder, pres. Korean Heritage Found., 1991—; amb. City of Phila., 1991. Recipient Phila. award Human Rights award, 1981, Disting. Cmty. Svc. award Phila. Dist. Atty., 1981, medal of Merit Presdl. Task Force, 1981, Medal of Nat. Order, Republic of Korea, 1984, Nat. Dong Baek medal Republic of Korea, 1987, award City Coun. Phila., 1987, Gov.'s Pa. Heritage awards, 1990, commendation award Pa. Senate, 1991, award Asian Law Ctr., 1991, Rep. Senatorial Medal of Freedom, 1994; named to Legion of Honor, The Chapel of Four Chaplains; named Amb. City of Phila., 1991. Mem. AMA, Am. Soc. Internal Medicine, Am. Coll. Cardiology, Am. Heart Assn. (mem. coun. on clin. cardiology), Pa. Med. Soc., Phila. County Med. Soc., Royal Soc. Health, Am. Coll. Internat. Physicians, World Med. Assn., Fedn. State Med. Bds., Am. Law Enforcement Officers' Assn., Am. Fedn. Police, Internat. Culture Soc. Korea (hon.), Am. Soc. Contemporary Medicine and Surgery. Home: 3903 Somers Dr Huntingdon Valley PA 19006-1913 Office: 60 Township Line Rd Elkins Park PA 19027-2220

YUN, JAE HOON, engineer; b. Suwon, Korea, Sept. 10, 1960; s. Bo-sup and Soon-ja (Chung) Y.; m. Bok-lan Lee, May 4, 1991; children: Chang-ho, Gin-yong. B, Chungang U., Seoul, Korea, 1984, M, 1986, PhD, 1999. Project leader Elec & Telecomm Rsch. Inst., Taejon, Korea, 1990—. Inventor, patentee in field. Recipient Tech. prize KEES, Korea, 1994. Avocations: mountain climbing, travel. Home: Gaeryong Apt Ladong 102, 127-1 Moonwha-dong, Taejon 131-130, Korea Office: Elecs & Telecomm Rsch Inst, 161 Kajong-Dong, Taejon 305-350, Korea

YUN, JAMES KYOON, electrical engineer; b. Andong, South Korea, Oct. 26, 1965; came to U.S., 1973; s. Joh Kyong and Karen Suk (Kim) Y. BSEE, U. Ill., 1987, MSEE, 1989. System engr. GE Co., Syracuse, N.Y., 1989-91, software engr., 1991-93; software engr. Martin Marietta Corp., Syracuse, 1993-95; sr. mem. engring. staff Lockheed Martin Corp., Moorestown, N.J., 1995—; cons. Silver Knight Co., Liverpool, N.Y., 1994—. Inventor seal indicator. Mem. IEEE, Assn. for Computing Machinery, Tau Beta Pi, Eta Kappa Nu.

YUN, MICHELLE WONHE, librarian; b. Seoul, South Korea, July 18, 1936; d. Tchi-Chang and Jinsil Virginia (Sohn) Y.; m. Myungsoo Chun, Aug. 22, 1955 (div. Mar. 1963); m. Yoon-Choo Kim, June 15, 1968 (div. Dec. 1972). Student, Purdue U., 1955-57; BA magna cum laude, U. Pitts., 1974; MLS, Columbia U., 1977. Registered profl. libr., N.Y. English instr. Korean Lang. Sch., N.Y.C., 1978-79; translator, synopsis writer Asian Bilingual Curriculum Devel. Ctr., Seton Hall U., N.J., 1979-82; journalist Korean East Asian Daily News, N.Y.C., 1981-82; translator, lang. officer, analyst U.S. Dept. of Army, 1982-95; ret., 1995; English tchr. Korean Ministry Edn., 1996-98. Vol. Friends of Librs. of Montgomery County, Md., 1995—; mem. Friends of Book Arts Press, Columbia U., 1977—; mem. Montgomery chpt. ARC, 1995. Colby Coll. dean grantee, 1955. Mem. NAFE, Internat. Women's Assn. World Peace, Alumni Assn. U. Pitts., Alumni Assn. Columbia U., Alumni Assn. Kyongki Girls H.S. Avocations: rare books, calligraphy, piano, opera, concerts. Address: 1121 University Blvd W Wheaton MD 20902-3356

YUN, PETER LOK WAI, dental researcher; b. Hong Kong, Aug. 3, 1965; arrived in Australia, 1995; s. Ding Wah and Ngan Nui (Chan) Y.; m. Yuen Yee Cheng, July 2, 1990; 1 child, Matthew Hong Yin. BS in Biomed. Sci., U. Ulster, Ireland, 1989; MS in Immunology, Brunel U., London, 1993; PhD in Dentistry, U. Sydney, Australia, 2000. Med. lab. sci. officer John Radcliffe Hosp., England, 1990-93; lectr. Hong Kong Polytech. U., 1993-95; rsch. scientist Inst. Dental Rsch., Sydney, 2000—. NHMRC Australia scholar, 1996. Fellow Inst. Biomed. Sci.; mem. Australian Inst. Med. Sci. Avocations: table tennis, badminton, swimming, reading. Office: Inst Dental Rsch, 2 Chalmers St, Sydney 2010, Australia

YUN, SEI-EOK, bioelectrochemistry and biotechnology educator; b. Ansong, Kyungki, South Korea, Feb. 16, 1948; s. Nam-Hon and Jong-Nye (Lee) Y.; m. Hee-Joo Lee, Sept. 22, 1985; 1 child, Hyoung-Seon. BA, Korea U., Seoul, 1971, MA, 1973; PhD, Nagoya (Japan) U., 1982. Asst. prof. Chonbuk Nat. U., South Korea, 1984-89, assoc. prof., 1989-94, prof., 1994—; vis. rschr. Osaka (Japan) U., 1993-94. Contbr. articles to profl. jours. including Jour. Biotech. Techniques, Electroanalytical Chemistry, Electro and Magnetobiology. Grantee Korea Sci. and Engring. Found., 1995, 97, Korea Rsch. Found., 1998. Mem. Korean Soc. Applied Microbiology, Korean Soc. for Biotech. and Bioengring. Soc. for Biosci. and Bioengring. Avocations: classical music, swimming, mountain climbing. E-mail: seyun@moak.chonbuk.ac.kr. Office: Chonbuk Nat U, 664-14, Dukjin-dong, Dukjin-ku, Chonju Chonbuk 561-756, South Korea

YUN, SOK-HON, food chemist, researcher; b. Seoul, Republic of Korea, Mar. 26, 1958; came to Australia, 1988; s. Chul-Jung Yun and Ok-Jin Jung; m. Son-Mi Pak, Oct. 25, 1988; children: Yojun, Youngmin. BSc, Yonsei U., Seoul, 1983; PhD, U. Sydney, Australia, 1993. Nat. technol. cert. in quality control, Republic of Korea. Tech. officer Oriental Brewery Ltd., Seoul, 1983-87; tutor, rsch. asst. U. Sydney, 1988-92; sr. rsch. scientist Bread Rsch. Inst. Australia Ltd., Sydney, 1993—; project leader Quality Wheat CRC Ltd., Sydney, 1995—; hon. overseas rsch. scientist Rural Devel. Adminstrn., Korea, 1999—; rschr. in field. Contbr. articles to profl. jours. Mem. Royal Australian Chemistry Inst., Korea Orgn. in Food Sci. and Tech., Korean Assn. in Sci. and Tech. in Australia (gen. sec. 1994-96), Korean Scholar Assn. in Australia (auditor 1994). Avocations: rock climbing, bush walking, tennis, golf. E-mail: hyun@wheatcrc.csiro.au. Fax: 9888 5821. Home: 28 Alison St Eastwood, Sydney NSW 2122, Australia Office: BRI Australia Ltd, PO Box 7 North Ryde, Sydney NSW 2113, Australia

YUN, SOO IN, physics educator, researcher; b. Kyungjoo, Korea, Nov. 6, 1937; s. Jang Suk and Kae Won (Son) Y.; m. Hyun Young Huh, June 30, 1968; children: Zee Sun, Hee Sun, Dong Joo. BS, Pusan (Korea) Nat. U., 1960, MS, 1962; MS, Carnegie-Mellon U., 1970; PhD, Okla. State U., 1972. From lectr. to assoc. prof. dept. physics Pusan Nat. U., 1966-79, prof., 1979—, chmn. dept. physics, 1977-81, 99—, prof. dept. physics, 1979-95, dean acad. affairs, 1987-89, pres., 1995-99; vis. asst. prof. Okla. State U., Stillwater, 1973, vis. scientist, 1976. Hon. fellow U. Wis., 1985-86, Cultural award Nulwon Found., Pusan, 1992, Rsch. award Pusan Nat. U., 1976. Fellow Korean Phys. Soc. (v.p. 1993, rsch. award 1982); mem. Am. Phys. Soc., Optical Soc. Am. Home: Lucky Apt 18-803, 707 Oncheon-Dong, Pusan 607 753, Republic of Korea Office: Pusan Nat Univ, Dept of Physics, Pusan 609 735, Republic of Korea

YUNG, ALEXEI VICTOROVICH, research physicist; b. Leningrad, USSR, Mar. 26, 1957; s. Victor Nicolaevich Yung and Ulia Stepanovna Zaitseva; m. Elena Nicolaevna Filatora, Apr. 30, 1978 (div. Nov. 1995); children: Tania, Igor; m. Olga Alexandrovna Khrapkina, Feb. 15, 1996; 1 child, Lev. PhD in Physics, U. Leningrad, 1980; postgrad. student, Inst. Nuc. Physics, St. Petersburg, Russia, 1982-86. Jr. rschr. Inst. Nuc. Physics, St. Petersburg, 1986-89, rschr., 1989-90; postdoctoral rschr. Internat. Sch. for Advanced Studies, Trieste, Italy, 1990-92; sr. rschr. Inst. Nuc. Physics, St. Petersburg, 1992—. Contbr. articles to profl. jours. Rsch. grantee Russian Found. Rsch., Moscow, 1993, 96, 99, Soros Found., Moscow, 1994, 95 Royal Soc. Kapitsa fellow, London, 1994. Office: Petersburg Nuc Physics Inst, Gatchina, 188350 St Petersburg Russia

YUNG, BABINGTON CHUN-KUEN, radiologist; b. Hong Kong, China, July 30, 1959; s. Kwan Yung and Yip Hin Yeung; m. Donna Yuk-king Mok, June 24, 1984; children: Eva, Helen. MB BChir, U. Hong Kong, 1983. Diplomate Am. Bd. Nuclear Medicine, Am. Bd. Radiology. Resident Med. and Health Dept., Hong Kong, 1984-90; clin. and rsch. fellow Johns Hopkins Med. Instns. Johns Hopkins U., Balt., 1990-93; resident, asst. clin. prof. U. South Ala., Mobile, 1993-96; med. and sr. med. officer United Christian Hosp., Hong Kong, 1996—; examiner Hong Kong Coll. Radiologists, 1998; mem. task group on clin. referral guideline on positron emission tomography Hosp. Authority, Hong Kong, 1999. Author: (book) Nuclear Imaging in Drug Discovery, Development and Approval, 1993; contbr. sci. articles to profl. publs. Mem. Soc. Nuclear Medicine. Baptist. Avocations: bodybuilding, soccer. Fax 852 2379 4139. E-mail: jcschan@ha.org.hk. Office: United Christian Hosp, 130 Hip Wo St Kwun Tong, Kowloon Hong Kong China

YUNG, EDWARD KAI-NING, engineering educator; b. Hong Kong, China, Feb. 7, 1947; s. Fung-Ping Chan; m. Winnie Ming-Fen Fu, Mar. 21, 1981; children: Kenneth Yung Kin-On, Kitty Yung Kin-Ting. BSEE, U. Miss., 1972, MSc, 1974, PhD, 1977. Rsch. assoc. U. Ill., 1977-78; from lectr. to sr. lectr. Hong Kong Poly., 1978-84; prin. lectr., prof., chmn. prof. City U. Hong Kong, 1984—, head dept. elec. engring., 1995—; chmn. electronics divsn. Hong Kong Inst. Engrs., 1996-97, v.p., 1999—; pres. Hong Kong Assn. for the Advancement of Sci. and Tech., 1998-99; chmn. Piers '97, Hong Kong, 1997; chmn. Asia Pacific Microwave Conf., Hong Kong, 1997. Founding mem. Progressive Party, Hong Kong, 1994—; chmn. Assn. Experts China's Modernization, 1989-90; mem. engring. panel Rsch. Grants Coun., 1994—, electronics panel Industry & Tech. Devel. Coun., 1994—. Centenary scholar Queen's Coll., Hong Kong, 1964. Fellow Inst. Elec. Engrs., Hong Kong Assn. Advancement Sci. & Tech., Hong Kong Inst. Engrs. (coun. mem.), Chinese Inst. Elect.; mem. Engring. Coun. (chartered engr.). Office: City U Hong Kong, Tat Chee Ave, Kowloon Hong Kong China

YUNG-SILVA, JOSE BAYAN, immunology educator; b. Buenaventura, Colombia, June 22, 1967; s. Jose Bayan Yung Valero and Maria Nelly de Yung; m. Maria-Rosario Navarrete-Nino, Mar. 14, 1992. B, Sem. San Buenaventura, 1983; BS, U. Andes, Santafe de Bogotá, Colombia, 1988; MSc, U. Javeriana, Santafe de Bogotá, Colombia, 1993; postgrad., U. Costa Rica, San Jose, 1991; MBA, U. Externado de Colombia, 2000. Bacteriologist Hosp. Infantil, Bogota, Colombia, 1988-90, Hosp. La Misericordia, Bogota, Colombia, 1990-93; chief clin. immunology lab. Hosp. San Jose, Bogota, Colombia, 1993-96; prof. U. Los Andes, Bogota, Colombia, 1990-94, asst. prof., 1994-96; lab. specialist, sales rep. Johnson & Johnson Ortho-Clin. Diagnostics, Bogota. 1995—; prof. Colombian Dentist Coll., Bogota, 1991-92. Contbr. articles to profl. jours. Mem. Am. Soc. Microbiology, Assn. Bacteriologists, Colombian Soc. Parasitology and Tropical Medicine, Am. Assn. for Clin. Chemistry. Avocations: movies, travel, theater, scuba diving. Home: Apt 205, Carrera 27 #45A-56, Bogota Colombia Office: Johnson & Johnson Med, Calle 94A # 13-74, Santa Fe de Bogota Colombia

YUNKER, TODD ELLIOTT, writer; b. Corvallis, Oreg., June 30, 1960; m. Robert Allen and Deborah Pauline (Lamb) Y.; m. Jennifer Ann Olsen, Apr. 13, 1990; 1 child, Alex Devin. Student, Chemeketa C.C., Salem, Oreg., 1978-79, 90—; BS in Comm., Oreg. State U., 1993. Author: The Alternate; writer film scripts including Miss Direction (Scouts Honor award, Pacific N.W. Writers Conf. Editors award), The Alternate (Kay Snow award), My Clone Sleeps Alone, Of Shoes and Ships and Sealing Wax (award), Winds of Chance. Home: 4784 Ravine Ct NE Salem OR 97305-2540

YUNQUAN, LUO, physician, surgeon, researcher; b. Huoqiu, Anhui, China, Oct. 10, 1963; s. Luo Benyou and Tu Guangying; m. Shen Jiazhen, Jan. 23, 1991; 1 child, Luo huining. B Medicine, Anhui Med. U., Hefei, China, 1987; M Medicine, 2d Mil. Med. U., Shanghai, 1992, MD, 1995. Specialist in hepatobiliary surgery. Physician-in-charge East Hosp. of Hepatobiliary Surgery, Shanghai, 1995-98, assoc. prof., 1998—. Contbr. articles to profl. jours. Mem. Chinese Med. Assn. Home: KM 101/No 2/Range 255, Changhai Rd, Shanghai 200438, China Office: East Hosp Hepatobil Surgery, No 225 Changhai Rd, Shanghai 200438, China

YUNSHAN, QIN, marine geologist; b. Shenyang City, Liaoning, China, June 1, 1933; m. Chen Lirong, Dec. 1, 1962; children: Xiao'en, Xiaoming. BS, Beijing Coll. Geology, 1956; PhD, Inha U., Incheon, South Korea, 1994. Asst. rschr. Inst. Oceanology, Chinese Acad. Scis., Qingdao, 1956-61, asst. prof., 1962-78, assoc. prof., 1978-86, prof., 1986—; academician Chinese Acad. Scis., Beijing, 1995—; chmn. China SCOR, Beijing, 1992-95. Author: Geology of the Bohai Sea, 1985 (2d prize on natural scis. Chinese Acad. Scis. 1986), Geology of the East China Sea, 1987 (1st prize on natural scis. of Chinese Acad. scis. 1988), Geology of the Yellow Sea, 1989 (2d prize on natural scis. of Chinese Acad. Scis.); chief editor Oceanologia et Limnologia, 1995—. Mem. Chinese Soc. Oceanology and Limnology (bd. chmn. 1992—). Home: 5 Qihe Rd, Qingdao 266071, China Office: IOCAS, 7 Nanhai Rd, Qingdao 266071, China

YUN-XIANG, DENG, chemistry educator and researcher; b. Xing ning, Guangdong, China, Oct. 25, 1935; s. Deng Shui-Lian and Huang Fu-Zhao; m. Yuan Xiang-Ying, Aug. 14, 1962; children: Deng Hai, Deng Hong. Grad., Zhongshan U., Guangzhou, China, 1958. Asst. Zhongshan U., Guangzhou, 1958-66, tchr., 1967-78, lectr., 1978-80, assoc. prof., 1983-85, prof. chemistry, 1985—, chmn. dept. chemistry, 1985-92; guest scholar Kyoto (Japan) U., 1980-82; mem. pedagogical guide com. of chemistry The Edn. Com. of Chinese U., 1990—. Author: Principles of Product on Poly(vinylchloride) Resin, 1982, Introduction of Polymer Chemistry, Physics and Applications, 1997, Ethylene and Its Fine Chemical, 2000; editor Synthetic Resin and Plastics Jour., 1985—, Guangzhou Chem. Industry and Tech. Jour., 1985—. Mem. Chem. Industry and Engring. Soc. of Guangdong (v.p. 1987—), Chemistry and Industry Soc. Guangzhou (v.p. 1988—). Avocation: Chinese chess. Address: Zhongshan Univ, Pu-Yuan-Qu 607-403, Guangzhou 510275, China Office: Zhongshan Univ, Dept Chemistry Kang-Yue, Guangzhou 510275, China

YUREGIR, GUNES T., biochemist, educator; b. Adana, Turkey, Dec. 26, 1930; d. Niyazi and Zeynep (Osmanovich) Tabakoglu; m. Yalcin Remzi Yuregir, May 21, 1955. BA, Am. Girls' Coll., Istanbul, 1950, Wellesley Coll., 1952; MS, Tufts U., 1955. Rsch. asst. Kresge Rsch. Ctr., Ann Arbor, Mich., 1955-56, U. Mich., Ann Arbor, 1956-58; chief clin. lab. Adana State Hosp., Turkey, 1961-68, Adana Numune Hosp., 1968-72; chief clin. lab. to chief dept. biochemistry Cukurova U. Med. Faculty, Adana, 1972-97; cofounder Med. Faculty, Kahramanmaraz Sutcu Imam U., Turkey, 1998—, vice dean, 1999—. Author: Clinical Biochemistry, 1987; editor: Trace Elements in Health and Disease, 1991, New Technology in Biochemistry, 1995. Mem. Am. Chem. Soc., Assn. Clin. Chemistry (U.K.), Biochem. Soc. (Turkey) Hematol. Soc. (Turkey), Hematol. Soc. (Europe). Avocations: travel, books, music, walking.

YURENEV, ALEXEI PAVLOVICH, cardiologist, researcher; b. Moscow, Jan. 20, 1945; s. Pavel Nikolaevich Yurenev and Nina Petrovna Obnorskaya; m. Lilia Grigorievna Lipkina; children: Yulia, Elena, Inna, Alexei. MD 2d. Moscow Med. Inst., 1967; Candidate in Med. Scis., Cardiology Rsch. Ctr., Moscow, 1972, D in Med. Scis., 1984. Prof. cardiology 1990—. Resident Cardiology Rsch. Ctr., Moscow, 1967-69, fellow, 1969-72, jr.-sr. rschr., 1972-84, chief outpatient clinic, 1984—; chief cardiologist Moscow Health Dept., 1987—; chief, chair. cardiology, Moscow Med. Acad., 1989—. Coauthor: The Hypertensive Heart, 1994; contbr. articles to profl. jours. and chpt. to book; inventor and patentee in field. Fellow Am. Coll. Cardiology, Am. Heart Assn.; mem. N.Y. Acad. Scis., Internat. Acad. Informatisation (pres. clin. medicine br. 1994—), Lions Club Internat. (charter mem.; Melvin Johns fellow, dist. gov. 1995-96). Avocations: history, music, literature, art. Home: Osennaya 2-130, 121609 Moscow Russia Office: Cardiology Rsch Outpatient, 3rd Cherepkovskaya 15A, 121552 Moscow Russia

YURI, YOSHIKAZU JOHN, computer company executive; b. Matsumoto, Nagano, Japan, Oct. 25, 1951; s. Yoshinobu and Noriko (Ota) Y.; m. Akemi Kokado, May 29, 1976; children: Masaki, Yasuhiro. B in Engring., U. Osaka, 1976. Sales engr. Marubun Corp., Tokyo, 1976-82; mktg. mgr. Marubun USA Corp., Menlo Park, Calif., 1982-86; dir. bus. devel. Marubun Corp., Tokyo, 1986-94; pres., rep. dir. AST Rsch. (Japan) K.K., Tokyo, 1994-95; v.p. Acer Japan Corp., Tokyo, 1995-96, Iomega Corp. USA, 1996-98; rep. dir. Iomega (Japan) Corp., 1996-98; pres., CEO Vertex Link Corp., Tokyo, 1998—; pres. Linksys Japan Corp., Tokyo, 1998—; chmn. VICS Tech., Inc., 1999—; pres. Vertex Axis Corp., 1999—; dir., gen. mgr. Marubun Taiwan, Inc., Taipei, 1989-94; dir., v.p. Marubun Singapore Pte. Ltd., 1991-94, Marubun USA Corp., Menlo Park, 1991-94. Avocations: glass art, photography, essayist, world travel, tennis. Home: 3-8-5 Takaido Higashi # 101, Suginami Tokyo 168, Japan Office: Vertex Link Corp, 1-8-11 Kanda Surugadai, Tokyo 101-0062, Japan

YURSO, JOSEPH FRANCIS, engineering manager; b. Hazleton, Pa., July 5, 1930; s. Joseph James and Anna (Payne) Y.; m. Helen Elizabeth Michel, Dec. 17, 1955 (dec. Aug. 1988); children: Joseph Michael, Joanne Elizabeth; m. Barbara Lee Bergen, Apr. 17, 1993. BSME, Pa. State U., 1952; MSME, U.S. Naval Postgrad. U., 1960; hon. degree, Carnegie Mellon U., 1973. Registered profl. engr., Va., Conn. Commd. ens. USN, 1955, advanced through grades to capt., 1975; planning and quality assurance officer, supr. shipbldg. USN, Groton, Conn., 1967-71; ship maintenance officer to comdr. in chief Atlantic Fleet USN, Norfolk, Va., 1971-75; dep. CEO to supr. of shipbldg. conversion and repair USN, Newport News, Va., 1975-77; prodn. officer Norfolk Naval Shipyard USN, Portsmouth, Va., 1977-79; supr. of shipbldg., CEO USN, Groton, Conn., 1979-81; shipyard comdr., CEO Portsmouth Naval Shipyard USN, 1981-84, ret., 1984; group mgr., chief engr. Q.E.D. Sys., Inc., Virginia Beach, Va., 1986-96, dir. tech. devel., 1996—; sr. investigator Naval Sea Sys. Command, Washington, 1974-75, 78-79, 83-84. Contbg. author: Naval Engineering and American Sea Power, 1989; contbr. to profl. publs. Pres. Atlantic Fleet Credit Union, Norfolk, 1974-79, Emmanuel Luth. Ch., Virginia Beach, 1985-87. Recipient Legion of Merit. Mem. ASME, Am. Soc. Naval Engring. (chmn. tidewater sect. 1990-91, mem. nat. coun. 1990-92, Presdl. award 1991, 92, Frank G. Law award 1994, nat. v.p. 1993-96, nat. pres. 1997-99), Am. Soc. Quality Control (vice chmn. 1991-92, chmn. 1992-95, Presdl. award 1992), Soc. Naval Archs. and Marine Engrs. (chmn. programs 1991-92). Achievements include providing leadership in improving industrial performance of Portsmouth Naval Shipyard, to improve utilization of fleet/U.S. Navy maintenance facilities, introduction of new concepts of quality assurance to U.S. Navy shipbuilding and repair. Home: 4629 Player Ln Virginia Beach VA 23462-4639

YURTSEVEN, OMER, marketing and business educator; b. Bursa, Marmara, Turkey; s. Mehmet and Meliha (Sayliman) Y. BA, Ankara (Turkey) Acad., 1974; MBA, U. New Haven, 1981; MA, U. Tex., 1984, PhD, 1988. Bus. analyst Pusan, Ankara, 1976-77; mgr. Ramada Inn, Conn., 1979-81; rsch. asst. U. Tex., 1983-88, rsch. assoc., 1988-89; mng. dir., owner Chelsea Internat./USA, 1989-93; vice chmn. dept. bus. adminstrn. Hacettepe U., Ankara, Turkey, 1993—; cons. Has Holding, Ankara, 1993-94, UNICEF, Ankara, 1994-95; instr. Cen. Bank, Republic Turkey, 1993—; instr. MBA program Bilkent U., Baskent U.; mem. exec. bd. Turkish Sci. Rsch. Couns. Turkish Industry Mgmt. Assn., Hacettepe Cleaning Corp. Coauthor: (book) Population Issues in Turkey, 1993; contbr. articles to profl. jours. Founding mem. Hacettepe U. Scholarship Fund, 1995—. Lt. Turkish Army, 1977. Tex. Pub. Edn. grantee, 1983; overseas scholar Turkish Govt., 1976, Merit scholar Belgian Govt., 1975. Mem. Bus. Adminstrn. Found. (treas. 1994—). Avocations: theater, soccer, jogging, classical music, philosophy. Office: Hacettepe U, 11BF Dept Bus Adminstrn, 06532 Beytepe Ankara Turkey

YURYEV, VLADIMIR ARTHUROVICH, physicist, researcher; b. Moscow, May 6, 1963; s. Arthur Nikolayevich and Lidia Alekseyevna (Snopova) Y.; m. Tatyana Valeryevna Krasnova, Sept. 23, 1995; children: Nikolay, Maria. Engr./Physicist, Moscow Inst. Physics/Tech., 1986, PhD, 1990. Engr./rschr. P.N. Lebedev Phys. Inst. of Russian Acad. Sci., Moscow, 1985-86; engr./rschr. Gen. Physics Inst. of Russian Acad. Sci., Moscow, 1986-89, jr. rsch. scientist, 1989-91, rsch. scientist, 1991-93, sr. rsch. scientist, 1993-98, sr. rsch. scientist Natural Sci. Ctr., 1998-99, head of lab., 1999—. Contbr. articles to profl. jours. Mem. Gen. Physics Inst. Russian Acad. Scis. Avocation: mountaineering. Office: Nat Sci Ctr Gen Physics Inst of RAS, 38 Vavilov St bldg L2, 117942 Moscow Russia

YUS, MIGUEL, organic chemistry educator; b. Zaragoza, Spain, Sept. 11, 1947; s. Miguel Yus and Angeles Astiz; m. Carmen Najera, Oct. 9, 1973; children: Eva, Miguel. BS, Faculty of Scis., Zaragoza, 1969, MS, 1971, DSc, 1973; postdoctoral, Max Planck Inst., Mülheim/Ruhr, Germany, 1974-75. Asst. prof. U. Oviedo (Spain), 1976-86, prof., 1987; prof. U. Alicante (Spain), 1988—; head dept. Organic Chemistry Alicante U., 1990—. 2d lt. Spanish Army, 1970. Avocations: sports, music, travel. Home: Llevant 9, 03110 Mutxamel Alicante Spain Office: Univ Alicante APDO 99, 03080 Alicante Spain

YUSHCHENKO, ALEXANDER GEORGIEVICH, radiophysicist, researcher; b. Lozovaya, Kharkov, Ukraine, July 22, 1955; s. Georgey Ivanovich and Lidiya Victorovna (Popova-Prints) Y.; m. Irene Vaycheslavovna Bondarenko, Apr. 18, 1960; children: Ann, Elias. BS, Kharkov State U., 1979, MS, 1981, PhD, 1989; sr. doctorates candidate, Nat. Tech. U. of Ukraine, Kiev, 1996. Engr. Microwave Devices Lab./Kharkov State U., 1981-83, rschr., 1983-90, sr. rschr., 1990-91, head of group, 1991-96; head of group Inst. radiophysics and Electronics/Nat. Acad. Scis., Kharkov, 1997—; mem. U.S.-Ukraine Sci. and Tech. Working Group, 1998—; engr. NII-Priborostroeniya, Zhykovskiy, Russia, 1982-83, rschr., 1983-90, sr. rschr., 1990-91; head band pass filters designer Leninetz Leningrad, Kiev Rsch. Inst. Radio-Measurement Equipment, Kiev, 1991-92; sci. advisor of Kharkov Dolphinarium, 1998—. Patentee in field; contbr. articles to profl. jours. Maj. Soviet Mil. Group, 1973-75. Grantee State Com. on Sci. and Tech. of Ukraine, 1993, Min. of Sci. and Tech. of Ukraine, 1997. Mem. IEEE, N.Y. Acad. Scis. Panteist. Achievements include contributions to design of filters, transmission lines and test fixtures; hypothesis of young dolphin intellect forming by human as a task of integrating the noossphaira consciousness. Avocations: philosophy, biology, dolphin intellect. Home: Kvartira 7, Symskaya 74, 310002 Kharkov Ukraine Office: Inst Radiophysics/Elect, Ulitsa Proskury 12, 310085 Kharkov Ukraine

YUSHCHENKO, VIKTOR, prime minister of Ukraine. Chmn. Nat. Bank of Ukraine; prime min. Ukraine, Kiev, Ukraine, 1999—. Office: Cabinet of Mins, 12/2 Hrushevskiy St, 01008 Kiev Ukraine

YUSHINA, LUDMILA DMITRIEVNA, chemist; b. Kazan, Russia, Oct. 14, 1929; d. Dmitrij Nicolaevich and Taisija Deomidovna (Anisimova) Y.; m. Semion Abramovich Brajnin, Oct. 18, 1954; 1 child. Diploma, Ural State U., 1952, diploma in chem. scis., 1958. Master shop Optical Plant, Sverdlovsk, Russia, 1952-53; scientist Inst. Electrochem., Russian Acad. Scis., Sverdlovsk, Russia, 1956-63, leader analytic lab., 1963-65, sr. rschr., 1965-86; scientific counsellor Inst. High-Temp Electrochem. Russian Acad. Scis., Ekaterinburg, 1986—; cons. in field. Contbr. articles to profl. jours.; inventor in field. Mem. N.Y. Acad. Scis., Internat. Soc. Solid State Ionics. Avocation: piano. Office: Inst High Tem Electrochem, Russian Acad Sci, 620219 Ekaterinburg Russia

YUSICHENKO, NIKOLAY YURY, immunologist, consultant; b. Lviv, Ukraine, Apr. 5, 1949; s. Yury Ivan and Olga Peter (Mandrykin) Y.; m. Elena Mikhail Pisartzeva, June 1970 (div. Sept. 1983); 1 child, Ekaterina; m. Natalia Alexander Gavinsky, Dec. 10, 1983. MD, Odessa (Ukraine) Med. Inst., 1972, State Sch. Electropuncture, Riga, Latvia, 1983, Dnepropetrovsk Med. Inst., Krivoi Rog, Ukraine, 1985, Odessa Mil. Dist., 1995, Moscow State AIDS Ctr., 1996, Kharkov (Ukraine) Med. Inst., 1997. Cert. in secondary immunodeficiency. Scientist State Inst. Marine Hygiene, Moscow, Odessa, 1976-83; doctor State Hosps., Odessa, 1983-93; doctor, acupuncturist Health Ctr. Sanatorium, Odessa, 1993-95; chief specialist clin. dept. State Odessa Regional AIDS Ctr., 1995-96; chief specialist cross infections and HIV/AIDS Dept. Health Odessa City Adminstrn., 1996-97; chief specialist HIV/AIDS med. cons. Dept. of State Out-Patient Clinic, Odessa, 1997-98; chief specialist infectious diseases and HIV/AIDS Odessa State Ctr. Pub. Health Promotion, 1998—; adviser Nongovt. Orgn. (med. adviser, con., provider of med. care, condr. sci. investigations, pub. rels.), UNITY Assn. HIV-infected persons of Odessa region, Odessa, 1995—; cons. Dept. Health Odessa City Adminstrn., 1997—; cons., tel. advising coord. non-govt. org. Hope, Faith, Love, Odessa, 1999—. Author: Manual of Clinic and Differential Diagnosis Knowledge in HIV/AIDS, 1996, Clinical Examinations and Observations on HIV/AIDS Drugusers, 1997, HIV-Infection, 1999. With Ukrainian Navy, 1972-76. Mem. Heraldic Dept. All-Russian Nobleman Assembly (hon. corr.), Brit. Coun., N.Y. Acad. Scis. Achievements include patent for method of therapy HIV opportunistic infections. Avocations: dogs, sailing. Office: PO Box 22, 65044 Odessa 44, Ukraine

YUSSOUFF, MOHAMMED, physicist, educator; b. Cuttack, India, Aug. 14, 1942; came to U.S., 1991; s. Haji and Nurunnisa Fakhruddin; m. Farhana Begum, Apr. 6, 1969; children: Ashraf, Zeenat, Mustafa. MSc, Delhi U., 1963; PhD, Indian Inst. Tech., Kanpur, 1967. Prof. physics Indian

Inst. Tech., Kanpur, 1967-90; vis. prof. physics Mich. State U., East Lansing, 1991—; guest scientist Ford Rsch., Dearborn, Mich., 1991-97, GM Tech. Ctr., Warren, Mich., 1997-98, Delphi Tech. Ctr., Warren, 1999—; vis. scientist U. Köln, Germany, 1972-74, U. Western Ont., London, Can., 1990-91; Humboldt scientist Atomic Energy Agy, Jülich, Germany, 1979-81; vis. prof. U. Konstanz, Germany, 1986-89; mem. com. physics examination Pub. Svc. Commn., Delhi, India, 1976-86, rsch. grants Univ. Grants Commn., Delhi, 1985-90; dir. Internat. Sch. on Band Structure, Indian Inst. Tech., 1986; creator Slow Pace program for tchg. sci. and engring. to deficient students with poor econ. or sch. backgrounds. Editor: Electronic Band Structure and Its Applications, 1987, The Physics of Materials, 1987. Mem. Am. Phys. Soc., Internat. Ctr. Theoretical Physics (assoc.). Islam. Achievements include patents for monitoring the catalytic converters in cars; rsch. in theory of freezing, kinetic model of catalysis, theory of disordered systems, chaneling, clusters, electronic structure, ionic conductors, exhaust gas sensors, superconductors, zeolites, fundamental rate constants of catalytic reactions and foundations of quantum theory. Home: 31011 Grandview St Westland MI 48186-5065 Office: Mich State U Dept Physics East Lansing MI 48824-1116 also: GM and Delphi Tech Ctr Warren MI 48090-9005

YUSSUF IZZUDDIN GHAFARULLAH-LAHU SHAH, SULTAN AZLAN MUHIBBUDDIN SHAH, Sultan of Perak; b. Batu Gajah, Perak, Malaysia, Apr. 15, 1928; s. Sultan Yussuff Izzuddin Shah; m. Tuanku Bainum binti Hohd, 1955; children: Raja Nazrin, Raja Azureen, Raja Ashman, Raja Eleen, Raja Yong Sofia. Student, Malay Coll., Nottingham U. and Lincoln Inn.; DLitt (hon.), U. Malaya, 1979, U. Sains Malaysia, 1980. Bar: Eng. 1954. Asst. sec. state Perak, 1954-55; magistrate Kuala Lumpur, 1955-56; session camp resident Perak, 1957-59, fed. counsel and Dy pub. prosecutory, 1959, state legal advisor, 1959-62; registrar high ct. Kuala Lumpur, Malaysia, 1962-63; chief registrar Fed. Ct., Kuala Lumpur, 1963-65, high ct. judge, 1965, fed. judge, 1973, chief justice, 1979; Lord Pres., 1982-83, 34th Sultan of Perak, 1984—, named King of Malaysia, 1989-94. Author: The Role of Constitutional Rulers. Co-chancellor U. Sains Malaysia, 1971; chmn. Higher Edn. Adv. Council, 1974; v.p. Olympic Council, Malayisa. Decorated PMN, 1979, SSM, 1983. Mem. Internat. Hockey Fedn., Malaysian Hockey Fedn. (pres.). Office: Istana Iskandarish, 33000 Kuala Kangsar, Perak Malaysia*

YUSTOVA, ELISAVETA NICOLAEVNA, physician, researcher; b. Warsaw, Russia, Oct. 29, 1910; d. Nikolai Lavrentievich Yustov and Maria Wladimirovna Sacharova; m. Michail Grigorievich Veselov, 1932 (dec. Nov. 1987); 1 child, Anna. Grad., Pedagog. Coll., Zaraysk, Moscow, 1927, Leningrad U., 1932; Candidate of Sci., All-Union Rsch. Inst. Metrol., Leningrad, 1947, DSc, 1976. Cert. in optica-colorimetry. Sci. worker State Optical Inst., Leningrad, 1932-38; aspirant All-Union Rsch. Inst. Metrology, Leningrad, 1938-47, Leningrad U., Elabuga, 1941-44; sr. rschr. Optical Inst., Leningrad, 1947-53, All-Union Rsch. Inst. Metrology, Leningrad, 1953; chmn. Among Dept. Com. Colorimetry, Leningrad, 1963-71; hon. mem. Acad. Metrology, Leningrad, 1994—. Author: (book) Colorimetry, 2000; contbr. articles to profl. jours. Recipient Hon. Sighn for achievements in standardization, 1967, Gold medal Exhbn. of Achievement of Nat. Industry and Agr., 1968, medal Vet. of Labor, 1979, medal Inventor of USSR, 1983. Home: Home 4 St Sovietskya, Tosno Shapki 187025, Russia Office: All Russian Rsch Inst Metro, Home 19 prospect Moskovsky, Saint Petersburg 198005, Russia

YUSUF, NASIM, endocrinologist, consultant; b. Lahore, Pakistan, Dec. 30, 1034; d. Mohammed Yusuf and Iqbal Begum; m. Mohammed Miyanoorwala Amin, Sept. 17, 1971. MB, BS, Fatima Jinnah Med. Coll., Pakistan, 1958. Diplomate in internal medicine Coll. Surgeons and Physicians Que., also diplomate in endocrinology and metabolism. Endocrinologist Reddy Meml. Hosp., Montreal, Que., Can., 1973-95; cons. endocrinologist Shifa Internat. Hosp., Islamabad, Pakistan, 1996—; lectr. McGill U., Monreal, 1977-1998. Bd. dirs. Muslim Cmtyo Que., Montreal, 1979—. Home: House 16A F8/3, Khayaban E I Q Bal, Islamabad Pakistan

YUSUF, SAMUEL, lawyer; b. Zangon Kataf, Nigeria, June 4, 1960; s. Yusuf Gwanzwang and Laraba Mutuah; m. Rebecca Machu, Dec. 18, 1993; 1 child, Faith Nwamayhi. LLB with honors, A.B.U. Zaria, Nigeria, 1988, LLM, 1998. Barrister at law, solicitor and advocate, Supreme Ct. Nigeria. Archives asst. Nat. Archives, Kaduna, 1981-82; prin. legal officer Nipost Hdqs., Kaduna, 1990—. Mem. Nigerian Bar Assn., Ind. Lawyers Assn. Nigeria, Bida Old Boys Assn. Nigerian Baptist Convention. Avocations: football, reading, arts and crafts, cross country, Scrabble. Home: # 3 College Rd Kurmi Mashi, Kaduna Nigeria Office: Nigerian Postal Svc, Yakubu Gowon Way, PMB 2308 Kaduna Nigeria

YUTILOV, YURI MICHAILOVITCH, chemist; b. Baku, USSR, Sept. 3, 1936; s. Michael Vasilievitch and Xenia Sergeevna Y.; m. Neonila Volnich, Feb. 9, 1964; 2 children. BS, U. Rostov-on-Don, 1960, MSc, 1966; DSc, Inst. Organic Chemistry, Ufa, Russia, 1994. Sr. scientific worker Inst. Reactive Chemistry, Donetsk, USSR, 1963-68, Br. Inst. Phys. Chemistry, Donetsk, USSR, 1968-73; from head lab. to head dept. Inst. Phys., Organic and Coal Chemistry, Donetsk, USSR, 1973—, prof., 1996—. E-mail: yutilov@infou.donetsk.ua. Home: R Luxemburg St 71 ap 29, 83114 Donetsk Ukraine Office: Inst Phys Org and Coal Chem, R Luxemburg 70, Donetsk Ukraine

YUU, SHINICHI, mechanical engineering educator; b. Osaka, Japan, Dec. 15, 1940; s. Takeshi and Miwako (Oohi) Y.; m. Michiko Imai, Apr. 27, 1969; 1 child, Misako. BS, Kyoto U., 1965, MS, 1967, DSc, 1970. Rsch. assoc. Kyoto U., 1970-72; assoc. prof. Kyushu Inst. Tech., Kita Kyushu, 1973-78, prof., 1979-96, dean prof., 1996—. Contbr. articles to profl. jours. Mem. Japan Assn. of Powder Tech., Japanese Soc. Mech. Engring., Soc. Chem. Engring. Japan. Office: Kyushu Inst of Tech, Sensui-cho Tobata, Kita Kyushu 804, Japan

YUZBEKOV, AKHMED KADIMALIEVICH, biologist; b. Hiv, Russia, Sept. 16, 1952; s. Kadimaly Nadouralievich and Sofia Abdulouseevna (Shahnabieva) Y.; m. Loudmila Alexandrovna Zaitzeva, Dec. 5, 1976; 1 child, Marat Akhmedovich. Student, St. Petersburg (Russia) U., 1974-79; D of Biol. Scis., Acad. Scis., Kiev, Ukraine, 1994. Vice-rector Acad. Agrl., Novgorod, Russia, 1986-87, asst. prof., 1987-89, from asst. prof. to prof., head biology dept., 1993-97; dean dept. biology Novgorod State U., 1997—; postgrad. supr. Norgorod State U., 1995—, spl. coun. session mem., 1997—. Author: Spectrophotometrical Methods of Detectind Enzymes of Photosynthesis, 1990; contbr. articles to profl. jours.; inventor in field. Adv. coun. Gov. Novgorod Region, 1997—. Capt. Russian mil., 1983. Dept. Sci. Novgorod Region grant, 1997. Mem. N.Y. Acad. Scis., Internat. Acad. Scis., Man and Nature Protection Scis., Acad. Natural (corres. mem.). Avocations: tennis, travel, music, theatre, museums. E-mail: uak@info.novsu.ac.ru. Home: 41 Kochetova Apt 15, 173025 Novgorod Russia Office: Novgorod State Univ, 41 Bolshaya St Petersburgs, 173003 Novgorod Russia

YZAGUIRRE, MARK RAMON, lawyer; b. Nov. 7, 1970. BA, Rice U., 1994; JD, Harvard U., 1997. Bar: Tex. 1997, U.S. Dist. Ct. (so. dist.) Tex. 1998, U.S. Ct. Appeals (5th cir.) 1998. Law clk. to hon. Reynaldo Garza U.S. Fifth Cir. Ct. Appeals, Brownsville, Tex., 1997-98; assoc. Vinson & Elkins LLP, Houston, 1998-2000, Jackson Walker LLP, Houston, 2000—.

YZERMAN, STEVE, professional hockey player; b. Cranbrook, B.C., Can., May 9, 1965. With Detroit Red Wings, 1983—. Recipient Lester B. Pearson award, 1988-89; named Sporting News NHL Rookie of Yr., NHL All-Rookie Team, 1983-84, 1988-93. Youngest person ever to play in NHL All-Star game, 1984; mem. Stanley Cup Champions, 1997. Office: Detroit Red Wings 600 Civic Center Dr Detroit MI 48226-4419

ŻABA, RICHARD, pediatrician, researcher, educator; b. Zabrze, Poland, Apr. 2, 1948; s. Roman and Lidia Zofia (Zajac) Ż.; m. Teresa Nowak, Sept. 7, 1974 (div. 1981); m. Alina Zofia Klisiewicz, June 23, 1984; children: Caroline, Sophie. Grad., Silesian Acad. Medicine, Katowice, Poland, 1974. Med. diplomate. Jr. asst. III Clinic Pediatrics Silesian Acad. Medicine, Bytom, Poland, 1974-77, sr. asst. III, 1977-83, adj. III, 1985—; asst. Children's Clinic Free U., Berlin, 1984-85; insp. pediatrics & sch. medicine, Bytom, 1990-2000; head. cons. Rehab. Unit, Bytom, 1993-2000. Author: Influence of Rehabilitation on Ventilatory Parameters and Function of Peripheral Respiratory Tract in Children with Mild Idiopathic Scoliosis, 1991; contbr. articles to profl. jours. Recipient Polish Silver Order award Polish Bd. Edn., 1978, 3d prize Polish Satirical Comp. Barbara's Smile, 1979. Mem. Polish Med. Assn., Sci. & Arts Soc., N.Y. Acad. Scis., IPPNW (Polish sect.). Roman Catholic. Avocations: philosophy, horses, dancing, travel. Office: Silesian Acad Medicine, ul Batorego 15, 41-900 Bytom Poland

ZABALGOITIA, JOSE ANTONIO, diplomat; b. Mexico City, Jan. 29, 1962; m. Lucia Villalobos, July 8, 1989; children: Santiago, Patricio. BA in Internat. Rels., El Colegio de Mexico, 1985; MS in Internat. Rels., London Sch. Econs./Polit. Sci., 1987; MA in Mil. Adminstrn., Colegio de Defensa Nat., Mexico City, 1990. Adv. to min. fgn. rels. Ministry of Fgn. Rels., Mexico City, 1990-91, dir. Mexico-U.S. Bilateral Affairs, 1991-94; counselor for pub. affairs Embassy of Mexico to Spain, Madrid, 1994-97; min. for info. and pub. affairs Embassy of Mexico to USA, Washington, 1997—. Recipient S.H. Bailey prize for Internat. Studies, London Sch. Econs. and Polit. Sci., 1987. Mem. Revolutionary Instnl. Party. E-mail: embmxeuaoid@compuserve.com. Office: Embassy of Mexico to USA 1911 Pennsylvania Ave NW Washington DC 20006-3403

ZABAROVSKY, EUGENE REONADOVICH, molecular biologist, researcher; b. Penza, Russia, Sept. 5, 1958; s. Reonad Vasilevich and Galina Grigorevna (Brilevska) Z.; m. Veronika Igorevna Kakaulina, Aug. 12, 1984; 1 child, Stanislava. MS in Molecular Virology, Moscow Lomonosov State U., 1980; PhD in Molecular Biology, Engelhardt Inst. Molecular Bio, Moscow, 1984; Docent, Karolinska Inst., Stockholm, 1995. Rsch. fellow Engelhardt Inst. Molecular Biology, 1980-82, young rschr., 1982-85, rschr., 1985-86, sr. rschr., 1986—; guest rschr. Microbiology and Tumor Biology Ctr., Karolinska Inst., 1989-91, rsch. group leader, 1991—. Contbr. over 110 articles to profl. jours. Chmn. young scientists coun. Engelhardt Inst. Molecular Biology, Moscow, 1986-90. Grantee Karolinska Inst., 1990, Swedish Cancer Soc., 1996, Swedish Acad. Scis., 1999, Swedish Technol. Rsch. Coun., 2000. Mem. AAAS, Human Genome Orgn., Am. Soc. Human Genetics. Office: MTC Karolinska Inst, 171 77 Stockholm Sweden

ZABECKI, DAVID TADEUSZ, engineer, editor, military historian; b. Springfield, Mass., Aug. 8, 1947; s. Julian Tadeusz and Virginia Charlotte (Luthgren) Z.; m. Marlies Schweigler, 1991; children: Konrad Josef, Jonathan Tadeusz. BA, Xavier U., 1972, MA, 1973; MS, Fla. Inst. Tech., 1976; PhD, Calif. Coast U., 1987; diploma, U.S. Army War Coll., 1995. Patrolman Xavier U. Campus Police, Cin., 1972-74; quality assurance specialist Rock Island (Ill.) Arsenal, 1974-77; quality engr. Deere & Co., Moline, Ill., 1977-84, Fed. Republic Germany, 1985-93; adj. instr. Fla. Inst. Tech., 1977-79; adj. lectr. European program City Colls. Chgo., 1986-89; asst. prof. Am. Mil. U., 1993—; dep. chief of staff for ops. 7th Army Res. Command, Schwetzingen, Germany, 1997-98, chief staff, 1998-2000; dep. chief USAR, Washington, 2000—; lectr. in field. Author: Karl Doenitz: A Defense, 1972, Field Artillery in the 1980's, 1983, American Artillery and the Medal of Honor, 1987, Steel Wind: Colonel Georg Bruchmueller and The Birth of Modern Artillery, 1994; editor-in-chief: WWII in Europe: An Ency., 1998; contbg. editor Mil. History mag., 1987-99, World War II mag., 1987-99; editor Vietnam mag., 2000—; series editor The Art of War, 2000—; book reviewer Mil. Rev., Jour. of Royal Artillery; developer contbn. margin differential concept of quality cost analysis. Served to col. U.S. Army, 1966-69, 96-97; with Res. Decorated Combat Infantryman's Badge, Bronze Star, Army Commendation medal, Meritorious Svc. medal with 4 oak leaf clusters, German Army Proficiency badge in gold; Knight Comdr. Order St. John Jerusalem, Gen. John J. Pershing award U.S. Army Command and Staff Coll., 1988, George Washington Honor medal Freedoms Found., 1988, Wm. Hornaday Dist. Svc. in Conservation award, 1963. Mem. Am. Soc. Quality Control (sr. mem., cert. quality and reliability engr.), U.S. Field Arty. Assn., Order of St. Barbara, Res. Officers Assn., German Philatelic Socs., Co. Mil. Historians, Royal Arty. Assn., N.Y. Acad. Scis., Nat. Eagle Scouts Assn., Masons, Scottish Rite, York Rite, Nat. Sojourners, Alpha Sigma Nu. Address: Guenterstal Strasse 86, D-79100 Freiberg Germany

ZABEL, HARTMUT, physics educator; b. Radolfzell, Germany, Mar. 21, 1946; s. Gerhard and Klara Zabel; m. Rosemarie Havers, Dec. 10, 1972; children: Cordula, Astrid, Julia. Vordiplom, U. Bonn, Germany, 1969; Hauptdiplom, Tech. U. Munich, 1973; PhD in Physics summa cum laude, U. Munich, 1978. Rsch. assoc. U. Houston, 1978-79; asst. prof. physics U. Ill., Urbana-Champaign, 1979-83, assoc. prof., 1983-86, prof., 1986-89; prof. Ruhr U. Bochum, Germany, 1989—, chmn. dept. physics and astronomy, 1993-96, vice chmn. rsch. project SFB 166, 1989-98; chmn. DFG project physics of novel materials Ruhr U., Bochum, Germany, 1996—, chmn. rsch. project SFB491: Magnetic Heterostrucures; fellow Inst. Advanced Studies, Urbana, 1982; program dir. Materials Rsch. Lab., Urbana, 1987-89; adj. prof. physics U. Ill., 1989—; guest scientist Brookhaven Nat. Lab., 1985, 88, Risoe Nat. Lab., Denmark, 1986; guest lectr. KTH, Stockholm, 1998-99; referee various jours. and funding agys. Editor: Graphite Intercalation Compounds, Vol. I, 1990, Vol. II, 1992; contbr. over 250 articles to profl. jours. Cusanus grad. fellow, Bonn, 1970-73, Japanese Soc. for Promotion of Sci. fellow, 1989, Volkswagenstiftung fellow, 1993. Fellow Am. Phys. Soc.; mem. German Phys. Soc., Materials Rsch. Soc. Home: Schloss Strasse 129, 44795 Bochum Germany Office: U Bochum Inst Exptl Physics, Universitätsstrasse 150, 44780 Bochum Germany

ZABEL, SHELDON ALTER, lawyer, law educator; b. Omaha, Apr. 25, 1941; s. Louis Julius and Anne (Rothenberg) Z.; m. Roberta Jean Butz, May 10, 1975; children: Andrew Louis, Douglas Patrick, Robert Stewart Warren. AB cum laude, Princeton U., 1963; JD cum laude, Northwestern U., 1966. Bar: Ill. 1966, U.S. Supreme Ct. 1976. Law clk. to presiding justice, Ill. Sup. Ct., 1966-67; assoc. Schiff, Hardin & Waite, Chgo., 1967-73, ptnr., 1973—; instr. environ. law Loyola U., Chgo. Mem. bd. dirs. Chgo. Zool. Soc. Mem. ABA, Chgo. Bar Assn., Chgo. Coun. Lawyers, Order of Coif. Jewish. Clubs: Union League, Metropolitan (Chgo.). Avocations: skiing, squash. Office: Schiff Hardin & Waite 7200 Sears Tower 233 S Wacker Dr Ste 7200 Chicago IL 60606-6473

ZABIELSKI, ROMUALD, physiologist, educator; b. Warsaw, Poland, Dec. 25, 1960; s. Jerzy and Wanda (Moscibrocka) Z.; m. Anna Maria Kulig, Aug. 31, 1985; 1 child, Marta. DVM, Warsaw Agrl. U., 1984, PhD, 1990, habilitation, 1995. Asst. prof. physiology Warsaw Agrl. U., 1984-91, assoc. prof., 1995-98, prof., 1998—; rsch. assoc. Rakuno Gakuen U., Ebetsu, Japan, 1991-94; dir. Kielanowski Inst. Animal Physiology and Nutrition, Polish Acad. Scis., Jablonna, 1999—; vis. rschr. INRA, Rennes, France, 1996-97; vis. prof. Lund (Sweden) U., 1997—. Author: The Biology of the Pancreas in Growing Animals, 1999. Recipient Sci. prize Prime Minister Poland, 1996, Sci. prize Polish Acad. Scis., 1999. Mem. Polish Soc. Vet. Sci. (prize 1990). Avocations: music, table tennis, mountain biking. Office: Kielanowski Inst, Polish Acad Scis, 05-110 Jablonna Poland

ZABOROWSKI, MICHAŁ, electronic technology engineer, researcher; b. Warsaw, Poland, Jan. 16, 1952; s. Zbigniew Stanisław and Krystyna Barbara (Switalska) Z.; m. Barbara Maria Szafijańska, Dec. 29, 1984; children: Bartosz Jakub, Grzegorz Maciej. MSc, Tech. U. Warsaw, 1974; D in Electronics, Inst. Electron Tech., Warsaw, 1998. Asst. Inst. Electron Tech., 1976-79, asst. lectr., 1979-82, specialist, 1982-88, sr. specialist, 1988—; project mgr. State Com. for Sci. Rsch. Poland, 1993-95, 99—; conf. presenter in field. Contbr. articles to sci. jours.; inventor semicondr. device mfg. method. 2d lt. arty. Polish Army, 1975. Recipient prize Polish Ministry Industry, 1982, 86. Mem. Polish Psychotronics Soc., Yacht Club Poland. Mem. Solidarity. Roman Catholic. Avocations: yachting, travel, skiing, television camera. Office: Inst Electron Tech, al Lotników 32/46, 02 668 Warsaw Poland

ZABRISKIE, GEORGE ALBERT, film, video maker; b. Evanston, Oct. 24, 1926; s. George Albert and Dorothy Joyce (Yonkers) Z.; m. Virginia Marshall, June, 1953 (div. Dec. 1961); m. Sherry LaFollette, Feb. 10, 1962; children: Oliver, Tavia LaFollette. BA in History, Princeton U., 1948. USN-V12 Yale U., New Haven, 1944-46; film assoc. Internat. Film Found., N.Y.C., 1949-52; 2d lt. writer Signal Corps ASPC, N.Y.C., 1952-54, U.S. Army civilian writer, 1954-56; film maker Zabriskie Prodns., N.Y.C., 1956-68, Buenos Aires, 1968-71, Ackworth, N.H., 1971-73, Salisbury, Conn., 1973-83, Bklyn. Heights, N.Y., 1983—. Writer, producer over 23 films including Summerdog, 1977, various books and videos. Campaign film Steven Minot/Congrl., Conn., 1962; pres. N.Y. State United World Federalists, N.Y.C., 1960-62; campaign comml. producer Former Congressman Paul McCloskey's Presdl. Quest, N.H., 1972; fund raising chmn.-films-Dem. Town Com., Salisbury, Conn., 1976-78. Blue Ribbon winner Am. Film Festival, 1960, Golden Eagle winner Coun. for Internat./Short, 1964; grantee The Josephine Bay Paul/C. Michael Paul Found., 1988. Democrat. Avocations: travel, walking, museums, theatre, books, gardening. Office: Zabriskie Prodns PO Box 21524 Brooklyn NY 11202-1524

ZABRODSKY, PAVEL FRANCEVICH, toxicologist, educator; b. Dubno, Russia, Aug. 20, 1951; s. France Pavlovich and Varvara Afanasyevna (Snegireva) Z.; m. Varvara Vladimirovna Guseva, Feb. 9, 1980; 1 child, Ekaterina. Student, Mil. Med. Acad., Leningrad, Russia, 1968-74, postgrad., 1982; MD, Mil. Med. Acad., St. Petersburg, Russia, 1991. Head fisiocological lab. Med. Inst., Orenburg, Russia, 1974-81; instr. Mil. Med. Acad., Leningrad, 1981-83, Mil. Med. Faculty, Saratov, Russia, 1983-88; docent Mil. Med. Faculty, Saratov, 1988-91, prof., 1991-92, prof., head dept. toxicology, 1992—; chief toxicologist, Saratov, 1986—. Author: First Aid by Poisoning of Tech. Liquids, 1985, Military Toxicology and Radiology, 1992, Postintoxic Immunodeficiencies, 1992, Toxicological and Radiological Aspects of Medical Catastrophes, 1993, Immunomodulate Properties of Chemical and Drugs, 1998, First Aid by Poisoning of Chemical, 1999. Served with Russian mil., 1968—. Recipient Excellent Pub. Health award Ministry of Health, USSR, 1987, award for excellence in mil. svc., Mil. Fedn., 1992, Order of Courage award Pres. of Russian Fedn., 1998. Mem. Soc. Toxicology (chmn. 1986—), Soc. Immunotoxicology (chmn. 1991—), Acad. Mil. Sci., Acad. Nat. Sci., N.Y. Acad. Scis. Avocations: tennis, fishing. Home: PO Box 1706, 410015 Saratov Russia Office: Saratov State Med U, 112 Bolshaya Kazachya GSP-71, 410701 Saratov Russia

ZABŻA, ANDRZEJ STANISŁAW, chemistry educator, researcher; b. Komarówka, Biala-Podl, Poland, Dec. 11, 1932; s. Stanisław and Kazimiera (Gołda) Z.; 1 child, Elżbieta. BSc in Engring., Tech. U. Wrocław, Poland, 1955, PhD, 1962, DSc, 1974. Cert. prof. chemistry, engring., Poland. From asst. to assoc. prof. chemistry Tech. U. Wrocław, Poland, 1955-1980, prof. chemistry, 1980—; coord. ctrl. rsch. prog. Low Molecular Bioregulators of Cellular Metabolism, Poland, 1985-90; vice chmn. Com. of Biotechnology at the Presidium, Polish Acad. Scis., Warsaw, Poland, 1990-96, chmn., 1996—. Co-editor: (conf. procs.) Regulation of Insect Development and Behaviour, 1981, Endocrinological Frontiers in Physiological Insect Ecology, 1988; mem. editorial bd. Springer-Verlag series Chemistry of Plant Protection, 1991; contbr. articles to profl. jours. Mem. Polish Chem. Soc. Roman Catholic. Avocations: sailing ships modelling, classical music, jazz. Home: Podwale 52/3, 50-039 Wroclaw Poland Office: Tech U Wrocław, WYB Wyspiańskiego 27, 50-370 Wroclaw Poland

ZACARIAS, ISABEL, nutritionist, researcher, consultant; b. Talca, Chile, Dec. 18, 1953; d. Julio and Victoria (Hasbun) Z.; m. Jaime Roberto Fuentes, Jan. 23, 1982; children: Rodrigo, Victoria. Nutritionist, U. Chile, 1976, MSc in Human Nutrition, 1989; postgrad., UNU, Netherlands, 1994. Nutritionist Caritas Chile/INTA U. Chile, Santiago, 1976-77; nutritionist INTA-U. Chile, Santiago, 1977-90, asst. prof., 1990—, sec., in charge extension, 1998—. Contbr. chpts. to books, articles to profl. jours. Am. Inst. Nutrition travel grantee, 1978; U. Moncton, Can. travel grantee, 1985; Am. Soc. for Nutritional Sci. travel grantee, 1997. Mem. Latin Am. Confedn. Nutrition (treas. 1987-92), Latin Am. Soc. Nutrition, Chilean Soc. Nutritian (sec. 1991-92). Roman Catholic. Office: Instn Nutrition and Tech, U Chile, Casilla 15138, Santiago Chile

ZACH, OTTO RUPERT FRANZ, molecular biologist; b. Linz, Austria, Nov. 24, 1964; s. Otto and Anna (John) Z.; m. Katharina Frank; 1 child, Lea. M in natural scis., U. Salzburg, Austria, 1991; D of Natural Scis., U. Salzburg, 1994. Asst. U. Salzburg, 1991-94; head of lab. Inst. Molecular Biology, Salzburg, 1994-95, Elisabethinen Hosp., Linz, 1995—. Contbr. articles to profl. jours. Avocation: music. Office: Elisabethinen Hosp, Fadingerstr 1, A-4010 Linz Austria

ZACHARAKIS, CHRISTOS, ambassador; b. Athens, Greece, July 28, 1939; married; 2 children. Degree in Law, U. Athens. Attache of embassy Ministry of Fgn. Affairs, 1964; vice consul Consulate Gen. of Greece, N.Y., 1965; sec. Embassy of Greece, Copenhagen, 1966; consul Consulate Gen. of Greece, Istanbul, 1969; first sec. Perm. Delegation Greece to NATO, 1971; consul gen. Greece, Alexandria, 1974; counselor Embassy of Greece, Nicosia, Cyprus, 1975; mem. Ministry Fgn. Affairs, Athens, 1978; amb. Greece Cyprus, 1979; perm. rep. of Greece NATO, 1985; amb. Greece U.S., 1989; sec. gen. Ministry Fgn. Affairs, Athens, 1993; perm. rep. Greece UN, 1994; mem. European Parliament, Brussels, Belgium. Address: European Parliament, Rue Wiertz, ASP 8E210 Brussels B-1047, Belgium*

ZACHARIA, ZACH GEORGE, mechanical engineer; b. Tirvulla, Kerala, India, July 14, 1961; came to U.S., 1995; s. George and Mariamma (Paul) Z.; m. Sunitha Kurian, Sept. 27, 1987; children: Keziah Maria, Aaron George Kurian, Mikhalia Elizabeth. BSME, U. Calgary, Alta., Can., 1985; MBA, U. Alta., Edmonton, 1993. Registered profl. engr., Alta. Equip. engr. Alta. Transp. and Utilities, Edmonton, 1985-89, sr. rsch. engr., 1989-95; sr. rsch. assoc. U. Tenn., Knoxville, 1995-96, dir. TTAP, 1996-98, asst. dir. transp. ctr., 1998-99, assoc. dir., 1999—. Co-author: Supply Chain Management, 2000; contbr. articles to profl. jours. Coun. of Logistics Mgmt. fellow, Toronto, Ont., 1999, Chgo., 1997. Office: Univ of Tennessee 309 Conference Center Bldg Knoxville TN 37996-0001

ZACHARIAH, THONDIATH JOHN, research scientist; b. Mulakuzha, Kerala, India, Nov. 30, 1956; s. Thondiath Scaria Yohannan and Aleyamma Zachariah; m. Kamalam Joseph, May 12, 1985; children: Tony, Tiju. BSc, U. Kerala, Trivandrum, 1977, PhD, 1985; MSc, U. Baroda, India, 1980. Scientist NRCS, ICAR, India, 1985-90, sr. scientist, 1990-98; sr. scientist IISR, ICAR, India, 1998—. Editor report in field. Mem. Indian Soc. Spices (exec. com. 1996—). Christian Orthodox. Avocations: reading, music, writing. Home: Chelavoor, 673 571 Kozhikode Kerala India Office: Indian Inst Spices Rsch, Marikunnu PO, 673 012 Kozhikode Kerala India

ZACHARIASSON, TOINI MARIA, computer educator; b. Hedenaeset, Norrbotten, Sweden, Mar. 14, 1943; d. Helge Karl and Aili Maria (Maeki) Z. Computer Degree, Scandinavian Sch., Goteborg, Sweden, 1974; Degree Philosophy, Stockholm U., 1980. Clk. exec. The Def. Office, Stockholm, 1962-64; sec. of bus. Ericsson, Stockholm, 1964-79; sec. of parliament Stockholm, 1979-82; dir., owner of bus. Hedenaesef, Sweden, 1982-88, 88—. Taxation profl. the Cen. Party, Stockholm, 1977-88. Vol. Marine Def., Sweden. Mem. The Cen. Party. Lutheran. Avocations: computering, reading, sporting, mktg. Office: Toinis Datasvc AB, PO Box 107, S-95090 Hedenaeset Sweden

ZACHARIOU, ZACHARIAS, pediatric surgery consultant; b. Limassol, Cyprus, Nov. 25, 1957; arrived in Germany, 1977; s. Artemios and Elenitsa (Varnava) Z.; m. Ulrike Hauf, Mar. 1, 1985; children: Zachariou, Johannes. MD, U. Heidelberg, 1985, specialist in gen. surgery, specialist in pediatric surgery, 1994. Jr. med. officer U. Heidelberg, 1985-89, sr. med. officer, 1991-93, cons., asst. prof., 1993—; sr. med. officer City Hosp. Tauberbuchofoheim, Tauberbischofsheim, Germany, 1989-91; cons., asst. prof., 1993-99, prof. pediatric surgery, 1999—. Author: Pediatric Surgery Memorix, 1995, (CD-ROM) Routine Operations in Pediatric Surgery, 1999; contbr. articles to profl. jours. Officer Nat. Guard Cyprus, 1974-77. Mem. German Assn. Pediatric Surgery (com. for postgrad. tng. 1994, com. for quality assurance 1994), German Assn. of Surgery. Greek Orthodox. Avocations: studies on byzantine medicine, Tifany stained glass.

ZACHAROPOULOS, DIMITRIS, civil engineering educator, researcher; b. Amfissa, Fokida, Greece, Apr. 17, 1948; s. Athanasios Ioannis and Anna Loukas (Kaliantzi) Z.; m. Lia Nestor Lomef, July 13, 1969; children: Athanasios, Maria-Niki. Degree in math., Aristoteles U., Thessaloniki, Greece, 1972; PhD in Engring., Democritus U. Thrace, Xanthi, Greece, 1989, degree in civil engring, 1991. Rsch. asst. in civil engring. Democritus U. Thrace, 1974-89, lectr. civil engring., 1989-94, asst. prof. civil engring., 1994-99; assoc. prof. Democritus U., 1999—; vis. scientist Inst. Fracture and

Solid Mechanics Lehigh U., Bethlehem, Pa., 1986. Contbr. articles to profl. jours. Mem. ESIS, Hellenic Soc. Theoretical Applied Mechanics, Tech. Chamber of Greece. Home: 40 Ekklision 39A, 671 00 Xanthi Greece Office: Democritus U Thrace, Dept Civil Engring, 671 00 Xanthi Greece

ZACHARY, LOUIS GEORGE, chemical company consultant; b. Aug. 14, 1927; s. George E. and Angelike (Hantsis) Zacharakis; m. Lillie Vletas, Apr. 20, 1955; children: Leslie A., Louis George. Prodn. supr. Dewey & Almy Co., Acton, Mass., 1951-52; salesman chem. divsn. Union Camp Corp., Wayne, N.J., 1952-59, sales mgr. chem. divsn., 1959-62, gen. mgr. chem. ops., 1962-66, gen. mgr. chem. divsn., 1970-78, v.p., 1974-78; v.p. Drake Mgmt. Co., N.Y.C., 1966-70; sr. v.p. GAF Corp., N.Y.C., 1978-82, mem. office of chmn., 1981-82; cons., 1983-84; chmn., CEO Universal Die Casting, Inc., Saline, Mich., 1984-90; acting pres. chem. divsn. Church & Dwight Inc., 1990-91; v.p. Nat. Exec. Svc. Corp., N.Y.C., 1993-96; mem. vis. com. chem. engring. dept. Johns Hopkins U., Balt., 1981-83. Co-editor: Tall Oil and Its Uses, 1965. With USN, 1945-46. Mem. Chem. Mfrs. Assn. (dir. 1979-83), Synthetic Organic Chem. Mfrs. Assn., Soc. Chem. Industry, Baltusrol Golf Club, Harvard Club. Home: 227 Oak Ridge Ave Summit NJ 07901-3258

ZACHAU, HANS GEORG, molecular biologist, researcher; b. Berlin, Germany, May 16, 1930; s. Erich Franz and Gertrud (Mengers) Z.; m. Elisabeth Irmgard Vorster, Apr. 16, 1960; children: Martin, Ulrich, Thomas. Diploma in Chemistry, U. Frankfurt, 1953; DSc, U. Tübingen (Germany), 1955. Postdoctoral fellow MIT, Cambridge, Mass., 1956-57, Rockefeller U., N.Y.C., 1957-58; researcher Max Planck Inst., Munchen, Germany, 1958-61, U. Koln, Cologne, 1961-66; prof. Munchen, Germany, 1967-99, prof. emeritus, 1999—; pres. Gesellschaft fur Biologische Chemie, Germany, 1975-77. Contbr. 300 publs. in scientific jours. and books in field. Mem. Deutsche Akademie der Naturforscher Leopoldina, Bayerische Akademie der Wisenschaften, Orden Pour le merite (chancellor 1992—), Osterreichische Akademie der Wissenschaften, Academia Europaea, Maximiliansorden, The Human Genome Orgn., Russian Acad. Scis., Am. Soc. Biochemistry and Molecular Biology (hon.). Home: Pfingstrosenstr 5A, D81377 Munchen Germany

ZACHEM, KATHRYN A., lawyer; b. Freedom, Pa., Apr. 16, 1958. BA, George Washington U., 1980; JD, Goerge Mason U., 1985. Bar: Va. 1985, D.C. 1987. Atty. Wilkinson Barker Knauer, LLP, Washington; lectr. FCC Tng. Ctr., Norfolk, Va. Vol. law student mentoring program George Mason U. Sch. of Law, Columbus Sch. Law-Cath. U. Mem. Fed. Comms. Bar Assn. (mem. exec. com.), co-chair land mobile practice com., mem. found. charitable distbns. com.), D.C. Bar Assn., Va. State Bar Assn., Women's Bar Assn. Fax: 202-783-5851. Office: Wilkinson Barker Knauer LLP 2300 N St NW Ste 700 Washington DC 20037-1191

ZACK, STEVEN JEFFREY, master automotive instructor; b. Middletown, Conn., Oct. 12, 1955; s. Mathias Charles and Sylvia Ann (Berkowitz) Z. AAS, Williamsport Area C.C., 1976. Cert. EPA instr. Automotive technician Bob Sharp Nissan, Danbury, Conn., 1976-79; svc. engr. Ingersoll Rand, Painted Post, N.Y., 1979-85; tech. svc. rep. Chrysler Motor Corp., Metairie, La., 1985-87; automotive instr. Hartford (Conn.) Tech. Inst., 1988-92; master automotive instr. SPX/Automotive Diagnostics, Kalamazoo, Mich., 1992-97, SPX/OTC, Owatonna, Minn., 1997—; tng. cons. Conn. DMV, North Haven, 1994—; with Coun. of Advanced Automotive Trainers, Lisle, Ill., 1995—; master instr. EPA/Coalition Safer Cleaner Vehicles, Albany, N.Y., 1994—. Contbr. articles to trade jours. Mem. Coalition for Safer Cleaner Vehicles. Achievements include designed electric car heat exchanger motor; designed, patent Zack cycle engine; holder 10 copyrights. Avocation: God. Home: PO Box 116 Deep River CT 06417-0116

ZACKEY, CHRISTOPHER ALBERT, mythologist, writer/poet, librarian; b. Brattleboro, Vt., June 12, 1949; s. Albert Walter Jr. and Thelma Eloise Zackey; m. Martha Ann Zackey, Dec. 16, 1973. BA in English, Brandeis U., 1971; MA in English, Ind. U., 1975; MLS, SUNY, Albany, 1987. Cert. libr., N.Y. Libr. tech. asst. Ind. U. Librs., Bloomington, 1974-76; mortgage loan closer and collector U.S. Nat. Bank Oreg., Portland, 1976-80; exam. asst. Nat. Coun. for Interior Design Qualification, N.Y.C., 1982-84; residential mortgage closer Citibank, Troy, N.Y., 1985-86; grad. asst. SUNY, Albany, 1986-87; adult svcs. libr. Jervis Pub. Libr., Rome, N.Y., 1989—. Author: Chandelier, 1998, (chapbooks) An Introduction to the Mythology, 1998, Overworld, 1998, Geodesic Reading, 1999; author poetry, fiction, creative nonfiction. Mem. Phi Beta Kappa. Democrat. Avocations: reading, writing, listening to music. Home: 19 Chenango Ave S Apt 3 Clinton NY 13323-1661 Office: Jervis Pub Libr 613 N Washington St Rome NY 13440-4203

ZACKHEIM, MARC ALLEN, child psychologist, editor; b. N.Y.C., Oct. 12, 1950; s. Seymour David and Blanche (Kalt) Z.; m. Victoria Fraginals. AA, U. Fla., 1970, BA with high honors, 1972; MS, Fla. State U., 1974, PhD, 1977. Lic. psychologist Fla., Ill., Ind., Ala. Intern Duke U. Med. Ctr., Durham, N.C., 1976; postdoctoral fellow in psychology Fla. State U., 1978; resident in psychology Rush-Presbyn. St. Luke's Med. Ctr., Chgo., 1970; attending child psychologist Assocs. in Adolescent Psychiatry, Chgo., 1979-85, dir. tng., 1981-85; v.p. Assocs. in Clin. Psychology, 1985—, Westlake Hosp., Orlando, Fla., 1985—, Linden Oaks Hosp., Naperville, Ill., 1989—; faculty Auburn (Ala.) U.; attending childpsychologist Riveredge Hosp., Forest Park, Ill., 1979—, Koala Hosp., Plymouth, Ind., 1992—, Lebanon, Ind., 1993—. cons. editor Ednl. and Psychol. Rsch.; contbr. articles to profl. jours., including Readins, A Jour. Am. Orthopsych. Assn. USPHS fellow, 1973-76; apptd. State of Ill. Guardianship and Advocacy Commn. Human Rights Authority, chmn., 1990-94. Fellow Am. Orthopsychiat. Assn.; mem. Am. Psychol. Assn., Ill. Psychol. Assn., Ala. Psychol. Assn., Midwest Psychol. Assn., Fla. Psychol. Assn., S.E. Psychol. Assn. for Psychoanalytic Psychology, Acad. Psychosomatic Medicine. Home: 1801 Shore Acres Dr Lake Bluff IL 60044-1340 Office: Riveredge Hosp 8311 Roosevelt Rd Forest Park IL 60130-2500

ZACKS, ROGER WILLIAM, orchestral musician, educator; b. Detroit, Oct. 1, 1958; s. Norman and Florence (Safran) Z.; m. Annette Jansen, Dec. 21, 1987; children: Joshua Andre, Lauren Michelle. MusB, Northwestern U., 1979; MusM, New Eng. Conservatory, Boston, 1982. Prin. trumpet Landestheater Orchester Detmold, Germany, 1983; assoc. prin. trumpet Hessiche Staatstheater Orchester, Kassel, Germany, 1983-87; prin. trumpet Duisburg (Germany) Philharm. Orch., 1987—; asst. prof. trumpet Folkwang Musikhochschule, Essen, Germany, 1992—. Jewish. Home: Schillerstrasse 14, 47226 Duisburg Germany

ŽADNÍKOVÁ, RAJA LODINOVÁ, pediatrician; b. Tel Aviv, Aug. 25, 1929; d. Arthur and Rosa (Abramowicz) Englander; m. Zdenek Lodin, June 30, 1951 (div. 1974); two children; m. Milos Zadnik, Sept. 29, 1979. MD, U. Prague, 1953; PhD, Charles U., 1962. Mem. European Soc. Pediat. Rsch., Internat. Soc. Mucosal Immunology, Am. Acad. Sci. Office: Inst Care Mother & Child, Podolske nabr 157, 147 10 Prague 4 Czech Republic

ZADOFF, EFRAIM, historian, researcher, publisher; b. Buenos Aires, June 1, 1948; arrived in Israel, 1969; s. Leon and Berta (Garfunkel) Z.; m. Diana Beatriz Kapelusznik, Oct. 13, 1971; children: Noam Ariel, Jonathan, Itamar. BA, Hebrew U., Jerusalem, 1973, MA, 1980; PhD, Tel Aviv U., 1993. Supr. Nat. Archives, Jerusalem, 1976-78; mgr. adult edn. programs World Zionist Orgn., Jerusalem, 1978-89; rschr. Sch. Edn. Tel Aviv U., 1989-93; rschr. History Inst. Jewish Nat. Fund, Jerusalem, 1993—; owner E.D.Z. Nativ Ediciones Ltd., Jerusalem, 1996—. Author: (in Hebrew) Jewish Education in Latin America, 1994, (in Spanish) Historia de la Educacion Judia en Buenos Aires 1935-57, 1995; chief editor: Judaica Latinoamericana III, 1997, Enciclopedia de la Historia y la Cultura del Pueblo Judio, 1998, A Century of Argentinean Jewry: In Search of a New Model of National Identity, 2000. Mem. Israeli Assn. Rschrs. on Latin Am. Jewry, Assn. for Promotion of Latin Am. Jewry Rsch. (treas.). Jewish. Fax: 972-2-5860829. Office: E D Z Nativ Ediciones, PO Box 23526, Jerusalem 91234, Israel

ZADOR, STEVEN, pathologist; b. Budapest, Hungary, Mar. 29, 1925; arrived in Australia, 1950; s. Max and Irene (Spiegel) Zador-Grunfeld; m. Patricia June Crowe, Oct. 28, 1956; children: Deborah Alice Irene, Michael William. MRCS, LRCP, West London Hosp., 1961; PhD, U. Paris, 1969. Resident med. officer Bethnal Green Hosp., London, 1961-62; relieving pathologist Taorama Hosp., Port Moresby, 1963; fellow in pathology Prince Alfred Hosp., Sydney, Australia, 1964-66; postdoctoral rsch. fellow Inst. Cancer, Paris, 1966-69; med. resident Êtr des Hôsp. de Paris, 1969; sr. lectr. bacteriology U. Sydney, 1969-70; dir. clin. rsch. various, 1970-82; v.p. Far East med. affairs Sterling-Winthrop, Manila, Singapore, 1983-90; cons. in field Sydney, 1990—; vis. lectr. in field, 1968-90; life governor Sydney Hosp., 1979. Dan Mason rsch. scholar West London Hosp., 1962. Fellow Royal Coll. Physicians Faculty of Pharmaceutical Medicine. Achievements include research work in contractile proteins (actin), automatic antibiotic sensitivity testing, respir. studies on normal, premalignant and malignant skin, aldose reductase inhibition therapy use. Home: 8/337 New Southhead Rd, Doublebay 2028, Australia

ZADOW, JOHN GREIG, food industry consultant; b. Melbourne, Victoria, Australia, Apr. 28, 1941; s. Harold Louis and Gladys Alexandra (Greig) Z.; m. Betty Josephine Rockliff, Aug. 10, 1963 (div. 1988); children: Kirsten, Simon; m. Susan Michelle Collins, June 14, 1988. BSc with hons., U. Melbourne, 1961, MS, 1973; D in Applied Sci., Victoria Inst. Colls., Melbourne, 1981. Research chemist Taubmans Indsl. Coatings, Melbourne, 1958-64, Australian Paper Mfrs., Melbourne, 1964-67; scientist Dairy Research Lab. Commonwealth Sci. and Indsl. Research Orgn., Highett, Victoria, 1967-86, head of lab., 1986-91; cons. J.G. Zadow and Assocs., Victoria, 1991—. Contbr. articles to profl. jours. Recipient Silver medal Australian Soc. Dairy Tech., 1978, 89, Australian Jour. Dairy Tech. award Australian Soc. Dairy Tech., 1986. Mem. Dairy Industry Assn. Australia (corp.), Internat. Dairy Fedn. (group experts). Club: Black Rock (Victoria) Yacht. (sail com. 1985-88). Avocations: windsurfing, skiing, organ playing, farming, travel. Home: 21a Kershaw St, Mordialloc Victoria 3195, Australia Office: 21A Kershaw St Mordialloc, Victoria 3195, Australia

ZAEPFEL, GLENN P., psychologist; b. Feb. 15, 1951; s. Walter Henry and Lillian Adair (Kovach) Z.; m. Linda Carrie Grinton, June 1, 1974; children: Peter, Caroline, Christine. BA, U. S.C., 1973; MEd, Ga. State U., 1980, PhD, 1986. Milieu therapist Peachtree-Parkwood Hosp., Atlanta, 1978-80; dir. Roswell St. Counseling Ctr., Marietta, Ga., 1980-84; dir. counseling and psychol. svcs. DeKalb Pain Control and Rehab. Ctr., Decatur, Ga., 1981-85; pvt. practice Columbia, S.C., 1985—; Columbia Counseling Center/Columbia Behavioral Medicine; founder, program dir. Bapt. Med. Ctr. Pain Mgmt. Program, Columbia, 1985-87; founder, pres. Columbia Counseling Ctr., P.A., 1986—; vis. prof. Reformed Theol. Sem., Orlando. Author: He Wins, She Wins, 1994. Mem. APA, AACD, Christian Assn. for Psychol. Studies, Am. Rehab. Counseling Assn., Am. Bd. Med. Psychotherapists, Sinfonia. Republican. Presbyterian. Avocations: sports, music. Home: 1153 Scotts Hill Rd Chapin SC 29036-8974 Office: 900 St Andrews Rd Columbia SC 29210-5816 also: 601 Polo Rd Columbia SC 29223-2905 also: 122 Powell Dr Lexington SC 29072-9203

ZAFONTE, ROSS D., physiatrist; b. Freeport, N.Y., Nov. 30, 1960. BS, U. Ga., 1981; DO, Nova Southeastern U., 1985. Instr. Thomas Jefferson U., Phila., 1989-90; asst. prof. U. Mo., Columbia, 1991-92; asst. prof. to assoc. prof. Wayne State U., Detroit, 1992—; interim chmn. physical med and rehab. Wayne State U.; med. dir. tramatic brain injury unit Rehab. Inst. of Mich., Detroit, 1990—, co-dir. residency tng. program, 1994-96; chief phys. medicine Detroit Receiving Hosp., 1992—; pres. Rehab. Inst. of Mich., 2000—. Recipient Frank Blumenthal award for tchg. excellence Wayne State/Rehab. Inst., 1994, Appled award for tchg. excellence U. Mo., 1991. Fellow Am. Acad. Phys. Medicine and Rehab., Am. Bd. Electrodiagnostic Medicine; mem. Am. Spinal Injury Assn., Brain Injury Assn. (program chmn. 1995-96, Young Investigator award 1994), Am. Assn. Acad. Physiatrists (program com. mem.). Avocations: baseball, running. Office: Rehab Inst of Mich 261 Mack Ave Detroit MI 48201-2495

ZAFRA, AMMIE ILANO, insurance company executive; b. Manila, May 18, 1957; d. Jose Sanchez and Virginia (Ilano) Z. BS in Biology cum laude, U. The Philippines, Quezon City, 1978; MD, U. The Philippines, Manila, 1982. Diplomate Philippine Bd. Internal Medicine. Postgrad. intern St. Luke's Med. Ctr., Quezon City, 1982-83, resident in internal medicine, 1984-86; asst. v.p., med. dir. Lincoln Philippine Life Ins. Co., Inc., Makati, The Philippines, 1988-93; v.p., med. dir. CMG Life Ins. Co., Inc., Pasig, The Philippines, 1995-98; sr. v.p., med. dir., dir. customer svc. The Prumerica Life Ins. Co., Inc., Makati, 1998—; cons. dept. internal medicine St. Lukes Med. Ctr., Quezon City, 1987—; med. cons. Manulife Fin., Makati, 1994; presenter in field. Contbr. articles to profl. jours. Fellow Philippine Coll. Physicians; mem. Philippine Soc. Ins. Medicine (pres. 1996-98), Home Office Life Underwriters Assn. The Philippines. Roman Catholic. Avocations: walking, stamp collecting.

ZAGALLO, MARIO JORGE LOBO (FORMIGUINHA), professional soccer coach, former player; b. Rio de Janeiro, Aug. 9, 1931. Forward Brazil Nat. Team; winner World Cup, 1958, 62; coach United Arab Emirates Nat. Team; winner Copa Am.; coach Brazil Nat. Team. Named only man to have been associated with four World Cup winning teams. Office: Confederacao Brasil Futebol, Rua de Alfandega 70, 20070001 Rio de Janeiro Brazil*

ZAGASKI, CHESTER ANTHONY, JR., author, researcher; b. Manchester, Conn., Mar. 28, 1949; s. Chester Anthony Sr. and Lenora (Zakrzewski) Z.; m. Suzanne M. Celata, Apr. 1979 (div. Apr. 1989); children: Jason Paul, Brian Matthew. BA, U. S.C., 1971; postgrad., Northeastern U., Wilbraham, Mass., 1971-72, U. Conn., 1973-75. Career trainee Hartford (Conn.) Ins. Co., 1971; spl. agt. Am. Group, Worcester, Mass., 1973-76; supr. underwriter Interstate Nat./Chgo. Ins., Boston; underwriting mgr. Interstate Nat./Chgo. Ins., Phila., 1977-79; reins. mgr. N.Am. Reins., Phila., 1979-80; asst. v.p. casualty lines Comml. Union Ins. Co., Boston, 1980-82; acct. exec. Frank B. Hall & Co., Boston, 1982-84; surplus lines broker Stewart Smith East (USA), Boston, 1984-86; sr. underwriting cons. CNA Ins. Co., Quincy, Mass., 1986-89; former ind. ins. and risk mgmt. cons. to several prominent firms and groups; organizational cons. Omnium Capital, Montreal, 1st Physicians Ins. Co. Vt., 1995, 96; instr., lectr. Inst. Libr. Assn. Boston, Tufts U., 1984-88; former advisor govt. and bus. groups, 1982-90, including New Eng. Coun., Inc., SBA New Eng., Commonwealth of Mass., Dept. Environ. Protection, Joint Ins. Com. of Mass. Legis., U.S. Congl. Subcom., U.S. SEC; lead organizer, cons. Port Royal Ins. Co., 1983; provider expert testimony before state and fed. legis. coms., among others; workshop and seminar leader; rschr., author Deer Island Sentinels. Author: Environmental Risk and Insurance, 1992; contbr. articles to profl. jours; involved in prodn. feature film A Civil Action, 1997. Mem. Quincy City Rep. Com., 1989-91; del. State Conv., Boston, 1990; advisor nat. Bush/Quayle Campaigns, 1989, 92; charter mem., sponsor WWII Meml., Washington, 1997. Recipient Citation of Merit Mass. Legis. Spl. Commn. Liability Release Hazardous Materials, 1986. Mem. Harvard Sq. Script Writers, Cape Cod Writers Ctr. Roman Catholic.

ZAGAZETA, OCTAVIO, psychologist, psychotherapist, consultant; b. Lima, Peru, Aug. 18, 1957; s. Octavio Juan and Raquel Eloisa (Atencio) Z.; m. Maritza Bertha Iturrizaga, Nov. 10, 1984; children: Carmen Rosa, Teresa Raquel. BA in Psychology, Pontificia U. Catolica Peru, Lima, 1995, MA in Psychology, 1997. Lic. psychologist, Peru. Psychol. counselor Naval War Sch., Lima, 1982-88, prof. social psychology, 1984-88, psychol. candidate evaluator, 1983-88; chief human resources Mill Co., Lima, 1985-91; pers. psychol. evaluator Caja de Ahorros de Lima Bank, Lima, 1987; prof. psychoanalytical psychopathology Escuela de Psicoterapia Psicoanalitica de Lima, Lima, 1988-89; pers. psychol. evaluator Procter & Gamble, Lima, 1989; chief pers. dept. Mill Co., Lima, 1990; pers. psychol. evaluator Coop. Mixta de Telefonos de Cochabamba, Bolivia, 1991; prof. sexual edn. Pontificia U. Catolica del Peru, Lima, 1994-96, asst. prof., 1996; pers. psychol. evaluator Internat. Fair of the Pacific, Lima, 1996; asst. prof. metapsychology Escuela de Psicoterapia Psicoanalitica de Lima, 1996, prof. metapsychology, 1996-97; pvt. practice Lima, 1985—; media psychoanalytical counselor TV and radio, Radio Programas del Peru, Panam. TV, CCN, Peru, 1987—; human resources cons. Pontificia U. Catolica del Peru, 1995—. Co-author: La Frigidez, 1992; contbr. articles to profl. jours. including Tientos y Diferencias, Revista de Psicoterapia y Psicoanalisis, among others. Mem. APA, Colegio de Psicologos del Peru, Escuela de Psicoterapia Psicoanalitica de Lima (libr. chief 1990-93). E-mail: ozagaze@hotmail.com. Office: Jr Independencia 570-2, Lima 18, Peru

ZAGHLOUL, DINA AMAL, quality assurance professional, consultant; b. Omaha, Oct. 6, 1975; d. F. Omar and Hoda Z. BS in Biochemistry, U. Nebr., 1996. Quality assurance chemist Cargill, Blair, Nebr., 1996-97; validation specialist PharmTech, Libertyville, Ill., 1997-98; cons. Interim Tech., Oak Brook, Ill., 1998-99; sr. cons. Whittman-Hart, Chgo., 1999; quality assurance mgr. U.S. Office Products IT, Des Plaines, Ill., 1999-2000; cons. Interim Tech. Cons., Scottsdale, Ariz., 2000—. Mem. Am. Chem. Soc., Alpha Lambda Delta, Phi Lambda Upsilon, Phi Eta Sigma. Avocations: sports, reading. E-mail: DAZaghloul@aol.com.

ZAGHLOUL, MOHAMED SAAD, radiation oncologist; b. Banha, Egypt, Aug. 22, 1951; s. Saad Zaghloul Moustafa and Effat Mohamed (Ayad) M.; m. Amina Mohamed Abdel-Wahab; children: Nahla, Noha, Tarek. MB BCh, Cairo U., 1976, MS, 1980, MD, 1985. Resident Nat. Cancer Inst., Cairo, 1977-80, asst. lectr., 1980-85, lectr., 1986-91; rsch. assoc. Stanford (Calif.) U. Sch. Medicine, 1987-88; asst. prof. Nat. Cancer Inst., 1992-94; head oncology dept. Dr. S. Fakeeh Hosp., Jeddah, Saudi Arabia, 1994-96; prof. Nat. Cancer Inst., 1996—; gen. dir. El Minia (Egypt) Oncology Ctr., 1998—. Fellow Netherlands Cancer Inst. Amsterdam, 1983-84, Stanford U., 1991-92. Mem. AAAS, European Soc. Therapeutic Radiology & Oncology, Am. Soc. Therapeutic Radiology & Oncology, Franco Arabian Assn. Against Cancer, Egyptian Soc. Cancer Sci., N.Y. Acad. Scis. Home: 20 Youssef El Gindy St, Bab El Louk 11111, Cairo Egypt Office: Nat Cancer Inst, Kasr El Aini St, Cairo Egypt

ZAGINAYLOV, GENNADIY IVANOVICH, engineer, physicist; b. Belgorodskaya, Russian Fedn., Aug. 4, 1958; s. Ivan Petrovich and Inessa Egorovna (Klevtsova) Z.; m. Lyudmila Ivanovna Svir, Feb. 21, 1981; children: Vladislav, Artem. MS, Kharkov (Ukraine) State U., 1981, PhD, 1984, DSc, 1994. Jr. rschr. Kharkov State U., 1984-86, rschr., 1986-88, sr. rsch. scientist, 1988-92, leading scientist, 1992—; asst. prof. Ukrainian Polytech. Inst., Kharkov, 1985-87; leader of the rsch. group Scientific Ctr. of Phys. Technologies, Kharkov, 1995—. Patentee in field. Travel grantee Civilian R&D Found., 1997, Sci. and Tech. Ctr., Ukraine, 1998, NATO Sci. Divsn. expert visit grantee, 2000, NATO collaborative linkage grantee, 2000; scholar German Acad. Exch. Svc., 1998; fellow Matsumae Internat. Found. fellow, Japan, 1999, Japan Soc. for Promotion Sci., 2000. Mem. IEEE (sr.), Ukranian Phys. Soc. Avocations: European football, table tennis, classical music, traveling, fishing. Home: Ul O Yarosha 16A kv 55, 310045 Kharkov Ukraine Office: Kharkov State U, Svobody Square 4, 310077 Kharkov Ukraine

ZAGINEY, APOLLINARIY OLEXIYOVICH, physicist, researcher; b. Rivne, Ukraine, Sept. 23, 1955; s. Olexiy Nykonovich and Anna Zacharivna (Nehoda) Z.; m. Liudmila Zagineya, Aug. 20, 1955; children: Olena, Volodymir. BS, MSc in Electronic Engring., State U. of Lviv, Ukraine, 1977; PhD in Laser Material Sci., State U., Tchernivtsi, Ukraine, 1994. Engr. Inst. Applied Problems of the Mechanics and Math. Nat. Acad. Scis. Ukraine, Lviv, 1977-81, rschr., 1981-94, sr. rschr., 1994—; asst. prof. State U., Lviv, 1995—. Contbr. articles to profl. jours. Mem. IEEE. Avocations: fishing, hunting, auto repairing, tennis. Home: P Pancha St 11/7, 290020 Lviv Ukraine Office: IAPMMNASU, Naukova 3B Str, 290601 Lviv Ukraine

ZAGOLSKI, FRANCIS, remote sensing expert, executive, researcher; b. Mazingarbe, France, Mar. 9, 1965; s. Casimir and Edwige (Janiak) Z. M in Math. and Physics, U. Lille, France, 1988; DEA degree in space tech., Paul Sabatier U., Toulouse, France, 1990, PhD in Remote Sensing, 1994, D in Remote Sensing (hon.), 1994. Rsch. assoc. fellow CESR, Toulouse, 1989-93; rsch. fellow CNES, Toulouse, 1994-96; sr. scientist CARTEL, Sherbrooke, Que., Can., 1996-98; exec. dir. PRIVATEERS (Pvt. Experts in Remote Sensing), St. Maarten, The Netherlands, 1998—. Referee, contbr. articles to sci. publs. Cpl. inf., French mil., 1988-89. Mem. Planetary Soc. Avocations: travel, sports, music. Home and Office: PRIVATEERS NV, 274 Rd # 216, Stoke, PQ Canada J0B 3GO

ZAGOREN, ALLEN JEFFREY, surgeon; b. Bklyn., May 17, 1947; s. Max and Harriett (Feldman) Z.; m. Gail Marie Sarcinella, Feb. 20, 1977. BA in Biology, Hofstra U., 1969; DO, Phila. Coll. Osteo. Medicine, 1975. Diplomate Am. Bd. Osteo. Surgery, Nat. Bd. Examiners Osteo.-Med. Surgery. Intern Stratford (N.J.) div. John F. Kennedy Meml. Hosp., 1975-76; resident Cherry Hill (N.J.) Med. Ctr., 1976-80; assoc. prof. surgery U. Medicine and Dentistry, Piscataway, N.J., 1980-82; practice osteo. medicine specializing in surgery Des Moines, 1982—, Capitol Hill Surgery, Des Moines, 1994—; mem. staff Mercy Hosp. Med. Ctr., Des Moines; practice osteo. medicine specializing in surgery Capitol Hill Surgery, Des Moines; chmn. dept. surgery Des Moines Gen. Hosp., 1985-91, Madison County Meml. Hosp., Winterset, Iowa, chmn. surgery dir. Specialty Clinic; clin. prof. surgery and nutrition Des Moines Univ. Medicine; assoc. prof. pharmacy Drake U.; lectr. in field; sec. Iowa Bd. Med. Examiners, 1997, sec. 1996-98, vice chmn., 1999—; program dir. Wound Care Ctr., 1993—, dir. med. edn., 1999—, dir. Des Moines Univ. post grad. edn. Contbr. articles to profl. jours.; creator videotapes (with others). Bd. dirs. Des Moines Gen. Hosp. Found., sec., 1986-95; chmn. bd. dirs. Des Moines Gen. Found., 1991-94, dir. med. edn., 1999; trustee Tiffereth Israel Synagogue, 1992. Grantee SKF Labs., Phila., 1986, Norwich (N.Y.) Eaton Labs., 1986, Ross Labs., 1995-99; recipient J. Swartz award for med. leadership Iowa Osteo. Med. Assn. Found., 1996. Fellow Am. Coll. Osteo. Surgeons (rsch., nutritional support, visual aids coms., chair rsch. com. 1991-92, 1st Prize awards 1982, 83), Am. Coll. Nutrition, Internat. Coll. Surgeons; mem. Am. Osteo. Soc., Am. Soc. Gastrointestinal Endoscopy, Iowa Osteo. Med. Assn. (pres. 1994-95, chmn. constrn. and v.p. bylaws coms. 1992, trustee), Polk County Med. Soc. (treas. 1991-93), Am. Soc. Parenteral and Enteral Nutrition (bd. dirs. 1986, chmn. various coms.), Rhoades Rsch. Found., Iowa and Nebr. Soc. Parenteral and Enteral Nutrition (pres. 1990-92), Iowa Health Leadership Consortium (CEO com., co-chair postgrad. edn. com.), Smithsonian Instn., Airplane Owners and Pilots Assn., Iowa Nebr. Nutrition Soc. (pres. 1990-92). Jewish. Avocations: flying, golf, swimming, skiing, writing. Office: Capitol Hill Surgery 1300 Des Moines St Des Moines IA 50309-5502

ZAGOREN, JOY CARROLL, health facility director, researcher; b. N.Y.C., Oct. 31, 1933; d. Murray Morris and Celia (Donner) Rossman; m. Robert H. Zagoren, June 29, 1958 (div. 1988); children: Glenn, Robin; m. Robert Henry Chester, Apr. 1, 1988 (dec. Mar. 1998); children: Peter, Lisabeth, Melinda, Cecily, Kate. BS, NYU, 1957; MS, Adelphi U., 1969; PhD with distinction, NYU, 1981. Sec. sch. faculty Great Neck (N.Y.) Pub. Schs., 1957-71; rsch. scientist Inst. Psychobiol. Studies, Queens Village, N.Y., 1968-71; rsch. assoc. Albert Einstein Coll. Medicine, Bronx, N.Y., 1971-84; asst. prof. SUNY Sch. Medicine, Stony Brook, 1984-86; dir. Seriatum, N.Y.C., 1991—; ptnr. Winter Tree Collection; chmn. Esrath Nashim Hosp., 1986—; med. bd. dirs. Sarah Herzog Meml. Hosp. Editor: The Node of Ranvier, 1984; contbr. articles to profl. jours. Chair Peace Corps Svc. Coun., Tri-State, 1965-75; pres. Kidney Found. L.I., N.Y., 1965-77; v.p. United Cmty. fund L.I., 1970-83; bd. dirs. Jerusalem Mental Health Ctr., N.Y.C., 1986—; med. bd. dirs. Sarah Herzog Meml. Hosp., hon. chair dinner, 1995, chair dinner, 1996, med. chair, 1998, chair membership cocktail party, 2000, chair bd. dirs., 2000—; chmn. mem. N.Y. Acad. Scis., 2000. NIH fellow, 1982-84, Svc. awards Kidney Found., Kiwanis, others, 1970-87; named Disting. Alumnus of Yr., Adelphi U., 1986. Mem. AAAS, Nat. Acad. Sci., N.Y. Acad. Sci., Am. Assn. Neuropathology, Esrath Nashim Hosp. (chair 1986—, apptd. med. bd. dirs. 1994, med. chair 1998). Democrat. Jewish. Avocations: art, literature, piano, swimming, gardening. Home: 405 E 82nd St New York NY 10028-6038 Office: Seriatum 405 East 82d St New York NY 10028

ZAGORIN, JANET SUSAN, legal firm administrator, marketing professional; b. Lakewood, N.J.; d. Irving C. and Dorothy (Tarshish) Z. BA, Douglass Coll., 1975; MLS, Rutgers U., 1977. Asst. law libr. N.J. Atty. Gen., Trenton, 1977-78; head of reference sect. Cardozo U. Law Sch., N.Y.C., 1978-79; law and legis. svcs. libr. FTC, Washington, 1979-81; dir. of reference Paul Weiss Rifkind, N.Y.C., 1981-82; libr. dir. Riker Danzig Scherer & Hyland, Morristown, N.J., 1982; libr., profl. devel. dir. Baker & McKenzie, N.Y.C., 1982-96; dir. practice devel. and info. svcs. Stroock & Stroock & Lavan LLP, N.Y.C., 1996-98; dir. practice devel. Cadwalader,

Wickersham & Taft, N.Y.C., 1998-99, Gibson, Dunn & Crutcher, N.Y.C., 1999—. Bd. dirs. N.Y. Cares, 1998—. Mem. ABA (vice chmn. standing com. Law Libr. Congress 1995-96, chmn. 1996—, mem. law 2000 steering com. Libr. Congress), Fin. Women's Assn. (mem. bd. dirs. 1993-95, 99—), Bus. Women's Network, Am. Assn. Law Librs. (chair fgn. comparative internat. law com. 1990-91, vice chair pvt. law librs. 1990-91, chair 1991—, chair com. on recruitment 1991), Spl. Librs. Assn., Hadassah. Fax: 212-351-5222. E-mail: jzagorin@gdclaw.com.

ZAGOROVA, LYDIA KONSTANTINOVA, psychologist, consultant, writer; b. Sofia, Bulgaria, June 5, 1956; d. Konstantin Petroff and Stefana Todorova (Jeliazova) Z.; m. Slavian Dimitroff Jeliazkov, Sept. 21, 1979 (div. May 1986); 1 child, Slavian. MA, St. Kliment Ohridski U., Sofia, 1981. Cert. psychologist. Rschr., specialist Nat. Inst. Youth Rsch., Sofia, 1974-92; lead expert Nat. Commn. for Prevention of Juvenile Deliquency, Sofia, 1993—; cons. various T.V. stas., 1993—, non-profit orgns., 1995—; lectr. Sofia Police Acad., 1997—. Author: The Flowers of Night: My Meetings with Prostitutes, Part I, 1995, Part II, 1999; author, editor: Children in Crisis and Crisis in Children, 1991, A Nationwide Situation Analysis of Bulgaria's Children and Family, 1992. Mem. Bulgarian Assn. Criminology, Soc. Neglected Children (pres.), Internat. Soc. Prevention of Child Abuse and Neglect, End Child Prostitution, Pornography and Trafficking Internat., Children Rights Info. Network, Balkan Coalition Children's Rights. Avocation: writing. Fax: 3592-981-1140. E-mail: lydia zag@yahoo.com. Home: Sveta Troitza Block 302, Entr B Apt 42, 1309 Sofia Bulgaria

ZAGORUIKO, YURIY ANATOLIEVICH, physicist, researcher; b. Kharkov, Ukraine, Mar. 1, 1949; s. Anatoliy Mikhailovich and Anna Petrovna (Shatalova) Z.; 1 child, Alexander; m. Olga Ivanovna Antyufeeva, Apr. 18, 1986. Engr., Kharkov State U., 1971; PhD (hon.), Inst. Semicondr. Physics, 1981. Engr., jr. rschr. Inst. Single Crystals, Kharkov, 1971-82, sr. rschr., 1983—. Contbr. articles to profl. jours. Mem. Internat. Soc. Optical Engring. Avocations: music, travel, ecology. E-mail: zagoruiko@isc.kharkov.com. Home: 37 Danilevskogo Str Apt 21, 61058 Kharkov Ukraine Office: Inst Single Crystals, 60 Lenin Ave, 61001 Kharkov Ukraine

ZAGREEV, BORIS VASIGOVICH, physicist, researcher; b. Pushkino, Russia, Sept. 13, 1961; s. Vasig Vasylovich and Anna Innokent'evna (Torbeeva) Z.; m. Anna Borisovna Vlas'uk, Dec. 19, 1987; 1 child, Audrey. PhD, Inst. Theoretical and Exptl. Physics, Moscow, 1992. Sr. rsch. worker Inst. Theoretical and Exptl. Physics, Moscow, 1992—. E-mail: Boris.Zagreev@itep.ru. Office: Inst Theoret Exptl Physics, B Cheremushkinskaya 25, 117218 Moscow Russia

ZAGRIADSKI, SERGEI VICTOROVICH, radiophysics educator, researcher; b. St. Petersburg, Russia, Feb. 19, 1954; s. Victor Pavlovich and Tatiana Michailovna (Deriy) Z.; m. Elena Alexandrovna Gordeeva Zagriadski, Sept. 19, 1987; 1 child, Alice. Diploma in Engr. Rsch. (hon.), Polytech. Inst., St. Petersburg, Russia, 1977; PhD, State Tech. U., St. Petersburg, Russia, 1987, DSc in Radiophysics, 1997. Cert. engr. Engr., sr. rschr., assoc. prof. State Tech. U., St. Petersburg, Russia, 1977-97, prof., 1997—; cons. Inst. Radio Measurement, Beijing, China, 1995-97. Inventor: Microwave tunable oscillator, 1984-92; contbr. articles to profl. jours. Grantee: Russian found. Fundamental Rsch., Moscow, 1995; recipient Honors Popov Telecommunications Soc., Moscow, 1978. Mem. IEEE, N.Y. Acad. Scis. Fax: 7-812-552-60-86. E-mail: zagr@radio.stu.neva.ru. Office: St Petersburg State Tech U, Polytekhnicheskaya 29, 195251 Saint Petersburg Russia

ZAHARIA, VALENTIN, pharmacist, educator; b. TG. Lapus, Maramures, Romania, Oct. 31, 1957; s. Victor and Elena (Hortopan) Z.; m. Daniela Viorica Stanciu, Oct. 29, 1983; children: Valentin Dan. Grad., Faculty of Pharmacy, Cluj-Napoca, Romania, 1982. Pharmacist Inst. Drug Control, Bucharest, Romania, 1982-86; pharmacist Inst. Hygiene and Pub. Health, Cluj-Napoca, 1986-89, rschr., 1989-92; sr. asst. Univ. Med. and Pharmacy, Cluj-Napoca, 1992-97, assoc. prof., 1997—, head organic chemistry dept., 1994—. Author: Natural Products, 1996, Heterocyclic Natural Products, 1998; contbr. more than 30 articles to profl. jours. Mem. Internat. Soc. Heterocyclic Chemistry, Soc. Romanian Pharm. Scis. Orthodox Christian. Avocations: music, opera. Home: Calea Manastur/72, 3400 Cluj-Napoca Romania Office: U Med and Pharmacy/Org Chem, V Babes 41, 3400 Cluj-Napoca Romania

ZAHERA, JUAN ANTONIO, industrial engineer; b. La Coruña, Spain, Oct. 26, 1949; s. Juan A. Zahera de Toledo and rosario Pérez Blanco; m. Maria Carmen Garcia, June 29, 1990; 1 child, Diana. Diploma in indsl. engring., E.T.S.I.I., Madrid, Spain, 1973; M in History Art, U. A.M., Madrid, 1981. Cert. engr. Hadrware design engr. I.T.T. Labs Spain, Madrid, 1973-75; instruments & control sys. engr. Initec-Process Plants, Madrid, 1975-81; sys. engr. INITEC, S.A., Madrid, 1981-85; project engr. Assn. Nuc. Vandellós, Barcelona, Spain, 1983-85; telecom. divsn. dir. S.A. Poulain, Barcelona, 1988-91; telecom. domestic market mgr. Pirelli Cables & Sys., Barcelona, 1992-99. Roman Catholic. Avocations: history of art, painting, philately. Fax: 34-93-417-49-97. Home: Rda. Gral Mitre No 145-8-2, 08022 Barcelona Spain Office: Pirelli Cables, Rambla Pirelli, 2, 08800 Barcelona Spain

ZAHIR, ZAFAR, social sciences researcher, population studies; b. Lahore, Punjab, Pakistan, Apr. 10, 1958; s. Zahir Uddin Khan and Tahira Zahir; m. Shahin Shamim Zafar, Nov. 6, 1988; children: Fatima Zafar, Ayesha Zafar. BSc, U. Punjab, Lahore, Pakistan, 1984, MA in Stats., 1988; MA in Applied Population Rsch., Exeter U., U.K., 1993. Rsch. assoc. Nat. Inst. Population Studies, Islamabad, Pakistan, 1988-93, assoc. fellow, 1993—; prin. investigator Nat. Inst. Population Studies, 1994-2000. Author: Population Growth and It's Implications on Socio-Economic Development in Pakistan, 1998, Strengthening, Monitoring and Evaluation of Reproductive Health in Pakistan, 1999. Mem. Islamabad Club. Avocations: reading books, playing squash. Office: NIPS Sector F-8/3, 8 St # 70, 44000 Islamabad Pakistan

ZAHN, HELMUT GUSTAV, retired chemistry educator; b. Erlangen, Bayern, Germany, June 13, 1916; s. Hermann Wolfgang and Irma Etelka (Brand) Z.; m. Ingrid Hildegard Fricke, Oct. 5, 1961; children: Alexandra, Roland. Diplomingenieur, Tech. Hochschule, Karlsruhe, Germany, 1939, Dr.-Ing., 1940; Privatdozent, U. Heidelberg (Germany), 1948; Dr. med. h.c., U. Düsseldorf (Germany), 1972; DSc, U. Leeds (Eng.), 1972, U. Belfast (No. Ireland), 1975, U. Bradford, 1976, U. Liege, Belgium, 1980, U. Barcelona (Spain), 1979. Rsch. asst. Inst. for Textile Chemistry Karlsruhe (Germany) U. and Badenweiler (Germany), 1940-49; sci. asst., lectr. Heidelberg U., 1949-57; dir. German Wool Rsch., Aachen, Germany, 1957-85; free sci. asst. German Wool Rsch., Aachen, 1986—; prof. textile chemistry and macromolecular chemistry U. Aachen, 1960-85, prof. emeritus; const. BASF, Ludwighafen, Germany, 1957-80, BAYER, Leverkusen, Germany, 1960-82, Freudenberg, Weinheim, Germany, 1958-70, Naturin, Weinheim, 1970—. Editor: Formation and Structure of Human Hair, 1997; contbr. articles to profl. jours. Mem. Am. Soc. for Biochemistry and Molecular Biology, Textile Inst. Manchester (Eng.), Protein Soc. San Diego. Lutheran. Avocations: puppet theater. Office: Deutsches Wollforschungsins, Veltmanplatz 8, D 52062 Aachen Germany

ZAHN, RUDOLF KARL, biochemist, educator; b. Bad Orb, Germany, Feb. 6, 1920; s. Jakob Simon and Maria Margarethe (Noll) Z.; grad. summa cum laude in Medicine, Johann Wolfgang Goethe Universitat, Frankfurt, Dr. med., PhD (hon.) U. Zagreb, 1988 ; m. Gertrud Daimler, Feb. 17, 1942; children: Matthias A.A., Isabel M. Rockefeller fellow Harvard U., 1949-50; mem. faculty dept. pharmacy U. Pa., Phila., 1950; chief kidney lab. dept. physiology, sci. assoc. dept. biochemistry U. Frankfurt (W. Ger.), 1950-56, docent, 1956-61, assoc. prof. physiology and biochemistry, 1961-67; chmn., dir. Inst. Biochemistry, Johannes Gutenberg U., Mainz, W. Ger., 1967-88; prof. Rudjer Boskovic, Zagreb, Croatia; head Joint Venture Lab. Marine Molecular Biology, Rovinji, Croatia and Mainz, W. Ger., 1971-94; prof. med. biochemistry U. Kurume-Fukuoka (Japan), 1981; cons. Bundesminister Forschung u. Technologie; full mem. Acad. Sci. and Literature; chmn. Commn. Molecular Biology, 1973—, Dr. honoris causa U. Zagreb, Yugoslavia, 1988; prof. emeritus U. Mainz, Fed. Republic Germany, 1988; honorary prof. U. Kurumue-Fukuoka, Japan, 1988. Mem. Gesellschaft für Biologische Chemie, Deutsche Gesellschaft für Klinische Chemie, Deutsche Gesellschaft für Elektronenmikroskopie, Deutsche Gesellschaft für Biophysik, European Assn. Cancer Research, Gesellschaft für Freunde des Deutsche-Amerikanischen Akademischen Austauschs, N.Y. Acad. Scis., Paul Ehrlich Gesellschaft für Chemotherapie, Internat. Soc. Research in Med. Edn., Medizinische Gesellschaft Mainz, Gesellschaft für Genetik Munchen, Deutsche Pharmakologische Gesellschaft, European Environ. Mutagen Soc., AAAS, Deutsche Gesellschaft für Gerontologie, Gesellschaft deutscher Chemiker, Croatian Acad. Scis. and Arts (corr.). European editor Mechanisms Aging Development; editor Research Molecular Biology, Acad. Sci. Lit., Mainz; chmn., organizer Karl August Forster lectures on Programmed Biosynthesis, 1968-90; contbr. articles to profl. jours. Office: Physiologische-Chemisches Inst, Obere Zahlbacher Str 63, D55101 Mainz Germany Home: Oderstr 12, D-65201 Wiesbaden Germany

ZAHNER, DOROTHY SIMKIN, elementary education educator; b. Chengdu, Szechuan, China, May 1; came to U.S. in the 1930s; d. Robert Louis and Margaret Isadore (Timberlake) Simkin; divorced; children: Mary de Avilan, Robert Louis. BA in Sociology, Whittier Coll.; MLS, U. So. Calif., L.A. Cert. tchr. Calif., Ariz. Tchr. L.A. and Pasadena (Calif.) Schs., 1969-93; dir., owner Betty Ingram Sch., North Hollywood, Calif., 1976-79; dir. Foothill Nursery Sch., La Crescenta, Calif., 1970s; tchr. L.A. Unified Sch. Dist.; guest tchr. Washington Unified Sch. Dist., Phoenix, 1994-97; guest tchr. Osborn Sch. Dist., 1998—, Madison Sch. Dist., Phoenix, 1999—. Author: (poetry) Yucca Poetry Workshop, 1993-94, Treasured Poems of America, 1993, internat. poetry publ., others; poems published in Eng., 1999, 2000. Bd. dirs. Ariz. Tenants Assn., Phoenix, 1994, 95; vol. Am. Friends Svc. Com., Phila., Calif., 1985—, Common Cause, L.A., 1990, Dem. Candidates, L.A. and Phoenix. Recipient award for a poem, Ariz. State Poetry Soc., Phoenix, 1995, 2000; honorable mention for poem published Sandcutters, 2000; named Poet Laureate, Pheonix Poetry Soc., 2000. Mem. Phoenix Poetry Soc. (com. mem., pres. 1998), Phoenix Writers Club (sec. 1998), Alameda Writers Group. Avocations: theatre, films, music, swimming, reading.

ZAHRADNIK, FREDRIC DOUGLAS, internet professional; b. Chgo., Sept. 11, 1956; s. Robert Joseph and Grace Eileen (Armstrong) Z.; m. Sally Smith, Oct. 25, 1980; children: Brent Alexander, Alice Janine. BA, Pa. State U., 1980; postgrad., Coll. of St. Francis de Sales, Allentown, Pa., 1998—. Assoc. editor Rodale, Inc., Emmaus, Pa., 1982-86, sr. editor, 1987-91; tech. editor Rodale Press, Inc., Emmaus, Pa., 1992-94, dir. new media, 1995-96, corp. web site adminstr., 1997, mktg. mgr. online, 1998-99; dir. internet programming men's health brand Rodale Inc., Emmaus, 2000—; invited spkr. Atlanta Super-Show NSGA, 1990, U. Wis., 1995; corr. Outdoor Life Network, 1996; expert, interviewee NBC Olympic Telecast, 1996; corr. bicycling ESPN, 1994; mem. industry adv. bd. for e-commerce Kutztown (Pa.) U., Dept. Computer Sci., 1998—. Editor: Bicycling on America Online, 1994-96; photos pub.: McDougal Littel Algebra 2: Explorations and Applications, 1996, Houghton Mifflin Integrated Math, 1993; Author: Cross Country Skiing Guide to Waxing, 1995. Soccer coach Lower Macungie Youth Assn., Allentown, 1996—; mem. industry adv. bd. for e-commerce Kutztown (Pa.) U. Dept. Computer Sci. Mem. Direct Mktg. Assn., The Assn. for Interactive Media, Internat. Mountain Biking Assn., Trout Unlimited. Avocations: bicycling, kayaking, skiing. Office: Rodale Press Inc 33 E Minor St Emmaus PA 18098-0099

ZAHRADNÍK, RUDOLF, chemist, researcher; b. Bratislava, Czechoslovakia, Oct. 20, 1928; s. Rudolf and Jindřiška (Vondráčková) Z.; m. Milena Bílková, Sept. 10, 1954; 1 child, Milena. Diploma in engring., Inst. Chem. Tech., Prague, Czech Republic, 1952; PhD, Czech Acad. Sci., Prague, 1956, DSc, 1968; DSc honoris causa, U. Dresden, 1992, U. Fribourg, 1993, U Pardubice, 1994, Georgetown U., 1996, Charles U., Prague, 1998, Clarkson U., 1998, Comenius U., Bratislava, 2000. Prof. phys. chemistry Charles U., Prague, 1967—; dir. J. Heyrovsky Inst. Phys. Chemistry Acad. Sci., Prague, 1990-93; pres. Acad. Scis. of Czech Republic, Prague, 1993—; cons Škoda-Plzeň, Czech Republic, 1996-2000. Author 9 books on applied quantum chemistry; mem. editl. bds. sci. jours. Recipient medal Slovak Inst. Tech., Bratislava, 1989, Heyrovsky Gold medal Czech Acad. Sci., 1990, Votoček medal, Inst. Chem. Tech., Prague, 1992, Charles U. Gold medal, Gold medal Slovak Acad. Scis., Austrian 1st Class Hon. Cross Sci. and Arts, 1999. Fellow World Assn. Theoretical Organic Chemists; mem. Czech Learned Soc. (pres. 1994-97), Internat. Acad. Quantum Molecular Scis., European Acad. Environ. Affairs, European Acad. Scis. and Arts. Avocations: baroque music, architecture, arts. Office: Acad Scis of Czech Republic, Národní 3, 117 20 Prague Czech Republic

ZAHRAN, MOHSEN MOHARRAM, architect, educator; b. Cairo, Aug. 8, 1938; s. Moharram M. and Dawlat (Sadek) Z.; m. Gayle McConaghy; children: Mona, Tamer. BArch, Ein Shams U., Cairo, 1959; MArch, MIT, Cambridge, 1962; MFA in Architecture, Princeton U., 1963, PhD in Environ. Planning, 1965. Prof. archiecture and urban planning faculty engring. U. Alexandria, Egypt, 1965—; chmn. Alexandria Comprehensive Plan 2005/2020 Alexandria Planning Commn., 1983-98; chmn. Gov. of Alexandria's Consultative Com. for Planning, 1986; exec. dir. Gen. Orgn. of Alexandria Libr., 1988—; project mgr. Bibliotheca Alexandrina, 1995—; head dept. architecture U. Alexandria, 1995-98; cons., expert various UN agys., UNESCO, CHBP, Habitat, WHO, ECWA, UNEP; mem. sci. com. Arab Cities Orgn. and Mediterrean Cities Orgn.; prof. practice urban planning, housing, museums, banks, hosps., pub. bldgs., others in U.S., Nigeria, Egypt and UAE. Author: College Housing: An Arena of Involvement and Conflict, 1972, Challenges of the Urban Environment, 1973, Philosophy of Design, 1977. Chmn. Housing and Planning Com., Alexandria City Coun., 1989-94, Nat. Dem. Party, 1995. Recipient Egyptian Arab Republic's medal of distinction of first order, 1986, Honor Shield, U. Alexandria, 1986; fellow Salzburg (Austria) Seminar, 1981, Award Legion d'Honour (France), Alexandria Univ., 1997; winner prizes of several archtl. competitions. Fellow Lebanese Pub. Health Assn.; mem. AIA, Eqyptian Soc. Archs., Egyptian Engring. Syndicate, Alexandria Yacht Club (mem. bd. 1984-89), Sporting Club Alexandria, West Alexandria Rotary (past pres. 1994). Home: 23 Roushdy St Apt 3 Roushdy, Alexandria 21529, Egypt Office: Gen Orgn Alexandria Libr, 116 El Horreya Ave, BabSharqi Alexandria Egypt

ZAHRAN, YASMINE, archeologist, writer; b. Ramallah, Palestine, Dec. 25, 1933; d. Yacub and Bahia (Khoury) Z. BSc, Columbia U., 1949; MA, U. London, 1954; Doctorate in Archeology, U. Sorbonne, Paris, 1962. Prof. Womens Tng. Coll., Ranallah, 1954-57; inspector all girls' sch. Ministry Edn. Jordan, Jerusalem, 1957-58; cons. womens edn. Govt. Libya, Benhezi, 1959; chief edn. opportunities for girls and women UNESCO, Paris, 1962-86; writer Paris, 1986—; dir. and prof. Inst. Islamic Archeology, U. Jerusalem, 1991-95. Author: Echoes of History, 1957, First Melody, 1992, A Beggar at Damascus Gate, 1994, Septimius Severus, 2000. Home: 33 Jaffa St, Ranallah Palestine

ZAHRT, MERTON STROEBEL, investor; b. Ellington, Wis., May 8, 1910; s. Francis Henry and Anna Barbara (Maves) Z.; m. Genevieve Rosalie Kottler, Aug. 20, 1932 (div. July 1952); children: Barbara Ann, Merton William (dec.), Sally Sue Zahrt-O'Leary; m. Hilda Elizabeth Bouck, Aug. 23, 1952; 1 child, Nancy Joanne Zahrt-Maxwell. MusB, Lawrence U., 1932; MusM, U. Rochester, 1943; EdD, Columbia U., 1950. Prof. music, head dept. Ft. Hays (Kans.) State Coll., 1949-50; assoc. prof. Ithaca (N.Y.) Coll., 1950-52; prof. music Chgo. Mus. Coll., 1952-58, acting chmn. music edn., 1957-58; asst. to dean of students U. Ill., Chgo., 1953-62, asst. dean of men, 1962-65; prof. music edn. U. So. Miss., Hattiesburg, 1965-71, coord. grad. studies in music edn., 1968-71; real estate salesman Hubbard Real Estate, Richmond, Va., 1971-78; prof. investor Zahrt Family Investments, Zahrt Revocable Trust U/A, Dunedin, Fla., 1978-88; trustee, 1988—; adjudicator sch. music competitions, Ark., Ill., Ind., Kans., Minn., Okla., Wis., 1940-65; conv. chmn. Ill. State Music Tchrs. Assn., Chgo., 1957; ch. choir dir. Coll. Ch., Hampden-Sydney, Va., 1978-79. Contbr. articles to profl. jours. Asst. dir. YMCA Men's Glee Club, Green Bay, Wis., 1935-36; dir. Hays (Kans.) Community Chorus, 1949-50; lay eucharistic min. Ch. Ascension, Clearwater, Fla., 1986-96; music com. mem. Episcopal Ch. of the Ascension, Clearwater, 1988-91. Community music programs grantee U. So. Miss., 1967-68. Mem. Am. Assn. Ret. Persons, State Univs. Annuitants Assn. (Ill.), Lawrence U. Legacy Circle, Guideposts Legacy Circle, The Inst. Econometric Rsch., Phi Gamma Delta, Phi Mu Alpha Sinfonia, Kappa Kappa Psi, Kappa Delta Pi. Republican. Episcopalian. Avocations: travel, golf, music, photography.

ZAIDAN, ELIE E., banker; b. Beirut, Lebanon, Oct. 25, 1963; s. Emile and Jennette Z.; m. Patsy Tasso, Sept. 2, 1989; children: Jennifer, Caroline, Marc. BA, U. Pierre & Marie Curie, 1983; MA in Strategy & Fin., Ecole Sup. d'Adminstrn. Ent., Paris, 1985; postgrad., Stanford U., 2000. N.Y. stock exch. analyst Nasco Karaoglan Group, Paris, 1985-87; portfolio mgr. Banque Indosuez, Geneva, 1987-89, Credit Comml. de France, Geneva, 1989-93; from adj. dir. to dir. Banque Francaise de l'Orient (Suisse) SA, Geneva, 1993-98; v.p. Bankers Trust, Geneva, 1998; gen. mgr. Exceed SA, Geneva, 1998—. Avocations: squash, skiing.

ZAIDAT, OSAMA O., neurologist; b. Zarqa, Jordan, Sept. 3, 1969; s. Othman M. and Anneh H. Z.; m. Sabreen O. Owais, Mar. 19, 1998; 1 child, Bashar O.O. MBBS, MD, Jordan U., 1993. Diplomate Am. Bd. Neurology. Intern in internal medicine and emergency rotation U. Hosp., Amman, Jordan, 1993-94; resident in internal medicine Seton Hall U., St. Joseph Hosps., 1994-95; resident in neurology Case Western Reserve U., U. Hosps. of Cleve., 1995-98; fellow in cerebrovascular disease and neurocritical care Case Western Reserve U., 1998-99, Case Western Reserve U., U. Hosps. of Cleve., 1999—; vis. fellow neurocritical care Cleve. Clinic Found., 1997, Johns Hopkins U., 1998. Author: (with others) Geriatric Neurosurgery, Muscles Diseases, Neuromuscular Disorders in Clinical Practice; jour. reviewer Neurology, Jou. Neurology Neurosurgery and Psychiatry; contbr. articles to profl. jours.; presenter in field. Mem. Am. Heart Assn., Am. Stroke Assn. Mem. AMA, ACP, Am. Acad. Neurology, Jordanian Med. Assn. Avocations: sports, reading, movies, travel. Fax: 216-844-5066. E-mail: ozaidat@hotmail.com. Office: CWRU U Hosp of Cleve Dept Neurology Hanna House 11100 Euclid Ave Fl 5 Cleveland OH 44106-1736

ZAIDFOUDIM, PAVEL CHASKELIEVICH, academic manager, researcher; b. Penza, USSR, Oct. 11, 1948; s. Chaskel Z. and Vera S. (Shouchman) Z.; m. Galina V. Rylkova, May 22, 1971; 1 child, Rylkova Xenia P. Historian, State Pedagogical Inst., Penza, 1974; PhD, State U. Leningrad (USSR), 1979; D in Biology, State Med. Acad., Arkhangelsk, Russia, 1995; Diploma, Diplomatic Acad., Moscow, 1998. Sr. fellow State Inst. Constrn., Penza, 1979-87; dir. gen. Far East Devel. Ctr., Chabarovsk region, USSR, 1987-91; dep. chmn. State Com. No. Devel., Moscow, 1991-94, first dep. chmn., 1996-98; dep. min. Ministry Nationalities, Moscow, 1994-96; chair no. studies State U., Petrozavodsk, Russia, 1999—. Author: Russian North Environment Rehabilitation, 1993, Strategy of Rehabilitation and Regulation of Russian North Environment, 1995; co-author, editor: Technoekopolis in Russian Far East, 1996; co-author, project leader: Feasibility Study of the Project "Arctic Bridge", 1998. Chmn. Fund Support No. Indigenous Peoples, Moscow, 1998—; chmn. bd. trustees Fund Support Technoekopolis in Far East, Chabarovsk region, Russia, 1996—; dep. chmn. Russian Peoples Assembly, 1998; bd. trustees Internat. Fund. Support Russian Cosmonautics, Moscow, 1999. Recipient Honorable Polar Researcher Russian Fleet Agy., 1996, Medal for svc. to cosmonautics Fund to Support Russian Cosmonautics, 1997. Mem. Russian Diplomatic Club, Russian Acad. Humanitaria Scis., Acad. No. Forum, Assn. Polar Rschs. Avocations: riding, extreme tourism. Home: Lomonosovski prospekt, 14 apt 96, 117496 Moscow Russia

ZAIDI, EMILY LOUISE, retired elementary school educator; b. Hoquiam, Wash., Apr. 20, 1924; d. Burdick Newton and Emily Caroline (Williams) Johnston; m. M. Baqar Abbas Zaidi, June 12, 1949 (dec. Dec. 1983). BA in Edn. and Social Studies, Ea. Wash. State U., 1948; MEd, U. Wash., 1964, EdD, 1974. Tchr. 4th grade Hoquiam Schs., 1948-49; tchr. grades 5-6 Lake Washington Sch. Dist., Kirkland, Wash., 1949-51; tchr. grades 2-3 Port Angeles (Wash.) Schs., 1951-54; tchr. grade 2 Seattle Schs., 1954-55; tchr., reading specialist Northshore sch. Dist., Bothell, Wash., 1955-69, Sacramento City Schs., 1969-87; ret.; mem. Calif. State Instructional Materials Panel, Sacramento, 1975. Mem. Sacramento Opera Assn., 1986—, Sacramento Ballet Assn., 1987—. Fulbright Commn. Exchange Tchr., 1961-62. Mem. Reading Club. Democrat. Avocations: writing, children's literature, reading, travel. Home: 4230 N River Way Sacramento CA 95864-6055

ZAIDI, RIAZ HAIDER, aircraft engineer, consultant; b. Baghdad, Iraq, Aug. 25, 1959; s. Syed Ghulam Haider and Ashraf (Razvi) Z.; m. Beenish Zehra, Aug. 17, 2000. AS in Aviation Maintenance Tech., Embry-Riddle Aero. U., Daytona Beach, Fla., 1982, BS in Aero. Studies, 1988, BS in Aircraft Engring., 1990, M in Aero. Sci., 1994; M in Engring. Mgmt., Washington U., St. Louis, Mo., 1998, MS in Tech. and Human Affairs, 1999, postgrad. in engring. and policy, 2000. Lic. FAA Airframe and Powerplant. Engr. T-45 structures McDonnell Douglas Aerospace, St. Louis, 1992-94, sr. engr. T-45 support equipment, 1994-95; sr. engr. F/A-18 mech. sys. Boeing Co., St. Louis, 1995-98, project engr. Phantom Works Joint Strike Fighter program, 1998—; mem. industry adv. bd. Embry-Riddle Aero. U., 1994—; engring. cons. Britech, St. Louis, 1995-98; bd. dirs. Art2Part Plastics Inc., St. Louis. Vol. Jr. Achievement, St. Louis, 1994—, Embry-Riddle Aero. U. Aces program, 1994—. Achievements include pending patent for heat blanket test panel and test process. Home: 1748 Wichmood Ct Saint Charles MO 63303-4657 Office: The Boeing Co PO Box 516 Saint Louis MO 63166-0516

ZAIDI, ZEENAT FATIMA, anatomist, educator; b. Kohat, Pakistan, Oct. 12, 1947; d. Ghulam Abbas and Kubra Fatima Zaidi; m. Syed Mansoor Akhter, Feb. 12, 1978; children: Simin, Bilal. BS, Frontier Coll., Peshawer, Pakistan, 1966; MB BS, Khyber Med. Coll., Peshawer, 1971; diploma in neuropsychology, U. Bergen, Norway, 1976; DPhil in Neuroscis., U. Oxford, Eng., 1992. Demonstrator anatomy Peshawer U., 1972-75; lectr., demonstrator anatomy King Saud U., Riyadh, 1976-86, asst. prof., 1995—; sr. instr. The Aga Khan U., Karachi, Pakistan, 1986-89, 93-94, asst. prof., 1995. Contbr. articles to profl. jours. Norwegian Agy. for Internat. Devel. fellow, 1975-76. Mem. The Anat. Soc. Gt. Britain & Ireland, The Anat. Soc. Pakistan, The Oxford Soc. Avocations: embroidery, rugmaking, painting, reading, listening to music. Office: Dept Anatomy, King Saud U PO Box 22452, Riyadh 11495, Saudi Arabia

ZAIM, SALIH, education specialist; b. Paphos, Aydin, Cyprus, Nov. 1, 1951; s. Emin and Remziye (Galuda) Z.; m. Aytüz Naciogli; children: Remziye, Nurten. BS in Math., Mid. East Tech. U., Ankara, Turkey, 1979; postgrad., Amherst (Mass.) Coll., 1998. Tchr. Kurtulus Lycee, Gudelyurt, Turkey, 1979-88; asst. headmaster G/yurt Turk Maarif Coll., Gudelyurt, 1988-92, headmaster, 1992-93; maths. inspector Ministry of Edn., Nicosia, Turkey, 1993-94; edn. specialist Ministry of Edn., Nicosia, 1994—; mem. tchrs. union Tchr. Union Orgn., Micosia, 1989-91. With Cyprus Army, 1971-74. Author: Revised Maths, 1988. Mem. Bagcil Football Team. Muslim. Avocations: swimming, football, basketball, reading, movies. Home: 19 Hasan Kahya St, Guzelyurt Nicosia, Cyprus Office: Ministry of Edn, Nicosia Cyprus

ZAIMAN, K(OICHI) ROBERT, dentist; b. Cin., Oct. 19, 1944; s. Noboru Gary and Toshiko (Matsuyama) Z.; m. Kimberly Ann Sass, Nov. 6, 1976; children: Kara Jean, Matthew Robert. Student, Creighton U., Omaha, 1962-64, DDS, 1968. Asst. prof. Creighton U. Sch. Dentistry, Omaha, 1971-73, assoc. prof., 1973-75; pvt. practice dentistry Omaha, 1971—; dir. Chicano and Native-Am. Free Clin., Creighton U., 1970-75. Past v.p., bd. dirs. Japanese-Am. Citizens League, Omaha, 1977-86; mem. bd. elders King of Kings Luth. Ch., 1990-95, deacon, 1995—. Lt. comdr. USN, 1964-71. Fellow Acad. Gen. Dentistry (pres. 1976-77, nat. del. 1971-76), Acad. Continuing Edn.; mem. ADA, Omaha Dist. Dental Soc. (treas. 1980-85, bd. dirs. 1968-92, peer review 1996—), Nebr. Dental Assn. (del. 1971-94, 96—), Omaha Dental Study Club (pres. 1999—), Delta Sigma Delta (pres. 1973-74). Office: 10841 Q St Ste 109 Omaha NE 68137-3741

ZAINUDDIN, DIAM, government executive; b. Alor Star, Malaysia, 1937. Degree in law, U. London, 1959; postgrad., U. Calif., 1977-79. Atty. Allen & Gledhill; ptnr. Daim & Gamani; chmn. Perembe Fleet Holdings; pro-chancellor U. Sains, Malaysia, 1994; magistrate, deputy pub. prosecutor; apptd. Senate, 1980-82; elected MP, 1982—; econs. advisor Office of Prime Min.; treas. UMNO; min. fin. Malaysia, 1984-91, 99—; exec. dir. Nat. Econ.

Coun., 1997—. Vis. scholar Harvard U., 1991-92. Office: Min Fin, Block 9 Khazanah, Kuala Lumpur 50592, Malaysia*

ZAITSEV, ALEXANDRE SERGEEVICH, meteorologist; b. Petrokrepost, Leningrad, USSR, July 13, 1939; arrived in Switzerland, 1992; s. Serge Yakovlevich and Valentina Alexseevna Zaitsev; m. Tamara Pavlovna Chernitsova, Jan. 13, 1966; 1 child, Ilya. Meteorologist, Hydromet Inst., Leningrad, 1961; PhD, State U., Tashkent, USSR, 1966. Cert. engr. Scientist Main Geophys. Obs., Leningrad, 1961-65; sr. scientist Hydromet Inst., Tashkent, 1965-66; chief of lab. Main Geophys. Obs., Leningrad, 1966-75, dep. dir. sci., 1975-77; dir. R&D World Meteorol. Orgn., Geneva, Switzerland, 1977-85; dep. dir. Main Geophys. Obs., Leningrad, 1985-92; asst. sec.-gen. World Meteorol. Orgn., Geneva, 1992—; editor WMO Bulletin, 1995—; mem. sci. coun. Main Geophys. Obs., Leningrad, 1975-77, 85-92, State Hydrological Inst., Leningrad, 1987-92; mem. task team World Bank, Minsk, Belarus, 1992. Editor: Trudy Glavnaia Geophys. Obs., vol. 521, 1991, vol. 543, 1991; co-author: (publs.) Methodology for Air Pollution Assessment, 1972 (Bronze medal 1972), Automatic Air Pollution Monitoring Stations, 1976 (Silver medal 1976); mem. editl. bd. Meteorol./Hydrology Jour., 1994—. Mem. Russian Soc. to Protect Nature, Leningrad, 1986-92, Soc. Znanie, Leningrad, 1986-91; chmn. bd. Sci. and Tech. Soc., Main Geophys. Observatory, Leningrad, 1986-91. Lt. Res., 1961-91. Recipient State medal for hon. travail USSR Supreme Soviet, 1970; named Vet. of Travail, City Coun., 1987, Hon. Hydrometeorologist, State Coun. for Hydromet, 1974. Avocations: alpine skiing, traveling. Office: World Meteorol Orgn, 7 bis Ave de la Paix 2300, CH-1211 Geneva 2, Switzerland

ZAITSEV, BORIS DAVYDOVICH, physicist, educator; b. Saratov, Russia, Mar. 26, 1949; s. Davyd Nikolaevich and Maria Stepanovna (Slaschilina) Z.; m. Natalia Grigorevna Heifets, Aug. 22, 1973; 1 child, Marina Borisovna. Diploma in Physics, Saratov State U., 1971, PhD in Physics and Math., 1978, ScD in Physics and Math., 1998. Engr. Inst. Mechanics and Physics of Saratov State U., 1971-72, sr. engr., 1972-75, sr. rsch. scientist, 1975-81; sr. rsch. scientist Inst. radio Engring. and Electronics, Saratov, 1981-86, leading rsch. scientist, 1986—; assoc. prof. Saratov State U., 1987-99, prof. 1999—; vis. scientist Marquette U., Milw., 1996-98. Author: Acoustic Waves in Solids, 1998; contbr. articles to profl. jours. Grantee Soros Found., 1994, Nat. Acad. Scis., 1996. Mem. IEEE. Avocations: growing plants., biking, literature. Home: Sokolovaya Str 44/62 Apt 44, 410030 Saratov Russia Office: Inst Radio Engring/Elec, Zelyonayastr 38, 410019 Saratov Russia

ZAITSEV, VALENTIN FEODOROVICH, mathematician, researcher; b. Uglovoye, Russia, Sept. 29, 1945; s. Feodor Epifanovich and Elena Ivanovna (Davidovich) Z.; m. Zilya Nailyevna Khakimova, Jan. 30, 1987; children: Elena, Svetlana, Oleg. Engr. radiophysics, Leningrad Poly. Inst., USSR, 1969; PhD in Math., Leningrad State U., 1983; DSc in Math., Inst. Math. and Mechanics, Russia, 1992; sr. rsch. scientist (hon.), Leningrad State U., 1991; prof. math. (hon.), Russian State Pedagog. U., 1998. Cert. scientist. Engr. Leningrad State U., 1971-83, rsch. scientist, 1983-96; prof. Russian State Pedagog. U., St. Petersburg, 1993—; cons. Oryol (Russia) State U., 1994-98, St. Petersburg State Conservatory, 1989-99. Author: (books) Discrete Group Methods for Integrating Equations of Nonlinear Mechanics, 1994, Handbook of Exact Solutions for Differential Equations, 1995, Handbuch der linearem Differentialgleichungen, 1996. Grantee ISF, 1994-95. Avocations: classical music, biorhythms of musical creation. Office: Russian State Pedagog U, Nab r Moyki 48, 191186 Saint Petersburg Russia

ZAITSEV, VIACHESLAV FIODOROVICH, vice-chancellor, science educator; b. Astrakhan, Russia, Oct. 2, 1948; s. Fiodor Georgievich and Nina Georgievna (Kartashova) Z.; m. Margarita Mihailovna Sineeva, July 21, 1974; children: Igor, Sergey. Masters degree, Inst. of Hydrobiology, Kiev, Ukraine, 1979; doctors degree, Agrl. U., Krasnodar, Russia, 1992. Asst. Tech. U., Astrakhan, 1972-74, asst. prof., 1980-92, prof., 1992—; dean agrl. faculty Tech. U., Astakhan, 1985-88; head dept. hydrobiology Tech. U., 1992—; vice chancellor on scientific problems, 1997-99, chmn. thesis coun. field environ. protection, 1997-99. Author: Trade Aguaculture, 1992. Res. lt. Ministry of Internal Affairs, 1971-72. Recipient Meritorious Sci. worker Pres. Russian Fedn., 1999; grantee Internat. Assn. for the Promotion of Cooperation with Scientists from the Ind. States of the Former Soviet Union Assn., 1995, Russian Found. Sci., 1996. Mem. U. Assn. of Caspian Region, Russian Acad. of Natural Scis., N.Y. Acad. Sci. Avocations: swimming, fishing, traveling in mountains. Home: St Tatisheva 16-3, Bldg 5 Apt 16, 414025 Astrakhan Russia Office: Astrakhan State Tech U, St Tatisheva 16, 414025 Astrakhan Russia

ZAITSEV, VIKTOR MIKHAILOVICH, surgeon, orthopedist, gynecologist; b. Pokrovshoe, Russia, Feb. 6, 1948; s. Michael Vasilievch and Ekaterina Titovna (Puchkova) Z.; m. Ludmila Alekseevna Bulgakova, Aug. 27, 1971; 1 child, Inna Viktorovna. MD, U. Krasnoyarsk, Russia, 1972, surgery course, 1973-74, thorax course, 1983; thorax course, U. Moscow, 1980. Cert. in surgery, orthopedics, gynecology. Commd. officer Russian Army, advanced through grades to maj.; dir. surgery svc. Hosp., Beli Yar, Russia, 1972-78; surgeon Regional Hosp., Abakan, Russia, 1978-87; dir. surgery svc. Hosp. Ctrl., Nampula, Mozanbique, 1987-91, 93-96, Abakan, 1991-93; dir. surgery svc. Inhambane, Mozambique, 1996—. Avocations: hunting, fishing, playing football, basketball and volleyball. Home: Ul Puskine 96-44, 662600 Abakan Russia Office: Ministry Health, Moscow Russia

ZAITSEV, VLADIMIR NIKOLAEVICH, chemistry educator, researcher; b. Kiev, Ukraine, Soviet Union, Oct. 11, 1958; s. Nikolai Fedorovich Zaitsev and Tatiana Markovna Kanivets; m. Galina Nikolaevna Chorna, Dec. 16, 1978; children: Elena, Olga. MSc, Kiev State U., 1981, PhD, 1984, docent, 1992, DS, 1997. Lab. asst. Kiev State U., 1975-76, rsch. asst., 1984-86, asst. prof., 1986-91, assoc. prof., 1991-94, prof., 1994—; vis. scientist Southampton U., U.K., 1990-91; vis. prof. Tex. A&M U., College Station, 1995; inventor in field. Author: Chemically Modified Silicas: Synthesis Structure of Bonded Layer and Surface Chemistry, 1997; contbr. articles to profl. jours.; patentee in field. Brit. Coun. scholar, London, 1990-91, J.W. Fulbright scholar Coun. Internat. Exch. Scholars, Washington, 1995; recipient Brit. Coun. award, 1994. Mem. European Rare Earth & Actinid Soc., Am. Chem. Soc., Mendeleev's Soc. Avocations: travel, badminton. Home: 25 Vasilenko St 139 Apt, Kiev 252124, Ukraine Office: Taras Shevchenko Kiev U, 60 Vladimirskaya St, Kiev 252033, Ukraine

ZAITSEV, VLADIMIR VLADIMIROVITCH, molecular physicist, educator; b. Kadui, USSR, Aug. 12, 1944; s. Vladimir Nikkolaevitch Muravkkin and Valentina Alekseevna Zaitseva; m. Natalia Borisovna Botchkarieva, June 21, 1977; 1 child, Vladimir. PhD, Inst. Chemistry and Physics, Moscow, 1975; docent in physics, Ivanovo (USSR) Chem.-Tech., 1978; DSc in Chem. Sci., Moscow State U., 1992; prof. molecular physics, Ivanovo State U., 1995. Engr., v.p. dept. tech. Transistor, Minsk, USSR, 1967-70; asst. docent Ivanovo Chem.-Tech. Inc., 1970-79; docent Ivanova State U., 1979-92, prof., 1993—, head molecular physics dept., 1994—, chmn. dissertation coun. on PhD in phys. chemistry rank, 1999—; vice chmn. XIV Russian Conf. Physics Segnetho-electrics, Ivanovo, 1995; pres., chair Conf. on Molecular Physics, Ivanovo, 1997-2000; vice chmn. 1st Internat. Conf. Ecology of Man and Nature, Ivanovo, 1997; chmn. The IX Internat. Symposium Thin Films in the Electronics, Ivanovo, 1998. Author: Physics and Technique Nonequilibrium Systems, 1983, Biophysical Aspects of Human Blood Plasma Structurization in Myocardial Infarction Diagnostics, 1999; editor: Molecular Physics of Nonequilibrium Systems, 1997, Ecology of Man and Nature, 1997; contbr. over 300 articles to profl. jours. Sr. lt., Chemie, 1970, Ivanovo. Soros Fund grantee, Moscow, 1994, 95, 97. Mem. Internat. Soc. Fibrinolysis and Thrombolysis, Internat. Soc. Thrombosis and Haemostasis, Internat. Info. Acad., N.Y. Acad. Sci., Phys. Soc. Ivanovo Chem. Tech. Inst., Ivanovo Acad. Informationology (pres. 1999). Avocation: horticulture. Home: Sacco 3-60, 153000 Ivanovo Russia Office: Ivanovo State U, Ermaca 39, 153025 Ivanovo Russia

ZAITSEVA, GANNA IVANOVNA, organic chemist, researcher; b. Krasnye Baki, Russia, July 11, 1940; d. Ivan Dmitrievich and Anna Nikolaevna (Solovieva) Potkin; m. Eugenyi Konstantinovich Zaitsev, July 22, 1966; 1 child, Zaitsev Kirill. Grad. in Organic Chemistry, Poly. Inst., Gorkii, Russia, 1963; D in Organic Chemistry, Techol. Inst., Leningrad, Russia, 1968. Engr. Plant of Synthetic Rubber, Volgograd, Russia, 1963-64; rschr. Polymer Inst., Dzerzhinsk, Russia, 1964-65; sr. rschr. Inst. Wood Hydrolisis, St. Petersburg, Russia, 1969-79; sr. rschr. Inst. Hisotry of Material Culture, St. Petersburg, Russia, 1979-89, head lab., 1989—; sr. lectr. Inst. Engring. for Cinema, St. Petersburg, 1972-74, Technol. Inst., 1976-77, St. Petersburg State U., 1998—. Contbr. articles to profl. jours.; patentee in field. Named Honorable Inventor of USSR, 1982. Mem. St. Petersburg Club Scientists. Avocation: skiing. Home: Podvoiskogo 35-1-224, 193231 Saint Petersburg Russia Office: Inst History Mat Culture, Dvortsovaya nab 18, 191186 Saint Petersburg Russia

ZAITZEFF, ROGER MICHAEL, lawyer; b. Detroit, June 25, 1940; s. Peter and Mary (Fedchenia) Z.; children: Zachary, Natasha, Zoe, Peter. BA with honors and distinction, U. Mich., 1962; MA with distinction, U. Calif., Berkeley, 1963, JD, 1969. Bar: N.Y. 1970, U.S. Dist. Ct. (so. dist.) N.Y. 1975, U.S. Ct. Appeals (2nd cir.) 1975, D.C. 1985. Assoc. Seward & Kissel, N.Y.C., 1969-77, ptnr., 1977-94; ptnr. Latham & Wakins, N.Y.C., 1994-2000, LaBoeuf. Lamb, Greene & MacRae, N.Y.C., 2000—. Contbr. articles to profl. jours. Mem. Tribar Opinion Com., 1990-93. Heller grantee U. Mich., 1962; recipient William Jennings Bryan Prize. Mem. ABA, Internant. Bar Assn., Assn. of Bar of City of N.Y., N.Y. State Bar Found., Southwestern Legal Found. (adv. bd.), N.Y. County Lawyers Assn. (spl. com. legal opinions in comml. transactions), Phi Beta Kappa. Office: LeBoeuf Lamb Greene & MacRae 125 W 55th St 16th Fl New York NY 10019-5369

ZAJAC, ALFRED, physicist, educator; b. Vienna, Austria, Feb. 18, 1917; came to U.S., 1948; s. Joseph and Frances (Nevrkla) Z.; m. Dorothy Chmielowiec, Sept. 2, 1950; children: Mark, Andrew. BS, St. Andrew's U., 1948; MS, NYU, 1952; PhD, Polytechnic Inst. Bklyn., 1957. Prof. physics Polytechnic Inst. Bklyn., 1957-64, Adelphi (N.Y.) U., 1964-87, Hofstra U., Hempstead, N.Y., 1987—. Author: Basic Principles and Laws of Mechanics, 1964; co-author: Optics, 1970. Mem. Polish Army Vets. Post 123 (treas.), Hejnal Chorus (co-dir.). Democrat. Roman Catholic. Avocations: choral singing, bee keeping. Home: 60-26 60th Rd Maspeth NY 11378 Office: Hofstra Univ Hempstead NY

ZAJC, BARBARA, chemist, educator, researcher; b. Ljubljana, Slovenia, Mar. 26, 1953; d. Alojz and Sonja (Baš) Z. BS, U. Ljubljana, 1977, MSc, 1982, PhD, 1989. Rsch. chemist Jožef Stefan Inst., Ljubljana, 1977-87; asst. prof. U. Ljubljana, 1987-93, asst. prof., 1993-99, assoc. prof., 1999—; vis. fellow NIH, Bethesda, Md., 1991-94. Contbr. articles to profl. publs. Fogarty fellow NIH, 1991; Rsch. grantee Ministry of Sci. and Tech. of Slovenia, 1993, 97. Mem. Am. Chem. Soc. Avocations: art appreciation, skiing, hiking. Home: Na Jami 11, 1000 Ljubljana Slovenia Office: U Ljubljana, Aškerčeva 5, 1000 Ljubljana Slovenia

ZAJÍCEK, PAVEL, parasitologist; b. Mladá Boleslav, Czechoslovakia, Apr. 14, 1960; s. Jaroslav and Jaroslava (Kordová) Z.; m. Zdena Konopová, Mar. 24, 1990; children: Tomáš, Libor. MSc, Charles U., Prague, Czech Republic, 1984; PhD, Inst. Parasitology, Ceské Budejovicě, Czech Republic, 1991. Rschr. Inst. Parasitology, Lab. Fish Protozoology, 1990-92; asst. to gen. sec. Škoda automobilová a.s., Mladá Boleslav, Czech Republic, 1992—. Avocation: painting. Home: Václava Klementa 1236, 29301 Mladá Boleslav Czech Republic Office: Škoda Auto as, Gen Sec, Václava Klementa 869, 29360 Mladá Boleslav Czech Republic

ZAK, JOSHUA, physics educator; b. Wilna, Poland, Sept. 26, 1929; arrived in Israel, 1957; s. Mendel and Tsima (Shabad) Z.; children: Ben-Zion, Shabad. MSc, Wilna U., 1955; DSc, Technion, Israel, 1960. Vis. prof. MIT, Cambridge, Mass., 1967-68, Northwestern U., Evanston, Ill., 1968-69; prof. physics Technion, Haifa, Israel, 1970—, dir. Solid State Inst., 1970-73, Eric and Sheila Samson chair in physics, 1989—; vis. prof. U. Calif., San Diego, 1974-75, NYU, 1974-75, U. Mich., Ann Arbor, 1978, U. Va., Charlottesville, 1979, U. Toronto, 1994-95, Argonne (Ill.) Nat. Lab., 1981-82, 89-90, Inst. des Hautes Etudes Scientifiques, Bures-Sur-Yvette, France, 1985-86. Editor: Irreducible Representations of Space Groups, 1969; author: kq Representation in Quantum Mechanics, 1967, Zak Transform in Signal Processing. With Soviet Red Army, 1945-48. Recipient New Eng. Acad. award Am. Tech. Soc., 1994. Mem. European Phys. Soc., Israel Phys. Soc. Avocations: kayaking champion of Lithuania. Home: 72 Horev St, 34343 Haifa Israel Office: Technion, Haifa 32000, Israel

ZAK, ROBERT JOSEPH, lawyer; b. Steubenville, Ohio, July 29, 1946; s. Joseph and Pearl (Munyas) Z.; m. Kristy Hubbard Winkler, Sept. 13, 1980; children: Elizabeth Adele, Robert Joseph Jr., Barbara Ann. BS, W.Va. U., 1968, JD, 1975. Bar: W.Va. 1975, U.S. Dist. Ct. (so. dist.) W.Va. 1975, U.S. Dist. Ct. (no. dist.) W.Va. 1989, U.S. Ct. Appeals (4th cir.) 1990. Staff atty. Pub. Svc. Commn. of W.Va., Charleston, 1975-76; assoc. Preiser & Wilson L.C., Charleston, 1976-81, ptnr., 1981-85; sr. ptnr. Zak & Assocs., Charleston, 1985—; hearing examiner W.Va. Bd. Regents, Charleston, 1987-90; spl. asst. atty. gen. State of W.Va., Charleston, 1980-87; chmn. civil svc. commn. City of Charleston, 1987-90; mem. State of W.Va. Worker's Compensation Appeals Bd., Charleston, 1991-97. With U.S. Army, 1969-71, Vietnam. Fellow Am. Acad. Matrimonial Lawyers; mem. Order of Barristers. Republican. Presbyterian. Office: Zak & Assocs 607 Ohio Ave Charleston WV 25302-2228

ZAKAI, HAYTHAM AHMED, parasitologist, educator, consultant; b. Jeddah, Saudi Arabia, Sept. 19, 1967; s. Ahmed Sazai Zakai and Hikmat Abdullah Bakhsh; m. Nadia Abdullah Aljirafi, Aug. 13, 1993; children: Ghadeer, Razan. BSc in Med. Tech., King Abdulaziz U., Jeddah, Saudi Arabia, 1989; MSc, Sch. Tropical Medicine, Liverpool, Eng., 1993, PhD, 1996. Med. technologist Univ. Hosp., Jeddah, 1989-90, sr. technologist, 1990-92; demonstrator King Abdulaziz U., Jeddah, 1992-96, asst. prof., 1996—. Mem. Royal Soc. Tropical Medicine and Hygiene, Am. soc. Clin. Pathologists, Am. Soc. Tropical Medicine and Hygiene, Brit. Soc. Parasitology. Avocation: diving. Office: Faculty Medicine, PO Box 9029, 21413 Jeddah Saudi Arabia

ZAKAKIS, DIMITRIOS PAUL, shipping company executive, shipowner; b. Athens, Greece, Apr. 8, 1945; s. Paul Pandelis and Polymnia (Vamvakas) Z.; m. Angelique-Theodosios Moschopoulos, Sept. 12, 1972; children: Paul, Polymnia. Grad., Mcht. Marine Acad., Hydra, Greece, 1965. 2d officer Valmas Bros. Shipping Co., Piraeus, Greece, 1970-72, chief officer, 1972-75, marine master, 1976-77; mng. dir. Endeavour Shipping, Piraeus, Greece, 1977-85, pres., 1986—. Served with Royal Hellenic Navy, 1968-70. Mem. Mcht. Marine Acad. Grads. Assn. Greek Orthodox. Club: U.S. Propeller. Avocation: yachting. Home: 12 Singrou St, 15232 Halandri Greece Office: Endeavour Shipping Co, 35 Possidonos Ave, GR 18344 Moschaton Greece

ZAKARIA, GOLAM ABU, medical physicist, radiological safety officer; b. Naogaon, Bangladesh, Dec. 31, 1953; arrived in Germany, 1972; s. Md. Baniz Uddin and Rahima Begum; m. Elke Birgit Barbara Jenkner, Oct. 18, 1980; children: Florian Polash, Rebecca Priyanka. MS, Halle/Saale U., Halle, Germany, 1978; PhD, Heidelberg (Germany) U., 1986. Qualified expert in radiophysics. Rsch. fellow Univ. Hosp., Göttingen, Germany, 1979-80; rsch. fellow, med. physicist Univ. Hosp., Heidelberg, 1980-85; chief med. physicist Gummersbach (Germany) Hosp., 1986-87, head dept. med. radiophysics, 1987—; adviser dept. physics Engring. U., Dhaka, Bangladesh, 1995—; v.p. Ctr. for Med. Physics and Cancer Awareness, Chittagong, Bangladesh, 1997—; adviser Bangladesh Med. Physics Assn., Dhaka, 1998—. Editor: Kazi Nazrul Islam, 1999; contbr. articles to profl. jours. Mem. Afro-Asian Student Fedn., Göttingen, 1979—; mem. Heinrich-Böll Found., Berlin, 1987—; pres. Bangladesh Study and Devel. Ctr., Wiehl, Germany, 1996—. Mem. European Soc. for Therapeutic Radiology and Oncology, German Soc. for Med. Physics, Am. Assn. Physicists in Medicine, Assn. Med. Physicists India. Avocations: essay writing, jogging, gardening, listening to music. Home: Margeritenweg 7, 51674 Wiehl Germany Office: Gummersbach Hosp, Wilhelm-Breckow-Allee 20, 51643 Gummersbach Germany

ZAKHARCHENKO, MIKHAIL PETROVICH, ecologist, educator; b. Gomel, Russia, Jan. 24, 1950; s. Petr Vasilievich and Valentina Mikhailovna (Lukashenko) Z.; m. Galina Vladimirovna Pevnaya, Nov. 6, 1976; children: Mikhail, Valentin. BS, Vitebsk State Med. Inst., 1971; MS, Kuibyshev Mil. Med. Faculty, 1973; D in Med. Scis., Mil. Med. Acad., 1987. Intern Mil. Med. Soc., Leningrad, Russia, 1973-74, resident, 1974-76; dep. chief lab. Ctr. Hygienic Diagnostics, Leningrad, 1973-76; instr. Mil. Med. Acad., Leningrad, 1979-84, head office of studies, 1984-90; head dept. human ecology St. Petersburg (Russia) State Med. Acad., 1990—; gen. dir. Internat. Inst. Human Ecology and Profl. Health, 1999—; scientific cons. Coun. Russian Acad. Med. Scis., Moscow, 1992—, Mil. Med. Acad., St. Petersburg, 1992—. Author: (monographs) Ecologic and Hygienic Problems of Investigation of Man's and Population Immune Status, 1992, Modern Problems of Ecohygiene, 1993, Hygienic Diagnostics under Extreme Conditions, 1995, Problems of Hygienic Diagnostics Today, 1995, Hygienic Diagnostics of the Water Environment, 1996, Ecology and Health: Time To Act, 1996, Diagnostics in Prophylactic Medicine, 1997, Electromagnetic Radiation and Health, 1998, Hygenic Diagnostics of the Hospital Surroundings, 1999, Radiation Factor at the Extreme North of Russia, 1999, Thermal Affections, 2000; mem. editl. bd. Geographia Medica, 1992, Jour. Problems of Rehab., 1999—; contbr. articles to sci. jours. Col. Russian Mil., 1973-90. Mem. Russian Acad. Scis. (St. Petersburg House of Scientists 1991—), St. Petersburg Union Scientific and Engring. Socs. (mem. ctrl. adminstrn. 1993—), All Russian Sci. Med. Soc. Hygienists and Sanitation Physicians (sci. sec. St. Petersburg city dept. 1989—), All Russian Ctr. Scis. on Man, Petrovskaya Acad. Scis. and Arts, Internat. Acad. Scis. Ecology, Safety of Man and Nature, Editl. Bd. (editorjours. 1999—). Avocations: football, basketball, ice hockey, chess, tennis. E-mail: zaharc@chat.ru and zaharc@mail.ru. Office: Saint Petersburg State Med, PO Box 148, Saint Petersburg 194356, Russia

ZAKHARIA, MANELL ELIAS, underwater acoustics scientist; b. Beirut, Feb. 8, 1955; arrived in France, 1976; s. Elias and Mountaha (Abouchahine) Z.; m. Dominique Brac de la Perriere, 1995. B, Coll. Notre-Dame, Jamhour, Lebanon, 1972; engring. diploma, Inst. Chimie et Physique Industrielles, Lyon, France, 1978; diploma in acoustics, Lab. Mechanics and Acoustics, Marseille, 1979; Docteur-Ingénieur en Acoustique (hon.), U. d'Aix-Marseille, 1982. Scientist Cath. U. Lyon, 1980-84; scientist, educator Ecole Superieure de Chimie, Physique, Electronique, Lyon, 1984—, Ecole Superiour de Chimie, Physique Electronique, CPE Lyon; dir. lab. Acoustique, Systemes, Signaux et SOnar, 1991—; chmn. 1st French conf. on acoustics, 1989. Contbr. articles to profl. jours. Mem. IEEE, European Acoustics Assn. (bd. dirs.), Soc. Francaise d'Acoustique (pres. 1991-95), Acoustical Soc. Am., Soc. des Electriciens et des Electroniciens, Acoustical Soc. Japan, Inst. Acoustics. Avocations: music, fine arts, photography, sightseeing. Office: CPE Lyon LiSA/LASSO, 43 Bd dull novembre 1918, BP 2077 69616 Villeurbanne cedex, France

ZAKHAROV, NIKOLAI D., physicist; b. Moscow, Nov. 5, 1944; s. Dmitri S. and Varvara P. (Platonova) Z.; m. Lidia S. Petrova, July 20, 1968; children: Dmitri, Philipp. PhD, Inst. Crystallography, Moscow, 1975. Jr. rschr. Inst. Crystallography, Moscow, 1970-75, sr. scientist, 1975-80, head lab., 1985-92; rschr. Lawrence Berkeley (Calif.) Lab., 1991-93, Max Planck Inst., Halle/Saale, Germany, 1993—. Contbr. articles to profl. jours. Mem. Material Rsch. Soc. Home: A Dikogo str 7 Bldg 80, 111396 Moscow Russia Office: Max Planck Inst, Weinberg 2, Halle Saale 06120, Germany

ZAKHAROV, VASILII, physicist, consultant; b. London, Jan. 2, 1931; s. Viktor Nikiforovich and Varvara Semyenovna (Krzak) Z.; m. Jeanne Hopper, 1959; children: Oleg, Anna. BS in Math. 1st class, London U., 1951, BS with honors in Physics, 1952, MS, 1958, DS, 1977; PhD in Physics, Royal Coll. Sci., London, 1960; Diploma, Imperial Coll., London, 1960. Head computer systems and elecs. divsn., directorate mem. Sci. Rsch. Coun. Daresbury Lab., Eng., 1965-78; dir., prof. U. London Computer Ctr., 1978-80; sr. assoc. CERN, Geneva, 1981-83; invited prof. informatics Geneva U., 1984-87; dir. info. procs. Internat. Stds. Orgn., Geneva, 1989-95; pvt. cons., 1996—; demonstrator Birkbeck Coll., others, London, 1953-56; rsch. fellow Imperial Coll., London, 1957-60; vis. prof. physics Queen Mary Coll., London U., 1968, Westfield Coll., London U., 1974-78; cons. Atomic Energy Rsch. Establishment, Harwell, eng., 1965; vis. scientist Joint Inst. Nuclear Rsch., Dubna, USSR, 1965; cons., mem. internat., govt. and univ. coms.; invited lectr. internat. schs.; cons. UNDP, UNESCO, others. Author, coauthor, contbr. several textbooks on sci. and tech.; contbr. articles to profl. jours. Recipient numerous grants from govt. agys., award. Avocations: collecting Russian miscellanea, viticulture and wine making, amateur radio, rough shooting. Address: The Firs, Old Castle, Malpas SY14 7NE, England

ZAKHAROV, VLADIMIR NIKOLAEVICH, cardiovascular surgeon; b. Rubtsovsk, Russia, Apr. 5, 1947; s. Nikolaj Petrovich and Alexandra Borisovna (Davidova) Kudar; m. Olga Genrikhovna Scoritskaia, Mar. 24, 1990; children: Inga, Tatiana, Ivan. Prof. Medicine in Surgery, Novosibirsk State Med. Inst., 1972; MS in Med. Scis., Med. Inst., Omsk, Russia, 1984; Prof. in Medicine, Inst. of Transplantation, Moscow, 1994. Gen. surgeon Ctrl. Clinic, Novosibirsk, 1972-75; cardiovasc. surgeon Rsch. Inst. of Pathology of Circulation, Novosibirsk, 1975-86; surgeon, rschr. Clin. Diagnostic Ctr., Novosibirsk, 1986-94; leading rschr. Novosibirsk State U., 1995-97; leading rschr. Inst. of Laser Physics SB RAS, Novosibirsk, 1997-99, chief rschr., 1999—. Patentee in field. Mem. World Soc. of Cardiothoracic Surgeons (congress participant 1993-94), Internat. Assn. Authors Sci. Discoveries (Diploma #87 of Discovery, 1998, Diploma # 130, 1999, medal 1998, medal 1999), N.Y. Acad. Scis. Achievements include scientific discovers of phenomenon of helical blood flow in cardio-vascular system of man and mammals; universal phenomenon of helical media flow in transport canals of an organism. Avocation: painting. Home: Tereshkova 46-31, 630090 Novosibirsk Russia Office: Inst Laser Physics, 13/3 Lavrentjev Ave, 630090 Novosibirsk Russia

ZAKHAROV, VYACHESLAV IOSIPHOVICH, physicist, researcher, consultant; b. Scherbakty, Kazakhstan, Oct. 9, 1955; s. Iosiph Alexandrovich Zakharov and Nadezhda Nikiforovna Puida; m. Olga Yurjevna Markova, Dec. 10, 1980; children: Galina, Serge. Student, Tomsk (Russia) U., 1973-78, PhD, 1984. Rschr. Inst. of Atmospheric Optics, Tomsk, 1978-84, sr. rschr., 1984-89; head of laser test lab. Sverdlovsk Br. R&D Inst. Power Engring., Zarechny, Russia, 1989-95, chief of rsch., 1995—, mem. sci. and tech. coun., 1992—; cons. SORUS Co. Ltd., Zarechny, 1990-95, Inst. of Ecoenergy, Moscow, 1998; prin. project investigator NASDA, Tokyo, 1994—. contbr. articles to sci. and profl. jours. Grantee Internat. Sci. Found., 1996, SORUS Co. Ltd., 1991; fellow Sci. Tech. Agy. of Jpan Meteorolog. Rsch. Inst., 1998. Achievements include author of explosive greenhouse effect conception. Avocations: sports, mountain skiing. Home: Kuznetsova 24A-37, 624051 Zarechny Russia Office: SB RDIPE, 624051 Zarechny Russia

ZAKHAROVA, VERA PETROVNA, physicist; b. Moscow, Feb. 5, 1927; d. Petr Dmitrievitch and Ludmila Vasilievna (Ermakova) Z.; m. Vladimir Stepanovitch Zenkevitch, Dec. 13, 1956 (dec. Sept. 1997); children: Andrey, Natalia. Physicist, Moscow State U., 1949, PhD, 1974. Physicist Russian Inst. Atomic Energy, 1950-91, Kurchatov Inst., Moscow, 1991—. Contbr. articles to profl. jours. Mem. Russian Nuclear Soc. Avocations: belles-lettres, knitting. Home: Marshala Novikova 7-38, 123098 Moscow Russia Office: Kurchatov Inst Rsch Ctr, Kurchatov Square 1, 123182 Moscow Russia

ZAKHEIM, BARBARA JANE, information management and marketing executive; b. London, Jan. 31, 1953; d. David Sloma and Sarah Frances (Leifer) Portnoi; m. Dov Solomon Zakheim, Aug. 20, 1972 (div. 1990); children: Keith Samuel, Roger Israel, Scott Elisha; m. Ronald Kleinfeldt, Dec. 13, 1992. BA, Oxford U., Eng., 1974, MA, 1978. Economist Maxima Corp., Silver Spring, Md., 1979, U.S. Dept. Energy, Washington, 1979-80; sr. project analyst Applied Mgmt. Scis., Silver Spring, 1980-83, staff assoc., 1983-85; prin. analyst NUS Corp., Gaithersburg, Md., 1985-87, cons. analyst, 1987-89; pres. Keith R. Scott Assocs., Inc., 1989-96, African Treasures, Inc., 1990-93; dir. policy and econ. studies Sanford Cohen & Assocs., Inc., 1993-96, v.p. info. & comm. svcs. divsn., 1996-2000, COO, 2000—; U.S. rep. Coll. Petroleum Studies, Oxford, 1984-93; N.Am. rep. Twirltrade Internat. Ltd., London, 1985—; mem. adv. com. on women in bus. Theodore Roosevelt Nat. Bank, Washington, 1991-92; profl. team mem. Venture Ptnrs. Internat., Inc., N.Y.C., 1990-94. Contbr. articles to profl. jours. Bd. dirs. SE Hebrew Congregation, Silver Spring, 1977-78; sec. Stonington Woods Homeowners' Assn., 1997-98, pres., 1998-99. Mem. NAFE, Nat. Assn. Environ. Profls. Republican. Avocations: reading, travel,

theater, music, ballroom dancing. Home: 11247 Watermill Ln Silver Spring MD 20902-3439 Office: 1355 Beverly Rd Ste 250 Mc Lean VA 22101-3649

ZAKI, ESSAM AHMED, molecular biologist, educator; b. Cairo, Egypt, Apr. 25, 1967; s. Ahmed Mourad and Aisha Mohamed (Oweiss) Z. BSc, Ain Shams U., Cairo, 1988; MSc, Manchester (Eng.) U., 1990, PhD, 1993. Tchr. English and sci. St. George Coll., Cairo, 1988-89; rsch. assoc. Manchester U., 1990-93; postdoctoral Mubarak City for Sci. Rsch., Alexandria, Egypt, 1993-95, sr. rschr., 1995-97, assoc. prof., 1997—; cons. IBI, N.C., 1997-98, Cairo, 1998—, Social Fund, Cairo, 1998—; dir. Nucleic Acid Program, Cairo, 1998—. Author: Market Assessment of Biotechnology, 1998, Egyptian Market Assessment Biotechnology, 1998; author, editor reports. Mem. Amnesty Internat., 1990—. Grantee GERRI, Alexandria, 1993. Mem. AAAS, European Molecular Biology Office, European Bioinformatics Inst. Avocations: music, football, internet, interactive learning, travel.

ZAKI, HASSAN ABBAS, bank executive; b. Portsaid, Egypt, Jan. 2, 1917; s. Abbas Zaki; m. Nagah Assadiah, 1945; children: Sawsan, Mona, Nadia. BSc in Econs., Cairo U., 1938; postgrad., Am. U., Washington, 1953. Cert. economist. Comml. sec. Egyptian Embassy, Washington, 1952; Min. Economy and Supply Egypt, 1958-62, Min. Economy and Trade, 1965-72; advisor to Pres. United Arab Emirates, 1972-85; chmn. Arab Soc Internat. Bank/Arab Internat. Co./Arab Medicine Co., Cairo, 1973—; chmn. El Horreye Pub. Co.; vice chmn. Arab Internat. Bank, Egypt; govt. rep. Alexandria Stock Exch., Egypt, 1954-56; mem. People's Coun., Egypt, 1957-70; dir. Ctrl. bank Egypt; mem. bd. Nat. Investment Bank Egypt. Contbr. articles to profl. jours. Dir. gen. Currency Control Adminstrn. Egypt, 1957; vice chmn. Abu Dhabi Fund for Arab Econ. Devel., 1971-85; pres. Negotiation Com. with Brit. Occupation, 1965; pres. Plan and Budget Com. in People's Coun. Recipient (in the period between 1959 and 1962) 1st degree Republic Decoration, Arab Republic of Egypt, 1st degree Al Neilein Decoration, Sudan, Knight of Honour, Congo, Romania, Greece, Yugoslavia, Somalia, Italy. Mem. Banking Club, Young Muslims Internat. (chmn.), Fathers and Sons Instns. (chmn.). Avocations: reading, alternative medicine, social studies, economics. Home: Zamalek, 12 El Saleh Ayoub St, Cairo Egypt Office: Arab Soc Internat Bank, 56 Gameat el-Dowal al Arabia St, Giza Egypt

ZAKI, KAMAL EL-DIN MAHMOUD, veterinarian, educator; b. Atbara, Sudan, Oct. 3, 1927; arrived in Egypt, 1933; s. Mahmoud Zaki Ahmed and Monira Yousef Ibrahim; m. Hayat Abdel Hadi, May 8, 1952; children: Hani, Mahmoud, Hanaa, Maha. BVSc, Cairo U., Giza, 1950; Dr Med Vet, Vet. H.S., Hanoover, Germany, 1959. Demonstrator ob/gyb. Faculty Vet. Medicine Cairo U., Giza, 1955-60, lectr., 1960-67, asst. prof., 1967-72, prof., 1972-78, vice dean, 1978, dean, 1978-82, head surgery & obstet. dept., 1986-88, prof. emeritus, 1988—; v.p. Cairo U., Khartoum, Sudan, 1982-86; univ. advisor Cairo U., 1974-78; cons. Ministry Local Adminstrn., Cairo, 1959-66. Editor Vet. Medicine Jour., 1978-82. V.p. Egyptian Vet. Medicine Syndicate, 1978-82, Egyptian Vet. Medicine Assn., 1979-81. Recipient First Grade Sci. & Arts award Pres. Republic Egypt, 1983. Mem. Staf Mems. Club. Avocations: sports, camping, travel. Home: Galal El Dessouky St 3 Pyramids, Giza 12111, Egypt Office: Cairo U, Faculty Vet Medicine, Giza 12211, Egypt*

ZAKINE, CARINE EMMA, materials science and engineering researcher; b. St. Maur des Fosses Val de Marne, France, Aug. 25, 1967; d. Jean and Nicole (Samama) Z. Grad. in engring., Orsay U., France, 1990, MA, 1991; PhD, Ecole Cen., Paris, 1994. Materials sci. and engring. rschr. Technion-Israe. Inst. Tech., Haifa, Israel, 1994-96; R&D engr. boilers unit V&M France, Aulnoye-Aymeries, France, 1997—; dir. jr. enterprise engring. sch. Orsay U., Paris, 1988-89; dir. alumni news jour., 1993-94. Avocations: tennis, swimming, piano, needlework. Home: 6 R Jules de la Bouliniere, 78530 Buc Yvelines, France Office: V&M France Aulnoye Tube Plt, 64 Rte de Leval BP 159, 59620 Aulnoye-Aymeries France

ZAKIS, EUGENE, electrical engineer; b. Chgo., June 12, 1940; s. Jack and Eva (Scharff) Z.; m. Carolyn F. Orth, May 11, 1968; 1 child, Susan Kay. BA, North Ea. Ill. U., 1990. Registered profl. engr., Ill. Chief elec. engr. Stephens-Adamson Mfg. Co., Aurora, Ill., 1964-70; divsn. head materials handling Sargent and Lundy Engrs., Chgo., 1970-77, asst. divsn. head elec. design, 1977-82, divsn. head elec. design, 1982-93; southeast region mgr. Sargent and Lundy, St. Petersburg, Fla., 1993—. Contbr. articles to profl. jours. Dist. pres. Muscular Dystrophy Assn., Aurora, 1978-84. With USN, 1958-62. Mem. IEEE, Tech. Design Assocs. (exec. 1988—), Nat. Fire Protection Assn., Elec. Assn. Avocations: baseball, running, football, basketball.

ZAKRZEWSKA, JOANNA MARIA, oral physician; b. London, Dec. 7, 1949; d. Mieczyslaw and Kazimiera (Lichota) Z.; m. Jan Wladimir Ledochowski, June 23, 1984; children: Konrad, Krystyna. BDS, U. London, 1972; MB BChir, U. Cambridge, 1979, MD, 1990. House officer Addenbrookes Hosp., Norwich, England, 1980-81; sr. house officer St. Mary's Hosp., London, 1981-82; registrar Eastman Dental, London, 1982-84, from rsch. fellow to sr. registrar, 1984-89; cons. Univ. Coll., London, 1989-95; dept. head Royal London Hosp. & Mortimer Market Camden Islington Cmty., 1995—; hon. cons. Nat. Hosp. Neurology, 1990—. Author: Trigeminal Neuralgia, 1995; contbr. articles to profl. jours., chpts. to books. Fellow Dental Surgery Royal Coll. Surgery, Faculty Dental Surgery Royal Coll. Surgeons Ireland, Royal Soc. Medicine; mem. Brit. Soc. Oral Medicine (treas., sec., pres.), Royal Coll. Surgeons (Eng.), Internat. Assn. Study of Pain. Avocations: theatre, Gothic architecture. Office: Oral Med and Dental Inst, Royal London Hosp/Turner St, London E1 2AD, England

ZAKRZEWSKI, JAKUB MACIEJ, physicist, researcher researcher; b. Cracow, Poland, Dec. 11, 1957; s. Witold Stefan and Helena Wanda (Maciejewska) Z.; m. Katarzyna Ewa Budzynska, June 18, 1983. MSc, Jagellonian U., Cracow, 1981, Habilitation, 1990; PhD in Physics, Polish Acad. Scis., Warsaw, 1985. Asst. Inst. Physics Jagellonian U., 1981-83, adj. Inst. Physics, 1985-96, prof., 1996—; postdoctoral fellow U. So. Calif., L.A., 1987-88, U. Pierre et Marie Curie, Paris, 1991-92; assoc. prof. U. Pierre et Marèe Curie, Paris, 1993-96; vis. prof. Ecole Normale Superieure, Paris, 1995; bd. dirs. European Phys. Soc., Atomic Molecular Physics divsn. Budapest, 1995-98. Contbr. over 70 articles to profl. jours. Mem. Polish Phys. Soc. Avocations: volleyball, table tennis, art, music. E-mail: kuba@order.if.uj.edu.pl. Office: Jagellonian U M Smoluchowski Inst Physic, Ul Reymonta 4, 30059 Cracow Poland

ZAKRZEWSKI, JAN MARIA, electrical engineering educator; b. Warsaw, Poland, Sept. 2, 1939; s. Jan Gaston and Maria Anna (de Pourbaix) Z.; m. Maria Sadek, June 21, 1980; children: Christopher, Daria, Peter. MSc in Engring., Tech. U. Szczecin, Poland, 1961; PhD, Tech. U. Lodz, Poland, 1971; DSc, Silesian Tech. U., Gliwice, Poland, 1981. Asst. Inst. Elec. Engring., Warsaw, 1961-63; assoc. prof. Tech. U. Szczecin, 1963-77; prof. Silesian Tech. U., 1977—. Author: (in Polish) Nonlinearity of Measuring Sensors, 1979 (Ministry of Edn. award 1981); co-author: Dynamical Measuremnts, 1984 (Ministry of Edn. award 1985); contbr. articles to profl. jours. and J. Wiley Encyclopedia of Electrical and Electronics Engineering, 1999. Mem. Measurement Commn. of Polish Acad. Sci. Roman Catholic. Avocations: photography, film, mountain climbing. Home: Kopernika 3 M34, 44-117 Gliwice Poland Office: Silesian U Tech, Akademicka 10, 44-100 Gliwice Poland

ZAKY, ASSER ALY, electrical engineering educator; b. Alexandria, Egypt, Aug. 11, 1932; s. Ibrahim Zaky and Aziza Abany; m. Aziza Abdelsalam Rashad, Aug. 11, 1959; children: Ahmed, Layla, Bahira. BSEE, U. Alexandria, 1954; MS, U. Ill., 1955; PhD, London U., 1959. Chartered engr., U.K. UN expert in elec. engring. U. Brasilia, Brazil, 1967-71; head elec. engring. dept. King Saud U., Riyad, Saudi Arabia, 1977-81; prof. elec. power engring. U. Alexandria, 1979-91, head elec. engring. dept., 1991-93; head elec. engring. dept. Sultan Qaboos U., Muscat, Oman, 1983-96; cons. Arab Acad. for Sci. and Tech., 1993—. Author, co-author 13 books and over 50 rsch. papers in field of insulating liquids. Recipient Nat. Engring. Sci. award Egyptian Govt., 1966, 74, Order of Merit 2d Class, Egyptian Govt., 1974. Fellow IEEE (life), Inst. Elec. Engrs. U.K., Inst. Physics U.K. Avocations: gardening, music, history of science. Home: 14 Rue Ahmed Yehia, Mazloum Raml, Alexandria 21411, Egypt

ZAKZUK, MAHMOUD HAMDI, government official; b. Dakahleya, Egypt, Dec. 27, 1933; married; 1 child. MA in Teaching, al-Azhar U., 1960; PhD in Philosophy, Munich U., Germany, 1968. Dean faculty fundamentals Islam, v.p. al-Azhar U.; head Islamic thought com. Supreme Coun. Islamic Affairs; min. Ministry Awqaf, Cairo. Contbr. articles to profl. jours. Mem. Islamic Rsch. Acad., Egyptian Soc. Philosophy (chmn.). Office: Min Awqaf, Sharia Sabri-Abul Alam, Cairo Egypt*

ZALABARDO, JOSE LUIS, philosopher, educator; b. Madrid, Mar. 5, 1964; arrived in Eng., 1994; s. Jose Luis Zalabardo and Matilde Garcia-Muro; m. Inma Alvarez, July 4, 1988; children: Clara, Alicia. BA, U. Autonoma, Madrid, 1987; MPhil, St. Andrews U., Scotland, 1988; PhD, U. Mich., 1994. Tchg. asst. U. Mich., Ann Arbor, 1988-94; lectr. U. Birmingham, 1994-2000, U. Coll., London, 2000—. Author: Introduction to the Theory of Logic, 2000; contbr. articles to profl. jours. Mem. Spanish Soc. for Analytical Philosophy, Mind Assn., Aristotelian Soc. Avocations: music, literature, medieval history, wine. Office: U Birmingham, Univ Coll London/Dept Phils, Gower Str, London WC1E 6BT, England

ZALAQUETT, CARLOS PATRICIO, psychology educator, psychotherapist; b. Valparaiso, Chile; came to U.S., 1987; s. Carlos José Zalaquett and Susana Olivia Montenegro; m. Jenifer Pualuan, July 10, 1982; children: Andrea, Christine. Grad. in Clin. Psychology, P. Cath. U., Santiago, Chile, 1981; MA in Clin. Psychology, Sam Houston State U., 1988; PhD, U. Tex., 1993; hon. diploma, Dept. Edn. Municipal County, Chile, 1998. Lic. clin. psychologist, Chile; cert. neurotherapist, U.S., counselor, Tex. Asst. prof. Cath. U., Santiago, 1981-87, chair clin. psychology, 1985, vice chmn. rsch., 1986-87; counselor Sam Houston State U., Huntsville, Tex., 1993—, asst. dir., 1994—, interim dir., 1999, coord. stress mgmt., 1999—; clin. supr. Sam Houston State U., 1994—; cons. UpBEATT Bilingual Program, Huntsville, 1994—, Nat. Inst. Tng., Santiago, 1996—. Editor: Evaluating Stress, vol. 1, 1987, vol. 2, 1988; author web pages. Founder, 1st pres. Found. for Prevention of Sudden Infant Death Syndrome, Santiago, 1984; counselor The Woodlands (Tex.) Group, 1997; counselor, vol. Cancer Counseling, Houston, 1999. Recipient Best Presentation award Southwestern Comparative Psychology Assn., 1991. Mem. APA, Biofeedback Soc. Tex. (adv. bd. 1999—, Diplomat 1999), Neurotherapy Assn., Chilean Assn. Psychologists (Best Rsch. 1981), Southwestern Psychol. Assn., Chilean Soc. Clin. Psychologists (editor jour. 1981—, Best Contbn. award 1979). Roman Catholic. Avocations: web page creations, painting, writing. E-mail: ccp cxz@shsu.edu. Office: Sam Houston State Univ 1902 Ave J Huntsville TX 77341-2059

ZALAZAR, CARLOS ANTONIO, engineering educator, researcher; b. Paraná, Argentina, Sept. 19, 1940; s. Blas Zalazar and Emilia Di Pretoro; m. Susana Margarita Bernal, June 23, 1967; children: Carlos, Cristina, Maria Cecilia. BSc, Coll. Nat. Paraná, 1958; diploma in engring., Faculty Engring. Quimica, Santa Fe, Argentina, 1965. Jefe de trabajos prácticos Faculty Engring. Quimica, 1965-70, prof., 1971—; rschr. Conicet, Argentina, 1982—. Author: Quimica y Tecnologia de los Productos Lácteos, 1994, A Coulour Guide t Cheese and Fermented Milks, 1995. Vice decano Faculty Engring. Qca, 1994-97. Mem. Am. Dairy Sci. Assn., Internat. Coll. Alexandre Tessier. Office: Facultad Engring Quimica, Santiago del Estero 2829, 3000 Santa Fe Argentina

ZALAZNICK, SHELDON, editor, journalist; b. Bronx, N.Y., Aug. 6, 1928; s. Samuel and Esther Leah (Schneiderman) Z.; m. Vera Altobelli, Apr. 4, 1953; 1 dau., Andrea. B.A., Univ. Coll. N.Y. U., 1948; M.A., Tchrs. Coll. Columbia, 1950. Tchr. English Benjamin Franklin High Sch., N.Y.C., 1950-52; assoc. editor Newsweek mag., 1952-56; v.p. Manning Pub. Relations Co., 1956-59; sr. editor Forbes mag., 1959-63, mng. editor, 1976-89; founding editor New York mag. sect. N.Y. Herald Tribune, N.Y.C., 1963-64; Sunday editor N.Y. Herald Tribune, 1964-66; staff writer Gen. Learning Corp., 1966-67; assoc. editor Fortune mag., 1967-69; v.p., editorial dir. New York mag., 1969-76. Home: 458 W 246th St Bronx NY 10471-3330

ZALDASTANI, GUIVY, business consultant; b. Tbilisi, Republic of Georgia, Nov. 1, 1919; arrived in Paris, 1925, came to U.S., 1948, naturalized 1953; s. Soliko and Mariam (Hirsely) Z.; m. Meredeth Fowler, May 1956 (div. Jan. 1982); children: Nicholas, Tamara, Nina; m. Micheline de Bievre, May 12, 1984; 1 child, Brian O'Connell. License en Droit, Sorbonne U., Paris, 1945, Diplome d'Etudes Superieures en Droit, 1946; MBA, Harvard U., 1951. Dept. mgr., buyer Federated Dept. Stores, Boston, 1957-62; founder, pres. Finishing Touch, Boston, 1962-80, Ryan & Elliott Internat. Real Estate, Boston, 1980-83; pres. Zaldastani Cons., Boston, 1982—; vis. prof. Tbilisi Tech. U. Editor Voice of Free Georgia, 1951-65, Iveria, 1970-80, periodical in Georgian lang. Cons. Ho. of Reps. crimes of Krushchev, 1960; pres. Georgian Youth Assn., Paris, 1942-47; founder, pres. Ga. Coastal Devel. Found., Inc., 1998—; charter mem. Rep. Presdl. Task Force, Washington, 1980; co-chmn. Harvard Bus. Sch. Reunion, Cambridge, 1961, 76, 86, 96. Served to lt. French Marines, 1940-41. Named Hon. Citizen, Rep. Georgia, 1997. Mem. Georgian Assn. in U.S. (pres. 1966-74, bd. dirs. 1974-95), Harvard Club (Boston), Sommerset Club (Boston), Harvard Faculty Club (Boston), Cercle de l'Union Interalliée (Paris). Republican. Avocations: piano, reading, travel. Home: 85 E India Row Apt 12F Boston MA 02110-3397

ZALDASTANI, OTHAR, structural engineer; b. Tbilisi, Republic of Georgia, Aug. 10, 1922; came to U.S., 1946; naturalized, 1956; s. Soliko Nicholas and Mariam Vachnadze (Hirsely) Z.; m. Elizabeth Reily Bailey, June 22, 1963; children: Elizabeth, Anne, Alexander. Diplome D'Ingenieur, Ecole Nationale des Ponts et Chaussees, Paris, 1945; Licencie es Scis., Sorbonne, Paris, 1946; MS in Geotech. Engring., Harvard U., 1947, DSc in Aerodynamics, 1950. Registered profl. engr., Mass., R.I., Tenn., Mo., N.H. Mem. faculty Harvard U., Cambridge, Mass., 1947-50; ptnr. Nichols, Norton and Zaldastani, Boston, 1952-63; pres. Nichols, Norton and Zaldastani, Inc., Boston, 1964-76, Zaldastani Assocs., Inc., Boston, 1976-88, chmn., 1988-97, dir., 1997—; dir. Georgia Coastal Devel. Found. Inc., Boston, 1998—; Gordon McKay vis. lectr. structural mechanics Harvard U., 1961; trustee, 1st v.p. Mass. Constrn. Industry Bd., 1973-76; mem. Mass. Designer Selection Bd., 1976-80. Contbg. author: Advances in Applied Mechanics, vol. 3, 1953. Patentee sound absorbing block, prestressed concrete beam and deck system. Trustee Wheelock Coll., Boston, 1975-81, mem. corp., 1984-93; trustee Boston U. Med. Ctr., 1976—; trustee Brooks Sch., North Andover, Mass., 1986-95. Recipient awards from various orgns. and agys. including Prestressed Concrete Inst., Cons. Engrs. Coun. New Eng., Am. Inst. Steel Constrn., Concrete Reinforcing Steel Inst., Dept. Transp., Am. Concrete Inst. Fellow ASCE (Ralph W. Horne award), AIAA (assoc.), Am. Concrete Inst.; mem. Georgian Assn. in the U.S. (pres. 1958-65, hon. citizen Republic of Ga. 1997), Sigma Xi, Harvard Club, Harvard Faculty Club (Cambridge), Somerset Club (Boston), Country Club (Brookline, Mass.), Rolling Rock Club (Ligonier, Pa.). Home: 125 Parkway Rd Apt 1304 Bronxville NY 10708-3694 Office: Zaldastani Assocs Inc 70 Federal St Boston MA 02110-1906

ZALESKI, JAMES VINCENT, electronics executive; b. Kenosha, Wis., Oct. 8, 1943; s. Louis Edward and Lena Louise (Bellotti) Zaleski; m. Beverly Rae Neumann, Nov. 8, 1969. BBA, U. Wis., 1966, BSME, 1966, MS, 1967. Project engr. AC Electronics div. GM, Milw., 1968-73; ops. mgr. Applied Computer Sci., Inc., Milw., 1970-72; sect. mgr. Delco Electronics div. GM, Santa Barbara, Calif., 1973-84, dept. mgr., 1984-85, chief engr., 1985-87; pres., chief exec. officer Vetronix Corp., Santa Barbara, Calif., 1984—; chief exec. officer Vetronix Japan, Ltd., Kawagoe, Japan, 1990—; pres., chief exec. Vetronix Sales Corp., Santa Barbara, CA, 1997—. Contbr. articles to profl. jours.; patentee in field. Named Entrepreneur of Yr. Greater L.A. Inc. mag., 1995. Mem. Soc. Automotive Engrs., Evans Scholars Assn., Mensa. Avocation: backpacking. Office: Vetronix Corp 2030 Alameda Padre Serra Santa Barbara CA 93103-1716

ZALESSKY, VIACHESLAV NIKOLAJEVICH, cardiologist, researcher; b. Kherson, Ukraine, July 24, 1949; s. Nikolaj Grigorievich and Alla Stepanovna (Melnicova) Z.; m. Elena Anatolievna Alingorskaha, Sept. 7, 1984; children: Ekaterina, Anatolij. B in phylosophy, Medical Acad., Zaporozhie, Ukraine, 1972; MD, Kavetsky Inst., Kiev, 1980; D in acupuncture, Inst Acupuncture Rsch., Colombo Sri Lanka, 1982; D military medicine, Medical Acad., Sanct Petersbourg, Russia, 1973. Staff oncologist Kavetsky Inst Problems Oncology Nat. Acad. Scis., Kiev, 1975-85; assoc. prof. cardiology Strazhesko Inst. Cardiology Min. for Health Protection, Kiev, 1986—; co-dir office Kavetsky Inst Problems Oncology Nat. Acad. Scis., 1980-85, cons. to laser medicine Strazhesko Inst Cardiology Min. Health Protection, 1986—; mem. editorial adv. bd. Scandinavian Jour. of Acupuncture & Electrotherapy, Finland, 1987. Contbr. articles to profl. jours. Recipient R.E. Kavetsky Meml. award, 1983. Mem. Ukrainian Oncology Sco., Ukraninian Cardiology Sco., Scandinavian Soc. Acupuncture, N.Y. Acad. Scis. Avocations: collecting pictures, hiking, fire purchase. Home: Ap 202, Bolevar Druzba narodov 10, 252103 Kiev Ukraine Office: Medinfo Acad Laser Rsch, Krasnoarmejskaja st 102, 252150 Kiev Ukraine

ZALEWSKI, KACPER JAN, physicist, researcher; b. Warsaw, Poland, Jan. 6, 1935; s. Andrzej Kazimierz and Hanna (Lutoslawska) Z.; m. Agnieszka Grazyna Bak, June 27, 1970; children: Anna, Andrzej, Lidia, Mikolaj. PhD, Inst. Phys. Chemistry, Warsaw, Poland, 1960. Asst. Inst. Phys. Chemistry, Cracow, Poland, 1956-69, docent, 1961-68; docent Inst. Nuclear Rsch., Cracow, Poland, 1968-70; docent Inst. Nuclear Physics, Cracow, Poland, 1970-72, prof., 1972-92; prof. Jagellonian U., Cracow, Poland, 1992—; divsn. leader Inst. Nuclear Physics, 1982-86. Author: Lectures About Phenomenological and Statistical Thermodynamics, 1966, Lectures About the Rotation Group, 1987, Lectures About Nonrelativistic Quantum Mechanics, 1997; contbr. articles to profl. jours. Mem. Polish Acad. Scis., Polish Acad. Arts and Scis., Warsaw Scientific Soc. Roman Catholic. Home: Ul Herzoga 5, 30252 Cracow Poland Office: Inst Physics Jagellonian U, Ul Reymonta 4, 30059 Cracow Poland

ZALEWSKI, KAZIMIERZ, biochemist; b. D—browa Cherubiny, Xomia, Poland, Sept. 27, 1951; s. Stanislaw and Stanislawa (D—browska) Z.; m. Janina Kętowska, Feb. 18, 1978; children: Mariusz, Anna. Grad., Agrl.-Tech. Acad., Olsztyn, 1976, PhD in Agr., 1980. Faculty dept. biochemistry Agrl.-Tech. Acad., Olsztyn, asst. prof. agr., prof. biochemistry. Contbr. articles to profl. jours. Mem. commn. Polish Hunter Assn., 1995—; active Polish Red Cross, Wysokie Mazoiechie, 1970; mem. Solidarity, Olsztyn, 1980-81. Mem. Polish Bot. Assn., Fedn. of European Socs. of Plant Physiology. Home: Malewskiego 7/3, 10-686 Olsztyn Poland Office: Agr Tech Acad Dept Biochem, Plac Kodzki 3, 10-957 Olsztyn Poland

ZALM, GERRIT, The Netherlands minister of finance; b. May 6, 1952. Min. of finance The Hague, The Netherlands, 1994—. Office: Ministry of Finance, PO Box 20201, 2500 VB The Hague The Netherlands*

ZALTA, EDWARD, otorhinolaryngologist, physician; b. Houston, Mar. 2, 1930; s. Nouri Louis and Marie Zahde (Lizmi) Z.; m. Carolyn Mary Gordon, Oct. 8, 1971; 1 child, Ryan David; children by previous marriage: Nouri Allan, Lori Ann, Barry Thomas, Marci Louise. BS, Tulane U., 1952, MD, 1956. Diplomate Am. Bd. Quality Assurance and Utilization Rev. Physicians. Intern Brooke Army Hosp., San Antonio, 1956-57; resident in otolaryngology U.S. Army Hosp., Ft. Campbell, Ky., 1957-60; practice medicine specializing in otolaryngology Glendora, West Covina and San Dimas, Calif., 1960-82; ENT cons. City of Hope Med. Ctr., 1961-76; mem. staff Foothill Presbyn.; past pres. L.A. Found. Cmty. Svc., L.A. Poison Info. Ctr., So. Calif. Physicians Coun., Inc.; founder, chmn. bd. dirs. CAPP CARE, INC.; founder Inter-Hosp. Coun. Continuing Med. Edn.; trustee U.S. Pharmacopeial Conv., Inc.; mem. adv. bd. Global Health Sys., Inc. Author: (with others) Medicine and Your Money; mem. editl. staff Jour. Assn. Managed Healthcare Orgns., Managed Care Interface, Mng. Employee Health Benefits; mem. editl. adv. bd. Inside Medicaid Managed Care, Disease Mgmt. News, Managed Care Outlook; contbr. articles to profl. jours. Pres. bd. govs. Glendora Unified Sch. Dist., 1965-71; mem. Calif. Cancer Adv. Coun., 1967-71, Commn. of Californias, L.A. County Commn. on Economy and Efficiency. Served to capt. M.C. AUS, 1957-60. Recipient Award of Merit Order St. Lazarus, 1981. Mem. AMA, Calif. Med. Assn., Am. Acad. Otolaryngology, Am. Coun. Otolaryngology, Am. Assn. Preferred Provider Orgns. (past pres.), Am. Coll. Med. Quality, L.A. County Med. Assn. (pres. 1980-81), Kappa Nu, Phi Delta Epsilon, Glendora CountryClub, Centurion Club, Sea Bluff Beach and Racquet Club; Center Club (Costa Mesa, Calif.), Pacific Golf Club (San Juan, Capistrano). Republican. Jewish. Home: 3 Morning Dove Laguna Niguel CA 92677-5331 Office: West Tower 4000 Macarthur Blvd Ste 10000 Newport Beach CA 92660-2526

ZAMAGNI, STEFANO, economics educator; b. Rimini, Italy, Jan. 4, 1943; s. Quarto and Jolanda Z.; m. Vera Negri, Oct. 13, 1968; children: Giulia, Elena. Laurea, Cath. U., Milan, 1966. Asst. lectr. Cath. U., Milan, 1966-69; prof. U. Parma, Italy, 1973-79, U. Bologna, Italy, 1979—; vis. prof. U. Bocconi, Milan, 1985—; adj. prof. Johns Hopkins U., Bologna, 1993—, assoc. dir., 1982—; chmn. dept. econs. U. Bologna, 1985-93, dean faculty econs., 1993-96; State Victoria Bank vis. prof. Deakin U., Australia. Author: Microeconomic Theory, 1987, Civil Economy and Paradoxes of Growth, 1997; co-author: History of Economic Thought, 1993; editor: World Development and Economic Institutions, 1994, The Economic of Altruism, 1995, Living in the Global Society, 1997, Non Profit As Civil Economy, 1998; co-author: Economics: An European Text, 1999. Mem. Pontif Coun. Justice and Peace, Vatican City, 1994—; pres. Internat. Cath. Migration Commn., Geneva, 1999—. McDonnell disting. scholar, Helsinki, 1992; Paul Harris fellow, Rotary Internat., 1995; recipient St. Vincent Econs. prize Aosta Valley Regional Govt., 1989, Capri Econs. prize Assn. or Devel. of Social Scis., 1996, Golden Sigismondo prize Municipality of Rimini, Italy, 1997, Gold medal Internat. Ctr. Pio Manzu, 1998. Fellow Acad. Scis. Milan, Acad. Scis. Bologna; mem. Internat. Econ. Assn. (exec.com. 1989—), Pontifical Acad. Social Scis. (steering com. 1994—). Avocations: classic music, sports, civic participation. Home: Boldrini 6, 40126 Bologna Italy Office: U Bologna, Zamboni 33, 40126 Bologna Italy

ZAMAN, GUIDO JENNY RUDOLF, molecular biologist, researcher; b. Hulst, Zeeland, The Netherlands, May 6, 1964; d. Ronald Albert and Thila (Smit) Z.; m. Heike Bohne, Oct. 18, 1989; children: Lisa, Linda. Doctoraal cum laude, U. Nijmegen (The Netherlands), 1987, PhD, 1991. Molecular biologist. Postdoct. researcher Netherlands Cancer Inst., Amsterdam, 1991-96, N.V. Organon, Oss, The Netherlands, 1996—. Contbr. over 20 articles to profl. jours. Office: NV Organon, PO Box 20, 5340 BH Oss The Netherlands

ZAMAN, MAKHDOOM KHALEEQ, agricultural scientist, legislator; b. Hala, Sindh, Pakistan, Feb. 13, 1949; s. Talibulmaula-Makhdoom Mohd Zaman; m. Shamsi Ikram; 3 children. BA, U. Karachi, Pakistan, 1970. Mem. Provincial Assembly, Karachi, 1977, Nat. Assembly, Islamabad, Pakistan, 1988-90, Senate, Islamabad, 1991-97. Author poetry, 1973-96. Mem. Les Ambassadeurs Club (London). Mem. Pakistan People's Party. Avocations: travel, hunting, swimming, hiking, yoga. Home: 12-D Mohammad Ali Housing, Sindh Karachi 75350, Pakistan

ZAMAN, MD. RAKIB-UZ, applied chemistry educator, researcher; b. Jhinidah, Jessore, Bangladesh, Nov. 26, 1955; s. Munshi Mujibar Rahman and Mst. Junnoon (Nessa); m. Rezina Aktar Banu, July 6, 1984; children: Md. Rumman-uz-Zaman, Sarah Fatima Sunny. BSc, Rajshahi U., Bangladesh, 1975, MSc, 1977; PhD, Banaras H. U., Varanasi, India, 1990. Cert. Chemist. Lectr. Rajshahi U., Bangladesh, 1981-85, from asst. prof. to assoc. prof., 1985-96, prof., 1996—. Author papers; presenter in field. Recipient Bangladesh Assn. for Advancement of Sci. award Bangladesh Sci. Conf., 1992; fellow Indian govt., 1987-90, DAAD (Deutscher Akademischer Austauschdienst), Germany, 1995, 99, STA, Japan, 1997, Germany, 1999. Mem. Indian Assn. of Nuclear Chemists and Allied Scientists (IANCAS award 1990, life), BCS (life), N.Y. Acad. Scis., Alumni Assn. German Univs. in Bangladesh. Islam. Avocations: readings from various disciplines, rsch. Home: Village Dakatia PO Gurdah, PS Maheshpur Dist Jhinidah, Jessore Bangladesh Office: Rajshahi Univ, Dept Applied Chem, Rajshahi 6205, Bangladesh

ZAMAN, MOHAMED NASIR, auditor; b. Shinghajhully, Jessore, Bangladesh, May 3, 1942; s. Mahabobor and Rowshanara (Chowdhury) Rahman; m. Parveen Rahman, Jan. 28, 1973; children: Sheemain, Shahnoun. BSc, Dhaka (Bangladesh) U., 1962. Chartered acct., England,

Wales. Audit sr. Pannell Fitzpatrick & Co., London, 1969-73; audit supr. Blick Rothenberg & Noble, London, 1974-75; audit mgr. Bright Grahme Murray & Co., London, 1976-78; adminstr. Gulfbeton, Dubai, United Arab Emirates, 1978-79; head internal audit Abu Dhabi Drilling Chems & PRoducts Ltd., Abu Dhabi, United Arab Emirates, 1979—. Treas. Bangladesh Relief Fund, London, 1971-72. Fellow British Inst. Mgmt., Assn. Chartered Cert. Accts.; mem. Inst. Internal Auditors. Avocations: reading, photography, music, tennis. Office: Abu Dhabi Drilling Chems, PO Box 46121, Abu Dhabi United Arab Emirates

ZAMAN, RASHID, psychiatrist, educator, neuroscience researcher; s. Badar and Roshan Ara Zaman. BSc with honors, St. Andrews U., Scotland; MB, BChir, Cambridge U., Eng., 1987; Diploma in Geriatric Medicine, Royal Coll. of Physicians, 1989. MRCGP, MRCPsych. Gen. practice trainee in family medicine Cambridge and Stevenage, 1988-91; rsch. registrar in psychiatry Charing Cross and Westminster Med. Sch., London, 1991-92, resident in psychiatry, 1993-96; lectr. in psychiatry Divsn. Neurosci. and Psychol. Medicine Imperial Coll. Sch. Medicine at St. Mary's Campus, London, 1997—; joint chmn. crisis team Barnet Hosp., London, 1994-95; tutor in psychiatry Charing Cross and Westminster Med. Sch., 1995-96; lectr. Imperial Coll. Sch. Medicine, 1997—. Author: Chuchill's Pocketbook of Psychiatry, 2000; contbr. articles to profl. jours. Mem. Internat. Soc. for Transcranial Stimulation, Royal Coll. Gen. Practitioners Eng., Royal Coll. Psychiatrists Eng., Brit. Med. Assn. Avocations: squash, soccer, cricket, photography, poetry. E-mail: r.zaman@ic.ac.uk. Office: Imperial Coll Sch Medicine, Paterson Ctr 20 S Wharf Rd. London W21PD, England

ZAMBELIS, NIKOLAUS, internist; b. Athens, Attika, Greece, July 7, 1936; s. Neofytos and Eleni (Karamiliotaki) Z.; children: Nikoletta, Marcella, Ekaterini; m. Ulla Goldgruber Waimann, Sept. 18, 1986. MD, U. Innsbruck, Austria, 1971; nuclear specialist, U. Klinik, Innsbruck; intern specialist, Gen. Hosp., Lienz, Austria, 1984; Dr. U. Med., Leopold-Franzes U., Innsbruck, Austria. Surgeon Inst. Exptl. Pathology, Innsbruck, 1966-74; asst., doctor U. Klinik Nuc. Medicine, Innsbruck, 1974-79; ward physician Gen. Hosp., Lienz, 1979-89; sr. physician Gen. Hosp., Zell am See, Austria, 1989—; commr. radiation protection Gen. Hosp., Zell am See, 1989. Editor Wiener Klinische Wochenschrift, 1971, Contraception, 1971, 72, Exptl. Pathology, 1974, Acta Endokrinologica, 1979 (höchst-Stiftung award 1980), Wiener Klinische Wochenschrift, 1981,. Mem. works coun. Gen. Hosp., Zell am See, 1989. Mem. Deutsche Arbeitsgemenschaft fur Klinische Nephrologie, Osterrechische Gesellschaft fur Nuclearruediziu, Deutsche Gesellschaft fur Eud., Kiwanis (pres.-elect 1999—). Greek Orthodox. Office: Gen Hosp Zell am See, Paracelsusstr 8, 5700 Zell am See Salzburg, Austria

ZAMBELLI, ANGELO, lawyer; b. Milan, Oct. 27, 1962; s. Alessandro Cristoforo and Gabriella (Gramiccia) Z. JD magna cum laude, U. Milan, 1987. Bar: Milan 1992. Assoc. Toffoletto & Assocs., Milan, 1989-94, ptnr., 1995-98; ptnr. Croze, Radice & Zambelli Studio Legale, 1998-99, Carnelutti Law Firm, Milan, 2000—; asst. prof. U. MIlan, 1987—; freelance prof. U. Castellanza, 1995-97, apptd. cons. labor min. Romania EEC. Author: La Disciplina dei Licenziamenti, 3rd edit., 1995, Dieci Temi di Diritto Del Lavoro, 1996; contbr. articles to profl. jours. Lt. Italian mil., 1987-88. Mem. Am. C. of C. Avocations: skiing, sailing, horseback riding, books, motor biking. Office: Carnelutti Law Firm, Via Principe Amedeo 3, 20121 Milan Italy

ZAMBOGLOU, NICOLAOS, physician; b. Limassol, Cyprus, May 2, 1949; s. Costas and Paraskevi Z.; m. Doris Nolden, Aug. 16, 1979; 1 child, Constantinos. M in Physics, Tech. U. of RWTH, Aachen, Germany, 1974; Dr.rer.nat., Univ. Dusseldorf, Germany, 1977; Venia Legendi, Univ. Dusseldorf, 1990; Dr.med., U. Essen, Germany, 1986; Venia Legendi, N.T. Univ., Athens, 1994. Resident dept. radiation oncology Alfried-Krupp-Hosp., Essen, Germany, 1985-86; resident dept. radiation oncology Univ. Dusseldorf, 1986-89, specialist in radiation therapy, sr. resident, 1990-92, Venia legendi in radiation oncology, 1990; chmn. radiation medicine Stadtische Kliniken Offenbach/Wolfgang Goethe U., Frankfurt, Germany, 1992; Venia legendi for discipline of radiation therapy/physics Ins. Comm. and Computer Systems of Nat. Tech. U. of Athens, 19946. Home: Staedt Kliniken Offenbach, Starkenburgring 66, Offenbach 63069, Germany

ZAMBOLDI, RICHARD HENRY, lawyer; b. Kittanning, Pa., Nov. 22, 1941; s. Henry F. and Florence E. (Colligan) Z.; m. Maria Therese Reiser, Aug. 12, 1967; children: Elizabeth M., Richard H. Jr., Margaret B. BBA, St. Bonaventure U., 1963; JD, Villanova U., 1966. Bar: U.S. Dist. Ct. (we. dist.) Pa. 1966, Pa. 1968, U.S. Ct. Appeals (3d cir.) 1970, U.S. Supreme Ct. 1981. Law clk. U.S. Dist. Ct. (we. dist.) Pa., Pitts., 1966-67; atty. Nat. Labor Rels. Bd., Pitts., 1967-68; assoc. Kanehann & McDonald, Allentown, Pa., 1968-69; ptnr. Elderkin Martin Kelly Messina & Zamboldi, Erie, Pa., 1969-90; ptnr. Knox McLaughlin Gornall & Sennett, Erie, 1990—, pres., 1997—; Author (student articles) Villanova Law Rev., 1964-65, editor, 1965-66. Mem. Pa. Bar Assn., Erie County Bar Assn. Republican. Roman Catholic. Home: 6206 Lake Shore Dr Erie PA 16505-1013 Office: Knox McLaughlin Gornall & Sennett 120 W 10th St Erie PA 16501-1410

ZAMBONE, ALANA MARIA, special education educator; b. Vineland, N.J., Sept. 17, 1952; d. L. Alan and Joyce (Bernero) Z. AB in Spl. Edn. and Elem. Edn., U. N.C., Chapel Hill, 1974; MS in Human Devel. Liaison, George Peabody Coll. Tchrs., 1978; PhD in Spl. Edn., Vanderbilt U., 1984. Cert. spl. edn., elem. edn., visual impairments, mental retardation, N.C. Tchr., counselor Orange County Assn. for Retarded Citizens, Chapel Hill, N.C., 1973-74; lead tchr. Shelbyville-Bedford (Tenn.) County Adult Svc. Ctr., 1974; program coord. Dickson (Tenn.) County Adult Svcs., 1974-75; dept. head, habilitative svcs. CloverBottom Devel. Ctr., Nashville, Tenn., 1975-76; exec. dir. Waves, Inc. Adult Svcs., Fairview, Tenn., 1976-77; from vocat. cons. to liaison, Peabody Tchrs. Coll. Vanderbilt U., 1977-80; chairperson, bd. dirs. Residential Svcs., Inc., Nashville, 1976-80; asst. prof., coord., dept. curriculum N.C. State U., Raleigh, N.C., 1981-84; coord. and asst. prof., div. spl. edn. Minot (N.D.) State U., 1984-86; coord. internat. outreach svcs. Hilton-Perkins Internat. Program Perkins Sch. for the Blind, Watertown, Mass., 1989-94; assoc. prof., dir. Inst. for Visually Impaired Pa. Coll. Optometry, Phila., 1994—; co-founder, sr. rsch. fellow Walker-Wheelock Inst. for Equity in Edn., sr. project dir. exceptional needs assessment devel. lab. Edn. Devel. Corp., Newton, Mass., 1998—; co-coord. grad. program tchrs. of students with spl. needs, mem. grad. faculty infant toddler program evaluator Danforth cmty. devel. project Wheelock Coll., 1995-98; nat. cons. Am. Found. for the Blind, N.Y.C., 1986-89; adj. asst. prof. div. spl. edn., Columbia U., 1987—; co-dir. model infant/toddler program, sch. medicine, U. N.C., Chapel Hill, 1983-84; project dir., mem. grad. faculty severe and multiple disabilities Simmons Coll., 1990—; bd. dirs. N.D. Coun. for the Arts; adv. bd. Blind Babies Found.; mem. adv. com. Robert E. Miller, Inc., Community Residential Svcs. for Disabled Children; bd. dirs. Specialized Svcs. for Children, Inc.; sch. edn. rep. to fac. N.C. State U., sch. edn. fac. senate, among others. Grantee Busch Found., N.D. Coun. Arts, Nat. Coun. on the Arts, Dean's Grant Program, Burlington/No. Found., Kate B. Reynolds Found., Nat. Rural Spl. Edn. Consortium, U.S. Office Human Devel. Svcs., U.S. Office of Spl. Edn. Mem. Coun. for Exceptional Children (past dir. div. visual handicaps), Assn. for Retarded Citizens, Assn. for Persons with Severe Handicaps, Am. Assn. Mental Deficiency, Am. Assn. for Applied Behavior Analysis, Nat. Assn. for Parents of the Visually Impaired, Internat. Assn. for the Edn. of the Deaf-Blind, Assn. for the Edn. and Rehab. of the Blind and Visually Impaired (pre-sch. div., multihandicaps div., chairperson multiple disabilities div.), Internat. Coun. Educators of Children and Youth Who Are Blinded or Visually Impaired (co-coord. functions curriculum devel. project 1993—). Avocation: scuba diving. E-mail: zambone790@earthlink.net. Office: Inst for Equity in Schs Affiliate Walker Home & Sch 1968 Central Ave Needham MA 02492-1410 also: Edn Devel Corp 35 Chapel St Newton MA 02458-1010

ZAMMA, HIDEKI, linguist, educator; b. Ono-cho, Gifu, Japan, May 15, 1969; s. Katsunori and Mitsuko (Komeyama) Z.; m. Yuko Yoshida, Aug. 21, 1999; 1 child,Jion. BA, Waseda U., Tokyo, 1991; MA, U. Tsukuba, Japan, 1993. Rsch. fellow Japan Soc. for Promotion of Sci., Tokyo, 1996-98; rsch. assoc. U. Tsukuba, 1998-99; lectr. Kobe City U. Foreign Studies, 1999—. Contbr. articles to profl. jours. Mem. English Linguistic Soc. Japan, Linguistic Soc. Japan, Phonetic Soc. Japan (internat. com.), Phonol. Soc. Japan. Office: Kobe City U Foreign Studies, 9-1 Gakuen-higashimachi, Nishi-ku Kobe City Hyogo 651-2187, Japan

ZAMMIT DIMECH, FRANCIS, Maltese minister of environment; b. St. Julian's, Malta, Oct. 23, 1954; s. George and Ann (Dimech) Zammit. Student, St. Aloysius Coll., Birkirkara, 1966-71, Jr. Coll., Valletta, 1971-73; LLD, U. Malta, 1979. Prodr. Radio Malta, 1974; asst. night editor In-Nazzjon Taghna, 1977; mng. dir. Lexprint Pubs., Ltd., 1978-82; internat. sec. Nat. Party Youth Movement, Malta, 1980-82, v.p., 1984, pres., 1985; M.P. Maltese Parliament, 1987-89, parliamentary sec. transp. and comm., 1990; min. Maltese Ministry Transp. and Comm., 1992-94, Maltese Ministry Environment, Floriana, 1994-96, 98; columnist In-Nazzjon Taghna, 1974—, The Sunday Times, 1996—, The People, 1997-98, The Times, 1997—, The Independent, 1997; parliamentary corr. The Times, Malta, 1980; Maltese del. Parliamentary Assembly Coun. Europe, 1987-92, cultural and edn. com., 1987-92, com. rels. with European non-mem. states, 1987-92. Author: Poll of 76, 1980, The Untruth Game: Broadcasting Under Labour, 1986, Eddie-The People's Choice, 1987; chmn. editorial bd. Zaghzugh, 1986-87; editor: Il-Poplu mag., 1988-90. Exec. com. Nationalist Party, 1987—, sec. info., 1988-90, pres. adminstrv. coun., 1997-99. Mem. Casino Maltese Club, Neptunes Waterpolo Club, World Class Club. Roman Catholic. Avocations: reading, broadcasting, theatre, swimming. Office: Ministry for Environment, Block B, Floriana CMR 02, Malta also: 87 Lapsi St, Saint Julian's STJ 08, Malta

ZAMOLODCHIKOVA, YELENA, olympic athlete; b. Moscow, Sept. 19, 1982. Mem. gymnastics team Russia; winner team silver European Championship, 1998; winner team silver World Championship, 1999, winner bronze all-around, 1999, winner gold in vault, 1999; winner gold in vault and floor exercise Olympics, Sydney, Australia, 2000. Office: Fedn Gymnastique de Russie, Lujnetskaya Nabereynaya 8, 119 871 Moscow Russia*

ZAMORA, ROMEO DISING, surgeon; b. San Nicolas, Philippines, Apr. 16, 1926; s. Felix Ibasco Zamora and Agripina Manarang Dising; m. Estela Francia Llenado, Nov. 21, 1963; children: Rene, Ruben, Tina. M in Hosp. Adminstrn. Diplomate Am. Bd. Surgery, Am. Bd. Thoracic Surgery. Dir. Adminstrn. Philippine Heart Ctr., Quezon City, 1994-97; v.p. Philippine Coll. of Surgeons, 1971-72, pres. Philippine Coll./Hosp. Adminstrn., 1988-90. Author: (book) Emergency Medicine Reference Handbook, 1992-93. Mem. Rotary, Med.-Surg. Missions Com., Soc. of Thoracic Surgeons, AHA, Royal Australian Coll. of Surgeons, Assn. Thoracic and Cardiovascular Surgeons Asia (founding pres. 1972-74). Roman Catholic. Office: Philippine Heart Ctr, East Ave 1100, Quezon City Philippines also: St Luke's Med Ctr, Quezon City The Philippines

ZAMORA, ROSARIO, chemist, biochemist, researcher; b. Zafra, Spain, Aug. 17, 1959; d. Agustin Zamora and Rosario Corchero; m. Francisco Javier Hidalgo, Apr. 21, 1990. BSc, U. Extremadura, 1981, PhD, 1985. Rsch. assoc. Consejo Superior de Investigaciones Cientificas, Seville, Spain, 1986-87, rsch. scientist, 1990—; rsch. assoc. U. Calif., Davis, 1988-89. Contbr. articles to profl. jours. Mem. Am. Oil Chemists' Soc. Office: CSIC-Inst de la Grasa, Ave Padre Garcia Tejero 4, 41012 Seville Spain

ZAMORANO, IVAN, soccer player; b. Santiago, Chile, Jan. 18, 1967. Forward Real Madrid, 1995-96, Inter Milan (Italy) Football Club, 1996—. Address: Internazionale FC, Via Durini 24, 20122 Milano Italy*

ZAMORA PATIÑO, GEORGINA, industrial designer, educator; b. Mexico City, May 5, 1961; d. Alfonso Zamora Reyes and Cristina Patiño Fuentes. Degree in Indsl. Design, U. Iberoamericana, Mexico City, 1982; postgrad., U. Nat. Autonoma Mexico, Mexico City, 1994-97. Designer Gomez-Biagi Diseñadores S.C., Mexico City, 1982-83; devel. dept. coord. Calzado Sandak S.A. de C.V., Mexico City, 1983-84; designer Grupo Indsl. Casa, S.A., Mexico City, 1984, Lamparas Yvonne S.A. de C.V., Mexico City, 1984-85; design dept. mgr. Condumex S.A. de C.V., Mexico City, 1985-87; designer, part owner Artpiel S.A., Mexico City, 1988-91; indsl. design career coord. U. Iberoamericana, 1991-95, rschr., 1995—. Recipient 2d place award Med. Soc. Gen. Hosp., Mexico City, 1982. Avocations: music, traveling. Office: U Iberoamericana, Prol Paseo la Reforma 880, 01210 Mexico City Mexico

ZAMOTRINSKY, ALEXANDER VLADIMIROVICH, cardiologist; b. Tomsk, Siberia, Russia, May 7, 1961; s. Vladimir Alekseevich and Ekatrina Alexandrovna (Zimina) Z.; m. Valentina Ilinichna Smokotina, Oct. 25, 1984; 1 child, Vladimir. MD, Med. Inst. Tomsk, 1985; PhD, Ctr. Med. Genetics Moscow, 1991. Med. diplomate Russia. Rschr. Inst. Nuclear Physics, Tomsk, 1985-87; postdoctoral rschr. Ctr. Med. Genetics, Moscow, 1987-90; rschr. Inst. Med. Genetics, Tomsk, 1991-95; fellow Erasmus U., Rotterdam, The Netherlands, 1996; cardiologist Inst. Cardiology, Tomsk, 1999—; prin. investigator Dutch-Russian Clinic on Neurocardiology, Tomsk, Russia, 1997—; head Pvt. Cardiol. Clinic, Tomsk, 1998—. Inventor in field; contbr. articles to profl. jours. Recipient award Internat. Soc. Heart Rsch., 1995, Russian Fund Fundamental Investigation, 1995, Russian Pres. Adminstrn. and Russian Acad. Med. Scis., 1996. Fellow European Soc. Cardiology; mem. Am. Heart Assn. Avocation: water tourism. Home: Elizarovuch str 50 rm 110, 634012 Tomsk Russia Office: Inst Cardiology, Kievskaya str 111, 634012 Tomsk Russia

ZAMPIELLO, RICHARD SIDNEY, metals and trading company executive; b. New Haven, Conn., May 7, 1933; s. Sidney Nickolas and Louise Z.; m. Helen Shirley Palsa, Oct. 10, 1961; 1 child, Geoffrey Richard. BA, Trinity Coll., 1955; MBA, U. Bridgeport, 1961. With Westinghouse Elec. Corp., Pitts., 1955-64; exec. v.p. Ullrich Copper Corp., subs. Foster Wheeler Metals, Inc., Stamford, Conn., 1964-71; sr. v.p. Gerald Metals, Inc., Stamford, 1971-85; group v.p. Diversified Industries Corp., St. Louis, 1985-90; pres. Plume and Atwood Brass Mill div. Diversified Industries Corp, Thomaston, Conn., 1985-90, Upstate Metals Corp., Canastota, N.Y., 1990—. Dir. Conn. Resource Recovery Authority. Mem. ASME, Soc. Mfg. Engrs., AIME, Yale, Mining (N.Y.C.), Lake Waramug Country (Washington, Conn.), Washington Country. Home: 277 Woodbury Rd Washington CT 06793-1814 Office: 99 E River Dr East Hartford CT 06108-3288

ZAMPIERI, GUILLERMO ENRIQUE, physicist; b. Macia, Argentina, July 13, 1956; s. Juan Bautista and Maria Dolores (Fernandez) Z.; m. Alejandra Lilian Schnebeli, Nov. 16, 1985 (div. Aug. 1991); 1 child, Emiliaus. MS in Physics, Inst. Balseiro, Bariloche, Argentina, 1979, D of Physics, 1985; postgrad., Eidgenossische Tech. Hochsch., Zurich, 1985-86. Rschr. Nat. Atomic Energy Commn., Bariloche, Argentina, 1983—, CONICET, Bariloche, Argentina, 1990—; prof. Inst. Balseiro, Bariloche, Argentina, 1992—. Contbr. over 45 articles to profl. jours. Mem. Assn. Fisica Argentina, Assn. Profesionales de la Comision Nacional de Energia Atomica. Office: Centro Atomico Bariloche, 8400 Bariloche Argentina

ZAMRAZIL, VÁCLAV, internist, endocrinologist, educator; b. Prague, Czech Republic, Sept. 28, 1936; s. Václav and Marie (Ružičková) Z.; m. Elvíra Simková, Aug. 25, 1960; children: Václav, Hana. MD, Charles U., Prague, Czech Republic, 1960, PhD, 1972, DSc, 1989. Physician County Hosp., Pisek, Czech Republic, 1960-65; rschr. Inst. Endocrinology, Prague, 1965-83, head clin. dept., 1983—; cons. Tchg. Hosp. Prague Motol, 1978—; tchr. med. sch. Charles U., 1980—, asst. prof. internal medicine, 1993, prof. internal medicine, 1997, head dept. endocrinology Postgrad. Med. Sch., 1999—. Author: Diabetes and Thyroid disorders, 1985, Proceedings in Endocrinology, 1989, Iondine Deficiency in Czech Republic: Therapeutic Uses of Trace Elements, 1996, Early Stages of Diabetes Mellitus, 1997; co-author: Diseases of the Thyroid, 1995, Endocrinology, 1995; contbr. articles to profl. jours. With med. mil. svc. Czech Army, 1960—. Mem. Internat. Com. for Control of Iodine Def. Disorders, Czech. Endocrinol. Soc., Czech. Soc. Diabetologists. Roman Catholic. Avocation: collecting ceramics and fine art articles. Fax: 420 2 24905 325. E-mail: vzamrazil@endo.cz. Home: Pod Terebkou 3, CZ 14000 Prague Czech Republic Office: Inst Endocrinology, Národní 8, 116 94 Prague Czech Republic

ZAMSKI, ELI, botanist; b. Tel Aviv, Sept. 19, 1942; s. Meir and Sara (Weiss) Z.; m. Shoshana Grovas, Sept. 13, 1965; children: Tamar, Oren, Nufar, Carmel, Maor. BS, The Hebrew U., Jerusalem, 1966, MS, 1967, PhD, 1971. Rsch. asst. Hebrew U., Jerusalem, 1966-71; lectr. Hebrew U., Rehovot, Israel, 1972-78, sr. lectr., 1978-85, assoc. prof., 1985-94, chair botany, 1994—; head dept. agrl. botany Hebrew U., Rehovot, 1998—; rsch. asst. Hebrew U., Jerusalem, 1966-71; vis. prof. Harvard U., Cambridge, Mass., 1977-78, Utah State U., Logan, 1982-83, Pa. State U., State College, U. Wis., Madison, 1990-91, N.C. State U. Raleigh, 1995-96, 2000. Author: Cell Biology, 1997; editor: Secretion and Secretory Structures in Plants, 1986, Photoassimilate Distribution in Plants, 1996; contbr. 100 articles to profl. jours. Head Mcpl. Com., Moshav Kidron, Israel, 1992-94. Fellow Am. Soc. Plant Physiologists. Home: 11, 70795 Moshav Kidron Israel Office: Faculty Agrl, 76100 Rehovot Israel

ZANAZZI, GEORGE JOHN, neuroscientist; b. N.Y.C., Apr. 26, 1971; s. Giuseppe and Marisa (Cavanna) Z. BS, Stanford U., 1993. Rsch. asst. Cornell U. Med. Coll., N.Y.C., 1989, Stanford (Calif.) U. Med. Sch., 1991-93, NYU Med. Sch., N.Y.C., 1993—. Contbr. articles to profl. jours. Vol. Alzheimer's Assn., Palo Alto, Calif., 1991-93. Mem. AAAS, Soc. for Neurosci., N.Y. Acad. Sci. Achievements include first to report that some growth factors cause demyelination and to investigate the intracellular pathways involved in growth factor-induced demyelination; contribution to the development of porphyrins as anti-cancer drugs; co-discovery of the first molecule to be identified at the septate-like paranodal junctions of myelinated axons; elucidated the roles of cell adhesion molecules in the development and maintenance of the node of Ranvier; helped to determine the basis for the neural tropism of mycobacterium leprae and arenaviruses.

ZANCHI, PERO, surgeon, researcher; b. Split, Croatia, Dec. 30; s. Simun and Ivan Zanchi; m. Vanja Kuzmic, Feb. 20, 1988; children: Ivo, Sime. MD, Zagreb U., 1988, degree in gen. surgery, 1995. Gen. practitioner Outpatient Dept., Trogir, 1989-91; resident in surgery Split U. Hosp., 1991-93, Zurich U. Hosp., 1993-94, Split U. Hosp., 1994-95, Zagreb U. Hosp. Sisters of Mercy, 1995; gen. surgeon Knin Gen. Hosp., 1996—, head surgery dept., 1997—; cons. Split Med. Sch., 1999—. Contbr. articles to profl. jours. Recipient award in field of medicine Coun. Town Knin, 1998. Mem. Croatian Assn. for Surgery, Croatian Med. Assn., Croatian Assn. for Endoscopic Surgery, Internat. Gastro-Surg. Club. Home: Trscanska 43, 21000 Split Croatia Office: Knin Gen Hosp, S Suronje 12, 22300 Knin Croatia

ZANCHINI, ENZO, physicist; b. Forli, Emilia, Italy, Aug. 14, 1948; s. Mario and Linda (Farneti) Z.; m. Rosa De Simone, Oct. 27, 1991; childlren: Antonio, Francesco. D Engring., U. Bologna, 1975. Asst. prof. U. Bologna, 1977-82, assoc. prof., 1983-99, prof., 2000—; lectr. U. Parma, Italy, 1994-98. Contbr. articles to profl. jours. Mem. Soc. Italiana di Fisica, Unione Italiana di Termofluidodinamica, Assn. Termotecnica Italiana. Roman Catholic. Avocations: tennis, table tennis, music, movies. Office: Dienca Univ Bologna, Viale Risorgimento 2, I-40136 Bologna Italy

ZANDER, ERNST OTTO FERDINAND, economist, lawyer; b. Buchholz, Germany, May 1, 1927; s. Ernst Karl Christian and Else Anna (Behrent) Z.; m. Erika Maria Heinrich, May 11, 1957; children: Karin, Petra. Diplom Polit. Econs./Social Scis., U. Köln, Germany, 1956, DrRerPol, 1959. Mem. bd. mgmt., pers. mgr. H E W, Hamburg, Germany, 1957-75; mem. bd. mgmt. Reemtsma Co., Hamburg, 1975-87; chmn. Reemtsma Found. Bochum, Germany, 1976—; chmn. bd. Securitas, Bremen, Germany, 1979-96; mem. bd. mgmt. Internat. Inst. for Econs., Hamburg, 1988-99; mem. bd. mgmt. Employers Assn., 1976-89; mem. Inst. for Mgmt. Devel. and Social Scis., Hamburg, 1979-97; prof. indsl. leadership U. Hamburg, 1986-98; mem. adv. bd. Aachen Münchener Ins. Co., 1976-96. Author: Wage and Salary Policy, 12th edit., 2000, Management Principles, 8th edit., 2000, more than 50 others; pub. (handbook) Handbook for Labour Relations, 1977; pub. monthly rev. Personal, 1980—; author numerous articles. Served with German Army, 1944-45, prisoner of Soviets, 1945-50. Recipient Gold medal German Assn. for Pers. Mgmt., 1985, Gold medal Assn. Sch. and Econs., 1987, Zander-award U. Bochum, 1995—. Mem. Rotary Hamburg (pres.). Avocations: writing books and articles, travel in Middle East, Far East, Africa, Russia. Home: PO Box 670 427, 22359 Hamburg Germany

ZANDER, JOERG KLAUS-PETER, automotive parts company executive; b. Berlin, Germany, Sept. 2, 1953; arrived in Japan, 1981; s. Wilfried and Ingrid (Brueckner) Z.; m. Etsuko Fujita, May 2, 1989; children: Yuen-Ha, Michiko, Thorsten, Yoshio. Engr., Porsche AC, Berlin, 1971, Aviation PA, Berlin, 1976. Mgr. Bueckner KG, Berlin, 1978-81, Alltec, Tokyo, 1981-87; pres. Nihon ESPA, Yokohama, Japan, 1987-92; cons. Bosch/Siemens, Tokyo, 1992-93; pres. C-Lux Co., Ltd., Kawasaki, Japan, 1993—; bd. dirs. ZK Hold Espana Alicante, Spain, 1996—, C-Lux Philippines, Manila, 1996—. Inventor, developer, audio navigation system, 1987,88, water proof connector, 1988. Mem. Amtomotive Parts Supplier Assn., German C. of C. Avocations: music, reading. Office: C-Lux Co Ltd, 6-10-6 Tsuchihashi MiyameKu, Kanagawa Kawasaki 216, Japan

ZANDER, MAXIMILIAN, industrial research chemist, educator; b. Berlin, Feb. 7, 1929; s. Karl and Margarete (Loewenstein) Z.; m. Marianne Plasswich, Dec. 28, 1955; children: Georg, Jochen. BSc in Chemistry, U. Greifswald, Germany, 1953; PhD in Chemistry, U. Münster, Germany, 1956. Rsch. group leader Rütgerswerke AG, Castrop-Rauxel, Germany, 1955-68, 88-92, rsch. dir., 1968-88, rsch. cons., 1992-94; hon. prof. U. Clausthal, Germany, 1971—. Author: Phosphorimetry, 1968, Fluorimetrie, 1981, Polycyclische Aromaten, 1995; editor: Polycyclic Aromatic Compounds, 1990-97; contbr. over 300 articles to profl. jours. Recipient Franck medal Internat. Tar Conf., Biarritz, France, 1983. Mem. Internat. Soc. Polycyclic Aromatic Compounds (bd. dirs. 1993-97, Rsch. award 1993). Avocations: poetry, philosophy. Home: Friedenstrasse 9, D-44579 Castrop-Rauxel Germany

ZANDIAN, BABAK, metallurgical engineer; b. Tehran, Iran, Apr. 4, 1970; s. Rostam and Guity (Bahmanian) Z. BS, Sharif U. Tech., Tehran, Iran, 1993; MS, Sharif U. Tech., 1997. Rschr. Razi Metallurgical Rsch. Cen., Tehran, 1994-97, head rsch. labs., 1997-99; rsch. engr. Niroo (Power) Rsch. Inst. (NRI), Tehran, 1999—; co-rschr. Sharif U. Tech., Tehran, 1997. Mem. Iranian Metallurgical Engrs., Iranian Founders Orgn. Zoroastrian. Avocations: photography, history. Home: Golha Sq Fatemi Ave, No 108 Zinavand Ln, 14139 Tehran Iran

ZANE, WILLIAM ANTHONY, chemicals executive; b. Hazleton, Pa., Oct. 15, 1950; s. William Richard and Mary An (Maylath) Z.; m. Jean Marie Holy, Feb. 22, 1975; children: William P., Michael J., Andrew A. BSChE, Pa. State U., 1972. Sales rep. Diamond Shamrock Chem. Co., Omaha, Pitts., Dayton, Ohio, 1972-77; mktg. mgr. chlorine Diamond Shamrock Chem. Co., Cleve., 1978-80, product mgr. internat., 1981-82, dist. sales mgr., 1982-84; Midwest regional mgr. splty. chem. divsn. Diamond Shamrock Chem. Co., Chgo., 1985-87; nat. sales mgr. Cognis Corp. (formerly Henkel Corp.), Chgo., 1988-89; N.Am. sales mgr. Cognis Corp. (formerly Henkel Corp.), Phila., 1989-94, bus. dir., 1993-94, bus. dir. coating resins and additives, 1994-95, v.p., gen. mgr. plastic and polymer chem. divsn., 1995-98, v.p. coatings and inks divsn. and plastic/polymer divsn., 1998—. Treas. Methacton H.S. Basketball Club, Fairview Village, 1995-96. Mem. Medinah Country Club (non-resident). Republican. Roman Catholic. Avocations: golf, skiing, running, family activities. Home: 3067 Sunny Ayre Dr Lansdale PA 19446-5828 Office: Henkel Corp 300 Brookside Ave Ambler PA 19002-3497

ZANECCHIA, THOMAS EDWARD, financial executive; b. Bklyn., Dec. 29, 1954; s. Armando Luigi and Irma Elda (Martinuzzi) Z.; m. Deborah Sue Newhouse, June 18, 1977; children: Natalie Newhouse, Katie Lynn. BS in Commerce, U. Va., 1976; MBA in Fin., U. Pa., 1981. CPA, Colo. Sr. acct. Coopers & Lybrand, Boston, 1976-79; staff cons. Wharton Applied Rsch. Ctr., Phila., 1979-81; pres., shareholder Asset Mgmt. Group, Denver, 1981-93; founder, pres. Wealth Mgmt. Cons., Inc., Denver, 1993—; mem. bd. advisors F&B Mfg., Inc., 1994—; bd. dirs. Am. Materials Corp., 1997—; spkr. nat. seminars for Family Firm Inst., Young Pres.' Orgn., other trade assns. Contbr. fin. articles to profl. and fin. publs.; recognized in J.K. Lasser's Estate Planning for Baby Boomers and Retirees. Bd. dirs. Hospice of Metro Denver, 1989-94, bd. advisers, Denver Entrepreneurship Acad., 1992-94; mem. Body of Knowledge com. Family Firm Inst., 1997-98. Named among Worth Mag.'s Best Fin. Advisors, 1998, 99. Mem. AICPA, Colo. Soc. CPAs, Family Firm Inst. Avocations: golf, skiing. Home: 4930 S

Gaylord St Englewood CO 80110-7129 Office: Wealth Mgmt Cons Inc 475 17th St Ste 570 Denver CO 80202-4015

ZANELLA, RENATO, artistic director, choreographer; b. Verona, Italy, June 6, 1961. Student, Ctr. Danse Classique Rosella Hightower, Cannes, France, 1979-81. Dancer Hainz Spoerli, Basel, 1982-85, Stuttgart Ballets, 1985-93; artistic dir. Vienna State Opera Ballet, 1995—; mem. jury Prix the Lausanne, 1995. Choreographer (ballets) The Other Page, 1989, One Day, 1990, Stati d'animo, 1991, Triptychon, 1991, Man in the Shadow, 1992, Voyage, 1992, Empty Place, 1992, Black Angels, 1993, Mata Hari, 1993, Konzertantes Duo (rev. version of Stati d'animo), 1993, Lx27 Enfantillage, 1994, Process Polka, Perpetuum mobile, 1995, Pieces of Earth, 1995, Mon Euridice, 1995, Strawinski Evening: Symphony, movements, Sacre, 1996, Louis XIV, 1996, Bunck Incontra Verdi, 1996, Everyone Celebration, 1996, Love Beyond, 1996, Cycle of Item (Thin Air, Watching Waters, Pieces of Earth), 1997, La Chambre, 1997, Creates Blood, 1997, Memmemto Mori, 1997; (operas) Soiree Polka, 1996, At The Beautiful Blue Danube, 1996, Carnevals Ambassadors, 1997; arranger Behind the Window Blinds of the Ballets, Rienzi, 1997; developer Watching Waters, 1994. Named One of Best Italian Choreographers Danza & Danza mag., 1995. Office: Vienna State Opera Ballet, Opernring 2, A-1010 Vienna Austria*

ZANETTI, UGO ACHILLE, theologist, educator, priest; b. Ougree, Belgium, Nov. 7, 1948; s. Armando and Elsa (Carnielli) Z. B in Theology, U. Gregoriana, 1979; M iin Classics, Cath. U. Louvain, 1974, D in OrientalLangs., 1985. Ordained Roman Catholic priest. From assoc. to full staff Soc. Bollandists, Brussels, 1982—; lect. Cath. U. Louvain, 1985-90; prof., 1990—. Home: Bd Saint-Michel 24, 1040 Brussels Belgium Office: Inst Orientaliste, Pl B Pascal 1, 1348 Louvain-La-Neuve Belgium

ZANEVSKY, YURI VATSLAVOVICH, nuclear physicist, researcher; b. Minsk, Russia, Jan. 1, 1939; s. Vatslav Adolfovich and Galina Nikolaevna (Shaikovskaja) Z.; m. Lubov Aleksandrovna Kostrova; children: Aleksandr, Dmitrii. Diploma in engring. physics, Leningrad Inst. Electronics, Leningrad (now St. Petersburg), Russia, 1962; PhD, Joint Inst. Nuc. Rsch., Dubna, Russia, 1968, DSc, 1975. Jr. scientist Joint Inst. Nuc. Rsch., 1962-64, postdoctoral rschr., 1964-68, sr. scientist, 1969-73, head detector dept. lab. high energies, 1973—, prof. physics, 1984; participant internat. adv. bd. Position Sensitive Detectors conf., Manchester, Eng., 1996, London, 1999; mem. sci. com. on application of nuc. physics methodology Russian Acad. Sci., Moscow, 1995; participant internat. schs. Internat. Com. Future Accelerators 1990, 91, 93, 95, 97. Mem. editl. bd. Jour. Phys. Med., Rome, 1989. Recipient prize Govt. of USSR, 1985. Avocations: snow skiing, travel. Office: Jt Inst Nuc Rsch Lab High E, Jolio Cuirie 6, 141980 Dubna Moscow, Russia

ZANFAGNA, PHILIP EDWARD, government executive, urban planner; b. Lawrence, Mass., Dec. 5, 1936; s. Philip Edward and Edna Edith (Hill) Z.; m. Joan Elizabeth Criswell, Sept. 9, 1961; children: Deborah Carol Bass, Gary Philip. BA, Ohio Wesleyan U., 1958; MDiv, Yale U., 1961; JD, George Washington U., 1964. Certified in sr. exec. svcs., acquisition profl. Sr. negotiator USN, Washington, 1964-72; dep. dir. contracts dept. Navy USMC, Washington, 1972-80, dir. contracts, 1980-90, asst. chief of staff installations and logistics, 1990—, dep. asst. commandant, 2000; pres. Lewinsville Inc., McLean, Va., 1980-95. Commr., vice chmn. Fairfax (Va.) County Planning Commn., 1973-77; active Dulles Airport Planning Com., Fairfax, 1975-76, Fairfax Blue Ribbon commn., 1986-87; pres. Dranesville Dist. Coun., McLean, 1982-83; chmn. bd. dirs. McLean Citizens Assn., 1979-81; trustee McLean Found., 1980-86; bd. dirs. McLean Citizen's Assn., 1996—. Recipient Presdl. Rank award for exceptional pub. svc., 1993 98, Disting. Civilian Svc. medal. Mem. Sr. Exec. Assn., Yale U. Alumni Assn., Fed. Exec. Inst. Assn., Nat. Def. U. Alumni Assn., Harvard U. Sch. Govt. Alumni Assn. Presbyterian. Avocations: travel, music, photography, sports, teaching theology. Office: HQMC I & L Dept Code LB 3033 Wilson Blvd # 725 Arlington VA 22201-3843

ZANG, ARNO HEINZ WERNER, geophysicist, researcher; b. Aschaffenburg, Germany, Oct. 1, 1961. Diploma in geophysics, U. Frankfurt/Main, Germany, 1987, PhD, 1991; Dr.rer.nat.habil., U. Potsdam, Germany, 1998. Scientist U. Frankfurt, 1986-92; postdoctoral fellow SUNY, Stony Brook, 1992-93; scientist GeoForschungs Zentrum, Potsdam, Germany, 1993—. Contbr. articles to profl. jours.; dir., cameraman: (video) Micro Quakes, 1995. Served with Germany Army, 1981-82. Recipient 1st prize Best Oral Presentation German Geophys. Soc., Leipzig, 1993. Mem. Am. Geophys. Union. Office: GeoForschungszentrum, Telegrafenberg, 14473 Potsdam Germany

ZANGGER, EBERHARD, geoarchaeologist; b. Kamen, Westfalen, Germany, Apr. 9, 1958; arrived in Switzerland, 1991; s. Günter and Gerda (Kiefer) Finke; m. Ines Zangger, Aug. 5, 1988; children: Martina, Andrea. Mus. designer, Senckenberg Schule, Frankfurt, Germany, 1976; preparator, restauer, Ruhr U., Bochum, Germany, 1978; M in Geology, Kiel (Germany) U., 1984; PhD, Stanford U., 1988. Cert. rsch. diver. Technician German Mining Mus., Bochum, Germany, 1978-80; rsch. student Kiel (Germany) U., 1980-84; rsch. asst. Stanford (Calif.) U., 1984-88; sr. rsch. assoc. U. Cambridge, Eng., 1988-91; rsch. fellow Clare Hall, Cambridge, 1989-91; founder, dir. Geoarchaeology Internat., Zurich, Switzerland, 1991—; head Argive-Plain project, Greece, 1984-88; co-dir. Berbati-Limnes Archaeol. Survey, Nauplion, Greece, 1988-91; co-dir., head phys. sci. ops. Pylos (Greece) Regional Archeaol. Project, 1991-97; chief scientist Monastiraki-Amariou, Crete-Greece, 1996-97. Author: (books) The Flood from Heaven, 1992, Atlantis, 1992, The Geoarchaeology of the Argolid, 1993, Ein Neuer Kampf Um Troia, 1994, Die Zukunft der Vergangenheit, 1998. Recipient awards and fellowship German Nat. Scholarship Found., TSONN, 1981, 84, 86, Rsch. fellowship Clare Hall, U. Cambridge, 1985. Mem. Am. Inst. Archaeology, Senckenbergische Naturforschende Gesellschaft. Avocations: mountaineering, canoeing, collecting contemporary art. Home and Office: PO Box 313, 8125 Zollikerberg Switzerland

ZANNIS, GEORGE, engineering consultant; b. Piraeus, Attica, Greece, Jan. 1, 1959. BS with honors upper 2nd class, Plymouth Poly., Eng., 1982; MS in Applied Energy Engring., Cranfield Inst. Tech., Eng., 1984. Designer Agroplants S.A., 1987-88; prodn. and maint. engr. Famar-Essex Pharma, Athens, Greece, 1988-90; asst. tech. mgr. Castrol Hellas S.A., Piraeus, Greece, 1990-96; tech. mgr., shareholder Speedy Ferries S.A., Liberia, Greece, 1996—; tech. cons. Thermoplan S.A., Athens, 1998-99, Dodecanese Prefecture, 1999—; rsch. assoc. U. Athens, 2000—; energy cons. EEC Bldg. 2000 Programme, Athens, 1988-89, SAVE Programme Ministry Transport, 1998; vis. lectr. Ciene-U. Athens, 1993-97; cons., auditor A-Axion Devel. S.A., Athens, 1997-99; environ. adv. Prometee S.A., Athens, 1998—; tech. cons. WRE Hellas S.A., 1998; cons. Agroklimatiki S.A., 1998—; total quality mgmt. Cons. ISO 9000 projects Quali-Sys. S.A., 1993-94. Contbr. articles to profl. jours. Petty officer Hellenic Navy, 1984-86. Mem. Tech. Chamber Greece, Inst. Mech. Engring., Convocation Cranfield Inst. Technology. Greek Orthodox. Avocations: sailing, swimming, reading, cinema, music. Fax: 30-1-32 41 049. E-mail: zannisg@yahoo.com. Home: 177A Voulgari St, 185 34 Piraeus Attica, Greece Office: Filellinon 22 Syntagma, 105 57 Athens Greece

ZANONI, UMBERTO, banker, consultant; b. Verona, Italy, Oct. 28, 1937; s. Massimiliano and Giustina (Rivoldini) Z.; m. Luciana Signorati, Oct. 8, 1962; children: Andrea, Valeria, Michele. Degree in econs. and commerce, U. Padua, Italy, 1967. Acct. Cassa Risparmio Vr Vi Bl An, Verona, Italy, 1957-67, head br. office, 1967-68, sr. auditor, 1968-80, head cash dept., 1980-83, audit mgr., 1983-88, head audit dept., 1988-90, head revenues dept., 1990-96; pres. Verisparmio Gestri spa, Verona, 1996—; cons. Centro Formazione Personale Casse Risparmio Italiane, Rome, 1976—, Società per l'Organizzazione e la Formazione Manageriale, Milan, 1978-79, Istituto Studi Bancari, Lucca, Italy, 1988-90, Istituto Superiore Direzione Aziendale, Rome, 1989-91; v.p. audit and control com. Internat. Savs. Banks Inst., Geneva, 1989—; bd. dirs. Consorzio Nat. Concessionari, Rome, 1990-95; lectr. nat. meetings, seminars and roundtables, Italy, 5th Internat. Auditing Conf., Amsterdam, The Netherlands, 1988, Internat. Seminar on Auditing in Banking, Paris, 1988; guest lectr. U. Pavia, 1985, U. Verona, 1988-91, Luiss Rome, 1990-91, SDA Bocconi Milan, 1989-91, U. Venice, 1990. Author: Internal Auditing in Italian Savings Banks, 1988; co-author: Principles in Internal Auditing in Banking, 1983; contbr. articles to profl. jours., chpt. to booK. Bd. dirs. Sindircasse, Rome, 1987-92, Federdirigenticredito, Rome, 1988-90, Confedn. Italian Dirigenti Azienda, Rome, 1988-92. Mem. Inst. Internal Auditors (bd. govs. 1979-82, v.p. 1982-84, pres. 1984-86, chmn. bank auditing com. 1979-90), Ascotributi (advisor 1990-97, bd. govs. 1996—), Istituto Per l'Automazione delle Casse di Risparmio Italiane (advisor 1986-90, com. on computer crime), Italian Banking Assn. (mem. com. computer crime 1986). Home: Via Luigi Mercantini 12, 37124 Verona Italy Office: Cassa Risparmio Vr Vi Bl An Verisparmio, Gestri Spa Piazza Cittadella 6, 37122 Verona Italy

ZANOT, CRAIG ALLEN, lawyer; b. Wyandotte, Mich., Nov. 15, 1955; s. Thomas and Faye Blanch (Sperry) Z. AB with distinction, U. Mich., 1977; JD cum laude, Ind. U., 1980. Bar: Ind. 1980, Mich. 1981, U.S. Dist. Ct. (so. dist.) Ind. 1980, U.S. Dist. Ct. (no. dist.) Ind. 1981, U.S. Ct. Appeals (6th cir.) 1985, U.S. Dist. Ct. (ea. dist.) Mich. 1987, U.S. Dist. Ct. (we. dist.) Mich. 1990. Law clk. to presiding justice Allen County Superior Ct, Ft. Wayne, 1980-81; ptnr. Davidson, Breen & Doud P.C., Saginaw, Mich., 1981—. Mem. ABA, Mich. Bar Assn., Ind. Bar Assn., Saginaw County Bar Assn. Roman Catholic. Home: 547 S Linwood Beach Rd Linwood MI 48634-9432 Office: Davidson Breen & Doud PC 1121 N Michigan Ave Saginaw MI 48602-4762

ZANOTTI, LUIZ ROBERTO, computer company executive, computer store owner; b. Sao Paulo, Brazil, May 29, 1954; s. Luiz and Florinda (Freitas) Z.;m. Maria Elisabete Correa, May 10, 1978; children: Pablo Luiz, Thiago Henrique. Degree in Prodn. Engring., Politecnica-U. Sao Paulo, Brazil, 1978, M in Adminstrn., 1983. Mgr. Starco, Sao Paulo, 1977-83; dir. Flebra, Sao Paulo, 1983-94, Lince-Toshiba, 1994-95, Tatung, 1995—. Home: R Brigadeiro Franco 2212, 80250 Curitiba Parana, Brazil

ZANTOPULOS, WILLIAM THEODORE, sales representative, small business owner; b. Canton, Ohio, Sept. 1, 1962; s. John and Despina Z.; m. Karen Louise Wyler, Sept. 26, 1987; children: William John, Deanna Lee. BSBA, U. Akron, 1986. Mgmt. Rent-A-Ctr., Inc., Newcastle, Pa., 1987-91; mgr. Dollar Tree, Inc., Boardman, Ohio, 1992-94; rt. sales rep. Entenmann's Bakery, Tallmadge, Ohio, 1994—; co-owner Computer Experts LLC, Canton, 1999—. Democrat. Avocations: computers, golf, bowling, family. E-mail:wzantopulos@neo.rr.com. Office: Computer Experts LLC 5770 Navarre Rd SW Canton OH 44706-3239

ZANUSSI, ANA AMALIA, audit manager; b. Quilmes, B.A., Argentina, Feb. 14, 1960; d. Ferdinando and Ida Rita (Serafini) Z. Music prof., Inst. Musical Santa Cecilia, Buenos Aires, 1976; CPA, U. Buenos Aires, 1983; cert. internal auditor, Inst. Internal Auditors, 1996; master internal auditor, U. Austral, Buenos Aires, 1996. CPA, Argentina. Mem. acctg. and treasury dept. Du Pont Argentina, Berazategui, Argentina, 1983-84; acctg. analyst Du Pont Argentina, Berazategui, 1984-85, cost control supr., 1985-89, sr. tax analyst, 1989-93; regional adminstrv. mgr. for Tierra Del Fuego Soc. Anónima Importadora y Exportadora de la Patagonia, Rio Grande, Argentina, 1993-95; gen. auditor Soc. Anónima Importadora y Exportadora de la Patagonia, Buenos Aires, 1995-98; audit mgr. Alto Palermo, S.A., 1999—; cost prof. Inst. Superior del Profesorado Espiritu Santo, Quilmes, Buenos Aires, 1985-88; treas. Du Pont's Non Profit Employee Assistance Assn., Berazategui, 1990-93. Account supr. Assn. Cultural Sanmartiniana de Quilmes, 1990. Mem. Inst. Internal Auditors USA (Buenos Aires chpt.). Avocations: music, philosophy, traveling. Home: Alvear 654 Piso 4 Depto G, 1878 Quilmes B.A., Argentina

ZANUSSI, KRZYSZTOF, film director, producer, scriptwriter; b. June 17, 1939; s. Jerzy and Jadwiga A.; ed. Warsaw and Cracow univ., Lodz Higher Film Sch. Dir. numerous short feature films; films include Death of a Provincial, 1967; Structure of Crystals, 1972; Family Life, 1972; Illumination, 1972; The Catamount Killing, 1973; Womens Decision (OCIC prize West Berlin), 1974; Camouflage (Spl. prize Teheran 1977; Grand prize Polish Film Festival 1977), 1977; Spiral (award Cannes 1978, OCIC prize), 1978; Wege in der Nacht, 1979; Constant Factor (Best Dir. award Cannes), 1980; Contract (Distbn. prize Venice), 1980; From a Far Country; Imperative (W.Ger., France, award 1984); Year of the Quiet Sun, 1984 (Golden Lion Venice Film Fest 1984); The Power of Evil (OCIC prize Montreal), 1985; Wherever You Are, 1988; The Inventory (Oekumenical prize Moscow) Grand Prix Strausbourg 1989; Life For Life, 1990, The Silent Touch, 1992 (Best Actor prize Tokyo), On Full Gallop, 1995 (spl. jury prize, Tokyo), Our God's Brother, 1997, Life as Fatal, Sexually Transmitted Disease, 2000; TV films: Face to Face, 1967; Gdansk Lions, 1968, Mountains at Dusk, 1970, Role, 1971, Behind the Wall, (Grand priz San Remo 1972), 1971, Nachtdienst, 1975, Anatomiestunde, 1975, Haus der Frauen, 1978; Versuchung, 1981, Unaproachable, Blaubart, 1984, Grand Prix Venezia TV, Napoleon et Mme. Walewska (TF.3), Lutoslawski (BBC) Long Conversation With a Bird (WDR), 1990, Portrait of Russia of B. Yeltzin, 1991, Sounds and Images, 1991, Weekend Stories, 1996, 97 (7x1H) TVP. Mem. Erlöschene Zeiten (ZDF), Yehudi Menuhin (ARD), Mia Varsavia (RAI), Polish Film Assn. (vice chmn. 1971-81). Author: Nowele Filmowe, 1976; Scenariusze Filmowe, 1, 2, 3, 4; Sei Film, 1979; Rigorista, 1982, Pora Umierac, 1997, Opowiesci Weekendowe, 1998, Propheta, 1998, Miedzy Tarmarkiem A Salonem, 1999, Miedzy Darmarkiem A Salonem, 1999. Address: 8 rue Richepance, 75001 Paris France Office: Tor-Film Prodn Co, Pulaska 61, 00-173 Warsaw Poland

ZAORAL, MILAN, organic chemist; b. Olomouc, Czech Republic, May 5, 1926; s. Bohumil Zaoral and Ružena Sekaninová Zaoralová; m. Libuše Ševerová, Sept. 15, 1964 (div. June 1969); 1 child, Libuše; m. Jaroslava Šmídová, Aug. 20, 1970. Degree, Tech. U., Prague, Czechoslovakia, 1949; Candidate Sci., Czechoslovak Acad. Scis., Prague, 1955, DSc, 1968. Aspirant of scis. Czechoslovak Acad. Scis., 1949-51, sci. co-worker, 1951-56, ind. sci. co-worker, 1956-64, leading sci. co-worker, head, 1964-82, leading sci. co-worker, head dept., 1982-88; ind. scientist Prague, 1988—; cons. in field, Prague, 1990—. Author: Adiuretin, 1972 (State prize); co-author: Oxytocin, 1958 (State prize), Preparation of Synthetic Oxytocin, 1958 (State prize); editor-in-chief Synthetic Immunomodulators and Vaccines, 1986; inventor way of obtaining anti-diuretically active peptides (prize Presidium of Czechoslovak Acad. Scis., 1971); contbr. more than 140 articles to profl. jours.; patentee in field. Recipient Gold medal Dept. Tech. and Investment Devel., 1982, Heyrovsky's Gold medal presidium Czechoslovak Acad. Sci., 1986. Mem. Czech Chem. Soc., N.Y. Acad. Scis. Avocations: travel, high mountain tourism, aeronautics.

ZAPAŁOWICZ, ZBIGNIEW, thermal laboratory scientist; b. Ostrów Mazowiecka, Poland, Aug. 5, 1954; s. Antoni Sylwester and Antonina Elżbieta (Hryniewicz) Z.; m. Kinga Anna Mazurkiewicz, Sept. 29, 1984; 1 child, Kamila. MSc in Mech. Engring., Tech. U. Szczecin, Poland, 1979; PhD, Polish Acad. Scis., Gdańsk, Poland, 1989. Design engr. Factory Bldg. Machines-Hydroma, Szczecin, 1979-81; asst. Dept. Heat Engring. Tech. U. Szczecin, 1981-89, tutor, 1989-94, head thermal lab., 1994—. Contbr. articles to profl. jours. Mem. Polish Acad. Scis. (sect. thermodynamics and combustion, subsect. multiphase flow, sect. fluid mechanics). Avocation: sports. Home: Kutrzeby 13/4, 71-296 Szczecin Poland Office: Tech U Szczecin Heat Engr, Al Piastów 19, 70-310 Szczecin Poland

ZAPATA, CARMEN ELENA, formation damage and environmental researcher; b. Medellin, Antioquia, Colombia, Aug. 10, 1951; d. Conrado and Rosa Margarita (Sanchez) Z. Degree in petroleum engring., Nat. U., Colombia, 1978; MSc in Water Environment, Bournemouth (Eng.) U., 1995. Diplomate in engring., Colombia. Engr. Ecopetrol, Tibu, 1978-79; plant chief SOCOL, Medellin, 1979-80; prof. Nat. U. Colombia, Medellin, 1981-85, rschr., 1986-90, rsch. head, 1990—, petroleum engring. dir., 1995—, oil and gas unit coord., 1987; oil and gas lab. coord. Nat. U., Colombia, 1987—; dir. Engrs. Soc. of Antioquia, 1979-82; prin. mem. Colombian Petroleum Engring. Coun., 1990-93, 95—. Author: Water Treatment for Waterflooding, 1985, Waste Water Treatment on Petroleum Industry, 1990, Oil Effects in Soil, Groundwater, and Rock Strata, 1994, Environmental, Health and Safety Auditing on Oil and Gas Industry, 1997; co-author: Relative Permeability Measuring Equipment, 1991 (award 1992). Pres. Medellin Youthful Club, 1969-75; mem. Liberal Youthful Party, Colombia, 1972-80; coord. Medellin Environ. Soc., 1985-90; mem. Disaster Prevention Office, 1990—. Recipient scholarship Edn. Soc. of Antioquia, 1965-69, Overseas Devel. Adminstrn., Eng., 1993-94. Mem. Soc. Petroleum Engrs., Soc. of Petroleum Engring., Colombian Soc. Petroleum Engrs. Liberal. Roman Catholic. Avocations: reading, music, jogging, traveling, stamp collecting. Home: PO Box 59520, Calle 42 # 81A-71, Medellín Antioquia, Colombia Office: Nat U Colombia Facultad de Minas, CRA 80X Calle 65 POB 1027, Medellín Colombia

ZAPATA, JOSE VICENTE, lawyer, educator; b. Cali, Colombia, Oct. 2, 1966; s. Vicente and Luz Marlen (Lugo) Z. Degree in law, Pontificia U. Javeriana, Santafé de Bogota, Colombia, 1990; LLM, McGill U., Montreal, Can., 1994. Legal sec. Consultorio Juridico, Pontificia U. Javeriana, 1988; asst. legal counsel Dow Chem. Colombia, Santafé de Bogota, 1989-92; rsch. asst. McGill U., 1993-96; sr. assoc. Posse, Herrera & Ruiz, Santafé de Bogota, 1996-97, Brigard & Urrutia, Santafé de Bogota, 1997—; assoc. prof. law U. Rosario, Santafé de Bogota, 1996—, Mil. U. Nueva Granada, Santafé de Bogota, 1996—; external legal counsel Colombian Ministry of Environment, 1997. Judge Greenshields Meml. scholar McGill U., 1992, 93. Mem. Inst. Colombiano de Derecho Ambiental (gen. sec. 1997—). Roman Catholic. Avocations: piano, reading, wines. Home: Apt 402, Carrera 1 Este No 70-46, Santafé de Bogota Colombia Office: Brigard & Urrutia Abogados, Calle 70 No 4-60, Santafé de Bogota Colombia

ZAPESOTSKY, ALEXANDER SERGEEVICH, rector; b. Kursk, Russia, Apr. 14, 1954; s. Segey Mihailovich and Elena Georgievna (Stepanenko) Z.; m. Alla Grigorievna Kuanezova; 1 child, Yuri. Engr., Leningrad Inst. Precision Mech, Russia, 1976; Candidate, Leningrad State Inst. Culture, 1986. Specialist in sci. State Inst. Optics, Russia, 1976-86; tchr. High Sch. of Culture, Russia, 1986-90, rector, 1991-92; rector U. Humanities and Social Scis., St. Petersburg, Russia, 1992—. Author: Music and Youth, 1988, This Understandable Youth: The Problems of Unformal Youth Unions, 1990, Youth in Modern World. Problems of Individualisation and Social-Cultural Integration, 1996, Humanitarian Culture and Humanitarian Education, 1996, Strategic Marketing in Tourism, 1999; contbr. articles to profl. jours. Mem. Com. Russian Intelligence; chmn. Com. of Congress of St. Petersburg Intelligence; mem. Com. inn field of culture of Mayor of St. Petersburg. Recipient medal for saving person Govt. Russia, 1974, order of friendship Govt. Russia, 1996. Mem. Peter's Acad. Scis. and Arts, Acad. Humanities, Acad. Tourism, Russian Union Rectors, Internat. Acad. Psychol. Scis. Avocations: sports (swimming, tennis, skiing), theatre, music. Home: Kammennoostzousky p 2 61-8, Saint Petersburg Russia Office: St Petersburg U Humanities, & Social Scis, Futchika 15, 192238 Saint Petersburg Russia

ZAPF, HERMANN, book and type designer; b. Nuremberg, Germany, Nov. 8, 1918; s. Hermann and Magdalene (Schlamp) Z.; m. Gundrun von Hesse, Aug. 18, 1951; 1 child, Christian Ludwig. Freelance designer, 1938—; type dir. D. Stempel AG, type foundry, Frankfurt, Fed. Republic of Germany, 1947-56; design cons. Mergenthaler Linotype Co., N.Y.C. and Frankfurt, 1957-74; cons. Hallmark Internat., Kansas City, Mo., 1966-73; v.p. Design Processing Internat. Inc., N.Y.C., 1977-86; prof. typographic computer programs Rochester (N.Y.) Inst. Tech., 1977-87; chmn. Zapf, Burns & Co., N.Y.C., 1987-91; instr. lettering Werkkunstschule, Offenbach, Fed. Republic Germany., 1948-50; prof. graphic design Carnegie Inst. Tech., 1960; instr. typography Technische Hochschule, Darmstadt, Fed. Republic Germany, 1972-81. Author: William Morris, 1948, Pen and Graver, 1952, Manual Typographicum, 1954, 68, About Alphabets, 1960, 70, Typographic Variations, 1964, Orbis Typographicus, 1980, Hora fugit/Carpe diem, 1984, Hermann Zapf and His Design Philosophy, 1987, ABC-XYZapf, 1989, Poetry Through Typography, 1993, August Rosenberger, 1996, (film) The Art of Hermann Zapf, German version Die Welt der Buchstaben von Zapf; designer types, Palatino, Melior, Optima, ITC Zapf Chancery, ITC Zapf Internat., Digiset, Marconi, Digiset Edison, Digiset Aurelia, Pan-Nigerian, URW-Roman and San Serif, Renaissance Roman, Linotype Zapfino. Hon. pres. Edward Johnston Found., Ditchling, Eng.; hon. curator Computer Mus., Boston. Recipient Silver medal Brussels, 1962, 1st prize typgoraphy Biennale Brno, Czechoslovakia, 1966, Gold medal Type Dirs. Club, N.Y., Frederic W. Goudy award Inst. Tech. Rochester, 1969, Silver medal Internat. Book Exhbn., Leipzig, 1971, Gold medal, 1989; Johannes Gutenberg prize Mainz, Fed. German Republic, 1974, Gold medal Museo Bodoniano, Parma, Italy, 1975, J.H. Merck award, Darmstadt, 1978, Robert Hunter Middleton award, 1987, Euro Design award, 1994, Golden Bee, Moscow, 1995, Golden Bee, Moscow, 1995, Wadim Lazursky award, Acad. of Graphic Arts, Moscow, 1996; named hon. citizen State of Tex., 1970, hon. royal designer for industry. Mem. Royal Soc. Arts, Am. Math. Soc., Alliance Graphique Internationale, Caxton Soc., Bund Deutscher Grafik Designer, Internat. Gutenberg Gesellschaft, Caxton Soc.; hon. mem. Type Dirs. Club N.Y.C., Soc. Typographique de France (Paris), Soc. Typographic Arts (Chgo.), Double Crown Club (London), Soc. Scribes and Illuminators (London), Friends of Calligraphy (San Francisco), Soc. Printers (Boston), Soc. Graphic Designers Can., Bund Deutscher Buchkünstler, Grafiska Inst. (Stockholm), Typophiles (N.Y.), Alpha Beta Club (Hong Kong), Soc. of Calligraphy (L.A.), Wynkyn de Worde Soc. (London), Monterey Calligrapher's Guild, Washington Calligraphers Guild, Eesti Kalligraafide Koondis (Tallinn, Estonia), Chgo. Calligraphers Guild, Typographers Internat. Assn., Art Dirs. Club Kansas City, Assocs. Stanford U. Librs., Alcuin Soc. (Vancouver), Goudy Internat. Ctr., Brno Biennale Assn., Soc. Scribes N.Y., Dante e.V. (German Tex. Group, Heidelberg), German Tex Group (Heidelberg), Caxton Soc. (Chgo.), Gamma Epsilon Tau.

ZAPFFE, NINA BYROM, retired elementary education educator; b. Independence, Mo., Aug. 17, 1925; d. Richmond Douglas and Nina Belle (Howell) Byrom; m. Robert Glenn Fessler, June 25, 1946 (dec. June 1947); 1 child, Robert Glenn Fessler Zapffe; m. Fred Zapffe, July 1, 1952 (dec. Dec. 1999); children: Paul Douglas, Carl Raymond. BA, So. Meth. U., 1946. Fin. sec. Tyler St. Meth. Ch., Dallas, 1948-49; tchr. Dallas Ind. Sch. Dist., 1949-52, Norman (Okla.) Pub. Schs., 1966-74; cert. chief reader for GED Writing Skills Test Part II GED Testing Svc., Am. Coun. on Edn., Washington, 1990-98; adv. com. (Acad. Resource Ctr.) Moore-Norman Tech. Ctr., 1988—. Adv. bd. Norman Salvation Army, 1978-90; organizer, historian Norman Salvation Army Womens Aux., 1983—; organizer, past pres. Norman Literacy Coun., 1976—; organizing com., past pres. Norman Interfaith Coun., 1974-93; organizing com., past treas. Friends of the Norman Libr., 1979—; mem. McFarlin Meml. United Meth. Ch., historian 2-in-1 Sunday Sch. class, 1990—, lay leader, 1980-81. Named to Literacy Hall of Fame Pioneer Libr. Sys., Norman, 1995. Mem. DAR (regent Black Beaver chpt. 1998-2000, state literacy chmn. 2000—), Nat. Soc. Daus. 1812 (state treas. 1996-2000), Old Regime Study Club (pres. 1998-99), Coterie Club (pres. 1996), Delta Delta Delta Alumnae (named Norman Bus. and Profl. Women's Woman of Yr. 1999). Republican. Avocation: genealogy. Home: 2717 Walnut Rd Norman OK 73072-6940

ZAPHIRIOU, GEORGE ARISTOTLE, lawyer, educator; b. July 10, 1919; came to U.S., 1973, naturalized, 1977; s. Aristotle George and Callie Constantine (Economos) Z.; m. Peaches J. Griffin, June 1, 1973; children: Ari, Marie. JD, U. Athens, 1940; LLM, U. London, 1950. Bar: Supreme Ct. Greece 1946, Eng. 1956, Ill. 1975, Va. 1983. Gen. counsel Counties Ship Mgmt. and R & K Ltd., London, 1951-61; practicing barrister, lectr. City of London Poly., 1961-73; vis. prof. Ill. Inst. Tech.-Chgo. Kent Coll. Law, 1973-76; pvt. practice Northbrook, Ill., 1976-78; prof. law George Mason U. Sch. Law, 1978-94, prof. law emeritus, 1994—; prof. internat. transactions George Mason U. Internat. Inst., 1992-94; mem. Odin, Feldman & Pittelman P.C., Fairfax, Va., 1994-96; mem. study group on internat. elec. commerce model law and other pvt. internat. law covs. U.S. Dept. of State. Author: Transfer of Chattels in Private International Law, 1956, U.S. edit., 1981, European Business Law, 1970; co-author: Declining Jurisdiction in Private International Law, 1995; joint editor: Jour. Bus. Law, London, 1962-73; bd. dirs. and bd. editors Am. Jour. Comp. Law of Am. Soc. Comparative Law, 1980-94; contbr. articles to law revs. and profl. jours. Mem. ABA (sect. internat. law and practice and dispute resolution), Ill. Bar Assn., Chgo. Bar Assn., Am. Arbitration Assn. (panel of comml. arbitrators), George Mason Am. Inn of Ct. (founder, mem. emeritus). Fax: 301-984-1164. Home: 400 Green Pasture Dr Rockville MD 20852-4233

ZAPLETAL, ALOIS, pediatrician, pulmonologist, educator; b. Březovky, Zlín, Czech Republic, Oct. 24, 1932; s. Alois and Ludmila (Londinová) Z.; m. Božena Ohlídalová, Oct. 14, 1961 (dec. June 1983); children: Jana, Petr. MD, Charles U., Prague, Czechoslovakia, 1957, Candidate of Sci.,

1966, DSc, 1990. Asst. prof. 2nd Dept. Pediat., Prague, 1960-73, rsch. worker, 1977, head Lung Function Lab., prof., 1977-96; rsch. worker Kardiocentrum, Prague, 1977-91; assoc. prof. Med. Faculty, Charles U., Prague, 1992-95, prof., 1995—. Author: Function of the Respiratory Tract in Children and Adolescents, 1984; Lung Function in Children and Adolescents, 1987; mem. editl. bd. Pediat. Pulmonology, 1985-96; contbr. some 300 articles to profl. jours. Mem. Pediat. Soc. Argentina (hon.), Pediat. Pneumology Soc. Poland (hon.). Avocation: classical music. Home: Pod Lipami 2568/40, 130 00 Prague 3, Czech Republic Office: Vúvalu 84, 150 18 Prague 5, Czech Republic

ZAPOROZHETS, OLGA ANTONOVNA, chemist, educator; b. Kharkov, Ukraine, Sept. 27, 1958; d. Anthon Gordeyevich and Aleksandra Michailovna Kuyan; m. Yurij Petrovich Zaporozhets, Mar. 23, 1980; 1 child, Oksana. Bachelor's degree, Taras Shevchenko Kiev U., Ukraine, 1979, Master's degree, 1982, PhD, 1985. Cert. analytical chemist, lectr. Scientist Taras Shevchenko Kiev U., 1985-89, from asst. prof. to assoc. prof., 1989-97, assoc. prof., 1999—; leader rsch. group analytical chemistry dept. Taras Shevchenko Kiev U., 1995. Contbr. articles to profl. jours. Mem. Trade Union of Taras Shevchenko Kiev U., 1976. Recipient Jaroslav Mudry award Internat. Found. Edn., 1995; grantee Internat. Soros Sci. Edu. Program, 1998. Mem. Mendeleev Chem. Soc. Avocations: tennis, music, animals. Fax: 038 044 417 87 61. E-mail: miox@i.com.ua. Office: Taras Shevchenko Kiev U, Volodymyrska 64, Kiev 01033, Ukraine

ZAPOROZHETS, VLADIMIR VASILIEVICH, aviation technology educator; b. Zaporizhzhe, Ukraine, July 28, 1936; s. Vasiliy Porfirievich and Alexandra (Kurilekh) Z.; m. Liudmila Alexandrovna Akseonova, July 30, 1960; children: Marina Taran, Vladimir. Diploma, Inst. Civil Aviation, Kiev, Ukraine, 1960; Cand. Sci. in Engring., Inst. Civil Aviation, 1965, DSc in Engring., 1981. Aviation plant engr. Kiev, 1960-62; asst. prof. Inst. Civil Aviation Engrs., Kiev, 1965-68, prin. lectr., 1968-82, prof., 1982-84; chief dept. Internat. U. Civil Avication, Kiev, 1984—; chmn. Aviation Ground Support Tng. Complex, 1993—. Author: Aircraft Repair, 1981, 2d edit., 1984, Handbook on Aviation Ground Support Equipment, 1989, Reliability of Aviation Ground Support Equipment, 1989, Non-Destructive Control and Diagnostics, 1996. Named Honor Rschr. of USSR, Kiev, 1980, Honored Tchr. of Ukraine, Kiev, 1993. Mem. N.Y. Acad. Scis., Materials Info. Soc., Minerals, Metals and Materials Soc., Ukrainian Acad. Tribology, Assn. Airports of Ukraine (bd. dirs. 1994—). Avocations: yachting, hunting. Home: 5/9 Cytadelnaya St Apt 88, 01015 Kiev 15, Ukraine Office: Internat U Civil Aviation, 1 Komarov Ave, 03058 Kiev Ukraine

ZAPOTOCZKY, JOHANN GEORG, psychiatrist; b. Linz, Austria, Sept. 24, 1932; s. Hans and Gertrude (Steinbrecher) Z.; m. Helga Dunkl, Sept. 14, 1968; children: Andrea, Stephan. MD, U. Vienna, 1958. Asst. physician Wilhelminen Spital, Vienna, 1958-59, AKH Linz, 1960, Dept. Psychiatry U. Vienna, 1961-90; head dept. psychiatry U. Graz, Austria, 1990-2000; univ. lectr. dept. psychiatry U. Vienna, 1976-90; dir. dept. psychiatry U. Graz, 1990-2000. Home: Wenisbucher Str 9, A-8044 Graz Austria Office: Psychiatry Univ Clinic, Auenbruggerplatz 22, A-8036 Graz Austria

ZAPUSKALOV, NIKOLAI MIHAILOVICH, engineering researcher; b. Magnitogorsk, USSR, Sept. 27, 1962; arrived in Australia, 1995; s. Mihail Mironovich and Maria Nikolaevna Zapuskalov. M of Engring., Mognitogorsk Inst., 1985; PhD in Phys. Metallurgy, TsNIIchermet, Russia, 1993. Engr. Magnitogorsk Inst., 1987-89; rschr. TsNIIchermet, Moscow, 1989-93, Commonwealth Sci. and Indsl. Rsch. Orgn., Australia, 1995-96, BHP Rsch., Australia, 1997, BHP Inst., Australia, 1997—; dir. KORS, Moscow, 1993. Contbr. articles to profl. jours.; patentee in field. Sr. lt. Army of the USSR, 1985-87. Office: BHP Inst, U Wollongong, Wollongong NSW 2522, Australia

ZARCONE, MICHAEL JOSEPH, experimental physicist, consultant; b. Danbury, Conn., Dec. 10, 1950; s. Michael Joseph Zarcone and Mary Elizabeth Belardinelli; children from previous marriage: Cassandra Marie, Sally Marie; m. Sheila Candelario, Feb. 21, 1981; children: Michael Joseph, Christopher Michael. BS in Physics, Fairfield U., 1973; MS in Physics, N.Mex. Inst. Mining and Tech., 1984; PhD in Physics, U. Conn., 1989. Rsch. asst. Radon Lab., Socorro, N.Mex., 1983-84, VandeGraaff Accelerator Lab., Storrs, Conn., 1985-89; physics instr. Cen. Conn. State U., New Britain, 1989-90; accelerator tech. fellow Brookhaven Nat. Lab., Upton, N.Y., 1990-91, asst. physicist, 1991-93, physics assoc. II, 1993-98; physics assoc. I Brookhaven Nat. Lab., Upton, 1998—, coord. environ. safety/health, rsch./devel., foil prodn. tng. coord., 1994-99; dir. prodn., cons. Separations divsn. Corning Inc., 1994-99, Whatman Nuclepore, 1999—; cons. Corning. Contbr. articles to profl. jours. including Phys. Rev. A, Nuclear Instruments and Methods in Phys. Rsch., Physics Rev. Letters, Atmospheric Environment, Semiconductor Internat. Mem. Internat. Nuc. Target Devel. Soc., Am. Phys. Soc., Sigma Xi. Avocations: mountain climbing, hiking. Home: 17 Jones St East Setauket NY 11733-2935 Office: Brookhaven Nat Lab Bldg 510A Upton NY 11973

ZAREBICKI, JAN A., securities company executive, dog breeder; b. Wilmington, Del., July 26, 1955; s. Aleksander Josef and Barbara Ann (Ludzkowska) Z.; m. Dawn Ann Disabatino, Oct. 1, 1979 (div. June 1988); 1 child, Aleksander; m. Susan Carol Munze, May 15, 1989; children: Kathryn, Kristyn. BA, U. Del., 1977, MPA, 1979. Lic. life ins. agt., Del., Pa., Ky., Tenn, Md.; lic. series 7, 63, 65, 9 & 10 Nat. Assn. Securities Dealers. Rsch. assoc. U. Del., Newark, 1977-78; sales assoc. Scholarly Resources, Wilmington, 1979; exec. asst. New Castle County Office County Exec., Wilmington, 1979-80; chief dep. New Castle County Clk. of Peace, Wilmington, 1980-84; chief planner Del. Emergency Mgmt. Agy., Smyrna, 1984-89; fin. cons. Merrill Lynch, Wilmington, 1989-94; v.p. 1st Union Securities, Kennett Square, Pa., 1994-99; 1st v.p. Prudential Securities, Wilmington, 1999—; mem. leadership coun. Mass. Fin. Svcs., Boston, 1995-99; mng. ptnr. Zarebicki, Fierro & Schulten Investment Group, Wilmington, 2000—. Contbg. author Am. Field, 1980-99. State committeeman Del. Rep. Com., 1977-89; publicity agt. Aid to Poland, Del., 1982. Mem. Ducks Unltd., Quail Unltd., Del. Pointer and Setter Club, Va. Assn. Field Trial Clubs, Caroline County Field Trial Club, Coun. Polish Clubs (bd. dirs. Del. 1977-89), Diamond State Bird Dog Club (sec. Del. 1970-85). Democrat. Roman Catholic. Avocations: outdoor sportsman, horseman, bird dog breeder, trainer and field trialer. E-mail: jan zarebicki@prusec.com. Home: Summit Point Farm 2327 Chesapeake City Rd Bear DE 19701-2332 Office: Prudential Securities Inc PO Box 2750 Wilmington DE 19805-0750

ZARËUS, JØRGEN SIMON WALLBERG, retired shipbroker; b. Harstad, Norway, Aug. 21, 1923; s. Haakon Odin Berg Sareussen and Signora Katharina (Bølgen) Z. Student, Stabekk Jr. Coll., Baerum, Norway, 1942, Otto Treiders comml. sch., Oslo, 1946; BA in Internat. Rels., UCLA, 1950. Asst. to chief picture dept. Norwegian Embassy, Washington, 1942; solicitor J.S. Sareussen Ship Supplies Co., New Orleans and Mobile, Ala., 1946-48; asst. shipbroker Funch, Edye & Co., Inc., N.Y.C., 1951-53; shipbroker, v.p. Rohner, Gehrig Shipping & Alpina S/S Co., N.Y.C., 1953-56, Conaty Marine Chartering Corp., N.Y.C., 1959-61; shipbroker Tricerri Grain Corp., N.Y.C., 1956-57, Shipowners Agy., N.Y.C., 1957-59, Herman J. Sørensen, Oslo, 1970-71; chief shipbroker, dir. Norse Broker Ltd., Oslo, 1961-70; pvt. practice shipbroker Høvik, Norway, 1971-73, 78-89; shipbroker, mgr., v.p. Eagle Maritime & Trading Co., Piraeus, Greece, 1973-78; censor Tromsø (Norway) Maritime Acad., 1987-89. Sec. gen., bd. dirs. Norwegian Club, Inc., Bklyn., 1952-61. With Royal Norwegian Air Force, 1942-45. Mem. Royal Airforces Assn., Reps. Abroad, The Am. C. of C. in Norway. Lutheran. Avocations: skiing, tennis, swimming, bowling, hiking. Home: Myrvollveien 2, 1363 Hovik Norway

ZAREVÚCKA, MARIE, biochemist, researcher; b. Prague, Czech Republic, Feb. 24, 1961; d. Vladimír and Zdenka (Mertlíková) Fiser; m. Fedor Zarevucky, Apr. 2, 1987; children Ondrej, Iva. MSc, U. Chem. Tech., Prague, 1984; PhD, Acad. Sci. Czech Republic, Prague, 1996; postgrad., U. La Rochelle, France, 1998. Cert. engring. and biochemistry. Scientist Inst. Organic Chemistry and Biochemistry Acad. Sci. Czech Republic, Prague, 1996—. Contbr. articles to profl. jours. Grantee Bioflavour 95, Dijon, France, 1995, 8th Internat. Symposium on Chiral Discrimination, Edinburgh, Scotland, 1996, 10th Internat. Symposium on Chiral Discrimination, Vienna, Austria, 1988. Mem. Czech Chem. Soc. Avocations: traveling, music. Office: Inst Organic Chemistry, Flemingovo nám 2, 160 00 Prague Czech Republic

ZARICZNYJ, BASILIUS, orthopedic surgeon; b. Ukraine, Aug. 31, 1924; came to U.S., 1951; m. Stefania Pidburny, Aug. 21, 1954; children: Marta, Stephanie Christine, Andrea Maria, Mark B. MD, U. Bonn, Germany, 1951; MD (hon.), Odessa State Med. U., Ukraine, 1996. Diplomate Am. Bd. Orthopedic Surgery. Resident St. Luke's Hosp., Chgo., 1954-56, Univ. Hosps., Oklahoma City, 1955-56; fellow in orthopedics Northwestern U., Chgo., 1957; asst. prof. Sch. Medicine U. Okla., Oklahoma City, 1957-58; orthopedic surgeon Springfield, Ill., 1958—; clin. prof. Sch. Medicine So. Ill. U., Springfield, Ill., 1973-85, acting chmn. divsn. orthopedic surgery, 1972-75, chief sports medicine sect., 1975-82, program chmn. sports injury symposium, 1977-79, 82, 83; mem. sports medicine com. Ill. State Med. Soc., 1979-80; chmn. dept. orthopedic surgery St. John's and Meml. Hosps., Springfield, 1970-79; program chmn. Med. Congress of World Fedn. of Ukrainian Med. Assn., Dniepropetrovsk, 1994, Odessa, Ukraine, 1996; presenter Am. Acad. Orthopedic Surgeons, Miami, Fla., 1961, N.Y., 1969, San Francisco, 1971, Washington, 1972, Las Vegas, 1973, 77, Anaheim, Calif., 1983, Chgo. Orthopedic Soc., 1967, 76, O'Donoghue Okla. Orthopedic Alumni Assn., Oklahoma City, 1972, 75, 78, Internat. Soc. for Orthopedic Surgery and Traumatology, XII World Congress, Tel Aviv, 1972, Copenhagen, 1975, Kyoto, Japan, 1978, So. Ill U. Sch. Medicine, Springfield, 1977, 79, 80, 82, Ill. State Orthopedic Soc., Chgo., 1978, ACS, Chgo., 1979, Am. Orthopedic Soc. for Sports Medicine, Atlanta, 1980, Big Sky, Mont., 1980,, Lake Tahoe, Nev., 1981, Clin. Orthopedic Soc., Chgo., 1987, World Fedn. Ukrainian Med. Assn., Kiev, Ukraine, 1990, U. Lviv, Ukraine, 1990, 11th Congress of Orthopedic Surgeons of Ukraine, Kharkiv, 1991, Congress of World Fedn. of Ukrainian Med. Assn., Kharkiv, 1992, Dnipropetrovsk, 1994, Odessa, 1996, Ukraine, among others. Mem. editl. bd. Jour. Ukrainan Med. Assn. N.Am., 1977-95; contbr. articles to profl. jours. and med. textbooks. Fellow Am. Acad. Orthopedic Surgery; mem. AMA, Ill. Orthopedic Soc., Internat. Soc. Orthopedic Surgery and Traumatology, Am. Orthopedic Soc. for Sports Medicine, Internat. Soc. of the Knee, Mid-Am. Orthopedic Assn., Ukrainian Acad. and Profl. Assn. Pres. 1985-89), Sangamon County Med. Soc., Chgo. Orthopedic Soc. Avocations: golfing, walking, chess. Home and Office: 125 Oakmont Dr Springfield IL 62704-3118

ZARIN, KAMAR, education educator; b. Dezpal, Khozestan, Iran, July 23, 1967; s. Ali and Efat Z.; m. Tahereh Hokamzadeh. BA, Isfahan U., Iran, 1991; MA, Shiraz U., 1994. Cons. in edn. Iran, 1991-92; dean of faculty Zau U., Dezfoul, Iran, 1993-99; head Iranian Psychol. Assn., Dezfould, 1997—; lectr. and rschr. in field, Iran; spl. presentations poster sect. ann. mtg. APA, Washington, 2000, China. Author books in field. Mem. APA, Iranian Psychol. Assn. Avocations: painting, climbing, writing, swimming. Office: Islamic Azud Univ, PO 113, Dezfoul Iran

ZARINS, PETER VILHELM, retired chemical company executive; b. Bene, Latvia, Mar. 27, 1939; s. Nikolajs and Marija Katrina (Tilgals) Z.; m. Austra Valerija Niedra, Dec. 28, 1968; children: Ilmar, Marit, Kristina. MSc, U. Oslo, 1972. Mgr. Behring Diagnostika, Oslo, 1972-81; prodn. group mgr. immunochemistry Behringwerke AG, Marburg, Germany, 1981-85; product specialist Hoechst, Oslo, 1985-87, project mgr., 1987-97; ret., 1997. Contbr. articles to profl. jours. Mem. Norwegian Soc. Immunology, Scandinavian Soc. Immunology, Acad. Soc. Austrums. Avocations: fishing, photography. Home and Office: Nordraaks Vei 49, 1320 Stabekk Norway

ZARITSKI, SERGUEI PETROVICH, engineering executive; b. Moscow, Jan. 21, 1939; s. Pete Afanasievich Zaritski and Ludmila Sergeevna Shehoyan; m. Raissa Fedorovna Gratcheva, July 2, 1997; 1 child, Kirill Sergeevich. Diploma in engring., Bauman Tech. U., Moscow, 1962; DSc, Aviation Inst., Moscow, 1969; PhD, Oil and Gas U., Moscow, 1987. Engr. Saturn enterprise, Moscow, 1962-65; sr. scientist Vniigaz of Gazprom, Moscow, 1969-76; head dept. diagnostics JSC Orgenergogaz of Gazprom, Moscow, 1976-82; gen. dir. Tech. and Engring. Ctr. Orgtechdiagnostika, Moscow, 1982—; pres. diagnostic divsn. Internat. Info. Acad., Moscow, 1997—; dep. chmn. diagnostic divsn. Russian Acad. Tech. Sci., Moscow, 1996—; mem. sci. coun. Oil and Gas U., Moscow, 1990—; dep. chmn. coordination diagnostics Ministry of Fuel and Energy, Moscow, 1997—. Author: Air and Gas Turbines with Some Nozzles, 1975, Diagnostics of Gas Transport Units with Gas Turbine Engines, 1987; inventor in field. Recipient prize Pres. of Russian Fedn., Moscow, 1985, named Deserved Person of Oil and Gas Industry, 1999. Mem. Internat. Info. Acad. (prize 1997), Russian Acad. Tech. Sci., N.Y. Acad. Sci. Avocations: chess, jazz, soccer. Home: Naberezhnaya T Shevchenko 1/2 app 89, 121059 Moscow Russia Office: Orgtechdiagnostika, Karamzina 13 1, 117463 Moscow Russia

ZARKADA-FRASER, ANNA, university lecturer; b. Athens, Greece, May 30, 1964; d. Konstantinos and Vassiliki Zarkada; m. Campbell Fraser, Mar. 1, 1994; 1 child, Isadora. BS with honors, Athens U. Econs. Bus., 1988; MS, Victoria U. Manchester, U.K., 1993; PhD, Queensland U. Tech., Brisbane, Australia, 1998. Mktg. analyst Fed. Mogul World Trade Inc., Elefsis, Greece, 1988-90; mktg. mgr. lo Sys. SA, Athens, 1990-92; lectr. Fgn. Svc. Tng. Inst., Tokyo, 1993-95, Queensland U. Tech., Brisbane, 1996-2000, Griffith Univ., Brisbane, 2000—; cons. Nexxuss Comm., Tokyo. contbr. articles to profl. jours. Queensland U. Tech. rsch. scholar, 1995-96; recipient several grants. Mem. Australian Mktg. Inst., Internat. Assn. Bus. Soc, Acad. Mktg. Sci. (track chmn. 1999-2000), Greek Inst. Economists, Australia-New Zealand Acad. Internat. Bus., Australia-New Zealand Mktg. Acad. Avocations: music, literature, gardening, swimming. Fax: 61 7 3864 1771. E-mail: a.zarkada@qut.edu.au. Office: Queensland U Tech Sch Mktg and Internat Bus, 2 George St PO Box 2434, Brisbane Q4001, Australia

ZARKOVIĆ, MILOŠ PERO, physician; b. Kraljevo, Serbia, Yugoslavia, Aug. 13, 1960; s. Pero Milos and Miroslava Obren (Jović) Z.; m. Ivana Jugoslav Todorović, June 30, 1991. Grad., U. Belgrade, 1984, MA, 1990, PhD, 1992. Physician Inst. Endocrinology, Belgrade, 1987—; lectr. in internal medicine U. Belgrade, 1994—. Contbr. chpts. to books in field. Mem. Soc. Endocrinology, European Assn. for Study of Diabetes, Serbian Med. Assn. Office: Inst Endocrinology, Dr Subotića 13, 11000 Belgrade Serbia

ZARMBINSKI, RICHARD ANTHONY, chiropractic physician; b. St. Paul, June 21, 1950; s. Raymond Joseph and Dorothy Marie (Wilson) Z.; m. Michele Ann Peters; children: Claire, Breanna. AA, U. Minn., 1979; DC, Northwestern Coll. Chiropractic, 1981. Pres., clinic dir. Ctr. Chiropractic and Alt. Medicine Russia State Med. U., Mendota Heights and Woodbury, Minn., 1981—; trustee, bd. chmn. Northwestern Health Sci. U., 1999; bd. dirs., mem. peer rev. com. Minn. Bd. Chiropractic Examiners, 1987-89. Trustee Northwestern Coll. Chiropractic, 1990; mem. med. com. Internat. Spl. Olympics, Mpls., 1991. Mem. Am. Spine Found. (bd. dirs. 1989-91), Minn. Chiropractic Assn. (pres. 1989-91, pres. 4th dist. 1987, presdl. award 1989), Dakota County C. of C. Avocations: golf, racquetball, family activities. Home: 916 Adeline Ct Mendota Heights MN 55118-3622 Office: Spinal Care Ctr 1803 Woodlane Dr Woodbury MN 55125-2910

ZARO, JUAN JESUS, educator; b. Malaga, Spain, Nov. 1, 1956; s. Juan and Francisca (Vera) Z. MA, U. Granada, Spain, 1978, PhD, 1983; MA, NYU, 1984. Dept. head I.B. Emilio Prados, Malaga, Spain, 1979-89; assoc. prof. U. Malaga, Spain, 1989-93, sr. lectr., 1993—. Author: Storytelling, 1995, Manual de Traducción, 1998; translator: Reflective Teaching, 1997, Oroonoko and The Fair Jilt, 2000; dir. TRANS, Jour. of Translation and Interpreting, 1997—. Fulbright grantee, N.Y.C., 1983-84. Office: U Malaga, Facultad de F y Letras, 29071 Malaga Spain

ZAROWSKI, ANDRZEJ JAN, otorhinolaryngologist, biomedical engineer; b. Gdynia, Poland, Jan. 24, 1968; s. Lubomir and Krystyna Barbara (Stupnicka) Z.; Katarzyna Brygida Wyrwiak, Aug. 22, 1995; children: Alicje, Jekub. Student, U. Antwerp, Belgium, 1990-91, Tech. U. Gdansk, 1989-93; MD, Med. U. Gdansk, Poland, 1993. Resident in dept. internal diseases, cardiology clinic Med. U. Gdansk, 1992-94; physician, rschr., Cochlear Ctr. Diagnosis, Treatment and Rehab. Ctr. for Deaf, Warsaw, Poland, 1994—; rschr. Lab. Med. Electronics, U. Antwerp, 1994—, U. Antwerp ORL Svc., 1994-99; ENT cons., surgeon Inst. Physiology and Pathology of Hearing, Warsaw, 2000—; surg. cons. Philips Hearing Implants Co., 1997-99. Inventor in field of cochlear implants; contbr. articles to profl. jours. Recipient Min. Health award, Warsaw, 1992, Primus Inter Pares, Rector Med. U. Gdansk, 1993, Found. for Polish Sci., 1999. Mem. Polish Otorhinolaryngology Soc., Belgian Otorhinolaryngology Soc., Belgian Audiol. Soc. Avocations: travel, computer networking, skiing, water sports. Home: Orchideeënstraat 9, 2610 Antwerp Belgium Office: Med Inst St Augustinus ORL, Ostervedlaan 24, 2610 Antwerp Belgium

ZARPAO, LUIZ FERNANDO, physician, researcher; b. Mogi Mirim, Sao Paulo, Brazil, July 10, 1961; s. Geraldo and Abelina (Trentini) Z.; m. Ana Elisa Santos, Oct. 24, 1988; children: Tuyla Ananda, Tullio Fernando. Quimical Tecnical, Imaculada, Mogi, Brazil, 1980; Med. Diplomate, São Francisco U., Brazil, 1987. Dr. in medicine S.A.M.A.M. Hosp., Americana, Brazil, 1988-91; chief dept. S.A.M.A.M. Hosp., Americana, 1997-99; intensivist various hosps. in region, Americana, 1991-97; chief ICU dept. Mogi Mirim and SAMAM Hosp., 1999—. Cpl. Brazilian Army, 1978-79. Mem. Soc. Critical Care Medicine, Brazilian Intensive Medicine Assn., N.Y. Acad. Scis. Messianic Jewish. Avocations: lecturing, games, fishing, running, chess. Home: Av Cillos 1110, 13465000 Americana Sao Paulo, Brazil Office: SAMAM Hosp, Av Brasil # 1110 Girassol, 13465000 Americana Sao Paulo, Brazil

ZARRINPOUR, ARASH, dental surgeon; b. Tehran, Iran, Sept. 13, 1968; arrived in France, 1983; s. Morteza and Susan (Mahdavi) Z. DDS, Reims, France, 1992; MS, Paris, 1994, PhD, 1997. Biomaterial rschr. U. Medicine, Reims, France, 1994-97, Biomolecules, Reims, 1996; asst. prof. Dental Sch., Reims, 1994; v.p. S.F.O., Paris, 1997. Contbr. articles to profl. jours.; inventor in field. Mem. N.Y. Acad. Scis. Avocations: spirituality, golf, tennis, skiing. Office: 236 Blvd Saint Germain, 75007 Paris France

ZARUDI, MOSES (MOSHE ZARUDI), research educator; b. Kiev, Ukraine, Aug. 11, 1928; arrived in Israel, 1991; s. Haim (Efim) Zarudi and Reba Leah Mayrgoyz; m. Izida Tchernina, Apr. 18, 1950; 1 child, Alexander. MSc in Engring., Moscow Power U., 1950; PhD, All-Union Electromech. Inst., Moscow, 1962; DSc, All-Union Elec. Engring. Inst., Moscow, 1972. Head elec. lab. Siberian Chem. Plant, Novosibirsk, Russia, 1950-53; rsch. group leader Energotchermet, Moscow, 1953-61; assoc. prof. Moscow Univ. Radio-Electronics and Automatics, 1964-72; prof. Moscow Univ. Radio-Electronics & Automatics, 1973-91; rsch. prof. Ctr. Technol. Edn. Tel Aviv U., Holon, Israel, 1992-95; dir. and R&D mgr. ELMATEC Ltd., Nazareth Illit, Israel, 1996-97; sci. cons. Nat. Ctr. Magnetic Measurements & Superconductiv. Bar-Ilan U., Israel, 1998—; sci. cons. Plasma Lab. Electroheating Inst., Moscow, 1962-90. Author: Combined Work of High-Frequency Inductor Generators, 1962; co-author: (with others) Modelling and Methods of Calculation of Physical-Chemical Processes in Low-Temperature Plasmas, 1974, Collected Problems in Applied Electricity for Engineers (3 edits.), 1988; contbr. articles to profl. jours. Mem. IEEE (sr.), N.Y. Acad. Scis. Avocation: chess. Home: PO Box 7456, 506/3 Ramat Menachem Begin, 13100 Zefat Israel

ZARZYCKI, PAWEL KONRAD, pharmacist, educator; b. Koszalin, Poland, Feb. 5, 1966; s. Rajmund and Weronika Leokadia (Zamorska) Z.; m. Magdalena Bronislawa Siewiora, Aug. 17, 1991; children: Piotr R., Klara M. BSc, Med. U. Gdańsk, U., 1988, PhD, 1993. Asst. Med. U. Gdańsk, Poland, 1988-93; tutor Med. U. Gdańsk, 1993—. Recipient Chromatography award Polish Ministry Health, 1995, 98. Roman Catholic. Avocations: diving, classical guitar playing. E-mail: pkzarz@farmecja@amg.gda.pl. Fax: 349-31-30. Home: Mickiewicza 1/3 m36, 80-425 Gdańsk Poland Office: Med Univ Gdańsk, Hallera 107, 80-416 Gdańsk Poland

ZASAVITSKII, IVAN IVANOVICH, physics researcher, educator; b. Village Goluboe, Moldova, USSR, Aug. 25, 1939; s. Ivan Ivanovich and Elizabeta Dmitrievna (Kolomiets) Z.; m. Antonina Alexeevna Zhukova, Dec. 22, 1972; children: Ivan, Natalya. Grad., State U., Kishinew, USSR, 1961; PhD in Physics and Math., P.N. Lebedev Physics Inst., Moscow, 1972, DSc in Physics, 1991. Jr. rschr. Metallurgy Inst., Donetsk, USSR, 1961-65, Inst. of Spectroscopy, Troitsk, USSR, 1970-74; jr. rschr. P.N. Lebedev Physics Inst., Moscow, 1974-78, sr. rschr., 1979-90, vice dir. solid state physics divsn., 1990-95, prin. rschr., 1995—; extraordinary prof. Phys.-Tech. Inst., Moscow, 1984—, Inst. Fine Chem. Tech., Moscow, 1996—. Contbr. articles to profl. jours. Recipient State Prize in Sci. and Tech., 1985. E-mail: zasavit@sci.lebedev.ru. Office: PN Lebedev Inst RAS, Leninski Pr 53, 117924 Moscow Russia

ZASSOURSKY, YASSEN NIKOLAYEVICH, media educator; b. Moscow, Oct. 29, 1929; s. Nikolai Vasilyevich Zassoursky and Tatyana Fedorovna Makarova; m. Svetlana Alexandrovna Sherlaimova; 1 child, Ivan. MA in English, Moscow Inst. Fgn. Langs., 1948; PhD in Lit., Moscow State U., 1951, DSc, 1966. Cert. journalism, literary criticism, media and lit. edn. Editor Fgn. Lit. Pub. House, 1951-53; sr. lectr. faculty journalism Moscow State U., 1953-55, assoc. prof. faculty journalism, 1955-58, prof. faculty journalism, 1968—, dep. dean faculty journalism, 1956-65, dean faculty journalism, 1965—. Mem. IAMCR (v.p. 1972-92), Union Journalists (mem. exec. bd. 1992—), Writers' Union. Avocation: jogging. Home: Apt 61, 35 Lomonosovskyy Prospect, Moscow Russia Office: Moscow State Univ, 9 Mokhovaya St, 103914 Moscow Russia

ZATLIN, PHYLLIS, Spanish language educator, translator; b. Green Bay, Wis., Dec. 31, 1938; d. Frank L. and Ellen Mary (Butler) Z.; m. George Boring Kelly, Aug. 20, 1962; children: William, Lee. BA, Rollins Coll., 1960; postgrad., U. Grenoble, France, 1960-61; MA, U. Fla., 1962, PhD, 1965. Cert. Spanish to English translator Am. Translators Assn. Instr. Rutgers U., New Brunswick, N.J., 1963-66, asst. prof., 1966-71, assoc. prof., 1971-79, assoc. dean, 1974-80, prof. Spanish, 1979—, chair dept. Spanish, grad. dir., 1980-87; mem. discipline adv. com. Coun. for Internat. Exch. of Scholars, 1990-93; spkr. in field. Co-author: Lengua y Lectura: Un Repaso y Una Continuación, 1970; author: Elena Quiroga, 1977, Víctor Ruiz Iriarte, 1980, Jaime Salom, 1982, Cross Cultural-Approaches to Theatre: The Spanish-French Connection, 1994, The Novels and Plays of Eduardo Manet: An Adventure in Multiculturalism, 2000; editor: (Francisco Ayala) El Rapto, 1971, (Víctor Ruiz Iriarte) El Landó de Seis Caballos, 1979, (Jaime Salom) La Piel del Limón, 1980, (Antonio Gala) Noviembre y un Poco de Yerba, Petra Regalada, 1981, (Francisco Nieva) Combate de Opalos y Tasia, Sombra y Quimera de Larra, La Magosta, 1990; co-editor: The Contemporary Spanish Theater, A Collection of Critical Essays, 1988, Homenaje A Tribute to Martha T. Halsey, 1995; co-editor: Entre Actos: Diálogos sobre teatro español, 1999, Un escenario propio A Stage of Their Own, 1998; coguest editor jour. Art Teatral. Cuadernos de Minipiezas Ilustradas, 1996; translator play edits.: (J.L. Alonso de Santos) Going Down to Marrakesh, 1992, (Paloma Pedrero) Parting Gestures (The Color of August, A Night Divided, The Voucher With, Tonight in the Subway, 1999, (Jaime Salom) A Bonfire at Dawn, 1992, (Jean-Paul Daumas) The Elephant Graveyard, 1994, (Eduardo Manet) Lady Strass, 1992, 97, Hostages in the Barrio, 1997, also performances. State pres. Women's Equity Action League, N.J., 1971-72, nat. bd. dirs., Washington, 1973, 76-77. Fellow Fulbright Found., 1960-61, Woodrow Wilson Found., 1961-62; recipient Profl. award Fgn. Lang. Educators of N.J., 1989. Mem. AAUP (mem. nat. coun. 1987-90), MLA (mem. commn. on status of women 1978-81), Dramatists Guild, Soc. Gen. de Autores y Editores (Profl. award 1997). Democrat. Avocations: biking, jogging, travel. E-mail: zatlin@rci.rutgers.edu. Home: 5 Timber Rd East Brunswick NJ 08816-2941 Office: Rutgers Univ 105 George St New Brunswick NJ 08901-1414

ZATONSKI, WITOLD ANTONI, epidemiology educator; b. Wolomin, Poland, June 11, 1942; s. Zygmunt and Bronislawa Zatonski; m. Jadwiga Lisa Zawarska; 5 children. MD, Med. Acad., Wroclaw, Poland, 1966, DSc, 1974, Habilitation in Internal Medicine, 1978. Asst. prof. Med. Acad., assoc. prof.; head cancer unit Marie Sklodowska Curie Cancer Control and Inst. Oncology, Warsaw, Poland, 1979-84; divsn. dir. dept. cancer epidemiology and prevention Marie Sklodowska Curie Cancer Ctr. and Inst. Oncology, Warsaw, Poland, 1984—, prof. epidemiology, 1989—; pres. Health Promotion Found., Warsaw, 1992—; cons. on chronic diseases WHO, 1985—; pub. health advisor to prime min. Poland, 1996-97. Author: Atlas of Cancer Mortality in Central Europe. Mem. nat. coun. Program for Cancer Prevention and Control, 1988—; vice chmn. San.-Epidemiol. Coun., 1995.

Decorated Cross of Rebirth of Poland; recipient medal WHO, 1991, medal for disease control Jacques Chirac, Paris, 1993. Mem. My Vote-My Choice Found. Achievements include research on health status of Poland, intervention programs and tobacco control and other risk factors to improve health in Poland, state of health, chronic disease control and tobacco control in Eastern Europe. Avocation: gardening. Fax: 48 22 643 9234. E-mail: canepid@akp.itm.com.pl. Office: Marie Curie Meml Cancer Ctr, ul Roentgena 5, 02-781 Warsaw Poland

ZATSEPIN, ANATOLY FEDOROVICH, physics and technology educator, researcher; b. Kamensk-Uralsky, USSR, May 29, 1947; s. Fedor Grigorjevich and Anastasia Ivanovna (Voronina) Z.; m. Alla Ivanovna Semjakova, June 3, 1967; children: Dmitry, Vladislava. Grad., Ural Poly. inst., Sverdlovsk, USSR, 1970, PhD in Physics and Tech., 1974. Scientist Ural Poly. Inst., 1974, sr. rsch. scientist, 1974-86, assoc. prof., 1986, 1986—; cons. Inst. Metal Physics, Ekaterinburg, 1990—. Contbr. over 250 articles to profl. publs.; over 40 patents in field. Recipient award Open Soc. Inst.-Soros Found., 1995. Mem. Russian Optical Soc. Avocations: research, jazz, saxophone, art. E-mail: zats@dpt.ustu.ru. Office: Ural State Tech U, Mira St 19, 620002 Ekaterinburg Russia

ZATYKÓ, JÓZSEF, biologist; b. Budapest, Hungary, Dec. 6, 1932; s. Imre and Anna (Kárász) Z.; m. Zsuzsanna Mágel, July 23, 1970; children: Zsuzsanna, Judit, Miklós. Degree, U. Horticulture, 1956. Rsch. asst. Agrl. Rsch. Inst., Cegléd, Hungary, 1956-57; rsch. co-worker, head of plant physiol. lab. Fruit Rsch. Sta., Fertöd, Hungary, 1957—. Contbr. articles to profl. jours. Grantee Ford-Found., U. Calif. 1967. Mem. Internat. Assn. for Plant Tissue and Cell Culture, Internat. Soc. for Hort. Sci. Mem. Alliance of Free Dems. Lutheran. Home: 5 Madách sétány, H-9431 Fertöd Hungary Office: Fruit Rsch St, 3-4 Madách sétány, H-9431 Fertöd Hungary

ZAUZICH, KARL-THEODOR, Egyptologist, educator; b. Plauen, Germany, June 8, 1939; s. Karl and Josephine (Jünemann) Z.; m. Gisela Kaul, Apr. 21, 1968; 1 child, Martin. PhD, U. Mainz, Fed. Republic Germany, 1966; Dr.phil.habil., U. Berlin, 1980. Prof. U. Mainz, 1980-81; prof., head Inst. U. Würzburg, Fed. Republic Germany, 1981—. Author: The Tradition of Egyptian Scribes, 1968 (award), Egyptian Manuscripts, 1971, Hieroglyphs without Mystery, 1980, Demotic Papyri from Elephantine, 1978, vol. 2, 1993; editor jour. Enchoria, 1971—, (series) Demotic Studies, 1988—. Office: U Würzburg, Residenzplatz 2, D-97070 Würzburg Germany

ZAVADA, BARBARA JOHANNA, artist; b. Jena, Thueringen, Germany, June 20, 1938; came to U.S., 1953; d. Paul Egon and Johanna Helene (Kuehlich) Weber; m. Gerhard Manfred Grote, Mar. 6, 1971 (div. Jan. 1975); 1 child, Erika Barbara. Cert., Traphagen Sch. Fashions, N.Y.C., 1960; studied with, Karl Bobeck, Berlin, 1962; Assoc., Rochester (N.Y.) Inst. Tech., 1966; postgrad., Art Students League, N.Y.C., 1970. Painter Europe and U.S.A., 1960—; fashion designer H & U Schmidt, Berlin, 1961-62, Dave Goldberg, N.Y.C., 1967-71; graphic designer Zavada Assocs., Stamford, Conn., 1974-90; now lectr. on abstract expressionism. One-person shows include Mus. Art Sci. and Industry, 1974, Bruce Mus., 1976, Conn. Women's Bank, Greenwich, 1985, Stamford (Conn.) Landmark Tower Rotunda, 1985, So. Conn. State U., New Haven, 1990, Edge of Cedars Mus., Blanding, Utah, 1996, 99, Western Colo. Ctr. for Arts, 1998, State of Utah, Iron Mission State Park, 2000. Prodr. Graphics for Scholarship Fund, Greenwich (Conn.) Acad., 1985-90; v.p. Ind. German Lang. Sch., Westport, Conn., 1981-83; search and rescue pilot CAP, Rochester, N.Y., 1964-68, Staten Island, N.Y., 1969-70. Recipient 1st prize N.Y.C. Fashion Competition, 1960, Faber Birren Color award, Stamford, 1981. Mem. Am. Acad. Women Artists, The Art Ctr. at Fuller Lodge, Friends of Contemporary Art, Mus. N.Mex. Found. Avocations: travel, hiking, skiing, gardening. Home: HC 64 Box 3001 Castle Valley UT 84532-9614 also: 24 Meyers Rd Espanola NM 87532-9888

ZÁVADA, JAN, molecular oncologist; b. Prague, Czechoslovakia, Dec. 10, 1933; s. Vilém and Jaroslava (Hrejsová) Z.; m. Zuzana Šumavská, Mar. 23, 1963; 1 child, Karin. D of Natural Scis., Charles U., Prague, 1956; PhD, Slovak Acad. Sci., Bratislava, 1963. Cert. in cancer rsch. Jr. scientist Inst. Virology, Bratislava, 1956-58, scientist, 1963-92; scientist Inst. Molecular Genetics, Prague, 1993—; univ. tchr. Comenius U., Bratislava, 1963-69, Charles U., Prague, 1993—; vis. scientist Imperial Cancer Rsch. Fund Labs., London, 1969-70, 76-77, Harvard Med. Sch., Boston, 1984-85. Author: (book) Mystery of Cancer, 1994 (Slovak Acad. of Sci. award 1994); patentee in field. Recipient State prize Govt. of Czechoslovakia, 1981. Mem. European Assn. for Cancer Rsch., European Molecular Biology Orgn., Learned Soc. Avocations: naturalism, music, literature, history. Home: Na Pekne Vyhlidce 1, 16200 Prague Czech Republic Office: Inst Molecular Genetics, Flemingovo N 2, 16637 Prague 6, Czech Republic

ZAVITSAS, ANDREAS ATHANASIOS, chemistry educator, researcher; b. Athens, Greece, July 14, 1937; came to U.S., 1954; s. Athanasios A. and Catherine K. Zavitsas; m. Lourdes Romanacce, Apr. 17, 1959; 1 child, Athanasios. BS magna cum laude, CCNY, 1959; MS, Columbia U., 1961, PhD, 1962. Rsch. assoc. Brookhaven Nat. Lab., Upton, N.Y., 1962-64; rsch. chemist Monsanto Chem. Co., Springfield, Mass., 1964-67; prof. L.I. U., Bklyn., 1967—, grad. dean, 1975-80; cons. in field. Contbr. articles to Jour. Polymer Sci., Jour. Am. Chem. Soc., Jour. Phys. Chemistry. Chmn. sch. bd. Holy Cross Sch., Bklyn., 1980-87. Mem. Am. Chem. Soc., N.Y. Acad. Scis., Phi Beta Kappa. Greek Orthodox. Office: LI U University Pla Brooklyn NY 11201

ZAVODNIK, ILYA BORISOVICH, biophysicist, educator, researcher; b. Grodno, Belarus, USSR, June 23, 1956; s. Boris L'vovich Z. and Zinaida Abramovna Polyakova. MS in Physics with honors, State Pedagog. Inst., Grodno, Belarus, USSR, 1977; PhD in Biophysics, Inst. Photobiology, Minsk, Belarus, USSR, 1985; DSc in Biophysics, Inst. Photobiology, Minsk, Belarus, 1997. Fellow researcher Inst. Biol. Physics, Pushchino, USSR, 1977-78; rsch. scientist Inst. Biochemistry, Grodno, Belarus, USSR, 1977-86, sr. rsch. scientist, 1986—, postgrad. fellow, 1980-84; prof. Grodno Agrl. U., 2000; vis. rschr. U. Lodz, Poland, 1994, 96, 98, 99, vis. adj. prof., 1995. Contbr. articles to profl. jours. Tchr. Hebrew history and culture Jewish Sch. Grantee Internat. Sci. Found., 1993, European Fellowship Fund, 1994, 95, 99, The Jozef Mianowksi Fund, 1996, 98, 2000, Pres. of Belarus, 1999-2000. Mem. Soc. Biophysics and Photobiology Belarus. Home: Gagarin st 10 Apt 17, 230011 Grodno Belarus Office: Inst Biochemistry, Lenin Kom Blvd 50, 230017 Grodno Belarus

ZAVRAS, GEORGE, radiologist; b. Kastorion, Laconia, Greece, Feb. 15, 1942; s. Menelaos and Kalliopi (Varvitsioti) Z.; m. Paraskevi Papadaki, July 7, 1989. Med. diploma, U. Athens, Greece, 1970; diploma in med. radiodiagnosis, U. Aberdeen, Scotland, 1978. Registrar in radiology Royal Infirmary, Aberdeen, 1975-78; sr. registrar in radiology hosps., Liverpool, Eng., 1978-83; sr. registrar radiology dept. U. Patras (Greece) Med. Sch., 1983-86; clin. dir. radiology dept. Chest Disease Hosp., Patras, 1986-95, Kat Gen. Hosp., Athens, 1995—; tutor in radiology U. Aberdeen Med. Sch., 1977. Contbr. articles to med. jours., including Investigative Radiology, Röfo, Nuclear Medicine Comm. Mem. Royal Coll. Radiologists, Brit. Inst. Radiology, Hellenic Radiol. Soc. Avocations: reading history, music, theater.

ZAVREL, B. JOHN, account executive, museum director; b. Kurim/Gurein, Czechoslovakia, Aug. 2, 1949; came to U.S., 1969; s. Bohuslav and Radoslava (Holubik) Z.; m. Sandra McCracken, May 20, 1972; children: Wesley, Christopher, Thomas. Student, Econ. Sch. Fgn. Trade, Brno/Brünn, 1968; BSBA in Fin., U. Buffalo, 1972; BS in Acctg., Millard Fillmore Coll., 1974; postgrad., U. Buffalo, 1996-97. CPA, N.Y. Dir. Mus. European Art, Clarence, N.Y.; ptnr. Freed Maxick Sachs & Murphy, P.C., Buffalo; spokesman German-Am. Nat. Congress (European Affairs); chmn. Internat. Com. Artists for Ecology (USA); speaker Art For Olympia; pres. Rishikesh Found.; advisor Himalayan Inst. Trust Hosp., Dehra Dun, India; owner West Art Gallery and Pubs. Author: Salute America! A Commemorative Portfolio, Art of Our Time. An Exhibition Catalog, Arno Breker: His Art and Life, Arno Breker: Divine Beauty in Art, The Primer for Those Who Would Govern, A Museum is Born. An Exhibition Catalog, others. Advisor Himalayan Inst. Trust Hosp., Dehra Dun, India, Düren Sch. Painting, Germany; pres. Rishikesh Found.; bd. dirs. Europäische Kulturstiftung e.V.; chancellor Order of Alexander the Great; hon. consul Czech Republic; founder, dir. Mus. European Art; spokesman German-Am. Nat. Congress; chmn. Internat. Com. Artists for Ecology. Mem. NRW Kunstkreis (hon., Germany), Hermann-Oberth Mus., Nürnberg (hon., Germany). Office: Museum of European Art 10545 Main St Clarence NY 14031-1624

ZAVRSKI, JOSIP, musician; b. Zagreb, Croatia, Feb. 12, 1917; s. Vjekoslav and Katarina (Škalic) Z.; m. Alojzija Grozdanic, June 1955; children: Velebit, Dinarka. Student, Acad. Music Art, Zagreb, 1952; student in music entertainment, Orff Instrumentarium, Fredeburg, 1978. Cons. Jadran Film, Zagreb, 1947-51; prof. music Tchr. Sch., Zagreb, 1951-55; condr. Croation Nat. Teatre, Zagreb, 1955-66; freelance artist, 1966—; prof. practical teaching methods music Acad. Pedagogy, 1968-73; cons. Republic Inst. for Edn. and Culture, Zagreb, 1961-82; lectr. Inst. for Cuture, Zagreb, 1963-83. Author: Methodological Instructions for Music Teachers and Children's Choir Conductors, 1951, 5th edit., 1999, History of Music, 1963, Theory of Music, 1973, rev. edit., 1995, 4th edit., 1997, School for Melodic, 1977, School for Recorders, 1983, Croatian Public-Spirited Songs Part One, 1991, Part Two, 1992, Songs for children "Daisies", 1995; condr. various radio and TV programs, Zagreb, 1949-61. Recipient award Mayor of Zagreb, 1969, award Pres. of Yugoslavia, Belgrade, 1969, Gold medal Sch. Book Pub. Co. Edn. House, Zagreb, 1980. Mem. Union Artists in Music Entertainment (presidentship 1962-72, award 1975, 87), Union Artists in Serious Music (presidentship 1981-87). Roman Catholic. Avocations: collecting African and Asian nat. instruments, hiking. Home: Ilica 65, 10000 Zagreb Croatia

ZAVRTANIK, DANILO, physicist, researcher; b. Nova Gorica, Slovenia, Aug. 15, 1953; s. Avgust and Alojzija Zavrtanik; m. Pia Bratina, Sept. 16, 1972; 1 child, Marko. BS in Physics, U. Ljubljana, Slovenia, 1979, MS in Physics, 1984, PhD in Physics, 1987. Sci. assoc. European Lab. for Particle Physics CERN, Geneva, Switzerland, 1990-92; postgrad. researcher Inst. Jožef Stefan, Ljubljana, 1979-87, researcher, 1987-90, 92—, dir. gen., 1992-96, gov. bd., 1996—; prof. physics U. Ljubljana, 1991-99; pres. Sch. Environ. Scis., Nova Gorica, 1995-98; pres. Nova Gorica Poly., 1998—, prof. physics, 1999—; mem. sci. com. Ctrs. of Excellence of Ctrl. European Initiative, 1992-96; commr. U.S./Slovene joint bd. sci. and tech. coop., 1993-96; mem. sci. and tech. coun. Slovenia, 1994-98; mem. gov. bd. Inst. Environ. Rsch., Velenje, 1995-97; mem. Coun. Higher Edn. Republic of Slovenia, 1998—; coun. Primorska Tech. Park. Contbr. numerous articles to sci. jours. Recipient state award Amb. Sci. of Republic of Slovenia, 1997. Mem. Slovene Soc. for Med. and Biol. Engring., Slovene Math., Physics and Astron. Soc., European Phys. Soc. (mem. Bd. Interdivsnl. Group on applied Physics, 1995-99), Slovene C. of C. (mem. governing bd. 1992-95), Slovene Nat. Sci. Found. (v.p. 1994-96). Office: Nova Gorica Poly, Vipavska 13, SI-5000 Nova Gorica Slovenia

ZAVTRAK, SERGEI TIMOFEEVICH, physicist, researcher; b. Minsk, Belarus, USSR, July 23, 1955; arrived in New Zealand, 1998; s. Timofei Maksimovich and Olga Makarovna (Klepatskaya) Z.; m. Elena Olegovna Skatchkova, Apr. 30, 1977; children: Marina, Ksenia. M in Physics, Belorussian State U., Minsk, 1977, PhD in Theoret. Physics, 1984, B in Linguistics, 1997; DSc in Theoret. Physics, Belorussian Acad. Sci., Minsk, 1991. Postgrad. fellow Belorussian State U., Minsk, 1977-80, sr. rsch. officer, 1980-91; rsch. dir. Inst. Nuclear Problems, Minsk, 1991-97; vis. scientist Brit. Aerospace, Bristol, 1997-98; R & D mgr. Vortec Energy Ltd., Auckland, New Zealand, 1999—. Contbr. numerous articles to profl. jours. Grantee Internat. Sci. Found., 1994, 96, Acoustical Soc. Am., 1996. Mem. N.Y. Acad. Scis. Home: 4/12 Raines Ave, Forrest Hill, Auckland New Zealand Office: Vortec Energy Ltd, Auckland City 563 Albert St, Auckland New Zealand

ZAV'YALOV, VLADIMIR PETROVICH, immunology educator; b. Simferopol, USSR, Apr. 22, 1946; s. Peter Michailovich and Nina Eremeevna (Ivanina) Z.; m. Galina Alexandrovna Zav'yalova, July 18, 1970; children: Anton Vladimirovich, Andrej Vladimirovich. Med. Diplomate, Crimean State Med. Inst., Simferopol, 1970, PhD in Biochemistry, 1971; Higher Doctorate Degree in Molecular Biology, Inst. Molecular Biology, Russian Acad. Scis., Simferopol, 1978; Prof. Biochemistry, Higher Cert. Com., Moscow, 1989. Sr. lab. asst. Crimean Med. Inst., USSR, 1973-77; head lab. molecular biology All-Union Rsch. Inst. Applied Microbiology, USSR, 1977-80; head lab. molecular immunology Inst. Immunology, USSR, 1980-81, head dept. molecular immunology, 1981-84, dir. dep., 1984-86; dir. gen. Inst. Immunology (now Inst. Engring. Immunology), USSR, 1986—; prof. molecular and engring. immunology Moscow Med. Acad., 1989-92; vis. prof. molecular and engring. immunology U. Turku (Finland), 1992—. Contbr. articles to profl. jours.; inventor. 2nd lt. Med. Troops, 1971-72. Grantee Internat. Scientific Found., 1993-94, 94-95, 95-97, INOC-Copernicus Found., 1996-97, Internat. Sci. and Tech. Ctr., 1995-97, 98—, Russian Found. Fundamental Rsch., 1995-97, 96-98, 97-99, 98—; recipient Disting. Work medal Supreme Soviet USSR, 1981. Mem. Russian Biotech. Acad. (academician, mem. academci bd. 1990—), Scientific Immunology Soc. (mem. presidium 1989—), Coun. Protein Engring., Inst. Applied Microbiology (mem. academic bd. 1998—), M.M. Shemyakin and Yu. A. Ovhinnikov Inst. Bioorganic Chemistry (mem. academic bd. 1990-96), Regional Coun. Dirs. Scientific Rsch. Inst. and Concers (mem. presidium, chmn. medicine and microbiology sect. 1999). Russian Orthodox. Avocations: history, track and field athletics, winter bathing. Office: Inst Immunol Engring, Lyubuchany, 142380 Chekhov Dist Moscow, Russia

ZAVYALOVA, LYDMILA VASILYEVNA, physicist, researcher; b. Uzbekistan, Ukraine, Sept. 24, 1942; d. Vasiliy Vasilievic and Nadezhda Vladimirov; m. Yuriy Georgievich Zavyalov, Nov. 5, 1963; 1 child, Evgeniy Yurievich. Magister, U. Rostov-na-Donu, 1965; PhD in Tech. Scis., Inst. Semiconductor Physics, Kiev, Ukraine, 1982. Engr. Inst. Physics of Semiconductors, Kiev, 1965-70; sr. engr. Spl. Design Bur. Relay and Automatic Plant, Kiev, 1970-73, Kiev State U., 1973-75; sr. engr. Inst. Physics of Semiconductors, Kiev, 1975-81, jr. sci. rschr., 1981-86, sci. rschr., 1986-88, sr. sci. rschr., 1988—. Contbr. articles to sci. jours. Recipient medal in Honor of 1500 Yrs. of Kiev, USSR Govt., 1980, Vte. of Labour medal, USSR Govt., 1985, 80 Yrs. of Nat. Acad. Scis. of Ukraine medal, 1999. Mem. Russian Orthodox Ch. Avocations: music, poetry, painting. E-mail: wol82325f. Office: Inst Semiconductor Physics, 45 Prospect Nauki, 03028 Kiev Ukraine

ZAWADA, EDWARD THADDEUS, JR., physician, educator; b. Chgo., Oct. 3, 1947; s. Edward Thaddeus and Evelyn Mary (Kovarek) Z.; m. Nancy Ann Stephen, Mar. 26, 1977; children: Elizabeth, Nicholas, Victoria, Alexandra. BS summa cum laude, Loyola U., Chgo., 1969; MD summa cum laude, Loyola-Stritch Sch. Medicine, 1973. Diplomate Am. Bd. Internal Medicine, Am. Bd. Nephrology, Am. Bd. Nutrition, Am. Bd. Critical Care, Am. Bd. Geriatrics, Am. Bd. Clin. Pharm., Am. Bd. Forensic Examiners, Am. Bd. Forensic Medicine; specialist Hypertension, Am. Soc. Hypertension. Intern UCLA Hosp., 1973, resident, 1974-76; asst. prof. medicine UCLA, 1978-79, U. Utah, Salt Lake City, 1979-81; assoc. prof. medicine Med. Coll. Va., Richmond, 1981-83; assoc. prof. medicine, physiology & pharmacology U. S.D. Sch. Medicine, Sioux Falls, 1983-86, Freeman prof., chmn. dept. Internal Medicine, 1987—, chief div. nephrology and hypertension, 1983-88, pres. univ. physician's practice plan, 1992—; chief renal sect. Salt Lake VA Med. Ctr., 1980-81; asst. chief med. service McGuire VA Med. Ctr., Richmond, 1981-83. Editor: Geriatric Nephrology and Urology, 1984; contbr. articles to profl. publs. Pres. Minnehaha div. Am. Heart Assn., 1984-87, pres. Dakota affiliate Am. Heart Assn., 1989-91. VA Hosp. System grantee, 1981-85, 85-88; Health and Human Svcs. grantee Pub. Health Scvs. Rsch. Adminstrn. Bureau Health Profl., 1993—. Fellow ACP, Am. Coll. Chest Physicians, Am. Coll. Nutrition, Am. Coll. Clin. Pharmacology, Internat. Coll. Angiology, Am. Coll. Angiology, Am. Coll. Clin. Pharmacology, Am. Coll. Forensic Examiners, Royal Soc. Medicine, Soc. for Vascular Medicine and Biology; mem. Internat. Soc. Nephrology, Am. Soc. Nephrology, Am. Soc. Pharmacology and Exptl. Therapeutics, Am. Physiol. Soc., Am. Inst. Nutrition, Am. Soc. Clin. Nutrition, Am. Geriatric Soc., Am. Soc. Transplant Physicians, Westward Ho Country Club. Democrat. Roman Catholic. Avocations: golf, tennis, skiing, cinema, music. Home: 2908 S Duchess Ave Sioux Falls SD 57103-4826 Office: U SD Sch Medicine 1400 W 22nd St Sioux Falls SD 57105-1505

ZAYAS-BAZAN, EDUARDO, foreign language educator; b. Camagüey, Cuba, Nov. 17, 1935; came to U.S., 1962, naturalized, 1969; s. Manuel Eduardo and Aida Modesta (Loret de Mola); children: Eduardo, Elena María. Dr. en Derecho, U. Nacional José Martí, 1958; MS, Kans. State Tchrs.' Coll., 1966. Social worker Cuban Refugee Asst. Program, 1962-64; Spanish tchr. Plattsmouth High Sch., 1964-65, Topeka West High Sch., 1965-66; Spanish instr. Appalachian State U., 1966-68; asst. prof. East Tenn. State U., Johnson City, 1968-73; assoc. prof. East Tenn. State U., 1973-79, prof., 1979-99, chmn. fgn. lang. dept., 1973-93, prof. emeritus, 1999—. Author: (with P. Ferreiro) Cómo dominar la redacción, 1989, (with G. Fernández de la Torriente) Cómo aumentar su vocabulario 3, Cómo escribir cartas eficaces, 1989, (with N.A. Humbach and José B. Fernández) Nuestro mundo, 1990, (with José Fernández) !Arriba!, 1993, 97, (with Carolyn M. Novak) No se equivoque con el inglés, 1993, El inglés que usted no sabe que sabe, Primera y Segunda Serie, 1993, (with Susan Bacon and Dulce García) Conexiones, 1999; editor: (with Anthony G. Lozano) Del amor a la revolución, 1975, (with L. Suárez) De aquí y de allá, 1980, (with G. J. Fernández Así somos, 1983; translator: Secret Report on Cuban Revolution, 1981. Pres. Sister Cities Internat., Johnson City, 1971-76. Recipient Disting. Faculty award E. Tenn. State U., 1978. Mem. Am. Coun. Tchrs. Fgn. Langs., AAUSC, Am. Assn. Tchrs. Spanish and Portuguese (pres. 1985), Tenn. Fgn. Lang. Teaching Assn. (pres. 1980, Jacqueline Elliott award 1989), Nat. Assn. Cuban-Am. Educators (pres. 1991-93, chair bd. dirs. 1994—), Sigma Delta Pi (Premio Martel 1984), Pi Delta Phi. Home: 265 Grapetree Dr Apt 122 Key Biscayne FL 33149-2749

ZAYATS, ANATOLY V., physicist; b. Volodymyr-Volynsky, Ukraine, Aug. 24, 1963; s. Volodymyr S. and Olga M. (Vitkovskaya) Z. MSc with honors, Moscow Inst. Physics and Tech., 1986, PhD in Physics, 1989. Jr. rsch. scientist Inst. Spectroscopy, Russian Acad. Scis., Moscow, 1989-90, rsch. scientist, 1990-92, sr. rsch. scientist, 1992-97; rsch. fellow U. Konstanz, Germany, 1998-99; lectr. in condensed matter physics Queen's U. Belfast, Northern Ireland, 1999—; vis. scientist U. Aalborg, Denmark, 1992-94; vis. prof. U. Algarve, Faro, Portugal, 1995-97. Alexander von Humbolt fellow, 1998. Mem. Am. Phys. Soc. Office: Queens U Belfast, Dept Pure & Applied Physics, Belfast BT7 1NN, Northern Ireland

ZAYED, SALEM EL-GOHARY, chemistry educator, consultant; b. Mit Ghamr, Mansoura, Egypt, Sept. 22, 1945; s. El-Gohary Salem and Nafisa Mustafa Zayed; m. Nagat Ibrahim, May 27, 1975; children: Marwa, Maali, Mayad, Mustafa. BSc in Chemistry and Botany, Assiut (Egypt) U., 1968; MSc in Chemistry, Cairo U., 1973, PhD in Chemistry, 1977. Asst. rschr. Nat. Orgn. for Drug Rsch., Cairo, 1969-73, rschr., 1973-77; lectr. chemistry South Valley U., Kena, Egypt, 1982-85, asst. prof., 1985-95, head chemistry dept., 1995-96; mem. sci. mission Man. U., Winnipeg, Can., 1996-97. Mem. N.Y. Acad. Scis. Home: Fesal-Takseem Amr, 5 El-Takadom St, Giza 12 111, Egypt

ZAYKO, YURIY NIKOLAYEVICH, engineering educator; b. Saratov, Russia, July 6, 1946; s. Nikolay Pavlovich and Pelageya Alexeevna (Bekreneva) Z.; m. Valentina Pavlovna Horol'skaya, June 6, 1970 (div. Oct. 1975); 1 child, Andrey Yur'evich; m. Olga Dmitriyevna Martynkina, Feb. 26, 1983; 1 child, Nikolay Yur'evich. Diploma in Physics, Saratov State U., 1969; postgrad., Moscow Physics/Technics Inst., 1971-75; PhD, Moscow Power Inst., 1985. Engr. Ctr. Sci. Rsch. Inst. of Measuring Equipment, Saratov, 1969-71; rschr. Sci. Rsch. Inst. Mechanics and Physics, Saratov, 1975-76; sr. engr. Sci. Rsch. Inst. Volna, Saratov, 1976-86; leading engr. Ctr. Sci. Rsch. Inst. Measuring Equipment, Saratov, 1986-94; assoc. prof. Volga Region Acad. State Svc., Saratov, 1994—, Internat. Soros Sci. Edn. Program, 1998; founder, chair Sci. and Trading Coop. Soliton, Saratov, 1987-88; sci. dir. Sci. and Trading firm Avers, Saratov, 1992-93; co-worker Ctr.. Sci. Rsch. Inst., 1994-98. Contbr. articles to profl. jours. Internat. Sci. Found. grantee, 1993. Fellow N.Y. Acad. Scis.; mem. Planetary Soc. Avocations: tennis, reading, skiing. Home: Oktyabrskaya St 10/12 45 ap, 410002 Saratov Russia Office: Volga Region Acad State Svc, Sobornaya St 23/25, 410031 Saratov Russia

ZAZHIGALOV, VALERY ALEKSEEVICH, engineer; b. Kyiv, Ukraine, Aug. 4, 1946; s. Aleksey Nikolaevich and Zinaida Iosiphovna (Beskrovnaya) Z.; m. Irena Vasilievna Bacherikova, Nov. 25, 1976; children, Aleksej, Sergei. Degree in engring., Polytechnic Inst., Lvov, Ukraine, 1969; PhD, Inst. Phys. Chemistry, Kyiv, Ukraine, 1974, DSc, 1993. Engr. Inst. Phys. Chem., Kyiv, 1972-74, sci. worker, 1974-77, sr. sci. worker, 1977-85, main sci. worker, 1985-93, head lab., 1993—; head dept. catal. proc. Inst. Sorbt. Probl. Endoecolog. Editor Catalysis and Catalysts 1999, 1978-92; patentee in field. Dep. Town Coun., Kyjiv, 1990-94. Capt. Ukraine Mil. Recipient medal Govt. Ukraine, 1983; grantee ISF, 1995. Mem. Coun. Ecology. Home: Teremkovskaya 5/44, 03187 Kiev Ukraine Office: Inst Sorbt/Problem Endoecol, NASU Gen Naumova 13, 03164 Kyiv Ukraine

ZBACNIK, RAYMOND ERIC, process engineer; b. Cleve., June 28, 1951; s. Eric Victor and Jeanette Beatrice (Brock) Z. BSChE, Purdue U., 1973; MEChE, Manhattan Coll., 1977; postgrad., Stevens Inst. Tech., 1977-78, Ind. U., Purdue U., 1985. Process engr. Foster Wheeler Corp., Livingston, N.J., 1974-78, sr. process engr., 1979-81, process supr., 1981-84; process engr. Norton Co., Stow, Ohio, 1988-90, Babcock & Wilcox, Barberton, Ohio, 1990—. Mem. AAAS, AIChE, Am. Chem. Soc., Instn. Chem. Engrs., N.Y. Acad. Scis. Roman Catholic. Avocations: prayer, reading, theomatics, writing. Home: 4388 Millburn Ave Stow OH 44224-2879 Office: Babcock & Wilcox Environ Equipment Div 20 S Van Buren Ave Barberton OH 44203-3522

ZBAR, LLOYD IRWIN STANLEY, otolaryngologist, educator; b. Jersey City, June 2, 1939; m. Margo Wally, Mar. 25, 1965; children: Ross I.S., Brett I.W. MD, Queen's U., Kingston, Ont., Can., 1964. Cert. in otolaryngology. Intern Beth Israel/Harvard, Boston, 1964; resident in surgery French Hosp., N.Y.C., 1965-66; resident in otolaryngology Bellevue Hosp. Ctr.-NYU, N.Y.C., 1966-69, fellow in otolaryngology, 1969-70; chmn. med. edn. com. Mountainside Hosp., Montclair, N.J., 1979-89, dir. otolaryngology, 1990-97, 99—; sec. med. bd. Mountainside Hosp., Glen Ridge, N.J., 1986-90, clin. assoc. prof. otolaryngology NYU Sch. Medicine. Contbr. rev. to New Eng. Jour. Medicine, 1988. Mem. exec. bd. Boy Scouts of Am., Essex County, N.J., 1984-95; pres. Mountainside Physicians Scholarship Loan Fund, 1972-85. Fellow ACS, Am. Acad. Otolaryngology-Head and Neck Surgery, Royal Soc. Medicine. Fax: 973-743-3111. Office: 200 Highland Ave Glen Ridge NJ 07028-1528

ZBICINSKI, IRENEUSZ, chemical engineer, educator; b. Lódź, Poland, Apr. 16, 1953; s. Jan Zbicinski and Helena Surowiec; m. Wioletta Anna Przybyl, Oct. 6, 1979; 1 child, Malgorzata. MS, Tech. U. Lodz, 1977, PhD, 1981; DS, Tech. U. Warsaw, 1995. Chemist Inst. Chem. Engring. Tech. U. Lodz, 1977-80, asst., asst. prof. Inst. Chem. Engring., 1980-98, assoc. prof. Inst. Chem. Engring., 1998—; dir. Ctr. Continuing Edn., Lodz, 1997-2000. Co-author: Thermal Processing of Bioproducts, 1998; contbr. articles to profl. jours. Recipient Best Achievements in Sci. award Min. Edn., 1996. Fellow Edustim; mem. Polish Cons. Soc. Avocations: sports, music, walking. Home: Ziemowita 2/13, 92-413 Lódź Poland Office: Tech Univ Lódź, ul Wolczanska 213/215, 90-924 Lódź Poland

ZBOINSKI, KRZYSZTOF BOLESLAW, mechanical engineering educator; b. Gdansk, Poland, May 11, 1954; s. Janusz and Miroslawa (Hrynkiewicz) Z.; m. Dorota Gryglewicz, Apr. 13, 1985; 1 child, Mariusz. ME, Gdansk U. Tech., 1978; D of Engring., Warsaw U. Tech., Poland, 1985. Sr. design asst. Shipyard Industry Designing Office, Gdansk, 1978-79; asst. Warsaw U. Tech., 1984-85, tutor, head rsch. projects, 1989-99; staff exch. mem. Brit. Rail Rsch., Derby, 1988-89. Author: The Methodology of Modelling Rail Vehicle Dynamics with Regard to a Given Transportation and Its Applications, 2000; co-author: Dynamics of Mechanical System Railway Vehicle Track, 1991, Advanced Railway Vehicle Systems Dynamics, 1991; contbr. articles to profl. jours. Rsch. grantee Ministry Nat. Edn. and State Com. Sci. Rsch., Warsaw, 1990-91, 91-94, 97-99. Fellow Internat. Assn. for Vehicle System Dynamics, Gesellschaft fur Angewandte Mathematik und Mechanik, Soc. Indsl. and Applied Math. Avocations: horseback riding, sailing, skiing, railway models. Home: Kazubow 6/14, 01-466 Warsaw Poland Office: Warsaw U Tech, Koszykowa 75, 00-662 Warsaw Poland

ZDANSKY, KAREL, physicist, researcher; b. Czech Republic, Mar. 20, 1934; s. Karel and Zdenka (Hojna) Z.; m. Ludmila Synackova, June 8, 1961; children: Petra, Marie, Daniel. Degree in engring., Czech Tech. U., 1957; PhD, Acad. Scis. Czech Republic, Prague, 1963. Sci. worker Inst. Radio Engring. and Electronics Czechoslovak Acad. Scis., Prague, 1963-69, 73—; sr. lectr. in physics U. Canterbury, Christchurch, New Zealand, 1969-73. Contbr. articles to profl. jours. Avocations: bee master, handwork. Office: Acad Scis Inst Radio Engrin, Chaberska 57, 18251 Prague 8, Czech Republic

ZDENEK, SEAN, English educator; b. Northridge, Calif., Oct. 19, 1968; s. Dale Frank and Linda Susan Zdenek; m. Denise Ann Dexheimer, Aug. 14, 1993; children: Liam James, Pierce Joseph. MA in English, Calif. State U. Stanislaus, Turlock, 1994-96; BA in English, U. Calif., Berkeley, 1994; postgrad., Carnegie Mellon U., 1996—. Instr. rhetoric and composition Calif. State U. Stanislaus, Turlock, 1995-96, Carnegie Mellon U., Pitts., 1996—. Contbr. articles to profl. jours. Recipient Outstanding Scholastic Achievement award in English, Antelope Valley Coll., Lancaster, Calif., 1992; H. Hill scholar U. Calif. Berkeley Faculty, 1994. Mem. Phi Beta Kappa. E-mail: szdenek@andrew.cmu.edu. Office: Carnegie Mellon U Dept English 5000 Forbes Ave Pittsburgh PA 15213-3890

ZDETSIS, ARISTIDES DIMITRIOS, physics educator; b. Nikaia, Piraeus, Greece, May 31, 1946; s. Dimitrios and Filareti (Xatzopoulou) Z.; m. Elpiniki Panagiotou, June 7, 1980; children: Dimitrios, Sotiria, Filareti. BS, U. Athens (Greece), 1969; MS, Thomas Jefferson U., 1972, PhD, 1976. Rsch. fellow Bartor Rsch. Found. Franklin Inst. Swarthmore (Pa.) Coll., 1973-77; rsch. assoc. U. Va., 1976-78; vis. researcher Nuclear Rsch. Ctr., Demokritos, Greece, 1977-79; assoc. researcher Rsch. Ctr. Crete (Greece), 1983-89; asst. prof. dept. physics U. Crete, 1985-89; assoc. prof. L.P.C.S., Grenoble, France, 1987-88; prof. U. Patras (Greece), 1989—; vis. prof. dept. physics U. Ill., Urbana-Champaign, 1979-89; vis. disting. prof. U. Crete, 1981-85, dir. Computer Ctr., Rsch. Ctr., Crete; acad. dir. Open U. Greece, 1997—. Author: Modern Physics, 2000, Quantum Mechanics, 2000; contbr. over 100 articles to profl. jours. Mem. Greek Solid State Phys. Soc., Am. Phys. Soc., AAAS, Sigma Xi. Greek Orthodox. Avocations: multi media creations, swimming, travel, reading poetry and science for the layman. Home: 12 Isidorou St, 26442 Patra Greece Office: U Patras, Dept Physics, 261 10 Patra Greece

ZDRAVISTCH, FRANZ, fluid mechanics engineer; b. Caracas, Venezuela, Jan. 11, 1961; arrived in Australia, 1992; s. Franz and Josefa (Fernandez) Z. Degree in mech. engring., U. Simon Bolivar, Caracas, 1983; M in Engring., Inst. Aeronautical Tech., San Jose dos Campos, Brazil, 1990; PhD, U. NSW, Sydney, Australia, 1998. Cert. computational fluid dynamics engr. Geophys. engr. Schlumberger, West Africa, 1983-86; sales engr. DANA, Caracas, 1986-88; aircraft maintenance engr. Aviasvc., Caracas, 1991-92; rsch. assoc. U. NSW, 1993—. Contbr. articles to profl. jours. Mem. Instn. Engrs. Australia. Avocations: glider pilot, tennis, swimming.

ZDROJEWSKI, ZBIGNIEW JOZEF, nephrologist; b. Radomno, Toruń, Poland, Feb. 9, 1953; s. Zygmunt and Anna (Piotrowicz) Z.; m. Grazyna Leniec, Sept. 19, 1981; 1 child, Lukasz. Degree in medicine, Med. U., Gdansk, Poland, 1978, MD, PhD, 1983. Asst. dept. nephrology Med. U., Gdansk, 1978-89, chief dialysis unit, 1993, sr. asst., 1999—, asst. prof., 1999—, dep. head dept. nephrology; chief dialysis unit, Gdansk, 1993. Mem. Polish Soc. Nephrology (sec. 1992), European Dialysis and Transplantation Assn. Roman Catholic. Avocation: travel. Office: Med Univ Dept Nephrology, Debinki 7, 80-211 Gdańsk Poland

ZEBROWSKA, JADWIGA IRENA, horticulture engineer, educator, researcher; b. Lublin, Poland, Oct. 14, 1959; d. Antoni and Irena (Jaworska) Z. MSc in Hort. Scis., Agrl. U., Lublin, 1983, PhD in Agrl. Scis., 1993. Rsch. technician Exptl. Sta., Lublin, 1983-87; lectr., rschr. applied genetics and hort. plant breeding Agrl. U., Lublin, 1987—. Contbr. articles to profl. jours. Roman Catholic. Avocations: playing the piano, choral music. Home: Pozytywistow 14A/9, 20-639 Lublin Poland Office: Agrl U, Akademicka 15, 20-950 Lublin Poland

ZECCA, ANTONIO, physics researcher; b. Morbegno, Italy, Jan. 12, 1944; s. Giovanni and Maria (Del Nero) Z.; m. Annamaria Forni, June 28, 1975; children: Chiara, Giovanni, Pietro. Laurea in physics, U. Milan, 1970, specialization in atomic/nuclear physics, 1979. Fellow E. Mattei Found., Milan, 1971; fellow Nat. Rsch. Ctr., Milan, 1972-74, assoc., 1979-83, 91—; contract in theoretical physics U. Milan, 1975-81, theoretical physics rschr., 1981—; assoc. Nat. Inst. Nuc. Physics, Milan, 1976—. Contbr. articles to profl. jours. Mem. Internat. Quantum Structure Assn. Roman Catholic. Home: Via Borelli 12, I-20146 Milan Italy Office: U Milan Physics Dept, Via Celoria 16, I-20133 Milan Italy

ZECCA, JOHN ANDREW, retired association executive; b. Bklyn., June 18, 1914; s. Joseph and Elvira (Orsi) Z.; m. Jean Ann Scott, June 27, 1964; 1 son, John Andrew. Student, Heffley Queensboro Coll., Ridgewood, N.Y., 1931, N.Y. U., 1933-36. Auditor ASCE, 1936-50, comptroller, 1950-60; registered rep. Goodbody & Co., 1960-61; pvt. cons. practice, 1961-64; sec., gen. mgr. United Engring. Trustees, 1965-81; trustee Engring. Index, Inc., 1967-81; sec. Engring. Found., 1965-81. John Fritz Medal Bd. Award, 1965-81; Daniel Guggenheim Medal Bd. Award, 1965-81. Mem. East Side Assn., ASCE, Council Engring. and Sci. Soc. Execs., Am. Soc. Assn. Execs. Home: 15 Hillside Ter Suffern NY 10901-2104

ZECCHINO, ORTENSIO, federal official; b. Asmara, Italy, Apr. 20, 1943. Min. Portfolio, Univ. and Scientific Rsch., Rome. Italian Popular Party. Office: Office of Prime Min, Piazza Kennedy 20, 00144 Rome Italy*

ZEČEVIĆ, MIODRAG DJ., former archives director; b. Topola, Serbia, Yugoslavia, Sept. 4, 1930; s. Djordje and Pava (Batričević) Z.; m. Ljubica Jezdimirović, Mar. 7, 1956; children: Pava, Srdjan. Grad. Faculty of Law, Belgrade U., 1956, specialist tng., 1961; MA, Faculty of Polit. Scis., Belgrade, 1967; PhD, Faculty of Law, Belgrade, 1970, Faculty of Philosophy, 1961. Officer Fed. Secretariat Internatl Affairs, Belgrade, 1955-59; scientist Inst. Social Scis., Belgrade, 1959-61; sec. Gen. Bd. Yugoslav Socialist Alliance, Belgrade, 1961-63; sec. orgnl. polit. coun. Assembly of Republic of Serbia, Belgrade, 1963-69, pres. legis. and juridical commn., 1969-74; pres. legis. and juridical commn. Assembly of Yugoslavia, Belgrade, 1974-82; high official Assembly of S.F.R. Yugoslavia, Belgrade, 1982-85; fed. cons. Govt. of Yugoslavia, Belgrade, 1985-87; dir. Archives of Yugoslavia, Belgrade, 1987-95; prof. Belgrade U., Sch. Polit. Scis., 1995-97. Author: Socio-political Organizations and Associations, 1976, Creation of General Enactments, 1978, Joint Interest in Federation, 1984, Contradictions in Yugoslav Law, 1987; editor-in-chief Archives, Law and Social Sci. Rev. and Self-Mgmt. Law; contbr. articles to profl. jours. Sec.-gen. SUBNOR of Yugoslavia. Mem. Assembly Yugoslav Assn. (pres. 1990-95), Assembly Yugoslav Ecology Fedn. (pres. 1990-94), Presidency of the Assn. for Constnl. Law, Presidency of the Assn. for Polit. Scis., Fedn. of Vets. Assns. of Peoples Liberation War of Yugoslavia (sec. ctrl. com.), Union of Vets. Orgns. and Anti-Fascist Movements of the Balkans. Avocation: hunting. Home: Njegoševa 56, 11000 Belgrade Yugoslavia Office: Braće Jugovića 19, 11000 Belgrade Serbia, Yugoslavia*

ZECHNER, JOSEF, finance educator; b. Judenburg, Austria, July 2, 1955; s. Josef and Maria (Glanzer) Z.; m. Cecilia Ingrid Monica Amelson, Oct. 4, 1980; children: Anna-Katharina, Kerstin, Nikolas. Mag rer soc oec, U. Graz, 1978, Dr rer soc oec, 1980, habilitation, 1987. Univ. asst. U. Graz, Austria, 1978-85; vis. scholar U. B.C., Vancouver, Can., 1982-83, asst. prof., 1985-90, assoc. prof., 1990-93; rsch. scholar grad. sch. bus. Stanford U., 1991-92; prof. finance U. Vienna, Austria, 1993—; dir. Ctr. Banking and Finance Donau Univ. Krems, 1996—; rsch. fellow CEPR, 1996—. Mem. Austria Acad. Sci. (corr.), European Finance Assn. (pres. 1997-98), German Finance Assn. (exec. mem. exec. com. 1998—). Avocations: running, skiing, opera, theater. Office: U Vienna Dept Bus Studies, Bruenner Str 72, 1210 Vienna Austria

ZECHNER, RUDOLF, biochemist; b. Graz, Austria, Aug. 25, 1954. PhD, Karl-Franzens U., Graz, 1980; Docent, Karl-Franzens-Univ., Graz, 1990. Assoc. prof. Inst. Med. Biochemistry Karl-Franzens U.; prof. biochemistry Inst. Molecular Biology, Biochemistry & Microbiology, U. Graz (Austria), 1998—. Office: Inst of Molecular Biology Biochem & Microbiology U Graz, Heinrichstrasse 31a, A-8010 Graz Austria

ZEDDA, ALBERTO, conductor; b. Milan, Jan. 2, 1928. Student, Milan Univ. and Conservatory. Tchr. Cin. Coll. Music, 1957-59; faculty Urbino U., Italy, 1981-87, Osimo Acad., Italy, 1988-92; coach winners of Am. vocal competitions, 1959-61; dir. Centro Studi Spontiniani, 1981-92, Accademia Rossniana, Pesaro, Italy, 1989—; debut Polytechnic Chamber Group of Milan, 1956, Covent Garden, 1975; condr. Italian operas Deutsche Oper Berlin, 1961-63, N.Y.C. Opera, 1963; guest condr. leading orchs. and opera cos. throughout U.S., Israel, and Europe; Covent Garden debut, 1975, Il Barbiere di Siviglia; condr. Il Barbieri with co. of Cologne Opera, Hong Kong, 1989, Il Turco, Teatro de la Zarzuela, Madrid, 1990, La Scala di seta 1990 Pesaro Festival, Semiramide, 1992; co-editor: (with Philp Gossett) complete edit. Rossini's works; author critical edit. Il barbiere di Siviglia, 1969; edits. of Torvaldo e Dorliska and La Gazza Ladra by Rossini; music advisor Rossini Opera Festival, Pesaro, 1981-92; music dir. Festival della Valle D'Itria, Martinafranca, Italy, 1980-89; artistic dir. Teatro Carlo Felice, Genova, 1992, Teatro alla Scalla, Milan, 1992-93, Early Barok Festival, Fano, Italy, 1998-99, Rossini Opera Festival, 2000—. Mem. editl. com. Rossini's Complete Edit., Rossini Found., 1970-93; author critical edits.: Il barbiere di Siviglia, Cenerentola, Semiramide, La gazza ladra, Adelaide di Borgogna by Rossini, Otello, Falstaff by Verdi, Elisir d'amore by Donizetti, I Puritani by Bellini, L'Incoronazione di Poppea by Monteverdi, Juditha Triumphans, La Senna festeggiante by Vivaldi; recordings include: Rossini: Il Barbiere di Siviglia, La gazza Ladra, Tancredi, Semiramide, Adelaide di Borgogna; Bellini: Sonnambula, Beatrice di Tenda; Donizetti: Rita; Auber: Fra' Diavolo; Leoncavallo: La Bohème; Spontini: Teseo riconosciuto, Li puntigli delle donne; Cimrosa: Le donne rivali; Pergolesi: La serva padrona; Paisiello: Il maestro di Cappella; Vivaldi: Juditha Triumphans; Prokofiev (Sinfonietta, Classic Symphony), Milhaud (Création du Monde), Debussy, Ravel, Albeniz, Bach, Vivaldi, Carissimi, Viotti, Boccherini, Süssmayr, Vogler, others. Office: Accademia Rossiniana, Via Rossini 37, I-61100 Pesaro Italy

ZEDELMAIER, HELMUT, historian, educator, editor; b. Ravensburg, Germany, Sept. 4, 1954; s. Josef and Gertrud (Friedmann) Z.; m. Gabriele Zedelmaier-Murrer; 1 child, Joseph. MA in History, U. Munich, 1984, PhD, 1989, Dr.phil.habil in history, 1996. Asst. Inst. History U. Munich, 1985-97, prof. Inst. History, 1998-99. Author: Bibliotheca universalis, 1992; editor: (with R. Häfner, M. Mulsow and F. Neumann) Johan Lorenz Mosheim, 1997, (with L. Boehm, W. Müller, W. Smolka) Biographisches Lexikon der LMU München, 1998, (with M. Mulsow) Skepsis und Providenz, 1998, (with M. Kamp) Nilpferde an der Isar, 2000; editor jour. Bayernspiegel, 1991—. U. Munich scholar, 1985-86; rsch. fellow Görres-Gesellschaft, 1994-95, Deutsche Forschungsgemeinschaft, 1998—. E-mail: murrer@lrz.uni-muenchen.de. Home: Neubiberger St 32, 81737 Munich Germany Office: Historisches Sem, Geschwister-Scholl Platz 1, 80539 Munich Germany

ZEDILLO PONCE DE LEÓN, ERNESTO, president of Mexico; b. Mexico City, Apr. 27, 1951; s. Rodolfo Zedillo Castillo and Martha Alicia Ponce de Leon; m. Nilda Patricia Velasco Nuñez; children: Ernesto, Emiliano, Carlos, Nild Patricia, Rodrigo. Student, Instituto Politécnico Nacional, Bradford U., U. Colo.; MA, Yale U., 1977, PhD, 1981. With Partido Revolucionario Institucional, 1971—, Instituto de Estudios Politicos, Económicos y Sociales; econ. rschr. Dirreción Gen. de Programación Económica y Social; lectr. Colegio de Mex., 1978-80; dep. mgr. finance and econ. rsch., advisor to bd. dirs. Banco de Mex.; dep. sec. for planning and budget Govt. Mex., Mexico City, 1985-88, sec. for planning and budget, 1988-92, sec. public edn., 1992-93, pres., 1994—; campaign mgr. presdl. nominee Luis Donald Colosio Partido Revolucionario Institucional, 1993-94. Campaign mgr. Luis Donaldo Colosio. Office: Office of the Pres, Puerti, Col San Miguel, Mexico City 11850, Mexico

ZEDROSSER, JOSEPH JOHN, lawyer; b. Milw., Jan. 24, 1938; s. Joseph and Rose (Zollner) Z.; m. Antonina Krass, Sept. 6, 1997. AB, Marquette U., 1959; LLB, Harvard U., 1963. Bar: N.Y. 1964, U.S. Dist. Ct. (so. dist.) N.Y. 1966, U.S. Dist. Ct. (ea. dist.) N.Y. 1971, U.S. Ct. Appeals (2d cir.) 1971, U.S. Ct. Appeals (D.C. Cir.) 1975, U.S. Supreme Ct. 1975. Assoc. William G. Mulligan, N.Y.C., 1964-67, Christy, Bauman, Frey and Christy and successors, N.Y.C., 1967-71; dir. cmty. devel. unit Bedford-Stuyvesant Cmty. Legal Svcs. Corp., N.Y.C., 1971-73; assoc. fed. defender svcs. unit Legal Aid Soc., N.Y.C., 1973-74; asst. atty. gen. Environ. Protection Bur., N.Y. State Dept. Law, N.Y.C., 1974-80; regional counsel EPA, N.Y.C., 1980-82; assoc. prof. St. John's U. Sch. Law, N.Y.C., 1982-86; ptnr. Rivkin, Radler, Dunne & Bayh, Uniondale, N.Y., 1986-89, Breed, Abbott & Morgan, N.Y.C., 1989-93, Whitman Breed Abbott & Morgan, N.Y.C., 1993-95; v.p. CPR Inst. for Dispute Resolution, N.Y.C., 1996; sr. investigative counsel com. on investigations, taxation, and gov. ops. N.Y. State Senate, 1998-99; asst. atty. gen. Environ. Protection Bur. N.Y. State Office Atty. Gen., N.Y.C., 1999—. Lectr., contbr. to course handbooks for courses sponsored by Practicing Law Inst. and other assns. Lt. USNR, 1965-74, USAR, 1963-65. Mem. ABA, Assn. of Bar of City of N.Y., N.Y. State Bar Assn. (mem. Environ. Law Sect. Exec. Com.), Alpha Sigma Nu. Roman Catholic. Home: 45 E End Ave Apt 11F New York NY 10028-7982

ZEE, SZE-YONG, botanist, educator; b. Shanghai, Peoples Republic of China, Jan. 19, 1943; married; one child. BS with honors, U. Melbourne, 1966, PhD, 1969. Lectr. U. Hong Kong, 1970-83, reader, 1983—, prof., 1996—; prof. South China Agrl. U., Guangzhou, 1985—; rsch. fellow South China Inst. Botany, Guangzhou, 1991—. Del. Chinese Nat. People's Congress, Beijing, 1989-98; mem. nat. com. People's Polit. Consultative Conf. Beijing, 1998—; active Basic Law Consultative Com., Hong Kong, 1985-90. Office: U Hong Kong Dept Botany, Hong Kong Hong Kong

ZEECK, AXEL, biomolecular chemistry, educator, researcher; b. Rummelsburg, Pommern, Germany, Mar. 31, 1939; s. Günther and Gertrude (Haufschild) Z.; m. Gisela Friederike Ruppenthal, 1964; children: Marion, Elisa. PhD, U. Göttingen, Germany, 1966, Habilitation, 1974. Wiss. asst. U. Göttingen, 1966-74, univ.-docent, 1974-80, prof., 1980—; dean faculty chemistry U. Göttingen, 1981-83, v.p., 1983-85, senator, 1989—. Author: Chemie für Mediziner, 1990, 4th edit., 2000; contbr. over 150 articles to books and profl. jours. on biologically active metabolites from microorganisms; 15 patents in field. Recipient Max-Planck-Forschungspreis, Humboldt-Stiftung, 1994. Mem. Gesellschaft Deutscher Chemiker, Am. Soc. Microbiology. E-mail: azeeck@gwdg.de. Office: Inst Organic Chemistry, Tammannstrasse 2, D-37077 Göttingen Germany

ZEGARLINSKI, BOGUSLAW JOSEPH, science educator; b. Mielec, Rzeszow, Poland, Nov. 13, 1955; arrived in Eng., 1993; s. Stanislaw and Leokadia Zegarlinski; m. Bożena Aniela Ziobro, June 12, 1976; children: Lukasz, Malwina. MSc, Silesian U., Katowice, Poland, 1979; PhD, Wroclaw (Poland) U., 1984. Rsch. asst. MIT, Cambridge, Mass., 1992-93; lectr. Imperial Coll., London, 1993-94, reader, 1994-96, prof., 1996-2000; chmn. ICMP, 2000—. Contbr. articles to profl. jours. Grantee EPSRC, U.K., 1994, 95, 96, 97, 2000. Fellow Am. Math. Soc., London Math. Soc. Roman Catholic. Office: Imperial Coll Math Dept, 180 Queens Gate, London SW7 2BZ, England

ZEGENHAGEN, JÖRG, research physicist, educator; b. Otterndorf, Germany, Aug. 14, 1950; s. Hermann Friedrich and Waltraut Marta (Saint-Paul) Z.; m. Christa Erna Gertrud Trautmann, Oct. 6, 1976 (div. 1980); 1 child, Christiane. Diploma, Hamburg (Germany) U., 1980, PhD, 1984; habilitation, Dortmund (Germany) U., 1993. Rsch. assoc. DESY, Hamburg, 1980-82, U. Hamburg, 1982-84; staff scientist SUNY, Albany, 1984-86; tech. staff AT&T Bell Labs., Murray Hill, N.J., 1986-89; staff scientist Max-Planck-Inst.-FKF, Stuttgart, Germany, 1989-99, European Synchrotron Radiation Facility, Grenoble, France, 1999—; lectr. École des Mines, St. Etienne, France, 1990—, U. Dortmund, 1994—. Editor issue Philos. Mag., 1994, issue Phys. Stat. Sol., 1999; contbr. over 130 articles to profl. physics jours. Mem. Am. Phys. Soc., German Phys. Soc. Mem. Socialdemocratic Party Germany. Avocations: guitar, sailing.

ZEH, HEINZ-DIETER, retired theoretical physics educator; b. Braunschweig, Fed. Republic Germany, May 8, 1932; s. Otto and Irmgard (Stöckner) Z.; m. Sigrid Besch, July 5, 1941. Diploma, U. Heidelberg, Fed. Republic Germany, 1960, D. in Natural Scis., 1962, D. Habilitation, 1966. Rsch. assoc. Calif. Inst. Tech., Pasadena, 1964-65, U. Calif. San Diego, La Jolla, 1965-66; from lectr. to prof. U. Heidelberg, 1966-89. Author: Physik der Zeitrichtung, 1984, Physical Basis of the Direction of Time, 1989, 92, 99, (with D. Giulini et al.) Decoherence and the Appearance of a Classical World in Quantum Theory, 1996. Home: Gaiberger Strasse 38, D-69151 Waldhilsbach Germany

ZEHEL, WENDELL EVANS, surgeon; b. Brownsville, Pa., Mar. 6, 1934; s. Michael and Emma (Evans) Z.; m. Joan Leasure, Nov. 1, 1958; children: Lori Ann, Wendell Charles. BA, Washington and Jefferson Coll., 1956; MD, U. Pitts., 1960; postgrad. in bioengring., Carnegie-Mellon U., 1968-75. Diplomate Am. Bd. Surgery. Intern Shadyside Hosp., Pitts., 1960-61; resident in surgery U. Pitts., VA Hosp., 1963-66, Wilmington (Del.) Med. Ctr., 1966-68; pvt. practice Pitts., 1968—; surgeon St. Clair Hosp., Pitts., 1968—. Served with USAF, 1961-63. Fellow ACS; mem. Assn. Advancement of Med. Instrumentation. Home: 553 Harrogate Rd Pittsburgh PA 15241-2028 Office: 110 Fort Couch Rd Ste 3D Pittsburgh PA 15241-1030

ZEHRING, PEGGY JOHNSON, artist; b. Hutchinson, Kans., Jan. 4, 1941; d. Phillip E. and Bernice (Ashley) Johnson; m. R. David Zehring, July 27, 1963; children: Lisa, Geoff. BS, U. Kans., 1963; BA, U. Ill., 1977. Instr. Bellevue (Wash.) C.C., 1979-93, Sch. Visual Concepts, Seattle, 1985-86, Seattle Ctrl. C.C., 1987-97, North Seattle C.C., 1987-97, Coupeville (Wash.) Art Ctr., 1993—; juror and lectr. Eastside Assn. Fine Art, Mercer Island Visual Arts League, Nat. League Am. Artists & Pen Women; lectr. Women Painters of Washington, Bellevue Art Mus., N.W. Watercolor Soc., Hutchinson Art Assn., Kans. One-woman shows include King County Arts Commn., Seattle, Blake Gallery, Seattle, Bellevue (Wash.) C.C., PACCAR, Bellevue, Pacific N.W. Bell, Seattle, U. Ill., Chgo., Hutchinson Art Assn.; exhibited in group shows at COCA Annual, Seattle, Seattle Art Mus. Sales & Rental Gallery, LewAllen Fine Art, Santa Fe, Bellevue Art Mus., Diablo Valley Coll., Elizabeth Prince Gallery, Prescott, Ariz.; represented in selected collections City of Lynnwood, Wash., Pacific NW Bell, PACCAR, Delitte, Haskins & Sells, Opti-Copy, Kansas City, Harper & Assocs., Bellevue and numerous other pvt. collections; work published in The Artistic Touch I, II and III, The Encyclopedia of Living Artists. Pres. The LaVeta (Colo.) Sch. of Arts. Recipient 1st pl. award Ariz. Internat., Snowgrass Art Inst., Cashmere, Wash., Kans. State Fair, Hutchinson, SPACe, La Veta, Colo., Honorable Mention award W. Wash. State Fair, 2d pl. award Ea. N.Mex. U., Portales, Snowgrass Art Inst., Cashmere, Wash., Merit award Mont. Inst. of the Arts, Butte; named finalist Pierce County Libr. Project, Gig Harbor, Wash., 3rd place Greeley Nat. Juried show. E-mail: zehrings@rmi.net. Home: PO Box 967 La Veta CO 81055-0967

ZEICHNER, ARIE, chemist; b. Riga, Latvia, July 2, 1947; arrived in Israel, 1960; s. Maximilian and Raya Zeichner. BSc in Chemistry and Physics, Hebrew U., Jerusalem, 1968; MSc in Chemistry, Weizmann Inst., Rehovot, Israel, 1974; PhD in Chemistry, Hebrew U., Jerusalem, 1979. Head R & D photographic chems. dept. Makhteshim Ltd., Beersheva, Israel, 1979-81; head criminalistic photographic lab. Divsn. Identification and Forensic Sci., Israel Police, Jerusalem, 1981-82, head Toolmarks and Materials Lab., 1982-94, head toolmarks and materials sect., 1994—. Contbr. articles to profl. jours. Office: Israel Police Hdqs, Identification & Forensic Sci, 91906 Jerusalem Israel

ZEID, PHILIP L., metal recycling executive; b. Chgo., July 27, 1943; s. Samuel P. and Mary S. (Stamler) Z.; m. Donna M. Winston, Dec. 16, 1966 (div. Feb. 1978); 1 child, Jason I.; m. Paula S. Klein, Oct. 13, 1991. BA, Drake U., 1966; postgrad., U. Kans., 1966. Sales mgr. Random House, Inc., Chgo., 1969-74; v.p., dir. mktg. dept. Coronet Films, Chgo., 1974-82; sr. mgr. MCI Communications, Chgo., 1982-84; pres. Universal Scrap Metals, Inc., Chgo., 1984—, also bd. dirs.; pres., bd. dirs. USM Processing Ltd., 1997—. Mem. exec. com. Jewish United Fund. Mem. Assn. Media Producers (statis. com. 1980-82, speakers bur., chmn. trade show com., lobbyist Washington chpt. 1981-82), Sales and Mktg. Execs. Assn., Inst. Scrap Recycling Industries. Avocations: photography, art collecting, skiing, tennis, travel. Home: 1908 N Dayton St Chicago IL 60614-5029 Office: Universal Scrap Metals Inc 2500 W Fulton St Chicago IL 60612-2104

ZEIDMAN, ALIZA, internist; b. Jerusalem, Nov. 14, 1955; d. Asher and Ada (Hazan) Dayan; m. Yosef Zeidman, Nov. 24, 1980; children: Adi, Michal, Hadas. MD, Ben Gurion U., 1985; splty. in internal medicine, Hashoron Hosp. Tel Aviv U., 1992; splty. in Chinese medicine, Bar-Ilan U., 1992. Trainee in internal medicine Hasharon Hosp., Petal Tikva, Israel, 1987-92, specialist in internal medicine, 1992-95, asst. head, 1995—; instr. med. sch. Tel Aviv U., 1993—, tutor, 1990-97; tchr. nursing sch. Haasharon Hosp., 1990-96, tchr. MD residents, 1992-97. Contbr. articles to profl. jours. Cpl. Israeli Def. Forces, 1973-75. Fellow Israel Soc. Infectious Diseases; mem. Israel Soc. Internal Medicine, Israel Soc. Hematology. Jewish. Avocations: reading, walking, hiking. Home: Meridor 8 Neve 02, Petah Tikua Israel Office: Rabin Med Ctr, Hasharon Hosp, Petah Tiqwa Israel

ZEIGEN, SPENCER STEVEN, architect; b. Bklyn., Oct. 11, 1924; s. David and Ethel (Katz) Z.; m. Mildred Weinman, Dec. 27, 1952 (dec. Sept. 1992); children: Steven, Scott; m. Lillian Glogau, Oct. 10, 1993; children: Jordan, Laurence, Alexander. BFA suma cum laude, U. Pa., 1952. Registered architect, N.J. Architect Leo Fischer Arch., South Orange, N.J., 1952-54, Frank Grad Sons Arch., Newark, 1954-64; staff architect Rutgers State U., New Brunswick, N.J., 1964-74; pvt. practice Highland Park, N.J., 1974-78, Jamesburg, N.J., 1978—; architect Collins, Uhl, Hoisington, Anderson Architech, Princeton, N.J., 1978-80; dir. of architecture Brown Hale Arch., Newark, 1980-82, Brown & Mathews, Fords, N.J., 1982-86; litigation expert witness, 1980—; bd. arch. High Rise Condominiums, Fort Lee, N.J., 1982-89; cons. roofing expert, litigation, expert witness Kipcon, Inc., North Brunswick, N.J., 1980—, bldg. materials analyst, 1988—; instr. arch. Newark Coll. Engring., 1963-69; lectr. Rutgers U., 1961-65. Prin. works include N.J. Divsn. Motor Vehicles Testing Facilities, N.J. Cultural Ctr., Rutgers U. Ednl. Facilities. Bd. dirs. Whittingham Homeowners Assn., Monroe Twp., N.J., 1990-93. Sgt. USAF, 1942-46. Mem. Am. Soc. Arch., Am. Soc. Planners. Democrat. Jewish. Avocations: bridge, tennis, bocci, reading, drawing. Home and Office: 19B Winthrop Rd Monroe Township NJ 08831-2666

ZEIGFINGER, HAROLD (HAL ZEIGFINGER), chemicals executive; b. N.Y.C., Aug. 28, 1921; s. Jack and Hilda Zeigfinger; div.; children: Adam, Michell; m. Dorothy Zeigfinger; 1 child, Cheryl Jalpion. BSME, U.S. Merchant Marine Acad. Commd. 2d. lt. U.S. Mcht. Marine, advanced through grades to lt. comdr.; ret.; pres. Equity Assocs. (subs. Maj. Chem Corp.), Houston; cons. State of Tex. rep. to Rep. Presdl. Rountable, 1997-98; mem. Rep. Senatorial Inner Cir. Adm. Tex. Navy, 1979—. Mem. Am. Soc. Naval Archs. and Marine Engrs., Nat. Assn. Corrosion Engrs., Propeller Club of U.S. Office: Maj Chem Corp 2015 Shadowbriar Dr Houston TX 77077-6010

ZEIGLER, EARLE FREDERICK, physical education-kinesiology educator; b. N.Y.C., Aug. 20, 1919; s. Clarence Mattison and Margery Christina (Beyerkohler) Shinkle; m. Bertha M. Bell, June 25, 1941; children—Donald H., Barbara A; m. Anne K. Rogers, Feb. 27, 1999. AB, Bates Coll., 1940; AM, Yale U., 1944, PhD, 1951; LLD, U. Windsor, 1975; DSc, U. Lethbridge, Alta, Can., 1997. Assoc. phys. dir., aquatic dir. Bridgeport (Conn.) YMCA, 1941-43; instr. German U. Conn., Storrs, 1943-47; coach, instr. phys. edn. Yale U., 1943-49; asst. prof. U. Western Ont. (Can.), London, 1949-50; prof., chmn. dept. phys., health and recreation edn. U. Western Ont. (Can.), 1950-56, assoc. prof. Sch. Edn.; supr. phys. edn. and athletics U. Mich., Ann Arbor, 1956-63; chmn. dept. phys. edn. Sch. Edn. U. Mich., 1961-63; prof. dept. phys. edn. for men Coll. Phys. Edn., U. Ill., Urbana, 1963-72; head dept. phys. edn. for men, chmn. grad. dept. Coll. Phys. Edn., U. Ill., 1964-68; prof. dept. phys. and health edn. U. Western Ont., London, 1971-89, prof. emeritus, 1989—; dean U. Western Ont. (Faculty of Phys. Edn.), 1972-77. Author: A History of Professional Preparation for Physical Education in the United States, 1951, Administration of Physical Education and Athletics, 1959, The Case Method Approach: An Instructional Manual, 1959, Philosophical Foundations for Physical, Health, and Recreation Education, 1964, A Brief Introduction to the Philosophy of Religion, 1965, (with H.J. VanderZwaag) Physical Education: Progressivism or Essentialism, 1968,

Problems in the History and Philosophy of Physical Education and Sport, 1968, (with M.L. Howell and M. Trekell) Research in the History and Philosophy of Physical Education and Sport, 1971, Personalizing Physical Education and Sport Philosophy, 1975, Physical Education and Sport Philosophy, 1977, Issues in North American Physical Education and Sport, 1979, Decision-Making in Physical Education and Athletics Administration, 1982, (with G.W. Bowie) Management Competency Development in Sport and Physical Education, 1983, Ethics and Morality in Sport and Physical Education, 1984, (with J. Campbell) Strategic Market Planning: An Aid to the Evaluation of an Athletics/Recreation Program, 1984 , Assessing Sport and Physical Education: Diagnosis and Projection, 1986, (with G. Bowie and R. Paris) Competency Development in Sport and Physical Education Management, 1988, (with A. Mikalachki and G. Leyshon) Change Process in Sport and Physical Education Management, 1988, Introduction to Sport and Physical Education Philosophy, 1989, Sport and Physical Education: Past, Present, Future, 1990, Professional Ethics for Sport Managers, 1992, Critical Thinking for the Professions of Health, Physical Education, Recreation, and Dance, 1994, A Selected, Annotated Bibliography of Completed Research on Management Theory and Practice in Physical Education and Athletics to 1972, 1995, (with G.W. Bowie) Developing Management Competency in Sport and Physical Education, 1995; author, editor: A History of Sport and Physical Education to 1900, 1973, A History of Physical Education and Sport in the United States and Canada, 1975, (with M.J. Spaeth) Administrative Theory and Practice in Physical Education and Athletics, 1975, History of Physical Education and Sport, 1979, rev. edit., 1988, Physical Education and Sport: An Introduction, 1982, Physical Education and Kinesiology in North America: Professionalism and Scholarly Foundations, 1994; contbr. articles to profl. jours. Recipient Outstanding Tchr. award U. Western Ont., 1987, Disting. Svc. award Internat. Soc. Comparative Phys. Edn. and Sport, 1988; inducted into Univ. Western Ont.'s Wall of Wrestling Fame, 1991, Univ. Western Ont.'s W Club Hall of Fame, 1995; named first Human Movement Scis. and Edn. scholar U. Memphis, 1994. Fellow Am. Acad. Kinesiology and Phys. Edn. (pres. 1981-82, Hetherington award 1989); mem. AAHPERD (charter, Alliance scholar 1977-78, Disting. Svc. award 1979, Honor award 1981, Gulick award 1990), Philosophy Edn. Soc., Internat. Assn. Profl. Schs. Phys. Edn., Can. Assn. Health, Phys. Edn. and Recreation (v.p. 1955-56, v.p. 1983-85, honour award 1975, spl. presentation citation 1986), Am. Philos. Assn., Nat. Assn. Phys. Edn. in Higher Edn., N.Am. Soc. Sport History (life), Philosophic Soc. for Study of Sport (pres. 1974-75), N.Am. Soc. for Sport Mgmt. (founding mem., hon. past pres. 1986-87), N.Am. Soc. Health, Phys. Edn., Recreation and Dance (charter), Canadian Profl. Schs. Conf. (pres. 1953-55), Ont. Recreation Assn. (v.p. and dir. 1955-56), Soc. Municipal Recreation Dirs. Ont. (Honor award 1956), Phi Epsilon Kappa (life). Achievements include N.Am. Soc. Sport Mgmt. creating the Annual Earle Zeigler Lecture, 1988. Fax: (604) 270-8414. E-mail: zeigrog@axion.net. Home: 105 8560 Currie Rd, Richmond, BC Canada V6Y 1M2 also: PO Box 630 Point Roberts WA 98281-0630

ZEIGLER, JUDY ROSE, law firm administrator; b. Monte Vista, Colo., Aug. 26, 1946; d. Orville Edgar Zeigler and Kathryn Genevieve (Parsons) Duncan. BA, U. Oreg., 1968; degree in spirituality health & medicine, Bastyr U., 2000. Asst. v.p., mgr. staff planning and devel. Rainier Nat. Bank, Seattle, 1979-81, asst. v.p., mgr. staff devel., 1981-83; v.p., mgr. staff planning Blue Cross of Washington and Alaska, Seattle, 1983-85, mgr. market research, 1985-86; pres. Strategies Unltd., Seattle, 1986-96; law firm adminstr. Law Offices of Judith A. Lonnquist P.S., Seattle, 1991—; workshop presenter Gov.'s Conf. Women on the Move, Seattle, 1984, Women Plus Bus Conf., Seattle, 1984, 85, 86, 88, 89; pres. Natalie Skeels Meml. Found. Trustees, Seattle, 1987-90; co-founder, dir. N.W. Women's Inst., 1995—. Vice chair Blue Ribbon Citizens Task Force of King County Assessor's Office, Seattle, 1984; chair mktg. com. Bellevue Community Coll. Telecommunications Ctr. Task Force, Seattle, 1985-87; mem. Women's Polit. Caucus, Seattle, 1987-88, co-chair fundraising com. Mem. ASTD (pres. Puget Sound chpt. 1984-85), Women's Profl. and Managerial Network (pres. 1987-88), N.W. Women's Law Ctr. (bd. dirs. 1988-90, pres. Leadership Synthesis 1991-92, mem. adv. coun. 1988-96), Internat. Women's Conf. (exec. bd. officer 1991-95), Pacific N.W. Writers Conf. (bd. dirs. 1998-99, mem. exec. com. 1999-99). Democrat. Avocation: student pilot. Home: 1523 11th Ave W Seattle WA 98119-3204 Office: Law Offices of Judith A Lonnquist PS 1218 3rd Ave Ste 1500 Seattle WA 98101-3021

ZEIHEN, LESTER GREGORY, geology educator; b. Stevensville, Mont., Feb. 8, 1913; s. Gregory Sylvester and Francis M. (Haigh) Z.; m. Jeannette A. McMahon, July 10, 1941; children: Marilyn, Nancy (dec.), Donna, Gregory. BS in Geol. Engring., Mont. Sch. Mines, 1935, MS, 1937; profl. degree, 1961. Jr. engr. Anaconda Copper Mining Co., Butte, 1937-38; mine geologist Chile Exploration Co., Chuquicamata, 1938-52; rsch. geologist The Anaconda Co., Butte, 1952-73; cons. mineralogist, 1973-79; adj. assoc. prof. geology, adj. curator mineral mus. Mont. Coll. Mining Sci. and Tech., Butte, 1979—. Author in field. Pres. Silver Bow Humane Soc., Butte, 1971—; bd. dirs. Butte Sheltered Workshop, 1968-96, Butte Silver Bow Arts Found., 1979-86, World Mus. Mining, Butte, 1984. Recipient UUHO Sahinen award, 1999. Mem. AAAS, AIME (chmn. sect. 1964, Legion of Honor award), Am. Mineral. Assn. (life), Soc. Econ. Geologists, Geochem. Soc., Mineral. Assn. Can., Mont. Tech. Alumni Assn. (sec.-treas. 1977-2000), Rotary (pres. Butte club 1980-81, Svc. Above Self award 1976, Paul Harris award 1990), Sigma Xi. Republican. Roman Catholic. Home: 834 W Silver St Butte MT 59701-1548 Office: Mont Coll Mineral Sci and Tech W Park St Butte MT 59701

ZEILE, CHRISTOF, electrical engineer, educator; b. Sindelfingen, Germany, 1963; s. Johannes Martin and Ursula (Ensslen) Z. Diploma Ingenieur, U. Stuttgart, Germany, 1988. Sci. asst. U. Stuttgart, 1988—. Contbr. articles to The Internat. Soc. for Optical Engring. Proceedings. Office: U Stuttgart Inst Netzwerk & Sys, Pfaffenwaldring 47, 70550 Stuttgart Germany

ZEILINGER, ANTON, physics educator; b. Ried, Austria, May 20, 1945; s. Anton and Gertrud (Krause) Z.; m. Elisabeth Benka, May 27, 1972; children: Anna, Anton, Matthias. PhD, U. Vienna, Austria, 1971; Habilitation, Tech. U. Vienna, 1979. Asst. prof. Atom Inst. Vienna, 1972-81; Fulbright fellow, rsch. assoc. MIT, Cambridge, 1977-78, assoc. prof., 1981-83; assoc. prof. Tech. U. Vienna, 1983-90; prof. physics U. Innsbruck, Austria, 1990-99, dir. Inst. for Exptl. Physics, 1990-99; adj. prof. Hampshire Coll., Amherst, Mass., 1986-89; prof. Tech. U. Munich, 1988-89; vis. prof. U. Melbourne, Australia, 1984, Coll. de France, Paris, 1995, also numerous others. Co-editor: Frontiers of Neutron Scattering, 1986, Matter-Wave Interferometry, 1988, Quantum Interferometry, 1994, Fundamental Problems in Quantum Theory, 1995; co-author: The Physics of Quantum Information, 2000, Quantum Computation and Quantum Information Theory, 2000; author: Experiments on the Foundations of Quantum Mechanics, 2000; mem. editl. bd. Founds. Physics-Letters, 1988—, Phys. Rev. A, 1994—; contbr. over 200 articles to sci. jours. Recipient sci. prize Cardinal Innitzer Found., 1979, prize Theodor Körner Found., 1980; Sir Thomas Lyle fellow U. Melbourne, 1984, prize Vinct d'Excellence Found., LVHM, Paris, 1995,, Austrian Scientist of the Yr., 1996, prize European Optical Soc., 1997, Order Pour le Mérite, 2000. Fellow Am. Phys. Soc.; mem. Austrian Acad. Scis., Austrian Phys. Soc. Roman Catholic. Office: U Innsbruck Inst Exptl Phys, U Vienna/Inst Exptl Physics, Boltzmanngasse 5, A-1090 Vienna Austria

ZEILINGER, ELNA RAE, elementary educator, gifted-talented education educator; b. Tempe, Ariz., Mar. 24, 1937; d. Clayborn Eddie and Ruby Elna (Laird) Simpson; m. Philip Thomas Zeilinger, June 13, 1970; children: Shari, Chris. BA in Edn., Ariz. State U., 1958, MA in Edn., 1966, EdS, 1980. Bookkeeper First Nat. Bank of Tempe, 1955-56; with registrar's office Ariz. State U., 1956-58; piano tchr., recreation dir. City of Tempe; tchr. Thew Sch., Tempe, 1958-61; elem. tchr. Mitchell Sch., Tempe, 1962-74, intern prin., 1976, personnel intern, 1977; specialist gifted edn. Tempe Elem. Schs., Tempe, 1977-86; elem. tchr. Holdeman Sch., Tempe, 1986-89; tchr. grades 1-12 and adult reading, lang. arts, English Zeilinger Tutoring Svc., 1991—; grad. asst. ednl. adminstrn., Iota Workshop coordinator Ariz. State U., 1978; presenter Ariz. Gifted Conf., 1978-81; condr. survey of gifted programs, 1980; reporter public relations Tempe Sch. Dist., 1978-80, Access com. for gifted programs, 1981-83. Author: Leadership Role of the Principal in Gifted Programs: A Handbook, 1980; Classified Personnel Handbook, 1977, also reports, monographs and paintings. Mem. Tempe Hist. Assn., liaison, 1975; mem. Tempe Art League; mem. freedom train com. Ariz. Bicentennial Commn., 1975-76; bd. dirs. Maple Property Owners Assn., 1994—; storyteller Tempe Hist. Mus., 1997—. Named Outstanding Leader in Elem. and Secondary Schs., 1976' Ariz. Cattle Growers scholar, 1954-55; Elks scholar, 1954-55; recipient Judges award Tempe Art League, 1970, Best of Show, Scottsdale Art League, 1976. Democrat. Congregationalist.

ZEIN, DAVID A., software company executive; b. Tripoli, Lebanon, Oct. 4, 1935; came to U.S., 1961; s. Abdul Raouf Khalil and Fatimah Z. (Haddad) Z.; m. Diane M. Darling, Aug. 23, 1965; children: Reem D. Tarantino, Nadiya D. Zein. BS in Elec. Engring., U. Ill., 1965, MS, 1967; PhD, Northwestern U., 1972. Elec. engr. IBM, Kingston, N.Y., 1967-69; sr. elec. engr. IBM, Fishkill, N.Y., 1972-93; pres., CEO Zein Custom Software, Tarpon Springs, Fla., 1993—. Contbr. articles to profl. jours., book chpt. Mem. IEEE (pres. 1984-85, sr., assoc. editor Circuits & Devices mag. 1984). Avocation: marathon running. Home and Office: Zein Custom Software 1825 Wood Haven St Tarpon Springs FL 34689-7534

ZEITOUN, IBRAHIM MOHAMED, surgeon; b. Idku, Elbohaira, Egypt, Feb. 11, 1949; s. Mohamed and Fathia Mohamed Zeitoun; m. Hoda Abdulhamid Kasem, Jan. 28, 1981; children: Sarah, Hend, Khaled. MB, Alexandria U., Egypt, 1973, CM, 1977, B in Dentistry, 1981, PhD in Plastic and Maxillofacial Surgery, 1983. Registrar Canniesburn Hosp., Glasgow, Scotland, 1988-92; cons. Riyadh (Saudi Arabia) Med. Complex, 1992-96; lectr. faculty dentistry Alexandria U., 1983-85, 86-88, asst. prof., 1988-92, prof., head dept. maxillofacial and plastic surgery, 1996—; vis. cons. Ministry of Health, Almadina, Saudi Arabia, 1983-84, 84-85; cons. Ministry of Health, Riyadh, 1992-96. Contbr. articles to profl. jours. Award recipient Ministry of Health, Riyadh, 1996. Mem. Egyptian Assn. Plastic Surgery, Egyptian Assn. Craniomaxillofacial Surgeons, Royadh Oral and Maxillofacial Surgery Club (v.p. 1993-96, award 1996). Avocations: drawing, poetry, jogging, music. Home: Opp 2 Elbohaira St, Alexandria Gianclis, Egypt Office: Alexandria U Fac Dentistry, Champlion St Elmessalla, 21521 Alexandria Egypt

ZEKKAR, PATRIK HALIM, export company executive; b. Stockholm, Aug. 11, 1972; s. Tahar Z. and Berit Ginilla Rondahl. BS, Stockholm U.; MS, Uppsala U. With Telia Fin. Svcs. Internat., Sweden, 1996; legal & transaction AB SEK, Sweden, 1996-98; project fin. AB Svensk Exportkredit, Sweden, 1998-2000; export and project fin. SEB Merchant Banking, Stockholm, 2000—. Home: Hornsgatan 4, 11820 Stockholm Sweden Office: SEB Merchant Banking, Vastra Tradgardsg 11B, 10640 Stockholm Sweden

ZEKMAN, TERRI MARGARET, graphic designer; b. Chgo., Sept. 13, 1950; d. Theodore Nathan and Lois (Bernstein) Z.; m. Alan Daniels, Apr. 12, 1980; children: Jesse Logan, Dakota Caitlin. BFA, Washington U., St. Louis, 1971; postgrad, Art Inst. Chgo., 1974-75. Graphic designer (on retainer) greeting cards and related products Recycled Paper Products Co., Chgo., 1970—, Jillson Roberts, Inc., Calif.; apprenticed graphic designer Helmuth, Obata & Kassabaum, St. Louis, 1970-71; graphic designer Container Corp., Chgo., 1971; graphic designer, art dir., photographer Cuerden Advt. Design, Denver, 1971-74; art dir. D'Arcy, McManus & Masius Advt., Chgo., 1975-76; freelance graphic designer Chgo., 1976-77; art dir. Garfield Linn Advt., Chgo., 1977-78; graphic designer Keiser Design Group, Van Noy & Co., Los Angeles, 1978-79; owner and operator graphic design studio Los Angeles, 1979—; art and photography tchr. Ctr. for Early Edn., L.A., 1996—, Buckley Sch., Sherman Oaks, 1996—. Recipient cert. of merit St. Louis Outdoor Poster Contest, 1970, Denver Art Dirs. Club, 1973.

ZEKO, MERSIN ABAZ, retired veterinary surgery educator; b. Gjirokaster, Albania, Dec. 10, 1935; s. Abaz Beqir and Ramize Arshi (Muço) Z.; m. Vera Abdyl Ademi, Aug. 4, 1964; children: Albana, Altin. Vet. degree, Tirana (Albania) U., 1958. Vet. Agrl. Coop., Laknas Tirana, 1961-67; chief vet. faculty clinic Vet. Faculty, Tirana, 1967-68; surgery asst. Faculty Clinic, Tirana, 1968-69; lectr. vet. surgery Vet. Faculty, Tirana, 1969-74, chief vet. dept., 1974-85, dean vet. faculty, 1983-90; ret.; vet. Mil. Compounds, Saranda, Albania, 1958-61; post-univ. lecturing Vet. Faculty, Tirana, 1983-90. Authro: (textbooks) Veterinary Surgery and Practice, 1981, The Science of Veterinary Operation, 1992, (monographs) The Cezarian Operation in Cows, 1983, The Operations in Internal Organs, 1985. Capt. Albanian Brigade, 1958-61. Recipient DSc Acad. Scis., Tirana, 1978; named docent Acad. Scis., Tirana, 1983, prof. High Commn. Acad. Scis., Tirana, 1995. Avocations: water sports, athletics, country music, pets, books. Home: RR Elbasanit P4 SH4 AP16, Tirana Albania

ZEL, JANA, plant physiologist, researcher; b. Ljubljana, Slovenia, Feb. 7, 1958; d. Anton and Dragica (Oblat) Z. PhD, U. Ljubljana, Slovenia, 1990. Rschr. Nat. Inst. Biology, Ljubljana, 1981-2000, head Plant Physiology Lab., 1995—; prof. U. Ljubljana, 1996—. Patentee in field; contbr. chpt. to book, articles to profl. jours. Recipient award Boris Kidric Found., 1989. Mem. Internat. Assn. Rsch. Plant Tissue Culture, Fed. European Soc. Plant Physiology, Phytochem. Soc. Europe. Avocations: playing synthesiser, skiing. Office: Nat Inst Biology, Vecna pot 111, 1000 Ljubljana Slovenia

ZELAC, RONALD EDWARD, physicist; b. Chgo., Jan. 22, 1941. BS in Engring. Physics summa cum laude, U. Ill., 1962, MS in Physics, 1964; MS in Environ. Health, U. Mich., 1965; PhD in Environ. Engring., U. Fla., 1970. Diplomate Am. Bd. Health Physics, Am. Bd. Medical Physics. Chief health physicist IIT Rsch. Inst., Chgo., 1965-68; radiation physicist Mercy Medical Ctr., Chgo., 1967-68; asst., assoc. prof. Temple U., Phila., 1970-92, radiation safety officer, 1970-91; adj. assoc. prof. U. Pa., Phila., 1980-86; assoc. vice provost Temple U., Phila., 1987-91; sr. physicist and mgr. tech. Landauer Inc., Glenwood, Ill., 1991-97; adj. prof. Northwestern U., Evanston, Ill., 1991-97, Temple U., 1992—, Purdue U., 1998—; health physicist, tech asst., sr. asst. to chmn. U.S. NRC, Rockville, Md., 1998—; cons. Wyeth-Ayerst Rsch., Radnor, Pa., Princeton, N.J., 1971-94, Presby. U. Pa. Med. Ctr., Phila., 1974-86, Mobile Rsch. Devel. Corp., Paulsboro, Princeton, 1977-95, Rhone-Poulenc Rorer Cen. Rsch., Ft. Washington, Collegeville, Pa., 1986-93. Editor: A Guide to Personnel Monitoring, 1993; contbr. articles to profl. jours. Fellow Phi Kappa Phi, 1962-63, U.S. AEC, 1964-65, USPHS, 1968-70. Mem. Health Physics Soc. (com. mem. 1978-79), Campus Safety Assn., Am. Assn. Physicists in Medicine (com. mem. 1995—), Am. Coll. Medical Physics, Sigma Xi (v.p., pres. 1984-88). Home and Office: 8150 New 2d St Elkins Park PA 19027-5773

ZELANO, LUIGI, economist, business consultant; b. Accadia, Puglia, Italy, Feb. 2, 1943; s. Pasquale Zelano and Teresa Nigro; m. Palma Savino, Dec. 30, 1978; children: Maria Teresa, Cesare. Degree in Econ., U. Pescara, Italy, 1970; Jurisprudence Degree, U. Naples, Italy, 1977; Hon. Cert., U. Seoul, 1993; Prof. Honoris Causa, U. Pro Deo, N.Y., 1993. Tax and tributary cons. Foggia, Italy, 1971-73; tchr. stats. Sociology Sch., Accadia, 1974-75; bus. cons. Foggia, 1974-76, 90-93, Foggia and Rome, 1977-89; judge cons. Tribunal Ct. of Justice, Ariano, Italy, 1980-82, Foggia, 1980-99; maths. tchr. Sch. A. Manzoni, Monteleone, Italy, 1970-71, Inst. D. Alighieri, Cerignola, Italy, 1972-75; banking tchr. Inst. Rosati, Foggia, 1976-82, law and econs. tchr. Inst. Giannone, Foggia, 1983-99; principi di Morale, Economia, Politica e Diritto, 1998; U. Foggia, 1999-2000. Author: Notes, 1984, Scripts, 1993, Quale Europa?, 1997. Councillor Town Coun., Accadia, 1973-78, Indsl. Devel. Area, Foggia, 1973-78, sec., Calaggio, 1973-78; councillor Directive Com. Christian Dem. Party, Accadia, 1983-88; mem. Italian Red Cross. Winner of Law and Econs. Tchrs.' Exam, Ministry of Edn., Rome, 1982, Banking, Acctng. Qualification Tchr., 1976; recipient Great Cross Merit, Italian-Am. Acad., Rome, 1985, Confirmatio Magna de Laboris Fide, Internat. Econ. Acad., Rome, 1980, Chevalier du Travail de L'Europe Unie, Internat. Bus. Corp., Rome, 1984; named Man of Yr., 1995. Mem. Internat. Biog. Assn. (Cambridge, Eng.), Am. Biog. Inst., Officer's Circle, Royal Honour Guard, Internat. Acad. Sci. Nature and Soc., Internat. Lions Club, Italy Mensa, Italian Cath. Worker's Assn. (pres. 1983-87), Tiberina Acad./Gold Legion Union, Union Circle, Ret. Union (sec. 1992-95, advisor 1996—), Knights of Teutonic Order, Knights of Malta (U.S. priorate), Noble Man, Societa Libera. Mem. Franciscan Order (councillor-sec.-coord. 1992-95). Mem. United Democratic Christian Party. Avocations: travel, chess, reading, music, sports. Office: Via Nicola Parisi # 20, Puglia 71100 Foggia Italy

ZELCER, ELANE, executive technology transfer; b. Melbourne, Victoria, Australia, June 15, 1950; d. Nathan and Rica Z. BSc (hons.), Monash U., Clayton, Australia, 1971, PhD, 1977, Grad. Diploma in Mktg., 1993. Info. officer Australian Tourist Commn., Melbourne, Australia, 1983-84; dist. sales mgr. Yellow Pages Australia, Melbourne, Australia, 1984-87; tech. svcs., tng. mgr. Miles Australia/Bayer Diagnostics, Melbourne, Australia, 1987-90; pvt. consulting practice Melbourne, 1990-92; bus. devel. mgr. Montech Pty Ltd., Melbourne, 1992-95, CEO, 1995-97; CEO Thrombogenix Pty. Ltd., 1998—; dir. Key Ctr. for Advanced Materials Tech, Melbourne, 1994-99, Ctr. for Bioprocess Tech., Melbourne, 1995-98; dir. Thrombogenix Pty Ltd., Melbourne, 1997-99. Contbr. over 14 articles to profl. jours. Recipient Nat. Heart Found. fellowship Australian Nat. Heart Found., 1981-83, Cameron Moors Watkins award David Syme Faculty of Bus, Monash U., 1991, Hoover award, 1993. Mem. Australian Biotech. Assn. (dir. 1998—), Australian Coun. Business Women, Licensing Execs. Soc., Internat. Women's Fedn. Commerce & Industry. Avocations: skiing, cycling, music, theatre, the arts. Office: 196 Williams Rd, Toorak VIC 3142, Australia

ZELDES, ILYA M., forensic scientist, lawyer; b. Baku, Azerbaidjan, Mar. 15, 1933; came to U.S., 1976; s. Michael B. and Pauline L. (Ainbinder) Z.; m. Emma S. Kryss, Nov. 5, 1957; 1 child, Irina Zeldes Rieser. JD, U. Azerbaidjan, Baku, 1955; PhD in Forensic Scis., U. Moscow, 1969. Expert-criminalist Med. Examiner's Bur., Baku, 1954-57; rsch. assoc. Criminalistics Lab., Moscow, 1958-62; sr. rsch. assoc. All-Union Sci. Rsch. Inst. Forensic Expertise, Moscow, 1962-75; chief forensic scientist S.D. Forensic Lab., Pierre, 1977-93; owner Forensic Scientist's Svcs., Pierre, 1977-93. Author: Physical-Technical Examination, 1968, Complex Examination, 1971, The Problems of Crime, 1981; contbr. numerous articles to profl. publs. in Australia, Austria, Bulgaria, Can., Eng., Germany, Holland, India, Ireland, Israel, Rep. of China, Russia, U.S. and USSR. Mem. Internat. Assn. Identification (rep. S.D. chpt. 1979-93, chmn. forensic lab. analysis subcom. 1991-98), Assn. Firearm and Tool Mark Examiners (emeritus). Avocation: travel. Home: 5735 Foxlake Dr Apt 1 Fort Myers FL 33917-5661

ZELENIN, KIRILL NIKOLAEVICH, chemist, educator; b. Leningrad, Russia, Aug. 25, 1938; s. Nikolai Jvanovich and Ekatherine Mihailovna (Turkova) Z.; m. Nathalya Lvovna Hahalina, Nov. 1, 1964 (div. Apr. 1971); m. Nathalya Dmitrievna Grigoryeva, Jan. 23, 1976; children: Alexander, Ekatherina. PhD, U. Leningrad, 1963, DSc, 1972. Asst. dept. chemistry Mil. Med. Acad., St. Petersburg, Russia, 1964-68, lectr. dept. chemistry, 1968-73, head dept. chemistry, 1973—; adv. bd. Zh. Obsch. Khim., Russia, 1995—, Targets in Heterocyclic Sys., Italy, 1997—. Author: Chemistry for Physicians, 1997; contbr. articles to profl. jours. Honored Scientist of Russian Fedn., 1991; recipient Gustav Vanag's medal Latvian Acad. Scis., 1991; Soros prof. Internat. Sci. Found., Moscow, 1995, 97, 98, 99. Mem. N.Y. Acad. Scis., Russian Acad. Natural Scis., Russian Chem. Soc. (head organic chemistry sect. of St. Petersburg divsn., Zinin's medal 1998), Russian Mil. Med. Acad. Avocations: fishing, tourism. Home: Maly prospekt 27 apt 5, 199161 Saint Petersburg Russia Office: Military Medical Acad, ulitsa Lebedeva 6, 199044 Saint Petersburg Russia

ZELENKA, JIŘÍ, agricultural educator; b. Ostrava, Czech Republic, Apr. 26, 1938; s. Jaromír and Helena (Schmidt) Z.; m. Maria Madron, Jan. 26, 1963; children: Jiří, Marie, Petr, Tomáš, Veronika. Degree in engring., U. Agr., Brno, Czech Republic, 1962, PhD, 1968. Lectr. Mendel U. Agr. and Forestry, Brno, 1962-89, prof. animal nutrition, 1990—, head dept. animal nutrition, 1990—, dean faculty agronomy, 1991-97, vice chancellor univ., 1997-2000. Cpl. Czechoslovac Army, 1962. Mem. World Poultry Sci. Assn. (mem. commn. on poultry nutrition), European Assn. for Animal Prodn. (commn. on animal nutrition), Czech Acad. Agrl. Sci. Roman Catholic. Office: Mendel U Agr and Forestry, Zemědělská 1, 613 00 Brno Czech Republic

ZELENKA, JOSEF, educator; b. Slany, Czech Republic, Jan. 29, 1960; s. Josef and Jirina (Tlusta) Z.; m. Lenka Kollerova, June 14, 1983; children: Martin, Tomas. Dipl.Phys., Charles U., Prague, Czech Republic, 1984; PhD, CVUT, Prague, Czech Republic, 1993. Rschr. Rsch. Inst. Electrotech. Ceramics, Hradec Kralove, Czech Republic, 1984-92; tchr. U. Edn., Hradec Kralove, Czech Republic, 1992—. Co-author: Antiviruses Protection, 1996, Computers in Tourism, 1998; patentee in field. Mem. Soc. Sustainable Life, Czech Soc. Quality, Czech Soc. Standardisation. Avocations: sports, chess, tourism, literature. Office: U Edn, Vita Nejedleho 573, 500 03 Hradec Kralove Czech Republic

ZELENY, MARJORIE PFEIFFER (MRS. CHARLES ELLINGSON ZELENY), psychologist; b. Balt., Mar. 31, 1924; d. Lloyd Armitage and Mable (Willian) Pfeiffer; m. Charles Ellingson Zeleny, Dec. 11, 1950 (dec.); children: Ann Douglas, Charles Timberlake. BA, U. Md., 1947; MS, U. Ill., 1949, postgrad., 1951-54. Vocat. counseling psychologist VA, Balt., 1947-48; asst. U. Ill., Urbana, 1948-50; rsch. assoc. Bur. Rsch., Urbana, 1952-53; chief psychologist dept. neurology and psychiatry Ohio State U. Coll. Medicine, Columbus, 1950-51; rsch. psychologist, cons. Tucson, Washington, 1954—. Mem. APA, AAAS, DAR, D.C. Psychol. Assn., Southeastern Psychol. Assn., Nat. Soc. Daus. Colonial Wars, Nat. Soc. Daus. Am. Colonists, Nat. Soc. Colonial Dames XVII Century, Nat. Soc. Descendants of Early Quakers, Nat. Soc. Dames of Ct. of Honor, Nat. Soc. U.S. Daus. of 1812, Sons and Daus. Colonial Bench and Bar, Washington Club (Washington), Johns Hopkins Club (Balt.), Mortar Bd., Delta Delta Delta, Sigma Delta Epsilon, Psi Chi, Sigma Tau Epsilon. Roman Catholic. Home: 6825 Wemberly Way Mc Lean VA 22101-1534

ZELEPUKIN, VALERI, hockey player; b. Vosdresensk, Russia, Sept. 17, 1968; married. Hockey player VOSK/USSR, 1984-87, 89-90, CSKA/USSR, 1987-88, SKA/USSR, 1987-88, KHIM/USSR, 1990-91, NJER/NHL, 1991-92, 93-97, 1997-98; hockey player EDMO/NHL, 1997-98, RUSS/OLYMP, 1997-98, PHIL/NHL, 1998—, Chgo. Blackhawks, 2000. Recipient ice hockey Silver medal Olympic Games, Nagano, Japan, 1998. Avocation: tennis. Office: Chgo Blackhawks United Ctr 1901 W Madison Chicago IL 60612*

ZELEZA, PAUL TIYAMBE, African studies educator; b. Harare, Zimbabwe, May 25, 1955; s. Abel Lamuel Zeleza and Agnes Zakunja; m. Cassandra Rachel Veney; 1 child, Natasha Thandile. BA, U. Malawi, Zomba, 1976; MA, U. London, 1978; PhD, Dalhousie U., 1982. Lectr. U. W.I., Kingston, Jamaica, 1982-84; sr. lectr. Kenyatta U., Nairobi, Kenya, 1984-90; prin., prof. Lady Eaton Coll., Trent U., Peterborough, Ont., Can., 1990-95; prof., dir. Ctr. for African Studies U. Ill., Champaign, 1995—; cons. Ontario Arts Coun., Can. Arts Coun., 1994-95, Blackside Inc., Boston, 1996-99. Author: Smouldering Charcoal, 1992, A Modern Economic History of Africa, 1993 9NOMA award 1994), The Joys of Exile: Stories, 1994; gen. editor Routledge Ency. on Africa, 1999—. Mem. shadow cabinet United Dem. Front, Blantyre, Malawi, 1994; mem. exec. com. Malawi Action Com., Toronto, 1992-94. Rockefeller fellow, Senegal, 1989-93; grantee Social Sci. and Humanities Rsch. Coun., Ottawa, Can., 1994-99. Mem. African Studies Assn., Can. Assn. of African Studies (exec. bd. 1991-95), Can. Artists Network: Black Artists in Action (exec. bd. 1992-97), Assn. of African Cmty. in Jamaica (pres. 1983-84). E-mail: Zeleza@uiuc.edu. Office: 210 Internat Studies Bldg 910 S 5th St Champaign IL 61820-6216

ZELEZNIKAR, ANTON PAVEL, electrotechnical engineer, researcher; b. Slovenjgradec, Slovenia, June 8, 1928; s. Vinko and Pavla (Rogina) Z.; m. Sofija Sonja Ribic, Sept. 1954; children: Irena, Darja. MS, U. Ljubljana, Slovenia, 1966, PhD, 1967. Head digital engring. dept. Inst. Jozef Stefan, Ljubljana, 1961-78, head elecs. divsn., 1968-78; head microcomputer lab. Iskra-Delta Computers, Ljubljana, 1980-82, advisor to gen. mgr., 1982-90; from asst. prof. to assoc. prof. U. Ljubljana, 1961-85, prof., 1985—; mem. adv. bd. Iskra Corp., 1982-90; mem. program com. IFIP Congress '71, 1969-71; invited spkr. Internat. Conf. Consciousness in Sci. and Philosophy, Ill., 1998. Author: On the Way to Information, 1990; editor-in-chief Informatica: Computing and Informatics, 1977—; contbr. articles to profl. jours., especially on informational theory, cybernetics, consciousness, communication. Chmn. Yugoslav com. info. processing Com. Electronic Automation & Nuc. Tech., 1966-72; rep. Internat. Fedn. Info. Processing, organizer Congress, 1971. Recipient Nat. Sci. Found. award, 1968, 80, 86, cert. appreciation for outstanding contbns. in field of informatics, Internat. Conf. on Consciousness in Sci. & Philosophy, 1998. Mem. N.Y. Acad. Scis., Internat. Acad. Scis. San Marino, Internat. Cybernetics Acad. S. Odobleja Lugano, Internat. Assn. Cybernetics, Slovene Assn. Informatika (hon. pres., founder). Roman

Catholic. Avocation: amateur radio. E-mail: s51em@lea.hamradio.si. Home: Volariceva Ulica 8, SI-1111 Ljubljana Slovenia

ZELEZNY, JAN, Olympic athlete; b. Mlada, Czech Republic, June 16, 1966. Winner Gold medal javelin Barcelona, 1992, Atlanta, 1996, Sydney, 2000. Set Olympic record, Seoul, 1988; established current world record for 323 ft. throw, Atlanta, 1996. Office: Cesky Atleticky Svaz, Mezi Stadiony PS 40, 160 17 Prague 6 Strahov, Czech Republic*

ZELLER, MICHAEL EUGENE, lawyer; b. Queens, N.Y., June 19, 1967; s. Hans Ludwig and Geri Ann (Schottenstein) Z. BA, Union Coll., 1989; JD, Temple Law Sch., 1992; LLM magna cum laude, U. Hamburg, Germany, 1994. Bar: N.Y. 1992, U.S. Dist. Ct. (so. and ea. dists.) N.Y. 1995, N.C. 1996. Fgn. intern Bryan Gonzalez Vargas y Gonzalez Baz, Mexico City, 1990; student law clk. Hon. Jane Cutler Greenspan, Phila., 1990-91; fgn. clk. DROSTE, Hamburg, 1991, fgn. assoc., translator, 1992-94; freelance translator Charlotte, N.C., 1995—; assoc. Internat. and Corp. Law Group of Moore & Van Allen PLLC, Charlotte, 1995—; owner, restaurateur Salad Garden, L.L.C. and Salad Garden Café, L.L.C., 1998-99; owner Nighttime Entertainment LLC, BGZ Properties, LLC; vol. atty. Children's Law Ctr. Mem. Charlotte World Affairs Coun., Charlotte Mayor's Internat. Cabinet; bd. dirs. Alemannia Soc., 1996-2000, Young Affiliates of Mint Mus., 1999-2000; bd. dirs., pres. Southgate Commons Homeowners Assn., 1998—. Recipient scholarship Fedn. German/Am. Clubs, 1987; named Vol. Lawyer of the Yr. Children's Law Ctr., 1998. Mem. ABA, N.Y. State Bar Assn., N.C. Bar Assn., Mecklenburg County Bar Assn., Gewerblicher Rechtsschutz und Urheberrecht e.V., European Am. Bus. Forum, Am. Translators Assn., Am. Immigration Lawyers Assn. Avocations: singing, theater, golf, fictional writing. Office: 100 N Tryon St Fl 47 Charlotte NC 28202-4003

ZELLES, LÁSZLÓ, biologist, researcher; b. Szombathely, Hungary, Jan. 31, 1938; arrived in The Netherlands, 1956; s. József and Mária (Hodászi) Z.; m. Frigga Steiner, Dec. 15, 1974; 1 child, Vajk Roland. Candidate, Utrecht (The Netherlands) U., 1960, DSc, 1963; PhD in Agriculture, Bonn (Germany) U., 1967. Rsch. staff I.V.T./Euratom, Wageningen, The Netherlands, 1963-64; asst. U. Bonn, 1967; rsch. asst. physiol. chemistry Marburg (Germany) U., 1967-69; rsch. staff for ecol. physic Inst. GSF, Hannover, Germany, 1969-82; rsch. staff Inst. for Ecol. Chemistry/GSF, Munich, 1982—, Inst. for Soil Ecology/GSF, Munich. Author: In Fertilization in Higher Plants, 1974, Current Advances in Plant Reproductive Biology, 1979, Methods in Applied Soil Microbiology and Biochemistry, 1995, Current Advances in Plant Reproductive Biology, 1979, The Significance and Regulation of Soil Biodiversity, 1995, Methods in Soil Biology, 1996, The Significance and Regulation of Soil Biodiversity, 1995; contbr. over 75 articles to profl. jours. and conf. procs. Home: Josef-Priller-Str 19, D-86159 Augsburg Germany Office: GSF-Nat Rsch Ctr Environ, Ingolstadter Landstr 1, D-85764 Neuherberg Germany

ZELLMER, DAVID BRUCE, minister; b. Mpls., Dec. 21, 1953; s. Bruce Edward and Ila Corrine (Johnson) Z.; m. LaDonna Jean Graves, Mar. 6, 1976; children: Christina, Joshua, Sarah, Michael. BS in Psychology, Southwestern Okla. State U., 1977; MDiv, Luther-Northwestern Theol Sem., 1981. Ordained to ministry Am. Luth. Ch., 1981. Pastor, chaplain Scandinavia/Bethany Luth. Parish and Bethesda Nursing Home, Aberdeen, S.D., 1981-85; pastor Trinity Luth. Ch., Mitchell, S.D., 1085—. sr. pastor, Luthran Meml. Ch., 1993—. Office: Lutheran Meml Ch 320 E Prospect Ave Pierre SD 57501-2533

ZELLNER, KENNETH KERMIT, elementary education educator; b. Allentown, Pa., Sept. 4, 1945; s. Mellis Myron and Thelma Amanda (Bortz) Z.; m. Jean Elizabeth Welsh, June 24, 1978; children: Todd Benjamin, Amanda Elizabeth. BS, Kutztown U., 1967, MEd, 1971. Cert. elementary and secondary edn., environ. edn., supervision elementary edn., Pa. Tchr. Parkland Sch. Dist., Allentown, 1967—, environ. lab. cons., 1980-97; cooperating tchr. East Stroudsburg (Pa.) U., 1973-97, Lehigh U., Bethlehem, Pa., 1992-94, sci. camp instr. SMART Ctr., 1993-94; faculty mentor Pa. Gov.'s Sch. of Excellence for Teaching Pa. Dept. Edn., Harrisburg, 1992. Contbr. articles to profl. jours. Mem. little Lehigh watershed curriculum task force Wildlands Conservancy, Emmaus, Pa., 1984-97; mem. newspapers in edn. adv. coun. Allentown Morning Call, 1988-89. Recipient Presdl. Award for Excellence in Sci. and Math. Teaching NSF, 1992, Regional Catalyst award for Excellence in Sci. Teaching Chem. Manufacturers Assn., 1994, Nat. Educators award Milken Family Found., 1994, Congrl. Citation for Outstanding Sci. Teaching Pa. Ho. of Reps., 1994. Mem. Pa. Sci. Tchrs. Assn., Nat. Sci. Tchrs. Assn., Coun. for Elem. Sci. Internat., Assn. Presdl. Awardees in Sci. Teaching, Soc. Elem. Presdl. Awardees, Masons (worshipful master 1985). Republican. Lutheran. Avocations: woodworking, antique and classic cars, snow skiing. Home: 9022 Reservoir Rd Germansville PA 18053-2731 Office: Parkland Adminstrn Bldg 1210 Springhouse Rd Allentown PA 18104-2119

ZELMER, A.C. LYNN, computing educator; b. Calgary, Alta., Can., Mar. 19, 1943; arrived in Australia, 1989; s. Hubert Adam and Winona Ella (May) Z.; m. Amy Mary Elliott; 1 child, Jennifer Lynne. BEd, U. Alta., Calgary, 1965; MS, Stout State U., 1969; PhD, U. Queensland, 1994. Tchr. Calgary Sch. Bd., 1964-68; asst. prof. ednl. media U. Alta., Edmonton, 1968-73; cons. Internat. Comm. Inst., Edmonton, 1973-88; sr. lectr., lectr. Ctrl. Queensland U., Rockhampton, 1989-99, hon. sr. fellow, 2000—. Author: Community Media Handbook, 1973, 1979; co-author: Organising Academic Conferences, 1991; editor: Computer Basics for Health Practitioners, 1993, 2d edit., 1996; found. editor: Camera Canada, 1969-70; contbr. articles to profl. jours. Mem. Assn. Computer Machinery, Health Informatics Soc. Australia (nat. info. mgr.), Australian Soc. for Computers in Learning in Tertiary Edn. Avocations: model railroading, photography. Office: Faculty Info Comm, Ctrl Queensland Univ, Rockhampton 4702, Australia

ZELNIK, JOSEPH, bank executive, lecturer; b. Haifa, Israel, May 19, 1948; s. Yzhak and Rachel (Neuman) Z.; m. Annette Meghira, Dec. 29, 1949; children: Jonathan, Yair, Yael, Yaron. BSc in Econs. and Mgmt., Technion, Israel, 1973. Dep. mgr. city br. Bank Hapoalim, London, 1980-85; mgr. fin. and ins. dept. Elbit Ltd., Haifa, 1985-91; mgr. main br. Ivestec Clali Bank, Tel Aviv, 1991—; lectr. Technion, Haifa, 1986-94, Galilee Coll., Tivon, Israel, 1986—. Home: 25 Wingate St, 43587 Raanana Israel Office: Israel Gen Bank, 38 Rothschild Blvd, Tel Aviv Israel

ŽEMAITIS, ALGIRDAS JONAS ALEKSIS, diplomat; b. Salniskiai Manor, Lithuania; s. Vincentas Petras and Bronislava (Rusecki-Ruseckas) Z. Prince de Druck; m. Vanda Jadvyga Kibort-Kybartas, Apr. 5, 1956; children: Alexis-Pius-Kestutis, Maria-Birute, Rita-Vilia, Paulus-Algirdas, Julia-Dalia. Grad. student, U. Bonn., Fed. Republic Germany, 1954-56; BA (hon.), Balliol Coll. Oxford (Eng.) U., 1959; MA, 1964. V.p. Union-Chretienne-Democrat d'Europe Cen. S/J, Paris, 1955-59; asst. to pres., sr. economist Borg-Warner Internat. Corp., Chgo., 1959-61; dir. gen. Market facts ROC Internat., Chgo., 1962-63; internat. economist Sears, Roebuck & Co., Chgo., 1963-66; sr. internat. trade officer U.S. Dept. State, Washington, 1966-68; functionary FAO UN, Rome, 1968-83 ; rep. So. Sudan Juba, 1983-86; functionary Rome, 1986-92; rep. Pres. of Lithuania to Grand Master of Sovereign Order Malta, Rome, 1991-93; amb., permanent rep. Lithuania to FAO, 1992-99; amb., advisor agr. embassy Lithuania to Italy, 2000—. Del. Internat. Christian Dem. Movement, Europe and Lat. Am., 1955-66. Decorated knight grand comdr. Equestrian Order Holy Sepulchre of Jerusalem. Mem. various profl. and acad. socs. Home: Adomo Jakšto gatve 8-3, 2600 Vilnius Lithuania Office: Villa Lithuania, Piazza Asti 25, 00189 Rome Italy

ZEMANEK, ALICJA, historian of botany, researcher; b. Bielsko-Biata, Poland, Aug. 2, 1949; d. Franciszek and Józefa (Wsiotkowska) Piekietko; m. Bogdan Zemanek, July 30, 1981. MSc, Jagiellonian U., Poland, 1972, PhD, 1977, DSc, 1990. Asst. Jagiellonian U., 1972-77, lectr., 1977-90, assoc. prof., 1990-00, prof., 2000—. Author: Historia Ogrodu Botanicznego UJ, 1983, Historia Botaniki, 1989, (poetry) Modlitwa do trczy, 1997; co-editor: Studies on the History of Botanical Gardens and Arboreta in Poland, 1993, Studies in Renaissance Botany, 1998. Mem. Polish Bot. Soc. (head history of botany sect. 1992), Brit. Soc. for History of Sci., Soc. History Natural History. Roman Catholic. Avocations: poetry, parapsychology. E-mail: zemaneka@ib.uj.edu.pl. Home: Reymonta 42/2, 30-073 Cracow Poland Office: Bot Garden/Jagiellonian UJ, Kopernika 27, 31-501 Cracow Poland

ZEMANEK, BOGDAN JÓZEF, botanist, educator, researcher; b. Lubawka, Poland, Jan. 14, 1947; s. Jerzy and Ewa (Rzepa) Z.; m. Alicja Piekietko, July 30, 1981. MSc, Jagiellonian U., Cracow, Poland, 1970, PhD, 1978, DSc, 1991. Asst. Jagiellonian U., Cracow, 1970-78, lectr., 1978-91, assoc. prof., 1991—, dir. Botanic Garden, 1991—. Co-editor: Studies on the History of Botanical Gardens and Arboreta in Poland, 1993; editor-in-chief Botanical News jour.; contbr. articles to profl. jours. Mem. Polish Botanical Soc. Roman Catholic. Avocations: classical music, opera, military technology. E-mail: zemanekb@ib.uj.edu.pl. Home: Reymonta 42/2, 30-073 Cracow Poland Office: Jagiellonian U Botanic Gard, Kopernika 27, 31-501 Cracow Poland

ZEMANEK, JAMES EDWARD, JR., marketing educator; b. Alton, Ill., June 4, 1963; s. James Edward Zemanek and Wendy Pamela Zemanek, Nov. 23, 1999; children: Drake, Kyler. BBA, Tex. A&M U., 1985, MS in Mktg., 1987, PhD in Mktg., 1992. Sales engr. Interconnect Comm. Co., Houston, 1985-86; grad. rsch. asst. Dept. Mktg. Coll. Bus. Adminstrn. Tex. A&M U., College Station, 1987-89, undergrad. advisor Dept. Mktg., 1987-91, grad. teaching asst. Dept. Mktg., 1986-91, asst. prof. indsl. distbn. program Dept. Engrng. Tech., 1991-94, dir. undergrad. edn. indsl. distbn. program, 1992-94; asst. prof. East Carolina U., Greenville, N.C., 1994-99, assoc. prof., 1999—; pres., CEO Carolina Webworks, Inc., Greenville, 1998—; founder, advisor Alpha chpt. Sigma Delta, Distbn. Mgmt. Honor Soc., 1992—; advisor, sponsor Profl. Assn. Indsl. Distributors, 1991—; dept. United Way fundraising com. chmn., 1993, student computing facility com. chmn., 1991—, social com. chmn., 1993, minority scholarship com. mem., 1991—, indsl. distbn. scholarship com. mem., 1991—; cons. Tex. A&M U., College Station, 1991-94. Author: (with others) Wholesale Distribution Channels, 1994; author refereed jours.. Co-chmn. Personnel Com., Greenville, N.C., 1995—; chmn. United Way, Texas A&M U., 1993, Sch. of Bus., Greenville, 1994. Recipient fellowship Grad. Coll. Bus., 1987-88; named Outstanding Teaching Asst. in Coll. Bus. Adminstrn. for Tex. A&M chpt. Alpha Kappa Psi, 1987-88; rsch. grant 3M, 1992, 1993 Mfg., 1993-94. Mem. Am. Mktg. Assn. (advisor 1994—), So. Mktg. Assn., Beta Gamma Sigma. Republican. Roman Catholic. E-mail: zemanekj@mail.ecu.edu. Home: 2017 Cherry Stone Ln Greenville NC 27858-9483

ZEMANEK, KARL, law educator, consultant; b. Vienna, Austria, Nov. 11, 1929; s. Franz and Josefa (Bambule) Z.; m. Christine Conrath, Feb. 26, 1960; children: Barbara, Therese. LLD, U. Vienna, 1952. Rsch. asst. U. of the Saar, Saarbrucken, 1954-56; lectr. U. Vienna, Austria, 1957-58, assoc. prof., 1958-64, prof., 1964-98, prof. emeritus, 1998—; cons. Austrian Ministry for Fgn. Affairs. Author: 10 books and more than 140 articles in scholarly jours. Decorated Knight Cmmdr. with Star Order of St. Sylvester, Holy See, 1978, Grand Officer Pro Merito Melitensi Order of Malta, 1978, Cmdr. (Gold) Austrian Order of Merit, 1986. Mem. Inst. de Droit Internat., Internat. Acad. Astronautics. Avocations: collector modern paintings and etchings. Home: Mariannengasse 28, 1090 Vienna Austria Office: Inst Internat Law & Rels, Universitätsstr 2, 1090 Vienna Austria

ZEMANN, JOSEF, mineralogy educator; b. Vienna, Austria, May 25, 1923; s. Josef and Maria (Semler) Z.; m. Anna Aloisia Hedlik, Oct. 20, 1951; 1 child, Josef Viktor. PhD, U. Vienna, 1946, lic. pvt. doc., 1951. Prof. mineralogy U. Göttingen, Fed. Republic Germany, 1953-67; asst. U. Vienna, 1946-52, prof., 1967-89, prof. emeritus, 1989—. Author: Kristalichemie, 1966. Recipient Abraham Gottlob Werner medal German Mineral. Soc., 1984, silver medal U. Brno, 1992, gold medal sci U. Bratislava, 1993, Emanuel Boricky medal U. Praha, 1995. Fellow Mineral Soc. Am. (hon.); mem. Deutsche Acad. Naturforscher Leopoldina, Austrian Acad. Scis. (Tschermak Seysenegg prize 1974, Erwin Schroedinger prize 1984), Acad. Scis. Goettingen, Mediterranean Acad. Sci., Hungarian Acad. Scis. (hon.), Croatian Acad. Scis. and Arts, Polish Acad. Scis. & Art, Mineral Soc. Austria (hon.), Mineral Soc. Soviet Union (hon.), Mineral Soc. Poland (hon.), Mineral Soc. Germany (hon.), Mineral Soc. Romania (hon.). Home: Weinberggasse 67/4/46, A-1190 Vienna Austria Office: U Vienna Geozentrum, Althanstrasse 14, A-1090 Vienna Austria

ZEMEL, NORMAN PAUL, orthopedic surgeon; b. Bklyn., Oct. 15, 1939; s. Nathan M. and Mary (Sklarevsky) Z.; m. Mary P. Kane. BSN, Rutgers U., 1961; MD, Thomas Jefferson Med. Sch., 1965. Bd. cert. orthopaedic surgery with added qualification in hand surgery Am. Bd. Orthopaedic Surgery. Orthopaedic surgery resident Northwestern U., Chgo., 1969-73; hand surgery fellow Boyes Hand Fellowship, L.A., 1973-74; hand surgery physician Boyes, Stark, Ashworth, L.A., 1974-88, Kerlan-Jobe Orthopaedic Clinic, Inglewood, Calif., 1989—; clin. assoc. prof. dept. orthopaedics U. So. Calif. Sch. Medicine, L.A., 1977—. Contbr. chpts. to books and articles to profl. jours. Lt. USNR, 1966-68, Vietnam. Mem. ACS, Am. Acad. Orthopaedic Surgery (bd. councilors), Am. Soc. for Surgery of the Hand, Western Orthopaedic Assn. (pres. L.A. chpt. 1993-94), Soc. Internat. de Orthopedique et de Traumatologie. Avocations: walking, reading, photography. Office: Kerlan Jobe Orthop Clinic 6801 Park Ter Los Angeles CA 90045-1543

ZEMLIAK, ALEXANDER MIKHAILOVICH, electronics specialist, educator; b. Vladivostok, Russia, USSR, Oct. 21, 1948; s. Mikhail and Galina (Evdokimova) Z.; m. Natalia Georgievna Kopylevich, Aug. 14, 1980; 1 child: Kirill. MS, Poly. Inst., Kiev, Ukraine, 1972, PhD, 1976, MS (hon.), 1972; MS, State U., Kiev, Ukraine, 1975; diploma (hon.), Inst. of Tech., Ecatepec, Mex., 1997. Cert. radio engr. Rschr. Poly. Inst., Kiev, 1972-75, asst. prof., 1975-83, assoc. prof., 1983-86, sr. rschr., 1985-94, prof., 1987-94; prof. Autonomous U., Puebla, Mex., 1994—; vis. prof. Nat. Inst. of Astrophysics, Optics and Electronics, Puebla, 1995, Inst. of Tech., Mexico City, 1997, Am. U., Puebla, 1997-98; vis. rschr. Electrotechnic Inst., Leningrad, Russia, 1984. Patentee in field (prize 1991); contbr. articles to profl. jours. Recipient state medal Supreme Soviet of USSR, Moscow, 1983, grant Mex. Nat. Coun. Sci. and Tech., 1999; hon. chair Mexican Nat. Coun. of Scis. and Tech., Mexico City, 1994. Mem. IEEE (sr.), Ukrainian Sci.-Tech. Soc. (hon. diploma 1980), Mexican Nat. System of Investigators, N.Y. Acad. of Scis. Avocations: music, literature, sports. Home: Rio Lerma 5933 Col San Manu, 72570 Puebla Puebla, Mexico Office: Autonomous U, Ciudad Univ Dept Physics, 72570 Puebla Puebla, Mexico

ZEMSKOV, ANDREI ILYCH, library director; b. Moscow, Jan. 2, 1939; s. Ilya Fedorovich and Olga Leonidovna Z.; m. Irina Sergeevna, Sept. 7, 1963; 1 child, Dmitri Andreevich. PhD, Moscow Inst. Tech. Physics, 1962. From rschr. to sr. rschr. Atomic Energy Kurchatov Inst., Moscow, 1958-81; supr. large scale program plasma physics, high energy physic CPSU, Moscow, 1981-83, 1st sec., 1983-90; dir. Russian Nat. Pub. Libr., Moscow, 1990—; Contbr. articles to profl. jours. Contbr. articles to profl. jours. Mem. Russian Libr. Assn., Acad. Info., Internat. Assn. Rsch. and Sci. Tech. Librs., Internat. Fedn. Libr. Assns. and Instns., Internat. Assn. Technol. Univ. Librs. Avocation: walking. Home: 16 Koneva Str ap 69, 123060 Moscow Russia Office: Russian Nat Pub Libr, 12 Kuznetsky most, 103919 Moscow Russia

ZEMSKOVA, SVETLANA MIKHAILOVNA, chemist, researcher; b. Novosibirsk, Russia, Mar. 29, 1957; d. Mikhail Antonovich and Nina Dmitrievna (Arendarskaya) Selitsky; m. Anatoly Stanislavovich Zemskov, May 25, 1980 (div. Feb. 1993); 1 child, Leonid. BS, St. Petersburg State U., Russia, 1977; MS, St. Petersburg State U., 1979; PhD, Inst. Inorganic Chemistry, Novosibirsk, 1994. Sr. lab. asst. Inst. Inorganic Chemistry, Novosibirsk, 1979-85, rsch. engr., 1985-87, jr. rschr., 1987-91, rschr., 1991-96, sr. rschr., 1996-98; NSF-NATO fellow Oak Ridge (Tenn.) Nat. Lab., 1998—; student rsch. supr. Inst. Inorganic Chemistry, Novosibirsk, 1996-98; tchg. asst. Novosibirsk State U., 1996-98. Patentee in field. Grantee Internat. Assn. for the Promotion of Cooperation with Scientists from the Ind. States of the Former Soviet Union, Brussels, Belgium, 1996, Dept. High Edn. Russian, Novosibirsk, 1997; fellow NSF-NATO, Arlington, Va., 1998. Mem. Russian Mendeleev's Soc., Electrochem. Soc. Office: Oak Ridge Nat Lab PO Box 2008 1 Bethel Valley Rd Oak Ridge TN 37831-6063

ZEMTSOV, ALEXANDER, dermatology and biochemistry educator, inventor; b. Baku, USSR, Nov. 9, 1959; came to U.S., 1977; s. Ilya and Marya (Dubinsky) Z.; m. Tali Giveon, Oct. 17, 1987; children: Raquel Karen, Gregory Ethan. BA magna cum laude, Temple U., 1981; MSc, U. Pa., 1982; MD with honors, NYU, 1986. Diplomate Am. Bd. Dermatology. Intern, then resident Cleve. Clinic Hosp. Found., 1989-90; assoc. prof. biochemistry and molecular biology Ind. U. Sch. Medicine, Muncie, 1995—. Editor Skin Rsch. and Tech. Jour.; contbr. articles to profl. jours. and books; patentee in field. Recipient Am. Soc. Dermatol. Surgery award, 1989; Cert. Appreciation, Ohio Dermatol. Soc., 1990. Fellow Am. Acad. Dermatology, Am. Contact Dermatitis Soc.; mem. Soc. Magnetic Resonance, Internat. Soc. for Digital Imaging of Skin (pres.), Kiwanis. Jewish. Avocations: stamp collecting, hiking, swimming. Office: University Dermatology Ctr 2525 W University Ave Ste 402 Muncie IN 47303-3409

ŽEMVA, BORIS, chemistry educator, researcher; b. Ljubljana, Slovenia, June 8, 1940; s. Franc and Valentina (Lenarčič) Ž.; m. Majda Marija Brus, Aug. 6, 1966; children: Nataša, Barbara. BSc in Chemistry, U. Ljubljana, 1964, MSc in Chemistry, 1968, PhD in Chemistry, 1971; BA in Econs., U. Maribor, Slovenia, 1983. Postdoctoral fellow U. Calif., Berkeley, 1972-73; cons. Lawrence Berkeley Lab., 1978, sr. rschr., 1992; head dept. Jožef Stefan Inst., Ljubljana, 1983—, rsch. councillor, 1989—; dep. dir. U. Ljubljana, 1996—, prof. chemistry, 1985—; vis. Miller rsch. prof. Miller Inst. for Basic Rsch. in Sci., Berkeley, 1993; mem. steering com. European and internat. fluorine symposia, 1983—; mem. mgmt. com. for cost projects Action D-6, 1993-97; chmn. 11th European Symposium on Fluorine Chemistry, Bled, Slovenia, 1995. Contbg. author: Ency. of Inorganic Chemistry, 1994; guest editor European Jour. Solid State and Inorganic Chemistry, 1991, 96, mem. sci. com., 1988—; contbr. articles to sci. jours.; patentee on multilayer, fluorine-containing polymeric material (in 43 countries). Recipient Boris Kidrič award Slovenian Sci. Cmty., 1989, Humboldt Rsch. award, 1999; Fulbright travel grantee U. Calif., 1972, 78. Mem. Engrng. Acad. Slovenia (exec. com. 1996—), N.Y. Acad. Scis. Avocations: classical music, skiing, mountain climbing. Home: Pod Kostanji 42, 1000 Ljubljana Slovenia Office: Jožef Stefan Inst, Jamova 39, 1000 Ljubljana Slovenia

ZENEA, ARECIA CLARA, allergist, consultant; b. Havana, Cuba, Oct. 12, 1951; d. Carlos and Olga (Capote) Z.; m. Omar Alberto Piñero, Oct. 19, 1960. MD, High Inst., La Habana, Cuba, 1977; Allergy Splty., William Soler Hosp., La Habana, Cuba, 1985; 2nd Degree Splty. in Allergy, William Soler Hosp., 1997. Dir. Antonio Maceo Clinic, Cacocum, Cuba, 1977-80; chief pediatric residents William Soler Hosp., La Habana, Cuba, 1980-82, chief allergy residents, 1982-85, vice head allergy dept., 1986—, prof. allergy, 1998; med. dir. Rehab. Asthmatic Ctr., La Habana, Cuba, 1986—; allergy med. dir. Jose Martí Pediatric Hosp., La Habana, Cuba, 1986—; allergy cons. William Soler Hosp., La Habana, 1985—, prof., 1986—. Contbr. articles to profl. jours. Recipient recognition for med. assistance of the Chernobil Nuclear Accident, 1990-95, recognition for the Ednl. Program of the Asthmatic Rehab., 1991. Mem. Nat. Asthma Commn., Cuban Allergy Soc., Cuban Pediatric Soc., Am. Acad. Allergy, Asthma and Immunology (corr. mem. 2000). Avocations: poetry, writer, classical music. Home: San Antonio # 21707, entre Alamo y Ponce, Rpto Ponce, Arroyo Naranjo Habana 19, Cuba Office: William Soler Hosp, Doble Via de San Francisco, 10800 Altahabana Cuba

ZENG, EDDY YONGPING, chemist; b. Guangzhou, China, Jan. 11, 1960; came to U.S., 1986; s. Li and Qiuzhen (Zhou) Z.; m. Angela Minhui Xie, Dec. 30, 1986 (div. Jan. 1993); m. Jun Zeng, Aug. 27, 1999. BS, U. Sci. and Tech. of China, Heifei, 1982; MS, Zhongshan U., Guangzhou, China, 1985; MA, U. So. Calif., L.A., 1989, PhD, 1991. Rsch./tchg. asst. dept. chemistry U. So. Calif., L.A., 1986-90; chemist Enviropro, Inc., Chatsworth, Calif., 1990-92; prin. scientist So. Calif. Coastal Water Rsch. Project, Westminster, 1992—; lectr. dept. chemistry Zhongshen U., 1985-86; adj. prof. State Key Lab. of Organic Geochemistry, Guangzhou, 1998—. Contbr. articles to profl. jours. Mem. Am. Chem. Soc., So. Calif. Environ. Chemist Soc. (pres. 1997-98), Soc. of Environ. Texicology and Chemistry (bd. dirs. So. Calif. chpt. 1999—). Home: 7 Deer Crk Irvine CA 92604-3058 Office: So Calif Coastal Water Rsch Project 7171 Fenwick Ln Westminster CA 92683-5218

ZENG, HONG, systems engineer, researcher; b. Changchun, Jilin, China, Feb. 20, 1958; arrived in France, 1990; s. Peiwei Zeng and Shige Chen; m. Yuzhi Guo, Jan. 14, 1983 (div.); 1 child, Yu. B in Elec. Engring., Changchun Coll. Geology; M in Elec. Engring., U. Pierre & Marie Curie, Paris, 1991, D in Physics, 1996. Asst. engr. Hangzhou (China) Applied Acoustics Rsch. Inst., 1982-85, rsch. engr., dir. magnetic signal processing sect., 1985-90; rsch. engr. French Nat. Sci. Rsch. Ctr., Paris, 1990-95; sys. engr. O1dB Co., Lyon, France, 1995-98; sr. software engr., project team leader ATI Technologies, Inc., Toronto, ON, Canada, 1998—. Contbr. articles to profl. jours.; inventor in field. Recipient Sci. and Tech. award China Shipbuilding Industry Corp., Beijing, 1989. Mem. IEEE. Home: 815 Grandview Way, Toronto, ON Canada M2N 6V5 Office: ATI Technologies Inc, 75 Tiverton Ct, Unionville, ON Canada L3R 9S3

ZENG, HUAIREN, physicist, neuroscientist; b. Huarong, China, Feb. 15, 1965; s. Yaoguang Zeng and Wangzeng Xiao; m. Zhi Wang. BS, Chinese Aerospace Ministry, Beijing, 1987; PhD, Kent State U., 1999. Rsch. scientist Chinese Aerospace Ministry, Beijing, 1990-94; postdoctoral staff Yale U., New Haven, 1999—. E-mail: zeng@boreas.med.yale.edu. Home: 544 Whitney Ave Apt 3 New Haven CT 06511-2227

ZENG, QIN, astrophysicist; b. Shanghai, China, Sept. 1, 1938; s. Xian-Yu and Min (Wang) Z.; m. Yuan Miao; children: Miao Zong, Miao Yanti. Grad., Jilin U., Chang Chun, China, 1960, 64. Tchg. asst. Jilin U., 1964-76; engr. Factory of Drilling and Detecting Tools, Wuxi, China, 1977-78; engr. Purple Mountain Obs., Academia Sinica, Nanjing, China, 1978-85, assoc. prof., 1986-92, prof., 1993—; vis. scholar MPI Radioastronomy, Bonn, Germany, 1982-84, 93, 96; fgn. prof. Inst. Space and Astronautical Sci., Kanagawa, Japan, 1988-89. Contbr. articles to profl. jours. Mem. Chinese Atomic and Molecular Physics Soc., Chinese Astronomy Soc., Pub. Lab. Radio Astronomy. Office: Purple Mountain Obs, 2 W Beijing Rd, Nanjing 210008, China

ZENG, QING BING, chemistry educator; b. Changsha, Hunan, China, Dec. 5, 1973; d. Hui Gao and Han Bing (Wen) Z. B Engring., Nat. U. Def. Tech., China, 1993, MS, 1996; PhD, Zhongshan U., China, 1998. Lectr. dept. chemistry 1st Med. U. of PLA, Guangzhou, China, 1996—. Contbr. articles to profl. jours. Avocations: music, tennis, swimming. E-mail: zengqingbing@163.net. Home: 1st Med U PLA, Dept Chemistry, 510515 Guangzhou China

ZENG, QINGCHUAN, research civil engineer, educator; b. Chengdu, Sichuan, China, July 15, 1961; arrived in Australia, 1995; s. Guangliang and Yusheng (Liu) Z. BEng, Sichuan Inst. Tech., Chengdu, 1982; MEng, Huazhong U. Sci. and Tech., Wuhan, China, 1986, PhD, 1993. Engr. Sichuan Bur. Hydraulic and Electric Power Engring., Chengdu, 1982-83; asst. rschr. Huazhong U. Sci. and Tech., 1983-88, lectr., 1988-95; rsch. fellow U. Queensland, Brisbane, Australia, 1995—. Contbr. articles to profl. jours. Mem. Internat. Assn. for Hydraulic Rsch., Chinsese Soc. Hydroelectric Engring. Office: PO Box 6085, St Lucia Queensland 4067, Australia

ZENG, QING-CUN, meteorologist, educator; b. Yang-jiang, Guangdong, China, May 4, 1935; s. Ming-yao; m. Pei-sheng Lu, 1961; 1 child, Xiao-dong. BSc, Peking U., Beijing, China, 1956; PhD, Russian Acad. Sci., Moscow, 1961. Rsch. scientist Inst. Geophysics and Meteorology Chinese Acad. Scis., Beijing, 1961-65, rsch. scientist, prof. Inst. Atmospheric Physics, 1966—, dir. Inst. Atmospheric Physics, 1984-93, dir. State Key Lab. Numerical Modeling for Atmospheric Sci./Geophysics al Fluid Dynamics, 1985-93; dir. Internat. Ctr. Climate and Environ. Scis. IAP, Beijing, 1991—; vis. sr. scientist Princeton (N.J.) U., 1981-82; vice chmn. Com. of Acad. Degree, Chinese Acad. Sci., 1987-96; mem. WMO/ICSU Joint Sci. Com. for World Climate Programme, 1993-96. Author: Principles of Infrared Sounding of the Atmosphere, 1974, Physical-Mathematical Basis for Numerical Weather Prediction, vol. 1, 1979. Fellow Third World Acad. Sci.; mem. Chinese Acad. Scis. (academician), Russian Acad. Scis. (fgn. mem.), China Assn. for Sci. and Tech. (v.p. 1996—). Office: Inst Atmospheric Physics, Qi Jia Huo Zi, Beijing 100029, China

ZENG, XINWU, physics educator, researcher; b. Changsha, Hunan, China, Mar. 9, 1963. BSc, Nat. U. Def. Tech., China, 1983, MSc, 1986; PhD, Edinburgh U., 1994. Lectr. Changsha Inst. Tech., China, 1986-90; assoc. prof. Nat. U. Def. Tech., China, 1995-97, prof., 1997—. Author: Shear-Wave VSP Data Processing for Anisotrophy, 1997; editor: Proceeding of the 6th Nat. Conf. on Explosion Mechanics, 1999; contbr. articles to profl. jours. Fellow Royal Astronomical Soc.; mem. Soc. Exploration Geophysicists, European Assn. Geoscientists and Engrs. Office: Nat U Def Tech, Dept Applied Physics, 410073 Changsha China

ZENG, YAN JUN, biomechanics educator; b. Rui-an, Zhejiang, China, Mar. 14, 1935; s. Mian and Xuan Mo (Lin) Z.; m. Yan Hui Chang; children: Dai, Lu. Grad., Tsinghua U., Beijing, 1957. Rsch. asst. Acad. Sci., Beijing, 1957-61; vis. prof. U. Calif., San Diego, 1981-84; lectr., then assoc. prof. Beijing Poly. Inst., 1961-81, prof., 1984—; hon. prof. Capital U. Med. Sci., Beijing, 1995—; bd. dirs. Biomechanics and Med. Info. Inst., Beijing. Author: (with Meng He) Biomechanics of Orthopaedics, 1991, (with Yang Gui Tong) Medical Biomechanics, 1995; also articles. Recipient award Chinese Nat. Sci. Conf., 1978, Sci. Tech. Progress award Beijing Municipality Govt., 1998. Fellow Chinese Nat. Biomechanics Com. Coun., Internat. Soc. Biorheology; mem. N.Y. Acad. Scis. Avocations: reading, cooking, travel, chess, swimming. E-mail: yjzeng@bpju.edu.cn. Home: Chaoyang Dist, Mo Fang Nan Li 28th Bldg, 1-201 Beijing 100021, China Office: Beijing Poly U Biomed E Ctr, 100 Ping Le Yuan, Chaoyang Beijing 100022, China

ZENG, YUNBO, mathematics educator; b. Fuzhou, China, Aug. 26, 1944; s. Yinsheng and Churu (Liu) Z.; m. Shanhui Wang, Jan. 27, 1972; 1 child, Xiaomu. Grad., U. Sci. & Tech. China, 1967. Technician Elec. Inst., Shichuan, 1967-78; lectr. U. Sci. & Tech., Hefei, Anhui, 1978-84; assoc. prof. U. Sci. & Tech. China, Hefei, Anhui, 1987-93, prof., 1993-94; prof. Tsinghua U., Beijing, 1994—; vis. scholar U. Ariz., Tucson, 1984-87; vis. prof. Linkoping U., Sweden, 1993-94, U. Turku, Finland, 1995, Sophia U. Japan, 1997, City U. Hong Kong, 1998, 2000. Contbr. articles to profl. jours. Mem. Chinese Math. Soc., Am. Math. Soc. Avocations: music, reading, jogging. Office: Tsinghua U, Dept Applied Math, Beijing 100084, China

ZENG, ZUOTAO, research scientist; b. Nanning, Guanxi, People's Republic of China, Sept. 2, 1963; s. Fuxian and Wenxi Z. BS, Wuhan (China) U., 1984; MS, Chinese Acad. Sci., Changchun, 1989; PhD, Rutgers U., 2000. Lectr. South-Ctrl. U. Nationalities, Wuhan, China, 1984-86; rsch. asst. Chinese Acad. Sci., Changchun, 1989-95; rsch. scientist Argonne Nat. Lab., Chgo., 2000—. Contbr. articles to profl. jours. Mem. AAAS, Materials Rsch. Soc. E-mail: zeng@anl.gov. Office: Argonne Nat Lab 9700 S Cass Ave Argonne IL 60439-4803

ZENGIL, ALI HÜSEYIN, plastic company executive; b. Istanbul, Turkey, Apr. 9, 1945; s. Ali Osman and Taliha (Kiziltan) Z.; m. Sidika Esin Aydogan, Aug. 4, 1972; children: Tufan, Meltem. BSME, Istanbul Tech. U., 1966; MBA, Uludag U., Bursa, Turkey, 1990. Gen. foreman asst. Machine Workshop, Kdz Eregli, Turkey, 1968-71, gen. foreman, 1971-75; dir. asst. Workshop, Kdz Eregli, 1975-78; plant maintenance dir. Eregli Iron and Steel Plant, Kdz Eregli, 1978-80; factory mgr., gen. mgr. asst. tech. Asil Celik Quality Steel Plant, Bursa, 1980-93; gen. mgr. asst. BPO Bplas Plastic Omium, Bursa, 1993—. Lt. Turkish Army, 1966-68. Mem. SAE (U.S.), International Rotary Club (ex-pres., Calgary Challenge award 1995-96), Horse Riding Club Bursa (ex-pres.). Democrat. Muslim. Avocations: tennis, animals, gardening, tracking. Office: BPO Bplas Plastic Omium, Yeni Yalova Yolu 8 KM, 16105 Bursa Turkey

ZENILMAN, MICHAEL E., surgeon, educator; b. Far Rockaway, N.Y., Mar. 14, 1958; s. David and Dorothy Zenilman; married. BS with highest honors, SUNY, Stony Brook, 1980; MD summa cum laude, SUNY, Bklyn., 1984. Diplomate Am. Bd. Surgery. Resident in surgery, fellow, then chief resident Barnes Hosp.-Washington U. Sch. Medicine, St. Louis, 1984-91; asst. prof. surgery, chief geriatric surgery Johns Hopkins U. Sch. Medicine, Balt., 1991-93; assoc. prof., chief of surgery Albert Einstein Sch. Medicine, Bronx, N.Y., 1993—, vice chmn. dept. surgery, 1998—. Editor: Geriatric Surgery; contbr. articles on surgery and basic sci. to sci. jours. Fellow ACS; mem. Assn. Acad. Surgery, Soc. for Surgery Alimentary Tract, Am. Gastroent. Assn., Soc. Univ. Surgeons, Am. Physiol. Soc., Am. Pancreative Assn., Phi Beta Kappa, Alpha Omega Alpha. Office: Montefiore Med Pk 1575 Blondell Ave Ste 125 Bronx NY 10461-2660

ZENKEVICH, IGOR GEORGIEVICH, research chemist; b. St. Krutaya, Komi, Russia, Oct. 2, 1951; s. Georgy Konstantinovich and Lidia Mikhailovna (Markina) Z.; m. Natalia Grigoryevna Rabinovich, Nov. 20, 1972; children: Svetlana, Tatiana. MS in Organic Chemistry, St. Petersburg U., Russia, 1973. Sr. asst. chemistry St. Petersburg U., 1973-76, rschr., Chem. Rsch. Inst., 1976-85, sr. rschr., Chem. Rsch. Inst., 1985-94, head of lab., Chem. Rsch. Inst., 1994—; head of lab. Chem.-Pharm. Acad., 1994-98; guest rsch. Nat. Inst. Standards and Tech., Gaithersburg, Md., 1999; cons. Sci. Ctr. Applied Chemistry, St. Petersburg, 1995—; mem. St. Petersburg U. dissertation bds. in organic chemistry, 1990—, analytical chemistry, 1995—. Co-author: (with V.A. Isidorov) Determination of Organic Compounds Rests in Atmosphere, (in Russian) 1982, (with B.V. Ioffe) Interpretation of Mass Spectra of Organic Compounds, (in Russian) 1986, (with A.N. Marinichev) Physical Chemical Calculations with Personal Computers, (reference book, in Russian) 1990; contbr. over 300 articles to profl. jours. and conf. procs.; assoc. editor (jour.) Ecol. Chemistry, 1990—; mem. editl. bd. Jour. Plant Resources, 1994—. Grantee Internat. Sci. Found. (ISF), 1994, ISF and Russian Govt., 1995. Mem. N.Y. Acad. Scis. Avocation: walking, bicycling. Office: Chem Rsch Inst St Peters U, Universitetsky pr 2, 198904 St Petersburg Russia

ZENKOV, ANDREI VIACHESLAVOVICH, physicist; b. Alapayevsk, Russia, Feb. 23, 1966; s. Viacheslav and Larisa (Chubarova) Z.; m. Tatiana Chebykina, Apr. 29, 1994 (div. Oct. 1996); 1 child, Gloria; m. Larisa Sazanova, Dec. 5, 1998. MSc, Ural State U., 1987, DSc, 1990. Asst. prof. Ural Poly. Inst., Sverdlovsk, Russia, 1990-91; from sr. lectr. to assoc. prof. Ural Tech. U., Ekaterinburg, Russia, 1992—. Co-author: Tu ne quaesieris..., 1997, The Freedom Concept, 1998; contbr. articles to profl. jours. Home: Lenin Ave 54/3-115, 620075 Ekaterinburg Russia

ZENNER, HANS PETER, otolaryngologist; b. Essen, Germany, Nov. 13, 1947; s. Hans and Eleonore (Lang) Z.; m. Birgit Zenner, 1977; 4 children. MD, U. Mainz, Germany, 1972, PhD, 1974; Dr.habil., U. Wuerzburg, Germany, 1981. Wiss. asst. U. Wuerzburg, 1974-81, dozent, 1981-86, prof., 1986-88; prof. orolaryngology, chmn. dept. U. Tübingen, Germany, 1988—; vis. scientist U. Mich., Ann Arbor, 1985, Washington U., St. Louis, 1987. Author: Allergologie, 1987, Therapie HNO, 1993, Physiologie; editor: All. Atemwegserkrank., 1988. Pres. Inst. Sonderhoerhilfe, Munich, 1990-95; advisor Govt. of Germany, 1992-99. Recipient Troeltsch award German Acad. Otolayngology, 1982, Sandor-Cseresmes medal Hungarian Triological Soc., 1985, Four Centennial prize, U. Würzburg, 1985, Leibniz award German Rsch. Coun., 1986, Haymann prize German Triological Soc., 1988. Mem. Rotary. Home: Silcherstr 5, W-72076 Tübingen Germany Office: U Tübingen Dept Otolaryngology, Silcherstraße 5, 72076 Tübingen Germany

ZENOPHON, FONDA, poet, writer, publisher. Founder, editor Matilda Mag., 1980-85; founder Brunswick Poetry Workshop, 1972. Author 4 books; contbr. articles, revs., poems to numerous books and periodicals; editor 3 poetry anthologies; appeared on radio programs, Melbourne and Sydney, Australia; read poetry at 1st Poets' Festival, Montsalvat, Victoria, Australia, 1977. Apptd. Hon. Poet Laureate City of Brunswick, Australia, 1983; recipient 2d pl. Lyric award Melbourne's Observer Nat. Anthem Competition, and hon. poetry diploma from Internat. Poets Acad. Fellow Internat. Poets Acad. (3d place Daffodil Day Arts award Anti-Cancer coun.); mem. Fellowship of Australian Writers. Address: 7 Mountfield St, Brunswick Victoria 3056, Australia

ZEN-RUFFINEN, MICHEL, athletic organization executive; b. Sion, Switzerland, Apr. 24, 1959. BS, U. Geneva, 1983; Barrister's Lic., 1985, Notary Diploma, 1985. Solicitor Daolleves & Allet, Geneva, 1985-86; lawyer Fedn. Internat. Foodtball Assn., Zurich, 1986-90, head legal svcs., 1990-98, gen. sec., CEO, 1998—. Office: FIFA House, PO Box 85, 8030 Zurich Switzerland

ZENTALL, THOMAS R., psychologist, educator; b. Bezier, Herault, France, Sept. 29, 1940; came to the U.S., 1942; s. Robert Sigmund and Elizabeth Aigner Zentall; m. Sydney Snider, Aug. 29, 1965 (div.); m. Melodie Rae, June 4, 1988; children: Gabriel Clay, Shannon Rae. BA, BSEE, Union Coll., 1963; PhD, U. Calif., Berkeley, 1969. Asst. prof. U. Pitts., 1969-75; prof. U. Ky., Lexington, 1975—. Editor: Social Learning, 1988, Animal Cognition, 1993, Stimulus Class Formation, 1996; assoc. editor Psychonomic Bull. and Rev., 1998—. Fellow APA (exec. com. divsn. 6 1998—, exec. com. divsn. 3 1999—), Am. Psychol. Soc., Midwestern Psychol. Assn. (sec.-treas. 1998—), Psychonomic Soc. E-mail: zentall@pop.uky.edu. Office: Dept Psychology Univ Ky Lexington KY 40506-0001

ZENTGRAF, MARTIN, editor, clergyman; b. Mainz, Germany, May 20, 1955; s. Hans-Joachim and Erika (Schwaiger) Z. DrTheol, U. Bonn, Germany, 1983. Ordained to ministry Luth. Ch., 1979. Vicar Luth. Ch., Steinbach, Germany, 1980-82; rschr. U. Bonn, 1982-83; pastor Luth. Ch., Frankfurt, Germany, 1983-90, dean, 1990-97; pres. Stiftung Friedenswarte, Bad Ems, Germany, 1998—; editor Pfarrerinnen und Pfarrerverein, Frankfurt, 1992—; v.p. Artheon, Stuttgart, Germany, 1993—; pres. Pfarr-Verein, Frankfurt, 1992—. Author: Theologische Institutionenlehre, 1983; editor: Unternehmensphilosophie, 1991, Stadt, Kirche, Historie, 1993, Frankfurter Paulskirche 1848, 1998. Mem. Rotary. Avocations: art, painting. Office: Stiftung Diakoniewerk Fried, Schanzgraben 3, 56130 Bad Ems Germany

ZEO, FRANK JAMES, health products company professional; b. Springfield, Mass., Jan. 9, 1910; s. Michael and Jennie (Acquavella) Z.; m. Dorothea Louise Duncan, June 27, 1942; children: Virginia D. Kriz, Cynthia J. Newell. AB, Yale U., 1932; postgrad., Syracuse U., 1935-37. Cons. Pub. Adminstrn. Svc., Chgo. and Boston, 1938-40; cons. Mass. Taxpayers Found., Boston, 1940-58, exec. v.p., 1959-71; cons. mgmt./pub. affairs Boston, 1971—; ind. distributor Reliv Internat., Inc., Chesterfield, Mo., 1998—. Bd. dirs. Greater Boston Salvation Army, 1970—; bd. dirs. Exec. Svc. Corps of New Eng., Boston, 1982-95, mem. devel. com., 1984—; bd. dirs. Operation Able, Boston, 1982—; chmn. Nat. Taxpayers Conf., Boston, 1970-71; trustee John Hancock Variable Series Trust I, Boston, 1968—; New Eng. peer support coord. Elizabeth Campbell Peer Support Program, Manly, N.S.W., Australia; bd. dirs. Ron Burton Tng. Village, Hubbardston, Mass., 1991—; hon. trustee East Boston Savs. Bank, 1971—, Mass. Taxpayers Found., Boston, 1985—. Lt. Col. USAF, 1942-45. Decorated Legion of Merit; recipient Founder's award Salvation Army. Mem. Govtl. Rsch. Assn. (hon.), Coun. Mem. Yale Club of Boston, Rotary (past pres. Boston club). Congregationalist. Avocations: photography, music, fishing, walking, writing. Home and Office: Reliv Internat Inc 90 Naugus Ave Marblehead MA 01945-1552

ZEON, SEOK KIL, medical educator; b. Taegu, Republic of Korea, Mar. 3, 1948; s. Sah Yong and Mal Joh (Kwon) Z.; m. Hei Sook Kim, Nov. 23, 1975; children: Yong Won, Ji Won, Kyu Won. MD, Kyungpook Nat. U., Taegu, 1972, MA, 1977, PhD, 1983. Intern, resident in radiology Kyungpook Nat. U. Hosp., Taegu, 1972-77; chmn. dept. radiology Taegu Armed Gen. Hosp., 1978-80; prof. radiology Keimyung U. Sch. Medicine, Taegu, 1980—, chmn. dept. nuclear medicine, 1993—. Maj., Korean Army, 1977-80. Mem. Soc. Nuc. Medicine, European Assn. Nuc. Medicine, Korean Radiol. Soc. (chmn. Taegu-Kyungpook chpt. 1994-95), Korean Soc. Nuc. Medicine (trustee 1990-98, auditor 1999—). Avocation: essay literature. Home: Chonggu Town 101-1307, Beommool-Dong Taegu 706-100, Republic of Korea Office: Keimyung U Sch Medicine, 194 Dongsan-Dong, Taegu 700-712, Republic of Korea

ZEPEDA, SUSAN GHOZEIL, foundation administrator; b. N.Y.C., Aug. 8, 1946; d. Harry S. and Anne (Golden) Kantor; m. Isaac Ghozeil, Jan. 29, 1967 (div. Oct. 1979); children: Daniel Jacob, Adam Leo; m. Fernando Zepeda, Jan. 2, 1983 (div. Feb. 1998); children: Paloma Andrea, Sofia Elisa. BA, Brown U., 1967; MA, U. Ariz., 1971, postgrad., 1971-75; PhD, Internat. Coll., 1985. Rsch. assoc. div. bus. and econ. rsch. U. Ariz., Tucson, 1971-73, rsch. assoc. Coll. Medicine, 1975-76; assoc. dir. Pima Alcoholism Consortium, Tucson, 1976-79, exec. dir., 1979-80; dep. dir. pub. health Orange County Health Care Agy., Santa Ana, Calif., 1980-89; dir. policy, planning Orange County Health Care Agy., Santa Ana, 1989-90; dir. pub. fin. Orange County, 1990-92; dir. San Luis Obispo County Health Agy., 1993-99; exec. dir. The Healthcare Found. for Orange County, Sant Ana, Calif., 1999—; cons. Tucson Sch. Dist. No. 1, 1973-75, U.S. Dept. Labor, Washington, 1976-79, Indian Health Svc., Rockville, Md., 1984-85; ptnr. Zepeda Assocs., Fullerton, Calif., 1987-93; presenter confs. Mem. Fullerton Planning Commn., 1984-91, chmn., 1990-91; mem. Calif. Task Force on Comparable Worth, 1984-85, Calif. Dist. Appeal Bd. No. 510, L.A., 1986—. Recipient Woman of Achievement award Orange County Bd. Suprs., 1988, Disting. Achievement awards Nat. Assn. Counties, 1985, 86, 87, 89. Mem. APHA, Health Funders Partnership of Orange County (chair 2000—), County Health Execs. Assn. Calif. (v.p. 1998-99), Nat. Assn. County and City Health Ofcls. (bd. dirs.), Ctrl. Coast Hosp. Coun. (chair 1996), County Alcohol Program Adminstrs. Assn. Calif. (v.p. 1983, pres. 1984-85), Rotary Santa Ana. Avocation: fiber arts. Home: 24 Birchwood Irvine CA 92618-3941 Office: The Healthcare Found for Orange County 1450 N Tustin Ave Ste 103 Santa Ana CA 92705-8653

ZEPF, THOMAS HERMAN, physics educator, researcher; b. Cin., Feb. 13, 1935; s. Paul A. and Agnes J. (Schulz) Z. BS summa cum laude, Xavier U., 1957; MS, St. Louis U., 1960, PhD, 1963. Asst. prof. physics Creighton U., Omaha, 1962-67, assoc. prof., 1967-75, prof., 1975—, acting chmn. dept. physics, 1963-66, chmn., 1966-73, 81-93, coord. allied health programs, 1975-76, coord. pre-health scis. advising, 1976-81; cons. physicist VA Hosp., Omaha, 1966-71; vis. prof. physics St. Louis U., 1973-74; program evaluator Am. Coun. on Edn., 1988—. Contbr. articles and abstracts to Surface Sci., Bull. Am. Phys. Soc., Proceedings Nebr. Acad. Sci., The Physics Tchr. jour., others. Recipient Cert. Recognition award Phi Beta Kappa U. Cin. chpt., 1953, Disting. Faculty Svc. award Creighton U., 1987, Excellence in Teaching award Creighton U., 1997. Mem. AAAS, Am. Phys. Soc., Am. Assn. Physics Tchrs. (pres. Nebr. sect. 1978), Nebr. Acad. Sci. (life, chmn. physics sect. 1985—), Internat. Brotherhood Magicians, Soc. Am. Magicians (pres. assembly #7, 1964-65), KC, Sigma Xi (Achievement award for rsch. St. Louis chpt. 1963, pres. Omaha chpt. 1993-94), Sigma Pi Sigma. Roman Catholic. Office: Creighton U Dept Physics Omaha NE 68178-0001

ZERAFA, LAURENCE VINCENT, industrial pharmacist; b. Floriana, Malta, Apr. 7, 1958; s. Joseph and Maria (Farrugia) Z. BPharm, U. Malta, 1979, MPhil, 1992. Mgr. apothecary Floriana Dispensary, Malta, 1979-85; quality control mgr. Pharmamed Ltd., Zejtun, Malta, 1985-87; chemistry tchr. St. Aloysius Coll., B'kara, Malta, 1987-91; product registration officer, libr., tng. officer Pharmamed Ltd., Zejtun, 1992-97; tng. and info. mgr. Pharamed Ltd., Zejtun, 1998—, mgr. human resources, 1999—; vis. lectr. U. Malta, Msida, 1993. Co-author: A Directory of Libraries and Information Units in Malta, 1996; contbr. articles to profl. jours. Mem. Libr. Assn. Malta (sec. 1995-96, chmn. 1996—), Malta Chamber of Pharmacists (coun. 1988-89), Drug Info. Assn., Malta Inst. Mgmt., Br. Soc. History of Pharmacy. Avocations: reading, outdoor life, gardening, photography. Home: Schwarzwald Triq Il-Qroll, ZRQ 04 Zurrieq Malta

ZERATH, ERIK, pathologist, physiologist, researcher; b. Casablanca, Morocco, Nov. 15, 1956; s. Roger Zerath and Fiby Bitton; m. Dominique Georges, Apr. 2, 1981; children: Myriam, Sylvia, Helena, Benjamin, Cosima. MD, U. Marseille, France, 1981; cert. pathologist, U. Paris VI, 1989, PhD, 1993; cert. rsch. dir., U. Paris V, 1997. Rsch. asst. Aerospace Med. Rsch. Ctr., Paris, 1985-89; head divsn. histophysiology Aerospace Med. Rsch. Ctr., Bretigny, France, 1989-92, head dept. gravitational physiology, 1992—. Flight surgeon French Air Force, 1982-85, from lt. to col. Health Svc., 1995. Recipient Bronze medal for rsch. Mil. Health Svc., 1990, Silver medal, 1997. Mem. Am. Soc. Bone and Mineral Rsch., Am. Soc. Gravitational and Space Biology, Internat. Bone and Mineral Soc., Alumni Assn. for MDs holding Aerospace Medicine Degree. Avocation: private pilot. E-mail: ezerath@imassa.fr. Office: IMASSA, BP 73, Bretigny 91223, France

ZERATI, EDSON, neurologist, neurosurgeon; b. São Paolo, Brazil, Nov. 7, 1951; s. Romeu and Maria (Costa) Z. MD, Med. Sch. Sã José, Rio Preto, Sã Paolo, 1981. Anatomy pathology monitor Med. Sch. Sã José Rio Preto, 1979; intern casaulty dept. Santa Casa de Misericordia de Votuporanga, São Paolo, 1981; resident in neurology and neurosurgery Rio Preto Neurology and Neurosurgery Inst., Sã Preto, São Paolo, 1981-83; resident in neurology; spkr. childhood neurol. distorbance Sch. Edn. Infantil Piconze, Voturporanga, 1986; participant numerous profl. confs., courses and symposia. Co-author: History of Neurology in State of São Paolo, 1996; contbr. articles to med. publs. Fellow Am. Acad. Neurology; mem. Brazilian Med. Assn., Brazilian Acad. Neurology (mem. XV congress neurology 1992, asst. modernization course in extra-pyramidal, epilepsy therapy for control of headaches), Brazilian Soc. Neurourgery, Brazilian Acad. Neurosurgery, Paulista Soc. Neurosurgery (participant rheumatology working day 1979), Med. Surg. Soc. Sã Josée Rio Preto (spkr. phys. congress 1985, 87), World Fedn. Neurology, World Fedn. Neurosurg. Socs., Rotary Internat. Fax: 55-17-4225760. Home: San Marino Bldg, Vila Marin, 416 Ivai St Apt 101, Votupora São Paolo 15500470, Brazil Office: 226 Santa Catarina St, Votupora São Paolo 15500260, Brazil

ZERBE, JERZY MARIUSZ, chemist, researcher, educator; b. Poznan, Poland, Jan. 11, 1937; s. Franciszek and Helena Zerbe; m. Teresa Maria Ogórkiewicz, July 1, 1960; children: Piotr, Joanna. M Chemistry, Poznan U., 1958, PhD in Chemistry, 1978. Asst. Inst. Mpcl. Economy, Poznan, 1958-65, sr. asst., 1965-74; head analytical lab. Inst. Environ. Devel., Warsaw, Poland, 1974-81; dep. dir. Inst. Phys. Planning and Mcpl. Economy, Poznan, 1981-90; assoc. prof. chemistry Poznan U., 1990—. Polish expert tech. com. water quality Internat. Orgn. for Standardization, 1975—; Polish expert tech. com. water analysis European Com. for Standardization, 1990—. Co-author: Application of Instrumental Methods in Water and Waste Water Analysis, 1997, Physical and Chemical Examination of Water, 1998. Roman Catholic. Avocations: chess, travel, hiking. Home: Piatkowska 39/45, 60-648 Poznan Poland Office: Poznan U Dept Water Anal, Drzmaly 24, 60-613 Poznan Poland

ZERBIB, ERIC, nuclear medicine physician; b. Paris, France, Feb. 7, 1963. MS, U. Paris 13, 1994; Nuclear Medicine Specialist, Cochin U., Paris, 1992; Med. Statis. Cert., Paris, 1993. Asst. Univ. Hosps. AP/HP, Paris, 1992-95; hosp. physician Marie Lannelongue Medecine Nucleaire, Le Plessis Robinson, France, 1995—; med. reporter Impact Medecin, Paris, 1988-92; med. dir. JBH Santé, Paris, 1996-97. Author: Hepatic and Biliary Tract Scintigraphies, 1998; editor-in-chief Octreographies, 1997; coord. Radio-isotropic investigations for digestive pathology (in French), Ency. Medico-Chirurgicale, 1998; mem. editor PCM, Paris, 1992-95; coord. Nuclear Medicine and Gastroeuterology, 2000. Recipient Silver medal for med. doctorate thesis, 1991. Mem. French Soc. Biophysics and Nuclear Medicine, European Assn. Nuclear Medicine. Office: Ctre Chir Marie LanneLongue, 133 Ave de la Resistance, 92350 Le Plessis Robinson France

ZERBIN-RUEDIN, EDITH, retired psychiatric geneticist, educator; b. Munich, May 2, 1921; d. Ernst and Edith (Senger) Ruedin; m. Adolf Zerbin, May 30, 1956. Interpreter, Translator Grade B, Mcpl. Lang. Sch., Munich, 1946; Translator I and II, Munich Translator Sem., 1947; MD magna cum laude, Ludwig-Maximilian U., Munich, 1950. Med. diplomate. Clin. asst. Psychiat. U. Clinic, Munich, 1950-51; rsch. worker Max-Planck-Inst. Psychiatrie, Munich, 1947-58, head rsch. group psychiat. genetics, 1958-86; lectr. med. genetics Bavarian Ministry Edn. and Culture, Munich, 1972-86, extraordinary prof. med. genetics, 1978—; lectr. nat. and internat. congresses, symposia and seminaries, Germany, U.S.A., Denmark, Italy, France, Norway, Switzerland, Japan, Mexico. Co-editor Archiv für Psychiatrie und Nervenkrankheiten, 1975-86, European Archives of Psychiatry and Neurol. Scis., 1986-88, Neuropsychobiology, 1975-91; translator 4 med. books and book chpts.; author; Nature and Nurture in the Origin of Psychiatric Disturbances, Schizophrenia; contbr. articles to profl. jours., chpts. to books. Mem. Am. Soc. Human Genetics, Behavior Genetics Assn., Soc. for Study Social Biology. Avocations: theater visits, study of history, skiing, mountaineering, gardening. Home: Besselstr 1 A, D-81679 Munich Germany

ZERBST, EKKEHARD WOLFGANG, retired university educator; b. Insterburg, Germany, Jan. 19, 1926; s. Erich Fritz-Waldemar and Lucie Anna-Adelheid (Dadags) Z.; m. Monika Hanig; children: Marion, Annette; m. Irene Lilly Boroffka, July 10, 1970; children: Juliane, Johannes. MD, Free U., Berlin, 1956, PhD, Habilitation, 1966. Staff physician Berlin Hosp., 1956-58; sci. asst. Free U., 1958-66, lectr., 1966-69, prof., 1969-88; mng. dir. dept. physiology Free U., 1971-73, 76-78, 80-83; cons. ptnr. Physionic GmbH, Berlin, 1983-86. Author: Progress in Experimental and Theoretical Biophysics, Vol. 17, 1973, Bionik, 1987; contbr. articles to internat. sci. jours., poems to books and lit. publs., patentee in biomed. field. Ensign, pilot German Air Force, 1944-45. Avocations: bionics research, literature, poetry.

ZERDA, ALVARO, university dean, economist; b. Bogota, Colombia, Apr. 1, 1953; s. Eduardo Zerda and Isabel Sarmiento; m. Francisca Escobar, Aug. 22, 1982. Degree in bus. mgmt., Escuela de Administracion de Negocios, Bogota, 1975; grad. in econs., Univ. Ctrl., Bogota, 1980; Magister, U. Nat. Bogota, 1985; PhD in Econs., 2000. Mgr. Depósito Dental, Bogota, 1976-85; prof. econs. U. Nat. Bogota, 1985-90, sr. rschr., 1990-92, dean econs., 1992—; cons. UN Devel. Program, Bogota, 1990—. Author: Cuentas Nacionales, 1990, Apertura y Nuevas Tecnologia, 1992, Mercado de trabajo industrial, 1993, Pacto Social, 1994, Human Resources and the Adjustment Process, 1995, Politica Activa de Empleo, 1997, Pequehay mediana Industria, 1998, Evaluacin de la gestion publica, 1999, Sistemas de Seguios en Salud y Acceso a Medicamentos, 2000. Office: Nat U Bogota, Ciudad Universitaria, Bogota Colombia

ZERILLI, ANDREA EUGENIO, geology researcher; b. Fiorenzuola d'Arda, Italy, July 28, 1952; s. Giuseppe and Olga (Belforti) Z. DSc in Earth Scis., U. Parma, Italy, 1979. Vis. fellow U.S. Geol. Survey, Denver, 1980-83, 85; rsch. asst. U. Parma, 1984; rsch. assoc. Macquarie U., Sidney, Australia, 1986-87, Colo. Sch. Mines, Golden, 1988-89; sr. rsch. mem. ENI/AGIP, Milan, 1990—, tech. leader, 1991—. Mem. IEEE, European Assn. Geoscientists and Engrs., Soc. Exploration Geophysicists. Roman Catholic. Avocations: music, Saab cars, computer graphics, virtual reality. Home: Via Liberazione 36, 29017 Fiorenzuola d'Arda Italy Office: AGIP GEBA, Via Unione Europea 1, 20097 San Donato Italy

ZERNIG, GERALD, addictions research educator; b. Graz, Styria, Austria, Feb. 22, 1960; s. Horst and Gertrude (Cebavs) Z.; children: Patrick, Bernhard. Md, U. Graz, 1984. Cert. in pharmacology and toxicology. Assoc. prof. U. Innsbruck, 1984, 90, 97, U. Graz, 1996; vis. asst. prof. U. Mich., Ann Arbor, 1992; rsch. fellow U. B.C., Vancouver, 1995; cons. in pharmacology and toxicology. With Austrian Arty., 1985. Mem. Coll. Problems on Drug Dependence. Avocations: reading, running, visual arts, sailing. E-mail: gerald.zering@uibk.ac.at. Office: Innsbruck U Divsn Neurochem, Dept Psychiat Anichstr 35, 6020 Innsbruck Austria

ZERUNYAN, FRANK VRAM, lawyer; b. Istanbul, Turkey, Sept. 17, 1959; came to U.S., 1978; s. Jack Hagop and Ayda (Yagupyan) Z.; m. Jody Lynn Forman, May 18, 1986; children: Daniel, Nicole. French Bacalaureat, Coll. Samuel Moorat, Paris, 1978; BA, Calif. State U., Long Beach, 1982; JD, Western State U., Fullerton, Calif., 1985; postgrad., U. Southern Calif., 1988. Bar: Calif. 1989, D.C., 1995, U.S. Dist. Ct. (cen. dist.) Calif. 1989, U.S. Ct. Internat. Trade 1994. V.p. law Internat. Mktg. Alliance, Torrance, Calif., 1985-89; pvt. practice L.A., 1989-92; mng. mem. Yacoubian & Zerunyan, P.C., L.A., 1992-95; mem. Sulmeyer, Kupetz, Baumann & Rothman, L.A., 1995—; instr. law Alex Pilibos Sch., L.A., 1993-99; judge pro tem, L.A. Mcpl. Ct. Editor SKB&R Newsletter, 1995—. Bd. dirs. Am. Youth Soccer Orgn., Palos Verdes, Calif., 1995—, referee adminstr., 1995—; bd. dirs., vice-chmn. Daniel Freeman Hosps. Found., 1998—; chmn. scholarship com. Orgn. Istanbul Armenians, Van Nuys, Calif., 1992-94; legal counsel and polity adv. com. Armenian Nat. Com. of Am., Washington, 1993; planning commr. City of Rolling Hills Estates, 2000—. Mem. ABA, Financial Lawyers Conf. Avocations: golf, soccer, tennis. E-mail: fzerunyan@skbr.com. Office: Sulmeyer Kupetz et al 300 S Grand Ave Ste 1400 Los Angeles CA 90071-3124

ZER-ZION, DANIEL, physicist; b. Buenos Aires, Aug. 29, 1961; arrived in Switzerland, 1996; s. Jose and Susana (Goldberg) Zer-Zion; m. Eynat Cohen, June 18, 1993; children: Shahaf, Nitzane, Shaked. BSc, Technion, Haifa, Israel, 1985; MSc in Theoretical Physics, Tel Aviv U., 1989, PhD in Exptl. High Energy Physics, 1994. Physicist Deutsches Elektronen Synchrotron, Hamburg, Germany, 1989-94; asst. prof. physics Sta. Cruz (U.S.) Inst. Physics, 1993-94; physicist Wiezmann Inst., Rehovot, Israel, 1994-96; sci. assoc. European Lab. for Particle Physics, CERN, Geneva, Switzerland, 1996—. Contbr. articles on high energy exptl. physics and detection of gravitational waves to sci. jours. European Lab. for Particle Physics fellow, 1996-99; Weizmann Inst. grantee, 1994-96, Minerva grantee Alexander von Humboldt Found., 1990-92. Mem. Am. Phys. Soc., Israel Phys. Soc. Avocations: painting, history and philosophy of science, teaching physics. Office: CERN, EP-Divsn 23, 1211 Geneva Switzerland

ZEUNER, LILLI, sociologist, researcher; b. Horsens, Jutland, Denmark, Mar. 13, 1948; d. Børge and Signe (Nielsen) Hansen; m. Steen Scheuer, Apr. 14, 1978; children: Pernille Zeuner, Klara Scheuer. MA, U. Copenhagen, 1977; PhD, Copenhagen Bus. Sch., 1988. Tchg. asst. U. Copenhagen, 1977-80; head office Govt. Youth Commn., Copenhagen, 1981-84; sr. rsch. fellow, rsch. asst. Nat. Inst. Social Rsch., Copenhagen, 1984-89, rschr., 1989—; mem. Danish Social Sci. Rsch. Coun., Copenhagen, 1995-99, grantee 1985, 88; mem. adv. bd. Danish Inst. Edni. Rsch., Copenhagen, 1995-96. Author: Kulturelle processer i ungdomsuddannelserne, 1988, Normer i skred, 1990, Fortjent otium, 1991, Den moderne tidsalder og de unge, 1994, Livsstrategier og uddannelsesvalg, 1997, Sociologisk Kulturteori, 2000; editor: Social integration, 1997. Grantee Danish Coun. Rsch. Planning, 1983. Mem. Danish Sociol. Assn. Office: Nat Inst Social Rsch, Herluf Trollesgade 11, 1052 Copenhagen Denmark

ZEUTHEN, JESPER, biologist, cancer researcher, venture capitalist; b. Copenhagen, Apr. 27, 1947; s. Erik and Elisabeth Zeuthen; m. Natalia I. Misuno. MSc, U. Copenhagen, 1971, DSc, 1984. Rsch. fellow Karolinska Inst., Sweden, 1972-74; assoc. prof. U. Aarhus, Denmark, 1974-82; mem. Basel (Switzerland) Inst. Immunology, 1980-81; head dept. Novo Industri A/S, Denmark, 1982-83, rsch. dir., 1983-88; head of dept. Danish Cancer Soc., 1988-2000; mng. dir. BI Technology, Inc., BankInvest Group, Copenhagen, Denmark, 2000—; cons. BankInvest Biotech, Copenhagen, 1989-2000; chmn. The Fibiger Inst., Denmark, 1989-93; adj. prof. U. Copenhagen, 1987-92; sec. Com. on Basic Cancer Rsch. of Danish Rsch. Coun., Copenhagen, 1980-82; mem. biotech. sect. Swedish Tech. Rsch. Coun., 1996-98; Nordic guest prof. Karolinska Inst., Sweden, 1997—; mem. adv. bd. BankInvest Biomed. Devel., 1998—; vice-chmn. Heme Biotech A/S, Copenhagen, 1998—; chmn. Genmab A/S, Copenhagen, 1999—; bd. dirs. FibroGen Europe Ltd., Oulu, Finland. Author: Epstein-Barr Virus, 1984; editor: Gene Expression, 1978, T-Cell Hybridomas, 1982; patentee in field. Recipient Cancer Rsch. prize The Boel Found., Copenhagen, 1981, Internat. prize Found. E. Nuti, Rome, 1992. Mem. Danish Biol. Soc. (sec. 1989-92), Danish Soc. for Cancer Rsch. (treas. 1989-92, Hon. Cancer Rsch. prize 1996), Danish Soc. Immunology (treas. 1995-98), Scandinavian Soc. Immunology (pres. 1998—), Royal Physiographic Soc. (Lund, Sweden). Office: BI Tech A/S Bank Invest Grp, Toldbodgade 33 POB 9011, DK-1022 Copenhagen K, Denmark

ZEVEN, ANTON CORNELIS, plant breeding research scientist; b. Malang, Indonesia, Mar. 9, 1933; arrived in The Netherlands, 1937; s. Herman Anton and Cornelia Gesina (de Haas) Z.; m. Nini Charlotte Hissink, Jan. 25, 1958; children: Harm Anton, Ninette Corine. Degree in engring., Wageningen Agrl. U., The Netherlands, 1959, PhD, 1967. Officer-in-charge West African/Nigerian Inst. for Oil Palm Rsch., Abak and Benin City, Nigeria, 1959-64; rschr. dept. plant breeding Wageningen Agrl. U., 1964-95. Author: Dictionary of Cultivated Plants, 1975, rev. edit., 1982; editor: Who Lived in the City of Wageningen 1550-1880, 1999; editor-in-chief Euphytica, Wageningen, 1967-95. Active Municipality Com. on Hist. Monuments, Wageningen, 1988-92; bd. dirs. Wageningen Mus., 1998—. Mem. Geneal. Soc. Veluwse Geslachten (pres. 1976-2000), History Soc. Oud Wageningen (pres. 1995-99). E-mail: anton.zeven@hetnet.nl. Home: Dassenboslaan 6, 6705 BT Wageningen The Netherlands Office: Agrl U Dept Plant Breeding, PO Box 386, 6700 AJ Wageningen The Netherlands

ZEVIAR-GEESE, GABRIOLE, stock market investor, writer; b. L.A., Apr. 10, 1948; d. Harry Lindstedt and Josephine (Conrad) Blom; m. Stephan Otto Geese, Nov. 22, 1992. BA, York U., 1991; JD, Calif. Pacific Sch. Law, 1999. Edn. specialist Honeywell, Kansas City, Mo., 1979; data base cons., edn. specialist Bull Internat., Toronto, 1982-91; Oracle programmer Sparta, Inc., Laguna Hills, Calif., 1992; arbitrator BBB, 1998—; small claims advisor, legal cons. Kern County Counsel, 1998-2000. Author: Introduction to COBOL, 1979, Advanced COBOL, 1981, Introduction to FORTRAN, 1987, Oracle for Application Developers, 1990, also jour. articles. Mem. ATLA, Kern County Bar Assn. Avocations: classical piano, painting, Tae Kwon Do, motivational speaking. Home: 4400 Country Club Dr # 17 Bakersfield CA 93306-7553

ZEWAIL, AHMED HASSAN, chemistry and physics educator, editor, consultant; b. Damanhour, Egypt, Feb. 26, 1946; came to U.S., 1969, naturalized, 1982; s. Hassan A. Zewail and Rawhia Dar; m. Dema Zewail; children: Maha, Amani, Nabeel, Hani. BS, Alexandria U., Egypt, 1967, MS, 1969; PhD, U. Pa., 1974; MA (hon.), Oxford U., 1991; DS (hon.), Am. U., Cairo, 1993, Katholieke U., Leuven, Belgium, U. Pa., U. Lausanne, Switzerland, 1997; DU (hon.), Swinburne U., Australia, 1999. Teaching asst. U. Pa., Phila., 1969-70; IBM fellow U. Calif., Berkeley, 1974-76; asst. prof. chem. physics Calif. Inst. Tech., Pasadena, 1976-78, assoc. prof., 1978-82, prof., 1982-89, Linus Pauling prof. chem. physics, 1990-94, Linus Pauling prof. chemistry and prof. physics, 1995—, dir. NSF Lab. for Molecular Scis., 1996—; cons. Xerox Corp., Webster, N.Y., 1977-80, ARCO Solar, Inc., Calif., 1978-81. Editor Laser Chemistry, 1980-85, Jour. Phyical Chemistry, 1985-90, Chem. Physics Letters, 1991—, Internat. Series Monographs on Chemistry, 1992—, Advances in Laser Spectroscopy Vol. I, 1977, Advances in Laser Chemistry Vol. III, 1978, Photochemistry and Photobiology, Vols. I and II, 1983, Ultrafast Phenomena VII, 1990, VIII, 1993, IX, 1994, The Chemical Bond: Structure and Dynamics, 1992, Femtochemistry-Ultrafst Dynamics of the Chemical Bond, Vols. I and II, 1994; contbr. numerous articles to sci. jours.; patentee in solar energy field. Recipient Tchr.-Scholar award Dreyfus Found., 1979-85, Alexander von Humboldt Sr. U.S. Scientist award, 1983, John Simon Guggenheim Meml. Found. award, 1987, King Faisal Internat. prize in sci., 1989, NASA award, 1991, 1st AMM Achievement award, 1991, Nobel Laureate Signature award, 1992, Carl Zeiss award, Cairo U. Medal and Shield of Honor, 1992, U. Qatar medal, 1993, Niles award of honor Bonner Chemiepreis, Germany, 1994, Order of Merit first calss Egypt, Coll. de France medal Leonardo Da Vinci award of excellence, France, 1995, J.G. Kirwood medal Yale U., Peking U. medal, China, 1996, Robert A. Welch award in chemistry, Pitts. Spectroscopy award, 1997, Benjamin Franklin medal, Paul Karrer gold medal, Zurich, Roentgen prize, Germany, E.O. Lawrence award U.S. Govt., Merski award U. Nebr.,Nobel Prize in Chemistry, 1999, Egypt Postage Stamp with portrait issued, 1999. Mem. NAS (Chem. Scis. award 1996), Am. Acad. Arts and Scis. (Royal Netherlands Acad. Arts and Scis. medal 1993), Am. Chem. Soc. (Buck-Whitney medal 1985, Harrison Howe award 1989, Hoechst prize 1990, Peter Debye award, Linus Pauling medal 1997, 1st E.B. Wilson award 1997, William H. Nichols award 1998, Richard C. Tolman Medal award 1998), Am. Phil. Soc., Am. Phys. Soc. (Herbert P. Broida prize 1995), European Acad. Arts, Scis., and Humanities, Third World Acad. Scis., Sigma Xi (Earle K. Plyler prize 1993, Wolf prize 1993). Office: Calif Inst Tech Divsn Chemistry & Chem Engring Mail Code 127 72 Pasadena CA 91125-0001

ZEWDIE, GENET, minister of education of Ethiopia; married; 2 children. Degree in bus. edn., Haile Sellassie I Univ., Addis Ababa, Ethiopia, 1971; BSc in Bus. Edn., Plymouth State Coll., 1973; MSc in Bus. Edn., Suffolk U., Boston, 1984. Asst. lectr. dept. tech. tchr. edn. Addis Ababa U., 1973-83, asst. prof., lectr., 1984-91, head dept. bus. edn., 1986-91; intern dept. office edn. Bunker Hill C.C., Boston, 1983; external examiner Kenyatta U., Nariobi, Kenya, 1990—; vice min. higher edn. Govt. Ethiopia, 1991-92, min. edn., 1992—. Office: Min Edn, PO Box 1367, Addis Ababa Ethiopia*

ZEZE, MASAFUMI, metal products executive, engineering researcher; b. Matama, Oita, Japan, July 22, 1957; s. Tsunenori and Junko (Hayata) Z.; m. Kaori Nakao, Apr. 27, 1997; 1 child, Koki. M in Engring., Osaka (Japan) U., 1982. Cert. metall. engring. Sr. rschr. Nippon Steel Corp., Kitakyushu, Japan, 1991—. Mem. Iron and Steel Inst. Japan, Iron and Steel Soc., Nippon Steel Ham Club (pres.). Avocations: amateur radio. Home: 2-6-2-106 Takami, Yahatahigashi-ku, Kitakyushu-City 805-0016, Japan Office: Nippon Steel Corp, 1-1 Tobihatacho Tobata-ku, Kitakyushu City 804-8501, Japan

ZEZINA, OLGA NIKOLAEVNA, biooceanologist, researcher; b. Moscow, Feb. 3, 1937. Fisheries engr., Moscow Tech. Inst. Fisheries, 1959; M of Biol. Scis., P.P. Shirshov Oceanology Inst., Moscow, 1971, D of Biol. Scis., 1984. Cert. hydrobiologist. Lab. asst. P.P. Shirshov Oceanology Inst.-Russian Acad. Scis., 1960-67, from jr. scientist to leading scientist, 1967-94, prin. scientist, 1994—. Author: Ecology and Distribution of Recent Brachiopods, 1976, Recent Brachiopods and the Problems of the Bathyal Zone of the Ocean, 1985, Recent Brachiopods in Natural Bottom Biofilter in the Seas of Russia, 1997; contbr. articles to sci. jours. Grantee Soros Found., Moscow, 1993-95, Russian Found. Fundamental Scis., 1996-98. Mem. Hydrobiol. Soc. Moscow, Paleontol. Soc. St. Petersburg. Avocations: travel, skiing, skating, swimming, oceanic expeditions. E-mail: kap@chip.sio.rssi.ru. Office: PP Shirshov Oceanology Inst, Nakhimovsky Prospect 36, 117851 Moscow Russia

ZGLICZYNSKI, STEFAN, endocrinologist, medical educator; b. Plock, Poland, Jan. 10, 1935; s. Stanslaw and Maria (Goscicka) Z.; m. Barbara Bojanowska, July 18, 1956; children: Wojciech, Joanna, Piotr, Stefan. MD, Med. Acad. Warsaw, Poland, 1957. Diplomate in internal medicine and endocrinology. Fellow in internal medicine and gen. practice Med. Acad. Warsaw, 1957-60; prof. asst., sr. asst. dept. internal medicine Med. Ctr. Postgrad. Edn., Warsaw, 1960-67, adj., 1967-74, assoc. prof. dept. endocrinology, 1974-80, prof. medicine, dir. dept. endocrinology, 1980—. Contbr. numerous articles to Jour. Clin. Endocrinology and Metabolism, Hormone and Metabolic Rsch., Clin. and Exptl. Hypertension, others. Mem. N.Y. Acad. Sci., Internat. Endocrine Soc., European Fedn. Endocrine Socs., European Neuroendocrine Assn., N.Am. Menopause Soc., Internat. Menopause Soc., Polish Endocrine Soc., Nat. Found. Endocrinology (founder), Polish Menopause and Andropause Soc. (pres., founder), European Menopause and Andropause Soc., Internat. Soc. for Study of Aging Male. Home: 10 Ciolkowskiego, 01-480 Warsaw Poland Office: Med Ctr Postgrad Edn, Dept Endocrinology, 01-809 Warsaw Poland

ZGRABLICH, GIORGIO, physics educator, researcher; b. Novi de Modena, Italy, Nov. 10, 1942; arrived in Argentina, 1957; s. Antonio Zgrablich and Maria Pia Pollio; m. Maria Ciacera, Mar. 3, 1964; children: Alejandro, Andres. BS, Nat. Coll., San Luis, Argentina, 1959; lic., Nat. U. San Luis, 1964, PhD in Physics, 1971. Prof. Met. Autonoma U., Mexico City, 1976-79; asst. prof. physics Nat. U. San Luis, 1965-70, prof., 1971-76, 1984—, dean Faculty Scis., 1974; rsch. asst. Argonne (Ill.) Nat. Lab., 1968-69; ind. rschr. CONICET, Argentina, 1985-92, prin. rschr., 1992—; vis. scientist Internat. Ctr. for Theoretical Physics, Trieste, Italy, 1989; vis. prof. U. Alicante, Spain, 1992; dddir. Centro Regional Estudios Avanzados, San Luis, 1992-95; dir. Laboratorio de Ciencias de Superficies y Medios Porosos, Nat. U. San Luis, 1997—; chmn. Internat. Symposium on Advances in Measurement and Modeling of Surface Phenomena, San Luis, 1992; mem. acad. coun. Centro L.Am. Estudios Ilyia Prigogine, San Luis, 1996—. Editor: Equilibria and Dynamics of Gas Adsorption on Heterogeneous Solid Surfaces, 1996, Fundamentals and Applications of Complex Systems, 1999; mem. editl. bd. Langmuir, 1998, Adsorption Sci. and Tech., 1996—; contbr. articles to sci. jours., including Jour. Phys. Chemistry, Surface Sci., Phys. Rev., also chpt. to book. Named Arquitectos del Prestigio, Diario de la Republica, San Luis, 1989; recipient award Nat. Acad. Sci. of Argentina in Theoretical Physics, 1998. Mem. Argentine Physics Assn., Internat. Adsorption Soc., Nat. Acad. Sci. of Argenina. Avocation: architecture design. Office: Nat U San Luis Dept Physics, Chacabuco 917, 5700 San Luis Argentina

ZHA, CHAO-ZHENG, physics educator; b. Lu-Cheng, Jiangsu, China, Oct. 10, 1932; s. Chang-Sheng and Yu-Lan Wu Zha; m. Ai-Ju Kou, Mar. 23, 1941; children: Li-Hang Zha, Wei-Hang Zha, Xiao-Hang Zha. Grad., Zhejiang U., Hangzhou, China, 1952. Lectr. Xinjiang U., Wulumuqi, China, 1980-86; prof. Xinjiang U., Wulumuqi, 1986—; dir. Xinjiang U. Physics Dept., 1989-92, Xinjiang U. Ctr. for Theoretical Physics, 1992—. Contbr. articles to profl. jours. Recipient Specialist of Outstanding Contbns. award Personal Ministry of China, 1986, Outstanding Specialist award Xinjiang Autonomous Region, 1988, 93, Spl. Allowance award State Coun. of China, 1991—. Mem. Phys. Soc. China (bd. dirs. 1991-94, edn. com. 1995-99), High Energy Phys. Soc. (bd. dirs. 1998—). Avocation: music. Home: 14 Sheng-li Rd, 830046 Wulumuqi China Office: Ctr Theoretical Physics, Xinjiang U, 830046 Wulumuqi China

ZHA, XUAN-FANG, engineering educator, researcher; b. Dongzhi, Anhui, China, Oct. 17, 1965; arrived in Singapore, 1996.; s. Cheng-Gen and Qiao-Lian (Lu) Z.; m. Ling-Ling Li, Feb. 1, 1993; 1 child, Jiali. BSME with honors, Wuhan (China) Transp. U., 1988; MSME, S.E. U., Nanjing, China, 1991; PhD in Mech. and Prodn. Engring., Nanyang Tech. U., 1999. Ednl. diplomate; profl. engr., China, Canada. Asst. lectr. Nanjing U. Aeronautics and Astronautics, China, 1991-92, 1992-94, assoc. prof., 1994-95, adj. assoc. prof., 1995—; rsch. asst. Wuhan U. of Tech., 1985-88, S.E. U. 1988-91, tchg. asst. 1989-91; sr. engr. Nanjing Tiandi Group Co., Nanjing, 1992-93. Author: (with others) Machine and Mechanism Design, 1992, Robot Mechanics, 1994, Computer Aided Design, Engineering and Manufacturing Systems, 1999, Knowledge-Based Systems, 2000. Recipient rsch. fellowship Hong Kong Polytechnic U., 1995-96, Nanyang Technol. U., 1996-99; recipient Best Paper award Chinese Soc. Automation, 1994, Second Rank prize Jiangsu Provincial Com. Sci. and Tech., 1995. Mem. IEEE (Best Paper award, 1998), Chinese Assoc. Automation, Robotics and Automation Soc. Avocations: reading, swimming, table-tennis.

ZHA, ZIZHONG, physics educator, researcher; b. Wu Hu, An Hui, China, Oct. 28, 1936; s. Funan and Shushi (Shu) Z.; m. Rui Liu, Apr. 2, 1968; children: Dong, Bin. BS, Harbin (China) Inst. Tech., 1964. Profl. cert. nuclear physics; tchr. cert. higher sch., China. Asst. Harbin Inst. Tech., 1964-78, lectr., 1979-86, assoc. prof., 1987-95, prof. physics, 1996—; head sci. rsch. group Harbin Inst. Tech., 1987—, master's tchr. sci. rsch., 1987—; consideration specialist in info. Com. Nature Scis. Fund China, Peking, 1993—, Heilongjiang province, China, 1992—. Contbr. articles to profl. jours. Recipient Third-Class award in nature sci. Acad. Sci. China, Peking, 1993, 2nd Class award in nature sci. Space Industry Chief Co., Peking, 1996. Mem. Soc. Physics and Optics of Heilongjiang province in China. Mem. Chinese Communist party. Avocations: journey, appreciating music and literature.

ZHADIN, MIKHAIL NIKOLAEVICH, biophysicist, researcher; b. Leningrad, USSR, Mar. 12, 1935; s. Nikolaj Petrovich and Valentina Petrovna (Goloshchapova) Z.; m. Svetlana Dmitrievna Zhidikh, Apr. 17, 1965; 1 child, Pavel Mikhajlovich. Master's degree, Moscow U., 1960; D of Physics and Math., Pushchino U., Moscow, 1970, D of Biology, 1982. Cert. prof. biophysics. Engr. Timpton-Uchur Biophys. Expedition, Yakut Republic, USSR, 1960-61; sr. engr. Rsch. Inst. No. 88, Moscow, 1961-63; rschr. Inst. Higher Nervous Activity and Neurophysiology, Moscow, 1964-68; rschr. Inst. Biol. Physics, Pushchino, 1968-80, head of lab. neurocybernetics, 1980-90; head of lab. neurocybernetics Inst. Cell Biophysics, Pushchino, 1991—; dep. dir. Inst. Biol. Physics, Pushchino, 1987-90, Inst. Cell Biophysics, Pushchino, 1990-97; mem. coun. biol. physics problems Acad. Scis. USSR, Moscow, 1988-99; head com. effects of EMI on biol. objects Russian Acad. Scis., Moscow, 1992-99. Author: (book) Biophysical Mechanisms of Electroencephalogram Formation, 1984; editor: Electrical Activity of the Brain: Mathematical Models and Analytical Methods Proc. Int. Symp., 1997; contbr. articles to profl. jours. Recipient hon. diploma Russian Acad. Scis., 1999. Mem. Russian Acad. Natural Scis. Cybernetics (assoc.). Home: Micro-dist B, House 24 Flat 6, 142292 Pushchino Moscow, Russia Office: Inst Cell Biophysics, Institute St, 142292 Pushchino Moscow, Russia

ZHAI, HONGCHEN, optical engineering educator; b. Tianion, China, Oct. 15, 1944; s. Baofu and Shufeng (Liu) Z.; m. Li Chen; 1 child, Yu. BD, Nankai U., Tianjin, China, 1967, MD, 1981; PhD, Münster (Germany) U., 1991. Tchr. Tianjin 57 H.S., 1970-75; engr. Tianjin Inst. of Laser Tech., 1975-79; prof. Tianjin Inst. of Tech., 1982-86; vis. scholar Münster U., 1986-91, CNRS, Paris, 1991-93; prof. Nankan U., Tianjin, 1994—; vice dir. Lab. of Info. Sci. and Tech., Tianjin, 1997. Author: Trends in Optics, 1996, Optical Pattern Recognition, 1998, Optical Signa Processing, Computing, and Neural Networks, 1997. Mem. Internat. Soc. for Optical Engring., Chinese Optical Soc. Info. Processing. (com. mem. 1995). Avocations: music instruments, swimming, painting, Chinese Peking opera. Office: Inst Optics Nankai U, Weijin Rd 94, Tianjin 300071, China

ZHAN, HONGBIN, hydrogeologist, geophysicist; b. Wuhan, China, June 5, 1966; came to U.S., 1991; s. Zhongxue Zhan and Xiaoqing Wu; m. Gangshan Jin, Apr. 10, 1990; 1 child, Edward Zhan. BS in Physics, U. Sci. and Tech. China, Hefei, Anhui, 1989; MS in Physics, U. Nev., Reno, 1993, PhD in Hydrology and Hydrogeology, 1996. Rsch. and tchg. asst. in physics U. Nev., Reno, 1991-93, rsch. asst. in geol. scis., 1993-95; cons. Desert Rsch. Inst., Univ. and C.C. Sys. Nev., Reno, 1995-96, George Burke Maxey fellow, 1995-96; asst. prof. geology and geophysics Tex. A&M U., College Station, 1996—; cons. Tex. Natural Resource Conservation Commn., Austin. Contbr. articles to profl. jours. Recipient scholarship Am. Petroleum Inst. and Nat. Ground Water Assn., 1995. Mem. Internat. Assn. Hydrogeologists, Geol. Soc. Am., Am. Geophys. Union, Nat. Ground Water Assn. Avocations: tennis, swimming, travel. Fax: 979-845-6162. E-mail: zhan@hydrog.tamu.edu. Office: Tex A&M U MS 3115 Dept Geol And Geophys College Station TX 77843-0001

ZHANG, AI-RONG, gynecologist, medical educator; b. Shanghai, Sept. 14, 1932; d. Huamin and Jing Lan (Yu) Zhang; m. Ruqing Shao, Dec. 30, 1957; children: Jing Shao, Ying Shao. BS in Medicine, Beijing Med. U., 1955. Med. diplomate, sr. gynecologist. Lectr., resident Tongji Med. U., Wuhan, Hubei, China, 1955-58; resident Jingzhou (China) Hosp., 1958-64, physician, 1964-81, assoc. sr. physician, 1981-87, sr. physician, 1987—; prof. dept. gynecology Tongji Med. U., 1993—. Contbr. articles to Chinese Jour. Ob-Gyn., Jour. Practical Ob-Gyn. Recipient award for honorable svc. Hubei Healthcare Adminstrn., 1982, Internat. Women's Day medal Jingzhou Prefectural Govt., 1984. Mem. Chinese Med. Assn. (mem. com. on gynecology Hubei br. 1984—, sr. com. mem. com. on gynecology Jingzhou br. 1985—). Avocations; music, piano, fiction. Office: Jingzhou Ctrl Hosp, 72 M Jingzhou Rd, 434100 Jingzhou Hubei, China

ZHANG, BANGWEI, materials science scientist, educator; b. Hunan, China, Apr. 1, 1936; s. Zhongshu Zhang and Yuanxin Liu; m. Jieyun Dai; 1 child, Xiaogang. Diploma, Jilin U., Changchun, China, 1958. Asst. dept. physics Jilin U., Changchun, 1958-59; rschr. Inst. Metal Rsch., Academia Sinica, Shenyang, China, 1959-62; from asst. lectr. to assoc. prof. dept. physics Hunan U., Changsha, China, 1962-91; prof. dept. physics Hunan U., Changsha, 1991—, head tchg. and rsch. sect. for applied physics, 1983-87; leader rsch. group Inst. Metal Rsch., Academia Sinica, Shenyang, 1960-62; vis. prof. Max-Planck-Inst. für Plasmaphysik, Munich, 1987-89; sr. scientist dept. materials sci. U. Va., Charlottesville, 1989. Contbr. articles to profl. jours.; inventor in field. Recipient The Prizes of Achievement in Sci. and Tech. of Hunan Province in the Sixth Five Year Plan, The Hunan Province, 1987, The Advanced Prize of Sci. and Tech., The Ministry of Machine and Electron Bldg. Industry, China, 1992, 96, 98, 99; fellow Max-Planck Soc., 1987. Mem. China Ctr. Advanced Sci. and Tech. (World Lab.), Phys. Soc. China, Internat. Ctr. for Materials Sci. (academia sinica), Am. Phys. Soc. Avocations: reading, traveling, photography. Home: Hunan U, Feng Lin Cun 4-102, Changsha 410082, China Office: Dept Physics, Hunan Univ, Changsha 410082, China

ZHANG, BAORUI, journalist; b. Beijing, Aug. 23, 1952; s. Hongyi Zhang and Guiying Wang; m. Chou Mo, Aug. 28, 1982; 1 child, Mo. Degree, People's U. of China, Beijing, 1992. Reporter Beijing br. Xinhua News Agy., 1992—. Contbr. articles to profl. publs. Mem. Golden Rose Salon (chmn. 1992—), Writers' Union (Excellent News Worker award 1991), On-the-Spot Report Lit. Assn. Home: Dongcheng Qu Jiaodokou, Ju Er Hutong, Beijing 100009, China Office: Xinhua News Agy, Dong Cheng Qu Dent Shi Kou, XiJie 18 Beijing 100006, China

ZHANG, BIN, engineering executive; b. Chongqing, China, Oct. 17, 1961; s. Chang Qing Zhang and Zheng Bi Weng; m. Ji Han Xiang; 2 children. BS, U. Sichuan, China, 1982; M Engring., U. Electronic Sci. and, Technology of China, Chengdu, 1985; PhD, U. Birmingham, 1993; MBA, U. Singapore, 2000. Tchg. asst. U. Electronic Sci. and Technology of China, Chengdu, 1985-87, lectr., 1987-89; sr. R&D engr. Watt Electronics Singapore PTE Ltd., 1993-94; sr. electronic design engr. Astec Custom Power PTE LTd., Singapore, 1994-95; sr. design engr. Apple Computer Ltd., Singapore, 1995-98; mgr. Philips Electronics Singapore Pte Ltd, 1998—. Author rsch. papers in field. Recipient Tech. Coop. scholarship Brit. Coun., State Edn. Ministry of China, London and Beijing, 1990-92. Mem. IEEE. Avocations: reading, study skills, sports, travel. Office: Philips Singapore Pte Ltd, 620A Lorong 1 Toa Payoh, Singapore 319762, Singapore

ZHANG, BO XUE, dental educator, researcher; b. Beijing, Sept. 1, 1944; s. Ze Yuan Zhang and Ze Fang Xie; m. Jia Ping Zhang, July 1, 1971; children: Zhang, Nam. BSc in Stomatology, Beijing Med. U., 1970. Diplomate in dental sci. Dentist, dir. Huade Hosp., China, 1970-79; chief dentist Zhang Jiakou (China) Hosp., 1979-84; prof., dir. Sch. Stomatology, Beijing Med. U., 1984—; dir.office Nat. Com. for Oral Health, Beijing, 1988—; sec.-gen. China. Oral Health Found., Beijing, 1995—. Author: Handbook of Oral Health Care, 1994; editor Jour. Modern Stomatology, 1993—, Chinese Jour. Sch. Health, 1995—, Jour. Dental Prevention and Treatment, 1995—. Mem. Chinese Assn. for Preventive Dentistry (standing com. 1996—), Chinese Assn. Stomatology, Asian Acad. Preventive Dentistry (exec. com. 1995—). Office: Beijing Med U Sch Stomatol, Haidian Weigongcun, Beijing 100081, China

ZHANG, CAI-LI, pharmacologist, educator; b. Shanghai, May 9, 1929; d. Bing-Sun Zhang and Cuei-Ling Wang; m. Zheng-Huei Chen, Aug. 25, 1954; children: Ping, Liang. Student, Ginling Coll., Nanjing, China, 1946; diploma in nursing, Peking Union Med. Coll., Beijing, 1952, postgrad., 1952-53. Asst. in pharmacology 1st Mil. Med. U., Tianjin, China, 1953-54; asst. in pharmacology Tianjin Med. U., 1954-63, lectr. pharmacology, 1963-81, assoc. prof., 1981-86, prof., 1986—, chmn. pharmacology dept., 1987-94; fellow U. Va., Charlottesvile, 1981-82; vis. prof. U. Louisville, 1990-91, Nankai U., Tianjin, 1997—. Contbr. articles to profl. jours., textbooks. Mem. Chinese Pharmacology Soc. (bd. dirs. 1993—), Chinese Clin. Pharmacology Soc. (bd. dirs. 1982—), Tianjin Pharmacology Soc. (vice-chmn. 1993—). Avocation: reading novels. Office: Tianjin Med U, 22 Qi Xian Tai Rd, Tianjin 300070, China

ZHANG, CE, mechanical engineering educator; b. Beijing, China, Apr. 8, 1941; s. Liyan Zhang and Jingxin Zhu; m. Wenshuang Ma, May 1, 1967 (wid. July 1976); 1 child, Xiaohui Zhang; m. Lina Feng, Jan. 30, 1978; 1 child, Xiaolai Zhang. BS, Tangshan Inst. Tech., Hebei, China, 1962; MS, Worcester Polytech. Inst., U.S., 1982. Tchr. Tangshan Inst. Tech., 1962-78, lectr., 1978-86, prof., 1986-92, v.p., 1984-89; prof. Tianjin U., China, 1992—, head dept., 1992-97; dean sch. mech. engring. Tianjin U., 1997—; chmn., mem. com. of China of Internat. Fedn. for Theory of Mechanisms and Machines. Author: Analysis and Synthesis of Elastic Linkages, 1989. Vice chmn. adv. com. basic courses of mech. engring. Nat. Commn. Edn. Mem. Chinese Mech. Engring. Soc. (mem. br. com. mech. transmission 1992—). Avocation: music. Office: Tianjin Univ, Weijin Rd, Tianjin 300072, China

ZHANG, CHENG-ZHI, astronomer, educator; b. Qingdao, Shandong, China, Jan. 10, 1936; s. Yan-Ting Zhang and Feng-Zhen Yu; m. Jinhua Zhao, June 30, 1967; 1 child, Xiao-Kui. Grad., Nanjing (China) U., 1957. From asst. to prof. Nanjing U., 1957—. Author: Astrometry, 1986; contbr. articles to profl. jours. including Earth, Moon and Planets, Icarus, others; mem. editl. bd. Earth, Moon and Planets. Mem. Am. Geophys. Union. Home: 52-1 Hankou Rd Apt C6, Jiangsu Nanjing 210008, China Office: Nanjing U, 22 Hankou Rd, Jiangsu Nanjing 210093, China

ZHANG, CHUHAN, civil engineer, educator; b. Meixian, China, Oct. 4, 1933; s. Zhuohu Zhang and Qingrong Yu; m. Guiqin Wang, Apr. 30, 1962;

children: Qing, Jin. PhD, Tsinghua (China) U., 1965, Bachelor's, 1957. Instr., lectr. Tsinghua U., 1957-65; chief engr. Miyun Hydro Project, Beijing, 1976-78; assoc. prof., divsn. chair Tsinghua U., 1983-88, prof., divsn. chair dept. hydraulic engring., 1988-94, prof. engring., 1994—; vis. scientist U. Calif., Berkeley, 1978-81; adj. prof. Concordia U., Montreal, Can., 1988—; v.p. univ. grad. sch. com. Tsinghua U., 1993-97. Prin. investigator Seismic Analysis for High Dams, 1981—; sec.-gen. (China U.S. workshop) Earthquake Behavior for Arch Dams, 1986; editor, chair (Chinese Swiss workshop proceedings book) Soil-Structure Interaction, 1997; contbr. over 100 articles to profl. jours. Recipient China State Natural Sci. Prize, 1999. Mem. Chinese Soc. Mechanics (mem. fluid structure coupling com. 1993). Avocations: singing, dancing, photography, traveling. Office: Tsinghua U, Dept Hydraulic Engring, Beijing 100084, China

ZHANG, CHUNFANG, molecular biologist; b. Lingshou, Hebei, China, Feb. 28, 1956; arrived in Australia, 1984; s. Zhenhai and Xirong (Wang) Z.; m. Fenglan Luo, Nov. 30, 1983; children: Laura Luo, Jessica Jing. BSc, Beijing (China) Agrl. U., 1982; PhD, Monash U., Melbourne, Australia, 1989. Teaching asst. Beijing Agrl. U., 1982-84; rsch. asst. Monash U., Melbourne, 1989-90, rsch. officer, 1990-94, sr. rsch. officer, 1994-99; rsch. fellow Epworth Med. Ctr., Richmond, Victoria, Australia, 1999—. Author various inventions. Office: Epworth Med Ctr, 185-187 Hoddle St, Richmond Victoria 3121, Australia

ZHANG, DANIAN, lawyer; b. Shanghai, China, July 25, 1958; s. Zhitao and Weimin (Xiao) Z.; m. Junlin Mao, 1986; children: Howard M., Catherine M. LLB, Fudan U., Shanghai, 1983, LLM, 1986; JD, Duke U., 1989. Law faculty Fudan U., Shanghai, 1986; atty. Sidley & Austin, Washington, 1989-93; ptnr. Baker & McKenzie, Hong Kong, Beijing, 1993—; rsch. mem. Shanghai People's Congress, 1984. Co-author: Trade and Investment Opportunities in China, 1992; contbg. author: International Environmental Law and Regulation, 1994; contbr. articles to profl. jours. Ford Found. scholarship, 1986-87. Mem. ABA, D.C. Bar Assn., Pa. Bar Assn. Avocations: hiking, travelling, music. Office: Baker & McKenzie, Ste 2526 China World Trade, 1 Jianguomenwai Dajie, Beijing 100004, China

ZHANG, DAO HUA, electrical engineering educator, scientist; b. Zhang Zhuang, Shandong, China, Apr. 29, 1956; s. Kexing Zhang and Guiying Lu; m. Liping Ye; children: Yi, Anna Xinyu. BSc in Physics, Shandong U., China, 1978, Msc in Physics, 1982; PhD in Physics, U. NSW, Australia, 1989. Tchg. asst. Shandong U., China, 1982-83, lectr., 1983-84; vis. fellow U. NSW, Australia, 1984-86, rsch. fellow, 1989-91; lectr. Nanyang Technol. U., Singapore, 1991-94, sr. lectr., 1995-98; assoc. prof., 1999—. Contbr. articles to profl. jours. Mem. IEEE (sr.). Avocations: music, singing, sports. Office: Nanyang Technol U Sch EEE, Block S2 Nanyang Ave, Singapore 639798, Singapore

ZHANG, DAVID YAMING, engineering educator; b. Shen Yang, China, May 18, 1956; s. Jian Yi Zhang and Qin Rong Zhu; m. Hong Shan Qu; children: Alice Yi Hui, Belinda Yi Yao. B in Engring., Dalian Univ. Tech., 1982, M in Engring., 1984; ME, U. New South Wales, 1997. Tech. Shenyang Brewer, China, 1975-77; from asst. lectr. to asst. to head of sch. Dalian U. Tech., China, 1982-89; tutor U. New South Wales, Sydney, 1991—; with Mosman IT, New South Wales, 2000; technical cons. to dir. Creative Uni-Net Tech. Co., Sydney, 1994—. Vice chmn. Auschina Hitech Comml. Assn., 1996—; exec. dir. Sino-Aust Watch, Sydney, 1992—; com. mem. Chinese Australian Forum, Sydney, 1994—. Mem. IEEE, IEEE Computer Soc., Australian Robotics Soc. Avocations: swimming, table tennis, jogging, music. Home: 31 Rosebery St, Mosman NSW2088, Australia Office: Mosman IT, 640 A Military Rd, Mosman NSW, Australia 2088

ZHANG, DAWO, artist, calligrapher; b. Shaanxi, China, July 23, 1943; came to Australia, 1995; s. Zhang Wanli and Ma Yan. BA, Beijing Capital U. Edn., China, 1969. lectr. U. Tienjing, China, 1997, German Embassy, Beijing, 1994, Queen Victoria Mus. and Gallery, Launcaston, Australia, 1992, Coun. C. of C., Hobart, Australia, 1992; major pub. media interviews conducted with China Daily, Bejing, 1997, ABC TV, Launceston, 1997, Darwin, 1995, Darwin Daily, 1995; co-founder Devil Art (gallery). Exhbns. include: 5th Australian Contemporary Art Fair, Melbourne, 1996, Darwin-Beijing Cultural Exch., Darwin, 1995, Thomas Hardy meml., Rochester, Eng., 1994, Contemporary Chinese Calligraphy Invitational Exhbn., Nanjing, 1991, China/Japan Taiwan Contest Exhbn., Beijing, 1990, Modern Artist Gallery, Paris, 1988, 2nd Exhbn. of Modern Calligraphy, Beijing, 1986; art works include (ink and paper medium): Nan (Male), 1990 (3rd prize), Dragon's Resplendence, 1994 (award Brit. Mus. Collection 1998), Labyrinth, 1993 (award Brit. Mus. Collection 1994), Ricefield, 1994 (Brit. Mus. Collection 1998); public collections include: The Brit. Mus., Mus. and Art, Gallery of Darwin and Launcaston, Art Coun. of No. Territory Australia, German Consulate Beijing; corp. collections in Am., Europe, Asia and Australia; initiator Dawo Black in White Miaomo (Oriental abstract art). Mem. China Calligraphy Assn., others.

ZHANG, DE-CHUN, chemistry educator; b. Changzhou, Jiangsu, China, Sept. 21, 1941; s. Xingyi Zhang and Xingru Qiu; m. Yan-Qiu Zhang; 1 child, Yuan. Grad., Peking U., Beijing, 1964. Asst. East-China Inst. Tech., Nanjing, 1964-78, asst. prof., 1978-87; assoc. prof. Suzhou U., 1987-97, prof., 1998—; vis. scholar U. Calif., Berkeley, 1982-84, Rutgers U., New Brunswick, N.J., 1984; rsch. assoc. U. Md., College Park, 1984-86; guest scientist Max-Planck Inst., Mulheim, Germany, 1991-92. Contbr. articles to profl. jours. including Jour. Energetic Materials. Recipient scholarships Dept. Edn. in China, 1981, 91. Mem. Chinese Chem. Soc., Am. Crystallization Assn. Avocations: chess, sightseeing, basketball, music. E-mail: dczhang@suda.edu.cn. Office: Suzhou U, Dept Chemistry, Suzhou Jiangsu 215006, Peoples Republic of China

ZHANG, DEHENG, physicist, educator; b. Donge, Shandong, China, Nov. 12, 1946; s. Jing Xi and Lumei (Liu) Z.; m. Yongqin Wang, July 17, 1971; children: Xun, Jian. BSc, Beijing Normal U., 1970; MSc, Shandong U., Jinan, 1981; PhD, U. Waterloo, Ont., Can., 1993. Tchr. Shenyang Edn. Inst., 1970-79; tchg. asst. Shandong U., Jinan, 1981-83, asst. prof., 1983-88, assoc. prof., 1988-96, prof. physics, 1996—; vis. prof. U. Waterloo, 1990-94. Contbr. over 70 articles to profl. jours.; invited referee Chinese Physics Letter, 1995—, Chinese Sci. Bull., 1996—, Jour. Material Sci. and Tech., 1994—, Acta Physica Sinica, 1996—. Mem. Electro Soc. of China (sr.), Electro-Soc. Shandong Province (exec. mem.). Avocations: reading, basketball, sports, travel. Office: Shandong Univ, Dept Physics, Jinan 250 100, People's Republic of China

ZHANG, DE-WEN, structural engineering educator, researcher; b. Wuhan, Hubei, China, Apr. 5, 1937; s. Shoukuai Zhang and Xianggu Zhu; m. Kangling Huang, Sept. 28, 1968; 1 child, Xiang. B of Tech., Northwestern Poly. U., Xi'an, China, 1962, M of Tech., 1965, PhD, 1967. Cert. sr. rsch. engr., cert. prof. Asst. engr. Shenyang (China) Aerocraft Mfr. Corp., 1962-64; assoc. engr. Aerocraft Strength Inst., Xi'an, 1968-69; engr. Seaplane Inst., Jingmen, China, 1970-80; sr. engr. Beijing Inst. Structure and Environment, 1981-96; prof. China Acad. Launch-Vehicle Tech., Beijing, 1997—; rschr. Aerocraft Strength Inst., Xi'an, 1981-82; vis. lectr. Peking U., Beijing, 1988; vis. lectr. rschr. Nanjing U. Aeronautics and Astronautics, 1989, 98—. Author: (with others) System Identification for Flight Vehicle, 1995, Model Updating and Damage Detection, 1999; contbr. articles to profl. jours. Recipient award for progress of sci. and tech. China Ministry of Aeronautics, 1982, 96, award for progress of sci. and tech. Nat. Com. Sci. and Tech., 1985. Fellow Chinese Soc. Aeronautics and Astronautics; mem. AIAA (rep. 26th structures, structural dynamics and materials conf. 1985), Chinese Soc. Astronautics. Avocations: basketball, soccer, table tennis, chorus, calligraphy. Fax: (8610) 68383130. E-mail: candyzhang 99@yahoo.com. Office: Beijing Inst Struct/Env Eng, PO Box 9210, 100076 Beijing China

ZHANG, FENGLING, instrument scientist; b. Manas, Xinjiang, China, Apr. 19, 1973; arrived in US, 1996; d. Jiansi and Shouying Zhang. BS, Beijing Normal U., 1994; MS, Miami U., Oxford, Ohio, 1998. Instr. Beijing Normal U., 1994-96; rsch. asst. Miami U., Oxford, 1997-98; staff scientist USA Instruments, Inc., Aurora, Ohio, 1998—; pres. Sigwa, Inc., Streetsboro, Ohio, 1999—.

ZHANG, FU-XUE, scientist; b. Yunnan, People's Republic China, Jan. 13, 1939; s. Zhang Wei-Qi and Duo-Ding (Liu); m. Xiu-Luan Wang, Oct. 1, 1967; children: Wei, Lei. BS in Physics, Yunnan U., 1961. Project vice-dir. 11th Lab. in the 10th Rsch. Inst. Sci. and Technol. Com. on Nat. Def., Beijing, 1961-66; project mgr. 10th Lab. in the 14th Rsch. Inst. Sci. and Technol. Com. on Nat. Def., Guangzhou, People's Republic China, 1966-74; vice-dir., sr. engr. 26th lab. 14th rsch. inst. Sci. and Technol. Com. on Nat. Def., Sichuan, People's Republic China, 1974-85; dir., prof. sensor electronics sect. Beijing Info. Tech. Inst., 1985—; cons. Beijing Mcpl. Govt. and Govt. of Sichuan Province, Sichuan; hon. prof. Nanjing (People's Republic China) Aero. and Astronautics U.; hon. dir. Bejing Zhonghui Sensing Tech. Applications Inst., Beijing Huigu High-Tech Application Inst. Author: Piezoelectricity (books I and II), 1988 (Excellent Sci. and Tech. Books award 1988); contbr. 234 papers to profl. jours.; author 19 books in field. Candidate exec. All-China Fedn. of Trade Unions, Beijing, 1979-84, exec., 1984-89. Named Advanced Individual in Guangdong, Govt. of Guangdong Province, 1973, Advanced Individual in Sichuan, Govt. of Sichuan Province, 1978, Nat. Advanced Sci. and Tech. Worker, China Sci. Coun., 1978, Nat. Model Worker, China State Coun. 1979, State Expert Making Great Contbn., State Ministry of Labor and Personal Affairs, 1984; recipient 6 Nat. Inventive and Progressive awards, 21 ministerial progressive awards including Nat. Sci. Conf., 1978, Nat. Inventive award, 1983, 84, Silver award Nat. High Quality Product, Spl. Allowance cert. Chinese State Coun., 1991. Sr. fellow China Assn. Electronics (v.p. electronic sensitive tech. br.); mem. IEEE (sr.), China Assn. Inertial Tech. (councillor), Sensor Assn. (permanent councillor), China Assn. Electronics Quality Mgmt. (councillor). Achievements include development of the piezo-crystal rate gyro, piezoelectric fluidic rate sensor, and other devices applied to navigations, weapons, and robotics fields, theory that the human body consists of electric dipoles which, under static electric fields, turn to the field direction and move along the field direction; invention of gas pendulum inclination sensor, gas pendulum acceletometer, electric field therapeutical device which can cut short the healing time of born wounded by 2-3 times and has remarkable curative effects on long-time bone fractures, unhealing born, soft-tissue injury, disease in cervical vertebra, inflamation in shoulder periphery and arthritis; 10 pantents in U.S., UK, and China. Office: Beijing Info Tech Inst, Dewai, Beijing 100101, China

ZHANG, G. Z. (GUANGZHI), opto-electronic engineer; b. Linqu, China, May 23, 1963; came to U.S., 1997; s. Sengjie Zhang and Zhaofend Zeng; m. Hong Gao, May 1, 1989; 1 child, Bohan. BSc, Shandong U., Jinan, China, 1983; MSc, Tsinghua U., Beijing, 1988; PhD in Sci., U. Electro-Comms., Tokyo, 1995. Elec. engr. Ministry Metallogical Industry, Beijing, 1983-91; postdoctoral fellow U. Toronto, Ont., Can., 1995-97; sr. opto-elec. engr. New Focus Inc., Santa Clara, Calif., 1997—. Contbr. articles to profl. jours. Recipient Sci. and Tech. award Ministry of Metallogical Industry, Beijing, 1992, 9. Mem. Optical Soc. Am. Achievements include pioneering a method to produce broad-band frequent tunable single-mode laser with external feedback and mode-hop free orientation; first experimental research on high-conversion efficiency nonlinear optical generations using electromagnetically induced transparency; development and engineering on single-frequency tunable diode/dye lasers, optical coating, nonlinear optics, and optoelectronic instruments for in-situ imaging and metrology. Avocations: sports, fishing, hiking. E-mail: gzhang@newfocus.com. Office: New Focus Inc 2630 Walsh Ave Santa Clara CA 95051-0905

ZHANG, GANG, oral radiologist, educator; b. Kun Ming City, China, May 30, 1953; s. Ke Chang and Bao Quan (He) Z.; m. Xiang Hong Huang; 1 child, Xiao Yuan. MB, Capital Med. U., Beijing, 1983; M of Oral Radiology, Beijing Med U., 1988. Diplomate in oral/maxillofacial surgery. Resident, dentist Faculty of Stomatology Tong Xian Hosp., Beijing, 1983-85; resident, gen. radiologist Beijing Med. U., 1986-87; resident, oral radiologist, oral maxillofacial surgeon Stomatology Hosp., Beijing Med. U., 1987-88, attending oral radiologist, 1988-93, dep. dir. dept. oral radiology, 1994—, lectr. oral radiology, 1988-93; vis. scholar dept. oral radiology Sch. Stomatology, Meikai U., Japan, 1993-94; assoc. prof. oral radiology Beijing Med. U., 1994—. Author: Imaging Diagnoses for Oral and Maxillofacial Diseases, 1996; contbr. articles to profl. jours. Mem. Chinese Med Assn., Chinese Stomatology Assn. Office: Beijing Med U Sch Stomatol, Dept Oral Radiology, 100081 Beijing China

ZHANG, GENG JI, petroleum educator, consultant; b. Haerbin, China, Mar. 23, 1930; s. Nian Kun and Guan Hua (Dong) Z.; m. Wei Wang, Jan. 2, 1975; 1 child, Zhan Ying. BS, Tsinghua U., Beijing, China, 1952. Tchr's. asst. Beijing (China) Petroleum Inst., 1956-69, lectr., 1969-80; lectr. East China Petroleum Inst., Dongying, Shandong, 1969-80, assoc. prof., 1980-87; prof. U. Petroleum, Dongying, Shandong, 1987—; cons. Rsch. Inst. Well-Logging, Qianjiang, Hubei Province, 1996—, Rsch. Inst. No. XXII, Xinxiang, Henan Province, 1990—. Author: Electric Well-logging, 1986; contbr. articles to profl. jours. Avocations: reading novels, watching soccer. E-mail address: gjzhang@hdpu.edu.cn. Fax: 0086-0546-8392262. Office: U Petroleum, 149 Tai'an Rd, Dongying Shandong 257062, Peoples Republic of China

ZHANG, GUMAN, genetics and vegetable breeding educator; b. Fuzhou, China, Sept. 6, 1931; s. Yihui Zhang and Huiying Cao; m. Qiwei Lu, Aug. 1, 1957; children: Weina Stucken, Lingna Ninphius, Dongxiao. Diploma in hort. sci., Fujian Agrl. Coll., Fuzhou, 1953. Asst. Fujian Agrl. Coll., 1953-60, lectr. genetics and vegetable breeding, 1961-80, assoc. prof., 1981-85, prof., 1985—, chmn. dept. horticulture, 1981-87; chmn. Chinese del. 23d Internat. Hort. Congress, Italy, 1990. Contbr. articles to Acta Horticulturae Sinica, Netherlands Jour. Plant Breeding. Recipient prize of sci. Fujian Sci. Congress, 1978; 1st prize sci. and tech. Fujian Provincial Govt., 1979, title of scientist with outstanding achievements, 1987, title of excellent expert, 1992. Mem. Chinese Soc. for Horticulture (coun.). Avocations: classical music, studying foreign languages. Office: Fujian Agrl U, Dept Horticulture, Fuzhou 350002, China

ZHANG, GUOQING (GREGORY ZHANG), mechanical engineer, researcher; b. Shexian, Anhui, China, Sept. 13, 1962; came to U.S., 1993; s. Dusheng and Lianzi (Wu) Z.; m. Xiaomiao (Shirley) Li, Nov. 18, 1987; children: Beiwei (Lisa), Connie. BS, Nanjing U. Sci. and Tech., 1983, MS, 1986; PhD, Chinese Acad. Scis., 1990; MBA, Ill. Inst. Tech., 2000. Asst. prof. Chinese Acad. Scis., Beijing, 1990-92; vis. scholar U. Ill., Urbana, 1993-94; rsch. faculty U. Mich., Ann Arbor, 1995-97; sr. devel. engr. Internat. Truck & Engine Corp., Melrose Park, Ill., 1997—. Contbr. articles to profl. jours. UN Devel. Program fellow, 1993. Mem. ASME (tech. paper reviewer ASME Jour. Engring. for Gas Turbines and Power 1999—), Soc. Automotive Engrs. (tech. paper reviewer SAE Transactions 1997—). Avocations: table tennis, basketball, travel. Office: Internat Truck & Engine Corp 10400 W North Ave Melrose Park IL 60160-1028

ZHANG, HAO, research scientist; b. Tianjin, China, Nov. 30, 1962; s. Feng-Ming and Shu-Ying (Liu) Z. BSc, Peking (China) U., 1984; PhD, Monash U., Australia, 1993. Rsch. assoc. Peking U., 1985-86; from rsch. assoc. to rsch. fellow Monash U., Australia, 1986-95; sr. rsch. scientist Comalco Rsch. Ctr., Melbourne, Australia, 1995—; cons. in field. Contbr. articles to profl. jours. Mem. Assn. Profl. Engrs., Scientists and Mgrs., South Cambellwell Tennis Club (com. mem. 1998—). Avocations: tennis, classic music, walking, cooking, movies. Office: Comalco Rsch Ctr, 3074 Melbourne Australia

ZHANG, HONG, pathologist; b. Changchun, China, Oct. 3, 1957; s. Zhixie and Xiujing (Jin) Z.; m. Xiaofeng Sun, Nov. 14, 1986; children: Daniel, Alexander. MD, Bethune Med. U., 1982; MSc, Hebei Med. U., China, 1988; PhD, Linköping U., Sweden, 1995. Pathologist Hebei Med. U., 1982-89; pathologist Norrköping Hosp., Sweden, 1995-96, with dept. cell biology and oncology, 1996-2000, with dept. dermatology, 2000—. Mem. European Assn. for the Study of Diabetes, Internat. Soc. for Free Radical Rsch., Swedish Free Radical Club. Office: Clin Rsch Ctr, Linköping U, 581 85 Linköping Sweden

ZHANG, HONG, mathematician; b. Beijing, Dec. 19, 1956; d. Bing Jian Zhang and Min Chen; m. Xian-He Sun, Sept. 1983; children: Alan Sun, Linda Sun. BS in Math., Beijing Normal U., 1982; MS in Applied Math., Mich. State U., 1985, PhD in Applied Math., 1989. Lectr. Capital U. Econs. and Bus., Beijing, 1982-83; rsch. asst. dept. elec. engring. sys. sci. Mich. State U., East Lansing, 1987-88, tchg. asst. dept. math., 1983-89; vis. asst. prof. dept. math. Iowa State U., Ames, 1991; vis. scientist Inst. Computer Applications in Sci./Engring. NASA Langley Rsch. Ctr., Hampton, Va., 1992-94, 95, 96; NSF VPW vis. prof. dept. math. La. State U., Baton Rouge, 1996-97; from asst. prof. to assoc. prof. dept. math. scis. Clemson (S.C.) U., 1989-97; assoc. prof. dept. math. La. State U., Baton Rouge, 1997—; spkr. in field. Contbr. articles and papers to profl. jours. Recipient NSF/AWM Travel Grant award, 1990; NSF grantee, 1991-93, 95-97, 98-2000, grantee Coun. on Rsch., La. State U., 1998. Mem. SIAM, AMS, AWM. Address: 8108 Wittington Ct Darien IL 60561-6620 Office: La State U Baton Rouge LA 70803-0001

ZHANG, HONG-YU, pharmacology educator; b. Jinan, China, June 30, 1970; s. Peng Zhang and Ming-Feng Li. BSc, Shandong U., Jinan, 1992; PhD, Chinese Acad. Scis., Beijing, 1997. Lectr. Shandong Tchrs.' U., Jinan, 1997-98, prof., 1998—. Contbr. articles to profl. jours. Recipient Shandong Sci. and Tech. award for Youth, Shandong Province, 1998. Fellow Chinese Soc. Pharmacology, Chinese Soc. Biophysics; mem. N.Y. Acad. Scis. Avocations: running, table tennis, chess, weiqi. Fax: 86-531-2960682. E-mail: zhysdtu@jn-public.sd.cninfo.net. Office: Shandong Tchrs U, Wenhua Donglu # 88, Jinan 250014, China

ZHANG, JIAN-GUO, optical communications educator, researcher; b. Chongqing, Sichuan, China, Jan. 27, 1964; arrived in Finland, 1999; s. Xue-Ming Zhang and Chang-Hui Huang; m. Li-Juan Chen, Dec. 31, 1998. BS, Shenyang Inst. Aero. Tech., China, 1985; MS, Beijing U. Aero/Astronautics, 1988; PhD, U. Parma, Italy, 1994. Rsch. engr. Chengdu (China) Aircraft Co., 1988-90; rsch. asst. U. Parma, 1990-94; vis. assoc. Chinese U. Hong Kong, 1994, rsch. assoc., 1994-95; asst. prof. Asian Inst. Tech., Bangkok, 1995-98, assoc. prof., 1998—; sr. rschr. Comms. Lab., Dept. Elec. and Comms. Engring. Helsinki U. of Tech., Espoo, Finland, 1999—; summer vis. scholar Princeton U., U. So. Calif., 1993; short-term vis. U. Essen, Germany, 1998, Helsinki U. Tech., Finland, 1999; short-term visitor Helsinki U. of Tech., 1999. Contbr. more than 55 articles to internat. profl. jours.; reviewer for IEE and OSA jours., Kluwer Acad. Pubs., Internat. Jour. Electronics, UK. Ing. Migliorini scholar U. Parma, scholar Alcatel Face Research Ctr.; recipient Young Scientist awards Internat. Symposium on Signals, Sys. and Electronics, 1995, XXVth Internat. Union of Radio Sci. Gen. Assembly, 1996, Twentieth Century Achievement award, 1998, 2000 Millenium medal of honor, 1999, Outstanding Achievement medal, 1999, Distinguished Leadership award, 2000; Spl. EMCSC scholar World Fedn. Scientists, 1993. Mem. IEEE, ISA, OSA, SAE, Internat. Soc. Optical Engring., N.Y. Acad. Sci. Office: Comms Lab Helsinki U Tech, PO Box 2300 Otakaari 8, FIN02015 HUT Espoo Pathumthani, Finland

ZHANG, JIN, information educator; b. Zheng Zhou, Henan, China, Dec. 3, 1959; came to U.S. 1994; s. Shi Zhang and Lily Yang; m. Yi Hong, Aug. 26, 1987; 1 child, Tian Run. BS, Wuhan (China) U., 1983, MS, 1986; PhD, U. Pitts., 1999. Prof. Wuhan U., 1986-95; asst. prof. U. Wis., Milw., 1999—. Author: Principle of Computerized Information Retrieval System Design, 1994; contbr. articles to profl. jours. Fulbright scholar U.S. Govt., 1994. Mem. Am. Soc. for Info. Sci. (Pratt-Severn Best Student Rsch. Paper award 1994). Avocations: music, reading. E-mail: jzhang@uwm.edu. Fax: 414-229-4848. Office: U Wis Milw Enderis Hall PO Box 413 Milwaukee WI 53201-0413

ZHANG, JIN WEN, engineering educator, consultant; b. Xian, Shaanxi, China, June 11, 1961; s. Zhi Yao and Shu Zeng (Miao) Z.; m. Xiao Hong Zhang, Oct. 27, 1962; 1 child, Qi. Bachelor, Nanking (China) Aviation U., 1983; master, N.W. Polytech. U., 1991, PhD, 1994. In charge of group Chinese Flight Test Establishment, Xian, China, 1984-88; class monitor NW Polytech.U, Xian, 1992-94; dir. dept. Chinese Flight Test Establishment, Xian, 1997-98, dir. inst., 1999—, assoc. chief engr., 1997—; mem. Sci. and Tech. Com. Chinse Flight Test Establishment, Xian, 1999—, mem. cons. com., 1999. Contbr. articles to profl. publs. Dep. People's Congress, Yanliang Divsn., 1998—. Mem. AAAS, Acoustic Soc. Am., N.Y. Acad. Scis. Avocations: music, football, basketball, traveling, reading. Office: Chinese Flight Test, PO Box 73 Ext 23, Xian 710089, China

ZHANG, JINGWU, immunologist; b. Shanghai, Feb. 2, 1956; came to the U.S., 1996; s. Yuzeng and Xiochin Zhang; m. Ying C. Q. Zang, Feb. 19, 1986; children: Linda, Peter. MD, Shanghai (China) Med. U., 1984; PhD, U. Brussels, 1990. Lic. MD. Head dept. Dr. Willems Inst., Diepenbeek, Belgium, 1990-96; assoc. prof. neurology, rsch. dir. MS Ctr. Baylor Coll. Medicine, 1996—; rsch. assoc. Harvard Med. Sch., Boston, 1991-92; vis. prof. Baylor Coll. Medicine, Houston, 1993; prof. Limburgs U. Ctr., Diepenbeek, 1994—, Shanghai Med. U., 1995. Contbr. articles to profl. jours.; patentee in field. Recipient Rsch. award Am. Multiple Slcerosis Soc., 1990, Achievement award Belgian Soc. Clin. Immunology, 1993, Internat. award Assn. Malattie Rare, 1994. Mem. AAAS, N.Y. Acad. Scis., European Immunology Fedn., Am. Assn. Immunologists, Am. Acad. Neurology. Avocations: painting, music, sports. Office: Baylor Coll Medicine Dept Neurology Houston TX 77030

ZHANG, JINYAN, process engineer, researcher; b. Yinchuan, Ning-Xia, China, Mar. 16, 1959; s. Xinling Z. and Meixiu Gao; m. Yanbing Zhang, apr. 18, 1985; 1 child: Xi. BS, Lanzhou U., China, 1982, MS, 1990; PhD, Kanazawa U., Japan, 1996. Rschr. Ningxia Inst. New Techs., Yinzhuan, China, 1982-87, 90-92; engr. Pacusma Enterprises Inc., Shenzhen, China, 1992-93; rschr. Kanazawa U., Japan, 1996; process engr. Ball Semiconductor Inc., Allen, Tex., 1998—; cons., dir. Hopream Enterprises, Vancouver, B.C., Can. Scholar Ministry Edn. and Sci. Japan, Tokyo, 1993-96. Mem. Materials Rsch. Soc., Am. Inst. Physics. Avocation: soccer. Office: Ball Semiconductor Inc 415 Century Pkwy Allen TX 75013-3673

ZHANG, JIZE, information management specialist, researcher; b. Gyuyang, Guizhou, China, Dec. 1, 1945; parents Guangding Zhang and Shiyu Zhao; m. Chuiying Shen, 1971; children: Ziyi, Qonghui. B, Guizhou Normal Sch., Guiyang, China, 1968. Master, vice dir. Guizhou Province Info. Ctr., Guiyang, 1995—; vice dir. China Future Assn., Guizhou, 1995—. Editor Information and Future, 1995—. Avocations: photography, hill climbing, singing. Office: Guizhou Info Ctr, Yan'an Middle Rd No 110-1, Guiyang 550001, China

ZHANG, JUN, pathologist, researcher; b. Shijiazhuang, China, Mar. 11, 1937; came to U.S., 1987; became citizen, 1999; s. Jing-Chen and Jing-Fang (Liang) Z.; m. Da-Ai-Liu Zhang, Sept. 21, 1972; children: Hua, Paul P. Chang. MD, Beijing (China) Med. U., 1961, MS in Med. Scis., 1964. Asst. Beijing (China) Med. U., 1964-65; assoc. prof. Xinjiang Med. Coll., Urumqi, China, 1985-87; sr. staff fellow Ctr. for Drug Evaluation & Rsch. FDA, Laurel, Md., 1988-2000, pharmacologist, 2000—; mem. of coun. Xinjiang subcom., Chinese Electron Microscope, Urumqi, China, 1985-87; mem. edtl. bd. Chinese Jour. Pathology, Beijing, China, 1986-87. Author: Recent Development of Electron Microscopy, 1985. Recipient Rsch. awards, Xinjiang Sci. and Tech. Coun., 1984-88, FDA award, 1997-00; named Outstanding Scientist Chinese Nat. Sci. and Tech. Com., Beijing, China, 1986. Achievements include anthracycline-induced cardiotoxicity, phosphodiesterase inhibitor-induced vasculitis, and drug-induced apoptosis. Office: FDA (HFD-910) Divsn Applied Pharm Rsch Laurel MD 20708

ZHANG, JUN, electrical engineer; b. Tianjin, China, Feb. 21, 1967; s. Lanjuzhang and Ai Ying (Liu) Z. BSc, Hebei U. Tech., Tianjin, 1989, MSc, 1995; postgrad., Zhejiang U., Hangzhou, China, 1995-96, City U. Hong Kong, 1996—. Asst. engr. Tianjin Auto Factory, 1989-92. Author articles. Recipient scholarships. Achievements include research in chaotic time series prediction, intelligent neural networks, fuzzy logic. Avocations: sports, travel, cooking, computer. Home: 14-4-301 Tao Hua Yuan Dong, Ding Zhi Gu, Hong Qiao Qu, Tianjin China Office: City U Hong Kong, Dept Elec Engring, Hong Kong China

ZHANG, JUNBIAO, computer scientist. BS in Computer Sci., U. Sci. and Tech. China, 1990; MS in Computer Sci., Rutgers U., 1994, PhD in Computer Sci., 1997. Rsch. staff mem. C&C rsch. lab. NEC, Princeton, N.J., 1997—; expert in multimedia, comm. networks and info. systems. Contbr.

articles to profl. jours. Office: NEC CCRL 4 Independence Way Ste 4 Princeton NJ 08540-6685

ZHANG, JUNHAO, physicist, educator; b. Shantou, China, Mar. 9, 1936; s. Zhishen Zhang and Zeshan Yang; m. Xiang Chen, Dec. 14, 1958; children: Li, Yue. Grad., Zhongshan U., 1958. Asst. Guangxi U., Nanning, China, 1958-62; asst. lectr. Guanxi Coll. Nationalities, Nanning, 1962-85; from lectr. to prof. Shantou U., Shantou, China, 1985—. Mem. Chinese Phys. Soc.

ZHANG, KANGDA, mechanical engineering educator, researcher; b. Hangzhou, Zhejiang, China, June 18, 1935; s. Zhanhua and Yuahua (Jin) Z.; m. Bietian Hu, Jan. 17, 1971; 1 child. B in Engring., Dalian (China) Inst. Tech., 1956. Lectr. Zhejiang Inst. Chem. Tech., Hangzhou, China, 1956-78; assoc. prof. Zhejiang Inst. Chem. Tech., Hangzhou, 1978-83; prof. Zhejiang U. of Tech., Hangzhou, 1984-93, head of mech. engring. dept., 1984-95; project head Rsch. into Fatigue and Fracture of Pressure Vessels, 1979, Zhejiang Sci. Com., The Assessment of Defect in Structures, 1986 (award Ministry Mech. Engring. 1987), Engring. Application of Fatigue Rsch. 1993 (award Nat. Edn. Com. 1993), The Assessment of the Integrity of Pressure Vessels and Piping Containing Pefects, 1996 (award Ministry Mech. Engring. 1997). Author: (book) The Equipment of Chemical Engineering, 1961; editor Zhejiang Gongxueyuan Xuebao, 1993-97. Mem. Chinese Mech. Engring. Soc. (sr.), Chinese Soc. Pressure Vessels (bd. dirs.), China Nat. Standards Com. Pressure Vessel (bd. dirs.), Zhejiang Mech. Design Soc. (pres.). E-mail: kdz@mail.hz.zj.cn. Home: 6 Dist Zhaohui 72# 2-502, Zhejiang Hangzhou 310014, China Office: Zhejiang U Tech, Zhejiang Hangzhou 310032, China

ZHANG, KEFEI, science and engineering educator; b. Heilongjiang, China, Apr. 11, 1964; arrived in Australia, 1999.; married, July 1, 1989; 1 child, Xi. B of Engring., Wuhan (China) Tech. U. Surveying and Mapping, 1985, M of Engring., 1988; PhD, Curtin U. Tech., Perth, Australia, 1997. Assoc. prof. Wuhan Tech. U. Surveying and Mapping, 1992-93; rsch. assoc. Curtin U. Tech., Perth, 1994-97; rsch. fellow U. Nottingham, U.K., 1997-99; sr. lectr. Royal Melbourne Inst. Tech. U., Melbourne, Australia, 1999—. Contbr. articles to profl. jours. Vice-sec. Chinese Inst. Astronomy, Hubei, 1992-94; pres. Chinese Scholar and Student Assn., Nottingham, 1997-98; hon. head Nottingham Chinese Sch., 1999. Recipient Rsch. Excellency award China Nat. Bur. Surveying and Mapping, 1994, Best Postgrad. Student Paper award Inst. Australia Surveyor, 1996; overseas postgrad. rsch. scholar Australian Govt., 1994-97. Mem. Internat. Assn. Geodesy, Am. Geophys. Union. Avocations: Go chess, basketball, playing cards, traveling. Fax: 61 3 96632517. E-mail: kefei.zhang@rmit.edu.au. Office: RMIT U Dept Land Info, Swanston St GPO Box 2476V, 3001 Melbourne Victoria, Australia

ZHANG, KEQIANG, metallurgical engineer; b. Beijing, Sept. 10, 1950; s. Y. Zhang and Deyu (Gu) Z.; m. Huicong Tong Mar. 7, 1979; 1 child, Ting. Diploma, U. Sci. and Tech. Beijing, 1976. Metall. engr. U. Sci. and Tech. Beijing, 1976-90, 1994—; vis. scholar Tech. U. Denmark, 1990-93; mgr. tech. divsn. Jinda New Tech. Devel. Co., China, 1993-94. Contbr. articles to profl. jours. Recipient Sci. and Tech. Improvement award Min. Metallurgy Industry China, 1988, China Econ. Com., 1986. Achievements include development of an apparatus for measuring heat transfer coefficient in continuous casting of steel, computer software in continuous casting of steel. Office: Univ Sci and Tech Beijing, 100083 Beijing China

ZHANG, LIANG-JIE, multimedia architect, computer scientist; b. Hubei, China, Sept. 22, 1969. BEE, Xidian U., Xi'an, China, 1990; MEE, Xi'an Jiaotong U., 1992; PhD in Computer Engring., Tsinghua U., Beijing, 1996. Lectr. Tsinghua U., 1992-96; rsch. staff IBM China Rsch. Lab., Beijing, 1996-97; rsch. fellow Poly. U., Hawthorne, N.Y., 1997-98; multimedia arch. IBM Watson Rsch. Ctr., Hawthorne, 1998—. Named to Outstanding Sci. People List, 1995; recipient Best Paper award Internat. Conf. on Neural Networks and Signal Processing, 1995. Mem. IEEE, Assn. Computing Machinery. Achievements include patents for IBM HotVideo, HotMedia related tracking, transaction and interaction technologies, info. appliances. Fax: 603-452-0786. E-mail: zhanglj@us.ibm.com. Home: 14 Westview Ave White Plains NY 10603-3549 Office: IBM Internet Media Group 30 Saw Mill River Rd Hawthorne NY 10532-1507

ZHANG, LIJUAN, molecular microbiologist, researcher; b. Herbin, China, Mar. 13, 1962; d. Shaoquan Zhang and XuZhi Ma; m. Quan Yu, July 20, 1985; 1 child, Vivian. BSc, Northwestern U., Xian, China, 1983; MSc, Chinese Acad. Sci. Tech., Beijing, 1986; PhD, Turku U., Finland, 1996. Rsch. asst. Nat. Inst. Control Pharm. Biol. Products, Beijing, 1986-90; rsch. assoc. U. Turku, 1990-96, U. British Columbia, Vancouver, Can., 1996—. Contbr. articles to profl. jours. Mem. Am. Soc. Microbiology. Avocations: traditional Chinese painting, swimming, classical music. Office: Dept Microbiol Immunol, # 300-6174 Univ Blvd, Vancouver, Canada

ZHANG, LIN-CHANG, electromagnetic compatibility educator; b. Tianjin, Hebei, China, Aug. 18, 1932; s. Jin-Qing and Xiang-Quan (Jin) Z.; m. Ju-Zhen Wang, Dec. 22, 1956; children: Lu. E. Bachelor, No. Jiaotong U., Beijing, China, 1953. Asst., lectr. No. Jiaotong U., Beijing, 1953-79, assoc. prof., 1979-86, prof., 1986—; dir. electromagnetic compatibility rsch. sect. No. Jiaotong U., Beijing, 1982-99, acad. com. mem., 1989-96, vice-chmn. acad. degree com., 1997—; cons. Beijing Radio Adminstrn. Com., 1984-85, 88—; mem. Nat. Tech. Com. Standardization on Radio Interference, 1987—; vice chmn. Nat. Tech. Com. Standardization on Electromagnetic Compatibility, 1998—. Author: Dispatching Radio Station for Train, 1979, (textbook) Radio Measurements, 2d edit., 1985 (award 1992); editor: (procs.) Internat. Symposium on Electromagnetic Compatibility, 1992, 97. Recipient Sci. and Technique awards Rlwy. Ministry of China, 1983, 86, Beijing Authority, 1988, Nat. Acad. and Technique award, 1989, Tian-You Jhan award Rlwy. Ministry China, 1994. Fellow Chinese Inst. Electronics; mem. IEEE (sr. mem., vice chmn. electromagnetic compatibility chpt. Beijing sect. 1992—, chmn. exec. com. Beijing sect. 1999-2000, Third Millennium medal 2000), Chinese Soc. Elec. Engring. (sr. mem.), Chinese Electrotech. Soc. (standing coun. mem. 1990-95, vice chmn. electromagnetic compatibility com. 1984—, v.p. 1995—). Avocation: classical music. E-mail: lczhang@center.njtu.edu.cn. Office: No Jiaotong Univ, Electromagnetic Compatibility Rsch Sect, Beijing 100044, China

ZHANG, LI-NING, metallurgy educator, researcher; b. Nanjing, China, Aug. 26, 1935; s. Ze Zhang and Min-Yuan Yang; m. Rui-Lian Ding, Oct. 1, 1959; 1 child, Joy Zhang. Grad., Nanjing (China) Inst. Tech., 1956. Lectr. Nanjing Inst. Tech., 1960-79; vis. rschr. dept. metallurgy and materials science Oxford U., 1980-82; assoc. prof. Nanjing Inst. Tech., 1983-86; prof. Southeast U., Nanjing, 1987—, head dept. material sci. and engring., 1988-90. Author, co-editor: Advanced Materials Technique, 1992; numerous research papers published: Stress Asymmetries in the Deformation Behaviour of Niobium Single Crystals, 1983, Resistance of Metals to Microstrain and its Influential Factors, 1990, The Extrusion of Zn-Al Alloy in Semisolid State, 1994, Fabrication and Properties of SiC/Zn Composites, 1995; patentee in field. Recipient Sci. and Tech. Progress 3d prize Nat. Edn. Com., China, 1995, 3d prize Nat. Sci. and Tech. Progress, 1996; named Outstanding Supr. Rsch. Students, Edn. Com. Jiangsu Province, China, 1993; recipient of special subsidy issued by Chinese govt. for researcher and educator with outstanding achievements, 1992—. Mem. Chinese Composite Material Soc. (bd. dirs.), Jiangsu Soc. Metals (chmn. metallic material acad. com.). Office: Dept Materials Sci and Engring, Southeast U, Nanjing 210018, China

ZHANG, MING, environmental geologist; b. Nantong, China, May 29, 1964; s. Guanghuan Zhang and Yuee Sun; m. Yiming Weng, Apr. 30, 1988; 1 child, Xianyi. BS, China U. Mining Technology, 1986, MS, 1989; PhD, Kyushu U., 1996. Tchg. asst. China U. Mining & Technology, Xuzhou, China, 1989-92; vis. scholar, vis. rschr. Kyushu U., Fukuoka, Japan, 1992-96; rschr. Geol. Survey Japan, Tsukuba, 1996-99, sr. rschr., 1999—; rsch. fellow Japan Sci. & Technology Corp., Kawaguchi, 1996-99. Author: Underground Construction, 1995; contbr. articles to profl. jours. Fax: 81 298 61 3578. E-mail: zhang@gsj.go.jp. Office: Geol Survey Japan, Higashi 1-1-3, Tsukuba Ibaraki 305-8567, Japan

ZHANG, MING, computer scientist; b. Shanghai, China, July 29, 1949; arrived in Australia, 1992; s. Changdong Zhang and Wenshao Zuo; m. Zhaoqing Zhang, Apr. 19, 1949; 1 child, Jean Xueqing. MS, East China Normal U., Shanghai, 1982, PhD, 1989. Vis. scholar U. Ill., Champaign, 1985-86; assoc. chmn., lectr. East China Normal U., 1986-89; assoc. prof., postdoctoral fellow Chinese Acad. Scis., Shanghai, 1989-91; postdoctoral fellow USA Nat. Rsch. Coun., Washington, 1991-92; project mgr., PhD supr. U. Wollengong, Australia, 1992-94; lectr., PhD supr. Monash U., Churchill, Australia, 1994-95; sr. lectr. U. Western Sydney, Campbelltown, Australia, 1995—. Patentee standard nonlinear signal wave generator based on the neural networks; author: Visual Cognition, 1992; contbr. articles to profl. jours. Mem. IEEE Computer Soc. (sr.). Office: U Western Sydney, Dept Computing Info Systems, Campbelltown 2560 New South Wales, Australia

ZHANG, MINQUAN, chemistry educator; b. Yixin City, Jiangshu, China, Jan. 29, 1945; s. Peijing Zhang and Fuzheng Cheng; m. Xiaoli Ding, Oct. 25, 1973; 1 child, Yan. BS, East China Normal U., Shanghai, 1967, MS, 1981, PhD, 1984; postgrad., So. Ill. U., 1987-90. Cert. tchr., China. Engr. Salt Base Factory, Alta, China, 1968-72; H.S. dir. Alta, 1972-76; lectr. Xinjiang Inst. Tech., Urumqi, China, 1976-81; asst. prof., assoc. prof. Xinjiang Inst. Tech., Urumqi, China, 1981-87, 91-94, prof., 1995—; vis. asst. prof. So. Ill. U., Carbondale, 1987-90; vis. prof. Okla. State U., Stillwater, 1997—. Editor Jour. Xinjiang Inst. Tech., 1994—; contbr. articles to profl. jours.; patentee in field. Scholar China Edn. Com., Beijing, 1987, China Scholarship Coun., Beijing, 1996; recipient Outstanding Profl. award Xinjiang Autonomous Region, Urumqi, China, 1996, New Century Asia 500 award, 2000. Mem. AAAS, China Chemistry Soc., N.Y. Acad. Scis., Xinjiang Internat. Assn. for Cooperation of Sci. and Tech., Am. Chem. Soc., Calif. Spearation Scis. Soc., Nat. Resources Def. Coun., Planetary Soc. Avocations: table tennis, Chinese chess. Home and Office: Xinjiang Inst Tech, 21 N Friendship Rd, Urumqi Xinjiang 830008, China Office: Okla State U Dept Chemistry Stillwater OK 74078-0001

ZHANG, NAI-XIAO, computer science educator, researcher; b. Zhenjiang, China, Aug. 1, 1942; s. Shao-Pu Zhang and Shu-Hua Bi; m. Su-Lan Zhao, Feb. 2, 1969; children: Mong Zhang, Yuan Zhang. Grad., Peking U., 1965, Hitachi U., Tokyo, 1981, Cornell U., 1990. Asst. prof. math. Peking U., 1965-69, software engr. elec. instrument factory, 1970-78, lectr. computer sci., 1979-86; assoc. prof. computer sci., 1987-91, prof. computer sci., 1992-95, prof. informatics, 1996—; vice gen. engr., GC-01 Computer Sys. Project, Beijing, 1975-78; head theoretical computer sci. group, Peking U., 1985-92, vice chmn. informatics dept., 1996-98. Author: (textbook) Data Structures, 1987. Mem. IEEE, Computer Sci. Soc. China (vice chmn. software theory sect. 1985—). Avocations: music, sports.

ZHANG, NIEN FAN, statistician; b. Shanghai, China, Aug. 25, 1943; came to U.S., 1981; s. Zhong Han Jiang and Ya Li Zhang; m. Di Cheng Sun, July 10, 1970; children: Ning, Jing Yuan. BS, East China Normal U., 1965; MS, Va. Poly. Inst. and State U., 1982, PhD, 1985. Asst. prof. U. Sci. & Tech., Hefei, China, 1978-81; rsch. assoc. So. Meth. U., Dallas, 1985-88; rsch. statistician Shell Oil Co., Houston, 1988-93; math. statistician Nat. Inst. Stds. and Tech., Geithersburg, Md., 1994—. Contbr. articles to profl. jours. Recipient Silver medal U.S. Dept. Commerce, 1999, award for excellence in tech. transfer Fed. Lab. Consortium, 2000. E-mail: zhang@nist.gov. Office: Nat Inst Stds & Tech Stop 8980 Gaithersburg MD 20899-0001

ZHANG, PEI-LIN, physics educator; b. Chefoo, Shandong, China, June 13, 1933; s. Jun-Shan and Yue-Xian (Liu) Z.; m. Ci-Hui He, May 12, 1956; children: Xiao-Yu, Zhong-Yu. B, Tsinghua U., Beijing, China, 1953, MS, 1956. Lectr. Tsinghua U., 1959-78, assoc. prof., 1979-83, prof., 1984—; dir. lab. modern optics Tsinghua U. Contbr. articles to profl. jours. Recipient Nat. Invention award, State Sci. and Tech. Commn. China, 1981, Award of Progress Sci. and Tech., State Edn. Commn. China, 1991. Mem. Optical Soc. Am., Chinese Optical Soc. Office: Tsinghua U, Dept Physics, Beijing 100084, China

ZHANG, QIANHUI, chemist, educator; b. Fangcheng, China, Apr. 18, 1956; parents Jun and Qingrong (Meng) Z.; m. Kai Zhang, Oct. 1, 1984; 1 child, Yi. BS, Dalian Instn. Tech., China, 1981, MS, 1984; PhD, U. Miami, 1995. Lectr. Xiangtan (China) U., 1984-88; postdoctor U. Miami Sch. Medicine, 1995-96, Am. Heart Assn. rsch. fellow, 1996-98; asst. scientist U. Miami, 1998—; asst. prof. Miami Dade Cmty. Coll., 1999—. Contbr. articles to profl. jours. Avocations: sports, collecting stamps. E-mail: qianhuiz@yahoo.com. Fax: 305-669-0506. Office: Miami Dade CC North Campus/Dept Chemistry 11380 NW 27th Ave Miami FL 33167-3418

ZHANG, RUICHAO, material scientist, researcher; b. Suzhou, Jiangsu, China, Apr. 13, 1966; came to the U.S., 1994; d. Yanming Zhang and Peiqiou Chen; m. Weidong Guo, Apr. 1, 1991. BS, Zhejiang U., Hangzhou, China, 1988, MS, 1991; PhD, U. Utah, 1999. Lectr. Nanjing (China) Inst. Sci. and Tech., 1988-89; rsch. asst. Zhejiang U., Hangzhou, 1989-91; rsch. engr. SINOPEC, Guangzhou, China, 1992-94; rsch. asst. U. Utah, Salt Lake City, 1994-99; postdoctoral rsch. fellow Rensselaer Poly. Inst., Troy, N.Y., 1999—. Contbr. articles to profl. jours. Mem. AAAS, Am. Chem. Soc., Materials Rsch. Soc., Minerals, Metals and Materials Soc. Avocations: bridge, swimming, music, reading. E-mail: zhangr@rpi.edu. Office: Rensselaer Poly Inst ECSE Dept JEC 6003 110 8th St Troy NY 12180-3522

ZHANG, RUICHONG, civil and mechanical engineer, educator; b. Shanghai, China, Dec. 6, 1962; s. Xiangting Zhang and Shoumei Wang; m. Min Zhou, July 1, 1987; children: Vincent, Vivian (Cynthia). BS, Tongji U., 1984, MS, 1987; PhD, Fla. Atlantic U., 1992. Asst. prof. Tongji U., Shanghai, 1987; rsch. asst. U. Colo., Boulder, 1987-88, Fla. Atlantic U., Boca Raton, 1988-92; rsch. assoc. Princeton (N.J.) U., 1992-95; rsch. asst. prof. U. So. Calif., L.A., 1995-97; asst. prof. Colo. Sch. Mines, Golden, 1997—. Recipient Jr. Rsch. prize Internat. Assn. Structural Safety Reliability, 1997. Mem. ASME, ASCE, Earthquake Engring. Rsch. Inst., Internat. Assn. Structural Safety Reliability (Jr. Rsch. prize 1997). Home: 16501 W Ellsworth Ave Golden CO 80401-6540 Office: Colo Sch Mines Divsn Engring Golden CO 80401

ZHANG, RUNING, engineer, researcher; b. Kunming, Yunnan, China, Aug. 28, 1958; came to U.S., 1990; s. Renqing and Cuiying (Gao) Z.; m. Bo He Zhang, Dec. 26, 1989. BS, Chendu (China) U. Sci. & Tech., 1982; MS, Colo. Sch. Mines, Golden, 1993; PhD, U. Colo., 1996. Engr. Chang Engring., Denver, 1997-98; rschr. U. Utah, Salt Lake City, 1998—. Address: 10530 Holyoke Dr Parker CO 80134-9136 Office: U Utah 2202 MEB Salt Lake City UT 84112

ZHANG, S., engineering educator; b. Bainiang County, Hebei, China, Oct. 1, 1962; s. Jichun Zhang and Wei Shi; m. Ling Zhang, Feb. 27, 1987; 1 child, Shiyi. B in Engring., Wuhan (China) U. Hydraulics, 1982; M in Engring., Dalian (China) U. Tech., 1988; PhD in Engring., Osaka (Japan) U., 1995. Asst. North China U. Electric Power, Baoding, 1982-85, lectr., 1988-95. Contbr. articles to profl. jours. Mem. Japan Soc. Corrosion Engring., Japan Inst. Metals, Iron and Steel Inst. Japan. Home: 110 Wusi Rd, Baoding 071000, China Office: Osaka Univ, 2-1 Yamada-oka, Suita 565-0871, Japan

ZHANG, SHAOWU, research scientist; b. Shanghai, China, Feb. 28, 1942; s. Y.W. Zhang and F.Y. Jiang; m. Hong Zhu, Sept. 23, 1967; children: P.J., G.J. Diploma, U. Sci. and Tech of China, Beijing, 1964. Rsch. assoc. Inst. Biophysics Chinese Acad. Sci., Beijing, 1964-78, asst. prof. Inst. Biophysics, 1978-79, 84-86, assoc. prof. Inst. Biophysics, 1986-91; Alexander von Humboldt fellow Inst. Zool. U. Darmstadt, Germany, 1980-81; Alexander von Humboldt fellow Max Plank Inst. fü Biologishe Kybernetik, Tübingen, Germany, 1981-82, postdoctoral fellow, 1982-83; guest assoc. prof. Nanjing (China) Inst. Tech., 1987-89, guest assoc. prof. grad. sch. Chinese Acad. Sci., 1989-91; vis. fellow Australian Nat. U., Canberra, 1991-92, rsch. fellow 1993-96, rsch. officer, 1996—. Co-editor: Visual Physiology & Bionics, 1980; mem. editl. bd. Advances in Biochemistry and Biophysics, 1987-91; contbr. more than 70 articles to profl. jours. Mem. AAAS, N.Y. Acad. Scis., Beijing Optic Soc. (coun. 1979-83), Australian Neurosci. Soc., Internat. Neuroethology Soc., Biophysics Soc. China (expert com. on info. and biocybernetics 1987-91), Australian Assn. von Humboldt Fellows. Avocations: photography, music. Home: 4 Kruse Pl, Melba, Canberra ACT 2615, Australia Office: Australian Nat U, PO Box 475, CVS RSBS, Canberra ACT 2601, Australia

ZHANG, SHI, business educator, consultant; b. Urumgi, Xijiang, China, 1961; s. Xiru Zhang and Quging Dou; m. Ellie Y. Fang. MA in English and Linguistics, Nankai U., Tianjin, China, 1985; PhD in Linguistics, U. Ariz., 1990; PhD in Mktg. Mgmt., Columbia U., 1997. From rsch. asst. to assoc. U. Ariz., Tucson, 1985-89, lectr., 1989-90; asst. prof. Duke U., Durham, N.C., 1990-93; rsch. asst. Columbia U., N.Y.C., 1993-97; asst. prof. UCLA, 1997—. Contbr. articles to profl. publs., including Jour. Mktg. Rsch., Jour. Consumer Rsch., Linguistic Inquiry, others. Pres. China Pro-Dem. Found., Tucson, 1989-92. Rsch. grantee Duke U., 1991-92, Columbia U., 1995, UCLA, 1997—. Mem. Assn. Consumer Rsch., Linguistic Soc. Am., Soc. Judgment and Decision Making. E-mail: shi.zhang@anderson.ucla.edu. Office: Anderson Sch UCLA 110 Westwood Plz B412 Los Angeles CA 90095-0001

ZHANG, SHI-QING, biologist, physiologist, obstetrician/gynecologist; b. Nan-Chang, China, Mar. 3, 1963; arrived in Japan, 1990; d. Wei-min and Hui-Wen (Fu) Z.; m. Yong Chen, Oct. 16, 1987; 1 child, Xu-Xiang Chen. MD, Nanjing Railway Med. Coll., 1985; PhD, Tokyo Med. and Dental U., 1997. Ob/gyn. Nanjing Railway Med. Coll., China, 1985-90; instr. Tokyo Med. and Dental U., 1997-99; postdoctoral assoc. Rutgers U., Camden, Mass., 1999-2000; postdoctoral fellow Tokyo U., 2000—. Contbr. articles to profl. jours. Recipient scholarship, Assn. Internat. Edn., 1996-97, asst. rschr./fellowship Ministry Edn., Sci. and Culture, 1996-97. Mem. Japanese Soc. Sleep Rsch., Physiol. Soc. Japan. Avocations: violin, calligraphy, travel, hiking. Home: Yamasaki-Dan Chi 2-1-409, Yamasaki-cho 2200, Machida City Tokyo 195-0074, Japan Office: Tokyo U Ob-gyn Dept, 7-3-1 Hongo Bunkyo-ku, Tokyo 113-8655, Japan

ZHANG, SHUANG, mathematics educator; b. Beijing, Mar. 17, 1956; came to U.S., 1983; m. Songping Guo, July 14, 1982; children: Linda S., Michael Y. PhD, Purdue U., 1988. Postdoct. researcher U. Kans., Lawrence, 1988-90; asst. prof. maths. U. Cin., 1990-93, assoc. prof. maths., 1993-97, prof. maths., 1997—. Author: book, 1989; contbr. 32 articles to math. jours. Mem. Am. Math. Soc. Office: U Cin Dept Math Cincinnati OH 45231

ZHANG, SHUANG-YIN, materials and mechanics scientist, educator; b. Gaocheng City, Hebei, China, Feb. 3, 1938; m. Cuifang Yang, Feb. 19, 1965. Diploma, Beijing U. Aeronautics/Astro., 1962; Diploma of PhD study, Inst. Mechanics, 1966; Cert. Advanced Studies, U. Manchester Inst. Sci./Tech., U.K., 1985. Rsch. asst. Inst. Mechanics, Chinese Acad. Scis., Beijing, 1966-79, rsch. assoc., 1979-86, assoc. prof., 1986-90, prof., 1990—, vice dir. divsn. material mechanics, 1979-84; part-time assoc. prof. Beijing Inst. Tech., Beijing, 1986-91; part-time prof. Grad. Sch., China U. Sci. and Tech., beijing, 1990-92. Author: Mechanical Behavior of Composite Structures, 1992; co-author: Stiffened Cylindrical Panels and Shells, 1983, Ency. for China GRP Industries, 1992; vice editor-in-chief Chinese Jour Composite Materials, 1994—; mem. standing com. Jour. of Advances in Mechanics (in Chinese), 1997—. Recipient Award of Nat. Congress for Sci. and Tech., Beijing, 1978, 3d prize for achievement of sci. and tech. Chinese Acad. Scis., 1987, 3d prize for achievement natural scis., 1991, Cert. of Achievement of Sci. and Tech. Chinese Nat. Com. for Sci. and Tech., 1997. Mem. Chinese Soc. Space Scis. (standing com. 1996—), Chinese Soc. Composite Materials (com. mem. 1992—). Avocations: sports, music, excursions, gardening. E-Mail: syzhang@cc5.imech.ac.cn. Office: Inst Mechanics CAS, 15 Zhong guan Cun Rd, Beijing 100080, China

ZHANG, SHUDA, science researcher; b. Tianjin, China, Jan. 3, 1941; s. Ziren and Xiangqian (Qian) Z.; m. Yaohua Zhu, Dec. 30, 1967; children: Wengang, Wenhao. Grad. Physics Bachelor, Beijing Normal U., 1964. Engr. Inst. Hunan 230, Changsha, China, 1964-79; sr. engr. Tianjin Synthetic Diamond Factory, 1979-89; group dir., sr. engr. Tianjin Radio & TV U., 1989—; cons. Specialist Coop. Hedong Dist., Tianjin, 1995—; prof. Acad. Sinica, Shenyang, China. Editor: The Directory on Mineral Radiometric Analyses, 1978; contbr. articles to profl. jours. Internat. Ctr. for Material Physics fellow Acad. Sinica, Shenyang, China, 1990—, Sci. and Tech. Coun. fellow Tianjin Radio & TV U.; named Outstanding Dir. Tiajin 2d Edn. Bur., 1995. Fellow China Assn. for Materials (bd. dirs. Tianjin coun. 1995); mem. AAAS, Am. Physics Soc., Sr. Rschr. Assn. (head dept. specific materials 1992—, 2d prize Tianjin Sci. and Tech. Progress 1998). Avocations: long distance running, musicals, swimming, collecting stamps, singing. Home: Hedong Dist, Fudong Li 23-2-210, Tianjin 300300, China Office: Tianjin Radio & TV Univ, PO Box 220, Tianjin 300191, China

ZHANG, SHUNIAN, mathematics educator, researcher; b. Shanghai, Aug. 29, 1940; s. Lianfang Zhang and Rixiang Sun; m. Xinglin Zhang, May 1, 1964; children: Hao, Liang. Grad., Anhui (China) U., 1962. Asst. dept. math. Anhui U., Hefei, China, 1962-78, lectr., 1978-84, prof., 1986-94; prof. dept. applied math. Shanghai Jiactong U., 1994—; rsch. assoc. U. Toronto, Ont., Can., 1980-82; vis. assoc. prof. So. Ill. U., Carbondale, 1984-86; vis. prof. U. R.I., Kingston, 1991-93; hon. mem. adv. bd. ABI Rsch. Bd., 1989—, IBC adv. coun., 1990—, academician of Acad. of Nonlinear Scis. Author: Asymptotic Behavior of Solutions of Periodic Delay Differential Equations, 1984, Fundamental Theory of Extended Functional Differential Equations, 1985, Razumikhin Techniques in Infinite Delay Equations, 1989, Unified Stability Theorem in RFDE and NFDE, 1990, Limiting Equations and Stability for FDE, 1991, Basic Theory of Topological Dynamics in FDE, 1993, Stability of Infinite Delay Difference Systems, 1994, Boundedness of Infinite Delay Difference Systems, 1994, Invariance Principle for Autonomous Delay Difference Systems, 1995, The Unique Existence of Periodic Solutions of Linear Volterra Difference Equations, 1995, Invariance Principle for Autonomous Delay Difference Systems, 1995, Stability Analysis of Delay Difference Systems, 1997, Qualitative Result on Stability for Delay Difference Systems, 1997, An Improvement in Stability of Delay Difference Systems, 1998, Estimate of Total Stability of Delay Difference Systems, 1999; editor Annals of Differential Equations, 1985; assoc. editor-in-chief Jour. Biomathematics, 1997. Academician, Acad. Nonlinear Scis.; recipient Outstanding Achievement award State Coun. China, 1993; named hon. citizen, State of Okla., 1985, Nat. Excellent Tchr., Ministry of Edn., China, 1989. Mem. N.Y. Acad. Scis., Math. Soc, China, Am. Math. Soc., Internat. Fedn. Nonlinear analysts, Acad. Nonlinear Scis. E-mail: snzhang@online.sh.cn. Office: Shanghai Jiaotong U, Dept Applied Math, Shanghai 200030, China

ZHANG, SHUZHONG, economics educator; b. Putuo, Zhejiang, China, Oct. 20, 1963; s. Liansheng Zhang and Chunhua Chen; m. Yin Li, Nov. 7, 1988; 1 child, Thomas. BS, Fudan U., Shanghai, 1984; PhD, Erasmus U., Rotterdam, The Netherlands, 1991. Lectr. U. Groningen, The Netherlands, 1991-93, Erasmus U., 1993-99; sr. lectr. Chinese U. of Hong Kong, 1999—. Fellow Tinbergen Inst., Stieltjes Inst.; mem. Math. Programming Soc. Avocation: reading. Office: Chinese U Hong Kong, Dept Sys Engring/Engr Mgmt, Hong Kong Hong Kong

ZHANG, THEODORE TIAN-ZE, oncologist, health association administrator; b. Shenyang, Liaoning, People's Republic of China, Apr. 2, 1920. MBChB, Christie Meml. Med. Coll., Shen-yang, People's Republic of China, 1943. Intern Christie Meml. Med. Coll. Hosp., 1944, resident, 1945-48; chief resident surg. dept. Cen. Hosp., Lanzhou, People's Republic of China, 1949-50; vis. surgeon Mackenzie Meml. Hosp., Tianjin, People's Republic of China, 1951-52; dep. chief surg. oncology People's Hosp., Tianjin, People's Republic of China, 1953-75; chief surg. oncology Cancer Hosp., Tianjin, 1975-85; dir. Tianjin Cancer Inst. and Hosp., 1983-92; sec. gen. China Anti-Cancer Assn., 1985-87; pres. China Anti-Cancer Assn., Tianjin, 1988-97; pres. Asian Pacific Fedn. Orgns. for Cancer Rsch. and Control, 1989-91, vice chmn. exec. com., 1991—. Contbg. author: Oncology, Chinese Medical Encyclopedia, 1983, Gastric Cancer, 1987, Recent Advances in Cancer Chemotherapy, 1987, Researches on Breast Cancer, vol. 1, 1987, vol. 2, 1989; editor-in-chief: Oncology, 1996; contbr. more than 130 articles to profl. jours. Mem. Bridge Assn. (v.p. Tianjin chpt.). Avocation: bridge. Office: Tianjin Cancer Inst and Hosp, Huan-Hu-Xi Rd, Ti-Yuan-Bei, Tianjin 300060, China

ZHANG, TIANXU, engineering educator, researcher; b. Chongqing, Sichuan, China, May 18, 1947; s. Lingji Zhang and Shibin Li; m. Zhurong

Liu, Sept. 3, 1974; 1 child, Yongping. BS, U. Sci. and Tech. of China, Hefei, 1970; MS, Harbin (China) Inst. Tech., 1983; PhD, Zhejiang U., Hangzhou, China, 1989. Engr. Xiangfan (China) Inst. Automation, 1970-78; instr. Huazhong U. Sci. & Tech., Wuhan, China, 1981-85; sr. instr. Huzahong U. Sci. & Tech., Wuhan, 1989-90, assoc. prof., 1991-92, prof., 1993—; rsch. asst. Zhejiang U., 1986-89; dir. Inst. for Pattern Recognition and Artificial Intelligence, Wuhan, 1994—, The State Key Lab. for Image Processing and Intelligent Control, Wuhan, 1996—; vis. prof. Bordeaux (France)-3 U., 1997, Chinese U. Hong Kong, 1999. Contbr. articles to profl. jours.; assoc. editor-in-chief bd. Jour. Infrared and Laser Engring., 1997—. REcipient 1st award of disting. tchrs. Bao-Gang Edn. Found., 1995, 3d award Kwang-Hua Sci. and Tech. Found., 1995, 2d award of sci. progress, The State Edn. Commn. of China, 1996, 1st award scientific progress Min. Edn. China, 1998. Mem. IEEE (computer soc., comm. soc.), Chinese Assn. Computer Vision (sr.). Avocations: table tennis, swimming, qigong, mountain climbing, photography. Home: Apt 102, F-30 N 2d Rd W 2d Quarter Yujiashan, Wuhan 430074, China Office: Huazhong U Sci & Tech, 1037 Luo Yu Rd Yujiashan, 430074 Wuhan China

ZHANG, TIEJUN, laser scientist; b. Changchun, China, June 11, 1962; s. Gonglei and Fengzhi (Liu) Z.; m. Zhuoying Yang, Sept. 4, 1987; 1 child, Yumeng. BS, Harbin Inst. of Tech., 1984; MS, Changchun Inst. of Optics and, Fine Mechanics, Chinese Acad. Sci., 1987; DEng, Osaka U., 1995. Educator Yamanashi U., Kofu, Japan, 1995—. Contbr. articles to profl. jours. Scholarship Japanese Ministry of Edn., Sci., Sports and Culture, 1991-95, grant-in-aids for scientific researches, 1996, 97-98, 1999-00. Mem. Japan Soc. of Applied Physics, Laser Soc. Japan, Optical Soc. Am. Avocations: music, basketball, photography, travel. Office: Faculty Engring Yamanashi U, 4-3-11 Takeda, Kofu 400-8511, Japan

ZHANG, WEI, radio propagation researcher, electrical engineer; b. Liaoning, China, June 1, 1956. MS in Elec. Engring., China Rsch. Inst. Radiowave, Propagation, Xinxing, China, 1986; D Tech. in Elec. Engring., Helsinki U. Tech., Espoo, Finland, 1994. Engr. Qingdao (China) Rsch. Ctr. China, Inst. Radio Propagation, 1986-89; rsch. engr. Helsinki U. Tech., Espoo, Finland, 1989-94; sr. rschr. Helsinki U. Tech., Espoo, 1994-98; guest rschr. advanced network tech. divsn. Nat. Inst. Standards and Tech., Gaithersburg, Md., 1999—. Contbr. articles to profl. jours. Recipient Young Scientist award 23d Gen. Assemby Internat. Union Radio Sci., 1990, Best Presentation award (with others) Joint IEEE Internat. Union of Radio Scis. Meeting, Internat. Geosci. and Remote Sensing Symposium, Espoo, Finland, 1991, Fin. Support Program award Internat. Symposium on Antennas and Propagation, Sapporo, Japan, 1992. Avocations: swimming, table tennis. E-mail: wzhang@antd.nist.gov. Office: Advanced Network Tech Divsn Nat Inst Standards and Tech 100 Bureau Dr Stop 8920 Gaithersburg MD 20899-8920

ZHANG, WEIPING, research scientist, educator; b. Zhejiang, China, June 24, 1962; arrived in Australia, 1992; s. Yuen and Wenli (Li) Z.; m. Yanling Xue, Feb. 24, 1989; children: Shuran, Shudan. BS, Anhui (China) Normal U., 1983; MS, Anhui Inst. Optics and Fine Mechanics, 1986; PhD, Shanghai Inst. Optics and Fine Mechanics, 1989. Rsch. assoc. Shanghai Inst. Optics and Fine Mechanics, 1989; postdoctoral rsch. fellow U. Auckland, 1989-92; rsch. assoc. U. NSW, Sydney, 1992-93; rsch. fellow Macquarie U., Sydney, 1993, Australian rsch. fellow, 1993-99, asst. prof., 1999—; vis. rsch. fellow U. Ariz., Tucson, 1994, vis. prof. Shanghai Inst. Optics and Fine Mechanics, 1995; vis. fellow Rice U., Houston, 1997-98; referee Phys. Rev. Letters and Phys. Rev. A., 1993—, Jour. of Physics B, 1993—. Contbr. articles to profl. jours. including Phys. Rev. Letters, Phys. Rev. A, Jour. Optical Soc. Am. B., Physics Letters A, and Jour. Physics B. Recipient scholarship Italian Soc. Physics; fellow Australian Rsch. Coun., 1993; grantee Macquarie U., 1994; grantee Australian Rsch. Coun. Mem. Optical Soc. Am., Am. Inst. Physics, Australian Optical Soc., Australian Inst. of Physics. Avocations: table tennis, poetry, music, stamp collecting. Office: Macquarie U Dept Physics, Sch Math Physics Computing and Elec, Sydney NSW 2109, Australia

ZHANG, WEI-QIANG, dancer. Grad. with highest honors, Beijing Dance Acad., 1979; postgrad., Houston Ballet Acad. Prin. dancer Beijing Dance Acad. Ballet Co., 1981-84, Ctrl. Ballet of China, 1984-92, Royal Winnipeg (Man., Can.) Ballet, 1992—; guest artist Houston Ballet, Star Dancers Ballet, Japan, Asami Maki Ballet Co., Universal Ballet Co. of Korea, The Hong Kong Ballet, Goh Ballet, Can., Gala performance in memory of Anton Dolin, London, 1984, 2nd Internat. Ballet Competition Gala, Paris, 1986, 2d Aoyama Ballet Festival, Tokyo, 1988, Gala performance in memory of Prix de Lausanne, Tokyo, 1989, Japan Ballet Festival, Tokyo, 1989, 91, 92, and numerous other festivals and galas. Prin. roles include Giselle, Don Quixote, Swan Lake, Nutcracker, Raymonda, La Fille Mal Gardee, Coppelia, The Leaves Are Fading, The Afternoon of the Faun, Scotch Symphony, Allegro Brillante, Romeo & Juliet, Sleeping Beauty. Recipient Bronze medal 2nd Internat. Ballet Competition, Jackson, Miss., 1982, 2nd prize 4th World Ballet Competition, Osaka, Japan, 1984, Bronze medal 5th Moscow Internat. Ballet Competition, 1985, Highest Honor award 1st Nat. Ballet Competition, Beijing, 1985. Office: Royal Winnipeg Ballet, 380 Graham Ave, Winnipeg, MB Canada R3C 4K2*

ZHANG, WEIYI, physicist; b. Changzhou, China, Jan. 20, 1960; s. Yuqing Zhang and Enhui Lü; m. Deming Kong, Oct. 20, 1987; 1 child, Sujie Zhang. Bachelor's, Nanjing U., Jiangsu, China, 1982; D of Physics, Helsinki (Finland) U. of Tech., 1988; postdoctorate, Free U. Berlin, 1988-93. Assoc. prof. physics Nanjing U., 1993-96, prof. physics, 1996—. Contbr. articles to profl. jours. Mem. Am. Phys. Soc. Avocations: reading books, travel. Office: Dept Physics Nanjing U, Hankoulu 22, Nanjing 210008, China

ZHANG, WEN, applied mechanics educator; b. Hangzhou, China, Aug. 15, 1940; s. Zulie and Biqiu (Zhou) Z.; m. Huiyun Luo; children: Haijing, Haihua. Bachelor, Fudan U., Shanghai, 1962. Asst. Fudan U., 1963-77, lectr., 1978-84, assoc. prof., 1985-90; vis. prof. MIT, Boston, 1989-90, Harvard U., Boston, 1990-91; prof. Fudan U., 1991—, chair prof., 1996-98, head dept. applied mech., 1997-2000. Author: Theory of Rotordynamics, 1990, Creep In Structure, 1990; contbr. articles to profl. jours. Recipient Natural Sci. award, Dynamics of Complex Rotor Sys., China, 1988, Sci. and Tech. Progress award, The Application of Complex Rotordynamics, Shanghai, 1986, 93, The Talent in Shanghai Sci. and Tech. Circles award Shanghai Mayor, 1995. Mem. ASME, Chinese Soc. Vibration Engring., Chinese Soc. Theoretical and Applied Mechanics. Avocation: stamp collecting. Office: Fudan Univ, Dept Applied Mechanics, 200433 Shanghai China

ZHANG, WENDONG, engineering educator; b. Taikang, Henan, China, Aug. 8, 1962; s. Yongran and LImei (Chen) Z.; m. Yanping Bai, Dec. 8, 1986; 1 child, Jiaqi. BS, Taiyuan Inst. Machinery, 1982; MS, North China Inst. Tech., China, 1986; PhD, Beijing Inst. Tech., 1995. From asst. prof. to prof. North China Inst. Tech., 1982—; dept. dean North China Inst. Tech., 1989—. Mem. IEEE, Instrumentation and Measurement Soc., Test and Measurement Soc. China (sec. gen. 1994—). Avocations: reading, swimming, chess. Home and Office: PO Box 13, 030051 Taiyuan Shanxi, China

ZHANG, WENHUI, computer scientist; b. Fuan, Fujian, China, June 3, 1963; arrived in Norway, 1979; s. Jigui and Youju (Liu) Z. Student, Beijing U., 1978-79; Cand. mag., U. Oslo, 1982, Cand. Sci., 1985, DSc, 1988. Rschr. Inst. Software, Beijing, 1988-89, 93-94; cons. Citibank, Hong Kong, 1989; rschr. U. Oslo, Norway, 1989-91; sr. lectr. Telemark Coll., Norway, 1991-93, 94-95; sys. analyst Achilles Systems AS, Tananger, Norway, 1995-97; rschr. Inst. Energy Tech., Halden, Norway, 1997—. Contbr. articles to profl. jours. Mem. Norwegian Soc. Chartered Engrs. Avocations: chess, go, swimming. Home: Froyasvei 45, 1782 Halden Norway Office: Inst Energy Tech, PO Box 173, 1751 Halden Norway

ZHANG, WURONG, research scientist; b. Guanghan, China, July 28, 1966; came to U.S., 1991; s. Shaoyu Zhang and Yonghui Wu; m. Fanmin Liu, Jan. 4, 1996; 1 child, Victor Gongjie. BS, Tsinghua U., Beijing, 1988, MS, 1991; PhD, MIT, 1998. R&D scientist Bruker Instruments Inc., Billerica, Mass., 1998—. Contbr. articles to profl. jours. Mem. AAAS, Am. Chem. Soc., Am. Phys. Soc., Alpha Nu Sigma. E-mail: wurong@alum.mit.edu. Office: Bruker Instruments Inc Fortune Dr Billerica MA 01821

ZHANG, XIANGTING, engineering educator; b. Wenzhou, Zhejiang, China, June 11, 1932; s. Minshan Zhang and Yanmei Xie; m. Shoumei Wang, Feb. 16, 1958; children: Ruili, Ruixin, Ruichong. BS, Tongji U., Shanghai, 1953, MS, 1966. Asst. prof. Tongji U., 1953-60, lectr., 1960-80, assoc. prof., 1980-86, prof., 1986—, chmn. dept. engring. mechs., 1984-92, dir. Inst. Structural Theory, 1985-88, dir. Inst. Engring. Mechs., 1990-92, dir. Rsch. Ctr. of Civil Infrastructure Systems, 1998—; dir. wind engring. divsn. Shanghai Inst. Disaster Mitigation and Relief, 1988—. Author: Theory of Wind Loading and Its Applications, 1990 (2d award China Constrn. Ministry 1992), Analysis of Wind-and Earthquake-Excited Responses for Tall Buildings, 1997, State-of-the-Art Development on Structural Wind Engineering and Its Applications, 1995. Recipient 1st prize China Edn. Com., 1990, 2d prize China Constrn. Ministry, 1990, 1st prize Shanghai Sci. and Tech. Com., 1995. Fellow CSCE (chmn. subcom. 1988—), China Aerodynamics Soc. (chmn. subcom. 1988—), China Soc. Vibration Engring. (mem. nonlinear vibration com. 1986—). Office: Tongji U, Siping Rd 1239, Shanghai 200092, China

ZHANG, XIAO GUANG, physics educator; b. Beijing, June 8, 1961; s. Shao Jun and Guang De Z.; m. Jun Wu, Oct. 2, 1989; 1 child, Meng Wen. BS, Peking U., Beijing, 1985; MS, Beijing U. Posts & Telecom., 1999. Asst. Beijing U. Posts and Telecomms., 1988-91, lectr., 1991-96, assoc. prof., 1996—; deputy dir. physics teaching sect. BUPT, Beijing, 1997—. Contbr. articles to profl. jours.; inventor in field. Mem. Chinese Phys. Soc., Chinese Optical Soc., Beijing Inst. Comm., Comm. Inst. China. Avocations: reading, painting, taijiquan. Office: Beijing U Posts & Telecomm, 10 Xitucheng Rd, Beijing 100876, China

ZHANG, XIAOYAN, engineering educator, researcher; b. Xian, Shaanxi, China, Oct. 23, 1959; m. Pu Zhang; 1 child, Yi. BSc, Xian Hwy. Transp. U., 1982, MSc, 1986; PhD, Middlesex U., London, 1996. Asst. hwy. engr. Shaanxi Inst. Hwy. Surveying and Designing, Xian, 1982-83; asst. lectr. of transport Xian Hwy. Transp. U., 1986-87, lectr. of transport, 1987-89; hon. rsch. assoc. Birmingham (Eng.) U., 1989-90; postdoctoral rschr. Sch. Built Environ., Napier U., Edinburgh, Scotland, 1995—. Contbr. articles to profl. jours. Avocation: music. Office: Napier U Sch Built Environ, 10 Colinton Rd, Edinburgh EH10 5DT, Scotland

ZHANG, XIAO-ZHANG, mechanical engineering educator; b. Puzhai, Guangdong, China, Oct. 8, 1958; s. Zhan-Hong and Lu-Ying Zhang; m. Yin Wu, June 15, 1986; 1 child, Shu. B of Engring., Tsinghua U., Beijing, 1983; M of Engring., S.E. U., Nanjing, China, 1986; D of Engring., Hohai U., Nanjing, 1989. From lectr. to prof. Nanjing Aeronautics and Astronautics U., 1988-94; postdoctoral rschr. Cranfield U., Bedford, Eng., 1991-92; assoc. prof. Tsinghua U., Beijing, 1994-99, prof., 1999—; vice dir. Nanjing Indsl. Furnance Test Ctr., 1991-94; cons. Huahui Co., Zhuhai, 1993-94; vis. prof. MIT, Cambridge, 1998. Author: Measurement in Thermal Engineering, 1993; contbr. articles to profl. jours. K. C. Wong fellow Royal Soc. U.K., 1992. Mem. Instrument Soc. of Am., Chinese Soc. of Aeronautics, Chinese Soc. of Metrology. Avocations: poems, music, cultural comparison. Office: Tsinghua U, Dept Engring Physics, 100084 Beijing China

ZHANG, XINGGUO, physics educator; b. Nanjing, China, Dec. 18, 1944; came to U.S., 1981; s. Qingzhi Z. and Ronghua Liu. BS in Physics, Nanjing (China) U., 1968; PhD in Physics, Pa. State U., 1988. Engr. Fuyang (China) Electronic Co., 1974-78; mem. faculty U. Sci. and Tech. of China, Hefei, 1978-81; assoc. prof. Pa. State U., Hazleton, Pa., 1997—. Recipient Anhui Province Scientific award, China, 1982. Mem. Am. Phys. Soc. Office: Pa State U Dept Physics Hazleton PA 18201

ZHANG, XIYAN, educator; b. Laoting, Hebei, China, Aug. 26, 1957; d. Wenkui and Yingjie (Zhao) Z.; m. Guang Cheng, Aug. 20, 1987; 1 child, Liqun. B, Changchun Inst. Optics & Mech., China, 1980, M, 1985. Asst. tchr. Changchun Inst. Optics and Fine Mechanics, 1980-82, lectr., 1985-92, assoc. prof., 1992-98, prof., 1998—; scholar UMIST U.K., Manchester, 1992-93. Author: Rare Earth Optical Glass, 1989; inventor photoluminescence glaze. Avocation: swimming. Office: Changchun Inst Optics, No 7 Weixing Rd, Changchun 130022, China

ZHANG, XUEJI, chemist, educator; b. Fengyang, Anhui, China, Feb. 10, 1964; came to U.S., 1998; p. Ruting Zhang and Sanwen Wang; m. Jie Lin, Oct. 8, 1989; children: Wenbo, Andrew. BSc, Wuhan (China) U., 1989, PhD, 1994. Asst. engr. Huainan(China) Inst. Coal Chem. Engring., 1981-87; asst. prof. Wuhan U., 1994-95; guest scientist Nat. Inst. Chemistry, Ljubljana, Slovenia, 1995-96; W. Simon fellow Swiss Fed. Inst. Tech., Zürich, 1997-98; rsch. fellow N.Mex. State U., Las Cruces, 1998-99; sr. scientist, sect. head World Precision Instruments, Sarasota, Fla., 1999—; Contbr. articles to profl. jours. W. Simon fellow to Internat. Ctr. Sci. and Culture-World Lab., 1997; Recipient Sao Yizhou Meml. medal in China, 1993, 1st prize nat. applied sci. and tech. and invention, 1995; named extraordinary scientist, 1999; Outstanding Overseas Chinese scholar in Switzerland, 1997. Mem. AAAS, Am. Chem. Soc., Soc. Electroanalytical Chemistry, N.Y. Acad. Scis. Achievements include inventor of nanosensors. E-mail: zxj001@hotmail.com and xueji@wpiinc.com. Fax: 941-377-5248. Office: World Precision Instruments Inc 175 Sarasota Center Blvd Sarasota FL 34240-8750

ZHANG, YANCHUN, computer scientist, educator; b. Tang Shan, Hebei, China, Feb. 1, 1958; arrived in Australia, 1988; s. Xuelun and Xiushen (Gao) Z.; m. Jinli Cao, June 28, 1982; 1 child, Dana. BSc, Hebei U., China, 1982; PhD of Computer Sci., U. Queensland, Australia, 1991. Lectr. HebeiU., Baoding, China, 1982-87; rsch. assoc., fellow U. Queensland, Brisbane, Australia, 1988-93; lectr. U. So. Queensland, Toowoomba, Australia, 1994-98, sr. lectr., 1998—. Editor-in-chief Internet and Web Information Systems, 2000; contbr. articles to profl. jours. Grantee Australian Rsch. Grant, 1994, 2000. Mem. IEEE, Assn. Computing Machinery, Australian Computer Sci. Assn., Web Info. Systems Engring. Soc. (chmn. 2000—). Avocations: travel, fishing, swimming. Home: 19 Kurtz St, Toowoomba Q4350, Australia Office: Dept Math and Computing, Univ So Queensland, Toowoomba 4350, Australia

ZHANG, YANWU, electrical engineer, oceanographer; b. Xianyang City, China, June 26, 1969; came to U.S., 1994; s. Hongen and Baochuan Zhang. BSEE, Northwestern Poly. U., 1989, MS in Underwater Acoustics Engring., 1991; postgrad., U. Wash., 1994-95; MSEE and Computer Sci., MIT, 1998; MS in Oceanographic Engring., MIT/Woods Hole Oceanog. Instn., 1998, PhD in Oceanographic Engring., 2000. Rsch. asst. U. Wash., Seattle, 1994-95; rsch. and tchg. asst. MIT, Cambridge, 1995-2000; systems engr. GE Rsch. and Devel. Ctr., Niskayuna, N.Y., 2000—. Summer rsch. fellowship Woods Hole Oceanographic Instn., 1997; scholarship 10th Internat. Symposium on Unmanned Untethered Submersible Tech., 1997. Mem. IEEE, Sigma Xi. Achievements include research on the technology of measuring water velocity from an autonomous underwater vehicle (AUV), study of adaptive AUV survey strategy. Avocations: sports, music, sightseeing. Office: GE Corp R&D KW-B605 One Rsch Cir Niskayuna NY 12309

ZHANG, YANXIN, optics educator, researcher; b. Gongxian, Henan, China, Nov. 5, 1937; s. Jinkui and Youzhi (Fu) Z.; m. Tianlun Chen, Feb. 17, 1968; 1 child, Ning. BS in Physics, Nankai U., Tianjin, 1960. Physics tchr. Nankai U., Tianjin, 1960-78, lectr., 1978-80, assoc. prof., vice chmn., 1982-84, assoc. prof. Inst. Modern Optics, 1985-88, prof. Inst. Modern Optics, 1988-89, prof., dep. dir., 1989—, PhD program adviser, 1990—, dep. dean Coll. Info. Sci., 1994—; dir. optical info. sci. lab. State Edn. Commn. China, Tianjin, 1995-98; vis. scholar physics U. Minn., Mpls., 1980-82; vis. scientist MIT, Cambridge, 1985. Mem. editl. bd. Chinese Jour. Infrared and Millimeter Waves, 1991-95, Opto-electronic Engring., 1993—; contbr. numerous articles to profl. jours. Recipient Advanced Researcher award Nat. Sci. and Tech. Com., 1993, 2nd class award of progress in sci. and tech. Edn. Ministry China, 1996, 1st class award of progress in sci. and tech. Edn. Ministry China, 1998. Mem. Internat. Soc. Optical Engring., Internat. Neural Network Soc., Chinese Neural Network Coun. (com. 1990—), Chinese Optics Soc. (photoelec. com. 1991—, holography com. 1990—). Office: Nankai U Inst Modern Optics, 94 Weijin Rd, Tianjin 300071, China

ZHANG, YAO-ZHONG, mathematical physicist, research scientist; b. Hunan, China, Dec. 14, 1962; s. Qian-Rong and Shu-Ying (Liu) Z.; m. Jie-Ying Chen, May 21, 1962; 1 child, Lai-Ying. BSc, Xidan U., Xi'an, China, 1982; MSc, Sichuan U., Chengdu, China, 1985; PhD, N.W. U., Xi'an, China, 1988. Postdoctoral fellow N.W. U., 1988-89, Internat. Sch. Advanced Studies, Trieste, Italy, 1989-90; Humboldt fellow Bonn U., 1991-92; rsch. assoc. Australian Rsch. Coun. U. Queensland, Australia, 1992-95, Queens Elizabeth II fellow, 1996—; rsch. scientist Japan Soc. for Promotion of Sci. Kyoto (Japan) U., 1995-96; regular assoc. Internat. Ctr. Theoretical Physics, Trieste, 1997—. Author: Introduction to Anomalous Guage Theories, 1990; contbr. articles to profl. jours. Recipient China Young Rschrs. Sci. and Tech. award, 1988, Ying-Tung Fok prize Ying-Tung Fok Edn. Found., 1989, Queen Elizabeth II fellow Australian Rsch. Coun., 1996, Japan Soc. for the Promotion of Sci. fellow, 1995, Humboldt fellow Alexander von Humboldt Found., 1990. Fellow Asia Pacific Ctr. Theoretical Physics; mem. Internat. Assn. Math. Physics, Australian Math. Soc., Am. Math. Soc., Chinese Phys. Soc. Office: U Queensland, Dept Math, Brisbane QLD 4072, Australia

ZHANG, YAPU, lawyer; b. Huai Yin, China, Sept. 9, 1963; s. Bao Shar and Xia (Zhu) Z.; m. Kai-Yuan Tao; 1 child, Zitao. LLB, Wuhan U., China, 1985, LLM, 1988. Atty. Guangdong Internat. Coop., China, 1988-90, deputy mgr., fgn. svcs. dept., 1990-93; atty. 2d Fgn. Econ. Law Office, Guangdong, China, 1988-93; ptnr. King Pound Law Firm, Guangdong, China, 1993-96; sr. ptnr. Leeda Law Firm, Guangdong, China, 1996—. Author: Comments on Commercial Cases, 1994, English-Chinese Dictionary of Commerical Law, 1996, Legal Professional System in Hong Kong, 1999. Mem. Guangdong Lawyers Assn., China Internat. Law Assn. Avocations: reading, hiking. Office: Leeda Law Firm, 836 Dong Feng Dong Rd, Guangzhou 510080, China

ZHANG, YIN-CHANG, retired medical institute administrator, educator; b. Shenyang, Liaoning, China, Apr. 26, 1923; s. Yu-Hai Zhang and Zhang-Su Si; m. Qian-Lan Wang, May 13, 1944; children: Kan, Qi-Yeng, Qi-Yu, Ji-Hong. Bachelor's degree, China Med. U., Shenyang, 1949. Asst. of pathology China Med. U., Shenyang, 1950-56, lectr., 1956-78, assoc. prof., chief of lab., 1978-83, prof., 1983-95; dep. dir. Cancer Inst., Shenyang, 1985-93; ret., 1993; cons. Cancer Inst. China Med. U., 1994—, Benxi Steel Co. Hosp.; vis. dr. Temple U., Phila., 1981, vis scholar, 1981-82. Author, editor: (monographs) Gastric Cancer, 1984 (award Province Govt. 1998), Pathology of the Stomach and its Biopsy, 1984, Precancerous Conditions and Lesions of the Stomach, 1994; editor: (photographic works) The Sun of Nature, 1998. Recipient Sci. Promotion award Pub. Health Ministry China, 1990; 6th and 7th State Cancer Rsch. grantee Nat. Sci. Com., 1982-84, 85-89. Mem. Chinese Med. Assn., Liaoning Province Cancer Soc. (vice-chmn. 1983-95), Chinese Anticancer Soc. (coun. 1990-99), Chinese Cancer Rsch. Found. (permanent coun. 1990-99), Chinese Photography Soc. Avocations: photography of landscapes, Chinese traditional painting. Home: # 243 Bldg 4, 178 Ave Hepingbei St, Heping Dist Shenyang 110001, China Office: Cancer Inst China Med Inst, # 155 Nanjingbei St, Heping Shenyang 110001, China

ZHANG, YING HUA, research scientist; b. Shanghai, Apr. 29, 1936; came to U.S., 1988; d. Han Liang and Xiang E. (Xing) Z.; m. Chu Kun Kuo, Apr. 12, 1960; children: Yale Y. Guo, Jia Guo. BS, East China Inst. Chem. Tech., Shanghai, 1956; PhD, Chinese Acad. Scis., Shanghai, 1978. Assoc. prof. Shanghai Inst. Ceramics Chinese Acad. Scis., 1957-91; sr. scientist, prin. engr., fiber engring. mgr. Polaroid Corp., Boston, 1991-98; sr. staff scientist SDL Inc., San Jose, 1999—; vis. scientist Rutgers U., Piscataway, N.J., 1989-91. Recipient Nat. Award for Developing Sci. and Tech., China Nat. Com. Sci. and Tech., 1985; named Shanghai Extraordinary Woman Scientist, Shanghai Women's Assn., 1984. Mem. Optic Soc. Am., Photonic Soc. Chinese Am., Polaroid Asia Assn. Achievements include patents and process development for industrial high power fiber lasers; research and development of the first optical fiber telecommunication system between local offices in China. Office: SDL Inc No 1 Upland Rd Bldg N1 Norwood MA 02062

ZHANG, YINGBO, materials engineer, researcher; b. Beijing, Nov. 15, 1963; came to U.S., 1990; s. Xin Yu and Jieshu (Yang) Z.; m. Yu Zhang, Aug. 14, 1990; children: Annie. BSEE, Tsinghua U., Beijing, 1986, MS in Physics, 1989; PhD in Physics, U. Nebr., 1995. Process engr. CVC Products Inc., Rochester, N.Y., 1995-96; sr. R&D engr. Applied Magnetics Corp., Santa Barbara, Calif., 1996—.

ZHANG, YONG MIN, chemistry educator; b. Ningbo, China, Feb. 19, 1932; s. Lu An and Bao Qin (Ye) Z.; m. You Yu Zhu, Oct. 1, 1956; children: Zhong Xing, Zhong Cheng. BS, St. John's U., 1952. Instr., lectr. dept. chemistry Henan Normal U., Sinsiang, China, 1952-64; lectr. dept. chemistry Hangzhou (China) U., 1965-78, assoc. prof., 1978-85, chmn. dept. chemistry, 1984-90, prof., 1986-98; chmn. dept. chemistry Zhejiang U., 1998—; vis. scholar Fudan U., Shanghai, 1956-58; vis. prof. U. Fla., Gainesville, 1988-89. Contbr. articles to profl. jours. Recipient 2d award of Progress of Sci. and Tech. State Edn. Commn. China, 1991, 3d award, 1992, 96, 2d award of Progress of Sci. and Tech. Edn. Commn. Zhejiang Province, 1991, 2d award, 1998, 1st award, 1999. Mem. Chinese Chem. Soc. (bd. dirs. 1990—, acad. com. phys./organic chemistry 1989—, acad. com. organic synthesis 1991—), Zhejiang Chem. Soc. (bd. dirs. 1985—). Avocations: classical music, volleyball, soccer, baseball. Office: Zhejiang U Xixi Campus, 34 Tian Mu Shan Rd, Hangzhou 310028, China

ZHANG, YONG ZHAO, engineering educator; b. Wuxi, China, Aug. 20, 1934; m. Cai Huifang, Sept. 1, 1960; 1 child, Hao. BS, Zhejiang U., Hangzhou, China, 1955. Technician Power Sta. Ministry, Beijing, 1955-56; asst. Tsinghua U., Beijing, 1956-58; prof., dean Xi'an Jiaotong U., 1958—; cons. numerous cos. and socs., China, 1980—. Editor 12 books; contbr. articles to profl. jours.; inventor inertia collector and hot-water boiler. Recipient Sci. Achievement award Sci. and Tech. Com. China, 1989, 92, Govt. of Shaanxi Province, 1989, 91, award Mech. and Electronic Indsl. Ministry, 1992. Mem. ASME, Environ. Protection Soc. Shaanxi Province (cons. 1987), Chinese Energy Soc., Shaanxi Boiler Sci. Assn. (v.p. 1980—), Energy Soc. Xi'an (pres. 1989). Avocations: fishing, Chinese chess, table tennis, badminton, Chinese mahjong. Office: Xian Jiaotong U, Xian ning W Rd 28, Xian 710049, China

ZHANG, YUCHEN, computer scientist; b. Beijing, Aug. 23, 1971; child of Shiqiang and Huili Zhang. M. in Computer Sys. and Application, Beijing U. Chemtech, 1994; M in Computer Sys., Chinese Acad. Sci., Beijing, 1996; MS in Computer Sci., Ind. U., 1998. Cert. internet security specialist. Tchg. asst. Ind. U., Bloomington, 1997; rsch. asst. Motorola Rsch. Partnership/ Ind. U., Bloomington, 1997-99; sr. engr. NEC Rsch. Inst., Princeton, N.J., 2000; facility rep. computer sci. dept. Ind. U., Bloomington, 1997-99. Rsch. grantee Motorola Univ. Partnerships Rsch., 1997-99. Office: Ind U Lindley Hall 328 Bloomington IN 47405

ZHANG, YU-WEN, research scientist; b. Fujian Province, China, Feb. 11, 1966; came to U.S., 1999; MD, Shanghai (China) Med. U., 1989; PhD, Kyoto (Japan) U., 1997. Resident Fujian Province Hosp., 1989-90; postdoctoral fellow Inst. for Virus Rsch., Kyoto U., 1997-99; rsch. fellow Van Andel Rsch. Inst., Grand Rapids, Mich., 1999—. Contbr. articles to profl. publs. Rsch. fellowship Van Andel Rsch. Inst., 1999, Postdoctoral fellowship Japan Soc. for the Promotion of Sci., 1997, Med. fellowship The Sumitomo Life and Social Welfare Found., 1996. Mem. Am. Soc. Cell Biology, Am. Soc. Biochemistry and Molecular Biology, The Japanese Cancer Assn., Japan Soc. of Molecular Biology. Fax: 616-235-7558. E-mail: ywzhang@earthlink.net. Home: 532 Briar Ln NE Grand Rapids MI 49503-2174 Office: Van Andel Rsch Inst 333 Bostwick Ave NE Grand Rapids MI 49503-2518

ZHANG, ZHENFANG JOHN, mechanical engineer, educator; b. Lulong, Hebei, China, May 4, 1963; arrived in Can., 1996; s. Mantang Zhang and Guizhen Zhao; m. Hao Zhang, Nov. 12, 1989; children: Yuezhuo, Jeffrey-Tian Liang. BSc in Mech. Engring., Shen Yang Inst. Tech., China, 1983; M in Mech. Engring., Northeastern U., China, 1988; PhD in Materials Engring., U. Sydney, 1996. Mech. engr. Jinshan Machinary Plant, China, 1983-85; lectr. Shen Yang Inst. Tech., China, 1988-91; postdoc. U. Sydney, 1996; mech. engring. educator U. Western Ont., London, Ont., Can., 1996—;

process devel. engr. World Heart Co., Ottawa, Ont., Can., 2000—. Equity and Merit scholar Autralian Internat. Devel. Assistance Bur., Sydney, 1991-95. Mem. ASME. Avocation: sports. Office: World Heart Co, 1 Laser St, Ottawa, ON Canada K2E 7V1

ZHANG, ZHENGGUO, biomedical engineering educator; b. Bejing, China, July 31, 1949; s. An and Qi (Fan) Z.; m. Qingping Liu, Jan. 5, 1976; 1 child, Lilei. M, Broadcast and TV U., Beijing, 1982; M in Medicine, Peking Union Med. Coll., Beijing, 1985. Rsch. asst. Inst. Basic Med. Sci., Chinese Acad. Med. Sci., Beijing, 1985-87, rsch. assoc., 1987-89, 1990-93, prof., 1993—; postdoctoral fellow U. Calif., San Francisco, 1989-90. Patentee (5) in field. Recipient Sci. Rsch. award Ministry of Pub. Health China, 1986, Sci. and Tech. Progress award Ministry of Civil Affair China, 1987, Sci. Rsch. award Bus. Pub. Health Beijing, 1990. Mem. IEEE (sr.), Chinese Soc. Biomed. Engring. (sr.), Chinese Assn. Acoustics (sr.). Home: 59 Wai Jiao Bu Jie St # 34, Beijing 100005, China Office: Inst Basic Med Sci, Chinese Acad Med Sci, 5 Dong Dan San Tiao, Beijing 100005, China

ZHANG, ZHI, education educator; b. Kunming, Yunnan, China, Apr. 16, 1955; d. Yiming and Hong (Lu) Z.; m. Minghua Zong, Oct. 5, 1983. BA, Kunming Medicine Coll., 1983; MA, Yunnan Tchrs. U., Kunming, 1990. Technician Yunnan Broad Bur., Kunming, 1975-78; resident in internal medicine Wuhua Hosp., Kunming, 1983-87; from asst. lectr. to lectr. Yunnan Tchrs. U., Kunming, 1990-97, assoc. prof., 1997—. Contbr. articles to profl. jours. Mem. Am. Psychol. Assn., Internat. Assn. for Cross-Cultural Psychology, Internat. Soc. for the Study Behavioral Devel., Chinese Psychol. Soc. Office: Yunnan Tchrs Univ, Inst Ednl Sci, 650092 Kunming China

ZHANG, ZHIWEI, research scientist; b. Wuhan City, China, Oct. 5, 1964; s. Lian Wen and Guang Ming (Tang) Z.; m. Mei X. Zhang, June 18, 1991; children: Jenny, Olivia. BS, Huangzhong U. Sci. and Tech., Wuhan, China, 1985; MS, Va. Commonwealth U., 1994; PhD, Va. Tech., 1999. Sr. rsch. analyst Nat. Opinion Rsch. Ctr., Washington, 1997-98; rsch. scientist Nat. Opinion Rsch. Ctr. U. Chgo., Washington, 1998—; author drug use and workplace programs and policies, 1999. Recipient Bur. of Justice Stats. award, 1997; Bur. Labor Stats./Dept. Labor grantee, 1999. Mem. Am. Sociol. Assn. (Clifford C. Clogg award 1996), Am. Stats. Assn. Avocation: tennis. Office: Nat Opinion Rsch Ctr 1350 Connecticut Ave NW Ste 500 Washington DC 20036-1736

ZHANG, ZHONGFEI, computer science educator, researcher, consultant; b. Hangzhou, Zhejiang, China; came to U.S., 1989; s. Yukun Zhang and Ming Song; m. Aiqun Du, Jan. 1, 1997; children: Henry, Andrew. BS magna cum laude, Zhejiang U., Hangzhou, China, 1984, MS, 1987; PhD, U. Mass., 1996. Mem. rsch. staff Zhejiang U., 1987-89; rsch. asst. U. Mass., Amherst, 1989-95; rsch. scientist SUNY, Buffalo, 1995-99, rsch. asst. prof., 1997-99; asst. prof. computer sci. SUNY, Binghamton, 1999—; tech. cons. Applied Artificial Intelligence, Inc., Amherst, 1995-96. Assoc. editor: Procs. Internat. Conf. on Imaging Sci. Systems and Tech., 1998; contbr. articles to sci. jours., including Jour. Robotics, IEEE Transactions on Pattern Analysis and Machine Intelligence, Info. Retrieval, IEEE Multimedia. Achievements include invention of computer based method and apparatus for object recognition. E-mail: zhongfei@cs.binghamton.edu. Office: Computer Sci Dept SUNY Binghamton NY 13902

ZHANG, ZHU LIN, physics educator; b. Chao Hu, Anhui, China, Sept. 5, 1945; s. Zong Ben Zhang and Shi Sheng Wang; m. Bin Chu Zhang; 1 child, Lei. BSc, U. Sci. and Tech. China, 1970; postgrad., Wayne State U., 1980-86. Tchr. Huainan (China) Inst. Tech., 1970-80, assoc. prof. physics, 1986—. Author: Nuclear Instruments and Methods in Physics Research, 1999. Office: Huainan Inst Tech, Dept Math & Physics, Anhui Huainan 232001, China

ZHANG, ZHUOMIN, mechanical engineering educator; b. Henan, China, Apr. 14, 1962; came to U.S., 1989, naturalized, 1999; s. Wenbin and Xueqin Zhang; m. Lingyun Wang, Nov. 24, 1988; children: Emmy, Angie, Bryan. BS, U. Sci. Technol. China, Hefei, 1982, MS, 1985; PhD, MIT, 1992. Lectr. U. Sci. Technol. China, Hefei, 1987-89; rsch. assoc. U. Md., College Park, 1992-95; asst. prof. U. Fla., Gainesville, 1995-2000, assoc. prof., 2000—; guest scientist Nat. Inst. Stds. and Tech., Gathersburg, Md., 1992-95. Contbr. articles to profl. jours., chpts. to books. Recipient NSF Career award, 1999, Presdl. Early Career Award for Scientists and Engrs. Mem. ASME, AIAA, Am. Phys. Soc., Am. Soc. Engring. Edn., Materials Rsch. Soc., Soc. Photo-Optical Instrumentation Engrs., Sigma Xi. E-mail: zzhang@cimar.me.ufl.edu. Fax: 352-392-1071. Office: U Fla Dept Mech Engring 336 MEB Gainesville FL 32611-6300

ZHANG, ZHUOYONG, analytical chemist educator, researcher; b. Jilin, Peoples Republic of China, June 24, 1956; s. Zhenhuan and Jingxian (Sun) Z.; m. Ke Xu, Apr. 30, 1984; 1 child, Zheng. BS, Jilin U., Changchun, China, 1982; MS, Changchun Inst. Applied Chem., Changchun, China, 1985, PhD, 1988. Rsch. assoc. Changchun Inst. Applied Chemistry, Changchun, 1988-92; postdoctoral fellow U. Waterloo, Can., 1993-94; dep. dir. chemistry N.E. Normal U., Changchun, 1995—, prof. chemistry, 1997—. Contbr. articles to profl. jours. including Spectroscopy Letters, Talanta, and Spectrochimica Acta. Recipient award Chinese Analysis and Instrumentation Assn., 1997. Mem. Chinese Chem. Soc., Can. Spectroscopy Soc. Avocations: reading, swimming. Office: NE Normal U Dept Chemistry, 138 Renmin St, Changchun 130024, Peoples Republic of China

ZHANG, ZONGGUI, engineer; b. Wugang, Hunan, China, Aug. 23, 1964; s. Wen Yu and Jin Xiu (Liu) Zhang; m. Qing Liu, June 6, 1991; 1 child. BS, Chengdu Inst. Geology, Beijing, MS; postgrad., China U. Geoscis., Beijing. Asst. engr. Ctr. Remote Sensing in Geology, Beijing, China, 1987-91, engr., 1992-97, sr. engr., 1998—. Contbr. articles to profl. jours. Mem. Chinese Geol. Assn., Beijing Surveying & Mapping Assn. Avocations: sports, folk music. Office: Ctr Remote Sensing Geology, 29 Inst Rd, Beijing 100083, China

ZHAO, ANPING, electrical engineer; b. Siping, China, Mar. 16, 1963; s. Yixian Zhao and Shuqin Ding; m. Xiuqi Han; 1 child, Junting. BSc, Changchun Optics & Fine Mechs., China, 1984; MSc, Changchun Inst. Physics, 1987; PhD, Brunel U., 1994. Assoc. rschr. Changchun Inst. Physics, 1987-89; vis. rsch. fellow Surrey U., Guildford, England, 1990-91; rsch. engr. Helsinki U. Technology, Espoo, Finland, 1994-97; sr. rsch. engr. Nokia Rsch. Ctr., Helsinki, Finland, 1997—. Mem. IEEE (sr. mem.). Office: Nokia Rsch Ctr Elec Lab, Itamerenkatu 11-13, FIN00180 Helsinki Finland

ZHAO, BAOLU, biophysicist; b. Bai Xiang, Heibei, China, Oct. 20, 1943; s. Qingfant Zhao and Xiuyin Chen; m. Chunai Zhang, Aug. 8, 1970; children: Yan, Li. BA, U. Sci. and Tech., Hefei, China, 1969; MA, Grad. Sch. Acad. Sinica, Beijing, 1981. Lectr. U. Sci. and Tech., Hefei, 1970-78; from asst. to assoc. prof. Inst. Biophysics Acad. Sinica, Beijing, 1981-91, prof. biophysics, 1992—, vice dir., 1999—; vis. asst. prof. Ohio State U., Columbus, 1985-87, vis. assoc. prof., 1991-92; vis. prof. Inst. Food Rsch., U.K., 1997. Author: Basic Principal of ESR and Spin Labeling, 1987, Oxygen Free Radical and Antioxidants, 1999; contbr. articles to profl. jours. Coun. mem. Com. for Free Radical Biology and Medicine China, Beijing, 1992-95, vice-chmn., 1997—; mem. Com. for Biol. Gerontology China, Beijing, 1987-95. Mem. Internat. Electron Spin Resonance Soc., Biophys. Soc. China. Avocations: swimming, taijiquan boxing, badmiton, volleyball, mountain climbing. Home: Datun Rd, 205 Bldg 310 Kexueyuan, ChaoYang Beijing 100101, China Office: Inst Biophysics Acad Sinica, 15 Datun Rd, ChaoYang Beijing 100101, China

ZHAO, CHONGBIN, engineering educator, researcher; b. Xian, Shaanxi, China, Sept. 16, 1956; arrived in Australia, 1989; s. Jimin and Xiuzhen (Wang) Z.; m. Peiying Xu, Jan. 26, 1984; 1 child, Guoliang. B Engring., Tsinghua U., Beijing, 1983; PhD, Tsinghua U., 1987. Postdoctoral fellow U. NSW, Sydney, 1989-92; rschr. U. NSW, 1992-94, sr. project scientist, 1996; rsch. fellow U. Sydney, 1994-96; rsch. scientist CSIRO, Perth, 1996-97; sr. rsch. scientist CSIRO, 1997—; prof. Xian U. Tech., 1993—; assoc. prof. Shaanxi Inst. Mech. Engring., 1991-92; lectr. Shaanxi Inst. Mech. Engring., 1988-90. Contbr. over 120 articles to profl. jours. and conf. proceedings, chpts. to books. Recipient Best Acad. Paper award Chinese Assn. Rock Mechanics and Engring., 1987, Postdoctoral Fellowship award U. NSW, 1989, Best Acad. Paper award Chinese Assn. Hydraulic Engring., 1990, Significant Paper award Internat. Assn. for Computer Methods and Advances in Geomechanics, 1994. Avocations: cycling, reading, basketball, walking. Office: CSIRO Divsn Exploration and Mining, PO Box 437, 6009 Perth Australia

ZHAO, CHUN-MEI, histologist; b. Nanjing, Jiangsu, China, Mar. 12, 1964; d. Shi-Rong and Shun-Ying (Pang) Z.; m. Duan Chen, July 26, 1986; 1 child, Moquan. M in Med. Sci., U. Lund, 1995, D Med. Sci., 1999. Fellowship The Med. Faculty of U. of Lund, 1993—. Contbr. articles to profl. jours. Recipient various grants. Avocations: fashion, dancing. E-Mail: ChunMei.Zhao@farm.lu.se. Home: Snogenödsva 3, S-243 95 Höör Sweden

ZHAO, CONG LONG, physicist; b. Shaanxi, China, Mar. 9, 1944; came to U.S., 1990; m. Diying Yang, Dec. 1971; children: Jean, Ming. BA in Physics, Northwestern U., China, 1970; MS in Atmospheric Physics, Chinese Acad. Scis., 1981, PhD of Atmospheric Physics, 1986. Rsch. asst. Chinese Acad. Scis., Beijing, 1980-82; vis. scientist Wave Propagation Lab. NOAA, Boulder, Colo., 1983-85; rsch. assoc. Chinese Acad. Meteorol. Scis., Beijing, 1986-90; rsch. scientist Climate Monitoring and Diagnostics Lab. U. Colo., Boulder, 1990—. Contbr. articles to profl. jours.; inventor in field. Recipient 1st class nat. award for sci. and tech. Nat. Com. of Sci., Beijing, 1990. Office: NOAA/Climate Monitoring Diagnostics Lab 325 Broadway St Boulder CO 80305-3337

ZHAO, DAPENG, seismologist, educator; b. Zhaodong, China, Apr. 30, 1963; arrived in Japan, 1998; s. Fulin and Baiqing (Qu) Z.; m. Yanhong Lucy Liu, Oct. 30, 1988; children: Max, Frank. BSc, Peking (China) U., 1984; MS, Tohoku U., Sendai, Japan, 1988, PhD, 1991. Post-doctoral seismologist U. Alaska, Fairbanks, 1991-92; Texaco rsch. fellow Calif. Inst. Tech., Pasadena, 1992-95; sr. rsch. scientist Washington U., St. Louis, 1995-97; rsch. faculty U. So. Calif., L.A., 1997-98; assoc. prof. Ehime U., Matsuyama, Japan, 1998—; convenor 29th Gen. Assembly, Internat. Assn. Seismology and Physics of the Earth's Interior, Thessaloniki, Greece, 1997. Contbr. articles to profl. jours.; inventor in field. Mem. Seismol. Soc. Japan, Am. Geophys. Union, Seismol. Soc. Am. Avocations: reading, traveling. E-mail: zhao@sci.ehime-u.ac.jp. Office: Dept Earth Scis, Ehime Univ, Matsuyama, Ehime 790-8577, Japan

ZHAO, HAI, communications educator; b. Shenyang City, Liaoning, China, Mar. 10, 1959; p. Zuofu Zhao and Xiangzhen Pan; m. Xiaoxue Zhang, Mar. 1987; 1 child, Yu. Bachelors Degree, Dalian (China) Maritime U., 1982; Masters Degree, Northeastern U., Shenyang City, 1987, Doctors Degree, 1995. Radio-transmissional engr. Bur. Liaoning Broadcasting & TV, Shenyang City, 1982-84; prof. comm. engring. Northeastern U. Computer Corp., Shenyang City, 1987—, gen. mgr., 1993-99, 99—; gen. mgr. The Computer and Network Comm. Inst., Shenyang City, 1993—; rschr. in field. Editor Edit. of the Nat. Std., The Protocol of Mfg. Automation, 1993. Mem. standing com. The Civilian League of Liaoning Province, 1993—; commr. Info. Port Com. Shenyang City, 1998. Recipient Advancement award sci. and tech. Govt. Shenyang City, 1991, Advancement award sci. and tech. The Metallurgy Dept. China, 1993; named Advanced Leaguer, The Civilian League of Liaoning Province, 1998. Mem. Soc. Mfg. Engrs. U.S. (sr., sr. computer and automated sys. assn.). Achievements include inventor and patentee for The Open Network Device Connection Model; research includes The Fieldbus and the Embedded Internet, Data Fusion and Information Fusion. Avocations: China chess, Chinese draught, playing tennis, reading, music. E-mail: zhhai@mail.neu.edu.cn. Office: Coll Info Northeastern Univ, 11 3rd Ln Wenhua St, Shenyang City 110006, China

ZHAO, HONGBIN, artist; b. Shanghai, China, Aug. 15, 1952; arrived in Australia, 1988; s. Chi-Zhen Zhao and Xue-Min Chen; m. Mei-Jun Gu; 1 child, Hui-Jie. Student in Fine Arts Rsch., Shanghi Jiao Tong U., China, 1984-85. Art editor, designer Science Life Mag., Mcpl. Sci. and Tech. Assn., Shanghi, China, 1979-85; chief editor Modern New Products Pictorial, Shanghi U. Tech., China, 1985-88; freelance artist Mulgrave, Australia, 1988—. Art works pub. in nat. and internat. newspapers, mags. and books including Portraits of Australia, 1992, 50 Australian Artists, 1994, Dictionary of the Achievements of World Chinese Artists, 1994, The Paintings of Zhao Hongbin, 1997, Zhao Hongbin, Monet of the Orient, 1999; art calendars include Emotion of the Native Land, Blossom, 1984; one man shows include sixteen in Australia, Japan, China, Singapore, Indonesia, Taiwan; group shows include China Nat. Art Gallery, Shanghai Nat. Art Gallery of Art, 1977-85, Victoria Art Ctr., 1991, Sydney Opera House (Doug Moran Nat. Portrait Prize top four finalists), 1992, Australian Nat. Maritime Mus., 1993, Chinese War Meml. Mus., 1993, Internat. Exhbn., London (award winning), 1993, Nat. Gallery Victoria, Australia, 1992, 94, Art Gallery of New South Wales (Archibald prize finalist), 1994, Art Gallery of South Australia, 1995, New Parliament House, Canberra, 1995, Shanghai World Trade Ctr., 1997-99, Dr. Sun Yet-Sen Meml. Hall, Taipei, 1997. Recipient cert. of Hon. Shanghai Mcpl. Gov., 1986, Macquarie award 2000, 1994, Ernest Henry Meml. Art Show 1st prize, 1992-94, Dick Ovenden Meml. Art show first prize, 1991, Victor Harbor Art Exhbn. first prize, 1991, Mulcahy Mazda award, 1991, Omega Contemporary Art award Royal Overseas League, 1992, Bronze medal China Famous Figures Works Exhbn. of Arts Circles, 1994. Fellow Internat. Biog. Assn. U.K. (life); mem. Chinese Celebrity's Assn. Avocations: dancing, writing poetry, Chinese calligraphy. Studio: 36 Fernbank Crescent, Mulgrave VIC 3170, Australia

ZHAO, HUIRU, surgeon; b. Jinzhou, China, Nov. 23, 1940; s. Dexing and Suzhi (Zhang) Z.; m. Xiufen Li; children: Fan, Wei, Liyang. BS in Medicine, China Med. U., Shenyang, 1965. Resident surgeon First Affiliated Hosp., Shenyang, 1965-78, resident surgeon dept. thoracic surgery, 1978-80, surgeon in charge, 1980-86, assoc chief surgeon, 1986-94, chief surgeon, 1994—; dep. dir. dept. Thoracic Surgery, China Med. U., 1991—. Editor: (books) Modern Surgical Treatment of Tumors, 1994, The Fundamental and Clinical Lung Cancer, 1993; assoc.-editor: (book) Treatment of Commonly Seen Tumors, 1998. Mem. China Med. Assn. Thoracic and Cardiovascular Surgery (head com., consul mem. 1992—),Internat. Assn. Study Lung Cancer, Chinese Anti-Cancer Soc. Avocations: swimming, ping-pong, tennis. Office: China Med U/1st Affl Hosp, 155 N Nanjing St, 110001 Shenyang China

ZHAO, JAY ZIJUN, communications engineer; b. Xian, Shanxi, People's Republic China, Jan. 28, 1962; came to U.S., 1986; s. Deyin and Ping (Mann) Z. BS, Beijing Inst. Aeronautics/Ast., China, 1982, MS, 1983; PhD, Academia Sinica, Beijing, 1986; MA in Math., Temple U., 1987; exec. edn. program, Columbia U., 1998. Postdoctoral fellow U. Pa., Phila., 1988-89, rsch. assoc., cons., 1990-91; sr. scientist FAA Tech. Ctr., McKee, N.J., 1992-94; sr. engr. Raytheon, Pleasantville, N.J., 1994; cons. AT&T Bell Labs., Whippany, N.J., 1994-96; tech. mgr. Bell Labs., Lucent Techs., Murray Hill, N.J., 1996-98; dep. gen. mgr. Guoxin Lucent Techs., Providence, N.J., 1998-99; mng. dir. Bell Labs, Asia Pacific and China, 1999—. Contbr. articles to profl. jours. Mem. IEEE, Soc. Indsl. and Applied Math., Soc. Am. Math., Optical Soc. Am.

ZHAO, JIAN, civil engineer, researcher; b. Shanghai, July 9, 1960; s. Han-Zhong and Feng-Xian (Zhang) Z.; m. Jenny Shen, Sept. 12, 1990. BS, U. Leeds, 1983; PhD, Imperial Coll., 1987. Chartered engr.; registered profl. engr., Singapore. Rsch. fellow Nanyang Tech. U., Singapore, 1990-93, lectr., 1993-94, sr. lectr., 1994—, assoc. prof., 1999—; founding sec. Tunnelling & Underground Constrn. Soc., Singapore, 1998—. Co-author: Construction and Utilization of Rock Caverns in the Bukit Timah Granite of Singapore, 1994, Underground Cavern Development in the Jurong Formation of Sedimentary Rocks, 1999, Mechanics and Stability of Excavations in Fractured Rocks, 2000; editl. bd. mem. Internat. Jour. Rock Mechanics and Minings Scis., 1997—, Tunnelling and Underground Space Technology, 1998—, Chinese Jour. Rock Mechanics and Engring., 1999—; contbr. articles to profl. jours. Recipient Richard Wolters prize Internat. Assn. Engring. Geology and the Environ. Fellow Geol. Soc. U.K.; mem. ASCE, Instn. Engrs. Singapore. Avocations: Chinese literature and history, theatre and ballet classics, badminton. Office: Sch Civil and Structural Engring, Nanyang Technol Univ, Singapore 639798, Singapore

ZHAO, JINSONG JASON, engineer, researcher, administrator; b. Beijing, July 14, 1966; came to U.S., 1990; m. Wen Chen. BSME, Tianjin U., 1989; MSME, N.C. A&T State U., 1997. Project mgr. Sinolummus, Inc., 1989-92; sr. mech. engr. Microdyne System, Inc., 1994; mgr. rsch. & engring. IKA Works, Inc., Wilmington, N.C., 1994-98; v.p. CAM Techs., Inc., Schaumberg, Ill., 1998—; vice-chmn. task com. 3A Sanitary Com., 1997—; bd. dirs. Rotor Stator Mixer Rsch. Adv. Bd. Inventor cleaning in place multistage high shear in-line mixer. Mem. ASME, ISPE, AIChE, NAMF. Office: CAM Techs Inc 1035 Peters Ct Lake Zurich IL 60047-1451

ZHAO, JINXI, computational mathematician, mathematics educator; b. Changzhou, JiangSu, China, July 28, 1950; s. Yusong Zhao and Yazheng Mu; m. Li Mei-Lan, May 1, 1978; 1 child, Jiang Zhao. BS, Nanjing (China) U., 1977; PhD, Nanjing U., 1987. Lectr. maths. Nanjing U., 1986-88, asst. prof., 1989-99, prof., 1999—, vice chmn. dept. math., 1987-91, 93—. Math. reviewer 1989—. Recipient Excellent Young Tchr. awards Kok Ying Tung Edn. Found., 1989, 90. Mem. Chinese Math. Soc. Home and Office: Dept Math, Nanjing Univ, Nanjing 210008, China

ZHAO, JUNLIANG, astronomer; b. Shanghai, Mar. 13, 1942; s. Tiyong Zhao and Shene Li; m. Minming Yao, Apr. 4, 1946; children: Jianhong, Xiaohong. Grad., Wuhan (China) Inst. Geodesy and Cartography, 1964. Shanghai Obs., 1968—. Dep. dir. Shanghai Obs., 1992-93, dir., 1993—. Avocations: bridge. Office: Shanghai Astronomical Obs, 80 Nandan Rd, Shanghai 200030, China

ZHAO, KE-YOU, electrical engineer, educator; b. Qingdao, Shandong, China, Oct. 28, 1945; s. En-Tong Zhao and Rui-Ai Chi; m. Ai-Hua Yang, Oct. 30, 1972; children: Gang, Yu. Math., Shandong U., 1968. Technician Power Co., Liangshan, China, 1970-78; lectr. Shandong U., Jinan, China, 1978-86; prof. Qingdao (China) U., 1987—; vis. prof. U. Tenn., Knoxville, 1988, U. Wis., Madison, 1988-89, U. Strathclyde, Scotland. Contbr. articles to profl. jours. vice chmn. Chinese Peoples Polit. Cons. Conf., 1992—. Mem. AAAS, Chinese Automation Assn., Chinese Sys. Engring. Assn. Avocations: basketball, swimming, music. Fax: 86-532-5882831. E-mail: kyzhao@gdu.edu.ca. Home: 103 Ningxia Rd, Shandong Qingdao 266071, China Office: Qingdao U Fac Elec/Auto Engring, 308 Ningxia Rd, Shandong Qingdao 266071, China

ZHAO, MING, English studies educator; b. Wei Fang, Shan Dong, China, July 14, 1957; d. Zhongquan and Jian Zhao Huang; m. Yi Tang; 1 child, Rui. BA, Xuzhou Tchrs. Coll., 1982; MA, Shanghai Internat. Studies U., 1992. Tchr. Xuzhou Tchrs. Coll., 1982-89, 92-95, China U. Mining and Tech., Xuzhou, 1995—. Author: The Rudiments of English Writing, 1993 (Works of Excellence award 1994); contbr. articles to profl. jours. including Shanghai Jour. Translators for Sci. and Tech., Chinese Sci. and Tech. Translators Jour. Mem. N.Y. Acad. Sci. Avocations: reading, singing. Office: China U Mining and Tech, Dept English, Xuzhou 221008, China

ZHAO, REN WEI, economics educator; b. Jinhua, Zhejiang, China, Mar. 23, 1933; s. Jian guang and Shu jun (Huang) Z.; m. An lin Zhu, Aug. 15, 1965; children: Wen jing, Wen wei. BA in Econs., Beijing (China) U., 1957. Rsch. asst., asst. prof. Inst. Econs., Chinese Acad., Beijing, 1957-79; assoc. prof. Inst. Econs., Chinese Acad. Social Scis., Beijing, 1979-85, dept. dir., prof., 1985-88, dir., prof., 1988-91, prof. econs., 1991—; vis. fellow St. Antony's Coll. Oxford (Eng.) U., 1982-83, Columbia U., N.Y.C., 1992-93, Duisburg (Germany) U., 1996, All Souls Coll. Oxford (Eng.) U., 1997. Chief editor Econ. Rsch. Jour., 1989-91; author: Outline of Target Model of China's Economic Reform, 1988; author, editor The Distribution of Income in China, 1993, 99. Recipient Sun Yefang Prizes of Econs. Com. of Sun Yefang Prize, Beijing, 1984, 86, 94; rsch. grantee Ford Found., N.Y.C., 1988, 94, St. Antony's Coll Oxford U., 1983. Mem. Chinese Assn. Hong Kong and Macau Econ. Studies (v.p. 1990-93, hon. cons. 1993—), Chinese Assn. Market Econ. Studies (mem. coun. 1993—), China Devel. Inst. (mem. coun. 1989—), Chinese Assn. Comparative Econ. Studies (v.p. 1986—). Avocations: swimming, gardening. Home: 1 Chang yun gong, Zizhuyan, Beijing 100044, China Office: Chinese Acad Social Scis Inst Econs, 2 Yuetan Beixiaojie, Beijing 100836, China

ZHAO, SHUMING, business educator, dean; b. Haian, Jiangsu, China, Dec. 15, 1952; s. Zhenquan Zhao and Xiufang Yan; m. Xiaomei Xu; 1 child, Yixuan Zhao. BA in English Lang. and Lit., Nanjing U., China, 1977; MA in Linguistics and Edn., Claremont (Calif.) Grad. Sch., 1983, PhD in Higher Edn. Adminstrn., HR Mgmt., 1990; post doctoral fell., Florida Atlantic U., 1990-91. Gen. mgr. Oiwan Farm, Haian, 1970-74; lectr. Nanjing U., 1977-80, dir. Office Internat. Exch. Programs, 1983-87, assoc. prof., assoc. dean Sch. Internat. Bus., 1991-94, prof., acting dean, 1995—; vis. prof. Whitworth Coll., Spokane, Wash., 1990, Fla. Atlantic U., 1990-91, Oklahoma City U., 1991, U. Hawaii, Monoa, 1992, York U., U. Toronto, Canada, 1993, U. Southern Maine, 1994, U. Mo., St. Louis, 1995, U. Southern Calif., 1996, Bond U., Australia, 1997, U. S. Calif., 1998—; cons. China Bao An Group, Shenzhen, 1994-96, Jiangsu Provincial Govt., Nanjing, 1994—, China Human Resources Group, 1995-96, Pacific Bridge, Inc., 1995-96, Nanjing Lopu Corp., 1995-96, Jiangsu Xuan Tian Internat. Corp., 1997—, Meierzi Group, 1997-99; mem. of the acad. adv. bd. Hang Lung Ctr. for Orgn. Rsch. of Hong Kong U. of Sci. and Technology, 1999—; ind. dir. in Yizheng Chem. Fiber Co., Ltd. Author: International Human Resources Management, 2d edit., 1995 (China State Edn. award), Into. International Business, 2nd edit. 1998, (Jiangsu Provincial Govt. award 1994), East & West Cultures and Business Management, 1995, Joint Venture Management, 1995, World Economy and Internationalization of Chines Enterprises, 1995, Am. Higher Education Administration, 1992 (First Price award Nat. Assn. Higher Edn., 1993), Human Resources Management and Development: International Comparison Beijing, 1999; translator Democracy and Economic Power-Extending the ESOP Revolution through Binary Economics, 1996, Knowledge Across Cultures: Univeristies East and West, 1996, Contemporary Australian Society, 1993; co-author: (with Zhong Yang) International Business: Cross Cultural Management, 1994; editor: Multinational Business and Overseas Investment, 1995; contbr. over 100 acad. papers and articles to profl. jours.; lectr., presenter in field; mem. editl. bd. Asia Pacific Human Resources, Australia, Advances in Competiveness Rsch., U.S., Coastal Economy, China. Recipient Transcentury Excellent Scholar of State Education Comm., China, 1996, Outstanding Scholar award State Coun. of China, 1995, Outstanding Internat. Scholar award Fla. Atlantic U., 1992, award Found. for Ednl. Futures for Rsch., 1988; fellow Claremont Grad. Sch., 1987-90, 1982-83, First Level Scholar Jiangsu 333 Project, 1998. Mem. China Human Resources Assn. (exec. mem.), Jiangsu Provincial Assn. of Bus. (v.p. 1995—), Jiangsu Provincial Assn. Human Resources Mgmr. (pres.). Avocations: tennis.E-mail: zhaosm@netra.nju.edu.ch; zhaosm@njnet.nj.ac.cn; szhao@bus.usc.edu. Office: Nanjing U, Nanjing U, Sch Bus, Nanjing 210093, China

ZHAO, TIANSHOU, science educator; b. He Yang, Shaan Xi, China, June 18, 1961; parents Jianye Zhao and Rexian Dong; m. Song Jing, June 18, 1987; 1 child, Jing. BS, Tianjin (China) U., 1983, MS, 1986; PhD, U. Hawaii, 1995. Cert. profl. engr. Rsch. asst. U. Hawaii, Honolulu, 1991-95; lectr. Tianjin U., 1986-91; asst. prof. Hong Kong U. Sci. & Tech., 1995—; cons. Broad Air Conditioning, Ltd., Changsha, China, 1996—. Author: (book) Annual Review of Heat Transfer, 1998; contbr. articles to profl. jours. Everett E. Black scholar U. Hawaii, 1994. Mem. ASME, ASHRAE. Avocations: music, basketball. Fax: (852)23581543. E-mail: metzhao@ust.hk. Office: Hong Kong U Sci & Tech, Clear Water Bay, Kowloon Hong Kong

ZHAO, TIANXIAN ROY, medical products executive, researcher; b. Shuanfeng, Hunan, China, Dec. 10, 1963; s. Haiyu Zhao and Qiuying Shu; m. Guangmin Julia Zhou, Mar. 30, 1988; children: Rebecca, Jenny. B in Engring., Hunan U., China, 1983; MS, Peking Union Med. Coll., 1987; PhD, Karolinska Inst., Sweden, 1993. Rsch. asst. Peking Union Med. Coll., China, 1987-88; rsch. assoc. Karolinska Inst., Sweden, 1988-94, Sheffield U., Eng., 1994-95, UMIST, Eng., 1995-97; R & D mgr. O-Two Sys., Can., 1997—. Contbr. articles to profl. jours.; inventor, patent device for determining sedimentation of blood, 1993, 98. Avocations: badminton, table tennis, chess. Office: O-Two Sys Internat, 7575 Kimbel St Unit 5, Mississauga, ON Canada L5S 1C8

ZHAO, WEI-PING, physiologist; b. Gongzhuling City, China, Apr. 8, 1931; m. Chang-xiao He, Jan. 1, 1957; children: Zhao Yi-hong, Zhao Yi-nong, Zhao Yi-qing. BS, N.E. Normal U., 1953; MS, E. China Normal U., 1955. Asst. prof. N.W. Tchr.'s Coll., Lanzhou, China, 1955-57; asst. prof. Beijing Tchr.'s Coll., 1957-78, assoc. prof., 1978-85; prof. Capital Normal U., Beijing, 1985—; agr. sci. cons. Beijing People's Govt., 1981-96. Author: (books) Crop Physiology, 1982, Wheat Physiology and Molecular Biology, 1993, Plant Genomes: Organization, Expression and Control, 1996; contbg. author: (books) History of Plant Physiology in China, Structure and Function of Plant Genes, 1995. Mem. Beijing Com. of China People's Polit. Cons. Conf., 1983-92. Recipient advanced individual award Nat. Sci. Plenary Session, Beijing, 1978, Sci. and Tech. Assn. of China, Beijing, 1987, Excellent Tchg. Achievement award in Higher Edn., Beijing People's Govt., 1993. Mem. Beijing Soc. Plant Physiologists (sec.-gen. 1978-95), Chinese Soc. Plant Physiologists (dir. 1986-94), China Soc. Life Scis. (dir. 1995—). Avocations: swimming, dancing. Office: Capital Normal U Dept Biology, 105 West Thirdcycle Rd, Beijing 100037, China

ZHAO, WU-SHU, immunologist, researcher; b. Lai Shi City, Shandong, China, Oct. 29, 1940; s. Ji-Quan and Rui-Lan (Gao) Z.; m. Hui-Zhen Ma, Feb. 6, 1973; children: Ya-Li, Lu-Ting. BS, Peking U., Beijing, 1964; MS, Peking Union of Med. Coll., Beijing, 1980. Asst. rschr. Chinese Acad. Med. Scis., Beijing, 1964-75, assoc. rschr., 1976-82; vis. prof. Osaka City (Japan) U., 1983-85; assoc. prof. China Japan Friendship Inst. of Clin. Med. Scis., Beijing, 1985-93, prof., 1993—, dep. dir. dept. immunology, 1986-89, dir. dept. immunology, 1990—. Author: Basis of Molecular Biology, 1990; editor: Modern Clinical Immunology, 1994. Mem. china Biochemistry Molecular Biology Soc., N.Y. Acad. Scis., Chinese Microbiology and Immunology Soc. (com. mem. 1991—). Office: China Japan Friendship Hosp, Ying Hua East Rd, 100029 Beijing China

ZHAO, XIAOBO, economics educator; b. Hubei, China, Nov. 16, 1962. BS, Dalian Railway Inst., China, 1983; MS, Wuhan Transp. U., China, 1988; PhD, Nagoya Inst. of Tech., Japan, 1996. Asst. engr. Wuhan Factory of Engrng., China, 1983-85; lectr. Wuhan Transp. U., China, 1988-92; rsch. fellow Tsinghua U., China, 1996-98, assoc. prof., 1998—. Contbr. articles to profl. jours. Mem. Inst. Indsl. Engrs. (U.S.). Office: Sch Econs and Mgmt, Tsinghua U, 100084 Beijing China

ZHAO, XINWEI, physicist; b. Baixing, Hebei, China, Feb. 10, 1960; s. Yunhai and Xiange (Fan) Z.; m. Zhongfang Li, Mar. 25, 1984; children: Meng, Ye. B electronics engring., Tianjin U., China, 1982; M electronics engring., Tokyo U., 1985, D electronics engring., 1988. Lectr. Nankai U., Tianjin, 1989-90; prof. Nanking U., Tianjin, 1991—; postdoctoral rschr. Tokyo U., 1990-91, vis. rschr., 1991-92; rschr. Inst Phys and Chem Rsch, Saitama, Japan, 1992-99; prof. Sci. U. Tokyo, 2000—. Contbr. articles in profl. jours. Inventor in field. Pres. Nankai Alumni Assn. in Japan, 1995. Recipient Nat. Natural Sci. Found. for Young Scientists award Nat. Found. of China, 1989-91, grant-in-aid for scientific rsch. Min. Edn., Sci., Culture and Sports of Japan, 1993, 1996-97. Avocations: reading, hiking, assn. football. Fax: 81-424-75-1685. Email address: xwzhao@rs.kagu.sut.ac.jp. Home: No 6-3 1-14-8 Chu-O-Cho, Higashikurume-shi Tokyo 203-0054, Japan Office: U Tokyo Dept Phys Sci, 1-3 Kagurazaka, Tokyo 162-8601, Japan

ZHAO, XIU SONG, chemical engineering researcher; b. Ju Xian, China, Apr. 12, 1965; s. Hong Mian and Qing Lan (Min) Z.; m. Yimin Xiao, Mar. 18, 1990; children: Qi, Bo. Diploma, Dalian U. Fgn. Lang.; BS, Shandong U., Jinan, China, 1987; PhD, U. Queensland, Brisbane, Australia, 1999. Asst. engr. Chinese Acad. Scis., Dalian, 1991-92, investigator, 1993-95; vis. scholar U. Queensland, 1995-96, PhD student, 1996-98, postdoctoral rsch. fellow, 1999—; supr. PhD students U. Queensland, 1999—. Author: (book) Advanced Zeolite Materials and Applications in Catalysis, 1996 (3rd prize Nat. Sci. Found. of China, 1997); investigator rsch. project, 1988-91 (2d prize Advancement in Sci. and Tech., 1992). Avocations: basketball, cooking. E-mail: xiusongz@checque.uq.edu.au. Home: 6/133 Eagle Terr, Bisbane Qld 4066, Australia Office: Dept Chem Engrng U Qld, St Lucia, Brisbane Qld 4072, Australia

ZHAO, YONG-QING, metallurgist; b. Luiyang, China, Apr. 16, 1966; s. Yan-Wa Z. and Fenglian Tian; m. Fang Li, Sept. 15, 1992; 1 child, Qin-Yang. B, Northwestern Polytech. U., Xi'an, China, 1988; M, Ctr. So. Polytech. U., Changsha, China, 1991; D, Northeast U., Shanyang, China, 1999. Asst. engr. Northwest Inst. Nonferrous Metal Rsch., Booji, China, 1991-93; engr. Northwest Inst. Nonferrous Metal Rsch., Xi'an, China, 1993-95, sr. engr., 1995-98, prof., 1998—. Patentee in field. E-mail: lps@hope.hit.edu.cn. Office: Harbin Inst Tech, PO Box 305, 150 001 Harbin China

ZHAO, YU MIN, physics educator, researcher; b. Qin Huang-Dao, He Bei, China, Jan. 2, 1967; parents Chun-Qiu Zhao and Jin-Ying Zhang; m. Hua Lu, Dec. 24, 1993; 1 child, Jing-Wei. BS, Nankai U., Tian-Jin, 1989; MS, Academia Sinica, Lan Zhou, 1992; PhD, Nanjing (China) U., 1995. Asst. S.E. U., Nanjing, 1995, from lectr. to assoc. prof., 1996-97, prof. physics, 1998—; sci. & tech. agy. fellow RIKEN, The Inst. of Phys. and Chem. Rsch., Wako-shi, Saitama, 1998-00. Author: Physics Review C52,1453, 1995 (C.S. Wu prize 1996). Buddhist. Fax: 81 48 462 1111. E-mail: ymzhao@rikaxp.riken.go.jp.

ZHAO, YUWEN, physiochemist, researcher; b. Xixia, Henan, China, Sept. 24, 1939; s. Liangchen and Yunqing (Shi) Z.; m. Xiangyun Chen, Oct. 1, 1969; children: Kai, Di. BS, Tianjin U., 1964. Technician Academica Sinica, Beijing, 1964-67; asst. engr. Minister of Space Industry of China, Beijing, 1967-78; dir. solar materials lab. Beijing Solar Energy Rsch. Inst., 1978-87, dep. dir. inst., 1987-94, chief engr. of inst., 1994—, dir. photovoltaic dept., 1992—, chmn. acad. com., 1994—; sr. vis. scholar Tuebingen (Germany) U., 1990-91; exec. dir. Nat. Rsch. Ctr. for renewable Energy, Beijing, 1992—; chief specialist Beijing Photovoltaic Rsch. Ctr., 1996—. Editl. bd. Jour. Functional Materials, 1993—, Acta Energiae Solaris Sinica, 2000—; contbr. articles to profl. jours.; inventor in field. Recipient two awards Beijing Sci. and Tech., 1981, two awards Major Sci. and Acad. Achievements for Chinese in the World, 1999. Mem. Internat. Solar Energy Soc., China Solar Soc. (mem. standing com. 1995—, vice chmn. photovoltaic session 1995-99, chmn. photovoltaic session 1999, vice-chmn. 1999—), China Sci. and Tech. Min. (specialist sci. and tech. econ. specialist com. 1999—). Avocations: reading, bridge, swimming, travel, table tennis. Home: Haidian Dist, 3 Huayuan Rd, Beijing 100083, People's Republic China Office: Beijing Solar Energy Rsch, 3 Huayuan Rd Haidian Dist, Beijing 100083, People's Republic China

ZHAO, ZHIYONG, developmental biology researcher; b. Dunhua, Jilin, China, Dec. 24, 1961; s. Hui Zhao and Shulan Yu; m. Hua Jiang, May 15, 1988; children: Stephen, Andew. BSc, Dalian (China) Coll., 1982; MSc, South China Normal U., Guangzhou, 1985; PhD, U. Manchester, Eng., 1994. Rsch. assoc. Chinese Acad. Scis., Beijing, 1985-89, Pa. State U., University Park, 1994-97; assoc. rsch. scientist Yale U. Sch. Medicine, New Haven, 1997—. Contbr. articles to sci. jours., encys., books. Exec. dir. Chinese Culture Club, University Park, 1993.

ZHAO, ZHONG WEI, demographer; b. Beijing, China, Sept. 29, 1954; s. Shu Nan and Qi Xiu (Wang) Z.; m. Yan Ping Zhang, 1982; 1 child, Kun. BA, Peking U., 1983; MA, Exeter U., 1987; PhD, Cambridge (U.K.) U., 1993. Fellow Australian Nat. U., Canberra, 1996—. Contbr. chpts. to books and articles to profl. jours. Fellowship United Nation's Fund for Population Activities, 1986. Mem. Internat. Union for the Scientific Study of Population, Australian Population Assn. Office: Australian Nation U, Demography Program RSSS, Canberra ACT 0200, Australia

ZHAO, ZHONGYUN, economist; b. Taian, China, Jan. 14, 1962; came to U.S., 1991; s. Liangxiang Zhao and Youngyu Jin; m. Jiali Sha; children: Amy, Angela. BS, East China Normal U., Shanghai, 1983, MS, 1986; MA, U. So. Calif., L.A., 1994, PhD, 1997. Economist State Planning Commn., Beijing, 1986-88, economist, sect. dir., 1988-91; rsch. assoc., asst. U. So. Calif., L.A., 1994-97; sr. mgr. Merck-Medco Managed Care, LLC, Franklin Lakes, N.J., 1997-99, assoc. dir., 1999—. Author: (book chpts.) Analysis of Panels and Limited Dependent Variable Models, 1999; contbr. articles to profl. jours. World Bank Grad. scholar, 1992-94. Mem. Internat. Soc. for Pharmacoecons. and Outcomes Rsch., Am. Econ. Assn., Am. Statis. Assn., Drug Info. Assn. E-mail: zjzhao@worldnet.att.net. Office: Merck-Medco Managed Care LLC 100 Parsons Pond Dr Franklin Lakes NY 07417

ZHAO, ZINGZHONG, research scientist, educator; b. Dancheng, Henan, Peoples Republic of China, Feb. 4, 1964; s. Tingming and Xiaoying (Dong) Z.; m. Ring W. Zhao, Oct. 1, 1991; 1 child, Jennifer. BSc, Henan U., Kaifeng, China, 1986; MSc, Lanzhou Inst. Chem. Physics, 1989; PhD, Tsinghua U., Beijing, China, 1997. Rsch. asst. Lanzhou Inst. Chem. Physics, 1986-89; rsch. assoc. Zhengzhou Rsch. Inst. Mech. Engring., 1989-94; rsch. fellow Tsinghua U., Beijing, 1994-97; rsch. scientist Ohio State U., Columbus, 1997—. Contbr. articles to profl. jours. Mem. ASTM, Soc. Tribologists and Lubrication Engrs., Am. Automotive Assn. Avocations: sports, tourism, mountain climbing. E-mail: zhao6@hotmail.com Fax: (614) 292-3163.

ZHAOXING, LI, diplomat; b. Shandong, People's Republic of China, 1940; married; one son. Grad., Beijing U., 1964; postgrad., Beijing Inst. Fgn. Langs., 1964-67. Staff mem. Chinese People's Inst. Fgn. Affairs, 1967-70; staff mem., attache Chinese Embassy, Kenya, 1970-77; staff mem., dep. divsn. chief info. dept. Chinese Ministry Fgn. Affairs, 1977-83, dep. dir. gen., dir. gen. info. dept., 1985-90; first sect. Chinese Embassy, Kingdom of Lesotho, 1983-85; asst. min. fgn. affairs, 1990-92; permanent rep., amb. extraordinary and plenipotentiary People's Republic China to the UN, 1992-95; vice min. fgn. affairs, 1995-98; amb. extraordinary and plenipotentiary People's Republic China to the U.S., 1998—; guest prof. Beijing U., Nankai U., 1993. Fax: 202-588-0032. E-mail: webmaster@china-embassy.org. Office: Embassy of the Peoples Republic China 2300 Connecticut Ave NW Washington DC 20008-1724

ZHARIKOV, ALEXANDER NIKOLAEVICH, trade union federation executive; b. Michailov, Rjazan, Russia, Jan. 2, 1945; s. Nikolaj Philippovich and Claudia Egorovna (Gorodnicheva) Z.; m. Olga Borisovna Sukhova, Mar. 1975; 1 child, Michail. Student, Shipbldg. Inst., Leningrad, Russia, 1969. Sec. Student Orgn. Shipbldg. Inst., Leningrad, 1967-70; dir. student dept. Leningrad City Youth Orgn., Leningrad, 1970-71, sec., 1971-74; vice chmn. Com. Youth Orgns. USSR, Moscow, 1974-76; chmn. Student Coun. USSR, Moscow, 1976-78; v.p. Internat. Union Students, Prague, Czechoslovakia, 1978-84; officer Internat. Dept. Ctrl. Com. CPSU, Moscow, 1984-88; dir. internat. dept. All Union Ctrl. Coun. Trade Unions, Moscow, 1988-90; gen. sec. World Fedn. Trade Unions, Prague, 1990—; Co-author: International Union of Students, 1978. Mem. City Com. Leningrad Youth Orgn., 1970-71, sec., 1971-74; mem. Ctrl. Com. Youth Orgn. USSR, Moscow, 1978-84. Capt. Russian mil., 1962-66. Office: Branická 112, 14000 Prague 4, Czech Republic

ZHARKOV, VLADIMIR NAUMOVICH, physicist, geophysicist, educator; b. Leningrad, Former USSR, Mar. 4, 1926; s. Naum Yakovlevich Pilyavin and Dveira Ruvimovna Zharkova; m. Lyudmila Nikolaevna Panfilova, Nov. 2, 1954; children: Elena, Vladimir. MS in Physics, Math. Sci., Kharkov U., 1954; D in Physics, Math. Sci., Inst. Physics, Moscow, 1964. Sr. scientist Lab. Radiography, Cinema-Photography Rsch. Inst., Moscow, 1949-56, 1956-70, head of lab., 1970-96; chief scientist Inst. Physics of the Earth, Moscow, 1996—; prof. Moscow-Physico-Tech. Inst., 1973-91. Author: Interior Structure of the Earth and Planets, 1986; co-author: Equation of State for Solids at High Pressures and Temperatures, 1971, Physics of Planetary Interiors, 1978, Helioseismology, 1989, Venus, Geology, Geochemistry and Geophysics; Research Results from the USSR, 1992, The Earth and Its Rotation, 1996. Mem. Am. Geophysics Union, IAU (Internat. Astronomical Union). Office: Inst of Physics of Earth, B Gruzinskaya 10, 123810 Moscow Russia

ZHDANKIN, VIKTOR VLADIMIROVICH, chemistry educator; b. Sverdlovsk, Russia, June 6, 1956; came to U.S., 1990; s. Vladimir M. and Rimma V. (Lukanina) Z.; m. Olga Y. Geraskina, Sept. 20, 1980; children: Vasiliy V., Vladimir V. BS, MS, Moscow State U., 1978, PhD, 1981, DSc, 1987. Rsch. fellow Moscow State U., 1982-86; vis. scientist U. Minn., Duluth, 1987-88; rsch. prof. Moscow State U., 1988-89; instr., sr. rsch. assoc. U. Utah, Salt Lake City, 1990-93; asst. prof. U. Minn., Duluth, 1993-96, assoc. prof., 1996-99, prof., 1999—; panel mem. Internat. Sci. Found., Washington, 1993-95. Contbr. articles to profl. jours.; mem. editl. bd. Russian Jour. Organic Chemistry, 1989-93, Jour. Mendeleev Chem. Soc., 1989-95, Mendeleev Comm., 1998—. Grantee Rsch. Corp., 1993-96, Petroleum Rsch. Fund/Am. Chem. Soc., 1994-96, NSF, 1995—, Dreyfus Found., 1997—. Mem. Am. Chem. Soc., Coun. Undergrad. Rsch., Sigma Xi. Achievements include discovery of new phenomena in physical-organic chemistry; preparation of new iodine reagents; development of organic chemistry of xenon. Avocations: traveling, skiing, reading fiction. Office: U Minn Dept Chemistry 10 University Dr Duluth MN 55812-2403

ZHDANOV, RENAD IBRAHIMOVICH, chemist, researcher; b. Kazan, Tatarstan, Russian Fedn., Oct. 11, 1944; s. Ibrahim Khasanovich and Banu Zinnurovna (Bagautdinova) Z.; m. Galina Viktorovna Litvinenko, July 13, 1968; children: Albert, Elena; m. Elena Lazarevna Pyatigorskaya, Dec. 12, 1985; 1 child, Anton. MSc, Kazan State U., 1967; PhD, Semenov Inst. Chem. Physics, Moscow, 1971; DSc, Lomonosov Inst Fine Chem. Tech, Moscow, 1986. Rsch. assoc. Inst. Chemistry of Natural Products, Moscow, 1971-73; sr. rsch. fellow, dep. dir. R&D Inst. of Biotech., Moscow, 1974-95; head gene therapy Inst. Biomed. Chemistry, Moscow, 1995—; chief scientist Inst. Theoretical and Exptl. Biophysics, Russian Acad. Scis., Moscow region, 1996—; vis. scientist Max-Planck-Inst. for Med. Rsch., Heidelberg, Germany, 1989-90; vis. prof. U. Guelph (Ont., Can.) Vet. Coll., 1989-90, U. Ancona, Italy, 1992-93; prof. dept. biology Middle East Tech. U., Ankara, Turkey, 1993-94; cons. plant prodn. of bacterial preparations, Moscow, 1999—. Author, editor: Bioactive Spin Labels, 1992; author, editor jour. issues. Pres., Gene and Cell Therapy Found., Moscow, 1996—. Recipient 1st prize Mendeleev Chem. Soc., 1973; A. von Humboldt Found. fellow, 1989. Mem. Nat. Biochem Soc., Am. Soc. Gene Therapy (corr.), Am. Topical Soc. (corr.), Tatar Acad. Soc. (co-dir. 1997—), Moscow A. von Humboldt Club (co-dir. 1992-98). Avocations: tennis, collecting scientific postage stamps, photography, travel. Office: Inst Biomed Chemistry, 10 Pogodinskaya St, 119832 Moscow Russia

ZHDANOV, RENAT ZUFAROVICH, mathematician; b. Balyshly, Russia, May 29, 1962; s. Zufar Sagitzyanovich and Gul'sina Abdulkhakovna (Mussalyamova) Z.; m. Gouzel Akhmetzievna Rafikova, June 24, 1988; 1 child, Alija. MSc in Math., Kiev (Ukraine) State U., 1984; PhD in Math., Inst. Math., Kiev, 1987, D in Math. and Physics, 1992. Rsch. fellow Tech. U. Clausthal, Germany, 1994-96; rsch. fellow Inst. Math., 1987-92, leading rsch. fellow, 1992-94, 96—. Author: Nonlinear Spinor Equations, 1992, Symmetries and Exact Solutions of Nonlinear Dirac Equations, 1997. Alexander von Humboldt Found. fellow, Bonn, 1994. Avocations: travel, foreign languages. Office: Inst Math, 3 Tereshchenkivska Str, 252004 Kiev Ukraine

ZHEBULEV, IGOR ANATOLIEVICH, physicist, researcher; b. St. Petersburg, Russia, Aug. 25, 1967; s. Anatoly Ivanovitch and Tamara Pavlovna (Grigorieva) Z. MS, Tech. U., St. Petersburg, 1992. Jr. rschr. Ioffe Inst., St. Petersburg, 1990-93, rschr., 1993—; cons. MT computers, St. Petersburg, 1997—. Contbr. papers in field. Home: D Bednogo, 195276 Saint Petersburg Russia Office: AF Ioffe Inst, Politerchnicheskaya 26, 194021 Saint Petersburg Russia

ZHELEZNYAKOV, VLADIMIR VASILYEVICH, astrophysicist, educator; b. Nizhny Novgorod, USSR, Jan. 28, 1931; s. Vasily Vladimirovich Z. and Vera Nikolayevna Okuneva; m. Lyudmila Petrovna Koryavova, July 14, 1956; 1 child, Inna. MS, Gorky (USSR) State U., 1949-54, postgrad., 1954-57, Candidate in Physics and Maths., 1959, D in Physics and Maths., 1965. Scientific researcher Gorky Radiophys. Rsch. Inst., USSR, 1957-65; head theoret. dept. Gorky Radiophys. Rsch. Inst., 1966-77, prof., 1968-91; head astrophysics and cosmic plasma dept. Inst. Applied Physics, 1977—; prof. Nizhny Novgorod State U., Russia, 1991—. Author: Radio Emission of the Sun and Planets, 1970, Electromagnetic Waves in Cosmic Plasma, 1977, Radiation in Astrophysical Plasmas, 1996; editor-in-chief Radiophysics and Quantum Electronics Jour. Recipient Belopolsky prize USSR Acad. Sci., 1984; named Soros Prof. Open Soc. Inst., 1994. Mem. Russian Acad. Scis. (academician), Internat. Astronom. Union, European Astronom. Soc. E-mail: zhelez@appl.sci-nnov.ru. Office: Inst Applied Physics, Ulyanov st 46, 603600 Nizhny Novgorod Russia

ZHELUDEV, NIKOLAY IVANOVICH, physicist, educator; b. Moscow, Apr. 23, 1955; arrived in Eng., 1991; s. Ivan Stepanovich and Galina Antonovna (Krasnikova) Z.; m. Tatiana Ilinichna Nousinova, July 20, 1979; children: Ilya, Ivan. MSc, Moscow State U., 1978, PhD, 1981, DSc (hon.), 1992. From rsch. to sr. rsch. faculty mem. physics Moscow State U., 1981-91; lectr. physics U. Southampton, Eng., 1991-94, reader physics, 1994—, prof. physics and astronomy, 2000—. Author: Susceptibility Tensors for Nonlinear Optics, 1995, Polarization of Light in Nonlinear Optics, 1998, Encyclopedia of Material Tensors, 1999; contbr. articles to profl. jours. Grantee Royal Soc., Engring. and Phys. Scis. Rsch. Coun., U.K., R.W. Paul Instrument Fund, NATO, Leverhulme Trust. Fellow Inst. of Physics (London); mem. Optical Soc. Am., Am. Inst. Physics. Office: U Southampton Dept Physics, Highfield, Southampton S017 1BJ, England

ZHEN, YONG-SU, pharmacology educator; b. Kaiping, China, Nov. 10, 1931; s. Zhao-Ren and Rui-Ying (Yu) Z.; m. Miao-Lan Chen, Nov. 19, 1955; children: Wei-Ping, Wei-Ning. MD, Sun-Yatsen U. Med. Sci., Guangzhou, China, 1954. Rsch. assoc. Chinese Acad. Med. Sci., Beijing, 1954-78, assoc. prof., dept. head, 1979-84, prof., dept. head Peking Union Med. Coll., 1985—; vice chmn., adv. com. biotech. Ministry Health, Beijing, 1987—; elected academician Chinese Acad. Engring., 1997. Contbr. articles to profl. jours.; inventor in field. Named Nat. Outstanding Scientist, China, 1986. Mem. Chinese Acad. Med. Scis. (acad. com. 1985—), Chinese Pharm. Soc. (bd. dirs. 1989-93), Chinese Soc. Biotech. (bd. dirs. 1993—), Chinese Assn. Med. Biotech. (bd. dirs. 1993—), Chinese Med. Assn. (bd. dirs. 1999—). Home: 2 Nanwei Rd Bldg 9 Apt 4202, Beijing 100050, China Office: Inst Med Biotech Chinese Acad Med Sci, Beijing 100050, China

ZHENDONG, HUANG, administrator; b. 1935. Deputy min. Ministry Comm., 1985-94; mem. CPC CC, 1992—; min. Ministry Comm. & Transport, Beijing, 1994—. Office: Min Comm & Transport, 11 Jiangoymennei Dalie, Beijing 100736, China*

ZHENG, CHENGSI, social scientist, educator; b. Kunming, Yunan, China, Dec. 22, 1944; s. Boke and Xioujuan (Zeng) Z.; m. Liying Du, Oct. 1, 1973; 2 children. LLM, Beijing Inst. Polit. Sci./Law, 1967; Diploma, London Sch. Econs., 1982. Prof. China Acad. Social Scis., Beijing, 1986—; part-time prof. Beijing U., Peking, 1990—, Qing Hua (Tsing Hua) U., Beijing, 1998—; law com. Nat. People's Congress, 1998—; mem. Nat. Congress, China, 1998—. Author: Chinese IPR and Transfer of Technology, 1987 (CASS High Level Acad. award 1993), General Review of IPR, 1984 (Chinese Bright Daily award 1990). Cons. com. mem. Chinese Supreme Ct., Beijing, 1996—; arbitrator Arbitration Ctr. World Intellectual Property Orgn., Geneva, 1994. Mem. Internat. Acad. Orgn. (exec. com. 1995—), Chinese Intellectual Property Studies Assn. (dep. pres. 1993), Chinese Copyright Soc. (dep. pres. 1990). Avocations: swimming, Chinese boxing, Qi-Gong. Home: Xi Zhi Men Nam DaJie 22 902, 100035 Beijing People's Republic of China Office: Law Inst of CASS/IPR Ctr, 15 Sha Tan Bei Jie, 100720 Beijing People's Republic of China

ZHENG, DAO SHENG, mathematics educator; b. Xinghua, Jiansu, China, Apr. 6, 1937; s. Da Zhong and Wen Ying (Qi) Z.; m. Miao Fu Sun, May 8, 1973; children: Lu, Zheng. BS, Peking U., 1962. Lectr. Fudan U., Shanghai, 1962-79; asst. prof. East China Normal U., Shanghai, 1979-86, assoc. prof., 1986-96, prof., 1996—; reviewer Math. Revs., 1988. Contbr. articles to profl. jours. Recipient Cert. Merit Soc. Shanghai Soc. and Tech., 1989. Mem. Math. Soc. China, Ops. Rsch. Soc. China, Am. Math. Soc. Office: East China Normal U, Dept Math, Shanghai 200062, China

ZHENG, FAN, quality assurance engineer, educator; b. Beijing, Mar. 6, 1936; s. Fan Ren and Sun Qi Jie; m. Shu Yi; children: Fan Gang, Shu Lei. B of Engring., Qing Hau U., Beijing, China, 1959. Group leader lectr. welding faculty 9th br. Shanghai Mech.-Elec. Industry Inst., 1959-68; worker Shanghai Boiler Works, 1968-78, PV welding engr.-in-charge, group leader tech. dept., 1978-87, quality assurance engr., sr. quality assurance engr., 1987-98; dir. pres. edn. com. China Coop. Network of ASME Code Items, Beijing, 1994-98. Editor: Pressure Vessel Welder, 1991; mng. editor: Senior Welder, 1992; contbr. papers and rsch. reports to profl. jours.; introducer ASME Code to China translate B31.1, sect. I, sect. II-C, 1998, Chinese version, 2000. Commr. China People's Polit. Consultative Conf. of Minhang, Shanghai, 1987, 90, 93, standing commr., 1993-98; dir. Minhang Dist. Com. Jiusan Soc., Minhang, 1988-88, v.p., 1988, 92, 97; invited procurator Minhang Dist. Procuratorite, 1994—. Recipient Advanced Personage award Jiu San Soc. Shanghai City Com., 1985, 89, 95, China People's Polit. Consultative Conf. of Minhang Dist., 1995. Mem. ASME, China Soc. Mech. Engring. (dir. Shanghai Minhang dist. 1984-97). Mem. Jiu San Soc. Avocations: reading, writing, dancing. Office: Shanghai Boiler Works, 250 Hua Ning Rd, Minhang Shanghai 200245, China

ZHENG, HANQING, research engineer; b. Daye, Hubei, China, July 16, 1964; s. S.S. and S.Q. (Deng) Z.; m. Guilan Tian, Jan. 22, 1992; 1 child. B Engring., Huazhong U. Sci. & Tech., Wuhan, China, 1984; M Engring., South China U. Tech., Guangzhou, 1990, Nat. U. Singpore, 1999. Tchg. asst. Huangshi (China) U., 1984-87; rsch. and devel. engr., lectr. Guangdong U. Tech., Guangzhou, China, 1987-90; rsch. scholar Tokhyo inst. Tech., 1996-97, Nat. U. Singapore, 1997-99; engr. Gtech Far East, Singapore, 1999—. Co-author: Industrial Robot Design, 1995; contbr. articles to profl. jours. Mem. Japan Soc. Precision Engring. Avocations: sports, surfing on internet, travel, reading, cooking, music. Office: Nat U Singapore, 10 Kent Ridge Crescent, Singapore 119260, Singapore

ZHENG, JI, electrical engineering researcher; b. Shanghai, China, Nov. 23, 1969; came to U.S., 1998; s. Dengyun and Wanru (Chen) Z.; m. Min Zhuo, Mar. 7, 1996. BS, East China Normal U., Shanghai, 1992, MS, 1995; PhD, Shanghai JiaoTong U., 1998. Rsch. assoc. dep. elec. and computer engring. Oreg. State U., Corvallis, 1998—. Contbr. articles to profl. jours.; presenter papers in field. Mem. IEEE. Avocations: swimming, calligraphy. E-mail: jizh@ece.orst.edu. Office: Oreg State U Dept Elec and Computer Engr Corvallis OR 97331

ZHENG, JIAN MING, engineer; b. Huang Gang, Hubei, China, Dec. 6, 1964; s. Gui Hua Zhao and Dao Sheng Zheng; m. Qiu Yuan Xiong; 1 child, Yu Cheng. B, Huazhong U. Sci. and Tech., Wuhan, China, 1985, M, 1988; postgrad., U. Hong Kong, 1996—. Lectr. Huazhong U. Sci. and Tech., 1988-96. Avocations: table tennis, football, badminton. Office: Dept Mech Engring, U Hong Kong, Hong Kong Hong Kong

ZHENG, JIANG YU, information science educator; b. Shanghai, Aug. 6, 1961; arrived in Japan, 1984; s. Zhihang and Jijuan (Yin) Z.; m. Ling Shou, Feb. 14, 1989; 1 child, Yiting. BS, Fudan U., Shanghai, 1983; MS, Osaka U., 1987, D engring., 1990. Rsch. assoc. ATR Communication Systems Rsch. Lab., Seika, Japan, 1990-93; asst. prof. Kyushu Inst. Tech., Fukuoka, Japan, 1993-94, assoc. prof., 1994—. Contbr. articles to profl. jours.; inventor digital panoramic image (Japan Info. Soc. Rsch. award 1991). Recipient Oogawa award Oogawa Info. Sci. Found., 1994, Asahi Glass Rsch. award Asahi Glass Found., 1998. Mem. IEEE, Inst. Electronic Info. and Communication, Japan Info. Processing Soc. Avocations: painting, photography, travel, ping pong. Email address: zheng@mse.kyutech.ac.jp. Office: Kyushu Inst Technology, 680-4 Kawazu, Fukuoka 820 8502, Japan

ZHENG, LEMIN, electronics educator; b. Yangzhou, Jianjsou, China, Aug. 27, 1925; s. Xueyuan Zheng and Nuchang Zhang; m. Wu Jinghua, May 1, 1955; children: Wei, Pei. BS, Cen. U., Nanjing, China, 1948; postgrad., Tzinhwa U., Beijing, 1950. Asst. Tzinhwa U., 1950-52; lectr. physics Peking U., 1952-59, assoc. prof. electronics, 1960-83, prof., 1984—. Author: Atomic Structure and Atomic Spectra, 1989, Atomic Physics, 2000; contbr. articles to sci. publs. Recipient 2nd rank Progress in Sci. and Tech., Nat. Com. Edn., China, 1988. Fellow Chinese Inst. Electronics; mem. IEEE (sr.), SPIE, Chinese Inst. Optics. Avocation: travel. Office: Peking Univ, Dept Electronics, Beijing 100871, China

ZHENG, LI PING, physicist; b. Shanghai, China, Apr. 23, 1941; s. Qi Zheng and Shi Liu; m. Yue Fan, Feb. 4, 1969; two children. BSc, Peking U., 1965. Asst. Suzhou Med. U., China, 1965-75; from asst. to prof. Shanghai Nuclear Rsch., China, 1975—; vis. prof. Lab. Atomic Imaging Solids, Shenyang, China, 1992—, Internat. Ctr. Materials Physics, Shenyang, 1992—. Mem. AAAS, N.Y. Acad. Scis. Avocation: music. Office: Shanghai Inst Nucl Rsch, PO Box 800-204, 201800 Shanghai China

ZHENG, MAGGIE (XIAOCI ZHENG), materials scientist, turbine coating specialist; b. Shanghai, Apr. 21, 1949; came to U.S., 1986; d. George and Helen (Chou) Cheng; 1 child, Dee. BS in Physics, Qufu Normal U., Shangdong, China, 1981; MSEE, U. Sci. and Tech. China, Beijing, 1984; MS in Materials Sci., U. Wis., 1988, PhD in Materials Sci., 1991. Asst. prof. Tsinghua U., Beijing, 1984-86; assoc. scientist United Techs., East Hartford, Conn., 1991-92; staff scientist Pratt & Whitney, TALEN, Rocky Hill, Conn., 1992-93; materials and coating process engr. Chromalloy Turbine Techs., Middletown, N.Y., 1993-94; sr. engr. GE Power Generation, Schenectady, N.Y., 1995-98; pres. Turbine Coatings Inc., Schenectady, N.Y., 1999—; rsch. asst. U. Wis., Madison, 1986-91. Contbr. articles in profl. publs.; patentee in field. Mem. NAFE, Am. Metal Soc., Minerals, Metals and Materials Soc. Office: PO Box 600 Schenectady NY 12301-0600

ZHENG, QIGUANG, optics educator; b. Heng Yang, Hunan, China, Dec. 4, 1944; s. Dosen and Fangsheng (Wang) Z.; m. Zhongying Tao, May 1, 1974; children: Jieru, Jisi. BS, Hua Zhong U., Wuhan, China, 1969. Asst. Hua Zhong U., Wuhan, 1971-79, lectr., 1980-89, assoc. prof., 1989-92, prof., 1993—. Editor: Laser Machining, 1995, Interaction of Laser and matter, 1996; contbr. over 150 articles to profl. jours. Recipient 1st award State Edn. Commn. China, 1989, 2d award Hubei Province, 1995. Mem. Isata Internat. Assn., Optic Assn. Avocation: swimming. Office: Hua Zhong U Sci and Tech, Wuhan Hubei 430074, China

ZHENG, RONGLIANG, biologist, educator, researcher; b. Changzhou, China, Nov. 4, 1931; s. Yongkang and Yu (Xu) Z.; m. Zhongjian Jia, Feb. 3, 1959; 1 child, Qi. BS, Beijing U., 1953, PhD, 1956. Assoc. prof. Lanzhou (China) U., 1978-85, prof., 1985—, chmn. dept. biology, 1983-91, dir. divsn. biophysics-dept. biology, 1959—; postdoctoral fellow Johns Hopkins U., Balt., 1981; vice-dir. Profl. Com. Free Radical Biology & Medicine of China, Beijing, 1985—; dir. Acad. Com. of Nuclear Inst., Academica Sinica, Shanghai, 1991-95; mem. biol. edn. consultation com. State Edn. Commn., China, 1990-95. Author: Biophysics, 1982, Free Radical Biology, 1992; editor: Advances in Free Radical Life Science, vol. 1-8, 1993-2000. Recipient 2nd prize for work on antitumor activity of natural products from Chinese herbs, State Edn. Commn., 1985, 1st prize for study on free radical mechanism in cells carcinogenesis and new conception of antitumor, State Edn. Commn., 1995, 3d prize for work on reverse transformation of tumor cells by natural products DeBio-CCRF, 1997; grantee Assn. for Nat. Found. for Cancer Rsch., Bethesda, Md., 1984. Mem. N.Y. Acad. Scis. Avocation: travel. Office: Dept Biology, Lanzhou University, 730000 Lanzhou China

ZHENG, SHU YING, optical engineer; b. Fuzhou, China; s. Jing Hua Zheng and Si Mei Chen; m. Ping Guo, Jan. 26, 1968; 1 child, Zheng Yi. BS, Fudan U., Shanghai, China, 1964; MS, U. Waterloo (Can.), 1983. Engr., dir. dept. engring. Beijing Glass Rsch. Inst., 1964-81, 83-86; vis. scholar dept. physics Wilfrid Laurier U., Waterloo, 1981-82; full sr. engr., dir. dept. engring. Beijing Inst. Optoelectronic Tech., 1986—; vis. scientist dept. physics Chalmers U. of Tech., Göteborg, Sweden, 1990-91. Patentee in field. Mem. Chinese Optical Soc. (sr.), Chinese Vacuum Soc., The Optical Soc. Am. Mem. Peasant Worker's Dem. Party. Avocations: Chinese chess, classical music, ping-pong, Chinese painting, reading. Office: Beijing Inst Optoelec Tech, A-20 Dong Huangchenggen Beijie, Beijing 100010, China

ZHENG, TAO, research scientist; b. Hangzhou, Zhejiang, China, Nov. 4, 1967; s. Xiangcai Zheng and Lanzhen Zhao; m. Qian Guan, Mar. 9, 1991; 1 child, Pauline. BSc, Nanjing (China) U., 1988; MSc, U. Toronto, Ont., Can., 1993; PhD, Simon Fraser U., Burnaby, B.C., Can., 1996. Postdoctoral fellow Dalhousie U., Halifax, N.S., Can., 1996-97; rsch. scientist Telcordia Technologies (formerly Bellcore), Red Bank, N.J., 1997—. Contbr. chpt. to book. Recipient Erich Vogt prize Sci. Coun. B.C., Vancouver, 1995, Grad. Rsch. Engring. and Tech. award Sci. Coun. B.C., Vancouver, 1994, 96; grad. fellow Simon Fraser U., Burnaby, 1995. Mem. Electrochem. Soc., Materials Rsch. Soc. Avocations: table tennis, tennis, travel. E-mail: tao.zheng@worldnet.att.net and tzheng@telcordia.com. Fax: 732-758-4372.

ZHENG, WEI XING, electronic and electrical engineering educator; b. Nanjing, Jiangsu, China, Aug. 31, 1957; arrived in Australia, 1992; s. Tian Ren Zheng and Shun Zhang Shen; m. Shao Ning Zhu; 1 child, Cindy Sulei Zheng. BSc, Southeast U., Nanjing, China, 1982, MSc, 1984, PhD, 1989. Lectr. Southeast U., Nanjing, China, 1984-90, assoc. prof., 1990-91; rsch. fellow Imperial Coll., London, 1991-92, U. Western Australia, Perth, 1992-93, Curtin U., Perth, 1993-94; sr. lectr. U. Western Sydney-Nepean, Kingswood, Australia, 1994—. Author: Linear Multivariable Systems, 1991; contbr. articles to prof. jours. Recipient 1st class sci. prize State Edn. Commn. China, 1986, Chinese Nat. Sci. prize Chinese govt., 1991. Mem. IEEE (sr.), Internat. Fedn. of Automatic Control (affiliate). Avocations: stamp collecting, bridge, table tennis, swimming. Fax: 61-2-47360713. Office: Univ Western Sydney-Nepean, Sch Sci, Kingswood NSW 2747, Australia

ZHENG, WEI-TAO, science educator; b. Jiu-tai City, Jilin, China, Mar. 25, 1963; s. De-Chun Zheng and Xiu-Zhen Li; m. Ai-Ping Xu, Oct. 1, 1988; 1 child, Wei-Jai. BS, Jilin U., 1984, MS, 1987, PhD, 1990. Lectr. dept. materials sci. Jilin U., 1990-92, assoc. prof., 1992-97, prof., 1997—, dep. dir. Inst. Materials Sci., 1998—. Author: Introductio of Materials Science and Engineering, 1999. Avocations: sports, music. Office: Jilin U Dept Materials Sci, No 119 Jie-Fang Rd, 1030023 Changchun Jilin, China

ZHENG, XIAOGU, statistician; b. Nanjing, Jiangsu, Peoples Republic of China, Dec. 6, 1949; s. Ruogu and Jingyuan (Liu) Z.; m. Meiyun Song, Sept. 16, 1977; 1 child, Yanyan. BS, Beijing Normal U., 1977, MS, 1981, PhD, 1985. Math. tchr. The Beijing 173 Mid. Sch., China, 1977-78; assoc. prof. Beijing Normal U., 1986-87; postdoctoral fellow Victoria U. of Wellington, New Zealand, 1987-90; rsch. scientist Nat. Inst. of Water and Atmospheric Rsch. Ltd., Wellington, 1990—; Can. internat. scientific and engring. found. fellow Carleton U., Ottawa, Can., 1988, 91; Ethel Raybould vis. fellow The U. of Queensland, Brisbane, Australia, 1992; Queen Victoria II vis. fellow The Australian Nat. U., Canberra, 1992; fellow Inst. of Stats. and Oper. Rsch., Victoria U. of Wellington, 1990—; vis. assoc. prof. Inst. Statis. Math., Tokyo, 1998. Achievements include study of pure jump-type Markov processes theory in abstract spaces and mean-field models; estimation of earthquake risk for China, Persia and Japan from the historical earthquake records; decomposition of interannual climatological covariability and its applications to validating general circulation models. Improvement of Kalman filter scheme for data assimilation. Office: Nat Inst Water & Atmos Rsch, PO Box 14-901 301 Evans Bay, Wellington New Zealand

ZHENG, XITE, theoretical physicist, educator; b. Wuhan, Hubei, China, Nov. 3, 1935; s. Yaofu and Guang (Geng) Z.; m. Qingying Guo, Jan. 24, 1963; children: Chengyu, Minxue. Student, Peking U., Beijing, China, 1952-53, Beijing Inst. Russian Lang., 1953-54; diploma of physics, Moscow (Russia) U., 1960. Asst. Xi-an (China) U. Engring. and Tech., 1960-62; teaching asst. Chengdu (China) U., 1963-73; lectr., assoc. prof. Chengdu (China) U. Sci. and Tech., 1973-80, assoc. prof. to prof., 1983-87, prof., 1987-95, chmn. dept. physics, 1986-95; vice dean coll of sci. Sichuan Union U., Chengdu, China, 1995-97; vis. assoc. prof. rsch. Brown U., Providence, R.I., 1981-83, vis. prof. rsch., 1987. Contbr. articles to profl. jours. Recipient awards for progress in sci. and tech. Nat. Edn. Com. of China, Beijing, 1987, 96, award for young and middle age experts with disting. accomplishments Chinese Govt., Beijing, 1988. Mem. Chinese Phys. Soc. (coun. mem. 1995-99), Assn. High Energy Physics China (coun. mem.), Sichuan Phys. Soc. (coun. mem. 1986-98). Avocations: music, tourism, Chinese calligraphy, reading. Office: Sichuan U Dept App Physics, West Sect, 24 S Sect 1 Yihuan Rd, Chengdu 610065, China

ZHENG, XIULIN, materials science and engineering educator; b. Nanjing, Jiangsu, China, Feb. 12, 1933; s. Yushu and Shujun (Liu) Z.; m. Yuxuan Xie, Aug. 4, 1962; children: Qingying, Qingxiong, Qinghao. BS, E. China Inst. Aeronautics, Nanjing, 1955. Tchg. asst. East-China Inst. Aeronautics, Nanjing, China, 1955-56, Northwestern Polytech. U., Xi'an, China, 1957-61; lectr. Northwestern Polytech. U., Xian, 1961-79, assoc. prof., 1979-85, prof., 1985—, PhD supr., 1986—; vis. prof. Swiss Fed. Inst. Tech., Lausanne, Switzerland, 1980-82; mem. Swiss Assn. Engrs. and Architects, 1980-82, tech. rev. com. Internat. Conf. Fatigue, Fracture Mechanics, Corrosion Cracking and Failure Analysis, Salt Lake City, 1985, China Nat. Com. for Unifying Natural Sci. and Tech. Terms, 1993-98. Author: (books) Quantitative Theory of Metal Fatigue, 1994, Mechanical Properties of Materials, 1990; author (with others) Handbook of Fatigue Crack Propagation in Metallic Structures, 1994; translator ECCS recommendations for fatigue design of steel structures; contbr. more than 200 papers in English and Chinese profl. jours. Dep. to Nat. People Congress of China, 1988-98. Named Excellent Tchr., People's Govt. of Shaanxi Province, China, 1985, Expert Making Outstanding Contbrns., Ministry Aero. and Astro. Industries of China, 1992. Avocations: reading, table tennis, walking. Fax: (0086) 029 5250199. E-mail: zxl@nwpu.edu.cn. Office: Northwestern Polytech U, 127 Youngi Xilu, Shaanxi Xian 710072, China

ZHENG, XU-GUANG, engineering educator; b. Nanlin, Anhui, China, Aug. 6, 1963; arrived in Japan, 1985.; s. Si-Xin Zheng and Jin-Lian Tan; m. Chao-Nan Xu, Feb. 23, 1987; children: Mei-Jia, Li-Jia. BS in Electronics, Xi'an Jiaotong U., China, 1984; MS in Engring., Kyushu U., Japan, 1988; PhD in Engring., Kyushu U., 1991. Asst. prof. Kyushu U., Fukuoka, Japan, 1991-95; assoc. prof. Saga U., Saga, Japan, 1995. Recipient Ceramographic award Ceramic Soc. Japan, 1998. Avocations: table tennis, gardening, weigi. Office: Saga U Dept Physics, Honjo-1, Saga City 840-8502, Japan

ZHENG, YADONG, geology educator; b. Nanjing, Jiangsu, China, Jan. 18, 1936; s. Mingxin and Xiufang Liu Z.; m. Husheng Ding, July 22, 1962; 1 child, Lin Zheng. BS, Beijing Coll. Geology, 1957. Tchg. asst. Peking U., Beijing, 1957-62, lectr., 1963-82, assoc. prof., 1983-88, prof., 1989—; mem. rev. group for geoscis. under NSF of China, 1994-97; hon. prof. U. Lanzhou, China, 1995—; cons. scientific rsch. inst. and petroleum exploration and devel., Beijing, 1993. Chief editor: (textbook) Finite Strain Measurement and Ductile Shear Zones, 1985 (2nd prize of excellent textbook Ministry of Geology and Mineral Resource), Procs. of 30th Internat. Geol. Congress, vol. 14: Structural Geology and Geomechanics, 1997; contbr. articles to profl. jours. Recipient 3rd prize sci. and technology, Liaoning, Shenyang City, 1978, 2nd prize of progress of sci. and technology, Nat. Com. of Edn. of China, 1991. Mem. Geol. Soc. of China (mem. com. on structural geology/tectonics 1982—), Internat. Assn. Structural/Tectonic Geologists. Avocations: singing, jogging, playing badminton. Home: Apt 56, Peking Univ, 100871 Beijing China Office: Dept Geology, Peking U/Haidianlu, 100871 Beijing China

ZHENG, YIBIN, electrical engineer; b. Guangzhou, Guangdong, China, Oct. 8, 1966; came to U.S., 1989; s. Qingzhang Zheng and Weiyin Luo; m. Ying Yao, Jan. 3, 1994; 1 child, Christopher. BS, Zhongshan U., Guangzhou, 1988; MS, SUNY, Buffalo, 1992; PhD, Purdue U., 1996. Sr. elec. engr. GE Co., Schenectady, N.Y., 1996—. Mem. IEEE. Office: GE CRD KWC-605 One Research Cir Niskayuna NY 12309

ZHENG, ZUOXING, food scientist; b. Linyi, Shandong, China, Sept. 19, 1965; s. Lianyin and Chongmei (Zhu) Z.; m. Qing Lu, Apr. 28, 1995. BS, Shandong Inst. Light Industry, China, 1985; MS, Tianjin Inst. Light Industry, China, 1988; PhD, U. Mass., 1999. Asst. prof. Tsinghua U., Beijing, 1988-95; rsch. asst. U. Mass., Amherst, 1995-99, tchg. asst., 1997-99; rsch. scientist Kraft Foods, Inc., Glenview, Ill., 1999—. Patentee in field; contbr. articles to profl. jours. Recipient Grad. Rsch. Paper award Inst. Food Technologists, Orlando, Fla., 1997, Atlanta, 1998, Chgo., 1999, fellowship, Chgo., 1998-99, UNESCO, Japan, 1992. Mem. Inst. Food Technologists, Am. Soc. Microbiology, Soc. for Indsl. Microbiology, Phi Kappa Phi, Sigma Xi. E-mail: zzheng@kraft.com. Office: Kraft Foods Inc R&D 801 Waukegan Rd Glenview IL 60025-4312

ZHENGSHENG, YU, Chinese government official. Min. of constrn. Chinese Govt., Beijing, 1998—. Address: Xijiao Baiwanshuang 11, Beijing 100835, China*

ZHENGTING, CAI, chemist, educator; b. Zibo, China, Dec. 27, 1944; parents Qinpu Cai and Wang Xincui; m. Ma Airong, Jan. 10, 1969; 1 child, Wei Cai. BA, Shandong U., 1969, MS, 1982. From assoc. prof. to prof. Shandong U., China, 1988—; vice-dean Inst. Theoretical Chemistry Shandong U., 1990—, vice-dean dept. chemistry, 1990-92. Mem. Chinese Chem. Soc. Office: Shandong U, 27 S Shanda Rd, Jinan Shandong China 250100

ZHIDKOV, ALEXEI GENNADIEVICH, physicist, engineer, researcher; b. Moscow, Mar. 30, 1956; s. Gennadii S. and Zinaida P. (Petrunina) Z.; m. Natalia Stanislavovna Barinova, Mar. 16, 1979; children: Daria, Dmitri. MD, Moscow Phys. Engring. Inst., 1979; PhD, Kurchatov Inst. Atomic Energy, USSR, 1983. Cert. in engring. Rschr. Kurchatov Inst. Atomic Energy, 1982-83; rschr. Gen. Physics Inst., Acad. of Scis. of USSR, Moscow, 1983-86, staff sr. rschr., 1986—; expert Korean Atomic Energy Rsch. Inst., Korea, 1995-96; vis. scientist Japan Atomic Energy Rsch. Inst., 1997—. Author: (books) Reviews of Plasma Physics, vol. 12, 1982, Radiation of Ions in Non-Equilibrium Dense Plasmas, 1986; contbr. articles and papers to profl. jours. Mem. IEEE. Avocation: dachshunds. Home: Sevastopol'sky prkt 31-1-4, Moscow Russia Office: Gen Physics Inst, 117942 Vavilov 38, Moscow Russia

ZHIGAL'SKII, GENNADII PAVLOVICH, physicist, educator, researcher; b. Nivnoe, Russia, Apr. 15, 1939; s. Pavel Timofeevich and Klavdiya Philippovna (Pavluchenkova) Z.; m. Albina Kirillovna, Nov. 6, 1964; 1 child, Dmitry Zhigalsky. Phys. Faculty, Moscow State U., 1962, Cand. of Phys. and Math. Scis., 1967, PhD in Phys. and Math. Scis., 1993. Engr. Sci. rsch. Inst., Moscow, 1962-64, jr. scientist, 1967-68, head of lab., 1968-73; sr. lectr. Moscow Inst. Electronics Tech., 1973-78, asst. prof., 1978-94, prof., 1994—. Author: Physical Phenomena in Thin Metal Films, 1996; contbr. articles to profl. jours. Named Internat. Man of the Yr., Internat. biog. Ctr., 1997-98. Mem. N.Y. Acad. Scis. Avocations: music, poetry. Home: Bldg 802 Flat 13, Zelenograd, 103 527 Moscow Russia Office: Moscow Inst Electronics Tec, 103498 Moscow Russia

ZHIHUAN, FU, Chinese government official. Ministry of railways Govt. of China, Beijing, 1998—. Mem. Communist Party. Address: Ministry of Rys, 10 Fu Xing Jie/Hai Dian Dis, Beijing China 100844*

ZHIKHAREV, ARKADY IGOREVICH, electrochemist; b. Sergiev Posad, Russia, July 11, 1939; s. Igor Sergeevich and Ksenia Jakovlevna Z.; m. Irene Georgievna Zhikhareva, Aug. 22, 1968. M Chem. Scis., Kazan Inst. Chem. Tech., Russia, 1970, D Chem. Scis., 1996; hon. diploma, All-Union Chem. Soc., 1980. Asst. Kazan Inst. Chem. Tech., 1966-70; reader in chemistry Tyumen (Russia) Indsl. Inst., 1970-94; prof. Tyumen State Oil and Gas U., 1995—, head lab., 1973—. Author monographs and articles in field. Named Soros Docent Internat. Soros Sci. Edn. Program, 1997; recipient Gold medal, diploma Internat. Biograph. Ctr., Cambridge, Eng., 1998. Mem. N.Y. Acad. Scis. Avocations: music, painting, geography. Home: Permjakova Str 24 Apt 50, 625013 Tyumen Russia Office: Tyumen State Oil and Gaz U, Volodarsky Str 38, 625000 Tyumen Russia

ZHILENKOV, EUGENI LEONIDOVICH, microbiologist, researcher; b. Dmitrovsk, Russia, Mar. 15, 1954; s. Leonid Philippovich and Anfisa Fedorovna (Ivanisheva) Z.; m. Tatyana Olegovna Makeeva, June 16, 1979; 1 child, Mikhail Eugenievich. Degree in virology, Moscow State U., 1977, postgrad., 1977-80; D of Molecular Biology, State Rsch. Ctr. Applied Microbiology, Obolensk, Russia, 1984. Rschr. State Rsch. Ctr. Applied Microbiology, 1981-91, head of lab. bacteriophages, 1991—; chief of grad. students' theses State Rsch. Ctr. Applied Microbiology, 1994-97. Contbr. articles to profl. jours. Grantee Internat. Sci. and Tech. Ctr., 1997—. Avocations: literature, wood sculpting, hunting, boxing. Home: Microregion G 31-56, 142292 Pushchino Russia

ZHILI, CHEN, Chinese government official. Min. Ministry Edn., Beijing, 1998—. Mem. Communist Party. Office: Ministry Edn, 37, Damucang Hutong, Beijing China 100816

ZHILIANG, DAI, engineering executive; b. Shanghai, Nov. 24, 1939; m. Hua Nanzhen, 1966; children: Dan, Jie. Grad., Ea. China Chem. Tech. U., 1964. Engr. Beijing Glass Design & Rsch. Inst., 1964—; v.p., sr. engr. Bengbu Glass Design & Rsch. Inst., 1982—, pres., professorship sr. engr., dir., 1993—; pres. China Triumph Internat. Engring. Consultation Co., Shanghai, 2000—; vis. prof. Wu Han Indsl. U.; mem. steering com. Internat. Commn. on Glass; dir. China Glass Devel. Ctr. Mem. Chinese Ceramic Soc. (vice dir. glass specialized commn.), China Archl. and Indsl. Glass Assn. (vice dir.). Office: Chin Triumph Internat, No 2000 Zhongshan Bei Rd, Anhui Shanghai 200063, China

ZHIMING, CHEN, electronics educator, academic administrator; b. Fuling, Sichuan, China, Oct. 25, 1945; s. Nanping Chen and Shujun Zhang; m. Kaiya Chen, Mar. 20, 1971; children: Song-gu, Meiying. BS, Beijing Inst. Mech. Engring., 1969; MS, Chinese Acad. Sci., Beijing, 1981. Rsch. assoc. Chinese Acad. Scis., Beijing, 1981-86; vis. scientist U. Western Ont., London, Can., 1982-84; vice head dept. Xi'an (China) U. Tech., 1987-90, head dept., 1990-91, v.p., 1991-95, pres., 1995—; vice chmn. edn. cons. com. of Ministry-run univs. Ministry of Machinery Industry of China, Beijing, 1994-98, mem. specialist cons. group for R&D in power electronics, 1991-95; organizer, designer rsch. project, 1981-95. Author: Amorphous Semiconductor Materials and Devices, 1991, Basis of Power Electronic Devices, 1992, Basis of Meterial Physics for Semiconductor Devices, 1999. Recipient Nat. Specialist in Machinery Industry award Ministry of Machinery Industry, 1995; grantee Chinese Govt., 1992—; named Outstanding Sci. and Tech. Specialist in Shaanxi Province Shaanxi Province Gov., 1999. Mem. IEEE (sr.), China Inst. Power Electronics (v.p. 1989), Shaanxi Power Electronics Com. (pres. 1988), Shaanxi Inst. Elec. Engrs. (v.p. 1998). Avocations: painting, writing poems. Home and Office: Xi'an U Tech, 5 Southern Jinhua Load, Xi-an Shaanxi 710048, China

ZHIRABOK, ALEXEY NIL, radio and electronics educator, researcher; b. Khabarovsk, Russia, Nov. 27, 1946; s. Nil Peter and Nina Yevgeny (Kazakevich) Z.; m. Nina Dmitry Belokon, Sept. 2, 1983; 1 child, Svetlana. Grad. in Engring., Far Ea. State Tech. U., Vladivostok, Russia, 1970; PhD, Electrotech. Inst., Leningrad, Russia, 1978; DSc, Russian Acad. Scis., Vladivostok, 1996. Asst. prof. Far Ea. State Tech. U., 1970-75, assoc. prof., 1979-83, head dept., 1983-92, postdoctoral trainee, 1992-95, prof., 1996—. Author: Principles of Technical Diagnostics, 1986; co-author: Structure Analysis of Decomposable Systems, 1988, Computer Aid Design of Control Systems, 1990, Controllability, Observability, Decomposition of Nonlinear Dynamic Systems, 1993. Recipient Soros Prof. award Soros Found., 1997, 98, 2000, named Higher Sch. Worker of Russia, 1999. Mem. IEEE, Russian Acad. Engring. (Far Ea. br. main sci. sec. 1993—). Avocations: track and field athletics, art, walking. Home: Okeansky Ave 102-25, 690002 Vladivostok Russia Office: Far Ea State Tech U, Pushkinskaya St 10, 690600 Vladivostok Russia

ZHIRINOVSKY, VLADIMIR VOLFOVICH, Russian government official; b. Alma-Ata, Kazakhstan, Apr. 25, 1946; m. Galina Zhirinovsky; 1 son. Student, Moscow State U. With USSR Ministry Def., Gen. Staff Transcaucasian Command; with com. peace Soviet Soc. Friendship and Cultural Rels.; legal cons. Mir Publs., 1983-89; founder Liberal-Dem. Party of Soviet Union (now of Russia), 1989, chair, 1990—; mem. State Duma, 1993—. Author: The Zhirinovsky Phenomenon, The Last Leap South, 1992, The Last Train to the North, 1994; contbr. articles to profl. jours. Candidate in Russian Presdl. Election, 1991. Avocations: volleyball, swimming. Office: Liberal-Dem Party Russia, Lukov per 9, 103045 Moscow Russia*

ZHITOMIRSKY, VLADIMIR, materials scientist, researcher, engineer; b. Lvov, Ukraine, USSR, Sept. 16, 1952; arrived in Israel, 1991; s. Naum and Evgenia (Kwatter) Z. MSc, Steel and Alloys Inst., Moscow, 1974; PhD, Physics and Mechanics Inst., Lvov, 1989. Process engr. Prodn. Electronic Devices Plant, Lvov, 1974-77; engr. G.V. Karpenko Inst. Physics & Mechanics, Ukrainian Acad. Sci., Lvov, 1977-82, sr. engr., 1982-83, lead engr., 1983-87, head lab., 1987-91; lead specialist Inteltech Enterprise, Lvov, 1991; sr. rschr. U. Tel Aviv, 1992—; cons. prodn. plants, USSR, 1985-91, Coating Technique Rsch., Israel, 1992-93, 96—; fellow Sci. Cmty. Lvov, Phys. Mech. Inst., 1986-89. Contbr. over 50 articles to profl. jours.; 4 patents, including multi-layer materials and coatings. Grantee Tel Aviv U./U. Hull, U.K., 1995-99, Israel Ministry of Sci., 1995-99, Israel Sci. Found., 1999—. Avocations: travel, stamps, Jewish history. E-mail: zhitom@eng.tau.ac.il. Home: 35 Zahal St, 35221 Haifa Israel Office: Tel Aviv U, Elec Discharge & Plasma Lab, 69978 Tel Aviv Israel

ZHIYU WILSON, XIA, research fellow, consultant; b. Yangzhou, Jiangsu, People's Republic of China, Oct. 17, 1966; s. Liren Xia; m. Siu-kam Ivis, Mar. 18, 2000. B in Engring., Tsinghua U., Beijing, 1989; M in Engring., Beijing U. Chem. Tech., Beijing, 1992; PhD in Chemistry, U. Queensland, Australia, 2000. Grad. rsch. asst. Beijing U. of Chem. Tech., 1989-92; rsch. engr. Beijing Gen. Inst. Mining and Metallurgy, 1992-94; rsch. asst. Hong Kong Poly. U., 1994-96; vis. scientist U. So. Miss., 1998; rsch. fellow Monash U., Melbourne, Australia, 2000—; cons. Du-zhuang Adv. Coating Co. Ltd., China, 1992-94. Mem. Royal Australian Chem. Inst. (charter mem.), Instn. Engrs., Am. Chem. Soc. Avocations: travel, sports, investments. Home: 906 Waverley Rd, Glen Waverley VIC 3150, Australia

ZHMUR, STANISLAV IOSIFOVICH, geologist, researcher; b. Kiev, Ukraine, Dec. 25, 1935; s. Iosif Akimovich and Evdokia Trofimovna (Shutko) Z.; m. Dehtyareva Ludmila Vadimovna, May 10, 1960 (div. Feb. 1965); 1 child, Svetlana; m. Alevtina Nikitichna Schoukina. PhD, Moscow State U., 1972, DSc, 1992. Sr. geologist Kievgeology, Kiev, 1958-68, Dept. Geology of Ctrl. Region, 1968-71; leading rschr. Inst. Lithosphere Geol. Inst. RAN, Moscow, 1975—; head sect. interbrs. com. on lithology Geol. Inst. RAN, 1998—; cons. Paleontol. Inst. RAN, 1995—. Contbr. numerous articles to profl. jours. Avocations: angling, chess, gardening. Home: 26 Bakinskich komissarov, 2/1 ap 93, 117526 Moscow Russia Office: Inst Lithosphere RAN, Staromonetny per 22, 109180 Moscow Russia

ZHONE, NING, mathematician, computer scientist; b. Chengdu, Sichuan, China; came to U.S., 1985; d. Lujun Zhong and Baoxian Luo; m. Bingyu Zhang, July 14, 1984; children: April Zhang, Catherine Zhang. BS in Math., Sichuan U., Chengdu, China, 1982, MS in Math., 1985; PhD in Math., U. Wis., 1990; postgrad., U. Minn., 1992-94. Asst. prof. dept. math. U. Conn., Storrs, 1994-97, U. Cinn., 1997—; actuarial analyst William Mercer, Inc., Cin., 2000—; guest scientist dept. computer sci. Fern U., Hagen, Germany, 1998. Reviewer Math. Abstract, 1997—; contbr. articles to profl. jours. Recipent Jr. Faculty Rsch. award U. Conn., 1995; Summer Faculty Rsch. fellow U. Cin., 1998. Mem. Soc. Actuaries (assoc., ednl. initiative 1994). E-mail: ning.zhong@uc.edu. Office: Univ Cin Clermont Coll 4200 Clermont College Dr Batavia OH 45103-1748

ZHONG, FAN, otolaryngologist, educator; b. Suchow, Jsiangsu, China, Dec. 24, 1928; s. Fan Sushan and Wei Euzheng; m. Yu Luchen, Apr. 16, 1954. MD, Cheeloo U., Jinan, China, 1953. Ear, nose, and throat dr. Shandong Provincial Hosp., Jinan, 1953-58; dr., dir. District Hosp., Heze, China, 1958-62; dr., prof. Shandong Provincial Hosp., Shandong Med. U., Jinan, 1982—. Author: Neurosurgery of Otolaryngology, 1992 (Outstanding author 1996); contbr. sci. articles to profl. jours. Mem. Chinese Med. Assn. Avocations: music, painting. Home: 324 Jin 5 Wei 7 Rd, 250021 Jinan China Office: Shandong Provincial Hosp, Jin 5 Wie 7 Rd, 250021 Jinan China

ZHONG, JI, mathematician, mathematics educator; b. Chaozhou, China, Sept. 24, 1921; s. Xiang Wu Aand Xian Niang Wu Z.; m. Chu-Yan Huang, Oct. 12, 1945 (dec. Aug. 1980); children: Lin, Pong, Tong-Wei, Lei; m. Xue Zhen Lin, Feb. 11, 1983; 1 child, Yang Hui. BS, Zhong Shan U., 1944. Asst. Zhong Shan U., Quangzhou, China, 1944-46; tchr. Chao-an 1st Mid.

Sch., Quangdong, China, 1946-52, Pu-ning 3d Mid. Sch., Quangdong, China, 1952-53; lectr. South China Normal U., Guangzhou, 1954-78, assoc. prof., 1978-83, prof., 1983—. Author: Higher Geometry, 1983, Methods of Plane Geometry, 1986; editor: (textbook) Math of Junior Middle School. Vice chmn. bd. Higher Geometry Soc. China, 1984—, Combinatorics Soc. China, 1988-92; standing dir. Astronomy Soc. China, 1985-87. Named Nat. Excellent Tchr., All-China Fedn. Trade Union. Home: 7401 Ctrl Dist, South China Normal U, Guangzhou 510631, China

ZHONG, JIAN-JIANG, biochemical engineering educator; b. Yuyao City, China, Apr. 6, 1965; s. Pin-Xing and Xing-Fen Fu; m. Miyoko Sho; 1 child, Takami Sho. BS, East China Inst. Chem. Tech., Shanghai, 1986; MS, Osaka U., Japan, 1990, PhD, 1993. Lectr. East China U. Sci. and Tech., Shanghai, 1993, assoc. prof., 1993-96, prof., 1996—, dep. dir. Biochem. Engring. Rsch. Inst., 1996—, dir. State Key Lab. Bioreactor Engring., 1997—; chair prof. Cheung Kong Scholars Program, 1999—; dep. dir. acad. com. Nat. Engring. Rsch. Ctr. Biotech., Shanghai, 1996—; co-chmn. 1st Conf. Young Chinese Biochem. Engrs., Dalian, 1996. Author: Advances in Plant Biotechnology, 1994; contbr. articles to profl. jours. Rsch. fellow Japan Soc. Promotion Sci., 1996; named Outstanding Young Investigator State Edn. Commn. China, 1995. Mem. Internat. Assn. Plant Tissue Culture, Soc. Biosci. & Bioengring. Japan. Avocations: walking, music, mountain climbing, swimming, movies. Office: ECUST State Key Lab Bio Eng, 130 Meilong Rd, Shanghai 200237, China

ZHONG, JINGCHANG, engineering educator; b. Changchun, Jilin, China, July 18, 1938; s. Rongjiu and Suyun (Hao) Z.; m. Baiyan Zhao, Nov. 3, 1967; children: Gang, Ling. Degree in Engring., Changchun Inst. Optics, 1963. Engring. diplomate. Prof. Changchun Inst. Optics, 1978-80, 83-90, 1993—; prof. U. So. Calif., L.A., 1980-83, 90-91, U. N.Mex., Albuquerque, 1991-93; dir. optoelectronics dept. China Nat. Key Lab., Changchun, 1993—, Rsch. Inst. Modern Optics, Changchun, 1984-90; advisor Chinese Scholars Fedn. of Optoelectronic Cirs., Albuquerque, 1991-93. Editor: Laser Experiments - Principles and Techniques, 1988; contbr. articles to profl. jours.; patentee in field; editor Chinese Jour. Lasers, 1989—. Recipient Nat. Sci. award China State Coun., 1978, Award for progress in sci. and tech. China Ministry of Machino-Electronics, 1991, 94, Guang Hua Found. award, 1995, China Nat. Invention award, 1996, Excellent Achievement award Changchun Inst. Optics, 1997, 99, Outstanding Expert award Jilin Provincial Govt., 1998. Fellow Chinese Optical Soc.; mem. Assn. of Chinese Scholars in So. Calif. (chmn. 1980-83), Soc. of Photo-Optical Instrumentation Engrs., Chinese Materials Rsch. Soc. Avocations: collecting postage stamps, chess, opera, reading, table tennis. E-mail: zjc@public.cc.jl.cn. Office: Changchun Inst Optics, Weixing Rd #7, Changchun 130022, China

ZHONG, NING, engineering educator; b. Beijing, Aug. 11, 1956; m. Ju Zhen Dong; 1 child, Jing-Guang. BS, Beijing Poly. U., 1982; PhD, U. Tokyo, 1995. Rsch. assoc. Beijing Poly. U., 1982-86, lectr., 1986-89; rschr. AOTS, Japan, 1985-86; rsch. fellow RCAST, U. Tokyo, 1995-97; asst. prof., then assoc. prof. engring. Yamaguchi (Japan) U., 1996—; guest prof. Beijing Poly. U., 1998—; head knowledge engring. lab. Yamaguchi U., 1996—; mem. adv. bd. Internat. Rough Set Soc., 1997—; mem. steering com. Pacific-Asia Conf. on Knowledge Discovery and Data mining, 1999—; assoc. prof. Maebashi Inst. Tech., Japan, 2000—, head knowledge of info. sys. lab., 2000—. Editor jours. Knowledge and Info. Sys., 1998—; mem. editl. bd. Info., 1998—; contbr. articles to tech. publs. Rsch. grantee KTISA, Japan, 1997; recipient 5th advanced Automation Rsch. award ASTEJC, Japan, 1993. Mem. IEEE (mem. steering com. internat. conf. on data mining 2000—), AAAI, Assn. Computing Machinery (mem. Sigkod internat. liaisons bd. 1998—). Avocations: travel, swimming. Office: Maebashi Inst of Tech, 460-1 Kamisadori-cho, Maebashi City 371-0816, Japan

ZHONG, SHUN-SHI, electromagnetist, electronics educator; b. Rui'an, Zhejiang, China, Sept. 1, 1939; s. Guang-Di Zhong and Ai-Wei Bao; m. Su-Ping Yang, Aug. 26, 1967; children: Charles Gang, Li. BSc, N.W. Telecomm. Engring. Inst., Xi'an, China, 1960. Asst. lectr. N.W. Telecomm. Engring. Inst., 1960-80; lectr., assoc. prof. Xidian U., Xi'an, 1982-88; EM lab. dir., assoc. prof., prof., advisor doctoral grads. Shanghai (China) U. Sci. and Tech., 1988—; vis. scholar U. Wash., Seattle, 1980-81, U. Ill., Urbana-Champaign, 1981-82; rschr. Shanghai Factory of Test Equipment, 1970-73, Purple Mountain Obs., Academia Sinica, Nanjing, China, 1975-79. Author: Microstrip Antenna Theory and Applications, 1991 (Outstanding Electronics Textbook award of China 1995), Foundation of EM Field Theory, 1995 (Outstanding Univ. Textbook award of Shanghai 1997); mem. standing editorial com. Jour. Shanghai U., 1991—; contbr. more than 120 articles to profl. jours.; co-patentee in field. Mem. Three-Mem. Ednl. Delegation from China, Pakistan, 1989. Recipient Nat. Sci. and Tech. award, 1985, 1st Class Sci. and Tech. award Ministry Electronics Industry, 1986, Govt. Spl. Allowance award Govt. of Peoples Republic of China, 1991, Bao-Gang Outstanding Tchr. award, 1998. Fellow Chinese Inst. Electronics; mem. IEEE (sr.), N.Y. Acad. Scis. Office: Shanghai U Dept Comm Engr, 149 Yanchang Rd, Shanghai Jiading 201800, China

ZHONG, WILLIAM JIANG SHENG, glass scientist; b. Fujian, China, Sept. 3, 1934; came to U.S., 1980; s. Lu Zai and Bertha (Fang) Djung; m. Baoru Liu Zhong, Sept. 14, 1964; children: Charles H., Joan H. BChemE, South China Poly. Coll., Guang Zhou, 1953; MS in Mineralogy, Geology, Miami U., Oxford, Ohio, 1982. Asst. rsch. scientist Rsch. Inst. Optics and Fine Mechanics, Changchun, China, 1953-62; lectr. Coll. of Optics and Fine Mechanics, Changchun, China, 1959-61; assoc. rsch. scientist Rsch. Inst. Optics and Fine Mechanics, Changchun, 1962-70; rsch. scientist Shanghai Light Ind. Bur., 1970-72; dep. chief engr. Xin Hu Glass Wks., Shanghai, 1972-80; tech. dir. Kigre, Inc., Toledo, 1982-86; prin. glass scientist Circon ACMI, Stamford, Conn., 1986-93; sr. glass scientist Detector Tech., Inc., Sturbridge, Mass., 1994-96, Pegasus Glassworks, Inc., Sturbridge, 1997-2000; prin. glass scientist Circon ACMI Maxxim, Stamford, Conn., 2000—. Co-author: Optical Glass (in Chinese), 1964; contbr. articles to profl. jours. Recipient Sci. & Tech. Achievement in high transmittance lead glasses, Shanghai Sci. and Tech. Com., 1978, in 2.3 meter telescope mirror disk, 1979. Mem. Am. Ceramic Soc. Achievements include joint establishment of optical glass production technologies in China; zero expansion glass ceramic large astronomic telescope mirror blank manufacture technology in China; long life microchannel plate glasses; specialty glasses for fiberoptics; patents in laser glass, microchannel plate glasses. Office: Circon ACMI Maxxim 330 Stillwater Ave Stamford CT 06902-3641

ZHONG, XIAO YAN, physician; b. Wuhan, China, Sept. 6, 1961; s. Xin and Yin Ke (Wu) Z.; m. Ding Ge, Sept. 10, 1985; 1 child, Xiang. MD, Tongji Med. U., Wuhan, China, 1983, U. Heidelberg, Germany, 1998. Physician Tongji U. Hosp., Wuhan, China, 1983-90, 90-94, vice prof., 1995—; rschr. dept. ob-gyn. U. Basel, 1998—. Contbr. articles to profl. jours.; patentee in field. Avocations: travel, music, computers, housework. Office: U Basel, Dept Ob-gyn, 4031 Basel Switzerland

ZHONG, YUANZHEN, research chemist; b. Guangzhou, China, May 2, 1947; came to U.S., 1984; s. Yuanfan and Sumei (Zhang) Z.; m. Susan Siying Chen, Nov. 2, 1972; children: Xin, Xun. BS, Jinan U., Guangzhou, China, 1970; MS, Zhongshan U., 1984; PhD, Rutgers U., 1990. Rsch. staff Rsch. Inst., Xin-Yi County, China, 1970-73, 75-78; rsch. asst. Zhongshan U., Guangzhou, 1979-82; rsch. lectr. So. China Normal U., Guangzhou, 1982-84; rsch. asst. Rutgers U., New Brunswick, N.J., 1984-90; rsch. chemist Internat. Specialty Products, Wayne, N.J., 1990-92, sr. rsch. chemist, 1992-96, rsch. scientist, 1996—; lectr. in field. Contbr. numerous articles to profl. jours.; patentee (8) in field. Mem. Am. Chem. Soc. Avocations: reading, running, collecting stamps. Office: Internat Specialty Products 1361 Alps Rd Wayne NJ 07470-3700

ZHONG, YUN RUO, wireless communications executive; b. Shanghai, Oct. 31, 1928; s. Yansheng Liu; children: Ming, Hong, Yong. Bachelor, Jiao Tong U., Shanghai, 1949. Registered sr. engr., China; registered prof., China. Dir. Radio Sta. for Internat. Comm., Beijing, 1950-59; dir. Microwave Lab. China Acad. Posts and Telecomms., Beijing, 1962-64; dir., chief engr. Fourth Rsch. Inst. of Ministry Posts and Telecomms., Beijing, 1964-73, dir. microwave dept., 1973-79; v.p., chief engr. China Acad. Posts and Telecomms., 1980-90, sr. adviser, 1990—. Recipient Outstanding Contbn. award Nat. Com. Sci. and Tech., Beijing, 1988. Fellow China Inst. Electronics; exec. mem. com. Sci. and Tech. Ministry of Posts and Telecoms.; mem. IEEE (sr., chmn. Beijing sect. 1993, 99), N.Y. Acad. Scis. Avocations: music, tour. Office: China Acad Posts & Telecomms, 40 Xueyuan Lu, Beijing 100083, China

ZHONG LIAN, LI, mathematics educator; b. Tangshan, China, May 11, 1938; d. Li Hua and Fan Shu Shen; m. Zhou Li, feb. 1, 1965; children: Jingshan, Zhe. BS, Hebei Tchr.'s Coll., China, 1961. Lectr. Tsinghua U., Beijing, 1979-87; assoc. prof. Inst. of Fin. and Banking, Beijing, 1987-94, prof., 1994—. Author: Probability and Statistics, 1987, Economic Mathematics, 1990. Mem. Assn. of Probability and Statistics. Avocations: music, watching TV, reading novels. Office: Inst Fin and Banking, #10 Hui Xin Dong Jie, 100029 Beijing China

ZHONGZHEN, ZHAO, medical educator; b. Beijing, Apr. 29, 1957; s. Zhao Shunan and Wang Qixion; m. Hu Mei, 1984; children: Peng, Zhao. BS, Beijing U. Traditional Chinese Medicine, 1982; MS, China Acad. Traditional Chinese Medicine, 1984; PhD, Tokyo U. Pharmacy and Life Sci, 1992. Rsch. asst. China Acad. Traditional Chinese Medicine, 1984-87, lectr., assoc. prof., 1988-90; vis. scholar Tokyo U. Pharmacy and Life Sci., 1987-88, 90; rsch. dir. Chinese Medicine Rsch. Ctr., ISKRA, Japan, 1992-99; assoc. prof. Chinese medicine, history of Chinese medicine Hong Kong Bapt. U., 1999—. Co-author: Medicinal Plants in China, 1989, The Authentic and Superior Medicinal herbal in China, 1989, A Glossary of Chinese-Japanese-Latin Names of Medicinal Plants in China and Japan, 1991, Present Situation and Trend of Traditional Medicine in Japan, 1998, A Colored Microscopic Atlas of the Powder Chinese Materia Medica Specified in Pharmacopoeia of the People, 1999; contbr. articles to profl. jours. Recipient Nat. prize China Nat. Sci. Com., Beijing, 1992. Achievements include a patent for a new method of identification of the tree age by tree bark. Office: Hong Kong Bapt Univ, Kowloon Tong, Hong Kong Hong Kong

ZHOU, BANG RONG, physicist, educator; b. Chengdu, Sichuan, China, Apr. 18, 1941; s. Fu Cheng and Ying Juan (Wang) Z.; m. Yong Pu Kang, Feb. 2, 1981; 1 child, Xiao Zhi. Grad., U. Sci. and Tech. China, Beijing, 1963, degree, 1966. Tchg. asst. U. Sci. and Tech. of China, Hefei, 1973-78, lectr., 1979-85, assoc. prof. Grad. Sch., Academia Sinica Beijing, 1985-87, 87-90, prof., 1990—; vis. scholar Fermi Nat. Accelerator Lab., Batavia, 1981-83, Stanford (Calif.) Linear Accelerator Ctr., 1983; assoc. vis. prof. Internat. Centre for Theoretical Physics, Trieste, Italy, 1992, 94, 98. Contbr. articles to profl. jours. including Atomic Energy, Nuclear Physics B, Physics Letters B, Phys. Rev. D, others. Recipient award Chinese Nat. Sci. Conf., 1978, Sci. Achievements award Chinese Acad. Scis., 1981, award Nat. Natural Sci. of China, 1982, Spl. Allowance Upon Contbn. to Chinese Advanced Edn. award The State Coun. of China, 1992. Mem. Chinese Learned Soc. of High Energy Physics, Chinese Ctr. of Advanced Sci. and Tech. (assoc.), Western Returned Scholars' Assn. Avocations: collecting stamps and coins, swimming, ping-pong, classical music, athletic competition, detective films on television. Office: U Sci & Tech of China, Academia Sinica Grad Sch, Beijing 100039, China

ZHOU, BING, process scientist; b. Shanghai, China, Dec. 11, 1961; s. Helin and Juxian (Shi) Z.; m. Ruyi Yan; children: Daoshun, Zhou. BSc, Fudan U., China, 1983, MSc, 1988; PhD, Macquarie U., Australia, 1997. Cert. engr. Asst. engr. Shanghai Med. Equipment Factory, China, 1983-85; rschr. Shanghai Inst. Tech. Physics, 1988-92; sr. process scientist Thin Film Device Inc., Anaheim, Calif., 1997-2000; sr. process engr. Internat. Rectifier, El Segundo, Calif., 2000—. Co-author: GaN and Related Materials, 1997. Mem. The Internat. Soc. for Optical Engring. Home: 2404 Nutwood Ave Apt H-24 Fullerton CA 92831-3162 Office: Internat Rectifier 233 Kansas St El Segundo CA 90245

ZHOU, CHENG JI, neuroscientist; b. Jinyun, Zhejiang, China, Mar. 8, 1966; arrived in Japan, 1993; BS, Waseda U., Tokyo, 1998, MS, 1999. Cert. med. engr., China. Med. technologist Lishui Bihu Hosp., Lishui City, Zhejiang, 1984-88; med. engr. Lishui Zhongyi Hosp., Lishui City, 1988-92; rschr. Showa U. Med. Sch., Tokyo, 1998—. contbr. to pro. jours. Mem. Japanese Assn. Anatomists, Clin. Electron Microscopy Soc. Japan, N.Y. Acad. Scis., Chinese Students Assn. Waseda U. (ex-pres. 1996). Avocations: playing flute, weiqi, go.

ZHOU, DE-QING, microbiologist; b. Zhenhai, China, Dec. 7, 1935; s. Bing-cai and A-ju (Wang) Z.; m. Shi-ju Xu; children: Ren-ling, Ren-gang. Grad., Fudan U., 1957. Assoc. prof. Fudan U., Shanghai, 1980-88, prof., 1988—. Author: Course of Microbiology, 1993 (1st award State Edn. Com. China 1995); co-author: Microbiology, 1987 (1st award State Edn. Com. China 1988); editor-in-chief: Experimental Handbook of Microbiology, 1987; contbr. articles to profl. jours. Recipient 1st award Outstanding Tchg. Achievement, Shanghai Mcpl. Govt., 1996, 2d award, 1995, 2d award Outstanding Tchg. Achievement, State Grade of China, 1997, 2d award Sci. and Tech. Progress, State Ednl. Com. of China, 1997. Mem. Chinese Soc. for Microbiology (coun. 1987-96). Office: Fudan U Dept Microbiology, 220 Han Dan Rd, Shanghai 200433, China

ZHOU, GUO-DING, electric power university professor; b. Shanghai, China, Apr. 5, 1938; s. Jing-Tang Zhou and Yue-Qing Yu; m. Shu-Dan Zhou, Oct. 31, 1987. Bachelor, Beijing U., 1960, master, 1981. Postgrad. Beijing U., 1978-81; lectr. Rsch. Inst. of Photgraphic Chemistry, Beijing, 1981-84, assoc. prof., 1985-86; assoc. prof. Shanghai (China) Inst. of Electric Power, 1986-92, prof., 1992—; vis. scholar U. Houston, 1984-85; mem. title-appraisal com. Electric Power Ministry China, 1993-99. Contbr. articles to profl. publs. Del. People's Congress of Yangpu Dist., Shanghai, 1993—. Recipient Excellent Tchr. award Bao Steel Corp. Found., 1996, hon. cert. and Spl. Subsidy by Chinese govt., 1991; hon. cert. Electric Power Ministry, 1996. Avocations: music, Peking opera. Office: Shanghai Inst Elec Power, Ping Liang Rd 2103, Shanghai 200090, China

ZHOU, HUA, analytical chemist, educator; b. Rongshui, Guangxi, China, Apr. 7, 1941; s. Hongji Zhou and Wuying Huand; m. Lin Zeng, Jan. 1, 1963; children: Wei, Ting. PhD, Zhongshan U., Guangzhou, China, 1972. Dir. instrumental analysis lab. Nat. Bldg. Material Inst., Beijing, 1965-81; dir. chromatography and mass spectrometry lab. Analysis and Rsch. Ctr. Zhongshan U., 1982-91; dir. dept. inspection Nat. Ctr. Imported Food Inspection, Guangzhou, 1992-99; vis. scientist mass spectrometry lab. dept. chemistry Swiss Fed. Inst. Tech., Lausanne, 1986-87; rsch. fellow mass spectrometry Washington U. Sch. Medicine, St. Louis, 1987-88; vis. scholar dept. chemistry Chinese U. of Hong Kong, 1983, dept. organic chemistry U. Liverpool, Eng., 1983. Author: Mass Spectroscopy and Its Applications in Inorganic Analysis, 1986; editor Jour. Chinese Mass Spectrometry Soc., 1978-84. Recipient Nat. Invention prize Sci. and Tech. Com. of People's Republic of China, Beijing, 1984. Mem. Phys.-Chem. Testing Soc. of Beijing (bd. dirs. 1980-82), Chinese Preventive Medicine Soc. (commn., com. phys.-chem. test of food), Am. Soc. Mass Spectrometry, Assn. Ofcl. Analytical Chemists. Avocations: travel, photography, computer application. Home: 8 Yunyuan Zhi St Apt 502, Guangzhou 510405, China

ZHOU, JIMING, transportation engineering researcher; b. Anshan, Liaoning, China, June 30, 1964; came to U.S., 1998; s. Huilin Zhou and Lianfeng Yu; m. Jingtong Gao, July 17, 1991; 1 child, Boxin. BS, Liaoning Inst. Tech., 1986; MS, Jilin U. Tech., Changchun, China, 1989; PhD, Jilin U. Tech., 1992. Lectr. Jinzhou (China) Inst. Tech., 1992-94, assoc. chair, assoc. prof., 1994-95, prof., 1995-97; vis. scholar Cranfield U., Bedford, Eng., 1995-97; postdoctoral fellow Carleton U., Ottawa, Ont., Can., 1997-98; engring. rsch. assoc. II U. Mich., Ann Arbor, 1998—. Contbr. articles to profl. jours. Mem. ASME, Internat. Assn. Vehicle Sys. Dynamics, Soc. Automotive Engrs. Office: U Mich Transp Rsch Inst 2901 Baxter Rd Ann Arbor MI 48109-2150

ZHOU, JULIET LIJUN, journalist; b. Shanghai, China, Oct. 29, 1963; arrived in Eng., 1990; BA in English Lit., Shanghai Fng. Langs. Inst., 1985; BA in Internat. Journalism, Shanghai U., 1987; MA in Arts Criticism, City U., London, 1992. Reporter Radio Beijing, 1987-89; cons. China Monitor, Eng., 1992-94; editor Siyu Chinese Times, Chinese Bus. Impact, U.K.-China Future, Manchester, Eng., 1994-98; Chinese market specialist Deloitte & Touche, London, 1998—. Author: MacMillan Dictionary of Art, 1994; editor: Investing in the UK—A Guide for Chinese Businesses, 2000. Mem. Fgn. Press Assn., Brit. Chinese Artists' Assn. (mem. mgmt. com. 1995—), Hong Kong Exec. Club, Dragon Club. Avocations: photography, cycling, tennis, mountain walking.

ZHOU, KANG-WEI, physics educator; b. Zhongxian, Sichuan, China, June 21, 1935; s. Cheng-Han Zhou and Zhi-Fang Xiong; m. Shi-Fang Dai, Sept. 24, 1961; 1 child, Zhou Bing. B in Physics, Sichuan U., Chengdu, China. Asst. lectr. Inner Mongolia U., Huhehaote, China, 1961-71; technician Chengdu 1st radio factory, 1971-78; asst. lectr. Sichuan U., 1979-80, lectr., 1981-85, assoc. prof., 1986-92, prof. physics, 1993—. Author: Diferential and Integral Calculus, 1987; contbr. over 50 articles to profl. jours. Recipient sci.-tech. award Nat. Edn. Com. of China, 1990, Govt. Sichuan, 1993. Mem. AAAS, Chinese Ctr. of Advanced Sci. and Tech., Internat. Ctr. for Materials Physics, Acad. Sinica, Am. Phys. Soc. Avocations: music, touring. Office: Dept Physics, Sichuan Univ, Chengdu 610064, China

ZHOU, LI, engineering educator, researcher; b. Yu Tian, Hebei, China, Apr. 22, 1936; s. Li Xisheng and Liu Rufen; m. Zhong-Lian Li, Feb. 1, 1965; children: Li Jing-Shan, Li Zhe. BS, Tsinghua U., Beijing, 1960. Asst. Tsinghua U., 1960-78, lectr., 1978-86, assoc. prof., 1986-92, prof., 1992—. Author: L-L Extraction Process and Equipment, 1981 (awad of excellence 1987), Handbook of Chemical Engineering, 1985; contbr. over 60 articles to profl. jours.. Mem. Non-Ferrous Assn., Nuc. Chem. Engring. Assn., Bio-Engring. Assn. Avocations: travel, sports, listening to classical music, Beijing opera. Home: Hai Dian Dist, Xi Wang Zhuang 4-604, 100083 Beijing China Office: Dept Chem Engring, Tsinghua U, 100084 Beijing China

ZHOU, MEILI, systems scientist, educator; b. Lujiang, Anhui, China, July 17, 1949; s. Jiguang Zhou and Jinhua Qian; m. Chunrong Guo, Jan. 8, 1977; children: Jiangyuan, Jiangquan. Student, China Textile U., Shanghai, 1972, Anhui Inst. Tech., Hefei, 1979, Shanghai Jiao Tong U., 1995; cert. prof., Hefei U. Tech. Cert. univ. tchr., China. Asst. Anhui Inst. Tech., 1982-87, instr., 1987-93, assoc. prof., 1993-97; prof. Hefei U. Tech., 1997—; bd. dirs. GT Rsch. Inst. China, Beijing. Author: Similology, 1993, Similarity System Theory, 1994; contbr. numerous articles to sci. jours., including Jour. Advances in Sys. Sci. and Applications, Internat. Jour. Gen. Sys., others. Mem. AAAS, N.Y. Acad. Scis., China Soc. Life Sci. (bd. dirs. 1995—). Mem. Communist Party of China. Home: 158 Lu An Rd, Anhui Hefei 230061, China Office: Hefei U Tech, 193 Tun Xi Rd, Anhui Hefei 230009, China

ZHOU, MING, engineering educator; b. Hebei, China, Sept. 16, 1956; came to U.S., 1989; s. Ziao-Shan Zhou and Jefang Han; m. Aiping Zhang, May 1, 1983; 1 child, Yuan. BSME, Wuhan (China) Inst. Tech., 1982; MS in Indsl. Tech., Ind. State U., 1991; PhD in Indsl. Engring., U. Ariz., 1995. Design engr. Wuhan Marine Machinery Co., 1982-85, process engr., 1985-87; project coord. Wuhan Assn. Sci. and Tech., 1987-89; asst. prof. Ind. State U., Terre Haute, 1995-2000, assoc. prof., 2000—. Contbr. numerous articles to profl. jours. (Best Paper Transactions award 1998). Lilly Found. fellow, 1998; Kellogg Co. grantee, 1999. Mem. Inst. Indsl. Engrs., Soc. Mfg. Engrs. Avocations: reading, travel, music. Office: Ind State U Dept Indsl And Mech Tech Terre Haute IN 47809-0001

ZHOU, MING DE, aeronautical scientist, educator; b. Zhejiang, China, June 26, 1937; s. Pin Xiang and Ang Din (Xia) Z.; m. Zhuang Yuhua, Aug. 12, 1936; children: Zhengyu, Yan Zhuang. BS, Beijing U. Aeros.-Astronautics, 1962; MS, Northwestern U. Tech., 1967; PhD, Internat. Edn. Rsch. Found., 1992. Tchr. Harbin (China) U. Tech., 1962-64, 67-73; from lectr. to prof. Nanjing (China) U. Aeronautics and Astronautics, 1973-86, 86—; dean bd. postgrad. studies Nanjing (China) U. Aeros. and Astronautics, 1985-89; nationally qualified PhD advisor China, 1989—; rsch. scientist U. Ariz., Tucson, 1991-93, rsch. prof., 1993—; vis. scholar Cambridge (England) U., 1980-82; guest scientist Inst. Exptl. Fluid Mechanics, Göttingen, Germany, 1983-84, 85, 87; sr. vis. scientist Tech. U. Berlin, 1988, 90, 99; rsch. assoc. U. So. Calif., L.A., 1989-90. Author: (with others) Viscous Flows and Their Measurements, 1988, (with others) Introduction to Vorticity and Vortex Dynamics, 1992; mem. editl. com. Chinese Jour. Exptl. Mechanics, 1986-89; contbr. articles to Jour. Fluid Mechanics, Physics of Fluids, Aero. Jour. U.K., Experiments in Fluids, AIAA Jour., Chinese Jour., Aeronautics. Co-recipient Nat. award Progress in Sci. and Tech. first class, Peoples Republic of China, 1985. Mem. AIAA (sr.), N.Y. Acad. Scis., Am. Phys. Soc., Chinese Soc. Aeronautics, Chinese Soc. Mechanics (mem. acad. group exptl. fluid mechanics 1986-89), Chinese Soc. Aerodynamic Rsch. (acad. group unsteady flow and vortex control 1985-89). Achievements include patent for techniques and device of artificial boundary layer transition.

ZHOU, MING YONG, electrical engineer, researcher; b. Chongqing, China, Apr. 16, 1966; arrived in Singapore, 1996; B in Engring., Beijing U. Aeronautics and Astronautics, 1986; M in Engring., Osaka City (Japan) U., 1991, D in Engring., 1994. Rsch. fellow Melbourne (Australia) U., 1994-96; R & D engr. Thomson Multimedia Singapore, Thomson Group, 1996-99; sr. engr. Philips Singapore Pty. Ltd., 1999—. Contbr. articles to profl. jours. Mem. IEEE. Buddhist. Avocations: mathematics, law, arts, football, travel.

ZHOU, PENG, physics researcher. BSc, Ctrl. China Normal U., 1983, MSc, 1989; PhD, Queen's U. Belfast, No. Ireland, 1996. Tchg. asst. Xinyang Tchrs. Coll., China, 1983-86; rsch. asst. Ctrl. China Normal U., 1988-89; asst. prof. Hubei (China) Coll. Edn., 1989-92, assoc. prof., 1992-93; vis. rsch. fellow Inst. Materials Structure, Spain, 1993; rsch. fellow Queen's U. Belfast, 1996-99; postdoctoral fellow Ga. Inst. Tech., Atlanta, 1999—; assoc. mem. China Ctr. Advanced Sci. and TEch., 1992-93. Mem. AAAS, Am. Phys. Assn., Inst. Physics (U.K.). Fax: 404-8949958. E-mail: peng.zhou@physics.gatech.edu. Office: Ga Inst Tech 837 State St Atlanta GA 30332-0001

ZHOU, PING, physical engineer; b. Beijing, Apr. 21, 1946; came to U.S., 1985; 1 child, Jie Yang. BA, Beijing Inst. Chem. Tech., 1964; postgrad., U. Sci. & Tech., China, 1978, Beijing U., 1982. Asst. prof. SUNY, Albany, 1985-87; engr. Chinese Acad. Scis., Beijing, 1970-90; rsch. assoc. Stanford (Calif.) U., 1990—; vis. porf. Stanford U., 1987-88. Mem. Am. Soc. Materials Internat., Materials Rsch. Soc., Am. Vacuum Soc., Am. Phys. Soc. Achievements include development of multilayer Ti-Cu thin films for gravity probe-B gyroscope housings, BSCCO thin films with Tc above 100K; development, manufacturing, and testing of the thin film coatings and the superconducting bearings for the accelerometer for the Satellite Test of Equivalence Principle (STEP) Project. Office: Stanford Univ Hansen Lab Stanford CA 94305

ZHOU, QIANG TAI, engineering educator; b. Yang Jiang, China, Feb. 1, 1935; s. Qi Di and Qi Fang (Don) Z.; m. Xue Yuan Qian, Feb. 1, 1935; children: Jian-Hong, Jian-Yong. BSc, Ctrl. China Sci. & Tech., 1956; MSc, Southeast U., 1960. From assoc. prof. to prof. Southeast U., Nanjing, China, 1983—; chief engr. Nanjing Sunlight Energy Tech. Ltd. Co., 1992—. Author: Principles of Boilers, 1986 (award 1992); patentee in field. Fellow Nanjing Soc. Boilers, Nanjing Soc. Labor. Home: Rm 309 Bldg 14, 33 Jin Xiang He Rood, 210008 Nanjing China Office: Southeast U Dept Power Eng, 2 Sipailou, 210018 Nanjing China

ZHOU, QIANZHI, electrical engineer educator, researcher; b. Chongqing, China, Mar. 20, 1945; d. Qingyi and Weili (Chen) Z.; m. Qinggue Li, Dec. 4, 1968; children: Xuemei Li, Xuelian Li. B, N.E. U., Shenyang, China, 1968. Practice engr. 14th Metall. Constrn. Co., Kunmimg, China, 1968-75, asst. engr., 1975-80; asst. prof. East China U. Metallurgy, Maanshan, China, 1980-87, lectr., 1987-92, assoc. prof., 1993-98, prof., 1998—; councilor China Power Supply Soc., Tianjing, 1997—, vice chairwoman Spl. Power Supply Inst., 1997—. Contbr. articles to profl. jours. Councilor Maanshan Fedn. Returned Overseas Chinese, 1995; del. Anhui Fedn. Returned Overseas Chinese, 1996. Recipient award Sci. and Tech. Com. Anhui, 1987, grants State Dept. Beijing, 1993, Maanshan City, 1999. Mem. IEEE (sr.). Avocation: music. Home: East China U Metallurgy, 243002 Maanshan Anhui China Office: Electronics Ctr ECIM, Hutong, 243002 Maanshan Anhui China

ZHOU, QIBO, research scientist; b. Changzhou, Jiangshu, China, Jan. 17, 1943; s. Ruinan Zhou and Qinfang Yu; m. Meijuan Zhu, Feb. 1, 1969; children: Xiaoyi, Xiaofeng. BS, Fudan U., China, 1964. Physics diplomate. Asst. rschr. Shanghai Inst. of Tech. Physics/Academia Sinica, 1964-87, sr. rschr., 1987-93, prof., sr. rschr., 1994—; vis. scholar Mich. Technol. U., Houghton, 1984-86, 95-96, U. Ala., Huntsville, 1986-87. Prin. scientist: Dual Band Infrared Staring Imaging Radiometer, Chinese Acad. of Scis., 1994, IR-100 Series Infrared Thermal Imaging System, 1993, PtSi Staring Infrared Imaing System, 1992, Multi-Element Infrared Imaging System, 1986. Grantee China Guanghua Sci. and Technology Assn., Beijing, 1994; recipient Spl. Allowance, China State Coun., Bejing, 1993, Vis. Scholar award Ctr. of Applied Optics, U. Ala., Huntsville, 1987. Mem. Soc. Infrared and Remote Sensing of Shanghai (head of speciality com. 1987—), Optical Soc. of China, Soc. of Space Sci. of China. Avocations: travel, sports, music. Office: Shanghai Inst Tech Physics, 500 Yu Tian Rd/Acad Sinica, 200083 Shanghai China

ZHOU, SAN-DUO, management consultant, educator; b. Yixing, Jiangsu, China, Nov. 7, 1933; s. Shuzhen Wang; m. Chor Siang Ong, Feb. 12, 1996; 1 child, Ester Zhou Enyu. BS, People's U. China, 1955; MS, Harbin Inst. of Technology, China, 1958. Asst. instr. Changchun Inst. Automobile and Tractor, China, 1955-56; lectr. and dir. Jilin Polytechnics U., Changchun, 1969-77; engr., dir. Changzhou Passenger Vehicles Plant, Changzhou, 1977-80; lectr. to assoc. and full prof. Nanjing U., China, 1980-87, chmn., Dean Soc. Internat. Bus., 1987-95, dir., chief prof. Rsch. Ctr. for All-China MBA Edn., 1995—; dir. Inst. for Bus. Strategy, Nanjing U.; exec. dir. Rsch. and Tng. Ctr. for Multinat. Bus., Nanjing; sr. cons. Jiangsu Provincial People's Govt., Nanjing; exec. mem. commanding com. of All-China MBA Edn., Peking, 1995—. Author: (book) The Business Forecasting and Decision-Making of Firms, 1984 (2d class award Jiangsu 1985), A Socialist Firm Science, 1988 (Excellent Publs. award of E. China Region 1988); chief editor: (books) An Introduction to Management on Manufacturing Enterprises, 1987 (2d class award State Edn. Commn. 1992), Management, 1993 (1st class award State Edn. Commn. 1995). Vice-pres. Assn. for Bus. Mgmt., Nanjing; vice-chancellor Rsch. Soc. for Modern Technol. Economy, Jiangsu. Recipient Key Rsch. Project on Humanities and Social Scis., State Ednl. Commn., Beijing, 1998-2000, named Excellent Chief of Acad. Specialties of Colls. and Univs. in Jiangsu, Jiangsu Provincial Edn. Commn., 1997, others. Communist. Avocations: climbing, travel, photography. Office: Sch Internat Bus/Nanjing U, Hankou Rd 11, 210093 Nanjing/Jiangsu China

ZHOU, SHAO-MIN, chemist, educator; b. Jin-Jiang, Fujian, Peoples Republic of China, Nov. 18, 1921; m. Fu Su-wen, Jan. 1, 1948; children: Lu-wen, Hai-wen, Yue. BS, Amoy U., 1945; MS, Mendeleev Coll., USSR, 1957. Asst. dept. chemistry Amoy U., Amoy, Peoples Republic of China, 1946-50, lectr., 1950-53, assoc. prof., 1957-78; prof. Xiamen (Amoy) U., Peoples Republic of China, 1978—; researcher Moscow D.I. Mendeleev Coll. Chem. Tech., 1954-57. Author: Electrodeposition of Metal-Principle and Experimental Methods, 1987; editor: Advances in Electrochemical Methods, 1988; contbr. numerous articles to profl. jours. Recipient 2d Rank Prize of Progress in Sci. and Tech. Nat. Edn. Com., 1988. Achievements include patents in iridescent chromium plating, plating additives concentration analyzer and electroplating of Zn-Ni alloy from alkaline baths. Office: Xiamen U, Dept Chemistry, 361005 Xiamen China

ZHOU, SHI-WEI, environmental chemist, environmental hygienist; b. Ning Bo, China, Oct. 14, 1939; s. Zhen-Hua and Cui-Ying (Zhu) Z.; m. Cui-Zhang Yang, Jan. 20, 1968; 1 child, Ying. BS, Fudan U., Shanghai, China, 1962; MS, Chinese Acad. Med. Scis., Beijing, 1981. Rsch. asst. Inst. of Health, Chinese Acad. Med. Scis., Beijing, 1962-71; asst. rschr. Second Provincial Hosp., Nan Chang, China, 1971-81; prof., rschr., chief environment chem. dept. Inst. Environ. Health and Engring./Chinese Acad. Prev. Med., Beijing, 1981-93; prof., rschr., dep. chief environ. health dept. Shanghai Acad. Preventive Medicine, 1994—; prof. Shanghai Med. U., 1999—; commr. Chinese Coun. Environ. Hygiene Standards, Beijing, 2000—; vice dir. Chinese Com. Cosmetics Hygienic Monitoring, Beijing, 2000—. Contbr. articles to profl. jours. Recipient Sci. Achievement award Ministry Pub. Health, Beijing, 1991, Sci. Achievement award Inst. Environ. Helath and Engring., Beijing, 1992, Sci. Achievement award Nat. Com. Patriotic Pub. Health Campaign, Beijing, 1994. Mem. Chinese Assn. Preventive Medicine, China Med. Assn. Avocations: swimming, gymnastics. E-mail: swzhou@guomai.sh.cn. Home: Rm 805 Bldg 91, Mei Long Si Chun, Shanghai China 200237 Office: Shanghai Ctr Disease Prev & Ctrl, 1380 Zhong Shan West Rd, Shanghai China 200336

ZHOU, SHUHUA, physicist, educator; b. Beijing, Oct. 19, 1941; s. Xianhong Zhou and Jihui Wu; m. Jingshu Xing, Dec. 10, 1970; children: Yuezheng, Xinlan. Grad., Peking U., Beijing, 1963. Rsch. assoc. China Inst. Atomic Energy, Beijing, 1978-87, assoc. prof., 1987-93, prof., 1993—, dep. dir. dept. nuc. physics, 1995—, contact person A Large Ion Co. experiment, 1999—; vis. scientist Ind. U. Cyclotron Facility, Bloomington, 1981-82, 86, Lawrence Berkeley Lab., U. Calif., Berkeley, 1982-83; vis. prof. Brookhaven Nat. Lab., Upton, 1992; mem. instnl. bd. Pioneer High Energy Nuclear Interation Experiment, Upton, 1996—. Contbr. articles to profl. jours. Recipient award China Nat. Sci. and Tech. Conf., Beijing, Sr. Scientist with outstanding contbn. award China Nat. Nuc. Corp., Beijing, 1996. Mem. China Nuc. Phys. Soc. (bd. dirs.), China High Energy Physics Soc., N.Y. Acad. Scis. Avocations: swimming, table tennis, music. Office: China Inst Atomic Energy, Beijang PO Box 275(80), Beijing 102413, China

ZHOU, SHUZI, mathematics educator; b. Changsha, China, Nov. 23, 1940; s. Renfu and Jin (Huang) Z.; m. Bichun Zhang, Mar. 18, 1970; 1 child, Hong. B, Hunan Univ., Changsha, 1962. Tchr. asst. Hunan Univ., Changsha, 1962-78, lectr., 1978-85, prof., 1985—; vis. scholar Univ. Wis., Madison, 1980-82, vis. prof. Chalmers Univ. Tech., Gotebog, 1993-94. Author: Variational Inequalities and FEM for Them, 1988; editor: Hunan Univ. Jour., 1988—, Hunan Math. Annals, 1988—. Recipient Sci. and Tech. award Hunan Edn. Com., 1981. Mem. Chinese Math. Soc. (coun. mem.), Hunan Soc. Computational Math. (chmn. coun.). Avocations: table tennis, walk on mountains, enjoy music, singing. Office: Inst Applied Math Hunan Univ, 410082 Changsha China

ZHOU, SOPHIA HUAI, biomedical engineer; b. Huaiyin, Jiangsu, China, Dec. 6, 1953. MS, Dalhousie U., Halifax, Can., 1987, PhD, 1991. Rsch. assoc. U. Alta., Edmonton, Can., 1991-93, asst. prof., 1993-94; asst. prof. St. Louis U., 1994-95; engring. scientist Hewlett-Packard Co., Andover, Mass., 1995-99, Agilent Techs. Inc., Andover, 1999—. Contbr. articles to profl. jours. Mem. N.Y. Acad. Sci., Soc. Women Engrs., Internat. Soc. Electrocardiology (Young Investigator's award 1993), Internat. Soc. Computerized Electrocardiology, Am. Heart Assn. Achievements include design and development of automated ECG interpretations. Office: Agilent Techs Inc 3000 Minuteman Rd Andover MA 01810-1032

ZHOU, TAILI, metallurgist; b. Guangzhou, Guangdong, China, Mar. 29, 1937; came to U.S., 1985; s. Bocheng and Huaichen (Xie) Z.; m. Lina Qun Xie, Aug. 28, 1963; children: Enning, Enyu, Enhong. BS in Chemistry, Peking U., Beijing, 1958; PhD in Metallurgy, U. Leeds (Eng.), 1984. Rsch. asst., chemist Guangzhou Rsch. Inst. Chemistry, Chinese Acad. Sci., 1958-62, rsch. metallurg. engr. Changsha Rsch. Inst. Mining and Metallurgy, 1962-79; co-supr. grad. student program Changsha Rsch. Inst. Mining and Metallurgy, 1978-79; project mgr. Guangzhou Rsch. Inst. Non-ferrous Metals, 1980-81; postdoctoral rsch. assoc., rsch. chemist and metallurgist U. Idaho, Moscow, Idaho, 1985-94; co-prin. investigator U. Idaho, Moscow, 1990-94; R&D metallurgist The Shepherd Chem. Co., Cin., 1995—. Contbr. numerous articles to profl. jours., chpts. to books. Achievements include development of substituted amide and hydroxamic acid type extractants, and the relevant processes for recovery of rare and scarce metals from numerous soruces; invention substituted pyrazolyl pyridine chelaing extractant, techniques of selective extraction and separtion of cobalt and nickel. Office: The Shepherd Chem Co 4900 Beech St Cincinnati OH 45212-2398

ZHOU, TIAN XIAO, mathematician, educator, administrator; b. Zhong Jiang, Sichuan, People's Republic of China, Aug. 25, 1938; s. Yao De and Tai Hui (Liu) Z.; m. Hui Gou, Aug. 1, 1971; children: Xiao Sui, Yu Heng. Scholar, Sichuan U., Chengdu, 1961; D in Computation Math., Acad. Sinica, Beijing, 1965. Prof. Sichuan U., 1987-89; asst. rsch. fellow Inst. Aeronautical Computing Tech., Xian, Shaanxi, People's Republic of China, 1977-81, rsch. fellow, 1981-84, v.p., 1984—; prof. Xian Jiaotong U., 1984—, supr. doctorate program, 1986—; prof. Northwestern Poly. U., Xian, 1988—; mem. sci. and tech. com. Ministry of Aerospace Industry, Beijing, 1981—; mem. acad. award commn. CAE, Beijing, 1985—; mem. specialist group Nat. Sci. Engring. Com., Beijing, 1991—; mem. acad. bd. state key Lab. Sci. Engring. Computer Acad., Sinica, 1993—. Co-patentee in field (3rd pl. Nat. Invention award 1983); reviewer U.S. Math. Rev. Dep. 5th Shaanxi Province People's Congress, 1977-82, 6th and 7th Nat. People's Congress, Beijing, 1982-92. Named Advanced Worker, Nat. Sci. Congress, Beijing, 1978-83, Model Worker, Govt. of Shaanxi Province, 1982-89, Nat. Level Specialist having Outstanding Achievement, Pers. Dept. of State, Beijing, 1984. Mem. Chinese Soc. Computer Math. (mem. coun.), Sci. Tech. Assn. Shaanxi Province (mem. standing com.), Acta Aeronautical and Astronautical Soc. (mem. editorial com.), Math. Numerical Soc. Mem. Chinese Communist Party. Avocations: swimming, music. Office: Inst Aero Computing Tech, PO Box 90 29 S Tabai Rd, Xian, Shaanxi 710068, China

ZHOU, WANCHENG, engineer, educator; b. Gongyi, Henan, Peoples Republic of China, Nov. 26, 1953; s. Zhenyong and Fengxian (Ren) Z.; m. Xiaomei Sun; 1 child, Bo. BS, Northwestern Polytech. U., Xian City, 1981, MS, 1985, PhD, 1990. Lectr. Northwestern Polytech. U., Xian City, 1985-90, prof., 1993—; vis. scholar Iowa State U., Ames, 1990-91, postdoctoral rsch. assoc., 1991-93. referee China Edn. Com., Beijing, 1995-96, Jour. Northwestern Polytech. U., 1995—. Contbr. articles to profl. jours. including Jour. Am. Ceramic Soc. (Progress in Sci. and Engring. awards 1991, 94), Jour. Materials Sci. (Progress in Sci. and Engring. award 1997), Jour. Chinese Ceramic Soc., among others. Recipient Progress in Sci. and Engring. award China Ministry of Aviation, 1987, 88, 91, 97, Progress in Sci. and Engring. award China Edn. Commn., 1994, Progess in Sci. and Engring. award Shaanxi Province Govt., 1991, State Govt. Spl. award State Coun. China, 1995. Mem. Am. Ceramic Soc., Shaanxi Composite Soc. (coun. 1995—), Shaanxi Ceramic Soc., China Aviation Soc. Avocations: Chinese chess, go, travel. Home: East 4-1-402, 127 Youyi Xi Lu, Xian Shaanxi 710072, China Office: Northwestern Polytech U, State Key Lab Solid Process, Xian Shaanxi 710072, China

ZHOU, WEN KAI, philosophy educator, researcher; b. Kunming, Yunnan, China, May 20, 1931; s. Sheng Pu Zhou and Duan Zhao; m. Shun Zhu Lei, Jan. 6, 1953; children: Gong Shi, Ming Dong, Fong Yue, Si Hai. BS, Yunnan U., Kunming, China, 1949; BA, Kunming (China) Tchrs. Coll., 1953; MA in Philosophy, Chinese People's U., Beijing, 1956. Asst., lectr. politics dept. Notheast Tchrs. U., Changchun, China, 1957-77; lectr. politics dept. Yunnan U., Kunming, China, 1977-81, assoc. prof., 1981-85, prof., 1985—, chief libr., 1981-92. Author: History of Chinese Philosophy, 1984. Mem. Yunnan Assn. for Sci. and Tech. (mem. com. 1992-97), Chinese Soc. Dialectics of Nature (mem. coun. 1981-96), Yunnan Soc. Dialectics of Nature (pres. 1981-96). Avocations: listening to classical music, swimming, writing poems, singing. Office: Yunnan U, 52 N Cuihu Rd, Kunming Yunnan 650091, China

ZHOU, XIANG, textile chemistry educator; b. Su Zhou, China, Sept. 26, 1934; d. Jiamin and Meizhen (Yang) Z.; m. Maojia Kui, Jan. 1, 1956; 1 child, Chen Kui. BS, East China Inst. Textile Sci. & Tech., 1955. With Cheng Tong Textile — Dyeing Mil, Ji Nan, Shan Dong, China, 1955-56; asst., lectr. East China Inst. Textile Sci. & Tech., Shanghai, 1956-59, 59-80, assoc. prof., 1980-86; prof. Dong Hua U., Shanghai, 1986—; vis. scholar USDA So. Regional Rsch. Ctr., New Orleans, 1981-83; vice chmn., Dept. textile Chemistry China Textile U., 1984-85, acting chmn., 1985-86, chmn., 1986-93. Mem. China Assn. Textile Engring., Shanghai Overseas Returned Scholars Assn., Shanghai Grads. Edn. Assn., Chinese Acad. Engring., Shanghai Overseas Returned Scholars Assn. (v.p. 1999—). Office: China Textile U, Dong Hua U, 1882 W Yan-an Rd, Shanghai 200051, China

ZHOU, XIAO HUA, electrical engineer, educator; b. Nancheng, China, Nov. 11, 1954; s. Guo An Zhou and Xin Feng Wang; m. Su Zhen Du, Jan. 24, 1981; 1 child. BA, Xidian U., Xian, China, 1977; MSc, N.W. U., Xian, 1986. Asst. Xidian U., Xian, 1982-87, lectr., 1987-94, assoc. prof., 1994—; vis. scientist Riso Nat. Lab., Roskilde, Denmark, 1995-96. Author: Basis on Oxide and Compound Semiconductors, 1991, Inorganic Semiconductors Physics, 1995. Mem. Electronic Soc. China (sr.), Sensors Soc. Shannxi (sec. 1990—). Avocations: watching TV, reading novels, playing basketball, swimming. Home: No 2 Taibai Rd, Xian 710071, China

ZHOU, XIAOSI, surgeon, educator, researcher; b. Nanchuan, Sichuan, China, Apr. 25, 1933; s. Longzxiao Zhou and Kaijun Huang; m. Shimei Zhou, Mar. 31, 1957; children: Qing, Li, Qingsheng. Grad., Beijing Med. Coll., 1955. Resident 1st Affiliated Hosp. Beijing Med. Coll., 1955-58; resident, vis. surgeon 3d Affiliated Hosp. Beijing Med. Coll., 1958-80, assoc. chief gen. surgery, 1983-85, chief, cons. gen. surgery, 1985—; assoc. prof. Beijing Med. Coll., 1980-85, prof. surgery, 1985—. Contbr. chpts. to book: (in Chinese) Gastroenterology, 2d edit., 1993; editor, co-author: (in Chinese) Current Biliary Surgery, 1998; patentee in field; mem. editl. bd. Chinese Jour. Practical Surgery, 1982—; Chinese Jour. of Gen. Surg., 1997—, Chinese Jour. of Hepatobiliary Surg., 1998—; contbr. over 140 articles to profl. jours. Recipient 2d pl. award for progress in sci. and tech. Pub. Health Ministry China, 1988, Nat. Ednl. Com. China, 1988, award for tchg. excellence Beijing City, 1989. Mem. Surg. Soc. Chinese Med. Assn. (mem. standing com. 1988—), Internat. Hepato-Pancreato-Biliary Assn. Avocation: computers. Home: 49 N Garden Rd Apt 3-209, Beijing 100083, China Office: 3d Hosp of BMU, 49 N Garden Rd, Beijing 100083, China

ZHOU, XING, researcher, educator; b. Beijing, People's Republic of China, June 21, 1959; Arrived in Singapore, 1992.; s. Shouchang and Heqi (Wang) Z.; m. Hong Chai, May 24, 1985; children: Christopher R., Christina X. BSEE, Tsinghua U., Beijing, 1983; MSEE, U. Rochester, 1987, PhD, 1990. Rsch. assoc. U. Rochester, 1990-91; sr. scientist ANAmation, Inc., Rochester, 1991-92; rsch. fellow Nanyang Technol. U., Singapore, 1992-95, lectr., 1995-98, asst. prof., 1998-99, assoc. prof., 2000—; cons. ANAmation, Inc., Rochester, 1991-92, National Supercomputing Rsch. Ctr., Singapore, 1996; vis. fellow Stanford U., 1997. Mem. IEEE (sr.). Avocations: music, swimming, skating, photography. Office: Nanyang Technol U-Sch Elec & Electronic Engring, Block S1-Nanyang Ave, 639798 Singapore Singapore

ZHOU, YI GANG, materials science and engineering educator; b. Jiangyin, Jiangsu, China, Oct. 18, 1930; s. Qing Yuan Zhou and Mei Zhen Gu; m. Hai Li, Feb. 5, 1964; children: Hong, Tie, Ying. BSc in Engring., Tsinghua U., Beijing, 1958; MS, Northwestern Poly. U., Xi'an, China, 1964, PhD (hon.), 1986. Asst. master Northwestern Poly. U., 1958-72, lectr. materials sci. and engring., 1973-80, vice prof., 1981-85, prof., 1986—; tech. cons. An Da Forging Plant, Anshun, China, 1980-85, Hong Yuan Forging and Casting Plant, Xi'an, 1984—. Author: Atlas of Defects in Aviation Forgings, 1980, Forging and Casting Technology of Titanium Alloys, 1991; inventor and patentee for high-temperature deformation tech. of strength toughening of ti-alloy. Recipient award Appraisal Com. of Nat. Sci. and Tech. Advancement Award, 1987; ministerial sci. and tech. achievement award Chinese Ministry Aviation Industry, 1983, 84, 87, 92, outstanding contbn. exert of ministry award, 1987; Nat. invention award, 1993. Mem. Assn. China Mech. Engring., Assn. China Inventors, N.Y. Acad. Scis. Avocations: reading, calligraphy, cooking. Office: Northwestern Poly U, Coll Materials Sci-Engring, Xi'an 710072, China

ZHOU, YUQING, physicist; b. Suining, Sichuan, China, May 1, 1940; parents Yucheng Zhou and Yongfang Liu; m. ShouXin Bai; 1 child, Hua. Diploma, N.W. Industry U., Xian, China, 1957; diploma in physics, Jilin U., Changchun, China, 1963. Tchr. Jilin U., 1960-61; asst. rschr. China Acad. Engring. Physics, Chengdu, 1963-86, assoc. prof., 1987-94, prof., 1995—, supr. PhD grad. students, 1989%. Contbr. articles to profl. publs. Recipient awards Com. of Def. Sci. and Tech. of China, 1992, 94, Dept. of Nuclear Industry of China, 1986, 87, 89. Mem. Chinese Nuclear Soc. Avocations: reading novels, music, dancing. Office: China Acad Engring Physics, PO Box 919-213, 621900 Mianyang Sichuan, China

ZHOU, YUZUE, psychiatric physician; b. Chuxiong, China, Jan. 4, 1958; m. Ping Li; 1 child, Rui. Grad., Kunming Med. Sch., China. Psychiat. physician Chuxiong Mental Health Ctr., 1975—. Recipient award for Excellent Thesis, Prefectural Govt., 1999. Mem. Assn. Physicians of China. Avocation: reading. Office: Chuxiong Mental Health Ctr, S Tuangjie Rd, 675000 Chuxiong, Yunnan China

ZHOU, ZHEN FENG, materials scientist, educator; b. Yujiang, Jiangxi, China, Nov. 22, 1927; s. Pi Xian Zhou and Cui Hua Peng; m. Xue Ping Zhang, May 11, 1958; children: Gang, Min. BS, No. Jiao Tong U., Beijing, 1950; MS, Harbin Inst. Technology, 1953. Asst. prof. Harbin Inst. of Technology, 1954-61; asst. prof. Jilin U. of Tech., Changchun, China, 1961-78, assoc. prof., 1978-79, prof., 1979—; vice-pres. Welding Engr. Edn. Com., China, 1978-94. Editor: (book) Welding Metallurgy, 1980 (Excellent textbook of China 1992); co-editor: (handbook) Chinese Welding Handbook, 1992; author: (book) Welding Metallurgy of Cast Iron, 1999; contbr. articles to profl. jours. Recipient model worker award Nat. Edn. Com., China, 1989, scientific awards Min. of Machine Bldg. and Govt. of Jilin Province, China, 1980-98. Mem. N.Y. Acad. Sci., Chinese Welding Soc. Office: Welding Divsn/Jilin U Tech, People Ave No 142, 130022 Changchun China

ZHOU, ZHEN-SHENG, petroleum engineer; b. Tianjin, Hebei, China, Dec. 30, 1930; s. E-Fu and Xue-Xian (Wei) Z.; m. Yu-Hua Sun, Feb. 25, 1957; children: Xiang-Xin, Xiang-Min. BS, Qinghua U., Beijing, 1953; postgrad., Baku, Azerbaijan, 1958-60. Engring. diplomate. Engr. Yumen (China) Oil Field, 1953-58; dep. chief engr. Daqing (China) Oil Field, 1960-69, Jianhan Oil Field, Qianjiang, China, 1969-72; chief engr. Rsch. Inst., Beijing, 1972—; dep. sec. gen. Com. on Standardization of Petroleum Industry, Beijing, 1984-94; fellow Editl. Com. Periodical of Petroleum Industry Standardization, Xian, China, 1985-94; fellow, dep. dir. Com. on Standardization of Prodn. Equipment, 1982-97. Author: Collected Works of Articles about Petroleum Industry Standardization, 1994.; inventor in field (Nat. Invention award, 1965). Mem. China Nat. Petroleum Corp. Trade Union, Beijing, 1954—. Recipient Spl. Subsidy cert. The State Coun., Beijing, 1992; named Prominent Contributive Specialist in Petroleum Industry, China Nat. Petroleum Corp., 1992. Mem. Petroleum Soc. Avocations: touring, dancing, reading newspaper, television, walking. Home: Xue Yuan Rd Shiyou Yard, 14 Jia Bldg 3-202, Beijing 100083, China Office: Rsch Inst Petroleum Exp/Dev, 20 Xue Yuan Rd, Beijing 100083, China

ZHOU, ZHIDE, civil engineer, researcher; b. Beijing, Oct. 20, 1933; s. Ruiting Zhou and Lianyun Wang; m. Wanzhi Feng, Jan. 22, 1963; 1 child, Zhixu. D Engring., Hokkaido U., Sapporo, Japan, 1989. Engr. China Inst. Water Resources and Hydropower Rsch., Beijing, 1958-70, 81-84, Bur. Water Resources, Dingxiang, China, 1971-76, Yellow River Conservancy Commn., Zhengzhou, China, 1977-80; sr. engr. Internat. Rsch. and Tng. Ctr. on Erosion and Sedimentation, Beijing, 1991-94, 95—, dep. sec. gen., 1991-94; cons. Water and Power Devel. Agy., Lahore, Pakistan, 1991, 95; assoc. project mgr. Regional Tng. Program on Erosion and Sedimentation for Asia, Beijing, 1990-93. Author: Fluvial Processes, 1987 (Best Engring. Book award 1992), Estuarine Processes in China, 1994. Mem. Internat. Assn. Hydraulic Rsch., N.Y. Acad. Scis. Avocations: soccer, music, history, literature. Office: Internat Rsch & Tng Ctr, 20 Chegongzhuang Xilu, Beijing 100044, China

ZHOU, ZHIYOU, information scientist; b. Chongqing City, China, Dec. 14, 1933; s. Huipai Zhou and Chenghui Liu; m. Siyi Ju, Feb. 1959; 1 child, Qiquang. D of Machinery, China U. of Mining Industry, Beijing, 1955. Dep. chief Mining Haulage Lab., China U. of Mining Industry, Beijing, 1955-58; rsch. asst. Inst. Sci. Tech. Info. China, Beijing, 1959-85, assoc. rsch. fellow, 1985-90, rsch. fellow, 1990-94; vis. prof. Peking U., Beijing, 1992—; mem. edit. bd. Info. Sci.; chief editor basic theory sect. Encyclopedia of China, 1983-93. Chief editor: Chinese Terminology of Documentation Dictionary, 1982, Selected Works of Zhou Zhiyou, 1988, Practical Handbook for Scientific Technical Information, 1982, Selected Works of Zhou Zhiyou, 1989; contbr. over 100 articles to profl. jours. Dep. pres. Beijing alumni br. mid. sch. Chongqing Tshing-Hwa, 1995—. Avocations: singing, violin, accordion, poetry, computers. Office: Inst Sci Tech Info China, PO Box 3827, Beijing 100038, China

ZHOU, ZHUAN, biophysicist, biomedical engineer, educator; b. Hefei, Anhui, China, Mar. 24, 1957; came to U.S., 1986; s. Je Zhou and Yu Yin Fan; m. Yan-Fang Hu, May 10, 1986; 1 child, Feng-Bo. BS, Tong-Ji U., Shanghai, 1984; PhD, Huazhong U. Sci. and Tech., Wuhan, China, 1990. Asst. inst. Anhui Coll. Electronics, Wuhou, 1984-86; instr. Huazhong U. Sci. and Tech., 1990; postdoctoral fellow Max Planck Inst., Göttingen, Germany, 1990-93; postdoctoral fellow Washington U., St. Louis, 1993-94, rsch. asst. prof., 1995—. Contbr. articles to Jour. Physiology, Neuron, Jour. Biol. Chemistry, also procs. Nat. sci. grantee, Wuhan, 1993; McDonald neurosci. fellow, 1993-95. Mem. Biophys. Soc., Neurosci. Soc. Achievements include discovery that 25 percent of endogenous Ca2 buffers in a cell is mobile with molecule weight 20K Doldon; at rest membrane potential, fractional Ca2 current through NMDA channel is 7-10 percent; first combined measurement of action-potential and quantal secretion; 1st quantal secretion from neuroterminal by a physical sensor CFE. Avocation: handworks. Office: Inst Neurosci, 320 Yue-Yang Rd, Shanghai 200031, China

ZHU, CHANG-LUO, chemical engineering educator; b. Shanghai, China, June 7, 1930; d. Zhai-Zhen and Dean-Gai (Sha) Z.; m. Shi-Mo Li, July 1, 1963; children: Ning, Qing. BS in Chem. Engring, Zhejiang U., Hangzhou, China, 1952, BSin Fuel Specialty, 1958. Cert. chem. engr., separation processes, membrane sci. and tech. Rschr., lectr. dept. physics Zhejiang U., Hangzhun, China, 1958-62; dir. cryogenic lab. Zhejiang U., Hangzhon, China, 1963-70, vice chmn. chem. engring. tchg. group, 1970-80, assoc. prof., prof. chem. engring. dept., 1982—; vis. scientist chem. engring. dept. U. Cin., 1980-82; mem. standing com. Zhejiang Assn. Sci. & Tech., China, 1984-96, v.p., 1984-91, v.p. Zhejiang Acad. Soc. Membrane, Sci. & Tech., Hangzhou, 1988—; v.p. Zhejiang Provincial People's Assn. for Friendship with Fgn. Countries, 1985-94; vice-chmn. European-Am. Assn. Zhejiang Province, 1985-95; com. mem. Zhejiang Acad. Soc. Chem. Engring., Hangzhou, 1984-98, com. mem. China Assn. Sci. and Tech., Beijing, 1987-91; vis. prof. Water Treatment Ctr., Hangzhou, 1999-2000; rsch. advisor dept. chem. engring. Zhejiang U., 1999—. Author, editor: Membrane Processes, 1987, Membrane Science and Technology, 1992; contbr. articles to profl. jours.; patentee in field. Mem. People's Congress Zhejiang Province, Hangzhou, 1978-92, com. mem., 1987-92. Mem. AAAS, AIChE, European Soc. Membrane Sci. & Tech. Avocations: music, singing, travel. Office: Zhejiang U, Dept Chem Engring, Hangzhou 310027, China

ZHU, CHAOYUAN, physicist; b. Hailaer, Nei Menggu, China, Sept. 24, 1956; s. Zhenghe and Xiaomei (Zhenghe) Z.; m. Yuanrong Wang, Dec. 3, 1981; children: Zhu Pu, Zhu Qi. BA, Sichuan U., China, 1982, MS, 1985; PhD, Inst. Nuclear Rsch., China, 1990, Grad. U. Advanced Studies, Japan, 1993. Lectr. theoretical physics Sichuan U., China, 1985-87; rsch. assoc. Inst. Molecular Sci., Japan, 1993—. Contbr. articles to profl. jours. Monbusho fellow Japanese Govt., Japan, 1990-93. Mem. Japan Phys. Soc., N.Y. Acad. Scis. Avocations: go, badminton, table tennis. Office: Inst Molecular Sci, Myodaiji, Okazaki 444, Japan

ZHU, DING-ER, biochemist, molecular biologust; b. Changsha, China, June 11, 1928; s. Yi and Shu-Shan (He) Z.; m. Le-Sui Dai, Jan. 14, 1954; 4 children. BS, MD, Hiang-Ya Med. Coll., Changsha, China, 1952; PhD, Hunan Med. U., Changsha, China. Asst. lectr. Hunan Med. Coll., Changsha, China, 1954-78, assoc. prof., 1978-84, prof., chief, 1984-91, prof., advisor, 1991—; cons. rschr. in fields of hemoglobinophathies, thalassemias, and globin gene structure and regulation, 1964—. Contbr. articles to profl. jours. Mem. Internat. Soc. Advancement Biotech., Chinese Soc. Biochemistry (bd. dirs. 1984-90, vice chmn. sub-soc. 1993—), Chinese Med. Acad. (com. biochemistry and molecular biology),. Avocations: exercise, TV, reading, history. Home: Hunan Med Univ, C303 Bldg 10 Hiang-Ya Rd, Changsha 410078, China Office: Hunan Med Univ Rsch Ctr Molecular, Biology 88 Hiang-Ya Rd, Changsha 410078, China

ZHU, DONG, acoustician, researcher; b. Han Dan, Hebei, China, May 20, 1966; arrived in Denmark, 1994; s. Jingyi Zhu and Yamin Wang; m. Hong Liu, Jan. 12, 1993; 1 child, Linna Zhu. BSc, Peking U., Beijing, 1987, MSc, 1993; PhD, Tech. U. Denmark, 1998. Elec. engr. TV & Elec. Acoustics, Beijing, 1987-90; vis. scientist Tech. U. Denmark, Lyngby, 1994-96; sr. rschr.

Ødegaard & Danneskiold-Samsøe A/S, Copenhagen, 1998—. Avocations: Chinese painting, music, sports. Fax: (45) 35311001. E-mail: dz@oedan.dk.

ZHU, FRANK XIANG, medical researcher, internist; b. Nanjing, China, Mar. 1, 1958; m. Dexi and Lijuan (Qian) Z.; m. Juliet Bei He, May 16, 1986; 1 child, David Hemu. MB, 2d Mil. Med. U., Shanghai, 1983, M in Med. Sci., 1989. Resident, asst. tutor Changhai Hosp/2d Mil. Med. U., Shanghai, 1983-89, physician in charge, lectr., 1989-92, dep. dir., physician, assoc. prof., 1992-95; rsch. fellow Royal Marsden Hosp./Inst. Cancer Rsch., London, 1995-97; rsch. scientist Baker Med. Rsch. Inst., Melbourne, Australia, 1997-99; physician Latrobe Regional Hosp., Victoria, Australia, 2000—; mem. com. hosp. infection adminstrn. Changhai Hosp., 1993-95. Editor-in-chief: Handbook of Practical Anti-infection Therapy, 1993; editor: Yearbook of Medicine of China, 1991-94; contbr. articles to profl. jours. Recipient award for sci. and tech. achievement Gen. Logistics Dept. of PLA, 1991; named Grade A Tchr., 2d Mil. Med. U., 1991; Marie Curie fellow, London, 1995; Prostate Cancer Rsch. Fund grantee, London, 1996. Mem. Soc. Internal Medicine, Chinese Med. Assn. (Shanghai br.), Australian Soc. for Med. Rsch. Avocations: swimming, stamp collecting. Home: 4/77 Wetherby Rd, Doncaster Australia 3108 Office: Emergency Dept Latrobe Reg, PO Box 424, Traralgon Victoria 3844, Australia

ZHU, GE-LIN (GE-LIN CHU), botanist; b. Yan-Liang, Shaanxi, China, Oct. 28, 1934; s. Wen-guang and Qiao-Ling Liu; stepmother Yu-min Liu; m. Shao-zhen Zhang, Feb. 1962; children: Jian-yun, Jian-feng, Jian-Qiu. Grad., NW Normal U., 1956. From asst. lectr. to assoc. prof. NW Normal U., Lanzhou, China, 1956-86, prof., 1987—. Mem. editl. bd. Higher Plants China, 1999—. mem. editl. com. Acta Phylotaxonomia Sinica, 1973-85; dir. Inst. Botany, NW Normal U., 1984-94; vis. prof. dept. Botanical and Range Sci., Brigham Young U., 1984, 1988-91, 1993-96;. Named Mercer fellow Arn. Arboretum, Harvard U., Cambridge, Mass., 1982-83. Mem. Chinese Botany Soc., N.Y. Acad. Sci., Calif. Bot. Soc. Avocations: photography, reading, music, swimming. Office: Inst Botany, NW Normal U, Lanzhou 730070, China

ZHU, GUO-ZHANG, cell biologist, researcher; b. Fujian, China, July 9, 1969. BS, Shanghai Med. U., 1992; PhD, Chinese Acad. Scis., 1996. Rsch. scientist Shanghai Inst. Biochemistry, Chinese Acad. Scis., 1997, U. Calif., Davis, 1997—. Inventor Genbank, NIH, 1999. Recipient fellowship Chinese Acad. Scis., Beijing, 1996. Mem. AAAS, Am. Soc. Cell Biology, Chinese Soc. Biochemistry and Molecular Biology, N.Y. Acad. Scis. E-mail: gzhu@ucdavis.edu. Office: U Calif Davis 1 Shields Ave Davis CA 95616-5270

ZHU, HUAI YONG, chemist; b. Baotou, China, Sept. 12, 1956; s. Ming-Shan and Xiu Ying (Wang) Z.; m. Yue Ying Lu, Apr. 10, 1982; children: You Nan, Jessie. BS, Innermongolia U., Huhehot, China, 1982; MS, Nankai U., Tianjin, China, 1986; PhD, Antwerp U., Belgium. Asst. engr. Inst. Sci. and Tech. Info. Inner Mongolia, Huhehot, China, 1982-83; lectr., dep. dir. divsn. inorganic material chemistry Xian Jiaotong U., Xian, China, 1986-91; rsch. assoc. lab. inorganic indsl. chemistry Hiroshima (Japan) U., 1994-96; rsch. assoc., sr. rsch. assoc. dept. chem. engring. U. Queensland (Austalia), 1996—, Queen Elizabeth II rsch. fellow, 1996—. Contr. articles to profl. jours.; patentee in field. Postgrad. rsch. scholar Govt. of Antwerp Province, Belgium, 1991-94; recipient Best Tech. award Nat. EPA China, 1992, Nat. Cert. for Scientific and Tech. Achievement Nat. Com. Sci. and Tech. China, 1995, Third award Shaanxi Province, 1998, J.G. Russell award Australian Acad. Sci., 2000. Avocations: travel, table tennis. Office: Dept Chem Engr, U Queensland, Saint Lucia Qld 4072, Australia

ZHU, HUI-CHAO, research scientist; b. Hunan, China, Oct. 24, 1957; s. JingCong Zhu and Liying Yang; m. XiaoLing Ling, Jan. 21, 1987; 1 child, Lingna. BSc, Ctrl.-South U. Tech., Changsha, China, 1982, MSc, 1985; PhD in Applied Scis., Faculte Poly. de Mons, Belgium, 1997. Asst., lectr. Ctrl.-South U. Tech., 1985-92; rsch. asst., rsch. assoc. Faculte Poly. de Mons Fonds Nat. de la Rsch. Scientifique, 1996—. Contbr. articles to profl. jours.

ZHU, JIANHUA, civil and transporation engineer, researcher; b. NanChang, JiangXi, China, Mar. 15, 1957; s. Yian Zhu and Zhilian Li; m. Xianhua Hou, June 13, 1984; 1 child, Zheng. BS, JiangXi Inst. Tech., Nanchang, 1982; M Engring., Chinese Acad. Sci., Beijing, 1985; MS, U. Hawaii-Manoa, Honolulu, 1995; PhD, U. Okla., 1998. Registered profl. engr., Tex. Rsch. assoc. Inst. Water Resources Rsch., Beijing, 1985-87, engr., 1987-93, sr. engr., 1993-95; rsch. asst. U. Hawaii-Manoa, 1993-95; rsch. engr. U. Okla., Norman, 1995-97; engring. Tex. Dept. of Transp., Bryan, Tex., 1998—; cons. engr. Bur. Hydropower, Liaoning, China, 1985-89, Bur. Water Resources, Taiyuan, China, 1990-92; supervising engr. Puchen Power Plant, Xian, China, 1991-92; project mgr. Inst. Water Resources Rsch., 1992-93; prin. investigator nat. key rsch. project Min. Water Power, 1993. Author: Theory and Practice in Hydraulic Structure Engineering, 1991 (Kexiejingbu prize 1992); contbr. articles to profl. publs. Recipient Yusiuluwen prize Assn. Hydropower of China, 1991. Avocations: martial arts, cooking, fishing. Office: Tex Dept of Transp 1300 N Texas Ave Bryan TX 77803-2760

ZHU, JIAN-MING, medical physicist, consultant, researcher; b. Hangzhou, Zhejiang, China, Feb. 27, 1963; s. Jasheng Zhu and Yuzhen Xu; m. Jianya Feng, July 10, 1989; children: Darren, Warren, William. BS, Zhejiang U., Hangzhou, 1983; MS, Chinese Acad. Scis., Shanghai, China, 1986, Saskatchewan U., Saskatoon, Can., 1992; PhD, U. Manitoba, Winnipeg, Can., 1997. Lectr. Zhejiang U., Hangzhou, 1986-89; vis. rschr. Nat. Rsch. Coun. Can., Winnipeg, 1992-97; sr. rsch. specialist U. ill., Urbana, 1997-98; sr. sys. engr. GE Med. Sys., Waukesha, Wis., 1998—; reviewer Magnetic Resonance Medicine, Phila., 1996-97. Mem. Internat. Soc. Magnetic Resonance Medicine (reviewer 1997, 98). Achievements include patents pending for New Signal Used in Magnetic Resonance Imaging, New Magnetic Resonance Systems Capable of Spectrosocpy. Fax: 262-521-6460. Home: 1107 Larchmont Dr Waukesha WI 53186-6765 Office: GE Med Sys 3000 N Grandview Blvd Waukesha WI 53188-1615

ZHU, JIZHONG, engineering educator; b. Sichuan, China, Jan. 17, 1965; married; 1 child. BSEE, Chongqing U., 1985, MSEE, 1987, PhD in Elec. Engring., 1990. Rsch. asst. dept. elec. engring. Chongqing (China) U., 1987-90, lectr., 1990-92, assoc. prof., 1992-96, prof. elec. engring., 1996—; vis. rsch. fellow Brunel U., U.K., 1995-96; postdoctoral fellow Nat. U. Singapore,1996-97; rsch. fellow Howard U., Washington, 1997—. Contbr. articles to profl. jours., chpts. to books. Recipient Sci. and Tech. Progress prize State Edn. Commn., 1992, 94, Sichuan Province Govt., 1992, 93, 94, Sci. and Tech. New Idea prize Sichuan Province Sci. and tech. Soc., 1992, An Excellent Youth Tchr. prize, Chongqing City Govt., 1992, Nat. Rsch. prize State Edn. Commn. and Huo Yingdong Edn Fund Commn., 1996, others. Mem. IEEE (sr.). Home: 115 150th Ave NE Apt C Bellevue WA 98007-5047

ZHU, JUN, agricultural engineering educator, researcher; b. Hangzhou, Zhejiang, China, Sept. 5, 1958; came to U.S., 1991; s. Congzhi Zhu and Yuanzhen Chen; m. Hong Yu, Jan. 1, 1987; 1 child, Tina. BS, Zhejiang U., 1982, MS, 1985; PhD, U. Ill., 1995. Structural engr. Zhejiang Bldg. Design and Rsch. Inst., Hangzhou, 1985-90; postdoctoral assoc. Iowa State U., Ames, 1995-97; rsch. assoc. U. Minn., St. Paul, 1997-98; asst. prof. U. Minn., Waseca, 1999—. Mem. Am. Soc. Agrl. Engrs. Avocations: jogging, fishing, travel. E-mail: zhuxx034@tc.umn.edu. Home: 2100 4th St NE Waseca MN 56093-2655

ZHU, KAICHENG, physics educator, researcher; b. Changde, Hunan, China, Apr. 5, 1958; s. Jing'an Zhu and Lagu Li; m. Huigin Tang, Jan. 1, 1987; 1 child, Jie. BS, Hunan Normal U., China, 1982; MS, Jiangxi Normal U., China, 1988. Tchr. primary sch., 1974-78; tchr. Jishou U., Hunan, 1978-82, assoc. prof., 1988-93; assoc. prof. Xiangtan Normal U. (formerly Xiangtan Tchrs. Coll.), Hunan, 1993-96, prof., 1997—. Contbr. articles to profl. jours. Recipient The Progressive Reward of Sci. and Tech. Jiangxi Province Sci. and Tech. Coun. Jiangxi Province, 1993. Mem. Hunan Phys. Soc. (dir. 1994—), Optical Soc. Am. Avocations: Chinese chess, bridge, music. Home: Xiangtan Normal U, 411201 Xiangtan Hunan, China Office: Xiangtan Normal U, Dept Physics, 411201 Xiangtan Hunan, China

ZHU, LING, naval architect, applied mechanics specialist; b. Nanjing, Jiangsu, China, June 18, 1962; arrived U.K., 1988; s. Kun and Hui Fang (Su) Z.; m. Hui Jiang, Nov. 25, 1987; children: James Yu, Henry Yu. BSE, Huazhong U., 1983, ME, 1986; PhD, Glasgow U., 1990. Rsch. asst. Naval Acad. Engring. and Huazhong U., Wuhan, China, 1983-86; lectr. Huazhong U., Wuhan, China, 1986-88; cons. Brit. Gas project Liverpool (Eng.) U., 1990; ICI rsch. fellow Reading (Eng.) U., 1990-93; project mgr. Glasgow (Scotland) U., 1993-95; specialist/sr. specialist Lloyd's Register of Shipping, London, 1995—; former mem. 12th Internat. Ship and Offshore Structure Congress. Co-editor, contbr.: Selected Research Topics on Applied Mechanics in UK, 1996; contbr. articles to profl. jours. Grantee Royal Soc., 1993; recipient ORS awards Com. Vice Chancellors and Prins., 1988-90; Glasgow U. postgrad. rsch. scholar, 1988-90. Mem. Royal Inst. Naval Architects (chartered engr.), European Engr. Avocations: volleyball. Home: 4 Sundial Ave S Norwood, London SE25 4BX, England Office: Lloyds Reg Ship HQ Dept R&D, 100 Leadenhall St, London EC3A 3BP, England

ZHU, LONGGEN, chemistry educator; b. Shanghai, Dec. 1, 1940; m. Wei Huang; children: Haibo, Haizhong. BS in Chemistry, Nanjing (China) U., 1963. Asst. prof. chemistry Nanjing U., 1963-78, lectr., 1978-85, assoc. prof., 1985-93, prof., 1993—; dir. State Key Lab. Coordination Chemistry, Nanjing, 1994—. Contbr. articles to sci. jours., including Jour. Am. Chem. Soc; patentee in field (U.S.). Recipient 2d class provincial award Jiang Su Province, Nanjing, 1990, 1st class ministerial award Nat. Edn. Commn., Beijing, 1990, 3d class nat. natural sci. award Nat. Sci. and Tech. Commn., Beijing, 1991. Office: Nanjing U, Coord Chemistry Inst, Jiangsu Nanjing 210093, China

ZHU, MENGZHOU, mechanical engineering educator, consultant; b. Xian, China, Aug. 14, 1933; s. B of Mfg. Engring., Tianjin U., China, 1955. Asst. prof. Tianjin U., 1955-62, instr., 1962-81, assoc. prof., 1981-88, prof., 1988—; investigator Emerson Electric Co., 1996-98; vis. rsch. Institut für Werkzeugmaschinen und Fertigungstechnik, Tech. U. Berlin, 1981-82; vis. prof. Mich. U., 1995; dir. dept. mech. engring. Tianjin U., 1988-92. Author: Machine Tool Test, 1985 (Outstanding Textbook award 1992); editor: Electronics Engrs. Handbook, 1995; editor-in-chief Handbook Mech. Engr., 2d edit., 1998-99; inventor in field of mech. noise control (Sci. and Technique Advanced award 1991). Recipient Spl. grant State Coun., China, 1992—. Mem. Chinese Mech. Engring. Soc. (sr.), Soc. Labor Protection and Safety (vice chmn. 1989-96), Tianjin Metal Cutting Soc. (chmn. 1991-96, Outstanding Mem. award 1991). Avocations: photography, music. Office: Tianjin Univ Dept Mech Engring, Qilitai, Tianjin 300072, China

ZHU, MIN, pharmacy educator, researcher; b. Beijing, China, Apr. 4, 1956; d. Wan-Li and Rong-Zhen Z. BS, Peking U., Beijing, China, 1982; MPhil, Peking Union Med. Coll., Beijing, China, 1988; PhD, U. London, 1994. Rsch. asst. Inst. Material Media, Beijing, China, 1982-85; lectr. Inst. Medcinal Plant Development, Beijing, China, 1988-91; asst. prof. The Chinese U. of Hong Kong, 1994—. Contbr. articles to profl. jours. Recipient Pfizer studentship Pfizer Ltd., U.K., 1991-94. Mem. Hong Kong Soc. for Traditional Medicine and Natural Product Rsch., China Pharm. Soc.m Am. Assn. Pharm. Scientists. Avocations: swimming, volleyball, gym, movies, ping pong. Office: Dept Pharmacy, Chinese U Hong Kong, Shatin Hong Kong China

ZHU, QIANG, mechanical engineer; b. Luoyang, Henan, China, June 14, 1962; came to U.S., 1995; s. Jiqiao and YingPu (Ye) Z.; m. Ya Dong, Apr. 19, 1993; 1 child, Ye-Hong. BSME, Luoyang Inst. Tech., 1985; MS in Aerospace Engring., Syracuse U., 1996. Cert. profl. engr., Beijing. Sr. foundry engr. Beijing No. 1 Machine Tool Plant, 1985-95; sr. process engr. Gen. Casting Co., Delaware, Ohio, 1997-98; mech. and Chinese liaison engr. Atlas Bolt and Screw Co., Ashland, Ohio, 1998—. Mem. AIAA, ASME, Am. Foundry Soc. Avocations: fishing, football, cars. Home: 1465 Mifflin Ave Apt B Ashland OH 44805-3675 Office: Atlas Bolt & Screw Co 1628 Troy Rd Ashland OH 44805-1398

ZHU, QI-XIANG, mechanical engineer, researcher; b. Jinan, Shangdu, China, Apr. 20, 1936; s. Zhu Lu-Qing and Mei Wen-Lin; m. He Shang-Fen; children: Hung-Tao, Ya-Min. Degree in mech. engring., Moscow Machine Tool and Small Tool Inst., 1960. Engr. Inst. Optics and Finemech. A.S., Cahgchueng, China, 1960-73; assoc. prof. Inst. Optics and Electronics A.S., Chengdu, 1980-89, prof., 1989—; dir. R & D Inst. Optics and Electronics, Chengdu, 1987-91, dir. lab., 1991—. Author: Applications of Photonic Technology, 1995; translator, editor: The Problems of Optical Measurement, 1996; compiler: Handbook of Optical Technology, 1994; patentee in field of dynamic measuring sys. Mem. IEEE, Internat. Soc. Optical Engring., Optical Soc. Am., Chinese Soc. Metrololgy, Chinese Soc. Cosmonautics, Chinese Optical Soc. Office: Inst Optics and Electronics AS, PO Box 350 Shuangliu, Chengdu 610209, China

ZHU, QUAN MIN, educator; b. Dan-Dong, China, Oct. 31, 1955; arrived in England, 1986; s. Yi and Shu (Qi) Z.; m. Yu Lian, Jan. 10, 1982 (div. Mar. 1996); m. Xin Gu, Dec. 23, 1996. BS, Qiqihaer Light Industry Inst., China, 1980; MS, Harbin Inst. Tech., China, 1983; PhD, U. Warwick, England, 1989. Lectr. Qigihaer Light Industry Inst., 1983-86; sr. lectr. U. Brighton (England), 1994-97; lectr. Aston U., Birmingham, U.K., 1997-2000; reader Univ. West of Eng., 2000—; guest prof. U. Sci. & Tech., Beijing, 1994—; cons. Brit. Steel, Middlesborough, 1994; pres.'s guest Nankai U., Tianjin, China, 1994—. Contbr. papers to profl. pubs. Vis. fellow U. Warwick, 1986-89; rsch. fellow U. Sheffield (Eng.), 1989-94; recipient Tech. prize Space Industry Ministry, China, 1984. Avocations: sports, coin collecting, ravel, music, ballroom dancing. Home: 3 Church Walk Fullwood Row, Preston PR2 6SZ, UK Office: Fac Engrg Univ West of Eng, Frenchay Camp Coldhabour Ln, BS16 1QY Bristol UK

ZHU, RONGJI, Chinese government official; b. Changsha City, Hunan Province, People's Republic of China, 1928. Grad. electical engring., Qinghua U., Beijing, 1951. Dep. head prodn. planning office Northeast China's Ministry of Industry, 1951-52; divsn. head dept. combustion State Planning Commn., China, 1952-58; prof. Inst. at State Planning Commn., 1958-69; engr. Elec. Power Comm. Co., Ministry of Petroleum Industry, 1975-78; dir. Indsl. Econ. Inst. Acad. Social Scis., 1978-79; dir. Tech. Transformation Bur. State Econ. Commn., 1982-83, vice minister, 1983-88; dep. sec. mcpl. com. Chinese Communist Party, 1988; mayor City of Shanghai, 1988-91; vice premier responsible for econ. affairs State Coun., 1991—; gov. People's Bank of China, 1991-95; sec. Shanghai Communist Party, 1989-91; dep. bur.dir. State Econ. Commn. Mem. Indsl. Econs. Soc. (v.p. 1984). *

ZHU, RUI LIANG, biologist, educator; b. Shengzhou, Zhejiang, China, Dec. 1, 1963; s. Yun Wen Zhu and He Hua Lou; m. Hong Qiang; 1 child, Yi Jie. Bachelor's degree, N.W. U., Xian, China, 1986; Master's degree, East China Normal U., Shanghai, 1989; PhD, Hong Kong Bapt. U., 1999. Asst. lectr. East China Normal U., Shanghai, 1989-91, lectr., 1992-93, assoc. prof., 1994-99, prof., 1999—. Author: (book) Mosses and Liverworts of Hong Kong, 1996; contbr. papers to sci. jours. Mem. Internat. Assn. Biologists, Am. Soc. Plant Taxonomists, Bot. Soc. Shanghai (councilor 1996-00). E-mail: ruilianghzu@yeah.net. Office: East China Normal U, 3663 Zhong Shan N Rd, Shanghai 200062, China

ZHU, RUO-GU, optical educator; b. Huzhou, China, Dec. 27, 1946; s. Jin-Jiang and Lian-Zhu (Yang) Z.; m. Yin-Qin Niu, Dec. 30, 1975; 1 child, Rei. BS, Zhejiang U., 1968; MS, China U. Scis. Tech., 1981. Technician Xiangtan (China) Chem. Fertilize, 1968-76, Huzhou (China) Chem. Fertilize Mill, 1976-78; lectr. China Inst. Metrology, Hangzhou, 1981-92, assoc.prof., 1992-99, prof., 1999—; cons. Nat. Natural Sci. Found., China, Beijing, 1992—. Contbr. papers to profl. publs.; inventor in field. Mem. Optical Soc. Am., Phys. Soc. China, Instrumental Soc. China. Avocations: computers, communication. Home: Cui Yuan 4th QU 19-2-502, Hangzhou 310012, China Office: China Inst Metrology, Jiaogong 3d Rd, Hangzhou 310034, China

ZHU, SHAOWEI, power machinery engineer; b. Xi'xa County, Henan, China, Oct. 6, 1963; s. Xianghei Zhu and Ruxin Li; m. Dan Li; 1 child: Jingwen. BS, Xi'an Jiaotong U., 1984, MS, 1987, PhD, 1990. Lectr. Xi'an Jiaotong U., 1990-92, assoc. prof., 1992-93; rschr. Daido Hoxan Inc, Tsukuba, Japan, 1994-97, Aisin Seiki Co., Ltd., Kariya, Japan, 1997—. Contbr. articles to profl. jours.; inventor in field. Office: Aisin Seiki Co Ltd, 2-1 Asahi-machi 2d Dev Dept, Kariya 448-8650, Japan

ZHU, SHENGJIANG, physics educator, researcher; b. Binghai, Jiangsu, China, Feb. 27, 1946; s. Luyuan Zhu and Heying Xia; m. Qing Fan, Oct. 1, 1974; 1 child, Zhu Qiang. BS, Tsinghua U., Beijing, 1970; MS, Tsinghua U., 1982. Rsch. assoc. Nuc. Energy Inst. Tsinghua U., Beijing, 1970-78; tchg. asst., engring. physics dept. Tsinghua U., 1978-82, lectr. physics, 1982-91, assoc. prof. physics, 1991-97, prof. physics, 1997—; rsch. assoc., Vanderbilt U., Nashville, Tenn., 1987-88, vis. scholar, 1994-95, 97-98. Contbr. articles to profl. jours.; inventor in field. Recipient Beijing Sci. Com. prize, 1985, Ministry of Edn. prize, 1998. Mem. Nuc. Physics Soc. China, Nuc. Structure Soc. China, High Energy Physics Soc. China. Avocations: travel, music, swimming. Office: Tsinghua U, Dept Physics, Beijing 100084, China

ZHU, SHIJIE, materials engineer, educator; b. Jilin, China, Aug. 28, 1961; parents Changan Zhu and Yuchun Su; m. E Cui, June 1, 1985; 1 child, Jianyuan. B in Engring., Dalian U. Technology, 1982, M in Engring., 1985, D in Engring. From rsch. fellow to assoc. prof. Inst. Metal Rsch. Chinese Acad. Scis., Shenyang, 1989-92; Humboldt rsch. fellow U. Karlsruhe, Germany, 1992-93; vis. scientist Tech. U. Berlin, 1993; prof. Dalian U. Technology, China, 1994—; vis. rsch. fellow U. Tokyo, 1994-96; rsch. assoc. Nagaoka U. Technology, Japan, 1996-98; assoc. prof. U. Electro-Comms., Tokyo, 1998—. Mem. Minerals, Metals & Materials Soc., Japan Soc. Mech. Engrs., Soc. Materials Sci., Japan Inst. Metals, Am. Ceramic Soc. Office: Dept Mech Engring U Electro-Comm, 1-5-1 Chofugaoka, Chofu Tokyo 182-8585, Japan

ZHU, SHOU-YI, biochemical engineer; b. Nanjing, Jiang-su, China, Mar. 23, 1928; m. Jin Zhi-chun, Apr. 4, 1960; children: Li-peng, Li-jing. BS, U. Nanking, China, 1951. Technician Shanghai Inst. of Ind., 1951-56; from engr. to sr. engr. and prof. Shanghai Inst. of Pharm. Industry, 1957—; mem. biotech. experts com. State Pharm. Adminstrn. of China, 1987—; mem. first session of Experts Com. of Hi-Tech in Biotechnological Field of State Sci. and Tech. Commn., 1986-91. Author: Chemical Engineering Handbook, Vol. 5, 1984, Biosafety and Decontamination, 1998; contbr. articles to profl. jours.; editor Chinese Jour. Biotech., 1985—. Recipient awards for Sci. and Tech. Progress, State Pharm. Adminstrn. of China, 1983, 92, State Sci. Tech. Com., 1993. Mem. Chinese Soc. Biotech. (dir. 1993—). Achievements include process development, equipment design and technical innovation of many important bio-pharmaceuticals for this country, especially anti-tumor antibiotics, steroidal family-planning drugs as well as some traditional Chinese medicine. Avocations: calligraphy, floriculture. Office: Shanghai Inst Pharm Ind, 1320 Beijing Rd W, Shanghai 200040, China

ZHU, SHOUZHENG, engineering educator, academic administrator; b. Shanghai, China, Aug. 16, 1949; child of Zhaochun and Jingmei Yu; m. Youli Wu, Dec. 15, 1976; 1 child, Wei. BSc, E. China Normal U., Shaghai, 1986, MSc, 1992, PhD, 1992. Tchg. asst. E. China Normal U., Shanghai, 1982-87, lectr., 1987-92, assoc. prof., 1992-94, prof., 1994—, dep. chmn. dept. electronic sci. and tech., 1997—; acad. visitor U. Coll. London, 1990-91; vice chmn. Inst. Microwave Power Application, 1997—. Contbr. articles to profl. jours. Mem. IEEE, Chinese Inst. Electronics. Avocations: reading, basketball, traveling. Fax: 86-21-62578792. Office: E China Normal U, 3663 N Zhonshan Rd, Shanghai 200062, China

ZHU, YAO-CHEN, mathematician; b. Zhenjiang, China, Jan. 15, 1942; s. Zai-xing and Xiang-zheng (Sun) Z.; m. Pei-hua Du, Feb. 2, 1970; 1 child. Grad., U. Sci. and Tech. China, Beijing, 1964. Tchr. 108th Middle Sch., Beijing, 1964-72, The 1st Tchrs. Coll., Beijing, 1972-78; from rsch. assoc. to prof. Inst. Applied Math. Acad. Sci., Beijing, 1978-92, prof., 1992—; vis. rsch. assoc. prof. U. Southern Miss., Hattiesburg, 1987. Mem. editl. bd. Advances in Math. (Shuzue Jinzhan), 1996—. Vis. scholar Inst. Henri Poincaré, Paris, 1983. Mem. Am. Math. Soc. Avocation: photography. Office: Inst Applied Math, Inst Applied Math, Zongguancun Haidian Divsn, 100080 Beijing China

ZHU, YONG, mechanical engineer, educator; b. Zhijiang, China, July 28, 1962; s. Yi Qing and Qi Nian (Xian) Z.; m. Mei Tian, Nov. 19, 1994; 1 child, Wending. BS, Jiangsu Inst. Tech., China, 1983; MS, Shanghai U. Mech. Engring., 1986; PhD, Shanghai U., 1991. Asst. lectr. Shanghai U., 1986-88, lectr., 1988-96, assoc. prof., 1996—. Inventor in field; editl. mem. Internat. Jour. of Nonlinear Scis. and Simulation, 2000—. Recipient Nat. Excellent Tchr. award Bao-Steel, 1995, Hu Ying-dong, 1998, Outstanding Resaerch award Chinese End. Commn., 1995,. Mem. Chinese Soc. Mechanics, Chinese Soc. for Indsl. and Applied Math. Office: U Wash Dept Mech Engring Seattle WA 98195-0001

ZHU, YUAN, research scientist; b. Yixing, Jiangsu, China, Sept. 4, 1960; arrived in Germany, 1995; p. Seng-Lin Dai and Jing-Zhuang Zhu; m. Xuming Luan, Sept. 22, 1988; 1 child, Siyang Luan. BS, China Pharm. U., Nanjing, 1982, MS, 1988; PhD, Philipps U., Marburg, Germany, 1998. Tchr. asst. physiology dept. China Pharm. U., Nanjing, 1982-85, lectr. rsch. divsn. pharmacology, 1988-93, assoc. prof. rsch. divsn. pharmacology, 1994-95; rschr. Inst. Pharmacology and Toxicology, Philipps U., Marburg, 1999—. Author: Modulation of Oncogene Expression and Induction of Neurotrophic Factors by A Beta 2-adrenoceptor Agonist Clenbuterol: A New Stratage To Interfere the Neuronal Apoptosis in Vivo; contbr. articles to profl. jours. Recipient Outstanding Sci. Rsch. award Industrie und Handelskammer, Hessen, Germany, 1999. Mem. Soc. for Neurosci. E-mail: zhu@mailer.uni-marburg.de. Fax: 49 6421 2828918. Home: Am Richtsberg 88/409, D-35039 Marburg Germany Office: Philipps U Inst Pharm & Tox, Ketzerbach 63, D-35032 Marburg Germany

ZHU, ZHI SHOU, materials scientist; b. Wenzhou City, Zhejiang, China, Mar. 28, 1966; s. Wei Ji and De Hua (Jiang) Z.; m. Ruo Yu Liu, July 7, 1994. BS, Tianjin (China) U., 1986, MS, 1989, PhD, 1995. Lectr. Tsinghua U., Beijing, 1991-94; rschr. Beijing Inst. Aero. Materials, 1995—; sales sr. exec. Beijing Clever Computer Co. Ltd., 1995-96. Author: Textures of Materials, 1996; contbr. articles to profl. jours. Recipient Award of Basic Rsch. Achievements, Tsinghua U., 1995; Baoshan Steels Corp. grantee, 1992. Mem. AAAS, Chinese Acad. Sci. (sec. 1996—), The Nonferrous Metals Soc. China, Mech. Engring. Soc. China., Chinese Materials Rsch. Soc. (vice dir. youth br. 1997—). Avocations: music, sports, travel, cuisine. Office: Beijing Inst Aero Materials, PO Box 81-15, Beijing 100095, China

ZHU, ZI QIANG, electrical engineer, researcher; b. Ninbao, Zhejiang, China, Sept. 23, 1962; s. Xiao Niao and Xin Hua (Chen) Z.; m. Zhen Ping Xia, Mar. 8, 1987; 1 child, Yeats. B in Engring., Zhejiang U., China, 1982, MS, 1984; PhD, Sheffield U., 1991. Chartered engr., U.K. Lab. officer Zhejiang U., 1984-86, lectr., 1986-88; rsch. sci. Sheffield (Eng.) U., 1989-92, sr. rsch. officer, 1992-97, sr. rsch. scientist, 1997—; vis. rsch. fellow Sheffield U., 1988-89; vis. prof. Hong Kong U., 1999-2000; adv. prof. Shanghai U., 1999—; referee Oxford U. Press, 1993—; co-chmn. Chinese Internat. Conf. on Elec. Machines, Hangzhou, 1995; cons. Control Techniques Dynamics Ltd., 1995—; exec. mem. Sheffield Ctr. for Advanced Magnetic Materials and Devices, 1994—. Author: Analysis and Control of Noise from Electrical Machines, 1987; contbr. articles to profl. jours. Recipient Rsch. Achievement award Chinese Ministry Mech. Industry, 1986, Design and Rsch. Achievement award Chinese Govt. of Zhejiang Province, 1988, Excellent Paper award Chinese Electrotech. Soc., 1992. Mem. IEEE, Inst. Elec. Engrs. (U.K., The Swan Premium award 1995). Avocations: painting, poetry, country music, travel. E-mail: z.q.zhu@sheffield.ac.uk. Home: 60 Alms Hill Rd, Sheffield S11 9RS, England Office: U Sheffield Dept Electronic and Elec Engring, Mappin St, Sheffield S1 3JD, England

ZHU, ZUPEI, chemical engineer, technical advisor; b. Shanghai, China, June 17, 1921; s. Mei Zhu and Huiche Cheng; m. Tianyun Wuou, Oct. 14, 1956; children: Zhu Yung, Zhu Fong. BS in Engring., Zhejiang U., Hangzhou, China, 1944. Asst. engr. North China Portland Cement Co., Beijing, 1945-46; engring. trainee Allis-Chalmers Mfg. Co., Milw., 1947-49; engr. North China Portland Cement Co., 1950-52, Beijing Cement Industry Design Inst., 1953-71; engr. in charge Shandong Cement Industry Design Office, Jinan, China, 1972-82; chief engr. Tianjin (China) Cement Industry

Design and Rsch. Inst., 1982—. Co-translator: R.H. Bogue: The Chemistry of Portland Cement, 2d edit., 1955; editor: Handbook of Process Design of Cement Plant, 1976; co-editor: Manufacturing and Application of Cement, 1994; chief editor Shiuni Jishu, 1982-00. Recipient Design Master award, Ministry Constrn., Beijing, 1989. Home: Beicheng dist, Tianjin 300 400, China Office: Tianjin Cement Industry, Design and Rsch Inst, Tianjin 300400, China

ZHUANG, BING CHANG, biologist, researcher; b. Changbai county, Jilin, China, Dec. 12, 1957; s. Zi Ting Zhunag and Fu Zhen Peng; m. Ling Jie Dong, Jan. 26, 1983; 1 child, Zhe. B, Agr. U., Changchun, China, 1982; M, Agr. U., 1985, PhD, 2000. Technician Agr. Sta., Changbai, China, 1982; asst. prof. Soybean Inst., Gongzhuling, China, 1987-92; assoc. prof. Soybean Inst., Gongzhuling, 1992-95; prof. Biotech. Lab., Gongzhuling, 1996—, dir., 1996—; dir. Physiol. Lab., Gongzhuling, China, 1992-95. Contbr. articles to profl. jours.; inventor in field. Recipient Spl. Allowance State Coun., 1994, 2nd prize State Sci. and Tech. Com., 1996, Ministry Agr., 1987, 1st prize Ministry Agr., 1994, 3rd prize Stae Edn.Commn., 1997, 2d prize Ministry Agr., 1998. Mem. China Soc. Agro-biotech. (mem. coun. 1997), Jilin (China) Soc. Agrl. Biochemistry, Jilin Soc. Botany, Jilin Soc. Genetics. Office: Jilin Acad Agrl Sci, 6 Xixinghua st, 136100 Gongzhuling Jilin, China

ZHUANG, WAN, mathematician, educator; b. Shanghai, China, May 5, 1936; d. Weizhong and Yuan Ying (Shen) Zhuang; m. Yubo Chen, Aug. 1, 1959; children: Yan Chen, Jie Chen. BS, Nanjing Normal U., Peoples Republic China, 1954; MS, Beijing Normal U., Peoples Republic China, 1958. Asst. prof. Shandong Normal U., Jinan, Peoples Republic China, 1954-56, '58-80; assoc. prof. Shandong Normal U., Jinan, 1980-85, prof., 1986—; vis. prof. U. Tex. at Arlington, 1985-86; reviewer Math. Reviews, Mich., U.S., 1987—; referee Acta Mathematica Scientia, Beijing, Annals of Differential Equations, Fuzhou. Author: Ordinary Differential Equations, 1987, Mathematics Physics Equations, 1988, Functional Analysis (with Yubo Chen), 1980, Differential Calculus, 1981, An Elementary Introduction to Calculus, 1983, A Handbook of College Mathematics (with others), 1985; contbr. articles to profl. jours. Dep. The VIIth and VIIIth and IXth Ann. People's Congress of China, Beijing, 1988—. Recipient Disting. Rsch. award, Edn. Com. Shandong Province, 1987, '88, '89, '90, 94, 96, 99, Tchr. prize Com. Edn. Fund of Zeng Xianzi, 1993; named Excellent Tchr. Shandong Normal U., 1985. Avocation: bridge. Office: Shandong Normal U, Math Dept, Shandong Jinan 250014, China

ZHUANG, WEN-YING, mycologist, educator, researcher; b. Beijing, July 27, 1948. MS, Grad. Sch. Academia Sinica, Beijing, 1982; PhD, Cornell U., 1988. Tchr. Shanxi Agrl. Coll., Taigu, China, 1976-78; vis. scientist Cornell U., Ithaca, N.Y., 1983-85, postdoctoral fellow, 1990-91; rsch. assoc. Inst. Microbiology, Academia Sinica, 1981-83, 88-89, assoc. rsch. prof., 1989-93, rsch. prof., 1993—, dir. Systematic Mycology and Lichenology Lab., 1993—. Second author: Flora: Fungorum Sinicorum Vol. 6 Peronosporales, 1998; author Flora Fungorum Sinicorum Vol. 8 Sclerotiniasear et Geoglossacere, 1998; contbr. articles to sci. jours. Mem. Mycol. Soc. China (standing com. 1993—), Internat. Assn. Plant Taxonomy, Brit. Mycol. Soc., Internat. Mycology Assn. (exec. bd. mem. 1998—). Office: Inst Microbiology, Chinese Acad Sc PO Box 2714, Beijing 100080, China

ZHUANG, ZHEN-WAN, chemical engineering educator; b. Shanghai, China, Mar. 31, 1937; s. Ze-Xian Zhuang and Yun-Yu Li; m. Xi-Wei Yu, Apr. 29, 1968; children: Wei, Yu. B in Engring., Tsinghua U., Beijing, 1960. Rsch. fellow Inst. Mechanics Acad. Sinica, Beijing, 1961-64; engr. Chem. Machinery Rsch. Inst., Beijing, 1964-65, Lanzhou, China, 1965-83; assoc. prof. Nanjing (China) Inst. Chem. Tech., 1983-90, prof. chem. engring., 1990—. Editor: English-Chinese Quality Control Dictionary, 1988; contbr. articles to profl. jours. Recipient Project Achievement prize Ministry Chem. Industry China, 1983. Mem. Chinese Soc. Chem. Industry and Engring. (Rsch. Project Achievement prize 1984), Chinese Soc. Engring. Thermophysics, N.Y. Acad. Scis. Office: Nanjing Inst Chem Tech, 5 New Model Rd, 210009 Nanjing Jiangsu, China

ZHUKHOVITSKII, DMITRY IGOREVICH, physicist; b. Magadan, Russia, Mar. 6, 1958; s. Igor Mikhailovich and Maya Mitrofanovna (Ponomareva) Z. Student, Moscow State U., 1981; PhD, Inst. High Temperatures, Moscow, 1986, D of Physics and Math., 1997. Rschr. Inst. High Temperatures, Russian Acad. Sci., Moscow, 1981—. Contbr. articles to profl. jours. Alexander von Humboldt Found. Rsch. fellow, 1991-92. Avocations: music, literature, sport. Home: ul Orshanskaya h8 bl 1 flat 18, 121552 Moscow Russia Office: Inst High Temperatures, ul Izhorskaya 13/19, 127412 Moscow Russia

ZHUKHOVITSKY, VLADIMIR GRIGORIEVICH, physician, researcher; b. Baku, Azerbaijan, USSR, Sept. 5, 1954; s. Grigoriy Yakovlevich Zhukhovitsky and Rogneda Vladimirovna Rabchevskaya; m. Lala Alimovna Zhukhovitskaya, Apr. 9, 1993; children: Vladimir, Yakov. MD, Semashko Moscow Med. Stomatological Inst., 1977; PhD, Sechenov 1st Moscow Med. Inst., 1985; sr. scientist, Cen. Rsch. Inst. Epidemiology, Moscow, 1991. Sr. rschr. Cen. Rsch. Inst. Epidemiology, Moscow, 1986-93; asst. prof. Semashko Moscow Med. Stomatol. Inst., 1978-86, assoc. prof., 1993-95; head of unit Botkin Hosp., Moscow, 1997—; head Russian Helicobacter pylori Study Group, Moscow, 1994-95; guest rschr. Uppsala (Sweden) U., 1995-97; cons. Sechenov Med. Acad., Moscow, 1998—; sr. rschr. Gamaleya Rsch. Inst. for Epidemiology and Microbiology, Moscow, 1999—. Co-author: (book) Helicobacter pylori and peptic ulcer disease. New aspects, 1993 (Botkin prize 1994); co-patentee in field. Personal grantee George Soros Found., 1993. Mem. Am. Soc. for Microbiology, N.Y. Acad. Sci. Avocations: classical music, Brodsky's poetry, chess. Fax: 7 095 945 9906. E-mail: zhukhovitsky@mtu-net.ru. Home: h 22 build 1 apt 133, Kantemirovskaya ul, Moscow 115522, Russia Office: Botkin Hosp, 2nd Botkinsky proezd, Moscow 125101, Russia

ZHUKOV, ANDREI ALEXANDROVITCH, materials scientist, educator; b. Prague, Czechoslovakia, Sept. 15, 1928; arrived in Soviet Union, 1950; s. Alexander Andrevitch and Liudmila Vladimirovna (Gorbunova) Z.; m. Valeria Nikolaievna Soorovova, May 12, 1951 (div. 1960); 1 child, Mikhail; m. Valentina Gruntenko, Aug. 9, 1978; 1 child, Victoria. Degree in chem. engring., Aurora U., Shanghai, 1949; degree in metall. engring. with hons., Moscow Evening Metall. Inst., 1954; PhD, Rsch. Inst. TSNIITMASH, Moscow, 1959; DSc in Tech., Moscow Inst. Steel Alloys, 1968; DSc in Chemistry, Leningrad (USSR) Inst. Tech., 1989. Diplomate engring. Metallurgist China Centrifugal Casting Co., Shanghai, 1949-50; sr. lab. worker, jr. scientific worker Moscow Evening Metall. Inst., 1950-52; rsch. engr. Liublino Foundry Mech. Plant, Moscow, 1952-56; asst. prof. Evening Machine Bldg. Inst., Bauman Inst., Moscow, 1956-60, prof., head of chair/vice-rector and rector ZIL auto-plant, 1971-77, 81-82; head of chairs Briansk (USSR) Inst. Transport Engring., 1977-81; head dept. metals tech., chemistry, tribology State Tech. U. (formerly Vinnitsa Poly. Inst.), Vinnitsa, Ukraine, 1982-98; prof. Moscow State Ind. U., 1998—; dep. head com. cast iron, head subcom. ductile iron Ctrl. Directorate Scientific Technical Soc. Machine Bldg. Industries, Moscow, 1960-80; head metall. lab. Ctrl. Scientific Rsch. Inst. Machine Bldg. for Light Textile Industry, Moscow, 1960-71; pres. sect. hot processing metals Scientific Technical Coun. All-Union Min. Machine Bldg. Light Food Industries and Domestic Appliances, Moscow, 1962-77; Tata Chair prof. Indian Inst. Tech., Kharagpur, 1993-94. Author: Geometrical Thermodynamics of Iron Alloys, 1971 (Lenin Gold medal 1970), 2d edit., 1979, Wear Resistant Castings from Complex-Alloyed White Irons, 1985 (Bronze medal Min. Higher Edn. Ukraine, 1984); author, editor: Cast Iron, 1991; mem. editl. bd. Cast Metals, 1988-97; contbr. more than 800 articles to profl. jours., books, publs.; patentee in field. V.p. Knowledge Soc., Moscow, 1972-76, Briansk, 1978-81. Red Army Res., 1950-80. Recipient Tchernov prize Ctrl. Directorate, 1962, 77, Sobolevsky prize, 1967, Prof. Banerjee Silver medals, 1994,95. Fellow Moscow Foundrymen's Soc. (pres.), All-Union Soc. Inventors Rationalizers; mem. Deutsche Gesellschaft Materialkunde, N.Y. Acad. Scis., Aurore Mondiale Assn. Avocations: music, poetry. Home: Flat 29 21a 1st Dombrovskaya St, 141200 Pushkino Moscow Reg Russia Office: Moscow State Indsl Univ, 16 Avtozavodskaya St, 109280 Moscow Russia

ZHUKOV, OLEG IVANOVICH, chemist, researcher; b. Engels, Russia, Feb. 5, 1969; s. Ivan Nikolaevich and Nina Viktorovna (Goncharova) Z.; m. Olga Borisovna Drozdova, Aug. 15, 1987 (div. Nov. 1991); Natalya Nikolaevna, Jan. 15, 1992. M, Saratov (Russia) State U., 1994, PhD, 1997. Rschr. Chem. Rsch. Inst. Saratov State U., 1989-98; chief engr. Sulfat Ltd., Saratov, 1994-98, Nita-Farm Co., Saratov, 1998—. Contbr. articles to profl. jours.; patentee in field. Mem. Russian Chem. Soc. Avocations: fishing. Fax: 7 8452 247554. E-mail: nita@overta.ru. Office: Nita-Farm Co, Pugachovskaya St 161, 410005 Saratov Russia

ZHUO, JIA LONG, physiologist; b. Nanning, China, Oct. 25, 1956; arrived in Australia, 1984, naturalized, 1994; s. Ju Tang and Feng Zhao (Luo) Z.; m. Xiao Chun Li; children: David, Freda. MD, Guangxi Medical Univ., Nanning, 1983; MSc, Univ. Melbourne, Melbourne, Australia, 1985; PhD, Univ. Melbourne, 1990. Medical officer Guangxi Medical Univ., Nanning, 1982-83, assoc. lectr., 1983-84; rsch. officer Nat. Health and Med. Rsch. Coun. Univ. Melbourne, 1991-92, postdoc. fellow Nat. Health and Med. Rsch. Coun., Austin and Repatriation Med. Ctr., 1993-96, sr. rsch. officer Howard Florey Inst. Exptl. Physiology and Medicine, 1997-99; vis. asst. prof. physiology Tulane U. Sch. Medicine, New Orleans, 1999—. Contbr. numerous articles to profl. jour., chpts. to books. Recipient Overseas Rsch. fellowship Guangxi Gov., 1984, Australian Postdoc. fellowship Nat. Health and Med. Rsch. Coun., Australia, 1993-96, Young Australian Investigators award Internat. Hypertension Soc., 1994; named hon. prof. physiology Guangxi Med. U., 1995. Fellow Australian High Blood Pressure Rsch. Coun.; mem. N.Y. Acad. Scis., Australian Pharmacology Physiology Soc., Australian New Zealand Soc. Nephrology. Avocations: movies, novel reading, gardening, Australian football. Office: Howard Florey Inst, U Melbourne, Parkville Victoria 3052, Australia

ZHUPLATOV, SERGEY BORISOVICH, medical educator, investigator; b. Izhevsk, Russia, May 3, 1961; s. Boris Petrovich Zhuplatov and Tamara Andreyevna Jacobleva; m. Irina Mihkailovna Buthnaryuck, June 3, 1983; children: Ilya, Roman. MD, Izhevsk Med. Acad., 1984; PhD in Medicine, Sverdlovsk Med. Acad., Ecaterinburgh, Russia, 1991. Cert. med. diplomate of top qualification. Clin. fellow internal medicine dept. Izhevsk Med. Sch., 1984-86; clin. rsch. fellow in cardiology Sverdlovsk Med. Acad., Ecaterinburgh, Russia, 1986-89; asst. prof. Izhevsk Med. Inst., 1989-96; dir. Invention Med. Ctr., Izhevsk, 1992—; assoc. prof. Izhevsk Med. Acad., 1996—; vis. prof. Louisville Med. Sch., 1994; mem. Spl. Supporting Bd., Izhevsk, 1995—; cons. Izhmash Hosp., Izhevsk, 1991—. Author: (book) The Hemosorbtion in the Treatment of Diabetes Mellitus with Complications, 1998; contbr. articles to med. jours.; inventor in field. Pres. Fund of Supporting to Lang. Sch., Izhevsk, 1998—. Recipient State Prize of Udmurt Republic of Russia, 1998; grantee Med. Acad. of Sci. of Russia, 1991. Mem. Nat. Soc. Nephrology, Nat. Assn. Endocrinology, Nat. Assn. Cardiology, N.Y. Acad. Scis. Avocations: traveling, photo/video shooting, arts. Fax: 7 3412 510367. E-mail: joe sergey@mail.ru. Home: Vorovsky St 117-29, Izhevsk 426063, Russia Office: Med Acad, S Covalevsky 4a-100, Izhevsk 426000, Russia

ZHURAVEL, ALEXANDER PETROVICH, engineering researcher; b. Kharkov, Ukraine, Nov. 11, 1953; s. Peter Nikolaevich and Antonina Nikitichna (Abraimova) Z.; m. Tatiana Ivanovna Lisitskaya, July 29, 1982; 1 child, Igor Alexandrovich. MS, Aviation Inst., Kharkov, 1977; PhD, B. Verkin Inst. Low Temp., Kharkov, 1990. Engr. B. Verkin Inst. Low Temp., 1977-81, sr. engr., 1983-91, rsch. assoc., 1992-94, sr. rschr., 1994—. Contbr. articles to profl. jours.; patentee in field. Sr. Lt. Russian Air Force, 1981-83. Mem. Ukrainian Phys. Soc. Home: 4 Jankovskaya, 310045 Kharkov Ukraine Office: B Verkin Inst Low Temp, 47 Lenin Ave, 310164 Kharkov Ukraine

ZHURAVLEV, LEONID TIKHONOVICH, physicochemist; b. Moscow, Dec. 6, 1928; s. Tikhon Andreevich and Alexandra Gerasimovna (Stepanova) Z.; m. Anthonina Petrovna Kuznetsova, July 17, 1952 (div. Aug. 1962); children: Igor, Olga; m. Inga Gerasimovna Markelova, Sept. 28, 1962; children: Inna, Yaroslava. Grad., State U. Moscow, 1952; PhD, Inst. Phys. Chemistry USSR Acad. Scis., Moscow, 1965. Engr., physicist Plant of Nuclear Fuel, Russia, 1953-56; jr. rschr. Inst. Phys. Chemistry, USSR Acad. Sci., 1959-67, sr. rschr., 1967—; dep. chief dept. phys. methods investigation Inst. Phys. Chemistry, USSR Acad. Scis., 1965-79, chief sci. group mass spectrometry, 1965-88, mem. sect. sci. coun., 1967-88, sci. cons., expert, 1988—. Author: The Zhuravlev Model of the Surface Chemistry of Silica, Science Book Translator; co-author: Experiment. Methods in Adsorption and Molecular Chromatography, 1973, The Colloid Chemistry of Silica, ACS, 1994; contbr. articles to profl. jours. Recipient prize USSR Coun. Mins., 1955, 84, medal USSR Exhbn. of Nat. Economy Achievements, 1970, 2 USSR medals, 1970, 88, a Russian Order, 1994, Tittle of USSR Inventor, 1984. Office: Russian Acad Scis, Leninsky Prospect 31, 117915 Moscow Russia

ZHURAVLYOV, ANATOLII FOMITCH, physicist; b. Njandoma, Archangel, Russia, Oct. 20, 1946; s. Foma Ivanovitch and Valentine Jakovlevna (Popova) Z.; m. Elena Georgievna Masic, June 6, 1970 (dec. Oct. 1994); childrern: Irina, Olga; m. Raisa Nikolaevna Kostuchenko, Dec. 29, 1995. M in Physics, Moscow State U., 1971; Candidate Phys. and Math. Scis., Nat. Acad. Scis. Ukraine, Kiev, 1977. Cert. sr. rschr. Acad. Scis. USSR. Sr. engr. Geophys. Inst., Acad. Sci. Ukraine, Kiev, 1972-73; rschr. Inst. for Metal Physics, Acad. Sci. Ukraine, 1972-80, sr. rschr., 1980-95; sr. rschr. Inst. for Magnetism Nat. Acad. Sci. Ukraine, 1995—; author, dir. Ukrainian TV, Kiev, 1979-92; cons. ency. dictionary Solid State Physics, Kiev, 1985-99. Grantee Jour. Soros, 1995; recipient Ukrainian Republic Premium award for Young Scis., 1979, USSR medal "In Memory of 1500 Years of Kiev", 1982. Mem., Soc. of Free Travellers of USSR, 1991—, Natl. Geographic Soc., 1998—. Avocations: mountaining, diving, alpine skiing. E-mail: zhur@im.imag.kiev.ua. Fax: 38 044 4441020. Office: Inst for Magnetism, Vernadskii 36-b, 252680 Kiev Ukraine

ZHVAKOLIUK, YURY V., economist; b. Armiansk, Ukraine, Aug. 18, 1970; s. Victor P. and Galina V. (Afonina) Z.; m. Aset Saidachmedovna Galtakova, Nov. 13, 1993 (div. June 30, 1995); 1 child, Yury; m. Elena V. Lobacheva, Dec. 29, 1995. B, Odessa Fin. Coll., Odessa, Ukraine, 1997. Jr. seargent Military Airforce, Odessa, 1989-91; fin. dir. Printing Co., Simferopol, 1992-93; odd jobs Form Express, Simferopol, 1991-92; pres. Printing House, Simferopol, 1993-97; currency trader Hanford Enterprises; fin. cons.; bus. cons. Am. Cons. League, 1997. Author: Businessman's Help, 1993, About George Soros' Reflection Theory, 1997, TVT School Book 1 Five Rarities, 1999, Business for the Beginners, 2000, The Internal Trade on the Market Forex, 2000. Recipient Hon. Acedemician award Energy Acad., 1997. Avocations: Alpinist, poetry. E-mail address: igor@form.crimea.ua. Office: Simferopol Form Express Co, 3 Bakhchisarayskaya Str, Simferpol Crimea 95015, Ukraine

ZHVANIA, ZURAB, Georgian government official; b. Tbilisi, Dec. 9, 1963; married; 1 child. Student, State U. Sr. lab. asst., petty sci. worker Dept. Human and Mammal Physiology, 1985-92; mem. Parliament Govt. of Georgia, Tbilisi, 1992—, chmn., 1995, spkr. Parliament, 1996—. Founder Greenpeace, Georgia; chmn. Ctrl. Coun. Georgia's Greens, 1988-93; spkr. Party of Greens, 1992-93; co-chmn. European Union Greens, 1992-93; sec. gen. Citizens' Union Georgia, 1993—. Office: Office of Govt Parliament, Rustaveli 8, 380018 Tbilisi Georgia*

ZIA, SOHAIL, design engineer, educator; b. Kasur, Punjab, Pakistan, Apr. 12, 1956; parents Hussain and Surayya Hussain Sheikh. BSc, Govt. Nat. Coll., Karachi, Pakistan, 1978; MSc, U. Karachi. Instrumentation design cons. Thal Jute Mills, Muzaffargarh, Pakistan, 1981-83, Nat. Fibres, Karachi, 1983-84; CEO, design engr. Approvision Rsch., Karachi, 1989—; Karachi, 1985-88; vis. instr. Petroman, Karachi, 1983-84, ICMA, Karachi, 1984, PNS JAUHAR, Karachi, 1983-85; designer Approvision Rsch., Karachi. Designer: (electronics design) Electronic Aid Instruments for the Blind, 1979, Electronic Aid Instruments for the Deaf by Birth, 1979; sr. reporter Computer News, 1998-99. Recipient Gold medal Pakistan Assn. Scientists and Sci. Professions, 1973, 74, Young Scientist award PYSO, 1973. Avocations: experimentation, rowing, wind surfing, ethical discussions. Office: Approvision Rsch, 216 Clifton Ctr, Karachi Sind 75600, Pakistan

ZIAJA, WIESLAW SZCZEPAN, geographer; b. Huwniki, Poland, Oct. 10, 1956; s. Jan and Stefania (Frankiewicz) Z.; m. Jadwiga Krystyna Ichas, Jan. 10, 1987; three children. MA in Geography, Jagiellonian U., 1979, PhD, 1988. From asst. rschr. to lectr. geography Jagiellonian U., Cracow, Poland, 1979—. Mem. Polish Geographical Soc., Internat. Glaciol. Soc., European Arctic Ecol. Rsch. Roman Catholic. Avocations: explorative travels, political history, cycling. Office: Jagiellonian U, Inst Geography Grodzka 64, Krakow 31-044, Poland

ZIARATI, REZA, dean; b. Sary, Gilan, Iran, Jan. 30, 1952; arrived in U.K., 1971; s. Javad and Robab (Lazempoor) Z.; m. Zena Rosemary Kendall, Nov. 2, 1973; 1 child, Martin Afshin. BSc with honors, Bath (Eng.) U., 1976, MSc, 1977, PhD, 1979; Cert. Edn., Portsmouth U., 1983. Rschr. Holset/Bath U., 1977-79; sr. engr. Lucas, Gloucester, Eng., 1979-81; sr. lectr. Highbury Coll., Portsmouth, Eng., 1981-83; head sch. West Glamorgan Inst. Higher Edn., Swansea, Eng., 1983-85; head dept. Southampton Inst. Higher Edn., Eng., 1985-89; dean, assoc. dean U. Ctrl. Eng., Birmingham, 1989-96; acad. dir. Dogus Inst., Istanbul, Turkey, 1996—; pro-rector Dogus U., Istanbul, 1996—; sr. specialist, advisor European Union/EMployment Dept. British Govt., 1985—; lead examiner Bus. and Tech. Edn. Coun., London, 1989—; prof. CIMTEL, Birmingham, 1991-93, DELCAM, Birmingham, 1991-93. Contbr. articles to profl. jours., chpts. to books. Advisor EU, Europe, 1985—, ED, London, 1985—, Oman Govt., 1989—, Gibraltar Govt., 1989-94. Recipient Eureka award Coun. Ministers, 1991, Enterprise award UKTECNET, 1988. Fellow Inst. Elec. Engrs. U.K., Inst. Mech. Engrs. U.K.; mem. Engring. Assembly (rep. 1994—), Bus. Tech. Edn. Coun. (engring. adv. com. 1989-94), European Commn. (Eurotechet project dir. 1985—). Avocations: swimming, football, martial arts, tennis, reading. Office: Dogus U, Zeamet Acibadem, 8010 Kadikoy Istanbul, Turkey

ZICK, LEONARD OTTO, accountant, manufacturing executive, consultant; b. St. Joseph, Mich., Jan. 16, 1905; s. Otto J. and Hannah (Heyn) Z.; m. Anna Essig, June 27, 1925 (dec. May 1976); children: Rowene Neidow (Mrs. A.C. Neidow), Arlene (Mrs. Thomas Anton), Constance Mae (Mrs. Hilary Snell), Shirley Ann (Mrs. John Vander Ley) (dec.); m. Genevieve Evans, Nov. 3, 1977 (dec. Nov. 1996); m. Vera H. Helscher, Dec. 6, 1997. Student, Western State U., Kalamazoo, Mich. Sr. ptnr. Zick, Campbell & Rose Accts. (and predecessor firms), South Bend, Ind., 1928-48; sec., treas. C.M. Hall Lamp Co., Detroit, 1948-51, pres., 1951-54; chmn. bd., 1954-56; pres., treas., dir. Allen Electric & Equipment Co. (now Allen Group, Inc.), Kalamazoo, 1957-61; fin. v.p., treas., dir., chmn. bd. Crampton Mfg. Co., 1961-63; mgr. corp. fin. dept. Manley, Bennett, McDonald & Co., Detroit, 1963-68; mgr. Leonard O. Zick & Assocs., Holland, Mich., 1968-88. Contbg. editor: Cost Accountants Hand Book. Former mem. Mich. Rep. Cen. Com.; trustee YMCA Found., Clearwater, Fla., Richard E. Byrd Ctr., Boston; vice chmn. Army-Navy Munitions Bd., 1941-42, asst. to vice chmn. War Prodn. Bd., 1941-43; chmn. Greater Holland United Fund. Mem. Inst. Mgmt. Accts. (past nat. v.p., dir.), Mich. Self Insurers Assn. (past pres.), Fin. Execs. Inst., Stuart Cameron McLeod Soc. (past pres.), Union League (Chgo.), Soc. Automotive Engrs. (chmn. lighting com.), Rotary (Paul Harris fellow), Holland Country Club, Macawtwa Bay Yacht Club. Lutheran. Home: 314 Hunters Run Cir Holland MI 49423-2208

ZICKFELD, ROGER, medical products executive; b. L.A., Nov. 20, 1955; m. Cahterine Zickfeld; three children. BS magna cum laude, U. So. Calif., 1977; MBA, UCLA, 1982. CPA, Calif. Cons. mgr. KPMG, L.A., 1982-87; sr. v.p., CFO Karl Storz Endoscopy, Culver City, Calif., 1987—; pres. Karl Storz Lithotripsy, Culver City, 1997—. Bd. dirs. L.A. Chamber Orch., 1999—. Mem. Fin. Execs. Inst. Fax: 310-559-3218.

ZIDARU, CONSTANTIN, transportation executive, petroleum engineer; b. Commune Gorgota, Prahova, Romania, Aug. 1, 1949; s. Ion and Elena (Andrei) Z.; m. Niculina Coman, Aug. 26, 1973; children: Marius, Felicia. Engr., Oil/Gas Drilling/Prodn. Fac., Bucharest, Romania, 1972; student oil entities mgmt., The Tng. Ctr., Bucharest, Romania, 1990. Investments dept. head I.T.T.C. (Conpet S.A.), Ploñesti, Romania, 1972-83; gen. mgr. I.T.T.C. (Conpet S.A.), Ploñesti, 1990—; engr. Petroleum Ministry, Ploñesti, 1984-90; mem. leading com. Romanian Oil Concordia Consortium, 1998, nat. com. Oil World Congrs., 1993. Author: Aspects of the Oil Pipeline Transporting History in Romania, 1999. Mem. leading com. Romania at Crossroads forum, 1997. Mem. Orthodox Ch. Avocations: football, Formula 1. Office: SC Conpet SA, # 7 Independentei Blvd, 2000 Ploñesti 2000, Romania

ZIDORN, CHRISTIAN HERMANN WILHELM, pharmacologist; b. Aachen, Germany, Dec. 23, 1968; s. Georg and Gertrud (Trachterna) Z.; m. Alexa Christine Kuhns, Dec. 19, 1998; 1 child, Julius. Grad., U. Dusseldorf, 1995; MSc, U. Innsbruck, 1998. From staff asst. to asst. U. Innsbruck, Austria, 1995—. Office: Inst Pharmacy U Innsbruck, Innrein 52, A-6020 Innsbruck Tyrel, Austria

ŽIDOVEC LEPEJ, SNEZANA KLEMENTINA, biological scientist; b. Zagreb, Croatia, Jan. 11, 1971; d. Zdravko and Lubica (Krajnovic) ŽZidovec; m. Renato Lepej, Sept. 18, 1999; 1 cild, Glorija. BA in Molecular Biology, U. Zagreb, 1993, MSc in Biol. Scis., 1997. Cert. in molecular biology. Head Lab. for Interferon, Inst. Immunology, Zagreb, 1993-98; head Lab. for Flow Cytometry, Univ. Clinic for Infectious Diseases F. Minalevic, Zagreb, 1998—. Mem. Internat. Soc. for Interferon Cytokine Rsch. Home: Bašjanova 54, 10000 Zagreb Croatia Office: Univ Clin Infectious Dis, Mirogojsva 8, 10000 Zagreb Croatia

ZIĘBIK, ANDRZEJ JÓZEF, energy engineering educator, researcher; b. Strzemieszyce, Poland, Oct. 19, 1939; s. Józef and Maria (Krzętowska) Z.; m. Anna Maria Bagińska; children: Katarzyna, Grzegorz. MSc, Tech. U. Silesia, Gliwice, Poland, 1963, PhD, 1969, DSc, 1976. Rsch. asst. Tech. U. Silesia, 1963-69, asst. prof. energy engring., 1970-76, assoc. prof. energy engring., 1977-86, prof. energy engring., 1987—; vice-dir. Inst. Thermal Tech., Gliwice, 1979-93, dir., 1993—; mem. cons. coun. of the Energy Regulatory Authority. Author: Mathematical Modelling of Energy Management Systems in Industrial Plants, 1990; main author: Industrial Waste Energy Utilization and Equipment, 1993 (in Polish); co-author: Selected Problems of Industrial Energy Management, 1976 (in German), Fundamentals of Thermal Engineering, 1998 (in Polish); contbr. articles to profl. jours. Mem. Solidarity, Gliwice, 1980—. Recipient rsch. grants. Polish Ministry Sci. and Edn., 1977, 78. Mem. Polish State Com. Scientific Rsch., Polish Acad. Scis. (v.p. com. thermodynamics and combustion 1993—, bd. dirs. com. energy problems 1993—). Roman Catholic. Avocations: classical music, mountaineering, skiing. Home: Szmaragdowa 16, 44-121 Gliwice Silesia, Poland Office: Tech Univ Silesia, Konarskiego 22, 44-101 Gliwice Silesia, Poland

ZIEGE, CHRISTIAN, soccer player; b. Feb. 1, 1972. Midfielder, defender Bayern Munich, to 1998; midfielder AC Milan, Italy, 1998-99, Liverpool (Eng.) FC, 2000—, German Nat. Team, Frankfurt. Office: German Football Assn, Otto-Fleck-Schneise 6 Postfach 710265, 60492 Frankfurt Am Main Germany*

ZIEGELMAYER, GERFRIED WILHELM, anthropology professor; b. Saarbrücken, Fed. Republic Germany, June 4, 1925; s. Karl and Katharina (Meyer) Z.; m. Eva-Marie Saller, 1953; children: Sebastian, Sabine, Stephan, Christoph, Cordula. Student, U. Berlin, 1943, U. Prague, Czechoslovakia, 1944, U. Hamburg, Fed. Republic of Germany, 1946; DrMed, U. Freiburg, Fed. Republic of Germany, 1949; DrRerNat, U. Munich, Fed. Republic Germany, 1952. Prof. anthropology and human genetics U. Munchen, Fed. Republic of Germany, 1963, mem. mgmt. team Inst. Anthropology and Human Genetics, 1969-83; dir. Anthropologische Staatssammlung, Munchen, 1983-90. Contbr. numerous articles to profl. jours. Mem. Gesellschaft fur Anthropologie und Human Genetik (pres. 1984-85, 86-87), Gesellschaft fur Human Genetics, European Anthropol. Assn. Avocations: art of painting, classical music. Home: Kuckuckweg 3, D-82152 Krailling Germany Office: Inst fur Anthropologie, Inst fuer Anthropologie, Richard Wagner Str 10, D-8033 Munchen Germany

ZIEGELMEIER, PATRICIA KAY, music educator, executive secretary; b. Colby, Kans., July 14, 1944; d. Lon Elmer and Mary Marie (Saddler) Sowers; m. Carl Ernest Ziegelmeier, June 9, 1963; children: Matt, Steve, Lisa, Amy, Lori. BA in Music Edn., U. Wyo., 1967; MS in Ednl. Adminstrn., Ft.

Hays State U., 1991. Tchr. music, sub. tchr. Golden Plains Schs., Rexford, Kans., 1969-72; pvt. piano instr. Gem, Kans., 1972-87; ch. organist Gem and Colby, Kans., 1968—; instr. music Colby C.C., 1988—. Cmty. leader 4-H, Gem, 1980-88, 99—; bd. dirs. Thomas County Ext. Coun., Colby, 1982-86, 94-95. Mem. NEA, Music Tchrs. Nat. Assn., Kans. Music Tchrs. Assn. (bd. dirs. 1981—, exec. sec. 1987—, Outstanding Tchr. award 1994), Western Plains Arts Assn. (exec. dir. 1989—), Northwest Kans. Piano Assn. (clinic chair 1973—). Methodist. Avocations: reading, music listening, playing piano, walking. E-mail: patz@colby.ixks.com. Office: Kans Music Tchrs Assn 2154 County Road 27 Gem KS 67734-9008

ZIEGERT, BURKHARD WERNER, government official; b. Berlin, Aug. 16, 1945; s. Egbert and Margot (Kierdorf) Z.; m. Eva-Maria Hormuth, June 4, 1987; 1 child, Svenja-Christina. Abitur, Canisius Coll., Berlin, 1965; law degree, Free U., Berlin, 1970; postgrad., Berlin Kammergericht, 1973. Faculty asst. law dept. Free U., Berlin, 1970-72; atty. Esso Ag, Hamburg, Fed. Republic Germany, 1973-75; pvt. practice Berlin, 1975-81; instr. Law Coll., Rhineland/Palatia, 1981-87; legal advisor State Govt. Berlin, 1987-91; fund mgr. (compensation fund) Fed. Treasury, Berlin, 1991—. Author: Local Tax System, 1986. Am. Field Svc. scholar, 1962. Avocations: tennis, golf. Home: Oberhaardter Weg 27, D-14193 Berlin Germany

ZIEGLER, FRANZ, mechanical engineer educator; b. Wiener Neustadt, Austria, Dec. 12, 1937; s. August and Elisabeth (Payer) Z.; m. Waltraud Eberlein, Mar. 31, 1962; children: Robert F., Eva C. Diploma in mech engring., Tech. U., Vienna, Austria, 1961, DS, 1964, dozent of mechanics, 1971; DS (hon.), St. Petersburg State Tech. U., 1996. Cert. engr. With Engr. Material Testing Sta., Vienna, 1961-62; asst. prof. Tech. U., Vienna, 1962-72; prof. Tech. U., 1972—; cons. European and US Industry, 1964—. Author: Tech-Mechanics of Solids and Fluids, 1985, 3d edit., 1998; editor: (sci jour.) Acta Mechanica, 1983—, (procs.) IUTAM-Symposium on Nonlinear Stochastic Engring. Sys., 1988. Chmn. Nat. Com. T & A Mechanics, Vienna, 1986-93; sec. gen. Internat. Union Theoretical and Applied Mechanics ICSU, 1992-96. Recipient fellowship Max Kade Found., Northwestern U., 1967-68. Fellow ASME, Russian Acad. Natural Scis. (fgn.); mem. Internat. Inst. Acoustics and Vibrations (dir. 1999—), Austrian Acad. Scis., Austrian Assn. Earthquake Engring. (chmn. 1980—), Assn. for Applied Math. and Mechanics, Russian Acad. Scis. (fgn., academician), Assn. Applied Math. and Mechanics (pres. 1996-99, v.p. 1999—), Österr. Math Assn. Avocations: sailing, skiing. Office: Tech Univ, Wiedner-Haupstr 8-10 E 201, A-1040 Vienna Austria

ZIEGLER, HOLGER, film scholar; b. Würzburg, Bayern, Germany, Feb. 17, 1966; s. Erwin Ziegler and Marianne Kirchner. Final exam., Hessenkolleg, Frankfurt, Germany, 1992. Film scholar Johann Wolfgang Goethe-U./Inst. Filmwissenschaft, Frankfurt, 1994—; participant ARCHIMEDIA Network; cons., ptnr. Filmtheater Valentin, Frankfurt, 1994—. Co-author: (book) Star Wars, 1999. Mem. Gesellschaft für Film und Fernsehwissenschaft. Avocation: cinema. Fax: 49 69 79828451. E-mail: h.ziegler@tfm.uni-frankfurt.de. Office: Inst Filmwissenschaft, Dantestr 5, 60325 Frankfurt Hessen, Germany

ZIEGLER, MARGARET SANBORN, recreation facility executive, educator; b. Boston, Apr. 2, 1943; d. Alfred and Margaret Elizabeth (Parker) Z. BA, Bates Coll., 1964; postgrad., Wheaton Coll., 1964-66; MS, Ind. U., 1972. Unit dir. supplemental recreation activities overseas ARC, Pleiku, Republic of Vietnam, 1966-67; dir. Camp Nawaka, Otis, Mass., 1970-71; vis. prof. U. Mass., Amherst, 1973-74; exec. dir. Highland Valley Elder Svc. Ctr., Northampton, Mass., 1975-77; infoline coord., acting dir. N.H. Social Welfare Coun., Concord, 1978-80; prof. Franklin Pierce Coll., Rindge, N.H., 1980—; owner, mgr. Field 'n Forest Recreation, Hancock, Harrisville, N.H., 1977—; com. mem. N.H. Joint Promotional Program, Concord, N.H., 1978-92. Chair bd. trustees Cathedral of the Pines, Rindge, 1990-94, chair exec. com., 1994-98, trustee, incorporator, 1987—. Mem. N.H. Travel Coun. (bd. dirs. 1978—), N.H. Camp Ground Owners Assn. (bd. dirs. 1977-84, pres. 1978-80), Monadnock Travel Coun. (pres. 1992-98), C. of C. Avocations: traveling, reading, cooking. Office: Franklin Pierce Coll College Rd Rindge NH 03461-0060

ZIEGLER, ROBERT FRANZ, oil company engineer; b. Vienna, Austria, Feb. 17, 1963; s. Franz and Waltraud Ziegler; children: Alexander Maximilian, Nina Sophia. MS, Leoben (Austria) Mining U., 1992. Cert. econ. engr., value engr. Asst. Leoben Mining U., 1988-90; rsch. engr. Shell Rsch. Rijswijk, Netherlands, 1990-91, 91-93; project engr. Thai Shell E&P, Bangkok, 1991; protection technologist Petroleum Devel. Oman, Muscat, 1993-96; offshore drilling specialist P.D.O.-Shell-Congo, Pointe-Noire, 1996-97; offshore sr. drilling engr. Chevron-Cabinda, 1997—. Gen. sec. Young Austrians for Nuclear Energy, Vienna, 1982-92. Served to capt., inf. Austrian Army, 1981-83. Decorated DSM (Austria); Austrian Industry Fedn. scholar, 1990. Mem. Soc. Petroleum Engrs. (pres. 1989-91, Disting. svc. award 1990, 91), Austrian Industry Fedn., Austrian Soc. Econ. Engring., MWD Soc., Soc. Profl. Well Log Analysts. Roman Catholic. Avocations: yachting, skiing, flying. Home: Peter Jordan St 145/2/5, Vienna A-1180, Austria

ZIEGLER, ROLF, biochemist, biologist; b. Goeppingen, Germany, Dec. 11, 1940; s. Friederich Heinerich and Klara Maria (Lang) Z. PhD, Koeln, Germany, 1971; Habilitation, Berlin, Germany, 1979. Asst. prof. Berlin, Germany, 1974-80, prof., 1980-84; rsch. assoc. Kingston, Ont., Can., 1985-86; rsch. asst. prof. dept. biochemistry U. Ariz., Tucson, 1986-97; with Wiss. Mitavbeiter, Halle, Germany, 1997—. Contbr. articles to Nature, Biochem. Biophys. Rsch. Communications, Pesticide Biochem. Physiology, Peptids. Mem. AAAS, Entomol. Soc. Am., German Soc. Biol. Chemistry, German Zool. Soc. Achievements include activation of glycogen phosporylase by cold for the formation of glycerol as an antifreeze; sequence of the adipokinetic hormone from Manduca sexta. Office: Martin-Luther U Halle Inst Zoology, Domplatz 4, 06108 Halle Sachsen-Auhalt, Germany

ZIEGLER, RONALD LOUIS, former association and government official, writer; b. Covington, Ky., May 12, 1939; s. Louis Daniel and Ruby (Parsons) Z.; m. Nancy Lee Plessinger, July 30, 1960; children: Cynthia Lee Charas, Laurie Michelle Albright. Student, Xavier U., 1957-58; BS, U. So. Calif., 1961; DSc (hon.), Mass. Coll. Pharmacy, 1989, L.I. U., 1993. With Procter & Gamble Distbg. Co., 1961; account rep. J. Walter Thompson Co., 1962-68; press dir. Calif. Rep. Central Com., 1961-62; press aide to Richard Nixon in Calif. gubernatorial campaign, 1962; press aide staff Richard Nixon, 1968-69; press sec. to Pres. Nixon, 1969-74, asst. to, 1973-74; mng. dir., sr. v.p. internat. services Syska and Hennessy, Inc., Washington, 1975-80; pres. Nat. Assn. Truck Stop Operators, Alexandria, Va., 1980-87; pres., CEO, Nat. Assn. Chain Drug Stores, Alexandria, 1987-98; ret., now writer, 1998—; mem. nat. adv. bd. U. Okla.; adv. coun. Pharm. Found. U. Tex. Bd. dirs. Nat. Coun. on Patient Info. and Edn., Nat. Conf. on Pharm. Assns., Richard Nixon Libr. and Birthplace. Mem. Am. Soc. Assn. Execs., Nat. Retail Fedn. (bd. dirs.), Pharmacists Against Drug Abuse, Assn. White House Press Secs., Nat. Orgn. Rare Disorders, Sigma Chi Alumni.

ZIEHEN, WOLFGANG, soil scientist; b. Frankfurt, Germany, Apr. 30, 1935; s. Moritz Theodor Eduard and Hertha Ziehen. Dr.rer.nat., Johannes Gutenberg U., Mayence, Germany, 1968. Aux. asst. Geog. Inst. U. Mayence, Germany, 1960-61; asst. editor lexicon staff Bibliograph Inst. AG, Mannheim, Germany, 1961-62; sci. vol. bot. sect. Natural History Mus. Senckenberg, Frankfurt, 1968-69; asst. editor lexicon staff F.A. Brockhaus AG, Wiesbaden, Germany, 1969; asst. editor Bundesforschungsanstalt fuer Landeskunde Raumordnung, Bad Godesberg, Germany, 1969-71; adminstrv. officer Natural History Mus. Senckenberg, Frankfurt, 1973-79; sci. investigator, 1980—. Author: Wald und Steppe in Rheinhessen, 1968, 70, The Sand-Patch of Ponta de São Lourenço Madeira, 1981, Thomas Erastus: Epistula de natura, materia, ortu atque usu lapidis sabulosi qui in Palatinatu ad Rhenum reperitur, Basileae 1572, Als Beitrag zur Geschichte der Bodenkunde zum 400, Todestag von Thomas Erastus im Faksimile neu herausgegeben, übersetzt, mit Anmerkungen versehen, eingeleitet von W.Z., 99 S., Aalen, 1984, Zur Biochemie und Biophysik der Migräne Erkenntnisse an meinem eigene Körper, Mit einem Exkurs: Zur Irrealität von Psyche, und zur Biochemie nd Biophysik der Schizophrenie, von Blau und Rot und der Paedasterie, 1998. Mem. Freies Deutsches Hochstift, Deutsche Bodenkundliche Gesellschaft, Internat. Union Soil Sci., Deutsche Quartärvereinigung, Rheinische Naturforschende Gesellschaft, Senckenberg Naturforschende Gesellschaft, Geologische Vereinigung, Deutsche Geologische Gesellschaft, Gesellschaft für Umweltgeowissenschaften, Planetary Soc. Avocations: photography, music, political life, economy media. Home: Georg-Philipp-Gail Str 11, 35394 Giessen Germany

ZIEL, WULFHILD ELISABETH, Slavonicist, philosopher, researcher; b. Leipzig, Saxony, Germany, May 20, 1942; d. Henrik Emil and Irmgard Martha (Laussmann) Denert; m. Freddy Bernard Ziel; children: Lars-Gunnar, Corrie Barbara. Grad., Coll. Potsdam, Germany, 1968, ednl. diploma, 1969; Doctorate, U. Humboldt, Berlin, 1974. Tchr. Secondary Sch., Glesien, Germany, 1960-63, Rostock, Germany, 1963-65; ednl. diploma tchr. Secondary Sch., Berlin, 1968-77; Slavonical rschr. Inst. for History, Berlin, 1978-91, Devel. Program, Berlin, 1992-93, Devel. Program for Dresden and German Rsch. Cmty., Leipzig, Germany, 1994-97. Author: Der russische Volksbilderbogen in Bild und Text-ein kultur-u kunsthistor Intermedium, 1996-98, überarbeitete u erweiterte Auflage, 1998; editor: Bibliographien zu V. Propp u N.J. Tolstoi, 1995, VCRW, 1995-98, Bibliographien zur ostslawisch-folkloristischen Volksdichtung, 1996, Ziukerarbiuerw Auflage, 1998. Mem. AJLA, LSP, SIEF. Avocations: geology, archeology, costumes, handcraft museum. Home: Mundolfstr 08, 12524 Berlin Germany Office: Inst Slavistic, Augustusplatz 09, 04109 Leipzig Saxony, Germany

ZIELIŃSKI, JERZY STANISŁAW, scientist, electrical engineering educator; b. Łódź, Poland, Oct. 27, 1933; s. Jakub and Janina (Bocheńska) Z.; m. Jadwiga Wesołowska, Sept. 1, 1961; 1 child, Wojciech. MSc CEng, Tech. U., Łódź, 1956, PhD, 1964, DSc, 1969. Asst. Tech. U. Łódź, 1956-60, asst. lectr. tech., 1960-64; lectr. Tech. U., Łódź, 1964-70, asst. prof. engring., 1970-80; asst. prof. engring. Tech. U., Lublin, Poland, 1976-82, assoc. prof., 1982-86; U. Łódź, 1982-90, prof., head dept. informatics, 1990—, dep. dean mgmt. faculty, 1994-96, prof. in Salesian Order Higher Sch. Econs. and Mgmt., 1996-97; prof. Coll. Informatics, 1997-98; cons. Power Inst., Warsaw, 1973, Rsch. Ctr. Automatic, Łódź, 1987-91, Power Co., Zamość, 1988—, rsch. dir., Rsch. Ctr. Automatic, Łódź, 1991—. Author: Trans. Analysis in Electrical Power Systems with Application of the Method of Characteristics, 1975, Overvoltage in Electrical Power Systems Computation with Application of Analog and Digital Computers, 1985; (textbook) Analog and Digital Modeling, 1980, System Engineering, 1984; co-author: Intelligent Knowledge Based Systems in Electrical Power Engineering, 1997; co-author, editor: Intelligent Systems in Management, 1999; editor Acta Universitatis Lodziensis, Folia Informatica; author, co-author more than 200 papers and reports. Recipient Sci. award Polish Acad. Sci., 1966, Sci. award Minn. Higher Edn., 1965, 76, Sci. award Polish Soc. Theoretical and Applied Electrotechnics, 1963-68, Sci. award Rectors of Univs., Tech. U., Łódź, 1969, 70, 73, Tech. U. Lublin, 1981-84, U. Łódź, 1985-88. Mem. IEEE, Assn. Polish Electricians (expert Disting. Silver and Gold decorations), Polish Soc. Informatics, Polish Soc. Theoretical and Applied Electrotechnics, Łódź Sci. Soc., Sci. Soc., Econ. Informatics. Roman Catholic. Avocations: music, cycling, walking, stamp-collecting. Home: 99/101 m 63 Narutowicza, 90-145 Łódź Poland Office: U Łódź, 39 Rewolucji 1905, 90-214 Łódź Poland

ZIELINSKI, PAUL BERNARD, grant program administrator, civil engineer; b. West Allis, Wis., Sept. 9, 1932; s. Stanley Charles and Lottie Charlotte (Pliszkiewicz) Z.; m. Monica Theresa Beres, July 13, 1957; children: Daniel Paul, Gregory John, Robert Mathias, Sarah Ann. BSCE, Marquette U., 1956; MS, U. Wis., 1961, PhD, 1965. Registered profl. engr., Wis., S.C. Asst. instr. engring. mechanics Marquette U., Milw., 1956-59, asst. prof., 1964-67; instr. civil engring. U. Wis., Madison, 1959-64; from asst. prof. to prof. Clemson (S.C.) U., 1967-78, prof. environ. and systems engring., 1978-82, prof. civil engring., 1982-90, prof. emeritus, 1991—; dir. S.C. Water Resources Rsch. Inst., Clemson, 1978-90; assoc. dir. associateship grant program Nat. Rsch. Coun., Washington, 1990—; cons. Am. Pub. Works Assn., Chgo., 1973-76, Nat. Coun. Examiners of Engring. and Surveying, Clemson, 1973—; cons. swirl devices for storm water separation; com. on exams for profl. engrs. Author numerous publs. on hydraulics and water resources rsch. Chmn. Clemson City Planning Commn., 1971-74; ex-officio mem. S.C. Water Resources Commn., Columbia, 1978-90. Mem. ASCE, Sigma Xi. Roman Catholic. Home: 2111 Wisconsin Ave NW Apt 717 Washington DC 20007-2278 Office: Nat Rsch Coun 2101 Constitution Ave NW Washington DC 20418-0007

ZIELKE, ROLAND JÜRGEN, mathematics educator, physician; b. Opladen, Germany, July 30, 1946; s. Edmund and Lieselotte (Wittke) Z.; 1 child, Andrea. MS, Ohio State U., 1969; PhD, U. Konstanz, Germany, 1971; MD, U. Munster, Germany, 1983. Asst. prof. U. Tubingen, Germany, 1971-75; prof. math. U. Osnabruck, Germany, 1975—; vis. prof. Math. Research Ctr., Madison, Wis., 1979. Author: Discontinuous Cebysev Systems, 1979; contbr. articles to profl. jours. Mem. Deutsche Mathematiker-Vereinigung, Hochschulverband. Home: Herderstrasse 7, 49078 Osnabrück Germany Office: Universitat Osnabrück, D-49069 Osnabrück Federal Republic of Germany

ZIELKIEWICZ, JAN BOGDAN, chemist, educator, researcher; b. Gdansk, Poland, June 12, 1952; s. Bogdan and Zofia (Cieszanowska) Z.; m. Janina Tryka, Apr. 22, 1982; 1 child, Magdalena. BS, Tech. U. Gdansk, 1977, PhD, 1986. Toxicologist Med. Acad. Gdansk, 1982-84; asst. prof. Tech. U. Gdansk, 1984—. Contbr. articles to profl. jours. Recipient Award of Edn. Min. of Polish Govt. for Doctoral Work, 1986, awards Pres. Tech. U. Gdansk for rsch. activity, 1990, 91, 92, 93, 94. Home: Piastowska 100c/110, 80-358 Gdańsk Poland Office: Technical Univ Gdansk, Narutowicza 11/12, 80-952 Gdansk Poland

ZIEMELE, VITA, agricultural company executive; b. Ogre, Latvia, Feb. 25, 1961; d. Ēriks and Irina (Dmitričenko) Z.; 1 child, Ugis. Diploma, Acad. Agr., Jelgava, Latvia, 1984, Pedagog. U., Daugavpils, Latvia, 1996; postgrad., U. Agr., Jelgava, 1996-98. Cert. engr. of agr. machinery; cert. tchr. English. Engr. Collective Farm, Staburags, Latvia, 1984-85, mgr., 1985-87; study dir. Agr. Sch., Viesite, Latvia, 1987-88, dir., 1988-94; tchr. Sala (Latvia) Secondary Sch., 1994-99, head fgn. lang. dept., 1996-98; vice mng. dir. Farm Plant Latvia Ltd., 1998—. Author: (lang. tchg. methodology) Our Thoughts, 1996. Mem. Nat. Geographic Soc., English Tchrs. Assn. Lutheran. Avocations: knitting, embroidery, folk dancing, traveling. Home: Viesturu Iela 4-11, LV-5230 Sala Latvia Office: Farm Plant Latvia Ltd, Alejas Iela-3, LV-5230 Sala Latvia

ZIEMIANSKI, STANISLAW, philosophy educator, priest, musician; b. Besko, Krosno, Poland, Sept. 7, 1931; s. Kazimierz and Magdalena (Szybka) Kaplon. PhB, Jesuit Faculty Philosophy, Cracow, Poland, 1956; MTh, Jesuit Faculty Theology, Warsaw, Poland, 1960; MPh, Cath. U. Lublin, Poland, 1963, PhD, 1978. Lectr. Jesuit Faculty of Philosophy, Cracow, 1963-91, prof., 1991-97, vice dean, 1994—; pres. Jesuit Sci. Soc., Cracow, 1982-88; v.p. Assn. Philosophy Lectrs., Poland, 1988-96; prof. Papal Theol. Acad., Cracow, 1993—. Author: Natural Theology, 1995, I Sing and Play to God, I-IV, 1989, V, 1995; contbr. articles to periodicals. Avocations: composing music, singing in choir. Fax: 012 429-20-95. E-mail: ziemian@jezu-ici.krakow.pl. Home: ul Kopernika 26, 31-501 Cracow Poland

ZIEMKE, FRANK SIEGFRIED HARTMUT, microbiologist; b. Helmstedt, Germany, Oct. 31, 1967; s. Willi and Elsbeth (Rapski) Z.; m. Maren Kaegeler, Sept. 18, 1998. Diploma in Biology, Tech. U., Braunschweig, Germany, 1993; PhD, Tech. U., 1998. Postdoctoral Nat. Rsch. Cen. Biotech., Braunschweig, Germany, 1997-98; mgr. quality control Roch, Penzberg, Germany, 1999—. Grantee Fed. European Microbiol. Socs., Norway, 1996. Mem. Vereinigung fuer Allgemeine und Angewandte Mikrobiologie. Avocation: soccer. Office: Hoffmann La Roche, Nonnenwald 2, 82377 Penzberg Germany

ZIERATH, JULEEN RAE, research scientist, educator, consultant; b. Milw., Sept. 29, 1961; d. Donald George and Janet Wilhamina (Klug) Z. BA, U. Wis., River Falls, 1984; MA, Ball State U., 1986; PhD, Karolinska Inst., Stockholm, 1995. Rsch. asst. Sch. Medicine Washington U., St. Louis, 1986-89; doctoral fellow Karolinska Inst., Stockholm, 1989-95, assoc. prof. physiology, 1996-97; rsch. fellow in medicine Harvard U., Boston, 1995-96; assoc. prof. Karolinska Hosp., Stockholm, 1996—. Recipient Jr. Investigator award Swedish Med. Rsch. Coun., 1996, Young Promising Investigator award, 1996, Wallenberg Found. award, 1996. Mem. Am. Diabetes Assn., European Diabetes Assn. Avocations: athletics, cycling, swimming, field hockey, skiing. Office: Karolinska Hosp, Dept Clin Physiology, SE-171 76 Stockholm Sweden

ZIERDT, CHARLES HENRY, microbiologist; b. Pitts., Apr. 24, 1922; s. Conrad Henry and Nancy Leora (Harshberger) Z.; m. Margaret May Wise, June 1, 1942 (div. 1962); children: Charles Henry, Jr., Carolyn, Douglas, Richard; m. Willadene Smith, Sept. 30, 1967. BS, Pa. State U., 1943; MS, U. Mich., 1945; Ph.D., George Washington U., 1967. Rsch. assoc. Parke-Davis & Co., Detroit, 1945-48; microbiologist Henry Ford Hosp., Detroit, 1948-53, USPHS, Detroit, 1953-56; rsch. microbiologist NIH, Bethesda, Md., 1956—. Scientist sponsor U. Md., 1975—; instr. Found. Advanced Edn. Scis., Bethesda, 1978—. Author: Glucose Nonfermenting Gram Negative Bacteria in Clinical Microbiology, 1978; Non-fermentative Gram Negative Rods: Laboratory Identification and Clinical Aspects, 1985; McGraw-Hill Yearbook of Science and Technology, 1986; Diagnostic Procedures for Bacterial Infections, 1987; contbr. over 100 articles to profl. jours. Patentee in field. Active PTA. Fellow Am. Acad. Microbiology; mem. Am. Soc. Microbiology (chpt. pres. 1976), U.S. Fedn. Culture Collections (membership chmn. 1985), Avanti Owners Assn. Internat., Mensa, Model A Ford Club of Am. (Fairfax, Va. chpt. pres. 1985), Model T Ford Club Internat., Antique Auto Club Am. (pres. Sugar Loaf Mountain region 1997), Sigma Xi. Republican. Achievements include the classification and pathogenesis of Blastocystis Hominis, an intestinal protozoan parasite of man. Avocations: gardening; antique car restoration, church historian. Home: 4100 Norbeck Rd Rockville MD 20853-1869 Office: NIH Bethesda MD 20816

ZIERKE, ULRICH HANS HERMANN, bank executive; b. Bad Kreuznach, Fed. Republic Germany, June 24, 1944; s. Erwin and Elsbeth (kirschsieper) Z.; m. Kornelia Saur. MA, Johann-Wolfgang Goethe U., Frankfurt, 1972. Exec. Westdeutsche Landesbank, Duesseldorf, 1972-74; dir. Westdeutsche Landesbank, N.Y., Tokyo, Madrid, 1979-90; sr. v.p. Westdeutsche Landesbank, 1983; mgr. Libra Bank, London and Mexico City, 1974-78; dep. chief exec. Chartered WestLB Ltd., London, 1990-92; gen.mgr. WestLB, London, 1992-95; CEO, Thomas Cook Group Ltd., 1995-98; mng. dir. West LB Global Emerging Markets, 1999-2000; global head internat. trade and commodity fin. Westdeutsche Landesbank, London, 2000—. Avocations: travel, classical music, visual arts, skiing. Office: Westdeutsche Landesbank, 33-36 Gracechurch St, EC3V 0AX London Great Britain

ZIEROLF, MARY LOUISE, nurse anesthetist; b. Lima, Ohio, Dec. 12, 1946; d. Charles Peter and Agatha Cecilia (Jackman) Z. Diploma in nursing, St. Rita's Sch. Nursing, Lima, Ohio, 1967; diploma in anesthesia, Cin. Gen. Hosp., 1971; BS in Edn., U. Cin., 1974. RN, Ohio; cert. nurse anesthetist; cert. CPR instr., neonatal resuscitation. Staff nurse operating rm. St. Rita's Hosp., Lima, 1967-69; staff anesthetist, insvc. coord. Mercy Anesthesia Assocs Inc/Anesthesia & Intensive Care Cons, Cin., 1971—; staff anesthetist, specialist in obstet. anesthesia McCullough-Hype Hosp., Oxford, Ohio, 1993-96; staff anesthetist, specializing in obstet. anesthesia Mercy Fairfield, 1996—; staff anesthetist Intensive Care Consultants, Inc.; vis. lectr. Coll. Nursing, U. Cin., 1990-92; lectr. anesthesia in 3d world countries, 1992. Author papers. Mem. anniversary program to Russia, People to People/Citizen Amb. Program, Seattle, 1991, participant in 1st CRNA anesthesia exch. of tech. and sci. info. in China, 1989; active taking monthly blood pressures Fairfax (Ohio) Sr. Citizens, 1988—. Named one of Outstanding Young Women of Am., 1976. Mem. Am. Assn. Nurse Anesthetists, Ohio State Assn. Nurse Anesthetists (bd. dirs. 1981-83, 92—, pres. Greater Cin. Ednl. Dist. 1991—, chair fall Osana meeting 1995—, co-chair fall meeting 1997, sec. 1996-97), Am. Bus. Woman's Assn. (pres. 7 Hills chpt. 1982—, Woman of Yr. 1982), U. Cin. Alumni Assn., Gen. Hosp. Sch. Nurse Anesthesia Alumni, U. Cin. Sch. Nurse Anesthesia Alumni (treas. 1997—). Roman Catholic. Avocations: reading, traveling, volunteer work for needy and elderly. Home: 6 W Knoll Ct Fairfield OH 45014-3637 Office: Mercy Hosp Fairfield 3000 Mack Rd Fairfield OH 45014-5335

ZIERSKI, JAN TOMASZ, neurosurgeon; b. Lwow, Poland, Oct. 10, 1940; arrived in Eng., 1969.; s. Marian and Lina Hermine (Unger) Z.; m. Zofia Barbara Grochowska, Dec. 27, 1969; 1 child, Anne-Catherine. MD, Med. Acad., Lodz, Poland, 1969; Priv Doz, U. Giessen (Germany), 1986. Asst. Dept. Neurosurgery, Lodz, Poland, 1965-69; resident Dept. Neurosurgery, Lyon, France, 1967-68; registrar Dept. Neurosurgery, Hull, Eng., 1969-72; asst. rsch. Dept. Neurosurgery, Giessen, Germany, 1972-85, dep. head, 1985-87; head dept. neurosurgery Hosp. Neukoelln, Berlin, 1987—; prof. neurosurgery Giessen, Germany, 1987. Editor: Cerebral Aneurysms, 1979, Spontaneous Cerebral Haematomas, 1980, Intrathecal Treatment of Spasticity, 1986; contbr. articles to profl. jours. Decorated Officers Cross of Merit Pres. Polish Republic, 1996. Mem. German-Polish Med. Soc. (pres. 1994-96), German Soc. Neurosurgery, Polish Soc. Neurosurgery, Austrian Soc. Neurosurgery. Avocations: theater, languages. Home: Nelkenweg 1, 14532 Stahnsdorf Germany Office: Hosp Neukoelln Dept Neurosu, Rudowerstr 48, 12313 Berlin Germany

ZIETSCH, USCHI, writer, publisher; b. Munich, Aug. 3, 1961; d. Friedrich and Anna (Starringer) Z.; m. Gerald Jambor, Apr. 1, 1957. Grad. in Bus., Munich Bus. Sch., 1986. Mktg. asst. Control Data, Munich, 1986-89; sales asst. Cerberus, Munich, 1989-96; pub. Fabylon, Munich, 1987—. Author: Starcloud and Ice Magic, 1986, Wintersun's Dream, 1988 (Kurd-Laswitz award 1988), The Star of the Gods, 1989, Snowflaffy and the Major, 1997, Behind the Wall—Women in Jail, vol. 103, 11, 1998-2000, Peony Rhodan, 1993, Animals—Friends for Life, vol. 1-10, 1999-2000. Mem. WWF, Greenpeace. E-mail: fabylon@t-online.de. Home: Eichenstr 2, 86343 Konigsbrunn Germany Office: Fabylon Verlag, Forststr 10-12, 80997 Munich Germany

ZIETZ, KARYL LYNN KOPELMAN, writer, opera critic, television correspondent, producer, documentary filmmaker; b. N.Y.C., Oct. 11, 1943; d. Bernard and Vera Jean (Wantman) Kopelman; m. Neil J. Stone, Aug. 16, 1970 (div. 1975); m. Joachim Zietz, July 19, 1978 (div. 1994). BA in Chemistry, U. Pa., 1965; MA in Film and Broadcast Journalism, Am. U., 1980; spl. cert., Goettinger U., Germany, 1976. Researcher Columbia Coll. Physicians and Surgeons, N.Y.C., 1967-70, NIH, Bethesda, Md., 1971-72; producer, writer Am. Chem. Soc., Washington, 1976-78; producer,researcher Zweites Deutsches Fernsehen, Mainz, Germany, 1978-89; prodr ORF-Austrian TV, 1980-84; producer, reporter European Television Svc., Cologne, Germany, 1985-88; producer, dir., corr. KOPE Prodns., Washington, 1985—; Lectr. Smithsonian Inst., Arts Club, Chautauqua Instn., 1998, Italian Cultural Soc., 1999; site reporter NEA, 1994, 95. Author: Opera! Guide to Western Europe's Great Houses, 1991, Eastern Europe's and USSR's Great Opera Houses, 1992, Opera-Going in South America, 1993, Opera Companies and Houses of the United States: A Comprehensive, Illustrated Reference, 1994, The National Trust Guide to Great Opera Houses in America, 1996, Italian Opera Directory, 1998, Opera Companies and Houses of Western Europe, Canada, Australia, New Zealand: A Comprehensive Illustrated Reference, 1999, Storia dei Teatri d'Opera Italiani, 2000; prodr. (video) An Amish Portrait for USIA; prodr., dir., writer, interviewer documentary films; opera critic, contbr. articles to Opera Now, Orpheus Oper Internat., Toronto Globe and Mail, Opera News, Musica and Arte: Quaderno del Museo Teatrale alla Scala, Opera-Opera. Mem. Music Critics Assn., Coun. Internat. Nontheatrical Events, Internat. Platform Assn., Am. Women in Radio and TV, Author's Guild, Assn. Ind. Video and Filmakers, Washington Ind. Writers, Contemporary Authors, Cosmos Club. Avocations: sailing, jogging, bicycling, foreign languages. Office: KOPE Prodns Palisades Sta PO Box 40103 Washington DC 20016-0103

ZIFFER, GIORGIO, Slavic philologist; b. Genova, Italy, Nov. 11, 1960; s. Guido and Margherita (Mozzetti) Z.; m. Elisabetta Maria Cimmino, Sept. 23, 1991; 1 child, Giacomo. MA, U. Rome, 1985, PhD, 1991. Asst. U. Udine, Italy, 1990-99, prof. philology, 1999—. Contbr. articles to profl. jours. Recipient scholarship Humboldt-Stiftung, 1994-95. Roman Catholic. Avocations: swimming, tennis, music. Home: Via Duchi D'Aosta 1, 33100 Udine Italy Office: Univ Udine, Via Zanon 6, 33100 Udine Italy

ZIGLIN, SERGEY LVOVICH, mathematician, researcher; b. Tulskaya Oblast, USSR, Mar. 5, 1952; s. Lev Alexandrovich and Valentina Ivanovna

(Vasilyeva) Z.; m. Irina Nikolaevna Ziglina, Apr. 4, 1971 (div. Jan. 1979); 1 child, Tatyana. MA in Mechanics and Math., Moscow State U., 1973, Candidate Phys. and Math. Scis., 1976; D Phys. and Math. Scis., Superior cert. com., Moscow, 1985. Jr. rsch. worker Inst. Radiotechnics and Electronics, Acad. Scis. USSR (Russian Acad. Scis. 1991—), Moscow, 1976-81, sr. rsch. worker, 1981-86, leading rsch. worker, 1986—. Contbr. articles to sci. jours., including Funktsionalnyi Analiz i Ego Prilozheniya. Orthodox. Office: Inst Radiotech-Electronics, Acad Scis, Mokhovaya 11, 103907 Moscow Russia

ZIGLIOTTO, MAURO, electrical engineering researcher; b. Vicenza, Veneto, Italy, Nov. 20, 1963; s. Bruno Zigliotto and Marisa Bau; m. Maria Caterina Gonzato, Oct. 13, 1990; 1 child, Francesco. Degree in electronic engring., U. Padua, Italy, 1988. Dir. R & D Itaco srl, Vicenza, 1990-92; rsch. asst. U. Padua, 1992-95; asst. prof. of elec. drives, rschr. U. Padua, Italy, 1995—; lectr. U. Udine, Italy, 1995—, U. Padova, Italy, 1997—; lectr. U. Udine, Italy, 1995. Contbr. articles to jours. in field. Served with Italian mil., 1988-89. Grantee European Cmty., 1996. Mem. IEEE (sec. IEEE-IAS-IES-PELS North Italy joint chpt., 1998, jours. 1995, 96). Roman Catholic. Avocations: karate, skiing. Office: Dept Elec Engring, Via Gradenigo 6A, 35131 Padua Italy

ZIHA, KALMAN, engineering educator, researcher; b. Sombor, Vojvodina, Yugoslavia, July 24, 1948; s. Miklos and Anntonia (Slavikovic) Z.; m. Olga Tufegdzic; children: Milena, Mirko, Viktor. BSc, U. Zagreb, Croatia, 1973, MSc, 1978, PhD, 1989. Jr. rschr. Shipbuilding Industry, Split, Croatia, 1973-75; sys. engr. computing ctr. U. Zagreb, 1975-89, asst. prof. faculty mech. engring. and naval architecture, 1994-2000; sr. rschr. Naval Inst., Split, 1989-94; assoc. prof. U. Zagreb, 2000—. Contbr. articles to profl. jours. Mem. IEEE, Soc. Naval Archs. and Marine Engrs., N.Y. Acad. Scis. Home: Ljudevita Posavskog 15, 10000 Zagreb Croatia Office: U Zagreb, Ivana Lucica 5, 10000 Zagreb Croatia

ŽIHLA, ZDENĚK, avionics engineer, educator; b. Ostrava, Czech Republic, Oct. 25, 1936; s. Josef and Josefa (Maslowská) Ž.; m. Jindriska Pokorná, July 27, 1961; 1 child, Zdeňka. Diploma in engring., Mil. Acad., Brno, Czechoslovakia, 1961, PhD, 1974. Cert. avionics engr. Instr. Mil. Acad., Brno, 1961-67, assoc. prof., 1970-89, chief chair, 1990-91; assoc. prof. Mil. Tech. Coll., Cairo, 1968-69; dir. Inst. Fgn. Student Tng., Brno, 1992-93, Fgn. Lang. Inst., Brno, 1994-95; prof. U. Pardubice, Czech Replubic, 1996—; cons. Air Force Tech. Inst., Prague, Czech Republic, 1980-83, Brno Trade Fairs and Exhbns., 1993—. Author: (with M. Fišer) Servomechanisms of Guns, 1969; Control Fin Drives, 1982, Automatic Control of Aircraft, Part I, 1987, Part II, 1990; (with R. Jalovecky and J. Čižmár) Aircraft Avionics Systems, 1990. Col. Mil. Acad., 1961-95. Mem. Transport Acad. Ukraine (fgn.). Home and Office: Pšenik 7, 63900 Brno Czech Republic

ZIKA, BILL, psychologist; b. L.A., Jan. 16, 1946; s. Gilbert Francis Z. and Eleanor (Ames) Abranz; m. Sheryl Corinne Willis, Jan. 6, 1974; children: Kurtis (dec.), Shari, Danielle, Adam. BA, UCLA, 1969; MA, Calif. State U., Northridge, 1974; PhD, Massey U., Palmerson North, New Zealand, 1982. Lic. psychologist, Calif.; registered psychologist, New Zealand. Rehab. counselor New Horizons SFVAR, Panorama City, Calif., 1973-75; dir. counselling svc. Massey U., Palmerson North, New Zealand, 1975-97; clin., cons. psychologist Bill Zika, Dr. Psychol. Svcs., Palmerson North, 1993-97; sr. psychologist dept. corrections State of Calif., Soledad, 1997—; sec. med. bd. exec. com. Salinas Valley State Prison, 1998—; cons. psychologist Psychology Clinic Massey U., Palmerson North, New Zealand, 1991-97; provider Accident Comp. Commn., Wellington, New Zealand, 1992-97, Stratos, Ltd., Lower Hutt, New Zealand, 1993-97; clin. supr. Manline Men Against Violence, Palmerson North, 1993-97; clin. advisor Youth Line, Palmerson North, 1995-97; chairperson Marriage Guidance, Palmerson North, 1981. Contbr. articles to profl. jours. Lance cpl. USMC, 1966-67. Mem. New Zealand Coll. Clin. Psychologists. Office: Salinas Valley State Prison Hwy 101 Soledad CA 93960

ZIKAKIS, JOHN P., food scientist, consultant, educator, researcher; b. Piraeus, Greece; came to U.S., 1958; s. Philip J. and Salome J. (Moshou) Z.; m. Kiki K. Matrozos, Aug. 29, 1958; 1 child, Salome J. Assoc. engr., Pythagoras Coll., Piraeus, 1956; BA, U. Del., 1965, MS, 1967, PhD, 1970. Third merchant marine engr. Onassis Shipping Enterprises, Ltd., London, 1956-58; lab. asst. DuPont de Nemours and Co., Newark, Del., 1959-61; research asst. U. Del., Newark, 1965-70, asst. prof. animal sci. dept., 1970-75, assoc. prof. animal sci. dept., 1975-81, prof. animal sci. dept., coll. marine studies, 1981-89; acad. indust. consultant, 1986—; prof. food sci. U. Del., Newark, 1987-89, prof. emeritus, 1989; v.p. United Chitotechnologies, Inc., Newark, 1989-93; chief scientist, marine resource specialist Biopolymer Engring., Inc., St. Paul, 1997—, also bd. dirs.; cons. U. Thessaloniki, Greece, 1972-80; vis. prof. U. Panama, 1984-85, sci. advisor, 1985-89; sci. advisor Govt. of Greece, 1972-74; organizer numerous nat. and internat. sci. confs. and symposia over past 23 yrs. Author: Chitin, Chitosan and Related Enzymes, 1984, Advances in Chitin and Chitosan, 1992; mem. editorial bd. Jour. Agr. Food Chemistry, 1983-86; contbr. over 125 articles to profl. jours. Patentee in field. Trustee Riverside Hosp., Wilmington, Del., 1977-84; pres. bd. dirs. Maison Grande Condominium Assn., Inc., Miami Beach, Fla., 1990-92; bd. dirs. Holy Trinity Greek Orthodox Ch., Wilmington, 1971-73; pres. bd. govs. Commondore Condominium Assn., Ft. Lauderdale, Fla., 1993-94. 1st lt. Greek Air Force, 1952-56. Sr. Fulbright scholar, U. Panama, 1984-85; recipient Gold medal and cert. U. Patra, 1973, cert. recognition, commendation for excellence in rsch., edn., pub. svc. Pres. of U. Del., 1977. Mem. AAAS, Am. Chem. Soc. (historian div. agrl. and food chemistry 1980-84, chmn. pub. rels. com. 1980-85, chmn. disting. svc. award com. 1987-88, co-founder, editor div. agrl. and food chemistry membership directory 1980-86, chmn. div. agrl. and food chemistry 1986-87, Disting. Svc. award 1991), N.Y. Acad. Scis., Del. Acad. Sci., Inst. Food Technologists, Am. Inst. Biol. Sci., Am. Chitosci. Soc. (co-founder, trustee, pres. 1989—), Am. Dairy Sci. Assn., Sigma Xi. Avocations: tennis, sailing, swimming, gymnastics, travel. Office: 307 SE 14th St Fort Lauderdale FL 33316-1929

ZIKIC, ALEKSANDAR MIROSLAV, engineering educator, consultant; b. Beograd, Srbija, Yugoslavia, June 20, 1951; arrived in Scotland, 1986; s. Miroslav Aleksandar and Jovanka (Zaric) Z.; m. Borjana Subotic, June 1, 1993; children: Nikola A., Filip L. BSc in Physics with hons., U. Belgrade, Yugoslavia, 1973, MPh in Sci. Instruments, 1978, PhD in Control, 1984. Chartered engr., U.K. Lectr. in electronics U. Belgrade, Yugoslavia, 1974-86; lectr. in control U. Paisley, Scotland, 1986—; cons. Horn Engring., Johnstone, Eng., 1986-89, John Brown Engring., Clydebank, Eng., 1991—, Motorola, UK, East Kilbride, Eng., 1995—. Author: Practical Digital Control, 1989; contbr. articles to internat. profl. jours. Mem. IEEE, IEE (chartered engr.). Mem. Ea. Orthodox Ch. Avocations: fishing, painting, photography, exotic plants. Home: 3 Spinners Gardens, Paisley PA2 9PF, Scotland Office: U Paisley, High St, Renfrshr Paisley PA1 2BE, Scotland

ZILBERT, ALLEN BRUCE, education educator, computer consultant; b. Bronx, N.Y., May 26, 1957; s. Murray and Perla Z.; m. Barbara Dale Palley, July 1, 1984; children: Heather Robynne, Jared Lee. BA in Econ., CUNY, 1978; MBA, St. Johns U., 1980, advanced profl. cert., 1982; MEd in Adminstrv. Computer Systems Edn., Columbia U., 1986, EdD, 1988; post-grad., Kennedy-Western U., 1995—. Instr. bus. computer info. systems & quantitative methods Hofstra U., Hempstead, N.Y., 1981-83; asst. prof. info. systems Pace U. Sch. Computer Sci. and Info. Systems, N.Y.C., 1983-89; dir. ancillary systems Advanced Med. Systems, Rockville Ctr., N.Y., 1989-90; asst. prof. mgmt. Long Island U. Sch. Bus., Coll. Mgmt., Brookville, N.Y., 1990-94; asst. prof. mgmt. info. sys. Sy Syms Sch. Bus., David Zysman prof. of mgmt. info. sys. Yeshiva U., N.Y.C., 1994-2000; assoc. prof. math./computer sci. Molloy Coll., Rockville Ctr., N.Y., 2000—; mem. curriculum com. Pace U. Sch. Computer Sci. and Info. Sys., 1983-89; chmn. personal computer resources com. Advanced Med. Sys., 1989-90; mem. campuswide computer com. L.I. U., 1991-94, chmn., 1993-94, chmn. scholarship awards com., 1990-91; assembly collegiate schs. bus. curriculum planning com. Coll. Mgmt., 1993-94, chmn. computer needs, usage and stds. com., 1990-93, chmn. mgmt. dept. computer com., chmn. scholar awards com., 1992-93; book and software reviewer. Contbr. articles to profl. jours. Mem. IEEE, Assn. for Computer Tng. and Support, Assn. for Computing Machinery, Assn. of Info. Tech. Profls., Internat. Assn. for Computer Info. Sys., Internat. Assn. Mgmt., Info. Resources Mgmt. Assn. E-mail: azilbert@molloy.edu.

ZILBOORG, CAROLINE CRAWFORD, writer, English language educator; b. N.Y.C., May 17, 1948; d. Gregory and Margaret (Stone) Z.; m. Thomas Robert Nevin, July 27, 1977; children: Austin Nevin, Tobias Nevin, Elodie Nevin, Miranda Nevin. BA, Vassar Coll., 1970; MA, SUNY, Albany, 1972; PhD, U. Wis., 1976. Prof. English Lake Erie Coll., Painesville, Ohio, 1977-95; mem. faculty English Cambridge U., 1995—. Author: Women's Firsts, 1997; author, editor: Richard Aldington and H.D.: The Early Years in Letters, 1992, Richard Aldington and H.D.: The Later Years in Letters, 1995, also numerous articles; reviews editor Gravesiana, 1996-99. Life mem. Clare Hall, Cambridge U., 1993—. NEH fellow, 1995-96; H.D. fellow Beinecke Libr., Yale U., New Haven, 1991. Mem. MLA (life). Avocations: travel, writing. Office: Clare Hall, Cambridge Univ, Cambridge CB3 9AL, England

ZILGALVIS, PETERIS VIKTORS, lawyer; b. Inglewood, Calif., Apr. 10, 1964; s. Ansis and Aida Zilgalvis; m. Ilze Aramina, Aug. 3, 1996. BA in Polit. Sci., UCLA, 1986; JD, U. So. Calif., 1990. Bar: Calif. Chief legal counsel Latvian Min. Environ., Riga, Latvia, 1990-92; legal cons. Estonia, Latvia, Lithuania, 1992, Latvian Min. Fgn. Affairs, Riga, 1992-93, Commn. European Cmtys., Riga, 1992-93; environ. specialist The World Bank, Estonia, Latvia, Lithuania, 1993-96; sr. fgn. environ. law adv. CPPI, The World Bank, Fedn. Environ. Mgmt. Project, Moscow, 1996-97; mem. directorate of legal affairs Coun. of Europe, 1997—; of counsel Carroll, Burdick & McDonough, San Francisco, 1996-97. Author: (book) A Guide to the Latvian Environmental Communities, 1992; contbr. chpts. to numerous publs. Mem. bd. dirs. Latvian Environ. Protection Club, 1990-92. Recipient scholarship USC, 1987-90. Mem. Internat. Assn. Young Lawyers. Lutheran. Avocations: reading, snowboarding, surfing, mountain biking, skiing. Home: 15 Rue du Rhin, Plobsheim 67115, France

ZILGES, ANDREAS, nuclear physics educator, researcher; b. Moenchengladbach, Germany, Oct. 15, 1965; s. Franz-Josef and Gertrud (Wilms) Z. Diploma, U. Cologne, Germany, 1989, PhD, 1992. Rsch. assoc. U. Cologne, 1991-95; rsch. assoc., lectr. Yale U., New Haven, Conn., 1995; vis. asst. prof. Yale U., New Haven, 1996-97; prof. Darmstadt (Germany) Tech. U., 1997—. Contbr. articles to jours. in field. Mem. German Phys. Soc., European Phys. Soc., Am. Assn. Physics Tchrs. Avocation: sailing. Home: Moosbergstr 60, D-64285 Darmstadt Germany Office: Tech U Darmstadt, Schlossgartenstr 9, D-64289 Darmstadt Germany

ZILHAO, JOAO CARLOS, archaeologist; b. Lisboa, Portugal, Jan. 15, 1957; s. Adriano Antero Zilhao and Susana Alice Teiga; 1 child, Joao David. Lic., U. Lisbon, 1982, MA, 1988, PhD, 1995. Archaeologist Nat. Mus. of Archaeology, Lisbon, 1982-84; h.s. tchr. Escola Secundaria do Restelo, Lisbon, 1983-84; univ. tchr. U. Lisbon, 1984-97; dir. Coa Valley Archaeol. Park, Vila Nova de Foz Coa, Portugal, 1996-97, Portuguese Inst. Archaeology, Lisbon, 1997—. Author: (books) A Gruta da Feteira. Escavacao de emergencia de uma necropole neolitica, 1984, O Solutrense da Estremadura portuguesa, 1987, Gruta do Caldeirao. O Neolitico Antigo, 1992, O Paleolitico Superior da Estremadura Portuguesa, 2 vols., 1995, Arte rupestre e Pré-historia do Vale do Coe, 1997; contbg. author to edited vols.; contbr. articles to profl. jours. Rsch. grantee NSF, Portugal, 1988-93, 97, JNICT, Portugal and CNRS, France, 1996, 97, JNICT, 1993-95. Mem. Portuguese Assn. Archaeologists, European Assn. of Archaeologists, Soc. for Am. Archaeology, Paleonanthropology Soc., Union Internat. des Scis. Pre et Proto Historiques. Office: Inst de Arqueologia, Fac de Letras de Lisboa, 1500 Lisbon Portugal also: Portuguese Inst Archaeology, Av Da India 136, 1300 Lisbon Portugal

ZILLMER, HANS-JOACHIM, engineering company executive; b. Mölln, Germany, Sept. 20, 1950; s. Alwin and Lina (Jurkschat) Z.; m. Renate Stöcker, July 6, 1981; 1 child, Larissa. Diploma in Engring., Bergische U., Wuppertal, Germany, 1973, Technische U., Berlin, 1977; PhD in Politics, Technische U., Berlin, 1991. Registered profl. engr. Prin., owner Engring. Office Dr. Zillmer, Solingen, Germany, 1973—, Marco Investment and Devel., Inc., Naples, Fla., 1999—. Author: Darwin's Mistake, 1998. First chmn. TSG Solingen, 1993-99. Mem. N.Y. Acad. Scis., Am. Assn. for Advancement of Sci. Avocations: tennis, golf. Home and Office: RÜdigerstr 14, D-42653 Solingen Germany also: 200 Copperfield Ct Marco Island FL 34145-3520

ZIMA, MIROSLAV, biology educator, university official; b. Bukovec, Myjava, Slovakia, May 11, 1945; s. Juraj and Alžbeta (Holotíková) Z.; m. Lydia Kovárová, Apr. 23, 1973. Grad. engr., Slovak Agrl. U., Nitra, 1968, PhD, 1976. Asst. prof. biology Slovak Agrl. U., 1968-84, assoc. prof., 1984—, dep. head dept. plant physiology, 1978-90, head dept., 1994-96, rector, 1996—; dir. courses for tchrs. and rschrs. UNESCO, Nitra, 1984-90; mem. sci. bd. Crop Rsch. Inst. Piešťany, Slovakia, 1996—; sci. sec. plant physiology and biochemistry Commn. Acad. Agrl. Sci., Prague, Czechoslovakia, 1984-90. Author: Biological Principles of Irrigation, 1984, Plant Physiology, 1997; author, translator Ency. Gardening, 1995 (award Slovak Lit. Fund 1996). Bd. dirs. Alliance Univs. for Democracy, U. Tenn., 1996—. Named Excellent Young Scientist, Czechoslovak Acad. Scis., 1968; travel grantee UNESCO, The Philippines, 1980. Mem. Slovak Acad. Agrl. Sci. (v.p. 1998—), European Soc. for Agronomy (pres. 1996—), European Soc. Plant Physiology. Home: Štiavnická 18/1, 949 01 Nitra Slovakia Office: Slovak Agrl U, Tr A Hlinku 2, 949 76 Nitra Slovakia

ZIMA, PETER VÁCLAV, humanities educator; b. Prague, Czechoslovakia, Mar. 11, 1946; arrived in Austria, 1983; s. Miloslav and Anna (Seger) Z.; m. Veronica Smith, Aug. 11, 1984. MA with honors, U. Edinburgh, Scotland, 1969; Doctorat du 3e cycle, U. Paris (France) IV, 1971; Doctorat d'Etat, U. Paris (France) I, 1979. Asst. prof. U. Bielefeld, Germany, 1972-75, U. Groningen, The Netherlands, 1976-83; prof. U. Klagenfurt, Austria, 1983—. Contbr. short stories and literary criticisms to publs. Active European Movement, The Hague, 1974—. Recipient Woitschach Forschungs prize, Woitschach-Stiftung/Deutscher Stifterverband, Bonn, Germany, 1993. Mem. Comparative Lit. Assn., Austrian Acad. Scis. Office: Univ Klagenfurt, Universitatsstr 65-67, A-9020 Klagenfurt Austria

ZIMÁNYI, JÓZSEF, physicist, researcher; b. Budapest, Hungary, Dec. 5, 1931; m. Magdolna Györgyi, Oct. 15, 1956; 1 child, Gergely. MSc, Eötvös Loránd U., Budapest, 1955, PhD, 1965; acad. doctor, Hungarian Acad. Scis., Budapest, 1972. Rsch. fellow Ctrl. Rsch. Inst. Physics, Budapest, 1954-64, chief rsch. scientist, 1965-77, head of dept., 1975-86, scientific advisor, 1978-90, rsch. prof., 1990-93; head of dept. KFKI Rsch. Inst. for Particle and Nuclear Physics, Budapest, 1993—; titular prof. Eötvös Loránd U., Budapest, 1980—; co-chmn. Internat. Workshop Theoretical Physics, Budapest, 1983-86; pres. dept. natural scis. Nat. Sci. Rsch. Fund, Budapest, 1991-98; mem. Hungarian CERN Com., Budapest, 1992—. Contbr. articles to profl. jours. Recipient award Hungarian Acad. Scis., Budapest, 1981; named to Order of Hungarian Republic Officer's Cross, Pres. Republic, Budapest, 1992; recipient Széchenyi prize Pres. Republic, Hungary, 2000. Mem. Eötvös Loránd Phys. Soc. (Bródy Imre award 1962), European Phys. Soc., Hungarian Acad. Scis., European Acad. Arts, Scis. & Humanities. Avocations: philosophy, baroque music. Home: Dios arok 2, H-1125 Budapest Hungary Office: KFKI Rsch Inst Particle &, Nuclear Physics, PO Box 49, H-1525 Budapest Hungary

ZIMANYI, LASZLO, biophysicist, researcher; b. Pecs, Hungary, July 12, 1955; s. Laszlo Zimanyi and Judit Benedek. MS, Attila Jozsef U., Szeged, Hungary, 1979, PhD, 1982, DSc, 1999. Asst. rschr. Biol. Rsch. Ctr., Szeged, 1979-82, assoc. rschr., 1982-90, sr. rschr., 1990-99, sci. advisor, 1999—; postgrad. rschr. U. Calif., Irvine, 1986-88, asst. rschr., 1991-94. Contbr. articles to profl. jours. Mem. Hungarian Biophys. Soc. (Biophys. Edn. award 1995). Avocations: sports, hiking, music. Office: Inst Biophysics Biol Rsch Ctr, Hungarian Acad Scis POB 521, H-6701 Szeged Hungary

ZIMBLER, SIMON G., advertising agency executive; b. Leicester, Eng., Dec. 21, 1963; s. Lionel M. and Carla (Govoni) Z. BA in Natural Scis., Selwyn Coll., Cambridge U., 1985, MA in Computer Scis., 1986; BA in Mktg., Chartered Inst. Mktg., 1989. European marketer INMOS, Bristol, Eng., 1986-88; band mgr. Harvey's, Bristol, 1988-90; mng. dir. Anderson & Lembke, Bristol, 1991-96, Mason Zimbler, Bristol, 1997—. Avocations: snowboarding, climbing. Office: Mason Zimbler Ltd, Clifton Hts, Cifton Bristol BS8 1EJ, England

ZIMBROVSKAYA, NATALIA ARSENJEVNA, physicist, mathematics and physics educator; b. Ekaterinburg, Sverdlovsk, USSR, Sept. 28, 1947; d. Arsenii Nicolaevich Zhukov and Zinaida Alexandrovna Chekalova; m. Grigorii Michailovich Zimobovskii, Feb. 4, 1972; 1 child, Alexander. MA in Physics, Ural's State U., Ekaterinburg, USSR, 1970; PhD in Physics, Inst. Physics of Metals, Ekaterinburg, USSR, 1977; DSc in Physics, U. Nizhni-Novgorod (Russia), 1994. Asst. lectr. Ural's Mining Inst., Ekaterinburg, USSR, 1972-73; asst. prof. Ural's Mining Inst., Ekaterinburg, Russia, 1986-95; prof. Ural's State Mining and Geol. Acad., Ekaterinburg, 1995-99; rsch. prof. dept. physics City Coll. CUNY, N.Y.C., 1998—. Author: Local Fermi Surface Geometry and HF Effects in Metals, 1996; contbr. numerous articles to profl. jours. Mem. Am. Phys. Soc. Russian Orthodox. Office: City Coll CUNY Convent Ave at 138th St New York NY 10031

ZIMENKOVSKY, BORYS SEMENOVYCH, academic administrator, pharmaceutical educator; b. Berejan, Ukraine, Apr. 18, 1940; s. Semen Michailovich and Sophia Dmitrivna (Vishnevska) Z.; m. Ludmyla Yakivna Tkachenko, Mar. 11, 1961; 1 child, Andre. Diploma in gen. pharmacy, Lviv (Ukraine) Sch. Medicine, 1963, PhD in Organic Chemistry, 1966; DSc in Pharm. Chemistry, Moscow U., 1978. Asst. prof. Lviv State Med. U., 1964-72, assoc. prof., 1972-78, dean faculty pharmacy, 1977-79, chair dept. pharm., organic and bioorganic chemistry, 1978—, vice dir., 1979-98, dir., 1998—. Author textbook on organic chemistry, 3 vols., 1998; contbr. over 300 articles to profl. jours.; mem./fellow editl. coun. 5 profl. jours., 1972—. Col. mil. med. svcs. Recipient Internat. Man of Millenium Internat. Biog. Ctr., Cambridge, 1999, Man of Yr. scholar Higher Edn. Ukraine, 1980. Mem. Halytska Pharm. Assn. (pres. 1998—), Acad. Tech. Cybernetics Ukraine, Ukranian Acad. Higher Edn. (Yaroslav Mudryi medal 1999), Internat. Acad. Tech. and Engring., N.Y. Acad. Scis. Roman Catholic. Avocations: music, literature. Home: 29B Pasichna, 79033 Lviv Ukraine Office: Liv State Med U, 69 Pckarska St, Lviv Ukraine

ZIMET, GREGORY DAVID, clinical psychologist; b. Albany, July 13, 1956; s. Carl Norman and Sara Florence (Goodman) Z.; m. Lynne Anne Sturm, June 8, 1984; children: Patrick Daniel, Hannah Giselle. BA with honors, Vassar Coll., 1978; MA, Duke U., 1982, PhD, 1985. Lic. psychologist. Asst. prof. psychiatry Case Western Res. U., Cleve., 1986-87, asst. prof. pediat., 1987-93; assoc. prof. pediat. Ind. U., Indpls., 1993-99, prof., 1999—; sci. rschr. NIH, 1994-95, 97-00, 99—. Contbr. articles to profl. jours. Mem. APA, Soc. Pediat. Psychology, Soc. Personality Assessment, Soc. Adolescent Medicine, Soc. Pediat. Rsch., Soc. for Sci. Study of Sexuality, Phi Beta Kappa . Avocations: wine, music, reading, skiing.

ZIMET, MATTHEW, graphic arts and science educator; b. Bklyn., Aug. 29, 1947; s. Sidney and Rebecca (Wishnofsky) Z.; m. Yvonne Streisinger, Oct. 16, 1994; children: Timnah, Jacob, Abraham, Nathan. MS, U. Mass., 1976, PhD, 1976. Prof. Vt. Tech. Coll., Randolph, 1984—. Illustrator: Zero, 2000, Black Holes & Timewarps, 1996. Mem. Sigma Xi. Jewish. Avocations: art, canoeing, cross-country skiing. E-mail: mzimet.fac@night.vtc.vsc.edu. Office: Vt Tech Coll Main St Randolph VT 05061

ZIMIN, SERGEY PAVLOVICH, physics educator, researcher; b. Yaroslavl, Russia, June 18, 1954; s. Pavel Aleksandrovich and Tamara Dmitrievna (Mishueva) Z.; m. Olga Vladimirovna Kuzikova, Apr. 10, 1976; children: Dmitry, Anna, Ekaterina. DSc, State U., Yaroslavl, 1989. Engr. Electronpribor, Yaroslavl, 1976-77; sr. rschr. State U., Yaroslavl, 1977-90, assoc. prof., 1990-99, soros assoc. prof., 1999—; cons. postgrad. students U. Yaroslavl, 1996—. Contbr. articles to profl. jours. Grantee Russian Edn. Ministry, 1993-94, 96-97, 97-98, 99—. Mem. N.Y. Acad. Scis. Home: Komsomolskaya St 10-3, 150000 Yaroslavl Russia Office: Yaroslavl State U, Sovetskaya St 14, 150000 Yaroslavl Russia

ZIMMER, ALF CONRAD, psychology educator; b. Bevensen, Lower Saxony, Fed. Republic Germany, Nov. 2, 1943; s. Adolf and Margarete (Kleybolte) Z.; m. Margot Schürings, Dec. 16, 1970 (div. July 1980); m. Katharina Dahmen, Oct. 14, 1988; m. Sebastian, Fabian. Diploma in Psychology, Westf. Wilhelms U., Münster, Fed. Republic of Germany, 1971, PhD, 1973, PhD habilitation, 1982. Rsch. asst. Eberhard Karls U., Tübingen, Fed. Republic of Germany, 1971-73; asst. prof. Bayrische Landesuniv., Regensburg, Fed. Republic of Germany, 1973-76; assoc. prof. Ossietzky U., Oldenburg, Fed. Republic of Germany, 1976-80; visiting scholar Stanford U., Calif., 1980-83; assoc. prof. Westfälische Wilhelms U., Münster, 1980-84; full prof. Bayrische Landesuniv., Regensburg, 1984—; v.p. U. Regensburg, 1992-94, mem. steering bd., 1994—; mem. Acad. Senate of Univ., Regensburg, 1974-76, 90-94; chmn. dept. psychology, Münster, 1982-83, dept. philosophy II, Regensburg, 1988-90; chmn. Dept. Psychology, Regensburg, 1984-88, 96—; mem. adv. bd. Govt. Bavaria on Tech. Assessment & Risk, 1995—. Author: Multivariate Statistics, 1979; editor Wolfgang Köhler Centennial, 1988 (with R. Scholz); Qualitative Aspects of Decision Making, 1997, (with K. Dahmen-Zimmer) Criteria of Traffic Safety, 1997, (with R. Eckert) Rehabilitation Science-A Multidisciplinary Approach, 1999; co-editor Axiomathes; contbr. articles to profl. jours. Recipient Univ. medal Trieste U. dept. physics, 1990, Univ. medal U. Odessa, 1992. Fellow Gestalt Theory and Application (governing bd. 1982-86, mng. editor 1984-91); mem. Am. Psychol. Soc., Dt. Gesellschaft Psychology (Early Career award 1975), N.Y. Acad. Scis., Psychonomic Soc., Human Factors Soc. (European chpt.), Soc. German Engrs., Bayrische Elite-Akademie. Home: Muellerstr 4, d-93059 Regensburg Germany Office: Bayrische Landesuniv, Psychology Dept, D-93040 Regensburg Germany

ZIMMER, CHRISTOPH, retired biochemist; b. Dresden, Germany, Dec. 14, 1933; s. Gottfried and Margareta Z.; m. Lotti Riegel, Oct. 1961; children: Annette, Christiane. Diploma in chemistry, U. Jena, 1958, DSc, 1978. From asst. acad. scis. to dir. inst. molecular biology U. Jena, Germany, 1992-99; ret., 1999. Mem. Gesellschaft fur Biochemie und Molekularbiologie. Office: F Schiller U Inst Molecular Biology, Winzerlaer str 10, D-07745 Jena Germany

ZIMMER, HORST GUNTER, mathematics educator; b. Lubeck, Fed. Republic Germany, June 30, 1937; s. Erich Karl and Magdalene (Wilcken) Z.; m. Irmgard Schultes, July 12, 1968; children: Frank, Kathrin, Kirsten. Grundschulabschluss, Heine-Schule-Schule, Schwerin, German Democratic Republic, 1955; Abitur, Katharineum, Lubeck, Fed. Republic of Germany, 1957; Staatsexamen, U. Hamburg, Fed. Republic of Germany, 1963; PhD, U. Tubingen, Fed. Republic of Germany, 1966; habilitation, U. Karlsruhe, Fed. Republic of Germany, 1972. Asst. prof. Ohio State U., Columbus, 1967-69, U. Calif.-L.A., 1970-72, akademischer rat. U. Karksruhe, 1970-72; akademischer oberrat U. Karksruhe, Fed. Republic of Germany, 1972-74; prof. U. Saarbrucken, Fed. Republic of Germany, 1974—. Co-editor: Number Theory, 1972; editor: Number Theory, 1980, Computational Number Theory, 1991, Group Theory, Algebra, and Number Theory, 1996. Mem. Computer Algebra Group of Gesellschaft für Informatik, Deutsche Mathema iker-Vereinigung. Office: U Saarland, Fachberich Mathematik, Im Stadtwald, BAU 27, D-66386 Saarbrucken Federal Republic Germany

ZIMMER, IAN, dean. BBus, Swinburne; MCom, Liverpool U.; PhD, U. N.S.W., DSc. With Royal Melbourne Inst. of Technology, 1974-77; lectr. Warrnambool Inst. of Advanced Edn. (now Deakin Univ.), 1977-78; lectr., sr. lectr. in acctg. U. NSW, 1979-84; prof. acctg. Univ. Queensland, Brisbane, Australia, 1985, 86-98, head dept. of commerce, 1988-96; head TC Beirne Sch. of Law/U. Queensland, Brisbane, Australia, 1997-99; exec. dean, faculty bus. econs. and law U. Queensland, Brisbane, 1999—; mem. Specialist Assessment Panel of the Hong Kong Rsch. Grants Coun.; cons. in field; expert witness on work on appropriate acctg. practice. Contbr. articles to profl. jours.; editl. bd.: Acctg. Horizons jour., Asia Pacific Jour. of Acctg., The Brit. Acctg. Rev. and Acctg. and Bus. Rsch. Fellow Australian Soc. of Cert. Practising Accts., Inst. Chartered Accts. E-mail: feedback-about-uq@uq.edu.au. Office: Univ Queensland, Brisbane QLD 4072, Australia

ZIMMER, MICHAEL J., lawyer; married; 3 children. Student, Brown U., 1970; BA in Polit. Sci. cum laude, Providence Coll., 1971; JD cum laude, U. Md., 1975. Bar: D.C. 1975, Va. 1982. invited witness various energy and energy tax proposals before congrl. coms., various fed. depts. and agencies, and state commns. and agencies, 1977—; pres., gen. counsel Cogeneration and Independent Power Coalition Am., Inc. (now Electric Power Supply Assn.), 1980-90; active Am. Coun. Capital Formation, Am. Cogeneration Assn., Clean Coal Coalition, NAS, Energy Mich., Mid-Atlantic Independent Power Prodrs., Independent Power Prodrs. N.Y., Midwest Gas Assn.; active Am. Gas Assn., 1977-80, staff v.p. govt. rels.; group chair dept. and practice energy and project fin. various nat. law firms; nat. lectr. in field, including Va. Polytechnic Inst., U. Wis., Georgetown U.; invited spkr. N.Y. Soc. Security Analysts. Co-author: Energy Law Transactions, 1990; contbg. editor Independent Energy mag., 1986—, Electric Light and Power, 1999—; mem. adv. bd. programs McGraw-Hill, Internat. Bus. Forum, Fin. Times. Named Indsl. All-Star, Independent Energy mag., 1993, One of Top Leaders of IPP Industry, Independent Energy mag., 1996. Mem. ABA (mem. natural resources and pub. utility law sects.), Fed. Energy Bar Assn. (chmn. cogeneration small power prodn. com. 1986-87). Avocation: youth sports activities. Fax: 202-452-7074. Office: Baker & McKenzie 815 Connecticut Ave NW Washington DC 20006-4004

ZIMMER, PAUL GERALD, II, community care licensing professional; b. Detroit, Oct. 2, 1946; s. Paul Gerald and Beatrice Mae (Mitchell) Z.; m. Shelly Mardell Hallier, May 23, 1980; children: Paul Gerald III, Carrie Lea. BA in Religion/Social Work, Azusa Pacific U., 1973. Ordained to ministry So. Bapt. Conf., 1985. Vocat. rehab. counselor dept. vocat. rehab. State of Calif., Riverside, 1986-88, intake specialist social svc. cmty. care licensing, 1988-91, licensing program supr. dept. social svc. cmty. care licensing, 1991—; instr., adv. bd. mem. Riverside County Office Edn.-Family-to-Family, 1993—; mem. Riverside County Dept. Pub. Social Svcs. Child Advocacy Coun., 1994—; co-chair RICKI com. Riverside County Dept. Health-Immunizations, 1996-98; monthly music evangelist L.A. Union Rescue Mission, 1984—; mem. Fontana chpt. Am. Red Cross, 1983-87. Author (booklet) The Age of Becoming, 1977; author (music album) Day-A-Comin', 1989, (lyrics) Flashback Music, 1996. Dist. exec. Boy Scouts Am., Redlands/Victorville, Calif., 1981-83, mem. Order of Arrow, 1963—; mem./instr. Riverside County Office Edn. Child Care Initiative Project for Spanish Speaking Care Providers Indio, 1994—; appointed mem. State of Calif. Equal Employment Opportunity Adv. Com.-Disability Adv. Com., Sacramento, 1999-2000; min. Ch. in the Park, Hemet, Calif., 1996—. With U.S. Army, 1967-68. Recipient Youth Adv. of Yr. award Riverside County Office Edn., 1993. Mem. Inland Empire Parents Anonymous (group facilitator, crisis counselor 1990-93). Avocations: writing/performing Christian music, fitness walking, coin collecting. Home: 1188 Wilson Ave Perris CA 92571-4926

ZIMMER, REINHOLD GÜNTER, chemist, researcher; b. Wiesbaden, Hessen, Germany, Oct. 19, 1959; s. Günter Wolfgang and Maria Lydia (Pulger) Z.. Cert. chem. tech. asst., Kerschensteiner Sch., Wiesbaden, 1981; diploma in engring., Tech. U., Darmstadt, Germany, 1988, PhD in Chemistry, 1990. Rschr. Tech. U., Darmstadt, 1990-91; Karl-Landsteiner postdoctoral fellow Sandoz Rsch. Inst., Vienna, Austria, 1992-94; rschr. Tech. U., Dresden, Germany, 1994-2000, Freie U., Berlin, 2000—. Reviewer Jour. Organic Chemistry, U.S., Tetrahedron, Eng.; contbr. articles to profl. publs. Mem. Gesellschaft Deutscher Chemiker. Roman Catholic. Office: Freie U, Takustrasse 3, D-14195 Berlin Germany

ZIMMER, WOLFGANG MARTIN, periodontist; b. Einhausen, Hessen, Germany, Mar. 6, 1958; s. Lorenz and Gertrud (Freisens) Z.; m. Christa Maria Zechmeister, June 21, 1991; children: Anna-Kristina, Jacob Martin, Phillip B. DDS, U. Heidelberg, Germany, 1983, D Med. Dentistry, 1988; MSc in Periodontology, U. London, 1989; MS in Periodontics, Mayo U., Rochester, Minn., 1992. Stabsarzt German Bundeswehr, 1983-87; pvt. practice periodontics Munich, 1992—. Contbr. articles to profl. jours. Mem. Am. Acad. Periodontology, Germany Soc. for Periodontology, Alumni Assn. Mayo Grad. Sch. Medicine. Office: Praxis, Nibelungenstrasse 84, 80639 Munich Germany

ZIMMERLY, JAMES GREGORY, lawyer, physician; b. Longview, Tex., Mar. 25, 1941; s. George James and Irene Gertrude (Kohler) Z.; m. Nancy Carol Zimmerly, June 11, 1966; children: Mark, Scott, Robin; m. Johanna Bross Huffer, Feb. 14, 1991. BA, Gannon Coll., 1962; MD, U. Md., 1966, JD, 1969; MPH, Johns Hopkins U., 1968; LLD (hon.), Gannon U., 1998. Bar: Md. 1970, D.C. 1972, U.S. Ct. Mil. Appeals 1973, U.S. Supreme Ct. 1973. Ptnr. Acquisto, Asplen & Morstein, Ellicott City, Md., 1970—. Chmn. dept. legal medicine Armed Forces Inst. Pathology, 1971-91; prof. George Washington U., 1972-80; adj. prof. law Georgetown U. Law Ctr., 1972—, Antioch Sch. Law, 1977-80; assoc. prof. U. Md. Sch. Medicine, 1973—; mem. sci. adv. bd. Armed Forces Inst. Path., 1997—; cons. Dept. Def., Dept. Justice, HHS, VA, 1971-91. Fellow Am. Acad. Forensic Scis., Am. Coll. Legal Medicine, (pres. 1980-81), Am. Coll Preventive Medicine; mem. ABA, Md. Bar Assn., Am. Soc. on Law and Medicine, Am. Coll. Emergency Physicians, Md. Med. Soc. Editor: Legal Aspects of Medical Practice, 1978-88, Jour. Legal Medicine, 1975-78, Md. Med. Jour., 1977-88, Lawyers' Med. Ency., 1980-90, chmn. bd. dirs. Baltimore Rh Lab., 1984—; med. dir. Monumental Life Ins. Co., 1994—, Aegon Spl. Markets Group, Inc.; chmn. Am. Coll. Legal Med. Fdn., bd. dirs., 1996—. Home: 6300 Old National Pike Bluestone Overlook Boonsboro MD 21713 Office: Monumental Life Ins Co 2 E Chase St Baltimore MD 21202-2559

ZIMMERMAN, AARON MARK, lawyer; b. Syracuse, N.Y., Jan. 28, 1953; s. Julius and Sara (Lavine) Z. B.S., Syracuse U., 1974, J.D., 1976. Bar: N.Y. 1977, Pa. 1977, D.C. 1978, S.C. 1978, Fla. 1978, U.S. Dist. Ct. S.C. 1978, U.S. Dist. Ct. (no. dist.) N.Y. Corp. atty., asst. sec. Daniel Internat. Corp., Greenville, S.C., 1977-79; ptnr. Abend, Driscoll & Zimmerman, 1979-81; Zimmerman Law Office, Syracuse, 1981—. Bd. dirs. Syracuse Friends Ametuer Boxing, 1982-92. Mem. Am. Arbitration Assn. (arbitrator), Workers Compensation Com. N.Y. State Bar (exec. com. 1984—), Workers Compensation Assn. of Cen. N.Y. (charter mem., dir., treas. 1980-95), N.Y. State Bar, S.C. State Bar, D.C. State Bar, Fla. State Bar, ABA. Lodge: Masons. Home: 602 Standish Dr Syracuse NY 13224-2018 Office: 117 S State St Syracuse NY 13202-1103

ZIMMERMAN, AMY J., producer, director; b. N.Y.C., Nov. 4, 1961; d. Arthur S. and Louise (Weild) Z. BA in Journalism and History, U. So. Calif., 1983. Writer, photographer Thoroughbred of Calif. Mag., Arcadia, 1981-85; prodr. Hammond Prodns., Lexington, Ky., 1985; assoc. prodr. NBC Sports, N.Y.C., 1986—; dir. broadcasting Santa Anita Park, Arcadia, 1986—; prodr., dir. Fox Sports Net, L.A., 1996—; cons. Fox Sports, L.A., 1998—. Assoc. prodr. The Breeders' Cup, 1992 (Emmy award Best Live Sports Spl. 1992); exec. prodr. Santa Anita Today, 1996 (Eclipse award honorable mention for local tv), Inside Santa Anita, 1998 (Eclipse award hon. mention for local tv), Santa Anita Tonight: One on One, 1993 (Eclipse award honorable mention for local tv); exec. prodr., dir. Best of Santa Anita, 1999 (Eclipse award for local tv); assoc. prodr., editor: A Cup of Courage, 1988 (Eclipse award honorable mention for local tv). Bd. dirs. U. So. Calif. Panhellenic, 1982-83, Sterling Assn. Aviva Ctr., Hollywood, Calif., 1998—. Mem. Turf Publicists Assn., Nat. Thoroughbred Racing Assn. (racing and TV task force), Alpha Gamma Delta. E-mail: ajzimmerm@aol.com. Office: Santa Anita Park 285 W Huntington Dr Arcadia CA 91007-3439

ZIMMERMAN, CAROLE LEE, public relations professional; b. Roxboro, N.C., Aug. 28, 1948; d. Ray Richard and Annie Theresa (O'Briant) Z.; m. Richard A. Hoehn, Oct. 26, 1991; 1 child, Kristin Nicole Sizemore. BS in Edn., Fla. State U., 1970; publs. specialist cert., George Washington U., 1980; MA in Pub. Comm., Am. U., 1993. Accredited in pub. rels. Tchr. Gadsden County Pub. Schs., Quincy, Fla., 1971-72, Am. schs., Kaiserslautern and Darmstadt, Germany, 1974-76; editor, writer USLICO Corp., Arlington, Va., 1980-84; dir. communications Bread for the World, Washington, 1984-95; dir. comms. Nat. Inst. for Environment, Washington, 1995-97; dir. comms. and mktg. Am. Pub. Health Assn., Washington, 1997—. Mem. Am. Soc. Assn. Execs., Pub. Rels. Soc. Am., Assn. for Women in Comms. (bd. dirs. 1996-98), Am. Soc. Assn. Execs. Office: Am Pub Health Assn 800 I St Washington DC 20001-3710

ZIMMERMAN, JANE D., healthcare executive, psychologist; b. N.Y.C., May 17, 1952; d. Irving I. and Jeanette I. Zimmerman. BA in Psychology magna cum laude, U. Ariz., 1974, MA in Clin. Psychology, 1978, PhD in Clin. Psychology, 1982. Lic. psychologist, N.Y. NIMH pre-doctoral fellow U. Calif., San Francisco, 1981-82; NIMH postdoctoral fellow CUNY and Albert Einstein Sch. Medicine, 1982-83; assoc. prodr., rschr. CBS News, N.Y.C., 1983-86; mktg. analyst Jesup & LaMont Securities, Co., 1987; dir. health & sci. TV projects Scientist's Inst. Pub. Info., N.Y.C., 1988-90; pvt. practice N.Y.C., 1990-92; assoc. commr. N.Y.C. Dept. Mental Health, 1992-95; sr. v.p. comm. & mktg. N.Y.C. Health & Hosps. Corp., 1995—; cons. VIACOM, N.Y.C., 1990-92, Grey Advt., N.Y.C., 1990-92, Coun. Advancement & Support Edn., Washington, 1990-92, Found. Global Broadcasting, Washington, 1990-92; adj. prof. NYU, 1987. Prodr. Choose to De-Fuse Pub. Svc. Announcements (Finalst award NATAS, Internat. Silver Cindy award, Nat. Vision award, Nat. Edn. Media award), Africa: Struggle for Survival (Emmy award, Overseas Press Club award), Whose America Is It? (Emmy award, George Foster Peabody award); prodr., writer Making the Tough Choice (N.Y. State Gilbert award); contbr. articles to profl. jours. Fellow AAAS; mem. APA, Nat. Assn. Pub. Hosps., Health Care Pub. Rels. and Mktg. Soc., N.Y. Press Club. Avocations: swimming, sailing, hiking, dancing, travel. Office: NYC Health and Hosps Corp 125 Worth St Ste 510 New York NY 10013-4006

ZIMMERMAN, JO ANN, health services and educational consultant, former lieutenant governor; b. Van Buren County, Iowa, Dec. 24, 1936; d. Russell and Hazel (Ward) McIntosh; m. A. Tom Zimmerman, Aug. 26, 1956; children: Andrew, Lisa, Don and Ron (twins), Beth. Diploma, Broadlawns Sch. of Nursing, Des Moines, 1958; BA with honors, Drake U., 1973; postgrad., Iowa State U., 1973-75. RN, Iowa. Asst. head nurse maternity dept. Broadlawns Med. Ctr., Des Moines, 1958-59, weekend supr. nursing svcs., 1960-61, supr. maternity dept., 1966-68; instr. maternity nursing Broadlawns Sch. Nursing, 1968-71; health planner, community rels. assoc. Iowa Health Systems Agy., Des Moines, 1978-82; mem. Iowa Ho. Reps., 1982-86; lt. gov., pres. of Senate, State of Iowa, 1987-91; cons. health svcs., grant writing and continuing edn. Zimmerman & Assocs., Des Moines, 1991—; dir. patient care svcs. Nursing Svcs. Iowa, 1996-98; nurse case mgr. Olsten Health Svcs. (now Gentiva Health Svcs.), 1998—; ops. dir. Medlink Svcs., Inc., Des Moines, 1992-96. Contbr. articles to profl. jours. Mem. advanced registered nurse practioner task force on cert. nurse mid-wives Iowa Bd. Nursing, 1980-81, Waukee, Polk County, Iowa Health Edn. Coord. Coun., Iowa Women's Polit. Caucus, Dallas County Women's Polit. Caucus; chmn. Des Moines Area Maternity Nursing Conf. Group, 1969-70, task force on sch. health svcs. Iowa Dept. Health, 1982, task force health edn. Iowa Dept. Pub. Instruction, 1979, adv. com. health edn. assessment tool, 1980-81, Nat. Lt. Govs., chair com. on Agrl. and Rural Devel., 1989; Dallas County Dem. Ctrl. Com., 1972-84, 98—; bd. dirs. Waukee Cmty. Sch. Bd., 1976-79, pres. 1978-79; bd. dirs. Iowa PTA, 1979-83, chairperson Health Com., 1980-84; mem. steering com. ERA, Iowa, 1991-92; founder Dem. Activist Women's Network (DAWN), 1992. Mem. ANA, LWV (health chmn. met. Des Moines chpt.), Iowa Nurses Assn., Iowa League for Nursing (bd. dirs. 1979-83), Family Centered Childbirth Edn. Assn. (childbirth instr., advisor), Iowa Cattleman's Assn., Am. Lung Assn. (bd. dirs. Iowa 1988-92), Dem. Activist Women's Network (founder 1992). Mem. Christian Ch. Avocations: gardening, sewing, reading, bridge, breeding British White cattle. Office: Gentiva Health Svcs 3737 Westown Pkwy Ste 2C West Des Moines IA 50266-1028

ZIMMERMAN, MARLIN U., JR., chemical engineer; b. Akron, Ohio, Aug. 2, 1923; s. Marlin Ulrich and Helen (Nelson) Z. BChemE, Johns Hopkins U., 1944; MBA, Harvard U., 1966. Registered profl. engr., Ohio. Jr. engr. Standard Oil Co. (Ohio), Cleve., 1944-46, engr., 1946-48, sr. engr., 1948-49; process engr. Lima (Ohio) refinery Standard Oil Co. (Ohio), 1949-50; group engr. Standard Oil Co. (Ohio), Cleve., 1951-55, group supr., 1956-60, supr. process sys. sect., 1961-63, head acrylonitrile task force, 1961, tech. specialist, 1964-66; mgr. long term planning Norton Co., Worcester, Mass., 1966-69; cons. John Van Der Valk & Assocs., N.Y.C., 1970-73; pvt. practice cons. chem. engr. ammonia-urea Hackensack, N.J., 1974—; head task force to help commercialize Sohio acrylonitrile process. Contbr. articles to profl. jours. Baker scholar, 1966. Mem. AIChE, Johns Hopkins Club, Tudor and Stuart Club, Tau Beta Pi, Omicron Delta Kappa, Beta Theta Pi. Methodist. Achievements include patent for process improvement of Tosco shale process for oil recovery, patent for pig handling for gasoline blender meter testing loop, others. Avocations: travel, photography, reading, investing, computer programming. Home and Office: 229 Union St Hackensack NJ 07601-4225

ZIMMERMAN, MIKAEL CHRISTER, medical science educator; b. Lidingö, Stockholm, Sweden, Oct. 16, 1953; s. Carl-Olof Hjalmar and Inga-Britt Matilda (Björeby) Z.; m. A. Margareta Stigsdotter Leijonhufvud, Apr. 24, 1951; children: Malin, Gabriella, Carl-Olof. Lic. Dental Surgeon, Karolinska Inst., Stockholm, 1979, PhD, 1993. Lectr. Karolinska Inst. Sch. Dentistry. Author: Hygiene, Infection Control and Ethics in Dentistry, 1995; inventor (with others) system for mobile dentistry. Recipient Dentist of Yr. award Swedish Dental Acad., 1995. Office: Karolinska Inst, Box 4064, S-141-04 Huddinge Sweden

ZIMMERMAN, ROBERT ALLEN See DYLAN, BOB

ZIMMERMANN, DIETER, physicist; b. Suttgart, Germany, July 23, 1939; s. Karl and Ilse (Loosch) Z.; m. Gisela Schmidthals, June 3, 1965; children: Cornelia, Stefan. Diploma in physics, Freie U. Berlin, 1963; DSc, Tech. U. Berlin, 1968. Asst. Tech. U. Berlin, 1964-70, prof. physics, 1970—, head dept. physics, 1979-82, 86-87; vis. prof. MIT, Cambridge, 1976, Pa. State U., 1998. Contbr. articles to profl. jours. Home: Holtheimer Weg 11b, D-12207 Berlin Germany Office: Inst Atomare Analyt Physik, Hardenbergstrasse 36 Tech U, D-10623 Berlin Germany

ZIMMERMANN, HANS, United Nations official; b. Zurich, June 9, 1942; s. Hans D. and Margaretha J. (Sulzer) Z. Grad. in polit. sci., U. Zurich, 1970. Sr. humanitarian affairs officer UN Office for Coord. Humanitarian Affairs, Geneva, Switzerland; chair Working Group on Emergency Telecomms., 1994—; trustee Internat. Inst. Comms. Office: United Nations, Palais des Nations, CH-1211 Geneva 10, Switzerland

ZIMMERMANN, HORST ERNST FRIEDRICH, economics educator; b. Krefeld, Germany, Mar. 11, 1934; s. Arthur and Elfriede Z.; m. Amrei Moehl, June 24, 1967; children: Roland, Anne, Lisa. Student, U. Munich, 1957-58, Northwestern U., 1958-59; Dr. rer. pol., U. Cologne, 1963; postdoctoral scholar, U. Pa., 1965-66. Asst. dept. pub. fin. U. Cologne, Germany, 1960-65; rsch. scholar U. Cologne, 1965-68; prof. econs. Philipps U., Marburg, Germany, 1969—; counsel Fed. Agy. Regional Rsch. and Area Planning, 1977-82, Coun. Experts on Environ. Problems, 1981-90, Adv. Coun. to Fed. Fin. Ministry, 1986—; with Fed. Govt. Global Change Coun., 1992—; vis. scholar Brookings Instn., Washington, 1972-73, Urban Inst., Washington, 1977—, Cambridge (Eng.) U., 1986. Author: Public Aid to Developing Countries, 1963, Public Expenditure and Regional Economic Development, 1970, Regional Preferences, 1973, Public Finance, 8th edit., 2000, Regional Incidence of Fiscal Flows, 1981, Studies in Comparative Federalism, 1981, Future of Government Finances, 1988, Environmental Charges, 1993, Welfare State between Growth and Distribution, 1996, Local Government Finances, 1999. Recipient August Loesch prize for regional rsch., 1976, Cross of the Order of Merit of the Fed. Rep. Germany, 1993. Mem. Acad. Regional Rsch. and Planning, Am. Econ. Assn., Soc. Econ. and Social Scis. Office: Am Plan 2, D-35037 Marburg Germany

ZIMMERMANN, INGFRIED LEONHARD, pharmaceutical educator; b. Villingen-Schwenningen, Germane, June 14, 1945; m. Marianne Van Schie; children: Birgit, Bjoern. D in Natural Scis., U. Freiburg, Germany, 1975; qualification in postdoctoral lecturing, U. Braunschweig, Germany, 1990. Tchr. Coll. St. Sebastian, Stegen and Freiburg, Germany, 1972-76; scientist Schering AG, Berlin, 1976-80, head pharm. dept., 1981-85; dir. pharm. rsch. and devel. Boehringer Ingelheim, Germany, 1985-89, dir. devel., 1989-90, dir. rsch. and devel., 1990-94; prof. pharm. tech. U. Wuerzburg, Germany, 1994—; cons. family planning program WHO, Geneva, 1978; sci. adv. bd. Boehringer Mannheim, Germany, 1995-98; dir. Farmerit S.A., Buenos Aires, 1985-94. Author: Pharmazeutische Technologie: Industrielle Herstellung und Entwicklung von Arzneimitteln, 1998. Mem. Gesellschaft Deutscher Chemiker, Deutsche Pharmazeutische Gesellschaft, Kolloid-Gesellschaft, Arbeitsgemeinschaft Pharmazeutische Verfahrenstechnik. Avocations: cooking, flying. Office: Univ Wuerzburg Pharm Tech, Am Hubland, D 97074 Würzburg Germany

ZIMMERMANN, JACQUES, bank executive; b. Paris, June 9, 1945; s. Zimmermann and Montclair; m. Marie-Christine Jully. Head fgn. dept. Rothschild Bank Group, Paris, 1969-79; exec. Rothschild Bank, Paris, 1979-89; rep. IBERCAjA, Paris, 1989—. Office: IBERCAJA, 15 rue de la Paix, F-75002 Paris France

ZIMMERMANN, KAREL, chemical engineer educator; b. Ceske Budejovice, Czechoslovakia, Apr. 19, 1946; arrived in France, 1985; s. Frantisek and Antonie (Stránská) Z.; m. Iva Andrejsová, Oct. 16, 1972; children: Jakub, Katerina, Ian. Grad., Charles U., Prague, Czechoslovakia, 1968, RNDr, 1979, Candidate Sci., 1979. Rschr. Phys. Inst. Charles U., Prague, 1968-70, Inst. Macromolecular Chemistry, Prague, 1970-85; lectr., rschr. U. P&M Curie, Paris, 1986—; cons. Nat. Inst. Informatics and Antomatics, Roquencourt, France, 1987-88; lectr. Univs. and Schs. Engring., France, 1987—. Recipient award Czechoslovakian Acad. Sci., 1985. Avocations: music, submarines, computer simulations. Home: 24 Rue du 8 Mai 1945, 78460 Chevreuse France Office: INRA, Math Info & Genome, RD 10, 78026 Versailles France

ZIMMERMANN, KLAUS F., economics educator; b. Göppingen, Germany, Dec. 2, 1952. Diplom-Volkwirt, U. Mannheim, Germany, 1978, PhD, 1985, Dr. rer. pol. habil., 1987. Rsch. fellow Univ. Catholique de Louvain, Belgium, 1985-86; sr. rsch. fellow Sci. Ctr. Berlin, Germany, 1986; vis. assoc. prof. U. Pa., Phila., 1987; Heisenberg fellow German Sci. Found., Germany, 1988-89; prof. U. Munich, Germany, 1989-98; dir. Inst. for the Study of Labor, Bonn, Germany, 1998—; pres. German Inst. for Econ. Rsch., Berlin, 2000—; prof. U. Bonn, 1998—; sec. European Soc. for Population Econs., 1986-92, pres., 1994; dean Faculty of Econs., U. Munich, 1993-95; co-dir. human resources programme Ctr. for Econ. Policy Rsch., London, 1991-98, co-dir. Labor Econs. program, 1998—; vis. prof. U. Tilburg, The Netherlands, 1990, Humboldt-U. Berlin, 1991, U. Kyoto, Japan, 1995, Dartmouth Coll., 1997, Simon Fraser U., Burnaby, Can., 1999. Mng. editor Jour. of Population Econs., 1988-95, Economic Policy, 1995-98; editor-in-chief: Jour. of Population Econs., 1996—; contbr. articles to profl. jours. Fulbright scholar, 1986-87; recipient Ruhrgas Rsch. fellowship, U. Bergen, 1987. Fellow Ctr. for Econ. Policy Rsch.; mem. Verein für Socialpolitik Coun., European Econ. Assn. (mem. coun.). Office: U Munich, IZA/Inst for Study of Labor, PO Box 7240, 53072 Bonn Germany also: DIW Berlin, 14191 Berlin Germany

ZIMMERMANN, REINHARD, educator; b. Hamburg, Germany, Oct. 10, 1952; s. Fritz and Inge (Hansen) Z. Dr.iur., U. Hamburg, 1978; LLD, U. Cape Town, South Africa, 1991; LLD (hon.), U. Chgo., 1997. Asst. prof. U. Cologne, Germany, 1980; W.P. Schreiner prof. Roman and comparative law U. Cape Town, 1981-88; prof. pvt. law, Roman law and comparative law U. Regensburg, Germany, 1988—; Max Rheinstein vis. prof. U. Chgo., 1993; vis. prof. Tulane U., Yale U., U. Edinburgh, Scotland, U. Stellenbosch, South Africa; A.L. Goodhart prof. U. Cambridge, Eng., 1998-99. Author: Richterliches Moderationsrecht, 1979, Römisch-Holländisches Recht in Südafrika, 1983, Law of Obligations, 3rd edit., 1996; editor: Southern Cross, 1996, Zeitschrift für Europäisches Privatrecht, 1993—, Schriften für Europäische Rechtsgeschichte, 1992—. Recipient Leibniz prize, Bonn, Germany, 1996. Mem. Bavarian Acad. of Sci., Dutch Acad. of Arts and Scis. (corr. mem.). Lutheran. Avocations: music (piano), sports (field hockey, tennis). Home: Dechbettener Str 5 a, 93049 Regensburg Germany Office: U Regensburg, Universitatsstr 31, 93053 Regensburg Germany

ZIMOLO, ARMANDO, insurance company executive; b. Trieste, Italy, Jan. 16, 1938; s. Edoardo and Norma (Daris) Z.; m. Daniela Camperi. D Law, U. Trieste, 1962. Reporter Il Globo, Rome, 1963-67; head rsch. dept. Assicurazioni Generali, Trieste, 1968-81; mgr. Assicurazioni Generali, Rome, 1981—; with Comm. Dept. Generali Group, Trieste, 1992—. Author: L'Europa Per Non Morire, 1967, Assicurare il Futuro, 1979; contbr. articles to profl. publs. Nat. sec. Italian Liberal Youth, Rome, 1963-67; councillor Municipality of Trieste, 1966-78, Dist. of Trieste, 1978-81; mem. Leaders Exchange Program, 1967, Ministerial Commns., 1985—; bd. dirs. United World Coll. Adriatic, 1981—; mem. exec. com. Istituto Italiano Di Credito Fondiario, 1990—. Recipient Gold Legion award Unione Della Legion D'Oro, 1967. Mem. Ins. Law Internat. Assn. (councillor Italian sect.), Rotary (Paul Harris fellow). Avocation: tennis. Home: Via della Scrofa 57, 00186 Rome Italy Office: Assicurazioni Gen, Piazza Venezia 11, 00187 Rome Italy also: Piazza Duca degli, Abruzzi 2, 34132 Trieste Italy

ZIMOLONG, BERNHARD MICHAEL, psychologist, educator; b. Breslau, Germany, Apr. 26, 1944; s. Hans Joachim and Hiltraud (John) Z.; m. Ursula Eva-Maria Herbst, Aug. 5, 1966; 1 child, Andreas. Diploma, U. Munster, Germany, 1970; PhD, U. Braunschweig, Germany, 1974, habilitation, 1981. Asst. prof. U. Braunschweig, 1972-82; prof. U. Bochum, Germany, 1984—; speaker Spl. Rsch. Ctr. 187, 1992-95; vis. prof. Purdue U., West-Lafayette, Ind., 1983-84, Decision Rsch., Eugene, Oreg., 1988-89. Author books on engring. psychology, human reliability, safety mgmt. and occupational health and safety; contbr. articles to profl. jours. Lt. German Army, 1964-66. Grantee Heisenberg Deutsche Forschungsgemeinschaft, 1982-84. Mem. Human Factors Soc., Deutsche Gesellschaft Psychologie, Gesellschaft Arbeitswissenschaft. Office: Ruhr U Bochum, Dept Psychology, 44780 Bochum Germany

ZINCKE, GERALD DIETMAR, software engineering consultant; b. Linz, Austria, Apr. 11, 1957; s. Hans Erich and Elenora Zincke; m. Evelyn M. Schmutz, June 6, 1983. Diplomingenieur, Kepler U., Linz, 1981; D in Tech., 1985. Rsch. asst. Kepler U., 1979-81, univ. asst., 1981-85; software engr. Voest Alpine Ag., Linz, 1985-86; vice mgr. Balzers Ag., Liechtenstein, 1986-89; project mgr. Servo Data GmbH, Linz, 1989-91; cons. Geseb GmbH, Vienna, Austria, 1991-93; tech. officer Fallmann u. Bauernfeind GmbH, Linz, 1993; sr. cons. GMO GmbH, Linz and Vienna, 1993-2000; mgr. process and quality engring. Axioma GmbH, Linz, 2000—; architect GMO Business Objects Framework. Contbr. articles to profl. jours., internat. confs. Mem. ACM, Austrian Soc. Informatics. Avocations: classical music, skiing, rowing. Office: Axioma Info Systems GmbH, Scharitzerstr 12, A-4020 Linz Austria

ZINEDINE, ZIDANE, professional soccer player; b. Marseille, France, June 23, 1972. With Cannes Football Club, France, Bordeaux Football Club, France; now midfielder Juventus Football Club, Torino, Italy; with French Nat. Team; winner two Serie A titles, World Club title, UEFA Cup (with Bordeaux), 1996, European Cup finals (with Juventus), 1997, 98. Named Third in European player of the year awards, 1997; winner World Cup with French Nat. Team, 1998. Office: Juventus Football Club SpA, Piazza Crimea 7, 10131 Turin Italy*

ZINGHER, HARRY LEE, chemical engineer; b. Rushville, Ill., Dec. 18, 1956; s. Henry Cherry and Dessie Z. BS in Chem. Engring., U. Ill., 1980; MS in Chem. Engring., U. Iowa, 1985; PhD in Chem. Engring., Ohio State U., 1989; MD, U. Ill., 1990. Registered profl. engr. Chem. engr. Nat. Starch & Chem., Meredosia, Ill., 1977, Marathon Oil Co., Robinson, Ill., 1979-80, Monsanto Chem., Texas City, Tex., 1980, Ill. EPA, Springfield, 1989-90; profl. cons. chem. engr. Rushville, Ill., 1990—. Recipient scholarship Marathon Oil Co., U. Ill., 1976-80, fellowships U. Iowa, 1984-85, Dow Chem., Ohio State U., 1985-89. Mem. AAAS, Am. Chem. Soc., N.Y. Acad. Scis., U. Ill. Alumni Assn., U. Iowa Alumni Assn., Pres.'s Club Ohio State U., Tau Beta Pi. Achievements include partial patenting including computer calculations of electrophoresis modeling and partial patenting on peristaltic pump. Office: Monsanto Chem Corp 417 W Washington St Rushville IL 62681-1355

ZINGIRIAN, MARIO, ophthalmologist, educator; b. Trieste, Italy, Jan. 16, 1932; s. Vahe and Dirce (Scandiuzzi) Z.; m. Astrid Uluhogian, Aug. 6, 1962; children: Alessandro, Matteo, Nicola. Degree in Medicine and Surgery, Univ., Parma, Italy, 1958; Degree in Ophthalmology, Univ., Genoa, Italy, 1961. Asst. Univ. Eye Clinic, Genoa, 1960-73; prof. of Ophthalmology Univ.

Eye Clinic, Sassari, Italy, 1973-75; prof. of Ophthalmology Univ. Eye Clinic, Genoa, 1976—, dir., 1976—. Avocations: music, restoration. Office: Clinica Oculistica-Ospedale S Martino, Pad 9 Largo R Benzi 10, 16132 Genova Italy

ZININ, PAVEL V., physicist; b. Moscow, Dec. 20, 1955; s. Valentin F. and Nailya G. (Zinina) Z.; m. Natalia O. Krokhina, Apr. 18, 1987; 1 child, Lisa. BS/MS, Moscow State U., 1973, 80; PhD, Moscow Inst. Physics/Tech., 1987. Rsch. engr. Scientific and Rsch. Inst. for Biol. Testing of Chem., Moscow, 1980-81, rsch. assoc., 1981-83; rsch. scientist N. Semienov Inst. of Chem. Physics/Russian Acad. Scis., Moscow, 1987-93; Alexander von Humboldt Found. Rsch. fellow Inst. for Material Sci. and Structure Rsch./U. Bremen, 1993-94; rsch. fellow U. oxford, 1995-97; asst. rschr. U. Hawaii, Honolulu, 1998—. Author: (with others) Handbook of the Elastic Properties of Solids, Liquids and Gases, 2000; contbr. more than 70 articles to profl. jours. Recipient fellowship Alexander von Humboldt, Germany, 1993; grantee NATO, Brussel, 1994-95, Caterpillar Inc., 2000. Mem. Optical Soc. of Am., Biomech. Soc. E-mail: zinin@soest.hawaii.edu. Office: Univ Hawaii 2525 Correa Rd Honolulu HI 96822-2219

ZINK, DAVID DANIEL, retired English educator, writer; b. Kansas City, Mo.; s. David Daniel and Virginia (Taylor) Z.; m. Joan Wilson (div. July 13, 1982); children: Laurie Wilson Zink, David Paul Zink; m. Joann Nelson Rocha, Oc.t. 29, 1982 (filed for dissolution of marriage Dec. 19, 1988); 1 child, Christopher Stewart. BJ, U. Tex., 1952; MA in English, U. Colo., 1957, PhD in Victorian Lit., 1962. Instr./assoc. prof. English USAF Acad., Colo. Springs, Colo., 1957-65; prof. English Lamar U., Beaumont, Tex., 1965-77; part-time English instr., Pasadena City Coll., Pasadena, Calif., 1984-89; exec. recruiter, L.A., 1980-84. Author: (book) The Ancient Stones Speak: A Photographic and Archaeological Atlas of the Megalithic Sites of the World, 1979, Stones of Atlantis, 1990, on camera cons. Leslie Stephen, 1972; co-author: (with wife Joan) You are the Mystery, 1976; in Bolivia for NBC series In Search of..., 1976, to Cousteau Soc. at Bimini Island for PBS special Calypso's Search for Atlantis, 1976; contbr. to TV specials on Atlantis, 1993-98; co-rschr. Kirlian photography project, 1973. Mem. Internat. Explorers Soc. expdn. to Mosquito Coast, NE Honduras, 1976; led 10 underwater projects (the Poseidia expdns.) to an archaeol. site off Bimini Island, 1974-79. With USAF, 1953-57. Explorer of Yr. Internat. Explorers Soc., 1976; appointed dir. of rsch. (hon.) Bahamas Antiquities Inst., Nassau, 1975; Poseidia project listed in Spirit of Enterprise from the Rolex Awards, 1978. Fellow Explorer's Club (N.Y.C.).

ZINK, KLAUS J., industrial management educator; b. Bad Mingolsheim, Germany, Mar. 13, 1947; m. Maria Zink; 4 children. PhD, U. Karlsruhe, Germany, 1975, Habilitation, 1978. Asst. prof. Inst. for Prodn. Mgmt. and Human Factors, U. Karlsruhe; prof. indsl. mgmt. U. Wuppertal, Germany, 1979-80, U. Kaiserslautern, Germany, 1980—; chairperson indsl. mgmt. and human factors, head rsch. inst. Tech. and Work, U. Kaiserslautern; mgmt. cons. various orgns.; jury rep. for Germany, European Quality Award, 1992—. Contbg. author books; contbr. articles to profl. publs. Mem. Internat. Ergonomics Assn. (mem. exec. com.), German Human Factors and Ergonomics Soc. (pres. 1997-99, past pres. 1999—). Avocations: travel, tennis, reading. Office: Univ Kaiserslautern, Gottlieb Daimler Str, D-67663 Kaiserslautern Germany

ZINK, LUBOR JAN, journalist, author; b. Klapy, Czechoslovakia, Sept. 20, 1920; naturalized Brit. citizen, 1949, Can. citizen, 1963; s. Vilem and Bozena (Wohl) Z.; m. Zora Nechvile, Apr. 1, 1942; 1 son, Alec Guy. Grad., Prague Sch. Econs. Info. officer Ministry Fgn. Affairs, Prague, Czechoslovakia, 1945-48; monitor, broadcaster BBC, Eng., 1948-51; polit. and econ. analyst Allied Authorities, W. Europe, 1951-57; editl. page editor Brandon (Man., Can.) Sun, 1958-62; polit. columnist Toronto (Ont., Can.) Telegram, 1962-71; syndicated columnist Toronto Sun, 1971-93; radio and TV commentaries. Author: The Uprooted, 1962, Under the Mushroom Cloud, 1962, Trudeaucracy, 1972, Viva Chairman Pierre, 1977, What Price Freedom?, 1981; also novels (2) and books of poetry (4) in Czech. Progressive Conservative candidate Parliament, 1972, 74. Served to 1st lt. (present rank Col.) Czechoslovak Brigade, Brit. Army, 1940-45. Decorated Mil. Cross, medal for Bravery; recipient Can. Nat. Newspaper award, 1961, Bowater award for Journalism, 1962, Latvian Pro Merito medal, 1968, Colin M. Brown Freedom medal and award, 1989, medal of merit 1st class, Pres. V. Havel, 1995, The Jan Masaryk prize, 1999. Mem. Parliamentary Press Gallery (life), Royal Can. Legion, Masaryk Meml. Inst. Toronto (hon.). Home: 47 Queensline Dr, Nepean, ON Canada K2H 7J3 Office: Ho of Commons, Parliamentary Press Gallery, Ottawa, ON Canada K1A 0A6

ZINKANN, PETER CHRISTIAN, business executive; b. Bremen, Germany, Sept. 17, 1928; s. Kurt Christian and Edith (Birkholz) Z.; m. Karin Elisabeth Rohe, Feb. 5, 1958; 1 child, Reinhard Christian. M in Engring., Tech. U. Darmstadt, Fed. Republic Germany, 1954, PhD in Econs., 1956. Co-ptnr. Miele & Cie, GmbH & Co. KG, Güterloh, Germany, 1957—; bd. dirs. Thyssen Krupp Steel AG, VGT, Grossalmerode Viessmann-Werke, Allendorf Hermann Heye, Obernkirchen. Mem. Technischer Überwachungsverein (bd. dirs. 1973—), Rheinland/Berlin Brandenburg, Köln. Lodge: Rotary (Gütersloh). Home: Thesings Allee 11a, D-33332 Gutersloh Germany Office: Miele & Cie, D-33325 Gutersloh Germany

ZINKERNAGEL, ROLF MARTIN, immunology educator; b. Basle, Switzerland, Jan. 6, 1944; s. Robert W. and Suzanne (Staehlin) Z.; m. Kathrin G. Lüdin, Mar. 11, 1968; children: Christine, Annelies, Martin. MD, U. Basel, 1968. Intern in surgery Claraspital, Basel, 1968-69; postdoctoral Inst. Biochemistry, Lausanne, 1970-72, Dept. Microbiology, ANU, Canberra, Australia, 1973-75; asst. prof. Dept. Immunopathology, Scripps U., La Jolla, Calif., 1975-80, mem., 1978-79; assoc. prof. Dept. Pathology, Div. Exptl. Pathology, U. Zurich, 1979-92; full prof. Dept. Pathology, Inst. Exptl. Immunology, U. Zurich, 1992—. Editorial bd. Exptl. Cell Biology, 1976-88, Immunogenetics, 1977—, Parasite Immunology, 1978-84, Jour. of Immunology, 1978-80, Thymus, 1979-89, Antiviral Rsch., 1980-88, Jour. of Exptl. Medicine, 1981-84, Cellular Immunology, 1983—, European Jour. of Immunology, 1981—, Jour. of Environ. Pathology Toxicology and Oncology, 1981—, Internat. Jour. of Microbiology, 1983—, and others. Recipient Albert Lasker Award for Basic Med. Rsch., 1995; Co-recipient Nobel Prize for medicine, 1996. Mem. Swiss Soc. of Allergy and Immunology, Australian Soc. for Immunology, Am. Assn. of Immunoloigsts, Am. Assn. of Pathologists, Scandinavian Soc. of Immunology (hon.), Soc. Française d'Immunolgie (hon.), Swiss Soc. of Pathology, Swiss Soc. of Microbiology, Swiss Soc. of Cell and Molecular Biology, Acadmia Euopea, Internat. Soc. for Antiviral Rsch., ENI European Network of Immunol. Instns., Deutsche Gesellschaft fur Immunologie, Deutsche Gesellschaft fur Virologie, others. Achievements include co-discovery of MHC-restricted T cell recognition; discovery of the tymus role in determining MHC-restricted T-cell specficity, NK-cell activity in virus infections, T-cell epitope escape virus mutants, tolerances to viruses; rsch. on role of virus-specific T-cells in causing immunopathology. Office: Univ Hosp Inst Exptl Immuno, Schmelzbergstr 12, CH-8091 Zurich Switzerland

ZINK-LORENZ, ANGELA MARIA, internist, researcher; b. Heidelberg, Germany, May 25, 1963; d. Franz Robert and Franziska (Wittmann) Zink; m. Wolfgang Adalbert Werner Lorenz, Dec. 17, 1993; children: Charlotte, Nicola. Grad., U. Heidelberg, 1989, MD, 1990. Lic. physician, Germany. Joinst resident and fellow dept. internal medicine U. Heidelberg, 1989-92, 93—; sr. house officer Royal Devon & Exeter Hosp., U.K., 1992-93, Torquay Gen. Hosp., U.K., 1993; rsch. fellow St. Vincent's Hosp., Melbourne, Australia, 1987. Mem. German Soc. Endocrinology (v. Recklinghausen award 1996), German Soc. Internal Medicine. Avocations: languages, scuba diving. Home: Trajanstrasse 24a, 68526 Ladenburg Germany

ZINN-JUSTIN, ANNE, genetic epidemiology researcher; b. Fontenay-Aux-Roses, France, Feb. 22, 1970; d. Jean and Nicole (Hallier) Zinn-J. Edn. cert., Acad. de Versailles, France, 1986; degree engring., Ecole Centrale de Paris, 1992; DEA of Pub. Health, U. Paris XI, 1996; PhD in Pub. Health, INSERM U436, France, 2000. Rsch. worker European Space Agy., Holland, 1991, Ecole des Hautes Etudes en Sciences Sociales, Paris, 1991-92; engr. Electricité de France, Chatillon, 1992-93; actress theatre cos., France, 1993-95; tchr. math. Mathematique Superieures, 1994-96, Med. U. Pitie-Salpetriere, Paris, 1996-97. Contbr. articles to profl. jours. Avocations: acting and directing. Home: 26 Rue Emile Lepeu, 75011 Paris France Office: Inserm U436, 91 BD De L'Hopital, 75013 Paris France

ZINOVIEV, YURY M., mathematician, researcher; b. Possiet, Russia, Jan. 5, 1948; s. Michael Dmitry Zinoviev and Alexandra M. Kushchenko; m. Tatyana P. Wadkowska, June 10, 1972 (dec. Sept. 1979); 1 child, Alexandra. MS, Moscow State U., 1971; PhD, Steklov Math. Inst., Moscow, 1974, DSc, 1994. Jr. rschr. Steklov Math. Inst., Moscow, 1974-84, sr. rschr., 1985-93, leading rschr., 1994—; cons. Russian Found. for Basic Rsch., Moscow, 1994—. Contbr. articles to profl. jours. Mem. Internat. Assn. Math. Physics. Office: Steklov Math Inst, Gubkin St 8, 117966 Moscow Russia

ZINSER, HARTMUT, philosophy educator; b. Tübingen, Germany, Nov. 1, 1944; s. Hans-Walter and Charlotte-Jenny-Louise (Eick) Z.; m. Herta-Erica Alten; children: Jenny, Charlotte. Abitur, Goethe Gymnasium, Berlin, 1965; MA, Freie U. Berlin, 1971, PhD, 1975, Habilitation, 1980. Assoc. scientist Freie U. Berlin, 1971-77, assoc. prof., 1980-84, prof., 1984-88; prof. U. Mainz, Federal Republic of Germany, 1989-90; bd. dirs. DVRG, Hanover, 1984-91; pres. Philosophy Soc. II, Freie U. Berlin, 1991. Author: Mythos und Arbeit, 1977, Mythos des Mutterrechts, 1981, Jugendokkultismus, 2993, Markt der Religionen, 1997; editor: Untergang von Religionen, 1986, Religionswissenschaft, 1988, Herausforderung Ethiku-Unterricht, 1991, Psychologische Aspekte neuer Formen der Religiosität, 1997, Zugendokkultismus, 1993. Mem. European Soc. for the Scientific Study of Religion (v.p.). Office: Freie U Berlin, Altensteinstr 40, 14195 Berlin 33, Germany

ZINTZEN, CLEMENS, science academy executive. PhD, U. Cologne, 1961, habilitation, 1963. Prof. classics U. Cologne, Mainz, Germany, 1968-69, U. Manheim, 1969-72, U. Saarbrücken, 1972-86; v.p. Acad. Scis. & Lit., Mainz, Germany, 1986-93, pres., 1993—. Office: Akademie der Wissenschaften und der Literatur, Geschwister-Scholl-str 2, 55131 Mainz Germany*

ZINZINDOHOUE, ABRAHAM, judge. Pres. Supreme Ct., Cotonou, Benin. Office: 01 BP 330, Cotonou Benin

ZIO, ENRICO, nuclear engineer; b. Milan, May 6, 1966; s. Cesare Augusto and Adriana (Sormani) Z. Laurea, Poly. Milan, 1991, PhD, 1995; MSc, UCLA, 1995; PhD, MIT, 1998. Rschr. dept. nuclear engring. Poly. Milan, 1996—. Mem. European Safety and Reliability Assn. (tech. com. 1997—, treas.), Internat. Assn. for Math. and Computers in Simulation, Sigma Xi. Avocations: soccer, tennis, biking, reading, music. Home: Via Giuseppe Meda 11, 20136 Milan Italy Office: Dept Nuclear Engring, Poly Milan Via Ponzio 34/3, 20133 Milan Italy

ZIÓŁKO, JERZY MACIEJ, civil engineering educator; b. Radom, Poland, Nov. 29, 1934; s. Mieczysław Oskar and Janina Zofia (Wecsile) Z. MSc, Tech. U., Gdańsk, Poland, 1957, PhD, DSc in Engring., 1964. Head bldg. contract Mostostal, Gdańsk, 1957-60, chief engr., 1961-63; sr. asst. Tech. U., Gdańsk, 1963-68, asst. prof., 1968-79, prof. civil engring., 1979—; cons. Gas Pipeline and Tanks Assembly, Warsaw, 1963-75, Oil Pipeline of Plock, Poland, 1984, Oil Pipelines Ops. Co. Friendship. Author: Tanks for Liquids and Gases (in Polish), 1970, 2d edit. 1986 (awards Min. Bldg. 1984, Min. Edn. 1971), Assembly of Steel Structures (in Polish), 1980, (in Russian), 1984 (award Ministry Bldg.); co-author: Durability of Steel Structures in Aspect of Reconstruction (in Russian), 1984, Special Steel Structures (in Polish), 1995, 7 other books; contbr. articles to profl. jours. Chmn. Commn. for Sci., Gdańsk Polish Bldg. Engrs. Assn., br. office, 1991—; mem. Polish Com. Standarization, Warsaw, 1994—. Mem. Polish Acad. Scis. (mem. civil engring. com. 1990—). Avocation: stamp collecting. Home: ul Pawła Gdańca 10B29, 80-336 Gdańsk-Oliwa Poland Office: Tech U Civil Engring Dept, ul Gabriela Narutowicza 11, 80-952 Gdańsk Poland

ZIOLKOWSKA-BOEHM, ALEKSANDRA, writer; b. Lodz, Poland, Apr. 15, 1949; came to U.S., 1990; d. Henryk and Antonina Zofia (Laskiewicz) Z.; m. C. Norman Boehm Jr., June 8, 1990; 1 child, Thomas J. Tomczyk. M in Lit., U. Lodz, 1973; PhD, U. Warsaw, Poland, 1978. Pvt. asst. Melchior Wankowicz, Warsaw, 1972-74; repertoire rsch. staff Warsaw TV Theater, 1977-81. Author: Blisko Wankowicza, 1975, 78, 88, Z Miejsca Na Miejsce, 1983, 86, 97, Senator Haidasz, 1983, Dreams and Reality, 1984, Kanada, Kanada, 1986, Diecezja Lodzka I Jej Biskupi, 1987, Moje I Zaslyszane, 1988, Kanadyjski Senator, 1989, Na Tropach Wankowicza, 1989, 99, Proces M. Wankowicza 1964, 1990, Nie Tylko Ameryka, 1992, Korzenie Sa Polskie, 1992, Ulica Zolwiego Strumienia, 1995, Amerykanie Z Wyboru, 1998, The Roots are Polish, 2000. Scholar Oxford (Eng.) Lang. Ctr., 1975, Ont. Ministry of Culture, Toronto, 1981-83, Can. Polish Rsch. Inst., Toronto, 1981-83, A. Mickiewicz Found., Toronto, 1981-83, Inst. Internat. Edn., Washington, 1985. Mem. Am. PEN Club, Polish Writers Union, Polish Writers Union Abroad, Polish Inst. Arts and Sci., Zaiks, Kosciuszko Found. (scholar 1990). Avocations: travel, birdwatching, domestic pets. Home: 11 Ridgewood Cir Wilmington DE 19809-2860

ZIOLKOWSKI, JOZEF JULIAN, chemistry educator; b. Husiatyn, Poland, Aug. 25, 1934; s. Wladyslaw and Helena (Matenczuk) Z.; m. Elzbieta Joanna Krohne, Sept. 28, 1960; 1 child, Piotr. MS, Tech. U., Wroclaw, Poland, 1957; PhD, U. Wroclaw, 1964, DSc, 1973; D (hon.), U. St. Petersburg, 2000. Asst. U. Wroclaw, 1956-61, sr. asst., 1961-64, adj. prof., 1964-68, asst. prof., 1968-76, assoc. prof., 1976-84, prof., 1984—; dep. dir. Inst. Chemistry, Wroclaw, 1969-79, dir., 1982-87, 93-94; vice rector U. Wroclaw, 1988-93, 99—, dean faculty of chemistry, 1995-99. Contbr. articles to profl. jours.; editor, co-editor: Advances in Chemical Education, Vol. 1, 1994, Vol. 2, 1996, Vol. 3, 1996; editor: Wiadomosci Chemiczne, 1993—. Pres. Found. for Wroclaw U., 1991—; chmn. Acad. Sport Union, Wroclaw, 1993—, Commn. Catalysis Acad. Sci., Wroclaw, 1986—. Recipient Scientific award Polish Acad. Sci., 1974, 76, 83, Ministry of Edn., 1964-86. Mem. Polish Chem. Soc., Wroclaw Scientific Soc., Internat. Union Pure and Applied Chemistry, Academia Europaea. Avocations: collecting, books, sports. Home: 7/2 Kazimierska, 51-657 Wroclaw Poland Office: U Wroclaw Faculty Chemistry, 14 F Joliot-Curie, 50-383 Wroclaw Poland

ZIÓLKOWSKI, TOMASZ, marketing executive; b. Czestochoua, Poland, Aug. 2, 1967; s. Józef and Kazimiera (Jedrecka) Z.; m. Julita Jaskowska, June 5, 1999. MS, Warsaw (Poland) Sch. Econs., 1992. Brand mgr. asst. Benckiser, Warsaw, 1993-95; sr. brand mgr. Tchibo, Warsaw, 1995-98; regional mktg. dir. Leaf Poland, Warsaw, 1998—. Avocations: windsurfing, tennis, photography, soccer, books. Home: Kaliskiego 35/76, Warsaw Poland Office: Leaf Poland, Topiel 12, 00-342 Warsaw Poland

ZION, MONTY M., cardiologist, researcher; b. Germiston, Transvaal, South Africa, Feb. 26, 1925; arrived in Israel, 1978; s. Abraham Moses and Rachel (Stern) Z.; m. Myra Michelow, Sept. 3, 1950; children: Sharon, Robyn, John. MBChB, U. Witwatersrand, South Africa, 1947; MD, U. Witwatersrand, 1958. Intern Baragwanath Hosp., Johannesburg, South Africa; resident Johannesburg Ge. Hosp. & London Chest Hosp.; cardiac cons. Johannesburg Gen. Hosp., 1956-78; chief cardiology Shaare Zedek Med. Ctr., Jerusalem, 1978-92; cardiac cons. Meuhedet Sick Fund, Jerusalem, 1992—; pvt. practice, Johannesburg, 1955-78; cons. Swiss-South African Reinsurance Co., 1956-78. Contbr. over 100 articles to profl. jours. Fellow Royal Coll. Physicians, Am. Coll. CArdiology. Jewish. Avocations: gardening, lawn bowls, music.

ZIPES, DOUGLAS PETER, cardiologist, researcher; b. White Plains, N.Y., Feb. 27, 1939; s. Robert Samuel and Josephine Helen (Weber) Z.; m. Marilyn Joan Jacobus, Feb. 18, 1961; children: Debra, Jeffrey, David. BA cum laude, Dartmouth Coll., 1961, B of Med. Sci., 1962; MD cum laude, Harvard Med. Sch., 1964. Diplomate Am. Bd. Internal Medicine (mem. subsplty. bd. cardiovascular disease 1989—, chmn., 1995—, chmn. com. cert. in clin. cardiac electrophysiology 1989-96, bd. dirs. 1995—, exec. com. 1999—). Intern, resident, fellow in cardiology Duke U. Med. Ctr., Durham, N.C., 1964-68; vis. scientist Masonic Med. Rsch. Lab., Utica, N.Y., 1970-71; asst. prof. medicine Ind. U. Sch. Medicine, Indpls., 1970-73, assoc. prof., 1973-76, prof., 1976-94, prof. pharmacology and toxicology, 1993—, disting. prof. medicine, 1994—; dir. divsn. of cardiology Krannert Inst. Cardiology, Ind. U. Sch. Medicine, 1995—; bd. dirs. Am. Bd. Internal Medicine, Inst. for Clinical Evaluation; cardiology adv. com. NIH, 1991-94; cons. in field. Author: Comprehensive Cardiac Care, 7th edit., 1991; editor: Slow Inward Current, 1980, Cardiac Electrophysiology and Arrhythmias, 1985, Nonpharmacological Therapy of Tachyarrhythmias, 1987, Cardiac Electrophysiology From Cell to Bedside, 1990, 3d edit., 2000; co-editor: Treatment of Heart Diseases, 1992, Ablation of Cardiac Arrhythmias, 1994, Antiarrhythmic Therapy: A Pathophysiologic Approach, 1994, Heart Disease, A Textbook of Cardiovascular Medicine, 6th edit., 2000; mem. editl. bd. Circulation, 1974-78, 83—, Am. Jour. Cardiology, 1979-82, 88—, Am. Jour. Medicine, 1979-90, Jour. Am. Coll. Cardiology, 1983, Am. Heart Jour., 1977-97, PACE, 1977—, Circulation Rsch., 1983-90, Am. Jour. Noninvasive Cardiology, 1985-89, Jour. Electrophysiology, 1987-89, Cardiovascular Drugs and Therapy, 1986-93, Japanese Heart Jour., 1989—, Jour. Cardiovascular Pharmacology and Therapeutics, 1994—, Jour. Cardiovascular Pharmacology, 1995—, Cardiovascular Therapeutics, 1995, Current Clin. Trials, 1995-98, Jour. Interventional Cardiac Electrophysiology, 1996—; editor-in-chief: Progress in Cardiology, 1988-92, Jour. Cardiovascular Electrophysiology, 1990—, Cardiology in Rev., 1992—, Contemporary Treatments of Cardiovascular Disease, 1996-98, Am. Coll. Cardiology Extended Learning, 1997—; contbr. articles to profl. jours.; patentee cardioverter, elec. prevention of arrhythmia, discrimination of atrial fibrillation, fixation of implantable devices, and periocardial delivery of therapeutic and diagnostic agents. Pres., bd. dirs. Indpls. Opera Co., 1983-85; mem. study sect. NIH, Washington, 1977-81; mem. nat. merit rev. bd. VA, 1982-85, Cardiology Adv. Com. NHLBL, 1991-98, chmn. steering com. AVID; chmn. Data and Safety Monitoring Bd. AFFIRM, 1996—. Recipient Disting. Achievement award Am. Heart Assn., 1989. Fellow ACP, Am. Coll. Cardiology (chmn. ACC/AHA subcom. to assess EP studies, chmn. young investigators award com. 1988-94, trustee 1992-97, mem. nominating com. 1993-95, Disting. Scientist award 1996, chmn. devel. com. 1996—, sci. sessions program com. 1996-98, v.p. 1999-00, pres.-elect 2000-01, pres. 01-02), Am. Heart Assn. (exec. com. 1980-88, sci. sessions program 1983-86, chmn. various coms., chmn. 1995, bd. dirs. Internat. Cardiology Found. 1993-98, bd. dirs. 1994-96, chmn. emergency cardiac care com. 1995-96; Herrick award 1997); mem. Am. Soc. Clin. Investigation, Assn. Univ. Cardiologists (v.p. 1994, pres. 1995), Assn. Am. Physicians, Am. Physiol. Soc., Cardiac Electrophysiology Soc. (pres. 1985-86), N.Am. Soc. Pacing and Electrophysiology (pres. 1988-90, trustee 1990—, Disting. Scientist award 1995), InterAm. Soc. Cardiology (1st v.p. 1995-98), Ind. Cardiac Electrophysiology Soc. (founder), Inst. Clin. Evaluation (bd. dirs. 1997—). Home: 10614 Winterwood Carmel IN 46032-9688 Office: Ind U Sch Medicine 1100 W Michigan St Indianapolis IN 46202-5208

ZIPF, MARK EDWARD, electrical engineer; b. Balt., Aug. 1, 1962; s. Edward Charles and Kate Hart (Fleenor) Z.; m. N. Renee Slaugenhoupt, July 27, 1984; 1 child, Michael David. BS in Elec. Engring., U. Pitts., 1984, MS in Elec. Engring., 1988, PhD in Elec. Engring., 1997. Rsch. asst. U. Pitts., 1983-88; rsch. fellow Ctr. Motion Control, 1988-89; chief engr. ISTcom, Inc., 1989-92; sys. design engr. Mill Equipment & Engring. Co., 1992-94, mgr. process automation, 1994-95, asst. v.p. control and automation, 1995-96, asst. to pres., 1996-97; prin. scientist Optomation, Inc., 1997—; rsch. cons. Laurel Ridge Observatory, Ligonier, Pa., 1989—; engring. cons. ISTcom, Inc., Pitts., 1992—, Dietrich Industries, Warren, Ohio, 1997—, World Class Processing, Ambridge, Pa., 1997—, Feralloy Corp., Chgo., 1999—, Huntco Steel, Inc., Blytheville, Ark., 2000—. Contbr. articles to profl. jours. Mem. IEEE, ASEE, ISA, Soc. Photo-Optical Instrumentation Engr., Assn. Iron & Steel Engrs., Tau Beta Pi. Avocations: golf, photography, seismology, digital photography and image processing.

ZIPFEL, ANDREAS JOSEF, biostatistician; b. Freiburg, Breisgau, Germany, Oct. 9, 1953; s. Leo and Marianne (Unverzagt) Z.; m. Sylvie Maryvonne Lapierre, Sept. 8, 1984; children: Tristan, Joseph. Student, Howard C.C., Columbia, Md., 1972; Diplome Math., Freie U., Berlin, 1981. Biostatistician Schering AG, Berlin, 1981-84; head biometrics Rhone-Poulenc Sante, Paris, 1984-87, Synthelabo, Paris, 1987-97, Bayer PLC, Berks, Eng., 1997—; spl. interest adv. com. Drug Info. Assn., 1994; pres. satellite meeting Internat. Statis. Inst. work session Statistical Methods in Biopharmacy, 1989. Guest editor: Statistics in Medicine Vol. 10, 1991; program chmn., invited spkr.: DIA Jour., 1995. Mem. European Fedn. Statisticians in the Pharm. Industry (first pres. 1992-95), Assn. Statistics and its Utilization (v.p. 1987-91, first pres. group biopharmacie 1987-91). Avocations: classical music, creative arts. Home: 17 Rue Beranger, F-75003 Paris France Office: Bayer Plc, Stoke Ct Stoke Poges, Slough SL2 4LY, England

ZIPFINGER, FRANK PETER, lawyer; b. Sydney, Australia, Feb. 27, 1953; s. Franz Johann and Annie Thea (Van Kooij) Z.; m. Susan Elizabeth Gulliver, Jan. 5, 1979; children: Sarah Elizabeth, Jonathan Francis, Nicholas James. BA in Econs., Macquarie U., Sydney, 1974; LLB, Sydney U., 1977, LLM, 1986. Bar: Australia 1977, High Ct. Australia 1977, N.Y. 1981. Assoc. Stephen Jaques and Stephen, Sydney, 1977-80, Winthrop, Stimson, Putnam & Roberts, N.Y.C., 1980-81, Stephen Jaques Stone James, Sydney, 1982-83; ptnr. Mallesons Stephen Jaques, Sydney, 1983—. Author: Australian Stamp Duties Law, 1982, Stamp Duty Aspects of Trusts Settlements and Gifts in Australia, 1984, The Stamp Duty Book - NSW, 1994. Mem. ABA, Law Soc. New South Wales, Killara Golf Club, Australian Club. Avocations: philately, tennis, golf. Home: 1 Arthur St, Killara Australia 2071

ZIPORI-BECKENSTEIN, PNINIT, business administration educator, researcher; b. Tel Aviv, Israel, Oct. 22, 1947; d. Shmaya and Tirza Beckenstein; m. Dov Zipori, June 1, 1971 (div. 1993); children: Sigal, Dan. MSc with honors, Tel Aviv U., 1970; PhD, Weizman Inst. Sci., Rehovot, Israel, 1976; MBA, Bar-Ilan U., Ramat-Gan, Israel, 1985; PhD (hon.), Weizman Inst. Sci., 1977. Researcher Leiden (The Netherlands) U., 1976-78; with software mktg. dept. Med. Corp., Palo Alto, Calif., 1985-87; dir. mktg. Orgenics Ltd., Yavne, Israel, 1987; health editor Globes Econs. Newspaper, Tel Aviv, 1988-90; exec. Med. Mktg., Rehovot, 1988-97; lectr. Sch. Bus. Adminstrn., Israel, 1990-97; researcher Sheba Med. Ctr., Tel-Hashomer, Israel, 1993-97. Author: Effective Interpersonal Communication, 1996, Effective Coping with Obstacles, 1997; contbr. articles to profl. jours. Mem. municipality edn. com., Rehovot, 1980; mem. leadership com. Meretz Polit. Party, Tel Aviv, 1997. Mem. Biochemistry Soc. Jewish. Avocations: solo travel, swimming. Home: 4 Hagra St, 76310 Rehovot Israel Office: Med Mktg Ltd, 23A Weizman St, 76282 Rehovot Israel

ZIPORYN, TERRA DIANE, writer; b. Chgo., June 1, 1958; d. Marvin Charles and Charlotte Weinberg Z.; m. James Harry Snider, Jun 22, 1986; children: Pallas Amita, Sage Tivona, Solon Abraham. BA summa cum laude, Yale U., 1980; MA, U. Chgo., 1981, PhD, 1985. Assoc. editor Jour. of the Am. Med. Assn., Chgo., 1984-86; freelance writer Severna Park, Md., 1986—; editl. cons./freelance Harvard Med. Sch./Harvard Sch. Pub. Health, Boston, 1986—. Co-author: (books) Alternative Medicine for Dummies, 1998 (AMWA Beth Fonda award for excellence), The Women's Concise Guide to Emotional Well-Being, 1997, The Women's Concise Guide to a Healthier Heart, 1997 (winner Nat. Health Info. award Health Info. Resource Ctr. 1998), The Harvard Guide to Women's Health, 1996 (various awards ALA, others), Future Shop: How New Technologies Will Change the Way We Shop and What We Buy, 1992; author: Nameless Diseases, 1992, Disease in the Popular American Press: The Case of Diphtheria, Typhoid Fever, and Syphilis, 1870-1920, 1988; contbr. articles to profl. jours. Recipient numerous awards including Marine Biol. Lab. Sci. Writing fellowship 1997, hon. mention Writer's Digest Mag. Writing Competition, 1996, artist devel. grant Vt. Coun. on the Arts, 1994, scholarship Old Chatham Writer's Conf., N.Y., 1994, writing fellowship Am. Chem. Soc., 1992, AAAS Mass Media Sci. fellowship, numerous others. Mem. Am. Assn. for History of Medicine, Nat. Assn. Sci. Writers, Am. Med. Writers Assn. (Beth Fonda award 1999), Authors Guild of Am., Phi Beta Kappa. Jewish. Avocations: playwriting, creative writing, cello, swimming. E-mail: ziporyn@megsinet.net.

ZIRKER, HANS, theologian, educator; b. Ludwigshafen, Germany, Mar. 17, 1935. ThD, U. Mainz, Germany, 1964. Tchr. Grunstadt (Germany) H.S., 1964-71; cons. Inst. Lehrerfortbildung, Mainz, 1971-74; prof. Coll. Edn., Neuss, Germany, 1974-80, U. Duisburg, Germany, 1980-93, U. Essen, Germany, 1993—. Author: The Cultic Recalling of the Past in the Psalms, 1964, Readings of God and World, 1979, Ekklesiologie, 1984, Christianity and Islam, 2d edit., 1992, Islam, 1993, Criticism of Religion, 3d edit., 1995, The Koran: Accesses and Readings, 1999. Home: Blumenstr 29, D-41564

Kaarst Nordrhein Germany Office: Univ Essen, Postfach, D-45117 Essen Nordrhein Germany

ZIRKIND, RALPH, physicist, educator; b. N.Y.C., Oct. 20, 1918; s. Isaac and Zicel (Lifshitz) Z.; m. Ann Goldman, Nov. 22, 1940; children: Sheila Zirkind Knopf, Elaine Zirkind Gorman, Edward I. B.S., CCNY, 1940; M.S., Ill. Inst. Tech., 1945; postgrad., George Washington U., 1946-47; Ph.D., U. Md., 1950; D.Sc., U. R.I., 1968. Physicist Navy Dept., 1945-50, chief physicist, 1951-60; physicist Oak Ridge Nat. Lab., 1950-51, Advanced Research Project Agy., Washington, 1960-63; prof. Poly. Inst. Bklyn., 1963-70; prof. U. R.I., Kingston, 1970-72, adj. prof., 1972—; physicist Advanced Research Projects Agy., Arlington, Va., 1972-74; cons. Advanced Rsch. Projects Agy., Arlington, Va., 1974—; lectr. U. Md., 1947-48, George Washington U., 1952-53, U. Mich., 1964; cons. ACDA, Jet Propulsion Lab., Calif. Inst. Tech.; cons. to industry, 1974—. Contbg. author: Jet Propulsion Series, 1952, FAR Infrared Properties of Materials, 1968; editor: Electromagnetic Sensing of Earth, 1967; mem. editorial bd.: Infrared Physics, 1963—; contbr. articles profl. jours. Recipient Meritorious Civilian Svc. award Navy Dept., 1957, Meritorious Civilian Svc. award Dept. Def., 1970, Outstanding Educator of Am. medal, 1972, Maj. Contbn. award BMDO/AIAA, 1994. Mem. Am. Phys. Soc., N.Y. Acad. Scis., Sigma Xi, Sigma Pi Sigma, Eta Kappa Nu. Home: 820 Hillsboro Dr Silver Spring MD 20902-3202 Office: 4001 Fairfax Dr Ste 700 Arlington VA 22203-1618

ZIRNITIS, PETERIS, publishing executive; b. Riga, Latvia, Nov. 28, 1944; s. Karlis Karlsons and Milda (Puke) Zirnite; m. Anita Erna Jansone, Sept. 19, 1975. Grad., U. Leningrad, Russia, 1971, Acad. Social Scis., Moscow, 1984. Chief editor Latvian State TV, 1969-72, Cultural Weekly, Latvia, 1972-75; sec. Writer's Union, Latvia, 1975-82; chief editor State News Agy., Latvia, 1984-86; dir. Nat. Archive Culture, Latvia, 1988-92; pres. NORDIK, Latvia, 1992—. Author 6 books; contbr. over 200 articles to profl. jours. Sgt. Soviet Army, 1964-69. Mem. Latvian Writer's Union, Bd. Latvian PEN, Lions. Lutheran. Avocations: nature, history. E-mail: nordik@nordik.lv. Fax: 371 7602 818. Home: Terbatas str 55-20, LV-1001 Riga Latvia Office: NORDIK, Daugavgrivas Str 36-9, LV 1007 Riga Latvia

ZISSER, MARTIN SHEPHERD, fur apparel manufacturer, investor and trader; b. Bklyn., Jan. 30, 1942; s. Irving and Jean (Shepherd) Z. Student, NYU, 1960-63. Wall St. invester and trader; sec. treas. Fur Dressers Union Local 2A, N.Y.C., 1989-92; v.p. UFCW Local 174, N.Y.C., 1992—. Mem. Internat. Soc. Philosophical Enquiry, Mensa. Republican. Jewish. Avocations: study of history, politics, world current events, economics. Home: 1219 E 80th St Brooklyn NY 11236-4165

ZITHA, PACELLI LIDIO JOSÉ, laboratory director, educator; b. Maputo, Mozambique, Oct. 19, 1961; s. Jose Eugenio and Maria Salome (Mulhui) Z.; m. Emrin Bovens, Apr. 5, 1997; 1 child, Edgar Ferdinand Pouleni. Lic. in fundamental physics, U. Pierre et Marie Curie, France, 1989, M in Fundamental Physics, 1990, DEA in Theoretical Fluid Physics, 1991, PhD in Physics, 1994. Jr. rschr. U. Orsay, France, 1990-91; asst. rsch. engr. French Petroleum Inst., Rueil-Malmaison, France, 1991-95; rsch. assoc. Delft (The Netherlands) U. Tech., 1995-97, asst. prof., 1997—, sci. dir. Dietz-Lab., 1997—. Contbr. articles to profl. jours. Marie Curie fellow European Commn., 1996. Mem. APS, SPE, Tijdnood Chess Club (sec. 1999—). Avocations: swimming, chess, reading, history, gardening. Office: Delft U Tech, Mijnbouwstraat 120, 2628 RX Delft The Netherlands

ZITTER, HERBERT HANS, chemistry educator; b. Bruck/Mur, Austria, Mar. 12, 1929; s. Herbert Hans and Maria (Schoberl) Z.; m. Helga Stix, June 8, 1957; children: Gerhard, Herbert. Dipl. Ing., Tech. U., Graz, Austria, 1952; Dr.Techn., Tech. U., 1955. Head chem. lab. Gebr Bohler, Kapfenberg, Austria, 1952-67; prof., head inst. gen. and analytical chemistry Montanuniversity, Leoben, Austria, 1967-94. Contbr. articles to profl. jours. Mem. Verein Eisenhutte Osterreich, Verein Deutscher Eisenhuttenleute, Verein Osterreichischer Chemiker. Roman Catholic. Home: Josef Stanekgasse 16, Kapfenberg Austria A-8605 Office: Montanuniversitat, Leoben A-8700, Austria

ZITTO, RICHARD JOSEPH, physics educator; b. Lisbon, Ohio, Sept. 1, 1945; s. Tony Joseph and Olive Lucille (Davison) Z.; m. Pamela Daryl Irons, July 22, 1967; children: Angela Marie, Elena Michelle. BS in Sci. Edn., Ohio State U., 1968, MA in Phys. Sci. Edn., 1978. Tchr. sci. Kenton (Ohio) Jr. H.S., 1968-70; tchr. physics and sci. Kenton Sr. H.S., 1970-76; tchr. physics Boardman H.S., Youngstown, Ohio, 1976-99; physics educator Youngstown State U., 1981—, coord. Physics Olympics, 1994—; dir. Youngstown Area Physics Alliance, 1987—. Trustee Hardin Meml. Hosp., Kenton, 1971-76; bd. dirs. Blue Cross of Lima, Ohio, 1973-76, Nat. Multiple Sclerosis Soc. N.E. Ohio, 1981-91; trustee Columbiana Pub. Libr., 1990—, pres., 1993-95, 2000—. Recipient Outstanding Young Educator award Kenton Jaycees, 1972, Outstanding Sci. Tchr. Youngstown State U. Sigma Xi, 1980, Career Educator award Ohio State U. Coll. Edn., 1997; A. Jennings scholar Martha Holden Jennings Found. Mem. ASCD, Am. Assn. Physics Tchrs. (physics teaching resource agt. 1986—, pres. Ohio sect. 1989-90, mem. physics in high schs. com. 1991-94, history and Philosophy com. 1999—), Ont. Assn. Physics Tchrs., Nat. Sci. Tchrs. Assn., N.E. Ohio Edn. Assn. (co-chmn. sci. workshop 1979—), Ohio Acad. Sci., Sci. Edn. Coun. Ohio, United Teaching Profession, Lions, Rotary (sec. 1978-79), Elks. Republican. Presbyterian. Avocations: woodworking, tennis, history of science, collecting antique physics apparatus. E-mail: rjzitto@cc.ysu.edu. Home: 332 W Park Ave Columbiana OH 44408-1242 Office: Physics & Astronomy Dept Youngstown State Univ Youngstown OH 44555-0001

ZIVAS, DIONYSIS, architecture educator, architect; b. Zakynthos, Greece, Jan. 4, 1928; s. Antonios and Angelica (Xenou) Z.; m. Helen Theodoropoulou, Sept. 16, 1956; children: Antonios, Angelica-Dionysia. MSc in Architecture, Nat. Tech. U. Sch. of Architecture, Greece, 1953, PhD in Architecture, 1970. Cert. arch. Instr. Nat. Tech. U., Athens, Greece, 1958-72, asst. prof., 1973-76, assoc. prof., 1977-79, prof., 1979-97, dean Sch. Architecture, 1979-83, 89-95, prof. emeritus, 1997; architect Ministry of Housing, Athens, Greece, 1955-57, Orgn. for Labor Housing, Athens, 1957, Nat. Tourist Orgn., 1958-61. Author: The Architecture of Zakynthos, 1970, 2 edit. 1984, Zante Architectural Miscellanies, 1976, the Monuments and the City, 1991, 2d edit., 1997; co-author, editor: Plaka the Old Town of Athens, 1978; contbd. numerous articles to profl. jours. Recipient Europa Nostra medal, 1982, G.V. Herder prize U. Vienna, 1993; Fulbright Found. scholar, 1975. Mem. Hellenic Soc. for Aesthetics (pres. 1982—), P.E. Michelis Found. (pres. 1984—), Soc. for Zakynthian Studies (pres. 1987-98). Christian Orthodox. Home: Karpathou 11, 112 52 Athens Greece

ZIVELONGHI, KURT DANIEL, computer graphics artist, art director, designer; b. Barstow, Calif., Oct. 3, 1960; s. Vincent Otto and Beverly Dean (Schwind) Z. Student, Pasadena (Calif.) City Coll., 1984-85, Art Students League, N.Y.C., 1988-89; BFA, Art Ctr. Coll. of Design, 1993. Mgr. Foothill Airplane Washing Svc., Claremont, Calif., 1980-82; sales rep. Valley Group Fin. Svc., Claremont, 1986-88; loan rep. Pacific Group Funding, Claremont, 1989-90; self employed fine artist Alhambra, Calif., 1990—; art dir. movies Seagull's Journey, Gizmo LLC, The Innocent Bystander, Mad Dogs Prodns., 1998. One-man show at Coll. of Design Art Ctr., Pasadena, Calif., 1993, two-man show at Flux Gallery, Eagle Rock, Calif., 1993, group show at Art Students League, N.Y.C., 1989. Mem. Ctr. for the Study of Popular Culture, Century City, Calif., 1994. Mem. Am. Soc. Portrait Artists. Avocations: pianist, weight lifter, theatre, cinema. Office: 957 Amador St Claremont CA 91711-3621 Address: The Print Merchants Pacific Design Ctr 8687 Melrose Ave West Hollywood CA 90069-5701

ZIVKOVIC, BORA DUŠAN, biologist, researcher; b. Belgrade, Yugoslavia, May 11, 1966; came to U.S., 1991, naturalized, 1998; s. Dušan and Rea Živković; m. Catharine Cella Zivkovic, Sept. 15, 1992; children: David Dusan, Ruth Bye. BS, U. Belgrade, 1991; MS, N.C. State U., 1998. Tchg. asst. N.C. State U., Raleigh, 1994-97, rsch. asst., 1997—. Contbr. articles to sci. jours., including Physiology and Behavior, Jour. Biol. Rhythms. E-mail: bdzivkov@unity.ncsu.edu. Office: NC State U PO Box 7617 Raleigh NC 27695-0001

ZIXIN, HOU, academic administrator. Pres. Nankai U., Tanjin, China. Office: Nankai U, 94 Weijin Rd, Tianjin 300071, China*

ZIYAL, BEKIR TURGUT, food products executive; b. Istanbul, Turkey, Feb. 23, 1956; s. Mahmut Sakir and Munevver (Duygun) Z.; m. Ferhan Dayigil, Nov. 3, 1983; 1 child, Omer. BA, Bosphorus U., Istanbul, 1977, MBA, 1978. Brand mgr. Dasa-Eczacibasi, Istanbul, 1980-82; mgr. sales and mktg. Sinangil Holding, Istanbul, 1982-84; mgr. mktg. MIS Dairy, Istanbul, 1984-86; asst. gen. mgr. ETI Biscuits, Istanbul, 1986-88; dir. sales Sanipak-P&G, Istanbul, 1988-90; comml. dir. Perfetti Turkey, Istanbul, 1990-97, mng. dir., 1997—. Lt. Turkish Army, 1978-80. Mem. Turkish Food Importers Assn. (bd. dirs. 1994-97), Rotary (club pres. 1998—, Istanbul Gayrettepe br. 1997-98). Avocations: collecting maps, golf. E-mail: tziyal@perfetti.com.tr. Home: Yaprak Mh 12 cd 1 sk No 4, Zekeriyaköy, Sariyer Istanbul Turkey Office: Perfetti Turkey, Kirac Atatürk St 17, 34900 B Cekmece Istanbul Turkey

ZIZI, NAJATE, science educator; b. Taza, Morocco, Jan. 10, 1941; d. Mohammed Zizi and Khnata Bennani; m. Ahmed Ben Sari, Sept. 10, 1964; children: Nawfel, Abdelhaq. BS in Physics, Faculty of Scis., Rabat, Morocco, 1965; MS, U. Paris-Sud, 1973, PhD in Molecular Physics, 1981. Tchr. h.s. Casablanca and Rabat, 1964-69; student rschr. Lab d'Infrarouge Orsay, Paris, 1970-73; lectr. Faculty of Scis., Rabat, 1973-76; rschr. Lab. Photophique Molèculaire Orsay, Paris, 1977-80; prof. Faculty of Scis., Rabat, 1981—; dir. Lab. Spectronomie Physique Appliquée, Rabat, 1993-96; rsch. dir. Unité de Formation et de Recherche, Rabat, 1997-2001; dir. PhD dissertation rsch., Rabat, 1982. Contbr. sci. articles to profl. jours. Fellow Nat. Ctr. Rsch., 1990; grantee Programme d'Appliu à la Recherche Sci., 1998. Avocations: walking, sewing, cooking, traveling. Office: Mohammed V U Sci Spectron Lab, Ave Ibn Batouta, BP 1014 Rabat Morocco

ZIZIC, THOMAS MICHAEL, physician, educator; b. Milw., Dec. 9, 1939; s. Michael Mitchell Zizic and Dorothy (Batas) Ciric; m. Karen Owens, June 15, 1962 (div. Sept. 1967); m. Martha Ann Ardos, Nov. 22, 1967; children: Lara Ann, Kristine Michelle. BS, U. Wis., 1961; MD, Johns Hopkins U., 1965. Intern Johns Hopkins Hosp., Balt., 1965-66, asst. resident, 1966-67, fellow in internal medicine, 1969-71, instr. dept. medicine, 1971-73, asst. prof. medicine, 1971-81, assoc. prof. medicine, 1981—; pvt. practice, Balt., 1988—; co-dir. Chesapeake Osteoporosis Ctr., Balt., 1988—; dir. med. affairs Murray Electronics, 1993—; v.p. med. quality care Physicians Quality Care, 1995—; pres. U.S. Osteoporosis Network, Inc., 1996—; co-founder, dir. Creative Environ. Solutions, Inc., 1996—; cons. in field. Contbr. numerous articles and abstracts to profl. jours. V.p. Md. chpt. Arthritis Found., Balt., 1976-77; chmn. Md. Commn. on Arthritis and Related Diseases, 1986-90. Fellow Am. Coll. Rheumatology, 1986; Md. Soc. Rheumatic Diseases (pres. 1975-76), D.C. Rheumatism Assn., Balt. City Med. Soc., Johns Hopkins Hosp. Med. Soc., Arthritis Found. (fellow 1971-73, v.p. 1976-77, med. and sci. com. 1977-79, chmn. profl. edn. com. 1977-78, govtl. affairs com. 1979-83), Phi Beta Kappa, Phi Kappa Phi, Phi Eta Sigma. Avocations: skiing, tennis. Office: 5601 Loch Raven Blvd Baltimore MD 21239-2905

ŽIŽKA, ZDENĚK, biologist, researcher; b. Prague, Czech Republic, Jan. 21, 1944; s. Bedřich and Ružena (Srámková) Ž.; m. Eva Nováková, Jan. 11, 1980; 1 child, Zdeněk. MS, Charles U., 1967, RNDr, 1970; PhD, Acad. Scis. Prague, 1975, DrSc, 1997. Scientist Inst. Entomology, Acad. Scis., Prague, 1967-84; scientist Inst. Microbiology, Acad. Scis., Prague, 1985—, head labor, 1988-90. Contbr. more than 150 articles to profl. jours. Head Youth Biol. Club in Youth Ctr. Neratovice, 1974—. Acad. Scis. and Ministry of Environment of Czech Republic grantee, 1992-95. Fellow Czech Zool. Soc., Czech. Soc. Microbiology, Czech. Soc. Electron Microscopy. Avocations: field zoology, herpetology, microscopy. Home: Blanická 13, 120 00 Prague 2, Czech Republic Office: Academy of Sciences, Inst of Microbiology, Vídeňská 1083, 142 20 Prague Czech Republic

ZLATANOV, ASSEN ILIEV, bank executive, consultant; b. Sofia, Bulgaria, July 27, 1935; s. Ilia Zlatanov Krastanov and Nevena Ivanova Kratsanova; m. Penka Slavi Mileva, Nov. 8, 1958; children: Veneta, Todor. M in Econs., Univ. of World, Sofia, 1959. Economist, dir. Bulgarian Nat. Bank, Sofia, 1959-64; dir., 1st v.p. Bulgarian Fgn. Trade Bank, Sofia, 1964-76; amb. Kuwait City, Kuwait, 1976-82, Bagdhad, Iraq, 1986-90; amb., head dept. Mininstry Fgn. Affairs, Sofia, 1982-86; head corr. banking Bank Fgn. Agrl. Credit, Sofia, 1992—; expert cons. UN Com. Contributions, N.Y.C., 1986-91; part-time lectr. Univ. World, 1968-74; bd. dirs. Tokuda Credit Express Bank, Ltd., Sofia, 1992-96. Author: Bulgaria's Foreign Economy Relations, 1984; co-author: Money, Credit and Banking Systems, 1974; co-author, editor: Encyclopedic Guide in Foreign Trade, 1977; co-author, cons.: International Organisations, 1987. Mem. Nat. Assn. Fgn. Rels. (bd. dirs. 1993), Bulgarian Diplomat Soc. Office: Bank Agrl Credit, Tokuda Credit Express Bank, 3 Graf Ignatiev Stz, 1000 Sofia Bulgaria

ZLATKIN, MICHAEL BRIAN, physician; b. Montreal, Que., Can., Mar. 20, 1957; came to U.S., 1986; s. Ralph and Gertrude (Rosen) Z.; m. Paula Roanne Ralph, May 30, 1982 (div. Jan. 1992); children: Nancy, Robert; m. Marilyn Judith Bohan, June 5, 1994; children: Alyssa, Chad. BSc with great distinction, McGill U., Montreal, Can., 1977; MD, Queens U., Kingston, Ont., Can., 1981. Intern Royal Victoria Hosp. McGill U., Montreal, 1981-82, resident diagnostic radiology Jewish Gen. Hosp., 1982-85, chief resident diagnostic radiology Jewish Gen. Hosp., 1985-86; fellow osteoradiology U. Calif., San Diego, 1986-87; asst. prof. radiology Hosp. U. Pa., 1987-89; dir. musculoskeletal imaging Memorial Healthcare System, Fla., 1989-99, Health S. Drs. Hosp., Coral Gables, Fla., 1995-97; pres. Specialists in Diagnostic Imaging. PA, Sunrise, Fla.; clin. assoc. prof. Sch. Medicine U. Miami, Coral Gables, 1989—. Author: Magnetic Resonance Imaging of the Shoulder, 1991, Clinical Magnetic Resonance Imaging, 2d. edit., 1996. Frances C. C. Lynch scholar Carleton U., 1974-75; Univ. Entrance scholar McGill U., 1975-76, Univ. scholar, 1976-77; named one of Best Drs. in Am., 1998, one of Outstanding Young Men of Am., 1998. Fellow Royal Coll. Physicians (Can.), Am. Bd. Radiology; mem. AMA, Internat. Soc. Magnetic Resonance Imaging Medicine, Internat. Skeletal Soc., Am. Roentgen Ray Soc., Radiologic Soc. N.Am., Am. Coll. Radiologists. Avocations: tennis, swimming, skiing, reading, movies. Address: 2689 Meadowood Ct Fort Lauderdale FL 33332-3434

ZLATOFF-MIRSKY, EVERETT IGOR, violinist; b. Evanston, Ill., Dec. 29, 1937; s. Alexander Igor and Evelyn Ola (Hill) Z.-M.; m. Janet Dalbey, Jan. 28, 1976; children from previous marriage—Tania, Laura. B.Mus., Chgo. Mus. Coll., Roosevelt U., 1960; M.Mus., Roosevelt U., 1961. Mem. faculty dept. music Roosevelt U., Chgo., 1961-66; founding mem., violinist, violist Music of the Baroque, 1971—. Violinist orch. Lyric Opera of Chgo., 1974—; concert master, pers. mgr., 1974—, violinist, violist, Contemporary Chamber Players U. Chog., 1964-82, solo violinist, Bach Soc., 1966-83; violist, violinist, Lexington String Quartet, 1966-81; rec. artist numerous recs., radio-TV and films; solo violinist appearing throughout U.S. Recipient Olive Ditson award Franklin Honor Soc., 1961. Mem. Nat. Acad. Rec. Arts and Scis. Republican. Roman Catholic. Home: 41w743 Hughes Rd Elburn IL 60119-9776 Office: Lyric Opera Chgo 20 N Wacker Dr Chicago IL 60606-2806

ZLOCH-CHRISTY, ILIANA HADJIGEORGIEV, economist; b. Sofia, Bulgaria, Mar. 3, 1953; arrived in Austria, 1980; d. Krastju T. and Jordanka G. (Paskova) Hadjigeorgiev; divorced; 1 child, Daniela Christy Zloch. MA in Bus. Adminstrn., Sofia Sch. Econs., Bulgaria, 1976; MA in Econs., U. Vienna, 1981, PhD in Econs., 1983. Cons. and dir. Bus. Cons., Vienna, 1983—; habilitations fellow Austrian Sci. Found., Vienna, 1993—; sr. assoc. mem. St. Antony's Coll., Oxford, U.K., 1988-89, 94; faculty assoc. dept. econs. Harvard U., 1984-85, 92-93, 1998; cons. UN Econ. Commn. for Europe, Geneva, 1990; cons. Internat. Monetary Fund, Washington, 1989, The World Bank, Washington, 1986-87, Austrian Bundeskanzleramt, Vienna, 1991, comml. and investment banks, 1983—; vis. scholar Hoover Instn., Stanford U., Calif., 1991, 95; fellow Bulgarian Acad. of Scis. Inst. of Fgn. Trade, Sofia, 1976-80. Author: Debt Problems of Eastern Europe, 1987, East-West Financial Relations: Current Problems and Future Prospects, 1991, Eastern Europe in a Time of Change: Economic and Political Dimensions, 1994; editor: Privatization and Foreign Investments in Eastern Europe, 1995, Bulgaria in a Time of Change: Economic and Political Dimensions, 1996, Eastern Europe and the World Economy: Challenges of Transition and Globalization, 1998, Economic Policy in Eastern Europe: Were Currency Boards a Solution?, 2000. Recipient E. Schroedinger award Austrian Sci. Found., Vienna, 1991, Theodor Koerner award Theodor Koerner Found., Vienna, 1994, Maria Schaumayer Scholarly prize, Vienna, 1997. Mem. Am. Assn. Advancement Slavic Studies, Assn. for Comparative Econ. Studies, Internat. Studies Assn. Bulgarian Orthodox. Avocations: reading, music, travel, yoga, tennis. Home: Auhofstrasse 164/1/4, 1130 Vienna Austria

ZLOTNICK, CHERYL, health services researcher; b. N.Y.C., Dec. 11, 1955. MS, Rush U., 1982; MPH, Johns Hopkins U., 1987, DPH, 1992. Dir. profl. svcs. Superior Care, Inc., Riverside, Ill., 1984-85; clin. nurse specialist, team coord. Travellers' and Immigrants Aid - Healthcare for Homeless, Chgo., 1985-86; rsch. asst. epidemiology Johns Hopkins U., Balt., 1986-87; supr. spl. projects Balt. County Dept. Health, Balt., 1987-90, dir. evaluations and rsch., 1990-92; post-doctoral fellow U. Calif., Berkeley, Calif., 1992-93; from rsch. analyst to assoc. rsch. scientist Children's Hosp. Oakland, Oakland, Calif., 1994—; from assoc. scientist to scientist alcohol rsch. group Western Consortium Pub. Health, Berkeley, Calif., 1994—; mem. rsch. com. Children's Hosp. Oakland, 1995—; grant reviewer Sigma Theta Tau,Indpls., 1994—. Author: Public Health Quality Assurance Manual, 1990. Recipient Otis Clapp Rsch. award Am. Assn. Occpul. Health Nurses, 1991. Mem. APHA, Am. Evaluation Assoc.

ZMITROWICZ, ALFRED PAWEL, engineer, researcher; b. Braniewo, Poland, Jan. 25, 1950; s. Marian and Halina (Boguslaw) Z. MSc in Civil Engring., Tech. U. Gdansk, Poland, 1973; PhD in Engring. Scis., Inst. of Fluid-Flow Machinery, Gdansk, 1980, DSc in Mechanics, 1994. Rsch. asst. Inst. of Fluid-Flow Machinery, Gdansk, 1973-75, sr. rsch. asst., 1975-80, asst. prof., 1980-94, assoc. prof., 1994—. Recipient Prof. W. Wierzbicki award Polish Soc. Civil Engrs. and Technicians, 1973, Sci. Sec. award Polish Acad. Scis., 1982; rsch. fellow Alexander von Humboldt Found., Bonn, Germany, 1984. Mem. Polish Soc. Applied and Theoretical Mechanics, Societas Humboldtiana Polonorum, Polish Acad. Scis. (mem. solid mechanics sect. of mechanics com.). Home: Oranska 1B/11, PL-80287 Gdańsk Poland Office: Inst Fluid-Flow Machinery, ul J Fiszera 14, PL-80952 Gdańsk Poland

ZMOOD, RONALD BARRY, control systems engineer, researcher, educator; b. Melbourne, Victoria, Australia, Aug. 15, 1942; s. Maurice and Ethel Bertha (Dabscheck) Z.; m. Devorah Loris Alperstein, Dec. 6, 1966; children: Simone, Daniel, Benjamin. B in Elec. Engring. with honors, U. Melbourne, 1964, M in Engring. Sci. with honors, 1967; PhD, U. Mich., 1971. Engr. Australian PMG Rsch. Labs., Melbourne, 1965-67; lectr. U. Queensland, Brisbane, 1971-74; sr. engr. Lohning Bros., Richmond, 1974-76; exptl. officer Aero. Rsch. Lab., Melbourne, 1976-80; sr. lectr. Royal Melbourne Inst. Tech., 1980-88, prin. lectr., 1988—; cons. Applied Dynamics, Ann Arbor, 1969-70, Ozy Dyn, Melbourne, 1980-95; vis. assoc. prof. U. Md., College Park, 1989-90, 95-98; contbr. numerous confs. Co-author: Introduction to Control Systems, 1995, Adaptive Control Systems, 1999; mem. editl. bd. Jour. Micromechanics & Microengineering; contbr. more than 40 articles to profl. jours. Mem. B'nai B'rith, 1978—. Henry E. Riggs fellowship, U. Mich., 1967-70; rsch. grantee Micro Machine Ctr., Japan, 1992—; recipient Oscar Weigel Exhbn. award U. Melbourne, 1962. Mem. IEEE. Avocations: music, theatre, reading, bushwalking. Office: Royal Melbourne Inst Tech, 124 Latrobe Street, Melbourne VIC 3000, Australia

ZMORA, OHAD, publisher; b. Tel-Aviv, July 23, 1933; s. Israel and Ada Olga (Kremianski) Z.; m. Zehara Poznanski, Sept. 9, 1952; children: Eran, Shachar, Hillay. Student, Hebrew U., Jerusalem, 1954-56. Journalist, 1955-86; mng. editor D'var Hashavua mag., 1956-64; editor in chief D'var Hashavva mag., 1964-86; mng. editor Davar (daily newspaper), 1970-71, dep. chief editor, 1985-86; pub. Zmora, Bitan Pubs., 1973—, Dvir Pubs., 1986—. Mem. Israeli Book Pubs. Assn. (chmn. 1994). Mem. Labour party. Jewish. Office: Zmora Bitan-Pubs House, 32 Schocken St PO Box 22383, Tel Aviv Israel

ŻMUDKA, KRZYSZTOF FELIKS, medical educator, physician, researcher; b. Bielsko-Biala, Poland, Mar. 2, 1954; s. Tadeusz Jozef and Marta Anna (Janicki) Z.; m. Jolanta Mria Uzar, June 25, 1977; children: Jadwiga, Małgorzata, Marta. MD, Med. Acad. Cracow, Poland, 1979; PhD, Med. Acad. Cracow, 1986. Med. diplomate. Asst. 2d Clin. Cardiology, Cracow, 1979-90; asst. dept. cardiology U. Leuven, Belgium, 1990-91; adj. prof. 2d Clin. Cardiology, Cracow, 1992-96; asst. prof. Inst. Cardiology Jagiellonian U., Cracow, 1996—, head dept. hemodynamics and angiocardiography, 1996—; Contbr. articles to med. jours.; inventor in field. Mem. Polish Soc. Cardiology, Polish Soc. Internal Medicine, Lions. Home: Jozefitou, 30-039 Cracow Poland Office: Jagiellonian U Inst Cardiol, Pradnicka 80, 31-202 Cracow Poland

ZMUDZKI, STEFAN, engineering educator, researcher; b. Gdynia, Poland, Sept. 3, 1939; s. Bronislaw and Genowefa (Saulewicz) Z.; m. Wanda Szumska Zmudzka, Dec. 25, 1965; 1 child, Piotr. ME, Tech. U., Szczecin, Poland, 1962; PhD, Tech. U., Poznan, Poland, 1971; DSc, Tech. U., Krakow, Poland, 1978. Cert. mech. engr. Asst. Tech. U., Szczecin, Poland, 1962-71, lectr., 1971-79, prof., 1979—; dir. Shipbuilding Inst., Szczecin, Poland, 1981-84; dean Faculty of Maritime Tech. U., Szczecin, Poland, 1983-99. Author: Railway Diesel Engines, 1982, Stirling Engines, 1993; patentee: 1999; contbr. articles to profl. jours. Chmn. Polish Assn. Mech. Engrs., 1975-78. Avocations: sports, touring, numismatics. Home phone: 48-91-4231822. Home: Kollataja 11/6, 71-525 Szczecin Poland Office: Tech U, Piastow 41, 71-065 Szczecin Poland

ZNOJIL, MILOSLAV IVAN, mathematical physicist; b. Prostějov, Czech Republic, Apr. 30, 1946; s. Miloslav and Libuše (Kubíčková) Z.;m. Jarmila Formánková, Oct. 31, 1948; 1 child, Kateřina. BSc, Czech Tech. U., Prague, 1968; MSc, Charles U., Prague, 1969, PhD, 1977; postgrad., Inst. Nuclear Rsch., Řež, Czech Republic, 1970-71. Rsch. worker Inst. Nuclear Physics, Řež, 1972-77, rsch. scientist, 1978—. Contbr. articles to profl. jours.; referee peer revs. in sci. jours. Mem. Czech Union Math. and Physicists, Internat. Assn. Math. Physicists, Am. Math. Soc., Doppler Inst. Prague. Avocations: crossword puzzles, cross-country walk. Home: 28 Října 1143/6, 277 11 Neratovice Czech Republic Office: Nuclear Physics Inst, Acad. Scis. Czech Republic, 250 68 Řež Czech Republic

ZNYSHEV, VALENTIN VASIL'EVICH, physicist, researcher; b. Nizhny Novgorod, Russia, Dec. 11, 1935; s. Vasily Vasil'evich and Alexandra Leont'evna (Zvereva) Z.; m. Ludmila Nikoaevna Zviagina, Aug. 16, 1978; children: Alla Valentinovna, Tatiana Valentinovna. MS, Lobachevsky State U., Nizhny Novgorod, Russia, 1959, PhD, 1975. Jr. rsch. worker Lobachevsky State U., Nizhny Novgorod, 1959-60, sr. engr., 1960-62, sr. engr.-designer, 1962-65, chief engr.-designer, 1965-70, sr. rsch. worker, 1970-75, lab. head, 1975—; mem. diagnostic com. State Std. Russia, 1990—. Contbr. articles to profl. jours. Recipient medal for disting. pub. svc., USSR, 1970, Vet. of Labor medal, 1985, Vet. of Sport medal, 1986; named Swimming Champion of Russia, 1955, Honoured Culture Worker of Russia, 1978. Mem. Hunters and Fishermans Soc. Russia, Nuc. Soc. Russia. Achievements include patentee in field. Avocations: singing, fishing, versification. Office: Lobachevsky U Rsch Inst, Gagarin Ave 23 Korp 6, Nizhny Novgorod Russia

ZOBEL, GUENTER, German language and literature educator, comparative and Japanese theatre researcher; b. Duisburg, Germany, Feb. 7, 1939; s. Lorenz and Helene Emma (Semper) Z. PhD, U. Cologne, Germany, 1967. Fgn. lectr. in German lang. and lit. Tohoku U., Sendai, Japan, 1967-73; fgn. lectr. in German lang. and lit. Waseda U., Tokyo, 1973-76, univ. lectr., 1976-79, assoc. prof., 1979-84, prof. German lang. and lit., 1984—. Author: Noh-Theater: Stage and Dramaturgy, Folklore & Ethnological Backgrounds, 1987; co-author, co-editor: Gold in Wax, 1988; co-author: Richard Strauss: The Woman Without a Shadow, 1993, Japanese Theater in the World, 1997; co-translator, co-editor; Kunio Yanagita: From Festival to Celebration, 1975; co-curator exhbns. N.Y.C., Munich, 1997-98. Recipient scholarship German Rsch. Coun., Japan-Germany, 1979-80. Mem. Japanese Theatre Soc., German E. Asiatic Soc. (mem. scientific com. 1983—), Kabuki Soc. Office: Waseda U Politics/Econs Fac, Nishi-Waseda 1-6-1, Tokyo 169-8050, Japan

ZOBEL, JILL ANNE HAUSRATH, journalist, editorial consultant; b. Lancaster, Pa., Jan. 8, 1949; d. Gordon Lewis and Karolyn Margareth (Kindt) Hausrath; m. Konrad Zobel; 1 child, Laura Kim. B.A., Mary Washington Coll., U. Va., 1971. Editl. sec. Bantam Books, 1971, editl. asst., 1972, asst. editor, 1972, editor, 1972-73; sr. editor, exec. editor Ballantine Books, Inc., N.Y.C., 1974-75; N.Y. rep. to Nat. Enquirer, 1975-77; editor M. Evans & Co., 1976; freelance editl. cons., 1976-78, 79—; assoc. pub. 21st Century Comm., Inc., N.Y.C., 1978-79; journalist Austrian Radio, Blue Danube Radio, Vienna, 1980—; editor "Today at Six" Blue Danube Radio, Vienna, 1998—; editor English programming FM4 Radio, Vienna, 2000—. Home: Rembrandtstrasse 9/5 A-1020, Vienna Austria

ZOBEL, JON D., JR., electrical engineer; b. Colorado Springs, July 7, 1961; s. Jon D. Zobel and Yolanda Jean Billingiere; m. Catherine Anne McKamie, July 21, 1990; 1 child, R.J. BSEE, U. Colo., 1986, MSEE, 1991. Rsch. asst. U. Colo. Control Sys. Lab., 1985-86; rsch. fellow Frank J. Seiler Rsch. Lab., USAF Academy, Colo., 1986; R&D engr. Ford Aerospace Corp., Colorado Springs, 1986-91; sr. electrical engr. TRW Electromagnetic Sys., Sunnyvale, Calif., 1991—. Pubs. chmn. Santa Clara Valley IEEE Electromagnetic Compatibility Soc. EMC '98, Santa Clara, Calif., 1998. Recipient cert. of merit Colo. Engring. Coun., 1986; named Outstanding Young Man of Am., 1987. Mem. IEEE, IEEE Electromagnetic Compatibility Soc., Nat. Assn. Radio and Telecomms. Engrs. (cert. electromagnetic compatibility engr.), Eta Kappa Nu (chpt. v.p. 1985-86). Republican. Roman Catholic. Avocations: cycling, golf. E-mail: emc.xprt@ieee.org. Fax: 408-743-6029. Office: TRW Electromagnetic Sys PO Box 3510 1330 Geneva Dr Sunnyvale CA 94088-3510

ZOBEL, LOUISE PURWIN, author, educator, lecturer, writing consultant; b. Laredo, Tex., Jan. 10, 1922; d. Leo Max and Ethel Catherine (Levy) Purwin; m. Jerome Fremont Zobel, Nov. 14, 1943; children: Lenore Zobel Harris, Janice A., Robert E., Audrey Zobel Dollinger. BA cum laude, Stanford U., 1943, MA, 1976. Cert. adult edn. and community coll. tchr., Calif. Freelance mag. writer and author Palo Alto, Calif., 1942—; writer, editor, broadcastor UP Bur., San Francisco, 1943; lectr. on writing, history, travel No. Calif., 1964—; lectr., educator U. Calif. campuses, other colls. and univs., 1969—; writing cons. to pvt. clients, 1969—; editorial asst. Assn. Coll. Unions Internat., Palo Alto, 1972-73; acting asst. prof. journalism San Jose State U., 1976; keynote speaker, seminar leader, prin. speaker at nat. confs.; cruise/shipboard enrichment lectr. and presenter of travel slide programs; coord. TV shows; TV personality publicity and public rels. campaigns; tchr. corr. classes Writer's Digest Sch. Author: (books) The Travel Writer's Handbook, 1980, (hard cover), 1982, (paperback) 83, 84, 85, rev. edits., 1992, 94, 97; author, narrator (90 minute cassette) Let's Have Fun in Japan, 1982; contbr. articles to anthologies, nat. mags. and newspapers; writer advertorials. Bd. dirs., publicity chair Friends of Palo Alto Libr., 1985—; officer Santa Clara County Med. Aux., Esther Clark Aux., others; past pres. PTA. Recipient award for excellence in journalism Sigma Delta Chi, 1943, awards Writers Digest, 1967-95, Armed Forces Writers League, 1972, Nat. Writers Club, 1976, All Nippon Airways and Japanese Nat. Tourist Orgn., 1997. Mem. Am. Soc. Journalists and Authors, Travel Journalists Guild, Internat. Food, Wine and Travel Writers Assn., Pacific Asia Travel Assn., Calif. Writers Club (v.p. 1988-89), AAUW (v.p. 1955-57, Nat. writing award 1969), Stanford Alumni Assn., Phi Beta Kappa. Avocations: travel, reading, writing, photography. Home and Office: 23350 Sereno Ct Unit 30 Cupertino CA 95014-6543

ZOËGA, TÓMAS, psychiatrist; b. Reykjavik, Iceland, July 3, 1946; s. Jóhannes and Gudrun (Benediktsdottir) Z.; m. Frida Bjarnadottir, June 29, 1968; children: Kristin, Gudrun, Helga, Jóhannes. MD, U. Iceland, Reykjavik, 1973. Diplomate Am. Bd. Psychiatry and Neurology. Rotating intern Univ. Hosp., Beykjavik, 1973-74; dist. physician Patreksfjordur, Iceland, 1974-76; resident in psychiatry Strong Meml. Hosp., U. Rochester, N.Y., 1976-79; fellow in psychiatry Mass. Gen. Hosp., Harvard U., Boston, 1979-81; pvt. practice Boston, 1980-82; psychiatrist Nat. Univ. Hosp., Reykjavik, 1982-91, chief psychiatrist, 1991—; cons. affiliated hosps., Reykjavik, 1982—. Contbr. numerous articles to med. jours., chpts. to books. Chmn. State Youth Homes, 1985-92. Grantee Icelandic Sci. Found., 1986. Mem. Icelandic Med. Assn. (chmn. ethics com. 1992—), Icelandic Psychiat. Assn. (chmn. 1987-91), Am. Psychiat. Assn. (corr.). Avocations: reading, travel, sports, political activities. Home: Vidjugerdi 8, 108 Reykjavik Iceland Office: Nat Univ Hosp, Dept Psychiatry, Reykjavik Iceland

ZOELLNER, HANS, research scientist, educator; b. Rotenburg, Germany, Jan. 26, 1960; arrived in Australia, 1960; s. Reinhold and Inge (Genseleiter) Z.; M. Helen Cox, Mar. 18, 1984; children: Sophie, Mark. B dental surgery, Sydney U., 1983, PhD, 1990. Dental surgeon Wagga Wagga, Australia, 1983-85; vis. and hon. dental officer Calvary Hosp., Wagga Base Hosp., Wagga Wagga, 1983-85; sr. rsch. officer, dept. medicine Melbourne U., 1990-92; postdoctoral rsch. fellow, dept. physiology U. Vienna, 1993-94; lectr. in oral pathology Sydney U., 1995-96, sr. lectr. in oral pathology, 1997—. Contbr. articles to profl. jours. Recipient dental postgrad. rsch. scholarship Nat. Health & Med. Rsch. Coun., Inst. Dental Rsch., Sydney, 1986-89, Lise Meitner postdoctoral rsch. fellowship Austrian Found. for the Promotion of Scientific Rsch., Dept. Physiology, U. Vienna, 1993-94, project grant Nat. Health & Med. Rsch. Coun., Dept. Oral Pathology, U. Sydney, 1996-98, project grant U. Sydney Rsch. Grants Scheme, Sydney U., 1995-96. Mem. Australian Soc. for Med. Rsch., Australia Vascular Biology Soc., Australian and New Zealand Soc. for Oral Pathology. Office: U Sydney/Westmead Hosp, Dept Oral Pathology, 2120 Sydney Australia

ZOFFER, DAVID B., lawyer; b. N.Y.C., 1947. BA, Hofstra U., 1969; JD, Fordham U., 1972. Bar: N.Y. 1973, U.S. Dist. Ct. (so. and ea. dists.) N.Y. 1974, U.S. Ct. Appeals (2d cir.) 1974, U.S. Supreme Ct. 1978, N.C. 2000; cert. mediator. Asst. dist. atty. frauds bur. N.Y. County Dist. Atty.'s Office, N.Y.C., 1972-76; spl. asst. atty. gen. State of N.Y., N.Y.C., 1976-79; sr. v.p. USAU, Inc. (subs. Gen. Reins. Corp.), N.Y.C., 1979-90; exec. v.p. Internat. Claims and Litig. Mgmt. Group Inc., Chapel Hill, N.C., 1990—; mem. faculty Fordham Crisis Mgmt. Strategies Program, N.Y.C., 1994, 7th Annual Tenn. Corp. Counsel Inst., Nashville, 1999, 5th Annual FICC Litig. Mgmt. Coll., Evanston, Ill., 1999; litig. strategies panelist Am. Trucking Assns., New Orleans, 1998; lectr. in field. Mem. Fordham Urban Law Jour., 1971; contbr. articles to profl. jours. Mem. ABA (moderator and chmn. tort and ins. practice conf. 1997, 98, 99), N.Y. Bar Assn., Fedn. Ins. and Corp. Counsel, Def. Rsch. Inst., Am. Corp. Counsel Assn. (chief legal officers' club 1998—), N.C. Bar Assn. (task force on Multidisciplinary practice), N. Hempstead Country Club, Carolina Club, Pi Gamma Mu. Fax: 919-419-7366. E-mail: dbz@icalmgroup.com. Home: 150 Meadow Run Dr Chapel Hill NC 27514-7786 Office: ICALM Group 6320 Quadrangle Dr Ste 230 Chapel Hill NC 27514-7815

ZOGHBI, MARIA DAS GRAÇAS BICHARA, scientist; b. Igarapé-Açú, Pará, Brazil, Aug. 24, 1951; d. Abibe Bechara and Hermogênia Araújo Bichara; m. Ibrahim Hassan Zoghbi; children: Nadia, Soraia, Raquel, Débora. Bachelor's degree, U. Fed. Pará, 1973; Doctorate, U. São Paulo, Brazil, 1979. Pesquisadora INPA, Manaus, Brazil, 1974-94, Museu Paraense Emílio Goeldi, Belém, Brazil, 1994—; chief dept. INPA, Manaus, 1985-88, 93-94, dir. de área pesq., 1988, 89. Contbr. numerous articles to profl. jours. Avocation: swimming. Office: PO Box 399, Av Perimetral S/N, Belém Brazil

ZOGU, VELI, cardiovascular surgery educator; b. Zerqan, Albania, Sept. 10, 1940; s. Sadik and Sude (Kuka) Z.; m. Violeta Berxolli, Sept. 3, 1967; children: Aida, Iljan. Med. diploma, Faculty Medicine, 1963; cardiovascular surgeon, Acad. Med. Scis., 1969. Prof. human anatomy Faculty Medicine, Tirana, Albania, 1963-64; gen. surgeon Hosp. Nr.2, Tirana, Albania, 1964-66; cardiovascular surgeon U. Clinic Surgery, Tirana, Albania, 1970-90; head dept. cardiovascular surgery U. Hosp. Ctr., Tirana, Albania, 1991—; dean Medicine Faculty, Tirana, 1983-89; chmn. Scientific Coun. Faculty Medicine, 1983-89; mem. State Com. Scis., Tirana, 1983—, Scientific Coun. Tirana U., 1984—. Author: Replacement if the Heart Valves, 1991; co-author: General Surgery, 1974, Surgical Diseases, 1981; contbr. 33 articles to profl. jours. Mem. Coll. Sanitary Ministry, Tirana, 1984-90; candidate for deputy Parliament of Albania, 1991. Mem. European Soc. Cardiology, Med. Balcanic Union, Balcanic Assn. Vascular Surgery, Ital-Albanian Assn. Mini-Vascular Surgery. Avocations: reading, travel, chess. Home: Rruga GJON BUZUKU P 100, Shk 3 Ap 7, Tirana Albania Office: U Hosp Ctr Tirana, Univ Hosp Ctr Tirana, RRuga DIBRA 370, Tirana Albania

ZOHADIE, MUHAMAD, engineering educator; b. Klang, Selangor, Malaysia, Dec. 29, 1950; s. Bardaie Hassan and Sumanah Yusof; m. Umi Kalsom Hussein; children: Zahrina Azian, Zaireen Aliza, Zuliana Azrin. Diploma, Coll. of Agr., Malaya, 1971; BS, U. Calif., Davis, 1974, MS, 1976; PhD, Cornell U., Ithaca, N.Y., 1979. Cert. profl. engr., Malaysia. Assoc. prof. engring. U. Putra Malaysia, Selangor, 1982-92; dept. head power and machinery engring. U. Putra Malaysia, 1982-88, dean faculty of engring., 1988-93, prof. engring., 1993—, dep. vice chancellor, 1993-99. Author: Energy and Agriculture in Malaysia, 1981; contbr. articles to profl. jours. Conferred title Dato' His Royal Highness Sultan of Selangor, 1996. Mem. N.Y. Acad. Sci., Inst. Indsl. Engrs. (sr.), Club Bologna, U. Putra Malaysia Golf Club (pres.). Avocation: golf. E-mail: zohadie@eng.upm.edu.mc. Office: Faculty Engring, U Putra Malaysia, 43400 UPM Serdang Malaysia

ZOHAR, MATTANYAH, archaeology educator; b. Berlin, May 6, 1938; arrived in Israel, 1971; s. Vladimir and Agnes (Prange) Von Lobza/Goldmann; m. Brigitte Klein, 1972; 1 child, Tobia David Prange. Student, Alliance Israelite, Istanbul, Turkey, 1957; PhD, Hebrew U., Jerusalem, 1994. Studied and lived with pastoral nomads, Turkey, Iran, India, 1958-65; electronic engr. Can. Aviation, Stolberg, Germany, 1966-70; instr. archaeology Hebrew U., 1975—. Contbr. articles to Israel Exploration Jour., Anchor Bible Dictionary, Monographs in World Archaeology, New Ency. of Archaeology, Excavations in Holy Land, numerous others. Jewish. Achievements include research in problem of nomadic intrusions and the role of pastoral nomads in cultural development of ancient Near East and in Mediterranean countries, specializing in megalithic monuments in Near East and Mediterranean countries. Home: PO Box 82548, Hamishlat 12, 90805 Ma'oz Tsion Israel Office: Hebrew U, Inst Archaeology, Jerusalem Israel

ZOHLNHÖFER, WERNER FERDINAND, economic policy educator; b. Lichtenau, Bavaria, Germany, Nov. 19, 1934; s. Karl and Pauline (Rogner) Z.; m. Ingeborg Duday, Aug. 27, 1965; children: Burkhard, Dietlind, Reimut. Diploma in econs., U. Freiburg, Germany, 1958, PhD, 1965; diploma in internat. rels., Johns Hopkins U., Bologna, Italy, 1960; MA in Polit. Sci., U. N.C., 1963. Asst. prof. U. Freiburg, 1965-72; prof. econs. U. Dortmund, Germany, 1972-80, chmn. dept. econs. and social scis., 1974-76, v.p., 1976-78; prof. econ. policy U. Mainz, Germany, 1981—, chmn. dept. law and econs., 1984-86, bd. dirs. Inst. for Econ. Policy Rsch., 1983—. Author: Wettbewerbspolit im Oligopol, 1968, Die Wirtschaftspolitische Willens-und Entreheidingsbildung in der Demokratie, 1999; editor: Wachstumsminderung u. WI-System, 1982, Wirtschaftswissenschaft in Dienste der Politikberatung, 1992; Zukunftsprobleme der Welt-wirtschaftsordnung,1996, Tarifautonomie auf dem Prüfstand, 1996, Europa auf dem Weg zur Politischen Union?, 1997, Perspektiven der Osterweiterung und Reformbedarf der EU, 1998. Mem. assembly Luth. Ch., Hessen-Nassau, Germany, 1992—. Fellow Govt. of Germany, 1959-60, German Rsch. Assn., 1969-71, Japan Soc. for Promotion Sci., 1979. Mem. List Gesellschaft (exec. bd. 1992—), Verein für Socialpolitik (exec. bd. 1993-99), Am. Econ. Assn., Rotary (pres. Mainz). Avocations: music, literature, fine arts. Home: Bahnweg 33, D-55129 Mainz Germany Office: U Mainz, Saarstrasse 21, D-55099 Mainz Germany

ZOIS, CONSTANTINE NICHOLAS ATHANASIOS, meteorology educator; b. Newark, Feb. 21, 1938; s. Athanasios Konstantinos and Asimina (Speros-Blekas) Z.; m. Elyse Stein, Dec. 26, 1971; children: Jennifer, Jonathan. BA, Rutgers U., 1961; MS, Fla. State U., 1965; PhD, Rutgers U., 1980. Draftsman Babcock and Wilcox Corp., Newark, 1956; designer Foster Wheeler Corp., Carteret, N.J., 1956; instr. Rutgers U., New Brunswick, N.J., 1961-62; grad. asst. Fla. State U., Tallahassee, 1962-65; rsch. meteorologist Nat. Weather Svc., Garden City, L.I., N.Y., 1965-67; prof. Kean Coll. N.J., Union, 1967—; founder meteorology program Kean Coll., N.J.; cons. Connell, Foley and Geiser, Roseland, N.J., 1986-88; chmn. Kean Coll. All-Coll. Promotion com., 1991-93. Author, editor: Papers in Marine Science, 1971; author: Observation of the Newark N.J. Nocturnal Heat Island and Its Consideration in Terms of a Physical Model, 1980, Dynamical and Physical Oceanography, 1988, Atmospheric Dynamics: Exercises and Problems, 1988, Climatology Workbook, 1988, Weather Map Folio, 1989; contbg. author: Outcomes Assessment at Kean College of N.J., 1992, Synoptic Meterology-Exercises and Readings, Vols. 1-3, 1995. Mem. AAAS, Nat. Weather Assn., Am. Meteorol. Soc. (pres. N.J. chpt. 1980-81), N.Y. Acad. Scis. (vice chmn. atmospheric scis. sect. 1986-87, chmn. 1987-88, adv. com. atmospheric sci. sect., 1988—), N.J. Marine Scis. Consortium, Phi Beta Kappa. Republican. Greek Orthodox. Avocations: guitar, banjo, fishing, baseball, snorkeling. Home: 2798 Carol Rd Union NJ 07083-4831 Office: Kean Coll of NJ Dept Meterology Morris Ave Union NJ 07083-7117

ZÖLDHELYI-DEÁK, ZSUZSANNA MÁRIA, historian of literature; b. Budapest, Hungary, Jan. 27, 1928; d. Sándor and Sándorné (Susitzky) Z.; m. Sándor Deák, Apr. 14, 1954; children: István, Imre. BA, Leningrad (Russia) State U., 1951; PhD, Hungarian Acad. Scis., Budapest, 1961, DSc, 1991. Cert. philologist. Lectr. Budapest U. Eötvös Lóránd, 1951-63, reader, 1963-92, cons., 1992—, titular prof., 1992-96; ret. Author: Turgenev, 1964, Turgenyev Világa,1978, Turgenyev Prózai költeményei, 1991; editor: Tolsztoj L. N. 1-10, 1964-67. Mem. Edn. Bd. Studia Slavica Hungary Acad. Sci. Hungary (com. modern phylology), Internat. Slavonic Commn. (Hungarian divsn.). Avocations: travel, contacts with people of different countries. Home: Kárpát 12, 1133 Budapest Hungary Office: Eötvös Lóránd Tudományegyetem Keleti, Szláv Tanszék, 1052 Budapest Hungary

ZOLOTARYOVA, TATYANA ANANEVNA, rehabilitation physician; b. Odessa, Ukraine, Jan. 15, 1948; d. Ananij and Valentina (Prokopeva) Z.; m. Vladimir Grubnik, Apr. 27, 1979; 1 child, Alexandra. MD, Med. U. Odessa, 1973; PhD, Inst. Med. Rehab., Odessa, 1980; DSc, Scientific Ctr. Rehab., Moscow, 1992. Rural physician Dist. Hosp. Odessa, Ukraine, 1973-75; from jr. rschr. to chief rschr. Inst. Med. Rehab., 1975-98, prof., 1998—. Author: (with V. Zaporojan, V.V. Grubnik, B. Podubny, Yu. Kuvshinov, P. Shipulin) Lasers for Endoscopy, 1998, Physical Agents: Basic Mechanism of their Action on Hepatic Biotransformation, 2000; editor-in-chief: Jour. Med. Rehab. Balneology, Physiotherapy, 1995—; contbr. articles to profl. jours.; patentee in field. Mem. Ukrainian Scientific Assn. Phys. Therapy, N.Y. Acad. Scis.

ZOLOTUKHIN, ANATOLY BORIS, petroleum engineering educator; b. Moscow, Mar. 11, 1946; s. Boris Konstantin and Ekaterina Fedor (Garanina) Z.; m. Alla Nickolai Gladkova, July 26, 1968; children: Alexey. MS in Reservoir Engring., State Gubkin Acad. Oil and Gas, Moscow, 1969, PhD in Fluid Mechanics, 1973, D Tech. Sci. Reservoir Engring., 1990; MS in Math., Moscow State U., 1977. Diplomate reservoir engring., fluid mechanics, applied math. Jr. rschr. State Gubkin Acad. Oil and Gas, Moscow, 1972-78, sr. rschr., 1979-85, assoc. prof., 1985-90, prof., 1985-90; fellow Stanford U., 1978-79; head lab. Oil & Gas Rsch. Inst., Moscow, 1987-95, chief rsch. specialist, 1995—; prof. Stavanger (Norway) Coll., 1991—; project mgr. Statoil, Norway, 1999—. Author: Forecasting Methods for the Oil and Gas, 1991; co-author: Fundamentals of Petroleum Reservoir Engineering, 1997, Basics of OffShore Petroleum Engineering and Development of Marine Facilities, 1998; contbr. articles to profl. jours. Grantee Norwegian Rsch. Coun., Oslo, 1992, 96, Stavanger (Norway) Coll., 1996-97. Mem. Soc. Petroleum Engrs., Norwegian Petroleum Soc. Avocations: music, painting, tennis, mountain skiing. Office: Stavanger Coll, Ullandhaug, PO Box 2557, N-4004 Stavanger Rogaland, Norway

ZOLTIE, NIGEL, physician; b. Leeds, Eng., June 12, 1954; s. Jack and Betty (Wolfson) Z.; m. Julie Anne Ramsden, Dec. 4, 1981 (dec. Dec. 1989); children: Jonathan, Timothy; m. Lindsay Michelle Stein, June 12, 1994. M.B.,Ch.B., Bristol (Eng.) U., 1977. Cons. in emergency medicine Leeds Gen. Infirmary, 1993—. Fellow Royal Coll. Surgeons Edinburgh. Faculty Accident and Emergency Medicine. Office: Leeds General Infirmary, Accident/Emergency Dept, Leeds LS1 3EX, England

ZOMAYA, ALBERT YOUSIF, electrical and computer engineering educator; b. Rasafa, Iraq, July 16, 1964; arrived in Australia, 1990; s. Yousif H. and Elizabeth H. Z. B of Engring., Kuwait U., 1987; PhD, Sheffield (Eng.) U., 1990. Registered profl. engr. Rsch. engr. Kuwait U., Kuwait City, 1987; tutor Sheffield U., 1987-90; prof. U. Western Australia, Perth, 1990—; vis. prof. Waterloo U., 1996, U. Mo., Rolla, 1997—; assoc. editor IEEE Transaction on Parallel and Distributed Sys., 1997—; prof. dept. elec. and electronic engring. U. Western Australia, 1994—. Author: Modelling and Simulation Robot Manipulators: A Parallel-Processing Approach, 1992; editor: Parallel and Distributed Computing Handbook, 1996, Parallel Computing: Paradigms and Applications, 1996; co-author: Neuro-Adaptive Process Control: A Practical Approach, 1996, Collision Avoidance in Multi Robot Systems, 1998, Scheduling in Parallel Computing Systems: Fuzzy and Annealing Techniques, 1999; founding editor: Wiley Book Series on Parallel and distributed Computers, 1997—; assoc. editor IEEE Transactions on Systems, Man and Cybernetics, 1997—, Jour. of Future Generation Computer Systems, 1997—, Internat. Jour. on Parallel and Distribution Systems nad Networks, 1996, IEEE Transactions on Parallel and Distributed Systems, 1998—; contbr. numerous papers to profl. jours. and confs. Kuwait U. scholar, 1982, Sheffield U. scholar, 1988; grantee Australian Rsch. Coun., 1992—. Mem. IEEE (sec. Western Australia sect. 1993-94, computer sect., robotics and automation sect., bd. dirs. tech. com. on parallel processing), Inst. Elec. Engrs., Internat. Fedn. Automatic Control (algorithms and archs. for real-time control com. mem.), Assn. for Computing Machinery, N.Y. Acad. Scis., Sigma Xi. Assyrian Orthodox. Avocations: chess, squash, soccer, reading. Office: U Westn Australia Nedlands, Dept Elec Engring, Perth 6907, Australia

ZONG, RUHOU, telecommunications engineer; b. Beijing, Feb. 13, 1929; parents Zhixin Zong and Rongjuan Zheng; m. Peijun Lu, Oct. 1, 1961; children: Xiaorong, Yuchen. Grad., Utopia U., Shanghai, 1951. Cert. engr. at prof. level. Engr. radio dept. Shanghai Telecom. Bur., 1951-57; project mgr. Shanghai Telecom. Rsch. Inst., 1957-66; dir. satellite comm. lab. First Rsch. Inst. of MPT (Ministry of Posts and Telecom.), Shanghai, 1974-82, chief engr., 1984-89, sr. advisor to pres., 1990—; assignee INTELSAT (Internat. Satellite Comm. Orgn.), Washington, 1982-83; nat. project dir. of digital satellite comm. project UN Devel. Program, Washington, 1991-96; head Chinese del. to Study Group IV (Fixed Satellite Svc.), Internat. Radio Cons. Com., Internat. Telecom. Union, Geneve, 1987-90; part-time prof. Shanghai Jiao-Tong U., 1986-97; mem. acad. com. Chinese Acad. of Posts and Telecomm. Sci., 1986-94, mem. eval. com. for sr. level techn. qualification, 1987-91. Organizer, tech. writer transmission plan for Chinese domestic satellite system, 1981-85; project dir. several satellite comms. expts. mem. editorial panel of the Wiley-Interscience pub.--Internat. Jour. of Satellite Com. 1986—. Recipient award of Sci. and Tech. Advancement, Chinese MPT, 1985. Fellow Chinese Inst. of Comms. (chmn. satellite comms. profl. com. 1984-96), Shanghai Inst. of Comms. (chmn. radio comms. com. 1984-92); mem. IEEE (sr.). Avocation: Chinese weiqi. E-mail: rhzong@pub-lic.sta.net.cn. Home: 25 Ping Jiang Lu 1305, Shanghai 200032, China Office: 1st Rsch Inst of MPT, 48 Ping Jiang Lu, 200032 Shanghai China

ZONG, ZHI, research engineer; b. Lingyuan, Liaoning, China, Apr. 30, 1964; arrived in Singapore, 1995; s. Zheng Yu Zong and Shu Qin Wei; m. Li Zhou, Oct. 14, 1989; children: Xue Zhou, Xue Ting. B of Engring., Dalian (China) U. Tech., 1986, M of Engring., 1989; PhD, Hiroshima (Japan) U., 1995. Lectr. Dalian U. Tech., 1989-92; rsch. fellow Nat. U. Singapore, 1995-97; sr. rsch. engr. Inst. High Performance Computing, Singapore, 1997-99, prin. rsch. engr., 1999—. Contbr. articles to profl. jours. Recipient Best Paper award Internat. Soc. Offshore and Polar Engrs., The Netherlands, 1995, Devel. of Underwater Shock Tech. award Singapore Navy, 1996-99, Def. Tech. prize Singapore Govt., 1998. Mem. Soc. Naval and Marine Architects, Soc. Naval and Marine Architects Japan, Nat. U. Singapore Faculty Club. Avocations: table tennis, soccer. Home: Teck Whye Ln #11-614, 680 111 Singapore Singapore Office: IHPC The Rutherford, 89C Science Park Dr 02-1112, Singapore 118261, Singapore

ZONN, SERGEI VLADIMIROVICH, soil scientist, consultant; b. Vladikavkas, Russia, Mar. 20, 1906; s. Vladimir Ivanovich and Nadegeda Mihavlovna (Popova) Z.; m. Vera Gerasimovna Ananyeva Zonn, 1928; 1 child, Vladimir; m. Valentina Vladimorovna Kellerman Zonn, 1933; children: Marina, Igor. PhD, Moscow, Russia, 1935. Main soil scientist Dagvodhos, Mahachckala, Russia, 1928-31; sr. scientist Agrl. Acad., Lenningrad, Russia, 1932-41; chief of lab. Inst. of Forest, Moscow, Russia, 1941-62; head of sect. Inst. Geography, Moscow, Russia, 1962-83, cons., 1983—; prof. Ąain Inst., Leningrad, USSR, 1938-41, Forest Tech. Inst., Moscow, USSR, 1946-48, U. Friendship, Moscow, USSR, 1962-88. Author: Mountain Forest Soils of the NW Caucases, 1950, Tropical Soil Science, 1980, Soil Map of the N. Caucases, 1975 (gold medal 1978). editor-in-chief magazin Soil Sci., Moscow, Russia, 1947-99; v.p. of All Union Of USSR Soil Scientists Soc., Moscow, Russia, 1940-60. Mem. Ukranian Ecol. Acad. Sci., ISSS, Dokuchaeu SSS. Home: Dm Ulianova 4-2-322, 117333 Moscow Russia Office: Inst Geography, Staromonetny 29, 109017 Moscow Russia

ZOOK, MERLIN WAYNE, meteorologist; b. Connellsville, Pa., July 2, 1937; s. Ellrose Durr and Frances Adeline (Loucks) Z.; m. Maxine Beatrice Hartzler, May 1, 1965; children: Kevin Ray, Kathleen Joy. BA, Goshen (Ind.) Coll., 1959; MS, Pa. State U., 1961. Cert. consulting meteorologist. Rsch. assoc. U. Mich., Ann Arbor, 1958; grad. asst. Pa. State U., University Park, 1960-61; audio-visual asst., staff meteorologist Mennonite Cen. Com., Akron, Pa., 1961-63; air quality program specialist Pa. Dept. Environ. Protection, Harrisburg, 1963-2000; ret., 2000; book reviewer Sci. Edn. Dept. Boston U., 1990-92, Nat. Weather Assn., Temple Hills, Md., 1983-88, book rev. editor, 1988-92; scientist, participant AAAS-Bell Atlantic Found., Washington, 1989-90. Author, contbr.: (chpt.) Behind the Dim Unknown, 1966. Guest lectr. Millersville (Pa.) State U., 1988, 90, Boy Scouts Am., Camp Hill, Pa., 1990, Pa. State U., Middletown, 1990, 91—, Cub Scouts Am., Camp Hill, 1991—. Mem. Am. Meteorol. Soc., Union of Concerned Scientists. Achievements include development of models for the daily prediction of the Air Quality Index of Pa.; collection of cloud type photographs with classifications for study of cloud characteristics/physics; research in meso-scale meteorology and localized forecasting, on the relationship between solar radiation and formation of ozone in urban areas in Pa., research and development of mathematical models for the prediction of ozone episodes in urban areas; on migratory patterns of local birds influenced by meteorological conditions. E-mail: mwzook@itech.com. Home: 105 June Dr Camp Hill PA 17011-5069

ZOOK, THERESA FUETTERER, gemologist, consultant; b. Barberton, Ohio, Mar. 12, 1919; d. Charles Theodore and Ethel May (Knisely) Fuetterer; m. Donovan Quay Zook, June 21, 1941; children: Theodore Alan, Jacqueline Deborah Zook Cochran. AB, Ohio U., 1941; MA in Pub. Adminstrn., Am. U., 1946. Adminstrv. intern Nat. Inst. Pub. Affairs, Washington, 1941-42; mgmt. intern USDA, Washington, 1941-42; adminstrv. analyst Office Emergency Mgmt., Washington, 1942-43, Office Price Adminstrn., Washington, 1943-45; founder Zook and Zook Mgmt. Cons., Arlington, Va., 1945-47; tchr. ancient history and U.S. govt. Fairfax County (Va.) Pub. Schs., 1963-64; founder, pres. Associated Gem Cons. Lab., Alexandria, 1974—, Alpha Gate Crafts Ltd., Alexandria, 1977—; color cons. Internat. Com. on Color in Gems, Bangkok, 1983. Author: Directory of Selected Color Resources Annotated Guide, 1982, Reunion of Descendants of David and Magdalena (Blough) Zook, 1983, Basic Machine Knitting, 1979; contbr. articles to profl. jours. Bd. dirs. Am. Embassy Com. on Edn., Montevideo, Uruguay, 1962; co-founder Workshop of Arts, Santiago, Chile, 1958; mem. Nat. Trust for Hist. Preservation, Nat. Mus. Women in Arts, Nat. Mus. Am. Indian, Am. Horticulture Soc., Textile Mus. Fellow Gemmological Assn. of Gt. Britain (diplomate); mem. AAUW, DAR, Nat. Geneal. Soc., Inter-Soc. Color Coun. (chmn. com. color in gemstones 1982-84, Appreciation cert. 1984), Accredited Gemological Assn. (co-founder, v.p.), Phi Beta Kappa, Tau Kappa Alpha, Kappa Delta Pi. Avocations: garden design, knitting, fabric creation, genealogy, music. Home: PO Box 6310 Alexandria VA 22306-0310

ZOPFI, HANS JAKOB, secondary education educator, botanist; b. Schwanden, Glarus, Switzerland, Aug. 26, 1960; s. Hanspeter and Rosa (Elmer) Z.; m. Melitta Buechel, July 9, 1983; children: Lukas, Elias, Theres. Diploma, U. Zurich, Switzerland, 1987, D degree, 1991, cert. tchr., 1996. Asst. U. Zurich, 1987-91, lectr. botany, 1996—, postgrad. rschr. Swiss Nat. Found., 1991-95; tchr. Kantonsschule Glarus, 1995—. Author: Geschuetzte

Pflanzen und ihre Lebensraeume, 1997; contbr. articles to sci. jours., including Plant Systematics and Evolution, Flora, Biol. Jour. Linnean Soc. Mem. Naturforschende Gesellschaft des Kantons Glarus (pres. 1999). Avocations: botany, hiking. E-mail: euphrasia@bluewin.ch. Home: Im Thon 43, CH-8762 Schwanden Glarus, Switzerland Office: Kantonsschule Glarus, Winkelstrasse 1, CH-8750 Glarus Switzerland

ZOPPO, CIRO ELLIOTT, retired political science educator, consultant; b. Caserta, Campania, Italy, Aug. 21, 1923; came to U.S., 1936, naturalized, 1943; s. Romualdo and Romilda (Veccia) Z.; m. Rosemary Pampalone, June 25, 1949; children: Adriana, Gian. BA, Montclair State U., 1948; MA, Columbia U., 1959, PhD, 1963. Rschr. Rand Corp., Santa Monica, Calif., 1960-63, 66-68, cons., 1968-83; rsch. assoc. Ctr. for Internat. Affairs, Harvard U., Cambridge, Mass., 1963-66; assoc. dir. Security Studies Project, UCLA, 1968-70; prof. polit. sci. UCLA, 1969-91, prof. emeritus, 1991—. Author, editor: Geopolitics: Classical and Nuclear, 1985, Nordic Security and 21st Century, 1992; contbr. articles to profl. publs. Assoc. rsch. coun. Inst. Civil-Mils., Toulouse, France, 1982-87; mem. World Affairs Coun., L.A., 1995—; acad. assoc. Atlantic Coun. U.S., Washington, 1986. Lt. U.S. Army, 1943-45, ETO. Decorated Bronze star; grantee Ford Found., 1970-75, U.S. Dept. State, 1972, UCLA, 1976—. Mem. Internat. Inst. Strategic Studies (London), Istituto Affari Internazionali (Rome), Istituto Cuestiones Internacionales (Spain). Avocations: painting, languages, travel. E-mail: czoppo@polisci.ucla.edu. Office: UCLA Dept Polit Sci Hilgard Ave Los Angeles CA 90095-0001

ZORC, DAVOR, electrical and computer engineering educator; b. Zagreb, Croatia, Dec. 7, 1954; s. Zvonimir and Dragica (Travašić) Z.; 1 child, Marina. BSEE, U. Zagreb, 1978, MSc, 1986, PhD in Elec. Engring., 1990. Electronics researcher Rade Koncar Inst., Zagreb, 1978-82; prof. elec. engring. faculty mech. engring. U. Zagreb, 1982—; computer rschr. IPSEN Industries Internat., Kleve, Germany, 1989—. Mem. IEEE, IEEE Computer Soc. Roman Catholic. Avocation: literature. Home: Bosihevska 34, 10 000 Zagreb Croatia Office: U Zagreb Fac Mech Engring, Ivana Lucica 5, 10 000 Zagreb Croatia

ZORIN, SERGEI MICHAIL, optical theater director, artist; b. Poltava, Ukraine, Feb. 27, 1944; s. Michail Vasili and Serafina Timghei (Makazenko) Z.; m. Helena Vladimir Zorina; 1 child, Daniel. Degree, Poly. State Inst., Kharkov, 1968. Chief of dept. Elec.-Mech. Concern, Poltava, Ukraine, 1970-73; dep. chief of lab. Ctrl. Rsch. Sci. Inst. of the Connection, Moscow, 1973-77; sci. rschr. Moscow State U., 1977-83; chief of dept. Sci. Rsch. Inst. Ekos, Moscow, 1983-89; dir. optical theater Moscow, 1989—. Author: The Light-Musical Environment in Intense Education, 1977, Integrative Art and Education, 1983. Mem. Assn. Russian Painters, Soc. Indians' Culture. Home: Konnekov St Apt 7, 127560 Moscow Russia Office: Internat Rerich's Ctr Optical Theatre, mal Znamensky per 3/5, 121019 Moscow Russia

ZORN, GUNTHER JOSEPH, human resources consultant; b. Vienna, Mar. 3, 1932; s. Rudolf Otto and Friederike (Rosenblatt) Z. BA in Polit. Sci., U. Calif., L.A., 1956; diploma in pub. affairs, Coro Found., L.A., 1962; cert. in program mgmt., U. Calif., Davis, 1970; MA in Urban Studies, Occidental Coll., 1971. Asst. dep. dir. legis. Calif. State Dept. Health, Sacramento, 1975-76; chief establishments group Food and Agr. Orgn. of the UN, Rome, 1976-90, chief human resources planning svc., 1991-94; internat. cons. in human resources UN, 1994—; pers. specialist Calif. State Dept. Mental Hygiene, Sacramento, 1962-69, orgn. and manpower specialist, 1969-71; chief pers. svc. Calif. State Dept. Health, Sacramento, 1971-73, chief mgmt. cons. sect., 1973-75. Lt. comdr. USNR, 1956-61. Mem. Am. Soc. for Pub. Adminstrn. (chpt. treas. 1973-75), Internat. Pers. Mgmt. Assn. E-mail: gzorn@tiscalinet.it. Office: Casella Postale 10355, 00144 Rome Italy

ZORN, REINER, physicist, researcher; b. Cologne, Germany, June 3, 1960; s. Jakob and Anna Maria (Schmitz) Z. Diplom Physik, U. Cologne, 1985, PhD, 1989; habilitation, U. Münster, 1996. Rsch. scientist IFF Forschungszentrum, Jülich, Germany, 1990-92, 94—; guest scientist Nat. Inst. of Stds. and Tech., Gaithersburg, Md., 1993. Editor: (with B. Frick and H. Büttner) International workshop on dynamics in confinement, 2000; contbr. articles to profl. jours. Deutsche Forschungsgemeinschaft fellow, 1993-95; Studienstiftung des deutschen Volkes scholar, 1980-89. Mem. German Phys. Soc., Rheological Soc. Avocations: Chinese culture and language, hang-gliding. Home: Gereonswall 5a/b, 50668 Cologne Germany Office: IFF Forschungszentrum, PO Box, 52425 Jülich Germany

ZORYCHTA, ANDRZEJ, rock mechanics and mining engineering educator; b. Karwina, Poland, May 14, 1945; s. Henryk and Zofia (Filipowska) Z.; m. Mieczyslawa Golik, Oct. 8, 1975; 1 child, Barbara. MSc, U. Mining and Metallurgy, Cracow, Poland, 1969, PhD, 1973, DSc, 1985. Sr. lectr. rock mechanics and mining engring. U. Mining and Metallurgy, 1969-85, prof., 1985—, vice dir., 1985-88, vice dean, 1990-93; vice com. Commn. Rock Bursts, State Mining Office, Katowice, Poland, 1993—, chmn. Commn. Underground Mining Support, 1996—. Author: Opinions and Solutions Concerning Rock Bursts in Coal Mines, 1984, Criterion of Rock Burst During Exploitation of Coal Seams, 1985. Avocations: skiing, swimming. Home: Grzegórzecka 76a/29, 31-559 Cracow Poland Office: U Mining and Metallurgy, Al Mickiewicza 30, 30-059 Cracow Poland

ZOSIMO-LANDOLFO, GUIDO, publisher, chemist, pharmacist; b. Beirut, Lebanon, Jan. 1, 1956; s. Armando Zosimo-Landolfo and Maria Nahas. MS in Pharmacy, St. Joseph U., Beirut, Lebanon, 1981; DEA in Chemistry, Paris U., 1981; PhD in Pharm. Chemistry, Geneva U., Switzerland, 1986. Pharmacist Am. Hosp., Beirut, Lebanon, 1981; lectr. U. Geneva, Switzerland, 1981-86, sr. lectr., 1986-88; prof. Lebanese U., Beirut, Lebanon, 1989-90; acquisitions editor Elsevier Science, Lausanne, Switzerland, 1991-95, sr. product mgr., 1995-96; assoc. pub. Elsevier Science, Lausanne, 1997-98, pub., 1998-99; pub. dir. Editions Scientifiques et Mèdicales Elsevier, Paris, 2000—; cons. Eagle SA, Beirut, Lebanon, 1989. Contbr. numerous articles to profl. jours. Mem. ASP, ACS, Soc. Phys. Nat. History, Soc. Chimica Italiana. Avocations: reading, soccer, rugby, stamp collecting, travelling. Home: 5 Rue de Lyon, 1201 Geneva Switzerland France Office: Elsevier Science SA, Editions Elsevier, 23 Rue Linois, 75015 Paris France

ZOTALEY, BYRON LEO, lawyer; b. Mpls., Mar. 18, 1944; s. Leo John and Tula (Koupis) Z.; m. Theresa L. Cassady, Sept. 7, 1969; children: Nicole, Jason, Krisanthy. BA in Psychology, U. Minn., 1966; MATC, U. St. Thomas, St. Paul, 1968; JD, William Mitchell Coll. of Law, 1970. Bar: Minn. 1970, U.S. Dist. Ct. Minn. 1971, U.S. Ct. Appeals (8th cir.) 1972, U.S. Supreme Ct. 1975. Pres. LeVander, Zotaley & Vander Linden, Mpls., 1970-99, Zotaley Law Offices, Ltd., Hopkins, Minn., 1999—; arbitrator Minn. No Fault Panel, 1974—; cons. Marthe Properties, Mpls., 1980-90, Theron Properties, Mpls., 1985—. Bd. dirs. Minn. Consumer Alliance, 1994-95; mem. adv. bd. Benilde-St. Margaret's Jr. H.s., 1993-95; bd. trustees St. Mary's Greek Orthodox Ch. Mpls., 1997—, v.p., 1998, pres., 1999—. Mem. ABA, ATLA, Minn. Bar Assn., Hennepin County Bar Assn., Minn. Trial Lawyers Assn. (chmn. Amicus Curiae com. 1980-87, bd. govs. 1982-93, mem. exec. com. 1987-89, emeritus, 1994—). Fax: 612-933-9034. E-mail: b zotaley@worldnet.att.net. Home: 5504 Parkwood Ln Minneapolis MN 55436-1728 Office: 310 Wells Fargo Bank Bldg 1011 1st St S Hopkins MN 55343-9413

ZOTIKOV, EVGENIL ALEXEEVICH, immunohematologist, researcher; b. Moscow, Dmitrov, USSR, Dec. 25, 1928; s. Alexei Vasilievich and Natalia Ivanovna (Suchanova); m. Anna Georgieyna Babaeva, Feb. 23, 1954; 1 child, Andrey Evgnievich. Student, First Med. Inst., Moscow, 1953; cand. Med. Scis., U. Moscow, 1958, D in Med. Scis., 1966, Prof. Hematology and Blood Transfusion, 1970. Postgrad. fellow Inst. Exptl. Biology, Moscow, 1953-56, rschr., 1956-60; sr. rschr. Inst Blood Transfusion and Hematology, Moscow, USSR, 1960-62; head of lab. Inst. Blood Transfusion and Hematology, Moscow, 1982—; mem. expert adv. panel on immunology, WHO, 1969-78. Inventor in field: 1965 (Bronze medal at All Union Exhbn. Nat. Economy USSR, 1977, Gold medal); Author: (book) Human Antigen Systems and Homeostasis, 1982 (Silver medal at All-Union Exhbn. Nat. Economy, 1984; co-inventor, 1996 (Diploma of Sci. Discovery). Mem. Acad. Med. Scis. Moscow. Avocations: art, lierature, skiing, swimming. Office: Sci Hematology Ctr, Novozikovsky Pr 4A, 125 165 Moscow Russia

ZOTT, REGINE JOHANNA, historian; b. Zassnitz, Germany, Oct. 15, 1938; d. Heinz Hermann and Johanna Margarete (Behla) Wolf; m. Hans-Jörg Heinrich Zott, May 3, 1937; children: Antje Johanna, Ulrike Annemarie. MS, U. Greifswald, Germany, 1961; PhD, U. Berlin, 1976. High sch. tchr. Oschatz, Germany, 1962-66; rschr. Acad. Sci., Berlin, 1969-91, Orgn. for Scientist's Integration Programme Tech. U., Berlin, 1991—. Author, editor: Wilhelm Ostwald-Zur Geschichte der Wissenschaft. Vier Manuskripte aus dem Nachlass von W. Ostwald, 1985; editor: (with Emil Heuser) Justus Liebig und A.W. Hofmann ihren Briefen, 1988, Die steitbaren Gelehrten. Justus Liebig und die preussischen Universitaeten, 1992; editor: Wilhelm Ostwald und Walther Nernst in ihren Briefen, 1994, Wilhelm Ostwald und Paul Walden in ihren Briefen, 1994, Wilhelm Ostwald und Fritz Haber in ihren Briefen, 1997, Briefliche Begegnungen, Korrespondenzen von Wilhelm Ostwald, Friedrich Kohlrausch und Hans Landolt. Recipient Liebig-Woehler-Freundschaftspreis Goettinger Chemische Gesellschaft, 1996. Mem. Gesellschaft Deutscher Chemiker, Gesellschaft fur Wissenschaftsforschung. Avocations: classical music, drawing, history of arts, literature. Home: Am Sportplatz 2, D-15366 Dahlwitz-Hoppegarten Germany Office: Inst for Philosophy Theory, Sci History Sci Tech U, D-10587 Berlin Germany

ZOTZ, VOLKER HELMUT MANFRED, philosophy historian; b. Landau, Pfalz, Germany, Oct. 28, 1956; arrived in Austria, 1978; arrived in Japan, 1994; arrived in Luxembourg, 1999; s. Helmut Georg Severin and Ines Dagmar (Aehle) Z.; m. Simone Marie Johann, Apr. 25, 1986; children: Philippe Mitsuya, Yvonne Mitsuka, Akemi Sophie, Claire Mei. PhD, U. Vienna, Austria, 1987. Rschr. Mehrdimensionale Ursachenforschung, Vienna, 1987-92; rschr. Inst. Buddhist Cultural Studies Ryukoku U., Kyoto, Japan, 1989-90; lectr. dept. cultural history U. Applied Arts, Vienna, 1990-91; lectr. dept. philosophy U. Vienna, 1991-95; rschr. Inst. Buddhist Cultural Studies Ryukoku U., Kyoto, 1994-97; vis. prof. Buddhist Comprehensive Rsch. Inst. Otani U., Kyoto, 1997-98; dir. Internat. Inst. Buddhist Studies, Hong Kong and Kyoto, 1998—; founder, pres. Eurasischer Humanismus, Kyoto, 1995; curator Monsignore Agostino Sépinski Soc., Luxembourg, 1998; appointed prof. ancient history Centre U. Luxemburg, 1999. Author 17 books including (in German) Liberty and Bliss, 1987, André Breton, 1990, Buddha, 1991, A History of Buddhist Philosophy, 1996; editor 3 jours.; contbr. articles to profl. jours. Mem. Internat. Assn. Shin Buddhist Studies (mem. steering com. 1988), PEN Club (Austria), Hokkekyo Bunka Inst., Rissho U., Tokyo. Fax: 352-26530028. Home: Yabunouchi-cho 634 Chudoji, 600-8374 Shimogyo-ku Kyoto, Japan Office: Internat Inst Buddhist Studies, 44 rue Xavier Brasseur, L-4040 Esch-sur-Alzette Luxembourg

ZOU, DUO-XIU, chemist, researcher; b. Changzhou, Jiangsu, China, Nov. 29, 1934; d. Ming-Da Zou and Yin-Di Jiang; m. Long-Xiang Tao, Oct. 22, 1960; children: Xue-Heng Tao, Xue-Ming Tao. Student, Tianjin (China) U., 1958, Dalian (China) Inst. Petroleum, 1960. Assoc. rschr. Dalian Inst. Chem. Physics., Chinese Acad. Scis., 1979-85, sr. rschr., 1985-94, pres. project of Chinese Nat. Com. of Scis. and Tech., 1991-95, adviser sci. rsch. group, 1995—. Contbr. articles to sci. jours. Recipient Achievement award of scis. and tech. Chinese Acad. Scis. Mem. Chinese Chem. Soc. Home: 161 Zhongshan Rd PB 100, 116012 Dalian Liaoning, China Office: Dalian Inst Chem Physics, 457 Zhongshan Rd, 116023 Dalian Liaoning, China

ZOU, HUIJUN, engineering educator; b. Jiaxing City, Zhejiang, China, Oct. 8, 1934; s. Shunlin Zou and Abao Zong; m. Meili Li, May 1, 1964; children: Hong, Jian. Engring. scholar, Shanghai (China) Jiao Tong U., 1958. Tchr. Shanghai Jiao Tong U., 1958-82, assoc. prof., 1982-88, prof., 1988—, PhD advisor, 1993—. Author: (book) Design of Mechanism Systems, 1996; chief editor, author: (books) Advance Theory of Machinery, 1990 (2d award 1996), Design Theory of Machinery, 1995 (Top Grade award 1997); contbr. papers to profl. jours. Mem. Soc. of Sci. Technique (bd. dirs. 1984-88), Chinese Soc. Mech. Engring. (sr., vice-chmn. Mech. Transmission Inst. 1996—, chmn. mechanisms com. 1996—). Avocations: drawing, reading. Home: Rm 5-02 # 12 Ln 50, Guang Yuan W Rd, 200030 Shanghai China Office: Shanghai Jiao Tong U, 1954 Hua Shan Rd, 200030 Shanghai China

ZOU, LYU-FAN, physicist, researcher; b. Wuhan, Hubei, China, Mar. 23, 1959; arrived in Can., 2000; s. Zhulian Zou and Peixun Lu; m. Qin Yao, Dec. 29, 1984; 1 child, Wendi. BSc, Wuhan (China) U., 1982; MSc, Huazhong U. Sci. and Tech., 1988; PhD Inst. Semiconductors, Chinese Acad. Scis., Beijing, 1996. Editor HUST Press, Wuhan, 1982-85; asst. prof., asst. rschr. East China Jiaotong U., Nanchang, 1988-93; asst. prof. Inst. Semiconductors, Chinese Acad. Scis., 1993-96; postdoctoral rsch. asst. Inst. Microelectronics, Tsinghua U., Beijing, 1996-97; sr. rschr. Centro de Investigaciones en Optica, Aguascalientes, Mex., 1997—. Contbr. articles to profl. jours. Mem. Optical Soc. Am., Sistema Nacional de Investigadores. Home: Reforma Agraria No 120, Lazaro Cardenas, Aguascalientes 20256, Mexico Office: CIO Loma del Bosque No 115, Lomas del Campestre, León 37150, Mexico

ZOU, ZHEN, English and Chinese educator, translator and critic, computer technologist; b. Ganzhou, Jiangxi, China, Sept. 12, 1954; came to U.S., 1998; s. Xunqing and Jilie (Li) Z.; m. Ling Wang, Sept. 4, 1982; 1 child, Jia. BA, Jiangxi Normal U., 1982; MA, Peking U., Beijing, 1989, PhD, 1999. Lectr. Jiangxi Normal U., Nanchang, 1982-86; tchg. asst. Peking U., Beijing, 1986-89, asst. prof., 1989-95, assoc. prof., 1997—, dir. grad. English tchg. divsn., 1989-91; vis. scholar SUNY, New Paltz, 1991-92; tchg. asst. Purdue U., West Lafayette, Ind., 1995-97, tchr. and rsch. asst., coord., 1998—. Chief editor: An English Listening and Speaking Course for Graduate Students, 1996; contbr. articles to profl. jours. Grantee Purdue Rsch. Found., 1999; Winner Translation Contest, English Rev. Mag., 1983; Guanghua award Peking U., 1993-94. Mem. MLA, Chinese Lang. Tchrs. Assn., Peking U. Lit. and Translation Rsch. Soc. (v.p.). Avocations: swimming, skating, table tennis. Office: Dept Fgn Langs Stanley Coulter Hall Purdue University IN 47907

ZOUBOULIS, ANASTASIOS I., chemical and environmental technology educator; b. Thessaloniki, Greece, Feb. 10, 1959; s. Ippokratis A. and Garyfallia P. (Paraskevopoulou) Z.; m. Paraskevi P. Paraschiakou, Apr. 11, 1988; children: Eftichia, Garyfallia, Ippokratis. Diploma in chemistry, Aristotelian U., Thessaloniki, 1980, PhD in Chem. Tech., 1986; specialization in environ. sci., Technol. Inst. Thessaloniki, 1984. Rsch. and tchg. asst. dept. chemistry Aristotelian U., 1981-86, lectr., 1987-91, asst. prof. chem. tech. divsn. dept. chemistry, 1991-95; assoc. prof. environ. tech. dept. chemistry, 1996—; mem. adv. com. on environ. protection of indsl. area Ministry of Macedonia-Thrace, Thessaloniki, 1987—; vis. scholar German Acad. Exch. Svc., 1988, European Cmtys., 1989-91, USIA, 1994; invited visitor, lectr. Imperial Coll., U. London, U. Newcastle-upon-Tyne, Eng., Tech. U. Wroclaw, Poland, Tech. U. Karlsruhe, Germany, Tech. U. Berlin, U. Chem. Tech., Burgas, Bulgaria, U. Sofia, Bulgaria; participant, presenter numerous seminars, workshops, confs., and symposia. Contbr. articles and revs. to profl. jours. With Greek Army, 1986-87. Scholar State Scholarship Found., 1977-79. Mem. Greek Chem. Soc., Internat. Assn. on Water Quality, Water Environ. Fedn., Am. Water Works Assn., Mediterranean Assn. for Environ. Protection, Chemists Union No. Greece (gen. sec. 1985-87). Avocations: collecting books, gymnastics, table tennis, chess, travel. E-mail: zouboulis@chem.auth.gr. Office: Aristotelian U, Aristotelian U, Dept Chemistry Box 116, 54006 Thessaloniki Greece

ZOUFONOUN, AMIR H., electrical engineer; b. Nov. 6, 1959. BSEE, San Jose State U., 1982; MSEE, Santa Clara U., 1986. Devel. engr. Harris Group, 1979-84, engring. mgr., 1985-89; v.p. engring. Glenayre Western Multiplex, Sunnyvale, Calif., 1989-97, gen. mgr., 1998—.

ZOUMADAKIS, MICHAEL, molecular biologist; b. Kitchener, Ont., Can., May 21, 1964; s. Nick and Triantafillia (Panagiotidou) Z.; m. Antigoni Andrikidou, Dec. 27, 1992; 1 child, Mary-Helen. BSc, U. Patras, 1986; MSc, McMaster U., 1989; PhD, U. Crete, 1995. Head pub. rels. Mcpl. Enterprise Water and Sanitation of Chania (Greece), 1997—. Contbr. articles to profl. jours. Mem. Greenpeace, 1997. Soldier Med. Unit, 1995. Mem. Internat. Soc. Plant Molecular Biology, N.Y. Acad. Scis. Avocations: studying, fishing, mount climbing, music. Home: Milonogianni 124, 73135 Chania Greece

ZRUST, JAROMÍR, plant physiologist; b. Polička, Czech Republic, May 19, 1936; s. Jaromír and Jiřina (Brutarová) Z.; m. Božena Jilková, June 20, 1961; children: Božena, Alena, Jaromira. MSc in Engring., Agrl. U., Prague, Czech Republic, 1960; PhD, Ctrl. Rsch. Inst. Crop Prodn., Prague, 1980. Rsch. asst. dept. physiology Potato Rsch. Inst., Havlíčkuv Brod, Czech Republic, 1960-64, head dept. physiology, 1964-72, head dept. physiology chemistry and tech. potato processing, 1972-94, head dept. physiology chemistry and quality, 1994—. Contbr. articles to profl. jours. Grantee Plant Prodn. Genetics and Breeding, 1995, Quality and Agrl. Food Products, 1996, 99. Mem. Fedn. European Socs. Plant Physiology, Plant Exptl. Biology Assn. Avocations: recreational sports activities, reading. Home: Na sadech 744, 539 01 Hlinsko v C Czech Republic Office: Potato Rsch Inst, Dobrovského 2366, Havlíčkuv Brod Czech Republic

ZRUST, JIRI, financial executive; b. Prague, Czech Republic, Nov. 16, 1974; s. Jiri Josef and Alena (Stastna) Z. Diploma in mgmt., Open U., U.K., 1999. Asst. to CEO TNT Chech Republic, Prague, 1994-95, fin. and adminstrv. cupr., 1995-97, county FZA mgr., 1998—; county FZA mgr. TNT SK, Bratislava, Slovakia, 1997-98. Mem. Civil Dem. Party. Avocations: reading, history, economics, sports, driving.

ZSCHUNKE, WILLMUT ROLF, communications technology educator; b. Wuppertal, Germany, Feb. 29, 1940; s. Rolf and Maria (Groen) Z.; m. Rita Maria Ehlen, Oct. 15, 1965; children: Inken, Dirk. Degree in Engring., Tech. U., Stuttgart, 1964, Doctor Engring., 1968, Degree in Habilitation, 1972; D (hon.), Polytech. U., Bucharest, 1997. Head Broadband Lab. Standard Elektrik Lorenz AG, Stuttgart, Germany, 1972-75, head lab. for advanced devel., 1975-79, head Main Dept. for Adv. Product Devel., 1976-87; prof. comm. tech. Darmstadt U. Tech., Germany, 1987-90; mem. study commn. CCIR of UIT, Geneva, 1973-79; mem. VDE/NTG Expert Commn., 1975-84; mem. VDE/NTG Expert Commn., 1975-89; sci. dir. Rsch. Inst. German Telekom, Darmstadt, 1987-90; mem. VDE/NTG (ITG) Expert Commn., 1985-97. Patentee in field. Roman Catholic. Avocations: ski instructor, radio amateur. Office: Darmstadt U Technology, IfNT-Merckstrasse 25, D-64283 Darmstadt Germany

ZS-NAGY, IMRE, medical educator; b. Balassagyarmat, Hungary, Oct. 28, 1936; s. Imre and Imréne Vilma (Huszovszky) Z-N.; m. Valéria Tóth, Aug. 30, 1958; children: Imre, Ildikó. MD, U. Med. Sch., Debrecen, Hungary, 1961. Resident U. Med. Sch., Debrecen, 1960-63; sr. scientist U. Med. Sch., 1976-81, dir., 1981-96; chair gerentol. dept. U. Med. Sch. (now U. Debrecen Med. and Health Sci Ctr.), 1997—; scientist MTA Biol. Inst., Tihany, Hungary, 1963-73; dir. INRCA, Ancona, Italy, 1973-76; vice-dir. MTA Biol. Inst., 1969-73. Author: The Membrane Hypothesis of Aging, 1994; editor-in-chief: Archives of Gerontology and Geriatrics, 1982—. Recipient Sub Auspiciis Rei Publ. Pop. award pres. of Hungary, 1962, Acad. award MTA, 1971. Mem. Internat. Assn. Biomed. Gerontology (pres. 1993-95), Hungarian Gerontology Soc. Avocations: electronics, stamp collecting. Office: U Debrecen Med Health Sci, PO Box 50, H-4012 Debrecen Hungary

ZSOLDOS, FERENC, plant physiologist; b. Sarkad, Hungary, Mar. 24, 1927; s. Ferenc and Margit (Nagy) Z.; m. Ildikó Jerémiás, Aug. 28, 1962; children: Gábor, Ildikó. MS, Eötvös U., Budapest, Hungary, 1952, PhD, 1958; DSc, Hungarian Acad. Scis., Budapest, Hungary, 1983. Rsch. assoc. József A. U., Szeged, Hungary, 1957-67; sr. rsch. assoc. József A U., Szeged, 1968-73, assoc. prof., 1974-82, prof., 1983-84, chairholder prof., 1985-95, prof. emeritus, 1996—; Internat. Atomic Energy Agy. postdoctoral fellowship, Seibersdorf, Austria, 1962. Mem. editl. bd. Physiol. Plantarum, Lund, Sweden, 1980-92. Mem. Hungarian Biol. Soc., Fedn. European Socs. Plant Physiology, Hungarian Acad. Scis (mem. plant physiol. com. 1996—, award 1992). Avocations: photography, gardening. E-mail: zsoldos@bio.u-szeged.hu. Home: Boldogasszony sgt 7, H-6722 Szeged Hungary Office: U Szeged Dept Plant Physiol, Egyetem u 2, H-6722 Szeged Hungary

ZSOLNAI, LASZLO, economics educator; b. Szentes, Csongrad, Hungary, May 5, 1958; s. Jozsef Zsolnai and Margit Dobo; m. Julianna Farkas, June 12, 1982. M in Econs., Budapest U. Econ. Scis., 1982, PhD in Econs. and Sociology, 1984. Rsch. assoc. Budapest U. Econs. Scis., 1984-90, assoc. prof., 1991—; vis. scholar U. Calif., Berkeley, 1990-91; founding dir. Bus. Ethics Ctr., Budapest, 1993—; coord. ethics interfaculty group Communities of European Mgmt. Schs., 1995. Author: (book) Making of a Meta-Economics, 1985; editl. bd.: Internat. Jour. Social Econs., 1993—; contbr. articles to profl. jours. and publs. Fellow Netherlands Inst. for Advanced Study, Wassennaar, 1996-97; rsch. grantee Soros Found., 1987-88, Hungarian Nat. Sci. Found., 1993-95; tempus vis. European U. Inst., Firenze, 1993. Mem. N.Y. Acad. Scis., Soc. for Advancement of Socio-Econs. (country rep. 1995—), Internat. Soc. Ecol. Econs. Avocations: visual arts, nature.

ZU, DONGLIN, physicist, educator; b. Shandong Province, China, Mar. 21, 1946; s. Yongzeng and Hongxi (Wang) Zu; m. Wu Yunyuan, May 6, 1974; 1 child, Xuemin Zu. Mem. Particle Accelerator Soc. China, Am. Physics Soc. Office: Beijing U, Dept Tech Physics, Beijing 100871, China

ZUBAIRI, SALIM AHMAD, banker; b. Kanpur, Pakistan, Sept. 20, 1932; arrived in Eng., 1977; s. Munir Ahmad and Islam Fatima Zubairi; m. Zakia Hafeezulla, Mar. 31, 1967; children: Fatima S., Ahmad S., Sara S. BA, U. Karachi, Pakistan, 1952. From officer to sr. v.p. Habib Bank, Ltd., Pakistan, 1953-73, exec. v.p., 1974-76; exec. v.p. to sr. exec. v.p. Habib Bank A.G. Zurich, London, 1977-83, chief exec. v.p., 1984-93; assoc. dir. Habib Bank A.G. Zurich, 1994—; dir. Metropolitan Bank, Ltd., 1993—; bd. dirs. Habib European Bank, Ltd., Isle of Man. Home: 115 The Reddings Mill Hill, NW7 4JP London Eng. Office: Habib Bank AG Zurich, 42 Moorgate, EC2R 6JJ London England

ZUBAIR MOHAMED, MAHAMOOD, information scientist, educator, computer consultant; b. Bangalore, Karnataka, India, Jan. 31, 1957; d. Abdur Serigere and Zahara (Khanum) R.; m. Nishbath Zubair Mohamed, Aug. 17, 1980; children: Farhan, Abrar, Zakriya. BS in Engring., Bangalore U., 1979; MS in Engring., U. Ky., 1989, Doctorate Bus. Adminstrn., 1991. Engr. Wildia (India) Ltd., Bangalore, 1979-83; rsch. asst. U. Ky., Lexington, 1984-89; asst. prof. Western Ky. U., Bowling Green, 1989-1995, assoc. prof., 1995-2000, prof., 2000—; cons. Fruit of the Loom, Bowling Green, 1995-97, Scott Health Care, Bowling Green, 1994; manuscript reviewer Decision Scis. Inst., 1990—. Liaison Bowling Green C. of C., Bangalore C. of C., Bowling Green and Bangalore, 2000. Recipient Coll. award for rsch. scholarship, 1998, Don and Suzanne Vitale award for innovation, initiative, and leadership, 2000; merit scholar Bangalore U., 1974-79. Mem. Decision Scis. Inst., Prodn. and Mgmt. Soc., Nat. Assn. Purchasing Mgmt. Avocations: gardening, reading, tennis. Fax: 270-745-6376. E-mail: Zubair.mohamed@wku.edu. Home: 1529 Greenmeadow Ct Bowling Green KY 42104-4707 Office: Western KY U Dept Mgmt & Info Sys Bowling Green KY 42101

ZUBER, LIANNE CAROL, elementary school educator; b. Independence, Mo., Nov. 23, 1968; d. Jeffry Lane and Carol Yukuko Glauner; m. Michael John Zuber, Dec., 1990; children: Mikala Johoku, XoeAnne Yukukomari. BA in Edn., Park Coll., 1990; MA in Edn., Ctrl. Mich. U., 1998. Lic. tchr. Hawaii, Mo. Summer program coord. Hawaii Preparatory Acad., Kamuela, Hawaii, 1989-97; art tchr. k-6 Hawaii Preparatory Acad., Kamuela, 1990-91; counselor Honoka'a (Hawaii) Elem. and H.S., 1991-92, career guidance tchr., remedial tchr., 1992-93, grade 2 tchr., 1993-94; grade 1 tchr., computer tchr. Waikoloa (Hawaii) Elem. Sch., 1994-2000, summer sch. coord., 1999; grade 3 tchr. Milton Moore Elem., Kansas City, Mo., 2000—; summer sch. coord. Waikoloa (Hawaii) Elem. Sch., 1999; mem. tech. com., curriculum com. Waikoloa Elem. Sch., 1994-2000, workshop presenter, at local schs. and at convs. Recipient Perkins award, 1987; grantee Good Idea, 1994, 95, 98, Environmental grant, 1996, Hawaiian Studies grant, 1996. Mem. NEA (del. 2000), Nat. Coun. Tchrs. English (testing and evaluation com. 1999—, instrnl. tech. com. 2000—), Hawaii State Tchrs. Assn. (v.p. Hamakua chpt. 1994-95, state conv. del. 1994, 95, co-chair 1996-98, mem. tech. sub-com. 1996-2000, state chair 1998), Delta Kappa Gamma (sec. Nu chpt. 1998-2000, presenter, com. mem. fall workshop).

ZUBER, NORMA KEEN, career counselor, educator; b. Iuka, Miss., Sept. 27, 1934; d. William Harrington and Mary (Hebert) Keen; m. William Frederick Zuber, Sept. 14, 1958; children: William Frederick Jr., Michael,

Kimberly, Karen. BS in Nursing, U. Southwestern La., 1956; MS in Counselling, Calif. Luth. U., 1984. Nat. cert. counselor, nat. cert. career counselor; registered profl. career counselor, Calif. Intensive care nurse Ochsner Found. Hosp., New Orleans, 1956-59; career devel. counselor BFC Counseling Ctr., Ventura, Calif., 1984-87; founder, prin., counselor Career & Life Planning-Norma Zuber & Assocs., Ventura, 1987—; instr. adult continuing edn. Ventura C.C., 1987—; instr. Calif. State U., Northridge, 1988-89; instr. U. Calif. Santa Barbara, Antioch U.; mem. adv. coun. on tchr. edn. Calif. Luth. U., Thousand Oaks, 1984-87; mem. adv. bd. for development of profl. career counseling cert. program U. Calif., San Diego, 1991—. Co-author: The Nuts and Bolts of Career Counseling: Setting Up and Succeeding in Private Practice, 1992. Chmn. bd. dirs. women's ministries Missionary Ch., Ventura, 1987-90. Recipient profl. contbn. award H.B. McDaniel Found.-Stanford U. Sch. Edn., 1988, Govt. Rels. Com. Cert. of Appreciation, Am. Assn. for Counseling and Devel., Career Devel. Practitioner of the Year award Internat. Career Conf., 1998. Mem. NAFE, ACA, Nat. Career Devel. Assn. (western region trustee 1994-97), Calif. Assn. Couseling and Devel. (chmn. legis. task force 1987-89, Jim Saum govt. rels. award 1989), Internat. Platform Assn., Nat. Career Devel. Assn. (western regional trustee 1995—), Internat. Career Conf. (Career Devel. Practitioner of Yr. 1998), Calif. Career Devel. Assn. (bd. dirs. 1985-98, membership dir. 1991-92, pres. 1992-93, Leadership and Professionaliam award 1988, 89), Calif. Career Conf. (program chair 1993), Ventura County Profl. Women's Network (dir. membership 1990-91, pres. 1998-99), Calif. Registry Profl. Counselors and Paraprofls. (bd. dirs. 1990-94, chair 1995-97), Chi Sigma Iota. Republican. Home: 927 Sentinel Cir Ventura CA 93003-1202 Office: Career and Life Planning Norma Zuber and Assocs 3585 Maple St Ste 237 Ventura CA 93003-9117

ZUBER, RAYMOND FRANCOIS, international relations consultant; b. Paris, Sept. 24, 1946; s. Michel Henri and Anna Marie (Laporte) Z.; m. Marta Spranzi, July 13, 1985; children: Thomas Julien, Martin Simon. BA in History, Sorbonne, Paris, 1968; M in History, Sorbonne-Paris 1, 1971, Agregation in History, 1975, PhD in History, 2000. Author: (with others) Ency. de L'Europe, 1993, Actualite Strategique, 1992; contbr. articles to profl. jours. Avocations: skiing, sailing. Home and Office: 17 rue des Fosses St Marcel, 75005 Paris France

ZUBEREK, WACLAW MARIAN, geophysicist; b. Cieszyn, Poland, Oct. 24, 1940; s. Jozef and Maria Z.; m. Barbara Placzek; three children. MSc, U. Mining and Metal, Cracow, 1962, DSc, 1984; PhD, Polish Inst. Mining, Katowice, 1972. Rsch. asst. Polish Inst. Mining, 1962-79; lectr. U. Silesia, 1979-80, deputy dean, 1987-93, prof. geophysics, 1991—, head dept. applied geology Faculty Earth Sci., 1979—. Mem. Am. Geophys. Union, Polish Soc. Rock Mechanics, Polish Assn. Friends of Earth Sci. Roman Catholic.

ZUBRICZKY, LÁSZLÓ, civil engineering executive, consultant; b. Budapest, Hungary, Oct. 10, 1942; s. Ireneusz and Ireneeuszné (Grensó Sára) Z.; m. Lászlóné Molnár Edit, Aug. 14, 1974; children: Barbara, Levente. MSCE, U. Budapest, 1966. Cert. civil engr. Prodn. engr. Gravel Mining Co., Hungary, 1966-69; design engr. UVATERV, Hungary, 1969-81; bus. promotion Transinvest, Budapest, 1981—; project mgr. AMER, Kuwait, 1989-90; dir. Transinvest-Bp, 1991; chmn. Magyar Transroute Ltd., Hungary, 1995—; advisor Gravel Mining Co., Hungary, 1966-69; cons. UVATERV, 1969-81. Avocations: music, skiing. Home: Marvany 33, 1126 Budapest Hungary Office: Transinvest, Hungaria krt 113, 1143 Budapest Hungary

ZUBRILOV, ANDREI SERGEEVICH, physicist, science consultant; b. St. Petersburg, Russia, Feb. 13, 1958; s. Sergei Pavlovich and Lidia Oskarovna (Neiman) Z. MS, St. Petersburg Electro-Tech. U., Russia, 1981; PhD, A.F.IOFFE Phys.-Tech. Inst. of Russian Acad. Scis., St. Petersburg, 1991. Jr. sci. rschr. Ioffe Phys.-Tech. Inst., St. Petersburg, 1981-89, sci. rschr., 1989-95; sr. sci. rschr. Cree Ed Inc., St. Petersburg, 1994-96, Ioffe Phys.-Tech. Inst., 1995—; rsch. assoc. Howard U., Washington, 1994. Contbr. articles to profl. jours.; Russian patentee in field. Recipient grant Russian Found. for Basic Rsch., 1995, 97. Mem. N.Y. Acad. Scis. Avocations: alpine skiing, tourism. Fax: 7(812) 247-6425. Office: AF Ioffe Phys Tech Inst, 26 Polytechnicheskaya St, 194021 Saint Petersburg Russia

ZUBRITSKY, ALEXANDER NICKOLAEVICH, pathologist; b. Severo-Kurilsk, Sakhalin, Russia, Mar. 14, 1949; s. Nickolay Alexandrovich and Kaleriya Andreevna (Chechulina) Z.; children: Vladimir, Sergey Yashin. MD, Med. Inst., 1974. Hosp. attendant dept. pathology City Hosp. N21, Sverdlovsk, Russia, 1965-67; hosp. attendant Medico-Legal Morgue N1, Sverdlovsk, 1967-68; nurse Sta. of Emergencies Care N1, Sverdlovsk, 1971-72; head pathology dept. Ctrl. Regional Hosp., Neviyansk, Russia, 1975-76; chief pathology dept., head pathologist Sverdlovsk Rd. Hosp., 1976-83; lectr. path. anatomy Med. Sch. Sverdlovsk Rd., 1976-77; chief dept. pathology Taldom (Russia) Territorial Med. Union, 1983—. Contbr. articles to profl. jours. Recipient award Am. Coll. Chest Physicians, 1990, Pathology Rsch. Pract award , Taldom-Innsbruck, 1993; named International Man of Yr., 1994-95. Mem. European Soc. Pathology, Internat. Union Against Tb and Lung Disease, Internat. Soc. Heart Rsch. (European sect.), Internat. Soc. Diagnostic Quantitative Pathology, N.Y. Acad. Scis. Avocations: music, walking. Home: Microraion Yubileynyi 12/26, 141900 Taldom Moscow, Russia Office: Taldom Territorial Med Unio, Ulitsa Pobedy 19, 141900 Taldom Moscow, Russia

ZUBROFF, LEONARD SAUL, surgeon; b. Minersville, Pa., Mar. 27, 1925; s. Abe and Fannie (Freedline) Z. BA, Wayne State U., 1945, MD, 1949. Diplomate Am. Bd. Surgery. Intern Garfield Hosp., Washington, 1949-50, resident in surgery, 1951-55, chief resident surgery, 1954-55; pvt. practice medicine specializing in surgery, 1958-76; med. dir. Chevrolet Gear and Axle Plant, Forge Plant, GM, Detroit, 1977-78; divsnl. med. dir. Detroit Diesel Allison divsn., Detroit, 1978-87; regional med. dir. GM, 1987-89; ret., 1989; chief of surgery, chief profl. svcs. N.E. Air Command, Pepperell AFB, Newfoundland. Trustee LeVine Found. With USAF, 1956-58. Fellow ACS, Coll. Occupl. and Environ. Medicine, Mich. Occupl. Med. Assn. (ret., pres. 1990-91), Detroit Occupl. Physicians Assn. (past pres.), Masons (33 degree), Phi Lambda Kappa. Home and Office: 22511 S Bellwood Dr Southfield MI 48034-2116

ZUBRZYCKI, JERZY, retired sociology educator; b. Krakow, Poland, Jan. 12, 1920; arrived in Australia, 1955.; s. Jozef and Zofia (Madeyska) Z.; m. Alexandra Krolikowska, Oct. 23, 1943; children: Thomas, Anna, John, Joanna. BS in Econs., Sch. Econs. U. London, 1948, MS in Econs., 1952; PhD, Polish U. Abroad, London, 1954; D (hon.), U. Poznan (Poland), 1998. Asst. lectr. sociology U. London, 1949-52; research fellow Australian Nat. U., Canberra, 1955-58, sr. sociology fellow, 1959-64, profl. fellow, 1965-70, found. prof. sociology, 1970-86, prof. emeritus, 1986—. Served to capt. spl. ops. exec., Brit. army, 1941-46. Decorated Polish Cross of Valor; mem. Order of Brit. Empire, Pontifical Acad. Social Scis., Vatican City; comdr. Order of Brit. Empire; officer Order of Australia. Fellow Acad. Social Scis. in Australia.

ZUCCARELLI, EMILE, mayor; b. Bastia, France, Aug. 4, 1940; married; 3 children. Student, Ecole Polytech. Mem. nat. com. Movement of Radical Left, 1980, vice chmn., 1983-89; mem. Regional Assembly Corsica, 1982-84; elected to Nat. Assembly, Deputy Haut-Corse, 1986, 88, 93,97; chmn. Movement of Radical Left, 1989-92; mayor City of Bastia, 1989, 97, 2000—; chmn. del. PRS, 1989—; min. Ministry Postal Svcs. & Telecomm., 1992-93, Ministry Civil Svc., Adminstrv. Reform & Decentralization, 1997-2000; mem. regional assembly Consica, 1999—. Office: Maririe de Bastia, Ave Pierre Giudicelli, 20200 Bastia France

ZUCKA, GEORGES, international patent official; b. Anderlecht, Belgium, June 9, 1962; s. Jan and Veronique (Van Rooy) Z. BS in Physics, U. Leuven, 1983, MS in Physics, 1985, MS Computer Sci., 1987. Computer engr. Agfa-Gevaert, Antwerp, Belgium, 1986; scientific cons. Belgian Air Force, Koksijde, 1987-88; tech. expert European Patent Office, Munich, 1988-94; B.E.S.T. tng. officer European Patent Office, The Hague, The Netherlands, 1994-2000, dep. B.E.S.T. project leader, 2000—. Author: Brehmsstrahlung of Spin-O Bosons at High Energies, 1985, How to Emulate SQL-Commands on the DEC-20, 1987. Mem. N.Y. Acad. Scis., Mensa Internat., Alumni Lovanienses. Avocations: personal computers, flying. Office: European Patent Office, Patentlaan 5 Rm S01F46, 2288 EE Rijswijk The Netherlands

ZUCKER, HOWARD ALAN, pediatric cardiologist, intensivist, anesthesiologist; b. N.Y.C., Sept. 6, 1959; s. Saul and Phyllis (Goldblatt) Z.. BS, McGill U., Montreal, Quebec, Can., 1979; MD, George Washington U., 1982; JD, Fordham U., 2000. Diplomate Am. Bd. Pediatrics, subspecialties in pediatric critical care, pediatric cardiology, Am. Bd. Anesthesiology, subspecialty in anesthesia critical care. Pediatric intern Johns Hopkins Hosp., Balt., 1982-83, pediatric resident, 1983-85; anesthesiology resident Hosp. of U. Pa., Phila., 1985-87; pediatric critical care fellow Children's Hosp. of Phila., 1987-88; asst. prof. anesthesiology and pediatrics Yale U. Sch. Medicine, New Haven, Conn., 1988-90; pediatric cardiology fellow Children's Hosp., Harvard Med. Sch., Boston, 1990-92; assoc. prof. clinical pediatrics, clinical anesthesiology Columbia U. Coll. Physicians and Surgeons, N.Y.C., 1992—; dir. pediatric transport Columbia Presbyn. Med. Ctr. Babies & Children's Hosp. N.Y., N.Y.C., 1992—; involved with crew tng. of NASA Space Shuttle STS-1 Mission, 1978-80; rsch. affiliate, Man-vehicle Lab, MIT; chmn. bd. dirs. Terre Verte Found., Inc. Chmn. bd. Terre Verte Found., Inc.; participant med. missions to China, Children of China Pediat. Found.; bd. dirs. Pediat. Found. Named Person of Week ABC World News Tonight, 1993, one of Best Doctors in Am., Woodward & White, 1996, 98-99. Fellow Am. Acad. Pediatrics, Am. Coll. Cardiology, Am. Coll. Chest Physicians; mem. AMA, Am. Soc. Anesthesiologists, Am. Heart Assn., Soc. Critical Care Medicine. Jewish. Achievements include research in adaptation to zero gravity, cardiac critical care. Home: 100 Winston Dr Apt 12G Cliffside Park NJ 07010-3240 Office: N Y-Presbyn Hosp Babies & Childrens Hosp NY 3959 Broadway New York NY 10032-1551

ZUCKER, LEONARD CHARLES, trucking executive, rabbi; b. Bronx, N.Y., June 13, 1933; s. Ralph Gilbert and Elsie (Himmelstein) Z.; m. Elaine Trachtman, Dec. 25, 1955 (dec. Aug. 1998); children: Anne, Esther Lynne, Rhea Miriam, Ronald Gary; m. Marilyn Stennstien, Dec. 12, 1999. BA, Yeshiva U., 1951; postgrad., Acad. Advanced Traffic, 1955. Ordained rabbi, 1957. With Charlton Bros. Transp. Co., Inc., Phila., 1953-58; sales mgr. Phila.-Pits. Carriers, Phila., 1958-61; dist. sales rep. Preston Trucking Co., Inc., 1961-65; v.p. Drake Motor Lines Inc., Cherry Hill, N.J., 1965-76; exec. v.p., COO Pinto Trucking Svc., Inc., Phila., 1976-83, pres., 1984-86; pres. L. Zucker Assocs., 1986—; rabbi Congregation B'nai Tikvah, Turnersville, N.J., 1975-97, Golden Lakes Temple, West Palm Beach, Fla., 1998—; chaplain Fedn. Jewish Agys. of Atlantic County, 1987-93; pres. Tri County Bd. Rabbis, 1995-97; mem. Phila. Bd. Rabbis, Palm Beach County Bd. Rabbis. Author: Why Be a Transportation Specialist, 1971, Safety Guide for the Motor Carrier, 1973. Bd. dirs. Motor Transport Labor Rels., Phila., 1973-76. With U.S. Army, 1953-55. Mem. Assn. ICC Practitioners, Transp. Law Practitioners U.S., Air Cargo Club, Nat. Fedn. Men's Clubs, Fifth Wheel Club, Traffic and Transp. Club, Delta Nu Alpha. Democrat. Jewish. Home: 119 Lake Nancy Dr West Palm Beach FL 33411-9202 Office: PO Box 210064 Ryl Palm Bch FL 33421-0064

ZUCKER, STEFAN, tenor, writer, editor, radio broadcaster; b. N.Y.C.. BS, Columbia U., 1967; postgrad., NYU, 1967-72. Freelance tenor concerts and operas in U.S. and Europe, 1965—; tenor RCA Records, N.Y.C., 1972-77; guest singer radio and TV programs U.S. and Europe, 1975—; radio producer, host WKCR-FM, N.Y.C., 1980-94; opera critic N.Y. Tribune, 1983-84; philosophy lectr. Coll. Ins. N.Y.C., 1972. Author: The Origins of Modern Tenor Singing, 1997; appeared in film Opera Fanatic: Stefan and the Divas, 1998; record producer including Rossini's Rivals: Music By Then-Famous, Now-Obscure, Italian Composers, 1984; restorer films of opera singers, 1987—; singer, producer, stage dir., adminstr. various operas, 1967—; editor Opera Fanatic mag., 1986—; commentator and singer (TV series) Bel canto: Tenors of the 78 Era, 1996-97; contbr. articles to Internat. Dictionary of Opera, Opera News, The Opera Quar., Am. Record Guide, Opera Fanatic, News World, Professione Musica, others. Pres. Bel Canto Soc., Inc., 1985—. Named Worlds Highest Tenor by Guinness Book of World Records, 1979—; subject of record Stefan Zucker: The World's Highest Tenor, 1981. Mem. NYU Philosophy Assn. (pres. 1969-72, v.p. 1968), Music Critics Assn., Assn. Furtherment Bel Canto (pres. 1967-80). Office: Bel Canto Soc Inc 11 Riverside Dr New York NY 10023-2504

ZUCKERMAN, MATTHEW IAN STANLEY, writer, editor, educator; b. Berlin, Nov. 7, 1956; s. Stanley Allen and Nancy Georgina (Howell) Z.; m. Mieko Kitazume, Apr. 28, 1984; children: Naomi, Cecil. Diploma in English lit., Bath Coll. of Further Edn., 1977. English instr. Time-Life Ednl. Svcs., Tokyo, 1980-85; cons., mgr. Waseda Mgmt. Acad., Tokyo, 1987-89; English instr. Tokyo Women's Med. Coll., 1990-92, Kyoritsu Women's U., Tokyo, 1992-95, Chuo Univ. H.S., 1995-97; freelance writer Eng., 1997—; English instr. Toita Women's Coll., Tokyo, 1990-97; fiction editor Wingspan, Tokyo, 1986—; music reviewer Asahi Evening News, Tokyo, 1994—; editor Tels Press, Tokyo, 1982-94; test examiner UN, Tokyo, 1985-97; blues and comedy reviewer Bath Chronicle, 1998—. Columnist Isis, 1998—; author: Okinawa by Road, 1985; editor: Imitating Flight, 1986, Hanashimasho!, 1987, Trog, 1992, In Daylight, 1995, Monumenta Nipponica, 1995; author of numerous short fiction and travel articles. Chmn. Young Liberals, 1975. Named Poet of Yr. (spl. commendation) BBC Wildlife, 1994. Mem. Labour Party. Avocation: songwriting. Home: 13 Audley Grv Lower Weston, Bath BA1 3BS, England

ZUCKERMAN, RICHARD ENGLE, lawyer, law educator; b. Yonkers, N.Y., Aug. 2, 1945; s. Julius and Roslyn (Ehrlich) Z.; m. Denise Ellen Spoon, July 14, 1968; children: Julie Ann, Lindsay Beth. BA, U. Mich., 1967; JD cum laude, Southwestern U., 1974. Bar: Calif. 1974, Mich. 1976, Nev. 1986, U.S. Dist. Ct. (ea. and we. dists.) Mich. 1977, U.S. Ct. Appeals (6th cir.) 1977, U.S. Ct. Appeals (9th cir.) 1982, U.S. Ct. Appeals 2d and 7th cirs.) 1994, U.S. Tax Ct. 1980, U.S. Supreme Ct. 1985. Spl. atty. organized crime and racketeering sect. U.S. Dept. Justice, Detroit, 1974-77; sr. ptnr. Raymond, Rupp, Wienberg, Stone & Zuckerman, P.C., Troy, Mich., 1977-87; sr. ptnr. Honigman, Miller, Schwartz & Cohn, Detroit, 1987—, chair litigation dept., 1996—, also bd. dirs., 1999—; adj. prof. Detroit Coll. Law, 1978-98; mem. Mich. Atty. Grievance Commn. (Mich. supreme ct. appointee), 1995—, vice chair, 1999—; trustee Detroit Metropolitan Bar Found., 1999-2000. Served to lt. USN, 1967-71, Vietnam. Mem. ABA (grand jury com. criminal justice sect.), Fed. Bar Assn. (chmn. criminal law sect. Detroit chpt. 1985-90, bd. dirs. 1985-94, co-chair criminal def. com. 1990-95), Knollwood Country Club (West Bloomfield, Mich.), Std. Club, Am. Inns Ct. (master of bench 1995-97). Republican. Jewish. Office: Honigman Miller Schwartz & Cohn 2290 First National Bldg Detroit MI 48226

ZUCKERMAN, STUART, psychiatrist, forensic examiner, educator; b. Syracuse, N.Y., Feb. 18, 1933; s. George and Cassie (Kolsan) Z. Student, U. Kans., 1950-51; BS, U. Ala., 1954; DO, Phila. Coll. Osteo. Medicine, 1958. Diplomate Am. Osteo. Bd. Neurology and Psychiatry, Am. Nat. Bd. Psychiatry, Am. Coll. Forensic Medicine, Bd. Forensic Medicine, Bd. Forensic Examiner; cert. correctional health profl. Rotating intern Hosps. Phila. Coll. Osteo. Medicine, 1958-59; psychiat. fellow, resident Phila. Mental Health Clinic, 1959-62, Psychoanalytic Studies Inst., Phila., 1959-62; chief resident, 1962; chief div. neuropsychiatry Grandview Hosp., Dayton, Ohio, 1962-65; asst. med. dir., chief children's and adolescent's unit N.J. State Hosp., Ancora, 1967-70; chief outpatient dept. Atlantic City, 1970-72; practice specializing in neuropsychiatry Atlantic City, 1965—; founding prof. psychiatry, chmn. dept. Ohio U. Coll. Osteo. Medicine, Athens, 1976-77; psychiatry, chmn. dept. Ohio U. Coll. Osteo. Medicine, 1977—; mem. faculty U. Pa. Sch. clin. prof. Ohio U. Coll. Osteo. Medicine, 1977—; mem. faculty U. Pa. Sch. Medicine, Phila. Coll. Osteo. Medicine, 1972-76; lectr. U. Pa., 1977-79; prof. dept. psychiatry, charter faculty Sch. Medicine, Marshall U., 1977-78, clin. prof., 1979-80; clin. prof. N.Y. Coll. Osteo. Medicine, 1979—; chief mental hygiene VA Hosp., Huntington, W.Va., 1978-79; liaison psychiatrist, acting chief VA Med. Center, Perry Point, Md., 1979-80; med. dir. Mental Health Clinic of Ocean County, Toms River, N.J., 1980-85, Ventnor (N.J.) Mental Health Ctr.; chief psychiatrist N.J. Dept. Corrections So. State Correctional Facility, 1985-96; physician Atlantic City Beach Patrol, 1961-63; attending psychiatrist Atlantic City, Shore Meml., Kessler Meml., Washington Meml., Atlantic County Mental hosps., 1965-76; attending psychiatrist, asst. dir. dept. psychiatry Phila. Gen. Hosp., 1972-76; med. dir. Shawnee Mental Health Center, (Adams, Lawrence, Scioto counties), Portsmouth, Ohio, 1977-78; cons. psychiatrist Athens Mental Health and Mental Retardation Ctr., 1976-77, Scioto Meml., So. Hills, Mercy hosps., Portsmouth, 1977-78, Lansdowne Cmty. Mental Health Center, (Greenup, Carter counties), Ashland, Ky., 1977-78, Atlantic City Med. Ctr., 1984-97, Cmty. Meml. Hosp., Toms River, N.J., 1984-91, So. Ocean County Hosp., Manahawkin, N.J., 1984-91, Paul-Kimball Med Ctr., Lakewood, N.J., 1984-97, Obleness Meml. Hosp., Clin. Services of Athens, Vinton, Hocking Counties, Hudson Health Ctr., Ohio U., 1976-77; cons. Bayside State Prison, Leesburg, N.J., 1989-96, Atlantic County Justice System, Mays Landing, N.J., 1992-93, child study spl. svcs. S. Jersey sch. systems; chmn. profl. adv. com. Atlantic County Mental Health Bd., 1969-71; mem. nominating com. Mental Health Assn., Atlantic County, 1972-75; exam. psychiatrist Jersey Police and Fire depts.; mem. Atlantic County Mental Health Bd.; mem. profl. adv. com. N.J. Dept. Corrections; cons. N.J. Dept. Pub. Advocate; mem. panel med. cons. N.J. State Med. Bd., 1998—. Mem. adv. bd. Osteo. Physician, 1975-98; assoc. editor Bull. Am. Coll. Neuropsychiatrists, 1963-70, Jour. Corr. Health Editl. Bd.; contbr. articles to profl. jours. Bd. dirs. Atlantic County Family Svcs. Assn., 1968-74, Cape May County Drug Abuse Coun., 1973-76, Nat. Comm. Correctional Health Care, 1988-97; mem. Ventnor City Beautification Com., 1996—; sponsor, house physician Friends of the Pops Ocean City (N.J.) Music Pier. Fellow Am. Coll. Forensic Psychiatry, Am. Coll. Neuropsychiatrists (bd. reps.), Am. Acad. Disability Evaluating Physicians (charter), Acad. Psychosomatic Medicine, Acad. Medicine N.J., Coll. Physicians of Phila.; mem. AMA (Physicians Recognition award 1985—), AAUP, Am. Bd. Forensic Examiners (cert. 1994), Am. Coll. Forensic Medicine (bd. cert. 1996), World Psychiat. Assn., Am. Psychiat. Assn., N.J. (confidentiality, pub. psychiatry com., gen. hosp. psychiatry com., law com., mkgt. benefits com.) Psychiat. Assn., Am. Assn. Psychiatrists in Alcohol and Addictions (founder), Am., N.J. pub. health assns., Am. Osteo. Assn. (hosp. inspection team 1971-75, bd. reps.), Am. Assn. CMHC Psychiatrists, Am. Assn. Psychiatrists in Pvt. Practice, Internat. Assn. Med. Specialists, Am. Soc. Law and Medicine, Am. Acad. Clin. Psychiatrists, Corp. Advancement Psychiatry, Am. Med. Writers Assn., Nat. Council Community Mental Health Ctrs., Nat. Alliance Mentally Ill (profl. assoc. mem.), Met. Coll. Mental Health Assn., Am. Soc. Criminology., South Jersey Neuropsychiat. Soc., Psychiat. Outpatients Ctrs. Am., Am. Coll. Legal Medicine, Acad. Psychiatry and Law (pub. info. com., edn. com., internat. affairs com.), Am. Acad. Forensic Scis., Am. Assn. Acad. Psychiatry, Am. Coll. Emergency Physicians (charter mem.), Am. Acad. Psychotherapists, Am. Assn. Mental Deficiency, Am. Assn. Psychiat. Services for Children, N.J. (chmn. com. on confidentiality, liaison com. health human svcs., corrections), Fla. assns. osteo. physicians and surgeons, N.J. Hosp. Assn., Am. Vocat. Assn., Am. Assn. Group Therapy, Am. Soc. Clin. Psychopharmacology, Assn. Mil. Surgeons U.S., Nat. Assn. VA Physicians, Am. Assn. Psychiat. Adminstrs., Am. Assn. Adolescent Psychiatry, World Med. Assn., Am. Assn. Mental Health Adminstrs., Am. Assn. Gen. Hosp. Psychiatrists, Human Factors Soc., Orthopsychiat. Assn., Am. Physicians Fellowship, Assn. for Research Nervous and Mental Diseases, Atlantic County Osteo. Med. Soc. (pres. 1970-72), N.J. Assn. Mil. Surgeons U.S. (v.p.), Am. Assn. Correctional Health Care, Am. Coll. Forensic Psychiatry (diplomate 1984), charter mem. Soc. of Correctional Physicians. N.J. State bd. of Med. Examiners Specialty Adv. Panel, 1998—. Home: 6700 Atlantic Ave Ventnor City NJ 08406-2618

ZUEHLSDORF, MICHAEL THEODOR, pharmacist; b. Cologne, Germany, Oct. 28, 1959; s. Theodor Franz and Anneliese (Schmitz) Z. Degree, U. Bonn, Germany, 1985, PhD, 1991. Rsch. asst. U. Bonn, Germany, 1985-91; fellow Bayer AG, Wuppertal, Germany, 1992-94, lab. head, 1994—; bd. dirs. Arbeitsgemeinschaft for Angewandte Humanpharmakologie. Contbr. articles to profl. jours. Mem. Am. Soc. Microbiology, European Soc. Clin. Microbiology and Infectious Diseases, Paul Ehrlich Assn., Assn. for Biologische Chemie, N.Y. Acad. Scis. Home: Brauweiler Weg 38, 50933 Cologne Germany Office: Bayer AG, Aprather Weg, 42096 Wuppertal Germany

ZUFFARDI, PIERO, retired economic geology educator; b. Turin, Italy, Nov. 10, 1916; s. Pietro and Rosa (Comerci) Z.; m. Hedyth Ferro, May 12, 1946; 1 child, Orsetta. Degree in mining, Polytechnic, Turin, Italy, 1939, degree in aeronautics, 1942; degree in geology, U. Cagliari, Italy, 1994. Asst. prof. Polytechnic, Turin, 1939-41, 44-45; geologist Italian Geo-Survey, Rome, 1941; mine officer Montevecchio, Sardinia, 1946-62; lectr. Polytechnic, Milan, Italy, 1950-57; from lectr. to full prof. U. Cagliari, Italy, 1956-73; full prof. U. Milan, Italy, 1973-92; cons. Montevecchio, Sardinia, 1962-70, Ente Nazionale Idzocarburi, Milan, 1962-75, Unesco and Oece, Paris, 1967-70, Province, Bergamo, Italy, 1989-95; councillor Nat. Rsch. Coun., Rome, 1972-77, Superior Mining Coun., Rome, 1976-80. Author: L'Uranio, 1956, Giacimentologia, 1985; co-author: Strata-Bound Ore Deposits, 1976; contbr. articles to profl. jours. Lt. Italian Mil. Svc., 1942-43, 44-45. Recipient Gold medal Ministry of Edn., Rome, 1981, award for geology and mineraology Acc. Lincei, Rome, 1986. Mem. Soc. Econ. Geologists (v.p. for Europe 1969-71), Internat. Assn. Genesis Ore Deposits (councillor 1963-72), Internat. Fedn. Soc. Econ. Geologists (councillor 1969-71), Soc. Geology Applied to Mineral Deposits, (founder., pres. 1975-76), Osterreikische Akademie der Wissenshaften, Accademia Nationale Lincei, Assn. Sarda (pres. 1968-69, councillor), Associazione Mineraria Sub-Alpina (v.p. 1972-73), Acc. Scienze G. Capellini, Soc. Italiiana di Mineralogia e Petrografia (pres. 1972-73), Soc. Geologica Italiana. Avocations: reading, traveling, hiking, tennis, skiing. Home: via Fratelli Cervi, Residenza Spiga, 20090 Segrate Milan, Italy Office: Dip Scienze Terra, Via Botticelli 23, 20133 Milan Italy

ZUGIBE, FREDERICK THOMAS, pathologist; b. Garnerville, N.Y., May 28, 1928; s. Benjamin and Anna (Zarick) Z.; m. Catherine Frances O'Leary, Apr. 7, 1951; children: Frederick T., Thomas P., Cathryn T. Blaber, Theresa A. Mandracchia, Mary E. Raleigh, Matthew M., Kevin J. BS, St. Francis Coll., 1951; MS, U. Chgo., 1954, PhD, 1960; MD, W.Va. U., 1968. Diplomate Am. Bd. Pathology-Anatomic, Am. Bd. Pathology-Forensic, Am. Bd. Family Practice. Rsch. histologist Lederle Labs., Pearl River, N.Y., 1950-52, rsch. chemist, 1953-55; rsch. assoc. ophthalmic rsch. Columbia U., N.Y.C., 1955-56; dir. cardiovascular rsch. U.S. VA, Pitts., 1956-65; chief med. examiner County of Rockland, Pomona, N.Y., 1969—; adj. assoc. prof. pathology Columbia U., 1972—; bd. dirs. Hudson Techs. Inc., Hillburn, N.Y., Rockland Westchester Found. for Sudden Infant Death, White Plains, N.Y.; med. dir. Rockland County Emergency Med. Svcs. N.Y.S. Dept. Health, Pomona, 1990—; supervising med. officer disaster med. assistance team Nat. Disaster Med. Assistance, Pomona, 1992—. Author: Eat, Drink and Lower Your Cholesterol, 1964, Diagnostic Histochemistry, 1970, The Cross and Shroud: A Medical Inquiry into Crucifixion, 1988, 14 Days to a Healthy Heart, 1986; contbr. numerous articles to profl. jours. and chpts. to books. Recipient Disting. Citizens award Assn. Visually Impaired, 1998, also numerous awards for svc. legis., proclamations, physician recognition awards, continuing edn. awards, law enforcement awards and others. Fellow Coll. Am. Pathologists, Am. Coll. Cardiology, Am. Acad. Forensic Scis., N.Y. Cardiology Soc., Coun. Arteriosclerosis, Am. Heart Assn., Assn. Scientists and Scholars Internat. for the Shroud of Turin (pres., founder), Sigma Xi. Roman Catholic. Achievements include first to describe glycoprotein storage disease (Zugibe-Gilbert Syndrome), the defect in the syndrome of the sea blue histocyte and arthrodentoosteodysplasia. an acroosteolysis syndrome, a mask to eliminate odors of putrefaction, and a demummifaction technique for fingerprinting; invented ac/dc cardiopulmonary resuscitator, many others. Home: 1 Angelus Dr Garnerville NY 10923-2022 Office: Rockland County Health Comp Office Med Examiner Pomona NY 10970

ZUGRAV, MARIA ITTU, chemist; b. Sibiu, Romania, Apr. 26, 1945; came to U.S., 1988; d. Valeriu and Maria (Badila) Ittu; m. Sylvester Ilie Zugrav, Jan. 22, 1975; children: Dan, Christian. MS in Chemistry, U. Bucharest, 1968; PhD in Chemistry, Poly. Inst., Bucharest, 1982. Rsch. assoc. Inst. Atomic Physics, Bucharest, 1968-72; sr. rsch. scientist Nat. Ctr. Physics, Bucharest, 1972-80, rsch. group leader, 1980-87; rsch. scientist Consortium for Materials Devel. in Space, Huntsville, Ala., 1989-98; rsch. team leader Ctr. for Microgravity and Materials, Huntsville, 1998—; reviewer manuscripts Jour. Crystal Growth. Contbr. articles to profl. jours.; patentee in field. Recipient Cert. of Appreciation, U. Ala., 1995, 996. Named NASA Female Role Model for Contbns. made to NASA Microgravity Rsch. and Space Product Devel. Programs, 1999. Mem. Am. Assn. Crystal Growth, Internat. Soc. Photo-Optical Instrumentation Engrs. Achievements include design of a solution crystal growth technique with gradual addition of a

reactant and application for ammonium dihydrogen phosphate; development of a unique natural buoyancy-driven multi-zone crystallizer; growth of non-linear optical organic single crystals and thin films by effusive ampoule physical vapor transport aboard the U.S. Space Shuttles on STS-40, STS-57, STS-59, STS-69 and STS-77. Avocations: hiking, swimming, reading. Office: Univ of Ala in Huntsville RI D-29 301 Sparkman Dr NW Huntsville AL 35805-1911

ZUHDI, NABIL (BILL ZUHDI), lawyer, litigator, consultant, producer; b. N.Y.C., June 8, 1955; s. Nazih and Lamya Zuhdi; child from previous marriage: Noah; m. Darla L. Boyd, May 19, 1984. BS, U. Ctrl. Okla., 1979; JD, U. Okla., 1982. Bar: Okla. 1982, U.S. Dist. Ct. (we. dist.) Okla. 1982, U.S. Ct. Appeals (10th cir.) 1989, U.S. Supreme Ct. 1990, Tex. 1991, U.S. Dist. Ct. (no. dist.) Tex. 1998. Assoc. Linn & Helms, Oklahoma City, 1982-85; ptnr. Zuhdi & Denum, Oklahoma City, 1985-87; assoc. Law Firm Darrell Keith, Ft. Worth, 1994; pvt. practice Oklahoma City, 1987—; pres. Zuhdi Entertainment Group, Inc., Okla. City, 1986—, Amerisphere, Inc., Okla. City, 1996—, criminal justice act panel We. Dist. Okla., 1985—, spl. death penalty habeas corpus panel, 1998, criminal justice act voluntary panel No. Dist. Tex., 1998. Producer: (concerts) Frank Sinatra, Julio Igleas. Patron Okla. Heart Ctr., Oklahoma City, 1994—. Mem. ABA, ATLA, State Bar Tex., Oklahoma Bar Assn., Oklahoma County Bar Assn., Phi Alpha Delta, Alpha Chi. Republican. Avocations: boxing, film, prodr. of concerts including Frank Sinatra and others. Office: PO Box 1077 Oklahoma City OK 73101-1077

ZUHDI, NAZIH, retired surgeon, administrator; b. Beirut, May 19, 1925; came to U.S., 1950; s. Omar and Lutfiye (Atef) Z.; children by previous marriage: Omar, Nabil; m. Annette McMichael; children: Adam, Leyla, Zachariah. BA, Am. U., Beirut, 1946, MD, 1950. Diplomate Am. Bd. Surgery, Am. Bd. Thoracic Surgery. Intern St. Vincent's Hosp., S.I., N.Y., 1950-51, Presbyn.-Columbia Med. Ctr., N.Y.C., 1951-52; resident Kings County SUNY Med. Ctr., N.Y.C., 1952-56; fellow SUNY Downstate Med. Ctr., Bklyn., 1953-54; resident Univ. Hosp., Mpls., 1956; resident Univ. Hosp., Oklahoma City, 1957-58, practice surgery specializing in cardiovascular and thoracic, 1958-87, adminstr., 1985-99, retired, 1999; founder, dir. Oklahoma Transplantation Inst. (renamed Nazih Zuhdi transplant Inst., Aug., 1999) Bapt. Med. Ctr., 1984-99, chmn. dept. transplantation, 1994-99; transplantation surgeon in chief Bapt. Hosp., Oklahoma City, 1984-99; founder, chmn. Okla. Cardiovascular Inst., Oklahoma City, 1983-84, Okla. Heart Ctr., Oklahoma City, 1984-85. Contbg. author Cardiac Surgery, 1967, 2d edit., 1972; contbr. articles to profl. jours.; developer numerous med. devices, techniques, rsch. and publs. on cardiopulmonary bypass, internal hypothermia, assisted circulation, heart surgery and transplantation of thoracic organs; developer heart-lung machines; designer, use of exptl. plastic bypass hearts; originator use of banked citrated blood for cardiopulmonary bypass for open heart surgery, of clin. non-hemic primes of heart-lung machines producing intentional hemodilution, at present, the universally accepted principle of cardiopulmonary bypass for partial and total body perfusion; researcher in cardiovascular studies. Founder Islamic Ctr., Inc., Oklahoma City. Inducted into Okla. Hall of Fame, 1994. Fellow ACS; mem. AMA, NCCJ (Humanitarian award 1996), Am. Thoracic Soc., Okla. Thoracic Soc., So. Med. Assn., Okla. Med. Assn., Internat. Coll. Angiology, Am. Coll. Chest Physicians, Oklahoma City C. of C., Oklahoma County Med. Soc., Oklahoma City Clin. Soc., Okla. Surg. Assn., Oklahoma City Surg. Soc., Southwestern Surg. Congress, Am. Coll. Cardiology, Am. Soc. Artificial Internal Organs, Soc. Thoracic Surgeons (founding mem.), Am. Assn. for Thoracic Surgery, Internat. Cardiovasc. Soc., Okla. State Heart Assn., Osler Soc., So. Thoracic Surg. Assn., Lillehei Surg. Soc., Internat. Soc. Heart Transplantation, Dwight Harken's Founder's Group Cardiac Surgery, Internat. Soc. Cardiothoracic Surgery (Japan, founding mem.), Am. Soc. Transplant Surgeons, Milestones of Cardiology of Am. Coll. Cardiology, Okla. City Golf and Country Club, Okla. Hall of Fame. Achievements include originating use of banked citrated blood for cardiopulmonary bypass for open heart surgery; invention of clinical non-hemic primes of heart-lung machines producing intentional hemodilution. Home: 7305 Lancet Ct Oklahoma City OK 73120-1430

ZUIDERVAART, LAMBERT PAUL, philosophy educator; b. Modesto, Calif., Aug. 1, 1950; s. Martin and Tena (Beuving) Z.; m. Joyce Alene Recker, Jan. 8, 1977. BA, Dordt Coll., 1972; MPhil, Inst. Christian Studies, Toronto, Ont., Can., 1975; postgrad., Free U. Berlin, 1977-80; PhD, Free U. Amsterdam, The Netherlands, 1981. Asst. prof. philosophy King's Univ. Coll., Edmonton, Alta., Can., 1981-85, chmn., divsn. humanities, 1982-85; assoc. prof. philosophy Calvin Coll., Grand Rapids, Mich., 1985-89, prof., 1989—, chmn. dept., 1991-97, conf. dir., 1995, vice chair faculty senate, 1999—; dissertation supr. Free U., Amsterdam, 1996—; vis. prof. Inst. for Christian Studies, Toronto, Ont., Can., 1991, mem. senate, 1993—, chancellor, 1998—; treas. bd. dirs. King's Coll. Found., U.S., Grand Rapids, Mich., 1989-95, pres. bd. dirs., 1998—; pres., bd. dirs. Urban Inst. for Contemporary Arts, Grand Rapids, 1994-98, chmn. 2.75 Million Dollar Capital Campaign, 1996-99; chmn. organizing com. Art Talks, Toronto, 1996-97; founding secretary-treas., Calvin Coll. Chap., AAUP; pub. lectr. Kendall Coll. Art and Design, 1993, Free U., Berlin, 1994, St. Louis U., 1998, Loft Forum Detroit, 1999, Seattle Pacific U., 2000; seminar leader Lang., Truth and Postmodern Culture, Toronto. Author: Adorno's Aesthetic Theory, 1991; co-author: Dancing in the Dark, 1991; co-editor: Pledges of Jubilee, 1995, The Semblance of Subjectivity, 1997, The Arts, Community and Cultural Democracy, 2000; contbr. articles to profl. jours. Pres. bd. dirs. Inn Roads Housing Coop., Edmonton, Alta., Can., 1982-85; mem. Politics Meaning Discussion Group, Grand Rapids, 1994-97; mem. Internat. Critical Theory Seminar, 1995—; mem. Coalition to Combat Racism, Grand Rapids, 1997-98; workshop leader Leadership Grand Rapids, Mich., 1993, 94. Grantee STEP Prov. Alberta., Can., 1984, 85, Travel grant Am. Coun. Learned Socs., 1988, Rsch. Visit grant German Acad. Exch. Svc., 1994; NEH Summer Seminar grantee, 1997; rsch. fellow Calvin Coll., 1990, 93, 94, 96, 98, 99, McGregor Summer fellow, 1999. Mem. Am. Philosophical Assn., Am. Soc. Aesthetics, Can. Philosophical Assn., Can. Soc. Aesthetics, Internat. Assn. Aesthetics, Soc. Phenomenology and Existential Philosophy. Democrat. Avocations: international travel, music, film, hiking. Office: Calvin College Department of Philosophy Grand Rapids MI 49546

ZUKERMAN, LARRY WILLIAM, lawyer; b. Pitts., Nov. 11, 1960; s. Robert Allen and Marlene (Maysels) Z.; m. Norma Friedman, July 8, 1990; children: Matthew, Shayna, Dara. BA, Washington & Jefferson Coll., 1982; JD, Case Western U., 1985. Bar: Ohio 1985, U.S. Dist. Ct. (no. dist.) Ohio 1985, U.S. Ct. Appeals (6th cir.) 1988, U.S. Supreme Ct. 1993. Atty. Greene & Hennenberg, Cleve., 1985-91; ptnr. Hennenberg Stuplinski & Zukerman, Cleve., 1991-93; proprieter Zukerman & Assocs., Cleve., 1993-96; mng. ptnr., shareholder Zukerman, Daiker & Lear Co. L.P.A., Cleve., 1996—; law dir., chief prosecutor Village of Moreland Hills (Ohio), 1996-98; adj. prof., trustee Case Western Res. U., Cleve., 1996—. Vice-chair Nat. Israel Bonds Orgn., 1996—; bd. dirs. Solomon Schechter Day Sch., 1996—, Cleve. ORT, 1997-99. Mem. ABA, Assn. Trial Lawyers Am., Ohio Assn. Criminal Def. Lawyers (v.p. 1996-98), Cleve. Acad. Trial Lawyers, Ohio State Bar Assn. (coun. dels. 1994-96), Cuyahoga Bar Assn. (judicial selection com. 1992-99), Nat. Assn. Criminal Def. Lawyers, Cleve. Bar Assn. (trustee, chair criminal law sect. 1994-95, vice chair fee dispute/arbitration com. 1992—, chair profl. ethics com. 1990-91), Cuyahoga Criminal Def. Lawyers Assn. (v.p. 1998-99, pres.-elect 1999-2000, pres. 2000—). Democrat. Jewish. Avocations: travel, skiing. Office: Zukerman Daiker and Lear Co LPA 2000 E 9th St Ste 700 Cleveland OH 44115-1301

ZUKERMAN, MICHAEL, lawyer; b. Bklyn., Oct. 3, 1940; s. Charles Morris and Gertrude Ethel Zukerman; m. Claire J. Goldsmith, June 25, 1961 (div. 1986); children: Steven, Amy; m. Elaine DeMasi, Nov. 21, 1986 (div. 1999); children: Jaclyn, Laura. BS, U. Fla., 1961; LLB, St. John's U., 1964; LLM, NYU, 1966. Bar: N.Y. 1965, Pa. 1983, U.S. Tax Ct. 1984. Credit analyst, loan officer Franklin Nat. Bank, 1964-66; assoc. Jaffin, Schneider, Kimmel & Galpeer, N.Y.C., 1966-67; ptnr. Zukerman, Licht & Friedman and predecessors, N.Y.C., 1967-79, Baskin & Sears, P.C., N.Y.C., 1979-85, Graubard, Moskowitz, Dannett, Horowitz & Mollen, N.Y.C., 1985-86, Gersten, Savage, Kaplowitz & Zukerman, N.Y.C., 1986-89; of counsel Olsham, Grundman, Frome & Rosenzweig, N.Y.C., 1990-95, Graham & James, N.Y.C., 1995-2000, Bryan Cave LLP, 2000—; exec. v.p. Brookhill Group, 1986-89; pres. First Ptnrs. Credit Corp., N.Y.C., 1988-93; bd. dirs. Interjurist LTD, internat. law firm, Dames Moore/Brookhill LLC; mng. dir. Colebrook Capital Corp., 1996—, Whitestone Realty Capital, Inc., 1997—. Contbg. editor Real Estate Taxation and Acctg., 1988-93; lectr. on various subjects, 1986—. Contbr. articles to profl. jours. Trustee Temple Beth Torah, Melville, N.Y., 1972-80, YMHA Suffolk County, Hauppague, N.Y., 1980-85; bd. dirs. Dayton Mgmt. Corp., 1974—, Suffolk Jewish Cmty. Planning Bd., Hauppague, 1982-85, Congregation Bnai Elohim, 1994, 2nd v.p., 1995; co-chmn. bus. adv. coun. Town of Greenburgh, 1992. Mem. ABA. Home: 500 E 77th St New York NY 10162-0025 Office: Bryan Cave LLP 245 Park Ave Rm 2801 New York NY 10167-2897

ZUKOWSKA, ZOFIA MARIA, cardiovascular physiologist, educator; b. Sosnowiec, Poland, July 16, 1949; came to U.S., 1980; d. Wladyslaw and Natalia (Kiewszynis) Zukowska; children: Anna Natalia, Wojtek Pawel Grojec. MD, Med. Acad., Warsaw, Poland, 1972, PhD, 1979. Med. diplomate. From resident to sr. resident dept. hypertension Med. Acad., Warsaw, 1972-74, asst. prof. dept. hypertension, 1974-80; vis. fellow NIMH/NIH, Bethesda, Md., 1980-83; vis. assoc. NINDS/NIH, Bethesda, 1983-85; asst. prof. dept. physiology Georgetown U., Washington, 1985-91, prof. dept. physiology, 1991—; cons. Astra Zeneca, Sweden, 1997—, dept. hypertension Acad. Med., Warsaw, 1990—; Polish-Am. sci. exch./vis. prof. Nat. Heart, Lung and Blood Inst./Cardiology Program, Bethesda and Warsaw, 1990—, prin. investigator R01, Bethesda, 1996—. Author: (book chpt.) The Biology of NPY, 1992; contbr. articles to Sci., Proc. NAS, Am. Jour. Physiology, Cir. Rsch. Recipient Adele Holmes Established Investigatorship award D.C. chpt. Am. Heart Assn., 1988. Fellow Coun. for High Blood Pressure Rsch. Am. Heart Assn.; mem. Polish Acad./Hypertension Soc. (hon.), Soc. Neurosci. Achievements include discovery of high sensitivity of males to vasoconstrictor effects of neuropeptide Y (NPY) and stress-induced release of NPY; beneficial effects of NPY in treatment of shock and mitogenic and angiogenic activities of NPY. Avocations: sailing, dancing, traveling, languages, literature. Office: Georgetown U Dept Physiology 3900 Reservoir Rd NW Dept Washington DC 20007-2188

ZULBERTI, CARLOS ALBERTO, planning executive; b. Bahia Blanca, Argentina, Jan. 22, 1944; s. Carlos and Maria Zulberti; m. Ester Nelida Costanzo, June 13, 1968; children: Florencia and Emiliano (twins). Ingeniero Agronomo, Universidád Catolica, Mar del Plata, 1968; MS, Cornell U., 1971, PhD, 1974. Advisor Internat. Devel. Rsch. Ctr., Bogota, Colombia, 1974-76, Can. Internat. Devel. Agy., Quito, Ecuador, 1976-78; project dir. The SNC Group, San Domingo, Dominican Republic, 1978-81; project assoc. Harvard U., Nairobi, Kenya, 1982-86; cons., advisor Internat. Devel. Rsch. Ctr., Nairobi, 1987-91; dep. chief, tech. cooperation UN Environment Programme, Nairobi, 1992-93; head planning UNEP, Nairobi, 1994-98; cons. Consultative Group on Internat. Agrl. Rsch., 1998—; cons. Winrock Internat., Nairobi, 1991, FAO, Rome, 1989, UNDP, Nairobi, 1989, World Bank, 1988. Co-author: Living Rural Development, 1978; contbr. articles to profl. jours. George F. Warren grantee, Cornell U., 1971; Ford Found. fellow, N.Y.C., 1968-73. Mem. Internat. Assn. Agrl. Economists, Soc. for Internat. Devel., Internat. Soc. for Ecol. Econs., Am. Agrl. Econs. Assn., Can. Agrl. Econs. and Farm Mgmt. Soc. Address: 2117 L St NW #113 Washington DC 20037-1524

ZU LOEWENSTEIN-WERTHEIM-FREUDENBERG, PRINCE RUPERT LOUIS FERDINAND, financial consultant; b. Palma, Majorca, Aug. 24, 1933; s. Prince Leopold and Countess Bianca H-M Fischler von Treuberg; m. Josephine Lowry-Corry, July 18, 1957; children: Rudolf, Konrad, Theodora. MA, Magdalen Coll., Oxford, 1953. With Bache & Co., London, 1953-62; with Leopold Joseph & Sons, Mcht. Bankers, Ltd., London, 1963-81, sr. mng. dir., 1966-81; ind. fin. cons. London, 1981—. Decorated knight grand cross of honor and devotion Sovereign Mil. Order of Malta, Constantine Order of St. George: Bailiff Grand Cross of Justice. Mem. Bucks Club, Boodles Club, Whites Club, Portland Club, Pratt's Club, Beefsteak Club, The Brook Club, Regency Club (N.Y.C.). Conservative. Roman Catholic. Address: Petersham Lodge, River Ln, Richmond Surrey, England

ZULUETA GREENEBAUM, JOHN DE, insurance company executive; b. Cambridge, Mass., Feb. 23, 1947; m. Carmen Castell Sala, May 4, 1989. BA, Stanford U., 1968; MBA, Columbia U., 1976. Cons. The Boston Consulting Group, San Francisco, 1976-78; asst. to pres. PepsiCo Foods Internat., Dallas, 1979; pres., gen. mgr. La Vienesa, Caracas, 1979-80, Productos PepsiCo, Barcelona, Spain, 1981-85; mng. dir. Schweppes, S.A., Madrid, 1985-91; v.p. Cadbury Beverages Europe, Madrid, 1989-91; mng. dir. Sanitas, Madrid, 1991—; dir. APD, Madrid, 1999, Bankinter, Madrid, 1998—; bd. dirs. Bankinter. Author: Buscando El Dorado, 1997. Dir. Found. Tierra de Hombres, Madrid, 1996—; v.p. Found. Sanitas, Madrid, 1996—. Recipient cert. appreciation U.S. Dept. Commerce, Washington, 1966. Office: Sanitas SA de Seguros, Serrano 88, 28006 Madrid Spain

ZUMA, JACOB G., deputy president of South Africa; b. Inkandla, South Africa, Apr. 12, 1942. Mem. African Nat. Congress, 1959—; polit. prisoner, 1963-73; underground organizer in the Natal African Nat. Congress, 1973-75, mem. exec. com., 1977-84, chief rep. in Mozambique, 1984, head underground structures, then chief of intelligence, chairperson So. Natal region, 1990-91, dep. chmn., 1991-94, cand. for KwaZulu-Natal premiership, 1994, chmn., 1996—, dep. pres., 1997—; dep. pres. Republic of South Africa, 1999—. Office: Office of Pres, Union Bldgs Pvt Bag X1000, Pretoria 0001, South Africa*

ZUMBRUN, KEVIN RONALD, mathematics educator; b. Walnut Creek, Calif., Aug. 11, 1959; s. Ronald Arthur and Ann Hartley Zumbrun. BS in Math., U. Calif., Davis, 1981, MS in Math., 1983; PhD in Math., NYU, 1990. Vis. asst. prof. SUNY, Stony Brook, 1990-92; postdoctoral rschr. Stanford (Calif.) U., 1992; asst. prof. Ind. U., Bloomington, 1992-96, assoc. prof., 1996-99, prof., 1999—; vis. scholar Mittag-Leffler Inst., Stockholm, 1997, Ecole Normale Superieure, Lyon, France, 1998; lectr. in field. Contbr. articles to profl. jours. Named Navy Young Investigator, Office Naval Rsch., 1994-97; Postdoctoral fellow NSF, 1991-93; grantee NSF, 1994-2000. Mem. Am. Math. Soc., Soc. for Indsl. and Applied Math., Sigma Xi. E-mail: kzumbrun@indiana.edu. Office: Dept Math Ind Univ Bloomington IN 47405

ZUMERCHIK, JOHN, urologist; b. Chgo., Nov. 29, 1932; s. John and Anna (Marchuk) Z.; m. Eileen Heraty, June 14, 1958; children: Cheryl ann, John Francis, David Lee, Steven Jay, Patricia Eileen, James Jacob, Janine Marie. AA, Wilson Jr. Coll., Chgo., 1953; student, U. Ill., Chgo., 1953-54; MD, Loyola U., 1958. Diplomate Am. Bd. Urology. Rotating intern Cook County Hosp., Chgo., 1958-59, urology resident, 1960-63; gen. surg. resident MacNeal Meml. Hosp., Berwyn, Ill., 1959-60; pvt. practice Drs. Ross-Zumerchik Partnership, Evergreen Park, Ill., 1964-67, Drs. Ross, Zumerchik, Boctor, Evergreen Park, 1970-83, Southwest Urology Assocs., Evergreen Park, 1983—; staff urologist Little Co. of Mary Hosp., chmn. divsn. urology, dept. surgery, 1977-80, 82-84; staff urologist Ingalls Meml. Hsop.; mem. resident edn. attending staff dept. urology Cook County Hosp., 1961-85, grad. edn. asst. prof., 1963-85; clin. instr. urology med. student edn. Loyola U. Chgo., 1962-72. Pres. 98th and Kedzie Corp., Evergreen Park, 1988, 96-97. Lt. col. M.C. U.S. Army, 1968-70. Fellow ACS (mem. examining com. 1978-84, 92-96); mem. AMA, Am. Urol. Assn. (north ctrl. sect.), Am. Assn. Clin. Urologists, Chgo. Urol. Soc. (exec. com. 1987), Ill. Urol. Soc., Ill. Med. Soc., Chgo. Med. Soc., Pan-Pacific Surg. Assn., Royal Soc. Medicine, Am. Soc. Andrology, Am. Fertility Soc., Am. Inst. Ultrasound in Medicine, Endourology Soc. Avocations: tennis, skiing, biking, photography, carpentry. Office: Southwest Urology Assocs 9760 S Kedzie Ave Evergreen Park IL 60805-3123

ZUMKELLER, WALTER, pediatrician, researcher; b. Bad Säckingen, Germany, May 15, 1961; s. Oswald and Katharina (Stillinger) Z.; m. Natalia Liakhova, Mar. 21, 1991; children: Alexander Frederick, Michael Anthony. MD, U. Berlin, 1989. Rsch. asst. Karolinska Inst. and Hosp., Stockholm, 1988-90, Inst. Child Health, London, 1990-91, U. Cambridge, Eng., 1991-92; pediatrician, sr. scientist Univ. Hosp. Eppendorf, Germany, 1992-97; pediatrician Children's U. Hosp., Heidelberg, 1997-98, German Cancer Rsch. Ctr., Heidelberg, 1998—, Children's U. Hosp., Halle/Saale, 1998—; mem. Insulin-like Growth Factor-binding Protein study group. Contbr. numerous articles, revs. to profl. publs. in field. Mem. Marburger Bund, Hamburg, 1994. Grantee Nat. Kidney Rsch. Fund, Eng., 1991-92. Mem. N.Y. Acad. Scis., Endocrine Soc., Am. Assn. Cancer Rsch. Avocations: opera, ballet, classical music. Office: Childrens U Hosp, Ernst-Grube-Str 40, 06097 Halle Saale, Germany

ZUMWINKEL, KLAUS, management consultant. MS, U. Pa. Cons. McKinsey & Co., Dusseldorf, N.Y.C., 1974-79; ptnr. McKinsey & Co., 1979-85, dir. worldwide mgmt., 1984-85; mem. exec. bd. Quelle, Furth, Germany, 1985-87, exec. chmn., 1987-89; chief exec. Deutsch Bundespost POSTDIENST, Bonn, Germany, 1990-95; CEO Deutsche Post, Bonn, 1995—, chmn. bd. mgmt., CEO. Office: Deutsche Post, Heinrich von Stephan Str 1, Bonn 53175, Germany*

ZUNA, JAN, physician, researcher; b. Praha, Czechoslovakia, Sept. 13, 1971; s. Petr and Marie (Krusinová) Z.; m. Jana Havlová, July 29, 1995; 1 child, Eliska. MD, 2nd Med. Sch.-Charles U., 1995, PhD, 1999. Physician 2nd dept. pediatrics 2nd Med. Sch., Charles U., Praha, 1995-96, rsch. fellow, 1996—. Contbr. articles to profl. jours. Mem. Czech Paediatric Haematology Working Group, Childhood Leukaemia Investigation Prague. Avocation: sports, games. Office: 2nd Med Sch Charles U, Vuvalu 84, 150 06 Praha Czech Republic

ZUNA, PETR JOSEF OTAKAR, university dean, materials science educator; b. Prague, Czechoslovakia, Mar. 21, 1943; s. Jiri and Vera (Srdinková) Z.; m. Marie Krušinová, Aug. 27, 1964; children: Pavel, Jan. MSc in Mech. Engring., Czech Tech. U. in Prague, 1963, CSc in Phys. Metallurgy, 1972. Rsch. worker CKD, heavy machinery works, Prague, 1985-86; tchg. asst. Czech Tech. U. in Prague, 1963-89, assoc. prof. materials sci., 1989-92, prof., 1992—, dean, 1991-97, rector, 1997-2000; dep. chmn. Czech Republic Grant Agy., Prague, 1991—; mem. adv. bd. Czech Republic Ministry Def., 1996—; mem. prep. com. for nat. metallographic confs., 1982—; mem. bd. Czech Rector's Conf., 1997-2000; mem. supervisory bd. CKD Holding, 1997-98; bd. dirs. Aero Vodochody; mem. Commn. for R and D of Union Trade and Transport Czech Republic, 1997—; mem. mng. coun. Found. for Human Biomechanics, 1995—. Co-author: (monograph) Recovery and Recrystallization, 1985; mem. editl. bd. Technik, 1995—; contbr. over 80 articles to Czech and internat. jours. Mem. mng. coun. Zvonicek Found., Prague, 1995—; sci. coun. Nat. Tech. Mus., Prague, 1997—. Mem. Czech Acad. Sci. (sci. bd. 1997—), Nuclear Rsch. Inst. (chmn. sci. bd. 1997—), Engring. Acad. Czech Republic (pres. 1995—), Czech Soc. New Materials and Techs. (v.p. 1990—), Assn. Mech. Engrs., Internat. Soc. for Engring. Edn. (gold medal 1995), Soc. for Sci. and Arts (v.p.). Avocations: classical music, theatre, literature, skiing, tennis. Home: Nad Šárkou 97, 160 00 Prague 6, Czech Republic Office: Czech Tech U in Prague, Technická 4, 166 07 Prague 6, Czech Republic

ZUNDER, WILLIAM LIMBERY, English educator; b. London, Dec. 10, 1938; s. Wilfred Hagen and Lilian Freda (Carr) Z.; m. Barbara Anne Golding, Sept. 1, 1984; m. Judith Butcher, July 14, 1962 (div. 1983); children: Thomas Hagen, Harriet Jane, Charlotte Lucy, Prudence Amy. BA, Oxford U., England, 1961; MA, McMaster U., Can., 1964; PhD, London U., 1969. Lectr. English London U., 1966-67; lectr. English Hull U., England, 1967-96, fellow English, 1996—; dir. Unity Press, Ltd., Cottingham, England, 1994—. Author: Poetry of John Donne, 1982, Elizabethan Marlowe, 1994, Diana: A Sonnet Sequence, 1998; co-author: Jacobean Poetry and Prose, 1988; co-editor: Writing and the English Renaissance, 1996; editor: Paradise Lost (John Milton), 1999; contbr. articles to profl. jours. Teaching fellow McMaster U., Can., 1963. Home: 34 Canongate, Cottingham HU16 4DG, England Office: Hull U, Cottingham Rd, Hull HU6 7RX, England

ZUNIGA, MIGUEL ANGEL, health care sciences professor; b. Minas de Oro, Comayagua, Honduras, Nov. 21, 1957; came to U.S., 1988; s. Miguel Angel Zuniga-Bonilla and Maria Antonia Donaire-Escoto; m. Genny T. Carrillo, Jan. 8, 1992; children: Miguel Angel, Gisela Lotzil. MD, U. Nacional Autonoma (Honduras), 1985; M in Health Adminstrn., Tulane U., 1990, PhD, 1994. Prof. U. Nacional Auronoma de Honduras, Tegucigalpa, Honduras, 1985-87; dist. health officer Ministerio de Salud Publica, Danli, El Paralso, Honduras, 1987-88; health svcs. planner Office Public Health, New Orleans, 1990-91; mktg. strategic planning assoc. Tulane U. Hosp., Clinic, New Orleans, 1991-93; rsch. physician, outcomes assesement Tulane U. Hosp., Clinic, 1994-97; adj. asst. prof. Tulane U. Med. Ctr., 1994-97, clin. asst. prof., 1997—; nat. prin. investigator, Internat. Quality Life Assessment Project, Merida, Mexico, 1995; cons. in field. Contbr. articles to profl. jours. Naturalist, Audobon Inst., New Orleans, 1993. Recipient Delta Omega hon. public health soc. award, 1991; Fulbright Scholar, U.S. Info. Agency., 1988-93. Mem. Assn. Health Svcs. Rsch., Assn. U. Programs Health Adminstrn., Med. Outcomes Trust. Avocations: photography, gardening, wilderness exploration, bicycling. Office: Tulane U Dept Health Systems Mgmt Med Ctr New Orleans LA 70112

ZUNINO, RODOLFO FRANCESCO LUIGI, electronic engineer; b. Genoa, Italy, Dec. 21, 1961; s. Giuseppe and Lucia (Mortari) Z. Laurea degree, U. Genoa, 1985. With San Paolo (Italy) Bank, 1981-89, mgr., 1989; rsch. cons. in electronic engring. U. Genoa, 1985-95; asst. prof. Genoa U., Italy, 1995-2000, assoc. prof., 2000—. Contbr. articles to profl. jours. Roman Catholic. Office: DIBE-Univ of Genoa, Via All Opera Pia 11A, 16145 Genoa Italy

ZUO, CHENGYE, psychiatrist, educator; b. Changsha, Hunan, China, Jan. 16, 1933; s. Dajie and Shan (Peng) Z.; m. Lingling Yang, Apr. 30, 1954; 1 child, Yang. Grad., Hunan Med. Coll., Changsha, China, 1955. Psychiatrist Hunan Med. Coll., Changsha, 1955-80, asst. prof., 1980-83, assoc. prof., 1983-89, prof., 1989—. Editor Fgn. Med. Scis. sect. of Psychiatry, 1980—. Mem. Chinese Med. Assn. Avocations: reading novels, travel. Office: Hunan Med Univ, 2d Affil Hosp Renming Rd 86, Changsha 410011, People's Republic of China

ZUO, HONGSHU, electric power designer, educator, consultant; b. Jingzhou, Hubei, China, Oct. 30, 1938; s. Kaize Zuo and Xinfeng Yao; m. Peizhen Li, Dec. 16, 1966; children: Xiaolu, Hailang. BSc, Huazhong Inst. Sci. and Tech., Wuhan, China, 1960. Engr. East China Electric Power Design Inst., Shanghai, 1981-86, sr. engr., 1987-92, prof., 1993—; sr. cons. Shanghai Sci. and Tech. Inst., 1995—. Author: Practical Mathematics for You-How To Find the Optimum Point, 1980, Design and Calculation of Practical Micropore Mufflers, 1983, How To Find the Optimum Decision in Planning, 1988, Micropore Muffler: Its Application in Fossil Power Plants, 1991. Recipient 3rd prize China Nat. Sci. and Tech. Com., 1985, Bronze medal Beijing Internat. Invention Exhbn., 1988, Gold medal China Internat. New Technol. Famous and Excellent Products Fair, 1995. Fellow Chinese Soc. Elec. Engring., Shanghai Engring. Thermal Physics Soc., Shanghai Solar Energy Soc. Avocations: literature, art, sports. Home: 805 No 3 Chang Feng Er Cun, Shanghai 200062, China Office: East China Elec Power De In, 409 Wuning Rd, Shanghai 200063, China

ZUOHI, ZHANG, Chinese government official. Min. labor and social security Govt. of China, Beijing, 1998—. Mem. Communist Party. Office: Ministry Labor, 12 He Ong Li Zhong Jie/East, Beijing 100716, China*

ZUPANETS, IGOR ALBERTOVICH, academic administrator, clinical pharmacist; b. Mikhaylovka Village, Khemel, Ukraine, June 23, 1958; s. Albert Rudolfovich and Lidia Grigoryevna (Budko) Z.; m. Irena Grigoryevna Dyakonova, Dec. 8, 1984; children: Dmitry, Igorevich. M in Medicine, Pharm. & Toxicol. Rsch. Inst., Kiev, USSR, 1988; MD, High Certifying Commn., Moscow, USSR, 1993. Dist. therapist City Hosp., Kharkov, USSR, 1982-84; lectr. in pharmacology Pharm. Inst., Kharkov, USSR, 1984-88, asst. prof., pharmacology chair, 1988-92; head of physiology dept. Ukrainian Acad. Pharmacy, Kharkov, Ukraine, 1992-93, head clin. pharmacy, 1993—; vice rector Ukrainian Acad. Pharmacy, Kharkov, 1996—; asst. dean pharmacy faculty Ukrainian Acad. Pharmacy, Kharkov, 1987-91; presidium mem. Pharmacological Com., Ministry of Health, Ukraine Govt., Kiev, 1996—; head of clin. base of Pharmacological Com., Ministry of Health, 1996. Author (books) Osteoarthoses: Pharmacological Correction

Pathways, 1992, Osteoarthrosis: Conservation Therapy, 1999; (textbook) Pharmacology, 1984; contbg. author: Licensing in European Union, Pharmaceutical sector, 1998; patentee Medical Formulation; editor-in-chief Clin. Pharmacy, 1997; mem. editl. bd. Visnyk of Pharmacy, 1996, School of Fundamental Medicine, 1997. Rep. Com. in Narcotics, Ministry of Health, Ukraine, Kharkov, 1997. Major Ukrainian Med. Corps. Grantee Govt. Ukraine and Internat. Sci. Fund, 1995. Mem. Pharmacological Soc. Ukraine, Pharmacists' Soc. Ukraine. Avocations: chess, billiards, motor races, collecting art. Home: Apt 10 15 Chubar Str, 61003 Kharkov Ukraine Office: Nat Ukraninian Acad Pharmacy, 53 Pushkinskaya Str, 61002 Kharkov Ukraine

ZUPAN-RUSKOVIC, PAVE, travel agency executive; b. Trebinje, 1947; d. Ante and Ane (Bagovic) Zupan; m. Ivan Ruskovic; children: Antonia, Marinela. MS in Econs., U. Zagreb, Croatia. Guide Atlas Travel Agy., Dubrovnik, Croatia, 1968, head BPFA dept., head road traffic divsn., 1968-82, pres., 1982—; mem. coun. Croatian Tourist Bd., Zagreb. Bd. dirs. Rebuild Dubrovnik Fund, Washington, 1992-98. Mem. Croatian Assn. Travel Agys. (pres. 1983—), Croatian Assn. Mgrs., Am. C. of C. in Croatia, Croatian Coun. for European Movement, WITC (pres. chpt. 1998—), Am. Soc. Travel Agys. (pres. Croatian chpt. 1990-98). Office: Atlas Travel Agy, Brsalje 17, 2000 Dubrovnik Croatia

ZUPPARDI, GENNARO, aerodynamic educator; b. Naples, Italy, Nov. 30, 1950; s. Giovanni and Rosa (Cinque) Z.; m. Rita Crispino, Oct. 30, 1977 (div. Apr. 1996); children: Giovanni, Maura. Degree in aeronautical engring., U. Naples, Italy, 1977. Rschr. aerodynamics U. Naples, Italy, 1981—. Contbr. articles to profl. jours. Office: Dept Space Sci Engring, Tecchio 80, 80125 Naples Italy

ZU PUTLITZ, GISBERT, retired physics educator; b. Rostock, Germany, Feb. 14, 1931; s. Waldemar and Annalies (von Wolffersdorff) zu P.; m. Haide Beckers, July 9, 1960; children: Jasper, York, Julian. Diploma in physics, U. Heidelberg, Germany, 1961, PhD, 1962, habilitation, 1966; JD (hon.), Boston U., 1986; DSc (hon.), U. Md., 1986; Prof. (hon.), Fed. U. Rio Grande do Sul, 1987; PhD (hon.), Staatsuniv. Leningrad, 1990, U. Alisher Navoi, Samarkand, Usbekistan, 1992, Staatsuniv. Kalingrand, 1995, Jagiellonische U., Cracow, Poland, 1996. Asst. in physics U. Heidelberg, 1962-66, docent, 1966-70, assoc. prof., 1970-72, prof., 1972-99, prof. emeritus, 1999, rector, 1983-87; sci. dir. Assn. for Schwerionenforschung, Darmstadt, Germany, 1978-83; chmn. Assn. German Nat. Labs., Bonn, Germany, 1981-83, Gottlieb Daimler and Karl Benz Stiftung, Ladenburg, Germany, 1986—; pres. Heidelberg Acad. Scis., 2000—; chmn. confs. including Linear Accelerator Conf., Darmstadt, Internat. Conf. on Particles and Nuclei, Heidelberg, others. Contbr. over 250 articles to profl. jours. Recipient Order of Merit 1st class Fed. Rep. Germany, 1984, Gold medal of Honor, State of Baden-Württemberg, 1988, Leo Baeck prize Ctrl. Coun. Jews in Germany, 1989. Fellow Am. Phys. Soc., World Acad. Art and Sci., N.Y. Acad. Scis.; mem. German Phys. Soc., German Acad. Art and Sci., European Phys. Soc., Heidelberg Acad. Scis. (pres. 2000—), Berlin-Brandenburg Acad. Scis. Evangelical. Office: U Heidelberg, Philosophenweg 12, 69120 Heidelberg R Neckar, Germany

ZURABOV, ALEXANDER YURIEVICH, airline executive, bank executive, economist; b. Leningrad, Russia, Apr. 15, 1956; s. Yourij Georgievich Pupko and Enguelina Robertovna Z.; m. Elena Vladimirovna Smirnova, Apr. 4, 1953; children: Maria, Georgy. Diploma in Econ. Cybernetics, Moscow Acad. Mgmt., 1977; Postgrad. Diploma in Internat. Econs., Acad. for Fgn. Trade, Moscow, 1989; PhD, Inst. Marine Transp., Moscow, 1986. Lectr. Acad. Fgn. Trade, Moscow, 1989-91; dir. Konversbank, Moscow, 1991-94; CEO and chmn. Trust and Investment Bank, Moscow, 1994-95; pres., chmn. bd. dirs. Menatep Bank, Moscow, 1995-99; chmn. bd. dirs. Russian Standard Bank, Moscow, 1999—; 1st dep. gen. dir., commerce and fin. Aeroflot, Moscow, 1999—. Office: Aeroflot/Russian Airlines, 37 Bld 9, Leingradsky Prosp, 125167 Moscow Russia

ZURAK, IVICA, clinical microbiologist, educator, inovator; b. Split, Croatia, June 13, 1938; s. John and Ljubica (Blazicevic) Z. Vocational High Medic Lab. Diagnostic Sch., Zagreb, Croatia, 1970, U. Pharmacy and Biochemistry, Zagreb, Croatia, 1980. Histology tech. Med. U., Rijeka, Croatia, 1959-60; clin. hematology and biochemistry U. Hosp., Rijeka, Croatia, 1963-65; clin. hematology U. Hosp., Beograd, Yugoslavia, 1967; clin. biochemistry U. Hosp., Zagreb, Croatia, 1970-73, clin. microbiology, 1973—; spkr. in field; assoc. asst. U. of Pharmacy and Biochemistry, Zagreb, Croatia, 1980—. Mem. Am. Soc. Microbiology, Croatian Pharm. Soc.

ZURKOWSKI, STANISLAW, engineering researcher; b. Warsaw, Feb. 1, 1955; s. Zbigniew Henryk and Aurelia (Szpiro) Z.; m. Katarzyna Ewa Heidrich, Oct. 11, 1980; 1 child, Aleksander. MScME, Warsaw U. Technology, 1979; postgrad., Inst. of Math./Polish Acad. of Scis., 1979-80; PhD, Warsaw U. Technology, 1989. Probationer Inst. of Aviation, Warsaw, 1979, mechanic, 1979-83, asst. prof., 1983-87; sr. asst. prof. Inst. of Aviation, 1987-89, chmn. bd. aeroengines dept., 1992—; project mgr., 1994-96; adj. prof. Inst. Aviation, 1989—; mem. main commn. aircraft accident investigation Min. Transport & Maritime Economy, Warsaw, 2000—; mem. accreditation commn. of profl. edn., Min. of Edn., Warsaw, 1998—, com. on multilingual terminology data base Internat. Acad. of Astronautics, Paris, 1997—; sec. astronautical commn. The Space Rsch. Com. of the Polish Acad. of Scis., Warsaw, 1990—; expert rep. Polish Aerospace Industry, Polish Pavilion Expo '93, Korea, 1993. Lang. coord.: IAA Multilingual Space Dictionary, 1996; tech. and scientific asst. to lang. coord.: IAA Space Dictionary, 1992; patentee in field; contbr. over 45 articles to profl. jours. and pubis. Recipient state com. for scientific rsch. award 1994-96, joint indsl. and comml. tng. programme, Confedn. of Brit. Industry, Rolls-Royce, Derby, 1993, Fulbright Found. Sr. Rsch. grant U. Calif. Berkeley, 1991, 92. Mem. N.Y. Acad. Scis., Polish Soc. of Mech. Engrs. (com. on profl. devel. 1998—), Polish Astronaut. Soc. (dep. chmn. 1992— Golden award 1995, Silver award 1987), Polish Fulbright Alumni Assn. Avocations: mem. bd. of condominium residents, biking, electronic music, mountain hiking, theater. Office: Inst of Aviation, Al Krakowska 110/114, 02-256 Warsaw Poland

ZÜRN, MICHAEL, political science educator; b. Esslingen, Germany, Feb. 14, 1959. MA, U. Denver, 1984; grad., U. Tübingen, Germany, 1987, PhD, 1991. Asst. prof. Inst. for Polit. Sci. U. Tübingen, 1989-93; prof. polit. sci. and internat. rels. U. Bremen, 1993—, co-dir. Inst. for Intercultural and Internat. Studies, 1995—, co-dir. Ctr. for European Law and Policy, 1996-00; vis. prof. Grad. Sch. Internat. Studies U. Denver, 1991; Thyssen rsch. fellow Ctr. for Internat. Affairs Harvard U., 1992-93; rsch. assoc. Internat. Inst. for Applied Sys. Analysis, Laxenburg, Austria, 1993-96, Ctr. for Advanced Studies, Oslo, Norway, 1999. Author books and book chpts.; editor Jour. for Internat. Rels., 1997—; contbr. articles to profl. jours. including Internat. Studies Quar., World Politics, among others. Grantee German Rsch. Assn., 1994—, German Am. Acad. Coun., 1995-96. Mem. Internat. Studies Assn., German Polit. Sci. Assn. (curricula bd. 1993—), German Peace and Conflict Rsch. Assn. Avocations: music, squash, soccer. Office: U Bremen Inst Intercul Stud, Postfach 330440, 28334 Bremen Germany

ZUROFF, EFRAIM YAAKOV, war crimes researcher, historian; b. N.Y.C., Aug. 5, 1948; s. Abraham N. and Esther Pearl (Sar) Z.; m. Elisheva Bannett, Aug. 1972; children: Avigayil, Itamar, Elchanan, Ayelet. BA, B Hebrew Lib., Yeshiva Coll., N.Y.C., 1970; MA, Hebrew U., Jerusalem, 1975, PhD, 1997. Asst. editor Yad Vashem Studies Yad Vashem, Jerusalem, 1973-77, dir. dept. for contacts with Diaspora, 1977-78; dir. Simon Wiesenthal Ctr., L.A., 1978-80; rschr. Office Spl. Investigations U.S. Dept. Justice, Jerusalem, 1980-86; dir. Israel Office, coord. Nazi war crimes rsch. Simon Wiesenthal Ctr., Jerusalem, 1986—; delegate Third Way, 33rd Zionist Congress, 1998. Author: Occupation: Nazi-Hunter, 1994, The Response of Orthodox Jewry in the United States to the Holocaust: The Activities of the Vaad Ha-Hatzala Rescue Committee 1939-45, 2000; editor: Rescue Attempts During the Holocaust, 1977. Mem. Efrat (Israel) City Coun., 1984-85, 87-90; mem. secretariat Third Way, polit. party, Israel, 1996-99; mem. coun. Meimad, Israel, 1997—. With Israel Def. Forces, 1980. Recipient Shimshon Junichman prize World Jewish Congress, 1972, cmty. svc. award Yeshiva U. Israel Alumni, 1997; Egit grantee for Holocaust and Jewish Resistance Lit., 1998. Office: Simon Wiesenthal Ctr, 1 Mendele St, 92147 Jerusalem Israel

ZU SAYN-WITGENSTEIN, LUDWIG-FERDINAND PRINCE, company executive; b. Rosendahl, Westfalen, Germany, Jan. 25, 1942; s. Ludwig-Ferdinand Prince and Frederike Juliane Princess zu Sayn-Wittgenstein-Princess Salm Hortsmar; m. Yvonne Jaquette Countess Wachtmeister/Princess Wittgenstein, Sept. 6, 1975; children: Karl, Anna, August, Theodora. Diploma forestry, U. Munich, Bavaria, Germany, 1966, diploma econs., 1969; MBA, Insead, Fontainebleau, France, 1971. Attache de direction Banque Parisbas, Paris and Frankfurt, Germany, 1971-74; bus. cons. Munich, 1974-80; mng. dir. Louis Sayn, Bad Laasphe, France, 1980—; mng. owner forest estates Forstgut Ditzrod, Bad Laasphe, Germany, 1986—; bd. mem. Fürst Wittgenstein'sche Waldbesitzergesellschaft, Westfalen, Germany, 1966-86. Head European Federalist Studentsorganis, Munich, 1964-66; mem. environ. mcpl. com., Bad Laasphe, 1989-95; mem. local bds. Christian Democrat Party 1989-95, Bad Laasphe, 1989-94; head parents assn. Gymnasium Schloss Wittgenstein, Bad Laasphe, 1988-95. Mem. Lions Club (Siegen), Union Club (Frankfurt). Avocations: shooting, tennis, modern art, literature. Office: Louis Sayn, Schloss Wittgenstein 1, 57334 Bad Laasphe Germany

ZUSCHLAG, NANCY HANSEN, environmental and nature resources educator; b. Montclair, N.J., Dec. 12, 1954; d. Irving Djalmar and Carmen (Del Grippo) Z.; m. Jeffrey Jon Miller, Sept. 21, 1991. BA in Biology cum laude, Coe Coll., 1977; MA in Biology, U. Kans., 1982. Regional conservation educator and coord. Mo. Conservation Dept., Jefferson City, 1982-84; coord. sch. programs Denver Mus. Natural History, 1986-87; program dir. dept. natural resources and environ. edn. Coop. Ext. Colo. State U., 1988-98; dir. ops. and edn. Mad Sci. of Denver, 1998-99; pres. Green Triangle Assocs. Internat., 1997—; instr. environ. educator Mus. Natural History, U. Kans., Lawrence, 1976-82, assoc. pub. edn. dept. , 1986-89; lectr. William Woods Coll., 1982-84; mem. study, rsch. rev. group Canary Islands, 1985; cons. Kongskilde Field Study Edn. Ctr., Soro, Denmark, 1985; bd. dirs. Foothills Nature Ctr., Boulder, Colo., 1987-89; assoc. zool. Denver Mus. Natural History, 1988; cons. and educator Mus. Zool., U. Copenhagen, 1984-85, 95-96; co-dir., sci. coord., instr. Lower Sch. Colo. Acad., 2000—. Author, editor: Back to Ancient Egypt, 1987; (with others) Science - Natur/Teknik, Assessment and Learning Studies and Educational Theory Curriculum, Vol. 22, 1995; editor: (with others) Contributions to Vertebrate Ecology and Systematic; a Tribute to Henry S. Fitch, 1983; contbr. articles to profl. jours. state edn. coord. Colo. Earth Day is Every Day campaign, Boulder, 1990; bd. dirs. Colo. Found. Agr., Denver, 1992-95, mem. edn. bd., 1993; facilitator and presenter UN Program Youth in the Environment, U. Colo., Boulder, 1993; chair environ. and natural resources future's task force com., Colo. State U. Coop. Ext., 1993; mem. nat. natural resources and eviron. mgmt. support team coop. states, rsch. ext. edn. sys., USDA, 1993-96; mem. synthesis team and original document writing team, Colo. Environ. Edn. Master Plan, 1994; mem. state steering com. Denver Urban Resources Partnership, 1996—, Denver Youth Naturally Project, 1995. Recipient N.J. award AUW, County Achievement award Nat. Assn. Counties, 1989, Environ. Scholar award USEPA, 1990, region 8 Outstanding Women's Contbns. in Environ. Edn. award, 1992, Nat. Environ. Coun. award, 1992, 94, Celebrate Colo. Environ. Leadership award Colo. State Gov., 1993; scholar Coe Coll., 1973-74; Virginia Harkness-Sawtelle Found. scholar Coe Coll. and U. Kans., 1976-78; Fulbright scholar U. Copenhagen Zool. Mus., 1984-85, Fulbright scholar assoc. Royal Danish Sch. Edn., 1995-96. Mem. Am. Assn. Biol. Scis., Nat. Wildlife Fedn. (mem. steering com. Naturlink 1993), North Am. Assn. Environ. Edn., Alliance Environ. Edn., Nat. Assn. Interpreters, Am. Arachnological Assn., Colo. Alliance Environ. Edn. (bd. dirs. 1988-92, pres. 1990-91, adv. bd. 1997), Colo. Assn. Tchrs., Fulbright Alumni Soc., Phi Sigma, Epsilon Sigma Phi (State Early Career Excellence award 1990). Avocations: hiking, writing on myth, nature and culture, jewelry-making, traveling. E-Mail: nhzgreentri@hotmail.com. Office: Green Triangle Assocs Internat PBM 223 4255 S Buckley Rd Aurora CO 80013-2951

ZUTLER, BRUCE B., marketing executive, consultant; b. N.Y.C., Dec. 7, 1960; s. Aaron and Barbara (Reganbagen) Z.; m. Barbara Krug, Dec. 28, 1991; children: Brooke, Benjamin. BS, Skidmore Coll., 1982. From territory mgr. to asst. product mgr. Am. Home Products, Inc., Albany, N.Y., 1982-84; product mgr. Internat. Playtex, Inc., Stamford, Conn., 1984-85; dir. mktg. Marketing Congress, Inc., Plainview, N.Y., 1986-90; mktg. mgr. Franklin Mint, Franklin Center, Pa., 1991-94; pres., CEO, MCI Products Group, Inc., Plainview, 1995—; bd. dirs. Aris Technologies, Inc., Cambridge, Mass. Patentee printed light switch plate, bottled water ice cubes. E-mail: bzmcjpg@aol.com. Office: MCI Products Group Inc 80 Skyline Dr Plainview NY 11803-2518

ZUZOWSKI, ROBERT, political scientist, educator; b. Kherson, Ukraine, USSR, Sept. 22, 1945; arrived in South Africa, 1990; s. Marian and Felicia (Tug) Z.; divorced. M Econs., Acad. of Econs., Wroclaw, Poland, 1968; MA, Australian Nat. U., Canberra, 1981; PhD, LaTrobe U., Melbourne, Australia, 1990. Tutor LaTrobe U., 1983-85; lectr. Royal Melbourne Inst. Tech., 1989-90; lectr. U. Witwatersrand, Johannesburg, Republic of South Africa, 1990-93, sr. lectr., 1994-99, assoc. prof., 2000—. Author: Political Dissent and Opposition in Poland, 1992, Social Self-Defence Committee, 1996, Political Change in Eastern Europe Since 1989: Prospects for Liberal Democracy and a Market Economy, 1998; contbr. articles to profl. pubis. Hon. vis. fellow Sch. Slavonic and East European Studies, London, 1996. Mem. South African Polit. Sci. Assn., South African Inst. Internat. Affairs. Avocations: hiking, tennis, golf, cycling, sailing. Fax: +27-11-339 4605. E-mail: 161rober@cosmos.wits.ac.za. Office: U Witwatersrand, Dept Internat Rels Pvt Bag 3, WITS 2050 Johannesburg South Africa

ZVÁROVÁ, JANA, statistician, educator; b. Prague, June 30, 1943; d. Karel and Ludmila (Kolinská) Sladká; m. Karel Zvára, Feb. 5, 1966; children: Marie, Karel. MS, Charles U., 1965, Dr., 1970, PhD, 1978, DSc, 1999. Asst. med. faculty Charles U., Prague, 1965-68, sr. lectr., 1977-87, head med. informatics dept., assoc. prof., 1987-98, prof., 1999—; rschr. Inst. Haematology and Blood Transfusion, Prague, 1969-76, Inst. Social Medicine and Health Care Mgmt., Prague, 1976-77; cons. in statistics Inst. Rhematology, Prague, 1977-87; rsch. specialist Acad. Sci. Inst. Computer Sci., Prague, 1992—; chair internat. confs. Assn. Czech Med. Socs., 1985, 90; dir. EuroMISE Ctr. Charles U. and Acad. Scis., Prague, 1994—. Editor: Medical Decision Making: Diagnostic Strategies and Expert Systems, 1985, Medical Informatics and Medical Education, 1990; mem. editl. bd. Medical Informatics, 1988; chief editor: Physician and Technology, 1982. Mem. Med. Soc. J.E. Purkyně (head med. informatics sect. 1977—), Internat. Med. Informatics Assn. (rep. Czechoslovakia/Czech Republic 1987—), Czech Soc. for Med. Informatics and System Sci. (pres. 1991-93), European Fedn. Med. Informatics (rep. Czech Rep. 1995—), Soc. Biomed. Engring. and Med. Informatics (bd. dirs. 1977—), Czech Statis. Soc., Biometric Soc., Czech Soc. Cybernetics and Informatics (bd. dirs. 1997—). Avocations: music, sports. Office: EuroMISE Ctr, Pod vodárenskou věží 2, 182 07 Prague Czech Republic

ZVEREV, VALENTIN PETROVICH, geochemist; b. Moscow, Aug. 2, 1933; s. Peter Mikhailovitch and Maria Vasilievna (Malfygina) Z.; m. Valentina Alexandrovna Novikova, Jan. 2, 1960; 1 child, Mikhail. MS in Hydrogeology, Geol. Prospecting Inst., Moscow, 1957; PhD in Hydrogeology, USSR Acad. Sci., Moscow, 1966, DSc in Geochemistry, 1987. From jr. to leading researcher Geol. Inst. USSR Acad. Sci., Moscow, 1957-91; main sci. researcher, chief lab. Inst. Environ. Geosci. Russian Acad. Sci., Moscow, 1991—. Author: Hydrogeochemistry investigation of Gypsum-subsurface water system, 1967, Role of subsurface water in the migration of Chemical Elements, 1982, The Energetic of Hydrogeochemistry Process of Recent Sedimentogenesis, 1983, Hydrogeochemistry of sedimentary process, 1993, Massflows of the Subsurface Hydrosphere, 1999. Famous scientist state grantee Presidium Russian Acad. Scis., 1994, 97, 2000; named Honored Scientist of Russia, 1998. mem. Scientific Coun. Engring. Geology and Hydrogeology, 1991, Internat. Assn. Geochem. Cosmochem. (mem. working group water-rock interaction 1974—). Russian Orthodox. Avocations: walking with grandchildren, reading, classical music. Home: Dekabristov 10-1-153, 127562 Moscow Russia Office: RAS Inst Environ Geosci, Ulanskii per 13-2 PO Box 145, 101000 Moscow Russia

ZVETINA, JAMES RAYMOND, pulmonary physician; b. Chgo., Oct. 14, 1913; s. John and Jennie (Albrecht) Z.; m. Florence Courtney, Feb. 4, 1944. BS, Loyola U., 1940; MD, U. Ill., 1943. Intern West Suburban Hosp., Oak Park, Ill., 1944, resident physician, 1944-45; asst. ward med. officer USNH, NOB, Norfolk, Va., 1945; staff physician Pulmonary TB Svc. VA Med. Hosp., Hines, Ill., 1946-54; asst. chief Pulmonary Svc. VA Med. Hosp., Hines, Ill., 1954-68, sect. chief, 1968-88, attending physician, 1988-91, cons., 1992—; clin. prof. medicine Coll. Medicine, U. Ill., Chgo., 1978—; mem. adv. bd. Coll. Medicine, U. Ill., 1985—; rep. Rsch. Conf. in Pulmonary Disease, VA Armed Forces, 1946-74. Contbr. articles to profl. jours. V.p. Chgo. Cath. Physicians, 1979, pres., 1978. Comdr. USNR, 1945-46, med. officer USNR, ret. Recipient Svc. award 40 Yrs. VA Adminstrn., 1985, Svc. award 30 Yrs. U. Ill. Med. Sch., 1978. Fellow Am. Coll. Chest Physicians; mem. AMA, Ill. State Med. Soc. (Fifty Yr. club), Chgo. Med. Soc., Third Order of St. Dominic. Roman Catholic. Achievements include research in area of pulmonary infections. Avocation: travel. Home: 96 Forest Ave Riverside IL 60546-1977 Office: VA Hines Hines IL 60141

ZVEVEVA, ELLINA, Olympic athlete. Winner Gold medal discus Sydney, 2000. Office: Track & Field Athletics Fed, F Skorina prospect 49, Minsk 22005, Belarus*

ZVIDRINS, PETERIS, demographer, researcher; b. Kraslava, Latvia, May 31, 1943; s. Pavels and Juzefa Zvidrins; m. Mara Zauere, Mar. 23, 1968; 1 child, Sanita. CandSci in Stats., U. Latvia, Riga, 1970, DrHabilEcon, 1992; PhD in Demography, Moscow State U., 1981. Chief Dept. of Censuses Ctrl. Statis. Office, Riga, 1965-67; sr. rschr. Rsch. Statis. Inst., Riga, 1967-70; sr. lectr. U. Latvia, Riga, 1970-72, assoc. prof., 1972-79, head dept. stats. and demography, 1979—, prof., head Ctr. Demography, 1982—, chmn. commn. of univ. senate, 1995-98; mem. Govtl. Commn. of Demography, Riga, 1985-99; chmn. Baltic Assn. for Population Studies, Riga, 1990-93; vice chmn. Latvian Coun. Sci., Riga, 1993-94, chmn., 1994-95. Author: Investigation of Fertility, 1973, Population of Great Britain, 1979, Population and Economics, 1987, Latvians: A Statistical and Demographic Portrait, 1992, (textbook) Demography, 1983, 2d edit., 1989, 3d edit., 2000; editor, co-author: Population Replacement in Latvia, 1996, Family and Fertility in Latvia, 1996, Fertility and Family Surveys in Countries of the ECE Region. Latvia, 1998, Population Development in Latvia (On the Eve of 21st Century), 1999. Dep., City Coun., Jurmala, Latvia, 1990-94; mem. Parliamentarian Commn., Riga, 1996-98. Population Coun. fellow, 1990; NATO fellow, 1996-98. Mem. Latvian Statis. Assn. (pres.), Internat. Union Sci. Study of Population, European Assn. for Population Studies, Latvian Acad. Sci. (bd. dirs., mem. senate, Karlis Balodis prize 1996). E-mail: zvidrins@lanet.lv. Office: U Latvia, 19 Rainis Blvd, LV-1586 Riga Latvia

ZVONOVA, ALEVTINA NICKOLAYEVNA, publisher, consultant; b. Moscow, Mar. 24, 1937; d. Nickolay Kuzyamich and Maria Stepanovna (Abrashina) Truchanov; m. Anatoly Michaylovich Zvonov, Aug. 5, 1967; 1 child, Valentina. Grad., Fin. Inst., Moscow, 1958, PhD in Econs., 1977. Editor Statistika Pub. House, Moscow, 1961-64, chief of textbook dept., 1964-66, dep. editor-in-chief, 1966-73, editor-in-chief, 1973-87; mng. dir., editor-in-chief Finansy i Statistika Pub. House, Moscow, 1987—. Editor numerous textbooks and dictionaries; contbr. articles to profl. jours. Former mem. Communist Party of Soviet Union, 1961-91. Recipient Hon. Master of Culture medal State Com. on Printing and Pub. Affairs, 1987, Order of Honour, 1998. Mem. Pubs. Assn. (chief supr. dept.), Assn. Russian Book Distbrs. Avocations: reading, numismatics. Fax: 095 925 0957. Office: Finansy i Statistika Pub House, Pokrovka 7, 101000 Moscow Russia

ZVULUNOV, ALEXANDER, pediatric dermatologist; b. USSR, May 31, 1959; arrived in Israel, 1974; s. Yair and Raya Z.; m. Irit Yogev, Jan. 7, 1985; children: Noa and Yael. MD, Sackler Sch. Med., Tel Aviv, 1984. Resident in pediatrics Beilinson Med. Ctr., Petah-Tigwa, Israel, 1986-91; sr. pediatrician Yoseftal Med. Ctr., Eilat, Israel, 1991-93; fellow in pediatric dermatology Med. Coll. Wisc., Milw., 1993-94; resident in dermatology Soroka Med. Ctr., Beer-Sheva, Israel, 1994-97; pediat. dermatologist Soroka Med. Ctr. Ben Gurion U., Beersheba, Israel, 1997-98, sr. lectr. the Faculty of Health Scis., 1997—; head dept. pediatrics Josephtal Hosp, Eilat, Israel, 1998—. Home: 3 Saharon Ln, Eilat 88000, Israel Office: Joseftal Hosp Med Ctr, Dept Pediatrics, Eilat 88000, Israel

ZWAHLEN, BEAT JÜRG, automotive executive; b. Berne, Switzerland, Feb. 13, 1960; m. Margarita Aeberhard; two children. Grad. in econs., Sch. Economy & Bus. Adminstrn., Berne, 1985; CPA, Berne & Zurich Swiss CPA Sch., 1990. Audit asst., auditor Allgemeine Treuhand AG Ernst & Young, Berne, 1985-89; head mgmt. consulting VISURA, Burgdorf, Switzerland, 1989-91; M&A cons. STG Coopers & Lybrand, Zürich, Switzerland, 1992; head corp. bus. controlling Landis & Gyr Corp., Zug, Switzerland, 1992-94; head fin. and controlling Landis & Gyr (Europe), Zug, 1994-96; CFO, sr. v.p. Rieter Automotive, Winterthur, Switzerland, 1996—. Pres. Nat. Profl. Orgn., Zürich, 1992-97. Capt. Swiss Tank Force, 1989-94. Mem. Round Table. Avocations: family activities, sailing, cars, politics, music. Office: Rieter Automotive Mgmt, Schlosstalstrasse 43, 8406 Winterthur Switzerland

ZWARTZ, GORDON JOSEPH, research scientist; b. Portage, July 16, 1964; m. Sally Seidel. BSc in Physics, U. Winnipeg, 1986; MSc in Physics, U. Toronto, 1989, PhD in Physics, 1996. Tchg. asst. U. Toronto, 1986-90, rsch. asst., 1986-95; vis. scholar U. N.Mex., 1991-96; fellow Lovelace Respiratory Rsch. Inst., Albuquerque, 1996-2000; NRSA fellow U. N.Mex., Albuquerque, 1999—. Contbr. articles to profl. jours. E.C. Stevens scholar U. Toronto, 1989-91; recipient Young Invest. Travel award Biomed. Engring. Soc., 1997. Mem. Internat. Soc. for Aerosols in Medicine, Am. Assn. for Aerosol Rsch. E-mail: gzwartz@salud.unm.edu. Office: U NMex Sch Medicine Cancer Ctr/Cytometry 900 Camino De Salud NE Albuquerque NM 87131-0001

ZWECKER-LAZAR, IRINA, physiatrist; b. Bucharest, Romania, Sept. 7, 1961; d. Osy and Lianne Solange (Spaier) Lazar; m. Manuel Zwecker, Nov. 1, 1992; 1 child, Raphael. MD, U. Bucharest, 1987. Gen. practitioner Outpatient Clinic Jewish Cmty., Bucharest, 1987-89, dept dir., 1989; gen. practitioner Emergency Hosp., Bucharest, 1987-89; resident in plastic surgery Soroka Hosp., Beer-Sheva, Israel, 1990; resident in urology Ichilov Hosp., Tel-Aviv, Israel, 1991-93; resident in phys. medicine & rehab. Loewenstein Hosp., Raanana, Israel, 1993-2000; specialist phys. medicine and rehab. Loewenstein Rehab. Hosp., Raanana, 2000—. Mem. Israeli Soc. Phys. Medicine & Rehab., Israeli Soc. Sports Medicine, Internat. Classification Com. Sports for Disabled. Avocations: sports, traveling, music, dancing.

ZWEIFEL, FRANCOISE, international organization administrator. Sec. gen. Internat. Olympic Com., Lausanne, Switzerland. Office: Internat Olympic Committee, Chateau De Vidy Case Postale 356, 1007 Lausanne Switzerland

ZWERIN, MICHAEL, musician, business executive. BA in Music, U. Miami. Bus. mgr. Barzeverin Steel Co., Haifa, Israel, 1951-53; v.p. Capitol Steel Corp., N.Y.C., 1953-58, pres., 1961-66; jazz columnist Sounds, Village Voice, 1964-69, European editor, 1969-71; freelance journalist for various publs. including Esquire, Playboy, Vogue, New Republic, Vanity Fair, Madamoiselle, Elle, Rolling Stone, Eye, others; monthly columnist Down Beat, State of Mind, 1966-69; restaurant columnist Playbill Mag., 1967-69; pop music critic Internat. Herald Tribune, 1977—. Author: The Silent Sounds of Needles, 1968, A Case for the Balkanization of Practically Everyone, 1976, Close Enough for Jazz, 1983, Swing Under the Nazis, 1985; musician, trombonist with big bands inlcuding Claude Thornhill, Sonny Dunham, Urbie Green, Billy May, others, Maynard Ferguson big band, 1959-61, Earl Fatha Hines, 1967; recording Archie Shepp, Magic of Ju-Ju, 1968; musician orchestra USA Gunther Schuller, John Lewis, 1963-66; recorder, prodr., musical dir., arranger, trumpet soloist for recording Mack the Knife, Jazz Versions of the Berlin Theatre Songs of Kurt Weill; musician Mike Zwerin Quartet, 1982. Recipient Chevalier de L'Ordre Des Arts Et Des Lettres Min. Jack Lang, 1992. Fax: 33-1-4348-4525. E-mail: mzwer-in@compuserv.com. Home: 11 Rue Jean Mace, F-75011 Paris France

ZWEYNERT, MANFRED, mathematics consultant; b. Grethen, Germany, Aug. 20, 1932; s. Georg and Margaretha (Schindler) Z.; Christine Bär, Dec. 21, 1962; children: Matthias, Ulrike. Dipl.math., T.U., Dresden Saxony, 1962, Dr.rer.nat., 1984. Tchr. Sch. of Engring., Reichenbach, Germany,

1959-70; rschr. ROBOTRON Dresden, Germany, 1970-86, Transformatoren Werk, Germany, 1986-91; cons. Mathematik-Beratung, 1991—. Mem. IG Radverkehr Dresden, 1987; leader ADFC-IG Radverkehr Dresden, 1990-97. Fachschuldozent Ingsch., Reichenbach, 1967. Avocations: organ, genealogy. Home and Office: Kaitzer Strasse 103, D-01187 Dresden Germany

ZWIAUER, KARL F.M., pediatrician; b. Niedernondorf, Austria, Mar. 18, 1955; s. Karl M. and Herta (Riemer) Z.; m. Gabriele Frantsich, May 1, 1988; children: Valentina, Victoria. DrMed, U. Vienna, 1980. Bd. cert. pediatrician, 1988. Mem. dept. pediatrics U. Vienna, 1981-91, head dept. pediatrics, 1992—, prof. pediatrics, 1991; head dept. pediatrics Gen. Hosp., St. Poelten, 1991. Contbr. more than 80 articles to med. jours. Mem. Austrian Soc. Pediatrics (head of the nutrition com.), German Soc. for Pediatrics (pres. com. for food), European Soc.for Pediatric Rsch., German Soc. for Obesity Rsch., Euroepan Soc. for Study of Obesity, Austrian Working Group for Clin. Nutrition, Austrian Assn. for Nutrition, Rotary Club. Roman Catholic. Avocations: golf, skiing, climbing, scuba diving. Home: Mahlergasse 9, 3100 Saint Poelten A-3100, Austria Office: Gen Hosp St Poelten, Propst-Fuehrer Str 4, Saint Poelten A-3100, Austria

ZWICK, KEITH R., landscape architect; b. Hutchinson, Kans., Aug. 18, 1943; s. Harry and Marjory Ann Zwick; m. Virginia Sue Zwick, Nov. 20, 1976; children: Brian, Justin; m. Sandy Zwick, Nov. 25, 1996. BS, Kans. State U., 1966. Landscape arch. Oblinger Smith Corp., Wichita, Kans., 1966-70, Dallas, 1970-78; dir., project mgr. Downtown Devel. Authority, City of Loveland, Colo., 1978-84; project mgr., landscape arch. EDAW, Inc., Ft. Collins, Colo., 1984-90; planning mgr. The Earth Tech. Corp., Colton, Calif., 1990-95; pvt. practice planning/design cons. Phoenix, 1995—. Designer Restoration of Downtown Lancaster, Tex., 1972 (numerous design awards 1976); dir. Loveland Downtown/Cmty. Arts Program, 1978. Recipient Numerous Design awards Am. Assn. Nurseryment, Washington, 1977-86, Maxwell AFB Design award USAF, Washington, 1986. Mem. Nat. Trust for Historic Preservation. Avocation: restoration of houses. Home: 9048 N 14th Dr Phoenix AZ 85021-2986

ZWICKY, JULIA FAY, writer, educator; b. Melbourne, Victoria, Australia, July 4, 1933; d. Clifford Leslie and Iris Naomi (Rothstadt) Rosefield; m. Karl Thomas, Mar. 19, 1957 (div. 1980); children: Karl, Anna; m. James A.C. Mackie, Feb. 23, 1990 (div. 1991). MA, U. Melbourne, 1956. Tutor Univ. Women's Coll., Melbourne, 1955-56; sr. lectr. U. Western Australia, Perth, 1973-87, ret., 1987; writer in residence Macquarie U., Sydney, 1982, Rollins Coll., Fla., 1984, La Trobe U., Melbourne, 1985, Tasmania U., Sydney, 1985, Melbourne U., 1987; mem. lit. bd. Australia Council, Sydney, 1978-81, Western Australia Theatre Co., 1991—. Author: Isaac Babel's Fiddle, 1975, Kaddish and Other Poems (Premier of N.S.W. award) 1982, Hostages and Other Stories, 1983, The Lyre in the Pawnshop (Western Australia Lit award), 1986; editor: Patterns, 1973-78, Westerly, 1973-96, Ask Me, 1990 (Premier of W.A. award), Poems 1970-92, 1993, The Gatekeeper's Wife, 1997 (Premier of W.A. award). Mem. Australian Bi-Centennial Reference Group, 1982—. Avocations: music, reading.

ZWIERZAK, ANDRZEJ KAROL, chemistry professor, researcher; b. Warsaw, Poland, Mar. 17, 1931; s. Andrzej and Jadwiga (Krantz) Z.; m. Krystyna Godlewska, Dec. 21, 1957. MSc, Tech. U., Lodz, Poland, 1955, PhD, 1959, Habilitation, 1964. From instr. to assoc. prof. Tech. U., Lodz, 1953-72, prof., 1972—. Contbr. articles to profl. jours. Recipient three awards Polish Ministry of Sci., Higher Edn., Tech., 1965, 1974, 1978; Polish Acad. Scis., 1969. Mem. Polish Chem. Soc. (Kostanecki medal 1980), Union Polish Tchrs. Avocations: qualified tourism, travelling, photography. Home: Lokatorska 4/27, 93-024 Lódź Poland Office: Inst Organic Chem Tech U, Zeromskiego 116, 90-924 Lódź Poland

ZWIESLER, HANS-JOACHIM HERMANN, actuarial science educator; b. Heidenheim, Fed. Republic Germany, Mar. 2, 1957; s. Werner Friedrich Otto and Erika Waltraud Elisabeth (Hellwig) Z.; m. Centa Schwarz, Jan. 23, 1982; children: Julia, Maximilian. Diploma, U. Ulm, Fed. Republic of Germany, 1980, PhD in Math., 1983, Habilitation, 1990. Vis. prof. Syracuse (N.Y.) U., 1985, San Diego State U., 1995; dir. student exch. programs U. Ulm, 1981—, prof. actuarial scis.; exec. dir. Inst. for Actuarial Sci., 1992—. Contbr. articles to profl. jours. Sport's dir. Heidenheim (Fed. Republic of Germany) Fencing Club, 1977-85. Recipient Silver medal Wuerttemberg Fencing Fedn., Heidenheim, 1985. Fellow Studienstiftung des deutschen Volkes; mem. Internat. Fencing Fedn. (internat. referee 1977—, mem. commn. statutes 1985-89), German Youth Fencing Fedn. (pres. 1984-95), German Fencing Fedn. (v.p. 1984—, Gold medal 1996). Avocations: classical music, fencing. Office: U Ulm, Helmholtzstr 18 E11, D-89069 Ulm Germany

ZWINKELS, JAN H., Aruban government official. Atty. gen. Govt. of Aruba, Oranjestad. Office: care Ministry of Justice, 76 LG Smith Blvd, Oranjestad Aruba*

ZWIRN, HERVÉ, engineer; b. Marseille, France, Oct. 6, 1954; s. Paul Henri and Paulette (Mselati) Z.; m. Helene Marie Kowalski, June 29, 1985; children; Adeline, Claire. Engr., Polytechnique, France, 1978, Ecole Nat. Superieure Tele., France, 1980; Doctor es scis., U. Paris VI, France, 1988. Engr. Thomson, Paris, 1980-84; vice gen. mgr. MNEF, Paris, 1984-96; pres. Prestintel, Paris, 1987-96; gen. mgr. Steria, Paris, 1996-99, Eurobios, Paris, 2000—. Author: The Age of Science, 1989, Logic Methods for Cognitive Sciences, 1995; contbr. articles to profl. jours. Pres., Assn. pour Faciliter l'Insertion professionnelle des Jeunes, Paris, 1994-99. Mem. History of Scis. Inst. Avocations: photography, tennis.

ZYBILL, CHRISTIAN ERICH, chemist, physicist, materials scientist; b. Bremen, Germany, Apr. 1, 1956; s. Hermann and Erika (Freitag) Z.; m. Ellen Magareta Krüger, May 28, 1982; children: Thomas Felix, Martin Jakobus. B.Sc., Philipps U., Marburg, 1977; M.Sc., Tech. U. Munich, 1980, Dr. rer. nat. Ph.D., 1983, Dr. rer. nat. habil., 1992; postgrad., U. Wis., 1984-85. Tutorial phys. chemistry Philipps U. Marburg, 1976-78; rsch. asst. Tech. U. Munich, 1980-84; postdoctoral asst. U. Wis., Madison, 1984-85; akad. Rat. Tech. U. Munich, 1986-92, asst. chemistry, 1993-94; vis. lectr. Nat. U. Singapore, 1994-96; pubs. cons. Quelle & Meyer Co., Wiesbaden, Germany, 1993; prof. chemistry Ludwig-Maximilians U. Munich, 1994. Author: Coordination Chemistry of Subvalent Silicon Ligands in: Topics in Current Chemistry, 1992, Metal-Silicon Multiple Bonds in: Advances in Organometallic Chemistry, 1994; contbr.: (with W.A. Hermann) Synthetic Methods of Organometallic and Inorganic Chemistry, Vol. 1, Vol. 2, 1996, (with W.A. Herrmann) Vol. 4, Vol. 7, (with W.A. Hermann and F. Kreissl), Vol. 8, 1997, (with N. Auner and J. Weis) Organosilicon Chemistry-From Molecules to Materials, 1994; contbr. over 70 sci. articles to profl. jours.; contbr. over 80 papers to sci. confs. Mem., 1st violin Siegen Youth Orch., Germany, 1966-74. Recipient Jugend Forscht medal Stern Pubrs. Co., Hamburg, 1970, Erasmus-Sacerius medal Gymnasium in Lôhrtor, Siegen, 1974; named Internat. Man of Yr., Cambridge Biog. Inst., 1995, 96, Erice Vaciago award, 1999. Mem. Am. Chem. Soc., German Chem. Soc. (ADUC-Jahrespreis award 1989), Singapore Nat. Inst. Chemistry, N.Y. Acad. Scis., Deutsche Physikalische Gesellschaft. Lutheran. Achievements include research on chemical vapour deposition of transition metal silicides for use in micro-electronics, in-situ UPS, study of domain structure of ferroelectric thin films (PZT, SBT, BST), single domain switching, non-volatile data storage, devices with Gbit/square inch storage density. Home: Muenchener Str 25, 85748 Garching Germany Office: Tech U Munich Dept Physics, Dept E16/James-Franck-Str 1, D-85747 Garching Germany also: Nat U Singapore, Lower Kent Ridge Rd, Singapore 119260, Singapore

ZYBLIKIEWICZ, LUBOMIR WSEWOŁOD, international relations educator; b. Przemyśl, Poland, July 4, 1943; s. Włodzimierz and Olga (Wasylkiewicz) Z.; m. Danuta Maria Czyżowicz, Nov. 9, 1968; children: Lidia, Marta, Maria Magdalene. MA, Jagiellonian U., Cracow, Poland, 1966, PhD, 1973, D Habilitation, 1984. Asst. prof. dept. polit. sci. Jagiellonian U., Cracow, 1967-70, asst. prof. dept. social sci., 1970-84, head dept. social sci., 1973-81, assoc. prof., chair internat. rels., 1985-93, prof., chair internat. rels., 1993—, head doctoral sch. polit. scis., 1988—, chair internat. rels. Inst. Polit. Scis.; mem. Commn. Polit. Studies, Polish Acad. Scis., Cracow, 1985—; fellow NATO, Brussels, 1992-93; prof. Jean Monnet Project, Brussels, 1996—. Author: The U.S. and British Policies Towards Poland in the Years 1944-49, 1984 (prize Polist Inst. Internat. Rels. 1984), The U.S. Policies Towards Latin America and the Caribbean, 1981-1988, 1992; co-author: (with Erhard Cziomer) An Introduction Into Contemporary International Relations, 2000; editor: Unidad, diversidad y dependencia de America Latina, 1991, Repercussions of Malvin/Falklande Conflict for the Foreign Policies of Latin America, 1991. Mem. Polish Assn. Latin Am. Studies (pres. 1985-89), Polish Assn. Polit. Studies (chmn. 1984-87), Polish Tchrs. Assn. (rep. to coun. of faculty of law 1993—). Avocation: walking. E-mail: UHZYBLIK@IF.UJ.EDU.PL. Home: Mogilska 19/14, 31-542 Cracow Poland

ZYCZKOWSKI, KAROL WOJCIECH, physicist, researcher; b. Cracow, Poland, Apr. 27, 1960; s. Michal Jozef and Teresa Maria (Heydel) Z.; m. Jolanta Maria Kulczycka, Apr. 30, 1994; 1 child, Jan. MS, Jagiellonian U., Cracow, 1983, PhD, 1987. Asst. S. Inst. Physics, Cracow, 1983-89; Humboldt fellow U. Essen, Essen, Germany, 1989-90; adjunct S. Inst. Physics, Cracow, 1991-93, assoc. prof., 1994—. Author: (book) Notatki szeregowca, 1990. Recipient Award for Outstanding Habilitation Polish Prime Minister, 1994; sr. Fulbright fellow U. Md., 1997-98. Mem. Polish Physical Soc. Roman Catholic. Avocations: skiing, fencing, history, politics. Office: Inst Physics-Jagiellonian U, ul Reymonta 4, 30-059 Cracow Poland

ZYGLIDOPOULOS, STELIOS CHARALAMBOS, management educator; b. Athens, Feb. 10, 1960; arrived in Canada, 1988; s. Leandros Zyglidopoulos and Dimitra (Hondrodimitriou) Zyglidopoulou. MSc, U. Piraeus, Athens, 1982; MBA, Mc Gill U., Montreal, 1991, PhD, 1999. Distbn. mgr. 2-v S.A., Athens, 1985-87; credit sales supr. Toyota Hellas, Athens, 1987; gen. mgr., founder Ionikon, Athens, 1987-88; project mgr. Delta SA, Athens, 1988; mktg. liaison Crane Can., Montreal, 1989-90; faculty lectr. McGill U., Montreal, 1991-99; asst. prof. Erasmus U., Rotterdam, The Netherlands, 1998-2000; prof. Rochester (N.Y.) Inst. Tech., 2000—. Contbr. articles to profl. jours. With Grecian Navy, 1982-84. Recipient doctoral fellowship SSHRC, 1992-94, doctoral fellowship FCAR, 1992. Avocations: swimming, kendo. E-mail: szyglidopoulos@yahoo.com. Home: 195 Harvard St Apt 1 Rochester NY 14607 Address: Erasmus U Sch Mgmt, POB 1738, NL 3000 Rotterdam The Netherlands

ZYGLOWICZ, DANIEL T., librarian; b. N. Charleroi, Pa., Jan. 13, 1962; s. Tadeusz and Dolores Agnes Z. BS in Edn., Calif. U. of Pa., 1985; MLS, U. Pitts., 1988. Cert. Commonwealth of Pa. pub. libr. Cataloging asst. 2 Calif. U. of Pa., 1986-2000, govt. documents asst., 2000—; ref. libr. Monessen (Pa.) Pub. Libr. and Dist. Ctr., 1989—. Cons. Monessen Centennial, 1998. Mem. Monessen Centennial Cmty., 1997-98, Greater Monessen Hist. Soc., Hist. Soc. of We. Pa., Geneal. Soc. of Southwestern Pa. Mem. ALA, Phi Delta Kappa, Kappa Delta Pi. Democrat. Roman Catholic. Avocations: antiques, historical research, gardening. E-mail: zyglowicz@cup.edu. Home: 1229 Patton Ave Monessen PA 15062-1914 Office: Calif U of Pa Louis Manderino Libr 250 University Ave California PA 15419-1341

ZYGMUNT, MARCZENKO, chemistry educator, researcher; b. Warsaw, Poland, Feb. 15, 1922; s. Michal and Maria (Osinska) M.; m. Zofia Stepien Marczenko, Aug. 2, 1952. M in Chemistry, Tech. U., Warsaw, Poland, 1948, MD, 1959. Asst. Indsl. Inst. Chemistry, Warsaw, Poland, 1948-61; asst. Tech. U., Warsaw, Poland, 1949-65, asst. prof., 1965-71, prof., 1971-92; vice chmn. Com. Analytical Chemistry, Warsaw, Poland, 1980-89; dean Faculty Chemistry Tech. U., Warsaw, Poland, 1982-83. Author: Spectrophotometric Determination of Elements, 1976, Separation and Spectrophotometric Determination of Elements, 1986, Dictionary of Analytical Reagents, 1993, Encyclopedia of Analytical Science, 1995, Spectrochemical Trace Analysis for Metals and Metalloids, 1996, Separation, Preconcentration and Spectrophotography in Inorganic Analysis, 2000; contbr. articles to profl. jours. Home: ul Korsykanska 7-48, 02-761 Warsaw Poland Office: ul Noakowskiego 3, pl00-664 Warsaw Poland

ZYKOV, BORIS GEORGIEVICH, physicist, researcher; b. Ufa, USSR, Nov. 26, 1949; s. Georgy Konstatinovich and Tamara Tihohovna (Gorbachova) Z.; m. Ludmila Mihailovna Holueva, Dec. 7, 1979; 2 children. Higher edn., Bashkirian U., Ufa, USSR, 1972; Diploma of Candidate of Ph. Mat. Scis., St. Petersburg U., 1986. Jr. rsch. worker Inst. Chemistry, Ufa, USSR, 1974-80; rsch. worker Dept. Physics, Ufa, 1980-86; sr. rsch. worker Dept. Physics, Ufa, Russia, 1986-92; head lab. Inst. Phys. Molecular and Crystals, Ufa, 1992—. Contbr. articles to profl. jours. Capt. Ministry Def. USSR, 1972-74. Grantee Russian Fund Fundamental Investigations, 1996-97. Mem. Internat. EPR (ESR) Soc., Ill. EPR Rsch. Ctr. (U. Ill.). Russian Orthodox. Avocations: sports, games. Home: Prospekt Oktybrya 63/5-36, 450083 Ufa Russia Office: Russian Acad Scis, Prospekt Oktybrya 147, 450065 Ufa Russia

ZYLICZ, TOMASZ, economics educator; b. Lublin, Poland, Sept. 22, 1951; s. Marek Roger and Teresa Maria (Zmigrodzka) Z.; m. Barbara Stankiewicz, Jan. 17, 1976; children: Anna, Marta. MA in Econs., Warsaw (Poland) U., 1974, MA in Math., 1977, PhD in Econs., 1979. Asst. and lectr. Warsaw U., 1974-88; Fulbright vis. fellow U. Colo., Boulder, 1988-89; dir. econs. Ministry of Environment, Poland, 1989-91; prof. Warsaw U., 1991—, chair microecons., 1995—; Valfrid Paulsson prof. Royal Swedish Acad. Sci., Stockholm, 1992-93; dir. Warsaw Ecol. Econs. Ctr., 1993—; project assoc. Harvard U., Cambridge, Mass., 1995-98; mem. Green Forum European Commn., Brussels, 1997—. Author: Lectures on Differential and Difference Equations, 1987, Costing Nature in a Transition Economy. Case Studies in Poland, 2000; editor: Markets and Prices in a Sustainable Society, 1997; contbr. articles to profl. jours. Pew scholar in conservation and the environment, 1993. Mem. European Assn. Environ. and Resource Economists. Roman Catholic. Avocations: classical music, hiking, skiing. Office: Warsaw Ecol Econs Ctr, 44-50 Długa St, 00-241 Warsaw Poland

ZYTKO, KAZIMIERZ SIGISMUND, geologist, researcher; b. Niewachlow, Poland, Apr. 29, 1930; s. Stephen and Sophia (Szrek) Z. Student, Jagiellonian Univ., Cracow, Poland, 1952; D, Inst. Geology, Warsaw, 1969; habilitation, Jagiellonian Univ., 1982. Asst. State Geological Inst., Cracow, Poland, 1952-62, divsn. chief, 1962-64, 68-86; editor of maps State Geological Inst., Krakow, Poland, 1962-67, 78-94, project mgr., 1962—; cons. State Geological Svc., Warsaw, 1969—; commn. chief Carpatho-Balkan Geological Assn., 1965-89. Contbr. articles to profl. jours. Mem. Soc. Geologorum Poloniae. Office: State Geological Inst, Skrzatow 1, 31-560 Cracow Poland

ZYUGANOV, ALEXANDER NICKOLAEVICH, physicist; b. Orel, Russia, Oct. 3, 1940; arrived in Germany, 1991; s. Nickolai Georgievich and Natalie Georgievna Surzova; m. Tamara Michailovna Liebman, May 5, 1965; 1 child, Victor. Diploma in physics, Kiev (Ukraine) State U., 1962; D of Tech. Scis., Acad. Scis., Kiev, 1968, prof. dr. math. and physics (hon.), 1984. From engr. to leading engr. Inst. Semicondrs. Acad. Scis., Kiev, 1962-65, leading rsch. worker Inst. Semicondrs., 1970-86, vice-chief optoelectronic dept. Inst. Semicondrs., 1986-91; sci. cooperator Max-Planck-Inst., Heidelberg, Germany, 1993—; dir. dissertations on phys.-math. scis. Inst. Semicondrs., Acad. Scis., Kiev, 1973, 77, 81, 90. Co-author: (monographs) Photopotentiometers, 1970, Injection-contact Phenomena in Semiconductors, 1981; contbr. numerous sci. articles to profl. jours.; inventor in field. Recipient State Prize of Ukraine for inventions in sci. and tech. Coun. of Mins. of Ukraine, 1973. Avocations: music, literature, sports. Home: Römerstrasse 60A, 69115 Heidelberg Germany Office: Max-Planck-Inst Med Forsch, Jahnstr 29, D-69120 Heidelberg Germany

ZYWIETZ, MARTIN MICHAEL, physician; b. Dorsten, Germany, Mar. 18, 1954; s. Erwin and Margarete (Hauske) Z.; m. Cornelia Broéschen-Zywietz, Sept. 3, 1976 (div. 1993); children: Daniel, Miriam, Jenny; m. Lizzie Rolon Roth, Aug. 5, 1994; children: Paula, Jose Miguel, Laüra. MD, U. Bonn, Germany, 1979. Physician Univ. Hosp., Bonn, 1978-85; pvt. practice Bonn, 1986—. Co-author: Echocardiography, 1984. Active Internat. Physicians for Prevention Nuc. War, 1983—. Capt., flight surgeon German Army, 1993-94. Evangelist. Avocations: music, piano, keyboards. Home: Auf Dem Steinchen 1, 53127 Bonn Germany Office: Auf Dem Steinchen 3, 53127 Bonn Germany

Professional Index

AGRICULTURE

Ahmed, Sheikh Sarfuddin plant breeder
Akingbade, Adebayo Abel agricultural studies educator, nutritionist
Alarcon Vera, Antonio Luis agricultural educator, counselor, researcher
Aleixo da Silva, José A. forestry educator, researcher
Amir, Jonathan agriculture educator
Antoun, Gamal George agricultural researcher
Arya, Roshan Lal agricultural researcher
Asante-Wiafe, Isaac farming director
Bálint, Andor agricultural studies educator emeritus
Balnave, Derick agricultural studies educator
Bawden, Richard John agricultural studies educator
Bennett, John Charles farmer, former engineering-construction executive
Bergquist, Gene Alfred farmer, rancher, county commissioner
Blakers, Kenneth Roger farmer, former military officer
Boussard, Jean-Marc research director
Bull, Kenneth Winson retired rancher
Burmeister, Paul Frederick farmer
Burnett, Raymund Carmi retired rancher, agricultural researcher
Callahan, James Robert retired agricultural products administrator
Campbell, John Stephen agricultural consultant
Cannon, David C. aquaculture company executive, mechanical engineer
Cattier, Jean Jacques champagne and wine company executive
Charley, Robert Clive agricultural products company executive
Chen, Lan Zhuang agricultural studies educator
Cox, Berry Gordon rancher
Crescimanno, Giuseppina Maria Giulia agricultural studies educator
Creswell, John Lewis agricultural studies educator
de Mouchy, Duchesse vineyard executive
Diab, Kamel Tawfik agricultural products company executive
Dimitrijevic, Momcilo Dusan agriculture educator, researcher
Dohy, János agricultural studies educator
Doku, Emmanuel Victor crop scientist, educator
Eler, Joanir Pereira animal breeding educator, researcher, consultant
El Soda, Morsi Abou El Seoud agricultural studies educator
Farkas, István agricultural studies educator
Fischer, Eugene Randolph farmer
Frazer, Stuart Harrison, III cotton merchant
Gates, Ronald Cecil retired beef cattle breeder
Gilboa, David agricultural economist, consultant
Govindasamy Dasamy, Ramu marketing educator, assistant professor
Gregg, Billy Ray seed industry executive, consultant
Gregg, Marie Byrd retired farmer
Gregson, Anthony Knight farmer
Hicks, Peter Alastair agroindustry specialist
Hillman, John Richard agricultural and biotechnological studies educator, researcher
Hodgson, John agricultural educator
Hutton, Angus Finlay cattle breeder, consultant
Isirimah, Nnaemaka Ogu agricultural studies educator
Ismail, Saad Mohamed agricultural studies educator
Jadhav, Jayawant Dadaji agro-meteorology educator
Kadiata, Bakach Dikand agriculture educator
Karamanos, Andreas J. agriculture educator, agronomist
Kobliha, Jaroslav tree breeder, educator
Koshibe, Heihachiro agricultural company executive
Kozák, János agriculture educator, researcher
Lee, Yong-Hwan agricultural biology educator
Leiby, Robert E. county agricultural agent
Li, Rongbai agricultural studies educator, researcher
Lindteigen, Susanna rancher, state official
Loskutov, Igor Gradislavovich agricultural industry executive
Mapel, Patricia Jolene farmer, consultant
Martinez-de-toda, Fernando agricultural studies educator
Martynenko, Alexey Ivanovich agricultural executive
Matras, Jan Wiesław agriculture educator
McDonald, Angus Wheeler farmer
Messing, Sten Ingmar agricultural studies educator
Mouazen, Abdul Mounem agricultural studies educator
Mulley, Robert Claude agricultural studies educator, researcher
O'Brien, (Michael) Vincent horse trainer, owner, breeder
Orpen, Michael Gerald farmer
Papantonis, Antony wine company executive
Paul, Catherine J. Morrison agricultural educator
Pavlin, Zdenko forestry educator, researcher
Pelekassis, Constantine Eustathius retired agricultural educator
Petty, Scott, Jr. rancher
Powles, Stephen Bruce agricultural educator, researcher
Prajapati, Jashbhai B. dairy microbiologist
Ram, Hari Har vegetable breeder, researcher, educator
Rankin, Helen Cross cattle rancher, guest ranch executive
Roberts, Eric Hywel retired agriculture educator
Rostad, Lee B. rancher, writer
Scatena, Lorraine Borba rancher, women's rights advocate
Schilling, Günther agricultural chemistry educator
Sechman, Andrzej agricultural studies educator
Serlachius, Gustaf Fredrik forest industry company executive
Shauman, Wendell L. farmer
Shaw, James Derek farmer, agribusiness company executive
Simmons, Carl Kenneth cooperative executive
Smith, Michael Allen rangeland management educator
Smith, William Raymond farmer, thoroughbred owner, breeder and trainer, retired history educator, philosophy educator
Sokolov, Pjotr Alexejevitch agricultural studies educator
Sood, Kamal Kishor forestry educator
Stanley, Marlyse Reed horse breeder
Steelhammer, Page Miller dairy farmer
Stella, Clara agricultural educator, researcher
Streibig, Jens Carl agricultural studies educator
Takahashi, Tadashi agricultural studies educator
Tolera, Adugna agricultural studies educator, researcher
Upton, Martin agriculture educator
Weaver, Peggy (Marguerite McKinnie Weaver) plantation owner
Wollpert, Sandra Cox horse breeder
Xu, Shizhong agricultural educator
Yang, Xin-Mei mycology educator, phytopathology researcher
Yonekawa, Satoshi agricultural engineering and agro-biology educator
Yoshizawa, Kiyoshi agricultural studies educator
Zelenka, Jiří agricultural educator
Ziemele, Vita agricultural company executive

ARCHITECTURE AND DESIGN

Abram, Joseph architect, painter
Abramovitz, Max architect
Agnew, Kenneth Malcolm design educator
Ahmad, Adil Mustafa architect, educator
Ahmad, Nazar Othman architect, urban planner, consultant
Ahrens, William Henry architect
Akkor, Gundogdu hospital architect, architectural and engineering services executive
Anderson, Paul Scott architect
Ando, Tadao architect
Ankrom, Charles Franklin golf course architect, consultant
Antony, Jeff architect
Arango, Jorge Sanin architect
Archer, Richard Earl product designer, alternative energy design consultant
Ardalan, Nader architect
Armistead, Katherine Kelly (Mrs. Thomas B. Armistead, III) interior designer, travel consultant, civic worker
Arrigone, Jorge Luis architect, housing and development consultant
Ashihara, Yoshinobu architect, educator
Ataman, Orol Sadrettin consultancy firm executive
Aung-Khin, Cherie antique dealer, designer, owner
Aybar, Fehmi architect, real estate developer
Azuma, Takamitsu architect, educator
Badgley, John Roy architect
Baggs, Sydney Allison architect, educator, environmental impact consultant
Balcells, Santiago Gorina architect
Banerjee, Arup Kumar landscaping and agro-chemical consultant
Barrie, Thomas architecture educator, architect, writer
Beckett, Martyn Gervase architect, artist
Beckmann, John architect, designer, writer
Bedoire, Fredric Kurt architectural history educator and researcher
Beeby, Thomas H. architect
Benedetti, Sandro architect
Bereder, Frédéric Laurent architect
Bergholm, Ernst Tauno Herman (Baron of Amida) architect, company director, author
Bernard, Bess Mary interior designer, consultant
Beusan, Mario architect, educator
Bextermiller, Theresa Marie Louise architect, computer graphics
Björkman, Anders B. naval architect
Blanton, John Arthur architect
Bobic, Milos architect
Bonutti, Alexander Carl architect, urban designer
Borrelli, John Francis architect
Botsai, Elmer Eugene architect, educator, former university dean
Bowen, Richard Lee architect
Boyer, Lester Leroy, Jr. architecture educator, consultant
Bradley, Charles MacArthur architect
Bredholt, Sverre architect
Brems, David Paul architect
Broadbent, Geoffrey Haigh architecture educator
Brown, Denise Scott architect, urban planner
Brown, Shirley Margaret Kern (Peggy Brown) interior designer
Buckley, Richard George architect, educator
Budaev, Vladimir Michailovich architect, designer
Buranakarn, Vira architect
Burggraf, Frank Bernard, Jr. landscape architect, retired educator
Bustamante, Acona Manuel architect, consultant
Buszko, Henryk Bronisław architect
Caivano, Jose Luis architect
Callmeyer, Ferenc architect
Candia, Rene Contreras architecture educator
Canepa, Giacomo Giovannini architect
Case, Gerard Ramon drafting technologist, paleontologist
Caston, Philip Stewart Charles architect, researcher, educator
Catroux, Francois Philippe interior designer
Celentano, Linda industrial designer
Cengizkan, Ali architectural design educator
Cernosek, Kitty interior decorator
Chang, Te Lin architect
Chang, Walter Tuck, Sr. drafting and autoCAD educator, real estate agent, national defense instructor
Chao, James Min-Tzu architect
Chatterjee, Ashok Kumar naval architect
Chevalier, Barbara Lansburgh interior designer
Cho, Kyunam marine architect and engineer, educator
Claassen, Wynand architect, editor
Coffin, Robert Parker architect, engineer
Cooke, R(ichard) Caswell, Jr. architect
Correa, Charles M. architect
Costa, Xavier architect, curator
Cowles, Walter Curtis naval architect
Curl, James Stevens (E. B. Keeling; Adytum) architect, educator, writer
Czerner, Olgierd Władysław architect, educator
Dahinden, Justus architect
Daum, Johannes Peter architecture educator
Dean, Robert Bruce architect
Dementis, Katharine Hopkins retired interior designer
Demerly, Mark architect
Dick, Neil Alan architecture executive
Diebel, Gary R. architect
DiLorenzo, Sharon Hiestand architect, real estate professional
Divakarla, Shailaja ecological architect, researcher
Diwakar, Deepti architect, dancer
Dobbelmann, Reinier Petrus Hubertus Maria windsurf design company executive, naval architect
Dobrin, Sheldon L. architect
Dokmeci, Vedia architect, educator
Dowd, Michael Burke architect
Dranger, Jan industrial designer
Droege, Peter F. designer, planner, educator
Duda, Richard Frank architect, engineering executive
Dumont, Edward Abdo architect, interior designer
Eddison, John F. P. naval architect
Edwards, F. (Frederick) Gary architect, health facility planner
Ehsan, Noushin architect
Elkins, Steven Paul architect
Ellis, James Jolly landscape resort official
End, Henry interior and industrial designer
Engel, Jürgen Josef Karl architect
Erickson, Arthur Charles architect
Erktin, Ayse Hasol architect
Fainsilber, Adrien architect
Fatouros, Dimitris architect
Ferrell, Gene Hilliard architect
Ferrin, Allan Hogate architect
Ferris, Roger Patrick architect
Field, Hermann Haviland architect, educator, author
Firehock, Barbara A. interior designer
Flansburgh, Earl Robert architect
Flint, Stephen Ernest architect
Flom, Robert Michael interior designer
Forbes, Peter architect
Fowler, Charles Allison Eugene retired architect, engineer
Fowler, George Selton, Jr. architect
Frank, Hartmut Friedrich Gustav architect
Frescura, Franco architect
Friedman, Yona architect
Fry, Louis Edwin, Jr. architect
Fuller, Robert Kenneth architect, urban designer
Fung, Stanislaus architecture educator
Garcia-Salgado, Tomas architect
Gardner, Donald Angus architect
Gehry, Frank Owen architect
Gibson, James Elliott architect
Gold, Allan Harold architect, structural engineer, educator
Goodman, Marvin David architect
Goodwin, Marcy architectural planner, consultant
Gorostiza López, Jorge architect
Gosling, David architect, urban design educator
Grandin, Temple industrial designer, science educator
Gregor, James Andrew architect
Grotta, Sandra Brown interior designer
Guggenheimer, Tobias Immanuel Simon architect
Guida, Harold Seymour architect
Gürçinar, Yusuf architect, educator
Haak, Alex Johan Henri architect, educator
Hadjipateras, Dimitris Constantine naval architect, marine consultant
Haenlein, Hans architect, educator
Hammer, Charles John cabinetmaker, architectural draftsman, designer
Harrington-Lloyd, Jeanne Leigh interior designer
Harter, Georges architect, urban planning consultant
Hayashi, Yoshihiro architect
Heine, Achim industrial designer, educator
Hertzberger, Herman architect, educator
Heynen, Hilde Maria architecture educator
Holt, Philetus Havens, III architect
Holzer, Richard architect, educator, consultant
Hopfer, Andrzej Jerzy surveying educator
Horiguchi, Toyota environmental design educator
Hower, Jeanne Louise landscape designer
Hoyt, Earl Edward, Jr. industrial designer
Huffman, Donna Lou interior designer
Hui, Desmond Cheuk-Kuen architecture educator
Hyderabadi-(Alikhan), Akbar retired architect, poet
Hyland, Anthony David Charles architecture educator
Ide, Hisato landscape architect
Imatake, Midori industrial design company executive
Jackson, Jane W. interior designer
Johnson, Charles Foreman architect, architectural photographer, planning architecture and system engineering consultant
Jones, Richard Wallace interior designer
Jorge, Nuno Maria Roque architect
Juvanec, Borut architecture educator, researcher
Kang, Jian architectural acoustician
Karlemo, Rolf Waldemar naval architect, consultant
Karyono, Tri Harso architect, researcher, educator
Kattan, Mohd Imad architect
Kenney, John Michel architect
Kephart, Larry Robert architect
Kido, Ewa Maria architect, consultant
Kienast, Hermann Josef architect, archaeologist
Kim, Jong-Kyu architect, educator
Kim, Won architect
Kinnear, John Kenyon, Jr. architect
Kobylanski, Pawel M. architect
Kobza, Dennis Jerome architect
Korpys, Konrad Karol industrial designer, educator
Kraft, Donald Eugene architecture and engineering company executive
Kuenzle, Robert Creed industrialist, architect
Kwik, King Han naval architect, researcher
Lasdun, Denys Louis architect
Lawrence, Roderick John architect, social science educator, researcher, consultant
Leavitt, David Livingstone architect
Lederer, Paul Edward landscape architect
Lee, Betty Redding architect
Leedy, Gene Robert architect
Li, Xiao dong architect, educator
Light, Pamela Delamaide interior designer
Little, R. Donald architect, administrator
Lopez, Remi architect
Lowe, Douglas Howard architect
Luckner, Herman Richard, III interior designer
Lugo, Octavio A. architect, executive
Mack, Alan Wayne interior designer
Mair, Bruce Logan interior designer, company executive
Marder, Abram Pavlovich architect, researcher, educator
Mathes, Edward Conrad architect
McCranor, Laurie S. residential designer
McKean, John Maule architecture educator, historian, critic
Meric, Rene Pierre, Jr. shipbuilding marine construction executive
Minar, Paul G. design consultant
Minkoff, Alice Sydney interior designer, showroom owner
Misu, Kunihiro planner, architect, engineer
Mitchell, Joseph Patrick architect
Mock, Robert Claude architect
Moe, Stanley Allen architect, consultant
Moffett, Frank Cardwell architect, civil engineer, real estate developer
Moggridge, Harry Traherne landscape architect
Moore, Sandy architect, environmental designer, urban strategist
Morey, Jeri Lynn Snyder architect
Morris, Calvin Curtis architect
Morrison, Murdo Donald architect
Mujica, Mauro E. architect
Munson, Virginia Aldrich interior designer, decorator
Murrelle, Ronald Kemp architectural firm executive
Murtiyoso, Sutrisno architect
Nary, John Henry interior designer
Navarro, Casas Jaime architect, educator
Nemcsics, Antal Károly architect, artist, educator
Nicolas, Marina Savvidou architect
Nohl, Werner landscape architect, researcher
Nomura, Kaneo architect
Nordin, Holger Zacharias naval architect
Nordling, Carl Olof architect, urban planner, retired, researcher
Obiora, Chris Sunny architect
Oelberg, Robert Nathan landscape architect
Ohsaki, Makoto architecture educator
Olsen, Donald Emmanuel architect, educator
Omholt, Bruce Donald product designer, mechanical engineer, consultant
Oommen, George architect, painter
Opie, Simon Andrew Robert lighting designer, mathematician, project manager
Ornstein, Sheila Walbe architect, educator
O'Toole, Shane architect, critic
Ottolenghi, Marinella architectural educator
Paik, Jeom Kee marine architect
Palermo, Robert James architect, consultant, inventor
Pallasmaa, Juhani Uolevi architect, educator
Pei, Ieoh Ming architect
Pelli, Cesar architect
Peppiatt, Nicholas Anthony product designer
Peters, Ralph Edgar architectural and engineering executive
Pfanstiel Parr, Dorothea Ann interior designer
Phipps, Lynne Bryan interior architect, clergywoman, educator
Pirkl, James Joseph industrial designer, educator, writer
Potente, Eugene, Jr. interior designer
Powell, Sir (Arnold Joseph) Philip architect
Pradhan, Kishore Dwarkanath landscape architect, consultant
Prosser, John Martin architect, educator, urban design consultant
Ptitchnikova, Galina Alexandrovna architect, educator, researcher
Puchkov, Andrew Alexander architecture educator, writer
Rahman, Shahid architect
Rallo, Harry architect, artist
Ramirez, Martin Ruben architect, engineer, educator, cognitive scientist, consultant
Ramirez-Portilla, Carlos Alfonso architect
Rams, Dieter industrial designer, architect
Rane, Ulhas architect, educator
Robertson, Donna Virginia architect, educator, dean
Roche, Kevin (Eamonn Roche) architect
Rogers, Kate Ellen interior design educator
Rosenlund, Hans Lennart architect
Ross, Terence William architect
Roth, Harold architect
Ruemler, Ruprecht Ernst landscape architect, educator
Scherer, József industrial designer, educator
Schiffner, Charles Robert architect
Schmeidler, Karel Robert architect, sociologist
Seehausen, Richard Ferdinand architect
Serraglio, Mario architect

Setzekorn, William David *retired architect, consultant, author*
Shonk, Scott Lamar *architect, educator*
Simon, Katalin Edith *interior architect, designer artist*
Siren, Heikki *architect, educator*
Siren, Kaija Anna-Maija Helena *architect*
Skoler, Louis *architect, educator*
Smithson, Peter Denham *architect*
Sorey, Thomas Lester, Jr. *architect, educator*
Springer, Floyd Ladean *architect*
Stahlschmidt, Per *landscape architect, educator*
Stanley, Duffy B. *architect*
Steel, Philip S. *architect, artist*
Steinmann, John Colburn *architect*
Steneroth, Erik Robert *naval architectural studies educator*
Stenros, Anne Kaarina *architect*
Stephens, Jeffrey Garett *architectural and construction management executive*
Stockenberg, Bo Peter *architect*
Stricker, Jack Maurice *architect, designer*
Sugawara, Michio *architectural company executive*
Sumers, Rebecca Ann *interior designer*
Sutter, Madeline Ann *landscape architect*
Szyszkowski, Antoni Walenty *architect*
Tabb, Phillip James *architect, educator, director, consultant*
Tachi, Douglas Paul *architect, interior designer*
Tadokoro, Teruo *interior design firm executive, architect*
Taipale, Kaarin Hanna Irene *architect*
Tarpgaard, Peter Thorvald *naval architect*
Tatai, Mária *architectural firm executive*
Taylor, Bruce Stevenson *architect, planner*
Tedin, Delia Marie *interior decorator*
Teixeira-Leite, Manuel Adalberto Leonardo *architect, consultant*
Tengbom, Anders *architect*
Teodorescu, George *industrial designer, educator, consultant*
Teramoto, Tetsu Satoshi *architect*
Terp, Dana George *architect*
Thalden, Barry R. *architect*
Thimian, Horst Julius *architect, engineer, researcher*
Tibbalds, Francis Eric *architect*
Toš, Igor Pegan *architect*
Traung, Jan-Olof *naval architect*
Trudnak, Stephen Joseph *landscape architect*
Turner, Peter John *naval architect, marine engineer*
Turtola, Risto Pekka *architect*
Unikel, Eva Taylor *interior designer*
Vago, Pierre *architect*
Vámossy, Ferenc *architecture educator, art critic, editor*
Van Arsdel, Thomas Paul *architect, engineering consultant*
Vandiver, Renee Lillian Aubry *interior designer, architectural preservator*
Van Geyt, Henri Louis *architect*
Venet, Claude Henry *architect, acoustic engineer*
von Klein, Michael Hans Ullrich *industrial designer*
von Seidlein, Peter C. *architect*
Voorsanger, Bartholomew *architect*
Voss, Werner Konrad Karl *architect, engineer*
Vries, Gerrit de *architect, consultant, educator*
Walden, Henry Russell *architect, educator*
Walton, Conrad Gordon, Sr. *architect*
Warburton, Ralph Joseph *architect, engineer, planner, educator*
Waters, Terrance J *architect*
Watney, Lynne Mountford *interior designer*
Webb, Lamar Thaxter *architect*
Weber, John Bertram *architect*
Wehdorn, Manfred *architect, educator*
Weill, Michael *architect*
Welling, Helen Geertruida *architecture educator*
Wenzler, Edward William *architect*
Wheatley, William Arthur *architect, musician*
Whitehead, Paul Felton *landscape consultant*
Wiberg, Krister Nils Gunnar *architect, educator, dean*
Wilkes, Delano Angus *architect*
Wilson, Blair Mansfield *architect*
Wilson, Peter *architect, civil engineer, management consultant*
Wolff, Arnold *architect, scholarly writer*
Wong, Lily Lim *interior design company executive, architect*
Woodman, Arthur Tullis *architect, consultant*
Woodring, Margaret Daley *architect, planner*
Ylinen, Jaakko Kristian *architect*
Zahran, Mohsen Moharram *architect, educator*
Zamora Patiño, Georgina *industrial designer, educator*
Zeigen, Spencer Steven *architect*
Zhu, Ling *naval architect, applied mechanics specialist*
Zivas, Dionysis *architecture educator, architect*
Zwick, Keith R. *landscape architect*

ARTS: LITERARY. *See also* COMMUNICATIONS MEDIA.

Aari, Jamiluddin *writer*
Abdulsalam, Rukaiyah Hill *writer*
Abramovitz, Anita Zeltner Brooks (Mrs. Max Abramovitz) *writer*
Achebe, Chinua *writer, humanities educator*
Ackroyd, Peter *writer*
Adams, Douglas Noel *writer*
Adams, Richard George *writer*
Aiken, Joan (Delano) *author*
Albee, Edward Franklin *author, playwright*
Albertsen, Ken *writer, philosopher*
Albizurez, Francisco *writer, educator*
Alborough, Jez *children's book author*
Albright, Judith Anne *writer*
Alcock, Vivien (Dolores) *children's author*
Aldiss, Brian (Wilson) *writer*
Aldrich, Yvette M. *writer, educator*
Aliki, (Aliki Liacouras Brandenberg) *author, illustrator children's books*
Al-Kharrat, Edwar *writer*
Allaby, John Michael *writer*
Allen, Fergus Hamilton *writer, retired government official*
Allende, Isabel Angelica *writer*
Allsebrook, Mary Nesbit *writer, researcher*
Alméras, Philippe Charles *writer, educator*
Aloff, Mindy *writer*
Al-Qatam, Abdulla Abdali *Arabic poetry educator*
al-Sawahri, Khalil Hussein *writer, publishing executive*
Alvarez, A(lfred) *writer*
Alvarez Gardeazabal, Gustavo *writer*
Amalsad, Meher Dadabhoy *writer, speaker, seminar leader*
Ambers, Henry John *writer*
Amis, Martin Louis *author*
Ammann, Lillian Ann Nicholson *writer, small business owner*
Anderson, Patricia Sue *writer*
Angell, Lois Louise *writer, speaker, poet, comedian*
Angelou, Maya *writer*
Anker, Charlotte Miriam *playwright, educator*
Antoine, Jacques *author, consultant*
Anton, Barbara *writer*
Appiah, James Peter King *writer*
Ararat, Nisan *writer, lecturer, educator*
Archdeacon, Sarajane *writer, photographer*
Arden, John *playwright*
Arlen, Michael J. *writer*
Arnold Hubert, Nancy Kay *writer*
Arrabal, Fernando *writer*
Arrowsmith, Joseph Bernard *writer*
Asadov, Eduard Arkadevich *poet*
Ashdown, Marie Matranga (Mrs. Cecil Spanton Ashdown, Jr.) *writer, lecturer*
Aslanides, Timoshenko John *poet*
As-Salaam, Jamaal (William Louis Williams, Jr.) *poet, film producer, writer*
Atwood, Margaret Eleanor *writer*
Atwood, Mary Sanford *writer*
Aubry, Cecile (Anne-José Bernard) *writer*
Auchincloss, Louis Stanton *writer*
Auel, Jean Marie *writer*
Auguste Le Breton, (Montfort) *author*
Ault, Phillip Halliday *author, editor*
Avery, Stephen Neal *playwright, author*
Avrett, Roz (Rosalind Case) *writer, advertising creative director*
Awdry, Christopher Vere *author*
Ayckbourn, Sir Alan *playwright*
Bahr, Jane Marie *writer, retired English educator*
Bailey, George Theodore *writer, liaison officer*
Bailey, William Waddell *writer, communications executive*
Bainbridge, Beryl *author*
Bajetta, Carlo Maria *literary scholar, educator, translator*
Baker, Mark Allen *author, historian, consultant, graphologist*
Baker, Mona *translator, educator*
Baklanov, Grigoriy Yakovlevich *writer*
Ball, Philip Charles *writer*
Bantelmann, Kurt C. *author*
Barba, Harry *author, educator, publisher*
Barfoot, Joan *writer, journalist*
Barker, Clive *artist, screenwriter, director, producer, writer*
Barker, Pat *writer*
Barnaby, Charles Frank *writer*
Barnett, Harold *writer*
Barnett, Ursula Annemarie *literary agent*
Barone, Rose Marie Pace *writer, retired educator, entertainer*
Barrett, Katherine *writer, multimedia producer*
Bartelski, Leslaw *writer*
Barth, John Simmons *writer, educator*
Barzun, Jacques *author, literary consultant*
Battle, Jean Allen *writer, educator*
Battles, Roxy Edith *novelist, consultant, educator*
Baumel, Joan Patricia French *educator, writer, lecturer*
Bawden, Nina (Mary) *author*
Bayley, Stephen *design consultant, author*
Beadel, Stephen Jay *author*
Beattie, Ann *writer*
Beatty, Grace Joely *author, consultant*
Beauchamp, Valdivia Vânia S. *translator*
Bedford, Sybille *writer*
Bekhor, Jamil Sion *writer*
Bell, Linda Gwenn *periodical and magazine writer*
Bellow, Saul C. *writer*
Belmonté, Kathryn (KiKi Belmonté) *writer, small business owner*
Benjamin, Ruth *writer*
Bennett, Velma Joyce (Joyce Williams) *writer, poet*
Benson, Judi Lamar *poet, magazine editor*
Bereczky, Erzsébet *literary advisor*
Berge, Hans Cornelis ten *author, poet*
Berger, John Peter *author, art critic*
Berger, Linda Fay *writer*
Berger, Thomas Louis *author*
Beusse, Jacqueline *writer, marketing company executive*
Bingham, Charlotte (Mary Therese) *writer*
Bingham, June *author, playwright*
Bitov, Andrei Georgevich *writer*
Black, Charlie J. *technical writer, author, educator, business consultant*
Black, David Luther *writer, consultant*
Blass, Elizabeth Victoria *writer, editor*
Blokh, Alexandre (Jean Blot) *writer*
Bly, Carol McLean *writer, educator*
Boersma, June Elaine (Jalma Barrett) *writer, photographer*
Borel, Jacques *writer*
Bortă, Elena *literary researcher*
Bottaccioli, Francesco *medical writer, journalist, consultant, educator*
Botti, John Lawrence *author*
Bouthillier, Russell Lee *writer*
Bowering, George Harry *writer, English literature educator*
Bowman, Raymond DeArmond, Sr. *writer, music critic*
Boyne, Walter James *writer, former museum director*
Bradbury, Sir Malcolm Stanley *scriptwriter, educator, author*
Bradford, Barbara Taylor *writer, journalist, novelist*
Bradley, James Michael *novelist*
Brady, Joan *writer*
Braman, Heather Ruth *technical writer, editor, consultant, antiques dealer*
Bredsdorff, Elias Lunn *writer*
Breslin, Mike Aloysius *writer, philosopher*
Breuer, Georg *writer, journalist, peace advocate*
Bringhurst, Robert *poet*
Brink, André Philippus *author, educator*
Brinkley, Shelia M. *poet*
Brissenden, Alan (Theo) *writer*
Bristow, Robert O'Neil *writer, educator*
Broadbent, J. Michael *wine writer, wine auctioneer*
Brooke, Tal (Robert Taliaferro) *writer*
Brookner, Anita *writer, educator*
Brooks, Gwendolyn *writer, poet*
Brophy, Kevin Thomas *writer*
Brown, James Franklin *political writer, consultant*
Brown, Kevin *writer*
Brown, Philip John *scientific author, publisher, computer consultant*
Brugioni, Dino Anthony *writer, lecturer, consultant*
Bruton, Eric Moore *author, publisher, diamond consultant*
Bryan, Felicity Anne *literary agent*
Bryant, John *author, publisher*
Buck, Pitman August, Jr. *writer*
Bucknell, Katherine *writer*
Budniakiewicz, Therese *writer*
Buehler, Evelyn Judy *poet*
Bullington, Gayle Rogers *writer, researcher*
Bunch, Richard Alan *writer, educator*
Burden, Jean (Prussing) *poet, writer, editor*
Burland, Brian Berkeley *novelist, poet, painter, scenarist*
Butcher, Russell Devereux *author, photographer*
Butler, David Dalrymple *screenwriter, actor*
Butler, Gwendoline Williams (Jennie Melville) *writer*
Butor, Michel *author, educator*
Buzo, Alexander John *writer*
Byfield, Bert A. *novelist*
Byron, Julie Anne *author*
Cabalquinto, Luis Carrazcal *freelance writer*
Cairnes, Margot Beresford *business writer, leadership expert*
Calder, Nigel David Ritchie *freelance writer*
Cameron, Lolita Ann *writer*
Camner, Howard *author, poet*
Campbell, Ramsey *writer*
Campos, Haroldo Eurico Browne de *poet, educator*
Campton, David *writer*
Camus, Michel *writer, poet, philosopher*
Capelle-Frank, Jacqueline Aimee *writer*
Carangelo, Lori *writer, publisher, social activist, not-for-profit executive*
Carew, Sir Rivers Verain *writer*
Carey, Ernestine Gilbreth (Mrs. Charles E. Carey) *writer, lecturer*
Carey, Peter Philip *novelist*
Carlson, Dale Bick *writer*
Carner, Charles Robert, Jr. *screenwriter, director*
Carpenter, Betty O. *writer*
Casas, Walter Mario de las *writer*
Cavarnos, Constantine Peter *writer, philosopher*
Cejpek, Jiří *art educator*
Cela, Camilo José *author*
Chandler, Juliette Anne *writer, communications executive*
Cheiten, Marvin Harold *writer, hardware manufacturing company executive*
Chopra, Deepak *writer*
Cicellis, Kay *novelist, translator, short story writer*
Civasaqui, Jose (Sosuke Shibasaki) *poet*
Clark, Fred *legal writer, editor*
Clarke, Sir Arthur Charles *author*
Clarke, George Elliott *writer*
Clarke, (Mary) Patricia *writer, editor, journalist*
Clavel, Bernard Charles Henri *writer*
Cleese, John Marwood *writer, businessman, comedian*
Cline, Charles William *poet, pianist, rhetoric and literature educator*
Clod, Bente *scriptwriter, screenwriter, educator, consultant*
Codnia, Juan Pablo *writer, teacher, technician*
Cohen, Leonard (Norman Cohen) *poet, novelist, musician, songwriter*
Cohen, Steven Arthur *writer*
Cohn, Linkie Seltzer *professional speaker, author*
Coil, Suzanne Magdalena *writer, artist*
Coleman, Wanda *poet, writer*
Colquhoun, Keith *writer*
Compagnon, Jean George Andre *writer*
Compton, Jennifer Lee *writer*
Connelly, Mark *writer, educator*
Conroy, Richard Timothy *writer, retired foreign service officer*
Cook, Robin *author*
Cooke, Chantelle Anne *writer*
Cooney, Patrick Louis *writer*
Cooper, Julia Clare *medical writer executive*
Cornish, Linda Sowa Young *children's books writer and illustrator, educator*
Cortright, Barbara Jean *writer*
Coste, Marion Louise *author, educational consultant*
Cousineau, Philip Robert *writer, filmmaker*
Cox, Clarice Robinson *writer*
Craig, Roy Phillip *writer, educator, rancher*
Cramer, Esther Ridgway *author, historian, retired supermarket executive*
Cresswell, Helen *children's writer*
Crichton, Michael (John Crichton) *author, film director*
Criqui, Fernand *scientific writer*
Cron, Theodore Oscar *writer, editor, educator*
Crossley-Holland, Kevin (John William) *poet, children's writer*
Crow, John Armstrong *writer, educator*
Cullen, Paula Bramsen *author*
Cummings, James William *poet*
Cupstid, Robert Jack, Jr. *writer*
Curry, Mary Earle Lowry *poet*
Dallemagne-Cookson, Elise Camille *writer*
Darke, Marjorie (Sheila) *writer*
Darr, Ann Russell *poet, educator*
David, Joseph Raymond, Jr. *writer, periodical editor*
Davidson, Mark *writer, educator*
Davis, Clayton *writer, pilot*
Day, Richard Somers *author, editorial consultant*
de Bourbon Busset, Jacques *writer, author*
De Cuyper, Frank Roger Florimond *translator, writer*
de Hartog, Jan *writer*
Deighton, Len *author*
Delgado, Ramon Louis *educator, author, director, playwright, lyricist*
Delibes, Miguel (Miguel Delibes Setien) *author*
Demas, Sophia Patty *poet, former secondary education educator*
DeMille, Nelson Richard *writer*
Dempster, Barry (Edward) *writer, poet*
Denker, Henry *playwright, author, director*
Denny, Richard William Geoffrey *writer, lecturer*
Derchin, Dary Bret Ingham *writer*
de Saint Phalle, Therese *author*
DeSmith, David W. *writer*
Detering, Heinrich *literary critic*
Deutch, Richard Michael *writer, poet*
Devlin, Wende Dorothy *writer, artist*
Dewlen, Alton LeRoy (Al Dewlen) *writer*
Didion, Joan *writer*
Dixon, Dougal *writer*
Dowdy, Homer Earl *writer, retired philanthropic foundation executive*
Doyle, Will Lee *writer, editor*
Drabble, Margaret *writer*
Drucker, Peter Ferdinand *writer, consultant, educator*
Dryansky, Gerald Y. *writer, editor, film producer, screenwriter*
Dunn, John Clinton *writer, editor, organization executive*
Durant, Penny Lynne Raife *writer, speaker, educator*
Duyck, Kathleen Marie *poet, musician, retired social worker*
East, Brenda Kathleen *writer*
Edwards, Michael Aubrey *writer, foundation executive*
Egleton, Clive (Frederick) (John Tarrant) *writer*
Eikenberry, Arthur Raymond *writer, service executive, researcher*
Elgin, Duane *writer, activist*
Elleström, Lars *comparative literature educator, critic*
Ephron, Nora *writer, director*
Esterházy, Peter *author*
Fader, Shirley Sloan *writer*
Fallaci, Oriana *writer, journalist*
Fallon, Peter *poet, editor, publisher*
Fammerée, Richard Arthur *poet, composer, performing artist*
Fehrenbach, T(heodore) R(eed) *author, businessman*
Fenton, Alexander *writer*
Ferrell, Paul Cleveland *writer*
Field, Amanda Katherine *writer, editor*
Fisher, Alan Hall *guidebook writer*
Fitzgerald, Gerald *writer, director, actor*
Fitzgerald, Tim K. *writer, political organizer*
Flagg, Helen Clawson *writer*
Fleming, Alice Carew Mulcahey (Mrs. Thomas J. Fleming) *writer*
Fleming, Marjorie Foster *freelance writer, artist*
Fleutry, Michel *technical translator*
Flink, Stanley Edgar *writer, public affairs consultant*
Fo, Dario *playwright*
Follett, Kenneth Martin *author*
Ford, Peter Fletcher *writer*
Foss, John Houston *writer, consultant, educator*
Fowles, John *author*
Francis, Dick (Richard Stanley Francis) *novelist*
Frankel, Jennie Louise *writer*
Fraser, Gordon Murray *science writer*
Fratti, Mario *playwright, educator*
Free, Ann Cottrell *writer*
Friedmann, Patricia Ann *writer*
Friel, Brian (Bernard Patrick Friel) *author*
Friesz, Mary Lee *poet*
Frost, Sir David (Paradine) *author, producer, columnist*
Frost, Helen Marie *writer*
Fry, Christopher *playwright*
Fuentes, Carlos *writer, former ambassador*
Fulder, Stephen John *author, educator*
Fuller, John (Leopold) *poet*
Furley, Peter A. *university educator, researcher*
Gallagher, Kevin Michael *writer, lyricist*
Gallant, Mavis *author*
Gallimore, Margaret Martin *poet*
Gallup, Donald Clifford *bibliographer, educator*
Gao, Xingjian *writer*
Garcia, Cristina *writer*
García Márquez, Gabriel José *author*
Garner, Fradley Hamilton *writer, editor, narrator*
Garrison-Finderup, Ivadelle Dalton *writer*
Gelb, Norman *writer*
Geller, Bunny Zelda *poet, author, publisher, sculptor, artist*
Gersoni-Edelman, Diane Claire *author, editor*
Gertis, Neill Allan *writer*
Gibson, Morgan *writer, educator*
Gifford, Heidi *writer, editor*
Gilbert, Marie Rogers *poet*
Gillan, Garth Jackson *writer, former educator*
Gillett, Grover *author*
Girling, John (Lawrence Scott) *writer*
Glazier, Lyle *writer, educator*
Goldman, William *writer*
Good-Black, Edith Elissa (Pearl Williams) *writer*
Goodman, Jeffrey Allan *poet, educator*
Gordimer, Nadine *author*
Goss, William Allan *author, speaker*
Gould, Lilian *writer*
Grady, Sean Michael *writer*
Grass, Günter (Wilhelm) *writer*
Graves, Richard Perceval *author*
Gray, Simon James Holliday *writer, educator*
Green, Phyllis Hartman *writer, playwright*
Greenblatt, Miriam *writer, editor, educator*
Griffiths, Josephine Ivy *writer*
Griffiths, Trevor *playwright*
Grisham, John *writer*
Gross, Michael Robert *writer, editor*
Grove, Noel Randall *writer*
Grzanka, Leonard Gerald *writer, consultant*
Gunn, S. Jeanne *writer, natural healer*
Gustafsson, Lars Erik Einar *writer, educator*
Guy, Eleanor Bryenton *writer*
Hacks, Peter *playwright*
Hadley, Leila Eliott-Burton (Mrs. Henry Luce, III) *writer*
Hagar, Audrey Spilker *playwright*
Hailey, Arthur *author*
Haines, Robert Emmett *technical writer, vocational educator*
Hakim, Seymour (Sy Hakim) *writer, artist, retired secondary education educator*
Hallengren, Anders *writer, historian*
Hamit, Francis Granger *freelance writer*
Hamlin, George L. *technical writer*
Hamlyn-Harris, Geoffrey *writer, publisher*
Hampton, Christopher James *writer*
Hanes, Frank Borden *author, farmer, former business executive*
Hare, David *playwright*
Harrell, Margaret Ann *writer, editor, dream researcher, photographer*
Harvey, Diana Karanikas *writer*
Harvey, Ronald K. *writer, researcher*
Hastings, John Jacob *writer, lyricist, consultant, activist*
Hawkins, John *writer*
Hayes, Stephen Kurtz *writer*
Heaney, Seamus Justin *poet, educator*
Heath, Mariwyn Dwyer *writer, legislative issues consultant*
Heath-Stubbs, John (Francis Alexander) *poet*
Hecker, Jutta *writer*
Helland, Sherman M. *writer*
Hendriks-Jansen, Horst Jurgen *author*
Henigson, Ann Pearl *freelance writer, songwriter, lyricist*
Herbert, James Alan *writer*
Herman-Sekulich, Maya B. (Maja Herman) *poet, essayist, editor*
Herndon, Venable *screenwriter, educator*
Heron, Frances Dunlap *author, educator*

Valette, Jean Paul *writer*
van Appledorn, E(lizabeth) Ruth *writer*
Van der Elst, Nicole *author, consultant, educator*
van Renterghem, Tonny *writer*
Varda, Agnes *screenwriter, director*
Varniene, Regina *bibliographer*
Vaughan, Gwen Morris *poet*
Venzke, Andreas Willi *author, journalist, translator*
Verma, Om Prakash *translator*
Vine, P. A. L. *author*
Vira, Soma *writer, publisher*
Vladem, Steven Allen *writer, motivational speaker*
Vlavianos, Haris *poet*
Volk, Patricia Gay *fiction writer, essayist*
Vonnegut, Kurt, Jr. *writer*
Von Randow, Gero *science writer, editor*
Vosevich, Kathi Ann *writer, editor, scholar*
Wachinger, Burghart *German literature educator*
Wager, Walter Herman *author, communications director*
Walcott, Derek Alton *poet, playwright*
Walker, Alice Malsenior *author*
Walker, Doris I. *writer, historian, educator*
Wallace-Crabbe, Christopher Keith *poet, English language educator*
Wallmann, Jeffrey Miner *author*
Walser, Martin *writer*
Warnke, Uwe *writer, publisher*
Warren, Bacil Benjamin *writer, publisher*
Watkin, Bruce Wykeham *writer*
Weaver, Kitty Dunlap *author*
Webster, Richard Edward *author, consultant, hypnotherapist*
Weeks, Christopher Henry Clark *writer, historian*
Wehner, Kay Y. *poet*
Weichslgartner, Alois Joseph *writer*
Weiser, Stanley *screenwriter*
Weldon, Fay *author*
Wells, Fay Gillis *writer, lecturer, broadcaster, aviation historian*
Welty, Eudora *author*
Wentworth, Diana von Welanetz *author*
Wenzel, Lynn *writer, editor*
Wesker, Arnold *playwright, director*
West-Hill, Gwendolyn *poet, educator*
Westrum, Helen Josephine *writer, retired educator*
Whitaker, Marsha Jones *author, educator*
White, W. Robin *writer*
Whiteman, Joseph Hilary Michael *writer, researcher*
Wiener, Solomon *writer, consultant, former city official*
Wiesel, Elie *writer, educator*
Wilbur, Richard Purdy *writer, educator*
Wilder, Amos Tappan *literary executor*
Wilding, Michael *writer, English and Australian literature educator*
Wilkinson, Rosemary Regina Challoner *poet, writer*
Williams, Edward Macon *poet*
Williams, Miller *poet, translator*
Williamson, Bruce Loomis *writer, retired journalist*
Wilson, Colin Henry *writer*
Wilson, Lanford *playwright*
Wilson, Robert Michael Alan *writer*
Wilson, Rosina *writer, editor*
Winebrenner, Susan Kay *writer, educational consultant*
Winebrenner, William Patrick *writer*
Winton, Calhoun *literature educator*
Wisse, Billy *writer*
Witman, Laura Kathleen *writer, security professional*
Wolf, Marilyn *freelance writer*
Wolfe, Thomas Kennerly, Jr. *writer, journalist*
Wolff, Diane Patricia *author, journalist, producer*
Wooley, Geraldine Hamilton *writer, poet*
Worley, Noelle Frances *poet*
Wormer, Eberhard Juergen *science writer, medical historian*
Worms, Jeannine Eliane *writer*
Wouk, Herman *writer*
Wright, Kirby Michael *writer, editor*
Wroble, Lisa Ann *writer, educator*
Wycoff, Charles Coleman *writer, retired anesthesiologist*
Yarborough, William Pelham *writer, lecturer, retired army officer, consultant*
Yarrow, Andrew Louis *writer, journalist, educator, international relations consultant*
Yeager, Anson Anders *writer, former columnist and newspaper editor*
Yehoshua, Abraham B. *writer, comparative literature educator*
Yglesias, Rafael Jose *novelist*
Young, (Arthur) Allen *writer*
Young, Bette Ann *writer*
Young, Chesley Virginia *writer, educator*
Yunker, Todd Elliott *writer*
Zagaski, Chester Anthony, Jr. *author, researcher*
Zenophon, Fonda *poet, writer, publisher*
Zietsch, Uschi *writer, publisher*
Zietz, Karyl Lynn Kopelman *writer, opera critic, television correspondent, producer, documentary filmmaker*
Zilboorg, Caroline Crawford *writer, English language educator*
Ziolkowska-Boehm, Aleksandra *writer*
Ziporyn, Terra Diane *writer*
Zobel, Louise Purwin *author, educator, lecturer, writing consultant*
Zwicky, Julia Fay *writer, educator*

ARTS: PERFORMING

Abah, Oga Steve *theater educator, researcher*
Abbado, Claudio *conductor*
Abraham, F(ahrid) Murray *actor, educator*
Abril, Victoria *actress*
Accardo, Salvatore *violinist*
Acosta, Antonio Monreal *composer*
Adams, Dean (Lewis Adams) *theater director*
Adams, Liliana Osses *music performer, harpist*
Adey, Christopher *conductor*
Adjani, Isabelle *actress*
Adoor, Gopalakrishnan *filmmaker*
Agajanian, Gilda *pianist*
Agutter, Jenny *actress, dancer*
Ahronovitch, Yuri *conductor*
Akhedjakova, Liya Medjidovna *actress*
Alain, Marie-Claire *organist*
Albarn, Damon *singer, songwriter*
Albery, Tim *theatre and opera director*
Albrecht, Joie *television and film producer, director, writer*
Alda, Alan *actor, writer, director*
Alenikoff, Frances *choreographer, performer, writer, dancer, artist*
Alexander, Bill *theater director*
Alexander, Roland E. *musician, educator*
Alexeev, Dmitri Konstantinovich *pianist*
Alldis, John *musical director*
Allen, Woody (Allen Stewart Konigsberg) *director, actor, writer*
Allman, William Berthold *musician, engineer, consultant*
Almodóvar, Pedro *filmmaker*
Almond, Paul *film director, producer, screenwriter*
Altman, Robert B. *film director, writer, producer*
Alvarez, Thomas *producer, performing company executive, consultant*
Andersen, Frank Angelius *principal dancer, ballet company artistic director*
Anderson, Gerry *television film producer*
Anderson, Gillian *actress*
Anderson, Jewelle Lucille *musician, educator*
Anderson, Reid Bryce *performing company executive*
Andrews, Anthony *actor*
Andrews, Ralph Herrick *television producer*
Andsnes, Leif Ove *concert pianist*
Angel, Steven *musician*
Angelopoulos, Theo *film director*
Angerer, Paul *musician, educator, composer, conductor*
Anhalt, Istvan *composer, writer, educator*
Annakin, Kenneth Cooper *film director, writer*
Annaud, Jean-Jacques *film director, screenwriter*
Ann-Margret, (Ann-Margret Olsson) *actress, performer*
Antonioni, Michelangelo *film director*
Apted, Michael David *film director*
Araiza, Francisco (José Francisco Araiza Andrade) *opera singer*
Archibeque, Charlene Paullin *music educator*
Argerich, Martha *pianist*
Arman Gelenbe, Deniz *concert pianist*
Armatrading, Joan *singer, songwriter*
Armstrong, Sheila Ann *classical vocalist*
Arnell, Richard Anthony Sayer *composer, conductor*
Arquit, Nora Harris *music educator*
Arrigo, Robin Jean Sempey *piano educator, accompanist*
Arthur, Thomas Hahn *theater educator, director*
Asahina, Takashi *conductor*
Asher, Jane *actor, writer, business owner*
Ashkenazy, Vladimir Davidovich *concert pianist, conductor*
Ashvil-Bibi, Sigalit *musician, artist*
Aston, Peter George *music educator, composer, conductor*
Astruc, Alexandre *director, writer*
Asylmuratova, Altynai *dancer*
Atcher, Randy *musician, narrator, entertainer, retired realtor*
Atkins, Richard Bart *film, television producer*
Atkinson, Rowan Sebastian *actor, writer*
Attenborough, Baron Richard Samuel *actor, producer, director, goodwill ambassador*
Aubery, Stephen Royston Edmund *film producer*
Audi, Pierre Raymond *artistic director*
Audren, Christophe (Chris Audren) *composer, musician*
Auteuil, Daniel *actor*
Avraamidou, Maria Lysandrou *television director*
Awodiya, Muyiwa Peter *theater educator, researcher, arts administrator*
Aznavour, Charles (Varenagh Aznavourian) *singer, actor*
Babbitt, Milton Byron *composer*
Bacall, Lauren *actress*
Backer, Matthew De Bracey *musician, educator*
Bacon, A. Smoki *television host*
Badinski, Nikolai I. *composer, pedagogue, violinist*
Baer, Olaf *vocalist*
Baerwald, Susan Grad *television broadcasting company executive producer*
Baez, Joan Chandos *folk singer*
Bailey, Derek *musician*
Bailey, Exine Margaret Anderson *soprano, educator*
Baker, Dame Janet *vocalist*
Baker, Rebecca Louise *musician, music educator, consultant*
Balassa, Sandor *composer*
Ballard, Louis Wayne *composer*
Ballou, Jeffrey Pierre *producer*
Balmuth, Bernard Allen *retired film editor*
Banbury, Frith (Frederick Harold Banbury) *theater director, actor*
Bancroft, Anne (Mrs. Mel Brooks) *actress*
Banderas, Antonio *actor*
Bandler, Vivica Aina Fanny *theater director*
Baranovich, Diana Lea *music educator*
Barba, Eugenio *theater director*
Barbee, Victor *ballet dancer*
Bardot, Brigitte *actress*
Barenboim, Daniel *conductor, pianist*
Barkworth, Peter Wynn *actor, writer*
Barreto, Bruno *film director and producer*
Barron, Paul Douglas *film producer*
Barsalona, Frank Samuel *theatrical agent*
Bartha, Daniela C. *music educator*
Bartoli, Cecilia *soprano*
Barton, John Bernard Adie *drama director and dramatic adaptor*
Baryshnikov, Mikhail *ballet dancer*
Baschung, Christina Maria *opera singer, voice educator*
Basinger, Kim *actress*
Bastien, Jane Smisor *music educator*
Bate, Jennifer Lucy *musician*
Bates, Alan (Arthur Bates) *actor*
Bates, Kathy *actress*
Battle, Kathleen Deanna *soprano*
Batty, Peter Wright *television and film producer, director, writer*
Bausch, Pina *dancer, ballet director, choreographer*
Beal, John Everett *composer, conductor*
Béart, Emmanuelle *actress*
Beatty, (Henry) Warren *actor, producer, director*
Becofsky, Arthur Luke *arts administrator, writer*
Bedford, Steuart John Rudolf *conductor*
Bee, Anna Cowden *dance educator*
Beechey, Gwilym Edward *musician, educator*
Beguin, Bernard Auguste *columnist, retired broadcasting company executive*
Behrens, Hildegard *soprano*
Belafonte, Harry *singer, concert artist, actor*
Bélai, István *film director, writer*
Bell, Joshua *musician*
Belmondo, Jean-Paul *actor*
Belohlavek, Jiri *conductor, educator*
Beltzner, Gail Ann *music educator*
Bencini, Sara Haltiwanger *concert pianist*
Benigni, Roberto *actor, writer, director, producer*
Bening, Annette *actress*
Benjamin, George William John *composer, conductor, educator*
Benner, Charles Henry *retired music educator*
Bergen, Christopher Brooke *opera company administrator, translator, editor*
Bergeron, Earleen Fournet *actress*
Berky, Albin Louis *music educator, musician*
Berman, Mona S. *actress, playwright, theatrical director and producer*
Berman, Sanford Solomon *motion picture sound designer, composer, arranger, artist*
Bertenshaw, William Howard, III *radio and television producer*
Bertolucci, Bernardo *film director*
Bhatia, Vanraj Anandji *composer*
Biasutti, Michele *composer, psychologist*
Bilger, Dorinne Potter *musician, educator*
Bintley, David *ballet company artistic director, choreographer*
Birkenhead, Thomas Bruce *theatrical producer and manager, educator*
Birtwistle, Sir Harrison *composer*
Bjørn, Dinna *choreographer, artistic director*
Black, Don *lyricist*
Black, Rilla Alma *violinist, library assistant, poet*
Blair, Betsy *actress*
Blake, David Leonard *composer*
Blakemore, Michael Howell *theatre and film director*
Blanchett, Cate *actress*
Blankson, Victor Emmanuel Roberts *music educator, researcher church and choral music*
Blau, Richard Miles (Dick Blau) *performing arts educator, photographer, filmmaker*
Bobo, Len Davis *musician*
Boddie, Don O'Mar *recording company executive, producer, recording artist*
Bodin, Lars-Gunnar *composer*
Bolotowsky, Andrew Ilyitch *flutist, composer*
Bond-Brown, Barbara Ann *musician, educator*
Bondebjerg, Ib *film and media studies educator*
Bone, Lawson Mitchell *songwriter, poet*
Bonham-Carter, Helena *actress*
Bonynge, Richard *opera conductor*
Boone, Walter Lee, Jr. *music educator*
Boorman, John *film director, producer, screenwriter*
Booth, Mark *broadcasting executive*
Borch, Christian *television correspondent, writer, educator*
Borg, Kim *basso*
Boughton, Ross Byron *composer, television producer*
Boulez, Pierre *composer, conductor*
Boxill, Edith Hillman *music therapist, educator, writer*
Boyarsky, Terry Linda *music educator*
Boyd, Liona Maria *musician*
Brabourne, Lord *film and television producer*
Bradley, Barbra Bailey *musician, educator, accompanist*
Bradley, Leon Charles *musician, educator, consultant*
Bradshaw, Richard James *conductor*
Bragg, Bernard *actor, educator*
Bragg, William David *film producer, screenwriter*
Branagh, Kenneth *actor, director*
Brand, Oscar *folksinger, writer, educator*
Brando, Marlon, Jr. *actor*
Bräuninger, Jürgen *composer, music educator*
Bream, Julian *classical guitarist and lutanist*
Brendel, Alfred *concert pianist*
Breton, Philip Joseph *musician*
Brewster, Robert Gene *concert singer, educator*
Brlek, Darko *managing and artistic director*
Brown, Charles Samuel *singer, composer, educator*
Brown, David *motion picture producer, writer*
Brown, Deborah Elizabeth *television producer*
Brown Leatherberry, Thomas Henry *gospel music company executive, clergy member*
Bruce, Christopher *artistic director*
Bruck, Daniel Stephen *producer, director*
Bull, Sandy (Alexander Benjamin Bull) *musician, composer*
Bumbry, Grace *soprano*
Burchard, Ellen Williams *actress, producer, artist, writer*
Burkhalter, Susan Shively *music educator, organist*
Burnett, Frances *concert pianist, music educator*
Burrell, Michael Philip *actor, writer*
Burton, Tim *film director*
Butuza, Octavian *radio producer, journalist*
Bychkov, Semyon *conductor*
Caine, Michael *actor*
Cameron, James *film director, screenwriter, producer*
Campbell, Ian David *opera company director*
Campbell, Naomi *model*
Campbell, Neal Franklin *music educator*
Campbell, Russell Drummond *filmmaker, educator*
Canessa, Francesco *theatre administrator, music critic*
Capalbo, Carmen *theater director and producer*
Caples, Richard James *dance company executive, lawyer*
Cardy, Patrick Robert Thomas *composer, educator*
Carey, Mariah *vocalist, songwriter*
Carmichael, Judy Lea *record industry executive, concert jazz pianist*
Carney, Karen Rose *music educator, pianist*
Carrey, Jim *actor*
Carroll, Charles Michael *music educator*
Carroll, David Joseph *actor*
Carroll, Lucy Ellen *choral director, music coordinator, educator*
Cary, Tristram Ogilvie *composer, writer*
Castro, Joseph Armand *music director, pianist, composer, orchestrator*
Caswell, Dorothy Ann Cottrell *arts administrator*
Chahine, Youssef *film director*
Chailly, Riccardo *conductor*
Chang, Helen Chung-Hung Hsiang *piano pedagogy specialist*
Chang, Marian S. *filmmaker, composer*
Charles, Walter *actor*
Charnin, Martin *theatrical director, lyricist, producer*
Chechenya, Kostyantyn Anatolijovych *musician, conductor*
Chen, Chin-Chin *music educator*
Chen, Patsy Fang *music educator*
Chéreau, Patrice *theater, opera and film director*
Chiarelli, Robert Charles *audio engineer*
Chierighino, Brianne Siddall *voice-over, actress, assistant location manager*
Chopra, Yash Raj *film director*
Chow, Yun-fat *actor*
Christian, Jackie Don, Jr. *television production executive*
Christie, Julie *actress*
Christing, Adam *performing company executive*
Chritton, George A. *theater producer*
Chukhrai, Pavel Grigoryevich *film director*
Clark, Faye Louise *drama and speech educator*
Clark, Keith Collar *musician, educator*
Clay, Clifton Ford *motion picture producer, writer*
Clayburgh, Jill *actress*
Cleary, David Michael *composer, critic, library assistant*
Cleary, James C. *audio-visual producer*
Cloonan, Patrick Michael *radio news producer, writer*
Close, Glenn *actress*
Codron, Michael Victor *theatrical producer*
Coe, Judith Anne *music educator, composer, performer*
Cohen, Robert L. *film producer*
Colbath, Brian (Brian Colbath Watson) *actor, script and live performance writer*
Cole, Carol Alma Tomlinson *classical musician*
Cole, Daniel *music educator, conductor, clinician*
Collier, Nathan Morris *musician, music educator*
Collignon, Stef G. *recording company executive*
Collins, Gordon Dent *recording company executive*
Collins, Joan Henrietta *actress*
Comissiona, Sergiu *conductor*
Connery, Sean (Thomas Connery) *actor*
Conrad, Richard A. *opera singer, educator*
Conti, Tom *actor, writer, director*
Cooke, Philip Howard *television director, producer*
Cooperman, Alvin *television and theatrical producer*
Copeland, Jacqueline Turner *music educator*
Copperfield, David (David Kotkin) *illusionist, director, producer, writer*
Corbitt, Gretchen Johnson *music educator*
Corman, Julie Ann *producer, director*
Costa-Gavras, (Konstaninos Gavras) *director, writer*
Cotrubas, Ileana *opera singer, retired lyric soprano*
Coukis, Peter George *musician, composer*
Couret, Keiron Leigh *performing arts presenter*
Crawford, Cindy *model, actress*
Crawford-Mason, Clare Wootten *television producer, journalist*
Cremer, Thomas Gerhard *music educator*
Cristofer, Michael *actor, screenwriter, playwright*
Crocker, Joy Laksmi *concert pianist and organist, composer*
Crocker, Ray Dean *musician, musical director*
Cronenberg, David *film director*
Cronyn, Hume *actor, writer, film director*
Cropp, Ben *film producer*
Crosby, John O'Hea *conductor, opera manager*
Crotty Guile, Julianne Marie *musician, composer, writer*
Crow, Laura Jean *design educator, costume designer*
Crowther, G. Rodney, III *television production company executive, writer, photographer*
Cruise, Tom (Tom Cruise Mapother, IV) *actor*
Curry, Daniel Francis Myles *filmmaker*
Cutshall, Brian Ervin *radio news director*
Dabrowski, Edward John *television technical director*
Dahl, Arlene *actress, writer, designer, cosmetic executive*
Danaher, Mallory Millett (Mallory Jones) *actress, photographer, writer, poet*
Daniel-Lesur, Jean Yves *composer*
Danilow, Deborah Marie *singer, songwriter, musician, rancher, realtor*
D'Arcangelo, Marcia Diane *educational media producer*
Dardenne, Jean-Pierre *film director*
Dardenne, Luc *film director*
Darion, Joe *librettist, lyricist*
Darnell, Doris Hastings *storyteller, antique clothing collector, exhibitor*
Davies, Dennis Russell *conductor, music director, pianist*
Davies, Sir Peter Maxwell *composer, conductor*
Davis, Sir Colin Rex *conductor*
Davis, Luane Ruth *theatrical director, performer*
Davis, Terri Judith *television producer, writer*
Dearnley, Christopher Hugh *organist, choral director*
Debus, Eleanor Viola *retired business management company executive*
Decker, Franz Paul *symphony conductor, educator*
Del Forno, Anton *classical guitarist, recording artist, composer, arranger, educator*
Delon, Alain *actor*
Dench, Judith Olivia *actress*
De Niro, Robert *actor*
Denke, Conrad William *motion picture producer*
De Pablo, Luis *composer*
Depardieu, Gérard *actor*
Depuydt, Xavier Christophe Laurent *film director*
Deutsch, Didier (Delaunoy Deutsch) *music producer, writer*
Deutsch, Herbert Arnold *music educator*
Deutsch, Nina *pianist*
De Waart, Edo *conductor*
DeWolfe, Martha *singer, songwriter, publisher, producer*
Diaz, Cameron *actress*
Di Chiera, David *performing arts company executive*
Dickinson, Peter *composer*
Dion, Celine *musician*
Diverrès, Catherine *choreographer*
Di Virgilio, Nicholas *voice music educator*
Dodson, Daryl Theodore *ballet administrator, arts consultant*
Dohnanyi, Christoph von *musician, conductor*
Domingo, Placido *tenor*
Donner, Jörn Johan *film director, writer, legislator, diplomat*
Doty, Shayne Taylor *organist*
Douglas, P.C. *producer, director, reporter, editor*
Dowell, Anthony James, Sr. *ballet dancer*
Dower Gold, Catherine Anne *music history educator*
Downs, Jon Franklin *drama educator, director, writer*
Drake, Laura *theater director, performer*
Druck, Mark *theater director, producer, writer*
Duff, James Michael *conductor, musical director*
Dumas, Charles *filmmaker, educator*
Dumont, Bruno *film director*
Dunlop, Frank *theater director*
Dunn, Craig Andrew *entertainer, conductor, composer, educator*
Dutoit, Charles *conductor*
Dutton, Leslie Ruth *music educator*
Dye, O. David *speech and theatre educator*
Dylan, Bob (Robert Allen Zimmerman) *singer, composer*
Eagan, Sherman G. *producer, communications executive*
Eastman, Donna Kelly *composer, music educator*
Eastwood, Clint *actor, film director, former mayor*
Ecklund, Peter Johnson *musician*
Edwards, Sian *conductor*
Egoyan, Atom *film director*
Ehrhart, Joseph Edward *retired television broadcast engineer*

Nelson, Winifred Harrison *singer, actress, computer programmer*
Nesterenko, Yevgeniy Yevgeniyevich *singer, vocal art educator*
Nettheim, Nigel Felix *musicologist*
Neuman, Maxine Darcy *cellist, educator*
Neumann, Alfred John *music director*
Neumeier, John *choreographer, ballet company director*
Neville, John *actor, director*
Nevins, Sheila *television programmer and producer*
Newell, Mike *film director*
Nichols, Leslie Carol *music educator*
Nichols, William J. *film studies educator*
Nicholson, Jack *actor, director, producer*
Nilles, Laila Padorr *musician, record producer*
Noble, Adrian *artistic director*
Norman, Jessye *soprano*
North, Robert (Robert North Dodson) *dancer, choreographer, artistic director*
Norton, Eunice *pianist*
Nowak, Grzegorz *conductor, music and artistic director*
Nugent, Nelle *theater, film and television producer*
Numano, Allen Stanislaus Motoyuki *musician, writer*
Nunn, Trevor Robert *theater director*
Nuridsany, Claude *filmmaker*
Nussbaum, Jeffrey Joseph *musician*
Nygaard, Jens *conductor, music educator*
Obe, Eric Moonman *radio educator*
O'Connell, Taaffe Cannon *actress, publishing executive*
Odnoposoff, Ricardo *violinist, educator*
Oh, Y. June Choi *pianist, music educator*
Ohira, Kazuto *theatre company executive, writer*
Oldman, Gary *actor*
Oliveira, Manuel de *film director*
Olson, Leslie *music educator*
Orledge, Robert Nicholas *music educator, researcher, musicologist*
Orphanides, Nora Charlotte *ballet educator*
Orr, Robin Kemsley *composer, emeritus educator*
Ortiz, Fernando, Jr. *film researcher, stage manager*
Ortlip, Stephen Jude *musician*
Oskarson, Peter O.H. *theatre director*
Osolsobě, Ivo *performing arts educator*
Ottaviani, Maria Gioia *performing arts educator*
Ottley, Jerold Don *retired choral conductor, educator*
Ouedraogo, Idrissa *film director*
Owen, Michael *ballet dancer*
Ozaki, Nancy Junko *performance artist, educator*
Padberg, Helen Swan *violinist*
Padmore, Elaine Marguirite *artistic director*
Page, Genevieve *actress*
Pagels, Jürgen Heinrich *balletmaster, dance educator, dancer, choreographer, writer*
Palin, Michael Edward *actor, screenwriter, writer*
Palmer, Christine (Clelia Rose Venditti) *operatic singer, performer, pianist, vocal instructor, lecturer, entertainer*
Palmer, Felicity Joan *mezzo-soprano opera singer*
Palmer, Willard Aldrich, III *magician, writer, actor*
Paltrow, Gwyneth *actress*
Pang, Ting Sun *music educator*
Pankov, Gradimir Krunislav *ballet artistic director*
Pardee, Margaret Ross *violinist, violist, educator*
Parker, Alan William *film director, writer*
Parker, Jim (James Mavin Parker) *composer*
Paro, Georgij *performing company executive*
Patterson, Mark Allan *musician*
Patteson, Charles Lynn *musician, retired music educator*
Pavarotti, Luciano *lyric tenor*
Paxton, Glenn Gilbert *composer*
Payne, Karen Suzanne *music educator*
Peck, Gregory (Eldred Gregory Peck) *actor*
Pede, Ron *film critic*
Peirson, George Ewell *film producer, writer, art director, educator*
Penderecki, Krzysztof *composer, conductor*
Pennington, Donald Harris *musician, retired physician*
Perahia, Murray *pianist*
Perennou, Marie *filmmaker, biologist*
Perry, André *recording industry executive*
Peters, Joseph Donald *filmmaker*
Peterson, Clark C. *announcer, writer*
Peterson, Douglas Robert *music educator*
Peterson, John Willard *composer, music publisher*
Petrić, Ivo *composer, artistic director*
Petrov, Nicolas *dance educator, choreographer*
Pfeiffer, Michelle *actress*
Phillips, Sian *actress*
Pinnock, Trevor *conductor, harpsichordist*
Pinschof, Thomas *flutist, conductor*
Pistone, Daniele *musicologist, educator*
Pizzamiglio, Albert Theodore (Al Pierson) *conductor*
Pizzuto, Emanuelina Maria *concert pianist, composer*
Pladevall, Tomàs *cinematographer, educator*
Plowright, Joan Anne *actress*
Plummer, Christopher (Orme) (Arthur Plummer) *actor*
Plummer, Graeme Leslie *television program director*
Pollack, Sydney *film director*
Ponné, Nanci Teresa *entertainment promoter, writer*
Popper, Felix *retired conductor, pianist*
Porter, Joyce Klowden *theatre educator and director*
Potts, Glenda Rue *music educator*
Poulsen, IB *mass communications educator, researcher*
Powell, Benjamin L. *entertainment company executive*
Pravdyuk, Yury Aleksyevich *composer, performer*
Preminger, Aner Hillel *film producer, director, writer*
Preysz, Sandra *music educator*
Price, Betty Jeanne *choirchime soloist, writer*
Price, Leontyne *concert and opera singer, soprano*
Price, Thomas Frederick *theatre educator*
Procaccini, Teresa *composer, music educator*
Pryce, Jonathan *actor*
Pugh, Kyle Mitchell, Jr. *musician, retired music educator*
Puttnam, Lord David Terence *film producer*
Quinn, Anthony Rudolph Oaxaca *actor, writer, artist*
Rabey, David Ian *theater educator*
Rainey, Terry Lee *music educator, director*
Rais, Mark *composer, musicologist, acoustician*
Ramaswamy, Mohan Krischke *cultural consultant*
Ramis, Harold Allen *film director, screenwriter, actor*
Ramovs, Primoz *composer*
Ramsey, Bill (William McCreery) *singer, actor, composer-lyricist, television executive*
Randle, Ellen Eugenia Foster *opera and classical singer, educator*
Rappeneau, Jean-Paul *film director, screenwriter*
Rea, Stephen *actor*
Redford, Robert (Charles Robert Redford) *actor, director*
Redgrave, Lynn *actress*
Redgrave, Vanessa *actress*
Redman, Cinda J. *music educator*
Redman, Joshua *jazz musician*
Reed, Lou *musician*
Regner, Hermann *music educationalist, composer*
Reid, Joyce Eleanor *musician, minister*
Renshaw, Peter *music educator*
Rex, Christopher Davis *classical musician*
Rhodd, Alice Jane Monica *producer, script writer, educator, broadcaster*
Rhodes, Lawrence *artistic director*
Richards, Keith *musician*
Richards, Kenneth Roland *drama and theater studies educator*
Richardson, Dana Roland *video producer*
Richardson, Ian William *actor*
Richardson, Miranda *actress*
Riche, Wendy *television producer*
Rigg, Dame Diana *actress*
Riggs-Hall, Carla Lynn *entertainer-performing arts educator, restaurateur*
Riley, Jack *actor, writer*
Roads, Curtis *music educator, composer*
Robards, Jason Nelson, Jr. *actor*
Robb, Thomas Lindsey Wyatt *theatre producer, set and costume designer*
Robbins, Timothy (Francis) *director, actor*
Roberts, Esther Lois *piano educator, composer, writer*
Roberts, Mark (Robert Ellis Scott) *actor, writer*
Roberts, Mel (Melvin Richard Kells) *retired film editor*
Roberts, William Richard, III *record company executive, fire fighter*
Robinson, Alice Jean McDonnell *retired drama and speech educator*
Roby, B. Andrew *music educator*
Roddam, Franc *film director*
Roeg, Nicolas Jack *film director*
Rogillio, Kathy June *musician, piano rebuilder, educator*
Rosa, Bobbie Carol *music educator*
Roscher, Wolfgang *composer, music educator, musicologist*
Roseanne, (Roseanne Barr) *actress, comedienne, producer, writer*
Rosegarten, Rory *talent manager, television and theater producer*
Rosenberg, Richard Mark *orchestral conductor, artistic director*
Rosenfeld, Steven Ira *artistic director, music publisher*
Rossellini, Isabella *actress, model*
Rostropovich, Mstislav Leopoldovich *musician*
Rowe, Bonnie Gordon *music company executive*
Royle, David Brian Layton *television producer, journalist*
Rozhdestvensky, Gennadi Nikolaevich *conductor*
Runnicles, Donald *conductor*
Russell, George Haw *video production company executive*
Russell, Robert Charles *drama educator, music director, actor, theater director*
Ryder, Hal *theater educator, director*
Ryder, Kenneth Stanley *organist, music educator*
Sabey, John Louis *pianist, song composer, beekeeper*
Saglimbeni, Rodolfo *conductor, educator*
Saied, James Guy *conductor, consultant*
Sallagar, Walter Hermann *musician, educator*
Saltzman, Philip *television writer, producer*
Salvatore, Richard John *cinematographer, company executive*
Salvatores, Gabriele *film director*
Samuelson, M. Kristin *music educator*
Sands, Camille *actress*
Saraste, Jukka-Pekka *conductor*
Scavarda, Donald Robert *composer, artist*
Schaffer, Candler Gareld *conductor, hornist, educator*
Schaffman, Karen Helen *performing company executive*
Schamus, James Allan *film producer, educator*
Schaufuss, Peter *dancer, producer, choreographer, ballet director*
Schepisi, Fred *producer, director, screenwriter*
Schepping, Wilhelm *music educator, ethnomusicologist*
Schläpfer, Martin *performing company executive*
Schlesinger, John Richard *film, opera and theater director*
Schmehl Morley, Susan Linda *performing arts educator*
Schnaus, Peter *musical history educator*
Schnepel, Birgit *pianist, educator*
Schoening, Ruth Irene *retired music educator, musician*
Scholz, Uwe *ballet director, choreographer, stage director*
Schrade, Robert Warren *classical pianist, educator*
Schrade, Rolande Maxwell Young *composer, pianist, educator*
Schroeder, Barbet G. *director*
Schultz, Klaus *theater administrator*
Schultz, Patricia Bowers *vocal music educator, performer*
Schwartz, Stephen Lawrence *composer, lyricist*
Schwarzkopf, Dietrich Guenter *television program director*
Sciannameo, Franco Ludovico Orlando *music educator*
Scofield, Paul *actor*
Scott, Derek Brian *music educator*
Scripps, Douglas Jerry *music educator, conductor, director*
Seaman, Arlene Anna *retired musician, educator*
Seary, Lawrence Anthony *cinematographer, news assignment editor*
Sedelmaier, J. J. *filmmaker*
Seiler, Ernst Friedrich *pianist*
Selwyn, Zachary Stephen *disc jockey*
Serov, Edward Afanasjevich *conductor*
Sesta, Hilary Sophia *actress, writer*
Severs, William Floyd *actor*
Sewell, Rufus *actor*
Shakibanasab, Lauren Vorwerk *music director, educator*
Sharif, Omar (Michael Shalhoub) *actor*
Sharpe, Robert Kent *writer, director, producer, photographer*
Sharvit, Uri *music educator*
Sheldrick, Katharyn Elizabeth *musicologist*
Shelgren, Richard Eric (Sven), Jr. *film and television producer*
Sheridan, Jim *director, screenwriter*
Sherlaw-Johnson, Robert *music educator*
Shivas, Mark *film and television producer*
Shuman, Earl Stanley *songwriter, music publisher*
Siddique, Imam Amir *creative consultant, casting director*
Siegel, Wayne Perry *composer, music studio director*
Sikes, Cynthia Lee *actress, singer*
Simmonds, Rae Nichols *musician, composer, educator*
Simms, Beverley Singleton *music educator, musician*
Simonds, Martha Muñoz *musician, educator*
Sinden, Sir Donald Alfred *actor*
Sitsky, Larry *composer, pianist, musicologist, educator*
Skoog, William Melvin *music/voice educator*
Skrobela, Katherine Creelman *music producer*
Skrowaczewski, Stanislaw *conductor, composer*
Sloane, J.P. *television producer, writer, entertainer, theologian*
Smith, Barbara Barnard *music educator*
Smith, Barry *organist, conductor, former music educator*
Smith, Betty Pauline *television producer*
Smith, James Edward *music educator, jazz guitarist*
Smith, Dame Maggie *actress*
Smith, Richard Emerson (Dick Smith) *make-up artist*
Smith-Epstein, Mary Kathleen *dancer*
Smith-Lombardini, Maryelizabeth Anne *opera singer, artistic director*
Snyder, David L. *film production designer*
Soderbergh, Steven Andrew *filmmaker*
Soederstrom, Elisabeth Anna *opera singer*
Solleveld, René Jacques *film producer*
Solyom, Janos Paul *concert pianist, conductor, consultant*
Sontag, David B. *producer, writer, communications executive*
Sorce, Richard *music educator, composer, writer*
Sorrell, Rozlyn *singer, recording artist, actress, educator, entrepreneur*
Spacey, Kevin *actor*
Spader, James *actor*
Spangler, David Sheridan *composer, director, creative arts educator, writer*
Speller, Robert Ernest Blakefield, Jr. *choreographer*
Spielberg, Steven *motion picture director, producer*
Spillman, Marjorie Rose *producer, dancer*
Spivakov, Vladimir Teodorovich *conductor*
Sprecher, Baron William Gunther *pianist, composer, conductor, diplomat*
Springer, Ashton, Jr. *theatrical producer*
Springer, Leonard *musician, educator*
Sprosty, Joseph Patrick *producer, writer, weapons specialist*
Stallone, Sylvester Enzio *actor, writer, director*
Stango, Juliette Mary *composer, music publisher, educator*
Stanley, Helen Camille *composer, musician*
Stanley, Margaret King *performing arts administrator*
Starr, Ringo (Richard Starkey) *musician, actor*
Steele, Robert Dennis *radio producer, announcer, actor*
Stefano, Joseph William *film and television producer, writer*
Stein, Julie Esther *piano instructor*
Stephan, Egon, Sr. *cinematographer, film equipment company executive*
Stern, Isaac *violinist, performing arts executive*
Stevenson, Robert Murrell *music educator*
Stewart, Roderick David *singer*
Stiller, Ben *actor, director, writer*
Stinchcomb, Albert Monroe *producer, designer/realtor*
Sting, (Gordon Matthew Sumner) *musician, songwriter, actor*
Stock, Kim H. *dance studio owner, choreographer*
Stockhausen, Karlheinz *composer*
Strautins, Vilnis *flute educator, past symphony orchestra executive*
Streep, Meryl (Mary Louise Streep) *actress*
Streisand, Barbra Joan *singer, actress, director*
Stretton, Ross *ballet dancer*
Stroud, Bradley Lyn *ballet company executive*
Stuart, James Fortier *musician, artistic director*
Sugar, Joseph Robert *educator, musician, conductor*
Suitner, Otmar *conductor*
Sundberg, Johan Emil Fredrik *music educator, researcher*
Susso, Alhaji Papa *musician*
Sutherland, Donald *actor*
Sutherland, Melanie Jan *theatre director and producer*
Sutowski, Thor Brian *choreographer*
Swank, Hilary Ann *actress*
Swartz, Christopher John *musician, instrument designer and builder*
Swenson, Kathleen Susan *music and art educator*
Swinson, Betty White *composer*
Swoger, James Wesley *magician*
Szabo, Istvan *film director*
Tabakin, Ralph *actor, communications executive, industrial engineer*
Tabakov, Emil *orchestra conductor*
Tacchella, Jean-Charles *film director, screen writer*
Taft, John Thomas *television producer, writer*
Tal, Josef *composer*
Talbot, Stephen H. *television producer, writer*
Talmi, Yoav *conductor, composer*
Taravella, Rosie *actress, writer*
Tarrant, Deirdre Elizabeth Anne *dancer, educator, dance company director*
Taylor, Elizabeth Rosemond *actress*
Teissonniere, Gerardo *musician, educator*
Te Kanawa, Kiri *opera and concert singer*
Thierry, Fouquet *opera administrator*
Thies, Julie Ann *music educator*
Thomas, Dale *film producer*
Thomas, John David *musician, composer, arranger, photographer, recording engineer, producer*
Thomas, Ouida Power *music educator*
Thomas, Paul Lindsley *composer, organist, music director*
Thompson, Barnaby David *film producer*
Thompson, Emma *actress*
Thompson, Larry Angelo *producer, lawyer, personal manager*
Thompson, Margaret Knowles *opera singer*
Thulin, Ingrid *actress, director, writer*
Thurman, Virgil Leon *voice educator*
Tilden, Ralph Fulton *retired music educator, organist*
Tilson Thomas, Michael *symphony conductor*
Tinturin, Noëlle Compinsky *pianist, music educator*
Toeplitz, Gideon *symphony society executive*
Tohver, Berit Ingrid Elsa *pianist, educator*
Tokunaga, Emiko *dancer*
Tompa, Gabor *theatre director*
Topol, Chaim *actor, producer, director*
Tornatore, Giuseppe *film director*
Townsend, Barbara *actress*
Trân, Quang Hai *ethnomusicologist*
Tregle, Linda Marie *dance educator*
Troup, Malcolm *music educator, concert pianist*
Trueba, Fernando *film director and producer, screenwriter*
Tucapsky, Antonin *composer, conductor, educator*
Tucker, Allan Marc *mastering engineer*
Tune, Tommy (Thomas James Tune) *musical theater director, dancer, choreographer, actor*
Turlington, Christy *model*
Turturro, John *actor*
Tutin, Dorothy *actress*
Twombly, Jean Sawyer *musician, educator*
Uchida, Mitsuko *pianist*
Unger, Gary Allen *recording industry executive, singer, lyricist*
Ustinov, Sir Peter Alexander *actor, director, writer*
Uzan, Bernard *artistic director*
Valenti, Frederick Alan *actor, screenwriter*
Vallegio, Giuseppe Eugenio *composer*
Vàmos, Youri Elemér *choreographer, ballet director*
van Appledorn, Mary Jeanne *composer, music educator, pianist*
van Diem, Mike *film director, writer*
Van Dusen, Blanche Baker *actress, sculptor*
van Geel, Maurits *artistic director*
Vanier, Jerre Lynn *art director*
Van Ness, Patricia Catheline *composer, violinist*
Varga, Deborah Trigg *music educator, entertainment company owner*
Vargas, Antonio Pinho *composer, musician, educator*
Vasary, Tamas *concert pianist, conductor*
Vavilov, Guennady Alekssevich *composer, music educator*
Vazsonyi, Balint *concert pianist, television producer, political philosopher*
Velasco-Mills, John Anthony *music publishing company executive*
Velazco, Jorge *orchestra conductor, research musicologist*
Villella, Edward Joseph *ballet dancer, educator, choreographer, artistic director, performing arts administrator*
Vizzini, Carol Redfield *symphony musician, music educator*
Vlad, Roman *composer*
Voight, Jon *actor*
von Trier, Lars *film director*
Wachmann, Eric James *music educator, symphony musician*
Wadsworth, Bill *producer*
Waidler, Beverly Mae *music teacher*
Waks, Nathan *music director*
Waldekranz, Rune *film educator emeritus*
Waldman, Alan I. (Alawana) *songwriter, composer, lyricist, computer programmer, emergency medicine provider*
Walker, Charles Dodsley *conductor, organist*
Wallace, Petter *television producer, director*
Walsh, Elizabeth Jameson *musician*
Walsh, Thomas Francis, Jr. *producer, writer, director*
Walter, Horst *musicologist*
Walters, Jefferson Brooks *musician, retired real estate broker*
Walton, John Michael *drama educator*
Wang, An-Ming *composer*
Wang, Wayne *film director*
Wang, Wenyi *music educator*
Warberg, Willetta *concert pianist, writer, piano educator*
Ward, Lillian Hazel *music educator*
Wargnier, Regis *film director*
Warrell, Ernest Herbert *organist, choir master, educator*
Warren, Raymond H.C. *music educator, composer*
Watters, Cora Tula *musician*
Waugh, Michael Brian *filmmaker, film editor*
Wayne, Jesse *actor/stuntman, film production manager*
Webb, Veronica *fashion model, journalist*
Webber, Peggy *actress, producer, director, writer*
Weber, Édith *music educator, critic, researcher*
Weber, Jeffrey Randolph *record producer*
Weeks, Clifford Myers *musician, educational administrator*
Wehr, James Paul *musician*
Weidaw, Kenneth Roe *musician, educator, consultant*
Weinzweig, Daniel *producer*
Weir, Dame Gillian Constance *concert organist, harpsichordist*
Weir, Peter Lindsay *film director*
Weisbrod, Neil L. *film and television director*
Weiskopf, Kim Robert *television producer, writer*
Wendelburg, Norma Ruth *composer, pianist, educator*
Wenders, Wim *film director*
West, James Reyenard *dance educator*
West, Timothy *actor, stage director*
Wester, Keith Albert *film and television recording engineer, real estate developer*
Wetterwald, Audrey Lynn *dance educator*
Whitaker, Forest *actor, director, producer*
White, Stephanie Darleen *dancer*
Whitener, William Garnett *dancer, choreographer*
Whyte, Nancy Marie *performing arts educator*
Wickbom, Kaj Sten Erik *media education scientist*
Wiedebusch, Mary Kathryne *dance educator*
Wilansky, Aleksandr Neal *director, actor, choreographer*
Wilcox, Roberta Moat *music educator*
Wilde, Patricia *retired artistic director*
Wilder, Valerie *ballet company administrator*
Wiley, David Cole *producer*
Willett, Anna Hart *composer*
Williams, Dan Edward *music company owner*
Williams, Julius Penson *composer, conductor*
Williams, Richard Glyn *singer, educator*
Williamson, Nicol *actor*
Willis, Walter Bruce *actor, singer*
Wilson, Keith Dudley *retired media and music educator, consultant*
Wilson, Michael Gregg *film producer, writer*
Wilson, Wanda Lee Davis *entertainment promotions professional, casting director*
Winner, Michael Robert *film director, writer, producer*
Winslet, Kate *actress*
Wise, Robert *film producer, director*
Woelfel, Robert William *broadcast executive, mayor*
Wolff Von Nattermoeller, Hans Jüergen *film director, script writer, producer*

Wollan, Curtis Noel theatrical producer and director
Wood, Vivian Poates mezzo soprano, educator, writer
Woodies, Leslie choreographer, dancer
Woodward, Joanne Gignilliat actress
Wooten, John J. artistic director, playwright
Wordsworth, Barry conductor
Workman, William Gatewood, Jr. educator
Wright, Alfred George James band symphony orchestra conductor, educator
Wright, Gladys Stone music educator, composer, writer
Wu, Yusen (John Woo) film director
Wyle, Noah actor
Wynne, Meredith W. musician, writer
Yamane, Naoko composer, lyricist, pianist, educator
Yannotta, Bernard Joseph musician
Yelin, Robert Bruce musician, recording artist, composer, lyricist
Yezerski, Danny special event producer
Yip, Wai-Hong music educator, composer, conductor
Young, Bryan Kendall radio announcer
Young, Sean (Mary Sean Young) actress
Young-Lyon, Kay Lynn dance educator, small business owner
Zabriskie, George Albert film, video maker
Zacks, Roger William orchestral musician, educator
Zanella, Renato artistic director, choreographer
Zanussi, Krzysztof film director, producer, scriptwriter
Zavrski, Josip musician
Zedda, Alberto conductor
Zhang, Wei-Qiang dancer
Ziegelmeier, Patricia Kay music educator, executive secretary
Ziegler, Holger film scholar
Zimmerman, Amy J. producer, director
Zlatoff-Mirsky, Everett Igor violinist
Zucker, Stefan tenor, writer, editor, radio broadcaster
Zwerin, Michael musician, business executive

ARTS: VISUAL

Abakanowicz, Magdalena artist, sculptor
Abbe, Elfriede Martha sculptor, graphic artist
Abbott, Beverly Stubblefield artist
Abid, Ali artist, caricaturist
Abrams, Faith (Faith White) sculptor
Abramson, Elaine Sandra graphic designer, crafts artist
Abul-Haj, Elizabeth art and antique appraiser
Acconci, Vito (Hannibal) conceptual artist
Ackroyd, Norman art educator
Adalbert, Per artist
Adams, Kim Hastings artist, sculptor
Adams, Norman artist, educator
Adams, Tracey Linden artist, educator
Adaskin, Gordon artist, educator
Adler, Adrienne Edna-Lois art dealer, gallery owner, publisher
Adler, Posy (Roslyn) artist, educator
af Trolle, Marika Elisabeth artist
Agam, Yaacov artist
Ahmad, M-Nor Azhari artist
Alaïa, Azzedine fashion designer
Albacete Carreira, Alfonso artist
Albert, Suzanne Dickson artist
Alexander, Anna Margaret artist, educator
Alexander, Marjorie Anne artist, hand papermaker, art consultant
Alexenberg, Mel artist, art educator
Alexis, Michel artist
Alfaro, Andrev sculptor
Alkire, Betty Jo artist, commercial real estate broker, marketing consultant
Allison, Brooke Hastings artist
Allman, Avis Asiye artist, poet, Turkish and Islamic culture educator, human rights activist
Amaral, Helena Galvão (Lenagal) artist
Ammann, Jean-Christophe art director
Amoah, James Kwame artist, educator
Amor, Simeon, Jr. photographer
Andersen, Mogens painter, author
Anderson, James R. photographer, multimedia producer
Andersson, Helen Demitrous artist
Andre, Carl sculptor
Andreyev, Vladamir Alekseyevich actor, stage director
Antes, Horst painter, sculptor
Anuszkiewicz, Richard Joseph artist
Arabas, Jan Mary artist, art educator
Arai-Abramson, Lucy artist
Armani, Giorgio fashion designer
Armbruster, Klaus electronic media artist, educator
Armfield, Diana Maxwell artist, educator
Armitage, Kenneth sculptor
Armstrong-Jones, Earl Antony (Antony Charles Robert Armstrong-Jones, Earl of Snowdon) photographer
Arndt, Dianne Joy artist, photographer
Aronson, Jan artist, educator
Aronson, Marc artist
Arrons-Lane, Marion Jean artist, educator
Aruj, Estrella fashion designer, artist
Aryan, Kishan Chand artist, art historian
Aska, Warabé artist, writer
Atkin, Edith artist, poet
Auerbach, Frank artist
August, June artist, educator
Auwarter, Brian William sculptor
Avedon, Richard photographer
Avery, Robert Newell sculptor
Baba, Junichiro glass artist
Babcock, Catherine Evans artist, educator
Bachmann, Bill photographer
Bachner, Barbara LaVerdiere artist
Badalamenti, Fred Leopoldo artist, educator
Bahnassi, Afif art history and architecture educator
Baily, Richard artist, music composer
Baird, Julian Thompson, Jr. art dealer
Baird, Ronald A. sculptor
Baladão, Ana artist, educator
Baladi, Roland artist
Baldassano, Vincent J. artist
Banach, Art John graphic artist
Banerjee, Bimal artist, educator
Banks, Allan Richard artist, art historian, researcher
Banks, Monica sculptor
Banks, Rela sculptor
Barboza, Anthony photographer, artist
Barnes, Patricia Ann art educator
Barnett, David Richard illustrator, designer
Barney, Christine J. artist
Barral, Susana G. artist, small business owner
Barry, Paula Jean artist
Bartkiw, Roman artist
Barton, John Murray artist, lecturer
Barton, Paul B. artist, sculptor
Bary, Etienne de artist, journalist
Basch, Richard Vennard photographer, producer, writer, director
Base, Graeme Rowland illustrator, author
Basilious, Nagi Moussa artist, painter
Bator, Martha Zachry Mayson artist
Baxter, Glen artist
Baxter, Jeffrey Q. graphic artist, sculptor
Bayefsky, Aba artist
Bayer, Jonathan Levy photographer
Baykam, Bedri painter, writer, politician
Bazaine, Jean artist
Beaumont, Mona artist
Beck, Christine Safford photographer, publisher, volunteer
Becker, Elisabeth Maria artist, educator
Beck-Friedman, Tova artist
Bednarski, Krzysztof sculptor
Behr, Marion Ray artist, writer, business executive
Beilis-Majerfeld, Rachel painter, graphic artist
Belić Weiss, Zoran artist, educator
Belsky, Franta sculptor
Belson, Patricia A. artist
Beltran, Felix graphic designer
Beltran, Lecy plastic artist
Bender, Janet Pines artist
Benish, Barbara Lucilla artist, educator
Bennett, Genevieve artist
Bensen, Annette Wolf graphic art company consultant
Bernay, Betti artist
Bernstein, Carl jewelry designer, artist
Berry, Glenn educator, artist
Besant, Derek Michael artist, educator
Betts, Barbara Stoke artist, educator
Bickel, Minnette Duffy artist
Bjørgeengen, Kjell artist, educator
Black, Lisa artist
Blair, Phyllis E. artist, sculptor, illustrator
Blair, Warren artist, educator
Blandino, Bayardo Martin artist
Blatt, Morton Bernard medical illustrator
Blitt, Rita Lea artist
Bloom, Julian artist, editor
Blum, Mordechai (Motke) painter, sculptor
Blumberg, June Beth artist
Blunk, Joyce Elaine artist, educator
Bolley, Andrea artist
Bonniere, Christophe Julien Jean Antoine artist
Borgatta, Isabel Case sculptor
Bornstein, Laura Lee artist
Borochoff, Ida Sloan artist
Bowman, Bruce art educator, writer, artist
Boyd, Donald Edgar artist, educator
Boyett, Joan Reynolds arts administrator
Boyle, John Bernard artist
Brackett, Prilla Smith artist, educator
Bradley, Marilynne Gail advertising executive, advertising educator
Brandt, Andreas artist
Braswell, Paula Ann artist
Braverman, Donna Caryn fiber artist
Bray, Charles artist
Brihat, Denis photographer
Brodhead, Quita artist
Brodie, Howard artist
Bronkar, Eunice Dunalee artist, art educator
Brook, Donald visual arts educator emeritus
Brower, James Calvin graphic artist, painter
Brown, Frances Louise (Grandma Fran) artist, art gallery owner
Brown, Sarah M. artist, gallery owner, educator, publisher
Bruce, George John Done portrait painter
Bruce, John Anthony artist
Brzozowski, Kenneth Charles artist, artistic studio executive
Buckley, Brian Burke artist, educator
Buckner, Melvin Daniel artist, designer, educator
Bull, Helen May artist, writer
Bullard, Roger Perrin artist
Burch, G. David sculptor
Burge, Larry Brady artist
Burger, Werner Carl retired art educator
Burkee, Irvin artist
Burke-Fanning, Madeleine artist
Burkett, Helen artist
Burnett, Patricia Hill portrait artist, author, sculptor, lecturer
Burns, Toni Anthony artist
Burtley, Calvin painter, educator, publisher
Burtt, Larice A.R. artist
Busch, Nancy Elizabeth artist, educator
Butzer, Gary William mural artist
Byington, Mary artist, designer
Byrd, Marc Robert florist, designer
Cabot, Hugh, III painter, sculptor
Cameron, Shawn Dee artist, cattle rancher
Camhy, Sherry Wallerstein painter
Cancino, Javier art director
Cane, Louis Paul Joseph sculptor
Cantwell, Christopher William artist
Cappello-Angellotti, Rita artist
Cardenas-Arroyo, Santiago painter
Cardin, Pierre fashion designer
Carez, Christian Charles-Marie photographer
Carmichael, Mary Alice artist, genealogist
Carrell, Hammel Lee jewelry designer
Carroll, Billy Price artist
Cartier-Bresson, Henri photographer
Casebeer, Douglas Kelley artist, ceramist, consultant
Casey, Thomas Warren graphic design company executive, architect
Cassidy, Denis Andrew artist, architect
Cattaneo, Jacquelyn Annette Kammerer artist, educator
Cattani, Dante Thomas artist, art educator, writer
Catullo, Doris Jane sculptor
Cerri, Robert Noel photographer
Cetin, Anton artist
Cetrulo, Jerry artist, sculptor
Chambers, Glenn Darrell wildlife photographer, artist
Chandler, Clifford photographer, airline company executive
Chandler, Elisabeth Gordon (Mrs. Laci De Gerenday) sculptor, harpist
Chang, Rodney Eiu Joon artist, dentist
Chen, James Tsing-fang artist, educator, cultural center administrator
Chen, Roger Lei fashion designer
Chin, Sue Soone Marian (Suchin Chin) conceptual artist, portraitist, photographer, community affairs activist
Chodes, John Jay photographer, writer
Chowe, Flory Fa-Long sculptor, art educator, consultant
Christ, Karyn Lynn clothing and swimwear designer, poet
Cia, Manuel Lopez artist
Clague, John Rogers sculptor
Clark, Thomas Fetzer sculptor, religious art educator
Clarke, Cathrine Sylvia jewelry designer
Claus, Jürgen visual artist, writer
Clergue, Lucien Georges photographer
Cockrille, Stephen art director, business owner
Colbert, Margaret Matthew artist
Collins, Harvey Arnold art educator, retired
Colp, Norman Barry photographic artist, curator
Colquhoun, Peter Lloyd artist, educator
Colta, Onisim painter, stage designer, educator
Conrader, Constance Ruth artist, writer, librarian
Cook, Jenik Esterm (Jenik Esterm Cook Simonian) artist, educator
Cooper, Elva June artist, writer
Copplestone, David Wesley artist, small business owner
Cote, Louise Roseann creative director, designer
Cotter-Smith, Cathleen Marie art educator, artist
Cousino, Joe Ann sculptor
Cowan, Rebecca Gail artist, illustrator
Cox, Pat artist
Coyne, John Michael artist, educator
Craver, Charles Henry illustrator
Craw, Freeman (Jerry Craw) graphic artist
Crawshaw, Alwyn painter
Creates, Marlene Ruth artist
Crilley, Joseph James artist
Crippa, Daniele modern art critic, lawyer
Cruz-Diez, Carlos painter
Cuba, Ivan artist
Curt, Denise Morris artist, limner, photographer
Czorniak, Andrew artist
Dabinett, Diana Frances visual artist
Dahl, Curtis Ray photographer
Dallas, Eugenia artist, writer
Daminato, Vanda artist
D'Angora, Kendra Marie artist, preschool educator
Dangremond, David W. fine arts educator
Dank, Leonard Dewey medical illustrator, audio-visual consultant
Danon, Ambra costume designer
Danson, Andrew photographer
Dantzic, Cynthia Maris artist, educator
Datcu, Ioana visual artist
Davidhazy, Andrew photography educator
Davis, Evelyn Marguerite Bailey artist, organist, pianist
Day, Melvin Norman artist, art historian
De Bary, Etienne artist, journalist
Decil, Stella Walters (Del Decil) artist
de Gerenday, Laci Anthony sculptor, educator
DeGuatemala, Joyce sculptor
DeJack, Jacqueline Elvadeana artist, educator
de la Renta, Oscar fashion designer
de Louville de Toucy, Francois-Eudes fine art investment consultant, import executive
Delph, Shirley Cox artist, designer, illustrator, consultant
Dennick, Lori Ann artist
Dennis, Wayne Allen graphic designer, photographer, advertising executive
De Olazabal, Eugenia commercial photographer
DeZurko, Edward Robert retired art educator
d'Hauterives, Arnaud Louis Alain painter
Di Cosola, Lois Bock artist, educator
Dierauer, Julie Dawn sculptor, secondary education educator
Dietrich, Melinda visual arts administrator
Dike, Rad (Edward Conrad Dike) artist
Ding, Ning art theory educator
di Nicolini, Conte di Theodor W. Conte fine arts and antiques dealer
Disle, Michel graphic designer
Dismukes, Valena Grace Broussard photographer, former physical education educator
Dittmer, Linda Jean photographer, computer artist, retired photojournalist
Dixon, Michael Wayne designer, writer, researcher
Dobay, Susan Vilma artist
Dobie, Jeanne H. artist
Dobry, Aliki Calirroe artist
Dolack, Monte A. artist
Dombrowski, Bob artist, publisher
Dompke, Norbert Frank retired photography studio executive
Donath, Therese artist, author
Donizetti, Mario painter
Donnelly, Barbara artist, educator
Doren, Henry J.T. artist, painter
Dorn, Gordon Joseph artist, art educator
Downing, Robert James artist
Dox, Ida medical illustrator, writer
Dressel, Margaret Jane artist, art educator
Drexler, Joanne Lee art appraiser
Drinnon, Janis Bolton artist, poet, author, volunteer
Du Boise, Kim Rees artist, photographer, art educator
Duffy, Irene Karen artist
Dumas, Michael Godfrey Joseph artist
Durani Nack, Claire Joyce artist, educator, author
Durehed, Lennart Nils photographer
Earle, Patricia Nelson artist
Earwood, Barbara Tirrell artist
Edelman, Janice artist, educator
Eden, F(lorence) Brown artist
Edgerton, Debra artist, educator
Edwards, Sylvia Ann artist
Ehrenhalt, Amaranth Roslyn artist, painter, print maker, sculptor
Elder, Richard Bruce artist, writer
Elliott, George Armstrong, III artist, journalist
Elliott, Virgil Irl, Jr. artist, writer
Elliott, Walter Albert artist
Ellison, Robert W. sculptor
Elloian, Peter artist, educator
Enders, Elizabeth McGuire artist
English, Ron Dale artist
Erdman, Barbara visual artist
Eren, Zeynep artist
Eriksson, Ulf artist, consultant
Erwin, Joan Lenore artist, educator
Evans, James Hays photographer
Falk, Gathie artist
Falkman, Susan Ann sculptor
Fallon, Pat artist, art educator
Falls, Kathleene Joyce photographer
Fan, Lily Xiaoming fashion designer
Fauntleroy, Don Edward photography director
Faxon, Alicia Craig art educator
Fearing, William Kelly art educator, artist
Feigen, Richard L. art dealer, collector, author
Ferre, Sylvie art agent
Fetter, William Allan computer graphics executive
Feuerherm, Kurt Karl artist, educator
Ficara, Robin fine art consultant
Fillmore, John Dillon artist
Finch, Ruth W. photographer
Fisher, Shirley Ida A. photography and humanities educator
Fitzsimmons, Debra C. art educator, artist
Flavin, D. Aeschliman artist, lecturer, educator
Flechner, Roberta Fay graphic designer
Fok, Dennis Wai-Kee design director, educator
Forest, Fred artist
Fowler, Jennefer Rae sculptor
Fowler, Terri (Marie Therese Fowler) artist
Fox, Carson Alexandra artist, educator
Fraser, Frances Marie artist
Frederick, Craig Matthew sculptor
French, Richard Paul artist
Fretz, Joseph Nelson art educator, artist
Frieden, Jane Heller art educator
Fukuhara, Henry artist, educator
Fullerton, Dorothy Mallan artist, modeling agency executive
Gaadt, Suzanne DeMott graphic designer
Gage, Beau artist
Galina, Sheetikoff plastic artist, watercolor painter
Gallegos, Maria Bennine artist
Gamaan, Hussein graphic designer, educator, illustrator, artist
Garey, Patricia Martin artist
Garvens, Ellen Jo art educator, artist
Gaultier, Jean-Paul fashion designer
Gelfand, Andrew design consultant
Geoffrey, Iqbal (Mohammed Jawaid Iqbal Jafree) art educator
George, Cedric Matthew artist, art educator
Gepp, David photographer, lecturer
Gerhart, Charles James art director, illustrator
Gerhartz, Steven Lewis artist
Gervits, Leonid artist, art educator
Giannetti, Claudia art historian, educator
Gibson, Michael Francis art critic, author
Giles, Patricia Cecelia Parker retired art educator, graphic designer
Gilliland, Thomas art gallery director
Gisondi, John Theodore theater and television designer
Givenchy, Hubert James Marcel Taffin de fashion designer
Givot, Winnie artist, educator
Glaser, David painter, sculptor
Glesmann, Sylvia-Maria artist
Goff, Kimberly art dealer, writer
Goff, William M., Jr. art director, graphic designer
Gold, Betty Virginia artist
Goldsmith, Barbara Cecile sculptor, curator
Gonzales, Froilan Tayag fashion designer
Gonzalez, Arthur Padilla artist, educator
Gonzalez, Richard Theodore photographer
Gonzalez, Rose A-Navarro artist
Goodyear, John L. artist
Gordon, Florence Irene graphic artist, illustrator
Goudy, Ken Gordon graphic designer
Graells, Francisco (Pancho Graells) painter, caricaturist
Grant, Joan Julien artist, poet
Grauer, Gay Sherrard Meredith (Sherry Grauer) artist
Gray, George mural painter
Greaves, Stanley Joseph artist, educator
Gredzens, Sandra May Pillsbury art educator
Greenaway, Paul Raymond gallery director
Greene-Mercier, Marie Zoe sculptor
Grimes, Margaret Whitehurst artist, educator
Grizzard-Barham, Barbara Lee artist
Gruliow, Agnes Forrest artist, educator
Grunbaum, Marianne Hettner artist
Guevarra, Manuel Robinson artist, retired military officer
Gugel, M. Sue artist
Guo, XuanChang sculptor, educator
Gura, Sarit artist
Guzak, Karen Jean Wahlstrom artist
Hakeem, Muhammad Abdul artist, educator
Hampton, Phillip Jewel artist, educator
Hanan, Laura Molen artist
Hanes, John Ward sculptor, civil engineer consultant
Hanes, Ursula sculptor
Hara, Mikae artist, educator
Haraguchi, Mikimaro artist, educator
Harlan, Susan Jordan artist, educator
Harris, Robert Gaylen art director, graphic designer, illustrator
Harvey, Andre sculptor
Hay, Kenneth Gordon artist, art educator
Headings, Reneé artist, sculptor
Heitsch, Leona Mason artist, writer
Helberg, Shirley Adelaide Holden artist, educator
Helioff, Anne Graile painter
Herranen, Kathy artist, graphic designer
Herrmann, Frank (Henry) painter, educator
Heyer, Carol Ann illustrator
Heywood, Anne artist, educator, writer
Hicken, Russell Bradford art dealer, appraiser
Hicks, Gerald artist
Higby, Wayne (Donald Higby) artist, educator
Hill, Catherine Stanton freelance artist
Hilt, Mary Louise artist
Hockney, David artist
Hodge, Ann Linton artist
Hoffman, Franklin Thomas artist, printmaker, retired army officer
Hoffman, Lorre C. fine art educator, sculptor
Hollands-Robinson, Phyllis artist
Hollinbeck, Ethel Lindell sculptor
Holtz, Laurence artisan, photographer
Honegger, Federico artist
Hopkins, Cathy sculptor, educator
Hopkins, Tom artist
Hosoe, Eikoh (Toshihiro Hosoe) photographer, educator
Howell, Frank Edward artist
Hsu, Pi Hua artist
Hu, Li art educator
Huber, Colleen Adlene artist
Huber, Lynn Manos artist, educator, administrator
Huber, Robert Louis art dealer
Hudson, Noel artist
Hughes, Sarah Farrell artist
Hug-Levy, Suzy artist
Hull, Lynne environmental artist
Hungate, Jay W. artist, sculptor
Hunsperger, Elizabeth Jane art and design consultant, educator

Hunter, Robert Douglas *artist*
Huo, Bonnie Kwan *artist*
Hurn, David *photographer, lecturer*
Huser, Joyce Marie *art educator*
Hutchens, Pat Mercer *art educator*
Huxley, Mary Atsuko *artist*
Igarashi, Masaru *art museum curator, consultant*
Ihamuotila, Kristiina *textile artist*
Ipousteguy, Jean *sculptor, designer, engraver, painter*
Iverus, Lennart Jan Gustaf *artist*
Jachna, Joseph David *photographer, educator*
Jacobs, Diana Pietrocarli *botanical illustrator*
Jacobs, Ted Seth *artist, educator*
Janice, Barbara *illustrator*
Janiga, Mary Ann *art educator, artist*
Jasen, J(une) E. *artist, designer, enamelist*
Jaworska, Tamara *painter, tapestry maker*
Jenkins, Earnestine L. *art history educator*
Jiwkow, Wasil *violin maker*
Jo, Sook Jin *artist*
Johnson, Lester Larue, Jr. *artist, educator*
Johnson, Morgan Burton *artist, writer*
Jones, Clyde Adam *art educator, artist*
Jones, John Harding *photographer*
Jones, Leon Herbert, Jr. (Herb Jones) *artist*
Jonsdottir, Aslaug *illustrator, author*
Joseph, Rodney Randy *artist, arts society executive*
Juan, I-Jong *photographer, publisher, editor*
Jungkind, Walter *design educator, writer, consultant*
Kachergis, Joyce W. *designer*
Kam, Jin G. *artist, educator*
Kamali, Norma *fashion designer*
Kamienska-Carter, Eva Hanna *designer, artist*
Kann, Isabel *artist*
Kaplan, Phyllis *computer artist, painter*
Karan, Donna (Donna Faske) *fashion designer*
Karnofsky, Mollyne *artist, poet, art educator*
Karsh, Yousuf *photographer*
Kato, Tomiko *artist*
Kaufer, Shirley Helen *artist, painter*
Kawada, Janet Hansen *artist, educator*
Kawakubo, Rei *fashion designer*
Kawashima, Takeshi *artist*
Keech, Ann Marie *training design and multimedia consultant*
Kehew, George Mansir *artist*
Keith, Pauline Mary *artist, illustrator, writer*
Kelekian, Lena *painter, art restorer, geologist, researcher*
Kellogg-Smith, Peter *sculptor*
Kellum, Betsy M. *artist, educator*
Kemp, James William *graphic artist*
Kendrick, Laurie Lynn *artist*
Kennedy, Mary Sussock *artist*
Kent, Jeanne Yvonne *artist*
Kenton, Mary Jean *artist, writer*
Khosla, Manoviraj *fashion designer*
Kilguss, Elsie Schaich *artist, gallery owner*
Killian, Lawrence Harding, II (Larry H. Killian) *sculptor*
Kim, Sook Cha *artist*
Kimura, Masashi *graphic design educator*
King, Stephen William Pearce *fine art dealer, journalist, writer*
King Hookham, Eleanor *artist*
Kingsley, Judith *artist*
Kinstler, Everett Raymond *artist*
Kircher, Lynn Francis *artist*
Kirk, Brian Douglas *sculptor, art educator*
Kissel, William Thorn, Jr. *sculptor*
Kitchel, Karen Emma *artist*
Kitching, Alan *typographic artist, educator*
Kitt, Olga *artist*
Kjok, Solveig *artist, art historian, linguist*
Klear, Julie Ann *artist, educator*
Klein, Calvin Richard *fashion designer*
Klevit, Alan Barre *fine art dealer, publishing executive, motivational speaker, writer*
Kline, Mary Frances *graphic artist, sales executive*
Knebel, Constance *potter, ceramist*
Knebel, Sven E. *artist, painter, sculptor, writer*
Knepper, Ronald Alan *sculptor, educator*
Koch, Robert *art educator*
Kodner, Martin *art dealer, consultant*
Koenigstein, Georg Friedrich *artist, educator*
Koller, Shirley Leavitt *sculptor*
Kooluris Dobbs, Linda Kia *artist*
Koulouvari, Panagiota *graphic art technologist, research scientist*
Koutroulis, Aris George *artist, educator*
Kozel, Ana *astronomical artist*
Kracke, Judy Sutton *sculptor*
Kramer, Norma Domenica Andrea *artist*
Krausz, Peter Thomas *artist, gallery director, educator*
Krebs, Rockne *artist*
Krementz, Jill *photographer, author*
Kristin, Karen *artist*
Kromka, James Thomas Michael *designer, illustrator*
Kuby, Selma Miller *artist, poet*
Kujawski, Mario Julio *artist, educator*
Kulyk, Karen Gay *visual artist*
Kutosh, Sue *artist*
Labriola, Norberto Luis *artist, designer*
Lahmann, Robert Oscar *artist, retired*
La Liberte, Ann Gillis *graphic artist, consultant, designer, educator*
LaMar, Jason Randolph *graphic designer*
Lanza, John Francis, Jr. *artist, educator*
LaPlantz, David Milton *artist, educator*
Lark, Raymond *artist, art scholar*
Laufer, William Hervey *artist, printmaker*
Lauren, Ralph *fashion designer*
Lauterbach, Michael Alan *artist*
Lauttenbach, Carol *artist*
Lavatelli, Carla *sculptor, weaver*
Lawler, John Griffin *graphic designer, educator*
Layton, Harry Christopher *artist, lecturer, consultant*
Leak, Nancy Marie *artist*
Lee, Dora Fugh *artist*
Lee, Kang S. *artist, educator*
Lee, Margaret Norma *artist*
Leepa, Allen *artist, educator*
Leites, Barbara L. (Ara Leites) *artist, educator*
Lem, Richard Douglas *painter*
Leslie, John *artist, designer, photographer, sculptor*
LeVasseur, Lee Allan *fine artist*
Levine, Jack *artist*
Lewis, Judith Susanna *artist*
Lewis, Sharyn Lee *sculptor*
Libensky, Stanislav *art educator*
Light, John Richard *sculptor*
Liman, Ellen *painter, writer, arts advocate*
Lindquist, Louis William *artist, writer*
Lipton, Jackie F. *artist, educator*
Lloyd, Sally-Heath Fahnestock *artist*
Lockspeiser, Nancy Flanders *artist, designer*
Lopata, Vasili Ivanovich *artist*
Lopes Cardozo Kindersley, Lydia Helena (Lida) (Lydia Helena (Lida) Kindersley) *letter cutter and designer, publisher*
Lopez, Jesus Martinez *artist*
Lord, John Vernon *art educator, illustrator*
Lord, Richard Dennis *photographer*
Lorenson, Robert Lawrence *sculptor, art educator*
Lorenz, Albert *illustrator, educator*
Lotta, Tom (Anthony Tom Lotta) *artist*
Low, Mary Louise (Molly Low) *documentary photographer*
Lowenthal, Susan *artist, designer, retired finance executive*
Lu, Tsan Fei *artist*
Lukas, Maya *art manager*
Lundy, Anstis Burwell *artist*
Lusher, Nicholas Crosson *art dealer*
Lydon, Mary Elizabeth *artist, poet*
Lynn, Midge *artist*
Lyon, Terry Sherill *artist, retired engineer*
Machell, Iain Hugh *artist educator*
Mac Whinnie, John Vincent *artist*
Maglione, Lili *fine artist, art consultant*
Magoni, Despo *artist*
Mag Walz, Günther *artist*
Mahfouz, Ilham Badreddine *artist*
Mahmud, Shireen Dianne *photographer*
Mallet, Jacques Robert *art dealer*
Malmanger, Magne *art educator*
Mangold, Robert L. *sculptor, retired educator*
Mann, Frank Bert *visual artist, painter*
Mannweiler, Mary-Elizabeth *painter*
Marable, Simeon-David *artist*
Maree, Wendy *painter, sculptor*
Margolin, Jean Spielberg *artist*
Marks, Shirley I. *artist*
Marlatt, Tom Owen *artist*
Marlow, Audrey Swanson *artist, designer*
Marlowe, Willie *artist, fine arts educator*
Marshall, Nathalie *artist, writer, educator*
Martin, Agnes *artist*
Mártonyi, Csaba Lászlo *ophthalmic photographer, imager*
Marvin, Freda Mary *art educator, nurse*
Maser, Siegfried *design educator, researcher*
Massey, Allyn F. *artist, educator*
Masson, Manju *graphic designer, scientist, daycare administrator*
Mathieu, Georges Victor Adolphe *artist*
Matteson, Clarice Chris *artist, educator*
Matthew, Neil Edward *artist, educator*
Mauney, Thomas Lee *theater designer*
Maxwell, George Russell *scenic designer*
Mayer, Joyce Harris *artist*
Mazzilli, Roslyn *sculptor*
McCann, Jean Friedrichs *artist, educator*
McCargar, Eleanor Barker *portrait painter*
McCoy, John Denny *artist*
McCray, Dorothy Westaby *artist, printmaker, educator*
McDonald Smith, Paul *artist*
McFarland, Willellyn Shaw *artist, educator*
McGrail, Jeane Kathryn *artist, educator, poet, curator*
McIntosh, Molly Jean *interior designer*
McKay, Renee *artist*
McKenzie, Kathleen Julianna *artist*
McKey, Winston Jackson (Jack McKey) *artist, boat designer, builder*
McKinley-Haas, Mary *artist*
McKinney, Charles Michael *artist, educator*
McMahon, Eileen Marie *art agent*
McNamara-Ringewald, Mary Ann Thérèse *artist, educator*
McPherson, Kenneth John *art director*
Mead, Carl Duane *gallery owner, educator*
Mellor, Marjorie Loth *art and museum education consultant*
Mendoza, Ryan *artist*
Merfeld, Gerald Lydon *artist*
Metzger, Philip William *artist, author*
Michaels-Paque, Joan Marie *artist, educator*
Miller, Jean Patricia Salmon *art educator*
Miller, Peter Daniel *artist, printmaker*
Mills, Susan C. *sculptor*
Milne-Kuhn, Michelle Dawn *artist*
Mitchell, Alison *textile artist*
Mizrahi, Isaac *fashion designer*
Mochizuki, Takeshi *artist, art critic*
Moeller, Susan Elaine *artist*
Moffett, Donald R. *artist, retired sales and marketing executive*
Molnar, Vera (Veronique Molnar) *visual artist, educator*
Monk, Diana Charla *artist, stable owner*
Moonie, Liana Maria *artist*
Moore, Mary French (Muffy Moore) *potter, community activist*
Moorhead, Rolande Annette Reverdy *artist, educator*
Morey, Jean W. *artist*
Morgan, Anne Margaret Barclay *artist, author, ambassador*
Morreau, Jacqueline *artist*
Morrison, Margaret L. *artist, educator, consultant*
Morton, Lee Jack, Jr. *graphic artist, designer, art educator*
Moyé, Dean *lighting design professional*
Mullins, W. Stan *artist, cultural ambassador*
Multhaup, Merrel Keyes *artist*
Mundschenk, Mark *photographer*
Muranaka, Hideo *artist, educator*
Mussi, Alessandro *painter, writer*
Myers, Adele Anna *artist, educator, nun*
Myers, Eugene Ekander *art consultant*
Naar, Harry I. *fine arts educator, artist*
Nack, Claire Durani *artist, author*
Napp, Gudrun F. *artist*
Neiman, LeRoy *artist*
Nelipovich, Sandra Grassi *artist*
Nelson, Carey Boone *sculptor*
Nemiroff, Maxine Celia *art educator, gallery owner, consultant*
Nery, Eduardo *painter*
Ness, Albert Kenneth *artist*
Neumann, Jeffrey Jay *photographer, minister*
Newman, Stacey Clarfield *artist, curator*
Newmark, Marilyn *sculptor*
Nguyen, Giang Dai (Dai-Giang) *artist, sculptor, graphic artist, muralist*
Nitsch, Carolina *art dealer, publisher*
Noakes, Michael *portrait and landscape painter*
Noble, Lawrence Alan *artist*
Noffke, Jane Bunge *sculptor*
Nogi, Tiaki *textile designer*
Noonan, Robert Harry *art and music educator*
Noone, Kathleen Mary *art educator*
Nuss, Joanne Ruth *sculptor, artist*
Nuzzo, Anne L. *artist*
Nyiri, Joseph Anton *sculptor, art educator*
O'Beil, Hedy *artist*
Ochs, Richard Wayne *artist, gallery owner*
Odom, Patrician Ann (Patt Odom) *artist, educator*
Odulio, Sheridoni Torres *illustrator*
O'Hara, Paul Anthony, Jr. *retired art educator, artist*
Oldenburg, Claes Thure *artist*
Olesen, Marie *fashion designer*
Oliver, Gilda Maria *sculptor, artist*
Olivere, Raymond Louis *illustrator, artist, portrait painter*
Olsen, Richard James *artist, art educator*
Olson, Lynn *sculptor, painter, writer*
Oman, Julia Trevelyan *theatrical designer*
O'Neill, Casteen *artist*
Ord, Linda Banks *artist*
O'Reilly, Myra Faith *artist*
Orlowska-Warren, Lenore Alexandria *art educator, fiber artist*
Orr, Carole *artist*
Ortlip, Mary Krueger *artist*
Ortlip, Paul Daniel *artist*
Osterhaus, Greg S. *artist, graphic designer*
Ovissi, Nasser *artist*
Owen, June Lois *artist*
Owen, Thomas James *artist, educator*
Ozaki, Yukio *artist, educator*
Palmieri, Samuel Nicolari *artist, educator*
Palser, Beth Anne *painter*
Papi, Liza Renia *artist, writer, educator*
Parineh, Parima *artist*
Park, Chung *painter, educator, computer software developer*
Park, Lee (Lee Parklee) *artist*
Pascual, Carlota *painter*
Pasquini, Antonio *sculptor, painter*
Passlof, Pat *artist, educator*
Paterson, Tony Ralph *sculptor, educator*
Pavlakos, Ellen Tsatiri *sculptor*
Payne, John D. *art educator, sculptor, consultant*
Peet, Caroline Linda *artist*
Peker, Elya Abel *artist*
Pellicone, William *artist, sculptor, writer, architect*
Peretz, Carol *fashion designer*
Perlmutter, Jack *artist, lithographer*
Perroni, Carol *artist, painter*
Perry, Sarah Hollis *artist, archivist*
Persche, Henry-Peter *art consultant, artist*
Peters, Andrea Jean *artist*
Peters, Evelyn Joan *artist*
Peterson, Dorothy Lulu *artist, writer*
Pettersen, Tor Arve *graphic designer*
Petterson, Margo *artist*
Phillips, Kimberly Sandra *artist*
Phillips, Ronald Edward *artist, sales executive*
Picasso, Maria Isabel *artist*
Pickering, Pollyanna *artist*
Pieper, Patricia Rita *artist, photographer*
Pippin, Ronald Gene *artist*
Piza, Arthur Luiz *painter*
Platus, Libby *artist, sculptor, speaker*
Plavinskaya, Anna Dmitrievna *artist*
Plawska-Jackiewicz, Kristina *sculptor*
Podesta, Robert Edward *artist*
Polaji, Sabaji Bhagwan *artist*
Poleskie, Stephen Francis *artist, educator, writer*
Pollaro, Paul Philip *artist*
Poloukhine, Olga *artist*
Pope, Ingrid Bloomquist *sculptor, poet*
Pope, Robert David *artist, philosopher*
Powell, John Constantine *artist*
Powers, Runa Skötte *artist*
Preuss, Roger E(mil) *artist*
Prince, Leah Fanchon *art educator and research institute administrator*
Provis, Dorothy L(ouise) *artist, sculptor*
Puckett, Richard Edward *artist, consultant, retired recreation executive*
Purcell, George Richard *artist, postal employee*
Pusey, Mavis Iona *artist, educator*
Qian, Zifen *artist, researcher*
Quant, Mary *fashion and cosmetics company executive, designer*
Quest, Kristina Kay *art educator, small business owner*
Raczka, Tony Michael *artist*
Rainey, Jocelyn Elizabeth *artist, educator*
Ralston, Lucy Virginia Gordon *artist*
Ramos, Theodore Sanchez de Piña *artist, educator*
Rankine, V.V. *sculptor, painter*
Rapaport, Richard J. *artist, researcher*
Rasmuson, Brent (Jacobsen) *photographer, graphic artist, lithographer*
Raviv, Ilana *artist*
Ray, Robert *educator, sculptor*
Read, Mark Everard *art dealer*
Reenpää, Olli *graphic arts company executive*
Reese, Claudia *artist*
Reinoehl, Richard Louis *artist, scholar, martial artist*
Rendl-Marcus, Mildred *artist, economist*
Reni, (Arlene Patricia Theresa Brown) *artist*
Renouf, Edda *artist*
Resnick, Kenneth *photography director*
Reynolds, Nancy Bradford duPont (Mrs. William Glasgow Reynolds) *sculptor*
Reynolds, Roy Ernest *artist, sculptor*
Rhodes, Ann Frances Bloodworth *artist, art history lecturer*
Richards, Jay Claude *commercial photographer, news service executive, historian*
Richards, Patricia Jones *artist, poet*
Richert, Robert A. *artist*
Rickett, Carolyn Kaye Master *artist, criminologist*
Rideout, Edna Baker *artist*
Ringgold, Faith *artist*
Ristow, Gail Ross *art educator, paralegal, children's rights advocate*
Rivas, Silvia *artist, educator*
Roald, Curt *banknote and securities designer, retired*
Robben, Mary Margaret *portrait artist, painter*
Roberts, Caryl *artist*
Robertson, Lorna Dooling *artist, real estate developer*
Robins, Betty Dashew *antiques and arts dealer*
Robinson, Kenneth Roger *art educator*
Robinson, Lynda Hickox *artist*
Robinson, Michael Francis *private art dealer and appraiser*
Roche, Joan I. *artist*
Rodriguez-Amat, Jordi *artist, educator, architect*
Rogers, Eva *artist, poet*
Rogers, Ruby Elizabeth *artist*
Roller, Marion *sculptor*
Roman, Patricia Ann *sculptor*
Rooney, Maria Dewing *photographer*
Rosalsky, Barbara Ellen *artist, home health aide*
Roseberg, Carl Andersson *sculptor, educator*
Rosenbaum, Belle Sara *appraiser, interior designer, museum director, educator*
Rosenberg, Alex Jacob *art dealer, curator, fine arts appraiser, educator*
Rosenberg, Carole *art dealer, real estate broker*
Rosenberg, Herb *sculptor, educator*
Rosenfeld, Sarena Margaret *artist*
Rosenthal, Randall Marc *artist*
Ross, Beatrice Brook *artist*
Ross, Molly Owings *gold and silversmith, jewelry designer, small business owner*
Rothermel, Joan Ashley *artist*
Rothschild, Jennifer Ann *artist, educator*
Rothwell, Elaine B. *artist*
Rowe, Michael Duane *artist*
Rowley, Frank Selby, Jr. *artist*
Ruffo, Michael *painter*
Rugala, Karen Francis (Karen Francis) *painter, television producer*
Rush, Julia Ann Halloran (Mrs. Richard Henry Rush) *artist, writer*
Rye, Marcy Louise *graphic designer, artist*
Saarelma, Hannu J. *graphic arts educator*
Sabelis, Huibert *artist*
Sacal Micha, José *sculptor, educator, consultant*
Sadek, Hassan Sadek *sculptor, educator*
Safer, John *artist, lecturer, banker, real estate developer*
Saghir, Adel Jamil *artist, painter, sculptor*
Sahler, Hildegard *art historian, journalist*
St. Lifer, Jane M. *art dealer, curator*
St. Pierre, Joyce Bourré *art educator*
Sainty, Guy Stair *art dealer*
Sakaoka, Yasue *artist, educator*
Saletta, Mary Elizabeth (Betty) *sculptor, rancher*
Samuels, Fern Jacqueline *artist, educator*
Samuels, Hanna *artist*
Sanabria, Sherry Zvares *artist*
Sanchez, Leonedes Monarrize Worthington (His Royal Highness Duke de Leonedes of Spain Sicily Greece) *fashion designer*
San Miguel, Manuel *painter, historian, composer, poet*
Sarnoff, Lili-Charlotte (Lolo Sarnoff) *artist, executive*
Saru, George *artist*
Sasaki, John Eric *art company executive, artist*
Satin, Claire Jeanine *sculptor, book artist*
Savedra, Jeannine Evangeline *art educator, artist*
Schabner, Dawn Freeble *artist, educator*
Schaefer, Marilyn Louise *artist, writer, educator*
Schafer, Ruth Erma *artist, educator*
Schellart-vanDeursen, Riky Hendrika Matthea *artist, educator*
Schiller, Sophie *artist, graphic designer*
Schrank, Shirley Ann *artist*
Schraufnagel, Tony *artist, educator*
Schreiber, Eileen Sher *artist*
Schrey, Manfred *lithography educator*
Schultz, Evelyn Ecale *artist*
Schütz, Helmut Georg *art educator*
Schwalb, Harry *artist*
Schwan, LeRoy Bernard *artist, retired educator*
Schwartz, Charles Robert, Jr. *photographer*
Schwebel, Renata Manasse *sculptor*
Searles, Edna Lowe *artist, illustrator*
Seddon, Priscilla Tingey *painter*
Seddon, Richard Harding *artist*
Sehgal, Amar Nath *sculptor*
Sehili, Mahmoud *artist*
Sehring, Adolf *artist, sculptor*
Seiden, Beatrice Rabin *artist*
Seiffer, Neil Mark *photographer*
Seigo, Satoru Nishi *artist, educator*
Selberg, Timothy Scott *artist*
Semple, Margaret Olivia *arts education director*
Sempliner, John Alexander *artist*
Senkarik, Mikki *oil painter*
Sensiba, Winifred J. *lighting designer*
Senter, Terence Arthur *art and design history educator*
Setien, Edwardo *artist*
Shackleton, Keith Hope *artist, naturalist*
Shaffer, Mary Louise *art educator*
Sheaff, Richard Dana *communications and graphic designer*
Shell, Robert Edward Lee *photographer, writer*
Shelley, Clyde Burton *artist*
Shinolt, Eileen Thelma *artist*
Shirayama, Sadao *art educator*
Shistle, Patricia Anne *fine artist*
Shpitalnik, Vladimir *set and costume designer*
Shryock, Verna E. *artist*
Shubart, Dorothy Louise Tepfer *artist, educator*
Shurtleff, Akiko Aoyagi *artist, consultant*
Shwayder, Elizabeth Yanish *sculptor*
Siegel, Mary Ann Garvin *author*
Siejka, George John *artist*
Siff, Marlene Ida *artist, designer*
Sigal-Ibsen, Rose *artist*
Simon, Robert Stephen *artist*
Simon, Teru *artist, sculptor, ceramist, educator*
Skinner, Delda Smith *artist, educator*
Skoor, John Brian *art educator, art consultant*
Slangal, Lovella Joeann *artist*
Slater, Jess Everett *artist*
Slavick, Ann Lillian *art educator, arts*
Slonem, Hunt *artist*
Smith, David Lyle *art educator, artist*
Smith, Dorothy *artist, actress*
Smith, Dorothy Ottinger *jewelry designer, civic worker*
Smith, Jack *artist*
Smith, Paul Brierley *fashion designer*
Smith, Peter Edward *sculptor, artist*
Smith, Ralph *artist*
Smith, Susan Porter *artist, environmentalist*
Smith, Terence Edwin *art historian*
Smittle, Nelson Dean *artist*
Smyth, Craig Hugh *fine arts educator*
Snider, Stephen William *art director, graphic designer*
Sobell, Nina R. *artist*
Soe, H.S. Sunny *painter*
Somuncu, Melek Tülin *artist*
Sorenson, Roxann *artist*
Sorrin, Mary Louise *artist, nurse*
Soulages, Pierre *painter*
Southworth, Linda Jean *artist, critic, educator, poet*
Sozzani, Laurent Steven George *art restorer, conservator*
Sparke, Penny Anne *history of design educator, writer, researcher*
Spears, Diane Shields *artist, retired art academy administrator*
Speck, Catherine Margaret *art historian*
Speranza, Linda M. *art educator, artist*

Stahr, Curtis Brent *photographer, art association administrator, educator*
Stassen, Willy *photographer, educator*
Stavans, Isaac *artist*
Steel, Kuniko June *retired artist*
Stermer, Dugald Robert *designer, illustrator, writer, consultant*
Stettner, Louis *photographer*
Stevens-Sollman, Jeanne Lee *artist*
Stewart, Arlene Jean Golden *designer, stylist*
Stewart-Bell, Leslie Ann *sculptor, moldmaker*
Stockdale, Sally Boyd *artist, realtor*
Stolpin, William Roger *artist, printmaker, retired engineer*
Stripling, Betty Keith *artist, nurse*
Strong, Karin Hjort *artist, educator*
Strong-Cuevas, Elizabeth *sculptor*
Stump, M. Pamela *sculptor*
Sullivan, Shirley Ross (Shirley Ross Davis) *art collector*
Sumida, Gregory Zio *artist, photographer, musician*
Sun, Chao *artist, consultant*
Sunderman, Robert Allen *artist, set designer*
Sunward, Justin Hugo *artist, writer*
Sutton, Kerry Peter *exhibition and graphic designer*
Sutton, Paul Robert *graphic designer, computer programmer*
Svendsen, Alf *artist, art educator*
Svoboda, Joanne Dzitko *artist, educator*
Sweet, Harvey *theatrical set designer, lighting designer*
Sylvester, Lynda Joann *product designer*
Szabo, Franz Georg *computer artist, science journalist, computer mathematician, pipe sculptor*
Szajna, Jozef *painter, stage designer, theater director*
Szyszka, Roswita Evelyn *artist*
Taft, Nellie Leaman *artist*
Tagliente, Josephine Marlene *artist*
Tandy, Jean Conkey *art educator*
Tanigawa, Atsushi *art educator*
Taranczewski, Pawel Maria *painter*
Tarsnane, Terence James *artist, educator*
Tatum, Arthur, III *educator, lexicographer, pianist*
Tawfik, Ruhiyah Mohamad Tawfik *artist*
Taylor, Gage *artist, writer*
Taylor, Margaret Turner *clothing designer, architectural designer, economist, writer, planner*
Tchaicovsky, Beny *artist, composer, musician*
Terpening, Virginia Ann *artist*
Terry, Elizabeth Hays *calligrapher, needlepoint designer*
Thies, Timothy R. *artist, gallery owner*
Thomas, Franklin Rosborough *retired animator*
Thompson, Mary Koleta *sculptor, non-profit organization director*
Thompson, Terrie Lee *graphic designer*
Thomson, Helen Louise *artist*
Thorpe, Samuel Stanley, Jr. *artist*
Tierney, Robert *artist, textile and graphic designer*
Tilson, Joe Charles *artist, sculptor*
Tisdale, Gregory Brokaw *artist*
Tisma, Marija Stevan *artist*
Todonai, Robert Paul *artist*
Tollifson, Thomas Gerald *retired art education consultant, teacher*
Tomkow, Gwen Adelle *artist*
Tonnellier, Michel Andre *art educator, architect, painter, engraver*
Treacy, Sandra Joanne Pratt *art educator, artist*
Treherne, Katherine Thamer *painter, illustrator*
Triggs, Teal Ann *design educator, historian*
Trone, Jacquelyn Lee *artist*
Tyler, Richard *fashion designer*
Tylevich, Alexander V. *sculptor, architect, educator*
Tzallas, Niove *painter*
Uehling, Judith Olson *artist, painter, printmaker, sculptor*
Ultes, Elizabeth Cummings Bruce *artist, retired art historian and librarian*
Ungaro, Emanuel Matteotti *fashion designer*
Unger, Howard Albert *artist, photographer, educator*
Urban, Alan Gene *painter, art executive*
Ushenko, Audrey Andreyevna *painter, art historian, educator*
Valdez, Nora *artist, educator*
Van Allen, Katrina Frances (Katrina Frances) *painter*
Van Bruggen, Coosje *artist*
Van Rensselaer, Miles *artist, sculptor*
Van Tiel, Dagmar Helga *retired designer, educator*
Varik, Matti *sculptor*
Vaugel, Martine Olga *sculptor, educator*
Verlinde, Claude *artist*
Versace, Donatella *fashion designer*
Vikhagen, Håvard *artist*
Villoch, Kelly Carney *art director*
Vitkine, Alexandre *computer sculptor*
Volmer, Suzanne *artist*
von Retyi, Andreas *artist, writer*
von Rydingsvard, Ursula Karoliszyn *sculptor*
Voorhees, Stephanie Robin Nee Faught *retired art educator*
Vreman, Anna Aurora *artist, technical writer*
Wachtel, Joseph H. *sculptor*
Waldner, Veryl Culver *artist*
Walotsky, Ron *illustrator*
Walters, Robert Frederick *illustrator, museum consultant*
Walton, Anthony John (Tony Walton) *theater and film designer, book illustrator*
Wandel, Sharon Lee *sculptor*
Warburton, Minnie *writer, art educator*
Wassmer, Theodore Milton *artist*
Watling, Michael Lee *sculptor*
Watson, Helen Richter *educator, ceramic artist*
Weaver, Jacquelyn Kunkel Ivey *artist, educator*
Webster, Jeffrey Leon *graphic designer*
Wechsler, Gil *lighting designer*
Weir, Sonja Ann *artist*
Weitz, Jeanne Stewart *artist, educator*
Wenegrat, Saul S. *arts administrator, art educator, consultant*
Wennberg, Teresa *artist*
Weresh, Thelma Faye *sculptor, artist*
Weston, Dawn Thompson *artist, researcher*
Wexler, George *retired art educator, artist*
White, Roger L., Jr. *graphic designer, art director*
Whitener, Carolyn Raye *artist*
Whitman, Kathy Velma Rose (Elk Woman Whitman) *artist, sculptor, art educator*
Wick, Tamara *photographer, artist, writer*
Wiley, William T. *artist*
Wilhoit, Susan Cassidy *artist*
Wilkins, H. Andrew *artist*
Williams, Adair L. *artist*
Williams, DeWayne Arthur, Jr. *artist, fish and wildlife biologist*
Williams-Steinwender, Karin Mae *artist*
Winer, Jessica Daryl *artist*
Winter, Mark Anthony *graphic designer, educator, filmmaker*
Winterer-Schulz, Barbara Jean *designer, author*
Wojnecki, Stefan *photographer*
Wolfe, Jon M *glass artist*
Wolfe, Mildred Nungester *artist*
Wood, Kenneth Anderson *artist, designer, consultant*
Woolard, Connie Ward *artist, retired art gallery manager*
Worden, Katharine Cole *sculptor*
Worden, Marny *artist, musician*
Wosk, Miriam *artist*
Woskow, Catherine Rose *artist*
Wostrel, Nancy Jo A.W.S. *painter, illustrator*
Wray, Geraldine Smitherman (Jerry Wray) *artist*
Wu, Wayne Wen-Yau *artist*
Yager, William Stewart *sculptor*
Yamada, Kohei *art educator*
Yamaguchi, Yuriko Fujita *artist*
Yampolsky, Phyllis *artist*
Yee, Steve *artist*
Yen, Joseph Chen-Ying *artist, educator*
Yost, Nancy Runyon *artist, designer, art educator*
Zapf, Hermann *book and type designer*
Zavada, Barbara Johanna *artist*
Zehring, Peggy Johnson *artist*
Zekman, Terri Margaret *graphic designer*
Zhang, Dawo *artist, calligrapher*
Zhao, Hongbin *artist*
Zimet, Matthew *graphic arts and science educator*
Zivelonghi, Kurt Daniel *computer graphics artist, art director, designer*

ASSOCIATIONS AND ORGANIZATIONS. *See also* specific fields.

Abdulai, Yesufu Seyyid Momoh *international agency executive*
Abouzayd, Shafiq Bahjat *educational foundation executive*
Agarwal, Ghanshyam Das *association executive*
Ahuja, Chander Shekhar *non-profit association administrator*
Aldridge, Sandra *civic volunteer*
Al-Hejailan, Jamil Ibrahim *international organization executive*
al-Meguid, Ahmad Esmat Abdel *international organization executive*
al-Omair, Saleh *trade association administrator*
Alper, Anne Elizabeth *professional association executive*
Altéus, Åke *foundation administrator*
Ambach, Gordon Mac Kay *educational association executive*
Ammerman, Gale Richard *organization executive, retired educator*
Amoako, Kingsley Y. *international organization administrator*
Anderson, Dale *philanthropist*
Anderson, Dana Cunningham *director, teacher, artist*
Anderson, Richard Theodore *association executive, urban planner*
Angermüller, Rudolph *music foundation executive*
Anthony, Sylvia *social welfare organization executive*
Anthony-Byng, Kimberly Ann *social services administrator, psychotherapist*
Appel, Marsha Ceil *association executive*
Aragona, Giancarlo *political organization executive*
Armson, Frederick Simon Arden *company executive, not-for-profit organization*
Arnold, Robert William *nonprofit corporation executive*
Arnold, Ronald Henri *nonprofit organization executive, consultant*
Arnold, William Edwin *health advocate, consultant*
Aron, Peter Arthur *charitable foundation executive, private investor*
Aronovich, Ilya *fraternity president, small business owner*
Arpino, Mario *NATO official*
Ash, Dorothy Matthews *civic worker*
Ashbrook, Kate Jessie *charitable organization director*
Ataman, Oktar *NATO official*
Augustine, Norman Ralph *organization executive, educator*
Aung San Suu Kyi *human rights activist, writer*
Ayres, Janice Ruth *social service executive*
Bahlman, David Arthur *cultural society administrator*
Ball, Samuel *educational administrator, psychologist*
Balter, Frances Sunstein *civic worker*
Balz, Frank Joseph *trade association executive, researcher*
Baptiste-Ahmed, Linda *social services professional*
Barbe, Yves *association administrator, consultant*
Barnes, William David *non-profit charities consultant, publisher*
Barnett, Eric Oliver *foundation administrator*
Barranco, Gregory Crofford *lobbyist*
Bartnicki, Karen Jo *social services administrator*
Bashore, Irene Saras *research institute administrator*
Bates, Lura Wheeler *trade association executive*
Beals, L(oren) Alan *association executive*
Beardsley, Theodore S(terling), Jr. *professional society administrator*
Beatty, Frances *civic worker*
Beck, Irene Clare *educational consultant, writer*
Beigbeder, Yves Bayard *international organization educator, researcher*
Belcher, Max *social services administrator, college dean*
Belfrage, Anna C. *executive club president*
Bellamy, Carol *international organization executive*
Benjamin, Adelaide Wisdom *community volunteer and activist*
Bergman, Charles Cabe *foundation executive*
Berna, Marie-Rose *international organization executive*
Berthelot, Yves M. *international organization administrator*
Betancourt Lopez, Antonio L. *association executive*
Bex, Brian William Louis *educational administrator*
Binder, Mildred Katherine *retired public welfare agency executive*
Bircher, Martin M(aximilian) *foundation director, German language educator*
Bjornson, Edith Cameron *foundation executive, communications consultant*
Black, Geneva Arlene *social services agency administrator*
Black, Page Morton *civic worker*
Blackie, Peter Antony *international administrator*
Blair, Kathie Lynn *social services worker*
Blanco, Josefa Joan-Juana (Jossie Blanco) *social services administrator*
Block, Francine Ellen *educational association administrator, consultant*
Blom, Aart *non-profit organization administrator*
Boersma, Lawrence Allan (Larry Allan) *animal welfare administrator, photographer*
Bogdansky, Betsy Bougess *professional society administrator*
Bompas, Donald George *charitable organization executive, consultant*
Bond, Julian *civil rights leader*
Bond, Niles Woodbridge *cultural institute executive, former foreign service officer*
Bonner, Charles William, III *community services executive, newspaper writer*
Boyd-Kjellen, Gia *social services administrator*
Brandt, Gene Stuart *fundraising consultant*
Brasington, Dyan Lingle *association executive*
Brawer, Catherine Coleman *foundation executive, curator*
Bricker, William Rudolph *organization executive*
Brierley, Peter William *charitable foundation administrator*
Bristow, Jamett LaGenia *not-for-profit developer*
Brooks, Gene (Leslie Gene Brooks) *cultural association administrator*
Brooksbank, Ray Stephen *retired professional society administrator*
Brooks Shoemaker, Virginia Lee *volunteer, librarian*
Brosnan, Carol Raphael Sarah *retired arts administrator, musician*
Brouse, Deborah Elizabeth *health association executive*
Brown, Janice Anne *political organization executive*
Brown, Joy Alice *social services administrator*
Brown, Judith Ann *association executive*
Bruck Lieb Port, Lilly *retired consumer advisor, broadcaster, columnist*
Bruton, John Macaulay *trade association executive*
Bryan, A(lonzo) J(ay) *retired service club official*
Buckley, Edgar *political organization worker*
Buckmaster, Christopher Meredith *business association executive*
Buhl, Cynthia Maureen *foreign policy educator and advocate*
Burdette, Jane Elizabeth *nonprofit association executive, consultant*
Burks, Rocky Alan *independent living center executive, consultant*
Burnett, Judith Jane *public relations consultant*
Busch, C. Thomas *fundraising executive*
Busfield, Roger Melvil, Jr. *retired trade association executive, educator*
Bush, Barbara Pierce *volunteer, former First Lady of the United States*
Byrne, Martha F.C. *education association executive*
Calder, Martin Charles *social welfare administrator*
Calhoun, John Alfred *social services administrator*
Campbell, Stewart Fred *foundation executive*
Carey, Ronald *former labor union leader*
Carine, James *association administrator*
Carlton, James Joseph *Australian Red Cross administrator*
Carrard, Francois Denis *international organization administrator, lawyer*
Carrington, Edwin Wilberforce *international organization administrator*
Carter, Michael Andrew *missionary center administrator*
Carter, Ruth B. (Mrs. Joseph C. Carter) *foundation administrator*
Cathomas, Bernard *arts council administrator*
Cawaling, Manuel Roberto *artist, cultural organization administrator*
Chacko, Samuel *association official*
Chadwick, Derek James *foundation administrator*
Chalker, Robert Phelps *retired association executive*
Chamberlain, Jean Nash *county government department director*
Chandler, James Barton *international education consultant*
Chapin, Maryan Fox *civic worker*
Charles, Cheryl *non-profit and business executive*
Chebez, Juan Carlos *foundation administrator*
Cherpitel, Didier J. *international organization executive*
Cheung, Fanny Mui-ching *educator, foundation administrator*
Chien, Francoise Fang-Lin *immigration and education consultant*
Chilcote, Samuel Day, Jr. *trade association administrator*
Christman, Irene Ranck *retired music education association administrator*
Christopher, James Roy *executive director*
Church, Jane Evelyn *executive director, counselor*
Cicerchi, Eleanor Ann Tomb *fundraising executive*
Clark, Alicia Garcia *political party official*
Clarke, Evelyn Woodman *volunteer*
Clarkson, Elisabeth Ann Hudnut *civic worker*
Clemons, Robert Earl *non-profit organization administrator*
Cline, Michael Patrick *association executive*
Coe, Margaret Louise Shaw *community service volunteer*
Colchester, Charles Meredith Hastings *charitable trust executive*
Coly, Lisette *foundation executive*
Combaldieu, Jean-Claude *trade organization executive*
Conner, James Hoyt *trade association executive*
Conway, Gordon Richard *foundation executive*
Cord, Steven B. *foundation administrator*
Corder, Steven Lee *non-profit organization executive*
Corrigan-Maguire, Mairead *peace worker*
Courshon, Carol Biel *civic worker*
Cowles, Elizabeth Hall *program consultant*
Craik, Wendy Jean *farm federation administrator*
Crist, Bainbridge *volunteer*
Crooke, Kenneth Warren *political party director*
Cucchi, Giuseppe *NATO official*
Cullom, William Otis *trade association executive*
Cutler, Morene Parten *civic worker*
Czékus, János *NATO official*
Dahlman, Roland Sven *advocate*
Daniels, Kathleen A. *educational administrator*
Danjczek, Michael Harvey *social service administrator*
Darnall, Roberta Morrow *association executive*
Decker, Harley S. *volunteer*
Deissler, Mary Alice *foundation executive*
De Jouvenel, Hugues Alain *think-tank executive, consultant*
de Kergorlay, Roland Marie *association executive*
De Lung, Jane Solberger *independent sector executive*
DeMarco, Roland R. *foundation executive*
de Marneffe, Barbara Rowe *volunteer*
Dembowski, Frederick Lester *educational administrator, educator, consultant*
Depan, Mary Elizabeth *civic volunteer, nurse*
de Pret, Lode Jean-Claude *engineering association executive, diplomat*
de Puig, Lluis Maria *international organization executive*
De Schutter, Krishna Serge *organization administrator*
Diakité, Madubuko Arthur R. *association administrator, consultant*
Diasio, Ilse Wolfartsberger *volunteer*
Dickinson, Jane W. *social services administrator*
DiConti, Michael Andrew *trade organization executive*
Didisheim, Count Michel George *foundation executive*
Dillon, Robert Morton *retired association executive, retired educator, architectural consultant*
Diouf, Jacques *intergovernmental organization administrator*
Docherty, Anne *association executive*
Dodd, Morgan Cary *fundraising executive*
Dolan, Thomas Christopher *professional society administrator*
Dole, Elizabeth Hanford *former charitable organization administrator, former secretary of labor, former secretary of transportation*
Dolk, Arthur Johan *advocate, solicitor*
Donoho, Tim Mark *charity executive, entrepreneur*
Drake, Stanley Joseph *association executive*
Drapalik, Betty R. *civic worker, artist*
DuBois, Paul Martin Joseph *non-profit organization executive*
du Bois-Reymond, Alard *foundation administrator*
Duhme, Carol McCarthy *civic worker*
Dundas, Charles Christopher *educational administrator*
Dunn, Anne Yvonne *advocacy organization executive*
Dvora, Susan (Susan Bernstein) *non-profit organization professional*
Eastman, Francesca Marlene *volunteer, art historian*
Eberhard, Franz Valentin *association executive*
Eberlie, Richard Frere *trade association director*
Ehlers, Eleanor May Collier (Mrs. Frederick Burton Ehlers) *civic worker*
El-Beblawi, Hazem Abdel Aziz *international organization administrator*
El Gammal, Hussein Mokhtar *organization official, researcher, consultant*
Elliot, Ligia Gomes *researcher, evaluator*
Elliott, Thomas Michael *association executive, educator, consultant*
Ellis, Anne Elizabeth *fundraiser*
Ellis, Raymond Clinton, Jr. *association executive*
Emely, Mary Ann *association executive*
Eppes, William David *civic worker, curator*
Ertl, Gerhard *institute director*
Espiroto Santo, Gabriel *NATO official, military officer*
Estievenart, Georges *executive director*
Evans, Valerie Marie *association executive*
Faller, Dorothy Anderson *international agency administrator*
Fawcett, Marie Ann Formanek (Mrs. Roscoe Kent Fawcett) *civic leader*
Ferree, John Newton, Jr. *fundraising specialist, consultant*
Ferreira, Carlos José Galamba *social foundation administrator*
Filippelli-DiManna, Leslie Pamela *fundraiser*
Fiore, Colleen Mary *professional society administrator*
Fisher, John Morris *association official, educator*
Fisk, Doris Rosalie Scanlan *volunteer*
Flanders, Eleanor Carlson *community volunteer*
Flood, Henry *non-profit organization executive*
Florian, Marianna Bolognesi *civic leader*
Floyd, Jeanne *professional society administrator*
Fobes, John Edwin *international organization official*
Fockler, Herbert Hill *foundation executive*
Foerst, John George, Jr. *fundraising executive*
Fogelberg, Paul Alan *continuing education company executive*
Folgate, Cynthia A. *domestic violence systems coordinator, educator*
Fordice, Patricia Owens *civic leader, former state first lady*
Foro, Lynda J. *humane organization director*
Forsythe, Patricia Hays *development professional*
Fourcard, Inez Garey *foundation executive, artist*
Fournel, Paul Lucien *writer, professional society administrator*
Frank, Gerald Wendel *civic leader, journalist*
Frankl, Jeanne Silver *association executive*
Freiha, Judith Anne Supple *volunteer*
Frey, James Severin *educational association executive*
Freyd, William Pattinson *fund raising executive, consultant*
Friedman, Miles *trade association executive, financial services company executive, university lecturer*
Fritz, Thomas Vincent *association and business executive*
Fuentes, Angel *health organization coordinator*
Funnell, Christina Mary *non-profit consultant*
Gadea, Raul *cultural foundation administrator*
Gale, Robert L. *educational association administrator, consultant*
Gandini, Umberto *organization director*
Garnett, Helen Margaret *professional organization executive*
Garrison, John Raymond *organization executive*
Gartz, Rolf Fritz *foundation administrator*
Geissler, Heiner *political leader*
Gervais, Paul Nelson *foundation administrator, psychotherapist, public relations executive, writer*
Gesch, Carl Bernard *research charity director*
Ghanem, Shokri *oil organization administrator*
Gibbons, Mary Peyser *civic volunteer*
Gibson, John Frederick *administrator*
Gilmartin, Clara T. *volunteer*
Ginocchio, Greg J. *social services professional*
Ginsberg, Judith *foundation administrator*
Gjermani, Linda *educational researcher, consultant*
Glickman, Marlene *non-profit organization administrator*
Gloss, Lawrence Robert *fundraising executive*
Gobeli, Virginia C. *national program leader*
Gogineni, Babu Rajaji Ramanadha *association executive*

Goldin, Milton *fund raising counsel, writer*
Gonzalez-Quijano Vazquez, Gustavo Ernesto *trade association administrator*
Goodman, Gertrude Amelia *civic worker*
Goodman, Sylvia Klumok *volunteer*
Goodwin, Felix Lee *retired educational administrator, retired army officer*
Gore, Madhav Sadashiv *social work educator*
Goulait, John Joseph *association professional*
Gould, D. Joy *social services administrator*
Grachov, Dimitry Dimitrievich *foundation executive*
Grand, Marcia *civic worker*
Grant, Donald Marcus *alcohol policy specialist*
Green, John Lafayette, Jr. *education executive*
Green, Laura Lorraine *foundation administrator*
Greenberg, Helaine Iris *volunteer*
Grell, Lewis Adam *association executive*
Grenfell, Gloria Ross *community volunteer*
Grose, Andrew Peter *foundation executive*
Grossman, Jerome *non-profit organization executive, educator*
Gruder, Yaron E. *foundation administrator*
Gruenwald, James Howard *association executive, consultant*
Guenther, Kenneth Allen *business association executive, economist*
Guthrie, Charles *NATO official, military officer*
Haas, Eileen Marie *homecare advocate*
Haddacks, Paul K. *NATO official*
Hadinoto, Kusudiarso *professional society administrator, engineering and business consultant*
Hajtman, Ladislav Michael *charitable foundation executive, educator*
Hall, Deborah Woodrick *social services administrator*
Hallak, Jacques *educational administrator*
Handling, Piers Guy Paton *arts executive*
Handy, Robert Truman *association administrator, finance consultant*
Hansen, Jay *professional organization executive*
Hansen, Peter *international organization executive*
Hanshew, Louisa Emily *fundraiser*
Harada, Yasuo *educational administrator*
Harberg, Albert Justus *association executive*
Hardy, Sally Jane *association director*
Harrington, Lori Lynn *social services administrator*
Harrington, Nancy Regina O'Connor *volunteer*
Harris, Penny Smith *fundraising consultant*
Harvey, Karen L. *professional organization administrator*
Harvey, Patricia Jean *special education administrator, retired*
Hastey, Shari Rose *nonprofit organization administrator*
Hathaway, Lynn McDonald *education advocate, administrator*
Hawley, Harold Patrick *educational consultant*
Hays, Mary Katherine Jackson *civic worker*
Hayward, Fredric Mark *social reformer*
Hazell, Robert John Davidge *policy institute director*
Heap, Sylvia Stuber *civic worker*
Heckler, Walter Tim *association executive*
Helton, Arthur Cleveland *advocate, lawyer, scholar, writer*
Hemley, Eugene Adams *trade association executive*
Henderson, Mary Louise *civic worker*
Henderson, William J. *association executive*
Hendricks, Edward David *speaker, educator, consultant*
Hense, Donald Langford *educational association administrator*
Hesselbein, Frances Richards *foundation executive, consultant, editor*
Hicks, Dolores Kathleen (De De Hicks) *foundation director*
Hiergesell, David Henry *association executive*
Himes, Diane Adele *buyer, fundraiser, actress, lobbyist*
Hinduja, Srichand Parmanand *association executive*
Hochbaum, Martin *trade association administrator*
Hochberg, Mark Stefan *foundation president, cardiac surgeon*
Hoffenblum, Allan Ernest *political consultant*
Hoffheimer, Minette Goldsmith *community service volunteer*
Hohman, Sharolyn Ann *chamber administrator*
Holcomb, Caramine Kellam *volunteer worker*
Holland, Ruby Mae *social welfare administrator*
Holloway, James Lemuel, III *foundation executive, retired naval officer*
Holowacz, Eric Vaughn *non-profit executive director*
Holt, Mavis Murial *parents group executive*
Hope, Margaret Lauten *civic worker*
Houlihan, Gail Lanier *child advocate, educator*
Howells, Muriel Gurdon Seabury (Mrs. William White Howells) *volunteer*
Howitt, Pamela Tesler *development and philanthropy consultant, association administrator*
Hoyt, John Arthur *humane society executive*
Hudec, Jaroslav *NATO official*
Hughes, Sharon Mary *trade association executive*
Humphrey, Diana Young *fund raiser, travel consultant*
Hunt, Mary Reilly *organization executive*
Hvidt, Christian *NATO official*
Iatropoulos, Michael John *health research executive, pathology educator*
Inokuchi, Hiroo *education administrator, escientist*
Iseux, Jean-Christophe *international relations specialist*
Jackson, Jesse Louis *civic and political leader, clergyman*
Jackson, Wynelle Redding *children's services educational administrator, tax preparer*
Jacobsen, Theodore H. (Ted H. Jacobsen) *labor union official, educator*
Janssen-Arts, Theodora J. F. *civic worker*
Jenger, Jean Antoine *civil servant*
Jens, Elizabeth Lee Shafer (Mrs. Arthur M. Jens, Jr.) *civic worker*
Jessup, Jan Amis *arts volunteer, writer*
Joa, Eugen Ernst *educational association administrator*
Johnson, Anne Hale *educational association administrator*
Johnson, Katharyn Price (Mrs. Edward F. Johnson) *civic worker*
Johnson, Marlene M. *nonprofit executive*
Johnson, Robert Bruce *historic preservationist*
Johnston, Bernard Fox *foundation executive, writer*
Jones, George Fleming *international consultant*
Jones, Mary Trent *endowment fund trustee*
Jones, Sydney *youth organization administrator*
Jonsen, Richard Wiliam *retired educational administrator*
Jordan, James Wallace, Jr. *trade association administrator*
Jordan, William *international organization administrator*
Jueschke, Rainie Bishop *non-profit organization administrator*
Kaggen, Lois Sheila *non-profit organization executive*
Kang, Byung Kyu *association administrator*
Kanno, Akira *professional society administrator*
Kaplan, Claudette S. (Claudia Kaplan) *civic leader, philanthropist, volunteer*
Kaya, Akira *association executive, real estate executive*
Kelly, Brian L. *lobbyist*
Keltz, Amy Lynn *foundation administrator*
Kennedy, David Boyd *foundation executive, lawyer*
Kerkyasharian, Stepan *foundation executive*
Khosla, Ashok *association executive*
Kidd, Darlene Joyce *social services administrator, nurse*
Kindermans, Jean-Marie *international medical organization executive*
King, James A. *NATO official*
King, Lea Ann *community volunteer and leader*
King, M. Jean *association executive*
Kinslow, Margie Ann *volunteer worker*
Kitt, Eugene Clark *organization administrator*
Kivrikoglu, Huseyin *NATO official, military officer*
Klaiber, Klaus-Peter *NATO official*
Klimczuk, Stephen John *business executive, foundation director*
Klimley, Nancy Lee *volunteer, civic leader*
Klot, Jennifer *children's fund administrator*
Knotts, Glenn R(ichard) *foundation administrator*
Kobayashi, Shoichi *think tank executive, economist*
Kohnert, Dirk *institute administrator, editor*
Kolb, Charles Chester *humanities administrator*
Koller-Andorf, Ida *professional society executive, editor*
Konkel, Harry Wagner *civic volunteer, retired career officer*
Kovner, Kathleen Jane *civic worker, portrait artist*
Kozlov, Leonid Yakowlevich *institute administrator*
Kreig, Andrew Thomas *trade association executive*
Kreutner, Shimshon Jacob *cultural organization administrator*
Kroon, Luuk *NATO official, military officer*
Kunstadter, Geraldine Sapolsky *foundation executive*
Lancellotta, John Jerry-Louis *public service administrator*
Landau-Crawford, Dorothy Ruth *local social service executive*
Landy, Joanne Veit *foreign policy analyst*
Larson, Charles Fred *trade association executive*
Laszewski, Boleslaw Tadeusz *civic volunteer*
Lawrence, Marilyn Edith (Guthrie) *association executive*
Lazar, John Edward *administrator non-profit organization*
Leal, Barbara Jean Peters *fundraising executive*
Leavey, Thomas Edward *international organization administrator*
Le Dentu, Charles *professional association administrator*
Lee, Blaine Nelson *executive consultant, educator, author*
Lenz, Guy *NATO official*
Leonard, Joseph Howard *association organization executive*
Lerner, Alexander Robert *association executive*
Lessey, Samuel Kenric, Jr. *foundation administrator*
Leung, Wing Tai *youth organization executive*
Levy, D.A. Finer *social services administrator*
Liddell, Jane Hawley Hawkes *civic worker*
Lim, Licarion Gorembalem *fraternal organization administrator*
Limpert, John H., Jr. *fund raising executive*
Lin, Jade Chen *art society administrator, dance educator, artist*
Lindegaard, Kirsten Kelstrup *retired advocate*
Lindsey, Jonathan Asmel *development executive, educator*
Littlefield, Roy Everett, III *association executive, legal educator*
Livers, Thomas Henry *fundraiser for nonprofit organizations*
Lockhart, Madge Clements *educational organization executive*
Lofgren, Erik Loyd *professional society executive*
Loin, E. Linnea *retired social work administrator*
London, Robert James *fraternal organization administrator*
Longin, Thomas Charles *education association administrator*
Lopez Canis, Francisco Jose *association executive*
Lott, Jason Edward *community service coordinator*
Lottes, Patricia Joette Hicks *foundation administrator, retired nurse*
Lovelace, Dorothy Louise *volunteer*
Lucas, Louis M. *former intergovernmental organization executive*
Luce, Henry, III *foundation executive*
Luckey, Doris Waring *civic volunteer*
Luers, Wendy Wilson Woods *non-profit foundation executive*
Luhman, William Simon *community development administrator*
Lüst, Reimar *foundation president*
MacCullagh, Bruce Scott *fund raiser, software designer*
Magnusson, Thor Astthor *cultural association administrator*
Magoon, Nancy Amelia *art association administrator, philanthropist*
Magrath, C. Peter *educational association executive*
Mahoney, Ann Dickinson *fundraiser*
Makins, Christopher James *foreign policy institute administrator*
Malek, Marlene Anne *cultural organization, foundation executive*
Mandel, Carola Panerai (Mrs. Leon Mandel) *foundation trustee*
Mankoff, Albert William *cultural organization administrator, consultant*
Mann, Simranjit Singh *political party official*
Marmolejo, Francisco J. *educational association administrator*
Maroy, Michel *European affairs consultant*
Marrian, Ian Frederic Young *professional society administrator*
Marschall, Miklós *civic organization executive, economist*
Marshall, Brian Laurence *trade association executive*
Marshall, Mary Jones *civic worker*
Marshall, Susan Lockwood *civic worker*
Martínez, Miguel-Angel *international organization executive*
Mason, Stephen Olin *nonprofit association administrator*
Masterson, Harold Thomas *social services administrator*
Mastrokostopoulos, Ioannis *NATO official*
Masujima, Toshiyuki *public administration educator*
Mathur, Veerendra Swarup *trade unionist, educator, social scientist*
Mattes, Robert Britt *civil rights advocate*
Maxwell, Dorothea Bost Andrews *civic worker*
Maxwell, Florence Hinshaw *civic worker*
Maxwell, Patricia Joy *fund raising executive*
Maynard, Virginia Madden *charitable organization executive*
Maynes, John Peter *retired trade union officer, accountant*
Mbadugha, Loretta Nkeiruka Akosa *social services administrator, consultant*
McAuliffe, Keith William *association administrator*
McAusland, Randolph M. N. *arts administrator*
McCobb, Allan Paul *not-for-profit organization executive*
McCrary, Eugenia Lester (Mrs. Dennis Daughtry McCrary) *civic worker, writer*
McDonald, Bronce William *community activist, advocate*
McGlue, Robert David *foundation administrator*
McInerney, James Eugene, Jr. *trade association executive*
Mc Kay, Emily Gantz *civil rights professional*
Mc Kinney, Michael Whitney *trade association executive*
McLauchlan, Sylvia June *charity organization executive*
McNulty, Robert Holmes *non-profit executive*
Means, George Robert *organization executive*
Melgar, Haroldo Rodas *associations executive*
Mellon, Gwen Grant *foundation executive*
Menses, Gerard *foundation executive*
Merrill, Mary Lee *professional society administrator*
Messere, Kenneth Charles *international civil servant*
Mestrallet, Gérard *professional society administrator*
Meyer, Danial Ronald *association executive*
Meyer, Rachel Abijah *foundation director, artist, theorist, poet*
Meyer, Rosalind Mae *community volunteer*
Michalik, John James *legal educational association executive*
Middelhoek, André J. *international organization administrator, auditor*
Middendorf, Alice Carter *volunteer*
Miller, Jerome M. *civic worker*
Miller, Woodburn Davidson *educational administrator, retired, consultant*
Miller, Zoya Dickins (Mrs. Hilliard Eve Miller, Jr.) *civic worker*
Mills, Gregory John Barrington *think-tank executive*
Miner, Jacqueline *political consultant*
Minow, Josephine Baskin *civic volunteer*
Mitchell, Janet Aldrich *fund raising executive, reference materials publisher*
Miyahara, Kenji *investment company executive*
Moltzau, Trond *NATO official*
Montgomery, Lynn Marie *professional association executive*
Monzel, Catherine Luise *international agency administrator*
Moore, Daniel Keith *scientific society executive, earth scientist*
Moral-Lopez, Pedro *international civil servant*
Morgan, Mary Louise Fitzsimmons *fund raising executive, lobbyist*
Morse, Jean Avnet *higher education administrator, lawyer*
Mouravieff-Apostol, Andrew *association executive*
Muir, Patricia Allen *professional association administrator*
Muirden, Geoffrey William Adelaide *institute assistant director*
Mullen, Rod *nonprofit organization executive*
Munger, Paul David *company executive, educational administrator*
Muranty, Wojciech *pastor, youth group administrator*
Murphy, Mary Ann *human services administrator*
Musil, Robert Kirkland *professional society administrator*
Myers, Norman Lewis *fund development consultant*
Nagda, Kanti *advice services administrator*
Neal, Leora Louise Haskett *social services administrator*
Neale, Gail Lovejoy *non-profit organization management consultant*
Neely, Marion Victoria *community volunteer*
Nelson, Elizabeth Hawkins *public association administrator*
Nenstiel, Susan Kisthart *fundraising professional*
Neufeld, Howard B. *foundation administrator*
Neuwald, Vera Littmann *association administrator*
Newkirk, Peggy Rose Wills *civic volunteer*
Nikkel, Ronald Wilbert *social services administrator*
Northrup, Stephen James *professional association executive*
Nowell, Linda Gail *organization executive*
Noxon, Margaret Walters *community volunteer*
O'Bryon, David Scott *association executive*
O'Connor, Sylvia Cannon *association legislative liaison, analyst, retired*
Odland, Barbara *medical association administrator*
O'Donnell, Kathleen Mary *social services administrator*
Öğütçü, Mehmet *organization administrator*
Ohayon, Maurice M. *research center administrator, psychiatrist*
O'Neill, Elizabeth Sterling *trade association administrator*
Orms, R. Norris *healthcare society administrator*
O'Rourke, Joan B. Doty Werthman *educational administrator*
Ortner, Evelyn Mavis Jacobs *organization executive*
Orvananos, Marcela De Rovzar *philanthropist*
Osborn, Frederick Henry, III *foundation executive*
Ostendorf, Joan Donahue *fund raiser, volunteer*
Owen, Gordon Peter *fundraising professional*
Owens, Luvie Moore *association consultant*
Paine, Eric *society executive*
Pak, Bo Hi *foundation administrator*
Paltridge, Rosemary *social welfare administrator*
Park, Won Kuk *foundation administrator*
Parthasarathy, Rajagopalan *trade and professional associations administrator*
Paru, Marden David *fundraising executive*
Pawliger, Caryn R. *think tank executive*
Payne, Winfield Scott *national security policy research executive*
Peck, Raymond Charles, Sr. *driver behavior research specialist and research consultant*
Pelavin, Sol Herbert *research company executive*
Pellaud, Bruno Francis *consultant*
Pendley, Donald Lee *association executive*
Perera, Liyanage Henry Horace *human rights advocate, educator*
Perez Esquivel, Adolfo *human rights activist*
Pettman, Barrie Owen *international institute executive*
Phelps, Dorothy Frink *civic worker*
Pine, William Charles *foundation executive*
Pinkham, Frederick Oliver *foundation executive, consultant*
Pironti, Lavonne De Laere *developer, fundraiser*
Plaks, Livia Basch *foundation executive*
Platthy, Jeno *cultural association executive*
Poblaciones, José *NATO official*
Pogue, Mary Ellen E. (Mrs. L(loyd) Welch Pogue) *youth and community worker*
Pontius, James Wilson *foundation administrator*
Potter, James Vincent *association executive*
Potter, John Buchanan *educational association director*
Potter, William Allen *trade association administrator*
Powell, Charles David (Lord Powell of Bayswater) *merchant*
Prescott, Barbara Lodwich *educational administrator*
Priddle, Robert *international organization director*
Probert, Edward Whitford *foundation executive, volunteer*
Purcell, James Nelson, Jr. *international organization administrator*
Purcell, Kathy Ann *business association administrator*
Purkis, Andrew James *memorial fund executive*
Pushkarev, Boris S. *research foundation director, writer*
Quigley, Kevin F. F. *nonprofit organization executive*
Rainey, Nancy L. *organization executive*
Raiser, Konrad *international organization executive*
Ramos-Horta, Jose *Indonesian political activist*
Randall, Catherine Horn *advocate*
Rasmus, John Charles *trade association executive, lawyer*
Rathke, Dale Lawrence *community organizer and financial analyst*
Rawson, Jessica Mary *educator*
Rayburn, Wendell Gilbert *educational association executive*
Rea, Desmond *labor relations director, consultant*
Read, Patricia Ellen *administrator non-profit organization, editor*
Reading, Phyllis Ann *social welfare administrator*
Reed, James (Rudolph) *foundation administrator*
Reed, Joyce Lasky *foundation administrator, writer*
Reinig, Gaston *NATO official*
Renyi, Judith A. *foundation administrator*
Ricciardi, Christine Secola *international trade consultant*
Richardson, William Russell *foundation executive*
Richie, Robert Douglas *foundation executive*
Richter, Ingo Karl Albert *director youth institute, law educator*
Riedy, Patricia Ann *international development specialist*
Riley, James Joseph *retired union executive*
Rinker, Ruby Stewart *foundation administrator*
Riordan, James Cornell *cultural association administrator*
Roach, William Russell *training and education executive*
Robbins, Pat Sweeney *political organization executive*
Robinson, Leonard Harrison, Jr. *international government consultant, business executive*
Rockefeller, Laurance S. *philanthropist*
Rogul, June Audrey *fundraising executive, government relations specialist*
Rooke, Stephen *bureau executive*
Rose, Joanna Semel *cultural activist*
Rosenstein, Peter D. *educational association administrator*
Ross, Thomas McCallum *professional society administrator*
Rossier, William *world trade organization*
Rotfeld, Adam Daniel *research institute director*
Roth, Kenneth *human rights advocate*
Rountree, Patricia Ann *youth organization administrator*
Routti, Risto Ilkka *advocate*
Rowell, Barbara Caballero *academic administrator*
Rózsa, György *academy library foundation president*
Rumbaugh, Max Elden, Jr. *professional society administrator*
Russell, Mary Wendell Vander Poel *non-profit organization executive, interior*
Ryder Richardson, Edward Colin *social services administrator*
Ryeo, Jeoung Dong *association administrator*
Ryerson, William Newton *non profit organization executive*
Saari, Juhani Heikki *social services administrator*
Sabathe, Emile *NATO official*
Sadruddin, Moe *foundation administrator*
Saffuri, Khaled Ahmad *cultural organization executive*
St. John, Shannon Elaine *foundation executive*
Saitoh, Akio *association administrator retired*
Salah-El, Tiyo Attallah *political society executive, newsletter editor*
Samples, Esther Louise Henrietta *political activist, animal rights activist*
Sánchez-Castelli, Engardo Primo *educational services company owner, educator*
Sanders, Verona Harbert *special events coordinator*
Sané, Pierre Gabriel Michel *international social welfare executive*
Sarmento, Arthur Junqueiro *NATO official*
Schanfield, Fannie Schwartz *community volunteer*
Schatz, Thomas Andrew *nonprofit organization executive, lawyer*
Scheier, Ivan Henry *volunteer, writer*
Schiazza, Guido Domenic (Guy Schiazza) *educational association administrator*
Schmidt, Martha Bubeck *educator, counselor*
Schrenk, Gary Dale *foundation executive*
Schwartz, John J. *association executive, consultant*
Schwarz, Susan Decker *development officer*
Scott, Alexander Robinson *engineering association executive*
Scott, Donald Michael *educational association administrator, educator*
Scott, Lottie Bell *retired civil rights administrator*
Searles, Thomas Daniel *society administrator*
Sedlak, James William *organization administrator*
Seggerman, Anne Crellin *foundation executive*
Seigel, Leila Ruth *activist organization representative, advocate*
Serventy, Caroline Mary *cultural organization administrator*
Sesow, Peter Alfred *social services administrator*

PROFESSIONAL INDEX 2497 ATHLETICS

Sha, Zong professional society administrator, educator
Shakely, John Bower (Jack Shakely) foundation executive
Sharansky, Natan (Anatoly Sharansky) human rights activist, mathematician, computer programmer
Sharif, Khalid educational association administrator
Shaw, Colin Don retired professional society adminstrator, writer
Shawdale, Brian John organization executive
Sheldon, William Frederick cultural institute administrator, consultant
Sheridan, Diane Frances public policy facilitator
Shevitz, Laurie Michelle social services administrator
Shiffert, Sarah Anne Idell association executive
Shipton, Sidney Lawrence non-profit association consultant, solicitor
Shoemaker, Helen E. Martin Achor civic worker
Sillard, Yves political organization worker
Silvester, Frederick John public affairs consultant
Simkin, Sandra Joan women's medical rights advocate, public relations
Simons, G. Willy NATO official
Simpson, Diane Jeannette social welfare administrator
Singh, Jyoti Shankar international organization executive
Singleton, Roger charitable association executive
Sipilä, Matti Kalevi professional society administrator
Skillingstad, Constance Yvonne social services administrator, educator
Slater, William Adcock retired social services organization executive
Smart, Mary-Leigh Call (Mrs. J. Scott Smart) civic worker
Smith, Barry Hamilton foundation administrator, physician
Smith, Elise Becket arts administrator
Smith, Jean Webb (Mrs. William French Smith) civic worker
Smith-Carroll, Myrtle civic worker, former journalist
Snyder, John Michael lobbyist, public relations director
Sohlman, Michael foundation administrator
Sommaruga, Cornelio humanitarian services organization administrator, diplomat
Spangler, Nita Reifschneider volunteer
Sparks, Kenneth R. association executive
Spence, Janet Blake Conley (Mrs. Alexander Pyott Spence) civic worker
Spencer, Mary Miller civic worker
Stackpole, Kerry Clifford association executive
Stahl, Hans Joachim Alexander youth organization administrator
Stallins, Ellen Rae trade development executive
Stamoulas-Karlas, Nick social welfare, recreation administrator
Starr, Charles Christopher foundation executive, priest
Stebbins, Gregory Kellogg foundation executive
Stern, John Peter association executive
Sternberg, Sir Sigmund foundation trustee
Stevens, Sheila Maureen teachers union administrator
Stevenson, Josiah, IV cultural arts administrator
Stewart, George Ray association executive, educator
Stone, Thomas Richardson cultural center president
Stout, Elizabeth West foundation administrator
Stringer, Gretchen Engstrom consulting volunteer administrator
Strong, Selden Rice advocate
Stuart, Joan Martha fund raising executive
Styron, Rose human rights activist, poet, journalist
Sumberg, Alfred Donald professional association executive
Swig, Roselyne Chroman community consultant
Szaz, Zoltan Michael association executive
Szepesy, Kenneth Stephen charity organization administrator
Szumski, Henryk NATO official, military officer
Tacik, Henryk M. NATO official
Tadros, Marlyn Ramzi human rights activist, feminist
Takin, Manouchehr think tank member
Tank, Andrew George association administrator, writer
Tarney, Karen organization executive
Teasley, Ella Loraine educational association administrator
Teich, Albert Harris professional society administrator
Tharp, David Wayne association executive
Theodore, Eustace D. educational advancement consultant
Thibaudeau, Mary Frances cultural organization administrator
Thirtle, Michael Robert community activist, consultant
Thompson, Pauline Anne charity administrator
Thornton, Edmund B. philanthropist
Thorpe, John Alden association executive, mathematician
Toke, Frederick K. J. social services executive, clergyman, psychologist
Toomey, Jeanne Elizabeth animal activist
Tophøj, Laurits NATO official
Touborg, Margaret Earley Bowers non-profit executive
Townsend, Susan Elaine religious organization officer
Trettin, Rosemary Elizabeth fraternal organization administrator
Tsuzawa, Masami association administrator
Turner, Gloria Townsend Burke social services association executive
Turner, John Freeland non-profit administrator, former federal agency administrator, former state senator
Turner, Mary Jane educational administrator
Uhde, Larry Jackson joint apprentice administrator
Vaccaro, Antoine fundraising company executive
Vail, Iris Jennings civic worker
Valderas, Santiago NATO official, military officer
van der Wal, Eelco foundation executive
van Gerwen, Lucas Joseph foundation executive, psychologist
Vanstan, Stephen Thomas business executive
Veatch, Elizabeth Wilson educational administrator
Verbruggen, L. A. J. NATO official
Vogelzang, Jeanne Marie professional association executive, attorney
Votaw, John Frederick educational foundation executive, educator
Wachtell, Esther non-profit management executive, consultant
Waldrep, Alvis Kent, Jr. non-profit foundation administrator
Walker, Eljana M. du Vall civic worker
Walker, Jennie Louise fundraising director
Walker, Nathan Belt trade association administrator
Waller, Ephraim Everett retired professional association executive
Waller, Wilhelmine Kirby (Mrs. Thomas Mercer Waller) civic worker, organization official
Washington, Dolores art association administrator
Washington, Valora non-profit administrator
Webb, Mark professional society administrator
Weber, George former international social welfare administrator
Weir, Michael Eckford Lind educational professional executive
Weisl, Edwin Louis, Jr. foundation executive, lawyer
Welte, A. Theodore chamber of commerce executive
West, Wallace Marion cultural organization administrator
Wetterberg, Per Gunnar professional society administrator
Whipple, William Perry foundation administrator
Whisnand, Rex James association executive
White, Emmet, Jr. retirement community administrator
White, Mary Ruth Wathen social services administrator
White, William Samuel foundation executive
Wieland, Carl non-profit organization executive
Wiesenthal, Simon cultural association executive, engineer
Wiesmann, Klaus NATO official
Wiesner, Louis Arnold social welfare organization executive
Williams, Betty peace activist
Williams, Jody political organization administrator
Williams, Walker Richard, Jr. social services administrator
Wills, Jean Marie professional association executive
Wilson, Doris H. volunteer
Wise, William Harvey, IV human service executive
Wolff, Henning Otto August private public school administrator
Wood, Jeanne Clarke charitable organization executive
Woods, Gwendolyn Lenar parole program administrator
Wooten, Austin Franklin lobbyist, educator, writer
Wright, Helen Kennedy retired professional association administrator, publisher, editor, librarian
Wright, Helen Patton professional society administrator
Wunstell, Erik James non-profit organization administrator, communications consultant
Xie, Yusheng foundation administrator, educator
Yano, Hironori organization executive
Yaroslavtsev, Andrew Borisovich foundation administrator
Yilmaz, Mesut political party administrator
Young, Ina Weinstein association administrator
Yun, Chang Hee management association administrator, researcher
Zecca, John Andrew retired association executive
Zepeda, Susan Ghozeil foundation administrator
Zharikov, Alexander Nikolaevich trade union federation executive
Ziegler, Ronald Louis former association and government official, writer
Zielinski, Paul Bernard grant program administrator, civil engineer
Zweifel, Francoise international organization administrator

ATHLETICS

Abdul-Rahim, Shareef professional basketball player
Agassi, Andre Kirk professional tennis player
Ahrenberg, Sven-Gosta Theodor retired athletics professional
Akebono, Taro (Chad Rowan) professional sumo wrestler
Albertini, Demetrio professional soccer player
Alekna, Virgilijus Olympic athlete
Alesi, Jean race car driver
Amanar, Simona olympic athlete
Andrade, William Thomas professional golfer
Andretti, Mario race car driver
Aowei, Xing olympic athlete
Appleby, Stuart professional golfer
Arsenault, Samantha Olympic athlete
Aspe, Alberto Garcia soccer player
Auch, Susan retired speed skater
Axelson, Joseph Allen professional athletics executive, publisher
Azinger, Paul professional golfer
Baggio, Dino soccer player
Baggio, Roberto professional soccer player
Bailey, Donovan Olympic athlete
Baker, Peter Alan professional golfer
Baker, Vincent Lamont professional basketball player
Baldini, Stefano long distance runner
Ballesteros, Severiano professional golfer
Barkley, Charles Wade retired professional basketball player
Barnett, Michael sports agent, business manager
Barrichello, Rubens race car driver
Barthez, Fabien professional soccer player
Batistuta, Gabriel Omar professional soccer player
Beard, Amanda swimmer, Olympic athlete
Beckenbauer, Franz former soccer player, professional soccer team executive
Becker, Boris retired professional tennis player
Beckham, David professional soccer player
Bedford, Barbara J. Olympic athlete
Behring, Kenneth E. professional sports team owner
Belfour, Ed professional hockey player
Belle, Albert Jojuan professional baseball player
Benko, Lindsay Olympic athlete
Bennett, Brooke Olympic athlete
Bergkamp, Dennis professional soccer player
Bertman, Skip baseball coach
Beunen, Gaston Prudence physical education educator
Beya, Zoubier soccer player
Bierhoff, Oliver professional soccer player
Binning, Bette Finese (Mrs. Gene Hedgcock Binning) athletic association official
Bird, Larry Joe professional basketball coach, former professional basketball player
Bjorkman, Jonas tennis player
Blanc, Laurent professional soccer player
Blatter, Joseph S. sports association administrator
Blazevic, Miroslav professional soccer coach
Boban, Zvonimir soccer player
Boboc, Loredana Olympic athlete
Bolton-Holifield, Alice Ruth basketball player
Bonds, Barry Lamar professional baseball player
Bonev, Hristo professional soccer coach, former player
Borden, Amanda gymnast, Olympic athlete
Borg, Bjorn professional tennis player
Botsford, Beth swimmer, Olympic athlete
Bowman, William Scott (Scotty Bowman) professional hockey coach
Bradley, Edward William sports foundation executive
Bradley, Patricia Ellen professional golfer
Brands, Tom Olympic athlete
Brind'Amour, Rod Jean professional hockey player
Brisson, Therese hockey player
Brodeur, Martin professional hockey player
Brown, Wendy Joan physical education educator
Buford-Bailey, Tonja Yevette track and field Olympic athlete
Bure, Pavel professional hockey player
Burton, Deon (Neon Deon Burton) soccer player
Bye, Karyn Olympic hockey athlete
Callus, Ashley Olympic athlete
Campbell, Cassie hockey player
Canseco, Jose professional baseball player
Carlos, Roberto de Silva (Roberto Carlos Da Silva) professional soccer player
Carter, Vince professional basketball player
Cerny, Harald soccer player
Chang, Michael tennis player
Cheever, Eddie formula I driver
Chen, Lu figure skater
Chilavert, Jose Luis professional soccer player
Chow, Amy gymnast, Olympic athlete
Clark, Shelia Roxanne sports association executive, legislative analyst
Clarke, Darren golfer
Clemente, Javier soccer coach
Coetzer, Amanda tennis player
Colander-Richardson, LaTasha Olympic athlete
Compagnoni, Deborah Olympic athlete
Corretja, Alex tennis player
Costacurta, Alessandro professional soccer player
Coulthard, David race car driver
Couples, Frederick Steven professional golfer
Crenshaw, Ben professional golfer
Crespo, Hernan soccer player
Crocker, Ian Olympic athlete
Crone, David Lloyd horse racing industry executive
Cronin, Paul David physical education educator, director
Cross, Kendall Olympic athlete
Csollany, Szilveszter Olympic athlete
Cushman, Valerie Jean athletic director
Daehlie, Bjorn Olympic athlete
Davenport, Lindsay professional tennis player
Davids, Edgar professional soccer player
Davidson, Bruce Olympic athlete
Davies, Laura professional golfer
Davis-Thompson, Pauline Olympic athletic
Deal, Lance Earl Olympic athlete
Dean, Christopher ice dancer
de Boer, Frank soccer player
de Boer, Ronald soccer player
de Bruijn, Inge olympic athlete
Deferr, Gervasio Olympic athlete
De La Hoya, Oscar Olympic athlete, professional boxer
Desailly, Marcel professional soccer player
Devers, Gail track and field athlete
Diebel, Nelson Olympic athlete, swimmer
Dieckert, Jürgen sports scientist
Diniz, Pedro race car driver
Dmitriev, Artur ice skater
Dolan, Tom Olympic athlete
Dragila, Stacy track and field athlete
Drechsler, Heike Olympic athlete
Drummond, Jon Olympic athlete
Duerr, Dianne Marie educator, sports medicine consultant
Duval, David Robert professional golfer
Edberg, Stefan former professional tennis player
Edwards, Jonathan Olympic athlete
Edwards, Teresa basketball player
Elkington, Steve professional golfer
Els, Theodore Ernest professional golfer
Erickson, Ralph D. retired physical education educator, small business owner, consultant
Ervin, Anthony Olympic athlete
Evert, Christine Marie (Chris Evert) retired professional tennis player
Ewing, Patrick Aloysius professional basketball player
Faldo, Nick (Nicholas Alexander Faldo) professional golfer
Faxon, Brad professional golfer
Ferguson, Debbie Olympic athlete
Fernandez, Mary Joe professional tennis player
Fioravanti, Domenico olympic athlete
Fish, Mark soccer player
Fisichella, Giancarlo race car driver
Forsberg, Peter professional hockey player
Franco, Carlos professional golfer
Freeman, Cathy Olympic athlete
Frentzen, Heinz-Harald race car driver
Frolander, Lars olympic athlete
Furyk, James Michael professional golfer
Fydler, Chris Olympic athlete
Fynes, Savetheda Olympic athlete
Gambill, Jan-Michael professional tennis player
Garcia, Anier Olympic athlete
Garcia, Sergio professional athlete
Garnett, Kevin professional basketball player
Gascoigne, Paul (Gazza) professional soccer player
Gebrselassie, Haile long distance runner
Geiberger, Brent Andrew professional golfer
Gerg, Hilde skier
Gimelstob, Justin professional tennis player
Graf, Steffi retired professional tennis player
Granato, Catherine (Cammi Granato) professional hockey player
Green, Tammie golfer
Greene, Maurice Olympic athlete
Gretzky, Wayne Douglas retired hockey team executive
Griffey, Ken, Jr. (George Kenneth Griffey, Jr.) professional baseball player
Griffith, Yolanda Evette professional basketball player
Guerrero, Julen soccer player
Gwynn, Anthony Keith (Tony Gwynn) professional baseball player
Hackett, Grant Olympic athlete
Hagi, Gheorge retired professional soccer player
Häkkinen, Mika race car driver
Hall, Gary, Jr. Olympic athlete
Hardaway, Timothy Duane basketball player
Harkes, John professional soccer player
Harrison, Alvin Olympic athlete
Harrison, Calvin Olympic athlete
Hasek, Dominik professional hockey player
Hattestad, Trine Olympic athlete
Havelang, Joao sports association administrator
Henman, Tim professional tennis player
Hennagan, Monique Olympic athlete
Herbert, Johnny Paul race car driver
Herron, Timothy Daniel professional golfer
Herzog, Andreas soccer player
Hill, Grant professional basketball player
Hingis, Martina tennis player
Hoch, Scott Mabon professional golfer
Holdsclaw, Chamique Shaunta professional basketball player
Holik, Bobby professional hockey player
Houston, Allan Wade professional basketball player
Hunter, John Stevenson sports sciences educator
Hurst, Patricia Ann professional golfer
Huston, John professional golfer
Hyman, Misty Dawn Olympic athlete
Hysong, Nick olympic athlete
Ikpeba, Victor soccer player
Ikulayo, Philomena Bolaji physical education educator
Ilyina, Vera Olympic athlete
Indurain Larraya, Miguel retired professional racing cyclist
Inkster, Juli professional golfer
Irvine, Edmund race car driver
Isarescu, Andreea olympic athlete
Jacklin, Anthony professional golfer
Jackson, Philip Douglas professional basketball coach
Jacobsen, Peter Erling professional golfer
Janzen, Lee professional golfer
Jarni, Robert soccer player
Johnson, Michael track and field Olympic athlete
Jones, Marion track and field athlete
Jonk, Wilhelm soccer player
Jordan, Michael Jeffrey professional sports team executive, retired professional basketball player, retired baseball player
Joyner Kersee, Jacqueline track and field athlete
Junfeng, Xiao Olympic athlete
Jurimae, Toivo physical education educator, researcher
Kafelinkov, Yevgeny tennis player
Kane, Lorie professional golfer
Kariya, Paul professional hockey player
Kasparaitis, Darius hockey player
Kasperczak, Henry professional soccer coach, former player
Kenteris, Konstantinos Olympic athlete
Kerrigan, Nancy professional figure skater, former Olympic athlete
Khorkina, Svetlana olympic athlete
Kidd, Jason professional basketball player
Kim, Pyung-Soo martial arts educator
King, Alma Jean former health and physical education educator
King, Betsy professional golfer
Kirby, William olympic athlete
Kite, Thomas O., Jr. professional golfer
Kjus, Lasse Olympic athlete
Klim, Michael Olympic athlete
Klochkova, Yana olympic athlete
Kluivert, Patrick professional soccer player
Koivu, Saku hockey player
Kovacs, Agnes olympic athlete
Krajicek, Richard tennis player
Krayzelburg, Lenny Olympic athlete
Krone, Julie jockey
Kucera, Frantisek ice hockey player
Kuehne, Kelli professional golfer
Kuerten, Gustavo professional tennis player
Kulik, Ilia Alexandrovich figure skater
Kwan, Michelle professional figure skater
Lai, Brendan martial arts professional
Lane, Barry professional golfer
Langer, Bernhard professional golfer
Lapuente, Manuel professional soccer coach, former player
Laskiewicz, Henryk Eryk physical education educator, researcher
Lauber, Christopher Joseph sports event promoter
Laudrup, Michael professional soccer player
Lazier, Buddy professional race car driver
LeClair, John Clark professional hockey player
Lehman, Tom (Thomas Edward Lehman) professional golfer
Lemay-Doan, Catriona speed skater
Lenzi, Mark Olympic athlete, springboard diver
Leonard, Justin (Justin Charles Garret Leonard) professional golfer
Leslie, Lisa DeShaun professional basketball player
Levy, Marvin Daniel retired professional football coach, sports team executive
Lewis, Brian Olympic athlete
Lewis, Carl (Frederick Carlton Lewis) Olympic track and field athlete
Lewis, Denise Olympic athlete
Lewis, Mark James tennis coach
Liang, Tian Olympic athlete
Lindros, Eric Bryan professional hockey player
Lopez, Nancy professional golfer
Love, Davis Milton, III professional golfer
Lowe, Gerald Scott former university athletic administrator, entrepreneur
Lueke, Donna Mae yoga instructor, Reiki practitioner, instructor
Mackey, Rick dog musher
Maddux, Gregory (Alan) professional baseball player
Maggert, Jeffrey Allan professional golfer
Magowan, Peter Alden professional baseball team executive, grocery chain executive
Maier, Hermann skier
Majoli, Iva tennis player
Malchow, Tom Olympic athlete
Maldini, Cesare professional soccer coach, former player
Maldini, Paolo professional soccer player
Mallon, Meg professional golfer
Malone, Karl professional basketball player
Maroney, Susie Jean swimmer
Marth, Fritz Ludwig sports association executive
Martin, Michael Townsend racing horse stable executive, sports marketing executive
Martin, Todd professional tennis player
Martinez, Conchita tennis player
Mboma, Patrick soccer player
McCarthy, Benedict professional soccer player
McCarthy, Jean Jerome retired physical education educator
McCray, Nikki Kesangame basketball player
McCurrach, James Crampton professional squash player
McDyess, Antonio professional basketball player

McEnroe, John Patrick, Jr. professional tennis player, commentator
McGann, Michael Geyer martial arts instructor, protection expert
McNulty, Mark professional golfer
Mickelson, Phil (Philip Alfred Mickelson) professional golfer
Mijatovic, Predrag soccer player
Miles-Clark, Jearl olympic athlete, track and field
Miller, Shannon Olympic athlete
Milton, DeLisha professional basketball player
Mingxia, Fu Olympic athlete
Mocanu, Diana Olympic athlete
Moceanu, Dominique gymnast, Olympic athlete
Modano, Michael professional hockey player
Moeller, Andreas soccer player
Montgomerie, Colin professional golfer
Moodie, Janice golfer
Moses, Ed Olympic athlete
Mourning, Alonzo professional basketball player
Mouzakidis, Christos Alexander physical education educator, basketball coach
Moya, Carlos professional tennis player
Munz, Diana Olympic athlete
Mutola, Maria Olympic athlete
Mutombo, DiKembe (Dikembe Mutombo Mpolondo Mukamba Jean Jacque Wamutombo) professional basketball player
Nakano, Shinji race car driver
Navratilova, Martina former professional tennis player
Nemchinov, Sergei hockey player
Nemov, Alexi Olympic athlete
Neumann, Liselotte professional golfer
Ngeny, Noah Kiprono Olympic athlete
Ni, Xiong Olympic athlete
Nicholas, Alison professional golfer
Nicklaus, Jack William professional golfer
Niemann-Stirnemann, Gunda speed skater
Nilsmark, Catrin professional golfer
Nomo, Hideo professional baseball player
Nool, Erki Olympic athlete
Norman, Gregory John professional golfer
Norman, Magnus pro tennis player
Novotna, Jana tennis player
O'Brien, Daniel Dion track and field athlete, Olympic athlete
O'Connor, Karen Lende Olympic athlete
Okada, Takeshi professional soccer coach, former player
Okano, Masayuki soccer player
Okocha, Augustine (Jay Jay Okocha) professional soccer player
Olajuwon, Hakeem Abdul professional basketball player
Olaru, Maria olympic athlete
Olazabal, Jose Maria professional golfer
Oliseh, Sunday soccer player
Olsen, Egil former soccer coach
O'Meara, Mark professional golfer
O'Neal, Shaquille Rashaun professional basketball player
O'Neill, Susie Olympic athlete
Owen, Michael James professional soccer player
Ozaki, Jumbo professional golfer
Pak, Se Ri professional golfer
Pakhalina, Yulia Olympic athlete
Pallen, Max Moratillo martial arts educator
Palmer, Arnold Daniel professional golfer
Panis, Olivier race car driver
Parnevik, Jesper Bo professional golfer
Parreira, Carlos Alberto soccer coach
Passarella, Daniel professional soccer coach, former player
Passey, Mark Lyman sports association executive
Pate, Stephen Robert professional golfer
Payton, Gary Dwayne professional basketball player
Pearson, Todd olympic athlete
Pechstein, Claudia Olympic athlete
Pedroso, Ivan Olympic athlete
Pepper, Dottie professional golfer
Perry, Chris professional golfer
Pettigrew, Antonio Olympic athlete
Philippoussis, Mark pro tennis player
Piazza, Michael Joseph professional baseball player
Pierce, Mary professional tennis player
Pioline, Cedric pro tennis player
Pippen, Scottie professional basketball player
Player, Gary Jim professional golfer, businessman, golf course designer
Polster, Anton retired soccer player
Postma, Ids speed skater
Presacan, Claudia olympic athlete
Price, Nick professional golfer
Privalova, Irina Olympic athlete
Prosinecki, Robert soccer player
Pyne, David Bruce sports scientist, researcher
Quann, Megan Olympic athlete
Radák, Zsolt physical education educator
Raducan, Andreea olympic athlete
Rafter, Patrick tennis player
Ramirez, Ramon soccer player
Ramos, Tabare professional soccer player
Rebagliati, Ross snowboarder
Reeve, Thomas Gilmour physical education educator
Reichel, Robert ice hockey player
Reinsdorf, Jerry Michael professional sports teams executive, real estate executive, lawyer, accountant
Rhode, Kim Olympic athlete
Riley, Patrick James professional basketball coach
Rincon, Freddy professional soccer player
Rios, Marcello tennis player
Ritsma, Rintje speed skater
Robbins, Kelly professional golfer
Robinson, David Maurice professional basketball player
Robitaille, Luc professional hockey player
Romme, Gianni Petrus Cornelis speed skater
Ronaldo, (Ronaldo Luiz Nazário da Lima) professional soccer player
Rosengren, Ulf Carl Gösta equestrian series director
Rosolino, Massimiliano olympic athlete
Roy, Patrick professional hockey player
Rubin, Chanda professional tennis player
Ruby, Karine snowboarder
Rusedski, Greg tennis player
Ruta, Thomas V. professional sports team executive, accounting executive
Safin, Marat pro tennis player
Sakic, Joseph Steve professional hockey player
Salo, Mika race car driver
Samaranch, Juan Antonio (Marqués de Samaranch) International Olympic Committee president
Sammer, Matthias professional soccer player
Sampras, Pete professional tennis player
Sampson, Steve former professional soccer coach
Sanchez-Vicario, Arantxa tennis player
Sanders, Ross Howard sports science educator
Sautin, Dmitry Olympic athlete
Savon, Felix Olympic athlete
Scherbo, Vitaly V. gymnast
Schmeichel, Peter professional soccer player
Schnyder, Patty professional tennis player
Schrempf, Detlef professional basketball player
Schumacher, Michael race car driver
Schumacher, Ralf race car driver
Schumann, Nils Olympic athlete
Seedorf, Clarence soccer player
Selanne, Teemu professional hockey player
Seles, Monica professional tennis player
Selinger, Andrew Joseph ice and roller rink development company executive
Shanahan, Brendan Frederick professional hockey player
Shealy, Courtney Olympic athlete
Shearer, Alan professional soccer player
Shimizu, Hiroyasu speed skater, office worker
Shishigina, Olga Olympic athlete
Shriver, Pamela H. retired professional tennis player, sports analyst
Shtalenkov, Mikhail hockey player
Simoes, Rene professional soccer coach
Singh, Vijay professional golfer
Sluman, Jeff (Jeffrey George Sluman) professional golfer
Smith, Edward Martin, III football player
Smith, Emmitt J., III professional football player
Smith, Katie basketball player
Smith, Steven Delano professional basketball player
Sobovitz, Iacov Ernest physical education administrator
Sorenstam, Annika professional golfer
Sosa, Samuel (Sammy Sosa) professional baseball player
Souza Faria, Romario professional soccer player
Spirlea, Irina tennis player
Staley, Dawn basketball player
Steinbrenner, George Michael, III professional baseball team executive, shipbuilding company executive
Steinhauer, Sherri professional golfer
Stelter, Reinhard Erich sports scientist, educator, psychotherapist
Stockton, John Houston professional basketball player
Stoichkov, Hristo professional soccer player
Stojko, Elvis ice skater
Street, Picabo Olympic athlete
Strug, Kerri former gymnast, Olympic athlete
Sturrup, Chandra Olympic athlete
Sundin, Mats Johan professional hockey player
Sutton, Hal Evan professional golfer
Svoboda, Petr hockey player
Swoopes, Sheryl Denise professional basketball player
Szabo, Gabriela Olympic athlete
Takahashi, Naoko Olympic athlete
Talebi, Jalal professional soccer coach, former player
Tauziat, Nathalie tennis player
Taylor, Angelo Olympic athlete
Thomas, Frank Edward professional baseball player
Thompson, Jenny Olympic athlete
Thorpe, Ian Olympic athlete
Thuram, Lilian professional soccer player
Tikkanen, Esa hockey player
Timmer, Marianne speed skater
Tomjanovich, Rudolph professional athletic coach
Torrance, Sam professional golfer
Torrence, Gwen Olympic athlete
Torres, Dara Olympic athlete
Torvill, Jayne ice dancer
Trevino, Lee Buck professional golfer
Troussier, Philippe (The White Witchdoctor) professional soccer coach
Trulli, Jarno race car driver
Tryba, Ted Nickolas professional golfer
Tueting, Sarah professional hockey player
Tulu, Derartu Olympic athlete
Turgeon, Pierre professional hockey player
Unser, Alfred, Jr. professional race car driver
Urzica, Marius Olympic athlete
Valkova, Hana physical education educator, psychologist
van den Hoogenband, Peter olympic athlete
van der Sar, Edwin soccer player
Van Dyken, Amy swimmer, Olympic athlete
Vihrovs, Igors Olympic athlete
Villeneuve, Jacques race car driver
Walker, Larry Kenneth Robert professional baseball player
Watson, Thomas Sturges professional golfer
Weah, George professional soccer player
Webb, Karrie professional golfer
Wei, Yang olympic athlete
Weicker, Helmut Georg sports medicine administrator
Westwood, Lee professional golfer
Whitaker, Pernell (Sweet Pea Whitaker) professional boxer
Wilkens, Leonard Randolph, Jr. (Lenny Wilkens) professional basketball coach
Wilkins, (Jacques) Dominique retired professional basketball player
Wilkinson, Laura Olympic athlete
Williams, Bernabe Figueroa professional baseball player
Williams, Bernard Olympic athlete
Williams, Serena professional tennis player
Williams, Ted Vaughnell physical education educator
Williams, Venus professional tennis player
Wilmots, Marc soccer player
Wilson, Stacy hockey player
Winn, Anthony W. chess player, poet, screenwriter
Witty, Christine (Chris Witty) speed skater
Wolde, Millon Olympic athlete
Wolters, Kara basketball player
Woods, Tiger (Eldrick Woods) professional golfer
Woosnam, Ian Harold professional golfer
Wrege, Julia Bouchelle tennis professional, physics educator
Wright, Helen Clare physical education educator, researcher
Wurz, Alexander race car driver
Wynalda, Eric professional soccer player
Xiaopeng, Li Olympic athlete
Xu, Huang olympic athlete
Xuan, Liu olympic athlete
Xue, Sang Olympic athlete
Yzerman, Steve professional hockey player
Zagallo, Mario Jorge Lobo (Formiguinha) professional soccer coach, former player
Zamolodchikova, Yelena olympic athlete
Zamorano, Ivan soccer player
Zeigler, Earle Frederick physical education-kinesiology educator
Zelepukin, Valeri hockey player
Zelezny, Jan Olympic athlete
Zen-Ruffinen, Michel athletic organization executive
Ziege, Christian soccer player
Zinedine, Zidane professional soccer player
Zveveva, Ellina Olympic athlete

COMMUNICATIONS MEDIA. See also ARTS: LITERARY.

Aabad, A. M. M. multi-media consultant
Aalbaek-Nielsen, Bent publishing executive
Abbott, Rick Joseph broadcast executive
Abel, Elie reporter, broadcaster, educator
Absmeier, Albert Franz publisher
Adamatzky, Igor Alekseevich publishing company
Adamczak, Eugeniusz publisher
Adams, Robert Edward journalist
Adams, Warren Lynn publisher, business consultant
Adanyina, John Elvis journalist
Adler, Edward I. media and entertainment company executive
Agazzi, Evandro journalist, educator
Aguirre-Baca, Francisco publisher, consultant
Åhlström, Per G. editor
Akelis, Vincas book publisher
Akutsu, Yoshihiro communications educator
Albertson, Christiern Gunnar (Chris Albertson) broadcaster, music critic, writer
Aldrich, Jorgen editor, writer
Alessandri, Francisca Cohn journalist, educator
Alexeenko, Ihor Rostislavovich publishing executive
Alexiadou, Vefa publisher
Alho, Olli broadcast executive
Allison, Stephen Galender broadcast executive
Alperin, Stanley I. publisher, writer, editor, consultant
Anchev, Panko Kirilov literary critic, publisher, journalist
Anderberg, Roy Anthony journalist
Anderson, Francis media director
Anderson, Karl Stephen editor
Anderson, Kenneth Norman retired magazine editor, author
Anderson, Parker Lynn editorial columnist, playwright
Andreose, Mario editor
Andrews, John Frank editor, author, educator
Andrillon, Pierre Jean editor, journalist
Angel, Heather Hazel wildlife photographer, author
Ankrah-Hoffman, Nii Adotey journalist, newspaper editor, minister
Ansari, Bashir editor
Ansel, Rene editor, photographer
Anthony, Edward (Ted) Mason, IV journalist, educator
Antoun, Annette Agnes newspaper editor, publisher
Ap Rees, Elfan Dyfed publisher, editor
Araki, Takaharu editor, mineralogist, crystallographer, consultant
Arana, Marie editor, writer
Arasteh, Kavouss communications specialist, consultant
Arcache, Jean publishing executive
Archambault, George Francis editor, pharmaceutical consultant
Archibald, Fred John newspaper executive
Aretova, Mariana Borisova publishing executive
Armentrout, Frederick Sherman publisher, editor
Arnett, Peter journalist
Arnold, Heinz Ludwig editor
Arnould, Henri-Laurent publishing executive
Aronson, Norman Leonard publishing executive, consultant
Arrhenius, Sara Anna critic, writer
Arrott, Elizabeth journalist
Aschoff, Gerd journalist
Ascott, Terence broadcast executive
Asher, Kathleen May communications educator
Ashton, Michael John magazine editor
Asirifi, Mary Magdalene publisher, author, consultant
Askew, William George publisher
Astley, Neil Philip book publisher
Attiyate-Schwarzenbach, Yvonne Hélène linguistics publishing executive, retired
Au, Bak Ling publisher
Augstein, Rudolf publisher
Augustithis, Stylianos-Savvas publisher
Austin-Kelley, Patricia Davis publishing executive
Avidor, Arie publisher
Axelrod, Glen Scott publishing company executive
Babson, Irving K. publishing company executive
Bachi, Ruth Kolodny broadcaster
Bae, Sung Nam cable television company executive
Bagchi, Gopa communication educator
Bagherzade, Iradj A. publisher
Bagla, Pallava journalist, photographer
Bahbah, Bishara Assad editor
Bal, Param Ajeet Singh broadcasting executive
Balaram, Thayanur Shivram editor-in-chief
Baldwin, Peter Alan Charles broadcasting consultant
Balk, Alfred William journalist
Ball, William Lee (Atley Fall) sportswriter
Balle, Annemarie Schack editor
Bandow, Douglas Leighton editor, columnist, policy consultant
Banks, O'drean Edythe publishing company executive
Banks, Robert Lee publisher, author, jazz guitarist, composer, arranger
Barataу, Claude Raymond Joseph consultant, educator
Barber, Charles Edward newspaper executive, journalist
Barber, Richard William publishing executive
Barbey, Adélaïde publisher
Barcys, Jonas publishing executive
Barfod, Jørgen Henrik Pagh editor
Barkhoff, Martin Kristian Tobias retired editor
Barnes, Larry Glen journalist, editor, educator
Barnes, Sandra Henley publishing company executive
Barnhurst, Christine Louise broadcast executive
Barry, James P(otvin) writer, editor
Bartley, Robert LeRoy newspaper editor
Bassoli, Massimo editor
Batchelder, Anne Stuart former publisher, political party official
Bauer, Antonie Gertrud journalist
Baumann, Thomas publishing company editor
Beaune, Patrick publisher
Beck, Angel C. columnist, screenwriter, educator
Beck, Ivan Gabriel publishing company executive
Beckerman, Milton Bernard retired media broker
Bednarik, Robert Gerhard scientific publisher
Bedrossian, Ursula Kay Kennedy editor
Beerekamp, Johannes Bernardus film critic
Begell, William publisher
Behar, Maxim journalist, public relations and advertising executive
Beisel, Dieter Erwin editor-in chief of periodical
Bell, William Jack journalism educator
Bellmer, Helmut Wilhelm Karl Johann editor
Beltran, Patria Antonieta Castro editor
Benal, Jolanta editor, dog trainer
Bender, John Henry, Jr. (Jack Bender) editor, cartoonist
Benedict, Helen journalism educator, writer
Benito, Miguel publishing executive
Bentley, John information, media and finance executive
Bergant, Boris Miran journalist, broadcasting researcher
Bergmann, Arthur M. writer, investor, former county official, former newspaperman
Bergsma, Ad journalist, psychologist
Berner, Joachim editor-in-chief, publisher
Bernfeld, Wendy Lynn media consultant company executive, lawyer
Bernhard, Manfred Eugen publisher
Bersia, John Cesar editorial writer, political science educator
Bertez, Bruno Jacques editor
Beyer-Enke, Siegfried magazine editor, publisher
Bhargava, Sunita Wadekar journalist
Bhatti, Zaheer broadcast company executive
Bickers, Patricia Evelyn editor, lecturer
Billeter, Robert James newspaper publisher
Bindé, Jérôme international official, educator, futurist
Birch, Diana Elizabeth publisher
Birt, Baron John broadcasting executive
Björnsson, Per Anders journalist
Black, Barbara Ann publisher
Black, Conrad Moffat publishing corporate executive
Blake, John Michael publisher, writer
Blakley, John Clyde telecommunications consultant
Bland, John Hannam editor
Blankfort, Lowell Arnold newspaper publisher
Blaser, Marco broadcasting executive
Blitzer, Wolf anchor, news correspondent
Bloch, Andrew Charles Danby publisher
Block, Alvin Gilbert journal executive editor
Blount, Gregory James publishing executive, consultant
Blue, Adrianne writer
Boccardi, Louis Donald news agency executive
Bocker, Hans Jurgen editor, analyst, consultant, management educator
Bode, Dietrich Karl Ernst publishing company executive
Bodiford, Vincent W. newspaper publisher, automotive journalist
Bodley, Harley Ryan, Jr. editor, writer, broadcaster
Boers, Rene editor
Bohannon-Kaplan, Margaret Anne publisher, lawyer
Böhme-Dürr, Karin communications educator
Bokor, Pal journalist
Bolanos, Michael Templeton new media executive
Bond, Frances Curtis retired editor
Boserup, Esther Malling editor
Bouchez, Jean-Antoine Pierre magazine publisher
Bouret, Alain publisher
Boutros, Antoine Edward journalist, writer
Bové, Robert Charles editor, writer, educator
Bowser-Nott, Carole Ann editor
Boyar, Jay Mitchell film critic
Boyd, Theophilus Bartholomew, III publishing company executive
Boykin, Arletha Faye speaker, publisher
Boyle, David Courtney journalist, writer, editor
Bradford, Judith Lynnell journalist, artist
Bradford, Susan Anne broadcast journalist
Bradford, Tutt Sloan retired publisher
Bradley, William Bryan cable television regulator
Brady, Conor Patrick newspaper editor
Bragança, Maria da Luz de Campos Pereira de editor, public relations professional
Brakel, Cornelius retired publishing executive
Brand, Stewart editor, writer
Brasher, Christopher William journalist, business executive
Bratcher, Juanita journalist
Bratzler, Mary Kathryn desktop publisher
Brauer, Harrol Andrew, Jr. broadcasting executive
Braverman, Jordan columnist
Breedin, Berryman Brent journalist, public relations, historian, consultant
Brett, James Clarence retired journalism educator
Brevetti, Francine Clelia journalist
Brewin, Keith Alan Frederick publisher, accountant
Brickey, Suzanne M. editor
Brinch, Niels foreign news correspondent
Brinkley, David McClure news commentator
Britt, David Van Buren retired educational communications executive
Britten, William Harry editor, publisher
Broadwater, James E. publisher
Brode, Andrew Stephen publisher, accountant
Brokaw, Thomas John television broadcast executive, correspondent
Bromberger, Dominique Jean Marie journalist, news correspondent
Bromley, Anna Lucy publications executive
Brook, Stephen journalist
Brown, Helen Gurley editor, writer
Brown, J'Amy Maroney journalist, media relations consultant, investor
Brown, Sir John (Gilbert Newton) publisher
Brown, Katherine Jane editor, retired, chamber of commerce executive
Brown, Lynette Ralya journalist, publicist
Brownson, Anna Louise Harshman publishing executive, editor
Brummer, Alexander editor
Brun, Bernard editor, researcher
Brune, Dag Kristen publishing executive
Bryant, Dennis Michael publisher, educator
Buchheim, Lothar-Günther publisher, writer
Buchwald, Art columnist, writer
Buckwalter, Roger Jerome editor, columnist, TV interviewer
Buhler, Jill Lorie editor, writer
Bulgin, Sally Ann publisher, editor
Bumgarner, Marlene Anne writer, editor, educator
Burello, Joseph Matthew publishing executive
Burke, Al publisher, editor
Burkhardt, Frederick Henry editor
Burlacu, Constantin journalist, educator
Burns, John F. reporter
Burr, Norman John journalist, researcher, technical writer
Burton, Sandra Jean journalist
Busck, Ole Arnold publishing company executive

Robins, Reed W. *music recording executive*
Robinson, Barbara Ellen *film production executive*
Robinson, Derek *medical editor*
Robinson, Francis John Gibson *publishing executive, bibliographer, historian*
Robinson, Gerrard Jude *television company executive*
Robinson, Richard M. *technical communication specialist*
Robinson, Spencer Cade *publishing company executive, author, editor*
Roces, Alejandro Reyes *journalist, educator*
Rodowick, David Norman *media educator*
Rodrigues, Adriano Duarte *communication educator*
Rojany, Lisa Adrienne *publishing company executive, writer*
Rolnik, Zachary Jacob *publishing company executive*
Romain, Pierre R. *commercial and television production executive, producer*
Roncarati, Christina *publisher*
Rosenberg, Göran J. *editor*
Rosenblatt, Julia Carlson *journalist, psychology educator*
Rosenthal, Irving *journalism educator*
Ross Stanton, Ronald *publisher, retired*
Rotem, Yaacov *editor, pediatrician*
Roth, Andrew *journalist*
Roth, Lane *communications educator*
Roy, Jean *film critic*
Roy, Kenneth Alfred *editor, publisher*
Roy, Kuldip Kumar *editor*
Rubin, Nancy Zimman (Nancy Rubin Stuart) *journalist, author, writer, producer*
Rudella, Gualtiero *publishing executive*
Rudman, Solomon Kal *magazine publisher*
Rudolf, Anthony *publisher, writer*
Rukeyser, Louis Richard *economic commentator*
Runck, Roger John *editor*
Rusling, Paul Alexander *broadcast executive, consultant*
Russell, Michael *publisher, author*
Russell, Michael Paul *entertainment industry executive, consultant*
Saadi, Ghazi Kamel *journalist*
Sabat, Khalil Yusuf *communications educator*
Sabbatini, Marcello *journalist, motor sports weekly director*
Sagara, Junji *editor*
Sager, Donald Jack *publisher, former librarian*
Sahel, Pierre *literary critic, educator*
Saini, Timo Olavi *publishing executive*
St. Pierre, Roger *communications specialist*
Saleh, Sameer Yasin *journalist, researcher*
Salojarvi, Pekka Tapani *publishing company executive*
Salvini, GianPaolo *editor, economist*
Salyer, Stephen Lee *media executive*
Samuelson, Sir Sydney Wylie *retired film commision administrator*
Sand, Johnny Jen-Nan *broadcasting company executive*
Sandal, Ejvind *publisher*
Sandelands, Eric Alan *publisher, educator, editor*
Sanders, Gerald Hollie *communications educator*
Sandler, Boris *editor, writer*
Sandum, Howard E. *literary agent*
San Juan, Enrico Abella *political analyst, journalist*
Saralegui, Cristina Maria *journalist*
Sarambei, Nicolae *editor*
Saraste, Heikki Juhani *publishing executive*
Sasser, Charles Wayne *journalist, educator, writer*
Sasu, Voichita Maria *literature educator*
Satin, Mark *editor, lawyer*
Scalza, Margaret T. *publishing executive*
Scannell, John R. *publishing consultant*
Scarborough, Charles Bishop, III *broadcast journalist, writer*
Schalkwijk, Johan Pieter *information and communication educator*
Schatken, Nancy Leah *medical editor*
Scheel, Kurt *editor*
Scherer, Barbara Elizabeth *publishing company executive*
Schiff, Judith Jenny *editor, proofreader, photographer*
Schilling, Mark Rea *film critic, journalist*
Schlagman, Richard Edward *book publisher*
Schmalbrock, Gerd *journalist*
Schmitz, Heinrich Walter *communications educator*
Schnibbe, Steven C. *media consultant*
Schnurr, Lewis Edward *telecommunications educator*
Schock, Axel *magazine editor, writer*
Schrader, Michael Eugene *columnist, editor*
Schrand, Richard Henry *broadcaster*
Schreuder, Rino Herman Christiaan *publisher, consultant*
Schrotta, Werner *newspaper publisher*
Schuck, Marjorie Massey *publisher, editor, author's consultant*
Schuemchen, Andreas *editor, educator*
Schulte-Hillen, Gerd *business executive*
Schurz, Franklin Dunn, Jr. *media executive*
Schutz, Robert Rudolph *retired editor*
Schwallie, John Alan *media company executive, certified public accountant*
Schwarz, Gerhard E. *journalist*
Schweickart, Russell Louis *communications executive, astronaut*
Schwier, Priscilla Lamb Guyton *television broadcasting company executive*
Scogin, Troy Pope *publishing company executive, accounts executive*
Scott, Frederick Isadore, Jr. *editor, business executive*
Scott, Marie Evelyn *publisher, journalist*
Seamans, Andrew Charles *editorial and public relations consultant, columnist, author*
Seingry, Georges-Francis *publishing company executive*
Selvey, Anthony Rochford *publishing executive*
Sen, Ananda *communications senior executive*
Seppalainen, Ugi Gerhard *journalist*
Serour, Aleya Aly *publishing executive, literary agent*
Sforza, Mario Vito *newspaper writer, retired surgeon*
Shaine, Frederick Mordecai *newspaper executive, consultant*
Shams-ud Doha, Aminur Rahman *publisher, editor-in-chief*
Sharma, Chandra Shekhar *editor, mathematics educator*
Sharma, Pawan Kumar *publishing executive*
Sharrock, John Timothy Robin *editor*
Shaw, Bernard *television journalist*
Shaw, Grace Goodfriend (Mrs. Herbert Franklin Shaw) *publisher, editor*
Shelton, James Keith *journalism educator*
Sherman, Robert *broadcaster*
Shier, Shelley M. *production company executive*
Shindler, Colin *editor, lecturer*
Shine, Neal James *journalism educator, former newspaper editor, publisher*
Shirane, Kunio *publishing executive*
Shreiner, Curt *educational technologist, consultant*
Shulman, Alon Hamilton *multimedia entertainment entrepreneur*
Shushurin, Gregory Sergeevich *publishing company executive, consultant*
Siddiqui, Athar *publishing executive, editor*
Siddiqui, Dilnawaz Ahmed *communications educator, international communication planning advisor, consultant*
Siegel, Ira T. *publishing executive*
Siemon-Netto, Uwe *journalist, theologian*
Sieveking, Vincent Jan *publishing executive*
Silva Martins, Joao Francisco *television company executive*
Silver, Eric *journalist, writer*
Simon, Robin John Hughes *magazine editor, publisher, writer*
Simons, Carol Lenore *magazine editor*
Simpson, John Andrew *lexicographer*
Sims, Calvin Gene *journalist*
Singh, Sheetla *journalist*
Singh, Surendra Nihal *journalist, writer*
Skierka, Volker H. *journalist, author*
Slater, John Ninis *journalist*
Sloan, Karen Leslie *journalist*
Smail, Derek James Richardson *publishing executive*
Smiley, Xan de Crespigny *journalist*
Smit, L. J.M. *editor, career officer*
Smith, Alexander Alan George *publishing executive*
Smith, Chester *broadcasting executive*
Smith, D(aisy) Mullett *publisher*
Smith, David Harold *communication educator*
Smith, Donald E. *broadcast engineer, manager*
Smith, Joseph Phelan *film company executive*
Smith, Louise Ellen *editor-in-chief, publisher*
Smith, W. Preston *publishing executive, educator, real estate broker*
Smyth, David *editor, author*
Smythe, Colin Peter *publisher*
Snip, Jerina Carla *periodical editor*
Snowden, Alan *editor, consultant*
Snyder, Arthur *publishing company executive*
Snyder, James P. *audio and digital television engineer, videographer, editor*
Snyder, Joseph John *editor, historian, author, lecturer, consultant*
Somers Cocks, Anna Gwenllian *publishing executive, editor*
Soni, Ramesh Kumar *publisher, journalist*
Soni, Shankarlal *editor in chief, consultant*
Soto, Roberto Fernando Eduardo *journalist*
Souchal, Francois Charles *editor*
Spangler, Ronald Leroy *retired television executive, aircraft executive, automobile collector*
Speck, Kurt Georg *publisher*
Speller, Robert Ernest Blakefield *publishing executive*
Sperlich, Thomas *journalist, consultant*
Spicer, Tim Simon *broadcasting executive, retired military officer*
Spirtos, Andrea C. *columnist, muralist, office manager*
Stack, Maurice Neville *journalist, consultant*
Staempfli, Rudolf Samuel *publisher*
Stafford, Matthew Jackson *newspaper writer*
Stahl, Günter *publisher, editor, writer*
Stalfelt, Sven Olov *publishing executive, writer*
Stamp, Robert Colin *media company executive*
Stamper, Malcolm Theodore *publishing company executive*
Stangos, Nicolas *publishing executive*
Stanton, John Jeffrey *editor, broadcast journalist, government programs director, analyst, professional society administrator*
Stapf, Karl R.G. *editor, researcher*
Stareva, Lilia Petrova *publisher*
Stenumgaard, Peter Frank *telecommunications researcher*
Stewart, Michael McFadden *professional speaker*
Stewart, Robert Arthur Churchill (Bob Stewart) *journal publisher, municipal official*
Stienstra, Stephani Ann *editor*
Stitt, Dorothy Jewett *journalist*
Stoilov, Dimitar Iliev *publishing executive*
Stolley, Richard Brockway *journalist*
Stone, Ingeborg Eda *recording industry executive*
Stone, John Owen *freelance journalist*
Stott, Robert Henry *journalist*
Strahilevitz, Meir *inventor, researcher, psychiatry educator*
Straka, Laszlo Richard *publishing consultant*
Stringer, Howard *media executive*
Stuart, Maxwell Charles *film and television distribution company executive*
Sturges, Sherry Lynn *recording industry executive*
Subrahmanya, Susheela *journalist, editor, publisher*
Sugita, Nobuo *publisher*
Sugiyama, Kazunori *music producer*
Sukun, Kamil Mehmet *publisher*
Suleski, Ronald *publishing executive*
Sullivan, John Fox *publisher*
Sullivan, Scott *journalist*
Suzuki, Toshio *publishing executive*
Sweeny, Donna Bozzella *writer, editor*
Swenson, L. Anne *publisher*
Switzer, Maurice Harold *journalist*
Szmyt, Przemyslaw Aleksander *media executive*
Taegi, Yu *publisher*
Tahir, Muhammad Aejaz Ali *editor*
Taifour, Majed Ghaleb *editor, journalist*
Taishoff, Lawrence Bruce *publishing company executive*
Tait, Richard *editor-in-chief*
Tait, Simon John Anderson *journalist*
Takahashi, Shotaro *retired communications executive, former ambassador*
Talley, Truman Macdonald *publisher*
Talmor, Sascha *editor*
Talvitie, Jyrki Kalevi *lexicographer*
Tankard, James William, Jr. *journalism educator, writer*
Tarr, Ian James *publisher*
Tast, Hans-Jürgen *book editor*
Temple, Christopher Lawrence *financial editor, publisher, foundation executive*
Terry, Elizabeth Joanna *publisher, editor*
Tetzner, Karl *editor*
Thalmann, Jörg (Arthur) *retired journalist*
Theis, Paul Anthony *publishing executive*
Therond, Dominique *publisher*
Thind, Sukhpal Singh *publishing company executive, investment executive*
Thomas, Anne Moreau *newspaper owner*
Thomas, Dana Fife *journalist, educator*
Thomas, Dwayne Allen *composer, publisher*
Thomas, Patricia Goodnow *journalist*
Thompson, Nicolas de la Mare *publisher*
Thomson, Derick Smith *editor, educator, poet*
Thomson, Kenneth R. (Lord Thomson of Fleet) *publishing executive*
Thornhill, Arthur Horace, Jr. *retired book publisher*
Thornton, Steven Rupert *patent examiner*
Tiede, Tom Robert *journalist*
Todorovic, Aleksandar *broadcasting educator*
Toms, Michael Anthony *broadcast journalist, editor, writer, producer*
Tondowidjojo, John Vincent *communication educator, priest*
Toni, Aldemaro *publishing executive*
Torella, Lucio *editor*
Toro, Hernan *communications educator*
Townsend, Terry *publishing executive*
Travis, Alice Dimery *journalist*
Traylor, William Robert *publisher*
Treglown, Jeremy Dickinson *writer, editor, educator*
Trembly, Cristy *television executive*
Trinco, Ornella Maria *publishing executive*
Tsuruta, Takuhiko *publishing executive*
Tufte, Thomas *communications researcher, educator*
Turk, Esin C. *public relations educator*
Turková, Vladimíra *editor-in-chief, consultant*
Turner, Ted (Robert Edward Turner) *television executive*
Ueda, Kenichi *journalism educator*
Uimonen, Risto Juhani *columnist*
Ulfkotte, Udo Konstantin *editor*
Ullmann, Bernard Francois *journalist, author*
Underwood, Steven Clark *publishing executive*
Uno, Hisashi *communications educator*
Utakapan, Chukiat *publishing executive, editor*
Utley, Jon Basil *think tank director, journalist*
Vail, Thomas Van Husen *retired newspaper publisher and editor*
Valagussa, Roberto Paolo *publishing executive, consultant*
Valentin, Beate *freelance journalist, art market expert*
Vallcorba, Jaume *publisher, editor, educator*
van Allen, Philip Andrew *interactive development company executive, educator*
Vance, Leslie Edwin *multimedia technologist*
van den Hoek, Kees *publisher*
Van Der Sluis, Wiebe *editor*
Van Duyse, Francis Donald *publisher*
VanMeer, Mary Ann *publisher, writer, researcher*
Vannier, Alain Robert *film company executive*
Van Puyvelde, Eric Michel *editor-in-chief, journalist*
van Rosendaal, John *journalist*
Van Susteren, Greta Conway *news anchor, lawyer*
Vardhan, Peeta Bobby *journalism educator*
Varner, Helen *communications educator*
Vartiovaara, Ilkka Juhani *publishing executive, medical writer*
Velics, Gabriella *journalist, sociologist*
Verghese, George Thomas *editor*
Vermaat, John Arthur Emerson *reporter*
Vernon, Doris Schaller *retired writer*
Vernon, Weston, III (Wes Vernon) *broadcaster, writer, actor*
Verstappen, Harrie *photographer, audio-visual director*
Vesa, Mikko Juhani *retired editor-in-chief*
Veshkurtsev, Juriy Mikhailovich *communications educator*
Vick, Frances Brannen *publishing executive*
Vinken, Pierre Jacques *publishing executive, neurosurgeon*
von Boehm, Gero *journalist, film director, producer*
Vonk, Gerrit Rokus *radio executive, consultant*
von Minckwitz, Bernhard Albert Roman *publishing house executive*
Waern, Rasmus Lennart *editor, architect*
Wafula, Richard Makhanu *literary critic, researcher*
Wagner, Phil *publisher, writer*
Walendy, Udo Bruno *publisher*
Walker, Ronald R. *writer, editor, educator*
Walls, Carmage Lee, Jr. *newspaper publisher/executive, consultant*
Walls, Martha Ann Williams (Mrs. B. Carmage Walls) *newspaper executive*
Walsh, Mary Noelle *publishing executive*
Walsh, Peter Joseph *multimedia marketing professional*
Walters, Barbara *television journalist*
Wang, Yu Liang *journal editor*
Wang, Yuhai *magazine editor-in-chief*
Wangchindorj, Langtai Baljinniam *periodical editor*
Ward, Hiley Henry *journalist, educator*
Warren, Albert *publishing executive*
Wasserman, Steve *editor*
Watanabe, Tsuneo *newspaper executive*
Watkinson, John Ronald *communications consultant*
Wayne, Donald *editor*
Webb, Pauline Mary *broadcaster, writer*
Webster, Richard *editor-in-chief*
Wechsler, Bradley J. *film company executive*
Wein, Hanns-Ulrich Herbert *editor, publisher*
Weinberger, Caspar Willard *publishing executive, former secretary of defense*
Weingartz, Hans *editor, educator*
Weir, Hugh William Lindsay *publishing executive, writer*
Welke, Elton Grinnell, Jr. *publisher, writer*
Wen, Ruilin *editor*
Wenge, Ralph *newscaster*
Weniger-Phelps, Nancy Ann *media specialist, photographer*
Wentworth, William Edgar *journalist*
Westermann, Maarten Huibert Joris *journalist, author*
Westin, David Lawrence *broadcasting executive, lawyer*
Westphal, Ruth Lilly *educational media company*
Weyel, Volker Alfred *editor*
Wham, William Neil *publisher*
Whitaker, Ruth Reed *retired newspaper editor*
White, Gregg Kenneth *writer*
White, Roderick Douglas Thirkell *editor, advertising and marketing consultant*
Whitehouse, Mark Edward *communications executive, small business owner*
Whitelaw, Kevin John *journalist*
Whitney, Paul Michael *publisher, import/export executive*
Whittell, Polly (Mary) Kaye *editor, journalist*
Wieder, Judy Sara *editor-in-chief*
Wiener, Hesh (Harold Frederic Wiener) *publisher, editor, consultant*
Wigart, Sture Bengt *publishing company executive*
Wilder, Robert David *publishing executive*
Wilkins, Adam Stanley *editor*
Wille, Volker *publishing executive*
Williams, Earl Patrick, Jr. *editor, freelance writer*
Williams, Ellis Keith *broadcast executive*
Williams, Joy Rhonda *publishing and entertainment company executive*
Williams, Kenyon Donald *inventor*
Williams, Susan A. *broadcast executive*
Williams, William Henry, II *publisher*
Willis, John Alvin *editor*
Willis, Laurel Eileen (Anna Livia Plulaurelbelle) *publishing executive*
Wilson, James Reid, Jr. *publishing executive*
Wilson, Johnny Lee *group publisher*
Wilson, Sanna Beth *managing editor, writer religious magazine*
Winfrey, Marion Lee *television critic*
Wintzek, Bernhard Christian *publisher*
Wirsig, Woodrow *magazine editor, trade organization executive, business executive*
Wiseman, Carter Sterling *editor, author*
Wittstadt, Thomas Peter *economic expert, media specialist, entrepreneur*
Wizard, Brian *publisher, author*
Woldt, Harold Frederick, Jr. *newspaper publishing executive*
Wolf, John Howell *retired publisher*
Wong, Wai Ming Otis *editor-in-chief*
Woodard, H. Tom *entertainment company executive*
Woodford, F. Peter *scientific editor*
Woodruff, Mark Reed *magazine editor*
Woon, Tai Ho *broadcasting executive*
Wordsman, Elizabeth Schmitt (Betsy Wordsman) *senior manager print production*
Wortmann, Hildegard Maria *global media executive*
Wössner, Mark Matthias *retired publishing company executive*
Yamaguchi, Shoko *journalist*
Yamamoto, Irwin Toraki *editor, publisher investment newsletter*
Yang, Chung-Chuan *communications educator*
Yao, Zhineng *publishing executive*
Yasnyi, Allan David *communications company executive*
Young, Jonathan Piers *editor*
Yu, Janice J. *journalist*
Yule, Andrew Morrison *broadcasting director*
Zalaznick, Sheldon *editor, journalist*
Zassoursky, Yassen Nikolayevich *media educator*
Zentgraf, Martin *editor, clergyman*
Zhang, Baorui *journalist*
Zhang, Jian-Guo *optical communications educator, researcher*
Zhao, Hai *communications educator*
Zhou, Juliet Lijun *journalist*
Zink, Lubor Jan *journalist, author*
Zirnitis, Peteris *publishing executive*
Zmora, Ohad *publisher*
Zobel, Jill Anne Hausrath *journalist, editorial consultant*
Zosimo-Landolfo, Guido *publisher, chemist, pharmacist*
Zvonova, Alevtina Nickolayevna *publisher, consultant*

EDUCATION. For postsecondary education, *See also* specific fields.

Aarestad, James Harrison *retired educational administrator, army officer*
Abdelsamad, Moustafa Hassan *dean*
Abe, Jin *admissions administrator*
Aboreshaid, Saleh *director, engineering educator*
Abraham-Frois, Gilbert *educator*
Adachi, Nobuhiro *educator*
Adams, Freddy *university rector*
Adams, Maerita Elaine Owen *early childhood educator*
Adams, Michael Fred *university president, political communications specialist*
Adams, Ronald G. *middle school educator*
Adcock, Muriel W. *special education educator*
Adkins, Gregory D. *higher education administrator*
Adler, Norman T. *dean, psychologist, educator*
Agnew, Janet Burnett *secondary education educator*
Agreen, Linda Kerr *secondary education educator*
Ahmad, Shakil *education educator, researcher*
Ahmed, Mubarik Rajpoot *secondary education educator*
Aitken, Ruth Elaine Willson *educational consultant*
Aitkin, Donald Alexander *university administrator*
Akbar, Sher *education educator*
Aker, Susan K. *elementary education educator*
Akhtar, Muhammad *education educator*
Al-Abed, Nazmieh Salim *principal*
Albe Fessard, Denise Gabrielle *educator*
Albury, William Randall *university administrator, educator*
Alcamo, Frank Paul *retired educational administrator*
Alderman, Charles Wayne *university dean*
Alderman, Geoffrey *academic administrator*
Al-Dhobaib, Ahmed Mohammad *academic administrator*
Aldrich, Richard Edward *education educator*
Alemdaroglu, Kemal *university official*
Alexander, John Andrew *academic administrator*
Alexander, William M. *educator, researcher, writer*
Alexandroff, Mirron (Mike Alexandroff) *retired college president*
Alhozab, Adel Abdulla *dean, educator*
Ali, Khayyam, Sr. *elementary education educator*
Alicias, Eduardo Rezonable, Jr. *education educator, researcher*
Allardt, Erik Anders *academic administrator, educator*
Allén, Sture *academic administrator, linguistics educator*
Allen-Meares, Paula G. *dean, social work educator*
Allman, Margaret Ann Lowrance *counselor*
Almore-Randle, Allie Louise *special education educator*
Al-Moshaikah, Mohamed Sulaiman *dean, education educator*
Al-Said, Anwar Ghalib *educational administrator, education educator*
Alvarez, Blanca Magrassi *educational director, psychotherapist*
Alzayed, Naser S. *academic administrator, educator*
Amal, Ichlasul *academic administrator*
Amos, Francis John Clarke *academic administrator*
Andacht, Herman William *retired educator and counselor*
Andenyang, Ikun Habu *education educator*
Anderson, Bruce Ray *school superintendent*

Anderson, Claire W. *computer gifted and talented educator*
Anderson, Francile Mary *secondary education educator*
Anderson, Joel E., Jr. *university administrator*
Anderson, Susan Elaine Mosshamer *education and organizational consultant, musician*
Anderson, Thomas *dean, computer engineering consultant*
Anderson, Brother Timothy Mel *academic administrator*
Andersson, Egil Anders Danold *education educator*
Andorfer, Donald Joseph *university president*
Andrews, Richard John *education educator*
Angeles, Rodolfo B. *elementary education educator*
Anicama Gomez, José Carlos *academic administrator*
Aoun, Georges Michel *university dean*
Aquino, Alfredo Fernandez *academic administrator*
Aramata, Shigeo *university administrator*
Arambel, Phyllis Ann *elementary education educator*
Arima, Akito *academic administrator*
Arimoto, Akira *education educator*
Armitage, John Vernon *academic administrator*
Armstrong, Lloyd, Jr. *university official, physics educator*
Armstrong-Law, Margaret *school administrator*
Arnold, Heinz *academic administrator*
Arnold, Mitylene B. *special education educator, consultant*
Arnold, Roslyn Mary *educator, education consultant*
Arnott, Geoffrey Dale *academic administrator*
Arshi, Gurcharan Singh *academic facility administrator*
Arsov, Yanko Boyanov *institute director*
Artémiadis, Nicolas K. *educator*
Asadi, Robert Samir *high school principal*
Ashley, Lynn *educator, consultant, administrator*
Atkinson, Richard Chatham *university president*
Aucella, Laurence Frank *counseling administrator, educator*
Austvik, Ole Gunnar *educator*
Auvenshine, William Robert *academic administrator*
Aversa, Dolores Sejda *educational administrator*
Azevedo, Joao Luis Toste *academic education educator*
Babayevsky, Peter Gordeevich *educational administrator*
Bacanli, Hasan *educational psychologist*
Bacow, Lawrence Seldon *academic administrator, environmental educator*
Badley, William J. *education program director, English language educator*
Baetz Reutergårdh, Lars Bertil *educator, consultant*
Bailey, James Curtis *college administrator*
Bailey, Philip Sigmon, Jr. *university official, chemistry educator*
Baird, Gregory Ross *university program director, theater educator*
Bajaj, Satinder Khurana *academic administrator, educator*
Baker, Ian Helstrip *university official*
Baker, Ruth Holmes *retired secondary education educator*
Bakhshiev, Nikolay Grigorievich *adult education educator, researcher*
Balan, Vladimir *adult education educator*
Baldi, Stéphane *education researcher, sociologist*
Baldwin, Dorothy Leila *secondary school educator*
Baltimore, David *university president, microbiologist, educator*
Balzer, Wolfgang *educator*
Ban, Tsunenobu *education educator*
Banas, Suzanne *middle school educator*
Baqi, Muhammad Abdul *education educator*
Barayuga, Petronio Jacosalem *college executive*
Barber, Benjamin R. *director, educator*
Barbour, Robert Angus *retired academic educator*
Barck, Karlheinz Rudolf *university administrator*
Baric, Josip *academic administrator*
Barksdale-Ladd, Mary Alice *education educator*
Barnard, John Michael *educator*
Barnes, Marylou Riddleberger *retired academic administrator, educator*
Barnes de Castro, Francisco Jose *academic administrator*
Barnett, Charles Thomas *retired secondary education educator*
Barnett, Marilyn Doan *secondary education business educator*
Barratt, Donna Lee *elementary school educator*
Barriskill, Maudanne Kidd *primary school educator*
Bartels, Siegfried Hans Murray *educator*
Bartnicka, Kalina Hanna *history of education educator, researcher*
Barton, Allan Douglas *retired university executive*
Bartow, Barbara Jené *university program administrator*
Baruch, Yehuda *educator*
Bascetincelik, Ali *academic administrator, engineering educator*
Bateman, Walter Samuel Grono *academic researcher*
Bates, James Earl *academic administrator*
Batho, Gordon Richard *education educator*
Bauernfeind, James C. *secondary education educator*
Baumann, Ernst Frederick *college president*
Baxter, Betty Carpenter *educational administrator*
Baxter, Roger George *boarding school consultant*
Bayer, Ernst *academic administrator, chemistry educator*
Bayliss, David *transport studies educator, consultant*
Beach, Sandra Marie Yudichak *secondary education educator*
Beals, Mark Graden *educator*
Bean, John Perrin *education educator*
Bean, Philip Thomas *educator*
Beanland, David George *academic administrator*
Beatty, Barbara Rachel *education educator*
Beck, Barbara Nell *elementary school educator*
Beck, Elaine Kushner *elementary and secondary school educator*
Beering, Steven Claus *academic administrator, medical educator*
Bekui, Sefiamor Kwadzo Mensah Dotse *technical educator*
Bell, Paul Burton, Jr. *academic administrator, zoology educator*
Bello, Joseph Yusuf *academic administrator*
Bencze, Lorant Anselm *college president, linguist, educator*
Benedict, Barry Arden *university administrator*
Benedict, Julius Niyi *education educator*
Bennett, Sister Elsa Mary *secondary education educator*
Bennett, Helen Donele *educator*
Benson, Joan Dorothy *secondary school educator*
Berceli, Tibor *education educator*
Beresford-Hill, Paul Vincent *headmaster, international educator*
Berezantseva, Maria Sergeyevna *education educator*
Berger, Deborah Kornbluth *educator, educational consultant*
Berger, Nathan Allen *dean, university administrator*
Bergeron, Lynn Henry *assistant principal, private school educator*
Bernardi, Mauro *educator, physician*
Berne, Michel *educator*
Bernik, France *science academy executive, literary historian*
Berntson, Kevin Anton Olof Martin *educational administrator, art historian, psychologist*
Berry, James Lee *retired educator*
Berry, Robert *secondary school educator, art educator*
Besch, Lorraine W. *special education educator*
Besenyi, Carlos Arón *academic administrator*
Bethel, David Percival *education professional*
Beverly, Laura Elizabeth *special education educator*
Beyene, Tilahun *educator, writer, researcher*
Beyer, Mary Edel *primary education educator*
Bhalerao, Sudhakar Kashinath *education educator*
Bi, Guangguo *education educator*
Billaz, André *education educator*
Binnion, John Edward *education educator*
Bird, Donald C. *college administrator*
Biróné-Nagy, Edit *education educator*
Biscoe, Timothy John *academic administrator, physiologist*
Bishop-Graham, Barbara *secondary school educator, journalist*
Bisquerra, Rafael *education educator*
Biziuk, Marek Karol *educator*
Black, Clinton Leander *education educator, author*
Black, Lavonne Patricia *special education educator*
Blake, Barry John *educator*
Blanco Lopez, Desiderio *secondary school educator, investigator*
Blessing, Maxine Lindsey *secondary education educator*
Bleumink, Eric *academic administrator, educator*
Bloch, Julia Chang *educator, former ambassador, former bank executive*
Block, Sandra Linda *special education educator*
Blomberg, Douglas Gordon *education educator*
Bloodworth, Gladys Leon *educator*
Blue, Robert Lee *secondary education educator*
Blumberg, Baruch Samuel *academic research scientist*
Blumhardt, Jon Howard *college official*
Bodmann, Hans Walter *education educator*
Boesch, Diane Harriet *elementary education educator*
Boggan, Jeffrey Scott *college administrator*
Böhm, Winfried Franz *education educator*
Boisjoly, Russell Paul *dean, educational consultant*
Boman, (John) Robert *educator*
Bonnaud, Olivier Andre *education educator*
Booth, Penelope Partridge *educator, school principal, author*
Bordelon, Carolyn Thew *elementary school educator*
Boreczek, Krzysztof Andrzej *history educator, editor*
Boren, David Lyle *academic administrator*
Bornstein, Rita *academic administrator*
Borntrager, John Sherwood *principal*
Boseker, Barbara Jean *education educator*
Bottoms, Stephen James *educator*
Bouchereau, Jean-Luc Marcel *educator, researcher*
Bouchillon, John Ray *education coordinator*
Bourgat, Robert Michel *educator, curator*
Bouton, Marshall Melvin *academic administrator*
Bowleg, Lisa Ingrid *education educator*
Bowlin, Lyle Lewis *educator*
Boyd, Richard Alfred *school system administrator*
Boyd, Willard Lee *academic administrator, museum administrator, lawyer*
Boykin, William Edward *retired principal, state legislator*
Brading, David Anthony *education educator*
Braekman, Willy Louis *retired educator*
Braksick, Leslie *academic administrator*
Branch, Michael Arthur *academic administrator*
Brandon, Peter Samuel *academic administrator, civil and structural engineer*
Brann, Donald Lewis, Jr. *school superintendent*
Brannan, Cleo Estella *retired elementary education educator*
Breedlove, Frances Burton *elementary educator*
Brewer, A. Bruce *university administrator*
Brewer, Nevada Nancy *elementary education educator*
Brezinka, Wolfgang *educator*
Bridges, Edwin Maxwell *education educator*
Broad, Cynthia Ann Morgan *special education educator, consultant*
Brock-Utne, Birgit *education educator*
Brodeur, Michael Stephen *dean*
Brooks, Lillian Drilling Ashton *adult education educator*
Broome, Kathryn *secondary education educator*
Brown, David Richard *school system administrator, minister*
Brown, Elmira Newsom *retired elementary school educator*
Brown, Felicia M. Jefferson *academic administrator*
Brown, Jay Marshall *retired secondary education educator*
Brown, Kathryn Lisbeth *secondary education educator*
Brown, Lillian Hill *retired educator*
Brown, Linda K. *secondary education educator, writer*
Brownson, Kenneth C. *university dean*
Broyles, Ruth Rutledge *principal*
Brunel, Pierre Denis *education educator*
Bryan, Lawrence Dow *college president*
Bryan, Thelma Jane *university administrator, English language educator*
Büchsel, Elfriede Elisabeth *retired secondary education educator, researcher*
Buckley, Robert John *academic research administrator*
Bui, Khoi Tien *college counselor*
Bullock, Donald Wayne *elementary education educator, educational computing consultant*
Bumgardner, Cloyd Jeffrey *school principal*
Buote, Rosemarie Boschen *special education educator*
Burgess, Robert George *academic administrator*
Burnett, Robert Adair *university administrator, history educator*
Burnley, June Williams *secondary school educator*
Burns, Bonnie *educator*
Burns, James Milton *retired educator*
Burrell, E. William *retired university adminstrator, educator*
Burridge, Richard Alan *college dean*
Burris, Craven Allen *retired college administrator, educator*
Bush, Gail *secondary school educator, librarian, consultant, writer*
Bush, Stanley Giltner *secondary school educator*
Buss, Gerald Vere Austen *educator, clergyman*
Butler, Marilyn Speers Evans *college rector*
Butler, Orton Carmichael *education educator*
Buzzelli, Charlotte Grace *educator*
Byeon, Jong Heon *education educator*
Cabahug, Susana Baring *educational administrator, consultant*
Cable, Richard Charles *education administrator, educator, consultant*
Caldwell, William Edward *educational administration educator, arbitrator*
Čalogović, Marko *engineering educator*
Campbell, Sir Colin Murray *university vice chancellor*
Campbell, F(enton) Gregory *college administrator, historian*
Campbell, Joan Virginia Loweke *secondary school educator, language educator*
Campbell, Robin *primary education educator*
Canham, Pruella Cromartie Niver *retired educator*
Cannon, Francis V., Jr. *former academic administrator, electrical engineer, economist*
Cantrell, Sharron Caulk *principal*
Caplan, Ann Patricia Bailey *education educator*
Cappel, Constance *academic administrator, author*
Caprio, Anthony S. *university president*
Carden, Joy Cabbage *educational consultant*
Carmichael, John Craig, Jr. *career counselor*
Carnesale, Albert *university chancellor*
Carney Nelson, Ellen B. *elementary school educator*
Carr, Bessie *retired middle school educator*
Carr, Sir (Albert) Raymond *retired educator*
Carr-Chellman, Alison Alene *education educator*
Carty, Heidi Marlene *educator, researcher*
Casler, Frederick Clair *academic administrator, law enforcement educator*
Caspersen, Sven Lars *academic administrator, statistician*
Cassidy, Jack *educator*
Casteen, John Thomas, III *university president*
Castenell, Louis Anthony *college dean*
Cattaneo, Anna Giulia *university technician*
Celis, Jean-Pierre P.J.C. *educator*
Chadwick, Alan Frank *adult educator*
Chadwick, Owen *historian, educator*
Chambers, Johnnie Lois (Tucker Chambers) *retired elementary school educator, rancher*
Chambers-Mangum, Fransenna Ethel *special education educator*
Champion De Crespigny, Richard Rafe *academic administrator, educator*
Chandler, Kimberley Lynn *gifted education resource specialist*
Chang, Chia-Cheng *educator*
Chang, Flora Chia-I *university administrator*
Chang, Hiang-Chu Ausilia *education educator, researcher*
Chang, Hsueh-Wen *educator*
Chang, Tai-Ping *educator*
Chapiro, Adolphe *education educator, consultant*
Charles, Blanche *retired elementary education educator*
Charlton, Shirley Marie *educational consultant*
Charp, Sylvia *educator, consultant*
Charters, Alexander Nathaniel *retired adult education educator*
Chartier, Pierre *educator*
Chase, Pearline *adult education educator*
Chattin-McNichols, John Patrick *education educator*
Chaudhry, Praveen K. *adult education educator, researcher*
Chen, Albert Hung-yee *academic dean*
Chen, Huitang *educator*
Cheng, Ting-Wong *academic administrator*
Cheng, Yiu-chung *academic administrator*
Cheong, Kenneth Keng-Liang *academic administrator*
Cheung, Gordon Chi Kai *education educator*
Cheung, Paul V.S. *dean, engineering educator*
Childers, Susan Lynn Bohn *special education educator, administrator, human resources and transition specialist, consultant*
Chirva, Vassily Yakovlevich *dean, researcher*
Choi, Jae Hoon *retired university administrator, legal educator*
Choi, Yearn-Ik *educator*
Choi-Cheung, Vivien L.F. *university administrator*
Chon, Kye-Sung (Kaye Chon) *educator*
Chook, Edward Kongyen *university administrator, disaster medicine educator*
Choue, Young Seek *university administrator, association executive*
Christensen, Donna Ray *educator*
Christian, Richard Carlton *university dean, former advertising agency executive*
Christie, Renfrew Leslie *dean*
Christodoulides, Andreas Demosthenes *educational administrator, researcher, editor*
Christopherson, Myrvin Frederick *college president*
Chu, Wang Bo *university administrator, educator, researcher*
Chudzikiewicz, Ryszard Jerzy *foundry educator*
Chung, Chi Yung *college administrator*
Chung, Stephen Yue Ping *academic dean*
Chung, Young Ryun *educator, research scientist*
Chung-Kwong, Poon *academic administrator*
Churilla, Barbara Ann Kuryan *secondary education educator*
Cicerone, Ralph John *academic administrator, geophysicist*
Cifoletti, Giovanna Cleonice *education educator*
Cioclov, Dragos Dumitru *education educator, researcher*
Cirilo, Amelia Medina *educational consultant, supervisor*
Cirone, William Joseph *educational administrator*
Cizek, Gregory J. *educator*
Claire, Dennis Daniel, Jr. *secondary education educator*
Clark, Gordon Leslie *educator*
Clark, Paul Ernest *university administrator*
Clarke, Lambuth McGeehee *retired college president*
Clemente, Patrocinio Ablola *secondary education educator*
Cleveland, Julia Lynn *elementary school educator*
Clifton, Bobbie Jean *elementary education educator*
Cline, Janet E. Safford *school district administrator, desktop publisher*
Clinkenbeard, James Howard *principal*
Coberly, Patricia Gail *elementary education educator, adult education educator*
Cocchi, Alessandro *education educator*
Cochrane, Walter E. *education administrator, writer*
Coello Valadez, Carlos Antonio *principal, researcher*
Coffey, David Thompson *guidance and counseling educator, consultant*
Coglianese, Kara Ann *elementary education educator, consultant*
Cohalan, John Robert *educator*
Cohen, David Walter *academic administrator, periodontist, educator*
Coker, Gurnelle Sheely *retired secondary education educator*
Cole, Joyce Macklin *mathematics educator*
Coleman, Brenda Forbis *gifted and talented educator*
Coleman, Gary William *elementary school educator, retired*
Coleman, Michael Christopher *educator*
Coll, John Charles *university administrator, chemist*
Collins, S(arah) Ruth Knight *education educator*
Colman, Charles Kingsbury *academic administrator, criminologist*
Compagna, Donna J. *preschool administrator, primary school educator*
Connell, Annie Mahan *educator*
Connellan, William Wesley *higher education administrator*
Connor, Leo Edward *special education administrator*
Conrad, Edgar William *educator*
Constantinou, Clay *dean, lawyer*
Contoli, Longino *biodiversity researcher, educator*
Cook, Edward David *institute executive director*
Cook, James Junior *academic administrator*
Cook, Mary Gooch *elementary school educator*
Cook, Sister M(ary) Mercedes *educator, educational administrator*
Cooke, Evelyn Kathleen Chatman *retired elementary education educator*
Cooley, Regina Kae *educational administrator*
Cooper, Christopher Donald *educator*
Cooper, Martin *education educator*
Coquery-Vidrovitch, Catherine M. *educator*
Corbitt, Eumiller Mattie *education educator, special education educator*
Cordell, Beulah Faye *special education educator*
Corey, Judith Ann *educator*
Corley, Jenny Lynd Wertheim *elementary education educator*
Cornelius, Jacquelyn H. *high school principal, educator*
Cornish, Brian Alexander *retired university dean*
Correa, Jaime Montalvo *university administrator*
Correu, Sandra Kay *special education educator*
Cosper, Sammie Wayne *educational consultant*
Cossée de Maulde, Guy Jean *education educator, consultant*
Costa Picazo, Rolando *education educator, translator*
Cox, Alma Tenney *retired English language and science educator*
Cox, Gregory Stevens *educator, lecturer, publisher, broadcaster*
Cox, Stephen James *educator*
Coy, Doris Rhea *counselor, educator*
Coyne, Edward James *international business educator*
Cozza, Eduardo Nestor *university executive, researcher*
Crawford, Sheila Jane *education educator, consultant*
Crean, Maureen Rose *educational consultant*
Creel, Sue Cloer *secondary education educator*
Creutzburg, Reiner *education educator*
Cromwell, Ronald R. *educator*
Crooks, Patricia Kay *counselor*
Crouzet, M.-J. Michel *educator*
Csapó, Benö *education educator*
Culton, Paul Melvin *retired counselor, educator, interpreter*
Cummins, Patricia Willett *academic administrator*
Cunningham, Marina *university program director*
Cunningham, William Hughes *academic administrator, marketing educator*
Cureton, Bryant Lewis *college president, educator*
Curry, David *guidance staff developer*
Curry, Everett William, Jr. *college official, minister*
Curtis, Paula Annette *elementary and secondary education educator*
Custodi, Paolo Antonio *secondary education educator*
Cutler, Sarah Taylor *educator, enamelist, writer*
Czabán, János *academic administrator*
Daghir, Nuhad Joseph *dean*
Dahm, Helmut Johannes *research institute administrator*
dal Covolo, Enrico *university dean*
Daley, Veta Adassa *educational administrator*
Danforth, William Henry *retired academic administrator, physician*
Dangelo, Eugene Michael *elementary education educator*
Darby, Anita Loyce *secondary school educator*
Darby, Marianne Talley *elementary school educator*
Darmon, René Yves *dean, research educator*
Das, Mamota *education educator, researcher*
Datkiewicz, Gregory *educator*
Daudel, Raymond *academic administrator, educator*
Daugherty, Linda Hagaman *private school executive*
Daukantas, George Vytautas *counseling practitioner, educator*
Davey, Alison *principal, educational consultant*
Davidson, Christopher *special education consultant*
Davidson, Shirley Jean *elementary and secondary educator*
Davidson, Vicky L. *university administrator*
Davidson-Burnet, Gaie *university administrator*
Davis, Cecelia Grace *elementary and secondary education educator*
Davis, Karen Ann (Karen Ann Falconer) *special education educator*
Davis, Lynn Harry *secondary education educator*
Davis, Patricia M. *educator*
Davis, Ronald P. *secondary school administrator*
Davison, Elizabeth Jane Linton *education educator*
Dawkins, Anthony Peter *educational trust administrator*
Dawson, Eugene Ellsworth *university president emeritus*
De, Abhijit *educational administrator*
de Abreu, Sue *elementary educator*
Dean, Virginia Agee *principal*
de Castro, Francisco Jose Barnes *academic administrator*
Dech, Ruth Lynn *academic administrator*
Deen, Alieu Swarray *registrar*
de Gamarra, Ahnal Marynika Criego *adult education educator*
Dehaan, Peter *educator*
Dehez, Pierre *educator*
de Jong Henricus, Cornelis Johannes *educator*
Delacato, Janice Elaine *learning consultant, educator*

Delahanty, Rebecca Ann *school system administrator*
de la Torre, Saturnino *education educator, researcher*
Delbouille, Paul *educator*
Del Duca, Rita *educator*
Della Paolera, Gerardo *rector, researcher*
Deman, Suresh *educator*
Demery, Dorothy Jean *secondary school educator*
Demirkan, Halime *academic administrator*
Demoulin, Robert-Léon *retired educator*
Deng, Tian-Bo *educator*
DePaolo, Rosemary *college dean, university president*
de Russy, Candace Uter *education reformer*
de Sá e Silva, Elizabeth Anne *secondary school educator*
de Silva, Eugene Lakshman *academic administrator, educator*
Dettinger-Klemm, Martin *retired academic administrator, legal practitioner*
DeVera, Gertrude Quenano *education educator*
De Vos, Luc Leo *educator, writer*
DeVoss, Evelyn Ida *retired elementary education educator*
DeWitt-Rogers, Johari Marilyn *community college administrator*
Diaz, Ande N. *academic administrator, educator, consultant*
DiBiaggio, John A. *university president*
Dickinson, Gail Krepps *educator*
Dickinson, John Philip *academic manager*
Die, Ann Marie Hayes *college president, psychology educator*
Diez, Juan Jose Badiola *academic administrator*
Dike, Margaret Hopcraft *retired education administrator*
Dimitry, John Randolph *academic administrator*
Di Nunzio, Dominick *educational administrator*
DiSalle, Michael Danny *secondary education educator*
Ditlevsen, Peter Dalager *educator*
Dixon, Charles Harwood *retired secondary education educator, clergyman*
Djerejian, Edward Peter *institute administrator, former diplomat*
Dluhy, Deborah Haigh *college dean*
Dockrill, Christopher Frederick *secondary education educator*
Dodge, Harry Leon *retired secondary educator*
Dodson, Michael Ivan George *international seminar company executive, photo journalist*
Doerr, Patricia Marian *elementary and special education educator*
Doiphode, Vijay Vishwanath *dean*
Dolui, Swapan Kumar *education educator*
Dong, Jin-Keun *education educator*
Donley, Dennis Lee *school librarian*
Donnithorne, Audrey Gladys *research scholar*
Doody, James Robert *educator, information technology consultant*
Dormeyer, LaVon *school counselor*
Dorst, Friedhelm *educator*
Douglas, Judith Ann *secondary educator*
Douglass, Enid Hart *educational program director*
Down, Ross William *secondary school educator*
Downes, Toni Irene *educator*
Dowton, S. Bruce *academic dean*
Doyle-Marino, Helen *special education educator*
Doz, Yves Lucien *researcher*
Drake, E. Maylon *academic administrator*
Dreyfus, Susan Kahn *elementary education educator*
Driskell, Claude Evans *college director, educator, dentist*
Drögemüller, Hans-Peter *academic administrator*
Drozdowski, Helen Elaine Cswaykus *retired educator*
Druhe Brandt, Iris Claire *retired elementary school educator*
Druliner, Marcia Marie *education educator*
Dubey, Kumudini *high school principal*
Dubin, Martin Steven *principal*
Duckett, Stephen John *university dean, economist*
Duderstadt, James Johnson *academic administrator, engineering educator*
Duffy, Louann C. *career counselor*
Dujon, Diane Marie *director, activist*
Dulzon, Alfred Andreevitch *university executive*
Dumbleton, Duane Dean *college president, educator*
Dumerer, Lorraine JoAnne *social studies educator, clinician*
Dumoulié, Camille Marc *education educator*
Dunn, Doris Marjory *retired educator, volunteer*
Dunnewijn-Bude, Marianne Hubertina *dean*
Dunphy, Steven *educator, real estate broker*
Duquoc, Christian *educator*
Durkin, Dorothy Angela *university official*
Dutta, Birendra Nath *former college principal*
Dwinell, Ann Jones *special education educator*
Dwyer, John Thomas, Jr. *educator, researcher*
Dyakonov, Vladimir Pavlovith *higher education educator*
Dyankov, Alexander Ivanov *technical education educator, mechanical engineer*
Dzelme, Juris *accreditations agency administrator, researcher*
Eastham, John Derek *comprehensive school principal, consultant*
Eastman, John Robert *educator*
Eastman, W. Dean *secondary school educator*
Ebenbauer, Alfred *university administrator*
Echols, Ivor Tatum *retired educator, assistant dean*
Eckel, Karl *education educator*
Edens, Betty Joyce *reading recovery educator*
Edfeldt, Ake Werner *information specialist, educator*
Edmund, Norman Wilson *educational researcher*
Edwards, Kathryn Inez *educational technology consultant*
Eekels, Johannes *retired educator, consultant*
Egertson, Thilda Wennes *retired librarian and secondary educator*
Egginton, Everett *educational administrator*
Eichman, Charles Melvin *career assessment educator, school counselor*
Einoder, Camille Elizabeth *secondary education educator*
Eisenberg, Eliyohu *academic researcher and administrator*
Eisermann, Walter Friedrich *education educator*
Eisler, David Lee *provost*
Elboim-Dror, Rachel *education educator*
El-Emary, Nasr Ahmed *adult education educator, researcher, consultant*
El-Khawas, Elaine *college educator*
Ellegard, Alvar *educator*
Ellingson, Mary *secondary education educator, city councilman*
Elliott, Michelle Catherine *special education educator*
Ellison, Betty D. *retired elementary educator*
Ellis-Vant, Karen McGee *elementary and special education educator, consultant*
El-Sowygh, Hamad Z. *education and science educator*
Emmanuel, Arghiri *educational consultant*
Emmert, Mark Allen *academic administrator, educator*
Encel, Solomon *education educator, consultant*
Engalytchev, Vali Fatekhovich *academic administrator*
Engle, Richard Mallory *academic administrator, civil engineer*
Erlander, Sven Bertil *academic administrator, educator*
Erskine, Sheena Christine *retired educator, researcher*
Ertas, Ismet *retired educator*
Essandoh, Hilda Brathwaite *kindergarten educator*
Essawi, Tamer Ahmad *education educator*
Estes, Laurie Lynn *educational program developer and administrator*
Eto, Shinkichi *educator*
Etzkowitz, Henry *educator, consultant*
Euvrard, George John *education educator*
Evans, Edward Frank *educator*
Evans, Michael Robert *educational consultant, writer*
Everhart, Thomas Eugene *retired university president, engineering educator*
Evers, Terry N. *university administrator, consultant*
Eyherabide, Juan Jose *education educator*
Facini, Christina J. *secondary education educator*
Fägerlind, Ingemar Emanuel *education educator*
Fair, Marcia Jeanne Hixson *retired educational administrator*
Fairchild, Phyllis Elaine *school counselor*
Faivre, Antoine *educator*
Falkowski, Mary Gerard *elementary principal*
Fan, Chong Cheng *educator, researcher*
Fan, Xijun *education educator*
Farmer, Martha Knight *academic administrator, executive*
Farquhar, Doris Irene Davis *academic administrator*
Fasol, Karl Heinz *educator*
Faust, Naomi Flowe *education educator, poet*
Fayed, Ramzi *academic administrator, educator*
Featherman, Sandra *university president, political science educator*
Fecanin, Mary Ellen *secondary education educator*
Feld, Thomas Robert *academic administrator*
Feldstein, Joshua *educational administrator*
Fellenius, Kerstin Birgitta *special education educator*
Felsenhardt, Philippe Gerard *educator*
Feola, David Craig *secondary school administrator*
Ferguson, Wendell *private school educator*
Ferry, Joan Evans *school counselor*
Fetters, Doris Ann *retired secondary education educator*
Feuillet, Jack *educator*
Fidelman, Uri *educator, philosopher, neuropsychologist*
Fielding, Elizabeth Brown *education educator*
Figgs, Linda Sue *educational administrator*
Figueiredo, Paulo Costa *educator*
Filby, Ivan Leonard *academic administrator*
Finger, Iris Dale Abrams *elementary school educator*
Fink, Gerhard *educational administrator, author*
Fink, Joseph Richard *academic administrator*
Finley, Margaret Mavis *retired elementary school educator*
Fischer, Klaus-Dietrich *educator*
Fischer-Appelt, Peter *academic administrator*
Fisher, William Henry *education educator*
Fisiak, Jacek *university administrator, educator*
Fitz-Carter, Aleane *elementary education educator, composer*
Fixen, Randall Robert *academic director*
Flagg, E(loise) Alma Williams *educational administrator*
Flaherty, David Peter *academic administrator*
Flannagan, Larnell Daniel *academic administrator*
Fleming, Horace Weldon, Jr. *higher education administrator, educator*
Fleming, Jane Williams *retired educator, writer*
Fletcher, Brady Jones *vocational education career specialist*
Fletcher, Sarah Lee *retired elementary education educator*
Flitner, Andreas H. *education educator*
Flodgren, Boel *university president, law educator*
Flood, Joe Emerson *secondary education educator*
Flood, Patrick Christopher *business educator, researcher, corporate speaker*
Florenzano, Francesco *academic administrator, psychologist*
Fløttre, Nils Henrik *secondary education educator*
Fong, Simon Chi Chiu *educator, research scientist*
Fontaine-Bayer, Lucette Blanche *educator*
Fordham, Christopher Columbus, III *university dean and chancellor, medical educator*
Fordham, Paul Ellis *adult education educator, consultant*
Forina, Maria Elena *gifted education educator*
Fortson, Laura Rogers *educational consultant*
Foster, Joseph Tennille, Jr. *school administrator, teacher*
Foster, Phillips Wayne *retired adult education educator*
Fowler, Carl *retired educator, boxing statistician*
Frame, Jean Groetz *educator, consultant*
Francard, Michel *educator*
Francis, Stewart Alexander Clement *secondary education educator, retired*
Franklin, Dorothy Ann *guidance counselor*
Franklin, Godfrey *adult education educator*
Franklin, Mary Ann Wheeler *educator, higher education and management consultant*
Franklin, Mary Elizabeth *special education educator*
Fraser, Barry John *university administrator*
Fraser, William Kerr *university official*
Frask, Robin Ann Kostanesky *secondary school educator*
Freed, Melvyn Norris *retired higher education educator, writer*
Freeston, Kenneth Russell *school system administrator*
Freire, Juan Jose *education educator*
Frend, William Hugh Clifford *emeritus educator, clergyman*
Fried, Vance Hoyt *educator*
Friedmann, Bernhard *educator*
Fritz, Judith Ann *special education administrator, educator*
Frolick, Patricia Mary *retired elementary education educator*
Frost, James Arthur *former university president*
Froyen, Ludo L.P. *educator*
Fuest, Clemens *educator*
Fuggi, Gretchen Miller *education educator*
Fukamachi, Masanobu *chancellor, chaplain*
Fultz, John Howard *middle school educator*
Fung, Rosaline Lee *educator*
Furuta, Katsuhisa *educator*
Gagné, Robert Mills *educator*
Gajic, Ranka Pejovic *educator*
Galeev, Albert Abubakir *academic director, educator*
Galima, Loreta Vivian B. Ramel *educator*
Gall, Jean-Claude *education educator*
Gall, Lenore Rosalie *educational administrator*
Galloway, David Malcolm *education educator*
Galyanov, Alexander Pavlovitch *academic administrator*
Gann, Laura Vera *educator*
Gantz, Suzi Grahn *special education educator*
Gardiner, John Graham *university dean, consultant, educator*
Gardner, Paul Leslie *education educator, educational researcher*
Garfinkel, Lawrence Saul *academic administrator, educator, television producer*
Garn, Susan Lynn *secondary education educator*
Garner, Doris Traganza *educator*
Gary, C. Ceci *primary school educator*
Gaston, Bonnie Faye James *elementary education educator*
Gautier, Maurice Paul *educator*
Gawrecki, Lechosław Kazimierz *education management educator*
Gaxer, Walter Peter *academic director, educator*
Gee, Chuck Yim *dean*
Geffen, Amy *education executive*
Geist, Karin R. *secondary education educator, realtor, musician*
Genesi, Susan Petrovich *educator*
Gennett, Timothy *academic administrator*
Gentilcore, Eileen Marie Belsito *elementary school principal*
Gerberding, William Passavant *retired university president*
Gerberich, Susan Goodwin *education educator*
Germroth, Peter *private school educator*
Geyer, Dennis Lynn *university administrator and registrar*
Giannakopoulos, Gabriel Basil *educator*
Gibbons, Robert Ebbert *university official*
Gibson, Gary Richard *educator*
Gibson, Jannette Poe *educator, consultant*
Gibson, John Willis *educator*
Gibson, William Thomas *university administrator*
Gilbert, Alan D. *university president*
Gilbert, Richard Keith *education educator, researcher*
Giles, Phyllis Lenore Williams *retired elementary educator*
Gillespie, Thomas William *theological seminary administrator, religion educator*
Giraud, René Ernest *academic administrator, economist, educator*
Girish, Kudhuvalli Purnaiah *education and management trainer, educator*
Girod, Christian Alphonse *educator*
Gladden, Garnett Lee *educator, psychologist*
Glaise, Joyce Elizabeth *secondary education educator, city councilor*
Glave, Adolfo Enrique *retired academic administrator*
Glenn, Cornelia Jarmon *education educator*
Glenn, Hugh Victor *educator*
Goertz, Roger Lamar *retired education counselor*
Goes, Kathleen Ann *secondary education educator, choral director*
Goh, Mark Keng H. *educator, researcher, consultant*
Goikhman, Oscar Jakovlevich *institute director*
Golding, Raymund Marshall *university administrator, retired*
Goldstein, Brenda Iris *retired elementary school educator*
Gomez Lopez-Egea, Jose Luis *university president*
Gomez-Skarmeta, Antonio F. *technology educator*
Gonzalez, Antonio *academic administrator, mortgage company executive*
Gonzalez, Rolando Noel *secondary school educator, religion educator, photographer*
Goode, Bobby Claude *retired secondary education educator, writer*
Goodheer, Wil Charles *academic administrator*
Gopal, Nakka *university official, poet*
Gorman, Lyn *educator, editor*
Gostiaux, Bernard *secondary education educator*
Gottschalk, Alfred *retired college chancellor, museum executive*
Goulding, Marrack Irvine *college administrator*
Graham, Lois Charlotte *retired educator*
Grainger, Inés Paulina *adult educator*
Granholt, Erling *retired educator*
Grant, Michael *retired university president, author*
Grant, Michael Ernest *educational administrator, institutional management educator*
Grant, Phyllis Moore *elementary education educator*
Graves, Karen Lee *high school counselor*
Gray, Nancy Ann Oliver *college administrator*
Gray, Paul Edward *academic official*
Gray, Paul Wesley *university dean*
Green, Betty Nielsen *education educator, consultant*
Green, Jens-Peter *academic administrator*
Green, Patricia Pataky *school system administrator, consultant*
Greenblatt, Deana Charlene *elementary education educator*
Gregorian, Vartan *academic administrator*
Gregory, Marian Frances *educator, counselor, principal*
Greisenegger, Wolfgang *university official*
Grenestedt, Joachim Lennart *educator*
Griffin, Betty Jo *elementary school educator*
Grigoroiu, Gabriela *educator, researcher*
Grigoryeva, Margaret Vasilyevna *academy administrator, linguist*
Grino, Rene Sudario *educator*
Grogan, Stanley Joseph *educational and security consultant*
Groombridge, Brian Hughes *retired adult education educator*
Grose, Elinor Ruth *retired elementary education educator*
Groseclose, Wanda Westman *retired elementary school educator*
Gros Louis, Kenneth Richard Russell *university chancellor*
Grove, Myrna Jean *elementary education educator*
Grugulis, Irena *educator*
Grumley, Larry Tyler *secondary education educator*
Guajardo, Elisa *counselor, educator*
Guangun, Gu *academic administrator*
Gubern, Roman *education educator*
Guglielmino, Lucy Margaret Madsen *education educator, researcher, consultant*
Gunn, Morey Walker, Jr. *secondary education educator, choir director, organist*
Gunther, William David *university administrator, economics educator*
Guy, David Maurice *academic administrator*
Guy, Mildred Dorothy *retired secondary school educator*
Guzman, Linda Ann *educator*
Guzy, Marguerita Linnes *middle school education educator*
Haders, Thomas Michael *elementary school educator, portrait painter*
Haeberle, Rosamond Pauline *retired educator*
Haff, Guy Gregory *college educator, researcher*
Hagedorn, Linda Serra *education educator, researcher*
Hagstrom, David Alan *educational consultant, educator*
Hain, Joan E. *secondary education educator*
Haine, Thomas William Nicholas *educator*
Hall, James Robert *secondary education educator*
Halperin, George Bennett *education educator, retired naval officer*
Halpern, David Rodion *special education administrator*
Hambardzumyan, Vemir *educator*
Hambrick, Arlene *school system administrator, minister*
Hamilton, Howard Henry *educational administrator*
Hamilton, Rhoda Lillian Rosén *guidance counselor, language educator, consultant*
Hammond, DeAnna *educator*
Hammond, Vernon Francis *school administrator*
Hammond-Blessing, DiAnn A. *elementary education educator*
Handlir, Jiri Vladimir *headmaster*
Haneke, Dianne Myers *education educator*
Hansen, Harold B., Jr. *principal*
Hansen, John Herbert *university administrator, accountant*
Hansen, Magnus Bang *special education administrator, consultant*
Hansford, Nathaniel *academic administrator, lawyer*
Hanson, Sir John Gilbert *academic administrator*
Hanson, Kaido *academic administrator*
Hanson, Marci Jill *educator*
Harden, Patricia Keegan *financial aid officer*
Hardie, James Carl *college administrator, consultant*
Harmon, George Marion *academic administrator*
Harrelson, Clyde Lee *secondary school educator*
Harrington, Donald James *university president*
Harris, Emily Louise *special education educator*
Harris, June Leatrice *education coordinator, administrator*
Harris, Marilyn *retired academic administrator*
Harris, Robert James *adult education educator*
Harris, Sidney Eugene *dean, management educator*
Hart, James Warren *university administrator, restaurant owner, former professional football player*
Hartman, Rosemary Jane *retired special education educator*
Hasselmo, Nils *academic administrator, linguistics educator*
Hastings, Chester Ray *education educator, director student services*
Hasumi, Shigehiko *academic administrator*
Haugland, Susan Warrell *education educator, consultant*
Hauser, Bernice Worman *inter-campus director*
Hauser-Cram, Penny *developmental psychologist*
Haussonne, F. Jean-Marie *educator*
Haviland, Marlita Christine *elementary school educator*
Hawkins, Loretta Ann *secondary school educator, playwright*
Hay, John A. *academic administrator*
Hayes, William *academic administrator*
Haynes, Janice Jaques Elizabeth *educator, editor*
Hazel, Mary Belle *university administrator*
Hearne, George Archer *academic administrator*
Heartt, Charlotte Beebe *university official*
Heath, Berthann Jones *education administrator*
Hegde, Belle Monappa *academic administrator*
Helfman, Carolyn Rae *middle school educator*
Hemby, James B., Jr. *college president*
Hemmes, Marcia Kay *special education educator*
Henderson, James Stuart *dean, medical educator, retired*
Hendren, Robert Lee, Jr. *academic administrator*
Hendrikse, George W. *educator*
Henry, Nicholas Llewellyn *college president, political science educator*
Hermann, Raphael Pierre *secondary education educator*
Herrera, Sandra Johnson *school system administrator*
Herzberg, Dorothy Crews *secondary education educator*
Hess, Dorothy Haldeman *college official*
Hester, Linda Hunt *university dean, counselor*
Hewitt, Paul Deane *headmaster*
Hildreth, Ethan Joe David *school principal, communications consultant*
Hill, Howard Darnell *education educator, dean*
Hill, Peter William *university official, educator*
Hill, Virgil Lusk, Jr. *academic administrator, naval officer*
Hillocks, George *education educator, researcher, consultant*
Hinitz, Blythe Simone Farb *early childhood and elementary school educator*
Hinton, Susan Frazier *secondary education educator*
Hirst, Paul Heywood *retired education educator*
Hisama, Tosiaki *special education psychologist, educator*
Hlengwa, Msawakhe Almon *educational administrator*
Hockey, Stuart William *retired headmaster*
Hodakievic, James Joseph *secondary education educator*
Hodapp, Shirley Jeaniene *curriculum administrator*
Hoerner, Wolfgang Peter *educator*
Hoffman, Philip Guthrie *former university president*
Hogan, John Donald *college dean, finance educator*
Hollingsworth, Abner Thomas *university dean*
Holmdahl, Svante Martin *university president, anesthesiology educator*
Holton, Samuel Melanchthon *education educator emeritus, consultant*
Holzner, Johann *educator*
Hong, Yang-Pyo *political ethics educator*
Hopkins, Laurie Boyle *academic administrator*
Hornblow, Andrew Reed *academic administrator, psychologist*

McDaniel, Carolyn Marie (Lynn) *secondary education educator*
McDaniel, Sara Sherwood (Sally McDaniel) *trainer, consultant*
McDonald, Lari *secondary education educator, small business owner*
McEniry, Robert Francis *education educator*
McGrory, Mary Kathleen *retired college president*
McIntire, Mary *university administrator*
McKenna, Margaret Anne *college president*
McKenzie, Stanley Don *academic administrator, English educator*
McLain, William Tome *principal*
McLean, Janelle Annette *elementary education educator*
McLeod, Stephen Glenn *education educator, language educator*
McVay, Barbara Chaves *secondary education mathematics educator*
McWilliams, Charles Henry (Sir Charles Henry McWilliam) *educational administrator, researcher*
McWilliams, Chris Pater Elissa *elementary school educator*
Medland, William James *college president*
Meincke, Jens Peter *university rector*
Meisalo, Veijo P. Juhani *education educator*
Mellis, Werner *education educator*
Meltebeke, Renette *career counselor*
Memory, Jasper Durham *academic administrator, physics educator*
Mendoza, George John *college administrator, public speaker*
Mermoz, Jorge Francisco *secondary education educator, researcher*
Merritt, John Howard *secondary school educator*
Merry, Bruce Carmichael *education educator, writer*
Meskill, Victor P. *college president, educator*
Messer, Janice Grabowski *academic administrator*
Messina, Paul Francis *education consultant*
Metzner, Barbara Stone *university counselor*
Meyer, George Rex *retired freelance educational consultant, author*
Meyers, Dorothy *education consultant, writer*
Meyers, John Thomas, Jr. *academic administrator*
Mia, Lokman *educator*
Micka, Jennifer Leigh *university program director*
Miguel, Paulo Cauchick *educator*
Miller, Audrey Thornton *vice principal elementary school*
Miller, Dorothy Eloise *education educator*
Miller, Harry Freeman *university administrator*
Miller, Jerry Huber *retired university chancellor*
Miller, Linda Karen *educator*
Miller, Sanford Arthur *academic administrator, biochemistry educator*
Miller, Stephen Warren *dean*
Millis, Nancy Fannie *university administrator*
Mills, Belen Collantes *early childhood education educator*
Mills, Helene Audrey *education educator*
Milne, Henry James Ogston *education educator*
Mindlin, Paula Rosalie *retired reading educator*
Miner, Mary Elizabeth Hubert *retired secondary school educator*
Ming, Ruisen *educator*
Minnerly, Robert Ward *retired headmaster*
Minor, Marian Thomas *elementary and secondary school educational consultant*
Mirk, Judy Ann *retired elementary educator*
Misawa, Giichi *special education educator*
Mitchell, Lucille Anne *retired elementary school educator*
Mittelstaedt, Arthur Howard, Jr. *educational educator*
Mitter, Partha *educator*
Mitter, Wolfgang Andreas *education educator, researcher*
Mitterand, Henri C. *education educator, writer*
Miyajima, Hideaki *education educator*
Miyazaki, Shigeki *university official*
Mobley, Tony Allen *university dean, recreation educator*
Mockler, Adele *educator*
Moen, Ole O. *American studies scholar*
Mohammad, Syed Younus *educator*
Mohr, Geoffrey Arnold *academic administrator, mathematics consultant*
Moler, Donald Lewis *educational psychology educator*
Moll, Clarence Russel *retired university president, consultant*
Moller, Marianne *retired primary school educator*
Monroe, Haskell Moorman, Jr. *university educator*
Montgomery, Anna Frances *elementary school educator*
Monyeki, Kotsedi Daniel *education educator*
Moore, Donald Walter *academic administrator, school librarian*
Moore, Mary Julia *educator*
Moore, Nancy Fischer *elementary school educator*
Moran, James D., III *child development educator*
Morecki, Adam *educator*
Morel, Mary-Annick Thérèse *educator*
Morgan, Mary Lou *retired education educator, civic worker*
Mori, Wataru *academic administrator, educator*
Morimoto, Masao *education educator*
Morreale, Joseph Constantino *higher education administrator, public administration educator, economic and financial consultant*
Morris, Robert *educator*
Morrison, Keith Robert Barclay *education educator, consultant*
Morrison, Michael Gordon *university president, clergyman, history educator*
Morrow, Martina A. *educator, cultural organization administrator*
Mortimore, Peter John *university administrator, education educator*
Mosa, Ali Abdullah *dean, education educator*
Moscowitz, Joyce Marla *elementary school educator*
Moseley, Karen Frances Flanigan *retired school system administrator, educator*
Moskal, Anthony John *former dean, professor, management and education consultant*
Mosley, David P. *school system administrator*
Moszkowski, Lena Iggers *secondary school educator*
Motoki, Ken *education educator*
Motonaka, Junko *educator*
Mott, June Marjorie *school system administrator*
Mousley, Judith Anne *educator*
Mowaiye-Fagbemi, Olufunmilayo Julian *educator*
Moxon-Browne, Edward Philip *educator*
Mthoko, November Ananias *adult education educator*
Mu, Guoguang *former university president, educator*
Mueller-Kohlenberg, Hildegard *social education educator, researcher*
Mugler, Josef Alois *education educator*
Muir, William Lloyd, III *academic administrator*
Mukhia, Harbans *educator*
Muladi, H. *university rector*
Mulder, Patricia Marie *education educator*
Mulford, William Richard *education educator*
Mullen, Terri Ann *special education educator*
Muller, John Bartlett *university president*
Müller-Merbach, Heiner Erich *educator*
Munir, Jamshed Aqil *retired educator*
Munlu, Kamil Cemal *educator*
Murakami, Yoshio *educator, editor*
Murez, John *music education director, educator*
Muriá, José Maria *academic administrator, researcher*
Murray, Bruce Alan *reading educator*
Murray-Harvey, Rosalind *education educator*
Muta, Taizo *academic administrator*
Mutinga, Mutuku John *university president, parasitologist, entomologist*
Mwendwa, Kyale *educational services executive*
Myers, Harold Mathews *academic administrator*
Myers, Kenneth L(eRoy) *secondary education educator*
Nabeya, Seiji *education educator*
Nagao, Makoto *academic administrator, engineering educator*
Nagi, Catherine Raseh *retired educational administrator, financial planner*
Nakayama, Hideaki *academic administrator*
Nakayama, Osamu *education educator*
Nánai, László *physics educator, principal*
Nance, Retha Hardison *reading specialist*
Narumi, Hideyuki *secondary education educator*
Nash, Robert John *materials educator*
Nash, William Lewis, III *retired music education educator*
Nathan, Samandam Shanmuga *principal, educational consultant*
Naugle, Charlotte June *principal, educator*
Neal, Joseph Lee *vocational school educator*
Neave, Guy Richard *education educator*
Negoita, Constantin Virgil *educator*
Neilson, Charles Bienvenu *education executive*
Neisler, Otherine Johnson *education educator, consultant*
Nenniger, Peter *education educator*
Nentwich, Michael Andreas Erhart *educator, consultant*
Neocleous, Kyriakos *school principal, writer*
Nettelhorst, Robin Paul *academic administrator, writer*
Neuberger, Herman Naftoli *college president, rabbi*
Newby, Earl Fernando *educator*
Newman, Judith Alice *education educator*
Newsome, David Hay *retired headmaster*
Nichols, Marci Lynne *gifted education coordinator, educator, consultant*
Nickels, Mavis Lanore *secondary education education, farmer*
Nielsen, Bonnie Belle *secondary school educator*
Niemeyer, Antonio Bilisoly, Jr. *school system administrator*
Nii, Shiro *college executive, virology educator*
Nissen, Lowell Allen *education educator*
Nkuebe, Joshua Sempe *education testing officer, evaluator*
Norris, Lonnie Harold *dean*
North, Alastair Macarthur *retired academic administrator*
North, Anita *secondary education educator*
North, Peter Machin *academic administrator, lawyer*
Novotny, Vladimir *educator, consultant*
Nowacki, Wojciech Krzysztof *solid mechanics educator*
Nuissl von Rein, Ekkehard *adult education educator*
Nwadiani, Mon *educational planner, education educator*
Nyagura, Levi Martin *mathematics and education educator, administrator*
Oak, H(elen) Lorraine *academic administrator, geography educator*
Obagah, Mamudu Omosah Nasiru *educational evaluator*
O'Brien, George Dennis *retired university president*
O'Brien, Kevin *college dean, consultant*
Ocal, Akar *academic administrator*
O'Connor, Bernard F. *academic administrator*
O'Connor, John *hotel management educator, consultant*
Odier, Pierre Andre *educator, writer, photographer, artist*
O'Donoghue, Heather *university educator*
Ogunmokun, Gabriel Olayinka *academic administrator, marketing educator*
Ohno, Keiichi *academic administrator, engineering educator*
Oikawa, Hiroshi *college president, materials science educator*
Ojeda-Castañeda, Jorge *academic administrator, researcher*
Oliveira, Rose Marie *elementary educator*
Oliver, Ann Breeding *secondary education educator*
Oliver, G(eorge) Benjamin *retired educational administrator, philosophy educator*
Olivieri, Dario *university administrator, educator*
Olsen, Haakon Andreas *educator*
Olson-Hellerud, Linda Kathryn *elementary education educator*
O'Malley, John Patrick *dean*
O'Neil, Robert Marchant *university administrator, law educator*
Opara, Ukachukwu Eugene *university administrator, researcher*
Opoku, Wisdom Komla *academic administrative assistant*
O'Reilly, Francis Joseph *academic administrator*
Oro, Felisa Panal *education supervisor*
Orr, Joseph Alexander *educational administrator*
Ortiz Ruiz, Aida M. *university administrator, educator*
Osman, Mohamed Sayed *dean, mathematics educator*
Ospina-Londoño, Oscar Francisco *educator*
Østergård, Patric Ralf Johan *educator*
Ostergren Baits, Marcia *elementary education educator*
Ostrom, Katherine Elma *retired educator*
Otal, Javier *secondary education educator*
Ou, Shan-Hwei *dean, engineering educator*
Outten, Kristina Marie *secondary education educator*
Oxley, Margaret Carolyn Stewart *elementary education educator*
Packer, Claude Montgomery *college president*
Page, Sally Jacquelyn *university official*
Paglini, Severo *educator*
Pagnotta, Mario-Augusto *educator*
Pal, Umapada *physics professor*
Palabay, Carmilita Llabres *principal*
Palm, Michael Martin *college administrator, artist*
Panawidan, Hadji Hasan Adiong *university chancellor, foundation administrator*
Panayiotis, Chinas *school psychologist, consultant*
Paolini, Claire Jacqueline *dean, educator*
Paonessa, M. Suzanne *financial aid administrator*
Papadakis, Constantine N. *university executive*
Papadias, Basil C. *education educator*
Papasolomontos, Christina *elementary educator, researcher*
Papastephanou, Marianna Kyriaki *educator*
Pappas, James Pete *university administrator*
Parekh, Kiran Laxmidas *early childhood care and education educator*
Parker, Theresa Ann Boggs *special education educator, music educator*
Parkhe, A. *educator, researcher*
Parks, Debora Ann *private school director*
Parks, Gerald Bartlett *educator*
Parmenter, Trevor Reginald *education educator*
Parrillo, Thomas Matthew *secondary education educator*
Parr-Johnston, Elizabeth *academic administrator*
Parry, Thomas Herbert, Jr. *school system administrator, educational consultant*
Parsons, Mark Frederick *college development officer*
Parsons, Martin Leslie *education educator*
Pascua, Reynaldo V. *education educator*
Paskin, Nancy C. *rehabilitation education director*
Pastin, Mark Joseph *association executive*
Patte, Dominique Marie *university administrator, physician*
Patterson, David *academic administrator, educator, scholar, retired*
Paul, Peter Andrew *academic administrator*
Paul, Rochelle Carole *special education educator*
Paxton, Juanita Willene *retired university official*
Payá-Bernabeu, Jordi *educator, researcher*
Payne, Antony John *retired academic administrator*
Payne, George Frederick *educational administrator*
Payne, Richard Harold *university research administrator*
Paz, Yehudah *university administrator*
Pearce, Patsy Beasley *elementary education educator*
Peck, Malcolm Cameron *educational exchange specialist*
Peckham, Colin Neil *academic administrator, minister, lecturer*
Pedersen, Norman Arno, Jr. *retired headmaster, literary club director*
Pellat, Bernard *dean*
Peltason, Jack Walter *foundation executive, educator*
Pena, Maria Geges *academic services administrator*
Penn, Maggie Scott *school counselor, small business owner*
Perez, Priego Miguel Angel *educator*
Perez Ipiña, Juan Elias *educator*
Perez-Latre, Francisco J. *educator, dean*
Perkins, John Helm *college administrator, educator*
Perry, William James *educator, former federal official*
Perteet, Icy D. *secondary education educator*
Peterkin, Albert Gordon *retired education educator*
Peters, Jacqueline Mary *secondary education educator*
Peterson, Erlend Dean *dean*
Peterson, Leroy *retired secondary education educator*
Peterson, Walter Fritiof *academic administrator*
Petersson, Birgit Holm *educator*
Petersson, Olof R. *policy studies administrator*
Petitan, Debra Ann Burke *educator, education counselor, design engineer, writer, author*
Pfeiffer, Erna *educator, literary translator*
Pfeuffer, Dale Robert *secondary school social studies educator*
Phillips, Patricia Jeanne *retired school administrator, consultant*
Phillips, Vicky L. *distance learning specialist*
Phillips, Winfred Marshall *dean, biomedical researcher, mechanical engineer, educator*
Philp, Ian *academic administrator, consultant physician*
Pickering, AvaJane *specialized education facility executive*
Pickering, Brian Thomas *university official*
Pickett, Stephen Wesley *university official, lecturer and consultant*
Pidgeon, John Anderson *headmaster*
Piele, Philip Kern *education infosystems educator*
Pierce Korte, Thresia (Tish Pierce) *primary school educator*
Pierzynowski, Stefan Grzegorz *educator*
Pikas, Anatol *education educator*
Pilling, Anita Randall *educator*
Pillot, Gene Merrill *retired school system administrator*
Piper, Fredessa Mary *school system administrator*
Pippin, James Adrian, Jr. *middle school educator*
Pirinccioglu, Necmettin *education educator*
Pitchforth, Roger John *educator, dispute resolutions administrator, arbitrator, mediator*
Pitts, Sadie Turner *retired educator*
Platis, Chris Steven *educator*
Platis, James George *secondary school educator*
Platti, Rita Jane *educator, draftsman, writer, inventor*
Plum, David Robert *educator*
Podewils, Ulrich *academic administrator*
Poland, Anne Spellman *counselor*
Poley, Janet Kathleen *consortium executive*
Polisi, Joseph W(illiam) *academic administrator*
Polkinghorne, John Charlton *retired academic administrator, clergyman*
Pollock, Gruselda Frances Sinclair *educator*
Polydorides, Georgia Kontogiannopoulou *educator*
Pont, Kenneth Graham *retired education educator*
Pool, Eugene Hunter *educator, writer*
Popenfoose, Sharren E. *school counselor*
Popov, Vadim Petrovich *academic administrator, engineering educator*
Potts, Billie Luisi *college administrator*
Power, Desmond John *special education educator, consultant*
Pratt, Raymond Burl *educator, researcher*
Pratt, Sharon L. *secondary and elementary education educator*
Preece, Peter Frederick William *education educator*
Premo-Hopkins, Blanche Lillie *university official, philosophy educator*
Pribbenow, Paul P. *higher education administrator, consultant*
Prichard, John Robert Stobo *academic administrator, law educator*
Prideaux, Bruce Richard *education educator, regional planner*
Pries, Janise Goff *counselor, secondary education educator*
Priestley, Holly *education educator*
Primm, David John *middle school educator*
Prince, Gregory Smith, Jr. *academic administrator*
Prior, Howard Grenfell *secondary school educator, acupuncturist*
Pritchard, Claudius Hornby, Jr. *retired university president*
Proctor, William Lee *college president*
Prodan, Augustin *educator*
Profillidis, Vassilios Aristidis *educator*
Pruitt, George Albert *college president*
Pukkila, Tarmo Mikko *academic administrator, educator*
Pulliam, Yvonne Antoinette *gifted education educator*
Pulverer, Gerhard *secondary education educator*
Purcell, Dale *college president, consultant*
Pushnykh, Victor Alexandrovich *education educator, researcher*
Pweddon, Nicholas *academic administrator, educator, researcher*
Qu, Bao-kui *education educator*
Quaintance, Alice Lynn *elementary school media specialist*
Quick, Jerry Ray *academic administrator*
Quigney, Theresa Ann *special education educator*
Quijada, Angélica Maria *elementary education educator*
Quinton, Lord Anthony Meredith *academic administrator*
Quirk, Lord Randolph *former academy president, educator, consultant*
Quiroz Velasco, Maria Teresa *dean, communications researcher*
Rada, Alexander *university official*
Rago, Ann D'Amico *university official, public relations professional*
Ragone, David Vincent *former university president*
Rahkonen, Ossi Juhani *educator*
Raines, Louis Edward *school administrator*
Raisian, John *academic administrator, economist*
Rajakovics, Gundolf Emil von *retired academic institute director, engineering educator*
Ramachandrachar, K. *education educator*
Ramaswami, Panchapakesan *educational administrator*
Ramer, Hal Reed *academic administrator*
Ramiro, Renald Peter Ty *college dean, physiatrist*
Ramón, Bagur *educational adviser, engineer*
Ramsay, John Gerard *academic administrator, writer*
Ranck, Edna Runnels *academic administrator, researcher*
Rao, Chintamani Nagesa *academic administrator, chemistry educator*
Rao, Kalya Jagannatha *education educator*
Rasmussen, Ebbe Gert *secondary education educator, researcher*
Ratcliffe, Frederick William *university librarian*
Rathburn, Robert Charles *retired educator*
Ratliff, Gerald Lee *academic administrator/speech and theater educator*
Rauch, Wolf Dietrich *rector*
Rawlings, Hunter Ripley, III *university president*
Ray, Stephen Alan *academic administrator, lawyer*
Raza, Agha Asad *academic administrator*
Read, Sister Joel *academic administrator*
Reavis, Susan Scott *elementary educator*
Reddel, Carl Walter *educational administrator*
Redlich, Shimon *educator*
Reece, Geraldine Maxine *elementary education educator*
Reed, Alfred Douglas *university administrator*
Reents, Larry G. *secondary education educator*
Rees, Brian *headmaster*
Regn Fraher, Bonnie *special education educator*
Reha, Rose Krivisky *retired business educator*
Reid, Mary Wallace *retired secondary education educator*
Reinalda, David Anthony *elementary education educator*
Reissman, Rose Cherie *elementary education educator*
Remick, Forrest Jerome, Jr. *former university official*
Retief, François Pieter *retired university administrator*
Reuthinger, Georgeanne *special education educator*
Rex, John Arderne *educator*
Rexed, Bror Anders *educator emeritus*
Reynolds, Ruth Carmen *school administrator, secondary school educator*
Rezin, Andrew Anthony *academic administrator, educator*
Rheinish, Robert Kent *university administrator*
Rhine, Kelly Anne *secondary education educator*
Rhoan, Chester D. *adult education educator*
Rich, Paul John *educator, political consultant*
Richard, Gisbert *educational director*
Rider, Robin *secondary education educator*
Ridler, Ann Margaret *retired registrar*
Riecke, Jörg *educator*
Riehl, Jane Ellen *education educator*
Rinehart, James Forrest *educator*
Ritchey, Kenneth William *administrator*
Ritchie, Anne *educational administrator*
Rittenhouse, Nancy Carol *elementary education educator*
Rivera, Robert LeRoy *university administrator, educator*
Rives, Stanley Gene *university president emeritus*
Rizk, Maher Farid Sami *university official, research consultant*
Robbins, Cornelius (Van Vorse) *educational administration educator*
Robbins, Eldora King *retired secondary education educator*
Robbins, Keith Gilbert *academic administrator*
Robbins-Wilf, Marcia *educational consultant*
Roberts, Kathleen Joy Doty *secondary education educator*
Robertson, Wyndham Gay *university official*
Robey, Sherie Gay Southall Gordon *secondary education educator, consultant*
Robinson, David *academic administrator*
Robinson, Earl James *academic administrator, information systems and statistics educator, consultant*
Robinson, Maureen Loretta *retired secondary school educator*
Robinson, William P. *academic administrator, consultant, speaker*
Robison, John Jeffrey *university official*
Rocha, Darrell Dean *dean*
Rochelle, Lugenia *academic administrator*
Rodenbaugh, Marcia Louise *elementary school educator*
Rodgers, Grace Anne *university official*
Rodgers, Sue Ann *academic counselor*
Rodrigues, Augusto Silveira *educator*

Rodrigues, Carol Maria secondary school educator
Roels, Harry A. educator
Roemer, Ronald educator, educational administrator
Roger, Jerry Lee school system administrator
Rogers, Brenda Gayle educational administrator, educator, consultant
Rogers, Richard Lee educator
Roloff, Hans-Gert educator
Roman, Marco Antonio educator
Romero, Alejandro Francisco academic administrator
Ronchi, Américo Roberto education educator
Roots, Keith Dyland academic administrator
Ropers-Huilman, Becky educator
Rorie, Nancy Katheryn elementary and secondary school educator
Rosado, Alvaro Jaime university administrator
Rosenberg, Raymond David secondary education educator, consultant
Rosenblum Grevéy, Estelle retired dean, nursing educator
Roshong, Dee Ann Daniels dean, educator
Ross, Mary Ann principal
Rosse, Therese Marie reading and special education educator, curriculum, school improvement and instruction consultant
Rossignoli, Jose Luis educator
Roth, Hermann Josef secondary school administrator
Rothermel, Dorothy G. Noak retired secondary education educator
Roueche, John Edward, II education educator, leadership program director
Roueche, Suanne Davis university administrator
Roulhac, Nellie Gordon retired special education administrator
Roversi-Monaco, Fabio academic administrator
Rovira, Antoni academic administrator
Rowe, Sung Man university executive, educator
Rowe, William Brian university director, mechanical engineering educator
Rubin, Cathy Ann retired educator
Ruch, Marcella Joyce retired educator, biographer
Rudenstine, Neil Leon academic administrator, educator
Rudraiah, Nanjundappa academician and university administrator
Rupp, Gary A. academic administrator
Rupp, George Erik academic administrator
Rutledge, Virgie Marilyn educator
Ruud, Jay Wesley dean
Ryabinin, Igor Alexeevich educator
Ryabinina, Nataliya Pavlovna university administrator, psychology educator
Ryan, Joseph F. educator
Rydberg, Anders Bo Lars educator
Ryder, Edward Francis secondary education educator
Sack, Richard education policy analyst
Sackey, James Kwao Narh education educator
Sacks, Robert D. educational administrator, fund raiser
Saenger, Hanns Hermann retired academic administrator
Saenger, Rudi Fred retired superintendent
Saengsook, Rangsan academic administrator
Sahin, Sami educator
Sakamoto, Yoshikazu educator
Sakou, Toshitsugu dean, educator
Salewski, Michael educator
Salgado-Gama, Maria Clara educational consultant
Salmenkallio, Kauko Alvar school counselor
Salmon, Michael John academic administrator
Sambo, Abubakar Sani academic administrator
Sample, Steven Browning university executive
Samson, Maria Elena educational administrator, counseling psychologist, sociologist
Sanchez, Mary Anne retired secondary school educator
Sanchez, Tomasa Calvo educator
Sandwell, Kristin Ann special education educator
San Lorenzo, Carmen Neri college dean
Saplin, Leonid Alexeevitch academic administrator
Sappington, Sharon Anne retired school librarian
Saraux, Henry Camille academic administrator, ophthalmologist, educator
Sarocchi, Jean education educator
Sarsfield, Luke Aloysius school system administrator
Sathaye, Bhaskar Vinayak university executive
Satterfield, John Roberts, Jr. retired college president and music educator
Sauer, Georg Heinrich education educator
Sawkins, John university administrator
Saxena, Arun Kumar educator, researcher
Scaffidi, Judith Ann academic administrator
Scala, Rita Nadine polytechnic institute official, health therapist
Scarpelli, Vito adult education educator, administrator
Schacker, Sarah Elizabeth educator
Schade, Wilbert Curtis education administrator
Schaefer-Wicke, Elizabeth reading consultant, educator
Scharfenberg, Margaret Ellan retired elementary educator
Scharlig, Alain Raymond educator
Schauenberg, Susan Kay educational counselor, educator
Schelp, Lothar Heinrich Walter program director, researcher
Schenck, David elementary education educator, director
Scherer, George Robert secondary education educator
Schieffer, Rudolf educator
Schiemenz, Rolf Bernd business educator
Schier, Rudolf educational administrator, educator
Schilperoort, Sharon Ann secondary education educator
Schmidli, Keith William vocational education administrator, educator, researcher
Schmincke, Hans Ulrich educator
Schmitt, Roland Walter retired academic administrator
Schmitz, Dolores Jean primary education educator
Schneider, Jayne B. school librarian
Schoen, Johann university administrator
Scholz, Otfried academic administrator
Schreiber, Judy Ann counselor
Schreuder, Deryek M. academic administrator
Schroeder, Erich Christian educator
Schuckman, Nancy Lee retired principal
Schulz, Wilfried educator
Schure, Alexander university chancellor
Schwabl, Franz educator
Schwartz, Michael university president, sociology educator
Schwarz, Barbara Ruth Ballou elementary school educator
Schwedes, Joerg university administrator, consultant
Sciame, Joseph university administrator
Scott, Charles Tolbert elementary educator, health care interviewer
Scott, Joyce M. C. academic administrator
Scott, Pamela secondary education educator
Scott, Quincy, Jr. dean, clergy
Scott, Robert Allyn academic administrator
Scriba, Johannes Hermann academic dean
Scudder, Charles A. primary and secondary education educator
Šebenik, Anton education educator
Seebold, Elmar retired educator
Sehnal, Frantisek administrator
Sekimoto, Mayako professor
Selberherr, Siegfried university dean, educator, researcher, consultant
Seller, Timothy John academic administrator, zoology educator
Sember, June Elizabeth retired elementary education educator
Senghas, Karlheinz retired university administrator
Serdyuk, Alexander Dmitrievich rector
Sessoms, Allen Lee academic administrator, former diplomat, physicist
Sexson, Stephen Bruce education writer, educator
Seyfert, Wayne George secondary education educator, anatomy educator
Seznec, Alain university dean, foreign language educator
Shadrick, Betty Patterson university administrator, consultant
Shaffer, Anita Mohrland counselor, educator
Shagam, Marvin Hückel-Berri private school educator
Shama, Mohamed Abdel Fattah dean, engineering educator
Shamsavary, Parisima academic admInstrator, educator
Shaner, Bronwyn Marian elementary education educator
Shapiro, Harold Tafler academic administrator, economist
Shapiro, Jerome Franklin educator
Sharma, Motilal senior education specialist
Sharma, Shuk Dev education educator
Sharman, Diane Lee secondary school educator
Sharp, Douglas Andrew secondary school educator
Shaver, Judson Rayford academic administrator
Shaw, Danny Wayne secondary education educator, consultant
Shaw, Josephine training consultant
Shaw, Roslyn Lee retired elementary education educator
Shearburn, Dudley Dovel retired education educator
Shearer, Derek Norcross international studies educator, diplomat, administrator
Shehab, Moufid university president
Shelby, Nina Claire special education educator
Shelby, Tim Otto secondary education educator
Shelton, Bessie Elizabeth school system administrator
Shelton, Olga-Jean school counselor
Shen, Qing education educator
Shengwu, Xie academic administrator
Shepherd, Lewis A., Jr. educational administrator, minister
Shepherdson, David school caretaker, tutor
Sheppard, Anne Deborah Raphael educator
Sheridan, Susan Margaret educator
Sherman, Garth Lyndon counselor administrator, consultant
Sherratt, Alan Frederick Cave college director
Sherratt, Gerald Robert retired university president
Sherriffs, Alexander Carlton higher education administrator
Shields, Martha Buckley middle school educator
Shiraiwa, Yoshihiro educator
Shkolnikov, Victor Alexeevitch academic administrator
Shoemaker, Cameron David James dean, educator
Shuberoff, Oscar Julio university administrator
Shubik, Philippe academic administrator
Shuhan, Janice-Lynn Nazziola educator
Shum, Ping educator
Siarry, Patrick educator
Siemon-Burgeson, Marilyn M. education administrator
Signorelli, Carlo university educator
Silva, Monica gifted education educator
Silver, Roberta Frances (Bobbi Silver) educator, writer
Simola, Liisa Kaarina educator
Simone, Albert Joseph academic administrator
Singleton, Robert Culton graduate school administrator, Bible educator
Sisselman, Murray educator, union executive
Sivakumar, Krishnamoorthy educator
Sjoden, Hilding Karl university administrator
Skelsey, Geoffrey Brian academic administrator
Skende, Dhimitri university rector, researcher
Skladal, Elizabeth Lee retired elementary school educator
Sklar, Gail Janice secondary special education educator
Skurnik, Joan Iris special education evaluator, educator, consultant
Slaughter, John Brooks former university administrator
Sliger, Bernard Francis academic administrator, economist, educator
Sloman, Albert Edward retired university administrator, consultant
Slynko, Basil technology education educator
Smagorinsky, Peter education educator
Small, Roger Steven middle school educator
Smalley, Stephen Stewart dean
Smiley, Frederick Melvin education educator, consultant
Smith, Abbie Oliver college administrator, educator
Smith, Brona Naomi educator
Smith, Clodus Ray retired academic administrator
Smith, David Langley education educator, consultant
Smith, David Robert university administrator
Smith, Dwyane university administrator
Smith, Karla Salge Jordan early childhood education educator
Smith, Martha Virginia Barnes retired elementary school educator
Smith, Roland Blair, Jr. university administrator
Smith, William Steven university financial administrator, consultant
Smithers, Alan George educator, researcher
Smorgon, Sam academic administrator
Snakenberg, Sharon Ann special education educator
Snitow, Virginia Levitt educator
Snyder, Carolyn Ann university dean, librarian
Snyder, George Morris, Jr. adult education educator, writer, consultant
Sobotka, Werner Karl dean, communication consultant
Sobralske, Barbara Nila educator
Soedarto, H. academic administrator
Sohlenius, Gunnar H. academic administrator, manufacturing educator and researcher
Soifer, Jack educational consulting company executive, engineer
Solari, Luca educator, consultant
Sonnenschein, Hugo Freund academic administrator, economics educator
Sonu, Jong-Ho academic administrator
Sorgdrager, Albert Johan educator
Sorgen, Herbert J. international education educator
Sorosky, Jeri Ruth academic administrator
Sorrell, Stephen A. principal
Sotamaa, Yrjö Kalervo university president, design educator
Southard-Bornyasz, Marjorie special education educator, consultant
Southworth, William Dixon retired education educator
Søvik, Nils education educator
Spahr, Clinton S., Jr. retired elementary education educator
Spangler, David Robert college administrator, engineer
Spangler, Stanley Eugene international relations educator
Sparks, Jack Norman college dean
Spencer, John Loraine retired headmaster
Speth, Gerald Lennus education and business consultant
Speth, James Gustave dean, environmental studies educator, lawyer
Spindler, Judith Tarleton elementary school educator
Spinner, Kaspar Heinrich educator
Spitze, Glenys Smith retired educator
Spoelders, Marc Hubert Paul education educator
Sprenger, Marilee Broms educational consultant
Sprintzen, David A. educator, community activist
Stafford, Rebecca academic administrator, sociologist
Stahl, Norman A. educator
Sta Maria, Felixberto Cangco retired university president
Stanford, Kathleen Theresa secondary school educator
Stanley, John educational administrator, financial consultant
Stanton, Sara Baumgardner retired secondary school educator
Starcher-Dell'Aquila, Judy Lynn special education educator
Stark, Norman secondary school educator
Starks, Florence Elizabeth retired special education educator
Stassen, Hendrik Gerard machine systems educator
Staub, Martha Lou retired elementary education educator
Steed, Michelle Elnora special education educator, counselor
Steere, Anne Bullivant retired student advisor
Stein, Dale Franklin retired university president
Steinberg, Stephen Phillip university administrator, philosopher
Steinberg, Warren Linnington school principal
Steindorf, Gerhard education educator
Steiner, Stuart college president
Stellar, Arthur Wayne educational administrator
Stenby, Erling Halfdan applied thermodynamics educator
Stephens, Helen Janssens principal
Stern, Geoffrey Howard educator
Stern, Joanne Thrasher elementary school educator
Stevens, Leota Mae retired elementary education educator
Stewart, George university dean
Stewart, Lucille Marie special education coordinator
Stewart, Mac A. educator
Stickeler, Stephan educator
Still, James adult education educator, writer
Stock, Jeffrey Kevin academic administrator
Stocker, Joyce Arlene retired secondary school educator
Stoffle, Carla Joy university library dean
Stoltzfus, Victor Ezra retired university president, academic consultant
Stopford, Michael John university administrator
Storer, Roy former dean of dentistry, educator
Stovall, Richard L. academic administrator
Stoyanov, Ivan Iliev rector
Stoyle, Peter Blin academic administrator
Stracher, Dorothy Altman education educator, consultant
Street, Brian Vincent education educator, consultant
Street, Patricia Lynn secondary education educator
Street, Robert retired academic administrator, physicist
Strejcek, Elizabeth Geierman reading specialist, educator
Striler, Ray distance education consultant
Stringer, Pamela Mary retired headmistress
Stromholm, Stig Fredrik university administrator, lawyer, educator
Stromnes, Aasmund Lonning education educator
Stuart, Cynthia Morgan university administrator
Stull, Frank Walter elementary school educator
Subramanian, Sermadevi Ramalingam university researcher, educator
Subramanya, Srikantia educator
Suchodolski, Henryk Szigniew primary school educator
Sugioka, Yoichi academic administrator
Sugiyama, Toku Mary retired school administrator
Sullivan, Debra Kae elementary education educator
Sullivan, Keith Frederick education educator
Sunderland, Eric university president
Surber, Joe Robert assistant superintendent of schools
Sutherland, David William educator
Sutherland, Sir Stewart university vice chancellor
Suttle, Helen Jayson retired education educator
Suttner, Jon Richard elementary education educator
Sutton, Betty Sheriff elementary education educator
Sutton, Gerard university administrator
Suzuki, Shin'ichi comparative education educator
Suzuki, Shinzo researcher
Swartz, James D. education educator
Sweet, William education educator
Swe-Khine, Myint educational technology educator, consultant, resea
Syms, Helen Maksym educational administrator
Syphers, Mary Frances music educator
Szegedy-Maszák, Mihály educator, editor, literary historian
Szolnoki, John Frank special education educator, administrator
Tabagari, Sergo Ilya dean
Taggart, Helen M. adult education educator, nurse
Taher, Zainab Abdulhusain educational administrator
Tai, Li-Ming school principal, consultant
Tajima, Hajime education educator
Tajon, Encarnacion Fontecha (Connie Tajon) retired educator, association executive
Takahashi, Katsuhisa school administrator
Takakuwa, Yasuo education educator
Takanishi, Lillian K. elementary school educator
Takeshige, Chifuyu university president, retired physiology educator
Takeuchi, Seiichi dean, engineering educator
Taleb, Ahsene Mebarek school administrator, criminologist, educator
Talluri, Srinivas education educator
Tam, Sheung Wai educational administrator
Tamayo, Eduardo Emiliano (Eddy Tamayo) college educator
Tammi, Olli Eino educator emeritus
Tammisto, Kalle Antero academic administrator
Tanaka, Junji educational administrator
Tanaka, Sachiko Sako educator
Tang, Grace W.K. dean
Tanguy, Yann university president
Tanner, Daniel curriculum theory educator
Tanti, Charmaine Caruana education educator
Tavman, Ismail Hakki education educator
Taylor, Carol Ann educational administrator
Taylor, Clifford Otis retired principal
Taylor, Jane Ellen elementary educator
Taylor, Richard Kenneth Stanley education educator
Tcha, Dong-Wan educator
Teichler, Ulrich Christian higher education educator, researcher
Tener, Carol Joan retired secondary education educator
Terenzio, Marion Ann college program executive
Terrell, Deane university vice chancellor
Terveer, Joyce Ann academic administrator, English language educator
Terwiliger, Gwen H. education educator
Tetsu, Nakamura education educator
Thangaraj, Manuel Amirthavasagam college administrator, higher education consultant
Theetranont, Choti academic administrator
Thomas, Beverly Irene special education educator
Thomas, Ellen Louise private school administrator
Thomas, Jeff Alan educator
Thomas, Norman education educator
Thomas, Virginia Vaudaline retired educator
Thompson, Ana Calzada secondary education educator, mathematician
Thompson, Bertha Boya retired education educator, antique dealer and appraiser
Thompson, Keith Bruce retired university administrator
Thompson, Larry James gifted education educator
Thompson, Loring Moore retired college administrator, writer
Thompson, Martha Parrish researcher, educator
Thrane, Henrik Carl Albert education educator
Thueme, William Harold educator
Timonen, Pertti Aarre Sulevi educational administrator
Tirado, Felipe Segura dean
Tizard, Barbara education and child development researcher
Tjosvold, Dean William university administrator, educator
Tlou, Thomas university vice-chancellor
Toca, Angel educator
Todd, Mary King university educator
Todd, Shirley Ann school system administrator
Toff, Maxine adult educator, business consultant
Toll, John Sampson university president, physics educator
Tollett, Kenneth Scrugs education educator
Tomaselli, Sylvana Palma academic fellow
Tombaugh, Dorothy Elve retired secondary school educator, author, lecturer
Tomich-Bolognesi, Vera educator
Tomoda, Hiroshi educational administrator, researcher
Tomoeda, Cheryl Kuniko academic researcher
Tomov, Boris Ivanov rector, mechanical engineer, educator
Tompkins, Curtis Johnston university president
Tonkin, Humphrey Richard academic administrator, educator
Tornberg, Claes Egmont university administrator
Torp, Arne educator
Torres-Labawld, Jose Dimas institutional research director, service company executive, educator
Townley, Julie B. high school counselor
Trachtenberg, Stephen Joel university president
Tracy, Tracy Faircloth special education educator
Travaglini, Joseph educational consultant
Travelstead, Chester Coleman former educational administrator
Trefts, Joan Landenberger retired educator, administrator
Trigeaud, Jean-Marc Daniel educator, author
Trobian, Helen R. retired college administrator, consultant
Trojanowski, Ford Alexander college adminstrator
Troupe, Bonnie Lee college program coordinator, educator
Trow, George Frederick college administrator
Truslow, Marion Archer secondary education educator
Trybul, Theodore Nicholas education educator
Tse, Chi-Wai Daniel university president
Tse, Man-Chun Marina special education educator
Tsunogae, Hiroshi education educator, administrator
Tsutsui, Yoshiro educator
Tugbiyele, Emmanuel Akande education consultant
Tuhkanen, Sakari Martti educator
Tumminelli, Roberto Vittorio R. educator, author
Turenko, Anatoliy Nikolaiyevitch academic administrator
Turmov, Gennady Petrovich academic administrator
Turnbull, Vernona Harmsen retired residence counselor, education educator
Turner, Elvin L. retired educational administrator
Turpin, Calvin Coolidge retired university administrator, educator
Tyllia, Frank Michael university official, educator
Tyson, Laura D'Andrea dean, economist, educator
Ueda, Yoshisuke education educator
Uehling, Barbara Staner educational administrator
Ueno, Kazue college president, microbiologist, researcher
Ullsten, Robert Stig Karl education administrator
Umeyama, Motohiko educator

Undy, Roger *management educator, academic administrator*
Upward, Christopher *academic researcher, orthographer*
Urbina, Febe Gloria *elementary school principal*
Ushakov, Vasilii *academic administrator*
Vacek, Jaroslav *rector*
Vaidyan, Kurian Varghese *educator*
Vajner, Ludek *educator*
Vance, Mary Lee *academic administrator*
Vandenberg, Donald *retired education educator, philosopher*
Van Der Cruysse, Dirk J.S. *educator, researcher, writer*
Vandiver, Frank Everson *institute administrator, former university president, author, educator*
Van Hoven, Jay *retired school system administrator*
Van Mingroot, Erik Alfons *educator*
Van Patten, James Jeffers *education educator*
van Roermund, Arthur H.M. *educator*
Van Schoote, Jean-Pierre *university president, priest*
Van Vuuren, Jan H. *education educator*
Vargas, Jose Israel *academic administrator*
Varghese, Mariamma *academic administrator*
Varwig, Freyr Roland *secondary educator*
Vasaikar, Babulal Fakira *principal*
Vasquez Martinez, Claudio Rafael *educator, university administrator, author*
Vatandoost, Nossi Malek *art school administrator*
Vauchez, André *school administrator, history educator*
Velano, Edson Antônio *university official*
Velazquez-Squeglia, Sharon Kathleen *elementary education educator, language educator*
Veldhuis, Johannes G. F. (Jan Veldhuis) *university president*
Ven Horst, Marie E. *retired university dean*
Veras, Marcia Pereira *educator*
Verbitskaya, L.A. *academic administrator*
Vercruysse, Jeroom August Johan Ghisleen *retired education educator*
Verde, Rui Alexandre *educator*
Verloop, Nico *education educator*
Verma, Surjit Kumar *retired school system administrator*
Vertiy, Alexey *educator*
Vest, Charles Marstiller *academic administrator*
Vichiola, Christopher Michael *educator, writer*
Virgili, Antonio *educator, consultant*
Viswanadha Rao, Tamvada *academic administrator, English studies educator*
Vita-Finzi, Claudio *university educator*
Vlokh, Iryna Josipivna *medical university administrator*
Vocelka, Karl Gerhard *university educator*
Vogt, Hartmut *education educator*
Voigt, Dawn A. *college program adminstrator, consultant*
von der Gablentz, Otto Martin *college rector*
von Hentig, Hartmut *education educator*
Vucelic, Dusan *education educator*
Vulliamy, (John-Na'vred) Graham *education educator*
Wachman, Marvin *former university chancellor*
Wackermann, Gabriel *education educator*
Wade, Henry William Rawson *legal scholar, author*
Wagner, Paul Anthony, Jr. *education educator*
Wagner, Peter Hans *educator*
Wagner, Wilfried *educator*
Waite, Ronald Scott *educator, tennis instructor*
Walford, Geoffrey *education policy educator*
Walker, Annette *counseling administrator*
Walker, Carolyn Smith *college services administrator, counselor*
Walker, Lucy Doris *secondary school educator, writer*
Walker, Stuart Carter *educator*
Walker, Will Earl *educator*
Wall, Patrick David *educator, scientist*
Wallen, Carl Joseph, Jr. *education educator*
Waller, Wilma Ruth *retired secondary school educator and librarian*
Walsh, Dolores Ann Gonczo (Lorry Walsh) *special education educator*
Walter, George Anthony *elementary education educator*
Walters, Kenneth C. *retired educator*
Walters, Sherwood G. *professor, consultant*
Wang, Aihe *educator*
Wang, Cheng Xu *education educator*
Wang, Lipo *educator, researcher*
Wang, Quan *university educator*
Wang, Ying-Luo *college dean, educator*
Wang, Zheng Ping *educator*
Wani, Ghulam Mohy-ud-Din *education director*
Ward, Mark Gordon *university dean, language educator*
Ward, Richard Hurley *university dean, writer*
Ware, Bennie *university administrator*
Warner, Malcolm *educator, author, social scientist*
Warner, Patricia Ann *secondary school educator*
Warren, John Coolidge *private school dean, history educator*
Wartiovaara, Jorma Juhani *educator*
Wassell, Richard Charles *educational consultant*
Watkins, Sherry Lynne *elementary school educator*
Watteau, John Francois *academic administrator*
Watts, Ross Wakefield *retired school principal, mayor*
Watts, Victor Ernest *university administrator, educator*
Watts, Vincent Challacombe *educational administrator*
Webb, Donna Louise *academic director, educator*
Weber, Arnold Robert *academic administrator*
Weber, Harald Wolfgang *educator*
Weber, Wilford Alexander *education educator*
Wedderburn, Dorothy Enid Cole *educational administrator*
Wedel, Millie Redmond *secondary school educator*
Wedgeworth, Robert *former dean, university librarian, former association executive*
Weicker, Jack Edward *educational administrator*
Weier, Winfried *educator*
Weinstein, Rhonda Kruger *elementary mathematics educator, administrator*
Weir, Morton Webster *retired academic administrator, educator*
Weller, Debra Anne *elementary educator*
Wells, Zella Faye *assistant school superintendent, consultant*
Welsh, Doris McNeil *early childhood education specialist*
Wendt, Alexander Edward *educator*
Werres, Karl Josef *university educator, academic administrator, lawyer*
Wertz, John Alan *secondary school educator*
West, Dana Renee *secondary education educator*
West, Linden Reginald *education educator, researcher*
West, Paul Gavin *educator, administrator*
Weston, Francine Evans *secondary education educator*
Weston, Richard *adult education educator, researcher*
Whalen, John Philip *retired educational administrator, clergyman, lawyer*
Wheeler, Susie Weems *retired educator*
Whelan, Raymond E. *educator, researcher*
Whitaker, Reginald Percy *educator*
Whitaker, Thomas Kenneth *former university chancellor*
White, Alice June *retired educator*
White, Gladys Hope Franklin *reading specialist*
White, Lynda Gayle Melton *reading specialist, educational diagnostician*
White, Warren Travis *educational consultant firm executive*
Whitehead, Maurice *education educator*
Whittington-Brown, Vanessa Elizabeth *educator*
Wiechert, Allen LeRoy *educational planning consultant, architect*
Wiederuh, Eckhardt Martin *educator*
Wielemans, Willy *education educator*
Wiesenberg, Jacqueline Leonardi *lecturer*
Wilbur, Barbara Marie *elementary education educator*
Wild, Ray *academic administrator*
Wilke, Constance Regina *elementary education educator*
Wilkinson, John Eric *education educator, broadcaster*
Wilkinson, Rupert Hugh *educator*
Wille, Rosanne Louise *higher education administrator*
Williames, Lee John *university official, history educator*
Williams, Carol Marie *secondary school educator*
Williams, Cheryl A. *secondary education educator*
Williams, Felton Carl *college administrator*
Williams, James Franklin, II *university dean, librarian*
Williams, Paul Robert *school system administrator*
Williams, Ross Alan *dean, educator*
Williams, Thomas B. *secondary school educator*
Williams, Vivian Lewie *college counselor*
Willoughby, John Wallace *former college dean, provost*
Wilpert, Bernhard Ottmar *educator*
Wilson, Arthur Theodore *education consultant*
Wilson, Esther Elinore *technical college educator*
Wilson, Imogene R. *counselor*
Wilson, Karen Jeanine *education educator*
Wilson, Sonja Mary *secondary education educator, consultant, poet*
Wilson-Webb, Nancy Lou *adult education administrator*
Winchell, George William *curriculum and technology educator*
Winter, Alan Thomas *university official, physicist*
Winter-Neighbors, Gwen Carole *special education/art educator, consultant*
Winterstein, James Fredrick *academic administrator*
Wire, Donald Richard, II *college administrator*
Wittig, Sigmar *academic administrator, researcher*
Wode, Henning *education educator*
Wodraschke, Georg Stephan *communications educator*
Wolf, Alois *educator*
Wolf, Frances Mary Guthrie *music therapist, teacher of the disabled*
Wolfe, Rose *academic administrator*
Wolff-King, Sally *college administrator, educator*
Wollenberg, Jörg *university educator*
Woo, Chia-Wei *academic administrator*
Woodfill, Christopher C. *secondary school educator*
Woods, Pendleton *college director, author*
Woods, Phyllis Michalik *retired elementary school educator*
Woodward, Sir (Albert) Edward *academic administrator, retired judge*
Woolworth, Susan Valk *primary school educator*
Wootson, Gerry Levon *preschool teacher, writer*
Wraga, William G. *educator*
Wright, C. T. Enus *former academic administrator*
Wright, Carole Dean *reading specialist*
Wright, John Spencer *school system administrator*
Wright, Katie Harper *educational administrator, journalist*
Wright, Pamela Jean *administrator*
Wu, Jihuai *dean, chemical engineer*
Wyatt, Brett Michael *secondary school educator*
Wylie, James Malcolm *educator*
Wyss, Ramon Alexander *educational administrator*
Xia, Yiben *college dean*
Xu, Lihao *education educator*
Yabunaka, Satoru *educator*
Yahaya, Mohamed Jamil *school system administrator*
Yalçineli, Melih *educational projects executive, physics educator*
Yamanaka, Chiyoe *institute president*
Yamashita, Yasumasa *educator*
Yan, Hong *university educator*
Yancey, Carolyn Dunbar *educational policy maker*
Yang, Chih-Hung *academic administrator*
Yao, John T.K. *school system administrator*
Yao, Leehter *educator*
Yaqub, Mohammed *educator*
Yaskawa, Katsumi *university administrator*
Yasukata, Toshimasa *educator*
Yerger, Linda F. *human resources administrator, educator*
Yett, Sally Pugh *elementary education educator, art specialist*
Yin, Baolu *educator*
Yoshida, Masami *university administrator, researcher*
Yoshida, Yoshio *dean, physical geography educator*
Yoshie, Hisaya *educator*
Yoshino, Toshihiko *education educator*
You, Ke-wei *educator*
Young, Charles Edward *university chancellor emeritus*
Young, Deidra Jane *educational researcher*
Young, Ian Robert *academic administrator, educator, researcher*
Young, Lauren Sue Jones *education educator*
Young, Sandra *adult education executive*
Young, Vera Lee Hall *educational administrator, association executive*
Yu, Jing Quan *educator*
Yu, Pei-San *business educator, marketing consultant*
Yu, Pufan *educational administrator*
Yuan, Chuan Rong *educator, academic administrator*
Yui, Daizaburo *educator*
Yukselen, Adil Mahmut *academic administrator*
Zahner, Dorothy Simkin *elementary education educator*
Zaidfoudim, Pavel Chaskelievich *academic manager, researcher*
Zaidi, Emily Louise *retired elementary school educator*
Zaim, Salih *education specialist*
Zaitsev, Viacheslav Fiodorovich *vice-chancellor, science educator*
Zambone, Alana Maria *special education educator*
Zapesotsky, Alexander Sergeevich *rector*
Zapffe, Nina Byrom *retired elementary education educator*
Zarin, Kamar *education educator*
Zarkada-Fraser, Anna *university lecturer*
Zaro, Juan Jesus *educator*
Zeilinger, Elna Rae *elementary educator, gifted-talented education educator*
Zelenka, Josef *educator*
Zellner, Kenneth Kermit *elementary education educator*
Zerda, Alvaro *university dean, economist*
Zhang, Lin-Chang *electromagnetic compatibility educator*
Zhang, Xiyan *educator*
Zhang, Zhi *education educator*
Zhou, Guo-Ding *electric power university professor*
Zhu, Quan Min *educator*
Ziarati, Reza *dean*
Zilbert, Allen Bruce *education educator, computer consultant*
Zimenkovsky, Borys Semenovych *academic administrator, pharmaceutical educator*
Zimmer, Ian *dean*
Zimmermann, Reinhard *educator*
Zixin, Hou *academic administrator*
Zopfi, Hans Jakob *secondary education educator, botanist*
Zuber, Lianne Carol *elementary school educator*
Zuber, Norma Keen *career counselor, educator*
Zuna, Petr Josef Otakar *university dean, materials science educator*

ENGINEERING

Aakjer, Thomas *electrical engineer*
Aarinola, Peter Kofoworola *chemical engineer, researcher*
Abadjiev, Valentin Ivanov *engineering educator, researcher*
Abak, Ali Toygar *engineering researcher*
Abaya, Efren Flores *engineering educator, telecommunication consultant*
Abbas, Husain *civil engineering educator, consultant, researcher*
Abbas, Khaled Abdelazim *engineering educator, researcher, consultant*
Abbasi, Ghaleb Yousef *engineering educator*
Abbott, John Rodger *electrical engineer*
Abdallah, Mayssa Amin *engineering educator*
Abdelgader, Hakim Salem *engineering researcher*
Abdel-Halim, Ibrahim Abdel-Moneim *electrical engineering educator*
Abd El-Salam, Mohamed El-Husseiny *engineering executive*
Abdul Ghani, Abdus Salam *electric company engineer*
Abe, Hiroyuki *mechanical engineering educator*
Abe, Masayuki *engineering executive*
Abecassis, Fernando Maria de Gamboa *engineering executive, educator*
Abedi, Mehrdad *electrical engineering educator*
Abhary, Kazem *mechanical and manufacturing engineering educator, researcher, consultant*
Able-Thomas, Uriel Lytton *engineering executive*
Abramowicz, Adam Zbigniew *electrical engineering educator, researcher*
Abrie, Pieter Lucas *engineering company executive, software developer, educator*
Abubakr, Said Mohammed *chemical engineering educator*
Abul-Azm, Ahmed Gamal *marine engineer*
Achi, Peter Benson Uchechukwu *mechanical engineer*
Achilles, Ricardo Alfredo *power system consultant, researcher, educator*
Ackerman, Brian Michael *marine engineer, consultant*
Ackerman, Robert Lloyd *chemical engineer, environmental tree farmer*
Ackerman, Roy Alan *research and development executive*
Ackermann, Juergen Ernst *research institute administrator, researcher*
Adams, Alfred Bernard, Jr. *environmental engineer*
Adams, Charles Paul *communications engineer*
Adams, Dee Briane *hydrologist, civil engineer*
Adams, Joseph Brian *operations research engineer, mathematics educator*
Adams, Robert David *mechanical engineering educator, consultant*
Adebayo, Stephen Oluyemi *engineering educator*
Aderoba, Adeyemi Adegbemisipo *mechanical engineer educator, industrial engineer*
Adesina, Adesoji Adediran *engineering educator*
Adetiba, Mayen Modupeola *civil engineer, consultant*
Adham, Samer *environmental engineer*
Adlershteyn, Leon *naval architect, engineer, educator, researcher*
Adrian, Jim *retired mechanical engineer*
Agarwal, G. *engineering educator, consultant*
Agbetoye, Leo Ayodeji *agricultural engineer, educator*
Agelidis, Vassilios Georgios *electrical engineer*
Aggarwal, Amrit Lal *engineer executive*
Aggarwal, Satish Kumar *electrical engineer, government official*
Aggarwal, Sudesh Kumar *mechanical engineer, educator*
Aghassi, William J. *mechanical engineer, consultant*
Agnew, John Broughton *chemical engineering educator, consultant*
Agrawal, Bijaya Krishna Das *chemical engineering educator*
Agrawal, Rakesh *industrial researcher*
Agrawal, Satyendra Kumar *metallurgical engineering educator*
Aguerrevere-R, Gonzalo *electrical engineer, management consultant*
Aguilar, Glenn *engineering educator*
Aguinaldo, Jorge Tansingco *chemical engineer, water treatment consultant*
Aguirre, Roberto Ramon Ignacio *engineering executive*
Aharoni, Herzl *engineering educator, researcher*
Ahmad, Manjur Sarwar *mechanical engineer*
Ahmad, Zaki X. *materials science and corrosion educator*
Ahmed, Shaikh Faiz Uddin *civil engineering educator*
Ahn, Jung-Ho *engineering educator, scientist*
Ahn, Young-Cheol *chemical engineer, educator*
Aichbhaumik, Dibyajyoti *metallurgical engineer*
Aihara, Ken-ichi *engineering educator*
Aindow, Mark *engineering educator*
Ajuria, Sergio *chemical engineer, researcher*
Akbar, Syed Ali *chemical engineer*
Akers, Nicolas Paul *electronics engineer, physicist*
Akhmetzianov, Marat Khalikovich *mechanical engineer, educator, research scientist*
Akhtar, Junaid *engineering researcher*
Akins, Vaughn Edward *retired engineering company executive*
Akintunde, Ifedayo *civil engineer*
Akiyama, Fuminori *educator*
Akramullah, Shahriar Mohammad *engineer*
Akurugoda, Sangadasa *electrical engineer, consultant*
Akyarli, Adnan Oguz *civil engineer, educator*
Alabi, Babatunde *mechanical engineer, educator*
Alaluf, Rafael *structural engineer, consulting company executive*
Alam, Mansoor *computer science and engineering educator*
Alam, Mohammad Jahangir *engineering educator*
Alam, S. Kaisar *electrical engineer*
Alappa, Rama Krishna *food products engineering executive*
Alatiqi, Imad Mohammad *chemical engineering educator*
Alcaraz, Jose Luis *engineering educator*
Aldahhan, Abdulmonem Abdullah *electrical engineer, consultant*
Aleissa, Khalid A. *nuclear engineering researcher*
Alekhin, Vladimir Nicholaevich *civil and structural engineering executive*
Aleksandrov, Aleksei Aleksandrovich *engineering educator*
Aleksandrov, Georgij Nikolaevich *electrical engineering educator, researcher*
Alencar, Marcelo Sampaio de *electrical engineering educator*
Alexa, Dimitrie *electrotechnical engineer, educator*
Alexander, Carl Albert *ceramic engineer, educator*
Alexiou, George Philip *computer engineer, educator, researcher*
Al-Falahi, Laith Abdulla *mechanical engineer*
Alfares, Hesham Kamal *engineering educator*
Alfonso-Faus, Antonio *engineering educator, researcher*
Alfstad, Tore *telecommunications engineer*
Al-Garni, Abdullah Mohammed *civil engineering educator, researcher, consultant*
Al-Garni, Ahmed Zafer *aerospace engineer, educator*
Al-Ghusain, Ibrahim Ahmad Nouri *engineering educator, researcher, consultant*
Alhabibi, Yasser Ali *mechanical engineer*
Alhamid, Abdulaziz A. *hydraulics specialist, educator, researcher*
Al-Homoud, Mohammad Saad *architectural engineer, educator, consultant*
Ali, Emadadeen M. *engineering educator*
Ali, Khwaja Mohammed *aeronautical engineer*
Ali, Syed Ahmed *chemical engineer, researcher*
Al-Ibrahim, Abdulrahman Mohammed *research educator*
Alkhadra, Fouad Fawzi *engineering consulting company executive*
Al-Kodmani, Nasser *civil engineer*
Allahverdi, Ali *engineering educator, industrial engineer, researc*
Allardice, David John *fuel technologist*
Allen, John Edward *engineering educator, plasma physicist*
Allen, John Elliston *aeronautical engineer, educator, consultant*
Allison, Robert Joseph *software engineer*
Allport, John Martin *mechanical engineer*
Al-Mahmeed, Ahmed Saleh *engineering educator*
Almahroos, Hussain Mohamed Hasan *engineering educator*
Almalik, Mansour Saleh *petroleum engineering educator, researcher*
Al-Modhhi, Adel Zaid *electrical engineer*
Alnahi, Haitham Ghalib *electrical engineering educator*
Alpan, Sadrettin H. *mining engineer*
Al-Ramahi, Wadee *engineering executive*
Al Shaye, Mohamed A. *engineering executive*
Altan, M(ustafa) Cengiz *mechanical engineering educator*
Altwegg, Peter *mechanical engineer*
Alves, Diógenes Salas *engineering researcher, engineer*
Alves, Fernando Jorge Lino *engineering educator, researcher*
Aly, Omar Fernandes *thermal power plant engineer*
Alzebdeh, Khalid Ibrahim *structural engineer, consultant*
Amati, Pietro *computer and video engineer*
Ambujam, N.K. *agricultural engineering educator*
Ametani, Akihiro *engineering educator*
Amin, Mohammad Ruhul *engineering educator, researcher*
Amin, Shahid *civil engineer*
Amini, Farshad *engineering educator, consultant*
Amon Parisi, Cristina Hortensia *mechanical engineering educator, researcher*
Amtmann, Hans Henry *aeronautical engineer, naval architect*
Anagnostopoulos, John Panagiotou *electrical engineer, researcher*
Anagnostou, Emmanouil Nikolaos *civil and environmental engineering educator*
Anastassiadis, Kyriakos *civil engineering educator*
Anbumozhi, Venkatachalam *environmental science educator, researcher*
Ancheyta-Juárez, Jorge *petroleum engineer, educator*
Anderson, Bruce James *electrical engineer, consultant*
Anderson, Clarence Axel Frederick *retired mechanical engineer*
Anderson, George Hugo *chemical engineer*
Anderson, Karl Richard *aerospace engineer, consultant*
Anderson, Robert John *electronic engineer*
Andersson, Helge Ingolf *mechanical engineering educator*
Andersson, Karl-Hugo Svante *mechanical engineer, consultant*

Andersson, Per Lennart *computer engineer, consultant*
Ando, Yasuhisa *mechanical engineer*
Andre, Jean-Michel *physical engineer*
Andreadis, Ioannis *engineering educator, researcher*
Andreiev, Yura (George) *electronics engineer*
Andrews, David Charles *energy and power consultant*
Andrievsky, Boris Rostislavich *engineering educator, researcher*
Andrus, James Brannon *electrical engineer*
Ang, Marcelo Huibonhoa, Jr. *mechanical engineering educator*
Angelle, Philippe Albert *retired electrical engineer*
Angelsky, Oleg Vyacheslavovich *optical engineer, educator, university dean*
Angierski, Bernd-Ruediger *process engineer, dialysis consultant*
Aniserowicz, Karol *electrical engineering educator, consultant*
Anjanappa, Muniswam Appa *engineering educator*
Anma, So *engineer consultant*
Annergren, Goran Erik *chemical engineer, consultant*
Anosov, Oleg Lwovich *bioengineer, researcher*
Antalffy, Leslie Peter *mechanical engineer*
Anton, Joan Mihai *engineering educator*
Antonenko, Alexander Nicholas *researcher*
Antonopoulos, Kimon Antoniou *engineering educator*
Antoun, Elie *engineering executive*
Antweiler, Dennis Francis *mechanical engineer*
Anwar, Habib-ollah *civil engineering, consultant*
Aoki, Hitoshi *engineering consultant*
Apelt, Colin James *civil engineering educator*
Apetrei, Constantin *engineer*
Apostolescu, Vlăstar Nestor *retired structural engineer*
Apostolico, Alberto *electrical engineer, educator*
Aprea, Jose Luis *process engineer*
Arai, Tamio *mechanical engineering educator*
Araki, Kenji *mechanical engineering educator*
Aranguren, Arthur *chemical engineer*
Arau, Jaime E. *electronics educator*
Aravindan, Palanisamy *mechanical engineer, educator*
Aravossis, Konstantin G. *mechanical engineer*
Arbogast, Gordon Wade *systems engineer, executive, educator, consultant*
Archer, John William *electrical engineer*
Ardash, Garin *mechanical engineer*
Arduino, Pedro *engineering educator*
Aref, Amjad Jalal-Eddin *structural engineer, educator*
Arefjev, Alexandre Sergeyevich *engineering educator, researcher*
Arena, Alejandro Pablo *mechanical engineer, educator*
Argaman, Yerachmiel *engineering educator*
Argentini, Alessandro *engineer*
Arghir, George *metallurgical engineering educator, researcher*
Argonz, Raquel *mechanical engineer, researcher*
Arif, Mustafa Kamal *electrical engineer*
Arimoto, Suguru *engineering educator*
Aristodemou, Loucas Elias *industrial engineer, manufacturing company executive*
Armentano, Ricardo Luis *biomedical engineering researcher*
Armstrong, Bruce Irving *mechanical engineer*
Armstrong, Keith Bernard *engineering consultant*
Armstrong, Otis Price *chemical engineer, environmental engineer*
Arnis, Efstathios Constantinos *mechanical engineer*
Arnold, Jay *retired engineering executive, educator*
Arnold, Rinee' Stephen *petroleum engineer*
Arntsen, Arnt Peter *engineer, consultant*
Arreguin-Cortes, Felipe *hydraulics engineer, researcher, educator*
Arroyave, Carlos Enrique *engineering educator, researcher*
Arsali, Mohammad *engineering consultant, realtor*
Arslan, Levent Mustafa *engineering educator, consultant*
Artisyuk, Vladimir Vasilyevich *nuclear engineer*
Arumugam, Murugesan *electrical engineering educator*
Arzi, Yohanan *industrial engineer, educator*
Asamoah, Joseph Kwasi *chemical engineer, energy and the environment consultant*
Asano, Hitoshi *engineering educator*
Asano, Shiro *nuclear engineer*
Asharif, Mohammad Reza *electrical engineer, educator*
Ashenberg, Joshua *aerospace engineer*
Askovic, Radomir Velimira *engineering educator*
Astrelin, Igor Mikhailovich *chemical engineering and technology educator*
Aswendt, Petra Gertraude *material engineer, researcher*
Atchison, Arthur Mark *industrial, research and development engineer*
Atherton, Philip Gwyther *chemical engineer*
Atilgan, Timur Faik *structural engineer*
Atkinson, Malcolm *engineering scientist*
Atkinson, Neil Norman *mechanical engineer*
Attipoe, Bloomfield Crosby *agricultural engineer*
Attoh-Okine, Nii O. *civil and environmental engineering educator*
Au, Tsien-Ming *electrical engineer*
Audenino, Alberto Luigi *engineering educator*
Augusti, Giuliano *structural engineering educator, consultant*
Austin, Fred *consultant mechanical engineer*
Averboukh, Elena *systems engineer, consultant*
Awaya, Nobuyoshi *electronics engineer, materials researcher*
Awbi, Hazim Bashir *engineering educator*
Axford, Roy Arthur *nuclear engineering educator*
Axsater, Sven Bertil *engineering educator*
Ayala-Ramirez, Victor *engineering educator, researcher*
Aye, Lu *mechanical engineering educator, researcher*
Aygun, Ilhami *electronics engineer*
Ayling, Laurence John *scientist, consultant*
Ayres, Raymond Maurice *mechanical engineer*
Azad, Abul Kashem Mohammod *engineer*
Azari, Zitouni *engineering educator*
Azegami, Hideyuki *mechanical engineer, educator*
Aziz, Sajid *electronics engineer, consultant*
Azizoglu, Meral *engineering educator*
Azodi, Djahangir *engineer*
Babich, Alexander *metallurgy researcher, educator, consultant*
Babitsky, Vladimir Ilyich *mechanical engineering researcher, consultant, educator*
Back, Lloyd H. *mechanical engineer, researcher*
Badawi, Mohamed El Sayed Mohammed *engineering manager*
Badell Yturriaga, Mariana *chemical engineer*
Badescu, Mihail Viorel *thermal engineering educator, researcher*
Badr, Ahmed Zaki *engineering educator*
Badran, Abdulkarim *biomedical engineer*
Bae, Young Chan *chemical engineering educator*
Baek, Won-Pil *nuclear engineer, researcher, educator*
Baerwald, John Edward *traffic and transportation engineer, educator*
Bagajewicz, Miguel *engineering educator*
Bahill, A. Terry *systems engineering educator*
Bai, Hsunling *environmental engineering educator*
Bai, Yong *engineering executive, educator*
Baier, Paul Walter *electrical engineering educator*
Baig, Hasib Tahir *aeronautical engineer, consultant*
Baig, Taqi M. *electrical engineer*
Bailey, Cecil Dewitt *aerospace engineer, educator*
Bailey, Larry Alan *mechanical engineer*
Bailey, Michael Wallace *aerospace engineer*
Bair, William Alois *engineer*
Bair, Yueih Jin *civil engineer*
Bakos, George Chris *engineering educator, consultant*
Bakoss, Stephen Lewis *civil engineering educator*
Bal, Anupam Deep Singh *information technology engineer*
Balachandran, Swaminathan *industrial engineering educator*
Balakrishnan, Arcot Ramachandran *engineering educator, researcher*
Ballard, Robert Clifford *automation engineer, failure analysis consultant*
Balme, Louis *electrical engineering educator*
Balnaves, Charles *petroleum engineer*
Baltz, Richard Arthur *chemical engineer*
Bandyopadhyay, Manas *environmental engineer*
Bangalore, Srinivas *computer engineering researcher*
Bangash, Mohammad Yusaf Hassan *structural engineering educator*
Baniotopoulos, Charalambos *civil engineer, educator*
Bankov, Banko Petkov *civil engineer, educator*
Banks, William McKerrell *mechanical engineer, educator*
Bannister, Michael Keith *materials engineer, researcher*
Bansal, Vishal *chemical engineer*
Bantekas, Demetrios *electrical engineer, researcher, educator*
Bányász, Csilla *electrical engineer*
Bao, Yiwang *engineering researcher*
Bao, Zhuojun *software engineer*
Barakat, Elhaj Elhussien *electrical engineer*
Barakzai, Myhammed Naeem *engineering executive*
Baran, Lubomir Wlodzimierz *engineering educator*
Barber, Pierre Yves *engineering executive*
Barbour, Blair Allen *electro-optical engineer, researcher*
Barboza, Angel Alberto *aerodynamics engineer*
Barbulescu, Sorin Adrian *electronic engineer, researcher*
Barbusinski, Krzysztof *environmental engineering educator, researcher*
Bardin, Boris Vasiljevitch *electrical engineer*
Bardos, Richard Paul *environmental scientist, educator*
Bari, Mohammed Abdul *civil engineer*
Barkanov, Evgeny *engineering educator*
Barker, Michael David *design engineer*
Barkhash, Vladimir Alexandrovich *chemical engineer*
Barko, Gyorgy *chemical and mechanical engineer*
Barnes, Howard Anthony *rheologist, engineer, educator*
Baron, Gino Victor *chemical engineering educator*
Barr, Spencer *opto-electronic engineer*
Barr, William Robert *industrial engineer, consultant*
Barrenechea, Ricardo Miguel *civil engineer*
Barrett, Michael John *engineer*
Barrett, Robert David *engineering executive*
Barringer, J. Michael *electrical engineer*
Barros, Ricardo Carvalho *nuclear engineering educator*
Barton, Nick *rock mechanics and tunneling engineer*
Bartosch, Thorsten *electrotechnical engineer, researcher*
Bartoszewicz, Andrzej Pawel *engineering educator, researcher*
Barua, Alok *engineering educator*
Barua, Gautam *environmental engineer educator*
Baruzdin, Sergey Anatolievich *radioelectronics educator, researcher*
Baryla, Jean-Michel Pierre *civil engineer*
Bashilov, Alexander Sergeyevich *mechanical engineer*
Baskakov, Albert Pavlovich *heat engineering educator*
Baskous, Athan A. *retired environmental engineer*
Basso, Christophe Paul *electrical engineer*
Bastawros, Ashraf F. *engineering educator*
Bastenhof, Dirk *retired mechanical engineer, researcher*
Bastiaans, Rob J.M. *mechanical engineering researcher*
Basu, Somnath *engineer*
Batchelor, Joseph Brooklyn, Jr. *electronics engineer, consultant*
Batterman, Steven Charles *engineering mechanics and bioengineering educator, forensic engineering and biomechanics consultant*
Bauchot, Frederic Jacques *telecommunications engineer*
Bauer, Jerome Leo, Jr. *chemical engineer*
Bauer, Maria Casanova *computer engineer*
Bauer, Pierre *electrical engineer*
Baum, Carl Edward *electromagnetic theorist*
Baum, Richard Theodore *engineering executive*
Baumann, Theodore Robert *aerospace engineer, consultant, army officer*
Baumann, Wolfgang Heinrich *electrical engineer*
Bautista, Reynaldo Yasay *civil and sanitary engineering educator,*
Baxter, Gene Kenneth *mechanical engineer, company executive*
Baxter, Glenn Austin *engineer*
Bayandor, Javid *aerospace engineer, researcher, educator*
Bayerl, Maximilian *electrical engineer*
Bažant, Zdeněk Josef *civil engineering educator, scientist*
Bazes, Melvin Israel *electronics engineer*
Beale, Jack Gordon *engineering consultant, water research foundation administrator*
Bear, Jacob *civil engineer, educator, consultant*
Beatty, Craig David *mechanical engineer*
Bechteler, Wilhelm *engineering educator*
Beck, Roland Herwig Friedrich *biotechnology engineer*
Beck, Vaughan Rodney *fire safety systems and risk engineer*
Beckwith, Larry Edward *mechanical engineer*
Becvarova, Věra *agricultural engineer, economist*
Béda, Gyula *mechanical engineer, educator*
Bedi, Rajan *electronics designer*
Been, Derek Craig *electrical engineer, consultant*
Beenackers, John A.W.M. *engineering consultant*
Behrend, William Louis *electrical engineer*
Beitinger, Gunter *electronic engineer*
Bell, Charles Eugene, Jr. *industrial engineer*
Bell, John Tedford *civil engineer*
Bell, Michael Geoffrey Harrison *civil engineering educator*
Bell, Robert Stanley *aerospace engineer*
Bellanger, Gilbert *nuclear engineer*
Bellas, Stelios Kirikos *information engineer*
Bellegarda, Jerome René *electrical engineer, scientist, consultant*
Beloborodow, Wladimir Witaljewitsch *chemical engineer*
Belyakov, Andrey Nikolaevich *metallurgical engineer*
Benam, Javid Feizollah *engineering educator, researcher, consultant*
Bengtson, Richard Lee *agricultural engineer, educator*
Ben-Haim, Yakov *mechanical engineering educator, researcher*
Benjamin, Ralph *electronics researcher*
Benkipur, Vidyashankar Sadasivarao *mechanical engineer, consultant, researcher*
Benn, Raymond Christopher *materials engineer*
Bensal, Moshe *electrical engineer*
Benson, Frank Atkinson *electrical engineer*
Benyamini, Dubi *mechanical engineer*
Benz, Carl Arvell *nuclear engineer, physics educator*
Beom, Hyeon Gyu *engineering educator*
Bera, Rajendra Kumar *aerospace engineer, researcher*
Beranek, Leo Leroy *acoustical consultant*
Berckmoes, Frederic-Benoit *environmental and mechanical engineer*
Berezyuk, Anatoliy Nikolaevich *civil engineer, educator, administrator*
Berg, Werner *agricultural engineer*
Berger, Frederick Jerome *electrical engineer, educator*
Berger, Per Erik *drilling service company manager*
Bergeron, Elmo P. *chemical engineer, consultant*
Bergfield, Gene Raymond *engineering educator*
Bergquist, Olof Bjarne Jörgen *process engineer, researcher*
Berlamont, Jean E. *engineering educator*
Berlin, Alexander Alexandrovich *polymer engineer, educator*
Bernasconi, Christian *chemical engineer*
Berndtsson, Gunilla Helen *acoustical engineer*
Bernet, Steffen *engineering executive, electrical engineer*
Bernhard, Andreas Paul *engineer*
Bero, Joseph Martin *manufacturing engineer*
Beroual, Abderrahmane *electrical engineering educator, researcher*
Berri, Mohamad Hussein *engineer, researcher*
Bertels, Guy Louis *electrical engineering company executive*
Bertolini, Enizo *engineering consultant*
Bertoti, Edgar Frigyes *mechanical engineer, researcher*
Bertram, Christopher David *engineering educator*
Beshir, Mohamed Youssef *industrial engineer, consultant*
Beskos, Dimitri E. *structural engineering educator*
Besley, Morrish Alexander (Tim Besley) *civil engineer*
Bessai, Horst Joachim *electrical engineering educator*
Besson, Raymond Jean *electronics engineering educator*
Bestaoui, Yasmina *electronic engineer, educator*
Bevc, Frank Peter *electrical engineer*
Beyreuther, Roland *mechanical engineer, scientist*
Bharadwaj, Balaji *automotive engineer*
Bhat, Niranjan Chidanand *inspections executive*
Bhatia, Suresh Kumar *chemical engineering educator*
Bhatt, Navinchandra Baldevram *electrical engineer*
Bhattacharjee, Ajit Kumar *mechanical engineer, engineering company executive*
Bhattacharyya, Souvik *engineering educator*
Bhattarai, Rishi R. *civil engineer, researcher*
Bhobe, Atul D. *structural engineer*
Bhongir, Madan Mohan *public health engineer*
Bhuiyan, Md. Shoaib *electronics engineer, computer engineer, educator*
Bi, Jia Ju *engineering educator, researcher*
Bianchi, Ettore Fulgenzio *textile engineer*
Bianchi, Giovanni Antonio *mechanical engineering educator*
Bicknell, Barbara Ann *mechanical engineer, executive, consultant*
Biechl, Helmuth *electrical engineer, educator*
Biener, Ernst *civil engineering educator, consultant*
Bies, David Alan *mechanical engineering educator*
Bilgin, Nuh *mining engineer, educator*
Billet, Reinhard *chemical engineer, consultant*
Billimoria, Rusi Peston *specifications engineer*
Billings, Stephen Alec *engineering educator*
Billingsley, John *electronics engineer, educator*
Bilston, Lynne Eckert *biomedical engineer, reseacher*
Bilston, Paul *engineering executive, consultant*
Bingham, Paris Edward, Jr. *electrical engineer, computer consultant*
Birca-Galateanu, Serban *electronics educator*
Bird, Trevor Stanley *electrical engineer*
Biswas, Dhrubes *electrical engineer*
Biswas, Dilip Kumar *engineering company executive*
Bjork, Jens Niklas Kristofer *systems engineer*
Björkman, Anders Erik Gustaf *retired engineering educator*
Blaabjerg, Frede *engineering educator, researcher*
Blachere, Gérard Pierre Henri *civil engineer*
Black, James Robert *industrial engineer*
Blackman, Deane Robert *engineering educator, consultant*
Blakeley, David *chemical engineer*
Blanchard, Bruce *environmental engineer, government official*
Blanchet, Jean-Didier François *civil engineer*
Blasco, Agustin *agricultural engineering educator*
Blechman, Isaak Haim *civil engineer*
Bloch, Erich *retired electrical engineer, former science foundation administrator*
Blockley, David Ian *civil engineer*
Blok, Harmen *mechanical engineer, consultant*
Bobco, William David, Jr. *consulting engineering company executive*
Bobin, Nikita E. *mining engineer*
Boccuzzi, Joseph *electrical engineer, educator*
Boche, Bernhard *process engineer*
Boczkaj, Bohdan Karol *structural engineer*
Boczkaj, Boleslaw Franciszek *electrical engineer, consultant*
Bodizs, Arpad Kalman *chemical engineer*
Boger, David Vernon *chemical engineering educator*
Boghosian, Soghomon B. *chemical engineer, educator*
Bogunovic, Nikola *computer engineering educator*
Bohn, Dieter Eugen *engineering educator, researcher*
Boileau, Jacques *engineer, scientific expert*
Boisjoly, Richard Thomas *plastics engineer, educator*
Bokhari, Shahid Hussain *electrical engineer, educator*
Bollinger, Kenneth John *aerospace engineer, computer and space scientist*
Bologa, Octavian Constantin *engineering educator*
Bolotin, Vladimir Vasilyevich *mechanical engineer, educator*
Bolz, George Michael *engineering executive, consultant*
Bon, Alexandr Ivanovich *chemical engineer*
Bond, Peter Desmond Rolland *civil engineer*
Bonnechere, Francois Joseph *civil engineer, educator*
Bontha, Jagannadha Rad *scientist, development engineer*
Bontozoglou, Vasilis *chemical engineering educator*
Boone, James Virgil *retired engineering executive, researcher*
Bor, Sheau-Shong *electrical engineer, educator, researcher*
Bordes-Bouret, Elisabeth Françoise *engineering and chemistry educator*
Borg, Robert Frederic *civil engineer*
Borisyuk, Andriy Olexandrovych *mechanical engineer, researcher*
Born, Robert Heywood *consulting civil engineer*
Borrego, Carlos Soares *environmental engineering educator*
Borrego, Jesus Garcia *engineer*
Borsa, Judit *engineering educator, researcher*
Børsting, Hakon *electrical engineer, researcher*
Borysyuk, Mykhaylo Demianovich *mechanical engineer*
Borzycki, Krzysztof Wacław *communications research engineer, interpreter*
Boscovic, Dragan Milos *electrical engineer*
Bose, Kingshuk *research engineer*
Bosma, Anne Adriaan *electrical engineer*
Boström, Anders Einar *mechanics educator*
Botsaris, Pantelis *electrical engineer*
Botsis, John *science and engineering educator*
Bouda, Václav František *engineering educator*
Boudouvis, Andreas G. *engineering educator, researcher*
Bouraou, Nadejda Ivanovna *engineering educator*
Bournazel, Jean Pierre Christian *civil engineer, educator*
Bowen, Richard Antony *retired computer engineer*
Bowers, Brian Peter *engineering historian, researcher*
Boychuk, Leonid Mikhailovich *control theory and system analysis explorer and educator*
Boyd, Darrell Wayne *electrical engineer*
Boyd, Ian William *research engineer, educator, consultant*
Boyd, John Addison, Jr. *civil engineer*
Boyer, Vincent Lee *engineering executive*
Bozeman, Ross Elliot *engineering executive*
Božičević, Katica *environmental engineer*
Braam, Ben C. *mechanical engineer*
Bradford, Mark Andrew *civil engineer, educator*
Branco, Paulo José Costa *electrical engineer*
Brandell, Sol Richard *electrical power and control system engineer, research mathematician*
Brandenstein, Hartmut *electrical engineer*
Braoude, Vadim Borisovich *radio engineer, educator*
Braun, Simon Georg *engineering educator*
Breitwieser, Karina Maria *civil engineer*
Brenner, Martin John *aerospace engineer*
Brent, Paul Leslie *mechanical engineering educator*
Brezeanu, Gheorghe Ion *engineering educator, researcher*
Bridges, Robert Seymour *environmental engineer*
Bridgwater, John *chemical engineering educator*
Briggs, James Henry, II *engineering administrator*
Briggs, Philip Harold *retired engineer, consultant*
Bright, Glen *mechanical engineer, researcher*
Brilman, Derk Willem Frederik *chemical engineer, educator*
Brito, Hector Hugo *aerospace engineer*
Broch, Einar *geological engineering educator, administrator*
Brodsky, Wesley George *electrical engineer*
Brodt, Burton Pardee *chemical engineer, researcher*
Brogan, Joseph William, Jr. *safety and health consultant*
Brøndum-Nielsen, Troels *engineering educator*
Brookes, Alan Thomas *civil engineer*
Brooks, Brian Walter *chemical engineering educator*
Brooks, William George *aeronautical engineer*
Broomfield, John Philip *corrosion engineer, consultant*
Brouse, John Ammon, Jr. *fiber optics engineer*
Brovchenko, Vladimir Grigorievich *nuclear engineering researcher*
Brown, Alexander *engineering educator*
Brown, E. Merritt *engineering technician*
Brown, Gardner Russell *engineering executive*
Brown, Ivor John *consulting minerals, land reclamation-planning engineer*
Brown, Kenneth John *nuclear engineer*
Brown, Robert Frederick *industrial systems engineer, technology applications, industrial systems and management systems consultant*
Brown, Ronald Malcolm *engineering corporation executive*
Brown, Stephen Frederick *civil engineering educator*
Brown, Teion O'Dell *engineering executive*
Browne, Perry James *electrical engineer, mathematician*
Bruen, Michael Patrick *civil engineer, researcher*
Brugger, Hans Johann Georg *engineer*
Bruhns, Otto Timme *mechanics educator*
Brunale, Vito John *aerospace engineer*
Brunda, Daniel Donald *retired aerospace engineer, consultant, inventor*
Brunold, Axel Manfred *mechanical engineer, consultant*
Bruns, Billy Lee *electrical engineer, consultant*
Brunton, Daniel William *mechanical engineer*
Bryant, James Mitchell *electronic engineer, consultant*
Bryant, Paul T. *electronics engineering manager*
Bryson, Vern Elrick *nuclear engineer*
Bublikov, Igor Albertovich *engineering educator*
Bubnicki, Zdzislaw *computer science and engineering educator*
Bucci, Reginaldo *engineering company administrator, educator*
Buddington, Patricia Arrington *engineer*
Budiningsih, Yusty *petroleum engineer*
Budisan, Nicolae Ilie *electrical and control engineering educator, consultant*

De Bruijn, Joost Dick *biomedical engineer*
Decamps, Freddy *chemical engineer, educator*
Deconinck, Geert Leopold *electrotechnical engineer*
Decreton, Marc Camille *electrical engineer, researcher*
de Franca, Francisca Pessoa *biochemical engineering educator, researcher*
Defrance, Jérôme *acoustics engineer, researcher*
Degauque, Pierre Jules *electronics educator*
Degrave, Alex G. *computer engineer, consultant*
De Grave, Dany Michel *biomedical engineer*
DeGroot, Loren Edward *engineering executive, consultant*
De Guio, Roland *electrical engineer, educator*
Dehays, Tarek Samir Abu *company executive*
de Hemptinne, Jean B. Charles *research engineer, educator*
Dehui, Song *engineering educator*
Deipser, Anna *waste management engineer, researcher*
de Jong, Rémy Lucien *water resources engineer*
De Klerk, Joseph Adrian *civil engineer*
Delahanty, Carlos Anthony *industrial engineer*
de la Houssaye, Brette Angelo-Pepe *electronics engineer, researcher*
de la Morena, Javier *engineering consultant*
De Lange, Philip Gerardus *mechanical engineer*
Delapalme, Bernard M.J. *naval architect, engineer*
Del Castillo, Jose Maria *mechanical engineer, educator*
Delhaes, Pierre Vincent *engineer, researcher*
DeLima, Lutero Carmo *engineering educator*
Delire, Philippe *automotive engineer*
Delport, Volker *telecommunications engineer*
Deltort, Bruno Jean Louis *engineering executive*
De Luca, Patrick *virtual manufacturing engineer, researcher*
Demarchi, Ernest Nicholas *aerospace engineering administrator*
de Martinis, Umberto *electrical engineering educator, consultant*
De Meester, Paul Jozef August *nuclear engineering educator, construction company executive*
De Meyer, Arnoud Cyriel Leo *engineering educator, dean*
Demić, Miroslav Dragoljub *mechanical engineering educator*
Demidova, Nadejda *engineering educator*
de Miguel Gonzalez, Rafael *avionics engineer, information systems consultant*
Demirer, Goksel Niyazi *environmental engineering educator*
De Moor, Bart L.R. *researcher*
Deng, Jiun-Shiou *electronic engineer, educator*
Deng, Tianquan *electrical engineering consultant, educator*
Denisov, Dmitri Alexeevich *chemical engineering educator*
Denisov, Nikolay Alexander *optical engineer*
Denke, Paul Herman *retired aircraft engineer*
D'Entremont, Edward Joseph *infosystems engineer, educator*
Deouline, Eugeny Alexeevitch *engineer, educator*
DePriest, C(harles) David *engineering executive, retired air force officer*
De Roy, Walter Lodewijk Vincent *engineering executive*
Desai, Sunil Chandrakant *civil engineer, consultant*
De Saive, Michel Jrms *commercial engineer*
De Schamphelaere, Lucien *engineer*
Deshmukh, Kishor Madhukar *electronics and telecommunications engineer*
Deshpande, Ajay Narayan *process engineer, engineering executive*
Desideri, Jean-Antoine *research scientist, aeronautical engineer*
Desjardins, Benoit Pierre *mining engineer, consultant*
Desrochers, Alan Alfred *electrical engineer*
Deswarte, Yves André *research director*
Detreköi, Ákos *engineering educator, university administrator*
de Wet, Jacobus Anthony *civil engineer, physicist*
Dey, Subhasish *hydraulics educator*
de Yeregui, Carlos Gilberto *engineering executive*
Dezhurny, Igor Ivanovich *radiocommunication engineer*
Dhariwal, H.C. *mechanical engineering educator, researcher*
Dhir, Vijay K. *mechanical engineering educator*
Dhondt, Guido Dominique *civil engineering researcher*
Diab, Hassan Bahaeddine *electrical and computer engineering educator*
Diao, Dongfeng *engineering educator, consultant*
Diaz-Zubieta, Agustin *nuclear engineer, engingeering executive*
Diederich, Joachim *computer technology educator, researcher*
Dierkes, Wilma Karola *chemical engineer*
Dietz, David William *structural engineer*
Dillinger, Stephan Alexander *structural dynamics engineer*
Dimas, John Dimitriou *metallurgical engineer*
Dimentberg, Mikhail Fyodorovich *mechanical engineering educator*
Dimitrienko, Irina Donatovna *mechanical engineer, applied mathematician*
Dimitriou, Stavros George *electronics educator*
Dimitry, Said *chemical engineer, researcher*
Dimova, Silvia Lubomirova *engineer, researcher*
Ding, Jack Jie *mechanical and structural engineer, lecturer*
Dinghua Guan *researcher, educational association administrator*
Diomin, Yury Vasilievich *engineering educator, researcher*
Dix, Gary Errol *engineering executive*
Dix, Samuel Morman *industrial engineer, physical economist, appraiser*
Dixit, Prakash Mahadeo *mechanical engineering educator*
Dixon, Phillip George *electrical engineer, consultant*
Dixon, Robert Clyde *systems engineer, consultant*
Djazmati, Sameh Mohamed *engineering educator*
Djukan, Petar *civil engineer*
Dluzewski, Pawel *mechanical engineer*
Dobrolyubov, Anatoli Ivanovich *engineering research facility administrator*
Doepper, Ronald Fridrich *chemical engineer*
Doersam, Charles Henry, Jr. *engineer*
Doetsch, Markus *communications/electrical engineer*
Doherty, Leslie Edward *electronic engineer, research scientist*
Dohrn, Ralf *chemical engineer*
Doi, Yutaka *electrical engineer*
Dolby, Ray Milton *engineering company executive, electrical engineer*
Dolce, Mauro *structural engineer, educator*
Dolecek, Quentin Edward *electronics engineer*
Dolejs, Vaclav *chemical engineering educator*
Doma, Eugène *engineering executive*
Dombrovsky, Leonid Alexandrovich *mechanical engineer, researcher*
Domschke, Alfred Gunther *mechanical and electrical engineering consultant*
Donahoo, Leonard E. *retired engineer*
Donevski, Bozin *mechanical engineering educator, researcher*
Donovan, Robert F. *senior safety specialist, construction consultant*
Dooge, James Clement Ignatius *civil engineer, hydrologist, former senator*
Dorato, Peter *electrical and computer engineering educator*
Dorn, Edward Harvey *design engineer, writer, illustrator*
Dorrah, Hassen Taher *engineering executive, educator*
Doss, Frank Allen *electronic technician*
Dou, Henri Jean-Marie *engineering educator*
Dou, Hua-Shu *mechanical engineering educator*
Doucakis, Nicolas P. *production engineer and executive*
Dougherty, Floyd Wallace *design engineer*
Doulai, Parviz *engineering educator*
Dragulin, Dan *engineering educator*
Dranchak, Lawrence John *retired mechanical engineer*
Drdácky, Miloš Ferdinand *civil engineer, researcher*
Dreifke, Gerald Edmond *electrical engineering educator*
Dreisbach, Mary Elizabeth *manufacturing engineer*
Drewry, Don Neal *safety engineer*
Dreyfus, Gérard *electronics engineering educator*
Drikakis, Dimitrios *mechanical engineer, educator*
Droese, Siegfried Otto *engineering educator, researcher*
Drozdov, Igor Alexeevich *metallurgical engineering educator, researcher*
Drozdziel, Marion John *aeronautical engineer*
Drung, Dietmar *electronics engineer, researcher*
Dryer, Richard *mechanical design engineer*
Du, Xiaoguang *mechanical engineer, engineering executive*
Du, Yanqing *electrical engineer*
Dubey, Chandra Varty *technical consultant*
Dubinsky, Anatoly *mechanical engineering researcher*
Duchon, Bedrich Milan *engineering and economics educator, researcher*
Duddeck, Fabian Emanuel Maro *engineering educator*
Dudziński, Piotr Antoni *mechanical engineering educator, consultant*
Duffy, Robert Edward *fluid dynamics engineer, consultant*
Dufour, Jacques Julien *mining engineer*
Duhovnik, Jože *mechanical engineer*
Dunnill, Peter *biochemical engineer*
Duong, Duy Quang *mechanical engineer, research scientist*
Du Peloux, Cyrille *communications engineer*
Durgin, Frank Herman, II *aeronautical engineer*
Durian, Stewart William *design engineer*
Dutta, Aloke Kumar *electrical engineering educator*
Dutta, Dipak *engineering consultant*
Dutta, Nirma Lendu *mining engineer*
Duvvur, Satyanarayana Rao *engineering company executive*
Dvorak, Bruce Irvin *environmental engineer, educator*
Dwivedi, Dinesh Chandra *engineering executive*
Dybczynski, Wladyslaw *electrical engineer, educator*
Dzieduszko, Janusz Wladyslaw *electrical engineer*
Dziopak, Józef *civil engineering educator*
E, Jisheng *engineer*
Eastburn, Martin Howard *engineer*
Eaton, George Wesley, Jr. *petroleum engineer, oil company executive*
Ebenezer, Duraisingh Diamond *acoustical engineer*
Eberhardsteiner, Josef Markus *civil engineer*
Ece, Mehmet Cem *engineering educator, researcher*
Echempati, Raghu *mechanical engineering educator, consultant*
Eckel, James J. *flight test engineer*
Eckelman, Richard Joel *engineering specialist*
Eckert, Ernst R. G. *mechanical engineering educator*
Edens, Fred Joe *petroleum engineer*
Edlund, Robert Mauritz *electrical engineer*
Edward, David Andrew *environmental engineer*
Edwards, Kenneth Neil *chemical engineer, consultant*
Edwards, Ross Alexander *aircraft systems engineer*
Edwards, Victor Henry *chemical engineer*
Efstathiadis, Stilianos George *transportation engineer and planner*
Ehrlacher, Alain *engineering educator*
Ehrlich, Margaret Isabella Gorley *systems engineer, mathematics educator, consultant*
Eick, Olaf J. *engineer, scientist*
Eigel, James Anthony *environmental engineer*
Ekel, Petr Yakov *electrical engineer, educator*
El Alfi, Mohamed Bahaa El Din *engineering company executive*
Eldada, Louay A. *fiber optic engineer*
El Gamal, Yousry Saber *engineering dean, computer consultant*
El Ganzory, Mohamed Ahmed *quality control engineer, inspector*
El-Hawary, Moetaz Maher *civil engineering educator*
Eliassen, Svein Leonard *engineer*
Elinson, Vera Matveevna *engineer*
Elishakoff, Isaac *engineering educator*
Ellerbusch, Fred *environmental engineer*
Ellero, Antonio Sergio Dutra *metallurgical engineer, planning executive*
Ellis, George Edwin, Jr. *chemical engineer*
Ellison, William Theodore *marine engineer*
El-Mahallawy, Nahed Abdel-Hamid *mechanical engineering educator, researcher*
Elmendorp, Jacob J. *engineering educator*
El Mhamedi, Abderrahman *engineering educator, researcher*
El-Midany, Tawfik *engineering educator*
Elms, David George *civil engineering educator, consultant*
Elnashai, Amr Salah *civil engineer*
El Sanafawy, Mohamed Ahmed *civil engineer*
El-Sayed, Khalil Mohamad *aerospace engineer*
Elsharkawy, Adel Mohamed *engineering educator*
El-Sherif, Mahmoud A. *electrical engineering educator*
Elsunni, Mohamed Eltayeb *electrical engineer, consultant*
El-Taji, Mohamed Sami Mahmoud Nadim *engineering executive, consultant*
El-Tatawy, Hesham Ibrahim *civil engineer*
Eltohami, Omer Ahmed *engineering educator*
Elwakil, Ahmed Elsayed *electronic engineer, researcher*
Embrechts, Jean Jacques *research engineer, educator*
Emi, Toshihiko *materials engineering educator, consultant*
Enache, Eduard *network engineer*
Enescu, Crisan *engineering executive, consultant*
Engelbart, Doug *engineering executive*
Engelmann, Rudolph Herman *electronics consultant*
Engin, Nur *engineer, researcher*
Engman, Ernst Rune *engineering executive*
Engstrom, Dan Bertil *structural engineer, researcher, consultant*
Enriquez, Ricardo Caburian, Jr. *electrical engineer*
Ensminger, Dale *mechanical engineer, electrical engineer*
Epple, Wolfgang Karl *computer science engineer*
Epright, Charles John *retired aerospace engineer*
Erdogdu, Ferruh *agricultural and biological engineering educator*
Eren, Halit *engineering educator*
Eriç, Rauf Hürman *metallurgical engineering educator*
Ericsson, Bernt Olof *chief engineer*
Erkan, Semih *agricultural engineer, researcher*
Erkmen, Aydan Müserref *electrical engineering educator*
Erlandsen, Thor Egil *marine engineering company executive*
Erling, Spencer *steel contracting executive, civil engineer*
Ernst, Kurt Wilhelm *retired chemical engineer, researcher*
Ernst, Randyl Allen *engineer*
Ervin, Patrick Franklin *nuclear engineer*
Escaron, Pierre Camille *engineering executive*
Esmailzadeh, Ebrahim *mechanical engineering educator, consultant*
Esposito, Antonio *physics engineer*
Essa, Mohammed Hussein *environmental engineer, researcher*
Essén, Hanno Fredrik Bengtsson *mechanical engineering educator*
Estrin, Genrikh Yakovlewitsh *structural engineer, researcher, administrator*
Evans, Alan George *electrical engineer*
Evans, John Winton *engineering educator, consultant*
Evans, Robin John *electrical engineer*
Evans, Walter Reed *retired engineering executive, consultant*
Excell, Peter Stuart *electronics and electrical engineering researcher*
Exe, David Allen *electrical engineer*
Eyraud, Henri Louis Charles *chemical engineer*
Ezell, James Norman, II *environmental engineer*
Ezhov, Yuri Vladimirovich *retired mechanical engineer*
Ezzine, Jelel *engineering educator, consultant*
Fabiano, Bruno *industrial engineer, researcher*
Fabre, Alain *electrical engineering educator*
Fadarishan, Stephen Robert *systems engineer*
Faghih, Nezameddin *engineering educator*
Faig, Wolfgang *civil engineer, engineering educator*
Fainberg, Valentin *chemical engineer, writer, playwright*
Fairbairn, Eduardo M.R. *civil engineer, educator, consultant, researcher*
Fakhro, Samir Qasim *technology educator, computer company executive*
Falconer, Roger Alexander *water engineering educator, consultant*
Fallet, Truls Rugland *electrical and petroleum engineer*
Fallmann, Wolfgang Franz *electronics educator*
Fan, Changxin *electrical engineering educator*
Fan, Honggang *mechanical engineer, researcher*
Fan, Yeuk Hon *John engineering executive*
Fanchi, John Richard *industrial technologist, educator, physicist*
Fang, Cui Chang *mechanics educator, scientist*
Fang, Hung-Yuan *educator*
Fang, Shu-Cherng *industrial engineering and operations research educator*
Fang, Yung-Show *civil engineering educator*
Fang, Zhaohong *engineering educator*
Fantana, Nicolaie Laurentiu *electrical engineer, researcher*
Fanuele, Frank John *engineering executive*
Farag, Mahmoud Mohamed *engineering educator*
Farine, Pierre Andre *microelectronics engineer*
Farkas, Jozsef Bela *chemical engineer, educator*
Farnham, Timothy *training and education administrator*
Farrell, Gregory Alan *biomedical engineer*
Farschtschi, Abbas *engineering educator*
Fasciotti, Vittorio *mechanical engineer*
Fassois, Spilios D. *mechanical engineering educator*
Fatta, Despo Costa *chemical engineer*
Fatullayev, Eldar Gurban *engineer, educator, researcher*
Faul, Gary Lyle *electrical engineering supervisor*
Faw, Richard Earl *nuclear engineering educator*
Fawcett, Christopher Babcock *civil engineer, construction and water resources company executive*
Fayet, Michel *mechanics educator*
Feavearyear, John Edgar *aerospace systems engineer*
Federico, Panfilo Benny *mechanical engineer*
Fedorov, Mikhail Petrovich *engineering educator*
Fedrowitz, Christian Harry *electrical engineer, educator*
Fehr, Manfred *engineering educator, researcher*
Fei, Lin *engineering educator, engineering executive*
Feichtinger, Friedrich *metallurgical engineer*
Fejes, Pal *chemical researcher*
Felber, Sonja Veronika *mechanical engineer*
Feliu, Vicente *electrical engineering educator, dean*
Felsburg, David F. *engineering executive, educator*
Felsch, Karl-Otto *mechanical engineering educator, scientist*
Felts, Margaret "George" Clemen *environmental engineer, consultant*
Feng, Chude *engineering educator, ceramics engineer*
Feng, Chunfeng *engineering researcher*
Feng, Xiao *chemical engineering educator*
Ferderber-Hersonski, Boris Constantin *process engineer*
Fereig, Sami M. *civil engineer*
Ferencz, Robert Mark *mechanical engineer*
Fernald, James Michael *professional engineer*
Fernandez, Patrick Joseph *engineering executive*
Fernandez del Rio, Jose Enrique *communications engineer, researcher*
Fernandez Long, Hilario *civil engineer*
Ferraioli, Armando *biomedical engineering company executive*
Ferrante, Augusto Vittorio *engineering educator, researcher*
Ferrari, Ronald Leslie *engineering educator*
Ferreira, Hendrik Christoffel *electrical and electronic engineering educator*
Ferreira, Isabel Maria Mercês *materials engineering researcher*
Ferreira, Joao Carlos Espindola *mechanical engineering educator*
Ferreira, Luis Jorge *engineering educator*
Ferrell, Charles Madison *retired nuclear engineer, health physicist*
Ferrigno, Giancarlo *bioengineering educator, researcher*
Fertner, Antoni *electrical engineer*
Fettweis, Gerhard Paul *engineering educator*
Fettweis, Günter Bernhard Leo *mining engineering educator*
Fiala, Alois *engineering educator*
Fiala, Pavel *electrotechnics educator*
Fidler, Charles Robert *electrical engineer*
Fiedler, Christian *aerospace engineer*
Figueroa Higueros, Juan Carlos *electrical engineer*
Figwer, Jarosław Piotr *control engineering researcher*
Filatov, Vladimir Victorovich *electrical and nuclear scientist, engineer*
File, Joseph *research physics engineer*
Finck, Jean-Daniel *bioengineering executive, researcher*
Finn, Shane Darren *product development manager, design engineer*
Fiolitakis, Emmanuel *chemical engineer, researcher*
Fiorini, Vittorio *airworthiness and engineering educator*
Fischer, Harald Robert *biomedical engineer, researcher*
Fischer, Peter *engineering researcher*
Fishe, Gerald Raymond Aylmer *engineering executive*
Fisk, Edward Ray *retired civil engineer, author, educator*
Fix, Douglas Martin *electrical engineer*
Flandre, Denis Georges *microelectronics researcher and educator*
Fleisher, Andrew Roy *engineer, investor, business consultant*
Fletcher, David Ralph *civil engineer*
Fliss, Albert Edward, Jr. *molecular neuroscientist*
Floyd, John Millice *engineering executive, educator*
Foda, Rabiz Nasir *industrial engineer*
Fogel, Irving Martin *consulting engineer*
Fok, Thomas Dso Yun *civil engineer*
Fokuo, Emmanuel Adu *mechanical engineer*
Folić, Radomir J. *structural engineering educator*
Folke, Peterson Karl *mechanical engineer, educator*
Fomichov, Sergiy Konstantinovich *engineering educator, consultant*
Fomine, Serguei *chemical engineer, educator*
Fontana, Mario H. *nuclear engineer*
Fontenot, Jackie Darrel *safety and health consultant*
Ford, Edwin Roe *engineering company executive*
Ford, Sir Hugh *mechanical engineer*
Ford, Mark Lee *aerospace engineer, scientist*
Foreman, John Patrick *electrical engineer*
Foreman, Philip Frank *mechanical engineer*
Forest, Samuel Christophe *mechanical engineer, researcher*
Forman, Edgar Ross *mechanical engineer*
Forsberg, K. Haakan *electronic design engineer*
Forster, Hamish *engineer*
Fort, Ivan *chemical engineer, researcher*
Fortney, Thomas Kent *cost and petroleum engineer, management consultant*
Fossati, Humberto Mario *electrical engineer, researcher*
Foster, Peter Reynolds *biochemical engineer, researcher*
Foster, Sydney William George *retired aerospace and aviation history consultant*
Foster, Walter Herbert, III *mechanical and manufacturing engineer, executive*
Fouad, Bachtouti *civil engineer*
Fourt, Bernard-Francois P. *retired engineer*
Fox, Joan Phyllis *environmental engineer*
Fox-Rabinovich, German Simonovich *engineering executive*
Francis, Joy N. *communications engineer*
Franetzki, Manfred *medical engineering executive, researcher, entrepreneur*
Frank, Judit *chemical engineer*
Frank, Paul Martin *engineering educator, scientist*
Frankenberger, Jane Rossing *soil and water engineer*
Frant, Grigory *electrical engineer, industrial consultant*
Frantzeskakis, John Michael *civil engineering educator*
Fraser, Gale William, II *civil engineer*
Frassinelli, Guido Joseph *retired aerospace engineer*
Freiman, Charles Visvald *engineering foundation administrator*
Freiman, Lener Josifovich *corrosion engineer*
Frene, Jean Baptiste Marie *mechanical engineering educator*
Freudenrich, David Robert *civil engineer, traffic engineer*
Freund, Eckhard *electrical engineering educator*
Fricks, Ernest Eugene *engineering company official*
Fridman, Boris Emmanuilovich *electromechanical engineer, mathematician*
Friebe, Michael Horst *biomedical engineer*
Fried, Joel Robert *chemical engineering educator*
Frimmer, Elliot M. *fluid mechanics engineer*
Fristacky, Norbert *computer engineering educator, researcher*
Fronzo, Victor Jonathan *manufacturing engineer*
Fuerst, Albert Alan *remote sensing engineer*
Fuerstenau, Douglas Winston *mineral engineering educator*
Fugate, Charles Royce, Sr. *civil engineer*
Fuhrman, Donald C. *systems engineer*
Fujii, Hironori Aliga *aerospace engineer, educator*
Fujii, Toshio *electrical engineering educator*
Fujioka, Yuichi *chemical engineer*
Fujita, Hideki *electrical research engineer*
Fukuda, Mitsuo *electronic engineering researcher*
Fukuhara, Mikio *materials engineer, physicist*
Fukui, Yukio *engineering educator*
Fukumoto, Brian Michael *mechanical engineer*
Fukumoto, Masahiro *engineering educator*
Fukuoka, Yutaka *biomedical engineer, researcher*
Fukushima, Masakazu *electronic engineering executive*
Furey, Keith W. *mechanical engineer*
Fursov, Vladimir Alexyevich *engineer, researcher*
Furukawa, Mutsuhisa *engineering educator, researcher*
Gabbert, Ulrich *engineering educator*
Gad, Emad Fakhry *engineering educator, researcher*

PROFESSIONAL INDEX 2511 ENGINEERING

Gaddis, Edward Shafik *engineering educator, researcher*
Gad-el-Hak, Mohamed *aerospace and mechanical engineering educator, scientist*
Gadre, Aniruddha Dattatraya *research engineer*
Gaidau, Carmen Cornelia *chemical engineer, researcher*
Gal, Richard John *industrial engineer*
Galdi, Vincenzo *electrical engineer, researcher*
Galiev, Shamil Usmanovish *mechanical engineer, researcher*
Galindo-Sanchez, Angel *engineering company executive, educator*
Galvez-Durand, Federico Humberto Arturo *electronic engineering educator, researcher*
Gambling, William Alexander *electrical engineering educator, administrator*
Gammon, Jonathan Robert Arthur *civil engineer*
Gammon, Malcolm Ernest, Sr. *surveying and engineering executive*
Ganan-Calvo, Alfonso Miguel *fluid mechanics educator, mechanical engineer*
Gangadharan, Nagendra *engineer, educator*
Gangriwala, Huned Ahmedi *engineering executive*
Gao, Ming *structures engineer*
Gaonkar, Gopal Hosabu *mechanical engineer, educator*
Gapes, James Richard *bioprocess engineer*
Garavelli, Eduardo Norberto *mechanical engineer, consultant*
Garbatov, Yordan Ivanov *marine engineer, educator, researcher*
Garber, Nicholas Jack *civil engineer, educator*
Garcia, Andrew B. *chemical engineer*
Garcia, Rafael Jorge *retired chemical engineer*
Garcia-Martinez, Reinaldo *engineering educator*
Gardiner, William Ralph *electrical engineer, consultant*
Gardissat, Jean-Louis *physical engineer*
Gardner, Alec Sydney *engineering training manager*
Gardner, Julian William *electronic engineering educator*
Garg, Vijay Kumar *telecommunications engineer*
Garretson, Owen Loren *mechanical and chemical engineer*
Garrett, Joseph Edward *aerospace engineer*
Garris, Charles Alexander *mechanical engineer, educator*
Garvick, Kenneth Ryan *broadcast engineer, announcer, educator*
Gary, Gerard Elie *mechanical engineer, educator*
G—sowski, Włodzimierz *mechanical engineering educator*
Gáspár, Zsolt *civil engineer*
Gatopoulos, Denis G. *computer science and electrical engineer*
Gaudeau, Claude Jules Michel *biomedical engineer*
Gaul, Lothar *educator, mechanical systems consultant*
Gavish, Motti *electronic systems engineer, researcher*
Gawthrop, Peter John *engineering educator*
Gaxiola, Enrique Humberto *electrical engineer, researcher*
Gaymard, Robert *petroleum engineer, retired*
Gazzetta, Moreno Augusto *engineer*
Gboney, William Kwasi *mechanical engineer*
Ge, Li-Feng *engineer, physics educator, researcher*
Ge, Shuzhi Sam *electrical engineering educator*
Ge, Zhenchang *retired engineering educator*
Geantă, Victor *engineering educator*
Gegus, Ernö *retired chemical engineer, researcher*
Géher, Károly *electrical engineering educator*
Gehlawat, Jagdish Kumar *chemical engineering educator, researcher*
Geiger, Harald *optoelectronics researcher*
Gela, George *electrical engineering researcher*
Geldart, Derek *retired chemical engineering educator*
Genain, Marc P. *engineering consultant*
Genieser, Lars Herbert *chemical engineer*
Gentry, James Walter *chemical engineer, educator*
George, Nelson Raj *electrical engineer, engineering executive*
Gera, Dinesh *mechanical engineer*
Geramani, Konstantina *biomedical engineer, researcher*
Gerasimov, Victor Grigorievich *engineering educator*
Gerey, Tamas *mechanical and environmental engineering educator*
Gérin, Vincent *civil engineer*
Gerlach, Thurlo Thompson *electrical engineer*
Gers, Juan Manuel *electrical engineer, consultant, educator*
Gershman, Alexei *electrical engineer, researcher*
Gervasio, Susana Graciela *chemical engineer*
Ghafoor, Abdul *civil engineer*
Ghanem, Shihab Muhammad Abduh *engineering and economics educator*
Ghannam, Mamdouh Taha *chemical engineering educator*
Ghassemlooy, Zabih *engineering educator*
Ghizawi, Nidal Awni *aerospace engineer, researcher*
Ghojel, Jamil Ibrahim *mechanical engineering educator, researcher*
Ghosh, Somnath *engineering educator*
Ghosh, Soumitra Kumar *electrical engineer*
Ghosh Moulic, Sandipan *mechanical engineering educator, researcher*
Ghouse, Mohammed *chemical engineering educator, researcher*
Ghwanmeh, Sameh Hussein *engineering educator*
Giambene, Giovanni *research associate*
Giannamore, David Michael *electronics engineer*
Giannopoulos, George Anastasios *transportation engineer, educator, consultant*
Gibbons, Allen Ray *production engineer, tooling consultant*
Gibbons, Larry Roland *civil engineer*
Gibbs, Barry Marshall *acoustical engineer, educator, researcher*
Gierzyńska-Dolna, Monika *engineering educator, science administrator*
Gies, Robert Jay *mechanical engineer*
Giglmayr, Josef *electrical engineer, researcher*
Gilbert, Paul Thomas *chemical development engineer*
Gill, Hardayal Singh *electrical engineer*
Gilleland, John Rogers *technology company executive*
Gilmore, Duncan Bartlett *mechanical engineer*
Gingu, Oana *mechanical engineer, educator*
Ginsztler, János *mechanical engineer, educator*
Girardi Schoen, Elizabeth Catherine *chemical engineer*
Gisonni, Corrado *civil engineer, educator, researcher, consultant*
Givhan, Steven Allen *engineering executive*
Gladki, Hanna Zofia *civil engineer, hydraulic mixer specialist*
Glaser, Tracy L. *manufacturing engineer, executive*
Gliksberg, Alexander David *engineering executive*
Glouschenkov, Vladimir Aleksandrovich *metallurgy engineer, educator*
Gluschenkov, Oleg *electrical engineer*
Gnaedinger, John Phillip *structural engineer, consultant*
Godard, Michel Paul *engineering educator*
Godec, Zdenko *electrical engineer, consultant, educator*
Godo, Einar *computer engineer*
Godoy, Luis A. *engineering researcher, educator*
Goggins, Jean *biomedical engineer, foundation administrator*
Goh, Ronald *audioengineer, engineering executive*
Göker, Mehmet Hayri *design engineer, research scientist*
Golas, Ashok *telecommunications engineer*
Goldaniga, Alessandro Edoardo *chemical engineer, researcher*
Goldfeld, Lev Naum *communication engineer*
Goldman, Charles *electromechanical engineer*
Goldman, Yacov *aerospace engineering researcher, educator*
Goldszal, Alberto Figueiredo *biomedical and electrical engineer*
Golenko-Ginzburg, Dimitri *industrial engineering educator, researcher*
Golic, Jovan *electrical engineering educator*
Gomes, Norman Vincent *retired industrial engineer*
Gomes, Vincent G. *chemical engineering educator*
Gómez, Luis Carlos *engineer*
Gomory, Fedor *electrical engineer, researcher*
Goncalves, Daniel Milstein *aircraft maintenance engineer*
Gonder, Atila *engineering executive*
Gong, Zhengquan *engineer*
González, Enrique *industrial engineer, consultant*
González-Rey, Gonzalo *engineering educator*
González Vidosa, Fernando Manuel *road bridge designer, civil engineer, educator*
Goodell, John Dewitte *electromechanical engineer*
Goodwin, Billy Wayne *chemical engineer*
Gooi, Hoay Beng *electrical engineer, educator*
Gookin, Thomas Allen Jaudon *civil engineer*
Goossens, Arie Gerhard *chemical engineering consultant*
Goovaerts, Pierre Etienne *agriculture engineering educator*
Gopalakrishnan, Srinivasan *civil engineer*
Gopalan, Mysore Narayana Iyengar *engineering educator*
Gopalaswamy, Srinivasan *electrical engineer*
Goras, Liviu *engineering educator*
Gorbunovs, Anatolijs *engineer, construction specialist, politician*
Gordon, James Maynard *marine and mechanical engineer, consultant*
Gorelik, Vadim Semenovich *metallurgical engineering educator, consultant*
Goryacheva, Irina Georgievna *mechanics educator, researcher*
Goto, Nobuyuki *engineering educator*
Goto, Toshio *engineering educator*
Göttig, José Maria *engineering executive*
Gouesbet, Gerard *systems and process engineering educator*
Govatsos, Panagiotis Aristidis *mechanical engineering consultant*
Govic, Rudolf *structural engineer*
Graae, Tapani Carl-Gustav *nuclear engineer, marketing consultant*
Graaf, Jan de *engineering executive*
Grabacki, Jan Kazimierz *engineering educator*
Grabchev, Ivo Kotsev *researcher*
Grabisch, Michel Jacques *electrical engineer, educator*
Gracia Nuñez, Sabas Luis *electrical engineer, consultant*
Grambow, Richard F. *construction engineer, consultant*
Granciu, Ioan *engineer*
Grant, John M. *civil engineer*
Grau, Manuel *mechanical engineer*
Grauer, Manfred *computer engineering educator, researcher*
Gray, Carol Hickson *chemical engineer*
Gray, Festus Gail *electrical engineer, educator, researcher*
Gray, Nicholas Frederick *environmental engineer*
Grebennikov, Andrei Viktorovich *radio engineer, researcher, educator*
Green, Harry Edward *electrical engineer, private consultant, educator*
Green, Mino *engineering educator*
Gregory, Cedric Errol *retired mining engineer*
Greitzer, Edward Marc *aeronautical engineering educator, consultant*
Grenzebach, William Southwood *nuclear engineer, consultant, historian*
Griffiths, Hugh Duncan *electrical engineer*
Grimble, Michael John *industrial engineering educator*
Grimes, Craig Alan *electrical engineering educator*
Grimm, Clayford Thomas *architectural engineer, consultant*
Grippa, Luigi *chemical engineer*
Grisham, Andrew Fletcher *aerospace engineer, consultant*
Grishin, Yuri Petrovich *electronics educator, researcher*
Grković, Vojin Radovan *engineering educator*
Grooms, Henry Randall *civil engineer*
Grootenhuis, Peter *mechanical engineer, educator*
Gros, Xavier Emmanuel *non-destructive testing engineer, consultant*
Groseclose, Jay C. *civil engineer, consultant*
Grossi, Filippo *industrial engineer*
Gruchalla, Michael Emeric *electronics engineer*
Grum, Janez *mechanical engineering educator*
Gruyitch, Lyubomir Tihomir *engineering educator*
Gu, Yuanchao *biomedical engineer, geneticist*
Guan, Dagao *metallurgical engineer*
Guan, Xiaojun *research computer scientist*
Guardia, Gilberto F. *civil engineer*
Gubaidullin, Amir Anvarovich *mechanical engineer, educator*
Gubaidullin, Damir Anvarovich *engineering educator*
Guernsey, Nancy Patricia *mechanical engineer*
Guethenke, Gunnar Karl-Heinz Hermann *engineering researcher*
Gueulle, Patrick *engineer, author*
Guezzane, Saïd *electrical engineer*
Guha, Abhijit *engineering educator, researcher*
Guine, Raquel Pinho Ferreira *chemical engineer, educator*
Guirardello, Reginaldo *engineering educator*
Güler, Inan *electrical engineer, lecturer*
Gullo, Louis Joseph *reliability engineer*
Gulyani, Bharat Bhushan *chemical engineer, educator, researcher*
Gunduz, Gonul *chemical engineer*
Gunsel, Selda *chemical engineer, researcher*
Guo, James Zhiqiang *engineer*
Guo, Qixin *scientist, electrical engineering educator*
Guo, Qizhong *engineering educator, researcher*
Guo, Yong-Ming *mechanical engineering researcher, educator*
Guo, Zhixiong *mechanical engineer*
Gupta, Ajit *civil engineer*
Gupta, Narendra Kumar *electrical engineering educator*
Gupta, Narinder Kumar *mechanical engineer, educator*
Gupta, Rohit Bhram *chemical engineer*
Gupta, Santosh Kumar *chemical engineer, educator*
Gupta, Satyandra Kumar *mechanical engineering educator, researcher*
Gurel, Cigdem Seckin *electronics engineer, researcher*
Gutierrez, Frias Marcelo Arturo *civil engineer*
Guttmann, Karl *consulting mechanical engineer*
Guyot, Alain M. *researcher, consultant*
Gy, Pierre Maurice *sampling consultant and expert*
Gyekenyesi, John Paul *mechanical engineer*
Ha, Quang Phuc *engineering educator, researcher*
Ha, Yeong-Ho *electrical engineering educator, consultant*
Haan, Chan-hoon *architectural engineering educator, acoustic design consultant*
Habel, Helmut Heinrich *electronic engineer*
Haberman, Charles Morris *mechanical engineer, educator*
Habibi, Soheil *electrical engineer*
Habon, Eduardo Vaño, Jr. *mechanical engineer*
Habuka, Hitoshi *engineering educator*
Hachichou, Nabil Mahmoud *engineering executive*
Haddad, Edward Raouf *civil engineer, consultant*
Hadfield, Mark *engineering educator*
Hadfield, Michael James *electrical engineer*
Hadgu, Teklu *mechanical research engineer, consultant*
Hadhoud, Mohiy Mohamed *electronic engineering educator, researcher*
Hadi, Muhammad Najib S. *civil engineer, lecturer*
Hadjicostas, Thyrsos *electrical engineer, consultant*
Hadjiev, Dimitre Emilov *chemical engineer, researcher*
Hadjimichael, Georghios Costa *civil engineer, consultant*
Hadjistamov, Dimiter *chemical engineer*
Haeberlin, Heinrich Rudolf *electrical engineering educator*
Hagan, Francis Kwesi *mechanical engineer*
Hagare, Prasanthi *engineering educator*
Hagel, Reinhold Anton *electrical engineer, researcher*
Hagen, Kirk Dee *mechanical engineer, educator*
Hager, Willi Hermann *hydraulics educator*
Haggblom-Ahnger, Ulla Marjut *engineering educator*
Hahn, Song-Yop *electrical engineer, educator*
Hai, Bai Yu *acoustical engineer, researcher*
Halabe, Udaya Bhatta *civil engineering educator, researcher*
Halang, Wolfgang Andreas *electrical engineer, educator*
Halawa, Edward E.H. *engineer, consultant*
Haldar, Subhas Chandra *mechanical engineering educator, researcher*
Halemane, Rajendra K. *engineering executive*
Halkias, Christos Constantine *electronics educator*
Hall, Teresa Joanne Keys *manufacturing engineer, educator*
Hallberg, Örjan Hans Olof *reliability engineer*
Halley, Peter John *research engineer, lecturer*
Halligan, Mary A. *mechanical engineer*
Hambley, Douglas Frederick *geological and environmental engineer*
Hamed, Mohamed *engineering educator*
Hamidzadeh, Hamid Reza *mechanical engineer, educator, consultant*
Hamlett, James Gordon *electronics engineer, management consultant, educator*
Hammad, Mahmoud Ahmad *mechanical engineer*
Hammond, Walter Edward *aerospace engineer*
Hammons, Thomas James *electrical engineering consultant, engineering educator*
Hamner, Marvine Paula *aerospace engineer, researcher*
Hamza, Günter *engineering company executive*
Han, Chingping Jim *industrial engineer, educator*
Han, Kwan-Hee *industrial engineer, educator*
Han, Kyongho *electrical engineering educator*
Hanamirian, Varujan *mechanical engineer, educator, journalist, publisher*
Hanamura, Toshihiro *engineer*
Hancock, William Marvin *computer security and network engineering executive*
Hands, Eric William *civil engineer, electrical engineer, researcher*
Hanika, Jiří *chemical engineering*
Hanisko, John-Cyril Patrick *electronics engineer, physicist*
Hankó, Zoltán György *hydraulic engineer, researcher*
Hanson, Dorene Kay *engineering draftsman*
Hanson, Wendy Karen *chemical engineer*
Hanzawa, Satoshi *industrial engineer, researcher*
Haque, Iftikhar *electrical engineer*
Haque, Mohammed Shahidul *electrical engineer*
Harave, Maheshappa Devanna *engineering educator*
Hardalupas, Yannis *engineering educator, researcher*
Harding, John Edmond *engineering educator, academic administrator*
Hare, Clare Kean *aeronautical and aerospace engineer, consultant*
Hargitai, Robert *mining engineer, consultant, educator*
Hariu, Takashi *engineering educator, researcher*
Har-Lev, Moti (Mordechai Har-Lev) *electrical engineer*
Harris, Guy Hendrickson *chemical research engineer*
Harris, John Leonard *chemical engineering educator, researcher*
Harris, LeRoy S. *mechanical engineer*
Harris, Rhodri *electronics engineer*
Harris, Stuart Innes *construction equipment engineer, marketing professional*
Harris, Warren Lynn *development engineer*
Harsanyi, Gabor *microelectronics educator, researcher*
Hartal, Oren Michael *engineering executive*
Hartman, Charles Edward *engineer*
Hasan Babu, Hafiz Mohammad *computer engineering educator, researcher*
Hasebe, Norio *civil engineering educator*
Hashimoto, Akihiro *engineering educator*
Hashimoto, Shigehiro *biomedical engineer*
Hashmi, Syed Azhar Rasheed *polymer engineer*
Hassan, Hany Ibrahim *engineering consultant*
Hasund, Svein Harald *mechanical engineer*
Hatch, Ross Riepert *weapon system engineering executive*
Hatfield, Jim Gail *safety engineer*
Hauggaard-Nielsen, Anders Boe *structural engineer*
Haun, Jacob, Jr. *electrical engineer*
Haupt, Guenther Kurt *chemical engineer*
Hauptman, Aharon *mechanical engineer, technology-foresight researcher*
Havner, Kerry Shuford *civil engineering and solid mechanics educator*
Haws, E. Thomas *civil engineer, consultant*
Hayashi, Hidetaka *engineering and marketing electronic products executive*
Hayes-Gill, Barrie Robert *electronic systems educator, consultant*
Hays, Herschel Martin *electrical engineer*
Haythornthwaite, Robert Morphet *civil engineer, educator*
Haywood, John William, Jr. *manufacturing engineering consultant*
He, Bin *biomedical engineer, educator*
He, Ji-Fan *mechanics educator, researcher*
He, Li *aerospace engineer*
He, Yaping *safety engineer, researcher*
Hearn, Charles Lee *petroleum reservoir engineer*
Heckel, Richard Wayne *metallurgical engineering educator*
Hedar, Per Anders *engineering educator*
Heder, Mats Olof *mechanical engineer, educator, automotive historian*
Heer, Ewald *engineer*
Hegazi, Hesham Ahmed *mechanical engineer, educator*
Heide, John Wesley *engineering executive*
Heimer, Hans *electric power engineering executive, consultant*
Hein, Robert Eldor *electrical engineer*
Heinz, Roney Allen *civil engineering consultant*
Helm, John Leslie *mechanical engineer, company executive*
Helsen, Lieve *chemical engineer, researcher*
Helsingius, Mika Petri *optical engineer*
Hemment, Peter Layton *microelectronics educator and researcher*
Henderson, Michael L. *engineering executive*
Henderson, Paul Lloyd *electrical engineer*
Henderson, William David *mechanical engineer*
Hendrickson, Chris Thompson *civil and environmental engineering educator, researcher*
Hepper, Dietmar *electronics engineer*
Heragu, Sunderesh Sesharanga *industrial engineering educator, consultant*
Herak, Jure *chemical engineer*
Herisanu, Nicolae Horatiu *engineering educator*
Herman, Elvin E. *retired consulting electronic engineer*
Herman, Leszek *electronics engineer*
Hernandez, Eulogio Jose *electrical engineer*
Hernandez, Hector Manuel *consulting engineer, engineering educator*
Hernandez Gress, Neil *engineering researcher*
Herpe, Georges *astronomy engineer, researcher*
Herridge, Alistair Frederick *retired engineer*
Herrin, Stephanie Ann *retired aerospace engineer, yachtsman*
Hersman, Fernando William (Ferd Hersman) *retired engineering executive*
Heumann, Klemens Richard *electrical engineering educator, researcher*
Hewel, Horst Ferdinand *retired electronics engineer*
Hicks, Harold Eugene *chemical engineer*
Hidaka, Mutsuo *superconductive electronics researcher*
Higby, Edward Julian *safety engineer*
Hilberg, Wolfgang *technology educator*
Hill, Richard Inglis *retired civil engineer*
Hillery, Robert Charles *naval engineer, management consultant*
Hillstrom, Thomas Peter *engineering executive*
Hinch, Edward John *fluid dynamics engineer, researcher*
Hinderliter, Richard Glenn *electrical engineer*
Hinkle, Muriel Ruth Nelson *naval warfare analysis company executive*
Hino, Taro *engineering educator*
Hipona, Cesar Dumpit *civil engineer*
Hirai, Michihiro *computer engineer, translator, educator*
Hirai, Toshiro *battery research engineer*
Hiramatsu, Mitsuo *engineering researcher*
Hirata, Tomio *engineering educator*
Hiroyuki, Hashimoto *engineering educator*
Hitzios, Georgios *chemical engineer*
Hiyama, Keiichiro *biochemical engineer, researcher*
Hlavička, Jan *electrical engineering educator*
Ho, Chu Eu *civil engineer*
Ho, Hwa-Shan *engineering executive, civil engineer, consultant, drilling engineer*
Ho, KC *electrical engineering educator*
Ho, Keang-Po *information engineering educator*
Ho, Kwok Chiang *transportation engineer*
Ho, Sa Van *chemical engineer, researcher*
Ho, Shiu Fai *marine design consultant*
Hoang, Loc Bao *electrical engineer*
Hockeimer, Henry Eric *business executive*
Hodge, Bobby Lynn *mechanical engineer, manufacturing executive*
Hoelderich, Wolfgang Friedrich *chemistry engineering educator*
Hoeptner, Norbert *engineering educator*
Hoffer, Roy Daniel *forensic electrical engineer, fire investigator*
Hoffmann-Petersen, Erik *civil engineer*
Hogan, Stephen John *electrical engineer*
Holcombe, Homer Wayne *nuclear quality assurance professional*
Holl, Helmut J. *engineering educator*
Holland, Phillip Kent *aerospace engineer*
Hollaway, Leonard Charles *engineering educator*
Holló, János *chemical engineer, educator, research director*
Hollowell, Monte J. *engineer, operations research analyst*
Holmes, Paul Arthur *polymer scientist, researcher*
Holmgren Hägg, Anna Maria *chemical engineer*
Holonyak, Nick, Jr. *electrical engineering educator*
Holst-Jensen, Ole *engineer, consultant*
Holtrop, Jan Fokke *petroleum engineering educator, consultant*
Holz, Dietmar Alexander *materials engineer, process development engineer*
Honda, Keizoh *research engineering executive*
Honda, Takuya *engineering educator*
Hong, Guang *mechanical engineer, educator*
Hong, Guowei *computer engineer*
Hong, Jae-Dong *engineering educator*
Hong, Jin-Long *engineering educator*

Hong, Keum-Shik engineer educator
Hong, Zuu-Chang engineering educator
Hongo, Kohei engineering educator
Honour, Osuwe drilling engineer
Hootman, Harry Edward retired nuclear engineer, consultant
Hopfe, Harold Herbert retired chemical engineer
Hopkins, Christopher Edward engineer
Hopkins, Herbert Ziegler (Zeke) retired aerospace engineering company executive
Hopkins, Robert Arthur retired industrial engineer
Hopkinson, Brian Eric engineering executive, consultant
Horáček, Jaromír mechanical engineer, researcher, educator
Horii, Kiyoshi mechanical engineer, educator
Horn, Petr Jan electrical engineer
Hornik, Joseph William civil engineer
Horta, José Carlos de Oliveira Sousa civil engineering consultant
Horvath, Arpad engineering educator
Horváth, Csaba chemical engineering educator, researcher
Hoschl, Cyril mechanical engineer, educator
Hoshide, Toshihiko mechanical engineering educator
Hoskins, William Andrew aerospace engineer
Hotta, Masashi electronics engineer and educator
Hou, Ho-Shong transportation engineer
Hou, Tung-Hsu industrial engineering educator, researcher
Hough, Robert Alan civil engineer
Houpert, Luc Gabriel engineer, educator
Hovdestad, Wayne Roy petroleum engineer
Howell, Alvin Harold engineer, company executive, educator
Hozayen, Hozayen A. engineering educator, consultant, researcher
Hsi, Morris Yu mechanical engineer, applied researcher
Hsiao, Ming-Yuan nuclear engineer, researcher
Hsieh, Shou-Shing mechanical engineering educator, researcher
Hsing, Yue Cheng aeronautical engineer
Hsu, Cheng decision sciences and engineering systems educator
Hsu, Frank Fu-Chang computer engineer
Hsu, Ming-Yu engineering educator
Hsu, Pao-Chiu water treatment engineer, educator
Hu, Bin mechanical engineering educator
Hu, Haiyan applied mechanics educator, consultant
Hu, Jin-Lin electrical engineering educator
Hu, Xiandeng engineering educator
Huang, Ben (Haibin) chemical engineer, researcher
Huang, Chih Yao electronics engineer
Huang, Chung lin engineering educator
Huang, Dading semiconductor materials administrator, researcher
Huang, Farong engineer, researcher, educator
Huang, Han-Pang electrical engineer, educator, researcher
Huang, Hsiang-Hsi industrial engineering educator
Huang, Hsien-Lu electrical engineer
Huang, Huan-Tsung electrical engineer, educator
Huang, Hung-chia microwave photonics researcher, educator
Huang, Jiadong electronic engineer
Huang, Joseph Chen-Huan civil engineer
Huang, Shouhua electronics engineer
Huang, Tiao-yuan engineering executive
Huang, Ting-Chia chemical engineering educator, researcher
Huang, Wei engineer, researcher
Huang, Yaqi biomedical and mechanical engineer, researcher
Huang, Yen Ti civil engineer
Huang, Yi-Cheng mechanical engineer, educator
Huang, Yung-Hui chemical engineer
Hubbard, Walter Bryan chemical engineer, consultant
Huber, John Charles fiberoptic executive
Hubert, John F. metallurgical materials and processes engineer
Huckins, Harold Aaron chemical engineer
Hudak, Paul Alexander retired engineer
Hudson, William John chartered electrical engineering consultant
Huffman, David George electrical engineer
Hugel, Rene Paul engineering educator
Huguenin, Denis research engineer
Huh, Hoon engineering educator
Hui, Ping electrical engineering educator
Hultquist, Paul Fredrick electrical engineer, educator
Humphreys, David Anderson research engineer
Hung, Hon Cheung George engineering executive
Hung, Tzu-Chen engineering educator
Hungerford, John Charles mechanical engineer
Hunsucker, Robert Dudley physicist, electrical engineer, educator, researcher
Hunter, Larry Lee electrical engineer
Hunter, William Schmidt engineering executive, environmental engineer
Hupfer, Robert engineering company executive
Husain, Rahat electrical engineer, researcher
Hussain, Kazi Fareeduddin engineering executive
Hussein, Adel Mokhtar nuclear engineer
Hutchison, James Arthur, Jr. architectural and engineering company executive
Hwang, Chang-Chou engineering educator
Hwang, Chi-Hung mechanical engineering researcher
Hwang, Ki-Young mechanical engineer, researcher
Hwang, Sung-Ho mechanical engineer
Hwang, Tae-Wook engineering researcher
Hwang, Weng-Sing materials engineer
Hyde, Thomas Horace mechanical engineering educator
Hylander, Walter Raymond, Jr. retired civil engineer
Hyyppa, Kalevi electrical engineering educator
Iannone, Eugenio communications engineer, researcher
Iaquinto, Joseph Francis electrical engineer
Ibrahim, Kimball Yusuf aerospace engineer
Ichino, Manabu engineering educator, college dean
Idrees, Muhammad engineering designer, consultant
Iemma, Umberto engineering educator
Ieremia, Mircea Constantin engineering educator
Iftar, Altug electrical engineering educator, researcher
Iglseder, Heinrich Rudolf space engineer, researcher
Ihm, Son-Ki chemical engineering educator, researcher
Ii, Jack Morito aerospace engineer
Iino, Hiroshi engineering educator
Ikawa, Hiroyuki ceramic science and engineering educator
Ikeda, Hiroaki retired engineering educator
Ikeda, Shuji semiconductor engineer
Ikegawa, Masato engineering researcher
Ikossi-Anastasiou, Kiki electrical and computer engineer
Ikuta, Nobuaki electrical engineering educator
Imado, Fumiaki mechanical, systems engineering educator
Imado, Keiji tribologist, researcher
Imam, Muhammad Hasan engineer educator
Imre, László energy engineering educator, designer, researcher
Inczédy, Janos Joseph retired chemical engineering educator
Inyang, Hilary Inyang geo-environmental engineer, researcher
Ionita, Maria Ileana chemical engineer, researcher
Iordache, Mihai engineering educator
Ippen, Erich Peter electrical engineering educator
Irandoust, Said chemical reaction engineering educator, scientist
Irarrazaval, Ismael Mendez engineering executive
Iri, Masao mathematical engineering educator
Irmay, Shragga engineering educator, lexicographer
Irudayaraj, Joseph agricultural engineering educator
Irwin, Richard Dennis electrical engineering educator
Isayev, Avraam Isayevich polymer engineer, educator
Isdale, Charles Edwin chemical engineer
Ishaq, Mousa Hanna materials engineer
Ishibashi, Eiichi engineering researcher and educator
Ishida, Masaru chemical engineer, educator
Ishigohka, Takeshi engineering educator
Ishiguro, Ryoji mechanical engineer
Ishikawa, Motoo electrical engineer, educator
Ishikawa, Nobutaka civil engineer, educator
Ishiwara, Hiroshi electronics engineer
Ishiwatari, Hiromasa biomedical electronics educator, researcher
Islam, Rafiqul chemical engineer, educator
Ismael, Nabil Fathy civil engineer, educator, consultant, researcher
Ismail, Kamal Abdel Radi mechanical engineering educator, consultant
Itaketo, Umana Thompson systems and control engineer
Ito, Koichi engineering educator, antenna researcher
Ito, Tomohiro mechanical engineer
Iuga, Alexandru Iuliu engineering educator
Ivanova, Ginka Georgieva chemical engineer
Ivanova, Pavlina Krasteva geophysical engineer
Ivanova, Tania Nenova electrical engineer
Iwahashi, Masahiro engineering educator
Iwai, Zenta engineering educator
Iwamoto, Souichi engineering educator, scientific researcher
Iwuh, Paschal Chinaenye petroleum and chemical engineer, researcher
Iyer, Ram manufacturing engineer
Izuchukwu, John Ifeanyichukwu industrial and mechanical engineer
Izzuddin, Bassam Afif computing in civil engineering, educator
Jachowicz, Ryszard Slawomir electronics educator, researcher
Jacobs, Harold Robert mechanical engineering educator, practitioner
Jacobson, Albert Herman, Jr. industrial and systems engineer, educator
Jacoby, Neil Herman, Jr. astronautic engineer, consultant
Jacqmin, Robert P. nuclear engineer
Jaeger, David Leonard chemical engineer
Jaeggi, Martin Niklaus Richard river engineer
Jaegle, Andre retired engineer
Jaffe, William J(ulian) industrial engineer, educator
Jaffrin, Michel Yves biomedical engineer, educator, consultant
Jäger, Jürgen research engineer
Jahkola, Kaarlo Antero retired engineering educator
Jaimoukha, Imad Mahmoud electrical and electronic engineering educator
Jain, Dil Sukh engineering executive
Jain, L. C. engineering executive
Jain, Prem Chand mechanical engineer
Jain, Ratan Lal business executive, consultant engineer
Jain, Sudhir Kumar civil engineering educator
Jakobson, Björn Anders research and development engineer
Jaksa, Mark Brian civil engineering educator, researcher
Jalili, Nader mechanical engineer, educator
Jaluria, Yogesh mechanical engineering educator
Jamalipour, Abbas electrical engineer, educator
Jamil, Tariq computer engineer, educator
Jan, Jiri electronics engineer, educator
Jandaghi Alaee, Majid civil engineer
Jandrell, Ian Robert electrical engineer, educator
Jang, Do-Hyun engineering educator
Jang, Hyun Myung materials engineering and science educator
Jangid, Radhey Shyam engineering educator
Janković, Slobodan aerodynamics educator, researcher
Jankowski, Robert civil engineering educator
Jano, Patrice Jose optical engineer
Jansson, Ake Roland engineer
Janushevskis, Alexander mechanical engineer, research administrator
Jaouen, Herve Jean electrical engineer
Jaramillo, Ricardo Mejia mechanical engineer
Jarbath, Hebert Michel civil engineer, consultant
Jàrmai, Karoly engineering educator
Jarnagan, Harry William, Jr. project control manager
Jasinski, Piotr electronic engineer, researcher
Jategaonkar, Ravindra Vinayak aeronautical engineer
Jedlicka, Miroslav electronic engineer, researcher
Jędrzejewski, Jerzy Witold mechanical engineering educator, consultant
Jeffredo, John Victor aerospace engineer, manufacturing company executive, inventor
Jeffreys, Elystan Geoffrey geological engineer, petroleum consultant and appraiser
Jelaska, Damir Tihomir mechanical engineering educator
Jelinek, Frantisek radio engineering and electronics researcher
Jellows, Tracy Patrick software engineer
Jeng, Dong-Sheng engineering educator
Jeng, Mu-Der electrical engineering educator
Jeng, Yann-Chyn quality engineer
Jenkins, William McLaren engineering educator, civil engineer, researcher
Jensen, Karsten Høgh engineering educator, researcher
Jeong, Jae-Jun nuclear engineer, researcher
Jeong, Ji Hwan mechanical engineering educator
Jeyaseelan, Sithamparapillai instrumentation/control systems engineer
Jezernik, Karel electrical engineer, educator
Jezowski, Jacek Maria chemical engineering educator
Ji, Minggang mechanical engineering educator
Ji, Yusheng computer engineering educator
Jia, Xingdong electrical engineering educator, researcher
Jia, Yumin engineer
Jiang, Chongjun chemical engineer
Jiang, Jia-Qian environmental engineer, chemist
Jiang, Lei mechanical engineer, researcher, consultant
Jiang, Zhao-Hui mechanical engineering educator, scientist
Jie-Qing, Wu engineering educator, consultant
Jimenez-Varona, Jose research engineer
Jin, Jian-Xun metallurgical and electrical engineer, researcher
Jin, Tae Eun mechanical engineer
Jin, Xuecheng engineering researcher
Jin, Yong chemical engineering educator
Jo, Won Ho engineeing educator
Johannessen, Erling Aarsand development engineer
Johansson, Alf Gunnar civil engineer, educator
Johnnerfelt, Bengt Åke electrical engineer, administrator
Johns, Allan Thomas electrical engineering educator
Johnson, Brian Keith electrical engineering educator
Johnson, Daniel Leon aeronautical engineer
Johnson, David Blackwell safety engineer
Johnson, Matthew Hill structural engineer
Johnson, Rufus Norman, Jr. electrical engineer
Johnson, Stewart Willard civil engineer
Johnston, John Thomas engineering executive
Jokl, Miloslav Vladimir mechanical engineer
Jolly, Richard Stephen engineering executive
Jones, Edward Allen engineer
Jones, John Clifford engineering educator
Jones, John T. ceramics engineer, writer
Jones, Mark Allen structural engineer
Jones, Norman mechanical engineer, educator
Jones, Roger Clyde retired electrical engineering educator
Jones, Roger H. mechanical engineer, music educator
Jones, Trevor Owen company executive
Jones, William Kinzy materials engineering educator
Jonna, Saindranath civil engineer
Joos, Felipe Miguel mechanical engineer, researcher
Jorgensen, Robert William product engineer
Joseph, William Nathaniel mechanical engineer, marine engineer
Joshi, Hemchandra Vinayak electronic engineer, consultant
Joshi, Jyeshtharaj Bhalchandra chemical engineering educator, researcher
Joshipura, Bhushit Pradyumna engineering executive
Josifovski, Vanja engineering educator
Joslyn, H. David turbomachinery research specialist, technology systems manager, consultant
Josyula, Eswar aerospace engineer
Jouvin, Jose-Vernaza paper products engineer
Jóźwiak, Lech technology educator
Juang, Miin-Horng electrical engineer, educator, researcher
Judycki, Jozef civil engineer, educator
Jue, Tswen-Chyuan vehicle engineering educator
Juhasz, George engineer
Juman, Mariam Ahmed electrical engineer
Jun, Byung Hwan computer engineering and pattern recognition educator
Jung, Jae Hak engineering educator, consultant
Jung, Peter electrical engineering researcher, educator
Juricic, Davor mechanical engineering educator
Jurkiewicz, Stanislas chemical engineer
Juston-Coumat, Denis Eugene engineering executive, educator
Juteau, Michel Hilaire communications engineer
Kabacik, Pawel research electrical engineer
Kaberger, Tomas Arne engineering researcher
Kaburlasos, Vassilis George electrical engineer, researcher
Kaczmarczyk, Andrzej Dariusz information technology educator
Kaczmarek, Zdzislaw environmental engineer, scientist, educator
Kagan, Val Alexander engineer, researcher, educator
Kagawa, Koji naval architectural engineering educator
Kahill, Armand George mechanical engineer
Kahre, Ragnar E. engineering executive
Kajander, Richard Emil chemical engineer
Kalaidjian, Berj Boghos civil engineer
Kalaus, György chemical engineer, educator
Kalay, Gurhan project engineer, materials scientist
Kalinin, Victor Alexandrovich engineering educator, researcher
Kalitkar, Kishan Rao engineering educator
Kaliyamurthy, Krishnaswamy engineer, educator, researcher, consultant
Kalliokoski, Pentti Juhani engineering educator, dean
Kalliontzis, Constantine civil engineer, consultant
Kalwara, Joseph John engineer
Kalyanaraman, Shivkumar computer engineering research and educator
Kam, Moshe electrical and computer engineering educator
Kamabe, Hiroshi engineering educator
Kamada, Masaru engineering educator
Kamenetskii, Valentine Robertovich engineering educator, researcher
Kamiyama, Shinichi engineering educator
Kampik, Marian Paul engineering educator, scientist
Kanai, Hiroshi electrical engineering educator
Kanai, Kimio engineering educator
Kanatas, Athanasios George electrical engineer, researcher
Kanda, Yozo electronics educator
Kandil, Mahmoud Saber electrical power engineering educator
Kaneff, Stephen electrical engineer, researcher, consultant, educator
Kanegaonkar, Hari Bhagwan structural engineer
Kaneko, Hisashi engineering executive
Kanematsu, Hideyuki materials science and engineering researcher
Kang, Hie Chan mechanical engineering educator
Kang, Leen-Seok engineering educator
Kang, Seong-Woo acoustical engineer
Kang, Won Ho engineering educator, researcher
Kanniah, Jagannathan engineering educator
Kao, Charles Kuen electrical engineer, educator
Kao, Tsair biomedical engineering educator, researcher
Kapadia, Yezad Sam retired engineering executive, consultant
Kappatos, Konstantinos Nicholas engineering executive
Kar, Ramesh Chandra mechanical engineer, educator
Kara, Aysun chemical engineer
Karakuzu, Ramazan mechanical engineer, educator
Karam, Anwar G. construction engineer
Karam, Vania Jose engineer, researcher, educator
Karasawa, Shinji electrical engineer, educator
Karayan, Harry J. electrical engineer
Kara-Zaitri, Chakib engineering educator
Karbowski, Ferdinand Ronald, Jr. engineer
Karczewski, Jan Antoni engineering educator, researcher
Karlos, George Efthimios chemical engineer, consultant
Karpiscak, John, III engineer, army officer
Karpisek, Ladislav Stephan engineering company executive, researcher
Karthikeyan, Janakiram engineering educator
Kasai, Naoki electronics engineer
Kasano, Hideaki mechanical engineering educator
Kasper, Erich Alex electrical engineering educator
Kasprowski, Zygmunt Jan engineering executive, consultant
Kasprzak, Wacław Antoni engineering educator, researcher
Katayama, Masaaki information electronics educator, researcher
Kato, Haruo electronics engineer, researcher
Kato, Kiyoshi civil engineering educator, researcher
Kauffeld, Michael engineer, researcher
Kawabata, Keishi engineering educator
Kawai, Yasuhito engineering educator
Kawakami, Shogo civil engineering educator
Kawamoto, Pauline Naomi information engineering educator
Kawamura, Hiroyuki structural engineer, educator
Kawanishi, Hidenori opto-electronics researcher
Kayaalp, N(esibe) Mehlika public health engineer
Kazandjiev, Robert Flavy mechanical engineer, mathematician, researcher
Kazi, Karoly microwave engineer
Kazumasa, Takei manufacturing and quality management engineer, consultant
Kažys, Rymantas Jonas electronics educator
Ke, Chih-Ming engineer, semiconductor company official
Kearns, Robert William manufacturing engineer, inventor
Keaton, Lawrence Cluer safety engineer, consultant
Keerthipala, Wickramaarachchige Weebadda Liyanage electrical engineering educator
Keh, Huan Jang chemical engineering educator, researcher
Keicher, William Eugene electrical engineer
Keil, Frerich Johannes chemical engineer
Kelly, John Joseph chemical engineer, educator
Kemble, James Richard engineering services executive, retired
Kemelhor, Robert E(lias) mechanical engineer
Ke Ming, Wang retired engineer, researcher
Kenji, Ueno electrical engineer
Kenkel, Jerome Bernard civil engineer
Kennedy, Michael Peter engineering educator, researcher
Kent, Sergei electrical engineer
Kerckaert, Pierre engineering executive
Kerh, Tienfuan civil engineer, educator
Kermani, Abdy structural engineering educator
Kerr, James Wilson engineer
Kerr, Walter Belnap retired missile instrumentation engineer, English language researcher, consultant
Kerr-Jarrett, Mark Newton mechanical engineer
Kesavadas, Thenkurussi mechanical engineering educator, researcher
Ketterling, Hans-Peter Alfred electrical engineer
Khairoun, Ibrahim materials engineer
Khalaf, Fouad Mohammed civil engineer, educator
Khaleeli, Ali Mohammad retired consulting engineer
Khalessi, Mohammad R. structural engineer, researcher
Khalid, Muhammad Wasim engineering executive
Khalifa, Yaser engineering educator
Khalil, Hussein Mohammad engineering company executive, electrical engineer
Khan, Ahmed Mukhtar Mohamed geotechnical engineer
Khan, Ali Yar mechanical and industrial engineer
Khan, Eakalak civil engineering educator
Khan, Ishtiaq Rasool electrical engineer, researcher
Khanani, Naeem Ilyas engineering executive
Khare, Mukesh Kumar environmental engineer, educator
Kharin, Vladimir Michaylovich engineering educator
Khasnabish, Bhumip telecommunications engineering executive, information scientist, educator
Khetagurov, Valery Nickolaevich technology educator
Khoo, Boo Cheong engineering educator
Khozeimeh, Issa electrical engineer
Kiatkamjornwong, Suda engineering educator, polymer engineer, consultant
Kice, John Edward engineering executive
Kielbasa, Wladyslaw engineering consultant
Kielmeyer, William Henry ceramic engineer, researcher
Kikuchi, Kiyokatsu (Kyohsha Kikuchi) electrical engineering educator
Kikuchi, Shigeaki architectural engineering educator
Kilby, Jack St. Clair electrical engineer
Kilpelä, Ari Juhani electrical engineering researcher
Kim, Chang-Jin mechanical engineer
Kim, Hee Chan biomedical engineering educator
Kim, Hyeonjae engineering educator
Kim, Hyo-Sung engineering educator
Kim, Jeong Du mechanical engineer, educator
Kim, Jin Young telecommunications engineer
Kim, Jin-Keun engineering educator
Kim, Jiyoung materials engineering educator
Kim, Ki Young engineering educator
Kim, Min-Huei electrical engineer, educator
Kim, Sang-Wook industrial and engineering chemistry educator
Kim, Seock-sam engineering educator
Kim, Yongmin electrical engineering educator
Kim, Yong-woo mechanical engineering educator
Kim, Young Ho electrical engineer
Kim, Young Kil aerospace engineer
Kim, Yung Kwon electrical engineer, educator
Kimbell, Marion Joel retired engineer
Kimura, Ichiro engineering educator
King, Robert Augustin engineering executive
King-Ning, Tu materials science and engineering educator
Kinloch, Anthony James mechanical engineering educator, researcher
Kinniment, David John electrical engineer, educator
Kinno, Hitoshi mechanical engineer, educator
Kinnunen, Sven retired structural engineering educator
Kinsella, Brian F. mechanical engineer, consultant
Kint, Arne Tonis industrial engineer, mechanical engineer
Kirchner, James William retired electrical engineer

PROFESSIONAL INDEX 2515 ENGINEERING

Mota, Oscar David Santos engineering educator, researcher
Motchalov, Igor Valentinovich optical engineer, educator
Motter, Gregg A. electrical engineer, consultant
Mourão, Paulo de Salles retired civil engineer, programmer
Moura-Relvas, Joaquim M.M.A. electrical engineer, educator
Moussa, Nabil Mohamed Ahmed engineering educator, mathematician
Moustafa, Mahmoud Mohamed civil engineer, researcher
Moustakis, Vassilis S. engineering educator
Mow, Van C. engineering educator, researcher
Mow, Wai Ho communications engineer, lecturer, researcher
Moynihan, Gary Peter industrial engineering educator
Mridha, Shahjahan materials engineering educator
Mroziewicz, Bohdan electrical engineer, researcher
Mudag, Salic Cadar civil engineer
Muehlemann, Rolf electrical engineer
Mueller, Joaquin Pablo agricultural engineer, researcher
Mueller, Lisa Maria chemical engineer
Muffoletto, Barry Charles engineering executive
Mugarra, Pedro M. engineering professional
Muhlenbruch, Carl W. civil engineer
Mujumdar, Arun S. chemical engineering educator, consultant
Mujumdar, Arun Sadashiv chemical engineering educator
Mujumdar, Vikas Sitaram engineering and construction management consultant
Mukherjee, Amalendu mechanical engineering educator
Mukherjee, Shib Prasad engineering executive
Mukhopadhyay, Rabindra engineering executive, researcher
Mukhopadhyay, Siddhartha electrical engineering educator, researcher
Mukhopadhyay, Sumit chemical engineering researcher
Mulcahy, Noel William consultant
Mulchandani, Kishanchand Balchand mechanical and industrial engineering educator, researcher
Mulford, Richard Albert mechanical engineer
Mulholland, Bernard James engineer
Muljadi, Paulus Benjamin electrical engineer, webmaster
Muller, Daniel Jean aeronautical engineer, experimental test pilot
Müller, Wolfgang Helmut engineering educator, researcher
Mulvihill, Peter James fire protection engineer
Munger, Elmer Lewis civil engineer, educator
Munoz, Mario Alejandro civil engineer, retired consultant
Munshi, Prabhat engineering educator, researcher
Munson, Janis Elizabeth Tremblay engineering company executive
Muntasser, Mohamed Abdulla engineering educator
Murakami, Masahide mechanical engineer
Murakami, Masato engineering educator, researcher
Murali Krishna, Srikanteswara Sharma mechanical engineering educator
Murayama, Tadashi automotive engineer, educator
Murgu, Alexandru N. engineering educator
Murkes, Jakob research engineer
Muromtsev, Juri Leonidovich engineering educator
Murphy, Thomas Michael civil engineer
Murray, Alan engineering executive
Murray-Smith, David James engineering educator
Murty, Hema S. aerospace engineer, researcher
Musalimov, Victor Michael mechanical engineer, researcher, educator
Muscato, Giovanni engineering educator
Musil, Vladislav electrical engineering educator
Muskett, David engineer, project management consultant
Muste, Marian civil engineer
Musuda, Wataru mechanical engineering educator
Muszyński, Robert engineering educator
Myrstad, Trond chemical engineer
Na, Man-Gyun nuclear engineering educator
Na, Suck-Joo mechanical engineer, educator
Nadarajah, Chithranjan mechanical engineer, consultant
Nafalski, Andrzej (Andrew Nafalski) electrical engineering educator, administrator
Nagalingam, Sev Verl mechanical engineer, consultant
Nagaraja, S.K. electrical engineer
Nagashima, Hideyo electronics educator
Nagata, Shoichi engineering educator, researcher
Nagatani, Takeshi aircraft engineer
Nagatsuma, Tadao electrical engineer, researcher
Nagisetty, Irena Aldona technical specialist
Naguib, Raouf Gorgui electrical engineering educator, researcher
Nagy, Endre László electrical engineer, researcher, educator
Nagy, Imre V. civil engineer, educator
Nagy, István engineering educator
Nahman, Norris Stanley electrical engineer
Naidoo, Pragalathan Dhanapalan engineering executive
Najafi, S. Iraj optical engineering executive
Najar, Jerzy engineering educator
Nakae, Hideo metallurgical engineering educator, researcher
Nakagawa, Tohru electronic company researcher
Nakai, Hiroshi civil engineering educator
Nakai, Sadao engineering educator
Nakamori, Seiichi electrical engineering educator
Nakamura, Kenichi engineering educator
Nakamura, Yasuaki electronics engineer, educator
Nakata, Yoshiki electrical engineering researcher
Nakra, Bahadur Chand mechanical engineering educator
Nam, Hyoung Gin electrical engineering educator
Nameda, Naoyoshi engineering educator
Namgung, Ihn engineer
Napau, Ioan mechanical engineer, mathematician, researcher
Narasimham, Prabhala Lakshmi civil engineering and management consultant
Narayanan, Ramaswamy biomedical engineer
Narda, Narinder Krishan agricultural engineering studies educator
Nash, Richard Eugene aerospace engineer
Nashawi, Ibrahim Sami engineering educator
Nassehi, Vahid chemical engineer, educator
Nasser, Mahmood Mohammed Khalil electrical engineer, researcher
Nasseri, Simin researcher
Nastac, Laurentiu materials and metallurgy engineer
Nasu, Kenichi engineering educator
Nasu, Shoichi electrical engineering educator
Nation, Earl Kelvin mechanical engineer
Navickas, John fluid dynamics engineer, researcher, consultant
Nawy, Edward George civil engineer, educator
Nayar, Chemmangot Velayudhan electrical engineering educator
Ndjountche, Tertulien engineer
Ndon, Udeme James civil engineering educator
Neale, Michael John engineering company executive
Neary, Vincent Sinclair engineering educator
Nedermark, Rikke mechanical engineer
Nedvěd, Rudolf retired building engineer, scientist
Negnevitsky, Michael electrical engineer
Negro, Paolo civil engineer
Neher, Leslie Irwin engineer, former air force officer
Nehmzow, Ulrich D.F. electrical engineer, educator
Neill, Robert D. engineering executive
Neirynck, Jacques Julien electrical engineering educator, writer
Nelson, Philip Arthur engineering educator
Nelson-Thorpe, Carlon Justine engineering and operations executive
Nemetz Mills, Patricia Louise engineer, educator
Nemoto, Shojiro engineering educator
Nepershin, Rostislav mechanical engineering educator, researcher
Neshyba, Victor Peter retired aerophysics engineer
Nesvijski, Edouard G. materials engineer, educator, researcher
Nethercot, David Arthur civil engineering educator, consultant
Neti, Sudhakar mechanical engineering educator
Neto, Luciano Martins engineering educator
Neto, Luiz Gonçalves electrical engineering educator, researcher
Netzer, Moshe Z electrical engineer
Netzer, Walther Alois Johann civil engineer, educator, consultant, researcher
Neuvo, Yrjö Aunus Olavi engineering educator
Neves, Joaquim Jose electrical engineer, educator
Nevill, Andrew John biomedical engineer
Neville, Adam Matthew civil engineer, consultant, arbitrator
Newby, John Robert metallurgical engineer
Newland, David Edward engineering educator
Neyin, Alexander Akumeme petroleum engineer, educator
Ng, Kim Chai electrical engineer
Ng, Tuck Wah engineering educator
Ngo, Nam Quoc electrical engineering educator
Nguyen, Dung Luong mechanical and aeronautical engineer, researcher
Nguyen, Han Van mechanical engineer
Nguyen, Uu Van lawyer, civil engineering consultant
Nickle, Dennis Edwin electronics engineer, church deacon
Nicolae, Paul metallurgical engineer
Nicolescu, Valeriu Norocel engineering educator, researcher
Nieh, T. G. materials scientist, researcher
Nightingale, Stephen James electronics engineer, consultant
Nikita, Konstantina S. electrical engineer, educator
Nikolskii, Iourii Gavrilov engineering educator
Nilsson, Gert E. biomedical engineer
Nimcevic, Dragan Ivan biochemical engineer
Nishimura, Akitoshi electronics engineer
Nishimura, Tatsuya materials engineer, investigator
Nishiyama, Hitoshi environmental engineer, consultant, researcher
Nissan, Moshe biomedical engineer and researcher
Niwa, Kiyoshi engineering educator
Nizamska, Marina Vladova nuclear engineer, consultant
Niznik, Carol Ann electrical engineer, educator, consultant
Noblitt, Nancy Anne aerospace engineer
Noda, Nao-Aki mechanical engineering educator, researcher
Nogata, Fumio engineering educator
Noguchi, Hiroshi structural engineering educator
Nogueira e Silva, Jose Afonso engineering executive
Nolan, Benjamin Burke retired civil engineer
Noll, Bernhard Friedrich food engineer, researcher
Nomoto, Shinichi telecommunications engineer
Nonaka, Taijiro structural engineering educator
Nordström, Olle mechanical engineer
Nosu, Kiyoshi communication science researcher
Novak, Darwin Albert, Jr. chemical engineer, consultant
Novak-Lyssand, Randi Ruth engineer, computer scientist
Novikov, Ilya engineering educator
Novokshchenov, Vladimir Ilich civil engineer
Novosad, Jan chemical engineer
Nowakowski, Tomasz Tadeusz technology educator
Nudurupati, Kishore Krishna engineering educator
Nugapitiya, Manoshantha Bandara civil and mining engineer, management consultant
Numbere, Daopu Thompson petroleum engineer, educator
Nunes, Raul civil engineer
Nunz, Gregory Joseph aerospace engineer, program manager, educator, entrepreneur
Nyfors, Ebbe Gustaf radio engineer, researcher
Nykänen, Timo Juhani engineering educator, researcher
Nykles, Oldrich retired engineering company administrator
Obaidat, Mohammed Taleb civil engineering educator
Obaya, Maria Cristina chemical engineer, researcher
Oberndorfer, Wolfgang Johannes engineering educator
Obrebski, Jan Bogdan civil engineer, educator
O'Callaghan, Donal Joseph engineering researcher
O'Connor, Clint Haynie electrical engineer
O'Connor, Kim Claire chemical engineering and biotechnology educator
O'Connor, Patrick Digby Taaffe engineer, consultant
Öfverholm, Stefan electrical engineer
Ogata, Katsuhiko engineering educator
Ogawa, Tohru electrical engineer, researcher
Ogawa, Toshio materials engineering educator
O'Geary, Dennis Traylor retired contracting/ engineering company executive
Ogiso, Ken engineering educator, researcher
Ogiwara, Hiroyasu electrical engineering educator
Oguzer, Taner Abdullah electrical and electronics engineer
Oh, Jongtaek telecommunications engineering researcher
Ohama, Yoshihiko architectural engineer, educator
O'Hare, Daniel John electrical engineer
Ohayon, Roger Jean aerospace engineering educator, scientific deputy
Ohira, Tatsuya research industrial engineer
Ohlsson, Niclas technical director
Ohmori, Hiromitsu electrical engineering educator
Ohnami, Masateru mechanical engineering educator
Ohsato, Hitoshi ceramic science educator
Ohsawa, Yasuharu engineering educator
Ohta, Isamu mechanical engineer
Ohta, Shozaburo engineering educator
Ohta, Tokio engineering educator, researcher
Ohtsuka, Toshiyuki engineering educator
Ohyama, Yoshishige mechanical engineer
Oi, Takao chemist, educator
Oida, Akira engineering educator
oim, Pill Soo electrical and automotive engineering educator
Ojha, Chandra Shekhar environmental engineer
Ojima, Toshio engineering educator
Okayama, Hideaki opto-electronic engineer, researcher
O'Kelly, Michael E. engineering educator
Okeya, Ephraim Nkem biomedical engineer
Olaño, Servillano San Buenaventura, Jr. chemical engineer, educator
Olariu, Ioan Vasile civil engineer, educator
Olaru, Radu electrical engineering educator
Oldfield, Frank Eugene retired aerospace engineering executive
Oldshue, James Y. chemical engineering consultant
O'Leary, Paul Alistair civil engineer
Oliva, Dominador Pagkalinawan engineering and technical educator
Olofsson, Kurt Stefan development engineer
Olsen, Flemming Ove mechanical engineer, educator
Oman, Henry retired electrical engineer, engineering executive
Omidvar, Bijan structural engineer, researcher
Omnes, Franck electrical engineering researcher
Onda, Kazuo engineering educator
O'Neill, Kevin plastic engineer, consultant
Onet, Traian I. civil engineering educator, researcher
Onukwuli, Okechukwu Dominic mechanical engineering educator, researcher
Öpik, Ilmar power engineering educator, thermal physicist
Opitz, Hans-Peter Manfred electrical engineer
Ördög, Adam mechanical engineer
O'Reilly, John James electronic engineer, educator
Ören, Ersin Emre materials engineer, physicist, researcher
Orgler, Yair E. engineer
Orhon, Mine civil engineer, educator, dams specialist
Ormezzano, Ugo mechanical engineering company executive
Orthwein, William Coe mechanical engineer
Ortiz-Conde, Adelmo Antonio electrical engineering educator, researcher
Orton, George Frederick aerospace engineer
Osborn, John Robert retired mechanical engineer
Osborn, Ralph J. retired electrical engineer
Oskouie, Ali Kiani chemical and environmental engineer
Ossikovski, Razvigor Bojidarov research and development engineer, physicist
Ostachowicz, Wiesław Mieczysław mechanical engineer, educator
Östberg, Gustaf metallurgical engineer, educator
Ostoja-Starzewski, Martin engineering educator
Ostrovsky, George Maximovitch engineering educator
Ota, Yorito electronics engineer, researcher
Otis, John James civil engineer
Otsterwald-Lenum, Carsten engineer
Otsuka, Kazuhiro engineering educator
Ottino, Julio Mario chemical engineering educator, scientist
Ouchi, Isuke engineering educator
Owczarek, Stefan engineering educator
Owuama, Chukwunonye Ozioma civil engineering educator, consultant
Oya, Takio engineering educator
Oyekanmi, Raffiu Adekunle maintenance engineer, consultant
Ozawa, Masaki nuclear chemical engineering scientist
Ozdilek, H. Goksel environmental engineer
Özgen, Mehmet Tankut electrical engineer, researcher
Özkaya, Erdogan engineer
Ozturk, Cengizhan biomedical engineer
Ozturk, Veli mechanical engineer
Paál, Zoltán chemical engineer, researcher
Paaswell, Robert Emil civil engineer, educator
Páca, Jan Václav bioengineering educator
Pace, George Ernest hospital engineer
Pacheco, Fernando Antonio Leal aquatic engineer
Pacheco, Marcos Tadeu engineering educator, researcher
Pacini, Glenn Allen electrical engineer
Pacoste, Costin Calmanovici civil engineer, educator
Padmanabhan, Mukund researcher company executive
Padmanabhan, Tattamangalam Ramachandran engineering executive
Padula-Pintos, Victor Horacio telecommunications engineer
Pagano, Nicholas Joseph materials engineer
Pagano, Patrick Joseph biomedical researcher
Pagendarm, Hans-Georg mechanical engineer
Pajalic, Oleg chemical engineer, consultant, researcher
Pakchung, Warren Gregory engineer consultant
Pal, Ranendra Nath engineering educator
Pal, Surendra communications engineer, electronics engineer, space technologist, educator, researcher
Palacio, Francisco Jose chemical engineer, researcher
Palacios-Pawlovsky, Alberto engineering educator
Palen, Peter Hasbrouck retired mechanical engineer, consultant
Pálfi, Tamás mechanical engineer
Palhoto, Glauco Bietrezatto electrical engineer
Paliwal, Shrikrishna Tarachand retired civil engineer, researcher
Palmason, Palmi Ragnar geotechnical engineer, consultant
Palmer, Andrew Clennel petroleum engineering educator, consultant
Palmiter, P. Russel mechanical engineer
Palotasi, Andras electrical engineer, researcher
Paloukis, Dimitrios chemical engineer
Pan, Don Xiao Dong engineering company executive, consultant
Pan, Feixia aeronautical engineeer
Pan, Huo-Hsi mechanical engineer, educator
Pan, Junzheng agricultural engineering educator
Pan, Lung Kwang educator
Panagiotou, George Nicolas mining engineering educator
Panchal, Chandrakant B. chemical engineer, researcher
Panda, Rajesh Kumar ceramics and materials engineer
Panda, Sarat Chandra chemical engineer
Pandit, Aniruddha Bhalchandra chemical engineering educator, consultant, researcher
Panigrahi, Bibhu Prasad engineering educator, researcher
Panner, Jeannie Harrigan retired electrical engineer
Pantelaras, Pantelis John chemical engineer
Panuszka, Ryszard acoustic engineer, educator
Panyasorn, Sawat mechanical engineer
Papadaki, Maria chemical engineer
Papadakis, Vagelis G. chemical engineer
Papadopoulos, Demetrios Panagiotou engineering educator
Papadopoulos, Evangelos engineering educator, consultant
Papadopoulos, George Aristides mechanics educator
Papadopoulos, Theoharis chemical engineer, consultant
Papageorgiou, Markos engineering educator
Papakostas, Achilleas telecommunications engineer, researcher
Papaspyrides, Constantine Dimitrios chemical engineering educator, consultant
Papathanasiou, Thanasis D. chemical engineer
Papoutsakis, Eleftherios Terry chemical engineering educator, consultant
Paracha, Muhammad Salim mechanical engineer
Parascos, Edward Themistocles engineering consultant
Paraskevas, Spyridon Michael chemical engineer
Parida, Basant Kumar aerospace engineer, researcher
Parienti, Raoul Saül engineering consulting company executive
Park, Byeong-Jeon engineering educator
Park, Daewon chemical engineering educator
Park, Hee Chan materials engineering educator
Park, HyunWook electrical engineer, educator
Park, Jong Chul engineering educator
Park, Joon Bu biomedical engineer, researcher, educator
Park, Kyihwan mechanical and electrical engineering educator
Park, Kyu Tae engineering educator
Park, Min-Soo engineer
Park, Seok-Kyun civil engineer, educator
Park, Song Hui system engineer, senior researcher
Park, Soo-Gil chemical engineer, educator
Park, Tae Joo engineering educator
Park, Warn-Gyu mechanical engineering educator
Park, Won-Hoon chemical engineer
Park, Young Taek industrial engineering educator
Park, Young-Moon electrical engineering educator
Parker, John Melvyn materials engineering educator
Parker, Michael Seth energy engineer
Parkvall, Stefan electrical engineer, researcher
Parman, Setyamartana engineering educator
Paromtchik, Igor Eugene computer engineer, researcher
Parrish, Norman Charles technical consultant, mechanical engineer
Parsley, George Michael James retired electrical engineering educator
Parsons, John David electrical engineering educator
Parsonson, Peter Sterling civil engineer, educator, consultant
Parvez, Saeed mechanical engineer
Pascall, Stephan Christian engineer, government official
Paschke, Fritz electronics engineer
Passerone, Alberto chemical engineer
Passlack, Matthias electrical engineer, researcher
Pastravanu, Octavian Cezar engineering educator
Pataki, Nándor engineer
Patel, Ketan research engineer
Patel, Madhu Purushottam engineering executive
Patel, Mrugank Maganbhai engineer, consultant
Patel, Mukund Ranchhodlal electrical engineer, researcher
Patwardhan, Vilas Shridhar chemical engineer, consultant
Paul, Binod Bihari engineering educator, researcher
Paulson, Raymond Arnold engineering executive
Paureau, Jean Julien mechanical engineer
Pavlov, Detchko chemical engineer
Pavlyuk, Yury aerospace engineer
Pawlus, Pawel Piotr mechanical engineering educator, researcher
Payatakes, Alkiviades Charidemos chemical engineering educator
Payens, Bernardus Theodorus electrical engineer, administrator
Pearce, Graham Lloyd petroleum engineer
Pearce, Joseph Huske industrial engineer
Pearcy, Mark John engineering educator
Peculea, Marius Sabin retired engineering executive, educator
Pedersen, Michael Stanley chemical engineer, researcher
Pedersen, Sven chemical engineer, researcher
Pedrero, José I. engineering educator, researcher
Peev, Georgi Angelov chemical engineering educator, researcher
Peklenik, Janez engineering educator
Peng, Liang-Chuan mechanical engineer
Penman, David William electrical engineer
Penner, Stanford Solomon engineering educator
Pennings, Engelbertus Caspar Maria engineering executive
Pennington, Theresa Sue engineer professional
Pereira, Carmo Joseph chemical engineer and researcher
Pereira, Michael engineering administrator
Pereira, Orlando José Barreiros Almeida civil engineer, educator
Perera, Dayantha Shreshta ceramic engineer
Perez, Reinaldo Joseph electrical engineer
Perez-Rios, Jose engineering educator
Perlman, Edwin Francis retired aeronautical engineer
Pernak, Juliusz industrial engineering and chemistry educator
Perry, John Grenville civil engineering educator, education director
Perry, Nelson Allen radiation safety engineer, radiological consultant
Perry, Robert Terrell, Jr. nuclear engineer, consultant
Perry, Stuart William electrical engineer, researcher
Pervez, Yaqub Raziq telecommunications engineer
Pescod, Mainwaring Bainbridge environmental engineering consultant
Peserik, James E. electrical, controls and computer engineer, consultant, forensics and safety engineer, fire cause and origin investigator
Pesquet-Popescu, Beatrice research engineer
Petermann, Jürgen chemical engineering educator
Petersen, Jill Renee Lekawa chemical engineer

Petersen, Ole Svenstrup *engineering educator, researcher*
Peterson, Robert Scott *electrical engineer*
Petersson, Carl Sture *scientist, electronics educator*
Petizon, Yves Pierre *civil engineer*
Petlyuk, Felix Boris *chemical engineer, researcher*
Petrasovits, Geza Laszlo *geotechnical engineering educator*
Petric, Nedjeljka *chemical engineering educator, researcher*
Petrou, Maria *researcher, educator*
Pettersson, Göran *aeronautical engineer*
Pettis, Francis Joseph, Jr. *electrical engineer*
Peyser, Michael John *chemical engineer*
Pfeffer, Robert *chemical engineer, academic administrator, educator*
Pfeifer, Howard Melford *mechanical engineer*
Phadke, Uday *mechanical and electrical engineer*
Pham, Duc Chinh *mechanical engineering*
Pham, Hoang *engineering educator, researcher*
Pham, Kinh Dinh *electrical engineer, educator, administrator*
Phan, Binh Cong *electrical engineer*
Phang, Jacob C.H. *engineering educator*
Phillip, Clyde Herman *electrical and electronic engineer educator*
Phillipps, Ian Hugh *retired civil engineer*
Phillips, Oliverio Michelsen *retired chemical engineer*
Phulé, Pradeep Prabhakar *engineering educator*
Piana, Zenório *agricultural engineer*
Piccoli, Humberto Camargo *engineering educator, researcher*
Pichler, Peter Johann *electrical engineer, researcher*
Pickering, Kim Louise *materials science, engineering educator*
Pierce, Francis Casimir *civil engineer*
Pieterse, Jan Karel *process engineer*
Pietkiewicz, Andrzej *electrical engineer*
Pietrobon, Steven Silvio *electronic engineer, researcher*
Piganiol, Pierre Guy Albert *science and development policies consultant*
Pilarczyk, Krystian Walenty *engineering company executive, consultant*
Pimentel-Gomes, Frederico *retired engineering educator, editor*
Pinho, Rui Antonio *engineering executive*
Pinkerton, Robert Bruce *mechanical engineer*
Pipal, Anil Kumar *electronics engineer*
Piper, Lloyd Llewellyn, II *engineer, government and service industry executive*
Piper, Samuel O'Dell *engineer*
Pirner, Miroš *civil engineer, researcher*
Pischinger, Franz Felix *engineer, researcher*
Pissakas, Sotiris *civil engineer*
Plaćković, Ratko *engineer*
Plate, Erich J. *civil engineering educator*
Platin, Bulent Emre *mechanical engineering educator*
Plazl, Igor *chemical engineering educator*
Plitt, Enrique Javier *electronic engineer, military officer*
Plough, Charles Tobias, Jr. *retired electronics engineering executive*
Plougonven, Christian Herve *semiconductor physics engineer*
Plumidakis, Nick Konstantinos *electronic engineer*
Podcameni, Abelardo *engineering educator, researcher*
Podporkin, Georgij Viktorovich *engineering executive, educator*
Polaert, Rémy Henri *electrical engineer, researcher*
Polites, Michael Edward *aerospace engineer*
Polkinghorne, Martyn Neal *control engineer, researcher*
Poll, Ruediger Michael Leander *biomedical engineer, educator*
Polley, William Alphonse *retired power systems engineer*
Polo, Richard Joseph *engineering executive*
Poloujadoff, Michel Eugene *electrical engineering educator*
Polychronakis, Stavros Alexander *chemical and environmental engineer*
Pomerene, James Herbert *retired computer engineer*
Pomeroy, Stephen John *electrical engineer*
Ponce, Victor Miguel *civil engineering educator*
Ponnambalam, Sivalinga Govindarajan *engineering educator, researcher*
Ponter, Alan Robert Sage *civil engineering educator, consultant*
Pook, Leslie Philip *mechanical engineering researcher*
Popescu, Mihail Ilie *engineer, researcher, educator*
Popov, Eugene Vladimirovich *mechanical engineer*
Popov, Kantcho Georgiev *applied mechanics educator*
Popov, Victor *engineering educator*
Porev, Volodymyr Andriyovich *structural engineer, educator*
Porteanu, Mircea Julian *electrical engineering educator, consultant*
Portela, Antonio Gouvea *retired mechanical engineer, researcher*
Portman, Vladimir *mechanical engineer, educator, researcher, consultant*
Poskrobko, Jan *chemical engineer, researcher*
Posten, Clemens Heinrich *electrical engineer, researcher*
Posvar, Jiri *civil engineer*
Potthoff, Matthias *process engineer*
Potti, Periyamana Kesavan Govindan *mechanical engineer, researcher*
Poulsen, Lars Kaergaard *chemical engineer*
Pounds, Gerald Autry *aerospace engineer*
Pourbeik, Peyam *communication engineer*
Pourbeik, Pouyan *applications engineer*
Pousada, Jose Eduardo *mechanical engineer*
Powell, Alan *acoustical engineer, aeronautical engineer, mechanical engineer*
Powell, John William *mechanical engineer, consultant*
Pozzi, Angelo *engineering executive, civil engineer*
Prabhu, Sasindran Madhava *communications engineer*
Prada, Ricardo Bernardo *electrical engineering educator, consultant*
Pradeep, Sreelatha *electronics engineer, researcher*
Prakash, Kunja Adhavan *biomedical engineer*
Prakash, Swatantra *engineering executive*
Prasad, Kodati Satya *electronics and communication educator, researcher*
Prasad, Mohit Kishore *electrical engineer*
Prasad, Subhash Chandra *engineering educator, researcher, consultant*
Prassianakis, Ioannis Nicolaos *mechanics educator, researcher*
Pratap, Siddharth *electromechanics researcher, educator*
Pratt, David Bruce *industrial engineering educator*
Prengle, Herman William, Jr. *chemical engineer*
Presser, Cary *research engineer*
Pressnell, Raymond Thomas *electronics engineer*
Price, Edward Warren *aerospace engineer, educator*
Priest, Melville Stanton *retired consulting hydraulic engineer*
Prieto, Fabio Romao *engineer, product manager*
Primdahl, Soeren *chemical engineer*
Prochaska, Charles Roland *aerospace engineer*
Procházka, Ales Bedrich Vaclav *electrical engineer, researcher, educator*
Procházka, Jaroslav *civil engineering educator, researcher*
Prochazka, Petr Pavel *structural mechanics educator*
Prommersberger, Klaus Hubert *mechanical engineer, researcher*
Psaltikidou, Maria *hospital engineer*
Psarianos, Basil *highway engineering educator, consultant*
Ptaszkowski, Stanley Edward, Jr. *civil engineer, structural engineer*
Puang, Melvin Kah Wei *aerospace engineer*
Pudlik, Wieslaw Wladyslaw *mechanical engineer, educator*
Puente, Jose Garza *safety engineer*
Puga, André Teixeira *engineering educator*
Puglisi, Filadelfio *engineer*
Pulkkinen, Jyrki Tuomo Juhani *structural engineer*
Pulkkis, Per-Göran Bernhard *computer engineering educator*
Pultorak, Jerzy *electronics engineer, educator*
Purnell, Charles G. *engineering executive*
Pushpalal, Game Kankanamge Dinilprem *research engineer*
Puskarz, Stanley John *engineering executive*
Pust, Ladislav *mechanical engineer*
Puthenkudy, Rajan Varghese *engineering executive*
Pype, Patrick Filip *electrical engineer, engineering company official*
Pytko, Stanislaw Jerzy *mechanical engineering educator*
Qi, Xicheng *civil engineer, researcher*
Qian, Feng *electrical engineer*
Qian, Jiang *engineering educator, researcher*
Qian, Rengji *engineering educator*
Qian, Shinan *optical engineer, researcher, educator*
Qian, Zhengfang *research scientist*
Qin, Qing Hua *mechanical engineer*
Qiu, Guo Yu *agricultural engineer*
Qiu, Hua *mechanical engineering educator*
Qiu, Sigang *telecommunications engineer*
Qiu, Sunqing *engineering educator*
Qu, Peng *engineer, researcher*
Que, Wen Xiu *engineer, researcher*
Queen, Daniel *acoustical engineer, consultant*
Queneau, Paul Blaisdell *metallurgical engineer, educator*
Quénec'hdu, Yves *electrical engineering educator, researcher*
Quentrall-Thomas, Peter *civil engineer*
Qureshi, Jahangir *mechanical engineer*
Raamachandran, Jayaraman *engineering educator*
Rabinovich, Boris Isaakovich *aerospace engineer, researcher*
Rabosky, Joseph George *engineering consulting company executive*
Racicovschi, Virgil Dan *electrical engineering company official*
Raczynski, Stanislaw *engineering educator*
Radhakrishnan, V.R. *chemical engineer, educator*
Radhamohan, Samprati Kalanidhi *engineer*
Radin, Shulamith *materials engineer*
Radonjic, Ljiljana *educator, researcher*
Radu, Adrian *civil engineer, consultant*
Ragsdale, Ralph Hairston *electrical engineer*
Ragulin, Alexei Jurievich *engineer, physicist, computer specialist*
Rahman, Mohammed Siddiqur *environmental engineer, researcher*
Rahman, Muhammad Abdur *mechanical engineer*
Rainal, Attilio Joseph *electronics engineer, researcher*
Raj, Baldev *engineering executive*
Rajagopal, Rathinam *electrical and communications engineer, researcher*
Rajaram, Ramachandran *electrical engineer, consultant*
Rajarao, Anantharamiah *electrical engineer*
Rajasekaran, Sundaramoorthy *civil engineering educator*
Rajasingh, John Samuel *engineering consulting company executive*
Rajiv, E(davan) P(uthalath) *corrosion engineer, researcher*
Raju, Konduru Nagabhushan *mechanical engineer*
Rakha, Karim Ahmed *civil engineer, educator, researcher*
Ramakrishna, Seeram *engineering educator*
Ramakrishnan, Angarai Ganesan *electrical engineer, educator*
Ramakrishnan, Venkataswamy *civil engineer, educator*
Ramirez, Carlos Eduardo *electrical engineer*
Ramos, Severino Monteiro *engineering executive*
Ramos-Sobrados, Juan Ignacio *engineering educator, researcher*
Ramsdell, Richard Adoniram *marine engineer*
Randive, Rajul V. *process engineer*
Ranganayakulu, Segu Venkata *electronics educator, researcher*
Rani, K. Yamuna *chemical engineer*
Ranieri, Marco *hydraulic engineer*
Rankilor, Peter Richard *geotechnical engineer, educator*
Rankin, Sir Ian, Baronet *textile manufacturer, real estate and oil company executive*
Ransom, Gaylord Rick *structural engineer*
Ransom, Victor Harvey *engineering educator*
Ranta-Maunus, Alpo Kalevi *timber engineering scientist*
Rao, D. S. Prakash *civil engineer, educator*
Rao, Ganti Prasada *engineering educator*
Rao, Katragadda Sarveswara *chemical and metallurgical engineer*
Rao, Nagaraja Bangalore *engineering educator*
Raoof, Mohammed *engineering educator*
Rapier, Pascal Moran *chemical engineer, physicist*
Raptis, Nikos *civil engineer*
Ras, Juan *engineer*
Rasmussen, Gunnar *engineer*
Rasskazov, Alexander Olegovich *mechanics educator*
Rasul, Mohammad Golam *engineer, researcher*
Ratner, Buddy Dennis *bioengineer, educator*
Raudkivi, Arved Jaan *civil engineering educator*
Rautenbach, Ernst Robert *chemical engineering educator*
Ravichandran, Mahalingam *environmental engineer*
Raymont, Warwick Deane *chemical engineer, environmental engineer*
Raymundo, Paulo Mansur *petroleum engineer, consultant, explorer, researcher*
Reagan, Lawrence Paul, Jr. *systems engineer*
Rebhun, Menahem E. *environmental engineer, consultant*
Rech, Wolf-Henning *electrical engineering educator*
Recuero, Alfonso *civil engineer, consultant*
Reddy, Iska Gopal *electrical engineer, educator, administrator*
Rees, David Andrew Sessler *mechanical engineer, educator*
Refaat, Hossam-Eldin, Ahmed Aly *engineering educator, researcher*
Reible, Danny David *environmental chemical engineer, educator*
Reich, Stefan *plastics engineer*
Reichel, Martin Manfred *biomedical engineer, researcher, educator*
Reinsma, Harold Lawrence *design consultant, engineer*
Reisch, Frigyes *nuclear engineer*
Reiter, William Martin *chemical engineer*
Reiver, Julius *mechanical engineer*
Remniov, Anatoliy Michailovitch *engineering educator*
Ren, Shou Ju *engineering educator*
Replogle, Michael A. *civil engineer, urban planner, environmentalist*
Restrepo, Daniel Esteban *engineering executive, engineering educator*
Retik, Arkady *civil engineering educator, researcher, consultant*
Rettedal, Arne *engineering educator*
Rettich, Thomas *electrical engineer*
Rew, William Edmund *civil engineer*
Rey, Boleslaw Ludwik *mechanical engineer*
Reyes, Carlito Abad *chemical engineer*
Reza, Ali *mechanical engineer, consultant*
Reznik, Leonid Carlovich *engineering and information technology educator, researcher*
Rhee, Young *engineering educator*
Rhimes, Richard David *civil engineer*
Ricard, Jean-Henry Georges *electromechanical and electronics engineer*
Ricard, Thomas Armand *electrical engineer*
Rich, Thomas Paul *engineering educator, administrator*
Richardson, Everett Vern *hydraulic engineer, educator, administrator, consultant*
Richardson, Melvin Orde Wingate *engineering educator*
Richardson, Peter John *software engineering consultant*
Richey, Marvin E(lden) *electrical engineer, administrator*
Richon, Dominique Jean-Francois *thermodynamicist*
Ricks, N(orman) Richard, Jr. *engineering executive*
Ricny, Vaclav *TV technology engineer, educator*
Riden, Michael David *nuclear engineer*
Ridgway, John William Thomas *engineering executive*
Riekels, Lynda Marie *materials engineer*
Riganti di Serres, Mario *reliability engineer*
Rikmanis, Māris Ints *engineering educator*
Rikoski, Richard Anthony *engineering executive, electrical engineer*
Riley, Ronald Jim *industrial engineer, consultant*
Rindel, Jens Holger *acoustical engineer, educator, researcher*
Riposan, Iulian *engineering educator*
Riskowski, Gerald L. *engineering educator*
Ritchey, Harold W. *retired chemical engineer*
Ro, Yong Man *electrical educator*
Roberts, Dwight Loren *engineering consultant, writer*
Robinson, Michael R. *aeronautical engineer*
Robinson, William Henry *industrial engineer*
Rocchi, Marc Christian *engineering educator*
Roche, Bernard Pierre *nuclear engineer*
Rodgers, Billy Russell *chemical engineer, research scientist*
Rodin, Peter Rodionovich *manufacturing engineer, educator, researcher*
Rodrigues Filho, Arlindo *electrical engineer*
Rodriguez, Jose Ernesto *environmental manager*
Rodriguez, Juan Francisco *chemical engineering educator*
Rodriguez-Leon, Jose Angel *chemical engineer*
Roefs, Hans Frans Albert *electrical engineer*
Roenningen, Ottar Nyhus *retired electronics engineer*
Rogachko, Stanislav Ivanovich *marine laboratory administrator*
Rogers, Benjamin Talbot *consulting engineer, solar energy consultant*
Rogers, David Freeman *aerospace engineering educator*
Rogers, Eric William Evan *aeronautical research consultant*
Rogers, Mal David, Jr. *chemical engineer*
Rogo, Kathleen *safety engineer*
Roif, Henry Irving *flight test engineer, electronic engineer*
Rollins, Albert Williamson *civil engineer, consultant*
Rollitt, Ian William *project manager*
Romanov, Igor Grigor'evich *engineering researcher, consultant*
Romero, Joaquim José Barbosa *engineering educator*
Romero, Murilo Araujo *educator*
Romero-Rojas, Jairo Alberto *civil engineering educator*
Ronchi, Alfredo Michele *engineering educator*
Rong, Yiming *manufacturing engineering educator*
Ronold, Knut Olav *geotechnical engineer, researcher*
Rosanov, Nikolay Nikolaevich *optical engineering educator, researcher*
Rosca, Radu Gheorghe *mechanical engineer educator*
Rose, Livingstone Murray *chemical engineer*
Rosen, Joseph *technical researcher, lecturer*
Rosenbach, Leopold *engineer, consultant*
Ross, Bernard *engineering consultant, educator*
Ross, Carlisle Thomas *mechanical engineer, educator, consultant*
Rossit, Carlos Adolfo *civil engineer, educator*
Rotella, Frédéric *engineering educator*
Roth, J(ohn) Reece *electrical engineer, educator, researcher-inventor*
Rousseau, Pieter Gerhardus *engineering educator*
Rovera, Giovanni Daniele *electrical engineer*
Rovinsky, Lev Abram *food engineer*
Rovison, John Michael, Jr. *chemical engineer*
Rowe, Harrison Edward *electrical engineer*
Rowe, Peter Noel *chemical engineering educator*
Roy, Tuhin Kumar *engineering company executive*
Rozenblat, Anatoly Isaacovich *manufacturing engineer, inventor*
Rozhdestvenskiy, Mikhail Georgievich *aeronautical engineer*
Rozinaj, Gregor *telecommunications engineer, educator, researcher*
Rozzi, Jay Christopher *mechanical engineer*
Ruan, Mingchuan *civil engineer*
Rubenstein, Leonard *engineering company executive*
Rubeša, Domagoj *mechanical engineering educator*
Rubin, Arnold Jesse *aeronautical engineer*
Rudas, Imre József *engineering educator*
Rudnev, Boris Ivanovich *marine engineer, educator*
Rudobashta, Stanislav Pavlovich *engineering educator*
Rudy, Yoram *biomedical engineer, biophysicist, educator*
Ruelas-Gomez, Roberto *electrical engineer*
Ruffing, Bernhard *acoustics company executive*
Ruigrok, Jaap *electrical engineer, researcher*
Ruiz de la Herran, Jose Antonio *engineering executive*
Rumane, Abdul Razzak Abdul Rehman *electrical engineer, consultant*
Ruokolainen, Janne Tapio *engineer*
Russell, Andrew Tarbet *materials engineer*
Russell, David Emerson *mechanical engineer, consultant*
Russell, Eugene Robert, Sr. *engineering educator, administrator*
Russo, Gilberto *engineering educator*
Rust, William David, Jr. *retired structural engineer*
Rustan, Agne Peter *mining engineer*
Ruys, Andrew John *ceramics and biomaterials engineer*
Ryan, Frank Savage *metallurgical engineer*
Ryan, John James *electronics executive, design engineer*
Rychetsky, Steve *civil and environmental engineer, consultant*
Rydahl, Allan Kim *engineering executive*
Ryssel, Heiner *electrical engineering educator*
Saad, El Sayed Mostafa *electrical engineering educator, consultant*
Sacadura, Jean François *engineering educator*
Sackett, David Harrison *electrical engineer*
Sadek, Alber Alphonse *metallurgical engineer, educator*
Sado, Kimiteru *hydrologist, researcher*
Sadowski, Tomasz Stanisław *mechanical engineering educator*
Saeed, Hayder Mohamed *structural engineering researcher*
Saegusa, Takeo *engineering educator, university president*
Saemann, Ernst-Ulrich *civil engineer*
Saev, Nikolai Iliev *engineering executive, mechanical engineer*
Saevarsson, Torfi Dan *electrical power engineer*
Sag, Yesim *engineering educator, researcher*
Sagayama, Shigeki *engineering educator*
Sagir, Abuzer *agricultural engineer*
Saha, Ujjwal Kumar *mechanical engineering educator*
Sahi, Muhammad Javed *electrical engineer*
Sähn, Siegfried *engineering educator*
Sahoo, Susanta Kumar *engineering educator, researcher*
Sahota, Gurcharn Singh *mechanical engineer*
Saida, Toyoyasu *chemical and biochemical engineer*
Saini, Jogindar Singh *mechanical engineering educator*
Saito, Norihisa *engineering researcher*
Saito, Yoshihiro *systems engineer, researcher*
Saka, Mehmet Polat *structural engineer, educator*
Sakaida, Takashi *agricultural engineer, educator*
Sakamoto, Munenori *engineering educator, researcher, chemist*
Sakata, Hiroe *civil engineer*
Sakata, Kimio *aerospace engineer, researcher*
Sakuma, Kazuhiro *aerospace engineer*
Sakuta, Masaaki *engineering educator, consultant*
Salah, Sagid *retired nuclear engineer*
Salahuddin, Ahmad *civil engineer, educator*
Salaita, Shawqi Jubriel *mechanical engineer*
Salama, Mohamed Said *petroleum engineer*
Salamon, Miklos Dezso Gyorgy *mining engineer, educator*
Salas, Henry Joseph *environmental engineer*
Salatino, Piero *chemical engineering educator*
Salek, Sergio Correa *communications engineer*
Salib, Maher Badie *civil engineer*
Saliba, Ricardo Ellera *engineering company executive, consultant*
Salik, Fouad Yaqub *computer and civil engineer*
Salmatzidis, Ioannis Dimitrios *electrical engineer*
Salminen, Hannu Antero *engineer*
Salo, Ahti Antero *management scientist, systems analyst, educator*
Sanchez, Isaac Cornelius *chemical engineer, educator*
Sanchez-Carrillo, Jesus *engineering educator, researcher*
Sánchez Peña, Ricardo Salvador *researcher*
Sánchez Proal, Ernesto *engineering executive*
Sanders, David H. *civil engineering educator*
Sandler, Ben Zion *mechanical engineer*
Sandu, Constantine *process development engineer*
Sangiovanni-Vincente, Alberto *engineering educator*
Sangsuk-Iam, Suwanchai *engineering executive*
San Juan, Luis *geotechnical engineer*
Sanner, George Elwood *electrical engineer*
Santa, Karoly *electrical engineer, researcher*
Santic, Ante *electrical engineering educator*
Santurjian, Ohanes Hrant *hydraulic engineering educator*
Sanz, Molina Alfredo *engineering educator, researcher*
Saraiva, Pedro Manuel *chemical engineering educator*
Sarangapani, Jagannathan *intelligent systems and controls engineer, educator*
Sarapa, Milan *pipeline engineer*
Saravacos, George Demetrios *engineering educator, researcher*
Sarbadhikari, Suptendra Nath *biomedical engineer, physician*
Sardos, Panayiotis Antoniou *electrical engineer*
Sargent, Roger William Herbert *chemical engineer, retired*
Saridis, George Nicholas *electrical, computers and system engineering educator, robotics and automation researcher*
Sarisley, Edward F. *engineering technology educator, consultant*
Sarkar, Tapan Kumar *engineering educator, researcher*
Sarkomaa, Pertti Juhani *engineering educator*
Sarlos, Peter *agricultural engineer*
Sartor, Joachim Friedrich *hydraulic engineering and water resources educator*
Sasakura, Hiroshi *retired engineering educator*
Sase, Sadanori *agricultural engineer, researcher*

Stephens, Larry Dean *engineer*
Stephens, Robert David *environmental engineering executive*
Stepniewski, Alfred Daniel *mechanics educator*
Stetson, LaVerne Ellis *agricultural engineer*
Stevens, Geoffrey Wayne *chemical engineer, educator*
Stevens, Robert Edward *engineering company executive*
Stevenson, James Laraway *communications engineer, consulting*
Stever, Horton Guyford *aerospace scientist and engineer, educator, consultant*
Stewart, David Witherington *aerospace engineer*
Stewart, Warren Earl *chemical engineer, educator*
Stieglitz, Thomas *biomedical engineering, researcher*
Stiller, Christoph *electrical engineer, researcher*
Stilwell, David William *engineering company executive*
Stirrat, William Albert *electronics engineer*
Stoica, Petre *engineering educator*
Storb, John William *civil engineer, consultant*
Storey, Bobby Eugene, Jr. *electrical engineer, engineering consultant*
Strachan, William John *optical engineer*
Strada, Mauro *engineering educator*
Straja, Sorin Radu *chemical engineer, mathematician, computer programmer*
Strand, Erling Petter *computer and electronic engineering educator*
Strataridakis, Constantine John *aeronautical and mechanical engineer, consultant*
Stratton, John Alfred *mechanical engineer, educator*
Straub, Johannes *mechanical engineer, educator*
Straub, Laszlo *engineering executive*
Straughan, William Thomas *engineering educator*
Strevett, Keith Anthony *bioenvironmental engineer, educator*
Strobl, Gerhard Franz Xaver *engineer*
Stroe, Ion *mechanical engineering educator*
Stroud, John Franklin *engineering educator, scientist*
Stubberud, Allen Roger *electrical engineering educator*
Stubos, Athanassios *chemical engineer, research consultant*
Stuck, Roger Dean *electrical engineering educator*
Studer, James Edward *geological engineer*
Stumpers, Frans Louis *retired electrical engineering educator*
Stumpf, Helmut *mechanical engineering educator*
Stusek, Anton *mechanical engineer, researcher*
Stutzman, Warren Lee *electrical engineer, educator*
Stylianopoulos, Leonidas Constantinos *civil engineer, educator, consultant*
Styrylska, Teresa Bronislawa *mechanical engineer*
Su, Ching-Tzong *engineering educator, researcher, consultant*
Su, Chiung-Chieh Jack *mechanical engineer, researcher*
Su, Daizhong *mechanical engineering educator, researcher*
Su, Fong-Chin *bioengineer, educator*
Suarez-Arriaga, Mario-Cesar *geothermal reservoir engineer, educator*
Subbiah, Veeranan *engineering educator, researcher*
Subramaniam, B. *metallurgical engineer*
Subramanian, Ravi *electrical engineer*
Suganthan, Ponnuthurai Nagaratnam *electrical engineering educator, researcher*
Sugawara, Satoshi *space systems engineer*
Sugianto *mechanical engineer*
Sugimura, Kazuhisa *bioengineering educator*
Sugiura, Nobuaki *electronic and mechanical engineer*
Suh, Dong Jin *chemical engineer, researcher*
Suh, Jung Ho *engineering educator*
Suh, Soong-Hyuck *chemical engineer, educator, researcher*
Suh, Suk-Hwan *manufacturing engineer, educator*
Suhara, Toshiaki *electronics engineering educator*
Sukhorukov, Anatoly Nikolaevich *mechanician, researcher*
Sukhov, Dmitry Lvovich *engineering executive, consultant*
Sullivan, Charles R. *engineering educator*
Sultan, Rana Muhammad *mining engineer, consultant*
Sulten, Philippe Fernand *engineering executive*
Sumanth, David Jonnakoty *industrial engineer, educator*
Sumi, Chikayoshi *medical engineer, educator*
Sumihara, Kiyohide *mechanical engineering researcher, consultant*
Summerscales, John *engineer, educator*
Sun, Da-Wen *engineering educator, researcher*
Sun, Haiyin *optical engineer, educator*
Sun, Siying *mechanical engineer, educator*
Sun, Yan *electrical engineer*
Sun, Zheng Ming *mechanical engineer*
Sundvall, Lars *materials science engineer*
Sundy, George Joseph, Jr. *engineering executive*
Surana, Chandra Singh *civil engineering educator, consultant, researcher*
Surber, Dan Clifford *system engineer*
Suri, Rama Subbaraya Sastri *engineer, researcher*
Surmann, Hartmut *electrical engineer*
Surveyor, Ratan Dinshaw *civil engineer*
Suryavanshi, Arvind Krishnajirao *research and development engineer*
Sutherland, John Bennett *chemical engineer*
Sutton, Ernest Shaw *chemical engineer*
Sutton, Nigel James *aeronautical engineer, test flight officer*
Suzuki, Hirokazu *electrical engineer, researcher*
Suzuki, Toshio *electrical engineer*
Svaricek, Ferdinand *control engineer*
Svoboda, Petr *polymer engineer, researcher*
Swallow, Peter George *engineering educator*
Swaminathan, Kumar *electrical engineer, researcher*
Swartzlander, Earl Eugene, Jr. *engineering educator, former electronics company executive*
Sweeting, Martin Nicholas *electrical engineer*
Swinerd, Graham George *astronautical engineer, educator*
Swisher, Stacey Elaine *mechanical engrineer*
Syed, Shahabuddin Husainy *electrical engineer, researcher*
Sykas, Efstathios D. *electrical and computer engineering educator*
Szaller, Zsuzsanna *chemical engineer and researcher*
Szántó, Borisz *nuclear engineer, educator, researcher*
Szczepaniak, Czeslaw *electrical engineer, educator*
Szczuraszek, Tomasz Wieslaw *engineering educator*
Szecsy, Richard Samuel *civil engineer*
Szefner, Zbigniew Piotr *welding engineering educator, researcher*
Szelényi, János *petroleum engineer, oil industry executive*
Szerletics Turi, Maria *chemical engineer*
Szuecs, Ervin *mechanical engineer, educator*
Szymczak, Edward Joseph *mechanical engineer*
Tabata, Yasuhiko *biomedical engineering educator*
Tabiei, Ala *aerospace and mechanical engineer, educator*
Tachau, Herman *structural engineer*
Taha, Zahari *engineering educator, consultant*
Taherzadeh, Mohammad J. *biochemical engineer*
Takacs, Gabor *engineering educator*
Takács, Jenö *research engineer, consultant*
Takahashi, Susumu *mechanical engineer, educator*
Takasaki, Akito *engineering educator, researcher*
Takata, Hitoshi *engineering educator, researcher*
Takeshita, Oscar Yassuo *engineering educator*
Takeuchi, Katsuhiko *chemical engineer*
Takhar, Harmindar Singh *scientist, engineering educator*
Talabattula, Srinivas *engineering educator, consultant*
Talášek, Vladimír Karel *engineering executive*
Tallent, Robert Glenn *chemical and environmental engineer, entrepreneur*
Tam, Paul Wing Ming *engineering consultant*
Tam, Wing Keung *engineering company executive*
Tamama, Tetsuo *electronics engineer*
Tamboli, Akbar Rasul *consulting engineer*
Tambouratzis, George Demetrius *electrical engineer, researcher*
Tanabe, Makoto *computational mechanics educator*
Tanaka, Kazuo *optical engineer*
Tanaka, Takeshi *electrical engineering educator*
Tanaka, Yoshihiro *engineering educator, researcher*
Tandon, Vinod Kumar *engineering educator*
Taneja, Dalip Singh *soil and water engineer, researcher*
Tang, Fang-Fu *civil and structural engineer, consultant*
Tang, Hansong *computational fluid dynamics researcher*
Tang, Jianming *electrical engineer, researcher*
Tang, Loon Ching *engineering educator, consultant*
Tang, Man-Chung *engineer, administrator*
Tang, Walter Zhonghong *environmental engineer*
Tang, Zhi-Lian *polymer engineering educator, researcher*
Tang, Zhi-ping *mechanical engineer, educator*
Taniguchi, Hiroshi *mechanical engineering and architecture educator*
Taniguchi, Keiji *engineering educator*
Taniuchi, Kiyoshi *retired mechanical engineering educator*
Tanner, Mauri Uuno Ensio *aerodynamicist*
Tanoue, Koji *engineering educator, researcher*
Tanthapanichakoon, Wiwut *chemical engineering educator*
Tao, Xue-heng *engineering educator*
Taprogge, Rainer Herbert *plastics engineer, consultant*
Taqieddin, Salah Abdulhamid *mining and civil engineer, educator*
Tari, Giuliano *ceramics engineer*
Tarifa, Enrique Eduardo *chemical engineer, educator, researcher*
Tarnopolskii, Yuri *mechanical engineer, researcher*
Tassi, Géza *civil engineer, educator*
Tassios, Theodossios Panayotis *engineering educator*
Tateiba, Mitsuo *communication engineering educator*
Tateishi, Ryutaro *engineering educator*
Tatipamula, Mallikarjun *telecommunications and networking engineer*
Tavare, Narayan Sanaba *chemical engineering educator, researcher*
Tawata, Shinkichi *agricultural engineering educator*
Tay, Tong-Earn *mechanical engineering educator, researcher*
Tayanc, Mete *engineering educator*
Taylor, Anthony Baldwin *civil engineer*
Taylor, Christopher Malcolm *mechanical engineer*
Taylor, William Brockenbrough *engineer, consultant, management consultant*
Tchuruk, Serge (Serge Tchurukdichian) *engineering executive*
Teague, Lavette Cox, Jr. *systems educator, consultant*
Teitelbaum, Joal *engineering executive, consultant*
Teixeira, Fernando Lisboa *electrical engineer, researcher*
Telfer, Max Leslie *engineering consultant*
Temiz, Mustafa *electrical engineering educator*
Temperley, Tom Groome *engineering executive, consultant*
ten Brink, Stephan *communications engineer, researcher, consultant*
Teng, Jianfu *electronics engineer, educator*
Tenno, Robert *electrical engineer, educator*
Teodorescu, Honoriu Dan *engineer, researcher*
Teodoru, George Vasile Marius *materials and structural engineer, consultant*
Tepfers, Ralejs Krišjānis *building technology educator*
Terada, Marco Antonio *electrical engineer*
Terakawa, Akira *solar cell engineer, materials scientist*
Terano, Toshiro *retired educator, mechanical engineering*
Terentjeff, Jorma Kalevi *engineering company executive*
Terutung, Hendra *mechanical engineer*
Tessler, Alexander *aerospace engineer*
Test, Stacy Marie *network engineer*
Tezcan, Semih Salih *civil engineering educator, consultant*
Thampi, Mohan Varghese *environmental health and civil engineer*
Thathachar, Mandayam A.L. *electrical engineering educator*
Thawait, Surendra Kumar *mechanical engineer, researcher*
Thayer, Keith Bayard *engineering company executive*
Theimer, Wolfgang Michael *telecommunications engineer*
Theodoridis, George Constantin *biomedical engineering educator, researcher*
Theodorou, Doros Nicolas *chemical engineering educator, researcher*
Theodoru, Stefan Gheorghe *civil engineer, writer*
Theofanous, Theo G. *engineering educator, consultant*
Theofylactos, Constantinos *energy engineer*
Theotokoglou, Efstathios Eleftherios *civil engineering educator*
Thiede, Andreas Alfred *information technology engineer*
Thim, Hartwig Wolfgang *engineering educator*
Thisayakorn, Chavalit *engineering executive*
Thoma, Manfred Hubert *electrical engineering educator*
Thomas, Bertram David *retired chemical engineer*
Thomas, John *mechanical engineer, research and development*
Thomas, William John *chemical engineer, researcher*
Thomason, Harry Jack Lee, Jr. *mechanical engineer*
Thomford, William Emil *engineer, consultant*
Thompson, David Alfred *industrial engineer*
Thompson, George Edward *corrosion science and engineering educator*
Thompson, Kevin Paul *optical engineer*
Thompson, LeRoy, Jr. *radio engineer, military reserve officer*
Thomsen, Ole Thybo *mechanical engineer, educator*
Thomsen, Ole Thybo *mechanical engineer, educator*
Thomson, Steven James *research agricultural engineer*
Thornely-Taylor, Rupert Maurice *acoustical consultant*
Thring, Meredith Wooldridge *chemical engineer, educator*
Tiblier, Fernand Joseph, Jr. *municipal engineering administrator*
Tica, Aldo Oscar *oil company process engineer*
Tichy, Milik Otakar *civil engineering educator, consultant, researcher*
Tien, Chang-Lin *engineering educator*
Tieng, Quang Minh *engineering researcher*
Tijmann, Willem Bert *civil engineer, consultant*
Tikhonov, Vadim Semenovich *mechanical engineer, researcher*
Tillman, Joseph Nathaniel *engineering executive*
Timm, Volker *engineer*
Timmermann, Claus Christian *electrical engineering educator*
Timofei, Simona Luminita *chemical engineer, researcher*
Tinaut, Francisco V. *engineering educator*
Ting, Joseph K. *mechanical engineer*
Tingsanchali, Tawatchai *engineering educator*
Tiong, Kwong-Kau *electrical engineer, educator*
Tisza, Miklos *mechanical engineering educator, researcher*
Tiwari, Gopal Nath *engineering educator*
Tizani, Walid M.K. *civil engineer, researcher*
Tkachenko, Yevgeniy Alexandrovich *engineering company administrator*
Toacse, George Radu *electrical engineering educator, researcher*
Toader, Ioan Horea Iosif *civil engineer*
Tocchetti, Andrea *transportation engineering educator, researcher*
Toda, Susumu *structural researcher*
Todorov, Todor Stoilov *theory mechanisms and machines educator, mayor*
Toeppe, William Joseph, Jr. *retired aerospace engineer*
Toerstad, Elisabeth Heggelund *engineer*
Tohmon, Ryoichi *optical engineer*
Tokarev, Vadim Ivanovich *aviation civics educator*
Tokerud, Robert Eugene *electrical engineer*
Tokura, Nobuyuki *electrical engineer, researcher*
Toliver, Lee *mechanical engineer*
Tolle, Melinda Edith *engineer, scientist*
Tolstoy, Nikolaj Theodorsson *civil engineer*
Tomaževič, Miha *civil engineer, educator*
Tomazi, George Donald *retired electrical engineer*
Tomczuk, Bronislaw Zbigniew *electrical engineering educator and researcher*
Tomczyk, Andrzej *aviation engineer, educator*
Tomlinson, James Lawrence *mechanical engineer*
Tomovic, Mileta Milos *mechanical engineer, educator*
Tondl, Aleš *retired engineering researcher*
Tönshoff, Hans Kurt *mechanical engineering educator*
Torii, Shuichi *mechanical engineer, educator, researcher*
Törmälä, Pertti Olavi *engineering educator, inventor*
Torres, Terry Terol *mechanical engineer, general contractor*
Torres, Vanessa De Macedo *chemical and minerals engineer, researcher*
Tosti, Silvano *chemical engineer, researcher*
Totoev, Yuri Zarevich *civil engineering educator*
Totsky, Alexander Vladimirovich *engineering educator, researcher*
Tourtellotte, Mills Charlton *mechanical and electrical engineer*
Toussaint, Patrick *materials engineering researcher*
Townsend, Miles Averill *aerospace and mechanical engineering educator*
Towry, Elisa Robinson *electronics engineer*
Toya, Masayuki *mechanical engineer, educator*
Tozzer, Jack Carl *civil engineer, surveyor*
Traina, Paul Joseph *environmental engineer*
Tran, Danh Xuan *mechanical engineer, educator*
Tran, Jack Nhuan Ngoc *gas and oil reservoir engineer*
Trasi, Dilip Sudhakar *electronic company executive, researcher, consultant*
Traub, Lance Wayne *research engineer, lecturer*
Travieso, Lissette *chemical engineer, researcher*
Trawinski, David Lee *aerospace engineer*
Trbojevic, Vladimir Milan *risk analyst and safety engineer*
Treacy, William Joseph *electrical and environmental engineer*
Treble, Frederick Christopher *electrical engineer, consultant*
Trelea, Ioan-Cristian *control engineer, researcher*
Tretz, Christophe Robert *electrical engineer*
Trevino, Mateo A. *mechanical engineer*
Tricoli, Vincenzo *chemical engineer*
Troch, Peter *civil engineer, researcher*
Troilo, Michele *engineering educator, consultant*
Troitzsch, Dirk *biomedical engineer*
Trommer, Gert Franz *engineering educator*
Troxel, Kent M. *engineering consultant, computer consultant*
True, Leland Beyer *civil engineer, consultant*
Trujillo-Cuthrell, Loretta Marie *chemical engineer*
Truong, Tuong Ngoc *engineering educator, researcher*
Trzynadlowski, Andrzej Maria *electrical engineering educator*
Tsahalis, Demosthenes Theodoros *engineering educator*
Tsai, Ching-Piao *civil engineering educator, researcher*
Tsai, Chong-Shien *engineering educator, consultant*
Tsakiroglou, Christos *chemical engineer, researcher*
Tsamopoulos, John *chemical engineer, educator*
Tsao, Chi-Yuan Albert *engineering educator*
Tsao, Shyh-Lin *electrical engineering educator*
Tsatsaronis, George *mechanical engineering educator, researcher*
Tse, Ka Kuen *engineering executive*
Tseesniex, Modris *mechanical engineer*
Tsekeridou, Sofia *electrical engineer*
Tseng, Ampere An-Pei *mechanical engineer, educator, administrator*
Tseng, Ching Shiow *mechanical engineer, educator*
Tseng, King-Jet *engineering educator, research scientist*
Tseng, Tseung-Yuen *engineering educator, researcher*
Tsenoglou, Christos *chemical engineer, educator*
Tsilingiris, Panayotis Theodore *mechanical engineer, electrical engineer, researcher, energy engineering consultant, educator*
Tsirkunov, Yury Mikhailovich *mechanical engineer, fluid mechanics specialist, researcher*
Tsitouras, Konstantinos *chemical engineer, educator, economist*
Tsitsos, Stelios *telecommunications engineer*
Tsitverblit, Naftali Anatol *fluid mechanics researcher*
Tsochatzidis, Nikolaos A. *chemical engineer, researcher*
Tsoulos, George Vasilios *electrical and electronics engineer*
Tsuda, Toru *communications engineering educator*
Tsui, Daniel C. *electrical engineering educator*
Tsunekawa, Yoshiki *engineering educator*
Tsung, Fugee *engineering educator, researcher*
Tsybakov, Boris Solomon *information theory researcher, educator*
Tsyfansky, Semyon Lyev *mechanical engineer, educator, consultant*
Tsyplakov, Oleg Georgievich *engineering educator, consultant*
Tu, Ji-Yuan *fluid mechanics engineer*
Tu, Yaqing *engineering educator, researcher*
Tugulea, Andrei *science educator*
Tuliszka, Edmund *combustion engineering researcher*
Tunay-Unsal, Nuran *geological engineer, researcher*
Tungsanga, Krai *civil engineer, engineering company executive*
Tuori, Timo Kustaa *engineering executive*
Tuovinen, Jussi J.A. *laboratory director*
Turchi, Peter John *aerospace and electrical engineer, physicist, educator*
Turner, David Lowery *system safety engineer*
Turner, Richard L. *retired computer software engineer*
Turrnberg, Bengt Lennart *nautical engineer*
Tutins, Antons *electrical and audio engineer*
Tyman, Adam Stefan *electrical engineer, educator*
Tyszer, Jerzy Stanisław *engineering educator, researcher*
Tzeng, Pei-Yuan *aeronautical engineering educator, researcher*
Uberoi, Mahinder Singh *aerospace engineering educator*
Ucan, Osman Nuri *electrical engineer, educator*
Uchida, Hirohisa *engineering educator*
Uchino, Kenji *electrical engineer*
Ücisik, Ahmet Hikmet *engineering educator*
Udupa, K. Manjunatha *aerospace structural design engineer*
Ueha, Sadayuki *engineering educator*
Uhlemann, Jens *chemical engineer*
Uike, Yasuyuki *chemical engineer*
Ujihara, Kikuo *engineering educator*
Ulgen, Kutlu Sefika *chemical engineer, educator*
Ulusoy, Özgür *engineering educator*
Ulybyshev, Yuri Petrovich *aerospace engineer*
Umeadi, Albert Nkuni *civil engineer, consultant*
Umemura, Teruyoshi *engineering educator*
Unbehauen, Heinz Dietrich *electrical engineering educator*
Underwood, Gerald Timothy *business consultant*
Underwood, John H. *research engineer*
Unsworth, Anthony *engineering educator*
Upadhye, Milind Dhundiraj *electronics engineer, educator*
Ural, Oktay *civil engineering educator*
Urata, Eizo *mechanical engineering educator*
Urdea, John *electromechanical engineer*
Uribe-Restrepo, Gustavo *civil engineer*
Ursic, Srebrenka *information technology researcher, manager, consultant*
Ushio, Masao *engineering educator*
Ushiō, Tetsuya *computer engineer*
Usov, Sergei Vadimovich *engineering company executive*
Vadlejch, Jan *nuclear engineer, consultant*
Vafiades, Pandelis *retired electrical engineering educator*
Vagelatos, Aristides Th *computer engineer*
Vahaviolos, Sotirios John *electrical engineer, scientist, corporate executive*
Vahlin, Anders *telecommunications engineer, research scientist*
Vaidya, Durgesh Shivram *chemical engineer, researcher*
Vaidya, Sadashiv Satish *electrical engineer*
Vaios, Christos Ioannis *systems engineer*
Vaireanu, Danut Ionel *chemical engineer, educator*
Vairis, Shtrauss *polymer engineer, researcher*
Valasquez, Joseph Louis *industrial engineer*
Valavanis, Nikitas K. *mechanical engineer*
Valdna, Vello *engineering researcher*
Valkovic, Zvonimir *electrical engineer*
Vallee, Rene Louis *nuclear research engineer, consultant*
Valles, Enrique Marcelo *engineering educator*
Valstad, Tor Nils *survey engineering manager*
Van Beckhoven, Dirk *design engineer*
Van Bladel, Jean Georges *engineering educator, retired*
Vance, Thomas Ray *engineer*
Van Den Akker, Harry E.A. *chemical engineering educator*
van der Meulen, Michael *electrical engineering educator*
Vander Sloten, Jos Edward August *biomechanical engineer, educator*
Van der Velden, Alexander Jacobus Maria *aerospace engineer, aerospace company executive*
Vander Vorst, André Sylvain Joseph *engineering educator*
van Deventer, Jannie Stephanus Jakob *engineering educator*
Vanhove, Dominique Michel *chemical engineering educator*
Van Jaarsveldt, Hendrik Jacobus *industrial engineer*
Van Kerckhove, Gilbert Rachel *engineering executive*
Vankov, Ivan Danailov *nuclear engineer, educator*
VanMarcke, Erik Hector *civil engineering educator*
van Nobelen, Robert *electrical engineer, researcher*
Van Vroonhoven, Jos Cornelis Walterus *mechanical engineer*
van Wijngaarden, Leendert *fluid mechanics engineering educator*
van Wissen, Gerardus Wilhelmus Johannes Maria *consulting engineering company executive*
Varadi, Janos *engineering educator*

Varghese, Parambeth George *production engineer, executive*
Varghese, Zubin Abraham *computer vision engineer, consultant*
Varias, Andrew George *research engineer, consultant*
Várkonyi-Kóczy, Annamária Rita *electrical engineer, educator, researcher*
Varma, Arvind *chemical engineering educator, researcher*
Varnish, Peter *engineering executive*
Varonos, Agamemnon *mechanical engineer, researcher*
Vasanta Ram, Venkatesa Iyengar *mechanical and aeronautical engineering scientist and educator*
Vashitz, Oded *biochemical engineer*
Vasile, Nicolae *electrical engineer, educator*
Vasilievici, Alexandru Petru *electrical engineer, educator*
Vassilev, Hristo Stoynov *engineer*
Vatavuk, William Michael *chemical engineer, author*
Vaughan, Otha H., Jr. *retired aerospace engineer, research scientist*
Vaughan, Rodney Grant *electrical engineer, communications scientist*
Vaurio, Jussi Kalervo *engineer and scientist*
Vayenas, Constantinos George *chemical engineering educator*
Veers, Paul Steven *mechanical engineer*
Vega-Carrillo, Hector Rene *nuclear engineer*
Végh, Ludevít *civil engineering educator*
Veit, Ivar Emils *engineer, acoustician*
Vejražka, František *radio engineer, educator*
Velu, Palani T. *materials processing engineer, researcher*
Vendik, Irina Borisovna *electrotechnology educator*
Vendik, Orest Genrikhovich *electronics educator*
Venkateswarlu, Paladugu *engineering educator*
Venugopal, Rayasam *educator*
Verboven, Peter Eric *engineering company executive*
Verdu, Sergio *engineering educator*
Vereshchagin, Igor Petrovich *electrical engineer, educator*
Vergilis, Joseph Semyon *mechanical engineering educator*
Vermeer, Martin *engineering educator*
Verschueren, Karel *environmental engineer*
Vibrans, Gerwig Ernst *retired material science educator*
Vicentin, Riccardo *project manager, consultant*
Vidal, Alain Jean Baptiste *agricultural and environmental engineer*
Viedma, Antonio *engineering educator*
Vienken, Joerg Hans *chemical engineer*
Viikki, Olli Jukka *electrical engineer*
Vijayaratnam, Kanapathipillai *chartered civil and environmental engineer, consultant, director*
Villamizar-C, Alvaro *civil engineer*
Villar, Eugenio *electronic system design, educator, researcher*
Villarreal, Carlos Castaneda *engineering executive*
Villaverde, Santiago *chemical engineer, educator*
Vinson, Roy Douglas *engineer*
Viravau, Philippe *engineering educator*
Virk, Gurvinder Singh *control systems engineering educator, consultant*
Virola, Juhani Seppo Anssi Pekka *bridge engineer*
Viscomi, B. Vincent *civil engineer*
Visvanathan, Kannuswamy *mechanical engineer*
Viteček, Antonin *engineering educator*
Vittal, Vijay *electrical engineer*
Viviani, Antonio *aerospace engineer, educator*
Vizcaino, Henry P. *mining engineer, consultant*
Vladimir Sergey, Pakhomov *chemical engineering educator*
Vlase, Ioan-Orest *electrical engineer*
Vlasov, Ivan Veselinov *microelectronic engineer*
Vogeley, Clyde Eicher, Jr. *engineering educator, artist, consultant*
Voges, Udo *systems engineer, researcher*
Volakis, John Leonidas *engineering educator*
Volberg, Herman William *electronics engineer, consultant*
Voleti, Shriram Murti *engineering educator*
Vonderbank, Ralf Sebastian *research engineer, energy executive*
Von Eschen, Robert Leroy *electrical engineer, consultant*
von Martens, Hans Jürgen *electrical engineer, researcher*
Von Roth, Walter Emil *civil engineer*
von Stockar, Urs C. *chemical engineering educator*
von Turkovich, Branimir Francis *engineering educator, researcher*
Voroncov, Vladimir *electronics engineer*
Voutsas, Epaminondas *chemical engineer*
Vovos, Nicholas Aneste *engineering educator*
Vrachas, Constantinos Aghisilaou *aeronautical engineer*
Vu, The Bao *engineering educator*
Vucak, Marijan *chemical engineer*
Vu-Dinh, Tuong *design engineer*
Vulic, Nenad *mechanical engineer*
Vunjak-Novakovic, Gordana *chemical engineer, educator*
Waage, Jan *retired engineering executive, researcher*
Waga, Mateusz Tomasz *engineer*
Wagner, Martin G. *chemical engineer, researcher*
Wahl, Michael Guenter *educator*
Wahlstrom, Lennart Stig *chemical engineer, scientist*
Wai, Ping-kong Alexander *engineering educator*
Wajand, Jan Aleksander *engineering educator, designer*
Wakabayashi, Hajimu *materials engineer, research center manager*
Wakamatu, Nobuyuki *environmental engineer*
Wakeman, Richard John *chemical engineering educator*
Wakuri, Yutaro *mechanical engineering educator*
Walczak, Zbigniew Kazimierz *polymer science and engineering researcher*
Walker, Clive Thomas *nuclear fuel technologist, microbeam analyst*
Wallace, Robert Bruce *environmental company executive*
Wallner, Franz *engineer*
Wallot, George Paul *electronics engineer*
Walser, Peter *mining engineer*
Walsh, John Breffni *aerospace consultant*
Walsh, Kenneth Joseph *design and engineering executive, consultant*
Walter, William Paul *retired bioengineer*
Walton, Clifford Wayne *chemical engineer, researcher*
Waltrich, Joseph Best *electronics engineer*
Wan Abas, Wan Abu Bakar *mechanical engineer, biomedical engineer, educator*
Wang, Anhua *solar energy educator*
Wang, Baoshan *electronic engineer*
Wang, Bu-Xuan *engineering educator*
Wang, Changjie *engineer*
Wang, Charles Ping *engineering executive*
Wang, Chien-Ming *structural engineer, educator, researcher*
Wang, Chi-Luen *fiber optics engineer*
Wang, Erqi *instrumentation engineering educator*
Wang, Francis Wei-Yu *biomedical materials scientist, researcher*
Wang, Guangqiu *aerospace engineer*
Wang, Haiming *research scientist*
Wang, Huining *engineer*
Wang, Jiangzhou *engineering educator*
Wang, Jung-Hua *electrical engineering educator*
Wang, Kesheng *engineering educator, researcher*
Wang, Ming De *engineer*
Wang, Qi *process engineer, materials scientist*
Wang, Qing *mechanical engineer, educator*
Wang, Ren *mechanical engineering educator*
Wang, Rong *chemical engineer, educator*
Wang, Rong-Ming *aeronautical engineer, researcher*
Wang, Sheng-De *engineering educator*
Wang, Shyh-Yau *engineering researcher*
Wang, Tahui *electronic engineering educator*
Wang, Tieguan *petroleum engineer, educator*
Wang, Wen Chuan *chemical engineering educator*
Wang, Xiaodu *engineering educator*
Wang, Xungai *engineering educator*
Wang, Yeong-Her *electrical engineer, educator*
Wang, Yixing *engineering educator*
Wang, Yongji *computer engineer*
Wang, Yu *telecommunication engineer*
Wang, Zhao Yin *hydraulic engineer, educator*
Wang, Zidong *electrical engineering and mathematics educator*
Wang, Zuobin *engineering educator*
Ward, Curtis William *process engineer*
Ward, Keith Albert *electronics engineer*
Ward, Keith Douglas *engineering research director*
Warfield, John Nelson *retired engineering educator, consultant*
Warnecke, Hans-Jürgen *engineering educator*
Warner, Frederick Edward *chemical engineer, educator*
Waseem, Mohammad *engineer*
Washington, Anthony Nathaniel *mechanical engineer*
Washington, Charles Henderson *laser systems designer, consultant*
Washiyama, Junichiro *chemical engineer*
Watabe, Tomiji *retired engineering educator, volunteer consultant*
Watanabe, Seiichi *electronics engineer*
Wataru, Weston Yasuo *civil engineer*
Waterfall, Roger Clive *engineering lecturer*
Watkins, Alan Keith *engineering executive*
Watson, Guy Edwards *mechanical engineer, consultant*
Watson, Neville Robert *electrical engineering educator*
Watson, Oliver Lee, III *aerospace engineering manager*
Wawszczak, Wlodzimierz Stanislaw *mechanical engineering educator*
Wazzan, Osama Ahmed *communications systems engineering executive*
Web, Shaw-Bing *engineering educator*
Webb, Colin *chemical engineering educator, consultant*
Webb, Robert Miles *civil engineer*
Weber, Wolfgang Hans *computer engineering educator*
Webster, George Arnold *mechanical engineer, consultant*
Wedenig, Harald Dieter *consulting plastics engineer*
Weeks, Robert Lee *electronic engineer, program manager*
Wei, Guanghua *mechanical engineer*
Wei, Shyue-Win *electrical engineering educator*
Weigold, Adam Mark *laser company executive, researcher*
Weilenmann de Tau, Maria Elisabet *agricultural engineer, researcher*
Weiner, Edward *civil engineer, federal agency administrator*
Weinmeister, Hanns-Wolfgang *forest engineer, educator*
Weinstein, Ilya Alexandrovich *engineer*
Weisbin, Charles Richard *nuclear engineer*
Weiss, Josef Johann *engineering educator, researcher*
Weissman-Berman, Deborah *composites engineer, researcher*
Wellen, Dana Thomas *engineering administrator*
Wells, Johnny Allen *electronics engineer*
Wellstead, Peter Eric *engineering educator*
Wen, Hungtao Joseph *management educator*
Wen, Xiaoqing *engineer, educator*
Weng, Cheng-Chiang *civil engineering educator, structural engineer*
Weng, Cheng-I *engineering educator*
Wessel, Peter Lorentz *telecommunication systems engineer*
Westerhoff, Heinz *thermodynamic engineer*
Westfall, Wayne Lynn *chemical engineer*
Westhaver, Lawrence Albert *electronics engineer, consultant*
Westveld, Belinda Joyce *reliability and quality engineer, educator*
Whipple, William, Jr. *engineering consultant, writer*
White, Calvin Lamont *engineer*
White, Charles Olds *aeronautical engineer*
White, Gary Richard *electrical engineer, plant operator*
White, Ian Frank *chemical engineer*
White, William Dudley *safety engineer*
Whitehurst, Brooks Morris *chemical engineer*
Whitelaw, Iain Edwin Baxter *operations engineer*
Whitlock, Brent Kevin *electrical engineer*
Whitmore, Raymond Leslie *retired mining-metallurgical engineering educator*
Whittle, Joseph F., Jr. *engineering executive, consultant*
Whitworth, Horace Algernon *mechanical engineer*
Wick, Hans Joachim *process automation engineer, consultant*
Widmann, Wolfgang *engineering executive*
Wiedermann, Alexander Richard *engineer, educator*
Wiegel, Markus *engineer*
Wieland, Paul Otto *environmental control systems engineer*
Wiercigroch, Marian *engineering educator*
Wiesbeck, Werner *electronics educator*
Wiese, Gerold Guenther *electrical engineer*
Wik, Torsten Erik Ingemar *chemical engineer, researcher*
Wild, Hans Jochen *former systems engineering executive*
Wilderer, Peter Adolf *engineering educator*
Wiley, Dianne Elizabeth *chemical engineering educator, researcher*
Wilhelm, Norbert Edwin *industrial engineer, structural engineer*
Wilhoit, Darrel Loel *chemical engineer*
Wilkinson, Chris D. W. *engineering educator*
Wilkinson, Gordon Thomas *retired chemical engineer, consultant*
Wilkomirsky, Igor A.E. *chemical and metallurgical engineer, educator*
Willgoose, Garry Raymond *environmental engineer, researcher*
Williams, Frederic Ward *structural engineering educator*
Williams, Jack Raymond *civil engineer*
Williams, Ronald Oscar *systems engineer*
Williamson, Stephen *electrical engineer*
Willis, André Maurice *electrical engineer, computing service executive*
Wilsdon, Thomas Arthur *product development engineer, administrator*
Wilson, Melvin Edmond *civil engineer*
Wilson, Robert Gordon *civil and mechanical engineer*
Wilson, Robert Ross *engineering manufacturing executive*
Wilson, William Alexander *manufacturing engineer, consultant*
Winand, René Fernand Paul *metallurgy educator emeritus*
Windhorst, Robert Dennis, II *aerospace engineer*
Winer, Ward Otis *mechanical engineer, educator*
Winkler, Wolfgang Georg *engineering educator, researcher*
Winn, C(olman) Byron *former mechanical engineering educator*
Wirasinha, Rohan Mahendra *electrical engineering consultant*
Wisnom, Michael Robert *aerospace engineer, educator*
Wisotsky, Serge Sidorovich *engineering executive*
Wiszniewski, Andrzej Józef *electrical engineer*
Wodzinski, Piotr *mechanical engineering educator, researcher*
Woinaroschy, Alexandru Eligiu *engineering educator, researcher*
Wojciechowicz, Boleslaw *machinery educator*
Wojciechowski, Jacek M. *electrical engineering educator*
Wojciulewitsch, Egon Servaz *aeronautical engineer, astrophysicist*
Wolff, Edwin Ray *retired construction engineer, consultant*
Wong, Albert Koon-Siu *mechanical engineer, research scientist*
Wong, Allan Wai Hoong *civil engineer, consultant*
Wong, Henry Hok-Yong *retired aerospace engineering educator*
Wong, Kin-Lu *engineering educator, electrical engineer*
Wong, Kon Max *electrical engineer educator*
Wong, Siu Kou *electronic engineer*
Wong, Stephen T.C. *radiology, neurology, computer scientist, and bioengineer educator*
Wong, Tommy Sai-Wai *civil engineering educator*
Wong, Wa Peng *engineering educator*
Wong, Wai On *mechanical engineer, educator*
Wongcharoen, Tiparatana *engineering educator*
Wongwises, Somchai *mechanical engineering educator*
Woo, Alex *process engineer*
Woo, Chunh-Ho *materials engineering educator, researcher*
Woo, Kwang-Sung *civil engineering educator*
Woo, Seong Ihl *chemical engineering educator*
Woodward, Clifford Edward *chemical engineer*
Woodward, John Frank *educator, consultant*
Workman, George Henry *engineering consultant*
Wörman, Anders Lars Edvard *civil engineering educator*
Woronoff, Georges D. *engineer*
Woxenius, Johan *engineering educator*
Wozniak, Richard Anthony *computer engineer*
Wright, Theodore Otis *forensic engineer*
Wrukowski, Krzysztof Władysław *engineering executive*
Wu, Chang-chun *mechanical engineering educator*
Wu, Chia-Ju *engineering educator*
Wu, Chih-Yang *mechanical engineering educator*
Wu, Daguan *aeroengine design engineer*
Wu, Dongping (Don Wu) *optical and electrical engineer*
Wu, Fu-Chun *environmental engineer*
Wu, Hai-Shan *electrical engineering educator*
Wu, Hsien-Jung *researcher*
Wu, Jing Long *electrical engineer*
Wu, Jung-Shyr *electrical engineering educator*
Wu, Nae-Lih *chemical engineering educator*
Wu, Shiming *materials scientist, researcher*
Wu, Thomas Xinzhang *engineering educator, researcher*
Wu, Tung-Chuan *mechanical engineer*
Wu, Wen-Fang *mechanical engineer, educator*
Wu, Xin Bao *engineering educator, researcher*
Wu, Xiying *mechanical engineering educator*
Wu, Yu-chi *engineering educator, consultant, researcher*
Wu, Zhen *opto-electronic engineering educator*
Wu, Zhen Yang *engineering educator*
Wu, Zhishen *engineering educator*
Wulf, Stanley Arthur *engineering executive*
Wuori, Paul Adolf *engineering educator*
Wylie, Richard Thornton *aerospace engineer*
Wyman, Richard Vaughn *engineering educator, exploration company executive*
Wynn, Robert Raymond *retired engineer, consultant*
Xeidakis, Georgios Stylianos *civil engineering educator*
Xi, Jiangtao *telecommunications engineer, educator*
Xi, Ning *engineering educator, researcher*
Xi, Yuyao *engineering educator*
Xia, An Bang *computer engineering educator*
Xia, Jiding *chemical engineering educator*
Xia, Renjie *civil engineer, researcher*
Xia, Xiang-Gen *electrical engineering educator*
Xiang, Guo Bo *engineering cybernetic educator*
Xiao, Zhongmin *engineering educator*
Xie, Shi-Leng *consulting engineer, educator*
Xie, Yi-Min *engineering educator*
Xie, Yu Jun *mechanical engineering educator*
Xoiculescu, Ionelia *engineer, educator*
Xu, Cheng *mechanical engineer, researcher*
Xu, Chunhui *systems engineer, educator*
Xu, Ding-Xin *structural engineer, consultant, educator*
Xu, Du *mechanical engineer, educator*
Xu, Guo Fang *design engineer*
Xu, Hua *engineering educator, researcher*
Xu, Jiefeng *industrial engineer*
Xu, Jingda *mining engineer*
Xu, Lixin *research engineer*
Xu, Min *mechanical vibration diagnosis engineer, educator*
Xu, Ronglie *civil engineer*
Xu, Shanjia *engineering educator*
Xu, Yangguang *acoustical engineer, system analyst*
Xu, Zhixiang *electronic engineering educator, consultant*
Xu, Zhong *mechanical engineering educator*
Xue, Lan *engineering educator*
Xue, Yusheng *engineering educator*
Xue-Qin, Cao *civil engineering educator*
Yabuki, Nobuyoshi *civil engineering educator*
Yackle, Albert Reustle *aeronautical engineer*
Yadav, Avinash *engineer, business educator*
Yadav, Sunil *mechanical engineer*
Yaghoubi, Mahmood *mechanical engineering educator, researcher*
Yamada, Hiroaki *engineering educator, chemist*
Yamada, Keiichi *engineering educator, university official*
Yamada, Shigeru *engineering educator*
Yamaguchi, Akira *engineering educator*
Yamamoto, Yousuke *electronics educator, scientist*
Yamane, Takashi *biomedical engineer*
Yamanouchi, Toyotoshi *civil engineer, educator*
Yamasaki, Hiroyuki *electrical engineer*
Yamayee, Zia Ahmad *engineering educator, dean*
Yamout, Hassan Mohammad *engineering executive*
Yan, Hua *microwave techniques educator*
Yan, Shangyao *civil engineering executive*
Yan, Wei Mon *mechanical engineering educator*
Yan, Zhenghua *combustion and fire researcher, safety engineer*
Yanagioka, Hiroshi *research company executive, consultant*
Yang, Bo-Suk *mechanical engineering educator*
Yang, Ching-Yu *mechanical engineer*
Yang, Di *aerospace engineer, educator*
Yang, En Ze *electronics engineering educator*
Yang, Hai-Yuan *engineering educator*
Yang, Hong-Sheng *electronics educator*
Yang, Jiaping *structural engineering researcher*
Yang, Jung Pil *engineer, researcher, consultant*
Yang, Kam Sang *electrical engineer*
Yang, Kelly *applications engineer*
Yang, Kuan-Hsiung *mechanical engineer, educator*
Yang, Naiheng *engineer*
Yang, Quanbing *materials engineering educator, researcher*
Yang, Shi-Ming *engineering educator*
Yang, Xianhua *systems engineer, researcher*
Yang, Xiaoping *engineering researcher*
Yang, Zane (Zhijia) *mechanical engineer*
Yang, ZhiCai *chemical engineering educator*
Yannas, Ioannis Vassilios *polymer science and engineering educator*
Yanovsky, Felix J. *radio-electronics and remote sensing scientist, educator, researcher*
Yanqui Murillo, Calixto *civil engineering educator, dean*
Yao, Jin *engineering educator, researcher*
Yao, Susu *electronics professor, researcher*
Yao, Y. Lawrence *engineering educator*
Yao, Zhenhan *engineering mechanics educator*
Yapijakis, Constantine *environmental engineering educator, consultant*
Yarar, Baki *mining and metallurgical engineering educator*
Yasuhara, Michiru *mechanical engineering educator*
Yates, Kenneth Lee *electro-optics engineer, flight instructor*
Yaxing, Wei *agricultural engineer*
Yazgan, Erdem *electronic engineering educator*
Ybarra, Kathryn Watrous *systems engineer*
Ye, Biqing *biomedical engineer, researcher*
Ye, Jianqiao *applied mechanics and structural engineering educator, researcher*
Ye, Meng *engineer, materials researcher*
Ye, Xudong *electrical engineering educator*
Yeh, Jung-Hua *senior mechanical engineer*
Yeh, Ying Chin *electrical engineer*
Yemelyanov, Svyatoslav Igorevich *aeronautical engineer, research*
Yen, Ben Chie *water resources engineering educator*
Yen, Shiow Kang *materials scientist, educator, consultant*
Yen, Wen Liang *aerospace engineer*
Yener, Aylin *electrical engineer, researcher*
Yeo, Allen Chiew Beng *mechanical engineer, consultant*
Yeo, Seung Tai *mechanical engineer, researcher*
Yeo, Tat-Soon *electrical engineer, educator*
Yeom, Choong Kyun *chemical engineer, researcher*
Yeryomin, Konstantin Isanosich *engineering educator, dean*
Yeung, Kwan Lawrence *electronics engineer*
Yeung, William Wai-Hung *technology educator*
Yevdayev, Nobert *retired engineer, art historian*
Yevi, Gilbert Yaovi *petroleum engineer*
Yi, Kyongsu *mechanical engineer, educator*
Yih, Yuehwern *engineering educator*
Yi-Jun, Qiu *electronic engineer*
Yin, Kewen Karen *chemical engineer, educator*
Ying, Jackie *chemical engineering educator*
Yinh, Victor Marius *electrical engineer*
Yip, Wing Chiu *electrical and electronic engineering researcher*
Yoda, Kentaro *biomedical engineering educator*
Yoeli, Pinhas (Guenther Aptekmann) *engineering educator*
Yokobori, Takeo *materials and mechanical engineering scientist, educator*
Yokobori, Toshimitsu *materials engineering researcher, educator*
Yokomizu, Yasunobu *engineering educator*
Yokota, Fumihiko *chemical engineer*
Yoneyama, Tsukasa *electrical communications educator*
Yong, Zhao *engineer*
Yoo, Hoseon *mechanical engineer, educator*
Yoo, Joo-Sik *mechanical engineer, engineering educator*
Yoo, Seong-Yeon *engineering educator*
Yook, Chong Chul *engineering educator*
Yoon, Soon Jong *civil engineering educator*
Yoon, Tae-Ho *materials science engineering educator*
Yoshimi, Yoshiaki *geotechnical engineer, consultant*
Yoshimura, Masataka *engineering educator, mechanical engineer*
Young, Danson *sanitary engineer, plumbing engineer, civil engineer, contractor*
Young, Kuu-young *engineering educator*
Young, Michael John *engineering executive*
Young, Nicholas Andrew *electrical engineering*
Youngdahl, Paul Frederick *mechanical engineer*

Youngquist, Carl William *environmental engineer*
Youngs, Robert Riggs *engineer*
Yu, Bingzhong *mechanical engineer*
Yu, Changtai *engineering educator*
Yu, Dahai *mathematics and engineering educator, researcher*
Yu, Han Qing *civil and structural engineer*
Yu, Kuo Tsung (Guocong) *chemical engineer educator*
Yu, Ming-Huei *mechanical engineering educator*
Yu, Qifeng *optical mechanics educator*
Yu, Qilian *engineering educator*
Yu, Shiu-lam *engineering educator*
Yu, Si Le *electronics educator*
Yu, Yong *engineering educator, robotics researcher*
Yu, Yue Qing *mechanical engineering educator, researcher*
Yuan, Pu *engineering educator*
Yuan, Shen-Chuan *civil and structural engineer, consultant*
Yuan, Xiao Jie *high technology professional, researcher*
Yuasa, Tetsuya *engineering educator*
Yudilevich, Isaac *engineering educator, management consultant, researcher*
Yue, Zhong Qi *civil engineer, educator, consultant*
Yuen, Shiu Yin Kelvin *engineering educator*
Yun, Jae Hoon *engineer*
Yun, James Kyoon *electrical engineer*
Yung, Edward Kai-Ning *engineering educator*
Yurso, Joseph Francis *engineering manager*
Yuu, Shinichi *mechanical engineering educator*
Zabecki, David Tadeusz *engineer, editor, military historian*
Zaborowski, Michał *electronic technology engineer, researcher*
Zacharia, Zach George *mechanical engineer*
Zacharopoulos, Dimitris *civil engineering educator, researcher*
Zahera, Juan Antonio *industrial engineer*
Zaidi, Riaz Haider *aircraft engineer, consultant*
Zakis, Eugene *electrical engineer*
Zakrzewski, Jan Maria *electrical engineering educator*
Zaky, Asser Aly *electrical engineering educator*
Zalazar, Carlos Antonio *engineering educator, researcher*
Zaldastani, Othar *structural engineer*
Zandian, Babak *metallurgical engineer*
Zannis, George *engineering consultant*
Zaporozhets, Vladimir Vasilievich *aviation technology educator*
Zapuskalov, Nikolai Mihailovich *engineering researcher*
Zaritski, Serguei Petrovich *engineering executive*
Zarudi, Moses (Moshe Zarudi) *research educator*
Zayko, Yuriy Nikolayevich *engineering educator*
Zazhigalov, Valery Alekseevich *engineer*
Zbacnik, Raymond Eric *process engineer*
Zbicinski, Ireneusz *chemical engineer, educator*
Zboinski, Krzysztof Boleslaw *mechanical engineering educator*
Zdravistch, Franz *fluid mechanics engineer*
Zebrowska, Jadwiga Irena *horticulture engineer, educator, researcher*
Zeile, Christof *electrical engineer, educator*
Zeleznikar, Anton Pavel *electrotechnical engineer, researcher*
Zeng, Hong *systems engineer, researcher*
Zeng, Qingchuan *research civil engineer, educator*
Zha, Xuan-Fang *engineering educator, researcher*
Zhai, Hongchen *optical engineering educator*
Zhang, Bin *engineering executive*
Zhang, Ce *mechanical engineering educator*
Zhang, Chuhan *civil engineer, educator*
Zhang, Dao Hua *electrical engineering educator, scientist*
Zhang, David Yaming *engineering educator*
Zhang, De-Wen *structural engineering educator, researcher*
Zhang, G. Z. (Guangzhi) *opto-electronic engineer*
Zhang, Geng Ji *petroleum educator, consultant*
Zhang, Guoqing (Gregory Zhang) *mechanical engineer, researcher*
Zhang, Jin Wen *engineering educator, consultant*
Zhang, Jinyan *process engineer, researcher*
Zhang, Jun *electrical engineer*
Zhang, Kangda *mechanical engineering educator, researcher*
Zhang, Keqiang *metallurgical engineer*
Zhang, Li-Ning *metallurgy educator, researcher*
Zhang, Ruichong *civil and mechanical engineer, educator*
Zhang, Runing *engineer, researcher*
Zhang, S. *engineering educator*
Zhang, Tianxu *engineering educator, researcher*
Zhang, Wei *radio propagation researcher, electrical engineer*
Zhang, Wen *applied mechanics educator*
Zhang, Wendong *engineering educator*
Zhang, Xiangting *engineering educator*
Zhang, Xiaoyan *engineering educator, researcher*
Zhang, Xiao-Zhang *mechanical engineering educator*
Zhang, Yanxin *optics educator, researcher*
Zhang, Yingbo *materials engineer, researcher*
Zhang, Yong Zhao *engineering educator*
Zhang, Zhenfang John *mechanical engineer, educator*
Zhang, Zhengguo *biomedical engineering educator*
Zhang, Zhuomin *mechanical engineering educator*
Zhang, Zonggui *engineer*
Zhao, Anping *electrical engineer*
Zhao, Chongbin *engineering educator, researcher*
Zhao, Jay Zijun *communications engineer*
Zhao, Jian *civil engineer, researcher*
Zhao, Jinsong Jason *engineer, researcher, administrator*
Zhao, Ke-You *electrical engineer, educator*
Zhao, Xiu Song *chemical engineering researcher*
Zheng, Fan *quality assurance engineer, educator*
Zheng, Hanqing *research engineer*
Zheng, Ji *electrical engineering researcher*
Zheng, Jian Ming *engineer*
Zheng, Shu Ying *optical engineer*
Zheng, Wei Xing *electronic and electrical engineering educator*
Zheng, Xiulin *materials science and engineering educator*
Zheng, Xu-Guang *engineering educator*
Zheng, Yibin *electrical engineer*
Zhiliang, Dai *engineering executive*
Zhiming, Chen *electronics educator, academic administrator*
Zhirabok, Alexey Nil *radio and electronics educator, researcher*
Zhong, Jian-Jiang *biochemical engineering educator*
Zhong, Jingchang *engineering educator*
Zhong, Ning *engineering educator*
Zhong, Shun-Shi *electromagnetist, electronics educator*
Zhou, Bing *process scientist*
Zhou, Jiming *transportation engineering researcher*
Zhou, Li *engineering educator, researcher*
Zhou, Meili *systems scientist, educator*
Zhou, Ming *engineering educator*
Zhou, Ming Yong *electrical engineer, researcher*
Zhou, Ping *physical engineer*
Zhou, Qiang Tai *engineering educator*
Zhou, Qianzhi *electrical engineer educator, researcher*
Zhou, Sophia Huai *biomedical engineer*
Zhou, Wancheng *engineer, educator*
Zhou, Xiao Hua *electrical engineer, educator*
Zhou, Zhen-Sheng *petroleum engineer*
Zhou, Zhide *civil engineer, researcher*
Zhu, Chang-Luo *chemical engineering educator*
Zhu, Jianhua *civil and transporation engineer, researcher*
Zhu, Jizhong *engineering educator*
Zhu, Jun *agricultural engineering educator, researcher*
Zhu, Mengzhou *mechanical engineering educator, consultant*
Zhu, Qiang *mechanical engineer*
Zhu, Qi-Xiang *mechanical engineer, researcher*
Zhu, Shaowei *power machinery engineer*
Zhu, Shijie *materials engineer, educator*
Zhu, Shou-yi *biochemical engineer*
Zhu, Shouzheng *engineering educator, academic administrator*
Zhu, Yong *mechanical engineer, educator*
Zhu, Zi Qiang *electrical engineer, researcher*
Zhu, Zupei *chemical engineer, technical advisor*
Zhuang, Zhen-Wan *chemical engineering educator*
Zhuravel, Alexander Petrovich *engineering researcher*
Zia, Sohail *design engineer, educator*
Ziębik, Andrzej Józef *energy engineering educator, researcher*
Ziegler, Franz *mechanical engineer educator*
Zieliński, Jerzy Stanisław *scientist, electrical engineering educator*
Zigliotto, Mauro *electrical engineering researcher*
Ziha, Kalman *engineering educator, researcher*
Žihla, Zdeněk *avionics engineer, educator*
Zikic, Aleksandar Miroslav *engineering educator, consultant*
Zillmer, Hans-Joachim *engineering company executive*
Zimmerman, Marlin U., Jr. *chemical engineer*
Zimmermann, Karel *chemical engineer educator*
Zincke, Gerald Dietmar *software engineering consultant*
Zingher, Harry Lee *chemical engineer*
Zio, Enrico *nuclear engineer*
Ziółko, Jerzy Maciej *civil engineering educator*
Zipf, Mark Edward *electrical engineer*
Zmitrowicz, Alfred Pawel *engineer, researcher*
Zmood, Ronald Barry *control systems engineer, researcher, educator*
Zmudzki, Stefan *engineering educator, researcher*
Zobel, Jon D., Jr. *electrical engineer*
Zohadie, Muhamad *engineering educator*
Zolotukhin, Anatoly Boris *petroleum engineering educator*
Zomaya, Albert Yousif *electrical and computer engineering educator*
Zong, Ruhou *telecommunications engineer*
Zong, Zhi *research engineer*
Zorc, Davor *electrical and computer engineering educator*
Zorychta, Andrzej *rock mechanics and mining engineering educator*
Zou, Huijun *engineering educator*
Zoufonoun, Amir H. *electrical engineer*
Zubriczky, László *civil engineering executive, consultant*
Zunino, Rodolfo Francesco Luigi *electronic engineer*
Zuo, Hongshu *electric power designer, educator, consultant*
Zuo, Mingjian *industrial engineering educator*
Zurkowski, Stanislaw *engineering researcher*
Zwirn, Hervé *engineer*

FINANCE: BANKING SERVICES. *See also* FINANCE: INVESTMENT SERVICES.

Abekawa, Sumio *bank executive*
Adegbite, Samuel Igbayilola *banker*
Afxentiou, Afxentis Costa *bank executive*
Agama, Godfried Kportufe *banker*
Agbetuyi, Segun *banker*
Agrellos, José Carlos *bank executive*
Ahmed, Abdalla Hassan *bank executive*
Ahmed, Ghiasuddin *banker*
Aho, Yao Messan *bank executive*
Aigrain, Jacques A. *banker*
Akanji, Omolara Ololade *banker, researcher*
Al-Assaf, Ibrahim Abdulaziz *banker*
al-Attiyah, Abdallah Khalid *banker*
Albert, Michel Maurice Louis Delphin *bank executive*
Aldrich, Frank Nathan *banker*
Aleinikov, Gennady *bank executive*
Alexandre du Portal, Luc Jean *banker*
Ali, Ahmad Mohamed *banker*
Ali, Djama Mohamed *bank executive*
Alimardonov, Murodali *bank executive*
Allen, Claxton Edmonds, III *investment banker*
Allen, William Anthony *banker*
al-Sabah, Sheikh Salem Abdul al-Aziz Al-Saud *banker*
al-Salami, Alawi Salih *banker*
al-Suwaydi, Sultan bin Nasir *banker*
Al-Zadjali, Hamood Sangour *banker*
Amusategui de la Cierva, José Maria *bank executive*
Anand, Pawan Kumar *bank officer*
Andersen, Bodil Nyboe *bank executive*
Anderson, Sir John Anthony *bank executive*
Andreoni, Piero Massimo *bank executive, consultant*
Aninat, Eduardo *international banking official*
Arhar, France *banker*
Arnold, Keith *banker*
Ashauer, Guenter *banker*
Attali, Bernard *bank executive*
Augustine, Jerome Samuel *merchant banker*
Ault, Jeffrey Michael *investment banker*
Austell, Edward Callaway *banker*
Aye, Kyi *bank executive*
Bäckström, Urban *banker*
Bajo, Momodou Clark *banker*
Baker, Dennis R. *bank officer*
Bansak, Stephen A., Jr. *investment banker, financial consultant*
Barátossy, Katalin *banker, economist*
Barbeosch, William Peter *banker, lawyer*
Baring, John Francis Harcourt (Lord Ashburton) *retired banker*
Bark, Theo J. *banker*
Barlow, Matthew Blaise Joseph *merchant banker*
Barnhill, Gregory Hurd *investment banker*
Baroli, Paolo *bank executive*
Barren, Bruce Willard *merchant banker*
Barrett, Robert James, III *investment banker*
Barry, Robert Hugh *banker*
Basagoiti, Antonio Garcia-Tuñón *banker, lawyer*
Basol, Mete M. *bank executive*
Bazoli, Giovanni *banker*
Bedrij, Orest *investment banker, scientist*
Beevor, Antony Romer *merchant banker*
Bellanger, Serge René *banker*
Benani, Saad Dyrar *investment banking associate*
Bergleitner, George Charles, Jr. *investment banker*
Biddle, Anthony Joseph Drexel, III *investment banker*
Billot, Eric Guy *bank executive*
Birchby, Kenneth Lee *banker*
Birmingham, Bruce R. *bank executive*
Bischoff, Winfried Franz Wilhelm *merchant banker*
Bitner, John William *banker*
Blain, Alexander David *merchant banker*
Blazin, Michael Joseph *banking executive*
Bloom, Jack Sandler *investment banker*
Blue, Delawrence Charles *investment banker, accountant, automobile dealer*
Blum, Georges *bank executive*
Boas, John Robert *banker*
Bodin, Manfred *banker*
Boehne, Edward George *banker*
Bohorquez, Joaquin *banker*
Bolduc, J. Emilien *bank executive*
Bond, John (Reginald Hartnell) *bank company executive*
Boudart, Yves Henry *banker*
Boulier, Jean-Francois *bank executive, researcher*
Bouton, Daniel *banker*
Braasch, Barbara Lynn *banker, consultant*
Brash, Donald Thomas *bank executive*
Brealey, Richard Arthur *bank official*
Brendsel, Leland C. *mortgage company executive*
Breuer, Rolf *bank executive*
Broaddus, John Alfred, Jr. *bank executive, economist*
Brokaw, Clifford Vail, III *investment banker, business executive*
Brown, G(lenn) William, Jr. *bank executive*
Brown, Gloria Vasquez *central banker*
Brown, William L. *banker*
Browne, Paul *banker*
Bruneel, Dirk *bank executive*
Brush, Martyn Thomas *bank executive*
Brydon, Donald Hood *investment management executive*
Bull, Nigel Russell *bank executive*
Burke, James Joseph, Jr. *investment banker*
Burke-Smith, Katrin Kandel *investment bank executive*
Burnett, David Henry *banker*
Buxton, Andrew Robert Fowell *bank executive*
Campbell, James Robert *banker*
Campbell, William Yates *investment banker*
Carballo, Jose Maria *banker*
Cardoso, Pedro Sousa *bank executive*
Carey, William Polk *investment banker*
Caruso, Anthony Ralph *mortgage banker, real estate developer*
Casey, Thomas Jefferson *investment banker, venture capitalist*
Castberg, Anders Stang *banking executive*
Cayne, James E. *investment banker*
Chang, Ying Kuang *banker*
Charalabous, Epaminondas *bank executive, stock derivatives consultant*
Charrier, Michael Edward *investment banker*
Chea, Chanto *banker*
Chen, Michael Shih-ta *banker*
Chen, Shu-Ying *bank executive*
Cheserem, Micah *bank executive*
Chester, Norman Charles *bank executive*
Chevrillon, Cyrille Louis *investment banking executive*
Chia, Pei-Yuan *banking executive*
Chikaonda, Mathew *bank executive*
Chong Song-taek *banker*
Choung, Jung Tae *investment banker*
Chu, Edward Kawah *bank administrator*
Chung, Che-shum *banker*
Citerne, Philippe *bank executive*
Cleghorn, John Edward *bank executive*
Clifford, Stewart Burnett *banker*
Cochran, George Calloway, III *retired bank executive, lawyer*
Cockrum, William Monroe, III *investment banker, consultant, educator*
Coleman, Lewis Waldo *bank executive*
Comper, Tony *banker*
Corcostegui, Angel *bank executive*
Coreth, Joseph Herman *bank executive*
Corluy, Walter Josephus *retired bank senior executive*
Cornick, Roger Courtenay *asset management company executive*
Corrigan, E(dward) Gerald *investment banker*
Coskuner, Sibel *bank executive*
Cossi, Paulin Laurent *bank executive, economics educator*
Coste, Thierry *bank executive*
Courcier, Jerome Claude *banker*
Crawley, Frederick William *banker, real estate company executive*
Crockett, Andrew Duncan *banker*
Croff, Davide *bank company executive*
Cromwell, Oliver Dean *investment banker*
Crutchfield, Edward Elliott, Jr. *banking executive*
Cunningham, James Archibald *bank executive*
Cuny, Stephane François *banker*
Curtin, John Paul, Jr. *investment banker*
Cytrycki, Slawomir Waclaw *bank executive*
Da, Thierry *bank executive*
Daberko, David A. *banker*
Dahlander, Pia Ywonne Maria *bank executive*
Dai Xianglong *banker*
Danielsen, Svend-Erik *bank executive*
Daridan, Dominique François *bank executive*
Dautresme, David Lucien *bank executive*
David, Ward S. *bank officer, retired federal agency executive*
Deans, Patricia Herrmann *investment banker*
Debs, Richard A. *investment banker*
DeGroff, Ralph Lynn, Jr. *investment banker*
de la Guardia, Dulcidio Jose *investment banker, financial consultant*
de la Rocha Marie, Javier *bank executive*
de Larosière de Champfeu, Jacques Martin Henri Marie *bank executive*
De La Selle, Alban *banker*
De Leonardis, Nicholas John *bank executive, financial lecturer, educator*
Del Rio-Herrera, Sergio *banking executive*
de Pourtalès, Christian Hubert *banker*
De Rothschild, Eric Alain Robert David *banker*
de Seze, Amaury-Daniel *bank executive*
de Sousa, Antonio Rebelo *bank executive*
Desprez, Christophe *investment bank administrator*
De Vabres, François Donnedieu *banker*
de Visscher, Francois Marie *investment banker*
de Ybarra y Churruca, Emilio *bank executive*
Dixon-Nielsen, Judy E(arlene) *loan officer*
Djordjevich, Miroslav-Michael *bank executive*
Dombret, Andreas Raymond *bank executive*
Donaldson, James Neill *banker*
Doubell, R.D. *investment banking executive*
Douglas, Cindy Holloway *mortgage company executive*
Douglass, Donald Robert *banker*
Douroux, Lucien *retired credit executive*
Dowd, David Joseph *banker, builder*
Droulers, Stephane Nicolas *investment banker*
Duisenberg, Willem Frederik *bank executive*
Duncan, Robert Michael *banker, lawyer, Republican national committeeman*
Duran, Michael Carl *bank executive*
Duval, Michael Raoul *investment banker*
Echaluse, Luella Hermosilla *banker*
Eckersley, Norman Chadwick *bank executive*
Eldin, Gérard *banker*
Elliott, Barry John *trust company executive*
Ellwood, Peter Brian *bank executive*
Elphick, Henry Richard Francis *investment banker*
Emerson, H. Garfield *investment banker, lawyer*
Enguehard, Jean-Luc *banker*
Ercel, Gazi *banker*
Fahs, John David *bank executive*
Fall, Cheikh Ibrahima *banking executive*
Faquih, Osamah Jaafar *bank executive*
Fares, Mikhael Issam *bank executive*
Fariz, Ziad *banker*
Fausti, Luigi *bank company executive*
Fazio, Antonio *bank executive*
Fees, James Richard *investment banker, corporate director, entrepreneur*
Fenaut, Jean-Michel *bank executive*
Ferreira, Paulo C. *bank executive*
Feuerstein, R. Horst *bank executive*
Finocchiaro, Alfonso G. *bank executive*
Fisher, Richard B. *investment banker*
Fitzmaurice, Laurence Dorset *bank executive*
Flood, A. L. (Al Flood) *retired bank executive*
Flores, Philip Joseph *bank executive*
Flugger, Penelope Ann *banker*
Fontana, Pedro *bank executive*
Ford, Gerald J. *bank executive*
Forrestal, Robert Patrick *banker, lawyer*
Francis, Julian W. *bank executive*
Francois, Eric Nicolas *investment banking executive*
Frangopoulos, Zissimos A. *banker*
Freeman, Richard Francis *banker*
Freytag, Richard Arthur *banker*
Fritz, Terrence Lee *investment banker, strategic consultant*
Fruitman, Frederick Howard *investment banker*
Fugate, Ivan Dee *banker, lawyer*
Fung, Kwok-King Victor *merchant banker*
Gamble, Theodore Robert, Jr. *investment banker*
Gameira, Antonia Cunha *banker, educator*
Garabiol, Dominique Yves *banker, economist*
Gavriisky, Svetoslav Veleslavov *bank executive*
Geipel-Faber, Ute Maja *banker*
George, Edward Alan John *banker*
Gerardin, Bernard *international banking consultant*
Geronzi, Cesare *bank executive*
Ghosh, Bimal *international consultant economic development*
Gifford, Charles Kilvert *banker*
Gjedrem, Svein *banker*
Godsoe, Peter Cowperthwaite *banker*
Goedschalk, Henk Otmar *banker, educator*
Goekjian, Christopher Allan *investment banking executive*
Goodison, Sir Nicholas Proctor *banker*
Gossett, Robert Francis, Jr. *merchant banker*
Graham, William Pierson *investment banker, entrepreneur*
Grant, Ross Alan *banker*
Gratalo, John, Jr. *mortgage banker, business owner*
Greene, Richard Thaddeus *bank executive*
Greenspan, Alan *central banker, economist*
Greenwood, John Edward Douglas *investment banker, lawyer*
Groenink, Rijkman Willem Johan *banker*
Gronchi, Divo *banker*
Gruffat, Jean-Claude *banker*
Guermonprez, Damien *banker*
Guiliani Cury, Hugo M. *economist, consultant*
Gumpel, Peter Eric *investment banker, lawyer*
Gunnarsson, Birgir Isleifur *bank executive, former parliamentarian*
Gut, Rainer E. *banker*
Hackl, Maximillian *banker*
Hadjiminas, Christian *investment banker*
Hager, Martin Hermann *bank executive*
Hagey, Walter Rex *retired banker*
Halifa, Mohamed *bank executive*
Hall, Bryan Howard *banking executive*
Hall, Robert Emmett, Jr. *investment banker, realtor*
Hamalainen, Sirkka *banker*
Hamda, Mohamed el-Beji *banker*
Handler, Kenneth Victor *banker*
Hans, Meyer *bank executive*
Haque, Mohammed Mominul *banking executive*
Hardy, David Malcolm *bank executive*
Harrison, William Burwell, Jr. *banker*
Harsev, Emil Manolov *bank executive*
Hart, Pamela Heim *banker*
Hashimoto, Toru *bank executive*
Hedelius, Tom Christer *banker*
Hendrickson, Alan Bryce *commercial banker*
Herregat, Guy-Georges Jacques *banker*
Heyn, William Burris *investment banker*
Hinkson, Gregory Evelyn *bank executive*
Hoedl, Heinz *banking executive*
Hoenig, Thomas M. *bank executive*
Hoffmeyer, Erik *former bank executive*
Hollis, Timothy Martin *bank executive*
Holmes, Timothy Alastair *mortgage banker*
Hon, Johnny Sei-Hoe *banker*
Hopkins, Colin *bank executive*

Horton, Michael L. mortgage company executive, publishing executive
Houenipwela, Rick banker
Huang, Wei-xin bank executive
Humann, L. Phillip bank executive
Hurley, Dean C. bank executive, lawyer
Ibbs, Sir (John) Robin retired bank executive
Ingraham, John Wright banker
IsArescu, Mugur banker
Israel, Edmond Sylvain banker
Issing, Otmar banking executive, economist
Istock, Verne George banker
Iversen, Benjamin Rupert Lars investment banker
Jacobs, Wilfried Desire Seraphin banker
Jacomb, Sir Martin banker
Jamal, Moez Ahamed banker
Janoski, Henry Valentine banker, former investment counselor, realtor
Janssen, Paul-Emmanuel bank executive
Jayawardena, A.S. banker
Jefferson, Joseph Murray banker
Jimenez, Valenka bank executive
Johnson, Everett Clark banker
Jourdren, Marc Henri investment banking company executive
Jusko, Marián banker
Kabbaj, Omar bank executive
Kaiho, Takashi bank executive
Kakudoh, Kenichi bank company executive
Kalff, Peter Jan former banker
Kambhato, Phumchai investment banker
Kane, Jay Brassler banker
Kantorowicz-Toro, Donald Manuel investment banker
Karasin, F. Banu bank executive
Karo, Tamas Andras investment banker, financial-economic adviser
Kasai, Kazuhiko banking executive
Kashiwagi, Yusuke bank executive
Kaufmann, Henry Mark mortgage banker
Kaufmann, Mark Steiner banker
Keehner, Michael Arthur Miller investment bank executive
Keller, J(ames) Wesley credit union executive
Kelly, Paul Knox investment banker
Keramane, Abdelouahab banker
Khokhlov, Vitaly Sergeyevich banker
Kikonyogo, Charles Nyonyintono bank executive
Kishi, Satoru bank executive
Kitsos, Petros banker
Klinger, Douglas Evan money management executive
Kluge, Holger retired bank executive
Knight, Robert Edward banker
Koffler, Stephen Alexander investment banker
Kohlhaussen, Martin banker
Kok, Frans Johan investment banker
Kolta, Sherif Zaher banker
Koning, J. banker
Koroma, James Sanpha banker, economist
Kovacevich, Richard M. banker
Kovalyov, Sergey Borisovich bank executive
Koyama, Hiromi Maria banker
Koyamba, Alphonse bank executive
Kraft, Vahur bank executive
Kurosawa, Yoh bank executive
Labrecque, Thomas G. bank executive
Laffineur, Gérard bank executive
Lai, Ricky K. M. banker
Lam, Kun Kin bank executive
Lance, David Harry investment banker
Landi, Giovanni banking executive
Lantis, Donna Lea retired banker, art educator, artist
Latibeaudiere, Derick Milton bank official
Latimer, Phil H. investment banker
LaWare, John Patrick retired banker, federal official
Le Blanc, Bart banker
Le Brun, Jean retired banker
Legaspi, Benedicto Cruz, Jr. banker, realtor
Leigh, Margie mortgage company administrator
Leighton, Lawrence Ward investment banker
Lein, Filip Marcel banker
Lemens, William Vernon, Jr. banker, finance company executive, lawyer
Leverkus, C. Erich banker
Lewin, Leif I. finance director
Lewis, Kenneth D. banker
Lewis, Sherman Richard, Jr. investment banker
Limhaisen, Mohammed Abdulraham banker
Ling, Robert Malcolm banker, publishing executive
Lipworth, Sir (Maurice) Sydney bank executive, solicitor
Lloyd, Brenda Averil bank executive, educator
Locke, Jennifer Lynne mortgage services professional
Loomis, Howard Krey banker
Lyons, Maureen Ann banker
Lyons, Terrence Allan merchant banking, investment company executive
Macfarlane, I. J. (Ian Macfarlane) banker
Mahy, Marcus John trust and estate practitioner
Maleiane, Adriano Afonso banker
Mallinckrodt, George W. bank executive
Mancera Aguayo, Miguel retired central banker
Mancini, Marcello banker
Mandell, Ross H. investment banker, stockbroker
Manges, James Horace investment banker
Maraye, Mitrajeet D. bank executive
Mårtensson, Arne Edward Georg bank executive
Maruping, Anthony Mothae bank executive
Masa, George John banker
Massad, Carlos bank executive
Mathews, Peter John bank executive
Mathewson, Sir George bank executive
Matsushita, Yasuo former banker
McCleary, Benjamin Ward investment banker
McColl, Hugh Leon, Jr. bank executive
McDonough, William J. banker
McGrath, Edward Leo investment banker
McGuirk, Ronald Charles retired banker, economic advisor
McNamara, Robert Strange former banking executive, cabinet member
McNaughtan, David Pringle investment banker
McTeer, Robert D., Jr. banker
Meachin, David James Percy investment banker
Meeker, Guy Bentley banker
Mehta, Ravi Ravinder Singh international trade finance consultant, banking trainer and researcher, trade specialist
Meijer, Wim bank executive
Menaker, Ronald Herbert retired bank executive
Meredith, Archibald L. banker
Middendorf, J. William, II investment banker
Middleton, Sir Peter (Edward) bank executive
Mieno, Yasushi Japanese central banker
Miller, Walter Richard, Jr. banker
Minkiewicz, Marian Rajmund banker
Miracle, Robert Warren retired banker
Mistry, Percy Shiavak investment banker
Mohamed, Ismail Hassan bank executive
Molinari, Sandro bank executive
Mondaini, Marco banker
Monroe, Melrose retired banker
Montgomery, James Fischer savings and loan association executive
Moores, Peter retired banker
Mooy, Adrianus bank executive
Morikawa, Toshio bank executive
Morrel, William Griffin, Jr. banker
Mosselmans, Carel Maurits investment banker
Moulaert, Jacques banker
Moussa, Pierre Louis banker
Mueller, Paul Henry retired banker
Mullajanov, Faizulla Makhsutjanovich bank executive
Mullan, Homi P.R. banker
Muñoz, Carlos Ramón bank executive
Muromachi, Kaneo bank executive
Murray, Brian Victor investment banker
Murray, Terrence banker
Mutawalli, Hisham bank executive
Mutemberezi, Francois bank executive
Mwanza, Jacob M. bank executive
Mwelwa, Jerry Baldwin bank executive
Myers, Bernard Ian merchant banker
Mylonas, Theodoros P. bank officer
Nair, M.P.K. banker
Najarian, Jack George investment banker
Namin, Mona Liza Caladiao banker
Naruse, Tomonori retired bank executive
Nash, Warren Leslie banker
Neiss, Hubert international banking executive
Nelissen, Roelof Johannus bank executive
Nemecek, Eduard bank educator
Neuber, Friedel banker
Nichols, C. Walter, III retired trust company executive
Nikolayev, Nikolay Nikolayevich bank executive
Nishida, Keiu bank company executive
Nishigaki, Satoru bank company executive
Nishikawa, Toshifumi bank executive
Nishimura, Masao banker
Nordal, Johannes banker
Noyer, Christian central banker
Nugée, John Francis bank executive
Nugent, Helen Marion bank executive
Nurbakhsh, Mohsen bank executive
Nurhalim, Purnomo Santoso banking executive
Oberrauch, Karl investment banker
O'Brien, Kevin James investment banking executive
O'Connell, Maurice banker
Ogasawara, Hideo bank executive
Ogata, Shijuro banker
Ogilvie, Donald Gordon bankers association executive
Okada, Akishige bank executive
Olmsted, Craig William mortgage banker
Olsson, Curt Gunnar banker
Ospel, Marcel bank executive
Ouedraogo, Boukary banker
Owens, John Robin finance company executive
Oyeh, Henry Kwashie bank officer
Palmer, Patrick Asa former banker, lecturer
Pane, Gerald Louis banker
Pantzaris, Christos Stavrou bank executive
Papadakis, Panagiotis Agamemnon financier, international business executive
Papademos, Loukas bank executive
Paracha, Samya Kadri investment banker
Parks, Grace Susan bank official
Parry, Robert Troutt bank executive, economist
Patel, Manubhai Darubhai retired banker
Patil, Jaysingrao Bhausaheb bank executive
Patpong-pibul, Kitti banking executive
Pébereau, Michel Jean Denis bank executive
Pereira Martins, Carlos Alberto banker
Perrin, Charles John banker
Pielak, Grzegorz Franciszek national investment fund executive
Pierson, Wayne George trust company executive
Pietruska, Alexander Michael investment banker
Piper, Kimberly A. bank cost analyst
Pitman, Sir Brian (Ivor) bank executive
Ponce Garcia, Jaime Alfredo bank executive
Poot, Theo bank executive
Potter, William James investment banker
Pou, Pedro bank executive
Powell, William Arnold, Jr. retired banker
Premi, Br banking executive
Prizzi, Jack Anthony investment banking executive
Propatto, Juan Carlos Aldo bank executive, educator
Que, Peter D., Jr. banking executive, consultant
Quint, David Paul investment banking executive
Quintos, Juan Gomez, Jr. bank executive
Raines, Franklin Delano company executive
Ramanauskas, Romas bank executive
Ramirez, Noel bank executive
Randall, William Brian mortgage banker
Ranuzzi (De Bianchi), Paolo bank executive
Rashid, Mamun Ur bank commission official
Rasmuson, Elmer Edwin banker, former mayor
Ravelojaona, Gaston bank executive
Raymond, Robert banker
Regenboog, Maurits Alexander banker
Reid Scott, David Alexander Carroll banker
Reintzel, Warren Andrew trust company executive
Repše, Einars banker
Rhodes, William Reginald banker
Ribeiro, Frank Henry banker, energy consultant
Ribeiro, Luis Candido banker
Rice, Joseph Albert banker
Risk, Thomas Neilson retired banker
Ritchie, Cedric Elmer banker
Robertson, Edwin Oscar banker
Rochette, Jean-François bank executive
Rockefeller, David banker
Roelants, Andre banking executive
Rogers, Alice Louise retired bank executive, writer, researcher
Rohlwink, Anthony bank executive
Rojo Duque, Luis Angel banker
Rolek, Ferenc bank executive, human resources professional
Roll, Lord Eric (Lord Roll of Ipsden) merchant banker
Rosenbaum, Greg Alan merchant banker, consultant
Rosenberg, Richard Morris banker
Ross, Wilbur Louis, Jr. investment banker
Rowland, David bank executive
Rubli, Federico bank executive, educator
Ruozi, Roberto banker
Rustamov, Elman bank executive
Ryan, Robert J. A. investment banker
Saif, Abdallah Hasan bank executive
Salameh, Riad Joseph banker
Samara, Marie-Therese bank executive
Sandler, Herbert M. retired savings and loan association executive
Sandler, Marion Osher retired savings and loan association executive
Sandler, Ron bank executive
Sanner, George Bradley bank executive
Santaella, Juan banker, investment advisor
Santini, Jean-Jacques Marie banker
Sarbanov, Ulan Kytaibekovich bank executive
Sargsyan, Tigran bank executive
Scanlan, Papali'i Tommy bank executive
Scaturro, Philip David investment banker
Schiff, David Tevele investment banker
Schlesinger, Helmut Franz banker
Schmidheiny, Thomas industrialist
Schmidt, Albrecht bank executive
Schmidt, Hartmut banking and finance educator
Schwingeler, Thomas Heinrich banker
Sease, Lynn D. mortgage company executive
Sedgwick, (Ian) Peter merchant banker
Sem, Richard Jorgen banker
Sennett, Paul William Gervase bank executive
Seqat, Mohamed banker
Shattuck, Mayo Adams, III investment bank executive
Shetty, Shridhara Mahabala bank executive
Shipley, Walter Vincent retired banker
Shresthra, Satyendra Pyara banker
Shukri, Sabih Mahmood banker, consultant
Sielemann, Gerhard retired bank clerk
Sievers, Reinhard banker, lawyer
Sigurdsson, Jon banker
Simonyi, Tamas Sander banker
Singaram, Ponnaiyan bank officer
Skånland, Hermod central banker
Skreb, Marko banker
Small, Parker Adams, III investment banker
Smith, James Herbert bank executive
Smith, Kathleen Tener bank executive
Smith, Lincoln Cain banking executive
Smith, Raymond W. investment banking executive
Smith, Richard Mark mortgage company executive
Smits, Hans N.J. bank executive
Snare, Carl Lawrence, Jr. business executive
Sondén, Erik Lars Nils investment banker
Songok, Daniel Kipsang bank executive
Sparber, Dale Paul banker
Spark, Andre Varouge investment banker
Spinks, Jeffrey Thomas bank officer
Spivak, Jacque R. bank executive
Stals, Christian Lodewyk retired bank executive
Stephens, Elton Bryson bank executive, service and manufacturing company executive
Stern, Gary Hilton bank executive, economist
Stewart, John Murray banker
Stewartby, Ian bank executive
Stricker, Andreas banking executive
Suarez, German banker
Subert, Edoardo Carlo banking executive
Sugisaki, Shigemitsu international bank official
Sugita, Katsuyuki bank executive
Sultan, H.E. Sheikh Faisal bin banking executive
Suranyi, Gyorgy bank executive
Surtani, Jackie Bhagwandas banker
Suslov, Alexander Victorovich bank executive
Sutherland, Peter Denis banker, lawyer
Svedberg, Bjorn Magnus Ivar bank executive
Svenson, Charles Oscar investment banker
Tabachuk, Emelia banker
Takagaki, Tasuku bank executive
Talen, William Claire bank executive, financial consultant
Talmaci, Leonid banker
Tang, Dawson private banker
Tanna, Shashi Jamnadas investment banking executive
Tanous, Peter Joseph banker
Tato, Antonio Carlos bank executive
Taylor, Allan Richard retired banker
Teem, Paul Lloyd, Jr. bank executive
Thacker, Peter James banker
Thain, John investment bank executive
Thaler, Richard Winston, Jr. investment banker
Thiessen, Gordon George banker
Thomas, René François bank executive
Thomson, Richard Murray retired banker
Thornburgh, Richard E. bank executive
Tibbs, Christopher Stanley banker
Tietmeyer, Hans banker, former government official
Tily, Stephen Bromley, III bank executive
Tisserand, Jean-Paul Philippe (Jean Hautepierre) bank executive
Tissot, Jean-Louis Antoine banker
Tošovsky, Josef bank official
Tous de Torres, Luz M. banker
Trachtenberg, Matthew J. bank holding company executive
Tranchimand, Henri-Michel François investment banking executive
Tregenza, Norman Hughson investment banker
Trichet, Jean-Claude banker
Tromp, Emsley D. bank executive
Trowbridge, Thomas, Jr. mortgage banking company executive
Tsumba, Leonard Ladislas banker
Tubbs, Edward Lane banker
Unwin, Sir (James) Brian bank executive
Urrutia, Miguel banker
Vagliano, Alexander Marino banker
Valentine, Michael Robert banker, director
van der Wyck, Herman Constantyn investment banker
Van Hovell tot Westerflier, Baron Zweder Otto Hubert Marie banker
Van't Veer, Anne banking executive
Vassallo, Francis bank executive
Vassilacos, Dimitri George bank advisor
Veniard, Jose M. bank officer
Vermilye, Peter Hoagland banker
Verplaetse, Alfons Remi Emiel bank administrator
Vilcassim, Mohamed Nawaz Jiffry bank officer
Villat, Claude Max Charles Henri retired banker
Vogt, Evon Zartman, III (Terry Vogt) merchant banker
von Liphart, George mortgage company executive
Wait, Charles Valentine banker
Wallander, Jan Rickard banker
Wallenberg, Peter banker, investor
Walter, Bernhard bank executive
Walther, Johannes Peter banker, financial consultant
Wang, Xuebing banker
Wanless, Derek bank executive
Warden, James Bryce bank executive
Warner, Douglas Alexander, III banker
Warner, Scott Dennis investment banker
Watkins, Richard Valentine investment banker
Watkins, Russell L. banker
Wayland-Smith, Robert Dean retired banker
Weill, Sanford I. bank executive
Weiner, Walter Herman banker, lawyer
Wellink, Nout bank executive
Welman, Jo Mark Pole banker
Weskamp, Kelley S. loan account manager, real estate company executive
Whitehead, John Cunningham bank executive, diplomat, philanthropist
Whiting, Gordon James investment banker
Wilson, Paul Lowell mortgage company executive, lawyer
Woodard, Nina Elizabeth banker
Wouters, Chris banker
Yamamoto, Yoshiro bank executive
Yamamoto, Yusho bank executive
Ybarra, Emilio bank company executive
Yeh, Kuo Hsing bank executive
Young, Robert Craig banker
Zaidan, Elie E. banker
Zaki, Hassan Abbas bank executive
Zanoni, Umberto banker, consultant
Zelnik, Joseph bank executive, lecturer
Zierke, Ulrich Hans Hermann bank executive
Zimmermann, Jacques bank executive
Zlatanov, Assen Iliev bank executive, consultant
Zubairi, Salim Ahmad banker

FINANCE: FINANCIAL SERVICES

Abdelrahman, Talaat Ahmad Mohammad financial executive
Abdelsayed, Wafeek Hakim accounting educator
Adeola, Anthony Olukemi management educator, researcher, management consultant
Adkins, Fredrick Earl, III financial consultant, educator
Afterman, Allan B. accountant, educator, researcher, consultant
Aga, Naozer Jamshed financial executive
Agboruche, William accountant, educator, philosopher, biologist
Agrawal, Hari Narayan finance educator, researcher
Aguirre, Francisco business educator
Ahlstrom, Theresa P. accountant
Aida, Ichiro production and operations management educator
Ajmera, Aroon financial company executive, management consultant
Akbari, Shaheen Ahmed financial executive
Akimaru, Haruo university educator
Akpakpan, Bassey Akpan accounting educator
Alam, Badrul accountant
Alam, Syed Mahbubul finance executive, accountant
Albano, Pasquale Charles management educator, management and organization development consultant
Al-Braikan, Hazem Khalid global fund manager
Albrecht, Ronald Lewis financial services executive
Alexander, Ellin Dribben financial marketing company executive
Alexander, Elmore Rosebur, III business educator, dean
Alkhateeb, Arwa business educator
Allan, Percy consultant
Allegre, Maurice retired public company executive
Allen, Charles Richard retired financial executive
Allhusen, James J. financial servies executive
Allison, Laird Burl business educator
Alnakhli Almuzani, Abdulkareem Ali auditor
Altenburger, Otto Andreas accountant, educator
Altfest, Lewis Jay financial and investment advisor
Amadasun, Patrick I. financial consultant, author
Amanze, Chinenye Dom business educator, procurement consultant
Amarchand, Deepchand commerce educator
Anderson, James Donald pension company executive
Anderson, Rex Albert accountant
Anderson-Gingold, Rosalind Gaye accountant
Andone, Ioan Ioan accountant, educator
Andrade, Armando auditor, consultant
Andrisani, Paul J. business educator, management consultant
Anjaria, Shailendra J. international finance official
Ankarcrona, Henric Th. asset management company executive
Arakawa, Yoshizo business educator
Armstrong, Robert William marketing educator
Arnold, Desmond Claude financial executive
Aronoff, Craig Ellis management educator, consultant
Arundell, Victor Charles accountant, international business consultant
Assen, Nigel St. Dennis travel writer and investment consultant
Assini, Vincent Paul financial executive
Atcheson, Sue Hart business educator
Athanasiadis, Spiros economic studies educator, consultant
Auslander, Kelly Boyce financial planner
Awasthi, Vidya Nidhi accounting educator
Axel, Bernard finance executive
Ayadi, Olusegun Felix finance educator
Ayano, Katsutoshi management educator
Ayub, Yacub financial consultant
Babbel, David Frederick finance and insurance educator
Badalamenti, Anthony financial planner
Bai, Charles Xiaoshu finance company executive
Baig, Mirza Mujeeb controller
Baker, J. A., II executive management advisor and consultant, monetary architect, financial engineer
Baladi, André international financier
Ball, Kenneth James independent financial advisor
Banks, Sandy B. accountant
Bannelier, Florence Anne financial analyst
Barbee, George E. L. financial services and business executive
Barlow, William Pusey, Jr. accountant
Barnard, Rollin Dwight retired financial executive
Barney, Austin Dunham, II estate planner
Baron Cohen, Gerald accountant, writer
Barr, Michael Charles financial consultant
Barratt, Eric George accountant
Barredo, Rita M. auditor
Barrett, Peter Stephen management educator
Barrington-Ward, Francis Miles accountant
Barry, James Albert, Jr. financial planner
Bartelds, J.L.M. (Hans) finance company executive
Barton, Noel accountant
Bassoul, Aziz Michel financial executive
Bauerly, Ronald John marketing educator
Bayor, Bernard Kofi financial company executive
Bayot, Marc investment consultant, finance educator
Becker, Horst-Vincent Daniel financial executive

Behrens, Henry William international business educator, investment executive
Bellemans, Michel Dominique financial services company executive
Belvedere, Marie accountant, stock broker
Benito, Gabriel R. Garcia management educator
Benoidt, Jean Victor Georges financial consultant
Benson, Donald Erick holding company executive
Berg, Anthony Richard finance company executive
Bergley, Bruce Allen certified public accountant
Bergman, Bo quality management educator, researcher
Bergsma, Syb financial executive
Berman, Barry marketing educator
Berman, Richard Andrew financial company executive
Bertrand, Jean-Louis financial company executive, lecturer
Bessis, Hugh Joel finance educator, consultant
Betts, James William, Jr. financial analyst, consultant
BetzJitomir, Susan Marie financial consultant, lawyer, adult education educator
Bevc, Carol-Lynn Anne advertising executive
Bezuidenhout, Pieter Jacobus Schalk investment consultant, researcher
Bhattacharya, Sukumar accountant
Bissa, Raman accountant, editor
Black, Raymond Alexander financial director
Blackwell, Julie Abbott financial analyst
Bland, Teresa P. financial analyst, consultant
Blausey, Jeanne Martha accountant, financial systems analyst, fraud examiner
Blazevich, Leslie Matthew financial consultant
Blinkova, Olga I(gor) financial educator
Bloemer, Rosemary Celeste bookkeeper
Bloomberg, Michael Rubens finance and information services company executive
Bly, James Charles, Jr. financial services executive
Bobbitt, Juanita Marilyn Crawford international organization executive
Bobillo Martinez, Alfredo international business educator
Boggs, David Jerome business educator, consultant
Bolt, Dawn Maria financial coach
Bonniel, Charles Eric accountant, educator
Bonugli, Beulah Evelyn finance company executive
Booth, Anna Belle accountant
Boronico, Jess Stephen management science educator, academic dean
Boross, Zoltán accountant, educator
Börsig, Clemens finance executive
Bourn, Alan Michael accounting educator, computer company executive
Bouvier, Christian René audit manager, administration educator
Bovee, Courtland Lowell business educator
Bowden, Elbert Victor banking, finance and economics educator, author
Bowden, Howard Kent accountant
Bowles, David Christopher finance executive, economist
Boyce, Daniel Hobbs financial planning company executive
Boyd, David Preston business educator
Brackner, James Walter accounting educator, consultant
Braden, Sarah Ergle financial aid manager
Brafman, Lionel finance company executive
Brah, Shaukat A. business educator
Braham, Delphine Doris supervisory government accountant
Branson, Harley Kenneth finance executive
Brickhill, William Lee international finance consultant
Brigham, John Allen, Jr. financial executive, environmentalist, polition
Brinker, Thomas Michael finance executive
Brizuela de Avila, Maria Eugenia financial and insurance company executive, lawyer
Broad, Eli financial services executive
Bröder, Ernst-Günther financial executive, economist
Bromwich, Michael accounting and finance educator
Bronson, Christopher Herbert financial service company executive, planner
Brouwer, Adriaan financial executive
Brown, Clifford Bryant financial consultant
Brown, L(arry) Eddie tax practitioner, real estate broker, financial planner
Bruner, Robert Frank business educator
Bryan, Robert Fessler former investment analyst
Bryant, James William management educator, consultant
Bryant, Timothy Clark investment brokerage executive
Bubnov, Sergey Igorevich financial analyst
Buckley, Adrian Arthur finance educator
Bughin, Jacques Rene business executive, educator
Bühler, Nicolas financial executive
Bullock, Peter Bradley company director
Bump, Rebecca Ruth financial analyst, accountant
Burgel, Hans Dietmar management educator, researcher
Burkhardt, Thomas Dirk Ralf finance educator
Burlaud, Alain Jean management educator, consultant
Byer, Theodore Scott accountant
Byres, Marshall Henry financial executive
Byrne, Ross Leon accountant
Cabatic, Ed accountant
Cabrera, Eduardo M. diversified financial services company executive
Caen, Jean-Bernard financial executive
Cagandahan, Sabino Magno accountant
Caldwell, Thomas Howell, Jr. accountant, financial management consultant
Camp, Craig Charles financial analyst
Campbell, Andrew Eustace Clavering business strategy educator
Campbell, David Reed financial services executive
Campbell, Joseph John financial services executive
Campolettano, Thomas Alfred international contract manager
Caprio, Nicholas Frank pension fund administrator, accountant, educator
Capuzziello, Paul Thomas senior financial advisor
Carbonel, Jean retired benefits and pensions consultant
Cardenas, Raul Alfredo business educator, management consultant
Cardona, Jose N. financial company executive
Cargill, Barbara Joan management educator
Carlson, Richard Gregory accountant
Carmignato, Guilio financial company executive
Carnahan, George Richard business educator, consultant
Caron, Thomas James financial planner, estate planner
Carraher, Shawn Michael management educator
Carroll, James J. business educator, litigation support consultant
Casey, Micheal William portfolio manager
Caspersen, Finn Michael Westby diversified financial services company executive
Castleman, Harry Weissinger financial planner
Ceszkowski, Daniel David financial analyst
Cézard, Francois financial executive
Chan, Yoke Kai finance educator
Chan, Yuk-Shee finance educator
Chandler, John Andrew financial investor
Chandy, Rajesh K. business educator
Chang, Wung business advisor, researcher, lecturer
Chatterjee, Amitava finance educator, consultant
Chattopadhyay, Prithviraj management educator
Chen, Chao finance educator
Chen, Eric Yen-Po accountant, consultant
Chenault, Kenneth Irvine financial services company executive
Christensen, Karl-Christian Huldgaard finance manager
Christesen, John Denis business educator
Christiaans, Peter Albert financial consultant
Christian, Suzanne Hall financial planner
Chrzanowski, Lionel Michel financial executive
Chung, Jay Young business educator, researcher
Churchill, James Garton retired international finance consultant
Cimino, Carlo equity analyst
Clarke, J(ohn) Neil accountant
Clayton, Simon Anthony financial executive
Clement, Daniel Roy, III accountant, assistant nurse, small business owner
Codd, Henry Wallace, Jr. finance executive
Cody, Alan Morrow financial consultant
Cohen, Philip Herman accountant
Cohen-Sabban, Nessim auditor, accountant
Coldwell, David Alastair business administration educator
Coleman, Henry James, Jr. management educator, consultant
Collec, Jean-Claude group treasurer
Collier, Joyce Ann budget analyst
Collufio, Hector Fernando Ramon company executive
Conger, Cynthia Lynne financial planner
Connor, Joseph E. accountant
Conradie, Murray Neil financial executive
Constance, Barbara Ann financial planner, small business owner, consultant
Conti, Indalicio Palomar accountancy educator
Conway, Earl Cranston business educator, retired manufacturing company executive
Copans, Kenneth Gary accountant
Cordaro, Robert Anthony financial analyst
Corey, Gordon Richard financial advisor, former utilities executive
Corinaldesi, Marcelo Ruben accountant
Cornick, Michael F(rederick) accounting educator
Corp, Lester Desmond financial executive
Corts, Kenneth S. business educator
Coryell, Glynn Heath financial service executive
Cosandey, David Antoine financial risk specialist
Cox, Michael David chief internal auditor
Craig, Anna Maynard financial educator, consultant
Craig, Charles Samuel marketing educator
Crall, Dale Eugene accountant
Crane, Steven financial company executive
Creger, David Lee financial planner, insurance executive
Crider, Robert Agustine international financier, law enforcement official
Crilly, James A. retired accountant, tax specialist
Crovella, Carlo Umberto financial markets analyst, consultant
Crowston, Wallace Bruce Stewart management educator
Cunningham, Nancy Schieffelin business educator
Curnow, Philip Michael John financial planner
Cutt, Malcolm George accountant
Dacey, Robert Frank accountant, executive
Daidone, Lewis Eugene financial services company executive
Dalal, Mayur Thakorbhai charitable estate planner
Danforth, Arthur Edwards finance executive
Darde, Jean Delphin financial executive
Darling, John Rothburn, Jr. business educator
Darr, Walter Robert financial analyst
Daubert, Madeline J. accountant, educator
Davenport, Jeffrey Paton financial planner, investment advisor
Davidson, Amanda Margaret financial advisor
Davies, Joyce business consulting executive
Davis, Brian Lee finance company executive, consultant
Davis, Charles Elliot accounting educator
Davis, Mark Herbert Ainsworth financial analyst, mathematician
Day, Michael John actuary
Day, Ronald Richard financial executive
Dayme, Meribeth G. business educator, consultant, voice educator
de Cidrac, Charles-Etienne asset management executive
Declercq, Guido Victor Alfons (Baron Declercq) retired investment company executive
De Coen, André accounting educator
de Frondeville, Eric Charles portfolio manager
de Jesus, Carlito Gonzales financial services consultant
Delecourt, Philippe Maurice portfolio manager
Dell, Peter Lawson business educator
della Faille d'Huysse, Christian finance company executive
De Martino, Kenneth company executive
Denisov, Alexander Pavlovich financial company executive
Denoble, Robert business executive
Depangher, Michael Leon accountant
de Pury, David financial company executive
De Saint Seine, Guillaume Benigne financial executive
De Villenfagne De Vo, Baron Jean investment company executive
Dezell, James Edward finance company executive
De Zilwa, Mary Elizabeth finance company executive
Dibb, Caroline Sally management educator, consultant
Dillaber, Philip Arthur budget and resource analyst, economist, consultant
Divan, Gautam Ramanlal accountant
Docherty, William Thomas accountant
Doherty, Thomas Joseph financial services industry consultant
Dolan, Peter J. corporate financial consultant
Donaldson, William Henry financial executive, insurance company executive
Donev, Vassil Stefanov finance company executive, financial consultant
Donnelly, Augustine Stanislaus financial executive
Donnem, Sarah Lund financial analyst, non-profit and political organization consultant
Doody, Louis Clarence, Jr. accountant
Dornier, Philippe-Pierre consulting company executive, educator
Dorsett, Mary Alice business and tax consultant
Doto, Paul Jerome accountant
Dottarelli, Sergio accountant
Doty, Philip Edward accountant
Doughty, Michael Lee financial advisor
Douglass, John Angus financial adviser
Doyle, David Patrick marketing and cost management specialist, educator, writer
Dreze, Xavier Etienne Uriel Marie marketing educator
D'Souza, Alan S. tax consultant, real estate agent, pianist, writer
Dube, Rajesh financial consultant
Dubois, Marie-Astrid accountant
Duff, Grant William accountant
Duke, George Wesley financial executive
Duncan, Charles Howard business education educator
Duncan, Robert Bannerman strategy and organizations educator
Dunn, James Randolph corporate executive
Dunphy, Dexter Colboyd management educator
d'Ursel, Bernard tax specialist
Du Thoit, Pierre Gerard financial company executive
Earle, Paul W. financial executive, consultant
Echauz, Romeo R. finance company executive
Edleson, Michael Edward economist, finance educator, consultant, writer
Edwards, Bert Tvedt accountant
Edwards, Charles Mundy, III financial consultant
Edwards, James Benjamin accountant, educator
Eichler, Sylvia Maria auditor, international consultant
Eldroubi, Asma Abdel-Aziz Saleh business educator
Ellegard, Roy Whitney appraiser
Ellett, John Spears, II retired taxation educator, accountant, lawyer
Elser, Danny R. financial planner
Engdahl, Richard Alan management educator, consultant
Engwirda, Maarten Boudewijn auditor
Entriken, Robert Kersey retired management educator
Epperson, Eric Robert company executive, film producer
Erdelyi, Eileen Edith financial planner and advisor
Eriksson, Donald Gordon finance company executive
Espey, Linda Ann Glidewell accountant
Esteban, Hernani Patricio business administration educator
Ettl, Wolfgang Johann actuary, educator, researcher
Evans, Barry Craig financial services company exexutive
Evans, Martin G. management educator
Everett, Donna Raney business educator
Fairchild, Joseph Virgil, Jr. accounting educator
Farb, Thomas Forest financial executive
Farman-Farmaian, Ghaffar investment company executive
Farooque, Abujafar Mohammad financial educator
Farrall, Harold John retired accountant
Fayolle, Alain business educator
Feinzig, Stuart C. financial planner
Ferguson, Judith Lynne bookkeeper, poet, lyricist
Ferguson, Robert financial services executive, educator, writer
Feroz, Ehsan Habib accounting educator, researcher, writer
Field, Anthony accountant, theatre consultant
Fietsam, Robert Charles accountant
Finley, Lewis Merren financial consultant
Fischer, Aaron Jack accountant
Fischer, Jörg Gerard accountant
Fisher, Marshall Lee operations management educator
Fitzpatrick, Matthew Joseph financial services company executive
Flachsmann, Jean-Paul finance company executive
Fleisher, Jerrilyn financial planner
Fletcher, John Frederick accountant
Foley, Eugene Arthur accountant, consultant
Foley, Patricia Jean accountant
Forbes, John Edward financial consultant
Ford, Marcia Marie financial consultant
Forest, Philip Earle housing finance consultant
Form, Fredric Allan accountant
Forsythe, Velma Brown accountant, consultant, English language educator
Foss, Karl Robert auditor
Foulds, (Hugh) Jon diversified financial services company executive
Fountain, Desmond Hale sculptor, painter
Fraioli, Beverly bank auditor
Franklin, Paul Deane financial services executive, investor
Fredrick, Susan Walker tax company manager
Freeman, Charles J. financial executive, credit risk manager
Freeman, Kevin David portfolio management executive
Frenzel, Michael holding company executive
Freudenberg, Kurt accountant, finance executive
Freudenthal, Ernest Guenter technology and business educator
Frevert, James Wilmot financial planner, investment advisor
Friedlander, Paul Alan government tax programs advisor
Friedman, Robert Elliot equity analyst
Friedrich, Jean-Jacques accounting educator
Frye, Clayton Wesley, Jr. finance company executive
Fulscher, Mitch R. accountant
Fumaroni, Daniel Angel accountant, tax consultant
Gallagher, Lindy Allyn banker, financial consultant
Ganguly, Ananda Roop business management educator
Gass, Aileen retired accountant
Gaston, Margaret Anne retired business educator
Gasztowtt, Guillaume Pierre finance company executive
Gatewood, Robert Payne financial planning executive
Gauci-Maistre, John A. finance company executive
Gaul, Hans Michael diversified services company executive
Gauster, Christian Belrupt business administration educator, consultant
Gavian, Peter Wood investment banker
Geller, Jeffrey Lawrence financier
Gengor, Virginia Anderson financial planning executive, educator
George, Ernest Thornton, III financial consultant
Gerstner, Louis Vincent, Jr. diversified company executive
Ghauri, Pervez Nasim finance educator, consultant
Gibbs, Norman Charles William accounting and finance educator
Gibert, Thierry Michel merger and acquisition specialist
Gibson, Robert Van Rensselaer accountant, financial executive
Gibson, William Lee financial consultant
Giese, William Herbert tax accountant
Gijsen, Paul Hubertus finance administrator
Gillis, Nelson Scott financial executive
Gimbel, Alfred Adolf employee benefits professional
Gleijeses, Mario holding company executive
Glynn, Gary Allen pension fund executive
Gmeiner, Franz accountant
Goldberger, George Stefan finance executive
Goldie, Julian Dominic retired financial adviser, educator
Goldsmith, Stuart Andrew corporate finance company executive
Golub, Harvey financial services company executive
Gómez-Bezares, Fernando business educator
Goncalves, Paulo Alexandre De Jesus controller
Goodall, Arthur Alan accountant
Goodman, Neal Robert international management consultant and educator
Gorenberg, Charles Lloyd financial services executive
Gottfried, Mark Ellis accountant, consultant
Graham, Allister P. diversified company executive
Graham, Howard Lee, Sr. financial services company executive
Gratton, Robert diversified financial services company executive
Gray, Joyce tax specialist
Graydon, Frank Drake retired accounting educator, university administrator
Greaves, Irene Ethel international business educator
Greenshields, Raymond financial services company executive
Griffin, Jo Ann Thomas retired financial planner, tax specialist
Grimwade, Frederick Sheppard finance company executive
Grinyer, Peter Hugh business educator, management consultant
Gross, Stephen Randolph accountant
Gruber, George Michael accountant, financial systems consultant
Guckenheimer, Daniel Paul financial advisor
Guha-Thakurta, Rajeeb financial planner
Gulati, Vipin accountant
Gummesson, Evert Nils business educator
Gunawan, Bambang payment system executive
Gunnels, Lee O. retired finance and management educator, manufacturing/research company director, inventor
Gunther, Ellen Sozanne treasurer
Gupta, Dinesh Chandra accountant, educator
Gupta, Nirmal Kumar marketing educator, consultant
Gyllenhammar, Pehr Gustaf finance company executive, retired automobile company executive, writer
Haavardsson, Fridthjov finance executive
Hahn, Thomas Joonghi accountant
Hakala, Thomas J(ohn) financial planner, accountant
Halaby, Najeeb E. financier, lawyer
Haldar, Frances Louise business educator, accountant, treasurer
Hale, Danny Lyman financial executive
Hall, Merri Carol financial advisor
Hameed, Salman finance executive
Hamilton-Burke, Ian Douglas accountant
Hannink, D. Bradley financial company executive
Hanson, John Kow accountant
Harezi, Ilonka Jo financial company executive, consultant
Harkin, Daniel John controller
Harley, John Henry accountant, financial advisor
Harris, Wiley Lee financial services executive
Hart, Margareta audit director, researcher
Hartmann, Ann W. financial planner
Hartmann, Ulrich diversified financial services company executive
Hatcher, Stephanie D. accountant
Hau, Harald business educator
Haugland, Jerry Lee accounting educator
Havsteen, Jakob Henrik financial executive
Hawawini, Gabriel Alfred finance educator
Hays, William Grady, Jr. corporate financial and bank consultant
He, Xiaohong finance educator
Healy, Joanne P. accounting educator
Healy, Tom stock exchange executive
Hegazy, Ibrahim Abd-Elaziz marketing educator, consultant
Helmi, Dahli accounting educator and administrator
Helppie, Charles Everett, III financial consultant
Heneman, Robert Lloyd management educator
Henne, Andrea Rudnitsky business educator
Henry, Catherine financial communications executive
Henry, Roy Monroe financial planner
Herbert, Sally Mary accountant
Hernandez, Alejandro financial analyst
Herouin, Françoise finance executive
Herreros, Carlos accountant, consultant
Herringer, Frank Casper diversified financial services company executive
Hersh, Ira Paul tax and financial planning consultant
Hess, Donald Marc holding company executive
Heun, Werner law educator
Hewson, Donna Walters financial consultant
Higginbotham, Kenneth James financial services executive
Hihara, Katsuji accounting educator
Hilgenberg, John Christian financial executive, corporate director, consultant
Hill, Thomas Clarke, IX accountant, systems specialist, entrepreneur
Hinterhuber, Hans Hartmann management educator, researcher
Hites, Becky E. financial executive
Hlozek, Carole Diane Quast business executive
Hobbs, Guy Stephen financial executive
Hogan, Daniel John financial executive
Holland, Joseph John financial manager
Holland, Neila Anchieta business educator, consultant
Hollingsworth, John Arthur business education educator
Holman, James Lewis financial and management consultant

Holt, Michael Kenneth *management and finance educator, consultant, city councilman*
Holzkan, Silvia Jorgelina *accountant*
Honeyman, John Raymond *account manager, consultant*
Hornstein, Mark *financial executive*
Horton, Thomas Roscoe *business advisor*
Horwing, Joakim David Olof *financial consultant*
Hossfeld, Christopher *financial educator, researcher*
Hough, Lawrence A. *former financial organization executive*
Howard, Melvin *financial executive*
Hsee, Christopher K. *business educator*
Huang, Tao *financial analyst*
Huchant, Jean-Louis Raymond *financial executive*
Hueppi, Rolf *financial services executive*
Hughes, Arthur Hyde *accountant, consultant*
Hughey, David Vaughn *business administration educator, dean*
Hume, Alan James *accountant, management consultant*
Hunkin, John S. *financial company executive*
Hüppi, Rolf *financial company executive*
Hurlimann, Werner Stefan *actuary*
Hussain, Altaf *financial controller*
Hutchins, Edith Elizabeth *accountant*
Hyman, Leonard Stephen *finanical consultant, economist, author*
Hyman, Sigmund M. *benefits consultant*
Ibraimo, Ismael Mahomede *financial executive*
Ibssa, Seifu *accountant*
Ickis, John Cather *business administration educator*
Iles, Roger Dean *financial educator*
Innes, John *accounting educator*
Insardi, Nina Elizabeth *benefits administrator*
Ishikawa, Akira *global management educator*
Ismail, Michael Mohammed *financial consultant*
Ito Acosta, Javier Yutaka *financial consultant*
Ivy, Benjamin Franklin, III *financial and real estate investment advisor*
Iwasawa, Isoo (Francis) *accountant, management consultant*
Jaafar, Mohamed Ali *accountant, financial consultant*
Jackson, John Hermas *financial company executive*
Jacobsen, Søren Lange *financial consultant*
Jadin, Emile Joseph *finance company executive, consultant*
JaffrÈ, Eric *financier*
James, Annette L. *financial planner*
Jason, J. Julie *money manager, author, lawyer*
Jayson, Richard Andrew *accountant*
Jeanne, Pierre Paul *retired chief financial officer*
Jensen, Karsten Ulrik *management educator*
Jensen, Paul Edward Tyson *business educator, consultant*
Jessup, Joe Lee *business educator, management consultant*
Jimenez, Josephine Santos *portfolio manager*
Joaquin, Domingo Castelo *finance educator, management consultant*
Joergensen, Steen Bo *financial services executive*
Johanet, Olivier *finance executive, educator*
Johansen, Tor Fredrik *finance company executive*
Johnson, H. Thomas *business educator*
Johnson, James A. *financial organization executive*
Johnson, Robert Doheny *portfolio manager*
Johnson, Sondra Lea *accountant*
Jones, Larry Darnell *tax specialist*
Jones, Michael Lynn *financial consultant, branch operations manager*
Jönsson, Sten Arne *business administration educator*
Jordaan, Barend Daniel *management educator*
Kabat, Eduardo Esteban *actuary*
Kachos, George *financial analyst*
Kahalas, Harvey *business educator*
Kalas, Frank Joseph, Jr. *financial, information systems consultant*
Kandel, Donald Harry *financial analyst*
Kandil, Ahmed Amine *international financial consultant, entrepreneur*
Kao, Chiang *management educator*
Kaplan, Steven Mark *accountant*
Kapoor, Jagdish R. (Jack Kapoor) *marketing educator, writer*
Karapanchev, Georgi Lubomirov *treasurer*
Karnavat, Sumatilal Chhaganlal *educator, consultant*
Ka-shing, Li *finance company executive*
Katerndahl, Paul David *financial consultant*
Kaufman, Charles David *controller*
Keefe, Carolyn Joan *tax accountant*
Keehn, Neil Francis *investment banker, engineer, technologist*
Keim, Donald Bruce *finance educator*
Kelleher, Kathleen *financial services marketing specialist*
Kellogg, C. Burton, II *financial analyst*
Kennedy, Thomas Patrick *financial executive*
Kenney, Donna Denise *accountant*
Key, Helen Elaine *accountant, consulting company executive, educator*
Kherati, Rizwan Ullah *accountant*
Khor, Lian Huat *auditor*
Kilby, Theodore Morgan, Jr. *auditor, educator*
Kilmann, Ralph Herman *business educator*
Kim, Byung-Do *marketing educator*
Kim, E. Han *finance and business administration educator*
Kim, Jai-Beom *international business educator*
Kim, Kiseon *information and communications educator*
Kimishima, Akira *finance company administrator, educator*
Kimmel, Paul Robert *financial executive*
King, Ronald Lee *accountant, government agency official*
Kinnison, Robert Wheelock *retired accountant*
Kirsch, Donald *financial consultant, writer*
Kirschenbaum, Lisa L. *portfolio manager, financial advisor*
Klapper, Byron D. *financial company executive*
Klauber, James Shuler *financial consultant, state legislator*
Klein, Steven Douglas *financial planner, securities broker*
Klote, James Denver *financial consultant*
Kobayashi, Noritake *business educator*
Kocher, Juanita Fay *retired auditor*
Koda, Kazuo *management educator*
Koehl, Camille Joan *accountant*
Kohler, Fred Christopher *tax specialist*
KÖhler, Horst *finance company executive*
Köhler, Rodolfo *financial executive*
Kolb, John Conner *financial markets executive*
Komansky, David H. *financial services executive*
Komorowski, Stanislaw Maurice *finance educator, consultant*
Konola, Claudette June *finance company executive, financial analyst*
Koong, Lin Loong *accountant*
Koraua, Baoro Laxton *financial services company executive*
Korunič, David John *financial executive, consultant*
Kotolup, James Alexander *finance company executive, accountant*
Kovacs, Flora *financial executive, economist*
Kraut, William *financial executive*
Krintas, Theodore *finance company executive*
Kroeger, Susan Jean *accountant*
Kube, Harold Deming *retired financial executive*
Kuintzle, Audry Jane *financial executive*
Kulesza, Chester Stephen (Bud Kulesza) *finance executive*
Kullberg, Duane Reuben *accounting firm executive*
Kurish, James Brian *finance executive*
Kwong, Alvin Lin-Pik *financial controller*
Labaki, Salim E. *scheduling and cost control engineer*
Labrow, Christopher Reginald *investment advisor*
Ladimeji, Oladapo A. *accountant*
Ladjevardi, Hamid *fund manager*
Lam, Andrew *financial advisor*
Lam, Anthony Chi K. *financial executive*
Lam, Wai Kuen Alex *financial controller, accountant*
Lamaze, Jean-Hughes de *equity analyst executive*
Lamont, Alice *accountant, consultant*
Lampert, Shlomo Izhak *marketing and business strategy consultant*
Landrakis, John *business educator, consultant*
Langer, Horst *financial corporate executive*
Langermann, John W. R. *financial services executive*
La Noire, Alberto *finance administrator, consultant*
Lansford, Edwin Gaines *accountant*
Larmola, Eero Antero *business educator*
La Rosa, Giuseppe *accountant*
Larsen, Glen Albert, Jr. *finance educator*
Lastra, Rosa Maria *law and finance educator*
Laubach, Roger Alvin *accountant*
Lauletta, Francisco *accountant*
Laurent, Jean *credit company executive*
Laverge, Hendrik Johannes *finance company executive, investor, consultant*
Lavolpe, Antonio *accountant*
Lawson, Abraham Odartey *accountant*
Leavy, Brian Cahir *business educator*
Leckie, Stuart Hamilton *investment actuary*
Ledbetter, Linda Carol *pension fund executive, professional organization executive*
Lee, Chi-Wen Jevons *accounting educator, administrator, columnist*
Lee, Myung Woo *financial secretary, accountant*
Lee, Ronson Kwok Keung *accountant*
Lee, Sang Moon *management educator*
Leech, Stewart Andrew *accounting educator, researcher*
Leerberg, Per *accountant*
Lees, William Glenwood *finance executive, retail executive*
Le Goc, Michel Jean-Louis *business educator*
Lehmann, Steffen *financial counsulting company executive*
Leino, Deanna Rose *business educator*
Lelong, Pierre *auditor*
Leong, Choon-Chiang *business educator*
Leong, Sze Hian *finance company executive, financial planner*
Leraaen, Allen Keith *financial executive*
Lerner, Herbert J. *retired accountant*
Le Roux, Gerard Edouard *financial consultant, author*
Levin, Harvey Jay *financial institution design and construction specialist, developer, auctioneer*
Levinson, Shauna T. *financial services executive*
Lewis, W. Walker *strategic and financial advisory company executive*
Li, Kuan-Te Kevin *business educator, restaurateur, consultant*
Lienemann, Delmar Arthur, Sr. *accountant, real estate developer*
Lifschultz, Phillip *financial and tax consultant, accountant, lawyer*
Lilani, Pankaj Maganlal *financial controller*
Lim, Wei Shi *business educator, researcher*
Lin, Jiken *banking educator*
Lin, Thomas Wen-shyoung *accounting educator, researcher, consultant*
Lin, William Bing-Tsang *accountant*
Lincoln, Alexander, III *financier, lawyer, private investor*
Lindholm, Richard Theodore *economics and finance educator*
Lindquist, Richard James *portfolio manager*
Linnecar, Peter Charles Roland *financial services company executive*
Lintacker, Marcel Alphonse Sidney *finance company executive, consultant*
Lippens, Maurice *finance company executive*
Lis, Anthony Stanley *retired business administration educator*
Little, Mark McKenna *financial management executive*
Liu, Alcott K.P. *accountant, business consultant*
Liu, Kennedy Tat-Yin *accountant*
Llewellyn, David Thomas *financial services educator*
Lohmann, Leslie John *employee benefit consultant, actuary*
Lohse, Andrea *business and competition law educator*
Long, Susan Diane *management educator*
Longhi, Robert Leonard *chief financial officer*
Longin, Pierre E. *government affairs consultant*
Lorimer, Sir Desmond *retired chartered accountant*
Lotwala, Bhupendra Tulsidas *finance executive, tax consultant*
Lovell, Terry Jeffry *business educator*
Low, George Solon *business educator, consultant*
Lu, Lihjeng Maurice *finance company executive, consultant*
Lubash, Dan *financial executive*
Lueders, Carl L. *finance executive*
Lulat, Mohamed Gora Suleman *financial executive*
Luna, Barbara Carole *financial analyst, accountant, appraiser*
Lundblad, Eric Roy *finance executive*
Luo, Jessica Chaoying *actuary*
Luthans, Fred *management educator, writer, consultant*
LymBurner, James Richard William *financial services executive, economic financial adviser*
Lynn, Leonard Harvey *business educator*
Lysons, Arthur F. *management educator*
Macaya, Jose M. *strategy consultant*
MacCallan, James Michael Ferguson *corporate treasurer*
MacKenzie, Ian Donald *actuary*
Madariaga, Lourdes Mercedes *accountant*
Maffei Faccioli, Carlo Francesco *financial executive*
Magoon, Donald W. *retired business educator*
Mahenthiran, Sakthi *accounting educator, consultant*
Mahoney, Thomas Henry, IV *finance executive*
Major, Suzette *management sciences educator*
Makihara, Minoru *diversified corporation executive*
Malan, Jacques Daniel *actuary*
Malek, Frederic Vincent *finance company executive*
Malhotra, Yoginder Nath. *finance company executive*
Malkin, Moses Montefiore *employee benefits administration company executive*
Malone, Lisa R. *accountant, scheduler*
Mancillas-Perez, Eduardo José *business educator, consultant*
Mankin, Robert Stephen *financial executive*
Mann, Barlow Treadwell *financial consultant, lawyer*
Manu, Franklyn Achampong *business educator, consultant*
Marchand-Tonel, Maurice John *business executive*
Marcombes, Eric François *finance company executive*
Marconi, Peter Paul, Jr. *financial analyst*
Markou, Demetrios *accountant*
Markowitz, Harry M. *finance and economics educator*
Marlas, James Constantine *holding company executive*
Martin, Luan *accountant, payroll and timekeeping supervisor*
Martin Alonso, Olga *auditor*
Martiniere, Gerard de la *holding companies executive*
Massey, Sam Guerry *financial analyst*
Massura, Edward Anthony *accountant*
Mathews, George Meprathu *accounting executive*
Mathews, Martin Reginald *accounting educator*
Matschke, Manfred Juergen *finance educator*
Maury, Mireille *finance administrator*
May, Carl Emil *accountant*
Maystadt, Philippe *financial executive*
Mazaud, Jean-Francois *organization executive*
Mazzarella, James Kevin *business administration educator*
McAdoo, Michael Brendan *accounting consultant, lecturer, broadcaster*
McCall, Louis Charles John *chief financial officer, financial advisor and executive*
McCuen, John Joachim *building company and financial company executive*
McDonald, John Gregory *financial investment educator*
McElroy, Maurine Davenport *financier, educator*
McElyea, Jacquelyn Suzanne *accountant, real estate consultant*
McGraw, Bryan Kelly *financial company executive*
McGraw, Kenneth Wayne *financial executive*
McIntyre, Louise S. *income tax consultant*
McMahon, Paul Francis *finance company executive*
McNeil, Paul Joseph, Jr. *employment security interviewer*
McWhorter, Jerry Evan *accountant*
Melling, John Kennedy *accountant*
Menipaz, Ehud *business administration educator, engineer*
Menon, Sanjay Thekkecheruvath *management educator*
Merchant, Ruth Nelms *retired accountant*
Merrifield, Dudley Bruce *business educator, former government official*
Merville, Lawrence Joseph *finance educator*
Meyer, Robert Lewis *investment company executive*
Meyler, William Anthony *financial executive*
Mian, Waseem Shafiq *accountant*
Michelet, Jorgen Georg *financial executive*
Mijatovic, Miroslav *financial company executive*
Mikołajczyk, Zofia Stanisława *management educator*
Miles, John Bill *accountant, tax advisor*
Miller, L. Martin *accountant, financial planning specialist*
Miller, Renée Jacques *accountant, administrator*
Millett, Terry Brian *financial services executive*
Millns, Anthony Thomas Cowling *financial and maritime consultant*
Minehart, Jean Besse *tax accountant*
Miselson, Alex J. (Jacob) (Jacob Miselson) *portfolio manager, securities analyst, investment theorist*
Mishra, Chandra S. *finance educator, consultant*
Mitcham, Julius Jerome *accountant*
Mitchell, Charles Basil *accountant, company director*
Mitchell, John Campbell *financial broker*
Mitchell, Keith Ronald *accountant, politician*
Mitchell, Robert Lee, III *auditor*
Mitchell, Vincent-Wayne *management educator*
Mitra, Sunirmal *accountant, consultant*
Mittal, Dutt Kumar *commerce educator, researcher*
Mitte, Roy F. *finance company executive*
Mitty, Todd Jay *financial services company executive*
Mobley, William Hodges *management educator, researcher, author, executive*
Modena, Stefano Paolo Emilio *financial executive*
Moers, Joyce Ann *bookkeeper, day camp administrator*
Mohamed, Mohd-Zain Bin *management educator, consultant, researcher*
Moir, James Marcus *finance company executive*
Mokhtar, Mohamad *financial executive*
Monahan, Thomas Paul *accountant*
Monippally, Mathukutty Matthew *business communication educator*
Monod, Jérôme *diversified financial services company executive*
Montanus, Mary Rosamond *accountant*
Montero, Analia Haidee *accountant, educator, consultant*
Montgomery, Henry Irving *financial planner*
Moolla, Zulker Nain *accountant*
Moore, Brian Clive *actuary*
Moore, Herff Leo, Jr. *management educator*
Moore, Joyce Kristina *financial planner*
Moore, Peter David *finance director, accountant*
More, Philip Harvey Birnbaum *business administration educator*
Morgan, Frank T. *business educator, consultant*
Morgan, William J. *accounting company executive*
Morgan, William P., Jr. *financial planning and investment firm executive*
Moriya, Toshikazu *accountant*
Morrissey, Helena Louise *fund manager*
Mosler, John *retired financial planner*
Mosoloi, Thago Felix *accountant*
Mourgue D'Algue, Pierre Andre *finance company executive*
Mowat, Magnus Charles *company executive*
Moy, Helen Kwong *accountant*
Moyer, F. Stanton *financial executive, advisor*
Moyles, Philip Vincent, Jr. *financial services company executive*
Mudry, Michael *pension and benefit consultant*
Muhlemann, Lukas *financial executive*
Muldowney, Michael Patrick *finance executive*
Munkholt, Peer *fund executive*
Murray, Thomas James *financial planner, publisher*
Muscarella, Christopher James *finance educator*
Muthana, Dechu Palecanda *structured finance analyst*
Myers, Anthony Charles *accountant*
Naik, Prasad Anand *marketing educator*
Nakano, Isao *accounting educator*
Nartey, Ebenezer Jackson *accountant, finance manager*
Nasu, Yukio *business educator*
Neeley, James Kame *credit agency executive*
Neeter, Henry *financial analyst*
Negem, Helmi M. *accountant, lawyer*
Neki, Saichi *marketing educator*
Nelson, Dennis Lee *finance educator*
Nelson, Mary Ellen Dickson *retired actuary*
Neuhaus, Joan T. *finance company executive, private investigator*
Neves, João Adamor Dias *marketing educator, researcher*
Newton, David Alexander *holding company executive*
Neyt, Philip *pension fund executive*
Nicholls, Miles Grafton *business educator*
Nicholson, Nigel *business educator*
Ninke, Arthur Albert *accountant, management consultant*
Nirsimloo, Jay *financial company executive*
Niwa, Uichiro *financial company executive*
Nix, John Sydney *retired business management educator*
Nixon, Robert Obey, Sr. *business educator*
Njinu, Peter Kimani *controller*
Nold, Aurora Reyes *business and economics educator*
Nondi, Richard Owino *management educator*
Nordlinger, Gerson *investor*
Norlander, Jonas Rolf *treasury executive*
Norwood, Samuel Wilkins, III *financial consultant*
Notarte, Rommel de Guzman *accountant*
Nunez-Lawton, Miguel G. *international finance specialist*
Nwoye, May Ifeoma *accountant, business educator, consultant*
Nzomo, Nzele David *accounting educator*
Obereder, Erich Anton *financial analyst*
O'Brien, Kevin Patrick *business and management educator*
Odescalchi, Edmond Péry *international financial consultant, author*
Ogunc, Kurtay *investment advisor, manager*
Oh, Tai Keun *business educator*
Olayan, Suliman Saleh *finance company executive*
O'Leary, Teresa *controller*
Oliver, Dominick Michael *business educator*
Olsen, Jan Terje *corporate treasurer*
Olshen, Abraham Charles *actuarial consultant*
Öman, Pertti Juhani *auditor*
O'Mullain, Ciaran *accountant*
Önkal-Atay, Dilek *management educator*
Orpen, Christopher Edward *management educator*
Osborn, Kenneth Louis *financial executive*
Osburn, Hugh Jack *business valuation consultant, accountant*
Osei-Ofei, Emmanuel *auditor, accountant*
Osiegbu, Patrick Ife *finance educator, consultant, researcher*
Otto, Johan Lodewikus *financial executive*
Ozair, Syed Mohammad *business educator*
Ozer, Muammer *business educator*
Pagano, Filippo Frank *financial broker, commercial loan consultant*
Painter, Christopher *public management educator*
Palesky, Carol East *tax accountant*
Palin, Michael Gurdon *portfolio manager*
Pamensky, Joseph Leon *financial executive*
Papachatzis, Petros Nikolaos *finance, insurance executive*
Pappas, Michael *financial services company executive*
Park, Chul Am *finance educator*
Parker, Lee David *accounting and management educator, researcher, consultant*
Parmeggiani, Luca *asset management company executive*
Parrott, Dennis Beecher *accountant*
Parsons, John Seymour *accountant, trading company executive*
Pastor, Javier Lopez *marketing consultant*
Pataki, Béla *management educator*
Pate, John Gillis, Jr. *financial consultant, accounting educator*
Patel, Bharat *financial executive*
Patel, Vinod Motibhai *accountant*
Pattoo, Srinivasan *finance company executive*
Pavanelli, James Paolo *business executive, financial adviser*
Pawson, Kenneth Vernon Frank *farmer, former hotel company executive*
Pearson, Alan Wilfred *management educator*
Pearson, Barrie *finance executive*
Pearson, Conrad E. *financial services executive*
Pedlar, Arthur Peter *accountant*
Pendrill, David *accounting and financial management educator*
Pennington, Beverly Melcher *financial services company executive*
Pennington, Margaret Angela *financial consultant*
Pentin, David John *accountant, financial advisor*
Peow, Ong Toon *controller*
Peralta, Lionel *financial executive*
Perel, Mariano *finance executive, consultant*
Peters, Ann Louise *accounting administrator*
Petersen, Douglas Arndt *financial development consultant*
Petersen, Gladys *accounting clerk, writer*
Peterson, Randall Scott *management educator*
Pettersen, Thomas Morgan *accountant, finance executive*
Pettit, John Douglas, Jr. *management educator*
Pétursson, Gísli Ragnar *accountant, consultant*
Pfeister, Raymond Lynn *diversified financial services company executive*
Picard, Laurent A(ugustin) *retired management educator, administrator, consultant*
Picconatto, Evelyn Clara *accountant*
Pick, Robin Alexander *accountant*
Pietro, Jeremy *finance company executive*
Pike, Charles James *employee benefits consultant, financial planner*
Pilar, L. Prudencio R. *financial services executive*
Pinon, Eric Marie Daniel *finance company executive*

Pinto-Pereira, Berardo Francisco financial consultant, management consultant
Plaistowe, William Ian David accountant
Plimpton, Peggy Lucas trustee
Polemitou, Olga Andrea accountant
Pollak, Norman Lee retired accountant
Pomeranz, Felix accounting educator
Poot, Allan Arnold internet financial services company executive
Portal, Jonathan Francis (Sir Jonathan Portal Bt.) accountant
Post, Gerald V. business educator
Potworowski, Tadeusz Krzysztof accountant
Powell, Thomas Ervin financial consultant, small business owner
Poza, Ernesto Juan business consultant, educator
Prabu, R.S.K. Lakshmanan business educator
Pranada, Marfred Jandoc financial adviser
Price, David William James money manager, farmer
Price, Michael F. money management executive
Prosnitz, David J. unemployment cost control company executive
Prosser, Sir Ian M.G. financial executive
Prost-a-la-Denise, Bernard M. financial controller, industrial economist
Prot, Baudouin financial company executive
Prout, Carolyn Ann controller, personnel administrator
Pruitt, Stephen Wallace finance educator
Pugh, David John accountant, company director
Purcell, Philip James financial services company executive
Purcell, Stuart McLeod, III financial planner
Puri, Rajendra Kumar business and tax specialist, consultant
Purvis, John Robert international business consultant
Quandour, Mohydeen Izzat financial consultant, author
Quant, Harold Edward retired financial services company executive, ranc
Queen, Nathaniel Francis, Jr. financial executive, consultant
Quinn, Michael Desmond diversified financial services executive
Quirici, Daniel finance company executive
Raffegeau, Jean Michel audit and consulting company executive, editor
Rahn, Friedrich James financial executive and researcher
Raj, Mahendra business educator
Rajkovic, Vladislav management information systems educator
Rakower, Joel A. business appraiser, litigation consultant
Ralston, Steven Philip portfolio manager, financial analyst
Ramaseshan, Balasubramanian marketing educator
Ramchander, Sanjay finance educator
Ramík, Jaroslav operations research educator, researcher
Randall, Kay Temple accountant, real estate agent, retired
Rao, Vithala R. marketing educator
Rastegar-Djavahery, Nader E. private equities investor
Rawson, Jim Charles accountant, executive
Reddy, Chilakala Ramamuni business educator
Reech, Christophe Gilbert Daniel financial executive
Reedy, Harry Lee financial services executive
Reidy, Thomas Michael financial executive
Reilly, Frank Kelly business educator
Reps, David Nathan finance educator
Reser, Elizabeth May (Betty Reser) bookkeeper
Revin, Bengt financial executive
Rey, Jan Michal financial consultant
Ricci, Giovanni Mario finance company executive
Rich, David Barry financial executive, accountant, entertainer
Richards, David Gordon financial executive
Richardson, Arline Annette accountant, comptroller
Rickershauser, Paul E. benefits compensation director
Ritz, Stephen Mark financial advisor, lawyer
Robin, Donald P. business educator
Robinson, Kenneth Charles business educator
Rockwell, Elizabeth Dennis retirement specialist, financial planner
Rodarie, Denis financial company executive
Rodgers, Steven Edward tax practitioner, educator
Rodriguez Valero, Francisco Jose management consultant, accountant, international travelling consultant
Rogers, James Gardiner accountant, educator
Rogers, Jon Martin financial consultant, financial company executive
Rogers, Patrick R. management educator
Roland, Melissa Montgomery accountant
Ronald, Adhami financial expert and planner, advisor
Ronald, Thomas Iain retired financial services executive
Rorke, William Buckland (Paddy Rorke) accountant, consultant
Roseingrave, Janice Anne accountant
Rosenberg, Theodore Roy financial executive
Rosenheim, Elchanan Shimshon property consultants company executive
Rosmundsson, Olafur Ingi internal auditor
Ross, Steven Charles business administration educator, consultant
Roth, Gary Neal accountant
Rothman, Adam Alan financial consultant
Round, Tony independent financial adviser
Rovinelli, Judith Frances financial advisor
Roy, Barin Brian travel and financial services company executive
Royer, Thomas Jerry financial planner
Royle, Anthony William accountant
Rubinowicz, Claude Jean-Pierre financial consultant, inspector finances
Rufeh, Mark finance company executive
Ruff, Henri-Jacques credit card company executive
Ruggeri, Andrea Pietro auditor
Ruhlin, Peggy Miller investment adviser, financial planner
Rukodzi, Patrick Saniro accountant, secretary
Rupe, Gary E. controller
Ruppert, Edouard auditor
Rush, Richard Henry financial executive, writer, lecturer
Russell, Ian MacGregor accountant, utility company executive
Ruyle-Hullinger, Elizabeth Smith (Beth Ruyle) consultant, municipal financial advisor
Ryan, John Patrick consulting actuary, management consultant
Ryan, Leo Vincent business educator
Ryan, Michael John finalcial analyst
Rylander, Robert Allan financial service executive
Saaiman, Nolan auditor
Sacco, John Michael accountant
Saeed, Arshad financial consultant
Sagafi-nejad, Tagi business educator
Sahni, O.P. business educator, management consultant
Salama, Ali Gamal El Din audit firm executive, consultant
Samii, Massood international business educator, consultant
Sanborn, Anna Lucille pension and insurance consultant
Sandstrom, Alice Wilhelmina accountant
Sarther, Lynette Kay accountant
Sasaki, Edson Mitsuo financial services company executive
Saurazas, Julia Roberta business educator
Savage, Thomas Joseph executive development company executive, priest
Sawyer, Adrian John taxation educator, consultant
Saykiewicz-Sajkiewicz, Jan Napoleon marketing educator
Schechter, Clifford financial executive, lawyer
Schildbach, Thomas business administration educator
Schmadl, Franz Wilhelm financial management executive
Schmid, Stefan international management educator
Schmidt, Glen Kevin finance director
Schmitt, Bernd Herbert business educator
Schredelseker, Klaus finance educator
Schroeder, Kimberly Hudson financial auditor
Schunke, Hildegard Heidel accountant
Schwartz, Gerald Wilfred financial executive
Schwepker, Charles Henry, Jr. marketing educator
Schwister, Jay Edward portfolio manager
Schwyn, Charles Edward accountant
Scott, David Richard Alexander finance director, accountant
Scott, George Gallmann accountant
Scott, Ian James accountant
Scott, Sidney Buford financial services company executive
Scott, William Raymond accountant, financial director
Scozzari, Albert portfolio manager, inventor
Scruton, Robert accountant, management consultant
Seaman, Jerome Francis actuary
Selles, Robert Hendrikus actuary, consultant
Selšek, Cvetka stock exchange executive
Serota, Wendy Ellen tax officer
Séroux, Patrice Jean finance company executive
Servien, Louis-Marc, Comte De Boisdauphin, Lord of Quendon finance company and import-export executive
Sessions, Barbara C. business development director, lawyer
Sethi, Ramesh Kumar accountant
Sethi, Suresh P. management educator, researcher
Seto, William Roderick public accounting company executive
Sha, Zhen-Quan marketing educator
Shackleton, Robert James accounting executive
Shah, Shantilal Jamnadas accountant, educator
Sharov, Alexander Nick financial exchange executive
Sharp, J(ames) Franklin finance educator, investment portfolio manager
Sharpe, Kenneth Joseph financial services executive
Shaw, Richard Glenn financial analyst
Shayo, Stephen Mashindano accountant
Shenkman, Mark Ronald investment and finance executive
Sherman, Howard D. financial consultant
Sherman, Signe Lidfeldt portfolio manager, former research chemist
Shima, Hiromu management educator
Shmueli, Alfred accountant, educator
Shoecraft, Tim Henry tax minimization strategist
Shol, Kim Durand accountant, computer programmer
Showalter, David Scott accounting executive
Shrager, Robert Neil business executive
Shrimpton, David accountant
Shueh, John Wei-chung finance company executive, management educator
Shusterman, Peter Ivan Michael financial advisor
Siekmann, Donald Charles accountant
Sillanpdd, Jarkko financial professional, lawyer
Silver, Peter John accountant
Simmonds, Kenneth management educator
Simmons, John Derek financial consultant
Sinclair, David Grant accountant
Singer, Alan Evan management educator
Singh, Gangaram business educator
Singh, Malvinder financial executive
Singhal, Deepak finance executive
Sisson, Douglas Lee pension fund executive
Skou, Peder Noes financial executive
Skwiersky, Paul accountant
Smith, Harold Charles private pension fund executive
Smith, Jo Ann Costa comptroller
Smith, Michael Richard finance director
Smith, Robert Luther management educator
Smith, Stephen DeWitt finance educator
Smoot, David Paul finance company executive
Smunt, Timothy Lawrence management educator, business researcher, consultant
Smythe, Thomas Ira, Jr. finance educator, researcher
Solidum, James finance and insurance executive
Sonnier, Patricia Bennett business management educator
Soros, George fund management executive
Southwell, John Philip financial consultant
Spicer, Ronald L. financial services educator
Spinner, Lee Louis accountant
Springett, Peter Antony financial consultant
Stammler, Michael Hans portfolio manager, financial research executive
Stanton, William John, Jr. marketing educator, author
Stapleton, Nigel John financial executive
Starr-Glass, David Baruch management education educator, consultant
Steensma, Michael Eric controller
Stehle, Richard Eugen finance educator
Stein, Paul Clinton financial planner
Stenberg, Adam W. financial advisor, investment company executive
Stern, Ernest trust company executive
Sterrett, James Melville accountant, business consultant
Stevens, Wilbur Hunt accountant
Stevenson, Kevin Michael accountant
Stibbe, Austin Jule accountant
Stockmeyer, Rolf-Peter accountant
Stoever, William Alfred international business educator, lawyer, consultant
Stone, Philip James financial director
Storbeck, Matthew Lee finance director
Storey, Robert Clifton financial consultant
Street, Maryan industrial relations educator
Subrahmanyam, Avanidhar management educator
Surana, Prakash Chand accountant, consultant
Suryanarayanan, Ananthanarayanan finance company executive
Suster, Zeljan business educator, dean
Swamy, M. R. Kumara financial management researcher
Swanson, Leslie Keating financial services executive
SyCip, Washington accountant
Syron, Richard Francis financial executive, economist
Szabó, László financial executive, economist, chemical engineer
Szokoloczy-Syllaba, Philippe Bela tax and estate planning specialist
Talbot, Peter Jennings financial services executive
Talley, Richard Woodrow accountant
Talonov, Alexander V. management educator
Tan, Li-Su Lin accountant, insurance executive, investment consultant
Tan, Richie Reynan Chua finance officer
Tarapoom, Voravan mutual fund executive
Tarpeh-Doe, Linda Diane controller
Taylor, Frank Henry accountant
Taylor, John Patrick controller
Taylor, John Read, Jr. financial management company executive
Taylor, Martin Gibbeson accountant
Taylor, Richard Bertrom accountant
Taylor, Wilson H. diversified financial company executive
Teets, Walter Ralph accounting educator
Tegner, Ian Nicol financial executive
Telow, Susan Tan accountant, business executive
Tengen, Thomas L. financial planner, finance educator
Terták, Adam tax consultant
Thomas, James Edward accountant
Thomas, Kerry-Anne Abigail investment executive
Thomas, Michael James business educator
Thompson, G. Kennedy financial services company executive
Thompson, John Douglas financier
Tidwell, Paula Marcella business educator
Tiedemann, Henrik financial executive, consultant
Tiew, Daniel controller
Ting, Paul Wai-Tai auditor
Tofias, Allan accountant
Tombaugh, Richard L. financial aid consultant
Tomkinson, Robert Charles financial executive
Tomsett, Alan Jeffrey retired accountant
Toohey, Edward Joseph financial services company executive
Torkelund, Kay Robert financial executive
Tothfalusi, Andras finance company executive, consultant
Trasi, Giampaolo financial analyst, head of equity strategy
Trebing, David Martin financial executive
Tsuji, Akihiro finance company executive
Tsukiji, Richard Isao international marketing and financial services consultant
Tsutani, Motohiro accounting educator
Tucker, Matthew D. controller, systems administrator
Tugendhat, Baron Lord Christopher Samuel finance company executive
Tully, Daniel Patrick financial services executive
Turner, Henry Brown finance executive
Tyler, Richard James personal and professional development educator
Ukaegbu, David Okwukanmanihu accountant, management consultant
Urick, Dean W. tax and financial planner
Usui, Noriyuki finance educator
Val, Georges Antoine international financial development consultant, photographer
van Blerck, Marius Cloete tax consultant
Van Bulck, Hendrikus Eugenius accountant
van Bulck, Margaret West accountant, financial planner, educator
Van Dusen, Glenn T. controller, secretary, treasurer
Vangerven, Paul Marie financial executive
Vanniasingham, Samuel Kanagasabapathy accountant
Vannukul, Virachai management consultant
Van Rensburg, Botha Janse accountant, educator
Van Rompuy, Victor Maurice retired educator
Van Westen, Frans finance executive
Van Zijl, Piet-Hein finance company executive
Vecchio, Robert Peter business management educator
Velisaris, Chris Nicholas financial analyst
Verde, Juan accountant
Vermilya, Dale Nelson accountant
Vetter, Claus Johannes financial-real estate management company executive
Vinten, Gerald auditing and ethics educator
Vohra, S. Ray accountant
von Braun, Peter Carl Moore Stewart finance company executive
Vorobiev, Igor Andrejevich finance company executive, science educator
V. Wysocki, Klaus accounting educator
Wade, Royce Allen financial services representative
Walczak, Joanne Carol accountant
Waldegrave, Lord of North Hill financial services company executive
Wallace, Roger James educator, researcher
Wallenius, Ilkka Jyrki management educator
Wang, Ji Zu finance educator, economics researcher
Wang, Peter Tsing-Shih fund management company executive
Wankmueller, John Robert finance company executive
Warde-Norbury, William George Antony financial executive
Warner, Roberta Arlene accountant, financial services executive
Waskow, Mark Stuart financial planner
Watanabe, Kishichi retired business educator
Watford, Paul Stephen finance analyst
Watkin, Virginia Ruth financial professional
Watne, Donald Arthur accountant, educator
Watts, Ross Leslie accounting educator, consultant
Wayne, Jeanette Marie auditor
Webb, James R. finance educator, consultant
Wechter, Ira Martin tax specialist, financial planner
Weinstein, Larry B. business educator
Wellisch, Dietmar Franz public finance, taxation educator, tax consultant
Wells, Damon, Jr. investment company executive
Wells, Patricia Trent auditor
Welsch, Glenn Albert accounting educator
Wenzel, Loren Alvin accounting educator
Werring, Henri Tuxen management educator
Wesberry, James Pickett, Jr. financial management consultant, auditor, international organization executive
Weston, W. Galen, Sr. diversified holdings executive
Weston Smith, John Harry finance director
Wheeler, David Michael financial executive
Whitaker, Heidi Sue accountant, auditor, information systems specialist
White, Margit Triska financial advisor
White, Roberta Lee financial analyst
Whitson, Keith R. business executive
Whittington, Geoffrey accountant, educator
Wichmann, Henry, Jr. accounting educator, researcher
Wicker, Franklin Michael financial consultant
Widjaja, Indrajuwana Komala accountant, consultant
Wierup, Ola financial analyst
Wilder, Robert Allen finance and leasing company executive, leasing broker, consultant
Wilhelmsson, Mats Anders marketing executive
Wilkinson, Harry Edward management educator and consultant
Williams, Gregory Keith accountant
Willy, Alexander Kenneth controller, consultant
Wilson, Robert M. financial executive
Winford, Maria audit executive
Winter, Edwin Thomas, Jr. accountant, treasurer
Winter, Richard Lawrence financial and health care company executive
Wippern, Ronald Frank financial and corporate consultant
Wirtschafter, Irene Nerove tax consultant
Wist, Paul Gabriel accountant
Wittenberg, Jon Albert accountant
Wolf, Frank business educator, consulting executive
Wolfensohn, James David finance company executive
Wolff, Richard Carl financial planner, insurance agency and pension planning company executive
Won, Youkyung business administration educator
Wong, Elizabeth financial controller
Wong, Mary financial executive
Wong, Tin Hong finance administrator, accountant
Woodcock, Barrie accountant, consultant
Woodring, John Olmer, Jr. financial planner and advisor
Woods, Ivan K.J. financial executive
Workman, Norman Allan accountant, graphic arts consultant
Wright, Donald Gene accountant
Wuest, Larry Carl tax examiner
Wulker, Laurence Joseph portfolio manager, educator, financial planner
Wullaerts, Lode Rene Elisabeth finance executive
Wunderlich, Hermann diversified corporation executive
Wyatt, Wilson Watkins, Jr. communications and public affairs executive
Wyss, David Alen financial service executive
Xi, Jun Yang financial educator, academic advisor
Yagil, Joseph finance educator
Yam, Joseph Chi-Kwong financial executive
Yamanobe, Yoshimasa business educator
Yamashita, Kotaro financial executive
Yang, Sao-Ping (Daisy Yang) accountant
Yeh, Chung-Hsing business systems educator
Yeung, Allan Yun-leun accounting educator
Yong-Dal, Suh accounting educator
York, Christopher Rodney finance company executive
Young, Colin S. financial services executive
Yu, Chao Chuan business educator, consultant
Yurtseven, Omer marketing and business educator
Zaman, Mohamed Nasir auditor
Zanecchia, Thomas Edward financial executive
Zanussi, Ana Amalia audit manager
Zavrel, B. John account executive, museum director
Zechner, Josef finance educator
Zhang, Jin information educator
Zhang, Shi business educator, consultant
Zhao, Shuming business educator, dean
Zick, Leonard Otto accountant, manufacturing executive, consultant
Zrust, Jiri financial executive
Zu Loewenstein-Wertheim-Freudenberg, Prince Rupert Louis Ferdinand financial consultant
Zyglidopoulos, Stelios Charalambos management educator

FINANCE: INSURANCE

Abbott, William Thomas claim specialist
Achis, Christos George insurance company executive
Adams, Gregory James insurance company executive
Alexander, Harold Campbell insurance consultant
Amjad, Imran McSood insurance executive
Aptowitzer, Willi Zeev insurance executive
Austin, Michael Charles insurance company executive
Aven, Terje risk and safety educator
Baerga-Vaquer, Rafael Antonio insurance agent
Bakker, James Wessel insurance company executive
Barry, Richard Francis retired life insurance company executive
Barthley, Rolston Lushington insurance company executive
Bartholomay, William C. insurance brokerage company executive, professional baseball team executive
Bebear, Claude insurance company executive
Beck, Luke Ferrell Wilson insurance specialist
Beery, Roger Lewis, II risk management consultant
Berkley, William Robert insurance holding company executive
Beshears, Charles Daniel insurance executive
Bhalla, Chaman Lal insurance broker
Bickley, John S. insurance association executive, educator, writer
Biggs, John Herron insurance company executive
Bloomer, Jonathan insurance company executive
Boarts, Laird Speer retired insurance company executive
Bond, William Laurie insurance executive
Bowers, Edna Reece underwriter
Brown, Randall L. reinsurance company executive
Buck, Earl Wayne insurance investigator, private detective
Bunker, Beryl H. retired insurance executive, community volunteer
Burgess, Ian Glencross insurance company executive
Burton, Daniel G. insurance executive

FINANCE: INVESTMENT SERVICES

Fohl, Timothy *consulting and investment company executive*
Fortina, Fabio *entrepreneur*
France, Joseph David *securities analyst*
Frankel, Leslie Fritz Gunther *stockbroker*
Fredericks, Ward Arthur *venture capitalist, food industry consultant*
Frerejean, Pierre Edward *investment management company executive*
Frey, Dale Franklin *financial investment company executive, manufacturing company executive*
Friedenberg, Daniel Meyer *financial investor, writer*
Friedl, Richard Anton *international holding company executive*
Fuld, Richard Severin, Jr. *investment banker*
Gaffney, Thomas Francis *investment company executive*
Gale, Michael Jonathan *entrepreneur*
Galloway, Daniel Lee *investment executive*
Gambrell, Thomas Ross *investor, retired physician, surgeon*
Georgi, Stefan *venture strategist*
Giammarco, Mario J. *investment manager*
Giannini, Valerio Louis *investment banker*
Gilbert, Debbie Rose *entrepreneur*
Gilbert, Steven Jeffrey *venture capitalist, screenwriter, lawyer*
Giordano, Nicholas Anthony *stock exchange executive*
Girondi, Patrizio F. *investment company executive*
Glassell, Alfred Curry, Jr. *investor*
Goddard, Edward Dean *stockbroker, accountant*
Goenka, Harsh Vardhan *diversified company executive*
Gottlieb, Lester M. *entrepreneur*
Gray, James L. *investment company executive*
Green, Francis William *investment consultant, former missile scientist*
Greenberg, Alan Courtney (Ace Greenberg) *stockbroker*
Gregg, David, III *investment banker*
Groezinger, Leland Becker, Jr. *investment professional*
Groom, Jeremy Richard *stockbroker*
Guccione, Joyce E. *securities company executive*
Guggenheim-Boucard, Alan Andre Albert Paul Edouard *business executive, international consultant*
Gunter, Bradley Hunt *capital management executive*
Haering, Kurt Arnold *investment executive*
Haight, Warren Gazzam *investor*
Halliday, John Meech *investment company executive*
Halmos, Peter *entrepreneur*
Hambro, Charles Eric Alexander *investment company executive*
Hanau, Kenneth John, III *venture capitalist*
Hardenberg, Alexander Johan *entrepreneur*
Hargrove, Roy Belmont, III *stockbroker*
Harilela, David Jethanand *enterpreneur*
Harlow, Ernest *portfolio manager*
Hart, Gurnee Fellows *investment counselor*
Haug, Marius Nygaard *investment company executive*
Hawksworth, Brian Michael *investment company executive*
Healey, Thomas J. *former government official, brokerage house executive*
Heath, Donald Wayne *securities wholesale executive, financial planner*
Heaton, Larry Cadwalder *securities company executive*
Hedberg, John Charles *investor*
Heilborn, George Heinz *investor*
Heimann, John Gaines *investment banker*
Heine, Leonard M., Jr. *investment executive*
Heinonen, Jouko Ensio *investment advisor, trading company executive, strategic advisor*
Heizer, Edgar Francis, Jr. *venture capitalist*
Hellman, F(rederick) Warren *investment advisor*
Henderson, Ian Ramsay *investment company executive*
Henderson, Kenneth Atwood *investment counseling executive*
Henkel, Arthur John *investment banker*
Hennigar, David John *investment broker*
Hennion, Carolyn Laird (Lyn Hennion) *investment executive*
Herbert, Jeffrey William *investment company executive*
Herrmann, Lacy Bunnell *investment company executive, financial entrepreneur, venture capitalist*
Hewitt, William Harley *investment and marketing executive*
Hickel, Walter Joseph *investment firm executive, forum administrator*
Hickey, Jerome Edward *investment company executive*
Hidalgo-Quehl, Guillermo *investment executive*
Hillman, Rita *investor*
Hinds, Glester Samuel *financier, program specialist, tax consultant*
Hinrichs, Todd Aaron *securities executive*
Hinshaw, Ernest Theodore, Jr. *private investor, former Olympics executive, former financial executive*
Hirschfield, Alan James *entrepreneur*
Hjorth, Jan E. *retired entrepreneur, small business consultant*
Hoffmann, Carlo Jean *business executive*
Hogan, Pauline Adina *entrepreneur*
Holland, George Frank, II *investment company executive*
Holmes, Douglas Quirk *investment banker*
Hongchoy, George M. *investment banker*
Horning, Robert Alan *securities broker*
Horton, Kenneth *investor*
Houck, John Dudley *investment adviser, educator*
Howe, James Everett *investment company executive*
Howell, George Bedell *equity investing and managing executive*
Huberman, Jonathan Serge *venture capitalist*
Hudson, Donald J. *retired stock exchange executive*
Huffman, Patricia Nell *entrepreneur*
Humes, Willem J. *investment manager*
Hunter, John Graham *investment management company executive*
Hyun, Myung-Kwan *investment company executive*
Indirkas, Tayfun Abdulhalik *holding company executive*
Indjic, Drago *investment company executive*
Islam, Muhammad Nurul *securities trader*
Ivanov, Iolian Marinov *investment manager, consultant*
Jagtiani, Ram Alimchand *investment counselor*
James, Bruce Richard *investor*
Janke, Kenneth *investment consultant*
Jargiello, Przemyslaw *investment company executive*
Jay, Christopher Edward *stockbroker*
Jepson, Hans Godfrey *investment company executive*
Johnson, Michael Warren *international relations specialist*
Johnson, Richard Walter *entrepreneur*
Johnstone, C. Bruce *investment company executive*
Jones, John Wesley *entrepreneur*
Jørgensen, Claus *investment company executive*
Joukowsky, Artemis A. W. *private investor*
Kahn, Herta Hess (Mrs. Howard Kahn) *retired stockbroker*
Kahn, Ronald N. *investment researcher*
Kan, Elizabeth Ka Yee *investment company executive*
Karatzas, Basil Michael *holding company executive, consultant*
Keane, Philip Vincent *investment company executive*
Keating, Margaret Mary *entrepreneur, business consultant*
Keegan, James Joseph *financial executive*
Keenan, Beverly Owen *entrepreneur*
Keffler, Karl Joseph *investment company executive, lawyer*
Kelly, Arthur Lloyd *management and investment company executive*
Keough, Donald Raymond *investment company executive*
Khan, Salahuddin Kasem *industrialist, diplomat*
Khemka, Shiv Vikram *investment company executive, venture capitalist*
Kiam-Siew, Michael Yap *technology entrepreneur*
Kidd, David Paul *investment manager*
Kim, Hyun Jin *venture capitalist*
Kim, Ke Bom *stockbroker, financial planner*
Kimmel, Mark *writer, retired venture capital company executive*
Kinney, Paul William *investment company executive*
Knapp, George Robert *investment executive, business advisor, lawyer*
Koonce, John Peter *investment company executive*
Krejs, Franz Reinhard *venture capital executive*
Krylov, Andrei Anatolievich *business executive*
Kuhens, Brian Scott *investment company executive, publishing company exexcutive*
Kuljanin, Spasoje *international trading company executive*
Kulok, William Allan *entrepreneur, venture capitalist*
Lakatos, Susan Carol *investment banker, artist*
Landis, Robert Kumler, III *investment banker, lawyer*
Lanitis, Nicholas Constantine *investments and business executive, author*
Lecomte, Olivier *property investment executive*
Lee, Andrew Siu Woo *investment company executive*
Leighton, Robert Bruce *investment company executive*
Levens, Joseph David *investment company executive*
Levy, Matthew Degen *investment banking technology and operations company executive, consumer products business development and planning executive, management consultant*
Liebau, Frederic Jack, Jr. *investment manager*
Liebscher, Klaus *stock exchange executive, banker*
Lin, Lin *stock broker, insurance agent*
Lindström, Caj-Gunnar *asset management company executive*
Lipper, Kenneth *investment banker, author, producer*
Lipukhin, Yuri Viktordvich *investment company executive*
Lloyd, Matthew David *entrepreneur, actor*
Locklin, Kenneth Robert *international venture capitalist, merchant banker*
Loeb, John Langeloth, Jr. *investment counselor*
Lombardo, Gaetano (Guy Lombardo) *venture capitalist*
Lovejoy, Lee Harold *investment company executive*
Lovell, Francis Joseph *investment company executive*
Lowenthal, Norman Dror *stockbroker, financial consultant*
Lucas, Donald Leo *private investor*
Lucas, Peter Charles *investment company executive*
Lurton, Horace VanDeventer *brokerage house executive*
Lust, Herbert Cohnfeldt, III *securities trader*
Lynch, William Wright, Jr. *investment executive, engineer*
Mack, John J. *investment company executive*
Main, Patricia Englander *investor*
Mak, Ken Ping *brokerage executive*
Malm, Rita H. *securities executive*
Mamut, Mary Catherine *retired entrepreneur*
Mann, Nancy Louise (Nancy Louise Robbins) *entrepreneur*
Mansur, Miguel José *holding and investment company executive*
Markman, Sherman *investment banker, venture capitalist, corporate financier*
Markopolos, Harry M. *investment professional*
Marron, Donald Baird *investment banker*
Marshall, Conrad Joseph *entrepreneur*
Martinez, John Stanley *entrepreneur*
Mathias, Julian Robert *investment manager*
Maumus, Olivier Jean-Dominique *investment executive*
Mavrikos, Elias *market analyst, investment consultant*
May, Benjamin Tallman *securities specialist, administrator*
May, Jeffrey R. *business executive*
McCullen, Joseph T., Jr. *venture capitalist*
McDonald, Mary Ann Melody *investment management executive*
McGlynn, William Charles *brokerage house executive*
McIntosh, William Alan *financier*
McLachlan, John James *investment company executive*
McMullan, William Patrick, III *investment banker*
McReynolds, Allen, Jr. *investment company executive*
Mergler, H. Kent *investment counselor*
Miles, Philip Allington *stockbroker*
Mitchell, Sir Derek *company director*
Mobbs, Sir Gerald Nigel *property investment executive*
Montgomery, Joseph William *finance company executive*
Moon, Peter Geoffrey *investment executive*
Moran, Christa Ilse Merkel *investor, linguist, educator*
Morgenroth, Earl Eugene *entrepreneur*
Morrison, Gordon Mackay, Jr. *investment company executive*
Morse, Robert Parker *investment company executive*
Moulton, Jonathan Paul *venture capitalist*
Mounsey, Joseph Backhouse *investment consultant*
Mountcastle, Kenneth Franklin, Jr. *retired stockbroker*
Muller, Johan Tobias *investment company executive*
Nazem, Fereydoun F. *venture capitalist, financier*
Neale, Frank Leslie George *venture capitalist*
Neece, Olivia Helene Ernst *investment company executive, consultant*
Nelson, Allen F. *proxy solicitation company executive*
Newman, Claire Poe *private investor*
Nichols, Katie *investment company executive*
Niemi, Niko Timo *entrepreneur*
Niemistö, Kari Pertti Henrik *investment company executive*
Nik Mohamed Din *stock exchange executive*
Nowaczek, Frank Huxley *venture capital executive*
Ofner, William Bernard *investor*
O'Grady, Beverly Troxler *investment executive, counselor*
Ohlman, Douglas Ronald *commodities and securities trader, investment consultant, lawyer*
Oldham, Gavin David Redvers *brokerage house executive*
Olinger, Chauncey Greene, Jr. *investment executive, editorial consultant*
Olisa, Ken Aphunezi *venture marketing company executive*
Olson, Edward Charles *entrepreneur, conservationist, writer, business consultant, foundation administrator*
Omole, Gabriel Gbolabo *international venture capitalist*
Osias, Richard Allen *international financier, investor, real estate investment executive, corporate investor*
Othman, Talat Mohamad *financial consultant, investment banker*
Owen, Thomas Llewellyn *investment executive*
Ozbolt, Simone Tracy *investment company executive*
Paladino, Albert Edward *venture capitalist*
Papps, Bruce William *investment company executive*
Parekh, Deepak *housing development finance executive*
Parry, Roger George *entrepreneur*
Paulson, Henry Merritt, Jr. *venture capitalist, investment banker*
Paulson-Ellis, Jeremy David *investment management executive*
Penn, Dawn Tamara *entrepreneur*
Penny, Susan Caroline Voelker *investment manager*
Pereira Pinto, Carlos Manuel Azevedo *investment manager, consultant*
Pescarmona, Enrique M. *entrepreneur*
Pesut, Timothy Scott *investment advisor, professional speaker, consultant*
Phillips, Thomas Edworth, Jr. *financial advisor, senior consultant*
Pickerell, Blair Chilton *investment management executive*
Pilkington, Mary Ellen *stockbroker, trader*
Pinner, Stephen John *stockbroker*
Pollack, Stephen J. *stockbroker*
Polster, Leonard H. *investment company executive*
Potter, John Davis *investment banker*
Pottruck, David Steven *brokerage house executive*
Pouschine, John Laurence *private equity investment executive*
Preston, Letricia Elayne *financial planner*
Price, Frank *property investment consultant*
Priestley, Hugh Michael *investment manager*
Pritchard, James Patrick *investment company executive*
Proffitt, John Richard *business executive, educator*
Puricelli, Franco *investment company executive*
Ragan, Robert Allison *private investment executive, financial consultant*
Rainwater, Joan Lucille Morse *investment company executive*
Rand, Lawrence Anthony *investor and financial relations executive*
Raphael, Paul Michel *investment banker*
Reagan, Lester Franklin *securities executive*
Reaves, Charles Durham *investment company executive*
Redo, David Lucien *investment company executive*
Reese, David Jen *stockbroker*
Riccardo, Benny *day trader, stock broker*
Richards, Darrie Hewitt *investment company executive*
Richards, Leonard Martin *investment executive, consultant*
Rizk, Tareq Abdul Kareem *investment company executive*
Roberson, Robert S. *investment company executive*
Roberts, David Glen *prospector, investor*
Robertson, Sara Stewart *private investor, entrepreneur*
Roby, Joe Lindell *investment banker*
Rock, Rosalind *international business consultant, educator*
Rogers, Theodore Courtney *investment company executive*
Roland, Catherine Dixon *entrepreneur*
Rom, (Melvin) Martin *investor*
Rondeau, Doris Jean *entrepreneur, consultant*
Rose, Robert Neal *brokerage house executive*
Rosenzweig, Herbert Stephen *stockbroker*
Rosier, Frederick David Stewart *securities company executive*
Ross, Darius Alexander *merger and acquisition specialist*
Rotar, Tomaz *stock exchange executive*
Roth, Hans Rudolf *commercial and industrial ventures executive, consultant*
Roy, Ranodeb *bond trader, investment banker*
Rozłucki, Wiesław *stock exchange executive*
Russell, George *industrial investment company executive*
Rydén, Bengt Gunnar *stock exchange executive*
Sampson, Deborah *investment company executive*
Samuel, Graeme Julian *entrepreneur*
Santoro, Charles William *investment banker*
Sasson, Arley Alberto *investment company executive*
Scher, Joseph S. *investment company executive*
Schinnerer, Alan John *entrepreneur*
Schoen, J. Christopher *investment banker*
Schreyer, William Allen *retired investment firm executive*
Schwab, Charles R. *brokerage house executive*
Schwartz, Carol Ann *investment company executive*
Schwartzman, Michael Isaac *investment management firm executive*
Scott, James Hunter, Jr. *investment executive*
Scott, Kerrigan Davis *private investor, philanthropist*
Searson, John Eric *stockbroker*
Segal, Gary Stephen *investment and venture capital company executive*
Seidel, Joan Broude *stockbroker, investment advisor*
Serwitz, Marshall David *finance company executive*
Setlin, Alan John *entrepreneur*
Shigeru, Obara *trading company executive*
Shrier, Adam Louis *investment firm executive, consultant*
Shuler, Jon Emmett *securities industry professional*
Siddiqui, Alimuddin A. Rashid *investment company executive, consultant*
Simon, Francois Melchior *stockbroker*
Sinko, Otto *holding company executive*
Sipprelle, Dudley Gene *investor*
Sivany, Abdul Rauf Haji Ibrahim *investment company executive*
Skogen, Haven Sherman *investment company executive*
Smiddy, F(rancis) Paul *stockbroker*
Smith, Alan Howard *investment banker*
Smith, Albert Cromwell, Jr. *investments consultant*
Smith, Cece *venture capitalist*
Smith, Diane *investment manager*
Smith, Linda Zimbalist *investment research executive*
Smith, Robert Myron *investment company executive*
Sorte, John Follett *investment firm executive*
Spaulding, William Rowe *investment consultant*
Spears, Doris Ann Hachmuth *entrepreneur, writer, publisher, real estate and management consultant*
Stansell, Ronald Bruce *investment banker*
Stead, James Joseph, Jr. *securities company executive*
Steck, Brian Jason *brokerage house executive*
Steffens, John Laundon *brokerage house executive*
Stewart, Thomas Clifford *trading and investment company executive*
Stone, Edward Luke *private equity investor, realtor*
Storm, Ruth Ellen *venture capitalist*
Strasburg, Dudley *investment counselor*
Street, David Hargett *investment company executive*
Strickland, Robert Louis *former investment company executive*
Strong, George Hotham *private investor, consultant*
Suga, Hitoshi *investment company executive*
Sutton, Robert Edward *investment company executive*
Swanson, Barry Ernest *securities company executive*
Swanson, Lauren A. *consultant, entrepreneur, educator, researcher*
Szabo, Peter John *investment company executive, financial planner, mining engineer, lawyer*
Tallman, Robert Hall *investment company executive*
Tan, Kevin Yew-Lee *investment consultant*
Teig, Marlowe Gilman *investment banker*
Tener, George E. *investor*
Tengberg, John T.U. *investment company executive*
Tennenbaum, Michael Ernest *private investor*
Theocarakis, Basil *entrepreneur*
Thomas, James Edward, Jr. *brokerage house executive*
Thompson, Waite *investment company executive, researcher*
Thornley, Dale Jonathan *financial services company director*
Tizzio, Thomas Ralph *brokerage executive*
Trill, Pauline Maud *investment and financial planning executive*
Trott, John Francis Henry *investment banker*
Trumbull, Stephen Michael *entrepreneur*
Tsui, Alec Yiu Wa *stock exchange executive*
Tuck, Edward Fenton *venture capitalist*
Tucker, Howard McKeldin *investment banker, consultant*
Ueshima, Shigeji *investment company executive*
Ujiie, Junichi *investment company executive*
Underwood, Robert Leigh *venture capitalist*
Urciuoli, J. Arthur *investment executive*
Uribe, Javier Miguel *investment executive*
Utermann, Andreas Ernst Ferndinand *fund investment manager*
Valentine, Gene C. *securities dealer*
Van Dine, Vance *investment banker*
Van Loucks, Mark Louis *venture capitalist, business advisor*
Varnum, Keith Addison *entrepreneur*
Vaughan, Eugene H. *investment company executive*
Velde, John Ernest, Jr. *investment company executive*
Venitis, Basil *financial consultant*
Vermillion, Richard Dickens *investment securities company executive*
Veselinović, Draško *stock exchange executive*
Vladem, Paul Jay *investment advisor, broker*
Völgyes, Tamàs *investment company executive, consultant*
Volpe, Andrew Arnold *securities company executive, mathematician*
von Bauer, Eric Ernst *venture capital and investment banking executive*
von Brosda Kupferber, Baron Alexander Christian *investment banker*
von Campe, Hilmar A. *investment company executive, writer*
von Kohorn, Baron Ralph Steven *retired investment banker, author*
von Rosen, Rüdiger *stock exchange executive*
Wagner, William Michael *investment company executive*
Wallace, Matthew Walker *retired entrepreneur*
Walldal, Sigurd *investment company executive*
Wallinger, John D(avid) A(rnold) *investment banker*
Walsh, William Desmond *investor*
Ward-Howlett, Ronald Peter Henry *financial investment executive, consultant*
Warren, Russell James *investment banking executive, consultant*
Welch, J(oan) Kathleen *entrepreneur*
Wells, James T. *development and brokerage executive, consultant*
Wells, Simon John *global investment management executive*
Wertheim, John David *investment and manufacturing executive*
Westmacott, Richard Kelso *venture capitalist*
Wheeler, John Stuart *bookmaking company executive*
Whitney, William Gordon *investment management company executive*
Wilkes, Clem Cabell, Jr. *stockbroker*
Williams, Dave Harrell *investment executive*
Wilson, Michael Holcombe *investment banker, former Canadian government official*
Wong, Ling Wah *investment company executive*
Yasutake, Shiro *commodities trader*
Yeung, Eric Tsun Man *entrepreneur*
Young, Peter Francis *investment banker*
Yue, Nora Yik-Lo *entrepreneur, researcher*
Zahrt, Merton Stroebel *investor*
Zarebicki, Jan A. *securities company executive, dog breeder*
Zeviar-Geese, Gabriole *stock market investor, writer*

FINANCE: REAL ESTATE

Abernethy, Robert John *real estate developer*
Ackeret, Christoph Martin *real estate company executive, urban development consultant*
Addison, Jason Lawrence *retirement community development executive*
Agbonoga, John Edelefo *urban and regional planning educator, researcher*
Ahmed, Rasheed *environmental health executive*
Albers, Gerd *city and regional planner*
Aldrich, C. Elbert *real estate broker*
Alemán, Marthanne Payne *environmental planner, consultant*
Almy, Earle Vaughn, Jr. (Buddy Almy) *real estate executive*
Anthony, Harry Antoniades *city planner, architect, educator*
Arenson, Stanley *property manager*
Ariss, David William, Sr. *real estate developer, consultant*
Armstrong, Alfreda Juanita *real estate executive*
Arroyo, Rodney Lee *city planning and transportation executive*
Badman, John, III *real estate developer, architect*
Bagby, Martha L. Green *real estate holding company executive, novelist, publisher*
Balbi, Kenneth Emilio *environmental lead specialist, researcher*
Baran, Perver Korça *urban planner, educator, researcher*
Barnes, William Anderson *real estate investment executive*
Barrere, Jamie Newton *real estate executive*
Barter, Stephen Leslie *chartered surveyor, real estate investment banker*
Batey, Peter William James *urban planning educator, urban and regional analysis consultant*
Beal, Robert Lawrence *real estate executive*
Beck, John Roland *environmental consultant*
Bell, John Nigel Berridge *environmental pollution educator, researcher*
Bell, Nancy Lee Hoyt *real estate investor, middle school educator, volunteer*
Benyon, William *landowner*
Bergerac, Jacques *real estate investment company executive*
Berry, Clare Gebert *real estate broker*
Bertolini, Luca *urban planner, architect, artist*
Blackham, Ann Rosemary (Mrs. J. W. Blackham) *realtor*
Bodinson, Holt *conservationist*
Boedeker, Daniel Arthur *retired contractor*
Boeker, Herbert Ralph, Jr. *urban planner*
Bohoskey, Bernice Fleming *mineral-land owner, writer*
Borin, Jeffrey Nathan *real estate developer*
Borin, Ralph *real estate developer*
Borns, Robert Aaron *real estate developer*
Bosch, Anna *property manager*
Bourchier, Christopher Paul *agricultural estates manager*
Boustany, Fadi Nabil *real estate developer*
Branco, Vasco Novais *real estate executive*
Breipohl, Walter Eugene *real estate broker*
Breslin, Wilbur F. *real estate broker, developer*
Broughton, James Walter *real estate development executive, consultant*
Brown, Ann Lenora *community and business development professional*
Brown, Trevor Ernest *environmental risk consultant*
Buddensiek, Volker Wilhelm Hans Dieter *conservationist, journalist*
Burton, John Jacob *retired real estate company executive appraiser*
Byron, E. Lee *real estate broker*
Carlson, Paul Edwin *real estate developer, writer*
Cecil, Dorcas Ann *property management executive*
Cherry, Brad Charles *real estate sales professional*
Chesler, Doris Adelle *real estate professional*
Christensen, C(harles) Lewis *real estate developer*
Chua, Tuan Meng Hockchua *real estate developer, community leader*
Ciputra *real estate developer*
Clark, Philip Hart *retired urban and regional planner*
Clements, John Robert *real estate professional*
Clemons, Lynn Allan *land use planner*
Clyburn, Luther Linn *real estate broker, appraiser, ship captain*
Cobb, Rowena Noelani Blake *real estate broker*
Coffey, Nancy Ann *real estate broker*
Colgan, George Phillips *real estate developer, real estate analyst*
Compton, William Thomas *real estate investor*
Comstock, Robert Donald, Jr. *real estate executive*
Cooke, Fred Charles *real estate broker*
Copsetta, Norman George *real estate executive*
Cossé, R. Paul *realty company executive*
Coudert, Dale Hokin *real estate executive, marketing consultant*
Cox, Corey Lynn *urban planner*
Crawford, Joe Jay *real estate company executive*
Crawford, Susan A. *realtor, artist*
Crispin, Sam *property services administrator, researcher*
Crowley, Michael Ryan *real estate appraiser/analyst, educator*
Cupp, Steven Eugene *real estate executive*
Dale, Sharer Susan *real estate agent*
Daley, Vincent Raymond, Jr. *real estate executive, consultant*
Daly, Patrick F. *real estate executive, architect*
Dasso, Jerome Joseph *real estate educator*
Davis, Betty Bourbonia *real estate investment executive*
d'Empaire, Oscar Eduardo *real estate executive*
DeWitt, Sallie Lee *realtor*
Diemer, Arthur William *real estate executive*
Dijkmans, Roger *environmental researcher*
Donaldson, George Burney *environmental consultant*
Driscoll, Richard Stark *retired land evaluation and land use planner*
Duarte, Patricia M. *real estate and insurance broker*
Durrell, Lee McGeorge *conservationist*
Dwyer, William H. *real estate company executive*
Edin, Esat Rasim *real estate developer*
Estes, Moreau Pinckney, IV *real estate executive, lawyer*
Eyde, George F. *real estate developer*
Farkas, Abraham Krakauer *urban developer, educator*
Farrell, Sharon Elaine *real estate broker*
Fawcett, John Scott *real estate developer*
Ferguson, David Windsor Stuart *environmentalist*
Fiifi-Yankson, Alexander *quantity surveyor, researcher*
Fjerdingstad, Erik *environmentalist, educator*
Fleischer-Rieveschl, Ellen Lee *real estate agent*
Fluegel, Walter Geno *urban planner*
Foster, Walter Herbert, Jr. *real estate company executive*
Fournier, Walter Frank *real estate executive*
Fox, J. Charles *environmental adminstrator*
Frank, Martin Ernst *real estate executive, writer*
Friedman, Hugh Robert *land developer, soccer coach, lacrosse referee*
Frink, Eugene Hudson, Jr. *business and real estate consultant*
Furlotti, Alexander Amato *real estate development company executive*
Gasper, Ruth Eileen *real estate executive*
Gasperoni, Emil, Sr. *realtor, developer*
Gazzoli, Ruben Nestor *urban planner, researcher*
Gibb, Robert M. *real estate company executive*
Gilbertson, Steven E(dward) Satyaki *real estate broker, guidance counselor*
Gimenez-Dixon, Mariano *conservationist*
Glazer, Guilford *real estate developer*
Good, Sheldon Fred *realtor*
Good, Virginia Johnson *real estate executive*
Goray, Gerald Allen *real estate executive, lawyer*
Gott, Marjorie Eda Crosby *conservationist, former educator*
Gowa, Andrew *real estate developer, lawyer*
Graham, William Aubrey, Jr. *real estate broker*
Greenberg, Judith Ann *real estate developer*
Griffiths, Dale Charles *real estate executive*
Grimes, Ruth Elaine *city planner*
Grindley, Bruce Alan *real estate agency executive*
Groppenbacher, Douglas J. *real estate investment broker, consultant*
Grübler, Arnulf Marian *regional planner*
Gutstein, Carol Feinhandler *realtor*
Hall, Anthony Clive *land use planner, educator*
Hallett, Christopher R. *realtor*
Hánek, Pavel *surveying educator*
Harb, Phyllis *realtor*
Harbeck, William James *real estate executive, lawyer, international consultant*
Herbo, Preben *real estate agent*
Hershberger, Rudy Crist *real estate agent*
Hersley, Dennis Charles *environmentalist, software systems consultant*
Holland, James R. *real estate corporation executive*
Hollis, Linda Eardley *urban planning consultant*
Holtz, John William *property management executive*
Howell, William Page *real estate executive*
Hueting, Roefie *environmental economomist, consultant, researcher*
Hukkinen, Janne Ilmari *environmental management educator*
Innes-Brown, Georgette Meyer *real estate broker, insurance broker*
Jackson, Betty L. Deason *real estate developer*
Jain, Yatish *environmental educator*
Jan, Sardar Ahmed Shah *real estate agent*
Janes, William Sargent *real estate corporation executive*
Jarrell, Glenn *city planner, farmer*
Jennison, Brian Lester *environmental specialist*
Ji, Hanbing *property development merchant, information technology merchant and developer, neural network specialist, researcher*
Johannsen De Block, Anne Christine *real estate agent*
Jones, Vernon Quentin *surveyor*
Jordan, Andre Francisco *real estate developer*
Joseph, Steven W. *real estate executive, lawyer*
Karantokis, Nicolas Georgiou *contractor, developer*
Kee, Lee Shau *real estate developer*
Kelton, Arthur Marvin, Jr. *real estate developer*
Kennard, Edward Trevor *construction consultant*
Kibbe, James William *real estate broker*
Kim, Hyun-Soo *urban planner, educator*
Kinney, Carol Naus Roberts *real estate broker*
Klaits, Robert S. *real estate executive*
Klebba, Raymond Allen *property manager*
Klein, Didier *environmental educator*
Koppelman, Lee Edward *regional planner, educator*
Koproski, Alexander Robert *real estate executive*
Koury, Agnes Lillian *real estate property manager*
Kreiser, Frank David *real estate executive*
Krone, Norman Bernard *commercial real estate developer, lawyer*
Kuhle, Shirley Jean *real estate appraiser*
Lagerblade, Mary Helen *relocation director*
Lai, Shih-Kung *urban planning educator*
Lallo, Larry Jonathon *community developer*
Lamy, M(ary) Rebecca *land developer, former government official*
Lan, Zhang *conservationist, researcher, educator*
Lane, Margaret Anna Smith *real estate property manager, real estate developer*
Langfield, Raymond Lee *real estate developer*
Lapidus, Dennis *real estate developer*
Lavigne, Peter Marshall *environmentalist, lawyer, educator*
Lax, Philip *land developer, space planner*
Lazaris, Pamela Adriane *community planning and development consultant*
Lea Mond, Harold Joseph *urban planner*
Lee, Edward Brooke, Jr. *real estate executive, fund raiser*
Lee, James Jieh *environmental educator, computer specialist*
Lehrling, Terry James *real estate broker*
Lerner, Alfred *real estate and financial executive*
Leung, Chun-Ying *surveyor, consultant*
Levine, Steven Alan *real estate appraiser, environmental consultant*
Levitt, Jaren *real estate corporation officer*
Levy, Arnold S(tuart) *real estate company executive*
Li, Ka-Shing *property developer*
Ligon, Patti-Lou E. *real estate company executive, educator*
Lochmiller, Kurtis L. *real estate entrepreneur*
Locufier, Patrick Claude *city planner*
Louargand, Marc Andrew *real estate executive, financial consultant*
Lovejoy, George Montgomery, Jr. *real estate executive*
Lovett, Laurence Dow *retired real estate and steamship executive*
Lovett, Radford Dow *real estate and investment company executive*
Lundburg, Frank Leonard *conservationist*
Lundgren, Richard John *real estate executive, city planner*
Lupo, Robert Edward Smith *real estate developer and investor*
Lynch, Jacquelyn *environmental planner*
Mac Donald, Margaret Clark *retired real estate agent*
Mahayni, Riad Ghaleb *urban planning educator*
Malcuria, Sherry JoAnne *real estate company executive, interior designer*
Manger, Gerald H. *real estate broker*
Marking, T(heodore) Joseph, Jr. *transportation and urban planner*
Marsh, Carol K. *adult community administrator*
Marshall, Craig Tyler *urban planner*
Martinez, Anthony Joseph *real estate appraiser*
Mason, Ann Darlene *real estate broker*
Masunaga, Shigeki *environmental science educator*
Mathis, Robert Arthur *planner, rancher*
Matloff, Gregory Lee *consulting environmental, space and computer scientist*
McCarthy, John Robert *real estate firm officer*
McCarty, Terry Shane, Sr. *real estate developer*
McChesney, Samuel Parker, III *real estate executive*
McClendon, Fred Vernon *real estate professional, business consultant, equine and realty appraiser, financial consultant*
McCollum, Alvin August *real estate company executive*
McCuan, William Patrick *real estate company executive*
McDonald, Malcolm Willis *real estate company executive*
McGowan, Harold *real estate developer, investor, scientist, author, philanthropist*
McInerny, Austin T. *planner*
McKinnon, James Buckner *real estate sales executive, writer, researcher*
McLain, John Lowell *resource specialist, consultant*
McLean, Robert, III *real estate company executive*
McLemore, Harry Kimbrell *retired real estate developer*
McMichael, Jeane Casey *real estate company executive, educator*
McNeil, Edward Warren *real estate executive*
Meyer, Daniel Kramer *real estate executive*
Milk, Jared Marc *real estate company executive, writer*
Mirante, Arthur J., II *real estate company executive*
Moffett, Sean Patrick *property developer*
Morgan, Constance Louise *real estate executive*
Morley, Harry Thomas, Jr. *real estate executive*
Morosani, George Warrington *real estate developer, realtor*
Morris, John Theodore *planning official*
Morton, Craig Richard *real estate investor*
Mulckhuyse, Jacob John *energy conservation and environmental consultant*
Murphy, Patrick Gregory *real estate company executive*
Mwangi, Evans Mungai *conservation biologist, consultant*
Naess, Petter *urban planning researcher*
Nandan, Satya Nand *ecological organization executive*
Nash, John J(oseph) *real estate manager, computer programmer*
Nelson, Arthur Hunt *real estate management development company executive*
Nestor Castellano, Brenda Diana *real estate company executive*
Norman, Wyatt Thomas, III *landman, consultant*
Noss, Andrew Jay *conservationist*
Nutter, David George *urban planner*
O'Brien, Brian John *environmental and strategic consultant*
Ogawa, Makoto *environmentalist, mycologist*
Ogbuefi, Joseph Ugochukwu *real estate educator*
Ong, Giok Lim *real estate executive*
Osgood, Frank William *urban and economic planner, writer*
Palmer, John David *property manager*
Papa, Michael Joseph *real estate broker*
Payne, Malcolm D. *real estate broker, financial advisor*
Percival, Arthur John *environmentalist*
Pfeifer, Johan Peter *urban planner, architect, sculptor*
Pick, Miloš *surveyor, educator*
Pickford, David Michael *surveyor, business executive*
Pilcher, Alan Rodney *chartered surveyor*
Pinson, John Dennis *real estate broker*
Polk, Emily DeSpain *conservationist, writer, designer*
Polydorides, Nicos Demetriou *urban planner, educator*
Portnov, Boris A. *urban planner, researcher*
Potter, J(effrey) Stewart *property manager*
Powell, Louise Fox *real estate developer*
Pritchard, Paul William *environmental management scientist, consultant*
Proximo, Juan Fernandez *land developer*
Puig, Al A., Jr. *real estate broker*
Pulliam, Francine Sarno *real estate broker, real estate developer*
Purcell, Henry, III *real estate developer*
Rachow, Sharon Dianne *realtor*
Rains, Gloria Cann *environmentalist company executive*
Randman, Barry I. *real estate developer*
Rasmussen, Robert Dee *real estate appraiser*
Reed, Timothy Michael *conservationist*
Reutschler, Carl Thomas *real estate executive, consultant*
Ripma, Barbara Jean Stierle *realtor*
Ritson, Scott Campbell *real estate management and development consultant*
Rivoli, Louis John *economic development consultant*
Roberts, Thomas Andrew, II *urban development executive*
Rohlena, Robert Charles *retired, real estate manager*
Romero, Reghis M., II *port city and real estate developer*
Rommelaere, Carlo Leopold *land surveyor*
Rose, Daniel *real estate company executive, consultant*
Rosenberg, Jill *realtor, civic leader*
Ross, Matthew Alan *real estate company executive*
Rossini, Joseph *contracting and development corporate executive*
Rosvall, Jan Christer *conservation scholar scientist, educator*
Rowe-Maas, Betty Lu *real estate investor*
Saab, Deanne Keltum *real estate appraiser, real estate broker*
Sakai, Akiyoshi *urban redevelopment consultant*
Salamack, Laurice Sullivan *city planner*
Sallah, Majeed (Jim Sallah) *real estate developer*
Sams, James Farid *real estate development company executive*
Sasaki, Tsutomu (Tom Sasaki) *real estate company executive, international trading company executive, consultant*
Scheyd, Joseph Frederick *real estate broker*
Schindler, Norbert *land use planner*
Schlotfeldt, William West (Bill Schlotfeldt) *real estate investor*
Schnebelen, Pierre *resort planner and developer, consultant*
Schnur, James A. *real estate executive*
Scott, David *real estate professional*
Scott, Stanley DeForest *real estate executive, former lithography company executive*
Scott, Stuart L. *real estate company executive*
Seeger, Melinda Wayne *realtor*
Sella di Monteluce, Bina Indurkumar *real estate developer*
Selman, Paul Harry *environmental planner, educator*
Sendi, Richard *land use planner, researcher, architect*
Sethi, Naresh *property investor, accountant, management consultant, educator*
Shafer, Thomas W. *real estate executive*
Shen, Qing *urban planning educator, researcher*
Shorenstein, Walter Herbert *commercial real estate development company executive*
Simonis, Udo E. *environmental educator*
Simpson, Allan Boyd *real estate company executive*
Singh, Ram Dayal *regional planner, educator*
Skillman, Ernest Edward, Jr. *real estate sales and management executive*
Smith, Marie Edmonds *real estate agent, property manager*
Sokolov, Richard Saul *real estate company executive*
Spadora, Hope Georgeanne *real estate company executive*
Spencer, Mary Goldacre *real estate executive*
Spunt, Shepard Armin *real estate executive, management and financial consultant*
Squirrell, Maurice Denton *retired real estate valuation educator*
Stair, Wilson Alfred, Jr. *urban planner, landscape architect*
Staveley, Henry Scowcroft *building consultant, surveyor*
Stein, Ellen Gail *executive manager*
Stepanek, Joseph Edward *industrial development consultant*
Stephens, Steve Arnold *real estate broker*
Stepnowski, Piotr *environmentalist, consultant*
Stevens, George Alexander *realtor*
Stewart, Harold Sanford *real estate investment and supply executive*
Stith, W(illiam) Mark *real estate executive*
Stout, Donald Everett *real estate developer, environmental preservationist*
Stucley, Hugh George *land owner*
Stuebner, James Cloyd *real estate developer, contractor*
Subramanian, Vaidyanathan *environmental science educator*
Sullivan, Patricia W. (Terry Sullivan) *real estate trainer*
Sutton, David Ainsley *real estate company executive*
Tamai, Teruhiro *urban planner, architect, consultant*
Tamkin, Curtis Sloane *real estate development company executive*
Taylor, Ralph Orien, Jr. *real estate developer, investor*
Tedros, Theodore Zaki *real estate broker, appraiser, educator*
Thorsen, Nancy Dain *real estate broker*
Tipple, Allan Graham *town planning researcher*
Tookes, James Nelson *real estate investment company executive*
Tornabene, Phillip A.A. *real estate investor*
Toshach, Clarice Oversby *real estate developer, former computer executive*
Travis, Joyce Marie *real estate executive*
Urhausen, James Nicholas *real estate developer, construction executive*
Vincent, Carl G., Jr. *real estate portfolio manager*
Vora, Kirit H. *environmental consultant*
Walker, Margaret Smith *real estate company executive*
Walsh-McGehee, Martha Bosse *conservationist*
Wang, Nina *real estate executive*
Weisinger, Ronald Jay *government housing and economic development consultant*
Welch, Nancy L. *urban planner*
Wermuth, Manfred Jakob *urban engineering educator*
Wiggins, Nancy Bowen *real estate broker, market research consultant*
Williamson, Fletcher Phillips *real estate executive*
Williamson, Ian Philip *surveying and land information educator*
Willis, Harold Wendt, Sr. *real estate developer*
Willmer, Ralph Robert *environmental planner, consultant*
Wilson, Paul Wayne *retired real estate developer*
Wingert, Hannelore Christiane *real estate agent, chemical company executive*
Wood, Neil Roderick *real estate development company executive*
Worrell, Ernst *energy and environmental analyst, researcher*
Xie, Shang-Ping *environmental studies educator*
Xu, Alex S. *real estate development company executive*
Yang, Amanda *real estate agent*
Yang, Hyung-Jae *environmentalist*
Yeroulanos, Marinos *environmentalist, consultant*
York, James Orison *real estate executive*
Zapata, Carmen Elena *formation damage and environmental researcher*

GOVERNMENT: AGENCY ADMINISTRATION

Adli, Habib El *administrator*
Ainscow, Robert Morrison *former British government official, independent consultant*
Alberts, Bruce Michael *federal agency administrator, foundation administrator, biochemist*
Alexander, Jane *federal agency administrator, actress, producer*
Al-Sabah, Shaikh Saud Nasser *federal agency administrator, gas, oil industry executive*
al-Salih, Mohammed Maldi *minister of trade*
Alston, Richard *administrator*
Anderson, Mary Elizabeth *protection services official*
Apple, Daina Dravnieks *government agency official*
Arey, William Griffin, Jr. *former government official*
Arlacchi, Pino *protective services official*
Ausseil, Jean *government official*
Baird, Iain Stewart *federal agency executive*
Batton, Kenneth Duff *federal agency administrator, contractor, consultant*
Beale, Julian Howard *parliamentarian*
Begum, Forquan *government administrator*
Beilin, Joseph (Yossi) *member of parliament*
Bessero, Gilles Marie *government official*

Betzer, Roy James *retired national park service ranger*
Beurman, Albert Leroy *retired corrections officer*
Bhatti, Baqar Hussain *public sector executive, educator*
Biddle, Livingston Ludlow, Jr. *former government official, writer, consultant*
Bishop, Bronwyn *administrator*
Blix, Hans Martin *retired international atomic energy official*
Bloomfield, Sir Kenneth Percy *educational administrator*
Blumberg, Barbara Salmanson (Mrs. Arnold G. Blumberg) *retired state housing official, housing consultant*
Bogert, Tracy Joseph *adult probation officer*
Boly, Yéro *government official*
Boodhram, Pardhomun *police officer*
Bowdre, Paul Reid *protective services official, consultant*
Boyd, Linda Wharton *federal agency administrator*
Broadhurst, Violet Alison *safety consultant*
Brown, Betty Marie *government agency administrator*
Brown, Dale Susan *government administrator, educational program director, writer*
Brown, Nick *administrator*
Brye, Gary Melvin *chief of police, personnel consultant*
Bush, Mitchell Lester, Jr. *retired federal agency administrator*
Bush, William Arden *internal revenue agent*
Byrne, Shaun Patrick *law enforcement officer*
Camdessus, Michel (Jean) *international organization executive*
Cannaday, Kenneth D. *retired federal agency administrator*
Carino, Ledivina Vidallon *public administration educator*
Carter, Harry Robert *fire protection consultant*
Chaiken, Jan Michael *government agency official*
Chang, Rocson Chi Meng *government agency administrator*
Chen, Teh-Hsun Bean *government safety official*
Chester, Thomas Wayne *state agency administrator*
Christodoulou, Efthymios Nicolas *government official, banker*
Cicci, Rafael Alejandro *government agency financial executive*
Clark, Thomas Ryan *retired federal agency executive, business and technical consultant*
Compton, Dale Leonard *retired space agency executive, consultant*
Cook, Harvey Carlisle *law enforcement official*
Couig, Mary Patricia *federal agency administrator*
Crosbie, John Carnell *retired Canadian government official, university administrator, lawyer*
Culver, Dan Louis *federal agency administrator*
Cuomo, Andrew *federal agency administrator*
Daeubler-Gmelin, Herta *government official*
Dai, Peter Kuang-Hsun *government official, aerospace executive*
Davis, Cherry Dean *investigator, poet*
Day, Russell Clover *state agency administrator*
DeLucia, Gene Anthony *government administrator, computer company executive*
Dempsey, Noel *administrator*
Deneys, Keith Donald *protective services official*
de Wispeleir-Lely, Roger Alois Adelin *government agency administrator*
DeYoung, David Jeffrey *state official*
Diaz-Llanos, Antonio Ezequiel *government agency administrator*
Dibunda Kabuinji, Crispin-Medard *presidents commissioner*
Dill, C. Jerome *deputy premier of Bermuda, barrister*
Dominguez Mendoza, Boris *search and rescue technician, educator*
D'Onofrio, Dominick Anthony *police officer, acting police chief*
Dunning, Herbert Neal *government official, physical chemist*
Durand, Thomas Henry *government intelligence officer*
Dzakah, Mawunyo Francis *prison officer*
Eberling, George Gifford *federal agency administrator*
Edmiston, Joseph Tasker *state official*
Eltayeb, Salah Elzein *deputy director general, publisher, consultant*
Enggaard, Knud *former government official*
Entin, Stephen Jay *federal agency administrator*
Eversole, Kellye Anne *government relations and public affairs consultant*
Fall Creek, Stephanie Jean *state agency administrator*
Fefferman, Hilbert *government official, lawyer*
Fouchard, Joseph James *retired government agency administrator*
Franklin, Bonnie Selinsky *federal agency administrator*
Freeman, Chas. W., Jr. *government official, ambassador, author*
Freitag, Carol Wilma *state official, political scientist*
French, Richard Vaughn *federal agency administrator*
Frendo, Michael *parliamentarian, lawyer*
Funk, Sherman Maxwell *former government official, writer, consultant*
Gay, John Marion *federal agency administrator, organization-personnel analyst*
Gelb, Bruce Stuart *city commissioner, consultant*
Gentry, James William *retired state official*
Geweily, Said M.H. *police officer*
Gill, Sukhdev Singh *government agency technical director*
Giovannini, Jean François *federal agency administrator*
Glaenzer, Camille Henri *security consultant*
Gleichman, John Alan *safety and loss control executive*
Glen, Robert Alexander *state official*
Gober, Hershel W. *government official*
Goldin, Daniel S. *federal agency administrator*
Goodloe, James Edward *protective services official, emergency manager*
Goodson, Harlan Wayne *state regulator, educator*
Gossard, William H(erbert), Jr. *federal agency program administrator*
Graycar, Adam *federal agency administrator*
Griego, Juan Lawrence *federal agency administrator*
Grünewald, Björn Mikael *employers' organization administrator, educator, consultant*
Guear, Christopher Thomas *state agency administrator*
Gurgulino de Souza, Heitor *government organization consultant*
Haack, Richard Wilson *retired police officer*
Hafer, Thomas Paul *government official*
Hager, Laurie Vincent *federal agency executive*
Hailu, Solomon *international government official*
Halliday, Peter Ernest *police officer, researcher*
Hamadjoda, Adjoudji *government official*
Haque, Shahudul *protective service official*
Hardwick, Kevin Dale *protective services official*
Harkness, David Dalgleish *patent administrator*
Hellyer, Timothy Michael *protective services officer*
Henderson, William J. *postmaster general*
Henke, Shauna Nicole *police dispatcher, small business owner*
Heppell, (Thomas) Strachan *government agency administrator*
Herron, John *administrator*
Heseltine, Michael Ray Dibdin *retired government minister*
Heyman, Ira Michael *federal agency administrator, museum executive, law educator*
Hill, Jefferson Borden *regulatory oversight officer, lawyer*
Hill, Robert *administrator*
Hill, Robert Martin *retired protective services official, forensic document examiner, consultant, writer, lecturer*
Hobbs, Peter Thomas Goddard *trust administrator*
Hodsoll, Francis Samuel Monaise *government official*
Horwitz, Eleanor Catherine *information and education official*
Howard, Clive Jonathan *protective services official, consultant*
Hudak, Joseph David *forensic engineer, educator, police investigator*
Husbands, Sir Clifford Straughn *governor general of Barbados*
Ijäs, Teuvo Tapio *federal agency administrator*
Iklé, Fred Charles *former federal agency administrator, policy advisor, defense expert*
Iliescu, Mihai *military officer*
Iredale, Peter *health authority chairman*
Jackson, Stephen Eric *police official*
Jansen, Lambertus *state agency administrator, retired judge*
Jarman, Theresa Kay *fire chief*
Jiaxuan, Tang *government agency official*
Jilek, James Parker *state agency official*
Jiler, Linda Cerise *retired fire and aviation program technician, fire emergency dispatcher, consultant, researcher, writer*
Jin, Bo *government agency executive, engineering educator*
Jiya, Jonathan Yisa *national government official, preventive medicine*
Johnson, Arlene Lytle *government agency official*
Johnson, Ralph Raymond *ambassador, federal agency administrator*
Jonah, James O. C. *UN official*
Jones, Donald Kelly *state agency executive*
Jones, John Paul *probation officer, psychologist*
Joshi, Murli Manshar *administrator*
Joubert, Stanley *protective services official*
Kaboré, Joseph *government official*
Kalicki, Jan H. *federal official, banker, political scientist*
Kandra, Joseph *retired federal agency administrator*
Kawamura, Yoya *retired diplomat, correspondent, writer*
Kee, Walter Andrew *former government official*
Keene, Mary Ellen *federal agency executive*
Kelepecz, Betty Patrice *protective services official, lawyer*
Kelleher, Graeme George *natural resources manager, civil engineer*
Kelley, Edward Watson, Jr. *federal agency administrator*
Kell-Smith, Carla Sue *federal agency administrator*
Kemp, David, Jr. *administrator*
Khan, Mohammad Mohabbat *public administration educator*
Khosa, Hafiz Muhammad Ali *federal investigator*
Kirwin, Andrew Dean *protective services official*
Knowlton, William Allen *political and military consultant, educator*
Lacy, Gregory Lawrence *protective services official*
Lacy, John Russell *state government administrator*
Leckie, Carol Mavis *retired state government administrator*
LeLeux, John Allen *retired protective services official*
Lentini, Joseph Charles *government agency management analyst*
Lewis, George Douglas *federal agency administrator*
Lilan, Zhu *Chinese government official*
Llanos, Luis Socorro *retired public administrator, mediator, arbitrator, public affairs consultant*
Lloyd, George Peter *retired government administrator*
Logan, James Scott, Sr. *federal agency administrator*
Loginovsky, Oleg Vitalyevitch *state agency administrator*
Loose, Rodney Stewart *FBI agent*
Lowery, William Odell *protective services executive*
Luu, James Cuong Phu *correctional services educator*
Machicado Saravia, Flavio *government agency administrator*
Malungo, Albino *government official*
Marinho de Bastos, Joaquim L.F. *air transport policy administrator*
May, David A. *protective services official, public official*
McClinton, James Alexander *state agency administrator, councilman*
McInturff, Floyd M. *retired state agency administrator*
McKee, Margaret Jean *federal agency executive*
McLauchlin, Tammy Denise *protective services official*
Means, Tina *police officer, consultant*
Menguturk, Muhsin *government agency administrator*
Meridith, Denise Patricia *government official*
Metz, Steven Kent *federal agency administrator, writer*
Minchin, Nick *administrator*
Mitz, Nina *government communications advisor*
Mohammad, Ali Nasser *politician*
Molterer, Wilhelm *administrator*
Moniz, Ernest Jeffrey *government official, former physics educator*
Moser, Jeffery Richard *state agency administrator, public affairs and public management executive, artist, writer, former state official*
Mramor, James Plummer *security consultant*
Mthembi-Mahanyele, Sankie Dolly *government official*
Muslimov, Renat Khaliulllovich *state administrator, scientist, educator*
Nathanael, Muthu Paul *police officer*
Newman, Jocelyn *administrator*
Ngongi, A. Namanga *federal agency administrator*
Nichols, Dinah Alison *environmental agency official*
Novotny, Jaromir *federal agency administrator*
Odgers, Peta Michelle *fire and emergency services administrator*
O'Keefe, Kathleen Mary *state government official*
Opacich, Milan *protective services official, musician*
Ordoño, Adelino Valdez *retired goverment official, farmer*
Ouédraogo, Elie Justin *government official*
Outrata, Edvard *public information administrator, statistician*
Packa, Daniel E. *federal agency administrator*
Padden, Anthony Aloysius, Jr. *federal government official*
Pallett, Ray(mond) David *civil servant*
Parks, James William, II *public facilities executive, lawyer*
Paterson, Paul Charles *private investigator, security consultant*
Paul, Darrell Frederick *state trooper*
Pearson, Jennie Sue *retired government administrator*
Percival, Bernard S. *government official*
Port, Arthur Tyler *retired government administrator, lawyer*
Pradan, Dasho Om *government official*
Quinlan, Michael Edward *retired civil servant*
Rabadeau, Mary Frances *protective services official*
Rakusic, Spomenka Beker *federal agency administrator*
Ramdahl, Gunnar Halvor *security services professional*
Ramirez, Norberto Luis *public official*
Ramsey Lines, Sandra *forensic document examiner*
Rauchschwalbe, Renae *federal agency administrator*
Reith, Peter *administrator*
Revin, Valery Petrovich *government official*
Richardson, John *retired international relations executive*
Riza, Iqbal *United Nations agency administrator*
Rominger, Richard *federal agency administrator*
Rucker, Kenneth Lamar *law enforcement officer, educator*
Ruddock, Philip *government administrator*
St. Luce, John *government official*
Salih, Abd al-Mun'im Ahmad *Iraqi government official*
Sallai, Gyula *communications executive, educator*
Sasser, William Jack *retired federal agency administrator, consultant*
Schlogl, Karl *administrator*
Schroeder, Joyce Katherine *state agency administrator, research analyst*
Sedacca, Angelo Anthony *police officer, scholar, notary*
Selkowitz, Lucy Ann *security officer*
Severin, Cecile Francoise *retired protective services official*
Sheikh, Atique Zafar *public information officer*
Short, Clare *administrator*
Simpson, Linda Anne *retired protective services official, municipal official*
Smith, David Mitchell *fire and explosion consultant*
Smith, Rick Earl *law enforcement officer*
Smith, Waldo Gregorius *former federal agency administrator*
Sorter, Bruce Wilbur *federal program administrator, educator, consultant*
Spaulding, Wallace Holmes *retired federal agency professional*
Spooner, Donna *public administrator*
Springfeldt, Bjorn Eric *Swedish cultural official*
Stagliano, Vito Alexander *former government official, company executive, energy policy analyst*
Steensgaard, Anthony Harvey *federal agency administrator*
Stenbäck, Pär (Olav Mikael) *international agency administrator*
Stiver, William Earl *retired government administrator*
Stroetmann, Karl Antonius *company executive*
Sudarsono, Juwono *government administrator*
Suleman, Syed Mohammad *postmaster general*
Sullivan, Dorothy Rona *state official*
Taylor, Nicholas C. *state agency administrator, energy executive*
Telesetsky, Walter *government official*
Tenet, George John *government agency official*
Tomlinson, Michael John *British education official*
Torio, Melanio Saruca *government official*
Towey, Carroll Francis *senior education specialist*
Udjo, Eric Oghenerioborore *federal agency administrator*
Uttinger, Hans Walter *retired federal administrator*
Vaile, Mark *administrator*
Varela, Marta B. *city agency administrator, lawyer*
Varmus, Harold Eliot *health science administrator, educator, science researcher*
Vattilana, Joseph William *retired chief state safety inspector*
Vega, Steve *protective services official, poet*
Virdebrant, Carl-Erik *government administrator*
Volski, George *economist*
Wahlström, Bo Anders *government agency administrator*
Walpen, Laurent *chief of police, lawyer*
Walters, Jerry Willard *retired federal intelligence officer*
Wapner, Alan Dean *security professional, mayor pro tem*
Warner, Susan *federal agency administrator*
Washburn, Kathryn Hazel *government agency executive*
Weinberg, Daniel H. *federal agency administrator, economist*
Weiner, Robert Stephen *federal agency administrator*
White, Bonnie Havana *retired federal agency official*
Wieting, Gary Lee *federal agency executive*
Willis, Ralph Walker *retired firefighter*
Wilson, Stephen Rip *public policy consultant*
Wolfe, Deborah Cannon Partridge *government education consultant, educator, clergy*
Wood, Benjamin Carroll, Jr. *safety professional*
Wright, Nina Hornbuckle *police official*
Yakimenko, Roman Ivanovich *government agency administrator*
Yaou, Aissatou *government official*
Zhendong, Huang *administrator*
Ziegert, Burkhard Werner *government official*
Zimmermann, Hans *United Nations official*
Zucka, Georges *international patent official*

GOVERNMENT: EXECUTIVE ADMINISTRATION

Aaviksoo, Jaak *Estonian government official*
Abaza, Mohamed Maher *Egyptian government official*
Abdulatipov, Ramazan *Russian government official*
Abi-Sad, Sergio Caldas Mercador *diplomat*
Abitbol, William *foreign diplomat*
Abiyev, Safar *government official*
Aboul Gheit, Ahmed Al. *Egyptian diplomat*
Abudo, Jose Ibraimo *government official*
Abulhasan, Mohammad Abdulla *ambassador*
Abu Nimah, Hasan *former ambassador*
Acebes, Angel *federal official*
Achard, Pierre *international finance administrator*
Adam, André *ambassador*
Adamkus, Valdas V. *president of Lithuania*
Adamov, Yevgeniy Olegovich *Russian government official*
Adkins, William Lloyd *state official*
Advani, Lal K. *government executive, former journalist, social worker*
Afshar, Amir Aslan *former Iranian government official*
Afwerki, Isaias *president of Eritrea*
Agag Longo, Alejandro *member European parliament*
Agathocleous, Nicos *permanent delegate*
Aguiar, Cristina M. *diplomat, educator*
Ahern, Bertie *prime minister of Ireland*
Ahern, Dermot *government minister*
Ahmad, Toheed *diplomat, writer*
Ahmed, Shahabuddin *president of Bangladesh*
Aimé, Jean-Claude *United Nations official*
Ainardi, Sylviane H. *foreign diplomat*
Akayev, Askar *Kyrgyz government official*
Akihito, Emperor *Emperor of Japan*
Aksenenko, Nikolay Yemelyanovich *federal official*
Alam, Sultan Salahuddin Abdul Aziz Hishamuddin *Sultan of Selangor*
Al-Ashtal, Abdalla Saleh *ambassador*
Alathel, Abdullah M. *diplomat, commerce and trade consultant*
al-Bashir, Umar Hasan Ahmad *Sudanese president*
al-Beltagui, Mamdouh Ahmed *Egyptian government official*
Albert, His Majesty II *King of the Belgians*
Albright, Madeleine Korbel *U.S. secretary of state*
Alemán, (Jose) Arnoldo *president of Nicaragua*
Aleskerov, Murtuz Nadzhaf Oglu *Azerbaijan government official*
Alexander, Leslie M. *ambassador*
al-Hadi, Abd al-Rab Mansur *Yemenite government official*
Alhajri, Abdullah Dhaffer *government official*
Alhegelan, Faisal Al-Abdul-Aziz *Saudi Arabian government official*
Ali, Her Majesty Wijdan *Princess of Jordan, art historian*
al-Iryani, Abd al-Karim Ali *Yemeni prime minister*
Aliyev, Heydar *Azerbaijani government official*
Aliyev, Irshad *government official*
al-Jarallah, Mohammed bin Ibrahim *federal official*
al-Jihani, Ali bin Talal *Saudi Arabian government official*
al-Jihimi, Tahir *Libyan government official*
al-Junayd, Muhammad Ahmad *Yemeni government official*
Al-Khalifa, Abdallah bin Khalid *Bahraini government official*
Al-Khalifa, Sheikh Hamad bin Isa *Crown Prince of Bahrain*
Al-Khalifa, Sheikh Khalifa bin Salman *prime minister of Bahrain*
Al-Khalifa, Sheikh Muhammad Bin Mubarak *Bahraini government official*
Al-Khalifa, Sheikh Mohamed Bin Khalifa Hamid *Bahrain government official*
Allen, Algernon S.B.P. *government official*
Allen, Alpian *Saint Vincentian government official*
Allen, David *government official*
Allen, Donald George *retired diplomat*
Al-Mahayni, Mohamad Khaled *Syrian government official, finance educator*
Almakky, Ghazy Abdulwahed Makky *diplomat, geography educator*
Al-Maktum, Sheikh Hamdan bin Rashid *United Arab Emirian government official*
al-Maktum, Sheikh Maktum bin Rashid *United Arab Emirian government official, ruler of Dubai*
Almeida, Jose Jorge Alcazar *diplomat*
Almeida Bosque, Juan *Cuban government official, musical composer*
Al-Mogbel, Abdullah Abdulrahman *government executive*
Al-Moualem, Walid *diplomat*
al-Mousawi, Fasisal Rahdi *Bahraini government official*
Al Nahyan, Sheikh Zayed bin Sultan *president of United Arab Emirates, ruler of Abu Dhabi*
al-Naimi, Ali bin Ibrahim *government official*
al-Nuaymi, Rashid bin Abdallah *United Arab Emirian government official*
al-Nuhayyan, Hamdan bin Zayid *United Arab Emirian government official*
al-Qadhafi, Muammar Abu Minyar *Libyan government official*
al-Qasimi, Sheikh Sultan bin Muhammad (Sheikh Sultan bin Muhammad Al-Qasimi) *Emir of Sharjah*
al-Rasheed, Muhammad bin Ahmad *federal official*
Al-Sabah, Sheikh Jabir al-Ahmad al-Jabir *Emir of Kuwait*
Al-Sabah, Mohammed Sabah Al-Salim *ambassador*
Al-Sabah, Sheikh Saad al-Abdallah al-Salim *Crown Prince of Kuwait, prime minister of Kuwait*
Al-Saleh, Dawood Musaad *Kuwaiti government official*
al-Salih, Ali Salih Abdallah *Bahrain government official*
al-Salloum, Naser bin Mohammad *federal official*
Al-Samawi, Ahmed Abdulrahman *government official*
al-Saud, Prince Abdallah bin Abd al-Aziz *Saudi Arabian government official*
al-Saud, Fahd bin Abd al-Aziz *King of Saudi Arabia*
Al-Saud, Prince Nayif bin Abdul-Aziz Al bin Abdulrahman *Saudi Arabian government official*
Al-Saud, Prince Saud al-Faysal bin Abd al-Aziz *Saudi Arabian government official*
Al Saud, Prince Sultan Ibn Abdulaziz *Saudi Arabian government official*
Al-Sayyari, Hamad Saud *Saudi Arabian government official*
Al-Shaali, Mohammad bin Hussein *diplomat*

Deby, Idriss Chadian government official
de Charette, Hervé French political party executive
de Clercq, Willy C.E.H. member of European parliament, barrister
Decourriere, Francis foreign diplomat
De Croo, Herman Francis government official
de Dardel, Jean-Jacques Pierre diplomat
Dedeaux, Jules A. city official
Defago, Alfred Swiss ambassador
de Franchis, Amedeo Italian diplomat
DeGonia, Mary Elise government community relations executive, publisher
de-Grave, Frank federal official
de Gruben, Thierry Belgian ambassador
De Guenin, Jacques Vincent mayor
Dehousse, Jean-Maurice federal official
Deiss, Joseph Swiss government official
Dejammet, Alain diplomat
de Keghel, Alain Jean-Marie consul general of France, diplomat
de Klerk, Frederik Willem former state president
de la Fuente Ramirez, Juan Ramon Mexican government official
De La Rua, Fernando president of Argentina
Dell'Alba, Gianfranco member European Parliament
Della Vedova, Benedetto member European Parliament
Dell'utri, Marcello member European Parliament
Delors, Jacques former government official
del Pino, Gustavo A. government official
Del Turco, Ottaviano minister of finance
de Maria y Campos, Mauricio United Nations official
Demataki, Glykeria J. federal official
Demby, Albert Joe Sierra Leone vice president
De Mita, Luigi Ciriaco former prime minister of Italy
de Oliveira Maciel, Marco Antonio Brazilian vice president
de Palacio del Valle-Lersundi, Loyola government official
Desai, Nitin Dayalji federal official
De Sarnez, Marielle foreign diplomat
de Schoutheete de Tervarent, Philippe ambassador
Désir, Harlem foreign diplomat
de Soto, Alvaro diplomat
de Valera, Sile Irish government official
De Veyrac, Christine foreign diplomat
Devos, Jean-Marie general secretary, lawyer
de Vries, Klass government official
Dhanapala, Jayantha diplomat
Diatta, Joseph Nigerian diplomat
Dienstbier, Jiří diplomat, political scientist, journalist, writer
Diercks, Frederick Otto government official
Diez González, Rosa M. foreign diplomat
Dijkstal, Henry Frans (Hans Dijkstal) Dutch government official
Di Lello Finuoli, Giuseppe member European Parliament
Diliberto, Oliviero federal official, educator
Dimitrakopoulos, Giorgos member European Parliament
Dimitrov, Philip ambassador
Dingwall, David C. Canadian government official
Dini, Lamberto Italian government official
Dinkelspiel, Ulf Adolf Roger ambassador
Di Pietro, Antonio Italian government official
Djabir, Ahmed diplomat
Dlamini, Barnabas Sibusiso prime minister
Dlamini-Zuma, Nkosazana South African government official
Do Amaral, Diogo Freitas Portuguese politician, educator
Dodik, Milorad prime minister of Serb Republic
Doje Cering Chinese government official
Dömény, János ambassador
Dondukov, Aleksandr Nikolayerich Russian government official
Donnelly, Martin Eugene civil servant, lecturer
Donovan, Francis Patrick retired diplomat
Dorda, Abuzeid Omar Libyan government official
Dornelles, Francisco Oswaldo Neves Brazilian government official
do Rosario, Antonio Gualberto Cape Verdean government official
Dorrell, Stephen James British government official
Dos Santos, Carlos ambassador
dos Santos, Jose Eduardo president of Angola
Dougan, Serafin Seriche prime minister of Equatorial Guinea
Douglas, Denzil prime minister of Saint Kitts and Nevis
Dowiyogo, Bernard Nauruan government official
Downer, Alexander John Gosse Australian government official
Dragseth, Joyce Lynn county official
Dreifuss, Ruth Swiss government official
Drozda, Jeffery Allen government affairs administrator
Duff, Andrew Nicholas government official
Du Granrut, Claude diplomat
Duhamel, Olivier foreign diplomat
Dührkop Dührkop, Bárbara foreign diplomat
Dumont, Ivy L. government official
Dunion, Celeste Mogab consultant, township official
Dunnett, Dennis George state official
Dupuis, Olivier member European Parliament
Durrant, M. Patricia diplomat
Dusza, Raymond Kaspar county legislator
Dyvig, Peter P. ambassador
Eastmond, Rawle C. Barbadian government official
Ebeid, Atef Mohammed Egyptian government official
Ebeid, Nadia Riad Makram government official
Ebner, Michl member European Parliament
Ecevit, Bulent prime minister of Turkey, journalist, politician
Edgar, Jim former governor
Edward, Prince (Antony Richard Louis Edward) member of British royal family, television producer
Efthymiou, Petros member European Parliament
Egan, Wesley William, Jr. former ambassador
Egelund, Niels diplomat
Eggleton, Arthur C. Canadian government official, member of Parliament
Eichel, Hans federal official
Eickhoff, Ekkehard retired German ambassador, historian
Eiselsberg, Otto H. diplomat
Eisenstadt, G. Michael diplomat, author, lecturer, research scholar
Eizenstat, Stuart E. ambassador, lawyer
Ekeus, Rolf Carl diplomat
El Abridi, Omar diplomat
El-Amawi, Ahmed government official
Elaraby, Nabil A. Egyptian diplomat
Eldon, Stewart Graham diplomat
Eliasson, Ingemar E. Swedish government official
Eliasson, Nils diplomat, international organization executive
Elizabeth, Her Majesty (Elizabeth Angela Marguerite) The Queen Mother
Elizabeth, Her Majesty II (Elizabeth Alexandra Mary) Queen of United Kingdom of Great Britain and Northern Ireland, and her other Realms and Territories, head of the Commonwealth, Defender of the Faith
Eman, Henny Jan (J. H. A. Eman) prime minister of Aruba, lawyer
Enenbach, Mark Henry community action agency executive, educator
Engqvist, Lars Swedish government official
Enkhsaikhan, Jargalsaikhan ambassador
Ertur, Omer Selcukhan United Nations official, educator
Erwa, El-Fatih Mohamed Ahmed diplomat
Erwin, Alexander federal official
Esclopé, Alain foreign diplomat
Essy, Amara Ivorian government official
Esteve, Pere foreign diplomat
Estrada, Joseph Marcelo Ejercito Philippine government official
Etter, Christian financial and economic diplomat
Evangelou, Alecos Costa Cyprian government official
Evans, Gareth Australian government and international official
Ewing, Blair Gordon federal official
Eyadema, Etienne Gnassingbe president of Togo
Fabius, Laurent politician, former prime minister of France
Fahey, John Joseph Australian government official
Fakafanua, Tutoatasi Tongan government official
Falcam, Leo A. Micronesian government official
Fälldin, Nils Olof Thorbjörn former Prime Minister of Sweden, retired farmer
Farell Cubillas, Arsenio Mexican government official
Farley, Reginald R. minister of industry and international business
Farsi, Fuad Abd al-Salam federal official
Fassino, Piero Franco Rodolfo government official
Fasslabend, Werner Austrian government official
Fatuzzo, Carlo member European Parliament
Fava, Giovanni Claudio member European Parliament
Fenech, Joseph Maltese government official, lawyer
Fenech Adami, Edward prime minister of Malta
Ferber, Markus member European parliament
Ferguson, Sarah The Duchess of York
Fernandes, George federal official
Fernandes, Ulpio Cape Verde government official
Fernández Martin, Fernando foreign diplomat
Fernandez Mirabal, Jaime David government official
Fernandez Reyna, Leonel president of the Dominican Republic
Ferreira, Anne foreign diplomat
Ferrero-Waldner, Benita-Maria minister of foreign affairs
Ferri, Enrico member European Parliament
Fiebiger, Christel member of the European parliament
Filippov, Vladimir Mikhaylovich federal official
Filker, Hans Georg city administrator
Finauri, Graciela Maria foreign service professional
Fini, Gianfranco member European Parliament
Fiori, Francesco member European Parliament
Fischer, Andrea German government official
Fischer, Josef "Joschka" German vice chancellor
Fischer, Leni international association executive
Fischer, Timothy government official
Fishel, Andrew S. director, federal
Fitton, Harvey Nelson, Jr. former government official, publishing consultant
Flack, Ronald David diplomat, public service educator, banker
Flaten, Robert Arnold retired ambassador
Flautre, Hélène foreign diplomat
Fleisher, Eric Wilfrid retired foreign service officer
Florenz, Karl-Heinz member of European parliament
Flores Facusse, Carlos Roberto country president, publisher
Flosse, Gaston senator, French Polynesian federal official
Foglietta, Thomas Michael diplomat, former congressman
Foley, Thomas Stephen diplomat, former speaker House of Representatives
Folias, Christos member European Parliament
Fonseca, Gelson, Jr. diplomat
Fontaine, Nicole foreign diplomat
Ford, Betty Bloomer (Elizabeth Ford) former First Lady of United States, health facility executive
Ford, Gerald Rudolph, Jr. former President of United States
Forne, Marc Andorran government official
Forté, Debra Brooks municipal government official
Fourtou, Janelly foreign diplomat
Fowler, Robert Ramsay Canadian government official
Fowler, Wyche, Jr. ambassador
Fraga Estévez, Carmen foreign diplomat
Fraisse, Geneviève member of European Parliament
Frank, Sergei federal official
Frank, Sergey O. Russian government official
Franke, Wayne Thomas retired government affairs director, consultant
Fraser-Moleketi, Geraldine federal official
Frawley Bagley, Elizabeth government advisor, ambassador
Fréchette, Louise Canadian diplomat
Fredericks, J. Richard ambassador
Freeman, Lord Roger Norman former British government official
Freivalds, Laila Swedish government official, lawyer
Frick, Mario head of government of Liechtenstein
Fried, Daniel ambassador
Friedrich, Ingo member of European parliament
Fritsche, Claudia diplomat
Fritz, Jack government official
Fruteau, Jean-Claude foreign diplomat
Fujimori Fujimori, Alberto Kenyo president of Peru
Fulci, Francesco Paolo diplomat
Funke, Karl-Heinz government official
Gagliano, Alfonso Canadian government official
Gahler, Michael member of European parliament
Galante, Ann Muriel town official
Galeote Quecedo, Gerardo foreign diplomat
Galinsky, Deborah Jean county official
Gallagher, Dermot A. Irish diplomat
Galuska, Vladimir diplomat
Gandhi, Maneka government official
Gandhi, Sonia government official
Ganic, Ejup Bosnia-Herzegovina government official
Gao, Changli federal official
Garcia-Margallo Y Marfil, José Manuel foreign diplomat
Garcia-Orcoyen Tormo, Cristina foreign diplomat
Garot, Georges foreign diplomat
Garriga Polledo, Salvador foreign diplomat
Gasoliba i Böhm, Carles-Alfred foreign diplomat
Gatti, Gabriele San Marinese government official
Gaviria Trujillo, Cesar international organization administrator, former president of Colombia, economist
Gayoom, Maumoon Abdul president of Maldives
Gayssot, Jean-Claude government official
Gebhardt, Evelyne member of European parliament
Gehrer, Elisabeth government official
Geingob, Hage Gottfried prime minister of Namibia
Geisel, Harold Walter diplomat
Gelbard, Robert Sidney ambassador
Genscher, Hans-Dietrich German government official
Geremek, Bronislaw government official
Gervais, Jean-Marie Kacou ambassador
Ghaffar, Muhammad Abdul ambassador
Ghannouchi, Mohamed government official
Giannakou-Koutsikou, Marietta member European Parliament
Giffin, Gordon D. ambassador, lawyer
Gil-Delgado, Jose Maria Gil-Robles retired parliamentary president
Gil Lavedra, Ricardo Rodolfo minister of justice
Ginsberg, Marc C. former diplomat, investment company executive
Gladovsky, Sergey Aleksandrovitch governmental manager
Glante, Norbert member of European parliament
Glase, Anne-Karin member European parliament
Glaze, Michael (James) diplomat
Glenny, Robert Joseph Ervine retired civil servant, consultant
Glickman, Daniel Robert federal official
Godal, Björn Tore Norwegian government official
Goddard, Phillip C. Barbadian government official
Godfrey, Carl Franklin, Jr. government affairs consultant
Goepel, Lutz member of the European parliament
Goh, Chok Tong prime minister of Singapore
Goh, Kun mayor
Gold, Dore diplomat
Goldsmith, Jocelyn Stone state employment professional
Gomide, Aloysio Marés Dias diplomat
Gomolka, Alfred member of European parliament
Goncz, Arpad president of Hungary, writer
Gonzalez, Guillermo Enrique diplomat
González Alvarez, Laura foreign diplomat
Gonzalez Fernandez, Jose Antonio government official
Goodale, Ralph E. Canadian government minister
Gorbachev, Mikhail Sergeyevich former president of the former Union of Soviet Socialist Republics
Gordon, Pamela Felicity Bermuda government official
Gore, Albert, Jr. Vice President of the United States
Gore, Michael Edward John former governor, former ambassador, author
Gorita, Ion ambassador
Gorlach, Willi member of European parliament
Gorostiaga Atxalandabaso, Koldo foreign diplomat
Gosa, Noluthando Primrose telecommunications commissioner
Goulden, John diplomat, NATO official
Gradin, Anita former ambassador/European Commission member
Graefe zu Baringdorf, Friedrich-Wilhelm member European parliament
Graeve, Peter John county official
Graham, Douglas Arthur Montrose former New Zealand government official, consultant on indigenous people
Granic, Mate Croatian government official
Granillo Ocampo, Raul Enrique Argentine government official
Granqvist, Hakan Ragnar Axel Swedish diplomat
Grasser, Karl-Heinz minister of finance
Gray, Herbert Eser Canadian government official
Green, Guy Stephen Montague governor of Tasmania
Green, Rosario federal official
Greenidge, Carl Barrington international public servant, economist
Green Macias, Rosario United Nations official
Greenstock, Sir Jeremy diplomat
Gregori, José minister of justice
Griffiths, John Liebig retired foreign service officer, marketing consultant
Grignon, Gérard Eugène Joseph government official of Saint Pierre-et-Miquelon
Grimsson, Olafur Ragnar President of Iceland
Groner, Lissy member of European parliament
Grossman, Marc diplomat
Grueber, Nils Heinrich Augustin retired German diplomat, international law educator
Grzybowski, Andrzej Edward mayor, ophthalmologist
Guani, Alberto diplomat
Guelluy, Phillipe diplomat
Guigou, Elisabeth French government official
Gumppert, Karella Ann federal government official
Gurirab, Theo-Ben Namibian government official
Gurria Trevino, José Angel Mexican government official
Guterres, Antonio Manuel de Oliveira prime minister of Portugal
Gutierrez, Carl T. C. governor
Gu Xiulian Chinese government official
Guy, Matthew Todd county official
Gyenge, András diplomat
Haakonsen, Bent diplomat
Haavisto, Heikki Johannes retired Finnish government official
Habibi, Hassan Ebrahim Iranian government official
Hackney, Howard Smith retired county official
Haga, Vigleik Arnbjørn cultural affairs executive
Hague, William Jefferson British politician
Haig, Alexander Meigs, Jr. former government official, former army officer, business executive
Haile Weldensae Eritrean government official
Hakeem, Ahmed Ataul government executive
Hakuo, Yanagisawa government official
Hall, Kathryn Walt ambassador
Halonen, Tarja Finnish government official
Halsted, David Crane diplomat
Hama, Amadou prime minister
Hamm-Bruecher, Hildegard retired politician, writer
Hamylton-Jones, Keith diplomat, writer
Han, Seung-Soo diplomat
Hannay, David Hugh Alexander diplomat
Hannibalsson, Jon Baldvin Icelandic ambassador
Hans-Adam, II Prince of Liechtenstein
Hansenne, Michel European parliamentary administrator
Hanson, Gerald Warner retired county official
Hao, Lawrence Kaholo state official, clinical hypnotherapist
Harald V King of Norway
Hardie Boys, Sir Michael New Zealand governor-general
Harney, Mary government official
Harris, Joe Frank former governor
Harris, Marion Hopkins former government official
Harris, Raymond Jesse retired government official
Harrop, William Caldwell retired ambassador, foreign service officer
Hasle, Karl-Frederik ambassador
Hassan, Toghrille Peter governmental relations consultant
Hassanal Bolkiah, His Majesty Mui'zzaddin Waddaulah Sultan of Brunei
Hassan bin Talal Crown Prince of Jordan
Hassanein, Muhammad Medhat federal official
Hauer, Jerome M. city official
Havel, Vaclav Czech government official, playwright
Hawley, Donald Frederick retired diplomat
Hayden, William George (Bill Hayden) former Australian governor general
Healey, Lord Denis Winston politician, writer
Heap, Sir Peter (William) consultant, retired diplomat
Hecklinger, Richard E. ambassador
Hellström, Mats Swedish government official
Hempstone, Smith, Jr. diplomat, journalist
Hennekam, Bernardus Martinus Johannes government official
Hennicot-Schoepges, Erna government executive
Henry, David Howe, II retired diplomat
Henry, Geoffrey Arama prime minister of Cook Islands
Herdman, John Mark Ambrose retired British government official
Herfkens, Eveline government official
Herman, Alexis M. federal official
Hermannson, Steingrimur former prime minister of Iceland
Hermans, Loek government official
Hernandez Mollar, Jorge Salvador foreign diplomat
Herzog, Roman German government official
Hillery, Patrick John former president of Ireland
Hilton, Robert Parker, Sr. national security affairs consultant, retired naval officer
Hinds, Samuel Archibald Anthony president of Guyana
Hjelm-Wallén, Lena Swedish government official
Hodges, Raymond Gregg county official
Hoffman, Gary Rodger state government official
Hogg, Douglas Martin British government official
Holbrooke, Richard Charles Albert ambassador, government official
Holik, Josef Friedrich retired diplomat, consultant
Holloway, Jacqueline county commissioner
Holmes, Genta Hawkins diplomat
Holmes, Richard Bale county manager
Hong, Soon-young federal official
Hoon, Geoffrey federal official
Horn, Gyula former prime minister of Hungary
Horoi, Rex Stephen ambassador
Horton, Jeanette municipal government official
Hosni, Farouq Abdelaziz Egyptian government official, sculptor
Hostler, Charles Warren former ambassador, international affairs consultant
Hottenroth, Dawn Cathleen city official
Howard, John Winston Australian politician
Howard, Michael British government official
Howe, Brian Leslie government official
Howe, Lord Richard Edward Geoffrey (Baron Howe of Aberavon) former British government official
Hrinak, Donna Jean ambassador
Hu, Jintao vice president of China
Hubert, Jean-Paul ambassador
Huhn, Darlene Marie county official, poet
Hume, John politician of Northern Ireland
Hun Sen Prime Minister of Kampuchea
Hunt, Swanee G. public policy educator, former ambassador
Hunter, Patricia Rae (Tricia Hunter) state official
Hurd, Douglas Richard British legislator
Hurst, Lionel Alexander Antigua and Barduda diplomat, lawyer
Hussain, Mohamed Zahir Maldivian government official
Hussein, Saddam president of Republic of Iraq
Hutchins, Brian R. attorney general
Hu Tsu Tau, Richard Singapore government official
Huxley, Carole Corcoran state education commissioner
Ibraimova, Elmira diplomat
Ichikawa, Atsunobu Japanese government official
Ifvarsson, Carl-Anders Swedish government official
Iglesias, Enrique V. bank executive, former government minister
Ilkin, Baki diplomat
Ilves, Toomas Hendrik diplomat
Indyk, Martin S. diplomat
Ingolfsson, Thorsteinn diplomat
Ingraham, Hubert Alexander Bahamian government official
Insanally, Samuel Rudolph diplomat
Insulza, José Miguel Chilean government official
Irvine, Baron of Lairg Alexander Andrew Mackay Lord Chancellor of England and Wales
Ishmael, Mohammed Ali Odeen Guyana diplomat
Ismail, Amat Chinese government official
Ismail, Wan Azizch Wan government party leader
Itoh, William H. former ambassador
Ivanov, Igor Sergeyevich federal official
Ivry, David diplomat
Izetbegovic, Alija government official
Jack, David Emmanuel governor general
Jagan, Janet retired president of Republic of Guyana
Jagland, Thorbjørn member of parliament
Jai, Lee Hun government executive
Jameel, Fathulla government official
James, William Hall former state official, educator
Jammeh, Yahya Abdulaziz Jemus Junkung Gambian government official
Jansen, Eppo retired international government official
Japaridze, Tedo Zurab diplomat
Jaskiernia, Jerzy Polish government official
Jatiya, Satyanarayan government official
Jayakumar, Shunmugam Singapore government official
Jean, (Benoit Guillaume Marie Robert Louis Antoine Adolphe Marc D'aviano) Grand Duke of Luxembourg
Jeffords, Edward Alan former assistant state attorney general

Jelved, Marianne government executive
Jensen, Tom Risdahl diplomat
Jesseramsing, Chitmansing ambassador
Jeszenszky, Geza historian, politician
Jethmalani, Ram government official
Ji, Chaozhu United Nations official, diplomat
Jia, Chunwang Chinese government official
Jiang, Zemin Chinese government official
Jibin, Liu federal official
Jin, Nyum federal official
Johannsson, Kjartan politician
Johansen, Lars Emil Greenland government official
Johnsen, Sigbjørn governor
Johnson, Donald Harry, Jr. government official, educator
Johnson, Frank retired state official, educator
Johnston, David William city manager
Johnston, Donald James civic organization official
Jones, Raymond Moylan strategy and public policy educator
Jones, Robert Howard government official
Jong, Kim, II government official
Jonsson, Marita Laila research administrator
Joondeph, Marcia diplomat
Jorritsma-Lebbink, Annemarie Dutch government official
Jospin, Lionel prime minister of French Republic
Jouve, Bernard Alexandre public works researcher
Jovanovic, Vladislav Serbian government official, diplomat
Juan Carlos, His Majesty I (Juan Carlos de Borbón y Borbón) King of Spain
Juma, Omar Ali government executive
Juncker, Jean-Claude Luxembourg government official
Jungmann, Raul Brazilian government official
Jurkāns, Janis government official
Jusys, Oskaras former ambassador
Ka, Ibra Deguene diplomat
Kabbah, Ahmed Tejan government official
Kaberuka, William Ugandan government official
Kabila, Laurent Desire president Democratic Republic of the Congo
Kabir, Humayun ambassador
Kaczynski, Lech federal official
Kadirgamar, Lakshman minister of foreign affairs
Kalantari, Isa Iranian government official
Kalashnikov, Sergei Russian federal official
Kallas, Siim government official
Kalnins, Ojars Eriks Latvian diplomat
Kamali, Hossain Iranian government official
Kaminska, Teresa federal official
Kamman, Curtis Warren retired ambassador
Kamotho, Joseph minister of education
Kamzari, Hamim government executive
Kant, Krishnan Indian vice president
Kanya, Mary Madzandza diplomat
Kapanga, Andre diplomat
Karimov, Islam Abduganiyevich Uzbek government official
Karlsson, Ingmar Axel ambassador
Kasanda, Peter Lesa ambassador
Kaskarelis, Vassilis Greek diplomat to NATO
Kastrup, Dieter diplomat
Kasyanov, Mikhail M. federal official
Kato, Moriyuki governor
Katz, Abraham retired foreign service officer
Kausikan, Bilahari Singapore government official
Kauzlarich, Richard Dale ambassador, retired foreign service officer
Kavaldzhiev, Todor Bulgarian government official
Kawanishi, Tetsuya government official, researcher
Kelly, John Joseph, Jr. government executive
Kemp, Jack French association director, former United States secretary of housing and urban development, former congressman
Kendrick, Joseph Trotwood former foreign service officer, writer, consultant
Kennedy, Chester Ralph, Jr. former state official, director
Keobounphan, Sisavath prime minister of Laos
Kerekou, Mathieu (Ahmed) president People's Republic of Benin
Kerr, Duncan Australian government official
Kerr, Sir John diplomat
Keryczynskyj, Leo Ihor county official, educator
Khaddam, Abd al-Halim ibn Said Syrian government official
Khalilov, Erkin Uzbek government official
Khamenei, Ayatollah Ali Hoseini religious leader Islamic Republic of Iran
Khamouan Boupha Laotian government official
Khamzayev, Almaz N. diplomat
Kharrazi, Kamal A. diplomat
Khatami-Ardakani, Hojjat ol-Eslam Ali Mohammad president of Iran
Khuweiter, Abdul Aziz Abdallah al Saudi Arabian government official
Kikwete, Jakaya Tanzanian government official
Killion, Redley government official
Kim, Chung-kil Republic of Korea governent official
Kim, Dae-Jung president of Republic of Korea
Kim, Deok government official
Kim, Jae Ho government official
Kim, Jong-il leader of Democratic People's Republic of Korea
Kim, Song-hun federal official
Kim, Yong-Chu North Korean government official
Kim, Yong-Nam North Korean government official
Kinkel, Klaus German government official
Kinnock, Neil Gordon former British government and political leader
Kirchner, Emil Joseph political science educator
Kiriyenko, Sergei former prime minister of Russia
Kissinger, Henry Alfred former secretary of state, international consulting company executive
Kittikhoun, Alounkeo ambassador
Kiwanuka, Semakula Mathias Mulumba United Nations ambassador
Klaus, Vaclav Czech government official
Klepsch, Egon Alfred German government official
Klestil, Thomas president of Austria
Knight, Keith Desmond St. Aubyn Jamaican government official
Koba, Henri ambassador to UN
Kobayashi, Hideaki diplomat
Kocharyan, Robert president
Kohl, Helmut former chancellor of Germany
Kohli, Alka government official
Koirala, Girija Prasad government official of Nepal
Kok, Willem prime minister of The Netherlands
Koller, Arnold former Swiss government official
Kolodko, Grzegorz W. Polish government official, educator, researcher
Komilov, Abdulaziz Uzbek government official
Komolowski, Longin federal official
Komorowski, Bronislaw minister of defense
Konan, Lambert Kouassi Ivory Coast government official
Konare, Alpha Oumar Malian government official
Kongor Arop, George federal official
Kono, Yohei Japanese government official
Koolman, Olindo Aruban government official
Kornblum, John Christian ambassador
Korth, Penne Percy ambassador
Korthals, Albert Hendrik (Benk) Netherlands government official
Kostov, Ivan government official
Kotaite, Assad United Nations agency administrator
Kotil, Rostislav defense attache
Kouliev, Eldar ambassador
Kouomegni, Augustin Kontchou Cameroon government official
Kouros, Pantelis government official
Kovanda, Karel Czech Republic government official
Koziej, Stanislaw director defense ministry
Koźmiński, Jerzy ambassador
Kpotstra, Roland Yao diplomat
Kramer, Benjamin Robert sheriff's deputy, accident reconstructionist
Krasts, Guntars Latvian parliament official
Kristensen, Anders Buch diplomat
Kropiwnicki, Jerzy Janusz federal official
Kruimel, Jan Paul civil servant, consultant, sculptor
Kucan, Milan Slovenian government official
Kuchma, Leonid Danylovich Ukrainian government official
Kudrin, Aleksey Leonidovich federal official
Kukan, Eduard Slovakian government official
Kullenberg, Gunnar Erik B. international civil servant, researcher, educator
Kulstad, Guy Charles public works official
Kumalo, Dumisani Shadrack diplomat
Kumar, Ananth government official
Kumar, Nitish government official
Kumaratunga, Chandrika Bandaranaike Sri Lankan government official
Kunin, Madeleine May former ambassador to Switzerland, former governor
Kuntjoro-Jakti, Dorodjatun diplomat
Kuntoro, Mangkusubroto government official
Kurisaqila, Apenisa Neiori government executive, physician
Kurtzer, Daniel ambassador
Kwaśniewski, Aleksander president of Poland
Kwelagobe, Daniel K. government official
Kyi, Aung San Suu government official
Kyprianou, Spyros government official
Labastida Ochoa, Francisco government official
Lader, Philip government official, diplomat, business executive, university president
Lagasse, Charles-Etienne Belgian government official, law educator
Lahoud, Emile president of Lebanon
Laing, Edward Arthur government official, judge
Laksono, Agung government official
Laliotis, Konstandinos Greek government official
Lalumière, Catherine diplomat
Lamb, Robert Edward diplomat
Lampreia, Luiz Felipe Brazilian government official
Landman, Lawrence Bruce federal official
Landsbergis, Vytautas Lithuanian government official
Laney, James Thomas former ambassador, educator
Lang, Danny Robert municipal development official
Laraki, Azedine prime minister of Morocco
Larifla, Dominique Lucien Guadeloupean government official, cardiologist
Larsen, Vibeke Danish government official
Larsson, Kjell Swedish government official
Laun, Louis Frederick government official
Lavrov, Sergei Viktorovich ambassador
Leao Monteiro, Jose Luis Barbosa diplomat
Lee, Han Dong prime minister of Korea
Lee, Hongkoo diplomat
Lee, Jimmy Che-Yung city planner
Lee, Joung-binn minister of foreign affairs and trade
Lee, Kuan Yew Singapore government official
Lee, Teng-Hui president of Republic of China
Lee, Timothy Earl international agency executive, paralegal
Leekpai, Chuan prime minister of Thailand, lawyer
Legwaila, Legwaila Joseph ambassador
Lekota, Mosinoa Gerard Patrick federal official, writer
Lenoir-Freaud, Noëlle French government official
Lenzi, Guido diplomat
Le Pen, Jean-Marie politician
Le Pensec, Louis French politician
Letsie, III (Mohato Seeiso) King of Lesotho
Letta, Enrico Italian government official
Leuenberger, Moritz federal official
Leveque, Michel, Sr. diplomat
Levin, Herbert diplomat, foundation executive
Levitsky, Melvyn former ambassador, professor
Levy, David Israeli politician
Lewis, Delano Eugene ambassador, former broadcast executive
Lewis, Patrick Albert diplomat
Lian, Hans Jacob Bjørn Norwegian diplomat, NATO official
Licalzi, Michael Charles county official
Lichem, Walther G. diplomat
Liejon, Britta Swedish deputy minister of justice
Likphai, Chaun prime minister of Thailand
Lilley, Peter Bruce government official
Limón Rojas, Miguel Mexican government official
Lindh, Anna Swedish government official
Lino, Marisa Rose diplomat
Lipkin-Shahak, Amnon Israel government official
Lipponen, Paavo Finnish prime minister
Lise, Claude government official of Martinique, physician, politician
Lisinenko, Igor government official
Liu, Sung-Pan Taiwanese government official
Livingood, Wilson S. law enforcement official
Lodgaard, Sverre nuclear disarmament researcher
Lodhi, Maleeha diplomat
Loong, Lee Hsien government executive
Lorenzo Franco, José Ramón Mexican government official
Louisy, Pearlette governor general of Saint Lucia
Lovden, Lars Erik Swedish government official
Low, Donald diplomat, financial investor
Lozano Escribano, Tomás diplomat
Lubensky, Earl Henry diplomat, anthropologist
Lucinschi, Petru president of Moldova
Luis, Berenguer Fuster member of European parliament
Lukashenko, Aleksandr Grigoryevich president of Belarus
Lukashou, Alyaksandr Vasiljevich Belarus government official
Luong, Tran Duc president national assembly of Vietnam
Lyakh, Ivan A. Belarus government official
Lykketoft, Mogens Danish federal official
Lymberopoulos, Elias L. diplomat, researcher
Ma, Ying-Jeou mayor
Mabilangan, Felipe Hugo, Jr. Philippine diplomat
Macapagal-Arroyo, Gloria federal official, economist, educator, journalist
Maccanico, Antonio Italian government official
MacGregor, John Russell Roddick British government minister, businessman
Machinea, José Luis minister of economy
Macleod, Sir (Nathaniel William) Hamish former Hong Kong government official
Madelin, Alain French government official
Madison, Eddie Lawrence, Jr. public relations consultant, editor, writer
Madrazo Cuellar, Jorge Luis Mexican government official
Maduna, Penuell federal official
Magang, David Ntsimele government official
Magee, Charles Thomas international consultant, retired diplomat
Magnaga, Martin-Fidele government official
Magnussen, Jan Danish county administrator
Mahathir bin Mohamad prime minister of Malaysia
Major, John former prime minister of United Kingdom
Makarovs, Vladimirs Latvian government official
Malan, Pedro Brazilian government official
Malewezi, Justin Malawian government official
Malietoa Tanumafili, II Western Samoan government official
Malik, Gunwantsingh Jaswantsingh diplomat, physical chemist
Malk, Raul diplomat
Malley, Raymond Charles retired foreign service officer, industrial executive
Mamadou, Michel Koui supreme court president
Mandela, Nelson Rolihlahla South African government official, lawyer
Mandela, Nomzamo Winnie South African politician
Mangoaela, Percy Metsing diplomat
Manley, John Canadian government official
Manuel, Trevor Andrew South African government official
Manz, Johannes Jakob Swiss diplomat
Maope, Kelebone Albert Lesotho government official
Maraj, Ralph Trinidadian government official
Marchi, Sergio Sisto Canadian government official
Marehalau, Jesse B. ambassador
Marengo, Marc Michael Rogers diplomat, United Nations ambassador
Margaret, Princess (Rose Margaret) Countess of Snowdon
Margrethe, Her Majesty II (Margrethe Alexandrine Thorhildur Ingrid) Queen of Denmark
Marinich, Mikhail Afanasyevich diplomat
Markham, Clarence Matthew, III city administrator
Markham, J. David educator, writer, historical consultant
Marleau, Diane Canadian government official
Marsalis, Sherry H. municipal official
Martelli, Claudio Italian government official
Martin, Michael government official
Martin, Paul Canadian government official
Martin, Thomas Geoffrey government official
Martinez-Racines, Cesar P. agricultural products researcher
Martynov, Serguei Nikolaevich Belarus diplomat
Maruf, Taha Muhyi al-din Iraqi government official
Mascarenhas Monteiro, Antonio president of Cape Verde
Masefield, John Thorold government official
Masera, Rainer Stefano Italian government official
Mashariqa, Muhammad Zuhayr Syrian government official
Masri, Taher Nashat Jordanian government official
Masset, Jean-Pierre diplomat
Mathews, Mary Kathryn retired government official
Mattarella, Sergio minister of defense
Matute, Daul J. diplomat
Matza, Joshua government official
Mayanja-Nkangi, Joshua Sibakyalwayo Ugandan government official
Mayor Oreja, Jaime Spanish government official
Mazankowski, Donald Frank Canadian government official
Mbeki, Thabo South African government official
Mboumbou-Miyakou, Antoine Gabon government official
Mboweni, Tito T. South African government official
McAleese, Mary Patricia President of Ireland
McBee, Robert Levi retired federal government official, writer, consultant
McCarthy, George A. Cayman Islands government executive
McClinton, James Leroy city administrator
McCreevy, Charlie Irish government official
McDaid, Jim government official
McFarland, Jon Weldon retired county commissioner
McGauran, Peter Australian government official
McGuire, Roger Alan retired foreign service officer
McLean, John Bonwell, Sr. government official
McLellan, A. Anne Canadian government official
Mdladlana, Sheperd South African government official
Medgyessy, Peter Hungarian government official
Meguid, Ahmed Esmat Abdel government official
Meidani, Rexhep president of Albania
Meinander, Martin city official
Mejdoub, Noureddine diplomat
Mejia, Cecilia Colombian government official, publisher
Meles, Zenawi Ethiopian government official
Melkert, Ad P W Dutch government official
Melkonian, Armen consul general of Armenia
Mellandri, Giovanna government official
Mello-Franco, Affonso Arinos de diplomat
Mendez, Ruben Policarpio diplomat, educator
Mendouga, Jerome diplomat
Menendez Del Valle, Emilio ambassador
Menkerios, Haile diplomat
Merab, Julie Atieno administrator
Merafhe, Mompati S. Botswana government official
Meri, Lennart president of Estonia
Merimee, Jean-Bernard diplomat
Mesfin, Seyoum Ethiopian government official
Metzler-Arnold, Ruth federal official
Meyer, Sir Christopher J.R. diplomat
Michel, Alix James Seychelles government official
Micheli, Enrico federal official
Mifflin, Fred John Canadian government official
Mifsud, Francis Montanaro ambassador
Milam, William Bryant diplomat, economist
Milinaire, Gilles Jean French diplomat
Millares Rodriguez, Manuel Cuban government official
Miller, Billie Antoinette Barbadian government official
Miller, William Green ambassador
Millon, Charles Marie André Philippe French government official
Mills, John Evans Atta Ghanaian government official
Milstam, Karl Östen Swedish government official
Milutinovic, Milan A. President Republic of Serbia
Minger, Terrell John public administration and natural resource institute executive
Minoves-Triquell, Juli diplomat, economist, political scientist, writer
Mitchell, Austin Vernon member of parliament
Mitchell, George Charles diplomat, international consultant, mediator, educator, writer
Mitchell, Graham Richard government engineering executive
Mitchell, Sir James Fitzallen prime minister Saint Vincent and The Grenadines, agronomist, hotelier
Mitchell, Keith Claudius Grenada government official
Miyanda, Godfrey Zambian government official
Miyazawa, Kiichi Japanese government official
Mkapa, Benjamin William president of Tanzania
Mocumbi, Pascoal Manuel prime minister of Mozambique
Modrow, Hans German Democratic Republic government official
Mogae, Festus Gontebanye Botswana government official
Mohamad, Mahathir government executive
Mohammed Taib, Pehin Dato Haji Abdul Rahman bin Brunei government official
Moi, Daniel T. Arap president of Kenya
Mokkamakkul, Sakda supreme court president Thailand
Molyneaux, James Henry retired government official
Momin, Alhaj Babul Ahmed investigation bureau director
Mondale, Walter Frederick former Vice President of United States, diplomat, lawyer
Mönkäre, Sinikka Finnish government official
Montoro, Cristobal federal official
Mooney, Lori county official
Moore, John Colinton Australian government official
Moore, Michael Kenneth international organization executive
Morgan, David Gethin county treasurer
Mori, Yoshiro government official
Morris, Earle Elias, Jr. retired state official, business executive
Moscovici, Pierre government official
Mosisili, Pakalitha prime minister of Lesotho
Moss, Malcolm Douglas member parliament
Mottley, Mia A. Barbadian government official, minister of education, youth affairs and culture
Moussa, Amre Mahmoud Egyptian government official
Mowlam, Marjorie minister
Moxey-Ingraham, Theresa government official
Mpasu, Samuel John government of Malawi minister
Mswati, His Majesty III King of Swaziland
Muammar, Abdallah bin Abd al-Aziz federal official
Mubarak, Muhammad Hosni president of Egypt
Mubarak, Umid Midhat Iraq minister of health, internist
Mudenge, Stanislaus Zimbabwean government official
Mueller, Werner government official
Mufamadi, Sydney Fholisani South African federal official
Mugabe, Robert Gabriel president of Zimbabwe
Muja, Kathleen Ann state official, consultant
Mullings, Seymour Jamaican government official
Mulroney, Brian (Martin Brian Mulroney) former prime minister of Canada
Muluzi, Bakili Malawian government official
Munavvar, Mohammed Maldivian government official
Mungra, Soebhas Chandra Surinamese government official
Munshi, Aziz A. Pakistani government official
Muradov, Sakhat Nepesovich Turkmen government official, educator
Muratovic, Hasan diplomat
Murray, Kathleen municipal official
Musa, Abdul Abdulkadir diplomat
Museveni, Yoweri Kaguta president of Uganda
Musonge, Peter Mafany government official
Mustafa, Shawkat Issa government executive
Muzenda, Simon Vengai vice president of Zimbabwe
Mwakawago, Daudi Ngelautwa diplomat
Myrick, Bismarck diplomat
Nakamura, Kuniwo president of Palau
Nakayama, Masho diplomat
Naor, Gideon retired executive, developer
Napier and Ettrick, Lord (Knight Comdr.) member Royal household
Napolitano, Giorgio Italian government official
Narayanan, Kocheril Raman president of India
Narveson, Joyce Ann public services administrator
Nasir, Mohammed retired educator and diplomat
Nazarbayev, Nursultan Abishevich president of Kazakhstan
Nazarov, Talbak Tajik government official
Ndam, Shadrack Njah United Nations official, adviser
Negasso, Gidada president of Ethiopia
Neiditz, Andrew E. city administrator
Nejad-Hoseinian, Mohammad Hadi diplomat
Nelsen-Cudddeiro, Jeffrey Charles leadership consultant
Nelson, Eric Victor retired diplomat
Nemeth, Miklos politician
Nemfakos, Charles Panagiotis government official
Nes, David Gulick retired diplomat
Netelenbos, Tineke government official
Neumann, Hans-Adolf international governmental administrator
Ngenmune, Suthat Thai government official
Ngoenmun, Suthat federal official
Nguyen, Dinh Loc Vietnamese government official
Nguyen, Manh Cam Vietnamese government official
Nguyen, Thi Binh Vietnamese government official
Niinistö, Sauli Finnish government official
Nikkola, Antti Salomoni retired government official
Nish, Ian Hill political science educator
Nishida, Mamoru Japanese government official
Niyazov, Saparmurad Atayevich president of Turkmenistan
Noble, John Joseph diplomat
Nong Duc Manh Vietnamese government official
Nordenfelt, Johan foreign service official
Norrback, Johan Ole Finnish government official
Nothomb, Simon-Pierre government official
Novetzke, Sally Johnson former ambassador
Nujoma, Sam Daniel president of Namibia

Nyers, Rezso Hungarian politician
Obame, Paulin Gabonese government official
Obasanjo, Olusegun (Matthew Olusegun Fajinmi Aremu Obasanjo) president of Nigeria
Obasi, Godwin Olu Patrick United Nations agency administrator, scientific organization administrator, meteorologist
Obermann, Richard Michael governmental technology and policy analyst
Obiang Nguema Mbasogo, Teodoro president of Equatorial Guinea
Oddsson, David prime minister of Iceland
Odlum, George William government official
O'Donoghue, John government official, solicitor
Ogata, Sadako United Nations official
Ogi, Adolf government official
O'Huiginn, Sean diplomat
Ojeda Eiseley, Jaime de former Spanish ambassador, educator
Okawara, Yoshio former ambassador
Olechowski, Andrzej government official, economist
Oleksy, Jozef former prime minister of Poland
Oliveira Maciel, Marco Brazilian government official
Olljum, Alar J. Rudolf ambassador
Olsen, Erling Heymann Danish government official
Olson, Lyndon Lowell, Jr. ambassador
Olson, Roy Arthur government official
Olszak, Norbert lawyer, educator
Ondo Bile, Pastor Micha ambassador
Oppenheimer, Tamar Mariamne international government specialist
Oral, Sümer Turkish government official
Orbán, Viktor prime minister of Hungary
Orellana, Edmundo Honduran government official
Ornellaas, Waldeck Vieira Brazilian government official
O'Rourke, Mary public representative
Ortiz, Fernando, Jr. municipal budget official
Ortner, Gustav Austrian diplomat
Östros, Thomas federal official
O'Toole, Tara Jeanne federal official
Ouane, M. Moctar diplomat
Ouedraogo, Kadre Desire foreign government official
Ould Deddach, Mahfoudh diplomat
Owada, Hisashi government official
Owen, Arthur S. Barbados government official
Owen, Lord David Anthony Llewellyn former British government minister, physician
Oxenstierna, Maria Teresa Dorado Ortiz (Countess Maria Teresa Dorado Oxenstierna) political-military advisor
Oyarzabal, Antonio diplomat
Oyé-Mba, Casimir Gabonese government official, banker
Öymen, Onur Turkish diplomat, NATO official
Oyono, Ferdinand Léopold Cameroonian government official
Oyono Ndong, Miguel Equatorial-Guinean government official
Paasio, Pertti Kullervo Finnish government official
Padhila, Eliseu Brazilian government official
Pak, Song-Cho'ol vice president of Democratic People's Republic of Korea
Pak, Tae-Chun former prime minister of South Korea
Palsson, Gunnar diplomat
Palsson, Thorsteinn Icelandic diplomat
Pancha, Kesornthong federal official
Panday, Basdeo prime minister of Trinidad and Tobago
Papalexandrou, Christos Elias retired Greek government official, economist
PaPandoniou, Ioannis Greek government official
Pardee, Jeffrey Clark county government official
Park, Yeon-Soo government official
Parris, Mark Robert ambassador
Parrish, Lori Nance county commissioner
Pascoe, Nigel Spencer Knight Queen's counsel, recorder of Crown Court
Pashayev, Hafiz Mir Jalal diplomat, physics educator
Patasse, Ange Felix president of Central African Republic
Patten, Christopher Francis government official
Patterson, Percival James prime minister of Jamaica
Pavlov, Aleksandr Kazakhstani government official
Paye, Jean-Claude diplomat
Peaucellier, Patrick French Polynesian government official
Peck, Ellie Enriquez retired state official
Peiris, Gamini Lakshman Sri Lankan government official
Peliza, Sir Robert John former Gibraltar government official
Peña, Federico Fabian retired federal official
Pendleton, Miles Stevens, Jr. diplomat
Peng, Li government official
Peper, Bram government official
Peres, Shimon government official
Perez-Otermin, Jorge diplomat
Persow, Meyer Joseph federal official
Persson, Goran Swedish government official
Persson, Sten Erik Bertil member of parliament, physician
Peterle, Lojze Slovenian politician
Peters, Melanie Maria federal official
Peters, William ambassador
Petersen, Niels Helveg Danish government official
Peterson, Douglas Pete (Pete Peterson) ambassador, former congressman
Peterson, Thage G. retired Swedish politician
Petri, Carl Axel former Swedish government official
Petric, Ernest Slovenian ambassador
Petrovsky, Vladimir Fyodorovich United Nations administrator
Phan, Van Khai prime minister of Vietnam
Phieu, Le Kha government executive
Philip, Prince (Duke of Edinburgh) Prince of United Kingdom of Great Britain and Northern Ireland, Earl of Merioneth, Baron Greenwich
Phillips, Christopher Hallowell diplomat
Phillips, Mark Anthony Peter British official
Philo, Gordon Charles George retired diplomat
Phumiphon Adulyadej, His Majesty King of Thailand
Piacitelli, John Joseph county official, educator, pediatrician
Pibulsonggram, Nitya diplomat
Pickering, Thomas Reeve diplomat
Pierce, Samuel Riley, Jr. government official, lawyer
Ping, Jean Gabonese government official
Pique I. Camps, Josep Spanish government official
Pitsuwan, Surin minister of foreign affairs
Plaisted, Joan M. diplomat
Plantey, Alain Gilles French government official, writer
Pollack, Anita Jean civil servant, politician
Pongpol, Adireksarn federal official
Ponsonby, Frederick Edward Neuflize (10th Earl Bessborough) government executive
Poos, Jacques Francois member of European Parliament
Popova, Jasmine diplomat
Porter, Dwight Johnson former ambassador, former assistant secretary of state, former electric company executive, foreign affairs consultant
Poungui, Ange-Edouard former People's Republic of Congo government official
Powles, Michael John diplomat
Prabhu, Suresh government official
Prachuap, Chaiyasan federal official
Prescott, John deputy prime minister of Great Britain
Preval, Rene president of Haiti
Pritts, Kim Derek state conservation officer, writer
Prokopovich, Piotr federal official
Putin, Vladimir president of Russia
Putt, Jerry Wayne municipal official
Qian, Qichen Chinese government official
Qin Huasun diplomat
Quainton, Anthony Cecil Eden diplomat
Quayle, Dan (James Danforth Quayle) former vice president United States, entrepreneur
Quinn, Ruairi Irish government official
Quintao, Geraldo Magela da Cruz federal official
Quiroga Ramirez, Jorge Fernando vice president of Bolivia
Rabuka, Sitiveni Ligamamada Fijian government official, army officer
Radebe, Jeff T. South African government official
Radhakishun, Pretaapnarain Surinamese government official
Radmann, Michael Wolfdieter diplomat, geologist
Rahmani, Reza Mossaver writer, retired Iranian Air Force officer, banker, tour operator
Rainier, Prince III (Louis Henri Maxence Bertrand Rainier) Sovereign Prince of Monaco
Rajabov, Safarali Tajik government official
Rajaonarivelo, Pierrot J. Madagascar government official
Rajapov, Matkarim Rajapovich foreign government official
Rajoy Brey, Mariano Spanish government official
Rajpurohit, Kishan Singh government official, researcher, consultant
Rakhmonov, Emomili president of Tajikistan
Ramadan, Taha Yasin Iraqi government official
Ramdin, Albert Ramchand Suriname government official, ambassador
Ramelan, Rahardi government official
Ramgoolam, Navinchandra prime minister of the Republic of Mauritius
Ramiz, Alia former president of Albania
Ramsey, Sally Ann Seitz retired state official
Rana, Kashiram government official
Ranald, Ralph Arthur former government official, educator
Ransom, David Michael retired ambassador
Rashid Ubaydi, Amir Rashid Muhammad Al- Iraqi government official
Rasizade, Artur prime minister
Rasmussen, Poul Nyrup prime minister of Denmark, economist
Rato Figaredo, Rodrigo Spanish government official
Ratsiraka, Didier president of Madagascar
Rattley, Jessie Menifield former mayor, educator
Rau, Johannes German politician
Rawlings, Jerry John president of Ghana
Ray, Siddhartha Sankar former government official
Reagan, Nancy Davis (Anne Francis Robbins) volunteer, wife of former President of United States
Reagan, Ronald Wilson former President of United States
Redwood, John Alan member British parliament
Reich, Robert Bernard former federal official, political economics educator
Reilly, William Kane former government official, educator, lawyer, conservationist
Reiter, Wolfgang Leo national government official
Remengesau, Thomas, Jr. Palauan government official
Renato de Souza, Paulo government official
Rene, France Albert president of Seychelles
Reno, Janet attorney general
Renwick of Clifton, Lord Robin William former diplomat, banker
Rey, Pete F. city official
Reyes Heroles, Jesus Mexican government official
Reyn, Alex Belgian ambassador
Reynolds, Albert Martin Irish government official
Richard, Alain French government official
Richards, Simon Paul diplomat
Richardson, William Blaine federal official
Ricks, David Trulock cultural affairs administrator
Ricupero, Rubens Brazilian government official
Ridgway, James Mastin government official
Riester, Walter government official
Rifkind, Malcolm (Leslie) British government official
Riley, Richard Wilson federal official
Ringholm, Bosse federal official
Roach, Victor Randolph government official
Roberts, Monty A. Saint Vincentian government official
Robertson, George international organization official
Robertson, Paul Douglas Jamaican government official
Robillard, Lucienne federal official
Robinson, Arthur Napoleon Raymond president
Robinson, Mary high commissioner for human rights
Roble Olhaye Oudine ambassador
Robson, Brian Ewart retired British government official, historian
Rocard, Michel Louis Léon French politician
Rock, Allan Michael Canadian government official
Rodocanachi, Emmanuel A. government official
Rodriguez Garcia, Jose Luis Cuban government official
Rodriguez Giavarini, Adalberto minister of foreign relations
Rodriguez Parrilla, Bruno diplomat
Rodriquez, Miguel Angel federal official
Rogers, Stephen Hitchcock former ambassador
Rohatyn, Felix George ambassador
Rohee, Clement Guyanese government official
Rollason, Christopher Richard European Parliament official
Romero, Edward L. diplomat, environmental engineering executive
Ronish, Robert Ray retired civil service administrator
Roper, Michael retired governmental official
Rosengren, Björn Swedish government official
Rossello, Pedro governor
Rowell, Edward Morgan retired foreign service officer, lecturer
Royal, Segolene government official
Rubin, Robert E. former secretary of treasury
Ruiz Sacristán, Carlos Mexican government official
Rumore, Charlotte Fowler city official
Rupel, Dimitrij diplomat
Rusling, Barbara N(eubert) state commissioner, real estate broker
Russell, Brian Scotney retired government administrator, consultant
Ryan, Richard diplomat
Ryle, Lillian June municipal administrator
Ryu, Kwang-sok Republic of Korean diplomat
Sacirbey, Muhamed ambassador
Sadik, Nafis United Nations administrator
Sáenz, Gerardo Mexican government official
Said, Qaboos bin Sultan of Oman, prime minister of Oman
Saidy, Aisatou Njie federal official
Sai Hung, Henri Li postal officer
Sainovic, Nikola prime minister of Serbia
Sainsbury, David John British government official
St. Hilaire, David William county official, financial manager
Saito, Hideaki defense official
Saitoti, George Kenyan government official
SaKong, Il minister of finance
Salamé, Riad Lebanon government official, bank executive
Saleh, Ali-Abdullah president
Saleh, Jaime governor
Saleh, Mohammed diplomat
Saliba, George Maltese government official
Salih, Ali Abdallah president of Republic of Yemen
Salim, Salim Ahmed government official of Tanzania
Sallam, Ismail Awad-Allah government official
Salleo, Ferdinando Italian diplomat
Salolainen, Pertti Edvard Finnish diplomat, politician
Salomao, Tomas Mozambican government official
Sambat, Alexandre Gabonese government official
Sambuaga, Theo Leo government official
Samhan, Mohammad Jasim ambassador
Sampaio, Jorge president of Portugal
Sampas, Dorothy Myers retired government official
Sanders, Ronald Michael diplomat
Sanou, Baworo Seydou Burkina Faso government official
Sarac, Ahmet governor
Sardenberg, Ronaldo Mota ambassador
Sarros, P. Peter diplomat, consultant
Sasser, James Ralph (Jim Sasser) ambassador, former senator
Sato, Yukio Japanese diplomat
Sattar, Abdul minister of foreign affairs
Saunders, Barry Wayne state official
Savage, Francis Joseph Governor of the British Virgin Islands
Sayf al-Nasr, Faruq Egyptian government official
Scales, John Thomas state official
Scharping, Rudolf government official
Schäuble, Wolfgang German politician, lawyer
Scheibner, Herbert Austrian minister for national defense
Schily, žOtto government official
Schmidt-Jortzig, Edzard former member of parliament
Schneider, Cynthia Perrin ambassador, art history educator
Schoenbohm, Joerg government executive
Schori, Pierre Swedish government official
Schroeder, Gerhard Fritz Kurt chancellor of Germany
Schuessel, Wolfgang Austrian chancellor
Schutz, Emile Kiribati government official
Scognamiglio, Carlo economics and finance educator, financial consultant
Scott, Gerald Wesley retired American diplomat
Sebastian, Sir Cuthbert Montraville governor general
Seck, Mamadou Mansour ambassador, career officer
Sedlák, Mikuláš ambassador, educator
Seignoret, Sir Clarence (Henry Augustus Seignoret) former president of Commonwealth of Dominica
Selby, Jerome M. mayor
Semyonov, Viktor federal official
Sen, Samdech Hun prime minister Cambodia
Sene, Ibrahima diplomat
Sergeyer, Igor Dmitriyerich federal official
Sergeyev, Igor Dmitriyevich federal official
Serra, José Brazilian government official
Serudin, Mohammed Zain bin Brunei government official
Sezer, Ahmet Necdet president of Turkey
Shade, Kerryn Vincent city manager
Shafeen, Ismail Maldivian government official
Shaftesbury, Anthony former British government executive, company executive
Shah, Narendra M. Nepalese diplomat
Shahabudin, Syed Ahmad Mahmud government official
Shahbazian, Gagik government official
Shalala, Donna Edna federal official, political scientist, educator, former university chancellor
Shalkovsky, Volodymyr Valentinovich diplomat
Shamir, Yitzhak (Yitzhak Yezernitsky) statesman, former Israeli prime minister
Sharif, Mahmud Sayid Ahmad Egyptian government official
Sharif, Mohammad Nowaz former prime minister of Pakistan
Sharma, Kamalesh diplomat
Sharpless, Joseph Benjamin former county official
Shaykh, Abdallah Muhammed Ibrahim-Al federal official
Sherif, Mohamed Safwat Egyptian government official
Sherifo, Mahmud Ahmed Eritrean government official
Shevardnadze, Eduard Amvrosiyevich Georgian government official, former minister of foreign affairs of Soviet Union
Shihab, Alwi Abdurahman minister of foreign affairs
Shinn, David Hamilton diplomat
Shkolnikov, Vladimir David civil servant
Shlaudeman, Harry Walter retired ambassador
Shochat, Avraham Israel government official
Shoda, Empress Michiko Empress of Japan
Shpek, Roman Vassylyovich Ukrainian government official
Shuart, Tina Ward municipal official
Shubukshi, Usama bin Abd al-Majid federal official
Shucheng, Wang government official
Shultz, George Pratt former government executive, economics educator
Siazon, Domingo Lim, Jr. Philippine government official
Sieberichs, Thomas regional government official, lawyer
Sigcau, Stella N. South African government official
Sihanouk, Norodom King of Cambodia
Sihver Liljegren, Carl Henrik Swedish ambassador
Siimann, Mart prime minister
Silajdzić, Haris former prime minister of Bosnia-Herzegovina
Sim, Lee-Ling government official
Simao, Leonardo Mozambican government official
Simelane, Maweni Swazi government official
Simitis, Constantine prime minister of Greece
Simmons, David government official
Simms, John William retired foreign service officer, consultant
Simonyi, Andras Hungarian diplomat, NATO official
Simpson, Daniel H. ambassador
Sinamenye, Mathias Burundi government official
Singh, Jaswant federal official
Singh, Paban Bahadur federal official
Singhateh, Edward Gambian government official
Sinha, Yashwant Indian government official
Sipahioglu, Hatice Elcin diplomat, interpreter/translator
Siphandone, Khamtay Laotian government official
Sisulu, Sheila Violet Makate diplomat
Skelemani, Phandu T. C. Botswana government official
Skosana, Ben M. federal official
Skou, Bent diplomat, public information officer
Skubiszewski, Krzysztof Polish government official, educator, arbitrator
Skweyiya, Zola S. T. South African government official
Slade, Tuiloma Neroni Western Samoan diplomat
Slater, Rodney E. federal official
Smith, Andrew federal official
Smith, Andrew David member of parliament
Smith, Betty Denny county official, administrator, fashion executive
Smith, Cornelius A. government official
Smith, Jane Schneberger retired city administrator
Smith, Michael government official
Smith, Myron George former government official, consultant
Smith, Robert Grant, Jr. public official, retired hotel executive
Smith, Wayland Rufus retired county official
Snoussi, Ahmed ambassador
Soares, Mário Alberto Nobre Lopes political party official, lawyer, historian
Sober, Sidney retired diplomat, educator
Soberon Valdez, Francisco federal official
Söderman, Jacob-Magnus European ombudsman
Sohn, Chan-Joon diplomat
Soliman, Mohammad Ibrahim government official
Solinger, Uwe Wolfgang Thailand government official
Solomon, Petros Eritrean government official
Somsavat Lengsavad Lao government official
Song, Defu Chinese government official
Soong, James Chu Yul government official
Sorensen, Jens Adser parliamentary service administrator
Sorenson, Roger A. international relations consultant
Sorhaindo, Crispin Anselm former president of Dominica
Sorsa, Kalevi government representative
Sossa, Jose Antonio Panamanian government official, lawyer
Sounkur, Salha Syrian government official, education educator
Soutello-Alves, Lauro Eduardo diplomat
Southam, G(ordon) Hamilton former Canadian government official
Souza, Paulo Renato Brazilian government official
Souza dos Santos, Paulo Afonso Brazilian diplomat
Sow, Sy Kadiatou Malian government official
Spencer, John Burton, III state agency administrator
Spring, Dick Irish government official and diplomat
Stabreit, Immo Friedrich Helmut diplomat
Stănculescu, Victor Atanasie former Romanian government official, executive
Stanton, William Anthony diplomat
Steen Crawford, Andrea village manager
Stefan, Charles Gordon retired foreign service officer and educator
Stephanopoulos, Constandinos president of the Republic of Greece
Sternik, Alexander Vadimovich diplomat, historian, linguist
Stewart, Christine Susan Canadian government official
Stix, Gerulf government official
Stone, Michael William retired tax official
Stoyanov, Petar government official
Strauss-Kahn, Dominique Gaston André government official
Strazhav, Vassily I. Belarus government official
Streeb, Gordon Lee diplomat, economist
Strother, Sherrie Kaye Carter county official
Sudanowicz, Elaine Marie government executive
Sudharsono, Juwono federal official
Sudibyo, Bambang Indonesian minister of finance
Suissa, Eli Israeli government official
Sujudi Indonesian government official
Sukarnoputri, Megawati government official
Sullivan, Michael John ambassador, former governor
Sultonov, Otkir Uzbek government official
Sumaye, Frederick Tluway prime minister of Tanzania
Sun, Jiazheng Chinese government official
Supachai, Panitchaphak federal official
Surin, Phitsuwan federal official
Suseno, Giri Hadiharjono Indonesian government official
Süssmuth, Rita government official, education and French educator
Suthep, Thaugsuban federal official
Suwat, Liptapanlop politician
Swan, Sir John (William David) former premier of Bermuda
Sweis Mussa, Rafiq consular general, activist
Swihart, James W., Jr. diplomat
Sychov, Alyaksandr diplomat
Szabó, Iván Hungarian government official
Szemerey, John European Commission official
Szergenyi, Istvan diplomat
Szövényi, Eszter ministerial counselor, international specialist
Tabone, Censu former president of Malta, ophthalmic consultant, former diplomat, educator
Taha, Ali Osman Mohammed federal official
Talay, Mustafa Istemihan federal official
Talgo, Harrison chief administrator tribal government
Tambs, Lewis Arthur diplomat, historian, educator
Tang, Jiaxuan Chinese government official
Tantawi, Mohammed Hussein government official
Taplin, Mark Allard foreign service officer

Tarar, Muhammad Rafiq *president of Pakistan*
Tarrin, Nimmanhemin *federal official*
Tatham, David Everard *diplomatic consultant, retired government official*
Taya, Maaouya Ould Sid Ahmed *president of Islamic Republic of Mauritania*
Taylor, Ann (Winifred) *British government minister*
Taylor, Charles Ghankay *Liberia government president*
Teare, Richard Wallace *ambassador*
Teeke, Kataotika *Kiribati government official*
Teixeira, Gail *Guyanese government official*
Tellez Kuenzler, Luis *government official*
Tello Macias, Manuel *diplomat*
Tembo, Christon S. *federal official*
Tentoa, Tewareka *I-Kiribati government official*
Teo, Feleti Penitala *Tuvaluan government official*
Tesfai, Ghebreselassie *Eritrean government official*
Thalén, Ingela *Swedish government official*
Than Shwe *prime minister of Burma, military officer*
Tharin Nimmanhemin *Thai government official*
Thatcher, Margaret Hilda *former prime minister of United Kingdom*
Thawley, Michael *diplomat*
Thigpen, Mary Cecelia *city official, consultant*
Thomas, James Arthur *retired government official, electrical engineer*
Tiapani, Albert Kakou *Cote d'Ivoire government official*
Tinga, Beniamina *Kiribati government official*
Tin Tun *Burmese government official*
Tito, Teburoro *president of Kiribati*
Tiuri, Martti Eelis *member Parliament of Finland, scientist*
Tizard, Dame Catherine (Anne) *association executive*
Tjipilica, Paulo *Angolan government official*
Tjiriange, Ngarikutuke Ernest *Namibian government official, lawyer*
Tkachenko, Oleksandr M. *government official*
Tlass, Mustafa Abdul-Kader *government official, military officer*
Tobias, Kevin Richard *borough manager*
Todorow, Marko Markow *Bulgarian government official*
Tokaev, Kasymzhomart Kemel-uly *government official*
Tómasson, Tómas Ármann *ambassador*
Tomka, Peter *Slovakian diplomat*
Tong, Goh Chok *government executive*
Tonoukouin, Lucien *diplomat*
Torashima, Kazuo *federal official*
Törnudd, Klaus Mattias *diplomat, educator*
Toth, József *diplomat*
Toungui, Paul *Gabonese government official*
Touraine Moulin, Françoise *scientific attache*
Touzenis-Bendeck, George *director*
Towell, Timothy Lathrop *foreign service officer*
Towpik, Andrzej *Polish diplomat, NATO official*
Traore, Maurice Mélégué *Burkina Faso government official*
Trillo, Federico *federal official*
Trimble, David *first minister designate of Northern Ireland*
Trittin, Juergen *government official*
Trout, Maurice Elmore *foreign service officer*
Trovoada, Miguel *Sao Tome and Principe president*
Troyjo, Marcos Prado *diplomat*
Tsang, Donald *government official*
Tserenpilyn, Gombosuren *former Mongolian government official*
Tsering, Ugyen *diplomat*
Tshering, Ugyen *Bhutan diplomat*
Tshwete, Steve *South African government official*
Tsukamoto, Katsuichi *administrator Japanese research association*
Tucker, Alvin Leroy *retired government official*
Tuerk, Helmut *diplomat*
Tuila'epa Sailele Malielegaoi *Western Samoan government official*
Tu'ipelehake, Prince Fatafehi *Tongan government official*
Tulba, Abdallah *Syrian government official*
Tuomioja, Erkki Sakari *Finnish government official*
Tupou, His Majesty Taufa'ahau, IV *King of Tonga*
Tupou, Tevita *Tongan government official*
Tupouto'a, Prince *Crown Prince of Tonga, government official*
Turco, Livia *Italian government official*
Türk, Hikmet Sami *federal official*
Turner, John Napier *former prime minister of Canada, legislator*
Turner, Wilfred *diplomat*
Turney, Alan Harry *retired state official*
Turnquest, Orville A. *Bahamian governor general*
Twining, Charles Haile *ambassador*
Tzannetakis, Tzannis *Greek government official*
Ugur, Halil *ambassador*
Uhler, Walter Charles *government official, writer, reviewer*
Ulmanis, Guntis *former President of Latvia*
Ulufa'alu, Bartholomew *prime minister*
Ulvskog, Marita *Swedish government official*
ünver, Olcay Ismail Hakki *government official, water resources engineer, planner*
Uosukainen, Riitta Maria *government official, educator*
Ushakov, Yuri Viktorovich *diplomat*
Usubov, Ramil Idris ogly *government official*
Uteem, Cassam *president of Republic of Mauritius*
Vaea, Baron of Houma *Tongan prime minister*
Vajpayee, Atal Bihari *prime minister of India*
Valencia-Rodriguez, Luis *diplomat, lawyer*
van Aartsen, Jozias J. *Dutch government official*
Vanclief, Lyle *federal official*
Vandever, Judith Ann *county official*
Vanstone, Amanda *Australian government official*
van Walsum, Peter *diplomat*
Van Waning, Jacob Jan-Willem *parliamantarian, retired*
Vasile, Radu *Romanian politician, academic*
Vassiliou, George Vassos *former president of Cyprus, consulting company executive*
Vedrine, Hubert *French government official*
Veiga, Carlos Alberto Wahnon de Carvalho *prime minister of Cape Verde*
Veil, Simone *government official*
Venkataraman, Nangavaram Srinivasa *federal official*
Vermeend, Willem A. F. G. *government official, state secretary finance*
Vershbow, Alexander R. *diplomat*
Vibe, Kjeld *ambassador*
Vickers, John Stuart *government official*
Vidović, Davorko *social welfare administrator*
Villiger, Kaspar *Swiss government official*
Vohidov, Alisher *diplomat*
Voi, Mali *Samoa government official*
von Boetticher, Christian Ulrik *member of European parliament*
von Efans-Tarafdar, Quentin (Knight, Count von Vlore, Baron de Nares) *diplomat, real estate developer*
von Kyaw, Dietrich *diplomat*
von Lersner, Heinrich Freiherr *former German government official*
von Moltke, Gebhardt *diplomat*
Von Sydow, Bjorn *federal official*
von Wogau, Karl *member of European Parliament*
Voorhoeve, Joris *Dutch government official*
Vorontsov, Yuliy Mikhaylovich *ambassador*
Vos, Edgar J. (Watty Vos) *Aruban government official*
Vos, Joris Michael *diplomat*
Voynet, Dominique *government official*
Vranitzky, Franz *Austrian government official*
Vrhunec, Miha Marko *ambassador*
Vural, Volkan *Turkish representative to UN*
Wago, Mildred Hogan *municipal official*
Wahid, Abdurrahman *president of Indonesia*
Wajed, Sheikh Hasina *prime minister*
Wakeham, Lord John *former parliamentarian*
Wako, Amos *Kenyan government official, lawyer*
Walesa, Lech *former president of Poland, foundation administrator*
Walker, Anne Kathleen *state official*
Walker, Dale Maxwell *city official*
Walker, Lannon *foreign service officer*
Walker, Miles Rawstron *Isle of Man government member*
Wally, Youssef Amin *Egyptian government official*
Walsh, Joe *government official*
Walston, Roderick Eugene *state government official*
Wan Chat Kwong, Taye Wah Michel *diplomat*
Wang, Senhao *Chinese government official*
Wang, Zhongyu *Chinese government official*
Wangchuck, His Majesty Jigme Singye *King of Bhutan*
Ward, George Frank, Jr. *ambassador*
Wärnersson, Ingegerd *Swedish government official*
Warthman, Leslie *administrative assistant, writer*
Wasacz, Emil *federal official*
Wastberg, Olle M. *diplomat*
Wathelet, Melchior *Belgian government official*
Watson, Frank H. *government official*
Weber, Norman Joseph *Seychelles government official, banker*
Webster, Christopher White *foreign service officer*
Weekes, John *international organization executive*
Weffort, Francisco Correa *Brazilian government official*
Wehbe, Mikhail *diplomat*
Weinreich, Dan *federal official*
Weizman, Ezer *president of Israel, air force officer*
Weizsacker, Richard von *former president of Federal Republic of Germany*
Wells, Tennyson R. *government official*
Wendt, Robin Glover *retired public official*
Wenkang, Zhang *Chinese government official*
Wennar, Amí Ayne *foreign service officer program intern*
Wensley, Penelope *diplomat*
Westendorp y Cabeza, Carlos *diplomat*
Westlake, Martin Jerome *government executive*
Wettenhall, Roger Llewellyn *public administration educator*
Whitaker, C. Bruce *postal worker*
Whiteley, Rose Marie *city clerk, treasurer*
Wibisono, Makarim *diplomat*
Wickremasinghe, Ranil *former prime minister of Sri Lanka, lawyer*
Wieczorek, Norbert Georg Walter *government official, banker*
Wieczorek-Zeul, Heidemarie *German government official*
Wijdenbosch, Jules Albert *president of Suriname*
Wilk, Andrzej Jan *international consultant, journalist, educator*
Wilkey, Malcolm Richard *retired ambassador, former federal judge*
Willi, Andrea *Liechtenstein government official*
Williams, Daniel *government official*
Williams, Phillip Wayne *former state official and army officer, securities and diversified company executive, consultant*
Willoch, Kåre *former prime minister of Norway*
Wilmot, Jack Botwe *diplomat*
Wilson, Eleanor McElroy *county official*
Wilson, Joseph Charles, IV *ambassador*
Winberg, Margareta *Swedish government official*
Win Mra *ambassador*
Winn, U Tin *diplomat*
Win Tin *Burmese government official*
Wiranto, Gen. *federal official*
Wissmann, Matthias *German government official, lawyer*
Wolf, Dale Edward *state official*
Wolters, Curt Cornelis Frederik *foreign service officer*
Wong, Kan Seng *Singapore government official*
Wong, Walter Foo *county official*
Woods, Michael *government official*
Woolcott, Peter Richard *diplomat, lawyer*
Worth, Mary Page *mayor*
Wright, David *diplomat*
Wright, Patrick Richard Henry (Lord Wright of Richmond) *diplomat, retired*
Wu, Jichuan *Chinese government official*
Wu, Ming-yen *Republic of China diplomat*
Wu, Shaozu *Chinese government official*
Wu, Xi-jun *government official, chemistry educator*
Wu Yi *Chinese government official, engineer*
Wyatt, Edward Avery, V *city manager*
Wynmaalen, Hans Alexander *retired government official*
Wyzner, Eugeniusz *diplomat*
Xiang, Huaicheng *Chinese government official*
Xie, Linzhen *government executive*
Yaacobi, Gad *former Israeli ambassador*
Yahalom, Shaul *government official*
Yahya Petra, Ismail Petra *Sultan of Kelantan*
Yamani, Hashim bin Abdallah bin Hashim *federal official*
Yanai, Shunji *diplomat*
Yaobang, Chen *Chinese government official*
Yarga, Larba *government official*
Yasuoka, Okiharu *federal official*
Yates, John Melvin *ambassador*
Yeh, Chang-Tung *government official*
Yel'chenko, Volodymyr Yu *diplomat*
Yeltsin, Boris Nikolayevich *Russian government official*
Yeo, George Yong-Boon *Singapore government official*
Yeo, Ning-Hong *Singapore industrialist*
Yew, Lee Kuan *government executive*
Yong, He *Chinese government official*
Yongue, Xy *Chinese government official*
Younes, Nadia *United Nations official*
Young, Sir Colville *Belizean government official*
Young, Sir George *British government official*
Young, Herbert G. *ambassador*
Young, Warren Arthur *state official, researcher*
Youssoufi, Abderrahmane *Moroccan government official*
Yushchenko, Viktor *prime minister of Ukraine*
Yussuf Izzuddin Ghafarullahu-Lahu Shah, Sultan Azlan Muhibbuddin Shah *Sultan of Perak*
Zabalgoitia, Jose Antonio *diplomat*
Zacharakis, Christos *ambassador*
Zainuddin, Diam *government executive*
Zakzuk, Mahmoud Hamdi *government official*
Zalm, Gerrit *The Netherlands government official*
Zammit Dimech, Francis *Maltese government official*
Zecchino, Ortensio *federal official*
Zedillo Ponce de León, Ernesto *president of Mexico*
Žemaitis, Algirdas Jonas Aleksis *diplomat*
Zewdie, Genet *Ethiopian government official*
Zhaoxing, Li *diplomat*
Zhengsheng, Yu *Chinese government official*
Zhihuan, Fu *Chinese government official*
Zhili, Chen *Chinese government official*
Zhirinovsky, Vladimir Volfovich *Russian government official*
Zhu, Rongji *Chinese government official*
Zhvania, Zurab *Georgian government official*
Zuber, Raymond Francois *international relations consultant*
Zuccarelli, Emile *mayor*
Zuma, Jacob G. *deputy president of South Africa*
Zuohi, Zhang *Chinese government official*
Zwinkels, Jan H. *Aruban government official*

GOVERNMENT: LEGISLATIVE ADMINISTRATION

Abetz, Eric *senator*
Ajello, Edith H. *state legislator*
Allen, Maryon Pittman *former senator, journalist, lecturer, interior and clothing designer*
Angelilli, Roberta *parliament member*
Atkins, William Austin, Sr. (Bill Atkins) *former state legislator*
Barish, Lawrence Stephen *nonpartisan legislative staff administrator*
Bell, Martin *member of parliament*
Berman, Arthur Leonard *retired state senator*
Bilirakis, Michael *congressman, lawyer, business executive*
Boehner, John A. *congressman*
Bradley, Bill *former senator*
Bragman, Michael J. *state legislator*
Brauneder, Wilhelm *parliamentarian, law educator*
Brookes, Peter T. *legislative staff member*
Burton, Dan L. *congressman*
Buyer, Steve Earle *congressman, lawyer*
Castle, Michael N. *congressman, former governor, lawyer*
Chaney, Frederick Michael *senator, lawyer*
Chua, Maria Cora Y. *legislative counsel*
Ciannella, Joeen Moore *legislative staff member, small business owner*
Clayton, Eva M. *congresswoman, former county commissioner*
Cochrane, Betsy Lane *state senator*
Coleman, Edward Lawrence *councilman*
Combest, Larry Ed *congressman*
Conyers, John, Jr. *congressman*
Cook, Cathy Welles *state senator*
Corbett, Richard Graham *parliament member*
Coulter, John Richard *retired senator*
Crane, Philip Miller *congressman*
Desutter, Manu *senator*
Diez, John C. *state legislator, business owner*
Dmitrich, Mike *state senator*
Durbin, Richard Joseph *senator*
Evans, R. Mont *state legislator*
Eyton, John Trevor *senator, business executive*
Fazio, Vic *former congressman*
Fitzgerald, Peter Gosselin *senator, lawyer*
Fong, Hiram Leong *former senator*
Forbes, John Francis *government official*
Garaud, Marie-Françoise *European parliament official*
Gingrich, Newton (Leroy) (Newt Gingrich) *former congressman*
Gregg, Judd *senator, former governor*
Haarde, Geir Hilmar *government official*
Haler, Lawrence Eugene *councilman, communications educator*
Hamilton, Darden Cole *state legislator, flight test engineer*
Hart, Melissa Anne *state senator*
Hart, William Lee, IV *legislative staff member*
Harvin, Charles Alexander, III *state legislator, lawyer*
Hayner, Jeannette Clare *former state legislator*
Hess, Marilyn Ann *state legislator*
Hughes, William John *former congressman, diplomat*
Kennan, Stephanie Ann *legislative staff member*
Kennedy, Edward Moore *senator*
Kerr, Kleon Harding *former state senator, educator*
Kerry, John Forbes *senator*
Kirsh, Herbert *state legislator*
Klaer, Karl-Heinz *government official*
Knight, Alice Dorothy Tirrell *state legislator*
Kohring, Victor H. *state legislator*
Kynštetr, Petr *federal official*
Leighton, Robert Joseph *state legislator*
Loviagin, Andrey Yevgenyevich *legislative assembly member*
Matsui, Robert Takeo *congressman*
Matusow, Naomi C. *state legislator*
McIntyre, Douglas Carmichael, II *congressman*
Metz, Craig Huseman *legislative administrator*
Moore, Richard Thomas *state legislator*
Murray, Nicholas Joseph *councillor, compliance officer*
Nuciforo, Andrea Francesco, Jr. *state legislator, lawyer*
Papandreou, George Andreas *parliamentarian*
Patrick, Michele Mary *government official*
Pettigrew, Pierre S. *politician, member of parliament*
Pevear, Roberta Charlotte *retired state legislator*
Regula, Ralph *congressman, lawyer*
Risko, Katherine Jean *constituent services coordinator*
Roth, Toby *former congressman, political consultant*
St-Hilaire, Caroline *member of parliament*
Salah, Abdullah Amin *senator*
Sawyer, Thomas C. *congressman*
Schexnayder, Charlotte Tillar *state legislator*
Sinclair, William Donald *state legislator, former church official*
Smith, Carol Estes *retired city councilman*
Stewart-Cousins, Andrea Alice *legislator*
Tanner, Jordan *state legislator*
Terry, Lee R. *congressman, lawyer*
Upton, Frederick Stephen *congressman*
van Eekelen, Willem Frederik *senator*
White, Douglas Allan *legislative aide, data archivist*
Zanfagna, Philip Edward *government executive, urban planner*

HEALTHCARE: DENTISTRY

Abiko, Yoshimitsu *dental studies educator*
Aboalsamh, Duaá Abdulrahman *endodontist, researcher*
Adriaens, Patrick André *periodontist, consultant, educator*
Akimoto, Yoshiaki *oral and maxillofacial surgeon*
Al-shehry, Garamah-Yahya *surgeon, consultant, health facility administrator*
Amor, James Michael *dentist, actor*
Andersson, Lars Göran *oral maxillofacial surgeon, researcher, educator*
Armstrong, Edward Bradford, Jr. *oral and maxillofacial surgeon, educator*
Ash, Major McKinley, Jr. *dentist, educator*
Askinas, Samuel Walter *dentist, educator*
Astobieta, Inaki *dental educator*
Aulsebrook, William Alexander *dental surgeon, consultant, researcher*
Axelsson, Gudjon *prosthetic dentist, educator*
Aydin, Murat *dentist*
Bäcker, Annika E. *dentist, researcher*
Baillet, Gilles Pierre *orthodontist*
Barsan, Robert Blake *dentist*
Bass, Neville M. *orthodontist*
Baumann, Michael Alfons *dentist, scientist*
Beals, Clem Kip, III *dentist*
Bearn, David Russell *orthodontist*
Besimo, Christian Emanuel *dentist, department head, educator*
Bessho, Kazuhisa *oral surgeon*
Björkman, Lars *dental educator*
Bjorling, Ewa Helena *dental researcher*
Blanchaert, Remy Henry, Jr. *oral and maxillofacial surgeon*
Blanton, Patricia Louise *periodontal surgeon*
Block, Robert Michael *endodontist, educator, researcher*
Blum, Jean-Yves Marie *dentist, researcher*
Boltchi, Farhad Eslam *periodontist, researcher*
Bondemark, Lars Johan *dental surgeon, orthodontist, consultant*
Böning, Klaus Walter *dentist, educator*
Booher, Robert Bonke *dentist*
Borrman, Hélène Inger Maria *forensic odontologist, educator*
Brod, Morton Shlevin *oral surgeon*
Brown, Gerald James *dentist*
Bryant, Roland Warwick *dentist, educator*
Buchmann, Rainer *periodontology educator, researcher*
Caryl, William R., Jr. *orthodontist*
Catovic, Adnan *dentist, educator*
Cehreli, Zafer Cavit *dental educator, researcher*
Celebic, Asja *dentist*
Chance, Kenneth Bernard *endodontist, educator, university official*
Chang, Jeffrey Chai *dentist, educator, researcher*
Chawla, Harpinder Singh *pediatric dentist, consultant, researcher*
Chiari, Adriana *dentist, artist*
Christensen, Robert Wayne *oral maxillofacial surgeon, minister*
Cleaton-Jones, Peter Eiddon *physician, dentist*
Cohen, Steven Michael *orthodontist*
Cotti, Elisabetta *endodontist, educator, researcher*
Crawford, Felix Conkling *dentist*
Démogé, Paul Hugh *orthodontist, educator*
Dietschi, Didier *dentist, researcher*
Dobrescu, Mircea Virgil *veterinary dentist, scientist, owner, consultant*
Donado, Jaime Enrique *dentist, researcher*
Dorocka-Bobkowska, Barbara *dentistry researcher*
Dunne, Stephen Michael *dental surgeon*
Eger, Thomas *periodontist, researcher*
Etessami, Hirbod (Hiri Etessami) *endodontist, educator*
Eyman, Russell Gardner *periodontist*
Feifel, Hartmut *physician, dentist, researcher*
Feret, Adam Edward, Jr. *dentist*
Ferreira, Maryna Ras *dental educator*
Foster, Ruth Mary *dental association administrator*
Fradeani, Mauro *dentist*
Freire, Maria do Carmo Matias *dentist*
Fritz, Edward Lane *dentist*
Fujisawa, Seiichiro *dentist, educator*
Fusayama, Takao *dental educator*
Fyler, Carl John *dentist*
Gaengler, Peter Wolfgang *dentist, researcher*
Galgut, Peter Neil *periodontist*
Galkin, Samuel Bernard *orthodontist*
Gamboa, George Charles *oral surgeon, educator*
Gammal, Robert Maurice *dentist*
Garfunkel, Adi Adrian *educator in oral medicine, researcher*
Gausch, Kurt *retired prosthodontics educator, physician*
Gerard, Paul *oral surgeon*
Gilbert, Jan Wade *dentist, marketing professional*
Gist, William Claude, Jr. *dentist*
Glantz, Per-Olof Johan *dental researcher, dental educator, oral surgeon*
Glenner, Richard Allen *dentist, dental historian*
Goldstein, Leonard Barry *dentist, educator*
Greenspan, John S. *dental and medical educator, scientist, administrator*
Hall, Roger Kingsley *pediatric dental surgeon, educator*
Hall, Stanton Harris *dental educator, orthodontist*
Hammad, Ihab Adel *dentist, educator*
Hardaway, Ernest, II *oral and maxillofacial surgeon, public health official*
Hassona, Walid Hassan *dentist, surgical research scientist*
Hayashi, Yoshihiko *dental educator, researcher*
Hibi, Hideharu *oral and maxillofacial surgeon, researcher*
Hirsch, Martin Alan *dentist*
Hise, Mark Allen *dentist*
Hjortdal, Olav *retired oral surgeon*
Hollender, Lars Gösta *dental educator*
Honda, Masaki *oral surgeon*

Hong, Yu-Ching *dental educator, researcher*
Honkala, Eino Juhani *dental educator*
Hopf, Frank Rudolph *dentist*
Hosoya, Noriyasu *endodontist, educator*
Hotta, Masato *dental educator*
Hsu, Bilin Spring *orthodontic educator*
Isberg, Annika Maria *oral and maxillofacial radiologist, researcher, educator*
Ishikawa, Isao *periodontologist, educator*
Ishimaru, Takanori *dentist, educator*
Jandt, Klaus Dieter *dental materials and biomaterials science scholar, researcher, educator*
Jinbu, Yoshinori *dentist*
Johnson, Dewey E(dward), Jr. *dentist*
Jolly, Daniel Ehs *dental educator*
Joos, Ulrich Klaus *oral and maxillofacial surgeon, educator*
Kang, Ming-Yuan *dentist, researcher, educator*
Kaplan, Andrea Edith *dental educator*
Kassman, Andrew Lance *orthodontist*
Kastner, Michael James *dentist*
Kato, Ihachi *dentist, periodontology educator*
Kaufman, Samuel Leopold *dentist, educator*
Keller, Ulrich Otto *dentist, consultant*
Kern, Matthias *dentistry educator*
Khosla, Ved Mitter *oral and maxillofacial surgeon, educator*
Khullar, Shelley Godtfredsen *oral surgeon, researcher*
Kim, Han Pyong *dentist, researcher*
Kim, Hyung-Il *dental educator, metallurgist*
Klötzer, Walter T. *prosthetic dentistry educator*
Ko, Jea-Seung *dentist, educator*
Koga, Toshihiko *dental educator*
Kotschy, Peter *dentist*
Krakoff, Kenneth B. *dentist, consultant*
Kramer, Louis Deyong *dentist*
Kriebel, Ricardo *dentist*
Krishnamoorthy, Savitha *dental surgeon, educator*
Kruger, Gustav Otto, Jr. *oral surgeon, educator*
Kuebler, Norbert Rolf *oral and maxillofacial surgeon*
Kula, Katherine Sue *dentist*
Kunimatsu, Kazushi *dentist, educator*
Kurol, Jüri *orthodontist*
Kuwahara, Toshiya *dentist, prosthodontist*
Kvaal, Sigrid Ingeborg *dental surgeon*
Kyu-Moon, Kim *orthodontist*
Lampert, S. Henry *dentist*
Laskin, Daniel M. *oral and maxillofacial surgeon, educator*
Lawson-Baker, Neil Anthony *dental surgeon*
Leempoel, Peter J. B. *dentist*
Leite, Isabel Cristina *dentist*
Lim, Joseph Dy *oral surgeon*
Lin, Choung-Min *dentist, educator*
Liou, Eric Jein-Wein *orthodontist, researcher*
Lippert, Christopher Nelson *dentist, consultant*
Lloyd, Cecil Rhodes *pediatric dentist*
Lockhart, Charles Fredrick *dentist*
Logan, Lee Robert *orthodontist*
Lowe, Cameron Anderson *dentist, endodontist, educator*
Lucht, Erik Dan Tommy *dentist*
Lynch, Denis Patrick *dentist, educator*
Machtou, Pierre E. *endodontist*
Mack, Ronald Brand *pediatric dentist, clinician, educator, writer, lecturer*
Magnusson, Tomas Herbert *dentist, researcher*
Magowan, Arthur Kenneth Train *retired dentist*
Malpassi, Mauro *dentist*
Mathis, Remy Rene *orthodontist educator*
Mattila, Pauli Taneli *dental researcher*
McArdle, Barry Francis *dentist*
McCauley, H(enry) Berton *retired public health dentist*
McClelland, Richard Lee *dentist*
McNeely, Carol J. *dentist*
Medicus, Hildegard Julie *retired dentist, orthodontist, educator*
Melsen, Birte *orthodontics educator*
Memezawa, Masako *dentist, educator*
Metcalf, Roger Dale, Sr. *dentist*
Meyler, Mark Zinovyevich *dentist*
Mickenautsch, Steffen *dentist, consultant*
Miller, Neal Adrian *periodontist*
Misiek, Dale Joseph *oral and maxillofacial surgeon*
Mitsis, Fotis John *dentist, educator*
Miyagawa, Yukio *dentistry educator*
Möller, Åke Johan Richard *oral microbiologist, endodontist, educator*
Moral, Emrah *dentist*
Morelli, Anthony Frank *pediatric dentist*
Moscovich, Hila *dentist, dental researcher*
Murata, Masaru *oral surgeon, educator*
Murray, John Joseph *dentistry educator, academic dean*
Nabers, Claude Lowrey *retired periodontist, writer*
Nagesh, K.S. *oral surgeon*
Nagy, Gábor *dentist, educator*
Nakago-Matsuo, Chie *orthodontist*
Nelson, Dennis George Anthony *dental researcher, life scientist*
Nergiz, Ibrahim *dentist*
Newbury, Anthony Charles *dental surgeon*
Newman, Hubert Neil *periodontist, researcher, educator*
Ngang'a, Peter Macharia *orthodontist, consultant, researcher*
Nicopoulou-Karayianni, Kety *oral radiology educator*
Nweeia, Martin Thomas *dentist, musician, composer, anthropologist*
Ogden, Graham Richard *oral and maxillofacial surgery educator*
Olaitan, Ademola Abayomi *oral and maxillofacial surgeon*
Olasz, Lajos *dental surgeon, oncology researcher*
Oliet, Seymour *endodontics educator, dean, dentist*
Oliver, William Donald *orthodontist*
Olorunfemi, Babatunde Olatunde *dental surgeon*
Olsen, Steven Kent *dentist*
Opinya, Gladys Nabubwaya *dental educator, consultant*
Oro, Robert John *dentist, consultant, writer*
Oruç, Selçuk *dentist*
Osborn, Mark Eliot *dentist*
Osborne, Harry Alan *orthodontist*
Palmer, Hubert Bernard *dentist, retired military officer*
Parameswaran, Anantanarayanan *dental educator*
Parashos, Peter *endodontist*
Park, Jon Keith *dentist, educator*
Parker, Warren Andrew *public health dentist, consultant*
Parnes, Edmund Ira *oral and maxillofacial surgeon, educator*
Parodi, Renato Augusto *dentist, researcher*
Perlea, Paula *dentistry educator*
Perret, Gerard Anthony, Jr. *orthodontist*
Pietrokovski, Jaime *dental services administrator, educator*
Pilot, Taco *dentist, educator*
Plasschaert, Alphons Johannes Marie *dental educator, academic administrator, foundation executive*
Ponce, Eleanor Haight *dentist, researcher, educator*
Poulsen, Sven *dental educator*
Pripatnanont, Prisana *dentist, consultant*
Prowell, Roy Walters, Jr. *orthodontist*
Rabe, Richard Frank *dentist, lawyer*
Raibley, Parvin Rudolph *dentist*
Raja Rayan, Raj K. *dentist*
Rama, Natu *dentist, pain management specialist, researcher*
Razzano, Michael R. *dental and healthcare industry consultant*
Reed, Erbie Loyd *dentist*
Reid, David Earl *dentist, military officer*
Rodriguez y Baena, Ruggero *oral surgeon, educator*
Romînu, Mihai *dentist*
Rosen, Michel *retired prosthodontist*
Rota, Massimo Tommaso *oral surgeon*
Rotaru, Alexandru Isidor *maxillofacial surgeon, educator*
Rwenyonyi, Charles Mugisha *dentist*
Santangelo, Mario Vincent *dentist*
Sasaki, Kenichi *oral and maxillofacial surgeon*
Sasaki, Motomasa *oral surgeon, educator emeritus*
Sauveur, Gabriel Marie-Joseph *dental surgery educator*
Schiodt, Morten *dentist, oral surgeon*
Schlagenhauf, Ulrich *dentist*
Schmalz, Gottfried *dentist*
Schmuth, Gottfried Peter Franz *orthodontist*
Schroeder, Hubert Ernst *dentist, researcher*
Scott, Karen Ann *dentist*
Scully, John Robert *oral and maxillofacial surgeon*
Semergidis, Themistocles George *oral maxilofacial surgeon*
Shabana, El-Hassan *dentistry educator*
Shaw, Cheng-Kuang *dentist, epidemiologist, educator, administrator*
Shen, E-Chin *dentist, periodontist*
Shiau, Yuh Yuan *dentist, educator*
Shibata, Takanori *oral and maxillofacial surgeon, researcher*
Shillingburg, Herbert Thompson, Jr. *dental educator*
Sikora, Suzanne Marie *dentist*
Siqueira, José Freitas, Jr. *dentist, researcher*
Slaughter, Freeman Cluff *retired dentist*
Smith, Jerry Wayne *pediatric dentist*
Söderholm, Anna Lisa *maxillofacial surgeon*
Somayaji, Bantval Venkatramana *dental surgeon, periodontics educator*
Soory, Mena *periodontology educator*
Sousa-Neto, Mandel Damaio *dental educator*
Soyman, Asim Mübin *dental educator*
Speculand, Bernard *oral and maxillofacial surgeon*
Spiry, Jean Louis *oral surgeon*
Srivastaa, Anand Behari *dentistry educator*
Steadman, Robert Kempton *oral and maxillofacial surgeon*
Stegaroiu, Roxana *dentistry educator*
Stephanick, Carol Ann *dentist, consultant*
Strohecker, Leon Harry, Jr. *orthodontist*
Suenaga, Shigeaki *dentist, dental radiologist*
Sun, Andy *dentist*
Tellefsen, Georg *dentist*
Theodorou, John Spero *orthodontist, researcher*
Tolidis, Kosmas-Theodore *dentist, educator*
Tonn, Elverne Meryl *pediatric dentist, dental benefits consultant, forensic odontologist*
Tränkmann, Gert Joachim *orthodontist, educator*
Trisi, Paolo *dental researcher*
Tseng, Chuen-Chyi *periodontist, educator*
Uribe Echevarria, Jorge *dentist*
Utz, Karl-Heinz *dentist, educator*
Vaahtoniemi, Lauri Henrikki *dentist, researcher*
Valdez, Arnold *dentist, lawyer*
Vallittu, Pekka Kalevi *dentist, researcher*
Van Der Bijl, Pieter *dental and medical educator*
Verma, Mahesh *dentistry educator, consultant*
Vermilyea, Stanley George *prosthodontist, educator*
Virtanen, Jorma Ilmari *dentist, researcher*
Wachstein, Joan Martha *dental hygienist*
Walton, DeWitt Talmage, Jr. *dentist*
Wang, Songlin *dentist*
Warren, Paul Robert *dentist*
Watts, Paul Graham *oral and maxillofacial surgeon, consultant*
Wefers, Klaus Peter *dentist*
Weiss, Robert Michael *dentist*
Welton, Michael Peter *dentist*
Wenzel, Ann *dentist, researcher*
White, George Edward *pedodontist, educator*
Wiedemann, Charles Louis *dentist*
Williams, Benjamin Hayden, Jr. *orthodontist*
Witherspoon, Walter Pennington, Jr. *orthodontist, philanthropist*
Wu, Min-Kai *dentist, researcher*
Xue, Miao *dentistry educator, biomaterial scientist*
Yale, Seymour Hershel *dental radiologist, educator, university dean, gerontologist*
Yamada, Jason Masayoshi *periodontist, educator*
Yamaki, Masao *dentist, educator*
Yamaoka, Minoru *dentist*
Yarbrough, Isabel Miles *dentist, educator*
Yun, Peter Lok Wai *dental researcher*
Zaiman, K(oichi) Robert *dentist*
Zakrzewska, Joanna Maria *oral physician*
Zarrinpour, Arash *dental surgeon*
Zhang, Bo Xue *dental educator, researcher*
Zhang, Gang *oral radiologist, educator*
Zimmer, Wolfgang Martin *periodontist*

HEALTHCARE: HEALTH SERVICES

Abdel-Rahman, Susan M. *pharmacy and medicine educator*
Abubakar, Abbulsalami Aminu *pharmacist*
Achalu, Onuegbu Emmanuel *university administrator, health educator*
Acosta, Mario *pharmaceutical educator, consultant, researcher*
Acosta, Martha M. *physical therapist, educator*
Adams, Corlyn Holbrook *nursing facility administrator*
Adekson, Mary Olufunmilayo *therapist, counselor educator*
Adrounie, V. Harry *public health administrator, scientist, educator, environmentalist*
Aehlert, Barbara June *health services executive*
Agarwal, Suraj Prakash *pharmacy educator*
Ahmed, Ahmed Abdulla *medical administrator, ophthalmologist*
Aiache, Jean Marc *pharmaceutical educator*
Aiken, Linda Harman *nurse, sociologist, educator*
Ajiwo, Enoch Olufemi *laboratory technology educator*
Åkerblom, Malin Johanna Brändén *science administrator*
Akers, James Eric *medical practice marketing executive*
Akwar, Emmanuel C. *laboratory staff*
Alameda, Russell Raymond, Jr. *radiologic technologist*
Al-Ani, Majeed Rasheed *nutritionist*
Alexander, Lisa D. *nursing administrator*
Alghaferi, Muneera Younus *health facility administrator*
Al Hamdani, AbdulKarim Mohamed *health facility administrator, physician, internist, consultant, cardiologist*
Al-Herabi, Zaid M. Abbad *health facility administrator*
Al-Khawashky, Mohammad Ishaq Ahmad *health organization representative, consultant*
Allen, Robert Edward, Jr. *physician assistant*
Allen, Sheila Hill *nursing executive, counselor, consultant*
Al-Muhandis, Batool Ali *nurse educator*
Alperin, Richard Martin *clinical social worker, psychoanalyst*
Alpert, Martin Jeffrey *chiropractic physician*
Al-Qubati, Yasin Abdul Aleem *health association administrator*
Alsup, Karen *nurse*
Altenhofen, Katrina Beth *emergency medical services coordinator*
Alyoshin, Alexander M. *science organization executive*
Anagnostakis, Yannis Emmanuel *pharmacist*
Anderson, Allan Curtis *pharmaceuticals researcher*
Anderson, Allan R. *psychotherapist, educator*
Anderson, Ernest Robert, Jr. *pharmacist*
Anderson, Frances Swem *nuclear medical technologist*
Anderson, Linda Jean *critical care and psychiatric nurse*
Anderson, Stuart Charles *pharmacy researcher*
Andréasson, Gunnar Osborn *consultant in sport, biomechanics and textiles*
Andruzzi, Ellen Adamson *nurse, marital and family therapist*
Angus, Robert Carlyle, Jr. *naturopathic physician, health administrator*
Anisfeld, Michael H. *industrial pharmacist, consultant*
Ansari, Karim Ullah *pharmacology and therapeutics educator, researcher*
Antoun, Mikhail *medicinal chemistry and pharmacognosy educator*
Anukam, Kingsley Chidozie *lab administrator, pharmacologist, microbiologist*
Anyanwu, Chukwukre *alcohol and drug abuse facility administrator*
Aouizerate, Philippe Andre *pharmacist*
Arora, Vipin *laboratory administrator*
Arundale, C. Jean *psychotherapist*
Ashmead, Allez Morrill *speech, hearing, and language pathologist, orofacial myologist, consultant*
Ashmead, Harve DeWayne *nutritionist, executive, educator*
Atamian, Susan *nurse*
Atti, Roberta Maria *nutritionist, chef, educator*
Aubertin, Madeline Katherine *retired nursing educator, medical/surgical nurse, mental health services professional*
Baale, John Olalere *pharmacist*
Babao, Donna Marie *community health and psychiatric nurse, educator*
Babitzke, Theresa Angeline *health facility administrator*
Baeriswyl-Rouiller, Irène Andrée *psychologist, speech pathologist*
Bahl, Saroj Mehta *nutritionist, educator*
Baker, Lynn R. *health facility administrator*
Balaban, Murat Omer *food science educator*
Baldwin, Cynthia Ann *industrial hygienist*
Baldwin, Jeffrey Nathan *pharmacy educator*
Bali, Vishal *health services administrator*
Ballard, Joseph Raymond *nurse anesthesist*
Ballesteros, Paula M. *nurse*
Balt, Christine Ann *family nurse practitioner*
Banks, Melanie Anne *nutritionist, biochemist, educator, dietitian*
Barber, Elaine *social worker, psychotherapist*
Barker, Christopher David *audiologist, researcher*
Barker, Martha Smith *retired mental health nurse*
Barker, Virginia Lee *nursing educator*
Barkhan, Ronnie Cecil *psychotherapist*
Barlow-Stewart, Kristine Kay *public health service officer*
Barnes, Graham *psychotherapist, educator, consultant*
Barnes, Raymond D. *optometrist*
Barrett, Elizabeth Ann Manhart *nursing educator, psychotherapist, consultant*
Barry, Brian William *pharmaceutical technology educator*
Bartlett, Cheryl Ann *public health service administrator*
Baser, Kemal Hüsnü Can *pharmacist, educator*
Bas Ramallo, Francisco *psychotherapist, educator, researcher*
Bass, Lynda D. *medical/surgical nurse, educator*
Bassiladze, Sergey Gennadievich *laboratory administrator, nuclear engineer*
Bast, Kenneth George *healthcare executive*
Basten, Antony *health facility administrator*
Bastine, Reiner H. E. *psychotherapist, psychologist, mediator*
Bates, Christopher John *nutrition researcher*
Battin, R(osabell) Ray (Rosabell Harriet Ray) *audiologist, neuropsychologist*
Baumgartner, Hans Rudolf *retired pharmaceutical researcher, educator*
Bays, June Marie *counselor, social worker*
Beasley, John Julius *child and family development educator*
Beasom, Nancy Ann *occupational therapist, consultant*
Beaton, Meredith *enterostomal therapy clinical nurse specialist*
Beaton, Rebecca Andrea *psychotherapist*
Beatrice, Ruth Hadfield *hypnotherapist, retired educator, financial administrator*
Beavan, Eva Varie *social worker, therapist*
Bechtel, Sherrell Jean *psychotherapist*
Behbahani, Roya *clinical pharmacist*
Bekoff, Oscar *psychotherapist*
Beletz, Elaine Ethel *nurse, educator*
Belis, Vladimir *medical administrator, educator*
Bell, Donna Ledbetter *guidance counselor*
Bell, Frances Louise *medical technologist*
Bell, Rebecca *psychotherapist, journalist*
Bellomo, Jo *social worker, school administrator, educator*
Bender, Randi Laine *occupational therapist*
Bendheim, Leonore Caroline *psychotherapist*
Benter, Teresa Ann *health facility administrator*
Bentley, Helen *nursing educator*
Berg, Hermann Johannes *laboratory administrator, researcher*
Berger, Birgit *pharmacist*
Berger-Kraemer, Nancy *speech and language pathologist, artist*
Berkley-Carter, Deborah Lynne Hall *counselor*
Bernoth, Maree Anne *nursing educator*
Beveridge, Jo-Anne Fay *laboratory director*
Bezrukova, Alexandra Gennadievna *ecological optician, biophysicist*
Bhise, Satish *pharmacy educator*
Bianchi, Maria *critical care specialist, adult nurse practitioner, acute care nurse practitioner*
Bidan, Gérard Marie *laboratory director*
Billingsley, Mary Lee *health facility administrator, counselor*
Bilsky, Edward Gerald *clinical social worker*
Bircher, Andrea Ursula *psychiatric-mental health nurse, educator, clinical nurse specialist*
Birkbeck, John Addison *nutritionist, consultant*
Bischoff, Marilyn Brett *clinical social worker*
Biton-Poussin, Catherine Jeanne *health facility administrator*
Blackie, Spencer David *physical therapist, administrator*
Blanc, Darlita Judith *counselor*
Blasingim, Charlotte Oren DeShazor *counselor, consultant*
Blendon, Robert Jay *health policy educator*
Blossey, Maureen B. *mental health administrator*
Blume, Arthur Walter, IV *addictive behaviors researcher, therapist*
Boadella, David John *psychotherapist*
Boccia, Judy Elaine *home health agency executive, consultant*
Boffert, Joyce D. *chiropractor*
Boles-Carenini, Bruno *ophthalmologist, educator*
Bonci, Andrew S. *chiropractor*
Bonneterre, Jacques M. *health facility administrator, oncologist*
Bopanna, K. N. *pharmacist, marketing specialist*
Borah, Kripanath *pharmacist*
Borchgrevink, Hans Melchior *hospital administrator, research scientist*
Bordeleau, Lisa Marie *human services professional, consultant*
Borg, Ruth I. *home nursing care provider*
Borgstahl, Kaylene Denise *health facility administrator*
Boruchowitz, Stephen Alan *health policy analyst*
Bottini, Egidio *medical educator*
Bottone, JoAnn *health services executive*
Boufford, Jo Ivey *health and human services administrator*
Bougas, Efthemios *occupational health specialist*
Bower, Barbara Jean *nurse*
Braddock, David Lawrence *health science educator*
Bradford, Louise Mathilde *social services administrator*
Braillon, Alain Leopold Henri *health facility administrator*
Brainin, Constance Spears *psychotherapist, educator, social worker, counselor*
Bramwell, Marvel Lynnette *nurse, social worker*
Brancaleone, Salvatore Joseph *nutritionist, consultant*
Brange, Jens J.V. *biopharmaceutical scientist*
Brera, Giuseppe Rodolfo *physician, psychotherapist, educator, scientist*
Breslin, Evalynne Louise Wood-Robertson *retired psychiatric nurse*
Brewer, Barbara Bagdasarian *nursing administrator*
Briggs, Stella *optometry educator, researcher*
Bristow, Louise Alice *mental health nurse*
Britton, Monica Ena Louise *community health nurse, public health nurse*
Britton, Ronald Skirrow *psychoanalyst, psychiatrist*
Brock, Barry James *health services administrator, educator, consultant*
Brockway, Stephen Swift *health facility administrator, psychiatrist, addiction medicine specialist*
Brodie, Alice Velma *health and ethics advocate*
Brodie, David Alan *exercise science educator*
Bronaugh, Deanne Rae *home health care administrator, consultant*
Broselow, Linda Latt *medical office technician, aviculturist*
Brossman, Karen Rebeca *healthcare administrator*
Brotman, Richard Dennis *counselor*
Brown, Anne Sherwin *speech pathologist, educator*
Brown, Arnold *physical therapy consultant*
Brown, Doris Jane *nursing aide*
Brown, Eric N. W., Jr. *hospital administrator*
Brown, Frederick Lee *health care executive*
Brown, Lester B. *social work educator*
Brown, Millie Louise *mental health nurse*
Brown, Nancy Childs *marriage and family therapist*
Brown, Patricia Ann *child health nurse*
Brown, Stephen Hayze, Jr. *human services caseworker*
Bruce, Ian Waugh *health science association administrator*
Brumen, Vlatka *occupational and environmental health educator*
Brunell, Gerard Arthur *disability consultant*
Brunner, Janet Lee *physician assistant*
Bryner, Peter *chiropractor*
Buccafusco, Jerry Joseph *pharmacologist, educator*
Buccino, Daniel L. *psychotherapist, consultant*
Buckley, John Joseph, Jr. *health care executive*
Budnick, Thomas Peter *social worker*
Buehler, Thomas *psychotherapist, expressive therapist*
Buff, Margaret Anne *psychiatric nurse practitioner*
Bull, Dennis Lee *counselor*
Bullock, Weldon Kimball *health facility administrator, pathologist, pathology educator*
Bunce, Jillian Margery *therapy educator*
Buon, Tony *mental health services professional, educator*
Burney, Mary Ann *mental health nurse*
Burrows, Robert Paul *optometrist*
Bussino, Melinda Holden *human services administrator*

PROFESSIONAL INDEX 2535 HEALTHCARE: HEALTH SERVICES

Bustamante, Pilar pharmaceutics educator
Butz, Lori Gail nursing administrator
Byrd, Ellen Stoesser dermatology nurse
Cabrera, Katherine E. health facility administrator
Callanan, Margaret Mary clinical psychologist
Calodny, Alan Lee retired pharmacist
Camp, Delpha Jeanne counselor
Campbell, Robbi Elizabeth Margaret counselor, educator
Campbell, Simon John public company director
Campos, Paulo Campana health services executive
Canahuati, Judy lactation consultant
Canda, Edward R. social work educator
Carbonell, Josep Iluis medical administrator
Cardens, Jeanice Wynclare Maylen geriatrics nurse
Cardwell, Harold Douglas, Sr. retired rehabilitation specialist
Cardwell, Sandra Gayle Bavido hospital admissions professional
Cargill, Paula Marie social worker, gerontologist
Carle, Harry Lloyd social worker
Carlsen, Kai Hakon health facility administrator
Carlson, Robert Marshall hospital professional services official
Carman, Susan Hufert nurse coordinator
Carr, Bernard Francis hospital administrator
Carr, Larry Dean health care management company executive
Carreqo, Patricia pharmacy educator, researcher
Carrington, J(oe) P(eter) (Jossif Peter Bartolotti) nutritionist, psychoanalyst, research scientist, educator
Carter, Louvenia McGee nursing educator
Casolin, Armand health facility administrator
Cassidy, Barry Allen physician assistant, clinical medical ethicist
Cassirer, Christopher healthcare educator
Castleman, Breaux Ballard health management company executive
Catalano, James Anthony social worker
Catalfo, Betty Marie health service executive, nutritionist
Chait-Magen, Suzanne psychotherapist
Chan, Peter Wing Kwong pharmacist
Chan-Ling, Tailoi optometrist, neurobiologist, educator
Chapdelaine, Perry Anthony, Jr. public health physician, educator
Charles, Bruce Gordon pharmaceutical educator
Charles, Ruth Patricia nutritionist
Chase, Sandra Lee clinical pharmacist, consultant
Chavez, Mary Lynn pharmacy educator
Chen, Hong-I hospital administrator, educator
Chen, Peter Wei-Teh mental health services administrator
Chen, Te Tsaw healthcare executive
Chenvidhya, Dhiraphol Zalvino hospital executive, surgeon
Cherry, Barbara Waterman speech and language pathologist, physical therapist
Cheshire, Carolyn Irene personal trainer, fitness and health consultant
Chiu, Weihsueh Albert researcher
Chiverton, Patricia Ann nursing educator, dean
Choulis, Nicolas H. pharmacy educator
Chowdhury, Zafrullah A.T.M. healthcare activist, surgeon, consultant
Chowning, Orr-Lyda Brown dietitian
Chrai, Suggy Singh pharmacist
Christensen, Pamela Karen pediatric nurse
Christenson, Eileen Esther geriatrics nurse
Christophe, Armand Bruno nutrition educator, consultant
Chukwu, Umunneochi pharmacist, educator, researcher, consultant
Clampitt, Otis Clinton, Jr. health agency executive
Clark, Janet retired health services executive
Clark, Jessie Dona social worker
Clark, Mary Jo community health nurse
Clark, Teresa Watkins psychotherapist, clinical counselor
Clarke, H(arold) Digby clinical thanatologist, consultant
Clary, Roy hospital administration executive
Clausen, Amie Jo adult day center administrator
Clements, Lynne Fleming family therapist, programmer
Coffman, Patricia JoAnne school nurse, counselor
Coffman, Renee Elise pharmacy educator, pharmacist
Coghill, Davis Garold chiropractic physician, counselor, psychotherapist, educator
Cohen, Alan Barry educator, former foundation executive
Cohn, Lucile psychotherapist, nurse
Colangelo, James Joseph psychotherapist
Colibar, Olimpia Mihaela nutritionist
Collière, Marie-Françoise nursing educator, ethnohistory researcher
Collinet, Pierre Alain research associate
Condie, Vicki Cook nurse, educator
Connor, Paul Eugene social worker
Conover, Dorothy Nancy Lever medical practice administrator, nurse
Conte, Julie Villa nurse, administrator
Conway, Samuel Anthony retired chiropractor
Coogan, Frank Neil health and social services administrator
Cook, Judith Ruth administrative nursing supervisor
Cooley, Fannie Richardson emeritus educator, consultant
Cooper, James Melvin healthcare executive, consultant
Cope, Kathleen Adelaide critical care and parish nurse, educator
Coppock, Janet Elaine mental health nurse
Core, Harry Michael psychiatric social worker, mental health therapist and administrator
Corwin, Bert Clark optometrist
Courdi, Adel radiotherapist
Covault, Lloyd R., Jr. retired hospital administrator, psychiatrist
Crabtree, Ben C. home health care agency administrator
Crais, David R. healthcare consultant
Cranfill, Virginia May retired nursing administrator
Creede, Michael David nursing administrator
Crnkovic, Anise Elaine marriage and family therapist
Crocker, Barbara Jean infection control practitioner
Crosser, Carmen Lynn marriage and family therapist, clinical social worker, consultant
Croucher, Paul Harold optometrist, educator
Crystal, Stephen health care educator, researcher
Csango, Thomas Michael health organization executive
Csende, Ferenc pharmacist, researcher
Cummings Rockwell, Patricia Guilbault psychiatric nurse
Czerwinski, Thomas J. health facility administrator
Dabasy, Eva Anna educator, nutritionist
Daephenkhae, Phitak hospital development company executive
Dahlgren, Goran Erik public health expert
Dain, Stephen John optometrist, educator, researcher
Dallas, Daniel George social worker
Dalrymple, Christopher Guy chiropractor
Daly, John Patrick nurse educator and administrator, researcher, cons
D'Ambola, Lori Susan speech therapist
Dame, Catherine Elaine acupuncturist
Daniel, Somuah microbiology technician
Dann, Oliver Townsend psychoanalyst, psychiatrist, educator
Dato, Virginia Marie public health physician
Daus, Victoria Lynn nurse midwife
Davenport, Ann Adele Mayfield home care agency administrator
Davis, Ada Romaine nursing educator
Davis, Annalee Ruth Conyers clinical social worker
Davis, Arthur Columbus health facility administrator
Davis, Crystal Michelle health association administrator
Davis, Edgar Glenn science and health policy executive
Davis, June Fiksdal medical facility owner, floral designer
Davis, Margaret Thacker critical care, medical and surgical nurse
Davis, Richard Carlton rehabilitation consultant
Davis, Shirley Harriet social worker, editor
Davis, Troy Arnol reflexologist, hypnotherapist
Davoine, Françoise psychoanalyst
Day, Ralph Lawrence retired physician, abbot
Dear, Ronald Bruce social work educator
Dearborn, Maureen Markt speech and language clinician
Declerck, Paul Jules pharmaceutical biology educator
DeGraffenreid, Jeff Gordon paramedic, educator
de Kretser, David Morritz research institute administrator, endocrinologist
Delarge, Jacques Elie pharmacist, medical educator
De Luca, Anthony James psychoanalyst, theologian
Demeola, Richard Ingram critical care nurse, emergency room nurse
Denzler, James Wyatt pharmacist
Deppe, Hans-Ulrich medical sociology educator, researcher
Derstadt, Ronald Theodore health care administrator
De Saeger, Sarah Maria Diana Guido pharmacist
DeShazer, Ruth Shomler health facility administrator
Deuschle, Constance Joan counselor, educational consultant
De Valk, Maurice Michel Armand occupational medicine physician, consultant
de Vos, Dirk medical director
Díaz, César Rodolfo public health services officer
Dibble, Suzanne Louise nurse, researcher
Dicks, Patricia Delores counselor, educator
DiClaudio, Janet Alberta health information administrator
DiGeronimo, Diane Mary nursing educator, psychotherapist
Dik, Khaled health facility administrator, consultant
Dimeo, Sandra B. occupational therapist
Diorio, Eileen Patricia retired medical technologist, philosophy educator
Dishong, Diane Elizabeth medical/surgical nurse, rehabilitation nurse
Dixson, Jean social worker
Do, Thanh Xuan pharmacist educator
Donlon, Josephine A. diagnostic and evaluation counseling therapist, educator
Donovan, Anne nursing educator
Dorton, Truda Lou medical, surgical and geriatrics nurse
Dortunc, Betül Aran pharmaceutical technology educator, pharmacist
Dougherty, Geoffrey health science educator, researcher
Douglas, Kathleen Mary Harrigan psychotherapist, educator
Downing, Cynthia Hurst therapist, addiction and abuse specialist
Drachnik, Catherine Meldyn art therapist, artist, counselor
Draper, Robert William social worker
Driel, Bas Van laboratory manager
Driscoll, David Lee chiropractor
Driscoll, Diana Sanderson optometrist, consultant
Drummond, Frances psychotherapist, author
Dudek, Jaromir pharmacist, consultant
Duenas, Laurent Flores health and nursing consultant
Duffy, Mary Kathleen neonatal nurse
Duncan, Elizabeth Charlotte marriage and family therapist, educational therapist, educator
Dunlap-Williams, Nancy A. rehabilitation management company executive, nurse
Dunn, Dana-Lori counselor
Dupont, Eric laboratory administrator
Durr, Leslie Martina nurse, psychotherapist
Durrieu, Alain-Jacques diabetologist, nutritionist
Dvornik, Štefica laboratory administrator, biochemistry educator
Dwyer, Judith Margaret health service administrator
Dyomin, Victor Valentinovich optician, educator
Eagan, Marie T. (Ria Eagan) chiropractor
Early, Ames S. healthcare system executive
Ebbeson, Karen Ann retired social worker
Eby, Maureen Ann medical surgical nursing consultant
Eck, Kenneth Frank pharmacist
Eckenhoff, Edward Alvin health care administrator
Edelstein, Rosemarie (Hublou) nurse educator, medical and legal consultant
Edmonds, Velma McInnis nursing educator
Edson, Herbert Robbins retired foundation and hospital executive
Edwards, Teena Ann community health nurse, educator
Egito, Eryvaldo Socrates Tabosa do pharmacist, consultant, researcher, educator
Elander Lindberg, Noomi Christin psychotherapist, psychologist
El Ayouby, Nadia S. industrial hygienist
El Kamel, Ali chest physician, educator, researcher
Elliott, Holly Hall retired occupational therapist
Elliott, Rosalind May intensive care nurse
Ellis, Robert Jeffry health facility executive
Elmanama, Abdelraouf Ali laboratory administrator, medical educator
Elsinger, Julie Anne registered nurse, medical transcriptionist
Eng, Catherine health care facility administrator, physician, medical educator
Engs, Ruth Clifford health educator, historian
Evans, David Seamus health organization researcher
Evert, Sandra Florence (Wheeler) medical/surgical nurse
Evgenev, Michael Boris health facility administrator
Ewig, Brent Matthew health policy analyst
Ezenwa, Josephine Nwabuoku social worker
Fagan, Jay social work educator
Farkas, Carol Garner nurse, administrator
Farrar, Donna Beatrice hospital official
Farrington, Bertha Louise nursing administrator
Fasano, Anthony Vincent chiropractor
Faub, Kenneth James school nurse practitioner
Faulkner, Keith clinical scientist, consultant
Fava, Maurizio hospital administrator, researcher
Feighner, George Christy laboratory owner, chemist
Feinendegen, Ludwig Emil retired hospital and research institute director
Felhofer, Marylouise Katherine nursing administrator
Fennell, Christine Elizabeth healthcare system executive
Fernandez-Velazquez, Fernando Jose optometrist, consultant
Fernicola, Nilda Alicia Gallego Gándara de pharmacist, biochemist
Ferreri, Michael Victor optometrist
Ferson, Lu Ann medical and surgical nurse
Feuerlein, Wilhelm Egidius psychiatrist
Filip, Karel health facility administrator
Fisher, Donald Wayne medical association executive
Fitch, Rachel Farr health policy analyst
Fittro, Ronald G., Jr. healthcare executive, consultant
Fitzgerald, Harold Kenneth social work educator, consultant
Fleming, Steven Denis scientific director
Flick, Charlotte human services administrator
Flori, Anna Marie DiBlasi nurse anesthetist, educational administrator
Foerster, David Wendel, Jr. counselor, consultant, human resources specialist
Fogh-Andersen, Niels laboratory director
Foley, Virginia Sue Lashley counselor, international training consultant
Fondiller, Shirley Hope Alperin nursing educator, journalist, historian
Fore, Ann counselor, educator, country dance instructor
Foreman, Deborah Delores social work administrator, consultant
Fottler, Myron David health services educator
Foussard, Odette Blanpin retired pharmacy educator, researcher
Fowlkes, Nancy Lanetta Pinkard social worker
Fox, Thomas George health science educator
Fragell, Levi humanism consultant
Franc, Ales pharmacist, researcher
Francis, Lorna Jean nutritionist
Francis, Timothy Duane chiropractor
Franck, Helmut internal medicine and rheumatology consultant
Frank, Richard Daryl therapist
Franklin, Barry Allan health facility administrator, physiologist
Franklin-Griffin, Cathy Lou Hinson nursing educator
Fredericks, Sharon Kay nurse's aide
Freeman, Joy Lynn counselor, psychotherapist
Freese, Barbara Tapp nursing educator
Frenzel, Frances Johnson registered nurse, educator, lecturer, poet
Freund, Emma Frances medical technologist
Fricker, Jacques physician, nutrition specialist, researcher, consultant
Friedrich, Christoph Johannes pharmacist
Frogge, Beverly Ann nurse, consultant
Frokjaer, Sven pharmaceutical scientist
Froozani, Minodokht nutritionist, educator
Fry, Randy Dale emergency medical technician, paramedic
Fry, Sirpa-Raija psychoanalyst, researcher
Frye-Moquin, Marsha Marie social worker
Fuchs, Walter Stefan pharmacist, researcher, consultant
Fuller, Margaret Jane medical technologist
Fulton-Quindoza, Debra Ann nurse practitioner
Fulzele, Ratnakar Haribhau pharmacist, management consultant
Funkhouser, Arthur Taylor psychotherapist
Furuse, Mitsuhiro nutritionist
Gagliano, Mauro Antonio medical assistant
Gagnon, John Harvey psychotherapist, educator
Galembo, Alexander acoustician
Gallaher, William Marshall dental laboratory technician
Galuske, Michael Alfons social worker, educator
Gan, Woon Siong acoustician
Gandy, Gerald Larmon rehabilitation counseling educator, psychologist, writer
Gantz, Nancy Rollins nursing administrator, consultant
Ganzarain, Ramon Cajiao psychoanalyst
Garcia-Arieta, Alfredo pharmacist, drug assessment consultant
Garcia y Carrillo, Martha Xochitl pharmacist
Gardner, Clyde Edward healthcare executive, consultant, educator
Garel, Pascal hospital administrator, consultant
Garison, Brenda Mae forensic nurse
Garnett, Linda Kopec nurse, researcher
Garrahan-Masters, Mary Patricia retired social worker, volunteer
Garrett, Sinead Katherine research organization executive
Gavin, Mary Jane medical and surgical nurse
Gaylor, Barbara Gail Davis geriatric nurse
Gentile, Robert Dale optometrist, consultant
George, Sir Charles Frederick health facility administrator
Gerdner, Linda Ann nursing researcher
Gerede, R. Selcuk medical director
Getz, Morton Ernest medical facility director, gastroenterologist
Ghafourifar, Pedram pharmacologist
Ghaly, Evone Shehata pharmaceutics and industrial pharmacy educator
Ghorayeb, Fay Elizabeth nurse educator
Giakas, Giannis health services educator
Gianakos, Patricia Ann social programs administrator
Gibbs, Sydney Royston health facility administrator
Gibson, Frances nurse
Giebels, Sharon J. human services manager
Gil, David Georg social policy educator
Giles, Walter Edmund alcohol and drug treatment executive
Gillam, Ian Herbert nutrition consultant
Gillman, Mark Alfred medical research facility administrator, dentist
Gilmartin, Raymond V. health care products company executive
Gilmore, David Schneiter administrator
Gimbel, Hervey Willis medical administrator
Ginn, Connie Mardean retired nurse
Giridhar, Rajani pharmacy educator
Glashan, Constance Elaine retired nurse, civic worker
Gleich, Carol S. health professions education executive
Goh, Zenton researcher
Golden, Kimberly Kay critical care, flight nurse
Golomb, Gershon pharmaceutics educator, researcher
Gonzales, Richard Robert counselor
Gordon, Helen Tate nurse assistant
Gordon, Sandy Gale Combs medical/surgical nurse, community health nurse
Gortner, Susan Reichert nursing educator
Goudy, Josephine Gray social worker
Gould, Daniel Robert health services information professional
Gousopoulos, Stavros occupational health facility administrator
Grado-Wolynies, Evelyn (Evelyn Wolynies) clinical nurse specialist, educator
Graham, Denis David marriage and family therapist, educational consultant
Grahn, Gertrud Louise nursing educator
Granati, Diane Alane ophthalmic nurse
Grandolini, Giuliano pharmacy educator
Gray, Leonard Charles hospital administrator, geriatrician
Graziani, Jeanne Patricia healthcare administrator, consultant
Green, Suzanne nurse
Greer, Marsha Adair health facility administrator
Griffin, Christopher Oakley healthcare professional, humanities educator
Groh, Donna H. healthcare administrator
Gross, Mechthild Maria women's health nurse
Gross, Stanley Merhl chiropractor
Grützmeier, Sven Sahlgren health clinic administrator, physician
Guigov, Krassimir Borissov health management administrator, toxicologist
Guillama-Alvarez, Noel Jesus healthcare company executive
Gundu Rao, P. pharmacist
Gutheil, Irene Anderman social work educator, researcher
Guthrie, Diana Fern nursing educator
Gutman, Lucy Toni school social worker, educator, counselor
Haas, Lu Ann counselor
Habansky, Beth Judith speech language pathologist
Habicht, Jean-Pierre public health researcher, educator, consultant
Haertter, Sebastian Goetz pharmacist
Hahn, Klaus Jürgen pharmaceutical research executive
Haire, Marjorie Frances nurse
Haley, Patricia Ann psychiatric therapist, school counselor, administrator
Hambraeus, Leif Magnus nutritionist
Hamilton, T(homas) Stewart hospital administrator
Hanners, G(ary) Dale retired psychological mental health professional
Hansell, Phyllis Shanley nursing educator, researcher, consultant
Harden, Anita Joyce nurse
Hardin, Ann marriage and family therapist
Harllee, Mary Beth social worker, educator
Harman, Donald Lee nurse, educator, consultant
Harmon, David Eugene optometrist, geneticist
Harper, Shirley Fay nutritionist, educator, consultant, lecturer
Harrar, Richard Earle nurse
Harris, Michael Gene optometrist, educator, lawyer
Harvey, Gloria-Stroud physician assistant
Harvey, Jacqueline Mary Melrose health facility administrator
Hassel, James Craig counselor
Hauenstein, Karen physician's assistant, critical care nurse
Hauschild, Douglas Carey optometrist
Haustein, Knut-Olaf Friedrich clinical pharmacologist, researcher, educator
Hawken, Patty Lynn retired nursing educator, dean of faculty
Hector, Vivian Cleave social worker
Hedrick, Wyatt Smith pharmacist
Hedstrom, Susan Lynne maternal women's health nurse
Hegedüs, Mihály nutritionist
Heil, Mary Ruth former counselor
Heilig, Margaret Cramer nurse, educator
Heisler, Norma Boodman psychotherapist
Héjjas, István optoelectronics researcher
Henke, Jürgen institute administrator, forensic consultant
Henkind-Joslow, Janice Veronica family nurse practitioner
Henneman, Stephen Charles psychotherapist
Henry, Olga Elaine nursing educator, health care trainer
Henry, Richard Joseph, Jr. nursing home management executive
Henshaw, Beverly Ann Harsh women's health nurse, consultant
Herman, Larry Marvin psychotherapist
Hermet, Jean-Pierre, Henry healthcare company executive
Herold, Ivan anesthesiologist, educator
Heston, Renate nursing administrator
Hetlelid, Kjell Birger pharmacist
Hickcox, Leslie Kay health educator, consultant, counselor
Hickey, Maurice Robert pharmacist
Hidai, Hideo hospital administrator, educator
Higashi, Toshiaki occupational health educator
Higgins, Marika O'Baire nurse, philosopher, educator, writer, entrepreneur
Hilkemeyer, Renilda Estella nurse
Himburg, Susan Phillips dietitian, educator
Hinderlich, Horst Klaus health facility administrator
Hinshaw, Robert psychotherapist, publishing executive
Hiremath, Shobha Rani R. pharmaceutics educator
Hirning, Fredric Carl pharmacist
Hochstrasser, Barbara health facility administrator, consultant
Hocking, Clare Shelley occupational therapist, educator
Hodges-Robinson, Chettina M. nursing administrator

Hodnicak, Victoria Christine *pediatric nurse*
Hogan, Mark James *clinical pharmacist, pharmaceutical firm executive*
Hokenstad, Merl Clifford, Jr. *social work educator*
Holl, James Andrew *prehospital care administrator*
Holland, Rosemary Sheridan *program evaluation consultant*
Hollinger, Charlotte Elizabeth *medical technologist, tree farmer*
Hollis, Julia Ann Roshto *critical care and medical/surgical nurse*
Holmes, Harry Dadisman *health facility administrator*
Holmgren Öhman, Peggy Maria *study and career counselor, educator, researcher*
Honaker, Charles Ray *health facility administrator*
Horan, Mary Ann Theresa *nurse*
Hori, Yasushi *pharmacist, analytical chemist, toxicologist*
Horowitz, Ben *health facility administrator*
Horwath, Caroline Christine *nutritionist*
Hosny, Ehab Ahmed *pharmacist, educator*
House, Ann *home health nurse, administrator*
Hovenga, Evelyn Johanna *health administration executive*
Howe, John Prentice, III *health science center executive, physician*
Howe, Virginia Hoffman *nurse administrator*
Hudson, Geoffrey John *retired nutritionist, researcher*
Hugg, Geraldine Bertha Novotny *retired gerontology specialist, journalist*
Huggins, Elaine Jacqueline *nurse, retired army officer*
Hughes, Barbara Bradford *nurse, real estate manager*
Hui, Ho-Wah *pharmaceutical scientist*
Hull, Grafton Hazard, Jr. *social work educator*
Hung, Mei-Jong Chow *social worker*
Hunter, David James *health policy and management educator, researcher, analyst*
Hurlbut, Robert Harold *health care services executive*
Huttunen, Jussi Kalervo *health institute administrator*
Huysman, James David *healthcare executive, consultant*
Idänpään-Heikkilä, Juhana Eljas *health organization administrator, pharmacologist*
Ihara, Masataka *pharmacy educator*
Ikeda, Tadasu *diabetologist*
Illum, Lisbeth *pharmaceutical scientist, educator*
Imamura, Sadao *hospital administrator, retired educator*
Ingersoll, Gail Laura *nursing administrator, nursing educator, nursing researcher*
Irvine, Phyllis Eleanor *nursing educator, administrator*
Isaacs, Richard B. *investigative and protective services professional*
Isard, Phillip Isaac *medical nutritionist, consultant*
Isaza, Diana Maria *medical technologist, researcher*
Ishii, Masami *hospital director, neurosurgeon*
Islam, Sk Nazrul *pharmacist*
Itoh, Sonoe *medical technologist, cytologist*
Ivaturi, Rao *nutritionist, educator, consultant*
Iwamoto, Yoshihisa *biochemistry and microbiology educator*
Iyengar, Rajani Giridhar *pharmaceutical chemistry educator, researcher*
Jacobs, Karen Louise *medical technologist*
Jaiswal, Dinesh Kumar *pharmaceutical scientist, educator*
James, Barbara Frances *school nurse, special education educator*
Janes, Joseph Anthony, Jr. *optometrist*
Janzen, Norine Madelyn Quinlan *medical technologist*
Japp, Nyla F. *infection control services administrator*
Jarolmen, Josephine Tuzeo *social worker, psychotherapist, educator*
Jekunen, Antti Pekka *health facility administrator, oncologist*
Jensen, Robert Gordon *nutritionist, consultant*
Jensen, W. Lynne *family nurse practitioner*
Jew, Henry *pharmacist*
Jin, Shaohong *pharmacist*
Johanson, Gregory John *psychotherapy trainer, minister*
John, Gerald Warren *hospital pharmacist, educator*
Johns, David Peter *hospital administrator, medical researcher*
Johnson, Barbara Ann *health services educator*
Johnson, Carl Frederick *marriage and family therapist*
Johnson, Kenneth Owen *retired audiologist*
Johnson, Mattiedna *nurse, retired diaconal minister*
Johnson, Naomi Bowers *nurse*
Johnson, Sharon Marguerite *social worker, clinical hypnotherapist*
Johnson-Brown, Hazel Winfred *nurse, retired army officer*
Johnson-Lewis, Angela Dawn *therapist*
Johnstone, Megan-Jane *nursing educator*
Jones, Barbara Dean *substance abuse and family relations counselor*
Jones, Evelyn Gloria *medical technologist, educator*
Jones, Lucinda (Cindy Jones) *oncology nurse*
Jones, Renee Kauerauf *health care administrator*
Jonsdottir, Gudrun Sigridur *retired social worker*
Joseph, Stephen *nephrology and dialysis nurse*
Joshi, Harihar S. *medical laboratory executive*
Juarez, Maretta Liya Calimpong *social worker*
Juneby, Hans Bertil *medical consultant, health counselor, educator*
Jyot, Gurdarshan *counselor, researcher*
Kabanov, Modest Mikhailovich *health facility administrator*
Kafouros, George *physical therapist, consultant*
Kai, Masaaki *pharmacist, educator, researcher*
Kamalakshappa, Ravi Bhushan *physical therapist*
Kamerman, Sheila Brody *social worker, educator*
Kanazawa, Yasunori *medical facility administrator*
Kane-Villela, Grace McNelly *maternal, women's health and pediatrics nurse*
Karikas, George Albert *pharmacist, educator*
Karlstrom, Anders Rolf *laboratory professional, educator*
Karnanda, Bopanna *pharmacist*
Karp, Rosanne *oncology and women's health nurse*
Karrer, Carol Converse *nurse educator*
Kastanakis, Serafim *hospital administrator*
Katzin, Carolyn Fernanda *nutritionist, consultant*
Kavishe, Festo Patrick *nutritionist*
Keenan, Retha Ellen Vornholt *retired nursing educator*
Keeth, Betty Louise *geriatrics nursing director*
Keisel, Maurine Lilley *rehabilitation nurse*
Keller, Paul Raymond *health facility administrator*
Kelly, William E. *psychoanalyst*
Kendall, Katherine Anne *social worker*
Kent, Howard *health foundation director*
Kerc, Janez *pharmacist*
Kesel, Andreas Johannes *pharmacist, researcher*
Ketchledge, Kathleen A. *nurse*
Kets de Vries, Manfred Florian *psychoanalyst, educator*
Kevanishvili, Zurab Shamshe *audiologist, researcher, educator*
Kielczynski, Wojciech Edward *medical herbalist*
Kiely, Gabriel Martin *social policy and social work educator, college dean, researcher*
Kiley, Thomas *rehabilitation counselor*
Kim, Jinwoong *pharmacist, educator*
Kim, Shin-Kon *hospital administrator, surgeon, educator*
Kimura, Takanori *health facility administrator, family physician*
King, Barbara Jean *nurse*
King, Margaret René (Peggy Harris) *medical/surgical nurse*
King, Sheldon Selig *medical center administrator, educator*
Kingsley, Charon *nurse practitioner*
Kishi, Kyoichi *nutrition educator*
Klainman, Eliezer Isaak *health facility administrator, cardiologist, researcher, consultant*
Klein, Deborah Rae *health facility administrator*
Klein, Josephine F.H. *psychotherapist, writer*
Klein, Rosalyn Finkelstein *social worker*
Knapp, Mildred Florence *retired social worker*
Knight, Derek John *regulatory affairs professional*
Koch, Barbara Louise *foreign service family nurse*
Koehler, Carol Jean *nurse*
Koenig, Juergen *nutrition scientist*
Kogan, Gerald *psychotherapist*
Koida, Masao *pharmacology educator, researcher*
Kojima, Akinori *public health counselor, pathologist*
Kokubo, Hiroyasu *pharmacist, researcher*
Kolarz, Gernot *medical administrator, physician, researcher*
Kolb, John Carl *family therapist, minister*
Komprda, Tomáš *nutritionist, educator*
Kooima, Linda Kay *neonatal and pediatrics nurse*
Kopytko, Edwin Edward *nursing administrator*
Kowalczyk, Jan *nutritionist, biochemist, researcher*
Krall, Yung N. *health facility administrator*
Krauser, Robert Stanley *health care executive*
Krauss, Henry Frederick, Jr. *optometrist*
Kruger, Barbara *audiologist, speech and language pathologist*
Kubeczka, Karl Heinz *pharmacist, educator*
Kubelka, Wolfgang Leopold *pharmacy educator*
Kubli, Laurie Jean *social worker*
Kumanyika, Shiriki K. *nutrition epidemiology researcher, educator*
Kushner, Jack *retired physician executive*
Kyriakides, Constantinos Herod *pharmacist, marketing professional*
Läcis, Aris *health facility administrator, cardiac surgeon*
Ladd, Eric Justin *mental health services professional*
Laff, Jay Ellis *health facility acquisition executive, entrepreneur*
Laincz, Betsy Ann *nurse*
Laissy, Jean Pierre *health facility administrator, radiologist*
Lalla, Jogender Kishinchand *pharmacy educator*
Lambert, Jean Marjorie *health care executive*
Landino, Daniel *speech pathologist*
Lane, Dorothy Person *nursing educator*
LaPorte, Adrienne Aroxie *nursing administrator*
Larmour, Ian *pharmacist, pharmacologist*
Lasys, Joan *medical nurse, writer, educator, publisher*
Laszewski, Zofia K. *medical administrator*
Latimer, Hugh Scot *healthcare consultant, architect*
LaTourrette, Kathryn *family therapist, counselor, artist*
Laubscher, Leeann *medical and surgical nurse*
Lauck, Donna L. *adult psychiatric and mental health nurse*
Lawrence, (Robert) John *social work educator, consultant*
Lawson, Gerald Wilbur *health facility administrator*
Laycock, Anita Simon *psychotherapist*
Leake, Heather Alison *pharmacist, educator, minister*
Lechner, Jon Robert *nursing administrator, educator*
Leclercq, Guy *laboratory director*
Ledesma, Jose Fortunato Gamboa *health facility executive*
Lee, Heesoon *pharmacy educator*
Lee, Margaret Anne *psychotherapist, social worker*
Leek, Diane Webb *nurse*
Lefelhocz, Irene Hanzak *nurse, business owner*
Leffler, Carole Elizabeth *mental health nurse, women's health nurse*
Lefko, Jeffrey Jay *hospital administrator*
Leibetseder, Josef Leopold *nutritionist, educator*
Leigh, Vincenta M. *health administrator*
Leitzmann, Claus *retired nutritionist, writer*
Lemke, Sherry Ellen *therapist*
Lentz, Deborah Lynn *telemetry, thoracic surgery, and intensive care nurse*
Lentz, Edward Allen *consultant, retired health administrator*
Leonard, Mary Eileen *medical technologist, educator*
Leslie, Evelyn *psychotherapist*
Lev, Elise L. *nurse*
Levashov, Mikhail Ivanovich *laboratory administrator, researcher*
Levene, Shirley Schechter *psychotherapist*
Levin, Judith Maria *health science association administrator*
Levitt, Harry *speech and hearing scientist*
Lewis, Benjamin Pershing, Jr. *pharmacist, public health service officer*
Lewis, Corinne Hemeter *psychotherapist, educator*
Lignereux, Yves Guy *veterinary anatomy educator*
Likis, Frances Estes *nurse midwife, nurse practitioner*
Lilliehöök, J(ohan) Björn O(lof) *health science association administrator*
Lin, Chien-Chih *hospital administrator, thoracic surgeon*
Linde, Lucille Mae (Jacobson) *motor-perceptual specialist*
Lindner, Udo Klaus *medical director*
Lingel, Nada Jo *optometry educator*
Linn, Carole Anne *dietitian*
Lipsky, Linda Ethel *business executive*
Litchfield, Jean Anne *nurse*
Little, Gayle Anne *neonatal nurse practitioner*
Liu, Shing Hwa *pharmacy educator, pharmacologist*
Liukko, Anne Päivi Kristiina *psychiatric and medical nurse*
Llerandi Phipps, Carmen Guillermina *nutritionist and dietitian*
Loarie, Thomas Merritt *healthcare executive*
Lombardo, Fredric Alan *pharmacist, educator*
Long, Judith Ann *nurse anesthetist*
Long, Michael John *public health sciences educator, researcher*
Loomis, Norma Irene *marriage and family therapist*
Lopez, Sue Ann *nursing educator, nurse*
Loring, Richard William *psychotherapist*
Lothian, Scott Thomas *clinical pharmacist*
Love, Jamie L. *clinical therapist*
Lowrance, Muriel Edwards *program specialist*
Luick, Barbara Jean *physical therapist assistant*
Luini, Alberto *medical administrator, surgeon*
Lund-Adams, Margaret Grace *nutritionist, researcher*
Lunsford, Elizabeth Marshall *nurse*
Lustig, Susan Gardner *occupational therapist*
Luyben, Johanna (Ans) Gerarda *midwife, educator, researcher*
Luz, Virginia Olivar *dietitian, nutritionist*
Luzier, Aileen Bown *pharmacist, educator, researcher*
Lybeert, Marnix Lodewijk Maria *radiotherapist*
Lyle-Wilson, Trevor *clinical physiotherapist*
Lysne, Allen Bruce *laboratory director*
Lytton, Linda Rountree *marriage and family therapist, test consultant*
Macdonald, Karen Crane *occupational therapist, geriatric counselor*
MacKellar, Keith Robert *hospital administrator*
Macosko, Paul John, II *psychotherapist*
MacPherson, Shirley *clinical therapist*
Madden, Wanda Lois *nurse*
Madison, Andrea Pleshette *health educator*
Maeda, Hisatoshi *medical technology educator*
Maeda, Nobuo *health economist*
Maganto, Carmen *psychotherapist, educator, clinical psychologist*
Mahapatra, Rajat Kanti *medical administrator*
Mahon, Margaret M. *advanced practice nurse*
Maitland, Geoffrey Douglas *manipulative physiotherapist, consultant, educator, author*
Makarewicz, Rufin Jozef *acoustics educator, consultant*
Malsch, Reinhard Peter *pharmacist*
Manne, Deborah Sue *oncology nurse, consultant, dental hygienist*
Manthey, Merrily Ruth *psychotherapist, educator, consultant*
Marchioro, Carla *health facility administrator*
Marcos Barrado, Andres *food science educator*
Mařík, Ivo Antonín *health facility administrator, physician*
Mariner, William Martin *chiropractor*
Marohn, Ann Elizabeth *health information professional*
Marsh, Carla A. *document control group leader*
Marshall, Donald Thomas *medical technologist*
Martikainen, A(une) Helen *retired health education specialist*
Martin, James Grubbs *medical executive, former governor*
Martin, Virve Paul *licensed professional counselor*
Martinez, J. Alfredo *nutritionist, educator*
Martis, Leo *healthcare researcher*
Massey, W(ilmet) Annette *retired nurse, former educator*
Mateo-de-Acosta, Oscar *research institute director*
Matheson, Linda *retired clinical social worker*
Mathews, Charles Race Thorson *researcher*
Matsuda, Michiyuki *health facility administrator*
Matsui, Takayoshi *health facility administrator*
Matsuura, Yuichiro *medical school dean*
Maver, Andrew G. *optometrist*
Mavros, George S. *clinical laboratory director*
Mayer, Susan Lee *nurse, educator*
Mázzafero, Martin Vicente Enrique *public health administrator, researcher*
McBride, Wanda Lee *psychiatric nurse*
McCarthy, Charles R. *bioethicist, consultant*
McCaslin, Kathleen Denise *child abuse educator*
McClenahan, Roshan *speech and language therapist*
McClintock, William Thomas *health care administrator, retired*
McClurg, Robert James *emergency nurse practitioner, educator*
McConnon, Virginia Fix *dietitian*
McCreary, Deborah Dennis *oncology nurse*
McCulloch, Daphne Lynne *optometrist*
McCullough, Kathryn T. Baker *social worker*
McEwan, Robert Neal *health facility administrator*
McGrath, Pamela Della *psychosocial researcher*
McGuire, Sandra Lynn *nursing educator*
McHaffie, Hazel Esther *medical ethics researcher*
McLaren, Ian Kenneth *cardiovascular researcher*
McMenamin, Helen Marie Foran *home health care, pediatric, and maternal nurse*
McNeil, Helen Jo Connolly *nursing educator, public health administrator*
McPartland, Patricia Ann *health educator and administrator*
McWilliams, Nancy Riley *psychotherapist, educator*
Mealy, J. Burke () *psychological services administrator*
Medeiros, M. Joyce *community health educator*
Melendez, Joaquin *retired orthopedic assistant*
Mendeleev, Vladimir Yakovlevich *optician, researcher*
Mendoza, German David *nutritionist, educator*
Merchant, Roland Samuel, Sr. *hospital administrator, educator*
Merson, Michael Howard *public health physician, epidemiologist*
Meserve, John Shackford, II *retirement housing executive*
Metz, Laurent Dominique *health products company executive*
Metzger, Henry *federal research institution administrator*
Meyer, Roberta *mediator, communication consultant*
Michael, Jerrold Mark *public health specialist, former university dean, educator*
Middleton, Ellen Long *family nurse practitioner, educator*
Mikel, Thomas Kelly, Jr. *laboratory administrator*
Miles, Andrew *senior health scientist*
Miles, Edward Harry *optometrist*
Miller, Mary Lois *retired nurse midwife*
Miranda, Michele Renee *optometrist*
Mirkowski, Jan André *occupational safety and health manager*
Mirzaei, Siroos *health facility administrator*
Misan, Gary Michael *pharmacist, lecturer*
Mitchell, Edward William *mental health researcher*
Mitchell, Paula Rae *nursing educator, college dean*
Mitchell, Wayne Lee *health care administrator*
Mix, Eilhard *biomedical laboratory chief*
Miyake, Yoshio *health facility administrator*
Mizzi, Joann M. *nurse*
Moellering, Helen S. *retired social worker*
Mohl, Allan S. *social worker*
Mojica, Jose Alvin Pardiñas *rehabilitation medicine specialist*
Mok, Henry Tai Kee *social work educator*
Molden, A(nna) Jane *retired counselor*
Moldenhauer, Nancy A. *social worker, consultant, educator*
Molino, Gianpaolo *health facility executive*
Momah, David N. *physiotherapist*
Momah, Ethel Chukwuekwe *women's health nurse*
Moneer, Mohamed Mohamed *surgery educator*
Montague, Joel Gedney *public health officer*
Montanez, Mary Ann Chavez *counselor, consultant, writer*
Moore, Brian Cecil Joseph *auditory researcher*
Morehead, Annette Marie *disabled children's facility administrator, child advocate*
Morgan, Michael James *medical research administrator*
Morgan, Robert Miles *paramedic, educator*
Morley-Ball, Joyce Ann *psychotherapist, speaker, educational consultant*
Morris, Elizabeth Treat *physical therapist*
Morton, Ronald Lee *pharmacist*
Mowbray, Carol Beatrice Thiessen *mental health researcher, social work educator*
Mugglestone, Christopher John *health facility executive*
Muller, Patricia Ann *nursing administrator, educator*
Munic, Rachelle Ethel *health services administrator*
Muniruzzaman, Md *pharmaceutical scientist*
Muñoz, Romeo Solano *audio visual curator, educator*
Murata, Akira *nutrition educator*
Murphy, Margaret A. *nursing educator, adult nurse practitioner*
Murray, Julia Kaoru (Mrs. Joseph E. Murray) *occupational therapist*
Murray, Muz *metaphysician, artist, writer*
Musgrave, Catherine *nurse educator*
Mustafa, Seham M. Darwish *pharmacist, educator*
Muzychenko, Leonid A. *laboratory director*
Myers, Elmer *social worker, psychiatrist*
Myers, Libby Ann *retired nurse*
Myshlyaev, Leonid Pavlovich *research administrator*
Naasani, Imad *pharmacist, medical researcher*
Naegle, Madeline Anne *mental health nurse, educator*
Nagai, Tsuneji *pharmaceutics educator*
Nagarajan, Laxmi Priyadharshini *dietitian*
Nakagawa, Allen Donald *radiologic technologist*
Nakamura, Isao *acoustician, researcher*
Nakamura, Yashuhide *community health educator*
Nakanishi, Tsutomu *pharmaceutical science educator*
Nakano, Masahiro *pharmacist*
Nasser, Moes Roshanali *optometrist*
Naz, Mughal Muhammad Yousif *hospital administrator*
Neff, P. Sherrill *health care executive*
Nelson, James Harold *health sciences administrator*
Nelson, William Joseph *oncological and community health nurse*
Neumann, Heinz Dieter *occupational health engineer, researcher*
Newton, Sarah Elizabeth *nursing researcher, educator*
Ng, Kingsley King Kau *hospital pharmacy administrator, educator*
Nichols, Gerald *counselor, hypnotist*
Nicholson, Ellen Ellis *clinical social worker*
Nicklin, George Leslie, Jr. *psychoanalyst, educator, physician, author*
Nikiforov, Alexei Sergeevich *acoustician*
Nojima, Yoshiko *nursing educator*
Norman, Mary Marshall *educator, counselor, therapist*
Norton, Linda Lee *pharmacist, educator*
Novak, Alexej *speech pathologist*
Nusbaum, Geoffrey Dean *psychotherapist*
Nygaard, Lance Corey *nurse, data processing consultant*
Nys, Pauline S. *health facility adminstrator, educator*
Nzoika, Peter Ndalu *medical technologist*
Oak, Jeffrey Charles *ethicist*
Oakes, Ellen Ruth *psychotherapist, health institute administrator*
Oakes, Maria Spachner *nurse*
Oberstein, Marydale *geriatric specialist*
O'Brien, Nora Mary *nutrition educator*
O'Connell, Michael Alexander *social worker*
O'Donnell, John Joseph, Jr. *optometrist*
Odor, Richard Lane *mental health administrator, psychologist*
Oestmann, Mary Jane *retired senior radiation specialist*
O'Gorman, James Vivian *health executive*
O'Hara, Delia Iglauer *family nurse practitioner*
Ohara, Ikuo *nutrition educator*
Ohkoshi, Masaaki *medical company executive*
Ohno, Tadao *health science association*
Okeh, Samson Ewruje *psychiatric nurse*
Olafsson, Olafur *public health official, consultant*
Olego, Oscar *psychiatrist*
Oliver, William Edward, Jr. *mental health nurse*
Olson, Roger Norman *health service administrator*
Olsson, Elisabeth E.C. *physical therapist, educator*
Onnis, Luigi *psychotherapist, educator*
Ono, Hiroshi *health facility administrator*
Ono, Junji *acupuncturist*
Onuma, Naoki *audiologist, educator for hearing impaired*
Optale, Gabriele *psychotherapist, physician*
O'Quinn, Nancy Diane *nurse, educator, consultant*
Orlowski, Andrzej Jerzy *acoustician, educator*
Orner, Linda Price *family therapist*
Orr, Wendy Ann *occupational therapist, writer*
Osterhus, Elizabeth *pediatric academy administrator*
Ostrowski-Meissner, Henry *nutritional biochemist, educator, researcher, administrator*
Overcash, Shelia Ann *nurse*
Overland, Jane Elizabeth *nurse consultant*
Oxlade, Zena Elsie *retired nursing officer*
Oyler, Amy Elizabeth *medical/surgical nurse*
Ozawa, Kyosuke Samuel *retired medical company executive*
Özer, A. Yekta *pharmacist, researcher*
Ozimek, Edward *acoustician, researcher*
Paalman, Maria Elisabeth Monica *public health executive*
Pagliarulo, Michael Anthony *physical therapy educator*

Virgo, Katherine Sue health services researcher
Vitvitsky, Jack physician assistant
Vohs, James Arthur health care program executive
von Friederichs-Fitzwater, Marlene Marie health communication educator
Vormfelde, Stefan Viktor clinical pharmacologist, medical educator
Vuong, Larry Viet chiropractor
Wachewski, Robert Thomas health facility administrator
Waddington, Gordon Stuart physiotherapist, researcher
Waine, Colin director health programs
Waisbein, Héctor hospital administrator
Waisman, Warner pharmacist
Walker, Roderick Bryan pharmaceutical scientist
Walsh, James William mental health professional
Walsh, Marie Leclerc nurse
Walsh, Raoul Anthony behavioural medicine consultant
Wang, Guo Zhi optician, educator
Ward, Elizabeth Despard medical association administrator
Warren, Janet L. psychiatric medicine educator, psychotherapist
Watanachai, Kasem health services administrator, consultant
Watkins, Ted Ross social work educator
Watson, Mavis Pauline retired nurse
Watson, S. Michele home health nurse
Watts, Carolyn Sue nurse
Wdowiak, Leszek Hieronim public health physician, educator
Webster, John Kingsley Ohl, II health administrator, rehabilitation manager
Webster, Linda Jane clinical social worker, consultant
Weed, Roger Oren rehabilitation services professional, educator
Wehner, Henry Otto, III pharmacist, consultant
Weingast, Marvin laboratory executive
Weisbrot, Marvin Myron retired healthcare administrator, consultant
Weisman, Irving social worker, educator
Wells, Claudia Mae Ellis nutritionist, educator
Wells, Jonathan Charles Kingdon nutritionist, educator
Wells, Ronald Henry Cecil health sciences consultant
Weltermann, Birgitta M. health care administrator
Wendt, Karol Jean marriage and family therapist, consultant, trainer
Westheimer, Gerald optometrist, educator
Weuffen, Wolfgang Friedrich pharmacist, microbiologist, hygienist, researcher
Whildin, Leonora Porreca nurse midwife, nursing
Whitaker, Cynthia Ellen managed healthcare consultant
White, Elsie Pearl nurse, retired
White, James, Jr. psychiatric, mental health nurse, consultant
Whittemore, Ronald Paul hospital administrator, retired army officer, nursing educator
Whittingham, Wayne chiropractor
Whybrow, Peter Charles psychiatrist, educator, author
Wickner, Fran S. psychotherapist, educator
Widell, Susanne Christina Marie-Louise laboratory technologist
Wiedemann, Ramona Diane occupational therapist
Wieneke, Paul medical technologist
Wikman, Georg Karl institution administrator
Wilcox, Ian medical research scientist, cardiology consultant
Wilkes, Angela Biggs mental health consultant
Wilkes, David Ross therapist, social worker
Willcott, Earline Fay social worker
Williams, John Michael physical therapist, sports medicine educator
Williams, Michael James health care services consultant
Williams, Rynn Mobley community health nurse
Williams, Thelma Jean social worker
Williams Maddox-Brown, Janice Helen nurse
Williamson, William Allen retired optometrist
Wilson, Bruce Keith men's health nurse
Wilson, Johnnie Lou social work educator, retired
Wilson, William James healthcare executive
Win, Myo nutritionist, biochemist
Winstanly, Derek Miles medical practitioner, company executive
Winter, Joan Elizabeth psychotherapist
Winton, Howard Phillip retired optometrist
Wirsing, Rolf Lorenz public health educator, researcher
Wirth, Dyann Fergus public health educator, microbiologist
Withrow, Lucille Monnot nursing home administrator
Wittberger, Steven Duane nursing educator
Woie, Maren social worker educator, consultant
Wolensky, Joan occupational therapist, interfaith minister
Wolf, David Brian social worker, writer
Wolffsohn, James Stuart William optometrist
Wolfson, David John pharmacist, researcher
Wolinsky, Fredric David health services research educator
Womer, Charles Berry retired hospital executive, management consultant
Woo, Mi-Hee pharmacy educator
Wood, Julie Diane family therapist
Wood, Sandra Synhoff psychotherapist, corporate trainer, seminar leader
Woods, Rosalie Karen dietitian, researcher
Wurster, Dale Erwin pharmacy educator, university dean emeritus
Wyatt, Rose Marie clinical social worker
Wyber, Ronald John acoustic consultant
Yakisich, Juan Sebastian medical researcher
Yamamoto, Masahiro hospital director
Yokoyama, Shigeru science facility professional
Yoo, Vak Yeong health facility administrator
York, Janet Brewster nurse, family and sex therapist, sculptor
Yoshioka, Mieko hospital administrator, pediatrician, consultant
Youan, Bi Botti Célestin pharmacist, researcher
Young, Diane S. social work educator
Youssef, Diaa Tohamy pharmacist, researcher, educator
Yu, Chia-Peng health facility administrator
Yuasa, Hiroshi pharmacologist
Zacarias, Isabel nutritionist, researcher, consultant
Zagoren, Joy Carroll health facility director, researcher
Zaharia, Valentin pharmacist, educator
Zarmbinski, Richard Anthony chiropractic physician
Zarzycki, Pawel Konrad pharmacist, educator
Zernig, Gerald addictions research educator
Zhang, Yin-Chang retired medical institute administrator, educator
Zhou, Xing researcher, educator
Zhu, Dong acoustician, researcher
Zidorn, Christian Hermann Wilhelm pharmacologist
Zierolf, Mary Louise nurse anesthetist
Zimmer, Paul Gerald, II community care licensing professional
Zimmerman, Jane D. healthcare executive, psychologist
Zimmerman, Jo Ann health services and educational consultant, former lieutenant governor
Zimmermann, Ingfried Leonhard pharmaceutical educator
Zlotnick, Cheryl health services researcher
Zuehlsdorf, Michael Theodor pharmacist
Zupanets, Igor Albertovich academic administrator, clinical pharmacist

HEALTHCARE: MEDICINE

Aasuri, Murali Krishnamachary ophthalmologist
Abaza, Mohamed Hilmy physician, consultant, researcher
Abboud, Emad Bishara ophthalmologist, vitreotretinal specialist
Abbruzzese, Pietro Angelo cardiac surgeon
Abdel-Fattah, Moataz Mohammed medical statistician, educator
Abdel-Rahman, Abdel A. pharmacology educator
Abd Elrazak, Mohamed Aly rheumatologist
Abd El-Wahed, Moshira Mohamed physician, researcher
Abdo, Saad orthopedic surgeon, researcher
Abdulla, Walied Yousif anesthesiologist
Abdullaev, Yalchin G. neuroscientist, educator
Abdullah, Jafri Malin neurosurgeon, educator, researcher
Abdulrazzaq, Yousef Mohamed pediatrics educator
Abe, Kenji pathologist, researcher
Abe, Yumiko obstetrician-gynecologist, educator
Åberg, Torkel Hampus Johan cardio-thoracic surgeon
Ablin, Richard Joel immunologist, educator
Aboagye, Sampson Yaw medical educator
Aboulafia, Elie D. vascular surgeon
Abraham, Georgi Koodathummuriyil physician, medical educator
Abrahamsen, Pål psychiatrist, consultant
Abrahm, Janet Lee hematologist, oncologist, educator
Abram, Zoltan Samoil medicine educator
Abramov, Yoram obstetrician, gynecologist, researcher
Abramowitz, Israel vascular surgeon, educator, consultant
Abshagen, Ulrich Wolfgang Peter consultant, phamacology educator
Abu-Arafeh, Ishaq Ahmad pediatric neurology consultant, educator, researcher, lecturer
Abu-Arafeh, Wael Mahmud physician, consultant in urology
Abu Daia, Jehad Mohamad pediatric surgeon
Abu Esleih, Mahmoud Mohammad internist
Abul-Haj, Suleiman Kahil pathologist
Abu-moustafa, Adel H. medical educator, dean
Abu-Musa, Antoine Albert physician
Abushaban, Lulu M.T. pediatric cardiologist
Abu-Zidan, Fikri Mahmoud surgeon
Abyad, Abdulrazak M.B. geriatrician
Acero, Julio J. surgeon, educator
Acevedo, Guillermo pathologist, educator
Acharya, Vidya Narayan medical educator, consultant nephrologist
Achimastos, Aristarquos Ioannis hemobiologist
Achmadi, Umar-Fahmi public health physician, educator
Achrafi, Hadi cardiologist, consultant
Acierno, Louis Joseph medical educator, researcher
Ackermann, Lothar August radiologist
Adachi, Shinya surgeon, educator
Adachi, Yukihiko medical educator
Adam, George physician
Adamietz, Irenaeus A. physician, researcher
Adamkin, David Howard pediatric medicine educator
Adams, Christopher Bertlin neurosurgeon
Adams, Jimmy Wayne osteopath
Adams, Peter William diabetologist, endocrinologist, physician
Adamson, Joyce Roberts physician
Addai, Frederick Kwaku anatomy educator, research scientist
Ade, Wolfgang Roland physician, medical advisor
Adebimpe, Victor Rotimi psychiatrist
Adelt, Dieter physician, spine surgeon
Adeniran, Adeshola plastic and reconstructive surgeon, consultant
Adêyokunnu, Adetunji Ademuyiwa pediatrician, consultant
Adhami, Eftim Josif anesthesiologist
Adler, Charles Spencer psychiatrist
Adler, Yehuda cardiologist
Adolphs, Hans-Dieter urology educator
Aeberhardt, Andre Auguste physician radiobiologist
Afifi, Ashraf Mohamed El-Sadek neonatologist, pediatrician
Afridi, Muhammad Ali oncologist, consultant
Afshar, Farhad neurosurgeon
Afzal, Mohammad physician, consultant
Agarwala, Sanjay orthopaedic surgeon
Agarwalla, Vipin pediatrician
Agbenorku, Pius Thomas plastic surgeon, educator, consultant
Aggarwal, Narinder Kumar physician, educator
Aggarwal, Rajesh Kumar ophthalmic surgeon, consultant
Aggerbeck, Lawrence Paul medical researcher, research scientist, educator
Aglietta, Massimo medical educator
Agorastos, Theodoros obstetrics and gynecology educator
Agruss, Neil Stuart cardiologist
Ahlbeck, Karsten Magnus anesthesiologist
Ahlberg, Åke Karl Martin orthopedic surgeon, researcher
Ahlberg, Richard Eric physician, researcher
Ahmadi-Abhari, Seyed-Ali psychiatrist, educator
Ahmed, Akhtar neurologist, educator
Ahmed, Fathelrahman Elawad pediatric educator, consultant
Ahn, Duck Kyoon plastic surgeon, educator
Ahn, Ducksun plastic surgeon
Ahn, Sei-Hyun breast surgeon, educator, researcher
Ahn, Yong Chan radiation oncologist, educator
Aiba, Nobuyasu physician
Aigner, Thomas pathologist
Aikawa, Jerry Kazuo physician, educator
Aikawa, Naoki surgeon, educator
Airaksinen, Mauno Matti retired medical educator, researcher
Aizenberg, Alexander family practice physician
Aizyatulov, Rushan Fatichovich physician, educator
Akagbosu, Fidelis Thomas infertility consultant, gynecologist/obstetrician
Akahoshi, Kazuya gastroenterologist
Akane, Atsushi medical educator
Akhtar, Shamim obstetrician, gynecologist
Akira, Masanori radiologist
Akiwumi, Akiwusi Abiola physician, consultant
Akiyama, Kayo neuroscientist, researcher
Akkoyunlu, Mustafa physician, scientist
Akopov, Andrei surgeon, researcher
Akovbian, Vagan Armaisovich physician
Akpaka, Patrick Eberechi physician
Aksakoglu, Gazanfer Huseyin community medicine educator
Aktan, Samiye Gülderen ophthalmologist, consultant
Akyol, Fadil Husnu radiation oncologist
Alabsi, Jalal M. dermatovenerologist, researcher
Alam, Imtiaz gastroenterologist, hepatologist
Alam, Shahin hypertension physician
Al-Aqeel, Aida Ibrahim pediatrician
Al-Azzawi, Farook Abdul Latif gynecologist, consultant, educator
Albani, Roberto pediatrician, consultant
Albes, Johannes thoracic and cardiovascular surgeon
Albrecht, Heinz psychiatrist
Albrecht, Ronald Frank anesthesiologist
Albrecht, Walter urologist, researcher
Albrecht-Olsen, Peter Mikael orthopedic surgeon
Albu, Ion anatomist, educator
Albus, Margot Irene psychiatrist
Alcazar, Juan Luis physician
Alchorne, Maurício de Oliveira de Avelar physician
Al-Dawood, Kasim Mohd medical educator
Aldren, Christopher Philip otolaryngologist, surgeon, consultant
Al Duri, Zaid orthopaedic surgeon, researcher
Alejandro, Giraldo physician
Alexander, James Wesley surgeon, educator
Alexander, John Innis anesthesiologist
Alexandre, Gérard-Eugene orthopedic surgeon
Alfaro, Miguel E. plastic surgeon, surgery educator
Alfieri, Sergio surgeon, researcher
Al-Ismail, Saad Abdul-Daim hematologist, consultant
Allain, Herve Jean neurologist, pharmacologist, medical educator
Allain, Yves-Marie radiotherapist
Allal, Abdelkarim Said radiation oncologist, researcher
Allami, Shamsi pediatrician, educator
Allaouchiche, Bernard anesthesiologist
Allegra, Luigi Salvatore medicine educator, researcher
Allegri, Ricardo Francisco physician, researcher, consultant, educator
Allen, Howard Norman cardiologist, educator
Allen, Thomas Wesley medical educator, dean
Allescher, Hans-Dieter internist, gastroenterologist
Allikmets, Kristina cardiologist, researcher
Allison, Marvin Jerome pathologist, anthropologist
Allsop, John Leslie neurologist, consultant
Allums, James A. retired cardiovascular surgeon
Al-Madhi, Fahad Turki physician, medical attache
Almagor, Yaron cardiologist
Almane, Khalid Abdulatif pediatric radiologist, consultant
Almansa Pastor, Angel F. chest physician
Al-Mansouri, Hanaa Mohammed family physician
Almazan, Mauricio A. obstetrician/gynecologist
Almond, Richard J. psychiatrist
Almstrom, Harald Nils Haraldsson obstetrician, gynecologist
Al-Mutairi, Sajed Meteb occupational health physician
Al-Nahhas, Adil Moosa nuclear medicine physician
Alonso-Lej, Fernando cardiothoracic surgeon
Alpar, John J. ophthalmologist, educator
Alpern, Linda Lee Wevodau health agency administrator
Alpert, Jonathan Edward psychiatrist, researcher
Alpini, Dario Carlo otolaryngologist, researcher
Alrubaie, Talal Hamdi psychiatrist, psychotherapist, consultant
Als, Claudine physician, clinician, researcher
Al-Salman, Mussaad Mohammed Saleh medical educator, surgeon
Al-Saqat, Tarik Mohammad Arabi infectious diseases physician
Al-Sawwaf, Monqidh Mohammed surgeon
Al-Shabanah, Othman Abdullah pharmacologist, educator
Alshuaib, Waleed Baker neurobiology educator, researcher
Al-Sohaibani, Mohammed Omar pathology educator
Alt, Eckhard U. physician, educator
Altin, Sedat medical educator, medical administrator
Alton, Eric Walter Frederick Wolfgang respiratory medicine academic
Al Traif, Ibrahim Hamad physician, consultant
Al-Turaiki, Mohammed Homod biomedical technologist
Alusik, Stefan physician, rheumatologist
Alvarez, Rafael Gonzalez anesthesiologist
Alwasiak, Janusz Franciszek pathologist
Amagasa, Masaharu neurosurgeon
Amara, Fahmy El-Sayed endocrinologist, educator
Amato, Marisa Campos Moraes cardiologist
Ambache, Nachman medical researcher
Ambler, Zdeněk neurologist, educator
Ambros, Robert Andrew pathologist, educator
Ambrose, Thomas Albert, II orthopaedic surgeon
Ambrozaitis, Arvydas medical educator, researcher
Ambrus, Julian L. physician, medical educator
Ameen, Fawzi Abdulla physician
Amelar, Richard Daniel urologist, andrologist
Amer, Mohamed Amin dermatologist, educator
Amexo, Kwaku internist
Amiel, Michel Jean radiologist, educator
Amin, Prafull Bhogilal pathologist, consultant
Amir, Hassan surgeon
Amirou, Mustapha physician
Amler, Barbara physician
Ammaturo, Vincenzo physician
Ammon, Hermann Philipp Theodor pharmacologist, educator
Amr, Sherif Mamdouh orthopedist
Amsel, Bram Jules cardiologist
Amyes, Edwin Westby neurosurgeon
An, Yuehui Huey orthopaedic surgeon, educator
Anagli, John Yao biomedical research scientist, consultant
Anah, Christian Onyekpandu cardiologist, consultant, educator
Anapliotis, Spyros John physician, consultant
Anastasescu, Michael administrator
Anastassiades, Efthyvoulos George nephrologist
Anders, Norbert ophthalmologist, researcher, educator
Andersen, Jens Rikardt gastroenterologist
Anderson, Geraldine Louise medical researcher
Anderson, Kenneth Paul nephrologist, administrator
Anderson, Robert Henry pathology educator
Anderson, Stuart James neuropsychologist
Anderson, William Henry psychobiologist, educator
Anderson, William Robert pathologist, educator
Andersson, Sven-Olof physician
Ando, Hironobu medical educator, cardiologist
Ando, Yukio physician, biochemist, educator
Andonopoulos, Andrew P. physician, researcher, educator
Andrade-Paez, Pedro Enrique internist
Andre, Charles physician, researcher
Andreas, Stefan cardiologist
Andreé, Bengt Alof Lennart psychiatrist, researcher
Andreelli, Fabrizio physician
Andrews, Billy Franklin pediatrician, educator
Andrews, Christopher John registrar in anesthesiology
Andrews, John Thomas retired nuclear medicine physician, consultant
Andreyev, Michael Dmitrievich pathologist, health center administrator
Andrianov, Yuri Nickolaevich neurophysiologist, researcher
Andrijich, Vincent Benedict radiologist
Ang, Peng-Tiam physician, consultant
Ang, Swee Chai orthopedic surgeon, consultant
Angel, Carlos Alberto pediatric surgeon, urologist
Angelini, Gianni Davide surgeon, educator
Angelov, Lyuben Lazarov epidemiologist, researcher
Angulo, Mario radiology educator
Angus, James Alexander pharmacology educator
Anisimov, Vladimir Nikolaevich oncologist
Anna, Arkadjevna Moldavskay anatomy educator
Annane, Djillali cardiology educator, researcher, pharmacologist
Annerud, Carolyn Riederer emergency physician
Ansari, Ahmad Farooq pharmacology educator
Anschütz, Till Rainer ophthalmologist
Antakly, Marie-Claire anesthesiologist, educator
Antal, Albert gynecologist, obstetrician, anesthesiologist
Antell, Darrick Eugene plastic surgeon, educator
Anthopoulos, Lambros Prodromos cardiologist, educator
Antica, Mariastefania immunologist
Antoce, Georgiana Magdalena physician, psychiatrist
Antonatos, Panagiotis (Takis) cardiologist
Antonio, Artigas intensive care physician, researcher
Antuna de Alaiz, Ramiro diabetologist
Aoki, Hideo neurosurgeon
Aono, Jun anesthesiologist, educator
Aoun, Ragab Salem physician, consultant pediatrician
Aoyagi, Masaru otolaryngologist, educator
Aoyama, Hideyasu medical educator
Apahideanu, Octavian physician, consultant
Aparicio, Jorge oncologist
Apjok, Enikő pediatrician
Apostolopoulos, Vasso immunovaccinologist
Appel, Lawrence John physician, educator
Apud, Jose Antonio psychiatrist, psychopharmacologist, educator
Araga, Shigeru internist, neurologist
Arai, Yumiko public health physician, researcher
Arakgui, Jean Aziz retired obstetrician, gynecologist, consultant
Aranui-Faed, Julia Anne consultant psychiatrist
Arcasoy, Mufit Mazhar physician, pediatrician
Arce, A. Anthony psychiatrist
Archampong, Emmanuel Quaye surgery educator, university dean, consultant
Archer, Jonathan Robbins biomedical researcher
Arcot, Rangaraj Govindraj retired physician
Ardal, Bjorn pediatrician
Arenberger, Petr dermatologist
Arie, Thomas Harry David psychiatry educator
Arima, Eitoku surgeon, hospital administrator
Aritome, Teruchica physician
Arkossy, Otto nephrologist
Arleevsky, Igor Petr cardiologist
Armand, Jean Pierre oncologist
Armato, Ubaldo anatomist, cell biologist, researcher, educator
Armstrong, Peter radiologist
Arnala, Ilkka Olavi orthopaedic surgeon
Arnbjörnsson, Einar Ólafur pediatric surgeon
Arnold, William Parsons, Jr. retired internist
Arnott, Eric John ophthalmologist
Arnu, Thomas Joseph surgeon
Aronow, Wilbert Solomon physician, educator
Aronson, Jeffrey Kenneth pharmacologist
Arora, Shyam Sunder biomedical engineering and physics educator, researcher
Arriola-Isais, Carlos obstetrician-gynecologist, educator
Artigues, Jean Marie ophthalmologist
Artik, Suzan immunologist
Arvanitakis, Constantine S. gastroenterologist
Arvers, Philippe physician, researcher
Arya, Mohammad Javad pathologist
Asada, Kanji orthopedic surgeon, physician
Asano, Makishige medical educator
Asch, Leopold medical educator
Ascherman, Stanford Warren surgeon
Aschermann, Michael cardiologist, researcher
Aschoff, Alfred Walter neurosurgeon
Asero, Riccardo Salvatore physician
Ashley, Michael Matthew radiologist
Asikainen, Ilmari neurology specialist
Askanas-Engel, Valerie neurologist, educator, researcher
Aslam, Toqeer general practice physician
Asplund-Carlson, Anette Maria physician, researcher
Assaf, Ahmed Abdel-Rahman ophthalmic surgeon, consultant, educator
Assion, Hans-Jörg neurologist, psychiatrist
Assumpcao, Francisco Baptista, Jr. psychiatrist, educator
Astillero, Carlito Lapar physician, microbiologist, consultant
Ata, Khaled Ahmad physician, medical researcher
Atarashi, Hirotsugu cardiologist, educator
Atassi, Ghenem oncologist
Ates, Yalim orthopaedic surgeon
Ates, Yesim anesthesiologist, educator

Athanassiadi, Kalliopi cardiothoracic surgeon
Athanassiou, Athanassios E. medical oncologist, researcher
Athanassopoulos, Anastassios Andreas urologist, consultant
Ather, M. Hammad urologist
Atiba, Joshua Olajide O. internist, pharmacologist, oncologist, educator
Atkinson, Barbara Frajola pathologist
Atlas, Scott William radiologist
Atlay, Robert David gynecologist, administrator
Atlee, John Light physician
Attarian, Houshang rheumatologist
Au, Otto Yum-To plastic surgeon, educator
Aubier, Michel medical educator
Auer, Ignaz Oscar gastroenterologist, rheumatologist
Auewarakul, Chirayu medical educator
Auffermann, Wolfgang Friedrich Wilhelm radiologist, neuroradiologist
Augoustides, John George Themistocles cardiothoracic anesthesiologist, educator
Aurell, Mattias Nils nephrology educator
Auriacombe, Marc psychiatrist, educator, researcher
Aursnes, Ivar Andreas clinical pharmacologist
Austen, W(illiam) Gerald surgeon, educator
Austrian, Robert physician, educator
Au Yong, Ting Kun nuclear medicine physician
Avakoff, Joseph Carnegie medical and legal consultant
Avasthi, Ajit Kumar psychiatrist, educator
Avenarius, Stefan Michael pediatrician
Avery, Birthe Margit embryologist, educator, researcher
Avierinos, Christian Yves cardiologist
Avram, Morrell M. nephrologist, educator, consultant
Awad, Mahmoud Mohamed cardiologist, consultant
Awad El Karim, Rihab Abdel Magid immunologist
Awofeso, Niyi public health physician
Axel, Dorothea Ilse pharmacologist
Axelrod, Julius pharmacologist, biochemist
Axelson, Magnus E.G. medical educator, researcher
Axelsson, Uno Tore retired hematologist
Axler, Olivier Louis critical care physician, researcher, consultant
Aygun, A. Denizmen medical educator
Aymerich, Jose Gros oncologist
Ayoub, Adham Mohamed ophthalmology educator
Ayres, Jonathan Geoffrey respiratory medicine educator, physician, research
Ayus, Juan Carlos nephrologist
Azevedo, João Roberto Duff neurosurgeon
Aziz, Aasma family physician
Aziz, Lutful anaesthesiologist
Aziz, Samir Mohamed Fouad obstetrician-gynecologist, educator, consultant
Azpiroz, Fernando physician, researcher
Baaklini, Walid Antoine physician, educator
Baba, Hisamichi surgeon, health facility administrator
Babaeva, Anna Georgievna cytologist, researcher
Babuš, Vladimir epidemiologist, educator
Bacchus, Robby Ahmad metabolic physician
Bach, Christian Michael orthopedic surgeon
Bach, Heinz Jürgen physician, researcher
Bachmann, Gregor surgeon
Bachor, Edgar otolaryngologist, researcher
Backer, Carl L. pediatric cardiac surgeon, educator
Bacon, Andrew Kenneth anesthetist
Bacon, Paul Anthony rheumatology educator, consultant
Baczyk, Kazimierz Marian medicine educator
Badary, Osama Ahmed pharmacologist, educator
Bader, Hermann Joseph pharmacologist, educator
Badiu, Corin Virgil P. endocrinologist, educator
Badrek-Amoudi, Hassan Said pediatrician
Baev, Stanislav surgeon, consultant, researcher
Bafaqeeh, Sameer Ali otorhinolaryngologist, educator, consultant
Bagdy, Gyorgy pharmacologist, researcher
Bagolan, Pietro surgeon, consultant
Bagshaw, Malcolm A. radiation oncologist, educator
Bagshawe, Kenneth Dawson oncologist
Bahk, Jae-Hyon anesthesiologist educator
Bai, Jun medical researcher
Baig, Abdul Sattar physician, researcher
Baillou, Jean surgeon
Baird, Roger Neale surgeon
Bajcsay, Andras radiation and clinical oncologist
Bajoghli, Amir A. physician
Bakács, Tibor oncologist, immunologist, researcher
Bakari, Muhammad dermatologist
Baker, Bruce Edward orthopedic surgeon, consultant
Baker, Deborah Jane epidemiology and health services researcher
Baker, F. M. psychiatry educator
Baker, Timothy Danforth physician, educator
Baker, Timothy Holland physician, echocardiographer
Bakheit, Abdel Magid physician, medical educator, consultant
Bakos, Lucio dermatologist, educator
Bak-Romaniszyn, Leokadia gastroenterology, educator, pediatrician
Bakshi, Sandhya Arun anesthesiologist, consultant
Bala, Ovidiu Eugen surgeon
Balanescu, Serban Mihai cardiologist
Balaschevich, Leonid ophthalmologist
Balci, Sevin M. pediatrician, medical geneticist
Baldari, Marco physician
Baldi, Alfonso pathologist
Baldini, Edoardo surgeon
Baldonado, Celeste Bulan obstetrician/gynecologist, consultant
Baldwin, John Charles surgeon, researcher
Bale, Reto Josef physician
Balen, Adam Henry obstetrician, gynecologist
Balestrini, Aristóbulo Enrique cardiologist
Balik, Ismail medical educator
Balint, Gabor Alexander pharmacologist
Bálint, Géza Peter clinical rheumatologist, physiotherapy educator
Balldin, Ulf Ingemar medical researcher
Balleari, Enrico internist, rheumatologist, educator, researcher
Baller, Detlev physician, cardiologist, physiologist, researcher
Ballweg, Ruth Milligan physician assistant, educator
Balogh, Ferenc urologist
Baloyannis, Stavros Joannis neurologist, educator, researcher
Baltazar, Romulo Flores cardiologist
Baltkajs, Janis pharmacology educator
Balybin, Eugeni Sergeevich nuclear medicine physician, immunophysiologist
Bana, Ajeet cardiac surgeon, consultant
Bana, Dhiremdra Singh physician
Banafaa, Omar Saleh consultant obstetrician and gynecologist
Bandaranayake, Raja Christie anatomist, educator
Bandarchi-Chamkhaleh, Bizhan physician
Bandouvas, Emmanuel Jean surgeon, educator
Bandt, Paul Douglas physician
Banerjee, Anjan Kumar surgeon
Banerjee, Ashis physician
Banerjee, Ramendra Nath hematologist, consultant
Bang, Gisle pathologist, researcher
Bang, Moon-Suk medical educator
Bang, Rameshwar Lal physician
Bangasser, Ronald Paul physician
Bankl, Hans Christian physician, researcher
Bannister, Gordon Campbell orthopaedic surgeon
Bannister, Sir Roger Gilbert neurologist, college administrator
Bansal, Yash Pal physician
Bansinath, Mylarrao pharmacologist, educator
Bao, Katherine Sung pediatric cardiologist
Barac, Bosko Antun neurologist, educator
Baraczka, Krisztina neurologist
Barandun, Juerg physician
Baranowski, Andrew Paul anesthetist
Bárány, Peter Franz nephrologist
Barar, Kiran Vijay pharmacology educator
Barbadimos, Aris N. physician
Barbaro, Giuseppe physician
Barber, Ann McDonald physician
Barbieri, Sergio neurologist
Barclay, Alan Neil immunologist, researcher
Barclay, Thomas Laird plastic surgeon
Bard, David Roy medical researcher
Bardak, Yavuz Kamil ophthalmologist
Barer, Arnold medical educator
Bares, Ludek Francis neurologist, consultant
Barie, Philip Steven surgeon, educator
Barillari, Paolo surgeon, researcher
Barišić, Nina pediatrician, neurologist, educator
Barker, Barbara Ann ophthalmologist
Barker, Clyde Frederick surgeon, educator
Barker, David James medical researcher
Barker, Geoffrey Ronald physician, consultant, surgeon
Barley, Victor Laurence oncologist
Barlow, David John Harding psychiatrist
Barnes, Gary John psychiatrist
Barnes, Nicholas Mark medical researcher and lecturer
Barnes, Peter John thoracic medicine educator, consultant, physician
Barnes, Phillip Robert John neurologist
Barnes, Richard Charles psychiatrist, consultant
Barnett, Anthony Howard internist, medical educator
Barnett, Benjamin Lewis, Jr. retired physician
Barnett, Crawford Fannin, Jr. internist, educator, cardiologist, travel medicine specialist
Barnett, Gene Henry neurosurgeon
Barnhill, Larry Jarrett, Jr. neuropsychiatrist
Barnsley, Leslie rheumatologist, educator
Baroldi, Giorgio Cesare cardiovascular pathology educator
Baron, Jean-Claude neuroscientist, researcher
Barr, Geoffrey Samuel head and neck surgeon, research administrator
Barr, Lester surgeon
Barrett, Andrew William oral pathologist, educator
Bar-Sever, Zvi physician
Barsome, Michael Yassa pulmonarist, consultant
Barson, Anthony James perinatal pathologist, educator
Barták, Jaroslav Vladimír cardiologist, clinic administrator
Bartek, Gordon Luke radiologist
Barthelemy, Jean-Paul Francois orthopedic surgeon
Barthelet, Yves anesthesiologist, intensive care physician
Bartko, György Jenö psychiatrist
Bartoli, Ettore medical educator
Barton, Everard Nathaniel medical educator, consultant nephrologist
Barton, József retired physician, dentist
Barton, Nicholas James surgeon, educator
Bartos, Andres Esteban physician, educator
Bartoš, Pavel phytopathologist, geneticist, researcher
Bartsocas, Christos Spyros physician, educator
Bartunkova, Jirina immunologist
Baschat, Ahmet Alexander obstetrician, gynecologist
Bascil Tütüncü, Neslihan endocrinologist
Bashour, Fouad Anis cardiology educator
Basoğlu, Metin psychiatrist, researcher
Basra, Devinder Singh plastic surgeon
Bassano, Carlo cardiac surgeon
Bassili, Safwat Sobhy ophthalmologist
Bassler, Markus Sylvester medical researcher
Bassompierre, Patrice Joseph physician, health facility administrator
Bassot, Jacques aesthetic surgeon
Basta, Antoni obstetrician/gynecologist, educator
Bastin, Guy Sylvain Paul retired clinical laboratory physician
Bateman, Peter Patrick retired allergist
Batey, Robert Gordon hepatological specialist, educator
Batislam, Ertan urology educator
Batmanabane, Mounissamy anatomist, educator
Batt, Ronald Elmer gynecologist, scientist
Battistella, Linamara medical educator
Baú, Plínio Carlos surgeon, educator
Bauch, Karlheinz Gerold medical consultant
Baudis, Pavel psychiatrist, researcher
Baudoin, Tomislav otolaryngologist
Bauer, A(ugust) Robert, Jr. surgeon, educator
Bauer, Brent A. physician
Bauer, Gaston Egon cardiologist
Bauer, Viktor pharmacologist, researcher
Baufreton, Christophe cardiothoracic surgeon
Baum, Richard Paul nuclear medicine physician
Bauman, William Allen pediatrician, educator, health systems consultant
Baume, Peter Erne medical educator
Baumgarten, Stephen Robert physician, urologist
Baumgartner, Johann Franz radiochemistry scientist, educator
Bavbek, Murad neurosurgeon, educator
Baxter, Alan George immunologist
Baylac-Domengetroy, Frédéric Pierre Dominique cardiologist
Bayliss, Sir Richard Ian Samuel endocrinologist
Baynes, Roy Dennis hematologist, educator
Bayramlar, Huseyin ophthalmologist
Bazarbashi, Mohammad Shouki oncologist
Beachley, Michael Charles radiologist
Beahrs, Oliver Howard surgeon, educator
Beale, Sir Peter John medical advisor
Beales, Peter Frederick tropical diseases physician, consultant, educator
Beard, Jonathan David vascular surgeon, consultant, educator
Beattie, James Alexander Gordon physician
Beatty, Robert Alfred (R. Alfred) surgeon
Beauchamp, Harry internist, pulmonologist
Bechter, Karl psychiatrist
Beck, John Robert pathologist, information scientist
Beck, Michael Hawley dermatologist, consultant
Beck, Morris allergist
Becker, Bruce Carl, II physician, educator
Becker, Juergen Christian physician, researcher
Becker, Robert Jerome allergist, health care consultant
Beckers, Albert Marie endocrinologist
Beckett, Henry Dale consultant, psychiatrist
Bécouarn, Yves Henri oncologist, researcher
Bednarek, Francis John pediatrician and neonatologist
Bedworth, David Albert health educator
Beer, Michael Dominic psychiatrist, educator
Beerman, Joseph health educator
Behari, Madhuri neurologist, educator
Behnke, Roy Herbert physician, educator
Behrens, Georg Martin Norbert immunologist, researcher
Beier-Holgersen, Randi physician, surgeon
Beierwaltes, William Henry physician, educator
Beigl, William physician, naturopath, hypnotist, acupuncturist, consultant
Beischer, Norman Albert retired medical educator, editor
Bekassy, Albert Nandor pediatrician
Bekiesińska-Figatowska, Monika radiologist
Belaisch, Jean Gagou gynecologist
Belaïsch-Allart, Joëlle obstetrician-gynecologist
Belani, Kumar Girdharidas anesthesiologist
Belizán, José Miguel obstetrician, researcher
Belizario, Vicente Ylanan, Jr. tropical medicine physician
Bell, John Irving medical researcher, educator
Bell, Patrick Michael endocrinologist, researcher
Bell, Peter Frank surgeon, educator
Bell, Robert Charles retired plastic surgeon, author, civic worker
Bella, Jonathan Noriega cardiologist
Bellaiche, Guy gastroenterologist
Bellastella, Antonio endocrinologist, educator
Beller, Martin Leonard retired orthopaedic surgeon
Bellin, Howard Theodore plastic surgeon
Bellis, Carroll Joseph surgeon, educator
Bellows, A. Robert ophthalmologist, surgeon
Belmonte-Serrano, Miguel A. rheumatologist
Belovezhdov, Nicolay Ivanov physician, researcher, consultant
Belšan, Tomáš radiologist
Benacerraf, Baruj pathologist, educator
Benagiano, Giuseppe Pino medical institute director, medical educator
Benaim, Fortunato surgeon, educator
Benchimol, Marcos emergency physician, internal medicine educator
Bencko, Vladimir physician, researcher, educator
Bendeck-Nimer, Alberto Costa pediatrician
Bendell, Simon Neil radiographer
Bender, Tamas rheumatologist
Benderitter, Thierry Xavier pathologist
Bendtsen, Preben medical educator
Benes, Solomon biomedical scientist, physician
Benet, Leslie Zachary pharmacokineticist
Bengesser, Gerhard psychiatrist and neurologist
Bengtson, Sten Olof orthopedic surgeon
Ben-Haim, Shlomo Auraham medical educator, physiologist
Benigno, Mary Ann osteopath, surgeon
Benirschke, Kurt pathologist, educator
Benito-Ruiz, Jesus plastic surgeon
Benkovitch, Boris Ilich pharmacologist
Bennett, Edward Virdell, Jr. surgeon
Bennett, John Roderick consulting gastroenterologist
Bennett, Max Richard neuroscience
Bennett, Peter Norman physician
Bensahel, Henri pediatric orthopedics educator, researcher
Benson, John Russell surgeon, researcher
Bensussan, Denis radiologist
Bentdal, Øystein Hagen transplant surgeon
Bentley, Douglas Paul hematologist
Bentley, George orthopedics educator, researcher, consultant, surgeon
Benzer, Seymour neuroscience educator
Benziane, Khalid radiologist
Beran, Roy Gary neurologist
Beran, Samuel Jonathan plastic surgeon
Berardesca, Enzo educator, researcher
Berbary, Maurice Shehadeh physician, military officer, hospital administrator, educator
Bereczki, Daniel physician, consultant neurologist
Beregi, Edit retired gerontologist
Berendi, Erlinda Bayaua physician surgeon
Beretta, Giovanni urologist, andrologist, researcher
Berg, Gertrud Erika Birgitta oncology educator
Berga, Sarah Lee women's health physician, educator
Bergamini, Ettore pathologist
Bergel, Meny physician, researcher
Bergenheim, Anders Tommy neurosurgeon, educator
Berger, Gert Alexander neurologist
Berger, Richard obstetrician and gynecologist
Berghs, Hubert Theodoor rheumatologist
Bergin, Colleen Joan medical educator
Berg-Johnsen, Jon neurosurgeon
Berglund, Kåre Nils rheumatologist
Bergman, Reuven dermatologist
Bergmark, Tord psychiatrist, psychotherapist
Bergoglio, Remo Miguel infectious disease physician
Bergold, Orm medical educator
Bergquist, Nils Robert medical consultant
Bergsholm, Per psychiatrist, neurologist
Bergstein, Jack Marshall surgeon
Berk, Mehmet Caglar neurosurgeon
Berkarda, Bulent internist, hematologist, oncologist
Berkenblit, Scott Ira orthopaedic surgeon
Berki, Timea immunologist, researcher
Berkley, Reginald Maurice surgeon, art historian
Berkova, Nadejda Petrovna biochemist, medical researcher
Bern, Murray Morris hematologist, oncologist
Bernard, Claude Charles Andre neuroimmunologist
Bernard, Richard Montgomery retired physician
Bernays, René Ludwig neurosurgeon
Bernhard, Jeffrey David dermatologist, editor, educator
Bernheim, Jan L. medical scientific consultant, educator
Bernstein, Sol cardiologist, educator
Berra, Lodovico Edoardo psychiatrist, psychotherapist
Berrey, Bedford Hudson physician
Berrut, Gilles internist
Berseus, Olle Jan Olof pathologist
Bershitsky, Sergey Yurievich physiologist
Bertelsen, Aksel Brockhusen psychiatrist
Berthelsdorf, Siegfried psychiatrist
Berth-Jones, John consultant dermatologist, educator
Berthold, Frank pediatrician and oncologist
Berton, Giuseppe Stefano physician, cardiologist
Bertoncello, Ivan experimental hematologist, researcher
Besancon, Francois Jean internist, gastroenterologist, educator
Besancon, Roger R. pharmacologist
Bessell, Eric Michael medical practitioner, clinical oncology consultant
Bessell, Justin Raymond surgeon, researcher
Bessmeltsev, Stanislav Semionovitch physician, researcher
Besson, Philippe Gaston physician
Bessou, Jean-Paul thoracic surgeon, medical educator
Best, Lael-Anson Eliezer thoracic surgeon
Besuschio, Santiago Cesar pathologist, epidemiologist
Bethell, Hugh James Newton general practitioner
Bethoux, François Andre physiatrist, researcher
Betlejewski, Stanislaw physician
Betta, Pier-Giacomo pathologist
Betti, Roberto physician
Bettocchi, Carlo urologist
Bevers, Therese Bartholomew physician, medical educator
Beversdorf, David Quentin neurologist, researcher
Bewes, Peter Cecil surgeon
Bewley, Anthony Paul dermatologist
Bex, Jean-Pierre cardiovascular surgeon, consultant
Bexell, Anna Kerstin Elin physician
Bey, Pierre oncologist
Bezborodnyi, Sergei Dmitrievitch physician, researcher, journalist
Bezzaoucha, Abdeldjellil epidemiologist
Bhagia, Vasdev physician, consultant
Bharadwaj, Renu Satish educator, medical researcher
Bharucha, Nadir Eddie neurophysician
Bhatia, Arati pathologist
Bhatia, Vipan urologist, educator
Bhaumik, Sabyasachi psychiatrist
Bhigjee, Ahmed Iqbal neurology educator
Bhore, Jay Narayan psychiatrist
Bhugra, Dinesh Kumar Makhan Lal psychiatrist, educator
Bhunchet, Ekapot pathologist
Bhutto, Imran Ahmed ophthalmologist, researcher
Bialasiewicz, Alexander Arthur ophthalmologist, educator
Bialik, Viktor pediatric orthopediatric surgeon
Biary, Nabil M. neurologist
Biase, Francisco Di neurosurgeon, researcher
Bick, Rodger Lee hematologist, oncologist, researcher, educator
Biederman, Robert Wallace Williams cardiologist
Biellik, Robin Julian epidemiologist
Biers, Martin Henry physician
Biersack, Gertrud Maria obstetrician, gynecologist, hospital administrator
Biesbrouck, Maurits Albert Georges pathologist
Bifulco, Antonia Teresa psychiatrist, researcher
Bigazzi, Mario Amelio endocrinologist
Bignon, Yves-Jean oncologist, geneticist
Bihari, Imre physician
Bilaceroğlu, Semra pulmonary specialist
Bilfinger, Thomas Victor surgeon, educator
Bilgin, Yasar physician
Billé, Jean-Georges neurologist
Billing, Ronald James immunologist, researcher
Billson, Frank Alfred ophthalmologist, educator
Binder, Henry J. internist, educator
Bindman, Lynn Janice neurophysiologist
Bingham, James Stewart genitourinary physician
Bion, Julian Fleetwood intensive care and anaesthetist educator
Birabuza, André pediatrician
Birch, Nicholas John pharmacology consultant
Birk, Lee (Carl Birk) psychiatrist, educator
Birketvedt, Grethe Støa medical scientist, writer, musician
Birks, Doreen Ann retired ophthalmic surgeon
Birleson, Peter psychiatrist, educator
Bishop, Christopher C. R. surgeon, consultant
Bishop, John Michael biomedical research scientist, educator
Bishop, Malcolm Graham Hamilton medical essayist
Bismuth, Favre Chantal medical educator
Bissada, Nabil Kaddis urologist, educator, researcher, author
Bisset, Gordon Wood pharmacology educator, researcher, retired
Bitensky, Valeriy S. psychiatrist, educator
Bitran, Jacob David internist
Bittencourt, Paulo L. gastroenterologist, hepatologist
Biziulevichius, Gediminas Arvydas enzymologist, researcher
Bjenning, Christina Anna neuroscientist
Bjerke, H. Scott surgeon
Bjerneroth, Gunnel Birgitta anesthesiologist
Bjerregaard, Peter medical researcher, educator
Bjorck, Martin Gustaf vascular surgeon
Björk, Lars Mikael anesthesiologist, consultant
Björkelund, Cecilia family practice physician
Björkstén, Bengt H. medical educator, consultant
Black, Carol Mary rheumatologist, educator
Black, Sir James (Whyte) pharmacologist
Black, Mark D. neuroscientist
Black, Michael Darryl pediatric cardiac surgeon, educator
Bláha, Milan hematologist
Bláha, Vladimír internist, researcher
Blair, Robin Leitch otolaryngologist, educator
Blais, Bernard Raymond ophthalmologist, occupational health physician, educator
Blake-Inada, Louis Michael cardiologist, researcher
Blakemore, Colin (Brian) neuroscientist, writer, broadcaster
Blanchard, Benoit Marie-Regis cardiologist
Blancher, Antoine Pascal immunologist, educator
Blanck, J. Guillermo psychiatrist, philosopher
Blanco, Carlos allergist, researcher
Blanco, Jose medical educator
Blandy, John Peter retired urological surgeon
Blansjaar, Ben A. psychiatrist, researcher
Blanuša, Maja medical researcher, educator
Bläsius, Nikolaus Heribert Arnold (Klaus Bläsius) orthopedic surgeon, medical educator, researcher
Blau, Joseph Norman neurologist
Blauw, Gerard Jan physician
Bleehen, Norman Montague oncologist, educator
Bleiberg, Leon William surgical podiatrist
Bleicher, Sheldon Joseph endocrinologist, medical educator
Blendis, Laurence Morton internist, educator, consultant

Bleyn, Jacques Armand vascular surgeon
Blichert-Toft, Mogens professor of surgery
Bloch, Antoine cardiologist
Blomhoff, Heidi Kiil immunology educator
Blöndal, Thorsteinn internist
Blondin, Joan nephrologist educator
Bloodworth, J(ames) M(organ) Bartow, Jr. physician, educator
Bloom, Stephen Robert medical educator, biomedical researcher
Bloom, Victor Roy physician
Bloom, William Herman neurosurgeon, author
Blower, Peter Robin pharmacologist, educator
Bluefarb, Samuel Mitchell physician
Blumenreich, Martin Sigvart oncologist
Blundell, James Edward radiologist
Bo, Mario Edoardo geriatrician, cardiologist
Boal, Bernard Harvey cardiologist, educator, author
Bobrovnik, Sergey Afanasievich immunologist, researcher
Bocchi, Edimar Alcides physician, researcher
Bockeria, Leo Antonovich cardiac surgeon
Boda, Domokos István retired pediatrics educator
Boda, Zoltan internist
Bodanszky, Hedvig Eros pediatrician, educator
Boddie, Arthur Walker, Jr. surgeon, cancer researcher
Bode, Johann Christian internist, gastroenterologist
Bodemann, H(einz) Harm physician
Bodereau, Xavier Jacques ophthamologist, surgeon
Bodis, Jozsef Ferenc obstetrician/gynecologist
Bodis, Stephan B. radiation oncologist, educator, researcher
Bodmer, Walter Fred cancer research administrator
Bodner, Bruce Ira ophthalmologist
Boelaert, Marleen tropical medicine researcher
Bogadi-Sare, Ana occupational medicine specialist, researcher
Bogen, Bjarne immunologist, educator
Boggs, Joseph Dodridge pediatric pathologist, educator
Böhle, Andreas urologist, educator, research scientist
Bohman, Michael Carl child psychiatrist, researcher
Böhmer, Thomas internist
Bohuš, Ondrej anesthesiologist, consultant
Boismenu, Richard immunologist, researcher
Bokemeyer, Carsten physician, researcher, medical educator
Bokor, Magdolna neurologist
Boleslaw, Nagay physician and surgeon
Bolger, Graeme Barrett medical educator
Boling, Eldon Avery physician
Bolla, Michel Maurice physician, consultant
Bolliger, Eugene Frederick retired surgeon
Bollinger, Alfred internist, researcher
Bolós, Jordi chemist, pharmacist
Bolton, Thomas Bruce pharmacologist, educator
Bolzani, Luciano Guiseppe psychiatrist
Bom, Hee-Seung nuclear physician, educator
Bomhof, Martin A. M. neurologist, consultant
Bonaventura, Antonino oncologist
Boncoeur-Martel, Marie Paule neuroradiologist
Bond, Malcolm James medical educator
Bondeson, Jan physician
Bonding, Per otolaryngologist, researcher
Bonner, Jack Wilbur, III psychiatrist, educator, administrator
Bonnici, Albert Victor orthopedic surgeon
Bonora, Enzo medical educator, researcher, consultant
Bonsall, John Lytton medical officer
Boom, Willem Henry physician, biomedical researcher
Boonchai, Waranya dermatologist
Boran, Robert Paul, Jr. orthopedic surgeon
Borbola, George radiologist
Borel, Georges Antoine gastroenterologist, consultant
Boren, Kenneth Ray endocrinologist
Borger, Michael Hinton Ivers osteopathic physician, educator
Borghi, Battista anesthesiologist
Borgstein, Paul Justus surgeon, oncologist
Borman, Edwin Miles anesthetist consultant
Born, Gustav Victor Rudolf medical researcher
Borodin, Yuriy Ivanovish gynecologist, obstetrician
Borodina, Elena L'vovna physician, acoustical researcher
Borody, Thomas Julius gastroenterologist, consultant
Boronow, Richard Carlton gynecologist, educator
Borromeo, Romana Gonzalez obstetrician, gynecologist
Bose, Subash Chandra dermatologist
Bosio, Angelo pharmacologist, psychiatrist, scientific advisor
Bosl, George Joseph physician, oncologist
Bossuyt, Xavier Andre Anna pathologist
Bostick, Roberd Maner epidemiologist, family physician
Boswell, George Marion, Jr. orthopedist, health care facility administrator
Böszörményi, Miklós physician, pneumonologist
Botseas, Dionysios Sotirios surgeon
Botterman, Jacky A. oncologist
Bouchet, Alan vascular surgeon
Bouda, Jaromír physician
Bouffette, Patrick Pierre oncologist, hematologist
Bougas, James Andrew physician, surgeon
Bouju, Philippe Pierre Michel A. anesthesiologist
Boulis, Zoser Fouad radiologist, consultant
Boulton, Thomas Babington anesthesiologist, educator
Bound, John Pascoe pediatrician, consultant
Bourgeau, Jean-Paul Leonce pediatrician
Bourin, Michel Sylvain pharmacology educator
Bourmayan, Claude Vahan cardiologist
Bourne, Anthony John paediatric pathologist
Boutaric, Jean-Jose Etienne physician, writer
Bouwer, Johan Stefaan otolaryngologist
Bouziani, Ammar pathologist, consultant, educator
Boven, Katia pediatric immunologist, nephrologist
Bovingdon, Michael Edward pharmacology educator
Bower, Philip Jeffrey cardiologist
Bowsher, David Richard neurologist
Boyd, Katie medical consultant
Boyd, Robert David pediatrician
Boysen, Gudrun Margrethe neurologist, educator, researcher
Bozbuğa, Mustafa neurosurgeon, educator, consultant
Bozsik, Bela Pal retired physician
Braathen, Lasse Roger dermatologist, educator
Brabon, David Lawrence plastic reconstructive surgeon
Braciale, Vivian Lam immunologist
Brackett, Edward Boone, III orthopedic surgeon
Bradley, Charles William podiatrist, educator
Bradley, John immunology educator, pathologist, physician
Bradley, Patrick James otolaryngologist
Brady, Stephen R.P.K. physician
Braimbridge, Mark Viney cardiothoracic surgeon
Branch, William Terrell urologist, educator
Brandl, Richard vascular surgeon, consultant
Brandon, Gary Kent physician, health facility administrator
Brannen, George Elsdon surgeon
Bransford, Richard Samuel physician, missionary
Branski, David pediatrician, educator
Braszko, Jan Jozef pharmacologist, educator
Brathwaite, Alfred Fitzgerald pathologist
Bratt, Ola urological surgeon, researcher
Braun, Bennett George psychiatrist
Braun, Joseph Christian surgeon
Braun, Karsten physician, researcher
Braun, Ruediger Walther physician, virologist
Braunberger, Eric cardiac surgeon, researcher
Bräutigam, Peter physician
Brearley, Stephen surgeon
Bree, Remco de otolaryngologist
Bregman, Davis orthopedist, pain management specialist
Breinin, Goodwin M. physician
Breitbart, Arnold Sol plastic surgeon
Bremner, Fion Domnall ophthalmic surgeon
Brendler, Charles Burgess urologist
Brennan, Patrick Christopher radiographer, lecturer
Brennand-Roper, David Andrew cardiologist, consultant
Brennecke, Shaun Patrick obstetrician-gynecologist, educator
Brenowitz, Eliot A. neurobiologist, educator
Brewerton, Timothy David psychiatrist
Brew-Graves, Samuel Henry pediatrician, international health and management consultant
Breyer, Detlev Richard Hans ophthalmologist
Briasoulis, Evangelos medical oncologist, consultant
Brichon, Pierre-Yves cardiothoracic surgeon
Brickl, Rolf Stefan pharmacokineticist
Bridge, T(homas) Peter psychiatrist, researcher
Bridges, Paul Kenneth psychiatrist, consultant
Bridges, Ronald Claude medical records clerk
Brierly, Mary Carol physician, dermatologist, consultant
Brigino-Buenaventura, Emerita immunologist, allergist
Brilla, Christian Georg cardiologist, researcher, educator
Brimioulle, Serge intensive care physician
Brinck, Ulrich pathologist, researcher
Bringmann, Ingra Monique resident, researcher
Brinkhous, Kenneth Merle retired pathologist, educator
Brissot, Pierre Gabriel physician, medical educator
Bristow, Cynthia Lynn immunologist
Broadley, Kenneth John pharmacology educator
Brochier, Mireille L. cardiologist, educator
Brockenbrough, Edwin Chamberlayne surgeon
Brockington, Colin Fraser social and preventive medicine educator
Brocklebank, John Trevor pediatrician, consultant, educator
Brodie, Harlow Keith Hammond psychiatrist, educator, past university president
Brodine, Charles Edward physician
Brody, Eugene B. psychiatrist, educator
Brogard, Jean-Marie internist, physician
Brohammer, Richard Frederic psychiatrist
Broka, Serge Maurice anesthesiologist
Brölmann, Hans gynecologist
Broman, George Ellis, Jr. retired surgeon
Bronisch, Thomas Ernst psychiatrist
Broocks, Andreas psychiatry and psychology educator
Brook, Charles Groves Darville pediatric endocrinology educator
Brookes, Murray retired physician, anatomy educator
Brooks, John Samuel Joseph pathologist, researcher
Brossner, Clemens urologist
Brotchi, Jacques medical educator, neurosurgeon
Brountzos, Elias Nikolaos radiologist
Brouqui, Philippe Lucien infectious diseases and tropical medicine educator
Brown, Charles Alexander retired ophthalmic surgeon
Brown, Elizabeth Ruth neonatologist
Brown, Morris Jonathan clinical pharmacology educator, physician
Brown, Ricky medical consultant
Brown, Robert Stephen, Jr. physician
Brown, Steven Brien radiologist
Brown, Thomas Christopher Kenneth anesthesiologist
Brown, Thomas Huntington neuroscientist
Brown, William Michael scientist, consultant, writer, editor, lawyer
Browne, Roger Michael oral pathology educator, consultant
Browne, Thomas Reed neurologist, researcher, educator
Brox, Georg Alexander consultant histopathologist, researcher
Bruce, Thomas Allen physician, philanthropist, educator
Brue, Thierry Christian endocrinology educator
Brueren, Mark Mattheus general practice physician
Brueton, Martin John pediatrician
Bruggeman, Lewis LeRoy radiologist
Brugger, Hermann physician
Brugha, Traolach Sean psychiatrist
Brull, Sorin Joseph educator, physician
Brun, Georges Harris gynecologist
Bruna, Josef radiology educator
Brundage, Gertrude Barnes pediatrician
Brunel, Olivier dermatologist
Brunelli, Alessandro thoracic surgeon
Bruner, William Evans, II ophthalmologist, educator, researcher
Brunkwall, Jan Sigge vascular surgeon, consultant, educator
Brunner, Kirstin Ellen pediatrician, psychiatrist
Brunner, Sam Aage radiologist
Bruno, Guglielmo physician, educator, consultant, researcher
Brunt, Manly Yates, Jr. psychiatrist
Brusov, Pavel Georgievich surgeon, researcher
Brüstle, Oliver neuropathologist, researcher
Brüstmann, Hermann pathologist, researcher
Bruwier, M.W. internist
Bruynes, Eduard urologist
Bryant, Stewart James pathologist
Bryskier, André Julien physician, microbiologist
Brzosko, Witold Jozef physician, medical educator, researcher, scientist
Buadu, Lawrence Danso physician, researcher
Buanes, Trond Arnulf surgeon, researcher
Buc, Milan medical educator, researcher
Buchan, John physician
Buchan, Ronald Forbes internal and preventive medicine physician
Buchner, Amos oral pathologist, educator and researcher
Buckingham, John Michael surgeon
Buckingham, Julia Clare pharmacology educator
Buckler, John Michael retired medical educator
Bucknall, Clifford Adrian cardiologist
Bucove, Arnold David psychiatrist
Bucsky, Peter Pal pediatrician
Budde, Thomas cardiologist, educator
Budo, Camille Jean Raymond ophthalmologist, researcher
Budoff, Penny Wise physician, author, researcher
Buhac, Ivo gastroenterologist
Bui, Huong Quoc neuropsychiatrist
Bukvic, Nenad physician, researcher, educator
Bulbulyan, Mariana Antonovna physician, researcher
Buligescu, Lucian E. D. gastroenterologist, hepatologist, educator
Bull, Matthew James radiologist
Bull, Peter Townley consultant anesthetist
Bullard, Rickey Howard podiatric physician, surgeon
Bult, Hidde pharmacologist
Bundred, Nigel James surgeon
Bunker, Timothy David orthopaedic surgeon
Büntzel, Jens physician, researcher, oncologist
Burdach, Stefan E.G. pediatrics educator
Burdett-Smith, Peter emergency physician
Burdick, Claude Owen pathologist
Burge, Peter Sherwood internist, consultant
Burgen, Sir Arnold pharmacologist
Burger, Henry George endocrinologist
Burgess, John Richard endocrinologist
Burioni, Roberto immunologist, virologist, medical educator
Burke, Frank Desmond orthopedic surgeon, educator
Burke, John Patrick internist, educator
Burke, Michael Desmond pathologist
Burke, Robert Harry surgeon, educator
Burlaka, Dmytro Petrovych experimental oncologist, researcher
Burmester, Gerd Rüdiger medical educator, physician
Burn, John Philip neurologist
Burrell, Joel Brion neurologist, researcher, clinician
Burris, Boyd Lee psychiatrist, psychoanalyst, physician, educator
Burroni, Luca nuclear medicine physician
Burroughs, Andrew Kenneth internist, hepatologist, consultant
Burstein, Stephen David neurosurgeon
Bursten, Stuart Lowell physician, biochemist
Burt, Alastair David medical researcher
Burt, Paul Alexander oncologist
Burton, John Lloyd dermatologist, author
Burton, Richard Irving orthopedist, educator
Burton, Robert Charles public health physician
Burwood, Richard John nuclear medicine physician
Busard, Hubertus Lambertus neuro-psychiatrist, consultant, researcher
Busch, Martin radio oncologist, consultant
Bush, Eugene Nyle pharmacologist, research scientist
Butler, Ann Benedict neuroscientist, educator
Butler, Ian John neurologist
Butler, Leslie White epidemiologist
Butler, Robert Moore, Jr. podiatrist
Butrous, Ghazwan S. cardiologist, researcher
Buvat, Jacques Alain endocrinologist
Büyükünal, Cenk S.N. pediatric surgeon, pediatric urologist, educator
Buzov, Ian physician
Buzunov, Vladimir Afanasiyevich epidemiologist, researcher
Byeff, Peter David hematologist, oncologist
Bynes, Frank Howard, Jr. physician
Byrd, Benjamin Franklin, Jr. surgeon, educator
Bystritsky, Alexander psychiatry educator
Cabrera-Gomez, Jose Antonio neurologist researcher
Cabrijan, Tomislav Viktor internist, endocrinologist, educator
Cabrol, Christian Emile cardiologist
Cachia, Adrian Ralston anatomical pathologist
Cacic, Mirjana surgical pathologist
Cadiet, Laurent psychiatrist, anthropology researcher
Caen, Jacques Philippe physician
Caetano, Raul psychiatrist, educator
Cahana, Alex anesthesiologist, pain specialist
Cahill, Kevin Michael physician, educator
Caixia, Tu dermatologist, educator
Calandri, Cesare hematologist
Calçado, Antonio Celso pediatric gastroenterology administrator, educator
Calda, Pavel obstetrician-gynecologist, consultant
Calderon, Moises cardiothoracic transplant surgeon
Calenda, Emile anesthesiologist
Calin, Andrei rheumatologist, consultant
Calkins, Evan physician, educator
Callahan, Alston physician, author
Callahan, Daniel Joseph surgeon, consultant
Callans, David John cardiologist
Callaway, Clifford Wayne physician
Calnan, Arthur Francis ophthalmologist
Calò, Pietro Giorgio surgeon, researcher, educator
Calore, Edenilson Eduardo physician, researcher
Calverley, Peter Martin Anthony respiratory physician
Calvo, Víctor José thoracic surgeon
Camacho, Luis Hernando oncologist
Cambon-Thomsen, Anne M. medical researcher
Cammisa, Frank P., Jr. surgeon, educator
Camner, Per Jonas Hilding environmental medicine educator
Campagnoli, Carlo endocrinologist, gynecologist
Campanelli, Giampiero surgeon
Campbell, Craig John podiatrist
Campbell, Eugene Paul physician, retired public health administrator
Campbell, Ian Garth medical educator
Campbell, John Richard pediatric surgeon
Campbell, Magda child psychiatrist, researcher, educator
Campbell, William Ian physician, consultant
Campos-Christo, Marcelo surgeon, educator
Campo Sien, Carlos nephrologist
CÀndea, Vasile cardiovascular surgeon
Capão-Filipe, João Artur ophthalmologist
Capasso, Giovanni orthopedic surgeon
Capella, Giovanni Luigi dermatologist
Caplan, Gideon A. physician, researcher
Cappa, Stefano Francesco neurologist, researcher
Cappato, Riccardo Paolo physician
Cappuccio, Francesco Paolo internist
Capron, André immunologist, researcher
Carabin, Hélène epidemiologist, veterinarian
Carapancea, Mihai Titus ophthalmologist
Cardenas, Juan Carlos plastic surgeon, educator
Cardia, Giuseppe surgeon
Cardoso, Elie Patrick physician, researcher, toxicologist
Carlsen, Karin Cecilie Lødrup pediatrician
Carlson, Lars Anders physician, educator
Carlsson, Per Arvid Emil pharmacologist, educator
Carmichael, Paul Louis ophthalmic surgeon
Carneiro, Antonio Vaz internist, medical educator
Carney, Andrew Simon surgeon
Carniol, Paul J. plastic and reconstructive surgeon, otolaryngologist
Caron, Murielle Hellsten physician, researcher
Carpenter, Paul Lynn cardiologist
Carpentier, R physician, astronomer
Carr, Daniel Barry anesthesiologist, endocrinologist, medical researcher
Carrasquilla, Gabriel epidemiology educator, provincial health official
Carratú, Romano gastroenterologist
Carrera, Jose psychiatrist, child psychiatrist, psychoanalyst
Carroll, Frank Edward radiologist, researcher
Carroll, William MacEwan neurologist, researcher
Carter, John Norman endocrinologist, educator
Carter, Paul Richard physician
Cartwright, Theodor T. medical association administrator
Caruso, Calogero immunopathologist
Caruso, Rosario Alberto pathologist, researcher
Carvell, John Edward trauma and orthopaedic surgeon, consultant
Casati, Andrea anesthesiologist, researcher
Case, David Bartlett internist, educator
Casscells, Samuel Ward, III cardiologist, educator
Cassel, John Michael plastic surgeon
Casselman, Jacques A. Eduard urologist
Cassisi, Nicholas John otolaryngologist, dean
Cassorla, Fernando Goluboff physician, pediatric endocrinologist, researcher
Castelain, Pierre-Yves retired dermatologist
Castiglioni, Paolo researcher
Castilla, Carlos Eduardo surgeon
Castro, Luiz Guilherme Martins dermatologist
Castro, Maria Graciela medical educator, gene therapy researcher
Castro, Rafael pediatrician, hospital administrator
Catalano, Louis William, Jr. neurologist
Catoe, Bette Lorrina physician, health educator
Catsky, Jiri plant physiologist, researcher
Catz, Amiram physiatrist
Causey, G(eorge) Donald medical educator
Causse, Jean-Bernard R.M. otologist, surgeon
Cavaillon, Jean-Marc immunology researcher, educator
Cavanagh, John Barr neuropathologist
Cawood, Charles David urologist
Cazaubon, Chichéle Caroline physician, editor
Cazzullo, Carlo Lorenzo psychiatrist
Čecchi, Mario vascular surgeon, consultant
Čech, Svatopluk embryologist, educator, researcher
Cecil, Linda Marie obstetrician/gynecologist
Cekic, Osman ophthalmology educator
Celik, Gulfem Elif allergist, researcher
Cénac, Arnaud Guy internist, educator
Cerna, Marie physician, immunogeneticist
Cerny, Joseph Charles urologist, educator
Cerri, Giovanni Guido radiologist, educator
Cesa, Michael Peter cardiologist, consultant
Cete, Mükerrem surgeon, health facility administrator
Cha, Se Do internist
Chabane, Mohammed Habib allergist, immunologist
Chahinian, A(ram) Philippe oncologist
Chahl, Loris Avril pharmacologist, educator
Chakravarty, Nirmal Kumar pharmacologist, educator
Chalam, Kakarla Venkata physician, educator
Chamberlain, John Loomis, III retired pediatrician, educator
Chambonet, Jean-Yves physician
Champion, Pierre Dheilly surgeon, researcher
Chamuleau, Robert Antoine François Marie internist, educator
Chan, Bernard Wan Bun transplant physician, biomedical consultant
Chan, Carlyle Hung-lun psychiatrist, educator
Chan, David Moon Cheung physician, educator
Chan, Donald Pin-Kwan orthopaedic surgeon, educator
Chan, Kiong Kong gynecological oncologist, consultant
Chan, Nor Norman physician
Chan, Wing-Chung pathologist, educator
Chance, Graham Wilfrid pediatrician, emeritus educator
Chandakas, Stefanos medical researcher, military officer
Chandran, Chitra consultant pediatrician
Chandrasekhar, Kulangarezhathu P. physician, consultant, cardiologist, educator
Chang, Anne Bernadette pediatrician
Chang, Baochong Bolin oncologist
Chang, Byung-Chul surgeon, educator
Chang, Cheng-Jen surgeon, researcher
Chang, Chih Jen family physician, educator
Chang, Chi-Sen gastroenterologist
Chang, Deh-Ming rheumatologist, immunologist, medical educator
Chang, Hang emergency physician
Chang, Paul Chee My neurologist
Chang, Rei-Yeuh cardiologist, hospital administrator
Chang, Shan-Chwen medical educator, researcher, physician
Chang, Shi-Chuan chest physician, researcher
Chang, Sung-Goo urological oncologist
Chang, Winshih orthopedic surgeon
Chang, Yun Sil pediatrician, researcher
Chao, Tsai Chung physician, residency program director
Chao, Tzu-Chieh surgeon, researcher
Chaouat, Ari physician
Chaouat, Didier physician, rheumatologist
Chapa, Elia Kay health administration educator
Chapireau, François Pierre psychiatrist
Chapman, Anthony Bradley psychiatrist
Chapman, David intensive care physician
Chapman, Jeremy Robert renal physician
Chapoval, Andrei immunologist
Charabi, Samih Ahmed otolaryngologist
Charachon, Robert Louis medical educator
Chari, Sreemathi endocrinologist, researcher
Charles, Mbala Lhemba pediatrician, researcher
Charmes, Jean-Pierre physician, researcher
Charmot, Guy Denis epidemiologist, retired health officer

Derossi, Arnaud *medical services company administrator, physician*
De Roy, Luc Joseph *cardiologist*
Desai, Tushar Nandlal *pathologist, health facility administrator*
de Sanctis, Nando *pediatric surgeon*
Deschamps, Frederic Jacques *occupational medicine physician*
De Schryver, Antoon Augusta *epidemiologist*
Dési, Illés *physician*
Desjeux, Jehan-François *pediatrician*
De Souza, José Maria *physician*
De Soza, Pierre *surgeon*
DesRochers, Gerard Camille *surgeon*
Destandau, Jean *neurosurgeon*
Deura, Shigeyuki *anatomy educator, researcher*
Deuschl, Guenther *neurologist, educator, researcher*
Deutsch, Alexander Aaron *surgeon*
Deutsch, Andre *physician*
De Valk, Harold Wessel *internist*
Devane, Peter Andrew *orthopaedic surgeon, educator*
Devichenskii, Vyacheslav Mikhailovich *physician, biochemist*
De Villiers, François Pierre-Rousseau *pediatrician, educator, researcher*
DeVita, Marie N. *physician*
DeVita, Vincent Theodore, Jr. *oncologist*
Dexeus, Santiago *obstetrician-gynecologist*
Dexter, James Riley *internist, critical care specialist*
Dey, Radheshyam Chandra *cytologist*
Dhaliwal, Rajinder Singh *surgeon, educator*
Dhall, Dharam Pal *retired surgeon, consultant*
Dhande, Prakash Laxman *anatomy educator*
Dhar, Gauranga Chandra *tropical medicine physician*
Dhar, Sandipan *dermatologist, consultant*
Dhara, Venkata Ramana *physician, educator*
Dhong, Hun Jong *otolaryngologist*
Dhont, Marc *gynecologist*
Dhuley, Jayant Nilkanth *pharmacologist*
Diakomanolis, Yvonne Helen Claire *endocrinologist*
Diament, Aron Judka *pediatric neurologist*
Diamond, Gary Warren *physician, pediatrician*
Dianzani, Mario Umberto *pathology educator*
Diaz, Fernando *internist*
Diaz-Franco, Carlos *surgeon, anatomist, anesthesiologist*
DiBenedetto, Robert Lawrence *obstetrician, gynecologist, insurance company executive*
Di Cataldo, Andrea *pediatric oncologist, researcher*
Dick, Hans Burkhard *ophthalmologist*
Dickes, Robert *psychiatrist*
Dickey, William *gasteroenterologist*
Dieckmann, Klaus Peter *urologist, educator*
Diehl, Karl Friedrich *urologist*
Dienstbier, Zdeněk Josef *physician*
Dieter, Robert Sean *physician*
Dieterich, Klaus Dieter *molecular biologist, educator, writer*
Dietzfelbinger, Hermann *hematologist, oncologist*
Di Gesu, Giuseppe *surgery educator*
Digiesi, Vincenzo *internist, educator*
Dignani, Maria Cecilia *physician*
Di Guardo, Giovanni *veterinary pathologist*
Dillard, Robert Perkins *pediatrician, educator*
Dille, John Robert *physician*
Dimaano, Rowenda Dumlao *pediatrician, consultant*
Dimancescu, Mihai D. *neurosurgeon, researcher, educator*
DiMartino-Nardi, Joan *pediatric endocrinologist, educator*
Dimasi, Linda Grace *epidemiologist*
Dimsdale, Joel Edward *psychiatry educator*
Dinca, Petruta Luminita *physician, researcher*
Diner, Patrick Antoine *plastic surgeon*
Ding, Hueisch-Jy *radiologist, researcher*
Dinh, Tung Van *obstetrician, gynecologist, pathologist, educator*
Dinsmore, Wilbert Wallace *physician, consultant*
di Paola, Guillermo Rogelio *gynecologist*
Dirks, Kenneth Ray *pathologist, medical educator, army officer*
Dissen, Erik *immunologist, physician*
Distler, Wolfgang *obstetrician-gynecologist*
Divall, Paul William *psychiatrist, consultant*
Dixit, Udayan Madhukar *ophthalmic surgeon*
Dixit, Vijay K. *plastic surgeon*
Dixon, Shirley Lee *emergency physician*
Djapardy, Stefen Sutedjo *gynecologist, oncologist*
Djordjis, Farid *physician*
Dmitrieva, Natalia Vladimirovna *physician, researcher*
Dmochowski, Jan Rafal *surgeon, researcher*
Dmowski, W. Paul *obstetrician, gynecologist, endocrinologist, researcher*
Doartero, Carlos Maria *ophthalmologist*
Dobes, William Lamar, Jr. *dermatologist*
Dobrjakova, Olga Borisovna *plastic surgeon*
Dobrocky, Ivan *radiologist*
Döbrönte, Zoltán *gastroenterologist*
Dobrowolska, Ewa *surgeon, pediatrician*
Dobrusin, Michael *physician*
Dobrydnjov, Igor Leonti *anesthesiologist*
Do Carmo, Isabel *physician*
Dockhorn, Robert John *physician, educator*
Doczi, Tamas Peter *neurosurgery educator*
Doebbeling, Bradley N. *physician, epidemiologist*
Doehn, Christian *urologist, researcher*
Doehring, Ekkehard *medical association administrator, pediatrician*
Doershuk, Carl Frederick *physician, pediatrics educator*
Doery, James Clifford Gowar *pathologist, researcher*
Doganci, Levent *physician, career officer*
Dogra, Jaideep *physician*
Doherty, Peter Charles *immunologist*
Dohmen, Kazufumi *physician, educator*
Doi, Toshio *nephrologist*
Doig, Stephen Grant *orthopedist*
Dökmeci, Fulya *obstetrician-gynecologist, educator*
Dolan, James Patrick *surgeon*
Doll, Jacques Louis *physician*
Domanin, Andrei Alexandrovich *pathologist*
Domingo, Christian *physician, researcher*
Domingo, Faustino Teopaco *neurosurgeon*
Dominguez Ortega, Luis *medical educator, health facility administrator*
Dominiczak, Anna F. *medical educator*
Donaldson, David *pathologist*
Donaldson, Iain Malcolm Lane *physiologist, educator, researcher*
Donaldson, Sarah Susan *radiologist*
Donath, Tibor *anatomist*
Donati, Robert Mario *physician, educational administrator*
Donato, Rosario Francesco *neurologist, educator*
Donauer, Erich *neurosurgeon*
Donelan, Peter Andrew *dermatologist*
Donnan, Geoffrey Alan *neurology educator, researcher*
Donohugh, Donald Lee *physician*
Donovan, Christopher Ferrier *physician*
Doppalapudi, Samba Murthy *surgeon, educator*
Dor, Xavier Marie *medical researcher*
D'Orbán, Paul Theodore *psychiatrist*
Dorf, Guy Samy *physician, educator, consultant*
Dorfmann, Henri *physician*
Dörner, Gerd Günter *medical educator, researcher*
Dornfeld, Sylvia *radiologist*
Dornfest, Burton Saul *anatomy educator*
Dorsch, Nicholas William Caspar *neurosurgeon, educator, researcher*
Dorsch, Walter Janos M. *allergologist, pediatrician, researcher*
Dorta-Contreras, Alberto Juan *neuroimmunologist*
Dorward, Neil Lawrence *neurosurgeon, educator*
dos Anjos, Mario Negreiros *endocrinologist*
Dose, Matthias *medical director*
Dosios, Theodosios *thoracic surgeon*
Doss, Mirko *cardiac surgeon*
Doubleday, Charles William *dermatologist, educator*
Dougherty, James *orthopedic surgeon, educator, author*
Doughty, Robert Neil *cardiologist*
Douglas, James Frederick *nephrologist*
Douglas, Robert Matheson *medical educator, program director*
Doumas, Athanasios Apostolos *plastic surgeon*
Dourmishev, Assen Lyubenov *dermatologist, researcher*
Douzenis, Athanassios *psychiatrist*
Dowse, Gary Kenneth *medical epidemiologist*
Dowson, Jonathan Hudson *psychiatrist, educator*
Doyle, Anthony James *radiologist*
Doyle, Patrick James *pharmacologist*
Dracker, Robert Albert *physician*
Draganova, Nadejda Ivanova *physician, educator*
Drago, Joseph Rosario *urologist, educator*
Dragoljub, Kocić Aleksandar *physician, administrator*
Dratcu, Luiz *psychiatrist, psychopharmacologist, consultant, educator*
Draur, Ronald Alvin *retired cardiologist*
Dreinhöfer, Karsten Eberhard *orthopedic surgeon, educator, researcher, health economist*
Drenhaus, Ulrich Karl Gustav *anatomist, researcher*
Drepaul, Loris Omesh *internist, infectious diseases physician*
Drew, Jeanette Helen *medical scientist researcher*
Drewes, Asbjørn Mohr *internist, gastroenterologist*
Drolshagen, Leo Francis, III *radiologist, physician*
Dryjski, Maciej Lukasz *vascular surgeon, educator*
Drzezga, Alexander Eduard *nuclear medicine physician*
Dubernard, Jean-Michel *surgeon, educator*
Dubray, Bernard Maurice *radiation oncologist*
Du Buske, Lawrence M. *immunologist, allergist, rheumotologist*
Ducassou, Dominique *medical educator, nuclear medicine physician*
Ducreux, Christian Pierre *neuroscientist, educator*
Dudczak, Robert Wilhelm *internist*
Dudley, Samuel Calvert *physician*
Dudley-Robey, Edward Giles *public health physician, television host*
Duffin, Anthony Cecil *podiatrist, researcher*
Dufour, Thierry François *neurosurgeon, consultant*
Duggan, John Malcolm *gastroenterologist*
Duguid, Jennifer Karen Mary *hematologist*
Dühmke, Eckhart *radiation oncology educator*
Duinslaeger, Luc André *surgeon*
Dulguerov, Pavel *otolaryngologist-head and neck surgeon, educator*
Duliček, Petr *hematologist*
Dumitrescu, Constantin P. *internist*
Dumontier, Christian Alain *physician, consultant*
Dumortier, Renaud *plastic surgeon*
Duncan, Iain Jeffrey *physician*
Duncan, Sheila Longmuir Black *retired gynecologist*
Dungan, John Russell, Jr. (Titular Viscount Dungan of Clane and Hereditary Prince of Ara) *anesthesiologist*
Dunlop, James Montgomery *physician, consultant*
Dunn, Floyd Emryl *psychiatrist, neurologist, consultant*
Dunn, Jeffrey Edward *neurologist*
Dunne, John Walter *neurologist*
Dunne, Regis Mary *bioethics professional*
Dunnill, Michael Giles Simpson *dermatologist*
Dunovsky, Jiří *pediatrician, educator*
Dupuy, Patrick Francis *dermatologist*
Duque, Alberto *physician, clinical pharmacologist*
Durand, Pierre-Yves *physician, nephrologist*
Durant, Blondelle Angelia *dermatologist, educator*
Durbano, Federico *psychiatrist, researcher*
Durca, Eric Marcel *physician for addictions*
Durlach, Jean Pierre *endocrinologist, researcher*
Durmusoglu, Fatih *obstetrician-gynecologist, educator*
Durosinmi, Muheez Alani *hematologist consultant*
Dušková, Markéta *plastic surgeon, consultant*
Dutcher, Janice Jean Phillips *oncologist*
Dutkiewicz, Tomasz *physician*
Duval, Elisabeth L.I.M. *pediatric intensivist*
Duvall, Charles Patton *retired internist, oncologist*
Dvorkin, Edward *physician*
Dweik, Raed A. *physician, researcher*
Dwyer, John Michael *medical educator, medical administrator*
Dwyer, Richard Peter *physician*
Dy, Francisco Justiniano *public health consultant*
Dyauli, David Philipo *pediatrician*
Dyck, George *psychiatry educator*
Dyr, Wanda Stanislawa *biomedical researcher*
Dziewanowska, Zofia Elizabeth *neuropsychiatrist, pharmaceutical executive, researcher, educator*
Dzul, Paul J. *physician, medical journal editor*
Dzyak, Georgy Viktorovich *internist, educator, university official*
Earlam, Richard John *surgeon, consultant*
Eastman, Joseph Rilus, III *pathologist*
Eaton, Gary David *physician*
Eaton, Richard Gillette *surgeon, educator*
Ebbels, Bruce Jeffery *physician, health facility administrator*
Ebel, Klaus Dietrich *pediatric radiologist*
Ebenezer, Ivor Shadrack *neuropharmacology educator*
Eberhard, Goran U.O. *psychiatry educator*
Ebisu, Toshihiko *neurosurgeon, neuroscientist*
Ebrí, Bernardo Torné *physician, researcher*
Eckert, Anne *neuroscientist, researcher*
Eckstein, Karl Ludwig *anesthesiologist*
Economopoulos, George Christos *cardiothoracic surgeon*
Eden, Alvin Noam *pediatrician, author*
Eden, Osborn Bryan *pediatric oncology educator*
Edgar, Michael Alan *orthopaedic and spinal surgeon*
Edge, William E. Basil *retired pediatrician*
Edis, Anthony John *surgeon*
Edis, Gloria Toby *pediatrician*
Edmondson, Stephen John *cardiothoracic surgeon, consultant*
Edrees, Burhan Mohammed *pediatric nephrologist, consultant, researcher*
Edston, Erik Hampus *medical examiner, consultant*
Eduard, Serban *physician, researcher*
Edwards, Huw *psychiatrist, consultant*
Edwards, Janice G. *medical educator*
Edwards, Larry David *internist, educator*
Edwards, Samuel Roger *internist*
Eeles, Rosalind Anne *oncology consultant*
Efremidis, Anna Papastavrou *oncologist, hematologist, educator*
Efthimiou, John *physician, researcher*
Efthymiou-Vernadet, Marie-Louise *occupational medicine physician*
Egerton, Charles Pickford *anatomy and physiology educator*
Eggert-Kruse, Waltraud *physician*
Ehinger, Berndt Erik Johannes *ophthalmology educator*
Ehrengut, Wolfgang Franz *pediatrician, immunologist*
Ehrenpreis, Eli Daniel *physician, educator, biomedical researcher*
Ehrlich, Frederick *surgery consultant, orthopedist, rehabilitation specialist*
Ehrnst, Anneka Cecilia *immunologist, virologist*
Eichenbaum, Joseph Walter *ophthalmologist*
Eickelberg, Oliver *physician*
Eid, Zeina *physician, researcher*
Eid Antoun, Zeina *research physician*
Eidelhoch, Lester Philip *physician, educator, surgeon*
Eidelman, Arthur Isaac *pediatrician, neonatologist*
Eidsvold, Gary Mason *physician, public health officer, medical educator*
Eikelenboom, Pieter *psychiatrist, researcher*
Ein, Daniel *allergist*
Einarsson, Gisli *physiatrist, educator*
Einarsson, Gudmundur Vikar *urologist, educator*
Einhorn, Nina *gynecologic oncologist*
Eis, Sergio Ragi *orthopedic surgeon*
Eiselt, Michael *pathophysiologist, researcher*
Eisenmann-Klein, Marita *plastic surgeon*
Eiser, Arnold Robert *internist, bioethicist*
Ejercito, Napoleon Campos *otolaryngologist*
Ejzenberg, Bernardo *pediatrician, educator, researcher*
Ekbom, Karl Edvard *neurologist*
Ekdahl, Karl Gustaf *medical officer, educator*
Eke-Okoro, Sunday Theophilus *medical educator*
Ekici, Synan *physician*
Ekman, Gunnar Ernst Åke *psychiatrist*
El-ahl, Mohammad Hamza *pediatrician, educator*
El Bahri, Lotfi *pharmacologist, toxicologist, researcher*
Elbaz, Jean Sauveur *plastic and aesthetic surgeon*
El-Bedeiwy, Abd-El-Fattah Ahmed *pathology educator, consultant*
Elbein, Alan David *medical science educator*
Elbers, Armin Rudolf Wilfred *epidemiologist, educator*
El Bushra, Hassan El Mahdi *epidemiology, research scientist*
El Danaf, Ahmed Abdel-Hady *plastic surgeon*
Elder, Murdoch George *obstetrician, gynecologist, educator*
Eldrup, Ebbe *physician*
El Ebiary, Mustafa *physician, researcher*
Elenius, Valter Anton *retired ophthalmology educator*
Elequin, Cleto, Jr. *retired physician*
Eleraky, Mohammed Aly *neurosurgeon*
El Gharbawi, Mohamed Ahmed *consulting surgeon, physician, educator, poet*
Elguindy, Mohamed Sayed *medical educator, cardiologist, consultant*
El Hassan, Elhassan Sidahmed *consultant physician*
El Hemaly, Abdel Karim Mohamad Aly Ahmad *obstetrician, gynecologist, educator*
Elian, Marta *neurologist, medical counsellor*
Elibol, Orhan *ophthalmic surgeon*
Elibol, Tarik *gastroenterologist*
Elidan, Josef *otolaryngologist, educator*
Elleder, Milan *pathologist, educator*
Ellestad, Myrvin Harold *cardiologist*
Elliott, Virginia F. Harrison *retired anatomist, kinesiologist and educator, investment advisor, publisher, philanthropist*
Ellis, Brian William *surgeon*
Ellis, Eldon Eugene *surgeon*
Ellis, Frank *radiotherapeutic oncologist*
Ellis, Stephen Geoffrey *medical educator, physician*
Elma, Bayani Borja *physician*
El Malik, El Fadil Mohamed Ali *physician, surgeon, educator, consultant*
El Matri, Mohamed Aziz *medical educator*
El Miedany, Yasser Mahrous *rheumatologist, consultant*
El Molahez, Hegazi Hussein *plastic surgeon, consultant*
El-Naggar, Mostafa Mohammed *anatomy educator, researcher, clinician*
El Nahas, Abdel Meguid *nephrology*
Elperin, Louis Solomon *physician*
El Ridi, Rashika Ahmed Fathi *immunology educator, researcher*
El-Rufaie, Omer El-Farouk Ahmed *psychiatry educator, consultant*
El-Sebaie, Hisham Ismail *surgeon*
El Shakankiry, Hanan Mostafa *pediatrics educator, consultant*
El Shaker, Mohammed Mohammed Amin *physician, orthopedic surgeon*
El-Shanti, Hatem Isam *pediatric geneticist*
El-Shazly, Amr Essam *otolaryngologist, researcher*
Elsorougi, Mohamed Kamal Eldine *medical educator, pneumologist, physiologist*
Elte, Jan Willem Frederik *internist*
Eluf-Neto, José *physician, researcher*
Elwood, J. Mark *epidemiologist, researcher*
Ely, Scott Adams *heamtopathologist, researcher*
Emanuelsson, Hakan U. *cardiologist, researcher*
Embry, Ronald Lee *physician, diagnostic radiologist*
Emerson, Peter Albert *physician, consultant*
Emme, Stefan Peter *dermatologist*
Emmerson, Bryan Thomas *physician, educator*
Emmett, Michael *physician*
Emrich, Hinderk Meiners *neurologist, psychiatrist, educator*
Enarson, Donald Arthur *internist, educator*
Enchev, Ventzeslav Georgiev *pathologist, cytologist, researcher*
Endo, Norio *physician, educator*
Endoh, Ryohei *cardiologist*
Endres, Matthias *neurologist*
Enescu, Dan Mircea *physician*
Eng, Charis Eu Li *oncologist, geneticist*
Engel, William King *neurologist, educator*
Engelberg, Hyman *internist, researcher*
Engelhardt, Hugo Tristram, Jr. *physician, educator*
Engelmann, Uwe *medical informatics scientist, consultant*
Engqvist, Alice Birgitta *internist, gastroenterologist*
Engstrand, Beatrice C. *neurologist, educator*
Enriquez, Cristino Catud *radiologist, internist, cardiologist*
Enriquez, Juan Cabot *researcher*
Ensenat, Louis Albert *surgeon*
Epler, Gary Robert *physician, author, educator*
Epstein, Murray *medical educator*
Epstein, William Louis *dermatologist, educator*
Eraković, Vesna *pharmacologist, researcher*
Erb, Peter A. L. *immunology professor, researcher*
Erbsloeh, Joachim *retired obstetrician/gynecologist, educator*
Erceg, Damir *pharmacologist*
Erdem, Atilla *neurosurgeon, educator*
Erdmann, Christine Anne *epidemiologist*
Erdö, Sándor Lajos *pharmacologist*
Eregie, Charles Osatande *pediatrician, consultant*
Ergin, M.T. *physician and surgeon*
Ericson, Ruth Ann *psychiatrist*
Eriksen, Erik Fink *endocrinologist, osteoporosis researcher*
Eriksen, Poul Sindberg *medical consultant*
Erikson, G(eorge) E(mil) (Erik Erikson) *anatomist, archivist, historian, educator, information specialist*
Erikson, Uno Eugen *diagnostic radiology educator, dean*
Eriksson, Sven-Erik *neurologist*
Ermert, Leander *pathologist*
Erni, Dominique *plastic surgeon*
Ernst, Edzard *medical educator*
Ernst, Olivier Jean *radiologist*
Erntell, Mats Thore Henning *physician, consultant*
Ertl, Doris Elisabeth *anesthesiologist*
Erve, Ruud H.G.P. van *orthopaedic surgeon*
Erwin, Goodloe Y. *physician, land company executive*
Escaf, Safwan J. *surgery educator, urology educator*
Esche, Clemens *dermatologist, immunologist*
Escher, Robert F.A. *hematologist, researcher*
Eshagian, Joseph *ophthalmologist*
Ésik, Olga *radiation oncologist*
Espaldon, Ernesto Mercader *plastic surgeon, former senator*
Espar, William George *interventional cardiologist*
Espinola-Zavaleta, Nilda Gladys *cardiologist*
Esquenazi, Salomon *ophthalmologist*
Esquibel, Edward V. *psychiatrist, clinical medical program developer*
Esser, James Mark *cardiovascular and interventional radiologist*
Esterhai, John Louis, Jr. *surgeon, medical educator*
Estes, Nathan Anthony Mark, III *cardiologist, medical educator*
Eteng, Eno Ebri *psychiatrist*
Etkind, Paul *epidemiologist, health facility administrator*
Ettl, Armin *ophthalmologist, plastic eye surgeon*
Eu, Kong-Weng *consultant surgeon*
Eulderink, Frits *pathologist*
Evangelou, Grigorios Nikolaos *surgeon*
Evans, Andrew Lloyd *pediatrician*
Evans, David Alan Price *physician*
Evans, Mark Russell *physician, researcher*
Evans, Paul *osteopath*
Evdokimov, Valeri *andrologist, researcher*
Evett, Russell Dougherty *internist, educator*
Evrard, Sergio Gustavo *physician, psychiatrist, consultant*
Exergian, Florin Eduard *physician, surgeon, researcher*
Eybl, Vladislav *pharmacologist*
Eyden, Brian Philip *tumor diagnostician, medical researcher*
Eyskens, Erik Joannes *surgeon, educator*
Ezcurra, Maria Cristina *physician, researcher*
Eze, Friday Chinyere *gynecologist*
Ézsiás, András *consultant maxillofacial surgeon*
Faber, Josef Ivan *neurologist*
Fabinyi, Gavin Christopher Andrew *neurological surgeon*
Fabre, Serge Jean *physician*
Fabri, Peter Jeffrey *surgeon, educator*
Fachet, József *immunologist, pathophysiologist, educator*
Fadul, Jamal Makki *physician, nephrologist*
Fagan, Frederic *neurosurgeon*
Fagerström, Ritva Kyllikki *psychiatrist, psychotherapist, psychologist, researcher*
Fahed, Charbel Dawood *ophthalmologist*
Fahim, Ayman Ekram *physician, medical educator, researcher*
Fahimi, H. Dariush *medical educator, pathologist*
Fair, Alan Derek *physician*
Fajardo, Romeo Velasco *ophthalmologist, educator*
Falaschi, Paolo *internist, educator*
Falcone, Robert Edward *surgeon*
Falk, Robert Barclay, Jr. *anesthesiologist, educator*
Falkmer, Ursula Gerda *oncology educator, physician*
Faller, József *surgeon, gastroenterologist, educator*
Famà, Francesco *ophthalmologist, researcher*
Familusi, Julius Babashola *pediatrics educator, pediatric neurology consultant*
Fan, Yong-kang *surgeon, educator*
Fandino, Javier *physician*
Fang, Ji-Qian *medical statistics educator*
Fanos, Kathleen Hilaire *osteopathic physician, podiatrist*
Fanta, Jan *surgeon*
Fanti, Stefano *nuclear medicine physician*
Farah, Fuad Salim *dermatologist*
Farber, George Allan *dermatologist*
Farghali, Hassan *pharmacologist, administrator, educator*
Fariña, Juliana *pathologist*
Farkas, Attila *cardiologist*
Farkas, Gyula *surgeon, educator*
Farkas, Henriette *physician, researcher*
Farkas, Maria Margit *physician, educator*
Farkas, Michael Laszlo *plastic and reconstructive surgeon*
Farnsworth, Bruce Norman *obstetrician/gynecologist*
Farren, Conor Kevin *psychiatry educator, researcher*
Faruqui, Azhar Masood A. *cardiologist, educator*

Godeberge, Philippe Dominique gastroenterologist, proctologist, consultant
Godfraind, Theophile Joseph pharmacologist, educator
Godin, Christine physician
Godot, Thierry psychiatrist, consultant
Godoy, Arnaldo José clinical neurologist, educator
Godukhin, Oleg Viktorovitch neuroscientist, researcher
Goel, Atul neurosurgeon, educator, consultant
Goerttler, Klaus Juergen pathologist, researcher
Goff, Christopher Wallick pediatrician
Gögen, Sedat physician, consultant
Goilav, Béatrice Sarah physician, educator
Goin, Michel physician
Goktay, Ahmet Yigit radiologist
Golabek, Wieslaw surgeon
Golan, David Eric biophysicist, pharmacologist, hematologist
Gold, Jeffrey Philip cardiothoracic surgeon
Gold, Mark Stephen psychopharmacologist, physician
Goldberg, David Bryan biomedical researcher
Goldberg, Ivan ophthalmologist, surgeon
Goldberg, Jorge internist
Goldberg, Martin physician, educator
Goldberg, Paul Bernard gastroenterologist, clinical researcher
Goldenberg, David physician, computer/internet consultant
Goldenberg, Solomon Maurice family physician
Goldfarb, C. Richard radiologist
Goldman, Ira Steven gastroenterologist
Goldman, John Michael physician, consultant hematologist, educator
Goldner, Bruce Gary physician
Goldschmidt, Ernst Walter Matthias ophthalmology educator, ophthalmic surgeon
Goldsmith, Lowell Alan medical educator
Goldsmith, Michael Allen oncologist, educator
Goldstein, David oncologist, educator
Goldstein, Jerome Eric emergency physician surgeon, lawyer
Goldstein, Joseph Leonard physician, medical educator, molecular genetics scientist
Goldwurm, Gian Franco psychiatrist, psychologist, psychotherapist
Golledge, Jonathan surgeon
Golomb, Jacob S. urologist
Golovchiner, Gregory cardiologist
Goltzman, David endocrinologist, educator, researcher
Golumbeck, Carl Timothy forensic psychiatrist
Golusin, Millard R. obstetrician and gynecologist
Gomes, Romeu public health educator
Gomez, Alberto biomedical researcher
Gomez, Gonzalo A. physician, consultant
Gomez-Arbesu, Jesus immunologist
Gonçalves, Elisabeto Ribeiro physician, ophthalmology educator
Goncharov, Nikolai P. endocrinologist
Gonnering, Russell Stephen ophthalmic plastic surgeon
Gontier, Jean Roger medicine and physiology educator
Gönül, Bilge physiologist, educator
González, Domingo neurosurgeon
Gonzalez, Ricardo surgeon, educator
Gonzalez-Echeverria, Francisco pediatrician, researcher
Gonzalez-Gonzalez, Jesus Maria dentist, stomatologist, researcher in medicine
Gonzalez-Guerra, Miguel Geronimo medical educator
Gonzalez-Mendoza, Jorge E. infectious diseases physician, consultant
Gonzalez-Scarano, Francisco Antonio neurologist, virologist
Good, Robert Alan physician, educator
Goodacre, Selwyn Hugh physician
Goodhue, William Walter, Jr. pathologist, military officer, medical educator
Goodman, Edmund Nathan surgeon, pain management consultant
Goodman, Kenneth Joel radiologist
Goodrich, Isaac neurosurgeon, educator
Goodwin, Andrew Wirt, II radiologist
Goodwin, Gregory R. family physician with obstetrics subspecialty
Goodwin, Jean McClung psychiatrist
Goodyer, Ian Michael psychiatrist
Goon, Anthony Teik Jin dermatologist
Gopalakrishnakone, Ponnampalam medical educator
Gorard, David A. gastroenterologist
Gordon, Neil Stuart Ian urologist
Gordon, Richard Douglas physician, clinical researcher
Gore, Donald Ray orthopedic surgeon
Górny, Rafal Longin medical educator, researcher
Gorodischer, Rafael pediatrician
Gorsky, Meir clinical oral pathologist
Gosain, Arun Kumar physician, surgeon
Goslings, Johan Carel surgeon
Goss, J.B. psychopharmacologist
Goswami, Ajanta psychiatrist
Gosztonyi, Georg neuropathologist, educator
Göthert, Manfred pharmacologist
Goto, Fumio anesthesiologist
Gotta, Alexander Walter anesthesiologist, educator
Gottlieb, Julius Judah podiatrist
Gottrup, Finn gastroenterologist, surgeon
Gottsauner-Wolf, Florian orthopaedic surgeon, educator
Gottschall, Carlos Antonio Mascia cardiologist, medical researcher
Gotzoyannis, Stavros Eleutherios cardiologist
Gøtzsche, Peter Christian internist, biologist
Gough, Ian Ronald surgeon
Gouiry, Pierre Louis anethesiologist
Gourlay, Steven Geoffrey physician, clinical pharmacologist, epidemiologist
Gouteux, Jean-Paul biomedical researcher
Gouveia-Oliveira, Antonio Manuel physician, researcher
Gouveris, John George internist, angiologist
Govoni, Antonio Fortunato radiologist
Gozali, Victor Kartika physician, surgeon, consultant
Gozes, Illana neuroscientist, educator
Gözübüyük, Irfan otorhinolaryngologist
Grabosch, Alfons plastic surgeon
Graessmann, Adolf physician, biomedical researcher
Graham, Alan Morrison surgeon
Graham, Albert Cecil pediatrician, consultant
Graham, Anna Regina pathologist, educator
Graham, James Herbert dermatologist
Grangier, Rene Maurice ophthalmologist
Granström, Gösta P.B. physician, researcher
Granzotti, João Antonio pediatrics educator
Grardel, Bruno Edward physician
Graudal, Niels Albert medical researcher
Gravett, Peter James hematologist, medical administrator
Gray, Denis Pereira physician, educator
Grechko, Alexander Timofeevich pharmacologist
Green, Lora Murray immunologist, researcher, educator
Green, Pnina physician
Green, Stephen J. cardiovascular surgeon
Greenaway, John Moore physician, consultant
Greenberg, Benjamin physician
Greenberg, William Michael psychiatrist
Greene, Hinda Marsha osteopath, educator
Greene, Karl Anthony neurosurgeon
Greengard, Paul neuroscientist
Greenhalgh, Roger Malcolm vascular surgeon, medical educator
Greenidge, Charles Woseley surgeon
Greer, Mack Varnedoe physician
Gregor, Pavel cardiologist
Gregory, John Michael urologist
Gregory-Roberts, John Charles ophthalmologist
Grenier, Bernard pediatrician, infectious disease consultant
Grénman, Reidar Axel otorhinolaryngologist, head and neck surgeon
Griebel, Guy psychopharmacologist, researcher
Grieg, Eduard Emillian physician
Griesinger, Frank physician
Griesser, Gerd Hans-Werner surgeon, educator, retired
Griez, Eric Jacques psychiatrist, medical educator
Griffin, John Parry clinical pharmacologist
Griffith, Robert Charles allergist, educator, planter
Griffiths, Robert Irwin neuromuscular physiologist, researcher
Grigoriadis, Nikolaos Christos neurologist, researcher
Grigoryev, Peter Yakovlevich gastroenterologist
Grill, Valdemar Erik endocrinologist, educator
Grimby, Gunnar Lars physician, researcher
Grinstein, Yury Isayevich physician
Grivna, Michal epidemiologist, educator, administrator
Groch, Mark Walter medical physicist
Grodzki, Tomasz surgeon
Groisman, Vitaliy physician
Grollman, Julius Harry, Jr. cardiovascular and interventional radiologist
Grönemeyer, Dietrich H.W. radiologist, medical educator
Gronouwe-Hiddink, Riet Hendrica Jacoba Maria cytologist, hematologist
Grönroos, Matti obstetrician/gynecologist, educator, retired
Grøntvedt, Torbjørn orthopaedic surgeon, educator
Gross, Johann physician, biochemist
Gross, Lillian psychiatrist
Gross, Peter Alan epidemiologist, researcher
Gross, Richard Childrey radiologist
Grossmann, Hans Henning dermatologist
Grossmann, Vojtech Eduard pharmacologist, toxicologist
Grósz, Andor ophthalmologist
Groundstroem, Kaj Walter Edvard cardiologist, consultant
Grove, Jeffrey Scott family practice physician
Groves, Sheridon Hale orthopedic surgeon
Gruber, Doris Maria obstetrician/gynecologist, educator
Gruber, Eva Maria physician
Gruber, Ronald P. plastic surgeon, researcher
Grubnik, Vladimir Vladimirovich surgeon
Grunberg, Robert Leon Willy nephrologist
Grundmann, David surgeon
Grunenwald, Dominique Henri thoracic surgeon
Gu, Niu-Fan psychiatrist, educator
Guanzon, Ricardo Sotelo physician, educator
Guardiola, Philippe physician, researcher
Guder, Walter Georg physician
Gudkov, Alexander Vladimirovich urologist
Gudmundson, Claes Richard physician, researcher
Gudmundsson, Sigurdur physician, medical director
Guelinckx, Paul Julien plastic surgery educator
Guembel, Hermann Oskar Cornelius surgeon
Guerin, Christian Jean Marie ophthalmologist
Guerin, Daniel François ophthalmologist, surgeon
Guéritée, Nicolas endocrinologist
Guerrero-Igea, Francisco Javier physician, researcher
Guerrero-Romero, Jesus Fernando internist, researcher
Gueson, Emerita Torres obstetrician, gynecologist
Guffi, Michele Emilio Alfredo cardiothoracic surgeon, consultant
Guillausseau, Pierre Jean physician, educator
Guillermond, Gabriel Georges physician
Guillet, Jacques Andre physician, medical researcher
Guimaraes, Claudia Teixeira plant geneticist
Guimaraes, Rui Manuel cardiologist
Gulacsy, Istvan surgeon
Gulati, Kavita pharmacologist
Gulati, Sanjeev pediatric nephrologist
Güler, Erden pharmacy educator, consultant
Gulesen, Ozdemir medical educator
Gulubova, Maya Vladova pathologist, educator
Gulya, Ernö oncologist
Gümüsalan, Yakup anatomist
Gunalingam, Brinthapan Brendan cardiologist
Gunalp, Ilhan Riza ophthalmologist, educator
Gunczler, Peter pediatric endocrinologist
Gunderson, Steven Alan anesthesiologist
Gundlach, Karsten Kurt Helmuth maxillofacial surgery educator
Gündüz, Ahmet Kaan ophthalmologist
Gunduz, Mehmet otolaryngologist, cancer genetic researcher
Gunin, Andrei Germanovich reproductive endocrinologist
Gunn, Albert Edward, Jr. internist, educator, lawyer, administrator
Günther, Bruno Guillermo physiology educator
Guntinas Lichius, Orlando surgeon, otolaryngologist
Gupta, Braj Bansh Prasad endocrinology educator
Gupta, Nirmal gynecologist and obstetrician, educator
Gupta, Pratibha medical educator
Gupta, Ramesh Chandra medical educator, epidemiologist, researcher
Gupta, Rishab Kumar medical association administrator, educator, researcher
Gupta, Sanjay psychiatrist
Gupta, Sudhir immunologist, educator
Gupta, Vinod Kumar internist, researcher, ethicist
Gurland, Hans Juergen internist, nephrologist
Gurry, Desmond Leo pediatrician
Gurumurthy, Prema medical researcher
Gusdon, John Paul, Jr. obstetrics and gynecology educator, physician
Gustafson, Robert Allen pediatric cardiothoracic surgeon
Gusterson, Barry Austin pathologist
Guthrie, Randolph Hobson, Jr. plastic surgeon, consultant
Gutierrez-Carretero, Encarnacion cardiac surgeon, researcher
Gutierrez-Morlote, Jesús physician, cardiologist
Gutman, Haim surgical oncologist, researcher
Gutmann, Valentin physician
Gutowicz, Matthew Francis, Jr. radiologist
Guzman, Angel Esteban physician
Guzman, Miguel A. surgeon
Gyenes, Gábor physician
Győry, Ákos Zoltan medical educator
Hangody, Lászlo physician, orthopedic consultant, surgeon
Haas, Gilbert Alain physician
Haas, Robert Lance surgeon, consultant
Haase, Gerald Martin pediatric surgeon
Habib, Elias Edouard surgeon, researcher
Habib, Mir-Mohamed physician
Habib-Nassif, Anne-Marie internist
Hacker-Klom, Ursula Beate radiobiologist
Hackett, John Peter dermatologist
Hackl, Guido medical editor
Hackney, Jack Dean physician
Haddad, Menashe vascular surgeon
Hadden, Robert David Martin neurologist, researcher
Hadjiyannakis, Evagelos Yiannis surgeon
Hadzic, Nedim pediatric hepatologist, consultant
Haenen, Roger Edouard infection control practitioner
Hafeez, Zeba Hasan dermatologist
Hafner, Heinz psychiatrist, researcher
Hägg, Göran Mikael health science researcher
Haggerty, Arthur Daniel stress and chronic pain management specialist
Hagihara, Akihito epidemiologist, educator
Hagiwara, Keiji pediatrician
Hagmüller, Egbert surgeon
Haider, Zulfiqar physician, researcher, consultant
Hajivassiliou, Constantinos Argyrou pediatric surgeon, educator
Hakama, Matti Kaarlo epidemiologist, consultant, educator
Hakola, Hannu Panu Aukusti psychiatry educator
Halász, Béla anatomist, educator
Halasz, George psychiatrist, consultant
Halevy, Sima dermatologist
Hall, Bruce Milne physician, medical educator
Hall, Robert Joseph physician, medical educator
Hall, Timothy S. surgeon
Hallan, Stein Ivar internist, researcher
Hallberg, Leif Yngve Gustaf medical educator
Hallett, John William surgeon, educator, former career officer
Hallez, Jean Paul surgeon
Hallgrimsson, Jonas pathologist, educator
Halliday, Gary Mark immunology researcher
Halliday, William Ross retired physician, speleologist, writer
Hallworth, Robert Earl anesthesiologist
Halperin, Edward Charles physician
Halstensen, Trond Sundby immunology educator
Halvorsen, Fred-Arne internist, gastroenterologist, consultant
Halwig, J. Michael allergist
Hamakubo, Takao medical researcher
Hämäläinen, Mirja Liisa pediatric neurologist, researcher
Hamaoka, Takafumi preventive medicine educator
Hamar, Pèter physiologist, researcher
Hambye, Anne-Sophie Emmanuelle nuclear medicine physician
Hamdi, Anwar pharmacology educator
Hamed, Saab Khalil physician
Hameed, Kamran pulmonologist, consultant
Hamilton, Carlos Robert, Jr. internist, endocrinologist
Hamilton, Charles Richard oncologist
Hamlyn, Peter John neurosurgeon
Hammarström, Lars-Erik physician, consultant surgeon
Hammer, Terence Michael physician
Hammond, Charles Bessellieu obstetrician, gynecologist, educator
Hammond, Isaac William physician, epidemiologist
Hammond, Lisa A. oncologist, researcher
Hammond, Raymond William pharmacotherapy specialist
Hamori, Jozsef neuroscientist
Hamour, Abuobeida A. infectious diseases physician
Hampel, Klaus Erich retired gastroenterologist
Han, Buxin psychologist
Han, Huiwan physician, researcher, biochemist educator
Han, Rui pharmacologist
Han, Sehwan medical educator
Hanai, Fumihiko orthopedist
Handelsman, David Joshua endocrinologist, researcher
Handzel, Zeev Theodor immunologist, allergist
Haneke, Eckart dermatologist
Haninec, Pavel neurosurgeon, researcher, educator
Hanke, Hartmut physician
Hanna, Adel Shafik dermatologist, venereologist, consultant
Hannay, David Rainsford general practice physician, educator
Hannequin, Pascal Paul physician
Hansdottir, Helga geriatrician
Hanselaar, Antonius G.J.M. pathologist
Hansen, Hanne Sand radiotherapist, consultant, oncologist
Hansen-Flaschen, John Hyman medical educator, researcher
Hanson, Gerald Eugene oral and maxillofacial surgeon
Hansson, Carita G. dermatologist, educator, consultant
Hansson, Lars Magnus Nils physician
Hantschmann, Peer medical educator
Hanuš, Tomáš urologist, consultant
Hanuschak, Lee Nicholas physician
Harada, Teruichi medical educator
Harahap, Rustam Effendi gynecologist
Haraldsson, Per-olle physician
Harat, Marek neurosurgeon, researcher
Hardicsay, Gabor physician
Hardman, George Lynn psychiatrist
Hardy, John Denis paediatrician consultant
Harleman, Johannes Hendrikus experimental pathologist
Harlow, Timothy Neal physician
Harney, Jean Lenore physician
Haroun, Eltahir Mohamed veterinary pathology educator, researcher
Harries, Anthony David physician, consultant
Harris, Jeffrey Saul physician, executive, consultant
Harris, Matthew Nathan surgeon, educator
Harris, Pamela Sue rehabilitation physician
Harris, Rachel Louise therapeutic radiographer, researcher
Harrison, James Wilburn gynecologist
Harrison, Leonard Charles medical educator, researcher
Hart, Paul Vincent, Jr. emergency and family medicine physician, inventor
Hartmann-Johnsen, Olaf Johan internist
Hartnell, George Gordon radiologist
Harvey, John Collins physician, educator
Harvey, Peter Marshall podiatrist
Hasanoglu, Alper physician, physiologist
Hasegawa, Yukihiro physician
Hashida, Mitsuru pharmaceutical sciences educator
Hashimoto, Daijo surgeon, physician
Hashimoto, Paulo Hitonari anatomy educator, physician
Hashiro, Makoto dermatologist, psychodermatologist
Hashizume, Makoto surgeon
Hashmi, Farrukh Siyar psychiatrist
Haslegrave, Marianne medical association administrator
Haspl, Miroslav orthopedic surgeon
Hassan, Ezzeldin Osman obstetrics/gynecology educator
Hassan, Wajahat Ul rheumatologist, consultant
Hassanain, Ahmed Hany Abdel Hamid Kamal environmental chest physician, educator, consultant, researcher
Hately, William retired radiology consultant
Hatlevoll, Reidulv oncologist
Hattenbach, Lars Olof ophthalmologist, researcher
Hauber, Frederick August ophthalmologist
Hausser, Dominique public health physician
Haustgen, Thierry René Camille psychiatrist
Haverkos, Harry William epidemiologist
Havu, Niilo pathologist
Hawkins, David Ramon psychiatrist, writer, researcher
Hawkins, David Rollo, Sr. psychiatrist
Hay, David Russell retired cardiologist
Hay, Elizabeth Dexter embryology researcher, educator
Hayashida, Motoi psychiatrist, educator
Haycock, Christine Elizabeth medical educator emeritus, health educator
Haydon, John Ralph physician, retired military officer
Hayez, Jean-Yves child and adolescent psychiatrist, psychologist
Hazard, Jean endocrinologist, educator
He, Guo-Wei medical educator, cardiovascular scientist/surgeon
He, Lin dermatologist, medical educator, researcher
He, Shangkuan anatomist, educator
He, Xiao Yan Clara scientist, physician
Healey, Tim retired radiologist
Hebebrand, Johannes psychiatrist, geneticist
Hedley-Whyte, John anesthesiologist, educator
Hedrick, Marc Hamilton plastic surgeon
Heggie, Andrew Alistair Cromie surgeon
Heick, Alex physician, neurologist
Heidendal, Guido Alfons nuclear medicine physician
Heimburger, Irvin LeRoy retired surgeon
Heinemann, Lothar Alfred epidemiologist
Heininger, Ulrich Franz pediatrician, researcher
Heinle, Robert Alan physician
Heinz, Andreas psychiatrist, neurologist
Heiss, Markus Maria surgeon, educator, researcher
Heissmeyer, Hannes Hinrich physician
Heistaro, Sami Mikael medical researcher
Hejazi, Nedal Abdallah physician, consultant
Helander, Herbert D.F. anatomist
Helgason, Pall Bergsson physician
Hellsing, Anna-Lisa ergonomist
Hemachudha, Thiravat neurologist, educator
Hemmila, Heikki Matias physician, researcher
Hempel-Jørgensen, Anne medical researcher
Hendricks, Leonard D. emergency medicine physician, consultant
Hendrickse, Ralph George medical educator
Hendrikse, Frederik ophthalmologist, educator
Hendry, Jean Sharon psychopharmacologist
Heng, Lee-Kwang opthalmologist
Hengartner, Hans immunologist, educator
Hengeveld, Michiel Willem psychiatrist
Henneberg, Alexandra Ehrengard neuropsychiatrist, neuroimmunologist
Hennessey, William Joseph physician
Henriksen, Jens Henrik physician, educator, scientist
Henrotin, Yves Edgard medical educator
Henschke, Claudia Ingrid physician, radiologist
Hensel, Andreas pharmacist
Henter, Jan-Inge pediatrician
Herault, Yann embryologist, researcher
Herber, Steven Carlton physician
Herdson, Peter Barrie forensic pathologist, educator
Herman, Mary Margaret neuropathologist
Herman, Miroslav radiologist, educator
Hermann, Robert Ewald surgeon
Hermans, Johannes Jozef Robertus pharmacology researcher
Hermsteiner, Markus Gerard Josef obstetrician-gynecologist, researcher
Hernandez, Ramon Pomes physics educator
Hernandez-Ilescas, Juan Homero epidemiologist, educator
Herndon, James Henry orthopedic surgeon, educator
Herrera-Llerandi, Rodolfo Eduardo surgeon, educator
Herrerias, Carla Trevette epidemiologist, health policy analyst
Herrmann, Guenter surgeon
Herrmann, Karlheinz Siegfried cardiologist
Hershey, Linda Ann neurology and pharmacology educator
Hertzberg, Henry radiologist, educator
Hertzog, James Henry pediatrician, educator
Hertz Picciotto, I. epidemiologist, educator
Herxheimer, Andrew clinical pharmacologist
Heshiki, Atsuko S. physician
Hess, Darla Bakersmith cardiologist, educator
Hess, Jürgen immunologist
Hess, Walter Otto surgeon
Hesse, Volker pediatrician
Hewes, Robert Charles radiologist
Hewitson, William Craig physician, career officer
Heyd, Bruno surgeon
Heywang-Koebrunner, Sylvia H. radiologist, educator
Hickish, Gordon Walter physician

Jordan, Ruth Ann physician
Jorga, Karin Monika pharmacologist, researcher
Jorgensen, Peter Leth physiologist, physician, researcher
Josefsson, Göran Erik orthopedic surgeon, administrator
Joseph, Christopher Arthur ear, nose, and throat surgeon
Joseph, Thangam pharmacology educator
Joshi, Girish Premji anesthesiologist
Jósvay, János plastic surgeon, consultant
Joura, Elmar Armin gynecologist
Jousilahti, Pekka Juhani medical researcher
Joye, Frederic emergency medicine physician, researcher
Juarez Olguin, Hugo pharmaceutics educator
Judge, Rajinder psychiatrist
Judkins, Keith Charles anesthetist
Juhan-Vague, Irene Suzanne hematologist, educator, biologist
Juhl, Magne orthopedic surgeon, consultant
Juncos, Luis Isaias internal medicine educator
Jung, Hai Ryun ophthalmologist, educator
Jung, Jean-Luc surgeon
Jung, Roland Tadeusz physician
Jurczyszyn, Artur Jan hematologist
Jurkowski, Marek Kajetan neuroimmunologist, educator
Jurukova, Zanka Borissova pathologist, educator
Juzwa, Witold Julian medical educator
Kaasik, Ain Elmar neurology educator
Kabane, Sipho general medical practitioner, business consultant
Kabir, Shahjahan immunologist, biomedical researcher, consultant
Kad, Surinder Kumar physician, educator, researcher
Kádár, Anna pathologist, educator
Kadar, Avraham immunologist
Kader, Howard Aaron pediatrician
Kadota, Eiji pathologist, researcher
Kadota, Koichi pathologist, veterinarian
Kaelin, William George, Jr. physician, oncologist
Kaesemeyer, Wayne Harry internist, hypertension specialist
Kagawa, Sohei internist, anesthesiologist
Kähärä, Veikko Johannes physician, researcher
Kahn, Fredrick Henry internist
Kahn, Marc Leslie orthopedic surgeon
Kai, Tatsuya cardiologist
Kail, Konrad physician
Kainberger, Franz M. radiologist, researcher
Kainz, Christian physician, educator
Kaiser, Werner Alois radiology educator
Kajanti, Mikael Johannes radiotherapy and oncology specialist
Kajino, Akihide orthopedist
Kajiwara, Kagemasa neuroscientist, researcher
Kakar, Daisy Adarsh nutrition educator, consultant
Kakigi, Akinobu otolaryngologist, researcher
Kakizoe, Saburo surgeon
Kakosy, Tibor physician, consultant
Kakourou, Talia Tsivitanidou pediatric dermatologist
Kakuda, Naoyuki neurologist
Kala, Miroslav Michael neurosurgeon
Kalavrouziotis, Georgios cardiothoracic surgeon
Kaleli, Semih obstetrician-gynecologist, educator
Kalén, Johan Gunnar Ingemar internist, endocrinologist
Kališnik, Miroslav medical educator
Kalkhof, Thomas Corrigan physician
Kallee, Ekkehard Albert Hermann physician, educator
Kalman, Peter cardiologist
Kalmaz, Gulgun Durusoy physician, scientist
Kaltenbach, Martin Hans cardiologist, educator
Kamakura, Mitsuhiro epidemiologist, educator, researcher
Kamalakar, Kadali Venkata Nagaraja cardiologist, consultant
Kamalvand, Kayvan physician
Kamata, Katsuo pharmacologist
Kamath, Patrick Sequeira physician, educator, researcher
Kamei, Chiaki pharmacology educator
Kamei, Hideo surgeon, medical educator
Kamei, Tamio physician
Kamei, Tsutomu medical researcher
Kameyama, Osamu orthopaedic surgeon, educator
Kamisako, Toshinori physician, educator
Kamoi, Kyuzi physician, researcher
Kamso-Pratt, Jimmy Michael physician, administrator
Kanakoudi-Tsakalidou, Florence pediatrician, immunologist educator
Kanda, Tatsuo physician, surgeon
Kandel, Eric Richard neuroscience educator
Kandel, Joan Ellen osteopath
Kane, Thomas Jay, III orthopaedic surgeon, educator
Kaneda, Yasuhiro neuropsychiatrist
Kaneko, Takashi medical educator
Kaneko, Yoshihiro cardiologist, researcher
Kanekura, Takuro physician
Kaneoka, Koji orthopedic surgeon
Kang, Bann C. immunologist
Kang, Chang Il physician, educator
Kang, Juan pathologist
Kang, Moon Won physician, medical educator
Kang, Yoogoo anesthesiologist
Kanim, Linda Elie Aliea medical researcher
Kankare, Jyrki Heikki Antero orthopedic and trauma surgeon, spine consultant
Kannan, Anupama pathologist, consultant
Kanno, Hiroshi neurosurgeon
Kannourakis, George pediatrician, hematologist, oncologist, medical researcher
Kannus, Veli Pekka sports medicine physician, educator
Kanonowicz, Robert Peter obstetrician, gynecologist
Kanthraj, Garehatty Rudrappa dermatologist
Kao, Ming-Chien neurosurgeon
Kapasi, Faiyaz Mohamed urologist
Kapila, Kusum Angrish cytopathologist, pathologist, educator
Kapitola, Jiri endocrinologist
Kaplan, Marshall Myles gastroenterologist, researcher, educator
Kaplowitz, Lisa Glauser physician, educator
Kapnick, S. Jason oncologist
Kapoor, Vijay Kumar medical educator
Kapsambelis, Vassilis psychiatrist, psychoanalyst
Karabachev, Ivan otolaryngologist
Karak, Asis Kumar pathology educator, consultant
Karande, Sunil pediatrician, researcher
Karapetsas, Argyris neuropsychologist
Karayalçin, Ümit internist, endocrinologist, educator
Karayiannakis, Anastasios Ioannis surgeon
Karchev, Todor otorhinolaryngologist
Kardar, Abdul Hafeez urologist
Kardassis, Dimitrios physician
Karim, Mohammed Mohibul ophthalmologist
Kariotakis, Emmanuel surgeon
Karlsson, Nils Göran medical director
Karner, Ivan physician, researcher, medical educator
Kárpáti, Pál cardiologist
Karpe, Fredrik physician, researcher
Karpman, Diana Ora pediatrician, researcher
Karppanen, Heikki Olavi pharmacology educator
Karpukhin, Oleg Yurevich surgery educator
Kartha, Chandrasekharan Cheranellore medical educator
Kartsounis, Loucas Demos clinical neuropsychologist, consultant
Karunakaran, Nair Venugopal viral oncologist, researcher
Kasa, Peter medical educator
Kasai, Kohei surgeon
Kasarskis, Edward Joseph neurologist
Kasemsuwan, Lalida medical educator, otolaryngologist
Kashimoto, Satoshi anesthesiologist
Kashiwagi, Naoya pediatric orthopedic surgeon
Kashyap, Ajit Singh endocrinologist
Kasperlik-Zaluska, Anna Antonina medical educator, consultant, researcher
Kasprow, Barbara Anne biomedical scientist, writer
Kassem, Moustapha Saad El-Deen endocrinologist, educator
Kassianos, George physician, educator, editor
Kassubek, Jan Rainer physician, researcher
Kastanias, Isidoros surgeon
Kaste, Linda Marie medical educator, researcher
Kaste, Sue Creviston pediatric radiologist, researcher
Katabuchi, Hidetaka obstetrician/gynecologist, researcher
Katayama, Fumihiko physician
Katayama, Isao pathology educator
Kathuria, Nirmal Bhatia psychiatrist
Katibah, Daniel Daoud surgeon, administrator
Katila, Marja Leena medical educator
Katodritou, Angela Nicolas radiologist
Katoh, Shuji internist
Katoh, Yoshimitsu Yuki anatomist, educator
Katrana, David John plastic and reconstructive surgeon
Katsas, Aristoteles Gregory surgeon
Katschinski, Martin Kurt gastroenterologist, researcher
Kattenbeck, Klaus cardiologist
Katz, Alfred pharmacognosist
Katz, David gastroenterologist, educator
Katz, Michael Jesse orthopedic surgeon
Katz, Robert Irwin retired physician
Kaufmann, Charles Arthur psychiatrist, neuroscientist, educator
Kaufmann, Stefan Hugo Ernst immunologist
Kauhanen, Jussi Heikki physician
Kaukinen, Liisa Marjatta anesthesiologist, educator
Kaukinen, Seppo Antero anesthesiologist, educator
Kaul, Deepak biomedical scientist, educator
Kautzner, Josef physician, cardiologist, researcher
Kavanagh, John Joseph medical educator
Kawabata, Hidetaka surgeon, oncologist
Kawagoe, Koh physician
Kawahira, Youichi cardiovascular surgeon, researcher
Kawai, Chuichi medical educator, cardiologist
Kawai, Koichi endocrinologist
Kawakami, Masaya medical educator
Kawakami, Yutaka biomedical researcher, hematologist, educator
Kawamura, Hideto medical scientist, educator
Kawamura, Yutaka J. coloproctologist
Kawano, Michio Motto hematologist, physician
Kaya, Nusret psychiatrist
Kaye, Alan David anesthesiologist, researcher
Kaye, Georges Sabry physician
Kaye, Gerald Cyril physician, consultant
Kazan, Robert Peter neurosurgeon
Kazemian, Hossein scientist, researcher
Kazuma, Norio pediatrician
Kdolsky, Richard K. surgeon
Kebudi, Rejin pediatric oncologist, educator
Keck, Ernst Wilhelm pediatric cardiologist
Keefe, Deborah Lynn cardiologist, educator
Keeler, Bradford Richard surgeon
Keilmann, Annerose pediatric otolaryngologist, phoniatrician
Kelemen, Endre hematologist, researcher
Kelemen, John neurologist, educator
Kelemen, Jozsef consultant neuropathologist
Keller, Egon Heinrich Josef surgeon
Kelley, Joseph Frank retired allergist
Kellis, Michael John osteopathic physician
Kelly, Anne-Maree emergency physician, medical educator
Kelly, Maurice Paul internist, gastroenterologist, researcher
Kelly, Ralph Whitley emergency physician, health facility administrator
Kelmanson, Igor pediatrics educator
Kelsey, Jeffrey Easton psychiatrist, educator
Kemp, Hubert Bond Stafford orthopaedist
Kenawi, Mohammad surgeon, educator
Kendall, Harry Ovid internist
Kendall, Leigh Wakefield surgeon
Kendig, Edwin Lawrence, Jr. pediatrician, educator
Kenesi, Claude orthopedic surgeon
Keng, Tay Boon surgeon, consultant, health facility administrator
Kennedy, Charles retired medical educator
Kennedy, Linda Mann neuroscience educator, researcher
Kennedy, Roger I.L. psychoanalyst, child psychiatrist
Keogh, Anne Margaret clinical cardiologist, researcher
Kerbrat, Pierre medical educator
Keris, Valdis neurosurgeon, consultant
Kersten, Robert C. ophthalmic plastic surgeon
Keshavan, Matcheri psychiatrist
Kessel, Humberto Domingo physician
Kesseler, Michael Edward physician
Kestila, Matti Seppo radiologist
Kestlmeier, Ralph physician, researcher
Keutgen, Henri Antoine pediatrician
Khachadurian, Avedis physician
Khalef, Bachir physician, physicist, educator
Khalid, Ghulam Haider physician, educator, consultant
Khalil, Ahmad Khalil ophthalmologist, educator
Khan, Abu Sayed Serajul Islam neonatologist
Khan, Amanullah physician
Khan, Ejaz Ahmed pediatrician consultant
Khan, Khalid Saeed clinical epidemiologist, obstetrician-gynecologist
Khan, Mohammad Hussein Gameryani physician, consultant
Khan, Rafeeq Alam pharmacology educator
Khandelwal, Chiranjiva gastroenterologist
Khanjanasthiti, Priya physician
Khanna, Ajay Kumar surgeon, educator
Khanna, Yash Kumar family practice physician, pediatrician
Kharb, Simmi physician, consultant
Kharjrullin, Radik Magsinur physician, researcher
Khatamee, Masood Ahmad obstetrician, gynecologist
Khatib, Rustom Atfat endocrinologist, researcher, consultant
Khatim Mohd, Salah Sir hematologist
Khatter, Prithipal Singh radiologist
Khawaja, Xavier biochemical pharmacologist
Kho, Hing Gwan anesthetist, researcher
Khojasteh, Ali medical oncologist, hematologist
Khoo, Andrew Kian Ming plastic/reconstructive surgeon, researcher
Khozouei, Homayoun psychiatrist
Khuenl-Brady, Karin Sigrid anesthesiologist, researcher
Khurana, Ashok Kumar ophthalmologist, educator
Khurana, Atul physician
Kiani, Reza endocrinology and internal medicine educator
Kiba, Tetsuji anesthesiologist, hospital administrator
Kiczka, Witold medical researcher, educator
Kidd, James Marion, III allergist, immunologist, naturalist, educator
Kidd, Michael Richard medical educator, general practitioner
Kido, Tomoyuki physician
Kidwai, Zubair chemical pathologist
Kiefer, Helen Chilton emergency/trauma neurologist
Kiefer, Renata Gertrud physician, epidemiologist, economist, international health management consultant
Kiehn, Ole neurobiology educator, researcher
Kielstein, Rita physician
Kierkegaard, Asbjoern physician
Kiernan, Matthew Colm neurologist
Kiesewetter, Holger Heinz physician, consultant
Kigure, Teruaki urologist, researcher
Kihana, Toshimasa gynecological oncologist
Kihlstrom, Lars Lennart Grahl neurosurgeon
Kijlstra, Aize ophthalmology educator
Kikawa, Kazuhiko physician, educator
Kikuchi, Ken infectious disease physician, educator
Kikuchi, Kokichi pathologist, medical educator
Kilarski, Wincenty Michal cytology educator, department chairman
Kilhamn, Jan Erik physician, researcher
Kilickan, Levent physician, medical educator
Kilpatrick, David cardiologist, educator
Kim, Byung Soo physician, educator
Kim, Dal Soo medical educator
Kim, Dong Gyu neurosurgeon
Kim, Dong Ik surgeon, educator
Kim, E. Kitai pathologist
Kim, Edward William ophthalmic surgeon
Kim, Hak Yang gastroenterologist, educator
Kim, Hyo Katherine oncologist
Kim, Ji Yeul nuclear medicine physician, educator
Kim, Julian Anthony surgical oncologist
Kim, Kwang-Iel psychiatrist, educator
Kim, Yoon Berm immunologist, educator
Kimoto, Yasuhiko surgical oncologist
Kimura, Shigeru surgeon, educator
Kimura, Tokihisa endocrinologist
Kinder, Eugene J(oseph) psychiatrist, psychoanalyst
Kindermann, Gerhard Wilhelm internist
Kindermann, Wilfried physician, educator, researcher
King, Peter Tian-Lung physician
King, Roger Graham pharmacology educator
King, Walter Wing-Keung plastic surgeon, head and neck surgery consultant
Kingsnorth, Andrew Norman surgery educator
Kingwell, Bronwyn A. medical researcher
Kinnunen, Esko Sakari neurologist, researcher
Kinoshita, Akitoshi medical oncologist, pulmonologist
Kinoshita, Shinji cardiologist, educator
Kinzie, Jeannie Jones radiation oncologist, nuclear medicine physician
Kipman, Simon-Daniel psychiatrist, psychoanalyst
Kipshidze, Nodar Nicolaevich medical educator
Kirali, Mehmet Kaan cardiovascular surgeon
Kirby, Brian John physician, academic administrator, educator
Kiriike, Nobuo psychiatrist, educator
Kirila, Carol Elizabeth osteopathic physician, internist
Kirkos, John orthopedic surgeon, educator
Kirkwood, John Robert neuroradiologist
Kirshenbaum, Richard Irving public health physician
Kirsner, Robert Scott dermatologist
Kirvassilis, George V. anesthesiologist
Kishi, Koichiro medical educator, researcher
Kishida, Akihiro surgeon
Kishida, Yutaka physician, researcher
Kisner, Wendell Howard, Jr. plastic surgeon
Kiss, Peter pediatrician, geneticist
Kitagawa, Kazuo physician, strokologist
Kitahara, Shizuo allergist
Kitakoji, Takahiko orthopaedist, researcher
Kitamura, Akihide surgeon
Kitamura, Hironori anatomist, educator
Kitamura, Junichi medical educator
Kitamura, Toshinori psychiatrist
Kitazawa, Yoshiaki medical educator
Kito, Shozo medical educator
Kitua, Andrew Yona epidemiologist, medical researcher
Kivela, Sirkka-Liisa general practice medical educator
Kivikoski, Asko Ilmari obstetrician , gynecologist
Kivioja, Aarne orthopaedic surgeon, educator
Kivuls, Juris plastic surgeon
Kiyingi, Aggrey cardiologist, consultant, research scientist
Kjaer, Andreas physician, researcher
Kjellgren, Olle R.H. oncologist, educator
Klapan, Ivica otorhinolaryngologist, consultant
Klareskog, Lars Göran rheumatologist, educator
Klaus, Sidney Nathan dermatologist
Klee, Andreas Peter gynecologist
Klein, Arnold William dermatologist
Klein, Leo plastic surgeon
Klein, Michael Elihu physician
Kleine, Michael Werner physician
Kleine, Tilmann Otto neurochemist, educator
Kleiner, Hilda Feng-Kai Lin pediatrician, pathologist
Kleinman, Yosef internist
Kleinrok, Zdzislaw pharmacologist
Kleitman, Naomi neuroscientist
Klen, Rudolf medical researcher
Klener, Vladislav radiation protection researcher, consultant
Klezl, Zdenek orthopedic surgeon
Klima, Roger Radim physiatrist
Klimek, Joseph John physician, educator
Klimek, Marek obstetrician and gynecologist
Klimek, Rudolf obstetrics and gynecology educator
Klimovič, Michal pediatrician, anesthesiologist, internist
Klingenberg, Claus Andreas pediatrician
Klinger, Wolfgang Gottfried pharmacologist, toxicologist
Klitzman, Robert Lloyd physician, author
Klockner, Constantin orthopaedic surgeon
Kloehn, Ralph Anthony plastic surgeon
Klöppel, Günter Karl Paul pathology educator, hospital administrator
Kluger, Jeffrey cardiologist, health facility administrator
Klutzow, Friedrich Wilhelm neuropathologist
Knapp, Albert Bruce gastroenterologist
Knauff, Hans Georg physician, educator
Knecht, Ben Harrold surgeon
Knight, Edwin Walter occupational physician
Knight, Stella Catherine medical researcher
Knights, Kathleen Mary biochemical pharmacologist
Knisel, Werner physician
Knoell, Dieter Rudolf medical educator
Knottenbelt, John Duncan emergency physician
Knudsen, Aage gynecological oncologist
Knudsen, Bjarne Fredberg medical consulting company executive
Knudsen, Thor Andersen surgeon
Knyihár, Elizabeth neurologist
Kobak, Alfred Julian, Jr. obstetrician, gynecologist
Kobayashi, Fuminori physician
Kobayashi, Makio pathology educator
Kober, Gisbert Herbert cardiologist, clinician
Kobren, Steven Mark internist
Koch, Michael Gerhard epidemiologist
Koch, Olaf Manfred hematologist, educator
Kochar, Kanwal Preet physiologist, educator
Kochar, Mahendr Singh physician, educator, administrator, scientist, writer, consultant
Kocyigit, Hikmet rheumatologist
Kodaki, Nobuo retired medical educator, researcher
Kodama, Hiroko pediatrician, educator
Kodama, Junzo physician, researcher
Koelz, Anne Marie nephrologist
Koh, Jai Kyoung dermatologist, educator
Koh, Yongbok surgeon, educator
Kohl, Daniele Marguerite immunologist, vaccinologist
Kohlberger, Petra physician, researcher, educator
Köhler, Ekkehart cardiologist
Kohler, Lennart Ingemar pediatrician, educator
Kohli, Anil medical educator, researcher
Kohli, Rajesh marketing medical consultant
Kohno, Isao internist
Kohri, Kenjiro urologist, educator
Kohshi, Kiyotaka neurosurgeon, researcher
Kojima, Hiroshi hematologist, educator
Kokoszka, Andrzej Wlodzimierz psychiatrist, psychotherapist, psychologist
Kokot, Franciszek Józef nephrology educator
Kokuina, Elena immunologist, educator
Kolář, Jaromír Jan radiologist
Kolb, Lawrence Coleman psychiatrist
Kölbel, František Pavel physician, researcher
Kolek, Vítězslav internist, oncologist, pneumologist
Kolesar, Tibor Paul physician, researcher
Kolettis, Theofilos cardiologist
Kolh, Philippe Henry cardiothoracic and vascular surgeon, researcher
Kolker, Christopher Trent physician
Kolkin, Iakov Grigorevich surgeon, medical educator
Kollias, Costas Themistokleous psychiatrist
Kolmodin-Hedman, Birgitta Christine medical educator
Kolosovsky, Ernest Dmitrievich dermatologist
Kolstad, Jens food microbiologist
Komai, Hiroyoshi cardiovascular surgeon
Komarek, David pediatrician
Komori, Teruhisa psychiatrist, researcher
Komoroski, Richard Andrew medical sciences educator, spectroscopy researcher
Kompatscher, Peter plastic surgeon, consultant
Konermann, Martin physician, researcher
Kong, Tak-Kwan geriatrician, consultant
König, Rolf immunologist, educator
Konishi, Ikuo gynecologist, researcher
Kono, Takeshi dermatologist
Konstantinos, Tepetes surgeon, consultant
Konsten, Joop surgeon
Kontošić, Ivica occupational health physician, medical educator
Koo, Sun Hoe medical educator
Koo Ahn, Sun Hoe clinical pathology educator
Kook, Abraham Izhak neuroimmunologist
Kopatsis, Anthony surgeon
Kopera, Hans pharmacologist
Koppenbrink, Walter Edwin, III internist
Koprowska, Irena cytopathologist, cancer researcher
Korabiowska, Monika physician
Korać, Želimir surgeon
Koranda, Pavel nuclear medicine physician, educator
Korbitz, Bernard Carl retired oncologist, hematologist, educator, consultant
Korenev, Alexander Nicolaevich psychiatrist, researcher
Korenkov, Michael surgeon
Kořístek, Vladimir Joseph retired surgeon
Kornaros, Stylianos Evangelos surgeon, researcher, consultant
Kornbluth, Ralph Ross physician
Kornet, Ene obstetrician
Korshunov, Andrey neuropathologist
Korting, Hans Christian dermatology educator
Kosakovskyy, Anatoliy Lukianovich otolaryngologist
Kosasih, Eddi Niko internist, educator
Kosasky, Harold Jack fertility researcher
Kosel, Arnold Israilevich physician, neurosurgeon
Koshiyama, Masafumi gynecologist
Koskenvuo, Kimmo public health physician
Kosmas, Epaminondas N. chest physician, researcher
Kossmann, Stefan Antoni medical educator, researcher
Kostadinov, Dimitar Temelkov medical educator
Kostrzewski, Jan Karol epidemiologist, researcher
Kostyuk, Inna Fedorovna medical educator, department chair, consultant
Kotanko, Peter physician, researcher
Kotarski, Jan obstetrician-gynecologist, educator
Kotler, Ronald Lee physician, educator
Kotoulas, Othon Basil physician, educator
Kottow, Miguel Hugo ophthalmologist, educator
Kotwal, Prakash orthopaedic surgeon

Lotti, Torello M. dermatologist, educator
Lotz, Jean-Pierre oncologist
Lotze, Martin Philippe neuroscience researcher
Lou, Hans Christensen neuropediatrician, medical educator
Loubet, René Pierre Emmanuel pathologist
Loubrieu, Georges Louis radiologist, neurologist, consultant
Loughman, Barbara Ellen immunologist researcher
Louisy, Francis physician
Loulmet, Didier Felix cardiac surgeon
Lovren, Robert mechanical engineer, educator
Lowenstein, Pedro Ricardo gene therapy scientist
Loye, Ajibola radiologist, consultant
Loyke, Hubert Frank internist, cardiologist
Loza, Nasser Fathy psychiatrist
Lu, Wei medical researcher
Lu, Weibo physician
Lu, Weixin medical researcher
Lubkin, Virginia Leila ophthalmologist
Luchette, Frederick Albert surgeon
Luchins, Daniel Jonathan psychiatrist
Lucia, Marilyn Reed physician
Lucore, Charles Lee cardiologist
Lüdecke, Dieter Konrad neurosurgeon
Ludik, Paul Stefan clinical pharmacologist, consultant
Ludvigsson, Petur pediatric neurologist
Ludvik, Bernhard Heinrich medical educator, endocrinologist
Luepker, Russell Vincent epidemiology educator
Luessenhop, Alfred John neurosurgeon, educator
Luhr, Owe Robert physician, consultant
Luik, Antinus Johan internist, nephrologist
Luk, James Ka Hay geriatrician
Lukacs, Andreas dermatologist
Lukács, Géza László surgery educator
Lukas, Elsa Victoria radiobiologist, radiobiochemist
Lukauskas, Algirdas industrial hygiene researcher, educator
Luke, Tan Kim Siang otolaryngologist, educator
Lumsden, Andrew Gino neurobiologist, researcher
Lund, Peere Caroe anesthesiologist
Lundberg, Per Olov Magnus neurology educator
Lundbergh, Per Runo physician
Lund-Olesen, Knud physician, retired
Luntz, Maurice Harold ophthalmologist
Luo, Hong Yuan biomedical scientist, educator
Luo, Xizhang physician, educator
Luoma, Jukka Sakari physician, health facility administrator
Luong, Khanh Vinh Quoc nephrologist, researcher
Lupescu, Grigore cardiologist
Lupu, Amca Roxana Ilie physician, haematology educator
Lupulescu, Aurel Peter medical educator, researcher, physician
Lusch, Charles Jack oncologist
Luthra, Rita obstetrician/gynecologist, consultant
Lutz, Myron Howard obstetrician, gynecologist, surgeon, educator
Luus, George Aarne physician
Luzsa, George radiologist, educator
Lyden, Patrick Donovan neurologist, neuroscientist
Lyman, Donald Owen preventive medicine physician
Lynch, Gearoid retired surgeon, consultant
Lyons, Declan physician, educator
Ma, Hon Ming pulmonologist
Ma, Lijun endocrinologist, molecular biologist
Maache, Abdelhalim endocrinologist
Maak, Bernhard Rudi physician, pediatrician, professor
Maas, Anthony Ernst pathologist
MacAra, Alexander Wiseman (Sir) public health physician, educator
MacDougall, John Duncan surgeon
MacFarlane, Campbell surgeon, emergency physician
Machaczka, Maciej Jaroslaw medical educator, hematologist, researcher
Machave, Yeshavant Vasudeo hematologist
Machida, Yoshiharu pharmaceutical educator
Machleidt, Wielant psychiatrist, psychotherapist
Maciejewski, Ryszard Romuald anatomist
Mack, Doris Margarethe urologist, researcher, educator
Mackay, Eric Vincent medical practitioner
MacKintosh, Frederick Roy oncologist
Macklis, Roger Miton physician, educator, researcher
Mac Loughlin, Ernesto Santiago internist, intensivist
MacRorie, Roderick Andrew physician
Macura, Anna Barbara mycologist researcher, dermatologist
Madalinski, Kazimierz Z. immunologist, researcher
Madan, Ira occupational physician, consultant
Madathil, Sahadevan Govindan retired medical educator, neurology consultant
Madden, Brendan Patrick cardiothoracic and transplant physician, educator
Madebo, Tesfaye physician, researcher
Madei, Werner Ferdinand anesthesiologist, researcher, pharmacologist
Madianos, Michael George psychiatry educator
Madjirova, Nadejda Petrova psychiatrist, educator
Madlang, Rodolfo Mojica retired urologic surgeon
Madrigal, Jose Alejandro hematology, educator, researcher
Madsen, Bjørn Lindegaard orthopaedist
Maeda, Kenji medical educator
Maegaki, Yoshihiro pediatric neurologist
Maes, Michael psychiatrist, researcher
Maetani, Iruru medical educator
Magarelli, Nicola radiologist, researcher
Mager, Peter Paul pharmacologist, toxicologist, educator
Magid, Erik Jakob clinical chemist
Magnes, Harry Alan physician
Magnin, George Ernest physician
Magnússon, Hallgrimur physician
Magoha, George Albert medical educator, consultant
Magometschnigg, Heinrich vascular surgeon
Maguire, Charlotte Edwards retired physician
Maguire, Peter James family physician, medical educator
Mahatumarat, Charan plastic surgery educator, consultant
Mahendra Raj, S. gastroenterologist
Mahenthiran, Jothiharan physician, cardiologist, consultant
Mahenthran, Lakshmanan Veerabadran immunologist, immunogeneticist
Maher, Cornelius Creedon, III neurologist, toxicologist, army officer
Maher, Vincent Mary Gerard cardiologist
Mahesh, Virendra Bhushan endocrinologist
Mahla, Michael E. anesthesiologist, educator
Mahlknecht, Ulrich Rudolph physician, researcher
Mahran, Gamal El-Din Hussein pharmacognosy and pharmacology educator
Mahran, Maher Ahmed obstetrician, gynecologist, consultant
Maickel, Roger Philip pharmacologist, educator
Maiese, Kenneth neurologist
Main, Paul Graeme Neilson general practice physician, educator
Mainzer, Francis Kirkwood neurosurgeon, health facility consultant
Maioriello, Richard Patrick otolaryngologist
Maisin, Jean René Simon medical researcher, educator
Maitz, Manfred Franz physician, researcher
Maitz, Peter Karl-Maria surgeon
Maj, Jerzy Michał Józef pharmacologist, educator
Majeed, Gulnaz Syed gynecologist
Majeed-Saidan, Muhammad Ali pediatrician
Majji, Ajit Babu ophthalmologist, consultant
Majtenyi, Catherine neuropathologist
Mak, Kan Hing orthopedist
Mäkelä, Jirki Tapani gastroenterological surgeon, educator, consultant
Makhija, Sushil Kumar medical microbiologist, researcher
Makris, Nikolaos Dimitrios obstetrician-gynecologist, educator
Mala, Theodore Anthony physician, consultant
Malach, Monte physician
Maladry, David Henri plastic surgeon, hand surgeon
Malaterre, Henri Romain cardiologist
Malbran, Enrique S. ophthalmologist, consultant
Malca, Samuel Albert neurosurgeon
Malecka-Panas, Ewa Izabela gastroenterologist, educator
Maleika-Rabe, Annette obstetrician, gynecologist, researcher
Malekzadeh, Reza medical educator
Malendowicz, Ludwik Kazimierz medical educator
Malhotra, Vinay cardiologist
Malik, Iftikhar Hussain pathologist
Malin, Howard Gerald podiatrist
Malina, Jan Rudolf surgeon
Malina, Martin surgeon
Malinin, Theodore medical educator, researcher
Mallet, Michel Marie-Joseph ophthalmologist
Mallias, Alexius John physician
Mallouh, Ahmad Abdellatif pediatric hematologist, oncologist
Malluche, Hartmut Horst nephrologist, medical educator
Maloney, Milford Charles retired internal medicine educator
Malpas, James Spencer oncology consultant
Maluf, Miguel Angel surgeon, educator
Mamchenko, Galena Fyodorovna medical educator
Mamianetti, Arnaldo medical educator
Mamiya, Kikyo physician
Mamun, Kazi Zulfiquer physician
Manafi, Ali plastic surgeon
Manchanda, Dev Parkash physician, consultant
Mancini, Mary Catherine cardiothoracic surgeon, researcher
Mandal, Ashis K. cardiothoracic surgeon
Mandalaki-Yiannitsioti, Titica Emmanuel hematologist
Manders, Karl Lee neurosurgeon
Manderson, Lenore Hilda medical educator, medical anthropologist
Mandic, Zlatko Antun pediatrician
Mandysová, Eva cardiologist, researcher
Manfredini, Roberto internist, educator
Mangell, Charles Peter physician, colorectal surgeon, researcher
Manger, William Muir internist
Mangete, Eric Otorudigiyo surgeon, health facility executive
Mangola, Bruno Charles emergency physician
Maniatis, George Marinos medical educator, researcher
Manimtim, Winston Mendoza pediatrician
Mann, Oscar physician, internist, educator
Mann, Stefan Martin surgeon
Manna, Vincenzo psychiatrist
Manning, Martina Melitta urologist
Manning-Weber, Claudia Joy medical radiography administrator, consultant
Manns, Michael Peter physician
Mano, Yukio medical educator, physician
Manolis, Antonis S. cardiologist, electrophysiologist
Mansi, Mostafa Kamal urologist, educator
Manson, Roberto Ramon surgeon, educator
Mantegazza, Paolo pharmacology educator
Manto, Mario Ubaldo neurologist, researcher
Manusama, Eric Robert surgeon, researcher
Manvelov, Lev Sergeevich neurologist
Mao, JianHua pediatrician, researcher
Marano, Anthony Joseph cardiologist
Maranta, Christian Arturo otolaryngologist
Marazziti, Donatella psychiatrist, researcher
Marc, Bernard Robert physician, emergency medicine physician
Marchetti, Cristina medical physicist, hospital department director
Marchi, Marcello plastic surgeon, microsurgeon
Marciniak, Witold Lukasz orthopaedic surgeon
Marcinkowski, Tadeusz physician, retired educator
Marcos Sanchez, Oscar physician, surgeon
Marcotte, Paul John neurosurgeon, educator
Marcusson, Jan Anders dermatologist, researcher
Marecos, Edgardo Miguel physician, researcher
Maret, Karl Helmuth medical research corporation executive, consultant
Margolin, Solomon Begelfor pharmacologist
Mariani, Jean neurobiologist, psychiatrist
Marie, Jean-Pierre hematologist
Marin, Gilles Wilfred healing practitioner
Marino, Ignazio Roberto transplant surgeon, educator, researcher
Marino, Raul, Jr. neurosurgeon
Marin-Rojas, Rafael Angel immunohematologist, educator
Marion, Fabienne emergency medicine physician, researcher
Mariotti, Egidio cardiologist, researcher
Maris, Charles Robert surgeon, otolaryngologist
Mark, Richard Kushakow internist
Markham, Charles Henry neurologist
Markovic, Nenad S. internist, hematologist, oncologist, educator
Markoyannis, Niki psychiatrist
Marks, Isaac Meyer psychiatrist
Marks, Jon Owen physician
Marks, William H. organ transplant program director, pharmacognosist, director for laboratory transplantation biology
Marktl, Wolfgang physiologist, medical educator
Marlicz, Krzysztof gastroenterologist, educator
Marlow, Neil neonatology educator
Maronde, Robert Francis internist, clinical pharmacologist, educator
Marosi, Christine oncologist, cytogeneticist
Marotta, Francesco gastroenterologist
Marquez Campos, Alfredo surgeon, editor
Marsh, Ella Jean pediatrician
Marsh, Harold Michael anesthesiologist
Marshall, John ophthalmology educator, consultant, executive
Marshall, Wayne Keith anesthesiology educator
Marshall, Willis Henry psychiatrist
Marsot-DuPuch, Kathlyn physician
Marthak, Kiran Vithal physician, researcher
Martin, Clyde Verne psychiatrist
Martin, Daniel C. surgeon, gynecologist, educator
Martin, Didier Herman neurosurgeon, researcher
Martin, Donald William psychiatrist
Martin, Jean F. physician, consultant
Martin, John Thomas physician, author, educator
Martin, Joseph Boyd neurologist, educator
Martin, Leonardo S.J. urologist, surgeon
Martin, Lorna Jean forensic pathologist, specialist, consultant
Martin, Louis Frank surgery and healthcare outcomes analyst
Martin-Duverneuil, Nadine neuroradiologist
Martinek, Jan physician
Martinez, Joe Louis, Jr. neurobiologist, educator
Martinez, Luis Osvaldo radiologist, educator
Martinez, Miguel Acevedo urologist, consultant, lecturer
Martinova, Elena Alexandrovna immunologist, consultant, researcher
Martin-Paredero, Vicente vascular surgeon
Martire, Maria Concetta pharmacology educator
Marty, René Pierre obstetrician/gynecologist
Marusic, Ana anatomy educator, researcher
Maruyama, Koshi pathologist, educator
Marvisi, Maurizio internist, researcher
Marzo, Amanda Lee immunologist, researcher
Marzo, Antonio Pietro pharmacologist
Masaki, Ishizaka physician
Masci, Joseph Richard medical educator, physician
Masdeu, Jose Cruz neurologist, medical school administrator
Mashonganyika, Charles anesthesiologist, consultant
Maslov, Alexander K. medical researcher
Maslowski, Andrew Henry interventional cardiologist
Mason, Dean Towle cardiologist
Mason, Gregg Claude orthopedic surgeon, researcher
Mason, Malcolm David oncologist, researcher
Masquelet, Alain Charles orthopaedic surgeon, educator
Massad, Malek George surgeon, researcher
Massarrat, Sadegh physician
Masson, Jean Philippe radiologist
Masud, Ahmad Ijaz radiation oncologist
Masunaga, Shin-ichiro radiology educator, researcher
Mataringa, Mihaela Irina physician, neuropsychiatrist
Materson, Richard Stephen physician, educator
Matheson, Thomas neuroscientist, researcher
Mathews, William Edward neurological surgeon, educator
Mathewson, Hugh Spalding anesthesiologist, educator
Mathias, Christopher Joseph physician, educator, researcher, consultant
Mathiesen, Lars R. physician, researcher
Mathieu, Henri-Pierre physician, business executive
Mathieu, Michele Suzanne medical association administrator
Matijevic, Ratko gynecologist
Matos, Arnaldo José Duarte otolaryngologist
Matousek, Michael geriatrician
Matsuda, Takayoshi surgeon, educator, biomedical researcher
Matsuhashi, Nobuyuki physician, researcher, educator
Matsumine, Hiroto neurologist, researcher, educator
Matsumoto, Mitsuomi physician, educator
Matsumoto, Tsukasa orthopedic surgeon
Matsuoka, Masato occupational and environmental physician, researcher
Matsushima, Yoshiharu neurosurgeon, educator
Mattelaer, Johan Jozef urologist
Matthys, Heinrich medical educator
Mattie, Herman internist
Matusiewicz, Ryszard physician
Matweev, Leonid Vladimirovich physician
Matz, Dieter Rudolf clinical neurologist, educator
Mätzsch, Thomas Winfried surgeon
Maudgal, Prabhat Chander ophthalmologist
Maughan, Willard Zinn dermatologist
Maulion, Richard Peter psychiatrist, neurolinguist
Maurer, Hans Hilarius pharmacology educator
Mautalen, Carlos Alfredo medical researcher
Mautner, Branco cardiologist, researcher
Maweu, David pathologist, consultant
Max, Theodore Conrad surgeon
May, Donald Robert Lee ophthalmologist, retina and vitreous surgeon, educator, farmer
Maya, Jose Maria physician, medical educator, rector
Mayatepek, Ertan Hilmi physician, researcher
Mayer, Heinz Michael orthopedic surgeon and neurosurgeon
Mayer, Michal medical educator
Mayock, Robert Lee internist
Mayr, Georg Wilhelm physician, biochemist, biologist, researcher
Mayumi, Makoto immunology educator
Mazariegos, George Vincent pediatric transplant surgeon
Mazeyrat, Roseline pediatrician
Mazo, Evsey Borisovitch urologist
Mazuranic, Ivica physician
Mazzio-Moore, Joan L. radiology educator, physician
McAlister, Hugh Francis consultant cardiologist
McAnally, James Francis nephrologist
McAnena, Oliver James general surgeon, consultant
McCarthy, Denise Marie radiologist
McCarthy, Mary Frances medical foundation administrator
McCarthy, William Henry surgeon, educator
McCawley, Austin psychiatrist, educator
McCleane, Gary John physician
McCollum, Charles Nevin surgery educator
McConaghy, Nathaniel (Neil) psychiatrist, researcher
McConnell, Archibald Allison chemical pathologist consultant, educator
McDaniel, John Stephen psychiatrist, educator
McDonnell, Gavin Vincent physician
McDouall, Rhoda Mary immunologist, researcher
McEniery, Paul Timothy cardiologist
McFadden, James Frederick, Jr. surgeon
McFadden, P. Michael physician, surgeon
McFadden, Robert Stetson hepatologist
McFarland, Robert Bruce physician
McGeown, Mary Graham physician
McGovern, John Hugh urologist, educator
McHarg, James Fleming retired psychiatrist
McHenry, Martin Christopher physician, educator
McIntosh, Edwin David George pediatrician, educator, pharmaceutical physician
McKenzie, Harry James cardiothoracic surgeon, surgical researcher
McMurry, William Scott retired allied health educator
Mc Murtry, James Gilmer, III neurosurgeon
McNab, Alan Angus ophthalmologist
McNaughton, Peter Anthony pharmacology educator, neuroscience researcher
McVie, John Gordon research administrator, oncologist
Meagher, David James psychiatrist, researcher
Mealie, Carl A. physician, educator
Mechl, Zdenek oncologist
Meddens, Marc Johannes medical association administrator, virologist
Medhus, Asle Wilhelm physician, researcher
Medicus, Gerhard psychiatrist
Medina, Fernando Hector physician, oncologist, researcher
Mee, Aeneas David urologist
Meengs, William Lloyd cardiologist
Meerpohl, Hans Gerd obstetrics and gynecology educator
Meessen, Michel Joseph surgeon
Megahy, Diane Alaire physician
Megarbane, Bruno physician
Mehnert, Hellmut physician
Mehrotra, Naveen pediatrician
Mehrotra, Seema anesthesiologist
Mehta, Rakesh Kumar physician, consultant
Mehta, Yatin anesthesiology consultant
Meier, Paul Daniel psychiatrist, writer
Meier-Ruge, William Alfred pathologist
Meignan, Francis Georges rheumatologist
Meijler, Frits Louis cardiologist, educator
Meikan, Seki gynecologist, educator
Meinders, Arend Edo internal medicine educator
Meirelles, Ricardo Martins da Rocha endocrinologist
Meistas, Mary Therese endocrinologist, diabetes researcher
Mejia, Luis Fernando ophthalmologist
Melberg, Atle neurologist
Meldrum, Brian Stuart neuroscientist, educator
Melegh, Béla pediatrician, geneticist, researcher
Melendez, Edwin Manuel orthopaedic hand surgeon
Melichercik, Juraj cardiologist
Meling, Torstein R. neurosurgeon, researcher
Mellbring, Göran Olof Lennart surgeon
Mellors, Robert Charles physician, scientist, educator
Meluzín, Jaroslav cardiologist
Memezawa, Hajime physician, educator
Memon, Aamir Aziz dermatologist, consultant, educator
Menanteau, Bernard Paul medical educator
Menck, Johannes Herwig physician, researcher
Mendel, Tadeusz Andrzej neurologist
Mendes, Nelson Figueiredo physician, educator, researcher
Meng, Xianmin dermatologist, researcher
Mennen, Ulrich hand surgery and orthopaedics educator, surgeon
Mennin, Gerald Stanley ophthalmologist
Menten, Johan Jozef radiotherapist
Mentzel, Thomas Dietrich Wilhelm histopathologist
Mentzelopoulos, Spyros Dennis anesthesiologist, researcher
Menzinger, Guido endocrinology educator
Mercado, Mary Gonzales cardiologist
Mercado-Bosch, Maria Carmen pediatrician
Mercer, Betty Deborah electrologist, poet, writer, proofreader
Mercier, Claude Paul vascular surgeon, educator
Merenda, Roberto surgeon
Merin, Saul Cvi ophthalmologist
Merkin, Donald H. internist
Merle, Michel Paul plastic surgeon, orthopedic surgeon, educator
Merolli, Antonio orthopedic surgeon, consultant
Mert, Ali physician, educator
Meschia, James Frederick neurologist, researcher
Meskhi, Apollo obstetrician, gynecologist, researcher, educator, manager
Messias, José Augusto Da Silva medical educator, physician
Messmer, Konrad Friedrich Wilhelm surgical researcher
Meštrović, Julije pediatrician
Metka, Wolfgang Ernst plastic surgeon
Metodiev, Krassimir Tihomirov medical educator, researcher
Meurman, Jukka Heikki medical educator
Meyberg-Solomayer, Gabriele Christine physician, researcher
Meyer, Carol Frances pediatrician, allergist
Meyer, Jean-Pierre psychiatrist
Meyer, Jon Keith psychiatrist, psychoanalyst, educator
Meyer, Lutz-Michael physician
Meyyanathan, Subramania Nainar pharmaceutical analyst, educator
Meziane, Moulay Ahmed physician
Michael, Cecil Francis, Jr. pediatrician
Michaelides, Doros Nikita internist, medical educator
Michalek, Hilma Adelheid Leonore histopathology educator, researcher, consultant
Michalopoulos, Christos Demetrius cardiologist
Michalowicz, Roman Piotr child neurologist
Michel, Olaf Gert surgeon, educator
Michelsen, Christopher Bruce Hermann surgeon
Michler, Markwart Waldemar orthopedist, surgeon
Michler, Robert E. heart surgeon
Middlemiss, Derek Neil pharmacologist, research scientist
Middleton, Anthony Wayne, Jr. urologist, educator
Midgley, John Morton pharmaceutical educator, researcher, consultant
Mieli-Vergani, Giorgina physician
Miermont, Jacques Georges Jean psychiatrist, researcher
Mietz, Holger ophthalmologist
Mihan, Richard retired dermatologist
Mihaylov, Dimiter Mihaylov surgeon
Mikhailidis, Dimitri Philip pathologist, educator, consultant
Miki, Yoshitsugu oncologist
Mikkelsen, Erich Olaf pharmacologist

Milch, Wolfgang E. *physician, researcher, analyst*
Miles, Arnold Ian *physician*
Milkov, Borys Olegovych *physician, educator*
Miller, Brian John *surgeon, educator*
Miller, Jacques Francis *medical researcher*
Miller, Michael James *radiation oncologist*
Millikan, Clark Harold *physician*
Milloy, Frank Joseph, Jr. *surgeon*
Mills, Don Harper *pathology and psychiatry educator, lawyer*
Milman, Nils *respiratory physician*
Miltenburg, Darlene Margaret *surgeon*
Mimica, Marko *gynecologist, researcher*
Mimica, Ninoslav *psychiatrist*
Mimura, Goro *medical educator, researcher*
Min, Geh *surgeon*
Min, Zheng *dermatology educator*
Minakami, Korebumi *medical school educator*
Minale, Carmine *cardiovascular surgeon*
Minami, Masaru *pharmacologist*
Mindermann, Thomas Friedrich Gerhard *neurosurgeon, researcher*
Mineev, Konstantin Peter *traumatologist, orthopedist*
Minkowski, Alexandre *neonatology educator, retired*
Minor, Thomas *medical researcher*
Minuth, Will Wolfgang *anatomist, educator*
Miossec, Pierre Jean *immunologist, rheumatologist*
Mirilas, Petros *pediatric surgeon*
Miroli, Alfredo Americo *immunologist*
Mirone, Luisa *rheumatologist, researcher*
Mirshahi, Massoud *biomedical researcher*
Misawa, Miwa *pharmacology educator*
Misery, Laurent *dermatologist, biologist*
Misra, Basant Kumar *neurosurgeon, consultant*
Missana, Liliana Raquel *oral pathologist*
Mistiaen, Wilhelm Peter *surgeon, researcher*
Mitchell, George Trice *physician*
Mitchell, Ian Moorhouse *consultant cardiac surgeon*
Mitchell, John Douglas *clinical neurologist, educator*
Mitchison, Sally *psychiatrist*
Mitsuoka, Masahiro *surgeon, researcher*
Mittal, Suneeta *obstetrics and gynecology educator*
Mittelman, Moshe *internist, hematologist, educator*
Mittendorf, Robert *physician, epidemiologist*
Mitterauer, Bernhard Josef *psychiatrist, educator, neuroscientist*
Miwa, Kunihisa *cardiologist, researcher*
Mixson, William Tunno *retired gynecologist*
Miyagawa, Masao *radiologist, researcher*
Miyaguchi, Shingo *physician*
Miyaishi, Satoru *forensic pathologist*
Miyamoto, Richard Takashi *otolaryngologist*
Miyamoto, Yoshiyuki *pharmacologist, toxicologist, researcher*
Miyauchi, Fumihisa *obstetrician and gynecologist, researcher*
Miyauchi, Jun *pathologist, researcher*
Miyoshi, Sakuichiro *retired anatomy educator*
Mizutani, Tomohiko *neurology educator*
Mladinic-Vulic, Denis *pediatrician, researcher*
Mlczoch, Johannes Karl *cardiologist*
Mldrum, Brian Stuart *research neuroscientist*
Mo, Loar Ka-Keung *geriatrician, consultant, educator*
Mo, Ning *medical educator*
Mochizuki, Yohichi *medical educator*
Mock, David Clinton, Jr. *internist*
Modéer, Thomas *pediatric dentistry educator*
Modell, Stephen Mark *medical researcher, educator*
Modlin, Charles Trevor *physician, medical hypnoanalyst*
Moelby, Lars *nephrologist, internist*
Moen, Bente Elisabeth *physician*
Moëne, Yves Paul *neurologist*
Moens, Guido Frans *epidemiologist, scientific director, educator*
Moezi, Amir-Naser *neuropsychiatrist*
Moffat, David Andrew *otologist, otoneurosurgeon, consultant*
Mogyorósy, Gábor *pediatric cardiologist*
Mohaideen, A. Hassan *surgeon, healthcare executive*
Mohammad, Tufail *pediatrician, child rights activist*
Mohammadian, Parvaneh *pharmacology educator*
Mohan, Harsch *pathologist*
Mohanty, Aaron *neurosurgeon, educator*
Mohanty, Kailash Chandra *physician*
Mohanty, Sureswar *neurosugeon, educator*
Möhler, Hanns *pharmacologist executive, biochemist educator*
Mohr, Janet Ann *psychiatrist*
Mohr, Lawrence Charles *physician*
Mohri, Hitoshi *surgeon, educator*
Mohri, Mitsunobu *pharmacologist, researcher*
Moises, Hans Werner *psychiatrist, molecular geneticist*
Moldavskay, Anna Arkadjevna *anatomy educator*
Molendijk, Leendert Willemminus *obstetrician, gynecologist*
Moll, Friedrich Heinrich *urologist*
Möller, Erna Birgitta Irmgard *immunologist*
Möller, Göran *immunology educator*
Moller, Svend Erik *pharmacology company executive*
Molnár, Gábor *psychiatrist, neurologist, researcher*
Molnar, Ildiko *internist, allergist, immunologist*
Molnar, Mark *psychophysiologist*
Molnar, Rowan Rustem *anesthesiologist*
Molnar, Thomas Ferenc *thoracic surgeon, consultant, educator*
Molnár, Zoltán *neuroscientist, anatomy educator*
Momčilović, Berislav *clinical research scientist, consultant*
Momen, Moojan *physician, researcher*
Mondadori, Cesare *neurobiologist, researcher*
Monge-Argiles, J. Antonio *neurologist*
Mongelli, Max *medical educator*
Monhart, Václav *nephrologist, consultant*
Mönkemüller, Klaus Erik *physician, researcher*
Monks, Paul Saville *anaesthetist, consultant*
Monninger, Robert Harold George *ophthalmologist, educator*
Monosson, Ira Howard *physician*
Monro, James Lawrence *cardiac surgeon*
Monson, Carol Lynn *osteopath, psychotherapist*
Monson, John Patrick *endocrinologist, educator*
Montandon, Denys *plastic surgeon*
Montasser, Amr M.K. *physician, anaesthesiologist consultant, researcher*
Monteiro, Brendan Thomas *psychiatrist, consultant*
Monteiro, Jose Maria Pereira *neurologist*
Monteiro, Victor Jerome *anatomy educator*
Montero, Antonio *internist, researcher*
Montgomery, Bruce Stewart *urological surgeon*
Montgomery-Davis, Joseph *osteopathic physician*
Monties, Jean-Raoul Emile *cardiac surgeon, educator*
Moon, Il Soo *medical educator*
Moon, Sang-Eun *dermatologist, educator*
Moore, Austen Peter *neurologist, educator*
Moore, Nicholas Delafon *pharmacologist, educator*
Moore, Ray *endocrinologist*
Moore, Richard Carroll, Jr. *family physician*
Moore, Wistar *cardiovascular surgeon*
Mooro, Hisham A.W. *surgeon, educator*
Moosa, Allie *pediatrics and pediatric neurology educator*
Morakinyo, Olufemi *psychiatrist, educator*
More, Ranjit Singh *cardiologist, consultant*
Moreau, Jean Claude *astrophysician*
Moreau, Patrick Marcel *thoracic and vascular surgeon*
Moreira, Milton Baggio *neurologist, researcher*
Morello, Daniel Conway *plastic surgeon*
Moreno, Fidela Llorca *physician, medical educator*
Moreno-Arias, Gerardo Antonio *dermatologist*
Moreno-Cabral, Carlos Eduardo *cardiac surgeon*
Moreno-Davila, Herman William *neurology educator*
Morenon, Jean *psychiatrist*
Morgan, Avanelle Proctor *physician*
Morgan, Clyde Nathaniel *dermatologist*
Morgan, Leslie Yarborough *physician*
Mori, Akio *immunologist, researcher*
Mori, Nozomu *medical educator*
Morishita, Tetsuo *physician, researcher in medical science*
Moritz, Timothy Bovie *psychiatrist*
Moriura, Shigeaki *surgeon*
Morooka, Hiroshi *neurosurgeon*
Morosetti, Roberta *hematologist, researcher*
Morozov, Vyacheslav Grigorievich *immunologist, researcher*
Morrell, David Cameron *medical practice educator*
Morris, John Carl *neurologist, educator, researcher*
Morris, Norman Frederick *gynecologist*
Morris, Raymond Gregory *pharmacology scientist*
Morrison, Francine Darlene *psychiatrist, massage therapist, herbal simplist*
Morse, Martin A. *surgeon*
Morsiani, Eugenio Antonio *surgeon*
Mortimer, Ann Margaret *psychiatrist, educator, consultant*
Morton, Anne Jennifer *neuroscientist*
Morys, Janusz *neuroanatomist, educator*
Mosbaugh, Phillip George *urologist, educator*
Mosbech, Holger *allergist, educator*
Mosekilde, Leif *endocrinologist, educator*
Moseley, Ivan Frederick *neuroradiologist*
Moser, Royce, Jr. *physician, medical educator*
Moses, Hamilton, III *medical educator, hospital executive, management consultant*
Moskowitz, Michael Arthur *neuroscientist, neurologist*
Mosli, Hisham Ahmed *urologist*
Mosqueda-Garcia, A. Rogelio *physician*
Moss, Veronica Ann *palliative care physician*
Mostafa, Badr Eldin *otolaryngologist, educator*
Most-Levin, Carol Lynn *physician, geriatrician*
Mostofi, Fathollah Keshvar *pathologist, educator, consultant*
Moszczyński, Paulin *hematologist*
Motoori, Shigeatsu *physician, researcher*
Motoyama, Satoru *medical educator*
Motson, Roger Wingfield *surgeon*
Mou, Thomas William *physician, medical educator and consultant*
Mougrabi, Mohammed Mostafa *cardiologist*
Moukarzel, Juan Carlos *internist*
Moul, Judd Wendell *urologist, surgeon*
Moulana, Abdulraheem *nephrologist*
Mourad, Jean-Jacques *physician, researcher*
Mourad, Walid A. *pathologist*
Moy, Ronald Leonard *dermatologist, surgeon*
Moyers, Sylvia Dean *retired medical record librarian*
Moyle, Graeme John *physician*
Moyle, Robert John *forensic psychiatrist*
Mózsik, Gyula *internist, gastroenterologist, educator*
Mraček, Zdeněk *neurosurgeon, educator*
Mrazek, David Allen *pediatric psychiatrist*
Mróz, Jan Kazimierz *physician*
Muangman, Debhanom *public health physician, administrator, researcher*
Muchnick, Richard Stuart *ophthalmologist*
Muckle, David Sutherland *surgeon, educator*
Muellbacher, Wolf *neurologist*
Muelleman, Robert Leo *physician, researcher medical educator*
Mueller, Charles Barber *surgeon, educator*
Mueller, Herwart *surgeon*
Mueller, Walter E. *pharmacologist, educator*
Mueller-Heubach, Eberhard *medical educator*
Mueller-Schimpfle, Markus Peter *radiologist*
Muguti, Godfrey Ignatius *surgeon, consultant*
Mui, Piu Cheung *internist*
Muir, John Robert *cardiologist*
Mujeeb, Syed Abudl *pathologist*
Mukai, Minoru *oncologist*
Mulic, Hazim A. *neurology and psychiatry educator*
Mullendore, Mark Edward *internist, educator*
Müller, Frank Robert *pharmacologist*
Müller-Schimpfle, Markus Peter *radiologist, researcher*
Müller-Schweinitzer, Else Elise *pharmacologist, researcher*
Mullings, Anthony Mortimer Alexander *medical educator, consultant*
Mumenthaler, Marco *neurologist, educator*
Munas, Fil A. *psychiatric physician*
Mune, Masatoshi *medical educator*
Mune, Ole *physician, rheumatologist, physiologist*
Mungan, Necmettin Aydin *urologist*
Mungiu, Ostin Costel *medical educator*
Munisamy, Thulasimani *pharmacologist, consultant*
Muniz, Javier *physician*
Munk, Zev Moshe *allergist, researcher*
Munker, Reinhold *physician*
Munoa, José L. *ophthalmologist, medical educator*
Muñoz, Ricardo *pediatrician, educator, researcher*
Muñoz-Hoyos, Antonio *pediatrics educator*
Munro, Donald Sinclair *endocrinologist, educator*
Munson, Paul Lewis *pharmacologist*
Muntaner, Carles *social epidemiologist, researcher, educator*
Munton, Charles Gregory *consultant ophthamalic surgeon*
Munz, Dieter Ludwig *nuclear medicine physician*
Mupanemunda, Richard Henry J. *pediatrician*
Murad, Ferid *physician*
Muranaka, Toru *radiologist*
Murashima, Yoshiya Luca *psychiatrist, neuroscientist*
Murata, Katsumi *physician*
Murata, Satoru *radiologist, researcher*
Muravskaya, Galina Vladimirovna *radiologist, oncologist*
Murch, Simon Harry *pediatric gastroenterologist*
Murcia Lora, Jose Maria *obstetrician/gynecologist, consultant*
Muretto, Pietro Aurelio *pathologist*
Muroff, Lawrence Ross *nuclear medicine physician, educator*
Murphree, Henry Bernard Scott *psychiatry and pharmacology educator, consultant*
Murphy, Edward Stack *pathologist*
Murphy, George Francis *pathologist, dermatologist, oncologist, educator*
Murphy, Ricardo *neuroscientist, plant physiologist*
Murphy, Robert Patrick *physician, ophthalmic researcher*
Murphy, Thomas Miles *pediatrician*
Murphy, Timothy Francis *physician, scientist*
Murray, John Frederic *physician, educator*
Murray, Joseph Edward *retired plastic surgeon*
Murray-Lyon, Iain Malcolm *gastroenterologist*
Murshid, Waleed Rida *neurosurgery educator*
Murugavel, S. *medical researcher, consultant, anesthesiologist*
Muscolino Emanuele, Giuseppe *thoracic surgeon*
Mussurakis, Stavros *radiologist, researcher*
Mustila, Anu Kristiina *physician*
Mustonen, Eila Marja Aulikki *neuro-ophthalmologist*
Muthukumar, Natarajan *neurosurgeon*
Muti, Paola Cornelia *physician, educator*
Mutoh, Tatsuro *neurologist, molecular neurochemist*
Mutter, Didier *surgeon, educator, researcher*
Mutziger, John Charles *physician*
Muyembe, Victor Mwanzi *surgeon, consultant*
Myers, Allan Arthur *physician*
Myers, Kenneth Arthur *vascular surgeon, antique dealer*
Myers, Richard Kelley *family physician*
Myers, William Osgood *thoracic and cardiovascular surgeon*
Myerson, Keith Roger *anesthesia and intensive care medicine consultant*
Myhre, Hans Olav *vascular surgeon, educator*
Myllykangas-Luosujarvi, Riitta Anneli *rheumatologist*
Myllylä, Vilho Valdemar *neurologist, educator*
Myo-Khin *physician, researcher*
Myrup, Bjarne *internist*
Myslinski, Norbert Raymond *medical educator*
Mysorekar, Viswanath Ramrao *anatomist, educator, researcher*
Nabae, Toshinaga *surgeon*
Naber, Dieter Helmut *psychiatrist*
Nachemson, Ann Kerstin *hand surgeon*
Nacul, Luis Carlos *epidemiologist*
Nadar, Thankayyan Sankaran *physician, researcher*
Nadas, John Adalbert *psychiatrist*
Nader, Nader Djalal *anesthesiologist, health science researcher*
Naef, Paul Andreas *thoracic surgeon*
Nafe, Reinhold *neuropathologist*
Nafeh, Mohamad Adawy *gastroenterologist, educator*
Nagarsenker, Mangal Shailesh *pharmaceutical technologist*
Nagase, Fumihiko *immunologist, researcher*
Nagase, Sohji *medical educator*
Nagata, Tetsuji *anatomist, biology educator*
Nagatsu, Masayoshi *cardiothoracic surgeon, researcher*
Nagayama, Masao *neurologist, neuroscientist, educator*
Nagele, Susan Lynn *physician*
Naidoo, Datshana Prakesh *cardiologist, researcher*
Naimi, Shapur *cardiologist, educator*
Nair, Velayudhan *pharmacologist, medical educator*
Naito, Kensei *otolaryngologist, researcher*
Naito, Masahito *cardiologist*
Naito, Masatoshi *orthopedic surgeon, educator*
Nakagami, Tomoko *internist, researcher*
Nakagawa, Hidemitsu *neurosurgeon, researcher*
Nakagawa, Koji *endocrinologist, educator*
Nakagawa, Yasuaki *orthopaedic surgeon, educator*
Nakagoe, Tohru *surgeon, researcher*
Nakahama, Hajime *physician, educator*
Nakai, Yuichiro *obstetrician and gynecologist*
Nakajima, Osamu *physician, cardiologist*
Nakajima, Sumio *physician, researcher*
Nakamura, Hiroshi *urology educator*
Nakamura, Kumi *anesthesiologist*
Nakamura, Masami *internist*
Nakane, Yoshibumi *psychiatry educator*
Nakano, Mineo *plastic surgeon*
Nakatani, Satoshi *cardiologist*
Nakatsuji, Tadako *medical researcher, educator*
Nakayama, Hideo *dermatologist, allergist*
Nakayama, Takeo *epidemiologist*
Nakayama, Tomohiro *internist, molecular biologist*
Nappi, Giuseppe *neurology educator*
Narang, Anil *neonatologist*
Narasimhamoorthy, Lalitha *oncologist, consultant, medical researcher*
Narayanan, Shridhar *pharmacology educator*
Narita, Mitsuo *pediatrician, microbiologist*
Naritomi, Kenji *pediatrician, clinical geneticist, educator*
Narramore, Christopher Llewellyn *orthopaedic surgeon*
Nassar, Faris Michael *physician, researcher*
Nassar, Munir Emile *retired cardiovascular physician*
Nassim, Michael Arnold *clinical pharmacologist*
Nast, Edward Paul *cardiac surgeon*
Naszlady, Attila Janos *physician, educator*
Nataloni, Andrew Hector *obstetrician, gynecologist*
Natarajan, Aruna *physician, educator, researcher*
Natello, Gregory William *cardiologist, educator*
Nathoo, Narendra *neurosurgeon, consultant*
Nauck, Matthias Alexander *internist*
Naumann, Gottfried Otto Helmut *ophthalmology educator*
Nauš, Antonin *occupational health educator*
Navaratnam, Visvanathan *medical educator*
Navarra, Giuseppe *surgeon, educator*
Navarro, Jose Tomas *physician, researcher*
Navrátil, Leoš *radiobiologist*
Nazaire, Michel Harry *physician*
Nazareth, Irwin Darryl Wilfred *general practitioner, educator*
Nazarov, Peter Grigorievich *immunologist*
Nazar-Stewart, Valle *epidemiologist, educator*
Nazli, Cem *physician, educator*
Neagu, Stefan Ilie *surgeon, educator*
Neal, Anthony James *oncologist*
Neal-Parker, Shirley Anita *obstetrician and gynecologist*
Neelam, Venkataramana Krishnan *neurosurgeon, consultant*
Neglen, Nils Peter *surgeon*
Neiman, Jack *neurologist, psychiatrist*
Neimark, Mikhail Izrailevich *anesthesiologist*
Nelson, Ed *medical educator, research scientist*
Nelzén, Olle Per *vascular surgeon*
Nemickas, Rimgaudas *cardiologist, educator*
Neoptolemos, John Phythohiannis *surgeon, educator*
Nermut, Milan Vladimir *biomedical scientist, researcher*
Nesbit, Gary Merlin *neuroradiologist, educator*
Nesbitt, Robert Edward Lee, Jr. *physician, educator, scientific researcher, writer, poet*
Nessa, John Nikolaus *physician*
Nettles, John Barnwell *obstetrics and gynecology educator*
Neuberger, James Max *physician, consultant*
Neuberger, Manfred Arthur *medical educator, researcher*
Neufang, Karl Friedrich Rudolf *radiologist, educator*
Neumayr, Guenther *medical educator*
Neundoerfer, Bernhard *neurologist*
Neutra, Raymond Richard *epidemiologist*
Neuwald, Christine Angela *physician*
Neves, Jayme *medical educator, consultant, researcher*
Neville, Alexander Munro *pathologist*
Newell, Christopher James *medical educator*
Newell, Simon James *medical educator, consultant*
Newell, William Keith *neurobiological researcher*
Newman, Anita Nadine *surgeon*
Newman, Barry Marc *pediatric surgeon*
Newman, Fredric Alan *plastic surgeon, educator*
Newman, Steven E. *neurologist*
Newman-Tancredi, Adrian *research neuroscientist*
Newstead, Charles George *renal physician*
Newton, David James *biomedical research scientist*
Newton, Kenneth Kurt *physician, educator*
Neylan, John Francis, III *nephrologist, educator*
Nezelof, Christian *retired pathologist, educator*
Ng, Chi-Sing *pathologist, consultant*
Ng, Eng-Hen *surgeon*
Ng, Heung-Tat *obstetrics and gynecology educator, hospital official*
Ng, Hon Wah *physician*
Ng, Lorenz K. *neurologist, educator*
Ng, Man-Lun *psychiatrist, educator*
Ng, Shu Hang *radiologist*
Ng, Tian Seng *internal medicine consultant*
Ngai, Yin Leung Stephen *dermatologist*
Ngugi, Elizabeth Njeri *medical educator*
Nguyen, Duc Dinh *physician*
Nguyen, Hieu Trong *physician*
Nguyen, Thach Ngoc *cardiologist*
Nguyen, Tien Manh *physician*
Nguyen-Trong, Hoang *physician, consultant*
Nguyen-Van-Tam, Jonathan Stafford *public health educator*
Ni, Yicheng *radiologist, educator and researcher*
Nicholas, Nick Sotiriou *consultant obstetrician and gynecologist*
Nichols, Ronald Lee *surgeon, educator*
Nichols, Trent Lee *physician, physicist*
Nicholson, William Noel *clinical neuropsychologist*
Nickelsen, Thomas Nikolaus *endocrinologist, internist, researcher*
Nicolaidis, Stylianos *neurosurgeon, institute director, former educator*
Nicolodi, Maria *neuropharmacologist, medical researcher*
Nidecker, Andreas Cornelis *radiologist, educator*
Niederman, James Corson *physician, educator*
Nieto, Juan Manuel *emergency medicine physician*
Nieto Diaz, Anibal *obstetrician, gynecologist*
Nieuwenhuys, Rudolf *retired neuroanatomy educator*
Niggebrugge, Arthur Henri Philips *surgeon*
Nigro, Giovanni *physician, researcher, medical educator*
Nihoyannopoulos, Petros *cardiologist, consultant*
Nii-Amon-Kotei, David *medical educator, surgeon, consultant, dean*
Nijevitch, Alexander Albertovich *pediatrician, researcher*
Nikl, János *neurologist*
Nikoevski, Nikolai Penchev *neurologist, lecturer, consultant*
Nikolenko, Vladimir Nikolaevich *anatomist, dean, educator*
Nikolic, Nebojsa *physician, educator*
Nikolopoulos, Thomas Panayotis *physician, consultant*
Nilsson, Bernt Ove *human anatomy educator*
Nilsson, Bo Ingvar *hematologist*
Nilsson, Holger *physiology/pharmacology educator and researcher*
Nilsson, Ralph Ingemar *occupational and environmental health physician*
Ning, John Tse-Tso *urologic surgeon*
Ning, Ke *neurosurgeon*
Ning, Shoucheng *cancer biologist, head and neck surgeon*
Nir, Isaac *medical educator*
Nirschl, Robert Phillip *orthopedic surgeon*
Nisce, Lourdes *radiologist*
Nishi, Okihiro *ophthalmologist, surgeon*
Nishimura, Toshikazu *anatomy educator*
Nishiyama, Yayoi *mycologist, educator*
Niskanen, Raimo Olavi *orthopedic surgeon*
Nisli, Güngör *pediatric hematologist, pediatrics educator*
Nissel, Martin *radiologist, consultant*
Nissenbaum, Gerald *physician, educator, inventor*
Nissenson, Allen Richard *physician, educator*
Nisticó, Giuseppe *pharmacology educator*
Nitta, Douglas *family practice physician*
Niveau, Gerard *psychiatrist, researcher*
Niwano, Sinichi *physician, researcher*
Nixdorff, Uwe *cardiologist, researcher, consultant*
Nizze, Horst Karl Gerhard *pathologist, educator*
Njokah, Joseph Munene Mbui *surgeon, educator, educator*
Nnodim, Joseph Ogbonna *biomedical researcher, educator*
Noach, Arthur Bernard Joseph *pharmacologist, pharmacist*
Noda, Mami *pharmacology educator*
Noda, Yutaka *physician, otolaryngologist*
Nógrádi, Antal *ophthalmology educator, researcher*
Nogueira, Diogo Pupo *occupational health educator*
Nollet, Franciscus *physiatrist*
Nolte, Wilhelm *physician*
Nomicos, Nicholas Eugene *emergency medicine physician*
Nomikos, Iakovos Nicolas *general surgeon*
Norcross, Keith *surgeon*
Norcross-Mehlman, Karyl *neurologist, educator*
Nordberg, Erik Magnus *physician, researcher*
Nordshus, Tore *pediatric radiologist*
Nores, Jean-Marc *rheumatologist*
Norrby, Klas Carl Vilhelm *pathology educator*
Norrgren, Hans Rikard *physician*
Norrid, Henry Gail *osteopathic physician and surgeon, biologist, researcher, human anatomy and physiology educator*

Norrie, Philip Anthony *family physician, historian*
Norstrand, Iris Fletcher *psychiatrist, neurologist, educator*
Northover, Basil John *pharmacologist, educator*
Nosko, Michael Gerrik *neurosurgeon*
Nosratian, Farshad Joseph *internist, cardiologist*
Nossal, Gustav Joseph Victor *medical research institute administrator, biologist, educator*
Notghi, Alp *physician*
Noto, Hiroshi *internist*
Nour, Bakr M. *surgeon, health facility administrator*
Nousia-Arvanitakis, Sanda *pediatrician*
Novaes, Luiza Helena Vinholes Siqueira *pediatrician, educator*
Novak, Helmut Franz *neurologist*
Novak, Ivan *pediatrician, consultant*
Novotny, Ladislav *experimental oncologist, educator*
Nowinski, Wieslaw Lucjan *medical researcher*
Nozaki, Ryoichi *gastroenterologist*
Nuebler-Moritz, Michael *oralmaxillofacial surgeon*
Nunez de Arco, Jorge Albert *psychiatrist*
Nunley, Julia Riley *physician, educator*
Nurhussein, Mohammed Alamin *internist, geriatrician, educator*
Nürnberg, Bernd E.R. *molecular pharmacology educator*
Nüsslein-Volhard, Christiane *medical researcher*
Nutton, Vivian *history of medicine educator*
Nyam, Denis Christopher *colorectal surgeon*
Nyborg, Helmuth *psychoneuroendocrinologist*
Nye, Edwin Richard *physician, writer*
Nyrke, Timo Jukka *neurophysiologist*
Nystrom, Fredrik Hans *endocrinologist, researcher*
Oates, Geoffrey Donald *surgeon, consultant*
Obamogie, Mercy A. *physician*
Obara, Marian Zygmunt *gynecologist, consultant*
Obeid, Lina M. *medical educator*
Öberg, Tommy Roland *biomechanic and orthopaedic educator*
Oberneier, Klaus Henner *health care executive*
Obiala, Raphael Uzodinma *pediatrician, family medicine physician*
O'Boyle, Patrick John *urologist, consultant*
O'Brien, Mark Stephen *pediatric neurosurgeon*
O'Brien, Michael Dermod *physician, consultant neurologist*
O'Byrne, Elizabeth Milikin *pharmacologist, researcher, endocrinologist*
O'Callaghan, Bryan Irvine *physician, radiologist, neuroradiologist*
Och, Mohamad Rachid *psychiatrist, consultant*
Ochiai, Masahiko *cardiologist, educator*
Ochoa, Manuel, Jr. *oncologist*
Ochsner, Seymour Fiske *radiologist, editor*
O'Connor, Brian Joseph *physician, consultant*
O'Connor, Brian Kevin *pediatric cardiac electrophysiologist, researcher*
O'Connor, Joseph Benedict *surgeon*
Odamtten, George Tawia *mycologist*
Odar-Cederlöf, Ingegerd Elisabet *internist, nephrologist, researcher, educator*
Odawara, Masato *physician, researcher*
Odlind, Bo Gunnar *physician, educator*
O'Donnell, Stella Rayner *pharmacology educator*
Oei, S. Guid *gynecologist*
Oeiria, David Sudarto *dermatologist, plastic and reconstructive surgeon, educator*
Oertel, Wolfgang Hermann *physician, neurologist*
Oesterling, Joseph Edwin *urologic surgeon*
Ofoefule, Sabinus Ifeanyi *pharmaceutical technology educator*
Ogawa, Yasuo *pharmacology educator, researcher*
Ogawa, Yoshihide *urologist*
Ogihara, Toshio *medical educator*
Ogita, Shuhei *surgeon, educator*
O'Grady, John Charles *forensic psychiatrist, consultant*
Ogunniyi, Adesola *neurologist, consultant, educator*
Ogura, Chikara *neuropsychiatry educator*
Oguz, Yasemin Neyyire *physician, medical educator*
Oh, Young-Taek *radiologist, oncologist, researcher*
O'Hanlon, Mary Teresa *consultant psychiatrist*
O'Hara, Hiroshi *internist*
Ohashi, Yoichi *surgeon, immunologist*
O'Higgins, Niall John *surgeon, educator*
Ohkoshi, Norio *neurologist*
Ohri, Sunil Kumar *surgeon*
Ohsaki, Katsuichiro *otolaryngologist researcher, and educator*
Ohshima, Tohru *legal medicine educator*
Ohta, Akihide *physician, researcher, educator*
Ohta, Hitoya *radiologist*
Ohtahara, Shunsuke *medical educator*
Ohtake, Eiji *radiologist*
Ohtani, Haruo *pathologist, educator*
Ohyanagi, Mitsumasa *physician, medical educator*
Ojebode, Jacob Olusoji *radiation therapist*
Ojewole, John Akanni Oluwole *pharmacology educator, pharmacist*
Okada, Hiroaki *pharmaceutical scientist, pharmacist*
Okada, Ryozo *educator, clinician and researcher*
Okada, Shigeru *pathology educator*
Okada, Shuichi *physician, researcher*
Okada, Yoshitaka *radiologist*
Okai, Osamu *physician, educator*
Okajima, Yasutomo *physiatrist*
Oken, Robert *neuroscientist, researcher, consultant*
Okere, Chuma Onyeaghala *neuroscientist*
Okonkwo, John Emewulu Nicholas *obstetrician-gynecologist, educator*
Okosun, Ike S. *epidemiologist, educator*
Okuda, Yukichi *medical educator, endocrinologist*
Okudaira, Masahiko *pathologist, researcher*
Okumura, Fukuichiro *anesthesiology educator*
Okuno, Tsutomu *medical researcher*
Olafsson, Jon Hjaltalin *dermatology educator*
Older, Jay Justin *ophthalmic plastic surgeon*
Oldham, John *family physician*
O'Leary, Robert Thomas *physiatrist*
Olesen, Ole Frilev *neurobiologist, researcher*
Oliphant, Charles Romig *retired physician*
Oliveira, Mario Martins *physician*
Oliveira, Tania Cristina *epidemiologist*
Oliver, David John *physician, consultant*
Oliver, Michael Francis *physician, consultant cardiologist, educator*
Olofsson, Jan Gunnar Vilhelm *otolaryngologist, educator*
Olson, Daniel Jay *surgeon, researcher, educator*
Olumide, Yetunde Mercy *dermatologist, educator, researcher*
Olver, Ian Norman *medical oncologist*
Omagari, Katsuhisa *internist, educator*
O'Malley, Patrick Pearse *neurologist, psychiatrist*
Omata, Ken *physician*
Omer, Mohamed Ibrahim Ali *pediatrician, educator*
Omland, Tov *physician, medical microbiologist*
Omori, Koichi *otolaryngologist, educator*
Omura, Emily Fowler *dermatologist, educator*
Omura, George Adolf *medical oncologist*
Onadeko, Babatunde Owolabi *medical educator, consultant*
Onat, Teoman *pediatric cardiologist*
Oneglia, Carlo *cardiologist*
Ong, Edmund Liang Chai *infectious diseases physician, consultant*
Oni, Olusola Olumide Akindele *orthopaedic surgeon, consultant*
Onischenko, Evgeni Fedorovish *physician, researcher*
Onishi, Tetsuro *urology educator*
Onitsuka, Hideo *radiologist, health facility administrator*
Onoé, Kazunori *immunologist, educator, pathologist*
Onsager, David Ralph *cardiothoracic surgeon, educator*
Onyemelukwe, Geoffrey Chukwubuike *physician, consultant*
Oonishi, Hironobu *orthopedic surgeon*
Oosterlinck, Willem *urologist, educator*
Oqbal, Syed Mohammed *otolaryngologist*
O'Rahilly, Stephen Patrick *clinical endocrinologist, researcher, educator*
Orallo, Francisco *pharmacologist, researcher, educator*
Orazi, Attilio *anatomic pathologist, researcher, educator*
Orchard, John William *sports physician, researcher*
Orda, Ruben *surgeon*
Ordonez, Nelson Gonzalo *pathologist*
Orefice, Umberto *clinical researcher*
Orihuela Nicolau, Rafael *urology educator*
Orliaguet, Gilles André *anesthesiologist, researcher*
Orlikov, Gregory Alexander *medical educator*
Orłowski, Tadeusz *medical educator*
Orman, Nanette Hector *psychiatrist*
Orme, Michael L'Estrange *pharmacologist, educator*
Ormerod, Lawrence Peter *thoracic physician, consultant*
Ormos, Jenö *pathologist*
Ornish, Dean *medical educator, administrator*
Ornoy, Asher *pediatrician, researcher*
Orr, Kevin Bridson *surgeon, educator*
Orrom, William John *surgeon*
Ortel, Thomas Lee *oncologist, hematologist, educator*
Ortiz, Juarez *medical diagnostic center director*
Ortiz de Zarate, Julio Cesar *physician*
Ory, Steven Jay *physician, educator*
Osen, Kirsten Kjelsberg *anatomy educator, researcher*
Osinsky, Sergey *oncologist, researcher*
Osman, Ali *medical educator, researcher*
Ospina, Julio Enrique *pathologist, medical education expert*
Oštádal, Oldřich *internist, educator*
Ostaszewska-Puchalski, Iwona *dermatologist*
Ostergren, Jan B. *physician, researcher*
Ostertun, Burkhard *radiologist*
Ostrowska, Teresa Halina *medical historian, researcher*
Osuchowski, Jacek Karol *neurosurgeon, consultant*
O'Sullivan, John Conor *gynecological surgeon, educator, consultant*
Ota, Hirotaka *gynecologist*
Oton, Claudio Antonio *radiology educator, oncologist*
Otte, Kjeld Erik *medical consultant*
Otto Buczkowska, Ewa *pediatrician, researcher*
Ottonello, Carlo Maurizio *radiologist*
Ouchterlony, Örjan Thomas *physician, educator*
Oura, Toshiaki *pediatrician, health facility administrator*
Out, Henk Jan *clinical scientist*
Out, Theo Anthonius *immunologist*
Overton, Caroline Elizabeth *obstetrician, gynecologist*
Oviasu, Efosa *medical educator, consultant physician*
Owen, Michael John *psychiatrist, geneticist*
Owen, Robert Frederick *internist, rheumatologist*
Owor, Raphael *histopathologist, educator*
Oxhøj, Henrik *pediatric cardiologist, consultant*
Oyama, Tsutomu *anesthesiologist*
Oyanagi, Mitsumasa *medical educator*
Ozdamar, Sukru *pathology educator*
Özdemir, Enver *urologic surgeon, researcher*
Ozdemir, Yildiz Emine *ophthalmologist*
Ozesmi, Mustafa *chest physician, consultant*
Ozet, Ahmet *medical educator*
Ozgür, Servet *public health educator, researcher*
Ozornek, Murat Hakan *obstetrician-gynecologist*
Pacifici, Gian Maria *clinical pharmacology educator, researcher*
Packard, Peter *medical educator, retired internist*
Pacurar, Vasile *oncologist, educator*
Padmachandran, Korambath Payyanadan *surgeon, consultant*
Padrón, Rubén Salvador *endocrinologist, educator*
Pagani, Olivia *oncologist*
Page, John Graham *emergency medicine educator, consultant*
Pagtalunan, Flora Zenaida Diaz *pediatrician*
Pagtalunan, Redentor Juan Guillermo *general surgeon, consultant*
Paguio-Torreyillas, Dimpna Duran *pediatrician, educator*
Pahor, Ahmes Labib *physician*
Pahor, Dušica *ophthalmologist, consultant*
Paintaud, Gilles *pharmacologist*
Pajno, Giovanni Battista *allergist, pediatrician*
Pakesch, Georg *psychiatrist, educator*
Pakkala, Seppo Tapio *hematologist, researcher*
Palacios, Ronald *immunologist*
Palacz, Olgierd Jan *ophthalmologist, educator*
Palatianos, George Michael *surgeon*
Palermos, John George *immunologist, military officer*
Pálffy, György Antal *neurologist, educator*
Palmedo, Holger *nuclear medicine physician*
Palmer, Alan Michael *neuroscientist*
Palmer, Ann Patricia *public health physician*
Palmer, Robert Marshall *geriatrician*
Palmstierna, Tom Krisman Kule *psychiatrist, researcher*
Paloczi, Katalin *haemoto immunologist, consultant*
Palva, Ilmari Pellervo *haematologist*
Pan, Cynthia X. *geriatrician, educator, researcher*
Pan, Henry Yue-Ming *clinical pharmacologist*
Pan, Wynn Hwai-Tzong *neuropharmacology educator, neurochemist*
Panas, Raymond Michael *pharmaceutical researcher*
Panasoff, Josef Hugo *allergist*
Panayeas, Sotirios George *flying surgeon, pathologist*
Panayi, Gabriel Stavros *medical educator*
Panayiotou, Barnabas Nicos *consultant physician, educator*
Pandey, Manoj *oncologist*
Pang, Herbert George *ophthalmologist*
Pang, Samuel Chow-Ern *reproductive endocrinologist, gynecologist-obstetrician*
Pang, Zhan-Jun *medical researcher*
Pangas, Julio Cesar *physician, educator*
Panitz, Lawrence *physician*
Panopoulos, George *internist*
Panotopoulos, George *internist, nutritionist*
Paolaggi, Joseph Antoine *physician, medical educator*
Paoletti, Rodolfo *pharmacology educator*
Paolino, Richard Gerald *physician, consultant*
Papadakis, Chariton E. *physician, consultant*
Papadopoulos, Constantine Denis *cardiology educator*
Papadopoulou, Alexandra *pediatrician*
Papageorgiou, Athanasios *thoracic surgeon, educator*
Papagiannis, John *pediatrician*
Papantoniou, Nicolas Elpidoforos *obstetrician, gynecologist, researcher*
Papay, Francis Anthony *plastic surgeon, researcher*
Papouin, Gérard *cardiologist*
Parameshvara, Vishvanathapura *internist, cardiologist*
Paraschivescu, Lucian *physician*
Parellada Cuadrado, Carlos Maria *surgeon, consultant, researcher*
Parikh, Sherwin Kirit *dermatologist, educator*
Parikh, Vinay *pharmacology scientist*
Parish, Anthony Royal *medical researcher*
Parisi, Mario Nestor *medical educator*
Pařizek, John Francis *pediatric neurosurgeon, consultant*
Park, Dong Soo *physician*
Park, Gilbert Richard *physician*
Park, Hae Sim *allergist*
Park, Hyosoon *clinical pathologist, educator*
Park, Jung-Han *medical educator*
Park, Lee Crandall *psychiatrist*
Park, Moon Suh *otolaryngologist*
Park, Soon J. *cardiovascular surgeon*
Parker, Andrew James *physiologist, researcher, writer*
Parker, Peter Joseph Jacques *medical researcher*
Parkes, Colin Murray *psychiatrist, educator*
Parkey, Robert Wayne *radiology and nuclear medicine educator, research radiologist*
Parkin, Donald Pysden *clinical pharmacologist, medical researcher*
Parnas, Josef Stefan Stanislaw *psychiatrist*
Parnell, Michael John *medical products executive*
Parnham, Michael John *pharmacologist*
Parpala-Spårman, Teija Mirjami *surgeon, urologist*
Parra-Mejia, Tulio E. *surgeon*
Parrish, Matthew Denwood *psychiatrist*
Parsonage, Maurice John *neurologist, retired*
Parsons, Anthony David *gynecology educator*
Pärssinen, Tahvo Olavi *ophthalmologist, educator, myopia researcher*
Partinen, Markku Mikael *neurologist*
Partonen, Timo Tapio *physician, researcher*
Partridge, Terence Anthony *medical researcher, educator*
Paruthikal, Louis Mathen *surgeon, consultant*
Parvathy, Usha *surgeon, educator*
Pascale, Jane Fay *pathologist*
Pascu, Oliviu *medical educator*
Pasini, Evasio *physician*
Pasternac, André *cardiologist*
Pasternak, Shai Sam *physician, nutritionist*
Pastorelli, Gianni *gynecologist, medical administrator*
Patel, Pravin Chaturbhai *physician, consulting surgeon*
Paterson, Iain MacKenzie *surgeon, consultant*
Paterson, John Kirkpatrick *retired physician, author*
Pathak, Rakesh Ranjan *internist*
Pathi, Vivek Lakshmi *cardiothoracic surgeon*
Patil, Naishadh Prabhakar *otolaryngologist*
Patinkin, Deborah *hematologist, developmental biologist*
Patole, Sanjay Keshav *pediatrician*
Paton, David *ophthalmologist, educator*
Patra, Bhagaban Chandra *gynecologist*
Patrocínio, Lécio Luíz Amaral *cardiologist*
Patterson, Alan Bruce *obstetrician, gynecologist*
Pattison, Neil Spencer *obstetrics educator, researcher*
Paty, Donald Winston *neurologist*
Patzakis, Michael J. *orthopaedic surgeon, educator*
Paul, Frank Allen *physician*
Paul, Norman Leo *psychiatrist, educator*
Paul, Robert *physician*
Paul, Sindy Michelle *preventive medicine physician*
Paule, Merle Gale *pharmacologist*
Paulley, John Wylmer *gastroenterologist*
Paulus, Christian *maxillofacial plastic surgeon*
Paumgartner, Gustav *hepatologist, educator*
Paus, Ralf *dermatologist*
Paventi, Saverio *anesthesiologist*
Paver, William Kenneth *dermatologist*
Pavlovic, Dragan *researcher, sports medicine physician, anaesthesiologist*
Pavlović, Draško *physician*
Payne, Meredith Jorstad *physician*
Payne-James, John Jason *physician*
Peach, Donald Frederick *medical educator*
Pearce, John Barber *psychiatry educator*
Pearn, John Hemsley *pediatrician, Australian military officer*
Peatfield, Richard Crompton *neurologist*
Pechan, Jiri Viktor *retired neurologist*
Peckitt, Ninian Spenceley *surgeon*
Pecori Giraldi, Francesca *endocrinologist, researcher*
Pedersen, Erling B. *physician, medical educator*
Pedersen, Niels Tinggaard *hematopathologist*
Pedley, Julian Eric *public health physician, consultant*
Pedley, Timothy Asbury, IV *neurologist, educator, researcher*
Peek, Giles John *cardiothracic surgeon, researcher, educator*
Peetermans, Willy Eduard *physician*
Peh, Wilfred Chin Guan *radiologist, researcher*
Peitsch, Werner Karl *surgeon, researcher*
Peitzman, Andrew Bertram *surgeon*
Peixoto Neto, Jose Ulysses *internist, researcher*
Pekmezci, Salih *physician, educator*
Pelikanova, Terezie *endocrinologist*
Pellegrini, Vincent D., Jr. *orthopaedic surgeon*
Pellegrino, Peter *surgeon*
Pelliniemi, Lauri Johannes *medical educator*
Pelosi, Marco Antonio *obstetrician and gynecologist*
Pena-Andreu, Jose Miguel *psychiatry educator*
Pendagast, Edward Leslie, Jr. *physician*
Pendergraft, Roy Daniel *medical educator, physician*
Pengelly, Andrew William *surgeon*
Pennell, Dudley John *cardiologist*
Penning, Donald Henry *anesthesiologist, obstetrician-gynecologist*
Pennington, D. Glenn *surgeon*
Pentelényi, Thomas John *neurosurgeon*
Pepine, Carl John *physician, educator*
Perani, Daniela *neuroscientist, researcher, educator*
Peräsalo, Juhani Olavi Sakari *retired physician*
Perea Carrasco, Rafael *physician, biochemist*
Pereira, Artur Torres *medical educator, microbiologist*
Perényi, András *psychiatrist*
Peretz, Tamar *oncologist*
Perez, Josephine *psychiatrist, educator*
Perez, Louis Anthony *radiologist*
Perez-Cruet, Jorge *physician, psychiatrist, psychopharmacologist, psychophysiologist, educator*
Pérgola, Federico Miguel *medical educator*
Perkin, George David *neurologist, consultant*
Perlik, František *pharmacologist, educator*
Perlmutter, Lynn Susan *neuroscientist*
Perlstein, Abraham Phillip *psychiatrist, educator*
Perna, Giampaolo Robert *psychiatrist, researcher*
Perng, Chin-Lin *gastroenterologist*
Perniciaro, Charles Vincent *dermatologist, educator, entrepreneur*
Pero, Margaretha Ida Lena *child and adolescent psychiatrist*
Peromingo, José-Antonio Díaz *physician, biologist*
Perotti, Daniela *cancer biology researcher*
Perret, Claude Henri *internist*
Perrin, Louis François *allergist-immunologist, medical educator*
Perry, Ian Charles *physician*
Perry, Lewis Charles *emergency medicine physician, osteopath*
Perry, Wayne *endocrinologist, consultant*
Persico, Antonio Maria *psychiatrist, physiologist*
Persson, Bjorn Mauritz *orthopaedist*
Persson, Jonas Karl Erik *physician, researcher*
Pesce, Maria Ester *medical educator*
Pesonen, Erkki Juhani *pediatric cardiology educator*
Pestell, George Stanley *retired surgeon, consultant*
Peszke, Michael Alfred *psychiatrist, writer*
Petelenz, Tadeusz Karol *cardiologist*
Peter, Ralf Uwe *dermatologist, radiobiologist*
Peter, Sebastian Augustine *endocrinologist*
Petersdorf, Robert George *physician, medical educator, academic administrator*
Petersen, Edward Schmidt *retired physician*
Petersen, Kitt Mia Falck *medical scientist*
Petersen, Kresten Rubeck *gynecologist*
Peterslund, Niels Anker *infectious disease physician, hematologist*
Peterson, Daniel Raymond *emergency management administrator, career officer*
Petrášek, Jan Václav *medical educator*
Petratos, Steven *neuroscientist*
Petrek, Martin *immunogeneticist*
Petrichko, Mikhail Ivanovich *urologist, nephrologist*
Petroianu, Andy *surgeon, educator*
Petroukhin, Andrey Sergeevich *pediatric neurologist, educator*
Petrovic, Mirko *geriatrician, consultant*
Petrunov, Bogdan Nikolov *medical educator, allergologist*
Pettee, Daniel Starr *retired neurologist*
Pettersen, Jan Sommerfelt *physician*
Pettersson, Gosta Bengt *thoracic surgeon*
Pettersson, Holger Tage Arthur *radiologist, educator*
Petty, Thomas Lee *physician, educator*
Petursson, Hannes *psychiatry educator*
Peus, Joseph Carl *orthopedic surgeon*
Peyman, Michael Anthony *medical researcher*
Pfeffer, Cynthia Roberta *psychiatrist, educator*
Pfeifer, Johann Gottfried *surgeon*
Pfeiffer, Michael *orthopaedic surgeon, educator*
Pflum, William John *physician*
Pfulg, Michel Edmond *plastic and aesthetic surgeon*
Phanjoo, André Ludovic *psychiatrist, educator*
Pharoah, Peter Oswald Derrick *epidemiologist educator*
Phelip, Xavier André *rheumatologist, educator*
Phelps, Carol Jo *neuroendocrinologist*
Philipp, Elliot Elias *consulting gynecologist*
Philippe, Bagros *nephrologist*
Philippon, Marc Joseph *orthopaedic surgeon*
Phillips, Michael Robert *psychiatrist*
Phillips, Robert Derrick *psychiatrist*
Phillips, Robin Kenneth Stewart *colorectal surgeon*
Piasek, Martina *physician, researcher*
Pick, Edgar *immunologist*
Pickens, William Stewart *cardiologist*
Picó-Aracil, Francisco *cardiologist*
Pieninkeroinen, Ilkka *neurologist, researcher*
Pienovi, Alberto Daniel *sports medicine physician, educator*
Pierce, Donald Shelton *orthopedic surgeon, educator*
Pierik, Engelbertus G.J.M. *surgeon, researcher*
Pieroni, Robert Edward *internist, educator, military officer*
Pierpont, Ross Z. *retired surgeon*
Pierquin, Bernard *oncologist*
Pierre, Bitoun *pediatrician, geneticist*
Pierson, R. Warren *retired surgeon, farmer*
Pietropaolo, Aniello *surgeon, ophthalmologist*
Pietrzak, Zbigniew *obstetrician-gynecologist*
Pietschmann, Peter *internal medicine educator, rheumatologist*
Pilch, Yosef Hayim *physician, retired educator*
Pile-Spellman, John Martin *radiology and neurosurgery educator*
Pilheu, Jorge Alberto *internal medicine educator*
Pilkerton, Arthur Raymond, Jr. *surgeon, educator*
Pilotto, Alberto *geriatrician*
Pimparkar, Bhalchandra Dattatraya *gastroenterologist, educator*
Pimpinella, Ronald Joseph *retired surgeon*
Pineda, Anselmo *neurosurgery educator*
Pinillos Ashton, Luis V. *radiologist, educator*
Pinsky, Michael Raymond *internist, educator, critical care physician*
Pinto, Claudio Ivan *anesthesiologist*
Pinto, Maria Cristina Rosamond *internal medicine and genetics educator*
Pinto, Olavo De Campos, Jr. *psychiatrist*
Pipic, Nedim *plastic surgeon*
Pires, Jose Guilherme Pinheiro *pharmacologist, educator*
Pires-Neto, Mario Ary *physician, medical educator*
Pirk, Jan *cardiac surgeon*
Pirodsky, Donald Max *psychiatrist, educator*
Pisarev, Mario Alberto *endocrinologist, medical researcher*
Pistolesi, Massimo *medical educator*
Pitchika, Prasada Rao Vignananda Vara *anatomist, educator*
Pitcock, James Allison *retired pathologist*

Pitr, Karel physician
Pitt, William Alexander cardiologist
Pittaluga, Paul cardiologist, consultant
Pittaway, Donald Edward endocrinology educator, gynecologist
Piver, M. Steven gynecologic oncologist
Pivovarov, Arkady Saulovich neurophysiologist, researcher
Plant, Gordon Terence neurologist
Platonov, Igor Aleksandrovitch pharmacology educator
Platz, Thomas Franz physician, researcher
Plch, Josef otorhinolaryngologist, educator
Plesan, Aida neurologist
Plesko, Ivan oncologist
Plesnicar, Stojan Josip oncologist, educator, consultant
Pless, Jorgen Emil plastic surgery consultant
Plettner, Jean-Louis Georges angiologist
Plockinger, Ursula endocrinologist, researcher
Plorde, James Joseph physician, educator
Plotkowiak, Zyta Maria pharmacist
Pluta, Ryszard neuropathologist, educator
Poch, Herbert Edward retired pediatrician, educator
Pocock, Stuart John medical statistics educator, consultant
Pocoski, David John cardiologist
Podani, Manuela physician, researcher
Podchernyaeva, Raisa Jakovlevna virologist, researcher
Podea, Delia Marina psychiatrist
Podskochy, Alexander physician, researcher
Pogue, John Marshall physician, editor, researcher
Poh-Fitzpatrick, Maureen B. dermatologist, educator
Pohjola-Sintonen, Sinikka Hannele internist
Pohl, Jürgen Ernst medicine educator, physician
Poissonnier, Marie-Helene obstetrician/gynecologist
Pokorny, Alex Daniel psychiatrist
Pokorny, Lajos radiologist, consultant, educator
Polascik, Mary Ann ophthalmologist
Polenaković, Momir Haralampie nephrologist, educator, scientist
Polenz, Joanna Magda psychiatrist
Poletto, Bernard physician
Polidori, Giancarlo pediatrician, intensivist
Polkowska, Jolanta neuroendocrinologist, researcher
Pollack, Robert William psychiatrist
Pollock, Bruce Godfrey psychiatrist, educator
Polosukhin, Vasiliy Vladimirovich anatomist
Poloy, Anna (Anna Polay) dermatologist
Polymenidis, Zafiris Panos pathologist, immunologist, nephrologist
Pombo, Manuel pediatric endocrinologist, researcher, educator
Pompei, Pierluigi neuropharmacologist
Pompidou, Alain Jacques medical educator
Ponomareva, Olga Victorovna epidemiologist
Pons, Jean-Claude obstetrician, gynecologist
Ponsonby, Anne-Louise public health physician
Pöntinen, Pekka Juhani anesthesiologist, consultant
Poon, Ronnie Tung-Ping surgeon, educator
Poon, Tak Lun orthopedic surgeon, photographer
Popa, Ioan physician
Pope, Harrison Graham, Jr. psychiatrist, educator
Popescu, Christian surgeon
Popescu, Gabriel-Adrian physician, educator
Popescu, Valerian medical educator, physician
Popiela, Tadeusz surgeon, educator
Popoli, Maurizio neuroscientist, pharmacologist
Porkert, Manfred (Bruno) medical sciences educator, author
Porschen, Rainer gastroenterologist, clinician
Portel, Laurent physician
Porter, John Maurice surgeon
Portilla, Eliseo surgical researcher
Portman, Ronald Jay pediatric nephrologist, researcher
Portmann, Bernard Claude pathology educator, consultant
Porto, Jarbas Anacleto retired physician
Portsmouth, Owen Henry Donald physician, consultant, medical ethics educator
Portwich, Philipp Otto physician
Posse, Margareta G. consulting psychiatrist, researcher, psychoanalyst
Postacchini, Franco orthopaedic surgeon, researcher, educator
Postaire, Eric R.R. biomedical researcher
Potter, John McEwen retired neurosurgeon and medical educator
Pousada, Lidia physician
Poussaint, Alvin Francis psychiatrist, educator
Povoa, Pedro Manuel physician, consultant
Powell, Deborah Elizabeth pathologist
Power, Michael W. physician, consultant
Powers, Karen Elizabeth medical research administrator
Powers, William Edward emergency physician, educator
Powles, Raymond Leonard oncologist
Powrie, James Kenneth endocrinologist, consultant
Poyser, John general practice physician
Poyser, Norman Leslie pharmacology educator
Pozzi, Maurizio gynecologist
Pracht, Denis radiodiagnostician
Pradella, Stephan Paul ophthalmologist, physician
Pradelli, John Mauricio physician, gerontologist, translator
Pradhan, Sunil neurology educator, consultant
Pradhan, Suresh Chandra pharamacologist, educator
Praetorius, Finn oral pathology educator
Praharaj, Shanti Shankar neurosurgeon
Prais, Dario physician, researcher
Prange, Arthur Jergen, Jr. psychiatrist, neurobiologist, educator
Prat, Frederic Pierre hepatogastroenterologist
Pratt, Hillel neurophysiologist
Pratt, Philip Chase pathologist, educator
Prayaga, Krishna Murai Mohan anestheesiologist, consultant
Preclik, Guenter Wolfgang gastroenterologist
Premasathian, Dilok plastic surgeon
Prescott, William Glenn psychiatrist
Press, Edward consulting physician
Prestar, Franz Jürgen neurosurgeon, researcher
Preston, Clive Ian palliative medicine consultant
Preston, William Leon family practice
Preti, Antonio psychiatrist, researcher
Prezzia, Charles Paul physician
Přibylová, Hana pediatrician, researcher
Price, James Melford physician
Price, Robin Murray retired medical librarian
Price, William Anthony psychiatrist
Priebe, Cedric Joseph, Jr. pediatric surgeon
Priest, Robert George psychiatrist, educator, author
Prieto, Victor Gerardo physician
Prigerson, Holly Gwen psychiatry researcher, educator
Prignot, Jacques Jules retired pneumology educator
Prinz, B. Beth physician
Prisant, L(ouis) Michael cardiologist
Prischl, Friedrich Cornelius nephrologist
Prisco, Douglas Louis physician
Probstfield, Jeffrey Lynn cardiology educator, consultant
Pronin, Alexander Vasilyevich immunologist, researcher
Proos, Lemm Artur pediatrician
Prosińska-Kibler, Maria Krystyna physician, consultant
Provan, Drew Benjamin hematologist, consultant
Prusiner, Stanley Ben neurology and biochemistry educator, researcher
Prydz, Hans Peter Blankenborg medical director, cell biologist
Pryor, John Pembro uroandrologist, consultant
Pshenisnov, Kirill Pavlovich surgeon, educator
Puccetti, Luca rheumatologist, researcher
Puchtler, Holde histochemist, pathologist, educator
Puckett, C. Lin plastic surgeon, educator
Puddu, Paolo Emilio cardiologist, educator, researcher
Puente Fonseca, Claudio Julio pediatric surgeon
Pugeat, Michel endocrinologist
Puig, Juan Garcia internist, researcher
Pukel, Clifford Stuart physician
Puliafito, Carmen Anthony ophthalmologist, healthcare executive
Pulimood, Benjamin Mani gastroenterologist, consultant, physician
Pullen, Julia M. psychiatrist
Puntis, John William Lambert pediatrician, consultant
Puolakkainen, Pauli Antero surgeon and educator
Puretić, Štefanija Košak pediatric dermatologist
Puri, Basant Kumar medical researcher, physician
Purvez, Akhtar otolaryngologist, researcher
Puschett, Jules B. medical educator, nephrologist, researcher
Puskás, Tamás radiologist, consultant
Putnam, Joe B., Jr. thoracic and cardiovascular surgeon
Puvaneswary, Murugasu radiologist and consultant
Puybasset, Louis Jean anesthesiologist, intensivist
Pylkkänen, Kari Eino K. psychiatrist
Pyrohova, Vera medical educator, dean
Pyrros, Demetrios G. orthopaedic surgeon
Pytkowski, Mariusz cardiologist
Pytsky, Victor Ivanovich allergist, educator
Qian, Liang neurosurgeon
Qiao, Qing pediatrician, researcher
Qin, Ling orthopedics educator, researcher
Qin, Yong-Mei medical sciences educator
Qu, Chengyi epidemiologist
Qu, Qiang surgeon
Quatrehomme, Gerald pathologist, researcher
Querleu, Denis obstetrics and gynecology educator
Quesada, Orlando internist, educator
Quillope, Jose Perez pathologist, consultant
Quinn, Michael John surgeon
Quintanilla, Antonio Paulet physician, educator
Qureshi, Shakeel Ahmed pediatric cardiologist
Qvarnstrom, Mari Johanna physician
Rabee, Hussein Mohammed surgeon, educator
Raber, Jacob neuroscientist
Rabin, Olivier Paul medical researcher
Raboch, Jiri psychiatrist, educator
Race, George Justice pathology educator
Rachkova, Mariana Ilieva physician, researcher
Racine, Eric pharmacology administrator, educator, researcher
Racz, Joseph George psychiatrist, researcher
Rademacher, David Jeffrey neuroscientist, psychology educator
Raden, Koestedjo surgeon, educator
Radevski, Ivelin Valtchev physician
Radovanovic, Zoran epidemiologist
Radulescu, Elena hematologist, immunocytochemist, researcher
Radvany, João neurologist
Radwan, Abdalla Gomaa pharmacologist
Radwi, Amer Naeem medical educator
Raev, Dimitar Christov cardiologist, educator
Raev, Michael Borisovich immunologist, educator, molecular biologist
Raeva, Svetlana Nikolayevna neurophysiologist, researcher
Rafael Aguilera, Julio Cesar surgery educator
Rafel, Enrique pathologist
Rafique, Syed Firoz Alfred physician, retired
Ragland, Thomas Eugene osteopath, prison medical director
Rahim, M. Abdur oncologist
Rahim, Sheikh Idris Abdel psychiatry educator
Rahman, Mahfuzar physician, researcher
Rahman, Mizanur ophthalmologist
Rahman, Rafiq Ur oncologist, educator
Rahman, Syedur A. H. ophthalmologist, consultant
Rahmathullah, Vijaya Laxmi physician
Rai, Gurcharan Singh physician, educator
Raichev, Ivan Todorov pathologist, consultant, medical educator
Raja, Ramesh Chandra radiologist
Rajagopalan, Mani psychiatrist, consultant, researcher
Rajakumar, Deshpande Vasudevarao neurosurgeon, consultant
Rajna, Peter psychiatrist
Raju, Kanthi Penmatch psychiatrist
Rak, Kalman internist
Rakhmanova, Aza Gasanovna physician, educator
Rako, Susan psychiatrist, author
Rakusic, Neven pulmonologist, consultant
Ramacciotti, Carla Emilia psychiatrist, educator
Raman, Poondy Gopalratnam medical educator
Ramaratnam, Sridharan neurologist
Rama Subbu, Raja Gopalan Ariyur surgeon, consultant
Ramazanov, Ramil neurosurgeon
Rammos, Kyriakos S. surgeon
Ramos, Hugo Roberto cardiologist
Ramos, Julio Antonio ophthalmologist, educator
Ramos-Alvarez, Manuel pediatrician, researcher
Ramos-Martínez, Ernesto pathologist
Ramos-Zúñiga, Rodrigo neurosurgeon, educator
Rampal, Marius urologist, surgeon, educator, retired
Ramsahoye, Walter Alan neurologist
Ramsdale, David Roland cardiologist
Ranade, Geetanjali Gajanan medical safety educator, researcher
Ranakusuma, Asman Boedisantoso physician, medical educator
Rani, Rajni immunologist, researcher
Ranjadayalan, Kulasegaram cardiologist, physician, consultant
Ransil, Bernard J(erome) research physician, methodologist, consultant, educator
Ransmayr, Gerhard N. neurology educator
Rantakallio, Paula Tuulikki medical educator
Rao, Akkinepalli Badri Narayan physician, educator
Rao, Arun P. physician
Rao, Chitaldroog Ramachandra physician
Rao, P. Syamasundar pediatric cardiologist
Rao, Rajesh P.N. neuroscientist, computer scientist
Raoult, Didier Alain medical educator
Rappaport, Raphael medical educator
Raschka, Christoph Josef sports physician, internist, anthropologist
Rašková, Helena pharmacologist
Rasmussen, Claus internist, rheumatologist
Rasmussen, Kjeld Leisgaard physician, consultant
Rasmussen, Michael Hojby clinical research physician
Rasmusson, Lars Gösta oral and maxillofacial surgeon, researcher
Rassam, Salwan M. B. ophthalmologist
Rau, Bhimanakunte surgeon, educator
Rau, Rolf retired rheumatologist
Raulic, Patrick gynecologist, consultant
Raunest, Juergen surgeon, educator
Rauschmeier, Hans urologist
Rautava, Päivi Tuire public health educator, pediatrician
Ravenscroft, Peter James anaesthesiologist, educator
Ravi, Govinda Panicker urologist, consultant
Ravi, Rajagopalan surgery educator
Ravitz, Leonard J., Jr. physician, scientist, consultant
Ravnskov, Uffe retired internist, nephrologist and researcher
Rawlins, Mark Ian surgeon
Ray, André Pierre orthopedic surgeon
Ray, Charles Dean neurosurgeon, spine surgeon, bioengineer, inventor
Ray, John Walker otolaryngologist, educator, broadcast commentator
Raymond, Azman Ali neurologist, consultant
Raymond, Nigel John consultant physician, educator
Rayner, Colin Robert plastic surgeon
Rea, Desmond Maurice Vincent plastic surgeon
Reach, Gérard endocrinologist, researcher
Reader, John Granville family practitioner
Reaman, Gregory Harold pediatric hematologist, oncologist
Reay-Young, Peter Shirley oncologist, consultant
Rebolledo, Gema ophthalmologist
Rechtman, David J. physician
Records, Raymond Edwin ophthalmologist, medical educator
Reddihough, Dinah Susan pediatrician
Reddy, Doodipala Samba pharmacologist, researcher
Reddy, Sasiragha Priscilla medical researcher, administrator
Reddy, Satti Sethu-Kumar physician, educator
Reddy, Vardhan Jonnala surgeon
Redman, Christopher Willard G. obstetric physician, educator
Redman, Robert Shelton pathologist, dentist
Redmond, Donald Eugene, Jr. neuroscientist, educator
Rednam, Krishna Rao Venkata ophthalmologist
Reed, Eddie pharmacologist
Reek, Jan Van epidemiologist, researcher
Rees, Gareth John Glyn oncologist
Rees, Gareth Mervyn cardiac surgeon consultant
Rees, John Elvan pharmaceutical consultant, researcher, educator
Rees, Peter John medical educator, consultant
Reeve, Jonathan physician, researcher
Reeves, Billy Dean obstetrics and gynecology educator emeritus
Regensberg, Claude digestive and general surgeon
Reginald, Daniel ophthalmic surgeon
Reginster, Jean-Yves Luc physician, researcher
Regös, László medical educator, cardiologist
Rehak, Jiri ophthalmologist
Rehany, Uri physician, ophthalmologist, lecturer
Rehman, Asif Bin pharmacologist, educator, researcher
Rehncrona, Stig Lennart neurosurgeon, researcher
Rehnqvist, Nina Anna Kristina physician
Reich, Oleg pediatric cardiologist, consultant
Reichen, Jürg hepatology and pharmacology educator
Reif, Thomas Henry internist, health products company executive
Reik, Rita Ann Fitzpatrick pathologist
Reilly, Paul Alexander rheumatologist, consultant
Reinecke, Leopold radiation oncologist
Reinecke, Martin neurologist, psychiatrist
Reinhardt, Kurt retired radiologist and nuclear physician
Reinoso, Luis Alberto retired physician
Reis, Ernane D. surgeon, researcher
Reissman, Petachia physician, general surgeon, researcher
Rello, Jordi epidemiologist, intensivist, researcher
ReMine, William Hervey, Jr. surgeon
Ren, Jian-Fang echocardiologist, medical educator
Ren, Lei-Ming pharmacology educator, dean
Renckens, Cees N.M. gynecologist, consultant
Renganathan, Radhakrishnan physician
Rennie, Janet Mary neonatal physician
Rennie, Morag Lilian retired psychiatrist
Reno, Joseph Harry retired orthopedic surgeon
Rentchnick, Pierre retired physician
Renwick, Andrew Gordon pharmacology educator
Renzulli, Attilio cardiothoracic surgeon
Repassy, Denes Laszlo urologist
Reron, Elzbieta otolaryngologist, researcher
Resnik, Harvey Lewis Paul psychiatrist
Restian, Adrian Gratiaö physician, researcher
Restori, Gabriele emergency medicine physician
Retsas, Spyros oncologist
Retterstol, Kjetil physician
Reuland, Peter nuclear medicine physician, researcher
Reus, Werner Alois physician
Révai, Tamás nephrologist
Reverte, Maria pharmacologist
Rewerski, Wojciech pharmacologist
Rey, Alix Charles psychiatrist
Rey-Bellet, Jean Julien physician
Reyers, Fred clinical pathologist, veterinary educator
Reyes, Raul Gregorio surgeon
Reyes-Noyla, Jose Godoy pediatrician, endocrinologist
Reymond, Jean Charles surgeon
Reynolds, Edward Osmund Royle neonatal pediatrician
Reynolds, Glenn G. rehabilitation medicine physician
Reynolds, Herbert Young physician, internist
Reynolds, Ronald Davison family physician
Rhiew, Francis Changnam physician
Rhim, Johng Sik physician, educator, medical researcher
Rhoads, George Grant medical epidemiologist
Rhoads, Jonathan Evans surgeon
Rhodes, Jonathan Michael physician
Rhodes, Lesley Elizabeth dermatologist, educator
Riantawan, Pratheep physician
Ribeiro, Isabela Quilelli Correa Rocha infectious disease physician, internist
Ribeiro, Joaquim Alexandre medical researcher, educator
Ricard, Philippe Olivier cardiologist, electrophysiologist
Ricci, Michael Anthony surgeon
Rich, Alan John medical educator, surgeon
Richard, Karl Eduard neurosurgeon, educator
Richardson, A(rthur) Leslie former medical group consultant
Richardson, Jonathan anesthesiologist, consultant
Richardson, Peter John cardiologist, consultant
Richert, Harvey Miller, II ophthalmologist
Richie, Rodney Charles critical care and pulmonary medicine physician
Richling, Bernd neurosurgeon
Richmond, David Eric geriatrician, consultant
Richter, Hans Peter neurosurgeon, educator
Richter, Jay Alan physician, educator
Rickels, Karl psychiatrist, physician, educator
Rickenbach, Mark Alan physician
Rickers, Carsten physician
Rickert, Robert Richard pathologist, educator
Rico Claros, Julio Alberto orthopaedic surgeon, educator
Ricordi, Camillo surgeon, transplant and diabetes researcher
Ridgway, Alan Edward ophthalmic surgery consultant
Ridley, Colin Charles Sheridan psychiatrist
Ridsdale, Leone Lorna physician, educator
Riecken, Ernst-Otto gastroenterologist, physician, educator
Riegel, Byron William ophthalmologist
Rieger, Gebhard physician, researcher, medical educator
Riess, Friedrich-Christian Edgar surgeon, researcher
Rietbrock, Norbert clinical pharmacology educator
Rietschel, Robert Louis dermatologist
Rifai, Ghassan Moutieh urologist, consultant
Rigg, Charles Andrew pediatrician
Riggs, Byron Lawrence, Jr. physician, educator
Rihmer, Zoltan psychiatrist, neurologist
Říhová, Blanka Jiřina immunologist, researcher
Riikonen, Raili Sylvia child neurologist
Rijal, Kiran Prasad orthopedic surgeon
Riley, Patrick Anthony pathologist
Rilling, David Carl surgeon
Rimar, Stephen pediatric anesthesiologist
Rimoldi, Reynold Louis orthopedic surgeon
Rimón, Ranan Hilel psychiatry educator
Rinck, Peter A. radiologist, research scientist
Riner, Ronald Nathan cardiologist, business consultant
Ringelstein, Erich Bernd neurology educator
Ringertz, Hans Gösta radiology educator
Ringoir, Severin Maria Ghislenus medical educator, physician
Rink, Thomas nuclear medicine physician
Rioux, Patrice medical facility administrator
Rioux, Pierre August psychiatrist
Ripandelli, Guido Alberto ophthalmologist, researcher
Ripka, Otto internal medicine educator
Rippere, Victoria retired psychologist, retired psychology educator
Ristich, Miodrag psychiatrist
Ristow, Brunno plastic surgeon
Ritsilä, Veijo Antti surgeon, researcher, consultant, educator
Ritter, Henning consultant in obstetrics and gynecology
Riva, Alessandro Lodovico anatomy educator, scientist
Rivas del Fresno, Manuel urologist, consultant
Rivera, Alejandro Flores surgeon, medical researcher
Rivner, Michael Harvey neurologist
Rizkallah, Marie-Therese Youssef pediatrician
Rizova, Elena dermatologist, consultant
Rizza, Charles Rocco hematologist
Rizzo, Vito physician, researcher in cardiovascular diseases
Ro, Dusik oriental medicine physician
Roach, John Michael gastroenterologist
Robakis, Nikolaos K. medical educator
Robberstad, Magnus Knutson neurology consultant
Robbins, Frederick Chapman retired physician, medical school dean emeritus
Roberts, Albert Dee internist
Roberts, Donald Wilson pathologist, consultant
Roberts, Doris Emma epidemiologist, consultant, nurse
Roberts, Eleanor Sterett (Ruth Eleanor Sterett Roberts) osteopathic physician
Roberts, Lynne Jeanine physician
Roberts, Peter Johan surgical oncologist, surgery educator
Roberts, Stanley Dwayne physician, medical educator
Roberts, William Lewis clinical pathologist
Robertson, Abel L., Jr. pathologist
Robertson, Andrew Geoffrey public health physician, naval officer
Robertson, James Ian medical educator, researcher
Roberts-Thomson, Ian Charles physician, gastroenterologist
Robinson, Charles Graham Francis radiologist, consultant
Robinson, Elizabeth Angela hematologist, consultant
Robinson, Joe Sam neurosurgeon
Robinson, John Richard retired psychiatrist
Robles, Alfredo neurologist
Robson, Martin Cecil surgery educator, plastic surgeon
Robson, Robert Howard pharmacologist
Robule, Vesma Herberta neurologist
Roch, Lewis Marshall, II ophthalmic surgeon, medical entrepreneur
Roch, Philippe Gerard developmental immunologist, researcher
Rocha, Paulo Roberto hemodynamicist, cardiologist
Rockswold, Gaylan Lee neurosurgeon
Rockwell, Don Arthur psychiatrist
Rodden, Appletree Frank neuroscientist
Roddie, Robert Kenneth otolaryngologist, educator
Roddie, Thomas Wilson retired obstetrician, gynecologist

Rodeck, Charles Henry obstetrician and gynecologist, educator
Rodeck, Heinrich F.J. pediatrician, educator
Rodrigues-Radischat, Margarida Pocinho physician, researcher
Rodriguez, Beatriz Lorenza epidemiologist
Rodriguez, Carlos Alberto pathologist
Rodriguez, Guillermo Gerardo physician, surgeon
Rodriguez, Maria Carmela physician
Rodriguez, William Julio physician
Rodriguez-Camps, Salvador plastic surgeon
Rodriguez Morales, Julio cardiologist
Roe, Francis J. Caldwell pathologist, consultant
Roel, José Enrique physician
Roger France, Francis Henri medical educator
Rogers, Fergus John medical association administrator
Rogers, Ian Munro surgeon, researcher
Rogiers, Xavier surgeon
Rognoni, Paulina Amelia cardiologist
Rogstad, Oddvin Moerch physician
Rohack, John James cardiologist
Röhl, Hardy Frode surgeon, consultant
Rohrer, Richard Jeffrey surgeon, educator
Rohrmann, Dorothea urologist
Roilides, Emmanuel John pediatrician
Rojas-Fernandez, Carlos H. geriatric medicine and pharmacology educator
Rokicka-Milewska, Roma pediatrician, hematologist, oncologist
Rokicki, Wladyslaw Stanislaw pediatrician
Rokstad, Kirsten Skinlo physician, educator
Roland, Jan Patrick nuclear medicine physician
Roldan-Moré, Alfonso physician, educator, dean
Rolfes, Leonard Joseph pediatrician
Rollin, Henry Rapoport psychiatrist
Romanelli, Anna Maria epidemiologist, researcher
Romano, Ennio oncologist, medical educator
Romas, Evangelos physician, health services administrator
Romics, Imre urology educator
Rónai, Zoltán allergist, immunologist, researcher
Rønningen, Kjersti Skjold physician
Rontoyannis, George Panayote sports medicine, researcher
Roomi, Riad cosmetic surgeon, physician
Roosendaal, Goris physician, researcher
Ropac, Darko Ivan epidemiologist, educator
Rosa, Nicola ophthalmologist
Rosales, Carlos immunology educator, researcher
Rosandić, Marija gastroenterologist, researcher
Rosario, Luis Bras cardiologist
Rosario, Manuel Tainha Ribeiro physician
Rose, Deborah epidemiologist
Rose, Noel Richard immunologist, microbiologist, educator
Rose, Stephen John pediatrician, consultant
Rosen, Arthur David neurology educator
Rosen, Harald Reinier physician, researcher
Rosen, Paul Peter pathologist
Rosen, Sidney Walter gastroenterologist
Rosenbaum, Dieter exercise scientist
Rosenbaum, Ernest Harold internist, oncologist, educator
Rosenbaum, Tomas Pedro surgeon
Rosenberger, Jean Alexandre radiologist
Rosenblatt, Michael medical researcher, educator
Rosenbloom, Mindy Sharon psychiatrist
Rosendal, Tage anesthesiologist, consultant
Rosengart, Todd Kenneth cardiothoracic surgeon, researcher
Rosenthal, Rafail Leon surgeon
Rosin, Arnold Jack physician, educator
Rosin, Richard David consultant surgeon
Rösler, Norbert Felix neurologist, neuroscientist
Ross, Edward cardiologist
Ross, Michael Wallis public health educator
Rossdeutscher, Reinhard Kurt Paul, Jr. radiologist, educator, nuclear medicine physician
Rossi, Giovanni Arturo pneumatologist
Rossitti, Sandro L. physician, researcher
Rossmann, Pavel pathologist
Rossof, Arthur Harold internal medicine educator
Rossor, Martin Neil neurologist
Rostaing, Lionel Paul-Emile transplant physician
Rostoker, Guy Pascal Francis nephrologist
Rostron, Chad Kenneth ophthalmologist
Roszkowska, Anna Maria ophthalmologist
Rotenberg, Vadim Semionovich psychiatrist, educator
Roth, Oliver Ralph radiologist
Rothenberger, Aribert psychiatrist
Rothenhausler, Hans-Bernd Matthaus psychiatrist
Rothman, Joel Harry medical educator, research scientist
Rothman, Ulf Sven Erik plastic surgery educator, inventor
Rotim, Krešimir neurosurgeon
Rotolo, Vilma Stolfi immunology researcher
Rott, Natalia Nikolaevna embryologist, researcher
Roulidis, Zeses Chris physician, medical educator
Rouot, Jacques retired physician, educator
Rouveix, Bernard Jean pharmacology educator
Rowell, Neville Robinson dermatologist, educator
Roy, Alec psychiatrist
Roy, Chunilal psychiatrist
Rozanov, Vsevolod Anatoliyevich neurochemist, biochemistry educator and researcher
Rozgonyi, Ferenc medical educator, microbiologist
Rozner, Leo plastic surgeon, writer
Rozsíval, Pavel ophthalmologist, educator, surgeon
Rozsos, István Imre general surgeon, researcher
Różyło, Teresa Katarzyna physician, educator
Rubay, Jean Etienne cardiac surgeon, educator
Rubens, Robert David physician, educator
Rubin, Theodore Isaac psychiatrist
Rubins, Andris Janis medical educator
Rudert, Cynthia Sue gastroenterologist
Rudnick, Abraham psychiatrist, philosopher
Rudofsky, Gottfried angiologist
Rudowski, Witold Janusz surgeon, educator
Rudy, David Robert physician, educator
Rueckert, Frederic plastic, reconstructive and hand surgeon
Ruehle, Charles Joseph pathologist, military officer
Rugarn, Olof obstetrician-gynecologist
Ruggiero, David A. neuroscientist
Ruichek, Yassine physician, educator
Ruiz, Robert physician, researcher, educator
Ruiz, Ulises medical educator
Ruiz-Cruces, Rafael radiology and medical physics educator, consultant
Rukavina, Daniel immunology and physiology educator
Rumberger, John Arthur cardiologist
Rümenapf, Gerhard vascular surgeon, educator
Rumyantsev, Sergey Nikolaevich immunology researcher
Rund, Deborah Gasner hematologist
Ruohonen, Jarkko Kalevi pharmaceutical researcher
Rupp, Henry Jacob physician
Rusalova, Margarita Nikolaevna psychophysiologist
Russell, John Robert neurosurgeon
Russell, Paul Sudhakar psychiatrist
Rusten, Gunnar physician
Rustomjee, Sabar psychiatrist
Rusznák, Zoltán Gyula physiologist, educator
Rutherford, John David forensic pathologist
Rutishauser, Wilhelm Jakob medicine educator
Rutter, Martin Kenneth endocrinologist, diabetologist, research physician
Rutty, Guy Nathan forensic pathologist, educator
Ružička, Miloš general and vascular surgeon, educator
Ryan, Francis Patrick physician, writer
Ryan, Terence John dermatologist, educator
Rychlik, Ivan nephrologist
Ryder, Kenneth William pathologist, educator
Rymsha, Sofia Vitalievna psychiatrist, consultant
Rywik, Stefan Ludwik cardiovascular epidemiologist, educator
Ryzhavskii, Boris Yakovlevitch histologist, consultant
Sa', Geraldo Matos de surgeon
Saadeddine, Monir Campos surgeon, military officer
Saari, Kaarlo Matias ophthalmology educator
Sabbaga, Jorge oncologist, educator
Sabbah, Alfred immunologist
Sabetian, Manuchehr consulting surgeon
Sabo, Edmond pathologist, researcher
Sabolic, Ivan physician, scientist
Sabra, Fuad neurology educator
Sabri, Osama nuclear medicine physician, researcher
Sabui, Tapas Kumar medical educator
Sachar, David Bernard gastroenterologist, medical educator
Sachdev, Harshpal Singh pediatrics educator, researcher
Sachdev, Perminder Singh neuropsychiatry educator
Sachdeva, Satya Pal retired consultant anaesthetist
Sackmann, Michael Franz medical educator
Sadan, Naum pediatrician
Sadaqa, Ahmad Saeed surgeon
Sadek, Sameh Saad El-Din physician, consultant
Sadikoğlu, Yilmaz medical educator
Saebo, Arve gastroenterological surgeon
Safai, Bijan physician, investigator
Sago, Haruhiko obstetrician, gynecologist, geneticist
Sah, Purushottam gynecologist, consultant
Saha, Asis Kumar cardiologist
Sahni, Pritam Singh general practice physician
Sahoo, Madan Mohan orthopaedic surgeon, educator
Saidi, Parvin hematologist, medical educator
Saifuddin, Abdul Bari obstetrics-gynecology educator, consultant
Saigol, Muhammad Younus physician
St George, Lourdes Ingrid obstetrician, gynecologist, consulant
Saito, Takashi immunologist, educator
Saito, Toshikazu medical researcher, educator
Saji, Madathiparambil Joseph orthopedist, surgeon
Sakaguchi, Sanae health educator, researcher
Sakakibara, Hisataka occupational hygiene educator, researcher
Sakakibara, Yuzuru medical educator
Sakamoto, Shinobu endocrinologist, gynecologist and obstetrician, educator
Sakanashi, Matao pharmacology educator
Sakhnovskii, Mikhailo Yurievich optics and spectroscopy educator
Šakić, Katarina anaesthesiologist, educator
Sakka, Samir George physician
Saku, Motonori surgeon, educator
Sala, Evis physician
Salatich, John Smyth retired cardiologist, internist
Salazar, Omar Mauricio radiation oncologist, educator
Saldanha, Leopoldo Frederico nephrologist, physician, educator
Saleh, Hesham otolaryngologist
Saleh, Khaled J. orthopaedic surgeon, educator
Salgo, Peter Lloyd internist, anesthesiologist, broadcaster, journalist, lecturer, consultant
Salicru, Bruno radiologist
Salih, Mustafa Abdalla Mohamed pediatric neurologist, educator
Salim, Kasim Abdul medical educator, researcher
Salimonu, Lekan Samusa immunologist, researcher
Salisbury, Jonathan Richard histopathologist, educator, consultant
Saljinska-Markovic, Olivera T. oncology researcher, educator
Sallah, Ahmed Sabah hematologist
Salles, Gilles medical educator
Salmasi, Abdul-Majeed cardiologist, consultant, hypnotherapist
Salmivalli, Marja Leena Kaarina occupational health physician
Saloga, Joachim dermatologist, allergist, researcher, educator
Salomone, Jeffrey Paul surgeon, educator
Salonen, Oili Laila Marjatta neuroradiologist, researcher
Salt, Alec Nicholas otolaryngology educator
Salt, Thomas Edgar neuroscientist, researcher
Saltykov, Konstantin Albertovich neurophysiologist
Salvatierra, Oscar, Jr. transplant surgeon, urologist, educator
Šámal, Martin biomedical physics educator, researcher
Šamánek, Milan pediatrics educator
Samarzija, Miroslav physician
Sambasivan, Mahadeva Iyer neurosurgeon, consultant
Samberger, Michael Antoni gynecologist, obstetrician, consultant, educator
Sambrook, Paul John oral and maxillofacial surgeon, educator
Samegy, Diviacante Cantilal Givane occupational health physician
Sames, Klaus Hermann anatomist, gerontologist, researcher, educator
Sames, Martin neurosurgeon
Samman, Juan M. prosthodontist
Sammon, Alastair Macnaughton surgeon, consultant
Samodelov, Leonid Feodor anesthesiologist
Samojlik, Eugeniusz medical educator, clinical researcher
Sampablo Lauro, Italo physician
Sampath Kumar, Arakalgud surgeon, educator
Sampino, Anthony F. physician, obstetrician and gynecologist
Sampson, Anthony Peter pharmacologist
Sampson, Jerome Mark pulmonologist
Samsioe, Goran Nils obstetrician, gynecologist, educator
Samter, Thomas Gustav retired pathologist, educator
San, Nguyen Duy psychiatrist, educator
Sanchez, Miguel Ramon dermatologist, educator
Sánchez, Pablo J. pediatrician, educator
Sanchez, Pedro Luis psychiatrist
Sanchez Alvarado, Alejandro embryologist, molecular biologist
Sánchez-Guerrero, Sergio Arturo hematologist
Sanchis-Alfonso, Vicente orthopaedic surgeon
Sandblom, Philip John retired medical educator, writer
Sandermann, Jes vascular surgeon
Sanders, Eric physician
Sandhu, Davinder Pal Singh urological surgeon, consultant
Sandhu, Sarbjinder Singh surgeon
Sandomir, Miller physician
Sándor, László surgeon
Sanger, Gareth John autonomic neuroscientist
Sankar, Madhu Nainar surgeon
Sanki, Soheir physician, surgeon
Santamarta, David neurosurgeon
Santarina, Rosita Borja pediatrician
Santelmo, Nicola surgeon
Santos, Juan Luis pediatrician, immunology researcher
Santos, Renato de Lima pathology educator
Santos Ocampo, Perla D. pediatrician, educator
Sanyal, Utpal scientist, medical researcher
Sanz, Pere medical educator
Sanz-Guajardo, Damaso physician, educator
Sapsford, Ralph Neville cardiothoracic surgeon
Sarac, Arif Murat surgeon
Sarai, Masakazu psychiatrist, researcher
Sarazin, Laurent radiologist
Sarg, Taha Mostafa pharmacognosist, educator
Saric, Marko physician, consultant
Sariola, Hannu Veikko pathologist
Sarkar, Michael Robindra surgeon
Sarramon, Jean-Pierre Fernand Louis urologist, educator
Sarrazin, Thierry Bernard medical physicist, researcher
Sarris, George Elias cardio-thoracic surgeon
Sarrot-Reynauld, Françoise internist, researcher
Sartani, Abraham endocrinologist, researcher
Sarti, Paolo pathologist
Sarwal, Virendar cardiac surgeon
Sasamoto, Yoichi ophthalmologist, immunologist
Sasse, Dieter anatomy educator
Sassolas, Bruno André dermatologist, researcher
Satake, Katsusuke surgeon, educator
Sathanandan, Muttukrishna Satha obstetrician gynecologist
Sathekge, Machaba Michael nuclear physician
Sato, Chifumi physician, educator
Sato, Yoshinobu clinical pathologist, otolaryngologist
Satoh, Tomohide pathologist
Satoyoshi, Eijiro neurologist
Satriano, Giuseppe Salvatore surgeon
Satsangi, Jack medical researcher, gastroenterologist
Satti, Idrees Ahmed physician, consultant
Satullo, Gaetano physician
Sauer, Gordon Chenoweth dermatologist, educator
Sauerbruch, Tilman internist, educator
Saugstad, Ola Didrik pediatric educator
Saunders, John Barrington medical educator
Saunders, Kenneth Barrett medical educator
Saunders, Roger Alletson epidemiologist
Saur, Petra physician, anesthesiologist
Sauvé, Georges surgeon
Savage, Seax Scott physician, educator
Savey, Lionel gynecologist and obstetrician
Savona-Ventura, Charles obstetrician, gynecologist
Saw, Ho-Suk oncologist
Sawada, Terufumi medical researcher
Sawhney, Harjeet Kaur obstetrician-gynecologist
Sawicki, Peter Thaddaeus physician, consultant
Sax, Daniel Saul neurologist
Saxen, Arno Erik Erkki pathologist, epidemiologist
Sayeed, (Abulfatah) Akram physician
Sayeed, Mohammed Abu endocrinologist, researcher
Scaglione, Francesco pharmacologist, researcher
Scambler, Peter James molecular medicine educator, researcher
Scarpinati, Marco neurosurgeon, consultant
Scasta, David Lynn forensic psychiatrist
Schaad, Urs B. pediatrics educator, hospital administrator
Schachner, Melitta medical educator
Schaeberle, Wilhelm surgeon
Schaefer, Franz Stefan pediatrician, research
Schaefer, Hans physiology educator, consultant
Schaefer, Hans Guenter pharmacokineticist
Schäfer-Korting, Monika pharmacology educator, university official
Schäffer, Michael Ralf physician, surgeon
Schaison, Gerard Simon physician, researcher
Schaller, Bernhard Jakob physician
Schally, Andrew Victor endocrinologist, researcher
Schanzlin, David J. ophthalmology educator, researcher
Schärer, Karl Othmar physician
Scharold, Mary Louise psychoanalyst, educator
Schattenberg, Peter-Joachim retired pharmaceutical research executive
Scheeren, Thomas Werner anesthesiology educator
Scheinmann, Pierre pediatrician, educator
Schellenberg, Rüdiger physician, researcher, therapist
Schenker, Joseph George physician, obstetrics and gynecology educator
Schepker, Renate child and adolescent psychiatrist, psychoanalyst
Schepp, Wolfgang internist
Schettini, Sergio Tomaz pediatric surgeon, educator
Scheule, Albertus Maria cardiothoracic surgeon
Scheving, Lawrence Einar anatomy educator, scientist
Schiavetta, Alessandro Edoardo vascular surgeon
Schiavi, Raul Constante psychiatrist, educator, researcher
Schicha, Harald nuclear medicine physician
Schifano, Fabrizio psychiatrist, pharmacologist
Schiffer, Randolph Brenton physician
Schild, Ralf Lothar physician, educator
Schildberg, Friedrich Wilhelm surgery educator
Schiller, Erich Karl Paul physician
Schimpf, Klaus physician
Schirren, Carl dermatologist, andrologist
Schleiffenbaum, Boris Eugen hematologist
Schlenska, Günter Kuno neurologist
Schlesinger, Philippe cardiologist
Schleusing, Michael anesthesiologist
Schmeller, Nikolaus Theodor surgeon, educator
Schmid, Lynette Sue child and adolescent psychiatrist
Schmid, Rudi (Rudolf Schmid) internist, educator, scientist
Schmidbauer, Georg Sebastian surgeon, researcher
Schmidt, Axel general practice physician, mycologist, researcher
Schmidt, Martin nephrologist
Schmidt, Robert Milton physician, scientist, educator, administrator
Schmidt, Waldemar Adrian pathologist, educator
Schmidt-Trucksäss, Arno internist
Schmitt, Wolfgang Georg I Hubertus radiologist
Schmoeckel, J. Michael cardiac surgeon
Schmolke, Cordula physician, anatomical researcher and educator
Schmoll, Hans Joachim internal medicine, hematology, oncology educator
Schmucker, Peter anesthesiologist
Schnabel, Ralf Paul Helmut neuropathologist, pathologist
Schnader, Jeffrey Y. physician, educator
Schneider, Calvin physician
Schneider, Frank psychiatrist
Schneider, Imre Gyula Ferenc dermatologist, educator
Schneiderka, Peter physician, biochemist
Schneidewind, Jana-Maria nephrologist
Schnuda, Daniel Nasr internist, pathologist
Schoenau, Eckhard pediatrician, endocrinologist, consultant
Scholes, Robert Thornton physician, research administrator
Scholz, Hasso pharmacologist, educator
Schomburg, Eike Dieter neurophysiologist
Schönberger, Winfried Josef pediatrics educator
Schott, John William psychiatrist
Schraeder, Peter Klaus orthopaedic surgeon, educator
Schraub, Simon oncologist, educator
Schreiber, Stefan Wolfgang gastroenterologist, immunologist
Schrell, Uwe Martin Heinrich neurosurgeon, educator, researcher
Schröder, J. Michael neuropathologist, medical educator
Schröder, Tom Martin surgeon
Schualler, Ulrich Christoph physician, researcher
Schubert, Guenther Erich pathologist
Schuchert, Andreas medical educator
Schück, Otto nephrologist, researcher
Schühlen, Helmut cardiologist
Schuleri, Erwin Wilhelm physician, consultant
Schulhof, Robert J. medical association administrator
Schulman, Claude Charles urologist, educator
Schulman, Sam hematologist
Schult, Marc physician, researcher
Schülz, Leo-Clemens pathologist
Schulz, Martin Wilhelm pharmacologist
Schulz, Rainer Maria physician, clinical pharmacologist
Schulzke, Jörg-Dieter gastroenterologist, educator
Schumacher, Stefan medical educator
Schumpelick, Volker surgeon, educator
Schupp, Wilfried Johannes physiatrist, neurorehabilitation specialist
Schuppan, Detlef Bruno physician
Schurek, Hans Joachim Franz nephrologist
Schürer, W(ilfried) Ralph physician
Schuster, Marvin Meier physician, educator
Schuurman, Hendrik Jan medical researcher
Schuz, Joachim Christoph epidemiologist
Schwaber, Evelyne Albrecht psychiatrist
Schwade, James Gary radiation oncologist
Schwartz, George R. physician
Schwartz, Gordon Francis surgeon, educator
Schwartz, Hedwiga physician
Schwartz, Louis Winn ophthalmologist
Schwartz, Sorell Lee pharmacologist, toxicologist, educator
Schwartze, Peter Heinrich physician, researcher
Schwartze-Köhler, Hannelore G. retired pathophysiologist
Schwarz, Joachim preventive medicine physician
Schwarz, Markus J. psychiatrist, neurochemist
Schwarzacher, Severin Paul physician, consultant
Schwehr, Udo cardiologist, internist
Schweiger, Ulrich psychiatrist, psychotherapist
Schweins, Michael Josef physician, surgeon
Schweitzer, Wolf physician, forensic medicine specialist
Schwilk, Bernhard physician, researcher
Sclafani, Anthony Paul plastic surgeon, educator, biomedical researcher
Scott, John Paul medical educator
Scott, Ralph C. physician, educator
Scuccimarra, Antonio Tommaso Gabriele physician, researcher
Scudla, Vlastimil hematology educator
Seaton, Anthony environmental and occupational medicine educator
Sebastianelli, Mario Joseph internist, nephrologist, health services administrator
Secher, Niels Henry anesthesiologist
Sedaghatian, Mohamad Reza pediatrician, neonatalogist
Sedláček, Dalibor immunologist, educator
Sedo, Aleksi scientist, physician
Seed, Michael Peter rheumatologist, researcher
Seedat, Yackoob Kassim medical educator
Seegenschmiedt, Heinrich Michael radiation oncologist
Seely, Robert Daniel physician, medical educator
Seeman, Philip pharmacology educator, neurochemistry researcher
Şeffer, István surgeon, plastic surgeon
Šefr, Roman Josef surgeon, endoscopist
Segawa, Daisuke surgeon
Seggev, Meir radiologist, educator
Seidell, Jacob Caesar epidemiologist, nutritionist
Seifert, Eberhard phoniatrician
Seiff, Stephen S. ophthalmologist
Seigel, Arthur Michael neurologist, educator
Seipelt, Maria Uta physician
Seitelberger, Franz neurologist, emeritus educator
Seitz, Rüdiger Jürgen neurology educator
Sekine, Joji George oral and maxillofacial surgeon
Sekizawa, Tsuyoshi medical educator, physician, neurologist
Selberg, Oliver physician
Selby, Roy Clifton, Jr. neurosurgeon
Seliem, Mohamed Abdel-Hamid pediatric cardiologist
Selivanov, Vasyl internist
Seliverstov, Vladimir Mikhailovich pediatrician
Sellar, Robin John neuroradiologist, magnetic resonance consultant
Selli, Cesare urologist, researcher
Sells, Robert Anthony surgeon

PROFESSIONAL INDEX 2553 HEALTHCARE: MEDICINE

Selmaj, Krzysztof Wojciech neurology educator, researcher
Selten, Jean-Paul Constant Jeroen psychiatrist, researcher
Seltzer, Vicki Lynn obstetrician, gynecologist
Semenova, Tatiana Pavlovna neurophysiologist, researcher
Semplicini, Andrea therapeutics educator
Semprini, Augusto Enrico physician, researcher
Sempuku, Takeo orthopedist
Semyonov, Alexey Vladimirovich immunologist, researcher
Senecal, Jean retired medical educator
Sener, Burcin physician, microbiology educator
Senior, Roxy physician
Seo, Dong Wan internist
Seo, Toru medical doctor
Seong, Jinsil physician, researcher
Seow-Choen, Francis colorectal surgeon
Seppala, Markku Tapio gynecologist, obstetrician, eductor
Seppälä, Matti Tapio neurosurgeon
Seppala, Pentti Olavi retired medical director, physician
Šercl, Miroslav radiologist
Seregard, Stefan Bjorn ophthalmologist, pathologist
Serenelli, Giovanna pathologist, researcher
Serfling, Edgar Albert Ernst pathology educator
Sergi, Consolato pediatric pathology researcher
Sergieva, Sonja Borissova oncologist
Sergin, Vladimir Yakovlevich cybernetician, brain scientist
Seri, Istvan physician, researcher
Serrano-Molina, Jose S. pharmacologist
Serratto, Maria E. pediatric cardiologist, educator
Servant, Christopher Terence Jackson orthopaedic surgeon
Seshan, Surya Venkata pathologist
Seshanarayana, Kolar Nagarajan radiologist, consultant
Sessa, Salvatore orthopaedic surgeon
Sestan, Branko orthopedic surgeon, consultant
Sethi, Prahlad Kumar neurologist, consultant
Seward, James Pickett internist, educator
Seymour, John Francis medical oncologist
Shade, Debra L. biomedical researcher
Shafiq, Muhammad surgeon, consultant, lecturer
Shah, Aashit K neurologist
Shah, Mukhtar Hamid surgeon
Shahid, Nigar Sayem epidemiologist
Shaikh, Saad physician
Shakir, Saad A. W. pharmacologist, physician, researcher
Shalita, Alan Remi dermatologist
Shand, William Stewart surgeon
Shanklin, Douglas Radford physician
Shapiro, Edward Muray dermatologist
Shaposhnik, Igor Iosifovich cardiologist
Shaposhnikov, Yakov David gastroenterologist
Sharland, Desmond Edward physician, anatomy educator
Sharma, Arjun Dutta cardiologist
Sharma, Harbans Lal nuclear medicine researcher, educator
Sharma, Kamal Kishore surgeon
Sharma, Madan Lal pharmacologist, researcher
Sharma, Manoj health educator, research physician
Sharma, Pankaj clinician scientist
Sharma, Tarun physician, consultant
Sharp, Christopher occupational physician
Sharpe, David Thomas plastic surgeon, consultant
Shatrov, Vladimir Anatoljevich immunologist, researcher
Shats, Vladimir Yakov retired physician, researcher
Shear, Mervyn oral pathologist, educator
Sheen, Portia Yunn-ling retired physician
Shefer, Olga Vladimirovna physician, mathematician, researcher
Shehabi, Yahya critical care physician
Shelby, James Stanford cardiovascular surgeon
Sheldon, Michael Graham physician
Shen, Edward Nin-Da cardiologist, educator
Shen, Hong pharmacologist, researcher
Shennak, Mustafa Mahmoud Musa internist, gastroenterologist, medical educator
Shepard, Kirk Van, Sr. physician, researcher
Shepherd, Donald Ray pathologist
Sheptulin, Arkady Alexandrovich medical educator
Sher, Phyllis Kammerman pediatric neurology educator
Sherban, Semen Dmitrievich oncology researcher, pathologist
Sherbet, Gajanan Venkatramanaya pathologist, cell biologist, research scientist
Sherwood, James Alan physician, scientist, educator
Shetty, Mambettu Vasanth Kumar consultant radiologist
Shetty, Mulki Radhakrishna oncologist, consultant
Shetty, Shivaram Narayan pharmacologist, toxicologist
Sheu, Wayne Huey-Herng diabetologist, educator, physician
Shi, Jialan pathologist, educator
Shibata, Motohiro pediatrician
Shibuya, Akira immunologist, researcher
Shidham, Vinod Baburao pathologist, cytopathologist, surgical pathologist
Shields, Robert surgery educator
Shigemitsu, Toshiro ophthalmologist, researcher, pathologist
Shih, Shin-Ru medical educator
Shiino, Masataka anatomy educator
Shikata, Yasushi physician
Shilling, Kay Marlene psychiatrist
Shima, Hiroki urology educator
Shimamoto, Kazuhiro radiologist
Shimao, Tadao epidemiologist
Shimizu, Ichiro hepatologist
Shimizu, Katsuji orthopaedic surgeon
Shimizu, Wataru cardiologist
Shimoji, Koki anesthetist, educator
Shin, Myung Hi physician
Shindo, Katsuhisa surgeon
Shindo, Masaomi neurologist
Shine, Kenneth Irwin cardiologist, educator
Shiner, Stephen Lewis anesthesiologist
Shinohara, Haruo anatomy educator
Shinton, Neville Keith retired hematologist, consultant
Shiota, Kohei anatomist, embryologist, teratologist, educator
Shirasaka, Yukiyoshi pediatric neurologist, pediatrician
Shirasawa, Takuji molecular biologist, researcher
Shires, George Thomas surgeon, educator
Shiu, Man Hei surgeon
Shlyakhov, Elie Nahum epidemiologist, researcher
Shmerling, David Haim pediatrician, educator, retired
Shneerson, John Michael medical educator
Shohieb, Moustafa Mohamed orthopedic surgeon, researcher
Shoji, Hiromu orthopedic surgeon, educator
Shoji, Shin'ichi medical educator, neurologist, anthropologist
Sholl, John Gurney, III physician
Shons, Alan Rance plastic surgeon, surgical oncologist, educator
Shore, Eric Eugene physician, consultant
Shore, Laurence Stuart reproductive endocrinologist
Shors, Clayton Marion cardiologist
Shorter, Nicholas Andrew pediatric surgeon
Shorvon, Philip John radiologist
Shou, Magang pharmacologist
Shrestha, Santosh Man hepatologist
Shrivastava, Sanjay physician, researcher
Shu, Changda endocrinologist, educator
Shudo, Ryushi physician
Shumake, James Martin emergency medicine physician
Shungu, Dikoma Cyrille radiology educator
Shurbaji, M. Salah pathologist
Shuster, Sam dermatology educator, consultant, researcher
Shuttleworth, Anne Margaret psychiatrist
Shwe, Tin tropical medicine physician
Si, Ying-Jie ophthalmologist
Sia, Alex Tiong-Heng anesthesiologist, educator, consultant
Sicard, André medical administrator
Siddiqui, Mohammad Shahid pathologist, consultant, researcher
Sieber, Hans-Peter orthopedist
Siebler, Mario physician
Siebzehnruebl, Ernst Robert gynecologist, consultant
Siede, Werner Heinrich physician
Siegel, Eberhard Gottfried endocrinologist, gastroenterologist, educator
Siegel, Michael Elliot nuclear medicine physician, educator
Siegenthaler, Walter Ernst internal medicine educator
Siennicki-Lantz, Arkadiusz physician, researcher
Sievert, Horst internist, cardiologist, angiologist
Siggeirsson, Einar Ingi phytopathologist, researcher
Signy, Mark cardiologist, consultant
Sigurdsson, Ragnar ophthalmologist
Sigwart, Ulrich cardiologist
Siklosi, Gyorgy Szilard obstetrician and gynecologist, educator
Sikora, Karol radiologist
Sikora, Sadiq Saleem gastrointestinal surgeon, oncologist, researcher
Sila, Cathy Ann neurologist
Silberg, Louise Barbara physician, anesthesiologist
Silberstein, Morry radiologist, educator
Silva, Paul Douglas reproductive endocrinologist
Silver, Ian Adair pathology educator
Silver, John Russell spinal injury consultant, researcher, consultant
Silver, Jonathan M. physician
Silver, Marc A. physician
Silverman, Charlotte epidemiologist, educator
Silverman, David Gary physician, anesthesiologist
Silverman, Michael pediatrician, educator
Silverman, Morton Mayer psychiatrist, educator
Silverman, Stanley Harry surgeon, consultant
Silverman, Warren physician
Sima, Anders Adolph Fredrik neuropathologist, neurosciences researcher, educator
Sima, Petr immunologist
Simader, Harald Maximilian physician
Şimbruner, Georg pediatrician, educator
Šimeček, Cyril Methodej physician, educator
Šimelyte, Egle medical researcher, physician
Šimhandl, Christian Alois physician
Šimić, Goran neuroscientist, researcher
Simionescu, Radu Ion anesthesiologist, consultant
Simkin, Benjamin retired endocrinologist
Simko, Robert hematologist, consultant
Simmermacher, Roger Karl surgeon, educator
Simmons, Geoffrey Stuart physician
Simoes, Eduardo Jardim epidemiologist, educator
Simoes, Eric Arun Francis pediatrics educator
Simon, Martin Lorenz internist, hematologist, oncologist
Simonetti, Francesco radiologist, Italian navy officer
Šimonić, Ante pharmacologist, educator, researcher
Šimonovsky, Václav radiologist, educator
Simonsson, Erik physician, researcher
Simovski, Constantin Rufovich medical educator
Sims, Andrew Charles Petter psychiatry educator
Sinclair, Robert anesthesiologist
Sinclair, Rodney Daniel dermatologist, educator
Singer, Donald Robert James medical researcher
Singer, Jeffrey Alan surgeon
Singer, Pierre physician
Singh, Manmohan orthopedic surgeon, educator
Singh, Prakash Rangilal surgeon, educator
Singh, Ram B. cardiologist
Singh, Shyam Pratap cardiologist, consultant
Singh, Yadhu Nand pharmacology educator, researcher
Singhal, Atul pediatrician, researcher
Singla, Sham Lal surgeon
Singletary, Sonja Eva surgeon, educator
Sinha, Nakul cardiologist
Sinha, Prabhat Kumar anesthesiologist, educator, consultant
Sinha, Satyajit Sahay ophthalmologist
Sinning, Mark Alan thoracic and vascular surgeon
Sinohara, Hyogo medical educator
Sion, Jean-Paul O.M. physician
Sipinen, Seppo Antero obstetrician, gynecologist
Sipr, Kvetoslav medical educator
Siragusa, Maddalena dermatologist, researcher
Sirtl, Clemens J.H. physician
Sisson, James C. medical educator
Sitzler, Paul James surgeon
Sivasubramanian, Kolinjavadi Nagarajan neonatologist, educator
Sizonenko, Pierre Claude pediatric endocrinology educator
Sjoberg, Gunnar pediatrician, researcher
Sjöberg, Jan Stefan physician
Sjöblad, Hans Sture Bernhard pediatrician, educator, researcher
Sjönell, Göran family physician
Sjöström, Anders Kjell ophthalmologist, clinician, researcher
Skari, Hans physician, researcher
Skeggs, David Bartholomew Lyndon radiotherapist, oncologist
Skinhoj, Peter medical educator
Skodlar, Jasna physician, researcher
Skordis, Nicos physician
Skov, Flemming Kobberøe hematologist, educator, consultant, researcher
Škovránek, Jan pediatric cardiologist
Skromne-Kadlubik, Gregorio nuclear medicine physician
Slaby, Adolf internal medicine educator
Slagle, Richard Corbin cardiologist
Slatopolsky, Mario nuclear medicine physician, political scientist
Slavickova, Alena Hana hematological oncology researcher
Slavit, David Hal otolaryngologist
Slavov, Vladimir Ionovich physician, researcher
Slee, Peter H. Th. J. oncologist
Sleeter, John William Higgs physician, health service administrator
Sleiman, Asaad Ali orthopedic surgeon
Slenczka, Werner Georg virologist
Slípka, Jaroslav histology and embryology educator
Sloan, Herbert Elias physician, surgeon
Smallridge, Robert Christian endocrinologist
Smeets, Joep L.R.M. cardiologist, electrophysiologist
Smellie, Jean McIldowie pediatrician
Smetana, Karel, Jr. anatomist, cell biologist, researcher
Smetana, Shmuel Sane nephrologist, researcher
Smirnov, Alexander Nikolaevich endocrinologist
Smith, Arlan Robert plastic and reconstructive surgeon
Smith, Craig Brenton plastic surgeon
Smith, Dale Cary medical historian, educator
Smith, David Elvin physician
Smith, Earl Charles nephrologist, educator
Smith, Irving gerontologist
Smith, Joseph Colin urological surgeon
Smith, Julia A. internist, oncologist, educator
Smith, Martin Jay physician, biomedical research scientist
Smith, Paul Mapleston physician
Smith, Randolph Relihan plastic surgeon
Smith, Raymond Leigh plastic surgeon
Smith, Selwyn M. psychiatrist
Smith, Selwyn Michael psychiatrist
Smith, Stephen Kevin obstetrician, gynecologist
Smith, Thomas Kent radiologist, viticulturist
Smith, Warren Morrison cardiologist
Smits, Helen Lida physician, administrator, educator
Smits, Jozef Franciscus Maria pharmacology educator
Smolewski, Piotr Pawel hematologist, educator
Smyth, Diane Patricia Lesley pediatric neurologist
Snaith, Richard Philip psychiatrist, educator
Snashall, David Charles physician
Snell, Noel James Creagh physician, researcher
Snitker, Soren biomedical researcher, educator, physician
So, Samuel Cho Yee therapeutic radiological physicist
Sobaci, Güngör medical educator, consultant
Sobel, Mark Esar physician, researcher
Sobel, Richard Jay physician
Šobue, Itsuro internist, neurologist, educator
Šochman, Jan cardiologist, researcher
Soedermark, Tore cardiologist
Soeparwata, Rasjid cardiovascular and thoracic surgeon
Soergel-Ahovi, Marianne pediatrician
Sofonio, Mark Vincent plastic and reconstructive surgeon
Sohn, Dong-Ryul clinical pharmacology educator
Soininen, Hilkka Sirkku neurology educator
Sokal, Etienne Marc pediatrician, consultant
Sokol, Adolf endocrinologist, researcher
Sokol, Robert Josef haematologist consultant
Soldo, Ivan epidemiologist, educator
Solheim, Bjarte Gees transfusion medicine physician, educator
Solionova, Liya Gennadievna epidemiologist
Solomon, Paul Wayne medical association administrator
Solomon, Robert Douglas pathology educator
Solvey, Pablo psychiatrist
Soma, Johannes cardiologist
Soma, Masayoshi endocrinologist, educator
Somjee, Shehnaz otorhinolaryngologist, surgeon, poet, writer
Šomlo, Peter internist, consultant
Sommer, Harald Leo physician, researcher
Sommer, Hartmut physician
Somoza, Manuel Jesús physician
Song, Gwan Gyu rheumatologist, educator
Song, Yeong Wook physician, researcher
Sonoda, Shigeru physiatrist
Sonoda, Takao urologist, educator
Sontacchi, Boris radiologist
Soothill, John Farrar immunologist, educator
Soothill, Peter William fetal medicine educator
Sopenta Quesada, Angel physician, veterinary resarcher
Sørensen, Flemming Brandt pathologist
Sørensen, Kaj Harry orthopaedic surgeon
Sorger, Karin pathologist
Sorrel, William Edwin psychiatrist, educator, psychoanalyst
Sorteberg, Angelika Gabriele physician, researcher
Sotomora-von Ahn, Ricardo Federico pediatrician, educator
Soubrane, Gisèle ophthalmologist, researcher
Souhami, Luis physician, radiation oncology
Soukup, Tomas neurophysiologist
Soulis, Athina medical research scientist
Souney, Paul Frederick pharmacist
Soussignan, Robert neuroscience and ethology educator
Souza Neto, Edmundo Pereira anesthesiologist
Spaar, Friedrich Wilhelm retired physician, neuropathology educator
Spacek, Josef Vaclav physician, neurobiologist, pathologist, educator
Spagnolo, Samuel Vincent internist, pulmonary specialist, educator
Spallek, Roswitha Hildegard pediatrician, psychotherapist
Spalton, David John ophthalmologic surgeon
Spandow, Odd physician, educator
Spanjer, Patricia Lawrence health consultant
Sparell, Gunilla Kerstin Anita laboratory technologist
Sparks, Charles Edward pathologist, educator
Sparks, Janet Lindsay Dehoff pathology educator
Sparr, Marie-Brigitte surgeon
Spathis, Gerassimos Spyros physician
Spear, Scott Lawrence plastic surgeon
Spearing, Ruth Lilian hematologist
Speck, Matthias orthopedic surgeon
Spector, Larry Wayne osteopath
Spellman, Mitchell Wright surgeon, academic administrator
Spencker, Friedrich-Bernhard physician, medical institute executive
Sperry, Len Thomas psychiatrist and preventive medicine educator
Spetzger, Uwe neurosurgeon
Spiller, Robin Charles gastroenterologist educator
Spinner, Robert Jay orthopedic surgeon
Spirin, Nikolai Nikolaevitch medical educator
Spirnak, John Patrick urologist, educator
Spiro, Theodore Erich physician, researcher, pharmaceutical executive
Spiteri, Joseph Francis, Jr. psychiatrist, educator
Spittle, Margaret Flora consultant clinical oncologist, radiotherapist
Spooren, Pieter internist
Spornitz, Udo Meinhard anatomist, researcher
Sprandel, Ulrich V. physician, educator
Sprauve, Margaret E. physician
Spray, Paul Ellsworth retired surgeon
Spreng, Manfred Peter neurophysiologist, researcher
Spriggins, Anthony John orthopedic surgeon
Springgate, Clark Franklin physician, researcher
Sprinkle, Robert Lee, Jr. podiatrist
Spruiell, Vann psychoanalyst, educator, editor, researcher
Spurrell, Roworth Adrian consultant cardiologist
Spyropoulos, George Nicholas physician
Srb, Vladimír biologist, hygienist
Srikiatkhachorn, Anan neurologist, researcher
Srinath, Latha physician
Srinivas, Krishnamoorthy neurologist
Srinivasa, Arehalli Muniswarlah emergency physician
Srivastava, Brijnandan physician, consultant
Srivastava, Rajendra Nath pediatrician, educator
S. Rózsa, Katalin neurobiologist, scientific adviser
Stadnick, Cyril obstetrician, gynecologist
Staffen, Alfred surgeon, educator, medical educator
Stafford, Arthur Charles medical association administrator
Stage, Key Hutchinson urologist
Stahle, Jan retired medical educator, researcher
Staland, (Johan Gustaf) Bertil retired gynecologist
Stålberg, Erik Valdemar clinical neurophysiologist, educator
Stalder, Hans medical educator
Stambaugh, John Edgar oncologist, hematologist, pharmacologist, educator
Stamminger, Gudrun Katharina physician, laboratory consultant
Stančić, Marin Frane neurosurgeon, educator
Stanger, Robert Henry psychiatrist, educator
Stanhope, Richard Graham pediatric endocrinologist, consultant, pilot
Stanton, Stuart Lawrence obstetrician/gynecologist
Stapleton, Thomas pediatrician, educator, advisor
Stav, Anatoli Ovsei anesthesiologist
Steele, Arthur David McGowan ophthalmic surgeon
Steele, Stuart James obstetrician-gynecologist, consultant
Stefanidis, Alexander physician, researcher
Stefánsson, Einar ophthalmology educator
Stefánsson, Jón Grétar psychiatrist
Stefenelli, George Edward physician
Stefos, Theodor obstetrics-gynecology educator
Stegemann, Burckart surgeon
Stegemann, Hermann chemistry educator
Steier, Michael Edward cardiac surgeon
Steigleder, Gerd Klaus dermatologist, dermatohistopathologist
Stein, Bernhard Otto anesthesiologist
Stein, Gerald Herbert medical educator
Stein, Michael Alan cardiologist, medical educator
Steiner, Hans Herbert physician
Steiner, Timothy John medical researcher
Steinert, Tilman psychiatrist, psychotherapist
Steinetz, Bernard George, Jr. endocrinologist
Steinhagen-Thiessen, Elisabeth Rosalie physician, medical educator
Steinhoff, Bernhard Jochen neurologist
Steinke, Berthold physician, educator
Steinmann, Gerhard Gustav immunopathologist
Steinschneider, Robert Henri pediatrician
Stellato, Giovanni physician
Stemmermann, Grant Nicholas pathologist, educator
Stenager, Elsebeth Nylev physician
Stendig-Lindberg, Gustawa physician, researcher, educator
Stenestrand, Ulf cardiologist
Stenfors, Lars-Eric otolaryngology educator
Stengård, Jari Hannu Johannes family physician, genetic epidemiologist, educator
Stenius-Aarniala, Brita Signe Maria medical educator, consultant
Stenvinkel, Peter Lars nephrologist, educator
Stepanik, Joseph Vinzenz retired physician, researcher
Stephan, Mark Tyler radiologist
Stephens, Heidi Multhopp physician, researcher
Stern, David Howard physician, journalist
Stern, Kurt pathologist, educator
Stern, Robert C. physician, educator
Stern, Thomas Lee physician, educator, medical association administrator
Sternberg, Ahud surgeon, surgical oncologist, educator
Sternberg, Esther May neuroendocrinologist, immunologist, rheumatologist
Steurer, Wolfgang physician, surgeon, researcher
Stevens, Stephen Edward psychiatrist
Stevenson, David John Douglas physician, educator
Stevenson, Edward Ward retired physician, surgeon, otolaryngologist
Stevenson, James Richard radiologist, lawyer
Steward, Lester Howard psychiatrist, academic administrator, educator
Stewart, Alice Mary epidemiologist, researcher
Stewart, Ralph David Huston medical educator
Stibler, Helena Elisabeth Christina neurologist
Stief, Christian Georg urologist, consultant
Stiel, Georg Marian physician, engineer
Stierlin, Helm psychiatry educator
Stilgenbauer, Stephan physician, researcher
Stillman, Michael Allen dermatologist
Stine, Susan Marie psychiatrist, health science facility administrator
Stingl, Georg dermatologist, scientist
Stinner, Benno surgeon
Stipic Markovic, Asja physician, researcher
Stoebner, John Martin physician
Stoian, Ionela Marinela internist, researcher
Stoker, Dennis James consultant radiologist
Stokroos, Robert Jan otorhinolaryngologist
Stoliar, Leonid Michael family physician
Stolinsky, David C. physician
Stoll, Wolfgang plastic surgeon, educator
Stolzy, Sandra Lee anesthesiologist
Stone, Herman Hull internist
Stone, James Robert surgeon

Stone, Linda Chapman *physician, consultant, medical educator*
Stone, Ross Gluck *orthopedic surgeon*
Stone, Trevor William *medical educator, researcher*
Stonnington, Henry Herbert *physician, medical executive, educator*
Stoopler, Mark Benjamin *physician*
Storm-Mathisen, Jon *neuroscientist, educator*
Storr, Anthony *psychiatry consultant*
Storr, Martin Alexander *physician, gastroenterology*
Storr-Paulsen, Allan *ophthalmologist, educator, researcher*
Stothard, John *orthopaedic surgeon*
Stott, David James *physician*
Stoupel, Elijah *medical educator*
Stozicky, Frantisek Vaclav *pediatrician*
Straka, John Anthony *otolaryngologist*
Stranadko, Eugeny Philippovich *oncologist, educator*
Strang, Peter Mikael *oncologist, researcher*
Strassburg, Hans-Michael *pediatrician*
Straub, Rainer Hans *internist, rheumatologist, researcher*
Straube, Richard Hermann-Paul *physician, clinical supervisor, researcher, inventor*
Strauch, Berish *plastic surgeon, hand and cosmetic surgeon*
Strauer, Bodo Eckehard *internal medicine educator*
Strauser, David Ross *healthcare educator*
Strauss, Raymond Bernard *otolaryngologist*
Street, Dana Morris *orthopedic surgeon*
Streeten, Barbara Wiard *ophthalmologist, medical educator*
Streeten, David Henry Palmer *internist, educator*
Streifinger, Wolfgang *surgeon*
Streitman, Charles Michael *pediatrician*
Strejan, Gill Henric *immunologist, educator*
Strek, Pawel *surgeon, educator*
Strelkov, Rostislav Borisovich *physician, radiologist*
Stretton, John Edward Hallyburton *surgeon, consultant, writer*
Strobel, Stephan *pediatric immunologist, researcher, medical educator*
Strohm, Wolf Dieter *medical administrator*
Strohmaier, Walter Ludwig *urologist, educator*
Strohmeyer, Georg W.W.F. *physician*
Strutz, Frank Manfred *nephrologist*
Stuardo P., Jaime *ophthalmologist*
Stukalov, Serge Yephimovich *ophthalmologist, researcher*
Stupp, Roger *physician, clinical researcher*
Sturdee, David William *obstetrician-gynecologist*
Sturdevant, Charles Oliver *retired physician, neuropsychiatrist*
Suarez, Carlos *otolaryngologist, educator, hospital administrator*
Suarez, Louis A. *cardiothoracic surgeon*
Subramani, Munirathinam *neuroscience researcher*
Such, Jose *physician, researcher*
Su Chee Chen, (Chan Duki) *obstetrician, gynecologist*
Sucupira, Maria Silva *endocrinologist, nuclear physician*
Sudre, Marguerite Josette Germaine *anesthetist*
Suess, Jochen Richard *gynecologist, obstetrician*
Sugár, János *consulting pathologist, researcher*
Sugasawa, Toshinari *pharmacologist, biochemist*
Sugiki, Shigemi *ophthalmologist, educator*
Sugita, Takaaki *surgeon*
Sugiyama, Satoru *cardiologist, researcher*
Sugumaran, Samuel Thomson *physician*
Suh, Hwal *medical materials educator*
Suhadi, F.X. Budhianto *pathologist*
Sukpanichnant, Sanya *pathologist, consultant*
Süle, Tamás Gyula *physician, researcher*
Suleman, Amer *internist, cardiologist*
Suliman, Fawzi A. *pediatrician, immunologist*
Sulimani, Riad Abbas *endocrinologist*
Sulkes, Aaron *physician*
Sullebarger, John Thompson *physician, educator*
Sullivan, Gary *psychiatrist*
Sullivan, Ian Douglas *pediatric cardiologist*
Sultan, Abdul Hameed *obstetrician and gynecologist, consultant*
Sultan, Abdurazzaq Mohammed Nour *medical educator, biochemist, researcher*
Sumers, Anne Ricks *ophthalmologist, museum director*
Sumiyoshi, Tomiki *psychiatrist, researcher*
Summerfield, John Arthur *gastroenterologist, educator*
Sun, Jennifer Katherine *physician*
Sun, Ji-Yao *immunologist, researcher*
Sun, Junhong *surgeon, educator*
Sun, Tung-Tien *medical science educator*
Sun, Vincent Chingwen *medical educator, scientist*
Sun, Xue-Zhi *physician, researcher*
Sundnes, Knut Ole *physician, consultant*
Sung, Mi Sook *radiologist, educator*
Sungur, Mehmet Zihni *psychiatrist, educator, consultant*
Suomalainen, Tauno Olavi *orthopaedic surgeon*
Suphioglu, Cenk *medical researcher*
Suramo, Ilkka *radiologist, educator*
Surber, Christian *pharmacologist, researcher*
Sureau, Claude Guy *obstetrician, gynecologist, educator*
Suri, Deepika *nephrologist, internist*
Surman, Owen Stanley *psychiatrist*
Surucu, Huseyin Selcuk *physician, researcher*
Suryapranata, Haryanto *cardiologist*
Suter, Ludwig Hermann *dermatologist, educator*
Sutoo, Den'etsu *neuroscientist, researcher*
Sutton, John Andrew *physician, business executive*
Sutton, Richard *cardiologist*
Suwanjutha, Subharee *pediatrician, educator*
Suzuki, Hidekazu *medical educator*
Suzuki, Jiro *psychiatry*
Suzuki, Jun-ichi *cardiologist*
Suzuki, Tsutomu *pharmacology and toxicology educator*
Svanborg, Catharina *clinical immunology educator*
Svardsudd, Kurt Folke *internist, educator*
Svendsen, Ole Lander *physician*
Svensson, Lars Georg *cardiovascular and thoracic surgeon*
Svensson, Peter Johnny *physician*
Svenungsson, Bo David *physician, researcher*
Svirnovski, Arcadi Iosifovich *hematologist, researcher*
Svirskii, Alexey Victorovich *neurologist, educator*
Svoboda, Petr *gastroenterologist*
Svoboda-Beusan, Ivna *immunologist, researcher*
Swafford, Leslie Eugene *physician assistant, consultant*
Swaim, John Franklin *physician, health care executive*
Swaim, Mark Wendell *hepatologist, molecular biologist, gastroenterologist, educator, photographer*
Swaiman, Kenneth Fred *pediatric neurologist, educator*
Swales, John Douglas *medical educator, scientist*
Swanson, Jerry William *neurologist*
Swash, Michael *neurologist, educator*
Swedberg, Karl Birger *cardiologist, scientist*
Sweeney, Rosemarie *medical association administrator*
Swierż, Jerzy Wiktor *urologist, oncologist, consultant*
Swinson, Angela Anthony *physician*
Sxrensen, Thorkild Ingvor Arrild *epidemiology educator, administrator*
Sycip-Wale, Fe Lee *physician*
Syed, Amin Tabish *medical scientist*
Syed, Ibrahim Bijli *medical educator and physicist, writer, philosopher, theologist, public speaker*
Syed, Mubin Akhtar *psychiatrist, consultant*
Syka, Josef Nicholas *neuroscientist, educator*
Sykes, Nigel Philip *palliative medicine physician, consultant*
Sykova, Eva *neuroscientist, researcher*
Syvälahti, Erkka Karl *pharmacology educator*
Syvänne, Mikko Sakari *cardiologist, consultant*
Szabó, Dezsö *retired physician, medical research administrator*
Szabó, Gyula *physician, educator*
Szabó, István *obstetrician-gynecologist, educator*
Szabo, Jenö Imre *endocrinologist, immunologist, educator*
Szafrański, Andrzej *surgeon, researcher*
Szarewski, Anne *gynecologist*
Szatmári, Marianne *physician, consultant*
Sze, Daniel Yung-Ho *medical educator*
Sze, Frank Kai-Hoi *physician, researcher*
Szekeres, Maria *medical physiologist*
Széll, Kálmán Elemer *anesthesiologist, educator*
Szende, Béla *pathologist*
Szentmiklosi, Andras Jozsef *pharmacologist*
Szepielow, Włodzimierz Jerzy *neurologist, researcher*
Sziklai, Istvan *surgeon*
Szmitkowski, Maciej *medical researcher*
Szufladowicz, Marek *cardiac surgeon, educator*
Szymański, Zbigniew *endocrinologist, medical educator*
Szyszkowitz, Rudolf Hans Georg *physician, educator*
Tabatznik, Bernard *retired physician, educator*
Tabau, Robert Louis *rheumatologist, researcher*
Tabbah, Khaldoun *immunologist, educator*
Tabutin, Jacques *orthopaedic surgeon*
Tachakra, Spitman Savak *physician, consultant*
Tachauer, Allan Dinu *internist*
Tada, Tomio *immunologist, researcher*
Tagaya, Nobumi *surgery educator*
Taggart, Hugh McAllister *geriatrician*
Taguchi, Kiichiro *otolaryngologist*
Taguchi, Shinichi *cardiovascular surgeon*
Tahara, Eiichi *pathologist, educator*
Tahvanainen, Esa Petri *physician, researcher*
Tahvanainen, Pia Johanna *medical researcher, physician*
Tait, Sylvia Agnes Sophia *retired endocrinologist*
Tajti, János *neurologist*
Tak, Tahir *cardiologist, researcher*
Takács, Sándor *public health physician*
Takada, Goro *pediatrician, educator*
Takahashi, Koji *physician, radiologist*
Takahashi, Masao *cardiac surgeon*
Takahashi, Susumu *internist, educator*
Takahashi, Takeo *anesthesiology educator emeritus*
Takaishi, Noboru *psychiatrist, educator*
Takano, Susumu *gastroenterologist*
Takao, Kunori *surgeon*
Takase, Kensaku *neurosurgeon, neurosonologist*
Takebayashi, Shigeo *radiologist, educator*
Takeda, Tsunehiro *brain science educator*
Takei, Noriyoshi *psychiatrist, epidemiologist, educator*
Takekawa, Shoichi Daniel *radiologist, researcher*
Takemura, Katsumi *nephrologist*
Takeuchi, Akira *neurophysiologist, educator*
Takizawa, Hideaki *gastroenterologist*
Takumida, Masaya *medical educator*
Tala, Eero Otto *internist, chest diseases educator*
Talamantes, Roberto *developmental pediatrician*
Talisman, Ran *plastic surgeon*
Talvik, Tiina *pediatric neurologist*
Tam, Alfred Yat-Cheung *pediatrician, consultant*
Tam, Frederick Wai Keung *medical researcher, physician*
Tamaoki, Bun-Ichi *retired endocrinology biochemistry educator*
Tan, Alexander Junior Uy *internist, nephrologist, educator*
Tan, Kim Leong *pediatrician, neonatologist, medical educator*
Tan, Kong-Meng *radiologist*
Tan, Masaki *surgeon*
Tan, Siauw Koan *radiologist*
Tan, Tjiauw-Ling *psychiatrist, educator*
Tanaka, Kazuhiro *orthopaedic surgeon, educator*
Tanaka, Noboru *pathologist, educator, laboratory administrator*
Tanaka, Shigeki *neurologist*
Tanaka, Yasuo *otorhinolaryngology educator*
Tanakawa, Nobuo *pediatrician, hospital administrator*
Tanakol, Refik *endocrinologist, educator*
Tandon, Om Prakash *neurophysiologist, educator, researcher*
Tang, Tuckhon Alex *pediatrician*
Tang, Yi *radiologist, researcher*
Tanga, Ravindra J. *gynecologist-obstetrician, consultant*
Tanigawa, Nobuhiko *medical educator*
Taniguchi, Tadaaki *oncologist*
Tanimura, Takashi *anatomist, teratologist*
Tanous, Helene Mary *radiologist, educator*
Tanparsert, Srivilai *physician*
Tanphaichitr, Kongsak *rheumatologist, allergist, immunologist, internist*
Tanphaichitra, Deja *internist, educator, consultant, clinician, researcher*
Tao, Wang *ophthalmologist*
Taper, Henryk Stanislaw *pathologist*
Tarazov, Pavel Gadelgaraevich *radiologist, researcher*
Targhetta, Rémi Dominique *internist*
Tarlow, Michael Jacob *retired pediatrician, researcher*
Tarnow, Jörg *anesthesiologist educator*
Tartter, Paul Ian *breast surgeon, educator*
Tasman-Jones, Clifford *physician, gastroenterologist, hepatologist*
Tataranni, Pietro Antonio *research endocrinologist, educator*
Tatarelli, Roberto *psychiatrist, researcher*
Tatarintseva, Raisa Yakovlevna *physician, manual therapy healer*
Tateno, Yukio *physician, researcher*
Tateyama, Ichiro *gynecologist*
Tatsumura, Toshiki *thoracic and abdominal surgeon*
Tattevin, Pierre *physician, researcher*
Taub, Stanley *plastic surgeon, sculptor*
Taubøll, Erik *neurologist*
Tavartkiladze, George Abel *otorhinolaryngologist*
Taveras, Juan Manuel *physician, educator*
Tavormina, Vincenzo Antonio *surgeon*
Tawil, George *psychiatrist*
Tay, John Sin Hock *pediatrics educator*
Tayar, Rene Benedict *radiologist, consultant*
Taylor, Doris Denice *physician, entrepreneur*
Taylor, Irving *surgeon, educator*
Taylor, James Francis Nuttall *pediatric cardiologist*
Taylor, Richard Thomas *rheumatologist*
Taylor, Robert Murray Ross *surgeon*
Taylor, William Halstead *chemical pathologist, metabolic medicine physician*
Teather, Derek *medical statistician, educator*
Teder, Priit *physician*
Tedroff, Joakim Mihkel *neuroscientist*
Tegos, Sterghios Michalis *neurosurgeon*
Tekin, Mustafa *physician, geneticist*
Telleria, Carlos Marcelo *reproductive endocrinologist*
Tellez-Minor, Saul *physics educator and researcher*
Tello, Richard J. *radiologist, researcher*
Templeton, John Marks, Jr. *pediatric surgeon, foundation executive*
Ten Have, Henk AMJ *medical ethicist, educator*
Tenyi, Jeno *physician, researcher*
Teping, Christian *ophthalmologist educator*
Terao, Toshio *physician, educator*
Terao, Yasuo *physician, researcher*
Tergau, Frithjof *neurologist*
Terjung, Birgit *internist, researcher*
Terra, Jean-Louis *psychiatrist, educator*
Tervahartiala, Pekka Olavi *radiologist, researcher*
Teschemacher, Hansjoerg *medical educator, pharmacologist*
Tescher de Cranley, Michel (Baron de Farney) *gynecologist, obstetrician, surgeon*
Tesfaye, Solomon *physician*
Testori, Tiziano N. *physician, oral surgery educator*
Tetik, Cihangir *orthopedic surgeon, educator*
Teuscher, Arthur *diabetologist*
Tewari, Ashutosh *urologist, oncologist*
Thacker, Marise Anne *retired anesthetist*
Thadani, Udho *physician, cardiologist*
Thajeb, Peterus (Tai Tau-En) *neurologist*
Than, Gabor Nandor *obstetrician and gynecologist, researcher*
Thangavelu, Sellappan *physician, orthopaedic surgeon*
Thanikachalam, Mohan *surgeon*
Thapar, Anita *psychiatry educator, physician*
Thappa, Devinder Mohan *physician*
Thatte, Urmila Mukund *pharmacology educator*
Thayer, Walter Raymond *internist*
Theobald, Holger *physician, researcher*
Theodossiadou, Evangelia Konstantinos *internal medicine physician*
Theoharides, Theoharis Constantin *pharmacologist, physician, educator*
Thernlund, Gunilla Margarethe *child/adolescent psychiatrist*
Thiebauld, Charles Marie *physician*
Thiel, Eckhard *internist, educator*
Thiel, Walter *anatomy educator*
Thienpont, Louis Achiles *surgical pathologist, cytologist*
Thigpen, James Tate *physician, oncology educator*
Thinkhamrop, Jadsada *obstetrician-gynecologist*
Thomalske, R.E. Günther *neurosurgeon, educator*
Thomann, Klaus-Dieter *orthopaedic surgeon*
Thomas, Barbara Ann *medical sciences consultant*
Thomas, Claudewell Sidney *psychiatry educator*
Thomas, Colin Gordon, Jr. *surgeon, medical educator*
Thomas, Edward Donnall *physician, researcher*
Thomas, Nihal Jacob *endocrinologist, physician, researcher*
Thomas, Peter Kynaston *neurologist*
Thomas, William Ernest Ghinn *consulting surgeon, health facility administrator*
Thome, Johannes Ulrich Vinzenz *psychiatrist researcher*
Thompson, Byron Gregory *neurosurgeon, researcher*
Thompson, David George *gastroenterologist, educator*
Thompson, Geoffrey Stuart *physician, consultant*
Thompson, Gilbert Richard *physician, educator*
Thompson, John Albert, Jr. *dermatologist*
Thompson, Richard Paul Hepworth *physician, consultant*
Thompson, William Benbow, Jr. *obstetrician/gynecologist, educator*
Thomsen, Per Hove *psychiatry educator*
Thomson, Alistair Peter James *pediatrician, consultant*
Thomson, Graeme Arthur *hematologist*
Thorarinsson, Hjalti *surgeon, educator*
Thorgeirsson, Gudmundur *physician, cardiologist*
Thorn, Patrick Arthur *retired physician, researcher*
Thornton, Yvonne Shirley *physician, author, musician*
Thorsteinsson, Adalbjörn *anesthesiologist*
Thorsteinsson, Leifur *immunologist, researcher*
Thulin, Lars Ingemar *cardiac surgeon, researcher*
Tian, Zeng Min *neurosurgery educator, chief physician*
Tiefenbrun, Jonathan *vascular surgeon*
Tienari, Pekka Johannes *psychiatrist, educator*
Tierney, William Michael *internist, educator*
Tiihonen, Jari Arto Tapani *forensic psychiatry educator*
Tikal, Kamil Josef *psychiatrist, psychopharmacologist*
Tikhonov, Nikolay Gavrilovich *medical researcher*
Tikkakoski, Tapani Antero *radiologist, neuroradiologist*
Tiliacos, Michael Apostolos *physician*
Tillett, Grace Montana *ophthalmologist, real estate developer*
Tillil, Hartmut Hermann Ludwig *internist*
Timi, Jorge Ribas *surgeon*
Timmons, Gerald Dean *pediatric neurologist*
Timonen, Kirsi Liisa *epidemiologist, researcher*
Tischendorf, Frank Walter *internist, clinical chemist, immunologist*
Tiselius, Hans Göran *urology educator*
Tiszlavicz, Laszlo Istvan *physician, pathologist*
Titrud, Oliver George *retired medical educator*
Tiziano, Jean-Paul *plastic surgeon, researcher*
Tjandra, Joe Janwar *surgeon, educator*
Tjuvajev, Juri *surgery educator, researcher*
Tlaskal, Tomas *pediatric cardiac surgeon*
Tlaskalova-Hogenova, Helena *immunologist*
Tobey, Martin Alan *cardiologist*
Tobias, Jeffrey Stewart *radiotherapist consultant*
Todd, Ian Pelham *retired surgeon, consultant*
Todorov, Vasil Velichkov *nephrologist, educator*
Toghill, Peter James *medical association administrator, physician*
Toivanen, Auli Marjaana *internal medicine educator*
Toivanen, Paavo Uuras *immunologist, microbiologist, educator*
Tokuda, Haruhiko *endocrinologist, educator*
Tokumasu, Koji *medical educator*
Tokura, Yoshiki *dermatologist, educator*
Toledo, Frederico Granchi Steidel *physiologist*
Tollemar, Jan Gustav *surgeon, researcher*
Toma-Rednic, Carmen Dorina *physician, researcher*
Tomassoni, Maria-Letizia *pathologist, researcher*
Tomer, Gitit *pediatrician*
Tomiya, Tomoaki *internist, gastroenterologist, medical educator*
Tommasino, Concezione *anesthesiologist*
Tomonaga, Susumu *anatomy educator*
Tong, Alex Waiming *immunologist*
Tonkens, Solvin William *retired physician*
Tonkin, Ina Lynn Dyer *cardiovascular radiologist, educator*
Tönshoff, Burkhard *pediatrician, nephrologist*
Toole, James Francis *medical educator*
Toomes, Heikki *thoracic surgeon, educator*
Topliss, Duncan Jake *endocrinologist*
Torffvit, Ole John *physician, researcher*
Torfoss, Dag *physician*
Tori, Carlos A. *pediatrician*
Tornhage, Carl-Johan Anders *pediatrician*
Török, Béla *surgeon*
Torrens, Michael John *neurosurgeon, medical researcher*
Torres, Alberto Manuel *physician*
Torres, Arturo *physician*
Torring, Ove *endocrinologist*
Tos, Mirko *physician, educator*
Tosheff, Julij Gospodinoff *psychiatrist*
Toth, Kalman *cardiologist*
Toth, Pal *anatomist, educator, neuroscientist*
Touzeau, Olivier Jean-Marc Thierry *ophthalmologist, clinical researcher*
Tovey, Frank Ivor *retired surgeon*
Towers, Bernard Leonard *medical educator*
Tozawa, Yumiko *medical researcher*
Tracey, Irene Mary Carmel *neuroscientist*
Traczyk, Zdzisława *hematologist, consultant*
Trafimow, Jordan Herman *orthopedist*
Trager, Gary Alan *endocrinologist, diabetologist*
Tran, Minh Son *physician*
Trandaburu, Tiberiu *endocrinologist, researcher*
Tranquilino, Francisco Pascual *internist, cardiologist*
Tran-Viet, Tu *cardiovascular and thoracic surgeon*
Traube, Charles *internist, cardiologist*
Traupe, Heiko *dermatologist, educator*
Travers, Vincent Marie Georges *surgeon*
Travis, Simon P.L. *gastroenterologist*
Traynelis, Stephen Francis *neuroscientist, educator*
Trebichavsky, Ilja *immunologist*
Trefzger, Richard Charles *surgeon*
Treichel, Jürgen Klaus *radiologist*
Trejos, Franklin Anthony *physician assistant*
Trelles, Luis Antonio *neurology educator*
Tresguerres, Jesus A.F. *endocrinologist, edcator*
Treska, Vladislav *surgeon*
Trikha, Ajit *psychiatrist*
Tringer, László *psychiatrist, educator*
Tripp, John Howard *pediatrician, consultant, educator*
Trivedy, Chetan Rameschandra *head and neck oncologist, researcher*
Trkanjec, Zlatko *physician, consultant*
Trompeter, Richard Simon *pediatrician*
Trott, Edward Ashley *reproductive endocrinologist*
Trott, Justina A. *physician, medical association administrator, internist, medical educator*
Trotta, Vincenzo *gynecologist*
Trouillard, Laurent *radiologist*
Trouillas, Paul *medical educator*
Truelle, Jean Luc *neurologist, educator*
Trupo, Frank John *plastic surgeon*
Trushinsky, Zdislav Kazimirowitch *internist, educator*
Tryba, Michael *anesthesiologist, researcher*
Trzeciak, Henryk Ireneusz *pharmacologist, educator*
Tsai, Li Felländer *orthopaedist, educator*
Tsai, Shang-Ying *psychiatrist*
Tsai, Shih-Chuan *nuclear medicine physician*
Tsai, Tsu-Min *surgeon*
Tsai, Tung-Hu *pharmacologist, researcher, educator*
Tsai, Wu-Fu *ophthalmologist, educator*
Tsai, Yung-Chieh *gynecologist, educator*
Tsambaos, Dionysios *dermatologist, educator*
Tsang, Reginald C. *pediatrician*
Tschoepe, Diethelm *physician, consultant*
Tse, Harley Y. *immunologist, educator*
Tseng, Chin-Hsiao *internist, diabetologist, medical educator*
Tsien, Joe Z. *neurobiologist, educator*
Tsindos, Spero Perry *naturopathic physician, writer*
Tso, Mark On-man *ophthalmologist*
Tsochas, Constantinos *physician*
Tsuge, Kenya *retired medical educator, social service executive*
Tsuji, Fumio *pharmacologist*
Tsuji, Koh *radiation oncologist*
Tsuji, Shingo *physician*
Tsuji, Shuichi *physician, health facility administrator*
Tsukada, Yutaka *medical educator, researcher*
Tsunezuka, Yoshio *surgeon*
Tsunoda, Hajime *obstetrician-gynecologist*
Tsurumi, Yukio *cardiologist*
Tsushima, Toshio *endocrinologist, researcher, medical educator*
Tsutani, Kiichiro *clinical pharmacologist, physician*
Tsutsui, Kazuyoshi *medical educator*
Tu, Gui Yi *surgeon*
Tuccari, Giovanni *pathologist, educator*
Tucek, Stanislav *neurochemist*
Tucker, Sam Michael *pediatrician*
Tucker, William Morris *psychiatric educator*
Tuddenham, Edward George *pathologist*
Tudor, John Colin *ophthalmic surgeon*
Tuesta, Ignacio Diaz *cardiac surgeon, computer consultant*
Tumani, Hayrettin *physician, neuroscientist*
Tun, Zaw *forensic medicine researcher*
Tunbridge, William Michael Gregg *physician, consultant*
Tunc, Mustafa *pathologist*
Tuncer, A. Murat *physician*
Tuncer, Meral *pharmacologist, educator, pharmacist*
Tunner, William Sams *urological surgeon*

HEALTHCARE: MEDICINE

Werbitt, Warren gastroenterologist, educator
Wernick, Justin podiatrist, educator
Werry, John Scott physician, educator
Wessel, Karl Friedrich Maria neurologist
Westendorp, Iris C.D. cardiologist, epidemiologist
Wester, Knut Gustav physician, educator
Weström, Lars Vilhelm obstetrician, gynecologist, educator, researcher
Wetzel, Franklin Todd spinal surgeon, educator, researcher
Wever, Chris child psychiatrist
Weyerer, Siegfried Bernhard epidemiologist
Weyers, Wolfgang dermatopathologist
Whang, Kyu-Kwang medical educator
Wharton, Ralph Nathaniel psychiatrist, educator
Wheatley, Joseph Kevin physician, urologist
Wheless, James Warren neurologist
Whinery, Michael Albert physician
White, Leslie paediatric oncologist, clinician, researcher, hospital executive
White, Martha Vetter allergy and immunology physician, researcher
White, Richard Thomas radiologist
Whiteley, Mark Steven consultant vascular surgeon
Whitsell, John Crawford, II retired general surgeon
Whittle, Martin John obstetrician
Whitworth, Judith Ann medical educator
Wiberg-Jorgensen, Finn anesthesiologist
Wichmann, H.-Erich epidemiologist, researcher
Wichmann, Matthias Wilhelm surgeon, researcher
Wichrzycka-Lancaster, Elzbieta Jadwiga pathology educator
Widder, Joachim radio-oncologist, researcher
Widdison, Adam Lewis surgeon, consultant
Widhalm, Kurt Maria pediatrician, researcher
Widholm, Olof Eric Bernhard obstetrician, gynecologist, educator
Widimsky, Jiri cardiologist, medical educator
Widimsky, Jiří, Jr. internist, educator
Wiebe, Richard Herbert reproductive endocrinologist, educator
Wied, George Ludwig physician
Wiedenmann, Bertram physician, internist, gastroenterologist
Wiedow, Oliver dermatologist, researcher
Wielondek, Miroslaw gastroenterologist
Wienert, Peter physician
Wiernik, Peter Harris oncologist, educator
Wiersbitzky, Siegfried Karl Wilhelm pediatrician
Wierzbieta, Wojciech anesthesiologist, medical facility administrator
Wiesel, Frits-Axel Tage psychiatrist, educator, researcher
Wiesel, Torsten Nils neurobiologist, educator
Wiesinger, Guenther Franz physiatrist
Wikner, Johan Nils Pontus physician, researcher
Wikström, Arne Karl dermatologist, researcher
Wilailak, Sarikapan physician, researcher
Wilbur, Andrew Clayton radiologist, educator
Wilczek, Hanus internist, researcher
Wild, John Julian surgeon, director medical research institute
Wildenthal, C(laud) Kern physician, educator
Wildt, Ludwig gynecologist, endocrinologist
Wilensky, Robert J. plastic surgeon, historian
Wilhelm, Jane T. physical therapist
Wilhelm, Klaus Peter dermatologist, consultant
Wilkens, Ludwig Bernhard physician
Wilkins, Denis Charles surgeon, consultant, educator
Wilkinson, Timothy James geriatric physician
Willard, Ralph Lawrence surgery educator, physician, former college president
Willauschus, Wolfgang Guenter orthopedic surgeon
Willen, Roger pathology consultant
Williams, Carole Ann retired cytotechnologist
Williams, Drew Davis surgeon
Williams, Joan Elaine podiatric surgeon, educator
Williams, Larry Ross surgeon
Williams, Samuel Jeyakumar venerologist
Williams, Thomas Lloyd psychiatrist
Willis, Gladden Williams pathologist
Willis, Isaac dermatologist, educator
Willis, William Harris internist, cardiologist
Willoughby, William Franklin, II physician, researcher
Wilmer, Harry Aron psychiatrist
Wilson, Adel Michel plastic surgeon
Wilson, James Miller, IV cardiovascular surgeon, educator
Wilson, James Noel orthopaedic surgeon
Wilson, Mary Elizabeth physician, educator
Wilson, Myron Robert, Jr. retired psychiatrist
Wilson, Peter Wyman internist, cardiovascular, metabolic epidemiology
Wilson, Robert Godfrey radiologist
Wilson, Ronald Gene physician
Wilson, Samuel Eric vascular and general surgeon
Wilson, William Robert surgeon
Windler, Eberhard Ernst Theodor internist
Winer, Conrad Edward Robert osteopath, rehabilitation medicine physician
Wing, Lorna psychiatrist, consultant, researcher
Winkel, Elaine Marie physician, transplant cardiologist
Winkler, Ulrich Horst gynecologist, researcher, consultant
Winland, Denise Lynn physician
Winn, Francis John, Jr. medical educator
Winter, Martin physician, ophthalmologist
Winter, Steven internist, cardiologist
Winterhalter, Bernd Rainer internist, pharmaceutical company administrator
Wirsching, Michael Hilmar medical educator
Wischnik, Arthur physician
Wisdom, Peggy J. neurologist
Wisnicki, Jeffrey Leonard plastic surgeon
Witorsch, Philip internist, educator
Witte, Hartmut Friedrich anatomist, biomedical engineer
Witte, Otto Wilhelm neurologist, physiologist
Wittenberg, Ralf Hermann orthopaedic surgeon, educator
Wittrup, Hans Hechmann cardiologist
Witzel, Lothar Gustav physician, gastroenterologist
Wöckel, Werner Friedrich pathologist
Wojciechowski, Piotr Kazimierz pediatric surgeon
Wojczys, Romualda Maria surgeon, researcher
Wolbach, Albert Bogh, Jr. family practice physician
Wolcott, Hugh Dixon obstetrics and gynecology educator
Wolday, Dawit immunologist
Wolf, David Cary gastroenterologist, medical educator
Wolf, Hellmut Rudolf D. internal medicine educator
Wolf, Jörn Henning medical historian, educator
Wolf, Peter Traugott epileptologist, researcher
Wolf, Stewart George, Jr. physician, medical educator
Wolfensberger, Christoph plastic and reconstructive surgeon
Wolff, Klaus dermatologist, educator, researcher
Wolfhagen, Franciscus Hubertus Joseph internist, researcher
Wolf-Klein, Gisele Patricia geriatrician
Wolkoff, Peder occupational health research scientist
Wolkov, Harvey Brian radiation oncologist, researcher
Wollenhaupt, Jurgen H. rheumatologist
Wolozin, Benjamin Labe biomedical researcher
Wolters, Ulrich physician, educator
Wong, Cheuk Wah neurosurgeon
Wong, Chih-Shung anesthesiologist
Wong, Dennis Ka-Cheong physician, physical therapist
Wong, Felix Wu-Shun obstetrics and gynecology educator
Wong, James Robert oncologist, educator
Wong, Joseph Chee-Hoe nuclear medicine physician
Wong, Olivier physician, educator
Wong, Otto epidemiologist
Wong, Phillip Allen osteopathic physician
Wonnacott, James Brian physician
Woo, Jean medical educator
Woo, Patricia pediatric rheumatologist
Wood, Alexander Sandford retired urologist
Wood, David Bruce naturopathic physician
Wood, Dirk Gregory surgeon, physician, forensic consultant
Wood, Edwin Carlyle gynecologist
Wood, Frances Diane medical secretary, artist
Woodhouse, Stan Peter cardiology educator
Woodle, E. Steve transplant surgeon
Wood-Smith, Donald plastic surgeon
Woodward, Michael Clifford geriatrician, researcher
Woolcock, Ann Janet physician
Woolf, Anthony Derek consulting rheumatologist
Woolling, Kenneth Rau vascular internist
Woolston-Catlin, Marian psychiatrist
World, Michael John military medicine educator
Worner, Theresa Marie internist, educator
Worth, Peter Herman Louis consultant surgeon
Woscoff, Alberto dermatologist
Wozniak, Witold Stanislaw anatomist, researcher
Wren, Barry George gynecological endocrinologist, educator, researcher, consultant
Wright, Richard Oscar, III pathologist, educator
Wright-Pascoe, Rosemarie Angela endocrinologist
Wronski, Ian physician, educator
Wu, Lawrence Mg Hla Myin physician
Wu, Shi-Qi (Samuel Wu) medical geneticist
Wu, Wei cardiologist, educator
Wu, William Chien Lin cardiologist
Wuellner, Ullrich neurologist
Wulf, Hans Christian dermatology educator
Wunderlich, Peter retired pediatrician, educator
Wuolijoki, Erkki Ensio Fredrik pharmacologist
Würfel, Wolfgang Johann gynecologist
Wurzberger, Bezalel psychiatrist
Wyatt, Harold Vivian medical researcher
Wydra, Frank Thomas healthcare executive
Wyrost, Piotr anatomist, educator, researcher
Wyrwicka, Wanda research anatomist
Wysocki, Jarosław otolaryngologist
Xia, Harry Hua-Xiang medical researcher, microbiologist
Xiao, Chuanguo urologist
Xiao, Mao physician, consultant
Xicai, Cao radiologist
Xie, Ailiang medical scientist, writer
Xie, Liangdi physician, researcher
Xu, Gang medical researcher, educator
Xu, Guang-Yin neuroscientist, researcher
Xu, Qi Wu neurosurgeon
Xu, S. Liang pediatrics educator
Xu, Zhi-Biao physician, educator
Xue, Qi-Ming neurologist, educator, researcher
Xuexian, Qian cardiovascular physician
Yagi, Hiroshi surgeon, hospital administrator
Yakasai, Bashir Adam neuropsychiatrist, consultant
Yakoun, Maurice surgeon, researcher
Yam, Constance Shuk-Chee dermatologist
Yamada, Ryo rheumatologist, researcher
Yamagata, Kanato neuroscientist, researcher
Yamagata, Kenji internist
Yamaguchi, Toru internist
Yamamoto, Tadashi pathologist, educator
Yamamura, Mitsuhiro cardiovascular surgeon
Yamana, Hideaki surgeon
Yamauchi, Kunihiko hematologist
Yan, Zhongshu surgeon
Yanaga, Katsuhiko surgeon, researcher
Yanagawa, Tatsuo internist
Yanaka, Akinori medical researcher, educator
Yancy, William Samuel pediatrician
Yang, Chun-Yuh medical educator
Yang, Ping gastroenterologist
Yang, Ten-Fang cardiologist, medical educator and researcher
Yang, Victor Ting Hsun retired physician, gastroenterologist, educator
Yang, Xi Qiang medical association administrator, pediatrician
Yankah, Abraham Charles cardiothoracic and vascular surgeon, educator
Yano, Michitami gastroenterologist, health facility administrator
Yanovsky, Sergey Stepanovich psychiatrist, health facility administrator
Yao, Chung-Chin physician
Yao, John Sen physician
Yao, Tito Go pediatrician
Yaqub, Basim Abdul Rauf neurologist, consultant
Yarbrough, Terry Pinckney physician
Yarzábal, Luis biomedical researcher, university educator
Yasuda, Yuzuru neurologist
Yavelov, Igor Semenovich cardiologist, researcher
Yawata, Yoshihito hematologist, oncologist educator
Yazan, Yasemin pharmaceutical technologist, cosmetic researcher
Ybert, Jean-Paul Gustave occupational medicine physician, anthropologist
Ye, Shitai allergist, educator
Yee, Henry Chan Myint cardiologist
Yee, Kuo Chiang neuroscientist, neurologist
Yeh, John Sho-Ju neurosurgeon, educator
Yeh, Ming-Neng obstetrician, gynecologist
Yeh, Ming-Yang immunology educator
Yeh, Wen Ling orthopaedist, consultant
Yew, David T. anatomy educator
Yildiz, Bülent Okan physician
Yim, Anthony Ping-Chuen cardiothoracic surgeon
Yin, Beatrice Wei-Tze medical researcher
Yin, LiXue cardiologist, physician, educator
Yip, William Chin-Ling pediatric cardiologist, consultant, educator
Yip, Yu Lap surgeon, medical administrator
Yogesan, Kanagasingam telemedicine center director
Yokoe, Takao medical educator
Yokoi, Tsuyoshi pharmaceutical educator
Yokota, Mitsuhiro cardiologist educator
Yokota, Shouhei internist, researcher
Yondemli, Fuat medical educator
Yoneda, Ikuo anesthesiologist
Yoneda, Masashi gastroenterologist, scientist, educator
Yonei, Yoshikazu gastroenterologist
Yong, Weng Kwong biomedical scientist
Yoo, Byung Chul internal medicine educator
Yoon, Jay Myoung oncologist, hematologist, internist
Yoon, Tae-Young dermatologist, educator
Yordanova, Juliana psychophysiologist
Yorozu, Atsunori physician
Yoshida, Junichi surgeon
Yoshikawa, Kunihiko dermatologist, educator
Yoshikawa, Toshikazu medical educator
Yoshimoto, Tetsuyuki neurosurgeon
Yoshiura, Kazunori oral radiologist, researcher
Yoshizawa, Nobuyuki medical educator, nephrologist
Yosipovitch, Gil dermatologist, researcher
Young, Chainllie physician
Young, Daniel Greer surgical pediatrics educator
Young, Iven Hunter physician, educator, researcher
Ypma, Alphons Fgvm urologist, consultant
Ytterstad, Børge surgeon, educator, researcher
Yu, Chack Yung pediatrics educator
Yu, Dao-yi ophthalmologist
Yu, Fushun physiologist, researcher
Yu, Hsin-Su dermatologist, educator
Yu, Jack Chungkai plastic surgeon, researcher
Yu, Jeong-Sik physician
Yu, John Yuh-Lin endocrinologist, veterinary medicine and zoology educator
Yu, Peter Legaspi rehabilitation physician
Yu, Wansik medical educator
Yuan, Jason Xiao-Jian medical researcher, educator
Yuan, Yi Quan physician
Yüceer, Nurullah neurosurgeon
Yuhara, Takamichi rheumatologist
Yun, Daniel Duwhan physician, foundation administrator
Yung, Babington Chun-kuen radiologist
Yung-Silva, Jose Bayan immunology educator
Yunquan, Luo physician, surgeon, researcher
Yurenev, Alexei Pavlovich cardiologist, researcher
Yusichenko, Nikolay Yury immunologist, consultant
Yustova, Elisaveta Nicolaevna physician, researcher
Yusuf, Nasim endocrinologist, consultant
Žaba, Richard pediatrician, researcher, educator
Zachariou, Zacharias pediatric surgery consultant
Žadníková, Raja Lodinová pediatrician
Zador, Steven pathologist
Zafonte, Ross D. physiatrist
Zaghloul, Mohamed Saad radiation oncologist
Zagoren, Allen Jeffrey surgeon
Zaidat, Osama O. neurologist
Zaidi, Zeenat Fatima anatomist, educator
Zaitsev, Viktor Mikhailovich surgeon, orthopedist, gynecologist
Zakharov, Vladimir Nikolaevich cardiovascular surgeon
Zalessky, Viacheslav Nikolajevich cardiologist, researcher
Zalta, Edward otorhinolaryngologist, physician
Zaman, Rashid psychiatrist, educator, neuroscience researcher
Zambelis, Nikolaus internist
Zamboglou, Nicolaos physician
Zamora, Romeo Dising surgeon
Zamotrinsky, Alexander Vladimirovich cardiologist
Zamrazil, Václav internist, endocrinologist, educator
Zanazzi, George John neuroscientist
Zanchi, Pero surgeon, researcher
Zapletal, Alois pediatrician, pulmonologist, educator
Zapotoczky, Johann Georg psychiatrist
Zaricznyj, Basilius orthopedic surgeon
Zarković, Miloš Pero physician
Zarowski, Andrzej Jan otorhinolaryngologist, biomedical engineer
Zarpao, Luiz Fernando physician, researcher
Zatonski, Witold Antoni epidemiology educator
Závada, Jan molecular oncologist
Zavras, George radiologist
Zav'yalov, Vladimir Petrovich immunology educator
Zawada, Edward Thaddeus, Jr. physician, educator
Zbar, Lloyd Irwin Stanley otolaryngologist, educator
Zdrojewski, Zbigniew Jozef nephrologist
Zehel, Wendell Evans surgeon
Zeidman, Aliza internist
Zeitoun, Ibrahim Mohamed surgeon
Zeldes, Ilya M. forensic scientist, lawyer
Zemel, Norman Paul orthopedic surgeon
Zemtsov, Alexander dermatology and biochemistry educator, inventor
Zenea, Arecia Clara allergist, consultant
Zeng, Yan Jun biomechanics educator
Zenilman, Michael E. surgeon, educator
Zenner, Hans Peter otolaryngologist
Zeon, Seok Kil medical educator
Zerafa, Laurence Vincent industrial pharmacist
Zerati, Edson neurologist, neurosurgeon
Zerbib, Eric nuclear medicine physician
Zgliczynski, Stefan endocrinologist, medical educator
Zhang, Ai-rong gynecologist, medical educator
Zhang, Cai-Li pharmacologist, educator
Zhang, Hong pathologist
Zhang, Hong-Yu pharmacology educator
Zhang, Jingwu immunologist
Zhang, Jun pathologist, researcher
Zhang, Theodore Tian-ze oncologist, health association administrator
Zhao, Huiru surgeon
Zhao, Wu-Shu immunologist, researcher
Zhen, Yong-Su pharmacology educator
Zhong, Fan otolaryngologist, educator
Zhong, Xiao Yan physician
Zhongzhen, Zhao medical educator
Zhou, Cheng Ji neuroscientist
Zhou, Xiaosi surgeon, educator, researcher
Zhou, Yuzue psychiatric physician
Zhu, Frank Xiang medical researcher, internist
Zhu, Min pharmacy educator, researcher
Zhuplatov, Sergey Borisovich medical educator, investigator
Zierski, Jan Tomasz neurosurgeon
Zimmerman, Mikael Christer medical science educator
Zingirian, Mario ophthalmologist, educator
Zinkernagel, Rolf Martin immunology educator
Zink-Lorenz, Angela Maria internist, researcher
Zinn-Justin, Anne genetic epidemiology researcher
Zion, Monty M. cardiologist, researcher
Zipes, Douglas Peter cardiologist, researcher
Zizic, Thomas Michael physician, educator
Zlatkin, Michael Brian physician
Żmudka, Krzysztof Feliks medical educator, physician, researcher
Zoëga, Tómas psychiatrist
Zogu, Veli cardiovascular surgery educator
Zolotaryova, Tatyana Ananevna rehabilitation physician
Zoltie, Nigel physician
Zotikov, Evgenii Alexeevich immunohematologist, researcher
Zs-Nagy, Imre medical educator
Zubritsky, Alexander Nickolaevich pathologist
Zubroff, Leonard Saul surgeon
Zucker, Howard Alan pediatric cardiologist, intensivist, anesthesiologist
Zuckerman, Stuart psychiatrist, forensic examiner, educator
Zugibe, Frederick Thomas pathologist
Zuhdi, Nazih retired surgeon, administrator
Zukowska, Zofia Maria cardiovascular physiologist, educator
Zumerchik, John urologist
Zumkeller, Walter pediatrician, researcher
Zuna, Jan physician, researcher
Zuniga, Miguel Angel health care sciences professor
Zuo, Chengye psychiatrist, educator
Zvetina, James Raymond pulmonary physician
Zvulunov, Alexander pediatric dermatologist
Zwecker-Lazar, Irina physiatrist
Zwiauer, Karl F.M. pediatrician
Zywietz, Martin Michael physician

HUMANITIES: LIBERAL STUDIES

Aaserud, Finn science historian
Abádi-Nagy, Zoltán English language educator
Abellan, José Luis humanities educator
Abelshauser, Werner Ludwig educator
Abraham, Arthur history educator
Abramson, Edward Allan American literature educator
Absalom, Douglas John linguistics educator
Abu-Mansour, Mahasen Hasan linguistics educator
Achin, Milos Kosta historian, writer
Achkar, Maria language professional, educator
Acton, Edward David Joseph historian, educator
Adamec, Přemysl Russian linguistics educator
Adams, Barbara English language educator, poet, writer
Adams, Bernard Stanley Hungarian-English literary translator
Adler, Jacques history educator
Adler, Mortimer Jerome philosopher, author
Adler, Raphael educator emeritus, speech pathologist
Adler-Karlsson, Gunnar philosopher, social scientist
Agli, Stephen Michael English language educator, literature educator
Agnew, Theodore Lee, Jr. historian, educator
Aguirre-Batty, Mercedes Spanish and English language and literature educator
Ahmed, Peshimam Nisar Arabic educator
Ahrends, Günter English language educator
Ahvenainen, Jorma Juhani history educator
Ainsworth, James Peter art historian
Aizawa, Shiro English and comparative literature educator
Ak, Coskun foreign language educator
Akase, Masako humanities educator
Akiyama, Masayuki educator
Akula, Surya Kumari history educator, department head
Al-Abed Al-Haq, Fawwaz M. English studies educator
Alam, Qaiser Zoha English educator, researcher
Al-Attas, Syed Muhammad al-Naquib philosopher, educator
Albini, Umberto humanities educator
Alcock, Antony Evelyn international relations educator
Aleksandrowicz, Dariusz Leopold philosopher
Alexander, Manfred history educator
Alfvegren, Lars Bertil foreign language educator
Alia, Valerie humanities educator, writer
Aline, David Paul language educator
Alkalay-Gut, Karen Hillary lecturer, poet
Al-Khatib, Mahmoud Abed language educator
Allain, Louis literature educator, scientific advisor
Allam, Schafik Egyptology educator
Allan, Jonathan David autograph dealer, pop culture historian
Alleyne, Mervyn (C.) linguist
Alptekin, Cem linguistics and foreign language educator
Alqannoor, Nasser Muhammad linguist, educator
Alt, Karin philology educator
Amat Le Coz, Jacqueline Latin educator
Amerasinghe, Terence Percival English educator
Amphoux, Christian-Bernard research philologist, educator
Andersen, Paul Kent linguist, educator
Anderson, David Daniel retired humanities educator, writer, editor
Anderson, David Gaskill, Jr. Spanish language educator
Andersson, Thorsten retired language educator
Andrés-Gallego, José (J.A. Andrés-Gallego) history researcher, educator
Andrews, Carol Ann Ray Egyptologist, researcher
Andrews, Malcolm Yardley English educator
Andrews, Richard Antony Italian language educator
Ang, Minni Kim-Huai music educator, musician
Angermeier, Heinz history educator
Ansari, S. M. Razaullah historian of science, former physics educator
Ansbro, John Joseph philosophy educator
Ansen, Alan Joseph retired poetry educator
Antoine, Fabrice bilingual lexicography, researcher
Anton, Hans Hubert history educator, researcher
Anton, John Peter philosopher, educator
Antonopoulos, Constantin John philosophy educator
Antsyferova, Olga Yurievna English language and literature educator
Aoki, Reiko Japanese linguist
Aoki, Reiko Therese history educator
Aoley, Prakash Vithalrao literature and philosophy educator
Appatov, Semen Josifovich historian
Aquilecchia, Giovanni Italian studies educator
Arabatzis, Theodore science history educator
Arac, Jonathan English language educator
Araki, Toru French and comparative literature educator
Arfe, Gianpaolo philosopher, physicist
Ariesan, Claudiu philologist, researcher

Dvoichenko-Markov, Demetrius history educator
Dwyer, Richard Anthony retired English educator
Dyck, Andrew Roy philologist, educator
Eagleton, Terence (Francis) English literature educator
Eaton, Charles Edward English language educator, author
Ecole, Jean Joseph philosophy and metaphysics researcher
Eddleman, Floyd Eugene retired English language educator
Egri, Peter English and comparative literature educator
Ejituwu, Nkparom Claude history educator, researcher
Ekbladh, David Karl Francis historian, researcher
É Kiss, Katalin linguist, researcher
Ekmann, Bjoern foreign language educator
Elam, Diane Michele English literature educator
Eldredge, Charles Child, III art history educator
El-Enany, Rasheed Arabic literature educator
El-Hakamy, Abdulwahab A. English educator
Elia, Annibale linguist, educator
El-Sakkout, Hamdi Sayyid Ahmed arabic literature educator
Elsesser, Brian D. historian, educator
Elsness, Johan English language educator
Elvin, Mark historian, educator, translator
Engber, Cheryl Ann language educator, linguist
Englebert, Annick Regine linguist
Enomoto, Ryokichi English literature educator
Eörsi, Anna art historian
Erikson, Richard Alan history educator, artist
Erlich, Haggai historian, educator
Eshkoli, Hava Wagman historian, educator
Esmein, Jean Charles Japanologist
Espenlaub, Margo Linn women's studies educator, writer, artist
Essler, Wilhelm Karl philosophy educator
Esterhammer, Angela literary theorist, educator
Estor, Annemarie literature and science researcher, poet
Etherington, Norman Alan history educator
Evans, Richard John historian
Everaert-Desmedt, Nicole semiotics educator
Facchi, Paolo language philosophy educator
Faessler, Peter Ernst historian, educator
Faingold, Eduardo Daniel language and linguistics educator, researcher
Falkner, Noreen Margaret English language educator
Faller, Thompson Mason philosophy educator
Falola, Toyin history educator
Fang, Joong philosopher, mathematician, educator
Farnham, Thomas Javery historian
Farooqi, Zubair Ahmad language educator, journalist
Farrar-Hockley, Anthony Heritage defense consultant, historian
Fatemi, Saeid Khan language educator, writer
Fears, Jesse Rufus historian, educator, academic dean
Fedulin, Aleksander Alekseevich historian, educator
Feher, Istvan M. philosopher, educator
Fein, Patrick Louis-Marie French language educator
Feingold, Mordechai historian, researcher, educator
Ferrell, Robert Hugh historian, educator
Ferro, Marc Roger historian
Fetzer, James Henry philosopher, educator
Feyten, Carine Marie foreign language educator, translator, researcher
Fiechter, Jean-Jacques historian
Field, Heather Kathleen humanities educator
Figueira, Thomas John classics educator
Finney, Frank William, Jr. literature educator, poet
Fiorato, Adelin Charles Romance languages educator
Fischer, Bernd Jurgen history educator
Fishkin, Shelley Fisher English language educator
Fite, Gilbert Courtland historian, educator, retired
Fix-Bonner, Hans educator
Fizer, John literature educator
Fleming, Donald Harnish historian, educator
Flew, Antony (Garrard Newton) philosophy educator emeritus
Flindell, Edwin Frederick, III retired musicologist, choral conductor, organist
Florescu, Radu Radu East European history educator
Foeldes, Csaba linguist, educator
Fogelmark, Staffan J.H. Greek studies educator
Fokkema, Douwe Wessel literature educator
Foley, John Miles English language and classical studies educator
Folk, Katherine Pinkston English language educator, writer, journalist
Folks, Cathalin Buhrmann English language educator
Föllmi, Beat A. musicologist, theologian
Foltinek, Herbert language and literature educator
Fontaine, Piet Franciscus Maria retired history educator
Fontinoy, Charles-Marie retired Oriental studies educator
Foot, Michael Richard Daniell historian
Forceville, Charles Joseph humanities educator
Ford, Gordon Buell, Jr. English language, linguistics, and medieval studies educator, author, retired hospital industry accounting financial management executive
Ford, Harriet-Lynn English educator
Ford, Jean Elizabeth former English language educator
Ford, Jonathan Marcus historian, educator
Forsbach, Ralf historian
Forson, Barnabas English language educator
Förster, Eckart Heribert philosophy educator
Forsyth, Elliott Christopher French language educator
Forteza, Bartomeu philosophy educator
Foxcroft, Nigel Howard humanities educator
Franca, Jose-Augusto art historian, educator, author
Franca-Deal, Judith Jean language educator
Francis, Richard Andrew French language educator
Frangeskou, Vassiliki academic librarian
Frank, Tibor historian
Franke, Jack Emil foreign language educator
Franklin, H. Bruce language educator, writer
Franz, Gerhard Heinrich art historian
Frazier, Lyn psycholinguist
Fredericks, Robert Joseph language company executive
Freebody, Peter Raymond literacy and language educator
Fried, Morris Louis retired humanities educator
Friederichs, Michelle Maack English educator
Friedland, Klaus Dietrich Eberhard historian, researcher
Friedmann, Yohanan Islamic studies educator
Friesel, Evyatar historian
Frost, Molly Spitzer Chinese culture educator
Frumkina, Revekka Markovna linguist, essayist
Frye, Roland Mushat literary historian, theologian
Fues, Wolfram Malte German literature and culture educator
Fugmann, Nicole Elisabeth English studies scholar
Fujimoto, Koji linguistic researcher, educator
Fukatsu, Tanefusa retired Chinese classics educator
Fukuda, Setsuko translator
Furley, William David classics educator
Furomoto, Atsuko literature educator
Fuzes, Endre ethnologist, museum director
Galactéros-de Boissier, Lucie art historian, educator
Gallix, Françcois English literature educator
Galvani, Christiane Mesch English as a second language educator, translator
Gamboni, Dario Libero art historian, educator
Gamkrelidze, Thomas Valerian linguist, educator
Gantar, Kajetan classicist, educator
Garay, Jesús de philosopher, educator
Garbaty, Thomas Jay retired English language educator
Garcia Landa, José Ángel English educator
Garcia Moriyon, Felix philosophy educator
Garnot, Benoît history educator
Garrido, Miguel-Ángel philologist, researcher
Garrigus, Charles Byford retired literature educator
Gart, Jason H. historian
Gartman, Max Dillon language educator
Garvie, Alexander Femister classics educator
Gascoigne, John history educator
Gat, Azar history educator
Gateau, Jean-Charles literature educator
Gatt-Rutter, John Arthur Italian studies educator, literary translator
Gattullo, Francesca Elena language educator, trainer, consultant
Gaucher, Elisabeth Marie French language and literature educator
Gaudart, Hyacinth Marie educator
Gaut, Berys Nigel philosophy educator
Gava, Giacomo Mario philosophy educator
Gazda, Grzegorz Józef humanities educator
Gehler, Michael Karl Milon historian, educator
Gehrke, Hans-Joachim historian
Gelzer, David Georg English educator, missionary
Genin, Jean-Claude history and legal educator
Genini, Ronald Walter history educator, historian
Georgiev, Pavel Stefanov history educator
Gera, Dov ancient historian
Gert, Heather J. philosophy educator
Ghymn, Esther Mikyung English educator, writer
Giardina, Giancarlo classics educator
Gidley, Gustavus Mick American literature educator
Giesemann, Gerhard Russian literature educator
Gilbert, Creighton Eddy art historian
Gillett, Paula humanities educator
Gimeno Sanz, Ana Maria philology lecturer, researcher
Ginter, Valerian Alexius urban historian, educator
Giunti, Marco philosophy educator
Glaab, Charles Nelson educator, historian
Glahn, Esther humanities educator
Goble, Alan Reginald Stanley compiler
Godwin, Denise Ann languages educator
Goetschel, Willi foreign literature educator
Goetz, Thomas Hall English educator
Golczewski, Frank history educator
Goldberg, Maxwell Henry retired humanities educator
Golden, Herbert Hershel retired Romance languages educator
Golden, Leon classicist, educator
Golder, Herbert Alan classics educator
Goldston-Morris, Maurine Gertrude historian
Goldt, Rainer Slavic studies educator
Gomber, Drew Joseph historian, writer
Gombrich, Sir Ernst (Hans Josef) art historian, educator
Gomez-Gonzalez, Carmen English as second language educator
Gonzalez, Wenceslao Jose philosopher, educator
Gonzalez Calleja, Eduardo history educator, researcher
Goodenberger, Mary Ellen English educator
Goodrich, Norma Lorre (Mrs. John H. Howard) French and comparative literature educator
Goodrow, Gerard Andrew art historian, contemporary art specialist
Goonetilleke, Devapriya Chitra Ranjan Alwis English language educator
Gopal, Sarvepalli history educator
Gordon, Cyrus Herzl Orientalist, archaeologist, educator
Gordon, Ian Lewis history educator, academic administrator
Gorilovics, Tivadar literature educator
Gorman, Jonathan Lamb philosopher, educator
Górniak-Kocikowska, Krystyna Stefania philosopher, educator
Gossett, Philip musicologist
Goswami, Kanan Bihari foreign language educator
Gotovska-Henze, Teodoritchka Ilieva historian, educator
Gottfried, Paul Edward humanities educator, editor
Gougher, Ronald Lee foreign language educator and administrator
Gounaris, Basil historian
Graff, Henry Franklin historian, educator
Graham, Diane Shafer art and architectural history educator
Graham, Lanier art historian, curator, cultural planner
Granasztoi, Gyorgy historian
Graniela-Rodriguez, Magda educator, writer
Granqvist, Raoul Johannes English literature educator, writer
Granrose, John Thomas philosophy, psychology and religion educator
Grasthu, Lakshminarayana retired English educator
Gray, Clarence Jones foreign language educator, dean emeritus
Gray, Vivienne Joan classicist, educator
Grcic, Joseph philosophy educator
Green, Louis Ferdinand historian, educator
Grgas, Stipe literature and sociology educator
Griffin, Larry Don English language educator, poet, college administrator
Griffin, Miriam Tamara history educator
Griffin, Roger David history educator, researcher
Gross, Hanns history educator
Gross, Jonathan poetry educator
Gross, Stefan literary historian
Gruber, Loren Charles English language educator, writer
Guichemerre, Roger French literature educator
Gulgowski, Paul William German language, social science, and history educator
Gungwu, Wang historian, academic administrator
Guo, Sheng Ming retired history educator
Gupta, Baldev Raj linguistics educator, writer
Gurevich, Aaron Ja historian
Gurley, Elisabeth Anne art historian, educator, writer
Gushue, Peter Boland historian, educator
Gusmani, Roberto linguist
Gussenhoven, Carlos Henricus linguist
Gustavson, Royston Robert musicologist, consultant
Guthke, Karl Siegfried foreign language educator
Gutiérrez, Elisa de León languages educator
Guyard, Marius-Francois French literature educator
Gyalpo, (Nyilog-Gyari) Pema international relations educator, TV commentator
Habakkuk, John Hrothgar economic historian
Habermas, Jürgen philosopher, sociologist
Hagiwara, Nathaniel Tsutomu educator
Hagland, Jan Ragnar philology educator
Hahn, Lewis Edwin philosopher, retired educator
Hale, Cecil communications educator
Hall, Marcia Brown art historian, educator
Hall, Marie-Joyee Faith Spanish and English language educator
Hall, Ralph Frederick social science educator
Hall, Roland philosopher, researcher
Hallchurch, Timothy Thomas genealogist, consultant
Halliwell, Francis Stephen foreign language educator
Hamajima, Bin English and Japanese educator
Hamarneh, Sami Khalaf historian of pharmacy, medicine and science, author
Hamburger, Clara musicologist
Hamid, Mohammad Urdu language educator, university official
Hamlin, Wilfrid Gardiner retired literature and philosophy educator
Hancock, Eleanor Iris Margarete history lecturer
Hanhimaki, Jussi Markus historian, researcher
Hansen, Barbara L. English educator
Hansen, Deirdre Doris ethnomusicologist, educator, researcher
Hansen, Klaus English language educator
Haq, Ihsan Ul Arabic language educator
Haq, Kaiser Mohamed Hamidul English educator, author
Hara, Yoriko Japanese literature researcher
Hardy, Barbara Gladys English literature educator, critic, writer
Harig-Kollesch, Jutta philologist, researcher, retired
Harmond, Richard Peter historian, educator
Harnisch, Rüdiger linguist, educator, researcher
Harrell, David Edwin, Jr. history educator
Harris, Frederick John foreign language and literature educator
Harris, Jocelyn Margaret English educator
Harris, Mary Emma art historian, landscape designer
Harris, Robert Dalton history educator, researcher, writer
Harris, Sandra Jean linguist, educator
Harrison, Jonathan philosophy educator
Harrison, Steven J. English educator
Hartman-Irwin, Mary Frances retired language professional
Hartmann, Peter Claus historian, educator
Hasegawa, Yasuji French language educator
Hastings, Elisa Kipp English language educator
Hatano, Masami humanities educator
Hau, Michel historian, educator
Hauer, Thomas philosopher
Hauner, Milan Lothar historian
Hausser, Michel Jean literature educator
Hawke, Paul Henry historian
Hayden, Albert A. retired historian, educator
Hayes, John Trevor art historian, writer, exhibition organizer, retired museum administrator
Haynes, Barbara Judith language educator
Hayoun, Maurice-Ruben educator
Heald, Bruce Day English and music educator, historian
Heefner, Reginald Lee linguist, entertainer, author
Heffer, Jean historian, educator
Heffernan, Thomas Carroll English literature and American studies educator
Heilbron, John L. historian
Heitner, John A. (Jack Heitner) English language educator, writer
Heizer, Ruth Bradfute philosophy educator
Hell, Judit philosophy educator
Helmes, Günter German educator, researcher
Hemeliková, Blanka literary history researcher
Hemmersam, Flemming Peter Danish folklorist, researcher
Herbers, Klaus historian, educator
Herbert, Catherine Deming English educator
Herbert, Kevin Barry John classics educator
Heres Diddens, Johanna Geurtina translator
Hermes, Katherine Ann historian, history educator
Heroux, Erick J. languages educator
Herren, Michael Wayne classical studies educator
Herzstein, Robert Edwin history educator, author
Hess, Heinz-Juergen science historian
Hidai, Hoichi Asian studies educator
Hiebel, Hans Helmut German studies educator
Higgins, Ian Kevin English educator
Hila, Antonio Calleja historian, educator, researcher, writer
Hilfstein, Erna science historian, educator
Hinkle, Douglas Paddock retired languages educator
Hirano, Yorio English language and literature educator
Hirsch, Erhard educator
Hirschhorn, Bernard educator, historian, researcher, writer
Hiskes, Dolores G. educator
Hjärpe, Jan Östen religion and history educator
Ho, Hsiu-Hwang philosophy educator
Hoeffe, Otfried Gerhard philosophy educator
Hoeflin, Ronald Kent philosopher, intelligence test designer, newsletter publisher
Hoeltgen, Karl Josef English literature educator
Hoenigswald, Henry Max linguist, educator
Hoffmann, Achim Albert humanities educator
Hoffmann, Kathryn Ann humanities educator
Hoke, Rudolf legal history educator
Holland, Roy William Henry retired liberal studies educator
Hollar, Jeffrey Allen foreign language educator, biologist
Holtug, Nils philosophy and ethics educator
Holy, Jiri literature educator
Holz, Hans Heinz philosophy educator
Hon, Giora philosopher of science
Honda, Baku linguist
Hong, Jeesun interpreter, educator
Hongladarom, Soraj philosopher, educator
Hood, Ronald Chalmers, III historian, writer
Hoppen, Karl Theodore history educator
HorÁk, Petr philosophy educator, journal editor
Hori, Keiko English literature educator
Horii, Reiichi foreign language educator, library director
Horn, Michiel Steven Daniel history educator
Horne, Francis Philip English literature educator
Horning, Ross Charles, Jr. historian, educator
Horst, Samuel Levi history educator, researcher, writer
Horvath, Suzanne Korn historian
Hosking, Geoffrey Alan history educator, literary critic
Hosking, Richard Frank English language educator
Houziaux, Mutien-Omer linguistics educator
Howard, Lillie Pearl English language educator, academic administrator
Howard, Michael Eliot historian, educator
Hroch, Jaroslav philosophy educator
Hsu, Kylie language and linguistics educator, researcher
Huang, Cheng-Teh James linguistics educator
Hubík, Stanislav philosopher, researcher
Hughes, Kaylene historian, educator
Hughes, Stephen Ormsby foreign correspondent
Hult, Susan Freda history educator
Hund, Barbara Maurer English educator and speech broadcasting
Huning, Alois Konrad philosophy educator
Hunnecke-Enfert, Evelyn German language and literature educator
Hunt, Alan John English educator
Hunt, John J. historian, educator
Hunt, Maurice Arthur English educator, researcher
Hurley, Susan Lynn philosopher, educator
Husar, Alexandru Miciu humanities educator, writer
Huston, John Dennis English educator
Hutchinson, George Bain English and American studies educator
Hutchinson, Joseph Candler retired foreign language educator
Hutchison, Jane Campbell art history educator, researcher
Hutchison, Keith Robert history and philosophy of science educator
Hutto, Daniel Douglas philosopher, educator
Iamandi, Petru English educator, translator
Ichimura, Takahisa history educator, philosophy educator
Igarashi, Yasuo (David) language educator
Iguchi, Haruo history educator
Ihde, Aaron John history of science educator emeritus
Ilari, Virgilio history educator
Ilies, Beatrice Georgeta English language educator
Illés, László literary historian, educator
Im, Kaye Soon humanities educator
Imakita, Atsuko English language educator
Imre, László literature educator
Ineichen, Gustav linguistics educator
Ingenkamp, Heinz Gerd philologist, educator
Innes, Catherine Lynette English studies educator
Isaacs, Harold history educator
Iser, Wolfgang English and comparative literature educator, writer
Ishida, Masaharu political history educator
Ishihara, Kousai English language educator
Ito, Sadamoto American literature educator
Itoh, Isao humanities educator
Itoh, Shoko American literature educator
Ives, Margaret Christyne foreign language educator
Iwańczak, Wojciech Józef historian
Izquierdo, Luis Salvador literature educator
Jacob, Pierre philosophy educator
Jacqmain, Monique Hermance Julienne Italian language educator
Jaenen, Cornelius John history educator, consultant
Jäger, Ludwig philology educator
Jagirdar, Mohd Iqbal Yasznkhan foreign language educator
James, Gregory Cyril linguist
Jamindar, Rasesh Chaturbhai historian
Janson, Tore linguist
Janssens, Marcel literature educator
Jäntti, Ahti Johannes German language educator
Jaroszewski, Verda M. English educator
Jaumann, Herbert literary educator
Jechova-Voisine, Hana humanities educator
Jeet, Surjit Singh historian, research scholar
Jeffreys-Jones, Rhodri history educator
Jelínek, Milan linguist
Jennings, John Mark historian, writer
Jensen, Hans Frandsen historian, educator
Jettmarová, Zuzana linguist
Joensen, Jóan Pauli ethnology and history educator, academic administrator
Johansen, Hans Christian economic historian, educator
John Peter, Gibbons linguistics educator, linguist
Johnson, Alex Claudius English language educator
Johnson, Clifton Herman historian, archivist, former research center director
Johnson, Edna Scott English language educator, volunteer
Joly, Jacques humanities educator
Jonasson, Kerstin Maria romance languages educator
Jones Davies, Marie-Thérèse Louise educator
Joppen-Hellwig, Sandra linguist, researcher
Jorgensen, Paul Alfred English language educator emeritus
Joseph, John E. linguistics educator
Judd, Denis historian, educator
Jürgensen, Frank Dietrich Walter museum educator
Kabdebó, Lóránt historian
Kadir, Djelal literature educator, writer, translator, editor
Kaelble, Hartmut social history educator
Kaelin, Eugene Francis philosophy educator
Kagan, Constance Henderson philosopher, educator, consultant
Kageyama, Taro theoretical linguist, educator
Kalaga, Wojciech Henryk literature educator
Kalinowski, Konstanty art historian
Kamiyama, Yasushi humanities educator
Kanior, Marian historian
Kantawala, Sureshachandra Govindlal humanities educator, researcher
Kaplan, Francis philosophy researcher
Kasten, Wendy Christina literacy educator, writer, consultant
Kastovsky, Dieter English language educator
Kato, Fumihiko English and American literature educator
Katz, Steven Barry English educator, writer
Kautman, František library historian, writer
Kawai, Tokuharu philosophy educator
Kawashima, Kohei history scholar
Kazakevitch, Olga Anatolievna linguist, researcher

Kazama, Toshio *humanities educator*
Kazantseva, Tatayana Ivanovna *English educator*
Keesom, Cornelis H.A. *translator*
Keiger, John Frederick Victor *history educator*
Keil, Gundolf *medical historian, medievalist, Germanist*
Kelemen, Janos *philosopher, educator*
Kelley, Lynne Dhionis *language educator*
Kemiläinen, Aira Tellervo *historian, educator, researcher*
Kemp, Martin John *art history educator, history of science educator*
Kemp, Torben Peter *philosopher, educator*
Kempcke, Günter Rudolf *linguist*
Kenesei, István *linguist, educator*
Kerem, Yitzchak *historian, researcher*
Kerkhof, Maximiliaan Paul Adriaan *Spanish language and philology educator*
Kern, Alfred M. *English language educator, writer*
Kertesz, Andras Lajos *linguist*
Kervégan, Jean-François *philosophy educator, researcher*
Ketcham, Ralph *history and political science educator*
Khanzhina, Helen P. *English educator, translator*
Khrenova, Natalia Fjodorovna *English educator*
Khushu-Lahiri, Rajyashree *English educator, researcher*
Kiefer, Ferenc *linguist, educator*
Kiening, Christian Werner *German literature educator*
Kienzle, John Fred *history educator*
Kilanowski, Dana Marcotte *historian, writer, filmmaker, archaeologist*
Kilner, Ursula Blanche *genealogist, writer*
Kim, Elaine Haikyung *humanities educator, writer*
Kim, Tae-Chang *public philosopher, educator*
Kim, Yangho *language educator*
Kimura, Shigenobu *art historian*
King, (Robert) Thomas *linguistics and computer science educator*
Kingery, Sandra Lynn *Spanish language educator, translator*
Kinjo, Seiki *humanities educator*
Kirby, Ian John *English educator*
Kirkinen, Heikki *retired history educator*
Kirscht, Judith Mary *English educator*
Kiteley, Brian Alan *English literature educator, writer*
Kizuka, Masataka *English educator*
Kleinert, Annemarie Elisabeth *historian*
Klimbacher, Wolfgang *literary historian*
Klimowicz, Tadeusz *philologist*
Klinkenberg, Jean-Marie *humanities educator, researcher, consultant*
Knapp, Éva *literary historian*
Knight, Doris Rathbun *retired government and history educator*
Knipping, Detlef *art historian*
Knobloch, Hans-Joerg *German literature educator*
Knowles, Richard Alan John *English language educator*
Knox, George *art historian*
Knudsen, Laura Georgia *linguist*
Kobayashi, Seiei *English literature educator*
Koenen, Ludwig *classical studies educator*
Koenig, Yvan Henri *Egyptologist, researcher*
Kohák, Erazim Václav *philosophy educator, writer*
Köhler, Theodor Wolfram *philosophy educator*
Koizumi, Masatoshi *linguist*
Kojevnikov, Alexei Borisovich *historian, educator*
Kolak, Czeslawa *language professional, educator*
Kolsky, Stephen Derek *humanities educator*
Kom, Ambroise *literature educator*
Komárek, Miroslav *linguist, educator*
Komatsu, Eisuke *linguistics and French literature educator*
Konakov, Nikolai Dmitrijevich *ethnologist, educator*
Konno, Koichi *English language educator*
Konovalova, Liudmila Vasilievna *philosopher, educator*
Konrad, Helmut *history educator*
Kontra, Miklós *linguist, educator*
Konvitz, Josef Wolf *history educator, international civil servant*
Kooijman, Arthur *linguist, translator*
Kopf, David *history educator*
Kordić, Snježana *linguist, educator, researcher*
Korobeinikova, Larisa Aleksandrovna *philosopher, educator*
Korom, Michael *historian, educator*
Korshak, Yvonne *art historian*
Kortlandt, Frederik Herman Henri *Slavic languages and comparative linguistics educator*
Kosáry, Domokos *historian*
Kositchev, Anatoly *philosophy educator*
Kospartov, Stefan Dimitrov *English educator*
Kosyk, Wolodymir *history educator*
Kotin, Mikhail Lvovich *linguistics educator*
Koutkova, Alice Semyenovna *English language educator, researcher*
Kovásznai, Viktória Lukács *art historian, museologist, researcher*
Kowal, Rebekah Jane *English language educator*
Kra, Pauline Skornicki *French language educator*
Krajčovič, Rudolf *linguistics educator*
Krakover, Shaul *philosophy educator, researcher*
Kramer, Frank Raymond *classicist, educator*
Kramer, Matthew Henry *legal philosopher, law educator*
Krasteva, Yonka Kroumova *English and Russian language educator*
Kraus, Christina Shuttleworth *classics educator*
Kraus, Jiři *linguist, researcher*
Krebs, Pierre *philosopher, humanities educator*
Krier, Fernande Germaine *linguist, educator, researcher*
Krifka, Manfred *linguist, educator*
Kripke, Saul Aaron *philosophy educator, researcher*
Kritz, Reuven Rudolf *humanities educator, writer*
Krob, Josef *philosophy educator*
Krol-Dobrov, Charel B. *European studies and Dutch language educator*
Kruithof, Bernardus *historian, education*
Krymskii, Sergey Borisovich *philosophy educator*
Kryński, Andrzej *humanities educator*
Krzyzanowski, Jerzy Roman *Polish literature educator*
Kucera, Henry *linguistics educator*
Kucha, Ryszard *history of education educator*
Kuesters, Hanns Juergen R. *historian, political scientist, educator*
Kuhn, Anne Naomi Wicker (Mrs. Harold B. Kuhn) *foreign language educator*
Kujawińska, Courtney Krystyna Joanna *Shakespeare scholar*
Kula, Jan Marcin *historian*
Kulkarni, Madan *literature educator*
Kurtz, Paul *philosopher, educator, publisher*
Kvalheim, Olav Martin *educator, industrial consultant*
Kyrtatas, Dimitris *historian*
Labunka, Miroslav *history educator*
Lacy, Terry Goodwin *retired educator, translator, editor, author*
Laczkó, Tibor *English and Hungarian linguistics educator*
Lahvis, Sylvia Leistyna *art historian, educator, curator*
Lakritz, Esther *retired English language educator*
Lalithamba, Bhaskaram Yagneshwar *literature educator*
Landau, Iddo *philosopher, educator*
Landauer, Elvie Ann Whitney *humanities educator, writer*
Landauer, Michelle Deborah *English literature researcher*
Lane, David Gerald *classics educator*
Lansdowne, Karen Myrtle *retired English language and literature educator*
Lanzinger, Klaus *language educator*
Larsen, Erik *art history educator*
Larson, David Mitchell *English studies educator, writer*
Laska, Vera *history educator*
Lathrop, Thomas Albert *language educator*
Laufer-Dvorkin, Batia *English educator, applied linguist*
Lautner, Peter *historian of ancient philosophy*
Lavine, Thelma Zeno *philosophy educator*
Lawrence, Christopher John *historian*
Leavitt, Charles Loyal *English language educator, administrator*
Lederer, Herbert *foreign languages educator*
Lee, Cho-Sik *philosophy educator*
Lee, Chungmin *educator, linguist*
Lee, Eun Ji *linguist, educator*
Lee, Jay *foreign language educator*
Lee, Kiyong *linguistics educator*
Lee, Patsy L. *English educator, legal representative*
Lee, Su Kim *language educator*
Lee, Thomas Hong-Chi *historian, educator*
Lee, Ton-ju *Korean language and literature educator*
Leech, Geoffrey Neil *English language educator*
Lehmann, Winfred Philipp *linguistics educator*
Lehmkuhl, Ursula *history educator*
Leikola, Anto Heikki Albert *history of science educator*
Leinieks, Valdis *classicist, educator*
Leistner, Maria-Verena Helene *literary scholar*
Leitsch, Walter *historian, educator*
Lejosne, Roger *retired English language educator*
Lencek, Rado Ludovik *Slavic languages educator*
Lendinara, Patrizia *humanities educator*
Lendvai, Ferenc L(eimdörfer) *philosophy educator*
Lenk, Richard William, Jr. *history educator*
Lenman, Bruce Philip *historian, educator*
Lennard, John Chevening *literature educator*
Leonhardt, Jürgen Hans Karl *philologist*
Leon-Portilla, Miguel *historian, educator*
Leontidou, Lila (Triantafyllia) *humanities educator*
Lepschy, Anna Laura *Italian language educator*
Le Roy Ladurie, Emmanuel Bernard *historian, educator*
Leško, Vladimír *philosopher, researcher, educator*
Leslie, William Bruce *history educator*
Lethbridge, Robert David *French language educator, university official*
Letoublon, Francoise Vuillemin *Greek language and literature educator, researcher*
Levey, Michael (Vincent) *art historian, author*
Levinson, Jerrold *humanities educator*
Lewis, Victor Bradley *philosopher, educator*
Li, Qishu *English educator*
Lichtman, Allan Jay *historian, educator, consultant*
Lickindorf, Elisabeth Teresa *English educator, freelance journalist*
Liebertz-Gruen, Ursula *philologist, educator*
Lindgren, Charlotte Holt *English language educator*
Lindgren, J. Ralph *philosophy educator, writer*
Lindgren, Nelly Naila *linguist, educator, researcher*
Lindsey, Roberta Lewise *music researcher, historian*
Linters, Adriaan J. J. A. *heritage consultant, lecturer*
Liponski, Wojciech Adam *Anglosaxon cultures historian, sport historian*
Lippert-Rasmussen, Kasper *philosopher*
Lisovska, Evita *English educator*
Liste, Hartmut *language professional, researcher*
Livingston, Jeffery C. *history educator*
Lloyd-Jones, Sir (Peter) Hugh (Jefferd) *Greek language educator*
Löbel, Elisabeth *scientific researcher in linguistics*
Lock, Christopher Peter *English educator*
Lockett, Landon Johnson *retired linguistic educator, researcher*
Lodge, David John *English literature educator, author*
Loewe, Raphael James *retired humanities educator*
Lohrli, Anne *retired English language educator, writer*
Lönnqvist, Barbara *Russian language and literature educator*
Lope, Hans-Joachim *romance philology educator*
Lope-Blanch, Juan M. *philology educator, researcher*
Low, Frederick Emerson *English educator*
Low, Morris Fraser *foreign language and history educator*
Low, Victor N. *historian*
Lowe, Rodney *historian, educator*
Lowenthal, David *historian, geographer*
Lowry, Montecue Judson *military historian*
Lu, Shih-Peng *history educator*
Lübcke, Poul *philosopher*
Lucas, George Ramsdell, Jr. *philosophy educator*
Luna, Florencia *humanities educator bioethics, researcher*
Lundestad, Geir *historian, educator*
Luutonen, Jorma Kalervo *linguist*
Lyakhovitsky, Yuri Mikhailovich *historian, researcher*
Lyon, Gordon William *philosophy educator*
Macaku, Eleni Ioannou *language educator*
Macdonald, Ian Robert *Spanish educator, university administrator*
Mack, Jane Barnes *English and American studies educator*
MacKenzie, Craig Hugh *English language educator*
Mackenzie, J(ohn) Lachlan *English language educator, researcher*
Mac Kenzie, Norman Hugh *retired English educator, writer*
MacMahon, Michael Kenneth Cowan *phonetics educator*
Maddock, Lawrence Hill *retired language educator*
Maddox, Marilyn Coleman *literature and composition educator*
Maddy-Weitzman, Bruce Alan *historian, political analyst*
Magnani, Lorenzo *philosopher, educator*
Magyar, László András *historian*
Maienschein, Jane Ann *historian, philosopher, educator*
Makarenko, Victor *philosopher, political scientist, educator*
Malinovsky, Milan *linguistics educator, researcher, musician*
Mannath, Joe *philosopher*
Manning, Roberta Thompson *historian, educator*
Marchessou, Helene Daisy *English and American literature educator*
Marchione, William Philip *historian, writer*
Marcus, Kenneth Hearne *historian, educator*
Marcus, Laura Kay *literature educator*
Margolis, Howard *public policy studies educator*
Marko, Kurt Johannes *historian, educator*
Markus, Manfred Wilhelm *English language and literature educator*
Marovitz, Sanford E. *English language and literature educator*
Marsh, Dwight Chaney *English educator, editor*
Marshall, Linda Murphy *linguist, government official*
Martens, Maximiliaan Pieter Jan *art history educator*
Martensen-Larsen, Britta Tanja *art historian, researcher*
Martin, Mary Coates *genealogist, writer, volunteer*
Martin, Mary Laura *language educator, literature educator*
Martin, Mircea Aurelian *literary critic, educator*
Martin-Stern, Claudia Maria *interpreter, educator*
Mason, Peter *visual historian, analyst*
Masselos, Jim Cosmas *history educator, researcher*
Master, Peter Antony *educator, author, editor*
Mastrodimitris, Panayotis *literature educator*
Masuda, Sumiko *language and literature educator*
Mata, Elizabeth Adams *English language educator, land investor*
Mathews, Kuruvilla *African studies educator*
Mathis, Franz *historian, educator*
Mathur, Vishnu Dayal *historian, educator, researcher*
Matsumoto, Kazuko *linguistics and second language learning researcher*
Matsuoka, Kazumi *linguist, educator*
Matsuura, Naomi *English and American poetry educator*
Maxwell, Kenneth Robert *historian*
May, Georges (Claude) *French language and literature educator, university official*
Mazzotti, Massimo *history of science educator, consultant*
McAleer, John Joseph *English literature educator*
McCarthy, Thomas Anthony *philosophy educator*
McCutcheon, Marie Burgess Arlouine *town historian, retired*
McDevitt, Brian Peter *history educator, educational consultant*
McDonald, Marianne *classicist*
McDougal, Stuart Yeatman *comparative literature educator, author*
McEvoy-Jamil, Patricia Ann *English language educator*
McFarland, Thomas *English educator*
McGann, Lisa B. Napoli *language educator*
McGibbon, Ian Callum *historian, editor, educator*
McLaren, John David *literature educator, editor*
McMahon, William Edward *philosophy educator*
McNaughton, William Frank *translator, educator*
Means, John Barkley *foreign language educator, association executive*
Megone, Christopher Bruce *philosophy educator*
Mehrtens, Herbert *history educator*
Melandri, Pierre Christian *history educator*
Mencwel, Andrzej *literature and culture educator*
Mende, Michael *historian, educator*
Mendola, Louis André Mantegna *genealogist*
Menezes, Sister Mary Noel *religious organization administrator, history educator*
Méral, Jean *educator*
Merini, Rafika *foreign language and literature educator*
Merisalo, Outi Kaija *romance philologist*
Merl, Stephan *historian, history educator*
Merten, Klaus Rainer *humanities educator*
Meshke, George Lewis *drama and humanities educator*
Messmer, Marietta E. *English educator*
Mey, Jacob Louis *linguistics educator*
Meyer, Michel Bernard *philosophy educator*
Meyer, Norva *history educator*
Meyers, Peter *retired history educator*
Michailidis, Sousana *English educator, history educator*
Microyannakis, Emmanuel John *history educator*
Middell, Matthias *comparative history educator, researcher*
Miernowski, Jan *foreign language educator*
Migone, Gian Giacomo *history educator, Italian senator*
Mihaylova, Larisa Grigoryevna *humanities educator, researcher*
Miklas, Heinz Franz Alfred *Slavonic philology educator, scientist*
Mildner, Vesna *speech educator*
Miller, Charles Wallace *historian, environmental geologist, educator*
Miller, Genevieve *retired medical historian*
Miller, Jeanne-Marie Anderson (Mrs. Nathan J. Miller) *English language educator, academic administrator*
Miller, Philip Harold *linguistics educator*
Miller, Walter James *English and humanities educator, writer*
Mills, Alice Catherine *literature educator, writer*
Mills, Elizabeth Shown *genealogist, editor, writer*
Milton, Corinne Holm *art history educator*
Mintz, Samuel Isaiah *English language educator, writer*
Mirabello, Mark Linden *history educator*
Mishra, Vijay Chandra *English literature educator, researcher*
Mitchell, Mozella Gordon *English language educator, minister*
Mitsakis, Kariofilis *humanities educator*
Miura, Kiyohiro *English language educator, writer*
Miura, Tokuhiro *English and American literature educator*
Miyamae, Kazuhiro *linguist, language educator*
Miyoshi, Masao *English literature educator, writer*
Moeliono, Anton Moedardo *retired linguistics educator*
Mohamed, Yasien Alli *language educator*
Mohanan, Tara Warrier *linguistics educator, researcher*
Mollenkott, Virginia Ramey *English literature and language educator, author, guest lecturer*
Monson, Dianne Lynn *literacy educator*
Montanari, Franco *classicist, educator*
Montefiore, Alan Claude *retired philosophy educator*
Montgomery, Maureen Elizabeth *American studies educator*
Moody, Anthony David *literature educator*
Moore, Dennis Duane *English educator*
Moorhead, John Anthony *historian*
Morales Florez, Martin Carlos *philosophy educator*
Moran, Ronald Wesson *retired English educator, dean, writer*
Moreau, Jean-Pierre *history educator*
Morgan, Leslie Talbot *English language educator*
Morimoto, Toyotomi *humanities educator*
Mork, Gordon Robert *historian, educator*
Morozkina, Eugenia Alexandrovna *philology educator, consultant*
Morrell, Jack Bowes *science history educator*
Morrill, Penny Chittim *art historian*
Morrison, Barbara Sheffield *Japanese translator and interpreter, consultant, educator*
Morrow, Walter Eugene *philosophy educator*
Mortensen, Christian Edward *philosopher*
Morton, Eric *liberal arts educator*
Moses, Claire Goldberg *history educator*
Mosley, Derek John *classicist, retired educator*
Motte, Peter *translator*
Moulines, Carlos Ulises *philosopher, educator*
Moure, Nancy Dustin Wall *art historian*
Mousseux, Renate *language educator*
Muchembled, Robert Pierre *historian, educator*
Muchiri, Mary Nyambura *linguist, educator*
Müller, Beate Susanne *German language and literature educator*
Muller, Frederik Archibald *philosopher, physicist, writer*
Mulvey-Roberts, Marie Elizabeth *English educator*
Munk Olsen, Birger *medieval philology and culture educator*
Munslow, Alun *historiographer, educator*
Muraki, Masatake *retired linguistics educator, researcher*
Murata, Itaru *international relations educator*
Murata, Tatsuo *humanities educator*
Murdoch, Brian Oliver *German language educator*
Murphy, John Joseph *educator in English literature, critic, editor*
Murray, Joel N. *English educator*
Murti, Mulakaluri Srimannarayana *sanskritist, linguist, educator, researcher*
Mutschler, Hans-Dieter *philosophy educator*
Myers, Jack Elliott *English educator, poet*
Myllyniemi, Seppo Juhani *historian*
Na, Tsung Shun (Terry Na) *Chinese studies educator, writer*
Naeser, Margaret Ann *linguist, medical researcher*
Nagasaka, Francis Genichiro *retired philosophy educator*
Nagl-Docekal, Herta *philosopher*
Naiditch, Larissa *linguistics educator*
Nakanishi, Osamu *historian*
Nam, Myeong-jin *philosophy educator*
Nandi, Tapasvi Shambhuchandra *language educator*
Naumann, Horst Bruno *linguist*
Navarro, Juan Jesús Moreno *foreign language educator*
Navarro Durán, Rosa *philology educator*
Nazarova, Tamara B. *English educator*
Negley, Floyd Rollin *genealogist, retired army officer and civilian military employee*
Neitzel, Soenke *historian*
Nemesio, Aldo Severino *linguist, humanities educator*
Neubauer, Fritz *linguistics educator*
Neuenschwander, Erwin *science historian, mathematician, educator*
Neutatz, Dietmar *historian*
Newbould, Brian Raby *musicologist*
Newburger, Caryn Lason *English educator*
Nguyen, The Anh *historian, educator*
Nida-Rümelin, Julian Thomas *philosopher*
Niederhauser, Emil Károly *history educator*
Nigam, Prakash Kumar *historian, consultant*
Nighoskar, Mahesh Vishnu *language educator*
Niiniluoto, Ilkka Maunu Olavi *philosophy educator*
Nischik, Reingard Monica *literature educator*
Niven, Alastair Neil Robertson *literature director*
Noble, Peter Scott *language educator*
Nochman, Lois Wood Kivi (Mrs. Marvin Nochman) *retired educator*
Nommela, Mari *art history educator*
Nordenfelt, Lennart *philosophy educator*
Nordmark, Dag K. *comparative literature researcher, educator*
Norling, Bernard *retired history educator*
Norris, Todd D. *speech and theatre educator, actor*
Northcutt, Wayne *history educator*
Nöth, Winfried Maximilian *semiotics and linguistics educator, researcher*
Nott, David Owen *French educator*
Noutsos, Panagiotis Christos *philosophy educator*
Nowell-Smith, Patrick Horace *philosophy educator*
Nowicka-Jeżowa, Alina Maria *philology educator*
Ntlola, Peter Makhwenkwe *retired translator*
Nugent, Walter Terry King *historian*
Nussbaum, Laureen *retired foreign language educator*
Nussbaum, Norbert *architectural historian, researcher*
Nwogu, Kevin Ngozi *linguist, educator*
Obinaju, Joseph Nwabueze *foreign language educator*
O'Brien, Eugene Patrick *humanities educator*
Ochs, Robert David *history educator*
O'Connell, Richard (James) *English literature educator, poet*
Odamtten, Helen Mary *English language educator*
Ogbaa, Kalu *English literature educator*
Ogbar, Jeffrey Ogbonna Green *history educator*
Ogée, Frédéric *English literature and art educator*
Oh, Ju-Hwan *history educator*
Ohkado, Masayuki *linguistics educator*
Ohzeki, Toshiaki *English studies educator, prison chaplain*
Okada, Sumie Mary *educator, author*
Okasha, Sarwat *art historian, educator, writer*
Oldenziel, Ruth *history educator, researcher*
Oldroyd, David Roger *historian of science*
Olnas, Felix J. *retired Slavic language educator*
Olsen, Stein Haugom *humanities educator*
Olsson, Karl Anders *American literature educator, researcher*
Oltean, Stefan *English educator*
Omara-Otunnu, Amii *history and human rights law educator*

Ombaka, Christine Oduor humanities educator, researcher
Omi, Makoto speech communication educator
O'Neill, Robert John historian
Opat, Jaroslav historian, carpenter
Oppenheim, Frank Mathias S.J. philosophy educator
Oprisan, Ionel literary historian, folklorist
Orel, Vladimir linguist, educator
Ormond, Leonee English literature educator
Ormsby, Eric Linn educator, researcher, writer
Osborne, John German language educator
Oscarson, Mats Åke foreign language educator, researcher
Osen, Lynn M. women's studies educator, writer
Ota, Takao American literature and studies educator
Otani, Yasuteru linguist, educator
Ottlinger, Claudia English educator
Oueijan, Naji Boulos English literature educator, researcher
Overgaauw, Eef paleographer, researcher, educator
Ozawa, Katsumi Japanese literature educator, researcher
Pabisch, Peter Karl German and European studies educator
Pabito, Beatriz Vargas foreign language educator
Pach, Zsigmond Pal historian, educator
Paige, Anita Parker retired English language educator
Paikeday, Thomas M. lexicographer and language consultant
Palmer, Frank Robert linguist, educator
Palmer, Mona Gene humanities educator
Palomäki, Jari Juhani philosopher, librarian, educator
Paltridge, Brian Richard applied linguistics educator
Palumbo-Fossati Casa, Isabella humanities educator, writer, researcher
Paman, Urbana Jose linguistics educator, researcher, consultant
Pande, Hem Chandra Russian language educator
Panek, Jaroslav historian
Pang-White, Ann A. philosophy educator, researcher
Panichas, George Andrew English language educator, critic, editor
Panov, Branko Mito historian, educator
Papakonstantino, Stacy English language educator
Pape, Helmut Wolfgang philosopher
Parada, Arturo foreign language and literature educator
Parker, Harold Talbot history educator
Parrinder, John Patrick English literature educator, literary critic
Pärssinen, Martti Heikki historian, archeologist
Paschoud, François university educator
Pastré, Jean-Marc Medievalist, educator
Pauw, Dirk Anton Greek and Latin studies educator
Pavlowitch, Stevan K. historian
Payne, John Philip German educator
Pazandak, Carol Hendrickson liberal arts educator
Peacocke, Christopher Arthur Bruce philosopher, educator
Peck, John Frederick poet, English language educator
Pečman, Rudolf musicologist, aesthetist
Peet, Howard David English educator, writer
Peeters, Willem Johannes Maria German language and literature educator
Pekkanen, Tuomo Antero Latin educator
Pelz, Manfred Franz-Josef foreign language educator
Peng, Frederick Che-Ching linguistics educator
Penny, Ralph John Spanish language educator
Penttinen, Hannu Kalevi humanitarian educator
Peonidis, Filimon philosophy educator
Percival, Ray Scott philosophy educator
Perez Laraudogoitia, Jon philosophy educator
Perrin, Ronald Frederic retired humanities educator
Perry, Thomas Amherst English literature and language educator
Peter, Agnes English educator
Peter, Mihaly Russian philologist, educator
Petersen, Ib Damgaard historian, educator
Peterson, Barbara Ann Bennett retired history educator, television personality
Peterson, Pamela Carmelle English language educator
Petránsky, Ludovít art history educator
Petrucciani, Mario Italian literature educator
Pettersson, Anders Swedish literature educator
Pettit, Philip Noel philosopher, educator
Pfister, Lauren Frederick Chinese studies educator, researcher, philosopher
Pfister, Manfred Max English literature educator
Phillipson, Robert Henry Lawrence linguistics educator
Pierard, Richard Victor history educator
Pihlström, Sami Johannes philosopher, researcher, educator
Pilbeam, Pamela May history educator
Pina de Silva, Fernando Antonio tribology educator, researcher
Pineri, Riccardo Italian literature and philosophy educator
Pirjevec, Joze history educator
Pirozynski, Jan historian, librarian, educator
Pitt, Joseph Charles philosophy educator
Plag, Ingo linguistics educator
Plumb, Sir John (Harold) historian, educator
Pogačnik, Jože literature educator
Pogner, Karl-Heinz linguist, researcher
Poirson, Brigitte English language educator
Polák, Stanislav historian
Poláková, Jolana philosopher, researcher
Pole, Jack Richon historian
Poledňák, Ivan musicologist, educator, researcher
Polemis, Demetrios Ioannou historian
Polito-Shuffer, Robin Marie language educator
Polukhina, Valentina Platonovna Russian studies educator, author
Pomirko, Roman linguist, educator, researcher
Pompa, Leonardo philosophy educator, university dean
Ponelis, Friedrich Albert language educator
Pons, Xavier Jean Paul English educator, writer
Pontara, Giuliano philosophy and peace
Porat, Dina historian
Porcelli, Gianfranco language educator
Porter, Gerald David English educator
Posner, Rebecca Reynolds Romance language educator
Potter, David Stone Greek and Latin educator
Poulot, Dominique Pierre history educator
Powrie, Philip Peter French cultural studies educator
Pozzo, Riccardo philosophy educator
Prasad, Veena Rani English language educator
Prasad, Yamuna English educator
Prawer, Siegbert Salomon author, Germanic language and literature educator
Predota, Stanislaw foreign language educator
Prest, Wilfrid Robertson historian, educator
Preston, Paul historian educator
Prestwich, Michael Charles historian, educator
Prettyman, Alfred Emerson English language and social and behavioral sciences educator, publishing executive
Profit, Vera Barbara German language and literature educator
Pryor, William Daniel Lee humanities educator
Pstruzina, Karel philosopher, educator
Puha, Elena humanities educator
Puranen, Kristina retired translator
Putseys, Yvan Frans Louis retired language educator
Qazi, Firdous Anwer humanities educator
Quann, Joan Louise French language educator, real estate broker
Quarcoo, Emmanuel Auuley language educator, researcher
Quasem, Muhammad Abul philosophy educator
Quinn, David Beers retired history educator
Raaberg, Gloria Gwen literature educator
Rabanales, Ambrosio linguistics educator, researcher
Rabe, Horst historian
Radkau, Joachim history educator
Radrizzani, Ives philosophy researcher, writer, educator
Rafique, Mohammad philosophy educator
Raftery, Margaret Mary English educator, editor, translator
Railey, Kevin James English educator
Rajaraman, Vaidyanath English educator
Ramakrishna, Devarakonda English educator, researcher
Rambaux, Claude Henri Latin educator, researcher
Raphael, David Daiches academic philosopher, political theorist
Rath, R. John historian, educator
Rathkolb, Oliver Robert historian
Rathmayr, Renate Felicitas Slavonic language educator
Rattansi, Pyarally Mohamedally history of science educator
Ravaux-Kirkpatrick, Francoise language professional
Raz, Joseph philosophy educator
Razin, Alexander Vladimirovich philosopher, educator
Reading, Martin translator
Real, Reinerio Augusto English educator, consultant
Reardon, Stephen James, Jr. retired English speech educator
Rebelo, Luis De Sousa literary historian, researcher
Reber, Michael F. English educator, consultant
Reckert, Stephen researcher
Reddy, Dandu Jayaprakshnarayan English educator, researcher
Reece, Sydney Lorraine English composition educator
Reed, Berenice Anne art historian, artist, government official
Reeve, Lawrence John historian, educator
Reid, Brian Holden historian, educator
Reif, Stefan Clive Hebrew and Jewish studies educator, researcher
Reilly, John Marsden English language educator
Reiss, Hans Siegbert German language educator
Renshaw, Patrick Richard George history educator, writer
Resnik, David Benjamin medical humanities educator, researcher
Ressetar, Nancy foreign language educator
Restaino, Giovanni Franco philosophy educator
Rey-Coquais, Jean-Paul ancient history educator
Reynolds, Eva Mary Barbara foreign language educator
Rheinheimer, Martin historian, educator
Riback, Estelle Posner independent art historian
Ricci, Graciela Nilbet linguist
Richardson, Roger Charles history educator, author
Ricketts, Virginia Lee historian, researcher
Rickman, Hans Peter philosopher, educator, writer
Rieber, Alfred Joseph historian, educator, researcher
Riedweg, Christoph Anton classics educator
Riepe, Dale Maurice philosopher, writer, illustrator, educator, Asian art dealer
Riley-Smith, Jonathan Simon Christopher history educator
Rinsler, Norma Sybil French educator
Riordan, Sheilagh Margaret literature and language educator
Rippy, Frances Marguerite Mayhew English language educator
Ritter, Gerhard Albert historian, educator
Rittner, Leona Phyllis comparative literature scholar
Rivera-La Scala, Gladys Mary Romance languages educator, researcher
Riverso, Emanuele philosophy educator, researcher
Rivosh, Victor philologist, translator
Rizk, Laila Galal English lecturer
Robbins, Thomas Landau humanities researcher
Roberts, Priscilla Mary history educator
Roberts, Ricky Elias linguist, educator
Roberts-Parast, Ann Talbot English, foreign language educator
Robinson, Alice Helene English language educator, administrative assistant
Robinson, Michael Finlay musicologist, educator
Rochette, Bruno Robert Jean Armand Ghislain classicist, researcher, educator
Rodriguez, Ricardo Vélez philosopher educator
Rodriguez, Timothy Allen language educator
Roe, Nicholas Hugh English educator
Rogers, Graham Allan John philosophy educator
Rogister, John Marie Julien history professor
Röhl, John Charles Gerald educator, historian
Roisman, Hanna Maslovski classics educator
Rojas, Gonzalo historian
Roland, Grete language educator
Rolater, Frederick Strickland history educator, consultant
Rollo-Koster, Joëlle history educator
Romano-Magner, Patricia R. English studies educator, researcher
Römer, Franz Josef philologist, educator
Roos, Anna Marie history educator
Roraback, Erik Sherman English educator
Rose, Norman Anthony history educator
Rose, Paul Lawrence history educator
Rosemann, Philipp Wolfram philosopher, educator
Rossel, Sven Hakon literature educator
Roulet, Georges-Eddy linguistics educator
Rouman, John Christ classics educator
Rowen, Ruth Halle musicologist, educator
Roy, Joaquín humanities and international affairs educator
Rozbicki, Michal Jan American history educator
Rozenbaum, Najman languages educator, counselor
Rozumnyj, Jaroslav literature educator, researcher
Ruben, David-Hillel philosophy educator, administrator
Rubio, Patricia Ines literature educator, researcher
Rudy, Willis historian
Rueegg, Walter H(enri) humanities educator
Ruepke, Joerg religion historian, educator
Ruffieux, Roland retired history and political science educator
Ruffin, Paul Dean English language educator
Ruiz-Zúñiga, Angel historian, philosopher of science, mathematician, educator
Rumpler, Helmut history researcher, educator
Runciman, Sir Steven (James Cochran Stevenson Runciman) historian
Runggaldier, Edmund philosopher, educator
Ruoff, A. LaVonne Brown English language educator
Rupke, Nicolaas science history educator
Ruppert, Karsten historian, educator
Rüschoff, Bernd linguist
Russell, Sharon D. English educator, writer
Russo, Giovanni bioethics educator
Ruthven, Kenneth Knowles English language educator
Rychlík, Jan historian, researcher, educator
Rydén, Lennart Vilhelm retired Byzantine studies researcher
Ryder, Timothy Thomas classics educator
Rykov, Vladimir Vassiljevich linguist
Sabato, Hilda Iris historian, educator
Sabra, Afaf Sayed historian
Sagan, Alex Philip history educator, consultant
Sahu, Dharani Dhar English language educator, writer
Saikia, Nagen humanities educator
Sainsbury, Richard Mark philosophy educator
Saito, Hidetsune translator
Saito, Takafumi humanities educator
Saitoh, Mamoru English educator
Saizu, Ioan I. retired history educator
Sakamoto, Tadanobu English literature educator
Sakelliou-Schultz, Liana poet, critic
Sakharov, Vsevolod I. Russian and European literature educator
Salajczyk, Janina Russian literature educator, translator
Saltmarsh, John Albert historian, educator
Salvaneschi, Enrica humanities educator, writer
Sams, Eric musicologist
Samsonowicz, Henryk historian
Sands, Christine Louise English educator
Santoni, Ronald Ernest philosophy educator
Sasaki, Miyuki applied linguistics educator
Sasaki, Tsuyoshi Samuel linguistics educator
Sassoon, Adrian David art historian, antique dealer, art advisor
Sato, Kazuhiko English educator
Sato, Mitsuo retired philosophy educator
Sato, Yasushi linguist, educator
Satofuka, Fumihiko history of science and technology educator
Saukkonen, Pauli linguistics researcher
Saunders, Alison French educator
Saunders, Kay Elizabeth Bass history educator
Saunders, Matthew John architectural historian, conservationist
Scammell, Geoffrey Vaughan historian, educator
Scanlon, Lawrence Eugene English language educator
Scannone, Juan Carlos philosophy educator, priest
Schade, Richard Erich foreign language educator
Schadewaldt, Hans medical history educator
Schaefer-Weiss, Dorothea L. literary researcher
Schaeffner, Christina linguistics educator
Schafer, Elizabeth Diane historian, writer
Schäferdiek, Knut church history educator
Schaller, Helmut Wilhelm philology educator
Schcolnik, Miriam language educator
Scheler, Manfred philologist
Schenda, Rudolf Wilhelm classicist, educator
Schenkel, Elmar English educator, writer
Schereck, William John retired historian, consultant
Scherpe, Klaus Rüdiger literature educator
Schichler, Robert Lawrence English language educator
Schiffler, Ludger French language and literature methodology educator
Schlicke, Paul Van Waters English educator, writer
Schlobach, Jochen French literature educator
Schmale, Wolfgang historian
Schmid-Bortenschlager, Sigrid humanities educator
Schmider, Mary Ellen Heian American studies educator, academic administrator
Schmidt, Joanne (Josephine Anne Schmidt) language educator
Schmidt, Lawrence Kennedy philosophy educator
Schmidt, Paul Gerhard humanities educator
Schmidt, Sigurd Ottovich historian, educator, researcher
Schmidt-Biggemann, Wilhelm philosophy educator, dean
Schmied-Kowarzik, Wolfdietrich philosophy educator
Schmitt, Christian Karl W. romance linguist, educator
Schmitz, Hermann philosophy educator
Schneider, Hans Julius philosophy educator
Schneider, Valerie Lois speech educator
Schnepel, Roland English educator
Schnitzler, Günter Heinz German literature educator, music educator
Schofield, Malcolm philosopher educator
Scholz, Hans-Joachim linguistics educator
Schott, Heinz Gustav history of medicine educator, author
Schott, Rüdiger ethnology educator
Schourup, Lawrence Clifford linguist, educator
Schroeder, Klaus H. Romance philology educator
Schröter, Ulrich Hans philologist, educator, researcher
Schulenburg, Rosamunde Maria Graefin von der (Rosamunde Neugebauer) art historian, educator
Schultz, Helga historian, educator
Schulz, Gerhard Johann Ernst historian, educator
Schulze, Martin Samuel Paul English and American studies educator
Schupp, Volker literature educator
Schutz, John Adolph historian, educator, former university dean
Schwanauer, Francis philosopher, educator
Schwartz, Alexander translator, interpreter
Schwartz, Michael historian
Schwartz, Yves Raymond philosopher, educator
Schweid, Eliezer philosopher
Scott-Carroll, Kevin Michael conference interpreter
Scruton, Roger Vernon aesthetics educator, writer
Seaman, Gerald Roberts musicology educator, writer
Sebeok, Thomas Albert linguistics educator
Sedgwick, Mark John historian, educator
Seelbach, Karl Ulrich foreign language educator, literary historian
Segre, Cesare romance philology educator
Sehnal, Jiří musicologist
Seidel-Dreffke, Björn Birgit Slavist, educator
Seidensticker, Edward George Japanese language and literature educator
Seidler, Grzegorz Leopold historian, educator
Seiler, Charlotte Woody retired English language educator
Sekimoto, Mayaka English literature educator
Sekulic, Ante educator
Selig, Karl-Ludwig language and literature educator
Selmeczi, Joseph retired philosopher, researcher
Selting, Margret linguistics educator, researcher
Senft, Gunter psycholinguistics researcher, educator
Severin, Dorothy Sherman Spanish language and Hispanic studies educator
Sgall, Petr linguist, educator
Shaffer, Elinor Sophia English/comparative literature educator, writer
Shalif, Ruth English educator
Shanahan, Daniel Augustus foreign language educator
Sharkey, Michael Francis literature educator
Sharma, Dharma Dutta English educator
Sharma, Laxminarain language educator
Sharma, Prem Sagar foreign language educator
Sharma, Vasudena Subramonia literature educator, dean, editor
Sharon, Moshe Islamic history educator
Shavitsky, Ziva Hebrew language and literature educator
Shawcross, John Thomas English educator
Shchukin, Vasilii Georgievich literature historian, educator
Shea, William Rene historian, science philosopher, educator
Sherover, Charles M. retired philosophy educator
Shidehara, Francesco Eichi musicologist, educator
Shim, Jung-Soon English educator, theater critic
Shimamura, Totaro English educator
Shipley, D(onald) Graham J. historian
Shlapunov, Gennady Semyonovich historian
Sicking, Louis Henricus Joannes historian, researcher
Siegmund-Schultze, Reinhard historian
Siller, Max literature educator
Silva, Deonisio Daboit da literature educator
Silverman, Hugh J. philosophy educator
Simek, Rudolf humanities educator
Simmons, Richard Clive American history educator
Simmons, Robert Burns history and political science educator
Simon Diaz, Jose bibliography educator
Simons, Thomas W., Jr. history educator
Sinclair, Leon R. (Pete) retired literature educator, writer
Singer, Armand Edwards foreign language educator
Singer, Marcus George philosopher, educator
Singh, Sarva Daman historian, educator
Sinisgalli, Rocco classicist
Sitesh, Aruna English educator
Sixdenier, Guy-Dominique orientalist philologist, monk
Skinner, James Lister, III English language educator
Skinner, Quentin Robert Duthie historian, educator
Skorna, Hans Juergen literature educator
Skorna, Hans Jurgen literature studies educator
Skřivan, Aleš historian
Skrzypczak, Henryk Alfons historian
Skutnabb-Kangas, Tove Anita sociolinguistics researcher
Skvorecky, Josef Vaclav English literature educator, novelist
Skyllstad, Kjell Müller musicology educator
Slater, Barry Hartley philosophy educator
Slavin, Morris historian, educator
Slawinski, Christopher Mark sinologist, interpreter
Slinn, Errol Warwick language educator
Small, Michael Ronald English educator, writer
Small, Michele Geslin English studies and modern languages educator
Smart, John Jamieson Carswell retired philosopher, educator
Smith, Bonnie Gene historian, educator
Smith, Christopher Norman French language and literature educator
Smith, Gerrit Bruce foreign language educator
Smith, Grant William English language educator, civic fundraiser
Smith, Neil Colin military historian
Smith, Vivian Brian English literature educator, poet
Smits, Ronald Francis English educator, poet
Smulders, Ben retired historian
Smyth, Stuart John history educator
Snell-Hornby, Mary Adams Carruthers translation studies educator, researcher, consultant
Śnieżyńska-Stolot, Ewa Maria art historian, educator
Snow-Smith, Joanne Inloes art history educator
Sodei, Rinjiro historian, educator
Soderberg, Dale LeRoy English language educator, drama director, producer
Soderlind, Johannes literature educator
Sodeur, Wolfgang R. educator
Solbrig, Ingeborg Hildegard German literature educator, writer
Solin, Heikki Latin educator
Somerville, James Middleton, III retired philosophy educator, writer
Sommer, Andreas Urs philosopher, historian
Sommer, Manfred philosophy educator, writer
Sordi, Marta historian, educator
Soubrenie, Elisabeth Marie English literature educator, translator
Specht-Jarvis, Roland Hubert fine arts and humanities educator, dean
Spence, Nicol language educator
Spencer, Charles Samuel art historian, educator
Spicer, Harold Otis retired English educator, communications educator
Spires, Robert Cecil foreign language educator
Splett, Jochen Germanic philology educator
Splett, Jörg philosophy educator
Sproat, John Gerald historian
Stackelberg, John Roderick history educator
Stanberry, D(osi) Elaine English literature educator, writer
Starr, Joseph Barton history educator
Stasiak, Halina language educator
Stauffer, John William cultural historian
Stegenga, James Alan political scientist, ethicist, author, educator
Steindl, Michael Paul Armin linguist, author
Steiner, Richard C. semitic linguist, educator
Stemans, Werner German language educator, artist
Stempel, Wolf-Dieter Romance philology educator
Stenstroem, Thure Oscar humanities educator
Stenzl, Jürg Thomas musicologist, music critic

Stephens, Christopher Luke *writer, translator*
Sterling, Richard Leroy *English and foreign language educator*
Stevenson, William Edward, III *language educator*
Stevenson, William Robert *retired military historian, genealogist*
Stewart, Jon Bartley *philosophy educator*
Stewart, Michael Alexander *philosophy educator*
Stimpson, Catharine Roslyn *English language educator, writer*
Stock, Rodney Clifford *musicologist, editor*
Stocker, Arthur Frederick *classics educator*
Stockwin, James Arthur Ainscow *Japanese politics and modern studies specialist*
Stoddart, Leyland Kling *stamp dealer, correspondence club director*
Stoichita, Victor Ieeromim *art historian, writer*
Stokstad, Marilyn Jane *art history educator, curator*
Stolt, Birgit *foreign language educator*
Stoltzfus, Nathan A. *history educator, documentary and film consultant*
Stone, Gerald Charles *Slavonic studies researcher and educator*
Stoner, Joyce Hill *art conservator, art history educator, songwriter*
Stowasser, Barbara R.F. *foreign language and culture educator*
Strassler, Jurg *linguist, researcher*
Strawson, Sir Peter Frederick *philosophy educator*
Strelau, Renate *historical researcher, artist*
Strnad, Ernst *translator, writer*
Ströker, Elisabeth *philosophy educator, administrator*
Strong, Sir Roy Colin *historian, garden writer, diarist, former museum director*
Struna, Nancy L. *social historian and American studies educator*
Strunk, Klaus Albert *educator*
Stubbs, Michael Wesley *English linguistics educator*
Stuermer, Michael *historian*
Sturma, Michael Thomas *historian, educator*
Suchojad, Henryk *modern history educator, librarian*
Suckale, Robert *art historian*
Suda, Minoru *liberal studies educator*
Sudo, Shinji *languages educator, historian*
Suenobu, Mineo *applied linguistics educator*
Suiffet, Norma Julieta *language professional*
Suseendirarajah, Swaminathan *language educator, researcher*
Susla, Jeffrey Jonathan *English language educator*
Suzuki, Akira *language educator*
Svoboda, Olga *linguist, information professional, educator*
Swales, Martin William *German language educator*
Swaminathan, Natarajan (Sam Swaminathan) *storyteller*
Swan, Susan Linda *history educator*
Swanson, Roy Arthur *classicist, educator*
Swetman, Glenn Robert *English language educator, poet*
Swinburne, Richard Granville *philosopher, educator*
Sylvester, Nancy Katherine *speech educator, management consultant*
Szabadi, Judith *art historian, educator*
Szabo, Tibor *philosophy educator*
Szabolcsi, Miklos *Hungarian literary historian, educator*
Szarota, Tomasz Marceli *history educator, researcher*
Szèkely, La'szlo' *philosophy educator*
Szekeres-Varsa, Vera *linguistics educator, translator*
Szubka, Tadeusz *philosophy educator*
Tachiiri, Masayuki *art historian, assistant curator*
Tada, Toshio *literature classicist*
Taillefer de Haya, Lidia *English educator, translator*
Tairako, Tomonaga *philosophy educator*
Takahashi, Yasunari *English literature educator*
Takamiya, Toshiyuki *language educator*
Takayama, Machiko *humanities educator*
Takeda, Masako *English educator*
Tallár, Ferenc *philosopher, educator*
Tanahashi, Junji *historian science and technology, educator*
Tanaka, Takaji *English educator*
Tang, Paul Chi Lung *philosophy educator*
Tann, Jennifer *innovation studies educator*
Tanner, Norman Philip *clergyman, educator*
Tännsjö, Torbjörn *philosopher, educator*
Tarnopolsky, Oleg Borisovich *English educator*
Tarone, Elaine Elizabeth *linguistics educator*
Tarrant, Desmond *English and American literature educator*
Tatár, Béla *English and Russian educator*
Tate, Robert Brian *retired Renaissance studies educator*
Taylor, Margaret Wischmeyer *retired English language and journalism educator*
Taylor, Robert Edward *foreign language educator*
Temperley, Howard Reed *historian, educator*
Tenfelde, Klaus *historian*
Tengelyi, László *philosophy educator*
Tenkotte, Paul Allen *history and international studies educator*
Teramura, Shoji *linguist, educator*
Terauchi, Hajime *language educator*
Terry, Arthur Hubert *literary critic, educator*
Tersman, Folke Bengt Runesson *philosophy educator, researcher*
Tevzadze, Guram *philosopher educator*
Tezla, Albert *English educator*
Thacher, Barbara Auchincloss *history educator*
Thalassinos, Eleftherios *maritime studies educator*
Thanarak, Pimonpan *English educator*
Thesleff, B. Holger *retired philology educator*
Theunissen, Michael Heinrich *philosophy educator*
Thevoz, Michel *art history educator, curator*
Thibault, Paul John *linguistics educator*
Thiel, Manfred *philosopher, poet, publisher*
Thielen, Peter Gerrit *history educator*
Thirsk, (Irene) Joan *historian*
Thomaneck, Jurgen Karl Albert *German language educator*
Thomas, Helen Lee *linguistics educator*
Thomas, Hugh (Lord Thomas of Swynnerton) *historian*
Thomas, Keith Vivian *historian, former college president*
Thompson, Annie Laura Anne *foreign language educator*
Thompson, David Michael *historian, educator*
Thompson, Jan Newstrom *art historian, educator*
Thompson, Wayne Wray *historian*
Thompson-Cager-Strand, Chezia *literature educator, writer, performance artist*
Thomson, Heidi *English literature educator*
Thondhlana, Juliet *linguist, educator, consultant*
Thornton, Robert Kelsey Rought *English language educator*
Thürer, Georg *humanities educator*
Tice, Bradley Scott *humanities educator*
Tilby, Michael John *French language and literature educator*
Tilliette, Xavier *philosophy educator, priest*
Tiwary, Kapil Muni *English educator*
Todd, Malcolm *Roman literature and language educator*
Toland, John Willard *historian, writer*
Tomaszewski, Jerzy *history educator*
Tomomatsu, Atsunobu *international development specialist, educator, consultant*
Tønnesson, Stein Dorenfeldt *historian*
Toplin, Robert Brent *history educator, television producer*
Topolski, Jerzy *historian, educator*
Torii, Kiyoshi *English literature educator*
Torretti, Roberto *retired philosophy educator, editor*
Torstendahl, Rolf *history educator*
Tortarolo, Edoardo *historian, educator*
Toyonaga, Akira *English educator*
Trabant, Juergen *linguistics educator*
Tracey, Andrew Travis Norman *ethnomusicologist, musician*
Traeger, Claus *literature educator*
Trapp, Joseph Burney *classics educator*
Trevor-Roper, H(ugh) R(edwald) (Baron Dacre of Glanton) *historian, author, educator*
Trier, Else *humanities educator*
Tritle, Lawrence Alan *history educator*
Trosborg, Anna *English and linguistics educator*
Trunz, Erich *humanities educator*
Trusina, Pavel *translator, interpreter*
Tschiedel, Hans Jürgen *classical educator*
Tsirpanlis, Zacharias *humanities educator*
Tsuchiya, Tetsu Satoru *humanities educator*
Tsunematsu, Masao *English educator*
Tu, Guangnan *ethnologist*
Tung, Jeffrey Chao-hui *linguist, educator*
Turner, Ralph Vernon *historian educator*
Tüskés, Gábor *literary historian, researcher*
Tyler, Maurice Stanley *language educator*
Udolph, Jürgen *linguist, educator*
Ueda, Reed Takashi *historian, educator*
Ueding, Gert *humanities educator*
Uhlenbrock, Stefan *musicologist, editor*
Ullendorff, Edward *orientalist, educator*
Umeda, Iwao *English language educator*
Umeh, Marie Arlene *English language educator*
Underwood, Richard Allan *English language educator*
Unglaub, Erich *philologist, institute administrator*
Ünlü, Selcuk *German language and literature educator*
Unosawa, Kazuko *English language educator*
Urbina, Manuel, II *legal research historian, history educator*
Uriarte Rebaudi, Lia Noemi *literature educator*
Vail, Van Horn *German language educator*
Vajda, Mihály *philosopher, educator*
Vale, Peter Christopher Julius *humanities educator*
Valentine, Andrew Dominic *English language consultant*
Valero-Garces, Maria Carmen *language educator, translator, researcher*
Vallduvi, Enric *linguist*
Van Beek, Ursula Jolanta *historian, researcher*
van Benthem, Johan Franciscus Abraham Karel *philosophy, mathematics-computer science educator*
van der Dussen, Willem Johannis *philosophy educator*
van der Heyden, Ulrich *historian, political scientist, journalist, editor*
Van der Walt, Barend Johannes *philosophy educator*
van Gelderen, Elly *linguistics educator, researcher*
van Kemenade, Ans Maria Cornelia *linguistics educator*
Vanstapel, Maryse *French language educator*
Varga, Nicholas *historian, archivist, retired educator*
Varis, P. Tapio *media studies educator*
Varzegar, Minoo *English educator, reading specialist*
Vasić, Voislav *natural history educator, researcher*
Vasta, Edward *humanities educator*
Vater, Heinz *linguist*
Vecchiotti, Julius *philosophy educator*
Veiga, Manuel M.M. Alte Da *philosophy educator*
Veisbergs, Andrejs *linguistics educator, lexicographer, interpreter*
Velcic-Canivez, Mirna *linguist, university scholar*
Velez, Diana *historian, educator*
Velz, John William *literature educator*
Verhofstadt, Edward Cornelius *foreign language educator*
Verkruijsse, Pieter Jozias *classicist, educator*
Vernant, Jean-Pierre *philosophy educator*
Verolla, Steven Michael *French language educator*
Verrill, John Howard *museum director*
Vest, James Murray *foreign language and literature educator*
Vice, Roy Lee *history educator*
Vieira, David Gueiros *retired history educator*
Viereck, Wolfgang Wilhelm *linguist*
Vietor-Englander, Deborah Judith *foreign languages educator, researcher*
Vigne, (James) Randolph *historian, researcher*
Vijayakrishnan, Kumaralingam Gopalakrishnan *linguistics educator*
Vilanova, Mercedes *history educator*
Vincent, Julie *Russian literature educator*
Vinge, Louise *literature educator*
Viola, Mary Jo *art history educator*
Viquez, Eduardo Antonio *historian, geographer*
Vogel, Claus *Indology educator*
Vogt-Spira, Gregor *classics educator*
Volczer, Arpad *retired philosophy educator*
von Leyden, Wolfgang Marius *retired philosophy educator, author*
von Raffler-Engel, Walburga (Walburga Engel) *linguist, cross-cultural communications specialist, lecturer, writer*
Von Wright, Georg Henrik *philosopher, writer*
Vošahlíková, Pavla *historian, researcher*
Vossen, Rainer *linguistics educator*
Vowles, Richard Beckman *literature educator*
Vyplel, Zdeněk *language educator, translator*
Wagner, Donald B(lackmore) *historian*
Wagner, Ewald *orient language educator*
Wagner, Frank *literature educator*
Wåhlin, Vagn *history educator*
Wahsner, Renate Merkel *philosopher, researcher*
Walden, David Michael *historian, consultant*
Walder, Dennis Jean *literature educator, author*
Waldren, William Henre *historian, museum administrator*
Walker, Brigitte Maria *translator, linguistic consultant*
Wallace, William John *history educator*
Wallas, Armin Alexander *German literature researcher*
Waller, Philip John *history educator*
Wallman, Charles James *historian*
Wallner, Friedrich *philosopher, educator*
Walravens, Jan *foreign language educator*
Walter, Hugo Günther *humanities educator*
Walter, John Frederick *historical researcher, genealogist*
Walther, Helmut G(erhard) *medieval history educator*
Walther, Manfred Odo *philosopher, educator*
Walton, (Delvy) Craig *philosopher, educator*
Wandschneider, Dieter Fritz Erich *philosopher, educator*
Wang, Xueming *English educator, translator*
Wang, Zhong-Han *history educator*
Ward, Brian Ernest *historian, educator, writer*
Ward, Douglas Andrew *Spanish and special education educator*
Ward, Harry Merrill *history educator*
Ward, William Reginald *modern history educator*
Ward Jouve, Nicole Anne *English educator*
Warner, Anthony Rowland *linguistics educator, researcher*
Warner, Martin Michael *philosophy educator*
Warnke, Martin *art history educator*
Warren, Joyce Williams *English language educator, writer*
W—sik, Zdzisław *linguistics educator*
Watanabe, Mamoru *music historian*
Watkins, Lois Irene *English educator*
Watson, John Richard *English educator*
Watson, Seosamh *linguist, educator*
Watts, Cedric Thomas *English literature educator, author*
Waxenberger, Gabriele Maria *historical linguist*
Weber, Horst Hans Edward *musicologist, educator*
Weber, Jean Jacques *English educator*
Weber, Nico *linguist, researcher, educator*
Weber, Ralph Edward *history educator*
Webster, Jill Rosemary *historian, educator*
Wegener, Heide *linguist, educator*
Wegner, Guenter Peter *prehistorian, history educator*
Weigley, Russell Frank *history educator*
Weimann, Robert Karl *cultural historian, critic, educator*
Weinberg, Félix *historian, educator*
Weis, Eberhard *modern history educator*
Weiss, Paul *philosopher, educator*
Weiss, Wolfgang *English language educator*
Weisser, Ursula Brigitte *medicine historian*
Welch, Charles Edgar, Jr. *retired English language educator, writer*
Welden, Alicia Galaz-Vivar *foreign language educator*
Weller, Rainer *language educator, writer*
Wells, David Arthur *German language educator*
Wells, Keiko *humanities educator, folksong researcher*
Wenskus, Otta Helene *philologist*
Wenzel, Peter *English literature educator*
Wessel, Ingrid *history educator*
West, Martin Litchfield *classical scholar, educator*
Westendorf, Wolfhart Heinrich *Egyptologist*
Whallon, William *literature educator*
Wheeler, Geraldine Hartshorn *historian*
Whelpton, John Francis *English language educator*
White, Lana Joyce *English language educator*
Wichmann, Søren *linguist*
Wieland, Wolfgang *philosophy educator, physician*
Wiggins, David *philosophy educator*
Wigglesworth, Gillian *linguist, educator*
Wilcox, Wilma Blanche *English language educator*
Wilenius, Reijo Valfrid *philosophy educator*
Wilhelm, Hans Rudolf *medical historian, researcher*
Wilke, Alfred Walter *language educator*
Willauer, George Jacob *English literature educator*
Willems, Klaas Björn *Belgian language researcher*
Willemse, Heinrich Stephen *humanities educator, journalist*
Williams, David *French language educator*
Williams, Glanmor *history educator, retired*
Williams, Mukesh Kumar *humanities educator, researcher*
Williams, William Anthony *language and classics educator*
Willies, Walter Harry *language educator, arts/medicine specialist*
Wilson, Trevor Gordon *historian, educator*
Wimmel, Walter Erwin *philologist*
Wimmer, Clemens Alexander *garden historian*
Winnington, G. Peter *English educator, editor*
Winter, Werner *linguistics educator*
Wisniewski, Bohdan *philologie educator, researcher*
Wlosok, Antonie Elisabeth *classics educator*
Wojtilla, Gyula *ancient history educator*
Wolf, Werner Winfried *English and general literature educator*
Wolff, Heinrich Ekkehard *linguist, educator*
Wolfová, Eva *humanities educator*
Wood, Charles Tuttle *history educator*
Wood, Thomas Wesley *humanities educator, editor*
Woodbridge, John Dunning *history and church history educator*
Woods, Gregory *liberal studies educator, literary critic, poet*
Wortham, Christopher John *literature educator*
Wright, Barbara *foreign language educator*
Wright, Beth Segal *art historian, educator*
Wright, Donald Ian *history educator*
Wrightson, Keith Edwin *historian*
Wu, Chu-hsia Patricia *foreign language educator, linguistics educator*
Wucherer-Huldenfeld, Augustinus Karl *philosopher*
Wulf, Herwig *language educator*
Wunderli, Peter Franz Albert *romance linguistics educator*
Wussing, Hans *historian of science*
Wuttke, Dieter *philology and art history educator*
Wylder, Delbert E(ugene) *English educator*
Wyrobisz, Andrzej *historian, educator*
Xholi, Zija *philosopher*
Yajima, Kyoshiro *social philosophy educator*
Yakut, Atilla *linguist*
Yamaguchi, Kazuyuki *history educator*
Yamakura, Akihiro *English educator*
Yamamoto, Eriko *historian, educator*
Yamanaka, Mitsuyoshi *literature educator*
Yamanaka, Nobuhiko *linguist*
Yamauchi, Edwin Masao *history educator*
Yang, Peiran *tribologist*
Yang, Yonglin *linguist, educator*
Yao, Huey-Fen Fay *English language educator*
Yapp, Malcolm Edward *historian*
Yasuda, Takako *literature educator*
Yates, Mildred Campbell *retired literature educator*
Yegorov, Valery Pavlovich *heraldic expert and artist*
Yen, Wen-Hsiung *language and music professional, educator*
Yngve, Victor H. *linguist, researcher*
Yoon, Nae-Hyun *historian, educator*
Yoshida, Keiko *linguist*
Yoshida, Takashi *history researcher*
You, Sung-Keun *philosophy educator, statesman*
Young, James Harvey *historian, educator*
Yousef, Fathi Salaama *communication studies educator, management consultant*
Yue, Daiyun *literature educator*
Zackey, Christopher Albert *mythologist, writer/poet, librarian*
Zadoff, Efraim *historian, researcher, publisher*
Zalabardo, Jose Luis *philosopher, educator*
Zamma, Hideki *linguist, educator*
Zatlin, Phyllis *Spanish language educator, translator*
Zauzich, Karl-Theodor *Egyptologist, educator*
Zayas-Bazan, Eduardo *foreign language educator*
Zdenek, Sean *English educator*
Zedelmaier, Helmut *historian, educator, editor*
Zhao, Ming *English studies educator*
Zhou, Wen Kai *philosophy educator, researcher*
Ziel, Wulfhild Elisabeth *Slavonicist, philosopher, researcher*
Ziemianski, Stanislaw *philosophy educator, priest, musician*
Ziffer, Giorgio *Slavic philologist*
Zima, Peter Václav *humanities educator*
Zink, David Daniel *retired English educator, writer*
Zinser, Hartmut *philosophy educator*
Zobel, Guenter *German language and literature educator, comparative and Japanese theatre researcher*
Zöldhelyi-Deák, Zsuzsanna Mária *historian of literature*
Zott, Regine Johanna *historian*
Zotz, Volker Helmut Manfred *philosophy historian*
Zou, Zhen *English and Chinese educator, translator and critic, computer technologist*
Zuckerman, Matthew Ian Stanley *writer, editor, educator*
Zuidervaart, Lambert Paul *philosophy educator*
Zunder, William Limbery *English educator*
Zuroff, Efraim Yaakov *war crimes researcher, historian*

HUMANITIES: LIBRARIES

Abulkairova, Evgenia Dzhumadilovna *library director*
Adkins, Thomas Samuel *library director*
Adrianopoli, Barbara Catherine *librarian*
Afonin, Eduard Andriyovych *librarian, sociologist*
Alberani, Vilma *library and editorial service director*
Albright, Kendra Suzanne *research professional*
Al-Dobaian, Saad Abdullah *library science educator, researcher*
Ali, Mahjabeen *librarian*
Allen, Norma Ann *librarian*
Allmand, Linda F(aith) *retired library director*
Alpay, Meral *library science educator, library director*
Alperin, Goldie Green *consulting librarian, lawyer*
Ammar, Magda *librarian*
Andrews, Charles Rolland *library administrator*
Andrews, Michael William *librarian, information specialist*
Ariens, Karla Rae *library director*
Auh, Yang John *librarian, educational administrator*
Ball, David John *librarian*
Bassnett, Peter James *retired librarian*
Bautier, Robert-Henri *archivist, curator*
Bazin, Patrick *library director*
Beck, Helmut *retired librarian*
Becker, Nancy Jane *information science educator*
Belliveau, Gerard Joseph, Jr. *librarian*
Benvenuti, Alberto Guglielmo *library director, archaeologist*
Berning, Robert William *librarian*
Bestehorn, Ute Wiltrud *retired librarian*
Bethel, Marilyn Joyce *librarian*
Billings, Harold Wayne *librarian, editor*
Bimková, Anna *librarian*
Bishop, Rosalinda Matubis *information manager, choreographer*
Bloch, Thomas Anthony *librarian*
Bogza, Nadezhda Fedorovna *librarian, bibliographer*
Bolos, Adoracion Mendoza *librarian*
Bonnelly, Claude *library director*
Borei, Karin Elisabet *librarian*
Bostic, Mary Jones *librarian*
Botello Corte, Ricardo *information specialist, administrator*
Bourneuf, Henri Joseph, Jr. *librarian*
Brady, Donald Marian *librarian*
Brandis, Tilo *librarian, retired researcher in German studies*
Brechtel, Unda Jurka *library director*
Bredikhina, Nelina Alexandrovna *bibliographer, library director*
Brian, Robert Francis *parliamentary librarian*
Brower, Janice Kathleen *library technician*
Brown, Elizabeth Eleanor *retired librarian*
Browne, Joseph Peter *retired librarian*
Brudvig, Glenn Lowell *retired library director*
Bryant, Josephine Harriet *library executive*
Buholte, Agnese *library director*
Bulavas, Vladas *library director*
Burnett, Alfred David *librarian*
Burton, Barry Lawson *librarian, educator*
Bury, Stephen John *librarian, lecturer*
Busch, Sally J. *librarian, accounting clerk*
Butkevičienė, Birute *librarian*
Butorac, Frank George *librarian, educator*
Caccamise, Genevra Louise Ball (Mrs. Alfred E. Caccamise) *retired librarian*
Caldwell, Rossie Juanita Brower *retired library service educator*
Casey, Carol Ann *librarian*
Castillo López, Victor *librarian, educator*
Cavaleri, Piero *librarian*
Cernajsek, Tillfried *librarian, geologist*
Chang, Shirley Lin (Hsiu-Chu Chang) *librarian*
Chaudhry, Riaz Ahmad *librarian*
Chepesiuk, Ron Joseph *librarian, educator*
Chevrillon, Olivier *research company executive*
Chowdhury, Gobinda Gopal *library and information science educator*
Christensen, Karin *librarian*
Christopher, Irene *librarian, consultant*
Clayton, Peter Robert *library educator*
Clement, Richard Wolcott *librarian, educator*
Cline, Fred Albert, Jr. *retired librarian, conservationist*

Cloulas, Ivan archivist
Cohen, Selma reference librarian, researcher
Conover, Robert Warren retired librarian
Covington, Veronica Pro librarian, educator
Craig, David Victor archivist
Cress, Cecile Colleen retired librarian
Crisman, Mary Frances Borden librarian
Cylke, Frank Kurt librarian
D'Andrea, Astrid archivist
Daňkova, Helena chief librarian
Darden, Barbara L. library director
Day, Susan librarian, art historian
Deakyne, William John library director, musician
Deering, Ronald Franklin librarian, minister
De Gennaro, Richard retired library director, library advisor
de Joux, Christopher Joseph Brian consultant foreign affairs, library administrator
Demmitt, Joyce Miller library administrator
De Petro, Thomas Gerard librarian, educator
De Swart, Johannes Hermanus library director
Devarajan, G. library and information science educator
DeWeese, Eldonna Rose librarian, editor
Domzella, Janet retired library director
Donaldson, Penny LeeAnne library director
Donovan, William Alan retired librarian
Drescher, Judith Altman library director
Durbin, Margot Jane librarian
Durey, Peter Burrell retired librarian
Eaton, Nancy Ruth Linton librarian, university dean
Edwards, Ralph M. librarian
Eeber, Ludmilla acquisition librarian
Elder, Mary Louise librarian
Ernesta, L. library director
Evans, Brian David librarian
Falk, Diane M. research director, librarian, editor, writer
Fanus, Pauline Rife librarian
Fedorov, Victor Vasilievich library director
Ferriby, Peter Gavin librarian
Fishbein, Meyer Harry archivist
Fisher, Nancy DeButts library director
Fletcher, Homer Lee librarian
Fligge, Jörg librarian, library director
Fogerty, James Edward archivist, state official
Fountain, Joanna F. library consultant, business owner
Fox, Peter Kendrew librarian
Frank, Lawrence J. library director
Freeland, Robert Frederick retired librarian
Freeman, Patricia Elizabeth library and education specialist
Frühauf, Wolfgang librarian
Fry, James Wilson retired state librarian
Fry, Roy H(enry) librarian, educator
Füredi, Mihály librarian, researcher
Garcia, Jovencia Taroja librarian
Gardner, Frederick Boyce library director
Gardner, Roberta Joan retired library director
Gartner, Ian Richard librarian
Geh, Hans-Peter retired library director, consultant
Gerdes, Neil Wayne library director
Gibson, Charles Anthony archivist
Giebel, Miriam Catherine librarian, genealogist
Gill, Gerald Lawson librarian
Gilliland-Swetland, Anne Jervois archivist, educator
Goggin, Margaret Enid (Knox) librarian, educator
Gossage, Wayne library director, management consultant, entrepreneur, executive recruiter
Gough, Carolyn Harley library director
Green, Joal Fekete Stafford library media specialist
Greenberg, Hinda Feige library director
Gregor, Dorothy Deborah librarian
Griffin, Robin Henry archivist
Grimes, Joyce Metts librarian
Gruhl, Andrea Morris librarian
Gudmundsson, Finnbogi library administrator
Habeeb, Habeeba Hussain library director
Haeuser, Michael John library administrator
Hall, Alan Craig library director
Hanley, Fred William librarian, educator
Hanrahan, Fionnuala M. librarian
Hansson, Ulrika Tressa librarian
Harkness, Mabel Gleason retired librarian
Harwood, Eleanor Cash librarian
Haselden, Clyde LeRoy librarian
Haverly, Douglas Lindsay librarian, historian
Hayton, Bernard Quentin, Jr. library media specialist
Heanue, Anne Allen retired librarian
Helsley, Alexia Jones archivist
Henington, David Mead library director
Herold, Jeffrey Roy Martin retired library director
Hershenson, Miriam Hannah Ratner librarian
Heystek, Kristen Margaret librarian
Hill, Carol Koelling library director
Hill, Leda Katherine librarian
Hill, Michael William library director
Hill, Norma Louise librarian
Hoch, Ivo library director
Hoffmann, Frank William library science educator, writer
Hogensen, Margaret Hiner librarian, consultant
Holmes, Sue Ellen library director
Honsa, Vlasta retired librarian
Hopkinson, Shirley Lois library and information science educator
Howard, Joseph Harvey retired librarian
Hubbard, William James library director
Huthloff, Christa Rose library and information science educator
Hymas, June Hopper librarian
Idahosa, Patricia Okiemute librarian
Irgens, Kaya Mowinckel retired library director
Ishikawa, Tetsuya information science educator
Jackson, Andrew Preston library director
Jacquesson, Alain L. librarian
Jaffe, Katharine Weisman retired librarian
James, Stuart librarian
Jauslin, Jean-Frédéric library director
Johannsen, Carl Gustav library information scientist, educator
John, Nancy R. librarian, writer
Johnson, Ian Martin information and library science educator,
Johnson, Letha E.(velyn) archivist
Jordan, Pamela Carole librarian
Kabdebo, Thomas George library director
Kaliher, Michael Dennis librarian, historian
Kan, Lai-Bing librarian
Kapoor, Malti librarian
Kappenberg, Marilyn Kascius library director
Karetzky, Joanne Louise librarian
Karetzky, Stephen library director, educator, researcher
Karpinski, Huberta Elaine library trustee
Kaufman, Paula T. librarian
Kendall, Susan Haines library director
Kent, Susan library director, consultant
Kesseler, Matthew John librarian
Ketelaar, Frederick Cornelis Johannes archivist, educator
Kilpatrick, Clifton Wayne book dealer
Kimlička, Štefan information scientist, educator
King, Richard Joslin librarian
Kiser, Joy Marian librarian, writer, historian
Kiser, Nagiko Sato retired librarian
Kiyanitza, Lubov Denisovna library director
Klauber, Julie B. library director
Knöppel, Hans-Armin librarian
Kolczynski, Charlotte Ann music librarian
Köstler, Hermann librarian
Kratzsch, Konrad Adolf Richard librarian
Krishan, Kumar retired information scientist
Kristiansen, Kari Helene librarian
Krull, Jeffrey Robert library director
Krysiak, Ewa Janina librarian
Kuznetsova, Klaudia Prokofjevna librarian, library director
Laabs, Rainer archivist, art historian
Lambert, Deborah Nolan library administrator
Larsen, René conservator, educator
Larson, Larry librarian
LeClerc, Paul library director
Lee, Harrison Hon naval architecture librarian, consultant
Legler, April Arington librarian, educator
Lehmann, Klaus-Dieter library director
Lehner-Quam, Alison Lynn library administrator
Leo, Maggie Penina librarian
Lesaffre, Odile Ramette librarian
Leskien, Hermann Adalbert library director
Lewis, Robert John Cornelius Koons university library director, consultant
Lidman, Tomas Erik national librarian
Liu, Rhonda Louise librarian
Loh, Gerhard librarian
Loughridge, Frederick Brendan information science educator
Luft, Eric v.d. librarian, educator
MacDonald, Alan Hugh librarian, university administrator
Mack, Douglas Stuart librarian, educator
Magro, Emanuel Paul cataloger, priest
Malinkovskaja, Sofija Sergej library director
Maltby, Florence Helen library science educator
Manville, Stewart Roebling archivist
Marco, Guy Anthony librarian, educator, musicologist
Marquardt, Steve Robert library director
Martin, Susan Katherine librarian
Martindale, Carla Joy librarian
Marwinski, Konrad Ferdinand librarian, historian
Mason, Marilyn Gell library administrator, writer, consultant
Matheson, Ann librarian, writer
Maynard, Michael librarian
McCanless, Christel Ludewig library consultant
McGarry, Dorothy librarian
McGowan, Ian Duncan librarian
McLain, Thelma Louise retired college librarian, artist
Meder, Cornel national archives director
Mehta, Rajendraprasad Manilal librarian
Meng, Guang Jun librarian, educator
Meredith, Meri Hill reference librarian, educator
Mesa, Maria Elena librarian
Miller, Dwight Merrick archivist, historian
Miller, Robert Carl retired library director
Miller, Uri information specialist
Mintz, Kenneth Andrew librarian
Mobley, Emily Ruth library dean, educator
Moore, Carole Irene librarian
Moore, Everett LeRoy library administrator
Moore, Woodvall Ray librarian
Moran, Elizabeth Ames library director
Morehouse, Valerie Jeanne librarian
Morrison, Samuel F. library administrator, chief librarian
Mosley, Shelley Elizabeth library administrator
Mountz, Louise Carson Smith retired librarian
Muller, William Albert, III library director
Muñoz-Solá, Haydeé Socorro library administrator
Musiker, Reuben library director
Musmann, Klaus librarian
Musso, Louis Albert librarian, bibliographer
Mutschler, Herbert Frederick retired librarian
Nerkowa, Lyman Wilbur bookseller, consultant
Nielsen, Flemming archivist
Niggeman, Elisabeth library director
Nougaret, Roger archivist
Null, Elisabeth Higgins librarian
O'Brien, Elmer John librarian, educator
O'Brien, Marlys Carol Howe retired library director
Ochsenbein, Peter Engelbert library administrator, educator
Oddoye, David Emmanuel Michael library and archival studies educator
Oliver-Warren, Mary Elizabeth retired library science educator
Ospelt, Alois archivist, state librarian
Ostrow, Rona Lynn librarian
Otey, Rheba L. librarian
Owens, Marsha library director
Oyabu, Takashi information science educator
Palmer, Paul Richard librarian, archivist
Panneton, Jacques librarian
Park, Soyeon library science educator
Parry, Victor Thomas Henry retired librarian
Pepol, Anna Teresa librarian
Peters, Tim library administrator
Peterson, Fred McCrae retired librarian
Peterson, Trudy Huskamp archivist
Phillips, Dorothy Reid retired medical library technician
Pierik, Marilyn Anne retired librarian
Pillsbury, Penelope DeLaire library director
Pinder, Eric James archivist
Poad, Flora Virginia retired librarian and educator
Poprády, Géza librarian
Prchalová, Lea library director
Pritchatt, Diane Joy librarian
Quarg, Gunter librarian
Qureshy, Jamil Ahmad librarian
Raina, Roshan Lal educator
Rait, Satwant Kaur librarian
Ramos, Pedro de Paula Nogueira information science educator
Ramsden, Michael John library professional, consultant
Rasmussen, Anne-Mette Riis librarian, writer
Rasmussen, Jan William librarian
Razoharinoro archivist, historian, researcher
Ren, Jiyu library director
Retzer, Mary Elizabeth Helm retired librarian
Reveal, Arlene Hadfield retired librarian, consultant
Revuelta, Maria Dolores library director, methodology educator
Riggs, Donald Eugene librarian, university official
Roach-Reeves, Catharyn Petitt librarian, educator
Roberts, Nancy Mize retired librarian, composer, pianist
Rochman-Halperin, Arieh Pinhas archivist
Rodrigues, Manuel Augusto educator, archive administrator
Romi-Levin, Rivka information center head, librarian
Rosar, Virginia Wiley librarian
Roselle, William Charles librarian
Ross, Philip Rowland retired library director
Rothman, Moses library administrator
Runge, Kay Kretschmar library director
Runkle, Martin Davey library director
Russon, David library director
Sadykova, Vera Philippovna librarian, educator
Saiful-Islam, K.M. information scientist, edcuator
Santoro, Marco bibliography educator, researcher
Sareen, Tilak Raj historian, researcher
Sargsyan, David library director
Sarhan, Mansoor Mohamed library director
Sarkisian, David library director
Satija, Mohinder Partap library and information science educator, researcher, writer
Satterwhite, Robert Lee library director
Satzik, Julie Ann archivist
Saunders, Diane Gail archive director, author
Savolainen, Reijo Ilmari educator
Schaefer, Patricia librarian
Schon, Isabel library science specialist, educator
Sebastian, Njarakad Joseph librarian
Seela, Torsten library educator
Sessions, Judith Ann librarian, university library dean
Shabaka, Nabil El-Mongy Muhammad library director
Shank, Russell librarian, educator
Sharify, Nasser educator, author, librarian
Sharrow, Marilyn Jane library administrator
Shaw, Dennis Frederick retired library director, chartered physicist, consultant
Shaw, Joyce M. librarian
Sherman, Mary Angus public library administrator
Sigurdsson, Einar librarian
Sikora, Barbara Jean library director
Simpson, Jerome Dean librarian
Simpson, William George university librarian
Singh, Shashi Prabha library and informations science educator
Skalski, Detlef retired library and information science educator
Skinner, Robert Earle librarian, writer
Slawsky Leon, Donna Susan librarian, singer
Snapp, Elizabeth librarian, educator
Sordylowa, Barbara Lucja librarian
Soultoukis, Donna Zoccola library director
Spyers-Duran, Peter librarian, educator
Starovoytov, Alexander Fyodorovich library director
Stelzle, James Joseph library administrator
Stephens, Brenda Wilson librarian
Stevens, Norman Dennison retired library director
Stigall, Phyllis Graham retired librarian
Strait, Viola Edwina Washington librarian
Studer, William Joseph library educator
Stüssi-Lauterburg, Jürg Fred librarian, historian
Sumsion, John Walbridge information scientist
Sutton, Anne Frances archivist
Száva-Kováts, Endre library and information scientist, researcher
Tabler, Shirley May retired librarian, artist
Tabor, Curtis Harold, Jr. librarian, minister
Taddey, Gerhard archivist, historian
Tai, Elizabeth Shi-Jue Lee library director
Takacs, Miklos librarian
Thamm, Jochen Walter library director
Thomas, Jacquelyn May librarian
Thomas, Mary Augusta library administrator
Thompson, Sandra Lee library administrator
Tillie, Willy archivist, educator
Tomaiuolo, Nicholas Gregory librarian, educator
Traue, James Edward library science educator
Treyz, Joseph Henry librarian
Triipan, Maive library director
Tu, Susan retired librarian
Tull, Willis Clayton, Jr. librarian
Turetsky, Judith librarian, researcher
Turková, Helga library director
Turkulin, Branka librarian
Turock, Betty Jane library and information science educator
Utley, F. Knowlton library director, educator
Vaisey, David George librarian, archivist
Valmas, Anne library director
van der Wateren, Jan Floris librarian, psychotherapist, consultant
van Velzen, Johannes Henricus Matteus library director
Varma, Promod Kr information scientist
Vellucci, Sherry Lynn library and information science educator
Vernon, Lawrence Gordon librarian
Vibar, Belen Matias librarian
Vilchez, Ricardo S. library supervisor
Villanueva, Lucrezia Jacinta Garcia librarian
von Fettweis, Yvonne Caché archivist, historian
von Ungern-Sternberg, Sara Margareta information scientist
Vuksanović, Miro library director, writer
Wagner, Pater Benedikt Franz archivist, librarian
Wallot, Jean-Pierre archivist, historian
Walter, Kenneth Gaines library director
Wanderman, Miriam library studies educator
Wang, Sing-wu retired librarian
Warner, Julian Charles information science educator
Watson, Georgianna librarian
Wefers, Sabine Hildegard librarian, historian
Weiler, Dorothy Esser librarian
Werner, Gloria S. librarian
Wetherall, Robert Shaw librarian
Whalen, Mary Romance library director
White, Cecil Ray librarian, consultant
White, Joyce Louise librarian
Williams, John Troy librarian, educator
Williams, William Gwyn librarian
Willis, Paul Allen librarian
Willson, David Allen reference librarian, writer
Wilson, C. Daniel, Jr. library director
Winzenried, Arthur Paul library administrator, historian
Wyllie, Stanley Clarke retired librarian
Yants, Svetlana Vladimirovna librarian, lecturer
Yavarkovsky, Jerome Harold library director
Young, Julia Anne librarian, elementary education educator
Young, Susan Babson retired library director
Yu, May Huang librarian, educator
Yun, Michelle Wonhe librarian
Zemskov, Andrei Ilych library director
Zubair Mohamed, Mahamood information scientist, educator, computer consultant
Zyglowicz, Daniel T. librarian

HUMANITIES: MUSEUMS

Achkasova, Valentyna Nykyforivna curator
Adriansen, Inge O. museum curator, historian
Aizpuru, Juana de art gallery director
Albert, James Spurling curator, zoology educator
Anderson, Maxwell L. museum director
Anderson, Robert Geoffrey William museum director
Andersson, Göran Sven Arne museum director
Armstrong, Thomas Newton, III art and garden specialist
Arons, Karl Erik museum administrator
Backhouse, Sue art curator, writer, publisher
Bailey, Colin Barry curator
Barkley, William Donald museum administrator
Bartholomai, Alan retired museum director
Basquin, Mary Smyth (Kit Basquin) museum administrator
Battenberg, Friedrich archive director
Bayer, Fern Patricia curator, writer
Belsey, Hugh Graham museum curator
Berglund, Joel museum curator and director, researcher
Bibb, Daniel Roland antique painting restorer and conservator
Blackmore, Stephen garden director, botanist
Bogle, Michael MacLaine curator
Bolton, Bruce Douglas museum director
Borg, Alan Charles Nelson museum director
Bothmer, Dietrich Felix von museum curator, archaeologist
Brisebois, Marcel museum director
Brown, Godfrey Norman retired educator, small business owner
Brunhammer, Yvonne Suzanne curator
Burmeister, Helmut museum director, secondary education educator
Burnett, David Grant curator, writer
Buxton, Barry Miller museum director, historical author, educator
Buzinkay, Géza historian, curator
Carlén, Staffan Carl museum director
Casellas, Joachim art gallery executive
Castile, Rand (Jesse Randolph, III) retired museum director
Catano, Lucy Baca gallery manager
Chacon Arias, Virginia national archives director
Chilton, Meredith curator, museum administrator
Chruścicki, Tadeusz Jerzy museum director, museology researcher
Cohen, Mildred Thaler art gallery director
Conley, Susan art director, writer
Cossons, Sir Neil museum director
Crowston, Catherine Miya curator
Curtis, John Edward museum curator, archaeologist
Danilov, Victor Joseph museum management program director, consultant, writer, educator
Delluc, Brigitte museum curator
de Montebello, Philippe Lannes museum administrator
Doumenge, François André museum director
Elliott, Billie R. gallery owner, art educator
Escalet, Frank Diaz art gallery owner, artist, educator
Fisher, Wesley Andrew research administrator, Eurasian studies specialist
Forni, Gaetano museologist, historian
Forsberg Warringer, Gunnel retired museum director, writer
Frelinghuysen, Alice Cooney museum curator
Gabriel, Jeanette Hanisee curator, art historian
Gates, Laura Daignault museum executive
Gedai, István retired museum administrator, numismatist
Genden, Tserendulam museum director, physician
Gervereau, Laurent curator
Gilkey, Gordon Waverly curator, artist
Glynn, Kathleen Deary museum director
Gosselin, Claude A(lphonse) R(ené) curator
Granath, Olof Erik Tryggve museum administrator
Granlund, Lis curator
Guillaume, Philippe museum administrator
Hansley, Lee art gallery owner, curator
Haskell, Barbara curator
Holthuis, Lipke Bijdeley curator
Hough, Melissa Ellen curator, museum director
Indahl, Trond Marinus museum curator
Inman, Edward Oliver museum director
Janes, Robert Roy museum executive, archaeologist, museum consultant
Janousek, Ivo Petr museum director
Jervis, Simon Swynfen historic buildings director
Jones, Mark Ellis Powell museum director
Jones, Schuyler museum director, anthropologist
Josey, Donna Pearson art gallery director
Kahn, James Steven retired museum director
Kehoe, Thomas Francis curator
Kjaergaard, Thorkild museum director, historian, administrator
Koch, Rainer Philipp museum director
Kochta, Ruth Martha art gallery owner
Koepke, Wulf museum director
Kolltveit, Bård Johannes museum director
Köppen, Thomas Matthias museum adminstrator, researcher
Kornicker, Louis Sampson museum curator
Krogh, Thomas Edvard curator, geochronologist
Kuhler, Renaldo Gillet museum official, scientific illustrator
Kuhnen, Hans-Peter museum director, archaeologist
Kujawski, Elizabeth Szancer art curator, consultant
Lauer, Bernhard museum director
Lecher, Belvadine (Reeves) (Reeves Lecher) museum curator
Lemoine, Serge educator, museum director
Lin, Cheng-Shing entomology curator, researcher
Luria, Gloria art gallery executive, art consultant
Lytkin, Vladimir Vladimirovich space history museum administrator
Manndorff, Hans museum director, educator
Matthews, Eric Glasswell museum curator, researcher
Meadows, Patricia Blachly art curator, civic worker
Messer, Thomas Maria museum director
Mikkola, Kauri Eino Fredrik museum curator, entomologist
Morgan, Dahlia museum director

Naumann zu Königsbrück, Clas Michael *museum director, zoology educator*
Nikiforov, Victor Sergeevich *museum director*
O'Brien, Catherine Louise *museum administrator*
Oddy, William Andrew *museum official, author, editor*
Oldenburg, Richard Erik *auction house executive*
Pagel, Theo *curator*
Parrish, Maurice Drue *museum executive*
Persegati, Walter Angelo *museum director, educator*
Petersen, Henning *museum laboratory director, curator, researcher*
Piqué, Fernando Rafael *international art dealer*
Reimer, Charles Wilson *curator*
Reuterswärd, Patrik Anders Adolf *curator, educator*
Rexine, John Efstratios, Jr. *museum registrar, artist*
Rheinwald, Goetz *curator*
Rivin, Roberta *art gallery director*
Robson, Maureen Anne *museum conservation consultant*
Rosenberg, Pierre Max *museum director*
Rylands, Philip Brome *museum director, art historian*
Sato, Takeshi (Ken Sato) *retired planetarium director*
Saunders, Gillian Marguerite *museum curator*
Savours, Ann Margaret (Ann Shirley) *museum officer, historian, writer*
Sawhney, Shalini Harjit *art dealer, investment consultant*
Self, Dana R. *museum curator*
Serota, Nicholas Andrew *art gallery director*
Shestack, Alan *museum administrator*
Sidamon-Eristoff, Anne Phipps *museum official*
Silcox, Frances Eleanor *museum and exhibits planning consultant*
Simopoulos, Dionysios P. *planetarium director*
Simpson, William Kelly *curator, Egyptologist, educator*
Sjöström, Ingrid Cecilia *curator*
Skoler, Celia Rebecca *art gallery director*
Small, Lawrence M. *museum executive*
Smith, Lawrence Barrett, IV *art gallery director, curator*
Sooprayen, Paul Henry *archives director*
Soos, Sandor *museum director*
Souckova-Siegelova, Jana *museum director*
Spalding, Julian *museum director*
Sperber, Helmut *museum director*
Spur, Inga Birgitta *museum director, educator*
Steinhauser, Janice Maureen *arts administrator, educator, artist*
Stevens, Jane *curator*
Stevenson, Frances Kellogg *museum program director, inventor*
Stevenson, Nancy Nelson *museum executive*
Thorkildsen, Åsmund *art institution director*
Thorndahl, Jytte *curator, anthropologist*
Thue, Anniken *museum director, art historian*
Urban, Martin *retired museum director*
Urroz Arancibia, Carlos *gallery director, consultant*
Vadstrup, Wibeke *gallery owner*
Vail, Mary Barbara *publicist*
Van Noten, Francis *museum director*
Ward, William Edward *museum exhibition designer*
Wetenhall, John *museum director*
Williams, Robert Joseph *museum director, educator*
Wilson, Sir David Mackenzie *retired museum director*
Wilson, Marc Fraser *art museum director*
Wirgin, Jan Christer *educator, museum director emeritus*
Zečević, Miodrag Dj. *former archives director*

INDUSTRY: MANUFACTURING. *See also* FINANCE: FINANCIAL SERVICES.

Aadahl, Jorg *business executive*
Aall, Christian Bergengren *software company executive*
Aanenson, Eric Evan *food products executive*
Aban, Jeffrey Derick Christopher *executive*
Abbey, Karen Diane *clothing company executive*
Abeng, Tanri *diversified industry executive*
Abreu, Gregorio Benito *pharmaceutical executive*
Adam, Christopher *retired pharmaceuticals executive*
Adamo, Mario Antonio *beverage company executive, pharmacist*
Adamski, Peter J. *automotive executive*
Addy, Tralance Obuama *healthcare company executive*
Adelt, Bruno *automotive company executive*
Adrees, Muhammad *chemical industry executive*
Aeugle, Thomas *semiconductor development researcher*
Aga, René L. *retired petrochemical company executive*
Agnelli, Giovanni *industrial executive*
Agnelli, Umberto *industrialist*
Ahedo, Alejandro *electronics executive*
Ahmed, Syed Manzoor *chemicals company executive*
Aizenberg, Gustavo Elias *electronics research specialist*
Akeel, Hadi Abu *robotics executive*
Akiba, Ryojiro *aerospace institute administrator, engineering educator*
Al-Banawi, Mohammed Ismail *industry executive*
Albanese, Thomas *food industry executive, consultant*
Albani, Thomas J. *manufacturing company executive*
Aldag, Jorn P. *manufacturing executive*
Aldrees, Abdulmohsen Mohammed *manufacturing executive*
Alexakhin, Roudolf Mikhailovich *agricultural executive*
Al-Husseini, Ameen Abdullah *automobile trading company executive*
Ali, Mohammad Saber *fertilizer company executive*
Allaire, Paul Arthur *office equipment company executive*
Allars, Peter David *retired contractor*
Allawala, S.M. Idrees *cosmetics executive*
Allegretti, Edward Philip *electrical construction company executive*
Allen, Gerald (Gerry Allen) *spirits company executive*
Allen, Leon Robert *food products executive*
Alliance, David *apparel executive*
Allmer, Stephen Dale *agricultural products executive*
Almoayyed, Farouk Yousuf *conglomerate executive*
Al-Mubarak, Ahmed I. *chemical company executive*
Al Namlah, Abdulaziz Mohamed *construction executive*
Alonso, Ignacio Francisco *manufacturing executive*
Alperin, Irwin Ephraim *clothing company executive*
Al-Rasheed, Turki Faisal *agricultural products company executive*
Alshehabi, Ali Saleh *contractor*
Al-Tameemi, Amer Theyab *manufacturing executive*
Althaus, David Steven *chemical research company executive, controller*
Alván, Gunnar *medical products executive, researcher*
Alvine, Robert *industrialist, entrepreneur, international business leader*
Anbe, Yoshiharu *control system executive*
Ancheta, F. E. Caldito *fragrance company manager*
Anderson, Jack Roy *health care company executive*
Anderson, Jerry William, Jr. *technical and business consulting executive, educator*
Anderson, Michael Stuart *rubber company executive*
Anderson, Paul Milton *steel company executive*
Anderson, Raymond Quintus *diversified company executive*
Andreas, Dwayne Orville *business executive*
Andreasen, Charles Peter *retired electronics executive*
Angus, Sir Michael Richardson *chemical company executive*
Anscher, Bernard *manufacturing executive, investor, management consultant*
Anton, Bruce Norman *textile company executive*
Anton, Harvey *textile company executive*
Antonelli, Pierluigi *pharmaceutical executive*
Anwar, Chaudhry Muhammad *fertilizer plant administrator*
Apestegui, Alfredo *fresh fruit company executive*
Apostolakis, Constantine Nicolas *paint company executive*
Armstrong, Billie Bert *retired highway contractor*
Arnold, Leonard Joseph *construction executive*
Arnold, Patrick Jules Antoine *bridge company executive*
Arpi, Magnus Harald *greeting card company executive*
Arts, Theo Albert *chemicals production manager*
Arunanondchai, Surat *construction and trading company executive*
Asano, Hiroyuki *cosmetic company researcher*
Ascher, James John *pharmaceutical executive*
Aseer, Ghulam Nabi *business executive*
Ashek, Ullah Mohammed *apparel executive*
Ashkar, Abraham Charbel Seraphim *medical products executive*
Ashton, Simon Mark *food products executive*
Asmussen, Nils Wirenfeldt *pharmaceutical executive*
Atchison, Joseph Edward *pulp and paper industry consultant*
Athanasopoulos, Panagiotis Evangelos *food science educator*
Atkin, Louis Phillip *business executive, screenwriter, media producer*
Attebury, William Hugh *construction company executive*
Aussel, Jean-Paul *aluminum company official*
Awua, Paul Kwame *food products executive, biochemist*
Azar, Raza *chemicals executive*
Azzato, Louis Enrico *manufacturing company executive*
Baba, Isamu *construction company executive*
Backer, William Earnest *food products executive*
Baer, William Harold *business executive*
Baey, Lian Peck *manufacturing executive*
Bagley, William Evan *application technology specialist*
Bain, Lowell Sherman *automotive company executive*
Bain, Neville Clifford *company executive, consultant*
Bainton, Donald J. *diversified manufacturing company executive*
Baird, Malcolm David *company executive*
Bais, Ashok Singh *shoe company executive*
Baker, Charles DeWitt *research and development company executive*
Baldwin, Ralph Belknap *retired manufacturing company executive, astronomer*
Ballester Olmos, Vicente-Juan *automobile manufacturing company executive*
Banerjee, Jyoti Prasad *electronics educator*
Banka, Baldeo Prasad *steel producing company executive*
Banno, Hisao *ceramist*
Bantzis, Constantine *pharmaceutical company executive*
Baraket, Edmund S., Jr. *general contractor, contracting consultant*
Barber, Edward Bruce *medical products executive*
Barber, Salvador *food company executive*
Barbey, Georges Simon *chemical company executive*
Barca, George Gino *winery executive, financial investor*
Barchard, John Harley *timber importing company executive*
Barkes, Geoffrey Rogerson *electrical distributor*
Barlow, F(rank) John *mechanical contracting company executive*
Barnard, Timothy Charles *managing director*
Barnevik, Percy Nils *electrical company executive*
Barr, Mark David *food products executive*
Barrios, Marcelo Bernardo *health and medical products executive*
Bartlett, Michael John *swimming pool company executive*
Bartolic, Juraj *microwave electronics educator*
Baslé, Jean-Luc Louis *apparel manufacturing executive*
Basson, Henry Hawksworth *chemical company executive*
Batcho, Ronald Frank *automotive company executive*
Bauknight, Clarence Brock *consultant*
Bauman, Robert Patten *diversified company executive*
Baxter, Janet Schwartz *motivational company executive, cinematographer*
Beall, Donald Ray *multi-industry high-technology company executive*
Beare, Gene Kerwin *electric company executive*
Beaujean, Jacques Eugene *aviation products company executive*
Beaumarie, Carlos Fabian *food products executive*
Becherer, Hans Walter *retired agricultural equipment executive*
Beckett, William Alan *plastics company executive, air safety campaigner*
Beckman, Bjorn Ingemar *food products executive*
Belcher, Samuel L. *plastics engineer, manufacturing executive*
Beldotti, Dennis Jason *retired company executive*
Bell, Robert Matthew *pharmaceutical company consultant*
Bellinzoni, Rodolfo Cesar *medical manufacturing company executive*
Beltrao, Alexandre Fontana *coffee organization executive*
Benatar, Leo *packaging company executive*
Benchoff, James Martin *manufacturing company executive*
Bender, Harold *beverage company consultant*
Benetton, Gilberto *clothing manufacturing company executive*
Benetton, Luciano *clothing manufacturing company executive*
Benito, Roberto Patricio *pulp and paper company executive*
Bensaou, Mustapha Ben *management science educator, researcher*
Berger, Charles Martin *lawn and garden company executive*
Berger, Daniel Philippe *defense company executive*
Berggren, Bo Erik Gunnar *paper company executive*
Berghmans, Jean-Pierre *lime and dolomite company executive*
Bergstrom, Rolf Olof Bernhard *manufacturing company executive*
Berthon, Rene Max *corporate executive*
Berti, Giovanni *diagnostics company executive*
Bestwick, Warren William *retired construction company executive*
Bethmont, Michel *manufacturing executive, materials engineer, consultant*
Bettencourt, Liliane *cosmetics company executive*
Beutler, Arthur Julius *manufacturing company executive*
Bezares, Eduardo *brewery company executive, educator*
Bezuidenhout, Pieter Jacobus *construction company executive*
Bhatnagar, Surendra Prasad *company executive*
Bhattad, Sitaram Manikalal *food industry technical executive*
Bhogal, Charanjiv Singh *automotive company executive*
Bhosle, Ushadevi Narendra *math educator, researcher*
Bible, Geoffrey Cyril *tobacco company executive*
Bingham, J. Peter *electronics research executive*
Biren, Isik *project development and construction executive*
Bishop, Kim Irene *pharmaceutical executive, psychopharmacologist*
Bito, Janos Ferenc *corporate executive, educator*
Bivas, Robert *chemical company executive*
Biyari, Khaled Husain *electronics company executive*
Bjercke, Alf Richard *business executive, publisher*
Blakeway, John Murray *cosmetic company executive*
Blanckaert, Johnny François *manufacturing executive*
Blinken, Robert James *manufacturing and communications company executive*
Blutel, Xavier Hervé *cement group executive*
Boeck, Harald Christian Anando von Hamm *cement company executive, consultant*
Bogsch, Erik *pharmaceutical company executive*
Boguslavskii, Ilya Zelikovich *machine manufacturing executive*
Bollen, L(ambertus) J(acobus) *semiconductor laser industry executive*
Bombet, Jean-Pierre *executive*
Bompart, Francois Rene *pharmaceutical company executive*
Bonatti, Carlo Alberto *air conditioning company manager*
Bonsignore, Michael Robert *electronics and computer company executive*
Boonstra, Cornelius *electronics company executive*
Borletti, Maurizio *metals company executive*
Bosler, Lawrence M., III *retired manufacturing engineer*
Bost, John Rowan *retired manufacturing executive, engineer*
Boudville, Rodney John *manufacturing administrator, general manager*
Bougie, Jacques *aluminum company executive*
Boysanoglu, Erhan *construction executive*
Brabeck-Letmathe, Peter *food products company executive*
Bradshaw, Haydon Leigh *food products executive, consultant*
Brady, Sheila Ann *manufacturing company executive*
Brake, Cecil Clifford *retired diversified manufacturing executive*
Bratton, William Edward *electronics executive, management consultant*
Brauer, Stephen Franklin *manufacturing company executive*
Bray, William Otis, IV *diversified electronics company executive*
Brennan, Walter Matthew, Jr. *construction sales consultant*
Brettenthaler, Martin Stefan *wood and forestry products industry executive*
Brézillon, Olivier *license company executive*
Bridgwater, Roden John *chemical company executive*
Brinken, Frank *manufacturing executive*
Brinkerhoff, Peter John *manufacturing company executive*
Britt, Ronald Leroy *manufacturing company executive*
Broadhurst, Norman Neil *foods company executive*
Brody, Aaron Leo *food and packaging consultant*
Bronfman, Edgar Miles *beverage company executive*
Brown, Janet Lee *defense electronics company executive*
Brown, John Fred *steel company executive*
Browning, Peter Crane *packaging company executive*
Brullo, Robert Angelo *chemical company executive*
Brust, Edwin H. *automotive executive*
Bruzzone, Raul Alberto *engineer, manufacturing executive*
Bryan, John Henry *food and consumer products company executive*
Bryden, William Donald, Jr. *manufacturing executive, retired military officer*
Bucy, J. Fred, Jr. *retired electronics company executive*
Bullock, Francis Jeremiah *pharmaceutical research executive*
Burini, Sonia Montes de Oca *apparel manufacturing and public relations executive*
Burnham, Daniel Patrick *manufacturing company executive*
Burnouf, Thierry Pierre *pharmaceutical executive*
Burns, Dan W. *manufacturing company executive*
Busch, August Adolphus, III *brewery executive*
Bushue, Sherlyn Jean *wallpapering group executive, writer*
Bustani, Myrna *business executive*
Butcher, Jack Robert (Jack Risin) *manufacturing executive*
Byström, Bengt-Olov *wood processing equipment company executive*
Cabot, Lewis Pickering *manufacturing company executive, art consultant*
Cadbury, Sir Dominic *food products executive*
Caldwell, William Mackay, III *business executive*
Calvo De Dios, Juan Jose *pulp and paper manufacturing executive*
Cameron, Nicholas Allen *diversified corporation executive*
Camfield, Ronald Frederick *manufacturing and engineering company executive*
Campbell, Robert David *minerals and metals executive*
Campos, Fábio *electronics company executive*
Candiani, Carlos Luis *electronics executive*
Candido, A. Michael *contracting company executive, real estate manager*
Cantarella, Paolo *automotive executive*
Capdevila, Mariano Lazo *electro-mechanical company executive, industrial engineer*
Capomasi, Luis Antonio *plastic industry executive*
Cardó, Andrés Soria *publishing company executive*
Carey, Dean Lavere *fruit canning company executive*
Carmosino, Giancarlo *pharmaceuticals company executive*
Carnegie, Roderick H. *technological company executive, mining executive*
Cartella, Paolo *electronics company executive*
Carter, James Thomas *contractor, pilot*
Carter, Jane Foster *agriculture industry executive*
Carvalhaes, Affonso Luiz De Barros *steel products company executive*
Cassidy, James Mark *construction company executive*
Castel, Philippe *executive*
Catabelle, Jean-Marie Henri *industrial company executive*
Catling, Douglas George *product development company executive*
Cawthon, Frank H. *retired construction company executive*
Cazalet, Peter Grenville *business executive*
Cazes, Jean-Michel *food products executive*
Cedervall, Goesta Hugo *metallurgical company executive, management consultant*
Cerovsky, Nevenka *pharmaceuticals company executive*
Cevetillo, Gerri Marie *manufacturing company executive*
Chabra, Om Parkash *heavy electrical equipment company executive*
Chain, Bobby Lee *electrical contractor, former mayor*
Chakraborty, Asit Kumar *biotechnology products executive, scientist*
Cham, Jesus C. *food distribution company executive*
Chami, Roger Louis *heavy construction company executive*
Chan, Dwight Kung-Sang *automobile accessories company executive, musician*
Chan, Xianglin *automotive executive*
Chandra, Sheel *textiles executive*
Chang, Joseph Sylvester *electronics executive, engineering educator*
Chang, Kuang-Yeh *microelectronics technologist*
Chastain, James William *construction professional*
Chaudhari, Ghanashyam Narayan *pharmaceutical professional*
Chaudoir, Jacques *company executive*
Chaykin, Robert Leroy *manufacturing and marketing executive*
Chernin, Ralph *construction executive*
Chéron, Bruno Jean Michel *manufacturing executive*
Chiapparelli, Marco *pharmaceutical company executive*
Ch'ien, Raymond Kuo-fung *industrialist*
Chihorek, John Paul *electronics company executive*
Ch'in, Michael Kuo-hsing *international conference and travel management executive*
Chiu, Stephen Ka Wai *chemicals company executive*
Cho, Fujio *automobile company executive*
Choay, Patrick Henri *pharmaceutical executive*
Choi, Chong Whan *construction company executive*
Choquette, William H. *construction company executive*
Chowdhury, Humayun Quader *executive scientific instrument company*
Chung, Hui-Suk *company executive, educator*
Cicolani, Angelo George *research company executive, operating engineer*
Ciesielski, Jacek *toy manufacturing company executive*
Cieszewski, Sandra Josephine *manufacturing company manager*
Citrin, Yale *light industry executive*
Cizik, Robert *manufacturing company executive*
Clark, Robert Henry, Jr. *holding company executive*
Clayton, Marvin Courtland *engineering, manufacturing sourcing and health wellness consultant*
Clemens, T. Pat *manufacturing company executive*
Clewlow, Warren A. M. *manufacturing company executive, sugar cane farmer*
Closset, Gerard Paul *forest products company executive*
Clowes, Garth Anthony *electronics executive, consultant*
Coburn, Richard Joseph *company executive, electrical engineer*
Cochran, Earl Vernon *retired manufacturing company executive*
Cocolis, Peter Konstantine *business development executive*
Cohen, Gordon S. *health products executive*
Cohen, Mark N. *business executive*
Cohen, Robert *medical device manufacturing and marketing executive*
Coisne, Henri Paul *electrical wholesaling executive*
Colaiannia, Louis Mario *construction executive, dentist, composer, pianist*
Colburn, Richard Dunton *business executive*
Coleman, Deborah Ann *electronics company executive*
Collier, Duaine Alden *manufacturing and distribution company executive*
Collins, Christopher Carl *manufacturing executive*
Collins, Francis Winfield *chemical company executive*
Colpaert, Roger Achille Jacques *steel wire/steel cord company executive*
Constain, Alberto *food products executive*
Cooper, Norton J. (Sky Cooper) *liquor, wine and food company executive*
Coopersmith, Jeffrey Alan *distribution corporation executive*
Corbin, Krestine Margaret *manufacturing company executive, fashion designer, columnist*

Coren, Lance Scott consulting firm executive
Corio, Mark Andrew electronics executive
Cormier, Jacques manufacturing executive
Corna, Mark Steven construction company executive
Corness, Sir Colin (Ross) business executive
Correll, Alston Dayton, Jr. forest products company executive
Corson, Thomas Harold manufacturing company executive
Cortez, Alfredo Durval Villela food products executive
Corun, Ronald Lewis asphalt refining executive
Corwin, Joyce Elizabeth Stedman construction company executive
Cottingham, Richard Sumner paper company executive
Covino, Charles Peter chemicals executive
Cresson, Pierre-Arnaud F. J. manufacturing executive
Crompton, Kenneth Charles lawyer
Crooke, Stanley Thomas pharmaceutical company executive
Crowe-Hagans, Natonia manufacturing executive, engineer
Crundwell, Duncan James electronics executive
Cryer, Dennis Robert pharmaceutical company executive, researcher
Culp, Joe C(arl) electronics executive
Cuneo, Dennis Clifford automotive company executive
Curry, Thomas James manufacturers representative
Curtin, John Dorian, Jr. chemical company executive
Dacoutros, John George food and drink technologist, business executive
Dahle, Egil Oddvar brewmaster
Dahlmann, Niels Friedrich business executive, honorary consul
Dakas, Christos John pharmaceutical company executive
Dalboge, Henrik company executive
Dalby, Alan James pharmaceutical company executive
Dalmia, Jai Hari cement company executive
Dalton, Robert Issac, Jr. textile executive, consultant, researcher
Dalwadi, Thakor Shankerbhai company executive
Daniel, Kenneth Rule former iron and steel manufacturing company executive
Danjczek, David William manufacturing company executive
Danziger, Glenn Norman chemical sales company executive
Da Rocha Neto, Miguel Mauricio construction executive, consultant
Darrow, William Richard pharmaceutical company executive, consultant
Darwish, El Sayed Younis chemical company administrator, consultant
D'Ascanio, Vincenzo Maria chemical company executive
Daudet, Jean-Louis pharmaceutical executive
Daughenbaugh, Terry Lee steel industry executive
Davalos-Guevara, C. Mauricio agroindustrial company executive
Davey, Alan Edwin advanced composites and armour executive
David, F. Jorge food association executive
David, George Alfred Lawrence industrial company executive
Davies, Gareth retired steels and engineering company executive
Davis, Christopher Kevin equipment company executive
Davis, Darrell L. automotive executive
Davis, True corporate executive
Dawson, Edward Joseph merger and acquisition executive
Debbané, Andrea beverage company executive
De Boer, Uilke F. contracting company executive
de Bouchard d'Aubeterre, Count Hubert Guy former company executive, sculptor
de Clerck, Hervé Charles food products executive
DeCrosta, Edward Francis, Jr. former paper products company executive, consultant
Deeg, Emil Wolfgang manufacturing company executive, physicist
Degoix, Christophe Nicolas manufacturing executive
De Laat, Gilbert automotive executive
de La Motte Bouloumi, Guy Noël beverage company executive, mayor
Delano, Jimmy Gboyega business executive, accountant
Delest, Philippe Francis retired food company executive, consultant
Dell, Michael S. computer company executive
Del Vecchio, Leonardo manufacturing executive
Demetriou, Basil Philip food products executive, consultant
Demicoli, Charles company director
Demuth, Pavel pharmaceutical company executive, consultant
De Muynck, Johan Julien Lodewyck construction company executive
Dennehy, Leisa Jeanotta pharmaceutical executive
Dennison, Stanley Scott retired lumber company executive, consultant
Deoul, Neal electronics company executive
Depeyrot, Michel Yves-Louis engineering company executive
De Poorter, Pierre-Emmanuel technology executive
Derrick, William Dennis retired physical plant administrator, consultant
Dervieux, Frederic food products executive
Desimone, Livio Diego diversified manufacturing company executive
Dettman, Ian Christopher pharmaceutical manufacturing director
Devereux, Alan Robert industrialist
Devol, George Charles, Jr. manufacturing executive
De Wree, Eugene Ernest manufacturing company executive
Dewulf, Lode W.A. healthcare industry executive
Dial, N(athaniel) Victor industrialist
Diamond, Harvey Jerome machinery manufacturing company executive
Dickstein, Harvey Leonard pharmaceutical company executive
Diemer, Jean Claude textile company executive
Dikken, Jacob Jan manufacturing company executive
Di Sambuy, Vittorio Balbo Bertone retired electronics company executive
Disberger, Dennis Jay manufacturing executive
DiSerio, Frank Joseph pharmaceutical company executive, consultant
D'Lower, Del manufacturing executive
Dobbs, Herbert Hotaling automotive executive, consultant, engineer, scientist, retired army officer
Dobrzański, Lech Jan electronics executive
Dodds, Dale Irvin chemicals executive
Dodge, Arthur Byron, Jr. business executive, marketing professional
Dogramatzis, Dimitris pharmaceutical company executive
Dolan, Dermot Vincent pharmaceutical company executive
Dooley, Michael Leigh medical equipment company executive
Doppelfeld, Volker automotive company executive
Dor, Christian automotive company executive
Dormann, Jurgen chemical company executive
Doron, Tamar pharmaceutical company executive
Dorris, Joe Miller electronics company executive
Dorsey, Jeremiah Edmund pharmaceutical company executive
Doshi, Viul Praful pharmaceutical executive
Dos Santos N., Miguel Valle chemical company executive, consultant
Douglas, Kenneth Jay food products executive
Drexler, Heinrich Jurgen food product executive
Dugar, Chand Ratan textiles executive
Duncan, George chemicals executive, accountant
Dunn, Robert Riddell air conditioning company executive
Dupps, John Avery, Jr. machinery company executive
Duquesne, Stephan P. textiles executive, consultant
Durand, Lourens Gerhardus manufacturing executive
Dye, Robert Harris retired manufacturing company executive
Dykstra, William Dwight business executive, consultant
Eberbach, Steven John retired electronics company executive
Eccles, John Dawson textiles executive
Eckersten, Christer Curt automotive company manager
Ecklin, Robert Luther materials company executive
Eckman, Charles Clarke food company executive
Egner, Berthold Karl business executive
Ehlinger, Thierry pharmaceutical company executive
Einarsson, Gudfinnur seafood products company executive
Eitan, Raphael chemical company executive
Elabd, Mohamed Yehia metal products executive
El Gabaly, Sherif-Mostafa chemical company executive
Elliott, Gary Wayne forest products company executive
Elliott, John Dorman business executive
El-Turk, Said Nejam contracting and trading company executive
Endriz, John Guiry electronics executive, consultant
Engelke, Joanna Dember health products executive
Engelking, Ellen Melinda pattern company executive, real estate broker, manufacturing company
Engler, Eva Kay dental and veterinary products company executive
Enomoto, Makoto biotechnology company executive
Enrico, Roger A. soft drink company executive
Erasmus, Desmond manufacturing executive
Errickson, Barbara Bauer component based software company executive
Esmael, Haresad manufacturing executive
Evers, Robert James real estate sales and development executive
Fachnie, H(ugh) Douglas film manufacturing company official
Fagerström, Björn Robert company executive
Fajardo, Herminia Rosales company executive
Falk, Heinz Fred company executive, physicist
Falus, Ferenc health care company executive, consultant
Farabet, Tristan beverage company executive
Farooqui, Ishtiaq Uddin company executive
Farre Gomis, Antonio J. pharmaceutical company executive
Farrell, George Kevin manufacturing executive
Farrell, John Lindsay construction executive
Farrell, John Stanislaus manufacturing company executive
Faurre, Pierre Lucien business executive
Favreau, Donald Francis corporate executive
Featherman, Bernard steel company executive
Feinberg, Robert S. plastics manufacturing company executive, marketing consultant
Felcht, Utz-Hellmuth pharmaceutical executive, chemist
Fell, Samuel Kennedy (Ken Fell) infosystems executive
Ferraro, John Francis business executive, financier
Ferreira Fernandes, Elis Simone agricultural products executive
Fiechter, Georges Andre multinational company executive
Finder, Robert Andrew pharmaceutical company executive
Finger, David manufacturing executive, marketing professional
Fink, Aaron Herman box manufacturing executive
Finney, John Edgar, III food products executive
Fisher, Paul Cary writing supplies company executive
Fites, Donald Vester retired tractor company executive
FitzGerald, Niall food products executive
Flaschen, Steward Samuel high technology company executive
Floratos, Evangelos Jacob coffee company executive
Folz, Jean-Martin automotive company executive
Ford, William Clay, Jr. automotive executive
Forti, William Bell business executive, inventor
Fosseen, Neal Randolph business executive, former banker, former mayor
Foster, David Ramsey soap company executive
Foster, Edward Paul (Ted Foster) process industries executive
Fox, Brian L. (Monty Fox) automotive executive
Fox, Duke Melvin manufacturing company executive
François-Poncet, Jean André business executive, French senator
Frank, Thomas design, construction and management executive
Franklin, William George manufacturing executive
Franson, Timothy Raymond pharmaceutical company executive, physician
Frasch, Werner William manufacturing professional
French, Harold Stanley food company executive
Friedel, Paul Edmond electronics company executive
Fries, Raymond Sebastian manufacturing company executive
Frigo, James Peter Paul industrial hardware company executive
Fritze, James Napier automotive executive
Frölander, Ulf manufacturing company executive
Frostic, Gwen paper company executive
Fuchs, Manfred lubricant company executive
Fuchs, Patrick Eugene perfume company executive
Furrer, John Rudolf retired manufacturing business executive
Gaillard, Jean-Paul consumer products company executive
Galiatsatos, Christos G. bottling company executive
Galie, Louis Michael electronics company executive
Galitzine, Georges Pierre company executive
Galvin, Christopher B. electronics company executive
Gamet, Donald Max appliance company executive
Gan, Chaying chemicals company executive
Gandois, Jean Guy steel company executive
Garana, Maria Luisa communications company executive
Garcia, Lopez Rodolfo construction executive
Garcia, Lourdes Guerra manufacturing company executive, chemical engineer
Garcia, Mercedes pharmaceutical company executive
Garcia-Gonzalez, Francisco polymers company executive
Gardner, James Richard pharmaceutical company executive
Gargour, Allenby Toufic automotive company executive
Gary, James Frederick business and energy advising company executive
Gault, Thomas Emerson healthcare business executive, accountant
Gaunt, Bobbie automotive executive
Gentz, Manfred automotive company executive
Georgakis, Kyriakos furniture company executive
George, David technology company executive
Georgin, Michel Hubert information technology company executive
Gerardot, Mark Steven construction executive
Gerber, Fritz pharmaceutical company executive, insurance company executive, diversified financial services company executive
Gerrish, Catherine Ruggles retired food company executive
Gerstein, David Brown hardware manufacturing company executive, professional basketball team executive
Gertz, David Lee homebuilding company executive
Geurts, Theodorus Bernardus pharmaceutical executive
Ghanem, Joseph Dib mill executive
Giacona, Corrado Anthony II container company executive
Gibson, Ian Bennett retired business executive
Gibson, Joseph Whitton, Jr. retired chemical company executive
Gifford, John Irving retired agricultural equipment company executive
Gilat, Avraham defense company executive
Gill, Ronald Scott technology company executive
Ginzburg, Vladimir B. metal products company executive
Giordano, Richard Vincent chemicals executive
Glinianowicz, Krzysztof manufacturing executive
Glomski, Edward Earl electronic company executive, bookseller
Gockley, Barbara Jean business executive
Goldberg, Lee Winicki furniture company executive
Goldberg, Ron plastics broker executive
Goldenberg, George retired pharmaceutical company executive
Goldmann, Thomas management consultant
Gonzales, Richard Daniel manufacturing executive
Gonzalez, Luis A. medical equipment company executive
Gooch, Don A. manufacturing executive
Goodin, Leonard Charles plumbing and drainage contrator
Gorman, Joseph Tolle corporate executive
Gottesman, Roy Tully chemical company executive
Gottlander, Robert Jan Lars dental company executive
Gottwald, Floyd Dewey, Jr. chemical company executive
Gough, John Bernard former manufacturing company executive
Gould, Alvin R. international business executive
Gould, Harry Edward, Jr. paper company executive
Gouldey, Glenn Charles manufacturing company executive
Gow, Alan James automotive executive, consultant
Graham, William B. pharmaceutical company executive
Grant, Sir Matthew Alistair food products company executive
Grasset, Etienne Alfred pharmaceutical executive
Gray, Donald Allan computer software technical recruiting
Greaser, Constance Udean automotive industry executive
Greaves, Stuart agrochemical company executive
Green, David manufacturing company executive
Green, Edward Francis manufacturing executive
Greener, Anthony food and beverage company executive
Grenell, James Henry retired manufacturing company executive
Griffin, Donald Wayne diversified chemical company executive
Griffin, Luanne Marie automotive corporation executive
Gross, Ronald Martin forest products executive
Guiot, Pierre business development director in life sciences
Guizol, Christian Yves Marie manufacturing company executive
Gulli, Christian Andre Marie electronics company executive
Gunnoe, Nancy Lavenia food executive, artist
Gyulev, Vladimir Genkov manufacturing executive
Haertel, Rainer Maria chemical company executive
Haines, William Joseph pharmaceutical company executive
Hall, Robert Alan construction company executive
Halleux, Albert Martin Julien motor vehicle inspection company executive
Halluitte, Blaise chemical company executive
Hamada, Hiroshi electronics executive
Hamai, James Yutaka business executive
Hammergren, John H. health/medical products executive
Hammersley, David Alan retired chemical company executive
Hampel, Sir Ronald (Claus) retired chemicals executive
Hanassab, Shahram Samuel electronics executive, engineer
Hanawa, Yoshikazu automotive executive
Haneda, Hisao construction company executive
Hanes, Ralph Philip, Jr. former textiles executive, arts patron, cattle farmer
Hanna, Murad Sami industrial minerals company executive, financial consultant
Hanson, David Bigelow construction company executive, engineer
Hanson, Milton manufacturing executive, consultant
Hardie, Alan food products company executive
Harlan, Norman Ralph construction executive
Harrell, Samuel Macy agribusiness executive
Harriett, Judy Anne medical equipment company executive
Harsanyi, Kalman pharmaceutical company executive, educator
Hart, Sean Lee pharmaceutical executive, consultant
Hartough, Howard Dale, Jr. pharmaceutical company executive
Haskins, Christopher Robin food products executive
Haughey, Edward Enda pharmaceuticals executive
Havens, Edwin Wallace manufacturing executive
Hawe, David Lee manufacturing consultant
Hawkins, Ellis Delano manufacturing executive, insurance executive, gaming executive
Hawrylyshyn, Bohdan business educator
Head, William Iverson, Sr. retired chemical company executive
Heck, John Kevin construction manager
Hegde, Mijar Radhakrishna brewery company official, researcher
Heiberg, Jens Gerhard retired company executive
Heilmann, Christian Flemming corporate executive
Heimbold, Charles Andreas, Jr. pharmaceutical company executive
Heiskanen, Tomi Pentti chemical company executive
Hellebo, Olav business executive
Hellman, Per Ingvar metal products executive
Hemma, Sherif Mohamed Fathy pharmaceutical executive
Henderson, Sir Denys Hartley business executive
Henderson, John electronics executive
Henley, Joseph Oliver manufacturing company executive
Henych, Ivo metal processing consultant
Herlitz, Gunter company executive
Herman, Robert Lewis cork company executive
Hermant, Pierre Claude equipment company executive
Hernández, Jehú food products executive
Hernandez, Ramon medical products company executive
Hicks, J. Robert industrial packaging executive, retired
Hijlkema, Sjouke Lambertus Anna drilling manager
Hillion, Herve Pierre supply chain consultant
Hills, Robert O. retired pharmaceutical company executive
Hind, Harry William pharmaceutical company executive
Hiraga, Masaharu heating and cooling products company advisor
Hirayama, Masahiro electronics executive
Hirsh, Bernard supply company executive, consultant
Ho, Gek Mui chemicals executive
Hodgson, Thomas Richard retired healthcare company executive
Hoel, Robert Fredrick, Jr. construction executive, civil engineer
Holland, John Ben clothing manufacturing company executive
Holleaux, Jean-Marc Maurice business executive
Holliday, Charles O., Jr. chemical company executive
Holman, J(ohn) Leonard retired manufacturing corporation executive
Holton, J(erry) Thomas concrete company executive
Holtz, Gilbert Joseph steel company executive
Holtzman, Arnold Harold chemical company executive
Homsy, Christian Cherif medical devices company executive
Hoo, Sim Wang electronics executive
Hooker, James Todd manufacturing executive
Hopkins, David Lee medical manufacturing executive
Horchler, Frigyes (Fred) S. automotive executive
Hortaleza, Rolando Bonifacio manufacturing company executive
Horwell, David Christopher pharmaceutical company executive
Horwitz, David Larry pharmaceuticals company executive, researcher, educator
Hoshino, Yoshiro industrial technology critic
Hoshiyama, Tadafumi optoelectronics executive, researcher
Hoskison, George Arthur farming executive
Hosono, Toshio electronics educator
Houghton, James Richardson retired glass manufacturing company executive
Housova, Jirina food service executive, researcher
Howell, James Burt, III agricultural products company sales consultant
Hsu, Sing Rong manufacturing executive, marketing professional
Hudson, William Jeffrey, Jr. manufacturing company executive
Hulstaert, Frank pharmaceutical company executive
Humphrey, Albert S. business development executive
Hurd, Richard Nelson pharmaceutical company executive
Hurley, Jeffrey Scott fabric company administrator
Hussain, Liaqat pharmaceutical company manager
Huybrechts, Guy Henri food products executive
Hyde, Michael Arthur chemical company executive
Iacovides, Alkis automotive company executive
Iannicelli, Joseph chemical company executive, consultant
Ibrahim, M. Medhat Soliman chemical company executive
Ichikawa, Yoshio wood trade company executive
Idei, Nobuyuki electronics executive
Iida, Itsuo precious metal catalyst company executive
Iizuka, Hisakazu electronics company laboratory administrator
Ilker Geli en, Mehmet pharmaceutical company executive
Ilozumba, Kris Chinyere ceramics company executive
Imai, Takashi steel manufacturing executive
Imhof, Rene pharmaceutical company executive, researcher
Inaba, Kosaku heavy manufacturing executive
Inoue, Takashi food products executive
Irani, Ray R. oil, gas and chemical company executive
Irwin, Robert Hugh Crawford manufacturing company executive
Ishimoto, Coe electronics company executive
Islas Yepez, Oscar Alberto healthcare company executive, educator

Nordsieck, Karen Ann *custom apparel company executive*
Norris, John Steven *healthcare company executive*
Nuckols, William Marshall *electrical goods manufacturing executive*
Nye, John Robert *furniture company executive, transportation consultant*
Oakes, Tim Simon Neville *manufacturing company executive*
O'Connor, Francis David *automotive company executive*
O'Dell, William Francis *retired business executive, writer*
O'Donnell, William David *retired construction firm executive*
Ogg, Robert Danforth *corporate executive*
Ohashi, Mitsuo *chemical company executive*
Ohba, Hiroshi *manufacturing executive*
Ohga, Norio *electronics and entertainment executive*
Ohno, Eiichi *electronics company executive*
Okazaki, Masami *manufacturing company executive*
Okuda, Hiroshi *automotive executive*
O'Neill, Paul Henry *aluminum company executive*
Onorato, Giovanni *company executive*
Opoku-Mensah, Edward *construction company administrator, real estate developer, contractor*
Orlova, Ludmila Vladimirovna *agricultural management company executive*
Orona, Ernest Joseph *real estate and construction company executive*
Otto, Harry Claude *manufacturing executive*
Oussani, James John *stapling company executive*
Owen-Jones, Lindsay *cosmetics executive*
Oxley, Roland Ross *construction executive, food service executive*
Ozgorkey, Selim M. *food processing company executive, auto dealer*
Özmen, Yasar *construction executive*
Paefgen, Franz-Josef *automotive executive*
Paillet, Alain *automotive executive*
Pakarinen, Arvo Juhani *metals manufacturing company executive*
Pamplin, Robert Boisseau, Jr. *manufacturing company executive, minister, writer*
Pandia, Rajeev Mahendra *petrochemical company executive, chemical engineer*
Panganiban, Teresita Macatangay *manufacturing executive*
Panic, Milan *pharmaceutical and health products company executive*
Park, Jong Woo *electronics executive*
Park, Young-Suk *hospital equipment company executive*
Parker, John Henry *building society executive*
Parkhurst, Charles Lloyd *electronics company executive*
Parkin, Malcolm Hirst *chemical company executive*
Parmanand, Nari (Larry) *textile company executive*
Parniere, Paul *automotive company executive*
Parrott, Michael Verne *manufacturing company executive*
Patel, Chimanbhai Revadas *petrochemical company executive*
Patel, Sharif Ahmed *food executive, consultant*
Patel Fürstenberg, Carin Maya *steel company executive*
Pathak, Kailash Chandra *manufacturing executive*
Pathak, Satish Ramnarayan *pesticide company executive*
Patrawalla, Aspi Eruch *manufacturing executive*
Patton, Jeffrey *plastics company executive*
Peck, Charles Edward *retired construction and mortgage executive*
Peebles, Allene Kay *manufactured housing company executive*
Peinado, Arnold Benicio, Jr. *consulting engineer*
Pekin, Ahhmet Vasfi *manufacturing executive*
Peltonen, Keijo Kalervo *manufacturing executive*
Pendleton, Andrew H. *produce company executive*
Perissich, Riccardo *manufacturing executive*
Perissin, Aldo Arrigo *scientific instruments company executive*
Perlick, Richard Allan *steel company executive*
Perlman, Gary Alessandro *construction company executive*
Perosch, Tony Anthony George *corporate executive, consul*
Persson, Mats Kurt Uno *international heavy machinery dealer*
Pesses, Marvin *metal products executive, consultant*
Peterson, H(arry) William *chemicals executive, consultant*
Peterson, Robert L. *meat processing executive*
Petrik, Gerd *pharmaceutical executive*
Petsiavas, Demetre N. *industrial company executive*
Petzel, Florence Eloise *textiles educator*
Peugeot, Roland *automobile and holding company executive*
Peyruseigt-Marti, Pierre *electronics executive*
Pfeiffer, Johan Fredrik *company official*
Picard, Dennis J. *retired electronics company executive*
Pichler, Joseph Anton *food products executive*
Piëch, Ferdinand *automotive executive*
Pirelli, Leopoldo *industrialist*
Pittas, George Panayiotis *food products executive*
Plancher, Robert Lawrence *former manufacturing company executive*
Plat, Francis Raymond *pharmaceutical company executive*
Platt, Lewis Emmett *retired electronics company executive*
Pognonec, Yves Maurice *steel products executive*
Polizotto, Michael James, Jr. *technology executive, consultant*
Pollicove, Harvey Myles *manufacturing executive*
Pólya, Kálmán *pharmaceutical company executive*
Ponka, Lawrence John *automotive executive*
Pontarolo, Valerio *building and hardware company executive*
Poon, Hoh Fun Geoffrey *chemical company executive*
Popoff, Frank Peter *chemical company executive*
Popp, Joseph Bruce *manufacturing executive*
Possati, Stefano *electronic gauge company executive*
Powell, Thomas Edward, III *biological supply company executive, physician*
Powell, William Council, Sr. *service company executive*
Prabhu, Giridhar Gurupur *food products executive*
Pratley, Kimleigh George Montague *manufacturing and mining company executive*
Prescott, John Barry *business executive*
Prest, Nicholas Martin *company executive*
Preston, Seymour Stotler, III *manufacturing company executive*
Price, David B., Jr. *manufacturing executive*
Primeaux, Henry, III *automotive executive, author, speaker*
Prior, William Allen *electronics company executive*
Pritzker, Robert Alan *manufacturing company executive*
Procos, Costas *paper company executive*
Pryde, Neil Frederick *manufacturing company executive*
Psomas, Marselo Ignatio *food service executive*
Puckett, Paul David *electronics company executive*
Pugh, Richard Forrest *food product company executive*
Pulido, Mark A. *pharmaceutical and cosmetics company executive*
Pundmann, Ed John, Jr. *automotive company executive*
Purdon, Richard Alan *food products executive*
Purdy, John Edgar *manufacturing company executive*
Purrer, Siegfried *trading company executive*
Purwanto, Agus *pharmaceutical machinery manufacturer, company executive*
Quarta, Roberto *manufacturing company executive*
Quaye, Samuel Wilkinson *manufacturing executive*
Quinn, Lochlann Gerard *manufacturing executive, bank executive*
Rabe, Alita *manufacturing company executive*
Rabin, Brian Robert *biotechnology company executive, consultant*
Racamier, Henry *metal products executive*
Raden, Louis *tape and label corporation executive*
Radhakrishnan, Tarur Venkatasubramanian *research company executive*
Raghavan, Venkatesan V. *pharmaceuticals company executive, consultant*
Raininko, Kyösti Kalevi *sugar company administrator*
Ramadan, Nabih M. *pharmaceutical companyofficial, educator*
Ramay, Bilal Ahmad *pharmaceutical company executive, consultant*
Ramer, Lawrence Jerome *corporation executive*
Ramesh, Jalligampala *metals company executive*
Randall, William B. *manufacturing company executive*
Randolph, Roger Brooke *manufacturing executive*
Rao, Devdas *chemical executive*
Rao, Rama Krishna R. *pharmaceutical company executive*
Rao, Srinath Jayram *electronics professional*
Ratcliffe, Simon Toby *electronics executive*
Rauh, John David *manufacturing company executive*
Rautala, Pekka Juhani *cosmetics company executive*
Raymond, Lloyd Wilson *machinery company executive*
Raz, Moti *electronics company executive*
Reavis, Hubert Gray, Jr. *metal products executive*
Rebello Da Silva, Luis A. *glass company executive*
Recordati, Andrea Alessandro *chemical and pharmaceutical company executive*
Reeder, Michael S. *consulting firm executive*
Rees, David Roy *aerospace company executive*
Reeves, Ronald Victor *construction engineering company executive*
Regan, Paul Jerome, Jr. *manufacturing company executive, consultant*
Regazzi, John Henry *retired electronic distributor executive*
Reid, David Corey *manufacturing executive*
Reisinger, Karl *manufacturing executive*
Renkar-Janda, Jarri J. *retired paint manufacturing executive*
Rhee, Dae-Yeon *manufacturing executive*
Rhee, Sung Kyu *steel company executive*
Rheinstein, Peter Howard *health care company executive, consultant, physician, lawyer*
Rice, Victor Albert *manufacturing executive, heavy*
Rich, Albert Clark *solar energy manufacturing executive*
Richard, Patrice *food and cosmetic company executive*
Riggs, Rory *pharmaceutical executive*
Riley, William *corporate executive, writer*
Ritterhoff, C(harles) William *retired steel company executive*
Riva, Amadeo *general contractor, airline executive and owner*
Roach, Donald Arthur *manufacturing company executive*
Robbins, Ray Charles *manufacturing company executive*
Robert, Vincent Marie *chemicals executive*
Robertshaw, John Desmond *company executive*
Robertson, Charles Morven *electronics company executive*
Robertson, Joseph Edmond *grain processing company executive*
Robins, Sir Ralph *manufacturing executive*
Robinson, Robert Earl *chemical company executive*
Robleto, Randy E. *pharmaceutical company director*
Robson, Barry *biopharmaceutical and computer company executive, biochemist*
Roche, Gilles *pharmaceutical company executive*
Roddick, David Bruce *construction company executive*
Rodero, Joseph Santiago *electronics executive*
Rodrigues, Allan *chemicals executive*
Rogers, Leonard John *business executive*
Rohrbaugh, Wayne Joseph *chemical company executive*
Rosenberg, Rudy *chemical company executive*
Rosenthal, Milton Frederick *minerals and chemical company executive*
Ross, Edwin William *rubber company executive*
Rossbach, Volker Wilhelm *textile and polymer chemistry educator*
Rosson, Dennis McKinley *manufacturing company executive*
Roth, Georg Franz *pharmaceutical company executive*
Roude, Jean-Claude Maurice *road construction company executive*
Routson, Clell Dennis *manufacturing company executive*
Ruggiero, Anthony William *chemical company executive*
Ruhlman, Herman C(loyd), Jr. *manufacturing company executive*
Ruiseco, Juan Manuel *cement company executive*
Ruskin, Ryan Scott *packaging company executive*
Russell, Marjorie Rose *manufacturing company executive*
Russell, Robert James *biotechnology and chemical company executive*
Ruthman, Thomas Robert *manufacturing executive*
Ryan, George William *manufacturing executive*
Rydin, Bo Goran *industrial executive*
Saba, Shoichi *manufacturing company executive*
Safarian, Alek *pharmaceutical industry executive, consultant*
Sahney, Sandeep *pharmaceuticals executive*
Sako, Teiyu *electronics executive, researcher*
Salas, Randall Nouel *automotive company executive*
Salvini, Luca *electronics systems educator*
Samuels, Fred *biotechnology company executive*
Sanderson, Polly Elaine *pharmaceutical company executive*
Sapoff, Meyer *electronics component manufacturer*
Saran, Adarsh *business executive, finance company executive*
Sargious, Nagy Albear *pharmaceutical executive*
Saribekir, Nuzhet Esra *packaging company executive*
Sasayama, Makoto *food science executive*
Sato, Shigeru *computer research company executive*
Satoh, Yasuhiro *food products executive*
Sauer, Fernand Edmond *pharmaceutical evaluation organization executive*
Saunders, Joseph Arthur *office products manufacturing company executive*
Savakoor, Ashok Umesh *company executive*
Savin, Ronald Richard *chemical company executive, inventor*
Savouchkine, Serguei Nick *pharmaceutical company manager*
Sawada, Hideo *polymer chemistry consultant, chemist*
Saxena, Alok Jagdish *pharmaceutical executive*
Sayed, Nisar Ahmad Shah *manufacturing company executive, consultant*
Scannell, Thomas John *cold metal forming company executive*
Scaperdas, Agnes Costas *distillery executive*
Schadt, Dieter *manufacturing executive*
Schapiro, Jerome Bentley *chemical company executive*
Scharlack, Ronald Stuart *medical device company executive*
Schaus, Philippe Paul *luxury products executive*
Schindler, Alfred N. *manufacturing executive*
Schlensker, Gary Chris *landscaping company executive*
Schlumberger, Jean Francois *pharmaceutical company administrator*
Schmidt, Klaus Walter *fiber manufacturing company executive*
Schmitt, Ralph George *manufacturing company executive*
Schmitz, Justus Michael *textile company executive*
Schneider, Carl Christoph *pharmaceutical company executive*
Schneider, Carlos Rodolfo *manufacturing company executive*
Schneider, Dennis Eugene *manufacturing company executive*
Schneider, Manfred *chemical and pharmaceutical company executive*
Schoen, Michael David *manufacturing executive*
Schrempp, Jürgen *automotive executive*
Schuijt, Chris *pharmaceutical executive*
Schultz, Finn Peder *paper company executive*
Schulze, Andreas J. *pharmaceutical company executive*
Schumann, Debraoh Kay *construction company executive*
Schusser, František *construction executive*
Schweitzer, Louis *automotive industry executive*
Seachrist, William Earl *holding company executive*
Seal, John S., Jr. *manufacturing company executive*
Sebring, Marjorie Marie Allison *former home furnishings company executive*
Sedaghati, Ramin *manufacturing consultant, researcher*
Seelenberger, Sergio Hernan *clinical and diagnostic company executive*
Seiler, Robert Kurt *textile company executive, consultant*
Sekimoto, Tadahiro *electronics company executive*
Seppanen, Hanneli Kirsti *chemical company executive*
Seth, Andrew *industry executive, educator, writer*
Seth, Shashikant Surajmal *plastic industry executive*
Setty, Viswanath B. R. *chemical company executive*
Seya, Hiromichi *glass products company executive*
Sganga, John B. *furniture holding company executive*
Shackley, Douglas John *fire alarm company executive*
Shaffer, Clarence F. *retired electronics executive*
Shah, Aashit Amritlal *automotive executive*
Shah, Chittranjan *automobile company executive*
Shah, Madhu Chinubhai *textiles executive, risk management consultant*
Shah, Nitin Vinaychand *paper company executive*
Shapiro, Robert B. *manufacturing executive*
Shapovalova, Viktoriya Alexeevna *pharmaceutical company executive*
Sharf, Stephan *automotive company executive*
Sharkey, Leonard Arthur *automobile company executive*
Sharma, Krishan Kumar *retired computer company executive, physicist, oncologist, immunotherapist*
Sharma, Niyam Charan *pharmaceuticals company executive*
Shaw, Trevor Henry Montague *food company executive*
Sheikh, Ahsan Imdad *company executive*
Shen, John Jianyue *fuel cell company executive*
Shepherd, Alan Arthur *electronics company executive, consultant*
Sheu, Steve Chao-Kae *food products company executive*
Shibata, Taira *construction company executive*
Shih, Stan *electronics manufacturing executive*
Shirokov, Felix V. *electronics executive, researcher*
Sholto-Douglas, Ian Gordon *manufacturing company executive*
Shoyama, Etsuhiko *electronics executive*
Shrem, Charles Joseph *metals corporation executive*
Shrontz, Frank Anderson *airplane manufacturing executive*
Sibley, Anthony Robert *retired meter manufacturing company executive*
Sidiqi, Ghiasuddin *holding company executive*
Sidney, William Wright *retired aerospace company executive*
Sim, Jai-hoon *electronics researcher*
Simes, Stephen Mark *pharmaceutical products executive*
Simicevic, Velimir Nicholas *pharmaceutical executive, research scientist*
Simpson, George *manufacturing executive*
Singal, Suresh Kumar *manufacturing executive*
Singh, Bajrang Bali *chemical company executive*
Singh, Maharaj Kumar Manvijai *property, industry and business executive*
Singh, Rajinder *chemical company executive*
Sjolin, Christer K.G. *energy executive*
Skellern, David James *electronics educator*
Skerritt, John Howard *agricultural research executive*
Slaughter, Dorothy Elizabeth, Jr. *construction and engineering firm executive*
Slusser, Eugene Alvin *electronics manufacturing executive*
Smeltzer, Steven A. *manufacturing executive*
Smick, Susan Schnee *tile designer and manufacturer, airline strategic, marketing planner*
Smith, Charles Anthony *business executive*
Smith, Frederick Orville, II *wood products manufacturer, retired naval officer*
Smith, Hans Jurie *minerals and metals company executive*
Smith, John Francis, Jr. *automobile company executive*
Smith, Orin Robert *chemical company executive*
Smith, Roger Graham *company executive*
Smith, Sir Roland *company executive*
Smith, Van P. *holding company executive*
Smith, Zachary Taylor, II *retired tobacco company executive*
Snook, Quinton *construction company executive*
Sobey, Donald Rae *industrialist*
Sora, Sebastian Antony *business machines manufacturing executive, educator*
Sparks, Wilfred *plastics company executive, consultant*
Spector, Michael Joseph *agribusiness executive*
Spencer, Ivor *company executive*
Spencer, Thomas Melvin, III *soft drink company executive*
Spiller, Joan Marilyn *company executive*
Stafford, James Edwin Harry *pharmaceutical information management consultant*
Stafford, John Rogers *pharmaceutical and household products company executive*
Stahl, Francis *automobile manufacturing company executive*
Stall, Alan David *packaging company executive*
Stamps, Peter David *manufacturing administrator*
Starkov, Rinat Anverovich *pharmaceutical company executive*
Stavropoulos, William S. *chemical executive*
Stefens, Paul Edouard *defense electronics company executive, consultant*
Steinback, Michael A. *electronic component company executive*
Steiner, Jeffrey Josef *industrial manufacturing company executive*
Stephan, Bodo *retired manufacturing company executive*
Stern, Harold Peter *business executive*
Steyaert, Jan Karel Marie-Antoon *corporate executive*
Stiritz, William P. *food company executive*
Stokes, John Gérard *forest products company executive*
Stokes, Kerry Matthew *company executive*
Stone, Franz Theodore *retired fabricated metal products manufacturing executive*
Stonebridge, Jerry Bert *construction company executive, consultant*
Stonecipher, Harry Curtis *manufacturing company executive*
Storey, Keith *forest products company executive*
Stowe, Robert Lee, III *textile company executive*
Strack, Harold Arthur *retired electronics company executive, retired air force officer, planner, analyst, author, musician*
Straub, Gerhard Herbert *manufacturing company executive*
Strenger, Hermann Josef *chemicals executive*
Strength, Robert Samuel *manufacturing company executive*
Stroble-Thompson, Colette Mary Houle *plastering and stucco company executive*
Stronach, Frank *automobile parts manufacturing executive*
Strube, Juergen F. *chemical company executive*
Stryker, James William *automotive executive, former military officer*
Stuart, (Charles) Murray *manufacturing executive*
Stubbing, Thomas John *airless drying technology executive, inventor*
Stureson, Johan Bengt Anders *lubricating grease company executive*
Sudarsky, Jerry M. *industrialist*
Sugar, Alan Michael *company executive*
Sugiyama, Toru Tom *automotive executive*
Sukul, Lomash *power generation equipment and design manufacturing executive*
Sullivan, Jerry Stephen *electronics company executive*
Sullivan, Thomas James *retired manufacturing company executive*
Sumino, Koji *steel company executive, educator*
Sun, Robert Zu Jei *manufacturing company executive, inventor*
Sutter, John Richard *manufacturer, investor*
Suzuki, Hiroshi *manufacturing company executive*
Suzuki, Kazushige *cosmetics company executive*
Suzuki, Kunihiro *microelectronics company executive, researcher*
Suzuki, Osamu *automotive industry executive*
Svanholm, Poul Johan *former brewing company executive*
Swanson, David Heath *agricultural company executive*
Swanson, Thomas Richard *manufacturing, supply chain and systems executive*
Sykes, David Michael *office supplies executive*
Syron, Martin Bernard *business executive*
Takeda, Yasutsuga *manufacturing executive*
Tal, Jacob *electronics executive*
Talbă, Liviu-ioan N. *electronics company executive*
Talgam, Yoav *electronics manufacturing company executive*
Tanaka, Norihito *manufacturing executive*
Tang, Dechao *manager of computer software company*
Tang See Kiong, Adrian *electronic company executive, marketing consultant*
Taniguchi, Ichiro *electrical and electronics industry executive*
Taniishi, Naotoshi *food company executive*
Taracena, Antonio *cement company executive*
Tató, Francesco *company executive*
Taudien, Edward Paul *retired construction executive*
Taylor-Williams, Bonnie Jean *cosmetics executive*
Ten, Jeffrey Ronald *cosmetics executive*
Terneyre, Gerard M. *metallurgical company executive*
Terzopoulos, John E. *electrical company executive*
Tewari, Ranjan *company executive*
Thanawall, Khurshed Meherwanit *textile company executive*
Theis, Steven Thomas *executive safety director*

INDUSTRY: SERVICE

Barnes, Sally Anderson *human resources consultant, organization effectiveness and employee involvement facilitator*
Barnett, David Philip *funeral administrator, horticulturist*
Barnett, Marilyn *advertising agency executive*
Barnich, Michel *finance marketing advisor*
Bar-On, Raphael Raymond *tourism consultant*
Baron, Theodore *public relations executive*
Barrett, Craig R. *computer company executive*
Barrett, James Edward, Jr. *management consultant*
Barron, Peggy Pennisi *management consultant*
Barry, Bernard Anthony *management consultant*
Barsoe, Claus *marketing executive*
Bartels, Joachim Conrad *marketing and publishing corporation executive*
Bartlett, Arthur Eugene *franchise executive*
Bartlett, Thomas Foster *international management consultant*
Bartoli, Ivan Renzo *scientific marketing service executive*
Barzov, Yuri Nikolaevich *executive recruiter*
Basden, Andrew *information technology educator*
Basri, Meer S. *business executive*
Bassett, Tina *communications executive*
Bassily, Elijah Sarwat *management executive*
Bassy, Alain Marie *sales executive*
Bates, Charles Walter *human resources executive, lawyer*
Bathgate, Liam Donald *communication executive*
Bauer, Raymond Gale *sales professional*
Bauer, Thomas Günther *travel and tourism educator, consultant*
Baum, Sandra Beattie *executive secretary*
Beaumesnil, Arnaud J. *sales and marketing professional*
Beaver, Allan *travel and tourism educator, travel agency director*
Becker, Seymour *hazardous materials and wastes specialist*
Beckmann, Suzanne C. *business executive, researcher, educator*
Beckwith, George E. *computer company executive*
Beemster, Joseph Robert *risk management consultant*
Behl, Prem *exhibitions organizer*
Beiman, Yong Ling Sun *management consultant*
Beit-Or, Ben-Zion *company executive*
Belcourt, Alain Bernard *research director*
Beleson, Robert Brian *marketing executive*
Bellarosa, Aaron James *computer company executive*
Bellin, Howard *management consultant company executive*
Benabbes-Taarji, Jalil Abbes *hotel executive*
Benello, David *management consultancy director*
Benes, Daniel Markus *computer company executive, consultant*
Benhoff, Edward Spreng *marketing professional*
Benmbarek, Jilani *business executive*
Benn, Douglas Frank *information technology and computer science executive*
Bennett, John Makepeace *information systems specialist, consultant*
Bennett, Mark *software company executive*
Benson, Steven Donald *sheet metal research and marketing executive, sheet metal mechanic, programmer, author*
Bentata, David Joseph *company executive*
Benveniste, Xavier *computer company executive*
Benz, Jochen Walter *business administration educator, management consultant*
Beraho, Enoch Karobe *management educator*
Berce, Jaro *information and management consultant*
Bercovitz, George Edward *international marketing consultant*
Bergelt, Philip Robert, Jr. *printer, antiques dealer*
Berger, Jerome Morris *communications executive*
Berggren, Eric Griffith *consulting company executive*
Bergstrom, Betty Howard *consulting executive, foundation administrator*
Berinstein, William Paul *business executive*
Berman, Geoffrey Louis *management company executive*
Berman, Steven Richard *computer company executive*
Bernabeu, Patrick Thierry *communications executive*
Bernard, Norman Paul *management consultant*
Bernatowicz, Frank Allen *management consultant, expert witness*
Bernstein, Robert Geoffrey *business consultant*
Berouard, Gilles *advertising company executive*
Bertone, Thomas Lee *management consultant*
Bethell, John *company executive*
Beuerlein, David Lewis *executive recruiter*
Beyer, Suzanne *advertising agency executive*
Bhojwani, Romy Laxmikant *hotel executive*
Biasi, Mariapaola *personnel recruitment company executive*
Biddle, Dan A. *human resources executive*
Bierly, Shirley Adelaide *communications executive*
Biffa, Richard Charles *waste management company executive*
Bilginoglu, Faruk *marketing professional, human resources specialist*
Billick, L. Larkin *marketing executive*
Billis, Euripides Christos *communications executive*
Bingham, George Walter Chandler *sales executive*
Bin Mahfouz, Mahfouz Marei *company executive*
Binning, Gene Barton *computer company executive*
Bird, Stephen Christopher *microcomputer company executive, consultant*
Birken, Joseph GHM *marketing executive*
Birtwistle, David Thomas *computer company executive, consultant*
Bisanzo, Mark Thomas *sales executive*
Bishop, Susan Katharine *executive search company executive*
Bisiachi, Irene Maria Giulia *press office consultant*
Bissell, Brent John *advertising and direct marketing executive*
Bissler, Richard Thomas *mortician*
Bjerne, Matts Gösta *business executive*
Bjerre, Mikkel Berg *marketing executive*
Black, Kris Susan Lynn *marketing company executive, speaker, author, poet*
Blaha, Verle Dennis *golf course executive, electrical engineer*
Blakemore, John Stewart *international management consultant*
Blanchard, Richard Emile, Sr. *retired management services executive, consultant*
Blanchard, Ronald Joseph *food service executive*
Blank, Arthur M. *home and lumber retail chain executive*
Blankenship, Richard Eugene *communications company executive*
Bloustein, Peter Edward *entertainment management consultant, producer*
Boateng, Kwame Osei *information system engineer*
Boccon-Gibod, Dominique Christian *communications executive, consultant*
Bodenham, Martin Francis *sales executive*
Bodharamik, Adisai *communications executive*
Bodkin, Ruby Pate *corporate executive, real estate broker, educator*
Boedt, Philippe *management consultant*
Boice, Craig Kendall *management consultant*
Bojin, Jacques *management executive, consultant*
Boles, Eric Paul *staffing company executive*
Bolin, Richard Luddington *industrial development consultant*
Bolster, Jacqueline Neben (Mrs. John A. Bolster) *communications consultant*
Boner, Donald Leslie *information systems executive*
Bonometti, Robert John *technology management and strategy executive*
Bonomi, Ferne Gater *public relations executive*
Boom, Hans *information, communications specialist*
Booth, Benjamin Keith Willoughby *information systems specialist*
Boreen, Henry Isaac *computer company executive*
Borel, Joseph Paul Andre *retired business executive*
Borel, Richard Wilson *communications executive, consultant*
Borwick, Richard *management consultant*
Bosman, Michael John *business executive*
Botkin, James W. *knowledge business executive*
Bottomley, F. David *advertising executive*
Bouilly, Frederic C. *sales executive*
Boulte, Patrick *consultant*
Bourcier, Catherine Elizabeth T. *communications company executive*
Bourgeon, Jean-Marc Victor Pierre *sales executive*
Bourgery, Marc Edmond Clement *advertising executive*
Boussagol, Claire Reine *public affairs specialist*
Boutagy, George *tourism executive*
Boutterin, Emmanuel *public relations executive*
Bowd, Ronald Gregory *information systems executive, statistician*
Bowen, Charles John *executive*
Bowen, Paul L. *information systems and accounting educator*
Bower, Marvin *management consultant*
Bower, Shelley Ann *business management consultant*
Boyd, Lynne Kaplan *software company executive*
Brackenridge, N. Lynn *public relations and development specialist*
Bradetich, Robert William *advertising executive*
Bradley, Nolen Eugene, Jr. *personnel executive, educator*
Bradley, Philip Stephen *management consultant*
Bradshaw, James Edward (Jim Bradshaw) *consultant*
Bradstreet, Bernard Francis *computer company executive*
Braendlin, Christopher *business development administrator*
Bragason, Pall *executive*
Branch, David Alan *business development executive*
Brandmeir, Christopher Lee *hotel and tourism management educator*
Brandt, William Arthur, Jr. *consulting executive*
Brankovich, Mark J. *restaurateur*
Brashear, Jerry Paul *management consultant*
Braun, Reto *computer systems company executive*
Braunagel, Alfred *research and development company executive*
Bravi, Jean Luc *advertising executive*
Brecher, Bernd *management consultant*
Bredemeyer, Loretta Jeane *public relations, vocational and academic consultant*
Brenner, Michael Edward *executive search consultant*
Brent, Hal Preston *sales executive*
Brett, John Brendan, Jr. *corporate advertising and public relations executive*
Brevik, J. Albert *communications consultant*
Bricel, Mark Leon *marketing executive*
Briem, Sigurdur *personnel director*
Brilman, Jean Frans *management consultant*
Brisard, Jean-Charles *business intelligence executive*
Brito, José *planning executive, management consultant*
Brock, Kerry Lynn *internet executive*
Brook, Elaine Isabel *travel guide, writer*
Brown, Arnold *management consultant*
Brown, Laveda Page *consultant*
Brown, Roxanne (Jerene Roxanne Brown) *sales executive*
Brown, Stephanie C. *credit and collections manager*
Bruesewitz-LoPinto, Gail C. *marketing professional*
Brunello-McCay, Rosanne *sales executive*
Brunette, Herve *business executive*
Brunhes, Bernard *executive*
Bruski, Paul Steven *marketing executive*
Bruyn, Kimberly Ann *public relations executive*
Bryan, John Rodney *management consultant*
Bryant, Robert John *consultant*
Brynjolfsson, Erik *management educator, researcher*
Brzozowska-Ryczer, Malgorzata *management consultant*
Bucciero, Joseph Mario, Jr. *executive consultant*
Buchan, Craig Norman *technical officer*
Buchin, Stanley Ira *educator, management consultant*
Buck-Emden, Ruediger *software company executive, computer scientist*
Buckholtz, Thomas Joel *computer and telecommunications executive*
Budhiraja, Shashi Bhushan *management consultant*
Buehler, Martin *hotel executive*
Buhalis, Dimitrios *tourism and hospitality educator, consultant*
Buist, Richardson *corporate executive, retired banker*
Bull, Sir George *food service executive*
Bunditjaroenpun, Somchet *information systems specialist*
Bundschuh, Manfred Otto *insurance company executive, educator*
Bunning, Richard Leslie *management consultant*
Bunt, Marion Adams *retired administrative secretary/coordinator*
Buntrock, Dean Lewis *retired waste management company executive*
Burak, Markus René *communications executive*
Buras-Elsen, Brenda Allynn *retired public affairs executive*
Burd, Steve *food service executive*
Burdus, Julia Ann *marketing researcher*
Burga, Luisa R. *marketing researcher*
Burgard, Ralph *cultural/education planner*
Burgess, Anthony Reginald Frank *consultant*
Burgess, Marvin Franklin *human resources, management specialist, consultant*
Burgess, Robert Ronald *human resources executive*
Burgess, Steven Michael *marketing professional, educator*
Bürgi-Schmelz, Adelheid Hildegard *software company executive, computer scientist*
Burke, James Edward *consumer products company executive*
Burke, Thomas John *communications executive*
Burke-Kennedy, Desmond B. *marketing executive*
Burnham, J. V. *sales executive*
Burnham, Patricia White *consultant advocate, writer, business executive*
Burns, Neal Murray *advertising agency executive*
Burns, Pat Ackerman Gonia *information systems specialist, software engineer*
Burridge, Simon St. Paul *advertising executive*
Bush, Larry Don *communications company administrator*
Butera, Ann Michele *consulting company executive*
Byington, S. John *retained search executive, lawyer*
Bystrand, Fredrik Vilhelm *information systems executive*
Byth, Simon Harold *marketing analyst, consultant*
Cabrera, Luiz Carlos de Queirós *executive search consultant*
Cachalia, Ghaleb Kaene *management consultant*
Caffarelli, Arturo Jorge *commercial executive*
Cahana, Michael *quality assurance and engineering consultant*
Cajueiro, Marcelo Santos de *communications company executive, correspondent*
Calooy, Sonya Renee *advertising executive, consultant*
Calvin, Dorothy Ver Strate *computer company executive*
Cameron, Janice Carol *executive assistant*
Camilli, Carlo *management consultant*
Camlibel, Dizdar *marketing professional, advertising consultant*
Cammas, Thierry *media company executive*
Camoro, Simeon Fernandez *human resources and public relations executive*
Campbell, Stewart Clawson *retired sales executive, artist*
Campbell Davis, Trevor Fraser *communications company executive*
Campman, Christopher Kuller *consulting company executive*
Canta Yoy, Carlos Andrés *business executive, trade consultant*
Cantor, Alan Bruce *management consultant, computer software engineer*
Capellas, Michael D. *computer company executive*
Capone, Lucien, Jr. *management consultant, former naval officer*
Capponi, Gianfranco *company manager*
Cardyn, George Deon *marketing educator*
Careatti, Daniel M. *information systems specialist*
Careless, Simone *company executive*
Carino, Linda Susan *business consultant*
Caristo-Verrill, Janet Rose *international management consultant*
Carmichael, Richard Ardean *marketing professional*
Carney, Robert Arthur *restaurant executive*
Carro, Carl Rafael *executive search consultant*
Carroll, Patrick Thomas *communications executive*
Carter, David Edward *communications executive*
Carter, H. John *sales executive, consultant*
Carter, William Allen *sales executive, insurance company executive*
Carter, Willie Lee *quality management professional*
Carthew, Christopher David *software development executive*
Carty, John Charles Anthony *advertising executive*
Casavantes, Rita *defense electronics and engineering professional*
Case, Clyde Willard, Jr. *sales and marketing executive*
Case, Ric *computer company executive, consultant*
Casey, Barbara Jeanne *marketing professional*
Casey, James Francis *management consultant*
Cassal Abujder, Yusef Sleiman *business executive*
Cassim, Sirajuddin Akbarally *management consultant, stock broker*
Castell, William Martin *company executive*
Castille, Jean-Paul Gilbert *researcher, innovation and management consultant*
Castillo, Demetrio *management educator, researcher*
Castor, Jon Stuart *electronics company executive*
Cavanagh, Richard Edward *business policy organization executive*
Caveney, Robert John *quality assurance professional*
Cawthon, William Connell *operations management consultant*
Cayer, Joanne M. *sales executive*
Cech, Petr *communication executive*
Cerbone, Robert *sales and marketing executive*
Cernea, Minerva *executive search company executive*
Cerri, Alberto *management consultant executive*
Cerruti, Roberto *executive*
Chambel, Manuel Matos *airline official, consultant*
Chambers, Clytia Montllor *public relations consultant*
Chambers, Robert William *marketing professional, consultant*
Champion, Terence John *marketing professional*
Chan, Chak-Fu *hotel executive, real estate investment company executive*
Chan, Kar Ming Henry *administrator*
Chandler, Robert Leslie *public relations executive*
Chang, Edward H. *computer company executive*
Chang, Su Hui *executive*
Chaput, Eugene Michael *advertising executive*
Charles, Joel *forensic audio and video tape analyst, voice identification consultant*
Charles, Kwame Richard *management consultant, educator*
Charles, Lyn Ellen *marketing executive, commercial artist, photograph*
Charlier, Etienne Bernard *telecommunication equipment executive*
Charlier, Jean Pierre *management consultant*
Charlson, David Harvey *executive search company professional*
Charters d'Azevedo, Ricardo *management executive*
Chedore, Adrian Genge *marketing professional*
Chen, Kenneth Ting *information systems specialist*
Cheng, Kevin Hon-Kit *marketing professional*
Cheser, Raymond Norris, III *medical devices company executive*
Chesney, Robert Henry *communications executive, consultant*
Chew, David K. M. *company executive*
Chhabra, Tarlok Singh *advertising company executive*
Childs, Rand Hampton *data processing executive*
Chin, Janet Sau-Ying *data processing executive, consultant*
Ching, Chiao-Liang Juliana *development company executive, physician*
Chinn, Sir Trevor (Edwin) *business executive*
Chlamtac, Imrich *computer company executive, educator*
Choa, Walter Kong *technical service professional*
Chow, Raymond *entertainment company executive*
Choy, Kim Fun *human resource consultant*
Christie, David Thomas *information systems specialist, conductor*
Christodoulou, Chris *management professional, educator*
Chu, Allen Yum-Ching *automation company executive, systems consultant*
Chu, Patrick Tak-Long *marketing professional*
Chung, Jen-King *communications executive*
Church, Graham Jasper *communications educator*
Chyung, Chi Han *management consultant*
Cirlinci, Massimo *consulting company executive*
Citron, Richard Ira *management consultant*
Clackson, Stephen Gregory *communications executive*
Clark, James S. *marketing executive*
Clark, Merrell Mays *management consultant*
Clark, Oliver Nicholas Huntingdon *management consultant*
Clarke, Theo *management consultant*
Clauss, Frederic *sales executive*
Claverie, Christine *marketing specialist*
Clayton, Raymond Arthur *purchasing executive*
Cleary, Sean Michael *executive*
Clement, Paul Platts, Jr. *performance technologist, educator*
Clergue, Yolande *executive*
Clermont, Charles M. *entrepreneur, consultant*
Clinch, Nicholas Bayard, III *business executive*
Close, Melanie Jane *disability information and advice service coordinator*
Coad, Noel Kenneth *private country club administrator*
Coates, John Peter *technical executive*
Cobb, John Cecil, Jr. (Jack Cobb) *communications specialist and executive*
Coble, Paul Ishler *advertising agency executive*
Cochenour, Mark David *nuclear electronics*
Cochran, Jacqueline Louise *management executive*
Cogert, Harmon Ian *management executive*
Cohen, Cheryl Diane Durda *communications executive*
Cohen, Perry D. *management consultant*
Colangelo, Rocco, Jr. *sales executive*
Colas, Gilles F. *company executive*
Cole, Kristine Louise *human resources professional*
Coleman, Claire Kohn *public relations executive*
Coletta, Gerard Charles *management consultant*
Collins, Richard Stratton (Dick Collins) *retired public relations executive*
Colom, Nyani Iisha *payments company executive*
Colonna, Denis Auguste *tourism business executive, consultant*
Colvin, Clark Sherman *educator, management consultant*
Conidi, Daniel Joseph *private investigation agency executive*
Conlon, Brian Thomas *promotion executive*
Connaughton, David Michael *management consultant*
Connelly, Theodore Sample *communications executive*
Conole, Richard Clement *management consultant*
Conrads, Bernhard Wilhelm *management executive, editor*
Conway, Eileen *quality manager*
Cooksey, Ray Wagner *human resource management educator*
Cooley, Andrew Lyman *corporation executive, former army officer*
Coons, Barbara Lynn *public relations executive, librarian*
Cooper, James Robert, III *computer software company executive, mobile communications consultant*
Cooper, John Ambrose *management coordinator, international marketer*
Cooper, Penny *retired administrative assistant, writer, artist*
Copeland, John Howard *communications executive, television producer*
Copley, Gordon *executive search company administrator*
Coppieters, Kristiaan Hendrik Justin *computer company executive*
Cornell, Anna Claire *advertising executive*
Cortes, John Emmanuel *botanical garden administrator, consultant*
Costello, John H., III *business and marketing executive*
Costello, Robert Michael *public relations executive*
Cotting, Patrick *marketing professional, consultant*
Coughlin, William James Raymond *administrative associate*
Courson, Marna B.P. *public relations executive*
Courtaud, Bernard Jean-Jacques *human resource consulting executive*
Coutermarsh, Eva Marina *personnel executive*
Cover, Norman Bernard *retired electronic data processing administrator*
Cowden, Jere Lee *management consultant*
Cozier, Jeffrey Patrick *management professional*
Craig, Elizabeth Coyne *marketing executive*
Craig, Sandra Kay *sales executive*
Crandell, K(enneth) James *management and strategic planning consultant, entrepreneur*
Crane, Kent Bruce *international investments executive*
Cranois, Nicole Simone *communications executive*
Crehalet, Yves *advertising executive*
Crevelt, Dwight Eugene *computer company executive*
Criado, Jose Fernando *business executive*
Crittenden, Sophie Marie *communications executive*
Crosby, Lynn A. *business developer, owner*
Crosby, Ralph Wolf *communications executive*
Cuatt, John Edward *sales executive*
Cubitt, Sally Anne *administrative assistant*
Culley-Foster, Anthony Robert *international business consultant*
Culpepper, Warren Leigh *management consultant*
Cupp, Marilyn Marie *sales executive*
Curle, Robin Lea *computer software industry executive*
Curlook, Walter *management consultant*
Currie, Christopher Charles *database administrator*
Cvetkovic, Zorko *secretary*
Czajkowski-Barrett, Karen Angela *human resources management executive*
Dabbs Riley, Jeanne Kernodle *retired public relations executive*

Dace, Karen Yvette *executive assistant, travel consultant*
Dagit, Deborah Lynne *high technology executive*
Dahlgaard, Jens Jørn *business educator*
Dai, Ivan Nap Kwan *interior design company executive*
Daiya, Pravin Chaturbhuj *marketing professional, consultant*
D'Alene, Alixandria Frances *human resources professional*
Dalla Maria, Gabriele Felice *water industry executive*
D'Ambrosio, Daniele Attilio *marketing professional*
Dandapani, S. *management consultant*
D'Angelo, Andrea *business company executive*
Dangoor, David Ezra Ramsi *consumer goods company executive*
Daniel, Ronald Overton *management consultant*
Daniels, Marcel Ludolphe C.M. *communications executive*
Danter, Glyn E. *healthcare industry official*
Daoedsyah, Teuku Moh *personnel director*
Dapron, Elmer Joseph, Jr. *communications executive*
Dargan, John Henry *business executive*
Darien, Steven Martin *management consulting company executive*
Darlington, David William *management consultant*
Darrouzet, Jean-Claude *home furnishings distribution business executive*
Das, Dillip Kumar *business executive*
Das, Samir Kumar *software company executive*
Daschuta, Miguel Ismael Alejandro *advertising executive*
Da Silveira, Guilherme *business consultant, actor*
Datz, Israel Mortimer *information systems specialist*
Daum, Julie Hambrock *executive recruiter*
Daumen, Gustavo J. *company executive*
Dauvrin, Thierry *researcher*
David, Morgan Renan *business consultant*
Davidson, Per *marketing professional, researcher*
Davidson, Richard Alan *data communications company executive*
Davis, Alan Mark *software executive*
Davis, Alvin G. *company executive*
Davis, Connie Waters *public relations and marketing executive*
Davis, Julie Kramer *communications executive*
Davis, Lourie Irene Bell *computer education and information systems specialist*
Davis, Loyd Evan *defense industry marketing professional*
Davis, Rex Darwin *business consultant*
Davis, Stephen Clive *managment consultant*
Davis, Susan Gloria *sales representative, consultant*
Dawids, Richard Greene *business executive*
Dawson, Charloe H.O. *management consultant*
Dawson, Terance D. *data processing specialist, city councilman*
Day, Melvin Sherman *information and telecommunications company executive*
Day, Ronald Elwin *consulting executive*
Dayton, Deane Kraybill *translation company executive*
DCamp, Kathryn Acker *human resources director*
Dean, Thomas Joseph *management educator*
Deane, Christopher Philip *company executive, corporate consultant*
De Benedetti, Enzo *management consultant*
de Boer, Perry H.G. *data communications professional*
DeBow, Thomas Joseph, Jr. *advertising executive*
de Cicco, Francis *business consultant, religious administrator*
Decker, James Ludlow *management consultant*
De Curtis, Mauro Augusto *company executive*
De Deken, Jean *marketing professional*
Dedman, Robert Henry *sales executive*
Dee, James Phillip *human resources consultant*
Deerman, Ruth Gillett *sales professional, flying instructor*
de Fauconval, Baron Jean *retired companies director*
de Gastines, Brigitte *business executive*
Degutis, Mindaugas *marketing research company executive*
de Haas, Jan Hendrik Derk *management consultant*
De Hertogh, Hendrik Pieter Wim *outsourcing company executive*
deJesus-Burgos, Sylvia Teresa *information systems security manager*
Dekens, Alexander Leon Jean *computer company executive*
De Koning, Peter Hans *marketing executive*
De Lagabbe, Arnaud *sales company executive, consultant*
De La Garza, German *company executive*
De La Garza, Laura *human resources professional*
Delage, Gilles Pascal *international company sales executive*
Delannoy, Eric *advertising executive*
Delano-Condax, Kate (Kate Delano Condax Decker) *marketing and public relations executive*
Delcroix, Jean-Claude *management consultant*
Delena, Oscar *industrial consultant*
Delfino, Louis Joseph *sales representative*
de Liedekerke, Charles A. *industrial company executive*
De Luca, Jean Pierre *sales and marketing professional*
DeLuca, Ronald *former advertising agency executive, consultant*
Deluhery, Allison *marketing specialist*
del Valle, Marcelo Gustavo *information systems specialist, consultant*
de Margitay, Gedeon *acquisitions and management consultant*
De Marino, Donald Nicholson *international business executive, former federal agency administrator*
Demeester, Francky *consulting company executive*
Demidow, Maciej Adam *trade company executive, consultant*
DeMonte, Cynthia Maria *investor relations and management consultant*
Dempsey, Jerry Edward *retired service company executive*
Denning, Samantha *advertising executive*
Deoul, Kathleen Boardsen *executive*
de Pontbriand, Gael Jean *international consultant*
de Pouzilhac, Alain Duplessis *advertising executive*
Deppisch, Paul Vincent *data communications executive*
DePrez, Gene Edward *management consultant*
de Rosa, Mirio *marketing professional, consultant*
de Roux, Patrick *development and communication specialist*
Dersh, Rhoda E. *management consultant, business executive*
De Ruyver, Dirk Andre *business development manager*
Derzai, Matthew *retired telecommunications company executive*
De Sanctis, Nicola *environmental services company executive*
Desaulniers, Marcel Andre *food service executive*
Desmet, Stephane Joseph *sales company executive*
De Sofi, Oliver Julius *data processing executive*
Detschel, Frederick William *management consultant*
DeVaney, Carol Susan *management consultant*
De Vecchis, Michel Pierre *marketing professional*
De Veirman, Georges H. G. E. *sales and marketing executive*
Devendorf, Louise Marie *promoter, writer*
De Vlugt, Willem *packaging industry executive*
Devouge, Catherine *advertising executive*
Deysher, Paul Evans *training consultant*
Deza, Ricardo Juan *research and development company executive*
Dhanabalan, Suppiah *organization executive, business executive*
Dhankhar, J. N. *business executive*
Dhiman, B. S. *management consultant*
Dias, Sergio Antonio C. C. Da Pena *company financial executive*
Diaz, Lourdes Magdayao *human resource professional*
Diaz, Luis Cruz *management corporation president*
Direske, Peter Hans *communications executive*
Di Spigno, Guy Joseph *international management consultant, industrial psychologist*
Divatia, Parikshit Jayendrabhai *consultant*
Divjak, Tatjana Tanja *marketing executive*
Dixon, John Spencer *international executive*
Dobbs, George Albert *funeral director, embalmer*
Dobes, Richard *consulting company executive*
Doescher, William Frederick *communications executive*
Doetsch, Virginia Lamb *former advertising executive, writer*
Doherty, Barbara Whitehurst *chemical purchasing manager*
Dokoutchaev, Vladimir Anatolievich *communications company executive*
Dolan, Regina *security firm executive*
Doland, Judy Ann *administrative assistant, retired financial rating company associate*
Dolansky, Vaclav *marketing educator*
Dole, Trux *high technology marketing executive*
Dolezal, Jaroslav *research and development manager*
Dolgin, Kevin John *strategy consultant*
Domarkas, Vladislavas *public relations administrator*
Domeniconi, Reto *business executive*
Dommermuth, William Peter *marketing consultant, educator*
Donaldson, John Cecil, Jr. *consumer products company executive*
Doorley, Thomas Lawrence, III *management consulting firm executive*
Dore, Jagdish Viswanath *management executive*
Dorn, Norman Philip *management consulting firm executive*
Dornbush, K. Terry *former ambassador, consulting company executive, educator*
Dorrell, Juliet Louise *business consultant, writer*
Dosayla, Alberto Dequito *construction company sales executive, consultant*
Dostál, Jan *hotel, tourist and gaming industry executive*
Doucette, David Robert *computer systems company executive*
Doughty, David William *marketing executive*
Doull, Adrian Monteith *executive*
Doumlele, Ruth Hailey *communications company executive, broadcast accounting consultant*
Doyle, El Marques Declan *tourism professional*
Draeger, Kenneth W. *retired high technology company executive*
Drakes, David Hedley Foster *marketing consultant*
Draper, Steven Scott *laundry manager*
Drozdeck, Steven Richard *management consultant*
Droze, J. Tom *market researcher*
Dru, Jean-Marie Paul *communications executive*
Drummer, Dorothy Jean *executive search consultant, lawyer*
Drury, James Joseph, III *management consultant*
Drutchas, Gerrick Gilbert (Baron Khabarovsky) *investigator*
Dubrule, Paul Jean-Marie *hotel and restaurant company executive, wine producer*
Duelfer, Eberhard J.C. *business educator*
Duffield, David *computer company executive*
Duggan, Joseph Patrick *public affairs executive*
Duke, Ellen Kay *planned giving administrator*
Dunham, Joan Roberts *administrative assistant*
Dunlap, Donald Kelder *rental company executive*
Du Preez, Rose *management consultant*
Durek, Thomas Andrew *computer company executive*
Durham, James Michael, Sr. *marketing consultant*
Durlabhji, Yogendra *gem and jewelry company executive*
Duroux, Axel Renaud *communications company executive, journalist*
Dutton, Frank Elroy *data processing executive*
Duverger, Patrick *executive*
Dvorak, Kathleen S. *business products company executive*
Dwinfour, Kofi Antwi *marketing executive*
Dykstra, David Charles *management executive, consultant, accountant, author, educator*
Eaton, Amos Jorge *management consultant*
Ebbers, Bernard J. *communications executive*
Eby, Michael John *marketing research and technology consultant*
Echu, Ibrahim *civil service professional*
Eddins, James William, Jr. *marketing executive*
Eddy, Frank Sterling *human resources manager, teacher*
Ede, Fred Okotchy *marketing educator*
Edelman, Daniel Joseph *public relations executive*
Edmonds, Warren S. *patent agent*
Edwards, C. Karen *consultant company executive*
Edwards, Carolyn Mullenax *public relations executive*
Edwards, Doris Porter *computer specialist*
Edwards, Sir Llewellyn Roy *company executive*
Edwards, Patrick Michael *sales consultant*
Edwards, Paul Arthur *quality assurance company executive*
Edwards, Scott *human resource specialist*
Edwards, William Bennett *firearms industry consultant, gun dealer*
Edwards-LeBoeuf, Renee Camille *public relations professional, logistics engineer*
Egberts, Marvin E. *management consultant, psychologist*
Eggers, James Wesley *executive search consultant*
Eggleston, Claud Hunt, III *company executive, venture capitalist*
Eggleston, G(eorge) Dudley *management consultant, publisher*
Egi, Norihiko *computer software company executive*
Ekue, Foli *marketing executive*
Ekunno, Emmanuel Princewill *sales and marketing executive*
Elber, Ron *computer science educator*
Elix, Douglas Thorne *computer company executive*
El Khateeb, Gaber Kadry *quality assurance executive*
Ellig, Bruce Robert *personnel executive*
Ellis, June B. *human resource consultant*
El-Nadi, Fathi Ali *management consultant, management educator*
Eltgen, Jean-Jacques Pierre *digital printers manufacturing executive*
Emerson, Diane Marie *marketing executive*
Engelhardt, Regina *cosmetologist, artist, small business owner*
English, Marlene Cabral *management consultant*
Ennis, Thomas Michael *management consultant*
Erasmus, Louisa Helena *director human resources consulting firm*
Ernst, John Louis *management consultant*
Erskine Favre, Barbara L. *media relations executive*
Erumsele, Andrew Akhigbe *development policy analyst*
Esmieu, Dominique M. *market research executive*
Espino, Martin *business consultant*
Espinoza, Roberto Carlos *advertising agency executive*
Estefan, Nabil *business and finance executive*
Estes, Douglas Lee *motel owner*
Etterer, Sepp *industrial relations consultant*
Ettighoffer, Denis Charles *management and organization consultant*
Ettwig, Volker *management consultant*
Evans, Franklin Bachelder *marketing educator emeritus*
Evans, Joyce Evans *administrative assistant*
Evans, Pamela R. *marketing executive*
Evans, Paul Anthony Lee *management educator, consultant*
Evans, Robert Vincent *sales and marketing executive*
Evans, Thomas Passmore *business and product licensing consultant*
Ewing, Michael Thomas *marketing educator, consultant, researcher*
Eymieu, Alex *management consultant*
Fabian, Laszlo *marketing and public relations executive*
Fabris, Francesco *information specialist, educator*
Fabry, Alain *business executive*
Fahner, Harold Thomas *marketing executive*
Falangas, Costas *hotel executive*
Falco, Gérard *economic information manager*
Fallin, Barbara Moore *human resources director*
Faltejsek, Jiří *quality assurance professional*
Faluyi, Akinsola Olusegun *human resources development consultant, corporate professional*
Famiglietti, Nancy Zima *computer executive*
Faraone, Ted *public relations executive, consultant*
Faraone, Teri *public relations executive*
Faraut, Jean-Pierre *hotel owner and developer*
Farias Bouvier, Nestor *consulting company executive*
Faron, Fay Cheryl *private investigator, writer*
Farrell, Paul Noel *communications company executive*
Fassoulis, Satiris Galahad *communications company executive*
Faulkner, Herbert William *tourism management educator*
Faulkner, Robert Lloyd *advertising executive, graphic designer*
Favreau, Susan Debra *management consultant*
Fay, Toni Georgette *communications executive*
Fedotov, Vasiliy Ivanovich *technical specialist*
Fehér, Ottó *management consultant*
Fehr, Ury Ernst *marketing executive*
Feiner, Ava Sophia *public affairs and management consultant, economist*
Feldman, Javier *communications executive*
Feng, Sarah *international relations director*
Feran, Russell G. *sales executive*
Ferguson, Andrew Simon Crocker *holistic enterprise development consultant, author*
Fernandes, Jeanne Mary *human resource administrator*
Fernández, Alberto Antonio *security professional*
Ferretti, Fulvio *purchasing manager*
Fertig-Dykes, Susan Beatrice *communications executive, human resources professional, community and civil society facilitator*
Fessas, Theodore Demetrios *information technology executive*
Fetteroll, Eugene Carl, Jr. *human resources professional*
Fibiger, Bo *media researcher*
Fickinger, Wayne Joseph *communications executive*
Fiedler, Andreas Erich *mamagement consultant*
Fields, Stuart Howard *labor relations specialist*
Fierheller, George Alfred *corporate director*
Fierro, Alfredo Emilio *marketing professional, consultant*
Figueroa, Kimberly Susan *hotel and recreation executive*
Fila, Joseph Duncan *marketing and sales executive, public relations executive, real estate broker*
Filjar, Renato *information technology specialist, consultant*
Fine, Jo Renée *management executive*
Finger, Robert Roy *marketing executive*
Finger, Wilfried Bernd *marketing professional*
Fiorina, Carleton S. (Carly Fiorina) *computer company executive*
Fischer, Peter Heinz *public affairs and communications specialist*
Fischer, Russell Leonard *public relations executive*
Fiscus, James Ronald *telecommunications consultant*
Fisher, Eugene *marketing executive*
Fisher, George Myles Cordell *photographic imaging company executive, mathematician, engineer*
Fisher, James W., Jr. *management consultant*
Fitzgerald, Paul *business executive, consultant*
Flaschen, David Jenkin Steward *marketing executive*
Fleharty, Mary Sue *administrative assistant*
Fleisher, Frederic Elliott *communications executive*
Fletcher, Kenneth Boyd *business executive, entrepreneur*
Flood, Diane Lucy *marketing communications specialist*
Flood, Gregory Charles *human resources management specialist*
Florey, Jerry Jay *aerospace and management consultant*
Flueckiger, Claude René *marketing executive*
Flynn, Elizabeth Anne *advertising and public relations company executive*
Flynn, Ralph Melvin, Jr. *sales executive, marketing consultant*
Folter, Roland *book historian, rare books company executive, bibliographer*
Fontana, Olivier Frederic *marketing manager*
Fontani Thomas, Laura *consultant*
Fontès, Béatrice Liliane *marketing professional*
Foo, Siang Heng *human resource director*
Fookes, Eric Geoffrey Vincent *software developer*
Forester, Jean Martha Brouillette *innkeeper, retired librarian, educator*
Forkin, John Richard *company director*
Formo, Brenda Terrell *travel company executive*
Forrest, Gail *human resources executive*
Forshay, Steven R. *marketing professional, consultant*
Forster, Jean-Charles *consumer products company executive*
Forte, Lord Charles (Baron Forte) *hotel and catering company executive*
Forti, Lenore Steimle *business consultant*
Fortunato, Jose Manual Cardoso *marketing executive*
Foster, Thomas William *management consultant, entrepreneur*
Foster, William Anthony *management consultant, educator*
Fouad, Fouad Abdulla *business administrator*
Foulds, Leslie Richard *management educator*
Fousse, Jean-Louis Michel *management executive*
Foxman, Boris *consulting company executive, financial advisor*
Frame, Lawrence Milven, Jr. *inventor*
Franck, Antoine Maurice *marketing executive*
Frank, Michael John *training and development company executive*
Frank, Robert Allen *advertising executive*
Frank, William Fielding *computer systems design executive, consultant*
Frankenfeld, Miguel Harry *information specialist, journalist*
Franklin, Benjamin Barnum *dinner club executive*
Fransson, Ivar S.F. *marketing professional*
Fraser, John Foster *management company executive*
Frear, Jon S. *pet services company executive*
Freidheim, Cyrus F., Jr. *management consultant*
Freij, Ghassan Jamil *executive*
Freitas, Luis Carlos da Conceicao *computer company executive*
Fremon, Richard C. *retired infosystems specialist*
French, Michael Bruce *marketing consultant*
Freund, Ronald S. *management consultant, marketing company executive*
Friedman, Maria Andre *public relations executive*
Friedman, Marla Lee *media and investor relations coordinator*
Fries, Thomas *company executive, physicist*
Froessl, Horst Waldemar *business executive, data processing developer*
Fuchs, Andreas *marketing manager*
Fuchs, Gregory Oskar *marketing communications executive*
Fuess, Billings Sibley, Jr. *advertising executive*
Fuia, Stelian *business executive*
Fujita, Hiromichi *printing company executive*
Fukuda, Shigeru *business consultant*
Fukuda, Yoshihiro *advertising company executive*
Fulker, Edmund Norman *management consultant*
Fuller, Edwin Daniel *hotel executive*
Fulton, Guy Charles *company executive*
Fulton, Norman Robert *credit manager*
Funakawa, Atsushi *management consultant*
Furcon, John Edward *management and organizational consultant*
Gabbay, Marcel *management consultant*
Gabelgaard, Bent *telecommunications executive*
Gaborit, Ariane *media professional*
Gacnik, Darja *travel agency executive, tourism administrator*
Gagne, Armand Joseph, Jr. *business administration and computer science educator, consultant*
Gagnet, Grace *safety consultant, translator*
Gaither, George Manney *marketing consultant*
Galaly, Enan *corporate executive*
Galbraith, Nanette Elaine Gerks *forensic and management sciences company executive*
Gamble, (George) Alvan *retired marketing consultant, former Canadian government official*
Gandolfo, Robin Ragsdale *management analyst*
Gans, Erna Irene *printing company executive*
Gans, Samuel Myer *temporary employment service executive*
Gao, Hongsheng *data analyst*
Garcia-Cano, Pedro M. *advertising agency executive*
Gärdin, Karl Olov *customer service executive*
Gardner, Mary Josephine *management development consultant*
Gardner, Nord Arling *management consultant administrator*
Garingalao, Carlos Victor, Jr. *glass and aluminum dealer*
Garlick, Stephen Edwin *advertising executive*
Garlot, Joel Jean *consulting firm executive*
Garnaut, Michelle Anne *restaurateur*
Gart, Herbert Steven *communications executive, producer*
Gartner, Joseph Charles *business systems administrator*
Garvin, Florence Ward *management consultant*
Gasper, Richared Joseph *printing company executive*
Gates, Bill (III William Henry Gates) *software company executive*
Gaucher, Donald Holman *public opinion research company executive*
Gaw, Robert Bruce *sales executive*
Gawler, Ross Andrew *consulting company director*
Gazay, Henry G. *company executive*
Geary, David Leslie *communications executive, educator, consultant*
Geary, Patrick Joseph *naval security administrator*
Geisler, Johannes Andreas *hospitality service professional*
Geller, Robert James *advertising agency executive*
Gellert, Edward Bradford *advertising agency executive*
Genders, Keith Duncan *winery proprietor, viticulturist*
Georgieva, Vesselina *marketing executive, consultant*
Ger, Güliz *marketing/consumer research educator, researcher*
Gerstner, Lonise *Internet company executive*
Ghaffar, Mohammad Asif *food service executive*
Ghaith, Hisham Ahmad *management professional, mechanical engineer*
Ghatalia, Kim Shah *management consultant*

Ghazal, Michel process negotiation consultant, mediator
Ghazal, Samir Saaduddin human resources professional
Giammetti, Luca fashion company marketing professional
Giannakis, Ioannis Stavrou information systems specialist, educator
Gibbons, Robert Philip management consultant
Gidwitz, Teri Lynne marketing professional
Giffin, Margaret Ethel (Peggy Giffin) management consultant
Gilbert, Douglas Wayne environmental services administrator, inspector
Gilder, Richard Earl clinical information system administrator, data analyst
Gill, Roger William Thomas leadership specialist
Gillice, Sondra Jupin (Mrs. Gardner Russell Brown) sales and marketing executive
Gilmore, Fiona Catherine consultant
Gilmore, Jennifer A.W. computer specialist, educator
Gilpatric, Lawrence hospitality management educator
Gior, Fino (Serafino Giordano) electrology company executive
Gjurić Smrevar, Iva deputy director
Glacel, Barbara Pate management consultant
Glassman, Jon David business executive
Gleeson, Dermot James construction company executive
Glémet, François Jean management consultant
Glines, Stephen Ramey software industry executive
Gluzman, Paula human resources administrator, orgnization consultant
Gobba, Mostafa Abdelhakim Mamdouh marketing professional
Goedings, Eduard Clemens Maria sales professional
Goh, Kuang Huah business consulting company administrator
Gokhale, Srikant operations manager, management consultant
Goldberg, Pamela Winer business manager
Golden, James Leslie information technology executive
Goldfarb, Muriel Bernice marketing and advertising consultant
Goldin, Ian Andrew executive
Goldin, Jacob Isaak software executive
Gomez, Francis D(ean) corporate executive, former foreign service officer
Gonzalez, Richard quality performance professional
Goodacre, Jason Dean informations system specialist
Goode, Charles Barrington company director
Goodson, Frederick Brian business consultant
Goralski, Donald John public relations executive, counselor
Gordon, Judith communications consultant, writer
Gore, Prasanna management consultant
Gorman-Gordley, Marcie Sothern personal care industry franchise executive
Gornall, Alastair Charles public relations executive
Gorup, Gregory James marketing executive
Gosper, Brett advertising agency executive
Gosselin, Derrick-Philippe business company executive
Gould, R(ichard) Martin (Richard Martin Goldman) marketing consultant, researcher
Gould, Taffy Internet company executive, real estate executive
Govare, Pierre marketing professional
Gow, Neil Milne executive
Grafstrom, Nils E.G. pulp and paper industry company executive
Graham, David Maxwell computer company executive
Granath, Per Magnus Internet business executive
Grant, Nancy Marie marketing professional, journalist
Greco, Adolph Mario retired management consultant
Green, RuthAnn marketing and management consultant
Greenberg, Lenore public relations professional
Green-Dorsey, Jean Audrey information systems executive
Greene, Edward Allen retired public affairs executive
Gretz, Karl Frederick training consultant, writer
Greve, Henrich Rollef management educator, researcher
Grey, George Christopher technology company executive
Griesche, Robert Price hospital purchasing executive
Griffin-Rollo, Jean (Barbara Jean Griffin-Rollo) marketing professional
Griffith, Clark Dexter risk management professional
Griffith, Gary Ernest public affairs executive
Griggs, Emma management executive
Grigsby, Marvell A., Jr. security company administrator, consultant
Grimes, Colin management consultant
Grimes-Frederick, Dorothea D. communications executive
Grimsell, Colin Peter hotel executive, consultant
Grisi, Jean-Yves sales and marketing executive
Grobler, Jan Petras company executive
Groen, Bernie Gerardus computer specialist
Grose, Vernon Leslie corporation executive
Gross, Franck René Claude marketing professional
Gross, Laura Ann marketing and communications professional, acupuncturist, herbalist
Gross, Patrick Walter business executive, management consultant
Gross, Stanley Carl marketing consultant
Gross, Susan Lynn administrative assistant
Grubbs, Conway E. marine company executive
Gruol, Mary Catherine Schuetz human resources executive
Gruss, Ralf strategy consultant
Gualazzini, Giuseppe Ernesto human resources executive
Guan, Joseph Seng Kee corporate trainer, consultant
Guan, Ming product development manager
Guarno, Peter Gary consumer products company executive
Guerrero, Jose advertising executive
Guers, Christian Alain information systems specialist
Guez, Jean-Claude management consultant
Guichard, Andre Pierre direct mail order executive
Guida, Pat information broker, literature chemist
Guido, Gianluigi consumer researcher, consultant
Guijun, Zhuang marketing specialist, educator
Guinier, Daniel security firm executive
Gulledge, Sandra Smith publicist
Gulliksson, Anders Gunnar executive search firm executive
Gülsoy, Tanses Yasemin advertising agency executive
Gunnarsson, Magnus consulting company executive, economist

Gustafson, Eric William business consultant, conservationist
Gustafsson Hempel, Christina jewelry company executive
Gutthal, Stephan Dirk management consultant
Guy, Keith William Arthur marketing professional, engineering executive
Gyll, John Sören company executive
Haar, Ana Maria Fernández advertising and public relations executive
Haarman, Herman Roelof management consultant, real estate advisor
Habanec, Ivan Paul management consultant
Hacek, Laura I. Garcia administrative assistant
Haddad, Edmonde Alex public affairs executive
Hadisuwarno, Rudy Harsojo hairstylist, educator
Hadley, Paul Burrest, Jr. (Tabbit Hadley) domestic engineer
Haeffner, Erik Axel executive
Hagenbuch, Rodney Dale computer company executive, financial consultant
Hai, Syed M. Abdul executive
Haigh, Robert William business administration educator
Haines, David H. consulting executive
Hairald, Burney LeShawn (Shawn Hairald) marketing professional
Haizet, Patrick Felix management consultant
Hakoshima, Shin-ichi business executive
Hale, David Fredrick health care company executive
Hall, Christopher George Longden management consultant
Hall, Pamela S. environmental consulting firm executive
Hall, Roger David management consultant, educator
Halley, Paul-Louis food service executive
Hallissey, Michael strategic consultant
Halloran, Mike software company executive, music publishing executive
Halt, James George advertising executive, graphic designer
Hambleton, George Blow Elliott management consultant
Hamdy, Ihab Abdel Hamid business manager
Hammann, Peter J.C. management and marketing educator
Hammond-Parker, Stephen business executive
Hamper, Robert Joseph marketing executive
Hampson, Thomas R. investigations company executive
Hamway, Sary M. management consultant
Hamza, Milos hotel executive
Han, Youngyearl communication theory educator
Hanauer, Carl Morton storage company executive
Hancock, William Frank, Jr. management consultant
Handa, Junichi management consultant
Handel, William Keating advertising and sales executive
Hangen, William J. retired business executive
Hannaford, Peter Dor public relations executive, writer
Hannum, David Lawrence business consultant, training specialist
Hansen, H. Jack management consultant
Hansford, Stephen John marketing executive
Hanson, Diane Charske management consultant
Hanson, Lord James Edward industrialist
Hanton, E. Michael public and personnel relations consultant
Hardie, George Graham casino executive
Harding, Wayne Edward, III software company executive, accountant
Hardjo, Eliezer Hernawan business and educational consultant
Hardwich, Gerald Carlton marketing research executive
Hardy, David William executive
Harencak, Paul, III quality assurance professional
Hargrave, Robert Warren hair styling salon chain executive
Hargreaves, David William communications company executive
Harker, Debra P. marketing educator
Harkness, R. Kenneth restaurant chain executive
Harlan, Raymond Carter communication executive, writer, consultant
Harley, Ian executive
Harrer, Klaus Dieter management consultant
Harrigan, Richard George salesperson
Harrington, Peter Tyrus emergency management company executive, public relations consultant, author, photographer
Harrington, Robert Dudley, Jr. printing company executive
Harris, James Ridout retired communications executive
Harris, Mark Stephen telecommunications executive
Harris, Susan A. travel agent
Harris, Thomas Sarafen management consultant
Harrison, David J. sales professional
Harrison, Derek retired personal care industry executive, inventor, journalist
Harrison, Judith Anne human resources executive
Harvan, Sean C. marketing executive
Harvey, Susan company executive
Hasan, Masood company executive
Hasapis, Xenophon marketing professional
Hasegawa, Hiroshi marketing professional educator
Hashem, Hashem Hussein computer systems executive
Haskell, Paul Heger executive recruitment company executive
Hasner, Rolf Kaare management consultant
Hastings, David John management consultant
Hata, Ira Francis technology company executive
Hatcher, Joe Branch executive search consulting company executive
Hatfield, Jessica Lynn media company executive
Hatzialexandrou, Elena leisure center director
Haug, Thomas Peter communications executive
Hauser, Thomas marketing executive
Hausman, William Ray fund raising and management consultant
Havass, Miklós computer company executive
Hawes, Justin Alexander corporate executive
Hawthorne, Nan Louise Internet resources consultant, web designer, writer, editor
Hay, Julie training company executive
Hayden, Harrold Harrison information company executive
Hayes, Cynthia Ann administrative assistant, writer
Hayes, Eric James consulting company executive
Hayman, James Leslie Baddock executive search consultant
Hays, Diana Joyce Watkins consumer products company executive
Hayward-Williams, Carolyn Rose management and technology consultant

Haywood, Roger communications executive
Hazard, Christopher Wedvik international business executive
He, Susan Li business development executive
Heath, Ernie Thomas tourism management educator
Heatter, Joseph John material handler
Heck, Debra Upchurch information technology, procurement professional
Heeb, Hans-Rudolf software company executive
Heick, Leon Joseph data processing executive
Heidkamp, Mary Louise leadership management consultant
Heimbuch, Susanne Sebesta public relations, marketing executive
Heinamann, Paul Lindsay non-executive director of companies
Heinig, Norman Thomas consulting company executive
Helstein, Ivy Rae communications executive, psychotherapist, writer
Hemphill, William Alfred, III marketing executive
Hemsing, Josephine Claudia public relations professional for performing arts
Henderson, George Poland publisher
Henderson, James Gary marketing executive
Hendrickson, William George business executive
Hengels, Charles Francis management consultant, educator
Henley, Terry Lew computer company executive
Henning, William Clifford cemetery consulting company executive
Henninot, Jean-Pierre information systems specialist
Henry, Philip Lawrence marketing professional
Henry, Richard Charles communications executive
Henslowe, Philip Francis public relations and training consultant
Hentschel, Eberhardt Cedric cultural relations administrator
Hentsell, David management consultant
Heptinstall, Debra Lou marketing professional
Herbert, Marilynne public relations executive, freelance photographer
Herbits, Stephen Edward strategic consultant
Herford, Mark John communications executive
Hergenhan, Joyce public relations executive
Hering, Solange training business consultant
Herndon, John Laird consulting firm executive
Hershey, Colin Harry management consultant
Hetzel, Patrick Louis marketing educator
Heuer, Martin temporary services executive
Heuser, Gerd technical inspection company researcher, educator
Heuskel, Dieter consulting company executive
Heydrick, Linda Carol consulting company executive, editor
Heyerdahl, Jens P. business executive
Heyninck, Jean-Marie personnel executive
Hezir, Joseph S. energy and environmental company executive
Hick, Kenneth William marketing company executive
Hickey, Elizabeth Louise advertising agency executive, limousine company executive
Hickman, Charles Wallace Internet executive
Hicks, Roger George information systems consultant, educator
Hickson, Gary Wayne communications executive
Higgens, William John, III (Trey Higgens) sales executive
Highsmith, Anna Bizzell executive secretary
Hildebrand, Theodor Lorenz software and service company executive, consultant
Hildebrandt, Frederick Dean, Jr. management consultant
Hildebrandt, Janelle Diner sales executive
Hill, La Joyce Carmichael marketing professional
Hill, Larkin Payne real estate company data processing executive
Hill, Lawrence Sidney management educator
Hine, Scott Terrence business executive
Hinner, Paul Georg sales executive
Hinson, Robert William advertising executive, consultant
Hinz, Shirley Sorensen administrative secretary
Hirahara, Patti public relations executive
Hirano, Ko store automation, import/export company executive
Hirvelä, Antti Juhani (Jussi Hirvelä) marketing professional
Hixon, Robin Ray food service executive, writer
Hjorth, Niels environmental service company executive
Hochhalter, Gordon Ray advertising communications executive
Hochman, Judith L. executive recruiter
Hochreiter, John Allen computer company owner, firefighter
Hock, Morton entertainment advertising executive
Hodara, Ralph Leon consulting company executive
Hofert, Jack consulting company executive, lawyer
Hoffman, Darnay Robert management consultant
Hoffman, Fred L. human resources professional
Hoffman, Janet N. psychic counselor
Hofmeyr, Jan Hendrik marketing professional
Hofrichter, David Alan management consultant
Hogeland, Richard Wright executive, lawyer
Høie, Tore A. management consultant
Holcepl, James Robert sales professional
Hollander, Lawrence Jay marketing executive
Hollar, Michael John customer service representative
Hollinshead, Alan George company executive, financial advisor
Holmes, Robert Wayne service executive, consultant, biological historian
Holsgrove, Gareth John consultant
Holub, Jan Hubert radioactive waste company executive
Holwell, Peter management consultant
Hood, Alastair Sheridan product manager
Hook, Michael John advertising executive
Hoover, Lola Mae retired communications company executive
Hope, Gerri Danette telecommunications management executive
Horner, Harry Charles, Jr. sales executive, theatrical and film consultant
Hornstein, Florian Freiherr von advertising executive
Horowitz, Joseph marketing professional
Hoskie, Lorraine consumer products representative, poet
Hosoya, Yasuo management consultant
Hosri, Fernand Antoine corporate executive
Hossain, Mohammed Musharaf business management educator
Houtzagers, Gys business consultant
Hovell, Simon Alexander systems consultant
Hoving, John Hannes Forester consulting firm executive

Howard, Eric Sevan conservationist, environmental manager
Howe, John Kingman manufacturing, sales and marketing executive
Howes, Alfred S. business and insurance consultant
Howlett, Stephanie Ann home care equipment sales representative, nurse
Huang, Jian Ping company executive
Huber, Clayton Lloyd marketing professional, engineer, construction executive
Huda, Mirza Najmul development and management specialist
Hudson, Edward Voyle linen supply company executive
Hudson, Stanton Harold, Jr. public relations executive, educator
Huff, Dennis Lyle marketing professional
Huff, Richard G. recreational facility administrator
Huff, Ricky Wayne sales executive
Huff, Russell Joseph public relations and publishing executive
Hughes, Craig Martin management consultant
Huidobro, Fernando López marketing professional
Huizer, Jos marketing professional, consultant
Hull, LeAnne von Neumeyer public relations and communications executive, research consultant, writer
Hulse, Robert Douglas high technology executive
Hulseberg, Paul David financial executive, educator
Hultin, Sven Olof consulting company executive
Hultman, Gunnar W. communications consultant
Hunjan, Taljeet Singh hotel executive, consultant
Hunsberger, Roger Moore web developer, writer, lumber company executive
Hunt, Garry Edward management consultant
Hunt, Martha sales executive, researcher
Hunt, Robert William Gainer color consultant, educator
Hunter, Douglas Lee media executive, former elevator company executive
Hunter, John Hilton telecommunications company executive
Hunter, Leland Clair, Jr. management consultant
Hunter, William John European commission director
Hur, Jin Ho high technology company executive
Hurlock, James Bickford, III marketing executive
Husain, Ajmal marketing consultant
Husband, William Swire computer industry executive
Husted, William Armstrong sales executive
Hutcherson, Christopher Alfred marketing, recruiting and educational fundraising executive
Hutcheson, Jerry Dee manufacturing company executive
Hutchinson, Jerry James medical products executive
Hutton, Winfield Travis management consultant, educator
Huypens, Jozef Maria Alfons communication consultant
Iatropoulos, Theodore technical consultant
Ibarra, Silvia marketing professional
Ibn Alfred, Shareef marketing professional
Ichikawa, Tadayuki language institute executive
Ido, Yoshimitsu communication company executive
Iglehart, Patricia Ann strategy and market planning executive
Ignat, Adorian Nicolae information and telecommunications professional
Ignozzi, Bryan K. management consultant
Ikeo, Kyoichi marketing researcher, educator
Ilson, Bernard public relations executive
Imbardelli, Amedeo Patrick marketing professional
Imming, Marie Elizabeth public relations professional
Ingersoll, Ted Meriam advertising executive
Ingham, Kenneth Dale communication educator
Ingle, Sud Ranganath management consultant
Iordanow, Paul Stanislas marketing professional
Ip, Francis hotel executive
Ipekci, Ahmet holding company executive
Irazustabarrena, Miguel Angel marketing professional
Irvine, William Burriss management consultant
Irving, Jeffrey Alan management consultant, educator, lawyer
Irwin, Linda Belmore marketing consultant
Ishikawa, Kosuke management consultant
Ishizaka, Kazuyoshi electronics company executive
Ismiel, Mothafar Abdul-Ghafoor marketing professional
Itami, Yoshihiko communications executive
Ivanitz, John Michael operations supervisor
Iyengar, Narayana Rangachar administrator, researcher
Iyer, Viswanath advertising company executive
Jackson, Elijah, Jr. communication executive
Jackson, Patrick John public relations counsel, editor, author, public speaker
Jacobs, Alicia Melvina account executive
Jacobs, Ivor Mark administrator
Jacobs, Richard Alan management consultant
Jaffe, Jay M. company executive, management consultant
Jaggernauth, Rabindra management consultant
Jain, Ranjan executive
Jain, Vijay Prakash international marketing executive
Jakacki, Diane Katherine web production and marketing executive
Jamard, Michel Hubert corporate communications specialist
Janczak, Andrew Anthony executive
Jans, Robert Maciej environmental company executive, consultant
Janssen, Herman marketing and sales executive
Jardim, Luis Eduardo electronics industry executive
Jasinski-Caldwell, Mary L. company executive
Javeri, Sultanali Mahomedali fire protection consultant
Jeffrey, Francis software developer, forecaster
Jenkins, Bernard Louis parking lot company executive, consultant
Jenkins, William E. business executive
Jennings, Wirt Holman, Jr. retired marketing executive
Jensen, Beverly Ann communications specialist
Jernigan, Alvin, Jr. retired automobile sales executive
Jeyasothy, Selvadurai hotelier, actor
Jiménez, Blanca waste water treatment specialist, researcher
Jiménez-Beltran, Domingo executive
Jimenez Lora, Felix Antonio tourist company executive
Jinadu, Yusuf management consultant
Joaquim, Richard Ralph hotel executive
Jobs, Steven Paul computer corporation executive
Joffe, Barbara Lynne computer management professional, computer artist
Johansen, Sharon Frances tourism company executive

Maltese, Giulio information technology company professional, historian of science
Manara, James Anthony software executive, consultant
Mancel, Claude Paul household product company executive
Mandabach, Keith H. chef, educator
Mank, Edward Warren marketing professional
Mankarious, Ramsey N. hotel developer
Mantegazza, Sergio executive
Manuel, Vivian public relations executive
Mapps, Desmond James information science educator, researcher
Marchant, Frank Richard database administrator, state official
Marcovitch, Myles Joseph human resources executive
Marder, Carol advertising specialist and premium firm executive
Marenghi, Alberto business executive
Mareth, Paul David communications consultant
Marighetti, Luca P. business executive
Mark, Reuben consumer products company executive
Markham, Stephen Keith management consultant, educator
Marquis, Ronald James sales executive
Marriott, John Willard, Jr. lodging and senior living executive
Marsden, Andrew Charles marketing professional
Marsh, Mary Elizabeth Taylor recreation administrator, dietician, nutritionist
Marshall, Allen Wright, III communications executive, financial consultant
Marten, Lutz information management specialist
Martin, Claude Raymond, Jr. marketing consultant, educator
Martin, Donald James marketing professional
Martin, Karine Aline quality assurance professional
Martin, Raymond Edward management consultant
Martinen, John A. travel company executive
Martinez, Andre Georges Joseph corporate officer
Martinez, Arthur C. retail company executive
Martinez, Jose Maria business executive
Martino, Donna Frances newspaper sales administrator
Maruyama, Fumihiro computer company executive, researcher
Maruyama, Koyo marketing consultant
Marwaha, Jay management consultant
Marzloff, Georges M. management company executive
Masayoshi, Son Internet company executive
Mason, Craig Watson corporate planning executive
Massacane, Armando Luis communications company executive, consultant
Masselos, Vassilis business executive
Massey, William Walter, Jr. sales executive
Masterson Raines, Judith Amanda marketing executive
Mathis, Donald Hilliard chief operating officer, naval reserve officer
Mathis, Jack David advertising executive
Mathis, Laurelle Sheedy executive recruiter, volunteer
Mathon, Stephane Roger data processing company executive
Matisonn, Joanne Rona executive secretary
Matsuura, Koichiro business executive
Matthew, Lyn sales and marketing executive consultant
Matys, Václav communications company executive, journalist
Mauck, William M., Jr. executive recruiter, small business owner
Maul, Arthur Benjamin management consultant
Maurandy, Jean-Pierre J. sales professional
Maurice, Don personal care industry executive
Mayer, Charles Arthur management consultant, musician
Mayo, Louis Allen corporation executive
Mazzarella, Rosemary Louise business administration executive
McBride, Thomas Dwayne management consultant
McCallum, Emma Margaret sales executive
McCarthy, Daniel William management consultant
McCarthy, John Gilman, Jr. international executive search consultant
McClain, Thomas Emerson communications executive
McConnell, Gary Albert business executive, research consultant
McConnell, John Howard personnel management consultant, writer
McConnell, John Hunter marketing professional
McConnell, Malachy James programme executive
McCoy, William Earl, Jr. economic development training consultant
McCrae, Sean Christoph project manager
McCree, Paul William, Jr. systems design and engineering company executive
McCreight, Susan Buckley human resources executive
McCrickard, Eric Eugene customer service representative
McCullen, Michael John advertising executive
McCullough, Richard Lawrence advertising agency executive
McCully, Patrick William campaign director
McDade, James Russell management consultant
McDonald, Ian Archie sugar company executive, writer
McDonald, Peggy Ann Stimmel retired automobile company official
McFarland, Walter Gerard management consultant
McGervey, Teresa Ann technical information specialist
McGuire, John W., Sr. advertising executive, marketing professional, author
McGuire, Michael William communications executive
McIntosh, Amy Bennett telecommunications company executive
McIvor, Lee public relations consultant
McKelvey, Gerald public relations executive
McKenzie, Donald Cyril management consultant
McKeown, Lorraine Laredo travel company executive, writer
McLaren, Archie Campbell, Jr. marketing executive
McLaren, Karen Lynn advertising executive
McLarty, Thomas F., III (Mack McLarty) business executive
McLean, Ephraim Rankin information systems educator
McLean, Michael Johnson quality assurance professional
McMahon, Robert Lee, Jr. (Bob McMahon) semi-retired investor, retired aerospace and information systems executive
McMillan, Helen Berneice sales executive
McMiller, Anita Williams logistics management consultant
McMurray, David Gordon compliance and financial regulation expert
McMurry, William Mortimer retired sales executive
McWhorter, Sharon Louise business executive, inventor, consultant
Meador, Charles Lawrence management and systems consultant, educator
Meads, Donald Edward management services company executive
Means, Rosaline business executive, business educator
Mecke, William Moyn public affairs consultant
Medin, A. Louis computer company executive
Medin, Lowell Ansgard management executive
Medney, Tania Levy advertising agency executive
Meeker, David Anthony public relations executive
Megyer, Ors communication company executive
Mehan, Julie Ellen information systems specialist, consultant
Mehraj, Muhammad Ilyas company executive
Mehta, Narinder Kumar marketing executive
Mehta, Nirbhay Kumar computer software developer
Meinrath, Günther nuclear waste disposal consultant
Meira, Dilmar Malheiros telecommunications executive, system engineer, consultant, researcher, educator
Meis, Nancy Ruth marketing and development executive
Meleshko, Evgueni Alekseevich electronician
Mellendorf, Patricia Jean retired personnel professional
Mendelevich, Tamara Maria secretary, accountant
Menefee, Frederick Lewis advertising executive
Menton, Arthur Francis information services specialist
Mercer, James Lee management consultant
Merkuryev, Yuri computer modeling and simulation and industrial logistics managment educator
Merna, Gerald Francis advertising executive, retired marine officer, retired postal executive
Merritt, Joe Frank industrial supply executive
Messner, Sabine technology executive
Metzdorff, Carl Heinrich executive search executive
Metzger, Catherine Z. global marketing administrator
Meyer-Hentschel, Gundolf management consultant, futurist
Miano, James Gikonyo information systems specialist
Michaels, Alan J. safety, occupational health and training executive
Miclat, Augusto Nelmida, Jr. business executive
Middleton, John Albert retired communications executive
Miles, Francis James management consultant
Miles, Ray telecommunications executive, educator
Miller, Beverly marketing consultant
Miller, Dwight Richard personal care industry executive, cosmetologist, consultant
Miller, Joseph Alfred printing executive
Miller, Lia Verena Reyes management services executive
Miller, Luther Gordon, III tourism executive
Miller, Mary Jeannette office management specialist
Miller, Randy M. marketing professional
Miller, Susan Janet business educator, researcher
Milligan, Robert Lee, Jr. computer company executive
Mills, Carol Margaret business consultant, public relations consultant
Mills, Lois Jean company executive, former legislative aide, former education educator
Milo, Hjalmar Taeke arbiter, forensic data processing auditor
Mimikos, Michail George marketing, advertising agency executive
Minasi, Anthony software company executive
Mindin, Vladimir Yudovich information systems specialist, chemist, educator
Minkler, Blate Jones information technology consultant
Minner, Thomas O. marketing executive
Miracle, Gordon Eldon advertising educator
Miranda, Brinston Adrian communications executive, management consultant
Miscovich, Peter John consulting company executive
Mitchell, Andrew John advertising agency executive
Mitchell, Lee Mark communications executive, investment fund manager, lawyer
Mitchum, Beth bookstore manager, freelance editor, author
Mitelman, Bonnie Cossman editor, writer, lecturer
Mitman, Stewart Phipard retired purchasing officer
Mitrany, Devora marketing consultant, writer
Mizer, Richard Anthony technology company executive
Modi, Jagdish Jamnadas computer company executive
Moe, Ronald Chesney public administration researcher
Moehring, Fred Adolf fastener distribution company executive
Moeller, Robert Charles (Bud Moeller) management consultant
Mogensen, Charles Ray, Jr. food service administrator
Mohammad Mokhtar, Haitham Kamal food services executive
Mohammed, Hussein Raafat public relations executive
Moitra, Deependra software company executive, researcher
Mokwena, Cisco Frans Lesuira promotions company executive
Möller, Henrik Einar business executive, acoustics consultant
Molz, Philip Jack management consultant
Monclaro, Antonio Carlos Menna Barreto communications security company executive
Monplaisir, Malcolm Harold maintenance and management specialist
Montemayor, Carlos Rene advertising executive
Montes, Jorge Aramayo consulting company executive
Moore, Bob Stahly communications executive
Moore, Helen Lucille recruiting company executive
Moore, Justin Edward data processing executive
Moore, Linda Kathleen personnel agency executive
Moore, Patricia Chandler hair stylist
Moore, William Grover, Jr. management consultant, former air freight executive, former air force officer
Morales, Gustavo Adolfo business executive
Morano, Gerard John marketing executive
Morden, John Reid security-business intelligence company executive
Moreira, Marcio Martins advertising executive
Morgan, Alan William management consultant
Morgan, Anthony John health, safety and environmental executive
Morgan, Gary Cordell market research company executive
Morgan, Marianne corporate professional
Morgan, Robert Edward marketing and strategic management educator, consultant
Morice, William Daniel business and tax counselor
Morison, Niall Maclaine business executive
Moriyama, Hiroyoshi technical institute administrator
Morley, Roger Hubert company executive, consultant
Morosanu, Ion-Christian management executive
Morozov, Vladimir P. communications professional
Morrione, Melchior S. management consultant, accountant
Morris, Frederick William (Fred William Morris) technology management executive
Morrow, Monty Ramsey marketing and advertising executive
Moszkowicz, Virginia Marie quality administrator
Motlatle, Reshoketswe Maria human resources executive, psychologist
Mowbray, Robert Norman natural resource management consultant, ecologist
Mracky, Ronald Sydney marketing and promotion executive, travel consultant
Muccini, Gianni communications executive
Mueller, William Glennon, Jr. recruiting company executive
Mueller-Heumann, Guenther emeritus educator, business advisor
Muganga, Albert business executive
Müller, Klaus-Jürgen advertising executive
Mulligan, Timothy Hayden public relations executive, writer
Mulondo, Larry Yawe management consultant, educator, researcher
Mulvey, Gerald John telecommunication engineering administrator, meteorologist educator
Muniain, Javier P. computer software company executive, theoretical physicist, researcher
Mura, Gérard Paul Pacifique company executive
Murage, Stanley Karuthai quantity surveyor
Murayama, Michiko executive
Murphy, Dennis Patrick hotel business entrepreneur
Murphy, Randall Kent training consultant
Murphy, Robert search firm executive
Murphy, Robert Blair management consulting company executive
Murray, Graeme Douglas travel company executive
Murray, Lawrence management consultant
Murthy, Narayana N.R. software company executive
Musich, Robert Lorin motivational speaker
Mwanza, Frederick Kamnongona management consultant
Myers, Carol McClary retired sales administrator, editor
Myers, Mary A. public relations executive, consultant
Nabil, Mohamed computer company executive, legal consultant
Nag, Rajendra Gopal aerospace technology and management adviser
Nagazumi, Yasuo electronics researcher, software company executive
Nagpurkar, Ajit Dattatreya management consultant
Naimark, George Modell marketing and management consultant
Nakazawa, Takao marketing professional
Naor, Daniel management consultant
Napuk, Kerry F. management executive
Naqshband, Ghulam travel and tourism company executive
Naquin, Patricia Elizabeth employee assistance consultant
Narita, Yutaka advertising executive
Nascimento, José Pedro communications company executive
Nasim, Yousaf executive
Naylor, John Thomas telephone company executive
Nebenzahl, Israel D. marketing and business educator
Neel, Elisabeth company director
Neff, Thomas Joseph executive search firm executive
Nehra, Sanjeev consulting company executive
Neiman, Norman aerospace business and marketing executive
Neisen, Hans Josef management consultant
Neiser, Brent Allen public affairs and personal finance consultant, speaker
Nekman, Donald John communications company executive
Nelson, Robert Eddinger management and development consultant
Nelson, Walter Henry communications consultant, author
Nelson-Walker, Roberta management software company executive
Nemenyi, Ben aerospace marketing company executive
Nerney, Amanda Elizabeth management trainer and coach
Nesbitt, Veronica A. management executive
Neu, Carl Herbert, Jr. management consultant
Neukirchen, Kajo industry executive
Neuman, Robert Harold communication executive
Neumann, Linda Kay marketing executive
Neurgaonkar, Milind Madhukar information systems manager
Neuschel, Robert Percy management consultant, educator
Neveux, Denis marketing executive
Neville, Thomas Lee food service company executive
Nevling, Harry Reed human resources consultant
New, Anne Latrobe public relations, fund raising executive
Newcomb-Hodgetts, Barry John media company executive
Newkirk, Raymond Leslie management consultant
Newman, Geraldine Anne advertising executive, inventor
Newman, Paul Joseph communications executive
Newton, Hugh C. public relations executive
Neyeloff, Alejo travel agency executive
Ngcobo, Thembekile Thelma human resources executive
Nickerson, Richard Gorham research company executive
Nicolson, John Alick business executive
Niechoy, Detlev Heinz Thomas fiscal officer
Niefeld, Jaye Sutter advertising executive
Nielsen, Louisa Augusta broadcast association executive
Nielsen-Jones, Ian Richard lottery and gaming executive
Nienhaus, Adrianus Gerardus information technology company executive
Nijnens, Frans Andreas Maria marketing executive
Nikogiannis, Nikolas Stylianos food company executive
Nilsson, Per Gustan Ragnar business executive, management consultant
Nir, Raphael communication educator
Nishi, Hitoshi corporate communications consultant, critic
Nishioka, Shuzo environmental systems analyst
Nishita, Eiji management consultant, planning executive
Nnolim, Dorothy Adaku E. management consultant, educator
Noel, Trey Leonard, III strategic planning executive
Nogueira, Carlos Maia computer company executive
Nojarov-Isselhard, Roland Michailov management consultant
Nolan, Garry Francis company director and secretary
Norden, Karl Elis management consultant
Norfolk, David Hugh business executive, consultant
Norlin, Malcolm Carl leasing company executive
Normie, Lawrence Robert technologist
Norris, Tracy Hopkins retired public relations executive
Notowidigdo, Pri executive search consultant
Novak, Andreas Robert acoustic consultant, educator
Novak, Gregory marketing professional
Novotny, Deborah A. management consultant
Nowe, Dennis Anthony chef
Nowik, Henry Ian marketing executive, consultant
Nue, Steen management educator, consultant
Nuzzo, Anthony Gerald banking executive
Nyberg, Riitta Helinä communications and advertising manager
Nyer, Raymond Jean Pierre quality and environment executive
Nyide, Thabisile Gracious communications company executive
Nziramasanga, Chenjerai Samboku marketing professional
Oakley, Wanda Faye management consultant, educator
Oates, Jeremy John management consultant
Obermayer, Michael Erik Max management consultant
Obot, Patrick Enefiok workshop manager
O'Brien, Mary Devon communications executive, consultant
Obudho, Robert Abackuck communications company executive
Ocansey, Aaron Akrofi game designer
Ochs, Robert Hanson marketing professional
O'Connor, Betty Lou service executive
O'Connor, James Patrick Mel advertising agency director
Oda, Chikashi consultant
Oda, Jun hotel company executive
O'Dea, Sandra Renee sales professional
Ödman, Claes Sture Bertil communications company executive
O'Donoghue, Daniel Francis advertising agency executive
O'Dwyer, Tony corporate secretary, accountant
Ogbechie, Chris Ike marketing consulting executive
Ohi, Yoshiharu consulting company executive
Ohnishi, Minoru film company executive
Ohrt, Karsten company executive
Oka, Milind Madhukar information systems specialist
Okada, Hideaki information technology company executive
Okada, Takuya retail executive
Okafor, Okechukwu Michael Chukwu forwarding agency executive
Okamura, Tadashi business executive
Okemwa, Obiri Luke purchasing agent, consultant
Okenfuss, Ronald Joseph brand manager
Okrepilov, Vladimir Valentinovich business executive, quality management specialist
Oku, Shoichiro sales and marketing executive
Okubote, Amos Olakunle computer company executive, consultant
Olbrick, Valerie Lyn management consultant, information technologist
Oldham, Christopher Russell communications executive
Oler, Wesley Marion, IV executive
Oliver, Bruce Lawrence information systems specialist, educator
Oliver-Simon, Gloria Craig human resources advisor, consultant, lawyer
Olman, Maryellen human resources administrator
Olson, Donald George computer services administrator
Olson, Jeanne Innis technology and technical management executive
Olstead, Christopher Eric consulting executive, talent manager
Olujobi, Tola Abimbola advertising and marketing executive
Oppedahl, Phillip Edward computer company executive
Oppenheim, Robert beauty industry executive
Orlu, Levent Özcan business executive, management consultant
O'Rourke, Vincent John management consultant
Ortinau, David Joseph marketing specialist, educator
Ortiz Santoscoy, Raul human resources consultant
Osawa, Paula Mariani trading company executive
Osborne-Gollop, Margaret Beverley administrator
O'Shea, Lynne management consultant, educator
Otero, Kevin A. consumer products executive
Otsubo, Mayumi management educator, writer, commentator
Otto, Michael sales executive
Ottone, Jorge Antonio marketing management executive, consultant
Oudendijk, Alex P. communications executive
Ouellet, André business executive
Overgard, Robert Shawn database marketing professional
Ovitz, Michael S. communications executive
Ozaki, George Tadashi patent agent
Ozeki, Tomoyasu outsourcing company executive
Paajanen, Erkki Matti consultant company executive
Padget, John E. management professional
Pai, Tonse Ramesh Upendra business executive
Paintsil, Robert marketing professional
Pajares, Ramon hotel company executive
Palecek, Peter Vaclav management consultant
Paliwoda, Stanley Joseph marketing educator

Palola, Harry Joel *international affairs executive, consultant*
Palom Izquierdo, Francisco Javier *management consultant, educator*
Palumbo, Matthew Aloysius *marketing executive*
Pan, Cheng-Lieh *management executive, educator*
Pant, Muktesh *marketing professional*
Papaconstantinou, Adonis Miltiades *computer company executive*
Papakonstantinou, Zoe *marketing professional*
Parameswaran, Subramanian *tour company executive, accountant*
Parera Biosca, Alberto *business executive*
Paresky, Linda K. *travel company executive*
Park, Roy Hampton, Jr. *advertising executive*
Parkash, Wadia Vikram *hotel facility executive, consultant*
Parke, John Shepard *marketing consultant*
Parker, Diana Lynne *restaurant manager, special events director*
Parkhurst, Edwin Wallace, Jr. *healthcare management consultant*
Parrick, Gerald Hathaway *communications and marketing executive*
Parsons, Andrew John *management consultant*
Partnow, Susan Lee *consultant*
Pasher, Edna *management consultant*
Pashko, Valery Alexander *marketing director*
Passano, E. Magruder, Jr. *corporate philanthropist*
Passantino, Benjamin Arthur *medical marketing executive*
Passmann, John Walter *management consultant*
Patel, Chandra Kumar Naranbhai *communications company executive, educator, researcher*
Pathanasophon, Pornpen *civil service officer*
Pather, Sandy *consultant*
Patra, Eleni *personnel administrator, educator, mediator*
Patri, Erwin *human resources professional*
Patrick, Georgia O'Brien Lakaytis *communications executive*
Patstone, Cheryl *public relations executive*
Patten, Richard E. *personnel company owner*
Patterson, Denis W. *economic development official*
Patton, Warren Andre *public relations executive, journalist*
Paul, Julian Braithwaite *media and entertainment company executive*
Pavone, Gerardo Piero *advertising company executive*
Payne, Gregg Alan *communications consultant, educator*
Payton, Roger Louis *consultant*
Pazos, Walter Adrian *marketing specialist*
Peace, William Henry, III *management consultant*
Peacock, Graham Rex *business, financial consultant*
Pearce, Joan DeLap *research company executive*
Pearson, Clarence Edward *management consultant*
Pearson, Colin Bamford *information systems specialist*
Pearson, David Sadler *management consultant*
Pearson, Jim Berry, Jr. *human resources specialist*
Pearson, John R. Anthony *oil service consultant*
Pearson, Patricia Kelley *marketing representative*
Pechmann, Cornelia Ann Rachel *marketing professional*
Pecht, Shunia *computer professional*
Peck, George Holmes *public relations executive*
Pedersen, Jan Anders *amusement park manager*
Pedersen, Wesley Niels M. *public relations and public affairs executive*
Pedretti, Anthony D. *information systems specialist*
Pekki, Seppo Sakari *power plant worker*
Pellegrini, Alfredo *management consultant*
Peluffo, Franco Vinicio *trade company executive*
Penhall, Geoffrey Kenneth *human resources executive*
Penn-Tonkin, Lewis Montague *retired solicitor*
Pepper, John Ennis, Jr. *consumer products company executive*
Perera, Vimal Marcelline *practicing management consultant, accountant*
Pérez-Salgado, Ignacio *management consultant, educator*
Perier, Philippe *communications executive*
Perkins, James Winslow *international business consultant, builder, contractor*
Perkins, Roger Barton *company director*
Perrett, John Edmund *motel owner, farmer, butcher*
Perrone, Bruce L. *sales executive*
Perry, Sir Michael (Sydney) *industrialist*
Perry, Randall A. *business executive*
Pesec, David John *data systems executive*
Pesola, William Ernest *restaurant management executive*
Peter, Christian *computer company executive*
Peters, LeRoy Richard *materials management consulting company executive*
Peters, Robert James, Sr. *draftsman*
Petersen, Martin Ross *public affairs executive*
Petersen, Maureen Jeanette Miller *management information consultant, former nurse*
Peterson, William Gene *public affairs executive*
Petito, Margaret L. *public relations executive, consultant*
Petropoulos, Stathis *advertising company executive*
Pfeiffer, Leonard, IV *executive recruiter, consultant*
Pfendt, Henry George *retired information systems executive, management consultant*
Pham, Kim *aesthetician*
Phan, Seamus Ching-Chia *technology strategist, educator, consultant, researcher*
Philipsen, Flemming *management consulting executive*
Philpotts, Paul Barrington *public relations consultant*
Phonanan, Tanya *human resources manager*
Picache, Josefina Reyes *travel service company executive, marriage counselor*
Picard, Jacques Jean *retired business development executive*
Pidd, Michael *management science educator, consultant*
Pierguidi, Giuliano Francesco Luciano *logistic services and record management executive*
Pierre-Benoist, Jean (Baron de Vaubuzin) *retired international trade specialist*
Pillai, Palanikkumar Ayasamy *advertising executive*
Pillai, Parmeshwaran Govinda *private detective*
Pine, Martin E. *management consultant, technology consultant*
Pineau-Valencienne, Didier *industrialist*
Pineda, Rosemarie del Rosario *communications executive*
Piñeiro, Enrique Luis *dairy company executive*
Pines, Wayne Lloyd *public relations counselor*
Pinkerton, James Saunders *travel company executive, consultant*
Pinto, Eduardo dos Santos *marketing consultant*
Pinto Araya, John *marketing executive*
Pitayataratorn, Janewit *international business consultant*
Plath, Jennifer Lynn *marketing manager*
Plevyak, Thomas Joseph *communications executive*
Plotch, Walter *management consultant, fund raising counselor*
Plouvier, Philippe Antoine *retired management consultant*
Plunier, Guy Albert *public relations executive*
Poe, Randall Ellsworth *public relations executive, author*
Poggi, Silvano Nicoló *communications company executive*
Polich, John Elliott *marketing consultant, educator, writer*
Polillo, Roberto *software and information technology executive*
Pong, Wai Chung *computer hardware and software research company executive*
Pont, Anthony Michael *management consultant, writer*
Ponte, Carlos Manuel *computer company executive*
Ponzi Kay, Marylou *human resources specialist*
Pope, Lena Elizabeth *human resources specialist*
Popescu, Tiberiu T. *business executive*
Portelli, Vincent George *business executive, consultant*
Porvaznik, Pamela Ann *public relations specialist*
Posada, Juan Emilio *executive*
Posey, Robert B. *marketing and human resources executive*
Poteev, Oleg Gennady *warehouse executive*
Potia, Ismail Fidaali *company executive*
Potter, Lillian Florence *business executive secretary*
Potts, William Frederick *consultant*
Potvin, William Tracey *management consultant*
Poupard-Walbridge, Gloria Patricia *strategic planning consultant*
Pouraryan, Siamak Michael *management consultant*
Povzner, Dmitry Markovich *executive*
Powell, Simon Edward Meredith *management and business consultant*
Powers, David Murphy *consumer products company executive*
Powers, Ronald George *management consultant*
Prashad, Har *company executive, researcher*
Pratley, David Illingworth *management consultant*
Pratt, Alan John *business and marketing consultant*
Preis, Carl Otto *company executive, mechanical engineer*
Prescott Thomas, John Desmond *broadcasting executive, media consultant*
Pressman, Thane A. *consumer products executive*
Prestanski, Harry Thomas *public relations executive*
Pridmore, Elizabeth Ann *marketing professional*
Priestley, Clive *former management consultant*
Prieto Vial, Daniel *international relations consultant, educator*
Primas, Vinson Bernardi *management consultant*
Prior, Roger Arnold *executive search consultant*
Pritchard, Robert Jerome *resort owner, retired*
Probasco, Dale Richard *management consultant*
Protheroe, Alan Hackford *communications executive*
Provencher-Kambour, Frances *public relations executive*
Provost, Cheryl Louise Winters *account executive*
Pu, Hongjun *systems architect*
Pudlo, Frances Theresa *executive assistant*
Pugh, Revella *executive assistant*
Pulsifer, Edgar Darling *leasing service and sales executive*
Punkari, Yrjö Mauno *computer software company executive, programmer*
Purcell, Steven Richard *international management consultant, engineer, economist*
Purchase-Brown, Francena *human resources specialist, educator*
Purepong, Wichit *company executive, marketing researcher*
Puri, Adip Ramesh *communications company executive*
Puri, Shamlal *news agency executive, editor*
Qazi, Manzar Moin *advertising executive*
Qu, Hailin *hospitality and tourism professional*
Quella, James Andrew *management consultant*
Quellmalz, Henry *printing company executive*
Quester, Pascale Genevieve *marketing educator, consultant*
Quinn, Barry Michael *marketing educator*
Quinn, Tom *communications executive*
Radchenko, Arcadi Nicolaevich *information processing specialist*
Radice, Frank J. *communications executive*
Raghavan, Ramasubramanian *quality assurance professional, researcher*
Rahman, Mustaqur *travel representative*
Rajagopalan, Ravi *management consultant*
Raman, Venkata *communications company executive*
Rambabu, Karumudi *communications company executive*
Ramin, Gilles F. *business executive*
Ramirez, Ramon *database company executive*
Ramis, Pla Joaquim *communications company executive, consultant*
Ramos, Liliana Lacambra *information systems specialist*
Ramos-Cano, Hazel Balatero *caterer, chef, innkeeper, entrepreneur*
Ramqvist, Lars Henry *communications company executive*
Ramsey, Joanne Marie *data processing executive*
Ramsey, William Dale, Jr. *marketing and technology consultant*
Randall, Elizabeth Ellen *press clippings company executive*
Randle, Peter *communications company executive*
Randrup, Nils L. *communications executive, business educator*
Ránki, Zsuzsanna *management consultant*
Raper, Charles Albert *retired management consultant*
Rasch, David Gerard *customer service representative*
Rashid, Abdul *drug delivery systems consultant*
Raskovic, Alexander *sports agent, yacht broker*
Rasmussen, Robert *advertising executive*
Ratiu, Indrei Stephen Pilkington *management consultant*
Ratiu, Liviu Gabriel *management consultant*
Räty, Hannu Olavi *management consultant*
Raver, Miki *recruiter, writer*
Raynaud, Guillaume Roger *sales executive, marketing professional*
Reading, Alan William *marketing executive, graphic designer*
Reast, Deborah Stanek *executive assistant*
Reda, James Francis *business consultant*
Reddish, John Joseph *management consulting company executive*
Redstone, Sumner Murray *entertainment company executive, lawyer*
Reece, David Bryson *information systems administrator*
Reece, Monique Elizabeth *marketing, advertising and sales consultant*
Reed, David Patrick *infosystems specialist*
Reed, William Gerald *consulting firm executive*
Rees, Petra *management consultant*
Řehulka, Pavel *training company executive*
Reid, Richard Alfred *manufacturers representative*
Reilly, Robert Frederick *valuation consultant*
Reis, Jean Stevenson *administrative secretary*
Reis, Luis Rocha dos *marketing professional*
Reitan, Harold Theodore *management consultant*
Renkens, Jack H. *seminar speaker*
Reshetnikov, Michael Evgenievitch *company executive*
Ress, Charles William *management consultant*
Reyes, Perla Fandino *hotel management educator*
Rhodes, Karren *public information officer*
Richter, Anthony John *artificial intelligence company executive*
Ridley, Keith Alexander, IV *funeral director*
Riegnell, Göran Alvar *information consultant*
Rieke, Ronald Alfred *computer company executive*
Riggulsford, Michael James *public relations consultant*
Rimbotti, Francesco Mauro *management consultant*
Ring, Clare Charlotte *information systems specialist*
Ritacco, Patsy Richard *sales executive*
Rittner, Luke Philip Hardwick *arts administrator, marketing/communications executive*
Rix, Gerald *public relations consultant, archeologist*
Rizopoulos, Andreas C(hristos) *public relations consultant, journalist*
Roazzi, Vincent Michael *marketing professional*
Robbins, Jeanette Lee *sales and manufacturing executive*
Roberts, David Alun *construction industry consultant, expert witness, arbitrator*
Robertson, John Maxwell *service company executive*
Robins, Mitchell James *management consultant*
Robinson, Samira E. Watson *marketing executive, writer*
Robles, Eliodoro Gonzales *consulting company executive, educator*
Roche, Gerard Raymond *management consultant*
Rochford, Patricia Anne *executive search organization executive*
Roddam, Peter Leopold Baber *communications executive, accountant*
Rodolff, Dale Ward *sales executive, consultant*
Rodotà, Antonio *executive*
Rodrigues, José Dionisio *advertising executive*
Rodriguez, Marino *management assistant*
Rogers, Frank Andrew *restaurant, hotel executive*
Rohde, James Vincent *software systems company executive*
Roisler, Glenn Harvey *quality assurance professional*
Rojas, Leonardo Garcia *integration technology administrator*
Rombout, Luc Erna Theo *management consultant*
Romburgh, Alan Desmond Michael *hotel executive*
Ronan, William John *management consultant*
Ronc, Michael Joseph *company executive*
Ronell, Stanley L. *sales executive*
Root, Laura Lee *personal care industry executive*
Rose, Charles Robert *internet communications company executive*
Rose, David Semel *internet executive, entrepreneur*
Rose, Hugh *management consultant*
Rose, Merrill *public relations counselor*
Rosen, Wendy Workman *marketing professional*
Rosenblad, Elsa Fritze Susanne *technology educator, researcher*
Rosenfeld, Edward *travel company executive*
Rosenfeld, Martin Jerome *executive recruiter, educator*
Rosensaft, Lester Jay *management consultant, lawyer, business executive*
Roslow, Sydney *marketing educator*
Rossi, Pierre Marie *consultancy company executive*
Rossman, Robert Harris *management consultant*
Ross-Petersen, Jakob *company executive*
Rote, Nelle Fairchild Hefty *business consultant*
Roth, John Andrew *internet communications executive*
Rothman, Steve Andrew *advertising executive*
Rotunda, Donald Theodore *public relations consultant*
Rouse, Prudence Alison *security services executive*
Roux, Michel Andre *restaurateur*
Roy, J(ames) Stapleton *former secretary*
Royere, William Randolph, III *computer company executive*
Rubin, Martin N. *meeting planner, consultant*
Rudolph, Ronald Alvin *human resources executive*
Rufli, Kurt *hotel executive*
Ruiz, Javier *sales executive*
Ruppert, Armin *sales executive*
Rurak, Zbigniew Tadeusz *executive search consultant*
Russell, Carol Ann *personnel service company executive*
Russell, George Edward Bacheler *management consultant*
Russell, Henry Richard, Jr. *business communication adviser, educator*
Russell, Mervyn Keith *international marketing executive*
Russell, Timothy Paul *management consultant, engineer*
Ruth, Edward Keith *information systems specialist, management consultant*
Ruthchild, Geraldine Quietlake *training and development consultant, writer, poet*
Ruud, Arne Oddbjørn *marketing professional*
Ruvalcaba, Roberto Alejandro *marketing executive*
Ryan, James Herbert *retired security and retail services company executive*
Ryan, Susan Schaffer *electronic products developer*
Saatchi, Charles *communications and marketing company executive*
Saatchi, Maurice (Lord Saatchi) *communications and marketing company executive*
Sabbah Bensimon, Raymond *marketing executive*
Sabhaney, Aarti Harnam *public relations executive, journalist*
Sabino, Larrea Ereno *agricultural economic company executive/researcher*
Sachs, Freeman *retired management consultant, volunteer*
Sack, Brian George *hotel executive*
Sacksteder, Thomas Michael *corporate executive, entrepreneur, writer*
Sadek, Blland Niaz *marketing executive*
Sadler, David Gary *management executive*
Sadoun, Henry H. *international business developer*
Saenger, Bruce Walter *consulting firm executive*
Sahgal, Ash *marketing professional, consultant*
Saini, Vasant Durgadas *computer software company executive*
Sainsbury of Preston Candover, Lord (John Davan Sainsbury) *food retailer executive, art patron*
Saint-Martin, Estelle Marie Reine *communications executive*
Saito, William Hiroyuki *software company executive*
Saji, K. B. *management educator, consultant*
Sakuda, Akira Tony *travel agent*
Salama-Baroum, Magdi *management consultant*
Saleem, Mohammad Abdul *hotel executive*
Salem, Susanne Frances *consulting executive*
Salerno, Kerstin Ute *marketing professional*
Salino, Jeffrey Alan *leasing executive*
Saltzman, Irene Cameron *perfume manufacturing executive, art gallery owner*
Salvaggio, Salvino Anthony *internet strategy consultant, company director*
Salveson, Melvin Erwin *business executive, educator*
Sams, David Ronald *Internet marketing specialist, music producer*
Samuel, Sergiu *quality assurance professional*
Samuelson, Douglas Alan *information systems company executive*
Sanchelli, Charles Raymond (Chuck Sanchelli) *tennis company executive*
Sanchez-Camara, Antonio Alba *company executive, consultant*
Sanderson, Arthur Norman *international cultural relations specialist*
Sandifer, Kevin Wayne *archival services executive*
Sandler, Ian Martin *travel, tourism and leisure company executive*
Sandler, Kenneth Bruce *advertising executive*
Sandoval, Rik (Charles Sandoval) *broadcasting executive*
Sandy, Arthur Edward *retired sales executive*
Sanger, Stephen W. *consumer products company executive*
Santander, Danny R. *marketing and sales executive, consultant*
Santanera, Laura *marketing professional, researcher*
Santiago-Fandiño, Vicente *waste management administrator*
Sarantoglou, Menelaos Harry *general director*
Sareh, Mustafa Bin *e-commerce entrepreneur*
Sargeant, Adrian *marketing educator*
Sarkis, J. Ziad *management consultant*
Sarreals, Sonia *data processing consultant*
Sarvanto, Kari Tapani *management consultant, business executive*
Satchit, Balan *marketing educator*
Sato, Toshiaki *executive*
Satterthwaite, George, II *security director*
Saul, Ann *public relations executive, medical writer*
Saunders, Brian Keith *consulting company executive*
Saunders, Kathryn A. *retired data processing administrator*
Savage, Richard Nigel *travel firm executive*
Savage, Terry Richard *information systems executive*
Sawtell, Olga *marketing executive*
Saxonis, Anthony *marketing executive*
Sayles, Ronald Lyle *computer executive*
Sceiford, Mary Elizabeth *retired public television administrator*
Schaefer, Charles James, III *advertising agency executive, consultant*
Schaeffer, Barbara Hamilton *retired rental leasing company executive, writer*
Schellekens, Maarten Petrus Godefridus *marketing consultant*
Schersten, H. Donald *retired oil company executive*
Schirra, Walter Marty, Jr. *business consultant, former astronaut*
Schlageter, Kurt Edward *consultant*
Schlegelmilch, Bodo Bernd *marketing educator*
Schleifer, Thomas C. *management consultant, author, lecturer*
Schmidt, Frank Broaker *executive recruiter*
Schmidt, Sascha Leonard *strategic management consultant*
Schmidt, William Max *management consultant, business executive*
Schmitt, Robert Lee *computer scientist*
Schmitz, Shirley Gertrude *marketing and sales executive*
Schneider, Dieter *business administration educator*
Schneider, Sharon M. *systems administrator, information technologist*
Schneider Gower, Cindy Elaine Lones *electronic technician*
Schoenfelder, Eva Luise *ergonomics and organization business educator*
Schorpion, Wilfried Anna *information systems specialist*
Schott, John (Robert) *international consultant, educator*
Schreff, David Jonathan *marketing professional*
Schreiber, Harry, Jr. *management consultant*
Schriever, Fred Martin *management consultant, financial investor*
Schroeder, Bent *information technology executive*
Schulz, Ekkehard *business executive*
Schuster, Bertram *recruiter, management consultant, publisher*
Schwartz, Gerald *public relations and fundraising agency executive*
Schwartz, Robert William *management consultant*
Schweiker, Ulrich *management consultant*
Schwella, Erwin *management educator, consultant*
Scott, Adam *telecommunications consultant, educator, clergyman*
Scott, Debbie Ann *recreational facility executive*
Scott, Howard Winfield, Jr. *temporary help services company executive*
Scott-Buczak, Alma *human relations executive*
Scroggs, Deb Lee *communications professional*
Seadler, Stephen Edward *business and computer consultant, social scientist*
Seara, Ines Martins *business executive*
Sebastian, Phylis Sue *real estate broker*
Seddon-Brown, William Geoffrey *environmental services company executive*
Seemann, Rosalie Mary *international business and foreign policy association executive*
Sehgal, Jagjeet Singh *trading company executive*
Seiden, Henry (Hank Seiden) *advertising executive*
Seidman, Glenn Elliott *sales and marketing professional*
Seif Al Nasr, Waleed Mehmoud *advertising, communication and marketing executive*
Seigell, Man Mohan *marketing professional*

INDUSTRY: TRADE

Rodman, Sue A. *wholesale company executive, artist, writer*
Roushdi, Karim *import/export company executive*
Runge, Donald Edward *food wholesale company executive*
Rusher, George *small business owner*
Sabanci, Sakip *holdings company executive*
Sacranie, Iqbal Abdul Karim Mussa *business executive*
Sadh, Gulab Mohan *export company executive*
Sagmeister, Edward Frank *retired military officer, business owner*
Salem, Joseph John *jeweler, real estate developer*
Salén, Sven Hampus *trading company executive*
Sanden, Christer Eugen *company executive*
Sasaki, Mikio *trading company executive*
Saudi, Ashraf Hussein *retail executive*
Schilling, Franklin Charles, Jr. *retail management professional*
Schlussel, Joseph Lazar *diamond dealer, publisher*
Schnell, Roger Thomas *business owner, retired state official and career officer*
Schnitzer, Moshe *exporting company executive*
Schonfeld, Walter Tibor *retired jewelry importer, writer*
Schun, Laurent André *export company executive*
Scott, H. Lee *retail store company executive*
Seelenfreund, Alan *distribution company executive*
Serna Aristizabal, Juan Alberto *business owner*
Seufert, Janet Arlene *small business owner, consultant*
Shaffner, Randolph Preston *shop owner, educator, writer*
Shamdasani, Haresh Ramchandra *export company executive*
Sharples, Winston Singleton *automobile importer and distributor*
Shevade, Pratap Dattatray *bookseller*
Sidar, Thomas Wilson *retail executive*
Simmons, Warren Hathaway, Jr. *retired retail executive*
Simpson, H. Richard (Dick Simpson) *retailer*
Singer, Andrew Lawrence *export expansion consultant*
Smith, Barbara Anne (Bobbie Smith) *book seller, researcher*
Smith, Jack Carl *foreign trade consultant*
Snellen, Deborah Sue *training consulting company executive*
Solomon, Hilda Pearl *wholesale executive*
Sood, Davinder Nath *import/export executive*
Spartz, Alice Anne Lenore *retired retail executive*
Spazier, Reinfried Wilhelm *sporting goods executive*
Spitzer, Matthew *retired retail store executive*
Stafford, Jeffrey S. *small business owner*
Stallard, George Thomas (Duke Stallard) *retired retail store owner*
Stearns, Susan Tracey *lighting design company executive, lawyer*
Steffen, Maxine Lynn *small business owner*
Stenback, Guy Olof *import company executive*
Stewart, Rebekah Brooke *retired small business owner*
Strijdom, Peter *import-export company executive*
Stuart, Alan Edward *retail executive*
Stutz, Rolf Harry *trading company executive*
Suzuki, Barnabas Tatsuya *import/export manufacturing company executive*
Swenson, Richard Allen *business owner, animal trainer*
Tammivuori, Juhani Tapio *wholesale company executive*
Tan, Chin Kian *freight forwarding merchant*
Tateyama, Yoshiyuki *vegetables grower and exporter*
Terence, Sim Chet Hong *trade specialist*
Thwing, Bonnie J. *retail executive, nurse*
Tocantins, Paulo *trading company executive*
Toorabally, Naeem Salahuddin *import-export company executive*
Toriumi, Iwao *trading company executive*
Trombold, Walter Stevenson *supply company executive*
Trutter, John Thomas *consulting company executive*
Uffner, Michael S. *retail automotive executive*
Ulfves, Björn Olav *import company official*
Ulrich, Robert J. *retail discount chain stores executive*
Vandenburg, Kathy Helen *small business owner, career counselor*
Vander Naald Egenes, Joan Elizabeth *business owner, educator*
Vassilopoulos, Yerassimos George *marketing and merchandising company executive*
Vidal, Hector Marcelo *foreign trade manager*
Virgo, Muriel Agnes *swimming school owner*
Vu, Khoa *construction import/export company executive*
Wagner, Charlene Brook *publishing consultant*
Walton, S. Robson *discount department store chain executive*
Ward, Nina Gillson *jewelry store executive*
Watari, Akira *trading company executive*
Weber, Rabbe Johan *small business owner, consultant*
Weldon, Theodore Tefft, Jr. *retail company executive*
Werries, E. Dean *food distribution company executive*
Wiggins, Mary Ann Wise *small business owner, educator*
Wilson, Stanley Leif *small business owner*
Winata, Ken Omar *small business owner*
Winslow, Norman Eldon *business executive*
Winter, Richard Samuel, Jr. *computer training company owner, writer*
Wojcik, Cass *decorative supply company executive, former city official*
Wolf, Monica Theresia *small business owner, inventor*
Wood, Leslie Ann *retail administrator*
Wood, Peter John *small business owner*
Woodhouse, John Frederick *food distribution company executive*
Wright, Michael William *wholesale distribution and retail executive*
Yu, Kwan Lung *trading company executive*
Zaldastani, Guivy *business consultant*
Zekkar, Patrik Halim *export company executive*

INDUSTRY: TRANSPORTATION

Aadnesen, Christopher *railroad company executive, consultant*
Abdul, Mannan *airline executive*
Abraham, Jacob *delivery service executive*
Alatzas, George *delivery service company executive*
Allsop, Richard Edward *transport educator*
Anand, Arun Veer *airport executive*
Andreasson, Ingmar Joel *transportation scientist*
Ansary, Hanson Jaber *transportation and telecommunications executive*
Armstrong, Neil A. *former astronaut*
Ashby, Lindsey Gordon *railroad transportation executive*
Baddour, Anne Bridge *pilot*
Bangsund, Edward Lee *former aerospace company executive, consultant*
Barnhart, Larry Leroy *transportation executive*
Baskys, Paul John *airport manager*
Bean, Alan LaVern *retired astronaut, artist*
Bergrun, Norman Riley *aerospace executive*
Berthillier, Marc Jean *aircraft engine company researcher*
Beyer, Morten Sternoff *airlines executive*
Bigelow, Daniel James *aerospace executive*
Bishop, Mark Alan *airline pilot, flight instructor*
Bjerregaard, Ena *defense and aerospace industries association executive*
Blackney, Arthur Bruce *Middle East defense and aviation consultant*
Bland, Sir Christopher (Francis Buchan Bland) *freight company executive*
Boehnstedt, Susan *transportation executive*
Bolorinos, Jose *airline executive, researcher*
Bore, Clifford Lester *aircraft designer*
Borman, Frank *former astronaut, laser patent company executive*
Born, Gunthard Karl *aerospace executive*
Borton, George Robert *retired airline captain*
Bouley, Joseph Richard *pilot*
Bourgeault, Jean-Jacques *air transportation executive*
Boyer, Yves Maurice *aerospace company executive*
Bragg, Albert Forsey *retired airline captain*
Brice, Charles Steven *airline executive*
Brown, Janiece Alfreida *pilot*
Brown, Ronald William *airline executive*
Burkhardt, Edward Arnold *railway executive*
Cairns, Alan Joseph *transportation executive*
Campbell, James R. *transportation executive*
Campbell, Lewis B. *aerospace technology executive*
Camus, Phillippe *aerospace company executive*
Carleone, Joseph *aerospace executive*
Carlyle, Richard Stanley *water transportation executive*
Carr, Charles Anthony Bowrinc *aerospace company executive*
Carter, Thomas Smith, Jr. *retired railroad executive*
Carty, Donald J. *airline company executive*
Casanovas, Federico Valderrama *aviation executive*
Charalambides, Charalambos A. *shipping executive*
Chartier, Janellen Olsen *airline service coordinator*
Chaudhary, Naeem Sarwar *helicopter pilot*
Checchi, Alfred A. *airline company executive*
Childs, Donald Samuel *truck driver*
Chung, Caroline *airline professional*
Clark, Paul *airline analyst*
Clarkson, Lawrence William *airplane company executive*
Coffman, Vance D. *aerospace company executive*
Cole, Michael William Henry *aerospace executive*
Coln, William Alexander, III *pilot*
Conaway, Charles *retail company executive*
Conder, Jimmie Lee *commercial pilot, farmer*
Condit, Philip Murray *aerospace executive, engineer*
Cosulich, Antonio Felice *shipping company executive*
Cox, David A. *rail transportation executive*
Crew, Aubrey Torquil *aerospace inspector*
Curto, Daniel Alberto *airline transport pilot, flight instructor*
Daly, Cotton *air transportation executive*
Dasburg, John Harold *air transportation executive*
Davidson, Richard K. *railroad company executive*
Davis, H. Alan *retired airline captain, consultant*
Davis, Michael Chase *aerospace industry executive, consultant, retired naval officer*
de Murat de Lestang, Hervé *aeronautics general manager*
Deniau, Isabelle *delivery service executive*
De Pauw, Daniella Augusta *company executive*
Derilo, Rosalio Osip *airport ground equipment mechanic*
Dewar, James McEwen *marketing, aerospace and defense executive, developing nations consultant*
Dobler, Bruno *transportation executive*
Doherty, Robert Francis, Jr. *aerospace industry professional*
Downing, Darrell W. *aviation educator, department chair*
Droussiotis-Burns-Cowan, Sarah A. *transportation company executive*
Dunas, Etienne *space industry executive*
Eddington, Rod *air transportation company executive*
Eie, Leif *retired air transportation executive*
Ellis, Andrew John *airline pilot*
Erikson, Thomas (Karl Pehr) *shipbroker*
Ervin, Billy Maxwell *aerospace executive*
Evans, Richard H. *aerospace executive*
Ezzat, Emile Michel *airline company executive*
Fagerman, Peter Wilhelm *transportation and logistics consultant*
Fain, Richard David *cruise line executive*
Fakoussa, Thomas Awad *pilot, safety educator*
Farnworth, Alan *pilot*
Fedosov, Eugeni Alexandrovich *aviation system company executive*
Fellner, Andrzej *navigator, educator*
Fish, Howard Math *aerospace industry executive*
Fisher, Allan Campbell *railway executive*
Fisher, King *retired marine contracting company executive*
Fitch, Edward Harold *industry consultant*
Focas, Caralampo *transport advisor*
Foros, Markos Apostolos *shipping company executive, real estate company executive*
Foschi, Pier Luigi *cruise company executive*
Fotsis, Stavros Spyros *mariner*
Fournier, Marc *foundation executive*
Fowler, Hugh Charles *rail transportation executive*
Frew, Allan M. *aerospace executive*
Fugazy, William Denis *transportation company executive*
Gallardo, Roberto Baltazar *shipping industry executive, consultant*
Gasich, Welko Elton *retired aerospace executive, management consultant*
Gendre, Pierre Emile *airline passengers consultant*
Golanka, Stanley Richard *airline executive*
Goodwin, James E. *air transportation executive*
Gottfeld, Gunther Max *retired urban mass transit official, consultant*
Gourley, James Walter, III *airport executive*
Graham, John Hamilton, II *airborne delivery service company official*
Gutzman, Philip Charles *aerospace executive, logistician*
Hafstad, Helge Andreas *aviation administrator*
Haghighi, Vahid *airline pilot*
Hagrup, Knut *aviation consultant*
Hails, Robert Emmet *aerospace consultant, business executive, former air force officer*
Hanappe, Paul Clement *transportation executive, consultant*
Harmant, Michael Jean *aerospace executive*
Hassett, Patrick John *airline pilot*
Heald, David James *aerospace executive*
Heitz, Edward Fred *freight traffic consultant*
Hemann, Raymond Glenn *research company executive*
Hendricks, Susan Costinett *transportation planner*
Hielm, Borje Gustav *airline captain, historian, journalist*
Hirschmann, Franz Gottfried *aerospace executive*
Holfeld, Donald Rae *railroad consultant*
Homer, Thomas Keith *transportation consultant*
Hooper, Kelley Rae *delivery service executive*
Hsiung, Tai-Ping Jacob *avionics executive, researcher*
Hugues, Tourvieille de Labrouhe *air transportation executive*
Janssens, Danny Denis *transportation company executive*
Jerram, James *rail transportation executive*
Johnson, Evelyn Bryan *airport terminal executive*
Johnson, Gregory Carl *pilot, astronaut, career officer*
Johnson, Peter Forbes *transportation executive, business owner*
Jung, Philippe *aerospace executive, historian*
Kallakis, Achilleas Michalis S. *shipping company executive*
Kamm, Thomas Allen *air transportation company executive*
Kaneko, Isao *air transportation executive*
Kasai, Yoshiyuki *rail transportation executive*
Katsikas, Michael D. *air transportation executive*
Kawamoto, Hiroshi *maritime safety educator*
Kempston Darkes, V. Maureen *transportation company executive*
Kerbs, Wayne Allan *transportation executive*
Khanna, Rajendra Pall *marine services company executive*
Kilbourne, Krystal Hewett *rail transportation executive*
Kim, Chuljoo *air transportation executive*
Klein, Tiberiu Aladar *truck company executive*
Koch, Eberhard Georg Johann *shipping executive, ship owner*
Kolesov, Sergey Mikhailovitch *merchant marine officer, shipping consultant*
Kondas, Nicholas Frank *shipping company executive*
Kong, Cheong Choong *airline executive*
Korfiatis, Con *air transport executive*
Krissel, Susan Hinkle *transportation company executive*
Kristmannsson, Thorsteinn *airline pilot*
Krymsky, Victor Grigorievich *control systems researcher*
Küehne, Klaus-Michael *freight forwarding and logistics executive*
Kyotani, Yoshihiro *railway executive*
Leite, João Verdi Carvalho *aerospace executive*
Lenngren, Carl Anders *transportation executive*
Lerner-Lam, Eva I-Hwa *transportation executive*
Lewis, Martin Edward *shipping company executive, foreign government concessionary*
Lindsey, Joanne M. *flight attendant, poet*
Ljøstad, Torstein Torberg *retired airline company executive*
Loete, Steven Donald *pilot*
Logan, Henry Vincent *transportation executive*
Lorentzen, Fridtjof *water transportation executive*
Luhta, Caroline Naumann *airport manager, flight educator*
Lüning, Fredrik N son *transportation executive*
MacPhail, Sir Bruce (Dugald) *navigation company executive*
Maggiore, Maurizio *aeronautic company executive*
Marshall, Sir Colin *airline executive*
Martens, Gerd *transportation executive, consultant*
Mason, Raymond E., Jr. *distributing company executive*
Matalon, Norma *travel and public relations executive*
Materna, Petr Jan *air navigation services administrator*
Matsuda, Masatake *rail transportation executive*
Mavridoglou, Nicholas Isidore *shipping and trading company executive*
Mazarakis-Baltsavias, Phédon *international and maritime consultant, publicist*
Mbu, Matthew Tawo *shipping executive, legal consultant*
Metzgen, Frederick William *communications company executive*
Moreau, Claude Olivier *retired aircraft industry executive*
Morgan, John Phillip *rail transportation executive*
Morton, Sir Alastair *business executive*
Moss, Elizabeth Lucille (Betty Moss) *transportation company executive*
Mu, Chundi *control theory educator, researcher*
Mullin, Leo Francis *airline executive*
Murphy, Pat Gordon *aviation educator*
Murrin, Denis Roland *aviation consultant*
Nair, Krishnadas C.G. *aerospace company executive*
Nan-Ya, Shojiro *rail transportation executive*
Nashida, Atsuhiro *astronautical science administrator*
Nasirullah, Mohammed *port executive*
Neal, Michael DeWayne *company executive*
Nguyen-Duy, Phi *railway expert*
Nielsen, Jorgen *air transportation executive*
Nilsson, Nils Johnny *aviation executive*
Nobuyuki, Onimura *transportation executive*
Noethling, Victoria Ann *delivery service executive*
Nomura, Kichisaburo *air transporation company executive*
Nygren, Lars Johan *transportation executive*
Oliveira, Haroldo de Castro *aviation company executive, consultant*
Oztugran, Ali Okyay *air express executive*
Paloda, Martin *aircraft company executive*
Parker, T. John *shipping and shipbuilding company executive*
Parui, Ramen Kumar *airport executive, astrophysicist*
Pearlman, Louis Jay *aviation and entertainment company executive*
Pemberton, Gary *air transportation executive*
Pera, Carlos Alberto *airline pilot*
Pereira, Renato Claudio Costa *air transportation executive*
Petersen, Henning *air transportation executive*
Peterson, Gerald Joseph *aerospace executive, consultant*
Pierides, Demetrios Zeno *shipping company executive, entrepreneur*
Polensky-Ksi—żek, Henryk *pilot, educator*
Porzenheim, Clifford J. *business executive*
Poulterer, William Taylor, III *river pilot*
Prakasarao, Andra Surya *retired aerospace executive*
Prananto, Beni *shipping executive*
Prokhorenko, Victoria Ivanovna *space mission situation analyst, researcher*
Qasim, Syed Shah Abul *transportation planner*
Radina, Alejandro *airline pilot*
Rechtin, Eberhardt *retired aerospace executive, retired educator*
Reid, Sir Robert Paul *rail transportation executive*
Richards, Martin Gomm *transportation planner*
Roitsch, Paul Albert *pilot*
Rollain, Richard Andre *airline company administrator*
Rucker, Zena *retired flight school administrator*
Ruf, Donnie Lee *delivery service provider, fashion model, designer*
Ryan, Randel Edward, Jr. *airline pilot*
Salamah, Mohammad Abdul Latif *transportation company executive*
Scannell, William Edward *aerospace company executive, consultant, psychologist*
Schaupp, Joan Pomprowitz *trucking company executive, writer*
Seiler, Otto J. *retired shipping company executive*
Shamrikov, Boris Mikhailovich *aviation educator, researcher, engineer*
Shen, Chia Theng *former steamship company executive, religious institute official*
Shovelton, (Walter) Patrick *shipping and aviation company adviser*
Silve, Jean Paul *retired shipping and mining company executive*
Skogö, Ingemar *aviation company executive*
Smith, Frederick Wallace *transportation company executive*
Smith, Gordon Eugene *pilot*
Snow, John William *railroad executive*
Soutos, Nicolaos *ship owner, industrialist*
Spinetta, Jean-Cyril *airline executive*
Steiling, Daniel Paul *retired railroad conductor, writer*
Stenson, Henry Orjan *airline executive*
Sterling of Plaistow, Baron Jeffrey Maurice *transportation company executive*
Stokes, Donald William *shipping industry company executive*
Stults, Laurence Allen *airline pilot*
Suda, Hiroshi *rail transportation executive*
Takahashi, Yoshindo *retired transport company executive*
Tan, Lucio C. *airline, tobacco and beer company executive*
Tellier, Paul M. *railway transportation executive*
Tennyson, Edson Leigh *transportation administrator, consultant*
Terry, John Joseph *transportation investor*
Tessun, Franz *aerospace executive*
Tether, Anthony John *aerospace executive*
Thomas, Mitchell, Jr. *aerospace company executive*
Thompson, Dayle Ann *aerospace company executive*
Trabitz, Eugene Leonard *aerospace company executive*
Tsakos, Nikolas Panagiotis *shipping company executive*
Tsuchihashi, Tatsuhiko (Jack Tsuchihashi) *shipping company executive*
Tsutsumi, Yoshiaki *transportation executive*
Turcat, André *former test pilot, consultant, educator*
Tuscai, Shawnna Suzanne *transportation executive*
Unterman, Eugene Rex *aviation sales and manufacturing company executive*
Unverzagt, John Gerald *airline captain*
Uyeno, Takashi *oil shipping company executive*
Van Dijk, Robert Peter Adriaan *aerospace company executive*
Veniamis, Theodore Eleftherios *ship owner, business executive*
Vij, Satish Kumar *rail transportation company executive*
von Bernuth, Carl W. *rail transportation executive, lawyer*
von Haartman, Harry Ulf *international transportation consultant*
von Samson-Himmelstjerna, Armin *retired shipping executive*
Waldock, William David *aeronautical science and aviation safety educator*
Walland, Jakob *master mariner*
Wanglee, Thamnoon *airline executive*
Weber, Juergen *airline executive*
Weed, Melvin L. *retired railroad conductor, small business owner*
Weh, Allen Edward *airline executive*
Welborne, John Howard *railway company executive, lawyer*
Welsby, John Kay *rail transportation executive*
Weston, John *aerospace executive*
Widigsson, Olle *transport company executive*
Wigan, Marcus Ramsay *transportation research scientist*
Williams, David Alexander *retired chief pilot*
Williams, Eric Joseph *transportation executive*
Williams, Walter David *aerospace executive, consultant*
Winstanley, Derek *water resource executive*
Witkowski, Ryszard *test pilot, consultant*
Wolf, Stephen M. *airline executive*
Wong, Chin Wah *quantity surveyor*
Wu, Bruce Chung Dan (Bruce Chung Dan Ng) *steamship company executive, investor*
Yamazaki, Yoshio *rail transportation executive*
Yao, Zukang *transportation engineering education*
Zack, Steven Jeffrey *master automotive instructor*
Zarèus, Jørgen Simon Wallberg *retired shipbroker*
Zidaru, Constantin *transportation executive, petroleum engineer*
Zucker, Leonard Charles *trucking executive, rabbi*
Zurabov, Alexander Yurievich *airline executive, bank executive, economist*

INDUSTRY: UTILITIES, ENERGY, RESOURCES

Aakvaag, Torvild *petroleum company executive*
Abbas, Ali El-Sayed *oil company executive, researcher*
Ackerman, F. Duane *telecommunication industry executive*

INDUSTRY: UTILITIES, ENERGY, RESOURCES 2578 WHO'S WHO IN THE WORLD

Sarma, Amardeo Christian *telecommunications executive*
Sarropoulos, Constantin *utilities company executive*
Savage, Michael John Kirkness *oil company and arts management executive*
Savarirayan, Kantharaj *oil company executive*
Savino, Giovanni Maria *telecommunication executive, educator*
Schafer, William Harry *loss prevention consultant*
Schaller, Hans Nikolaus *telecommunications industry executive*
Schanzer, Mark Joseph *petroleum company executive*
Schaper, Dirk Wilhelm *telecommunications administrator*
Schneider, Martin Max *energy executive*
Scoates, Wesley Marvin *mining company executive*
Scott, Stephen Gregory *telecommunications company executive*
Seaman, Daryl Kenneth *oil company executive*
Sforna, Marino *utilities/energy executive*
Sham, Samuel Yat-wah *oil and transport executive, trade executive*
Shaw, Roland Clark *oil company executive*
Shibata, Susumu *electric company researcher*
Shultz, Delray Franklin (Lucky Shultz) *management consultant*
Sigelle, Marc Olivier *telecommunications researcher*
Silas, Cecil Jesse *retired petroleum company executive*
Sims, George Edward *electronics company executive*
Skala, Gary Dennis *electric and gas utilities executive management consultant*
Slavinski, Antoni Dimitrov *telecommunications executive, consultant*
Slawter, John David, Jr. *oil company and manufacturing executive*
Smith, David Kingman *retired oil company executive, consultant*
Sommer, Ron *telecommunications executive*
Sophusson, Fridrik Klemenz *Icelandic power company executive*
Sopko, Michael D. *mining company executive*
Sorensen, Per Morch *oil company executive*
Southern, Ronald D. *diversified corporation executive*
Stage, Richard Lee *consultant, retired utilities executive*
Stamati, Aleksi *oil industry executive*
Stankiewicz, Andrzej *telecommunications company executive*
Starkey, Russell Bruce, Jr. *utilities executive*
Stead, Jerre L. *telecommunications company executive*
Stead, Ronald *energy industry executive*
Sterckx, Luc Marie Jan *oil company executive*
Stetter, Joseph Robert *electric power industry executive*
Stonehill, Lloyd Herschel *gas company executive, mechanical engineer*
Strohal, Petar *Energy company executive*
Strong, Liam *telecommunications executive*
Struzak, Ryszard *radio scientist*
Sugiyama, Takashi *electric company executive*
Sundberg, Carl-Erik Wilhelm *telecommunications executive, researcher*
Suzuki, Yoshihiko *industrial gas company executive*
Sweeney, George Bernard *petrochemical industry executive, investor, broadcast executive, travel agency executive*
Taylor, Leslie George *mining and financial company executive*
Taylor, Russell Benton *mining executive*
Taylor, Vicky Ann *telephone company executive*
Tobias-Jones, Brian *oil field technology company executive*
Todd, Zane Grey *retired utilities executive*
Toivonen, Jarkko Kalevi *telecommunication executive*
Tollan, Arne *water and environmental management executive*
Townsend, Thomas Perkins *former mining company executive*
Tyurkyan, Raffi Armenakovich *mining executive*
Uematsu, Kunihiko *nuclear energy agency executive*
Underweiser, Irwin Philip *mining company executive, lawyer*
Upadhyay, Prem Chandra *oil company executive*
Uzawa, Kiyoshi *oil company executive, mechanical engineer*
Vallance, Iain David Thomas *telecommunications executive*
VanderLinden, Camilla Denice Dunn *telecommunications industry manager*
Van Dyke, Gene *oil company executive*
van Vlissingen, P. Fentener *gas, oil industry executive*
Van Wachem, Lodewijk Christiaan *petroleum company executive*
van Wamelen, Joop *technical assessment consultant*
Vassilakos, Nicholas *energy consultant*
Vasudevan, M. K. *petroleum company executive*
Venn, William Frederick *petroleum industry engineer/manager*
Verseput, Johannes Piet *retired oil company executive*
Virk, Gurdev Singh *power company executive*
Voigt, Hans-Dieter *oil company executive, researcher, educator*
Wali, Anil *petrochemical company executive*
Walsham, Bruce Taylor *mining company executive*
Walters, Peter Ingram *petroleum company executive*
Wang, De-Jung (Dejuan Wang) *telecommunications educator*
Ward, Llewellyn Orcutt, III *oil company executive*
Wéber, Kati *computing company executive*
Wedgwood, Ian Duncan *power company executive*
Weeks, William Rawle, Jr. *oil company executive*
Weil, Witold Andrew *energy company executive*
Weinzierl, Klaus *utilities company executive*
Welch, Jerry *oil company executive*
Wessner, Deborah Marie *telecommunications executive, computer consultant*
Weymuller, Bruno *oil and gas industry executive*
Whitacre, Edward E., Jr. *telecommunications executive*
Whyatt, Anthony Stewart *oil company executive*
Wilckens, Henrich *utility company executive*
Wilkerson, Theodore L. *electrician, county commissioner*
Williams, Joseph Scott *energy and natural resources company executive, city commissioner*
Williams, Neville *international solar energy corporation executive*
Williams, Robert Henry *oil company executive*
Willson, John Michael *mining company executive*
Wilson, David Clive (Baron Wilson of Tillyorn) *utilities executive, former British diplomat*
Wilson, Lynton Ronald *telecommunications company executive*
Wistrand, Richard Rhode *electric and gas utility executive*
Wood, Willis Bowne, Jr. *retired utility holding company executive*
Woodward, Richard H. (Woody Woodward) *electric power industry executive*
Wright, David John *telecommunications systems specialist, educator*
Wright, Malcolm Sturtevant *nuclear facility manager, retired career officer*
Wyatt, Oscar Sherman, Jr. *retired energy company executive*
Xu, Chang-Qing *electrical company researcher*
Yammine, Riad Nassif *retired oil company executive*
Yan, Gao *power company executive*
Yashimi, Toshiaki *electric power industry executive*
Yau, Tien Yau *telecommunications products company executive*
Yoshida, Takehito *electric industrial company researcher*
Yu, Teling *telecommunications company executive*
Ziegler, Robert Franz *oil company engineer*

LAW: JUDICIAL ADMINISTRATION

Abeba, Kadidja *court of appeals president*
Adamovich, Ludwig *judge*
Alber, Siegbert *international justice*
Aldrich, George Hoover *judge, arbitrator*
Al-Khaliq, Mustafa Abd *judge*
Al-Khasawneh, Awn Shawkat *judge*
al-Mahmoud, Sheikh Abdullah Bin Said *judge*
al-Mubarak, Ahmad Bin Abdul Al-Aziz *judge*
Amet, Sir Arnold K. *judge*
Anand, Adarsch Sein *judge*
Andreu-Garcia, Jose Antonio *territory supreme court chief justice*
Apsitis, Romans *judge, court official*
Arbour, Louise *judge*
Aruwa, Abdulkareem Ayikoye *magistrate, consultant*
Ashford, Clinton Rutledge *judge*
Astwood, Sir James Rufus *court administrator*
Atteya, Ahmad Mamdouh *judge*
Audouard, Christian *judge*
Auld, Robin Ernest *judge*
Austin, John DeLong *judge*
Bailhache, Sir Philip Martin *judge*
Banda, Richard Allen *chief justice*
Barak, Aharon *judicial administrator*
Barnett, John Henry *judge*
Barrio, Francisco Javier Delgado *Spanish supreme court justice*
Bartnoff, Judith *judge*
Basbas, Monte George *judge*
Bayekova, Cholpon *judge*
Beaumont, Bryan Alan *Australian federal court*
Beddow, Richard Harold *judge*
Beer, Peter Hill *federal judge*
Bierce, James Malcolm *retired judge*
Bingham, Thomas Henry (Lord Bingham of Cornhill) *judge*
Bladen, Edwin Mark *lawyer, judge*
Blom, Birgitta *judge*
Bonney, Hal James, Jr. *federal judge*
Boobekov, Kachkynbai D. *judge*
Boudin, Michael *federal judge*
Bowden, George Newton *judge*
Boyd, Lauri Louise *lawyer, judge*
Boyko, Vitaliy *judge*
Brackett, Colquitt Prater, Jr. *judge, lawyer*
Brennan, Sir Gerard *judge*
Breyer, Stephen Gerald *United States supreme court justice*
Bristow, Walter James, Jr. *retired judge*
Brock, David Allen *state supreme court chief justice*
Brosky, John G. *judge*
Brown, George E. *judge, educator*
Brown, Harold Eugene *magistrate*
Brown, Michael John *judge*
Brown, Sir Stephen *judge*
Buchwald, Naomi Reice *judge*
Bumin, Mustafa *judge*
Byk, Christian Jacques *judge, law educator*
Cain, Thomas William *judge*
Calabresi, Guido *federal judge, law educator*
Callow, Keith McLean *judge*
Campbell, Edward Adolph *judge, electrical engineer*
Campbell, Vincent Bernard *judge, lawyer*
Canivet, M. Guy *judge*
Capshaw, Tommie Dean *judge*
Choe Won Ik *judge*
Cijan, Rafael Victor *judge*
Connolly, Thomas Edward *judge*
Connors, Richard F. *judge*
Contu, Marco Enrico *judge*
Cook, Julian Abele, Jr. *federal judge*
Cooke, John P. *judge*
Cooke, Robin Brunskill (Lord Cooke of Thorndon) *judge*
Corbett, Michael McGregor *retired judge*
Corell, Hans *Swedish judge, diplomate*
Corrada del Rio, Baltasar *supreme court justice*
Crnic, Jadranko *judge*
da Cruz Vilaça, José Luís *judge, government executive, law educator, legal counsel*
Dasho Sonam Tobgye *judge*
Davies, Gillian *judge, writer, educator*
Davis, Marguerite Herr *judge*
Davlatov, Ubaidullo *judge*
Deane, Richard Hunter, Jr. *federal judge*
de la Bastide, Michael *judge*
Dela Cruz, Jose Santos *retired state supreme court justice*
Dembereltseren, Dashdorjiyn *judge*
de Puget, Albert Borg Olivier *magistrate*
de Silva, G. P. S. *judge*
D'Haenens, J. *judge*
Dinsmoor, Robert Davidson *judge*
Domingo Mendez, Jose *supreme court president*
Donne, Sir Gaven (John) *chief justice*
Due, Ole *judge, educator*
Early, Alexander Rieman, III *judge*
Edward, David Alexander Ogilvy *judge*
Eichelbaum, Sir (Johann) Thomas *retired chief justice of New Zealand*
Endziņš, Aivars *chairman Latvian constitutional court*
Epedo, Emmanuel *judge*
Eskew, Benton *judge*
Ezratty-Bader, Myriam *judge*
Fallon, Eldon E. *judge*
Fathy, Moosa *judge*
Feinberg, Robert Julian *judge*
Felizardo, João *judge*
Fennelly, Nial *international justice*
Ferrari Bravo, Luigi *judge*
Fisher, Ann L. *pro tem judge*
Fisk, Merlin Edgar *judge*
Fitzpatrick, Philip J. *judge, lawyer*
Flaherty, John Paul, Jr. *state supreme court chief justice*
Flori, Jean-Baptiste *judge*
Fogel, Jeremy Don *judge*
Franks, Herschel Pickens *judge*
Fuad, Khutu Tekin *judge*
Gandy, H. Conway *retired judge, state official*
García-Valdecasas Y Fernández, Rafael *judge*
Gens de Moura Ramos, Rui Manuel *judge*
Gleeson, Anthony Murray *judge*
Glover, Sir Victor Joseph Patrick *former chief justice*
Golden, Elliott *judge*
Goldstone, Richard Joseph *judge*
Gomes, Óscar *judge*
Grandhenry, Francis Henri *judge*
Grant, Isabella Horton *retired judge*
Greene, Clayton, Jr. *administrative judge, educator*
Greene, Jimmie Walker *county judge*
Gregow, Torkel *federal judge*
Grévisse, Fernand *judge*
Gribbs, Roman S. *judge, former mayor of Detroit*
Gubbay, Anthony Roy *judge*
Guillaume, Gilbert *judge*
Guljans, Andrejs *judge*
Hallberg, Pekka Ilmari *chief justice*
Hamblen, Lapsley Walker, Jr. *judge*
Hamilton, Liam *high court official*
Han, Zhubin *federal judge*
Harding, Ray Murray, Jr. *judge*
Harhut, Chester T. *judge*
Harre, George *retired chief justice*
Harrington, Walter Howard, Jr. *judge*
Hart, Kevin Arthur *justice of the peace*
Hartnett, Maurice A., III *state supreme court justice*
Hausner, John Herman *judge*
Heinonen, Olavi Ensio *judge*
Henrysson, Haraldur *judge*
Herczegh, Géza *judge*
Hinojosa, Federico Gustavo, Jr. *judge*
Holmes, Sven Erik *federal judge, educator*
Holtz, E. M. Catarina *judge*
Hope of Craighead, Lord (James Arthur David Hope) *lord of appeal in ordinary, life peer of Bamff*
Hunt, J. Robin *judge*
Hyatt, Dan Richard *judge*
Hytner, Benet Alan *barrister*
Jacobs, Jack Bernard *judge*
Jaeger, Marc M. *judge*
Jallin, Francois *judge*
Jann, Peter *international justice*
Jarvis, Donald Bertram *judge*
Jelin, Sheldon C. *judge*
Jennings, Sir Robert Yewdall *judge*
Johns, Timothy Robert *judge*
Johnson, Barbara Jean *retired judge, lawyer*
Johnson, Clarence Traylor, Jr. *state judge*
Johnson, Philip Wayne *judge*
Johnston, Elliott Frank *retired supreme court judge*
Kapteyn, Paul Joan G. *judge*
Katzmann, Robert Allen *judge*
Kayser, Paul *judge*
Kerman, David D. *judge*
Kirby, Michael Donald *judge*
Kneller, Alister *former chief justice of Gibraltar*
Knutsson, Anders *retired judge*
Kohlegger, Karl *judge*
Kowalski, Thaddeus Lawrence *judge*
Kuhn, James E. *judge*
Kūris, Pranas *judge*
Kwan, Yun *judge*
Lamer, Antonio *retired Canadian supreme court chief justice*
Langton, Jeffrey H. *judge*
Lashman, Shelley Bortin *judge*
Lay, Donald Pomeroy *federal judge*
Lebedev, Vyacheslav M. *judge*
Lenaerts, Koen *judge*
Leonie, Andrew Drake, III *judge, lawyer*
Lewis, Gerald Jorgensen *judge*
Liben, Asefa *judge*
Limbach, Jutta *judge*
Lindh, Pernilla *judge*
Lloyd, Leona Loretta *judge*
Low, Harry William *judge*
Macken, Fidelma O'Kelly *federal justice*
Mahomed, Ismail *judge*
Mangaze, Mario *judge*
Marino, Ruche Joseph *retired district court judge*
Martin, John Randolph *judge*
Maruste, Rait *judge European Court*
Mason, Sir Anthony Frank *judge*
Matia, Paul Ramon *federal judge*
McClure, Ann Crawford *judge, lawyer*
McLachlin, Beverley *Canadian supreme court chief justice*
McLelland, Malcolm Herbert *retired judge*
McManus, Clarence Elburn *judge*
Meader, John Daniel *judge*
Megarry, Sir Robert *retired judge, writer, lecturer*
Meyers, Hannes, Jr. *judge*
Miller, Charles E. (Chuck Miller) *judge*
Miner, Roger Jeffrey *federal judge*
Mirabelli, Cesare *judge, member of parliament*
Mischo, Jean *international justice*
Miyoshi, Toru *retired chief justice*
Moe, Henry Stanley Rawle *supreme court justice*
Moitinho de Almeida, J. C. *judge*
Mortimer, Wendell Reed, Jr. *judge*
Mosk, Stanley *state supreme court justice*
Moskowitz, Karla *lawyer, judge*
Mouelle, Alexis Dipanda *judge*
Mounla-Haydar, Nasrat *judge*
Muldoon, Francis Creighton *Canadian federal judge*
Murray, John Loyola *judge*
Nassar, Amin *judge*
Nazareno, Julio *judge*
Ndiaye, Youssoupha *judge*
Newman, James Michael *judge, lawyer*
Ngiraklsong, Arthur *judge*
Ngulube, Mathew M. S. W. *judge*
Nyalali, Francis Lucas *chief justice*
Oda, Shigeru *judge*
O'Malley, Carlon Martin *judge*
Ordonez, Ulises Schmill *Mexican supreme court justice*
Painter, Mark Philip *judge*
Pambou-Kombila, Benjamin *judge*
Patrick, H. Hunter *judge*
Payne, Mary Libby *judge*
Percy, Rodney A. *retired circuit judge*
Peters, Ellen Ash *trial referee, retired state supreme court justice*
Phillips, J(ohn) Taylor *judge*
Pietruszka, Michael F. *judge*
Pikis, Georghious M. *judge*
Pontoppidan, N. E. *judge*
Pope, Andrew Jackson, Jr. (Jack Pope) *retired judge*
Pope, John William *judge, law educator*
Powell, Stephen Walter *judge*
Prince, Dick *circuit judge, educator*
Puissochet, Jean-Pierre *judge*
Purnell, Oliver James, III *judge*
Puscas, Victor *judge*
Qayyum, Malik Mohammad *judge, agriculturist*
Raffalli, Henri Christian *retired judge, educator, criminologist*
Ragnemalm, Hans *international justice*
Ranjeva, Raymond *international court of justice judge*
Rehnquist, William Hubbs *United States supreme court chief justice*
Renda, Thomas Anthony *judge*
Reno, Ottie Wayne *former judge*
Ries, Peter *judge, educator*
Rigos, George *judge*
Riley, Patrick John *judge*
Rivera Portillo, Miguel Angel *judge*
Roberts, Sir Denys (Tudor Emil) *chief justice*
Rodriguez Iglesias, Gil Carlos *judge*
Ruiz-Jarabo Colomer, Dámaso *international justice*
Russell, David L. *federal judge*
Sack, Robert David *judge*
Saffels, Dale Emerson *federal judge*
Saggio, Antonio *judge*
Saleh bin, Mohammed al-Luhaldaan *judge*
Sarwata *Indonesia supreme court justice*
Satter, Raymond Nathan *judge*
Schintgen, Romain *judge*
Schoonover, Jack Ronald *judge*
Schwarz, Paul Winston *judge*
Schwebel, Stephen Myron *judge, arbitrator*
Seiler, James Elmer *judge*
Sevón, Leif Jörgen Arvidsson *judge*
Shafer, Robert Tinsley, Jr. *judge*
Shahabuddeen, Mohamed *judge, international arbitrator*
Shamgar, Meir *judge*
Shehu, Avni *judge*
Shi, Jiuyong *judge*
Sidime, Lamine *judge*
Skouris, Vassilios *international justice*
Skretny, William Marion *federal judge*
Slattengren, Linn *judge*
Smith, Carsten *judge*
Smith, James W., Jr. *state supreme court justice*
Smith, Ralph Wesley, Jr. *federal judge*
Solt, Pál *judge*
Standish, William Lloyd *judge*
Steininger, Herbert *judge*
Stephen, Ninian Martin *judge*
Stewart, Melinda Jane *judge*
Strzembosz, Adam Justyn *chief justice*
Suviranta, Antti Johannes *retired judge*
Tao, Kaiyuan *judge*
Tapper, Una Reid *administrative law judge*
Taylor, Alan Broughton *judge*
Thornsbury, Michael *judge*
Tiavaasue Falefatu Maka Sapolu *judge*
Tidball, Jane Alison *judge*
Tiili, Virpi *judge*
Tillman, Massie Monroe *federal judge*
Tjoflat, Gerald Bard *federal judge*
Tonello, Luis *judge*
Towery, Curtis Kent *judge*
Truche, Pierre *French federal judge*
Tuivaga, Sir Timoci (Uluiburotu) *judge*
Turnbull, E. R. (Ned Turnbull) *state judge*
Ugrekhelidze, Mindia *judge*
Van Antwerpen, Franklin Stuart *federal judge*
Vilhjalmsson, Thor *judge*
Vitruk, Nikolai Vasilievich *judge, lawyer, educator*
Vohrah, Lal Chand *judge, barrister*
Waldman, Jay Carl *judge*
Walton, Reggie Barnett *judge*
Wambuzi, Samson William Wako *chief justice Uganda*
Watts, Victor Brian *circuit judge*
Webster, Peter David *judge*
Wellings, Victor Gordon *retired judge*
Wells, Hugh Albert *retired judge*
West, William Brent *judge*
White, Renee Allyn *judge*
Wicker, Thomas Carey, Jr. *judge*
Wilkes, E.M., III *judge*
Williams, Sir Denys Ambrose *chief justice*
Woolf, Harold *judge*
Yager, Thomas C. *judge*
Yakovlev, Veniamin Fedorovich *judge*
Yamaguchi, Shigeru *judge*
Yamin, Dianne Elizabeth *judge*
Yong, Pung How *judge*
Zinzindohoue, Abraham *judge*

LAW: LAW PRACTICE AND ADMINISTRATION

Aaron, Benjamin *law educator, arbitrator*
Aarons, Stephen D. *lawyer*
Aarons-Holder, Charmaine Michele *lawyer*
Aaronson, David Ernest *law educator, lawyer*
Abbott, Charles Favour *lawyer*
Abbott, William Saunders *lawyer*
Abell, Richard Bender (Richard Lon Welch) *lawyer, federal judicial official*
Abramo, Miguel Angel *lawyer*
Abramovsky, Abraham *law educator, lawyer*
Ackerman, Bruce Arnold *law educator, lawyer*
Ackley, Robert O. *lawyer*
Adamantopoulos, Konstantinos *lawyer, consultant*
Adamany, David Walter *law and political science educator*
Adams, Deborah Rowland *lawyer*
Adams, George Bell *lawyer*
Adams, Jo-Ann Marie *lawyer*
Adams, Peter Gordon *solicitor*
Adams, Thomas Tilley *lawyer*
Adaniya, Kevin Seisho *lawyer*
Addington, David John *legal administrator, arbitrator*
Adler, Erwin Ellery *lawyer*
Adler, Sara *arbitrator, mediator*
Adler, Saul *lawyer*
Adlercreutz, Karin Elsa Inga *legal educator*
Aerts, Luc M.T.K. *barrister*

Carney, T. J *lawyer*
Carpenter, David Allan *lawyer*
Carpenter, Edmund Nelson, II *retired lawyer*
Carpenter, Gordon Russell *lawyer, banker*
Carpenter, Randle Burt *lawyer*
Carpenter, Richard Norris *lawyer*
Carr, Cynthia *lawyer*
Carr, Edward A. *lawyer*
Carr, Oscar Clark, III *lawyer*
Carrera, Victor Manuel *lawyer*
Carrere, Charles Scott *law educator, judge*
Carrió, Alejandro Daniel *lawyer, educator*
Carroll, Lewis Andrew *legal and management consultant*
Carroll, Thomas Colas *lawyer, educator*
Carrow, Milton Michael *lawyer, educator*
Carson, Ellen Godbey *lawyer*
Carter, Barry Edward *lawyer, educator, administrator*
Carter, James Alfred *lawyer*
Carter, Jeanne Wilmot *lawyer, publisher*
Carty, John Wesley *lawyer*
Case, David Leon *lawyer*
Casella, Peter F(iore) *patent and licensing executive*
Casey, Bernard J. *lawyer*
Casey, Patrick Anthony *lawyer*
Cashman, Gideon *lawyer*
Cassiday, Benjamin Buckles, III *lawyer*
Castagnola, George Joseph, Jr. *lawyer, mediator, secondary education educator*
Castano, Gregory Joseph *lawyer*
Castle, Louise Margaret *anti-trust lawyer*
Castrataro, Barbara Ann *lawyer*
Castro, Francisco Ferreira de *lawyer, educator*
Castro, Leonard Edward *lawyer*
Catanzariti, Joseph John *solicitor*
Caughfield, Lance Eric *lawyer*
Cavaliere, Frank Joseph *lawyer, educator*
Çavuşoğlu, Ibrahim Erfüs *lawyer, economist*
Cayea, Donald Joseph *lawyer*
Cazalas, Mary Rebecca Williams *lawyer, nurse*
Cederholm, Marita Brita Viktoria *lawyer*
Cermak, Josef Rudolf Cenek *lawyer*
Chaffin, William Michael *lawyer*
Chakarov, Anton Gotchev *barrister*
Chan, Thomas Tak-Wah *lawyer*
Chang, Janice May *lawyer, administrator, notary public*
Chanin, Michael Henry *lawyer*
Chansay Wilmotte, Philippe *lawyer*
Chapin, Mary Q. *arbitrator, mediator, writer, performing artist*
Chapman, Hilton Eveleigh *legal counsel*
Chappell, Milton Leroy *lawyer*
Charles, Robert Bruce *lawyer*
Chase, Eric Lewis *lawyer*
Chau, Kai Bong *lawyer, consultant*
Cheek, Michael Carroll *lawyer*
Chen, Andrea Ya-Huei *lawyer, arbitrator*
Chen, Kok-Choo *lawyer, educator*
Chen, Wesley *lawyer*
Cheong, Ella Shuk Ki *lawyer*
Cherney, James Alan *lawyer*
Cherny, David Edward *lawyer*
Chesley, Stanley Morris *lawyer*
Chesnut, Carol Fitting *lawyer*
Chesnutt, William James *barrister*
Chettle, A(lvin) B(asil), Jr. *lawyer, educator*
Chetty, Ravindra *barrister*
Chiacchiere, Mark Dominic *lawyer*
Chiang, Yung Frank *law educator*
Chidnese, Patrick N. *lawyer*
Chilton, Bradley Stewart *law educator*
Chin, Davis *lawyer*
Chinn, Mark Allan *lawyer*
Chisholm, Tommy *lawyer, utility company executive*
Cho, Byung-Sun *law educator*
Cho, Sung Yoon *law librarian*
Choate, Edward Lee *lawyer, educator*
Chong, Stephen Chu Ling *lawyer*
Chopin, Susan Gardiner *lawyer*
Chou, Yung-Ming *lawyer*
Choukas-Bradley, James Richard *lawyer*
Chow, Amy Hau Kuen *lawyer, contract negotiator, consultant*
Chow, Charn Ki Kenneth *lawyer*
Chrisant, Rosemarie Kathryn *law library administrator*
Christian, Gary Irvin *lawyer*
Christiansen, Roy Hvidkaer *lawyer*
Christol, Carl Q(uimby) *lawyer, political science educator*
Christopher, Warren *lawyer, former government official*
Christy, Arthur Hill *lawyer*
Chudzinski, Mark Adam *lawyer*
Chung Teh, Lee *lawyer*
Chynoweth, W. Edward *retired lawyer, farmer*
Cicconi, Christopher M. *lawyer*
Cinque, Dean Anthony *lawyer*
Cioffi, Michael Lawrence *lawyer*
Clark, Alastair Trevor *barrister, museum administrator*
Clark, David McKenzie *lawyer*
Clark, Grant Lawrence *corporate lawyer*
Clark, Joseph Francis, Jr. *lawyer*
Clark, Mark Jeffrey *paralegal, researcher*
Clark, Ross Bert, II *lawyer*
Clark, R(ufus) Bradbury *lawyer*
Clarke, Philip H. *law educator, university administrator*
Clary, Bradley G. *lawyer, educator*
Clary, Richard Wayland *lawyer*
Clements, Robin Edward *lawyer, company director*
Clemons, Bill *lawyer*
Clergerie, Jean-Louis *law educator, researcher*
Closson, Walter Franklin *prosecutor*
Clouse, John Daniel *lawyer*
Clubb, Bruce Edwin *retired lawyer*
Clyne, Patrick Francis *solicitor*
Coates, Glenn Richard *lawyer*
Cobb, Ty *lawyer*
Cobbett, Stuart Hanson *lawyer*
Cobey, Christopher Earle *lawyer*
Cobey, John Geoffrey *lawyer*
Coburn, Niall Francis *lawyer, educator, author*
Cochran, John M., III *lawyer*
Cody, Daniel Schaffner *lawyer*
Coffield, Conrad Eugene *lawyer*
Cohen, Cynthia Marylyn *lawyer*
Cohen, Edwin Samuel *lawyer, educator*
Cohen, Jeffrey Michael *lawyer*
Cohen, Joshua Robert *lawyer*
Cohen, Martin David *lawyer*
Cohen, Robert Stephan *lawyer*
Cohen, Ronald J. *lawyer*
Colbey, Richard *barrister, writer*
Cole, Charles Dewey, Jr. *lawyer*
Cole, Charles DuBose, II *law educator*
Cole, Phillip Allen *lawyer*
Coleman, James Julian *lawyer*
Coleman, James Julian, Jr. *lawyer, industrialist, real estate executive*
Coleman, Rexford Lee *lawyer, educator*
Coleman, Robert J. *lawyer*
Coleman, Roderick Flynn *lawyer*
Colen, Frederick Haas *lawyer*
Colessides, Nick John *lawyer*
Coletti, John Anthony *lawyer, furniture and realty company executive*
Colfin, Bruce Elliott *lawyer, video producer*
Colin, Jean-Pierre *law educator*
Collins, Don Cary *lawyer*
Collins, James Slade, II *lawyer*
Cologne, Gordon Bennett *lawyer*
Colson, Earl Morton *lawyer*
Combe, Michel *lawyer*
Combs, W(illiam) Henry, III *lawyer*
Condo, James Robert *lawyer*
Congalton, Christopher William *lawyer*
Conkel, Robert Dale *lawyer, pension consultant*
Conner, Michael Timothy *lawyer*
Conner, Warren Wesley *lawyer*
Connolly, K. Thomas *lawyer*
Conrad, John Regis *lawyer, engineering executive, consultant*
Conradsen, Keld Ole *associate lawyer*
Cook, Eugene Augustus *lawyer*
Cook, Harry Clayton, Jr. *lawyer*
Cook, Helena Mary *lawyer, researcher*
Cooke, Kevin George *lawyer, consultant, executive*
Cooney, J(ohn) Gordon, Jr. *lawyer*
Cooper, Margaret Leslie *lawyer*
Cooper, Michael Lee *lawyer*
Cooper, Richard Alan *lawyer*
Cooper, Stephanie R. *lawyer*
Copeland, James E. *lawyer*
Copeland, Roy Wilson *lawyer*
Cordell, Hilary Margaret *solicitor*
Cordwell, Nigel Martin *advocate, solicitor*
Cornaby, Kay Sterling *lawyer, former state senator*
Correale, Givlio *public administrator educator, lawyer*
Corson, Kimball Jay *lawyer*
Cosmas, Georges *legal administrator*
Costello, Kelly Lynn *lawyer*
Costello, Kenneth R. *lawyer*
Costenbader, Charles Michael *lawyer*
Costiglio, Lawrence U. *lawyer*
Cotchett, Joseph Winters *lawyer, author*
Cotter, James Michael *lawyer*
Cotter, Richard Timothy *lawyer*
Cotterrell, Roger Brian Melvyn *law educator*
Coukos, Stephen John *lawyer*
Courteau, Girard Robert *prosecutor*
Cousins, William Joseph *lawyer, litigation consultant*
Coutrelis, André *lawyer*
Covitz, Akiba J. *law educator*
Cowan, Stuart Marshall *lawyer*
Cowart, T(homas) David *lawyer*
Cowles, Frederick Oliver *lawyer*
Cowles, Robert Lawrence *lawyer*
Cowperthwait, Lindley M. *lawyer*
Cowser, Danny Lee *lawyer, mental health specialist*
Cox, John Thomas, Jr. *lawyer*
Cox, William Martin *lawyer, educator*
Craig, William Emerson *lawyer*
Cramer, Mark Clifton *lawyer*
Crane, Roger Ryan, Jr. *lawyer*
Cranford, James Michael *lawyer*
Crapon de Caprona, Count Noël François Marie *lawyer, historian*
Crassweller, Robert Doell *retired lawyer, writer*
Crawford, John Fort *lawyer*
Creed, Christian Carl *lawyer, investigator*
Creenan, Katherine Heras *lawyer*
Creggy, Stuart *retired lawyer*
Creighton, William Breen *lawyer, educator*
Cremin, Susan Elizabeth *lawyer*
Cribbet, John Edward *law educator, former university chancellor*
Croce, Paul W. *lawyer*
Crocker, Saone Baron *lawyer*
Cromley, Jon Lowell *lawyer*
Crommelin, Michael *law educator, university dean*
Crookenden, Simon Robert *barrister*
Crosby, William Duncan, Jr. *lawyer*
Crosio, Stefano *lawyer*
Cross, Milton H. *lawyer*
Crossan, John Robert *lawyer*
Crotty, Robert Bell *lawyer*
Crowell, Kenneth E. *lawyer, chemical engineer*
Crown, Nancy Elizabeth *lawyer*
Crum, Henry Hayne *lawyer*
Crumpton, Charles Whitmarsh *lawyer*
Cruz-Mayor, Antonio Manuel *lawyer, real estate and shipping executive*
Cuevas de Dolmetsch, Angela *lawyer*
Cuiffo, Frank Wayne *lawyer*
Cullen, Mark Kenneth *lawyer*
Culp, Nathan Craig *lawyer*
Cummings, Anthony William *lawyer, educator, banker*
Cummings, John Patrick *lawyer*
Cunningham, Craig Neil *lawyer*
Cunningham, Gary H. *lawyer*
Cunningham, Pierce Edward *lawyer, city planner*
Cunningham, Tom Alan *lawyer*
Curley, Robert Ambrose, Jr. *lawyer*
Curran, William P. *lawyer*
Curtis, James Theodore *lawyer*
Curtis, Karen Haynes *lawyer*
Cutchins, Clifford Armstrong, IV *lawyer*
Czaczkes, Morris *lawyer*
Czajkowski, Frank Henry *lawyer*
Dagtoglou, Prodromos *lawyer, educator*
Daily, Frank J(erome) *lawyer*
Dalgaard-Knudsen, Frants *lawyer*
D'Amico, Andrew J. *lawyer*
Danas, Andrew Michael *lawyer*
Dane, Stephen Mark *lawyer*
Dang, Marvin S. C. *lawyer*
Daniel, George Paul *lawyer, consultant*
Danielson, Derek Arthur *lawyer, barrister*
Dann, Alexander William, Jr. *lawyer*
Danneskiold-Samsoe, Ulrik Otto Hubert Viggo *lawyer*
Danziger, Peter *lawyer*
Dapello, Joseph J. *lawyer*
d'Aquino, Thomas *lawyer, business council chief executive*
Dariotis, Terrence Theodore *lawyer*
Darke, Richard Francis *lawyer*
Darling, Scott Edward *lawyer*
Daroff, William Clayton *lawyer*
Dauses, Manfred Albert *law educator*
David, Reuben *lawyer*
Davidson, James Joseph, III *lawyer*
Davis, Alan Jay *lawyer*
Davis, Andrew Neil *lawyer, educator*
Davis, Creswell Dean *lawyer, consultant*
Davis, Dai *solicitor*
Davis, Earon Scott *environmental health law consultant, lawyer*
Davis, E(dward) Marcus *lawyer*
Davis, Ferd Leary, Jr. *law educator, lawyer, consultant*
Davis, J. Alan *lawyer, writer*
Davis, Martin Clay *lawyer, professor*
Davis, Michael C. *law educator, commentator, activist, speaker*
Davis, Michael Steven *lawyer*
Davis, Muller *lawyer*
Davis, Robert Lawrence *lawyer*
Davy, Denis *lawyer*
Day, Christopher Mark *lawyer*
Daynard, Richard Alan *law educator*
Dazey, William Boyd *retired lawyer*
Dean, Martha Anne *lawyer*
De Boos, Rodney Malcolm *lawyer*
de Feydeau de Saint-Christophe, Henri *lawyer*
de Gaulle, Charles *lawyer, politician*
De Goff, Victoria Joan *lawyer*
de Holmsky, Dmitry *lawyer*
de la Garza, Luis Adolfo *lawyer, energy company executive*
Delgado Barrio, Francisco Javier *president supreme court of Spain*
Delgado Rivera, Flavio *lawyer, consultant*
Delo, Ellen Sanderson *lawyer*
de Lousanoff, Oleg *lawyer*
Delp, Ludwig *solicitor, consultant*
Demoyen, Christian André Jean *lawyer*
Dempsey, Bernard Hayden, Jr. *lawyer*
Dempsey, Edward Joseph *lawyer*
DeMuro, Paul Robert *lawyer*
Denger, Michael L. *lawyer*
Denoon Duncan, Russell Euan *solicitor, consultant*
Densmore, Douglas Warren *lawyer*
Denten, Christopher Peter *lawyer*
De Pfyffer, Andre *lawyer*
Derdenger, Patrick *lawyer*
Derrington, Sarah Catherine *barrister*
Desai, Aashish Y. *lawyer*
Desai, Jignasa *lawyer*
de Souza, William Jeremy *solicitor*
de Villiers, Ingrid Barbara *lawyer*
Devine, Antoine Maurice *lawyer*
Devine, Eugene Peter *lawyer*
Devins, Robert Sylvester *retired lawyer*
Devlin, John Gerard *lawyer, author*
DeVries, Donald Lawson, Jr. *lawyer*
Dewey, Anne Elizabeth Marie *lawyer*
Dexter, Deirdre O'Neil Elizabeth *lawyer*
Diamond, Paul Steven *lawyer*
Diamond, Richard S. *lawyer*
Dib, Albert James *lawyer*
Dickson, Gregory John *lawyer*
Diel, Mark A.C. *barrister*
Dierks, Christian *attorney, physician, consultant*
Diez de Velasco, Manuel *barrister, educator*
Dignan, Thomas Gregory, Jr. *lawyer*
Dillard, John Robert *lawyer*
Dilling, Kirkpatrick Wallwick *lawyer*
Dillon, Joseph Francis *lawyer*
Dilts, Jon Paul *law educator*
Di Mascio, John Philip *lawyer*
Dinerstein, Robert Charles *lawyer, bank executive*
Dingemans, Jan Johan *lawyer*
Diodosio, Charles Joseph *lawyer*
DiPietro, Mark Joseph *lawyer*
Dissen, James Hardiman *lawyer*
Dixon, E. A., Jr. *lawyer*
Dixon, Giles Clifford *solicitor*
Dockrell, John Henry *lawyer*
Dockterman, Michael *lawyer*
Dodd, Hiram, Jr. *lawyer*
Doerries, Chantal-Aimée *barrister*
Doherty, Glen Patrick *lawyer*
Dokurno, Anthony David *lawyer*
Dolan, Andrew Kevin *lawyer*
Dole, Robert J. *lawyer, former senator*
Doleac, Charles Bartholomew *lawyer*
Dolin, Lonny H. *lawyer*
Domiano, Joseph Charles *lawyer*
Donegan, Charles Edward *lawyer, educator*
Donnally, Robert Andrew *lawyer, real estate broker*
Donnelly, James Corcoran, Jr. *lawyer*
Donnici, Peter Joseph *lawyer, law educator, consultant*
Dopf, Glenn William *lawyer*
Doremus, Ogden *lawyer*
Dorkey, Charles Edward, III *lawyer*
Dost, Mark W. *lawyer*
Doswald-Beck, Louise *lawyer, international association executive*
Doubinskiy, Michael Illich *lawyer*
Douchkess, George *lawyer*
Doughty, Mark Anthony *lawyer*
Douginsky, Michael Illich *lawyer*
Dowling, Vincent John *lawyer*
Downer, Robert Nelson *lawyer*
Downey, Brian Patrick *lawyer*
Doyle, Anthony Peter *lawyer*
Doyle, David Anthony *barrister, solicitor*
Doyle, Gerard Francis *lawyer*
Draper, Gerald Linden *lawyer*
Dressel, Henry Francis *retired lawyer*
Dressen, Freddy Simeon *lawyer*
Driessen, Bart *lawyer*
Drinko, John Deaver *lawyer*
Drucker, Alison R. *lawyer*
Dubé, Lawrence Edward, Jr. *lawyer*
DuCanto, Joseph Nunzio *lawyer, educator*
Duczynski, Margaret Schilt (Margaret Schilt Austin) *lawyer*
Dudley, George Ellsworth *lawyer*
Dulaney, Richard Alvin *lawyer*
Dulles, Frederick Hendrik *lawyer*
DuMontier, Clarissa W. *lawyer*
Dunaway, Bridget *lawyer*
Dundas, Philip Blair, Jr. *lawyer*
Dunér, Karin Gunilla *lawyer*
Dunham, Frank Willard *lawyer*
Dunkley, Philip Christopher *lawyer*
Dunlay, Catherine Telles *lawyer*
Dunn, Herbert Irvin *lawyer*
Dunn, William Bradley *lawyer*
Du Plessis, Jean Jacques *law educator*
Dupont, Wesley David *lawyer*
DuPriest, Douglas Millhollen *lawyer*
Duquette, Donald Norman *law educator*
Durham, Harry Blaine, III *lawyer*
Du Rocher, James Howard *lawyer*
Duus, Gordon Cochran *lawyer*
Duyen, Vo Ha *lawyer*
Dworkin, Michael Leonard *lawyer*
Dye, Bradford Johnson, Jr. *lawyer, former state official*
Dyer, Charles Arnold *lawyer*
Dyer, Cromwell Adair, Jr. *lawyer, international organization official*
Eaby, Christian Earl *lawyer, small business owner*
Earle, Victor Montagne, III *lawyer*
Early, Bert Hylton *lawyer*
Early, James H., Jr. *lawyer*
Eason, Marcia Jean *lawyer*
Eastland, S. Stacy *lawyer*
Eaton, Joel Douglas *lawyer*
Ebel, Friedrich *law educator*
Ebell, C(ecil) Walter *lawyer*
Ebiner, Robert Maurice *lawyer*
Echeveverria, John D. *lawyer*
Eck, Matthias Heinrich *lawyer*
Eckbo, Eivind Higford *lawyer, deputy member of parliament*
Eckl, William Wray *lawyer*
Edelbaum, Philip R. *lawyer*
Edelman, Bernard Paul *lawyer, counselor*
Eden, Nathan E. *lawyer*
Eder-Rieder, Maria Anna *law educator*
Edmondson, Frank Kelley, Jr. *lawyer, legal administrator*
Edson, Charles Louis *lawyer, educator*
Edwards, Carl Norman *lawyer*
Edwards, Carl Ray, II *lawyer*
Edwards, Harry LaFoy *lawyer*
Edwards, James Alfred *lawyer*
Edwards, Priscilla Ann *paralegal, business owner*
Eekelaar, John Michael *law educator*
Eggert, Russell Raymond *lawyer*
Ehlermann, Claus-Dieter *law educator*
Ehlinger, Ralph Jerome *lawyer*
Ehmann, Anthony Valentine *lawyer*
Ehrlich, Thomas *law educator*
Eisele, John Eugene *lawyer*
Eisen, Eric Anshel *lawyer*
Ejiri, Takashi *lawyer*
Eldridge, Douglas Alan *lawyer*
Eldridge, Richard Mark *lawyer*
Elfers, Thomas Earl *lawyer, educator*
El-Helw, Maged Ragheb *law educator*
Elkins, Robert Neal *lawyer*
Elkins-Elliott, Kay *law educator*
Elkinson, Jeffrey Philip *barrister*
Ellickson, Robert Chester *law educator*
Ellin, Marvin *lawyer*
Elliott, Edwin Donald, Jr. *law educator, federal administrator, environmental lawyer*
Elliott, Richard Howard *lawyer*
Elliott, Thomas Clark, Jr. *lawyer*
Elliott, Warren G. *lawyer*
Ellis, Alfred Wright (Al Ellis) *lawyer*
Ellis, Donald Lee *lawyer*
Ellis, James Alvis, Jr. *lawyer*
Ellmann, Douglas Stanley *lawyer*
Ellmann, William Marshall *lawyer, mediator, arbitrator, researcher*
Elmer, Michael Bendik *legal administrator*
Elrod, Eugene Richard *lawyer*
Elsen, Sheldon Howard *lawyer*
Elsener, G. Dale *lawyer*
Elson, Charles Myer *law educator*
Eltgroth, George Vincent *lawyer*
Elwin, James William, Jr. *lawyer*
Embry, Stephen Creston *lawyer*
Emhardt, Charles David *lawyer*
Emmanouel, Andrew John *barrister*
Emvalomenos, Dimitris *lawyer*
Ence, Matthew Duane *lawyer*
Engel, David Lewis *lawyer*
Engel, Ralph Manuel *lawyer*
Engel, Tala *lawyer*
England, John Melvin *lawyer, clergyman*
Englert, Roy Theodore, Jr. *lawyer*
Ensenat, Donald Burnham *lawyer, former ambassador*
Enslen, Pamela Chapman *lawyer*
Epperson, Joel Rodman *lawyer*
Eppes, Walter W., Jr. *retired lawyer*
Epps, James Haws, III *lawyer*
Epstein, Judith Ann *lawyer*
Epstein, Michael Alan *lawyer*
Erauw, Johan Achiel *lawyer, educator, commercial arbitrator*
Ergec, Rusen *law educator, lawyer*
Ergenç, Mustafa Nida *lawyer*
Erma, Reino Mauri *lawyer, university chancellor emeritus*
Ernst, Daniel Pearson *lawyer*
Escarraz, Enrique, III *lawyer*
Escudero, Juan *solicitor*
Esser, Carl Eric *lawyer*
Essien, Prince Uwem Ekpo *lawyer, consultant*
Essmyer, Michael Martin *lawyer*
Estes, Andrew Harper *lawyer*
Estes, Carl Lewis, II *lawyer*
Estes, Richard Martin *lawyer*
Esty, Daniel Cushing *lawyer*
Etherington, Edwin Deacon *lawyer, business executive, educator*
Ettinger, Joseph Alan *lawyer*
Eubank, Stephen Reid *lawyer*
Eubanks, Ronald W. *lawyer, broadcaster*
Evans, Douglas Hayward *lawyer*
Evans, G. Anne *lawyer*
Evans, Lawrence E. *lawyer, educator*
Evans, Lawrence Jack, Jr. *lawyer, judge*
Evans, Paul Vernon *lawyer*
Evans, Trevor Mills *retired solicitor, retired coroner*
Even, Francis Alphonse *lawyer*
Everbach, Otto George *lawyer*
Everett, James Joseph *lawyer*
Ewell, A. Ben, Jr. *lawyer, businessman*
Ewen, Pamela Binnings *lawyer*
Ewing, Ky Pepper, Jr. *lawyer*
Eyzaguirre, Jose Maria *lawyer*
Faber, Robert Charles *lawyer*
Faerman, Silvia Fabiana *lawyer*
Fahlbeck, Reinhold Hans *legal studies educator*
Faiss, Robert Dean *lawyer*
Fajardo, Beda Gavino *lawyer*
Falco, Mathea *lawyer, educator*
Falkner, William Carroll *lawyer*
Faller, Rhoda Dianne Grossberg *lawyer*
Falvey, Patrick Joseph *lawyer*
Farber, Donald Clifford *lawyer, educator*
Faricy, John Hartnett, Jr. *lawyer*
Farina, John *lawyer*
Farjat, Gérard *law educator*
Farley, Thomas T. *lawyer*
Farnham, Clayton Henson *lawyer*

Long, Thad Gladden lawyer
Lopez, David Tiburcio lawyer, educator, arbitrator, mediator
Lopez, Reynaldo Galvez lawyer, partner, educator
Lopez-Guevara, Carlos Alfredo lawyer
Lorch, Amnon lawyer
Lordi, Katherine Mary lawyer
Lorenzo, Nicholas Francis, Jr. lawyer
Loubet, Jeffrey W. lawyer
Loughridge, John Halsted, Jr. lawyer
Louit, Christian Georges law educator, solicitor
Love, Jeffrey Benton lawyer
Lovell, Carl Erwin, Jr. lawyer
Lowder, Charles Lynn lawyer
Lowe, Alan Vaughan legal educator, barrister
Lowell, Stanley Herbert lawyer
Lowenfels, Lewis David lawyer
Lowenhaupt, Charles Abraham lawyer
Lowery, William Herbert lawyer
Lowndes, John Foy lawyer
Lowry, David Burton lawyer
Lozada, Salvador Maria lawyer, educator
Lubar, Charles Gordon lawyer
Lubic, Robert Bennett lawyer, arbitrator, law educator
Lucas, Rhett Roy mediator, arbitrator, lawyer, chemical engineer, artist, photographer
Lucas, Steven Mitchell lawyer
Luckey, Alwyn Hall lawyer
Lumbard, Eliot Howland lawyer, educator
Lund, James Louis lawyer
Lunde, Asbjorn Rudolph lawyer
Lundman, Ulf Peter Michael lawyer, composer, writer
Lunt, Jennifer Lee lawyer
Lupert, Leslie Allan lawyer
Lutz, John Shafroth lawyer
Luxton, Jane C(harlotte) lawyer
Luzzatto, Edgar lawyer
Lybecker, Martin Earl lawyer
Lyden, John Michael Ernest arbitrator, surveyor
Lyerla, Bradford Peter lawyer
Lyman, David lawyer
Lynch, Douglas Sir lawyer
Lynch, John James lawyer
Lynch, Paul Patrick corporate lawyer
Lyon, Bruce Arnold lawyer, educator
Lyon, James Burroughs lawyer
Ma, Alan Wai-Chuen lawyer
MacCormack, Geoffrey Dennis lawyer, researcher
MacDonald, Kirk Stewart lawyer
Macdonald, Lenna Ruth lawyer
Mace, Stephen Alan investment advisor
MacFarlane, Anne Bridget retired court master
Mackall, Henry Clinton lawyer
Mackey, Leonard Bruce lawyer, former diversified manufacturing corporation executive
MacLean, Babcock lawyer
Macleod, John Amend lawyer
MacRae, Cameron Farquhar, III lawyer
Madden, Ian Beresford lawyer, historian
Madsen, H(enry) Stephen retired lawyer
Madu, Leonard Ekwugha lawyer, human rights officer, newspaper columnist, politician, business executive
Maffei, Rocco John lawyer
Magid, Per lawyer
Maguire, Kevin Jerome lawyer
Maguire, Raymer F., Jr. lawyer
Mahar, Ellen Patricia law librarian
Maher, Stephen Trivett lawyer, educator
Mahmood, Adnan Baquar lawyer
Mahoney, Kathleen Mary lawyer
Maier, Peter Klaus lawyer, business executive
Mailander, William Stephen lawyer
Maitland, Guy Edison Clay lawyer
Malinowski, Arthur Anthony lawyer, labor arbitrator
Malm, Roger Charles lawyer
Maloney, Pat, Sr. lawyer
Maloon, Jerry L. trial lawyer, physician, medicolegal consultant
Malorzo, Thomas Vincent lawyer
Mancuso, Eva-Marie lawyer
Mandel, Maurice, II lawyer, educator
Mandelker, Daniel Robert law educator
Mangum, John K. lawyer
Manire, James McDonnell lawyer
Manley, David Bott, III lawyer
Mannino, Edward Francis lawyer
Mannino, Robert lawyer
Mannix, Charles Raymond law educator
Manoogian, William lawyer
Manson, Keith Alan Michael lawyer
Mapes, William Rodgers, Jr. lawyer
Mar, Eugene lawyer, financial consultant
Marambio Núñez, Alejandro Octavio lawyer, consultant
Marcusa, Fred Haye lawyer
Marger, Edwin lawyer
Margolin, Abraham Eugene lawyer
Marinis, Thomas Paul, Jr. lawyer
Mark, Michael David lawyer
Mark, Timothy Ivan lawyer
Markham, Jesse William, Jr. lawyer
Marlin, Richard lawyer
Marlow, James Allen lawyer
Marlow, Orval Lee, II lawyer
Marques, Hector Nestor lawyer
Marshall, Enid Ann law educator
Marshall, William Taylor lawyer
Marstrand-Jorgensen, Mads lawyer
Martens, S.K. legal administrator, retired
Martin, Andrew Ayers lawyer, physician, educator
Martin, Dallas Rea lawyer
Martin, Jay Griffith lawyer
Martin, Paul Edward lawyer
Martin, Quinn William lawyer
Martin, Walter retired lawyer
Martin-Smith, Nicholas lawyer, consultant
Martori, Joseph Peter lawyer
Martucci, William Christopher lawyer
Marvin, Charles Rodney, Jr. lawyer
Marvin, Monica Louise Wolf lawyer
Marx, Peter A. lawyer
Mason, David Charles lawyer
Massey, Kathleen Marie Oates lawyer
Masters, Jon Joseph corporate governance consultant, mediator
Mastronardi, Corinne Marie lawyer
Mateer, Don Metz lawyer
Materna, Joseph Anthony lawyer
Mathews, Elizabeth lawyer, healthcare administrator
Mathis, Samuel Mark lawyer
Matic, Tin lawyer, journal editor
Matteson, William Bleecker lawyer
Matthews, Andrew Julian Morton solicitor
Matug, Alexander Peter lawyer
Mauldin, John Inglis public defender
Maule, James Edward law educator, lawyer
Mavrellis, Christos Demosthenes lawyer
Maxwell, Richard Callender lawyer, educator
May, Alan Alfred lawyer
Mayne, Wiley Edward lawyer
Mazo, Mark Elliott lawyer
McAfee, William Gage lawyer
McAlhany, Toni Anne lawyer
McAlpin, Kirk Martin lawyer
McAmis, Edwin Earl lawyer
McAndrew, Paul Joseph, Jr. lawyer
McBride, Kenneth Eugene lawyer, title company executive
McBroom, Thomas William, Sr. lawyer
McBurney, Charles Walker, Jr. lawyer
Mc Callum, Charles Edward lawyer
McCarty, William Michael, Jr. lawyer
McClain, William Andrew lawyer
McClaugherty, Joe L. lawyer, educator
McClellan, Janet Elaine law educator
McClure, William Pendleton lawyer
McCoid, Nancy Katherine lawyer
McCollum, James Fountain lawyer
McCombs, Mark James lawyer
McConnell, David Kelso lawyer
McCormick, David Arthur lawyer
McCormick, Homer L., Jr. lawyer
McCrery, David Neil, III lawyer
McCullough, Edward Eugene patent agent, inventor
McCullough, Frank Witcher, III lawyer
McCune, Philip Spear lawyer
McCurley, Mary Johanna lawyer
McDaniel, Donald Hamilton lawyer
McDaniel, James Edwin lawyer
McDaniel, Jarrel Dave lawyer
McDermott, Kevin R. lawyer
McDermott, Thomas John, Jr. lawyer
McDiarmid, Robert Campbell lawyer
McDonald, Michael Scott lawyer
McDonell, Neil Edwin lawyer
McDougall, Gerald Duane lawyer
McElvein, Thomas Irving, Jr. lawyer
McFarland, Robert Edwin lawyer
McGee, James Francis lawyer
McGinnis, Thomas Michael lawyer
McGlamry, Max Reginald lawyer
McGovern, David Carr lawyer
McGovern, Theresa M. law educator
McGrath, Thomas J. lawyer, writer, film producer
McGuane, Frank L., Jr. lawyer
McGuire, Edward David, Jr. lawyer
McGuire, James Grant lawyer
McHale, Michael John lawyer
McHugh, James Joseph lawyer
McIntyre, Anita Grace Jordan lawyer
McIntyre, Bernice Kay lawyer, management consultant
McKay, John Judson, Jr. lawyer
McKay, Michael Wendell lawyer
McKean, Roderick Hugh Ross solicitor
McKenna, Frederick Gregory lawyer, consultant
McKenzie, Paul Douglas lawyer
McKeown, H. Mary lawyer, educator
McKinney, Bridget McArdle lawyer
McKinney, Dennis Keith lawyer
McKinstry, Ronald Eugene lawyer
McKinzie, Carl Wayne lawyer
McKittrick, Neil Vincent lawyer
McLain, William Allen lawyer
McLean, Susan Ralston lawyer
McLees, John Alan lawyer
McLellan, John Paul lawyer
McLendon, Susan Michelle lawyer, nurse
McLeod, Walton James lawyer, state legislator
McLeod, William Lasater, Jr. lawyer, former judge and state legislator
McManis, James lawyer
McManus, Francis law educator
McMeen, Elmer Ellsworth, III lawyer, guitarist
McNulty, William Joseph solicitor
McQuaid, John Gaffney lawyer
McReynolds, Mary Armilda lawyer
McVeigh, Joseph lawyer, geologist
Meador, Daniel John law educator
Medalie, Susan Diane lawyer, management consultant
Medearis, Miller lawyer
Meehan, Richard Thomas, Jr. lawyer
Meer, Farooq Amjad lawyer
Meessen, Karl M. commercial law educator
Mehta, Eileen Rose lawyer
Mekeel, Robert K. lawyer
Melbardis, Wolfgang Alexander lawyer
Melican, James Patrick, Jr. lawyer
Mellis, Michael J. lawyer
Meltzer, Bernard David law educator
Mendelsohn, Stuart lawyer, elected official
Menefee, Samuel Pyeatt lawyer, anthropologist
Mengel, Christopher Emile lawyer, educator
Mentz, Barbara Antonello lawyer
Mentz, Lawrence lawyer
Mercau Saavedra, Andres Juan lawyer
Meroni, Rudolf lawyer
Merrill, George Vanderneth lawyer, investment executive
Mersel, Marjorie Kathryn Pedersen lawyer
Mersman, Richard Kendrick, III lawyer
Merwin, John David retired lawyer, former governor
Meschkow, Jordan M. lawyer
Meshbesher, Ronald I. lawyer
Messina, Bonnie Lynn lawyer
Mestel, Mark David lawyer
Metchik, Mortimer J. retired lawyer
Meyer, Irwin Stephan lawyer, accountant
Meyer, J. Theodore lawyer
Meyer, Paul A. lawyer
Meyer, Philip Gilbert lawyer
Meyers, Jan E. lawyer
Meyers, Tedson Jay lawyer
Meyerson, Christopher Cortlandt law scholar
Mezvinsky, Edward M. lawyer
Mian, Ajmal chief justice
Micale, Frank Jude lawyer
Michaelis, Karen Lauree law educator
Michel, Keith solicitor, author
Michelstetter, Stanley Hubert lawyer
Michenfelder, Albert A. lawyer
Middendorf, Henry Stump, Jr. lawyer
Middleton, James Boland lawyer
Midkiff, Kimberly Ann paralegal
Mihaylov, Nikolay lawyer
Mikels, Richard Eliot lawyer
Miley, Stefany Ann lawyer
Milkey, James R. environmental lawyer
Milks, William Woods lawyer
Millar, Richard William, Jr. lawyer
Millard, Neal Steven lawyer
Miller, Arthur Harold lawyer
Miller, Arthur Madden lawyer, investment banker
Miller, Douglas Andrew lawyer, educator
Miller, Dwight Whittemore lawyer
Miller, Gary H. lawyer
Miller, Herbert H. lawyer
Miller, John T., Jr. lawyer, educator
Miller, J(ohn) Wesley, III lawyer, writer
Miller, Joseph Bayard lawyer
Miller, Louis H. lawyer
Miller, Randal J. lawyer, educator
Miller, Stephen Ralph lawyer
Miller, Stephen Wiley lawyer
Miller, Suzanne Marie state librarian, educator
Miller, Thomas Eugene lawyer, writer
Millett, John Antill lawyer, accountant, poet
Mills, Barbara barrister
Milne, David, IV lawyer
Milton, Harold W., Jr. lawyer
Milton, Joseph Payne lawyer
Mimms, Thomas Bowman, Jr. lawyer
Minna, Anthony Joseph lawyer
Minsky, Bruce William lawyer
Minter, Alan Huntress lawyer
Mintz, Jeffry Alan lawyer
Mintz, Ronald Steven lawyer, photojournalist
Mintzer, Edward Carl, Jr. lawyer
Mitchell, Ada Mae Boyd legal assistant
Mitchell, Allan Edwin lawyer
Mitchell, Charles Edward lawyer
Mitchell, Paul England solicitor
Mitchell, Ronnie Monroe lawyer, educator
Mitchell, William Graham Champion lawyer, business executive
Miyamoto, Yasumi law educator
Miyashita, Yoshiyuki lawyer
Mody, Zia Jaydev lawyer
Moeller, Floyd Douglas lawyer
Moerbeek, Stanley Leonard lawyer
Moerdler, Charles Gerard lawyer
Moessner, Joerg Manfred law educator, tax court judge
Moffatt, Michael Alan lawyer
Moffett, J. Denny lawyer
Moize, Jerry Dee lawyer, government official
Moldoff, William Morris retired lawyer
Molnar, Lawrence lawyer
Monaghan, Jessine Adrienne lawyer
Monateri, Pier Giuseppe law educator
Mondul, Donald David patent lawyer
Mónica, António De Carvalho Godinho lawyer
Monohan, Edward Sheehan, IV lawyer
Monroe, Murray Shipley lawyer
Monson, John Rudolph lawyer
Montgomery, Charles Harvey lawyer
Montgomery, John Warwick law educator, theologian
Monya, Nobuo law educator, arbitrator
Monypeny, David Murray lawyer
Moody, Willard James, Sr. lawyer
Mooney, Thomas Robert lawyer
Moore, Christopher Minor lawyer
Moore, Edward Warren lawyer
Moore, Hugh Jacob, Jr. lawyer
Moore, John Cordell retired lawyer
Moore, Marianna Gay law librarian, consultant
Moore, Rodney Gregory lawyer
Mord, Irving Conrad, II lawyer
Morgan, Kermit Johnson lawyer
Morgan, Richard Greer lawyer
Morganroth, Fred lawyer
Moroney, Michael John lawyer
Morpeth, Iain Cardean Spottiswoode solicitor
Morphonios, Dean B. lawyer
Morris, Gary Wayne lawyer
Morris, James Malachy lawyer
Morris, Roy Leslie lawyer, electrical engineer, venture capitalist
Morrison, John Martin lawyer
Morrison, Michael Dean lawyer, law educator
Morse, Christopher George John law educator
Morse, M. Howard lawyer
Mosenson, Steven Harris lawyer
Moser, Michael Joseph lawyer
Mosk, Richard Mitchell lawyer
Moss, Bill Ralph lawyer
Mossinghoff, Gerald Joseph patent lawyer, educator
Mount, Christopher John solicitor
Mousel, Craig Lawrence lawyer
Moya, Olga Lydia law educator
Moynihan, John Bignell lawyer
Mucci, Gary Louis lawyer
Mueller, Shirley Anne lawyer, real estate broker
Mugridge, David Raymond lawyer, educator, writer
Mull, Gale W. lawyer
Mulroy, Thomas Robert, Jr. lawyer
Mundheim, Robert Harry law educator
Mungia, Salvador Alejo, Jr. lawyer
Munson, Nancy Kay lawyer
Murai, Rene Vicente lawyer
Muraski, Anthony Augustus lawyer
Murchison, David Claudius lawyer
Murphy, Daniel Ignatius lawyer
Murphy, Daniel J. lawyer
Murphy, Deborah Jane lawyer
Murray, Daniel Richard lawyer
Murray, Stephen James lawyer
Murry, Harold David, Jr. lawyer
Murtaugh, John Patrick lawyer
Mwenda, Kenneth Kaoma legal consultant, educator
Myers, Rodman Nathaniel lawyer
Myers, Sidney Albert lawyer
Myhand, Wanda Reshel paralegal, legal assistant
Myles, Travis Olen, Jr. lawyer
Myllynen, Olli-Pekka lawyer, Finnish government official
Nachwalter, Michael lawyer
Nacol, Mae lawyer
Nadasen, Sundrasagaran law educator
Naftalis, Gary Philip lawyer, educator
Nagle, Mark Earl lawyer
Nagy, Boldizsár lawyer, educator
Nakata, Gary Kenji lawyer
Nally, Edward solicitor
Nance, John Joseph lawyer, writer, air safety analyst, broadcaster, consultant
Narayan, Beverly Elaine lawyer
Narmont, John Stephen lawyer
Nassar, William Michael lawyer
Nast, Dianne Martha lawyer
Nath, Ravi lawyer
Nations, Howard Lynn lawyer
Natori, Jeffrey Kazuo lawyer
Nayak, Rajendra Kumar lawyer
Naylor, Paul Donald lawyer
Nazaryk, Paul Alan lawyer, environmental consultant
Neff, Fred Leonard lawyer
Neff, Michael prosecutor
Neff, Robert Clark, Sr. lawyer
Neill, Sir (Francis) Patrick lawyer, educator, college administrator
Neira Archila, Luis Carlos legal consultant, accountant
Nelson, Robert Louis lawyer
Nelson, Roy Hugh, Jr. lawyer, mediator, arbitrator
Nelson, Steven Dwayne lawyer
Nelson, William Eugene lawyer
Neltner, Michael Martin lawyer
Nesland, James Edward lawyer
NeSmith, Kimblin Eugene law educator
Newburg, Andre lawyer
Newman, Lawrence Walker lawyer
Newman, Michael Rodney lawyer
Newsom, James Thomas lawyer
Newsome, Burton Wheeler lawyer
Nexsen, Julian Jacobs, Jr. lawyer
Neykov, Ivan law educator
Nicely, Andrew Abbott lawyer
Nicholas, Frederick M. lawyer
Nicholls, Dale William lawyer
Nicholls, John Anthony solicitor
Nickels, Christopher lawyer
Nicolai, Paul Peter lawyer
Niehuss, John Marvin lawyer
Nielsen, Linda lawyer
Nihoul, Paul Louis law educator
Nijboer, Johannes Fredrikus law educator, judge
Nishimura, Toshiro lawyer
Nisser, Carl Gustav lawyer
Nixon, Scott Sherman lawyer
Nobel, Peter lawyer, researcher
Noddings, Sarah Ellen lawyer
Nohrden, Patrick Thomas lawyer
Nolen, Roy Lemuel lawyer
Nolte, John Michael lawyer, consultant
Nomer, Ergin Nami law educator, university administrator
Noonan, William Donald lawyer, physician
Noorlander, Peter Jan Leendert lawyer, human rights advocate
Nordenberg, Mark Alan law educator, university official
Nordling, Bernard Erick lawyer
Norgaard, Carl Aage law educator
Norman, Albert George, Jr. lawyer
Norris, Charles Head, Jr. lawyer, manufacturing executive
Norris, Glenn L. lawyer
Norris, William Vernon Wentworth lawyer
North, Gerald David William lawyer
Norton, Christopher David legal assistant
Norton, Jay Lewis lawyer, recording company executive
Norton, William Alan lawyer
Norton-Larson, Mary Jean lawyer, planned giving officer
Novak, Joseph Anthony lawyer
Novak, Leslie Howard lawyer
Novak, Mark lawyer
Nowak, John E. law educator
Nugee, Edward George Queen's counsel
Nugent, Lori S. lawyer
Nunez-Mora Fernandez, Maribel lawyer
Nussbaum, Howard Jay lawyer
Nyman, Sven Åke Börje legal administrator, judge
Oakley, John Bilyeu law educator, lawyer, judicial consultant
Oberdank, Lawrence Mark lawyer, arbitrator
Oberin, Colin J. patent lawyer
Oberman, Steven lawyer
O'Brien, Daniel Robert lawyer
O'Brien, David A. lawyer
O'Brien, David Michael law educator
O'Brien, Joan Susan lawyer, educator
O'Connell, Brian Michael lawyer
O'Connell, Daniel James lawyer
O'Connell, Francis Joseph retired lawyer, arbitrator
O'Connell, Margaret Sullivan lawyer
O'Connor, Gayle McCormick law librarian
O'Connor, Kathleen Mary lawyer
O'Dell, Joan Elizabeth lawyer, mediator, business executive, educator
Odza, Randall M. lawyer
Oehler, Richard Dale lawyer
Oellers-Frahm, Karin law educator
Ogden, David William lawyer
Ogg, Wilson Reid lawyer, poet, retired judge, lyricist, curator, publisher, educator, philosopher, social scientist, parapsychologist
O'Higgins, Paul law educator
Okada, Haruo lawyer
Okinaga, Lawrence Shoji lawyer
Olaosebikan, Ebikaboere Bolanle law educator
Oldenburg, Ronald Troy lawyer
Oleisky, Robert Edward lawyer
Oles, Stuart Gregory lawyer
Oliver, Rodney John solicitor
Olschwang, Alan Paul lawyer
Olsen, M. Kent lawyer, educator
Olson, Dennis Oliver lawyer
Olson, Harriett Jane corporate lawyer
Olson, William Jeffrey lawyer
O'Meara, John Francis lawyer
O'Neill, Bradford Knight lawyer, legal translator
Ophof, Henri P. J. lawyer, law educator
Oquendo, Sergio lawyer
Orberson, William Baxter lawyer, educator
Ordoñez-Jonama, Ramiro lawyer
Oriana, Federico Filippo lawyer, educator
Orlovsky, Donald Albert lawyer
O'Rorke, James Francis, Jr. lawyer
O'Rourke, James Louis lawyer
Orth, Paul William lawyer
Osakwe, Christopher lawyer, educator
Osborn, John Edward lawyer, pharmaceutical and biotechnology industry executive, former government official, writer
Osborn, Malcolm Everett lawyer
Osborne, Duncan Elliott lawyer
Osborne, Frank R. lawyer, educator, lecturer
Osborne, Jerry Ramon lawyer
Osharova, Irina A. lawyer
O'Shields, June Cruce lawyer
Oshima, Michael W. lawyer
Ostendorf, Lance Stephen lawyer, investor, financial consultant and planner
Otis, Roy James lawyer
O'Toole, William George lawyer
Otorowski, Christopher Lee lawyer
Otsuka, Akio lawyer, consultant
Ott, Gilbert Russell, Jr. lawyer
Ough, Richard Norman lawyer, physician
Oulton, Richard James lawyer, entrepreneur
Outman, William Dell, II lawyer
Ovsepian, Zhanna Iosifovna law educator

von Hahn, Baron Karl lawyer
von Kalinowski, Julian Onesime lawyer
Von Mandel, Michael Jacques lawyer
von Quitzow, Carl Michael law educator, consultant
Voremberg, Rhoderick Peter Grosvenor solicitor
Vörös, Imre educator
Vorys, Arthur Isaiah lawyer
Vranicar, Michael Gregory lawyer
Vreeland, Victoria Lynn lawyer
Vukić, Zoran lawyer, banking and corporate law consultant
Vukmir, Mladen lawyer
Wachsman, Harvey Frederick lawyer, neurosurgeon
Wächtershäuser, Günter patent lawyer, researcher
Waddles, Lori Bobbitt lawyer
Wade, Robert Alan lawyer
Wagner, Arthur Ward, Jr. lawyer
Wagner, Michael Duane lawyer
Wagner, Wolfgang Heribert patent lawyer
Wahlgren, Mikael Ulf Lennart legal counsel
Waisanen, Christine M. lawyer, writer
Waite, Andrew Jonathan lawyer
Waldeck, John Walter, Jr. lawyer
Walker, Betty Stevens lawyer
Walker, Edward Fahey lawyer, honorary consul
Walker, George Kontz law educator
Walker, John Sumpter, Jr. lawyer
Walker, Lee E. lawyer
Walker, Randall Wayne lawyer
Walker, Woodrow Wilson lawyer, cattle and timber farmer
Wallace, Franklin Sherwood lawyer
Wallace, Ian Norman Duncan barrister
Wallace, Keith lawyer
Wallgren, Carita Christina Helena lawyer
Wallis, Ben Alton, Jr. lawyer
Walsh, David James lawyer
Walsh, Francis R. law educator
Walsh, James Joseph lawyer
Walsh, J(ohn) B(ronson) lawyer
Walsh, Thomas J., Jr. lawyer
Walter, Jeremy Canning lawyer
Walter, Michael Charles lawyer
Walters, David McLean lawyer
Walton, Anthony Michael lawyer
Walton, Dan Gibson lawyer
Wang, Albert Huai-En lawyer
Wang, Charleston Cheng-Kung lawyer, engineer
Wapler, Vincent legal auctioneer
Warburg, Richard Jeremy patent lawyer
Ward, Anthony John lawyer
Ward, Joe Henry, Jr. retired lawyer
Ward, Robert Richard lawyer
Warden, John L. lawyer
Waris, Michael, Jr. lawyer
Warner, Frank Shrake lawyer
Warnock, William Reid lawyer
Wasko, Steven E. lawyer
Wasserman, Stephen Alan lawyer
Watanabe, Hajime lawyer
Waterman, David Moore lawyer
Watmore, Leslie John retired solicitor
Watson, George William lawyer, legal consultant
Watson, Robert Francis lawyer
Weadon, Donald Alford, Jr. lawyer
Weatherup, Roy Garfield lawyer
Weaver, Judith Ann lawyer
Webb, Thomas Irwin, Jr. lawyer
Weber, Arnold I. lawyer
Wedderburn of Charlton, Lord Kenneth William law educator
Weeks, Tresi Lea lawyer
Weil, Cass Sargent lawyer
Weinberg, Robin Sue lawyer
Weiner, Kenneth Brian lawyer
Weiner, Lawrence lawyer
Weinmann, Eric retired lawyer
Weinschelbaum, Emilio lawyer
Weinstein, Alan Edward lawyer
Weinstein, Harris lawyer
Weinstein-Bacal, Stuart Allen lawyer, educator
Weisberg, Adam Jon lawyer
Weisberg, David Charles lawyer
Weiser, Frank Alan lawyer
Weisert, Kent Albert Frederick lawyer
Weisgall, Jonathan Michael lawyer
Weiss, Andrew Richard lawyer, mediator, educator, optician
Weiss, Arnold Hans lawyer, consultant
Weiss, Jonathan Arthur lawyer
Weiss, Ronald Phillip lawyer
Weissbard, Samuel Held lawyer
Welch, David William lawyer
Welch, Joseph Daniel lawyer
Weld, Jonathan Minot lawyer
Weller, Douglas LaFontaine patent lawyer
Weller, Keith A. lawyer, corporate officer
Wells, Benjamin Gladney lawyer
Wells, David Merlin lawyer
Wells, Steven Wayne lawyer
Welsh, Sir Alfred John lawyer, consultant
Welt, Philip Stanley lawyer, consultant
Welton, Charles Ephraim lawyer
Welz, Christian law educator
Wen, Carson lawyer, politician
Wender, Ira Tensard lawyer
Wenner, Charles Roderick lawyer
Wentworth, Larry Marshall lawyer
Wentworth, Theodore Sumner lawyer
Wesel, Uwe law educator
West, John Carl lawyer, former ambassador, former governor
Westerberg, Siv Öman lawyer, physician
Westerhaus, Douglas Bernard lawyer
Wheatley, Charles Henry, III lawyer, biomedical technology company executive
Wheeler, Mark Andrew, Sr. lawyer
White, Bruce David law and ethics educator, consultant
White, Edward Alfred lawyer
White, James Richard lawyer
White, Jeffery Howell lawyer
White, John Jameson solicitor
White, Walter Hiawatha, Jr. lawyer
Whiteside, William Anthony, Jr. lawyer
Whitson, Lish lawyer
Wick, Lawrence Scott lawyer
Wicker, R. David, Jr. lawyer
Wicki, Jodok Eugen lawyer
Wicklund, David Wayne lawyer
Widmayer, Warren J. lawyer
Wieder, Bruce Terrill lawyer, electrical engineer
Wigger, Jarrel L. lawyer
Wilcox, Mark Dean lawyer
Wilde, William Richard lawyer
Wilder, Roland Percival, Jr. lawyer
Wilkinson, Albert Mims, Jr. lawyer
Willey, Charles Wayne lawyer
Williams, Charles Judson lawyer
Williams, Clay Rule lawyer
Williams, Howard Russell lawyer, educator
Williams, John Michael solicitor
Williams, Ronald Doherty lawyer
Williamson, Douglas Franklin, Jr. lawyer
Willingham, Clark Suttles lawyer
Wilske, Stephan lawyer
Wilsman, James Michael lawyer
Wilson, Evelyn L. legal educator
Wilson, Hugh Steven lawyer
Wilson, John Pasley law educator
Wilson, Joseph Morris, III lawyer
Wilson, Julia Ann Yother lawyer
Wilson, LeVon Edward law educator, lawyer
Wilson, Michael Gerald solicitor
Wilson, Michael Moureau lawyer, physician
Wilson, Robert Foster lawyer
Wilson, Thomas Matthew, III lawyer
Wiltshire, William Harrison Flick lawyer
Wimbrow, Peter Ayers, III lawyer
Winder, Richard Earnest legal foundation administrator, writer, consultant
Wing, James David lawyer
Wingfield, Thomas Christopher lawyer
Winkler, Charles Howard lawyer, investment management company executive
Winship, Blaine H. lawyer
Winstead, George Alvis law librarian, biochemist, educator, consultant
Winston, Harold Ronald lawyer
Winterer, Philip Steele lawyer
Winthrop, Sherman lawyer
Winzenreid, James Ernest lawyer, entrepreneur
Wise, Aaron Noah lawyer
Wiswall, Frank Lawrence, Jr. lawyer, educator
Withers, Carl Raymond lawyer
Witherwax, Charles Halsey lawyer, arbitrator, mediator
Witkin, Eric Douglas lawyer
Witmeyer, John Jacob, III lawyer
Witt, Alan Michael lawyer, accountant
Wittels, Barnaby Caesar lawyer
Wittig, Raymond Shaffer lawyer, technology transfer advisor
Wolf, Cyd Beth lawyer, entrepreneur
Wolf, Martin Eugene lawyer
Wolfe, Deborah Ann lawyer
Wolfe, James Ronald lawyer
Wolff, Elroy Harris lawyer
Woller, James Alan lawyer
Wong-Diaz, Francisco Raimundo lawyer, educator
Wood, Malcolm James lawyer
Woodhouse, Thomas Edwin lawyer
Wood Kahari, Brenda Marie lawyer
Woodley, Ann E. lawyer, educator
Woods, Richard Dale lawyer
Woods, Winton D. law educator
Woody, Donald Eugene lawyer
Wooldridge, William Charles lawyer
Worenklein, Jacob Joshua lawyer
Worthington, Carole Yard Lynch lawyer
Worthington, Sandra Boulton lawyer
Wray, Robert lawyer
Wrede, Rabbe Kenneth lawyer
Wright, Charles Alan law educator, author
Wright, Frank Beverley law educator
Wright, Robert Joseph lawyer
Wright, Robert Ross, III law educator
Wright, Robert Thomas, Jr. lawyer
Wright, William Gordon foundation executive
Wrobleski, Jeanne Pauline lawyer
Wuori, Matti Ossian lawyer, environmental affairs consultant
Wuyts, Koenraad Maria lawyer
Wyatt, Robert Lee, IV lawyer
Wynn, Stanford Alan lawyer
Wynstra, Nancy Ann lawyer
Xu, Guojian lawyer, educator
Yaffa, Andrew Bryan lawyer
Yamada, Takao educator, lawyer
Yamakawa, David Kiyoshi, Jr. lawyer
Yamasaki, Yukuzo lawyer
Yambrusic, Edward Slavko lawyer, consultant
Yamin, Michael Geoffrey lawyer
Yang, Anja lawyer
Yang, Norris Hong-Ching lawyer, consultant
Yano, Chiaki lawyer
Yegge, Robert Bernard law educator, dean
Yelenick, Mary Therese lawyer
Yerrid, C. Steven lawyer
Yetter, R. Paul lawyer
Yonkman, Fredrick Albers lawyer, management consultant
Yoshino, Hajime law educator, knowledge engineer
Yost, Gerald B. lawyer
Young, Barney Thornton lawyer
Young, David Bradley lawyer
Young, Dean Anthony solicitor
Young, Martin Ford barrister
Young, Sheldon Mike lawyer, author
Youngblood, Deborah Sue lawyer
Yu, Benita Ka Po solicitor
Yücel, Yonca Fatma lawyer
Yusuf, Samuel lawyer
Yzaguirre, Mark Ramon lawyer
Zabel, Sheldon Alter lawyer, law educator
Zachem, Kathryn A. lawyer
Zagorin, Janet Susan legal firm administrator, marketing professional
Zaitzeff, Roger Michael lawyer
Zak, Robert Joseph lawyer
Zambelli, Angelo lawyer
Zamboldi, Richard Henry lawyer
Zanot, Craig Allen lawyer
Zapata, Jose Vicente lawyer, educator
Zaphiriou, George Aristotle lawyer, educator
Zedrosser, Joseph John lawyer
Zeigler, Judy Rose law firm administrator
Zeller, Michael Eugene lawyer
Zemanek, Karl law educator, consultant
Zerunyan, Frank Vram lawyer
Zhang, Danian lawyer
Zhang, Yapu lawyer
Zilgalvis, Peteris Viktors lawyer
Zimmer, Michael J. lawyer
Zimmerly, James Gregory lawyer, physician
Zimmerman, Aaron Mark lawyer
Zipfinger, Frank Peter lawyer
Zoffer, David B. lawyer
Zotaley, Byron Leo lawyer
Zuckerman, Richard Engle lawyer, law educator
Zuhdi, Nabil (Bill Zuhdi) lawyer, litigator, consultant, producer
Zukerman, Larry William lawyer
Zukerman, Michael lawyer

MILITARY

Abu-Haimid, Abdulrahman Ibrahim civilian military deputy
Açimuz, Metin Osman naval officer
Adams, Michael John air force non-commissioned officer
Adams, Michael Keith military officer
Ahlberg, Lars Åke military officer
Albano, Anthony William retired career officer, secondary school educator
Albright, Joseph William army officer
Alexandrakis, George military officer, model
Alexopoulos, Argyrios Dimitrios career officer
Allen, James Charlton career officer
Allred, Keith Johns naval officer
Alves, Harley military officer
Andriano-Moore, Richard Graf career officer
Astriab, Steven Michael army officer
Aultman, William Robert career officer
Badders, Rebecca Susanne military officer, educator, writer
Banker, Joe Dan naval officer, educator
Baril, Maurice career officer
Barrie, Christopher Alexander military officer
Beldecos, George John Hellenic air force officer, planning consultant
Bezerra, Marcio L. S. military officer
Biely, Debra Marie retired military officer
Bingeman, John Mervyn retired military officer, nautical archaeologist
Blackwell, Thomas George military police officer
Blashford-Snell, John Nicholas career officer, explorer, author, broadcaster
Bloch, Rene M. naval officer, high technology and political economy consultant
Blomjous, Dré J.G.M. army officer
Boncu, Simion military officer
Borovikov, Valeriy Vasiljevich military officer, aerospace engineer, researcher
Borrini, Francesco military officer, writer
Bosler, Charles Walter, Jr. retired military officer, engineer
Bowen, Clotilde Marion Dent retired career officer, psychiatrist
Bulkeley, Thomas Foster Rivers retired military officer
Burhan, Halis career military officer
Caine, Philip David retired military officer, author
Campbell, Troy David officer
Camporini, Vincenzo air force officer
Carney, Roger Francis Xavier retired army officer
Carr, James McLeod naval officer
Carr, Kenneth Monroe naval officer
Caudill, Delana Renee civilian military employee
Chaibi, Mohamed Ben M'Barek military officer, researcher
Chand, Prem career officer
Conti, Massimo career officer, consultant
Corrigan, Paula Ann career officer, internist
Cosentino, Michele navy officer, researcher
Costa, Paulo Roberto military officer, engineer, educator
Crow, John Downing United States Army officer
Crucioli, Piergiorgio air force officer
Demirkiliç, Uruk military career officer, surgeons, educator
DiCocco, Marc career officer, flight test engineer
Dingemans, Peter George Valentin retired rear admiral, benefits administrator
Doerzbacher, Ralph Elmer, Jr. career officer
Dominguez, David Alan army reserve medical officer
Downey, Gary Neil marine corps officer
Drews, Rudeiger military officer
Dube'-Odell, Dorice Suzanne career officer
Dunkle, Keith Allen military officer
Durrenberger, William John retired army general, educator, investor
Eberwein, Jeffrey Robert military officer
Edholm, Sten G. career officer
Eldridge, Charles Ray military officer, military science educator
Ellison, Henry Phillips military officer
Emmett, Peter Charles air force officer
Enqvist, Ove Teodor career military officer
Erickson, Lynn Edward non-commissioned officer, human resource manager
Fanuel, Bonginkosi military officer
Feland, John Morgan, III military officer, educator
Figueroa, Dorys military officer
Filho, Waldir Silva military educator
Fluckey, Eugene Bennett retired navy officer, author
Frazho, Gregory John non-commissioned officer
French, Uri Smith, III career officer, actor
Gales, Samuel Joel retired civilian military employee, counselor
Gallagher, Thomas French career officer, strategist
Galvin, John Rogers educator, retired army officer
Garlette, William Henry Lee army officer
Garner, Charles Larry retired military officer, human resources educator
Gawronski, Elizabeth Ann retired army officer
Grace, Thomas William, Jr. military officer, dentist
Griffith, Robert Dean military careerman, registered nurse
Grytsenko, Anatoliy retired military officer, researcher
Gurul, Aydin naval officer
Halpin, Timothy Patrick former air force officer
Hamilton, Richard A. retired military officer, aeronautical engineer
Heiser, Rolland Valentine former army officer, foundation executive
Henry, Charles Howard non-commissioned officer
Herteleer, Willy Maurits career officer
Hester, Paul V. career officer
Hodbod, Ludek career officer, engineering educator
Hodges, Carroll Broadus retired army officer
Hokborg, Sven-Olof military officer
Hollo, Ilkka Pentti Finnish military officer
Holshek, Christopher John civil-military relations consultant
Howe, Jonathan Trumbull naval officer
Ieko, Tohru military officer, researcher
Illi, Esko Antero military career officer
Jetley, Surrinder Kumar career officer
Johnson, Wallace retired army officer
Kasperkowiak, Stanislaw Kazimierz career officer
Kavanagh, John Joseph naval officer
Kayode, Oyewumi Abiwonleko military officer, aircraft technician
Kelley, Larry Dale retired army officer
Kerwin, Walter Thomas, Jr. career officer, consultant
Kilgore, Joe Everett, Jr. army officer
Kinay, Nadir Osman military officer
King, Joseph, Jr. government administrator, educator, consultant
Kirkbride, Max Verlyn retired career officer
Klain, David Richard naval officer
Kojac, Jeffrey Stanley military officer
Laari, Jouni Seppo career officer, researcher
Laikanok, Pramoat military officer
Lawlis, Patricia Kite air force officer, computer consultant
Less, Anthony Albert retired naval officer
Linwood, Russell John Australian army officer and state official
Lippiett, Richard John military officer
Liu, Ta-Tsai former military officer, maritime consultant
Lucchetti, Lynn L. career officer
Lungu, Angela Maria career officer
Mackenzie, James Frederick career military officer
MacMillan, Angus Campbell English military officer
Malishenko, Timothy Peter military
Markopoulos, Petros retired career officer, consultant
Marlow, Edward A. former army officer
Martin, James Victor, Jr. foreign service officer, writer
Matheny, Charles Woodburn, Jr. former army officer, civil engineer, city official
Matzouranis, George Greek army aviation officer
McCarthy, Sean Michael air force officer, pilot
McClendon, Dennis Edward retired air force officer
McGuinn, Michael Edward, III retired army officer
Mehmood, Khalid career officer, diplomat
Meigel, David Walter retired career officer, retired musician
Mendez, José Sanchez military officer
Messerschmidt, William Harclerode army noncommissioned officer, percussionist
Mirick, Robert Allen military officer
Mohammad, Islam Amirul Dalim career officer, economist, educator, researcher
Momani, Omar Hamid military officer, pilot instructor
Moser, Gregg Anthony retired career officer
Murdock, Robert McClellan air force officer
Musharraf, Pervez military officer
Novosad, Tomaš armed forces officer
O'Connor, Edward Cornelius army officer
Oppey, Mark Ofosy military employee
O'Reilly, Kenneth William military officer
Oren, John Birdsell retired coast guard officer
Palazzi, Ruben Oscar career military officer
Panwar, Surendra Singh military officer
Pastinica, Nicolae career officer
Patton, George Smith military officer
Peluffo, Angel Octavio military officer
Pickett, George Bibb, Jr. retired military officer
Pilkus, Joseph Edward, III career officer
Pittaras, Constantine coast guard officer
Pongsiri, Sangkorn Thai marine officer
Price, Joseph Sterling air force officer
Prueher, Joseph W. military officer
Randolph, Leonard McElRoy, Jr. career officer
Ratanasri, Taweesak military officer
Riddle, Wesley Allen army officer, writer
Roadarmel, Stanley Bruce civilian military employee
Robison, Kenneth Gerald former naval officer, national security consultant, historian
Rogers, Bernard William military officer
Rollins, James Gregory air force officer
Rosenfeld, David defense research and development executive
Ryder, Gene Ed retired United States Air Force training administrator
Saalfeld, Fred Erich naval researcher
Sannom, Jens military officer
Scholes, Edison Earl army officer
Schoups, Jozef Jan Belgian army officer
Schunicht, Shannon Anthony retired army officer, politician
Schwartz, Thomas A. military officer
Schwarzkopf, H. Norman retired army officer, public speaker
Schwartztrauber, Sayre Archie former naval officer, maritime consultant
Seiberlich, Carl Joseph retired naval officer
Shalikashvili, John Malchase retired military career officer
Sheargold, Ronald Harry engineer, military officer
Sherard, Rodney Merle retired military officer, educator
Sherman, Roger Anthony air force officer
Skora, Wayne Philip retired air force officer
Slaff, Allan Paul naval officer, university administrator, educator, entrepreneur
Slaihem, Ameer Abdullah career officer
Slater, Sir Jock naval officer
Slowik, Richard Andrew air force officer
Smyth, Dacre Henry Deudraeth retired naval officer
Snyder, Arnold Lee, Jr. retired air force officer, research director
Sparks, Bennett Sher retired military officer
Spooner, David Eric military officer
Starink, Dirk career officer
Stewart, J. Daniel air force official
Strean, Bernard M. retired naval officer
Subhirun, Preecha military officer
Suciu, Emil military officer
Thakur, Shashi Sjeljer career officer
Thapa, Kishor Jung military attache
Thathong, Suriyant military officer
Thomashow, Steven Roy military officer, intelligence officer
Thompson, Robert Frank, Jr. career officer
Tiantong, Thitichai Thai army officer
Tolbert, Clinton Jame army officer, machinist
Tyrrell, Patrick John career military officer
Valderas-Cañestro, Santiago career officer
Valencia, Angel Alejandro career officer
Vartiainen, Ahti Toimi Paavali military officer
Verhulst, Michel Joseph Julien naval officer
Voznica, Petr army officer
Wagemaker, Allard J. military officer
Walden, Joseph Lawrence career officer
Wallberg, Börje Carl-Gustaf retired Swedish army officer, philately consultant
Warme, Pierre Marie military officer engineer
Washington-Knight, Barbara J. career officer, nurse
Watts, Helena Roselle military analyst
Weisman, David S. military officer
Weyandt, Daniel Scott naval officer, engineer, physicist
Weyman, Steven Aloysius military officer, retired
Wheeler, Frank Knowles Blasdell retired military officer, business consultant
Wilkins, Peter Ivan career officer, helicopter pilot
Wilson, Kelce Steven air force officer, electrical engineer
Wineland, Desiree Claire Ann career military officer
Yoon, E. Yul retired career officer

Yoshinori, Miyamoto *medical officer*

RELIGION

Abante, Bienvenido Mirando, Jr. *missionary, pastor*
Abu-Akel, Fahed Labeeb *religious organization executive*
Ackerson, Charles Stanley *minister, social worker*
Agnew, Christopher Mack *minister, historian*
Agreiter, Anton Josef *priest*
Agustoni, Gilberto Cardinal *archbishop*
Akins, Martin T. *clergyman*
Aland, Barbara Edith *religious studies educator*
Al-Azmeh, Aziz *history of religion educator*
Alberigo, Giuseppe *religious studies educator*
Albertz, Rainer *religious studies educator*
Alcorn, Wallace Arthur *minister, writer*
Alexy, Patriarch II (Alexei Mikhailovich Ridiguer) *patriarch of Moscow and Russia*
Al-Hafeez, Humza *minister, editor*
Allen, William Jere *minister*
Almen, Lowell Gordon *church official*
Alvis, Joel Lawrence, Jr. *minister*
Ambrozic, Aloysius Cardinal (His Eminence Aloysius Cardinal Ambrozio) *cardinal archbishop*
Anderson, Danita Ruth *minister*
Anderson, Fred Richard *minister*
Anderson, Joan Balyeat *religion educator, minister*
Anderson, Vinton Randolph *bishop*
Andrews, Lawrence Wayne *priest, educator*
Angelini, Fiorenzo Cardinal *archbishop*
Angell, Kenneth Anthony *bishop*
Apassa, Cyril Omo-Osagie *clergyman, educator*
Ap Gwilym, Gwynn *clergy member*
Aponte Martinez, Luis Cardinal *archbishop emeritus*
Apuron, Anthony Sablan *archbishop*
Araújo Sales, Eugénio de *archbishop*
Arden, Donald S(eymour) *bishop*
Ariarajah, Wesley Seevaratnam *clergyman, church administrator*
Arinze, Francis Cardinal *archbishop*
Arisalya, Harish Chandra *missionary, administrator*
Armogathe, Jean-Robert *clergyman, educator*
Armstrong, Hart Reid *minister, editor, publisher*
Arns, Paulo Evaristo Cardinal *archbishop emeritus*
Assel, Heinrich Georg *theologian*
Assis, Moshe *Jewish studies scholar, educator*
Austin, James Grover, Jr. *theologian, pastor, telecommunications manager*
Austin-Thorn, Cynthia Kay *religious organization administrator, poet*
Austriaco, Nicanor Pier Giorgio *clergy member, researcher*
Bachelder, Robert Stephen *minister*
Bachmann, Michael *theologian, educator*
Baker, Josephine L. Redenius (Mrs. Milton G. Baker) *minister, civic leader, retired career officer, former public relations company executive*
Baker, Mary Evelyn *former church librarian, retired academic librarian*
Ball, David Terry *university chaplain, academic administrator*
Ballesteros, Juventino Ray, Jr. *minister*
Balslev-Clausen, Peter *theologian, clergyman, educator*
Baltakis, Paul Antanas *bishop*
Banks, Robert J. *bishop*
Barbour, Claude Marie *minister*
Barlow, August Ralph, Jr. *minister*
Barrett, John Charles Allanson *minister*
Barwig, Regis Norbert James *priest*
Basri, Hasan *religious organization leader*
Bates, Gerald Earl *bishop emeritus*
Bathersby, John Alexius *archbishop*
Battisti, Alfredo *archbishop*
Batule, Robert John *priest*
Baum, William Wakefield Cardinal *archbishop*
Baumann, Martin *religious studies educator*
Baumann-Hoelzle, Ruth Ella *theologian, ethics consultant*
Beals, Paul Archer *religious studies educator*
Beaupere, Rene Maurice *religious center administrator*
Bechert, Heinz Helmut *religious studies educator*
Beck, Edward Nelson *minister*
Beck, Robert Raymond *priest*
Beentjes, Pancratius Cornelis *religious studies educator*
Bell, John Perry *minister, religious organization administrator*
Belo, Carlos Felipe Ximenes *apostolic administrator*
Beltran, Eusebius Joseph *archbishop*
Berki, Feriz *Hungarian Orthodox priest, journal editor*
Beuken, Willem André *retired theology educator, priest*
Bevan, Richard Justin William *retired canon, church executive*
Bevilacqua, Anthony Joseph Cardinal *archbishop*
Bewes, Richard Thomas *minister, writer*
Bier, Louis Henry Gustav *minister*
Biffi, Giacomo Cardinal *archbishop*
Bitran, Leonardo Alejandro *rabbi*
Black, Cora Jean *evangelist, wedding consultant*
Blackmore, James Herrall *clergyman, educator, author*
Blackwood, James Hiram *retired pastor*
Blanchet, Bertrand *archbishop*
Bodycomb, John Francis *minister, consultant, theologian, sociologist*
Bohrer, Richard William *religious writer, editor, educator*
Boland, Raymond James *bishop*
Bolognesi, Pietro *theologian, editor*
Bommarco, Antonio Vitale *former archbishop of Roman Catholic Church*
Bonino, Serge Thomas *priest*
Bonner, Gerald *theologian, educator*
Booker, Bruce Robert *theology educator, author, educational consultant*
Borisov, Alexander Ilyich *priest*
Borrmans, Maurice Albert Charles *priest, Arabic and Islamic studies educator*
Bosco, Anthony Gerard *bishop*
Bowen, Gilbert Willard *minister*
Bowen, Mary Lu *ecumenical developer, community organizer*
Bowen, Michael George *archbishop*
Bowie, Alexander Glen *minister, military chaplain*
Boyd, H. Glenn *missionary agency executive*
Boyd, Miles Farris *minister*
Brandt, Robert Barry *lay worker*
Braulik, Georg Peter *religious studies educator*
Braun, Eunice Hockspeier *religious order executive, author, lecturer*
Bray, Gerald Lewis *minister, educator*
Braybrooke, Marcus Christopher Rossi *vicar*
Brito, Emilio *priest, educator*
Broglio, Timothy Paul *priest, administrator*
Brooks, Edward Charles *retired priest*
Brothers, Fletcher Arnold *minister, religious organization founder, director*
Brown, Laurence David *retired bishop*
Brown, Nan Marie *clergywoman*
Brown, Tod David *bishop*
Browne, Denis George *Roman Catholic bishop*
Browning, Don Spencer *religious educator*
Browning, Wilfrid Robert *Anglican clergyman*
Brownlee, Judith Marilyn *priestess, psychotherapist, psychic*
Brunori Pagliano, Pedro Alberto *priest, media executive, consultant*
Bruskewitz, Fabian W. *bishop*
Buechlein, Daniel Mark *archbishop*
Bui, Long Van *church custodian, translator*
Bullock, William Henry *bishop*
Burch, Francis Floyd *clergyman, educator*
Burrows, Elizabeth MacDonald *religious organization executive, educator*
Butler, Thomas Frederick *bishop*
Byrne, Brendan Joseph *theology educator, priest*
Byrskog, Samuel Per-Erik *theology educator*
Cacciavillan, Agostino *archbishop*
Camomot, Oscar Llanos *priest*
Campbell, Iain Donald *minister, editor*
Camps, Petrus Henricus J.M. (Arnulf Camps) *retired religious studies educator, researcher*
Capps, Richard Henry *minister*
Carey, George Leonard *archbishop of Canterbury*
Carey, Lindsay Brian *minister, researcher*
Carles Gordo, Ricardo Maria Cardinal *archbishop*
Carnes, Joseph Sydney *clergyman*
Carstens, Johann Christiaan *minister*
Carter, Gerald Emmett *retired archbishop*
Carter, Samuel Emmanuel *archbishop*
Casiano Vargas, Ulises Aurelio *bishop*
Cassidy, Edward Idris Cardinal *cardinal deacon*
Cassidy, Michael *evangelist, missionary, author*
Castillo Lara, Rosalio Jose Cardinal *archbishop*
Cé, Marco Cardinal *patriarch of Venice, former bishop of Bologna*
Cedar, Paul Arnold *church executive, minister*
Celier, Odile Marie *religious organization administrator*
Ceresko, Anthony Raymond *Old Testament educator*
Charron, Joseph L. *bishop*
Chavis, Eric Noel *religious organization executive, minister*
Chen, George Min-Yen *minister*
Christodoulos, Archbishop *archbishop*
Chrysostomos, (Christoforos Aristodimou) *archbishop of Cyprus*
Church, Frank Forrester *minister, author, columnist*
Cikrle, Vojtěch *bishop*
Clancy, Edward Bede Cardinal *archbishop*
Cohen, Jack Joseph *religious educator, rabbi, retired*
Collard, Eugene Albert *clergyman, publisher*
Collins, Rose Ann *minister*
Connolly, Thomas Joseph *retired bishop*
Conway, David Martin *theologian*
Cooley, Robert Earl *religion and archaeology educator*
Coolidge, Robert Tytus *deacon, historian, educator*
Cooney, Patrick Ronald *bishop*
Costa, Paolo *rector, educator*
Coste, René Jean-H. *theologian*
Couture, Jean Guy *bishop*
Couture, Maurice *archbishop*
Couve de Murville, Maurice Noël Léon *archbishop*
Cronin, Daniel Anthony *archbishop*
Croteau, Denis *bishop*
Crowley, Maurice Anthony *bishop*
Csiha, Kálmán *bishop*
Csontos, József György *minister, counselor*
Curlin, William G. *bishop*
Curtiss, Elden F. *bishop*
Daily, Thomas V. *bishop*
Dalai Lama, (Tenzin Gyatso) *supreme temporal and religious head of Tibet*
Daloz, Lucien Charles Gilbert *archbishop*
Daly, Cahal Brendan Cardinal *retired archbishop*
Daniel, George Francis *archbishop*
Danneels, Godfried Cardinal *archbishop*
D'Antonio, Enzio *archbishop*
Daoud, Basile Moussa *archbishop*
D'Arcy, John Michael *bishop*
Darmaatmadja, Julius Riyadi Cardinal *archbishop*
Dattilo, Nicholas C. *bishop*
Davidson, Robert *religious studies educator*
Davis, Esther Yvonne Butler *religious studies educator*
Davis, Francis Raymond *priest*
Davis, John James *religion educator*
De Celles, Charles Edouard *theologian, educator*
Defois, Gérard *archbishop*
de Jonge, Henk Jan *New Testament educator, editor*
Delaney, Joseph P. *bishop*
Delaney, Mary Anne *pastoral educator*
Delaporte, Jacques *archbishop*
De Pauw, Gommar Albert *priest, educator*
Deskur, Andrzej Maria *archbishop*
De Villiers, Pieter Gideon *theologian, educator*
Di Berardino, Angelo *religious organization administrator*
Diodoros, I (Damianos George Karivalis) *patriarch of Jerusalem*
Docherty, Robert Kelliehan, II *minister*
Dodaro, Robert John *priest, theology educator*
Doi, Kenji *theologian, educator*
do Nascimento, Alexandre *archbishop*
Donoghue, John Francis *archbishop*
Dormeyer, Detlev Robert *religious studies educator*
Douty, Robert Watson *minister, educator*
Down, William John Denbigh *bishop*
Drinan, Robert Frederick *priest, law educator*
D'Rozario, Michael Atul *bishop*
D'Souza, Gregory *priest, educator*
Duffy, Joseph Augustine *Roman Catholic bishop*
Dunderberg, Ismo *theology educator, researcher*
Duval, Joseph Marie Louis *archbishop*
Dziuba, Andrzej Franciszek *priest, religious studies educator*
Eames, Robert Henry Alexander *archbishop, primate*
Early, Pianapue Kept *pastor, writer*
Ebacher, Roger *archbishop*
Edwards, Otis Carl, Jr. *theology educator*
Egan, Edward M. *archbishop*
Eijk, Willem Jacobus *religious studies educator, bishop*
Emilsen, William Wayne *church historian, minister*
Etchegaray, Roger Cardinal *archbishop*
Etsou-Nzabi-Bamungwabi, Frederic Cardinal *archbishop*
Etzold, Herman Albert *clergyman, theology educator*
Ewing, Elisabeth Anne Rooney *priest*
Ewing, James E. *priest*
Eyt, Pierre Etienne Louis *archbishop*
Fager, Everett Dean *minister*
Fagiolo, Vincenzo Cardinal *archbishop*
Falcão, José Freire Cardinal *archbishop*
Famerée, Joseph Florent *theologian, educator*
Farley, Benjamin Wirt *religious studies educator, writer*
Feldkämper, Ludger Bernhard *religious organization executive*
Felici, Angelo Cardinal *religious organization executive*
Felix, Kelvin Edward *archbishop*
Fernando, Frank Marcus *bishop*
Finigan, Timothy Joseph *priest, editor*
Fischer, Georg Johann *priest, theology educator*
Fisher, Anthony Colin Joseph *priest, ethicist*
Fisher, Edgar Jacob, Jr. *religious organization administrator*
Fjeld, Bjorn Oyvind *religious organization executive*
Flory, Margaret Martha *retired religious organization administrator*
Floyd, John David *theology educator, minister*
Folk, Jerry Lee *ecumenical leader*
Ford, Austin McNeill *clergyman*
Foreman, Alfred G. *theologian, philosopher*
Fort, Robert Bradley *minister*
Fortier, Jean-Marie *retired archbishop*
France, Dorothy Daniel *minister*
Francis, Leslie John *theology educator, psychology researcher*
Frankemölle, Hubert *theological educator*
Franklin, Roosevelt *minister*
Freedman, David Noel *religious studies educator*
Freeman, Joel Arthur *author, organizational change facilitator*
Friedlander, Edward Robert *pathologist*
Frost, Linda Gail *clergyman, hospital chaplain*
Fry, Lowell Lawrence, Jr. *minister*
Furno, Carlo Cardinal *archbishop*
Gagnon, Edouard Cardinal *ecclesiastic*
Gallups, Ordice Alton *diaconal minister*
Gantin, Bernardin Cardinal *archbishop, dean*
Garland, James H. *bishop*
Garrione, Robert Michael *clergy member*
Gates, Brian Edward *religious studies educator*
Geisendorfer, James Vernon *religious writer, researcher*
Gemayel, (Edmond) Boutros *archbishop*
Geoghegan, William Davidson *religion educator, minister*
George, Francis Cardinal *archbishop*
Gepford, William George *minister*
Gerber, Jeffrey Robert *pastor*
Gerostergios, Asterios Nicholas *priest, writer, translator*
Gervais, Michel *theology educator, hospital executive*
Giardini, Fabio *theologian, educator*
Gil, Fernando Miguel *Catholic priest, historian*
Gilbert, Patrick Nigel Geoffrey *organization executive*
Gillett, James Walter *minister, missionary*
Gillispie, Harold Leon *minister*
Giordano, Michele Cardinal *archbishop*
Glazemaker, Antonius Jan *retired archbishop*
Glemp, Jozef Cardinal *archbishop*
Gonzáles Martín, Marcelo Cardinal *archbishop*
Gonzalez Zumarraga, Antonio Jose *archbishop*
Gouyon, Paul Cardinal *archbishop*
Graffy, Adrian Joseph *priest*
Green, Gerard Leo *priest, educator*
Greenacre, Roger Tagent *priest*
Greenstein, Edward L. *biblical studies educator*
Gregory, Myra May *religious organization administrator, educator*
Gregory, Wilton D. *bishop*
Grey, Mary Cecilia *theologian*
Griffin, James Anthony *bishop*
Groth, John Henry Christopher *pastor, author, academic administrator*
Gubler, Marie-Louise Elisabeth *theology educator*
Gulbinowicz, Henryk Roman Cardinal *archbishop*
Gunner, Murray *Jewish organization administrator*
Gushee, David Paul *religious studies educator*
Habgood, John Stapylton *archbishop*
Hager, Louise Alger *retired chaplain*
Haldane-Stevenson, James Patrick *minister*
Hallet, Charles Joseph *Jesuit priest, educator, academic administrator*
Hamlin, Ernest Lee *religious organization administrator, Christian education consultant*
Hanifen, Richard Charles *bishop*
Hansen, Wendell Jay *clergyman, gospel broadcaster*
Hardmeier, Christof Felix *religious studies educator*
Harmelink, Herman, III *clergyman, author, educator, ecumenist*
Harrington, Donald Szantho *clergy member*
Harrington, Mary Evelina Paulson (Polly Harrington) *religious journalist, writer, educator*
Harris, Curtis W. *minister, mayor*
Harris, E(leanor) Lynn(e) *religious studies and literature educator*
Harris, Mildred Clopton *clergy member, educator*
Harris, Wardell W. *minister*
Harrison, Richard Dean *minister, counselor*
Hart, John William *theology and ecology educator*
Hart, Richard Wesley *religious organization administrator, pastor*
Hartman, Jeffrey Edward *pastor*
Hayden, John Carleton *priest, history educator*
H Cardinale Paul, Poupard *archbishop*
Heim, Bruno Bernard *archbishop*
Heine, Susanne *religious studies educator*
Helmick, Raymond Glen *priest, educator*
Helve, Helena Marketta *religious studies educator*
Henrich, Rainer *theologian, researcher*
Hermisson, Hans-Jürgen *theologian, scientist*
Herranz Casado, Julián *archbishop*
Hezel, Francis Xavier *clergy member, educator*
Hickey, Barry James *archbishop*
Hickey, James Aloysius Cardinal *archbishop*
Higi, William L. *bishop*
Hill, Alfred DeWayne *religious studies educator*
Hilt, Thomas Harry *minister*
Hofius, Otfried *theologian*
Holladay, Carl R. *New Testament educator*
Holland, Tristam Keith *friar, liturgist*
Hollenweger, Walter Jacob *religious studies educator*
Holm, Nils Gustav *comparative religion educator*
Holter, Knut *religious studies educator*
Hood, Thomas Gregory *minister*
Hope, David Michael *bishop*
Houghton, Graham Whitfield *religious studies educator*
Howard, Gerald Kenneth *minister*
Howden, Frank Newton *Episcopal priest, humanities educator*
Hoy, George Philip *clergyman, food bank executive*
Hubbard, Howard James *bishop*
Hudson, David M. *minister*
Hudson, Richard L. *retired educator, clergyman*
Huebner, Ulrich *theologian*
Huet, Patrick L. *sports educator*
Hughes, Alfred Clifton *bishop*
Hughes, Edward T. *retired bishop*
Hunsberger, Alice Chandler *religion educator, human rights activist*
Hunt, T(homas) W(ebb) *retired religion educator*
Hurley, Francis T. *archbishop*
Hurowitz, Victor-Avigdor Benedict *Biblical and Ancient Near Eastern studies educator*
Hurtado, Larrry Weir *religious studies educator*
Hwang, Tzu-Yang *minister*
Iakovos, (Demetrios A. Coucouzis) *retired archbishop*
Iby, Paul *Roman Catholic bishop*
Innocenti, Antonio Cardinal *retired archbishop*
Jackson, Bernard Stuart *legal and religious studies educator*
Jaffe, Evan *rabbi*
Jakubowsky, Frank Raymond *religious writer*
James, Graham Richard *bishop*
Javierre Ortas, Antonio Maria Cardinal *archbishop, writer, educator*
Jebanesan, Subramaniam Sebanesan *bishop*
Jenkins, Keith Pellow *religious organization executive*
Jesse, Horst *minister*
Jeziorowski, Jürgen *retired theologian, journalist*
John Paul, His Holiness Pope, II (Karol Jozef Wojtyla) *bishop of Rome*
Johnson, Adrian *religious organization executive*
Johnson, Constance Ann Trillich *minister, internet service provider, small business owner, lawyer, writer, researcher, lecturer*
Johnson, Ora J. *clergyman*
Jones, Gerald Edward *religion educator*
Jones, James Edwards, Sr. *religion educator*
Jones, Laura Mead *religion educator*
Jones, Oscar Calvin *minister, dean*
Jones, Vernon Keith *minister, educator*
Joommal, Ali Sarfaraz Khan *retired religious studies educator*
Joseph, Thomas Erinjery *priest, religious organization administrator*
Juarez, Martin *priest*
Junghans, Helmar Paul *pastor, theology educator*
Kang, Chin Huat *minister*
Karekin, II *religious leader*
Kaufman, Luna Amalia *musicologist*
Kay, James Franklin *religion educator*
Keding, Reinhard Christian *bishop*
Keeler, Cardinal William H. *archbishop*
Keeling, Joe Keith *religion educator, college official and dean*
Kelly, Thomas Cajetan *archbishop*
Kenway, Ian Michael *clergyman, researcher*
Keown, William Arvel *minister, educator*
Ker, Ian Turnbull *priest, scholar*
Kern, William Bliem, Jr. *minister*
Kerr, Donald Craig *retired minister*
Kerr, Nancy Karolyn *pastor, mental health consultant*
Khalka, Jetsun Dhampa *head of religious order*
Kidd, James Lambert *retired minister*
Kiehl, Judith E. *pastoral associate*
Kikama, Yasuo *religion educator, translator*
Kim, Chin-Sam Sam-Woo *zen master, seminary president, publisher*
Kim, Sou-Hwan Stephen *cardinal, retired archbishop*
Kinahan, Timothy Charles *priest, writer*
Kinzig, Wolfram Ulrich *Protestant theologian, church historian*
Kitbunchu, Michael Michai Cardinal *archbishop of Bangkok*
Kjaer, Niels *theologian, scholar*
Klauck, Hans-Josef *theology educator*
Klein, Hans *theology educator, priest*
Knapp, Gary Alan *minister, psychotherapist*
Knudsen, Raymond Barnett *clergyman, association executive, author*
Koenig, Robert August *clergyman, educator*
Koenig, Robert Emil *clergyman*
Kong-Hi Youn, (Victorinus) *archbishop*
Konig, Franz Cardinal *cardinal, archbishop emeritus of Vienna*
Kooij, Arie Van Der *religious studies educator*
Korec, Jan Chryzostom Cardinal *bishop*
Korff, Y. A. *grand rabbi*
Kragnes, Earl Newton *retired minister*
Kreiner, Armin *theology educator*
Kristiansen, Roald Ernst *religion educator, researcher*
Krummacher, Johann-Henrich Karl *minister, writer*
Kruyf, Gerrit G. de *theology educator*
Kucera, Daniel William *retired bishop*
Kufeldt, George *biblical educator*
Kuftaro, Ahmad *religious leader*
Kuharić, Franjo Cardinal *archbishop of Zagreb*
Kuhn, Heinz-Wolfgang *biblical studies educator*
Kung (Gong) Pin-Mei, Ignatius Cardinal (Ignatius Kung (Gong) Cardinal Pin-Mei) *bishop*
Laghi, Pio *archbishop*
Laham, Lutfi *patriarchal vicar*
Lai, John Christopher *minister, educator, consultant*
Lamar, William Fred *chaplain, educator*
Land, Richard Dale *minister, religious organization administrator*
Langley, Timothy Michael *minister*
Langlinais, J. Willis *priest, theology educator*
Lansdale, H. Parker *minister, historian, non-profit administrator*
La Rocque, Eugene Philippe *bishop*
Larrea Holguin, Juan Ignacio *archbishop*
Larsen, Lawrence Bernard, Jr. *priest, pastoral psychotherapist*
Larsen, Samuel Harry *minister, educator*
Lathon, Sheraine *clergyman*
Lau, Israel Meir *chief rabbi of Israel*
Law, Bernard Francis Cardinal *archbishop*
Lawson, Carole Jean *religious educator, author, poet*
Leake, David *bishop*
Lee, Richard Francis James *evangelical clergyman, media consultant*
Leonard, Graham Douglas *priest*
León Villegas, Braulio Rafael *bishop*
Levi, Lester Wright *retired religion educator*
Levine, Amihud *rabbi*
Lewis, Cecil Dwain *minister*
Lewis, Ronald Hugh *religious organization administrator*

Lienhard, Marc theology and church history educator
Lightfoot, Albert J. clergyman
Linderman, Jeanne Herron priest
Lipscomb, Oscar Hugh archbishop
Liu, Luke Hsien-Tang bishop
Livingston, Margery Elsie missionary, clinical psychologist
Liwanag, Rodel Mora minister
Loader, James Alfred religious studies educator, minister
Lobinger, Frederich Josef bishop
Loenning, Per bishop
Logan, Thomas Wilson Stearly, Sr. priest
Logan, Vincent Paul bishop
Lohse, Eduard religion educator
Lonergan, James Barry priest
Lopez Lozano, Carlos bishop
Lopez Rodriguez, Nicolas de Jesus Cardinal archbishop
Lopez Trujillo, Alfonso Cardinal archbishop
Lorscheider, Aloisio Cardinal archbishop
Loubser, Johannes Albertus religious studies educator
Lourdusamy, D. Simon Cardinal archbishop
Loux, Gordon Dale religious organization administrator
Lovingood, Vivian Ann religious organization executive
Lowe, J. Allen minister
Lowe, Malcolm Frederick religious studies educator
Lowentrout, Peter Murray religious studies educator
Lundy, Robert Fielden minister
Lustiger, Jean-Marie Cardinal archbishop
Macchi, Jean-Daniel Old Testament and Biblical Hebrew educator
Macdonald, Fergus religious organization executive
Macharski, Franciszek Cardinal archbishop
Mackenzie, Donald Matthew, Jr. minister
Mac Kenzie, James Donald clergyman
MacLeod, James L. minister, finance executive, gallery owner
Macquiban, Timothy Stuart Alexander Methodist minister, educator
Mádr, Oto theologian, researcher, editor
Mahony, Cardinal Roger Michael archbishop
Maida, Cardinal Adam Joseph cardinal
Maire, Thierry theologian, educator
Malloy, Edward Aloysius priest, university administrator, educator
Margéot, Jean Cardinal bishop
Maria dos Santos, Alexandre José archbishop
Marjanczyk, Joseph Anicetus priest
Marrett, Michael McFarlene chaplain
Martinez Somalo, Eduardo Cardinal archbishop
Martini, Carlo Maria Cardinal archbishop
Marty, Martin Emil religion educator, editor
Marx, Alfred Rodolphe theology educator
Maser, Frederick Ernest clergyman
Massey, Donald Wayne clergyman, small business owner
Mather, George Ross clergy member
Matthews, Melvyn William priest
Maximos V Hakim patriarch
Mayes, Ila Laverne minister
Mc Auliffe, Michael F. retired bishop
McCann, Thomas Ryland, Jr. minister
Mc Carthy, John Edward bishop
McClain, Gregory David minister
McClelland, Patricia G. minister
McCormick, Queen Esther Williams clergyman
Mc Donald, Andrew J. bishop
McGary, Betty Winstead minister, counselor, individual, marriage, and family therapist
McGowan, Thomas Randolph retired religious organization executive
McHugh, James T. bishop
McLoughlin, James Patrick bishop
McNabb, Talmadge Ford religious organization administrator, retired military chaplain
McNaughton, William John bishop
McQuillan, William Robert association administrator, minister, lecturer
Medley, Alex Roy executive minister
Meisner, Joachim Cardinal archbishop
Menamparampil, Thomas S.D.B. archbishop
Meneses, Ernesto religious educator
Menezes, Ignatius bishop
Mensah, Samuel Kwame clergyman, educator
Mercieca, Joseph archbishop
Metz, Ronald Irwin retired priest, addictions counselor
Meyer, Hans Bernhard liturgy educator, priest
Meynet, Roland religious studies educator
Miceli, Mother Ignatius retired nun, missionary
Mikloshazy, Attila bishop
Milone, Anthony M. bishop
Miloro, Protopresbter Frank church official, religious studies educator
Miskimen, Robert Ivan retired pastor
Mixer, Ronald Wayne minister
Mohney, Nell Webb religion educator, speaker, author
Molinari, Todd Michael priest
Montalvo, Gabriel archbishop
Montgomery, Cleothus minister
Moore, Beatrice religious organization administrator
Moore, John Sterling, Jr. minister
Moore, Lester Leland clergy, financial consultant
Moreton, Thomas Hugh minister
Morrison, Glenn Leslie minister
Mortimer, Anita Louise minister
Mounayer, Joseph Ayoub archbishop
Mukanga, Paul Mambe bishop
Müller, Gerhard bishop
Munoz Nunez, Rafael bishop
Murphy-O'Connor, Cormac archbishop
Murray, Iain Hamish clergy member
Nakamoto, Mitsu-haru Kosei religious studies educator
Netters, James LaVirt pastor
Neves, Lucas Moreira Cardinal archbishop
Nevius, Richard Cassels religious studies educator, priest
Newell, Byron Bruce, Jr. pastor
Nichols, Anthony Howard bishop
Nichols, Clyde Richard clergyman, company executive
Nichols, George Leon, Jr. minister
Nineham, Dennis Eric retired theology educator
Noe, Virgilio Cardinal archbishop
Nolan, Richard Thomas clergyman, educator
Nordheim, Eckhard von clergyman
Noro, Yoshio Hayashi theological educator, writer
Novak, Michael (John) religion educator, author, editor
Noyer, Jacques bishop
Nurser, John Shelley retired religious organization administrator
Obando Bravo, Miguel Cardinal archbishop
Obloy, Leonard Gerard priest
O'Brien, Keith Michael Patrick archbishop
O'Connell, Anthony J. bishop
O'Connor, Kevin Thomas religious organization administrator
Oddi, Silvio Cardinal archbishop
O'Donnell, Edward Joseph bishop, former editor
Oke, Festus E. minister, religious organization administrator
O'Keefe, Fredrick Rea bishop, consultant, educator, writer
Olayiwola-Olosum, Bola Adigun priest
O'Malley, Sean bishop
Onwu, Emmanuel Nlenanya religious studies educator
Opocensky, Milan church alliance official
Ortega Y Alamino, Jaime Lucas Cardinal archbishop
Osborn, La Donna Carol clergywoman
Otčenášek, Karel archbishop of Roman Catholic church
Otunga, Maurice Michael Cardinal archbishop
Ouzts, Eugene Thomas minister, secondary education educator
Overton, Edwin Dean campus minister, educator
Ozorowski, Edward theology educator
Padakandla, John Sunder Rao clergy member
Paisley, Ian Richard Kyle clergyman, political activist
Panikkar, Raimon priest
Pappalardo, Salvatore Cardinal archbishop
Pappas, Barbara Estelle Biblical studies educator, author
Parker, Robert Chauncey Humphrey clergyman, publishing executive, psychic
Paskai, László Cardinal archbishop
Passoni Dell'Acqua, Anna Maria religious studies educator
Pastrana, Ronald Ray Christian ministry counselor, Biblical theology educator, former school system administrator
Pathrapankal, Joseph theology educator
Patten, Bebe Harrison minister, chancellor
Pauley, Shirley Stewart religious organization executive
Paulsen, Reidar pastor
Pavle Patriarch, Stojcevic Gojko head religious order
Payne, Sidney Stewart retired archbishop
Peers, Michael Geoffrey archbishop
Pehlke, Helmuth Bruno theology educator
Pelotte, Donald Edmond bishop
Pena, Raymundo Joseph bishop
Penchansky, David religious studies educator
Perez, Maaravi theologian, religious studies educator
Perrot, Charles theologist, educator
Pesce, Cesare priest missionary
Phelan, Thomas clergyman, academic administrator, educator
Phelps, Dennis Lane minister, educator, author
Pilarczyk, Daniel Edward archbishop
Pilick, Eckhart Rudolf clergyman, editor
Pilla, Anthony Michael bishop
Pimenta, Simon Ignatius Cardinal retired archbishop
Pinckaers, Servais Théodore theologian
Piovanelli, Silvano Cardinal archbishop of Florence
Piper, Thomas Samuel minister, consultant
Pirkle, Estus Washington minister
Piseddu, Antioco bishop
Plaster, George Francis Roman Catholic priest
Podemann Sørensen, Jørgen religious studies educator
Poggi, Luigi Cardinal archbishop
Poindexter, Richard Grover minister
Ponder, James Alton clergyman, evangelist
Poole, Clifford George Anglican priest, secondary school educator
Poswick, Reginald-Ferdinand Bible and computer scholar
Potgieter, Pieter Cornelius theologian, educator
Potocnak, Joseph James bishop
Pottmeyer, Hermann Josef theology educator
Povish, Kenneth Joseph retired bishop
Prescott, William Bruce minister
Presley, Kevin Patrick minister of music
Pressman, Jacob rabbi
Preston, Ronald Haydn theologian, retired educator
Price, John Edward religion educator
Primatesta, Raúl Francisco Cardinal archbishop
Puckett, Robert Marion clergyman
Puljic, Vinko Cardinal archbishop
Puljic, Želimir bishop
Ramirez, Ricardo bishop
Ratcliffe, Kermit Herman theology educator
Ratzinger, Joseph Alois Cardinal prefect, former archbishop
Ratzlaff, David Edward minister
Raub, Donald Wilmer minister, author
Razafindratandra, Armand Gaétan archbishop
Reaves, Bob H. pastor, counselor
Reber, Calvin Henry theological studies educator, minister
Reems, Ernestine C. minister
Reese, Martha Grace minister, lawyer
Reich, Karl Helmut religion educator, psychology educator
Reid, Benjamin Franklin bishop
Reinhardt, Linda Kay minister
Renn, Stephen Donald religious studies educator
Rex, Lonnie Royce religious organization administrator
Rice, David Preston minister, educator
Rice, Delbert retired missionary, anthropologist
Richardson, Paul Joseph pastor
Ridley, Betty Ann religous educator, church worker
Rigali, Justin F. archbishop
Riggle, Mary Lou missionary educator, academic adminstrator
Rivera Carrera, Norberto Cardinal archbishop
Robb, John Wesley religion educator
Robertson, Ian William Church of Scotland parish minister
Robillard, Edmond priest
Robinson, Ida LaFosse minister, broadcaster
Robinson, Jack Fay clergyman
Robinson, James M. religious studies educator
Robinson, William David priest
Rodriguez, Placido bishop
Rolston, Holmes, III theologian, educator, philosopher
Ronchino, Pedro Luis bishop
Rose, Robert John bishop
Rosen, Moishe religious organization founder
Roth, Sol rabbi
Rothenberger, Jack Renninger clergyman
Rotter, Hans theology educator
Rouco Varela, Antonio Ma archbishop
Rozario, Michael archbishop
Ruble, Bernard Roy minister, labor relations consultant
Ruini, Camillo Cardinal archbishop
Russell, Horace Orlando dean of chapel, theology educator
Russell, John Fintan theology educator, editor
Ruston, Alan Robert religious organization administrator, consultant
Sabatini, Lawrence bishop
Saier, Oskar archbishop
Saldarini, Giovanni Cardinal archbishop
Sales, Eugenio de Araujo Cardinal archbishop
Salt, Alfred Lewis priest
Sanchez, Jose T. Cardinal archbishop
Sandoval Iñiguez, Juan Cardinal archbishop
Satterthwaite, John Steven bishop
Saudreau, Michel Marie Paul bishop
Savoy, Douglas Eugene bishop, religious studies educator, explorer, writer
Schenk, Wolfgang Oskar Max theologian, researcher
Scherch, Richard Otto minister, consultant
Schilson, Arno history of religion educator
Schmid, Hans Heinrich theology, educator, educational administrator
Schmidt, Andreas pastor
Schmitz, Charles Edison evangelist
Schnabel, Eckhard Johannes theologian, educator
Schneider, Susan Ellen Judaism and Kaballah educator, writer, scientist
Scholtissek, Klaus Ludwig theologian
Schotte, Jan P. cardinal
Schrick, Jerry L. minister
Schroer, Silvia religious studies educator
Schultz, Arthur LeRoy clergyman, educator
Schüngel, Paul retired theology educator
Schupp, Ronald Irving clergyman, missionary, civil and human rights leader
Schwab, Ulrich theology educator
Schwery, Henri Cardinal bishop
Schwietz, Roger L. bishop
Scicluna, Charles Jude priest
Scott, David Irvin minister
Seaford, John Nicholas clergyman, dean
Searle, Robert Ferguson minister
Seckler, Max apologetics educator
Seybold, Klaus Dieter theology educator
Sfeir, Nasrallah Pierre Cardinal archbishop
Shaw, Maxwell Kenneth Christian school administrator
Shearlock, David John dean
Sheehan, Michael Jarboe archbishop
Shelby, Charles Francis priest, fundraising executive
Shelton, Kenneth N. bishop
Shelton, Thomas Alfred pastor
Shenouda, Pope III patriarch
Sherlock, John Michael bishop
Shim, Sang-Tai theologist, educator
Shirayanagi, Peter Seiichi retired archbishop
Shoemaker, Mark T. minister
Shriver, Donald Woods, Jr. theology educator
Shurin, Aaron Ben-Zion rabbi, Judaic studies educator
Sievers, Joseph Jewish studies educator
Sigrist, R. Marcel religious education educator
Sigurbjornsson, Einar theology educator
Silvestrini, Achille Cardinal archbishop, prefect
Simon, Werner Franz Heinz theology educator
Simonis, Adrianus Johannes Cardinal archbishop
Simpson, John Berchman, Jr. clergy member, chaplain, retired law enforcement officer, retired newspaper editor, retired military officer
Šimundža, Drago Roman Catholic priest, literature educator
Sin, Jaime Lachica Cardinal archbishop
Singh, Garnish Benedict bishop
Sit, Hong Chan minister
Skelly, John Joshua retired clergyman, fundraiser
Slaattè, Howard Alexander minister, philosophy educator
Slocum, Robert Boak minister, educator
Smend, Rudolf theologian
Smetana, Pavel Amos religious organization administrator
Smith, Axel retired theology and social ethics educator
Smith, Christopher Hughes minister
Smith, Clive John minister
Smyth, Malachy missionary priest, magazine editor
Snyder, Travis Carroll evangelist
Sodano, Angelo Cardinal cardinal, Vatican official
Sorscher, Marvin Loeb religious studies educator, rabbi
Southern, Lonnie Steven minister
Spann, James William, II minister
Sparer, Malcolm Martin rabbi
Spehr, Christopher clergyman
Spence, Francis John archbishop
Speyrer, Jude bishop
Sprenger, Ernest Henry pastor, translator
Sprengler-Rüppenthal, Anneliese Brünhilde retired ecclesiastical history and law educator
Stachel, Günter Max Albert religious studies educator
Stafford, James Francis archbishop
Stanislaw, Tkocz priest, editor
Stead, (George) Christopher retired divinity educator
Stedge-Fowler, Joyce retired clergywoman
Steinbock, John Thomas bishop
Stensether, John Eldon minister
Sterzinsky, Georg Maximilian Cardinal archbishop
Stokes, John Lemacks, II clergyman, retired university official
Stubbe, Ray William minister, chaplain, author
Stuhlmacher, Peter Otto Johannes religion educator
Stutzman, L. Lee pastor
Suarez Rivera, Adolfo Antonio archbishop
Suin de Boutemard, Bernhard religion educator, clergyman, publisher
Sullivan, James Stephen bishop
Sulyk, Stephen archbishop
Sunderaraj, Francis religious organization administrator
Šuštar, Alojzij retired bishop
Suttner, Ernst Christoph religious studies educator
Sutton, Peter Alfred former archbishop
Swanson, Dennis Michael religious institution librarian, pastor
Swiatek, Kazimierz Cardinal archbishop
Szoka, Edmund Casimir Cardinal archbishop
Takagi, Takako Frances theology educator
Tali, Tom clergyman
Tamminen, Kalevi Reino retired religion educator, researcher
Tan, Daniel Yunan minister
Tanquary, Oliver Leo minister
Taofinu'u, Pio Cardinal archbishop
Taylor, John Calvin missionary, dentist
Taylor, Lewis Jerome, Jr. priest
Taylor, Maurice bishop
Taylor, Thomas Fuller religious society administrator
Teissier, Henri archbishop
Tetlie, Harold priest
Thatcher, Adrian theology educator
Theissen, Gerd New Testament educator
Thiandoum, Hyacinthe Cardinal archbishop
Thomas, Elliott G. former bishop
Thompson, David B. bishop
Thompson, Robert Jaye minister
Thottupuram, Kurian Cherian priest, college director, educator
Thuemmel, Hans Georg theologian, educator
Timms, Richard Brian education consultant
Tolmie, Donald Francois religious studies educator
Tomko, Jozef Cardinal archbishop
Tonini, Ersilio Cardinal archbishop
Tonnos, Anthony bishop
Touati, Charles religious studies educator
Towne, Edgar Arthur theologian, educator
Townsend, Kenneth Ross retired priest
Toy, John priest
Trautman, Donald W. bishop
Trevijano, Ramon theology educator
Trindade, Armando archbishop
Truesdell, Walter George minister, librarian
Truitt, Charlotte Frances clergywoman
Trulear, Harold Dean minister, theological educator, social researcher
Tumi, Christian Wiyghan Cardinal bishop
Tung, Pham Dinh (Paul Joseph Pham Dinh Tung) Roman Catholic cardinal
Turcotte, Jean-Claude Cardinal archbishop
Tutu, Desmond Mpilo retired archbishop
Tworuschka, Udo religious historian
Tyagananda, Swami religious educator
Tzadua, Paulos Cardinal archbishop
Umbehocker, Kenneth Sheldon priest
Vachon, Louis-Albert Cardinal archbishop
Vandergriff, Kenneth Lynn minister
Van der Watt, Jan Gabriel religious studies educator
Van Der Woude, Adam Simon religious studies educator
Vanhoye, Albert Felix religious educator
Van Voorst, Robert E. theology educator, minister
Van Zyl, Hermias Cornelius religous lecturer, clergyman
Vasko, Peter Theodore Frederick priest
Veitch, James Alexander religious studies educator
Vermasvuori, Juha Kalevi religious studies educator
Vermes, Geza religious studies educator
Vicary, Douglas Reginald priest, headmaster
Vidal, Ricardo Cardinal archbishop of Cebu
Virkler, Mark William religious educator
Vlk, Miloslav archbishop
Voss, Gerhard Maria monk, theologian
Wagner, Donald Edward minister
Wainwright, Elaine Mary religious studies educator
Waldenfels, Hans theologian
Walker, Jewett Lynius clergyman, church official
Wall, Leonard J. bishop
Walls, James Douglas minister
Walter, Nikolaus religious studies educator
Wamala, Emmanuel Cardinal archbishop
Ward, Archbishop John Aloysius archbishop
Watson, JoAnn Ford theology educator
Weakland, Rembert G. archbishop
Weaver, E(lvin) Paul minister
Weder, Hans theology educator
Weible, Diane Lynn minister
Weigl, Michael religious studies educator
Weiss, Daniel Edwin clergyman, educator
Weitlauff, Manfred ecclesiastical history educator
Weld, Roger Bowen clergyman
Wells, Ronald John, Jr. clergyman
West, Daniel Charles lay worker, dentist
Wetter, Friedrich Cardinal archbishop
White, Lerrill James clinical pastoral educator
White, Nelson Henry writer, publisher, realtor
Whitlow, William La Fond minister, theology school planter
Wick, Lawrence Wayne clergyman
Willans, Jean Stone bishop, religious organization executive
Willans, Richard James bishop, religious organization executive
Williams, James Kendrick bishop
Williams, Rhys minister
Williams, Thomas Stafford Cardinal archbishop
Williamson, Thomas Michael pastor, civil servant
Willingham, Edward Bacon, Jr. ecumenical minister, administrator
Willmes, Bernd religious studies educator
Wills, Lois Elaine religious education educator
Wilson, Eldon Ray minister
Wilson, Robert Rutherford religious studies educator
Wingenbach, Gregory Charles priest, religious-ecumenical agency director
Winning, Thomas J. Cardinal archbishop
Winslow, David Allen chaplain, retired naval officer
Winter, William Paul, Jr. ministry director
Wirt, Sherwood Eliot minister, writer
Wismar, Gregory Just minister
Wittenbrink, Boniface Leo priest
Woestmann, Heribert theologian, university administrator
Wold, Margaret Barth religion educator, author
Wonneberger, Reinhard theology educator, computer scientist
Woods, J. P. minister
Worden, William Patrick deacon
Wright, David Frederick religious studies educator
Wright-Riggins, Aidsand F., III religious organization executive
Wu Cheng-Chung, John Baptist Cardinal bishop
Xiong, Tousu Saydangnmvang minister
Yalamov, Yuri Ivanovich vice rector, educator
Yule, Alexander theologian
Zanetti, Ugo Achille theologist, educator, priest
Zellmer, David Bruce minister
Zirker, Hans theologian, educator

SCIENCE: LIFE SCIENCE

Aarkrog, Asker radioecologist, researcher
Aas, I. H. Monrad researcher
Aaviksaar, Aavo research institute administrator, researcher
Abasaeed, Ahmed Elhag science educator
Abbas, Adel Mohammed Ali microbiology consultant
Abdel-Fattah, Kamal Ibrahim physiologist, researcher
Abdel Hadi, Ahmed veterinarian

SCIENCE: LIFE SCIENCE 2590 WHO'S WHO IN THE WORLD

Boughton, Geoffrey Neville *forestry educator, civil engineer, consultant*
Boulton, Ian Charles *microbiologist*
Boulyjenkov, Victor Edmundovich *geneticist*
Bouranis, Demetrios Lambros *plant physiologist, educator*
Bourgeois, Claude Fernand *science lab manager*
Bourne, Frederick John *veterinary medicine educator, researcher*
Bousfield, Edward Lloyd *biologist*
Bouthet, Catherine Francoise *cell biologist*
Boyd, David Gerald *technologist*
Braasch, Helen *biologist*
Brading, Alison Frances *physiologist, educator*
Bradley, John M(iller), Jr. *forestry executive*
Bradshaw, Anthony David *plant ecologist, biology educator*
Brain, Paul Fredric *zoology educator*
Braitenberg, Valentino *scientist*
Brändén, Carl Ivar *research scientist*
Brandl, Heinz *research scientist, consultant, educator*
Brauch, Hiltrud Beatrix *research scientist, consultant*
Breathnach, Caoimhghín Seosamh *physiologist, medical historian*
Brede, Andrew Douglas *research director, plant breeder*
Bredenkamp, Brian Victor *forester, educator*
Breed, Helen Illick *ichthyologist, educator*
Bregliano, Jean-Claude *geneticist, educator*
Brenner, Frederic James *biology educator, ecological consultant*
Breymeyer, Alicja Irena *ecologist*
Briley, Michael *research scientist*
Brim, Hassan *microbiologist, researcher*
Bringel, Françoise *microbiologist, researcher*
Bristow, John Leslie *science consulting company executive*
Britt, David Paul *biomedical sciences educator*
Britton, Paul *molecular biologist, researcher*
Broadhurst, Matthew Kenyon *research scientist, educator*
Brodey, Warren Mortimer *researcher*
Brodie, James William *marine scientist*
Bromley, Paul Douglas *exercise physiologist, educator*
Bromley, Stephen C. *zoology educator*
Bronner, Gary *science educator*
Brookes, Philip Charles *soil microbial ecologist*
Brooks, Gerald Thomas *toxicology educator*
Brooks, Peter Heath *agriculture educator, consultant, researcher*
Broom, Donald Maurice *animal scientist, educator*
Bro-Rasmussen, Finn *educator*
Brotchie, John Frederick *research scientist*
Brown, Alistair James Petersen *microbiology educator*
Brown, Austin Duncan *research scientist, writer*
Brown, Derek John Finlay *plant nematologist*
Brown, Lester Russell *research institute executive*
Brown, Michael Stuart *geneticist, educator, administrator*
Brown, Nigel Leslie *research molecular biologist, educator*
Brown, Paul Dean *microbiologist, researcher*
Brown, Robert Thorson *retired forest ecology educator, researcher*
Brown, Valerie Kathleen *ecologist*
Brown, Walter Creighton *biologist*
Bruhns, Erika Luise (Hazmuka) *ethologist, horse educator*
Brunner, Paul Hans *science educator*
Brunson, Kenneth Wayne *cancer biologist*
Bryan, Frank Leon *microbiologist, consultant, researcher*
Bryant, John Allen *biology educator, researcher, consultant*
Bryson, Nigel Robert *veterinarian, researcher*
Bubán, Tamás *horticultural engineer, researcher*
Bubeník, Jan *cancer researcher, biology educator*
Buc, Henri Christophe *molecular biologist*
Buchala, Antony Joseph *plant biology educator*
Büchen-Osmond, Ulla Maria Cornelia *biologist, consultant*
Bucio, Espinoza Miguel Angel *microbiologist, researcher*
Buckley, Ralf Christopher *research scientist*
Bueckmann, Detlef Georg *biologist, educator*
Bukenya, Remigius Ziraba *biology educator*
Bukhkalo, Sergey Petrovich *biologist, researcher*
Bullecer, Edgar Ladera *agriculturist*
Bullock, Peter *soil scientist*
Bullough, Ronald *research consultant*
Bunger, Rolf *physiology educator*
Burchenal, Joan Riley *science educator*
Burd, Genrich Israel *microbiologist*
Burda, Hynek *zoologist, researcher*
Burda, Renate Margarete *biologist, researcher*
Burdett, Barbra Elaine *biology educator*
Burdon, Douglas William *medical microbiologist*
Bureš, Stanislav *ornithologist, educator*
Burganos, Vasilis Nikolaos *researcher*
Burgoyne, Leigh Alexander *biology educator*
Burja, Adam Martin *marine microbiologist, epidemiologist*
Burkiewicz, Krystyna *plant physiologist*
Burmeister, Margit *research scientist, educator*
Burnie, James Peter *medical microbiologist, educator*
Burns, Paul Yoder *forester, educator*
Burr, Brooks Milo *zoology educator*
Burris, Kenneth Wayne *biologist, educator*
Burrows, John Philip *atmospheric research scientist, educator*
Burrows, Malcolm *zoology educator*
Bury, Jo B.J. *research institute administrator*
Buschiazzo, Daniel Eduardo *agronomist*
Bussmann, Rainer Willi *vegetation ecologist*
Butkevich, Irina Pavlovna *physiologist, researcher*
Buttin, Gérard *science educator*
Buyya, Rajkumar *research scholar*
Bye, Erik *scientific advisor*
Byron, H. Thomas, Jr. *veterinarian, educator*
Cabeza, Marisa *reproductive biochemist, educator*
Cabibbo, Nicola *scientific academy executive, physicist, educator*
Cabrera-Febola, Walter *ecologist, natural structuralist*
Café Filho, Adalberto Correa *plant pathologist*
Cai, Baoli *molecular biology educator*
Cai, Khiem Van *technologist, researcher, administrator*
Cai, Mingjie *scientist*
Cailliez, Jean-Charles *biologist*
Cain, Michael Dean *research forester*
Caldas, Carlos M. *physician, researcher*
Caldecott, Keith William *science educator*
Calderon, Reyna Olga *science educator, researcher*
Caldiz, Daniel Osmar *plant physiology educator*
Caligari, Peter Douglas Savaria *geneticist, researcher*
Calow, Peter *biology educator*
Cal-Vidal, José *food scientist, educator*
Calvo, Julio Cesar *forestry educator*
Camicas, Jean-Louis *entomologist*
Camlitepe, Yilmaz *biologist, researcher*
Campbell, Bruce Donald *biologist, researcher*
Campbell, David George *ecologist, researcher, author*
Campbell, Ella O. *botanist*
Campione-Piccardo, José Alfonso Domingo *virologist, educator*
Canning, Elizabeth Ursula *zoologist*
Cantell, Carl-Erik *zoologist*
Cantley, Mark Flett *biotechnology adviser*
Cao, Chang Qing *physiologist, researcher*
Cao, Heping *biologist, researcher*
Cao, Tong *botanist, educator*
Cao, Xinmin *molecular biologist*
Carbis, Colin Richard *toxicologist, immunologist*
Carlberg, Ulf Bertil *entomologist*
Carlile, Michael John *microbiologist, researcher*
Carlsson, Peder Ulf *science educator*
Carniel, Elisabeth *microbiologist*
Carrillo, Bernardo Jorge *veterinarian, researcher*
Carrillo, Leonor *microbiology educator, researcher*
Carrive, Pascal Luc *neuroscientist*
Carroll, Ray Dean, Sr. *veterinarian*
Carstairs, Kari Sigrid *clinical psychologist*
Carter, Anthony Michael *physiology educator*
Carvajalino, Mario Rafael *agroecological company executive*
Cary, John William *resource management educator, consultant*
Casal, Jorge José *plant physiologist*
Case, Charles Patrick *histopathologist, researcher, musician*
Cassidy, David C. *science educator, historian*
Castagnaro, Massimo *science educator*
Castaño, Fernando Daniel *agronomist, educator*
Castro, Marcia Salustiano de *marine biologist*
Castro-Vazquez, Alfredo *physiology educator, researcher*
Catach, Nina Abignoly *research director, deceased*
Cate, Peter Carl *zoologist, researcher*
Cavallaro, Joseph John *microbiologist*
Cavalli, Pietro *geneticist, consultant, researcher*
Cayot, Philippe *food scientist, reseacher*
Celichowski, Jan Stefan *science educator*
Çerchez, Lidia Cecilia *science researcher*
Čermák, František *science educator*
Cerny, Frantisek *science educator, researcher*
Certik, Milan *scientist in biotechnology, educator*
Cervantes, Emilio *biologist, scientist*
Cervinkova, Zuzana *physiology educator*
Chadeganipour, Mostafa *science educator, microbiologist, mycologist*
Chahal, Sukh Mohinder Singh *human genetics researcher, educator*
Chakrabarti, Subhash Ranjan *dairy technology educator, researcher, consultant*
Chakrabarty, Ananda Mohan *microbiologist*
Chalupsky, Josef (Jiri) *parasitologist, educator*
Chambers, David Wade *science educator*
Chan, Harvey Thomas, Jr. *food technology researcher*
Chan, Hsiao Chang *physiology educator*
Chan, Ken *ecology and physiology educator, researcher*
Chan, Kwong Yin *soil scientist*
Chan, Paul Kay-Sheung *clinical virologist, educator*
Chand, Suresh *life science educator*
Chandra, Kirtunia Juran *fish biology educator*
Chandra, Prakash *molecular biologist, educator*
Chandrashekaran, Maroli Krishnayya *biologist*
Chandromoni *veterinarian, educator*
Chang, Chao-Fu *microbiologist, educator*
Chang, Shu Ting *fungal geneticist, mushroom biologist*
Chang, Zong-Liang *biochemist*
Chaouat, Gerard Charles Paul *researcher*
Chapman, Audrey *science association executive, clergywoman*
Chapouthier, Georges *biologist, writer*
Chaput, Michel Albert *science educator, researcher*
Charity, Julia Anne *research scientist*
Charles, Jean-François Miguel *entomologist*
Charnock, John Stewart *biologist*
Chartier, Germain Henri *science educator*
Chartres, Colin John *soil scientist*
Chatelain, Peter John *research scientist*
Chater, Keith Frederick *microbiologist*
Chatterjee, Amar *physiologist, educator*
Chattopadhyay, Subrata *medical physiologist, researcher*
Chaudhari, Pradip Ramdas *veterinarian, scientist*
Chaudhary, Zafar Iqbal *pathologist, consultant*
Chauret, Christian Pierre *microbiologist, educator*
Chavancy, Gérard Jean *research scientist*
Chawla, Harvinder Singh *science educator*
Chawla, Santa *research scientist*
Cheah, Peh Yean *research scientist*
Cheido, Margarita Aleksandrovna *physiologist, researcher*
Chelidze, Tamaz Lucka *science administrator*
Chellappa, Naithirithi Tiruvenkatachary *environmental science educator, consultant*
Che Man, Yaakob Bin *food technology educator, researcher*
Chen, Chenggang *research scientist*
Chen, Feng *mechanics educator*
Chen, Guodong *scientist, chemical engineer*
Chen, Nian *toxicologist, government official*
Chen, Yih Ming *botany educator*
Chen, Zueng-Sang *soil science educator, researcher*
Cheney, David Warren *science and technology policy analyst, executive*
Cheng, I-Jiunn *marine biology educator*
Cheng, Yue *molecular geneticist, pathologist*
Cheour, Marie Katariina *research scientist*
Chep, Alain *science educator, researcher*
Chepurnov, Alexandr Alexei *virology and biotechnology researcher*
Chermann, Jean Claude *virologist*
Chermiti, Amor *agronomist, researcher*
Chertnetsof, Nikita *zoologist, researcher*
Chertkov, Victor Yakov *research scientist*
Cheruku, Srinivasa Rao *research scientist*
Chetverin, Alexander Borisovich *molecular biologist*
Chew, Fook Tim *research scientist*
Chew, Jessica Allen *genetics researcher*
Chibuzo, Gregory Anenonu *veterinary educator*
Chicco, Bruno *research scientist*
Chieffi, Giovanni *biology educator*
Chihara, Goro *biologist*
Chilliard, Yves *research scientist*
Chilton, St. John Poindexter *retired plant pathology educator, farm owner*
Chilukuri, Nageswararao *biochemist*
Chinabut, Supranee *fisheries scientist*
Chindah, Alex Chuks *biologist*
Chin-Dusting, Jaye Pui Fong *research scientist*
Chineme, Chijioke Nwankwo *veterinary pathologist, educator*
Chinnala, Ayodhya Ramulu *biotechnologist, researcher*
Chintalapati, Sasikala *microbiology researcher, educator*
Chiran, Aurel *agronomics educator*
Chirgadze, Yuri Nickolaievich *biologist*
Chiron, Jean-Paul Michel André *microbiology educator*
Chirvase, Ana Aurelia *research scientist*
Chitsomboon, Benjamart *science educator*
Chizzola, Remigius Karl *biologist, plant physiologist*
Chmielarz, Pawel *scientist*
Chmurzyński, Jerzy Andrzej *ethologist*
Chock, Alvin Keali'i *retired botanist*
Chockalingam, Mary Juliana *research and development executive*
Choi, Byung Han *plant breeder, researcher*
Choi, In-Ho *life science educator*
Choi, Sing-Ki Xavier *research scientist*
Choi, Yong-Eui *plant biologist, researcher*
Chojnacki, Juliusz C. *hydrobiologist, oceanographer, educator*
Chok, Timothy Kon Fui *microbiologist, researcher*
Choo, Yen *molecular biologist, researcher*
Choob, Vladimir Victorovich *biologist, educator*
Chopade, Balu Ananda *microbiologist, researcher, educator*
Choppin, Purnell Whittington *research administrator, virology researcher, educator*
Chou, Louis Sheng-Tsi *science administrator, educator*
Choubey, Veerendra Kumar *research scientist*
Choudhuri, P.C. *veterinarian educator*
Chow, Lung-Hen Henry *laboratory project manager*
Chow, Vincent Tak-Kwong *biomedical scientist, educator*
Chowdhary, Brahma Ram *veterinarian*
Chowdhury, Nirmalendu *veterinary, educator*
Christensen, Allen Clare *agriculturist, educator*
Christensen, Jens Jørgen Elmer *clinical microbiologist*
Christensen, Kaare *geneticist, epidemiologist*
Christoffersen, Martin Lindsey *evolutionary theory educator, researcher*
Christy, Alfred Antony *research scientist*
Chuang, Shou-Hwa *zoologist*
Chung, Gyuhwa *plant geneticist, educator*
Chung, Hai Won *geneticist, educator*
Chute, Harold LeRoy *veterinary pathologist, former chemical company executive*
Chvála, Milan *entomologist, educator*
Cicero, Silvio Moure *educator, researcher*
Ciereszko, Andrzej *science educator*
Cierniewski, Jerzy Leszek *soil science and remote sensing educator*
Ciesielska, Joanna Krystyna *science educator*
Ciftcioglu, Neva *microbiologist*
Çîrlan, Marius-Paul Vasile *veterinarian, educator*
Čítek, Jindřich *agriculture sciences educator, geneticist*
Clamann, York H. *biologist, educator*
Clark, Joseph Floyd *research scientist*
Clark, Noel Bryan *chemist, forester*
Clarke, Gary Norman *reproductive biologist*
Clarke, Peter Geoffrey Hatherley *neurobiologist, educator*
Clausen, Claus Andreas *marine biologist*
Cleeton, David Lawrence *economist, educational administrator*
Clemedson, Ulrika Cecilia *toxicologist, researcher, consultant*
Clement, Christophe *plant biologist, researcher*
Cliet, Isabelle Marie *biologist*
Clifford, Steven Francis *science research director*
Clode, William Henry *microbiologist*
Cloudsley-Thompson, John Leonard *retired zoology educator, author*
Clozel, Martine *research scientist*
Cochrane, Robert Lowe *biologist*
Cociu, Vasile *agriculture researcher*
Cockcroft, Shamshad *physiology educator, researcher*
Codoban, Alexandru *science educator*
Coe, Malcolm James *retired animal ecologist, consultant*
Cogălniceanu, Dan *ecology educator*
Cogdell, Richard John *botanist, biochemist, educator*
Cohen, Patricia Townsend Wade (Lady Patricia Townsend Wade Cohen) *molecular biologist*
Cohn, David V(alor) *oral biology and biochemistry educator*
Colak, Dilek *researcher*
Coleman, Bernell *physiologist, educator*
Colin, Blakemore *physiology educator*
Coloe, Peter John *biotechnology educator*
Colombo, Armando Walter *manufacturing automation researcher, educator*
Colwell, Rita Rossi *microbiologist, molecular biologist, educator, federal agency administrator*
Conand, Chantal *biologist, educator*
Conrad, Joseph Henry *animal nutrition educator*
Conrad, Melvin Louis *biology educator*
Conrath, Uwe *plant physiologist, educator*
Conway, John Bell *environmental biologist, educator*
Cooke, Louise Rene *plant pathologist, educator*
Cooper, Chester Lawrence *research administrator*
Cooperrider, Tom S. *botanist*
Corbet, Philip Steven *zoology educator, consultant ecologist*
Corbier, Philippe *physiologist educator*
Cordonnier-Pratt, Marie-Michèle *molecular biologist, researcher*
Corneanu, Gabriel Constantin *science educator*
Cornegliani, Luisa *veterinarian, researcher*
Corrêa, Iran Carlos Stalliviere *marine geology educator*
Correia, Joao Pedro Santos *marine biologist*
Corti, Giuseppe *soil scientist, researcher*
Cosson, Louis *retired botany educator*
Costa, Andrew Michele *geotechnics technologist, consultant*
Costa, Cleide *biologist, researcher*
Costa, Jefferson Luis da Silva *agronomer*
Costaneto, Eraldo Medeiros *biologist, educator*
Costanza, Vicente *science educator, researcher*
Cother, Eric John *plant pathologist*
Cotón, Eduardo *science researcher, educator*
Couplan, François Jean-Marie *ethnobotanist, writer*
Courtois, André Georges *microbiologist*
Coutard, Olivier *research scientist*
Coviello, Alfredo *physiology educator*
Coxam, Veronique Martine *physiologist, researcher*
Crailsheim, Karl Eberhard Richard *biologist, researcher, educator*
Cramp, David Christopher *agriculturist, consultant*
Crane, Alfred Charles, Jr. *scientist*
Creasia, Donald Anthony *toxicologist, researcher*
Cremers, Georges Alexis *botanist, researcher*
Crick, Francis Harry Compton *science educator, researcher*
Croghan, Gary Alan *cancer research scientist, physician*
Crouzet, Joël Jean *research scientist*
Crowl, Robert Mitchell *research scientist*
Crumbly, Isaac J. *biology educator*
Cruz, Emmanuel Manuel *scientist*
Cruz e Silva, Joaquim Alberto *science administrator*
Csányi, Vilmos *biologist, researcher, educator*
Csopaki, Gyula *science educator*
Culik, Boris Michael *marine zoologist*
Cullmann, Wolfgang Walter *microbiologist*
Cunningham, Edward Patrick *geneticist*
Cure, Graham Lewis *food scientist*
Curran, Michael Walter *management scientist*
Czaplewski, Lloyd George *biotechnology educator*
Czapowski, Grzegorz *geologist, researcher*
Czarnowski, Marian *plant physiologist, researcher, educator*
Czauderna, Marian *animal scientist*
Czihak, Gerhard *biologist*
Czirók, Eva *microbiologist*
Czyz, Zbigniew Henryk *research scientist, educator*
Dabbousi, Bashir Osama *research scientist*
Dadgari, Farzad *soil scientist, environmental specialist*
Daesety, Vishnuvardhan *biologist, researcher*
Daguzan, Jacques Jean Edmond *research biologist, educator*
Dahm, Erik *microbiologist*
Dai, Liming *research scientist*
Dai, Wei *research scientist*
Dale, Torbjørn *marine biologist, educator*
Dandashi, Fayad Alexander *operations research scientist, consultant*
Dang, Duc Can *biologist*
Daniel, Milan *parasitologist, researcher*
Daniel, Rolf *microbiologist, researcher*
Danielová, Vlasta *biologist, researcher*
Danzin, Charles Marie *enzymologist*
Darevsky, Ilya S. *zoologist, herpetologist, researcher*
Dart, Edward Charles *biotechnology and bioscience consultant*
Das, Aniruddha Mathuranath *veterinary microbiologist, educator*
Das, Mukul *toxicologist*
Dasgupta, Santanu *biological scientist, researcher, educator*
Daskalov, Georgi Mihaylov *scientist*
DasSarma, Shiladitya *geneticist, educator, research scientist*
Dastidar, Manisha G. *research scientist*
Datiri, Benjamin Chumang *soil and environmental scientist*
Datta, Debatosh *biotechnology and bioengineering educator*
Daudt, Carlos Eugenio *agronomist, educator*
Daugaard, Holger *food scientist*
Dauvalter, Vladimir *ecology researcher*
David, Bonnie Premkumar *veterinary microbiologist, researcher*
David, J(ames) Barry *equine veterinarian*
Davies, John Huw *science educator*
Davy, John Laurence *research scientist*
Dawson, Jeffrey Owen *forester, educator*
Dawson, Raymond Murray *research scientist*
Day, Ian *genetics educator*
Day, Michael Denny *entomologist, researcher*
Day, Peter Rodney *geneticist, educator*
Day, Roger William *research executive*
Dayal, Ram *retired science educator*
Dean, Peter Duncan Goodearl *molecular biologist*
DeAngelis, Paula Mary *cell biologist, researcher*
DeBakey, Lois *science communications educator, writer, editor*
DeBakey, Selma *science communications educator, writer, editor, lecturer*
de Belle, John Steven Cole *biologist*
Debeyssey, Mark Sammer *molecular and cellular biologist*
Debieve, Jean-Francois *research scientist*
De Bont, Antoon Frans *biologist, educator, consultant*
de Cataldo, Mark Andrea A. *science researcher*
Dedek, Wolfgang *research scientist*
Dedysh, Svetlana Nicolayevna *scientist, researcher*
Deetjen, Peter Henrich *physiology educator*
Degener, John Edward *medical microbiologist*
Deglise, Xavier Marcel *science educator, researcher*
De Groote, Patrick *science educator*
Deinzer, Renate Irene *psychologist*
De Iohgh, Hendrik Huibert *ecologist*
de Jesus, Julio Enrique *science educator*
Dejoux, Claude *retired hydrobiologist*
De Kesel, Toon *safety, health and environmental executive*
de-la-Rosa, Jorge Luis *biologist, researcher*
Delaveau, Pierre Georges *biologist, pharmacologist, educator*
Delille, Daniel *microbiologist, researcher*
Delpech, Rene Georges *science educator*
Delsol, Michel *biology educator*
Delville, Michel E. *research scientist*
Dely, Matthias Alexander *biologist, researcher*
De Maeyer, Edward *virologist*
De Maeyer-Guignard, Jaqueline Athénais *retired virologist, consultant*
Demaison, Luc *researcher*
Dematteis, Massimiliano *biology researcher, educator*
Dembiński, Artur Bogdan *physiologist, urologist, researcher*
De Mey, Bart *integrated circuits expert*
Deng, Ming-Qi *microbiologist, researcher*
Deniz, Günnur *science educator*
De Oliveira, João Serpa *retired biology educator*
Depauw, Hugo Hendrik *scientific researcher*
Derera, Nicholas Frederick *agricultural research scientist*
Derin, Ivanova *biologist, researcher*
DeRoo, Sally Ann *biology, geology and environmental science educator*
Desai, Pragna Dilip *microbiology educator*
Descamps, Michel Marcel *animal biology educator*
de Serres, Mark *research scientist*
Deshmukh, Prakash Ramchandra *scientist*
Deshpande, Rajendra V. *research scientist*
Desmouliere, Alexis *research scientist*
Dessaux, Yves *microbiologist*
Desvignes, Jean-Claude *virologist*
de Swart, Rik Ludolf *biologist, researcher*
Dev, Vas *biologist, researcher*
Deverall, Brian James *plant pathology educator*

Kahane, Simona Esther virology researcher
Kaila, Lauri Jaakko entomologist, curator, researcher
Kaiser, Robin researcher
Kaissling, Karl-Ernst zoophysiologist, researcher
Kaitera, Juha Antero forest pathologist, researcher
Kakkar, Virender Kumar scientist, researcher
Kalabukhova, Tatyana Nikolaevna biophysician, writer
Kalantzopoulos, George Costas food microbiologist
Kalimo, Esko Antero research institute administrator, educator
Kalisińska, Elżbieta biologist, educator
Kalms, Ian Charles plant company executive
Kalra, Alok plant pathologist
Kaman, Jiří František veterinary morphology educator, researcher
Kamata, Yoshiro food scientist
Kameda, Hisao science educator
Kamenir, Yury Gregory scientist, researcher
Kaminski, Franciszek science educator
Kamlage, Beate microbiologist
Kanal, Arno soil scientist, educator
Kang, Chil-Yong virology, immunology educator
Kang, Ke Won molecular geneticist
Kang, Manjit Singh geneticist, plant breeder
Kang, Shin-Sung biologist, educator
Kaninski, Pavel Sergeyevich research scientist
Kankofer, Marta Elizabeth veterinary biochemist, educator
Kanninen, Markku Tapani ecologist
Kapp, Gerald Bernhard agrosilviculturist, researcher
Kar, Supriya research scientist
Karaali, Artemis Fatma food engineering educator
Karakas, Ucan Nuray microbiologist
Karakaya, Sibel food engineer, researcher
Karathanassis, Athanassis research center administrator, educator
Karczmarzyk, Stanisław research scientist, educator
Karem, Kevin Lee microbiologist, educator
Karino, Kenji educator
Karp, Gerald Charles biologist, educator, writer
Karpenko, Larisa Ivanovna molecular biologist, researcher
Karpinski, Stanislaw biologist
Kartha, Ravindranathan K.P. research scientist
Kasaikina, Olga Tarasovna scientist, health facility administrator
Kashiwazaki, Hiroshi human sciences educator
Kasparek, Max biologist
Kassa, Jiří toxicologist, researcher, educator
Kassai, Tibor parasitologist
Kassam, Amirali Hassanali agricultural scientist
Kast, W. Martin microbiology and immunology educator
Kasuya, Toshio whale biologist
Kasyanov, Vladimir Leonidovich biologist
Kathju, Shyam plant physiologist
Kato, Kenji plant breeding educator
Kato, Nobuo bacteriology educator
Katow, Shigetaka virologist
Katsifis, Spiros Panagiotis biological sciences educator, researcher
Katsura, Isao molecular biologist
Katti, Muralidhar Kotleshachar microbiologist, researcher, consultant
Katz, Sir Bernard physiologist
Kaul, Chaman Lal science administrator
Kaul, Dhananjaya Kumar physiologist
Kaul, Pran Nath veterinarian
Kaul, Victor veterinarian, researcher
Kaustová, Jarmila microbiologist
Kavanaugh, Kevin Patrick research analyst, consultant
Kavsan, Vadim Moiseevich molecular biologist
Kawakatsu, Masaharu zoology educator
Kawamura, Haruki science educator
Kawiak, Jerzy Wladyslaw cell biologist, educator
Kayane, Isamu science educator
Kazi, Shahnaz science educator
Kaziae, Nikola veterinarian, beekeeper
Kazinczi, Gabriella horticulturist
Kearney, Marianne biologist, researcher
Kedves, Miklós József biologist, researcher
Keem, Michael Dennis veterinarian
Keevil, Charles William microbiologist, researcher
Kehayias, George marine biologist, researcher
Keleti, Georg retired microbiologist, researcher
Kelman, Lorraine Macellaro biology educator, molecular biology researcher
Kempken, Frank molecular biologist
Kence, Aykut biologist, educator
Kennedy, Clive Russell zoologist, educator
Kenrick, Paul botanist
Kerckhoffs, Eugene Jules Hubert science educator
Kern, Manfred Jakob biologist, researcher
Kerzhentsev, Anatoly Semenovich ecologist
Kessel, Brina ornithologist, educator
Kessler, Daniel Solomon biologist, educator
Keszthelyi, Lajos science educator
Kettle, Douglas Stewart teritiary educator, researcher
Kevelaitis, Egidijus physiologist, educator
Kevrekidis, Theodoros marine biologist, researcher
Keydar, Iafa virology educator
Khalequzzaman, Mohammad zoology educator
Khan, Hafiz Wasi agronomist, consultant
Khan, Ijaz Jamil microbiologist
Khan, Mahbubar Rahman microbiologist, educator
Khan, Mohammad Khairul Alam science educator
Khan, Mukhlesur Rahman agricultural educator, researcher
Khanuja, Suman Preet Singh molecular biologist and biotechnologist
Kharazipour, Alireza biotechnologist
Khatri, Tikam Chand zoology educator
Kheddar, Abderrahmane research scientist, educator
Kher, Sanjay scientist
Khin-Nwe-oo microbiologist
Khlgatian, Svetlana Vaginakovna physiologist, researcher
Khmurchik, Vadim Tarasovich biologist, researcher
Khodier, Soraya Abd-El-Aziz science educator
Khokhlova, Ludmila Petrovna biologist, physiologist, biology educator
Khugaeva, Valentina Kargoevna pathophysiologist, researcher
Khurana, Satyendra Mohan Paul food scientist, editor, researcher
Khush, Gurdev Singh geneticist
Kidd, Robert science educator
Kieser, Arnd molecular biologist
Kihlstroem, Jan Erik ecotoxicology educator, writer
Kikichi, Tateki science association director
Kille, John William, Jr. toxicology and biomedical product consultant
Kim, Bong Hwan veterinary educator, swine consultant
Kim, Byung-Dong molecular biology educator
Kim, Chul Geun science educator
Kim, Han-Do molecular biologist, educator
Kim, Hyun-Joong scientist, educator
Kim, Kyu-Jin research scientist
Kim, Seock-Ho educator
Kim, Sun-Jang engineer, construction company executive
Kim, Yoon Soo wood biology educator
Kimbeng, Collins Anye research scientist
Kimemin, Joseph Kangara agronomist researcher
Kimura, Shigenobu microbiology educator, dentist
Kindlmann, Pavel ecologist
Kinigakis, Panagiotis research scientist, engineer, author
Kinne, Rolf K.H. research scientist
Kinsman, Oonagh Susan microbiologist
Kirick, Daniel John agronomist
Kirkebo, Arne physiology educator, scientist
Kirkham, M. B. plant physiologist, educator
Kirsta, Yuri Bogdanovich research scientist, educator
Kishek, Rami Alfred scientist
Kishimoto, Hiroshi research institute executive
Kiss, Ferenc science educator, researcher
Kitabatake, Yoshifusa environmental policy educator
Kitagawa, Teizo molecular biology educator
Kitamoto, Yutaka microbiologist, educator
Kitano, Kazuaki microbiologist, researcher
Kittel, Agnes cell biologist
Klapper, Helmut Karl biologist, researcher
Klar, Daniela biologist
Klein, George research scientist
Kleinsmith, Lewis Joel cell biologist, educator
Klekowski, Romuald Zdzisław ecologist, researcher
Klemmer, Konrad Gerhardt zoologist
Kleven, Mark S. research scientist
Klimov, Alexander Ivanovich virologist
Klitzing, Klaus von research facility administrator, physicist
Klug, Aaron molecular biologist
Knegtel, Ronald Marcel Alphons research scientist
Kniest, Frans M. biologist
Kniewald, Jasna toxicologist, educator, scientist
Knight-Jones, Phyllis Kathleen marine biologist, consultant
Knussmann, Rainer human biology educator
Knyazev, Sergey P. biologist
Kobanov, Nikolai Illarionovich research scientist
Koblet, Hans Rudolf retired virologist
Kobrin, Vladimir Isaakovich physiology educator, researcher
Koch, Jørn Erland geneticist, researcher
Kocka, Frank Edward microbiologist
Kocum, Esra biologist, educator
Kodama, Fumio science educator
Kodama, Tohru biotechnology educator
Koganezawa, Hiroki plant pathologist
Koh, Seok Joo researcher
Köhler, Piotr Sebastian botany historian
Kohring, Gert Wieland microbiologist
Koivukangas, Eino Olavi scientific research director
Koizumi, Hideaki research scientist, educator
Kola, Ismail genetics educator
Kolacz, Jacek Tomasz research scientist
Kolb, Erich Friedrich veterinary biochemist
Kolbasov, Grigory Alexandrovich zoologist, researcher
Kolbe, Hartmut Reinhold agronomist, researcher
Kolesnichenko, Anatoly Fedorovich research scientist
Koley, Alok Ranjan physiology educator
Kolman, Ada scientist, educator
Kolmes, Steven Albert biologist, educator
Kolobov, Alexander V. research scientist
Kolomoets, Nikolay Vasilievich research scientist
Kolomytz, Erland Georgievich ecologist, science administrator
Kolozyn-Krajewska, Danuta Maria food technologist, educator
Komarova, Emilia Nicolaevna biologist, researcher
Kommedahl, Thor plant pathology educator
Kommonen, Bertel Wilhelm veterinarian, researcher
Kompanichenko, Vladimir Nicolajevich research scientist, educator, researcher
Kondo, Katsuhiko botanist
Kondo, Michio research scientist
Kong, Ling Xue scientific researcher, consultant
Kong, Mei Ying science educator
Kong, Xiang Yan science educator, researcher
König, Helmut microbiologist, researcher
Konishi, Eiji virologist, vaccinologist, researcher
Kononovich, Alexander Lvovich ecologist
Konrad, Jaroslav veterinarian
Kónya, József clinical microbiologist, researcher
Koopman, Peter Anthony developmental biologist, researcher
Kopec, John William research scientist
Kopec, Karel Emil horticulture educator
Korányi, Pál cell and molecular biologist
Korb, Jan molecular biologist, researcher
Kordyum, Elizabeth Lvovna botanist
Korge, Paavo cell physiologist
Korhonen, Kalle-Heikki soil mechanics educator
Kormanec, Jan molecular biologist
Kormas, Konstantinos Aristomenis biologist, researcher
Koronakis, Demetrios Eystathios biologist, astrologer
Kosachevskaya, Elena Aleksandrovna science administrator
Kosarov, Dimiter neurophysiologist
Koscielak, Jerzy scientist, science administrator
Koss, Peter research management consultant
Kostina, Marina Nikolaevna biologist, scientist
Kosuge, Sadao marine scientist, consultant
Koszinowski, Ulrich Helmut virologist, educator
Kosztolányi, György geneticist, educator
Kothari, Shanker Lal botany educator, researcher
Kotter, Ludwig food scientist
Kouri, Gustavo Pedro virologist
Kovač, Maja physiologist, researcher
Kovač, Miroslav agriculturist, consultant
Koval, Adolf Grigorievich research scientist, laboratory director
Kovarski, Alexander L. scientist, educator
Kozai, Toyoki horticulture educator, researcher
Kozhevnikov, Yuri Pavlovicz botanist
Kozlov, Mikhail Vasilievich entomologist, researcher
Kozlov, Yuri Pavlovich ecologist, educator
Krafft, Fritz Adolf science and pharmacy educator
Krakowski, Leszek Bronisław veterinarian, researcher, educator
Kralj, Metka biology and science educator, researcher
Kramer, Allan Franklin, II researcher, botanical garden official
Kranepool, Harry Anthony science educator
Krassa, Kathy Boltrek molecular biologist
Kratka, Jirina Elizabeth plant pathologist, researcher
Kraus, Otto Heinrich zoology educator
Krause, Maria Wichura physiotherapist
Kravec, Cynthia Vallen microbiologist
Krell, Frank-Thorsten zoologist, researcher
Kremer, Kurt research scientist, administrator
Kreppner, Kurt research scientist
Krettli, Antoniana Ursine parasitologist, educator
Krimbas, Costas B. evolutionary genetics educator
Krishna, Gopal scientist, pharmacokineticist
Krishna, Simile Srinivasan entomologist, educator
Krishnamurthi, M. research scientist
Kristensen, Reinhardt Moebjerg invertebrate zoology educator
Kristjansdottir, Ingileif Steinunn molecular biologist
Kroh, Jerzy retired science educator
Kruglyak, Semyon geneticist, researcher
Krupatkin, Alexander Ilyich clinical physiologist researcher, neurologist
Krupp, Guido molecular biology educator, researcher
Kuba, Miroslav neurophysiology educator, researcher
Kudeyarova, Agniya Yulievna soil scientist, researcher
Kudo, Shinichi molecular geneticist
Kudryashova, Irina Vladimirovna neurophysiologist, researcher
Kufidis, Dimitris Charilaos veterinary medicine educator
Kuhl, Patricia K. science educator
Kuhlmann, Hans-Werner research protozoologist
Kuhns, Larry J. horticulturist, educator
Kuitunen, Markku Tapio biologist, consultant
Kujawski, Daniel science educator
Kukielczak, Barbara Mariola research scientist
Kula, Emanuel forestry educator, researcher
Kulemin, Gennady Petrovich research scientist
Kulkarni, Meghaasham Dattatraya veterinarian, educator, researcher
Kumar, B. Mohan silvicuture and agroforestry educator
Kumar, Sanjay S. neuroscientist
Kumar, Sivanappan solar energy educator
Kumarasinghe, Gamini microbiologist, consultant
Kunes, Josef science educator, consultant, researcher
Kung, Shain-dow molecular biologist, academic administrator
Kunhardt, Martin Gerald plant breeder, researcher
Kunii, Akira human science educator
Kuo, Tsong-Teh biologist, botanist, educator
Kurane, Ryuichiro microbiologist
Kurashov, Evgenij Alexandrovitch hydrobiologist, researcher
Kurilo, Ivan Vasylovych science educator
Kuroda, Toshiro ceramic laboratory administrator
Kuroli, Géza entomologist, educator
Kurosawa, Tsutomu Miki science educator
Kuroshima, Akihiro environmental physiology educator
Kurtanjek, Zelimir Frank food science educator, researcher
Kurth, Reinhard H. virologist, educator
Kurvonen, Timo Lauri research scientist
Kuryszko, Jan Jozef histologist
Kuschinsky, Wolfgang physiologist
Kushalapa, Kodira Achappa forester, researcher, consultant
Kutilek, Miroslav soil science educator
Kutlakhmedov, Yuri Alexeevich radioecologist, radiobiologist, researcher, educator
Kutle, Ante environmentalist
Kuyer, Astrid Desirie Theresia Maria research scientist
Kuzian, Roman Oganesovich research scientist
Kuźnicki, Leszek biologist, cell biologist
Kuzyakov, Yakov Victorovich soil scientist, consultant
Kuzyukov, Anatoliy Nikolayevich research scientist, educator
Kwak, Ju-Won molecular biologist, researcher
Kwon, Byoung-Mog research scientist, educator
Kwon, E Hyock science academy executive
Kyung, Kyu Hang food microbiology educator
La Barre, Stephane Christian research scientist
Labarthe, Norma Vollmer science educator
Labes, Gabriele Marina molecular biologist, researcher
LaBrecque, John Joseph scientist, researcher
Lacal, Juan-Carlos biologist, biochemist, researcher
Lachance, Paul Albert food science educator, clergyman
Ladiges, Pauline Yvonne botanist
Ladygin, Vladimir Georgievich biologist, geneticist, researcher
Lafield, Karen Woodrow science educator, demographer
Lagerspetz, Kari Yrjö Henrik biologist, educator
Lagneborg, Rune Gunnar research institute executive, material scientist
Lagunez-Otero, Jaime researcher, scientist
Lahti, Markku Sakari research scientist
Lai, Yeong-Kang science educator
Lainson, Ralph parasitologist, researcher
Lakritz, Jeffrey veterinary educator
Lakshminarayana, Karri microbiology educator, researcher
Lamb, Christopher John research scientist
Lamb, James Warner biology educator
Lambers, Johannes Thieo biologist, educator
Land, Geoffrey Allison science administrator
Lane, Simon John wildlife biologist, researcher
Lang, Bohumir Alfons molecular biologist, researcher
Langdon, Simon Peter biologist
Langer, Glenn Arthur cellular physiologist, educator
Langmeier, Milos physiologist
Langner, Gerald science educator
Lanher, Bertrand Simon biological spectroscopist, corporate manager
Lansimies, Esko Antero clinical physiologist, physician, educator
Laporte, Yves Michel neurobiologist
Lara, Francisco botany educator, researcher
Largo, Danilo Basnillo biology educator
Larionov, Oleg Alekseevich biologist, researcher
Larotonda, Gerardo Julio veterinary pathologist
Larsen, Jan science educator
Larsen, Peder Olesen research foundation executive
Larsson, Per-Olov fish biologist, researcher
Lasmézas, Corinne Ida veterinarian
Last, Donald conservationist, educator
Lastra, Jose Ramon plant virologist, eductor
Laštuvka, Zdenek zoology educator, researcher
Laszczka, Andrzej Konstanty biologist, journal editor
Latorre, Cristina microbiologist
Lau, George Ka-Kit hepatologist
Laude, Jean-Pierre Robert scientific director
Laufer, Hans developmental biologist, educator
Laurent, Guy biology educator
Lauridsen, Søren Tindgard food scientist
Laurin, Michel zoologist
Lavado, Raul Silvio soil scientist, educator
Laws, Richard Maitland biology educator, scientist, government agency director
Laxminarayana, Dama geneticist, researcher, educator
Layson, William McIntyre retired research consulting company executive
Lázár, George pathophysiologist, researcher
Lazarides, Michael botanist
Lazzarotto, Marcio science educator
Leakey, Roger Richard Bazett research scientist, consultant
Le Berre, Michel science educator
Lebre, Maria Manuela A. Azevedo biologist, researcher
Le Coustumier, Alain medical microbiologist
Lederberg, Joshua geneticist, educator
Lederman, Frank L. scientist, research center administrator
Ledin, Maria Eva microbiologist, researcher
Le Duff, Yves science educator, laboratory administrator
Lee, Arthur Virgil, III biotechnology company executive
Lee, Baek Rak microbiologist, educator
Lee, Chien-Hsiung research scientist, educator
Lee, Daniel Kam-Len molecular biologist
Lee, Hyung Hoan science educator, researcher, director
Lee, Jungho botanist, researcher
Lee, Ki-Young research scientist
Lee, Kyoung microbiologist, educator
Lee, Yeonhee research scientist
Lee, Yu-May molecular biologist, educator
Leek, Barry Frank veterinarian, educator
Lefranc, Marie-Paule immunogenetics educator, researcher
Legovic, Tarzan ecologist
Lehman, Niles E. science educator
Leifsson, Bjorgvin Runar biology educator
Leistner, Otto Albrecht botanist, scientific editor, researcher
Lelek, Antonin fishery scientist
Lelord, Gilbert Francois physiologist and psychiatrist
Lemoine, Michel Jules research scientist, educator
Lemus-Deschamps, Lilia Lemus research scientist
Lénárd, László Csaba physiology educator, neuroscientist
Lengy, Jacob Israel parasitologist, educator
Lennon, Stephen John research scientist, executive
Leon, Nelson genetics educator, endocrinologist
Le Pair, Cornelis research organization executive, retired
Le Pecq, Jean-Bernard Rene biotechnologist, business executive
Le Quéré, Jean François Marie scientific instrumentation researcher
Lequeu, Bruno biologist, consultant
Lervik, John Markus research scientist
Leschonsky, Bernd molecular biologist, educator
Lesseva, Magdalena Ivanova microbiologist, researcher, consultant
Lestienne, Patrick Pierre molecular biologist
Letalick, Alf Dietmar scientist
Leung, Po Sing physiology educator
Leuschner, Ruth Maria biologist
Levi-Montalcini, Rita neurobiologist, researcher
Levin, Norman Lewis biology educator
Levinsen, Henrik biologist, researcher
Levison, Steven William scientist, educator
Levitzky, Michael Gordon physiology educator, researcher
Levy, Pierre-Yves microbiologist, health facility administrator
Levy-Leboyer, Claude research scientist, consultant
Lewald, Joerg neurobiologist
Lewinson, Dina cell biologist, anatomist, researcher, educator
Lewis, Edward B. biology educator
Lewis, JulianHart developmental biologist, author
Lewis, Kim microbiologist
Lewis, Thelma Agnes medical laboratory scientific officer
Li, ChangAn entomologist, educator
Li, David Wan-Cheng cell biologist
Li, Fengkui research scientist
Li, Jinghai science educator
Li, Mengfeng molecular biologist, virologist, educator
Li, Mingqi plant physiologist
Li, Peng biologist, researcher
Li, Qin research scientist
Li, Shibo medical genetics educator
Li, Shushen science administrator, environmental scientist
Li, Taiwu marine biologist, educator
Li, Xiankui research scientist
Li, You-Chun geneticist
Li, Zhengang molecular geneticist
Liang, Hua research scientist
Liang, Wei technology educator
Liang, Weiwen biological researcher
Liang, Xin-Gang science researcher, educator
Liao, Martha geneticist
Lichter, Peter geneticist, researcher
Lichtstein, David physiologist, researcher
Lidbury, Brett Andrew research virologist and immnologist
Liew, Soo Chin research scientist
Ligeti, Erzsébet Katalin physiology educator
Lin, Meei-Yn food microbiology/biotechnology educator
Lin, Shouyuan science educator
Lincoln, Edward Palmer biologist, research scientist
Lindberg, Uno Mårten biologist educator
Lindborg, Keihan food technologist
Linderholm, Håkan Per Gustaf physiology educator
Lindl, Toni biotechnologist, educator
Lindsay, Dale Richard research administrator
Ling, Jian researcher, consultant
Linga, Venkateswar Rao microbiologist, educator
Link, Gerhard Gottfried botany educator
Lipa, Jerzy Jozefat plant protection educator
Lipnitsky, Anatoly Vasilievich microbiologist
Lister, Bruce Alcott food scientist, consultant
Litster, Annette Lorna veterinarian
Liu, De Li agronomist
Liu, Jiankang K. freshwater biologist, research scientist
Liu, Jian-Xin science educator
Liu, Maw-Shung physiologist, dentist
Liu, Tai-Feng physiologist
Liu, Yi-Xun reproductive biologist, researcher
Liu, Yong-Yu molecular biologist

Lloyd, John Anthony *research scientist, consultant*
Lo, Hoi-Kwong *research scientist*
Lo, Kam Wah *research scientist*
Lochter, André *biosciences researcher*
Lodolo, Elizabeth Jacoba *research scientist*
Loesch, Andrzej Witold *biologist*
Loewenstein, Werner Randolph *physiologist, biophysicist, educator*
Loewer, Johannes K. *virologist, educator*
Loewy, Erich Hans *bioethicist, educator*
Loget, Olivier Marcel *toxicologist, ophthalmologist*
Loh, Wolfgang F.W. *virologist, biotechnologist, consultant*
Lohiya, Nirmal Kumar *zoology educator*
Lojda, Ladislav *veterinarian*
Lomakin, Eugene Victorovich *mechanician, educator*
Lomonte, Bruno *microbiology educator*
Londner, Mauricio Vladimiro *biologist, immunologist, researcher, educator*
Lone, Farooq Ahmad *scientist, researcher*
Lonza Ricci, Laura *researcher*
Lopes, Artur Oscar *mathematician, researcher*
Lopez, Genaro *biology educator*
Lorenço, Sergio Oliveira *biology educator*
Loria, Antonio *scientist, consultant*
Lorito, Matteo *biology educator*
Los, Marek Jan *scientist, physician*
Losano, Gianni Alberto *cardiovascular physiologist, educator*
Losos, Jonathan B. *biologist, educator*
Lossovsky, Eugene Kazimirovich *research scientist, science administrator*
Lotha, Stephen *science educator*
Louchev, Oleg Anatolievich *researcher, consultant*
Loucks, Terry Lee *writer, retired biosystems executive*
Louër, Daniel *research scientist*
Louvard, Daniel François *cell biologist, researcher*
Lowbury, Edward Joseph Lister *microbiologist, writer*
Lowe-McConnell, Rosemary Helen *biologist*
Lowseth, Lisa Anne *veterinarian*
Lu, Qi Keng *mathematics educator*
Lucà-Moretti, Maurizio *research scientist, nutrition researcher*
Lucic, Davor *biologist, researcher*
Lugovy, Mykola Ivanovich *scientist, consultant*
Luijendijk, Teus *scientist*
Luis, José Antoine *science educator, researcher*
Lukac, Josip *biologist*
Lumeij, Johannes Thomas *veterinarian*
Luna, Maria das Graças *microbiologist*
Lundblad, Roger Lauren *biotechnology consultant*
Lundin, Lena Gunhild Margareta *science educator, researcher*
Lüttge, Ulrich Ernst *botany educator*
Lvssl, Andreas G. *geneticist, philosopher*
Lyakh, Viktor Alekseevich *biologist, researcher*
Lyalikova, Natalia *microbiologist, researcher*
Lyapustin, Alexei Ivanovich *research scientist*
Lyshede, Ole Birger *plant anatomist, educator*
Ma, Hai-Fei *research scientist*
Ma, Jianzhong *science educator*
Mabro, Robert Emile *energy studies educator*
Macar, Francoise Jeanne *research scientist*
Macdonald, Brian Alexander *aquarium administrator*
Macek, Milan, Jr. *molecular geneticist*
Macer, Darryl Raymund Johnson *biology educator*
Macey, David John *animal physiologist*
Maciá, Enrique Barber *research institute executive, educator, researcher*
MacIntyre, Iain *scientist, research institute administrator*
Mack, Hananel *researcher*
MacKenzie, Ann Haley *science educator*
Madan, Mira *science educator, technology administrator*
Madhyastha, Nagappayya Mattu *bioscience educator*
Mae, Tadahiko *plant physiologist*
Maeda, Masanobu *physiology educator, researcher*
Maeda, Yasuo *biologist, educator*
Maeland, Johan Andreas *microbiologist, researcher*
Magee, John Francis *research company executive*
Magos, László Paul *toxicologist, consultant*
Magura, Igor Silvestrovitch *neurophysiologist, educator*
Mahadevappa, Madappa *rice breeder, university vice chancellor*
Maheshwari, Hari Krishna *palaeobotanist, researcher*
Mahmoud, Yehia Abdel-Galele *microbial biochemistry educator, researcher*
Mahmoudian, Mahmoud *biotechnology microbial physiologist, biotechnologist*
Mahner, Martin *biologist*
Mahunka, Sándor *acarologist, researcher, museum official*
Mailachalam, Babu *research scientist*
Maimusov, Dmitry Fedosovich *soil scientist, educator*
Maingi, Naichu *parasitology educator*
Maire, Jean-Claude *science educator, consultant*
Maiti, Ratikanta *botanist, research scientist*
Maitra, Arindam *molecular biologist*
Majer, Jozsef Mihaly *ecologist, educator*
Majumder, Parimal *researcher*
Makinde, Martin Oladiran *veterinary physiologist*
Malaka, Rainer *research scientist, project manager*
Malakhov, Vladimir Vasil'evitch *zoology educator*
Malavolta, Euripedes *agriculture educator, consultant*
Malcata, Francisco Xavier *science educator*
Maldonado-Lopez, Rafael *life sciences researcher*
Malek, Mohammed Abdul *scientist*
Malik, Rakesh Kumar *veterinary and animal science educator, researcher*
Malik, Ramesh Chander *geneticist, researcher, veterinarian, educator*
Malinin, Vladimir Viktorovich *scientist*
Malkov, Sergej Viktorovich *geneticist, researcher*
Malkusch, Wolf Peter *biologist*
Malling, Heinrich Valdemar *geneticist*
Malmuth, Norman David *research scientist, program manager*
Maloof, Joan E. *biologist, educator*
Malyshev, Igor Yurjevich *pathophysiologist*
Mamcarz, Andrzej *ichthyologist*
Mandal, Abul *agriculture educator*
Mandelker, Lester *veterinarian*
Mankertz, Annette *virologist, biochemist*
Mann, Bruce Quintin *biologist*
Mannheim, Adie *dairy products researcher, food engineer*
Mannion, Philip Thomas *medical microbiology consultant, disease control consultant*
Manolescu, Nicolae Manolache *veterinary science researcher*
Mansour, Mohamed Magdy Fahim *botany educator*
Mao, Jifang *biologist, researcher*
Maozhong, Yi *science educator, engineering educator*
Marai, Ibrahim Fayez Mahmoud *agronomist, educator, researcher, consultant*
Maravelias, Christos *marine and fisheries biologist, educator*
Marcellan, Olga Noemi *geneticist, researcher*
Marchionni, Mark Andrew *neurobiologist, researcher*
Marcström, Arne Oscar Emanuel *physiology educator, researcher*
Margallo, Agnes Atutubo *biology educator*
Marić, Jasmina *oenologist, researcher*
Marin-Garcia, Jose *researcher*
Mark, Alan Francis *plant ecologist, educator*
Mark, Jorgen *agronomist*
Markl, Hubert *zoology educator*
Marks, Andrew Robert *molecular biologist*
Markus, Miles Berkeley *parasitologist, researcher*
Maroto, Federico Garcia *molecular biology educator, researcher*
Marquardt, Otfried Hellmut *molecular biologist*
Marques, Otavio Augusto Vuolo *biologist, researcher*
Marrè, Erasmo *plant physiologist, researcher*
Marsalek, Jaroslav *microbiologist*
Marschall, Marianna *biologist, educator*
Marshall, Christopher John *molecular cell biologist*
Martin, Eva Viktoria *research scientist*
Martin, Joan *botanist, educator*
Martinelli, Alberto Piero *research scientist*
Martinelli, Lucia *biologist, researcher, laboratory manager*
Martinex-Padilla, Laura Patricia *food scientist, educator, researcher*
Martinez, Richard Isaac *science administrator*
Martino, Joseph Paul *research scientist*
Martin Sanchez, Juan Antonio *plant breeder*
Márton, László *agriculturist, researcher*
Marton, Sandor Istvan *ecology educator, consultant*
Martrenchar, Arnaud *veterinarian*
Maruyama, Ichiro *biologist, educator*
Marvan, Petr *phycologist, researcher*
Maselli, Fabio *research scientist*
Maseng, Torleiv *research scientist*
Mash, Robert Frank *biology educator*
Masilamani, Subramaniam *sericulturist, researcher*
Maslansky, Carol Jeanne *toxicologist*
Mason, Joan *research scientist*
Mason, Roger Maxwell *molecular pathology educator*
Masover, Gerald Kenneth *microbiologist*
Mastrangelo, Victor *science educator*
Masum, Mohammed Abdullah-El *microbiologist, researcher*
Matasa, Claude George *researcher, science administrator, educator*
Matassino, Donato *animal geneticist*
Mates, Abraham *microbiologist, immunologist*
Mathews, Rita White *retired research scientist, educator*
Mathie, Robert Taylor *physiologist*
Mathur, Premendu Prakash *life sciences educator, researcher*
Matsumoto, Jiro *biology educator, editor*
Matsumura, Kendo *marine biologist, researcher*
Matthes, Heide-Dörte *agriculturist, researcher, educator*
Mattoon, James Richard *biology educator*
Matuschek, Markus *biologist, research scientist*
Matveev, Vladimir Fiodorovich *aquatic ecologist, research scientist*
Matveyev, Valentin Volodymyrovich *research scientist*
Matyaš, Zdeněk *food hygiene and technology educator*
Mayr, Ernst *retired zoologist, philosopher*
Mazilu, Petrisor *research scientist*
Mazur, Peter *cell physiologist, cryobiologist*
McCallister, Gary Loren *biology educator*
McClure, William Owen *biologist*
McColm, George Lester *international agricultural consultant, journalist*
McCrindle, Cheryl Myra *veterinarian*
McCulloch, Alistair John *research scientist, educator*
McDonald, Carl Peter *microbiologist*
McDowell, Robert E. *animal science educator*
McGarvey, Brian *research scientist*
McGinnis, Michael Boyd *chemistry educator*
McHale, Anthony Patrick *biological sciences educator, researcher*
McIlwain, Thomas David *fishery administrator, marine biologist, educator*
McInerney, John Peter *agricultural economist, educator*
McIntosh, Dennis Keith *veterinary practitioner, consultant*
McKinnell, Robert Gilmore *zoology, genetics and cell biology educator*
McLean, Robert James Cameron *microbiologist, educator*
McNeill, John *botanist*
Mead, Frank Waldreth *taxonomic entomologist*
Mécs, Imre Gyula *biotechnologist, researcher*
Medeiros, Walter Eugenio *science educator*
Medina Filho, Herculano Penna *agronomist*
Mehendale, Harihara Mahadeva *toxicologist, educator*
Mehta, Nawzer Hoshang *science foundation director*
Mehta, Peshotan Rustom *magnetotherapist and holisticologist*
Meisner, G. Michael *researcher, anesthetist*
Mejia, Carmen *biologist*
Mejsnar, Jiří Antonín *physiologist, educator*
Mekalanos, John J. *microbiology educator*
Melchinger, Albrecht Eugen *science educator*
Melchior, Stefan *soil scientist, environmental engineer, consultant*
Melling, Jack *biotechnologist*
Mello, Maria Luiza Silveira *cell biologist, educator*
Melnick, Igor Vasilyevich *researcher*
Melnik, Boris Efim *science educator*
Mendenhall, Harlan Vincent *research veterinary surgeon*
Mendgen, Kurt Walter *plant pathologist, educator, researcher*
Mennicken, Lothar *animal and poultry scientist, researcher*
Menzies, James Ian *retired science educator*
Mergner, Hans Konrad *zoology educator*
Mesa Orama, Jesús de la Caridad *research scientist*
Meschede, Dieter H.K. *geneticist, researcher*
Meskauskas, Arturas *molecular geneticist, researcher*
Messenger, Nigel James *molecular biologist, researcher*
Messner, Paul *microbiologist, educator*
Mester, Tünde *microbiologist, researcher*
Metcalf, Dean Andrew *plant pathologist, researcher*
Metssalu, Rein *microbiologist*
Mettler, Norma Evangelina *research scientist*
Metz, William Clinton *program manager*
Metzlaff, Michael Heinz *plant molecular biologist, researcher*
Metzler, Ruth Horton *genealogical educator*
Meybeck, Alain Louis *research director*
Meyer, Alvin Felix *environmental consultant*
Meyer, Axel *science educator*
Meyer, Robert Ernest *veterinary educator*
Meyers, Marc Andre *research center administrator*
Mezhzherin, Vitaliy *zoologist, researcher*
Mezzina, Mauru *research scientist*
Michael, Milad Ishak *biologist, educator*
Michel-Briand, Yvon *microbiologist*
Michels, Richard Stephen *microbiologist*
Micklin, Philip Patrick *science educator, consultant*
Mihai, Dumitru Grigore *veterinary medicine educator*
Mihailov, Radu Mihail *agricultural company executive*
Mikhailov, Alexander Trofimovich *biologist, researcher*
Mikhalevich, Valeria-Alla Josiphovna *zoologist, poet*
Miki, Kenju *physiologist, educator*
Mikkola, Kari Juhani *scientist*
Mikla, Victor *science laboratory administrator, educator*
Mikulik, Karel *microbiologist*
Milburn, Harry George William *science educator*
Miller, G(erson) H(arry) *research institute director, mathematician, computer scientist, chemist*
Miller, Nicholas *business development executive, scientist*
Miller, Peter James *zoologist, educator*
Miller, Ronald Wright *pharmaceutical scientist*
Mills, Helen Rachel *biotechnologist*
Mills, Paul Christian *research scientist, veterinarian*
Milnes Coates, Anthony Robert *medical microbiology educator*
Miloszewska, Joanna Jozefa *biologist, researcher*
Milstein, César *molecular biologist*
Milyaeva, Elvina Leonidovna *biologist*
Mina, Mikhail Valentinovich *zoologist*
Minagawa, Teiichi *molecular biologist*
Minchey, Samuel Bone *research scientist*
Ming Zhong, Xia *agricultural educator, researcher*
Minkov, Dorian Asenov *science educator*
Mino De Kaspar, Herminia *microbiologist, researcher*
Miodoński, Adam Jan *biology researcher, otorhinolaryngologist*
Mironova, Antonina Petrovna *cell biologist, cytoecologist, researcher*
Mishra, Kaushala Prasad *biologist*
Misra, Ajit Kumar *dairy microbiology educator, researcher*
Misra, Rabindra Kumar *root scientist, soil scientist*
Misztal, Genowefa *science educator*
Misztal, Tomasz *zoologist, researcher*
Mitchell, John Daniel *taxonomist, ecologist*
Mitchell, Malcolm Stuart *physician, researcher*
Mitchison, John Murdoch *retired zoology educator*
Mitrofanova, Irina Vjacheslavovna *biotechnologist*
Mitsányi, Attila *physiologist*
Mittermayer, Helmut Wolfgang *physician, clinical microbiologist*
Mittwoch, Ursula *genetics educator*
Miura, Hajime *physiology educator*
Miyake, Akio *biologist, educator*
Miyamoto, Tadaomi-Alfonso Matsumoto *neurobiologist*
Miyata, Hideo *science educator, researcher*
Miyawaki, Shigeki *geneticist*
Mizrach, Amos *scientist*
Mleko, Stanislaw Waclaw *food scientist*
Mlinaric-Galinovic, Gordana *microbiologist*
Młynarska, Maria Stanisława *physiologist, researcher*
Mobasheri, Ali *cell biologist, educator*
Mockary, Peter Ernest *clinical laboratory scientist, researcher, medical writer*
Modi, Vinod *microbiologist*
Moeckel, Regina *research scientist*
Moeljopawiro, Sugiono *plant breeder, researcher*
Moen, Jon Peter Gunnar *research scientist*
Moenke-Wedler, Thurid Cora *scientist, researcher*
Mohanan, Parayanthala Valappil *toxicologist, researcher*
Mohr, Thomas *research scientist*
Mohsen, Zohair Husein *entomologist, research scientist*
Moida, Ramana Murty Venkata *research scientist*
Mokry, Jaroslav *histologist*
Molina, Misael *biologist, educator*
Molnar, Laszls Giza *microbiologist, researcher*
Molodtsov, Serguei L'vovich *educator*
Molokanova, Natalia Aleksandrovna *nuclear research scientist*
Momba, Maggy Ndombo-Beneteke *microbiology educator, researcher*
Momose-Sato, Yoko *physiology educator*
Momotaz, Aliya *plant breeder*
Monakhov, Vladimir Genrikhovich *biologist, researcher*
Monge-Najera, Julian Antonio *ecologist*
Monsen, Tor Johan *bacteriologist, researcher*
Montagnier, Luc Antoine *virologist*
Montasser, Magdy Shaban *molecular virologist, educator*
Montgomery, John Charles *biology educator*
Moon, Gun-Woo *researcher*
Mooney, Harold Alfred *plant ecologist*
Moore, Jeannette Aileen *animal nutrition educator*
Moore, Timothy Michael *physiologist*
Morais, Alcina Maria M. Bernardo *food science educator and researcher*
Morales-Peralta, Estela *clinical geneticist, educator*
Mordvinov, Viatcheslav Alekseyevich *molecular biologist*
Morehouse, Lawrence Glen *veterinarian, educator*
Morimoto, Masanori *science educator, researcher*
Morris, Brian James *physiologist, educator*
Morris, Norma *research scientist*
Morris, Trevor Raymond *biology educator*
Morrison, Nigel Alexander *molecular biologist*
Morrissey, Joseph James *biologist*
Morriss-Kay, Gillian Mary *embryologist*
Morse, Stephen *agronomist*
Moskalenko, Yuri Eugenij *human physiologist*
Mosquera-Losada, María Rosa *agricultural/forestry science researcher, educator*
Moss, Stephen J. *neuroscience and pharmacology educator*
Mostovaya, Irina Vladimirovna *science administrator*
Motokawa, Tatsuo *biology educator*
Mouchaty, Suzette Kay *biologist*
Mousseau, Timothy Alexander *biology educator*
Moustacchi, Ethel E. *geneticist*
Moutafchiev, Dimiter Andonov *biologist, biochemistry researcher*
Moyer, Jack Thomson *science administrator, ecologist, writer, consultant*
Mozharov, Oleg Tikhon *geneticist*
Mráček, Zdeněk *entomologist*
Mrozińska, Teresa Maria *botany educator*
Mu, Yongke *research scientist*
Mueller, Othmar *forensic expert*
Muić, Vladimir *microbiologist, parasitologist, researcher*
Mukasyan, Alexander Sergeevich *science administrator*
Mukherji, Mridul *biotechnologist, educator*
Mukhopadhyay, Arnab *biologist*
Mukkai, Lalitha Kesavan *microbiology educator, consultant, researcher*
Müller, Torsten *soil scientist, educator*
Mullins, Obera *retired microbiologist*
Mumcuoglu, Kosta Yani *medical entomologist*
Munda, Ivka Maria *marine biologist, phycologist, researcher*
Munroe, Paul Richard *electron microscopy educator*
Mura, Patrick *toxicologist, researcher*
Murali, Krishnamurthy *research scientist*
Murariu, Dumitru Toader *biologist, zoologist, researcher*
Murarka, Shyam Prasad *science and engineering educator, administrator*
Muravsky, Leonid *research scientist, lecturer*
Muravyov, Sergey Vasilyevich *research scientist, educator*
Murfet, Ian Campbell *retired botany educator*
Murphy, Julie Ann *zookeeper, consultant, educator, zoologist*
Murray, Sandra Ann *biology research scientist, educator*
Murrenhoff, Hubertus Josef *research institute executive*
Murthy, Hanumappa Shivananda *aquaculture educator, researcher, consultant*
Murthy, Prakhya Balakrishna *geneticist, toxicologist, researcher*
Musaev, Musa Abdurakhman oglu *science association director*
Muscatello, Gary *veterinary surgeon*
Muschiolik, Gerald Franz Wilhelm *food technologist*
Muskó, Ilona B. *biologist, researcher*
Musshoff, Frank *forensic toxicologist, researcher*
Mutwally, Hamed Mohammed A. *science educator*
Mwamba, Charles Kennedy *soil scientist*
Mwatha, Wanjiru Elizabeth *microbiologist, educator*
Mwethera, Peter Gichuhi *research scientist*
Myrberg, Arthur August, Jr. *marine biological sciences educator*
Naarala, Jonne Tapio *cell biologist, educator*
Nadagoudar, Babagouda Shankaragouda *forestry researcher, educator*
Naeveke, Rolf J. F. *science educator*
Naftalin, Richard Julian *physiologist, educator*
Naganagowda, Gowda Ajjappa *research scientist*
Nagarajan, Balasubramanyam *microbiologist*
Nagatomi, Akira *entomologist, educator*
Nagothu, Duaya Sekhar *forester, researcher*
Nagy, Balint *biologist*
Nagy, Endre Andrew *microbiologist, consultant, researcher*
Nagy, Janos *agricultural sciences educator*
Nagy, József *horticulture educator*
Nah, Seung-Yeol *veterinary medicine educator, neuroscientist*
Naidu, Kamatham Akhilender *scientist, researcher*
Nair, Shamila *research scientist, consultant*
Nair Govindapillai, Achuthan *biologist, ecologist*
Naitoh, Ken *scientist, researcher*
Nakagawa, Takeo Ryusui *science educator, poet, writer, priest*
Nakagawa, Yasuyoshi *microbiologist, researcher*
Nakao, Toshihiko *veterinary medicine educator*
Nakatsu, Ryohei *research company executive*
Nakaya, Rintaro *microbiologist, consultant*
Nakazato, Hiroshi *molecular biologist*
Nánási, Péter Pál *physiologist*
Nandi, Owi Ivar *botanist, quality control professional*
Nangju, Dimyati *agronomist, banker*
Narain, Prem *agricultural scientist, educator, researcher*
Narath, Albert *retired laboratory administrator*
Narayan, Shashi Prakash *research scientist*
Narayanan, Arumugakannu *plant physiologist, educator, researcher*
Narita, Tadashi *science educator*
Narwal, Ram Phal *soil scientist, researcher*
Naskar, Syamal *scientist*
Nasledov, Grigory Alexandrovich *laboratory administrator, muscle physiologist, educator*
Näslund, Ingemar *fish biologist, researcher*
Nász, István *microbiologist, educator, researcher*
Natcheff, Natcho Donkoff *physiologist*
Naumov, Gennadi Ivanovich *biologist, geneticist*
Navarro, Hector Alejandro *veterinarian*
Nayak, Ganga Dhara *science educator, researcher*
Nazarenko, Sergey Andreevich *biologist, researcher*
Nazina, Tamara Nikolaevna *microbiologist, researcher*
Ndon, Bassey Asuquo *agronomist, educator*
Ndukuba, Patrick Ifeanyichukwu *physiologist, biomedical researcher*
Neagu, Gabriel *research scientist*
Nedvídek, Josef *biologist, educator*
Nee, Michael H. *botanist*
Neeteson, Jacques J. *agronomist*
Nefedieva, Elena Edwardovna *plant physiologist, educator*
Nefyodov, Igor Yurievich *radiobiologist, researcher*
Negi, Rohit *researcher*
Negru, Traian *pathophysiology educator, physician*
Neidhardt, Frederick Carl *microbiologist*
Neilson, Roy *agriculturist, researcher*
Nejedli, Srebrenka *veterinarian, researcher*
Nelson, Paul Netelenbos *soil scientist*
Nelson, Stephen Glen *biologist, researcher*
Nemec, Marija *veterinarian*
Németh, Károly *chemistry educator*
Neophytou, Pavlos Ioanni *molecular geneticist*
Nepalia, Virendra *agriculture educator*
Nesis, Kir Nazimovich *marine biologist*
Nesmelova, Irina Vladislavovna *research scientist, physicist*
Nesturi, Dionis *agronomist, educator*
Neuhaus, David *structural biologist, researcher*
Neumann, Katharina *archaeobotanist*
Neunzig, Herbert Henry *entomologist, educator*
Newman, Michael Charles *ecotoxicologist*
Newman, Raymond Melvin *biologist, educator*
Neymeyer, Valerie R. *research scientist*
Nezer, Carine *animal geneticist*
Nguyen, Thien Ngoc *science administrator*

Nicaud, Jean Marc Jacques *microbiologist, researcher*
Nichols, Michael Adair *horticulture educator*
Nicolas, François *biologist*
Nicoletti, Rosario *research scientist*
Nie, Zhongnan *research scientist*
Niedermuller, Hans *science educator*
Nielsen, Jennifer Lee *molecular ecologist, researcher*
Nielsen, Ole Lerberg *veterinary surgeon, researcher*
Nielsen, Peder Bo *clinical microbiologist*
Niemann, Heiner Julius *reproductive biotechnologist, researcher*
Niemitz, Carsten *zoologist and medical researcher*
Niepmann, Michael *molecular biologist*
Nieto-García, Fernando Javier *science educator*
Niewiadomska, Ewa Maria *plant physiologist, researcher*
Niewiarowski, Stefan *physiology educator, biomedical research scientist*
Nikoshkov, Andrej *biologist, researcher*
Nilius, Bernd *physiologist, educator*
Nilsson, Bengt Olof *physiologist*
Nilsson, Ove *biologist*
Nilva, Leonid *scientist, researcher*
Nindl, Ingo *molecular biologist*
Ning, Xue-Han (Hsueh-Han Ning) *physiologist, researcher*
Nishida, Hiromi *biologist, researcher, educator*
Nishiyama, Toshimasa *parasitologist*
Nizami, Wajih Ahmad *parasitologist*
Njoroge, Ernest Mwangi *veterinarian*
Noamesi, Seewu Komla *food scientist*
Nofuentes, Gustavo *science educator*
Nogueira, Guilherme De Paula *veterinary educator, researcher*
Noireaud, Jacques Michel Rene *physiologist*
Noitsakis, Basile *agronomy educator*
Noldin, José Alberto *agricultural researcher*
Nomura, Setsuzo *microbiologist, researcher*
Noor, Mohamed Ahmed *biology educator, researcher*
Nordberg, M. Monica *science educator*
Nordeide, Jarle Tryti *biologist, educator*
Nordenfors, Helena Erica *biologist, researcher*
Nordenstam, (Rune) Bertil *botanist, educator*
Nores, Carlos *biologist, researcher, educator*
Norrby, Erling Carl Jacob *virology educator*
Norrild, Bodil *molecular biologist, educator*
Norris, Thomas Friedrich *marine biologist*
Nosaka, Tetsuya *molecular biologist*
Notarbartolo di Sciara, Giuseppe *marine biologist*
Nott, Jonathan Freeman *science educator, researcher*
Novak, Karel *entomologist*
Novelo-Gutiérrez, Rodolfo *biologist, researcher*
Nozaki, Hisayoshi *biologist, educator*
Nultsch, Wilhelm *botany educator, plant physiologist*
Nunez-Escobar, Roberto *soil science educator*
Nvodaru, Ion *zoologist*
Nye, Peter Hague *soil scientist, researcher*
Nylin, Britta *veterinarian*
Obal, Ferenc Francis *science educator*
O'Banion, Michael Kerry *molecular neurobiologist*
Obel, Nils Johan *veterinary surgeon, educator*
Ochi, Kozo *microbiologist*
O'Connell, Michael *quaternary palaeoecologist, botanist, educator*
Odening, Klaus *zoologist, parasitologist, researcher*
Odintsova, Nelly Adolphovna *marine biologist, researcher*
O'Donoghue, Philip Nicholas *zoologist*
Oechel, Walter Clarence *ecologist*
Oei, Hok Liang *immunobiologist, researcher*
Oelmüller, Ralf *plant physiologist, researcher*
Oelofse, Jan Harm *game rancher, wildlife management consultant*
Oester, Paul Thomas *forestry educator*
Oga, Seizi *toxicology educator*
Ogawa, Toru *science laboratory administrator, educator*
Ogbeibu, Anthony Ekata *zoologist, researcher*
Ogle, Roy Clinton *molecular biologist*
Ogunsola-Bandele, Mercy Funice *science educator*
Ogutu, Joseph Ochieng *ecologist, educator, researcher*
Oh, Deok Kun *microbiologist*
Oh, Yung-Hwan *science educator*
Ohhashi, Toshio *physiology educator, researcher*
Ohhira, Iichiroh *microbiologist, educator*
Ohlsson, Bertil Gullith *molecular biologist*
Ohto, Chikara *molecular biologist, biochemist*
Oikawa, Hiroshi *parasitologist, researcher*
Ojeniyi, Stephen Olusola *soil scientist, researcher, educator*
Ok, Ülgen Zeki *microbiologist, parasitologist*
Okada, Hakuyu *science educator*
Okamura, Hideki *research scientist, physicist*
Okarma, Henryk *zoologist, researcher*
Okazaki, Tsuneko *molecular biology educator*
Okere, Chigozie *microbiologist*
Okikiolu, George Olatokunbo *scientific and industrial company executive, mathematician*
Okino, Yoshihiro *science educator*
Okoh, Anthony Joseph *veterinarian, educator*
Okolodkov, Yuri Borisovich *marine botanist researcher*
Oksa, Juha Ah *scientist*
Old, John Michael *molecular geneticist*
Olejnicek, Jiri *entomologist, researcher*
Oliger, Tatiana Ivanovna *research scientist*
Oliveira Lima, Ronaldo Mattos *maritime official*
Ollier, William Ernest Royce *immunogeneticist*
Olney, Peter James Stephen *zoologist*
Olopade, Olufunmilayo Falusi *oncologist, geneticist, educator*
Olov, Hallenberg Nils *mycology educator, researcher*
Olsen, David Magnor *chemistry and astronomy educator*
Olsson-Liljequist, Barbro Elisabet *microbiologist, researcher*
Olszewska, Maria Joanna *biologist, researcher*
Olufolaji, David Babatunde *pathologist, microbiologist*
Om, Hari *agronomist, researcher*
O'Mahony, George Barry *hospitality educator, researcher*
Omata, Yoshiaki *research educator*
Omura, Minoru *toxicologist*
Oniang'o, Ruth Khasaya *food scientist, educator*
Onipchenko, Vladimir Gertrudovich *biologist, educator*
Ono, Elizabeth Orika *science educator*
Onoue, Yoshio *marine biology educator*
Ooi, Hong-Kean *veterinary parasitologist*
Opitz-von-Boberfeld, Wilhelm *agriculturist, researcher*
Orban, Guy Angèle *neurophysiology educator*
Orban, Laszlo *biologist*
Orlova-Bienkowskaya, Marina Yakovlevna *zoologist*
Oros, Gyula *biologist, researcher*
Orskov, Egil Robert *agriculturalist*
Ortiz-Pulido, Raul *ornithologist, researcher, educator*
Ortiz Vera, Luis Tomas *biologist, educator*
Örvell, Claes Gunnar *virologist, researcher, physician, educator*
Osawa, Akira *ecologist*
Oshima, Toshiyuki *science educator*
Osmak, Maja *biologist, researcher, educator*
Osmanov, Saladin Kamilovitch *microbiologist*
Ossei-Anto, Theophilus Aquinas *science educator*
Östling, Mikael Lars *microelectronics researcher*
Ostrovoy, Dmytriy Yuriyevich *research scientist*
Ostrovskaya, Larisa Anatolievna *biologist, researcher*
Osuntogun, Caleb Adeniyi *agricultural economist*
Oswald, Winfried *veterinarian*
Otazú, Ivone Beatriz *geneticist, researcher*
Otero González, Anselmo Jesus *microbiologist*
O'Toole, Desmond Keith *microbiologist, food scientist*
Ottoro, Zeleke Wolde Tenssay *microbiology educator*
Otubusin, Samuel Olu *aquaculturist educator, consultant*
Ou, Jonathan Tsien-hsiong *microbiology educator*
Ouchi, Seiji *plant pathology educator*
Ovadia, Michael *toxicology and anatomy educator*
Ovchinnikov, Lev Pavlovich *molecular biology educator*
Owadowska, Edyta Maria *forester, researcher*
Owens, Vivian Ann *plant science educator, researcher*
Oyenuga, Victor Adenuga *agricultural scientist, educator*
Oyoshi, Keiji *research scientist*
Ozawa, Hikaru *retired science educator, editor*
Ozbun, Michelle Adair *science educator*
Ozolins, Peteris *physiologist, researcher*
Ozols, Antons Edmunds *animal physiologist, educator*
Padisak, Judit *biologist, researcher*
Pagala, Murali Krishna *physiologist*
Pages, Montserrat *biologist*
Paik, Hyun-Dong *microbiologist*
Paiva, Melquiades Pinto *marine biologist, educator*
Pal, Haridas *scientist, researcher*
Pal, Mahendra *veterinary public health educator, researcher*
Palade, George Emil *biologist, educator*
Paladugu, Ramamohanarao *botany and biotechnology educator, researcher*
Palm, Maud Eva *veterinarian*
Palta, Jairo Alberto *plant scientist*
Palta, Prabhat *reproductive biologist, researcher*
Pályi, István *biologist, researcher*
Pan, I. Hung *microbiologist, geneticist*
Pan, Jixing *science history educator*
Pan, Tzu-Ming *biotechnologist*
Panchin, Yuri *research scientist*
Pande, Hari Krishna *agronomist, educator*
Pandey, Girja Shanker *researcher, veterinary pathologist, educator*
Pandey, Lakshman *physics, materials science educator, researcher*
Pane, Luigi *biologist, researcher*
Panek, Marek *wildlife biologist, researcher*
Paniagua, Ricardo *cell biologist, educator*
Panicker, Girish Kumar *agricultural scientist, consultant*
Panighi, Mónica Patricia *biological marketing professional*
Panigrahi, Debadatta *microbiology educator*
Panikov, Nicolai Sergeyevich *microbiologist, researcher*
Pankov, Yuri Alexandrovich *molecular biologist, biochemist*
Pant, Hem Chandra *veterinarian*
Pantić, Vladimir Radivoje *cytologist, neuroendocrinologist*
Panz, Vanessa Rose *medical scientist, researcher*
Paolicchi, Fernando Alberto *veterinary educator*
Papavassiliou, Athanasios George *molecular biologist, educator*
Papini, Roberto Amerigo *veterinary scientist, researcher*
Papp, Ferenc *scientific consultant, educator*
Papp, Thilo *molecular biologist*
Pappas, Christophoros *agriculturist, researcher*
Paquay, Raymond *agronomist, educator*
Paradi, Elemer *geneticist, researcher*
Paranich, Anatoly Valentinovich *biology and biophysics educator, researcher*
Paranjpe, Akalpita Shriniwas *research scientist*
Parija, Subash Chandra *microbiologist, researcher, educator*
Paris, Harry Stuart *plant geneticist, researcher*
Park, Bong-Woo *science educator*
Park, Choon-Keun *biology educator*
Park, Jong Kun *molecular cell biologist, educator*
Park, Kuk-Tae *science educator, researcher*
Park, Sang-Dai *molecular biologist, educator*
Park, SeungJoon *research scientist*
Park, Wondong *science company administrator*
Park, Yoondong *research scientist*
Parker, Andrew Richard *biologist*
Parmer, Dan Gerald *veterinarian*
Parnichkun, Manukid *technology educator*
Parodi, André Laurent Marie *veterinary medicine educator*
Parr, Wendy V. *science educator*
Parresol, Bernard Ross *research biometrician, statistician*
Parsons, Walter Aubrey *food scientist*
Pärssinen, Janne Henrik *research scientist, chemical engineer*
Partridge, Lloyd Donald *physiologist, educator*
Parvez, Mohammad Masud *plant biologist, researcher*
Parvez, Simone Marazzato *science educator*
Parys, Jean-Baptiste Therese Gaston *molecular physiologist*
Pascoe, Michael William *conservation consultant*
Paspatis, Mihalis *research biologist*
Pasten, Laura Jean *veterinarian*
Pásztor, Károly *plant breeder, researcher*
Patel, Bhagwandas Mavjibhai *research scientist*
Patel, Jyotindra Dahyabhai *botany educator*
Patil, Jawahar Govindappa *molecular geneticist*
Pattanayak, Debasis *research scientist*
Pattison, Graham Anthony *horticulturist*
Patton, Michael Alexander *medical geneticist*
Paul, Małgorzata Maria *parasitologist, immunologist*
Pauw, Anton *biologist, photographer*
Pavcnik, Dusan *researcher, educator*
Pavlicek, Tomas *biology researcher*
Pavlik, Ivo *microbiologist, veterinarian researcher*
Pavlov, Dimitri Alexandrovich *biologist*
Pawley, Ray Lynn *zoological park and environmental consultant*
Pawlikowski, Tadeusz *entomologist*
Pawlowski, Boguslaw Zbigniew *science educator*
Payevsky, Vladimir Alexandrovich *zoologist*
Pearincott, Joseph Verghese *educator, physiologist*
Pedersen, Michael *research scientist*
Pei-Ing Wu *agricultural economics educator*
Peixoto Filho, Jose Ulisses *agronomist, educator*
Pener, Meir Paul *biologist*
Peng, Min *molecular biology*
Pennington, Thomas Hugh *bacteriology educator*
Penteriani, Vincenzo *ornithology researcher, educator*
Pénzes, László Géza *retired biologist, educator*
Pepper, Gordon Terry *research center administrator, educator*
Peralta de Merida, Ana Maria *parasitologist, researcher*
Perea, Evelio José *microbiology educator*
Pereira, Sir (Herbert) Charles *agricultural scientist*
Pereira, João Louis *plant diseases specialist, scientist*
Pereira-Netto, Adaucto B. *botany educator*
Perez-Fernandez, Maria Angeles *biologist*
Pérez-Ramos, Santiago *microbiology educator*
Perin, Romeo Vittorio *research scientist*
Perk, Cem *veterinarian, educator*
Perkalskis, Benjamin *science educator*
Perlshtein, Gueorgui Zakharovich *geocryology researcher*
Pershin, Alexander Fedorovich *geneticist, researcher, sunflower breeder*
Persson, Hans Åke *ecologist, researcher*
Perthuisot, Jean-Pierre *science educator*
Perutz, Max Ferdinand *molecular biologist*
Petchenev, Alex *scientist*
Peter, Roland *biologist and educator*
Petermann, Hans Jürgen *research scientist*
Peters, D. Stefan *research scientist*
Petkov, Orlin *physiologist, researcher*
Petrak, Michael Johannes *biologist, educator*
Petrakovskii, Guerman Antonovich *research scientist, educator*
Petráš, Petr Enrico *microbiologist, researcher*
Petrini, Björn Sven *bacteriologist, researcher*
Petrovic, Alexandre Gabriel *physician, physiology educator, medical research director*
Pettersson, Olle *agricultural researcher*
Pettoello-Mantovani, Massimo *pediatrician, educator, microbiologist, researcher*
Petty, Elizabeth Marie *geneticist*
Pfersmann, Otto *science educator*
Pfister, Herbert Johannes *virology educator*
Phillis, John Whitfield *physiologist, educator*
Pichat, Louis Jean *retired research director*
Pichereau, Vianney Jean Denis *microbiologist, educator*
Piepenbring, Meike *botanist, mycologist*
Pierce, Sidney K., Jr. *biology educator, department chair*
Pietkainen, Iija Sisko Inkeri *science educator, researcher*
Pietkiewicz, Jerzy Jan *biotechnologist, educator*
Pietrzykowski, Jerzy *research scientist, civil engineer*
Piiper, Johannes *physiologist*
Pilch, Józef *cytogeneticist*
Pillai, C.K.S. *scientist*
Pillai, Raveendran K. *cytologist, researcher*
Pillay, Marrimuthoo *nuclear medicine consultant*
Pimentel, Márcia Mattos Gonçalves *human geneticist, educator*
Pinault, Louis Pierre *veterinarian, educator*
Pinheird, Patricia Rodriguez *science educator*
Pinna, Graziano *biologist, researcher*
Pishchik, Veronika Nikolaevna *microbiologist, researcher*
Piskin, Ayse Kevser Özden *scientist, educator*
Plaisant, Paola *microbiologist researcher*
Plant, William James *research scientist*
Platz, Ole *research scientist, consultant*
Plavsic, Mark Zelimir *veterinary virologist*
Płażek, Agnieszka Maria *plant physiologist, researcher, educator*
Plekhanov, Anton Yourievič *biologist, researcher*
Ploghaus, Alexander *research scientist*
Plotkin, Stanley Alan *medical virologist*
Plummer, Gayther L(ynn) *climatologist, ecologist, researcher*
Plummer, John Lewis *medical scientist, researcher*
P'mpols, Teresa *geneticist*
Pochet, Roland *science educator*
Podolski, Igor Yacovlevich *psychobiologist, neuroscientist, researcher*
Poertner, Hans Otto *zoologist, ecophysiologist, educator, researcher*
Pogribny, Wlodzimierz *science educator*
Pohlit, Adrian Martin *chemistry educator, researcher*
Pohtila, Eljas Heikki Pietari *forestry researcher, educator*
Pokorny, Jan *food science educator, nutrition consultant*
Pokorny, Jaroslav *physiologist*
Poletika, Michael Fedorovich *research scientist, educator*
Polidori, Paolo *veterinarian, researcher*
Polischuk, Valery Petrovich *virologist, educator*
Polishchuk, Leonard V. *ecologist, researcher*
Pollard, Irina *biology and bioscience ethics educator, researcher*
Pollmer, Jost Udo *food chemist*
Pollock, Michael Robert *horticulturist*
Polmear, Andrew Fraser *research fellow*
Polo, Olli Juhani *pulmonary physician, physiology educator*
Polshakov, Vladimir Ivanovich *scientist*
Polubesova, Tamara *soil scientist, researcher*
Pomfrett, Chris John *neurophysiologist*
Pommier, Patrick *veterinarian*
Pommier, Yves Georges *laboratory administrator*
Pompeiano, Ottavio *physiologist, educator*
Ponder, Bruce Anthony John *cancer geneticist*
Pongrantz, Ingemar Göran *research scientist*
Ponomarenko, Vasily Petrovich *ichthyologist, consultant*
Pope, Rodney Peter *physiotherapist, researcher*
Popescu, Theodor-Dan *research scientist, educator*
Popov, Sergei Yurievitch *research scientist*
Popova, Elida Nicolaewna *neuromorphologist, researcher*
Popova, Elka Borislavova *physiology educator*
Porath, Dan *biologist*
Porta-Puglia, Angelo *plant pathologist, researcher*
Porterfield, James Stuart *medical virologist*
Portiansky, Enrique Leo *veterinarian*
Poschwitz, Hartmut *biologist*
Pospisil, George Curtis *biomedical research administrator*
Pospisil, Leopold *microbiologist*
Pospíšil, Zdeněk *veterinary medicine educator, researcher*
Pospisilova, Jana *physiologist*
Postgate, John Raymond *microbiology professor*
Postlethwaite, Roy *retired microbiologist*
Potemkin, Alexey Dmitrievich *botanist*
Potenko, Vladimir Vladimirovich *science administrator*
Pouckova, Pavla Miloslava *biologist*
Poulsen, Emil *toxicological advisor*
Poulsen, Jens Kristian *ultrasonics researcher*
Poumellec, Bertrand Gilbert *researcher, consultant*
Pournoor, K. John *scientist*
Power, Edward Gerard Martin *microbiologist*
Powers, Robert William *biologist*
Pozdnyakov, Dmitry Victorovich *science educator*
Pozo-Lora, Rodrigo *food scientist, educator*
Prach, Karel *plant ecologist, researcher, educator*
Prahm, Lars Philipsen *director general, science institute administrator, atmospheric scientist*
Prakash, Thazha Purathiyath *research scientist, chemist*
Prance, Sir Ghillean Tolmie *botanical gardens administrator, botanist*
Prasad, Dasika Hanumantha Lakshminatha *research scientist*
Prasad, Shailendra Krishna *animal scientist, educator*
Pratt, William Frederic *radiomedical scientist*
Predeleanu, Mircea *research science educator*
Preisig, Hans Rudolf *botany educator*
Prejmerean, Cristina Alexandra *research scientist, chemist*
Procházka, Stanislav *plant physiologist, educator*
Prokeš, Jaroslav *toxicologist, educator*
Prokofiev, Vladimir Victorovich *zoology educator, researcher*
Prokop, Ludwig *sports medicine physician, physiologist*
Prokop, Otto *microbiologist*
Prosperi, Carlos Hugo *biologist, educator, researcher*
Prout, Timothy *retired genetics educator*
Prukner-Radovčic, Estella *microbiologist, researcher*
Pruszak, Zbigniew *scientist*
Przybojewska, Barbara *microbiologist, researcher*
Psychoudakis, Asimakis Demetrios *agricultural economy educator, consultant*
Puente, Yolanda *biochemist, allergist*
Pukahuta, Charida *microbiologist*
Pullin, Andrew Stuart *conservation biologist, educator*
Pumpens, Paul *molecular biologist, researcher*
Punčochář, Pavel *limnologist, researcher*
Puppala, Vijaya Kumar *agroclimatologist*
Puri, Sunil *forest scientist, researcher, educator*
Purwono, Albertus Soegiarto *biologist*
Pušcaš, Iuliana Carmen *internist, gastroenterologist, researcher*
Pushpavanam, Malathy *research scientist*
Puska, Pekka Matti *public health institute official*
Putilov, Arcady Alexandrovich *chronobiologist, researcher*
Puttlitz, Donald Herbert *medical microbiologist*
Pykh, Yuri Alexander *ecological modelling, researcher*
Qadar, Ali *scientist*
Qian, Kun-Xi *science and technology educator*
Qiu, Zeyuan *researcher, educator*
Quadrat, Otakar *research scientist*
Quezada-Euan, Jose Javier Guadalupe *veterinarian, researcher*
Qureshi, Sohail Asif *molecular biologist, researcher*
Rab, Abdur *soil physicist*
Raboch, Jan *sexologist, educator*
Rabsch, Wolfgang *bacteriologist, researcher*
Rabuffett, Armando *science administrator, soil science educator*
Rackham, Oliver *botanist, historical ecologist*
Racz, Zoltan Gabor *biologist*
Radcliffe, Edward Bruce *entomologist*
Radosevic-Stasic, Biserka *physiology, immunology, pathophysiology educator*
Rady, Mohamed Ramadan *research scientist*
Raeburn, John Alexander *medical geneticist, educator*
Ragab, Ragab *research scientist, hydrologist*
Raharinaivo, André Léon *research executive, educator*
Rahman, Shaikh Mizanur *agriculturist, educator*
Raina, Ravinder *botanist, educator*
Rainbow, Philip Stephen *marine biologist, museum zoologist*
Rainsford, Kim Drummond *biomedical scientist, educator*
Raisman, Geoffrey *neurobiologist*
Rajagopal, Sanjeevi *biologist, researcher*
Rajaram, Govindarajan *researcher*
Rallis, Timoleon Stavros *veterinary medicine educator*
Ralls, Katherine *zoologist*
Ramachandrappa, B.K. *agronomy educator*
Ramaseshan, Sivaraj *physicist, researcher, editor, retired educator*
Ramesh, Atmakuru *research scientist*
Ramesh, K.H. *geneticist, researcher*
Ramesh, Saraf Rajagopalaiahsetty *zoology educator*
Ramos, Lopes Kleyde Mendes *biologist, general practitioner*
Ramsey, Kathleen Sommer *toxicologist*
Rana, Bhupendra Kumar *accreditation officer, researcher*
Randlane, Tiina *botanical educator*
Rane, Koyar Sanlo *science educator*
Ranta, Raimo Olavi *science administrator, electronics engineer, researcher*
Rantsios, Apostolos Triantafyllos *military veterinarian, researcher, consultant*
Rao, Annangi Subba *soil scientist, research administrator*
Rao, Aratla Trivikrama *veterinary pathologist*
Rao, Desiraju Lakshmi Narsimha *microbiologist*
Rao, Govind P. *plant pathologist*
Rao, Gutti Madanmohan *physiologist, educator, researcher*
Rao, Meka Ramamohana *agronomist, researcher*
Rao, Naraharisetty Muralidhara *retired microbiologist*
Rapacz, Marcin *plant physiologist, researcher, educator*
Rapallino, Maria Vittoria *neurobiologist, researcher*
Rapley, Christopher Graham *research institute director*
Rapoport, Eduardo Hugo *ecology educator, researcher*
Rappoport, Yuri Moisevich *research scientist*
Rar, Andrei *research scientist*
Rasmussen, Jens Bødtker *zoologist researcher*
Raspopov, Igor Mikhajlovich *hydrobotanist*
Rautenstrauss, Bernd Walter *molecular biologist*

Singh, Ranjan *veterinarian*
Singh, Sukhchain *agriculturist*
Singh, Surinder Pal *molecular biologist, researcher*
Singh, Thakur Prasad *zoology educator, researcher*
Singh, Zora *agricultural researcher, educator*
Singha L., Rakesh Kumar *molecular biology educator, consultant, researcher*
Sinha, Abinash Kumar *science administrator*
Sinha, Bikash Chan *science administrator*
Sinha, Rajeshwar Prasad *scientist, researcher*
Sipilä, Tero Seppo *biologist*
Sitnov, Mikhail I. *research scientist*
Siva-Jothy, Michael Trevor *zoologist*
Sjögren, Erik *botanist, educator*
Sjolander, Sverre *zoologist, educator*
Skarpetis, Michael George *research scientist*
Skibsted, Leif Horsfelt *food chemistry researcher*
Skipetrov, Vadim Petrovich *physiologist, hematologist*
Skovmand, Ole *researcher*
Skowronek, Krzysztof Jerzy *microbiologist, molecular biologist*
Skrabka Błotnicka, Teresa *animal food technologist*
Slavik, Bohumil *botanist*
Sleigh, Michael Alfred *biology educator*
Slepukhina, Tatyana Dmitrievna *hydrobiologist*
Şluiman, Hans Jan *biologist, researcher*
Šmarda, Jan Jiří *biology educator*
Smiecinski-Salkowski, Alicia *genetic counselor*
Smietana, Walter *educational research director*
Smirnov, Nikolai Nikolaevich *research scientist*
Smirnov, Yuri Alexandrovich *virologist*
Smirnova, Olga Vyacheslavovna *biologist, researcher*
Smit, Willem Adriaan *plant pathologist, microbiologist, researcher*
Smith, Christopher Upham Murray *biology educator, philosopher, writer*
Smith, Crosbie Wimperis *science historian*
Smith, Eric Morgan *virology educator*
Smith, Geoffrey Lilley *scientist*
Smith, Hamilton Othanel *molecular biologist, educator*
Smith, Jared Russell William *research executive*
Smith, Kenneth George Valentine *retired entomologist, magazine editor*
Smith, Michael Kevin *plant biotechnologist, researcher*
Smither-Kopperl, Margaret Lydia *plant pathologist*
Smits, Paul H.M. *biologist*
Smutkupt, Sumin *plant breeder, educator, legume researcher*
Sneath, Peter Henry Andrews *microbiologist, researcher*
Snetkov, Vladimir *physiologist, researcher*
Snibson, Kenneth John *cell biologist*
Snow, Pamela Claire *researcher*
Soares-Costa, Manuel José Dias *animal science educator*
Sobhi, Fatma Saleh *microbiologist, educator*
Sobieszczuk, Peter (Piotr Sobieszczuk) *molecular biologist*
Sobotková, Eva *scientist*
Sohn, Jae-Keun *agronomist, educator*
Sokari, Tokuibiye Graeme *science educator*
Sokmen, Atalay *biologist, educator, researcher*
Sokoloff, Dmitry Dmitrievich *biologist, researcher, educator*
Soldatenkov, Viatcheslav Alexandrovich *cell and molecular biologist, researcher*
Soliman, Atef Shafik *geneticist, educator*
Sologoub, Elena Borisovna *physiology educator, researcher, consultant*
Sologoub, Mikhail Ivanovich *physiology educator, researcher, consultant*
Song, Jian *scientist, science administrator*
Song, Sihong *science educator*
Sonohara, Toyoji *research company executive*
Sonoike, Kintake *biologist, educator*
Sood, Ashok Kumar *pathologist, hematologist, microbiologist*
Sood, Seema *microbiologist*
Soremi, Sodipo Olugbemiga *mycologist, biologist, researcher*
Soria, Bernat Escoms *physiology educator*
Soriano-Santos, Jorge *science educator*
Sorokin, Yuri Ivanovich *aquatic microbial ecologist*
Sorokina, Elena Mikhaylovna *research scientist*
Soucek, Branko *research scientist*
Souček, Pavel *toxicologist*
Souilhac, Dominique Jacques *optical engineering researcher*
Sousa, Mário *cell biology educator*
Southgate, Vaughan Robert *parasitologist*
Southwood, Thomas Richard Edmund *zoologist, educator*
Soyfer, Valery Nikolayevich *molecular geneticist and biophysicist*
Spandidos, Demetrios *virologist, educator*
Spannagel, Alan Wayne *physiologist*
Spanò, Marcello *cytologist, toxicologist*
Sparholt, Henrik *fishery biologist, researcher*
Speedy, Eric Dawson *biologist*
Spencer, John Francis Theodore *microbiologist, consultant*
Spencer-Phillips, Peter Tyrell Nelson *mycologist, plant pathologist*
Sperelakis, Nicholas, Sr. *physiology and biophysics educator, researcher*
Sperlich, Diether *biology educator*
Spichak, Vjacheslav Valentinovich *science administrator*
Spiller, Susan Coates *plant physiologist-biologist*
Spitzer, Karel *entomologist*
Spízek, Jaroslav Pavel *microbiologist, institute executive*
Spohn, Bryan Gordon *entomologist*
Spona, Jurgen *scientist, educator*
Spranger, Joerg *veterinarian, researcher*
Sprent, John Frederick Adrian *retired parasitology educator, researcher*
Spring, Stefan *microbiologist, researcher*
Springfeldt, Bengt Daniel *health researcher, engineer*
Spyer, Kenneth Michael *physiology educator, university dean*
Squires, Richard Felt *research scientist*
Srebotnik, Ewald *research scientist*
Sree, Usha *research fellow*
Sreenivasan, Kunnatheery *scientist*
Srinivasan, Durairaj *microbiology educator*
Srivastava, Naresh Chandra *scientist*
Srivastava, P. N. *research scientist, educator*
Srivastava, Radhey Shyam *scientist, researcher*
Ssenyonga, Gustavus Stephen Zziriddamu *veterinarian*
Ştacey, Glyn Nigel *clinical scientist*
Ştalc, Anton *physiologist, researcher*
Štambuk, Nikola *research scientist*
Stamminger, Gudrun Mathilde *microbiologist*
Stanberry, Lawrence Raymond *virologist, vaccinologist, pediatrician, educator*
Stanchi, Nestor Oscar *microbiology educator*
Stange, Luise Magdalene Christine *plant physiology educator*
Stangler, Ferdinand *natural sciences educator, dean of faculty*
Stanhill, Gerald *agricultural climatologist, researcher*
Stanley, Andrew Philip *scientist, chemistry researcher*
Stanley, John Richard *virologist, research scientist*
Stansbery, David Honor *biology diversity educator, molacologist*
Staskon, Francis C. *research scientist*
Stastny, Miroslav *research scientist*
Stavroulakis, Anthea Merrie *biology educator*
Stazhevskiy, Stanislav Borisovich *research laboratory administrator*
Steding, Gerd *embryologist, educator*
Steenberg, Börje Karl *forester*
Steentoft, Anni *forensic toxicologist*
Stefan, Vladislav *research scientist*
Steffen, James Richard *science educator, optometrist*
Steffens, Werner Ludwig *fishery scientist*
Steger, Klaus *biologist, researcher*
Steiner, Adolf Martin *seed science educator*
Steinhausen, Michael Wilhelm Emil *physiologist, researcher*
Stepanichev, Mikhail Yurevich *biochemist*
Stepnowski, Andrzej *science educator*
Sterba, Oldrich Josef *veterinary surgeon, researcher*
Stetter, K. O. *microbiologist, educator*
Stevenson, Miranda Faye *zoologist*
Stewart, Alan Vincent *plant breeder, executive*
Stewart, B(obby) A(lton) *soil scientist, educator*
Stewart, T. Bonner *parasitology educator*
Stickle, David Walter *microbiologist*
Stimpert, Alison Kendra *marine biologist, researcher, ecologist*
Stöcker, Michael Wilhelm *science educator, editor*
Stoilova, Krasimira Petrova *science educator*
Stokke, Trond *geneticist*
Stol, Miroslav Bohuslav *biomaterials researcher*
Stoll, Peter *ecologist*
Stoll-Keller, Françoise *biologist, educator*
Stopler, Traian Iosef *microbiologist, researcher*
Stoppani, Andres Oscar Manuel *research center director, educator*
Storms, Lester C. (C Storms) *retired veterinarian*
Storz, Johannes *veterinary microbiologist, educator*
Straede, Christen Andersen *research center administrator*
Straka, Herbert Karl *botany educator*
Straka, Thomas James *forester, educator*
Stratil, Antonín *animal geneticist, researcher*
Straub, Otto Christian *veterinarian*
Stravoravdi, Pelagia *biologist, researcher*
Strawa, Anthony Walter *research scientist*
Streckert, Hans Juergen *virologist*
Strehlitz, Beate *research scientist*
Streiblova, Eva *microbiologist, educator*
Streit, Bruno *biologist, ecotoxicologist, ecologist*
Strelets, Valeria Borisovna *neurophysiologist, researcher*
Strelkov, Leonid ALekseevich *biologist, researcher*
Strena, Robert Victor *university research laboratory manager*
Strizhalo, Volodymyr Olexandrovych *science administrator*
Strobel, Stefan Michael *technical development director*
Struff, Richard Heinrich *science administrator*
Struik, Paul Christiaan *agronomy educator*
Strysick, Michael Otto *terrestrial ecologist, researcher*
Stuhl, Oskar Paul *scientific and regulatory consultant*
Stühmer, Walter *medical institute scientist*
Stylianopoulou, Fotini *biology educator*
Stynen, Dirk Edmond *biologist*
Suárez, Horacio Guillermo *biologist, researcher*
Subbaraj, Ramanujam *biology educator*
Subramaniyan, S. *biotechnologist*
Sudakov, Sergey Konstantinovich *neurobiologist, researcher*
Südi, Janos *biologist, researcher*
Suen, Shing-Yi *science educator*
Sueyoshi, Shuzo *forester, researcher*
Sugathan, Sheela Kanddenkattil *microbiologist*
Sugaya, Eiichi *physiology educator*
Sugiharta, Asep *national park administrator, educator*
Sugimoto, Seiji *biochemist*
Suh, Hak Soo *agronomist*
Suh, Yoo-Hun *molecular neurobiology educator, administrator*
Sukernik, Rem *geneticist, researcher*
Sulaiman, Sallehudin Bin *medical entomology educator*
Suleiman, Mohammed-Saadeh *physiologist*
Sultanbawa, M. U. S. *science academy executive*
Sun, Xuechuan *physiologist, educator, researcher*
Sun, Zheng *research scientist*
Sundaram, Ramakrishnan *research consultant*
Sundareshan, Tambarahalli Subramaniam *cytogeneticist, educator*
Sundstøl, Frik *agronomy and agricultural sciences educator*
Sunil, Mukaluvilayil Samuel *zoology educator*
Sunwoo, Myung Hoon *science and technology educator*
Suresh Kumar, Sivanpillai *science educator*
Suri, Jasjit S. *research scientist*
Surikov, Igor Michaelovitch *biologist, politician*
Suris, Josep M. *science educator, administrator*
Suskind, Sigmund Richard *microbiology educator*
Sutherland, William James *ecologist*
Suthers, Hannah Louise Bonsey *biologist*
Sutter, Jane Elizabeth *educator, writer*
Suvorov, Nickolai Fedorovitch *physiologist, researcher*
Suwanto, Antonius *microbiologist, researcher*
Suzuki, David Takayoshi *geneticist, science broadcaster*
Sveshnikov, Peter Georgievich *science administrator, researcher*
Svetina, Ante Stipe *pathophysiologist, researcher*
Sviridov, Andrei Valentinovitsh *entomologist, researcher*
Svoboda, Miroslav *veterinary medicine educator*
Swaminathan, Monkombu Sambasivan *agricultural researcher*
Swannell, Richard Paul *research and development administrator*
Swenson, Ulf *botany educator, researcher*
Symons, Hugh Williams *food technologist*
Szajdak, Lech Wojciech *soil scientist, researcher*
Szalai, Csaba *molecular biologist*
Szathmáry, Eörs *biologist, educator*
Szeberényi, József *physician, cell biologist, educator*
Szeleczky, Zoltán *biologist*
Szenci, Otto Ferenc *veterinarian*
Szirtes, László *nuclear scientist*
Szlachetko, Dariusz Lucjan *botanist*
Szodfridt, István *forestry engineering educator*
Szumiel, Irena *radiation biologist, researcher*
Szuts, Gabor György *agricultural science educator*
Tabaqchali, Soad *medical microbiology educator, consultant*
Tadi-Uppala, Padma Pauline *toxicologist*
Tadmouri, Ghazi Omar *molecular biologist, geneticist, agriculture engineer*
Tafani, Jean-Pierre J. *physiologist*
Taha, Ali Abdalla Mohamed *veterinary science educator*
Tai, John Jen *biostatistician*
Tairbekov, Murad Garun *cell biologist*
Takacs, Andras *veterinarian*
Takahashi, Kiyoshi *research educator*
Takenaka, Toshifumi *physiologist*
Tam, Nora Fung-yee *science educator*
Tambourin, Pierre Edmond *science administrator, researcher*
Tamin, Azaibi *molecular virologist, researcher*
Tamm, Carl Olof Sebastian *ecology educator*
Tamuzs, Vitauts *mechanics educator, researcher*
Tan, Roland Kim Chay *research scientist*
Tan, Xuelin *geneticist*
Tan, Y. *research scientist*
Tanaka, Kazunori *science educator*
Tande, John Olav Giaever *research scientist*
Tandon, Veena *parasitology educator, researcher*
Taneya, Shin'ichi *food science and technology consultant, rheologist*
Tang, Ben Zhong *science educator, researcher*
Tanigami, Akira *researcher*
Tantaoui-Elaraki, Abdelrhafour *agronomy engineer, microbiology educator*
Tao, Xu Tang *research scientist*
Tarakanov, Boris Vasiljevich *microbiologist*
Tarba, Corneliu *science educator*
Tarro, Giulio *virologist*
Tartes, Urmas *science institute director*
Tata, Jamshed Rustom *researcher, consultant*
Taulavuori, Kari Mikko Juhani *plant physiologist, researcher*
Taylor, Aubrey Elmo *physiologist, educator*
Taylor, David Marshall *radiotoxicology educator, consultant*
Taylor, David Mathieson *microbiologist*
Taylor, Kendrick Jay *microbiologist*
Taylor, Patrick Jonathan *researcher*
Taylor-Robinson, Andrew William *immunoparasitologist*
Tazawa, Masashi *biologist, educator, researcher*
Tchesnova, Larissa Vassilievna *zoologist, science historian, researcher*
Tchurikov, Nickolai Andreevich *molecular geneticist*
Teaci, Dumitru M. *soil scientist, researcher*
Teittinen, Pentti Johannes *retired agriculturist*
Teixeira, Paula Cristina Maia *microbiologist, researcher*
Telegdy, Gyula *physiologist, educator*
Tell, Leonid *pathophysiologist, writer, inventor, researcher*
Telnov, Vitaliy Ivanovitch *radiobiologist, researcher*
Temanel, Billy Estoque *agronomy director, educator, consultant*
Tembo, Sydney Douglas *science educator, researcher*
Tembrock, Günter Erwin Franz *zoologist, ethologist, researcher*
Tenter, Astrid Margareta *parasitologist, researcher, educator*
Terradas, Jaume *ecologist*
Terzolo, Horacio Raul *veterinarian, researcher*
Tewari, Vindhya Prasad *forester*
Thalacker, Victor Paul *research scientist*
Thauer, Rudolf Kurt *microbiologist and researcher*
Theede, Hans Johannes *marine zoologist, researcher*
Theyse, Lars Frederik Herman *veterinary orthopedic surgeon, researcher*
Thiagarajan, Tangavelu *science attache, researcher*
Thibier, Michel F. *veterinary medicine educator*
Thiede, Walther *researcher, publisher, consultant*
Thiele, Detlef Ferdinand *microbiologist*
Thierfelder, Tomas Karl Ernst *science educator*
Thierry, Bernard *ethologist, researcher*
Thiess, Alfred Michael *occupational medicine physician, toxicologist*
Thomas, Daniel Jean *biologist, researcher*
Thomas, Martin Vincent *scientific research company executive*
Thomas, Teresa Ann *microbiologist, educator*
Thomm, Michael Wolfgang *microbiologist*
Thompson, Guy Allen, Jr. *biology educator*
Thompson, Peter Allan *science educator, researcher*
Thomson, Jennifer Ann *microbiology educator*
Thormar, Halldor *microbiologist, educator*
Thorsell, James Westvick *ecologist*
Thorsen, Rune Asbjørn *researcher*
Thorstensen, Ketil *scientist*
Thulesius, Knut Olav *physiologist, researcher*
Thulin, Jan Einar *biologist*
Thuraisingham, Ranjit Arulnayagam *research scientist*
Thurau, Klaus Walther Christian *physiologist*
Thuries, Edmond Emile *science administrator*
Thurm, Ulrich *zoology educator*
Thuróczy, Julianna *veterinarian*
Thurston, Sidney Walter, III *marine scientist*
Tian, Xiuchun *research scientist*
Tibes, Ulrich *physiologist, educator, pharmacologist*
Tiburcio, Antonio Fernandez *plant physiology educator, researcher*
Tien, Po *virologist, biotechnologist*
Tikhonov, Vilen Nikolay *geneticist, researcher, educator*
Tilgner, Siegfried Johann *biologist, ophthalmologist*
Timofeev, Andrei Victorovitch *virologist*
Timofeev, Oleg Yakoulevich *science educator, researcher*
Timothy, David Harry *biology educator*
Tipikin, Dmitriy Sergeevich *research scientist, secondary education educator*
Titlyanova, Argenta Antoninovna *ecologist, researcher*
Tiunov, Mikhail Petrovitch *mammalogist*
Tochikura, Tatsurokuro *applied microbiologist, home economics educator*
Toda, Tatsushi *molecular geneticist, researcher, educator*
Toddywalla, Villi Sam *medical biologist, researcher*
Togo, Hisatake *research institute administrator*
Toh, Kok-Aun *science educator*
Tohno, Yoshiyuki *cell biologist, educator*
Toivanen, Helli Maria *psycho-physiology educator*
Tokarskaya, Zoya Borisovna *radiobiologist, researcher*
Tokatlidis, Ioannis *agricultural sciences educator*
Tokimoto, Keisuke *mycologist*
Tokin, Ivan B. *biologist, researcher*
Tolivia, Delio Ruben *cell biologist, researcher*
Tollit, Dominic John *marine biologist, researcher*
Tolman, Richard Robins *zoology educator*
Tomioka, Noboru *molecular biologist, researcher*
Tomkos, Ioannis *research scientist, communications educator*
Tonegawa, Susumu *biology educator*
Tonkopii, Valerii Dmitrievitch *toxicologist, researcher*
Torii, Tetsuya *retired science educator*
Toriizuka, Kazuo *research scientist, pharmacist*
Toru, Eguchi *microbiologist, researcher*
Toschi, Romano *thermonuclear fusion expert, engineering educator*
Tou, Stephen Kwok Woon *science educator*
Touwaide, Alain Jacques André *science educator, researcher*
Toyama, Hideo *biotechnologist*
Toyoda, Tetsuya *virologist, educator*
Traavik, Ingemar Terje *virology educator, consultant*
Trape, Jean-François *parasitologist, entomologist*
Trayhurn, Paul *research biologist, educator*
Treasurer, James Watt *fish biologist*
Treiber, Hubert *administrative sciences educator*
Trexler, Thomas W. *research scientist*
Trigg, Timothy Elliot *biotechnology executive*
Trimeche, Abdesselem *veterinarian researcher*
Trinajstić, Nenad *research scientist*
Tripathi, Shri Kant *ecologist, researcher*
Trivedi, Hitesh K. *research scientist*
Trojan, Stanislav *neurophysiologist, educator*
Troshin, Sergey Mikhailovich *research scientist, educator*
Trowsdale, John *research scientist*
Trubetskov, Michael Kirillovich *researcher*
Truong, Khuong Trong *biologist, researcher*
Truve, Erkki *molecular biologist*
Tryland, Morten *veterinary virologist, researcher*
Tsaknis, John Panagiotis *food science educator*
Tsalolikhin, Semyon Iakovlevich *biologist, zoologist, researcher*
Tsaturyan, Andrey Kimovich *researcher*
Tscharntke, Teja *ecologist, educator*
Tschermak-Woess, Elisabeth *botany educator*
Tselutin, Vladimirovich Konstantin *agriculturist, researcher*
Tseng, Cheng Kui *marine biologist*
Tsipis, Kosta Michael *science educator*
Tsubota, Toshio *veterinary science educator*
Tsui, Kan-Ming *clinical geneticist*
Tsuneoka, Yutaka *molecular geneticist*
Tsunogai, Shizuo *marine/atmospheric geochemistry educator/research*
Tsuyumu, Shinji *molecular plant pathologist*
Tu, Shan-Tung *science educator*
Tuba, Zoltán *botanist, educator*
Tubiello, Francesco Nicola *research scientist*
Tudzynski, Paul *biologist*
Tuğrul, Beril Asiye *science administrator, educator*
Tulyakova, Tatyana Vladimirovna *biotechnologist, researcher*
Tumová, Bela *retired microbiologist, virologist, educator*
Tung, Yeishin *research scientist*
Tur-Mari, Josep Antoni *physiologist*
Turner, Anne Marguerite *medical geneticist*
Turner, Anthony Peter Francis *biotechnologist, educator*
Turner, Neil Clifford *agricultural scientist, research scientist*
Turner, Thomas Bourne *retired microbiology educator*
Turnpenny, Peter Douglas *clinical geneticist*
Turtoi, Dumitru *science educator*
Tuteja, Renu *biologist*
Twidell, John William *energy educator, consultant*
Twohy, Cynthia Howard *research scientist*
Tyrrell, David Arthur John *retired virologist*
Tyystjärvi, Esa *plant scientist*
Tzen, Tze-Cheng Jason *biotechnology educator*
Tzortzakakis, Emmanuel A. *agriculturalist*
Ubbink, Johan Bernard *research scientist, laboratory administrator*
Uchida, Tatsuo *science educator*
Uchino, Takashi *research scientist*
Uchiyama, Katsumi *scientist, educator*
Udeh, Kenneth Ogbonna *food biotechnologist, researcher*
Udina, Irina Gennad'evna *geneticist*
Ugodchikov, Andrey Grigoryevich *science educator*
Uhitil, Sunčica *microbiologist, researcher*
Uhlig, Birgit A. *scientist, researcher*
Ukai, Yasuo *retired agronomy educator*
Ullén, Fredrik *researcher, concert pianist*
Ullmann, Uwe *microbiologist*
Ullrich, Sören *biologist, researcher*
Ulrich, Radomír *forester, educator*
Ungaro, Maria Regina *agronomist, researcher*
Ungerer, Dietrich Albrecht *safety scientist, educator*
Ungureanu, Ernest M. *parasitology educator, consultant*
Unsworth, Philip Francis *microbiologist, consultant*
Uozumi, Takeshi *biotechnology researcher and educator*
Urade, Yoshihiro *molecular biologist, researcher*
Usherwood, Peter Norman Russell *science educator*
Utvik, Toril Inga Røe *research scientist, environmental chemist*
Uusitalo, Mikko Aleksi *research scientist*
Uwah, Edet Johnnie *science educator*
Uyehara, Catherine Fay Takako (Yamauchi) *physiologist, educator, pharmacologist*
Vahidy, Ahsan Ahmad *genetics educator*
Valentine-Thon, Elizabeth Anne *biologist*
Valkonen, Jari Pekka Tapani *virology educator, researcher*
Van Arendonk, Johannus Antonius Marie *genetics educator, researcher*
Vanatta, John Crothers, III *physiologist, physician, educator*
Van Belzen, Nico *molecular cell biologist, consultant*
Van Damme, Els Jeanine *scientific researcher*
van den Berg, Henk *entomologist*
van der Walt, Johann George *veterinary physiologist, educator*
Van De Ven, Willem Jan Marie *molecular genetics educator, researcher*
Van de Voorde, Andre *scientific officer*
van Dijl, Jan Maarten *molecular biologist, educator*
Van Dongen, Hans Philemon Anna *research scientist, educator*
Van Dooren, Rene *mechanics educator*
Vaneček, Jiří *physiologist, researcher*

Van Klink, Ed Gerardus Maria *veterinarian*
van Meerwijk, Joost P.M. *research scientist, educator*
van Tets, Ian Gerard *ecophysiologist*
Van Tiel, Frank Herman *medical microbiologist*
Van Veldhoven, Paul Philip *biology educator*
Van Zandwijk, Jan Peter *scientific researcher*
Van Zutphen, Lambertus F. M. (Bert Van Zutphen) *geneticist, educator*
Várallyay, György *soil scientist, research educator*
Varga, Csaba *biologist, educator*
Varga, Janos Miklos *molecular immunologist, biochemist*
Vargas, Vera Maria Ferrão *biologist*
Varilo, Teppo Tapio *geneticist, researcher*
Varis, Anna-Liisa *entomologist*
Varju, Dezsoe *biologist, educator*
Varma, Anupam *virologist*
Várnagy, László Elek *veterinarian*
Varni, David Grant, Sr. *arborist*
Varshaver, Nina Borissovna *geneticist*
Varughese, Kuruvilla *agronomy educator, researcher*
Vasconcellos, Carlos Alberto *agronomist, researcher*
Vasconcelos, Vitor Manuel *biology educator*
Vashisth, Punit *research scientist*
Vasilev, Victor Sergeevich *scientific researcher*
Vasiliev, Gleb Alexandrovich *toxicologist, researcher*
Vasiliu-Oprea, Cleopatra Timofte *science educator*
Vayda, Andrew P. *human ecology and anthropology educator*
Veerapaneni, Sunaina *plant pathologist*
Vehmaanpera, Jari Olavi *molecular biologist*
Veijalainen, Heikki Sakari *forester*
Velardo, Joseph Thomas *molecular biology and endocrinology educator*
Vences, Miguel *zoologist*
Venizelos, Lily Therese E. *sea turtle conservationist*
Venkatesh, Byrappa *molecular biologist, researcher*
Venkov, Pencho Vassilev *molecular biology educator*
Venugopal, Pankajalakshmi Vellore *microbiologist*
Verberne, Anthony Johannes *scientist*
Verbitskii, Vladimir Boris *ecologist, educator*
Verburg, Peter *research scientist*
Verde Gonzalez, Luis S. *agronomy educator*
Verdonck, Patrick Bernard *researcher, science educator*
Veresegyházy, Tamás Péter *veterinarian, educator*
Veress, György *microbiologist, researcher*
Vergara, Patrocinio (Patri Vergara) *physiology educator, researcher*
Vergos, Evangelos-Apostolos *agriculturist, educator*
Verleger, Rolf *psychophysiologist, neuropsychologist*
Verma, Chaman Lal *building materials research institute official*
Verma, Ramtej Jayram *zoology educator, researcher*
Vermes, Laszlo Peter *agronomist*
Vershinin, Vladimir Leonidovich *ecologist, researcher*
Vertes, Alain Andre Guy *microbiologist*
Vestergaard, Peter *plant ecologist, researcher, educator*
Vetter, János *biologist*
Vetter, Ralf-Achim Horst *physiologist*
Vicherkova, Miroslava *plant physiologist*
Victor, Tetz Veniamim *microbiologist*
Vidal, Carlos Eugênio Soto *veterinarian, immunologist, researcher*
Vié, Jean Christophe *veterinarian*
Vieira, Luiz Carlos *microbiologist, consultant*
Vieira da Silva, Jorge *agronomy researcher and consultant*
Vietor, Ilja *molecular biologist, researcher*
Vijayakumar, T. *research scientist*
Vijayamohanan, Kunjukrishnapillai *scientist, educator*
Vilček, Štefan *molecular biologist, researcher*
Vimpani, Graham Vernon *pediatrician*
Vincent, James Louis *biotechnology company executive*
Vink, Jos Pièrre Marie *soil scientist, researcher*
Vinogradov, Alexander Evgenievich *biologist*
Vinuesa, Julio Hector *biologist, researcher*
Virbickas, Juozas *ecologist, researcher*
Virgós, Emilio Cantalapiedra *biologist, researcher*
Virkkala, Raimo Olavi *scientist, ecologist*
Virtanen, Simo Kasper *microbiologist*
Visser, Johannes *research scientist, biographer*
Viswanathan, Nurni Neelakantan *research scientist, educator*
Vit, Patricia Antonella *biologist, educator, researcher*
Vital Brazil, Oswaldo *research scientist, physician*
Vítek, Jiří Aleš *cell biologist*
Vlad, Stan Melu *research and development manager*
Vlasinova, Helena *botanist*
Vögel, Hans-Jörg *technology researcher, educator*
Voglino, Gianfranco Luigi *biologist*
Vojnits, András Mátyás *zoologist, educator, researcher*
Vollmers, Heinz Peter *cell biologist*
Volodin, Vyacheslav Vladimirovich *science administrator*
von Bassenheim, Gustavo Marcelo *veterinary surgeon, consultant*
Von Hagen, Heinrich Otto *retired zoologist*
Von Hertzen, Leena Carita *microbiologist, researcher*
Vonka, Vladimir *virologist*
von Lawzewitsch, Irene *veterinary science educator*
von Meyer, Ludwig Kurt *forensic toxicologist*
von Proschwitz, Ted Jörgen *zoologist*
Voronov, Victor Ivanovitch *science educator*
Vorontsov, Alexandre Valeryevich *research scientist*
Vorster, Pieter *botanist, researcher, educator*
Voves, Jan *electronics educator, researcher*
Vranes, Jasmina *microbiologist, researcher, educator*
Vysekantsev, Igor Pavlovich *research scientist, physician*
Wackermann, Jiri *research scientist*
Wade, Claire Margaret *animal scientist, educator*
Wadher, Bharat Jivraj *microbiology educator*
Wägele, Johann Wolfgang *zoologist*
Wagih, Mohamed-Rashead Elsayed *biotechnology researcher, research manager*
Wahl, Martin *marine biologist, researcher*
Waid, John Saville *ecologist*
Wailly, Alain Jamyl de *biologist*
Wainwright, Cherry Lindsey *science educator, researcher*
Waldrup, Kenneth Arlen *veterinarian, researcher*
Walenta, Kurt *retired mineralogy educator*
Walker, Brian Wilson *former field science foundation director*
Walker, John *molecular biologist*
Walker, John Ernest *molecular biologist*
Walker, Peter John *research scientist*
Walker-Brown, Andrew Belsham *science tertiary educator*
Wall, Brian Raymond *forest economist, business consultant, researcher*
Walla, Peter *biologist*
Waller, Geoffrey Nicholas Hugh *biologist, zoologist*
Walters, Keith Frederick Arthur *applied insect ecologist, researcher*
Walton, James Stephen *research scientist*
Wandrasz, Janusz Wladyslaw *science educator, research scientist*
Wanek, Wolfgang *plant physiologist, researcher*
Wang, Cheng-i *parasitologist, researcher in tropical medicine*
Wang, Huimin *science educator*
Wang, Jie *research scientist, science administrator*
Wang, Jiedong *cell biologist, reproductive biologist*
Wang, Lin-Fa *molecular biologist*
Wang, Long Huei *microbiologist*
Wang, Tsuey Tang *science educator, venture capitalist*
Wang, Wen-Xiong *science educator*
Wang, Xian Hui *researcher*
Ward, Alister Curtis *molecular biologist, researcher*
Ward, Katherine Nora *medical virologist, educator*
Ward, M. Neil *research scientist*
Warren, Graham Barry *cell biology educator*
Warrlich, Anne Carolina *veterinarian, journalist*
Wasserman, Irene *research scientist, educator*
Wassman, E. Robert, Jr. *geneticist, medical educator, management consultant*
Watanabe, Toshiharu *ecologist, educator*
Waterhouse, James Maris *physiologist educator*
Watkin, John Raymond *ecologist, writer*
Watson, James Dewey *molecular biologist, educator*
Watt, Kenneth Edmund Ferguson *zoology educator*
Wax, Naomi *science educator and researcher*
Webb, Ann Ruth *scientific researcher*
Webb, Emily *retired plant morphologist*
Webley, Simon *research administrator*
Weder, Juergen Kurt *food chemistry educator*
Weekley, Leslie Bruce *veterinarian, pharmacologist*
Weeks, Jason Mark *ecotoxicologist*
Węgrzyn, Grzegorz *biologist, researcher, educator*
Wegulo, Stephen Ngakhala *plant pathologist, researcher*
Wehnert, Manfred Siegfried *human molecular geneticist, educator*
Wehrmeyer, Walter Claus Heinrich *ecological management educator*
Wei, Guang-Pu *science educator*
Weickmann, Dirk Udo *toxinologist, arachnologist*
Weidekamm, Erhard *pharmacokineticist, pharmaceutical researcher*
Weidner, Stanisław Marian *biochemist, plant physiologist, educator*
Weinstein, Harel *physiologist, biophysicist, educator*
Weiser, Jaroslav *entomologist, researcher, consultant*
Weiss, Christoph Johannes *physiologist, educator*
Weiss, Eugen Franz Josef *veterinary pathology educator*
Weissmann, Charles *molecular biologist*
Welling, Michael Theo *biologist*
Wellington, Karl Everard *animal geneticist, researcher, agriculturist*
Wells, Martin John *zoology educator*
Wendelberger, Gustav *ecology educator*
Wendt, Hans W. *life scientist*
Wenseleers, Tom Hilaire *biologist, researcher*
Werner, Yehudah Leopold *zoologist, educator*
Wernig, Anton *neurophysiology, educator*
Wessing, Armin Richard Everhard *biologist*
West, Richard Gilbert *botany educator*
Westhoff, Victor *vegetation ecologist*
Westlund, Hans Gustav *researcher*
Weston, Peter Henry *plant systematist, research scientist, curator*
Westwood, Melvin Neil *horticulturist, pomologist*
Weyhenmeyer, Gesa Antonie *ecologist, researcher*
Whalley, Ralph Derwyn Broughton *grassland ecologist*
Whateley, Tony Louis *pharmaceutical science educator*
White, David Hodge *agricultural scientist, consultant, researcher*
White, Doris Gnauck *science educator, biochemical and biophysics researcher*
White, Saxon William *physiology educator*
Whitehouse, Frank, Jr. *microbiologist*
Whittington, Ian David *parasitologist*
Wiebe, Michael Eugene *microbiologist, cell biologist*
Wiemann, Marion Russell, Jr. (Baron of Camster) *biologist*
Wierzchos, Jacek *geobiologist, researcher*
Wieschaus, Eric F. *molecular biologist, educator*
Wieslander, Lars E. I. *biology educator*
Wietasch, Klaus Wilhelm *marine technologist, educator*
Wijaya, Christofora Hanny *food chemist, educator*
Wild, Thomas Fabian *virologist, researcher*
Wilhelm, Christian *biologist*
Wilkie, Andrew Oliver Mungo *clinical geneticist*
Wilkins, Malcolm Barrett *botany educator, consultant*
Wilkins, Peter William *plant breeder, researcher*
Willetts, Neil Stanley *biotechnologist, consultant*
Williams, Christopher Maxwell J. *agricultural scientist*
Williams, Craig Lester Cranage *microbiologist, educator*
Williams, Philip Gladstone *research mycologist*
Williams, Robert Joseph Paton *science educator*
Williams, Simon Christopher *science educator*
Williamson, Samuel Chris *research ecologist*
Willis, Arthur John *botany educator, researcher*
Willis, John *retired research scientist, consultant*
Wills, Ronald Baden Howe *food technology educator*
Wilmut, Ian *biologist*
Wilson, Alan Martin *veterinary educator and researcher, consultant*
Wilson, Edward Osborne *biologist, educator, writer*
Wilson, Thomas Woodrow, III *research scientist, consultant*
Wink, Michael *biologist, educator, scientist*
Winkel, Wolfgang *ornithologist*
Winkler, Rosita Alice *research scientist*
Winter, Hans *veterinary pathologist*
Wirthensohn, Michelle Gabrielle *botany researcher*
Wischmeyer, Erhard *neurobiologist, researcher*
Wiskich, Joseph Tony *botany educator, researcher*
Wiśniewski, Adam Bogusław *scientist*
Wisniewski, Zbigniew *geodesist, educator*
Withers, Robert Thomas *exercise physiologist, educator*
Wittner, Michal *physiology educator*
Wobus, Ulrich *biology researcher*
Woelkerling, William James *botanist, educator*
Wolf, E. Dan *veterinary ophthalmologist*
Wolf, Hans Joachim *medical microbiology educator*
Wolf, Norman Sanford *cell biologist*
Wolfe, Ralph Stoner *microbiology educator*
Wong, Ming Hung *biology educator, environmentalist, consultant*
Wong, Po-Keung *environmental microbiologist, toxicologist*
Woo, Norman Ying Shiu *zoologist, educator*
Woods, David Brian *soil scientist, consultant*
Woodside, John Moffatt *marine geology educator*
Woodward, Frank Ian *botany educator, ecologist*
Woolhouse, Mark Edward John *research scientist*
Wouters, Jan T. M. *microbiologist*
Wouters, Johan *research scientist*
Wu, Chengbin *biologist, researcher*
Wu, Guang *research scientist*
Wu, Hai-Ping *science educator, consultant*
Wu, Hongmin *research scientist*
Wu, Min *cell biologist, researcher, educator*
Wu, Rongling *geneticist, researcher*
Wu, Rudolf Shiu-Sun *biology educator*
Wu, Suh-Chin *science educator*
Wu, Zhonghu *reserach scientist*
Wu, Zu-Wang *science educator*
Wubah, Daniel Asua *microbiologist, educator, dean*
Wulff, Daniel Lewis *molecular biologist, educator*
Wüthrich, Kurt *molecular biologist, biophysical chemist, educator*
Wyatt, Kenneth Mark *veterinarian, consultant*
Wyatt, Philip Richard *geneticist, physician, researcher*
Wycherley, Paul Renoden *retired botanist*
Wyke, John Anthony *cancer researcher, research institute official*
Wynberg, Inge Dagmar *veterinarian*
Wyrick, Priscilla Blakeney *microbiologist*
Wysoczanski, Dariusz *science educator*
Xia, Kang *agronomy educator*
Xia, Xuhua *biology educator*
Xiadlan, Song *research fellow*
Xiang, Yun-Yan *molecular biologist, researcher*
Xiang, Zhonggui Gordon *research scientist*
Xiao, Jingping *plant biochemist, physiologist, scientist-educator*
Xiao, Yongshun *biomathematician, animal population dynamicist, marine biologist*
Xie, Min *scientist, lecturer*
Xiong, Fusheng *biologist, researcher*
Xiong, Shaojun *ecologist, educator*
Xu, Fu-Lui *science educator*
Xu, Huai-Shu *microbiologist, educator*
Xu, Hui-Lian *plant scientist*
Xu, You-Heng *physiology educator, cellular biology researcher*
Xu, Zhihong *soil scientist*
Xue, Yongbiao *plant molecular biologist*
Xue, Zhong Tian *plant molecular biologist, educator*
Yaalon, Dan Hardy *soil scientist*
Yablokov, Alexey Vladymirovich *biologist*
Yacout, Maged Mahmoud *physiologist, educator, researcher*
Yakobson, Emanuel Aharon *research scientist*
Yamada, Mamoru *molecular biologist, researcher*
Yamada, Shoji *electronics educator, administrator, retired*
Yami, Kayo Devi *microbiologist, researcher*
Yan, Jerry Jinyue *scientist, educator, researcher*
Yang, Czau-Siung *medical microbiologist, educator*
Yang, Dong-Seok *science educator, physicist*
Yang, Fengjie *science educator*
Yang, Gang *physiology educator*
Yang, Jiachi *research scientist*
Yang, Jingan *science educator*
Yang, Ruikang *research scientist*
Yang, Shang-Shyng *science educator, editor*
Yang, Yinhua *molecular biologist, researcher*
Yang, Yufeng *hydrobiologist, researcher*
Yang, Yuh-Shyong *science educator*
Yaniv, Moshe *molecular biology educator*
Yanov, Vitaly Georgievith *biologist, researcher*
Yarmola, Elena Georgiyevna *research scientist*
Yarovoi, Leonid Konstantinovich *research scientist*
Yarovoi, Serge V. *molecular biologist, researcher, interpreter, writer*
Yasui, Yukio *biologist*
Yazami, Rachid *research scientist, consultant*
Ye, Rongbin *researcher*
Ye, Yimin *research scientist*
Yegorov, Yegor Eugenevich *biologist*
Yeh, An-I *food engineering educator, researcher*
Yeh, Patrice Alain *geneticist, researcher*
Yim, Louis Wai Keung *research scientist*
Yin, Chang-Min *biology educator*
Yonehara, Shin *cell biologist, educator*
Yoo, Young Sook *research scientist, educator*
Yoon, Hyung-seok *technology educator, consultant*
Yoshinaga, Fumihiro *microbiologist*
Yoshizaki, Shiro *research scientist, consultant*
Young, Bruce Arthur *animal production scientist, educator*
Young, Celia Noreen *biologist, consultant*
Young, Judith Anne *animal conservationist*
Young, Michael Warren *geneticist, educator*
Youssef, Haroun Ali *veterinary surgery educator*
Youssef, Mahmoud Mohamed Ahmed *nematologist, plant pathologist, researcher*
Yu, Jiang W. *research scientist*
Yu, Qingchang *science educator*
Yu, Robert Kuan-jen *biochemistry educator*
Yu, Wen *science educator*
Yuan, (David) Aidong *cell biologist, researcher*
Yuchun, Wang *science educator*
Yufik, Yan Mark *director research development*
Yui, Nobuhiko *science educator*
Yumoto, Takakazu *tropical ecologist, educator*
Yun, Sok-Hon *food chemist, researcher*
Yuzbekov, Akhmed Kadimalievich *biologist*
Zabarovsky, Eugene Reonadovich *molecular biologist, researcher*
Zabielski, Romuald *physiologist, educator*
Zabrodsky, Pavel Francevich *toxicologist, educator*
Zach, Otto Rupert Franz *molecular biologist*
Zachariah, Thondiath John *research scientist*
Zachau, Hans Georg *molecular biologist, researcher*
Zadow, John Greig *food industry consultant*
Zajícek, Pavel *parasitologist*
Zakai, Haytham Ahmed *parasitologist, educator, consultant*
Zakharchenko, Mikhail Petrovich *ecologist, educator*
Zaki, Essam Ahmed *molecular biologist, educator*
Zaki, Kamal El-Din Mahmoud *veterinarian, educator*
Zaman, Guido Jenny Rudolf *molecular biologist, researcher*
Zaman, Makhdoom Khaleeq *agricultural scientist, legislator*
Zamski, Eli *botanist*
Zapałowicz, Zbigniew *thermal laboratory scientist*
Zatykó, József *biologist*
Zee, Sze-Yong *botanist, educator*
Zegarlinski, Boguslaw Joseph *science educator*
Zeko, Mersin Abaz *retired veterinary surgery educator*
Zel, Jana *plant physiologist, researcher*
Zelles, László *biologist, researcher*
Zemanek, Alicja *historian of botany, researcher*
Zemanek, Bogdan Józef *botanist, educator, researcher*
Zeng, Zuotao *research scientist*
Zerath, Erik *pathologist, physiologist, researcher*
Zerbin-Ruedin, Edith *retired psychiatric geneticist, educator*
Zerbst, Ekkehard Wolfgang *retired university educator*
Zeuthen, Jesper *biologist, cancer researcher, venture capitalist*
Zeven, Anton Cornelis *plant breeding research scientist*
Zezina, Olga Nikolaevna *biooceanologist, researcher*
Zhang, Chunfang *molecular biologist*
Zhang, Fu-Xue *scientist*
Zhang, Guman *genetics and vegetable breeding educator*
Zhang, Hao *research scientist*
Zhang, Kefei *science and engineering educator*
Zhang, Lijuan *molecular microbiologist, researcher*
Zhang, Shaowu *research scientist*
Zhang, Shi-Qing *biologist, physiologist, obstetrician/gynecologist*
Zhang, Shuda *science researcher*
Zhang, Weiping *research scientist, educator*
Zhang, Wurong *research scientist*
Zhang, Ying Hua *research scientist*
Zhang, Yu-Wen *research scientist*
Zhao, Chun-Mei *histologist*
Zhao, Tianshou *science educator*
Zhao, Wei-ping *physiologist*
Zhao, Zhiyong *developmental biology researcher*
Zhao, Zingzhong *research scientist, educator*
Zheng, Rongliang *biologist, educator, researcher*
Zheng, Tao *research scientist*
Zheng, Wei-Tao *science educator*
Zheng, Zuoxing *food scientist*
Zhilenkov, Eugeni Leonidovich *microbiologist, researcher*
Zhiyu Wilson, Xia *research fellow, consultant*
Zhou, De-qing *microbiologist*
Zhou, Qibo *research scientist*
Zhou, Zhen Feng *materials scientist, educator*
Zhu, Ge-Lin (Ge-lin Chu) *botanist*
Zhu, Guo-zhang *cell biologist, researcher*
Zhu, Hui-Chao *research scientist*
Zhu, Rui Liang *biologist, educator*
Zhu, Ruo-Gu *optical educator*
Zhu, Yuan *research scientist*
Zhuang, Bing Chang *biologist, researcher*
Zhuang, Wen-Ying *mycologist, educator, researcher*
Zhuo, Jia Long *physiologist*
Židovec Lepej, Snezana Klementina *biological scientist*
Ziehen, Wolfgang *soil scientist*
Ziemke, Frank Siegfried Hartmut *microbiologist*
Zierath, Juleen Rae *research scientist, educator, consultant*
Zierdt, Charles Henry *microbiologist*
Zikakis, John P. *food scientist, consultant, educator, researcher*
Zima, Miroslav *biology educator, university official*
Zimmer, Christoph *retired biochemist*
Zintzen, Clemens *science academy executive*
Zivkovic, Bora Dušan *biologist, researcher*
Zizi, Najate *science educator*
Žižka, Zdeněk *biologist, researcher*
Zoellner, Hans *research scientist, educator*
Zoghbi, Maria Das Graças Bichara *scientist*
Zonn, Sergei Vladimirovich *soil scientist, consultant*
Zoumadakis, Michael *molecular biologist*
Zrust, Jaromír *plant physiologist*
Zsoldos, Ferenc *plant physiologist*
Zurak, Ivica *clinical microbiologist, educator, inovator*
Zuschlag, Nancy Hansen *environmental and nature resources educator*
Zwartz, Gordon Joseph *research scientist*
Zwierzak, Andrzej Karol *chemistry professor, researcher*

SCIENCE: MATHEMATICS AND COMPUTER SCIENCE

Aanderaa, Stål Olav *retired mathematics educator*
Abadie, Jean M. *mathematician, educator, researcher*
Abadir, Karim Maher *econometrics and statistics educator*
Abbott, Stephen John *secondary education educator*
Abd-El-Barr, Mostafa Ibrahim *computer science educator, computer engineering educator, researcher, educator*
Abdel-Megied, Mohamed *mathematician, educator*
Abdullah, Abdullah Ahmad *mathematics educator*
Abe, Kanji *statistics educator*
Abels, Herbert *mathematics educator*
Abramovich, Felix *statistics researcher*
Accardi, Luigi *mathematics educator*
Achatz, Hans *computer science researcher*
Acker, Andrew French, III *mathematics educator, researcher*
Aczél, János Dezsö *mathematics educator*
Adams, Martin David *robotics research scientist, educator*
Adler, Irving *mathematician*
Adum, Davorin Mate *geometry researcher, artist, engineer*
Aebischer, Nicholas John *biometrician, researcher*
Aggarwal, Nand Lal *computer sciences educator*
Aggarwal, Neal *medical information scientist*
Agnihotri, Rohit *information technology executive, consultant*
Aguirre, Manuel Antonio *mathematical researcher, educator*
Ahluwalia, Daljit Singh *mathematics educator*
Ahmad, Khalil *mathematician, educator*
Ahn, Joong Ho *systems analyst, educator*
Ajit, Channagiri *computer scientist*
Akazawa, Kohei *statistician*
Akgun, Kemal *computer support professional, consultant*
Akimasa, Sakano *computer scientist*
Albracht, Manfred *software developer*
Albrecht, Gudrun *mathematician, researcher, adult educator*
Al-Dakhil, Badr Yousef *computer programmer*
Alderton, Ian William *mathematics educator*
Alfonseca, Manuel *computer scientist, educator*
Alias, Luis Jose *mathematician, educator, researcher*
Allan, George William *computer scientist, educator*

Lange, Frederick Edward, Jr. *computer information systems architect*
Langlands, Robert Phelan *mathematician*
Lanter, Sean Keith *software engineer*
Lantsman, Meir Haimovitch *mathematician*
LaPorte, Eric *computer science educator*
Lara-Rosano, Felipe *systems engineer*
Larkin, Nelle Jean *computer programmer, systems analyst*
Larsen, Gwynne E. *computer information systems educator*
Larsen, Jens Christian *mathematician, researcher*
Larsson, Per Erik Roland *biomathematician, statistician*
Lashley, Virginia Stephenson Hughes *retired computer science educator*
Lasry, Jean-Michel *mathematics educator*
Latypov, Roustam Khafizovich *mathematician, educator*
Lauterbach, Bernd Guenter *software engineer, researcher*
Lawson, Harold Wilbur *computer engineering company executive, consultant*
Lawton, Wayne Michael *mathematician, educator*
Lazarescu, Mihai Mugurel *computer scientist, researcher*
Le, Thang Kim *computer science educator*
Lee, Do-hoon *computer science educator*
Lee, Jintae *computer science educator, researcher*
Lee, Jong-Hyeon *computer and communications security researcher, mobile communications researcher*
Lee, Ruby Bei-Loh *multimedia and computer systems architect*
Lee, Woo Jong *logistics company executive*
Lee, Yun Bae *computer science educator*
Leeds, Harold Mitchell *computer consultant, director*
LeFloch, Philippe Gerard *mathematician*
LeGates, John Crews Boulton *information scientist*
Leindler, Laszlo *mathematics educator*
Lemanska, Miriam *mathematician, researcher*
Lennon, Douglas Raymond *management information systems executive*
Leong, Helen Vanessa *systems programmer*
Leopold-Wildburger, Ulrike *mathematician educator*
Lescot, Paul Edmond *mathematics educator*
Lesieur, Marcel Robert *mathematician*
Leung, Karl Richard Ping Hung *computer scientist*
Leung, Yiu Wing *computer science educator*
Levin, Leonid A. *computer science educator*
Levinson, Robert Arlen *computer science educator, consultant*
Li, Keqin *computer scientist, educator*
Li, Meng Ru *mathematics educator*
Li, Shujie *mathematician*
Li, Tien-Yien *mathematics educator*
Li, Zhi-Ping *mathematician, educator*
Liebers, Ralf Thorsten *mathematician, educator*
Liflyand, Elijah *mathematician*
Lin, Frank Chiwen *computer science educator*
Lin, Li Cong *mathematics educator*
Lin, Xihong *statistician*
Lin, Zong-Chi *mathematician educator*
Lindner, Daniel George *program analyst*
Lins, Romulo Campos *mathematics educator*
Lions, Jacques Louis *mathematician, educator*
Lions, Pierre Louis *mathematician*
Little, Richard Allen *mathematics and computer science educator*
Liu, Fawang *mathematics educator*
Liu, Jiming *computer scientist*
Liu, Yanpei *mathematician*
Lloyd, John Anthony *analyst*
Loginov, Boris Mikhailovich *mathematician, educator*
Loginov, Boris Vladimirovich *mathematician, educator, researcher*
Løkketangen, Arne *information science educator*
Loman, Mary LaVerne *retired mathematics educator*
Lopez-Gomez, Julian *mathematician, educator*
Lord, John Robert (HRH John Robert Lord, Prince of Judah) *computer consultant*
Lou, Der-Chyuan *computer science educator, researcher*
Love, Eric Russell *retired mathematics educator, researcher*
Low, Arnold Kinman *systems executive*
Low, David J. *mathematician*
Lozinskii, Eliezer Leonid *computer scientist*
Lu, Dan *systems analyst, mathematician, consultant*
Lu, Hsueh-I *mathematician, computer scientist, educator*
Lu, Jian *computer science educator*
Lu, Xiao-Yun *mathematician, researcher, control engineer*
Lu, Zhikang *mathematics educator, researcher*
Lubbe, Samuel Izak *information science educator*
Luc, Dinh The *mathematician, researcher*
Luding, Stefan *physics computer science educator*
Lukáčová, Mária Medvidová *mathematician, researcher*
Lund, William Boyce *computer analyst, project leader*
Lupo, David Emory *computer scientist*
Luque, Emilio Eugenio *computer science educator*
Lütkepohl, Helmut *econometrics educator, researcher*
Lynch, James Walter *mathematician, educator*
Lyons, Veronica Margaret *senior software engineer*
Lyubich, Mikhail *mathematician*
Lyubich, Yuri Illich *mathematics educator*
Lyz, Sergei Alexandrovich *computer operator*
Ma, Jiang-Hong *mathematician, statistician*
Ma, Wen-Xiu *mathematician, educator*
Macfarlane, Alison Jill *statistician*
Mache, Detlef Hauke *mathematician, educator*
Machover, Carl *computer graphics consultant*
Macias-Virgos, Enrique *mathematician, educator, researcher*
Mackevičius, Vigirdas *mathematician, researcher*
Madievski, Anton *applied mathematician, researcher*
Magidor, Menachem *mathematics educator, academic administrator*
Magidson, Jay *statistician*
Mahakuteshwar, Hebballi Yallappa *information scientist, educator*
Mahmoud, Hosam M. *statistics educator, academic administrator*
Maier, Burkhard *data processing consultant*
Makhover, Mikhail Sergeevich *mathematician, educator*
Malafeyev, Oleg Alexeyevich *mathematician*
Malawski, Andrzej Jerzy *mathematical economist, researcher*
Malik, Nazar-Muhammad *mathematics educator*
Malone, Nicholas Sherlon *systems analyst, consultant*
Mansfeld, Fredrik Nils *software developer*
Mansfield, Lois Edna *mathematics educator, researcher*
Manstavičius, Eugenijus *mathematics educator*
Manzhirov, Alexander Vladimirovich *mathematician*
Marandjian, Hrant Babkeni *mathematician and researcher*
Marcu, Dănut Ion *mathematician, researcher*
Mardare, Cristinel *mathematician, researcher*
Marek, Ivo Karel *mathematics educator*
Maričic, Andrija *computer science educator*
Marijuan, Pedro Clemente *information scientist, educator*
Marino, Louis J(ohn) *mathematics educator*
Marinos, Louis *software engineer*
Marinoschi, Gabriela *mathematician*
Marinov, Milko Todorov *software engineering educator*
Marranghello, Norian *computer science educator*
Marrocco, Thomas Michael *software engineer*
Marsden, Jerrold Eldon *mathematician, educator, engineer*
Martinez Finkelshtein, Andrei *mathematician, educator, researcher*
Marzocchi, Alfredo *mathematician*
Maslen, David Keith *mathematician*
Mason, Robert Marion *mathematician, musician*
Matelan, Mathew Nicholas *software engineer*
Mathéus, Frédéric Pierre *mathematician, educator*
Matkowsky, Bernard Judah *applied mathematician, educator*
Matskin, Mihhail *computer scientist*
Matúš, František *mathematician, computer science researcher*
Maxwell, Katrina Diane *information scientist*
Mayr, Ernst W. *computer scientist, educator*
Mazumdar, Ravi Rasendra *engineering and mathematics educator*
Maz'ya, Vladimir G. *mathematician, educator*
Mazzer, Maurizio *statistician, researcher*
McAllister, Marialuisa Nicosia *mathematics educator, editor, consultant*
McCann, Chris (Christian David McCann) *software engineer, educator*
McClanahan, Michael Nelson *systems analyst*
McCleery, Winston Theodore *computer consulting company executive*
McClinton, Travis Victor, II *mathematics educator*
McKinney, George Harris, Jr. *training systems analyst*
McKusick, Marshall Kirk *computer scientist*
McPherson, Samuel Dace, III *computer scientist, instructor, consultant*
Medin, Julia Adele *mathematics educator, researcher*
Megan, Mihail *mathematician, researcher*
Meher, Pramod Kumar *computer scientist, educator*
Meidanis, Joao *computer scientist*
Melnik, Roderick V. Nicholas *mathematician*
Mendez, Celestino Galo *mathematics educator*
Merikoski, Jorma Kaarlo *mathematics educator*
Merrington, Oliver J. *information scientist*
Merry, Paul Robert *statistics educator*
Mestechkin, Mikhail Markovich *math physicist*
Meszéna, George *mathematics educator*
Meznik, Ivan *mathematician, educator*
Micca, Giorgio *researcher*
Michaelis, Bernd *computer science educator*
Michelacci, Giacomo Adriano *mathematician, researcher*
Mihal, Sandra Powell *distance learning specialist*
Mihalache, Valeria *software engineer*
Miklavcic, Stanley Joseph *mathematician, educator*
Mikolajczak, Boleslaw *computer science educator, researcher, consultant*
Miller, Cynthia Ann *mathematics educator*
Milman, Vitali D. *mathematics educator*
Milner, Fabio Augusto *mathematics educator*
Minagawa, Sitiro *applied mathematics educator*
Minker, Wolfgang Manfred *computer science researcher, educator*
Mirotin, Adolf *mathematics researcher*
Mishchenko, Alan *computer scientist and engineer*
Mishuris, Gennady *applied mathematician, educator*
Mitrovic, Dragisa *mathematics educator*
Mitsch, Heinz *mathematician*
Mitsui, Taketomo *mathematician, educator*
Mittal, Ramesh Chand *mathematics educator, researcher*
Miyachi, Jun-ichi *mathematics educator*
Miyakawa, Toru *computer science educator*
Miyake, Yasuji *computer science educator*
Miyazaki, Nobuyoshi *computer scientist, educator*
Modis, Theodore *technological forecaster*
Moffatt, Henry Keith *applied mathematician, educator*
Mohan, Chander *mathematics educator*
Mohri, Mehryar *computer scientist*
Moia, Patricia Ines *mathematician, educator, researcher*
Moiseyev, Aleksey *software engineer*
Molenberghs, Geert *biostatistics educator, consultant*
Mollison, Denis *mathematics educator, conservationist*
Molodtsov, Dmitri *mathematician*
Mones, Reynaldo Amigan *information technology professional, consultant*
Montanus, Hans *mathematics educator*
Monteiro, Luiz Fernando *mathematician, researcher*
Moore, Karen Celyn *systems analyst*
Moraitis, Michael *information systems analyst*
Moran, Siegfried *mathematics educator*
Moreno, Ana Maria *software engineer, researcher*
Morey, Philip Stockton, Jr. *mathematics educator*
Morgenstern, Matthew *computer scientist*
Mori, Kinji *computer science educator*
Moroianu, Andrei M. *mathematician*
Morrison, Ann Marie *information systems specialist*
Morrow, Steven Roger *computer scientist*
Morton, Michael James *software engineer*
Morton, Richard Hugh *statistician, educator*
Moser, Kathleen Anne *systems analyst and data modeling educator, consultant*
Moson, Peter *mathematician, educator*
Mostafa, Javed *information scientist, edcuator*
Mostow, George Daniel *mathematics educator*
Moudatsou, Argiro *statistician*
Moulder, David Stephen *information scientist, librarian*
Mousa, Amany Mohamed *statistics educator, consultant, researcher*
Moussa, Mohamed Ahmed Amin *biostatistics educator, consultant*
Moutselos, Euthimios Cristos *information scientist*
Movsisyan, Yuri *mathematics educator*
Muehlbach, Guenter W. *mathematics educator*
Muffatto, Moreno *technology educator*
Muggleton, Stephen Howard *computer scientist, educator*
Mukhopadhyay, Satya Narayan *mathematician, educator*
Müller, Detlef Horst *mathematician, educator*
Mullery, Geoffrey Patrick *computer consultant*
Multon, Franck *computer scientist*
Mulvey, Christopher John *mathematics educator, researcher*
Mumick, Inderpal Singh *computer scientist, engineer*
Mumolo, Enzo *computer science educator, researcher*
Munetake, Tanaka *computer engineer, consultant*
Muranov, Yuri Vladimirovich *mathematics educator, researcher*
Murayama, Misao *statistical researcher*
Murray, Neil Vincent *computer science educator*
Musti, Narasimha Murty *computer science educator*
Mutafov, Christo Georgiev *medical information specialist*
Mworia, Steve Kyara *information technology executive*
Myers, Kimberly Ann *mathematics educator*
Mykhalevych, Volodymyr Markusovych *mathematics educator, researcher*
Nádeník, Zbyněk *mathematician*
Nagashima, Takashi *retired mathematician, educator*
Nagy, Attila *mathematician*
Nah, Fiona Fui-Hoon *information technology educator, researcher*
Nair, Krishnakumar R. *software engineer, researcher*
Nair, Murali *software engineering consultant*
Nakagawa, Hideki *computer science educator*
Nakao, Mitsuhiro *mathematician, educator*
Namba, Kanji *mathematics educator*
Nance, Richard Earle *computer science educator*
Narin'yani, Alexander Semyonovich *artificial intelligence researcher*
Narukawa, Kimiaki *mathematician, educator, researcher*
Narula, Pornthep *network technology researcher*
Nash, Alicia *computer programmer, physicist*
Nash, John Forbes, Jr. *research mathematician*
Nasri, Ahmad Hachem *computer science educator, consultant, researcher*
Nauroschat, Juergen Thomas *biosystems researcher, mathematician, educator*
Nauth, Peter Matthias *information technology educator*
Navara, Mirko *mathematician, educator*
Navrat, Pavol *software engineer, educator*
Neal, Leslie Robert *computer science educator*
Neave, Henry Robert *mathematician, statistician, management consultant*
Neimark, Juri Isaakovich (Yuri Neimark) *mathematician*
Nelder, John Ashworth *statistician*
Nerukh, Alexander Georgievich *mathematics educator, researcher*
Nesetril, Jaroslav *mathematics educator*
Nesterov, Yurii Eugenievich *mathematician, researcher, educator*
Neubauer, Hugo Duane, Jr. *software engineer*
Neumann, Bernhard Hermann *mathematician*
Nevyjel, Alexander *scientist*
Newell, Alan Francis *computing researcher, educator*
Nguyen, Phong Chau *biomathematics educator*
Niane, Mary Teuw *mathematician*
Nicholls, Frank Gordon *computer scientist, consultant*
Niederreiter, Harald Guenther *mathematician, researcher*
Nielsen, Soren Krag *software product development executive*
Niemiec, Wacław Stanisław *mathematics educator*
Nieto-Roig, Juan Jose *mathematics educator*
Nikitin, Yakov Yurievich *statistics and probability educator, researcher*
Niroma, Timo I. *systems analyst*
Nishigaki, Toru *information scientist, educator, science writer*
Nissan, Ephraim *computer scientist*
Niyogi, Partha *computer scientist, educator*
Nobel, Joris Roelof *civil servant, statistician, researcher*
Nogami, Yoshiko *mathematics and statistics educator*
Norenkov, Igor Petrovich *computer educator, researcher*
Notaris, Sotirios E. *mathematics educator*
Novak, Erich *mathematician, educator*
Novák, Vilém *mathematician, educator*
Novikov, Roman Gennadievich *mathematician, researcher*
Novotny, Miroslav *mathematics educator*
Novozhilov, Vasily Borisovich *mathematician, researcher*
Nowakowski, Andrzej Maria *mathematician*
Nuijten, Wim *computer scientist*
Nürnberger, Günther *mathematician*
Nwana, Hyacinth Sama *computer scientist*
Oberguggenberger, Michael Bernd *mathematician, educator*
Oberst, Ulrich Herbert Günter *mathematics educator*
Obrubov, Yuri Victor *mathematics educator*
O'Donnell, Teresa Hohol *software development engineer, antennas engineer*
Oganyan, Victor K. *mathematics educator*
Ogawa, Hidemitsu *computer science educator*
Ogiela, Marek Romuald *computer science educator*
Ohkuro, Shigeru *mathematics educator*
Ohlendorf, Thomas Charles *systems analyst*
Ohno, Yutaka *information sciences educator*
Oja, Eve *mathematician, educator*
Ojanen, Eetu Samuli *computer scientist*
Ojeda-Ramirez, Mario Miguel *statistician, researcher*
Okamoto, Jiro *information scientist, educator*
Olesen, Dorte Marianne *mathematician, educator*
Oliva-Lopez, Eduardo *information scientist, educator, consultant*
Olufsen, Mette Sofie *mathematician*
Onyszkiewicz, Janusz *mathematics educator, former federal official*
Oosthuizen, Berendien Laurika *information scientist, educator*
Orman, Gabriel V. *mathematician, educator*
Ortiz, Eduardo Leopoldo *mathematician, historian*
Osipenko, Konstantin Yur'evich *mathematician, educator*
Osipov, Yurii Sergeyevich *mathematician, mechanical scientist, educator*
Osman, Frederick *mathematics educator, researcher*
Ostasiewicz, Walenty *statistics educator*
Otto, Carl *statistical sciences educator, researcher*
Overill, Richard Edward *computer scientist, researcher*
Owaki, Kenichi *computer scientist, inventor*
Owolabi, E. Amole *computer scientist*
Oxley, James Grieve *mathematics educator*
Ozhigov, Yuri Igorevich *mathematician, educator, researcher*
Pach, János *mathematician, computer scientist, researcher*
Pajak, Marcin Ireneusz *information scientist*
Pajitnov, Andrei Vladimirovich *mathematics educator*
Palakkandy, Arun *computer program educator, researcher*
Palis, Jacob *mathematics educator*
Pallini, Andrea *statistician, educator*
Palm, Enok Johannes *mathematician*
Palmer, Christopher Ralph *medical statistician*
Pan, Ping-Qi *mathematician*
Paoli, Laetitia Aline *mathematics educator, researcher*
Papadopoulos, Constantinos Vassilios *systems analyst*
Pareja-Heredia, Diego *mathematics educator, bookseller consultant*
Parhi, Narahari *mathematician educator*
Parikh, Shrikant Navnitlal *computer scientist*
Parinov, Ivan Anatol'evich *mathematician*
Paris, Steven Mark *software engineer*
Parker, Simon *software design consultant*
Parmeley, Jerry Paul *software support specialist*
Parthasarathy, Koduvayur Ramaiyer *mathematician*
Parvatham, Rajagopalan *mathematician, educator*
Parviainen, Pekka Eino Olavi *mathematician, educator*
Pasetta, Vesna *mathematical economics educator*
Passi, Inder Bir Singh *mathematics educator*
Pauli, Josef *computer scientist*
Paun, Gheorghe *mathematician, researcher*
Pavelka, Elaine Blanche *mathematics educator*
Pedley, Timothy John *mathematics educator*
Peleg, Bezalel *mathematician*
Pelikant, Adam *electric researcher and educator*
Pelinovsky, Dmitry Efim *mathematics educator*
Peng, De-chun *computer researcher, educator*
Penm, Jack Hlung-wen *statistician, researcher*
Pennisten, John William *computer scientist, linguist, actuary*
Pepper, Jon V. *mathematics historian, educator*
Perfilieva, Irina *mathematics educator, researcher*
Perko, Walter Kim *computer engineer, songwriter, poet*
Perry, Joe Nelson *biometrician*
Peterson, Bonnie Lu *mathematics educator*
Peterson, Elmor Lee *mathematical scientist, educator*
Petersons, Haralds Freds *mathematics educator, geophysics researcher*
Pettinaro, Giovanni Cosimo *robotics and artificial intelligence researcher*
Pettorossi, Alberto *computer science educator*
Petty, James Alan *mathematics educator, consultant*
Petz, Dénes *mathematician, educator*
Peyerimhoff, Norbert *mathematician, researcher*
Pflug, Georg C. *statistician, educator*
Pham, Loi Vu *mathematician, educator*
Phat, Vu Ngoc *mathematician, researcher*
Phillips, Roger *software engineering educator*
Pickett, Harry Eldon *mathematician*
Pilz, Uwe *medical computer scientist*
Pitteway, Michael Lloyd Victor *computer science educator*
Plaskacz, Edward John *computational scientist, engineer*
Pohjola, Pekka Tapani *systems analyst*
Poland, Sydney Wade *software designer*
Pollock, Karen Anne *computer analyst*
Polyanin, Andrei Dmitrievich *mathematician, researcher*
Popa, Constantin Victor *mathematician, educator*
Pope, Mark L. *counseling psychologist, educator*
Popescu, Dan Corneliu *information science researcher*
Popkov, Yury Solomonovich *systems analyst, educator*
Porath, Jan-Erik *software engineer*
Porter, Hayden Samuel *computer science educator*
Posey, Eldon Eugene *mathematician, educator*
Postolică, Vasile *mathematics educator, researcher, professor*
Pottenger, Mark McClelland *computer programmer*
Pour-El, Marian Boykan *mathematician, educator*
Povstenko, Yuriy Zinoviy *mathematics educator, researcher*
Powell, Christopher Robert *systems engineer, executive, computer scientist*
Prabhakaran, Balakrishnan *computer science educator*
Prasad, Krishna Chandra *mathematics educator, consultant*
Preiss, Mitchell Paul *mathematics educator*
Preusser, F. Albrecht *computer scientist, consultant*
Priestley, Maurice Bertram *statistics educator*
Prikryl, Petr *mathematician*
Prince, Stephen *software developer, researcher*
Prokhorov, Dmitri Valentinovich *mathematician*
Prokhorov, Igor Vasilievich *mathematics educator*
Pryce, John Derwent *mathematics educator*
Przytycki, Jozef Henryk *mathematician*
Puckett, Stanley Allen *consultant, software engineer, business educator*
Pumariega, JoAnne Buttacavoli *mathematics educator*
Puninskij, Gennadij Evgeńevich *mathematics educator, researcher*
Purdea, Ioan *algebra educator*
Putz, Barbara *computer scientist*
Qian, Bohai *statistics and economics educator*
Qian, Fang *software engineer*
Quegan, Shaun *mathematician*
Quick, Danny Richard *computer systems engineer*
Qureshi, Azhar K. *biostatistician, research scientist*
Radzievskii, Grigori Vadimovich *mathematician*
Rai, Lallan Prasad *mathematician*
Raikes, Robert Timothy *computer consultant*
Raja-Rayan, Raja-Vigneshwaran *computer programmer*
Rajwade, Anant Ramchandra *mathematician, educator*
Ramalingam, Ganesan *computer scientist*
Ramani, K. V. *computer and information systems educator*
Rampacher, Hermann Hans *computer science executive*
Rampone, Salvatore *computer scientist*
Rao, Kakaraparti Visweswara *statistician, researcher*
Räsänen, Mika *information systems specialist*
Rasvan, Vladimir B. *mathematics educator, consultant*
Rathie, Pushpa Narayan *statistician, mathematician*
Rathore, Rupak *computer consultant*
Raudys, Sarunas *computer science researcher*
Rautenberg, Robert Frank *statistical advisor, stochastic process specialist*
Ravindran, S.S. *mathematician, educator*
Ravn, Anders Peter *computer science educator*

Ray, Kumar Sankar *computer science educator, researcher*
Ray, Pradeep Kumar *computing and information systeme educator*
Rayward-Smith, Victor John *computing educator*
Razpet, Marko *mathematics educator and researcher*
Reade, John Brian *mathematics educator*
Recski, András *mathematician, educator*
Reich, Axel Manfred *mathematics educator, actuary*
Reichmann, Péter Iván *mathematician*
Reijswoud, Victor Emil Van *information systems educator*
Reiley, T. Phillip *consultant*
Renaud, Peter Francis *mathematician, educator*
Revesz, Pal *retired mathematics educator*
Revina, Svetlana Vasilievna *mathematician, educator*
Reynier, Claude *mathematician, engineer*
Rhyne, Theresa-Marie *computer graphics and university executive*
Ribas-Xirgo, Lluís *computer science educator, researcher*
Ricca, Renzo Luigi *mathematician, researcher*
Ridley, Dennis *computer scientist, educator, consultant*
Riedi, Rudolf Hermann *mathematics researcher*
Riedrich, Thomas *mathematician, researcher*
Rieiro-Marín, Ignacio *mathematics educator*
Riemenschneider, Oswald Wilhelm *mathematician, educator*
Riha, Karel *information systems educator*
Riihentaus, Leo Juhani *mathematics educator*
Riley, Norman *applied mathematics educator*
Ritter, Gunter *mathematician, researcher, educator*
Roach, David Giles *information technology administrator*
Roberts, Michael *computer consultant*
Robertson, Ruth Ann *systems analyst, engineer*
Robles-Austriaco, Lilia Sinogba *information specialist*
Rochford, Christopher Eric *computer consultant, educator*
Rockart, John Fralick *information systems researcher*
Rodrigues, Waldyr Alves, Jr. *mathematical physics educator*
Rodríguez Avila, Eduardo René *information systems analyst*
Rodriguez-Seijo, José Manuel *mathematician, educator*
Rohn, Jiri *mathematician, researcher, educator*
Rokita, Przemyslaw Stefan *computer scientist, researcher*
Romanov, Vladimir Alexandrovich *computer engineering*
Romanov, Volodymyr Alexeevich *computer science educator, researcher*
Romanovski, Mikhail Rem *mathematician*
Ronse, Christian *information science educator*
Ronto, Miklós *mathematician, educator, researcher*
Rose, George Andrew *software developer, information systems specialist*
Rosenberg, Jonathan Micah *mathematics educator*
Rosenberger, Gerhard *mathematics educator*
Rosenblatt, David *mathematical statistician, research consultant*
Rosenknop, John *mathematician*
Rossi, Guido A(ntonio) *mathematics educator, researcher*
Ross-Langley, Richard S. *software engineer, consultant, researcher*
Roubíček, Tomáš *mathematician*
Rozenblum, Gregory (Gregory Vladimirovich Rozenblyum) *mathematics researcher, educator*
Rubin, Stuart Harvey *computer science educator, researcher*
Rudeanu, Sergiu *mathematician, educator*
Rudolph, Ekkart *software engineer, researcher*
Rukhin, Andrew Leo *mathematics and statistics educator*
Rus, Ioan A. *mathematics educator, researcher*
Rusan, Laurentiu Virgil *software engineer*
Russell, Dennis Charles *mathematics educator*
Ryjacek, Zdenek *mathematician, educator*
Rylski, Andrzej *electrical measuring educator, researcher*
Sabharwal, Ranjit Singh *mathematician*
Sacco, Riccardo *mathematician, researcher*
Sadun, Lorenzo Adlai *mathematician*
Sagalovich, Yuri Lvovich *mathematician, researcher*
Saha, Debashis *computer science and engineering educator*
Saint-Amand, David Cyrias Homberto *computer programmer, geologic consultant*
Sakia, Remi Mrume *biometrician, educator*
Salakhitdinov, Makhmud *mathematics educator*
Salanskis, Jean-Michel *logic and epistemology educator*
Salem, Shawky M.A. *information science educator*
Sampat, Dharmesh *computer consultant*
Samwald, Hans-Joachim *computer consultant*
Sánchez, José Salvador *computer scientist, educator*
Sanchez-Palencia, Evariste *mechanics and applied mathematics researcher*
Sánchez Ruiz, Luis Manuel *mathematician, researcher*
Sandefur, James Tandy *mathematics educator*
Sandergaard, Theodore Jorgensen *information technology director*
Santhannam, M.S. *computer operator*
Santos, Ara De Jesus *retired mathematics educator*
Sarfraz, Muhammad *computer scientist, educator*
Sari, Jonathan Paavo *software engineer*
Sarker, Shamsul Alam *mathematics educator, researcher*
Sattar, Abdus *mathematician, educator*
Satyanarayana, Bhavanari *mathematics educator*
Sauvan, Xavier Martial *computer scientist, consultant, researcher*
Savolainen, Vesa Valter *information systems educator, scientist*
Saworotnow, Parfeny Pavlovich *mathematician, educator*
Scedrov, Andre *mathematics and computer science researcher, educator*
Schaal, Werner Georg Hans *mathematician*
Schaar, Günter *mathematician, retired educator*
Schabe, Hendrik Kurt *computer scientist, consultant*
Schaich, Georg Eberhard *statistics educator*
Schamanek, Andreas *systems theory and computer science educator*
Schappert, Albert *mathematician, researcher*
Scheffler, Barbara Jane *statistician, business executive*
Schelhowe, Heidi *computer scientist*
Schelp, Richard Herbert *mathematics educator*
Scherb, Hagen Heinrich *mathematics, statician*
Scheurle, Jurgen Karl *mathematician, researcher, educator*
Scheutzow, Michael K.R. *mathematician, educator*
Schilders, Willy H.A. *mathematician*
Schilling, Klaus Jürgen *computer science researcher, educator*
Schimek, Michael Georg *statistics and biometrics educator*
Schinas, Christos J. *mathematician, researcher*
Schlee, Walter *mathematician, educator*
Schlesinger, Karl-Georg *mathematician, researcher*
Schliffer, Wolfgang *computer scientist*
Schmid, Hubert Martin *software developer*
Schmid, Karl Hermann *mathematician, educator*
Schmidt, Hans-Jürgen Reinhold *mathematician*
Schmidt, Klaus D. *mathematician, educator*
Schöning, Uwe *computer scientist, educator*
Schreiber, Martin Fritz Bruno *computer scientist*
Schreur, Barbara *computer science educator*
Schribman, Shelley Iris *database engineer, consultant*
Schubert, Axel *computer scientist*
Schubert, Per Johan Fredrik *computer scientist*
Schueth, Dorothee *mathematician, educator, researcher*
Schuiski, Larry Leroy *information scientist*
Schulhoff, Karen L. *information specialist*
Schultz, Jan Roger *computer scientist, software engineer*
Schulz, Ralph-Hardo *mathematician, educator*
Schulzrinne, Henning G. *computer science educator*
Schuster, Reinhard Gottfried *mathematician, researcher*
Schwabe, Rainer *mathematical statistician*
Schwartz, Ilany Calonimus *mathematician, institute director*
Schwarze, Jochen *applied computer science educator*
Sciriha Aquilina, Irene *mathematics educator, researcher*
Sears, Sandra Lee *computer consultant*
Seda, Anthony Karel *mathematics educator, researcher*
Sedlar, Milan *mathematician*
Segeth, Karel *mathematician*
Seifter, Norbert *mathematics educator*
Selbmann, Hans Konrad *medical information processing educator*
Selkirk, Keith Edward *mathematician*
Sellers, Peter Hoadley *mathematician*
Senac, Patrick Gabriel *computer science educator*
Şendov, Blagovest Hristov *mathematician, educator*
Šerbedžija, Nikola *computer scientist*
Sergeev, Yuri Alexandrovich *mathematician, educator*
Sestier, Andrés *mathematician, educator*
Setford, George A. *information systems company executive*
Sevastianov, Sergey Vassilyevich *mathematician*
Shaffer, Dorothy Browne *retired mathematician, educator*
Shah, Rajesh Chimanlal *mathematics educator*
Shah, Shirish Kalyanbhai *computer science, chemistry and environmental science educator*
Shahidi, Freydoon *mathematician, mathematics educator*
Shaikhet, Leonid Efimovich *mathematician, researcher*
Shaiwalla, Aliasger Yusufali *computer scientist, educator*
Shall, Basil *systems analyst*
Shapiro, Boris Z. *mathematician*
Sharan, Maithili *mathematician, educator*
Sharma, Neeraj K. *computer engineer, educator*
Shary, Sergey Petrovich *mathematician*
Shaw, Ronald *mathematical physics educator*
Sheehy, Brendan Matthew *systems engineer*
Shen, Jun *computer science educator, researcher*
Sheng, Dongyuan *software engineer*
Shepherdson, John Cedric *mathematics educator*
Sherman, Alan Theodore *computer science educator*
Sherstyuk, Andrei *computer programmer*
Shevchenko, Valery Nikolaevich *mathematics educator*
Shi, Feng Sheng *mathematician*
Shi, Peng *mathematics researcher*
Shi, Yong *information science educator*
Shi, Zhongzhi *computer science researcher*
Shier, Gloria Bulan *mathematics educator*
Shikhmurzaev, Yulii Damir *mathematician, researcher, consultant*
Shilepsky, Arnold Charles *mathematics educator, computer consultant*
Shimada, Nobuo *mathematician, researcher*
Shimamura, Tetsuya *computer and information sciences educator*
Shingareva, Inna Konstantinovna *mathematician*
Shinkin, Vladimir Nikolaevich *mathematician, educator*
Shionoiri, Hideo *computer technologist*
Shirai, Yasuto *information science educator, researcher*
Shirokova, Elena *mathematics educator, translator*
Shiryaev, Vladimir Mikhailovich *mathematics educator*
Shi-Zhong, Bai *mathematics educator*
Shohoji, Takao *statistician*
Shoji, Isao *statistician, educator*
Sholukha, Victor Anatolievitch *applied mathematics and biomechanics educator*
Shulcloper, José Ruiz *mathematician, researcher*
Shvartsman, Alexander Allister *computer scientist*
Shvidler, Mark Joseph *mathematician*
Sibeyn, Jop Frederik *computer scientist*
Siddiqi, Jawed Iqbal Ahmed *software engineer, research consultant, educator*
Sidelsky, Patricia Loney *science educator*
Siegelmann, Hava Tova *information systems educator*
Sills, Richard Reynolds *scientist, educator*
Silverman, Bernard Walter *statistics educator, priest*
Şim, Kwang Mong *computer scientist*
Šima, Jiří *theoretical computer scientist*
Şimalarides, Anastasios *mathematician, educator*
Šimić, Diana *statistics educator*
Simionescu-Badea, Claudia Lidia *mathematics educator*
Simis, Aron *mathematician, researcher*
Sinai, Yakov G. *theoretical mathematician, educator*
Singer, Julia *mathematician*
Singh, Gagan Deep *engineering software consultant*
Singh, Gautam B. *computer science researcher, educator, consultant*
Singh, Gulab *statistician, accountant*
Singmaster, David Breyer *mathematics educator*
Sinha, Pradeep Kumar *computer scientist, researcher*
Sinitsyn, Igor Nikolaevich *information scientist, educator*
Sivashinsky, Gregory *mathematics educator*
Skea, Alan David *computer scientist*
Skeppstedt, Jonas *computer science educator*
Skoularidou, Victoria E. *software engineer*
Skovoroda, Andrei Radionovich *mathematician*
Skurnick, Joan Hardy *biostatistician*
Slapal, Josef *mathematician, educator, researcher*
Sleeman, Brian David *mathematics educator*
Sloane, Andy *computer scientist, educator*
Sloman, Aaron *computer science educator, philosopher, cognitive scientist*
Slusanschi, Anca Eugenia *computer scientist, researcher*
Slusanschi, Horia Cristian *computer scientist, researcher*
Smagin, Valery *mathematician*
Smarandache, Florentin *mathematics researcher, writer*
Smith, John LeRoy *mathematics educator*
Smith, Ole Da Silva *systems administrator, engineer*
Smith, Peter *computer sciences educator*
Smith, Raoul Normand *computer science educator*
Smith, Thomas Raymond, III *software engineer*
Smith, Woollcott *statistician, educator*
Snášel, Václav *computer scientist, educator*
Soben, Robert Sidney *systems scientist*
Sobol, Ilya M. *mathematician, educator*
Soga, Hideo *mathematics educator*
Sohmer, Bernard *mathematics educator, administrator*
Sokol, Barnett Jerome *electronics educator, consultant*
Sokolichin, Alexander Alexandrovich *statistician, fluid dynamics researcher*
Sokolov, Victor Fedorovich *mathematics and control theory educator, researcher*
Solecki, Dieter *mathematician, consultant*
Soloviev, Igor Alexeevitch *mathematician, educator*
Solymosi, Tamás István *mathematics educator*
Sontag, Eduardo D. *mathematics educator, director*
Souplet, Philippe Pierre *mathematician*
Sövegjarto, Andras *mathematics educator, researcher*
Sowa, Artur *mathematician, researcher*
Spansky, Robert Alan *computer systems analyst, retired*
Sperling, Scott Edward *software consultant, Bible expositor*
Speros, Martha Chris *mathematics and science educator*
Spiegel, Wolfgang *mathematician*
Spinadel, Vera Winitzky de *mathematics educator*
Spohn, William Gideon, Jr. *mathematician, musician*
Squire, Vernon Arthur *mathematics educator, researcher*
Sridharan, Varadachari *mathematician, educator*
Srimani, Pradip K. *computer science educator*
Stadel, Manfred Peter *information systems administrator*
Stadje, Wolfgang *mathematician, educator*
Stahl, Herbert Robert *mathematics educator, consultant*
Stanchev, Walter Miklosh *computer science educator*
Stanciulescu, Florin S. *information scientist, educator*
Standish, Russell Kim *computational scientist*
Stanek, Bruno L. *software developer, author, commentator*
Stanuch, Helena *biostatician*
Stark, Heather Alexandra *electronic commerce industry analyst*
Starov, Victor Mikhilovich *mathematics educator*
Stata, Raymie *computer science researcher, investor*
Stavrinos, Panayiotis *mathematics educator*
Stavroudis, Orestes Nicholas *mathematician, educator*
Stefaniak, Jaroslaw Eryk *mathematician*
Stefanics, Barbara Zumbrun *computer educator, information technology consultant*
Stefanov, Stefan Minev *mathematics educator, researcher*
Steiner, Hans-Georg *mathematician*
Steinparz, Franz Xaver *information scientist, consultant, educator*
Štěpánek, Petr *computer science educator*
Stewart, Ian Nicholas *mathematics educator*
Stifter, Sabine Anna Maria *software developer*
Stone, Alexander Paul *mathematics educator*
Stormes, John Max *instructional systems developer*
Stoyan, Dietrich Kurt *statistics educator*
Strassen, Volker *retired mathematics educator*
Strazdins, Indulis *mathematician, researcher, educator*
Stuart, John Trevor *mathematics educator*
Stuart, Sandra Joyce *computer information scientist*
Stubbs, Susan Conklin *statistician*
Stucky, Wolffried *computer science educator*
Subramanian, Ramachandran *applied mathematician, researcher, educator*
Sudar, Subbiah *mathematician educator, researcher*
Sum, John Pui-Fai *computer science educator*
Sun, Dongchu *statistics educator*
Sun, Huafei *mathematics educator*
Sun, Jie *mathematics educator, researcher*
Sun, Ron *computer scientist, cognitive scientist*
Sun, Xian-He *computer science educator*
Suthaharan, Shanmugathasan *computer science educator*
Sutton, Louise Nixon *retired mathematics educator*
Switzer, Brian Carl *strategic systems designer*
Swyers, Donald G. *information scientist*
Syropoulos, Apostolos *computer scientist, educator*
Szabados, Tamas *mathematician, educator*
Szabó, Sándor *mathematician, researcher*
Szalek, Benon Zbigniew *logistics and heuristics educator*
Szczepaniak, Piotr Stanislaw *computer scientist, educator*
Szép, Jenö *mathematician, educator*
Szirányi, Tamás *computer science researcher, educator*
Sztandera, Les Mark *computer science educator*
Tagliaferri, Roberto *computer science educator and cybernetics researcher*
Takagi, Hideaki *computer scientist, mathematician*
Takahashi, Ryuichi *computer science educator*
Takizawa, Makoto *computer science educator*
Talati, Khushroo Jamshed *software applications architect*
Tam, Rosaline *payment industry management executive*
Tamura, Saburo *mathematics educator*
Tang, Shuang *computer programmer, researcher*
Tang, Yuan Yan *computer science educator*
Tang, Yuan-Liang *technology educator*
Tansey, Lisa Rebecca *database administrator, dancer, masseuse, musician*
Tapanes, Edward Eduardovich *fiber optic sensing company executive, physicist, research engineer*
Taran, Evgeny Yurievich *mathematician*
Tarzia, Domingo Alberto *mathematics researcher, educator*
Tatrov, Alexander Sergeevich *information analyst, educator, researcher*
Taylor, Frank Edward *forensic computer and communication consultant*
Taylor, Martin John *mathematics educator*
Tchaban, Vasyl Joseph *mathematics, modelling & electrodynamics educator*
Tecklenburg, Helga Anna *mathematics educator*
Teghem, Jacques *mathematics educator*
Temam, Roger M. *mathematician*
Tetlow, William Lloyd *infotech consultant*
Thangaraj, Venu *educator, researcher, probabilist*
Thawonmas, Ruck *computer scientist, educator*
Theys, Philippe Paul *data quality professional*
Thiébaux, H. Jean *mathematical statistician, researcher*
Thoma, Elmar Herbert *mathematician*
Thomas, Glanffrwd Powell *mathematician, computer scientist, educator*
Thomas, Tarquin Craig *computer scientist, writer*
Thompson, Walter David, Jr. *systems analyst*
Tian, Zhiyu *software and medical device engineer*
Tian, Zongshu *mechanics and applied mathematics educator*
Tichenor, Charles Beckham, III *operations research analyst*
Tichy, Robert Franz *mathematician, researcher*
Tichy, Walter Franz *computer science educator*
Tietjen, Scott Phillips *computer programmer, analyst*
Tietz, Dietmar Juergen *computer Web engineer, scientist*
Tikhonov, Nikolai Ivanovich *computer design educator*
Tillmann, Ulrike Luise *mathematician*
Timonin, Jury Alexandrovich *information science researcher*
Timpka, Toomas *computer scientist, physician, educator*
Tirao, Juan Alfredo *mathematician, educator*
Tisdale, Phebe Alden *cryptographer*
Tkadlec, Josef *mathematics educator*
Togasaki, Shinobu *computer scientist*
Toh, Chai *information science educator*
Toledano, Alicia Y. *statistician, educator*
Tolle, Henning *control theory and robotics educator*
Tomescu, Ioan *mathematician, educator*
Tong, Siu Wing *computer programmer*
Törn, Aimo Alf *computer science educator*
Torpey, Robin Lee *computer science and information systems educator*
Torra Reventós, Vicenc *computer scientist, educator*
Tóth, János *applied mathematician*
Towghi, Nasser M. *mathematician*
Townsend, James Willis *computer scientist*
Toyoshima, Noboru *virtual world researcher*
Tralle, Aleksy *mathematician*
Tran, Duong Hien *computational numerician*
Tran, Trung Van *mathematics educator, researcher*
Traub, J(oseph) F(rederick) *computer scientist, educator*
Traylor, Donald Reginald *mathematics educator*
Trench, William Frederick *mathematics educator*
Trenogin, Vladilen Alexandrovich *mathematician, educator*
Tretiakov, Aleksei Anatoliy *mathematician*
Trier, Oivind Thorvald Due *software engineer*
Trockel, Walter *mathematics and economics educator*
True, Hans Christian Godskesen *applied mathematics educator*
Truss, John Kenneth *mathematics educator*
Tsai, Jingpha (Jeffrey Tsai) *computer scientist, educator*
Tsapenko, Nikolai Evgenievich *mathematician, educator*
Tsodikov, Alexander David *biostatistician, educator*
Tsouros, Constantin Claude *computer science educator*
Tulya-Muhika, Sam *statistician, consultant*
Turaev, Vladimir Georgievitch *mathematician, researcher*
Turakainen, Paavo Kalevi *mathematics educator*
Turner, Malcolm Elijah *biomathematician, educator*
Turnwald, Gerhard *mathematician*
Tutschke, Wolfgang *mathematician*
Tyrl, Paul *mathematics educator, researcher, consultant*
Tyutyunnik, Vyacheslav Mikhajlovich *information scientist*
Tzafestas, Spyros Georgiou *robotics and control educator, researcher*
Udriste, Constantin Nicolae *mathematics educator*
Uhrik, Carl Thomas *computer scientist, educator*
Ullmann, Julian Richard *computer science educator*
Umoinyang, Imo Edet *mathematics educator, researcher*
Upton, Graham John Gilbert *statistics educator*
Urabe, Tohsuke *mathematics educator, researcher*
Üstünel, Ali Süleyman *mathematician, researcher*
Vainshtein, Peter *applied mathematics educator*
Vaisman, Izu *mathematics researcher, educator*
Válas, György *information specialist*
Valcher, Maria Elena *mathematics educator*
Vallée, Robert Gilbert *mathematician, educator*
Valverde, Llorenc *computer science educator, researcher*
Vámos, Tibor *computer scientist, educator*
van de Geer, Sara Anna *mathematician, educator, researcher*
Vandeman, Michael Joseph *computer programmer, environmental activist, writer*
Vanden-Broeck, Jean-Marc *mathematician*
Van Dyke, Joseph Gary Owen *computer consulting executive*
Vanhecke, Lieven Noel Adolf *mathematics educator*
Vanicek, Jiri *computer science educator, government advisor*
Van Osdol, Donovan Harold *mathematics educator*
van Rienen, Ursula Helga *mathematician, educator*
Van Tuyl, Otto Arie *technical director, quality systems auditor*
Varadharajan, Vijay *computer scientist, educator*
Vargas, Jorge Antonio *mathematician, educator*
Vass, Jozsef *software developer, researcher*
Vasudevan, Thirumalai Chakravarthi *mathematician, educator*
Vasylyev, Oleksiy Vsevolod *information brokering company executive*
Vázquez-Abad, Felisa Josefina *operations research educator, electrical engineer*
Veloso, Paulo Augusto Silva *computer science educator, researcher*
Vensel, Vello *statistics educator*
Verma, Babu Lal *biostatistics professional*
Verma, Rakesh Mohan *computer science educator*
Vermani, Lekh Raj *mathematics educator*
Vesely, Vítězslav *mathematician, educator, researche*
Vezvaei, Mahbobeh *mathematics educator*
Vierheller, Todd *software engineering consultant*

Viertl, Reinhard Karl Wolfgang statistician, educator, consultant
Viglianco, Ricardo Alberto computer scientist, educator
Vinnichenko, Sergey Victorovich mathematician, researcher
Vlada, Marin information educator
Vlamos, Panayiotis research mathematician, educator
Vogel, Silvia Angelika Emma mathematician, educator
Vogt, Carsten computer scientist
Voitovich, Nikolai Nikolayevich mathematician, researcher
Vojta, Paul Alan mathematics educator
Volk, Wolfgang Friedrich mathematician
Volkmann, Bodo mathematician, researcher
Voller, Rudolf Lambert mathematician, researcher
Voloshinov, Alexander Victorovich mathematics and philosophy educator
Von Der Mosel, Heiko mathematician, researcher
von Wolfersdorf, Lothar mathematics educator
Vorotnikov, Vladimir Il'ich mathematician, educator
Vougiouklis, Thomas Nicholaos mathematics educator
Vu Hoai, Chuong statistician, researcher
Vuorinen, Matti Keijo mathematician
Wabnig, Harald Werner systems analyst, researcher
Wahl, Bernt Rainer mathematician, writer, software engineer
Wain, Geoffrey Thomas academic administrator, mathematics educator
Wakid, Shukri Abu information technology director
Walbesser, Henry Herman computer science educator
Walden, Johan mathematician
Walker, Andrew Morris retired statistics educator
Wall, Charles Terence Clegg mathematics educator, researcher
Walter, Rolf Wilhelm mathematician, educator
Walter, Wolfgang Ludwig mathematics educator
Walters, Kenn David computer scientist, computer company executive
Walther, Gerd Erwin mathematics educator
Wang, Junqiang software developer and programmer
Wang, Peiguang mathematics educator, researcher
Wang, Pinchao mathematics educator
Wang, Zheng computer scientist, researcher
Wassell, Stephen Robert mathematics educator, researcher
Wasserman, Stanley statistician, educator
Watanabe, Hitoshi information technology educator, researcher
Watson, Alan Gordon software engineer, consultant, statistician
Webb, Geoffrey Ian computer scientist, educator
Weber, Michael computer science educator
Weck, Gerhard computer scientist
Wedeniwski, Sebastian software engineer
Wee, In-Suk mathematics educator
Wegener, Ingo computer science educator
Wegert, Elias mathematics educator
Wegmann, Rudolf mathematician
Wei, Guo-Qing computer scientist
Wei, Yuchuan mathematician, electrical engineer, physicist, researcher
Weichselberger, Kurt Franz statistics educator
Weisz, Ferenc mathematician
Wells, Raymond O'Neil, Jr. mathematics educator, researcher
Wells, Roger Stanley software engineer
Welsh, Charles Edwin mathematician, educator, EMT
Weng, John Juyang computer science educator, researcher
Wenzel, Vera Stepanowna mathematician
Werner, Peter Johann mathematics educator
Wernick, Edward Raymond company executive, computer consultant
Westberry, John Elliott mathematics educator
Wetherhorn, Aryeh (Lee Murray) computer analyst
Wetsch, John Robert information systems specialist
Wette, Eduard Wilhelm mathematician
Whitehouse, John Harlan, Jr. systems software consultant, diagnostician
Whitten, Ruth Ann mathematician
Wiegandt, Richard mathematician, educator
Wiesenberg, Russel John statistician
Wiesner, Anatol signals intelligence specialist, researcher
Wijayarathna, Pathirage Gamini computer scientist
Wilde, Alan Conrad mathematician
Williams, Gilbert Thomas systems engineer, consultant
Williams, Marsha Rhea computer scientist, educator, researcher, consultant
Williams, Morgan Howard computer science educator, researcher
Williams, Thomas Arthur biomedical computing consultant, psychiatrist
Willis, Ralph Houston mathematics educator
Wills, Joerg Michael mathematician
Wilson, Brian Eugene computer scientist
Wilson, Susan Ruth statistician
Winkler, Franz mathematics educator, researcher
Winskel, Glynn computer science educator, researcher
Wirszup, Izaak mathematician, educator
Wirth, David Eugene software designer, consultant
Witherow, Peter Kent geographic information systems analyst
Woike, Lynne Ann computer scientist
Wong, Patricia Jia-Yiing mathematician, educator
Wong, Roderick Sue-Cheun mathematics educator
Wouters, Dirk Constantia network management and software development administrator
Wright, Robert John mathematics educator, researcher
Wu, Ching-mu mathematician
Wu, Chuan Kun cryptographer, mathematician
Wu, Hong Ren computer science and engineering educator
Wu, Zongmin mathematics educator and researcher
Wulff, Gerhard mathematician
Wünsch, Volkmar Norbert mathematics educator
Xi, Changchang mathematician
Xia, Chang Yu mathematician
Xiang, Limin computer science researcher
Xiao Feng, Guo mathematics educator
Xie, Xianya computer control and signal processing scientist
Xu, Ruo Ning mathematics educator
Xu, Xue Jun mathematician, researcher
Xu, Zhong Ling mathematician, educator
Xue, Weimin mathematics educator, researcher
Yamada, Shin-Ichiro computer services company executive
Yamamoto, Hideo computer science educator
Yanagi, Kenjiro mathematics educator
Yang, Chung-Chun mathematics educator
Yang, Miin-Shen statistics educator
Yang, Xiao Qi mathematician
Yang, Xingjian computer software scientist, educator
Yang, Zhihong computer scientist
Yao, Andy Shunchi computer science educator
Yatsalo, Boris Ivanovich mathematician, researcher
Ye, Sanyu software engineer
Ye, Weichun information scientist, educator
Ye, Xiu mathematician, educator
Ye, Yiming computer scientist, researcher
Yeadon, Tammy Pamela information specialist
Yevtushenko, Alexander Alexej mathematician, researcher
Yin, Chunyong metrology educator
Yin, Weiping mathematics educator
Yonda, Alfred William mathematician
Yoo, Changsik integrated circuit designer, researcher
Yoshida, Norihiro Prince mathematician
Yoshise, Akiko mathematical programming researcher, educator
You, Hong mathematics educator
You, Suya computer scientist
Yu, Huiming computer scientist
Yu, Jia-rong mathematics educator
Yu, Jietai mathematician, educator
Yu, Shiaw-Shian computer engineer
Yuan, Xue-Ming applied mathematics researcher and educator
Yuan, Zeng Ren computer science educator, researcher
Yuechiming, Roger Yue Yuen Shing mathematics educator
Zachariasson, Toini Maria computer educator
Zaitsev, Valentin Feodorovich mathematician, researcher
Zelmer, A.C. Lynn computing educator
Zeng, Yunbo mathematics educator
Zhang, Hong mathematician
Zhang, Jize information management specialist, researcher
Zhang, Junbiao computer scientist
Zhang, Liang-Jie multimedia architect, computer scientist
Zhang, Ming computer scientist
Zhang, Nai-Xiao computer science educator, researcher
Zhang, Nien Fan statistician
Zhang, Shuang mathematics educator
Zhang, Shunian mathematics educator, researcher
Zhang, Wenhui computer scientist
Zhang, Yanchun computer scientist, educator
Zhang, Yao-Zhong mathematical physicist, research scientist
Zhang, Yuchen computer scientist
Zhang, Zhongfei computer science educator, researcher, consultant
Zhao, Jinxi computational mathematician, mathematics educator
Zhdanov, Renat Zufarovich mathematician
Zheng, Dao Sheng mathematics educator
Zheng, Jiang yu information science educator
Zheng, Xiaogu statistician
Zhone, Ning mathematician, computer scientist
Zhong, Ji mathematician, mathematics educator
Zhong Lian, Li mathematics educator
Zhou, Shuzi mathematics educator
Zhou, Tian Xiao mathematician, educator, administrator
Zhou, Zhiyou information scientist
Zhu, Yao-chen mathematician
Zhuang, Wan mathematician, educator
Zielke, Roland Jürgen mathematics educator, physician
Ziglin, Sergey Lvovich mathematician, researcher
Zimmer, Horst Gunter mathematics educator
Zinoviev, Yury M. mathematician, researcher
Zipfel, Andreas Josef biostatistician
Zumbrun, Kevin Ronald mathematics educator
Zvárová, Jana statistician, educator
Zweynert, Manfred mathematics consultant
Zwiesler, Hans-Joachim Hermann actuarial science educator

SCIENCE: PHYSICAL SCIENCE

Aaron, Francisc Dionisie physicist
Aaron, Jean-Jacques chemist, educator
Abakumov, Georgy Aleksandrovich physicist, researcher
Abdel-Latif, Ata Abdel-Hafez biochemistry and molecular biology educator
Abdel Wahab, Samiha Mohamed chemistry educator, researcher
Abdulagatov, Ilmutdin Magomedovich thermophysics researcher
Abdulsamad, Esam Omar paleontologist, researcher
Abe, Hiroki marine biochemistry educator
Abel, Edward William chemist and educator
Abhyankar, Krishna Damodar retired astronomy educator
Abken, Hinrich Johann biochemist, immunologist, researcher
Aboul Gheit, Ahmed Kadry chemist, educator
Abraham, Tonson chemist, researcher
Abramenko, Valentina Izosimovna astronomer, educator
Abramova, Ludmila Arkadievna chemist, researcher
Abramović, Biljana Franja chemistry educator
Abramovitch, Rudolph Abraham chemistry educator
Abrashev, Miroslav Vergilov physicist, educator
Abrikosov, Aleksei Alekseyevich physicist
Abrukov, Victor Sergeyevich physicist, educator
Absar, Nurul biochemistry educator
Acera, Manuel Martin-Merino physics educator
Acevedo, Roberto chemistry educator, researcher
Aceves-Pastrana, Patricia chemistry educator, researcher, editor
Achtziger, Norbert Rainer physics educator, researcher
Ackers, Gary Keith biophysical chemistry educator, researcher
Adam, Gunter Ernst Kurt chemist
Adamenko, Victor Gregory biophysics researcher and educator
Adamia, Shota geologist, researcher
Adamov, Moisey Naumovitch physicist, chemist, consultant
Adams, Jay Willette chemist, consultant
Addy, Marian Ewurama biochemist
Adebayo, Yinka Rotimi environmental scientist, diplomat
Adegbuyi, Olatunde geologist, geochemist, educator
Ademoroti, Christopher M. Aderemi chemistry educator
Adhikari, Raju molecular scientist
Adikane, Harshvardhan Vishvanath research biochemist
Adurodija, Ojo Frederick physicist, educator, researcher
Aerts, Diederik Emiel physics educator, science center administrator
Afanasev, Igor Borisovitch chemist
Afanas'ev, Valery Vasilijevitch physicist
Afanasyev, Boris Nikolaevich chemist, researcher
Agar, Robert Alexander geologist, consultant
Agarwal, Ashutosh chemist, researcher
Agarwal, Ram Kumar chemistry educator, researcher
Agarwal, Shiv Kumar chemist, researcher
Aggarwal, Madan Mohan physics educator, researcher
Agnon, Amotz earth science researcher
Agrawal, Jai Prakash chemist, researcher
Agrawal, Yadvendra Kumar chemistry educator, researcher
Aguiar, Adam Martin chemist, educator
Ahavi, Atsu Koku physicist, researcher
A'Hearn, Michael Francis astronomer, educator
Ahmad, Irshad physicist, nuclear chemist
Ahmad, Mohammad physicist, researcher
Ahmad, Salahuddin nuclear scientist
Ahmad, Sheikh Rafi optics scientist, educator
Ahmed, Iqbal chemist
Ahmed, Kazi Matin Uddin hydrogeologist
Ahmed, Mainuddin astrophysicist
Ahn, Changhyun physicist, researcher
Ai, Hsiao-bai (Xiao-bai Ai) theoretical physicist
Aiginger, Johannes physics educator
Aihara, Jun-ichi chemistry educator
Ai-lian, Ling chemistry educator
Aim, Karel Vaclav chemist
Aistov, Andrey Valentinovich physics and economics educator
Akal-Strader, Ayca chemistry and biochemistry educator
Akchurin, Rauf Khamzinovich material science and engineering educator
Akhatov, Iskander Shaukat physicist, educator
Aki, Keiiti seismologist, educator
Akimov, Mikhail Nikolaevich physicist
Akira, Toshiaki scientist
Akopyan, Valentin Babken biophysicist, educator
Akulin, Vladimir Mikhailovich physicist
Akutsu, Hideo biophysical chemist, educator
Al-Adel, Fida Fouad physics educator, laser spectroscopy researcher
Alajbeg, Anda chemist, researcher
Al-Alawi, Saleh Mahdi physics educator
Alavi, Ghasem biogeophysicist, researcher
Al Bakri, Dhia environmental geoscience educator
Albanese, Domenico chemist, researcher
Albanis, Triadafyllos Athanasios chemistry educator, researcher
Albeck, Michael chemist, educator
Alberts, Laurence physicist
Albini, Adriana chemist, researcher
Alblas, Bernard Pieter physical chemist, researcher
Al-Chalabi, Mahboub geophysicist, consultant
Aldaz, Antonio physical chemistry educator
Aldén, Erik Magnus physics researcher, educator
Aleksandrovskii, Anatolii Nikolaevich physicist, researcher
Alekseev, Boris Federovich physics educator, researcher
Alekseyev, Igor Evgenievich chemist
Aleshin, Andrei Nikolaevich physicist
Aleshin, Vladimir Pavlovich nuclear physicist
Alex, Volker Ernst physicist, researcher
Alexakis, Alexandre chemistry educator
Alexander, Vedhamonickom chemistry educator, researcher
Alexandratos, Spiro Dionisios chemistry educator
Alexandrov, Boris Sergeevitch physicist, researcher
Alexandrov, Eric Leonidovich physicist
Alexandrov, Yuri Andreevich physicist
Alexandrovich, Seregin Artur physicist, researcher
Alexandru, Horia V. physicist, educator, researcher
Alexeev, Boris Vladimirovich physicist, educator
Aleynikov, Sergey Mikhaylovich geotechnics educator
Alfaro, Guillermo Hanne geology educator, consultant
Alferov, Zhores I. physicist, researcher
Ali, Ahmed physicist
Ali, Md Mohsin radiation chemist
Ali, Mohammed chemistry educator
Ali, Syed Abid chemist
Ali, Syed Saeed chemist, researcher
Aligia, Armando Angel physicist, researcher
Alijah, Farhang Alexander chemistry educator
Al Khadhrawi, Mohammad Radhi chemist, geochemist
Al-Kofahi, Mahmoud Mejalli physicist, educator
Alkuhaimi, Siham Abdulaziz physicist, educator
Allakhverdov, Grant Rantovich chemist, researcher
Allavena, Marcel physical-chemistry researcher
Allen, Barry John physicist
Allen, Brian Philip physicist
Allen, John organic chemist
Allen, John Polk environmental scientist
Allen, Keith William retired chemist, educator
Allen, Leslie physics educator
Allen, Myles Robert climate researcher
Allen, William Douglas physicist
Allende, Jorge Eduardo biochemist, molecular biologist
Allenmark, Stig Gerhard chemistry educator, researcher, consultant
Alma'r, Ivan Ferenc astronomer
Almohandis, Ahmed A. geology educator, consultant
Al-Nasser, Ibrahim Abdulrahman biochemist, educator
Alonso-Amelot, Miguel Enrique chemistry educator
Alpen, Edward Lewis biophysicist, educator
Alperovich, Mark chemist
Alpert, Pinhas atmospheric scientist
Alsharif, Adnan A. geologist
Alstrøm, Preben physicist, researcher
Alt, Helmut Guido chemistry educator, researcher
Altadill-Felip, David geophysicist, researcher
Altaisky, Mikhail Victorovich nuclear scientist, physicist
Altarelli, Guido theoretical physicist
Altenberger, Andrzej Ryszard physical chemist
Altshuler, Nina Semenovna physics educator, researcher
Altukhov, Pavel Dmitrievich physicist
Alvarez-Estrada, Ramon Fernandez physicist, physics educator
Alves, Jürgen biochemist, educator
Amand, Jean-Claude Henri chemist
Amaravadi, Vedadri Narasimham physicist
Ambarisha, Babu Mullangi scientist
Ambartsoumian, Eugenia Nickolaevna physicist, researcher
Ameduri, Bruno Michel materials researcher
Ames, James Benjamin biochemistry educator, researcher
Ames, Susan astrophysicist
Amin, Mohammed Nurul chemist, researcher
Amory, Christine Marie Eugenie physicist, researcher
Ampel, Roman astronomer, researcher, educator
An, Junling environmentalist
Anagnostakis, Emmanuel Alexander physicist, educator
Anam, Edet Matthew chemistry educator, researcher
Anbar, Michael biophysics educator
Anderer, Friedrich Alfred biochemist, researcher
Andersen, Jens Ulrik physics educator
Andersen, Torben Brender optical researcher, astronomer, software engineer
Anderson, Barry chemist
Anderson, Gloria Long chemistry educator
Anderson, Paul Alexander environmental scientist, biochemist
Anderson, William Robert physicist
Andersson, Lennart N.E. chemist, researcher
Andersson, Per Sune geologist
Ando, Masanori chemist, researcher
Andor, Gyorgy physicist
Andrade-Garda, Jose Manuel chemist
Andreev, Aleksandr Fyodorovich physicist
Andreev, Alexander Vladimirovich physicist
Andreev, Igor Vasilievitch physicist
Andreeva, Lidiya Nikolaevna chemist
Andreini, Pierangelo engineer, educator
Andrejtscheff, Wenzeslav H. physicist, researcher
Andrenko, Andrey Stanislavovich radiophysicist, researcher
Andreou, Doros physicist, technoeconomic consultant
Andrews, Peter Ronald chemist, researcher
Andrianov, Dmitry Glebovich physicist, researcher
Andriesh, Andrei Mihail physicist, researcher
Andrillat, Henri retired astronomy educator
Andritsopoulos, George retired physical science educator
Andrushchenko, Zhanna physicist, researcher
Andrzejewski, Bartlomiej physicist researcher
Anevsky, Sergey Iosifovich physicist
Anfossi, Domenico physicist, researcher
Angel, Martin Vivian biological oceanographer
Anghileri, Leopoldo José researcher
Angyal, Stephen John chemist
Anischenko, Gennady Yakovlevich physicist, researcher
Anisimov, Oleg Alexandrovitch climatologist, educator, researcher
Anisimov, Sergei I. physicist, researcher
Anisovich, Vladimir Vladislavovich physicist, researcher
Anongba, Patrick Norbert physicist
Anselmi, Damiano physicist, researcher
Antia, H.M. astrophysicist
Anton, Gisela Hedwig physicist, educator, researcher
Antoniadis, Ignatios physicist
Antonov, Igor Nickolaevich radiophysicist, researcher
Antonova, Irina Veniaminovna physicist, researcher
Antonyuk, Volodimir Oleksandrovitsh scientific production executive
Antunes, Alexander Kolstad computational astrophysicist, web programmer
Anulov, Oleg Vyacheslav biochemist, researcher
Anumakonda, Varada Rajulu physicist, educator
Aoki, Ichiro theoretical biophysics, systems science educator
Aotmane, En Naciri physics educator
Apak, M. Resat chemistry educator, researcher
Apanasenko, Alexander Leonidovich physicist, researcher
Aparicio, Antonio astrophysicist
Apestegui-Barzuna, Alvaro biochemist
Aplesnin, Sergei Stepanovich physicist
Apostolov, Anton Atanassov physicist, researcher
Appel, Helmut nuclear physicist
Appenzeller, Immo Julius astronomy educator
Applewhite, Thomas Hood retired chemist
Appukuttan, Padinjaradath Sankunny biochemist, researcher
Aqrawi, Adnan A. M. sedimentologist, geologist
Arabczyk, Walerian chemistry editor, researcher
Arain, Ghulam Shabir chemist
Arakawa, Hideo biophysics researcher and educator
Aramaki, Kunitsugu chemist, educator
Arata, Kazushi chemist
Arav, Marc corrosionist
Arbona, Antonio physicist, educator
Arbuzov, Valerii Ivanovich physicist, researcher
Archakov, Alexander Ivanovich biochemist, researcher
Archwichai, Laa geologist
Arendt, Josephine biochemist
Arenhövel, Hartmuth physicist
Argiriou, Athanassios A. physicist, researcher
Arglebe, Christian retired biochemist
Aringazin, Ascar Kanapievich physicist, researcher
Aristov, Yurii Ivanovich chemist
Arkadiev, Vladimir Alexandrovich physicist
Arlt, Thilo chemist, mineralogist
Armand, Georges Jules physicist, consultant
Armannsson, Halldor geochemist, researcher
Arnold, Walter Konrad physicist
Aronin, Alexander Semenovich physics researcher
Arp, Halton Christian astronomer
Arriaga, Edgar Augusto chemistry educator
Arrigoni, Enrico physicist
Arsene, Melania-Liliana biochemist, researcher
Arsenyan, Tatiana Ishkhanovna physicist, researcher
Arshady, Reza chemistry educator, research director, author
Arst, Helgi geophysicist
Arykov, Anatoly Alexandrovich physicist
Asada, Toshi seismologist, educator
Asaoka, Hisatoshi chemist, educator
Ashmore, Jonathan Felix biophysicist, researcher
Ashokkumar, Mathupandian chemistry educator, researcher
Ashraf, Chaudhri Muhammad chemist, researcher, consultant
Aslanian, Daniel Laurent marine geologist
Assaad, Jamal Sami physicist
Assimakopoulos, Panayotis Adam physics educator
Assimiti, Daniela clinical biochemist, researcher
Astakhov, Valery Ivanovich research geologist, educator
Astakhova, Irina Sergeevna chemistry educator, researcher
Aszódi, András chemist
Atanov, Gennadiy Alexeevich physicist, educator

Athota, Rao Rama biochemistry educator
Atkins, Peter William chemistry educator
Atsarkin, Vadim Aleksandrovich physicist, educator
Attenborough, Keith physics educator
Atuchin, Victor Valerievich physicist, researcher
Au, Peter Chak Tong chemist, educator
Aubert, Andre Ernest biophysicist, educator, biology researcher
Aubry, Serge Jean theoretical physicist, researcher
Aucar, Gustavo Adolfo physics educator, researcher
Aue, Walter Paul chemist, senior researcher chemical disarmament
Auffermann, Gudrun chemist, researcher
Augusto, Walter Ruiz chemist, researcher
Auleytner, Julian Jan physicist
Aulitzky, Herbert climatologist, educator, forester
Ausloos, Marcel Raymond physics educator and researcher
Ausmees, Andrus physicist
Auzel, François-Emile physicist, educator
Avenhaus, Rudolf physics educator, research scientist
Avery, John Scales chemistry educator
Avila, Carlos Alberto physics researcher, inventor
Avinash, Khare physicist, researcher
Avissar, Nelly Emanuella biochemist, researcher
Avksentyuk, Boris Petrovich physicist, researcher
Avvakumov, Evgenii Grigorievich chemist, researcher
Awaji, Mitsuhiro physicist, researcher
Axelsen, Nils Holger biochemistry educator, administrator
Ayache, Jeanne Gilberte materials scientist, electron microscopist
Ayrapetyan, Sinerik Nerses biophysicist
Azcarate, Ismael Norberto physicist
Azcárraga, José Adolfo de theoretical physics educator
Azimi, Dariush physicist, researcher, educator
Azimioara, Mihai Dumitru chemistry researcher
Azzopardi, Marc Antoine astrophysicist, scientist
Baag, Czango geophysics educator
Baars, Franciscus Jacobus geologist
Babailov, Serguey Pavlovitch chemist
Babani, Fatbardha biophysics researcher
Babanin, Alexander Vladimirovitch physical oceanographer, researcher
Babel, Dietrich chemistry educator
Bach, Thomas Jörg Anton plant biochemist
Bachiller, Rafael astronomer
Bachmann, Peter Klaus chemist
Badal, José Ignacio geophysics educator
Badanian, Shaliko Hovakim chemistry researcher, educator
Baddiley, Sir James biochemist
Baerns, Manfred G.O. chemistry educator, science administrator
Baeuerle, Dieter Willy applied physics educator
Bagneid, Ali Abdalla physics educator
Bahadur, Aruna material scientist
Bahgat, Alaaeldin Abdelhamied physicist, educator, researcher
Bai, Bin physicist
Baibich, Mario Norberto physicist
Baican, Roman Horatiu physicist, project engineer
Baik, Seung-Chul metallurgist, researcher
Baikov, Yurii Mikhailovich physical chemist, researcher
Baimakova, Olga Arkadyevna physicist, educator
Baines, Peter George meteorologist, researcher
Bairamov, Bahish Haliloglu physicist
Baitsar, Roman Ivanovych physics educator, researcher
Bajkova, Anisa Talgatovna radio astronomy imaging and digital signal processing researcher
Bajusz, Sándor chemistry educator
Baker, David Eric Dale physicist, consultant
Bakharev, Boris Vasilievitch radiophysicist, researcher
Bakhchadjyan, Robert physical chemist, researcher
Bakhterev, Vladimir Vassilievich geophysicist, researcher
Bakonyi, Imre physicist
Bakos, József chemist, researcher
Baksht, Fedor Grigoriy physicist
Balagurov, Boris Yakovlevich theoretical physicist, researcher
Balarew, Christo Christov chemist, educator
Balassanian, Jean-Marie François Haïg astronomer
Balaya, Palani physicist
Balázs, András biophysicist, consultant
Balbolov, Entsho Christov chemistry educator, researcher
Balchin, Anthony Arthur physicist, research consultant
Balčiúniene, Milda Leonarda physicist, researcher
Balcou, Yves retired physicist, educator
Bald, Edward chemistry educator, researcher
Báldi, Tamás geology educator, researcher
Baldwin, Sheryl Denise chemist, writer, editor
Baleanu, Dumitru physicist, researcher
Balek, Vladimir materials scientist, educator, nuclear chemist
Balepin, Vladimir Vladimirovich aerospace propulsion scientist
Balian, Roger physicist
Ball, William Paul physicist, engineer
Balsiger, Hans Rudolf physics educator
Baltas, Michel chemist, researcher
Baluev, Anatolii Victorovich chemist, consultant, researcher
Balzar, Davor physicist
Balzarotti, Adalberto physicist, educator
Bamberg, Elmar biochemistry educator
Ban, Gábor physicist, researcher
Banaszkiewicz, Marek Władysław physicist
Bancewicz, Malgorzata Magdalena physicist, educator
Banciu, Axente Constantin chemist
Bandgar, Babasaheb Pandurang chemist, educator, researcher
Bando, Masayasu biochemist, researcher
Banegas, Estevan Brown environmental biotechnology executive
Banerjee, Basu Dev biochemist, educator
Banerjee, Prabir nuclear physicist
Banerjee, Sanjay geoscientist
Banfalvi, Gaspar biochemist, researcher
Bang, Hu Er nuclear scientist, educator
Banister, Arthur James chemistry educator
Bannach, Burkhardt medical physicist
Banno, Susumu chemist
Banskalieva, Veneta Borissova chemist, educator
Baquer, Najma Zaheer biochemistry, educator
Baquero-Parra, Rafael physicist, researcher
Barabás, Miklós physicist, researcher
Barabash, Alexander Stepanovich physicist
Barachevsky, Valery Alexander physicist researcher
Barakat, Khaled Jamil chemist, researcher
Barale, Vittorio oceanographer, researcher
Baran, Enrique José inorganic chemist
Baranov, Andrey Olegovich chemist, researcher
Baranov, Serguei Pavlovitch physicist, researcher
Baranov, Vladimir Borisovich physicist, educator
Baranowski, Paul Joseph instrumentation technician
Baratta, Giovanni Battista astronomer
Barbashov, Boris Mikhailovich physicist, researcher, educator
Barber, Anthony John geology educator, geological researcher
Barber, David John physics educator
Barber, James biochemist, educator
Barbieri, Renato retired chemistry educator
Barcelos, Eduardo Dorneles space company executive
Barcza, Szabolcs astrophysicist, educator
Barczyk, Grzegorz Rafal hydrogeology researcher, educator
Bard, Allen Joseph chemist, educator
Bardan, Virgil geophysicist
Bares, Jan physicist
Barford, Norman Charles retired physics researcher, educator
Barletta, Antonio physicist
Barlik, Marcin geodesist, educator
Barmore, Frank Edward physics educator
Barna, Peter B. physicist
Barnes, Diana Marion biochemist, consultant
Barr, John Baldwin chemist, research scientist
Barron, Jeffrey Lawrence chemist, consultant, educator
Barron, Thomas Hugh Kenneth retired physics educator
Barry, Aliou Hamady chemist, researcher
Bárta, Josef metallurgist, research scientist
Bartenev, Georgii Mikhailovich physicist, physicochemist, researcher
Barth, Andreas chemist
Barth, Tomislav biochemist, researcher, educator
Barthel, Josef M.G. chemistry educator
Barthes-Labrousse, Marie-Genevieve surface scientist, researcher
Barthová, Jana Kaiferová biochemist, educator
Bartoschewitz, Rainer chemist
Bartram, Ralph Herbert physicist
Bartsch, Christian Reinhard biochemist
Bartzokas, Aristides meteorologist, climatologist
Bar-Yam, Yaneer physicist
Baryshevsky, Vladimir Grigorievich physicist, researcher
Baryshnikov, Fedor Fedorovich physicist, researcher
Basavaiah, Deevi chemistry educator, researcher
Baschnagel, Jörg H. physicist, educator, researcher
Basdevant, Jean-Louis Henri physicist, educator
Baskerville, Charles Alexander geologist, educator
Basov, Nikolai Gennadievich physicist
Bass, Fridrich Gershon physicist, educator
Bassalo, Jose Maria Filardo physics educator, researcher
Bassford, Lynn Foster physicist, engineer
Bässler, Heinz chemistry educator
Basu, Jaydeep Kumar physicist
Basu, Sukumar materials science educator, researcher
Basumallick, Amitava metallurgy educator
Batamack, Patrice Theodore Desire chemistry educator, researcher
Bates, Colin Arthur physics educator
Bates, Edna Jean biochemist, researcher
Bathias, Claude materials science educator, consultant
Batisse, Michel physicist, international civil servant
Batley, Graeme Edward environmental analytical chemist, researcher
Batygin, Yuri Konstantinovich accelerator physicist
Bauchspiess, Karl Rudolf physicist
Baudet, Monique Marie chemistry educator
Baudin, Bruno biochemist, educator
Baudler, Marianne chemistry educator, researcher
Bauer, Ernst Georg physicist, educator
Bauersfeld, Walter Wolfram clinical chemist, laboratory professional
Baum, Edward Joseph chemistry educator, consultant
Baumann, Christopher Anthony chemist, educator
Baumann, Gerd physics educator, researcher
Baumann, Pierre Konrad biochemist, psychopharmacologist, educator
Baumann, Winfried retired physics educator, researcher
Baurov, Yuriy Alexeevich physicist, researcher
Baxter, Murdoch Scott nuclear geochemist, editor-in-chief, environmental consultant
Bayer, Edward Allen biochemist, researcher
Baykut, Fatma Sacide physical chemistry educator
Bazylak, Grzegorz Bohdan analytical chemist, educator
Beattie, James Kenneth chemist
Becherer, Richard Joseph science consulting firm executive, physicist
Bechert, Dietrich Wolfgang aeronautics scientist, acoustician
Beck, Hans physicist
Beck, Wolfgang Maximilian inorganic chemistry educator
Becker-Heidmann, Peter M. physicist, researcher
Beckhaus, Ruediger W.H. chemist, educator
Bederski, Krzysztof physicist
Bedford, Colin Thomas bio-organic chemistry educator
Bednar, Jaromir biochemist
Bednorz, J. Georg crystallographer
Beechey, Ronald Brian biochemist, researcher
Beekman, Freek J. research physicist
Beeley, Josie Ann biochemistry educator
Behr, Arno chemist, educator
Behrendt, John Charles geophysicist, writer
Behrens, James William physicist, administrator, author
Behrman, Edward Joseph biochemistry educator
Beiter, Thomas Albert crystallographer, research scientist, consultant
Beitner, Rivka biochemistry researcher, educator
Bejlegaard, Niels Martin retired metallurgy educator
Beker, Haluk physicist, educator
Bekyarova, Elena Borissova chemist, researcher
Belashov, Vasily Yurievich physics educator, researcher
Belenkaya, Elena Semenovna physicist, researcher
Belikova, Tatjana Pavlovna physicist, computer scientist, researcher
Bell, Roger Alistair astrophysicist
Bellamine, Aouatef biochemist
Bellelli, Andrea biochemist
Bellenger, George Collier, Jr. physics educator
Beller, Matthias Heinrich chemist, educator, researcher
Bellier, Olivier geologist
Belloni-Cofler, Jacqueline Dolorès Thérèse physical chemist, radiation chemist, photographer
Bellucci, Giancarlo planetary scientist, researcher
Belmares, Hector chemist
Belousov, Valery Vasilyevich physicist
Belousova, Anna Pavlovna geology researcher
Belyaev, Igor Yaroslavovich scientist
Belyavskiy, Evgeniy Danilovich radio-physicist, researcher
Ben-Amotz, Ami oceanographer, marine biologist, educator
Bencze, László chemist, educator
Bendl, Jiri scientist
Bendorius, Rimgaudas Adolfas physics educator, scientist
Beneš, Ivan chemist
Bénière, François Jean-Marie physicist
Benisti, Didier Leon physicist, researcher
Benjamin, Arlin James physicist
Benkhoff, Johannes chemist, researcher
Ben-Menahem, Ari geophysics educator, researcher
Benna, Carlo astrophysicist, researcher
Bennett, Harold Earl physicist, optics researcher
Benoit, Henri physicist, educator
Benoit a la Guillaume, Claude Joseph physicist
Ben-Tal, Nir biochemist
Bente, Lynn Alan chemist
Bentley, Robin Eric physicist
Berdowska, Ewa Danuta physicist, researcher, educator
Berdowski, Janusz Marek physicist, educator, researcher
Berezhnoy, Yuri Anatoliyovich physicist
Berezin, Andrey Alexandrovich physicist, researcher
Berg, Paul biochemist, educator
Berg, Stanton Oneal firearms and ballistics consultant
Berger, André Léon geophysics educator
Bergmann, Ralf B. physicist
Bergstrom, Robert chemist
Bergström, Sune K. D. retired biochemist
Beridze Giorgi, Thengiz biochemist, educator
Berkov, Dmitri Vladimirovitch physicist
Berlin, Yuri Alfredovich physicist, educator
Berman, Sylvia biochemist, researcher
Bernard, Jan Hus mineralogist, researcher
Berryhill, Henry Lee, Jr. geologist
Berset, Daniel analytical chemist
Bersin, Richard Lewis physicist, plasma process technologist
Berthon, Guy René chemistry researcher, consultant
Bertolami, Orfeu physicist
Besenhard, Jürgen Otto chemistry educator
Beshtoev, Khamidbi Mukhamedovich physicist, researcher
Bessonov, Evgueni Grigorievich physicist
Bethe, Hans Albrecht physicist, educator
Betinis, Emanuel James physics and mathematics educator
Betz, Jochen Nicolay physicist, researcher
Beygelzimer, Yakiv Efimovich materials science researcher, educator
Beysens, Daniel André-Marie physicist
Bezlepkin, Anatoliy Andreevich physicist, researcher
Bezuglov, Vladimir Vilenovich chemist, researcher
Bharadwaj, Prem Datta physics educator
Bharati, Sunil Yoveshchandra geologist, geochemist, educator
Bhardwaj, Anil astrophysicist
Bhaskarwar, Ashok Niwritti chemical engineer, educator
Bhat, Rajiv biophysical chemist, educator
Bhatnagar, Deepak biochemist, researcher
Bhatnagar, Ved Prakash physicist, researcher
Bhatt, Devendra Kumar geologist
Bhatt, Devendra Prakash chemist, researcher
Bhatt, Harish Chandra astrophysicist, educator
Bhosale, Chandrakant Hari physics educator, researcher
Bhushan, Shashi physics educator
Bhutani, Kamlesh Kumar chemist, researcher, educator
Bhutta, Amjad Pervaiz chemistry educator
Bi, Ru-Chang crystallographer, educator
Biallozor, Svetlana chemistry educator, researcher
Biasci, Andrea chemist
Bibby, Thomas Frederick Allen physicist
Bickelhaupt, Friedrich Matthias chemistry educator
Biederman, Edwin Williams, Jr. petroleum geologist
Bieganowska, Maria Lucyna chemistry educator
Bielińska-Waż, Dorota Joanna physicist
Bieron, Jacek physicist
Bietenholz, Wolfgang Peter physicist
Bigerelle, Maxence material science educator
Bigger, Stephen William chemistry educator
Bijnens, Johan L. theoretical physics researcher
Bikales, Norbert M. chemist, science administrator
Bilgic, Attila Michael physics researcher
Billard, Aude Gemma physicist, researcher
Billig, Franklin Anthony chemist
Bilyalov, Renat physicist
Bimbot, Rene physicist, researcher
Binder, Kurt educator in theoretical physics
Binder, Leo Otto chemistry educator
Bingham, Richard George physicist, optical designer, consultant
Binnemans, Koen chemist, researcher
Binnig, Gerd Karl physicist
Bird, Eric Charles Frederick environmental adviser
Birman, Alexander physicist, researcher
Birshtein, Tatiana Maximovna physicist, educator, researcher
Bishai, Augenie Mikhail physicist
Bisht, Prem B. physics educator
Bisnovatyi-Kogan, Gennadi Semyonovich astrophysicist, researcher
Biswas, Mukul retired chemistry educator, researcher
Bittencourt, Jose Augusto space science researcher, physics educator
Bittner, Michael physicist
Bjørkum, Per Arne geologist, educator, scientist
Bjornsdottir, Ingibjorg Elsa environmental scientist
Björnsson, Olafur Grimur biochemistry researcher
Black, John Harry astronomer
Blackwell, Dale Bascom physicist
Blackwell, Donald Eustace retired astrophysicist, educator
Blaih, Salah Moustafa chemist, pharmacist, educator
Blais, Roger Nathaniel physics educator
Blaive, Bruno Jean chemistry researcher, numerical analysis educator
Blanc-Talon, Jacques scientific manager
Blaz, Ludwik Marian metallurgist, educator
Blazhevich, Sergey Vladimirovich physicist, educator, researcher
Blázovics, Anna biochemist, researcher
Bleck, Wolfgang Peter metallurgy educator
Blinov, Michael Nikolaevich biochemist, researcher
Blin-Stoyle, Roger John physicist
Bloch, Konrad Emil biochemist
Bloembergen, Nicolaas physicist, educator
Blomhoff, Rune biochemist educator, researcher
Bloor, David physics educator, researcher
Blosser, Henry Gabriel physicist
Blundell, Derek John environmental geology educator
Blyakhman, Yefim Moisei chemist, researcher
Blyuman, Boris Alexandrovich geologist, researcher
Boakye, Francis physicist, educator, researcher
Bobier, Claude-Abel scientist, educator
Bockserman, Robert Julian chemist
Boddupalli, Sadasivudu biochemistry consultant
Boddy, Keith medical physicist, educator
Bode, Juergen biochemistry educator, researcher
Bódi, Alexander Charles physics educator
Bodner, George Michael chemistry and education educator
Bodoky, Tamás János geophysicist, researcher
Bodor, Géza chemistry educator, researcher
Bogatov, Alexander Petrovich physicist, educator
Bogaturov, Alexey Nicolaevich physicist, researcher
Bogatyrev, Vladimir Lvovich inorganic chemist
Bogdanov, Roman Vasilievith radiochemist, researcher
Bogod, Yuri Abraham physicist
Bogolubov, Nikolai Nikolaevich, Jr. mathematics physicist
Bogomolov, Edward Alexandrovich physicist, researcher
Bogusławski, Piotr physicist
Bohacek, Jaroslav metrologist, educator, researcher
Bohan, Thomas Lynch physicist, lawyer
Bohley, Peter biochemistry educator
Bohr, Aage Niels physicist, educator
Boichenko, Alexander Mikhailovich physicist, researcher
Boiko, Vitaly Petrovich chemist, researcher
Boillat, Guy Maurice Georges mathematical physicist
Boisset, Nicolas biochemist, researcher
Bojariu, Roxana climatologist
Boklund, John Uno chemist, educator, researcher
Bolin, Vladimir Dustin chemist
Bolmaro, Raul Eduardo physicist
Bolotin, Adolf Borisovich physics educator
Bolotin, Herbert Howard physics educator, consultant
Bolotov, Vladimir Nikolai physicist, educator, researcher
Bolshakov, Vladimir Ivanovich metallurgist, educator
Bolt, Michael Gerald metallurgist
Boman, Hans G. biochemist, educator
Bombicz, Petra Alexandra crystallographer, researcher
Bonciocat, Nicolae Ulpiu chemist, educator
Bond, Alan Maxwell chemist, educator
Bond, Andrew H. research chemist
Bond, Geoffrey Colin chemistry educator
Bondarenka, Vladimiras physicist
Bondarev, Victor N. physicist, educator
Bondarevskii, Svjatoslaw Igorevich physics educator
Bondybey, Vladimir Edmund chemistry educator
Bonhoeffer, Sebastian physicist, researcher
Bonitz, Michael Manfred physicist
Bonmatí-Pont, Manuel chemistry educator
Bonnett, Raymond organic chemist
Bonotto, Daniel Marcos geochemistry educator
Bonvoisin, Jacques Jean chemist, researcher
Boon, Jean Pierre physicist, researcher
Boopathy, Ramaraj environmental scientist
Boos, Herman theoretical physicist
Booth, John Graham physicist, educator
Bordin, Ninel physicist, researcher
Bordo, Vladimir Georgievich physicist, researcher
Bordusa, Frank scientist, biochemist
Borg, Gunnar Anders Valdemar psychophysics educator
Borgaonkar, Hemant Prabhakar meteorologist
Borie, Bernard Simon, Jr. physicist, educator
Borisov, Victor Vasil'evich physicist, researcher
Bormontov, Evgeny Nikolaevich physicist, consultant
Borneas, Marius physics educator
Bornhardt, Cristian chemical engineer, environmental engineering educator
Bornmann, William Gerard organic chemist
Borodin, Lev Sergeevich geologist
Borovička, Jiří astronomer
Borovtsov, Pyetr Vasiljevich physicist, educator
Börresen, Torger Andreas biochemist, researcher, science administrator
Boruah, Romesh Chandra research scientist, chemist
Borysenko, Valentin Oleksiyovych scientist, researcher, academic administrator
Boryski, Jerzy chemist
Bos, Annemarie Gerredina geophysicist
Bosanac, Miroslav physicist, researcher
Boschi, Enzo physicist, educator
Bose, Subhasis physicist, researcher
Bott, Andreas Benno meteorologist, educator
Bottu, Guy chemist
Bouas-Laurent, Henri Claude chemist, educator
Bouchal, Zdenek physicist, educator
Bouchareine, Patrick retired physics educator
Bougeard, Daniel Roger A.M. chemistry researcher
Boulaud, Denis Georges physicist, researcher
Bourasseau, Serge physicist
Bourdeau, Philippe environmental scientist
Bourilkov, Dimitri Todorov physicist
Bourkine, Serguei Pavlovich metallurgist, educator
Bourova, Tatiana Gennadievna physics educator
Bouška, Vladimír Jan geochemist, mineralogist
Boutaud, Olivier Gilles biochemistry research educator
Bouteville, Anne physicist, educator
Bouzat, Cecilia Beatriz biochemist
Bovey, Leonard physicist
Bowden, Keith chemistry educator
Bowell, Robert John geochemist, consultant
Bowen, David R. science and technology educator, consultant
Bowes, Donald Ralph geologist, educator
Bowie, John Hamilton chemistry educator
Box, Vernon George S. experimental and theoretical organic chemist, educator, researcher
Boyarchuk, Alexander A. astronomer
Boyarchuk, Kirill Alexandrovich physicist, researcher
Boyd, Derek Raymond organic chemistry educator
Boyd, Thomas James Morrow physicist
Boyer, Paul D. biochemist, educator
Boyle, Peter Howard chemistry lecturer
Bradbury, James Howard chemistry educator, researcher
Braddock, Joseph Vincent physicist
Bradford, Henry Francis neurochemistry educator

Bradford, Wesley Lamont *environmental scientist, consultant*
Bradley, Donal Donat Conor *physics educator, consultant*
Bradshaw, Alexander Marian *chemical physicist*
Bradshaw, Tony Kerry *chemistry educator*
Braese, Stefan *chemistry researcher, educator*
Braine, Raymond Germaine Marie Henri *chemistry educator*
Brainina, Khiena Zalmanovna *chemistry researcher*
Braithwaite, Wilfred John *physics educator*
Brandenburg, Albrecht *physicist, researcher*
Brandes, Tobias *theoretical physicist*
Brändström, Arne Elof *retired chemist*
Brandt, Oliver *physicist*
Branger, Hubert Vincent *oceanography researcher*
Brantley, Lee Reed *chemistry educator*
Brassington, Frederick Charles *hydrogeologist, consultant*
Bratman, Vladimir L'vovich *radiophysicist, physics educator*
Bratvold, Thomas Erik *physicist*
Braun, Tibor *chemist*
Braunstein, Samuel Leon *physicist*
Bravina, Svetlana Leonidovna *physicist, researcher*
Brazdes, Livia *medical physicist*
Brdička, Miroslav *retired physicist*
Breck, Howard Rolland *geophysicist*
Breedon, Richard *research physicist*
Bremner, John Barnard *chemistry educator*
Bressler, Barry Lee *theoretical physicist, systems analyst*
Briand, Frederic *environmental scientist*
Bribes, Jean-Luc *chemistry educator*
Bridger, Alison Frances Colvill *meteorologist, researcher, educator*
Bridgman, Howard Allen *environmental scientist, geography educator*
Briggs, George Andrew Davidson *materials science educator*
Brill, Michael Henry *physicist, vision scientist*
Brink, David Maurice *physicist*
Brink, Nils Erik *ecohydrologist*
Briskin, Madeleine *paleo-oceanographer, paleoclimatologist, micropaleontologist*
Brito, Adelson Silva de *physicist, educator, producer, entertainer*
Brito-Cruz, Carlos Henrique *physicist, researcher, science administrator*
Brizuela, Graciela Petra *chemical physics researcher*
Broca, Laurent Antoine *aerospace scientist*
Brockhouse, Bertram Neville *physicist, retired educator*
Brockhurst, Peter John *retired materials scientist*
Brodsky, Allen *radiological and health physicist, consultant*
Broekaert, Jose Alfons C. *chemistry educator*
Bronge, Christian Åke Olof *hydrology and climatology researcher*
Bronk, J(ohn) Ramsey *biochemistry educator*
Brookes, Hugh Clive *chemistry educator, researcher*
Brorson, Sverre Henning *biochemist*
Brosse, Jean-Claude *polymer chemistry educator, consultant, researcher*
Brown, Eric Joseph *chemist, educators*
Brown, Herbert Charles *chemistry educator*
Brown, Keith Spalding, Jr. *chemistry and ecology educator*
Brown, Michael Ewart *chemistry educator*
Brown, Richard Colin *physicist*
Brown, Ronald Drayton *chemistry educator*
Brown, Wyn *physical chemist, educator, researcher*
Browning, Keith Anthony *meteorology educator*
Brownlee, Donald Eugene, II *astronomer, educator*
Broyles, Michael Lee *geophysics and physics educator*
Bruce, Ian James *biochemist, researcher*
Bruce, Michael Ian *chemistry educator*
Bruce, Riitta Pia Kaarina *chemist*
Bruckner, Thomas Johann Christian *physicist, researcher*
Brueckner, Rolf Albert Otto *materials science educator, researcher*
Brusilovskij, Boris Arkadjevich *physicist*
Bruskin, Leonid Gregory *physicist, researcher, educator*
Bruss, Dagmar *physicist*
Bruynseraede, Yvan Julien *physics educator*
Bryknar, Zdenek *physics educator*
Bucala, Richard *biochemistry educator, immunologist*
Buch, Tomas *chemical physicist*
Buchanan, John Grant *chemistry educator*
Buchert, Thomas *cosmology educator*
Buck, Richard Pierson *chemistry educator, researcher*
Buckingham, Amyand David *chemistry educator*
Buckingham, Michael John *oceanography educator*
Bucur, Romulus Vasile *chemist*
Bucurescu, Dorel Amedeu *nuclear physicist*
Budnikov, Herman Constantinovich *chemistry educator, researcher*
Budrugeac, Petru *chemist, researcher, educator*
Budzikiewicz, Herbert M. A. *organic chemistry educator*
Buemi, Giuseppe *chemist, educator*
Builo, Sergey Ivanovich *physicist*
Buis, Patricia Frances *geology educator, researcher*
Bujarrabal, Valentin *astronomer*
Bujdosó, Georgette *biochemist, researcher, actor*
Bukin, Kirill Victorovich *geophysicist, educator*
Bukry, John David *geologist*
Bulanov, Sergei Vladimirovich *physicist, physics educator*
Bulman Page, Philip Charles *chemistry researcher*
Bumagin, Nikolay Alexandrovich *chemist*
Bunin, Mikhail Alekseevitch *physicist, researcher, educator*
Bunkov, Yuriy Michailovich *physicist*
Burbank, Robinson Derry *crystallographer*
Burczyk, Bogdan Wojciech *chemist, educator*
Burdyuzha, Vladimir Vladimirovich *astrophysicist*
Burge, Ronald Edgar *physics educator, consultant*
Bürgi, Hans-Beat *crystallography educator*
Burkhard, Dorothee J. M. *geology educator*
Burkin, Alfred Richard *extractive metallurgy educator*
Burkina, Rosa Semyonovna *physics educator*
Burnett, Jean Bullard (Mrs. James R. Burnett) *biochemist*
Burns, Douglas Alan *hydrologist*
Burri, Betty Jane *research chemist*
Burriel, Ramon *physicist, researcher*
Burrows, Philip Nicholas *physicist, researcher*
Bursa, Milan *geodesist educator*
Burton, Anthony David *environmental education consultant, writer*
Burukhin, Sergey Borisovitch *chemistry educator*
Buryan, Petr *chemical technology educator*
Burylev, Boris Petrovich *chemist, educator*
Bushuev, Vladimir Alekseevich *physics researcher*
Busson, Georges *geology educator*
Bustin, DuŠan *chemistry educator, academic administrator*
Butterworth, David *engineering consultant*
Buzea, Calin Gheorghe *physicist, researcher*
Byrdwell, William Craig *chemist, educator*
Cabeza, Javier Angel *chemistry educator*
Cabo Montes de Oca, Alejandro *physicist*
Cackovic, Hinko *physicist, researcher, artist*
Cafferata, Lazaro F.R. *chemistry educator, organic chemistry researcher*
Caglioti, Giuseppe *physicist, researcher*
Cahen, David *materials chemist, educator*
Cahn, Robert Wolfgang *physical metallurgist*
Cai, Weiping *physicist, material scientist*
Cai, Zhigang *physics educator, researcher*
Caldentey, Javier *biochemist, researcher*
Caldwell, Wallace Caughey *physicist, engineer*
Callaghan, Paul Terence *physicist, researcher*
Cameron, William Duncan *plastics company executive*
Cammenga, Heiko Karl *chemist, educator, consultant*
Campbell, Eleanor Elizabeth Bryce *chemical physicist, educator*
Campbell, George, Jr. *physicist, administrator*
Campbell, Jonathan Wesley *astrophysicist, aerospace engineer*
Campbell, Peter Nelson *biochemist*
Canas, José Antonio *physics educator*
Canestri, Franco *biophysicist, researcher*
Cao, Bisong *physics educator, researcher*
Cao, Fu Tian *physicist, educator*
Cao, Jinan *polymer scientist*
Cao, Wenji *chemist*
Cao, Zheng Yuan *mechanics and optics educator and researcher*
Čapek, Vladislav *physicist, educator*
Capella, Alphonse *physics researcher*
Cappiello, Achille *chemist, educator*
Cárabe, Julio *applied physicist, researcher*
Carbó-Dorca, Ramon *chemistry educator, researcher*
Carbognani, Lante Antonio *research chemist*
Cardone, Fabio *physicist*
Cardwell, David Anthony *physicist, educator*
Carey, Roy *physicist*
Carignan, Claude *astronomer, educator*
Carlow, John Sydney *research physicist, consultant*
Carlsmith, Roger Snedden *chemistry and energy conservation researcher*
Carmeli, Moshe *theoretical physicist*
Carmesin, Hans-Otto *physicist, educator*
Carneiro, Celso Del Ré *geology educator*
Carniani, Carlo *chemist*
Carrasquero, Armando *chemist, educator*
Carrington, Alan *chemistry educator*
Carter, William Harold, Sr. *physicist, researcher, electrical engineer*
Casalbuoni, Roberto *physics educator*
Casas, Alberto *physics educator*
Casati, Giulio *theoretical physics educator*
Casaubon, Juan Ignacio *physicist*
Case, Eldon Darrel *materials science educator*
Casella, Russell Carl *physicist*
Caselles, Vicente *physics educator*
Caser, Serge Joseph *physicist*
Cashion, John Dixon *physicist, educator*
Casiraghi, Giovanni *organic chemistry educator*
Cassar, JoAnn *stone conservation scientist, researcher*
Cássia-Moura, Rita De *biophysicist, educator, researcher*
Cassing, Wolfgang *physicist, researcher*
Castadeda-Sepulveda, Roman Eduardo *physicist*
Castano Pineda, Jorge Ivan *chemist*
Castellano, Joseph Anthony *chemist, management consulting firm executive*
Castro, Eduardo Alberto *theoretical chemist and educator*
Castro, Enrique Alfonso *chemist, educator, researcher*
Castro, Guillermo Raul *chemist and researcher*
Casu, Benito *biochemist*
Cata-Danil, Gheorghe *physicist*
Catalan, Cesar Atilio *chemistry educator*
Cataldo, Franco *chemist, researcher, educator*
Catoire, Valery *chemist, educator*
Cavalcanti, Solange Bessa *physicist, educator*
Cavallo, Francesca Romana *physicist*
Cavazza, William *geologist, educator*
Cech, Thomas Robert *chemistry and biochemistry educator*
Čejka, Jiří *chemist, researcher, museum director*
Celebi, Gurbuz *biophysics educator*
Celikel, Ayla *physicist, researcher, educator*
Celis, Julio Enrique *biochemist and educator*
Cerdà, A. *geologist, researcher*
Cerny, Radovan *physicist, researcher*
Çerny, Robert *physicist educator*
Çerny, Slavoj *physical chemist, researcher*
Červinka, Otakar *chemistry educator*
Cesari, Eduard *physics educator, materials science researcher*
Cetto, Ana Maria *physicist, researcher*
Chabrillat, Sabine *geophysicist, researcher*
Chacon, Graciela Gomez *chemistry educator, consultant*
Chadderton, Lewis Taylor *physicist, educator, researcher*
Chakrabarti, Bikas Kanta *nuclear physicist*
Chakraborty, Supriya *chemistry researcher*
Chalmers, John Murdo *vibrational spectroscopist, researcher*
Chama, Christopher Chambula *physical metallurgy educator, consultant*
Chamberlain, Owen *nuclear physicist*
Chambers, Donald Arthur *biochemistry and molecular medicine educator*
Chambolle, Thierry Jean-Francois *environmental scientist*
Chamis, Christos Constantinos *aerospace scientist, educator*
Champion, Kenneth Stanley Warner *physicist*
Chan, Andrew Yiu Chung *environmental scientist*
Chan, Paul S.L. *scientist, researcher*
Chandezon, Jean Gabriel *electromagnetism educator*
Chandra, Sulekh *chemist, educator*
Chandrasekharam, Dornadula *earth sciences educator*
Chang, Ching-jer *medicinal chemistry educator*
Chang, Ding-Kwo *biophysicist*
Chang, Leroy L. *physicist*
Chang, Ni-Bin *environmental pollution control educator*
Chang, Sam Shifeng *meteorologist*
Chang, Woong-Seong *metallurgist, researcher*
Chang, Yih *materials science educator, researcher*
Chang, Yoon-Young *geoenvironmentalist*
Chapman, Gilbert Bryant *physicist*
Chapman, Kenneth Maynard *retired workforce development specialist*
Charalambous, Stefanos *nuclear physics educator, laboratory director*
Charmandaris, Vassilis *astronomer*
Charnaya, Elena Vladimirovna *physics educator, researcher*
Charpak, Georges *physicist, nuclear scientist*
Charrier, Jacques Robert *materials educator*
Charvatova, Ivanka *geophysicist, astronomer*
Chatterjee, Smriti Narayan *biophysicist, researcher, educator*
Chatterjee, Tapan Kumar *astrophysics researcher*
Chatterjee, Udit *physics educator, researcher*
Chattopadhyay, Nitin *chemistry educator, researcher*
Chau, Foo-Tim *chemistry educator*
Chau, Hoi Fung *physicist, astrophysicist*
Chaudhary, Sujeet *physicist, research scientist*
Chaumba, Jefferson Brighton *geologist*
Chaves, Carlos Mauricio G.F. *physicist, educator, researcher*
Chaves, Wilson Luiz Caetano *metallurgist*
Chechin, Valery Andreevich *physicist*
Chekanov (Chakanau), Sergei Vladimirovich *physicist*
Cheltsov, Vladislav Feodorovits *physicist, theorist*
Chen, Changkang *physico-chemist, researcher*
Chen, Du-Xing *physicist*
Chen, I-Shin *physicist*
Chen, Jen-Ping *atmospheric sciences educator*
Chen, Jiabi *educator*
Chen, Ju-chin *oceanography educator*
Chen, Lin Xiang-Qun *chemist*
Chen, Mei-Lien *environmental studies educator*
Chen, Ming-Der *biochemist, researcher*
Chen, Robert Kuo-Cheng *environmental science educator, consultant*
Chen, Ruey-Hwa *biochemistry educator*
Chen, Shan-Tarng *physics educator*
Chen, Wen-Ping *astronomy educator*
Chen, Wenting *chemist*
Cheng, Cheanyeh *chemistry educator, researcher*
Cheng, Chuen Yan *biochemist, educator*
Cheng, Chunwei *physicist*
Cheng, Hsing-Hsien *biochemist, educator*
Cheng, Jin-Pei *chemistry educator, academic administrator*
Cheon, Il-Tong *physicist, educator*
Chepel, Vitaly Yurievich *physicist, researcher*
Cheremisin, Aleksander Alekseevich *physicist, educator*
Cherginets, Victor Leonidovitch *chemist, researcher*
Chermashentsev, Valerij Michailovich *chemist*
Chernenko, Vladimir Andreyevich *physicist, researcher, educator*
Cherniak, Saul Samuilovich *materials science educator*
Chernitskii, Alexander Aleksandrovich *physicist*
Chernogubovsky, Michael Alexandrovich *physicist, researcher*
Chernov, Stanislav *physicist*
Cherns, David *physicist, educator*
Chernyakov, Sergei Mikhailovich *physicist, researcher*
Chernykh, Valentin Petrovich *chemist, educator*
Chernyshev, Evgenii Andreevich *chemistry researcher, chemistry educator*
Cherry, Richard John *biophysicist*
Chesney, Antony *chemist, research scientist*
Chesnokova, Natalja Borisovna *biochemist*
Chester, Michael Alan *biochemist*
Cheung, Hee Tai Andrew *pharmaceutical chemistry educator, researcher*
Cheung, Man Ken *chemist, chemical engineer, educator*
Chevrolle, Françoise *chemist*
Cheynet de Beaupre, Bertrand Constantin *thermochemist, researcher*
Chi, Tong Chini *materials scientist*
Chiang, Albert Chinfa *polymer chemist*
Chiang, Kin Seng *optical physicist, engineering educator*
Chiarotti, Gianfranco *physics educator*
Chi-Chu, Lo *pesticide educator*
Chiew, Francis Hock Soon *hydrologist, researcher*
Chih, Chung-Ying *physicist, consultant*
Chin, Chi Chung *physicist, electrical engineer, researcher*
Ching, Shuk Chi Emily *physicist*
Chipara, Mircea *physicist*
Chirkin, Anatoly Stepanovich *physicist, educator*
Chiu, Yishu (Isu Kyu) *environmental educator, researcher*
Chivas, Allan Ross *geosciences, educator, research scientist*
Chlupáč, Ivo *geologist, paleontologist, educator*
Chmela, Pavel *physics educator, researcher*
Chmil, Vitaly Danilovich *chemist, researcher*
Cho, Yanglai *physicist*
Choe, Seungho *physicist, researcher*
Choh, Sung Ho *physics educator*
Choi, Sang Don *physics educator, researcher*
Chojnowski, Julian Jozef *chemist, educator*
Chong, Paul Joe *chemist*
Chopelas, Anastasia *geophysicist*
Chou, Jason Lucas *chemist, technology company executive*
Chou, Kuo-Chen *biophysical chemist*
Choudhury, Dilip Kumar *physicist, educator*
Choudhury, Namita Roy *polymer scientist, educator*
Chow, Celia Chung *physics educator*
Chow, Yuk-Tak *physicist, educator*
Christe, Karl Otto *research chemist*
Christensen, Per Rex *astrophysicist*
Christiaen, Hubert Georges T. *physics educator*
Christian, John Wyrill *metallurgy educator*
Christiansen, Erling N. *biochemist, educator*
Christoffel, David Alec *geophysicist, educator*
Chrysos, Michael George *physics educator, researcher*
Chu, Chung Kwang *medicinal chemistry educator*
Chu, Hsien-Kun *chemist, researcher*
Chu, Steven *physics educator*
Chua, James Hai-Joo *nuclear scientist*
Chubykalo, Andrew Evgenievich *physics researcher, educator*
Chukova, Yulia Petrovna *physicist*
Chung, Man Chin *medicinal chemistry educator, researcher*
Chuprina, Valentyna Grygoriyivna *physicist, researcher*
Churchill, Thomas John *broadcast meteorologist*
Cid, Consuelo *physicist, educator*
Cieslak-Golonka, Maria Teresa *chemist, educator*
Ciferri, Alberto *chemist, educator*
Cigna, Arrigo Angelo *physicist, consultant*
Cini, Marcello *physicist, educator*
Cini, Michele *physicist, educator*
Ciosek, Jerzy Feliks *physicist*
Ciufolini, Ignazio *physicist*
Ciugureanu, Constantin Teodor *chemistry educator, researcher*
Ciulli, Sorin *theoretical physicist, educator*
Clanet, Frank Emile *physicist, educator*
Claramma, Narivelil-Mathew *chemist*
Claramunt-Vallespi, Rosa Maria *chemistry educator*
Clare, Brian William *computational and medicinal chemist, researcher*
Clariá, Juan José *astrophysics researcher, educator*
Clark, Kenneth James *astronomer, educator*
Clarke, Adrienne Elizabeth *biochemist*
Clarke, Robert R. *biochemist, researcher*
Clarke, Ronald James *chemist, chemical engineer, consultant*
Clauberg, Rolf *physicist*
Clausen, Thomas Hans Wilhelm *chemist*
Clemens, Daniel *physicist*
Clemens, Peter Claus *physicist*
Clunies-Ross, Christopher Myles *environmental company executive*
Coecke, Bob *physics, mathematics and philosophy researcher*
Coffey, Helen Elizabeth *physicist*
Coffey, Mark William *theoretical physicist, applied mathematician*
Cognard, Jacques Jean *chemist*
Cohen, Philip *biochemistry educator*
Cohen, Stanley *biochemistry educator*
Cohen Addad, Jean-Pierre *physicist, educator*
Cohen-Tannoudji, Claude Nessim *physics educator*
Cohn, Daniel Ross *physicist*
Colacino, Michele *physicist*
Colbert, Edward James M. *astronomer*
Coldewey, Wilhelm Georg *geologist, educator*
Coleman, Paul Jerome, Jr. *physicist, educator*
Coles, Gerald Vivian *occupational hygienist*
Collins, David John *chemistry educator, researcher*
Collins, John Clements *physicist, educator*
Combes, Fransoise Marie *astronomer*
Combescure, Monique *physics researcher*
Compere, Pierre *retired psychologist*
Compton, Charles Daniel *chemistry educator*
Condé, Henri Paul Louis *retired physicist*
Conditt, Margaret Karen *scientist, policy analyst*
Condon, Francis Edward *retired chemistry educator*
Condrate, Robert Adam, Sr. *spectroscopy educator*
Connell, Desley William *chemist, educator, administrator*
Conoby, Joseph Francis *chemist*
Cook, Paul Fabyan *chemistry educator*
Cook, Peter John *geologist, foundation executive*
Cooper, Leon N. *physicist, educator*
Cooperstock, Fred Isaac *physics educator, researcher*
Coppens, Philip *chemist*
Coppin, Pol R. *spatial data sciences educator*
Cordani, Umberto Giuseppe *geosciences educator*
Cordeiro, Cecilia *chemist, educator*
Corey, Elias James *chemistry educator*
Corgier, Monique Marie-Claude *chemistry/biology educator*
Cornelia, Vasile *chemist, researcher*
Cornell, Hugh James *biochemist, researcher*
Cornet, Albert *physics educator*
Cornforth, Sir John Warcup *chemist*
Cornwall, John Michael *physics educator, consultant, researcher*
Corry, Charles Elmo *geophysicist, consultant*
Cortazar, Osvaldo Daniel *physicist, educator*
Cosandey, Maurice Roger *chemistry educator*
Cossa, Daniel Jacques *research oceanographer, educator*
Coste, Jean Georges *physicist*
Coster, Hans Gerard Leonard *biophysicist, educator*
Costes, Claude Roger *biochemistry educator, consultant*
Cotterill, Rodney Michael *biophysics researcher*
Cotton, Jean-Pierre Aimé *physicist*
Coughtrey, Peter John *environmental consultant*
Courtillot, Vincent Emmanuel *geophysics educator, consultant*
Courtin, Alfred *environmental management consultant*
Courty, Philippe Robert *chemist, petroleum association professional*
Coussement, Romain *physicist, educator*
Coutaz, Jean-Louis *optical sciences educator*
Couteau, Paul *astronomer*
Coutinho, Evans Clifton *chemist, educator, researcher*
Coutrot, Philippe *chemist, researcher*
Cowley, Stanley William Herbert *solar-planetary physics educator*
Cox, Robert Hames *chemist, scientific consultant*
Craciun, Constantin *geologist, researcher*
Craig, David Parker *retired chemistry educator*
Craig, Jonathan *petroleum geologist, researcher*
Cram, Donald James *chemistry educator*
Cronin, James Watson *physicist, educator*
Cronström, Christofer Eigeson *physicst, educator*
Crosby, Ian Travers *chemistry educator and researcher*
Cruickshank, Arthur Richard Ivor *paleontologist*
Cruikshank, Dale Paul *astronomer*
Crummett, Warren Berlin *analytical chemistry consultant*
Crutzen, Paul Josef *research meteorologist, chemist*
Cruz e Silva, Edgar Figueiredo *biochemist, researcher*
Csakvari, Bela *chemist*
Császár, Géza *geologist*
Csendes, Ernest *chemist, corporate and financial executive*
Csillag, Laszlo *physicist*
Csoregh, Ingeborg *crystallographer*
Csörgö, Tamás *physicist, researcher*
Cua-Christman, Florence Tansy *radiation and environmental protection consultant*
Cui, Fuzhai *materials scientist*
Culea, Monica *physics educator*
Cuney, Michel Louis *geologist, researcher*
Cunnigaipur, Anuradha Dhanasekaran *biochemist, researcher*
Curic, Mladjen B. *meteorology educator*
Curir, Anna *astronomer, researcher*
Curl, Robert Floyd, Jr. *chemistry educator*
Cutispoto, Giuseppe *astronomer*
Cutrone, Luigi Cutrone *chemist*
Cuypers, Johan Peter *physicist*
Cybulski, Zygmunt Alojzy *chemist, educator*
Czajkowski, Gerard Zygfryd *physicist, educator*
Czernilofsky, Armin Peter *biochemist*

Czernuszenko, Wlodzimierz environmental hydraulics professional
Czobor, Francisc chemist, researcher
Czochralska, Barbara chemist, researcher, educator
Czyzak, Stanley Joachim astronomy educator, researcher
Czyzewski, Jerzy Julian physicist
Dabbagh, Abdallah E. geology educator, research center administrator
Dadák, Vladimir Jan biochemistry educator
Daden, Bradley Francis geologist, petroleum engineer
Daehne, Lars Siegfried chemist
Daescu, Constantin chemist, educator
Dagar, Surender textile chemist
Dagaut, Philippe chemist, researcher
Dai, Jinxiang materials scientist, electrochemist
Dai, Le Rong chemistry educator
Dai, Li-xin chemistry researcher, educator
Dai, Zhenxue geologist, researcher, consultant
Dajani, Sami Wafa chemist, economist, consultant
Dakin, Vladimir Ivanovich radiation physics and chemistry researcher
Dale, Roger Graham physicist
Damay, Pierre Louis physics and chemistry educator
Damour, Thibault physicist
Dams, Richard chemistry educator, researcher
Dams, Rudolf research and development chemist
Dan, Douglas Kosloff geophysics educator
Dang, Nguyen Dinh physicist, painter
Daniewski, Wlodzimierz Maria chemistry educator, consultant
Danilov, Gennady Stepanovich physicist, researcher
Danko, Gene Andrew materials scientist
Daoud, Mohamed physicist
Darby, Barbara Ann-Lofthouse chemical technician
Darmanyan, Sergey research physicist
Darsey, Jerome Anthony chemistry educator, consultant
Das, Arabinda Kumar chemistry educator
Das, Baidya Nath physics educator, researcher
Das, Nachiketa geochemist, consultant
Das, Shankar Prasad physicist
Das, Subhajyoti hydrogeologist, consultant
Dasgupta, Goutam physics educator
Dasgupta, Samir scientist
Dasgupta, Tara Prasad chemistry educator
Dash, Madhab Chandra ecology educator
Dashevskii, Veniamin Yakovlevich scinetist/ metallurgist
Da Silva, Luis Fernando physicist and researcher
Dathe, Margitta Else Anna biophysicist, educator
Datka, Jerzy chemistry educator
Datta, K. P. metallurgist, materials scientist
Datta, Ramen metallurgist
Daub, Henrik Hannes biochemist, researcher
Daugherty, Kenneth Earl research company executive, educator
David, Pathikulangara Joseph physicist, researcher
David, Serge Michel chemistry educator
Davídek, Jiří chemistry educator
Davidson, Donald Allen environmental sciences educator
Davidson, Ernest Roy chemist, educator
Davidson, Ronald Crosby physicist, educator
Davier, Michel physicist, educator
Davies, Huw Cathan physicist, educator
Davies, Merton Edward planetary scientist
Davies, Noel William chemist, researcher
Davies, Roger geoscience educator
Davis, Jeremy Matthew chemist
Davis, Richard Lee chemist
Dawe, Richard Alan reservoir physics educator, petroleum engineering, educator, researcher
Dawicki, Doloretta Diane research biochemist, educator
Dawson, James Clifford environmental science educator, geologist
Day, John H. physicist
Dazlich, Donald Anthony, Jr. atmospheric science researcher
Deacon, Nigel chemistry educator, researcher
De Almeida, Wagner Batista chemistry educator, researcher
Dean, John Aurie chemist, author, chemistry educator emeritus
Dean, John Francis astronomer, researcher
De Angelis, Francesco chemistry educator, consultant
De Arruda Campos, Ivan Persio chemist, educator, researcher
de Bettignies, Bertin Jean-Marie chemistry educator
de Biasi, Ronaldo Sergio materials science educator
Debney, George C. mathematical physicist
de Boer, Fokke Wander Nicolaas physicist, researcher
de Certaines, Jacques Donald biophysicist
Decker, Christian Lucien research chemist
Deco, Gustavo Ricardo physicist, computer scientist
de Cosmo, Vittorio physicist
de Duve, Christian René chemist, educator
Deelstra, Hendrik Andries chemistry educator
DeFacio, W. Brian theoretical physicist
De Flora, Antonio Cesare biochemistry educator
de Gennes, Pierre-Gilles physicist, educator
Deghenghi, Romano chemist
DeGraffenried, John Willie chemist, researcher
De Groot, Paul Franciscus geophysicist
de Groot, Rudolf Steven environmentalist
Dehareng, Dominique chemist, researcher
Dehmelt, Hans Georg physicist
Deisenhofer, Johann biochemistry educator, researcher
Deiss, Erich chemistry and physics researcher
de Jager, Cornelis retired astronomer
de Jongh, Wilhelmus Karel (Willy K. de Jongh) physicist
Deka, Dibakar Chandra organic chemist, educator
Deka, Suresh microbiologist, educator
De Keukeleire, Denis chemist
Dekhtyar, Yuri David physicist, biophysicist
Dekker, David Lindsay geophysicist
de Koning, Charles Bernard chemistry educator, researcher
De la Lanza Espino, Guadalupe chemist, researcher
Delanghe, Joris Richard chemistry educator
De La Peña, Luis Auerbach physicist, educator
Delbeke, Frans T.M.C. chemistry educator
Delbourgo, Robert physics educator
Delibasis, Nicholas Demetrius geoscientist
Delion, Doru Sabin physicist
Dellagiarino, George Francis geologist
Della Valle, Francesco chemist
Delli Colli, Humbert Thomas chemist, product development specialist
Delmas, Michel Pierre chemist, educator, researcher
Delmon, Bernard chemistry educator
del Moral, Agustín physics educator, researcher
De Los Santos, Hector José solid state device scientist, researcher
Demacker, Pierre Nicolaas biochemist, researcher
De Marco, Roland chemistry educator
De Mello, Fernando Garcia biophysics educator, researcher
Demény, Attila geologist, researcher
Demetriades, Alecos geologist, geochemist, researcher
Demidenko, Serge Nikolayevich electronics educator, research manager
Demin, Dmitry L'vovich physics experimentalist, educator
Demjanenko, Milos physical chemistry researcher, consultant
Demoli, Nazif physicist, researcher
deMonsabert, Winston Russel chemist, consultant
De Morais, Paulo César physics educator, researcher
Demoulin, Pascal Noel astronomer
Demyanov, Sergey Evgenievich physicist, researcher
De Napoli, Lorenzo chemistry educator, researcher
De Neijs, Eduard Otto physicist
Deng, Min materials scientist
Deng, Zhaojing physics educator
Dengel, Ottmar Hubert physicist
Dengiz, Murat physics engineer, consultant
Deniard, Philippe Andre chemist, researcher
Denisov, Evguenii Timofeevich chemist
Deo, Brahma metallurgist, educator
Dera, Jerzy physics educator
De Ranter, Camiel Joseph chemist, educator
Dergunov, Alexander Dmitrievich biophysicist, researcher
Dergunov, Yuziy Ivanovich chemist, educator
DeRose, Paul Christian research chemist
DerVartanian, Daniel Vartan biochemistry educator
Derzhko, Oleg Volodymyrovych physicist, educator
Desai, Mahesh Dahyabhai geotechnologist, consultant
Desbrieres, Jacques chemistry educator, researcher
Descotes, Gérard Louis organic chemistry educator
De Silva, Handunnetti Sakuntala V. physicist
De Silva, Kuruneruge Tuley Dayanand chemist, educator
Desmurs, Jean Roger chemist, researcher
Desoize, Bernard biochemistry and molecular biology educator
Dessler, Alexander Jack space physics and astronomy educator, scientist
Detert, Miriam Anne chemical analyst
Deutsch, Claude David physicist, educator
Deutsch, Tibor Ivan chemist, researcher
Devanarayanan, Sankaranarayanan physics educator
Deviatkin, Evgeny Aleksandrovich physicist, researcher
Devínsky, Ferdinand chemist, educator
Devreese, Jozef Theofiel physicist, researcher
De Wachter, Rupert biochemical scientist
Dewar, Robert Leith research physicist, educator
Dewey, John F. geologist, educator
De With, Gijsbertus materials science educator
Dey, Kamalendu chemistry educator
Dey, Nibaran Chandra chemist
de Zeeuw, Pieter Timotheus astronomer
Dezhu, Wu chemist
Dhamelincourt, Paul Andre chemistry educator, researcher
Dharmaprakash, Sampyady Medappa physics educator
Dhoble, Nirupama Sanjay science educator, researcher
Dhoble, Sanjay Janraoji physics educator
Diamandescu, Lucian Constantin physicist, researcher
Dibo, Gabor chemist
Dick, Wolfgang Rudolf scientist
Didukh, Leonid Dmytrovych physicist, educator
Dieny, Bernard physicist
Dietrich, Klaus physicist, educator
di Jeso, Duke don Fernando biochemistry educator
Dikarev, Boris Nikolaevich physicist, educator
Dikovski, Vladlen physicist, researcher
di Lauro, Carlo physical chemistry educator, researcher
Dils, Raymond Ronald biochemistry educator
Dimitriou, Petros Panagiotis seismologist
Dimoglo, Anatoly Serafimovich chemistry researcher
Dimotakis, Paul Nicholas chemistry educator, researcher
Dinariev, Oleg Jurievich physicist
Dinesen, Lars Lundgard environmental consultant
Dineva-Vladikova, Petia Simeonova physicist, researcher
Ding, Dajun physicist, educator
Dingwell, Donald Bruce geoscientist, educator
Dinkova-Kostova, Albena Todorova biochemist
Dintcheva, Nadka Tzankova physicist, engineer, researcher
Dionne, Gerald Francis research physicist, educator, consultant
Diósi, Lajos physicist
Ditrói-Puskás, Zuárd geologist, educator
Dittberner, Gerald John meteorologist, space scientist, engineer
Divin, Yuri Y. physicist
Djabourov, Madeleine Daria physicist educator
Djakovic-Sekulic, Tatjana Ljubomir chemistry educator
Djavadi-Ohaniance, Lisa biochemist, researcher
Dmitriev, Sergey physicist
Dnestrovskij, Yurij Nicolaevich physicist, scientist, educator
Do, Giu Dang physicist, researcher
Dobrian, Anca Dana E. biochemist, researcher
Dobrzynski, Leonard physics researcher
Dobrzyński, Ludwik Roman physicist
Dobson, John Francis physics educator, researcher
Dodd, Robert Hugh medicinal chemistry researcher
Dodge, Clifford Howle geologist
Dodonov, Victor Vasilievich physicist, educator
Doe, Hidekazu chemistry educator
Doerre, Werner Heinz physicist
Dojahn, Julie Goodman chemist, educator
Dojlido, Jan Ryszard hydrochemist, educator
Doktorov, Alexander Borisovich physicist, researcher, educator
Dokuchaev, Vladimir Platonovich physicist, educator
Dolan, Louise Ann physicist
Dolenko, George Nikolaevich physicist
Dolezal, Ladislav biophysicist
Dolgoborodov, Alexander Yurievich chemical physicist, research scientist
Dollfus, Audouin Charles astronomer
Dolmatov, Valeriy Konstantinovich physicist, researcher
Dolocan, Voicu Dragomir physics educator, researcher
Domingos, Joaquim Maria physics educator, researcher, retired
Dominguez, Cesáreo Augusto physicist, educator
Domonkos, Jenő biochemist, researcher
Donahue, Thomas Michael physics educator
Donald, Athene Margaret physicist educator
Dondo, Eliakim Arackha water purification director, consultant
Donhoffer, Dieter Karl physicist
Donin, Valery Il'ych physicist, researcher
Donlon, Craig James oceanographer, researcher
Donnelly, Russell James physicist, educator
Donnet, Jean Baptiste physical chemist, educator, consultant
Donth, Ernst-Joachim physicist, educator
Donya, Alexander polymer chemist, educator
Doong, Ruey-An research chemist
d'Oreye de Lantremange, Nicolas Frederic physicist, researcher
Dorland, Elizabeth M. chemistry educator
Doroshenko, Tatyana Fyodorovna chemistr, researcher
Dorozhkin, Sergey Veniaminovich chemistry researcher
Dos Santos, Carlos Alberto physics educator
Dou, Kai physicist
Dou, Wenbin millimeter wave researcher, educator
Douillet-Breuil, Anne-Céline biochemistry researcher
Dow, John Davis physicist
Doweidar, Hamdy Doweidar physics educator, researcher
Downs, Hartley H., III chemist
Drabant, Bernhard mathematical physicist, researcher
Dragoun, Otokar physicist, researcher
Drake, Richard Paul physicist, educator
Drawin, Hans-Werner physicist
Drchal, Vaclav physicist, researcher
Drebushchak, Valeri Anatolievich physicist, researcher
Dreischuh, Alexander Alexandrov physics educator, researcher
Drescher, Kurt Walter physicist, educator
Dreyfuss, Patricia chemist, researcher
Drobyshev, Anatoly Ivanovich chemist, educator
Druker, Alexandru-Erminiu physicist, researcher
Dryga, Alexander Iosifovitsch physicist
Dryzek, Jerzy physicist, researcher
Du, Tengda researcher, engineer, physicist
Duan, Taizhong petroleum geologist, educator
Duatti, Adriano chemist, radiochemist
Dubief, Jean climatologist
Dubochet, Jacques biophysics educator
Dubois, Jacques-Emile chemistry and information science educator, researcher
Dubovski, Boris Grigorij nuclear physicist
Duburs, Gunars chemist
Ducháček, Vratislav chemistry educator
Duclohier, Hervé Pierre biophysicist
Duda, Seweryn Jozef geophysicist, educator
Dudkowiak, Alina physicist, researcher, educator
Dudnikov, Vadim G. physicist, researcher
Duff, Michael James physicist
Dugaev, Vitalii Konstantinovich physicist, researcher
Dugdale, John Sydney retired physics educator
Dumitrescu, Michel Paul aerospace researcher
Dumitru, Rodica Stănescu chemist, researcher
Duncan, Robert Allan astronomer
Dunn, Horton, Jr. organic chemist
Duplij, Stepan Anatolievich physicist, researcher
Duque, Ricardo German analytical chemist
Durand-Delga, Michel geologist, educator
Durbin, Thomas D. physicist
Durieux, Eric environmentalist
Durieux, Sylvain materials science researcher, educator
Durlu, Tahsin Nuri physics educator
Durrant, Steven Frederick physicist, chemist
Durrer, Ruth theoretical physicist
Durup, Jean physical chemistry educator
Dusane, Rajiv Onkar materials science educator, researcher
Dusatko, Drahomir geodesist, researcher
Dušek, Karel macromolecular chemist
Dušek, Miloslav physicist, researcher
Dutta, Anand Swaroop medicinal chemist, pharmaceutical researcher
Dutta, Naba Kumar polymer scientist, educator
Duveneck, Gert Ludwig physicist
Duysens, Louis N.M. biophysicist
Düzbastilar, Musa Kazim micropaleontologist, marine scientist, researcher
Dvoeglazov, Valeri Vladimirovich physicist, educator
Dvurechenskaya, Serafima Yakovlevna chemist
Dvurechenskii, Anatoly Vasil'evich physicist
Dwiggins, Claudius William, Jr. chemist
Dwivedi, Upendra Nath biochemistry educator
Dworzanski, Jacek Pawel analytical biochemist, researcher
Dyachenko, Peter physicist, researcher
Dyachenko, Vladimir Danylovich chemistry educator
Dyadkin, Yuriy Dmitrievich earth sciences educator
Dybczynski, Rajmund Stanislaw chemistry educator
Dye, James Louis chemistry educator
Dyer, Alan chemist, educator
Dymicky, Michael retired chemist
Dymnikova, Irina physicist
Dypvik, Henning geologist, educator
Dyson, Norman Allen physicist, educator
Dyson, Peter Lawrence physicist, educator
Dzido, Tadeusz Henryk chemist, educator
Dzuba, Vladimir Andreyevich physicist, researcher
Dzyaloshinskii, Igor Ekhielievich physicist
Dzyublik, Alexey Yaroslav physicist, physics educator
Eaker, David Leslie biochemist, educator
Eastoe, John Eric chemist
Eaton, Gordon Pryor geologist
Ebisuzaki, Yukiko retired chemistry educator
Echenique, Pedro Miguel physicist, educator
Eckolt, Klaus Rudolf physicist
Economou, Anastasios chemist, researcher
Edelman, Gerald Maurice biochemist, neuroscientist, educator
Edet, Aniekan Effiom geologist
Edge, David Owen science educator
Edgell, Henry Stewart geologist, educator
Edwards, Sir Samuel Frederick physicist, educator
Eerkens, Jeff W. nuclear scientist, laser engineer, educator
Efimov, Alexander Vasilievich chemist
Efimov, Andrei Markovich spectroscopist, researcher
Efremov, Anatoli Vasilievich physicist
Efremov, Roman Gerbertovich biophysicist, researcher
Efremova, Slava Viktorovna geologist, petrologist, researcher
Efros, Victor Danilovich physicist researcher
Egeland, Einar Skarstad organic chemist, researcher
Eggleston, Gillian research chemist, scientist
Eghbal, Morad geologist, lawyer
Egloff, Julius, III geologist
Egolf, Peter William physicist
Egorov, Vladimir Valentinovich theoretical physicist, researcher
Egorov, Vladislav Victorovitch chemist, researcher
Egry, Ivan Tamas physics educator
Ehnholm, Paul Christian biochemistry educator
Ehrenfreund, Pascale astrochemist
Ehrenstorfer, Siegmund Albert chemist, consultant
Ehrlich, Charles David physicist
Eichel, Rüdiger-Albert physicist, researcher
Eichhorn, Gunther Louis chemist
Eichler, David Steven physics educator
Eiderman, Boris Alexandrovich scientist, researcher
Eigen, Manfred physicist
Einaga, Yoshiyuki chemist
Eisenberg, Adi chemist
Ekambaram, Rajasekaran chemist, researcher
Ekblad, Ulf Staffan physicist, researcher
Ekdawi, Nagi chemist, researcher
Ekkundi, Vadiraj Subbanna chemist, researcher
Ekpo, Bassey Offiong environmental educator, researcher, consultant
Eksperiandova, Ljudmila Petrovna chemistry researcher
Ekvall, Tomas Ingemar environmental scientist, consultant
El-Adawi, Mohamed Abdelhady Kamel Baumy physicist, educator
Elagöz, Sezai physicist
El-Amri, Fathi Ali chemistry educator
El-Bahrawi, Mohammed El-Sayed physics educator, researcher
Elemes, Yiannis Eyaggelos chemistry educator, researcher
Elgavish, Gabriel Andreas physical biochemistry educator
Elhaddad, Mervet Ahmed mineralogy educator
Elizalde, Emilio mathematical physicist
Elizarov, Alexander Ivanovich physicist, researcher, educator
Elkomoss, Sabry Gobran physicist
Elling, Lothar biochemist, researcher
Ellis, Emory Leon retired biochemist
Ellis, George Francis Rayner astronomy educator
Ellis, John Heywood materials testing specialist
El Masri, Youssef M.I. nuclear physicist
Elodi, Pál biochemist, educator
El-Saied, Houssni Ali Mohamed chemist, educator, researcher
El-Sakhawy, Mohamed Mohamed Ahmed chemist, researcher
El-Sayed, Emad chemistry educator
El-Shennawy, Khamies Mohammed physical science educator
Elste, Guenther Heino Erich astrophysicist
El-Tawil, Samir Zaky metallurgist, educator, researcher
Emandi, Ana chemist
Emelchenko, Gennadi Anatol'evich physicist, researcher
Emelyanov, Alexander Alexandrovitch physicist, researcher
Emerson, Cherry Logan retired chemist
Emmanuel, Bosco chemistry researcher
Emons, Hans-Heinz chemist
Emtsev, Vadim Valentinovich physicist, researcher
Encinas San Martin, Juan Pablo microbiologist, research
Endacott, John Brendan chemist
Endale, Tamrat geophysicist, educator
Endo, Tamio engineering physicist, educator
Endrys, Jiri chemistry researcher
Engeland, Uwe physicist
Engelhardt, Rolf-Udo chemistry educator
Engle, Susan Ann chemist
English, Bruce Vaughan environmental consultant
Entsch, Barrie biochemist, molecular biologist
Epikhin, Vyacheslav Mikhailovich physicist, researcher
Eppelbaum, Lev Vilen geophysicist, researcher, educator
Erbatur, Oktay chemistry educator
Erbil, Husnu Yildirim surface and polymer physical chemist, researcher
Erdelyi-Toth, Valerie Agatha chemist, reseacher
Erdmann, Wlodzimierz Stefan biomechanist, researcher
Eremeev, Igor Petrovich physicist, researcher
Ergenzinger, Klaus physicist
Ericson, Magda Vera physicist
Erlanger, Bernard Ferdinand biochemist, educator
Erlykin, Anatoly Dmitrievich physicist
Ernst, Richard Robert chemist, educator
Eröss, Klára chemistry educator, researcher
Erostyak, Janos physicist
Eryomin, Alexander Nikolaevich bio-organic chemistry researcher
Esaki, Leo physicist, foundation executive
Escalante-Ramirez, Vladimir astronomer
Eschenmoser, Albert chemist
Eshel, Re'uven researcher, mechanical engineering educator
Eškinja, Ivan chemistry educator
Eskov, Alexei Grigorevich physicist
Esposito, Larry Wayne planetary astronomer
Esselbach, Matthias physicist
Esser, Franz Martin chemist
Essex, Elizabeth Annette physicist, researcher
Estefan, Selim Fahmy chemistry educator
Estrin, Emmanuil Isaakovich physicist
Eto, Morifusa chemistry educator
Euthymtou, Paraskevi physics educator
Evans, Billy Joe chemistry educator, consultant
Evans, Morgan D. physicist
Evans, Myron Wyn physicist
Evesque, Pierre Henri physics researcher
Evgeny, Pozhidaev physical chemistry educator, university dean
Evseeva, Lyudmila Evgeniyevna physicist, researcher
Ewen, H.I. physicist
Exner, Otto chemist
Exner, Pavel Vladimir physicist, researcher, educator
Ezeanyika, Lawrence Uchenna Sunday biochemistry educator
Ezeonu, Francis Chukwuemeka biochemist, educator
Ezerskaya, Elena Vladimirovna physicist
Fábián, István chemist, educator
Fabre, Claude P. physicist, researcher, educator
Fabrikesi, Eugenia-Theodora physicist
Fadnavis, Nitin Wasantrao chemist, researcher
Fadner, Willard Lee physics educator, researcher
Fagan, Ciaran Pius biochemist, educator
Faggiani, Sergio Maria physics educator
Fahmy, Sherif Medhat chemist, educator

PROFESSIONAL INDEX 2607 SCIENCE: PHYSICAL SCIENCE

Faifman, Mark Petrovich physicist, researcher
Fair, Kimberly Rollins chemist
Fairall, Anthony Patrick astronomer, planetarium director, writer
Fairbridge, Rhodes Wo. geologist, educator
Fairhead, James Derek geophysics educator, university director
Faisal, Farhad physics educator
Faissner, Helmut Carl physics educator
Faiz, Mohamed M. physicist, researcher
Falk, Heinz organic chemistry educator
Falkowski, Theresa Gae chemistry educator
Fan, Z. Hugh chemist, biomedical engineer
Fang, Remi (Rong Fang) physicist, educator
Fang, Yun-Zhong biochemist, educator
Fang, Zhenhe physics educator, academic administrator
Fara, Laurentiu Vladimir physics educator, researcher
Farag, Radwan Sedkey chemist, educator
Farias, Robson Fernandes de chemistry educator
Farooq, Afgan chemistry educator, researcher
Farré, Jean Antoine physical science educator
Fathauer, Theodore Frederick meteorologist
Faulkner, Donald Jack astronomer
Faulques, Eric Claude physicist, researcher
Fauser, Bertfried physicist, researcher
Faust, William Roscoe physicist
Fausto, Rui chemistry educator, researcher
Faustov, Rudolf Nikolaevich theoretical physicist, researcher
Favors, Willie James chemist
Fawcett, Brian Charles atomic physicist, researcher
Fayard, Thierry Hubert radio astronomy engineer, inventor
Fayzilberg, Emanuil physicist
Feast, Michael William astronomer, researcher
Fedorenko, Olga A. physicist
Fedorowski, Jerzy Andrzej paleontology educator, university official
Fedulina, Tatiana Germanovna chemist
Fei, Minrui automation educator
Feinstein, Alejandro astronomer educator
Fejfar, Antonin physicist
Feklisova, Olga Vladimirovna physicist, researcher
Felcman, Judith chemistry educator
Feldman, Eduard Benjaminovich chemical physicist, researcher
Feldtkeller, Ernst (Johannes) retired solid-state physicist
Felix, Julian physicist, educator
Feller, Winthrop Bruce physicist
Felton, Samuel Page biochemist
Fend, Thomas physicist
Feng, Qi-yuan physicist, educator, researcher
Feng, Wenqing physicist
Feng, Xiangdong (Shawn) (Shawn Feng) chemist
Feng, You-Min biochemist, researcher
Fényes, Tibor retired nuclear physicist
Feofilov, Grigori Alexandrovitch physicist, researcher
Ferber, Robert Rudolf physics researcher, educator, science administrator
Fergusson, David Andrew Napier ethicist, physician
Feringa, Ben Lucas chemist, educator
Ferlan, Igor biochemist
Fernández, Jorge Eduardo radiation physicist
Fernández, Julio Angel astronomer, educator
Fernandez-Prini, Roberto José chemist
Ferrara, Sergio physicist, educator
Ferrari, Attilio astronomy educator
Ferrari, Leonardo physics educator, researcher
Ferrari, Luca geologist, researcher
Ferretti, Gabriele physicist
Ferreyra, Elida Virginia Cignoli de chemistry researcher
Ferrier, Joseph John atmospheric physicist
Fetisova, Zoya Grigorievna physicist
Feughelman, Max biophysicist
Fezia, Corrado chemist
Ficker, Tomáš physics educator
Figadere, Bruno Alain Marie chemist, educator
Figgis, Brian Norman chemistry educator
Filakovsky, Karol aerodynamics educator, researcher
Filatova, Nadezhda Ivanovna geologist, laboratory administrator, researcher
Filevich, Alberto physicist, researcher, educator
Filip, Henry (Henry Petrzilka) physicist
Filippov, Boris astrophysicist
Filippov, Gennadiy Mikhailovich physicist, educator
Fillaux, Francois Joseph research chemist
Filonov, Michail Rudolf chemist, researcher
Fimreite, Norvald environmental science educator
Fincher, Geoffrey Bruce biochemist
Findley, Gary Lee chemistry educator
Finet, Jean-Pierre Bernard chemist, researcher
Fink, Anthony Lawrence chemistry educator, researcher
Fink, James Brewster geophysicist, consultant
Fink, Jörg Hermann physicist, educator
Finkel, Federico physicist, educator
Finkel, Vitaly Alexandrovich physicist, researcher, educator
Finks, Robert Melvin paleontologist, educator
Finnis, Michael William physics educator
Fišar, Zdenek biophysicist, researcher
Fischer, Edmond Henri biochemistry educator
Fischer, Ernst Otto chemist, educator
Fischer, Fred Walter physicist, engineer, educator
Fischer, Jan Marie Cyril physicist
Fischer, Wolfgang Bernd chemist
Fisher, Charles Harold chemistry educator, researcher
Fisher, Peter physics educator
Fisun, Oleg Ivanovich physicist
Fitch, Val Logsdon physics educator
Fiziev, Plamen Petkov theoretical physics educator
Flandrois, Serge Eugene chemist
Flatté, Stanley Martin physicist, educator
Fleming, Ian chemistry educator, researcher
Flemming, Gunther meteorologist
Flerov, Vladimir Ilja physicist, researcher
Fletcher, Neville Horner physicist
Floratos, Emmanuel physicist
Florey, André Bernard chemical laboratory administrator, consultant
Florez, Juan Bautista physics educator
Floris, Frans geoscientist
Fodor, Gábor Béla chemistry educator, researcher
Föger, Karl chemistry scientist
Foglizzo, Thierry Nicolas astrophysicist
Földes, Enikö chemist
Földes, István B. physicist, researcher
Folke, Jens chemist, consultant, educator
Fomel, Boris Mark physicist, consultant
Fomin, Valery Prokopievich astrophysicist
Fomin, Vladimir Mikhailovich physicist, researcher, educator
Fonseca, Jose Luis Cardozo chemistry educator, researcher
Fontana, Josi Domingos scientist, educator
Fookes, Peter George engineering geologist, educator
Foote, Nathan Maxted retired physical science educator
Ford, Kenneth William physicist
Formánek, Jiří physicist, educator
Formoli, Tareq Ahmad environmental research scientist, consultant
Forshaw, Jeffrey Robert physics educator, researcher
Forslind, Bo biophysicist, educator
Forssell-Aronsson, Eva Birgitta physicist, researcher
Fortelny, Ivan polymer physicist
Fortey, Richard Alan paleontologist
Fortner, Rosanne White environmental science educator
Fortov, Vladimir E. physicist, researcher
Fortunato, Mario David Cardoso scientific researcher
Fossel, Eric Thor medical biophysicist
Fottrell, Patrick biochemistry educator, university president
Foulke, Judith Diane health physicist
Fournier, Josette chemistry educator
Fowler, Scott Wellington biological oceanographer
Fragoulis, Emmanuel George biochemistry educator
Fraissard, Jacques Paul chemistry educator, researcher
Franco, Jose astrophysicist, researcher
Franconi, Florence physicist
Frank, Alejandro physicist, educator
Frank, Anna Glebovna physicist, researcher
Frank, Hartmut Gottlieb chemistry educator, environmental scientist
Frank, Ronald chemist, researcher
Franke, Rainer Siegfried biochemist
Frankevich, Eugene Leonidovich molecular physics educator, researcher
Frauenkron, Helge physicist
Freeman, John Clinton meteorologist, oceanographer
Freese, Katherine physicist, educator
Freiherr zu Putlitz, Gisbert physics educator, foundation executive
Freiwald, David Allen physicist, mechanical engineer
Frenk, Carlos Silvestre physics educator, consultant
Frenkel, Peter chemist
Freund, Hans-Joachim physical chemist
Frey, Andreas biochemist, researcher
Frey, Holger chemistry educator, researcher
Friedel, Jacques physics educator
Friedl, Peter biochemist
Friedl, Randall Raymond environmental scientist
Friedman, Gerald Manfred geologist, educator
Friedman, Jerome Isaac physics educator, researcher
Friedrich, Fabian biochemist
Frimmel, Hartwig Egbert geologist, educator, researcher
Fritsch, Albert Joseph director environmental demonstration center
Fritzsche, Hartmut biophysical chemist, educator
Froehlich, Wojciech Antoni geomorphologist, researcher
Frojdh, Per Anders theoretical physics educator
Frolov, Sergei Vladimirovich physicist, educator, researcher
Frolov, Vladimir Alexandrovich physicist
Frumkin, Amos Alexander geomorphologist, educator
Fu, Baopu meteorology educator, researcher
Fu, Shoukuan polymer chemist, educator
Fu, Xiao Yuan chemistry educator, researcher
Fuchs, Owen George chemist
Fuentes, Nestor Osvaldo physicist, researcher
Fuhrer, Thomas chemist, educator
Fuhs, G(eorg) Wolfgang environmental research manager
Fujii, Minoru physicist, researcher
Fujii, Toshihiro chemistry educator, researcher
Fujimoto, Masatoshi physicist, researcher
Fujino, Takeo solid state chemistry educator
Fujinoki, Akira chemist, laboratory manager
Fujioka, Manabu nuclear physics researcher and educator
Fujisaki, Haruo physicist
Fujisawa, Akihide physicist
Fujita, Miho chemistry educator, researcher
Fujita, Toshio chemist, researcher
Fujita, Yoshio astronomer
Fukada, Eiichi physicist, researcher
Fuks, Robert chemistry educator
Fuksman, Irma Ludvigovna chemist
Fukuda, Atsuo physicist, materials science researcher
Fukuzawa, Kenji physicist
Fukuzumi, Kazuo fats chemist
Fulco, Armand John biochemist
Funayama, Shinji chemist, educator
Funck-Brentano, Christian Jacques physician, researcher
Fung, Kwok Wing Sherman chemist
Funk, Christiane biochemistry educator, researcher
Furda, Ivan chemist, consultant
Furer, Victor Lvovich physicist, educator, researcher
Furic, Miroslav physics educator
Furman, Gregory Borisovich physicist, educator, researcher
Furrer, Albert Fridolin physicist, researcher, educator
Furrer, Patrick Bernard biophysicist, consultant
Futrell, Jean H. research scientist, administrator, educator
Füzes, Iván biophysicist, researcher
Fyodorov, Anatoly Andreewich chemist
Fyodorov, Yan V. theoretical and mathematical physicist, educator
Gaardhoje, Jens Jorgen physics educator, researcher
Gabel, Connie chemistry educator
Gabovich, Alexander Markovich physicist, researcher
Gabr, Yousry Ahmed biochemistry educator, consultant
Gadiyak, Grigorii V. physicist
Gadjieva, Riza Magomedovna physicist, researcher
Gainutdinov, Khalil Latypovich physicist, researcher
Gairola, Suresh Chandra physics educator, researcher
Gait, Michael John biochemist
Gal, Yeong Soon chemistry educator
Galatenko, Nataliya chemist
Galaz, Gaspar Antonio astronomer
Galkin, Nickolay Gennadiy physicist, educator, researcher
Gallardo Lancho, Juan Fernando biogeochemist, soil science educator, ecologist
Gallego, Stephane scientist, consultant
Galloway, Eilene Marie space and astronautics consultant
Galper, Alexander Rem physicist, researcher
Galperin, Yuri Ilich physics educator
Gamarnik, Moisey Yankelevich solid state physicist
Gamba, Zulema Beatriz chemical physics researcher, educator
Gan, Wei-Qun physicist
Gancherenok, Igor Ivanovich physicist, educator, researcher
Gandy, James Thomas meteorologist, entrepreneur
Ganguly, Ashit Kumar organic chemist
Ganguly, Gautam materials scientist, research administrator
Gantla, Vidyasagar Reddy chemist
Ganugapati, Subba Rao Sree Rama organic chemist educator, researcher
Gao, Hua materials science researcher, educator
Gao, Lingbiao physics educator, researcher
Gao, Vincent Chun Xin chemist, researcher
Gao, Yingjun physicist
Gao, Zhiqiang chemistry educator
Gaponenko, Sergei Vasilevich physicist, researcher
Garab, Győző biophysicist
Garbar, Isaac Joseph physicist, researcher, educator
Garbayo, Ines chemist
Garcia-Bach, Maria Angels physicist, educator, researcher
García Gómez, Antonio oceanographer
Garecki, Janusz mathematical and theoretical physics educator
Garmanov, Maksim Evgenievich electrochemist
Garnovskii, Alexander Dmitrievich chemist, academic administrator
Garr, Cheryl Denise research chemist
Garrett, Charles Geoffrey Blythe physicist
Garrett, Thomas Monroe chemist
Gartz, Jochen Ernst Friedrich chemist, mycologist
Gaspar, Vilmos Zoltan chemistry educator
Gasperini, Maurizio physicist
Gassan-zade, Salim Gulerzaevich physicist, researcher
Gatinsky, Yury George geologist, researcher
Gatt, Shimon biochemistry educator
Gatt, Suzanna physics educator
Gattupalli, Nareshkumar biochemistry educator
Gavella, Mirjana biochemist, researcher
Gavrilyuk, Vladimir Illich physicist, electronics educator, researcher
Gawalek, Wolfgang physicist
Gawrońska, Grażyna Teresa astronomer, researcher
Gazarian, Irina Georgievna biochemist
Gearing, John William polymer testing consultant
Gegeliya, Dmitriy Ilich chemist, researcher
Gehlaut, Balbir Singh veterinarian medicine educator
Gehrels, Tom astronomer
Gehringer, Peter chemist
Geissler, Erik physics researcher, educator
Gell-Mann, Murray theoretical physicist, educator
Gelman, Leonid Moiseevich scientist, vibroacoustician, educator
Gendel, Leonid Yakovlevich biophysicist, researcher
Georgescu, Emilian Ion chemist, researcher
Georgii, Robert Heinrich physicist, researcher
Georgiou, Christos Dimos biochemistry educator, researcher
Georgiou, Constantinos Andreas chemist, educator
Geranios, Athanassios nuclear physicist, educator
Gerard, Manju physicist, researcher
Gerasimchuk, Victor Semenovich physics educator, mathematician
Gerasimov, Oleg Ivanovich physicist, theorist, researcher
Gerber, Richard physicist, educator, researcher
Gerhardsson, Lars Gerhard environmental scientist
Gerholm, Tor Ragnar physics educator
Gerke, Jorg chemist
Gerken, Manfred chemist
Germinario, Louis Thomas materials scientist
Gernik, Vladislav Valerianovich geophysicist, researcher
Gershtein, Elena Sergeyevna biochemist, researcher
Gerward, Leif Ingemar physicist
Geyer, Gerd paleontologist
Ghanashev, Ivan Petrov physicist, educator, engineer
Ghebrebrhan, Ogubazghi M. geophysicist
Ghelmez, Mihaela Dimitru physics educator, lecturer
Ghelmez, Mihaela (Dumitru) physics educator
Ghetti, Roberta physicist, educator
Ghita, Rodica engineer-physicist, researcher
Ghomashchi, Reza materials scientist
Ghosh, Suchita physicist
Ghulghule, Jayant Ramchandra physics educator
Giacconi, Riccardo astrophysicist, educator
Giacomelli, Giorgio Maria physics educator
Giacomelli, Luiz Roberto Bigco biochemical researcher
Giacopello, Sergio chemist
Giaever, Ivar physicist
Gibson, David Mark biochemist, educator
Giedke, Geza Koloman physicist, consultant
Gielen, Marcel chemist, educator
Gienapp, Hans Reinhard physicist, researcher, educator
Giessauf, Andreas chemist
Gilardi, Gianfranco biochemist, biomedical engineer, educator
Gildberg, Asbjorn biochemist, writer
Gillet, Vincent Paul physicist, researcher, retired
Gillette, P. Roger physicist, systems engineer
Gilmutdinov, Albert Kharisovich physicist, educator
Ginos, James Zissis retired research chemist
Ginoza, William retired biophysics educator
Ginzburg, Lev Pavlovich physicist, educator
Ginzburg, Vitaly Lazarevich physicist
Giordano, Roberto chemist, researcher
Girdler, Ronald William research geophysicist, educator
Gisin, Boris physicist
Gitman, Dmitry Maximovich physicist
Giubbilini, Pierluigi Vittorio physics educator
Gladfelter, Harry Foster chemist, researcher
Gladkov, Peter Stefanov physicist, researcher
Gladyshev, Georgi Pavlovich research chemist
Gladysheva, Inna biochemist, researcher
Glaeser, William A. materials scientist, consultant
Glaser, Bruno Josef chemist, researcher
Glaser, Donald Arthur physicist
Glaser, Roland biophysicist, educator
Glaser, Steffen Johannes physicist, educator
Glashow, Sheldon Lee physicist, educator
Glassburn, Tracy Ann geochemist, researcher
Glavič, Peter chemical engineering and material science educator
Gleispach, Helmut biochemist, educator
Glesk, Ivan physicist, educator, researcher
Glibin, Evgenii Nikolaevich chemist, researcher
Glick, Jane Mills biochemistry educator
Gliner, Erast Boris theoretical physicist
Glover, Claiborne Van Cortlandt, III biochemistry and molecular biology educator
Glushko, Eugene Yakovlevich physics educator, researcher
Gluskin, Emanuel physicist, engineer, researcher
Gmachowski, Lech Zbigniew chemical physicist, researcher
Gnatchenko, Sergiy Leonidovych physicist, researcher
Gniazdowski, Marek Andrzej biochemistry educator
Goc, Jacek Przemslaw physicist, researcher
Gocan, Simion Gavril chemistry educator
Godfrey, John Carl medicinal chemist
Goel, Rajnish Kumar geologist, mining engineer, consultant
Goff, James Franklin physicist, consultant
Gogolashvili, Edward Laurentyevich chemist, researcher
Gogotsi, Yury materials science educator
Gokel, George William organic chemist, educator
Golan, Rachel biochemistry educator
Goldanskii, Vitalii Iosifovich chemist, physicist
Goldberger, Marvin Leonard physicist, educator
Goldfinch, Edward Peter physicist
Goldman, Richard Graybell physicist, psychologist
Goldreich, Yair climatologist, geographer
Goldsmith, Paul Felix physics and astronomy educator
Goldstein, David Arthur biophysicist, educator
Goldstein, Mark Kingston Levin high technology company executive, researcher
Golenetsky, Serguei Innokentjevitch seismologist, researcher
Gołkiewicz, Władysław Bogdan chemist, educator
Golobič, Amalija chemistry researcher, educator
Goloby, George William, Jr. environmental scientist, ornithologist, aviculturist
Golombek, Matthew Philip planetary geologist
Golovanevskiy, Vladimir Arkadievich thermophysicist, researcher
Golovashkin, Aleksander Ivanovich physicist, educator
Golovinski, Pavel Abramovich physics educator
Goloviznin, Vladimir Vasiljevich physicist
Golovkin, Boris Georgievich chemist, researcher
Golovko, Vitali Anatolievich physicist, educator
Golovneva, Elena Igorevna theoretical physicist, researcher
Golshani, Alireza physicist, researcher
Goltsov, Alexey Nikolaevich physicist, educator
Goltsov, Victor Alexeevich physics educator, technology administrator
Golub, Michael Aronovich optical company scientist, executive, educator
Gomankov, Alexey Vladimirovich paleontologist
Gombocz, Erich Alfred biochemist
Gomes, José Alberto chemistry educator, university official
Gomez C., Dora Maria chemist, physicist
Gómez-Pineda, Edgardo Alfonso chemist, researcher, educator
Goncalves Da Silva, Cylon E.T. physicist
Goncharov, German Arsen'evich physicist
Gonzalez-Pradas, Emilio Fernando chemistry educator
Gonzalez-Prieto, Serafin biochemist
Gooden, Robert chemist
Gopalakrishnan, Iyyani Kunjappu chemist, researcher
Gopalan, Vaidyanathan physics educator
Gopych, Petro Mykhaylovych physics educator, researcher
Gorbachev, Valery Nikolaevich physics educator
Gorbunov, Leonid Mikhailovich physicist
Gorbunov, Mikhail Evgenievich physicist
Gordeev, Alexander Vasilievich physics researcher, editor
Gordeev, Evgenii Iljich physicist, science administrator
Gordetsov, Alexander Sergeyevich chemistry educator, researcher
Gorelov, Igor Pavlovich chemist, educator
Gorodnij, Mikola Michailovich chemist, ecologist, researcher
Görög, Sándor analytical chemist, researcher
Gorokhov, Igor M. isotope geochemist, researcher
Gorski, Tadeusz Stanislaw climatologist, researcher
Goryaev, Mikhail Alexandrovich physicist
Gorynov, Yuri Vladimirovitch physicist, researcher
Gosalvez, Mario biochemist, biophysicist
Gose, William Christopher retired chemist
Goth, Laszlo chemistry educator
Goto, Masahiro chemist
Gott, Yuri Vladimirovich physicist, researcher
Gottardi, Waldemar Arthur chemist, hygienist, researcher
Goudis, Christos astrophysicist
Gough, Mark Adrian chemistry educator
Goulko, Gennadi physicist, researcher
Gourbesville, Philippe Marcel hydrology educator, consultant
Gourley, John Terry physicist, research administrator
Gowenlock, Brian Glover retired chemistry educator, researcher
Goyal, Rameshwar Prasad physicist
Gozani, Tsahi nuclear physicist
Góźdź, Andrzej physics educator, theoretical physics researcher
Gozdz, Antoni S. chemistry researcher
Gözükara, Engin M. biochemistry educator
Gozzo, Franco organic chemist, educator
Graack, Hanns-Üdiger Friedrich Wilhelm biochemist
Graber, Werner Karl atmosphere physicist, researcher
Grabner, Erich Walter physical chemistry educator
Gracin, Davor physicist
Grădinariu, Lăcrămioara chemist
Gradov, Oleg Mikhaelovich physicist
Graham, James mineralogist
Gramsch, Ernesto Vicente physics educator
Gránásy, László physicist
Grandini, Carlos Roberto physicist, researcher
Grandpierre, Attila astrophysicist
Granser, Harald geophysicist
Grantsev, Vladimir Ivanovich physicist
Graschew, Georgi Borislawow natural scientist, chemist, coordinator
Grashchenkov, Sergey Ivanovich physics educator
Grashin, Anatoliy Feodorovich physicist, educator
Gratier, Jean-Pierre geology educator
Grau, Gérard oceanographer
Grayeski, Mary Lynn chemist, foundation administrator
Greco, Mario physicist, educator
Gredel, Roland astrophysicist
Gredeskul, Sergey Andrew physicist, educator
Greenberg, Jacob Haskelevich chemist
Greenwell, Roger Allen scientist
Greger, Janusz Stefan biochemist, educator
Greiner, Walter Albin Erhard physicist
Greis, Ortwin scientist

Griesche, Joachim *materials researcher, crystallographer*
Griesinger, Christian *chemist, educator*
Grigas, Jonas *physicist*
Grigorescu, Marius *physicist, researcher*
Grigorieva, Galina Miron *physicist*
Grigoryev, Vladimir Alexandrovich *space communication systems educator*
Grijalva-Chon, Jose Manuel *oceanologist, researcher*
Grimes, James Gordon *geologist*
Grip, Carl-Erik *research metallurgist*
Grisar, Johann Martin *retired research chemist*
Grisham, Larry Richard *physicist*
Grishin, Anatoly Mikhailovich *mechanics educator*
Grismore, Roger *physics educator, researcher*
Grisogono, Branko *atmospheric physics educator, researcher*
Groeger, Viktor *physicist, educator*
Grögler, Thomas *materials scientist, researcher, manager*
Gromet-Elhanan, Zippora *biochemist, researcher*
Gromov, Evgeny Mikhailovich *physicist, researcher, educator*
Gromov, Vladimir Vsevolodovich *physical chemist*
Gromova, Elizaveta Sergeevna *chemist, researcher, educator*
Grøn, Øyvind *physicist, educator*
Grönig, Hans Ernst *physicist*
Grosjean, Henri J.E. *biochemist, researcher*
Gross, Axel *physics educator*
Grosse, Harald *theoretical physicist, educator*
Groves-Gidney, Gavrielle *consultant geophysicist*
Grozdova, Irina Dmitrievna *biochemist, researcher*
Gruber, Jonas *chemistry educator, researcher*
Grubmuller, Helmut *physicist*
Gruendler, Peter *chemistry educator*
Gruhl, James *energy scientist, artist*
Grümm, Johann J. *physicist, international officer*
Grundland, Jgnacy Marek *biochemist, astrophysicist*
Grunenberg, Alfons *chemist*
Gruner, Elissa L. *meteorologist*
Grünfeld, Veronica *physicist, educator*
Grupp, Hariolf Wolfgang *physicist, economist*
Gruzberg, Ilya A. *physicist, researcher*
Grygar, Jiri *astrophysicist*
Gryning, Sven-Erik Gorm *air pollution scientist*
Gryzodub, Oleksandr Ivanovich *chemist*
Gu, Benxi *physics educator, researcher*
Gu, Qu-Ming *chemist*
Guan-Rong, Qi *astronomy educator*
Gucer, Seref *chemsistry educator, researcher*
Guczi, Laszlo *educator*
Guerra, Vasco Leitão *educator, researcher*
Guerrero, Ariel Heriberto *chemist, educator, scientist, industrial consultant*
Guillaumont, Robert *retired chemist, educator*
Guillet, Jean Pierre *physicist*
Guiraldenq, Pierre-Henri *physical metallurgy educator*
Guirguis Saleh, Osiris Wanis *biophysicist, researcher*
Gulacsi, Miklos *physicist, researcher*
Gulacsi, Zsolt *physicist*
Gulkis, Samuel *astronomer*
Gulyakevich, Olga Vladimirovna *chemist, researcher*
Gumerov, Farid Muhamedovich *physicist, researcher*
Gumiński, Cezary *chemistry educator, researcher*
Gun'ko, Vladimir Moiseevich *research physicist*
Günter, Peter *physics educator*
Gunter, William Dayle, Jr. *physicist*
Guo, Houyang *physicist researcher*
Guo, Jian Dong *chemist, educator*
Guo, Kang-Xian *physicist, educator*
Guo, Min-Liang *biochemist, educator*
Guo, Xin *materials science educator*
Guo, Xin-Heng *physicist*
Guo, Yizhu *chemist*
Guozhang, Xie *physicist, educator*
Gupta, Ashok Kumar *physicist, researcher*
Gupta, Bal K. *physicist, researcher*
Gupta, Hari Mohan *physicist, educator*
Gupta, Manoj *materials scientist, educator*
Gupta, Munishwar Nath *biochemistry educator, researcher*
Gupta, Radha Raman *chemistry educator, editor, researcher*
Gupta, Raj Kumar *physics educator, researcher*
Gupta, Rajendra Kumar *meterologist, remote sensing technologist educator*
Gupta, Satya Prakash *chemistry educator, researcher*
Gupta, Suraj Narayan *physicist, educator*
Gupta, Suresh Chand *physicist, researcher*
Gur'ev, Nikolai Victorovich *chemist*
Gurevich, Alexander Victor *physicist, researcher*
Gurevich, Grigory Manovich *physicist, researcher*
Gürs, Karl August *physicist*
Gürses, Metin *physics educator*
Gurvich, Victor Alexander *physicist, engineer*
Guse, Andreas H. *biochemist*
Gusev, Alexander *geophysicist*
Gusev, Anatoly Alexandrovitch *space physicist, software analyst*
Gusev, Nikolai Borisovitch *biochemist, researcher*
Gusev, Vitalyi *physicist*
Gusev, Vladimir Georgiyevich *physicist, researcher*
Gustafson, Gösta *physicist*
Gustafson, Lewis Allan *engineering geologist*
Gut, Wlodzimierz *chemist*
Guthrie, Frank Albert *chemistry educator*
Gutowski, Juergen *physics educator*
Gutsol, Alexander Fyodorovich *physicist, researcher*
Gutzow, Ivan Stoyanov *chemist*
Guyon, Etienne Marie *physics educator*
Györgydeák, Zoltán Barnabás *chemistry educator*
Ha, Dong Han *physicist, researcher*
Ha, Hyun-Joon *chemistry educator*
Haag, Rudolf *theoretical physicist*
Haarer, Dietrich *physicist, educator*
Haas, Alois *retired chemistry educator, researcher, consultant*
Haase, Gunter *optics scientist educator*
Haberhauer, Georg Franz *chemist, educator*
Hack, Alberto German *chemistry educator, consultant*
Hadjicostas, Evsevios Petrou *chemist*
Hadjidemetriou, John Demetrios *physicist educator*
Hadjiolov, Dimiter Hristov *histochemist, oncology educator*
Haefelinger, Guenter *chemist, educator*
Haegi, Marcel *scientist, physicist*
Hafez, Abdel-Fattah *physics educator, researcher*
Hafner, Jürgen *scientist, physics educator*
Haga, Tatsuya *neurochemist, researcher*
Hagebø, Einar *chemistry educator*
Hagenmaier, Hanspaul *chemistry educator*
Hagfeldt, Anders Ulf *chemist, educator*
Haggard, William Henry *meteorologist*
Hagiwara, Naoto *materials scientist, researcher*
Hagoort, Jacques *physicist, educator*
Hahn, Hoh-Gyu *chemistry researcher*
Hahn, Jeong Sang *hydrogeologist, educator, consultant*
Hähnel, Roland *biochemistry educator, consultant*
Hajos, Zoltan George *chemist*
Hakim, Rémi Joèl *physics and astrophysics educator, researcher*
Hakimelahi, Gholam Hosein *chemistry educator, researcher, consultant*
Halas, Stanislaw *physicist, researcher*
Hale, Kenneth Frank *physicist*
Hale, Monica *environmental scientist*
Hall, Grace Rosalie *physicist, educator, literary scholar*
Hall, Margaret Jean (Margot Hall) *biochemistry educator*
Halliday, Ian *astronomer*
Halliday, Ian Gibson *physics educator*
Hallmann, Armin *biochemist*
Halmshaw, Ronald *retired physicist*
Halpern, Jack *chemist, educator*
Halpern, Vivian Haim *physicist, educator*
Hamasaki, Keita *chemistry educator*
Hamdi, Suhaila Talib *chemistry educator, researcher*
Hameka, Hendrik Frederik *chemist, educator*
Hamelin, Joël Hubert *space scientist*
Hamelin, Michel *planetary science researcher*
Hamilton, Leslie James *oceanographer*
Hamilton, Phillip Alexander *physicist*
Hamilton-Kemp, Thomas Rogers *organic chemist, educator*
Hammarstrom, Sven Robert *biochemistry educator*
Hampl, Jaroslav Alois *biochemist, researcher*
Han, Bo-ying *material scientist, researcher*
Han, Liying *physics educator*
Han, Man Jung *chemistry educator*
Han, Zhi-quan *physicist, researcher*
Handerek, Jan Michal *physicist, educator*
Handrich, Klaus Dieter *physicist, researcher, educator*
Hangartner, Thomas Niklaus *medical physicist, educator*
Hanjalic, Kenal *physics educator, researcher*
Hann, William Mathis *chemist, researcher*
Hansen, Charles Medom *chemist*
Hansen, Glen Arthur *scientist, researcher*
Hansen, Hans Christian *environmental chemist*
Hansen, Jorn Dines *physics educator*
Hansen, Lars Maersk *geologist, consultant*
Hanumaiah, B(eligiraiah) *physics educator*
Hardie, David Grahame *biochemist, educator*
Hardy, Jackie Norman *physics educator*
Hardy, Ralph W. F. *biochemist, biotechnology executive*
Hargett, David Raymond *gemologist*
Harmanec, Petr *astronomer*
Harmatz, David *biochemist*
Harper, David Benjamin *microbial biochemistry researcher*
Harrington, Michael Gerard *biochemistry educator, researcher*
Harris, Alan William *physicist, researcher*
Harris, Brian Nicholas *surveyor*
Harris, Miles Fitzgerald *meteorologist*
Harrison, Michael Jay *physicist, educator*
Harrison, Richard Anthony *solar physicist*
Harshman, Dale Richard *physicist*
Hart, Dabney Gardner *environmental scientist*
Hartley, David Minor *physicist, research scientist*
Hartmann, Ervin *physicist, researcher*
Hartquist, Thomas Wilbur *astrophysicist*
Harvey, John Arthur *nuclear physicist*
Haschke, Michael Roger *geologist*
Hase, Masashi *physicist, researcher*
Hase, Muneaki *physicist, researcher*
Hase, Tsunao *chemistry educator, researcher*
Hashimoto, Tsuneyuki *materials scientist*
Hashimoto, Yoshikazu *chemist, educator*
Hassan, Aladin Abdel-Aziz *biochemist, toxicologist, researcher*
Hassan, Sayed Mohammed *analytical chemist*
Hassan, Shawky Mohamed *chemistry educator*
Hasue, Kazuo *chemistry educator*
Hatada, Koichi *polymer chemistry educator*
Hategan, Cornel *physicist, researcher*
Hausel, William Dan *economic geologist, martial artist*
Hausler, Rudolf Heinrich *research chemist*
Hausmann, Michael *physicist*
Hausselt, Jürgen Heinrich *materials science educator, research administrator*
Havens, Timothy John *physicist*
Haverkamp, Richard Gerard *chemistry educator*
Hawkins, Pamela Leigh Huffman *biochemist*
Hawthorne, Marion Frederick *chemistry educator*
Hayashi, Koya *chemistry educator*
Hayashi, Kyozo *neurobiochemist, researcher*
Hayashi, Mitsuhiko *retired physics educator*
Hayashi, Takemi *physics educator*
Hayward, Mary Mavis *retired chemist*
He, Chaolai *meterologist, researcher*
He, Qingping *environment researcher*
He, Xu-Chang *chemist*
Hebling, Janos *physicist, educator*
Hedin, Lars Tore *physicist, researcher*
Heeger, Alan Jay *physicist*
Hegedüs, Tibor *astronomer*
Heggland, Roar Asbjørn *geophysicist, researcher*
Heidt, Frank Dietrich *physicist, educator*
Heiduschka, Peter *bioelectrochemist, researcher*
Heikkinen, Jari Olavi *medical physicist, researcher*
Heilig, Uwe Jens Gerhard *physicist*
Heilmann, Gerhard Max *retired physicist, educator*
Heindel, Ned Duane *chemistry educator*
Heinicke, Joachim Werner *chemistry educator, researcher*
Heinisch, Gottfried *pharmaceutical chemistry educator*
Heinrich, Christoph Andreas *geochemistry and economic geology educator*
Heinz, Ulrich Walter *theoretical physics educator*
Helas, Günter *chemist*
Held, Gerhard *environmental consultant, meteorologist*
Helene, Claude Michel *professor of biophysics*
Hellerqvist, Carl Gustaf *biochemist, educator*
Helling, Claudia Kristine *geologist*
Hellingwerf, Robert Hendricus *geology educator*
Hellsing, Bo *physics educator*
Hellstrom, Thomas Gert *environmental scientist*
Hemilä, Harri Olavi *biochemist, epidemiologist, researcher*
Hemmersbach, Peter *chemist*
Hempelmann, Alexander Michael *astrophysicist, researcher*
Hempelmann, (Carl) Ernst *biochemist*
Hendley, Coit Taylor, III *chemistry educator*
Hendolin, Minna Leena *biochemist*
Henkel, Andreas Wolfram *biochemist, researcher*
Henkel, Malte *physics educator*
Henriksson, Anders Sten *geologist*
Hepworth, John Leonard *chemist, researcher*
Herak, Janko N. *biophysics educator*
Herdendorf, Charles Edward, III *retired oceanographer, limnologist, consultant*
Hergert, Herbert Lawrence *consultant*
Hering, Ekbert *physics/management educator, university president*
Héritier, Michel *physicist*
Hermann, Robert Bell *physical chemist, consultant*
Herr, Werner Friedrich *physicist, researcher*
Herrick, Elbert Charles *chemist, consultant*
Herring, Jackson Rea *physicist*
Herrmann, Dieter Bernhard *astronomer*
Herschbach, Dudley Robert *chemistry educator*
Hertwig, Manfred Hans Friedbert *physicist, researcher*
Herve, Thierry Jean *physicist, researcher*
Herz, Werner *chemist, educator*
Herzel, Frank *research physicist*
Herzfeld, Charles Maria *physicist*
Hesse, Michael *chemist*
Hesthammer, Jonny *geologist*
Hestholm, Stig Ottar *scientist, consultant*
Hetflejš, Jiří *chemist, researcher*
Hetzheim, Annemarie Magdalena *organic chemistry educator*
Heudier, Jean-Louis Fernand *astronomer, educator*
Hewett, Kevin Brian *environmental chemist*
Hey, Richard Noble *marine geophysicist*
Heyn, Arno Harry Albert *retired chemistry educator*
Hibi, Nozomu *biochemist, researcher*
Hibino, Ken *chemist, researcher*
Hickey, Robert James, III *geologist, geographer, educator*
Hidalgo, Francisco Javier *chemist, biochemist, researcher*
Higatsberger, Michael Josef *physics educator emeritus*
Higginbotham, Carol A. *chemistry educator*
Hildmann, Eckart *environmentalist*
Hilgertová, Jirina *biochemist*
Hill, George Arthur *physicist*
Hill, Sir John McGregor *physicist, corporate executive*
Hill, Paul Windwood *geophysicist*
Hillion, Pierre Théodore Marie *mathematical physicist*
Hillis, Richard Ralph *geology and geophysics educator*
Hilscher, Helmut *physics educator*
Hilton, Richard Paul *geology educator, paleontological consultant*
Hiltunen, Jukka Kalervo *biochemist, educator*
Himbert, Marc Emile *metrologist, educator*
Himpsel, Franz Josef *physicist, educator*
Hinrikus, Hiie *physicist, physics educator*
Hirabayashi, Atsumu *physicist, researcher*
Hirasawa, Eiji *biochemist, researcher*
Hirashima, Hiroshi *chemistry educator*
Hirokawa, Shoji *chemistry educator*
Hirose, Chiaki *chemist, physicist, educator*
Hirose, Masaaki *biochemist, educator*
Hirsch, Peter Bernhard *metallurgist*
Hittmair, Otto Heinrich *physics educator*
Hiyama, Tamejiro *research chemist, chemistry educator*
Hjertén, Stellan Vilhelm Einar *biochemist*
Ho, Chih-Ming *physicist, educator*
Ho, Chung-Ru *oceanographer, educator*
Hoang, Ngoc Cam *physicist*
Hobbs, Marcus Edwin *chemistry educator*
Hobson, Art S. *physicist*
Hocquellet, Pierre *chemist, researcher*
Hoefling, Ronald Walter *physicist*
Hofacker, Ludwig Georg *chemistry educator*
Hoffman, Ronald Bruce *biophysicist, life scientist, human factors consultant*
Hoffman, Roy Emanuel *chemist, researcher*
Hoffmann, Günter Georg *chemist*
Hoffmann, Hans Juergen *physicist*
Hoffmann, Roald *chemist, educator*
Hoffstaetter, Georg Heinz *research physicist*
Hogarth, Cyril Alfred *physicist, consultant*
Högberg, Lars Gustaf *physics researcher, administrator*
Hogrefe, Henning *physicist*
Hojo, Junichi *chemistry educator*
Hojo, Masashi *chemistry educator*
Hokamoto, Kazuyuki *materials scientist, educator*
Hokin, Lowell Edward *biochemist, educator*
Holder, Neville Lewis *chemist*
Holland, Leslie Arthur *physicist, editor, educator*
Hollander, Lewis E., Jr. *physicist, consultant*
Holmes, Richard Brooks *mathematical physicist*
Holovko, Myroslav *physicist, educator*
Holt, William Henry *physicist, researcher*
Holtappels, Peter *chemist, research scientist*
Holub, Karel *seismologist, researcher*
Holz, Dietrich Adolf *materials scientist*
Holzapfel, Wilfried Bernd *physics educator*
Holzapfel, Wolfgang *physicist, industrial researcher*
Homeier, Herbert Hans Heinrich *chemistry educator, computer software researcher*
Homma, Teiichi *applied physics researcher*
Hönerlage, Bernd *physicist, educator*
Hong, Chang Yong *chemist*
Hong, Chu-Wan *materials scientist, researcher*
Hong, Feng-Lei *physicist*
Hong, Min *biochemistry and molecular biology educator*
Hong-Yi, Lee *chemistry educator*
Honig, William Martin *electronics/physics/math/bioengineering researcher*
Honjo, Tasuku *biochemist, educator*
Hoodbhoy, Pervez Amirali *physicist, educator*
Hoogenraad, Johannes Herman *physicist*
Hoogenraad, Nicholas J. *biochemist, researcher, educator*
Hoppe, Andreas *geologist, administrator*
Hoppe, Ulf-Peter Jürgen *atmosphere physicist*
Hora, Heinrich *physicist*
Horak, Jaromir *chemistry educator*
Horányi, György *chemist, researcher*
Hořejší, Jiří *physicist*
Horhoianu, Grigore *physicist, researcher*
Horiuchi, Noboru *biochemist, educator*
Horká, Marie *analytical chemist*
Horner, Carl Matthew *chemistry educator*
Hornung, Volker *chemist, management consultant*
Horsky, Jan Josef *theoretical physics educator, scientist*
Horváth, Ferenc *geophysics educator, researcher, consultant*
Hoshino, Sadao *physicist*
Hotokka, Matti *chemist, educator*
Hou, Chun-Kan *materials scientist*
Houghton, Andrew Julian Nicolas *scientific administrator*
Hounkonnou, Mahouton Norbert *physics educator*
Hovanessian, Ara Giragos *biochemist*
Hovland, Martin Torvald *marine geologist, engineer, researcher, educator*
Hovsepyan, Yuriy Ivanovich *physicist*
Howard, Christopher John *research scientist*
Howarth, Graham Alistair *research chemist*
Howe, Lyman Harold, III *chemist*
Hoz, Shmaryahu *chemist, researcher, educator*
Hrabovsky, Milan *physicst*
Hrdy, Jaromír *physicist, researcher, consultant*
Hsieh, Shyu-Hsien *physics educator*
Hsiung, Luke Lieh-Ming *metallurgist, electron microscopist*
Hsu, Baysung *physics educator*
Hsu, Rue Ron *physics educator*
Hsu, Tzu Yao *materials scientist, educator*
Hu, Chang Wei *chemist, educator*
Hu, Chun Pu *chemist, educator*
Hu, Jianguo *biochemist, researcher*
Hu, Xing *physics educator*
Hu, Zhi Bin *chemistry educator, researcher*
Hua, Tong-Wen *chemistry educator, researcher*
Huang, Chao-Shang *physicist*
Huang, Chein-Ho *chemistry educator*
Huang, Chun-Hui *chemist, educator*
Huang, Hesheng *physicist, educator*
Huang, Junlian *chemist, researcher*
Huang, Kai Hui *chemist, researcher*
Huang, Te-Hsiang *astrologist, consultant, researcher*
Huang, Wung Hong *physicist, educator*
Huang, Xiang-Yu *meteorologist*
Huang, Zhiwei *physicist, researcher, educator*
Hubáček, Milan *chemist, researcher*
Hubbard, Gregory Scott *physicist*
Huber, David Lawrence *physicist, educator*
Huber, Paul William *biochemistry educator, researcher*
Huber, Robert *biochemist, educator*
Hudak, Ondrej *physicist, consultant*
Hue, Jean Bernard *physicist*
Huh, Hyung-Tack *oceanoprapher*
Huheey, James Edward *chemist, herpetologist and educator*
Huisgen, Rolf K.J. *chemist*
Hulse, Russell Alan *physicist*
Hultman, Eric Helmer *clinical chemist*
Hums, Joseph Erich *chemist, chemical engineer, consultant*
Huntelaar, Mark Eduard *chemist, researcher*
Huntoon, Robert Brian *chemist, food industry consultant*
Huot, Nicolas *physicist*
Hurlburt, Harley Ernest *ocean modeling and prediction scientist*
Hurle, Donald Thomas James *physicist, researcher*
Hurwic, Jozef *physical chemist*
Husek, Petr Ivan *chemist, researcher*
Hussain, Manwar *research chemist*
Hussain, Moinuddin Syed *geologist, reservoir engineer, consultant*
Hussain, Tajammul *chemist*
Huston, Daniel Cliff *geophysicist*
Hwang, Chang-Sing *physicist*
Hwang, Seong Sik *materials scientist, researcher*
Hwang, Woei-Yann Pauchy *physics educator*
Hyun-Min, Kim *material scientist, educator*
Ibarra, Baldemar *astrophysicist, educator*
Ibrahim, Hisham Radwan *biochemist educator*
Idla, Katrin *chemist, educator*
Idol, James Daniel, Jr. *chemist, educator, inventor, consultant*
Igarashi, Kazuei *biochemist*
Igarashi, Takashi *chemist*
Ignatovich, Vladimir Kazimirovich *physicist, researcher*
Iguchi, Kazumoto *theoretical physicist, researcher*
Iida, Shuichi *physicist, educator*
Ikeda, Kazuyosi *physicist, poet*
Ikegami, Hidetsugu *physicist, educator*
Ikeyama, Masami *scientific researcher*
Ilavsky, Michal *physicist, researcher, educator*
Illés-Almár, Erzsébet Rozália *astronomer, researcher*
Ilyushin, Boris Borisovich *physicist, researcher*
Ilyushin, Yaroslaw Alexandrovich *physicist, researcher, consultant*
Imam, M. Ashraf *materials scientist, educator*
Imamura, Masashi *chemist, educator, researcher*
Imamura, Taira *chemistry educator*
Imamura, Tohru *physicist*
Inada, Yuji *biochemistry and biotechnology educator, researcher*
Indira, C.J. *electrochemical research scientist*
Infeld, Eryk *theoretical physicist*
Ingel, Lev Khanaanovich *geophysicist, researcher*
Inlow, Rush Osborne *chemist*
Inoue, Hisayuki *chemist*
Inoue, Naohisa *physicist, educator*
Inoue, Yoshiharu *biochemistry educator*
Intriligator, Devrie Shapiro *physicist*
Ioannou, Panagiotis *chemistry educator*
Ion, Dumitru Barbu *physicist, researcher*
Iordanskii, Alexey Leonidovich *polymer chemist*
Iosifova, Ekaterina Konstantinovna *paleontologist*
Iroh, Jude Onwuegbu *chemistry educator*
Irshad, Mohammad *biochemistry educator*
Irurre Perez, Jose *chemistry educator, researcher*
Irwin, William Edward, III *health physicist*
Isaak, George Richard *physicist, researcher*
Isakaev, Emin Khasaevich *physicist*
Isakov, Sergey Leonidovich *physicist*
Isbister, Dennis John *physicist, educator*
Ise, Norio *chemistry educator*
Ishchenko, Michail Alexeevich *chemistry educator*
Ishibashi, Akira *physicist, laboratory administrator, educator*
Ishii, Akihiko *chemist, educator*
Ishii, Sakae *physicist, researcher*
Ishii, Yoshinori *environmental science educator*
Ishikawa, Ikuo *metallurgist, researcher*
Ishikawa, Toshihisa *biochemist, educator*
Ishimaru, Kanji *plant biochemist*
Ishmaev, Sergey Nikolayevich *physicist, researcher*
Iskander, George Mina *chemistry educator, researcher*
Iskra, Maria *chemist, researcher*
Ismail-Zadeh, Ali Tofik *geophysicist, researcher*
Isobe, Syuzo *astronomer, educator*
Isolani, Paulo Celso *chemistry educator, researcher*
Israelit, Mark *general relativity and cosmology physics educator*
Isupov, Vladislav Aleksandrovich *physicist, researcher*
Itina, Tatiana Eugenievna *physicist, researcher*
Itoh, Kazuyoshi *educator*

Rauschenbach, Bernd Hans physicist, educator
Ray, Asim Kumar physics educator
Ray, Bradley Stephen petroleum geologist
Ray, Clayton Edward paleontologist, curator
Ray, Terrill Wylie physical scientist
Raynal, Jose Angel hydrologist, educator
Raynor, Susanne chemical physics educator
Read, Kenneth Francis, Jr. physics educator, researcher
Rechenberg, Wolfram Joachim Friedrich chemist, researcher
Reddy, Benjaram Mahipal chemist, researcher
Reddy, C. Devendranath chemist, educator
Redhead, Michael Logan Gonne history and philosophy of science educator
Reed, Mark Arthur educator, researcher
Reed, Ronald Keith oceanographer, researcher
Reese, Colin Bernard chemistry educator
Regnell, Gerhard retired geology educator
Reich, Robert Claude metallurgist, physicist
Reichelt, Rudolf biophysics educator
Reichenbach, Jürgen R. physicist
Reichert, Leo Edmund, Jr. biochemist, endocrinologist
Reid, Richard Dawson chemist
Reimers, Jeffrey Robert chemist
Reineker, Peter physics educator, researcher
Reinemund, John Adam geologist, geoscience consultant
Reinert, Karl-Ernst Wilhelm physicist, researcher
Reinhardt, Birgit Hedwig Elfriede chemist
Reinhardt, Hugo physicist, educator
Reissig, Hans-Ulrich chemist, educator
Reistad, Ragnhild biochemist
Rejzek, Martin organic chemist, entomologist, researcher
Relyea, Carl Miller hydrologist
Remko, Milan chemist, educator
Remo, John Lucien physicist, business executive
Ren, Xiaobing materials scientist, researcher, applied physicist
Rendic, Dubravko nuclear physicist
Rendic, Slobodan Petar biochemistry and chemistry educator
Renoux, André physicist, educator
Renshaw, Amanda Frances retired physicist, nuclear engineer
Rentzeperis, Panayiotis Ioannis physicist
Renz, Alfons scientist
Repa, Petr physicist, researcher, educator
Reshetov, Vladimir Alexandrovich physics educator
Residori, Stefania physicist, researcher
Resnick, Paul R. research chemist
Respondek-Liberska, Maria physician
Retey, Janos biochemistry educator
Rettori, Carlos physics educator
Reuben, Bryan Godel chemical technology educator, consultant
Reusch, Rosetta Natoli biochemistry educator, researcher
Revenga, Jorge Eduardo aquaculture researcher
Revillon, André chemistry researcher, educator
Revol, Jean-Pierre Charles physicist
Reyes-Trejo, Benito chemist, researcher
Rezchikov, Victor Grigorievich physicist, researcher
Rhee, Suh-Bong chemist
Rho, Mannque theoretical physicist, researcher
Riad, Bahia Yehia organic chemistry educator
Ribes, Jean-Claude Henri astronomer, writer
Rich, Charles Anthony hydrogeologist, consultant
Richards, Edward Graham retired physics educator
Richards, Randal William chemist, educator
Richardson, Jasper Edgar nuclear physicist
Richardson, Mervyn Lewis chemist, biologist, toxicologist
Richardson, Robert Coleman physics educator, researcher
Richter, Burton physicist, educator
Rickards, Richard Barrie palaeontologist, educator, curator
Rickayzen, Gerald physics educator
Ridd, John Howard chemistry educator
Ridley, Brian Kidd physicist, educator
Ried, Walter Georg chemistry educator, researcher
Riedel, Gerhardt Frederick oceanographer
Riege, Hans Karl physicist
Ries, Edward Richard petroleum geologist, consultant
Riggin, Leh-daw Alice analytical chemist
Rikvold, Per Arne physics researcher and educator
Riller, Ulrich Peter geologist
Rinkevich, Anatoly Bronislavovich physicist, educator
Rissanen, Kari Tapani organic chemistry educator
Ristic, Ramir Daroslav physics educator
Rittich, Bohuslav chemistry educator, researcher
Rizk, Assaad Toufic surgeon, urology educator
Rizvi, Mohammad Sadiq chemistry educator
Roberson, Mark Allen physicist, educator
Roberts, Bernard applied mathematician, solar physicist
Roberts, Thomas George retired physicist
Robinson, James Lawrence biochemistry educator, researcher
Robock, Alan meteorology educator
Robson, Geoffrey Robert geologist, seismologist, consultant
Rocca, Mario Agostino physics educator
Roček, Zbyněk J. paleontologist, researcher
Rochette, Pierre Eugene geophysicist, educator
Rochev, Vladimir Efimovich physicist, educator
Rock, Peter Alfred chemistry educator, researcher, consultant, dean
Rockenbauer, Antal István physicist, researcher
Rocks, Bernard Francis clinical chemist
Rockwell, R(onald) James, Jr. laser and electro-optics consultant
Rode, Bernd Michael theoretical chemistry educator
Rodgers, Robert Aubrey physicist
Rodhe, Henning atmospheric science educator
Rodin, Victor Vasilievich physicist
Rodinkov, Oleg Vasiliy chemist, researcher
Rodriguez, Guillermo physicist, secondary education educator
Rodriguez-Pasqués, Rafael Héctor chemist, educator
Roehle, Ingo aerospace scientist
Roehr, Max biochemist
Roengsumran, Sophon chemist, educator, researcher
Roesky, Herbert Walter chemistry educator
Roessler, Jochen physicist, researcher
Rogalski, Antoni physicist
Rogalski, Mircea Serban physics researcher
Rogers, James Edwin geology and hydrology consultant
Rogozkin, Victor Alexeevitch biochemist, researcher
Rogueda, Philippe Guy Auguste physical chemist
Rogulski, Witold biochemist
Rohatschek, Hans Bruno physicist
Rohlena, Karel physicist
Rohrer, Heinrich physicist
Rohwer, Klaus aerospace researcher
Rokhmanov, Nickolai Yakovlevich physicist, researcher
Rokhvarger, Anatoly Efim materials science and ceramic technology scientist
Rokita, Hanna Kasperczyk biochemist
Rokushima, Katsu optical science and engineering educator
Romaniv, Oleh materials scientist, educator
Romanova, Liya physicist
Romeo, Mario Francesco physics researcher
Romm, Freddy Alexandre chemist, researcher
Rona, Peter Arnold oceanographer, researcher, educator
Rosa, Joao Willy Correa physicist
Rosander, Reine physicist, science educator
Rose, Keith biochemist, researcher
Rose, Malcolm Edward novelist, chemist
Roselle, Paul Lucas material scientist
Rosenblith, Walter Alter scientist, educator
Rosenstock, Wolfgang Hans physicist
Rosenthal, Isadore Irving chemist
Rosich, Ronald Steven water and environmental scientist, researcher, consultant, educator
Rösner, Peter chemist
Rosochacki, Stanislaw Józef scientist, biochemist
Ross, Ian Norman research physicist
Rosseinsky, David Reuben chemist, educator
Rossell, John Barry chemist
Rotblat, Sir Joseph physicist, educator
Roudnicky, Dunja Soldo physicist, researcher
Rougeot, Henri Max medical imaging engineer, physicist
Rourke, William Bernard aerospace science educator, consultant
Routray, Jayant Kumar science educator
Roux, Didier Charles chemist
Rowinski, Pawel Mariusz hydrologist, scientist, educator
Rowland, Frank Sherwood chemistry educator
Rowley, William Richard Charlton experimental physicist, consultant
Rowlinson, John Shipley chemistry educator
Roxburgh, Ian Walter astronomy and mathematics educator
Roy, Kalyan Kumar geophysics educator
Roy, N.K. chemist
Roychoudaury, Rajkumar physicist, researcher
Rozelot, Jean Pierre astronomy educator, consultant
Rozental, Iosif Leonid physicist, researcher
Rozhansky, Vladimir Alexandrovich physicist, educator
Rozovskis, Gregory chemist, researcher
Rubaszek, Anna physicist, researcher
Rubel, Marek Jan chemist, physicist, researcher
Rubin, Lawrence Gilbert physicist, laboratory manager
Rubinstein, Boris Yakovlevich physicist, researcher
Rubinstein, Israel chemistry educator, researcher
Rubio, Angel theoretical physics educator
Rudakov, Elisey Sergeevich physical chemist
Rudd, Pauline Mary biochemist, researcher
Rüdiger, Günther Erhard astronomer, educator
Rudland, Philip Spencer biochemist, educator
Rudoi, Valentine Michailovich chemist
Rudolph, Peter material scientist, researcher
Ruedenberg, Klaus theoretical chemist, educator
Ruff, Ferenc chemist, educator
Ruffini, Remo Jacopo physics educator
Rühl, Werner physicist, educator
Runkle, Robert Scott environmental company executive
Ruoff, Heinz Peter chemistry educator
Rusanov, Anatoly Ivanovich chemist
Ruset, Christian Constantin physicist, researcher
Russakovich, Nikolai Artemjevich physicist, educator, researcher
Russell, Robert Bonnell petroleum geologist
Rutkevich, Igor Max physicist, fluid mechanics researcher
Ruzdjak, Vladimir astrophysicist
Ryabov, Vladimir Borisovich physicist, educator
Ryan, Matthew F. chemistry educator, consultant
Rybakov, Kirill Igorevich physicist, educator
Rybaltowski, Adam physicist, engineer
Rybová, Renata retired biochemist, researcher
Rychkov, Alexander Dmitrievich researcher and lecturer
Rycroft, Michael physicist
Ryde, Simon John Scrivener medical physicist
Ryde, Ulf Sigurd Bror theoretical chemist
Rydstrom, Carlton Lionel chemist, paint and coating consultant
Rynkowski, Jacek Michał chemist, educator
Ryttel, Anna Marta chemist, educator, researcher
Rytwo, Giora physical chemistry educator, researcher
Ryu, Chang-Mo physicist, educator
Ryzhak, Eugene physics educator, researcher
Ryzhikov, Gennady Antonovich geophysicist, researcher
Ryzhikov, Vladimir Diomidovich physicist, educator
Ryzhov, Vyacheslav Anatolyevich physics researcher
Sa, Ben-Hao physicist, researcher, educator
Saad, Massoud Abdel-Rahman oceanographer, researcher
Saadallah, Faycel Ben Habib physics educator, researcher
Saakes, Michel electrochemist
Sabatier, Jean-Marc André biochemist
Saber, Hafid structural geology educator, researcher
Sabin, John Rogers physics educator
Sabine, Peter Aubrey retired geologist, consultant, researcher
Sabinin, Konstantin Dmitrievich oceanographer
Sabnis, Ram Wasudeo research chemist
Sabry, Mohamed Montaser Foad physicist, educator
Sacak, Mehmet chemistry educator, researcher
Sachanska, Teodora Georgieva biochemist, educator
Sackmann, Inge-Juliana astrophysicist
Sacris, Eduardo Milan metallurgist, consultant
Sadofsky, Moshe J. biochemist
Sadofyev, Yuri Grigorievitch physicist
Sadovskii, Michael V. physicist
Sadun, Alberto Carlo astrophysicist, physics educator
Sáenz, Albert William theoretical physicist, researcher, consultant
Saenz-Ramirez, Alejandro physics educator, researcher
Safrany, Agnes physical chemist
Safta, Marius Mircea retired organic chemistry researcher
Sagar, Ram astrophysicist, researcher
Saha, Bidhan Chandra physics educator
Saha, Manoranjan chemistry educator
Sahade, Jorge astronomer, researcher
Sahagia, Maria Constantin physicist, researcher
Sahay, Pradosh Prakash physics educator, researcher
Sahrawat, Kanwar Lal chemist
Sahu, Surendra Nath physicist, researcher
Saifullin, Renat Salyakhovich inorganic technology educator, researcher
St-Onge, Denis Alderic geologist, research scientist
Saito, Teijiro nuclear physicist and educator
Sajgo, Mihaly biochemist, educator
Sakaguchi, Masato chemistry educator
Sakai, Hitoshi geochemist, scientific writer
Sakai, Taku metallurgist educator
Sakhibullin, Nail Abdullovich astrophysicist, educator
Sakka, Sumio chemistry educator
Sakkopoulos, Sotirios Angelos physics educator
Sakra, Tomas chemistry educator and researcher
Sakurada, Yutaka chemist
Sala, Martin Andrew biophysicist, inventor
Salagean, Maria N. physicist
Salama, Farid astrophysicist, spectroscopist, research scientist
Salatić, Dušan retired mineral processing educator
Saleem, Rubeena chemistry researcher
Saleh, Mahmoud Abbas chemistry educator
Salibian, Alfredo physiological and environmental sciences scientist
Salikhov, Kev Minullinovich physicist
Salimullah, Mohammad physics educator, researcher
Salk, Sung-Ho Suck physics educator and researcher
Sallay, Peter chemistry educator
Salmon, Neil Anthony research physicist
Salnikova, Ekaterina Borisovna geologist, researcher
Salo, Vitaly Ivanovich physicist, researcher
Salonen, Jarno Juhani physicist
Salvato, Matteo physicist
Sam, Richard Chung physicist
Sambasivan, Eswaran Venkat chemistry educator
Samios, Nicholas Peter physicist
Samman, Samir biochemistry educator
Samoilov, Naum Alexandrovich chemist, educator
Samoilov, Valery Samuel petrologist-geochemist, researcher
Samson, Sten Otto x-ray crystallographer, consultant, researcher
Samsonov, Alexander Mikhailovich physicist
Samuel, Clint David analytical chemist
Samuelsson, Bengt Ingemar medical chemist
Samukov, Vladimir Vasilyevich chemist, research scientist
Sanadze, Tengiz Ivanes-dze physicist, researcher
Sanchez, Enrique Pablo environmental pollution educator
Sanchez, Norma Graciela physicist, astrophysicist, educator
Sanchez-Cabeza, Joan-Albert physics educator, researcher
Sanchezgil, Jose Antonio physicist
Sanchez-Pozo, Antonio biochemistry educator
Sánchez Ruiz, Jorge physicist, educator
Sanchez-Soto, Pedro Jose chemist, researcher
Sander, Wolfram Willy chemist, educator
Sanders, Jeremy Keith Morris chemistry educator, author
Sandhu, Jagir Singh chemist
Sandler, Merton chemical pathology educator, researcher
Sandovskii, Vladimir Aaron physicist, researcher
Sandulescu, Aureliu Emil physicist, educator, politician
Sandulli, Roberto environmental sciences educator
Saner, Salih petroleum geologist, educator
Sanjeeviraja, Chinnappanadar physics educator, researcher
Sanjinés, Diego Ignacio physicist
Sano, Edson Eyji geologist, researcher
Sano, Masahito polymer physicist
Sant'Anna, Adonai Schlup physicist, mathematician, educator
Santos, Filipe Duarte physics educator
Santos, Gabriel Del Prado, Jr. geochemist
Sapna, Gupta chemist
Saqib, Mohammad materials scientist
Saranin, Alexander Alexander physicist, researcher, educator
Saranin, Vladimir Aleksandr physicist, educator
Saraswathy, Ariamuthu chemist, educator
Sarbey, Oleg Georgij physicist, researcher
Sardanashvily, Gennadi Aleksandre physicist, researcher
Sarin, Vinod Kumar materials scientist
Saris, Nils-Erik Leo biochemistry educator
Sarkar, Amitendra Nath geoscientist
Sarmientos, Paolo chemical company executive
Sarna, Marian physics and environmental science educator, designer
Sasabe, Shigeru theoretical physicist
Sasaki, Teikichi Akira materials scientist, researcher
Sasane, Akinobu chemist, educator
Satava, Vladimir chemistry educator, researcher
Satir, Ahmet physicist
Sato, Motoaki geologist, researcher
Sato, Noboru chemist
Sattel, Daniel geophysicist
Sauro, Joseph Pio physics educator
Savage, Martha Kane physics and geophysics educator
Savaniu, Cristian-Daniel chemist
Savchenko, Konstantin Vasilyevich physicist, researcher
Savenko, Oleg Mikhailovich physicist, educator, researcher
Savko, Konstantin Arkadyevich geology educator, researcher
Savrin, Victor Ivanovich physicist, educator
Saxena, Arjun Nath physicist
Saxena, Narendra Sahai physicist, educator
Saxton, John Edwin chemistry educator, writer
Sayko, Gennadiy physicist
Scanio, Charles John Vincent chemist
Şcarlat, Florea physicist, educator, research scientist
Ščedrov, Oleg biochemistry, organic chemistry educator
Schade, Heinz Fritz Georg physicist, fluid dynamics educator
Schaedeli, Ulrich P. chemist
Schaefer, Juergen Alois physics educator
Schaeffer, Evelyne biochemist, molecular biologist, researcher
Schaerpf, Otto Wilhelm physicist
Schäfer, Karola chemist, researcher
Schäfer, Ludwig Otto metallurgist, researcher
Schaffner, Kurt Walter chemistry researcher
Schapink, Frederik Willem metallurgist
Schaumann, Ernst O. chemistry educator
Schay, Zoltan chemist
Schebesta, Ingo physicist
Scheblykin, Ivan Gennadevich physicist, researcher
Scheck, Florian Alfred physicist, educator
Scheid, Werner Fritz physics educator
Scheirs, John polymer chemist, scientist
Schelev, Mikhail Yakovlevich physicist, researcher
Schellenberg, Juergen Bernd chemist
Schellenberger, Alfred Hermann biochemistry educator
Scheringer, Martin environmental scientist, researcher
Schewe, Tankred biochemist, researcher
Schidlowski, Manfred geochemist and earth sciences educator
Schiffer, Marcus Josef physicist, researcher
Schiffmann, Yoram research scientist
Schilling, Andreas Johan physicist, educator
Schilling, Frederick Augustus, Jr. geologist, consultant
Schipanski, Dagmar physicist
Schirmann, Jean-Pierre Henri chemist, researcher
Schirmer, Wolfgang retired physical chemist, researcher
Schlag, Edward William chemistry educator
Schlager, Walter August physicist
Schlaile, Hans Gerd physicist, researcher
Schlarb, Bernhard chemist
Schlatterer, Bert biochemist, educator
Schlenker, Claire physicist, educator
Schlichting, Frank physicist, researcher
Schluter, Robert Arvel physicist
Schmalisch, Gerd Heinz biophysicist, researcher
Schmeidler, Felix Bernhard astronomer
Schmid, Friederike Gertrud physicist, researcher
Schmid, Hans-Peter biochemistry educator, researcher
Schmidbaur, Hubert chemistry educator, consultant
Schmidpeter, Alfred chemistry professor
Schmidt, Alfred chemistry educator
Schmidt, Hartmut chemist, researcher
Schmidt, Maarten astronomy educator
Schmidt, Sebastian Martin physicist, researcher
Schmidt, Volker Reinhard chemist
Schmidtke, Hans-Herbert chemistry educator
Schmitt, Hans Juergen physics educator, researcher
Schmitz, Rudolf Peter physicist
Schneider, Gisbert research biochemist
Schneider, Uwe physicist
Schneider, Wolfgang Johann biochemical educator, biochemist
Schneiter, Roger biochemist
Schnitzler, Gavin Reinhardt biochemist, researcher, educator
Schnöckel, Hansgeorg chemist, educator
Schoeck, Gunther C. physics researcher
Schoeller, Wolfgang Wilhelm chemistry educator
Schoenborn, Benno P. biophysicist, educator
Schoenfeld, Nili Aviva biochemist, researcher
Schoentgen, Françoise Marie Laure biochemist, researcher
Schoepe, Klaus Bernhard chemist, pharmacist
Schoknecht, Guenter medical physicist, educator
Scholz, Roland W. environmental science educator
Schommers, Wolfram physicist, educator
Schoner, Wilhelm biochemist
Schönfeld, Eckart Albert Robert physicist, researcher
Schonhorn, Harold chemist, researcher
Schönwiese, Christian-Dietrich climatologist, educator
Schopper, Erwin Wilhelm retired physicist
Schreiber, Gerhard Hans biochemistry educator
Schreier, Gunter remote sensing data specialist, researcher
Schrieffer, John Robert physics educator, science administrator
Schröder, Heinz Christoph biochemistry educator, researcher
Schröder, Wolfgang Peter biochemist researcher
Schröecke, Helmüt Heinrich mineralogist, geologist, physical chemist, educator
Schroeder, Manfred Robert physics educator
Schroeder, Wilfried geophysicist
Schroetter, Heinz Wilhelm physics educator
Schubert, Ulrich chemistry educator
Schuberth, Erwin Arthur physicist, educator
Schuepbach, Evi environmental scientist, consultant
Schuhbauer, Heidi scientist
Schulien, Sigurd physicist, educator
Schulte, Jurgen physics educator
Schultze, Hans-Peter E.R. paleontology educator, researcher
Schultze, Joachim Walter chemistry educator
Schulz, Georg Eberhard biochemistry educator, researcher
Schulz, Max Joachim physics educator
Schulz, Pablo Carlos chemist, educator
Schulze-Hagenest, Detlef physicist, researcher
Schumann, Hans research chemist
Schumpe, Adrian chemistry educator
Schurig, Frank Volker chemistry educator, researcher
Schürmann, Hans Werner physicist, educator
Schutz, Bernard Frederick physics educator, astrophysics researcher
Schütz, Gunter Markus physicist, researcher
Schwahn, Dietmar Gerhard Jürgen physicist
Schwartz, A(lbert) Truman chemistry educator
Schwartz, Melvin physics educator, laboratory administrator
Schwartzberg, David B. chemical industry executive
Schwarz, Dominik Johannes physicist
Schwarz, Sigfrid Alfred chemist
Schwegler, Helmut theoretical physics educator
Schweikhard, Lutz Christian physics educator
Schweizer, Anette limnologist, researcher
Sciunnach, Dario Andrea geologist
Scoles, Giacinto chemistry educator
Scorei, Ion Romulus biochemist, educator
Scott, David Knight physicist, university administrator
Scott, Gerald chemistry, educator
Scott, John Ernest chemical morphologist
Scott, Thomas Gordon chemistry educator, writer
Scrutton, Nigel Shaun biochemistry educator
Sculfort, Jean-Lou chemistry and physics educator, researcher
Scurlock, Ralph Geoffrey cryogenics educator, consultant
Sczakiel, Georg Alois biochemist
Seab, Charles Gregory astrophysicist
Searle, Edward retired analytical chemist
Searle, Roger Clive geophysicist educator
Seba, Petr physicist, researcher
Sechovsky, Vladimir physicist
Sedano, Luis Angel physics educator, researcher
Sedlak, Antonin radiation biophysicist researcher
Seeds, Alwyn John opto-electronics researcher, educator
Segal, Vladimir M. metallurgist, researcher
Segal, Yossi biochemist, association executive

Stenkin, Yuri Vasilievich physicist
Stepanenko, Vladimir Danilovich meteorologist, researcher
Stepanov, Igor Aleksandrovich physicist, researcher
Stepanov, Nikita Vladimirovich physicist
Stepanov, Victor Georgievich chemical researcher, chemical engineer
Stephenson, Anthony Edgar (Tony Stephenson) geoscientist, researcher
Stephenson, Francis Richard astronomer
Stepto, Robert Frederick Thomas chemistry educator, consultant
Sterling, David Akiba environmental and occupational health science educator
Stesmans, Andre Leopold physicist, educator
Steudel, Heinz physicist
Steur, Peter P. M. physicist
Stevens, Derrick John research chemist
Stevens, Geoff(rey) chemist, writer
Stigebrandt, Anders Gösta oceanography educator
Stilp, Alois Josef retired physicist
Stirling, Charles James Matthew organic chemistry educator
Stockwell, William Ross atmospheric chemist
Stoev, Stoytcho Mitrev mineralurgist, educator
Stokes, Peter Hedley space debris analyst, researcher
Stoll, Heather Marie geochemist, researcher, educator
Stolyarova, Valentina Leonidovna physical chemist
Stone, Edward Carroll physicist, educator
Stoneley, Robert petroleum geologist, consultant
Störi, Herbert physics educator, consultant
Stork, Gilbert chemistry educator, investigator
Störmer, Horst Ludwig physicist
Storozhev, Vladimir physicist, researcher
Stortz, Carlos Arturo chemistry researcher, educator
Story, E(ugene) Jack physicist
Stoyanov, Eugenie Stepanovich chemistry researcher, educator
Stoylov, Stoyl Peshev biophysics educator, researcher
Stoytchev, Luben Ivanov geologist
Straka, Ronald Morris physicist
Strasser, Patrick physicist
Strauch, Friedrich paleontologist
Strazewski, Peter Marcin chemistry educator, researcher
Strehblow, Hans-Henning Steffen chemistry educator
Strehlow, Hans chemistry educator
Streit, Ludwig P. physics educator
Streitwolf, Hans Waldemar retired physicist
Strelniker, Yakov Mikhailovich physicist, researcher
Strel'nitskij, Vladimir Evgen'evich physicist
Strezh, Petr Evgenyevich physicist, educator
Striebel, Hans-Martin biochemist
Strinati, Giancarlo physics educator, scientist
Stringer, Christopher Brian paleontologist, educator
Stroh, Rüdiger Joachim physicist
Strücker, Gerhard analytical chemist, educator
Struckmeier, Juergen physicist, researcher
Strunk, Horst Paul physicist
Strunk, Martin atmospheric chemist, researcher
Strupczewski, Witold Gustaw hydrologist, educator
Strzalkowski, Ireneusz physicist, educator
Stubičar, Nada Kristina physical chemistry, researcher, chemistry educator
Stuchebrukhov, Alexey Alexandrovich chemistry educator
Stuermer, Hans-Dieter chemist
Ştuetz, Anton chemist, researcher, educator
Štulík, Karel chemical researcher, educator
Sturm, Gerhard chemistry educator, chemist
Stüwe, Hein Peter physicist, educator
Su, Ching-Hua materials scientist
Su, Ninghu hydrologist, research scientist
Su, Sheng-Hui (George S. Su) medicinal chemist, researcher
Suárez Batista, Lilia Esther chemist, researcher
Subasic, Damir environmental program and project manager, consultant, environmentalist
Subramanian, Ganapathy chemist, consultant, editor
Subramanian, Ramaswamy physicist, educator, researcher
Suceska, Muhamed chemist, researcher
Sudakov, Michael Yurievich physicist, researcher
Suffczynski, Maciej Jozef physicist
Suga, Shigemasa material physics educator
Sugimoto, Tadao chemistry educator
Sugimoto, Yukihiro chemist, educator
Suharta, Herliyani physics engineer, materials engineer
Sukhanov, Victor Alexandrovich biochemist, researcher
Sukhorukov, Victor Lev physicist
Sukmono, Sigit geology and geophysics educator
Sukumaran, Gopu Kumar electrochemist
Sulaiman, Afsar Mohammed environmentalist, consultant
Suleiman, Bashir Mohamed physicist, educator, researcher
Sullivan, Edwin Percy Albert retired chemistry and physics educator, researcher
Sullivan, James F. physicist, educator
Sullivan, Mark Hubbard Fitzmaurice biochemist, researcher
Sultan, Gilbert David physicist, researcher
Sultan, Rabih Fayez chemist, educator
Summers, Gabriel Jeffrey chemistry educator, consultant
Sun, Ching-Cherng optics science edcuator
Sun, Luorui physics educator, researcher
Sun, Rongqi organic chemistry educator, researcher
Sun, Siao Fang chemistry educator
Sun, Zhen-Dong laser and physics researcher
Sunandana, Channappayya Shamanna physics educator, researcher
Sund, Bengt Christian chemistry researcher, educator
Sundar Rajan, Asokan physicist, educator
Sunderland, Norman Ray (Norm Sunderland) health physicist, nuclear engineer educator
Sundius, Tom Robert physicist, educator, researcher
Sundstrom, Bernt Olof fiber optics researcher, consultant, educator
Sung, Dae Dong chemistry educator
Suoninen, Eero Juhani retired materials science educator
Suraud, Eric physicist, educator
Surin, Vitaly Ivanovich physicist, researcher, educator
Surján, Péter physicist, educator
Surma, Stanisław Antoni physicist
Surowiec, Andrew Julius biophysicist, researcher
Surpateanu, Gheorghe chemist, educator
Susic, Michael marine chemist, researcher, consultant
Suski, Jan physicist, researcher
Sutcliffe, Haydn chemistry educator, European education consultant
Suter, Robert Merle physicist, educator
Suvorova, Anna Isaakovna chemistry educator, researcher
Suwalsky, Mario chemistry educator
Suzdalev, Igor Petrovitch physicist
Suzuki, Akira physics educator
Suzuki, Hitomi organic chemistry educator, researcher
Suzuki, Isao physical chemist
Suzuki, Shigeru mineralogist
Svarc, Alfred physicist, researcher, consultant
Svasti, Jisnuson biochemistry educator
Svestka, Zdenek F. solar physicist
Svetitsky, Benjamin physicist, educator
Svettsov, Vladimir Vladimirovich physicist, researcher
Sviridov, Konstantin Nikolaevich physicist
Svoboda, Ladislav chemistry educator
Svoboda, Petr biochemist, educator
Svyazhin, Anatoly Grigorievich metallurgy educator, researcher
Sweeny, Charles David chemist
Sweeting, Linda Marie chemist
Swithinbank, Charles Winthrop glaciologist, consultant
Sy, Dalisay Chionglo biochemistry educator
Sydorova, Ludmilla Victorovna chemist, research scientist
Sye, Wen Fa chemistry educator
Sykes, Alfred Geoffrey chemist, educator
Symons, Martyn Christian chemistry educator
Synek, Miroslav physicist, chemist, world affairs independent consultant, researcher
Syromyatnikov, Vladislav Genrikhovich physicist
Syros, Constantin Elias physics educator
Sytko, Vladimir physicist, educator, researcher
Szalapski, Robert Francis theoretical physicist
Szalewicz, Krzysztof physics educator
Szantay, Csaba chemist
Szasz, Andras physicist, educator, researcher
Szasz, György pharmaceutical chemist
Szentgyorgyi, Paul nuclear chemist, researcher
Szentpáli, Béla physicist, researcher
Szepesy, László Elek chemist, researcher
Szigeti, János physicist
Szmaja, Witold physicist, researcher
Szondy, Zsuzsanna Julianna biochemist, researcher
Sztaniszlav, Anna Danielne chemical science company administrator, researcher
Szucs, Mihaly soil science educator
Szumiec, Maria Anna geophysicist, researcher
Szurkowski, Janusz Wiktor physicist, educator
Szuszkiewicz, Ewa astronomer, educator
Szuta, Marcin physicist
Szwajczak, Elzbieta Teresa physicist educator
Taalas, Jukka Petteri atmospheric scientist
Tabagari, Sergi Ilyich biochemist, educator
Tabaksblat, Lazar Sigizmundovich geochemistry educator
Tabata, Tatsuo physicist, researcher
Tabidze, Vazha biochemist
Tachiwaki, Tokumatsu chemistry educator
Tadasa, Koji biochemistry educator
Tadić, Dubravko physics educator, research scientist
Tadros, Aida Botros chemist, educator
Taggart, Keith Anthony physicist, systems analyst
Tagliaferri, Guido Alfonso physics educator
Tahirov, Tahir Haji oglu crystallographer
Taimuty, Samuel Isaac physicist
Taira, Kazunari chemistry educator
Tait, James Francis retired biophysicist, endocrinologist
Tajiri, Masayoshi physicist
Takami, Michio physicist, chemist, researcher
Takase, Kenji biochemist, researcher
Takase, Shigehiro chemist
Takashima, Shiro biophysics educator
Takeda, Takeshi chemistry educator
Takemoto, Kiichi chemistry educator
Takeoka, Yukikazu chemist, researcher
Takigawa, Tadahiro physicist
Takizawa, Kuniharu optoelectronics researcher, educator
Talandier, Jacques Marcel geophysicist, consultant
Talbot, David Keith environmental geochemist
Talbott, George Robert physicist, mathematician, educator
Tallent, William Hugh chemist, research administrator
Talukdar, Bandana biochemistry educator, researcher
Tam, Kin Yip chemist
Tamburrini, Maurizio biochemist, researcher
Tammet, Hannes physics educator, researcher
Tamulis, Arvydas physicist, researcher
Tan, Andy H.M. physicist, educator
Tan, Benjamin Yen-Jing physics educator, researcher
Tanabe, Setsuhisa material scientist, glass researcher
Tanabe, Tadashi biochemist, educator, researcher
Tanaka, Hideyuki physicist, researcher
Tanaka, Hiroshi L. atmospheric scientist
Tanaka, Toshijiro physicist
Tang, Kaluo chemistry educator
Taniewski, Marian chemist, educator
Taniguchi, Yoshihiro chemist, educator
Tanner, Brian Keith physics educator
Tao, Mariano biochemistry educator
Tara research chemist, publishing executive, writer
Tararin, Igor Aleksandrovich petrologist, researcher
Tarasenko, Alexander Alexeevich physicist, researcher
Tarasiewicz, Helena Puzanowska chemist, researcher
Tarasiewicz, Mikolaj chemist, researcher
Tarasov, Aleksandr physicist, researcher
Tarassoli, Abbas chemist, researcher
Tarin, Pere chemist
Tasset, Francis Joseph Emmanuel physicist
Tasso, Henri theoretical research physicist
Tatarenko, Valentin Andriyovych physicist, researcher
Tatarskii, Valerian Il'Ich physics researcher
Tatera, James Frank chemist, process analysis specialist
Tatikolov, Alexander Sergeevich chemist, researcher
Tatlonghari, Carmelito Arellano health physicist
Tatsumi, Kouichi radiation biologist, internist
Taube, Henry chemistry educator
Täuber, Uwe Claus physicist
Taur, Yuan physicist, researcher
Taylor, Fredric William physicist
Taylor, Joseph Hooton, Jr. radio astronomer, physicist
Taylor, Lawrence Dow geologist, educator
Taylor, Richard Edward physicist, educator
Taylor, Stuart Ross geochemist, author
Taylor, William Ramsay computational molecular biophysicist
Tebby, John Caesar chemist, researcher
Tegze, Miklos physicist
Teige, Scott Werner physicist
Tejada, Silvia chemistry educator, researcher in microbiology corrosion
Telišman, Spomenka biochemist, scientific consultant
Telnov, Valery Ivanovich physicist, educator
Temnikov, Aleksei Nikolaevich physics educator
Tendler, Michael physics educator, scientific association executive
Teng, Yonghong chemist, researcher, translator
Teoreanu, Ion solid state chemistry educator, researcher
Teoule, Robert Auguste biochemist
Teplykh, Vissarion chemistry educator
Terazawa, Hidezumi physicist, educator
Terblanche, Petro environmental scientist, consultant
Terentjeva, Alexandra K. astronomer, researcher
Tereshko, Irene Vasiljevna physicist, educator
Terez, Edward Ivan astrophysics and atmospheric physics educator
Terpugov, Eugeni L'vovich biophysicist, researcher
Terry, Glenn A. retired nuclear chemist
Tesner, Pavel Alexandr chemist, researcher
Tessler, Nir physicist, electrical engineer, educator
Teterin, Yury Alexandrovich physicist, researcher, educator
Tewari, Harish Chandra earth scientist
Teze, Andre Guy chemist, educator
Theile, Burkhard physicist
Theis, Werner R. physics educator
Theng, Benny Kian Goan clay-organic chemist
Theodore, Ares Nicholas research chemist
Theodorsson, Pall physics scientist
Theophanides, Theophilos chemistry educator, consultant
Thevik, Haavard Jan materials scientist, researcher, consultant
Thiede, Jorn paleoceanographer
Thiel, Walter chemistry educator, researcher
Thielheim, Klaus Oswald physicist
Thiemann, Wolfram Hans-Peter chemist
Thissell, James Dennis physicist
Thøgersen, Henning chemist, researcher
Thoma, Kallirroe-Andriane Theodorou physics educator
Thoman, Charles James chemistry educator
Thomas, David Jeffrey physicist, mathematician, researcher, editor, financier
Thomas, Edward John physicist, educator
Thomas, Helmut Jakob biochemist, educator, researcher
Thomas, Robert Kemeys chemistry educator, researcher
Thomason, Peter Frank materials scientist, educator, educator
Thompson, David Thomas consulting chemist, researcher
Thompson, John Michael chemist
Thomsen, Richard hydrologist
't Hooft, Gerardus physics educator
Thordarson, William retired hydrogeologist
Thornsberry, Willis Lee, Jr. chemist
Thrush, Brian Arthur physical chemist, educator
Thullner, Martin Christian physicist
Tibaldi, Alessandro geologist, educator
Tichy, Josef chemistry educator, researcher
Tichy, Miloš Antonín biochemist, educator
Tickell, Sir Crispin environmentalist
Tiedemann, Albert William, Jr. retired chemist
Tiederle, Viktor Chris physicist, microelectronic technician
Tien, Cheng physicist, educator
Tietze, Klaus Dieter physicist
Tigyi, Jozsef biophysicist
Tikhonov, Yuryi Vladimirovich biochemist
Tilbury, Rodney Neil chemistry educator
Tilinin, Igor Stanislavovich physicist, educator
Tilquin, Bernard chemistry educator
Timcenko, Lydia Teodora biochemist, chemist
Timmer, Cornelis Johannes chemist, researcher
Timofeevski, Sergei Leonidovich biochemistry and chemistry researcher
Timus, Clementina Alexandrina physicist
Ting, Samuel Chao Chung physicist, educator
Tipler, Frank Jennings, III physicist
Tirelli, Nicola chemistry researcher
Tisdale, Michael John biochemistry educator
Tishkov, Alexander Arkadevich chemist
Titov, Alexander Ivanovich physicist, researcher
Titov, Alexandre Nickolayevich physicist, researcher
Titov, Valentin Alexandrovich physical chemist, researcher
Tittmann, Karsten physicist
Titulaer, Urbaan Maria physics educator
Tjornelund, Jette scientist
Tjurin, Vladimir Alexandrovich physics educator
Tkach, Volodimir physicist, educator
Tkachenko, Nikolai Vladimirovich physicist
Tkachuk, Zenoviy Yuriyovych biochemist, consultant
Todinov, Michael Todorov materials scientist, researcher
Todorov, Nickola Stefanov physicist
Toennies, Jan Peter research chemical physicist
Tokar, Mikhail physicist, theoretician
Tőke, László chemistry educator
Tokheim, Robert Edward physicist
Tokousbalides, Paraskevas T. chemist
Tolman, Vladimír Břetislav chemist, researcher
Tolstoguzov, Vladimir Borisovich chemistry researcher
Tolstorukov, Michael Y. biophysicist
Toman, Rudolf Ludovit biochemist, researcher
Tomaselli, Michele chemist
Tomasz, Palewski physics educator, researcher
Tomaszewski, Jeremiasz Jerzy biochemist
Tombácz, Etelka chemist, educator
Tomé, Wolfgang Axel physicist, researcher, educator
Tomilov, Andrey Petrovich electrochemist, consultant
Tominaga, Shin-ichi biochemist, educator
Tomita, Akihiko astronomer
Tomomatsu, Hideo chemist
Tomson, Ilmar Nicolaevich geologist researcher
Tonchev, Svetlen Hristov physicist, scientist, researcher
Tong, Tanjun biochemist, educator
Tong, Zhi Shen physics educator
Tonnisson, Teofilus optics scientist, physicist
Tooming, Heino Ülo agrometeorologist, researcher
Toperverg, Boris P. physicist
Topkaya, Yavuz Ali metallurgy educator
Torché, Mark David physics educator
Torchynska, Tetyana Victorivna physicist
Torkelsson, Ulf Joakim astronomer
Tormen, Giuseppe astrophysicist
Tornqvist, Stefan program manager
Török, István physicist, researcher
Toro-Labbe, Alejandro Miguel chemist, educator, researcher
Torrades Carné, Francesc chemist, researcher, educator
Torrens, Francisco physical chemistry educator
Toste, Anthony Paim chemistry educator, researcher
Tosto, Sebastiano materials scientist
Tóth, Imre chemist, researcher
Toth, Istvan medicinal organic chemistry educator
Touret, Jacques Leon Robert geology educator
Tout, Christopher Adam astronomer, consultant
Townes, Charles Hard physics educator
Townsend, Peter David physicist, educator
Toyota, Naoki physicist
Trache Apostol, Andreea physicist
Träger, Frank Reiner physics, educator
Trautmann, Norbert Günter chemist
Trautwein, Alfred Xaver biophysics educator
Tretinnikov, Oleg Nikolayevich physicist
Trifonova, Emilia Petrova educator, researcher
Triftshäuser, Werner physics educator
Trigunayat, Govind Chandra physics educator
Trinh, Cam-Tu T. chemist
Tripathi, Yamini Bhusan biochemist, educator, researcher
Tristo, Gastone chemist
Tritt-Goc, Jadwiga physicist, researcher
Trivelpiece, Alvin William physicist, educator, consultant
Trkal, Viktor physical chemist, researcher
Trocewicz, Jerzy chemistry educator
Trocki, Linda Katherine geoscientist, natural resource economist
Troemel, Martin retired chemistry educator
Trofimov, Vladimor Isakovich physicist, researcher
Trofimova, Natalia Nikolaevna chemist, researcher
Troitski, Yuri Vladimirovich physicist, researcher
Troitzsch, Ulrike geologist, mineralogist, researcher
Trojer, Lena chemist, gender researcher
Trotsenko, Alexander Vladimirovych thermophysicist, researcher
Trowbridge, Charles William physicist, engineer, researcher
Trozzolo, Anthony Marion chemistry educator
Trsic, Milan chemistry educator, researcher
Trubetskoy, Vladimir Sergeevich polymer chemist
Trubitsyn, Michael physicist, educator
Trubko, Sergey Vladimir optical designer, researcher
Trueb, Beat biochemist, researcher
Truesdale, Geoffrey Ashworth former environmental chemist
Trulsen, Karsten wave hydrodynamicist, researcher
Trunkovsky, Evgenij Markovich astronomer, researcher
Truong, Thanh Nguyen chemistry educator, researcher
Truong, Van-Tan materials scientist
Tsai, Sheng-Yi physics educator, researcher
Tsang, Chi Fo chemist, researcher
Tsangaris, George Michael physicist, educator, researcher
Tsangaris, John Michael chemistry educator
Tschalaer, Christoph physicist, researcher
Tschesche, Harald chemist, scientist, educator
Tsekov, Roumen Tsvetanov chemistry educator
Tselepi-Mitrelias, Marina physicist, researcher
Tsendin, Konstantin Damdin physicist, researcher
Tseng, Tien-Jiunn physics educator
Tsidilkovski, Isaac Michailovich physicist
Tsipenyuk, Dmitry Yurievich physicist, inventor
Tsipenyuk, Yuri Mikhailovich physicist, educator
Tsitolovsky, Lev neurobiologist, researcher
Tsolas, Orestes Erofilos biological chemistry educator
Tsubomura, Hiroshi chemistry educator
Tsuchi, Ryuichi geoscientist, researcher
Tsuchiya, Masahiko chemist
Tsuda, Ichiro physicist, mathematician
Tsukamoto, Osamu meteorologist, educator
Tsunashima, Yoshisuke physical chemist, researcher, educator
Tsutsumi, Osamu chemist
Tsvetkov, Oleg Boris themophysicist, researcher
Tsymbalenko, Vladimir Leonidovich experimental physicist, researcher, consultant
Tu, Chuanyi space physics educator, researcher
Tufaile, Alberto physicist, researcher
Tuháčková, Zdena biochemist, researcher
Tuleta, Marek physicist, educator, researcher
Tulub, Alexander Alexandrovich physicist, researcher, educator
Tumakov, Vladimir Leonidovich physicist, researcher
Tuninskaya, Galina M. chemist
Tunitskaya, Vera Leonidovna chemist, researcher
Tur, Anatoli research physicist
Turanek, Jaroslav biochemist
Turcu, Ion Cristian Edmond physicist
Turki, Abd El-Mohsen Mohamed physical chemistry educator, researcher
Turnbull, Alan corrosion scientist, researcher
Turner, Robert physicist, researcher
Turovets, Sergei Ivanovitch laser physicist
Turovska, Baiba chemist, researcher
Tütem, Esma chemist, educator
Tuul, Johannes physics educator, researcher
Twardowski, Andrzej physics educator, researcher
Tyagi, Anand K. materials scientist
Tyagi, Som Dev physics educator
Tyman, John Henry Paul chemistry educator
Tyrer, Hugh engineering metallurgist, consultant
Tyschenko, Ida physicist
Tzanakos, George Stefanos physicist, educator
Tzartos, Socrates biochemist
Ubelis, Arnolds physicist
Ubuka, Toshihiko biochemistry educator, dean
Uchida, Tsuneko biochemist, researcher, educator
Uchrin, Christopher George environmental engineer and scientist
Udagawa, Takeshi physicist, educator
Udalov, Yuri Borisovitch physicist
Udem, Thomas physicist
Udoev, Yuri Pavlovich physicist, educator
Ue, Makoto chemist, researcher
Ueki, Masanori materials scientist
Uemoto, Michihisa chemistry educator, researcher
Ueno, Edward Isao environmental scientist
Ueoka, Ryuichi chemistry educator
Ugajin, Ryuichi physicist, inventor
Ugarov, Michael V. physics researcher
Ugrozov, Valery Vycheslavovich physical chemist, mathematics educator
Uhlenbrook, Stefan hydrologist
Uhlendorf, Volkmar Hans Friedrich research physicist
Uhlig, Egon chemistry educator
Uicich, Raul Eduardo biochemist, researcher
Ukerun, Sylvester Ohwevwo chemistry educator
Ukshe, Alexander Evgenievich physicist, researcher
Ulehla, Ivan physics educator
Ulmschneider, Peter Hermann astrophysics educator

SOCIAL SCIENCE

Amawattana, Emavardhana Tipawadee psychology educator
Ambirajan, Srinivasa economics educator
Ambrosi, Gerhard Michael economics educator
Amin, Abu Taher Mohammed Nurul economics educator, researcher
Amin, Mohammad Nurul political science educator
Amir, Rabah economist, educator
Anati, Emmanuel archaeologist, educator
Andelman, Fani neuropsychologist, speech therapist
Andersen, Ib sociologist, researcher, educator, consultant
Anderson, Arthur J. clinical psychologist, researcher
Anderson, Kym economics educator
Andersson, David Sten economist
Andrada, Luis economist
Andrain, Charles Franklin political science educator
Andrews, Adrienne Paine psychologist
Andrews, Melinda Wilson human development researcher
Angadi, Veeranna Basavantappa economist, administrator, researcher
Angelini, Paolo economist
Angell, Wayne D. economist, banker
Aniya, Masamu geographer, educator
Antonopoulou, Christina psychology educator
Anyanwu, Victor O(nye) criminologist, political scientist
Aono, Katsuhiro economist, educator
Appel, Antoinette Ruth neuropsychologist
Appleton, Rodney Lewis Claude economist, publisher, consultant
Appolinario, Fabio psychologist, researcher
Aranguren, Querejeta Mari Jose economics educator, researcher
Aratow-Kulaksiz, Kayan clinical psychologist
Arber, Sara Lynne sociology educator, researcher
Archer, Brian Harrison economics educator, consultant
Archer, John Ernest psychology educator
Argandoña, Antonio economics educator
Argyle, John Michael psychology educator, researcher
Ariffin, Yohan political scientist, researcher
Arita, Tatsuo economist, educator
Arlinghaus, Sandra Judith Lach mathematical geographer, educator
Armitage-Woodward, Fiona Louise educator, researcher in social sciences
Armstrong, Patrick Hamilton geography educator
Arndt, Heinz Wolfgang economics educator
Arnold, J(ames) Barto, III marine archaeologist
Arnon, Arie economist
Aronow, Edward psychologist, educator
Arouca Marques dos Santos, Luiz Frederico economics educator, civil engineering consultant
Arrow, Kenneth Joseph economist, educator
Arsebük, Güven anthropoarchaeologist, educator
Asano, Keiko psychology educator
Ashford, Nigel John Gladwell political scientist, educator
Asiedu, Thomas Kofi political scientist
Assink, Egbert Maria psychology educator
Athanassoglou, Panayotis Pantelis economist
Atherton, June Christina analytic psychologist, educator
Atkinson, Robert G. human development educator
Atlas, Jeffrey A. psychologist, educator
Auerbach, Anita L. clinical psychologist
Aukutsionek, Sergej Pavlovich economist, researcher
Aurada, Klaus D. physical geography educator
Aviles, Alice Alers psychologist
Ayad, Joseph Magdy psychologist
Azad, Nirmal Singh economics educator
Aziz, Shagufta psychologist, educator, researcher
Baales, Michael archaeologist
Baba, Marietta Lynn business anthropologist
Baborski, Andrzej Jozef economist
Bach, Christian Friis economics educator
Bachman, Jerald Graybill psychologist, researcher
Baddeley, Alan David psychologist
Bae, Hyung economist
Baehr, Juergen geographer
Baer, Michael Alan political scientist, educator
Baez, JoAnne Marie school psychologist
Bag, Orhan Ozlem economist
Bahiri, Simcha economist
Bailey, Michael Stewart political science educator
Bailey, Norman Alishan economist
Baird, Abigail Alicia psychologist
Bakirtzis, Charalambos archaeologist
Bakis, Henry Gerald Hubert geographer, sociologist, communications educator
Balcerowicz, Leszek economics educator
Baldaccini, Natale Emilio ethology educator, researcher
Baldrachi, Ryan Michael psychologist
Ball, Sir (Robert) James economics educator
Bammé, Arno social science educator
Banerjee, Jyotirmoy science educator, researcher
Bangha, Martin Wultoff demographer
Bannock, Graham Bertram economist
Banyar, Jozsef economist
Bara, Bruno Giuseppe psychology educator
Barahona de Brito, Alexandra political scientist
Barak, Azy psychologist, educator
Baranano-Martinez, Ana Maria management educator
Barbotko, Alexander Ivanovitch gerontologist
Barceló Mezquita, José Luis political scientist
Barkat, Abul economist educator, researcher
Barlybaev, Adigam Agzamovich economist, educator
Barrett, Scott Alexander environmental economics educator, consultant
Barron, Susan clinical psychologist
Barry, Herbert, III psychologist
Bartee, James William psychologist
Barthel, Günter Germany
Barthélemy, Luc geographer and researcher
Barthold, Thomas A. economist
Bashkirova, Elena Ivanovna public opinion administrator, consultant
Bastos, Suelena Vieira de Melo psychologist
Bate, Brian R. psychologist
Bateman, Ian Julian economist, researcher
Batnick, Michael Arnold political economist, political consultant
Batson, David Frederick Edward social studies educator
Battiau-Queney, Yvonne geography educator
Battigalli, Pierpaolo ecomomics educator
Batygin, Gennady Semyonovitch sociologist, researcher
Bauchet, Pierre Paul retired social science educator
Baudet, Francis Andre sociologist, educator
Bauman, Zygmunt sociologist
Bawn, Kathleen political science educator
Beck, Tamás economic expert
Becker, Gary Stanley economist, educator
Beckford, James Arthur sociologist, educator
Beckman, James Wallace Bim economist, marketing executive, educator
Beelmann, Andreas psychology educator, researcher
Belfiglio, Valentine John political science educator, pharmacist
Bell, Donald William experimental psychologist
Bell, Robert Trevor economics researcher, educator
Bellows, Thomas John political scientist, educator
Benes, Ivan economist
Bénézech, Michel Henri criminologist, researcher
Bennett, Robert John geography educator
Benon, Jean Francois economist, French local government official
Benos, Theofanis Evangelos economics educator
Benson, Lucy Wilson political and diplomatic consultant
Benthall, Jonathan Charles Mackenzie anthropologist, writer
Bentley, Raymond social studies of technology educator
Berardi, Jorge Enrique economist
Beraud, Alain economics educator
Berent, Stanley psychologist, educator, researcher, consultant
Berg-Schlosser, Dirk political science educator
Bergsten, C. Fred economist
Berliant, Marcus Craig economist
Bermudez Sokolich, Diana Lourdes psychologist
Bernard, Deryck Milton geographer, minister
Bernat, Tivadar retired geography educator
Berner, Boel sociology educator
Bernholz, Peter Ferdinand economics educator
Bernieri, Frank John social psychology educator
Bernstein, Basil Bernard sociology educator
Berrington, Hugh Bayard political science educator
Bertsch, Gary Kenneth political scientist, educator
Besançon, Alain Justin political scientist, historian
Betancourt, Hector Mainhard psychology scientist, educator
Betbeze, Jean-Paul economist
Beversdorf, Anne Elizabeth astrologer, author, educator
Bevir, William Mark political science educator
Bezic, Irena psychologist
Bezrukov, Vladislav Viktorovich gerontologist, researcher
Bhatta, Gambhir political science and management educator
Bhattacharya, Debesh economics educator
Bhattacharya, Purusottam political science educator
Bhuyan, Muhammad Ayubur Rahman economics educator
Biddle, Martin archaeologist
Bienaymé, Alain M. economics educator
Bierschenk, Bernhard Friedrich psychologist, researcher
Bih, Herng-Dar environmental psychologist
Bilinsky, Yaroslav political scientist
Billig, Michael social psychologist, educator
Binswanger, Hans Christoph economist, educator
Birkelbach, Klaus W. sociologist
Birnbaum, Philip development economist
Bishop, George David psychology educator
Biskup, Joachim psychoanalyst, psychologist
Björkman, Jan Olof sociology educator, researcher, administrator
Blaikie, Piers Macleod social studies educator
Blake, Gerald Henry geography educator
Blakey, Michael Louis anthropologist, educator
Blandy, Richard John economics educator
Blankenburg, Erhard R. sociology of law educator
Blaser, Arthur Weston political science educator, writer
Blauw, Pieter Wilhelmus sociologist
Bloch, Peter Conrad economist, educator
Block, Michael Kent economics and law educator, public policy association executive, former government official, consultant
Blondel, Jean Fernand political science educator
Blondiaux, Jokl forensic anthropologist, educator
Bloom, Gordon Allan psychologist, educator
Bloomfield, Lincoln Palmer political scientist
Bluestone, Barry Alan economics educator
Blumberg, Herbert Haskell psychology educator
Blumstein, Alfred urban and public affairs educator
Blundell, Richard William economics educator
Boardman, Sir John classical archaeology educator, historian, art educator
Bob-Duru, Robert C. geography and environmental sciences educator
Bobich, Zeljko psychologist, psychotherapist
Bodenhoefer, Hans Joachim economics educator
Bodenstedt, Andreas retired sociologist, educator
Boger, Dan Calvin statistical and economic consultant, educator
Boglar, Luiz anthropology educator
Boguslavsky, George William psychologist, educator
Bohannon, John Neil, III psychology educator, researcher
Bohner, Gerd Walter psychologist, educator
Boltho, Andrea economics educator
Bombelles, Joseph Thomas economics educator, consultant
Bonabello, Pietro political scientist
Bonatti, Luca Lorenzo psychology educator, researcher
Bond, Alma Halbert psychoanalyst, author
Bond, Nigel William psychologist
Bong, Mimi psychologist
Boor, Myron Vernon psychologist, educator
Boorstein, Laurence economist
Booth, David Allenby psychology educator
Boralli Rocha, Eduardo psychologist
Borelli, Giorgio economic history educator
Borg, Mark Gerard psychology educator, consultant
Borg, Olavi Allan political scientist
Borjas, George J(esus) economics educator
Borrelli, Mario Alfredo sociologist
Borsdorf, Axel geographer, educator, researcher
Boucher, Wayne Irving policy analyst
Boudon, Raymond sociologist, educator
Bouhdiba, Abdel Wahab sociologist, philosopher, educator, researcher
Bouillon, Rayan Gabriel development economist, international consultant
Boukaraoun, Hacene economist
Boudrieu, Pierre Felix sociology educator
Bouvry, Brigitte economics educator
Bowen, William Gordon economist, educator, foundation administrator
Bowman, Larry Wayne investigator, English and criminal justice educator
Bowman, Sheridan Gail Esther archaeological scientist
Boyan, A. Stephen, Jr. political science educator
Boyle, Gregory John psychology educator, research consultant
Brace, C. Loring anthropologist, educator
Bracewell-Milnes, John Barry economic consultant, writer
Bracey, Earnest Norton political science educator
Brada, Jaroslav economist
Bradburn, Robert Easton economics educator
Bradley, Jonathan economics educator
Braehler, Elmar psychology and medical sociology educator
Braeutigam, Ronald Ray economics educator
Braga de Macedo, Jorge Avelino economics educator
Braguinsky, Serguey economist
Bramsen, Inge psychologist, researcher
Branan, John Maury psychology educator, counselor
Brandão, Ana Paula Lima Pinto political science educator, researcher
Brandstätter, Eduard Johann psychology educator, researcher
Branigan, Keith archaeologist, educator
Brauers, Willem Karel economist, educator
Breakwell, Glynis Marie psychology educator
Brebner, John Main psychologist, educator
Bredenkamp, Juergen psychologist
Bredfeldt, John Creighton economist, financial analyst, retired air force officer
Breed, Ria anthropologist
Breen, Faith Fei-Mei Lee economist, management consultant
Bregnsbo, Henning political scientist, researcher
Brender, Anton economist
Brennan, H(arold) Geoffrey social sciences educator, researcher
Brennan, Teresa Mary Isabel social theory educator, writer
Brewer, Dominic James economist, researcher, administrator
Bridges, Julian Curtis sociologist educator, department head
Brigaldino, Glenn social scientist, consultant
Briggs, Philip James political science educator, author, lecturer
Brislain, Judy Ann psychologist
Briz, Julian E. economics educator
Brkić, Luka political scientist, educator
Brodbeck, Felix Claus psychology educator
Brodkin, Adele Ruth Meyer psychologist
Bronkhorst, Johannes Indologist, educator
Brown, Dennis Geoffrey psychoanalyst, psychotherapist, consultant
Brown, Edgar Cary retired economics educator
Brown, Eric Herbert geography professor
Brown, Eric Moite economist
Brown, Laurence Binet retired psychology educator
Brown, Mahlon Carl social science educator
Brown, Seyom international relations educator, government consultant
Brown-Jones, Valerie economist
Bruderl, Josef sociologist
Brus, Wlodzimierz retired economics educator
Brustein, William Irving sociology educator
Bryant, Edward Arnot geoscience educator
Buchanan, Ann Hermione social studies educator
Buchanan, James McGill economist, educator
Buckley, Peter Jennings economics educator
Buckner-Reitman, Joyce psychologist, educator
Bucky, Peter Stern psychologist
Budge, Ian political science educator
Bufon, Milan geographer, educator
Buggle, Franz psychology educator
Bull, Peter Joseph retired economic consultant
Bulmer, Martin sociologist, educator
Bunda, Stephen Myron political advisor, consultant, lawyer, classical philosopher
Bunkše, Edmunds Valdemārs geographer, educator, consultant
Buranelli, Francesco archaeologist, museum director
Burchardt, Jørgen ethnologist, consultant
Burchell, Brendan Joseph social and political science educator
Burcroff, Richard Tomkinson, II economist
Burger, Anna agricultural and geographical economics educator
Burisch, Matthias psychologist, educator
Burke, Paul Edmund social scientist, activist
Burke, Randy Scott psychologist
Burley, Peter Campbell urban economist, researcher
Burnham, Lem psychologist
Burris, B. Shane economist
Burrough, Peter Alan physical geographer
Burroughs, Susan Marie psychologist, professor
Buscaglia, Adolfo Edgardo economist, educator
Busch, John A. sociologist
Busjahn, Andreas psychologist
Busygina, Irina Markovna geographer, educator
Butler, Gillian clinical psychologist, consultant
Butler, Michael Ward economics educator
Butler, Nicholas Jones economist
Butterfield, Bonnie Sue psychology educator, librarian, researcher, university webmaster
Butz, Otto William political science educator
Buyst, Erik Cesar economic history educator
Byrne, Noel Thomas sociologist, educator
Caan, Albert Woodburn psychologist
Cabrera, Elizabeth Fraser educator, consultant
Caccomo, Jean-Louis economist, consultant
Cadogan, Peter William retired educator, activist
Cadwalder, Hugh Maurice psychology educator
Cagiano de Azevedo, Raimondo demographer, educator
Cagney, William Robert psychologist
Cahill, Neil economics educator, chaplain
Calder, Kent Eyring political science educator, diplomat
Caldwell, Dan Edward political science educator
Caldwell, Willard E. psychologist, educator
Calhoun, Thomas C. sociology and African American studies educator
Caltabiano, Marie Louise psychologist
Calvert, Peter Anthony Richard political science educator
Calvez, Jean Yves political science and theology educator
Calvin, Allen David psychologist, educator
Cameron, Rondo economic history educator
Canavesi Rimbaud, Marie Lissette E. anthrologyst
Canivez, Gary Lynn psychologist, educator
Canjar, Patricia McWade psychologist
Cannon, J. Timothy psychology educator, neuroscientist
Cannon, June A. social worker
Canterbury-Counts, W. Douglas psychologist
Cantoni, Louis Joseph psychologist, poet, sculptor
Cantor-Graae, Elizabeth Reva psychologist
Cantril, Albert H(adley) public opinion analyst
Capaldi, Elizabeth Ann Deutsch psychological sciences educator
Capie, Forrest Hunter economics educator
Caputo, Daniel Vincent psychologist
Carbonell, Eudald anthropologist, archaeologist, paleoanthropologist
Carey, Alida Livingston political scientist, writer, reporter
Carleson, Robert Bazil public policy consultant, corporation executive
Carlson, Laura Anne psychology educator
Carman, Janice Faller (Kit Carman) psychology educator, consultant
Carr, C. Lynn sociology educator, researcher
Carrillo-de-la-Peña, Maria Teresa psychologist
Carro, Domingo economist, consultant
Carsello, Carmen Joseph psychologist, educator
Carter, John Dale organizational development executive
Carter, Kathleen Janet Jan (Jan Carter) sociologist
Carty, Mary Ellen psychologist
Carvalho, Julie Ann psychologist
Casanova, Jean-Claude political science educator
Cash, Carol Vivian sociologist
Casonato, Marco Mario Alberto psychology educator, psychoanalyst
Castañeda, Marina psychologist, writer
Castano, Emanuele psychology educator
Caudill, Steven Brent economics educator
Cazabat, Eduardo Horacio psychologist
Cazan, Matthew John political science educator
Cebula, Richard John economist, educator
Ceci, Ruggero Lennart psychology researcher
Cerny, Philip George political scientist, educator
Cha, Jae-Ho psychology educator
Chabot, Jean-Luc political science educator
Chacholiades, Miltiades economics educator
Chaiken, Shelly L. psychologist, educator
Chakrabarti, Subir Kumar economics educator
Chalaby, Jean Karim sociologist
Champion, Anthony Gerard population geography educator
Chang, Eugene Yu-sheng political science educator
Chang, Gene Hsin economics educator, humanities educator
Chang, Hyoun Kab psychology educator
Chang, Theodore Chien-Hsin psychologist
Chang, Yongsung economist
Chanley, Virginia Ann political science educator
Chant, Sylvia Hamilton geography educator
Chapman, Bruce James academic economist
Chapman, Hope Horan psychologist
Charles, Ron archaeologist, researcher
Charlton, Bruce Graham psychology educator, physician
Charny, Israel Wolf psychologist, educator
Chatt, Allen Barrett psychologist, neuroscientist
Chaves, Francisco de Paula, Jr. criminalist
Chazine, Jean Michel ethno-archaeologist
Cheblakova, Elena Anatol'evna mathematician, researcher
Cheek, Howard Lee, Jr. political science and philosophy educator
Chelstrom, Marilyn Ann political education consultant
Chen, Esther Eva psychologist, educator
Chen, Hsuan-Chih psychologist
Cheng, Chu Yuan economics educator
Cheng, Joseph Yu-shek political scientist, educator
Cheng, Mei-Fang psychobiology educator, neuroethology researcher
Cheng, Stephen Kin Kwok psychologist, consultant, business consultant
Cherian, Varghese Iepen psychologist, educator
Cherkaoui, Mohamed sociologist
Chetty, Girija M. economics and computers educator, researcher
Chiegboka, Patricia Chinyere psychology administrator, consultant
Chiesa, Maria Donatella economics educator
Chimura, Akira economist
Chinn, Menzie David economics educator
Chinnian, Rajaratnam Rawlin psychologist
Cho, In-Koo economist, educator
Chobanova, Rossitsa Dobreva economist, researcher
Chodorow, Nancy Julia sociology educator
Chong, Tai-Leung Terence economist, educator
Chorot, Paloma clinical psychologist, lecturer
Chu, David S. C. economist
Chu, Szu-Te economics educator
Chughtai, Selina psychologist
Chukhlomin, Valeriy Dmitrievich economics educator, academic administrator
Chunze, Jiang economist, educator
Cilardo, Agostino political scientist, educator
Ciola, Egidio psychologist, consultant
Ciriaco, Sergio financial consultant
Cirrito, Joseph James geographer
Clagett, Arthur F(rank) psychologist, sociologist, qualitative research writer, retired sociology educator
Clark, Alfred William retired sociology educator
Clark, Andrew Eric educator of economics
Clark, Kathleen Margaret Claire political scientist
Clark, Susan Jeanne economics educator
Clark, William Arthur V. geographer, demographer
Clavero, Antonio economist, educator
Cliffe, Mark Alan economist
Cline, John Carroll clinical psychologist
Clinton, Richard Lee international relations educator
Clottes, Jean Jose archaeologist, researcher
Cludts, Stephan economist
Coase, Ronald Harry economics educator
Coats, Warren L., Jr. economist
Cobham, Vanessa Elise psychologist
Coché, Judith psychologist, educator
Cochran, John P. economics educator
Cochrane, James Louis economist
Cockerham, William Carl sociologist, professor
Coenraets, Andre Jean psychosociologist
Cohen, Benjamin Jerry political economy educator
Cohen, Irwin economist
Cohn, Ellen Gail criminologist
Coker, Sally Jo sociology educator
Cole, Donald Powell anthropology educator
Cole, Julio Harold economics educator
Cole, Leonard Aaron political scientist, dentist
Coles, Bryony Jean archaeologist, educator
Collins, Fuji clinical psychologist
Colombini, Fabiano economist, educator, consultant, researcher
Comunian, Anna Laura psychologist, educator
Condren, Conal Stratford political science educator
Connolly, Janet Elizabeth retired sociologist and criminal justice educator
Connor, John Murray agricultural economics educator
Conrad, Peter sociology educator
Conway, Dorothy Jean Williams economist
Conway, Lesley psychologist

Greenberg, Ira Arthur *psychologist*
Greene, Kay C. *psychologist, author*
Greene, Renee Judith *industrial psychology consultant*
Greene, William Henry *economics educator, software engineer*
Greene Oster, Selmaree *medical anthropologist and researcher*
Greenwood, Joen Elizabeth *economist, consultant*
Gregson, Robert Anthony Mills *mathematical psychologist*
Greifeld, Kathrin *anthropologist, consultant*
Greiffenhagen, Martin O.W. *retired political science educator*
Grekova, Maya Dimitrova *sociology educator*
Greven, Michael Thomas *political science educator*
Grieves, Forest Leslie *political science educator*
Grigoriev, Sergei Aleksandrovich *political scientist, researcher*
Grim, Patrick Neal *philosopher, educator*
Grinde, Turid Vogt *psychologist, researcher*
Grindea, Daniel *international economist*
Groenheim, Henri Arnold *psychologist, consultant*
Grønmo, Sigmund Harold *sociology educator*
Groom, Arthur John Richard *political science educator*
Groshev, Vladimir Pavlovitch *economics educator, bank executive*
Gros-Pietro, Gian Maria *economics educator*
Grosser, Alfred *retired political science educator*
Grossin, William *sociology educator, researcher*
Groves, Colin Peter *anthropologist, educator*
Grundhoefer, Horst Peter *sociologist, educator*
Gubert, Renzo *sociology educator*
Guderjan, Thomas Harold *archaeologist, educator*
Guhathakurta, Meghna *social science educator, researcher, writer*
Guilmet, George Michael *cultural anthropologist, educator*
Guinsburg, Philip Fried *alcohol and substance abuse counselor*
Gulyas, Loran *sociology educator*
Gunning, Jan Willem *economics educator*
Gupta, Girdharilal Saduram *economics educator*
Gupta, Kishan Chand *psychologist*
Gupta, Uma *psychology researcher, consultant*
Gurevitch, Pavel Semenovich *anthropologist, educator*
Gurri, Garcia Francisco Delfin *research anthropologist*
Gurvitz, Milton Solomon *psychologist*
Gutmann, Ramon Maximo *gerontologist*
Gutwirth, Jacques *anthropologist*
Guyer, Charles Grayson, II *psychologist*
Gwartney, Patricia Anne *sociology educator*
Gyohten, Toyoo *economist*
György, Lovász *geographer, educator*
Haag, Ralph-Gerald *economist, diplomat*
Haas, Peter M. *political science educator*
Habbe, Karl Albert *retired geography educator*
Hachet, Pascal André *psychologist, writer*
Hackett, Ian James *social science educator, charity administrator*
Haeberle, Erwin Jakob *sexologist*
Haemmerle, Markus *economist, educator, consultant*
Hafsi, Mohamed *clinical psychology educator, psychotherapist*
Hägg, Claes *economist, educator*
Haggett, Peter *geographer, researcher*
Hahn, Frank Horace *economics educator*
Hajnis, Karel *physical anthropology educator*
Hakogi, Masumi *economist, educator*
Halbardier, Sheryl Linette *social studies educator, counselor*
Hale, William Wallace, III *psychologist, researcher*
Halford, Graeme Sydney *psychology educator*
Hall, Miriam Elizabeth Lewis *psychologist, educator*
Hall, Richard Clayton *retired psychologist*
Haltom, Cristen Eddy *psychologist*
Hamada, Jiro *psychologist, educator*
Hamdar, Bassam Charif *agri-economics educator, consultant*
Hamilton, Jack Richard *retired social psychologist*
Hamilton, James Douglas *economics educator*
Hamilton-Smith, Elery *sociologist*
Hampe, Johannes A. *economist, educator*
Hampton, James Antony *psychologist, educator*
Han, Shaowei *geomatics educator*
Hanawa, Toshiya *economics educator*
Hanihara, Kazuro *anthropologist, educator*
Hansen, Flemming *economics educator, marketing consultant*
Hansen, Gerd *economist*
Hansjurgens, Bernd *economist*
Hanson, Rick *psychologist*
Hanushek, Eric Alan *economics educator*
Hara, Kazuo *retired psychologist, educator*
Harberger, Arnold Carl *economist, educator*
Harbeson, John Willis *political science educator*
Harding, Ann Margaret *economics educator*
Harner, Michael James *anthropologist, educator, author*
Harnisch, Jörg-Henner *economist*
Harris, Chauncy Dennison *geographer, educator*
Harris, Ian Louis *economist, writer, accountant*
Harris, Sandra M. *psychology educator*
Harrison, Russell Sage *political science educator, consultant*
Harsanyi, John Charles *economics educator*
Hart, John Fraser *geography educator*
Harter, John J. *economic analyst*
Harter, Lafayette George, Jr. *economics educator emeritus*
Hartshorne, Timothy Scotford *psychology educator*
Hartzell, Irene Janofsky *psychologist*
Haruta, Hisayoshi *economist, educator, consultant company executive*
Haseeb, Khair El-Din *economist, statistician*
Hashimoto, Hiroaki *economics educator*
Hassan, Rashid Mekki *economics educator*
Hassmén, Peter Karl *psychology educator, researcher, author*
Hatcher, Peter John *educational psychologist, researcher*
Hattori, Akira *economics educator*
Haugaard, Mark *social theorist*
Hay, Iain Mill *geographer, educator*
Hayakawa, Tatsuji *economist*
Hayashi, Yoshiko *economist, educator*
Hayes, Charles Austin *economic development executive, consultant*
Hayes, Durrie Allan *economic development coordinator*
Häyrynen, Yrjo-Paavo *psychologist*
Hazard, Heather Alison *economist, educator*
Hazuda, Helen Pauline *sociologist, educator*
He, Baogang *political scientist, educator*
Heady, Ferrel *retired political science educator*
Heal, Geoffrey Martin *economics educator*
Heath, Richard Albert *psychology educator*
Heckman, James Joseph *economist, econometrician, educator*
Hedges, Mark Stephen *clinical psychologist*
Heffner, Krystian Maria *economic geographer educator, urban planner*
Heininen, Lassi Kalevi *political scientist*
Heintz, Carolinea Cabaniss *retired home economics educator*
Helbrecht, Ilse *geographer, educator*
Heller, Kurt Alois *psychology educator*
Henken, Bernard Samuel *clinical psychologist, speech pathologist*
Henry, Lois Hollender *psychologist*
Hensel, Witold *archaeologist*
Hentze, Joachim *economist, educator*
Heo, Mane *international politics educator*
Herman, Barry Martin *international economist*
Hernadi, Andras *economist*
Herzmann, Jan *statistician*
Heskin, Kenneth Joseph *psychology educator*
Hesse, Christian Hermann *mathematics and economics educator*
Hester, Edward John *industrial psychologist, researcher*
Heurlin, Bertel *political scientist, eductor*
Heyman, Gene Morris *research psychologist, educator*
Higashiyama, Atsuki *psychologist*
Higinbotham, Harlow Niles *economist*
Hilberg, Raul *political science educator*
Hilbern, Sandra J. *social sciences educator, retired counselor*
Hilgers, Micha *psychoanalyst, consultant*
Hill, Edward William *economics educator, urban and regional planner*
Hill, Ronald James *political science educator*
Hillman, Arye Laib *economics educator, consultant*
Hilsabeck, Robin C. *neuropsychologist*
Himmelstrand, J. Ulf I. *sociology educator, writer*
Hiner, Gladys Webber *psychologist*
Hinloopen, Jeroen *economist, educator, researcher*
Hinterberger, Friedrich *economist*
Hirayama, Eiji *psychologist, educator*
Hirose, Eiko Ikeda *psychologist, educator*
Hirsch, Michael Lee *social studies educator, mayor*
Hiwaki, Kensei *economics educator*
Hlupić-Vidjak, Vlatka *economist educator*
Ho, Yan-Ki Richard *economics and finance educator*
Hoadley, Walter Evans *economist, financial executive, lay worker*
Hoc, Jean-Michel *psychology researcher*
Hoeckmann, Olaf Ottomar *archeology*
Hoffman, Bruce Robert *international relations educator, consultant*
Hoffman, Paul Jerome *psychologist, statistician*
Hoffmann, Lutz *economics educator*
Hohmeyer, Olav Hans *economist, educator*
Holden, Barry Barfield *political science educator*
Holm, Joy Alice *psychology educator, art educator, artist, goldsmith*
Holmén, Hans Gunnar *geographer, educator*
Holmes, Elizabeth *psychologist*
Holmgren, Myron Roger *social sciences educator*
Holowinsky, Ivan Zenove *psychologist, educator*
Holtmann, Everhard *political science educator*
Holtzman, Wayne Harold *psychologist, educator*
Holzman, Franklyn Dunn *economics educator*
Holzman, Philip Seidman *psychologist, educator*
Holzner, Burkart *sociologist, educator*
Hommel, Bernhard *psychologist, researcher*
Hommel, Manfred Rainer Wolfgang *geography educator*
Honegger, Claudia *sociology educator*
Hong, Sung Chick *sociology educator*
Honkapohja, Seppo Mikko Sakari *economics educator*
Hood, Roger Grahame *criminologist, educator*
Hoogerwerf, Andries *political scientist*
Hopf, Sigrid *retired psychologist, researcher, educator*
Hopmann, Philip Terrence *political science educator*
Hormess, Harald Andreas *economist, business executive*
Horne, David James *clinical psychologist, educator*
Horner, Althea Jane *psychologist*
Horner, Jeffrey Thomas *public policy researcher*
Horwill, Frank Merrick *retired psychologist*
Hoskovec, Jiri *psychologist, researcher*
Hosomi, Takashi *economist*
Høstaker, Roar *political science educator*
Ho Trieu, Luan Ngoc *energy economist, researcher*
Houghton, Ernest Leslie *economics educator*
Howard, Michael McGregor *economist, educator, school administrator*
Howe, Kathy Eleanor *geography educator, massage therapist*
Howell, Llewellyn Donald *management educator*
Hoxter, Curtis Joseph *international economic adviser, public relations and public affairs counselor*
Hradil, Stefan Klaus *sociologist, educator*
Hu, Yao-Su *economist, educator, author*
Hua, Shiping *political science educator*
Huang, Runhua *geography educator, researcher*
Hubálek, Slavomil *psychologist*
Hudson, Darril *political scientist, educator*
Hudson, Ray *geography educator*
Huetter, Bernd Otto *neuropsychologist, researcher*
Hufbauer, Gary Clyde *economist, lawyer, educator*
Huff, William Gregg *economics*
Huggett, Richard John *geography educator, writer*
Hughes, Brian Michael *psychologist, educator*
Hughes, Robert Norman *psychologist, educator*
Hughes, Stella Platt *sociology educator*
Huizinga, Harry Pieter *economics educator*
Hult, Gert Tomas Mikael *international business executive, educator*
Humlum, Ole *geography educator, researcher, consultant*
Humphries, Joan Ropes *psychologist, educator*
Hunter, John Thomas *biogeographer*
Hunyady, György *social psychologist, educator*
Huque, Ahmed Shafiqul *political science-public administration educator*
Hurtig, Christiane *political scientist, researcher, educator*
Hurtig, Serge *political scientist, educator, administrator*
Husemann, Kurt *psychoanalyst*
Hussain, Akmal *economist, manufacturing executive, consultant*
Huster, Ernst-Ulrich *political scientist, educator*
Hutnik, Nimmi *psychologist*
Huttin, Christine Claude *economist*
Iani, Ettore *sociologist*
Ibrahim, Abdulhamid S. *psychology educator, dean*
Ibrahim, Fouad Sayed *mathematician, researcher*
Idowu, Isiaka Adio *socio-economics consultant, agriculturist*
Igbineweka, Andrew Osabuohien *public administration, political science educator*
Illeris, Sven *geography educator*
Imamoğlu, Emine Olcay *social psychologist, educator*
Imanaka, Kuniyasu *psychologist*
Imani, Nikitah Okembe-Ra *anthropologist, sociologist*
Imhof, Margarete Lydia *psychology educator*
Inbar, Michael *social psychology educator, consultant*
Inchingolo, Giuseppe Martino *anthropologist*
Ingle, Stephen James *political science educator*
Inglehart, Ronald Franklin *political science educator*
Ingram, James Carlton *economist, educator*
Inoguchi, Takashi *political scientist, educator*
Inoue, Shun *sociologist*
Ioannidis, Dimitris Nikolaos *economist, marketing consultant*
Iritani, Toshio *psychology educator*
Irons, William George *anthropology educator*
Isbister, John William *economist, educator*
Ishikawa-Fullmer, Janet Satomi *psychologist, educator*
Ismagilova, Roza Nurgalievna *anthropologist, researcher*
Ismail, Gamal Ali Fouad *mathematics educator*
Ison, Mirta Susana *psychologist, researcher*
Israeli, Raphael *Asian studies educator*
Isshiki, Masayuki *sociologist*
Iyoda, Mitsuhiko *economics educator*
Jackson, Peter Anthony *psychology educator*
Jackson, Ryno Marshall *forensic psychologist, consultant*
Jacob, Teuku *bioanthropologist, educator*
Jacobs, Eleanor Alice *retired clinical psychologist, educator*
Jaeger, Adolf Otto *psychology educator, researcher, consultant*
Jagacinski, Carolyn Mary *psychology educator*
Jagtap, Krishna Kondiram *economics educator*
Jahn, Egbert Kurt *social scientist, educator*
Jahn, Jens-Eberhard P.W. *sociologist, linguist, educator*
Jahnke, Juergen *psychologist, educator*
Jain, B. M. *international political studies educator*
Jakee, Keith Eric *economics researcher, educator*
James, Gary Douglas *biological anthropologist, educator, researcher*
James, Milton Garnet *economist*
Jankowski, Tadeusz *mathematician, educator*
Jansen, Dennis William *economics educator, consultant*
Jaquette, Jane Stallman *foreign studies educator*
Järbe, Torbjörn Ulf Christian *psychologist, educator*
Jarvis, Darryl Stuart Leslie *social sciences educator, consultant*
Jasinski, Leszek Jerzy *economist, educator*
Jasso, Guillermina *sociologist, educator*
Javorska, Magda *psychologist*
Jawad, Abdul Jalil *anthropology educator, researcher*
Jawan, Jayum Anak *political science educator*
Jebsi, Khaileddine *economist, educator*
Jeffrey-Smith, Lilli Ann *biofeedback specialist, educator, administrator*
Jelinović, Zvonimir Stanko *economics educator*
Jenkins, J. Craig *sociology educator*
Jenny, Frederic Yves *economist, educator*
Jensen, Henrik *economics educator*
Jensen, Robert Granville *geography educator, university dean*
Jern, Nils Stefan *psychologist*
Jervis, David Thompson *political science educator, academic administrator*
Jesien, Leszek Antoni *political scientist*
Jiha, Jacques *economist*
Jilek, Jaroslav *economist*
Job, Raymond Franklin Soames *psychologist*
Joebstl, Hans Anton *forest economist, educator, scientist*
Joerger, Jay Herman *psychologist, entrepreneur*
Johansson, Gunn N.M. *psychology educator*
Johnson, Albert Wesley *consultant on governance*
Johnson, Alberta Clark *psychology educator*
Johnson, Badri Nahvi *sociology educator, real estate business owner*
Johnson, Cammarie *behavior analyst*
Johnson, David Gale *economist, educator*
Johnson, David Wolcott *psychologist, educator*
Johnson, J. Susan *psychologist*
Johnson, Neal Frederick *psychological scientist, educator*
Johnson, Robert Allan *psychologist*
Johnson-Laird, Philip Nicholas *psychologist*
Joireman, Jeffrey Alan *psychology educator*
Jonas, Ruth Haber *psychologist*
Jónasdóttir, Anna Gudrún *political science educator*
Joneken, Bertil *economist, consultant*
Jones, Frank Stuart *economist, educator*
Jones, Gavin Willis *demography educator*
Jones, Kenneth Van Leer *psychologist, medical educator*
Jones, Leslie Nicole *psychologist, educator*
Jones, Nigel Vincent *psychologist*
Jones, Robert Alonzo *economist*
Jonikis, Arvidas Anthony *psychologist*
Jonsson, Ernst Ossian *economics educator, researcher*
Jordan, Amos Azariah, Jr. *foreign affairs educator, retired army officer*
Jordan, Judith Victoria *clinical psychologist, educator*
Jordan, Robert Smith *political science educator*
Jorgensen, Gerald Thomas *psychologist, educator*
Joseph, Joseph Savva *political science educator*
Joshi, Rajendra Prasad *political science educator, researcher*
Jović, Tomislav *economist*
Jucker, Hans Konrad *retired economist*
Jung, Otmar *political scientist, researcher*
Jyrkila, Faina *sociology educator*
Kaase, Max Willi *political science educator*
Kaasik, Taie Aidula *health promotion and medical sociology educator, researcher*
Kabakchieva, Gergana Angelova *archaeology researcher*
Kabele, Jiri *sociologist*
Kaesler, Dirk Rudolf *sociologist, educator*
Kagan, Sioma *economics educator*
Kaiser, Florian Gabriel *psychologist, researcher, educator*
Kajitani, Motohisa *sociology educator*
Kaliski, Mary *psychologist*
Kalnins, Uldis *economist*
Kalof, Linda Henry *sociologist, educator*
Kaluger, George *clinical psychologist, educator*
Kameda, Tatsuya *psychologist, educator*
Kaminski, Włodzimierz *economist, researcher*
Kaminsky, Anatol *educator, writer*
Kanaan, Oussama *economist*
Kanazawa, Satoshi *sociologist*
Kanbargi, Ramesh Raghavendra *researcher, educator*
Kane, Kevin Patrick *economist*
Kane, Michael Barry *social science research executive*
Kane, Stephanie C. *social anthropologist, educator*
Kang, Shin Il *economist*
Kanin, Doris May *political scientist, consultant*
Kaplan, Howard Bernard *sociologist, educator*
Kaplan, Mitchell Alan *sociologist, researcher*
Kaptein, Adrian Arend *psychologist*
Kapur, Suman Omprakash *psychology educator*
Karageorghis, Vassos *archaeologist*
Karakitsos, Elias *economist*
Karavanić, Ivor *archaeologist*
Kareklas, Petros Michael *economist, association administrator*
Kark, Ruth *geographer, historian, educator, writer*
Karon, Bertram Paul *psychologist, educator*
Kasai, Makiko *psychologist*
Kaskarelis, Ioannis Alkiviades *economist, educator*
Kassem, Abir Abd-El-Mohsen *archaeologist, construction company official*
Kassin, Saul *psychology educator*
Kataja, Mirja Birgitta *psychologist*
Katakis, Charis *psychologist*
Kato, Peter Eiichi *political scientist, journalist, educator, university dean*
Kaufmann, Sylvia *economics educator, researcher*
Kavussanos, Manolis George *applied shipping economics educator, finance educator, researcher, consultant*
Kawaguchi, Kazuko Hirose *sociology of international law educator*
Kawakatsu, Heita *economic history educator*
Kawano, Toshiaki *economics educator*
Kazuya, Tetsuji *business educator*
Kebede, Bereket *economist, educator*
Kechroud, Ammar Tayeb *psychologist, educator*
Keck, Lois T. *anthropology educator*
Keel, Keith Garnett *economist*
Kegley, Charles William, Jr. *political science educator, author*
Kehal, Harbhajan Singh *economics educator*
Kelle, Udo *social science lecturer, researcher*
Keller, Heidi *psychologist, educator*
Kellermann, Peter Felix Natan *psychologist*
Kelly, Abesie Ogail *psychologist*
Kelly, Kathleen Dennis *international government affairs consultant*
Keloharju, Matti Raimo *economics researcher*
Kemp, Sarah (Sally Leech) *developmental psychologist, neuropsychologist*
Kenen, Peter Bain *economist, educator*
Kennedy, Marla Catherine *psychologist*
Kennedy, Robert *international affairs educator*
Kennett, Keith Franklin *psychologist, educator*
Kent, Martin *biogeography educator*
Kenyon, Daphne Anne *economics educator*
Keown, Lauriston Livingston, Jr. *consulting psychologist*
Kernstock, Elwyn Nicholas *political science educator, author*
Kerr, Allen Stewart *retired psychologist*
Kesavan, Sundararajo *sociology educator*
Kestenbaum, Richard *clinical and school psychologist, consultant adolescent, family and child psychology, biofeedback*
Ketcham, Warren Andrew *psychologist, educator*
Kevenhörster, Paul Johannes *political scientist, educator, consultant*
Khaleefa, Omar Haroon *psychologist, researcher*
Khan, Rahmattullah *psychologist, educator*
Khan, Shahana Saleem *psychologist*
Kharadia, Virabhai Chelabhai *economist, educator, researcher*
Kidd, Garry John *psychology educator*
Kidda, Michael Lamont, Jr. *psychologist, educator*
Kiesewetter, Hubert *economist, historian, educator*
Kim, Hak-Hoon *geographer, educator*
Kim, Hong Nack *polictical science educator*
Kim, Hongkeun *neuropsychologist*
Kim, Kee Young *economist, educator*
Kim, Kyeong-Won *economist*
Kim, Suk-Joon *political science educator*
Kimhi, Shaul *psychologist, consultant, educator*
King, Ambrose Yeo-chi *sociology educator, university official*
King, Anthony Charles *archaeologist, researcher*
King, Margaret Etukudo *educator in public policy and geography*
King, Mervyn Allister *economist, educator*
King, Preston Theodore *social science educator, writer, political philosopher*
Kingman, Elizabeth Yelm *anthropologist*
Kipp, Gisela Miller *anthropology and history of education educator*
Kirakowski, Jerzy Zdzisław Jozef *psychology educator*
Kirchgässner, Gebhard *economist, educator*
Kirezis, Nick Stamatios *economist, researcher, consultant*
Kirkaldy-Willis, Iain Dunbar *social sciences educator*
Kirkow, Peter Boris *economist, political scientist*
Kirkpatrick, Jeane Duane Jordan *political scientist, government official*
Kiselis, Algirdas Antanas *economist, researcher*
Kitromilides, Paschalis Michael *political scientist, educator*
Kivikari, Urpo Kalevi *international economics educator*
Kiyono, Ken *international relations educator*
Klauer, Karl Christoph *psychology educator*
Klein, Christopher Carnahan *economist*
Klein, Lawrence Robert *economist, educator*
Klemperer, Paul David *economics educator, consultant, researcher*
Klíma, Michal *political scientist*
Kliszcz, Joanna Elizabeth *psychologist*
Kloos, Peter *anthropology educator*
Klosterman, Richard Earle *city planning and geography educator, researcher*
Klotsvog, Felix Naumovich *economist, science administrator*
Knot, Klaas Henderikus Willem *economist, researcher*
Knotek, Petr *psychologist*
Knudsen, Olav Fagelund *international politics educator*
Knudson, Ruthann *environmental consultant*
Knutson, Ronald Dale *economist, educator, academic administrator*

Kobetz, Richard William criminologist, consultant
Kodym, Miloslav psychologist, researcher
Koenig, Louis William political science educator, author
Kofmehl, Kenneth Theodore political science educator
Kogiku, Kiichiro economics educator
Kohan, Dennis Lynn international trade educator, consultant
Kohli, Manorama political science educator
Kohout, Jaroslav sociologist, psychologist, researcher
Koht, Harald Sverdrup political scientist, educator
Kolla, Peter forensic scientist, consultant
Komaki, Junji psychologist
Komatsu, Kenji economics educator
Koo, Shou-Eng economics educator
Köörna, Arno economist, educator
Kornell, Ronald Frank economist
Kortmann, Walter economics educator, researcher
Kosinski, Leszek Antoni geography educator
Kostecki, Wojciech political scientist, researcher
Kostere, Kim Martin psychologist, consultant
Kothari, Swatantra Singh economist
Kottis, George Christopher economist, educator
Kottler, Raymond George Michael economist, researcher
Kouame, Nguessan sociology educator, researcher, consultant
Koulourianos, Dimitri Theodore economist
Kouyaté, Lansana economist, international official, diplomat
Kovács, Géza economics educator
Koyama, Mitsuto psychologist
Kozberg, Steven Freed psychologist
Kozulin, Alex psychology educator, researcher
Kramer, Karen Sue mind-body psychologist
Kramer, Martin Seth humanities educator, researcher
Kranjc, Andrej Aleksej geographer, researcher
Krasikov, Yurii Vladimirovitch psychologist, educator
Kratka-Schneider, Dorothy Maryjohanna psychotherapist
Krau, Edgar psychologist, researcher, educator
Krauss, John Landers public policy, urban affairs consultant, mediator
Krenek, Mary Louise political science researcher, educator
Kreps, Juanita Morris economics educator, former government official
Kresl, Peter Karl economist, educator
Kressel, Neil Jeffrey psychologist
Kressin, Nancy Ruth research health psychologist
Kristensen, Preben Sander economics educator
Kristmundsdottir, Sigridur Duna anthropology educator
Kristof, Ladis Kris Donabed political scientist, writer
Kritz, Mary Monica educator, demographer
Kritzas, Charalambos archaeologist
Kroeller, Edgar Hartmut retired economist
Kroger, Jane Elizabeth psychology educator
Krombholz, Heinz psychologist
Kronhausen, Phyllis C. psychologist, consultant
Krueger, Gerald Peter psychologist
Kruger, Louis Max economist, consultant
Kugler, Joachim psychologist
Kuhle, Matthias geography educator, researcher
Kula, Erhun Ibrahim economist, educator, writer
Kulik, Liat social science educator
Kulka, Jiri psychologist
Kumar, Kuderu B. psychologist
Kumashiro, Masaharu ergonomics educator
Kumazawa, Makoto economics educator
Kuniya, Nobuaki psychology educator
Kuper, Adam Jonathan anthropologist, educator
Kurata, Ayao political scientist, educator
Kurek, Nikolai Sergeevich psychologist, researcher
Kurke, David Samuel management executive, industrial psychologist
Kurz, Heinz Dieter economics educator
Kusy, Miroslav philosopher, political scientist, educator
Kuther, Tara L. psychology educator
Kuyvenhoven, Arie economics educator
Kuzmics, Helmut sociologist, researcher
Kverndokk, Snorre economist, educator
Kwek, Kian Teng economics educator
Kwon, Jung-Hye psychology educator, consultant
Kybal, Elba Gómez del Rey economist, non-profit organization executive
Labsvirs, Janis economist, educator
Lachmann, Frank Michael psychologist, psychoanalyst
Lack, Leon Colburn psychology educator
La Croix, Sumner Jonathan economics educator
LaFarga, Juan B. psychologist, psychotherapist
Lafrenz, Jürgen Hans Robert geography educator
Laine, Ale Matti Juhani neuropsychologist, researcher, educator
Lakov, Krassimir Ivanov economist
Lakshminarasaiah, Mandalapu economics educator, researcher
Lall, Amar Raj economist
Lalwani, Mahesh economist, educator, researcher
Lamberton, Donald McLean economics educator
Lambin, Eric FrançOIS geography educator
Lamm, Claus cognitive neuroscientist, psychologist, researcher
Lammerink, Marc Peter social scientist, consultant
Lamo de Espinosa, Emilio sociologist, educator
Lamonica, Sergio financial consulting company executive
Lancelot, Alain political science educator
Landon, William J. intelligence officer
Lane, Robert Edwards political scientist
Lang, Frieder R. psychologist, researcher
Langlois, Marilyn Sue psychologist
Langlois Immoos, Marilyn Sue psychologist, music therapist, singer, conductor, composer
Lant, Christopher Louis geographer, educator
Lantermann, Werner social scientist
Lapid, Koty economist, researcher
Larkin, Andrew economics educator
Larson, Lloyd Warren economist
Laska-Mierzejewska, Teresa anthropologist
Laskin, Mark Jeffrey psychologist
Latoni, Alfonso Rafael sociology and political science educator
Lau, Siu Kai sociology educator
Lauber, Volkmar political science educator
Laurent, John Angus social sciences educator
Lautmann, Ruediger sociology educator
Lawson, Thomas Cheney fraud examiner
Layder, Derek sociology educator
Layman, Emma McCloy (Mrs. James W. Layman) psychologist, educator
Lazarcik, Gregor educator, financial research company executive, economist
Lazarus, Arnold Allan psychologist, educator
Lazea, Valentin macroeconomist, researcher
LeCapitaine, John Edward counseling psychology educator, researcher
Leclant, Jean Egyptologist, archaeologist, philologist
Lee, Joseph Shing economics educator
Lee, Sanghack economist, educator
Lee, Sang-Ho economist, researcher
Lee, Stewart S. political scientist
Lee, Tong Hun economics educator
Lee, Yong-Joo sociologist, educator
Leeb, Charles Samuel clinical psychologist
Lehmann, Ines bank executive, economist, consultant
Lehtimäki, Pentti Johannes military and political scientist
Lehtonen, Heikki Antero social studies educator
Leidlmair, Adolf geographer
Len, Michael Wai Hin psychological consultant
Lengyel, György sociologist, educator
Lentner, Howard Henry political scientist
LeoGrande, William Mark political science educator, writer
Leoni, Francesco political science educator
Leontief, Rudolf Georievich economics educator
Leplow, Bernd psychologist, researcher
Leponiemi, Arvi Kalevi economist, educator
Lerman, Zvi economist, researcher
Lerner, Jennifer Susan psychology educator
Lesser, Ian O. foreign affairs expert
Lesthaeghe, Ron Jean sociologist, educator
Leung, Beatrice Kit Fun Benedict political studies educator
Leung, Jin Pang behavioral psychologist
Levin, Michael Martin John political science educator
Levin, Shana psychology educator
Levy, Daniel economics educator
Levy, Harold David psycholinguist
Lévy-Garboua, Louis Jacques economics educator
Lewandowski, Jerzy Boleslaw economist, educator
Lewis Mill, Barbara Jean school psychologist, educator
Li, Lei mathematics and computer science educator
Li, Ping psychologist, educator
Li, Qi economics educator, researcher
Li, Qing economics educator
Librová, Hana sociologist
Lichtig, Leo Kenneth health economist
Lidmar-Bergström, Karna Helena physical geographer, researcher, educator
Lidstone, John Graham geographer, educator
Lieberman, Lynn I. psychologist
Liebert, Ulrike political scientist, educator
Liebman, Nina R. economic developer
Lijewski, Teofil Zygmunt geographer, educator
Lim, Duck-Ho economics educator, university dean
Lim, Hyun-Chin sociologist
Liman, Adrian Mac political scientist
Limonero, Joaquim Timoteo psychologist, educator
Lincoln, Bruce Kenneth anthropology and history of religions educator
Lindgreen, Paul Theodoor Carolus business economist
Lindgren, Gunilla Karin social science educator, researcher
Lindsey, Linda Lee sociology educator
Liossi, Christina health psychologist, researcher
Lioubimtseva, Elena geography educator
Lisetskii, Fedor Nikolaevich geographer, educator
Lisienkov, Ivan Dmitrievich economist, agricultural engineer, researcher
List, Gudula psychology educator
Lister, (Margot) Ruth social science educator
Litvak King, Jaime archaeologist
Liu, Ben-chieh economist
Lo, Fu-chen economist, educator
Lobao, Joao Cortez de economist
Lobo, Crispino Simon economist
Lobocki, Mieczyslaw Henryk psychologist, educator
Loftus, Elizabeth F. psychology educator
Lo Iacono, Antonio psychologist, psychotherapist, educator
Lompscher, Joachim retired psychologist
London, Ray William consultant, mediator, arbitrator, researcher
Lonergan, Thomas Francis, III criminal justice consultant
Long, Clive Garry clinical psychologist, medical administrator
Long, Frank Leslie economist
Lopata, Helena Znaniecka sociologist, researcher, educator
Lopez Ayala, Jorge Napoleon economist, financial consultant
Lopez-Cachero, Manuel economist, educator
Lopez-Murphy, Ricardo Hipolito economist
Lopreato, Joseph sociology educator, author
Lörincze, Peter L. economist
Los, Cornelis Albertus economist, portfolio risk manager, educator
Losada-Paisey, Gloria psychologist
Lougheed, Alan Leslie economics educator
Löwe, Jürgen economist
Löwy, Michael sociologist, researcher, educator
Lu, Luo psychologist, researcher
Lu, Zhong-Lin cognitive psychologist
Lubin, Carol Riegelman political scientist
Lubke, Gitta Hildegard psychologist
Lucas, Marilyn Doreen psychologist, educator, researcher
Lucas, Robert Emerson, Jr. economist, educator
Ludden, John Franklin retired financial economist
Lüdtke, Hartwig archaeologist
Luepnitz, Roy Robert psychologist, consultant, small business owner, entrepreneur
Lüer, Gerd psychology educator
Lueschen, Guenther sociologist
Lukács, Peter sociology and education educator
Lundberg, Ulf Ingvar biological psychology educator
Lundy, Jackelyn Ruth consulting firm owner, economist, researcher
Lupiani, Donald Anthony psychologist
Lurie, Konstantin Anatoly mathematician, educator
Lynd-Stevenson, Robert MacKay psychology educator, clinical psychologist
Lyon, Jerry D. school psychologist
Lytle, Michael Allen criminologist, consultant
Mac Aulay, Thomas Gordon economics educator
MacDonald, Jerome Edward school psychologist, consultant
MacDonell, Herbert Leon criminalist, consultant, educator
MacDougall, Sir (George) Donald (Alastair) economist
Macek, Petr psychologist, educator
Macesich, George econmomics professor
Machanic, Mindy Robin psychologist, horticulturist, educator, consultant, writer
Machin, Barrie Michael anthropologist, filmmaker
Machonin, Pavel sociologist
Macík, Karel economist, educator, researcher
Macionis, John Johnston professor, writer
Mack, Judith Cole Schrim political science educator
MacKenzie, Donald Angus sociology educator
MacManus, Susan Ann political science educator, researcher
Macnicol, John Simson social policy educator, researcher
Madden, Bartley Joseph economist
Mades Milgram, Roberta psychology educator, researcher
Madian, Alan Leonard economist
Madsen, Kristen Bent retired psychologist, educator
Madžar, Ljubomir economics educator
Maennig, Wolfgang Georg Christoph economics educator
Maher, Michaeleen Constance parapsychologist
Mahncke, Dieter Martin political scientist, educator
Maiminas, Efrem Zalmanovitsh economist, educator
Mainwaring, Scott Patterson political scientist, educator
Majors, Richard George psychology educator
Makhanya, Edward Mbuyiselo geographer
Makhnach, Alexander V. psychologist
Maki, Atsushi economics educator
Makin, Anthony John economist
Malik, Munawar Iqbal economist
Malikiosi-Loizos, Maria psychologist, educator, researcher
Malmgren, Harald Bernard economist
Malone, Laurence Adams economist, consultant
Mamalakis, George psychologist, researcher
Mambo, Estêvão da Cruz economist
Manas, Miroslav economics educator, researcher
Manetsch, Dominic Claudius economist, bank executive, consultant
Manganello, James Angelo psychologist
Maniadaki, Katerina clinical child psychologist, researcher
Manjunath, Thitenamane Rajappa economics educator
Mann, Catherine L. economist
Manning, Peter Kirby sociology educator
Marbach, Joseph R. political science educator, consultant
Marchese, Ronald Thomas ancient history and archaeology educator
Marciniak, Tomasz sociologist
Marcus, Eric Colton social psychologist, organizational consultant
Mardon, Austin Albert geographer, writer, researcher
Maree, Jacobus Gideon educational psychology educator
Marias, Antal economist, educator
Marin, Emilio archaeologist
Markman, Arthur Brian psychology educator
Markopoulos, John S. economist
Markovits, Andrei Steven political science educator
Markowitsch, Hans Joachim neuropsychologist, researcher
Markowitz, Fran anthropologist, educator
Marks, David Francis psychologist, consultant, writer
Marques, José Ferreira psychology educator
Marta, Elena psychologist, researcher
Martella, Ronald Charles psychology educator, consultant
Martin, Paul Russell clinical psychologist, educator
Martin, Peter psychology educator
Martin, Philippe Marie Jean geography and physical geography educator
Martin, Tony geographer, educator
Martin, William Allen sociology educator
Martin, William Edward economist
Martinez, Ginez economist, consultant, educator
Martinez, Herminia S. economist, banker
Martinez, Manuela physician, psychobiologist, educator, researcher
Martínez Domínguez, Guillermo economist, financial executive
Martinez-Pons, Manuel psychology educator
Martinussen, Monica psychology educator
Martinussen, Willy Martin sociologist, educator
Martowski, Adam Stanislaw economist
Marx, Gary T. sociologist, writer
Marzetti, Silva economist, educator
Masai, Yasuo geography educator
Masataka, Nobuo psychologist
Maser, Jack D. psychology educator
Mashin, Vladimir Anatolevich psychophysiologist, educator
Masini, Eleonora Barbieri futurist
Mason, Robert Jeffrey geography educator
Massajoli, Pierleone Francesco W. anthropologist, dialectologist, researcher
Matejcek, Zdenek child psychologist, researcher
Mathai, George K. monitoring and evaluation expert, consultant
Matishov, Gennady Grigorjevitch geography educator
Matsushita, Keiichiro economics educator
Matthiasson, Thorolfur economics educator
Matthiessen, Christian Wichmann geography researcher and educator
Mátyás, Antal economist, educator
Matyas, Laszlo economist, educator
Matzner, Egon economics educator
Mau, Vladimir Alexandrovich economist, government official, researcher
Maury, René economics and history educator
Mavrogordatos, George Themistocles political scientist, educator
Maxwell, Sara Elizabeth psychologist, educator, speech pathologist, director
May, Philip Alan sociology educator
May, Ronald James political scientist, researcher
Mayer, Nonna political science researcher
Mays, Vickie M. psychology educator
Mazrui, Ali Al'Amin political science educator, researcher
Mazzucchelli, Trevor Gordon psychologist
McCafferty, James Arthur sociologist
McCarroll, Daniel geography educator
McCarthy, Barry Wayne clinical psychologist
McCarthy, Bill Darcy sociologist, criminologist
McCarthy, Jonathan Paul economist
McCluskey, Neil Gerard gerontologist, educator, literary agent
McCollum, William Franklin, Jr. sociology educator, private investigator
McConkey, Kevin Malcolm psychology educator
McCormack, Marjorie Guth psychology educator, career counselor, communications educator, public relations consultant
McCormick, Ken J. economics educator
McCoy, Valerie T. racial studies educator
McCrady, Barbara Sachs psychologist, educator
McCutcheon, Allan Lee sociology educator
McDivitt, Karen Louise psychologist, writer
McDonald, Craydon Dean psychologist
McEvoy, Pamela T. clinical psychologist
McFadden, Daniel Little economics educator
McGovern, Ligaya Lindio sociology and women's studies educator
McGowan, Joan Yuhas development researcher
McHugh, David psychology educator
McIntyre, John Andrew environmental and economic planner, geography educator
McKerracher, Daniel Wallace psychologist, consultant, researcher
McLean, Roger Fairbairn geographer, educator
McMillan, Thomas Murray psychology educator
Mc Nelly, Frederick Wright, Jr. psychologist
McQuaid, Ronald William economic development educator, consultant, researcher
Meagher, Robert Francis international economic law consultant
Medici, Rochelle psychologist, brain researcher
Meesters, Ybe psychologist, psychotherapist, researcher
Mehra, Jagdish economics educator
Mehran, Firouzeh psychologist, researcher
Meiner, Sue Ellen Thompson gerontologist, nurse practitioner, nursing educator and researcher
Meisel, John political scientist
Mejias, Cristina sociologist
Mékota, Karel anthropologist
Melcher, Jerry William Cooper clinical psychologist, army officer
Meleg, Csilla sociologist, educator
Melitz, Jacques economist, educator
Mellish, Gordon Hartley economist, educator
Mello Neto, Gustavo Adolfo Ramos psychology educator
Melotti, Umberto sociologist, educator
Melucci, Alberto sociologist, educator, clinical psychologist
Mena, F. Xavier economics educator, consultant
Mennin, Douglas Steven psychologist
Mentschl, Josef retired educator
Mercurio, Antonino Marco anthropologist, philosophy educator
Merenda, Peter Francis psychologist, emeritus educator
Merino, Fernando economist, researcher, educator
Merker, Richard J. economist, educator, consultant
Merriam, John Goodwin political scientist, educator
Merten, Thomas clinical neuropsychologist, researcher
Merton, Robert C. economist, educator
Merton, Robert K. sociologist, educator
Merz, Monika economics educator
Meseke, Cornelia Beate psychologist, researcher
Mesko, Ivan economist, mathematician, educator
Mesniaeff, Gregory economist
Messer, Andrea Elyse anthropologist, archaeologist, science writer
Messinis, Lambros clinical health psychologist
Mestre, Daniel economics consultant
Mészáros, Sándor agricultural economist
Metallo, Thomas Joseph language and political science educator
Mettler-von Meibom, Barbara Elisabeth political science educator
Meyer, Peter sociology educator
Michael, Diann Dee psychologist, educator
Michaelowa, Axel economist, researcher
Michalopoulou, Niovi psychologist, educator
Middleditch, Darren Paul economist
Middleton, George, Jr. clinical child psychologist
Mikhail, William Mesiha economist, educator
Mikkonen, Kauko Kalervo geographer, educator
Mili, Samir agricultural economist
Miller, Donald Andrew, II psychologist
Miller, James Clifford, III economist
Miller, Janel Howell psychologist
Miller, Margery Silberman psychologist, speech/language pathologist/educator
Miller, Sandra A. Caramela gerontologist, educator
Miller, Stephen Gaylord archaeology educator
Milliken, John Gordon research economist
Mills, Teheran L. (Terry Mills) sociology educator
Milner, Arthur David psychology educator
Minogue, Kenneth Robert political science educator, writer
Minor-Evans, Leslie psychology educator, writer
Mirrlees, Sir James Alexander economics educator
Mishra, Ashok Kumar economist, educator
Misner, Carol Dean mathematics educator
Mitchell, Peter Lawrence psychology educator
Mitchell, Rie Rogers psychologist, counselor, educator
Mittel, John J. economist, corporate executive
Mittenecker, Erich Felix Paul psychology educator
Miyazaki, Koichi economics educator
Mizen, Paul David economist researcher
Mizuno, Atsushi economist
Modigliani, Franco economics and finance educator
Moely, Barbara E. psychology researcher, educator
Mohammad, Yousuf Hasan J. economist, educator
Moix Queraltó, Jenny psychologist, educator
Molin, Eric Johannes Elisabeth social research educator, researcher
Monegro, Francisco psychology educator, alternative medicine consultant
Mongin, Philippe philosopher, economist, educator
Monna, Naoki sociology educator
Montenegro-Ferrão, Aura psychologist, researcher
Montiel, Eduardo Luis business and economics educator, consultant
Moodie, Graeme Cochrane political science educator
Moodley Kunnie, Thilo psychologist, educator
Moon, Byeong-Joon economist, educator
Moore, Dahlia psychologist, educator
Moore, Daniel Edmund psychologist, educator, retired educational administrator
Moore, Melanie sociology educator
Moore, Omar Khayyam experimental sociologist
Moore, Ruth Lambert Bromberg retired clinical psychologist
Moray, Neville psychology educator
Mora y Araujo, Manuel J. political sociologist, researcher
Mordecai, David K.A. financial economist, journal editor
Moretti, Lucia Helena Tiosso psychologist, educator
Morewitz, Stephen John behavioral scientist, consultant, educator
Morgan, Iwan Wyn political history educator
Moro, Beniamino economist
Moroney, John Rodgers economist, educator
Morris, Christopher David archaeology educator

Samuelson, Paul Anthony economics educator
Sanbar, Moshe Gustav economist, banker
Sanchez-Perez, Rosario economist
Sanders, David political scientist, educator, administrator
Sanders, Toon J.M. economist
Sandford, Cedric Thomas political economist and educator
Sandford, Herbert Adolphus cartographer
Sandoval, Maria Olga economics educator
Sanford, Anthony John psychology educator, researcher
Sanghavi, Girish Jayantilal psychologist, hypnotherapist, sexologist
Sangiorgi, Giorgio social sciences educator
Santamaria Carrasco, Alina Fabiola international relations and economics educator
Santilli, Nicholas Richard psychology educator
Sapra, Sunil K. economics educator
Sargent, John Richard economist
Sarma, Pulugurta Vyaghreshwara economics educator
Sarmela, Matti Eljas anthropology educator
Sartorius von Bach, Helmke Jens farming economics consultant
Sato, Hiroshi economics educator
Scanlon, Edward Charles clinical psychologist
Scarpa, Angela psychology educator
Schabert, Tilo Carl political studies educator, journalist
Schadlbauer, Friedrich Guenther geographer
Schafer, Donna Elizabeth gerontological educator, university administrator
Schäfer, Hans-Bernd economist, educator
Schauss, Alexander George psychologist, researcher
Schefold, Bertram economics educator
Schelling, Thomas Crombie economist, educator
Scherrer, Patrick economist
Schieb, Pierre-Alain Edouard economist
Schiffauer, Werner social anthropologist
Schilbred, Cornelius Mathias economics educator
Schimmelpfennig, Jörg economics educator
Schirrmacher, Thomas Paul ethics educator, publisher, periodical editor
Schlesinger, Izchak M. psychology educator
Schlesinger, James Rodney economist
Schlicht, Ekkehart Johannes economics educator
Schlotzhauer, Virginia Hughes parliamentary consultant
Schluter, Gerald Emil economist
Schmaehl, Winfried Arthur economist, educator
Schmelz, Bernd anthropologist
Schmid, Alfred Allan economist
Schmid, Holger psychologist
Schmidt, Gustav Friedrich political science educator
Schmidt, Ingo Lothar Ottokar retired economics educator
Schmidt, Volker Hermann social scientist
Schmieding, Holger economist
Schmitt, Karl M. political scientist
Schneider, Wolfgang Erich psychologist, educator, dean
Schobinger, Juan retired archaeology educator
Schofield, Roger Snowden historical demographer, research director
Scholz, Wolf-Ulrich psychologist, consultant
Schonpflug, Wolfgang Michael psychology educator
Schorr, Martin Mark forensic examiner, psychologist, educator, screenwriter
Schriefers, Heribert Johannes psychology educator
Schroeder, Friedrich-Christian criminal law and procedure educator
Schröger, Erich psychologist
Schuler, Heinz Friedrich psychologist, educator
Schuyler, Robert L. anthropologist, archaeologist
Schwab, George David social science educator, author
Schwantes, Robert Sidney international relations executive
Schwarting, Rainer Karl Willi psychologist
Schwartz, Lori Beth psychologist, educator
Schwarz, Rainer economics educator
Schweickert, Richard Justus psychologist, educator
Schweinfurth, Ulrich geography educator
Schweitzer, Carl-Christoph political science educator
Schweitzer, Marcell economics and business administration educator, researcher
Schwind, Hans-Dieter criminology educator
Scobie, Geoffrey Edward Winsor psychologist, clergyman
Scott, Allen John public policy and geography educator
Scott, Barbara Ann sociology educator, feminist, peace activist
Scott, Maurice FitzGerald economist
Scott, Nancy Ellen psychologist
Scott, Susan research demographer
Šebek, Michael psychologist, educator, psychoanalyst
Sechrest, Larry J. economist, educator
Segal, David Robert sociology educator
Segal, Geraldine Rosenbaum sociologist
Segal, Josylyn Chan cross-cultural clinical psychologist, musician
Seger, Martin geography scientist
Segre, Sandro sociologist, educator
Segui, Melissa Paula Reyes psychologist
Segura, Francisca Soledad geographer, educator
Seidenfus, Hellmuth Stephan retired economics educator
Seidenspinner, Gundolf O(tto) social science educator, writer
Seifer, Marc Jeffrey psychology educator
Seike, Atsushi labor economics educator
Selcher, Wayne A. political science educator
Selten, Reinhard retired economist, educator
Sempe, Henri Jean economics educator
Sen, Amartya Kumar economist, educator
Senda, Takashi economics educator
Senechal, Thierry J. economist, finance expert
Senesh, David clinical child psychologist, educator
Seppälä, Matti Kullervo physical geography educator
Serok, Shraga retired psychologist, social worker, educator
Serrie, Hendrick anthropology and international business educator
Serry-Kamal, Mordu political science/public administration educator
Seshamani, Venkatesh economics educator
Settis, Salvatore archaeologist, art historian
Shachmurove, Yochanan economics educator
Shafaeddin, Mehdi economist, educator
Shafer, Byron Edwin American government educator
Shafi, Muhammad geographer, educator
Shah, Muhammad Azher Zafar international relations educator
Shain, Yossi political scientist, educator
Shamsavari, Ali economist, researcher, lecturer
Shani, Esther medical sociologist, researcher
Shanin, Teodor sociology educator
Sharkansky, Ira political science educator
Sharpe, William Forsyth economics educator
Sharps, John Geoffrey retired psychologist, author
Shear, Ione Mylonas archaeologist
Shear, Theodore Leslie, Jr. archaeologist, educator
Shedyakov, Vladimir E. economic theory educator
Sheehan, Peter Winston psychology educator, researcher
Sheinbaum, Stanley K. economist
Shen, Jianfa geography educator
Sheridan, Richard Bert economics educator
Shi, Bolin political science educator
Shiller, Robert James economist
Shin, Eui-Soon economist, educator
Shiner, Rebecca Lynn psychology educator
Shmotkin, Dov psychologist
Shneidman, Edwin S. psychologist, educator, thanatologist, suicidologist
Shrestha, Hemanta Kumar economist, researcher, educator
Shubik, Martin economics educator
Sibaya, Patrick Themba psychologist, educator
Sicherl, Pavle economics educator
Siebert, Horst economics educator, foundation administrator
Siegel, Abraham J. economics educator, academic administrator
Sigmon, Scott B. psychologist
Signorino, Curtis Stephen political science educator, researcher
Silberston, (Zangwill) Aubrey economics educator
Silva, Zelmira Maria economist, consultant, researcher
Silverman, Lester Paul economist, energy industry consultant
Sime, James Thomson psychologist, consultant
Simon, Andras economist
Simon, Herbert A(lexander) social scientist
Simon, Jacqueline Albert political scientist, journalist
Simon, Katrin economist
Sinai, Allen Leo economist, educator
Sinclair, William Angus retired economics educator
Singer, George Milton clinical psychologist
Singer, J. David political science educator
Singh, Abha Lakshmi geography educator and researcher
Singh, Ajit economist
Singh, Amool Ranjan psychology educator, academic administrator
Singh, Rana P.B. cultural geographer, educator
Singh, Swaran political science researcher
Sinha, Dipendra Narayan economist, educator
Sinha, Prabhas Chandra political geographer, environmentalist, researcher, educator, consultant
Sinnott, Jan Marie Dynda psychologist
Sipos, Béla educator
Sisk, Fred Dean retired cartographer
Sisodia, Pratap economist, researcher
Sit, Victor Fung Shuen geography and geology educator
Siwicki, Michael cartographer
Sjoholt, Peter economic geographer
Sjöstrand, Sven-Erik business administration educator
Škare, Marinko economics educator
Skidmore, Jay Robert psychologist
Sklar, Richard Lawrence political science educator
Sklenář, Karel archaeologist
Skoe, Eva Elisabeth Aspaas psychology educator
Skouras, Thanos economics educator
Slater, Terence Richard geography researcher, educator
Slaven, Georgina Mary psychologist
Sloane, Peter James economics educator
Slonska, Zofia Antonina sociologist
Small, Kenneth Alan economics educator
Smedslund, Geir psychologist
Smit, Gertrude Nicolet psychologist
Smith, Barbara Mary Dimond retired urban and regional studies educator
Smith, David Horton social sciences educator
Smith, Donald Frederick research psychologist, neuropsychopharmacologist
Smith, Ethel Farrington retired social worker, genealogist, writer
Smith, Peter Kenelm psychology educator
Smith, Ross Lamont clinical psychologist, consultant, researcher
Smith, Willard Grant psychologist
Smolansky, Bettie Moretz sociology educator
Smoot, Skipi Lundquist psychologist
Snarey, John Robert psychologist, researcher, educator
Snooks, Graeme Donald political economist
Snower, Dennis James economics educator
Snyder, Jed C. foreign affairs specialist
Socher, Karl Friedrich economics educator
Söderström, Hans Tson economist
Sodhi, Nirmal Singh social work educator
Soh, Byung Hee economist, educator
Soldatos, Gerasimos Theodore economics educator
Solga, Heike sociologist, researcher
Soliman, Abdalla Mahmoud psychology educator, researcher
Solomon, Elinor Harris economics educator
Solow, Robert Merton economist, educator
Sommer, Gert psychology educator
Sondermann, Dieter Friedrich Wilhelm economic educator
Song, Shunfeng economist, researcher
Songsore, Jacob geographer, educator
Soubra, Yehia Muhieddine economist
Soudijn, Karel Adrianus psychologist
Souris, John Nickolas economist, accountant
Souzdaltsev, Igor Nikolayevich economist
Spangler, Edra Mildred clinical psychologist
Spash, Clive Laurence environmental economist
Spechler, Martin Charles economist
Spennemann, Dirk Heinrich Rudolph archeologist, cultural heritage administrator
Spindler, Konrad archaeologist
Spivak, Dmitri linguistic and psychological studies scientist
Spooner, Frank Clyffurde economic history educator
Spoonley, Paul sociologist, educator, researcher
Spragens, William Clark public policy educator, consultant
Sprainqs, Violet Evelyn psychologist
Spraos, John economics educator
Squires, Digby Peter Leighton economist
Staats, Thomas Elwyn neuropsychologist
Stabell, Ulf psychologist, researcher
Stacey, Margaret retired sociology educator
Stach, Alex G. retired sociology educator, social worker
Staffelbach, Bruno business economist
Stahel, Albert Alexander political scientist, educator
Stålhammar, Nils-Olov health economist
Stallworth, Charles Derotha, Jr. psychologist
Stamper, Ewa Szumotalska psychologist
Stassen, Jacques Marcel (Knight Stassen) emeritus political science educator, legal administration consultant, university director
Staudt, Erich Erwin labor economics educator
Steele, Howard L. psychology educator
Steele, Howard Loucks economic development consultant, author
Steerneman, Pim child psychologist, researcher
Steiger, Otto Martin Karl economics educator
Steininger, Karl W. economics educator
Stelzer, Irwin Mark economist
Stempel, John Dallas international studies educator
Stephan, Ed sociology educator
Stephan, Paula Elizabeth economist, school administrator
Stephen, Michael psychologist
Steptoe, Andrew Patrick Arthur psychologist, educator
Stern, Paul Clinton social scientist
Sternberg, Hilgard O'Reilly geographer, educator
Stevens, David Richard corporate psychologist
Stevens, Richard John psychology educator
Stewart, Chris economist, researcher, educator
Stewart, Jane psychology educator
Stewart, John Todd economist
Stewart, Malcolm William psychologist, researcher
Stewart, Patricia Rhodes retired clinical psychologist, researcher
Steyer, Rolf psychologist, educator
Stingel, Ana Maria psychology educator, psychotherapy researcher
Stockburger, David Webb psychologist, educator
Stoddard, William Bert, Jr. economist
Stoddart, Simon Kenneth archaeology educator
Stoetzel, Berthold psychologist, educator
Stokes, Jonathan Hugh organizational psychologist, psychotherapist
Stolnitz, George Joseph economist, educator, demographer
Stolzberg, Mark Elliott psychologist
Stone, Duane Snyder school psychologist, clergyman
Stoneman, Colin Frank economics educator, consultant, researcher
Storesletten, Kjetil economist, educator
Stout, David Ker economics educator
Strahler, Alan H. geography educator, author, researcher
Strano, Marco criminologist, researcher
Strasser, Helmut ergonomics, educator, researcher
Strasser, Hermann sociology educator
Strauss, Robert Philip economics educator
Streetman, Lee George sociology educator, criminology educator
Strempel, Ulrich political scientist
Strocka, Volker Michael archaeologist
Strømnes, Frode Jens psychologist
Strunk, Orlo Christopher, Jr. psychology educator
Stubbe, Michel Marie economist, statistician
Stufano, Thomas Joseph criminologist, author, inventor
Stumpf, István political scientist, academic administrator
Sturman, Andrew Philip geography educator
Su, Dongwei economist, educator
Subbotsky, Eugene Vasilevitch psychologist
Suchozebrski, Marek Jan economist
Suess, James Francis clinical psychologist
Sugawara, Masumi psychologist
Sugden, Robert economics educator
Suh, Chang-Jin health economist, researcher
Sulloway, Frank Jones psychologist, historian
Sumi, Shigemasa psychology educator
Summala, Heikki traffic psychology educator
Sun, Ji Wu energy economist, educator
Sunamura, Tsuguo coastal geomorphologist, coastal engineer
Suraci, Patrick Joseph clinical psychologist
Surgy, Albert de anthropologist
Suša, Oleg social science educator
Sutton, John E.G. archeologist
Şutton, L. Paul criminal justice educator
Švancara, Josef Stanislav psychology educator
Svebak, Sven Egil psychology medicine educator
Svensson, Palle political scientist
Swanke, Thomas Aquinas economist, educator
Swanson, Jack Elmer economist, investment consultant
Sweeney, Lucy Graham psychologist
Sweeney, Richard James economics educator
Sweller, John educational psychology educator
Swiger, Mark social studies educator
Swinson, Jeremy Mark psychology educator
Swope, Alan Joseph psychologist, educator
Symonds, Edward energy economist, consultant
Syristova, Eva psychologist, philosopher
Szabó, Máté political scientist, educator
Szapiro, Tomasz Jerzy economist, researcher
Szczepanik, Edward Franciszek economist, educator, government official
Szentes, Tamas economics educator, researcher
Tabatoni, Pierre economics educator, consultant
Tachiki, Dennis Shigeo sociologist, researcher
Taçon, Paul Stephen Charles anthropologist, archaeologist
Tafelski, Michael Dennis psychologist
Tagányi, Zoltán sociologist
Taha, Farag Abdil Kadir psychology educator, researcher
Taha, Hind Sayed psychology educator
Tainter, Joseph Anthony archaeologist
Tajima, Osamu psychiatrist, researcher
Takanaka, Kimio economist
Takashima, Shoji sociology educator
Takasuna, Miki psychology educator
Takekuma, Shinichi economist, educator
Takeuchi, Keiichi geography educator
Tan, Chee-Beng anthropology educator
Tan, Rodelene Penequito psychologist
Tanaka, Atsushi psychologist, researcher
Tanaka, Hisao economist, educator
Tanaka, Satoshi sociologist
Tang, Shengming sociology educator
Tange, Hiroyuki economics educator
Tanko, Adamu Idris geography educator
Tanno, Dai social sciences educator
Tannock, Charles psychiatrist, consultant, legislator
Tapscott, Christopher Peter sociologist
Taraszkiewicz, Margaret psychologist
Tarcă, Mihai economist, educator
Taris, Toon psychologist, researcher, consultant
Tarschys, Daniel political science educator
Tart, Charles Theodore psychologist, educator
Tasnádi, Attila economist, software developer
Tavecchio, Louis W(illem) C(ornelis) psychology educator
Taylor, Eldon psychological researcher
Taylor, Margaret Carol social studies educator
Taylor, William Jesse, Jr. international studies educator, research center executive
Teather, Elizabeth Kenworthy geography educator
Tedeschi, Richard Glenn psychologist, educator
Teikari, Veikko Olavi industrial psychology educator
Tenenbaum, Gershon psychologist
ten Raa, Thijs economist
Teodor, Dan G.H. archaeologist, researcher
Teodorescu, Nicolae Gheorghe economics researcher, educator
Tepper, Lynn Marsha gerontology educator
Teräsvirta, Timo economics educator
Terhal, Petrus Hendricus retired economist
Ternyik, Stephen economist, educator
Terris, Lillian Dick psychologist, association executive
Tester, Leonard Wayne psychology educator
Tezanos, Jose Felix sociology educator
Thanopoulou, Georgia Gina G. counseling psychologist
Tharakad, Saraswathi Subramanium child development educator
Thelin, Peter Carl economist, educator
Theodorou, Petros economist, consultant, researcher
Theodossiou, Ioannis economist, educator
Therborn, Göran Arne Axel social scientist
Thevenot, Maude Travis retired home economist
Thimotheose, Kadakampallil George psychologist
Thirlwall, Anthony Philip economist, educator
Thomas, Gale Denise psychologist
Thompson, Alan Eric economics educator
Thompson, George Brian psychologist, educator
Thompson, George Frederick, Jr. public management educator
Thomson, Marjorie Belle Anderson sociology educator, consultant
Thorne, Colin Reginald geography educator, consultant
Thorns, David Christopher sociology educator
Thraenhardt, Dietrich Joachim political science educator
Thranert, Oliver political scientist
Thrift, Nigel John geographer, educator
Thurman, Melburn D. anthropologist, researcher, consultant
Thurzo, Milan Henrich physical anthropologist, researcher
Tietz, Reinhard economics educator
Tietze, Wolf Rudolf geographer, editor, researcher, consultant
Tikkanen, Tuomo Aarne Juhani psychologist
Tilaar, Henry A.R. social planner educator
Tillema, Herbert Kendall political science educator
Tillman, Mary Norman urban affairs consultant
Timmons, Gordon David economics educator
Ting, Wai political science educator
Tiongson-Magno, Estrella Tanjutco psychologist, educator
Tismaneanu, Vladimir political science educator, researcher
Tobias, Phillip Vallentine anthropologist, anatomist, educator
Tobin, James economics educator
Tolins-Kaufman, Selma L. psychologist
Tom, C. F. Joseph economics educator
Toman, Walter Karl psychologist, educator
Toompere, Marika philologist
Torii, Shuko psychology educator
Torvi, Kai Antero economist
Tosti, Donald Thomas psychologist, consultant
Totten, George Oakley, III political science educator
Touyz, Stephen William clinical psychologist, educator
Towl, Graham John forensic psychologist, educator
Towler, Gary psychology educator
Trafimow, David A. psychology educator
Trainer, Frederick Edward economics educator
Trappe, Paul sociologist
Trasler, Gordon Blair criminologist, psychology educator
Treber, Salvador economist, educator
Treiman, Rebecca Ann psychologist
Trevor, Bronson economist
Troitzsch, Klaus Gerhard social science informatics educator
Trommsdorff, Gisela social sciences educator
Tsai, Diana Hwei-An economics educator
Tsao, Jiin-Wen psychologist, counselor
Tschacher, Wolfgang psychologist, researcher
Tsetskhladze, Gocha Revazi archaeologist, educator
Tsiamis, Athanassios psychologist
Tsotsoros, Stathis economist, management executive
Tsuji, Tadao economics educator
Tsuneyuki, Toshio economics educator, translator
Tullio, Giuseppe economist, researcher
Tung, Samuel Shui-Liang economics and business educator
Turan, Ilter Adil political science educator
Turcan, Robert Alain archaeology educator, historian
Turley, William Stephen political scientist, educator
Turner, Frederick Clair political science educator
Turner, John Andrew economist
Turnovec, František economist, educator
Turpin, Joseph Ovila counselor, educator
Tuthill, L. Lee economist
Twidale, C(harles) R(owland) geomorphologist, educator
Tykkyläinen, Markku Juhani geography educator
Tzelgov, Joseph psychologist, scientist
Tzuriel, David psychologist, educator
Uchiyama, Ichiro psychology educator
Uemura, Toshio economist, educator
Uggen, Christopher sociologist, criminologist
Uhlig, Harald F.H.V.S. economics educator, researcher
Ulijaszek, Stanley J. anthropologist
Ulrich, Rolf psychologist
Ulrich, Volker economist, researcher
Umezu, Toyoshi behavioral scientist
Undeutsch, Udo Heinz-Hermann psychology educator
Ungerer, Horst international economist, lecturer, writer
Ungurean, Pavel Vasile economist, educator
Unser, Guenther political science educator
Uphill, Eric Parrington archaeologist, educator
Uribe, Martin economics educator
Uribe Villegas, Oscar sociologist
Utens, Elisabeth Maria W. J. psychologist
Uzunidis, Dimitri Nicolas economist, journalist, sociologist
Vadus, Gloria A. scientific document examiner
Valckx, Nico economics educator
Valenčič, Ivan psychologist, writer, art critic, counselor